78TH EDITION

AMERICAN LIBRARY DIRECTORY™

2025-2026

American Library Directory™
78th Edition

Publisher
Thomas H. Hogan

Director, ITI Reference Group
Owen O'Donnell

Associate Editor
Jennifer Williams

Operations Manager, Tampa Editorial
Debra James

Project Coordinator, Tampa Editorial
Carolyn Victor

78TH EDITION

AMERICAN LIBRARY DIRECTORY™

2025-2026

VOL. 2

RHODE ISLAND–WYOMING & TERRITORIES

LIBRARIES IN CANADA

LIBRARY NETWORKS, CONSORTIA & SCHOOLS

ORGANIZATION INDEX

PERSONNEL INDEX

InformationToday

ISSN 0065-910X

Set ISBN: 978-1-57387-609-4

Library of Congress Catalog Card Number: 23-3581

Information Today, Inc.
143 Old Marlton Pike
Medford, NJ 08055-8750
Phone: 800-300-9868 (Customer Service)
800-409-4929 (Editorial)
Fax: 609-654-4309
E-mail: custserv@infotoday.com (Customer Service)
jwilliams@infotoday.com (Editorial)
Web Site: www.infotoday.com

Printed and bound in the United States of America

$449.50
ISBN 978-1-57387-609-4
44950>
9 781573 876094

CONTENTS

VOLUME 1

VOLUME 2

PREFACE

Welcome to the 78th edition of the *American Library Directory*, now in its 116th year. The *American Library Directory* is edited and compiled by Information Today, Inc. of New Providence, New Jersey.

ARRANGEMENT AND COVERAGE

The major section of the directory contains listings of public, academic, government, and special libraries in the United States and in Canada. Listings are arranged geographically by the U.S. and Canada, then alphabetized by states, provinces, cities, and finally by the library or organization name.

Each state and province chapter opens with statistical information regarding public libraries. These statistics were supplied by the state or provincial library authorities. Some are derived from public sources.

Entries include the name and address of the library, names of key personnel, and information on the library's holdings. In addition, the entries for the majority of libraries provide information on some or all of these additional areas: Income; Expenditures including salaries; E-Mail; Subject Interests; Special Collections; Automation; and Publications. Also included in each entry is a Standard Address Number (SAN), a unique address identification code used to expedite billing, shipping, and electronic ordering. For SAN assignments or questions, contact SAN@bowker.com. See the sample entry on page xi for a comprehensive guide to information that can be included in each entry.

Each library was provided its data to update via an e-mail and web data interchange application. If an update was not returned, the data were verified, as much as possible, through telephone outreach, direct e-mail, and web research. Entries verified from public sources are indicated by an asterisk (*) following the library name.

Non-listed libraries that have come to our attention since the previous edition are provided with questionnaires. If the library returns sufficient information, it is included. Entries new to the directory, are indicated by a section icon (§) to the left of the classification letter that precedes the entry.

Each library listed is identified by a code that indicates the type of library it is. The following codes are used:

A — Armed Forces
C — College or University
E — Electronic
G — Government, from local to federal
J — Community College
L — Law
M — Medical
P — Public and State Libraries
R — Religious
S — Special, including industry and company libraries as well as libraries serving associations, clubs, foundations, institutes, and societies.

ADDITIONAL SECTIONS

Library Award Recipients 2024. This section includes awards for outstanding librarianship or services, major development grants, and research projects.

Volume 2 of the directory provides auxiliary information to the Library industry, and includes a variety of specialized information:

1. *Networks, Consortia, and Other Cooperative Library Organizations* includes automation networks, statewide networking systems, book processing and purchasing centers, and other specialized cooperating organizations. Entries indicate the number of members and the primary functions of each.

2. *Library Schools and Training Courses* includes a variety of college, and university library science programs. Entries include entrance requirements, tuition, type of training, degrees and hours offered, and special courses offered. A dagger icon (†) indicates a program accredited by the American Library Association Committee on Accreditation.

3. *Library Systems* provides a listing of all state and provincial library systems as provided directly by those authorities. A brief statement indicating system functions within the state or province precedes the alphabetically arranged list of the state or

province's systems. Cities are also included so that the user can locate a system's entry in the Library Section of the directory, or in cases where the state is followed by (N), in the Network Section of the directory.

4. *Libraries for the Blind and Physically Handicapped* provides a listing of all libraries designated by the National Library Service for the Blind and Physically Handicapped as regional and sub-regional libraries serving print handicapped patrons. It also includes other specialty libraries and those with a significant amount of specialized equipment and/or services in these areas.

5. *Libraries Serving the Deaf and Hearing Impaired* provides a similar listing of all libraries that have a significant commitment to patrons who are deaf or hearing impaired as evidenced by the specialized equipment and services they have available. The list is arranged by state and then by library name. The city is included so the user can find the entry in the Library Section and determine the specialized services by reading the paragraph "Special Services for the Deaf" included in the library's entry.

6. *State and Provincial Public Library Agencies* indicates name, address, person-in-charge, and telephone number of the state agency that is responsible for public libraries.

7. *State School Library Agencies* indicates the same information for the state agency that is responsible for elementary and high school programs.

8. The *Interlibrary Loan Code for the United States* is reprinted with the kind permission of the American Library Association.

9. The *Organization Index* provides an alphabetical listing of all libraries, schools, and networks with the page number reference.

10. The *Personnel Index* is an alphabetical listing of individuals who are included within entries for libraries, consortia, and library schools. Entries include name, title, organization, location, and page number reference.

RELATED SERVICES

American Library Directory is also available online at **www.americanlibrarydirectory.com**. You can search and identify all libraries that meet certain specialty criteria such as legal, medical, religious, etc. You can also search by geographic criteria, vendors, holdings, staff size, expenditures, income, and more with a single search. We invite you to visit the site and take advantage of our free trial offer.

The editors and researchers have made every effort to include all material submitted as accurately and completely as possible within the confines of format and scope. However, the publishers do not assume and hereby disclaim any liability to any party for any loss or damage caused by errors or omissions in the *American Library Directory* whether such errors and omissions resulted from negligence, accident, or any other cause. In the event of a publication error, the sole responsibility of the publisher will be the entry of corrected information in succeeding editions.

ACKNOWLEDGEMENTS

The editors wish to thank all of those who responded to our requests for information; without their efforts, the *American Library Directory* could not be published.

The editors also wish to express their appreciation for the cooperation of the officers of the state, regional, and provincial libraries who have provided statistics and other information concerning libraries in their jurisdictions.

Return this form by e-mail or mail to:

aldsupport@infotoday.com

Information Today, Inc.

American Library Directory
121 Chanlon Road
New Providence, NJ 07974-2195

AMERICAN LIBRARY DIRECTORY EDITORIAL REVISION FORM

☐ Please check here if you are nominating this library for a new listing in the directory

☐ Please check if this library is already listed

Library Name: ____________________

Address: ____________________

City: ____________ State or Province: ________ Postal Code: ________

E-Mail: ____________ Web Site: ____________

Phone: ____________ Fax: ____________

Brief Description of Library: ____________________

Personnel

☐ Addition ☐ Deletion ☐ Correction

First Name: ________ Last Name: ________ Title: ________

☐ Addition ☐ Deletion ☐ Correction

First Name: ________ Last Name: ________ Title: ________

☐ Addition ☐ Deletion ☐ Correction

First Name: ________ Last Name: ________ Title: ________

(Continued on back)

Other Information

Indicate other information to be added to or corrected in this listing. Please be as specific as possible, noting erroneous data to be corrected or deleted.

____

____

____

____

____

____

____

Verification

Data for this listing will not be updated without the following information.

Your Name: ____________________ Your Title: ____________________

Organization Name: ____________________

Address: ____________________

City: ____________ State or Province: ____________ Postal Code: ____________

E-Mail: ____________________ Web Site: ____________________

Indicate if you are a: ☐ Representative of this organization ☐ User of this directory ☐ Other

If other, please specify: ____________________

Thank you for helping Information Today, Inc. maintain the most up-to-date information available.

SAMPLE ENTRY

(fictional)

[1]**P** [2]McNeil & Foster, [3]Prescott Memorial Library, [4]500 Terra Cotta Dr, 85005-3126. [5]SAN 360-9070. [6]Tel: 602-839-9108. Toll Free Tel: 800-625-3848. FAX: 602-839-2020. TDD: 602-839-9202. E-mail: mcneilfoster@prescott.org. Web Site: www.prescottlib.com. [7]*Dir* Michelle Trozzo; Tel: 602-839-5522; *Asst Dir* Brie Goodwin; *Tech Serv* Nina Silva; *Pub Servs* Katie Joyce; *Circ* Chris Joyce; *Children's Resources* Bobby Joyce. Subject Specialists: *Bus* Axel Abraham; *Fashion* Meg Trozzo; *Folklore* Ryan Joyce; *Paleontology* Casey Joyce; *Public Health* Mike Joyce; *Sports* Billy Goodwin; *Theology* Jessie Joyce.

[8]Staff 20 (MLS 15, Non-MLS 5)

[9]Founded 1903. Pop served 92,540; Circ 210,000

[10]July 2024-Jun 2025 Income (Main Library and Branch(es)) $750,500, State $600,000, City $150,500. Mats Exp $118,400, Books $53,400, Per/Ser (Incl. Access Fees) $60,000, Micro $2,000, AV Equip $3,000. Sal $53,000 (Prof $44,000)

[11]**Library Holdings:** Bk Vols 90,000; Bk Titles 87,000; Per subs 145

[12]**Special Collections:** Local History (Lehi College)

[13]**Subject Interests:** Child psychology, genetics

[14]**Automation Activity & Vendor Info:** (Acquisitions) Innovative Interfaces Inc.; (Cataloging) Innovative Interfaces Inc.; (Circulation) Gaylord

[15]Wireless access

[16]Mem of Southwestern Library System

[17]Partic in Amigos Library Services, Inc.; Library Interchange Network (LINK)

[18]Special Services for the Deaf-TDD. Staff member who knows sign language; projector & captioned films

[19]Friends of Library Group

[20]**Bookmobiles:** 1

[21]**Branches:** 1

EASTSIDE, 9807 Post St, 85007-3184. SAN 360-9083. Tel 602-839-9178; *Librn* Emily Trozzo; *Asst Librn* Andrew Trozzo.

Library Holdings: Bk Vols 23,000

1. Classification key (see "Arrangement & Coverage" in the Preface for explanation).
2. Official library name.
3. Other name by which library may be known.
4. Address.
5. SAN (Standard Address Number).
6. Communication information.
7. Personnel.
8. Number and professional status of staff.
9. Library background—Data on enrollment and the highest degree offered are included for academic libraries.
10. Income figures—Library income is broken down by source when reported.
    Expenditure figures—Material expenditure figures are requested for AV equipment, books, electronic reference materials (including access fees), manuscripts and archives, microforms, other print materials, periodicals/serials (including access fees), and preservation. In addition, salary figures are broken down by professional status when given.
11. Library holdings.
12. Special collections.
13. Subject interests.
14. Automation activity and vendor.
15. Library with wireless access.
16. Library system to which the library belongs.
17. Networks in which the library participates.
18. Special services.
19. Friends of Library Group.
20. Bookmobiles.
21. Branches (or departmental libraries for academic libraries)—Entries include library name, address, name of librarian, and number of book volumes. Branch libraries are listed under the library of which they are a part.

LIBRARY COUNT

Provided here are totals for major types of libraries in the United States and Canada. Included are counts for public, academic, armed forces, government, and special libraries. Excluded from the counts are branch, departmental, and divisional libraries not listed with a full address in the directory. Some categories, such as academic, provide counts for specialized libraries such as law or medical libraries. As counts for only certain types of libraries are given, these subcategories do not add up to the total count for each type of library.

PUBLIC—Each public library is counted once and then each branch is counted separately. Because the organization of systems varies from state to state, the method of counting these libraries varies also. In some cases, the libraries forming the systems were designated as member libraries, while in others they were given as branch libraries. In yet other instances, systems maintain branches as well as member libraries. If listed in this directory as a branch, the library was recorded in the branch count; however, member libraries were counted independently and recorded in the number of public libraries. Special public libraries are also included in the Total Special Libraries count.

ACADEMIC—The figure for academic libraries includes all libraries listed in the directory as part of academic institutions, whether they are main, departmental, or special. Specialized libraries and library departments at these colleges, such as law, medical, religious, or science libraries, are also counted in the Total Special Libraries figure.

GOVERNMENT and ARMED FORCES—Counts include all government and armed forces-related libraries listed in the directory, including specialized ones. Those libraries that are also defined as special libraries are included in the Total Special Libraries figure.

SPECIAL—The special libraries count includes only specialized libraries that are not public, academic, armed forces, or government institutions. The Total Special Libraries count includes all law, medical, religious, business, and other special libraries found in the *American Library Directory* regardless of who operates them.

LIBRARIES IN THE UNITED STATES

A. **PUBLIC LIBRARIES**....*16,979
- Public Libraries, excluding Branches....9,645
  - Main Public Libraries that have branches....1,442
- Public Library Branches....7,334

B. **ACADEMIC LIBRARIES**....*3,467
- Community College Libraries....1,087
  - Departmental....274
  - Medical....5
  - Religious....5
- University & College....2,380
  - Departmental....1,103
  - Law....187
  - Medical....236
  - Religious....246

C. **ARMED FORCES LIBRARIES**....*221
- Air Force....62
  - Medical....3
- Army....102
  - Medical....21
- Marine....12
- Navy....45
  - Law....1
  - Medical....8

D. **GOVERNMENT LIBRARIES**....*796
- Law....344
- Medical....92

E. **SPECIAL LIBRARIES** (Excluding Public, Academic, Armed Forces, and Government)....*3,976
- Law....555
- Medical....668
- Religious....317

F. **TOTAL SPECIAL LIBRARIES** (Including Public, Academic, Armed Forces, and Government)....5,123
- Total Law....1,087
- Total Medical....1,032
- Total Religious....716

G. **TOTAL LIBRARIES COUNTED (*)**....25,439

LIBRARIES IN REGIONS ADMINISTERED BY THE UNITED STATES

A. **PUBLIC LIBRARIES**...*16
Public Libraries, excluding Branches.................................8
Main Public Libraries that have branches..............3
Public Library Branches...8

B. **ACADEMIC LIBRARIES**..*38
Community College Libraries...3
Departmental...1
University & College...35
Departmental...18
Law..3
Medical...3
Religious..1

C. **ARMED FORCES LIBRARIES**..*2
Air Force...1
Army..1

D. **GOVERNMENT LIBRARIES**...*3
Law..1
Medical..1

E. **SPECIAL LIBRARIES** (Excluding Public, Academic, Armed Forces, and Government)..................................*4
Law...3
Religious..1

F. **TOTAL SPECIAL LIBRARIES** (Including Public, Academic, Armed Forces, and Government)...................13
Total Law...7
Total Medical..4
Total Religious..2

G. **TOTAL LIBRARIES COUNTED (*)**.................................63

LIBRARIES IN CANADA

A. **PUBLIC LIBRARIES**...*2,218
Public Libraries, excluding Branches.............................793
Main Public Libraries that have branches.............160
Public Library Branches...1,425

B. **ACADEMIC LIBRARIES**...*315
Community College Libraries..74
Departmental...14
Religious..1
University & College..241
Departmental...176
Law..16
Medical..11
Religious..32

C. **GOVERNMENT LIBRARIES**.....................................*141
Law...24
Medical..3

D. **SPECIAL LIBRARIES** (Excluding Public, Academic, Armed Forces, and Government)...............................*467
Law...79
Medical...110
Religious..19

E. **TOTAL SPECIAL LIBRARIES** (Including Public, Academic, Armed Forces, and Government)...........554
Total Law...119
Total Medical...124
Total Religious...64

F. **TOTAL LIBRARIES COUNTED (*)**.........................3,141

SUMMARY

TOTAL UNITED STATES LIBRARIES...............25,439

TOTAL LIBRARIES ADMINISTERED BY THE UNITED STATES..................................63

TOTAL CANADIAN LIBRARIES..........................3,141

GRAND TOTAL OF LIBRARIES LISTED............28,643

Library Award Recipients 2024

Listed below are major awards given to libraries and librarians in the calendar year 2023. These entries were selected from the more inclusive list of scholarships and grant awards found in the *Library and Book Trade Almanac*, 70th edition (Information Today, Inc., 2025). Included here are awards for outstanding librarianship or service, development grants, and research projects larger than an essay or monograph. Awards are listed alphabetically by organization.

American Association of School Librarians (AASL)

AASL/ABC-CLIO Leadership Grant (up to $1,750). To AASL affiliates for planning and implementing leadership programs at state, regional, or local levels. Donor: ABC-CLIO. Winner: Washington Library Association School Library Division.

AASL Chapter of the Year ($1,000). In recognition of the AASL Chapter most active and dynamic in achieving the goals of AASL at the state and local level. Winner: Not awarded in 2024.

AASL/Frances Henne Award ($1,250). To a school library media specialist with five or fewer years in the profession to attend an AASL regional conference or ALA Annual Conference for the first time. Donor: Libraries Unlimited. Winner: Gabriela Gualano, Paul Revere Middle School, Los Angeles, California.

AASL Innovative Reading Grant ($2,500). To support the planning and implementation of an innovative program for children that motivates and encourages reading, especially for struggling readers. Sponsor: Capstone. Winner: Wendy Gassaway, Alder Elementary School, Portland, Oregon.

AASL President's Crystal Apple Award. To an individual, individuals, or group for a significant impact on school libraries and students. Winners: All school librarians.

American Library Association (ALA)

ALA/INFORMATION TODAY, INC. LIBRARY OF THE FUTURE AWARD ($1,500). For innovative planning for, applications of, or development of patron training programs about information technology in a library setting. Donors: Information Today, Inc., and IIDA. Winner: Las Vegas-Clark County (Nevada) Library District for "Free to Be Connected," incorporating three programs to support underserved communities: Free high-speed Wi-Fi for households in southern Nevada; book vending machines, which provide 235 books in English and Spanish for all ages and reading levels to bilingual speakers of Las Vegas's Hispanic communities; and Hope for Prisoners Family Libraries, a program that facilitates educational support for the formerly incarcerated reentering society.

JULIA J. BRODY PUBLIC LIBRARIAN SCHOLARSHIP ($4,000). To a U.S. or Canadian citizen or permanent resident who is pursuing an MLS specializing public library services in an ALA-accredited program. Winner: Ana Soledad Santoyo.

DAVID H. CLIFT SCHOLARSHIP ($3,000). To worthy U.S. or Canadian citizens enrolled in an ALA-accredited program toward an MLS degree. Winner: Kara Jane Halden.

EQUALITY AWARD ($1,000). To an individual or group for an outstanding contribution that promotes equality in the library profession. Donor: Rowman & Littlefield. Winner: Felton Thomas Jr.

ELIZABETH FUTAS CATALYST FOR CHANGE AWARD ($1,000). A biennial award to recognize a librarian who invests time and talent to make positive change in the profession of librarianship. Donor: Elizabeth Futas Memorial Fund. Winner (2024): Not awarded in 2024.

MARY V. GAVER SCHOLARSHIP ($3,000). To a student pursuing an MLS degree and specializing in youth services. Winner: Sydney Keith.

MIRIAM L. HORNBACK SCHOLARSHIP ($3,000). To an ALA or library support staff person pursuing a master's degree in library science. Winner: Tyler Brady.

TONY B. LEISNER SCHOLARSHIP ($3,000). To a library support staff member pursuing a master's degree. Donor: Tony B. Leisner. Winner: Myla Grace Corn.

LEMONY SNICKET PRIZE FOR NOBLE LIBRARIANS FACED WITH ADVERSITY ($3,000 plus a $1,000 travel stipend to enable attendance at the ALA Annual Conference). To honor a librarian who has faced adversity with integrity and dignity intact. Sponsor: Lemony Snicket (author Daniel Handler). Winner: Patty Hector, former director of the Saline County Library, Benton, Arkansas.

JOSEPH W. LIPPINCOTT AWARD ($1,500). For distinguished service to the library profession. Donor: Joseph W. Lippincott III. Winner: Nicole A. Cooke.

SCHOLASTIC LIBRARY PUBLISHING AWARD ($1,000). To a librarian whose "unusual contributions to the stimulation and guidance of reading by children and young people exemplifies achievement in the profession." Sponsor: Scholastic Library Publishing. Winner: Rose Brock.

SULLIVAN AWARD FOR PUBLIC LIBRARY ADMINISTRATORS SUPPORTING SERVICES TO CHILDREN. To a library supervisor/administrator who has shown exceptional understanding and support of public library services to children. Donor: Peggy Sullivan. Winner: Susan Spicer, early learning program manager, Salt Lake County (Utah) Library.

Association for Library Service to Children (ALSC)

ALSC/BAKER & TAYLOR SUMMER READING PROGRAM GRANT ($3,000). For implementation of an outstanding public library summer reading program for children. Donor: Baker & Taylor. Winner: Hutchinson Memorial Library, Randolph, Wisconsin.

ALSC/CANDLEWICK PRESS "LIGHT THE WAY: LIBRARY OUTREACH TO THE UNDERSERVED" GRANT ($3,000). To a library conducting exemplary outreach to underserved populations. Donor: Candlewick Press. Winner: Kenosha (Wisconsin) Public Library.

Black Caucus of the American Library Association (BCALA)

BCALA TRAILBLAZERS AWARD. Presented once every five years in recognition of outstanding and unique contributions to librarianship. Winner (2021): Shirley A. Coaston.

CORE: Leadership, Infrastructure, Futures

JOHN COTTON DANA LIBRARY PUBLIC RELATIONS AWARDS ($10,000). To libraries or library organizations of all types for public relations programs or special projects ended during the preceding year. Donors: H. W. Wilson Foundation and EBSCO. Winners: Anchorage (Alaska) Public Library; Barrie (Ontario, Canada) Public Library; Curtis Memorial Library, Brunswick, Maine; Orange County (Florida) Library System; Richmond Hill (Ontario, Canada) Public Library; Salt Lake County (Utah) Library; Spokane (Washington) Public Library; Tacoma (Washington) Public Library.

CHRISTIAN LAREW MEMORIAL SCHOLARSHIP IN LIBRARY AND INFORMATION TECHNOLOGY ($3,000). Provides tuition help for library school students to follow a career in the library and information technology field. Winner: Madison Leigh Comer.

MARGARET MANN CITATION (includes $2,000 scholarship award to the U.S. or Canadian library school of the winner's choice). To a cataloger or classifier for achievement in the areas of cataloging or classification. Donor: Online Computer Library Center (OCLC). Winner: Robert L. Maxwell.

Ethnic and Multicultural Information and Exchange Round Table (EMIERT)

DAVID COHEN MULTICULTURAL AWARD ($300). A biennial award to recognize articles of significant research and publication that increase understanding and promote multiculturalism in North American libraries. Donor: Routledge. Winner (2024): Lisely Laboy, Dr. Rachael Elrod, Dr. Krista Aronson, and Brittany Kester.

Exhibits Round Table (ERT)

Christopher J. Hoy/ERT Scholarship ($5,000). To an individual or individuals who will work toward an MLS degree in an ALA-accredited program. Donor: Family of Christopher Hoy. Winner: Sarah Smith.

Freedom to Read Foundation

FREEDOM TO READ FOUNDATION GORDON M. CONABLE CONFERENCE SCHOLARSHIP. To enable a library school student or new professional to attend the ALA Annual Conference. Winners: Etana Laing and Tif Sutherland.

JUDITH KRUG FUND BANNED BOOKS WEEK EVENT GRANTS ($1,000 to $2,500). To support activities that raise awareness of intellectual freedom and censorship issues during the annual Banned Books Week celebration. Winners: Keller ISD Families for Public Education, Fort Worth, Texas; Georgia Southern University, Sa-vannah, Georgia; George Washington High School, Philadelphia, Pennsylvania; North Bergen (New Jersey) Free Public Library.

Reference and User Services Association (RUSA)

AWARD FOR EXCELLENCE IN REFERENCE AND ADULT LIBRARY SERVICES ($1,500). To recognize a library or library system for developing an imaginative and unique library resource to meet patrons' reference needs. Donor: Data Axle. Winner: Addison (Illinois) Public Library.

Federal Achievement Award. For achievement in the promotion of library and information service and the information profession in the federal community. Winners: Paula Laurita and D. Lynne Rickard.

MARGARET E. MONROE LIBRARY ADULT LIBRARY SERVICES AWARD ($1,250). To a librarian for his or her impact on library service to adults. Donor: NoveList. Winner: Not awarded in 2024.

ISADORE GILBERT MUDGE AWARD ($5,000). For distinguished contributions to reference librarianship. Donor: Credo Reference. Winner: Meg Smith, Physical Sciences Librarian and Head of Science Research Services at the New York University Division of Libraries.

KEY TO SYMBOLS AND ABBREVIATIONS

KEY TO SYMBOLS

A - Armed Forces libraries
C - College and University libraries
E - Electronic libraries
G - Government libraries
J - Community College libraries
L - Law libraries
M - Medical libraries
P - Public and State libraries
R - Religious libraries
S - Special libraries
* - No response received directly from the library; data gathered from other sources
§ - New library and/or listed for the first time
† - Library school program accredited by the American Library Association Committee on Accreditation

KEY TO ABBREVIATIONS

A-tapes - Audio Tapes
Acad - Academic, Academy
Acctg - Accounting
Acq - Acquisition Librarian, Acquisitions
Actg - Acting
Ad - Adult Services Librarian
Add - Address
Admin - Administration, Administrative
Adminr - Administrator
Adv - Adviser, Advisor, Advisory
Advan - Advanced, Advancement
Aeronaut - Aeronautics
AFB - Air Force Base
Agr - Agricultural, Agriculture
Ala - Alabama
Alta - Alberta
Am - America, American
Ann - Annual, Annually
Anthrop - Anthropology
APO - Air Force Post Office, Army Post Office
Approp - Appropriation
Approx - Approximate, Approximately
Appt - Appointment
Archaeol - Archaeology
Archit - Architecture
Ariz - Arizona
Ark - Arkansas
Asn - Association
Assoc - Associate
Asst - Assistant
AV - Audiovisual, Audiovisual Materials
Ave - Avenue
BC - British Columbia
Bd - Binding, Bound
Behav - Behaviorial
Bibliog - Bibliographic, Bibliographical, Bibliography
Bibliogr - Bibliographer
Biog - Biographer, Biographical, Biography
Biol - Biology
Bk(s) - Book(s)
Bkmobile - Bookmobile
Bldg - Building
Blvd - Boulevard
Bot - Botany
Br - Branch, Branches
Bro - Brother
Bur - Bureau
Bus - Business
Calif - California
Can - Canada, Canadian
Cap - Capital
Cat(s) - Cataloging Librarian, Cataloging, Catalog(s)
Cent - Central
Ch - Children, Children's Librarian, Children's Services
Chem - Chemical, Chemistry
Chmn - Chairman
Cht(s) - Chart(s)
Circ - Circulation
Cler - Clerical Staff
Co - Company
Col - College
Coll - Collection, Collections
Colo - Colorado
Commun - Community
Comn - Commission
Comt - Committee
Conn - Connecticut
Conserv - Conservation
Consult - Consultant
Coop - Cooperates, Cooperating, Cooperation, Cooperative
Coord - Coordinating
Coordr - Coordinator
Corp - Corporation
Coun - Council
CP - Case Postale
Ct - Court
Ctr - Center, Centre
Curric - Curriculum
DC - District of Columbia
Del - Delaware
Den - Denominational
Dent - Dentristry
Dep - Deputy, Depository
Dept - Department
Develop - Development
Dir - Director
Div - Division
Doc - Document, Documents
Dr - Doctor, Drive
E - East
Econ - Economic
Ed - Edited, Edition, Editor
Educ - Education, Educational
Elem - Elementary
Eng - Engineering
Enrl - Enrollment
Ent - Entrance
Environ - Environmental
Equip - Equipment
Est - Estimate, Estimation
Estab - Established
Excl - Excluding
Exec - Executive
Exp - Expenditure
Ext - Extension of Telephone
Fac - Faculty, Facilities
Fed - Federal
Fedn - Federation
Fel - Fellowship
Fla - Florida
Flr - Floor
Found - Foundation
FPO - Fleet Post Office
Fr - French
Ft - Fort
FT - Full Time

FTE - Full Time Equivalent
Ga - Georgia
Gen - General, Generated
Geog - Geographical, Geography
Geol - Geological, Geology
Govt - Government
Grad - Graduate
Hist - Historical, History
Hort - Horticulture
Hq - Headquarters
Hrs - Hours
Hwy - Highway, Highways
Hydrol - Hydrology
Ill - Illinois
ILL - Interlibrary Loan
Illustr - Illustrator, Illustration
Inc - Income, Incorporated
Incl - Including
Ind - Indiana
Indust - Industrial, Industry
Info - Information
Ins - Insurance
Inst - Institute, Institutions
Instrul - Instructional
Instr - Instructor
Intl - International
Jr - Junior
Juv - Juvenile
Kans - Kansas
Ky - Kentucky
La - Louisiana
Lab - Laboratories, Laboratory
Lang(s) - Language(s)
Lectr - Lecturer
Legis - Legislative, Legislature
Libr - Libraries, Library
Librn - Librarian
Lit - Literary, Literature
Ltd - Limited
Mag(s) - Magazine(s)
Man - Manitoba
Mass - Massachusetts
Mat(s) - Material(s)
Math - Mathematical, Mathematics
Md - Maryland
Med - Medical, Medicine
Media - Media Specialist
Mem - Member
Metaphys - Metaphysical, Metaphysics
Metrop - Metropolitan
Mgr - Manager, Managerial
Mgt - Management
Mich - Michigan
Micro - Microform
Mil - Military
Misc - Miscellaneous
Miss - Mississippi
Minn - Minnesota
Mkt - Marketing
Mo - Missouri
Ms - Manuscript, Manuscripts
Mus - Museum
N - North
NASA - National Aeronautics & Space Administration
Nat - National
NB - New Brunswick
NC - North Carolina
NDak - North Dakota
NE - Northeast, Northeastern
Nebr - Nebraska
Nev - Nevada
New Eng - New England
Newsp - Newspaper, Newspapers
Nfld - Newfoundland
NH - New Hampshire
NJ - New Jersey
NMex - New Mexico
Nonfict - nonfiction
NS - Nova Scotia
NW - Northwest, Northwestern
NY - New York
Oceanog - Oceanography
Off - Office
Okla - Oklahoma
Ont - Ontario
OPAC - Open Public Access Catalog
Ore - Oregon
Ornith - Ornithology
Pa - Pennsylvania
Pac - Pacific
Partic - Participant, Participates
Per(s) - Periodical(s)
Pharm - Pharmacy
Philos - Philosophical, Philosophy
Photog - Photograph, Photography
Phys - Physical
Pkwy - Parkway
Pl - Place
PO - Post Office
Polit Sci - Political Science
Pop - Population
PR - Puerto Rico
Prep - Preparation, Preparatory
Pres - President, Presidents
Presv - Preservation
Proc - Process, Processing
Prof - Professional, Professor
Prog - Program, Programming
Prov - Province, Provincial
Psychiat - Psychiatrist, Psychiatry, Psychiatric
Psychol - Psychological, Psychology
PT - Part Time
Pub - Public
Pub Rel - Public Relations Head
Publ(s) - Publisher, Publishing, Publication(s)
Pvt - Private
Qtr - Quarter
Que - Quebec
R&D - Research & Development
Rd - Road
Read - Readable
Rec - Record, Recording, Records
Ref - Reference
Relig - Religion, Religious
Rep - Representative
Reprod - Reproduction
Req - Requirement
Res - Research, Resource, Resources
RI - Rhode Island
Rm - Room
Rpt(s) - Report(s)
RR - Rural Route
Rte - Route
S - South
Sal - Salary
SAN - Standard Address Number
Sask - Saskatchewan
SC - South Carolina
Sch - School
Sci - Science, Scientific
Sci Fict - Science Fiction
SDak - South Dakota
SE - Southeast, Southeastern
Secy - Secretary
Sem - Semester, Seminary
Ser - Serials, Serials Librarian
Serv(s) - Service(s)
Soc - Social, Society, Societies
Sociol - Sociology
Spec - Special, Specialist
Sq - Square
Sr - Senor, Senior, Sister
St - Saint, Street
Sta - Station
Sub(s) - Subscription(s)
Subj - Subject, Subjects
Sup - Supplies
Supv - Supervising, Supervision
Supvr - Supervisor
Supvry - Supervisory
SW - Southwest, Southwestern
Syst - System, Systems
TDD - Telecomm. Device for the Deaf
Tech - Technical, Technician, Technology
Tel - Telephone
Tenn - Tennessee
Tex - Texas
Theol - Theological, Theology
Tpk - Turnpike
Treas - Treasurer
TTY - Teletypewriter
TV - Television
UN - United Nations
Undergrad - Undergraduate
Univ - University
US - United States
VPres -Vice President
V-tapes - Video Tapes
Va - Virginia
Vet - Veteran
VF - Vertical Files
VI - Virgin Islands
Vis - Visiting
Vols - Volumes, Volunteers
Vt - Vermont
W - West
Wash - Washington
Wis - Wisconsin
WVa - West Virginia
Wyo - Wyoming
YA - Young Adult Librarian, Young Adult Services
Zool - Zoology

78TH EDITION

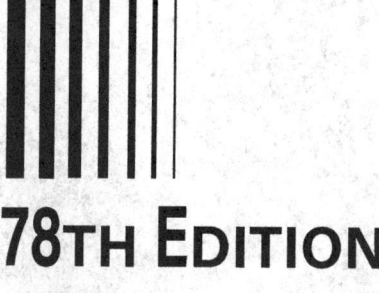

AMERICAN LIBRARY DIRECTORY™

2025-2026

RHODE ISLAND

Date of Statistics: FY 2024
Population, 2020 U.S. Census: 1,097,379
Population Served by Public Libraries: 1,097,379
Total Volumes in Public Libraries: 3,719,611
Total Public Library Circulation: 6,169,737
Digital Resources:
Total e-books: 221,676
Total audio items (physical and downloadable units): 201,201
Total video items (physical and downloadable units): 283,473
Total computers for use by the public: 1,397
Total annual wireless sessions: 1,082,129
Income and Expenditures:
Grants-in-Aid to Public Libraries:
Expenditure: $10,281,019
Construction: $1,909,317
Number of Bookmobiles in State: 1
Information provided courtesy of: Kelly Metzger, State Data Coordinator; Rhode Island Office of Library & Information Services

ASHAWAY

P ASHAWAY FREE LIBRARY*, 15 Knight St, 02804-1410. (Mail add: PO Box 70, 02804-0002), SAN 315-3924. Tel: 401-377-2770. FAX: 401-377-2770. Web Site: ashawaylibrary.org. *Dir,* Heather Field; E-mail: director@ashawaylibrary.org; Staff 1.8 (MLS 0.8, Non-MLS 1)
Founded 1907. Pop 3,500; Circ 25,225
Library Holdings: Audiobooks 216; CDs 305; DVDs 730; Large Print Bks 369; Bk Vols 23,103; Per Subs 41
Subject Interests: Fishing, Local hist
Wireless access
Function: Electronic databases & coll, ILL available, Mail & tel request accepted, Music CDs, Photocopying/Printing, Prog for adults, Prog for children & young adult, Summer reading prog, Tax forms, VHS videos
Partic in Library of Rhode Island Network; Ocean State Libraries
Open Mon & Fri 10-5, Tues & Thurs 4-8, Wed 10-8, Sat 9-1

BARRINGTON

P BARRINGTON PUBLIC LIBRARY*, 281 County Rd, 02806. SAN 315-3940. Tel: 401-247-1920. FAX: 401-247-3763. E-mail: information@barringtonlibrary.org. Web Site: www.barringtonlibrary.org. *Libr Dir,* Kristen Chin; E-mail: director@barringtonlibrary.org; *Asst Libr Dir,* Doug Swiscz; E-mail: doug@barringtonlibrary.org; *Head, Children's Servx,* Lisa Lesinski; E-mail: llesinski@barringtonlibrary.org; *Head, Info Serv,* Ben Hanley; E-mail: bhanley@barringtonlibrary.org; *Commun Engagement Librn,* Siobhan Egan; E-mail: segan@barringtonlibrary.org; *YA Librn,* Tanya Paglia; E-mail: tanya@barringtonlibrary.org; *Tech Coordr,* Patrick Elliot; E-mail: pelliot@barringtonlibrary.org; Staff 20 (MLS 6, Non-MLS 14)
Founded 1880. Circ 216,839
Library Holdings: AV Mats 9,137; Bk Vols 106,876; Per Subs 150
Automation Activity & Vendor Info: (Circulation) Innovative Interfaces, Inc
Publications: Calendar of Events (Monthly)
Partic in Library of Rhode Island Network
Open Mon-Thurs 9-9, Fri & Sat 9-4:30
Friends of the Library Group

BLOCK ISLAND

P ISLAND FREE LIBRARY*, Nine Dodge St, 02807. (Mail add: PO Box 1830, 02807-1830). Tel: 401-466-3233. FAX: 401-466-3236. E-mail: circ@islandfreelibrary.org. Web Site: www.islandfreelibrary.org. *Dir,* Kristin J Baumann; E-mail: kbaumann@islandfreelibrary.org; *Archives Librn, Tech Serv Librn,* Susan Gardner; Staff 1 (MLS 1)
Founded 1875. Circ 10,412
Library Holdings: Bk Vols 28,532; Per Subs 130
Subject Interests: Natural hist
Automation Activity & Vendor Info: (Acquisitions) SirsiDynix; (Cataloging) SirsiDynix; (Circulation) SirsiDynix; (Course Reserve) SirsiDynix; (ILL) SirsiDynix; (Media Booking) SirsiDynix; (OPAC) SirsiDynix; (Serials) SirsiDynix
Wireless access
Partic in Library of Rhode Island Network; Ocean State Libraries
Open Tues 11-7, Wed-Fri 10-5, Sat 10-3
Friends of the Library Group

BRISTOL

S BRISTOL HISTORICAL & PRESERVATION SOCIETY LIBRARY*, 48 Court St, 02809. (Mail add: PO Box 356, 02809-0356), SAN 372-9311. Tel: 401-253-7223. E-mail: info@bhps.necoxmail.com. Web Site: www.bhpsri.org/Library.html. *Curator, Librn,* Ray Battcher; E-mail: ray@bhps.necoxmail.com
Founded 1936
Library Holdings: Bk Vols 2,500
Restriction: Open by appt only

CL ROGER WILLIAMS UNIVERSITY*, School of Law Library, Ten Metacom Ave, 02809-5171. Tel: 401-254-4546. Interlibrary Loan Service Tel: 401-254-4537. Reference Tel: 401-254-4547. Administration Tel: 401-254-4530. FAX: 401-254-4543. E-mail: lawlibraryhelp@rwu.edu. Web Site: law.rwu.edu/library. *Asst Dean, Libr & Info Serv,* Raquel Ortiz; Tel: 401-254-4530, E-mail: rortiz@rwu.edu; *Head of Reference, Instruction & Engagement,* Nicole Dyszlewski; E-mail: ndyszlewski@rwu.edu; *Cataloging, Metadata & Archives Librn,* Kathleen MacAndrew; E-mail: kmacandrew@rwu.edu; *Assoc Law Librn,* Lucinda Harrison-Cox; E-mail: lharrison-cox@rwu.edu; *Asst Law Librarian, Collection Servs,* Artie W Berns; E-mail: aberns@rwu.edu; *Access Serv Coordr,* Erin Orsini; E-mail: eorsini@rwu.edu; *Faculty & Digital Services Asst,* Jessica L Silvia; E-mail: jsilvia@rwu.edu; Staff 7 (MLS 7)
Founded 1993. Enrl 550; Fac 60; Highest Degree: Doctorate
Library Holdings: AV Mats 580; CDs 384; DVDs 80; e-books 22,000; Microforms 1,084,369; Bk Titles 29,855; Bk Vols 115,397; Per Subs 3,365
Subject Interests: Law
Automation Activity & Vendor Info: (Acquisitions) Innovative Interfaces, Inc - Millennium; (Cataloging) Innovative Interfaces, Inc - Millennium; (Circulation) Innovative Interfaces, Inc - Millennium; (ILL) OCLC Connexion; (OPAC) Innovative Interfaces, Inc - Millennium; (Serials) Innovative Interfaces, Inc - Millennium
Wireless access
Publications: Legal Beagle Blog (Newsletter); Recent Acquisitions (Acquisition list); Rhode Island Bar Journal Index (Index to periodicals); TimeSavers Series (Research guide)
Partic in Consortium of Rhode Island Academic & Research Libraries; Library of Rhode Island Network; LYRASIS; NELLCO Law Library Consortium, Inc.
Open Mon-Thurs 7:30am-11pm, Fri 7:30-4:30, Sat 9-6, Sun 9am-11pm

C ROGER WILLIAMS UNIVERSITY LIBRARY*, One Old Ferry Rd, 02809. SAN 315-3975. Tel: 401-254-3031. Reference Tel: 401-254-3375. Toll Free Tel: 800-458-7144. FAX: 401-254-3631. Reference E-mail: libref@rwu.edu. Web Site: rwu.edu/library. *Dean, Univ Libr Serv,* Elizabeth Peck Learned; Tel: 401-254-3625, E-mail: elearned@rwu.edu;

Prog Dir, Adam Braver; Tel: 401-254-3720, E-mail: abraver@rwu.edu; *Libr Operations Mgr,* Thelma Dzialo; Tel: 401-254-3063, E-mail: tdzialo@rwu.edu; *Archit/Art Librn,* John Schlinke; Tel: 401-254-3833, E-mail: jschlinke@rwu.edu; *Coll Mgt Librn,* Position Currently Open; *Digital Scholarship & Metadata Librn,* Mary Wu; Tel: 401-254-3053, E-mail: mwu@rwu.edu; *Electronic Res Librn,* John Fobert; Tel: 401-254-3374, E-mail: jfobert@rwu.edu; *Instrul Serv & Campus Initiatives Librn,* Position Currently Open; *Res Serv & User Engagement Librn,* Susan McMullen; Tel: 401-254-3086, E-mail: smcmullen@rwu.edu; *Scholarly Communications Librn,* Lindsey Gumb; Tel: 401-243-3225, E-mail: lgumb@rwu.edu; *Circ Coordr, ILL,* Adam Riccitelli; Tel: 401-254-3458, E-mail: ariccitelli@rwu.edu; *Univ Archivist,* Heidi Benedict; Tel: 401-254-3049, E-mail: hbenedict@rwu.edu; *Web & Digital Spec,* Christopher Truszkowski; Tel: 401-254-5548, E-mail: ctruszkowski@rwu.edu. Subject Specialists: *Archit,* John Schlinke; Staff 10 (MLS 8, Non-MLS 2)
Founded 1946. Enrl 3,800; Fac 5; Highest Degree: Master
Library Holdings: e-books 535,186; Bk Vols 219,232; Per Subs 267,877
Special Collections: Roger Williams Family Association Papers; United States Census Coll. US Document Depository
Subject Interests: British hist, Marine biol, Poetry, Psychol, RI hist
Automation Activity & Vendor Info: (Acquisitions) OCLC Worldshare Management Services; (Cataloging) OCLC Worldshare Management Services; (Circulation) OCLC Worldshare Management Services; (Course Reserve) OCLC Worldshare Management Services; (Discovery) OCLC Worldshare Management Services; (ILL) OCLC Tipasa; (OPAC) OCLC Worldshare Management Services; (Serials) OCLC Worldshare Management Services
Wireless access
Partic in Helin; Library of Rhode Island Network
Open Mon-Thurs 7:30am-Midnight, Fri 7:30-6, Sat 10-8, Sun Noon-Midnight
Departmental Libraries:
ARCHITECTURE, One Old Ferry Rd, 02809-2921. Tel: 401-254-3679. *Archit/Art Librn,* John Schlinke; Tel: 401-254-3833, E-mail: jschlinke@rwu.edu; *Circ Coordr,* Claudia DeAlmeida; Tel: 401-254-3679, E-mail: cdealmeida@rwu.edu; Staff 2.5 (MLS 1, Non-MLS 1.5)
Library Holdings: Bk Vols 24,500; Per Subs 185
Subject Interests: Archit
Partic in Higher Educ Libr Info Network
Open Mon-Thurs 7:30am-Midnight, Fri 7:30-6, Sat 10-4, Sun Noon-Midnight

P ROGERS FREE LIBRARY*, 525 Hope St, 02809. (Mail add: PO Box 538, 02809-0538), SAN 315-3983. Tel: 401-253-6948. FAX: 401-253-5270. Web Site: rogersfreelibrary.org. *Dir,* Joan C Prescott; E-mail: prescottj069@gmail.com; *Asst Dir,* Jackie O'Brien; Staff 15 (MLS 1, Non-MLS 14)
Founded 1877. Pop 22,000; Circ 75,000
Library Holdings: Bk Titles 60,000
Special Collections: Portuguese Language Coll
Automation Activity & Vendor Info: (Acquisitions) Innovative Interfaces, Inc; (Cataloging) Innovative Interfaces, Inc; (Circulation) Innovative Interfaces, Inc; (Course Reserve) Innovative Interfaces, Inc; (ILL) Innovative Interfaces, Inc; (Media Booking) Innovative Interfaces, Inc; (OPAC) Innovative Interfaces, Inc; (Serials) Innovative Interfaces, Inc
Wireless access
Partic in Library of Rhode Island Network; Ocean State Libraries
Open Mon-Thurs 9-8, Fri & Sat 9-5
Friends of the Library Group

CAROLINA

P CLARK MEMORIAL LIBRARY*, Seven Pinehurst Dr, 02812. SAN 315-4688. Tel: 401-364-6100. FAX: 401-364-7675. E-mail: clarcirc@gmail.com. Web Site: www.clarklib.org. *Dir,* Lynn Thompson; *Asst Dir,* Johanna Wolke; Staff 6 (MLS 1, Non-MLS 5)
Pop 8,020
Library Holdings: Bk Vols 23,697; Per Subs 41
Special Collections: Emily Hoxie Archives; Richmond Conservation Commission Coll; Richmond Historical Society Archives; Richmond Historical Society Costume Coll
Subject Interests: Gardening, Local hist, RI
Wireless access
Function: ILL available, Prog for children & young adult, Summer reading prog
Publications: Newsletter
Partic in Library of Rhode Island Network
Open Mon, Wed & Fri 10-5, Tues & Thurs 1-7, Sat 10-2
Friends of the Library Group

CENTRAL FALLS

P ADAMS MEMORIAL LIBRARY*, 205 Central St, 02863. SAN 315-3991. Tel: 401-727-7440. Web Site: adamspubliclibrary.org. *Dir,* Lee Smith; E-mail: director@cflibrary.org; Staff 5 (MLS 1, Non-MLS 4)
Founded 1882. Pop 18,898; Circ 23,000
Library Holdings: Bk Vols 45,000; Per Subs 75
Special Collections: Civil War Coll; Local History Coll; Rhode Island Coll; Spanish Coll; Textile Special Coll. Oral History
Automation Activity & Vendor Info: (Acquisitions) SirsiDynix; (Cataloging) SirsiDynix; (Circulation) SirsiDynix; (Course Reserve) SirsiDynix; (ILL) SirsiDynix; (Media Booking) SirsiDynix; (OPAC) SirsiDynix; (Serials) SirsiDynix
Wireless access
Partic in Library of Rhode Island Network
Open Mon-Thurs 10-7, Fri 10-6, Sat 10-4

CHARLESTOWN

P CROSS' MILLS PUBLIC LIBRARY*, 4417 Old Post Rd, 02813. (Mail add: PO Box 1680, 02813-1680), SAN 315-4009. Tel: 401-364-6211. FAX: 401-364-0609. E-mail: staff@crossmills.org. Web Site: www.crossmills.org. *Dir,* Sarah Ornstein; *Asst Dir,* Nomi Hague; *Commun Serv Librn,* Amy Forbes; *Tech Librn,* Ray Brennan; Staff 3 (MLS 1, Non-MLS 2)
Founded 1913. Pop 7,900; Circ 56,802
Library Holdings: AV Mats 4,184; Bk Titles 29,932; Per Subs 176
Subject Interests: Eclectic approach to self improvement, Indians of NAm with local emphasis, Power resources incl alternate energy
Partic in Library of Rhode Island Network; LYRASIS; Ocean State Libraries; OCLC Online Computer Library Center, Inc
Open Mon 1-8, Tues 9-1, Wed 9-6, Thurs 9-8, Fri 1-6, Sat 9-3

CHEPACHET

P GLOCESTER LIBRARIES*, Glocester Manton Free Public Library, 1137 Putnam Pike, 02814. SAN 377-2047. Tel: 401-568-6077. FAX: 401-567-0140. E-mail: glocesterlibraries@gmail.com. Web Site: www.glocesterlibraries.org. *Dir,* Gayle Wolstenholme; *Head, Circ Serv,* Kathy Lawrence
Pop 10,283; Circ 35,211
Library Holdings: Bk Titles 28,322; Per Subs 25
Automation Activity & Vendor Info: (Acquisitions) Koha; (Cataloging) Koha; (Circulation) Koha; (Course Reserve) Koha; (ILL) Koha; (Media Booking) Koha; (OPAC) Koha; (Serials) Koha
Wireless access
Partic in Library of Rhode Island Network; Ocean State Libraries
Open Mon-Wed & Fri 10-8, Sat (Sept-June) 10-3
Friends of the Library Group
Branches: 1
HARMONY LIBRARY, 195 Putnam Pike, Harmony, 02829. (Mail add: PO Box 419, Harmony, 02829-0419), SAN 377-2063. Tel: 401-949-2850. FAX: 401-949-2868. *Librn, Adult Serv,* Brenda Fecteau; *Ref & Tech Librn,* Pat Kenny; *Cat Asst, Circ Asst,* Pat Svansson
Library Holdings: Bk Titles 48,000; Per Subs 45
Open Mon-Thurs 10-8, Sat (Sept-June) 10-4
Friends of the Library Group

COVENTRY

P COVENTRY PUBLIC LIBRARY*, 1672 Flat River Rd, 02816. SAN 315-4017. Tel: 401-822-9100. Reference Tel: 401-822-9105. FAX: 401-822-9133. E-mail: askreference@coventrylibrary.org. Web Site: www.coventrylibrary.org. *Libr Dir,* Megan Weeden; E-mail: megan@coventrylibrary.org; *Asst Dir,* Lauren Walker; E-mail: lwalker@coventrylibrary.org; *Head, Adult Serv,* Kiki Butler; E-mail: kbutler@coventrylibrary.org; *Head, Youth Serv,* Cara Delsesto; E-mail: cdelsesto@coventrylibrary.org; *Circ Mgr,* Deb Young; E-mail: dyoung@coventrylibrary.org; *Tech Serv,* Brenda Fecteau; E-mail: brecteau@coventrylibrary.org; Staff 26 (MLS 8, Non-MLS 18)
Founded 1972. Pop 35,000; Circ 250,000
Library Holdings: Audiobooks 4,300; DVDs 7,036; Bk Vols 84,000; Per Subs 135
Special Collections: Civil War Coll; High-Low Materials; Literacy Materials for Tutors & Students Including ESL
Subject Interests: Adult literacy, Local hist
Automation Activity & Vendor Info: (Cataloging) Innovative Interfaces, Inc; (Circulation) Innovative Interfaces, Inc; (OPAC) Innovative Interfaces, Inc
Wireless access
Function: Homebound delivery serv
Publications: Newsletter
Partic in Library of Rhode Island Network; Ocean State Libraries
Open Mon-Thurs 9-8, Fri & Sat 9-5, Sun 12-4
Friends of the Library Group

Branches: 1
GREENE PUBLIC, 179 Hopkins Hollow Rd, Greene, 02827. Tel: 401-397-3873. Web Site: www.coventrylibrary.org/greene-library. *Librn,* Lori Tait; E-mail: ltait@coventrylibrary.org
Founded 1929
Library Holdings: Bk Vols 11,000
Function: Adult bk club, Art exhibits, Audiobks via web, Bk club(s), Bks on CD, Children's prog, Computer training, Computers for patron use, Electronic databases & coll, Free DVD rentals, Holiday prog, ILL available, Internet access, Museum passes, Music CDs, Online cat, Online ref, OverDrive digital audio bks, Photocopying/Printing, Preschool reading prog, Prog for adults, Prog for children & young adult, Ref serv available, Res libr, Senior computer classes, Spoken cassettes & CDs, Spoken cassettes & DVDs, Story hour, Summer reading prog, Tax forms, Wheelchair accessible, Workshops
Open Tues & Thurs 1-7, Wed & Sat 9-1

CRANSTON

P CRANSTON PUBLIC LIBRARY, 140 Sockanosset Cross Rd, 02920-5539. SAN 359-7156. Tel: 401-943-9080. FAX: 401-946-5079. E-mail: central@cranstonlibrary.org. Web Site: www.cranstonlibrary.org. *Libr Dir,* Edward Garcia; E-mail: edgarcia@cranstonlibrary.org; *Asst Dir,* Julie Holden; E-mail: julieholden@cranstonlibrary.org; *Head, Circ Serv,* Dana Santagata; E-mail: dsantagata@cranstonlibrary.org; *Cat Librn,* Christine Hall; E-mail: chall@cranstonlibrary.org; *Teen Librn,* Alyssa Taft; E-mail: ataft@cranstonlibrary.org; *Coordr, Tech,* Corrie Alves; E-mail: calves@cranstonlibrary.org; *Coord, Ad Serv,* Dave Bartos; E-mail: davebartos@cranstonlibrary.org; *Coordr, Youth Serv,* Emily Brown-Suon; E-mail: emilybrown@cranstonlibrary.org
Founded 1983. Pop 83,000
Special Collections: Chinese Lang Coll; Local Cranston Hist; Spanish Lang Coll. State Document Depository
Automation Activity & Vendor Info: (Cataloging) Koha; (Circulation) Koha; (ILL) Koha; (Media Booking) Springshare, LLC; (OPAC) Koha
Wireless access
Function: 24/7 Electronic res, 24/7 Online cat, 3D Printer, Adult bk club, Art exhibits, Audiobks on Playaways & MP3, Audiobks via web, Bk club(s), Bks on CD, Children's prog, Computer training, Computers for patron use, Electronic databases & coll, ILL available, Internet access, Magazines, Makerspace, Mango lang, Meeting rooms, Museum passes, Notary serv, OverDrive digital audio bks, Photocopying/Printing, Scanner, Spanish lang bks, Tax forms, Wheelchair accessible
Partic in Library of Rhode Island Network; Ocean State Libraries
Special Services for the Blind - Talking bks plus
Open Mon-Wed 9-8, Thurs-Sat 9-5, Sun 1-5
Friends of the Library Group
Branches: 5
ARLINGTON BRANCH, 1064 Cranston St, 02920-7344, SAN 359-7180. Tel: 401-944-1662. *Asst Dir,* Julie Holden; E-mail: julieholden@cranstonlibrary.org
Open Mon-Wed & Fri 11-4:30
AUBURN BRANCH, 396 Pontiac Ave, 02910-3322, SAN 359-7210. Tel: 401-781-6116. E-mail: auburn@cranstonlibrary.org. *Br Librn,* Karen McGrath; *Ch,* Nomi Hague
Founded 1888
Special Collections: Auburn Local History
Open Mon-Wed & Fri 10-6, Thurs 2-6, Sat 10-5
Friends of the Library Group
WILLIAM H HALL FREE LIBRARY, 1825 Broad St, 02905-3599, SAN 322-5658. Tel: 401-781-2450. FAX: 401-781-2494. E-mail: hall@cranstonlibrary.org. *Br Librn,* Zach Berger; E-mail: zach@cranstonlibrary.org; *Youth Serv Librn,* Martha Boksenbaum; E-mail: mboksenbaum@cranstonlibrary.org
Founded 1897
Open Mon & Thurs 10-8, Tues & Wed 12-8, Sat 10-5
Friends of the Library Group
KNIGHTSVILLE BRANCH, 1847 Cranston St, 02920-4112, SAN 359-7245. Tel: 401-942-2504. E-mail: knightsville@cranstonlibrary.org. *Br Librn,* Nancy Gianlorenzo
Founded 1927
Open Mon-Wed & Fri 10-5
OAK LAWN BRANCH, 230 Wilbur Ave, 02921-1046, SAN 359-727X. Tel: 401-942-1787. E-mail: oaklawn@cranstonlibrary.org. *Br Librn,* Tayla Cardillo
Founded 1896
Special Collections: Local Oaklawn Hist
Open Tues, Wed, Fri & Sat 10-5

CUMBERLAND

P CUMBERLAND PUBLIC LIBRARY*, Edward J Hayden Library, 1464 Diamond Hill Rd, 02864-5510. SAN 359-7369. Tel: 401-333-2552. Circulation Tel: 401-333-2552, Ext 4. Reference Tel: 401-333-2552, Ext 2. FAX: 401-334-0578. Administration E-mail: administration@cumberlandlibrary.org. Web Site: www.cumberlandlibrary.org. *Libr Dir,* Celeste M Dyer; Tel: 401-333-2552, Ext 5, E-mail: cdyer@cumberlandlibrary.org; *Asst Dir,* Jacob Lotter; Tel: 401-333-2552, Ext 128, E-mail: jlotter@cumberlandlibrary.org; *Teen Serv Coordr,* Jillian Goss; Tel: 401-333-2552, Ext 208, E-mail: jgoss@cumberlandlibrary.org; *Adult Serv,* Elizabeth Karageorge; E-mail: ekarageorge@cumberlandlibrary.org; *Ch Serv,* Liz Gotauco; Tel: 401-333-2552, Ext 125, E-mail: liz@cumberlandlibrary.org; *Ref Serv, Ad,* Melissa Chiavaroli; Tel: 401-333-2552, Ext 201, E-mail: melissa@cumberlandlibrary.org; *Tech Serv,* Patricia Remavich; Tel: 401-333-2552, Ext 131, E-mail: premavich@cumberlandlibrary.org; Staff 37 (MLS 9, Non-MLS 28)
Founded 1976. Pop 36,405; Circ 2,025,944
Jul 2023-Jun 2024 Income $1,925,661, State $353,926, City $1,505,214, Locally Generated Income $20,000, Other $46,521. Mats Exp $136,587, Books $70,264, Per/Ser (Incl. Access Fees) $8,654, AV Mat $28,429, Electronic Ref Mat (Incl. Access Fees) $29,240. Sal $1,009,273 (Prof $425,514)
Library Holdings: AV Mats 67,894; Bks on Deafness & Sign Lang 67; DVDs 11,695; e-books 35,698; High Interest/Low Vocabulary Bk Vols 166; Bk Titles 80,691; Per Subs 109
Subject Interests: City hist, Cooking, Local hist, RI
Automation Activity & Vendor Info: (Cataloging) ByWater Solutions; (Circulation) ByWater Solutions; (OPAC) ByWater Solutions
Wireless access
Function: 24/7 Electronic res, 24/7 Online cat, 24/7 wireless access, Activity rm, Adult bk club, Adult literacy prog, After school storytime, Art exhibits, Audiobks via web, Bk club(s), Bks on CD, Chess club, Children's prog, Computer training, Computers for patron use, Digital talking bks, E-Readers, Electronic databases & coll, Free DVD rentals, Holiday prog, Home delivery & serv to seniorr ctr & nursing homes, Homebound delivery serv, Homework prog, ILL available, Internet access, Large print keyboards, Life-long learning prog for all ages, Literacy & newcomer serv, Magazines, Magnifiers for reading, Mail & tel request accepted, Makerspace, Mango lang, Meeting rooms, Movies, Museum passes, Music CDs, Notary serv, Online cat, Outreach serv, Outside serv via phone, mail, e-mail & web, OverDrive digital audio bks, Photocopying/Printing, Preschool outreach, Preschool reading prog, Printer for laptops & handheld devices, Prog for adults, Prog for children & young adult, Ref & res, Scanner, Senior computer classes, STEM programs, Story hour, Study rm, Summer & winter reading prog, Summer reading prog, Tax forms, Teen prog, Telephone ref, Wheelchair accessible
Publications: Off The Shelf (Newsletter)
Partic in Library of Rhode Island Network; Ocean State Libraries
Special Services for the Deaf - TDD equip
Open Mon-Thurs 9-8, Fri & Sat 9-5, Sun (Oct-May) 1-4
Friends of the Library Group

EAST GREENWICH

P EAST GREENWICH FREE LIBRARY*, 82 Peirce St, 02818. SAN 315-4033. Tel: 401-884-9510. Circulation Tel: 901-884-9511. FAX: 401-884-3790. E-mail: eastgreenwichlibrary@gmail.com. Web Site: www.eastgreenwichlibrary.org. *Dir,* Karen A Taylor; *Electronic Serv, Head, Ref,* Diane Hogan; *Ch Serv,* Jessica George; Staff 12 (MLS 7, Non-MLS 5)
Founded 1869. Pop 12,000; Circ 81,000
Library Holdings: Bk Vols 93,339; Per Subs 50
Subject Interests: Genealogy, RI hist
Automation Activity & Vendor Info: (Acquisitions) Innovative Interfaces, Inc; (Cataloging) Innovative Interfaces, Inc; (Circulation) Innovative Interfaces, Inc; (Course Reserve) Innovative Interfaces, Inc; (ILL) Innovative Interfaces, Inc; (Media Booking) Innovative Interfaces, Inc; (OPAC) Innovative Interfaces, Inc; (Serials) Innovative Interfaces, Inc
Wireless access
Publications: Friends (Newsletter)
Partic in Library of Rhode Island Network; Ocean State Libraries
Open Mon-Thurs 10-8, Fri & Sat 10-4
Friends of the Library Group

C NEW ENGLAND INSTITUTE OF TECHNOLOGY LIBRARY*, One New England Tech Blvd, 02818-1205. SAN 320-2291. Tel: 401-739-5000. Circulation Tel: 401-739-5000, Ext 3409. Reference Tel: 401-739-5000, Ext 3472. Interlibrary Loan Service E-mail: ill@neit.edu. Web Site: library.neit.edu. *Libr Dir,* Joseph Holland, Jr; Tel: 401-739-5000, Ext 3578, E-mail: jholland@neit.edu; *Cat,* Molly Jencks; Tel: 401-739-5000, Ext 3474, E-mail: mjencks@neit.edu; Staff 2.8 (MLS 2.8)
Enrl 1,900; Fac 300; Highest Degree: Doctorate
Library Holdings: Audiobooks 16; AV Mats 1,482; Bks on Deafness & Sign Lang 35; DVDs 428; e-books 28,806; Electronic Media & Resources 387; Large Print Bks 108; Bk Titles 43,364; Bk Vols 45,892; Per Subs 50; Videos 758
Subject Interests: Allied health, Archit, Electronics, Game design, Info tech
Automation Activity & Vendor Info: (Acquisitions) Koha; (Cataloging) OCLC; (Circulation) Koha; (ILL) OCLC; (OPAC) Koha; (Serials) Koha

Wireless access
Partic in Consortium of Rhode Island Academic & Research Libraries; Library of Rhode Island Network; OCLC Online Computer Library Center, Inc
Open Mon-Thurs 8-8, Fri 9-5, Sat 8-2

S NEW ENGLAND WIRELESS & STEAM MUSEUM INC LIBRARY*, 1300 Frenchtown Rd, 02818. (Mail add: PO Box 883, 02818), SAN 371-2559. Tel: 401-885-0545. E-mail: newsm@newsm.org. Web Site: www.newsm.org. *Pres,* Randy Snow
Library Holdings: Bk Vols 20,000

EAST PROVIDENCE

P EAST PROVIDENCE PUBLIC LIBRARY*, Weaver, 41 Grove Ave, 02914. SAN 359-7423. Tel: 401-434-2453. Reference Tel: 401-434-2520. Administration Tel: 401-434-2719. FAX: 401-434-3324. Administration FAX: 401-435-4997. E-mail: weaverlibrary@gmail.com. Web Site: www.eastprovidencelibrary.org. *Dir,* Joyce May; E-mail: mcarlozzi@eplib.org; *Digital Serv Librn, Head, Ref,* Catherine Damiani; E-mail: cdamiani@eplib.org; *Youth Serv Coordr,* Pamela Schwieger; E-mail: eplibrarypam@yahoo.com; *Adult Prog & Serv,* Joyce May; E-mail: eplibraryjoyce@yahoo.com; *Circ,* Paula Dubord; E-mail: pdubord@eplib.org; Staff 34 (MLS 15, Non-MLS 19)
Pop 50,000; Circ 471,415
Library Holdings: AV Mats 15,000; Bk Vols 303,551; Per Subs 320
Subject Interests: Lit, Literacy, Parenting, Portuguese, Psychol, Travel
Automation Activity & Vendor Info: (Circulation) SirsiDynix
Wireless access
Publications: Newsletter
Partic in Library of Rhode Island Network; Ocean State Libraries
Open Mon-Thurs 9-8, Fri & Sat 9-5, Sun (Sept-May) 1-5
Friends of the Library Group
Branches: 2
FULLER, 260 Dover Ave, 02914, SAN 359-7458. Tel: 401-228-3903. FAX: 401-434-3896. *Br Mgr,* Ryan McCauley; E-mail: rmccauley@eplib.org
Library Holdings: Bk Vols 62,000; Per Subs 150
Open Mon, Wed & Fri 9-5, Tues & Thurs 12-8
Friends of the Library Group
RIVERSIDE, 475 Bullocks Point Ave, 02915, SAN 359-7482. Tel: 401-433-4877. FAX: 401-433-4820. *Br Mgr,* Sharon Branch
Library Holdings: Bk Vols 55,000; Per Subs 115
Open Mon-Thurs 9-8, Fri & Sat 10-5
Friends of the Library Group

S READE INTERNATIONAL CORP*, Reade Advanced Materials Library, PO Drawer 15039, 02915-0039. Tel: 401-433-7000. FAX: 401-433-7001. E-mail: info@reade.com. Web Site: www.reade.com. *Dir, Mkt,* Elisabeth K Reade Law
Founded 1976
Subject Interests: Advertising, Ceramic compositions, Countertrade, Emerging tech, Export, High tech coatings, Metal alloy, Mkt, Powder metallurgy, Pub relations, Size reduction of metals, Size reduction of minerals
Wireless access
Restriction: Open by appt only, Restricted access
Friends of the Library Group

EXETER

P EXETER PUBLIC LIBRARY*, 773 Ten Rod Rd, 02822. Tel: 401-294-4109. FAX: 401-294-4796. E-mail: info@exeterpubliclibrary.org. Web Site: www.exeterpubliclibrary.org. *Libr Dir,* Tien Tran; E-mail: director@exeterpubliclibrary.org; *Youth Serv Librn,* Beth Robinson; E-mail: youth@exeterpubliclibrary.org
Library Holdings: Audiobooks 750; DVDs 2,700; Bk Vols 19,000
Automation Activity & Vendor Info: (Cataloging) Innovative Interfaces, Inc; (OPAC) Innovative Interfaces, Inc
Wireless access
Function: Computers for patron use, ILL available, Passport agency, Photocopying/Printing
Partic in Library of Rhode Island Network
Open Mon, Wed & Fri 10-5, Tues & Thurs 10-7, Sat 10-3
Friends of the Library Group

FOSTER

P LIBRARIES OF FOSTER, Foster Public Library, 184 Howard Hill Rd, 02825. SAN 315-4068. Tel: 401-397-4801. FAX: 401-392-3101. E-mail: libraries.of.foster@gmail.com. Web Site: fosterlibraries.org. *Exec Dir,* Jayne Lear; E-mail: jlear@fosterlibraries.org; Staff 8 (MLS 1, Non-MLS 7)
Pop 4,200; Circ 40,130
Library Holdings: Bk Vols 14,000; Per Subs 35
Automation Activity & Vendor Info: (Acquisitions) Innovative Interfaces, Inc; (Cataloging) Innovative Interfaces, Inc; (Circulation) Innovative Interfaces, Inc; (Course Reserve) Innovative Interfaces, Inc; (ILL) Innovative Interfaces, Inc; (Media Booking) Innovative Interfaces, Inc; (OPAC) Innovative Interfaces, Inc; (Serials) Innovative Interfaces, Inc
Wireless access
Publications: Newsletter (irregular)
Partic in Library of Rhode Island Network; Ocean State Libraries
Open Tues-Thurs 12-8, Sat 10-4, Sun 1-4
Friends of the Library Group
Branches: 1
TYLER FREE LIBRARY, 81A Moosup Valley Rd, 02825, SAN 315-4076. Tel: 401-397-7930. FAX: 401-397-5830. *Exec Dir,* Jayne Lear; *Youth Serv Coordr,* Lori Tait; *Spec Coll,* Eva Szosz; Staff 5 (MLS 1, Non-MLS 4)
Founded 1900. Circ 17,375
Library Holdings: Bk Vols 11,000; Per Subs 35
Automation Activity & Vendor Info: (Acquisitions) SirsiDynix; (Cataloging) SirsiDynix; (Circulation) SirsiDynix; (Course Reserve) SirsiDynix; (ILL) SirsiDynix; (Media Booking) SirsiDynix; (OPAC) SirsiDynix; (Serials) SirsiDynix
Open Mon 2-8, Wed 10-8, Fri 1-5, Sat 12-4
Friends of the Library Group

GREENVILLE

P GREENVILLE PUBLIC LIBRARY*, 573 Putnam Pike, 02828-2195. SAN 315-4084. Tel: 401-949-3630. FAX: 401-618-5513. TDD: 1-800-745-5555. E-mail: greenvillepubliclibrary@yahoo.com. Web Site: greenvillelibraryri.org. *Dir,* Dorothy J Swain; E-mail: dorothsn@yahoo.com; *Asst Dir,* Cassie Patterson; E-mail: greenvilleasstdirector@gmail.com; Staff 5 (MLS 5)
Founded 1882. Pop 21,000; Circ 200,709
Library Holdings: AV Mats 13,448; e-books 2,042; Bk Vols 75,966; Per Subs 140
Subject Interests: State genealogy
Automation Activity & Vendor Info: (Cataloging) Innovative Interfaces, Inc - Millennium; (Circulation) Innovative Interfaces, Inc - Millennium; (ILL) Innovative Interfaces, Inc - Millennium; (OPAC) Innovative Interfaces, Inc - Millennium
Wireless access
Function: After school storytime, Art exhibits, Audiobks via web, Bk club(s), Bks on CD, CD-ROM, Children's prog, Computers for patron use, Digital talking bks, Doc delivery serv, E-Reserves, Electronic databases & coll, Free DVD rentals, Home delivery & serv to seniorr ctr & nursing homes, Homebound delivery serv, Homework prog, ILL available, Instruction & testing, Internet access, Magnifiers for reading, Mail & tel request accepted, Museum passes, Music CDs, Notary serv, Online cat, Outreach serv, OverDrive digital audio bks, Photocopying/Printing, Preschool outreach, Prog for adults, Prog for children & young adult, Ref & res, Ref serv available, Scanner, Senior computer classes, Story hour, Summer reading prog, Tax forms, Teen prog, Telephone ref, VHS videos, Wheelchair accessible, Workshops
Publications: Happenings (Newsletter)
Partic in Library of Rhode Island Network
Open Mon-Thurs 9-8, Fri & Sat 9-5, Sun 1-5 (Oct-April); Mon-Thurs 9-8, Fri 9-5, Sat 9-1 (Summer)
Friends of the Library Group

HARRISVILLE

P JESSE M SMITH MEMORIAL LIBRARY*, 100 Tinkham Lane, 02830. Tel: 401-710-7800. E-mail: jmsreference@burrillville.org. Web Site: jmslibrary.org. *Libr Dir,* Beth Ullucci; E-mail: bullucci@burrillville.org; *Asst Libr Dir,* Jennifer Foster; E-mail: jfoster@burrillville.org
Pop 15,800; Circ 53,000
Library Holdings: Bk Vols 45,713; Per Subs 81
Automation Activity & Vendor Info: (Acquisitions) SirsiDynix; (Cataloging) SirsiDynix; (Circulation) SirsiDynix; (Course Reserve) SirsiDynix; (ILL) SirsiDynix; (Media Booking) SirsiDynix; (OPAC) SirsiDynix; (Serials) SirsiDynix
Wireless access
Partic in Library of Rhode Island Network
Open Mon-Thurs 9-8, Fri & Sat 9-4; Mon-Thurs 9-8, Fri 9-4, Sat 9-1 (Summer)
Friends of the Library Group

HOPE

P HOPE LIBRARY*, 374 North Rd, 02831. SAN 315-4106. Tel: 401-821-7910. E-mail: hopelibraryinfo@gmail.com. Web Site: www.hopepubliclibrary.org. *Dir,* Paula DiBiase
Founded 1875
Library Holdings: Bk Vols 26,000; Per Subs 40
Automation Activity & Vendor Info: (Acquisitions) Innovative Interfaces, Inc - Millennium; (Cataloging) Innovative Interfaces, Inc - Millennium;

(Circulation) Innovative Interfaces, Inc - Millennium; (Course Reserve) Innovative Interfaces, Inc - Millennium; (ILL) Innovative Interfaces, Inc - Millennium; (Media Booking) Innovative Interfaces, Inc - Millennium; (OPAC) Innovative Interfaces, Inc - Millennium; (Serials) Innovative Interfaces, Inc - Millennium
Wireless access
Publications: Newsletter
Partic in Library of Rhode Island Network; Ocean State Libraries
Open Mon & Fri 10-5, Tues-Thurs 10-8, Sat 10-2

HOPE VALLEY

P LANGWORTHY PUBLIC LIBRARY*, 24 Spring St, 02832-1620. (Mail add: PO Box 478, 02832-0478), SAN 315-4114. Tel: 401-539-2851. E-mail: langworthylibrary@gmail.com. Web Site: langworthylibrary.org. *Dir,* Margaret Victoria; *Asst Dir,* Martha Baton; Staff 7 (MLS 3, Non-MLS 4)
Founded 1888. Pop 5,080; Circ 25,514
Library Holdings: Bk Vols 26,876; Per Subs 37
Subject Interests: Genealogy, Local hist
Automation Activity & Vendor Info: (Acquisitions) Innovative Interfaces, Inc; (Cataloging) Innovative Interfaces, Inc; (Circulation) Innovative Interfaces, Inc; (Course Reserve) Innovative Interfaces, Inc; (ILL) Innovative Interfaces, Inc; (Media Booking) Innovative Interfaces, Inc; (OPAC) Innovative Interfaces, Inc; (Serials) Innovative Interfaces, Inc
Wireless access
Function: 24/7 Electronic res, 24/7 Online cat, Adult bk club, Archival coll
Partic in Library of Rhode Island Network; Ocean State Libraries
Open Mon & Wed 10-8, Tues & Thurs 4-8, Fri 10-5, Sat 10-2

JAMESTOWN

P JAMESTOWN PHILOMENIAN LIBRARY, 26 North Rd, 02835. SAN 359-7547. Tel: 401-423-7280. FAX: 401-423-7281. Web Site: www.jplri.org. *Dir,* Lisa Sheley; E-mail: jamlibdirector@gmail.com; Staff 5 (MLS 3, Non-MLS 2)
Founded 1874. Pop 5,600; Circ 76,000
Library Holdings: AV Mats 1,360; Bk Vols 42,000; Per Subs 84; Talking Bks 1,780
Automation Activity & Vendor Info: (OPAC) Innovative Interfaces, Inc
Wireless access
Function: 24/7 Electronic res, 24/7 Online cat, 3D Printer, Adult bk club, After school storytime, Art exhibits, Audiobks on Playaways & MP3, Audiobks via web, AV serv, Bk club(s), Bks on CD, Children's prog, Computer training, Computers for patron use, Digital talking bks, E-Readers, Electronic databases & coll, Free DVD rentals, Games & aids for people with disabilities, Holiday prog, Homebound delivery serv, ILL available, Internet access, Life-long learning prog for all ages, Magazines, Magnifiers for reading, Mango lang, Meeting rooms, Movies, Museum passes, Music CDs, Notary serv, Online cat, OverDrive digital audio bks, Photocopying/Printing, Preschool reading prog, Printer for laptops & handheld devices, Prog for adults, Prog for children & young adult, Ref serv available, Scanner, Senior computer classes, STEM programs, Story hour, Study rm, Summer reading prog, Tax forms, Teen prog, Wheelchair accessible, Workshops
Partic in Library of Rhode Island Network; Ocean State Libraries
Open Mon-Thurs 10-8, Fri 10-5, Sat 10-2
Friends of the Library Group

JOHNSTON

P MARIAN J MOHR MEMORIAL LIBRARY*, One Memorial Ave, 02919-3221. SAN 315-4130. Tel: 401-231-4980. FAX: 401-231-4984. TDD: 401-231-6709. E-mail: info@mohrlibrary.org. Web Site: www.mohrlibrary.net. *Dir,* Jon R Anderson; E-mail: director@mohrlibrary.org; *Assoc Dir,* Grayce J Moorehead; Staff 4 (MLS 4)
Founded 1961. Pop 28,195; Circ 81,500
Library Holdings: AV Mats 2,000; Bk Titles 65,000; Bk Vols 80,000; Per Subs 137
Special Collections: Local history
Subject Interests: Italian Am, Italy
Automation Activity & Vendor Info: (Circulation) SirsiDynix; (OPAC) SirsiDynix; (Serials) EBSCO Online
Partic in Library of Rhode Island Network; Ocean State Libraries
Special Services for the Deaf - TDD equip
Open Mon-Thurs 9-8, Fri 9-6, Sat 9-5, Sun (Oct-May) Noon-4
Friends of the Library Group

KINGSTON

S METASCIENCE FOUNDATION LIBRARY, PO Box 32, 02881-0032. SAN 324-3966. Tel: 401-294-2414. *Librn,* Marc Seifer; E-mail: mseifer@verizon.net
Founded 1977
Library Holdings: Bk Titles 600; Per Subs 12
Special Collections: Graphology Coll, articles, textbooks, translations, transparencies; Nikola Tesla Coll, articles, biographies, doc, patents; Parapsychology Journals
Subject Interests: Astrology, Gurdjieff, Lobsang Rampa, Palmistry, Parapsychol, Precognition, Psychics, Psychokinesis, Quantum physics of consciousness, Synchronicity, Tarot, Telepathy, Uri Geller, Wilhelm Reich
Wireless access
Restriction: Private libr

S SOUTH COUNTY HISTORY CENTER, Research Center & Library, (Formerly Pettaquamscutt Historical Society), 2636 Kingstown Rd, 02881. SAN 374-8464. Tel: 401-783-1328. Web Site: southcountyhistorycenter.org. *Exec Dir,* Erica Luke; E-mail: e@southcountyhistorycenter.org
Founded 1961
Library Holdings: Bk Titles 1,000
Special Collections: Washington County Coll
Subject Interests: County hist, Genealogy
Wireless access
Function: Ref & res, Res libr, Res performed for a fee
Restriction: Not a lending libr, Open by appt only, Open to pub for ref only, Open to qualified scholars, Open to researchers by request, Open to students, Pub use on premises

C UNIVERSITY OF RHODE ISLAND*, Robert L Carothers Library & Learning Commons, 15 Lippitt Rd, 02881-2011. SAN 359-7601. Tel: 401-874-2666. Circulation Tel: 401-874-2672. Reference Tel: 401-874-2653. FAX: 401-874-4608. TDD: 800-745-5555. E-mail: libadmin@etal.uri.edu. Web Site: www.uri.edu/library. *Dean of Libr,* Karim B Boughida; *Coll Mgt, Officer,* Joanna M Burkhardt; Tel: 401-874-4799, E-mail: jburkhardt@uri.edu; *Director, Distinctive Collections,* Karen Walton Morse; E-mail: kmorse@uri.edu; *Head, Access Serv,* Brian Gallagher; Tel: 406-874-9524, E-mail: bgallagher@uri.edu; *Head, Acq,* Andree J Rathemacher; Tel: 401-874-5096, E-mail: andree@uri.edu; *Head Govt Publ,* Deborah Mongeau; Tel: 401-874-4610, E-mail: dmongeau@uri.edu; *Head, Instrul Serv,* Mary MacDonald; Tel: 401-874-4635, E-mail: marymac@uri.edu; *Head, Libr Syst,* Laury Turkalo; Tel: 401-874-2820, E-mail: lturkalo@uri.edu; *Tech Serv Librn,* Michael Vocino; Tel: 401-874-4605, E-mail: vocino@uri.edu; Staff 41.5 (MLS 16.5, Non-MLS 25)
Founded 1892. Enrl 16,392; Fac 675; Highest Degree: Doctorate
Library Holdings: Electronic Media & Resources 16,000; Bk Titles 1,397,000; Bk Vols 1,020,000; Per Subs 18,641
Special Collections: Archives; Episcopal Diocese of RI Records; Fritz Eichenberg Coll; Manuscript Coll (Records of the Episcopal Diocese of Rhode Island); Oral Histories; Rare Books (Ezra Pound, Edna St Vincent Millay, Walt Whitman); Rare Books (Pound, St. Vincent Millay, Whitman); Rhode Island History & Literature; Rhode Island Oyster Bed Records 1844-1935); RI Political Papers; Senator Claiborne Pell Papers; Senator John Chafee Papers; Senator Pell Papers. Oral History; State Document Depository; US Document Depository
Subject Interests: Behav sci, Bus, Educ, Engr, Environ studies, Humanities, Indust, Marine, Natural sci, Pharm, Soc sci
Automation Activity & Vendor Info: (Acquisitions) Innovative Interfaces, Inc; (Cataloging) Innovative Interfaces, Inc; (Circulation) Innovative Interfaces, Inc; (ILL) Innovative Interfaces, Inc; (Media Booking) Innovative Interfaces, Inc; (OPAC) Innovative Interfaces, Inc
Wireless access
Publications: Bibliographies; Facility Publication
Partic in Consortium of Rhode Island Academic & Research Libraries; Library of Rhode Island Network; LYRASIS; New Eng Res Librs; OCLC Research Library Partnership
Open Mon-Thurs 7:30am-2am, Fri 7:30am-8pm, Sat 10-8, Sun 10am-2am

LINCOLN

J COMMUNITY COLLEGE OF RHODE ISLAND, Flanagan Campus Library, 1762 Louisquisset Pike, 02865. Tel: 401-333-7125. Reference Tel: 401-333-7054. Web Site: www.ccri.edu/library. *Asst Dean of Libr,* Lindsey Gwozdz; Tel: 401-825-1059, E-mail: lgwozdz@ccri.edu
Library Holdings: Bk Vols 33,000; Per Subs 750
Automation Activity & Vendor Info: (Acquisitions) Innovative Interfaces, Inc; (Cataloging) Innovative Interfaces, Inc; (Circulation) Innovative Interfaces, Inc; (Course Reserve) Innovative Interfaces, Inc; (OPAC) Innovative Interfaces, Inc; (Serials) Innovative Interfaces, Inc
Wireless access
Partic in Higher Educ Libr Info Network; LYRASIS
Open Mon-Thurs 8-8, Fri 8-4, Sat 10-2

P LINCOLN PUBLIC LIBRARY*, 145 Old River Rd, 02865. SAN 315-4149. Tel: 401-333-2422. Circulation Tel: 401-333-2422, Ext 10. Reference Tel: 401-333-2422, Ext 22. Toll Free Tel: 800-359-3090. FAX: 401-333-4154. E-mail: reference@lincolnlibrary.com. Web Site: www.lincolnlibrary.com. *Dir,* Becky A Boragine; Tel: 401-333-2422, Ext

13, E-mail: admin@lincolnlibrary.com; *Asst Dir,* Cassie Rainey; Tel: 401-333-2422, Ext 17; Staff 12 (MLS 5, Non-MLS 7)
Founded 1875. Pop 21,000; Circ 200,100
Library Holdings: AV Mats 15,000; Bk Vols 120,800; Per Subs 161
Special Collections: Descriptive Videos for Blind/Visually Handicapped
Subject Interests: Local hist
Automation Activity & Vendor Info: (Cataloging) Innovative Interfaces, Inc; (Circulation) Innovative Interfaces, Inc; (ILL) Innovative Interfaces, Inc; (OPAC) Innovative Interfaces, Inc
Wireless access
Publications: Newsletter (Quarterly)
Partic in Library of Rhode Island Network
Open Mon-Thurs 9-8, Fri & Sat 9-5
Friends of the Library Group

LITTLE COMPTON

P BROWNELL LIBRARY*, Little Compton Free Public Library, 44 Commons, 02837. (Mail add: PO Box 146, 02837-0146), SAN 315-4165. Tel: 401-635-8562. FAX: 401-635-9120. E-mail: info@brownell-libraryri.org. Web Site: www.brownell-libraryri.org. *Dir,* Susan Rousseau; E-mail: director@brownell-libraryri.org; Staff 4 (MLS 2, Non-MLS 2)
Founded 1879
Library Holdings: Bk Vols 27,500; Per Subs 41
Wireless access
Function: 24/7 Online cat, Adult bk club, After school storytime, Art exhibits, Audiobks on Playaways & MP3, Audiobks via web, Bk club(s), Bks on cassette, Bks on CD, Children's prog, Computer training, Computers for patron use, Free DVD rentals, Homebound delivery serv, ILL available, Internet access, Magazines, Magnifiers for reading, Mail & tel request accepted, Mail loans to mem, Museum passes, Music CDs, Online cat, Outside serv via phone, mail, e-mail & web, OverDrive digital audio bks, Photocopying/Printing, Preschool outreach, Preschool reading prog, Prog for adults, Prog for children & young adult, Scanner, Story hour, Summer & winter reading prog, Tax forms, Telephone ref
Partic in Library of Rhode Island Network; Ocean State Libraries
Special Services for the Blind - Bks on cassette; Bks on CD; Copier with enlargement capabilities; Home delivery serv; Large print bks; Large print bks & talking machines
Open Mon-Fri 10-5, Sat 10-3
Friends of the Library Group

MIDDLETOWN

P MIDDLETOWN PUBLIC LIBRARY*, 700 W Main Rd, 02842-6391. SAN 315-4173. Tel: 401-846-1573. E-mail: middletownpubliclibrary@gmail.com. Web Site: middletownpubliclibrary.org. *Dir, Libr Serv,* Theresa L Coish; E-mail: tcoish@middletownri.com; *Head, Children's Servx,* Candise Prewitt; *Head, Ref,* Heather Huggins; Staff 19 (MLS 5, Non-MLS 14)
Founded 1848. Pop 19,640
Library Holdings: AV Mats 2,956; Bk Vols 57,931; Per Subs 100
Special Collections: Rhode Island-Middletown History (Rhode Island Historical Coll)
Automation Activity & Vendor Info: (Acquisitions) Innovative Interfaces, Inc - Sierra; (Cataloging) Innovative Interfaces, Inc - Sierra; (Circulation) Innovative Interfaces, Inc - Sierra; (ILL) Innovative Interfaces, Inc - Sierra; (OPAC) Innovative Interfaces, Inc - Sierra
Wireless access
Function: Ref serv available
Publications: Friends of the Library (Newsletter)
Partic in Library of Rhode Island Network
Special Services for the Blind - Bks on cassette; Low vision equip
Open Mon-Thurs 9:30-8, Fri & Sat 9:30-5, Sun (Sept-May) 1-5
Friends of the Library Group

NARRAGANSETT

P MAURY LOONTJENS MEMORIAL LIBRARY*, 35 Kingstown Rd, 02882. SAN 315-419X. Tel: 401-789-9507. FAX: 401-782-0677. E-mail: circ@narlib.org. Web Site: www.narlib.org. *Dir,* Patti Arkwright; E-mail: pattiarkwright@narlib.org; Staff 4 (MLS 4)
Founded 1903. Pop 17,000; Circ 102,000
Library Holdings: AV Mats 2,100; High Interest/Low Vocabulary Bk Vols 75; Large Print Bks 575; Bk Vols 89,720; Per Subs 125; Talking Bks 2,565
Subject Interests: Local hist, Poetry, Travel
Automation Activity & Vendor Info: (Acquisitions) Baker & Taylor; (Cataloging) Innovative Interfaces, Inc; (Circulation) Innovative Interfaces, Inc; (ILL) OCLC FirstSearch; (OPAC) Innovative Interfaces, Inc; (Serials) EBSCO Online
Wireless access
Function: Adult bk club, Audiobks via web, Bks on cassette, Bks on CD, Children's prog, Computer training, Computers for patron use, Homebound delivery serv, ILL available, Mail & tel request accepted, Museum passes, Music CDs, Notary serv, Online cat, OverDrive digital audio bks, Photocopying/Printing, Prog for adults, Prog for children & young adult, Ref serv available, Summer reading prog, Tax forms, Teen prog, VHS videos, Wheelchair accessible
Partic in Library of Rhode Island Network; Ocean State Libraries
Special Services for the Deaf - Closed caption videos; High interest/low vocabulary bks; Videos & decoder
Open Mon-Thurs 9:30-8, Fri 9:30-6, Sat 9:30-5
Friends of the Library Group

G UNITED STATES ENVIRONMENTAL PROTECTION AGENCY*, ACESD Library, 27 Tarzwell Dr, 02882. SAN 315-4181. Tel: 401-782-3025. E-mail: acesdlibrary@epa.gov. *Librn,* Dale Sheehy; Staff 1 (MLS 1)
Founded 1967
Library Holdings: e-journals 25; Bk Vols 2,900; Per Subs 40
Special Collections: Narragansett Bay Project reports; Field Verification Project reports w/Army Corps Eng.
Subject Interests: Biological oceanog, Fisheries biol
Automation Activity & Vendor Info: (Cataloging) OCLC; (Discovery) ProQuest; (ILL) OCLC WorldShare Interlibrary Loan
Restriction: Badge access after hrs, Open to pub by appt only, Open to staff only

C UNIVERSITY OF RHODE ISLAND*, Pell Marine Science Library, 215 S Ferry Rd, 02882. SAN 359-7660. Tel: 401-874-6161. FAX: 401-874-6101. E-mail: pellib@etal.uri.edu. Web Site: web.uri.edu/library/pell. *Coordr,* Joyce A Downey; E-mail: jdowney@uri.edu
Founded 1959. Enrl 103; Fac 39; Highest Degree: Doctorate
Library Holdings: Bk Titles 65,857; Bk Vols 67,074; Per Subs 137
Special Collections: Barge North Cape Oil Spill; Marine & Polar Expeditionary Reports; Narragansett Bay; Quonset Point/Davisville (RI) Port Development.
Subject Interests: Marine biol, Oceanography
Automation Activity & Vendor Info: (Cataloging) Innovative Interfaces, Inc; (Circulation) Innovative Interfaces, Inc; (Course Reserve) Innovative Interfaces, Inc; (ILL) Innovative Interfaces, Inc; (OPAC) Innovative Interfaces, Inc; (Serials) Innovative Interfaces, Inc
Partic in Asn Col & Res Librs; Library of Rhode Island Network; OCLC Online Computer Library Center, Inc
Open Mon-Fri 9-5

NEWPORT

J COMMUNITY COLLEGE OF RHODE ISLAND, Newport Campus Library, One John H Chafee Blvd, 2nd Flr, 02840. Tel: 401-851-1600, 401-851-1696. Reference Tel: 401-851-1698. Web Site: www.ccri.edu/library. *Asst Dean of Libr,* Lindsey Gwozdz; E-mail: lgwozdz@ccri.edu
Wireless access
Partic in Higher Educ Libr Info Network
Open Mon-Fri 8-12 & 1-4

S INTERNATIONAL TENNIS HALL OF FAME & MUSEUM LIBRARY*, Information Research Center, 194 Bellevue Ave, 02840. SAN 315-4203. Tel: 401-849-3990. Web Site: www.tennisfame.com/museum-and-grounds/information-research-center. *Mgr, Research & Education,* Katie Harnett; Tel: 401-849-3990, Ext 1109, E-mail: kharnett@tennisfame.com; *Coll Curator,* Nicole Markham; E-mail: markham@tennisfame.com
Founded 1954
Library Holdings: Bk Vols 10,000
Subject Interests: Architects, Enshrinees, Gilded age, Newport Casino, Tennis, Tennis develop, Tennis hist, Tennis players
Wireless access
Publications: Hall of Fame News (Quarterly)
Restriction: Open by appt only

S NEWPORT HISTORICAL SOCIETY LIBRARY*, 82 Touro St, 02840. SAN 315-4211. Tel: 401-846-0813, Ext 106. Web Site: www.newporthistory.org. *Librn,* Bertram Lippincott, III; E-mail: blippincott@newporthistory.org. Subject Specialists: *Genealogy,* Bertram Lippincott, III
Founded 1854
Library Holdings: Bk Titles 6,000; Per Subs 3; Videos 20
Special Collections: Merchant Account Books; Newport Imprints. Municipal Document Depository; Oral History
Subject Interests: 18th Century colonial merchants, Archit, Church rec, Decorative art, Genealogy, Newport hist, Newport Town Council
Wireless access
Publications: Newport History (Quarterly)
Restriction: In-house use for visitors, Non-circulating, Open by appt only

P NEWPORT PUBLIC LIBRARY*, 300 Spring St, 02840. SAN 315-4238. Tel: 401-847-8720. FAX: 401-842-0841. E-mail: info@newportlibraryri.org. Web Site: www.newportlibraryri.org. *Libr Dir,* Joseph Logue; Tel:

401-847-8720, Ext 102, E-mail: jlogue@newportlibraryri.org; *Asst Dir & Head, Adult Serv,* Ann Amaral; E-mail: amaral@newportlibraryri.org; *Head, Coll Serv,* Kirby Lee; E-mail: klee@newportlibraryri.org; *Head, Patron Serv,* Moriah Hoefgen; E-mail: mhoefgen@newportlibraryri.org; *Head, Youth Serv,* Catherine Gould; E-mail: cgould@newportlibraryri.org; *Head, Property Mgmt & Security,* James Mass; E-mail: jmass@newportlibraryri.org; Staff 28 (MLS 15, Non-MLS 13)
Founded 1869. Pop 23,500; Circ 235,965
Library Holdings: AV Mats 39,842; Bk Vols 125,842; Per Subs 129
Special Collections: Chinese Artifact Coll; Cookbooks. US Document Depository
Subject Interests: Newport hist
Automation Activity & Vendor Info: (Acquisitions) Innovative Interfaces, Inc; (Cataloging) Innovative Interfaces, Inc; (Circulation) Innovative Interfaces, Inc; (Course Reserve) Innovative Interfaces, Inc; (ILL) Innovative Interfaces, Inc; (Media Booking) Innovative Interfaces, Inc; (OPAC) Innovative Interfaces, Inc; (Serials) Innovative Interfaces, Inc
Wireless access
Function: 24/7 Electronic res, 24/7 Online cat, 3D Printer, Activity rm, Adult bk club, Adult literacy prog, Archival coll, Audio & video playback equip for onsite use, Audiobks on Playaways & MP3, Audiobks via web, AV serv, Bk club(s), Bks on CD, Chess club, Children's prog, Computer training, Computers for patron use, Digital talking bks, E-Readers, Electronic databases & coll, Free DVD rentals, Games & aids for people with disabilities, Holiday prog, Home delivery & serv to seniorr ctr & nursing homes, Homebound delivery serv, Homework prog, ILL available, Internet access, Large print keyboards, Magazines, Magnifiers for reading, Mail & tel request accepted, Makerspace, Mango lang, Meeting rooms, Microfiche/film & reading machines, Movies, Museum passes, Music CDs, Notary serv, Online cat, Online ref, Outreach serv, OverDrive digital audio bks, Photocopying/Printing, Printer for laptops & handheld devices, Prog for adults, Prog for children & young adult, Ref & res, Ref serv available, Res assist avail, Res libr, Scanner, Senior computer classes, Senior outreach, Serves people with intellectual disabilities, Spanish lang bks, Spoken cassettes & CDs, Spoken cassettes & DVDs, STEM programs, Story hour, Study rm, Summer & winter reading prog, Summer reading prog, Tax forms, Teen prog, Telephone ref, Wheelchair accessible, Winter reading prog, Workshops
Partic in Library of Rhode Island Network
Open Mon 12:30-8:30, Tues-Thurs 9:30-8:30, Fri & Sat 9:30-5:30
Friends of the Library Group
Bookmobiles: 1. Coordr, Mary O'Neill Barrett. Bk vols 3,000

S REDWOOD LIBRARY & ATHENAEUM*, 50 Bellevue Ave, 02840. SAN 315-4246. Tel: 401-847-0292. Administration Tel: 401-847-0295. FAX: 401-847-5680. E-mail: redwood@redwoodlibrary.org. Web Site: www.redwoodlibrary.org. *Exec Dir,* Benedict Leca, PhD; E-mail: bleca@redwoodlibrary.org; *Dir, Admin & Finance,* David Thalmann; E-mail: dthalmann@redwoodlibrary.org; Staff 9 (MLS 6, Non-MLS 3)
Founded 1747
Library Holdings: CDs 1,481; DVDs 36; Large Print Bks 2,500; Bk Vols 200,000; Per Subs 221; Talking Bks 1,234; Videos 526
Special Collections: 18th & Early 19th Century American Portraits (Gladys Moore Vanderbilt Szechenyi Memorial Coll); 18th Century Fine & Decorative Arts Coll, furniture, paintings, sculpture; 19th Century Personal Libraries (Calvert, Greenvale & Perry Colls); 20th Century Personal Library (John P C Mathews Coll); Early 18th & 19th Century Furniture, Interior Design & Decoration (Cary Coll); Newportiana (Schumacher Coll); Original Coll-Mid 18th Century, bks, ms; Pre-1800 Imprints
Subject Interests: Arts, Gen, Humanities
Automation Activity & Vendor Info: (Cataloging) OCLC; (Circulation) Follett Software; (ILL) OCLC; (OPAC) Follett Software; (Serials) Follett Software
Function: Archival coll, Art exhibits, Bk club(s), Bks on CD, Children's prog, Holiday prog, ILL available, Jazz prog, Music CDs, Online cat, Orientations, Photocopying/Printing, Preschool outreach, Prog for adults, Prog for children & young adult, Ref & res, Story hour, Summer reading prog, Telephone ref, VHS videos, Wheelchair accessible
Publications: 1968: A Talk by the Honorable Marshall Brement; Annual reports; Booklist (Quarterly); Charles Bird King Catalog; Furniture in Print; Henry James, Edith Wharton & Newport; Newsletter (Quarterly); Pattern Books from the Redwood Library; Photographs of Lisette Prince; Recollection of Daniel Berkeley Updike; Redwood Papers: A Bicentennial Collection; The Viking Tower: A Finding Aid; Vetruvius Americanus Catalog
Partic in Library of Rhode Island Network; LYRASIS; OCLC Online Computer Library Center, Inc
Open Mon, Tues & Thurs-Sat 9:30-5:30, Wed 9:30-8, Sun 1-5
Restriction: Open to pub for ref & circ; with some limitations, Open to qualified scholars, Open to researchers by request, Sub libr

C SALVE REGINA UNIVERSITY*, McKillop Library, 100 Ochre Point Ave, 02840-4192. SAN 315-4254. Tel: 401-341-2330. E-mail: salvelibrarian@salve.edu. Web Site: library.salve.edu. *Dir, Libr Serv,* Dawn Emsellem; E-mail: dawn.emsellem@salve.edu; *Asst Director, Research & Instruction,* Lisa Richter; *Acq, Cat Librn,* Nancy Barta-Norton; *Colls Librn, Electronic Res,* Ingrid Levin; *Educ Librn,* Regina Connolly; *Archivist & Spec Coll Librn,* Liza Tietjen; *Special Programs & Instruction Librn,* Olivia Jones; *Tech & Syst Librn,* Edward Iglesia; *Access Serv Mgr,* Adam Salisbury; *Circ Mgr,* Beth Blycker Koll; *Evening Circ Supvr,* Bea Grimmitt; *Evening & Weekend Circ Supvr,* Katie Foley. Subject Specialists: *Logistics,* Beth Blycker Koll; Staff 12 (MLS 8, Non-MLS 4)
Founded 1947. Enrl 2,700; Fac 140; Highest Degree: Doctorate
Library Holdings: DVDs 4,000; e-books 56,000; e-journals 76,000; Bk Titles 120,000; Bk Vols 150,000; Per Subs 888
Special Collections: Jewish Holocaust (Dora & Elias Blumen Libr for the Study of Holocaust Literature); Whittaker Record Coll
Automation Activity & Vendor Info: (Acquisitions) OCLC Worldshare Management Services; (Cataloging) OCLC Worldshare Management Services; (Circulation) OCLC Worldshare Management Services; (Course Reserve) OCLC Worldshare Management Services; (Discovery) OCLC Worldshare Management Services; (ILL) OCLC Tipasa; (OPAC) OCLC Worldshare Management Services; (Serials) OCLC Worldshare Management Services
Wireless access
Function: Res libr
Partic in Higher Educ Libr Info Network; Library of Rhode Island Network; OCLC Online Computer Library Center, Inc
Open Mon-Thurs 8am-1am, Fri 8-8, Sat 10-6, Sun 10am-1am
Friends of the Library Group

A UNITED STATES NAVAL WAR COLLEGE LIBRARY*, Henry E Eccles Library, 686 Cushing Rd, 02841-1207. SAN 315-4262. Tel: 401-841-2641. Circulation Tel: 401-841-4386. Interlibrary Loan Service Tel: 401-841-6509. Reference Tel: 401-841-3052. FAX: 401-841-6491. Circulation FAX: 401-841-4804. Reference FAX: 401-841-6562. Reference E-mail: libref@usnwc.edu. Web Site: www.usnwc.edu/Learning-commons. *Dep Libr Dir,* Lori Brostuen; E-mail: lori.brostuen@usnwc.edu; *Head, Circ,* Robin A Lima; Tel: 401-841-6508, E-mail: robin.lima@usnwc.edu; *Head, Classified Library,* Wendy Kieron-Sanchez; Tel: 401-841-6504, E-mail: wendy.kieronsanchez@usnwc.edu; *Head, Infrastructure & Content,* Elizabeth G Holmes; Tel: 401-841-4307, E-mail: elizabeth.holmes@usnwc.edu; *Head, Res & Instruction,* Gina M Brown; Tel: 401-841-6500, E-mail: gina.brown@usnwc.edu; *Acq Librn,* Brenda Carr; Tel: 401-841-6494, E-mail: brenda.carr@usnwc.edu; *Copyright Librn,* Carolyn Wilk; E-mail: carolyn.wilk@usnwc.edu; *Electronic Res/Ser Librn,* William Corrente; Tel: 401-841-4345, E-mail: william.corrente@usnwc.edu; *Syst Librn,* Susan Chakmakian; Tel: 401-841-6492, E-mail: susan.chakmakian@usnwc.edu; *Head Cataloger,* Lydia Hofstetter; Tel: 401-841-6506, E-mail: lydia.hofstetter@usnwc.edu; *ILL Tech,* Jack J Miranda; E-mail: mirandaj@usnwc.edu; Staff 24 (MLS 14, Non-MLS 10)
Founded 1884. Enrl 723; Fac 194; Highest Degree: Master
Library Holdings: AV Mats 1,545; e-books 34,041; Microforms 1,451; Bk Titles 142,486; Bk Vols 184,546; Per Subs 413
Special Collections: Navy & Narragansett Bay (US Pre-1900 Geography, Manuscripts, Personal Papers & Oral Histories); US Pre-1900 Naval & Military History, Art & Science. Oral History; US Document Depository
Subject Interests: Area studies, Hist, Intl law, Intl relations, Mil art, Mil sci, Naval art, Naval sci, Polit sci
Automation Activity & Vendor Info: (Acquisitions) Ex Libris Group; (Cataloging) Ex Libris Group; (Circulation) Ex Libris Group; (Course Reserve) Ex Libris Group; (Discovery) Ex Libris Group; (ILL) OCLC; (OPAC) Ex Libris Group; (Serials) Ex Libris Group
Wireless access
Partic in Consortium of Rhode Island Academic & Research Libraries; Library of Rhode Island Network
Restriction: Open to students, fac & staff, Use of others with permission of librn

UNITED STATES NAVY

A ACADEMIC RESOURCES INFORMATION CENTER*, 440 Meyerkord Rd, 02841, SAN 359-7725. Tel: 401-841-4352, 401-841-6631. FAX: 401-841-2805. *Dir,* James F Aylward; E-mail: jim.aylward@navy.mil; *Asst Librn,* Robert S Wessells; *Circ,* Paul Cotsoridis; Staff 3 (MLS 3)
Founded 1917
Library Holdings: Bk Vols 100,000; Per Subs 275
Special Collections: Military Documents, fiche; Naval Training Manuals
Subject Interests: Adult educ, Educ, Leadership mgt
Automation Activity & Vendor Info: (Cataloging) Ex Libris Group; (Circulation) Ex Libris Group; (OPAC) Ex Libris Group; (Serials) Ex Libris Group
Partic in Defense Logistics Studies Info Exchange
Publications: Library Handbook; Special Interest Bibliographies
Open Mon-Fri 7-3:30
Restriction: Open to fac, students & qualified researchers

A NAVAL UNDERSEA WARFARE CENTER DIVISION, NEWPORT TECHNICAL LIBRARY*, 1176 Howell St, Bldg 101, 02841, SAN 320-2321. Tel: 401-832-4338. FAX: 401-832-3699. *Librn,* Mary N

Barravecchia; *Librn,* Allison Gardner; *Librn,* Marge Lacouture; *Librn,* Chuck Logan; *Librn,* Catherine Sloan
Founded 1970
Library Holdings: Bk Vols 11,000; Per Subs 212
Subject Interests: Acoustics, Engr, Underwater acoustics, Underwater ordnance
Partic in Consortium of Naval Libraries
Open Mon-Fri 7:45-4:15

NORTH KINGSTOWN

P DAVISVILLE FREE LIBRARY*, 481 Davisville Rd, 02852. SAN 315-4270. Tel: 401-884-5524. FAX: 401-884-9615. E-mail: staff@davisvillefreelibrary.org. Web Site: davisvillefreelibrary.org. *Dir,* Amanda Chapman
Founded 1916
Library Holdings: Bk Vols 10,853; Per Subs 19
Subject Interests: Genealogy, Local hist
Wireless access
Partic in Library of Rhode Island Network; Ocean State Libraries
Open Mon & Fri 9:30-5, Wed 1-6, Sat 10-3

P NORTH KINGSTOWN FREE LIBRARY*, 100 Boone St, 02852-5150. SAN 315-4289. Tel: 401-294-3306. FAX: 401-294-1690. Web Site: www.nklibrary.org. *Interim Dir,* Susan Aylward; E-mail: saylward@nklibrary.org; *Dep Dir,* Maggie Browne; E-mail: mbrowne@nklibrary.org; *Cat Librn, ILL,* Catie Angelo; E-mail: cangelo@nklibrary.org; *Ref Librn,* John Thresher; E-mail: jthresher@nklibrary.org; *Teen Serv Librn,* Lee-Ann Galli; E-mail: lgalli@nklibrary.org; *Commun Outreach Coordr,* Emily Goodman; E-mail: egoodman@nklibrary.org; *Reader's Serv Coordr,* Nancy Nadeau; E-mail: nnadeau@nklibrary.org; *Ref & Non-Fiction Serv Coordr,* Tom Frawley; E-mail: tfrawley@nklibrary.org; *Tech Serv Coordr,* Georgene Luttmann; E-mail: gluttmann@nklibrary.org; *Coordr, Teen Serv, Coordr, Youth Serv,* Jennifer Boettger; E-mail: jboettger@nklibrary.org; Staff 10 (MLS 9, Non-MLS 1)
Founded 1898. Pop 26,486; Circ 276,222
Library Holdings: AV Mats 5,244; DVDs 8,921; e-books 107,315; Bk Vols 88,873; Per Subs 145
Special Collections: State Document Depository
Subject Interests: Local interest
Wireless access
Publications: Among Friends (Newsletter)
Partic in Library of Rhode Island Network; Ocean State Libraries
Open Mon-Thurs 9-8:30, Fri & Sat 9-5, Sun (Oct-May) 1-5
Friends of the Library Group

NORTH PROVIDENCE

P NORTH PROVIDENCE UNION FREE LIBRARY*, Mayor Salvatore Mancini Union Free Public Library & Cultural Center, 1810 Mineral Spring Ave, 02904. SAN 315-4297. Tel: 401-353-5600. FAX: 401-353-1794. E-mail: nprlib@nprovlib.org. Web Site: nprovlib.org. *Libr Dir,* Stefanie Blankenship; *Head, Ch,* Jenny Duvant; *Head, Ref,* Joseph Uscio; *Circ Mgr,* Gina Marciano; Staff 7 (MLS 7)
Founded 1869. Pop 34,120; Circ 127,970
Library Holdings: Bk Vols 121,920; Per Subs 68
Special Collections: Careers-Vocational Guidance, vocational mat; Computer Software (Rhode Island Coll)
Subject Interests: Elderly concerns
Automation Activity & Vendor Info: (Cataloging) Innovative Interfaces, Inc; (Circulation) Innovative Interfaces, Inc; (Course Reserve) Innovative Interfaces, Inc; (ILL) Innovative Interfaces, Inc; (Media Booking) Innovative Interfaces, Inc; (OPAC) Innovative Interfaces, Inc; (Serials) Innovative Interfaces, Inc
Wireless access
Partic in Library of Rhode Island Network; Ocean State Libraries
Open Mon-Thurs 9-7:45, Fri 9-4:45, Sat (Sept-May) 10-5:45
Friends of the Library Group

M OUR LADY OF FATIMA HOSPITAL*, Health Science Library, Marian Hall, First Flr, 200 High Service Ave, 02904. SAN 359-8624. Tel: 401-456-3036. FAX: 401-456-3702. Web Site: www.fatimahospital.com/services/library-services. *Dir, Libr Serv,* Mary F Zammarelli; Tel: 401-456-2036; Staff 1 (MLS 1)
Founded 1954
Library Holdings: Bk Vols 5,065; Per Subs 129
Special Collections: Historical & Current Nursing Coll
Subject Interests: Allied health, Med, Nursing, Surgery
Automation Activity & Vendor Info: (ILL) OCLC WorldShare Interlibrary Loan
Partic in Association of Rhode Island Health Sciences Libraries; National Network of Libraries of Medicine Region 7
Open Mon-Fri 8:30-4:30

NORTH SCITUATE

P NORTH SCITUATE PUBLIC LIBRARY*, 606 W Greenville Rd, 02857. SAN 315-4300. Tel: 401-647-5133. FAX: 401-647-2206. E-mail: scituatelibrary@gmail.com. Web Site: scituatelibrary.org. *Dir,* Julie Lepore; E-mail: julie@scituatelibrary.org; *Youth Serv,* Alyce Robinson; E-mail: alyce@scituatelibrary.org; Staff 16 (MLS 3, Non-MLS 13)
Founded 1906. Pop 10,342; Circ 63,000
Library Holdings: Bk Vols 40,000; Per Subs 102
Special Collections: Scituate History Archives
Subject Interests: Local hist, Mysteries
Wireless access
Function: 24/7 Electronic res, 24/7 Online cat, Adult bk club, Archival coll, Art exhibits, Audiobks on Playaways & MP3, Audiobks via web, Bk club(s), Bks on CD, Children's prog, Computer training, Computers for patron use, E-Readers, Electronic databases & coll, Free DVD rentals, Holiday prog, Homebound delivery serv, ILL available, Internet access, Magazines, Mail & tel request accepted, Mango lang, Meeting rooms, Movies, Music CDs, Notary serv, Online cat, Online ref, OverDrive digital audio bks, Photocopying/Printing, Printer for laptops & handheld devices, Prog for adults, Prog for children & young adult, Ref & res, Ref serv available, Res assist avail, Scanner, STEM programs, Story hour, Summer & winter reading prog, Summer reading prog, Tax forms, Teen prog, Telephone ref, Wheelchair accessible, Workshops, Writing prog
Publications: NSPL (Monthly newsletter)
Partic in Library of Rhode Island Network; Ocean State Libraries
Special Services for the Blind - Talking bk serv referral
Open Mon-Thurs 10-8, Fri & Sat 10-4
Friends of the Library Group

PASCOAG

P PASCOAG PUBLIC LIBRARY*, 57 Church St, 02859. SAN 315-4319. Tel: 401-568-6226. FAX: 401-567-9372. E-mail: info@pascoaglibrary.org. Web Site: www.pascoaglibrary.org. *Libr Dir,* Gretchen H Hanley; E-mail: ghanley@pascoaglibrary.org
Founded 1871. Pop 16,279
Library Holdings: Audiobooks 160; DVDs 1,042; Bk Vols 15,220; Per Subs 4; Videos 1,042
Automation Activity & Vendor Info: (Acquisitions) Innovative Interfaces, Inc - Millennium; (Cataloging) Innovative Interfaces, Inc - Millennium; (Circulation) Innovative Interfaces, Inc - Millennium; (Course Reserve) Innovative Interfaces, Inc - Millennium; (ILL) Innovative Interfaces, Inc - Millennium; (Media Booking) Innovative Interfaces, Inc - Millennium; (OPAC) Innovative Interfaces, Inc - Millennium; (Serials) Innovative Interfaces, Inc - Millennium
Wireless access
Partic in Library of Rhode Island Network; Ocean State Libraries
Open Mon 1-8, Thurs 10-8, Fri 10-3, Sat 9-1

PAWTUCKET

P PAWTUCKET PUBLIC LIBRARY*, 13 Summer St, 02860. SAN 315-4351. Tel: 401-725-3714. Circulation Tel: 401-725-3714, Ext 201. Reference Tel: 401-725-3714, Ext 220, 401-725-3714, Ext 221. FAX: 401-728-2170. Reference E-mail: reference@pawtucketlibrary.org. Web Site: www.pawtucketlibrary.org. *Dir,* Susan L Reed; E-mail: sreed@pawtucketlibrary.org; *Asst Dir,* Christine Jeffers; E-mail: cjeffers@pawtucketlibrary.org; Staff 12 (MLS 11, Non-MLS 1)
Founded 1852. Pop 75,604; Circ 103,779
Library Holdings: AV Mats 8,950; Bk Vols 131,000; Per Subs 347
Special Collections: Local & Rhode Island History Coll
Automation Activity & Vendor Info: (Cataloging) Innovative Interfaces, Inc; (Circulation) Innovative Interfaces, Inc
Wireless access
Function: ILL available, Prog for adults, Prog for children & young adult, Ref serv available, Summer reading prog
Publications: City Program (Quarterly)
Partic in Library of Rhode Island Network; Ocean State Libraries
Open Mon-Thurs 9-8:45, Fri & Sat 9-4:45
Friends of the Library Group
Bookmobiles: 1

PEACE DALE

P SOUTH KINGSTOWN PUBLIC LIBRARY*, Peace Dale Library, 1057 Kingstown Rd, 02879-2434. SAN 359-7873. Tel: 401-783-4085, 401-789-1555. FAX: 401-782-6370. Reference E-mail: skiref@skpl.org. Web Site: skpl.org. *Libr Dir,* Laurel Clark; E-mail: lclark@skpl.org; *Ref Librn,* Jessica Wilson; E-mail: jwilson@skpl.org; *Mgr, Ref & Tech Serv,* Pamela Kaczynski; E-mail: pkaczynski@skpl.org; *Circ Supvr,* Janice Mark; E-mail: jmarks@skpl.org; *Ch Serv,* Tina Ladika; E-mail: tladkia@skpl.org; Staff 32 (MLS 9, Non-MLS 23)
Founded 1975. Pop 29,943; Circ 302,654
Library Holdings: Bk Vols 67,564; Per Subs 274
Special Collections: Rhode Island History Coll

Automation Activity & Vendor Info: (Cataloging) Innovative Interfaces, Inc; (Circulation) Innovative Interfaces, Inc; (ILL) OCLC; (OPAC) Innovative Interfaces, Inc
Wireless access
Partic in Library of Rhode Island Network; Ocean State Libraries
Special Services for the Blind - Bks on CD
Open Mon & Tues 9-8, Wed & Thurs 9-6, Fri & Sat 9-5; Mon 9-8, Tues-Thurs 9-6, Fri 9-5, Sat 9-1 (Summer)
Friends of the Library Group
Branches: 2
ROBERT BEVERLEY HALE LIBRARY, 2601 Commodore Perry Hwy, Wakefield, 02879, SAN 359-7938. Tel: 401-783-5386. FAX: 401-783-5386. *Br Mgr,* Mary Ann Comstock; E-mail: macomstock@skpl.org
Library Holdings: Bk Vols 13,813
Special Services for the Blind - Bks on CD
Open Mon 10-5, Tues 1-8, Wed-Fri 1-5
Friends of the Library Group
KINGSTON FREE BRANCH, 2605 Kingstown Rd, Kingston, 02881, SAN 359-7962. Tel: 401-783-8254. FAX: 401-783-8254. *Br Mgr,* Mary Ann Comstock; E-mail: macomstock@skpl.org; *Ch Serv,* Judith Munson; E-mail: jmunson@skpl.org
Founded 1975
Library Holdings: Bk Vols 18,277
Special Services for the Blind - Bks on CD
Open Mon & Tues 10-6, Wed 10-8, Thurs Noon-8, Fri & Sat 10-5; Mon & Tues 10-6, Wed 10-8, Thurs Noon-8, Fri & Sat 9-Noon (Summer)
Friends of the Library Group

PORTSMOUTH

P PORTSMOUTH FREE PUBLIC LIBRARY*, 2658 E Main Rd, 02871. SAN 315-436X. Tel: 401-683-9457. FAX: 401-683-5013. Web Site: www.portsmouthlibrary.org. *Dir,* Carolyn B Magnus; E-mail: porlibadult@gmail.com; *Asst Dir,* Nicole Carrubba; E-mail: porlibcirc@gmail.com; *Ch,* Olivia Seymour; E-mail: porlibchild@gmail.com; Staff 3 (MLS 3)
Founded 1898. Pop 17,149; Circ 137,431
Library Holdings: Audiobooks 3,022; DVDs 719; Bk Vols 69,960; Per Subs 115; Videos 1,819
Special Collections: Local History (John T Pierce Coll)
Subject Interests: RI
Automation Activity & Vendor Info: (Acquisitions) Innovative Interfaces, Inc; (Cataloging) Innovative Interfaces, Inc; (Circulation) Innovative Interfaces, Inc; (Course Reserve) Innovative Interfaces, Inc; (ILL) Innovative Interfaces, Inc; (Media Booking) Innovative Interfaces, Inc; (OPAC) Innovative Interfaces, Inc; (Serials) Innovative Interfaces, Inc
Wireless access
Partic in Library of Rhode Island Network; Ocean State Libraries
Open Mon & Tues 9-8, Wed-Fri 9-5, Sat 9-1, Sun (Sept-May) 1-5

PROVIDENCE

L ADLER POLLOCK & SHEEHAN PC LIBRARY*, One Citizens Plaza, 8th Flr, 02903. SAN 324-6043. Tel: 401-274-7200. FAX: 401-751-0604. *Mgr, Libr & Res Serv,* Brittany Strojny; Tel: 401-427-6103, E-mail: bstrojny@apslaw.com; Staff 1 (MLS 1)
Subject Interests: Law
Automation Activity & Vendor Info: (Cataloging) Softlink America; (OPAC) Softlink America

C BROWN UNIVERSITY*, John D Rockefeller Jr Library, Ten Prospect St, Box A, 02912. SAN 359-7997. Tel: 401-863-2165. Interlibrary Loan Service Tel: 401-863-2169. Administration Tel: 401-863-2162. FAX: 401-863-1272. Interlibrary Loan Service FAX: 401-863-2753. E-mail: rock@brown.edu. Web Site: library.brown.edu. *Univ Librn,* Joseph Meisel; E-mail: Joseph_Meisel@brown.edu; *Dep Univ Librn,* Nora Dimmock; E-mail: nora_dimmock@brown.edu; Staff 158 (MLS 47, Non-MLS 111)
Founded 1767. Enrl 7,435; Fac 577; Highest Degree: Doctorate
Library Holdings: Bk Vols 3,257,242; Per Subs 21,257
Special Collections: Abraham Lincoln (McLellan Coll); Alcohol & Temperance (Kirk Coll); American Poetry, Plays & Sheet Music (Harris Coll); American Sermons 18th & 19th Centuries; Archives; Broadsides Coll; Children's Books (Aldrich Pillar Coll); Comic Books; Dante (Chambers Coll); East Asia Coll; Edgar Allan Poe Coll; Fireworks Coll; G B Shaw (Albert Coll); Gay & Lesbian Literature (Katzoff Coll); H G Wells Coll; H P Lovecraft Coll; Henry D Thoreau (Lownes Coll); History of Medicine (Rhode Island Medical Society Library); History of Science (Lownes Coll); Humor, 19th & 20th Century (Miller Coll); Imperialism (Schirmer Coll); Incunabula (Annmary Brown Memorial); John Buchan (Bloomingdale Coll); John Hay Coll; Legend of the Wandering Jew (Louttit Coll); Lester Frank Ward Coll; Machiavelli Coll; Magic (Smith Coll); Mexican History Coll; Military History & Iconography (Brown Coll); Napoleon (Hoffman Coll); Napoleon Caricatures (Bullard Coll); Occult (Damon Coll); Pharmacopeia (Reitman Coll); Propaganda (Hall-Hoag Coll); Rhode Island History (Rider Coll); Silver (Gorham Archives); Small Press Archives; South America (Church Coll); St Martin's Press Coll; UNESCO, World Organization Document Depository; US Diplomatic History (John Hay & Jonathan Russell Colls); US Postage Stamps (Knight Coll); US Special Delivery Stamps (Peltz Coll); Walt Whitman Coll; Whaling (Morse Coll); William Blake (Damon Coll); Worldwide Postage Stamps (Champlin Coll). State Document Depository; UN Document Depository; US Document Depository
Automation Activity & Vendor Info: (Acquisitions) Innovative Interfaces, Inc; (Cataloging) Innovative Interfaces, Inc; (Circulation) Innovative Interfaces, Inc; (Course Reserve) Innovative Interfaces, Inc; (OPAC) Innovative Interfaces, Inc; (Serials) Innovative Interfaces, Inc
Wireless access
Publications: BiblioFile (Newsletter)
Partic in Boston Library Consortium, Inc; Center for Research Libraries; Greater NE Regional Med Libr Program; Library of Rhode Island Network; LYRASIS; OCLC Online Computer Library Center, Inc; OCLC Research Library Partnership; Research Libraries Information Network
Friends of the Library Group
Departmental Libraries:
JOHN CARTER BROWN LIBRARY, Brown University, 94 George St, 02906. (Mail add: PO Box 1894, 02912), SAN 359-8055. Tel: 401-863-2725. Reference Tel: 401-863-3923. FAX: 401-863-3477. E-mail: jcbl_information@brown.edu. Web Site: jcblibrary.org. *Dir & Librn,* Neil Safier; E-mail: neil.safier@brown.edu; *Dir of Develop,* Sarah Santos; *Head, Cat & Metadata Serv,* Susan Newbury; *Asst Librn, Res & Ref Serv,* Kimberly Nusco; *Curator,* Bertie Mandelblatt; *Cat,* Alison Rich; Staff 22 (MLS 10, Non-MLS 12)
Founded 1846
Library Holdings: Bk Titles 60,000; Per Subs 13
Special Collections: Colonial History of the Americas (North & South) 1492-1825, archives, bks, maps, mss & prints
Partic in Association of Research Libraries; Research Libraries Information Network
Publications: Bibliographies; Exhibition Catalogs; Facsimiles; Newsletters; Pamphlets
Open Mon-Wed & Fri 9-5, Thurs 9-7
Restriction: Authorized patrons
Friends of the Library Group
JOHN HAY LIBRARY, 20 Prospect St, Box A, 02912. Tel: 401-863-2146. E-mail: hay@brown.edu. Web Site: library.brown.edu/hay. *Asst Dir, Univ Archivist,* Jennifer Betts; Tel: 401-863-6414, E-mail: Jennifer_Betts@brown.edu
Open Mon-Thurs 10-10, Fri 10-5, Sun Noon-10
LIBRARY COLLECTIONS ANNEX, 10 Park Lane, 02907-3124. Tel: 401-863-5722. FAX: 401-867-3907. E-mail: annex@brown.edu. Web Site: library.brown.edu/info/about/annex/services. *Head, Library Annex & Stacks Maintenance,* Paul Magliocco; Tel: 401-863-5721, E-mail: paul_magliocco@brown.edu; *Head, Preservation, Conservation & Library Annex,* Michelle Venditelli; Tel: 401-863-3905, E-mail: michelle_venditelli@brown.edu; *Library Associate Specialist,* William Buzzell; E-mail: william_buzzell@brown.edu; *Library Associate Specialist,* Nadine McAllister; E-mail: nadine_mcallister@brown.edu
Function: 24/7 Online cat, Doc delivery serv, Microfiche/film & reading machines, Photocopying/Printing, Study rm
Open Mon-Fri 8:30-5; Mon-Fri 8-4 (Summer)
ORWIG MUSIC LIBRARY, Orwig Music Bldg, One Young Orchard Ave, 02912. (Mail add: Box A, 02912). Tel: 401-863-3759. E-mail: orwig@brown.edu. Web Site: library.brown.edu/about/orwig. *Librn,* Laura Stokes; E-mail: Laura_Stokes@brown.edu
Library Holdings: AV Mats 21,607; CDs 32,877; DVDs 1,041; Music Scores 24,000; Bk Vols 24,000; Per Subs 150; Videos 1,100
Open Mon-Thurs 8:30am-10pm, Fri 8:30-5, Sat 12-5, Sun 12-10
SCIENCES LIBRARY, 201 Thayer St, 02912. (Mail add: PO Box I, 02912). Tel: 401-863-3333. Circulation Tel: 401-863-3331. Interlibrary Loan Service Tel: 401-863-2750. FAX: 401-863-2753. E-mail: sciences@brown.edu. Web Site: library.brown.edu/about/scili. *Library Contact,* William Wood; E-mail: William_Wood@brown.edu
Library Holdings: Bk Vols 625,000
Open Mon-Thurs 8:30am-2am, Fri 8:30am-10pm, Sat Noon-10, Sun Noon-2am

M BUTLER HOSPITAL, Isaac Ray Medical Library, 345 Blackstone Blvd, 02906. SAN 315-4394. Tel: 401-455-6248. Web Site: www.butler.org/research. *Library Contact,* Celeste Caviness; E-mail: ccaviness@butler.org
Founded 1952
Library Holdings: Bk Titles 3,000; Per Subs 150
Special Collections: Early Psychiatry Archives (Pre-20th Century)
Subject Interests: Behav sci, Psychol, Soc sci
Partic in National Network of Libraries of Medicine Region 7
Restriction: Staff use only

J COMMUNITY COLLEGE OF RHODE ISLAND*, Liston Campus Library, One Hilton St, 02905-2304. Tel: 401-455-6078. Reference Tel: 401-455-6150. Web Site: www.ccri.edu/library. *Library Contact,* Laura Ryan; E-mail: ljryan@ccri.edu
Founded 1991
Library Holdings: Bk Vols 9,000; Per Subs 125
Automation Activity & Vendor Info: (Cataloging) Innovative Interfaces, Inc; (Circulation) Innovative Interfaces, Inc; (Course Reserve) Innovative Interfaces, Inc; (OPAC) Innovative Interfaces, Inc; (Serials) Innovative Interfaces, Inc
Wireless access
Partic in Library of Rhode Island Network
Open Mon-Fri 8-4

P COMMUNITY LIBRARIES OF PROVIDENCE, (Formerly Providence Community Library), PO Box 9267, 02940. Tel: 401-467-2700. E-mail: info@clpvd.org. Web Site: clpvd.org. *Libr Dir,* Cheryl Space; Tel: 401-467-2700, Ext 1616, E-mail: cspace@clpvd.org; *Mkt & Communications Mgr,* Janet Fuentes; Tel: 401-467-2700, Ext 1613, E-mail: jfuentes@clpvd.org; *Syst Coordr,* Aimee Fontaine; Tel: 401-272-3780, Ext 4406, E-mail: afontaine@clpvd.org; *Youth Serv Coordr,* Judanne Hamidzada; Tel: 401-467-2700, Ext 1611, E-mail: jhamidzada@clpvd.org
Founded 2009
Partic in Library of Rhode Island Network; Ocean State Libraries
Branches: 9
FOX POINT LIBRARY, 90 Ives St, 02906, SAN 359-8179. Tel: 401-331-0390. FAX: 401-331-0390. *Libr Mgr,* Julie Sabourin; E-mail: jsabourin@clpvd.org
Library Holdings: Bk Vols 17,924
Function: Wheelchair accessible
Open Mon, Wed & Thurs 9:30-5:30, Tues 1-8, Fri 1-5:30
Friends of the Library Group
KNIGHT MEMORIAL LIBRARY, 275 Elmwood Ave, 02907, SAN 359-8209. Tel: 401-467-2625. FAX: 401-467-2625. *Libr Mgr,* Michelle Freeman; E-mail: mfreeman@clpvd.org; Staff 4 (MLS 3, Non-MLS 1)
Founded 1915
Special Collections: Arnold Tombstone Records; Rhode Island History Coll
Subject Interests: Spanish lang
Function: 24/7 Electronic res, Archival coll, Audiobks via web, Bilingual assistance for Spanish patrons, Bks on CD, Children's prog, Computers for patron use, Electronic databases & coll, Equip loans & repairs, Free DVD rentals, ILL available, Magazines, Mango lang, Movies, Museum passes, Notary serv, Online cat, OverDrive digital audio bks, Photocopying/Printing, Preschool outreach, Preschool reading prog, Prog for adults, Prog for children & young adult, Ref serv available, Res libr, Scanner, Spanish lang bks, Story hour, Telephone ref
Open Mon-Thurs & Sat 9:30-8, Fri 1-5:30
Friends of the Library Group
MT PLEASANT LIBRARY, 315 Academy Ave, 02908, SAN 359-8233. Tel: 401-272-0106. FAX: 401-272-0106. *Libr Mgr,* Dhana Whiteing; E-mail: dwhiteing@clpvd.org
Founded 1906
Library Holdings: Bk Vols 36,120
Function: Wheelchair accessible
Open Mon-Thurs 9:30-8, Fri 1-5:30, Sat 9:30-5:30
Friends of the Library Group
OLNEYVILLE LIBRARY, One Olneyville Sq, 02909, SAN 370-9221. Tel: 401-421-4084. FAX: 401-421-4084. *Libr Mgr,* Kevin Veronneau; E-mail: kveronneau@clpvd.org
Library Holdings: Bk Vols 11,845
Function: Wheelchair accessible
Open Mon, Tues & Thurs 9:30-5:30, Wed 1-8, Fri 1-5:30
ROCHAMBEAU LIBRARY, 708 Hope St, 02906, SAN 359-8292. Tel: 401-272-3780. FAX: 401-272-3780. *Libr Mgr,* Aimee Fontaine; E-mail: afontaine@clpvd.org
Founded 1915
Library Holdings: Bk Vols 48,149
Subject Interests: Russian lang
Function: Wheelchair accessible
Open Mon-Thurs 9:30-8, Fri 1-5:30, Sat 9:30-5:30
Friends of the Library Group
SMITH HILL LIBRARY, 31 Candace St, 02908, SAN 359-8322. Tel: 401-272-4140. FAX: 401-272-4140. *Libr Mgr,* Alan Gunther; E-mail: agunther@clpvd.org
Library Holdings: Bk Vols 250,070
Open Mon, Tues & Thurs 9:30-5:30, Wed 1-8, Fri 1-5:30
Friends of the Library Group
SOUTH PROVIDENCE LIBRARY, 441 Prairie Ave, 02905, SAN 359-8357. Tel: 401-467-2619. FAX: 401-467-2619. *Libr Mgr,* Emily LeMay; E-mail: elemay@clpvd.org
Library Holdings: Bk Vols 29,386
Special Collections: Edna Frazier Coll
Function: Wheelchair accessible
Open Mon, Wed & Thurs 9:30-5:30, Tues 1-8, Fri 1-5:30
Friends of the Library Group
WANSKUCK LIBRARY, 233 Veazie St, 02904, SAN 329-5850. Tel: 401-274-4145. FAX: 401-274-4145. *Libr Mgr,* Denise Brophy; E-mail: dbrophy@clpvd.org; Staff 2 (MLS 1, Non-MLS 1)
Founded 1910
Library Holdings: Large Print Bks 57; Bk Vols 19,404; Per Subs 27
Special Collections: Spanish Coll
Function: Wheelchair accessible
Open Mon-Wed 9:30-5:30, Thurs 1-8, Fri 1-5:30
Friends of the Library Group
WASHINGTON PARK LIBRARY, 1316 Broad St, 02905, SAN 359-8411. Tel: 401-781-3136. FAX: 401-781-3136. *Libr Mgr,* Avelina Rocchio; E-mail: arocchio@clpvd.org
Library Holdings: Audiobooks 50; Bks on Deafness & Sign Lang 5; DVDs 700; High Interest/Low Vocabulary Bk Vols 200; Large Print Bks 50; Bk Vols 23,772; Per Subs 12; Videos 200
Special Collections: Rhode Island Coll
Function: Wheelchair accessible
Open Mon-Wed 9:30-5:30, Thurs 1-8, Fri 1-5:30
Friends of the Library Group

GM DEPARTMENT OF VETERANS AFFAIRS*, Health Science Library, Library Service, 830 Chalkstone Ave, 02908-4799. SAN 315-4629. Tel: 401-457-3001. FAX: 401-457-3097. *Dir, Libr Serv,* Cheryl R Banick; E-mail: cheryl.banick@va.gov; Staff 2 (MLS 1, Non-MLS 1)
Founded 1945
Library Holdings: AV Mats 170; e-books 69; e-journals 86; Large Print Bks 164; Bk Titles 680; Per Subs 65; Talking Bks 50
Special Collections: VA Medical Center History Coll
Subject Interests: Va hist
Function: Computers for patron use, Electronic databases & coll, ILL available, Internet access, Magnifiers for reading, Photocopying/Printing, Ref serv available, Res libr, Scanner, Telephone ref
Partic in Association of Rhode Island Health Sciences Libraries; Library of Rhode Island Network; National Network of Libraries of Medicine Region 7; Valpac
Special Services for the Blind - Assistive/Adapted tech devices, equip & products; Bks on cassette; Large print bks; Magnifiers; Ref serv; Talking bk serv referral
Open Mon-Fri 8-4:30
Restriction: Borrowing privileges limited to fac & registered students, Circ limited, Limited access for the pub, Non-circulating of rare bks, Non-circulating to the pub, Open to pub for ref only, Open to staff, patients & family mem, Open to students, fac & staff, Staff & patient use

SR DIOCESAN OF PROVIDENCE OFFICE OF FAITH FORMATION, Resource Center, 34 Fenner St, 02903. (Mail add: One Cathedral Sq, 02903), SAN 320-7382. Tel: 401-278-4646. FAX: 401-278-4645. Web Site: www.discovercatholicfaith.org/. *Dir,* Edward Trendowski; Tel: 401-278-4571; *Asst Dir,* Michelle Donovan; Tel: 401-278-4574, E-mail: mdonovan@dioceseofprovidence.org
Library Holdings: Bk Vols 2,000; Per Subs 30
Subject Interests: Relig
Open Mon-Fri 9-5

L HINCKLEY, ALLEN & SNYDER LLP*, Law Library, 100 Westminster St, Ste 1500, 02903. SAN 327-1242. Tel: 401-274-2000. FAX: 401-277-9600. Web Site: www.hinckleyallen.com. *Dir,* Carolyn Keery; Tel: 617-378-4380, E-mail: ckeery@hinckleyallen.com; Staff 5 (MLS 3, Non-MLS 2)
Library Holdings: Bk Titles 2,500; Per Subs 150
Subject Interests: Law
Automation Activity & Vendor Info: (Acquisitions) Inmagic, Inc.; (Cataloging) OCLC CatExpress; (Circulation) Inmagic, Inc.; (ILL) OCLC; (OPAC) Inmagic, Inc.
Wireless access
Function: Res libr
Partic in LYRASIS
Restriction: Not open to pub

C JOHNSON & WALES UNIVERSITY LIBRARY, Yena Ctr, 2nd Flr, 111 Dorrance St, 02903. (Mail add: Eight Abbott Park Pl, 02903), SAN 315-4424. Tel: 401-598-1722. Circulation Tel: 401-598-1098. Reference Tel: 401-598-1121. FAX: 401-598-1834. Web Site: pvd.library.jwu.edu. *Dir, Univ Libr,* Lisa Spicola; Tel: 401-598-1282, E-mail: lisa.spicola@jwu.edu; Staff 14.5 (MLS 10, Non-MLS 4.5)
Founded 1914. Highest Degree: Doctorate
Special Collections: Restaurant menus; US & Foreign Cookbooks
Automation Activity & Vendor Info: (Acquisitions) OCLC Worldshare Management Services; (Cataloging) OCLC Connexion; (Circulation) OCLC Worldshare Management Services; (Course Reserve) OCLC Worldshare Management Services; (Discovery) OCLC Worldshare Management Services; (ILL) OCLC WorldShare Interlibrary Loan; (OPAC) OCLC

Worldshare Management Services; (Serials) OCLC Worldshare Management Services
Wireless access
Function: 24/7 Electronic res, 24/7 Online cat
Partic in Association of Rhode Island Health Sciences Libraries; Docline; Higher Educ Libr Info Network; Library of Rhode Island Network
Special Services for the Blind - Assistive/Adapted tech devices, equip & products; Reader equip
Restriction: Authorized patrons, Not open to pub
Departmental Libraries:
HARBORSIDE LIBRARY, Friedman Ctr, 321 Harborside Blvd, 02905. (Mail add: Eight Abbott Park Pl, 02903), SAN 370-7679. Tel: 401-598-1466. *Head Librn,* Meika Matook; E-mail: mmatook@jwu.edu; Staff 3 (MLS 3)
Enrl 7,252; Highest Degree: Doctorate
Library Holdings: Bk Vols 60,000; Per Subs 200
Special Collections: International Menu Coll
Subject Interests: Culinary arts
Function: 24/7 Electronic res, 24/7 Online cat
Restriction: Authorized patrons

M MIRIAM HOSPITAL, Irving Addison Beck Library, Fain Bldg, Basement, 164 Summit Ave, 02906. SAN 359-808X. Tel: 401-793-2500. Web Site: brownhealth.org/locations/miriam-hospital. *Librn,* William Anger; E-mail: wanger@lifespan.org; Staff 1 (MLS 1)
Library Holdings: Bk Titles 1,300; Bk Vols 1,450
Subject Interests: Cardiology, Internal med, Nursing, Surgery
Publications: Annual reports; Library News; Orientation Brochure
Partic in Association of Rhode Island Health Sciences Libraries; National Network of Libraries of Medicine Region 7; North Atlantic Health Sciences Libraries, Inc
Restriction: Staff use only, Students only

S PROVIDENCE ATHENAEUM*, 251 Benefit St, 02903. SAN 315-4432. Tel: 401-421-6970. FAX: 401-421-2860. E-mail: info@providenceathanaeum.org. Web Site: www.providenceathenaeum.org. *Exec Dir,* Matt Burriesci; E-mail: matt@provath.org; *Coll, Dir, Libr Serv,* Kate Wodehouse; E-mail: kwodehouse@provath.org; *Ch,* Lindsay Shaw; E-mail: lshaw@provath.org; *Tech Serv Librn,* Brendan Ryan; E-mail: bryan@provath.org; Staff 6 (MLS 4, Non-MLS 2)
Founded 1753
Library Holdings: Bk Titles 167,000; Per Subs 100
Special Collections: Founders Coll; Holder Borden Bowen Coll; Rare Bk Library; Robert Burns Coll; Roycroft Coll; Voyage & Travel
Subject Interests: 19th Century Am lit, 19th Century English lit, Art, Biog, Exploration, Fiction, Hist, Natural hist, Travel
Automation Activity & Vendor Info: (Acquisitions) Innovative Interfaces, Inc; (Cataloging) Innovative Interfaces, Inc; (Circulation) Innovative Interfaces, Inc; (OPAC) Innovative Interfaces, Inc; (Serials) Innovative Interfaces, Inc
Wireless access
Publications: "Universal Penman" (Newsletter); Annual Report; Inquire Within - A Social History of the Providence Athenaeum since 1753; The Natural History Collection of the Providence Athenaeum (selected annotated bibliography); Travel & Exploration: A Catalogue of the Providence Athenaeum Collection
Partic in Library of Rhode Island Network
Open Mon-Fri 10-6, Sat 10-2
Restriction: Circ to mem only

C PROVIDENCE COLLEGE*, Phillips Memorial Library, One Cunningham Sq, 02918. SAN 315-4440. Circulation Tel: 401-865-1993. FAX: 401-865-2823. E-mail: library@providence.edu. Web Site: pml.providence.edu. *Libr Dir,* Mark J Caprio; Tel: 401-865-1996, E-mail: mcaprio1@providence.edu; *Assoc Libr Dir,* Sarah A Edmonds; Tel: 401-865-1622, E-mail: sedmond1@providence.edu; *Ser & Electronic Res Librn,* Janice Schuster; Tel: 401-865-2631, E-mail: janice.schuster@providence.edu; *Educ Librn, Research Librn,* David Bernardo; Tel: 401-865-2581, E-mail: dbernard1@providence.edu; Staff 12 (MLS 10, Non-MLS 2)
Founded 1917. Enrl 4,354; Fac 262; Highest Degree: Master
Library Holdings: e-books 8,450; e-journals 9,483; Bk Titles 234,777; Bk Vols 2,267,067; Per Subs 1,775
Special Collections: Aime J Forand Coll; Alice Lafond Altieri Coll; Blackfriars' Guild Coll; Bonniwell Coll; Cornelius Moore Papers; Coutu Genealogy Coll; Dennis J Roberts Papers; Edward J Higgins Coll; Edward P Beard Coll; English & Colonial 18th Century Trade Statistics Coll, IBM cards; Irish Literature; J Howard McGrath Coll; J Lyons Moore Coll; John E Fogarty Papers; John J Fawcett Coll; John O Pastore Coll; Joseph A Doorley Jr Coll; Louis Francis Budenz Papers, pamphlets, per; National Association for the Advancement of Colored People Coll; Nazi Bund Coll; Quonset Point Coll; Reunification of Ireland Clippings; Rhode Island Constitutional Convention, 1964-1968; Rhode Island Court Records Coll, 1657-1905; Rhode Island Library Association Coll; Rhode Island United States Colored Artillery (Heavy) 11th Regiment Coll; Rhode Island Urban League Papers; Robert E Quinn Papers & Oral History Project; Social Justice, 1936-1942; The Confederation Period in Rhode Island Newspapers Coll; The Limited Constitutional Convention, 1973; Thomas Matthes McGlynn, OP Coll; Walsh Civil War Diary; William Henry Chamberlin Papers, micro. State Document Depository; US Document Depository
Automation Activity & Vendor Info: (Acquisitions) Innovative Interfaces, Inc; (Cataloging) Innovative Interfaces, Inc; (Circulation) Innovative Interfaces, Inc; (Course Reserve) Innovative Interfaces, Inc; (OPAC) Innovative Interfaces, Inc; (Serials) Innovative Interfaces, Inc
Wireless access
Partic in Higher Educ Libr Info Network; Library of Rhode Island Network; NE Libr Network
Open Mon-Thurs 8am-Midnight, Fri 8-8, Sat 11-7, Sun 10-Midnight (Fall & Spring); Mon-Thurs 8-6, Fri 8-2, Sat Noo-6, Sun 10-6 (Summer)

P PROVIDENCE PUBLIC LIBRARY*, 150 Empire St, 02903-3283. SAN 359-8144. Tel: 401-455-8000. Circulation Tel: 401-455-8046, 401-455-8099. Reference Tel: 401-455-8005. FAX: 401-455-8080. Web Site: www.provlib.org. *Exec Dir,* Jack Martin; E-mail: jmartin@provlib.org; *Assoc Dir,* Aaron Peterman; E-mail: apeterman@provlib.org; *Dir, Info Serv, Dir, Tech Serv,* Beatrice Pullman; E-mail: beatrice@provlib.org; Staff 44 (MLS 14, Non-MLS 30)
Founded 1875. Pop 178,042
Library Holdings: AV Mats 24,293; Bk Vols 944,148; Per Subs 828; Videos 24,070
Special Collections: Architecture (Nickerson Coll); Band Music (David W Reeves Coll); Black History & Culture (Edna Frazier Coll); Checkers (Edward B Hanes Coll); Checkers Coll; Children's Books (Wetmore Coll); Civil War & Slavery (Harris Coll); Irish Culture (Potter/Williams Coll); Italian Coll; Jewelry Coll; Magic (Percival Coll); Printing (Updike Coll); Providence Journal (online access); Regional Foundation Coll; Rhode Island Coll; Textile Coll; US Patents & Depository; Whaling (Nicholson Coll). State Document Depository; US Document Depository
Subject Interests: Art, Music, RI
Automation Activity & Vendor Info: (Acquisitions) Innovative Interfaces, Inc; (Cataloging) Innovative Interfaces, Inc; (Circulation) Innovative Interfaces, Inc; (OPAC) Innovative Interfaces, Inc
Wireless access
Publications: Annual Report; Newsletter (Bimonthly)
Partic in Library of Rhode Island Network; Ocean State Libraries
Special Services for the Deaf - Bks on deafness & sign lang; Closed caption videos; TDD equip
Special Services for the Blind - ZoomText magnification & reading software
Open Mon & Wed 10-8:30, Tues & Thurs-Sat 10-5

C RHODE ISLAND COLLEGE, James P Adams Library, 600 Mt Pleasant Ave, 02908-1924. SAN 315-4475. Circulation Tel: 401-456-9617. Reference Tel: 401-456-8125. FAX: 401-456-9646. Web Site: library.ric.edu. *Libr Dir,* Carissa DeLizio; E-mail: cdelizio@ric.edu; *Asst Dir, Access Serv,* Sarah Sanfilippo; E-mail: ssanfilippo@ric.edu; *Asst Dir, Tech Serv,* Lisa Underhill; E-mail: lunderhill@ric.edu; *Electronic Resources & Tech Librn,* Kieran Ayton; E-mail: kayton@ric.edu; *Ref Librn,* Amy Barlow; E-mail: abarlow@ric.edu; *Ref Librn,* Dragan Gill; E-mail: dgill@ric.edu; *Digital Archivist, Spec Coll Librn,* Veronica Denison; E-mail: vdenison@ric.edu; Staff 14 (MLS 6, Non-MLS 8)
Founded 1854. Enrl 4,816; Fac 300; Highest Degree: Master
Library Holdings: Bk Vols 235,238; Per Subs 690
Special Collections: Curriculum Resource Center. State Document Depository; US Document Depository
Subject Interests: Educ, Soc work
Automation Activity & Vendor Info: (Acquisitions) OCLC Worldshare Management Services; (Cataloging) OCLC Worldshare Management Services; (Circulation) OCLC Worldshare Management Services; (Discovery) OCLC Worldshare Management Services; (ILL) OCLC Tipasa; (OPAC) OCLC Worldshare Management Services; (Serials) OCLC Worldshare Management Services
Wireless access
Partic in Higher Educ Libr Info Network; Library of Rhode Island Network
Open Mon-Thurs 7:45am-10pm, Fri 7:45-5, Sat 11-5, Sun 1-8
Friends of the Library Group

S RHODE ISLAND HISTORICAL SOCIETY*, Robinson Research Center, 121 Hope St, 02906. SAN 315-4491. Tel: 401-273-8107, Ext 410. FAX: 401-751-7930. Reference E-mail: reference@rihs.org. Web Site: www.rihs.org/locations/mary-elizabeth-robinson-research-center. *Dep Exec Dir, Dir, Coll & Interpretation,* Richard J Ring; Tel: 401-273-8107, Ext 419; *Assoc Dir,* Phoebe Bean; Tel: 401-273-8107, Ext 424, E-mail: psbean@rihs.org; *Cabinet Keeper & Library Colls Mgr,* Dana Signe Munroe; Tel: 401-273-8107, Ext 416, E-mail: dsmunroe@rihs.org; Staff 7 (MLS 4, Non-MLS 3)
Founded 1822
Library Holdings: CDs 20; Music Scores 500; Bk Vols 120,000; Spec Interest Per Sub 10; Videos 50

Special Collections: Film Coll; Graphics Coll; Manuscripts Coll; Map Coll; Museum Coll. Oral History
Subject Interests: Am hist, China, Genealogy, Hist of RI, New England, Slavery, Trade, Vital records
Automation Activity & Vendor Info: (Cataloging) OCLC; (OPAC) MINISIS Inc
Wireless access
Function: 24/7 Online cat, Archival coll, Bus archives, Electronic databases & coll, Internet access, Life-long learning prog for all ages, Magnifiers for reading, Mail & tel request accepted, Masonic res mat, Microfiche/film & reading machines, Online cat, Online ref, Outside serv via phone, mail, e-mail & web, Photocopying/Printing, Prog for adults, Ref & res, Ref serv available, Res assist avail, Res libr
Publications: Rhode Island History (Journal)
Partic in Consortium of Rhode Island Academic & Research Libraries; Library of Rhode Island Network; OCLC Online Computer Library Center, Inc
Special Services for the Blind - Aids for in-house use; Assistive/Adapted tech devices, equip & products; Audio mat; Copier with enlargement capabilities; Low vision equip; Magnifiers
Open Wed 1-7, Thurs & Fri 10-4
Restriction: Free to mem, In-house use for visitors, Non-circulating, Non-circulating coll, Non-circulating of rare bks, Non-circulating to the pub, Non-resident fee, Not a lending libr, Open to students, Photo ID required for access, Private libr, Registered patrons only

M RHODE ISLAND HOSPITAL, Peters Health Sciences Library, Aldrich Bldg, 593 Eddy St, 02902. SAN 359-8500. Tel: 401-444-4671. FAX: 401-444-8260. E-mail: llibrary@lifespan.org. Web Site: www.lifespan.org/providers/lifespan-libraries. *Libr Tech,* Cynthia Smith; Tel: 401-444-5450
Founded 1932
Library Holdings: Bk Vols 25,000; Per Subs 650
Wireless access
Publications: Peters Library Newsletter
Partic in Library of Rhode Island Network; OCLC Online Computer Library Center, Inc; Proquest Dialog
Restriction: Badge access after hrs, Open by appt only

R RHODE ISLAND JEWISH HISTORICAL ASSOCIATION LIBRARY*, 401 Elmgrove Ave, 02906. SAN 315-4505. Tel: 401-331-1360. FAX: 401-331-7961. E-mail: info@rijha.org, office@rijha.org. Web Site: www.rijha.org. *Exec Dir,* Kate-Lynne Laroche
Founded 1951
Library Holdings: Bk Titles 821; Per Subs 12
Special Collections: Jewish History of Rhode Island. Oral History
Function: Archival coll, Mail & tel request accepted, Online cat, Photocopying/Printing, Res libr, Scanner, Telephone ref
Publications: Rhode Island Jewish Historical Notes (Annual); RIJHA Newsletter (Quarterly)
Partic in Asn of Jewish Librs
Open Mon, Wed & Fri 9-5, Tues & Thurs 9-2
Restriction: In-house use for visitors, Non-circulating coll, Non-circulating to the pub, Not a lending libr, Open to pub for ref only, Pub use on premises, Ref only

§GL RHODE ISLAND OFFICE OF ATTORNEY GENERAL LIBRARY, 150 S Main St, 02903. Tel: 401-274-4400. FAX: 401-222-1331. E-mail: ag@riag.ri.gov. Web Site: riag.ri.gov/about-our-office/library. *Paralegal,* Aidan Giusti
Subject Interests: Constitutional law, Criminal justice, Educ, Environ law, Evidence, Fed law, Fed procedure, Health, RI, RI State Attorneys General
Wireless access
Partic in Library of Rhode Island Network
Restriction: Not open to pub, Open to staff only

G RHODE ISLAND PUBLIC EXPENDITURE COUNCIL LIBRARY, 225 Dyer St, 2nd Flr, 02903. SAN 372-9338. Tel: 401-521-6320. FAX: 401-751-1915. Web Site: ripec.org. *Pres & Chief Exec Officer,* Michael DiBiase; E-mail: m_dibiase@ripec.com
Library Holdings: Bk Vols 100; Per Subs 16
Wireless access
Open Mon-Fri 8:30-4:30

S RHODE ISLAND SCHOOL FOR THE DEAF LIBRARY*, One Corliss Park, 02908. SAN 315-4548. Tel: 401-222-3525. FAX: 401-243-1024. Web Site: rideaf.ri.gov/library. *Librn,* Chris Masiello; E-mail: cmasiello@rideaf.net; Staff 2 (MLS 1, Non-MLS 1)
Library Holdings: Bk Vols 10,000
Automation Activity & Vendor Info: (Cataloging) Chancery SMS; (Circulation) Chancery SMS
Wireless access
Partic in Library of Rhode Island Network
Special Services for the Deaf - Bks on deafness & sign lang; High interest/low vocabulary bks; Staff with knowledge of sign lang; TTY equip
Open Mon-Fri 8-3

C RHODE ISLAND SCHOOL OF DESIGN LIBRARY*, Fleet Library at RISD, 15 Westminster St, 02903. (Mail add: Two College St, 02903). SAN 315-4556. Tel: 401-709-5900. Circulation Tel: 401-709-5901. Interlibrary Loan Service Tel: 401-709-5904. Reference Tel: 401-709-5902. Administration Tel: 401-709-5909. FAX: 401-709-5932. Circulation FAX: 401-709-5903. E-mail: risdlib@risd.edu. Web Site: library.risd.edu. *Dir, Libr Serv,* Carol S Terry; *Cat/Ref Librn,* Marc Calhoun; Tel: 401-709-5941, E-mail: mcalhoun@risd.edu; *Res & Instruction Librn,* Ellen Petraits; Tel: 401-709-5905, E-mail: epetrait@risd.edu; *Spec Coll Librn,* Claudia Covert; Tel: 401-709-5927, E-mail: ccovert@risd.edu; *Tech Serv Librn,* Robert Garzillo; Tel: 401-709-5944, E-mail: rgarzill@risd.edu; *Visual & Mat Res Librn,* Mark Pompelia; Tel; 401-709-5935, E-mail: mpompeli@risd.edu; *Access Serv Mgr,* Gail Geisser; E-mail: ggeisser@risd.edu; *Archivist,* Andrew Martinez; Tel: 401-709-5920, E-mail: amartine@risd.edu; *Assoc Archivist,* Douglas Doe; Tel: 401-709-5922, E-mail: ddoe@risd.edu; Staff 10 (MLS 7, Non-MLS 3)
Founded 1878. Enrl 2,400; Fac 425; Highest Degree: Master
Library Holdings: AV Mats 639,714; e-books 143,200; e-journals 679; Bk Titles 124,735; Bk Vols 157,011; Per Subs 324; Videos 6,700
Special Collections: Artists' Bks; Gorham Design Library; Landscape Architecture (Lowthorpe Coll); Material Resource Center; Miniature Bks (Anne Jencks Coll)
Subject Interests: Archit, Art, Design
Automation Activity & Vendor Info: (Acquisitions) Innovative Interfaces, Inc; (Cataloging) Innovative Interfaces, Inc; (Circulation) Innovative Interfaces, Inc; (ILL) Clio; (OPAC) Innovative Interfaces, Inc; (Serials) Innovative Interfaces, Inc
Wireless access
Function: Art exhibits, Wheelchair accessible
Partic in Consortium of Rhode Island Academic & Research Libraries; Library of Rhode Island Network; LYRASIS; OCLC Online Computer Library Center, Inc; Providence Athenaeum-RISD Libr Consortium
Special Services for the Blind - Text reader
Open Mon-Thurs 8:30am-11pm, Fri 8:30-8, Sat 10-6, Sun Noon-11
Restriction: Open to researchers by request

G RHODE ISLAND STATE ARCHIVES*, 337 Westminster St, 02903. SAN 321-4192. Tel: 401-222-2353. FAX: 401-222-3199. E-mail: statearchives@sos.ri.gov. Web Site: www.sos.ri.gov/divisions/state-archives. *State Archivist,* Ashley Selima; E-mail: aselima@sos.ri.gov; Staff 8 (MLS 3, Non-MLS 5)
Founded 1647
Library Holdings: Bk Vols 1,000
Special Collections: Architectural Drawings; Charters & Proclamations; Colony Records; Correspondence (Governors); Legislative Records; Maps & Plans; Military Records; Photographs; State Censuses (1774-1935); Vital Records
Subject Interests: Genealogy, Govt, Graphics, Hist
Publications: Compilation of Rules of State Agencies
Open Mon-Fri 8:30-4:30

GL RHODE ISLAND STATE LAW LIBRARY*, Frank Licht Judicial Complex, 250 Benefit St, 02903. SAN 315-4572. Tel: 401-222-3275. FAX: 401-222-3865. E-mail: lawlibraryinfo@courts.ri.gov. Web Site: www.courts.ri.gov/programs-services/pages/state-law-library.aspx. *State Law Librn,* Colleen Hanna; E-mail: channa@courts.ri.gov; *Ref Librn,* Marcia Lakomsi Oakes; E-mail: moakes@courts.ri.gov; *Cat, Tech Serv,* Martha Moore; E-mail: mmoore@courts.ri.gov; Staff 6 (MLS 3, Non-MLS 3)
Founded 1827
Library Holdings: Bk Titles 12,600; Bk Vols 100,000; Per Subs 366
Special Collections: Rhode Island Colonial Laws. US Document Depository
Subject Interests: Am law
Automation Activity & Vendor Info: (Acquisitions) EOS International; (Cataloging) EOS International; (Circulation) EOS International; (ILL) OCLC; (OPAC) EOS International; (Serials) EOS International
Wireless access
Function: Computers for patron use, Electronic databases & coll, For res purposes, ILL available, Photocopying/Printing, Res assist avail, Scanner
Partic in Library of Rhode Island Network; NELLCO Law Library Consortium, Inc.; OCLC Online Computer Library Center, Inc
Special Services for the Blind - Closed circuit TV; Reader equip
Restriction: Circ limited, Open to govt employees only

P RHODE ISLAND STATE LIBRARY*, State House, Rm 208, 82 Smith St, 02903. SAN 315-4580. Tel: 401-222-2473. FAX: 401-222-3034. E-mail: statelibrary@sos.ri.gov. Web Site: www.sos.ri.gov/divisions/civics-and-education/state-library. *Dir, State Archives, Pub Info Officer,* Kaitlynne Ward Morris; E-mail: kmorris@sos.ri.gov; *State Librn,* Megan Hamlin-Black; E-mail: mblack@sos.ri.gov; *Govt Doc, Tech Serv,* Greg Facincani; E-mail:

gfacincani@sos.ri.gov; *Govt Doc,* Ann Teixeira; Staff 4 (MLS 3, Non-MLS 1)
Founded 1852
Special Collections: State Clearinghouse. State Document Depository; US Document Depository
Subject Interests: Legis
Automation Activity & Vendor Info: (OPAC) ByWater Solutions; (Serials) ByWater Solutions
Wireless access
Publications: Checklist of Rhode Island State Documents
Partic in Consortium of Rhode Island Academic & Research Libraries; Library of Rhode Island Network
Open Mon-Fri 8:30-4:30
Restriction: Non-circulating

P STATE OF RHODE ISLAND*, Office of Library & Information Services, Department of Administration, One Capitol Hill, 2nd Flr, 02908. SAN 359-8446. Tel: 401-574-9300. FAX: 401-574-9320. Web Site: www.olis.ri.gov. *Chief, Libr Serv,* Karen Mellor; Tel: 401-574-9304, E-mail: karen.mellor@olis.ri.gov; *Regional Librn,* Alicia Waters; Tel: 401-574-9315, E-mail: alicia.waters@olis.ri.gov; *Libr Prog Mgr,* Donna DiMichele; Tel: 401-574-9303, E-mail: donna.dimichele@olis.ri.gov; *Libr Prog Mgr,* Position Currently Open; *Adult Serv Coordr,* Nicolette Baffoni; Tel; 401-574-9316, E-mail: nicolette.baffoni@olis.ri.gov; *Digital Res Coordr,* Jason Ackermann; Tel: 401-574-9317, E-mail: jason.ackermann@olis.ri.gov; *Resource Sharing Coord,* Chaichin Chen; Tel: 401-574-9307, E-mail: chaichin.chen@olis.ri.gov; *State Data Coordr,* Kelly Metzger; Tel: 401-574-9305, E-mail: kelly.metzger@olis.ri.gov; *Youth Serv Coordr,* Danielle Margarida; Tel: 401-574-9309, E-mail: danielle.margarida@olis.ri.gov. Subject Specialists: *Blind-educ, Visually impaired,* Alicia Waters; Staff 12 (MLS 8, Non-MLS 4)
Founded 1964
Library Holdings: Bk Vols 4,800; Per Subs 110
Subject Interests: Libr sci
Automation Activity & Vendor Info: (Circulation) Innovative Interfaces, Inc; (Course Reserve) Innovative Interfaces, Inc; (ILL) Innovative Interfaces, Inc; (Media Booking) Innovative Interfaces, Inc; (OPAC) Innovative Interfaces, Inc; (Serials) Innovative Interfaces, Inc
Wireless access
Partic in Library of Rhode Island Network
Special Services for the Blind - Bks on flash-memory cartridges; Braille bks; Digital talking bk; Digital talking bk machines; Talking bk & rec for the blind cat; Talking bk serv referral; Talking bks; Talking bks & player equip
Open Mon-Fri 8:30-4
Restriction: Researchers by appt only
Branches: 1
P TALKING BOOKS LIBRARY, One Capitol Hill, 02908-5803, SAN 315-453X. Tel: 401-574-9310. FAX: 401-574-9320. E-mail: talking.books@olis.ri.gov. Web Site: www.olis.ri.gov/tbl. *Regional Librn,* Alica Waters; Tel: 401-574-9315, E-mail: alicia.waters@olis.ri.gov; *Readers' Advisory,* Neshmayda Calderon; Tel: 401-574-9313, E-mail: neshmayda.calderon@olis.ri.gov. Subject Specialists: *Spanish lang,* Neshmayda Calderon; Staff 3 (MLS 1, Non-MLS 2)
Founded 1967
Library Holdings: Bk Titles 85,000; Bk Vols 828,109; Per Subs 24
Automation Activity & Vendor Info: (Acquisitions) Keystone Systems, Inc (KLAS)
Partic in OCLC Online Computer Library Center, Inc
Publications: Regional Library Newsletter (Quarterly)
Special Services for the Blind - Braille equip
Open Mon-Fri 8:30-4

R TEMPLE BETH EL, CONGEGATION SONS OF ISRAEL & DAVID*, William G Braude Library, 70 Orchard Ave, 02906. SAN 315-4408. Tel: 401-331-6070. FAX: 401-331-8068. E-mail: info@temple-beth-el.org. Web Site: www.temple-beth-el.org/learning/library. *Librn,* Joanna Katsune; Fax: 401-521-6012, E-mail: librarian@temple-beth-el.org; Staff 1 (MLS 1)
Founded 1892
Library Holdings: CDs 45; Bk Vols 15,000; Per Subs 40; Talking Bks 100; Videos 40
Special Collections: Latin American Jewish Studies
Subject Interests: Bible studies, Childrens' bks, Hebraica, Holocaust, Judaica, Young adult bks
Automation Activity & Vendor Info: (Cataloging) Follett Software; (Circulation) Follett Software
Wireless access
Open Tues-Thurs 8-4, Fri 8-2
Restriction: Circ to mem only

R TEMPLE EMANU-EL LIBRARY*, 99 Taft Ave, 02906. SAN 315-4602. Tel: 401-331-1616. FAX: 401-421-9279. E-mail: library@teprov.org. Web Site: www.teprov.org/library. *Librn,* Maxine Wolfson; E-mail: mwolfson@teprov.org
Library Holdings: CDs 30; DVDs 70; Bk Titles 12,000
Subject Interests: Judaica
Wireless access
Open Mon-Thurs 7-6:15, Fri 7-2, Sat 8-1:30, Sun 8-12:30

GL UNITED STATES COURT OF APPEALS, First Circuit Satellite Library, One Exchange Terrace, Rm 430, 02903. SAN 371-9065. Tel: 401-752-7240. FAX: 401-752-7245. Web Site: www.rid.uscourts.gov. *Satellite Librn,* Ed Wallace; E-mail: edward_wallace@rid.uscourts.gov
Founded 1990
Library Holdings: Bk Vols 10,000; Per Subs 20
Wireless access
Partic in OCLC Online Computer Library Center, Inc
Restriction: Not open to pub

C UNIVERSITY OF RHODE ISLAND*, College of Continuing Education Library, 80 Washington St, 02903. SAN 315-4610. Tel: 401-277-5130. E-mail: uriccelib@etal.uri.edu. Web Site: web.uri.edu/library. *Dir,* Joanna M Burkhardt; E-mail: jburkhardt@uri.edu; Staff 4 (MLS 1, Non-MLS 3)
Founded 1964. Enrl 5,300; Highest Degree: Master
Library Holdings: Bk Vols 26,000; Per Subs 325
Subject Interests: Adult educ, Bus, English lit, Psychol
Automation Activity & Vendor Info: (Acquisitions) Ex Libris Group; (Cataloging) OCLC Online; (Circulation) Ex Libris Group; (Course Reserve) Ex Libris Group; (Media Booking) Ex Libris Group; (OPAC) Ex Libris Group
Wireless access
Partic in Boston Library Consortium, Inc; Library of Rhode Island Network; OCLC Online Computer Library Center, Inc
Open Mon-Thurs 8:30am-9pm, Fri 8:30-4, Sat 10-3

M ROGER WILLIAMS MEDICAL CENTER*, Health Sciences Library, 825 Chalkstone Ave, 02908. SAN 315-4637. Tel: 401-456-2036. FAX: 401-456-2191. Web Site: www.rwmc.org/for-caregivers/health-sciences-library. *Librn,* Mary Zammarelli; Staff 1.2 (MLS 1, Non-MLS 0.2)
Library Holdings: e-books 100; e-journals 150; Bk Vols 1,000; Per Subs 100
Subject Interests: Dermatology, Podiatry, Rheumatology
Wireless access
Function: Electronic databases & coll, Health sci info serv, ILL available
Partic in Association of Rhode Island Health Sciences Libraries; Basic Health Sciences Library Network; National Network of Libraries of Medicine Region 7
Open Mon, Tues & Thurs 8-4, Wed 12-4, Fri 8-Noon
Restriction: Hospital staff & commun, In-house use for visitors, Lending to staff only, Prof mat only

SAUNDERSTOWN

P WILLETT FREE LIBRARY*, 45 Ferry Rd, 02874. (Mail add: PO Box 178, 02874), SAN 315-467X. Tel: 401-294-2081. FAX: 401-294-2081. E-mail: willettfree@gmail.com. Web Site: willettfree.org. *Dir,* Jennifer Shaker; Staff 1 (MLS 1)
Founded 1886. Pop 6,000
Library Holdings: AV Mats 692; Bk Vols 9,400; Per Subs 10; Talking Bks 200
Special Collections: Local History Coll. Oral History
Subject Interests: Local hist, Nautical
Automation Activity & Vendor Info: (Acquisitions) Innovative Interfaces, Inc; (Cataloging) Innovative Interfaces, Inc; (Circulation) Innovative Interfaces, Inc; (OPAC) Innovative Interfaces, Inc
Wireless access
Function: Adult bk club, Archival coll, Audio & video playback equip for onsite use, Audiobks via web, Bks on CD, CD-ROM, Children's prog, Citizenship assistance, Computer training, Computers for patron use, Electronic databases & coll, Free DVD rentals, ILL available, Internet access, Museum passes, Music CDs, Online cat, OverDrive digital audio bks, Photocopying/Printing, Prog for adults, Prog for children & young adult, Ref serv available, Scanner, Spoken cassettes & CDs, Spoken cassettes & DVDs, Story hour, Summer reading prog, Telephone ref, VHS videos, Wheelchair accessible
Publications: The Ferry Whistle (Newsletter)
Partic in Library of Rhode Island Network; Ocean State Libraries
Open Mon-Fri 1-6, Sat 9-12
Friends of the Library Group

SLATERSVILLE

P NORTH SMITHFIELD PUBLIC LIBRARY*, 20 Main St, 02876. (Mail add: PO Box 950, 02876-0898), SAN 315-4696. Tel: 401-767-2780. FAX: 401-767-2782. E-mail: nsmlibrary@yahoo.com. Web Site: www.nspl.info. *Dir,* Susan Dubois; Staff 9 (MLS 3, Non-MLS 6)
Founded 1928. Circ 62,765
Library Holdings: AV Mats 5,825; Bk Vols 50,083; Per Subs 124

Subject Interests: Child care, Parenting
Automation Activity & Vendor Info: (Acquisitions) Innovative Interfaces, Inc; (Cataloging) Innovative Interfaces, Inc; (Circulation) Innovative Interfaces, Inc; (Course Reserve) Innovative Interfaces, Inc; (ILL) Innovative Interfaces, Inc; (Media Booking) Innovative Interfaces, Inc; (OPAC) Innovative Interfaces, Inc; (Serials) Innovative Interfaces, Inc
Wireless access
Function: 24/7 Electronic res, 24/7 Online cat, Activity rm, Adult bk club, Art programs, Audiobks on Playaways & MP3, Bk club(s), Bks on CD, Butterfly Garden, Children's prog, Computer training, Computers for patron use, Distance learning, Electronic databases & coll, Homebound delivery serv, Internet access, Mango lang, Movies, Museum passes, Notary serv, Online cat, Photocopying/Printing, Preschool outreach, Prog for adults, Prog for children & young adult, Ref & res, Ref serv available, Scanner, Story hour, Study rm, Summer & winter reading prog, Summer reading prog, Teen prog
Partic in Library of Rhode Island Network; Ocean State Libraries
Open Mon-Thurs 10-8, Fri 10-5, Sat 10-1

SMITHFIELD

C BRYANT UNIVERSITY, Douglas & Judith Krupp Library, 1150 Douglas Pike, 02917-1284. SAN 315-470X. Tel: 401-232-6125. Reference Tel: 401-232-6299. Administration Tel: 401-232-6298. E-mail: library@bryant.edu. Web Site: library.bryant.edu. *Dir, Libr Serv,* Laura Kohl; E-mail: lkohl@bryant.edu; *Asst Dir, Instruction & Research Mgr,* Allison Papini; E-mail: apapini1@bryant.edu; *Digital Services & Research Librn,* Rebecca Marcus; Tel: 401-232-6295, E-mail: rmarcus1@bryant.edu; *Res & Instruction Librn,* Dymond Bush; E-mail: dbush@bryant.edu; *Res & Instruction Librn,* Abby Dolan; E-mail: adolan1@bryant.edu; *Res & Instruction Librn,* Peregrine Macdonald; E-mail: pmacdonald1@bryant.edu; *Colls Mgr,* William Doughty; Tel: 401-232-6296, E-mail: wdoughty@bryant.edu; *Mgr, Borrower Serv,* Meagan Joseph; E-mail: mjoseph4@bryant.edu; Staff 13 (MLS 9, Non-MLS 4)
Founded 1955. Enrl 3,238; Fac 182; Highest Degree: Master
Library Holdings: AV Mats 1,964; e-books 30,076; e-journals 66,537; Bk Vols 146,246; Per Subs 147
Special Collections: U.S. Women & World War II Letter Writing Project
Subject Interests: Acctg, Finance, Gen bus, Intl bus
Automation Activity & Vendor Info: (Acquisitions) Innovative Interfaces, Inc; (Cataloging) Innovative Interfaces, Inc; (Circulation) Innovative Interfaces, Inc; (Course Reserve) Innovative Interfaces, Inc; (ILL) Innovative Interfaces, Inc; (OPAC) Innovative Interfaces, Inc; (Serials) Innovative Interfaces, Inc
Wireless access
Function: Computers for patron use, Photocopying/Printing, Ref serv available, Scanner
Partic in Consortium of Rhode Island Academic & Research Libraries; Higher Educ Libr Info Network; Library of Rhode Island Network; OCLC Online Computer Library Center, Inc
Open Mon-Thurs 7:30am-1:30am, Fri 7:30-7, Sat 9-5, Sun 10am-1:30am
Restriction: Open to fac, students & qualified researchers

P EAST SMITHFIELD PUBLIC LIBRARY*, 50 Esmond St, 02917-3016. SAN 315-405X. Tel: 401-231-5150. Circulation Tel: 401-231-5150, Ext 2. Reference Tel: 401-231-5150, Ext 8. FAX: 401-231-2940. E-mail: eastsmithfieldpubliclibrary@gmail.com. Web Site: www.eastsmithfieldpubliclibrary.org. *Libr Dir,* Cynthia Muhlbach; *Asst Dir,* Frank Floor; Tel: 401-231-5150, Ext 6; Staff 14 (MLS 5, Non-MLS 9)
Founded 1916. Pop 21,640
Jul 2019-Jun 2020 Income $713,918, State $133,069, Locally Generated Income $575,849, Other $5,000. Mats Exp $3,712
Library Holdings: Audiobooks 145,597; AV Mats 6,678; CDs 856; DVDs 4,518; High Interest/Low Vocabulary Bk Vols 78; Large Print Bks 4,003; Bk Vols 50,924; Per Subs 108; Videos 1,214
Special Collections: Local Smithfield & Rhode Island History Coll; Society of Friends or Quakers Coll
Subject Interests: Cooking, Disease information for the layman, Gardening, Gen med
Automation Activity & Vendor Info: (Cataloging) Innovative Interfaces, Inc - Sierra; (Circulation) Innovative Interfaces, Inc - Sierra; (ILL) Innovative Interfaces, Inc - Sierra; (OPAC) Innovative Interfaces, Inc - Sierra
Wireless access
Function: 24/7 Electronic res, 24/7 Online cat, 3D Printer, Activity rm, Adult bk club, After school storytime, Archival coll, Art exhibits, Audio & video playback equip for onsite use, Audiobks via web, AV serv, Bk club(s), Bks on cassette, Bks on CD, CD-ROM, Children's prog, Computer training, Computers for patron use, E-Reserves, Electronic databases & coll, Free DVD rentals, Holiday prog, Home delivery & serv to seniorr ctr & nursing homes, Homebound delivery serv, Homework prog, ILL available, Internet access, Magazines, Magnifiers for reading, Mail & tel request accepted, Mango lang, Meeting rooms, Movies, Museum passes, Music CDs, Online cat, Online ref, Outreach serv, OverDrive digital audio bks, Photocopying/Printing, Preschool outreach, Prog for adults, Prog for children & young adult, Ref & res, Ref serv available, Scanner, Senior computer classes, Senior outreach, Spoken cassettes & CDs, Story hour, Summer reading prog, Tax forms, Teen prog, Telephone ref, Visual arts prog, Wheelchair accessible, Workshops
Publications: East Smithfield Public Library's Happenings (Monthly newsletter)
Partic in Library of Rhode Island Network; Ocean State Libraries
Special Services for the Deaf - High interest/low vocabulary bks
Special Services for the Blind - Ref serv
Open Mon, Tues & Thurs 10-9, Wed & Fri 10-7, Sat (Sept-June) 10-3
Restriction: Internal use only, Non-circulating coll, Non-circulating of rare bks
Friends of the Library Group

TIVERTON

P TIVERTON PUBLIC LIBRARY, 34 Roosevelt Ave, 02878. SAN 320-460X. Tel: 401-625-6796. E-mail: staff@tivertonlibrary.org. Web Site: tivertonlibrary.org. *Dir,* Catherine Damiani; Tel: 401-625-6796, Ext 6, E-mail: director@tivertonlibrary.org; *Ad,* Debbie Estrella; Tel: 401-625-6796, Ext 5; *Ch, Ref & Acq Librn,* Elizabeth Aguiar; Tel: 401-625-6796, Ext 113, E-mail: eaguiar@tivertonlibrary.org; *Ch,* Meghan Paquette; Tel: 401-625-6796, Ext 3, E-mail: mpaquette@tivertonlibrary.org; *Teen Librn,* Jordyn Smith; Tel: 401-625-6796, Ext 4; *Tech Coordr,* Kristin Amaral; Tel: 401-625-6796, Ext 8; Staff 14 (MLS 6, Non-MLS 8)
Founded 1938. Pop 15,828; Circ 78,500
Jul 2015-Jun 2016 Income (Main & Associated Libraries) $701,000, State $124,000, City $565,000, Locally Generated Income $12,000. Mats Exp $43,350, Books $31,000, Per/Ser (Incl. Access Fees) $4,000, AV Mat $8,200, Presv $150. Sal $425,146
Library Holdings: AV Mats 3,900; DVDs 2,763; Bk Titles 44,483; Per Subs 200
Subject Interests: Local hist
Automation Activity & Vendor Info: (Cataloging) ByWater Solutions; (Circulation) ByWater Solutions; (OPAC) ByWater Solutions
Wireless access
Function: 24/7 Electronic res, Activity rm, Adult bk club, Audiobks via web, AV serv, Bk club(s), Bks on CD, Children's prog, Computer training, Computers for patron use, Digital talking bks, Electronic databases & coll, Free DVD rentals, Holiday prog, Home delivery & serv to seniorr ctr & nursing homes, Homebound delivery serv, ILL available, Internet access, Life-long learning prog for all ages, Magazines, Magnifiers for reading, Mango lang, Meeting rooms, Movies, Museum passes, Music CDs, Online cat, Online info literacy tutorials on the web & in blackboard, Outreach serv, Outside serv via phone, mail, e-mail & web, OverDrive digital audio bks, Photocopying/Printing, Preschool reading prog, Prog for adults, Prog for children & young adult, Ref serv available, Scanner, Spoken cassettes & CDs, Spoken cassettes & DVDs, Story hour, Study rm, Summer & winter reading prog, Summer reading prog, Tax forms, Teen prog, Telephone ref, Wheelchair accessible, Workshops
Publications: Friend to Friend (Online only)
Partic in Library of Rhode Island Network; Ocean State Libraries
Special Services for the Deaf - Adult & family literacy prog; Bks on deafness & sign lang; High interest/low vocabulary bks
Special Services for the Blind - Bks on cassette; Bks on CD; Home delivery serv; Magnifiers; Talking bks
Open Mon-Thurs 10-8, Fri 10-5, Sat 10-4
Friends of the Library Group
Branches: 1
UNION PUBLIC LIBRARY, 3832 Main Rd, 02878, SAN 320-4634. Tel: 401-625-6799. Web Site: tivertonlibrary.org/union-library. *Br Librn,* Dianna Parente; Tel: 401-625-6796, Ext 2, E-mail: dparente@tivertonlibrary.org; Staff 2 (Non-MLS 2)
Founded 1938
Function: 24/7 Electronic res, Adult bk club, Bks on CD, Computers for patron use, E-Reserves, ILL available, Internet access, Magazines, Music CDs, Photocopying/Printing
Open Tues 10-5, Sat 10-1
Friends of the Library Group

WARREN

P GEORGE HAIL FREE LIBRARY, 530 Main St, 02885. SAN 315-4734. Tel: 401-245-7686. FAX: 401-245-7470. E-mail: info@georgehail.org. Web Site: www.georgehail.org. *Dir,* Chris Matos; E-mail: director@georgehail.org; *Ad, Ref Librn,* Meredith Richards; *Youth Serv Librn,* Michaela Hutchinson; E-mail: youthservices@georgehail.org; Staff 10 (MLS 4, Non-MLS 6)
Founded 1888. Pop 11,500; Circ 51,345
Library Holdings: Bk Vols 28,000; Per Subs 60
Special Collections: Charles W Greene Museum; Whaling Industry Coll
Subject Interests: Local hist, Warren maritime hist
Automation Activity & Vendor Info: (Circulation) ByWater Solutions
Wireless access
Function: Telephone ref

Partic in Library of Rhode Island Network; Ocean State Libraries
Open Mon-Thurs 10-8, Fri 10-5, Sat 10-3
Friends of the Library Group

WARWICK

J COMMUNITY COLLEGE OF RHODE ISLAND*, Knight Campus Library, 400 East Ave, 02886-1807. SAN 359-8659. Tel: 401-825-2214. Reference Tel: 401-825-2215. FAX: 401-825-2421. Web Site: www.ccri.edu/library. *Interim Dean,* William Stargard; Tel: 401-825-1189, E-mail: wstargard@ccri.edu; Staff 8 (MLS 8)
Founded 1964. Enrl 5,210; Fac 297
Library Holdings: Bk Vols 54,000; Per Subs 750
Special Collections: Career & College Information CLSI; College Catalog Coll, micro
Automation Activity & Vendor Info: (Acquisitions) Innovative Interfaces, Inc; (Cataloging) Innovative Interfaces, Inc; (Circulation) Innovative Interfaces, Inc; (Course Reserve) Innovative Interfaces, Inc; (OPAC) Innovative Interfaces, Inc; (Serials) Innovative Interfaces, Inc
Wireless access
Partic in Higher Educ Libr Info Network; Library of Rhode Island Network
Open Mon-Thurs 8-8, Fri 8-4

S IN-SIGHT LIBRARY*, 43 Jefferson Blvd, 02888-9961. SAN 320-7420. Tel: 401-941-3322. FAX: 401-941-3356. E-mail: info@in-sight.org. Web Site: www.in-sight.org. *Dir,* Chris Butler; E-mail: cbutler@in-sight.org; Staff 1 (MLS 1)
Subject Interests: Blindness, Braille
Open Mon-Fri 8:30-4:30
Restriction: Mem only

M KENT HOSPITAL, Care New England Library Services, 455 Toll Gate Rd, 02886. SAN 320-7447. Tel: 401-737-7010. Web Site: www.kentri.org/for-physicians/library. *Librn,* Arline Dyer; Tel: 401-274-1122, Ext 42338, E-mail: adyer@wihri.org
Founded 1970
Library Holdings: Bk Vols 1,100; Per Subs 20
Subject Interests: Med, Nursing
Partic in Basic Health Sciences Library Network; National Network of Libraries of Medicine Region 7
Open Mon-Fri 8-4:30
Restriction: Open to staff, students & residents

P PONTIAC FREE LIBRARY*, 101 Greenwich Ave, 02886. SAN 315-4769. Tel: 401-737-3292. FAX: 401-737-3292. E-mail: info@pontiacfreelibrary.org. Web Site: www.pontiacfreelibrary.org. *Co-Dir,* Stacey Anter; *Co-Dir,* Joanne Tandy; Staff 5 (MLS 1, Non-MLS 4)
Founded 1884. Pop 3,000; Circ 12,056
Library Holdings: AV Mats 1,442; Bk Titles 16,448; Per Subs 26
Automation Activity & Vendor Info: (Cataloging) Innovative Interfaces, Inc; (Circulation) Innovative Interfaces, Inc; (OPAC) Innovative Interfaces, Inc
Wireless access
Partic in Library of Rhode Island Network; Ocean State Libraries
Open Mon 1-7, Tues 10-5, Thurs 2-7, Fri 1-5, Sat 10-2
Friends of the Library Group

P WARWICK PUBLIC LIBRARY*, 600 Sandy Lane, 02889-8298. SAN 359-8683. Tel: 401-739-5440. FAX: 401-732-2055. Web Site: www.warwicklibrary.org. *Dir,* Christopher LaRoux; Tel: 401-739-5440, Ext 9760, E-mail: laroux.chris@gmail.com; *Dep Dir,* Jana Stevenson; Tel: 401-739-5440, Ext 9759, E-mail: janalynnstevenson@gmail.com; *Coordr, Tech,* Evan Barta; Tel: 401-739-5440, Ext 9753, E-mail: evan.barta@gmail.com; *Adult Serv,* Mary Anne Quinn; Tel: 401-739-5440, Ext 9766; *Ch Serv,* Ellen O'Brien; Tel: 401-739-5440, Ext 9748; *Circ,* Kelly DiCenzo; Tel: 401-739-5440, Ext 9741; Staff 16 (MLS 16)
Founded 1965. Pop 80,619; Circ 570,575
Jul 2017-Jun 2018 Income (Main & Associated Libraries) $4,135,367, State $722,188, City $3,366,199, Other $46,980. Mats Exp $350,548, Books $176,379, AV Mat $63,559, Electronic Ref Mat (Incl. Access Fees) $110,610. Sal $1,978,076
Library Holdings: AV Mats 18,535; e-books 66,067; Electronic Media & Resources 73,156; Bk Vols 132,321; Per Subs 255
Special Collections: State Document Depository
Automation Activity & Vendor Info: (Cataloging) Innovative Interfaces, Inc; (Circulation) Innovative Interfaces, Inc; (OPAC) Innovative Interfaces, Inc
Wireless access
Function: 24/7 Electronic res, 24/7 Online cat, 3D Printer, Activity rm, Adult bk club, Art exhibits, Audiobks on Playaways & MP3, Audiobks via web, AV serv, Bk club(s), Bk reviews (Group), Bks on CD, Chess club, Children's prog, Computer training, Computers for patron use, Digital talking bks, E-Readers, E-Reserves, Electronic databases & coll, Equip loans & repairs, For res purposes, Free DVD rentals, Games & aids for people with disabilities, Genealogy discussion group, Govt ref serv, Health sci info serv, Holiday prog, Home delivery & serv to seniorr ctr & nursing homes, Homebound delivery serv, ILL available, Internet access, Jazz prog, Learning ctr, Life-long learning prog for all ages, Magazines, Magnifiers for reading, Mail & tel request accepted, Mango lang, Meeting rooms, Microfiche/film & reading machines, Movies, Museum passes, Music CDs, Notary serv, Online cat, Online info literacy tutorials on the web & in blackboard, Online ref, Outreach serv, Outside serv via phone, mail, e-mail & web, OverDrive digital audio bks, Photocopying/Printing, Preschool outreach, Preschool reading prog, Printer for laptops & handheld devices, Prof lending libr, Prog for adults, Prog for children & young adult, Ref & res, Ref serv available, Res libr, Scanner, Senior computer classes, Senior outreach, Serves people with intellectual disabilities, Story hour, Study rm, Summer & winter reading prog, Summer reading prog, Tax forms, Teen prog, Telephone ref, Visual arts prog, Wheelchair accessible, Workshops, Writing prog
Partic in Library of Rhode Island Network; Ocean State Libraries
Open Mon-Thurs 9-9, Fri & Sat 9-5, Sun (Sept-May) 1-5
Friends of the Library Group
Branches: 3
APPONAUG, 3267 Post Rd, 02886, SAN 359-8713. Tel: 401-739-6411. *Br Mgr,* Lois Mazzone
Library Holdings: Bk Vols 16,000
Open Mon & Fri 1-5, Wed 9-1 & 2-5, Sat 9-1
Friends of the Library Group
CONIMICUT, 55 Beach Ave, 02889, SAN 359-8748. Tel: 401-737-6546. *Br Mgr,* Jackie Petrarca
Library Holdings: Bk Vols 10,000
Open Mon, Tues, Thur & Fri 1-5 Wed 9-1 & 2-5
Friends of the Library Group
NORWOOD, 328 Pawtuxet Ave, 02888, SAN 359-8772. Tel: 401-941-7545. *Br Supvr,* Tina Travis
Library Holdings: Bk Vols 12,000
Open Mon, Wed-Fri 1-5, Tues & Sat 9-1
Friends of the Library Group

WEST GREENWICH

P LOUTTIT LIBRARY*, 274 Victory Hwy, 02817. SAN 315-4785. Tel: 401-397-3434. FAX: 401-397-3837. E-mail: louttitlibrary@gmail.com. Web Site: www.louttitlibrary.org. *Dir,* Annette Feldman; *Asst Dir, Youth Serv Librn,* Stephanie Barta; Staff 1 (MLS 1)
Founded 1951. Pop 6,520; Circ 31,730
Library Holdings: AV Mats 2,363; Bk Vols 23,450; Per Subs 43; Talking Bks 503
Subject Interests: W Greenwich hist
Automation Activity & Vendor Info: (Acquisitions) Innovative Interfaces, Inc; (Cataloging) Innovative Interfaces, Inc; (Circulation) Innovative Interfaces, Inc; (Course Reserve) Innovative Interfaces, Inc; (ILL) Innovative Interfaces, Inc; (Media Booking) Innovative Interfaces, Inc; (OPAC) Innovative Interfaces, Inc; (Serials) Innovative Interfaces, Inc
Wireless access
Partic in Library of Rhode Island Network; Ocean State Libraries
Open Mon-Thurs 10-8, Fri 10-5, Sat 10-2
Friends of the Library Group

WEST WARWICK

P WEST WARWICK PUBLIC LIBRARY*, 1043 Main St, 02893. SAN 359-8802. Tel: 401-828-3750. FAX: 401-828-8493. E-mail: info@wwpl.org. Web Site: www.wwpl.org. *Dir,* Tom O'Donnell; E-mail: tom@wwpl.org; Staff 12 (MLS 5, Non-MLS 7)
Founded 1967. Pop 29,581; Circ 139,238
Library Holdings: AV Mats 6,234; Bk Vols 94,198; Per Subs 142
Special Collections: Rhode Island; Science Fiction; West Warwick
Automation Activity & Vendor Info: (Cataloging) Innovative Interfaces, Inc; (Circulation) Innovative Interfaces, Inc; (ILL) Innovative Interfaces, Inc
Wireless access
Function: Homebound delivery serv
Publications: Newsletter (Monthly)
Partic in Library of Rhode Island Network; Ocean State Libraries
Open Mon-Wed 9-9, Thurs & Fri 9-5, Sat 9-1
Friends of the Library Group

WESTERLY

P MEMORIAL & LIBRARY ASSOCIATION*, Westerly Library & Wilcox Park, 44 Broad St, 02891. SAN 315-4815. Tel: 401-596-2877. Circulation Tel: 401-596-2877, Ext 300. Reference Tel: 401-596-2877, Ext 306, 401-596-2877, Ext 332. Toll Free Tel: 866-460-2877. FAX: 401-596-5600. Web Site: www.westerlylibrary.org. *Exec Dir,* Brigitte Hopkins; Tel: 401-596-2877, Ext 303, E-mail: bhopkins@westerlylibrary.org; *Asst Dir,* Bill Lancellotta; Tel: 401-596-2877, Ext 328, E-mail: wlancellotta@westerlylibrary.org; *Head, Youth Services & Education,* Rebecca Graebner; Tel: 401-596-2877, Ext 317, E-mail:

rgraebner@westerlylibrary.org; *Head, Adult Serv,* Caroline Badowski; Tel: 401-596-2877, Ext 307; *Head, Pub Serv,* Nick Engert; Tel: 401-596-2877, Ext 338, E-mail: nengert@westerlylibrary.org; *Ad,* Cassie Skobrak; Tel: 401-596-2877, Ext 312, E-mail: cskobrak@westerlylibrary.org; *Ch,* Melanie Fricchione; Tel: 401-596-2877, Ext 337, E-mail: mfricchione@westerlylibrary.org; *Spec Coll Librn,* Nina Wright; Tel: 401-596-2877, Ext 325, E-mail: nwright@westerlylibrary.org; *Teen Librn,* Colleen King; Tel: 401-596-2877, Ext 301, E-mail: cking@westerlylibrary.org; *Tween Librarian,* Ben Green; Tel: 401-596-2877, Ext 318, E-mail: bgreen@westerlylibrary.org; *Technology & Innovation Coord,* Maria Loughran; Tel: 401-596-2877, Ext 311, E-mail: mloughran@westerlylibrary.org. Subject Specialists: *Local hist,* Nina Wright; Staff 36 (MLS 10, Non-MLS 26)
Founded 1894. Circ 259,141
Library Holdings: Bk Vols 159,737; Per Subs 376
Special Collections: Art Gallery; Children's Literature (Margaret Wise Brown Coll), ms; Museum Coll, artifacts. US Document Depository
Subject Interests: Art, Genealogy, Granite indust, Local hist archives
Function: 24/7 Electronic res, 24/7 Online cat, 24/7 wireless access, Activity rm, Adult bk club, Art programs, Audiobks on Playaways & MP3, Audiobks via web, AV serv, Bi-weekly Writer's Group, Bk club(s), Bks on CD, Chess club, Children's prog, Computer training, Computers for patron use, Electronic databases & coll, Equip loans & repairs, Extended outdoor wifi, For res purposes, Free DVD rentals, Games, Govt ref serv, Holiday prog, Homebound delivery serv, ILL available, Instruction & testing, Internet access, Laptop/tablet checkout, Large print keyboards, Life-long learning prog for all ages, Magazines, Magnifiers for reading, Mail & tel request accepted, Makerspace, Mango lang, Meeting rooms, Microfiche/film & reading machines, Movies, Museum passes, Music CDs, Notary serv, Online cat, Outreach serv, OverDrive digital audio bks, Photocopying/Printing, Preschool outreach, Preschool reading prog, Printer for laptops & handheld devices, Prog for adults, Prog for children & young adult, Ref & res, Ref serv available, Res assist avail, Res libr, Scanner, Senior computer classes, Senior outreach, Serves people with intellectual disabilities, Spanish lang bks, STEM programs, Story hour, Study rm, Summer & winter reading prog, Summer reading prog, Tax forms, Teen prog, Telephone ref, Wheelchair accessible, Wifi hotspot checkout, Winter reading prog, Workshops, Writing prog
Publications: First Westerly Coloring Book; Life's Little Pleasures
Partic in Library of Rhode Island Network; Ocean State Libraries
Special Services for the Blind - Bks on cassette
Open Mon-Wed 9-9, Thurs & Fri 9-6, Sat 9-4
Restriction: Lending limited to county residents, Non-circulating of rare bks, Non-resident fee
Friends of the Library Group

M WESTERLY HOSPITAL*, Medical Library, 25 Wells St, 02891. SAN 315-4807. Tel: 401-348-3948. FAX: 401-348-3802. Web Site: www.westerlyhospital.org. *Libr Mgr,* Anne-Marie Kaminsky; Tel: 860-442-0711, Ext 2238, E-mail: anne-marie.kaminsky@lmhosp.org
Library Holdings: Bk Vols 640
Subject Interests: Med, Surgery
Wireless access

WOONSOCKET

S AMERICAN-FRENCH GENEALOGICAL SOCIETY LIBRARY, 78 Earle St, 02895. (Mail add: PO Box 830, 02895-0870), SAN 372-8587. Tel: 401-765-6141. E-mail: info@afgs.org. Web Site: afgs.org. *Pres,* Normand T Deragon; E-mail: nderagon@afgs.org
Founded 1978
Library Holdings: CDs 100; DVDs 25; Microforms 5,000; Music Scores 200; Bk Titles 12,000; Per Subs 120; Videos 60
Special Collections: Canadian Baptism, Marriage & Death Records from the Province of Quebec (Drouin Coll); Fabien File; Forget File; Loiselle Files; Rivest File. Canadian and Provincial
Wireless access
Function: Res libr
Publications: Je Me Souviens (Quarterly)
Open Tues 1-9, Sat 10-4

P WOONSOCKET HARRIS PUBLIC LIBRARY*, 303 Clinton St, 02895. SAN 315-4831. Tel: 401-769-9044. Reference Tel: 401-767-4124. FAX: 401-767-4120. Web Site: woonsocketlibrary.org. *Dir,* Leslie Page; E-mail: lpage@woonsocketlibrary.org; *Asst Dir,* Margaret McNulty; Tel: 401-767-4126, E-mail: mmcnulty@woonsocketlibrary.org; *Head, Ref,* Barbara Bussart; E-mail: bbussart@woonsocketlibrary.org; *Ch Serv,* Christine Wallace Goldstein; E-mail: cgoldstein@woonsocketlibrary.org; Staff 30 (MLS 7, Non-MLS 23)
Founded 1863. Pop 42,000
Library Holdings: Bk Vols 127,241; Per Subs 142
Special Collections: State Document Depository
Subject Interests: Local hist
Wireless access
Function: Meeting rooms, Notary serv, Photocopying/Printing
Partic in Library of Rhode Island Network; Ocean State Libraries
Open Mon, Wed & Thurs 9-9, Tues & Fri 9-5, Sat (Sept-May) 9-5
Friends of the Library Group

SOUTH CAROLINA

Date of Statistics: FY 2024
Population, 2020 U.S. Census: 5,118,425
Total Volumes in Public Libraries: 7,814,664
Volumes Per Capita: 1.53
Total Public Library Circulation: 16,610,711
Circulation Per Capita: 3.25
Digital Resources:
Total computers for use by the public: 3,835
Annual visits: 10,268,950
Registered Users: 2,433,876
Total annual wireless sessions 7,924,175

Income and Expenditures:
Total Public Library Income (including Grants-in-Aid):
Source of Income:
State Aid: $13,637,385
Formula for Apportionment: Per capita allocation to county libraries with a minimum allocation of $150,000
Number of County or Multi-county (Regional) Libraries: 42 county libraries; 2 regional libraries; 1 municipal library
Counties Served: 46
Number of Bookmobiles in State: 35
Information provided courtesy of: Leah Cannon, State Data Coordinator,

ABBEVILLE

P ABBEVILLE COUNTY LIBRARY SYSTEM*, 1407 N Main St, 29620. SAN 360-2702. Tel: 864-459-4009. FAX: 864-459-0891. Web Site: www.youseemore.com/abbeville. *Interim Libr Dir,* Faith Line; E-mail: fline@abbevillecounty.org; *Asst Libr Dir,* Lois Rhodes
Library Holdings: Bk Vols 58,365; Per Subs 81
Subject Interests: Genealogy, Local hist
Wireless access
Open Mon & Wed-Fri 9-5:30, Tues & Thurs 9-8, Sat 9-3
Friends of the Library Group
Branches: 2
AGNEW BRANCH, 429 W Main St, Donalds, 29638, SAN 360-2761. Tel: 864-379-8568. FAX: 864-379-8568.
Open Mon 10-1 & 2-8, Tues-Fri 10-1 & 2-5, Sat 10-1
Friends of the Library Group
CALHOUN FALLS BRANCH, 409 N Tugaloo St, Calhoun Falls, 29628, SAN 360-2737. Tel: 864-418-8724. FAX: 864-418-8724.
Open Mon, Tues, Thurs & Fri 10-1 & 2-5, Wed 10-1 & 2-8
Friends of the Library Group

AIKEN

P AIKEN-BAMBERG-BARNWELL-EDGEFIELD REGIONAL LIBRARY SYSTEM*, 314 Chesterfield St SW, 29801-7171. SAN 359-8861. Tel: 803-642-7575. FAX: 803-642-7597. Web Site: www.abbe-lib.org. *Dir,* Mary Jo Dawson; E-mail: maryjod@abbe-lib.org; *Dir, Tech Serv,* Holden Humphrey; *Syst Coordr,* Vic McGraner; E-mail: vicm@abbe-lib.org; Staff 15 (MLS 12, Non-MLS 3)
Founded 1958. Pop 207,014
Library Holdings: AV Mats 26,000; Bk Vols 232,544; Per Subs 367
Special Collections: South Carolina Coll
Automation Activity & Vendor Info: (Acquisitions) Ex Libris Group; (Cataloging) SirsiDynix; (Circulation) SirsiDynix; (ILL) OCLC Online; (OPAC) SirsiDynix
Wireless access
Friends of the Library Group
Branches: 13
AIKEN COUNTY, 314 Chesterfield St SW, 29801, SAN 359-8896. Tel: 803-642-2020. FAX: 803-642-7570. *Libr Mgr,* Jessica Christian
Open Mon, Wed, Fri & Sat 10-6, Tues & Thurs 10-9
Friends of the Library Group
BAMBERG COUNTY, 3156 Railroad Ave, Bamberg, 29003-1017. (Mail add: PO Box 305, Bamberg, 29003), SAN 359-8926. Tel: 803-245-3022. FAX: 803-245-2422. *Libr Mgr,* Jennifer Hiatt
Open Mon-Wed & Fri 10-6, Thurs 10-9, Sat 10-2
Friends of the Library Group
BARNWELL COUNTY, 40 Burr St, Barnwell, 29812-1917, SAN 359-8950. Tel: 803-259-3612. FAX: 803-259-7497. *Libr Mgr,* Tricia Gordon
Special Collections: South Carolina Genealogy
Open Mon-Wed & Fri 10-6, Thurs 10-9, Sat 10-2
Friends of the Library Group
BLACKVILLE BRANCH, 19420 Sol Blatt Ave, Blackville, 29817, SAN 359-8985. Tel: 803-284-2295. FAX: 803-284-2295. *Br Mgr,* Ruthie Hewitt
Open Mon, Tues & Thurs 10-1 & 2-6, Wed 2-6
Friends of the Library Group
NANCY BONNETTE - WAGENER BRANCH LIBRARY, 204 Park St NE, Wagener, 29164, SAN 359-9191. Tel: 803-291-6500. *Br Mgr,* LeWanda Fulmer
Open Mon-Thurs 10-1 & 2-6
NANCY CARSON - NORTH AUGUSTA LIBRARY, 135 Edgefield Rd, North Augusta, 29841-2423, SAN 359-9132. Tel: 803-279-5767. FAX: 803-202-3588. *Br Mgr,* Barbara Walker
Open Mon, Tues & Thurs 10-9, Wed & Fri 10-6, Sat 10-1
Friends of the Library Group
DENMARK BRANCH, 5122 Carolina Hwy, Denmark, 29042, SAN 359-9019. Tel: 803-793-4511. FAX: 803-793-4511. *Br Mgr,* Position Currently Open
Open Mon & Fri 10-1 & 2-6, Tues-Thurs 10-1
EDGEFIELD COUNTY, 105 Courthouse Sq, Edgefield, 29824, SAN 359-9043. Tel: 803-637-4025. FAX: 803-637-4026. *Libr Mgr,* Jalisha Adams
Open Mon-Wed & Fri 10-6, Thurs 10-9, Sat 10-2
JACKSON BRANCH, 106 Main St, Jackson, 29831-2616, SAN 377-0443. Tel: 803-471-3811. FAX: 803-471-3811. *Br Mgr,* Judy Rhinehart
Open Mon, Wed & Thurs 1-6, Tues 2-6
Friends of the Library Group
JOHNSTON BRANCH, 407 Calhoun St, Johnston, 29832, SAN 359-9078. Tel: 803-275-5157. FAX: 803-275-2754. *Br Mgr,* Patsy Mitchell
Open Mon, Tues & Thurs 12-6
Friends of the Library Group
MIDLAND VALLEY, Nine Hillside Rd, Warrenville, 29851, SAN 377-046X. Tel: 803-593-7379. FAX: 803-593-5253. *Br Mgr,* Linda Coffin
Open Mon, Wed & Thurs 1-6, Tues 2-6
NEW ELLENTON BRANCH, 113 Pine Hill Ave, New Ellenton, 29809, SAN 359-9108. Tel: 803-652-7845. FAX: 803-652-7845. *Br Mgr,* Susan Toole
Open Mon, Wed & Thurs 1-6, Tues 2-6
WILLISTON BRANCH, 5121 Springfield Rd, Williston, 29853-9762, SAN 359-9221. Tel: 803-621-6000. FAX: 803-266-3027. *Br Mgr,* Jo Crider
Open Mon-Thurs 10-1 & 2-6
Bookmobiles: 1. Supvr, Tracy Jackson

S SAVANNAH RIVER SITE*, Savannah River National Laboratory Applied Science Library, Bldg 773-A, A-1029, 29808. SAN 327-0815. Tel: 803-725-0069. Web Site: srnl.doe.gov, www.srs.gov. *Sr Librn,* Barry Bull; E-mail: Millard.Bull@srnl.doe.gov
Library Holdings: Bk Vols 34,000; Per Subs 1,750
Subject Interests: Nuclear, Safety, Training
Restriction: Staff use only

C UNIVERSITY OF SOUTH CAROLINA AIKEN*, Gregg-Graniteville Library, 471 University Pkwy, 29801. SAN 315-4866. Tel: 803-648-3465. Circulation Tel: 803-641-3286. Interlibrary Loan Service Tel: 803-641-3504. Reference Tel: 803-643-6808. FAX: 803-641-3302. Web Site: library.usca.edu. *Dean of Libr,* Dr Lisa Ennis; Tel: 803-641-3460, E-mail: lisa.ennis@usca.edu; *Circ Librn, Govt Doc Librn,* Susie O'Connor; Tel: 803-641-3261, E-mail: susano@usca.edu; *Instruction & Ref Librn,* Brandy R Horne; Tel: 803-641-3282, E-mail: brandyh@usca.edu; *Archives, Instruction & Ref Librn,* Deborah Tritt; Tel: 803-641-3589, E-mail: deboraht@usca.edu; *Instruction/Ref Serv, Syst Librn,* Robert Amerson; Tel: 803-641-3320, E-mail: ramerson@usca.edu; *Supvr, Per,* Willie Mae Dumas; Tel: 803-641-3284, E-mail: williemaed@usca.edu; *ILL Mgr,* Kelsey Crump; Tel: 803-641-3504, E-mail: kelseyc@usca.edu; *Coll Coordr,* Natalia Taylor Bowdoin; Tel: 803-641-3492, E-mail: nataliab@usca.edu; Staff 14 (MLS 6, Non-MLS 8)
Founded 1961. Enrl 2,722; Fac 147; Highest Degree: Master
Library Holdings: AV Mats 3,455; CDs 930; e-books 3,727; e-journals 41,643; Electronic Media & Resources 181; Microforms 76,276; Bk Titles 125,046; Bk Vols 135,810; Per Subs 1,328; Videos 385
Special Collections: Department of Energy Public Documents Coll; Gregg-Graniteville Historical Files; Southern History (May Coll); USC Aiken Archives. State Document Depository; US Document Depository
Automation Activity & Vendor Info: (Acquisitions) Innovative Interfaces, Inc - Millennium; (Cataloging) Innovative Interfaces, Inc - Millennium; (Circulation) Innovative Interfaces, Inc; (ILL) OCLC ILLiad; (OPAC) Innovative Interfaces, Inc - Millennium; (Serials) Innovative Interfaces, Inc - Millennium
Wireless access
Publications: Annual Report; Inter-Intra Library Loan Service Pamphlet; New Faculty Library Guide
Partic in Carolina Consortium; OCLC Online Computer Library Center, Inc; Partnership Among South Carolina Academic Libraries; SC Libr Network
Friends of the Library Group

ALLENDALE

P ALLENDALE-HAMPTON-JASPER REGIONAL LIBRARY*, Regional Office, 297 Main St, 29810. (Mail add: PO Box 280, 29810-0280), SAN 359-9256. Tel: 803-584-2371, 803-584-3513. FAX: 803-584-8134. Web Site: www.ahjlibrary.org. *Dir,* Scott Strawn; E-mail: ahjstrawn@gmail.com; Staff 1 (MLS 1)
Founded 1905. Pop 53,000; Circ 84,574
Library Holdings: Bk Vols 61,279
Automation Activity & Vendor Info: (Cataloging) Evergreen; (Circulation) Evergreen
Open Mon-Fri 9-5
Friends of the Library Group
Branches: 5
ALLENDALE COUNTY LIBRARY, 297 N Main St, 29810. (Mail add: PO Box 280, 29810-0280). Tel: 803-584-2371. FAX: 803-584-8134. *Br Mgr,* Bess Strong; E-mail: ahjbstrong@gmail.com; Staff 2 (Non-MLS 2)
Library Holdings: Bk Vols 20,000
Open Mon-Fri 9-5, Sat 10-2
ESTILL PUBLIC LIBRARY, 100 Peeples Ave, Estill, 29918-4827. (Mail add: PO Box 668, Estill, 29918-0668), SAN 359-9310. Tel: 803-625-4560. FAX: 803-625-3341. *Br Mgr,* Cynthia Deloach; E-mail: ahjcdeloach@gmail.com; Staff 1 (Non-MLS 1)
Library Holdings: Bk Vols 2,000
Open Mon-Thurs 10:30-5:30, Fri 10-5
HAMPTON COUNTY LIBRARY, 12 Locust St, Hampton, 29924, SAN 359-9345. Tel: 803-943-7528. FAX: 803-943-3261. *Br Mgr,* Chrissy Cook; E-mail: ahjccook@gmail.com; Staff 3 (Non-MLS 3)
Library Holdings: Bk Vols 16,279
Open Mon & Wed 9-5, Tues & Thurs 11-7, Fri 11-5, Sat 10-2
HARDEEVILLE COMMUNITY LIBRARY, 30 Main St, Hardeeville, 29927. (Mail add: PO Box 1837, Hardeeville, 29927-1837), SAN 359-937X. Tel: 843-784-3426. FAX: 843-784-5277. *Br Mgr,* Darlene Thomas-Burroughs; E-mail: ahjdburroughs@gmail.com; Staff 2 (Non-MLS 2)
Library Holdings: Bk Vols 5,000
Open Mon-Wed 10:30-5:30, Thurs 12-7, Fri 10-5, Sat 11-2
Friends of the Library Group
PRATT MEMORIAL, 451A Wilson St, Ridgeland, 29936. (Mail add: PO Drawer 1540, Ridgeland, 29936-1540), SAN 359-940X. Tel: 843-726-7744. Web Site: www.ahjlibrary.org/prattmemoriallibrary. *Br Mgr,* Marcia Cleland; E-mail: mceland@ahjlibrary.org; Staff 3 (Non-MLS 3)
Library Holdings: Bk Vols 18,000
Open Mon-Thurs 10:30-5:30, Fri 10:30-4:30, Sat 11-2
Bookmobiles: 1. Mgr, Joseph Harvey

C UNIVERSITY OF SOUTH CAROLINA*, Salkehatchie Library, 465 James Brandt Blvd, 29810. Tel: 803-812-7353. Web Site: uscsalkehatchie.sc.edu/home/library. *Head Librn,* Dan Johnson; E-mail: johns943@mailbox.sc.edu; Staff 2 (MLS 2)
Founded 1965. Enrl 820
Library Holdings: Bk Vols 55,725; Per Subs 153
Special Collections: South Carolina, Five County Area Coll (Allendale, Bamberg, Barnwell, Colleton & Hampton counties)
Subject Interests: African-Am, Women's studies
Automation Activity & Vendor Info: (Circulation) Innovative Interfaces, Inc
Wireless access
Publications: Newsletter
Partic in Association of Research Libraries; Association of Southeastern Research Libraries; Consortium of Southern Biomedical Libraries; LYRASIS; Partnership Among South Carolina Academic Libraries
Open Mon-Thurs 8-8, Fri 8-4:30; Mon-Fri 8-5 (Summer)
Departmental Libraries:
PEDEN MCLEOD LIBRARY, Salkehatchie East Campus, 807 Hampton St, Walterboro, 29488. (Mail add: PO Box 1337, Walterboro, 29488-1337), SAN 378-1607. Tel: 843-782-8627. *Librn,* Jessica Goodwin; E-mail: goodwij3@mailbox.sc.edu; Staff 1 (MLS 1)
Library Holdings: Bk Vols 13,000; Per Subs 25
Open Mon-Thurs 8-8, Fri 8-4:30; Mon-Fri 8:30-5 (Summer)

ANDERSON

P ANDERSON COUNTY LIBRARY*, 300 N McDuffie St, 29621-5643. SAN 359-9434. Tel: 864-260-4500. Circulation Tel: 864-260-4500, Ext 137. Interlibrary Loan Service Tel: 864-260-4500, Ext 110. Reference Tel: 864-260-4500, Ext 126. Administration Tel: 864-260-4500, Ext 102. FAX: 864-260-4510. E-mail: administration@andersonlibrary.org. Web Site: www.andersonlibrary.org. *Dir,* Faith A Line; E-mail: fline@andersonlibrary.org; *Asst Dir, Head, Ref,* Janet Price; E-mail: jprice@andersonlibrary.org; *Head, Access Serv,* Annie Sutton; E-mail: asutton@andersonlibrary.org; *Head, Children's Servx,* Diane Smiley; E-mail: dsmiley@andersonlibrary.org; *Head, Digital Serv,* Dan Bonsall; E-mail: dbonsall@andersonlibrary.org; *Head, ILL, Head, Per,* Sara Leady; E-mail: sleady@andersonlibrary.org; *Head, Spec Coll,* Laura Holden; E-mail: lholden@andersonlibrary.org; *Head, Tech Serv,* Susan Manalli; E-mail: smanalli@andersonlibrary.org; *Coordr, Prog,* Mary Lanham; E-mail: mlanham@andersonlibrary.org; *Coordr, Prog,* Jhanna Reck; E-mail: jreck@andersonlibrary.org; *Extn Serv,* Heather Bistyga; E-mail: hbistyga@andersonlibrary.org; *Ref Serv, YA,* Miriam Church; E-mail: mchurch@andersonlibrary.org; Staff 93 (MLS 15, Non-MLS 78)
Founded 1958. Pop 187,126; Circ 704,671
Library Holdings: AV Mats 24,594; e-books 101; Large Print Bks 6,983; Bk Vols 336,426; Per Subs 1,079
Special Collections: Foundation Center Cooperating Coll; South Carolina Coll, bks, microflm & newsp
Subject Interests: SC
Automation Activity & Vendor Info: (Cataloging) Evergreen; (Circulation) Evergreen; (ILL) OCLC; (OPAC) Evergreen; (Serials) Evergreen
Wireless access
Function: Adult bk club, After school storytime, Audiobks via web, Bk club(s), Bks on CD, Children's prog, Computer training, Computers for patron use, Electronic databases & coll, Free DVD rentals, Holiday prog, ILL available, Magazines, Movies, Music CDs, Online cat, Online ref, Outreach serv, Photocopying/Printing, Printer for laptops & handheld devices, Prog for adults, Prog for children & young adult, Ref serv available, Spanish lang bks, Spoken cassettes & CDs, Story hour, Summer reading prog, Tax forms, Teen prog, Telephone ref, Wheelchair accessible
Publications: Bookmarks (Newsletter)
Partic in DISCUS; LYRASIS; SCLENDS
Special Services for the Deaf - Assistive tech; TTY equip
Special Services for the Blind - Assistive/Adapted tech devices, equip & products; Audio mat; Talking bks
Open Mon-Thurs 9-9, Fri & Sat 9-6, Sun 2-6
Friends of the Library Group
Branches: 8
BELTON BRANCH, 91 Breazeale St, Belton, 29627, SAN 359-9469. Tel: 864-338-8330. FAX: 864-338-8696. E-mail: belton@andersonlibrary.org.
Open Mon 11-7, Tues-Fri 9:30-6, Sat 9:30-1:30
Friends of the Library Group
JENNIE ERWIN BRANCH, 318 N Shirley Ave, Honea Path, 29654, SAN 359-9493. Tel: 864-369-7751. FAX: 864-369-7751. E-mail: honeapath@andersonlibrary.org.
Open Mon & Wed-Fri 9:30-6, Tues 11-7, Sat 9:30-1:30
Friends of the Library Group
IVA BRANCH, 203 W Cruette St, Iva, 29655. (Mail add: PO Box 86, Iva, 26955-0086), SAN 359-9523. Tel: 864-348-6150. FAX: 864-348-6150. E-mail: iva@andersonlibrary.org.
Open Mon-Wed & Fri 9:30-6, Thurs 11-7, Sat 9:30-1:30

LANDER MEMORIAL REGIONAL, 925 Greenville Dr, Williamston, 29697, SAN 359-9558. Tel: 864-847-5238. FAX: 864-847-5238. E-mail: lander@andersonlibrary.org.
Open Mon, Tues & Thurs 9:30-8, Wed & Fri 9:30-6, Sat 9:30-1:30
Friends of the Library Group

PENDLETON BRANCH, 650 S Mechanic St, Pendleton, 29670. (Mail add: PO Box 707, Pendleton, 29670-0707), SAN 359-9612. Tel: 864-646-3045. FAX: 864-646-3046. E-mail: pendleton@andersonlibrary.org.
Open Mon, Tues & Thurs 9:30-8, Wed & Fri 9:30-6, Sat 9:30-1:30
Friends of the Library Group

PIEDMONT BRANCH, 1407 Hwy 86, Piedmont, 29673, SAN 359-9647. Tel: 864-845-6534. FAX: 864-845-6534. E-mail: piedmont@andersonlibrary.org.
Open Mon-Wed & Fri 9:30-6, Thurs 11-7, Sat 9:30-1:30
Friends of the Library Group

POWDERSVILLE BRANCH, Four Civic Ct, Powdersville, 29642. (Mail add: PO Box 51325, Powdersville, 29673-2017), SAN 328-7599. Tel: 864-295-1190. FAX: 864-295-2961. E-mail: powdersville@andersonlibrary.org.
Open Mon, Tues & Thurs 9:30-8, Wed & Fri 9:30-6, Sat 9:30-1:30
Friends of the Library Group

WESTSIDE COMMUNITY CENTER BRANCH, 1100 W Franklin St, 29624, SAN 378-1623. Tel: 864-260-4660. FAX: 864-260-4660. E-mail: westside@andersonlibrary.org.
Open Mon-Fri 9-4:30
Friends of the Library Group

Bookmobiles: Extension Librn, H Bistyga. Bk titles 6,085

C ANDERSON UNIVERSITY LIBRARY*, The Thrift Library, 316 Boulevard, 29621. SAN 315-4882. Tel: 864-231-2050. FAX: 864-231-2191. E-mail: library@andersonuniversity.edu. Web Site: www.andersonuniversity.edu/library. *Dir, Libr Serv,* Kent Millwood; Tel: 864-231-2049, E-mail: kmillwood@andersonuniversity.edu; *Head, Tech Serv,* Dana Whelchel; E-mail: Dwhelchel@andersonuniversity.edu; *Info & Tech Librn,* Betsy Elsner; E-mail: belsner@andersonuniversity.edu; Staff 7.5 (MLS 5, Non-MLS 2.5)
Founded 1911. Enrl 3,000; Highest Degree: Doctorate
Automation Activity & Vendor Info: (Cataloging) TLC (The Library Corporation); (Circulation) TLC (The Library Corporation); (Course Reserve) TLC (The Library Corporation); (Discovery) EBSCO Discovery Service; (ILL) OCLC; (OPAC) TLC (The Library Corporation)
Wireless access
Partic in DISCUS; OCLC Online Computer Library Center, Inc; Partnership Among South Carolina Academic Libraries

J FORREST COLLEGE LIBRARY*, 601 E River St, 29624. Tel: 864-225-7653. FAX: 864-261-7471. Web Site: www.forrestcollege.edu/library-coordinator. *Libr Coord,* Olivia Sparkman; E-mail: oliviasparkman@forrestcollege.edu
Founded 1946. Highest Degree: Associate
Library Holdings: AV Mats 1,082; Bk Vols 2,826; Per Subs 20
Wireless access
Partic in Library & Information Resources Network
Open Mon-Thurs 8am-9pm, Fri 8-5:30

BEAUFORT

P BEAUFORT COUNTY LIBRARY*, 311 Scott St, 29902. Administration Tel: 843-255-6465. E-mail: library@bcgov.net. Web Site: www.beaufortcountylibrary.org. *Dir,* Amanda Brewer Dickman; *Asst Dir,* Joshua Greer
Automation Activity & Vendor Info: (Acquisitions) Evergreen
Wireless access
Branches: 5

BEAUFORT BRANCH, 311 Scott St, 29902-5591, SAN 359-9825. Tel: 843-255-6456. Web Site: www.beaufortcountylibrary.org/beaufort-branch.
Subject Interests: Local hist
Automation Activity & Vendor Info: (Cataloging) SirsiDynix-Symphony; (Circulation) SirsiDynix-Symphony; (OPAC) SirsiDynix-Enterprise
Partic in Lowcounty Libr Fedn; SCLENDS
Friends of the Library Group

BLUFFTON BRANCH LIBRARY, 120 Palmetto Way, Bluffton, 29910, SAN 322-581X. Tel: 843-255-6501. Web Site: www.beaufortcountylibrary.org/bluffton-branch.
Friends of the Library Group

HILTON HEAD ISLAND BRANCH, 11 Beach City Rd, Hilton Head Island, 29926, SAN 359-985X. Tel: 843-255-6501. Web Site: www.beaufortcountylibrary.org/hilton-head-branch.
Friends of the Library Group

LOBECO BRANCH, 1862 Trask Parkway (Hwy17), Lobeco, 29931. Tel: 843-255-6479. Web Site: www.beaufortcountylibrary.org/lobeco-branch.
Founded 2003
Friends of the Library Group

SAINT HELENA BRANCH, 6355 Jonathan Francis Sr Rd, Saint Helena Island, 29920, SAN 375-5185. FAX: 843-255-6540. Web Site: www.beaufortcountylibrary.org/st-helena-branch.
Founded 2012
Friends of the Library Group

Bookmobiles: 2

J TECHNICAL COLLEGE OF THE LOWCOUNTRY*, Learning Resources Center, 921 Ribaut Rd, 29902. SAN 320-233X. Tel: 843-525-8304. Web Site: www.tcl.edu/library. *Dir, Learning Res,* Sasha Bishop; E-mail: sbishop@tcl.edu; Staff 4 (MLS 2, Non-MLS 2)
Founded 1961. Enrl 1,436; Fac 45; Highest Degree: Associate
Library Holdings: AV Mats 3,045; e-books 60,000; Bk Vols 23,576; Per Subs 185
Subject Interests: Health sci, Paralegal
Automation Activity & Vendor Info: (Cataloging) SirsiDynix; (Circulation) SirsiDynix; (Course Reserve) SirsiDynix; (OPAC) SirsiDynix
Wireless access
Publications: Check It Out; LRC Information Brochure
Partic in LYRASIS; OCLC Online Computer Library Center, Inc; Partnership Among South Carolina Academic Libraries; South Carolina Information & Library Services Consortium
Open Mon-Thurs 8-8, Fri 8am-11:30am

A UNITED STATES MARINE CORPS*, Air Station Library, Bldg 596, 29904. Tel: 843-228-7682. Interlibrary Loan Service Tel: 843-228-6131. FAX: 843-228-7596. Web Site; www.mccs-sc.com/mil-fam/libraries.shtml. *Librn,* Kevin Giampa; E-mail: kevin.giampa@usmc-mccs.org; Staff 5 (Non-MLS 5)
Founded 1957
Library Holdings: Bk Titles 24,000; Per Subs 90
Special Collections: Children's Stories, Fairytales, Classics; College Textbook; General Fiction & Non-fiction Coll
Subject Interests: City hist, Hist of aircraft, Maintenance of aircraft, Mil art, Mil sci
Wireless access
Open Mon-Thurs 8-8, Fri 8-3, Sat Noon-5

BENNETTSVILLE

P MARLBORO COUNTY LIBRARY SYSTEM*, Marian Wright Edelman Public Library, 203 Fayetteville Ave, 29512. SAN 315-4920. Tel: 843-479-5630. FAX: 843-479-5645. Web Site: www.edelmanpubliclibrary.org. *Dir,* Bobbie J Grooms; E-mail: mwelibrary@marlborocounty.sc.gov; Staff 1 (MLS 1)
Founded 1901. Pop 28,147; Circ 47,712
Library Holdings: AV Mats 2,900; Bk Vols 54,307; Per Subs 88
Automation Activity & Vendor Info: (Cataloging) Innovative Interfaces, Inc; (Circulation) Innovative Interfaces, Inc; (OPAC) Innovative Interfaces, Inc
Wireless access
Function: ILL available, Photocopying/Printing, Prog for children & young adult, Summer reading prog
Open Mon-Wed 9-7, Thurs & Fri 9-5, Sat 9-2
Friends of the Library Group
Bookmobiles: 1

BISHOPVILLE

P LEE COUNTY PUBLIC LIBRARY*, 200 N Main St, 29010. SAN 315-4939. Tel: 803-484-5921. FAX: 803-484-4177. E-mail: leecolibrary@gmail.com. Web Site: www.leecountylibrarysc.org/. *Dir,* Dawn Ellen; *Asst Librn,* Melissa Kiryen
Founded 1953. Pop 18,929; Circ 40,102
Library Holdings: Bk Vols 30,626; Per Subs 132
Automation Activity & Vendor Info: (Cataloging) TLC (The Library Corporation); (Circulation) TLC (The Library Corporation); (OPAC) TLC (The Library Corporation)
Open Mon-Fri 9-6, Sat 9-3, Sun 1-5
Friends of the Library Group

BLACKSBURG

G KINGS MOUNTAIN NATIONAL MILITARY PARK LIBRARY, 2625 Park Rd, 29702. SAN 323-7036. Tel: 864-936-7921. Web Site: www.nps.gov/kimo. *Superintendent,* Diana Bramble; *Librn,* Lamar Tate; Tel: 864-936-7921, Ext 3, E-mail: freeman_tate@nps.gov
Founded 1931
Library Holdings: Bk Titles 600
Open Wed-Sun 9-5

BLUFFTON

C UNIVERSITY OF SOUTH CAROLINA AT BEAUFORT LIBRARY, Eight E Campus Dr, 29909. SAN 315-4912. Tel: 843-208-8022. Interlibrary Loan Service Tel: 843-208-8160. FAX: 843-208-8296. Web

Site: www.uscb.edu/library. *Dir of Libr,* Kimberly B Kelley; Tel: 843-208-8025, E-mail: kk27@uscb.edu; *Access Serv & Electronic Res Librn,* Melanie Hanes-Ramos; Tel: 843-208-8023, E-mail: hanesml@uscb.edu; *Res & Instruction Librn,* Warren Cobb; Tel: 843-521-3122, E-mail: wc7@uscb.edu; *Res & Instruction Librn,* Victoria Neff; Tel: 843-208-8031, E-mail: vnneff@uscb.edu; *Res & Instruction Librn,* Emily Smith; Tel: 843-208-8028, E-mail: es47@uscb.edu; Staff 5 (MLS 5)
Founded 1959. Enrl 1,900
Library Holdings: e-books 25,299; Bk Vols 71,178; Per Subs 141
Special Collections: State Document Depository
Subject Interests: SC hist
Automation Activity & Vendor Info: (Acquisitions) Ex Libris Group; (Cataloging) Ex Libris Group; (Circulation) Ex Libris Group; (ILL) Ex Libris Group; (OPAC) Ex Libris Group
Wireless access
Partic in Association of Southeastern Research Libraries; LYRASIS; OCLC Online Computer Library Center, Inc; Partnership Among South Carolina Academic Libraries

BOILING SPRINGS

C SHERMAN COLLEGE OF CHIROPRACTIC*, Tom & Mae Bahan Library, 2020 Springfield Rd, 29316-7251. (Mail add: PO Box 1452, Spartanburg, 29304-1452), SAN 321-4842. Tel: 864-578-8770, Ext 253. FAX: 864-599-4860. Web Site: www.sherman.edu/library. *Dir, Learning Res,* Chandra Placer; Tel: 864-578-8770, Ext 258, E-mail: cplacer@sherman.edu; *Asst Dir, Learning Res,* Patricia Calhoun; E-mail: pcalhoun@sherman.edu; Staff 1 (MLS 1)
Founded 1973. Enrl 400; Fac 45; Highest Degree: Doctorate
Library Holdings: AV Mats 2,000; Bk Titles 3,100; Per Subs 48
Special Collections: Chiropractic (B J Palmer Green Coll)
Subject Interests: Biological, Chiropractic, Clinical sci
Automation Activity & Vendor Info: (Circulation) EOS International; (ILL) OCLC Worldshare Management Services; (OPAC) EOS International; (Serials) EBSCO Online
Wireless access
Function: Audio & video playback equip for onsite use, CD-ROM, Electronic databases & coll, ILL available, Internet access, Photocopying/Printing, Res libr, Spoken cassettes & CDs, VHS videos
Partic in Carolina Consortium; Chiropractic Libr Consortium; National Network of Libraries of Medicine Region 2; OCLC Online Computer Library Center, Inc
Open Mon-Thurs 7:30am-10pm, Fri 7:30-4:30, Sat 12-6

CAMDEN

S CAMDEN ARCHIVES & MUSEUM LIBRARY*, 1314 Broad St, 29020-3535. SAN 329-8582. Tel: 803-425-6050. FAX: 803-424-4053. E-mail: archives@camdensc.org. Web Site: www.classicallycarolina.com/what-do/museums-galleries/camden-archives-museum. *Dir,* Katherine Richardson; E-mail: krichardson@camdensc.org; Staff 2 (Non-MLS 2)
Founded 1975
Library Holdings: Bk Vols 5,100
Special Collections: South Carolina DAR Library; South Carolina Society Colonial Dames, XVII Century
Subject Interests: Genealogy
Wireless access
Open Mon-Fri 8-5, Sat 10-4
Restriction: In-house use for visitors. Non-circulating to the pub
Friends of the Library Group

P KERSHAW COUNTY LIBRARY*, Camden Branch, 1304 Broad St, 29020. SAN 359-9914. Tel: 803-425-1508. FAX: 803-425-7180. Web Site: www.kershawcountylibrary.org. *Dir,* Amy Schofield; Tel: 803-425-1508, Ext 3210, E-mail: amys@kershawcountylibrary.org; *Mgr,* Debbie Hemming; Tel: 803-425-1508, Ext 3207, E-mail: debbieh@kershawcountylibrary.org; *Ad,* Cris Wilson; Tel: 803-425-1508, Ext 3209, E-mail: cristib@kershawcountylibrary.org; *Ch,* Lauren Decker; Tel: 803-425-1508, Ext 3208, E-mail: laurend@kershawcountylibrary.org; Staff 21 (MLS 4, Non-MLS 17)
Founded 1936. Pop 52,647; Circ 108,928
Library Holdings: CDs 326; DVDs 300; Large Print Bks 4,280; Bk Titles 73,632; Bk Vols 87,995; Per Subs 190; Talking Bks 1,804; Videos 1,990
Subject Interests: SC
Automation Activity & Vendor Info: (Cataloging) SirsiDynix; (Circulation) SirsiDynix; (OPAC) SirsiDynix
Wireless access
Function: Adult bk club, Adult literacy prog, After school storytime, Bi-weekly Writer's Group, Bks on cassette, Bks on CD, Children's prog, Computers for patron use, E-Reserves, Electronic databases & coll, Home delivery & serv to seniorr ctr & nursing homes, ILL available, Internet access, Mail & tel request accepted, Orientations, Photocopying/Printing, Prog for adults, Prog for children & young adult, Senior computer classes, Summer reading prog, Tax forms, VHS videos, Wheelchair accessible
Open Mon-Thurs 9-8, Fri 9-6, Sat 10-5, Sun 2-5
Restriction: Off-site coll in storage - retrieval as requested
Friends of the Library Group
Branches: 2
BETHUNE PUBLIC, 206 S Main St, Bethune, 29009. (Mail add: PO Box 446, Bethune, 29009-0446), SAN 359-9949. Tel: 803-310-6006. *Mgr,* Jill Fleischman; E-mail: Jillf@kershawcountylibrary.org; Staff 1 (MLS 1)
Circ 5,091
Library Holdings: Large Print Bks 382; Bk Titles 6,784; Bk Vols 6,801; Talking Bks 63; Videos 56
Automation Activity & Vendor Info: (Circulation) SirsiDynix; (OPAC) SirsiDynix
Function: Bks on cassette, Bks on CD, Children's prog, Computers for patron use, ILL available, Internet access, Photocopying/Printing, Summer reading prog, Tax forms, VHS videos
Open Tues & Thurs 10-2 & 3-6, Wed & Sat 10-2
Friends of the Library Group
ELGIN BRANCH, 2652 Main St, Elgin, 29045. (Mail add: PO Box 725, Elgin, 29045-0725). Tel: 803-438-7881. FAX: 803-438-4428. *Mgr,* Rachael Sommer; Tel: 803-438-7881, Ext 3302; Staff 3 (MLS 1, Non-MLS 2)
Founded 1999. Circ 34,150
Library Holdings: CDs 48; Bk Titles 15,087; Bk Vols 15,329; Per Subs 25; Talking Bks 507; Videos 370
Automation Activity & Vendor Info: (Cataloging) SirsiDynix; (Circulation) SirsiDynix; (OPAC) SirsiDynix
Function: Accelerated reader prog, Bks on cassette, Bks on CD, Children's prog, Computers for patron use, Electronic databases & coll, ILL available, Photocopying/Printing, Tax forms, VHS videos, Wheelchair accessible
Open Mon-Thurs 10-7, Fri & Sat 10-6
Bookmobiles: 1. Coord, Hanna Gustafson

CENTRAL

C SOUTHERN WESLEYAN UNIVERSITY*, Claude R Rickman Library, 916 Wesleyan Dr, 29630-9748. (Mail add: PO Box 1020, 907 Wesleyan Dr, 29630-1020), SAN 315-4971. Tel: 864-644-5060. E-mail: library@swu.edu. Web Site: www.swu.edu/academics/library. *Dir, Libr Serv,* Shannon Brooks; Tel: 864-644-5072, E-mail: sbrooks@swu.edu; Staff 5 (MLS 4, Non-MLS 1)
Founded 1906. Enrl 1,200; Highest Degree: Doctorate
Library Holdings: Bk Vols 61,000; Per Subs 10
Special Collections: Genealogical Coll (Upstate South Carolina Families); Wesleyan Historical Coll
Wireless access
Partic in Partnership Among South Carolina Academic Libraries
Open Mon-Thurs 7:45am-10pm, Fri 7:45-4:30, Sat 1-4

CHARLESTON

G CENTER FOR COASTAL ENVIRONMENTAL HEALTH & BIOMOLECULAR RESEARCH*, NOAA Field Library, c/o College of Charleston, Marine Resources Library, 217 Ft Johnson Rd, Bldg 8, 29412. (Mail add: PO Box 12559, 29422-2559), SAN 315-5021. Tel: 843-953-9370. Interlibrary Loan Service Tel: 843-953-9373. FAX: 843-953-9371. Web Site: coastalscience.noaa.gov/about/centers/ccehbr. *Librn,* Geoffrey A Timms; E-mail: timmsgp@cofc.edu; Staff 3 (MLS 1, Non-MLS 2)
Library Holdings: Bk Vols 9,000; Per Subs 40
Subject Interests: Marine sci
Function: For res purposes
Partic in Federal Library & Information Network; NOAA Libraries Network; OCLC-LVIS
Open Mon-Fri 8:30-5

P CHARLESTON COUNTY PUBLIC LIBRARY*, 68 Calhoun St, 29401. SAN 359-9973. Tel: 843-805-6801. Reference Tel: 843-805-6930. Administration Tel: 843-805-6807. Administration FAX: 843-727-3741. E-mail: info@ccpl.org. Web Site: www.ccpl.org. *Exec Dir,* Angela Craig; *Dep Dir,* Darlene Jackson; E-mail: jacksond@ccpl.org; *Dir of Finance, Dir, Human Res,* Perry Litchfield; E-mail: litchfieldp@ccpl.org; *Br Mgr,* Nancy Lupton; *Mgr Fac,* Nancy Sullivan; E-mail: sullivann@ccpl.org; *IT Serv Mgr,* Thomas Wheeler; E-mail: wheelert@ccpl.org; *Project Mgr,* Toni Pattison; E-mail: pattisont@ccpl.org; *Tech Serv Mgr,* Amy Quesenberry; E-mail: amarala@ccpl.org; *YA Mgr,* Andria L Amaral; *Children's Coordr,* Pam Cadden; E-mail: caddenp@ccpl.org; Staff 219.8 (MLS 65.8, Non-MLS 154)
Founded 1931. Pop 350,209; Circ 3,090,479
Jul 2015-Jun 2016 Income (Main & Associated Libraries) $16,441,888, State $558,971, Federal $20,512, County $15,091,224, Other $771,181. Mats Exp $2,286,052, Books $1,281,495, Other Print Mats $15,327, AV Mat $407,511, Electronic Ref Mat (Incl. Access Fees) $581,719. Sal $7,510,706

Library Holdings: Audiobooks 21,128; Bks on Deafness & Sign Lang 75; Braille Volumes 30; CDs 6,584; DVDs 87,888; e-books 15,089; e-journals 177; Electronic Media & Resources 6,174; Large Print Bks 14,673; Bk Vols 690,345; Per Subs 1,117
Subject Interests: Ethnic studies, Local hist
Automation Activity & Vendor Info: (Cataloging) SirsiDynix; (Circulation) SirsiDynix; (ILL) OCLC ILLiad; (OPAC) SirsiDynix
Wireless access
Function: 24/7 Electronic res, 24/7 Online cat, Activity rm, Adult bk club, Adult literacy prog, Archival coll, Art exhibits, Audio & video playback equip for onsite use, Audiobks via web, AV serv, Bk club(s), Bks on CD, CD-ROM, Children's prog, Computer training, Computers for patron use, Electronic databases & coll, Free DVD rentals, Holiday prog, ILL available, Internet access, Life-long learning prog for all ages, Magazines, Mango lang, Meeting rooms, Microfiche/film & reading machines, Movies, Museum passes, Music CDs, Notary serv, Online cat, Outreach serv, Outside serv via phone, mail, e-mail & web, OverDrive digital audio bks, Photocopying/Printing, Prog for adults, Prog for children & young adult, Ref & res, Ref serv available, Scanner, Story hour, Summer reading prog, Teen prog, Telephone ref, Wheelchair accessible
Publications: Staff Connections (Newsletter)
Partic in LYRASIS
Special Services for the Deaf - Staff with knowledge of sign lang; TTY equip
Open Mon-Thurs 9-8, Fri & Sat 9-6, Sun 2-5
Restriction: ID required to use computers (Ltd hrs), Non-circulating, Non-resident fee
Friends of the Library Group
Branches: 15
COOPER RIVER MEMORIAL, 3503 Rivers Ave, 29405, SAN 360-0009. Tel: 843-744-2489. Web Site: www.ccpl.org/branches/cooper-river. *Br Mgr,* Rick Pelletier
Founded 1948. Circ 93,785
Automation Activity & Vendor Info: (Circulation) SirsiDynix
Function: Bks on CD, Children's prog, Computers for patron use, Electronic databases & coll, Free DVD rentals, Holiday prog, ILL available, Internet access, Mango lang, Meeting rooms, Notary serv, Online cat, Outreach serv, OverDrive digital audio bks, Photocopying/Printing, Prog for adults, Prog for children & young adult, Ref serv available, Summer reading prog, Wheelchair accessible
Open Mon-Thurs 10-8, Fri & Sat 10-6
Restriction: ID required to use computers (Ltd hrs), Non-resident fee
JOHN L DART BRANCH, 1067 King St, 29403, SAN 360-0068. Tel: 843-722-7550. Web Site: www.ccpl.org/branches/dart. *Br Mgr,* K'Lani Green
Founded 1968. Circ 48,968
Automation Activity & Vendor Info: (Circulation) SirsiDynix
Function: 24/7 Electronic res, 24/7 Online cat, Bks on CD, Children's prog, Electronic databases & coll, Free DVD rentals, ILL available, Internet access, Mango lang, Notary serv, Online cat, Photocopying/Printing, Prog for adults, Prog for children & young adult, Ref & res, Wheelchair accessible
Open Mon-Sat 10-6
Restriction: ID required to use computers (Ltd hrs), Non-resident fee
DORCHESTER ROAD REGIONAL, 6325 Dorchester Rd, North Charleston, 29418, SAN 370-9140. Tel: 843-552-6466. Web Site: www.ccpl.org/branches/dorchester. *Br Mgr,* Gerald Moore
Founded 1992. Circ 126,198
Automation Activity & Vendor Info: (Circulation) SirsiDynix
Function: 24/7 Electronic res, 24/7 Online cat, Bks on CD, Children's prog, Computers for patron use, Electronic databases & coll, Free DVD rentals, Holiday prog, ILL available, Internet access, Mango lang, Meeting rooms, Notary serv, Online cat, Outreach serv, OverDrive digital audio bks, Photocopying/Printing, Prog for adults, Prog for children & young adult, Ref & res, Summer reading prog, Wheelchair accessible
Open Mon-Thurs 10-8, Fri & Sat 10-6
Restriction: ID required to use computers (Ltd hrs), Non-resident fee
EDISTO BRANCH, Trinity Episcopal Church Hall, 1589 Hwy 174, Edisto Island, 29438, SAN 360-0017. Tel: 843-869-2355. Web Site: www.ccpl.org/branches/edisto. *Br Mgr,* Teri Blackberg
Founded 1991. Circ 10,647
Automation Activity & Vendor Info: (Circulation) SirsiDynix
Function: 24/7 Electronic res, 24/7 Online cat, Adult bk club, Bks on CD, Free DVD rentals, ILL available, Internet access, Mango lang, OverDrive digital audio bks, Prog for adults, Prog for children & young adult, Wheelchair accessible
Open Mon 10-6, Tues & Fri 2-6, Thurs 12-6, Sat 10-2
Restriction: ID required to use computers (Ltd hrs), Non-resident fee
FOLLY BEACH BRANCH, 55 Center St, Folly Beach, 29439, SAN 360-0025. Tel: 843-588-2001. Web Site: www.ccpl.org/branches/folly-beach. *Br Mgr,* Mary Bushkar
Founded 1941. Circ 17,561
Automation Activity & Vendor Info: (Circulation) SirsiDynix
Function: 24/7 Electronic res, 24/7 Online cat, Bks on CD, Computers for patron use, Free DVD rentals, ILL available, Internet access, Mango lang, Notary serv, OverDrive digital audio bks, Photocopying/Printing, Prog for adults, Prog for children & young adult, Ref & res, Wheelchair accessible
Open Mon & Fri 10-6, Wed 12-8
Restriction: ID required to use computers (Ltd hrs), Non-resident fee
CYNTHIA GRAHAM HURD SAINT ANDREWS REGIONAL, 1735 N Woodmere Dr, 29407, SAN 370-9167. Tel: 843-766-2546. *Br Mgr,* Jen McQueen
Founded 1991. Circ 356,223
Automation Activity & Vendor Info: (Circulation) SirsiDynix
Function: 24/7 Electronic res, 24/7 Online cat, Bks on CD, Children's prog, Computers for patron use, Electronic databases & coll, Free DVD rentals, Holiday prog, ILL available, Internet access, Mango lang, Meeting rooms, Notary serv, Online cat, Outreach serv, OverDrive digital audio bks, Photocopying/Printing, Prog for adults, Prog for children & young adult, Ref & res, Summer reading prog, Wheelchair accessible
Open Mon-Thurs 10-8, Fri & Sat 10-6
Restriction: ID required to use computers (Ltd hrs), Non-resident fee
JAMES ISLAND, 1248 Camp Rd, 29412, SAN 360-0033. Tel: 843-795-6679. Web Site: www.ccpl.org/branches/james-island. *Br Mgr,* Chris Johnston
Founded 1978. Circ 171,895
Automation Activity & Vendor Info: (Circulation) SirsiDynix
Function: 24/7 Electronic res, 24/7 Online cat, Audiobks via web, Bks on CD, Children's prog, Free DVD rentals, Holiday prog, ILL available, Internet access, Mango lang, Notary serv, Online cat, Outreach serv, OverDrive digital audio bks, Photocopying/Printing, Prog for adults, Prog for children & young adult, Ref & res, Summer reading prog, Wheelchair accessible
Open Mon-Thurs 10-8, Fri & Sat 10-6
Restriction: ID required to use computers (Ltd hrs), Non-resident fee
JOHN'S ISLAND REGIONAL, 3531 Maybank Hwy, Johns Island, 29455. Tel: 843-557-1945. Web Site: www.ccpl.org/branches/johns-island. *Br Mgr,* Linda Stewart
Founded 1986. Circ 154,646
Automation Activity & Vendor Info: (Circulation) SirsiDynix
Function: 24/7 Electronic res, 24/7 Online cat, Audiobks via web, Bks on CD, Children's prog, Electronic databases & coll, Free DVD rentals, Holiday prog, ILL available, Internet access, Mango lang, Meeting rooms, Notary serv, Online cat, Outreach serv, OverDrive digital audio bks, Photocopying/Printing, Prog for adults, Prog for children & young adult, Ref & res, Summer reading prog, Wheelchair accessible
Open Mon-Thurs 10-8, Fri & Sat 10-6
Restriction: ID required to use computers (Ltd hrs), Non-resident fee
Friends of the Library Group
MCCLELLANVILLE BRANCH, 222 Baker St, McClellanville, 29458, SAN 360-0041. Tel: 843-887-3699. Web Site: www.ccpl.org/branches/mcclellanville. *Br Mgr,* Pat Gross
Founded 1986
Open Mon 2-6, Tues, Thurs & Fri 9:30-1 & 2-6, Sat 9:30-2
MOUNT PLEASANT REGIONAL, 1133 Mathis Ferry Rd, Mount Pleasant, 29464, SAN 360-005X. Tel: 843-849-6161. Web Site: www.ccpl.org/branches/mount-pleasant. *Br Mgr,* Susan Frohnsdorff
Founded 1991
Function: 24/7 Electronic res, 24/7 Online cat, Audio & video playback equip for onsite use, Audiobks via web, AV serv, Bks on CD, Children's prog, Computers for patron use, Electronic databases & coll, Free DVD rentals, Holiday prog, ILL available, Internet access, Life-long learning prog for all ages, Magazines, Mango lang, Meeting rooms, Movies, Notary serv, Online cat, OverDrive digital audio bks, Photocopying/Printing, Prog for adults, Prog for children & young adult, Ref serv available, Summer & winter reading prog, Summer reading prog, Tax forms, Wheelchair accessible
Open Mon-Thurs 10-8, Fri & Sat 10-6
Restriction: ID required to use computers (Ltd hrs)
Friends of the Library Group
OTRANTO ROAD REGIONAL, 2261 Otranto Rd, North Charleston, 29406, SAN 370-9159. Tel: 843-572-4094. FAX: 843-572-4190. Web Site: www.ccpl.org/branches/otranto. *Br Mgr,* Ray Turner
Founded 1991
Function: 24/7 Electronic res, 24/7 Online cat, Adult literacy prog, Audiobks via web, AV serv, Bks on CD, Children's prog, Computers for patron use, Free DVD rentals, Holiday prog, ILL available, Internet access, Magazines, Mango lang, Meeting rooms, Movies, Notary serv, Online cat, OverDrive digital audio bks, Prog for adults, Prog for children & young adult, Ref serv available, Summer reading prog, Tax forms
Open Mon-Thurs 10-8, Fri & Sat 10-6
Restriction: ID required to use computers (Ltd hrs)
Friends of the Library Group
EDGAR ALLAN POE BRANCH, 1921 I'On Ave, Sullivan's Island, 29482, SAN 360-0076. Tel: 843-883-3914. Web Site: www.ccpl.org/branches/sullivans-island. *Br Mgr,* Marie Sollitt
Open Mon & Fri 10-6, Tues & Sat 10-2, Thurs 2-8

SAINT PAULS BRANCH, 5151 Town Council Dr, Hollywood, 29449. (Mail add: PO Box 549, Hollywood, 29449), SAN 360-0084. Tel: 843-889-3300. Web Site: www.ccpl.org/branches/hollywood. *Br Mgr,* Position Currently Open
Open Mon, Tues & Fri 10-6, Thurs 12-8, Sat 10-2

VILLAGE BRANCH, 430 Whilden St, Mount Pleasant, 29464, SAN 374-5236. Tel: 843-884-9741. Web Site: www.ccpl.org/branches/village. *Br Mgr,* Marvin Stewart
Founded 1948
Function: 24/7 Electronic res, 24/7 Online cat, Bks on CD, Children's prog, Free DVD rentals, Holiday prog, ILL available, Mango lang, Movies, Notary serv, Online cat, OverDrive digital audio bks, Prog for adults, Prog for children & young adult, Summer reading prog
Open Mon, Tues & Fri 10-6, Thurs 12-8, Sat 10-2
Restriction: ID required to use computers (Ltd hrs)
Friends of the Library Group

WEST ASHLEY, 45 Windermere Blvd, 29407, SAN 360-0092. Tel: 843-766-6635. Web Site: www.ccpl.org/branches/west-ashley. *Br Mgr,* Beth Bell
Founded 1964
Open Mon-Thurs 10-8, Fri & Sat 10-6

Bookmobiles: 1. Bookmobile Mgr, Gwen Wright. Bk vols 3,500

S CHARLESTON LIBRARY SOCIETY*, 164 King St, 29401. SAN 315-4998. Tel: 843-723-9912. E-mail: info@charlestonlibrarysociety.org. Web Site: www.charlestonlibrarysociety.org. *Exec Dir,* Ann Cleveland; E-mail: acleveland@charlestonlibrarysociety.org; *Head Librn,* Laura Mina; E-mail: lmina@charlestonlibrarysociety.org; *Librn & Archivist,* Trisha Kometer; E-mail: tkometer@charlestonlibrarysociety.org; *Ch,* Joyce Smith; E-mail: jsmith@charlestonlibrarysociety.org; *Asst Librn,* Janice Knight; E-mail: jknight@charlestonlibrarysociety.org; *Spec Coll Librn,* Lisa Hayes; E-mail: lhayes@charlestonlibrarysociety.org; Staff 11 (MLS 3, Non-MLS 8)
Founded 1748
Library Holdings: Audiobooks 780; DVDs 1,575; e-books 2,000; Large Print Bks 750; Bk Vols 15,000; Per Subs 90
Special Collections: 18th & 19th Century Manuscripts; Agriculture & Confederacy (Hinson Coll); Architecture (Staats Coll); Horticulture (Aiken Garden Club Coll); Igoe Shakespeare Coll; Letters, diaries, business papers relating to South Carolinians; Newspapers from 1732 to present; Timrod Scrapbooks (Courtenay Coll), books & photographs
Subject Interests: Am Jewish hist, Charlestonia, Civil War hist, Early 20th Century fiction, Elizabethan studies, Hist, Lit, Revolutionary war hist, SC
Automation Activity & Vendor Info: (Acquisitions) Baker & Taylor; (Cataloging) Innovative Interfaces, Inc - Sierra; (Circulation) Innovative Interfaces, Inc - Sierra; (OPAC) Innovative Interfaces, Inc - Sierra
Wireless access
Open Mon-Fri 9:30-4

C CHARLESTON SOUTHERN UNIVERSITY*, L Mendel Rivers Library, 9200 University Blvd, 29406. (Mail add: PO Box 118087, 29423-8087), SAN 315-498X. Tel: 843-863-7938. Reference Tel: 843-863-7946. Administration Tel: 843-863-7933. FAX: 843-863-7947. Web Site: library.csuniv.edu. *Libr Dir,* Eric Kistler; E-mail: ekistler@csuniv.edu; *Head, Ref & Instruction, Web Serv Librn,* Joe Fox; Tel: 843-863-7945, E-mail: jfox@csuniv.edu; *Ref & Instruction Librn,* Karen Meharg; Tel: 843-863-7937, E-mail: kmeharg@csuniv.edu; *Acq & Ser,* Dianne Boykin; Tel: 843-863-7925, E-mail: dboykin@csuniv.edu; *Archivist,* Enid Causey; Tel: 843-863-7940, E-mail: ecausey@csuniv.edu; *Syst & Electronic Res,* Delaina Zeinoun; Tel: 843-863-7951, E-mail: dzeinoun@csuniv.edu; Staff 8 (MLS 5, Non-MLS 3)
Founded 1966. Enrl 3,417; Fac 162; Highest Degree: Doctorate
Library Holdings: AV Mats 4,700; CDs 3,000; DVDs 800; e-books 421,000; e-journals 49,700; Microforms 23,000; Bk Titles 581,000; Per Subs 450
Special Collections: South Carolina History; US Document Depository. US Document Depository
Automation Activity & Vendor Info: (Acquisitions) Ex Libris Group; (Cataloging) Ex Libris Group; (Circulation) Ex Libris Group; (Course Reserve) Ex Libris Group; (Discovery) Ex Libris Group; (ILL) OCLC; (OPAC) Ex Libris Group; (Serials) Ex Libris Group
Wireless access
Function: 24/7 Electronic res, 24/7 Online cat, Archival coll, Art exhibits, Audio & video playback equip for onsite use, CD-ROM, Computers for patron use, E-Readers, Electronic databases & coll, Equip loans & repairs, Free DVD rentals, ILL available, Internet access, Laminating, Microfiche/film & reading machines, Music CDs, Online cat, Online info literacy tutorials on the web & in blackboard, Online ref, Orientations, Outreach serv, Outside serv via phone, mail, e-mail & web, Photocopying/Printing, Ref & res, Study rm, Telephone ref, Wheelchair accessible
Partic in Carolina Consortium; DISCUS; LYRASIS; Partnership Among South Carolina Academic Libraries
Open Mon-Thurs 7:30am-Midnight, Fri 7:30-5, Sat 9-5, Sun 3-Midnight (Winter); Mon-Thurs 8am-10pm, Fri 8-5, Sat 1-5, Sun 6pm-10pm (Summer)
Restriction: Circ limited, In-house use for visitors

C THE CITADEL*, Daniel Library, 171 Moultrie St, 29409-6140. SAN 360-0122. Circulation Tel: 843-953-6845. Reference Tel: 843-953-2569. FAX: 843-953-5190. Web Site: library.citadel.edu. *Libr Dir,* Aaron Wimer; E-mail: awimer@citadel.edu; *Dep Dir,* Position Currently Open; *Head, Pub Serv,* Danielle Moore; E-mail: emoore7@citadel.edu; *Head, Tech Serv,* Michele Ruth; E-mail: mruth@citadel.edu; *Admin Mgr,* Terri Johnson; E-mail: johnsont1@citadel.edu; Staff 16 (MLS 7, Non-MLS 9)
Founded 1842. Enrl 3,740; Fac 186; Highest Degree: Master
Special Collections: US Document Depository
Automation Activity & Vendor Info: (Acquisitions) Ex Libris Group; (Cataloging) Ex Libris Group; (Circulation) Ex Libris Group; (Course Reserve) Ex Libris Group; (Discovery) Ex Libris Group; (ILL) OCLC Tipasa; (Media Booking) Ex Libris Group; (OPAC) Ex Libris Group; (Serials) Ex Libris Group
Wireless access
Partic in Carolina Consortium; LYRASIS; Partnership Among South Carolina Academic Libraries
Open Mon-Thurs 7:30am-10:30pm, Sat 9-3, Sun Noon-10:30
Friends of the Library Group

C COLLEGE OF CHARLESTON*, Marlene & Nathan Addlestone Library, 205 Calhoun St, 29401-3519. (Mail add: 66 George St, 29424), SAN 360-0211. Tel: 843-953-5530. Circulation Tel: 843-953-8004. Information Services Tel: 843-953-8010. Web Site: library.cofc.edu. *Dean of Libr,* John White; E-mail: whitej@cofc.edu; *Dir, Admin Serv,* Tamara Rosas-Bossak; E-mail: bossaktc@cofc.edu; Staff 52 (MLS 26, Non-MLS 26)
Founded 1785. Enrl 11,531; Fac 988; Highest Degree: Master
Special Collections: Book Arts; College of Charleston Archives; Jewish Heritage Coll; John Henry Dick Ornithology Coll; South Carolina, books & per. Oral History; State Document Depository; US Document Depository
Subject Interests: Behav sci, Marine sci, Natural sci, Soc sci
Automation Activity & Vendor Info: (Acquisitions) Innovative Interfaces, Inc; (Cataloging) Innovative Interfaces, Inc; (Circulation) Innovative Interfaces, Inc; (Course Reserve) Innovative Interfaces, Inc; (ILL) OCLC ILLiad; (OPAC) Innovative Interfaces, Inc; (Serials) Innovative Interfaces, Inc
Wireless access
Publications: A Catalog of the Scientific Apparatus at the College of Charleston: 1800-1940; A History of the College of Charleston (1935); Introduction to Bibliography & Research Methods; Mendel; No Problems, Only Challenges: The Autobiography of Theodore S Stern; Proceedings of Southeastern Conferences on Bibliographic Instruction; St Michaels, Charleston 1751-1951 with Supplements 1951-2001; Tales of Charleston, 1930s
Partic in LYRASIS; Partnership Among South Carolina Academic Libraries
Special Services for the Deaf - Assistive tech
Friends of the Library Group

Departmental Libraries:

AVERY RESEARCH CENTER FOR AFRICAN AMERICAN HISTORY & CULTURE, 125 Bull St, 29424. Tel: 843-953-7609. FAX: 843-953-7607. E-mail: averyresearchcenter@cofc.edu. Web Site: avery.cofc.edu. *Exec Dir,* Tamara Butler, PhD; E-mail: tamarabutler@cofc.edu

MARINE RESOURCES LIBRARY, Bldg 8, 217 Fort Johnson Rd, 29412. (Mail add: PO Box 12559, 29422-2559), SAN 360-0246. Tel: 843-953-9370. FAX: 843-953-9371. E-mail: mrlcirc@cofc.edu. Web Site: www.mrl.cofc.edu. *Librn,* Geoffrey P Timms; E-mail: timmsgp@cofc.edu; Staff 1 (MLS 1)
Founded 1977
Special Collections: State Document Depository; US Document Depository
Subject Interests: Marine biol, Marine ecology, Marine genomics, Oceanography, Zoology
Automation Activity & Vendor Info: (Acquisitions) Innovative Interfaces, Inc - Millennium; (Cataloging) OCLC Connexion; (Circulation) Innovative Interfaces, Inc - Millennium; (Discovery) EBSCO Discovery Service; (ILL) OCLC ILLiad; (OPAC) Innovative Interfaces, Inc - Millennium
Function: Computers for patron use, E-Reserves, Electronic databases & coll, ILL available, Online cat, Photocopying/Printing, Ref serv available, Wheelchair accessible
Partic in NOAA Libraries Network; Partnership Among South Carolina Academic Libraries
Restriction: Badge access after hrs, Borrowing privileges limited to fac & registered students, Limited access for the pub, Open to fac, students & qualified researchers

S HUGUENOT SOCIETY OF SOUTH CAROLINA LIBRARY*, 138 Logan St, 29401. SAN 327-0858. Tel: 843-723-3235. FAX: 843-853-8476. E-mail: archivist@huguenotsociety.org. Web Site: www.huguenotsociety.org. *Research Historian,* Harriott Cheves Leland
Founded 1885
Library Holdings: Bk Vols 6,000
Special Collections: Quarto - Huguenot Society of Great Britain and Ireland (CD copies and hard copies)
Wireless access
Function: For res purposes, Internet access, Mail & tel request accepted, Online cat, Photocopying/Printing, Ref & res, Ref serv available, Res libr, Res performed for a fee
Publications: Transactions of the Huguenot Society of South Carolina
Open Mon-Fri 9-2
Restriction: Non-circulating

CM MEDICAL UNIVERSITY OF SOUTH CAROLINA LIBRARIES*, 171 Ashley Ave, Ste 419, 29425-0001. (Mail add: PO Box 254030, 29425-4030), SAN 360-0270. Tel: 843-792-9211. Circulation Tel: 843-792-2371. Reference Tel: 843-792-2372. FAX: 843-792-7947. E-mail: library@musc.edu. Web Site: www.library.musc.edu. *Dir of Libr,* Shannon D Jones; Tel: 843-792-8839, E-mail: joneshan@musc.edu; *Assoc Dir,* Heather N Holmes; Tel: 843-792-0065, E-mail: holmesh@musc.edu; *Dir, Digital Strategies & Innovation,* Erick T Lemon; Tel: 843-792-7672, E-mail: lemone@musc.edu; *Coll Serv, Dir, Info Res,* Jean Gudenas; Tel: 843-792-8309, E-mail: gudenas@musc.edu; *Dir, Pub Info & Commun Outreach,* David Rivers; Tel: 843-792-5546, E-mail: riversd@musc.edu; *Metadata Librn,* Jason Smith; Tel: 843-792-8727, E-mail: smijas@musc.edu; *Admin Coordr,* Ms Tasha Renfroe; Tel: 843-792-9211, E-mail: renfroej@musc.edu; *Info Res Coordr,* Tara Hay; Tel: 843-792-2811, E-mail: hayt@musc.edu; *Coordr, Learning Commons,* Joshua C Ivey; Tel: 843-792-6306, E-mail: iveyjc@musc.edu; *Prog Coordr,* Missy Anderson; Tel: 843-792-2369, E-mail: andersmp@musc.edu; *Pub Info Coordr,* Latecia Abraham; Tel: 843-792-5530, E-mail: abrahaml@musc.edu; *Univ Archivist,* Brooke Fox; Tel: 843-792-6477, E-mail: foxeb@musc.edu; *Digital Archivist,* Tabitha Samuel; Tel: 843-792-6749, E-mail: samuel@musc.edu; *Res & Educ Informationist,* Christine Andresen; Tel: 843-792-7183, E-mail: andresen@musc.edu; *Res & Educ Informationist,* Emily Brennan; Tel: 843-792-9275, E-mail: brennane@musc.edu; *Res & Educ Informationist,* Teri Lynn Herbert; Tel: 843-792-1370, E-mail: herbertl@musc.edu; *Res & Educ Informationist,* Emily Jones; Tel: 843-792-3364, E-mail: jonesmi@musc.edu; *Res & Educ Informationist,* Ayaba Logan; Tel: 843-792-4213, E-mail: loganay@musc.edu; *Res & Educ Informationist,* Irene M Lubker; Tel: 843-792-7648, E-mail: lubker@musc.edu; Staff 34 (MLS 11, Non-MLS 23)
Founded 1824. Enrl 2,996; Fac 1,725; Highest Degree: Doctorate
Library Holdings: e-books 340,460; e-journals 25,029
Special Collections: bks; History of Medicine (Waring Historical Library Coll); ms
Subject Interests: Allied health, Behav sci, Consumer health, Dentistry, Environ sci, Med, Natural sci, Nursing, Pharmacology, Soc sci
Automation Activity & Vendor Info: (Acquisitions) OCLC Worldshare Management Services; (Cataloging) OCLC Worldshare Management Services; (Circulation) OCLC Worldshare Management Services; (Course Reserve) OCLC Worldshare Management Services; (Discovery) OCLC Worldshare Management Services; (ILL) OCLC ILLiad; (Media Booking) OCLC Worldshare Management Services; (OPAC) OCLC Worldshare Management Services; (Serials) OCLC Worldshare Management Services
Wireless access
Partic in Consortium of Southern Biomedical Libraries; National Network of Libraries of Medicine Region 2; Partnership Among South Carolina Academic Libraries; South Carolina AHEC

Departmental Libraries:

WARING HISTORICAL LIBRARY, 175 Ashley Ave, 29425-0001. (Mail add: PO Box 250403, 29425-0403). Tel: 843-792-2288. FAX: 843-792-8619. Web Site: waring.library.musc.edu/index.php. *Curator,* Anna Schuldt; E-mail: schuldt@musc.edu; *Univ Archivist,* E Brooke Fox; Tel: 843-792-6477, E-mail: foxeb@musc.edu; *Digital Archivist,* Tabitha Samuel; Tel: 843-792-6749, E-mail: samuel@musc.edu; Staff 4 (MLS 3, Non-MLS 1)
Special Collections: Archives. Oral History
Subject Interests: Hist of med
Automation Activity & Vendor Info: (Discovery) OCLC Worldshare Management Services; (ILL) OCLC ILLiad
Publications: Waring Library Society (Newsletter)
Open Mon-Fri 8:30-5
Friends of the Library Group

S SOUTH CAROLINA HISTORICAL SOCIETY LIBRARY*, Addlestone Library, 3rd Flr, 205 Calhoun St, 29401. (Mail add: Fireproof Bldg, 100 Meeting St, 29401-2299), SAN 315-5056. Tel: 843-723-3225. E-mail: library@schsonline.org. Web Site: schistory.org. *Chief Exec Officer,* Faye Jensen; Tel: 843-723-3225, Ext 110; *Chief Operations Officer, VPres, Coll,* Virginia Ellison; Tel: 843-723-3225, Ext 114, E-mail: virginia.ellison@schsonline.org; *Sr Archivist,* Molly Silliman; Tel: 843-723-3225, Ext 112, E-mail: molly.silliman@schsonline.org; Staff 7 (MLS 5, Non-MLS 2)
Founded 1855
Library Holdings: Bk Vols 30,000
Special Collections: Civil War (R Lockwood Tower Coll); Manuscript Coll, includes family, business & organization papers
Subject Interests: Genealogy, Local hist, State hist
Automation Activity & Vendor Info: (OPAC) EOS International
Wireless access
Function: Res libr
Publications: Carologue; South Carolina Historical Magazine; South Carolina Historical Society Manuscript Guide
Open Mon-Fri 9-5
Restriction: Non-circulating

TRIDENT TECHNICAL COLLEGE

J BERKELEY CAMPUS LEARNING RESOURCES*, LR-B, PO Box 118067, 29423-8067, SAN 324-797X. Tel: 843-899-8055. FAX: 843-899-8100. Web Site: www.tridenttech.edu/library. *Dean of Libr,* Charnette Singleton; Tel: 843-574-6088, E-mail: charnette.singleton@tridenttech.edu
Founded 1982
Library Holdings: Bk Titles 4,025; Bk Vols 4,871; Per Subs 67
Subject Interests: Aircraft maintenance, Cosmetology, Veterinary tech
Publications: Annual Report

J MAIN CAMPUS LEARNING RESOURCES CENTER*, LR-M, PO Box 118067, 29423-8067, SAN 360-036X. Tel: 843-574-6089. Interlibrary Loan Service Tel: 843-574-6316. FAX: 843-574-6484. Web Site: www.tridenttech.edu/library. *Dean of Libr,* Charnette Singleton; Tel: 843-574-6087, E-mail: charnette.singleton@tridenttech.edu; *Ref & Coll Develop Librn,* Diane Lohr; E-mail: diane.lohr@tridenttech.edu; *Cat, Circ, Ser,* Patricia Vierthaler; E-mail: patricia.vierthaler@tridenttech.edu; *Circ & ILL,* Itaski Jenkins; *Syst,* Laura Barfield; Staff 15 (MLS 8, Non-MLS 7)
Founded 1964
Library Holdings: Bk Titles 85,000; Per Subs 175
Special Collections: Electronics (Sam Photofact Coll)
Partic in Partnership Among South Carolina Academic Libraries
Publications: Annual Report

J PALMER CAMPUS LEARNING RESOURCES CENTER*, 66 Columbus St, 29403, SAN 360-0335. Tel: 843-722-5540. FAX: 843-720-5614. Web Site: www.tridenttech.edu/library.htm. *Ref & Instruction,* Haley Hall; Tel: 843-722-5539, E-mail: haley.hall@tridenttech.edu; Staff 3 (MLS 1, Non-MLS 2)
Founded 1955. Enrl 1,800
Library Holdings: Bk Titles 20,492; Bk Vols 24,471; Per Subs 101
Subject Interests: Archives, Law
Publications: Annual Report
Open Mon-Thurs 7:30am-8pm, Fri 7:30-4:30

A UNITED STATES NAVY*, Naval Consolidated Brig Library, Bldg 3107, 1050 Remount Rd, 29406-3515. SAN 360-0459. Tel: 843-794-0074. FAX: 843-794-0325. *Supv Librn,* Vicki McGinnis; E-mail: vicki.mcginnis@navy.mil
Library Holdings: Bk Vols 10,000; Per Subs 41

CHARLESTON AFB

A UNITED STATES AIR FORCE*, Joint Base Charleston Library FL4418, 628 FSS/FSDL, 106 W McCaw St, Bldg 215, 29404. SAN 360-0548. Tel: 843-963-3320. E-mail: jbcharlestonlibrary@gmail.com. Web Site: www.jbcharleston.com/library. *Dir,* Maria Hernandez; *Prog Coordr,* Cynthia Sholtz; *Cat,* Carmen Alonso; *Circ Serv,* Luis Barcenas; *Tech Serv,* Position Currently Open; Staff 6 (MLS 2, Non-MLS 4)
Founded 1953
Library Holdings: Bk Vols 72,000; Per Subs 174
Subject Interests: Mil hist, Total quality mgt
Automation Activity & Vendor Info: (Acquisitions) Bibliomation Inc; (Cataloging) Bibliomation Inc; (Circulation) Bibliomation Inc; (ILL) OCLC Online; (OPAC) Bibliomation Inc
Wireless access
Partic in LYRASIS
Restriction: Not open to pub

CHERAW

J NORTHEASTERN TECHNICAL COLLEGE LIBRARY*, Harris Hall, Cheraw Campus, 1201 Chesterfield Hwy, Rm 506, 29520-7015. SAN 315-5099. Tel: 843-921-6953, 843-921-6954. Toll Free Tel: 800-921-6900. FAX: 843-537-6148. E-mail: librarian@netc.edu. Web Site: www.netc.edu/student_resources.php?Student-Resources-Library-4. *Head Librn,* Ron Stafford; E-mail: rstafford@netc.edu; Staff 2.4 (MLS 1, Non-MLS 1.4)
Founded 1968. Enrl 631; Fac 30; Highest Degree: Associate

Library Holdings: AV Mats 1,586; Bks on Deafness & Sign Lang 22; CDs 200; DVDs 572; e-books 300,000; Bk Titles 30,000; Per Subs 61; Videos 1,700
Automation Activity & Vendor Info: (Acquisitions) SirsiDynix; (Cataloging) OCLC Connexion; (Circulation) SirsiDynix; (Course Reserve) SirsiDynix; (ILL) OCLC FirstSearch; (OPAC) SirsiDynix; (Serials) SirsiDynix
Wireless access
Function: Audiobks via web, Bks on cassette, Bks on CD, Computers for patron use, Electronic databases & coll, Free DVD rentals, ILL available, Internet access, Music CDs, Online cat, Orientations, Outside serv via phone, mail, e-mail & web, Photocopying/Printing, Prof lending libr, Ref & res, Ref serv available, Tax forms, Telephone ref, VHS videos, Wheelchair accessible
Partic in Partnership Among South Carolina Academic Libraries; South Carolina Information & Library Services Consortium
Special Services for the Deaf - Bks on deafness & sign lang
Special Services for the Blind - Bks available with recordings; Bks on cassette; Bks on CD; Cassette playback machines; Cassettes; Closed caption display syst; Copier with enlargement capabilities; Integrated libr/media serv; Large print bks
Open Mon-Thurs 8-5, Fri 8-1:30
Restriction: Borrowing requests are handled by ILL, Open to pub for ref & circ; with some limitations, Open to students, fac & staff

CHESTER

P CHESTER COUNTY LIBRARY*, 100 Center St, 29706. SAN 360-0572. Tel: 803-377-8145. FAX: 803-377-8146. Web Site: www.chesterlibsc.org. *Mgr,* Carol Lewis; *Ch,* Kathryn Powell; E-mail: kpowell@chesterlibsc.org; *Ch Serv,* Beth Harris; E-mail: bharris@chesterlibsc.org; *Ref (Info Servs),* Judy Bramlett; E-mail: jbramlett@chesterlibsc.org; Staff 6 (MLS 1, Non-MLS 5)
Founded 1900. Pop 36,212; Circ 119,428
Library Holdings: AV Mats 4,836; CDs 1,126; DVDs 960; Large Print Bks 2,500; Bk Vols 108,247; Per Subs 90; Videos 35
Special Collections: Oral History
Subject Interests: Local hist, SC hist
Automation Activity & Vendor Info: (Acquisitions) Evergreen; (Cataloging) Evergreen; (Circulation) Evergreen; (Media Booking) EnvisionWare; (OPAC) Evergreen
Wireless access
Open Mon-Thurs 9:30-5:30, Sat 9-3
Friends of the Library Group
Branches: 2
GREAT FALLS BRANCH, 39 Calhoun St, Great Falls, 29055, SAN 360-0602. Tel: 803-482-2149. FAX: 803-482-3531. *Br Mgr,* Tally Johnson; E-mail: jfk5351@yahoo.com; Staff 2 (Non-MLS 2)
Founded 1927
Library Holdings: Bk Vols 10,000
Open Mon-Fri 10-6, Sat 10-2
Friends of the Library Group
LEWISVILLE COMMUNITY LIBRARY, 3771 Lancaster Hwy, Richburg, 29729. Tel: 803-789-7800. FAX: 803-789-7801. *Librn,* Valerie Taylor; Staff 2 (MLS 1, Non-MLS 1)
Founded 1997
Library Holdings: Bk Vols 10,000; Per Subs 10
Open Mon-Fri 10-6, Sat 10-2
Friends of the Library Group
Bookmobiles: 1

CHESTERFIELD

P CHESTERFIELD COUNTY LIBRARY SYSTEM*, 119 W Main St, 29709-1512. SAN 360-0637. Tel: 843-623-7489. FAX: 843-623-3295. E-mail: library@chesterfield.lib.sc.us. Web Site: www.chesterfield.lib.sc.us. *Dir,* Michael Kaltwang; E-mail: mkaltwang@chesterfield.lib.sc.us; *Br Mgr,* Samantha McCarn; E-mail: smccarn@chesterfield.lib.sc.us; *Ch Serv,* Gracie Williamson; E-mail: gwilliamson@chesterfield.lib.sc.us; *Tech Serv,* Shawn Wright; E-mail: swright@chesterfield.lib.sc.us; Staff 12 (MLS 2, Non-MLS 10)
Founded 1968. Pop 46,000
Library Holdings: Large Print Bks 991; Bk Titles 19,000; Bk Vols 23,000; Per Subs 229; Talking Bks 295
Special Collections: South Carolina History Coll
Wireless access
Partic in SCLENDS
Open Mon-Thurs 9-6, Fri 9-5, Sat 10-2
Friends of the Library Group
Branches: 4
FANNIE D LOWRY MEMORIAL LIBRARY, 500 N Main St, Jefferson, 29718. (Mail add: PO Box 505, Jefferson, 29718-0505), SAN 328-7149. Tel: 843-658-3966. FAX: 843-658-6695. *Br Mgr,* Kaye Penegar
Open Mon, Wed, Fri 10-1 & 2-5
MATHESON LIBRARY, 227 Huger St, Cheraw, 29520, SAN 360-0661. Tel: 843-537-3571. FAX: 843-537-6578. *Br Mgr,* Corina Esaw
Library Holdings: Large Print Bks 291; Bk Titles 17,993; Bk Vols 21,199; Per Subs 50; Talking Bks 333
Open Mon-Thurs 9-6, Fri 9-5, Sat 10-2
Friends of the Library Group
MCBEE DEPOT LIBRARY, 96 W Pine St, McBee, 29101. (Mail add: PO Box 506, McBee, 29101), SAN 328-7165. Tel: 843-335-7515. FAX: 843-335-6219. E-mail: library@cclssc.org. *Br Mgr,* Joe Elvington
Open Tues & Thurs 10-1 & 2-5
PAGELAND COMMUNITY LIBRARY, 109 W Blakeney St, Pageland, 29728, SAN 360-0696. Tel: 843-672-6930. FAX: 843-672-6670. *Br Mgr,* Kim Lowry; Staff 2 (Non-MLS 2)
Function: ILL available, Photocopying/Printing, Prog for children & young adult
Open Mon-Thurs 10-6, Fri 10-5, Sat 10-2

CLEMSON

C CLEMSON UNIVERSITY LIBRARIES*, R M Cooper Library, 116 Sigma Dr, 29631. (Mail add: Box 34-3001, 29634-3001). Tel: 864-656-3027. Circulation Tel: 864-656-1557. Toll Free Tel: 877-886-2389. FAX: 864-656-0758. Web Site: libraries.clemson.edu. *Dean of Libr,* Christopher Cox; E-mail: cnc2@clemson.edu; *Director, Learning Spaces,* Teri Alexander; Tel: 864-656-5172, E-mail: tajff@clemson.edu; *Head, Cat, Librn,* Lisa Bodenheimer; Tel: 864-656-1769, E-mail: bodenhl@clemson.edu; *Assoc Librn, Head, Spec Coll,* Brenda Burk; Tel: 864-656-5176, E-mail: bburk@clemson.edu; *Sci Librn,* Shelby Carroll; *Assoc Librn, Libr Tech,* Chris Vinson; Tel: 864-656-3622, E-mail: vinsonc@clemson.edu; *Assoc Librn, Info & Res Serv,* Suzanne Rook-Schilf; Tel: 864-656-6834, E-mail: rook@clemson.edu; Staff 104 (MLS 33, Non-MLS 71)
Founded 1893. Enrl 19,111; Fac 1,150; Highest Degree: Doctorate
Library Holdings: e-books 80,000; Bk Vols 1,388,093; Per Subs 47,150
Special Collections: National Park Service Directors' Papers; University Archives. US Document Depository
Subject Interests: Rare bks, Textile
Automation Activity & Vendor Info: (Acquisitions) Innovative Interfaces, Inc; (Cataloging) Innovative Interfaces, Inc; (Circulation) Innovative Interfaces, Inc; (OPAC) Innovative Interfaces, Inc; (Serials) Innovative Interfaces, Inc
Wireless access
Function: Res libr
Publications: In Touch
Partic in Association of Southeastern Research Libraries; Carolina Consortium; DISCUS; LYRASIS; Partnership Among South Carolina Academic Libraries
Departmental Libraries:
GUNNIN ARCHITECTURE LIBRARY, 2-112 Lee Hall, Clemson University, 29634, SAN 360-0750. Tel: 864-656-3933. FAX: 864-656-3932. *Archit/Art Librn, Dir,* Ann Holderfield; E-mail: kaholde@clemson.edu; *Libr Spec,* Ina Bottle; E-mail: inab@clemson.edu; *Circ Mgr,* Christopher Chapman; E-mail: chapma@clemson.edu; *Libr Spec,* Paula Smith; E-mail: pdunbar@clemson.edu; Staff 7 (MLS 2, Non-MLS 5)
SPECIAL COLLECTIONS & ARCHIVES, Strom Thurmond Inst Bldg, 230 Kappa St, 29634, SAN 373-7160. Tel: 864-656-3214. *Head, Spec Coll,* Brenda Burk; Staff 9 (MLS 8, Non-MLS 1)
Special Collections: Liberty Corporation Archives; National Park Service Directors
Subject Interests: SC hist, Textiles
Function: Archival coll, Computers for patron use, Ref serv available, Scanner, Wheelchair accessible
Restriction: Closed stack, Non-circulating, Open to pub with supv only

CLINTON

C PRESBYTERIAN COLLEGE*, James H Thomason Library, 211 E Maple St, 29325. SAN 315-5102. Tel: 864-833-8299. Reference Tel: 864-833-7080. FAX: 864-833-8315. E-mail: library@presby.edu. Web Site: www.presby.edu/library/. *Dir,* Position Currently Open; *Head, Circ,* Beverly Blalock; E-mail: bblalock@presby.edu; *Archivist, Spec Coll Librn,* Sarah Leckie; Tel: 864-833-8525, E-mail: smpaulk@presby.edu; *Coordr, Electronic Serv & Syst,* Abigail Rush; Tel: 864-833-7026, E-mail: asrush@presby.edu; *Ref Serv,* Betsy Byrd; E-mail: eebyrd@presby.edu; Staff 5.3 (MLS 5.3)
Founded 1880. Enrl 1,150; Fac 88; Highest Degree: Bachelor
Library Holdings: Bk Vols 137,314; Per Subs 684
Special Collections: Presbyterian denominational materials
Subject Interests: Caroliniana
Automation Activity & Vendor Info: (Acquisitions) Innovative Interfaces, Inc; (Cataloging) Innovative Interfaces, Inc; (Circulation) Innovative Interfaces, Inc; (Course Reserve) Innovative Interfaces, Inc; (ILL) OCLC WorldShare Interlibrary Loan; (OPAC) Innovative Interfaces, Inc; (Serials) Innovative Interfaces, Inc

Wireless access
Partic in LYRASIS; Partnership Among South Carolina Academic Libraries

COLUMBIA

CR ALLEN UNIVERSITY, J S Flipper Library, 1530 Harden St, 29204. Tel: 803-376-5719. Administration Tel: 803-765-6030. FAX: 803-765-6009. Web Site: www.allenuniversity.edu/current-students/j-s-flipper-library. *Dean of Libr,* Carol L Bowers; *Librn,* Katrine Leavy; E-mail: kleavy@allenuniversity.edu
Founded 1870
Library Holdings: Bk Vols 10,000; Per Subs 80
Special Collections: African Methodist Episcopal Church (AME) Coll; African-American Coll
Wireless access
Partic in Partnership Among South Carolina Academic Libraries
Open Mon-Fri 8-8, Sat 10-3

C BENEDICT COLLEGE LIBRARY*, Benjamin F Payton Learning Resources Center, 1600 Harden St, 29204. SAN 315-5137. Tel: 803-705-4364. FAX: 803-748-7539. Web Site: www.benedict.edu/library. *Dir,* Darlene Zinnerman-Bethea; Tel: 803-705-4773, E-mail: darlene.bethea@benedict.edu; *Ref Librn,* Brian R Crowley; Staff 11 (MLS 6, Non-MLS 5)
Founded 1870. Enrl 2,075; Fac 90; Highest Degree: Bachelor
Library Holdings: Bk Vols 125,500; Per Subs 320
Special Collections: State Document Depository; US Document Depository
Subject Interests: African-Am studies
Wireless access
Partic in Coop Col Libr Ctr, Inc; Partnership Among South Carolina Academic Libraries
Open Mon-Thurs 8am-11pm, Fri 8-5, Sat 1-5, Sun 3-10 (Fall & Spring); Mon-Thurs 8:30-8:30, Fri 8:30-5, Sun 3-7 (Summer)

M G WERBER BRYAN PSYCHIATRIC HOSPITAL LIBRARY*, 220 Faison Dr, 29203. SAN 315-5145. Tel: 803-935-5395. *Librn,* Theodora Richardson; E-mail: thr08@scdmh.org
Founded 1978
Library Holdings: Audiobooks 120; CDs 250; DVDs 125; Large Print Bks 100; Bk Vols 3,500; Per Subs 50; Videos 70
Subject Interests: Psychiat, Psychol
Partic in SC Health Info Network
Restriction: Staff & patient use
Friends of the Library Group

C COLUMBIA COLLEGE, J Drake Edens Library, 1301 Columbia College Dr, 29203-9987. SAN 315-5161. Tel: 803-786-3877. Reference Tel: 803-786-3703. Administration Tel: 803-786-3337. E-mail: refdesk@columbiasc.edu. Web Site: libguides.columbiasc.edu. *Libr Dir,* Laurel Whisler; E-mail: lwhisler@columbiasc.edu; *Educ Tech Librn,* Jesika Brooks; Tel: 803-786-3716, E-mail: jbrooks@columbiasc.edu; *Electronic Res & Cat Librn,* Daniel Stevens; Tel: 803-786-3570, E-mail: dstevens@columbiasc.edu; *Res & Instruction Librn,* Kala Dunn; Tel: 803-786-3338, E-mail: kdunn@columbiasc.edu; Staff 5 (MLS 4, Non-MLS 1)
Founded 1854. Enrl 1,200; Fac 65; Highest Degree: Master
Library Holdings: AV Mats 2,840; Bk Vols 83,909
Special Collections: Local Authors (Peggy Parish & Barbara Johnson Colls); Religious Literature for Children
Subject Interests: Women
Automation Activity & Vendor Info: (Cataloging) Ex Libris Group; (Circulation) Ex Libris Group; (OPAC) Ex Libris Group; (Serials) Ex Libris Group
Wireless access
Partic in LYRASIS; Partnership Among South Carolina Academic Libraries
Open Mon-Thurs 8am-10pm, Fri 8-5, Sat 10-5

CR COLUMBIA INTERNATIONAL UNIVERSITY*, G Allen Fleece Library, 7435 Monticello Rd, 29203-1599. SAN 315-5153. Tel: 803-807-5115. Circulation Tel: 803-807-5110. Reference Tel: 803-807-5102. FAX: 803-744-1391. E-mail: library@ciu.edu. Web Site: www.ciu.edu/library. *Libr Dir,* Cynthia Snell; Tel: 803-807-5107, E-mail: cynthia.snell@ciu.edu; *Access Serv,* Sue Konieczko; Tel: 803-807-5105, E-mail: sue.konieczko@ciu.edu; *Tech & Ref,* Kevin Flickner; Tel: 803-807-5112, E-mail: kevin.flickner@ciu.edu; *Evening Libr Asst,* Anna McElmurray; Tel: 803-807-5158, E-mail: anna.mcelmurray@ciu.edu; *Archivist,* Pattie Wheeler; Tel: 803-807-5106, E-mail: pattie.wheeler@ciu.edu. Subject Specialists: *Bus, Educ, Psychol,* Cynthia Snell; *English, Gen educ, Seminary,* Kevin Flickner; *Juv lit,* Pattie Wheeler; Staff 5 (MLS 3, Non-MLS 2)
Founded 1923. Enrl 931; Fac 65; Highest Degree: Doctorate
Library Holdings: AV Mats 8,000; e-books 15,000; Electronic Media & Resources 100; Microforms 50,000; Bk Titles 70,000; Per Subs 26
Subject Interests: Bus, Counseling, Educ, Intercultural studies, Theol
Automation Activity & Vendor Info: (Acquisitions) Innovative Interfaces, Inc; (Cataloging) OCLC; (Circulation) Koha; (Course Reserve) Koha; (ILL) OCLC FirstSearch; (OPAC) Koha; (Serials) Koha
Wireless access
Function: Wheelchair accessible
Partic in Christian Library Consortium; DISCUS; LYRASIS; OCLC Online Computer Library Center, Inc; Partnership Among South Carolina Academic Libraries
Special Services for the Deaf - Bks on deafness & sign lang; Closed caption videos
Special Services for the Blind - Internet workstation with adaptive software; Large screen computer & software
Open Mon-Sat 8am-Midnight
Restriction: Authorized patrons, Authorized personnel only, Authorized scholars by appt, Borrowing privileges limited to fac & registered students, Circ to mem only, ID required to use computers (Ltd hrs), Open to authorized patrons, Open to students, fac, staff & alumni, Registered patrons only

GM DEPARTMENT OF VETERANS AFFAIRS, William Jennings Bryan Dorn VA Medical Center - Medical Library, 6439 Garners Ferry Rd, 29209-1638. SAN 315-5315. Tel: 803-776-4000, Ext 57058. FAX: 803-695-7966. Web Site: www.va.gov/columbia-south-carolina-health-care/locations.
Library Holdings: e-books 20,000; e-journals 7,000; Bk Vols 1,187; Per Subs 224

M JOSEY HEALTH SCIENCES LIBRARY*, Prisma Health Richland, Five Richland Medical Park, 29203. SAN 315-5234. Tel: 803-434-6312. FAX: 803-434-2651. E-mail: phrlibrary@prismahealth.org. *Libr Mgr,* Cynthia D Garrett; *Coordr,* Marline C Robinson; Staff 3 (MLS 1, Non-MLS 2)
Founded 1957
Oct 2017-Sept 2018. Mats Exp $264,624, Books $2,000, Per/Ser (Incl. Access Fees) $72,750, Electronic Ref Mat (Incl. Access Fees) $74,900
Library Holdings: AV Mats 524; CDs 300; e-books 200; e-journals 2,000; Electronic Media & Resources 100; Bk Titles 2,145; Per Subs 275; Videos 100
Subject Interests: Allied health, Med, Nursing
Automation Activity & Vendor Info: (Acquisitions) EBSCO Online; (Cataloging) Marcive, Inc; (Circulation) EOS International; (ILL) SERHOLD; (OPAC) EOS International; (Serials) EOS International
Wireless access
Function: Computers for patron use, Electronic databases & coll, Health sci info serv, ILL available, Internet access, Mail & tel request accepted, Online ref, Orientations, Outside serv via phone, mail, e-mail & web, Photocopying/Printing, Prof lending libr, Ref & res, Ref serv available, Res libr, Res performed for a fee, Scanner, Spoken cassettes & CDs, Wheelchair accessible
Partic in National Network of Libraries of Medicine Region 2
Restriction: Badge access after hrs, ID required to use computers (Ltd hrs), Med & health res only, Med & nursing staff, patients & families, Med staff & students, Open to hospital affiliates only, Open to staff, students & ancillary prof, Open to students, fac & staff, Photo ID required for access, Restricted access, Restricted borrowing privileges, Restricted loan policy, Secured area only open to authorized personnel

R LENOIR-RHYNE UNIVERSITY*, Lineberger Memorial Library, 4201 N Main St, 29203. SAN 315-5218. Tel: 803-461-3220, 803-461-3269. FAX: 803-461-3278. Web Site: libguides.lr.edu/lineberger. *Assoc Dir,* Sandy Leach; E-mail: sandy.leach@lr.edu; *Instruction & Ref Librn,* Konni Shier; E-mail: konni.shier@lr.edu; *Libr Spec,* Lisa Antley-Hearn; E-mail: lisa.hearn@lr.edu; Staff 1.5 (MLS 1.5)
Founded 1830. Highest Degree: Master
Library Holdings: Bk Vols 100,000; Per Subs 474
Special Collections: 16th through 18th Century German Pietism
Subject Interests: Relig studies
Automation Activity & Vendor Info: (Acquisitions) Ex Libris Group; (Cataloging) Ex Libris Group; (Circulation) Ex Libris Group; (Course Reserve) Ex Libris Group; (OPAC) Ex Libris Group; (Serials) Ex Libris Group
Wireless access
Partic in Carolina Consortium; OCLC Online Computer Library Center, Inc
Open Mon-Thurs 8am-9pm, Fri 8-4, Sat 11-3, Sun 3-9

L NELSON, MULLINS, RILEY & SCARBOROUGH*, Law Library, 1320 Main St, Ste 1700, 29201. (Mail add: PO Box 11070, 29211-1070), SAN 323-6560. Tel: 803-255-9367. FAX: 803-255-7500. *Libr Mgr,* Monica Wilson; *Sr Res Spec,* Melanie DuBard; E-mail: melanie.dubard@nelsonmullins.com; Staff 13 (MLS 9, Non-MLS 4)
Founded 1982
Library Holdings: Bk Titles 3,500; Bk Vols 16,000; Per Subs 100
Subject Interests: Law
Wireless access
Restriction: Not open to pub, Staff use only

P RICHLAND LIBRARY*, 1431 Assembly St, 29201-3101. SAN 360-0939. Tel: 803-799-9084. Reference Tel: 803-929-3401. Administration Tel: 803-929-3422. FAX: 803-929-3448. Interlibrary Loan Service FAX: 803-929-3400. Web Site: www.richlandlibrary.com, www.richlandlibrary.com/main. *Exec Dir,* Melanie Huggins; E-mail: mhuggins@richlandlibrary.com; *Chief Customer Officer,* Georgia Coleman; *Chief Equity & Engagement Officer,* Tamara M King; *Chief Financial Officer,* Sarah Sullivan; *Chief Innovation Officer, Chief Programs Officer,* Tony Tallent; *Chief Operations Officer,* Steve Sullivan; *Dir of Digital Strategy, Dir, Mkt,* Phillips Higgins; *Dir of Libr Experience,* Caroline Hipp; *Develop Dir,* Tina Gills; Staff 280.8 (MLS 81.4, Non-MLS 199.4)
Founded 1934. Pop 384,504; Circ 4,404,707
Jul 2017-Jun 2018 Income (Main & Associated Libraries) $39,499,974, State $672,882, County $26,698,677, Other $1,630,080. Mats Exp $23,266,956, AV Mat $4,119,839. Sal $18,397,706
Library Holdings: Audiobooks 63,756; DVDs 86,422; e-books 21,940; e-journals 2; Electronic Media & Resources 1,006,974; Bk Titles 1,120,591; Per Subs 2,397
Special Collections: Oral History
Subject Interests: Local hist
Automation Activity & Vendor Info: (Acquisitions) SirsiDynix; (Cataloging) SirsiDynix; (Circulation) SirsiDynix; (OPAC) SirsiDynix; (Serials) SirsiDynix
Wireless access
Function: Adult bk club, Art exhibits, Audiobks via web, Bk club(s), Bks on cassette, Bks on CD, CD-ROM, Children's prog, Computer training, Computers for patron use, Digital talking bks, E-Reserves, Electronic databases & coll, Free DVD rentals, Holiday prog, Home delivery & serv to seniorr ctr & nursing homes, Homebound delivery serv, Homework prog, ILL available, Instruction & testing, Internet access, Learning ctr, Magnifiers for reading, Mail & tel request accepted, Music CDs, Online cat, Online ref, Outreach serv, Outside serv via phone, mail, e-mail & web, OverDrive digital audio bks, Photocopying/Printing, Preschool outreach, Prog for adults, Prog for children & young adult, Res libr, Senior computer classes, Senior outreach, Spoken cassettes & CDs, Spoken cassettes & DVDs, Story hour, Summer reading prog, Teen prog, Telephone ref, VHS videos, Wheelchair accessible, Workshops
Publications: Magazine (Bimonthly)
Special Services for the Deaf - TTY equip
Special Services for the Blind - Closed circuit TV magnifier; Computer access aids; Computer with voice synthesizer for visually impaired persons; Large print bks; Scanner for conversion & translation of mats; Talking bk serv referral
Open Mon-Thurs 9-9, Fri & Sat 9-6, Sun 2-6
Friends of the Library Group
Branches: 12
BALLENTINE BRANCH, 1200 Dutch Fork Rd, Irmo, 29063. Tel: 803-781-5026. Web Site: www.richlandlibrary.com/ballentine. *Mgr,* Kelly Jones; E-mail: kjones@richlandlibrary.com
Open Mon-Thurs 9-8, Fri & Sat 9-6
BLYTHEWOOD BRANCH, 218 McNulty Rd, Blythewood, 29016, SAN 373-7098. Tel: 803-691-9806. Web Site: www.richlandlibrary.com/blythewood. *Mgr,* Crystal Johnson; E-mail: cjohnson@richlandlibrary.com
Open Mon-Thurs 9-8, Fri & Sat 9-6
JOHN HUGHES COOPER BRANCH, 5317 N Trenholm Rd, 29206, SAN 360-0963. Tel: 803-787-3462. Web Site: www.richlandlibrary.com/cooper. *Mgr,* Heather Green; E-mail: hgreen@richlandlibrary.com
Open Mon-Thurs 9-9, Fri & Sat 9-6
EASTOVER BRANCH, 608 Main St, Eastover, 29044, SAN 360-1021. Tel: 803-353-8584. Web Site: www.richlandlibrary.com/eastover. *Mgr,* Kimberly Jones; E-mail: kjones1@richlandlibrary.com
Open Mon-Thurs 9-8, Fri & Sat 9-6
EDGEWOOD BRANCH, 2101 Oak St, 29204. Tel: 803-509-8355. Web Site: www.richlandlibrary.com/edgewood. *Mgr,* Chris Campbell; E-mail: chcampbell@richlandlibrary.com
Open Mon-Thurs 9-8, Fri & Sat 9-6
LOWER RICHLAND BRANCH, 9019 Garners Ferry Rd, Hopkins, 29061. Web Site: www.richlandlibrary.com/lowerrichland.
NORTH MAIN, 5306 N Main St, 29203-6114, SAN 360-1110. Tel: 803-754-7734. Web Site: www.richlandlibrary.com/northmain. *Mgr,* Dee Robinson; E-mail: drrobinson@richlandlibrary.com
Open Mon-Thurs 9-9, Fri & Sat 9-6
NORTHEAST REGIONAL, 7490 Parklane Rd, 29223, SAN 325-4372. Tel: 803-736-6575. Web Site: www.richlandlibrary.com/northeast. *Mgr,* Jake Duffie; E-mail: jduffie@richlandlibrary.com
Open Mon-Thurs 9-9, Fri & Sat 9-6
SAINT ANDREWS REGIONAL, 2916 Broad River Rd, 29210, SAN 360-1145. Tel: 803-772-6675. Web Site: www.richlandlibrary.com/standrews. *Mgr,* Michelle DuPre; E-mail: mdupre@richlandlibrary.com
Open Mon-Thurs 9-9, Fri & Sat 9-6, Sun 2-6
SANDHILLS, 763 Fashion Dr, 29229, SAN 373-7101. Tel: 803-699-9230. Web Site: www.richlandlibrary.com/sandhills. *Mgr,* Jim Staskowski; E-mail: jstaskowski@richlandlibrary.com
Open Mon-Thurs 9-9, Fri & Sat 9-6, Sun 2-6
SOUTHEAST REGIONAL, 7421 Garners Ferry Rd, 29209, SAN 373-711X. Tel: 803-776-0855. Web Site: www.richlandlibrary.com/southeast. *Mgr,* Sarah Maner; E-mail: smaner@richlandlibrary.com
Open Mon-Thurs 9-9, Fri & Sat 9-6, Sun 2-6
WHEATLEY, 931 Woodrow St, 29205, SAN 360-0998. Tel: 803-799-5873. Web Site: www.richlandlibrary.com/wheatley. *Mgr,* Elizabeth Barrett; E-mail: EBarrett@richlandlibrary.com
Open Mon, Wed, Fri & Sat 9-6, Tues & Thurs 9-8

GL SOUTH CAROLINA ATTORNEY GENERAL'S OFFICE LIBRARY*, 1000 Assembly St, Ste 519, 29201-3117. (Mail add: PO Box 11549, 29211), SAN 321-7604. Tel: 803-734-3970. FAX: 803-253-6283. Web Site: www.scag.gov. *Librn,* Tammie Wilson; E-mail: twilson@scag.gov; Staff 1 (Non-MLS 1)
Founded 1974
Special Collections: Attorney General's Opinions
Subject Interests: Law
Wireless access
Restriction: Open to pub for ref only

S SOUTH CAROLINA COMMISSION ON HIGHER EDUCATION LIBRARY*, 1122 Lady St, Ste 300, 29201-3240. SAN 371-4438. Tel: 803-737-2260. Web Site: www.che.sc.gov. *Librn,* Julie Housknecht; E-mail: julie.housknecht@pascalsc.org; Staff 1 (MLS 1)
Wireless access
Restriction: Staff use only

G SOUTH CAROLINA DEPARTMENT OF ARCHIVES & HISTORY*, 8301 Parklane Rd, 29223. SAN 327-0777. Tel: 803-896-6104. Automation Services Tel: 803-896-6100. FAX: 803-896-6198. Web Site: scdah.sc.gov. *Dir, Archives & Rec Mgt,* Patrick McCawley; E-mail: pmccawley@scdah.sc.gov
Founded 1905
Library Holdings: Microforms 20,000; Bk Vols 5,000
Special Collections: South Carolina Government Records, 1671-present
Wireless access
Publications: Colonial Records of South Carolina; Curriculum Resource Materials; Popular History Booklets; South Carolina Archives Micropublications; State Records of South Carolina; Technical Leaflets on Document Conservation, Historic Preservation & Records Management
Open Tues-Fri 8:30-5, Sat 8:30-12 & 1-5

P SOUTH CAROLINA STATE LIBRARY, 1500 Senate St, 29201. SAN 360-117X. Tel: 803-734-8666. Reference Tel: 803-734-8026. FAX: 803-734-8676. Reference FAX: 803-734-4757. Reference E-mail: reference@statelibrary.sc.gov. Web Site: www.statelibrary.sc.gov. *Dir,* Leesa M Aiken; E-mail: laiken@statelibrary.sc.gov; *Dep Dir,* Christopher Yates; Tel: 803-734-4618, E-mail: cyates@statelibrary.sc.gov; *Assoc Dep Dir,* Breanne Smith; Tel: 803-734-8626, E-mail: brsmith@statelibrary.sc.gov; *Dir, Finance & Grants,* Wendy Coplen; Tel: 803-734-0436, E-mail: wcoplen@statelibrary.sc.gov; *Dir, Libr Coll,* Sarah Pettus; Tel: 803-734-2841, E-mail: spettus@statelibrary.sc.gov; *Dir, Libr Serv,* Sarah Schroeder; Tel: 803-734-6061, E-mail: sschroeder@statelibrary.sc.gov; *Dir, Talking Book Services,* Jennifer Falvey; E-mail: jfalvey@statelibrary.sc.gov; *Human Res Dir,* Rashad Hickson; Tel: 803-734-4612, E-mail: rhickson@statelibrary.sc.gov; *IT Dir,* Paul Harmon; Tel: 803-734-8651, E-mail: pharmon@statelibrary.sc.gov; *Electronic Res Mgr,* Patricia Sinclair; Tel: 803-734-8851, E-mail: psinclair@statelibrary.sc.gov; Staff 35 (MLS 18, Non-MLS 17)
Founded 1943
Special Collections: Foundation Center Regional Coll; South Carolina Coll; South Carolina Government Publications, State Document Depository; US Document Depository
Subject Interests: Bus mgt, Info tech, Libr sci, SC hist
Automation Activity & Vendor Info: (Cataloging) SirsiDynix-Symphony; (Circulation) SirsiDynix-Symphony; (Discovery) EBSCO Discovery Service; (ILL) OCLC; (OPAC) SirsiDynix-Enterprise; (Serials) SirsiDynix-Symphony
Wireless access
Publications: Connect The Dots: Newsletter of the South Carolina State Library (Quarterly newsletter); Discus Monitor; More...The Newsletter for South Carolina Libraries; South Carolina Day by Day Family Literacy Calendar (Fifth Anniversary Edition (2014) (Quarterly newsletter); Talking Book Services (Monthly newsletter)
Partic in Association for Rural & Small Libraries; SCLENDS
Special Services for the Deaf - Bks on deafness & sign lang; TTY equip
Special Services for the Blind - Assistive/Adapted tech devices, equip & products; Computer with voice synthesizer for visually impaired persons; Open bk software on pub access PC
Open Mon-Fri 8:30-5

Branches: 1
TALKING BOOK SERVICES
See Separate Entry

P SOUTH CAROLINA STATE LIBRARY, Talking Book Services, 1500 Senate St, 29201. SAN 315-4963. Tel: 803-734-4611. Toll Free Tel: 800-922-7818. FAX: 803-734-4610. E-mail: tbsbooks@statelibrary.sc.gov. Web Site: www.sctalkingbook.org. *Dir,* Jennifer Falvey; Staff 8 (MLS 3, Non-MLS 5)
Founded 1973. Pop 6,000; Circ 221,338
Library Holdings: DVDs 1,006; Large Print Bks 15,697; Bk Titles 40,790; Bk Vols 173,753; Talking Bks 157,444; Videos 523
Special Collections: Descriptive DVDs
Subject Interests: Fiction, Non-fiction
Wireless access
Publications: Connect the Dots (Newsletter)
Special Services for the Blind - Assistive/Adapted tech devices, equip & products; Braille bks; Braille equip; Children's Braille; Computer with voice synthesizer for visually impaired persons; Digital talking bk; Digital talking bk machines; Home delivery serv; Info on spec aids & appliances; Internet workstation with adaptive software; Large print bks & talking machines; Large screen computer & software; Local mags & bks recorded; Machine repair; Magnifiers; Newsletter (in large print, Braille or on cassette); PC for people with disabilities; Reader equip; Screen enlargement software for people with visual disabilities; Screen reader software; Spec cats; Talking bk & rec for the blind cat; Talking bks & player equip; Tel Pioneers equip repair group; ZoomText magnification & reading software
Open Mon-Fri 8:30-5
Restriction: Registered patrons only

GL SOUTH CAROLINA SUPREME COURT LIBRARY, 1231 Gervais St, 29211. SAN 315-5293. Tel: 803-734-1080. FAX: 803-734-1499. Web Site: www.sccourts.org/courts/supreme-court. *Librn,* Janet F Meyer; Staff 2 (MLS 1, Non-MLS 1)
Founded 1871
Library Holdings: Bk Vols 49,500; Per Subs 115
Special Collections: Court Cases (1918 to present), micro
Subject Interests: SC law
Wireless access
Open Mon-Fri 8:30-5
Restriction: Non-circulating

C SOUTH UNIVERSITY*, Columbia Campus, Nine Science Ct, 29203. SAN 360-0815. Tel: 803-935-4336. Interlibrary Loan Service Tel: 803-935-4330. Web Site: libanswers.southuniversity.edu. *Libr Dir,* Van E Carpenter; E-mail: vcarpenter@southuniversity.edu; Staff 3 (MLS 2, Non-MLS 1)
Founded 1935. Enrl 1,000; Fac 55; Highest Degree: Master
Library Holdings: AV Mats 1,300; Bk Vols 15,000; Per Subs 100
Subject Interests: Acctg, Behav sci, Counseling, Econ, Hist, Nursing, Paralegal, Soc sci
Automation Activity & Vendor Info: (Acquisitions) Baker & Taylor; (Cataloging) Ex Libris Group; (Circulation) Ex Libris Group
Wireless access
Function: AV serv, CD-ROM, Computers for patron use, Electronic databases & coll, ILL available, Instruction & testing, Internet access, Learning ctr, Online cat, Online ref, Orientations, Photocopying/Printing, Ref & res, Ref serv available, VHS videos, Workshops
Open Mon-Fri 9-5
Restriction: Authorized patrons, Borrowing privileges limited to fac & registered students, Circ privileges for students & alumni only, Open to qualified scholars, Open to researchers by request, Open to students, fac, staff & alumni

C UNIVERSITY OF SOUTH CAROLINA*, Thomas Cooper Library, 1322 Greene St, 29208-0103. SAN 360-1234. Tel: 803-777-3142. Circulation Tel: 803-777-3145. Interlibrary Loan Service Tel: 803-777-2805. Reference Tel: 803-777-4866. FAX: 803-777-4661. Web Site: www.sc.edu/library. *Dean of Libr,* Thomas McNally; E-mail: tom@mailbox.sc.edu; *Assoc Dean,* Rebecca Gettys; E-mail: gettysr@mailbox.sc.edu; *Assoc Dean, Admin Serv,* Mary C Horton; E-mail: hortonmc@mailbox.sc.edu; *Head, Acq,* Christee Pascale; E-mail: cpascale@mailbox.sc.edu; *Head, Cat,* Scott Phinney; E-mail: phinney@mailbox.sc.edu; *Head, Circ,* Tucky Taylor; E-mail: tucky@mailbox.sc.edu; *Head, Coll Develop,* Paul Cammarata; E-mail: paul@mailbox.sc.edu; *Head, Res & Instruction,* Sharon Verba; E-mail: sharonv@mailbox.sc.edu
Founded 1801. Highest Degree: Doctorate
Special Collections: Archaeology (19th Century), rare bks; EEC; English & American Literature, rare bks; F Scott Fitzgerald, rare bks; Ornithology (18th-20th Century), rare bks; Robert Burns & Scottish Literature, Civil War, rare bks; Scottish Literature; South Carolina Political Coll. Oral History; US Document Depository
Automation Activity & Vendor Info: (Acquisitions) Innovative Interfaces, Inc; (Cataloging) Innovative Interfaces, Inc; (Circulation) Innovative Interfaces, Inc; (OPAC) Innovative Interfaces, Inc - Millennium
Wireless access
Publications: Reflections
Partic in Association of Research Libraries; LYRASIS; Partnership Among South Carolina Academic Libraries
Friends of the Library Group

Departmental Libraries:

DIGITAL COLLECTIONS, Hollings Special Collections Library, 1322 Greene St, 29208. Tel: 803-777-0735. Web Site: sc.edu/about/offices_and_divisions/university_libraries/browse/digital_collections/index.php. *Dir, Digital Serv,* Kate Boyd; E-mail: boydkf@mailbox.sc.edu

EDUCATIONAL FILMS, Thomas Cooper Library, Level 3, Main Level, 29208. Tel: 803-777-2858. Web Site: sc.edu/about/offices_and_divisions/university_libraries/browse/educational_films/index.php. *Library Contact,* Rebekah Lane; E-mail: lanerl@mailbox.sc.edu; Staff 1 (Non-MLS 1)
Library Holdings: Bk Titles 11,000
Subject Interests: Anthrop, Bus, English, Film studies, Hist, Humanities, Psychol, Sociol

ERNEST F HOLLINGS SPECIAL COLLECTIONS LIBRARY, 1322 Greene St, 29208. Tel: 803-777-0577. FAX: 803-777-0578. Web Site: sc.edu/about/offices_and_divisions/university_libraries/about/locations/hollings/index.php. *Assoc Dean, Spec Coll, Dir,* Elizabeth Sudduth; Tel: 807-777-5487, E-mail: esudduth@mailbox.sc.edu; Staff 4 (MLS 4)
Special Collections: Papers of South Carolinians holding state & national level office post-WWII
Open Mon-Fri 8:30-5

IRVIN DEPARTMENT OF RARE BOOKS & SPECIAL COLLECTIONS, Ernest F Hollings Special Collections Library, 1322 Greene St, 29208. Tel: 803-777-3847. E-mail: tclrare@mailbox.sc.edu. Web Site: sc.edu/about/offices_and_divisions/university_libraries/browse/irvin_dept_special_collections. *Assoc Dean, Spec Coll, Dir,* Elizabeth Sudduth; E-mail: esudduth@mailbox.sc.edu
Open Mon-Fri 8:30-5

CL LAW LIBRARY, 1525 Senate St, 29208, SAN 360-1269. Tel: 803-777-5942. Reference Tel: 803-777-5902. FAX: 803-777-9405. Reference E-mail: lawweb@law.sc.edu. Web Site: www.law.sc.edu/library. *Assoc Dean, Dir,* Duncan Alford; E-mail: alfordd@law.sc.edu; *Assoc Dir, Faculty Servs & Administration,* Candle Wester; E-mail: westercm@law.sc.edu; *Assoc Dir, Libr Operations,* Rebekah Maxwell; E-mail: rkmaxwel@law.sc.edu; *Asst Dir, Legal Res Instruction,* Terrye Conroy; E-mail: conroyt@law.sc.edu; *Head, Tech Serv,* Cornelius Pereira; E-mail: cpareira@law.sc.edu; *Acq & Electronic Res Librn,* Megan Brown; E-mail: lmbrown@law.sc.edu; Staff 9 (MLS 9)
Founded 1866. Enrl 657; Fac 50; Highest Degree: Doctorate
Library Holdings: e-books 41,088; Electronic Media & Resources 256; Microforms 1,496,676; Bk Titles 124,668; Bk Vols 567,708
Special Collections: Anglo-American Law; Coleman Karesh Reading Room; South Carolina Legal History. US Document Depository
Automation Activity & Vendor Info: (Acquisitions) Innovative Interfaces, Inc - Millennium; (Cataloging) Innovative Interfaces, Inc - Millennium; (Circulation) Innovative Interfaces, Inc - Millennium; (Course Reserve) Innovative Interfaces, Inc - Millennium; (ILL) OCLC; (OPAC) Innovative Interfaces, Inc - Millennium; (Serials) Innovative Interfaces, Inc - Millennium
Function: Art exhibits, Computers for patron use, Doc delivery serv, Electronic databases & coll, ILL available, Online cat, Online info literacy tutorials on the web & in blackboard, Photocopying/Printing, Ref serv available, Telephone ref
Partic in Law Library Microform Consortium; LYRASIS; Partnership Among South Carolina Academic Libraries
Open Mon-Wed 7am-11pm, Thurs 7am-10pm, Fri 7am-9pm, Sat 9-9, Sun 1-11
Restriction: Open to pub for ref & circ; with some limitations, Pub use on premises

MOVING IMAGE RESEARCH COLLECTIONS, 707 Catawba St, 29201. Tel: 803-777-6841. FAX: 803-777-4756. E-mail: MIRC@mailbox.sc.edu. Web Site: sc.edu/about/offices_and_divisions/university_libraries/browse/mirc/index.php. *Dir,* Heather Heckman; E-mail: heckmanh@mailbox.sc.edu; *Asst Dir,* Lydia Pappas; E-mail: pappasl@mailbox.sc.edu; *Curator,* Amy Meaney; E-mail: meanya@maibox.sc.edu; *Curator,* Greg Wilsbacher; E-mail: gregw@mailbox.sc.edu; Staff 8 (MLS 4, Non-MLS 4)
Special Collections: C E Feltner, Jr Coll, newsfilm; Chinese Film; Covington Coll of Commercials & Shorts; Fox Movietone News; Local Television News; Roman Vishniac Coll; SC Dept of Wildlife Films

MUSIC LIBRARY, 813 Assembly St, Rm 208, 29208. Tel: 803-777-5139. FAX: 803-777-1426. E-mail: musiclib@mailbox.sc.edu. Web Site: sc.edu/about/offices_and_divisions/university_libraries/browse/music_library/index.php. *Head Librn,* Ana Dubnjakovic; Tel: 803-777-5425, E-mail: ana@mailbox.sc.edu; Staff 5 (MLS 3, Non-MLS 2)

Library Holdings: Bk Vols 90,000; Per Subs 135
Special Collections: Center for Southern African American Music; Digital Sheet Music Project; Henry Cowell Coll; Mario Castelnuovo-Tedesco Coll

CM SCHOOL OF MEDICINE LIBRARY, Bldg 101, 6311 Garners Ferry Rd, 29209. Tel: 803-216-3200. Circulation Tel: 803-216-3213. FAX: 803-216-3213. Web Site: uscm.med.sc.edu. *Dir, Libr Serv,* Ruth Riley; E-mail: ruth.riley@uscmed.sc.edu; *Dep Dir,* Felicia Yeh; E-mail: felicia.yeh@uscmed.sc.edu; *Asst Dir, Educ & Outreach,* Roz McConnaughy; E-mail: roz.mcconnaughy@uscmed.sc.edu; *Asst Dir, Info Serv,* Laura Kane; E-mail: laura.kane@uscmed.sc.edu; *Head, Access Serv,* Karen McMullen; E-mail: karen.mcmullen@uscmed.sc.edu; *Coll Develop Librn,* Christine Whitaker; E-mail: christine.whitaker@uscmed.sc.edu; *Outreach Librn,* Steve P Wilson; E-mail: steve.wilson@uscmed.sc.edu; *Syst Librn,* Victor Jenkinson; E-mail: victor.jenkinson@uscmed.sc.edu; Staff 16 (MLS 9, Non-MLS 7)
Founded 1975. Enrl 556; Fac 263; Highest Degree: Doctorate
Special Collections: Rare Medical Books
Subject Interests: Disabilities
Automation Activity & Vendor Info: (Cataloging) Innovative Interfaces, Inc; (OPAC) Innovative Interfaces, Inc
Partic in Carolina Consortium; National Network of Libraries of Medicine Region 2; Partnership Among South Carolina Academic Libraries; South Carolina AHEC
Open Mon-Fri 8-6, Sat 11-5, Sun 1-5

SOUTH CAROLINIANA LIBRARY, 910 Sumter St, 29208. Tel: 803-777-3131. Interlibrary Loan Service Tel: 803-777-3132. FAX: 803-777-5747. E-mail: sclref@mailbox.sc.edu. Web Site: sc.edu/about/offices_and_divisions/university_libraries/browse/south_caroliniana/index.php. *Dir,* Henry Fulmer; E-mail: fulmerh@mailbox.sc.edu; Staff 9 (MLS 9)
Founded 1801
Library Holdings: Bk Vols 101,114; Per Subs 325
Special Collections: South Caroliniana & Southern Materials
Subject Interests: SC culture, SC hist
Publications: Caroliniana Columns; University South Caroliniana Society Annual Report of Gifts to the Collection
Open Mon-Fri 8-5
Friends of the Library Group

CONWAY

C COASTAL CAROLINA UNIVERSITY*, Kimbel Library & Bryan Information Commons, 376 University Blvd, 29526. (Mail add: PO Box 261954, 29528-6054), SAN 315-5331. Tel: 843-349-2400. FAX: 843-349-2412. Web Site: www.coastal.edu/library. *Univ Librn,* Melvin Davis; E-mail: mdavis10@coastal.edu; *Assoc Univ Librn,* Jennifer Hughes; E-mail: jhughes@coastal.edu; *Head, Coll, Head, Info Tech,* John Felts; E-mail: jfelts@coastal.edu; *Instruction Coordr, Librn,* Allison Faix; Tel: 843-349-2511, E-mail: afaix@coastal.edu; Staff 19 (MLS 9, Non-MLS 10)
Founded 1954. Enrl 4,500; Highest Degree: Master
Library Holdings: e-books 66,130; Electronic Media & Resources 38,900; Microforms 4,700; Bk Vols 130,800; Per Subs 493
Special Collections: Marine Science. State Document Depository; US Document Depository
Automation Activity & Vendor Info: (Acquisitions) Innovative Interfaces, Inc; (Cataloging) Innovative Interfaces, Inc; (Circulation) Innovative Interfaces, Inc; (ILL) Innovative Interfaces, Inc; (OPAC) Innovative Interfaces, Inc; (Serials) Innovative Interfaces, Inc
Wireless access
Partic in Partnership Among South Carolina Academic Libraries
Open Mon-Sun 6am-2am (Winter); Mon-Thurs 7:30am-10pm, Fri 7:30-3:30, Sat 9-5 (Summer)
Restriction: 24-hr pass syst for students only
Friends of the Library Group

P HORRY COUNTY MEMORIAL LIBRARY*, Administration, 1008 Fifth Ave, 29526. SAN 360-1382. Tel: 843-915-5285. FAX: 843-248-1548. Web Site: horry.ent.sirsi.net. *Dir,* Cynthia Thornley; E-mail: thornley.cynthia@horrycounty.org; *Asst Dir,* Tracey Elvis-Weitzel; E-mail: elvist@horrycounty.org; *Tech Serv Supvr,* Jody Gray; *Coll Develop,* Claire Campana; E-mail: 843-248-1550; Staff 8 (MLS 3, Non-MLS 5)
Founded 1948. Pop 210,000; Circ 903,583
Special Collections: Local History. Oral History
Automation Activity & Vendor Info: (Acquisitions) SirsiDynix; (Cataloging) SirsiDynix; (Circulation) SirsiDynix; (ILL) OCLC; (OPAC) SirsiDynix
Publications: HCML Report
Partic in DISCUS; LYRASIS; OCLC Online Computer Library Center, Inc
Special Services for the Deaf - Staff with knowledge of sign lang
Open Mon-Fri 8-5
Friends of the Library Group

Branches: 11

AYNOR BRANCH, 500 Ninth Ave, Aynor, 29511, SAN 360-1412. Tel: 843-358-3324. FAX: 843-358-1639. E-mail: aynorlibrary@horrycounty.org. *Br Mgr,* Cheral Thompson; Staff 2 (Non-MLS 2)
Founded 1948. Circ 30,354
Open Mon-Thurs 9-6, Fri 9-2
Friends of the Library Group

BUCKSPORT, 7657 Hwy 701 S, 29527, SAN 375-5703. Tel: 843-397-1950. FAX: 843-397-1951. E-mail: bucksportlibrary@horrycounty.org. *Br Mgr,* Veronica Singleton; Staff 1 (Non-MLS 1)
Founded 1995. Circ 14,848
Library Holdings: Bk Vols 16,726
Open Mon-Thurs 10-7, Fri 10-3
Friends of the Library Group

CAROLINA FOREST BRANCH, 2250 Carolina Forest Blvd, Myrtle Beach, 29579. Tel: 843-915-5282. FAX: 843-915-6282. *Librn,* Jennifer Silmser
Open Mon-Thurs 9-7, Fri 9-6, Sat 9-5

CONWAY BRANCH, 801 Main St, 29526. Tel: 843-915-7323. Interlibrary Loan Service Tel: 843-915-7434. Reference Tel: 843-915-7431. FAX: 843-248-1443. TDD: 843-248-1547. E-mail: conwaylibrary@horrycounty.org. *Librn,* Kim Cantley
Circ 183,528
Special Collections: Local History Coll
Open Mon-Thurs 8-8, Fri 8-6, Sat 9-5
Friends of the Library Group

GREEN SEA-FLOYDS BRANCH, 5331 Hwy 9, Green Sea, 29545. Tel: 843-392-0994. FAX: 843-392-0996. E-mail: gsflibrary@horrycounty.org. *Br Mgr,* Melissa Shenk; Staff 2 (Non-MLS 2)
Founded 2000. Circ 19,260
Library Holdings: Bk Vols 11,728
Open Mon-Thurs 9-6, Fri 9-2
Friends of the Library Group

LITTLE RIVER BRANCH, Ralph H Ellis County Complex Bldg, 107 Hwy 57 N, Little River, 29566, SAN 375-5711. Tel: 843-399-5541. FAX: 843-399-5542. E-mail: littleriverlibrary@horrycounty.org. *Br Mgr,* Sadina Lewis; Staff 2 (Non-MLS 2)
Circ 68,767
Library Holdings: Bk Vols 20,459
Open Mon-Fri 9-6
Friends of the Library Group

LORIS BRANCH, 4316 Main St, Loris, 29569, SAN 360-1501. Tel: 843-756-8101. FAX: 843-756-1988. E-mail: lorislibrary@horrycounty.org. *Br Mgr,* Renae Strickland; Staff 2 (Non-MLS 2)
Founded 1952. Circ 52,446
Library Holdings: Bk Vols 27,958
Open Tues-Fri 9-6, Sat 9-2
Friends of the Library Group

NORTH MYRTLE BEACH BRANCH, 910 First Ave S, North Myrtle Beach, 29582, SAN 360-1471. Tel: 843-915-5281. Reference Tel: 843-915-7452. FAX: 843-915-6280. E-mail: nmblibrary@horrycounty.org. *Librn,* Amanda Soles
Founded 1948. Pop 120,000; Circ 163,040
Function: Adult bk club, Art exhibits, Bi-weekly Writer's Group, Bks on cassette, Bks on CD, Children's prog, Computers for patron use, Digital talking bks, E-Reserves, Electronic databases & coll, Free DVD rentals, ILL available, Internet access, Magnifiers for reading, Mail & tel request accepted, Microfiche/film & reading machines, Music CDs, Online cat, Online ref, Photocopying/Printing, Preschool reading prog, Prog for adults, Prog for children & young adult, Ref serv available, Spoken cassettes & CDs, Spoken cassettes & DVDs, Story hour, Summer & winter reading prog, Tax forms, Teen prog, Telephone ref, Wheelchair accessible
Special Services for the Deaf - Bks on deafness & sign lang; Closed caption videos
Special Services for the Blind - Audio mat; Bks on cassette; Bks on CD; Closed circuit TV magnifier; Copier with enlargement capabilities; Digital talking bk; Extensive large print coll; Free checkout of audio mat; Large print bks; Magnifiers; Telesensory screen enlarger
Open Mon-Thurs 9-7, Fri 9-6, Sat 9-2
Friends of the Library Group

SOCASTEE, 141 707-Connector Rd, Myrtle Beach, 29588, SAN 372-7874. Tel: 843-215-4700. FAX: 843-215-2801. TDD: 843-215-6764. E-mail: socasteelibrary@horrycounty.org. *Librn,* Leona Brown; Staff 8 (MLS 3, Non-MLS 5)
Founded 2003. Circ 259,359
Library Holdings: Bk Vols 59,000
Function: Adult bk club, Art exhibits, Bk club(s), Bks on cassette, Bks on CD, Children's prog, Computers for patron use, Electronic databases & coll, Free DVD rentals, Holiday prog, ILL available, Instruction & testing, Internet access, Magnifiers for reading, Music CDs, Notary serv, Online cat, Online ref, Photocopying/Printing, Prog for adults, Prog for

children & young adult, Ref serv available, Scanner, Story hour, Summer reading prog, Tax forms, Telephone ref
Open Mon-Thurs 9-7, Fri 9-6, Sat 9-5
Friends of the Library Group
SURFSIDE BEACH BRANCH, 410 Surfside Dr, Surfside Beach, 29575, SAN 360-1536. Tel: 843-238-5280. FAX: 843-205-6281 (SC Only). E-mail: hcg.libraries@horrycountysc.gov. *Librn,* Allison Hucks; Staff 4 (MLS 1, Non-MLS 3)
Circ 135,856
Library Holdings: Bk Vols 36,956
Open Mon-Thurs 9-7, Fri 9-6, Sat 9-2
Friends of the Library Group
TECHNICAL SERVICES, Extension Bldg, 1603 Fourth Ave, 29526, SAN 374-4116. Tel: 843-915-5289. FAX: 843-248-1549. *Head, Tech Serv,* Jody Gray; Staff 4 (Non-MLS 4)
Founded 1948
Open Mon-Fri 8-5
Bookmobiles: 1. Br Mgr, Allyson Kirven

J HORRY-GEORGETOWN TECHNICAL COLLEGE*, Conway Campus Library, 2050 Hwy 501 E, 29526-9521. (Mail add: PO Box 261966, 29528-6066), SAN 315-5323. Tel: 843-349-5268. Reference Tel: 843-349-5394. FAX: 843-349-7811. Web Site: www.hgtc.edu/about_hgtc/library. *Dir, Libr Serv,* Dr Richard Moniz; E-mail: richard.moniz@hgtc.edu; *Assoc Librn, Ref Serv Coordr,* Chris Williams; E-mail: christopher.williams@hgtc.edu; *Libr Spec,* Stephanie Courtney; Tel: 843-349-7596, E-mail: stephanie.courtney@hgtc.edu; *Coordr, Tech Serv, Resource Sharing Coord,* Roberta Tyson; Tel: 843-349-5396, E-mail: roberta.tyson@hgtc.edu; Staff 8.5 (MLS 4.5, Non-MLS 4)
Founded 1966. Enrl 4,398; Fac 180; Highest Degree: Associate
Library Holdings: e-books 68,395; Bk Vols 25,233; Per Subs 180
Subject Interests: Civil engr, Computer sci, Cosmetology, Criminal justice, Culinary arts, Early child care, Golf course maintenance
Automation Activity & Vendor Info: (Acquisitions) Ex Libris Group; (Cataloging) Ex Libris Group; (Circulation) Ex Libris Group; (Course Reserve) SirsiDynix; (ILL) OCLC WorldShare Interlibrary Loan; (OPAC) Ex Libris Group; (Serials) Ex Libris Group
Wireless access
Function: Computers for patron use, Electronic databases & coll, Free DVD rentals, ILL available, Internet access, Online cat, Online info literacy tutorials on the web & in blackboard, Online ref, Orientations, Outside serv via phone, mail, e-mail & web, Photocopying/Printing, Printer for laptops & handheld devices, Ref & res, Ref serv available, Telephone ref, Wheelchair accessible, Workshops
Partic in OCLC Online Computer Library Center, Inc; Partnership Among South Carolina Academic Libraries
Open Mon-Wed 8am-8:30pm, Thurs 8-4:30
Restriction: Non-circulating of rare bks
Departmental Libraries:
ELIZABETH MATTOCKS CHAPIN MEMORIAL LIBRARY - GRAND STRAND CAMPUS, 3639 Pampas Dr, Myrtle Beach, 29577, SAN 372-5049. Tel: 843-477-2012. Reference Tel: 843-477-2018. *Electronic Res Librn,* J J Fickenworth; Tel: 843-477-2100, E-mail: jennifer.fickenworth@hgtc.edu; Staff 2.5 (MLS 1.5, Non-MLS 1)
Founded 1990. Enrl 1,800; Fac 105; Highest Degree: Associate
Library Holdings: Bk Vols 20,080; Per Subs 153
Subject Interests: Allied health, Dental, Nursing, Paralegal, Radiology
GEORGETOWN CAMPUS, 4003 S Fraser St, Georgetown, 29440, SAN 372-5030. Tel: 843-520-1424. *Ref & Instruction Librn,* Jo Henry; Tel: 843-520-1423, E-mail: jo.henry@hgtc.edu; Staff 1.5 (MLS 0.5, Non-MLS 1)
Founded 1978. Enrl 900; Fac 25
Library Holdings: Bk Titles 7,161; Per Subs 4
Subject Interests: Forestry, Licensed practical nursing
Open Mon-Thurs 8-4:30, Fri 8-12

DARLINGTON

S DARLINGTON COUNTY HISTORICAL COMMISSION & MUSEUM, 204 Hewitt St, 29532. SAN 370-2103. Tel: 843-398-4710. E-mail: dchc@darcosc.net. Web Site: darlingtoncountymuseum.org. *Dir,* Brian E Gandy; E-mail: bgandy@darcosc.net; *Asst Dir,* Ann F Chapman; E-mail: achapman@darcosc.net
Founded 1965
Library Holdings: Bk Vols 10,000
Subject Interests: Genealogy, Local hist
Wireless access
Open Mon-Fri 9-5

P DARLINGTON COUNTY LIBRARY SYSTEM*, 204 N Main St, 29532. SAN 360-1560. Tel: 843-398-4940. FAX: 843-398-4942. Web Site: www.darlington-lib.org. *Dir,* Jimmie Epling; E-mail: jimmie.epling@darlington-lib.org; *Br Mgr,* Michelle Wallace; E-mail: michellew.dar@darlington-lib.org; Staff 42 (MLS 3, Non-MLS 39)
Founded 1968. Pop 68,800; Circ 303,065
Library Holdings: Bk Vols 140,000; Per Subs 422
Automation Activity & Vendor Info: (Cataloging) Innovative Interfaces, Inc. - Polaris; (Circulation) Innovative Interfaces, Inc. - Polaris; (OPAC) Innovative Interfaces, Inc. - Polaris
Wireless access
Function: 24/7 Electronic res, 24/7 Online cat, 3D Printer, Activity rm, Adult bk club, After school storytime, Audio & video playback equip for onsite use, Audiobks via web, Bk club(s), Bks on CD, Butterfly Garden, Children's prog, Computer training, Computers for patron use, Doc delivery serv, E-Reserves, Electronic databases & coll, Free DVD rentals, Holiday prog, ILL available, Internet access, Laminating, Life-long learning prog for all ages, Magazines, Mail & tel request accepted, Meeting rooms, Microfiche/film & reading machines, Movies, Music CDs, Notary serv, Online cat, Outreach serv, OverDrive digital audio bks, Passport agency, Photocopying/Printing, Preschool outreach, Preschool reading prog, Prof lending libr, Prog for adults, Prog for children & young adult, Ref & res, Ref serv available, Scanner, Senior outreach, Spanish lang bks, STEM programs, Story hour, Study rm, Summer reading prog, Tax forms, Teen prog, Telephone ref, Workshops
Partic in Association for Rural & Small Libraries
Open Mon-Thurs 9-8, Fri 9-5, Sat 10-2, Sun 2-5
Friends of the Library Group
Branches: 3
HARTSVILLE MEMORIAL, 147 W College St, Hartsville, 29550, SAN 360-1595. Tel: 843-332-5115. FAX: 843-332-7071. *Br Mgr,* Martha Brown; E-mail: marthab.har@darlington-lib.org; Staff 8 (MLS 1, Non-MLS 7)
Founded 1930. Pop 44,747; Circ 164,416
Library Holdings: Bk Vols 90,200; Per Subs 110
Special Collections: Hartsville Messenger Newspaper 1894-present
Function: Adult bk club, Audiobks via web, Bks on cassette, Bks on CD, Children's prog, Computer training, Computers for patron use, Electronic databases & coll, Free DVD rentals, ILL available, Microfiche/film & reading machines, Music CDs, Online cat, OverDrive digital audio bks, Photocopying/Printing, Preschool outreach, Printer for laptops & handheld devices, Prog for children & young adult, Ref serv available, Story hour, Summer reading prog, Tax forms, Teen prog, Telephone ref, VHS videos, Wheelchair accessible
Partic in Palmetto Academic Independent Library System
Open Mon-Thurs 9-8, Fri 9-5, Sat 10-2, Sun 2-5
Friends of the Library Group
LAMAR BRANCH, 103 E Main St, Lamar, 29069, SAN 360-1625. Tel: 843-326-5524. FAX: 843-326-7302. *Br Mgr,* Kelly Shull; E-mail: Kellys.lmr@darlington-lib.org; Staff 6 (Non-MLS 6)
Library Holdings: Bk Vols 18,500; Per Subs 36
Open Mon-Thurs 10-7, Fri 10-5, Sat 10-2
Friends of the Library Group
SOCIETY HILL BRANCH, 114 Carrigan St, Society Hill, 29593. Tel: 843-378-0026. FAX: 843-378-0051. *Br Mgr,* Lynn Anderson; E-mail: lynna.sh@darlington-lib.org; Staff 5 (MLS 1, Non-MLS 4)
Founded 1822. Pop 10,000; Circ 10,500
Automation Activity & Vendor Info: (Acquisitions) Innovative Interfaces, Inc; (Course Reserve) Innovative Interfaces, Inc; (ILL) Innovative Interfaces, Inc
Function: 24/7 Electronic res, 24/7 Online cat, 24/7 wireless access, 3D Printer, Adult bk club, Art programs, Audiobks via web, AV serv, Bk club(s), Bks on CD, Children's prog, Computer training, Computers for patron use, Distance learning, E-Reserves, Electronic databases & coll, Family literacy, Free DVD rentals, Games, Govt ref serv, Holiday prog, ILL available, Instruction & testing, Internet access, Laminating, Magazines, Meeting rooms, Movies, Notary serv, Online cat, Online info literacy tutorials on the web & in blackboard, Online ref, Outreach serv, OverDrive digital audio bks, Photocopying/Printing, Prog for adults, Prog for children & young adult, Ref & res, Ref serv available, Scanner, Senior outreach, Story hour, Study rm, Summer reading prog, Tax forms, Wheelchair accessible, Workshops
Partic in Palmetto Academic Independent Library System
Open Mon-Thurs 10-7, Fri 10-5, Sat 10-2
Restriction: Circ limited, In-house use for visitors, Non-resident fee, Off-site coll in storage - retrieval as requested, Photo ID required for access
Friends of the Library Group

DENMARK

J DENMARK TECHNICAL COLLEGE*, Learning Resources Center, 113 Solomon Blatt Blvd, 29042. (Mail add: PO Box 327, 29042-0327), SAN 374-6232. Tel: 803-793-5215. Reference Tel: 803-793-5216. Administration Tel: 803-793-5213. FAX: 803-793-5942. Web Site: denmarktech.libguides.com. *Dean of Libr,* Carolyn Fortson; E-mail: fortsonc@denmarktech.edu; Staff 2 (MLS 1, Non-MLS 1)
Founded 1948. Enrl 250; Fac 36; Highest Degree: Associate
Library Holdings: Bk Titles 13,000; Per Subs 187

Automation Activity & Vendor Info: (Circulation) EnvisionWare; (ILL) Ex Libris Group; (OPAC) Ex Libris Group
Wireless access
Function: 24/7 Electronic res, 24/7 Online cat, Archival coll, Computers for patron use, ILL available
Partic in Partnership Among South Carolina Academic Libraries
Open Mon-Thurs 8-7

C VOORHEES UNIVERSITY, Wright-Potts Library, 213 Wiggins Dr, 29042. (Mail add: PO Box 678, 29042-0678), SAN 315-534X. Tel: 803-780-1220. FAX: 803-793-0471. Web Site: www.voorhees.edu/academics/library. *Libr Dir,* Herman Mason; Tel: 803-780-1229, E-mail: hmason@voorhees.edu; *Ref Librn,* Leroy Fogle; E-mail: lfogle@voorhees.edu; *Tech Serv Librn,* Shatarra Glover; E-mail: sglover@voorhees.edu; *Circ,* Position Currently Open; *Libr Asst, Media Serv,* Gwendolyn Timms; E-mail: gtimms@voorhees.edu; Staff 4 (MLS 2, Non-MLS 2)
Founded 1935. Enrl 600; Fac 44; Highest Degree: Master
Library Holdings: Bk Vols 110,000; Per Subs 213
Special Collections: African American; Historical Papers; Ten-Year Developmental Study of Episcopal Church Book of Common Prayer; Voorhees College Documents
Wireless access
Partic in HBCU Library Alliance; Partnership Among South Carolina Academic Libraries
Open Mon-Thurs 8-5

DILLON

P DILLON COUNTY LIBRARY*, 600 E Main St, 29536. Tel: 843-774-0330. FAX: 843-774-0733. E-mail: dilloncountylibrary@live.com, library@dilloncountysc.org. Web Site: www.dillon.lib.sc.us. *Interim Dir,* Christina Fowler; E-mail: christina_herring@hotmail.com; *Asst Mgr,* Mia McAlister; *Ch,* Tierney Alford; Staff 8 (MLS 2, Non-MLS 6)
Circ 76,479
Library Holdings: Bk Titles 42,110; Bk Vols 90,340; Per Subs 35
Subject Interests: Genealogy, Local hist
Automation Activity & Vendor Info: (Cataloging) Innovative Interfaces, Inc; (Circulation) Innovative Interfaces, Inc; (OPAC) Innovative Interfaces, Inc; (Serials) Innovative Interfaces, Inc
Wireless access
Open Mon & Tues 9-8, Wed-Fri 9-6, Sat 9-1
Friends of the Library Group
Branches: 2
LAKE VIEW BRANCH, 207 S Main St, Lake View, 29563, SAN 360-294X. Tel: 843-759-2692. FAX: 843-759-0061. *Br Mgr,* Mertis Barnett
Open Mon-Fri 10-6, Sat 10-1
Friends of the Library Group
LATTA BRANCH, 101 N Marion St, Latta, 29565-3597, SAN 360-2885. Tel: 843-752-5389. FAX: 843-752-7457. *Br Mgr,* Dixie Weatherly
Founded 1914
Open Mon-Fri 9-6, Sat 9-1
Friends of the Library Group
Bookmobiles: 1. Mgr, Rose Magyar

DUE WEST

CR ERSKINE COLLEGE & THEOLOGICAL SEMINARY*, McCain Library, One Depot St, 29639. SAN 315-5358. Tel: 864-379-8898. Toll Free Tel: 877-876-4348. FAX: 864-379-2900. E-mail: library@erskine.edu. Web Site: www.erskine.edu/library. *Assoc Dean of Libr,* John F Kennerly; Tel: 864-379-8788, E-mail: kennerly@erskine.edu; *Access Serv Librn,* Ellis Major; Tel: 864-379-8714, E-mail: emajor@erskine.edu; *Asst Prof, Librn,* Frederick W Guyette; Tel: 864-379-8784, E-mail: fguyette@erskine.edu; *Asst Prof, Librn,* Sara M Morrison; Tel: 864-379-8747, E-mail: morrison@erskine.edu; Staff 6 (MLS 3, Non-MLS 3)
Founded 1837. Enrl 778; Fac 83; Highest Degree: Doctorate
Library Holdings: AV Mats 1,963; e-books 36,267; e-journals 625; Bk Vols 177,877; Per Subs 1,333
Special Collections: Associate Reformed Presbyterian Church Records. US Document Depository
Subject Interests: Erskiniana, Genealogy, Local hist, Relig
Automation Activity & Vendor Info: (Acquisitions) Innovative Interfaces, Inc; (Cataloging) OCLC CatExpress; (Circulation) Innovative Interfaces, Inc; (Course Reserve) Innovative Interfaces, Inc; (ILL) OCLC; (OPAC) Innovative Interfaces, Inc; (Serials) Innovative Interfaces, Inc
Wireless access
Partic in Carolina Consortium; Council for Christian Colleges & Universities; LYRASIS; OCLC Online Computer Library Center, Inc; Partnership Among South Carolina Academic Libraries
Open Mon-Thurs 8am-11pm, Fri 8-5, Sat 1-5, Sun 7pm-11pm

EASLEY

P PICKENS COUNTY LIBRARY SYSTEM*, Captain Kimberly Hampton Memorial Library, 304 Biltmore Rd, 29640. SAN 360-1684. Tel: 864-850-7077. FAX: 864-850-7088. Reference E-mail: reference@pcls.fyi. Web Site: pickenscountylibrarysystem.com. *Dir,* Stephanie Howard; E-mail: showard@pcls.fyi; Staff 26 (MLS 12, Non-MLS 14)
Founded 1935. Pop 110,757; Circ 775,000
Library Holdings: Bk Titles 190,063; Bk Vols 210,527; Per Subs 326
Subject Interests: SC
Automation Activity & Vendor Info: (Cataloging) SirsiDynix; (Circulation) SirsiDynix; (OPAC) SirsiDynix
Wireless access
Open Mon-Thurs 9-9, Fri & Sat 9-6, Sun 2-6
Friends of the Library Group
Branches: 3
CENTRAL-CLEMSON REGIONAL BRANCH, 105 Commons Way, Central, 29630. Tel: 864-639-2711. FAX: 864-639-6643. E-mail: ccreference@pcls.fyi. *Br Mgr,* Jennifer Crenshaw; E-mail: jcrenshaw@pcls.fyi
Open Mon-Thurs 9-9, Fri 9-6, Sat 9-4, Sun 2:30-5:30
SARLIN BRANCH, 15 S Palmetto St, Liberty, 29658. Tel: 864-843-5805. *Br Mgr,* Kasey Swords; E-mail: kaseys@pcls.fyi
Open Mon 10-7, Tues-Fri 10-6, Sat 10-2
VILLAGE BRANCH, 124 N Catherine St, Pickens, 29671. Tel: 864-898-5747. FAX: 864-898-5750. *Br Mgr,* Jennifer Kolesar; E-mail: jenniferk@pcls.fyi
Open Mon & Thurs 10-8, Tues, Wed & Fri 10-6, Sat 10-4

EDGEFIELD

S TOMPKINS MEMORIAL LIBRARY*, 104 Courthouse Sq, 29824. (Mail add: PO Box 546, 29824), SAN 327-8646. Tel: 803-637-4010. FAX: 803-637-2116. E-mail: OEDGS85@gmail.com. Web Site: oedgs.org. *Libr Dir,* Tonya Browder
Library Holdings: Bk Vols 17,100
Open Mon-Fri 9-4, Sat 9:30-1:30

FLORENCE

P FLORENCE COUNTY LIBRARY SYSTEM*, Dr Bruce & Lee Foundation Library, 509 S Dargan St, 29506. SAN 360-1838. Tel: 843-662-8424. Reference Tel: 843-413-7074. Reference E-mail: reference@florencelibrary.org. Web Site: www.florencelibrary.org. *Dir,* Philip Alan Smith; E-mail: pasmith@florencelibrary.org; *Info Serv Mgr,* Aubrey Carroll; *Tech Serv Mgr,* Timothy Anderson; Staff 18 (MLS 12, Non-MLS 6)
Founded 1925. Pop 185,000; Circ 313,024
Library Holdings: AV Mats 15,121; Bk Vols 310,117; Per Subs 446
Special Collections: Caroliniana. US Document Depository
Subject Interests: Local hist
Automation Activity & Vendor Info: (Acquisitions) SirsiDynix; (Cataloging) SirsiDynix; (Circulation) SirsiDynix; (ILL) OCLC; (OPAC) SirsiDynix; (Serials) SirsiDynix
Wireless access
Partic in LYRASIS
Open Mon-Thurs 9-7, Fri 9-5:30, Sat 9-1
Friends of the Library Group
Branches: 5
BAKER MEMORIAL TIMMONSVILLE PUBLIC LIBRARY, 298 W Smith St, Timmonsville, 29161, SAN 360-1951. Tel: 843-346-2941. FAX: 843-954-3409. Web Site: sites.google.com/florencelibrary.org/tpl. *Br Mgr,* Rachel Liptak
Library Holdings: Bk Vols 8,000
Open Mon, Thurs & Fri 10-5, Tues 11-7, Wed 10-4, Sat 9-1
Friends of the Library Group
JOHNSONVILLE PUBLIC LIBRARY, 242 S Georgetown Hwy, Johnsonville, 29555, SAN 360-1862. Tel: 843-386-2052. FAX: 843-954-3133. E-mail: jvlibrary@florencelibrary.org. Web Site: sites.google.com/florencelibrary.org/jpl. *Br Mgr,* Cathy Pruett; Staff 3 (MLS 1, Non-MLS 2)
Open Mon & Wed-Fri 9-5, Tues 9-6:30, Sat 9-1
Friends of the Library Group
LAKE CITY PUBLIC LIBRARY, 221 E Main St, Lake City, 29560-2113, SAN 360-1897. Tel: 843-394-8071. FAX: 843-394-1033. Web Site: sites.google.com/florencelibrary.org/lakecitypubliclibrary. *Br Mgr,* Michael Cooper; Staff 1 (MLS 1)
Library Holdings: Bk Vols 13,000; Per Subs 35
Open Mon-Thurs 9-7, Fri 9-5, Sat 9-1
Friends of the Library Group
DOZIER M MUNN PAMPLICO PUBLIC LIBRARY, 100 E Main St, Pamplico, 29583, SAN 360-1927. Tel: 843-493-5441. FAX: 843-954-3043. Web Site: sites.google.com/florencelibrary.org/ppl. *Br Mgr,* Christina Stewart; E-mail: cstewart@florencelibrary.org; Staff 3 (MLS 1, Non-MLS 2)
Pop 1,150; Circ 12,000

Library Holdings: AV Mats 1,068; Braille Volumes 1; CDs 387; DVDs 68; Large Print Bks 183; Bk Vols 15,000; Per Subs 32; Videos 310
Special Collections: South Carolina Coll
Function: Children's prog, Computers for patron use, ILL available, Mail & tel request accepted, Music CDs, Online cat, Photocopying/Printing, Prog for children & young adult, Ref & res, Ref serv available, Spoken cassettes & CDs, Summer reading prog, Tax forms, Telephone ref, VHS videos, Wheelchair accessible
Special Services for the Blind - Audio mat; Bks on cassette; Bks on CD; Large print bks; Talking bk serv referral; ZoomText magnification & reading software
Open Mon, Wed & Fri 10-5, Tues & Thurs 10-7, Sat 10-1
Friends of the Library Group
DR JOHN M THOMASON PUBLIC LIBRARY, 210 E Hampton St, Olanta, 29114, SAN 360-1919. Tel: 843-396-4287. FAX: 843-954-3246. Web Site: sites.google.com/florencelibrary.org/opl. *Br Mgr,* Robert Slabaugh
Library Holdings: Bk Vols 1,889
Open Mon, Wed & Fri 9-5, Tues 11-5, Thurs 11-7, Sat 9-1
Bookmobiles: 1. Librn, Kitty Hinnant. Bk vols 5,000

J FLORENCE-DARLINGTON TECHNICAL COLLEGE LIBRARIES*, Wellman, Inc Library, 2715 W Lucas St, 29501. (Mail add: PO Box 100548, 29501-0548), SAN 315-5390. Tel: 843-661-8034. Circulation Tel: 843-661-8033. FAX: 843-661-8037. Web Site: www.fdtc.edu/academics/library. *Dir of Libr,* Jeronell W Bradley; Tel: 843-661-8032, E-mail: jeronell.bradley@fdtc.edu; *Librn,* Linda B Coe; E-mail: linda.coe@fdtc.edu; Staff 3 (MLS 2, Non-MLS 1)
Founded 1964. Enrl 2,121; Fac 99; Highest Degree: Associate
Library Holdings: AV Mats 1,257; e-books 588,518; Bk Vols 3,163; Per Subs 28
Automation Activity & Vendor Info: (Acquisitions) Ex Libris Group; (Cataloging) Ex Libris Group; (Circulation) Ex Libris Group; (OPAC) Ex Libris Group; (Serials) Ex Libris Group
Wireless access
Partic in Partnership Among South Carolina Academic Libraries
Open Mon-Thurs 8-5:30, Fri 8am-11:30am
Departmental Libraries:
SEGARS LIBRARY HEALTH SCIENCES CAMPUS, 320 W Cheves St, 29501. (Mail add: PO Box 100548, 29501-0501). Tel: 843-676-8575. *Dir of Libr,* Jeronell W Bradley; *Librn,* Linda Coe; *Media Spec,* Yvette Pierce; E-mail: yvette.pierce@fdtc.edu; Staff 4 (MLS 3, Non-MLS 1)
Founded 2001. Fac 99; Highest Degree: Associate
Open Mon-Thurs 8-3

C FRANCIS MARION UNIVERSITY*, James A Rogers Library, 4822 E Palmetto St, 29506. (Mail add: PO Box 100547, 29502), SAN 315-5412. Tel: 843-661-1300. Circulation Tel: 843-661-1311. Interlibrary Loan Service Tel: 843-661-1299. Reference Tel: 843-661-1310. FAX: 843-661-1309. Administration FAX: 843-661-4682. Web Site: www.fmarion.edu/rogerslibrary. *Dean,* Demetra T Walker; *Head, Access Serv, ILL Librn,* Steven C Sims; Tel: 843-661-1299, E-mail: ssims@fmarion.edu; *Archivist, Head, Ref, Librn,* Suzanne Singleton; Tel: 843-661-1319, E-mail: msingleton@fmarion.edu; *Head Ref/Govt Doc Librn,* Bernadette J Johnson; Tel: 843-661-1313, E-mail: bjjohnson@fmarion.edu; *Head, Syst, Librn,* Nathan Flowers; Tel: 843-661-1306, E-mail: nflowers@fmarion.edu; *Head, Tech Serv, Librn,* Mrs Demetra W Pearson; Tel: 843-661-1308, E-mail: dpearson@fmarion.edu; *Ref Librn,* Faith Keller; Tel: 843-661-1399, E-mail: fkeller@fmarion.edu; *Ref & Instruction Librn,* Virginia Pierce; Tel: 843-661-1302, E-mail: vpierce@fmarion.edu; *Media Cat Serv Librn,* Cindy Price; Tel: 843-661-1354, E-mail: cprice@fmarion.edu; Staff 21 (MLS 9, Non-MLS 12)
Founded 1970. Enrl 4,187; Fac 282; Highest Degree: Master
Library Holdings: DVDs 201; e-books 343,000; e-journals 34,499; Microforms 61,592; Bk Vols 674,983; Per Subs 583
Special Collections: South Caroliniana especially relating to Pee Dee Area, bks & microfilm. State Document Depository; US Document Depository
Automation Activity & Vendor Info: (Acquisitions) Innovative Interfaces, Inc; (Cataloging) Innovative Interfaces, Inc; (Circulation) Innovative Interfaces, Inc; (Course Reserve) Innovative Interfaces, Inc; (ILL) OCLC ILLiad; (OPAC) Innovative Interfaces, Inc; (Serials) Innovative Interfaces, Inc
Wireless access
Publications: The Axis
Partic in Carolina Consortium; LYRASIS; OCLC Online Computer Library Center, Inc; Partnership Among South Carolina Academic Libraries
Open Mon-Thurs 8am-11pm, Fri 8-5, Sat 9-5, Sun 2:30-11

M MCLEOD HEALTH*, Health Sciences Library, 144 N Ravenel St, 29506. (Mail add: PO Box 100551, 29502), SAN 315-5420. Tel: 843-777-2275. *Libr Dir,* Lorraine Reiman; E-mail: lreiman@mcleodhealth.org; Staff 1 (MLS 1)
Founded 1975
Library Holdings: Per Subs 20
Special Collections: Medical & Nursing Coll
Subject Interests: Allied health fields, Clinical med, Continuing educ in the health fields, Nursing
Publications: Journal List
Partic in National Network of Libraries of Medicine Region 2
Restriction: Employees only

FORT JACKSON

UNITED STATES ARMY
A FORT JACKSON MAIN POST LIBRARY*, Thomas Lee Hall Main Post Library, Bldg 4679, 29207, SAN 360-1986. Tel: 803-751-4816, 803-751-5589. FAX: 803-751-1065. *Chief Librn,* John Anthony Vassallo; *Tech Serv,* Sharon Backenstose; Staff 5 (MLS 2, Non-MLS 3)
Founded 1946
Library Holdings: Bk Vols 70,115; Per Subs 50
Subject Interests: Hist, Mil sci
Automation Activity & Vendor Info: (Cataloging) Follett Software
Function: ILL available
Partic in OCLC Online Computer Library Center, Inc
Open Mon-Thurs 11-8, Fri-Sun 11-5
Restriction: Non-circulating to the pub
AM MONCRIEF ARMY HOSPITAL MEDICAL LIBRARY*, 4500 Stuart St, 29207-5720, SAN 360-2044. Tel: 803-751-2149. FAX: 803-751-2012. *Librn,* Steven Leap; E-mail: steven.leap@us.army.mil
Founded 1950
Library Holdings: Bk Vols 2,000; Per Subs 170
Subject Interests: Dental, Med, Nursing
Automation Activity & Vendor Info: (Acquisitions) Ex Libris Group; (Cataloging) Ex Libris Group; (Circulation) Ex Libris Group; (OPAC) Ex Libris Group

A US ARMY INSTITUTE FOR RELIGIOUS LEADERSHIP LIBRARY*, 10100 Lee Rd, 29207. Tel: 803-751-8828. FAX: 803-751-8393. E-mail: atzjpao@jackson.army.mil. Web Site: usairl.tradoc.army.mil/library. *Chief Librn,* Kathy Thomas
Library Holdings: CDs 62; DVDs 393; Bk Titles 23,413; Bk Vols 30,164; Per Subs 26
Special Collections: World Religions Coll
Subject Interests: World relig
Automation Activity & Vendor Info: (Acquisitions) Baker & Taylor; (Cataloging) LibraryWorld, Inc; (Circulation) LibraryWorld, Inc; (ILL) OCLC; (OPAC) LibraryWorld, Inc; (Serials) LibraryWorld, Inc
Wireless access
Publications: Monthly New Books List (Current awareness service)
Open Mon-Fri 8-6

GAFFNEY

P CHEROKEE COUNTY PUBLIC LIBRARY*, 300 E Rutledge Ave, 29340-2227. SAN 360-2079. Tel: 864-487-2711. FAX: 864-487-2752. E-mail: info@cherokeecountylibrary.org. Web Site: www.cherokeecountylibrary.org. *Libr Dir,* Ben Loftis; E-mail: bloftis@cherokeecountylibrary.org; *Syst Adminr,* Dana Peeler; E-mail: dpeeler@cherokeecountylibrary.org; *Circ Mgr,* Kendra Bell; E-mail: kbell@cherokeecountylibrary.org; *Ch Serv,* Alyssa D'Angelo; E-mail: alyssadangelo@cherokeecountylibrary.org; Staff 6 (MLS 1, Non-MLS 5)
Founded 1902. Pop 44,506; Circ 184,022
Library Holdings: AV Mats 3,000; e-books 40,000; Bk Vols 11,000; Per Subs 141; Talking Bks 3,000
Special Collections: Arthur Gettys Genealogy Coll; Gladys Coker Fort Fine Arts Coll; Heritage Room Coll; June Carr Photography Coll; Raymond & Bright Parker Story Tape Coll; Ruby Cash Garvin South Carolina Coll
Subject Interests: SC genealogy
Automation Activity & Vendor Info: (Cataloging) Evergreen; (Circulation) Evergreen; (OPAC) Evergreen
Wireless access
Open Mon-Thurs 9-7, Fri 9-5, Sat 9-4
Friends of the Library Group
Branches: 1
BLACKSBURG BRANCH, 201 S Rutherford St, Blacksburg, 29702, SAN 360-2109. Tel: 864-839-2630. FAX: 864-839-2572. *Br Mgr,* Kenny Covington
Special Collections: James M Bridges Reference Coll
Open Mon-Thurs 10-6, Fri 10-5
Friends of the Library Group
Bookmobiles: 1

C LIMESTONE UNIVERSITY LIBRARY, (Formerly Limestone College), 1115 College Dr, 29340. SAN 315-5439. Tel: 864-488-4612. Toll Free Tel: 800-795-7151, Ext 4612. E-mail: library@limestone.edu. Web Site: libguides.limestone.edu, www.limestone.edu/library. *Dir,* Lizah Ismail; Tel:

864-488-4610, E-mail: iismail@limestone.edu; *Asst Dir,* Janet Ward; Tel: 864-488-8351, E-mail: jward@limestone.edu; *Outreach & Instruction Librn,* Chloe Hoyle; Tel: 864-488-4446, E-mail: cflournoy@limestone.edu; *Tech Serv Librn,* Steven A Smith; Tel: 864-488-4611, E-mail: ssmith@limestone.edu; *Mgr, User Serv,* Lauren Roberts; E-mail: lmroberts@limestone.edu; Staff 6 (MLS 4, Non-MLS 2)
Founded 1845. Highest Degree: Master
Library Holdings: e-books 276,240; Bk Vols 71,014
Special Collections: Personal Library of Former Limestone College President (Lee Davis Lodge & Harrison Patillo Griffith)
Automation Activity & Vendor Info: (Acquisitions) SirsiDynix; (Cataloging) SirsiDynix; (Circulation) SirsiDynix; (Course Reserve) SirsiDynix; (OPAC) SirsiDynix; (Serials) SirsiDynix
Wireless access
Partic in Carolina Consortium; LYRASIS; Partnership Among South Carolina Academic Libraries
Open Mon-Thurs 7:30am-10pm, Fri 7:30-2, Sun 4-10 (Fall-Spring); Mon-Thurs 8:30-5, Fri 8:30-Noon (Summer)

J SPARTANBURG COMMUNITY COLLEGE LIBRARY*, Cherokee County Campus, Peeler Academic Bldg, 1st Flr, 523 Chesnee Hwy, 29341. (Mail add: PO Box 4386, Spartanburg, 29305). Tel: 864-206-2656. Web Site: libguides.sccsc.edu/about/cherokeecampus. *Libr Spec,* Denise Faltermeier; E-mail: faltermeiers@sccsc.edu; *Libr Spec,* Beth Peterson; E-mail: petersonbe@sccsc.edu
Wireless access
Function: Computers for patron use, Photocopying/Printing, Res assist avail, Scanner, Study rm
Open Mon-Thurs 7:30-6, Fri 7:30-1

GEORGETOWN

P GEORGETOWN COUNTY LIBRARY*, 405 Cleland St, 29440-3200. SAN 360-2133. Tel: 843-545-3300. FAX: 843-545-3392. Web Site: georgetowncountylibrary.sc.gov. *Dir,* Dwight McInvaill; Tel: 843-545-3304, E-mail: dmcinvaill@gtcounty.org; *Asst Dir,* Trudy Bazemore; E-mail: tbazemore@gtcounty.org; *Adult Serv,* Patti Burns; *Ch Serv,* Sheila Sullivan; *Circ,* Sharea Drayton; Staff 24 (MLS 2, Non-MLS 22)
Founded 1799. Pop 60,000; Circ 169,305
Library Holdings: Bk Vols 141,906; Per Subs 201; Talking Bks 6,953; Videos 10,893
Special Collections: 18th & 19th Century Library Records & Plantation Documents; Bank of Georgetown Records, 1920-1930's; Georgetown County Life 1890-1915, photos; Georgetown Library Society Materials
Subject Interests: Archives, Local hist
Automation Activity & Vendor Info: (Cataloging) Innovative Interfaces, Inc; (Circulation) Innovative Interfaces, Inc; (OPAC) Innovative Interfaces, Inc
Wireless access
Function: Art exhibits, Audiobks via web, Bks on cassette, Bks on CD, Children's prog, Computer training, Computers for patron use, Electronic databases & coll, Free DVD rentals, Holiday prog, Home delivery & serv to seniorr ctr & nursing homes, ILL available, Internet access, Jail serv, Mail & tel request accepted, Music CDs, Notary serv, Online cat, Outside serv via phone, mail, e-mail & web, OverDrive digital audio bks, Photocopying/Printing, Preschool outreach, Prog for adults, Prog for children & young adult, Ref & res, Ref serv available, Res libr, Satellite serv, Scanner, Spoken cassettes & CDs, Spoken cassettes & DVDs, Summer reading prog, Tax forms, Teen prog, Telephone ref, Wheelchair accessible, Workshops
Publications: A View of Our Past; Books on Local History; Friends (Newsletter)
Open Mon-Thurs 8:30-7, Fri & Sat 8:30-5:30, Sun (Sept-May) 2-5
Friends of the Library Group
Branches: 3
ANDREWS BRANCH, 105 N Morgan St, Andrews, 29510, SAN 360-2168. Tel: 843-545-3621. FAX: 843-545-3622. *Br Mgr,* Hailey Davis; E-mail: hdavis@gtcounty.org
Open Mon, Wed & Fri 9-5, Tues & Thurs 1-6, Sat 9-1
Friends of the Library Group
CARVERS BAY, 13048 Choppee Rd, Hemingway, 29554-3318. Tel: 843-545-3515. FAX: 843-558-6680. Web Site: www.gtcounty.org/facilities/facility/details/carvers-bay-library-2. *Br Mgr,* Marilynn Robb; E-mail: mrobb@gtcounty.org; Staff 5 (MLS 1, Non-MLS 4)
Founded 2005
Function: 24/7 Online cat, Art programs, Audiobks on Playaways & MP3, Bks on CD, CD-ROM, Children's prog, Computer training, Computers for patron use, Digital talking bks, Games, ILL available, Internet access, Magazines, Meeting rooms, Movies, Music CDs, Outreach serv, Photocopying/Printing, Prog for adults, Prog for children & young adult, Senior computer classes, Senior outreach, Story hour, Study rm, Summer reading prog, Teen prog, Wheelchair accessible
Open Mon & Wed 9-5, Tues & Thurs 10-6, Fri 1-5, Sat 10-2
Friends of the Library Group
WACCAMAW NECK, 41 St Paul Pl, Pawleys Island, 29585, SAN 373-1944. Tel: 843-545-3623. FAX: 843-545-3624. *Br Mgr,* Tamara McIntyre; E-mail: tmcintyre@gtcounty.org; *Teen Serv,* Donald Dennis; E-mail: ddennis@gtcounty.org
Open Mon-Thurs 8:30-7, Fri & Sat 8:30-5:30, Sun (Sept-May) 2-5
Friends of the Library Group
Bookmobiles: 1

GOOSE CREEK

A UNITED STATES AIR FORCE*, Weapons Station Branch Library, 2316 Red Bank Rd, Bldg 732, 29445. SAN 360-0513. Tel: 843-794-7900. Web Site: www.jbcharleston.com/library.
Founded 1966
Library Holdings: Bk Vols 27,000
Special Collections: Books on Cassette; CD-ROM: Help Wanted USA Classified Ads, microfiche; Educational & Children's Videos; Large Print Coll
Subject Interests: Self develop, Soc issues
Wireless access
Open Mon-Fri 9-5

GRANITEVILLE

J AIKEN TECHNICAL COLLEGE LIBRARY, 2276 Jefferson Davis Hwy, 29829. (Mail add: PO Drawer 696, Aiken, 29802-0696). SAN 315-484X. Tel: 803-508-7430. Web Site: www.atc.edu/study/library. *Dir,* Katie Miller; E-mail: millerku@atc.edu; *Pub Serv Librn,* Newkirk Barnes; E-mail: barnescn@atc.edu; Staff 3 (MLS 2, Non-MLS 1)
Founded 1973. Enrl 3,926; Highest Degree: Associate
Library Holdings: AV Mats 1,824; e-books 27,812; Bk Vols 32,898; Per Subs 180
Subject Interests: Computer tech, Health, Indust tech, Occupational tech, Pub serv
Automation Activity & Vendor Info: (Cataloging) NOTIS; (Circulation) NOTIS; (ILL) OCLC; (OPAC) NOTIS
Wireless access
Function: ILL available, Internet access
Partic in Partnership Among South Carolina Academic Libraries
Open Mon-Thurs 7:30am-8pm, Fri 7:30-1
Restriction: Open to students, fac & staff

GREENVILLE

C BOB JONES UNIVERSITY*, J S Mack Library, 1700 Wade Hampton Blvd, 29614. SAN 360-2192. Tel: 864-370-1800, Ext 6000. Circulation Tel: 864-241-1625. Interlibrary Loan Service Tel: 864-370-1800, Ext 6030. Reference Tel: 864-370-1800, Ext 6015. FAX: 864-232-1729. E-mail: library@bju.edu. Web Site: library.bju.edu. *Dir, Libr Serv,* Patrick Randall Robbins; Tel: 864-370-1800, Ext 6015, E-mail: probbins@bju.edu; *Head, Tech Serv,* Bryan Tyson; Tel: 864-370-1800, Ext 6030, E-mail: btyson@bju.edu; *Instrul Serv Librn,* Nancy Ruth McGuire; Tel: 864-370-1800, Ext 6025, E-mail: ncmcguir@bju.edu; *Cataloger,* Jennifer Walton; E-mail: jwalton@bju.edu; Staff 5 (MLS 4, Non-MLS 1)
Founded 1927. Enrl 2,588; Fac 247; Highest Degree: Doctorate
Library Holdings: Audiobooks 210; AV Mats 17,832; Bks on Deafness & Sign Lang 344; Braille Volumes 2; CDs 6,774; DVDs 1,761; e-books 185,691; e-journals 7,013; Electronic Media & Resources 1,780,165; Large Print Bks 68; Microforms 47,144; Music Scores 11,213; Bk Titles 224,506; Bk Vols 279,871; Per Subs 735; Talking Bks 210; Videos 2,071
Subject Interests: Art, Relig
Automation Activity & Vendor Info: (Acquisitions) Innovative Interfaces, Inc; (Cataloging) Innovative Interfaces, Inc; (Circulation) Innovative Interfaces, Inc; (Course Reserve) Innovative Interfaces, Inc; (Discovery) EBSCO Discovery Service; (ILL) OCLC ILLiad; (OPAC) Innovative Interfaces, Inc; (Serials) Innovative Interfaces, Inc
Wireless access
Function: Photocopying/Printing, Ref serv available
Partic in Partnership Among South Carolina Academic Libraries
Open Mon-Thurs 7:30am-10:30pm, Fri 7:30-7, Sat 11-7; Mon-Fri Noon-5 (Summer)
Restriction: 24-hr pass syst for students only
Departmental Libraries:
MUSIC LIBRARY, 1700 Wade Hampton Blvd, 29614. Tel: 864-370-1800, Ext 2704. FAX: 864-467-9302. Web Site: libguides.bju.edu/musiclibrary. *Music Libr Supvr,* Stephanie Shelburne; Tel: 864-370-1800, Ext 2706, E-mail: sshelbur@bju.edu; Staff 6 (MLS 4, Non-MLS 2)
Library Holdings: DVDs 743; e-books 213; e-journals 67; Music Scores 14,276; Bk Vols 7,304; Per Subs 204
Open Mon 7:45am-10pm, Tues-Thurs 7:45am-10:30pm, Fri 7:45am-8pm, Sat 11-7; Mon-Fri 9-Noon (Summer)

C FURMAN UNIVERSITY LIBRARIES*, James B Duke Library, 3300 Poinsett Hwy, 29613-4100. SAN 315-5455. Tel: 864-294-2190. Circulation Tel: 864-294-2265. Interlibrary Loan Service Tel: 864-294-2198. Reference Tel: 864-294-2195. Administration Tel: 864-294-2191. Automation Services

Tel: 864-294-3204. Interlibrary Loan Service FAX: 864-294-3560. E-mail: libraryreference@furman.edu. Web Site: library.furman.edu. *Dir of Libr,* Dr Caroline Mills; E-mail: caroline.mills1689@furman.edu; *Asst Dir, Discovery Serv,* Christy Allen; Tel: 864-294-2258, E-mail: christy.allen@furman.edu; *Asst Dir, Outreach Serv,* Jenny Colvin; Tel: 864-294-3797, E-mail: jenny.colvin@furman.edu; *Cat/Metadata Librn,* Nancy Sloan; Tel: 864-294-2197, E-mail: nancy.sloan@furman.edu; *Music & Outreach Librn,* Patricia Sasser; Tel: 864-294-2192, E-mail: patricia.sasser@furman.edu; *Outreach Librn,* Laura Baker; Tel: 864-294-2277, E-mail: laura.baker@furman.edu; *Outreach Librn,* Mary Fairbairn; Tel: 864-294-3226, E-mail: mary.fairbairn@furman.edu; *Outreach Librn,* Steve Richardson; Tel: 864-294-3227, E-mail: steve.richardson@furman.edu; *Outreach Librn,* Libby Young; Tel: 864-294-2260, E-mail: libby.young@furman.edu; *Sci & Outreach Librn,* Paige Dhyne; Tel: 864-294-2342, E-mail: paige.dhyne@furman.edu; *Spec Coll Librn & Univ Archivist,* Jeffrey Makala; Tel: 864-294-2714, E-mail: jeffrey.makala@furman.edu; *Web Discovery Librn,* Scott Salzman; E-mail: scott.salzman@furman.edu; Staff 26 (MLS 13, Non-MLS 13)
Founded 1826. Enrl 2,808; Highest Degree: Master
Library Holdings: AV Mats 9,833; e-books 14,461; e-journals 249; Bk Titles 489,944; Bk Vols 569,593; Per Subs 1,150
Special Collections: Furman University Archives; Rare Books & Manuscript Colls; South Carolina Baptist History; South Carolina Poetry Archives. US Document Depository
Automation Activity & Vendor Info: (Acquisitions) Innovative Interfaces, Inc; (Cataloging) Innovative Interfaces, Inc; (Circulation) Innovative Interfaces, Inc; (Course Reserve) Innovative Interfaces, Inc; (OPAC) Innovative Interfaces, Inc; (Serials) Innovative Interfaces, Inc
Wireless access
Partic in Asn of College & Res Libr; Carolina Consortium; National Information Standards Organization; National Institute for Technology & Liberal Education; Partnership Among South Carolina Academic Libraries
Friends of the Library Group

Departmental Libraries:

MAXWELL MUSIC LIBRARY, Herring Music Pavilion, 3300 Poinsett Hwy, 29613. Tel: 864-294-3795. FAX: 864-294-3004. Web Site: libguides.furman.edu/music/home. *Music Librn,* Patricia Sasser; E-mail: patricia.sasser@furman.edu; Staff 1 (MLS 1)
Founded 1998
Library Holdings: CDs 4,158; Bk Titles 13,164; Per Subs 77; Videos 506

SANDERS SCIENCE LIBRARY, Plyler Hall, 3300 Poinsett Hwy, 29613. Tel: 864-294-2342. Circulation Tel: 864-294-2455. E-mail: sciencelibrary@furman.edu. Web Site: libguides.furman.edu/science/home. *Sci Librn,* Paige Dhyne; E-mail: paige.dhyne@furman.edu
Founded 1962
Library Holdings: e-journals 60; Bk Titles 3,654; Per Subs 138; Videos 184
Open Mon-Thurs 9:30-4:30, Fri 8:30-4, Sat 1-5, Sun 1-Midnight

P GREENVILLE COUNTY LIBRARY SYSTEM*, Hughes Main Library, 25 Heritage Green Pl, 29601-2034. SAN 360-2257. Tel: 864-242-5000. Circulation Tel: 864-242-5000, Ext 2213. Interlibrary Loan Service Tel: 864-242-5000, Ext 2276. Reference Tel: 864-242-5000, Ext 2258. Administration Tel: 864-242-5000, Ext 2231. FAX: 864-235-8375. Reference FAX: 864-232-9656. E-mail: maincirc@greenvillelibrary.org. Web Site: www.greenvillelibrary.org. *Exec Dir,* Beverly James; Tel: 864-527-9231, E-mail: bjames@greenvillelibrary.org; *Access Serv Mgr,* Brian Morrison; Tel: 864-242-5000, Ext 2257, E-mail: bmorrison@greenvillelibrary.org; *Commun Engagement Mgr,* Jimmy Wooton; Tel: 864-527-9235, E-mail: communications@greenvillelibrary.org; *Human Res Mgr,* Ann Bishop; Tel: 864-242-5000, Ext 2262; *Tech Serv Mgr,* Tracy Anderson-Hancock; Tel: 864-242-5000, Ext 2265, E-mail: tanderson@greenvillelibrary.org; *Youth Serv Mgr,* Karen Allen; Tel: 864-242-5000, Ext 2249; *Info Tech,* Jerry Osteen; Tel: 864-242-5000, Ext 4231; Staff 187.6 (MLS 51.6, Non-MLS 136)
Founded 1921. Pop 451,225; Circ 3,481,512
Special Collections: Foundation Center Cooperating Coll, bks, databases, per; Local History & Genealogy, audio tapes, bks, databases, diaries, ledger bks, maps, micro holdings, pamphlets, personal papers, photog, rare bks; Parenting & Early Childhood Coll, bks, DVDs, videos. State Document Depository; US Document Depository
Subject Interests: Genealogy, Law, Local hist, State hist, Textile hist
Automation Activity & Vendor Info: (Acquisitions) Innovative Interfaces, Inc; (Cataloging) Innovative Interfaces, Inc; (Circulation) Innovative Interfaces, Inc; (OPAC) Innovative Interfaces, Inc; (Serials) Innovative Interfaces, Inc
Wireless access
Function: Adult bk club, After school storytime, Archival coll, Art exhibits, Audiobks via web, Bk club(s), Bks on cassette, Bks on CD, CD-ROM, Children's prog, Computer training, Computers for patron use, Digital talking bks, Electronic databases & coll, Free DVD rentals, Govt ref serv, Health sci info serv, Holiday prog, Home delivery & serv to seniorr ctr & nursing homes, Homebound delivery serv, ILL available, Internet access, Magnifiers for reading, Mail & tel request accepted, Music CDs, Online cat, Orientations, Outreach serv, Photocopying/Printing, Prog for adults, Prog for children & young adult, Ref serv available, Satellite serv, Senior computer classes, Senior outreach, Spoken cassettes & CDs, Spoken cassettes & DVDs, Story hour, Summer reading prog, Tax forms, Teen prog, Telephone ref, VHS videos, Wheelchair accessible, Workshops, Writing prog
Partic in National Network of Libraries of Medicine Region 2
Special Services for the Deaf - ADA equip; Assisted listening device; Assistive tech; Bks on deafness & sign lang; Closed caption videos; Pocket talkers; Sign lang interpreter upon request for prog; Sorenson video relay syst; TDD equip; TTY equip; Video & TTY relay via computer; Video relay services
Special Services for the Blind - Accessible computers; Aids for in-house use; Assistive/Adapted tech devices, equip & products; Audio mat; BiFolkal kits; Bks available with recordings; Bks on cassette; Bks on CD; Braille alphabet card; Braille bks; Children's Braille; Closed caption display syst; Closed circuit TV magnifier; Computer access aids; Computer with voice synthesizer for visually impaired persons; Copier with enlargement capabilities; Digital talking bk; Extensive large print coll; Home delivery serv; Internet workstation with adaptive software; Large print & cassettes; Large print bks; Large screen computer & software; Low vision equip; Magnifiers; Micro-computer access & training; Networked computers with assistive software; PC for people with disabilities; Playaways (bks on MP3); Scanner for conversion & translation of mats; Screen enlargement software for people with visual disabilities; Screen reader software; Sound rec; Text reader; Videos on blindness & physical disabilties; ZoomText magnification & reading software
Open Mon-Thurs 9-9, Fri & Sat 9-6, Sun 2-6
Friends of the Library Group

Branches: 10

ANDERSON ROAD BRANCH, 2625 Anderson Rd, 29611, SAN 360-2524. Tel: 864-269-5210. FAX: 864-269-3986. E-mail: andersonroad@greenvillelibrary.org. *Br Mgr,* Laurel Hicklin; Tel: 864-527-9202
Open Mon-Thurs 9-9, Fri & Sat 9-6
Friends of the Library Group

AUGUSTA ROAD BRANCH, 100 Lydia St, 29605, SAN 360-2281. Tel: 864-277-0161. FAX: 864-277-2673. E-mail: augustaroad@greenvillelibrary.org. *Br Mgr,* Teresa Lanford; Tel: 864-527-9205
Open Mon-Thurs 9-9, Fri & Sat 9-6
Friends of the Library Group

BEREA BRANCH, 111 N Hwy 25 Bypass, 29617, SAN 360-2311. Tel: 864-246-1695. FAX: 864-246-1765. E-mail: berea@greenvillelibrary.org. *Br Mgr,* Andy Dykes; Tel: 864-527-9201
Open Mon-Thurs 9-9, Fri & Sat 9-6
Friends of the Library Group

FOUNTAIN INN BRANCH, 311 N Main St, Fountain Inn, 29644, SAN 360-2346. Tel: 864-862-2576. FAX: 864-862-6376. E-mail: fountaininn@greenvillelibrary.org. *Br Mgr,* Danielle Thornton; Tel: 864-527-9210
Open Mon-Thurs 9-9, Fri & Sat 9-6
Friends of the Library Group

GREER BRANCH, 505 Pennsylvania Ave, Greer, 29650, SAN 360-2370. Tel: 864-877-8722. FAX: 864-877-1422. E-mail: greer@greenvillelibrary.org. *Br Mgr,* Stephanie Maters; Tel: 864-527-9207
Open Mon-Thurs 9-9, Fri & Sat 9-6
Friends of the Library Group

MAULDIN BRANCH, 800 W Butler Rd, 29607, SAN 360-2400. Tel: 864-277-7397. FAX: 864-277-7389. E-mail: mauldin@greenvillelibrary.org. *Br Mgr,* Michael Evans; Tel: 864-527-9204
Open Mon-Thurs 9-9, Fri & Sat 9-6
Friends of the Library Group

PELHAM ROAD BRANCH, 1508 Pelham Rd, 29615, SAN 360-2338. Tel: 864-288-6688. FAX: 864-675-9149. E-mail: pelhamroad@greenvillelibrary.org. *Br Mgr,* Donna Heatherington; Tel: 864-527-9206
Open Mon-Thurs 9-9, Fri & Sat 9-6
Friends of the Library Group

SIMPSONVILLE BRANCH, 626 NE Main St, Simpsonville, 29681, SAN 360-2435. Tel: 864-963-9031. FAX: 864-228-0986. E-mail: simpsonville@greenvillelibrary.org. *Br Mgr,* Lina Bertinelli; Tel: 864-527-9216
Open Mon-Thurs 9-9, Fri & Sat 9-6
Friends of the Library Group

TAYLORS BRANCH, 316 W Main St, Taylors, 29687, SAN 360-2494. Tel: 864-268-5955. FAX: 864-268-4275. E-mail: taylors@greenvillelibrary.org. *Br Mgr,* Beth Atwood; Tel: 864-527-9203
Open Mon-Thurs 9-9, Fri & Sat 9-6
Friends of the Library Group

TRAVELERS REST BRANCH, 17 Center St, Travelers Rest, 29690, SAN 360-246X. Tel: 864-834-3650. FAX: 864-834-4686. E-mail: travelersrest@greenvillelibrary.org. *Br Mgr,* Amy Grubbs; Tel: 864-527-9208
Open Mon-Thurs 9-9, Fri & Sat 9-6
Friends of the Library Group
Bookmobiles: 1

J GREENVILLE TECHNICAL COLLEGE LIBRARIES*, Barton Campus, Bldg 102, 506 S Pleasantburg Dr, 29607. (Mail add: Mail Stop 1021, PO Box 5616, 29606-5616), SAN 315-548X. Tel: 864-250-8319. FAX: 864-250-8506. E-mail: gtclibrary@gvltec.edu. Web Site: www.gvltec.edu/library. *Dir, Acad Res,* Jason Reed; Tel: 864-236-6500, E-mail: Jason.Reed@gvltec.edu; *Info Literacy Librn, Outreach Librn,* Michelle Rubino; Tel: 864-236-6439, E-mail: Michelle.Rubino@gvltec.edu; *Info Literacy Librn,* Carole Williams; Tel: 864-236-6438, E-mail: Carole.Williams@gvltec.edu; *Pub Serv Librn,* Lillie Ruegg; Tel: 864-250-8321, E-mail: Lillie.Ruegg@gvltec.edu; *Tech Serv Librn,* Jan Daniel; Tel: 864-250-8320, E-mail: Jan.Daniel@gvltec.edu; Staff 13.2 (MLS 8.1, Non-MLS 5.1)
Founded 1962. Enrl 13,457; Fac 620; Highest Degree: Associate
Library Holdings: Audiobooks 111; CDs 2; DVDs 2,135; e-books 70,000; e-journals 6; Bk Vols 33,557; Per Subs 168; Videos 308
Automation Activity & Vendor Info: (Acquisitions) SirsiDynix-WorkFlows; (Cataloging) SirsiDynix-WorkFlows; (Circulation) SirsiDynix-WorkFlows; (Course Reserve) SirsiDynix-WorkFlows; (ILL) OCLC; (Media Booking) SirsiDynix-WorkFlows; (OPAC) SirsiDynix; (Serials) SirsiDynix-WorkFlows
Wireless access
Function: Archival coll, Art exhibits, Computers for patron use, Electronic databases & coll, Equip loans & repairs, Free DVD rentals, ILL available, Internet access, Magazines, Magnifiers for reading, Online cat, Online info literacy tutorials on the web & in blackboard, Online ref, Orientations, Photocopying/Printing, Ref & res, Scanner, Spanish lang bks, Study rm, Telephone ref, Wheelchair accessible
Partic in Partnership Among South Carolina Academic Libraries; South Carolina Information & Library Services Consortium
Departmental Libraries:
BENSON CAMPUS LEARNING COMMONS, Bldg 301, Rm 121, 2522 Locust Hill Rd, Taylors, 29687. Tel: 864-250-3010. *Campus Librn,* Stephanie Broker; E-mail: Stephanie.Broker@gvltec.edu
Open Mon-Thurs 8-6
BRASHIER CAMPUS, Bldg 202, Rm 103, 1830 W Georgia Rd, Simpsonville, 29680. Tel: 864-250-4162. *Campus Librn,* Deborah Rouse; E-mail: Deborah.Rouse@gvltec.edu
Open Mon-Thurs 8-6
NORTHWEST CAMPUS, Bldg 402, Rm 122, 8109 White Horse Rd, 29617. Tel: 864-250-8018. *Campus Librn,* Allison Read; E-mail: Allison.Read@gvltec.edu
Open Mon-Thurs 8-6

L NELSON, MULLINS, RILEY & SCARBOROUGH*, Law Library, 104 S Main St, Ste 900, 29601. SAN 323-6609. Tel: 864-250-2300. FAX: 864-232-2925. Web Site: www.nmrs.com/locations/greenville. *Librn,* Melanie Dubard; E-mail: melanie.dubard@nelsonmullins.com; *Librn,* Kristen Perev; E-mail: kristen.perev@nelsonmullins.com
Library Holdings: Bk Vols 13,930; Per Subs 20

M PRISMA HEALTH SYSTEM*, Greenville Health Sciences Library, 601 Grove Rd, 29605. SAN 360-2559. Tel: 864-455-7176. FAX: 864-455-5696. E-mail: library@prismahealth.org. Web Site: www.prismahealth.org. *Dir,* Fay Towell; Tel: 864-455-3099, E-mail: fay.towell@prismahealth.org; Staff 6 (MLS 4, Non-MLS 2)
Founded 1912
Library Holdings: e-books 500; e-journals 3,000; Bk Titles 3,000; Bk Vols 25,000; Per Subs 5
Subject Interests: Allied health, Med, Mental health, Nursing, Psychiat, Psychol, Rehabilitation med
Automation Activity & Vendor Info: (Cataloging) EOS International; (Serials) EBSCO Online
Wireless access
Partic in National Network of Libraries of Medicine Region 2; South Carolina AHEC
Open Mon-Thurs 8-6, Fri 8-5
Restriction: Circulates for staff only

GREENWOOD

P GREENWOOD COUNTY LIBRARY*, 600 S Main St, 29646. SAN 360-2672. Tel: 864-941-4650. Reference Tel: 864-941-4655. FAX: 864-941-4651. Web Site: www2.youseemore.com/greenwood. *Libr Dir,* Tracey Ouzts; E-mail: touzts@greenwoodcountylibrary.org; *Head, Circ,* Debbie Price; Tel: 864-941-4653, E-mail: dprice@greenwoodcountylibrary.org; *Ref Librn,* Stephanie Holden; E-mail: sholden@greenwoodcountylibrary.org; *Ref Librn,* Jessica Howard; E-mail: jhoward@greenwoodcountylibrary.org; *Tech Serv Supvr,* Tiffany Crayne; E-mail: tcrayne@greenwoodcountylibrary.org; *Coordr of Ref Serv,* Julie Horton; Tel: 864-941-3042, E-mail: jhorton@greenwoodcountylibrary.org; *Adult Literacy Coordr, ESL Coordr,* Pattie Fender; Tel: 864-941-3044, E-mail: pfender@greenwoodcountylibrary.org; *Children's Serv Coordr,* Mrs Jody Gable; Tel: 864-941-4659, E-mail: jgable@greenwoodcountylibrary.org; Staff 8 (MLS 6, Non-MLS 2)
Founded 1901. Pop 70,355; Circ 153,152
Jul 2016-Jun 2017 Income (Main & Associated Libraries) $1,975,099, State $141,449, Federal $3,300, County $1,711,156, Locally Generated Income $70,095, Other $49,099. Mats Exp $253,172. Sal $829,595
Library Holdings: Audiobooks 5,587; DVDs 6,307; e-books 86,166; e-journals 32; Bk Vols 105,502; Per Subs 35
Special Collections: Greenwood County Historical Society, bks, letters, diaries & photos; Star Fort Chapter DAR Coll
Subject Interests: Genealogy, Local hist
Automation Activity & Vendor Info: (Acquisitions) TLC (The Library Corporation); (Cataloging) OCLC WorldShare Interlibrary Loan; (Circulation) TLC (The Library Corporation); (Media Booking) EnvisionWare; (OPAC) TLC (The Library Corporation); (Serials) EBSCO Online
Wireless access
Function: 24/7 Electronic res, 24/7 Online cat, Adult bk club, Adult literacy prog, After school storytime, Archival coll, Art exhibits, Audio & video playback equip for onsite use, Audiobks via web, Bilingual assistance for Spanish patrons, Bk club(s), Bks on CD, Children's prog, Computer training, Computers for patron use, Family literacy, Free DVD rentals, Games & aids for people with disabilities, Holiday prog, Home delivery & serv to seniorr ctr & nursing homes, ILL available, Internet access, Laminating, Literacy & newcomer serv, Magazines, Mail & tel request accepted, Mango lang, Meeting rooms, Microfiche/film & reading machines, Movies, Music CDs, Notary serv, Online cat, Outreach serv, Outside serv via phone, mail, e-mail & web, OverDrive digital audio bks, Photocopying/Printing, Preschool outreach, Preschool reading prog, Printer for laptops & handheld devices, Prog for adults, Prog for children & young adult, Ref & res, Ref serv available, Scanner, Senior computer classes, Spanish lang bks, Story hour, Study rm, Summer reading prog, Tax forms, Teen prog, Telephone ref, Wheelchair accessible
Partic in DISCUS
Special Services for the Blind - Audio mat; Bks on CD; Large print bks
Open Mon-Wed 9-8, Thurs & Fri 9-5:30, Sat 12-4, Sun 2-5:30
Friends of the Library Group
Branches: 2
NINETY SIX BRANCH LIBRARY, 100 S Cambridge St S, Ninety Six, 29666, SAN 360-2826. Tel: 864-321-0754. FAX: 864-321-0754. *Br Mgr,* Shannon Rickert; E-mail: srickert@greenwoodcountylibrary.org; Staff 1 (Non-MLS 1)
Founded 1976. Pop 2,057; Circ 10,400
Function: 24/7 Electronic res, 24/7 Online cat, Adult bk club, Children's prog, Computers for patron use, Free DVD rentals, Internet access, Mango lang, Photocopying/Printing, Prog for children & young adult, Ref serv available, Summer reading prog, Wheelchair accessible
Special Services for the Blind - Bks on CD; Large print bks
Open Mon-Fri 9-5:30
WARE SHOALS COMMUNITY LIBRARY, 54 S Greenwood Ave, Ware Shoals, 29692, SAN 360-2850. Tel: 864-377-4440. FAX: 864-377-4440. *Br Mgr,* Melissa Crenshaw; E-mail: mcrenshaw@greenwoodcountylibrary.org; Staff 1 (Non-MLS 1)
Founded 1911. Pop 2,183; Circ 11,044
Function: 24/7 Electronic res, 24/7 Online cat, Adult bk club, Computers for patron use, Internet access, Mango lang, Meeting rooms, Online cat, Prog for adults, Prog for children & young adult, Wheelchair accessible
Open Mon & Wed-Fri 7:30-5, Tues 7:30-7
Bookmobiles: 1. Head Circ, Debbie Price. Bk titles 2,800

M GREENWOOD GENETIC CENTER LIBRARY*, 106 Gregor Mendel Circle, 29646. SAN 372-9486. Tel: 864-388-1708. Toll Free Tel: 888-442-4363. Web Site: www.ggc.org/education/resources/libraries.html. *Librn,* Rachel Collins; E-mail: rlewis@ggc.org
Library Holdings: Bk Vols 3,000; Per Subs 60
Special Collections: Genetics Rare Book Coll
Subject Interests: Genetics, Pediatrics
Open Mon-Fri 8-5

C LANDER UNIVERSITY*, Larry A Jackson Library, 320 Stanley Ave, 29649. SAN 315-551X. Tel: 864-388-8365. FAX: 864-388-8816. E-mail: library@lander.edu. Web Site: libguides.lander.edu/jlibmain. *Dir, Libr Serv,* Lisa Wiecki; Tel: 864-388-8043, E-mail: lwiecki@lander.edu; *Assoc Dir, Libr Serv,* David Mash, PhD; Tel: 864-388-8046, E-mail: dmash@lander.edu; Staff 7 (MLS 4, Non-MLS 3)
Founded 1872. Enrl 3,019; Fac 139; Highest Degree: Master
Special Collections: South Carolina History (Watson Coll). State Document Depository; US Document Depository

Automation Activity & Vendor Info: (Acquisitions) Innovative Interfaces, Inc; (Cataloging) Innovative Interfaces, Inc; (Circulation) Innovative Interfaces, Inc; (Course Reserve) Innovative Interfaces, Inc; (ILL) OCLC; (OPAC) Innovative Interfaces, Inc; (Serials) Innovative Interfaces, Inc
Wireless access
Partic in Carolina Consortium; DISCUS; LYRASIS; OCLC Online Computer Library Center, Inc; Partnership Among South Carolina Academic Libraries
Open Mon-Thurs 7:30am-Midnight, Fri 7:30am-9pm, Sat 1-9, Sun 1pm-Midnight

J PIEDMONT TECHNICAL COLLEGE LIBRARY*, Marion P Carnell Library, Bldg K, 2nd Flr, 620 N Emerald Rd, 29646. (Mail add: PO Drawer 1467, 29648-1467), SAN 315-5536. Tel: 864-941-8441. Administration Tel: 864-941-8442. Toll Free Tel: 800-868-5528, Ext 8441. FAX: 864-941-8558. E-mail: librarian@ptc.edu. Web Site: www.ptc.edu/library. *Head Librn,* Lola Bradley; E-mail: bradley.l@ptc.edu; *Librn,* Yvonne Hudgens; E-mail: hudgens.y@ptc.edu; *Circ Mgr, Mgr, Ser,* Kayla Leopard; E-mail: leopard.k@ptc.edu; Staff 4 (MLS 2, Non-MLS 2)
Founded 1966. Enrl 5,811; Highest Degree: Associate
Special Collections: Piedmont Technical College Archives
Subject Interests: Allied health, Bus, Criminal justice, Early childhood educ, Engr tech, Funeral serv, Hort, Indust tech, Nursing, Off syst tech
Automation Activity & Vendor Info: (Acquisitions) SirsiDynix-WorkFlows; (Cataloging) SirsiDynix-WorkFlows; (Circulation) SirsiDynix-WorkFlows; (ILL) OCLC; (OPAC) SirsiDynix-Unicorn; (Serials) SirsiDynix-WorkFlows
Wireless access
Function: Archival coll, Art exhibits, Audio & video playback equip for onsite use, AV serv, Bk club(s), Distance learning, Electronic databases & coll, Health sci info serv, ILL available, Internet access, Magnifiers for reading, Music CDs, Orientations, Outside serv via phone, mail, e-mail & web, Photocopying/Printing, Prof lending libr, Ref serv available, Spoken cassettes & CDs, Spoken cassettes & DVDs, Telephone ref, VHS videos, Wheelchair accessible, Workshops
Partic in LYRASIS; OCLC Online Computer Library Center, Inc; Partnership Among South Carolina Academic Libraries; South Carolina Information & Library Services Consortium
Special Services for the Deaf - Bks on deafness & sign lang; Closed caption videos
Special Services for the Blind - Audio mat; Bks on cassette; Bks on CD; Cassette playback machines; Cassettes; Computer with voice synthesizer for visually impaired persons; Text reader
Open Mon-Thurs 8am-8:30pm, Fri 8:30-4
Restriction: Authorized patrons, Circ limited, In-house use for visitors, Restricted borrowing privileges, Restricted loan policy, Restricted pub use
Departmental Libraries:
LIBRARY RESOURCE CENTER - NEWBERRY COUNTY CAMPUS, 1922 Wilson Rd, Rm 200NN, Newberry, 29108. Tel: 803-768-8167. E-mail: newberry@ptc.edu. *Coordr,* Katrina Gallman; E-mail: gallman.k@ptc.edu
Open Mon-Thurs 8-7:30
LIBRARY RESOURCE CENTER - ABBEVILLE COUNTY CAMPUS, 143 Hwy 72 W, Rm 07AA, Abbeville, 29620. Tel: 864-446-8324. E-mail: abbeville@ptc.edu. *Admin Operations Specialist,* Angela Clinkscales; E-mail: clinkscales.a@ptc.edu
Open Mon-Thurs 8-8
LIBRARY RESOURCE CENTER - LAURENS COUNTY CAMPUS, Laurens County Higher Educ Ctr, Rm 205LL, 663 Medical Ridge Rd, Clinton, 29325. Tel: 864-938-1539. *Coordr,* Eyvonne Rice; E-mail: rice.e@ptc.edu
Open Mon-Thurs 8-8, Fri 9-12
LIBRARY RESOURCE CENTER - MCCORMICK COUNTY CAMPUS, 1008 Kelly St, Rm 111MM, McCormick, 29835. Tel: 864-852-3191. *Library Contact,* Cecelia Maston; E-mail: maston.c@ptc.edu
Open Mon-Thurs 8-6:30
LIBRARY RESOURCE CENTER - SALUDA COUNTY CAMPUS, 701 Batesburg Hwy, Rm 111SS, Saluda, 29138. Tel: 864-445-3144, Ext 3102. *Coordr,* Wanda Shull; E-mail: shull.w@ptc.edu
Open Mon-Thurs 8-8
LIBRARY RESOURCE ROOM - EDGEFIELD COUNTY CAMPUS, 506 Main St, Office Area, Edgefield, 29824. Tel: 803-637-5388. *Support Serv,* Linda Favor-Dawkins; E-mail: dawkins.l@ptc.edu
Open Mon-Thurs 8:30am-1:30pm

M SELF REGIONAL HEALTHCARE*, Medical Library & Community Health Information Center, 1226 Spring St, 29646. SAN 315-5544. Tel: 864-725-4797, 864-725-4851. FAX: 864-725-4838. E-mail: library@selfregional.org. Web Site: www.selfregional.org/healthcare-information/medical-library-community-health-information-center. *Librn,* Mollie Titus; Staff 1 (MLS 1)
Founded 1976
Library Holdings: e-books 20; e-journals 20; Per Subs 5
Special Collections: Community Health Information Center (consumer health resources)
Subject Interests: Med, Nursing, Pharm, Therapy
Automation Activity & Vendor Info: (Cataloging) Follett Software; (Circulation) Follett Software; (Course Reserve) Follett Software; (Media Booking) Follett Software; (OPAC) Follett Software; (Serials) Follett Software
Wireless access
Function: Computer training, Computers for patron use, Doc delivery serv, Electronic databases & coll, Health sci info serv, ILL available, Internet access, Mail & tel request accepted, Mail loans to mem, Online cat, Online ref, Orientations, Outreach serv, Outside serv via phone, mail, e-mail & web, Photocopying/Printing, Prof lending libr, Ref & res, Ref serv available, Res libr, Res performed for a fee, Scanner, Wheelchair accessible
Partic in National Network of Libraries of Medicine Region 2; SC Health Info Network; SEND; US National Library of Medicine
Open Mon-Fri 8:30-5

HARTSVILLE

C COKER UNIVERSITY, Charles W & Joan S Coker Library-Information Technology Center, (Formerly Coker College), 300 E College Ave, 29550. SAN 315-5560. Tel: 843-383-8125. Toll Free Tel: 888-887-4526. FAX: 843-383-8129. E-mail: reference@coker,edu. Web Site: www.coker.edu/library. *Outreach & Instructional Serv Librn,* Jonathan Garren; Tel: 843-383-8126, E-mail: jgarren@coker.edu; Staff 1 (MLS 1)
Founded 1908. Enrl 740; Highest Degree: Master
Library Holdings: CDs 737; DVDs 1,955; e-books 400,000; e-journals 19; Electronic Media & Resources 103; Music Scores 2,232; Bk Titles 68,835; Bk Vols 87,000; Per Subs 103; Videos 1,868
Special Collections: Arents Tobacco Coll
Subject Interests: Music, Video
Wireless access
Function: 24/7 Online cat, Art exhibits, Computers for patron use, Online cat, Online info literacy tutorials on the web & in blackboard, Ref serv available, Res assist avail
Partic in LYRASIS; Palmetto Academic Independent Library System; Partnership Among South Carolina Academic Libraries
Special Services for the Deaf - Closed caption videos
Special Services for the Blind - Sound rec
Open Mon-Thurs 8am-10pm, Fri 8-5, Sun 2-10
Restriction: Badge access after hrs, Circ to mem only, Open to pub for ref & circ; with some limitations

KINGSTREE

P WILLIAMSBURG COUNTY LIBRARY*, 215 N Jackson, 29556-3319. SAN 315-5587. Tel: 843-355-9486. FAX: 843-355-9991. Web Site: www.mywcl.org. *Dir,* Benjamin Hall; E-mail: hallbenjamin@hotmail.com; *Circ Mgr,* Audrey Williams
Founded 1967. Pop 37,217; Circ 52,245
Library Holdings: CDs 927; DVDs 614; Large Print Bks 1,065; Bk Vols 54,553; Per Subs 99; Videos 400
Automation Activity & Vendor Info: (Cataloging) TLC (The Library Corporation); (Circulation) TLC (The Library Corporation); (OPAC) TLC (The Library Corporation)
Wireless access
Function: Audio & video playback equip for onsite use, Electronic databases & coll, ILL available, Photocopying/Printing, Preschool outreach, Prog for adults, Prog for children & young adult, Ref serv available, Serves people with intellectual disabilities, Spoken cassettes & CDs, Telephone ref, VHS videos, Wheelchair accessible
Open Mon-Thurs 9:30-6, Fri 9:30-4, Sat 10-4
Friends of the Library Group
Branches: 1
HEMINGWAY BRANCH, 306 N Main St, Hemingway, 29554, SAN 320-9695. Tel: 843-558-7679. FAX: 843-558-0743. *Br Mgr,* Wanda Baxley
Open Mon-Thurs 10-6, Fri & Sat 11-4
Friends of the Library Group
Bookmobiles: 1. Bookmobile Mgr, Stephanie Watson

J WILLIAMSBURG TECHNICAL COLLEGE LIBRARY*, 601 MLK Jr Ave, 29556. Tel: 843-355-4110. Toll Free Tel: 800-768-2021. FAX: 843-355-4291. Web Site: www.wiltech.edu/wtcs-library. *Dir,* Dr Brandolyn Love; Tel: 843-355-4131, E-mail: loveb@wiltech.edu
Library Holdings: Bk Vols 18,200; Per Subs 90
Automation Activity & Vendor Info: (Acquisitions) Ex Libris Group; (Cataloging) Ex Libris Group; (Circulation) Ex Libris Group; (Course Reserve) Ex Libris Group; (ILL) OCLC; (OPAC) Ex Libris Group; (Serials) Ex Libris Group
Wireless access
Partic in Partnership Among South Carolina Academic Libraries
Open Mon-Thurs 8-8, Fri 8-1

LANCASTER

P LANCASTER COUNTY LIBRARY*, 313 S White St, 29720. SAN 315-5609. Tel: 803-285-1502. FAX: 803-285-6004. Web Site: www.lanclib.org. *Dir,* April Williams; E-mail: aprilwilliams@lancastercountysc.net; *Mgr,* Sharon Hammond; E-mail: shammond@lancastersc.net; *Youth Serv,* Susannah Baker; E-mail: sbaker@lancastersc.net; Staff 15 (MLS 5, Non-MLS 10)
Founded 1907. Pop 76,652; Circ 145,885
Library Holdings: Bks on Deafness & Sign Lang 50; Large Print Bks 4,604; Bk Vols 124,372; Per Subs 275; Talking Bks 4,000; Videos 9,250
Subject Interests: Caroliniana, Genealogy, Local hist
Automation Activity & Vendor Info: (Cataloging) SirsiDynix-Enterprise; (Circulation) SirsiDynix-Enterprise; (OPAC) SirsiDynix-Enterprise
Wireless access
Partic in DISCUS; SC Libr Network
Open Mon-Thurs 9-7, Fri 9-5, Sat 9-1
Branches: 2
DEL WEBB LIBRARY AT INDIAN LAND, 7641 Charlotte Hwy, Indian Land, 29707. Tel: 803-548-9260. *Dep Dir,* Nancy Berry; E-mail: nberry@lancastercountysc.net
Open Mon-Thurs 9-7, Fri 9-5, Sat 9-1
Friends of the Library Group
KERSHAW BRANCH, 101 N Hampton St, Kershaw, 29067, SAN 325-3961. Tel: 803-283-1010. *Br Mgr,* Susan Gandy; E-mail: sgandy@lancastercountysc.net
Founded 1949
Open Mon 11-2 & 3-7, Tues-Fri 9-12 & 1-5
Bookmobiles: 1

C UNIVERSITY OF SOUTH CAROLINA LANCASTER*, Medford Library, 476-B Hubbard Dr, 29720. SAN 315-5625. Tel: 803-313-7060. FAX: 803-313-7107. E-mail: medford@mailbox.sc.edu. Web Site: www.sc.edu/about/system_and_campuses/lancaster/experience/library. *Dir,* Rebecca T Freeman; Tel: 803-313-7062, E-mail: rfreeman@mailbox.sc.edu; *Asst Librn,* McKenzie Lemhouse; Tel: 803-313-7061, E-mail: lemhouse@mailbox.sc.edu; Staff 4 (MLS 3, Non-MLS 1)
Founded 1959. Enrl 1,259; Fac 110; Highest Degree: Associate
Library Holdings: Electronic Media & Resources 170,000; Bk Vols 59,000
Special Collections: US Document Depository
Automation Activity & Vendor Info: (Acquisitions) Innovative Interfaces, Inc - Millennium; (Cataloging) Innovative Interfaces, Inc - Millennium; (Circulation) Innovative Interfaces, Inc - Millennium; (Course Reserve) Innovative Interfaces, Inc - Millennium; (ILL) OCLC ILLiad; (Serials) Innovative Interfaces, Inc - Millennium
Wireless access
Partic in Carolina Consortium; Charlotte Area Educ Consortium; DISCUS; Partnership Among South Carolina Academic Libraries
Open Mon-Thurs 8-8, Fri 8-Noon (Fall & Spring); Mon-Thurs 8-6, Fri 8-Noon

LAURENS

P LAURENS COUNTY LIBRARY*, 1017 W Main St, 29360. SAN 360-2974. Tel: 864-681-7323. FAX: 864-681-0598. Web Site: www.lcpl.org. *Libr Dir,* Renita Barksdale; E-mail: rbarksdale@lcpl.org; Staff 19 (MLS 4, Non-MLS 15)
Founded 1929. Pop 71,000; Circ 172,312
Library Holdings: AV Mats 10,200; Bk Vols 122,271; Per Subs 296; Videos 2,912
Special Collections: Laurens County History & Genealogy Coll; South Caroliniana Coll, bk & micro
Subject Interests: Local hist
Automation Activity & Vendor Info: (Acquisitions) TLC (The Library Corporation); (Cataloging) TLC (The Library Corporation); (Circulation) TLC (The Library Corporation); (OPAC) TLC (The Library Corporation)
Wireless access
Function: Archival coll, Home delivery & serv to seniorr ctr & nursing homes, Homebound delivery serv, ILL available, Internet access, Magnifiers for reading, Photocopying/Printing, Prog for adults, Prog for children & young adult, Ref serv available, Summer reading prog, Telephone ref, Wheelchair accessible
Partic in DISCUS; SC Libr Network
Special Services for the Blind - Large print bks; Talking bks
Open Mon-Thurs 9-6, Fri 9-5, Sat 9-1
Friends of the Library Group
Branches: 1
CLINTON PUBLIC, 107 Jacobs Hwy, Ste A, Clinton, 29325. (Mail add: 1017 W Main St, 293360), SAN 360-3008. Tel: 864-833-1853. FAX: 864-833-9666. *Dir,* Renita Barksdale; Tel: 864-681-7323, E-mail: rbarksdale@lcpl.org; *Dep Dir,* Jamie Lambert; E-mail: jlambert@lcpl.org; Staff 4 (MLS 1, Non-MLS 3)
Library Holdings: Bk Vols 25,000
Open Mon-Thurs 10-1 & 2-6, Fri 10-1 & 2-5
Friends of the Library Group
Bookmobiles: 1

LEXINGTON

P LEXINGTON COUNTY PUBLIC LIBRARY SYSTEM*, 5440 Augusta Rd, 29072. SAN 359-9671. Tel: 803-785-2600. Circulation Tel: 803-785-2613. Reference Tel: 803-785-2680. FAX: 803-785-2601. Web Site: www.lex.lib.sc.us. *Dir,* Kelly Poole; Tel: 803-785-2643, E-mail: kpoole@lex.lib.sc.us; *Sr Librn,* Mark Mancuso; Tel: 803-785-2673, E-mail: mmancuso@lex.lib.sc.us; *ILL,* Marie Jefferies; E-mail: mjefferies@lex.lib.sc.us; *YA Serv,* Ellen Stringer; Tel: 803-785-2632, E-mail: estringer@lex.lib.sc.us; Staff 100.5 (MLS 23, Non-MLS 77.5)
Founded 1948. Pop 262,391; Circ 2,129,120
Library Holdings: Audiobooks 20,445; DVDs 46,229; e-books 11,095; Bk Vols 585,440; Per Subs 1,346
Subject Interests: SC genealogy, SC hist
Automation Activity & Vendor Info: (Acquisitions) Innovative Interfaces, Inc; (Cataloging) Innovative Interfaces, Inc; (Circulation) Innovative Interfaces, Inc; (OPAC) Innovative Interfaces, Inc
Wireless access
Function: ILL available, Life-long learning prog for all ages, Meeting rooms, Photocopying/Printing, Scanner, Summer reading prog, Workshops
Open Mon-Thurs 8:30-8, Fri & Sat 8:30-5:30, Sun 2-5
Restriction: Non-resident fee
Friends of the Library Group
Branches: 9
BATESBURG-LEESVILLE BRANCH, 203 Armory St, Batesburg, 29006, SAN 359-9760. Tel: 803-532-9223. FAX: 803-532-2232.
Open Mon 10:30-7:30, Tues-Fri 8:30-5:30, Sat 9-5, Sun 2-5
Friends of the Library Group
CAYCE-WEST COLUMBIA BRANCH, 1500 Augusta Rd, Columbia, 29169, SAN 359-9795. Tel: 803-794-6791. FAX: 803-926-5383.
Open Mon-Thurs 8:30-8, Fri & Sat 8:30-5:30, Sun 2-5
Friends of the Library Group
CHAPIN BRANCH, 129 NW Columbia Ave, Chapin, 29036-9423, SAN 359-9701. Tel: 803-345-5479.
Open Mon & Thurs Noon-8, Tues, Wed & Fri 9-5, Sat 9-1
Friends of the Library Group
GASTON BRANCH, 214 S Main St, Gaston, 29053. (Mail add: PO Box 479, Gaston, 29053), SAN 359-9728. Tel: 803-785-9908. FAX: 803-791-3208.
Open Mon 11-7, Tues & Thurs 10-6, Wed 12-6, Sat 10-1
Friends of the Library Group
GILBERT-SUMMIT BRANCH, 405 Broad St, Gilbert, 29054. (Mail add: PO Box 341, Gilbert, 29054-0341), SAN 329-5753. Tel: 803-785-5387. FAX: 803-785-5387.
Open Mon & Wed 11-5, Tues & Thurs 10-7, Sat 9-Noon
Friends of the Library Group
IRMO BRANCH, 6251 St Andrews Rd, Columbia, 29212-3152, SAN 359-9736. Tel: 803-798-7880. FAX: 803-798-8570.
Open Mon-Thurs 8:30-8, Fri & Sat 8:30-5:30, Sun 2-5
Friends of the Library Group
PELION BRANCH, 206 Pine St, Pelion, 29123, SAN 359-9779. Tel: 803-785-3272. FAX: 803-785-7651.
Founded 1986
Open Mon 12-5, Tues, Wed & Fri 9-5, Thurs 1-8, Sat 9-1
Friends of the Library Group
SOUTH CONGAREE-PINE RIDGE, 200 Sunset Dr, West Columbia, 29172. Tel: 803-785-3050.
Founded 1912. Pop 262,000; Circ 2,000,000
Function: 24/7 Electronic res, 24/7 Online cat, Adult bk club, After school storytime, Art exhibits, Audiobks on Playaways & MP3, Audiobks via web, AV serv, Bk club(s), Bks on CD, Butterfly Garden, Children's prog, Computer training, Computers for patron use, Electronic databases & coll, Family literacy, Free DVD rentals, Games & aids for people with disabilities, Home delivery & serv to seniorr ctr & nursing homes, Homebound delivery serv, ILL available, Internet access, Large print keyboards, Life-long learning prog for all ages, Literacy & newcomer serv, Magazines, Magnifiers for reading, Mail & tel request accepted, Mango lang, Meeting rooms, Microfiche/film & reading machines, Movies, Online cat, Online ref, Orientations, Outreach serv, OverDrive digital audio bks, Photocopying/Printing, Preschool outreach, Preschool reading prog, Printer for laptops & handheld devices, Prog for adults, Prog for children & young adult, Ref & res, Ref serv available, Scanner, Senior computer classes, Senior outreach, Serves people with intellectual disabilities, Spanish lang bks, Spoken cassettes & CDs, Story hour, Study rm, Summer & winter reading prog, Summer reading prog, Tax forms, Teen prog, Telephone ref, Wheelchair accessible, Winter reading prog, Workshops, Writing prog
Open Mon & Fri 9-5, Tues 11-7, Thurs Noon-6, Sat 10-1
Friends of the Library Group

SWANSEA BRANCH, 199 N Lawrence Ave, Swansea, 29160. (Mail add: PO Box 130, Swansea, 29160-0130), SAN 359-9809. Tel: 803-785-3519. FAX: 803-785-3519.
Open Mon & Fri 10-6, Tues 11-7, Thurs Noon-6, Sat 10-1
Friends of the Library Group
Bookmobiles: 1

MANNING

P HARVIN CLARENDON COUNTY LIBRARY*, 215 N Brooks St, 29102. SAN 373-7535. Tel: 803-435-8633. FAX: 803-435-8101. E-mail: info@clarendoncountylibrary.com. Web Site: www.clarendoncountylibrary.com. *Dir,* Holly Cockfield; E-mail: hcockfield@clarendoncounty.gov.org; Staff 8 (MLS 1, Non-MLS 7)
Founded 1977. Pop 34,500; Circ 43,000
Special Collections: Grandfamily Resource Center; South Carolina Coll
Automation Activity & Vendor Info: (Cataloging) Evergreen; (Circulation) Evergreen; (OPAC) Evergreen
Wireless access
Function: 24/7 Electronic res, 24/7 Online cat, Adult bk club, Audiobks on Playaways & MP3, Audiobks via web, Bks on CD, Children's prog, Computers for patron use, Doc delivery serv, E-Readers, Electronic databases & coll, Family literacy, Free DVD rentals, Home delivery & serv to seniorr ctr & nursing homes, ILL available, Internet access, Magazines, Mango lang, Online cat, Outreach serv, Photocopying/Printing, Preschool outreach, Preschool reading prog, Prog for adults, Prog for children & young adult, Ref & res, Ref serv available, Story hour, Summer & winter reading prog, Summer reading prog, Tax forms, Telephone ref, Wheelchair accessible, Winter reading prog
Special Services for the Deaf - Bks on deafness & sign lang; Staff with knowledge of sign lang
Special Services for the Blind - Bks on CD; Closed circuit TV magnifier; Large print bks
Open Mon-Thurs 10-7, Fri & Sat 9-5
Friends of the Library Group
Bookmobiles: 1. Librn, Patrica Ragin. Bk vols 3,000

MARION

P MARION COUNTY LIBRARY SYSTEM*, 101 East Court St, 29571. SAN 360-3067. Tel: 843-423-8300. FAX: 843-423-8302. E-mail: info@marion-lib.org. Web Site: www.marioncountylibrary.org. *Dir,* Diann Smothers; *Head, Tech Serv,* Pamela Dunscombe; *Circ Supvr,* Debbie Floyd; *Bkmobile/Outreach Serv, Youth Serv,* Jean Townsend; *Circ & ILL,* Lois Williams; Staff 17 (MLS 4, Non-MLS 13)
Founded 1898. Pop 34,904; Circ 81,669
Library Holdings: AV Mats 2,423; Bk Vols 82,248; Per Subs 202
Special Collections: South Carolina, bks & micro
Subject Interests: Hist
Automation Activity & Vendor Info: (Cataloging) Innovative Interfaces, Inc; (Circulation) Innovative Interfaces, Inc; (OPAC) Innovative Interfaces, Inc
Wireless access
Function: Archival coll, Home delivery & serv to seniorr ctr & nursing homes, Homebound delivery serv, ILL available, Photocopying/Printing, Prog for children & young adult, Ref serv available, Summer reading prog, Telephone ref, Wheelchair accessible
Publications: History of Marion County
Partic in LYRASIS
Special Services for the Deaf - Closed caption videos
Special Services for the Blind - Computer with voice synthesizer for visually impaired persons
Open Mon & Wed 9:30-8, Tues & Thurs 9:30-6, Fri 9:30-5:30, Sat 9:30-1
Friends of the Library Group
Branches: 2
MULLINS BRANCH, 210 N Main St, Mullins, 29574, SAN 360-3091. Tel: 843-464-9621. FAX: 843-464-5215. *Br Mgr,* Kelley Springer
Open Mon-Wed & Fri 9:30-5:30, Sat 9:30-1
NICHOLS BRANCH, 514 W Mullins St, Nichols, 29581, SAN 360-3121. Tel: 843-526-2641. FAX: 843-526-2641. *Circ,* Joel Fowler
Open Tues 9:30-12:30 & 1-5:30, Thurs 1-5:30
Bookmobiles: 1

MCCORMICK

P MCCORMICK COUNTY LIBRARY*, 201 Railroad Ave, 29835. (Mail add: PO Box 1899, 29835-1899), SAN 315-5633. Tel: 864-852-2821. FAX: 864-852-2821. E-mail: mccormicklibrary@hotmail.com. Web Site: mccormicklibrary.org. *Dir,* Paul Brown
Founded 1953
Library Holdings: Bk Vols 30,000; Per Subs 72
Automation Activity & Vendor Info: (Cataloging) TLC (The Library Corporation); (Circulation) TLC (The Library Corporation); (OPAC) TLC (The Library Corporation)
Wireless access
Open Tues-Thurs 10-7, Fri 9-6, Sat & Sun 1-5
Friends of the Library Group

MONCKS CORNER

P BERKELEY COUNTY LIBRARY SYSTEM*, 1003 Hwy 52, 29461. (Mail add: PO Box 1239, 29461), SAN 360-3156. Tel: 843-719-4223. Circulation Tel: 843-719-4937, 843-719-4938. Reference Tel: 843-719-4235, 843-719-4936. Web Site: berkeleylibrarysc.org. *Dir, IT Dir,* Gene Brunson; Tel: 843-719-4223, E-mail: gene.brunson@berkeleycountysc.gov; *Children's Coordr, Dep Dir,* Sharon M Fashion; Tel: 843-719-4227, E-mail: sharon.fashion@berkeleycountysc.gov; *Digital Projects Librn,* Ramona L Grimsley; Tel: 843-719-4240, E-mail: ramona.grimsley@berkeleycountysc.gov; *YA Librn,* Mary Shannon Duffy; Tel: 843-719-4278, E-mail: mary.duffy@berkeleycountysc.gov; *Br Coordr,* Sharon Eels; Tel: 843-572-1376, E-mail: sharon.eels@berkeleycountysc.gov; *Br Coordr,* Florence Lewis-Coker; Tel: 843-719-4228, E-mail: florence.lewis-coker@berkeleycountysc.gov; Staff 11 (MLS 11)
Founded 1936. Pop 161,486; Circ 453,986
Library Holdings: Audiobooks 2,974; CDs 1,957; DVDs 5,698; Large Print Bks 2,816; Bk Titles 114,968; Bk Vols 228,850; Per Subs 240; Videos 3,041
Subject Interests: Berkeley County hist, Genealogy, SC hist
Automation Activity & Vendor Info: (Circulation) SirsiDynix; (OPAC) SirsiDynix
Wireless access
Function: Adult bk club, Audio & video playback equip for onsite use, Bk club(s), Bks on cassette, Bks on CD, Children's prog, Computer training, Computers for patron use, E-Reserves, Electronic databases & coll, Free DVD rentals, ILL available, Internet access, Music CDs, Online cat, Online ref, Orientations, Outreach serv, Photocopying/Printing, Prog for adults, Prog for children & young adult, Ref serv available, Story hour, Summer reading prog, Tax forms, Teen prog, Telephone ref, VHS videos, Wheelchair accessible
Open Mon-Thurs 9-7, Fri & Sat 9-5
Restriction: Circ to mem only, In-house use for visitors, Non-resident fee, Pub use on premises
Friends of the Library Group
Branches: 6
CANE BAY, 1655 Cane Bay Blvd, Ste A, Summerville, 29486. Tel: 843-719-4796.
Open Mon-Thurs 10-6, Fri & Sat 9-5
Friends of the Library Group
DANIEL ISLAND, 2301 Daniel Island Dr, Charleston, 29492. Tel: 843-471-2952.
Founded 2007. Circ 54,123
Function: Bks on cassette, Bks on CD, Children's prog, Computers for patron use, E-Reserves, Free DVD rentals, ILL available, Internet access, Music CDs, Online cat, Online ref, Photocopying/Printing, Prog for adults, Prog for children & young adult, Ref serv available, Story hour, Summer reading prog, Tax forms, Teen prog, VHS videos, Wheelchair accessible
Open Mon & Wed 10-6, Tues & Thurs 11-7, Fri & Sat 9-5
Restriction: In-house use for visitors
Friends of the Library Group
GOOSE CREEK BRANCH, 325 Old Moncks Corner Rd, Goose Creek, 29445, SAN 360-3180. Tel: 843-572-1376.
Founded 1971. Circ 174,729
Open Mon-Thurs 9-7, Fri & Sat 9-5
Friends of the Library Group
HANAHAN BRANCH, 1216 Old Murray Ct, Hanahan, 29410, SAN 360-3210. FAX: 843-553-0047.
Founded 1965. Circ 27,839
Function: Bks on cassette, Bks on CD, Computers for patron use, E-Reserves, Electronic databases & coll, Free DVD rentals, ILL available, Internet access, Music CDs, Online cat, Online ref, Outreach serv, Photocopying/Printing, Prog for children & young adult, Ref serv available, Summer reading prog, Tax forms, Telephone ref, VHS videos, Wheelchair accessible
Open Mon-Thurs 10-7, Fri & Sat 10-5
Restriction: In-house use for visitors
Friends of the Library Group
SAINT STEPHEN BRANCH, 113 Ravenell Dr, Saint Stephen, 29479, SAN 360-3245. Tel: 843-567-4862. FAX: 843-567-4862.
Founded 1955. Circ 13,985
Function: Bks on cassette, Bks on CD, Children's prog, Computers for patron use, E-Reserves, Electronic databases & coll, Free DVD rentals, ILL available, Music CDs, Online cat, Photocopying/Printing, Ref serv available, Story hour, Summer reading prog, Tax forms, Telephone ref, VHS videos, Wheelchair accessible
Open Mon-Thurs 10-6, Fri & Sat 9-5
Friends of the Library Group

SANGAREE, 595 Sangaree Pkwy, Summerville, 29483. Tel: 843-695-1208.
Founded 2007. Circ 59,781
Function: Bks on cassette, Bks on CD, Children's prog, Computers for patron use, E-Reserves, Electronic databases & coll, Free DVD rentals, ILL available, Internet access, Music CDs, Online cat, Online ref, Outreach serv, Photocopying/Printing, Prog for adults, Prog for children & young adult, Ref serv available, Story hour, Summer reading prog, Tax forms, Teen prog, VHS videos, Wheelchair accessible
Open Mon & Wed 10-6, Tues & Thurs 11-7, Fri & Sat 9-5
Restriction: In-house use for visitors
Bookmobiles: 1. Librn, Barbara Ash

MURRELLS INLET

S BROOKGREEN GARDENS LIBRARY*, 1931 Brookgreen Dr, 29576. (Mail add: PO Box 3368, Pawleys Island, 29585), SAN 320-5118. Tel: 843-235-6000. FAX: 843-235-6003. E-mail: info@brookgreen.org. Web Site: www.brookgreen.org. *Pres,* Robert Jewell; *Curator,* Robin Salmon; E-mail: rsalmon@brookgreen.org
Founded 1931
Library Holdings: Bk Titles 2,800; Bk Vols 3,000; Per Subs 75
Special Collections: American Sculptors, archives, clipping files, correspondence, exhibit cat, photogs, taped & transcribed interviews; Brookgreen Gardens, newsp, photogs; Plantation Records, Medical Accounts & Personal Correspondence
Subject Interests: 19th Century Am sculpture, 20th Century Am sculpture, 21st Century Am sculpture, Fauna of the SE US, Flora of the SE US, Hist of SC, Hort, Landscape archit
Restriction: Not open to pub, Staff use only

MYRTLE BEACH

P CHAPIN MEMORIAL LIBRARY*, 400 14th Ave N, 29577. SAN 329-787X. Tel: 843-918-1275. Circulation Tel: 847-918-1286. FAX: 843-918-1288. E-mail: website@chapinlibrary.org. Web Site: www.chapinlibrary.org. *Dir,* Jennifer Nassar; E-mail: jnassar@cityofmyrtlebeach.com; Staff 11 (MLS 3, Non-MLS 8)
Founded 1949. Pop 39,162; Circ 74,813
Library Holdings: Bk Vols 77,679; Per Subs 62
Special Collections: Oral History
Subject Interests: Local hist
Automation Activity & Vendor Info: (Cataloging) Innovative Interfaces, Inc; (Circulation) Innovative Interfaces, Inc; (OPAC) Innovative Interfaces, Inc; (Serials) Innovative Interfaces, Inc
Wireless access
Open Mon & Wed 9-6, Tues & Thurs 9-7, Fri 9-5, Sat 9-3
Friends of the Library Group

L NELSON, MULLINS, RILEY & SCARBOROUGH*, Law Library, Pinnacle Corporate Ctr, Ste 300, 3751 Robert M Grissom Pkwy, 29577. SAN 323-6587. Tel: 843-448-3500. Toll Free Tel: 800-237-2000. FAX: 843-448-3437. Web Site: www.nelsonmullins.com/locations/myrtle-beach. *Library Contact,* Lisa Riek; E-mail: lisa.riek@nelsonmullins.com
Library Holdings: Bk Titles 10,000; Per Subs 20
Automation Activity & Vendor Info: (Acquisitions) Inmagic, Inc.; (Cataloging) Inmagic, Inc.; (Circulation) Inmagic, Inc.; (Course Reserve) Inmagic, Inc.; (ILL) Inmagic, Inc.; (Media Booking) Inmagic, Inc.; (OPAC) Inmagic, Inc.; (Serials) Inmagic, Inc.
Restriction: Not open to pub, Staff use only

NEWBERRY

C NEWBERRY COLLEGE*, Wessels Library, 2100 College St, 29108-2197. SAN 315-565X. Tel: 803-321-5229. E-mail: wessels.library@newberry.edu. Web Site: newberry.libguides.com/wesselslibrary. *Dir,* Reid Austin; E-mail: reid.austin@newberry.edu; *Outreach Librn,* Dr Russ Conrath; E-mail: russ.conrath@newberry.edu; *Tech Serv Spec,* Janice Hudson; E-mail: janice.hudson@newberry.edu; Staff 6 (MLS 3, Non-MLS 3)
Founded 1856. Enrl 1,084; Fac 68; Highest Degree: Bachelor
Library Holdings: AV Mats 1,928; DVDs 300; Bk Vols 83,928; Per Subs 122
Special Collections: Newberry College Materials; Regional Lutheran Materials; South Caroliniana
Automation Activity & Vendor Info: (Cataloging) SirsiDynix; (Circulation) SirsiDynix
Wireless access
Partic in LYRASIS; OCLC Online Computer Library Center, Inc; Partnership Among South Carolina Academic Libraries; SC Found of Independent Cols Consortia
Open Mon-Thurs 7:30am-Midnight, Fri 7:30-6, Sat 10-4, Sun 6pm-Midnight; Mon-Fri 7:30-4:30 (Summer)
Restriction: Open to students, fac & staff

P NEWBERRY COUNTY LIBRARY SYSTEM*, Hal Kohn Memorial Library, 1100 Friend St, 29108-3416. SAN 360-330X. Tel: 803-276-0854. Circulation Tel: 803-276-0854, Ext 1. FAX: 803-276-7478. Web Site: www.youseemore.com/newberry. *Dir,* Abigail Fuller; E-mail: afuller@newberrycounty.net; Staff 1 (MLS 1)
Wireless access
Open Mon-Fri 10-6, Sat 10-2
Friends of the Library Group
Branches: 1
WHITMIRE MEMORIAL, 303 Church St, Whitmire, 29178, SAN 360-3369. Tel: 803-694-3961. FAX: 803-694-9945. *Br Mgr,* Christina Watts
Library Holdings: Bk Titles 13,639; Per Subs 25
Open Mon, Tues, Thurs & Fri 9-5
Friends of the Library Group

ORANGEBURG

C CLAFLIN UNIVERSITY*, H V Manning Library, 400 Magnolia St, 29115. SAN 315-5676. Tel: 803-534-2710. Circulation Tel: 803-535-5308. Interlibrary Loan Service Tel: 803-535-5306. FAX: 803-535-5091. Web Site: www.claflin.edu/academics-research/academic-resources-support/library. *Libr Dir,* Marilyn Y Gibbs; Tel: 803-535-5309, E-mail: mgibbsdrayton@claflin.edu; *Archives, Spec Coll,* Barbara Green; Tel: 803-535-5406, E-mail: bargreen@claflin.edu; Staff 9 (MLS 3, Non-MLS 6)
Enrl 1,701; Fac 9; Highest Degree: Master
Library Holdings: AV Mats 1,141; Bk Vols 161,726; Per Subs 450
Special Collections: Black Life & History (Wilbur R Gregg Black Coll) bks, microfilm; Claflin University Archives/Claflin University History, Minutes of the Methodist Episcopal Church, selected Civil Rights papers
Subject Interests: Hist, Music, Relig studies
Automation Activity & Vendor Info: (Cataloging) Innovative Interfaces, Inc; (Circulation) Innovative Interfaces, Inc; (Course Reserve) Innovative Interfaces, Inc; (OPAC) Innovative Interfaces, Inc; (Serials) Innovative Interfaces, Inc
Wireless access
Partic in Partnership Among South Carolina Academic Libraries
Open Mon-Thurs 8am-Midnight, Fri 8-6, Sat 10-2, Sun 3-10

J ORANGEBURG-CALHOUN TECHNICAL COLLEGE LIBRARY*, 3250 Saint Matthews Rd NE, 29118. SAN 315-5684. Tel: 803-535-1262. FAX: 803-535-1240. E-mail: library@octech.edu. Web Site: libguides.octech.edu. *Head Librn,* Jason Reed; E-mail: reedjt@octech.edu; *Librn,* Robin Pesko; E-mail: peskorm@octech.edu; *Media Res Coordr,* Timothy Felder; Staff 4.5 (MLS 2, Non-MLS 2.5)
Founded 1968
Library Holdings: AV Mats 2,171; e-books 71,342; Bk Vols 10,569; Per Subs 49
Wireless access
Partic in Partnership Among South Carolina Academic Libraries
Open Mon-Thurs 7:30-7, Fri 7:30-1:30

P ORANGEBURG COUNTY LIBRARY*, 510 Louis St, 29115-5030. SAN 315-5692. Tel: 803-531-4636. Reference Tel: 803-533-5856. FAX: 803-533-5860. Web Site: www.orangeburgcounty.org/161/library. *Dir,* Anna Zacherl; E-mail: azacherl@orangeburgcounty.org; *Asst Dir,* Debra Allen; E-mail: dallen@orangeburgcounty.org; Staff 35 (MLS 7, Non-MLS 28)
Founded 1937. Circ 354,000
Library Holdings: Bk Vols 151,700; Per Subs 310
Subject Interests: Local hist
Automation Activity & Vendor Info: (Cataloging) Innovative Interfaces, Inc; (Circulation) Innovative Interfaces, Inc; (OPAC) Innovative Interfaces, Inc
Wireless access
Function: Adult bk club, Archival coll, Audiobks via web, AV serv, Bks on CD, Children's prog, Citizenship assistance, Computer training, Computers for patron use, Digital talking bks, Distance learning, E-Reserves, Electronic databases & coll, Family literacy, For res purposes, Free DVD rentals, Govt ref serv, Health sci info serv, Holiday prog, Home delivery & serv to seniorr ctr & nursing homes, Homebound delivery serv, ILL available, Instruction & testing, Internet access, Life-long learning prog for all ages, Magazines, Magnifiers for reading, Mail & tel request accepted, Mango lang, Meeting rooms, Microfiche/film & reading machines, Movies, Notary serv, Online cat, Online info literacy tutorials on the web & in blackboard, Online ref, Orientations, Outreach serv, OverDrive digital audio bks, Photocopying/Printing, Preschool outreach, Preschool reading prog, Prof lending libr, Prog for adults, Prog for children & young adult, Ref & res, Ref serv available, Res libr, Scanner, Senior outreach, Serves people with intellectual disabilities, Spoken cassettes & CDs, Spoken cassettes & DVDs, Story hour, Summer reading prog, Visual arts prog, Wheelchair accessible, Workshops
Open Mon 9-7, Tues-Thurs 10-7, Fri 9-6, Sat 9-5
Friends of the Library Group

Branches: 5
HOLLY HILL BRANCH, 8423C Old State Rd, Holly Hill, 29059. Tel: 803-496-7177.
Open Mon-Thurs 1-5:30, Fri 9-1
Friends of the Library Group
MENTOR BRANCH, 2621 Cleveland St, Elloree, 29047. (Mail add: PO Box 510, Elloree, 29047-0510). Tel: 803-897-2162.
Open Mon & Wed 2-5:30, Tues 1:30-5:30, Fri 9-1
Friends of the Library Group
NORTH BRANCH, 9316 North Rd, Hwy 178, North, 29112. (Mail add: PO Box 10, North, 29112). Tel: 803-247-5880.
Open Mon, Tues & Fri 2-5:30, Wed 9-1:30
Friends of the Library Group
SANTEE BRANCH, 119 Dazzy Circle, Santee, 29142. Tel: 803-854-5300.
Open Mon 3-7, Tues & Thurs 2-6, Fri 10-1
Friends of the Library Group
SPRINGFIELD BRANCH, 210 Brodie St, Springfield, 29146. Tel: 803-258-1100.
Open Mon 3-7, Tues & Thurs 2-6, Fri 10-1
Friends of the Library Group
Bookmobiles: 1. Head, Extension Servs, David Parnell. Bk vols 3,000

M REGIONAL MEDICAL CENTER OF ORANGEBURG & CALHOUN COUNTIES*, Medical Library, Medical Staff Services, 3000 St Matthews Rd, 29118. SAN 371-618X. Tel: 803-395-3002. FAX: 803-395-2557. *Mgr,* Caroline Thornton; E-mail: cwthornton@regmed.com; Staff 2 (Non-MLS 2)
Library Holdings: Bk Titles 218
Wireless access
Restriction: Not open to pub

C SOUTH CAROLINA STATE UNIVERSITY*, Miller F Whittaker Library, 300 College St NE, 29115. (Mail add: PO Box 7491, 29117), SAN 315-5714. Tel: 803-536-7045. Circulation Tel: 803-536-8645. Interlibrary Loan Service Tel: 803-516-4508. Reference Tel: 803-536-8640. FAX: 803-536-8902. Reference E-mail: reference@scsu.edu. Web Site: library.scsu.edu. *Info Serv, Interim Dean of Libr,* Dr Ruth A Hodges; E-mail: rhodges@scsu.edu; *Archivist, Coll Coordr,* Mr Avery Daniels; Tel: 803-536-8627, E-mail: adaniel5@scsu.efu; *Govt Doc Coordr, Ref & Info Spec,* Doris J Felder; Tel: 803-536-8642, E-mail: lb_djohnson@scsu.edu; *Coordr, Tech Serv,* Cathi Cooper Mack; Tel: 803-536-8633, E-mail: ccoopermack@scsu.edu; *Ref & Info Serv,* Wanda L Priester; Tel: 803-536-8647, E-mail: wpriest3@scsu.edu; Staff 11.5 (MLS 5, Non-MLS 6.5)
Founded 1913. Fac 200; Highest Degree: Doctorate
Library Holdings: e-books 256,766; e-journals 19,886; Microforms 1,052,345; Bk Titles 317,485
Special Collections: Black Coll-Books by & about Blacks; South Carolina State Data Center; South Carolina State University Historical Coll, bks, papers, pictures & memorabilia. Oral History; State Document Depository; US Document Depository
Subject Interests: Educ, Engr, Humanities, Soc sci
Automation Activity & Vendor Info: (Cataloging) ProQuest; (Circulation) ProQuest; (Course Reserve) ProQuest; (Discovery) ProQuest; (ILL) OCLC; (OPAC) ProQuest; (Serials) ProQuest
Wireless access
Publications: Campus Heartbeat (1 per semester newsletter); Circulation Department Policy; Citing References Using APA; Collection Development Policy; Computer and Technology Service [Use Policy]; Finding Articles in Academic Search Complete; Finding Resources in the Miller F. Whittaker Library; Library Personnel Handbook; Library Resources in Education; Library Resources in Engineering; Library Resources in Social Work; Library Webpage; Library-Faculty Liaison Program; Orientation to the Miller F. Whittaker Library (Online only); Reference and Information Services Policy; South Carolina Historical Collection and Archives Policy; Technical Service Policy
Partic in Carolina Consortium; DISCUS; LYRASIS; Partnership Among South Carolina Academic Libraries
Special Services for the Blind - Braille bks; Magnifiers
Open Mon-Thurs 8:30am-10pm, Fri 8:30-5, Sat 12-5, Sun 3-9
Friends of the Library Group

CR SOUTHERN METHODIST COLLEGE*, Lynn Corbett Library, 541 Broughton St, 29115. SAN 315-5722. Tel: 803-534-7826, Ext 106. FAX: 803-534-7827. E-mail: lcl@smcollege.edu. *Dir,* Christine Gaskin; Staff 1 (MLS 1)
Founded 1964. Enrl 241; Fac 5; Highest Degree: Master
Library Holdings: AV Mats 40; CDs 52; DVDs 48; Electronic Media & Resources 84; Bk Titles 18,900; Bk Vols 21,550; Per Subs 49; Spec Interest Per Sub 12; Videos 194
Special Collections: Southern Methodist Room (Southern Methodist Denominational Information)
Subject Interests: Biblical studies
Wireless access
Function: Archival coll, AV serv, CD-ROM, ILL available, Internet access, Music CDs, Ref & res, Ref serv available, Telephone ref, VHS videos, Wheelchair accessible
Restriction: Mem only

PARRIS ISLAND

A UNITED STATES MARINE CORPS*, Recruit Depot Station Library, Bldg 283, 521 Blvd DeFrance, 29905. SAN 360-3393. Tel: 843-228-1672. Interlibrary Loan Service Tel: 843-228-1671. FAX: 843-228-3840. Web Site: www.mccs-sc.com/mil-fam/libraries.shtml. *Librn,* Kevin Giampa; E-mail: kevin.giampa@usmc-mccs.org
Founded 1940
Special Collections: General Gray Marine Warriors Library
Subject Interests: Biographies, Mil
Wireless access
Open Mon-Thurs 9-6, Sat & Sun 10-4
Friends of the Library Group

PENDLETON

S PENDLETON DISTRICT HISTORICAL, RECREATIONAL & TOURISM COMMISSION*, Reference Library, 125 E Queen St, 29670. (Mail add: PO Box 565, 29670-0565), SAN 327-0874. Tel: 864-646-3782. Toll Free Tel: 800-862-1795. FAX: 864-646-7768. Web Site: www.pendleton-district.org. *Curator,* Les McCall; E-mail: les@lakehartwellcountry.com; *Coordr,* Josh Johnson; E-mail: josh@lakehartwellcountry.com
Founded 1966
Library Holdings: Bk Vols 2,100; Per Subs 30; Videos 35
Special Collections: Black Heritage, tapes; Historic Photos of South Carolina; Records of Anderson Cotton Mill (SC, 1895-1963); Speaking of History, tapes. Oral History
Subject Interests: Genealogy
Function: Photocopying/Printing
Restriction: Non-circulating to the pub, Open by appt only

J TRI-COUNTY TECHNICAL COLLEGE LIBRARY*, 7900 Hwy 76, 29670. SAN 315-5730. Tel: 864-646-1750. FAX: 864-646-1543. E-mail: library@tctc.edu. Web Site: library.tctc.edu. *Dir,* Som Linthicum; *Asst Dir,* Hannah Fakoornajad; *Pub Serv Librn,* Marisa Reichert; E-mail: mreicher@tctc.edu; Staff 7 (MLS 4, Non-MLS 3)
Founded 1963. Enrl 4,087; Fac 172; Highest Degree: Associate
Library Holdings: e-books 75,000; Bk Vols 37,948; Per Subs 165
Subject Interests: Ethnic studies, Hist, Literary criticism
Automation Activity & Vendor Info: (Acquisitions) SirsiDynix-WorkFlows; (Cataloging) SirsiDynix-WorkFlows; (Circulation) SirsiDynix-WorkFlows; (ILL) OCLC; (OPAC) SirsiDynix-WorkFlows; (Serials) EBSCO Online
Wireless access
Function: ILL available, Online cat, Online ref, Ref serv available
Partic in OCLC Online Computer Library Center, Inc; Partnership Among South Carolina Academic Libraries; South Carolina Information & Library Services Consortium
Restriction: 24-hr pass syst for students only

ROCK HILL

J CLINTON COLLEGE LIBRARY*, 1029 Crawford Rd, 29730-5152. SAN 315-5765. Tel: 803-327-7402. Toll Free Tel: 877-837-9645. FAX: 803-327-3261. Web Site: clintoncollege.edu/academic-affairs/library-services. *Dir,* Angela Duckett; E-mail: asharper@clintoncollege.edu; Staff 3 (MLS 1, Non-MLS 2)
Founded 1894. Enrl 190; Fac 27; Highest Degree: Associate
Library Holdings: AV Mats 100; Bk Vols 10,551; Per Subs 27
Special Collections: African-African American Coll
Automation Activity & Vendor Info: (Acquisitions) Book Systems; (Cataloging) Book Systems
Wireless access
Function: Archival coll, AV serv, For res purposes, Homebound delivery serv, Photocopying/Printing, Ref serv available, Telephone ref, Wheelchair accessible
Publications: Campus Communique (Newsletter)
Partic in DISCUS; Partnership Among South Carolina Academic Libraries
Open Mon-Thurs 8am-9pm, Fri 8-5
Restriction: Authorized scholars by appt, Open to fac, students & qualified researchers, Open to pub for ref & circ; with some limitations
Friends of the Library Group

C WINTHROP UNIVERSITY*, Ida Jane Dacus Library, 824 Oakland Ave, 29733. SAN 315-5781. Tel: 803-323-2131. Interlibrary Loan Service Tel: 803-323-2304, 803-323-4501. Administration Tel: 803-323-2184. Web Site: libguides.library.winthrop.edu/dacus. *Dean, Libr Serv,* Kaetrena Davis Kendrick; E-mail: kendrickk@winthrop.edu; *Dir, Spec Coll & Archives,* Gina Price White; Tel: 803-323-2210, E-mail: whitegp@winthrop.edu; *Head, Govt Info,* Jacqueline McFadden; Tel: 803-323-2322, E-mail:

mcfaddenj@winthrop.edu; *Acq/Coll Develop Librn,* Martha Smith; Tel: 803-323-2274, E-mail: smithms@winthrop.edu; *Assessment Librn, ILL Librn,* Philip Hays; E-mail: haysp@winthrop.edu; *Metadata & Discovery Librn,* Tracy Pizzi; Tel: 803-323-2179, E-mail: pizzit@winthrop.edu; *Mgr, User Serv,* Nancy White; Tel: 803-323-2335, E-mail: whiten@winthrop.edu; *Archivist, Spec Coll Coordr,* Andrew Johnston; Tel: 803-323-2302, E-mail: johnstona@winthrop.edu; Staff 24 (MLS 11, Non-MLS 13)
Founded 1886. Enrl 5,174; Fac 523; Highest Degree: Master
Jul 2021-Jun 2022 Income $3,143,569, Parent Institution $3,102,762, Other $40,807. Mats Exp $3,102,762, Books $30,337, AV Mat $29,480. Sal $1,329,569
Library Holdings: CDs 60; DVDs 68; e-books 502,934; e-journals 106,987; Microforms 17,295; Bk Titles 296,376; Bk Vols 383,070; Per Subs 283
Special Collections: Catawba Indians, ms; Draper Manuscript Coll, microfilm; Education Resources Information Center Reports, microfiche; Genealogy, ms; General South Carolina History, ms; League of Nations Documents & Serial Publications, 1919-1946, microfilm; Library of American Civilization, ultrafiche; Library of English Literature, ultrafiche; Local South Carolina History, ms; Louise Pettus Archives; Rare Books; United Nations Publications, 1946-1980, microprint; Winthrop Universitiy History, archives, ms; Women's History, ms. Oral History; State Document Depository; US Document Depository
Automation Activity & Vendor Info: (Acquisitions) OCLC Worldshare Management Services; (Cataloging) OCLC Worldshare Management Services; (Circulation) OCLC Worldshare Management Services; (Course Reserve) Blackboard Inc; (Discovery) OCLC Worldshare Management Services; (ILL) OCLC WorldShare Interlibrary Loan; (OPAC) OCLC Worldshare Management Services; (Serials) OCLC Worldshare Management Services
Wireless access
Publications: A Guide to the Manuscript & Oral History Collections; A Guide to the Records Documenting the History of Winthrop College; Dacus Focus; Dear Ida (Newsletter); Retrospect (Monthly newsletter); Sources of Genealogical Research in the Winthrop College Archives & Special Collections; The Dean's Corner
Partic in Charlotte Area Educ Consortium; LYRASIS; OCLC Online Computer Library Center, Inc; Partnership Among South Carolina Academic Libraries
Special Services for the Blind - Aids for in-house use
Restriction: Open to pub for ref only, Open to students, fac & staff
Friends of the Library Group

P YORK COUNTY LIBRARY, Rock Hill Public Library, 138 E Black St, 29730. (Mail add: PO Box 10032, 29731), SAN 360-3423. Tel: 803-981-5858. Circulation Tel: 803-981-5860. Reference Tel: 803-981-5825. Administration Tel: 803-981-5831. FAX: 803-547-4886. E-mail: ycl.ill@yclibrary.org. Web Site: www.yclibrary.org. *County Libr Dir,* Julie Ward; E-mail: julie.ward@yclibrary.org; *Bkmobile/Outreach Serv Mgr,* Jennifer Strokis; Tel: 803-981-5841, E-mail: jennifer.strokis@yclibrary.org; *Br Mgr,* Kalyani Veeraraghavan; Tel: 803-981-5853, E-mail: kalyani.veeraraghavan@yclibrary.org; *Circ Mgr,* Alvina Jefferies; Tel: 803-981-5873, E-mail: alvina.jefferies@yclibrary.org; *Ref Mgr,* Donna Andrews; Tel: 803-981-5844, E-mail: donna.andrews@yclibrary.org; *Grant & Assessment Coord,* Luanne James; Tel: 803-981-5838, E-mail: luanne.james@yclibrary.org; *Ch Serv,* Ginger Sawyer; Tel: 803-981-5882, E-mail: ginger.sawyer@yclibrary.orgh; *ILL,* Judi Cousar; Tel: 803-203-9220; *YA Serv,* Abbie Townson; Tel: 803-981-5830, E-mail: abbie.townson@yclibrary.org
Founded 1884. Pop 226,073
Special Collections: Catawba Indian, bks, clippings & micro; Genealogical & Caroliniana (Local, State & General), bks, clippings & micro; Rock Hill & York County History, bks, clippings & micro
Automation Activity & Vendor Info: (Acquisitions) SirsiDynix; (Cataloging) SirsiDynix; (Circulation) SirsiDynix; (OPAC) SirsiDynix
Wireless access
Function: 24/7 Electronic res, 24/7 Online cat, Archival coll, Bk club(s), Computers for patron use, Electronic databases & coll, Extended outdoor wifi, Family literacy, Home delivery & serv to seniorr ctr & nursing homes, Homebound delivery serv, ILL available, Internet access, Large print keyboards, Life-long learning prog for all ages, Literacy & newcomer serv, Magnifiers for reading, Mail & tel request accepted, Microfiche/film & reading machines, Online cat, Online ref, Outreach serv, Outside serv via phone, mail, e-mail & web, Photocopying/Printing, Printer for laptops & handheld devices, Prog for adults, Prog for children & young adult, Ref serv available, Res performed for a fee, Senior outreach, Spanish lang bks, Summer & winter reading prog, Telephone ref, Wheelchair accessible, Wifi hotspot checkout
Partic in SCLENDS
Friends of the Library Group

Branches: 4
CLOVER PUBLIC, 107 Knox St, Clover, 29710, SAN 360-3458. Tel: 803-222-3474. FAX: 803-222-6695. *Br Mgr,* Amanda Antonacci
Function: 24/7 Electronic res, 24/7 Online cat, Bk club(s), Computers for patron use, Electronic databases & coll, Extended outdoor wifi, ILL available, Internet access, Large print keyboards, Life-long learning prog for all ages, Online cat, Photocopying/Printing, Printer for laptops & handheld devices, Prog for adults, Prog for children & young adult, Ref serv available, Res performed for a fee, Spanish lang bks, Summer & winter reading prog, Telephone ref, Wheelchair accessible, Wifi hotspot checkout
Friends of the Library Group
FORT MILL PUBLIC, 1818 Second Baxter Crossing, Fort Mill, 29708, SAN 360-3482. Tel: 803-547-4114. FAX: 803-547-4852. *Br Mgr,* Tom Holloway
Function: 24/7 Electronic res, 24/7 Online cat, 24/7 wireless access, Bk club(s), Computers for patron use, Electronic databases & coll, Extended outdoor wifi, Family literacy, ILL available, Internet access, Large print keyboards, Life-long learning prog for all ages, Magnifiers for reading, Online cat, Online ref, Photocopying/Printing, Printer for laptops & handheld devices, Prog for adults, Prog for children & young adult, Ref serv available, Res performed for a fee, Spanish lang bks, Summer & winter reading prog, Wheelchair accessible, Wifi hotspot checkout
Friends of the Library Group
LAKE WYLIE PUBLIC, 185 Blucher Circle, Lake Wylie, 29710, SAN 323-5548. Tel: 803-831-7774. FAX: 803-831-7943. *Br Mgr,* Rae Lavvorn
Function: 24/7 Electronic res, 24/7 Online cat, 24/7 wireless access, Bk club(s), Computers for patron use, Electronic databases & coll, Extended outdoor wifi, ILL available, Internet access, Large print keyboards, Life-long learning prog for all ages, Magnifiers for reading, Online cat, Photocopying/Printing, Printer for laptops & handheld devices, Prog for adults, Prog for children & young adult, Ref serv available, Res performed for a fee, Spanish lang bks, Summer & winter reading prog, Telephone ref, Wheelchair accessible, Wifi hotspot checkout
Friends of the Library Group
YORK PUBLIC, 21 E Liberty St, York, 29745, SAN 360-3512. Tel: 803-684-3751. FAX: 803-684-6223. *Br Mgr,* Jennifer Stanley
Function: 24/7 Electronic res, 24/7 Online cat, Bk club(s), Computers for patron use, Electronic databases & coll, Extended outdoor wifi, Family literacy, ILL available, Internet access, Large print keyboards, Life-long learning prog for all ages, Magnifiers for reading, Online cat, Photocopying/Printing, Printer for laptops & handheld devices, Prog for adults, Prog for children & young adult, Ref serv available, Res performed for a fee, Spanish lang bks, Summer & winter reading prog, Telephone ref, Wheelchair accessible, Wifi hotspot checkout
Open Mon-Thurs 9-7, Fri & Sat 9-6
Friends of the Library Group
Bookmobiles: 1

J YORK TECHNICAL COLLEGE LIBRARY*, Anne Springs Close Library, 452 S Anderson Rd, 29730. SAN 315-579X. Tel: 803-327-8025. E-mail: library@yorktech.edu. Web Site: www.yorktech.edu/library. *Libr Spec,* Doretha Ward; Tel: 803-323-5991, E-mail: dward@yorktech.edu; Staff 2 (MLS 1, Non-MLS 1)
Founded 1964. Enrl 3,700; Fac 302; Highest Degree: Associate
Jul 2021-Jun 2022 Income $488,430. Mats Exp $177,287, Books $105,000, Per/Ser (Incl. Access Fees) $23,987, AV Mat $4,300, Electronic Ref Mat (Incl. Access Fees) $44,000
Library Holdings: Audiobooks 300; CDs 10; DVDs 1,500; e-books 900,000; Large Print Bks 16; Bk Titles 19,422; Per Subs 65
Special Collections: Electric Vehicles/Alternative Fuel (Alternative Energy Coll); Instructional Development Coll
Subject Interests: Allied health, Bus, Computers, Engr, Engr tech, Liberal arts, Nursing
Automation Activity & Vendor Info: (Acquisitions) Ex Libris Group; (Cataloging) Ex Libris Group; (Circulation) Ex Libris Group; (Course Reserve) Ex Libris Group; (ILL) OCLC; (Media Booking) Ex Libris Group; (OPAC) Ex Libris Group; (Serials) Ex Libris Group
Wireless access
Function: 24/7 Electronic res, 24/7 Online cat, Bks on CD, Computers for patron use, Electronic databases & coll, Free DVD rentals, ILL available, Internet access, Magazines, Magnifiers for reading, Movies, Music CDs, Online cat, Photocopying/Printing, Scanner, Study rm, Wheelchair accessible
Partic in Partnership Among South Carolina Academic Libraries; South Carolina Information & Library Services Consortium
Special Services for the Deaf - Assistive tech; Bks on deafness & sign lang
Special Services for the Blind - Assistive/Adapted tech devices, equip & products; Bks on cassette; Bks on CD; Computer with voice synthesizer for visually impaired persons; Large print bks; Talking bks
Open Mon-Thurs 7:30-7, Fri 7:30-5
Restriction: Authorized personnel only

SAINT GEORGE

P DORCHESTER COUNTY LIBRARY*, 506 N Parler Ave, 29477. SAN 360-3547. Tel: 843-563-9189. Web Site: dorchesterlibrarysc.org. *Exec Dir,* Robert Antill; E-mail: rantill@dorchesterlibrarysc.org; *Mgr,* Chris Johnston; Staff 42 (MLS 8, Non-MLS 34)
Founded 1953. Pop 100,833; Circ 671,590
Library Holdings: Audiobooks 1,000; AV Mats 18,079; e-books 4,950; Bk Vols 147,568; Per Subs 305
Subject Interests: SC hist
Automation Activity & Vendor Info: (Acquisitions) Evergreen; (Cataloging) Evergreen; (Circulation) Evergreen; (OPAC) Evergreen
Wireless access
Open Mon-Thurs 10-7, Fri & Sat 10-5, Sun 1-5
Friends of the Library Group
Branches: 1
SUMMERVILLE BRANCH, 76 Old Trolley Rd, Summerville, 29485, SAN 360-3571. Tel: 843-871-5075. *Br Mgr, Mkt Mgr,* Jenn Gleber; E-mail: jgleber@dorchesterlibrarysc.org; *Asst Br Mgr,* Leslie Koller; E-mail: lkoller@dorchesterlibrarysc.org; *Youth Serv Librn,* Elizabeth Neal; E-mail: eneal@dorchesterlibrarysc.org; Staff 6 (MLS 6)
Founded 1978. Pop 100,000; Circ 600,000
Open Mon-Thurs 10-7, Fri & Sat 10-5, Sun 1-5
Friends of the Library Group
Bookmobiles: 1

SAINT MATTHEWS

P CALHOUN COUNTY LIBRARY*, 900 FR Huff Dr, 29135. SAN 315-5803. Tel: 803-874-3389. FAX: 803-874-4154. E-mail: calhouncountylibrary2@gmail.com. Web Site: www.calhouncountylibrary.org. *Dir,* Kristen Simensen
Pop 15,385; Circ 35,930
Library Holdings: Bk Vols 34,500; Per Subs 110
Special Collections: Julia Peterkin Coll
Automation Activity & Vendor Info: (Cataloging) Evergreen; (Circulation) Evergreen; (OPAC) Evergreen
Wireless access
Partic in LYRASIS
Open Mon & Wed 10-6, Tues & Thurs 10-8, Fri 10-5, Sat 10-3
Friends of the Library Group
Bookmobiles: 1

S CALHOUN COUNTY MUSEUM & CULTURAL CENTER*, Archives & Library, 313 Butler St, 29135. SAN 329-8507. Tel: 803-874-3964. FAX: 803-874-4790. E-mail: calhouncountymuseum@gmail.com. *Dir,* Debbie Roland; *Archivist,* Colby Causey
Library Holdings: Per Subs 5
Wireless access
Restriction: Pub by appt only
Friends of the Library Group

SALUDA

P SALUDA COUNTY LIBRARY*, 101 S Main St, 29138. SAN 360-3334. Tel: 864-445-4500, Ext 2264. FAX: 864-445-2725. E-mail: saludacountylibrary@saludacounty.sc.gov. Web Site: www.saludalibrary.org. *Libr Dir,* Heath Ward; E-mail: h.ward@saludacounty.sc.gov
Library Holdings: Bk Titles 19,000; Per Subs 30
Subject Interests: Folklore
Automation Activity & Vendor Info: (Cataloging) Follett Software; (Circulation) Follett Software
Wireless access
Open Mon, Wed & Fri 8:30-5, Tues 8:30-6

SHAW AFB

A UNITED STATES AIR FORCE*, McElveen Library, 400 Shaw Dr, Bldg 827, 29152. SAN 360-3601. Tel: 803-895-4518. Circulation E-mail: library@20thfss.com. Web Site: www.thebestfss.com/family-youth/mcelveen-library.
Library Holdings: Bk Vols 40,000; Per Subs 76
Special Collections: Transition Assistant Program-Military
Subject Interests: Govt res, Mil
Automation Activity & Vendor Info: (Cataloging) OCLC Online; (Circulation) SirsiDynix; (ILL) OCLC Online; (OPAC) SirsiDynix
Open Mon-Fri 9-7, Sat 10-3
Restriction: Limited access for the pub

SPARTANBURG

C CONVERSE COLLEGE*, Mickel Library, 580 E Main St, 29302. SAN 315-5811. Tel: 864-596-9020, 864-596-9071. Interlibrary Loan Service Tel: 864-596-9596. Reference Tel: 864-596-9076. Administration Tel: 864-596-9072. FAX: 864-596-9075. Web Site: www.converse.edu/academics/mickel-library. *Libr Dir,* Wade Woodward; E-mail: wade.woodward@converse.edu; *Music Librn,* Wendi Arms; Tel: 864-596-9074, E-mail: wendi.arms@converse.edu; *Acq, Supvr,* Rebecca Dalton; E-mail: becky.dalton@converse.edu; *Circ Supvr, Doc Delivery Supvr,* Dell Morgan; E-mail: dell.morgan@converse.edu; *Coordr, Ref & Coll,* Mark Collier; E-mail: mark.collier@converse.edu; Staff 4.3 (MLS 4, Non-MLS 0.3)
Founded 1889. Enrl 1,066; Fac 4; Highest Degree: Master
Library Holdings: AV Mats 21,668; e-books 288; e-journals 47,679; Microforms 87,519; Bk Vols 155,731; Per Subs 500
Subject Interests: Educ, Music
Wireless access
Partic in LYRASIS; Partnership Among South Carolina Academic Libraries
Open Mon-Thurs 8am-11pm, Fri 8-6, Sat 12-5, Sun 1-11

S SOUTH CAROLINA SCHOOL FOR THE DEAF & THE BLIND*, Jesse Franklin Cleveland Learning Resource Center, 355 Cedar Springs Rd, 29302-4699. SAN 315-5846. Tel: 864-577-7642, 864-585-7711. Circulation Tel: 864-577-7647. FAX: 864-577-7649. TDD: . Web Site: www.scsdb.org/Page/1095. *Dir,* Galena Gaw; E-mail: ggaw@scsdb.org; *Tech Serv,* Jennifer Scruggs; E-mail: jscruggs@scsdb.org. Subject Specialists: *Blindness, Deafness,* Galena Gaw; Staff 2 (MLS 1, Non-MLS 1)
Founded 1849
Library Holdings: Bk Titles 20,000; Per Subs 20
Special Collections: Captioned Videos
Subject Interests: Blindness, Deafness
Automation Activity & Vendor Info: (Cataloging) Follett Software; (Circulation) Follett Software; (OPAC) Follett Software
Wireless access
Function: Accelerated reader prog
Special Services for the Deaf - Am sign lang & deaf culture; Bks on deafness & sign lang; Coll on deaf educ; Deaf publ; High interest/low vocabulary bks; Sorenson video relay syst; Staff with knowledge of sign lang; Video relay services; Videophone (VP)
Special Services for the Blind - Accessible computers; Audio mat; Bks & mags in Braille, on rec, tape & cassette; Bks on CD; Braille & cassettes; Braille bks; Braille equip; Braille paper; Children's Braille; Closed circuit TV; Computer with voice synthesizer for visually impaired persons; Descriptive video serv (DVS); Extensive large print coll; Large print bks & talking machines
Open Mon-Thurs 7:30-4:30, Fri 7:30-2

SPARTANBURG COMMUNITY COLLEGE LIBRARY

J DOWNTOWN CAMPUS*, Evans Academic Ctr, 2nd Flr, 220 E Kennedy St, 29302. (Mail add: PO Box 4386, 29305). Tel: 864-592-4058. Web Site: libguides.sccsc.edu/about/downtowncampus. *Libr Spec,* Kate Durham; E-mail: durhamk@sccsc.edu; *Libr Spec,* Patrick Wolfe; E-mail: wolfep@sccsc.edu
Function: Computers for patron use, Photocopying/Printing, Res assist avail, Scanner, Study rm
Open Mon-Thurs 8-6, Fri 8-1

J GILES CAMPUS*, 107 Community College Dr, 29303. (Mail add: PO Box 4386, 29305), SAN 315-5854. Tel: 864-592-4764. Interlibrary Loan Service Tel: 864-592-4450. Information Services Tel: 864-592-4654. Toll Free Tel: 866-542-2779. FAX: 864-592-4762. Web Site: libguides.sccsc.edu/home. *Dir,* Katherine Stiwinter; E-mail: stiwinterk@sccsc.edu; *Tech Serv Librn,* Julie Gilmore; Staff 9.5 (MLS 4, Non-MLS 5.5)
Enrl 4,000; Fac 120; Highest Degree: Associate
Library Holdings: AV Mats 1,700; e-books 1,216,901; Bk Titles 29,000; Bk Vols 32,000; Per Subs 112
Automation Activity & Vendor Info: (Cataloging) Ex Libris Group
Partic in Partnership Among South Carolina Academic Libraries
Open Mon-Thurs 7:30am-8pm, Fri 7:30-1:30

P SPARTANBURG COUNTY PUBLIC LIBRARIES*, 151 S Church St, 29306. SAN 360-3636. Tel: 864-596-3500. Circulation Tel: 864-596-3503. Interlibrary Loan Service Tel: 864-596-3500, Ext 1248. Reference Tel: 864-596-3505. Administration Tel: 864-596-3507. Automation Services Tel: 864-596-3515. FAX: 864-596-3518. Web Site: www.infodepot.org. *County Librn,* Todd Stephens; E-mail: todds@infodepot.org; *Asst County Librn,* Jayne Moorman; E-mail: jaynem@infodepot.org; *Asst County Librn, Pub Serv,* Jennifer Wright; *Dir, Ch Serv,* Jessica Lopez; *Dir, Multimedia & Adult Serv,* Jess Herzog; *Dir, Teen Serv,* Susan Myers; Staff 146 (MLS 40, Non-MLS 106)
Founded 1885. Pop 284,300; Circ 1,493,174
Library Holdings: Bk Vols 585,183
Special Collections: State Document Depository; US Document Depository
Subject Interests: SC hist
Automation Activity & Vendor Info: (Acquisitions) Innovative Interfaces, Inc; (Cataloging) Innovative Interfaces, Inc; (Circulation) Innovative Interfaces, Inc; (ILL) Innovative Interfaces, Inc; (OPAC) Innovative Interfaces, Inc; (Serials) Innovative Interfaces, Inc
Wireless access

Publications: Directory of Clubs & Organizations (Spartanburg County)
Special Services for the Deaf - Captioned film dep; Closed caption videos; High interest/low vocabulary bks
Special Services for the Blind - Bks on CD; Home delivery serv; Large print bks; Playaways (bks on MP3); Recorded bks
Open Mon-Fri 9-9, Sat 9-6, Sun 1:30-6
Friends of the Library Group
Branches: 9
BOILING SPRINGS LIBRARY, 871 Double Bridge Rd, Boiling Springs, 29316, SAN 360-3652. Tel: 864-578-3665. E-mail: bspcirc@infodepot.org. Web Site: infodepot.org/locations/boiling-springs. *Librn,* Travis Sanford
Open Mon, Tues & Thurs 10-8, Wed, Fri & Sat 10-6, Sun 1:30-6
Friends of the Library Group
CHESNEE LIBRARY, 100 Pickens Ave, Chesnee, 29323, SAN 360-3660. Tel: 864-461-2423. E-mail: checirc@infodepot.org. Web Site: infodepot.org/locations/chesnee. *Librn,* Jack Underwood; E-mail: jacku@infodepot.org
Open Mon, Tues & Thurs 10-8, Wed & Fri 10-6, Sat 10-4
Friends of the Library Group
COWPENS LIBRARY, 181 School St, Cowpens, 29330, SAN 378-164X. Tel: 864-463-0430. E-mail: cwpcirc@infodepot.org. Web Site: infodepot.org/locations/cowpens. *Librn,* Charlie Sinclair
Open Mon & Tues 10-8, Wed-Fri 10-6, Sat 10-4
Friends of the Library Group
CYRILL WESTSIDE LIBRARY, 525 Oak Grove Rd, 29301, SAN 325-4046. Tel: 864-574-6815. E-mail: wescirc@infodepot.org. Web Site: infodepot.org/locations/cyrill-westside. *Librn,* Sheryl Mann
Open Mon-Thurs 9-9, Fri 9-6, Sat 10-6, Sun 1:30-6
Friends of the Library Group
INMAN LIBRARY, 50 Mill St, Inman, 29349, SAN 360-3695. Tel: 864-472-8363. E-mail: inmcirc@infodepot.org. Web Site: infodepot.org/locations/inman. *Librn,* Jennifer Little
Open Mon-Thurs 10-8, Fri & Sat 10-6
Friends of the Library Group
LANDRUM LIBRARY, 111 E Asbury Dr, Landrum, 29356, SAN 360-3725. Tel: 864-457-2218. E-mail: lancirc@infodepot.org. Web Site: infodepot.org/locations/landrum. *Librn,* Anna Pilston
Open Mon, Tues & Thurs 9-8, Wed & Fri 9-6, Sat 9-2
Friends of the Library Group
MIDDLE TYGER LIBRARY, 170 Groce Rd, Lyman, 29365, SAN 360-375X. Tel: 864-439-4759. E-mail: mtycirc@infodepot.org. Web Site: infodepot.org/locations/middle-tyger. *Librn,* Leverne McBeth
Open Mon, Tues & Thurs 10-8, Wed, Fri & Sat 10-6, Sun 1:30-6
Friends of the Library Group
PACOLET LIBRARY, 390 W Main St, Pacolet, 29372, SAN 375-491X. Tel: 864-474-0421. E-mail: paccirc@infodepot.org. Web Site: infodepot.org/locations/pacolet. *Librn,* Khalisah Harris
Open Mon & Tues 10-8, Wed-Fri 10-6, Sat 12-4
Friends of the Library Group
WOODRUFF LIBRARY, 270 E Hayne St, Woodruff, 29388, SAN 360-3784. Tel: 864-476-8770. E-mail: wdfcirc@infodepot.org. Web Site: www.infodepot.org/locations/woodruff. *Librn,* Cyn Massey; E-mail: cynm@infodepot.org
Open Mon, Tues & Thurs 10-8, Wed 10-6, Fri Noon-6, Sat 10-4
Friends of the Library Group
Bookmobiles: 1

JR SPARTANBURG METHODIST COLLEGE*, Marie Blair Burgess Library, 1000 Powell Mill Rd, 29301. SAN 315-5870. Tel: 864-587-4208. E-mail: smclibrary@smcsc.edu. Web Site: libguides.smcsc.edu/main/home, www.smcsc.edu/academics/library. *Dir & Head Librn,* Position Currently Open
Founded 1911
Library Holdings: Bk Vols 27,973; Per Subs 75
Wireless access
Partic in OCLC Online Computer Library Center, Inc; Partnership Among South Carolina Academic Libraries
Open Mon-Thurs 8am-10pm, Fri 8-3

M SPARTANBURG REGIONAL MEDICAL CENTER*, Health Sciences Library, 101 E Wood St, 29303. SAN 315-5862. Tel: 864-560-6220, 864-560-6770. FAX: 864-560-6791. Web Site: www.spartanburgregional.com/locations/spartanburg-medical-center. *Mgr, Libr Serv,* Tonia Harris; E-mail: toharris@srhs.com; Staff 1 (MLS 1)
Founded 1962
Library Holdings: Bk Titles 2,000
Subject Interests: Allied health, Clinical sci, Med, Nursing
Automation Activity & Vendor Info: (Cataloging) LibraryWorld, Inc; (Circulation) LibraryWorld, Inc
Wireless access
Function: Doc delivery serv, ILL available
Partic in National Network of Libraries of Medicine Region 2; SE Network of Hospital Librs on Docline
Open Mon-Fri 8:30-5
Restriction: Non-circulating to the pub

C UNIVERSITY OF SOUTH CAROLINA UPSTATE LIBRARY*, 800 University Way, 29303. SAN 315-5889. Tel: 864-503-5620. Circulation Tel: 864-503-5611. Reference Tel: 864-503-5638. FAX: 864-503-5601. Web Site: www.uscupstate.edu/library. *Dean of Libr,* Frieda Davison; Tel: 864-503-5610, E-mail: davison@uscupstate.edu; *Coordr of Ref Serv, Pub Serv Librn,* Virginia Alexander Cononie; Tel: 864-503-5735, E-mail: cononie@uscupstate.edu; *Pub Serv Librn,* Laura Karas; Tel: 864-503-5637, E-mail: karas@uscupstate.edu; *Coordr, Libr Support for Distance Educ, Pub Serv Librn,* James LaMee; Tel: 864-503-5991, E-mail: jlamee@uscupstate.edu; *Coordr, Coll Mgt, Pub Serv Librn,* Camille McCutcheon; Tel: 864-503-5612, E-mail: cmccutcheon@uscupstate.edu; *Coordr, Archives & Spec Coll, Pub Serv Librn,* Ann Merryman; Tel: 864-503-5275, E-mail: amerryman@uscupstate.edu; *Coordr, Info Literacy, Pub Serv Librn,* John Siegel; *Pub Serv Librn,* Erika Montgomery; Tel: 864-503-5530, E-mail: erikam@uscupstate.edu; *Pub Serv Librn,* Allison Read; Tel: 864-503-5613, E-mail: reada@uscupstate.edu; *Access Serv Mgr,* Jonathan Newton; Tel: 864-503-5679, E-mail: jdn3@uscupstate.edu; *Pub Serv Librn,* Mark Smith; Tel: 864-503-5672, E-mail: smith432@uscupstate.edu; *Coord, Content Management Services,* Kevin Shehan; Tel: 864-503-5639, E-mail: kshehan@uscupstate.edu; *Coord of Distributed Educ, Open Educ Sources,* Dr Andrew Kearns; Tel: 864-503-5403, E-mail: kearns@uscupstate.edu. Subject Specialists: *Music, Nursing,* Dr Andrew Kearns; Staff 26.5 (MLS 12, Non-MLS 14.5)
Founded 1967. Enrl 6,000; Fac 310; Highest Degree: Master
Library Holdings: AV Mats 5,042; Braille Volumes 18; CDs 1,048; DVDs 4,419; e-books 502,194; Microforms 48,274; Bk Vols 154,449; Per Subs 401; Videos 503
Special Collections: Archives of the Upstate; Pre-1900 Publications; Thomas Moore Craig Coll of Southern History & Literature; University Publications
Automation Activity & Vendor Info: (Acquisitions) Innovative Interfaces, Inc; (Circulation) Innovative Interfaces, Inc; (Course Reserve) Innovative Interfaces, Inc; (ILL) OCLC ILLiad; (OPAC) Innovative Interfaces, Inc
Wireless access
Partic in Carolina Consortium; DISCUS; LYRASIS; Partnership Among South Carolina Academic Libraries
Special Services for the Deaf - ADA equip; Assistive tech
Special Services for the Blind - Aids for in-house use; Assistive/Adapted tech devices, equip & products
Open Mon-Thurs 7:30am-10pm, Fri 7:30-5, Sat 10-5, Sun 2-10
Restriction: Badge access after hrs, Borrowing requests are handled by ILL, ID required to use computers (Ltd hrs), Open to students, fac & staff
Departmental Libraries:
UNIVERSITY CENTER OF GREENVILLE LIBRARY, 225 S Pleasantburg Dr, Greenville, 29607-2544. Tel: 864-250-1111. FAX: 864-250-8905. Web Site: greenville.org/library-services. *Assoc Dean,* Andrew Kearns; Tel: 864-503-5615, E-mail: akearns@uscupstate.edu; *Pub Serv Librn,* James LaMee; Tel: 864-503-5991; Staff 1.5 (MLS 1.5)
Highest Degree: Master
Library Holdings: Bk Vols 218
Partic in South Carolina AHEC

C WOFFORD COLLEGE, Sandor Teszler Library, 429 N Church St, 29303-3663. SAN 315-5897. Tel: 864-597-4300. Web Site: www.wofford.edu/academics/library. *Dean of Libr,* Lisa Roberts; E-mail: robertsew@wofford.edu; *Access Serv Librn,* Erin Davis; E-mail: davise@wofford.edu; *Colls Librn,* Carmanita Turner; E-mail: turnercr@wofford.edu; *First Year Interaction Librn, Instruction Librn,* Timothy Brown; E-mail: browntе@wofford.edu; *Res Librn & Instruction Serv Coordr,* Emily Witsell; E-mail: witseller@wofford.edu; *Spec Coll Librn,* Luke Meagher; E-mail: meagherla@wofford.edu; *Student Success Librn,* April Grey; E-mail: greyae@wofford.edu; *Archivist,* Phillip Stone; E-mail: stonerp@wofford.edu; Staff 8 (MLS 8)
Founded 1854. Enrl 1,596; Fac 130; Highest Degree: Bachelor
Library Holdings: AV Mats 6,821; e-books 192,970; e-journals 43,572; Bk Vols 184,715; Per Subs 203
Special Collections: 16th & 17th Century Books; Geography & Travel; History of the South & South Carolina (Broadus R Littlejohn Jr Coll); Hymns & Hymnody; Press Books; Richard B Harwell Leonard Baskin Coll, bks, ephemera, prints, sculpture; South Caroliniana
Automation Activity & Vendor Info: (Cataloging) Innovative Interfaces, Inc
Wireless access
Partic in LYRASIS; OCLC Online Computer Library Center, Inc; Partnership Among South Carolina Academic Libraries
Open Mon-Thurs 8am-1am, Fri 8-7, Sat 10-5, Sun 11am-1am

SUMMERVILLE

S TIMROD LITERARY & LIBRARY ASSOCIATION*, Henry Timrod Library, 217 Central Ave, 29483. SAN 315-5919. Tel: 843-871-4600. E-mail: timrodlibrary@att.net. Web Site: www.thetimrodlibrary.org. *Dir,* Cindy Koontz; Staff 4 (MLS 1, Non-MLS 3)
Founded 1897
Library Holdings: Bk Vols 40,000
Subject Interests: SC hist
Wireless access
Open Mon-Fri 10-5, Sat 10-2
Restriction: Mem only

SUMTER

J CENTRAL CAROLINA TECHNICAL COLLEGE LIBRARY*, 506 N Guignard Dr, 29150. SAN 315-5935. Tel: 803-778-6647. E-mail: library@cctech.edu. Web Site: www.cctech.edu/resources/library. *Head Librn,* Denise K Robinson; Tel: 803-778-7851, E-mail: robinsondk@cctech.edu; *Libr Spec,* Johnette Brewer; Tel: 803-778-7884, E-mail: brewerjh@cctech.edu; Staff 2 (MLS 2)
Founded 1963. Enrl 3,000; Fac 88; Highest Degree: Associate
Library Holdings: AV Mats 2,770; e-books 53,288; Bk Titles 20,924; Bk Vols 26,157; Per Subs 174
Subject Interests: Early childhood develop, Law, Nursing
Automation Activity & Vendor Info: (Acquisitions) SirsiDynix; (Cataloging) SirsiDynix; (Circulation) SirsiDynix; (Course Reserve) SirsiDynix; (ILL) OCLC; (OPAC) SirsiDynix; (Serials) SirsiDynix
Wireless access
Partic in LYRASIS; OCLC Online Computer Library Center, Inc; Partnership Among South Carolina Academic Libraries; South Carolina Information & Library Services Consortium
Open Mon-Thurs 8am-9pm
Restriction: Circ to mem only

C MORRIS COLLEGE*, Richardson-Johnson Learning Resources Center, 100 W College St, 29150-3599. SAN 315-5927. Tel: 803-934-3230. Reference Tel: 803-934-3438. FAX: 803-778-2923. Web Site: www.morris.edu/library. *Dir,* Janet S Clayton; *Dir & Head Librn,* Margaret N Mukooza; E-mail: mmukooza@morris.edu; *Ref Serv,* Carol Fleury; E-mail: cfleury@morris.edu; *Ser Librn,* Mary Dow; E-mail: mdow@morris.edu; Staff 11 (MLS 3, Non-MLS 8)
Founded 1920. Enrl 970; Fac 52; Highest Degree: Bachelor
Library Holdings: CDs 300; DVDs 250; High Interest/Low Vocabulary Bk Vols 1,700; Bk Vols 74,819; Per Subs 300; Videos 1,760
Special Collections: African American Coll
Automation Activity & Vendor Info: (Acquisitions) SirsiDynix; (Cataloging) OCLC Connexion; (Circulation) SirsiDynix; (Course Reserve) SirsiDynix; (ILL) OCLC WorldShare Interlibrary Loan; (OPAC) SirsiDynix; (Serials) SirsiDynix
Wireless access
Function: ILL available
Partic in LYRASIS; OCLC Online Computer Library Center, Inc; Partnership Among South Carolina Academic Libraries
Open Mon-Thurs 8am-10pm, Fri 8-5, Sat 9-12 & 1-4, Sun 3-5 & 6-9; Mon-Thurs 8am-9pm, Fri 8-5, Sat 9-12 & 1-4, Sun 3-5 & 6-9 (Summer)
Restriction: Open to students, fac & staff

P SUMTER COUNTY LIBRARY*, 111 N Harvin St, 29150. SAN 315-5943. Tel: 803-773-7273. FAX: 803-773-4875. Web Site: www.sumtercountylibrary.org. *Dir,* Robert Harden; E-mail: director@sumterlibrary.net; *Head, Children's Servx,* Julie Hynes; E-mail: sumchild1@gmail.com; *Ref Librn,* Charles Higham; E-mail: highamc@gmail.com; *Ref/ILL,* Susan Smith; E-mail: sumref1@gmail.com; *Ref & Info Serv Coordr, Webmaster,* Greg Johnson; E-mail: infoservices@sumterlibrary.net; Staff 7 (MLS 5, Non-MLS 2)
Founded 1917. Pop 107,457; Circ 266,471
Library Holdings: Bk Titles 150,000; Bk Vols 175,000; Per Subs 250
Automation Activity & Vendor Info: (Acquisitions) Innovative Interfaces, Inc; (Cataloging) Innovative Interfaces, Inc; (Circulation) Innovative Interfaces, Inc; (OPAC) Innovative Interfaces, Inc; (Serials) Innovative Interfaces, Inc
Wireless access
Function: Adult bk club, Adult literacy prog, After school storytime, Audiobks via web, Bks on cassette, Bks on CD, CD-ROM, Children's prog, Computer training, Computers for patron use, Electronic databases & coll, ILL available, Music CDs, Online cat, Photocopying/Printing, Prog for children & young adult, Ref serv available, Spoken cassettes & CDs, Story hour, Summer reading prog, Tax forms
Friends of the Library Group
Branches: 2
SOUTH SUMTER BRANCH, 337 Manning Ave, 29150, SAN 374-745X. Tel: 803-775-7132. FAX: 803-775-7132. E-mail: ssumter@sumterlibrary.net. *Br Supvr,* Margo Stukes
Library Holdings: Bk Vols 7,000
Open Mon-Fri 10-6
WESMARK BRANCH LIBRARY, 180 W Wesmark Blvd, 29150, SAN 371-9545. Tel: 803-469-8110. FAX: 803-469-8347. *Br Mgr,* Mary Pack; E-mail: branchmgr@sumterlibrary.net
Library Holdings: Bk Vols 10,000
Friends of the Library Group

C UNIVERSITY OF SOUTH CAROLINA SUMTER*, J C Anderson Library, 200 Miller Rd, 29150-2498. SAN 315-596X. Tel: 803-938-3736. FAX: 803-938-3811. Web Site: sc.edu/about/system_and_campuses/sumter/experience/library. *Libr Mgr,* Constance Pender; Tel: 803-938-3797, E-mail: penderc@uscsumter.edu; *Head Librn,* Sharon Chapman; Tel: 803-938-3810, E-mail: hamptons@uscsumter.edu
Founded 1966. Enrl 1,500
Library Holdings: Bk Vols 100,000; Per Subs 125
Automation Activity & Vendor Info: (Circulation) Innovative Interfaces, Inc - Millennium
Wireless access
Partic in Partnership Among South Carolina Academic Libraries
Open Mon-Thurs 8:30-6, Fri 8:30-1
Friends of the Library Group

TIGERVILLE

C NORTH GREENVILLE UNIVERSITY, Hester Memorial Library, 100 Donnan Blvd, 29688. (Mail add: PO Box 1892, 29688), SAN 315-5978. Tel: 864-977-7091. Reference E-mail: reference@ngu.edu. Web Site: ngu.libguides.com/home. *Dean of Libr,* Carla McMahan; E-mail: Carla.McMahan@ngu.edu; *Instruction Librn,* Lian Warner; E-mail: Lian.Warner@ngu.edu; *Ref & ILL Librn,* Leslie Brown; E-mail: Leslie.Brown@ngu.edu; *Archivist, Tech Serv Librn,* Joanna Beasley; E-mail: Joanna.Beasley@ngu.edu. Subject Specialists: *Info literacy,* Leslie Brown; *Historic presv, Oral hist,* Joanna Beasley; Staff 14 (MLS 4, Non-MLS 10)
Founded 1892. Enrl 2,200; Fac 200; Highest Degree: Doctorate
Library Holdings: Bk Titles 46,000; Bk Vols 52,000; Per Subs 426
Special Collections: Archives; Edith Duff Miller Bible Museum Coll
Wireless access
Partic in Partnership Among South Carolina Academic Libraries
Open Mon-Thurs 7:30am-Midnight, Fri 7:30-4, Sat Noon-5, Sun 6pm-11pm (Fall & Spring); Mon & Tues 8am-9pm, Wed & Thurs 8-5, Fri 8-Noon (Summer)

UNION

P UNION COUNTY CARNEGIE LIBRARY*, 300 E South St, 29379. SAN 315-5986. Tel: 864-427-7140. FAX: 864-427-4687. E-mail: info@unionlibrary.org. Web Site: www.unionlibrary.org. *Dir,* Ms Taylor Atkinson; E-mail: tatkinson@unionlibrary.org; Staff 1 (MLS 1)
Founded 1904. Pop 30,000; Circ 45,900
Library Holdings: Bk Vols 39,700; Per Subs 93
Special Collections: South Caroliniana Coll, bks & micro
Wireless access
Partic in SCLENDS
Open Mon-Thurs 8:30-12 & 1-6, Fri 9-3
Friends of the Library Group

C UNIVERSITY OF SOUTH CAROLINA AT UNION LIBRARY*, Union County Carnegie Library, 300 E South St, 29379. (Mail add: 309 E Academy St, 29379-1932), SAN 315-5994. Tel: 864-424-8016. Toll Free Tel: 800-768-5566. Web Site: sc.edu/about/system_and_campuses/union/experience/library. *Libr Dir,* Taylor Atkinson; Tel: 864-427-7140, E-mail: tatkinson@unionlibrary.org; Staff 1 (MLS 1)
Founded 1965. Enrl 930; Fac 77
Library Holdings: Bk Vols 35,000
Partic in LYRASIS; Partnership Among South Carolina Academic Libraries
Open Mon-Thurs 8:30-Noon & 1-5, Fri 9-3

WAGENER

J CHRIST CENTRAL INSTITUTE*, Library & Research Center, 110 Park St NW, 29164. (Mail add: PO Box 387, 29164). Tel: 803-564-5902, Ext 5000. Web Site: www.ccins.org. *Library Contact,* Janet Perrigo; E-mail: jperrigo@ccins.org; Staff 1 (MLS 1)
Founded 2010. Highest Degree: Associate
Library Holdings: Bk Titles 35,000; Per Subs 5
Special Collections: Greg Humphries Church History Library
Subject Interests: Relig
Wireless access

WALHALLA

P OCONEE COUNTY PUBLIC LIBRARY*, 501 W South Broad St, 29691. SAN 360-3814. Tel: 864-638-4133. FAX: 864-638-4132. Web Site: www.oconeelibrary.org. *Dir,* Blair Hinson; E-mail: bhinson@oconeesc.com; *Br Mgr,* Quientell Walker; E-mail: qwalker@oconeesc.com; *Br Librn,* Sue Andrus; E-mail: sandrus@oconeesc.com; *Tech Serv Librn,* Michael Metzger; E-mail: mmetzger@oconeesc.com; *Youth Serv Librn,* Darcy Arnall; E-mail: darnall@oconeesc.com; Staff 28 (MLS 6, Non-MLS 22)
Founded 1948. Pop 74,000; Circ 348,500
Library Holdings: Bk Vols 202,317; Per Subs 368
Special Collections: South Carolina Coll
Subject Interests: Local hist
Automation Activity & Vendor Info: (Circulation) TLC (The Library Corporation)
Wireless access
Open Mon & Tues 10-6, Wed-Fri 10-4
Friends of the Library Group
Branches: 3
SALEM BRANCH, Five-B Park Ave, Salem, 29676, SAN 360-3849. Tel: 864-944-0912. *Br Mgr,* Dan Polk; E-mail: dpolk@oconeesc.com
Open Mon 10-6, Tues-Fri 10-12 & 1-4
SENECA BRANCH, 300 E South Second St, Seneca, 29678, SAN 360-3873. Tel: 864-882-4855. FAX: 864-882-5559. *Br Mgr,* Emily Whitmire; E-mail: ewhitmire@oconeesc.com
Open Mon & Thurs 10-6, Tues, Wed & Fri 10-4
WESTMINSTER BRANCH, 112 W North Ave, Westminster, 29693, SAN 360-3903. Tel: 864-364-5760. FAX: 864-647-3233. *Br Mgr,* Leah Price; E-mail: leahprice@oconeesc.com
Open Mon 10-6, Tues-Fri 10-4
Bookmobiles: 1. Mgr, Brenda Lee

WALTERBORO

P COLLETON COUNTY MEMORIAL LIBRARY*, 600 Hampton St, 29488-4098. SAN 315-6001. Tel: 843-549-5621. FAX: 843-549-5122. E-mail: ccoffin@colletoncounty.org. Web Site: www.colletonlibrary.org. *Libr Dir,* Carl K Coffin; E-mail: ccoffin@colletoncounty.org; *Asst Dir,* TJ Grant; E-mail: tjgrant@colletoncounty.org; Staff 14 (MLS 4, Non-MLS 10)
Founded 1820. Pop 40,610; Circ 99,869
Library Holdings: CDs 369; DVDs 1,328; e-books 5,000; Electronic Media & Resources 37; Bk Vols 122,645; Per Subs 145
Special Collections: Oral History
Subject Interests: SC hist
Automation Activity & Vendor Info: (Acquisitions) Evergreen; (Cataloging) Evergreen
Wireless access
Partic in SCLENDS
Open Mon-Thurs 9-8, Fri 9-6, Sat 9-5
Friends of the Library Group
Branches: 2
COTTAGEVILLE BRANCH LIBRARY, 72 Salley Ackerman Dr, Cottageville, 29435. Tel: 843-835-5621. *Br Mgr,* Rhonda Kierpiec; Tel: 843-835-5621, E-mail: rkierpiec@colletoncounty.org
Open Tues & Thurs 4-8, Sat 10-5
EDISTO BEACH BRANCH, 71 Station Ct, Edisto Beach, 29438. (Mail add: PO Box 760, Edisto Beach, 29438). Tel: 843-869-2499. *Br Mgr,* Sherry Shipes; E-mail: sshipes@colletoncounty.org
Open Tues & Thurs 1-5, Wed 10-12:30 & 1-5
Bookmobiles: 1

WEST COLUMBIA

J MIDLANDS TECHNICAL COLLEGE LIBRARY*, Airport Library, 1260 Lexington Dr, 29170-2176. (Mail add: PO Box 2408, Columbia, 29202-2408). SAN 360-0874. Tel: 803-822-3530. FAX: 803-822-3670. E-mail: libstaff@midlandstech.edu. Web Site: www.lib.midlandstech.edu/student-resources/library. *Libr Dir, Pub Serv,* Laura Baker; Tel: 803-822-3533, E-mail: bakerl@midlandstech.edu; *Cat Librn,* Marilyn Green; Tel: 803-822-3616, E-mail: greenm@midlandstech.edu; *Serials & Database Librarian,* Brad Whitehead; Tel: 803-822-3535, E-mail: whiteheadb@midlandstech.edu; *Ref Serv,* Evelyn Burger; Tel: 803-822-3537, E-mail: burgere@midlandstech.edu; *Ref Serv,* Aleck Willians; Tel: 803-822-3674, E-mail: williamsa@midlandstech.edu; Staff 18 (MLS 10, Non-MLS 8)
Founded 1963. Enrl 12,115; Fac 233; Highest Degree: Associate
Library Holdings: AV Mats 1,249; e-books 428,000; Bk Vols 61,141; Per Subs 152
Automation Activity & Vendor Info: (Acquisitions) Ex Libris Group; (Cataloging) Ex Libris Group; (Circulation) Ex Libris Group; (OPAC) Ex Libris Group; (Serials) Ex Libris Group
Wireless access
Partic in LYRASIS; Partnership Among South Carolina Academic Libraries
Special Services for the Deaf - Closed caption videos
Special Services for the Blind - ZoomText magnification & reading software
Open Mon-Thurs 7:30-7, Fri 7:30-1:30
Departmental Libraries:
BELTLINE LIBRARY, 316 S Beltline Blvd, 2nd Flr, Columbia, 29205. (Mail add: PO Box 2408, Columbia, 29202). Tel: 803-738-7629. FAX: 803-738-7719. *Instruction Librn,* Rachel Zitzman; Tel: 803-738-7847; *Syst Librn,* Shawn Carraway; Tel: 803-738-7734, E-mail: carraways@midlandstech.edu; *Coll Develop,* Georgina Dempsey; Tel: 803-738-7626, E-mail: dempseyg@midlandstech.edu; *Pub Serv,* Erica Huff; Tel: 803-738-7762, E-mail: huffe@midlandstech.edu; *Ref Serv,* Maluck Huyen; Tel: 803-738-7812, E-mail: maluckh@midlandstech.edu; Staff 18 (MLS 10, Non-MLS 8)
Founded 1963. Enrl 10,852; Highest Degree: Associate
Library Holdings: AV Mats 1,689; e-books 22,176; Bk Vols 97,562; Per Subs 423
Special Services for the Blind - ZoomText magnification & reading software

WINNSBORO

P FAIRFIELD COUNTY LIBRARY*, 300 W Washington St, 29180. SAN 360-3938. Tel: 803-635-4971. FAX: 803-635-7715. E-mail: library@fairfieldcountylibrary.com. Web Site: fairfieldcountylibrary.com. *Dir,* Eric Robinson; E-mail: werobinson@fairfield.lib.sc.us; Staff 2 (MLS 2)
Founded 1938. Pop 23,956; Circ 63,344
Library Holdings: Audiobooks 1,814; CDs 785; DVDs 1,139; Large Print Bks 1,965; Bk Vols 77,605; Per Subs 162; Videos 3,347
Subject Interests: Hist
Automation Activity & Vendor Info: (Cataloging) Evergreen; (Circulation) Evergreen; (OPAC) Evergreen
Wireless access
Open Mon, Tues, Thurs & Fri 10-5
Friends of the Library Group
Bookmobiles: 1

YORK

S MUSEUM OF YORK COUNTY, Historical Center, 210 E Jefferson St, 29745. SAN 326-3665. Tel: 803-329-2121. Web Site: chmuseums.org/myco. *Dir, Archives,* Nancy Sambets; E-mail: nsambets@chmuseums.org; *Archives Specialist,* Rylee Aquilanti; E-mail: raquilanti@chmuseums.org; *Archives Specialist,* Carleigh Isbell; E-mail: cisbell@chmuseums.org; Staff 3 (Non-MLS 3)
Founded 1987
Library Holdings: Bk Titles 2,000; Per Subs 102
Special Collections: Hart Family Names Coll; Southern Revolutionary War Institute; York County Court Records
Subject Interests: Am Revolution, County hist, Deeds, Family hist, Local genealogy, Local newsp, Maps, Native Am of the SE
Automation Activity & Vendor Info: (Acquisitions) PastPerfect; (Cataloging) PastPerfect; (Circulation) PastPerfect
Wireless access
Function: Res libr, Res performed for a fee
Open Mon-Fri 10-4
Restriction: Non-circulating

SOUTH DAKOTA

Date of Statistics: FY 2023
Population, 2020 U.S. Census: 919,318 (Census PEP)
Population Served by Public Libraries: 829,185
Underserved: 90,133
Total Volumes in Public Libraries: 8,383,519 (total collection size includes e-materials) 2,614,983 (total book volumes)
Volumes Per Capita: 10.11 (total collection includes e-materials) 3.15 (total book volumes)
Total Public Library Circulation: 5,536,339
Circulation Per Capita: 6.68
Digital Resources:
Total e-books: 3,814,082
Total audio items (physical and downloadable units): 1,634,006
Total video items (physical and downloadable units): 181,529
Total computers for use by the public: 930
Total annual wireless sessions: 1,303,785
Income and Expenditures:
Total Public Library Income: $34,099,567
Expenditure Per Capita: $39.07
Number of Bookmobiles in State: 6 (public libraries)
Information provided courtesy of: Shawn Behrends, Data Coordinator/Outreach; South Dakota State Library.

ABERDEEN

P K O LEE ABERDEEN PUBLIC LIBRARY*, 215 S E Fourth Ave, 57401. SAN 315-6060. Tel: 605-626-7097. FAX: 605-626-3506. E-mail: library@aberdeen.sd.us. Web Site: www.aberdeen.sd.us/22/Library. *Dir,* Shirley Arment; Tel: 605-626-7997, E-mail: shirley.arment@aberdeen.sd.us; *Asst Dir, Commun Serv,* Cara Romeo; E-mail: cara.romeo@aberdeen.sd.us; *Ad,* Kim Bonen; E-mail: kim.bonen@aberdeen.sd.us; *Tech Serv Librn,* Charlene O'Malley; E-mail: charlene.omalley@aberdeen.sd.us; Staff 13 (MLS 2, Non-MLS 11)
Founded 1884. Pop 35,580; Circ 237,334
Library Holdings: Bk Vols 108,144; Per Subs 364
Special Collections: Genealogy Coll; Germans from Russia Coll; L Frank Baum Coll; Local History Coll; Railroad History Coll
Automation Activity & Vendor Info: (Cataloging) Ex Libris Group; (Circulation) Ex Libris Group; (ILL) Ex Libris Group; (OPAC) Ex Libris Group; (Serials) Ex Libris Group
Wireless access
Function: Archival coll, Bk club(s), Bks on CD, Children's prog, Computers for patron use, Electronic databases & coll, Holiday prog, Homebound delivery serv, ILL available, Magnifiers for reading, Music CDs, Notary serv, Photocopying/Printing, Prog for adults, Prog for children & young adult, Story hour, Summer reading prog, Tax forms, Teen prog
Publications: AMPL News
Partic in OCLC Online Computer Library Center, Inc; South Dakota Library Network
Special Services for the Deaf - TDD equip
Special Services for the Blind - Bks on cassette; Bks on CD; Large print bks; Magnifiers
Open Mon-Thurs 9-9, Fri 9-6, Sat 10-2

C NORTHERN STATE UNIVERSITY, Beulah Williams Library, 1200 S Jay St, 57401. SAN 315-6079. Tel: 605-626-3018. E-mail: reference@northern.edu. Web Site: northern.edu/library. *Libr Dir,* Robert Russell; Tel: 605-626-7770, E-mail: robert.russell@northern.edu; *Librn,* Lynn Klundt; E-mail: lynn.klundt@northern.edu; *Syst Librn,* Nicole Christiansen; E-mail: nicole.christiansen@northern.edu; Staff 5 (MLS 4, Non-MLS 1)
Founded 1901. Enrl 2,555; Fac 102; Highest Degree: Master
Library Holdings: Bk Titles 250,000; Per Subs 172
Special Collections: Dorothea Kerr Germans from Russia Coll; Harriet Montgomery Water Resources Coll; SD History Coll; SD National Guard Coll. Oral History; State Document Depository; US Document Depository
Subject Interests: Educ
Automation Activity & Vendor Info: (Acquisitions) Ex Libris Group; (Cataloging) Ex Libris Group; (Circulation) Ex Libris Group; (Course Reserve) Ex Libris Group; (ILL) Ex Libris Group; (Media Booking) Ex Libris Group; (OPAC) Ex Libris Group; (Serials) Ex Libris Group
Wireless access
Function: Adult bk club, After school storytime, Archival coll, Art exhibits, Audio & video playback equip for onsite use, Computers for patron use, Distance learning, Doc delivery serv, Electronic databases & coll, ILL available, Online cat, Online info literacy tutorials on the web & in blackboard, Photocopying/Printing, Ref serv available, Wheelchair accessible
Partic in Minitex; OCLC Online Computer Library Center, Inc; South Dakota Library Network
Open Mon-Thurs 7:30am-10pm, Fri 7:30-5, Sun 1pm-10pm (Fall-Spring); Mon, Wed & Fri 7:30-4:30, Thurs 7:30am-9pm (Summer)

C PRESENTATION COLLEGE LIBRARY*, 1500 N Main, 57401-1299. SAN 360-4020. Tel: 605-229-8546. Administration Tel: 605-229-8468. FAX: 605-229-8430. E-mail: pclibrary@presentation.edu. Web Site: www.presentation.edu/library.htm. *Libr Dir,* JoAnne Freitag; E-mail: JoAnne.Freitag@presentation.edu; *Tech Serv,* Karen Maier; Tel: 605-229-8498, E-mail: Karen.Maier@presentation.edu; Staff 3 (MLS 1, Non-MLS 2)
Founded 1951. Fac 60; Highest Degree: Master
Library Holdings: AV Mats 1,972; CDs 14; DVDs 125; e-journals 38,970; Bk Titles 14,275; Per Subs 6
Special Collections: 225 Music (Vinyl LPs Titles Coll)
Automation Activity & Vendor Info: (Cataloging) OCLC Worldshare Management Services; (Circulation) OCLC Worldshare Management Services; (Discovery) OCLC Worldshare Management Services; (ILL) OCLC Worldshare Management Services; (OPAC) OCLC Worldshare Management Services; (Serials) OCLC Worldshare Management Services
Wireless access
Function: 24/7 Electronic res, 24/7 Online cat, Archival coll, Computers for patron use, Distance learning, Doc delivery serv, Electronic databases & coll, Equip loans & repairs, For res purposes, ILL available, Instruction & testing, Internet access, Learning ctr, Literacy & newcomer serv, Magazines, Online cat, Online info literacy tutorials on the web & in blackboard, Orientations, Outside serv via phone, mail, e-mail & web, Photocopying/Printing, Printer for laptops & handheld devices, Prof lending libr, Ref & res, Ref serv available, Res assist avail, Res libr, Scanner, Study rm, Telephone ref, Wheelchair accessible
Partic in South Dakota Library Network
Open Mon-Thurs 7:45am-9pm, Fri 7:45-5, Sun 1-9 (Fall & Spring); Mon-Fri 8-5 (Summer)
Restriction: Authorized patrons, Borrowing requests are handled by ILL, Free to mem, ID required to use computers (Ltd hrs), Open to students, fac & staff

S SOUTH DAKOTA SCHOOL FOR THE BLIND & VISUALLY IMPAIRED*, Library Media Center, 605 14th Ave SE, 57401. SAN 325-4909. Tel: 605-626-2580. Toll Free Tel: 888-275-3814. FAX: 605-626-2607. Web Site: sdsbvi.org/Resources/SDSBVI-Resources/Library (URL won't work without caps). *Librn,* Pat Geditz; Tel: 605-626-2675, E-mail: pat.geditz@sdsbvi.northern.edu
Founded 1900
Library Holdings: Bk Vols 18,311; Per Subs 50
Special Collections: Local School Archive
Subject Interests: Blind, Deaf, Educ of the blind, Learning disabled, Mentally retarded blind, Physically handicapped, Visually handicapped

Partic in South Dakota Library Network
Special Services for the Blind - Assistive/Adapted tech devices, equip & products; Talking bks
Open Mon-Fri 8-3

ARLINGTON

P ARLINGTON COMMUNITY LIBRARY*, 306 S Main St, 57212. (Mail add: PO Box 345, 57212-0345), SAN 315-6095. Tel: 605-983-5741, Ext 230. *Librn,* Jill Christensen; E-mail: jill.m.christensen@k12.sd.us
Pop 992; Circ 2,394
Library Holdings: Bk Vols 20,000
Open Mon, Wed & Fri 8:30-6, Tues & Thurs 8:30-8, Sat 9-Noon

ARMOUR

P ARMOUR PUBLIC LIBRARY*, 915 Main St, 57313. SAN 315-6109. Tel: 605-724-2743. E-mail: citylibrary@unitelsd.com. Web Site: facebook.com/armourcarnegielibrary.
Founded 1915. Pop 1,200; Circ 9,350
Library Holdings: Bk Titles 10,400
Wireless access
Function: ILL available
Open Mon, Tues, Thurs & Fri 2-6, Wed & Sat 10-2

BELLE FOURCHE

P BELLE FOURCHE PUBLIC LIBRARY*, 905 Fifth Ave, 57717. SAN 315-6117. Tel: 605-892-4407. E-mail: library@bellefourche.org. Web Site: bellefourche.yoursdlibrary.org. *Dir,* Wanda Nelson; *Asst Librn,* Betty Casper; Staff 4 (MLS 1, Non-MLS 3)
Founded 1906. Pop 10,240; Circ 64,230
Library Holdings: Bk Titles 46,500; Per Subs 110
Special Collections: Genealogy; History of South Dakota
Automation Activity & Vendor Info: (Cataloging) Follett Software
Wireless access
Function: Bks on CD, Children's prog, Computers for patron use, Free DVD rentals, Genealogy discussion group, Home delivery & serv to seniorr ctr & nursing homes, Homebound delivery serv, ILL available, Mail & tel request accepted, Microfiche/film & reading machines, OverDrive digital audio bks, Photocopying/Printing, Prog for adults, Prog for children & young adult, Scanner, Story hour, Summer reading prog, Tax forms, Telephone ref
Partic in South Dakota Library Network
Open Mon-Thurs 10-6, Fri & Sat 10-2
Friends of the Library Group

BERESFORD

P BERESFORD PUBLIC LIBRARY*, 115 S Third St, 57004. SAN 315-6133. Tel: 605-763-2782. FAX: 605-763-2403. E-mail: books@bmtc.net. Web Site: beresfordlibrary.com. *Libr Dir,* Jane Norling; *Ch,* Annie Crist; *Asst Librn,* Barb Bailey; Staff 2 (Non-MLS 2)
Founded 1923. Pop 2,320; Circ 49,070
Library Holdings: CDs 390; DVDs 473; Bk Titles 32,300; Per Subs 72; Videos 1,000
Special Collections: South Dakota Coll
Automation Activity & Vendor Info: (Cataloging) Book Systems; (Circulation) Book Systems; (OPAC) Book Systems
Wireless access
Function: AV serv, ILL available, Photocopying/Printing, Prog for children & young adult, Summer reading prog, Workshops
Partic in Minitex
Open Mon, Wed & Fri 1-6, Tues & Thurs 10-8, Sat 9-5

BOWDLE

P BOWDLE PUBLIC LIBRARY*, 3043 Main St, 57428. (Mail add: PO Box 280, 57428-0280), SAN 315-615X. Tel: 605-285-6464. E-mail: rmbpubliclibrary@yahoo.com. *Librn,* Lydia Schnaible
Founded 1971
Library Holdings: Audiobooks 60; AV Mats 10; DVDs 423; Large Print Bks 380; Bk Vols 11,729
Wireless access
Special Services for the Blind - Bks on CD; Cassettes; Large print bks; Talking bks from Braille Inst
Open Tues-Fri 12-6, Sat 1-5
Friends of the Library Group

BRITTON

P BRITTON PUBLIC LIBRARY*, 759 Seventh St, 57430. (Mail add: PO Box 299, 57430-0299), SAN 315-6168. Tel: 605-448-2800. FAX: 605-448-2497. E-mail: brittonlibrary@venturecomm.net. Web Site: www.brittonpubliclibrary.com. *Libr Mgr,* Peggy Satrang; *Asst Librn,* Rhonda Hardina
Pop 1,393; Circ 21,970
Library Holdings: AV Mats 250; Bk Vols 15,000; Per Subs 30
Wireless access
Open Mon-Fri 9-6, Sat 9-2

BROOKINGS

P BROOKINGS PUBLIC LIBRARY*, 515 Third St, 57006. SAN 315-6176. Tel: 605-692-9407. Web Site: www.brookingslibrary.org. *Dir,* Ashia Gustafson; E-mail: agustafson@cityofbrookings.org; *Ad,* Nita Gill; E-mail: ngill@@cityofbrookings.org; *Children's Serv Coordr,* Katherine Eberline; E-mail: keberline@cityofbrookings.org; Staff 19 (MLS 5, Non-MLS 14)
Founded 1913. Pop 31,965; Circ 297,940
Library Holdings: AV Mats 16,455; e-books 8,855; Bk Titles 105,561; Per Subs 199
Special Collections: South Dakota History & Literature (South Dakota Coll)
Automation Activity & Vendor Info: (Cataloging) Ex Libris Group; (Circulation) Ex Libris Group; (ILL) Ex Libris Group; (OPAC) Ex Libris Group; (Serials) Ex Libris Group
Wireless access
Function: Adult bk club, Audiobks via web, Bk club(s), Bks on CD, CD-ROM, Computers for patron use, Digital talking bks, Free DVD rentals, Home delivery & serv to seniorr ctr & nursing homes, Homebound delivery serv, ILL available, Microfiche/film & reading machines, Music CDs, Notary serv, Online cat, OverDrive digital audio bks, Photocopying/Printing, Preschool reading prog, Prog for adults, Prog for children & young adult, Story hour, Summer & winter reading prog, Tax forms, Teen prog
Publications: News & Events at Brookings Public Library (Newsletter)
Partic in OCLC Online Computer Library Center, Inc; South Dakota Library Network
Open Mon-Thurs 9:30-9, Fri & Sat 9:30-5:30, Sun 1-5
Friends of the Library Group

C SOUTH DAKOTA STATE UNIVERSITY, Hilton M Briggs Library, 1300 N Campus Dr, Box 2115, 57007. SAN 360-408X. Tel: 605-688-5106. Reference Tel: 605-688-5107. Toll Free Tel: 800-786-2038. Reference E-mail: blref@sdstate.edu. Web Site: www.sdstate.edu/hilton-m-briggs-library. *Dean of Libr,* Kristi Tornquist; E-mail: kristi.tornquist@sdstate.edu; *Head, Pub Serv,* Position Currently Open; *Head, Tech Serv,* Enerel Dambiinyam; Tel: 605-688-5565, E-mail: enerel.dambiinyam@sdstate.edu; *Archives & Spec Coll Librn,* Michele Christian; Tel: 605-688-4906, E-mail: michele.christian@sdstate.edu; *Discovery Librn, Syst Librn,* Shari Theroux; Tel: 605-688-5560, E-mail: shari.theroux@sdstate.edu; *E-Resources Librn, Scholarly Communications Librn,* Michael Biondo; Tel: 605-688-5567, E-mail: michael.biondo@sdstate.edu; *Libr Operations Mgr,* Emmeline Elliott; Tel: 605-688-5564, E-mail: emmeline.elliot@sdstate.edu; *Digital Initiatives Coordr,* Anthony Sax; Tel: 605-688-5576, E-mail: anthony.sax@sdstate.edu; *Access Serv,* Adam Hybbert; Tel: 605-688-4049, E-mail: adam.hybbert@sdstate.edu; *Cat,* Lisa Lindell; Tel: 605-688-5561, E-mail: lisa.lindell@sdstate.edu; *Govt Doc,* Elizabeth Fox; Tel: 605-688-5569, E-mail: elizabeth.fox@sdstate.edu; *Info Serv,* Robin Daniels; Tel: 605-688-5955, E-mail: robin.daniels@sdstate.edu; *Info Serv,* Kristin Echtenkamp; Tel: 605-688-5958, E-mail: kristin.echtenkamp@sdstate.edu; *Info Serv,* Annisija Hunter; Tel: 605-688-5571, E-mail: annisija.hunter@sdstate.edu; *Info Serv,* Linda Kott; Tel: 605-688-5957, E-mail: linda.kott@sdstate.edu; *Info Serv,* Nancy Marshall; Tel: 605-688-5093, E-mail: nancy.marshall@sdstate.edu; Staff 28 (MLS 13, Non-MLS 15)
Founded 1884. Enrl 12,065; Fac 550; Highest Degree: Doctorate
Library Holdings: Bk Titles 508,955; Bk Vols 781,548
Special Collections: Elizabeth Cook-Lynn Coll; George Norby Coll; Marghab Rare Book Coll; Rep. Ben Reifel Coll; Rep. Frank Denholm Coll; Senator Tom Daschle Papers; South Dakota Cookbook Coll; South Dakota Farm Bureau & Farmers Union Locals Records. State Document Depository; US Document Depository
Automation Activity & Vendor Info: (Acquisitions) Ex Libris Group; (Cataloging) Ex Libris Group; (Circulation) Ex Libris Group; (Discovery) Ex Libris Group; (ILL) Ex Libris Group; (OPAC) Ex Libris Group; (Serials) Ex Libris Group
Wireless access
Function: 24/7 Electronic res, 24/7 Online cat, Archival coll, Art exhibits, Art programs, Computers for patron use, Doc delivery serv, Electronic databases & coll, Equip loans & repairs, Free DVD rentals, Games, Govt ref serv, Health sci info serv, ILL available, Internet access, Laptop/tablet checkout, Magazines, Meeting rooms, Microfiche/film & reading machines, Movies, Online cat, Online Chat, Online ref, Orientations, Outside serv via phone, mail, e-mail & web, Photocopying/Printing, Printer for laptops & handheld devices, Ref serv available, Res libr, Scanner, Study rm
Partic in LYRASIS; Minitex
Open Mon-Thurs 7:45am-Midnight, Fri 7:45am-9pm, Sat 10-9, Sun 1-Midnight

Restriction: Non-circulating of rare bks
Friends of the Library Group

BUFFALO

P NORTHWEST REGIONAL LIBRARY*, PO Box 26, 57720-0026. SAN 315-6125. Tel: 605-375-3835. E-mail: hclibrary@sdplains.com. Web Site: www.nwrlibrary.com. *Librn,* Vicki Anderson; Staff 1 (Non-MLS 1)
Founded 2005. Pop 1,353; Circ 10,000
Library Holdings: Bk Vols 25,000
Wireless access
Partic in South Dakota Library Network
Open Mon 10-6, Tues 9:30-5:30, Fri 3-5:30; Mon & Tues 9:30-5:30, Fri 3-5:30 (Winter)
Bookmobiles: 1

CANTON

P CANTON PUBLIC LIBRARY*, 225 N Broadway, 57013-1715. SAN 315-6184. Tel: 605-987-5831. FAX: 605-764-5831. E-mail: cpl@midconetwork.com. Web Site: www.cantonpubliclib.com. *Dir,* Tracy Zylstra; Staff 5 (MLS 1, Non-MLS 4)
Founded 1912. Pop 4,000
Library Holdings: Bk Vols 35,548; Per Subs 73
Automation Activity & Vendor Info: (Circulation) Follett Software
Wireless access
Open Mon-Wed & Fri 9-5:30, Thurs 9-7, Sat 9-1
Friends of the Library Group

CENTERVILLE

P CENTERVILLE COMMUNITY LIBRARY*, 421 Florida, 57014. (Mail add: PO Box 100, 57014-0100), SAN 315-6192. Tel: 605-563-2540. FAX: 605-563-2615. E-mail: centervillecommunitylibrary@gmail.com. *City Librn,* Linda Holmberg; *Sch Librn,* Jamie Edberg
Founded 1935. Pop 921; Circ 3,300
Library Holdings: CDs 600; DVDs 580; Large Print Bks 400; Bk Titles 27,138; Bk Vols 28,212; Per Subs 47; Talking Bks 800; Videos 700
Special Collections: Centennial Book - History of Centerville, 100 yrs; Centerville Journal Newspapers since 1903; High School Annuals
Subject Interests: Pioneer hist of Turner Co
Automation Activity & Vendor Info: (Acquisitions) Follett Software; (Cataloging) Follett Software; (Circulation) Follett Software
Function: Homebound delivery serv
Open Mon & Wed 8:30-8:30, Tues, Thurs & Fri 8:30-5:30, Sat 10-Noon

CLEAR LAKE

P CLEAR LAKE CITY LIBRARY*, 125 Third Ave S, 57226. SAN 315-6206. Tel: 605-874-2013. E-mail: library@itctel.com. Web Site: www.clearlakesd.com/directory/library. *Libr Dir,* Patti Ruby; Staff 1.4 (Non-MLS 1.4)
Founded 1899. Pop 4,522; Circ 9,396
Library Holdings: Bk Titles 17,300; Per Subs 48
Special Collections: State Document Depository
Wireless access
Function: 24/7 Electronic res, 24/7 Online cat, Accelerated reader prog, Art exhibits, Audio & video playback equip for onsite use, Audiobks via web, Bk club(s), Bks on CD, Children's prog, Computer training, Computers for patron use, Digital talking bks, Electronic databases & coll, Equip loans & repairs, Free DVD rentals, Games & aids for people with disabilities, Govt ref serv, Health sci info serv, Home delivery & serv to seniorr ctr & nursing homes, Internet access, Laminating, Large print keyboards, Magazines, Magnifiers for reading, Mail & tel request accepted, Makerspace, Online cat, Online info literacy tutorials on the web & in blackboard, Online ref, Outreach serv, Outside serv via phone, mail, e-mail & web, OverDrive digital audio bks, Photocopying/Printing, Preschool outreach, Preschool reading prog, Printer for laptops & handheld devices, Prog for children & young adult, Res assist avail, Scanner, Senior outreach, Serves people with intellectual disabilities, STEM programs, Story hour, Summer reading prog, Tax forms, Teen prog, Wheelchair accessible, Writing prog
Open Mon & Wed Noon-8, Thurs & Fri 4-8
Restriction: Borrowing privileges limited to fac & registered students, Circ to mem only, Free to mem

CRAZY HORSE

S CRAZY HORSE MEMORIAL LIBRARY*, 12151 Avenue of the Chiefs, 57730-8900. SAN 315-6141. Tel: 605-673-4681. FAX: 605-673-2185. E-mail: memorial@crazyhorse.org. Web Site: crazyhorsememorial.org. *Librn,* Marguerite Cullum; Tel: 605-673-4681, Ext 285, E-mail: marguerite.cullum@crazyhorse.org; Staff 1 (MLS 1)
Founded 1973
Subject Interests: Art, Art hist, Hist, Native North American Indians, Western US hist
Automation Activity & Vendor Info: (Acquisitions) Follett Software; (Cataloging) Follett Software; (Circulation) Follett Software
Wireless access
Publications: Newsletter (Quarterly)
Restriction: Authorized scholars by appt, By permission only, Circ privileges for students & alumni only, Circulates for staff only, External users must contact libr, Non-circulating to the pub, Researchers by appt only, Restricted borrowing privileges, Secured area only open to authorized personnel, Visitors must make appt to use bks in the libr

CUSTER

P CUSTER COUNTY LIBRARY*, 447 Crook St, Ste 4, 57730. SAN 315-6214. Tel: 605-673-4803. FAX: 605-673-2385. E-mail: cuslib@gwtc.net. Web Site: custercountylibrary.org. *Libr Dir,* Jessica Phelps
Founded 1943. Pop 8,217; Circ 37,711
Special Collections: Black Hills Area History Coll; George Armstrong Custer Coll
Automation Activity & Vendor Info: (Acquisitions) Follett Software; (Cataloging) Follett Software; (Circulation) Follett Software; (OPAC) Follett Software
Wireless access
Partic in Black Hills Library Consortium
Open Mon, Tues, Thurs & Fri 11-5:30, Wed 3-7, Sat 10-3
Branches: 1
HERMOSA BRANCH, 234 Main St, Hermosa, 57744. (Mail add: PO Box 288, Hermosa, 57744). Tel: 605-255-5597. FAX: 605-255-5597. E-mail: hermosalib@custercountysd.com. *Br Dir,* Roberta Phillip
Open Mon, Wed & Fri 12:30-6:30

DE SMET

P HAZEL L MEYER MEMORIAL LIBRARY*, 114 First St, 57231. (Mail add: PO Box 156, 57231-0156), SAN 315-6222. Tel: 605-854-3842. FAX: 605-854-3842. E-mail: hlmlib@mchsi.com. Web Site: www.cityofdesmet.com/library. *Dir,* Mary Purintun
Founded 1937. Pop 1,800; Circ 30,887
Library Holdings: Bks on Deafness & Sign Lang 10; High Interest/Low Vocabulary Bk Vols 50; Bk Titles 19,797; Bk Vols 20,395; Per Subs 72; Spec Interest Per Sub 20
Special Collections: Harvey Dunn Original Paintings (5); Laura Ingalls Wilder Memorabilia
Wireless access
Special Services for the Blind - Audio mat; Large print bks
Open Mon, Tues, Thurs & Fri 12:30-5, Wed 12:30-6

DEADWOOD

P DEADWOOD PUBLIC LIBRARY*, 435 Williams St, 57732-2821. SAN 315-6230. Tel: 605-578-2821. FAX: 605-578-2071. E-mail: deadwoodlibrary@outlook.com. Web Site: www.cityofdeadwood.com/library. *Dir,* Patricia Brown; Staff 4 (MLS 1, Non-MLS 3)
Founded 1895
Library Holdings: High Interest/Low Vocabulary Bk Vols 256; Bk Titles 14,481; Bk Vols 14,652; Per Subs 61
Special Collections: Black Hills History; Centennial Archive Coll, black & white photog; Historic Local Newspapers, micro/newsp; Round Table Club scrapbooks; South Dakota History
Subject Interests: Local hist, SDak
Automation Activity & Vendor Info: (Cataloging) Koha; (Circulation) Koha; (ILL) PALS; (OPAC) Koha
Wireless access
Function: 24/7 Electronic res, 24/7 Online cat, Activity rm, Adult bk club, After school storytime, Audio & video playback equip for onsite use, Audiobks via web, Bks on CD, Children's prog, Computer training, Computers for patron use, Digital talking bks, Electronic databases & coll, Free DVD rentals, Govt ref serv, ILL available, Internet access, Laminating, Life-long learning prog for all ages, Magazines, Magnifiers for reading, Mail & tel request accepted, Microfiche/film & reading machines, Movies, Online cat, OverDrive digital audio bks, Preschool outreach, Preschool reading prog, Printer for laptops & handheld devices, Prog for adults, Prog for children & young adult, Ref & res, Res assist avail, Res performed for a fee, Scanner, Story hour, Summer reading prog, Tax forms, Wheelchair accessible
Publications: Index to Deadwood Newspapers (Local historical information)
Partic in Black Hills Library Consortium
Special Services for the Blind - Large screen computer & software
Friends of the Library Group

DELL RAPIDS

P CARNEGIE PUBLIC LIBRARY*, 513 N Orleans Ave, 57022-1637. SAN 315-6249. Tel: 605-428-3595. FAX: 605-428-3735. E-mail: plibrary@siouxvalley.net. Web Site: www.cityofdellrapids.org/departments/dell_rapids_carnegie_library. *Libr Dir,* Brittany Moeller; Staff 4 (Non-MLS 4)
Founded 1910. Pop 5,000; Circ 35,818
Library Holdings: Bk Titles 19,520; Bk Vols 21,688; Per Subs 60
Subject Interests: SDak hist
Wireless access
Open Mon-Thurs 8:30-7, Fri 8:30-5, Sat 9-Noon
Friends of the Library Group

EDGEMONT

P EDGEMONT PUBLIC LIBRARY*, 412 Second Ave, 57735. (Mail add: PO Box A, 57735), SAN 315-6257. Tel: 605-662-7712. FAX: 605-662-7922. E-mail: edgemont@gwtc.net. Web Site: www.edgemontlibrary.org. *Libr Dir,* Samantha Miller; *Asst Librn,* Agnes Reecy
Founded 1917. Pop 870; Circ 7,539
Library Holdings: Bk Titles 22,855; Bk Vols 23,440; Per Subs 12
Special Collections: South Dakota Coll
Subject Interests: Local hist
Automation Activity & Vendor Info: (Circulation) Follett Software
Wireless access
Partic in Black Hills Library Consortium
Open Mon-Fri 10-12 & 1-5

ELLSWORTH AFB

A UNITED STATES AIR FORCE*, Holbrook Library, Ellsworth Air Force Base FL4690, 28 FSS/FSDL, 2650 Doolittle Dr, Bldg 3910, 57706-4820. SAN 360-4144. Tel: 605-385-1686, 605-385-1688. FAX: 605-385-4467. Web Site: www.ellsworthfss.com/funandfood/holbrook-library. *Libr Dir, Supvry Librn,* Jeanne M Stoltenburg; E-mail: jeanne.stoltenburg@us.af.mil; *Syst Spec,* Tim Herdt; E-mail: tim.herdt@us.af.mil; Staff 2 (MLS 1, Non-MLS 1)
Founded 1969. Pop 4,659
Library Holdings: Audiobooks 1,095; AV Mats 2,563; CDs 500; DVDs 1,000; e-books 5,971; Bk Titles 40,000; Bk Vols 42,180; Per Subs 25; Videos 250
Automation Activity & Vendor Info: (Acquisitions) SirsiDynix; (Cataloging) SirsiDynix-WorkFlows; (Circulation) SirsiDynix-WorkFlows; (Course Reserve) SirsiDynix; (ILL) OCLC FirstSearch; (Media Booking) SirsiDynix; (OPAC) SirsiDynix-iBistro; (Serials) SirsiDynix
Wireless access
Function: Audio & video playback equip for onsite use, Audiobks via web, Bks on CD, Children's prog, Computer training, Computers for patron use, Electronic databases & coll, Free DVD rentals, Holiday prog, Homework prog, ILL available, Internet access, Music CDs, Online cat, Orientations, Outreach serv, OverDrive digital audio bks, Preschool outreach, Prog for adults, Prog for children & young adult, Ref & res, Ref serv available, Scanner, Story hour, Summer & winter reading prog, Summer reading prog, Tax forms, Teen prog, VHS videos, Wheelchair accessible
Publications: LARP (Annual report)
Open Mon-Fri 8:30-4:30

EUREKA

P KATHRYN SCHULKOSKI LIBRARY*, 613 Seventh St, 57437. (Mail add: PO Box 655, 57437-0655), SAN 315-6273. Tel: 605-284-2863. E-mail: kslibrary@valleytel.net. *Librn,* John R Nelson; Tel: 763-439-4093, E-mail: desktoptypography@gmail.com
Founded 1932. Pop 2,900; Circ 10,232
Library Holdings: Large Print Bks 65; Bk Vols 13,311; Per Subs 15; Talking Bks 49; Videos 281
Open Mon & Wed 6pm-9pm, Thurs & Sat 2-5

FAITH

P FAITH PUBLIC & SCHOOL LIBRARY*, 204 W Fifth St, 57626. (Mail add: PO Box 172, 57626-0172), SAN 326-5587. Tel: 605-967-2262. FAX: 605-967-2264. Web Site: faithsdlibrary.weebly.com. *Librn,* Heather Van Der Linden; E-mail: heather.vanderlinden@k12.sd.us; Staff 1 (Non-MLS 1)
Founded 1924. Pop 576; Circ 24,059
Library Holdings: Bk Titles 17,500
Special Collections: South Dakota. Oral History
Automation Activity & Vendor Info: (Cataloging) Follett Software; (Circulation) Follett Software
Wireless access
Partic in South Dakota Library Network
Open Mon-Thurs 8-6; Mon-Thurs 9-5 (Summer)
Friends of the Library Group

FLANDREAU

P MOODY COUNTY RESOURCE CENTER*, 610 W Community Dr, 57028. SAN 315-6281. Tel: 605-997-3326. Web Site: www.flandreau.k12.sd.us/mcrc. *Commun Librn,* Erica Rorvik; E-mail: erica.rorvik@k12.sd.us
Founded 1988. Circ 21,800
Library Holdings: Bk Titles 25,000; Per Subs 37
Special Collections: South Dakota Author Coll
Subject Interests: Local newsp
Wireless access
Open Mon & Fri 9-5, Tues-Thurs 9-8, Sat 9-2
Branches: 1
COLMAN BRANCH, 120 N Main Ave, Colman, 57017. (Mail add: PO Box 64, Colman, 57017), SAN 321-8740. Tel: 605-534-3154. *Librn,* Susan Brende
Open Wed 2-7, Sat 10-3

FREEMAN

P FREEMAN PUBLIC LIBRARY*, 322 S Main St, 57029. (Mail add: PO Box I, 57029), SAN 315-6311. Tel: 605-925-7003. FAX: 605-925-7127. E-mail: freemanlibrary@goldenwest.net. Web Site: www.freemanlibrary.org. *Libr Dir,* LeAnn L Kaufman; Staff 1 (Non-MLS 1)
Founded 1939. Pop 1,317; Circ 16,155
Library Holdings: DVDs 1,200; Bk Titles 14,326
Special Collections: Freeman, SD materials
Subject Interests: Germans in Russia from SDak, Hutterites, Mennonites, SDak hist
Automation Activity & Vendor Info: (Cataloging) Follett Software; (Circulation) Follett Software
Wireless access
Function: Adult bk club, Bks on CD, Children's prog, Computers for patron use, Electronic databases & coll, ILL available, Photocopying/Printing, Story hour, Summer reading prog, Wheelchair accessible
Partic in South Dakota Library Network
Open Mon, Wed & Fri 9-5:30, Tues & Thurs 9-7, Sat 9-2:30
Friends of the Library Group

GETTYSBURG

P POTTER COUNTY LIBRARY*, 205 W Commercial Ave, 57442. SAN 315-6338. Tel: 605-765-9518. E-mail: pclibrary@venturecomm.net. Web Site: pottercounty.yoursdlibrary.org. *Dir,* Barbara Vander Vorst; *Librn,* Connie Pearman
Founded 1923. Pop 3,400; Circ 35,000
Library Holdings: Large Print Bks 900; Bk Vols 25,700; Per Subs 35; Talking Bks 800
Special Collections: Potter County Obituaries 1883-2006
Wireless access
Special Services for the Blind - Large print bks; Talking bks
Open Mon-Wed & Fri 10-5, Thurs 10-6, Sat 10-1
Bookmobiles: 1. Libr, Holly Wright

GREGORY

P GREGORY PUBLIC LIBRARY*, 112 E Fifth, 57533-1463. (Mail add: PO Box 306, 57533), SAN 315-6346. Tel: 605-835-8531. FAX: 605-835-9575. E-mail: gregorylibrary@gmail.com. Web Site: www.gregorylibrary.com. *Dir & Head Librn,* Tara Engel
Founded 1926. Pop 1,384; Circ 14,000
Library Holdings: AV Mats 1,100; Large Print Bks 200; Bk Titles 10,327; Bk Vols 11,705; Per Subs 11; Talking Bks 75
Special Collections: Oral History
Subject Interests: Local hist
Wireless access
Open Mon & Tues Noon-5, Wed 10-5, Thurs Noon-7, Sat 10-2
Friends of the Library Group

HIGHMORE

P HYDE COUNTY LIBRARY, 107 Commercial SE, 57345. (Mail add: PO Box 479, 57345-0479), SAN 315-6354. Tel: 605-852-2514. E-mail: hydelib2@venturecomm.net. Web Site: hydecounty.yoursdlibrary.org. *Libr Dir,* Tina Hamlin; Staff 2 (Non-MLS 2)
Founded 1918. Pop 1,318; Circ 18,307
Library Holdings: Bk Vols 13,457; Per Subs 27
Wireless access
Function: After school storytime, Art programs, AV serv, Bks on CD, Children's prog, Computers for patron use, For res purposes, Free DVD rentals, Holiday prog, Homebound delivery serv, ILL available, Internet access, Magazines, Movies, Preschool reading prog, Prog for adults, Prog for children & young adult, Ref & res, Ref serv available, Res assist avail, Story hour, Summer reading prog

Special Services for the Blind - Bks on cassette; Large print bks
Open Mon-Fri 12-5

HILL CITY

P HILL CITY PUBLIC LIBRARY*, 341 Main St, 57745. (Mail add: PO Box 88, 57745). Tel: 605-574-4529. FAX: 605-574-4529. E-mail: hcpubliclibrary@hillcitysd.org. Web Site: www.hillcitysd.com/city-government/departments/public-library. *Dir,* Tammy Alexander
Library Holdings: Bk Vols 11,852; Per Subs 18
Automation Activity & Vendor Info: (Cataloging) Follett Software; (Circulation) Follett Software; (OPAC) Follett Software
Wireless access
Open Mon-Thurs 9:15-6, Fri 9-5, Sat 9-2

HOT SPRINGS

P HOT SPRINGS PUBLIC LIBRARY*, 2005 Library Dr, 57747-2767. SAN 315-6362. Tel: 605-745-3151. FAX: 605-745-6813. E-mail: hsplib@hs-sd.org. Web Site: www.hotspringspubliclibrary.com. *Libr Dir,* Mary Terrones
Founded 1898. Circ 16,278
Library Holdings: Bk Vols 25,000
Subject Interests: SDak hist
Automation Activity & Vendor Info: (Cataloging) Follett Software; (Circulation) Follett Software; (OPAC) Follett Software; (Serials) Follett Software
Wireless access
Open Mon, Thurs & Fri 10-5:30, Tues & Wed 11:30-7, Sat 10-2
Friends of the Library Group

HURON

P HURON PUBLIC LIBRARY*, 521 Dakota Ave S, 57350. SAN 315-6400. Tel: 605-353-8530. FAX: 605-353-8532. E-mail: myhpl@libraryhuronsd.com. Web Site: hpl.huronsd.gov. *Libr Dir,* Angela Bailey; E-mail: librarydirector@libraryhuronsd.com; *Asst Dir/Tech Librn,* Alex Gigov; E-mail: tad@libraryhuronsd.com. Subject Specialists: *Admin,* Angela Bailey; Staff 9 (MLS 3, Non-MLS 6)
Founded 1907. Pop 13,696; Circ 168,118
Jan 2021-Dec 2021 Income (Main Library Only) $1,012,013, City $944,280, Other $67,733. Mats Exp $145,000, Books $82,000, Per/Ser (Incl. Access Fees) $6,000, AV Mat $22,000, Electronic Ref Mat (Incl. Access Fees) $35,000. Sal $496,017
Library Holdings: Audiobooks 3,761; DVDs 3,745; e-books 46,886; Large Print Bks 6,256; Microforms 566; Bk Titles 56,111; Per Subs 108; Talking Bks 350
Special Collections: Local Newspaper, 1888-present on microfilm; South Dakota Coll, bks, mats
Subject Interests: SDak hist
Automation Activity & Vendor Info: (Acquisitions) Book Systems; (Cataloging) Book Systems; (Circulation) Book Systems; (ILL) OCLC ILLiad; (OPAC) Book Systems; (Serials) Book Systems
Wireless access
Function: 24/7 Electronic res, 24/7 Online cat, 3D Printer, Activity rm, Adult bk club, After school storytime, Archival coll, Art exhibits, Audiobks on Playaways & MP3, Audiobks via web, AV serv, Bk club(s), Bks on CD, Children's prog, Computers for patron use, Digital talking bks, E-Readers, E-Reserves, Electronic databases & coll, Equip loans & repairs, For res purposes, Free DVD rentals, Genealogy discussion group, Health sci info serv, Holiday prog, Home delivery & serv to seniorr ctr & nursing homes, Homebound delivery serv, ILL available, Instruction & testing, Internet access, Large print keyboards, Magazines, Magnifiers for reading, Mail & tel request accepted, Meeting rooms, Microfiche/film & reading machines, Movies, Notary serv, Online cat, Online ref, Orientations, Outreach serv, Outside serv via phone, mail, e-mail & web, OverDrive digital audio bks, Photocopying/Printing, Preschool outreach, Preschool reading prog, Prog for adults, Prog for children & young adult, Ref & res, Ref serv available, Res assist avail, Res libr, Res performed for a fee, Scanner, Spanish lang bks, STEM programs, Story hour, Summer & winter reading prog, Summer reading prog, Tax forms, Teen prog, Telephone ref, Wheelchair accessible, Winter reading prog, Workshops, Writing prog
Open Mon-Thurs 9-8, Fri & Sat 9-5
Friends of the Library Group

IPSWICH

P MARCUS P BEEBE MEMORIAL LIBRARY*, 120 Main St, 57451. SAN 315-6427. Tel: 605-426-6707. E-mail: mpblibrary@abe.midco.net. Web Site: ipswichsd.yoursdlibrary.org, www.facebook.com/mpblibrary. *Librn,* Ruby Bosanko
Founded 1886. Pop 2,000; Circ 17,580
Jan 2021-Dec 2021 Income $38,500. Mats Exp $4,000. Sal $18,000
Library Holdings: Bk Vols 19,542; Per Subs 12
Wireless access
Open Tues-Sat 2-6

KADOKA

P JACKSON COUNTY LIBRARY, 910 Main St, 57543. (Mail add: PO Box 368, 57543-0368), SAN 360-4381. Tel: 605-837-2689. E-mail: jclibrary2000@gmail.com. Web Site: jacksoncounty.yoursdlibrary.org. *Dir,* Arlene Hicks
Founded 1962. Pop 3,031; Circ 4,465
Wireless access
Open Tues-Thurs 8:30-12:30 & 2-5 or by appointment
Friends of the Library Group

KENNEBEC

P KENNEBEC PUBLIC LIBRARY, 203 S Main St, 57544. (Mail add: PO Box 111, 57544-0061), SAN 315-6435. Tel: 605-869-2207. E-mail: kennebeclibrary@kennebectelephone.com. Web Site: kennebec.yoursdlibrary.org. *Dir,* Angelique Hickey
Pop 700; Circ 12,810
Library Holdings: AV Mats 156; Bk Vols 13,575
Wireless access
Open Mon, Tues & Thurs 8-1, Wed 2-7

KEYSTONE

P KEYSTONE TOWN LIBRARY*, 1101 Madill St, 57751. Tel: 605-666-4499. E-mail: keystone@mt-rushmore.net. Web Site: keystone.yoursdlibrary.org.
Automation Activity & Vendor Info: (Cataloging) Koha; (OPAC) Koha
Wireless access
Function: Computers for patron use, Magazines, Photocopying/Printing, Ref & res, Summer reading prog
Partic in Black Hills Library Consortium
Open Tues, Wed & Fri 12-6, Thurs 2-7, Sat 10-4

KYLE

J OGLALA LAKOTA COLLEGE*, Woksape Tipi Academic/Public Library & Archives, Three Mile Creek Rd, 57752. (Mail add: PO Box 310, 57752), SAN 321-2319. Tel: 605-455-6069. FAX: 605-455-6070. Web Site: library.olc.edu. *Dir,* Michelle May; Tel: 605-455-6064, E-mail: mmay@olc.edu; *Asst Dir,* Sharon Janis; Tel: 605-455-6067, E-mail: sharonrjanis@olc.edu; *Archivist,* Tawa Ducheneaux; Tel: 605-455-6065, E-mail: tducheneaux@olc.edu; *Asst Archivist,* Ellen White Thunder; Tel: 605-455-6063, E-mail: ewhitethunder@olc.edu; *Circ & ILL,* Darlene Bear Killer; Tel: 605-455-6069, E-mail: dbearkiller@olc.edu; Staff 3 (Non-MLS 3)
Founded 1970
Library Holdings: Bk Titles 46,000; Per Subs 80
Special Collections: Oral History
Subject Interests: Archives
Wireless access
Publications: Policy & Procedures Manual (Library instruction & skills); Specialized Bibliographies of North American Indians & Related Archival Materials
Partic in American Indian Higher Education Consortium; OCLC Online Computer Library Center, Inc; South Dakota Library Network
Open Mon-Fri 8:30-5

Departmental Libraries:

EAGLE NEST COLLEGE CENTER, PO Box 476, Wanblee, 57577, SAN 321-5407. Tel: 605-462-6274. FAX: 605-462-6105. Web Site: www.olc.edu/centers/eagle_nest.htm. *Dir,* Georgia Rooks; E-mail: grooks@olc.edu
Library Holdings: Bk Vols 1,500
Open Mon-Thurs 8:30-8, Fri 8:30-5

EAST WAKPAMNI COLLEGE CENTER, PO Box 612, Batesland, 57716, SAN 321-5857. Tel: 605-288-1834. FAX: 605-288-1828. Web Site: www.olc.edu/centers/east_wapamni.htm. *Dir,* Colleen Provost; E-mail: cprovost@olc.edu
Library Holdings: Bk Vols 1,100
Open Mon-Thurs 8:30-8, Fri 8:30-5

HE SAPA COLLEGE CENTER, 127 Knollwood Dr, Rapid City, 57709. Tel: 605-342-1513. FAX: 605-342-8547. Web Site: www.olc.edu/centers/he_sapa.htm. *Dir,* Jackie Alcantar; E-mail: jalcantar@olc.edu
Library Holdings: Bk Vols 1,500
Open Mon-Thurs 8:30-8, Fri 8:30-5

LACREEK COLLEGE CENTER, PO Box 629, Martin, 57551, SAN 321-5881. Tel: 605-685-6407. FAX: 605-685-6887. Web Site: www.olc.edu/centers/lacreek.htm. *Dir,* Keely Clausen; E-mail: kclausen@olc.edu
Library Holdings: Bk Vols 1,300
Open Mon-Thurs 8:30-8, Fri 8:30-5

NURSING COLLEGE CENTER, PO Box 861, Pine Ridge, 57770, SAN 321-592X. Tel: 605-867-5856. FAX: 605-867-5724. Web Site: www.olc.edu/centers/pine_ridge.htm. *Chairperson,* Robin White; E-mail: rwhite@olc.edu
Library Holdings: Bk Vols 2,000
Open Mon-Fri 8:30-5

OGLALA COLLEGE CENTER, PO Box 19, Oglala, 57764, SAN 321-5903. Tel: 605-867-5780. FAX: 605-867-1243. Web Site: www.olc.edu/centers/ogala.htm. *Dir,* Paulina Fast Wolf; E-mail: pfastwolf@olc.edu
Library Holdings: Bk Vols 1,000
Open Mon-Thurs 8:30-8, Fri 8:30-5

PAHIN SINTE COLLEGE CENTER, PO Box 220, Porcupine, 57772, SAN 321-589X. Tel: 605-867-5404. FAX: 605-867-1242. Web Site: www.olc.edu/centers/pahin_sinte.htm. *Dir,* Avanelle No Braid; E-mail: anobraid@olc.edu
Library Holdings: Bk Vols 1,200
Open Mon-Thurs 8:30-8, Fri 8:30-5

PASS CREEK COLLEGE CENTER, PO Box 630, Allen, 57714, SAN 321-5849. Tel: 605-455-2757. FAX: 605-455-2428. Web Site: www.olc.edu/centers/pass_creek.htm. *Dir,* Leslie Heathershaw; E-mail: lheathershaw@olc.edu
Library Holdings: Bk Vols 1,300
Open Mon-Thurs 8:30-8, Fri 8:30-5

PEJUTA HAKA COLLEGE CENTER, PO Box 370, 57752-0370, SAN 321-5865. Tel: 605-455-2450. FAX: 605-455-2671. Web Site: www.olc.edu/centers/pejuta_haka.htm. *Dir,* Stephanie Sorbel; E-mail: stephsorbel@olc.edu
Library Holdings: Bk Vols 1,400
Open Mon-Thurs 8:30-8, Fri 8:30-5

PINE RIDGE COLLEGE CENTER, PO Box 1052, Pine Ridge, 57770, SAN 321-5911. Tel: 605-867-5893. FAX: 605-867-1241. Web Site: www.olc.edu/centers/pine_ridge.htm. *Dir,* Lena Goings
Library Holdings: Bk Vols 2,500
Open Mon-Thurs 8:30-8, Fri 8:30-5

WOUNDED KNEE COLLEGE CENTER, PO Box 230, Manderson, 57756, SAN 321-5873. Tel: 605-867-5352. FAX: 605-867-1245. Web Site: www.olc.edu/centers/wounded_knee.htm. *Dir,* Brian Dodge; E-mail: bdodge@olc.edu
Library Holdings: Bk Vols 1,100
Open Mon-Thurs 8;30-8, Fri 8:30-5

LAKE ANDES

P LAKE ANDES CARNEGIE PUBLIC LIBRARY*, 500 Main St, 57356. (Mail add: PO Box 248, 57356-0248), SAN 315-6443. Tel: 605-487-7524. E-mail: lalibrary@hcinet.net. *Head Librn,* Mary Jo Parker; *Asst Librn,* William Pontius
Founded 1912. Pop 1,500; Circ 6,358
Library Holdings: AV Mats 167; Bk Vols 10,866; Per Subs 23
Wireless access
Open Mon, Tues & Thurs-Sat 1-5:30, Wed 10-12:30 & 1-5:30

LEAD

P PHOEBE APPERSON HEARST LIBRARY - LEAD LIBRARY*, 315 W Main, 57754. SAN 315-6451. Tel: 605-584-2013. E-mail: library@cityoflead.com. Web Site: lead.yoursdlibrary.org. *Dir,* Cyndie Harlan
Founded 1894. Pop 3,500; Circ 12,744
Library Holdings: Bk Titles 17,574; Per Subs 60; Talking Bks 1,157; Videos 766
Special Collections: Curran Coll; Foreign Language Coll; Local History & Mining Records; Ralph G Cartwright Coll
Automation Activity & Vendor Info: (Cataloging) Koha; (Circulation) Koha
Wireless access
Partic in South Dakota Library Network
Open Mon, Thurs & Fri 10-5, Tues & Wed 10-6, Sat 9-12

LEMMON

P LEMMON PUBLIC LIBRARY*, 303 First Ave W, 57638. (Mail add: PO Box 120, 57638-0120), SAN 315-646X. Tel: 605-374-5611. E-mail: lemmonlibrary@sdplains.com. Web Site: www.lemmonsdlibrary.com. *Dir & Librn,* Raven Christman; Staff 1 (Non-MLS 1)
Founded 1919. Pop 1,500; Circ 14,200
Library Holdings: Bk Vols 35,000; Per Subs 33
Automation Activity & Vendor Info: (Circulation) Follett Software
Wireless access
Function: 24/7 Online cat, Audiobks via web, Bk club(s), Bks on CD, Children's prog, Computers for patron use, Electronic databases & coll, Free DVD rentals, Home delivery & serv to seniorr ctr & nursing homes, Homebound delivery serv, ILL available, Internet access, Laminating, Magazines, Mail & tel request accepted, Makerspace, Online cat, Photocopying/Printing, Prog for adults, Prog for children & young adult, Ref & res, Res assist avail, Scanner, Story hour, Study rm, Summer & winter reading prog, Summer reading prog, Tax forms, Teen prog
Open Mon, Tues & Thurs Noon-6, Wed Noon-8, Fri 9-5 (Winter); Mon-Thurs 9-5, Fri 9-1 (Summer)

LEOLA

P LEOLA PUBLIC LIBRARY, 802 Main St, 57456. SAN 315-6478. Tel: 605-439-3383. E-mail: leolalibrary@valleytel.net. Web Site: www.leolasd.com/leola-library.html. *Head Librn,* Pam Walz
Founded 1968. Pop 521; Circ 28,500
Library Holdings: Bk Vols 8,400
Special Collections: Oral History
Wireless access
Open Mon 1-5:30, Tues-Thurs 1-6

MADISON

C DAKOTA STATE UNIVERSITY, Karl E Mundt Library, 820 N Washington Ave, 57042. SAN 315-6494. Tel: 605-256-5203. Interlibrary Loan Service Tel: 605-256-5205. Reference Tel: 605-256-7128. FAX: 605-256-5208. Reference E-mail: reference@dsu.edu. Web Site: library.dsu.edu. *Libr Dir,* Mary Francis; E-mail: mary.francis@dsu.edu; *Ref & Instruction Librn,* Rachelle McPhillips; E-mail: rachelle.mcphillips@dsu.edu; *Research & Scholarship Librn,* Abbie Steuhm; E-mail: abbie.steuhm@dsu.edu; *Tech Serv Librn,* Ellen Hoff; E-mail: ellen.hoff@dsu.edu; Staff 6 (MLS 3, Non-MLS 3)
Founded 1881. Enrl 3,003; Fac 93; Highest Degree: Doctorate
Library Holdings: Bk Titles 77,117; Bk Vols 178,240; Per Subs 382
Special Collections: Senator Karl E Mundt Archives; South Dakota Coll; University Archives. Oral History
Automation Activity & Vendor Info: (Acquisitions) Ex Libris Group; (Cataloging) Ex Libris Group; (Circulation) Ex Libris Group; (ILL) Ex Libris Group; (Media Booking) Ex Libris Group; (OPAC) Ex Libris Group; (Serials) Ex Libris Group
Wireless access
Function: Adult bk club, Archival coll, Art exhibits, Audio & video playback equip for onsite use, AV serv, Bk club(s), Bks on CD, Computers for patron use, Digital talking bks, Distance learning, Doc delivery serv, Electronic databases & coll, Equip loans & repairs, Free DVD rentals, ILL available, Instruction & testing, Internet access, Mail & tel request accepted, Mail loans to mem, Online cat, Online info literacy tutorials on the web & in blackboard, Online ref, Orientations, Outreach serv, Photocopying/Printing, Ref & res, Ref serv available, Satellite serv, Scanner, Tax forms, Telephone ref, Workshops
Partic in OCLC Online Computer Library Center, Inc; South Dakota Library Network
Open Mon-Thurs 8am-11pm, Fri 8-5, Sat & Sun 5pm-11pm (Fall-Spring); Mon-Fri 7:30-4:30 (Summer)
Restriction: 24-hr pass syst for students only, In-house use for visitors, Open to pub for ref & circ; with some limitations, Open to students, fac & staff

P MADISON PUBLIC LIBRARY*, 209 E Center St, 57042. SAN 315-6508. Tel: 605-256-7525. FAX: 605-256-7526. E-mail: madisonpubliclibrary@gmail.com. Web Site: www.madisonpubliclibrarysd.com. *Libr Dir,* Nancy Sabbe; E-mail: nancy.sabbe@cityofmadisonsd.com; *Ch,* Lisa Martin; E-mail: lisa.martin@cityofmadisonsd.com; *ILL,* Melanie Argo; E-mail: melanie.argo@cityofmadisonsd.com; Staff 2 (MLS 1, Non-MLS 1)
Founded 1906. Pop 11,276; Circ 80,000
Library Holdings: Audiobooks 4,597; AV Mats 5,239; DVDs 3,898; Bk Titles 51,645; Per Subs 151
Special Collections: South Dakota-Lake County (Dakota Coll)
Automation Activity & Vendor Info: (Cataloging) OCLC Connexion; (Circulation) Ex Libris Group; (ILL) Ex Libris Group; (OPAC) SerialsSolutions
Wireless access
Function: Art exhibits, Bks on cassette, Bks on CD, Children's prog, Computers for patron use, Electronic databases & coll, Free DVD rentals, ILL available, Microfiche/film & reading machines, Online cat, Outreach serv, OverDrive digital audio bks, Photocopying/Printing, Preschool outreach, Preschool reading prog, Printer for laptops & handheld devices, Prog for adults, Prog for children & young adult, Ref serv available, Spoken cassettes & CDs, Story hour, Summer reading prog, Tax forms
Partic in South Dakota Library Network
Open Mon-Thurs 10-9, Fri 10-5, Sat 10-5; Mon-Thurs 10-9, Fri 10-5, Sat 10-1 (Summer)
Friends of the Library Group

MARTIN

P BENNETT COUNTY LIBRARY*, 101 Main St, 57551. (Mail add: PO Box 190, 57551-0190), SAN 315-6516. Tel: 605-685-6556. FAX: 605-685-6311. *Librn,* Belinda Ready; E-mail: belinda.ready@k12.sd.us
Founded 1951. Pop 4,000; Circ 19,304

Library Holdings: Audiobooks 900; Bk Vols 30,000; Per Subs 30
Automation Activity & Vendor Info: (Circulation) Follett Software
Wireless access
Open Mon-Fri 8-5, Sat 9:30-4
Friends of the Library Group

MILBANK

P GRANT COUNTY PUBLIC LIBRARY*, 207 E Park Ave, 57252. SAN 315-6532. Tel: 605-432-6543. FAX: 605-432-4635. E-mail: gclibrary21@hotmail.com. Web Site: grantcountylibrary.com. *Dir,* Jody Carlson; Staff 7 (Non-MLS 7)
Founded 1979. Pop 8,200; Circ 108,137
Library Holdings: Audiobooks 1,324; AV Mats 2,898; Bks on Deafness & Sign Lang 15; DVDs 1,380; e-books 16,000; Large Print Bks 4,870; Microforms 143; Bk Titles 59,500; Per Subs 64
Special Collections: Old County Newspapers on Microfilm
Subject Interests: Maps
Automation Activity & Vendor Info: (Acquisitions) Auto-Graphics, Inc; (Cataloging) Auto-Graphics, Inc; (Circulation) Auto-Graphics, Inc; (ILL) Auto-Graphics, Inc
Wireless access
Function: 24/7 Electronic res, 24/7 Online cat, Activity rm, Audio & video playback equip for onsite use, Audiobks via web, AV serv, Bks on CD, Children's prog, Computers for patron use, E-Readers, Electronic databases & coll, Free DVD rentals, Home delivery & serv to seniorr ctr & nursing homes, ILL available, Internet access, Large print keyboards, Magazines, Meeting rooms, Microfiche/film & reading machines, Online cat, Photocopying/Printing, Preschool reading prog, Printer for laptops & handheld devices, Prog for adults, Prog for children & young adult, Ref serv available, Res performed for a fee, Satellite serv, Senior outreach, Summer reading prog, Tax forms, Telephone ref, Wheelchair accessible, Winter reading prog
Partic in South Dakota Library Network
Special Services for the Deaf - Assistive tech; Bks on deafness & sign lang
Special Services for the Blind - Accessible computers; Audio mat; Bks on CD; Large print bks; Talking bks; Talking bks & player equip
Open Mon-Thurs 10-7, Fri 10-5, Sat 10-1
Restriction: Non-resident fee
Friends of the Library Group

MILLER

P HAND COUNTY LIBRARY*, 402 N Broadway, 57362-1438. SAN 315-6540. Tel: 605-853-3693. FAX: 605-853-3693. E-mail: library@handcountysd.org. Web Site: handcounty.yoursdlibrary.org. *Dir,* Mary Breitling; Staff 3 (MLS 1, Non-MLS 2)
Founded 1947. Pop 4,948; Circ 57,345
Library Holdings: Bk Titles 26,000; Bk Vols 35,000; Per Subs 108
Special Collections: Local Newspapers, micro
Subject Interests: Authors, SDak bks
Automation Activity & Vendor Info: (Cataloging) Follett Software; (Circulation) Follett Software; (OPAC) Follett Software
Function: ILL available
Open Mon & Thurs 11-6, Wed 11-7, Fri 11-5, Sat 11-3
Friends of the Library Group

MISSION

C SINTE GLESKA UNIVERSITY LIBRARY*, 1351 W Spotted Tail St, 57555. (Mail add: PO Box 107, 57555-0107), SAN 315-6559. Tel: 605-856-8100, 605-856-8112. FAX: 605-856-2011. Web Site: www.sintegleska.edu/library. *Dir,* Position Currently Open; *Cataloger, Interim Dir,* Diana Dillon; Tel: 608-856-8182, E-mail: diana.dillon@sintegleska.edu; *Secy Gen,* Elsie Hollow Horn Bear; *Cataloger, Ref Serv,* Mike Dillon; *ILL,* Ken Wike; *Youth Library Tech,* Position Currently Open
Founded 1972. Enrl 850; Fac 60; Highest Degree: Master
Library Holdings: Bk Vols 50,000; Per Subs 372
Special Collections: Unkiciksuyape (Native American Coll). Municipal Document Depository; State Document Depository
Subject Interests: Educ, Environ, Law, Native Am studies
Automation Activity & Vendor Info: (Cataloging) Ex Libris Group
Function: Adult literacy prog, After school storytime, Audio & video playback equip for onsite use, CD-ROM, Health sci info serv, Homebound delivery serv, ILL available, Internet access, Orientations, Photocopying/Printing, Prog for children & young adult, Ref serv available, Spoken cassettes & DVDs, Summer reading prog, VHS videos, Wheelchair accessible, Workshops
Partic in American Indian Higher Education Consortium; Ex Libris Aleph
Open Mon-Thurs 8am-10pm, Fri 8-5; Mon-Fri 8-5 (Summer)

MITCHELL

C DAKOTA WESLEYAN UNIVERSITY*, George & Eleanor McGovern Library, 1200 W University Ave, 57301. SAN 315-6567. Tel: 605-995-2618. E-mail: library@dwu.edu. Web Site: library.dwu.edu. *Dir,* Alexis Becker; Tel: 605-995-2617, E-mail: alexis.becker@dwu.edu; *Acq, Supvr, Circ Supvr,* Judy Lehi; Tel: 605-995-2894; E-mail: judy.lehi@dwu.edu; *Univ Archivist,* Laurie Langland; Tel: 605-995-2134, E-mail: laurie.langland@dwu.edu; Staff 3 (MLS 2, Non-MLS 1)
Founded 1885. Enrl 900; Fac 51; Highest Degree: Master
Library Holdings: AV Mats 1,179; CDs 625; DVDs 3,525; e-books 155,500; e-journals 64,900; Electronic Media & Resources 24,675; Microforms 64,397; Music Scores 206; Bk Titles 63,500; Bk Vols 72,400; Per Subs 353
Special Collections: Senator Francis Case Coll, political papers; Senator George McGovern Coll, personal papers & political photog; Western History & Literature (Jennewein Western Library Coll)
Automation Activity & Vendor Info: (Acquisitions) OCLC; (Cataloging) OCLC; (Circulation) OCLC; (Course Reserve) OCLC; (ILL) OCLC WorldShare Interlibrary Loan; (OPAC) OCLC; (Serials) OCLC
Wireless access
Function: 24/7 Electronic res, 24/7 Online cat, Archival coll, Art exhibits, Audio & video playback equip for onsite use, AV serv, Computers for patron use, Distance learning, Electronic databases & coll, Equip loans & repairs, For res purposes, Free DVD rentals, ILL available, Instruction & testing, Internet access, Laminating, Magazines, Microfiche/film & reading machines, Movies, Music CDs, Online cat, Online info literacy tutorials on the web & in blackboard, Online ref, Orientations, Photocopying/Printing, Printer for laptops & handheld devices, Ref & res, Ref serv available, Scanner, Study rm, Telephone ref, VHS videos, Wheelchair accessible
Partic in Minitex; OCLC Online Computer Library Center, Inc
Special Services for the Deaf - Assistive tech
Open Mon-Thurs 7:30am-11pm, Fri 7:30-5, Sat 11-4, Sun 5pm-11pm; Mon-Fri 7:30-5 (Summer)

P MITCHELL PUBLIC LIBRARY*, 221 N Duff St, 57301. SAN 315-6583. Tel: 605-995-8480. Web Site: www.cityofmitchell.org/Library. *Dir,* Kevin Kenkel; E-mail: kkenkel@cityofmitchell.org; *Ad,* Zackery North; E-mail: znorth@cityofmitchell.org; *Ch Serv Librn,* Jean Patrick; Tel: 605-995-8480, E-mail: jpatrick@cityofmitchell.org; *Cataloger, Tech Serv,* Michele DeVries; E-mail: mdevries@cityofmitchell.org; *Circ Asst,* Ada Morales; E-mail: amorales@cityofmitchell.org; *Circ Asst,* Rachel Soulek; E-mail: rsoulek@cityofmitchell.org; Staff 4 (MLS 2, Non-MLS 2)
Founded 1903. Pop 15,254; Circ 80,550
Library Holdings: Audiobooks 2,633; CDs 122; DVDs 939; Large Print Bks 1,938; Microforms 614; Bk Vols 67,444; Per Subs 25
Special Collections: Mitchell Area Archives, newspapers; South Dakota Coll
Automation Activity & Vendor Info: (Acquisitions) Book Systems; (Cataloging) Book Systems; (Circulation) Book Systems; (ILL) OCLC WorldShare Interlibrary Loan; (OPAC) Book Systems; (Serials) Book Systems
Wireless access
Function: 24/7 Electronic res, 24/7 Online cat, Adult bk club, Archival coll, Audiobks on Playaways & MP3, Audiobks via web, Bilingual assistance for Spanish patrons, Bk club(s), Bks on CD, Children's prog, Computer training, Computers for patron use, Electronic databases & coll, Free DVD rentals, ILL available, Internet access, Laminating, Magazines, Magnifiers for reading, Meeting rooms, Movies, Online cat, OverDrive digital audio bks, Photocopying/Printing, Preschool outreach, Printer for laptops & handheld devices, Prog for adults, Prog for children & young adult, Ref serv available, Scanner, Spanish lang bks, Story hour, Summer reading prog, Tax forms, Teen prog, Wheelchair accessible
Partic in Minitex; OCLC Online Computer Library Center, Inc
Open Mon-Thurs 10-9, Fri & Sat 10-6, Sun 2-5 (Winter); Mon 10-8, Tues-Sat 10-6 (Summer)
Restriction: Non-circulating of rare bks
Friends of the Library Group

MOBRIDGE

P A H BROWN PUBLIC LIBRARY*, 521 N Main St, 57601. SAN 315-6591. Tel: 605-845-2808. E-mail: ahbrown@westriv.com. Web Site: mobridge.org/library. *Libr Dir,* Karla Bieber
Founded 1930. Circ 10,132
Library Holdings: Bk Vols 20,000; Per Subs 43
Special Collections: South Dakota Coll
Subject Interests: Local hist
Open Mon-Fri 9-6, Sat 9-12

NEW HOLLAND

R CHRISTIAN REFORMED CHURCH LIBRARY, 100 Church Ave, 57364. (Mail add: PO Box 3, 57364), SAN 315-6613. Tel: 605-243-2346. *Librn,* Sharon Hofstee
Founded 1947
Library Holdings: Bk Vols 3,000

NEWELL

P NEWELL PUBLIC LIBRARY*, 208 Girard Ave, 57760. (Mail add: PO Box 54, 57760-0054), SAN 315-6621. Tel: 605-456-2179. E-mail: NPL@sdplains.com. Web Site: townofnewell.org/index.php/town-govnernment/dept/npl. *Libr Dir,* Lisa Parker Wonderly
Founded 2009. Circ 4,000
Library Holdings: Bk Vols 18,000; Per Subs 25; Videos 571
Automation Activity & Vendor Info: (Cataloging) ComPanion Corp
Wireless access
Open Mon, Wed, Fri, 10-12 & 12:30-5

ONIDA

P SULLY AREA LIBRARY*, 500 S Eighth St, 57564. SAN 315-663X. Tel: 605-258-2133. FAX: 605-258-2361. E-mail: sullyarealibrary@facebook.com. Web Site: sullyarealibrary.weebly.com. *Librn,* Jackie Aspelin; E-mail: jackie.aspelin@k12.sd.us
Pop 800; Circ 16,000
Library Holdings: Bk Vols 20,000; Per Subs 30
Automation Activity & Vendor Info: (Cataloging) Winnebago Software Co; (Circulation) Winnebago Software Co; (OPAC) Winnebago Software Co
Wireless access
Open Mon 9-1, Tues 12:30-3:30, Wed Noon-7, Fri 1-5

PARKER

P PARKER PUBLIC LIBRARY*, 290 N Main, 57053. (Mail add: PO Box 576, 57053-0576), SAN 315-6648. Tel: 605-297-5552. E-mail: parkerlib@iw.net. Web Site: parkerpublic.yoursdlibrary.org. *Dir,* Kathy Rand
Founded 1904. Pop 1,022; Circ 14,443
Library Holdings: Audiobooks 375; CDs 300; DVDs 348; Large Print Bks 700; Bk Vols 10,980; Videos 750
Special Collections: Vietnam Conflict Coll
Subject Interests: Christian fiction, SDak hist
Wireless access
Special Services for the Blind - Audio mat; Bks on cassette; Bks on CD; Large print bks
Open Mon-Fri 8:30-12:30 & 1:30-5:30, Sat 9-Noon

PHILIP

P HAAKON COUNTY PUBLIC LIBRARY*, 140 S Howard Ave, 57567. (Mail add: PO Box 481, 57567). Tel: 605-859-2442. E-mail: library@gwtc.net. Web Site: www.haakoncountypubliclibrary.yoursdlibrary.org. *Dir,* Sara Buls
Library Holdings: Bk Vols 10,000
Wireless access
Open Mon-Thurs 10-5
Friends of the Library Group
Branches: 1
MIDLAND COMMUNITY LIBRARY, 401 Russel Ave, Midland, 57552. Tel: 605-843-2158. E-mail: midlandlibrary@goldenwest.net. Web Site: midland.yoursdlibrary.org. *Librn,* Karel Reiman
Function: Computers for patron use, Photocopying/Printing, Scanner, Story hour, Summer reading prog
Special Services for the Blind - Large print bks
Open Wed & Thurs 2-5 (Sept-May); Wed & Thurs 9-Noon (June-Aug)

PIEDMONT

P PIEDMONT VALLEY LIBRARY*, 111 Second St, 57769. (Mail add: PO Box 101, 57769). Tel: 605-718-3663. E-mail: piedmont.library@hotmail.com. Web Site: www.piedmontlibrary.net.
Founded 2006
Function: Computers for patron use, Genealogy discussion group, Summer reading prog, Workshops
Partic in Black Hills Library Consortium
Open Tues 10-7, Wed-Fri 10-6, Sat 9-1
Friends of the Library Group

PIERRE

P RAWLINS MUNICIPAL LIBRARY*, 1000 E Church St, 57501. SAN 315-6656. Tel: 605-773-7421. FAX: 605-773-7423. Web Site: rawlinslibrary.org. *Libr Dir,* Abby Edwardson; E-mail: abby.edwardson@ci.pierre.sd.us; *Cat Librn,* Lisa Pfeiffer; E-mail: lisa.pfeiffer@ci.pierre.sd.us; *Ch,* Virginia Kaus; E-mail: virginia.kaus@ci.pierre.sd.us; Staff 8 (MLS 1, Non-MLS 7)
Library Holdings: Audiobooks 6,400; Bks on Deafness & Sign Lang 30; Braille Volumes 3; CDs 650; DVDs 9,600; e-books 26,000; Large Print Bks 3,400; Bk Titles 71,000; Per Subs 110
Special Collections: History (South Dakota Coll); Lewis & Clark Coll
Automation Activity & Vendor Info: (Acquisitions) Book Systems; (Cataloging) Book Systems; (Circulation) Book Systems; (ILL) Auto-Graphics, Inc; (OPAC) Book Systems; (Serials) Book Systems
Wireless access
Function: 24/7 Electronic res, 24/7 Online cat, Activity rm, Adult bk club, Adult literacy prog
Open Mon-Thurs 9-8, Fri & Sat 9-5, Sun 12-5
Restriction: Authorized patrons, Authorized personnel only, In-house use for visitors, Internal use only, Non-circulating coll, Non-resident fee, Restricted borrowing privileges
Friends of the Library Group

G SOUTH DAKOTA STATE HISTORICAL SOCIETY, State Archives, 900 Governors Dr, 57501. SAN 315-6664. Tel: 605-773-3804. FAX: 605-773-6041. Reference E-mail: archref@state.sd.us. Web Site: history.sd.gov/archives. *Librn,* Kimberly Smith; Tel: 605-773-4233, E-mail: KimberlyA.Smith@state.sd.us; *State Archivist,* Chelle Somsen; E-mail: Chelle.Somsen@state.sd.us; Staff 1 (MLS 1)
Founded 1901
Library Holdings: Bk Titles 7,164; Bk Vols 13,770; Per Subs 188
Special Collections: Dakota & Western Indians Coll, photog, newsp
Subject Interests: Plains Indians, SDak hist, SDak Western Am
Automation Activity & Vendor Info: (OPAC) Ex Libris Group
Partic in OCLC Online Computer Library Center, Inc; South Dakota Library Network
Library closed for renovations. Set to reopen in 2025
Restriction: Non-circulating

P SOUTH DAKOTA STATE LIBRARY, 800 Governors Dr, 57501-2294. SAN 360-4500. Tel: 605-773-3131. Circulation Tel: 605-773-5068. Reference Tel: 605-773-5070. Administration Toll Free Tel: 800-423-6665 (SD only). Administration FAX: 605-773-6962. E-mail: library@state.sd.us. Web Site: library.sd.gov. *State Librn,* George Seamon; E-mail: george.seamon@state.sd.us; *Coll Serv Librn, Res & Ref Serv,* Brenda Hemmelman; E-mail: brenda.hemmelman@state.sd.us; *Automation Serv, Cat, Metadata Librn,* Nina Mentzel; E-mail: nina.mentzel@state.sd.us; *Accessible Library Services Mgr,* Slocum Kathleen; E-mail: kathleen.slocum@state.sd.us; *Coordr, Ch & Youth Serv,* Amanda Raiche; E-mail: amanda.raiche@state.sd.us; *Continuing Educ Coordr,* JoAnne Freitag; E-mail: JoAnne.Freitag@state.sd.us; *Digital Res Coordr, Electronic Res,* Kim Bonen; Tel: 605-295-3174, E-mail: kim.bonen@state.sd.us; *Sch Libr Coordr,* Scottie Bruch; E-mail: scottie.bruch@state.sd.us; *Cat, ILL Assoc,* Position Currently Open; *State Data Coordr,* Shawn Behrends; E-mail: shawn.behrends@state.sd.us; Staff 21.5 (MLS 10, Non-MLS 11.5)
Founded 1913
Library Holdings: AV Mats 27; CDs 2,455; DVDs 487; e-books 2,233; e-journals 18; Microforms 10,044; Per Subs 64; Videos 111
Special Collections: State Document Depository; US Document Depository
Subject Interests: Educ, Librarianship, Native Am hist, SDak hist
Automation Activity & Vendor Info: (Acquisitions) Auto-Graphics, Inc; (Cataloging) Auto-Graphics, Inc; (Circulation) Auto-Graphics, Inc; (Course Reserve) Auto-Graphics, Inc; (Discovery) Auto-Graphics, Inc; (ILL) Auto-Graphics, Inc; (Media Booking) Auto-Graphics, Inc; (OPAC) Auto-Graphics, Inc; (Serials) Auto-Graphics, Inc
Wireless access
Function: 24/7 Online cat
Partic in OCLC Online Computer Library Center, Inc; Western Council of State Libraries, Inc
Special Services for the Blind - Audio mat; Bks & mags in Braille, on rec, tape & cassette; Braille bks; Dep for Braille Inst; Digital talking bk; Newsletter (in large print, Braille or on cassette); Production of talking bks; Radio reading serv; Talking bk & rec for the blind cat; Talking bk serv referral; Talking bks; Talking bks & player equip; Textbks & bks about music in Braille & large print
Open Mon-Fri 8-5
Restriction: Authorized patrons, Borrowing requests are handled by ILL
Branches: 1
P BRAILLE & TALKING BOOK PROGRAM, McKay Bldg, 800 Governors Dr, 57501-2294, SAN 315-6699. Tel: 605-773-3131. Toll Free Tel: 800-423-6665 (South Dakota only). E-mail: talkbkreq@state.sd.us. *Prog Asst, Braille & Talking Bks,* Connie Sullivan; Staff 6 (MLS 1, Non-MLS 5)
Founded 1968
Library Holdings: Braille Volumes 1,448; DVDs 895
Special Collections: Dakota Language Coll; South Dakota Coll

Automation Activity & Vendor Info: (Cataloging) Keystone Systems, Inc (KLAS); (Circulation) Keystone Systems, Inc (KLAS); (OPAC) Keystone Systems, Inc (KLAS)
Publications: Prairie Trails
Open Mon-Fri 8-5

GL SOUTH DAKOTA SUPREME COURT, Law Library, 500 E Capitol Ave, 57501. SAN 315-6702. Tel: 605-773-4898. *Librn,* Brigid Hoffman
Library Holdings: Bk Vols 30,000
Wireless access
Open Mon-Fri 8-5

PLANKINTON

P PLANKINTON COMMUNITY LIBRARY*, 404 E Davenport St, 57368. (Mail add: PO Box 190, 57368), SAN 315-6710. Tel: 605-942-7600. Web Site: cityofplankinton.com/library.html. *Librn,* Carrie Brink; E-mail: carrie.brink@k12.sd.us
Pop 750; Circ 5,380
Library Holdings: Bk Vols 6,000
Wireless access
Open Mon, Tues & Thurs 4-6, Sat 10-1

PRESHO

P PRESHO PUBLIC LIBRARY*, 108 N Main Ave, 57568. SAN 315-6737. Tel: 605-895-2443. E-mail: presholibrary@kennebectelephone.com. Web Site: www.facebook.com/presholibrary. *Librn,* Michelle Schindler
Pop 950; Circ 4,379
Library Holdings: Bk Vols 9,000
Open Mon 1-5, Tues-Thurs 10-1, Wed 10-12 & 4-6

RAPID CITY

P RAPID CITY PUBLIC LIBRARY*, 610 Quincy St, 57701-3630. SAN 315-6761. Tel: 605-394-6139. Administration Tel: 605-394-4171. Web Site: www.rapidcitylibrary.org. *Dir,* Terri Davis; Tel: 605-394-6713, E-mail: tdavis@rcplib.org; *Asst Dir, Circ & Tech Serv Librn,* Sean Minkel; E-mail: sminkel@rcplib.org; *Digital Serv & Emerging Tech Librn,* Sam Slocum; *Coordr, Outreach Serv,* Laurinda Tapper; *Vols Coordr,* Stephanie Jenner; *Spec Serv,* Danielle Wood; E-mail: dwood@rcplib.org; Staff 38 (MLS 12, Non-MLS 26)
Founded 1903. Pop 90,000; Circ 424,642
Library Holdings: AV Mats 12,970; e-books 9,471; Bk Vols 157,892; Per Subs 392; Videos 12,970
Special Collections: Rapid City Society for Genealogical Research Coll. State Document Depository
Automation Activity & Vendor Info: (Acquisitions) Ex Libris Group; (Cataloging) Ex Libris Group; (Circulation) Ex Libris Group; (OPAC) Ex Libris Group
Wireless access
Partic in Black Hills Library Consortium; OCLC Online Computer Library Center, Inc; South Dakota Library Network
Open Mon-Thurs 9-8, Fri & Sat 9-6, Sun 12-6
Friends of the Library Group

C SOUTH DAKOTA SCHOOL OF MINES & TECHNOLOGY*, Devereaux Library, 501 E Saint Joseph St, 57701-3995. SAN 360-456X. Reference Tel: 605-394-2419. Reference E-mail: library.reference@sdsmt.edu. Web Site: www.sdsmt.edu/library. *Dir,* Patricia M Andersen; E-mail: patricia.andersen@sdsmt.edu; *Assoc Librn, Colls Mgr, Syst Librn,* Cindy L Davies; E-mail: cindy.davies@sdsmt.edu; *Bus & Finance Mgr, Coordr, Outreach Serv, Coordr, Pub Serv,* Janet L Taylor; E-mail: janet.taylor@sdsmt.edu; *Circ Supvr,* Karen M Vieira; E-mail: karen.vieira@sdsmt.edu; *ILL Supvr,* Josh Wilkinson; E-mail: josh.wilkinson@sdsmt.edu; *Ref Serv,* Renee Ponzio; E-mail: Renee.Ponzio@sdsmt.edu; Staff 6 (MLS 2, Non-MLS 4)
Founded 1885. Fac 2; Highest Degree: Doctorate
Library Holdings: AV Mats 4,310; e-books 88,329; e-journals 23,917; Electronic Media & Resources 57,777; Microforms 39,000; Bk Titles 122,737; Bk Vols 160,087; Per Subs 417
Special Collections: Black Hills & Western South Dakota Mining History, (Black Hills Special Coll Area), maps; School History, 1885 to date. State Document Depository; US Document Depository
Subject Interests: Engr, Mining, Sci, Tech
Automation Activity & Vendor Info: (Acquisitions) Ex Libris Group; (Cataloging) Ex Libris Group; (Circulation) Ex Libris Group; (Course Reserve) Ex Libris Group; (ILL) Ex Libris Group; (Media Booking) Ex Libris Group; (OPAC) Ex Libris Group; (Serials) Ex Libris Group
Wireless access
Function: 24/7 Electronic res, 24/7 Online cat, Archival coll, Bks on cassette, Bks on CD, Computers for patron use, Doc delivery serv, Electronic databases & coll, Free DVD rentals, ILL available, Learning ctr, Microfiche/film & reading machines, Music CDs, Online cat, Online ref, Orientations, Photocopying/Printing, Ref & res, Spoken cassettes & CDs, Telephone ref, Wheelchair accessible
Partic in Minitex; OCLC Online Computer Library Center, Inc
Open Mon-Thurs 7am-Midnight, Fri 7-5, Sat 12-5, Sun Noon-Midnight
Friends of the Library Group

J WESTERN DAKOTA TECHNICAL INSTITUTE LIBRARY*, 800 Mickelson Dr, 57703. SAN 320-9849. Tel: 605-718-2904. FAX: 605-718-2537. E-mail: library@wdt.edu. Web Site: www.wdt.edu/student-life/library. *Libr Coord,* Jennifer Williams-Curl; E-mail: Jennifer.Williams-Curl@wdt.edu; Staff 2 (Non-MLS 2)
Founded 1968. Enrl 1,053; Fac 78; Highest Degree: Associate
Library Holdings: Bk Titles 4,000
Special Collections: Departmental Coll; Teen Prep
Subject Interests: Agr, Biographies, Bus mgt, Career, Carpentry, Computer network specialist, Electronics, Fiction, Law enforcement, Native Am, Nursing, Paralegal, SDak, State law, Vocational
Automation Activity & Vendor Info: (Acquisitions) Ex Libris Group; (Cataloging) Ex Libris Group; (Circulation) Ex Libris Group; (Course Reserve) Ex Libris Group; (ILL) Ex Libris Group; (Media Booking) Ex Libris Group; (OPAC) Ex Libris Group; (Serials) Ex Libris Group
Wireless access
Partic in South Dakota Library Network
Open Mon-Fri 7:30-5

REDFIELD

P REDFIELD CARNEGIE LIBRARY*, Five E Fifth Ave, 57469. SAN 315-6788. Tel: 605-472-4555. FAX: 605-472-4559. E-mail: carnegie2@hotmail.com. Web Site: www.city.redfield-sd.com/carnegie-library. *Head Librn,* Sarah Jones; *Asst Librn,* Linda Keller
Founded 1902. Pop 2,500
Library Holdings: DVDs 242; Bk Vols 26,000; Per Subs 30
Automation Activity & Vendor Info: (Cataloging) Follett Software; (Circulation) Follett Software; (OPAC) Follett Software
Wireless access
Function: 24/7 Online cat, Accelerated reader prog, Activity rm, Audiobks via web, Bks on CD, Children's prog, Computer training, Computers for patron use, Digital talking bks, Electronic databases & coll, Free DVD rentals, Homebound delivery serv, ILL available, Photocopying/Printing, Ref serv available, Wheelchair accessible
Open Mon 12-8, Tues 10-12 & 1-8, Wed & Fri 12-5, Thurs 10-12 & 1-5, Sat 10-4

G SOUTH DAKOTA DEVELOPMENTAL CENTER*, Redfield Library, 17267 W Third St, 57469-1001. SAN 328-4786. Tel: 605-472-4210. FAX: 605-472-4457. E-mail: dhs.redfld.info@state.sd.us. *Dir,* Barb Abeln
Library Holdings: Bk Vols 500
Subject Interests: Spec educ
Partic in South Dakota Library Network
Restriction: Private libr

SIOUX FALLS

C AUGUSTANA UNIVERSITY*, Mikkelsen Library, 2001 S Summit Ave, 57197-0001. SAN 315-6796. Tel: 605-274-4921. FAX: 605-274-5447. E-mail: augielibrarians@augie.edu. Web Site: library.augie.edu. *Dir, Libr Serv,* Ronelle Thompson; E-mail: ronelle.thompson@augie.edu; *Access Serv,* Krista Ohrtman; E-mail: krista.ohrtman@augie.edu; *Digital Initiatives,* Kelly Thompson; E-mail: kelly.thompson@augie.edu; *Media Serv,* Craig Johnson; E-mail: craig.johnson@augie.edu; *Pub Serv,* Lisa Brunick; E-mail: lisa.brunick@augie.edu; *Tech Serv,* Ana Olivier; E-mail: ana.olivier@augie.edu; Staff 11 (MLS 6, Non-MLS 5)
Founded 1860. Enrl 2,022; Fac 219; Highest Degree: Master
Library Holdings: Audiobooks 443; AV Mats 7,942; CDs 4,278; DVDs 3,124; e-books 267,799; e-journals 54,191; Electronic Media & Resources 152,149; Microforms 7,663; Bk Vols 181,022; Per Subs 115; Videos 23
Special Collections: Center for Western Studies; Norwegian Coll. US Document Depository
Automation Activity & Vendor Info: (Acquisitions) OCLC Worldshare Management Services; (Cataloging) OCLC Worldshare Management Services; (Circulation) OCLC Worldshare Management Services; (Course Reserve) OCLC Worldshare Management Services; (Discovery) OCLC; (ILL) OCLC WorldShare Interlibrary Loan; (Media Booking) OCLC Worldshare Management Services; (OPAC) OCLC; (Serials) OCLC Worldshare Management Services
Wireless access
Partic in Minitex; OCLC Online Computer Library Center, Inc
Open Mon-Thurs 7:30am-11pm, Fri 7:30-6, Sat 10-5, Sun 11am-11pm
Friends of the Library Group

Departmental Libraries:
CENTER FOR WESTERN STUDIES, 2201 S Summit Ave, 57197. (Mail add: PO Box 727, 57197-0727), SAN 329-3033. Tel: 605-274-4007. FAX: 605-274-4999. E-mail: cws@augie.edu. *Libr Dir,* Ronelle Thompson
Founded 1970. Enrl 1,800; Highest Degree: Master
Library Holdings: Bk Titles 32,000; Bk Vols 35,000; Per Subs 30; Spec Interest Per Sub 20
Special Collections: Episcopal Diocese of SD Archives; United Church of Christ SD Conference Archives; Upper Great Plains. Oral History
Subject Interests: Hist, Lit, Northern Prairie Plains
Publications: A New South Dakota History; CWS Newsletter; The Geography of South Dakota; Yanktonai Sioux Water Colors & Other Books About Plains Indians & Western History
Open Mon-Fri 8-12 & 1-5, Sat 10-2
Restriction: Non-circulating to the pub
Friends of the Library Group

R FIRST LUTHERAN CHURCH LIBRARY*, 327 S Dakota Ave, 57104. SAN 315-6818. Tel: 605-336-3734. FAX: 605-336-8370. E-mail: info@flcsf.org. Web Site: www.flcsf.org.
Founded 1920
Library Holdings: Bk Titles 6,600; Per Subs 3
Subject Interests: Relig studies
Wireless access
Open Mon-Thurs 8-5, Fri 8-4

S PETTIGREW HOME & MUSEUM LIBRARY, 131 N Duluth Ave, 57104. (Mail add: 200 W Sixth St, 57104), SAN 315-6907. Tel: 605-367-4210. FAX: 605-367-6004. E-mail: museum@minnehahacounty.gov. Web Site: siouxlandmuseums.com. *Dir,* William Hoskins; Staff 3 (Non-MLS 3)
Founded 1926
Library Holdings: Bk Titles 10,000; Per Subs 10
Special Collections: Local & Regional History Coll; Populism, Bimetalism, Maverick Politics 1880-1920; R F Pettigrew Papers & Private Library, bks, pamphlets, pvt papers
Subject Interests: Hist of Sioux Falls, Pioneering, SDak state, Surrounding region
Function: Archival coll, Photocopying/Printing, Res libr
Publications: Siouxland Heritage Museums Report (Newsletter)
Special Services for the Deaf - TTY equip
Restriction: Not a lending libr, Open by appt only

P SIOUXLAND LIBRARIES*, 200 N Dakota Ave, 57104. (Mail add: PO Box 7403, 57117-7403), SAN 315-6885. Tel: 605-367-8700. Interlibrary Loan Service Tel: 605-367-8720. FAX: 605-367-4312. Web Site: www.siouxlandlib.org. *Dir,* Jodi Fick; Tel: 605-367-8713; *Asst Dir,* Monique Christensen; Tel: 605-367-8723, E-mail: mchristensen@siouxfalls.org; *Sr Librn,* Alysia Boysen; Tel: 605-367-8702, E-mail: aboysen@siouxfalls.org; *Sr Librn, Staff Develop,* Dan Neeves; Tel: 605-367-8718, E-mail: dneeves@siouxfalls.org; *Librn, Adult Serv,* Amber Fick; Tel: 605-367-8703, E-mail: afick@siouxfalls.org; *Ch Serv Librn,* Stephanie Bents; Tel: 605-367-8719, E-mail: sbents@siouxfalls.org; *Coll Mgt Librn,* Elizabeth Berg; Tel: 605-367-8732, E-mail: eberg@siouxfalls.org; *Digital Res Librn,* Justin Stevenson; Tel: 605-367-8734, E-mail: jstevenson@siouxfalls.org; *Early Childhood Librn,* Jenna Neugebauer; Tel: 605-367-8708, E-mail: jneugebauer@siouxfalls.org; *Librn, Staff Develop,* Sabina Mustic; Tel: 605-367-8730, E-mail: smustic@siouxfalls.org; *Teen Serv Librn,* Lucy Steiger; Tel: 605-367-8712, E-mail: lsteiger@siouxfalls.org; *Communications Coordr, Mkt Coordr,* Betsy Rice; Tel: 605-367-8701, E-mail: brice@siouxfalls.org. Subject Specialists: *Communications, Tech,* Alysia Boysen; *Training,* Sabina Mustic; Staff 17 (MLS 16, Non-MLS 1)
Founded 1886. Pop 225,916; Circ 2,114,823
Jan 2019-Dec 2019 Income (Main & Associated Libraries) $8,066,171, City $6,776,325, County $1,135,000, Locally Generated Income $154,846. Mats Exp $906,040, Books $389,484. AV Mat $121,482, Electronic Ref Mat (Incl. Access Fees) $395,074. Sal $4,081,299
Library Holdings: Audiobooks 25,103; AV Mats 2,037; CDs 11,094; DVDs 20,457; e-books 20,630; e-journals 107; Large Print Bks 6,955; Bk Vols 221,080; Per Subs 447
Special Collections: State & Regional History & Genealogy (Caille Room). State Document Depository
Subject Interests: SDak hist
Automation Activity & Vendor Info: (Acquisitions) Innovative Interfaces, Inc; (Cataloging) Innovative Interfaces, Inc; (Circulation) Innovative Interfaces, Inc; (ILL) OCLC ILLiad; (Media Booking) Innovative Interfaces, Inc; (OPAC) Innovative Interfaces, Inc; (Serials) Innovative Interfaces, Inc
Wireless access
Function: 24/7 Electronic res, 24/7 Online cat, Activity rm, Adult bk club, After school storytime, Art exhibits, Audiobks on Playaways & MP3, Audiobks via web, AV serv, Bk club(s), Bk reviews (Group), Bks on CD, Children's prog, Computer training, Computers for patron use, Digital talking bks, Electronic databases & coll, Free DVD rentals, Govt ref serv, Health sci info serv, Holiday prog, Home delivery & serv to seniorr ctr & nursing homes, Homebound delivery serv, ILL available, Internet access, Large print keyboards, Life-long learning prog for all ages, Magazines, Magnifiers for reading, Meeting rooms, Microfiche/film & reading machines, Movies, Music CDs, Online cat, Outreach serv, Outside serv via phone, mail, e-mail & web, OverDrive digital audio bks, Photocopying/Printing, Preschool outreach, Preschool reading prog, Printer for laptops & handheld devices, Prog for adults, Prog for children & young adult, Ref & res, Ref serv available, Scanner, Senior outreach, STEM programs, Story hour, Study rm, Summer & winter reading prog, Summer reading prog, Tax forms, Teen prog, Telephone ref, Wheelchair accessible, Winter reading prog, Workshops, Writing prog
Partic in Minitex; OCLC Online Computer Library Center, Inc
Special Services for the Deaf - Closed caption videos; Sign lang interpreter upon request for prog; Staff with knowledge of sign lang; TTY equip
Special Services for the Blind - Accessible computers; Aids for in-house use; Bks on CD; Computer with voice synthesizer for visually impaired persons; Copier with enlargement capabilities; Descriptive video serv (DVS); Digital talking bk; Digital talking bk machines; Free checkout of audio mat; Home delivery serv; Internet workstation with adaptive software; Large print bks; Magnifiers; Recorded bks; ZoomText magnification & reading software
Open Mon-Thurs 9-8, Fri 9-6, Sat 9-5, Sun 1-5
Restriction: Non-resident fee
Branches: 12
BALTIC BRANCH, 213 St Olaf Ave, Baltic, 57003. (Mail add: PO Box 326, Baltic, 57003-0326), SAN 329-577X. Tel: 605-529-5415. FAX: 605-529-5415. *Br Librn,* Sharon Hall; E-mail: shall@siouxfalls.org; Staff 1 (MLS 1)
Open Mon & Thurs 2:30-6:30, Wed & Sat 9-Noon
BRANDON BRANCH, 305 S Splitrock Blvd, Brandon, 57005-1651, SAN 327-960X. Tel: 605-582-2390. FAX: 605-582-8760. *Br Librn,* Sharon Hall; E-mail: shall@siouxfalls.org; Staff 1 (MLS 1)
Open Mon 12-8, Tues-Thurs 9-8, Fri 9-5, Sat 9-3
CAILLE BRANCH, 4100 Carnegie Circle, 57106-2320, SAN 375-5606. Tel: 605-367-8144. FAX: 605-362-2816. *Br Librn,* James Borchert; E-mail: jborchert@siouxfalls.org; Staff 1 (MLS 1)
Open Mon & Fri 9-6, Tues-Thurs 9-8, Sat 9-5, Sun 1-5
COLTON BRANCH, 402 S Dakota Ave, Colton, 57018, SAN 322-6115. Tel: 605-446-3519. FAX: 605-446-3519. *Br Librn,* Sharlene Lien; E-mail: slien@siouxfalls.org; Staff 1 (Non-MLS 1)
Open Tues 3-7, Thurs 2-6, Sat 9-1
CROOKS BRANCH, 900 N West Ave, Crooks, 57020-6402, SAN 360-4179. Tel: 605-367-6384. FAX: 605-367-6383. *Br Librn,* Charlene Lien; Staff 1 (MLS 1)
Founded 1984
Open Mon 3-7, Tues & Fri 1-5, Wed, Thurs & Sat 10-1
GARRETSON BRANCH, 649 Main Ave, Garretson, 57030. (Mail add: PO Drawer N, Garretson, 57030-0392), SAN 322-6107. Tel: 605-594-6619. FAX: 605-594-6619. *Br Librn,* Sharon Hall; E-mail: shall@siouxfalls.org
Open Tues & Thurs 3-6, Wed 3-7, Fri 9-Noon
HARTFORD BRANCH, 119 N Main Ave, Ste A, Hartford, 57033. (Mail add: PO Box 607, Hartford, 57033), SAN 322-6093. Tel: 605-367-6380. *Br Librn,* Sharlene Lien; E-mail: slien@siouxfalls.org; Staff 1 (MLS 1)
Function: 24/7 Online cat
Open Tues 9-1, Wed 2-5, Thurs 3-7, Sat 10-1
HUMBOLDT BRANCH, 201 S Main St, Humboldt, 57035. (Mail add: PO Box 166, Humboldt, 57035-0166), SAN 322-6085. Tel: 605-363-3361. FAX: 605-363-3361. *Br Librn,* Sharlene Lien; E-mail: slien@siouxfalls.org; Staff 1 (MLS 1)
Open Mon 2-6, Wed 3-7, Fri 10-1
OAK VIEW BRANCH, 3700 E Third St, 57103. Tel: 605-367-8060. FAX: 605-367-4343. *Br Librn,* James Borchert; E-mail: jborchert@siouxfalls.org
Open Mon, Tues & Thurs 9-8, Wed 9-6, Sat 9-5, Sun 1-5
RONNING BRANCH, 3100 E 49th St, 57103-5877, SAN 375-5614. Tel: 605-367-8140. FAX: 605-371-4144. *Br Librn,* Jane Taylor; Staff 1 (MLS 1)
Open Mon-Wed 9-8, Thurs & Fri 9-6, Sat 9-5, Sun 1-5
VALLEY SPRINGS BRANCH, 401 Broadway Ave, Valley Springs, 57068. (Mail add: PO Box 277, Valley Springs, 57068), SAN 322-6123. Tel: 605-757-6264. FAX: 605-757-6730. *Br Librn,* Sharon Hall; E-mail: shall@siouxfalls.org; Staff 1 (Non-MLS 1)
Open Tues 3-6, Fri 9-Noon

S SOUTH DAKOTA STATE PENITENTIARY, Donald M Cole & Jameson Annex Library, 1600 North Dr, 57104. (Mail add: PO Box 5911, 57117-5911), SAN 315-6915. Tel: 605-367-5171.
Library Holdings: Bk Vols 8,000
Restriction: Staff & inmates only

G UNITED STATES GEOLOGICAL SURVEY*, Earth Resources Observation & Science (EROS) Center Library, Mundt Federal Bldg, 47914 252nd St, 57198-0001. SAN 315-632X. Tel: 605-594-2611,

605-594-6511. FAX: 605-594-6589. Web Site: www.usgs.gov/centers/eros. *Communications, Advocacy & Outreach Serv Coordr,* Michelle Bouchard; E-mail: mbouchard@usgs.gov; Staff 1 (MLS 1)
Founded 1973
Library Holdings: Bk Vols 5,600; Per Subs 6
Subject Interests: Aerial remote sensing in conjunction with geog, Computer graphics, Computer tech, Geog info systs, Geol, Hydrol, Land use planning, Satellite
Wireless access
Partic in OCLC Online Computer Library Center, Inc
Open Mon-Fri 8-4

CR UNIVERSITY OF SIOUX FALLS, Norman B Mears Library, 1101 W 22nd St, 57105. SAN 315-6842. Tel: 605-331-6660. E-mail: library@usioux falls.edu. Web Site: usiouxfalls.libguides.com. *Dir, Libr Serv,* Annie Sternburg; Tel: 605-331-6661, E-mail: annie.sternburg@usiouxfalls.edu; Staff 1 (MLS 1)
Founded 1883. Highest Degree: Master
Library Holdings: DVDs 400; Electronic Media & Resources 75; Bk Vols 49,000; Per Subs 12
Automation Activity & Vendor Info: (Cataloging) OCLC Worldshare Management Services; (Circulation) OCLC Worldshare Management Services; (Course Reserve) OCLC Worldshare Management Services; (ILL) OCLC WorldShare Interlibrary Loan; (OPAC) OCLC Worldshare Management Services; (Serials) OCLC Worldshare Management Services
Wireless access
Partic in Minitex; OCLC Online Computer Library Center, Inc
Open Mon-Thurs 8am-10pm, Fri 8-5, Sat 11-3, Sun 5pm-10pm

M UNIVERSITY OF SOUTH DAKOTA*, Wegner Health Science Information Center, 1400 W 22nd St, Ste 100, 57105. (Mail add: 414 E Clark St, Vermillion, 57069), SAN 377-6263. Tel: 605-357-1400. Toll Free Tel: 800-521-2987. FAX: 605-357-1490. E-mail: wegner@usd.edu. Web Site: www.usd.edu/wegner. *Health Sci Librn, Research Servs Librn,* Anna Simonson; Tel: 605-658-3388, E-mail: anna.simonson@usd.edu; Staff 6 (MLS 3, Non-MLS 3)
Founded 1998
Library Holdings: AV Mats 2,291; Bk Vols 16,011; Per Subs 545
Special Collections: Children's Coll; Ethics Coll; History of Medicine
Subject Interests: Health, Spec educ
Automation Activity & Vendor Info: (Acquisitions) Ex Libris Group; (Cataloging) Ex Libris Group; (Circulation) Ex Libris Group; (ILL) Ex Libris Group; (OPAC) Ex Libris Group; (Serials) Ex Libris Group
Wireless access
Function: Audio & video playback equip for onsite use, AV serv, Doc delivery serv, Health sci info serv, Homebound delivery serv, ILL available, Internet access, Photocopying/Printing, Ref serv available, Wheelchair accessible
Publications: Wegner Wellness (Newsletter)
Partic in National Network of Libraries of Medicine Region 4; OCLC Online Computer Library Center, Inc; South Dakota Library Network
Open Mon-Thurs 8am-9pm, Fri 8-5, Sat 10-5, Sun 2-9

SISSETON

P SISSETON MEMORIAL LIBRARY*, 305 E Maple St, 57262. (Mail add: PO Box 289, 57262-0289), SAN 315-694X. Tel: 605-698-7391. E-mail: sislib@venturecomm.net. Web Site: sissetonmemorial.yoursdlibrary.org. *Dir,* Jayne Nieland
Founded 1907. Pop 5,008; Circ 10,309
Library Holdings: Bk Vols 20,000; Per Subs 72
Special Collections: Bing & Grondahl Christmas Plate Coll; South Dakota History
Automation Activity & Vendor Info: (Cataloging) Winnebago Software Co; (Circulation) Winnebago Software Co
Wireless access
Open Mon & Thurs 10-8, Tues & Wed 10-6, Fri 10-5, Sat 9-Noon; Mon 10-8, Tues-Fri 10-5 (May-Sept)

C SISSETON WAHPETON COLLEGE LIBRARY*, Agency Village, PO Box 689, 57262-0698. SAN 322-9483. Tel: 605-742-1104. Web Site: www.swcollege.edu/newswcollege/student-life/campus-amentities. *Head Librn,* Delphine Hagel; E-mail: dhagel@swcollege.edu; Staff 1 (MLS 1)
Founded 1979. Enrl 227; Fac 17; Highest Degree: Associate
Library Holdings: Bk Titles 9,000; Videos 782
Special Collections: Native American Coll
Automation Activity & Vendor Info: (Cataloging) TLC (The Library Corporation); (Circulation) TLC (The Library Corporation)
Wireless access
Partic in American Indian Higher Education Consortium; South Dakota Library Network
Open Mon-Fri 8-4:30
Restriction: Pub use on premises

SPEARFISH

P GRACE BALLOCH MEMORIAL LIBRARY, 625 N Fifth St, 57783. SAN 315-6958. Tel: 605-642-1330. Web Site: www.cityofspearfish.com/836/library. *Dir,* Amber Wilde; E-mail: amber.wilde@cityofspearfish.com; *Ad,* Stephanie Kaitfors
Founded 1945. Pop 13,250; Circ 136,500
Library Holdings: Bk Titles 55,247; Per Subs 146
Special Collections: South Dakota History Coll. Oral History
Automation Activity & Vendor Info: (Circulation) Koha
Wireless access
Partic in Black Hills Library Consortium; South Dakota Library Network
Open Mon-Thurs 9-7, Fri & Sat 9-5, Sun 1-5
Friends of the Library Group

C BLACK HILLS STATE UNIVERSITY*, E Y Berry Library-Learning Center, 1200 University St, Unit 9676, 57799-9676. SAN 315-6966. Tel: 605-642-6250. Circulation Tel: 605-642-6834. Web Site: library.bhsu.edu. *Dir, Ref Librn,* Scott Ahola; Tel: 605-642-6359, E-mail: librarydirector@bhsu.edu; *Spec Coll Librn,* Lori Terrill; Tel: 605-642-6361, E-mail: lori.terrill@bhsu.edu; *Cat, Govt Doc,* Michael Tolan; Tel: 605-642-6356; *Circ,* Nikki Didier; *ILL,* Sarah Freng; Staff 5 (MLS 3, Non-MLS 2)
Founded 1883. Enrl 3,800; Fac 122; Highest Degree: Master
Library Holdings: DVDs 1,700; e-books 13,000; e-journals 26,000; Electronic Media & Resources 2,000; Bk Vols 288,000; Per Subs 175
Special Collections: ARROW, Inc Coll; Congressman E Y Berry Papers; Leland Case Western Historical Studies. State Document Depository; US Document Depository
Wireless access
Partic in Minitex; South Dakota Library Network
Open Mon-Thurs 7:30am-11pm, Fri 7:30-5, Sat & Sun 2-11; Mon-Fri 7:30-4:30 (Summer)
Friends of the Library Group

SPRINGFIELD

S MIKE DURFEE STATE PRISON, Carl G Lawrence Library, 1412 Wood St, 57062. SAN 370-5412. Tel: 605-369-2201. FAX: 604-369-2813. *Librn,* Brian Foley
Library Holdings: Bk Vols 30,000

STURGIS

P STURGIS PUBLIC LIBRARY*, 1040 Harley-Davidson Way, Ste 101, 57785. SAN 315-6990. Tel: 605-347-2624. FAX: 605-720-7211. E-mail: sturgispubliclibrary@gmail.com. Web Site: sturgispubliclibrary.blogspot.com, www.sturgis-sd.gov/library. *Libr Dir,* Christopher Hahn; E-mail: chahn@sturgisgov.com; *Ch Serv,* Kathy Dykstra; Staff 3 (Non-MLS 3)
Founded 1922. Pop 24,253; Circ 77,652
Library Holdings: Bk Titles 31,000; Bk Vols 38,000; Per Subs 140
Special Collections: Dakota Coll. Oral History
Subject Interests: SDak Black Hills region
Wireless access
Publications: Audiovisual Catalog
Partic in Black Hills Library Consortium; South Dakota Library Network
Open Mon-Thurs 8-7, Fri 8-5, Sat 8-4
Friends of the Library Group
Bookmobiles: 1

TIMBER LAKE

P DEWEY COUNTY LIBRARY*, 712 Main, 57656. (Mail add: PO Box 68, 57656-0068), SAN 360-4624. Tel: 605-865-3541. E-mail: deweybookgnome@gmail.com. *Head Librn,* Ramona Flying By
Pop 5,300; Circ 15,000
Library Holdings: Bk Titles 21,500; Bk Vols 23,000; Per Subs 15
Special Collections: Regional History Coll
Wireless access
Function: Wheelchair accessible
Open Mon-Fri 9-12 & 1-5

TYNDALL

P TYNDALL PUBLIC LIBRARY, 110 W 17th Ave, 57066. (Mail add: PO Box 26, 57066-0026), SAN 315-7008. Tel: 605-589-3266. E-mail: tynlibrary@hcinet.net. Web Site: tyndall.yoursdlibrary.org. *Librn,* Joan Johnson
Founded 1917. Pop 1,500; Circ 14,930
Library Holdings: Bk Vols 13,098
Wireless access
Open Mon-Thurs 12-5

VERMILLION

S W H OVER MUSEUM*, 1110 N University St, 57069. (Mail add: 414 E Clark, 57069), SAN 371-4446. Tel: 605-659-6151. E-mail: whover@usd.edu. Web Site: www.whovermuseum.org. Staff 17 (MLS 5, Non-MLS 12)
Founded 1883. Pop 10,500
Jan 2017-Dec 2017. Mats Exp $105,000. Sal $50,000
Library Holdings: Bk Vols 2,000
Wireless access
Function: Activity rm
Open Mon-Sat 10-4
Friends of the Library Group

P EDITH B SIEGRIST VERMILLION PUBLIC LIBRARY*, 18 Church St, 57069-3093. SAN 315-7024. Tel: 605-677-7060. FAX: 605-677-7160. E-mail: vplstaff@vermillionpubliclibrary.org. Web Site: vermillionpubliclibrary.org. *Libr Dir,* Daniel Burniston; *Tech Serv Librn,* Wendy Nilson; *Youth Serv Librn,* Amanda Raiche; *Circ Supvr,* Jeff Engeman; *Circ Asst,* Nicole Andrews; *Libr Asst,* Sophia Wermers; *Programming Spec, Pub Relations,* Rachelle Langdon; *Adult Serv,* Linda Calleja; Staff 4 (MLS 3, Non-MLS 1)
Founded 1903. Pop 14,300; Circ 98,752
Library Holdings: Audiobooks 5,678; AV Mats 2,954; CDs 970; DVDs 926; Large Print Bks 2,500; Microforms 250; Bk Titles 80,062; Per Subs 117; Videos 2,965
Automation Activity & Vendor Info: (Cataloging) Book Systems; (Circulation) Book Systems; (ILL) Auto-Graphics, Inc; (OPAC) Book Systems; (Serials) Book Systems
Wireless access
Function: 24/7 Electronic res, 24/7 Online cat, Activity rm, Adult literacy prog, After school storytime, Archival coll, Art programs, Audio & video playback equip for onsite use, Audiobks on Playaways & MP3, Audiobks via web, AV serv, Bk club(s), Bk reviews (Group), Bks on CD, Children's prog, Computers for patron use, Digital talking bks, Electronic databases & coll, Equip loans & repairs, For res purposes, Free DVD rentals, Holiday prog, Home delivery & serv to seniorr ctr & nursing homes, Homebound delivery serv, ILL available, Internet access, Life-long learning prog for all ages, Magazines, Meeting rooms, Movies, Online cat, Online ref, Outreach serv, OverDrive digital audio bks, Photocopying/Printing, Preschool outreach, Printer for laptops & handheld devices, Prog for adults, Prog for children & young adult, Ref & res, Res assist avail, Scanner, Story hour, Summer reading prog, Tax forms, Teen prog, Wheelchair accessible, Workshops, Writing prog
Publications: EAI Index, General Periodical Index, MGI, RapidCity, Journal Index, Health Index, Business Index (Index to educational materials)
Special Services for the Deaf - TDD equip
Special Services for the Blind - Audio mat; Bks on cassette; Bks on CD; Cassette playback machines; Cassettes; Copier with enlargement capabilities; Extensive large print coll; Home delivery serv; Large print bks; Lending of low vision aids; Magnifiers; Playaways (bks on MP3); Rec; Recorded bks; Ref serv; Screen enlargement software for people with visual disabilities; Sound rec
Open Mon-Thurs 8-9, Fri 8-6, Sat 10-5, Sun 1-5
Friends of the Library Group

S SOUTH DAKOTA ORAL HISTORY CENTER*, University of South Dakota, I D Weeks Library, Rm 231, 414 E Clark St, 57069. SAN 329-9228. Tel: 605-658-3382. FAX: 605-658-3366. Web Site: www.usd.edu/library/sdohc. *Curator,* Sam Herley; E-mail: samuel.herley@usd.edu
Library Holdings: Bk Vols 5,000; Per Subs 35
Special Collections: American Indian Research Project Coll; South Dakota Oral History Project Coll, recordings & oral histories. Oral History
Subject Interests: Agr, Ethnic groups, Hist, Music, Native American Culture, Native American issues, Politics, Rapid City flood, Relig, Veterans
Publications: Index to the American Indian Research Project; Index to the South Dakota Oral History Collection
Open Mon-Thurs 7:30am-Midnight, Fri 7:30am-10pm, Sat 10-10, Sun 10am-Midnight

C UNIVERSITY OF SOUTH DAKOTA*, University Libraries, I D Weeks Library, 414 E Clark St, 57069. SAN 360-4713. Tel: 605-677-5373. E-mail: library@usd.edu. Web Site: www.usd.edu/library. *Dean of Libr,* Dan Daily; Tel: 605-658-3369, E-mail: dan.daily@usd.edu; *Head, Res Mgt,* David Alexander; Tel: 605-658-3374, E-mail: david.alexander@usd.edu; *Sr Librn,* Diane Frigge; Tel: 605-677-6091, E-mail: diane.frigge@usd.edu; *Librn,* Caroline Bates; Tel: 605-658-3390, E-mail: caroline.bates@usd.edu; *Librn,* Michael Boring; Tel: 605-658-3364, E-mail: michael.boring@usd.edu; *Librn,* Anne Hinseth; Tel: 605-658-3392, E-mail: anne.hinseth@usd.edu; *Librn,* Catherine Paltz; Tel: 605-658-3371, E-mail: catherine.paltz@usd.edu; *Librn,* Doris Peterson; Tel: 605-658-3380, E-mail: doris.peterson@usd.edu; *Archives & Spec Coll Librn,* Michael Seminara; Tel: 605-658-3379, E-mail: michael.seminara@usd.edu; *Business & Distance Education Librn,* Stephen Johnson; Tel: 605-658-3387, E-mail: stephen.johnson@usd.edu; *Fine Arts & Technology Librn,* Danielle Loftus; Tel: 605-658-3386, E-mail: danielle.loftus@usd.edu; *Health Science & Research Servs Librn,* Anna Simonson; Tel: 605-658-3388, E-mail: anna.simonson@usd.edu; *Health Sci Librn,* Timmi Johnson; Tel: 605-658-3389, E-mail: timmi.johnson@usd.edu; *Instrul Serv Librn,* Alan Aldrich; Tel: 605-658-3384, E-mail: alan.aldrich@usd.edu; *Metadata/Cat Librn,* Kathleen McElhinney; Tel: 605-658-3367, E-mail: kathleen.mcelhinney@usd.edu; *Asst Librn,* Samuel Herley; Tel: 605-658-3382, E-mail: samuel.herley@usd.edu; *Information Literacy Coord,* Carol Leibiger; Tel: 605-658-3383, E-mail: c.leibiger@usd.edu; Staff 29 (MLS 11, Non-MLS 18)
Founded 1882. Enrl 9,243; Highest Degree: Doctorate
Library Holdings: AV Mats 19,686; CDs 5,491; DVDs 746; Microforms 740,794; Bk Titles 362,262; Bk Vols 550,778; Per Subs 1,509; Videos 6,220
Special Collections: Country Schools Survey; Herman P Chilson Western Americana Coll; Mahoney Music Coll; South Dakota History (Richardson Coll); USD Archives; USD Photograph Coll. State Document Depository; US Document Depository
Automation Activity & Vendor Info: (Acquisitions) Ex Libris Group; (Cataloging) Ex Libris Group; (Circulation) Ex Libris Group; (ILL) OCLC ILLiad; (OPAC) Ex Libris Group
Wireless access
Publications: Coyote Connection (Newsletter); Extension Express (Newsletter); Guide to the I D Weeks Library for USD Faculty & Staff; Guide to the I D Weeks Library Resources; I D Weeks Library Serials List; USD Internet Guide: Navigating Internet Services; Volante Index
Open Mon-Thurs 7:30am-Midnight, Fri 7:30am-10pm, Sat 10-10, Sun 10am-Midnight

Departmental Libraries:

CL MCKUSICK LAW LIBRARY, Knudson School of Law, 414 E Clark St, 57069-2390, SAN 360-4772. Tel: 605-658-3520. Reference Tel: 605-658-3525. FAX: 605-677-3544. E-mail: llibrary@usd.edu. Web Site: www.usd.edu/law/law-library. *Asst Dean, Dir,* Eric Young; Tel: 605-658-3524, E-mail: eric.young@usd.edu; *Head, Instrul Serv,* Courtney Segota; Tel: 605-658-3523, E-mail: courtney.segota@usd.edu; *Head of Public, Faculty & Student Servs,* Sarah Kammer; Tel: 605-658-3522, E-mail: sarah.kammer@usd.edu; *Head, Technical & Collection Services & Serials,* Sue Benton; Tel: 605-658-3521, E-mail: susan.benton@usd.edu; Staff 4 (MLS 3, Non-MLS 1)
Founded 1901. Enrl 225; Fac 17; Highest Degree: Doctorate
Library Holdings: Bk Vols 84,855
Subject Interests: Agr law, Family law, Health law, Indian law, South Dakota Law, Water law
Partic in Mid-America Law Library Consortium; NELLCO Law Library Consortium, Inc.; OCLC Online Computer Library Center, Inc
Open Mon-Fri 8-5
Restriction: 24-hr pass syst for students only, Open to pub for ref only

NATIONAL MUSIC MUSEUM LIBRARY, Corner of Clark & Yale St, 414 E Clark St, 57069-2390, SAN 326-7695. Tel: 605-658-3450. FAX: 605-677-6995. E-mail: nmm@usd.edu. Web Site: www.nmmusd.org. *Dir,* Dwight Vaught; Tel: 605-658-3454, E-mail: dwight.vaught@usd.edu; *Assoc Dir,* Margaret Downie Banks, PhD; E-mail: margaret.banks@usd.edu; Staff 11 (MLS 1, Non-MLS 10)
Founded 1973. Enrl 6; Fac 4; Highest Degree: Master
Library Holdings: AV Mats 50; CDs 1,200; DVDs 80; Microforms 100; Music Scores 59; Bk Titles 10,000; Per Subs 50; Videos 200
Subject Interests: Ethnomusicology, Music, Musical instruments, Musicology
Publications: National Music Museum (Newsletter)
Restriction: Non-circulating, Not a lending libr, Open by appt only, Open to pub by appt only, Open to qualified scholars, Open to researchers by request, Researchers by appt only

CM WEGNER HEALTH SCIENCES LIBRARY, Sanford School of Medicine, 1400 W 22nd St, Ste 100, Sioux Falls, 57105, SAN 315-7016. Tel: 605-357-1400. FAX: 605-357-1490. E-mail: wegner@usd.edu. Web Site: usd.edu/wegner. *Librn,* Mark Schroeder; E-mail: mark.schroeder@usd.edu; *Health Sci Librn,* Layal Hneiny; Tel: 605-658-1540, E-mail: layal.hneiny@usd.edu; *Assoc Librn,* Shelie Vacek; Tel: 605-357-1319, E-mail: shelie.vacek@usd.edu; Staff 6 (MLS 2, Non-MLS 4)
Founded 1907. Enrl 860; Fac 190; Highest Degree: Doctorate
Library Holdings: AV Mats 271; e-journals 14,500; Bk Titles 28,036; Bk Vols 91,247; Per Subs 677
Special Collections: History of Medicine Archives; Rare Books. US Document Depository
Subject Interests: Allied health, Basic sci, Clinical med, Nursing
Automation Activity & Vendor Info: (Acquisitions) Ex Libris Group; (Cataloging) Ex Libris Group; (Circulation) Ex Libris Group; (Course Reserve) Ex Libris Group; (ILL) Ex Libris Group; (Media Booking) Ex Libris Group; (OPAC) Ex Libris Group; (Serials) Ex Libris Group
Partic in Mid-America Law Library Consortium; Minitex; South Dakota Library Network

Publications: Accession List; Library Handbook
Open Mon-Thurs 8am-9pm, Fri 8-5, Sun 2-9

VIBORG

P VIBORG PUBLIC LIBRARY*, 114 N Main St, 57070. (Mail add: PO Box 172, 57070). Tel: 605-326-5481. E-mail: vpsdlibrary@gmail.com. Web Site: viborgpublic.yoursdlibrary.org. *Dir,* Becky Nutley
Library Holdings: Bk Vols 13,000; Per Subs 1
Wireless access
Open Mon-Fri 10-5:30

WAGNER

P WAGNER PUBLIC LIBRARY, 106 Sheridan Ave SE, 57380. SAN 315-7032. Tel: 605-384-5248. FAX: 605-384-5248. E-mail: wagpblb@hcinet.net. Web Site: www.cityofwagner.org/wagner-library. *Librn,* Anne Podhradsky
Founded 1914. Circ 14,000
Library Holdings: AV Mats 95; Large Print Bks 950; Bk Titles 16,877; Bk Vols 17,390; Per Subs 53; Talking Bks 165
Automation Activity & Vendor Info: (Cataloging) Book Systems; (OPAC) Book Systems
Wireless access
Partic in South Dakota Library Network
Open Mon-Fri 9-5

WALL

P WALL COMMUNITY LIBRARY*, 407 Main St, 57790. (Mail add: PO Box 131, 57790-0131). Tel: 605-279-2929. E-mail: wallcomlib@gwtc.net. Web Site: wall.yoursdlibrary.org, www.wallsd.us/library. *Libr Dir,* Ester Johannesen
Founded 1978
Library Holdings: Audiobooks 70; Braille Volumes 5; DVDs 100; Large Print Bks 107; Bk Vols 10,000; Per Subs 2
Wireless access
Function: 24/7 Electronic res, 24/7 Online cat, Audiobks via web, Bks on CD, Children's prog, Computers for patron use, Free DVD rentals, ILL available, Internet access, Mail & tel request accepted, Movies, Online cat, OverDrive digital audio bks, Photocopying/Printing, Preschool reading prog, Prog for children & young adult, Ref serv available, Story hour, Summer reading prog, Wheelchair accessible
Partic in Black Hills Library Consortium
Open Wed 12-7, Thurs 10-12:30 & 1:30-5, Fri 8-Noon, Sat 9-11
Restriction: Non-resident fee

WATERTOWN

S LAKE AREA TECHNICAL INSTITUTE LIBRARY*, L H Timmerman Library, 1201 Arrow Ave, Rm 210, 57201. (Mail add: PO Box 730, 57201-0730), SAN 327-0955. Tel: 605-882-5284, Ext 231. FAX: 605-882-6299. E-mail: library@lakeareatech.edu. Web Site: www.lakeareatech.edu/campus/library. *Librn,* Jenna Jewell; E-mail: jenna.jewell@lakeareatech.edu
Library Holdings: Bk Vols 1,500; Per Subs 113
Subject Interests: Agr
Wireless access
Open Mon-Fri 7:30-4

P WATERTOWN REGIONAL LIBRARY*, 160 Sixth St NE, 57201-2778. (Mail add: PO Box 250, 57201-0250), SAN 315-7040. Tel: 605-882-6220. FAX: 605-882-6221. E-mail: watadmin@watertownsd.us. Web Site: www.watertownsd.us/852/watertown-regional-library. *City Librn,* Deirdre Whitman; *Asst City Librn,* Maria Gruener; Staff 8 (MLS 4, Non-MLS 4)
Founded 1899. Pop 27,227
Jan 2016-Dec 2016 Income $1,048,350, City $998,100, Other $50,250. Mats Exp $129,100, Books $95,000, Electronic Ref Mat (Incl. Access Fees) $34,100. Sal $516,200 (Prof $324,200)
Special Collections: Dakota Territory Coll
Subject Interests: Watertown hist
Automation Activity & Vendor Info: (Acquisitions) Baker & Taylor; (Cataloging) OCLC; (Circulation) Beacon - TLC (The Library Corporation); (ILL) OCLC; (OPAC) Beacon - TLC (The Library Corporation)
Wireless access
Function: 24/7 Electronic res, 24/7 Online cat, Adult bk club, Art exhibits, Audiobks via web, Bk club(s), Bks on cassette, Bks on CD, CD-ROM, Children's prog, Computer training, Computers for patron use, Digital talking bks, Electronic databases & coll, Free DVD rentals, Holiday prog, Home delivery & serv to seniorr ctr & nursing homes, Homebound delivery serv, ILL available, Internet access, Magazines, Mango lang, Meeting rooms, Microfiche/film & reading machines, Music CDs, Online cat, Outreach serv, Outside serv via phone, mail, e-mail & web, Photocopying/Printing, Preschool outreach, Prog for adults, Prog for children & young adult, Ref serv available, Res performed for a fee, Scanner, Senior computer classes, Serves people with intellectual disabilities, Spoken cassettes & CDs, Spoken cassettes & DVDs, Story hour, Study rm, Summer & winter reading prog, Summer reading prog, Tax forms, Teen prog, Telephone ref, Wheelchair accessible
Partic in OCLC Online Computer Library Center, Inc
Open Mon-Thurs 9:30-9, Fri 9:30-6, Sat 9:30-5, Sun 1-5
Friends of the Library Group

WAUBAY

P WAUBAY PUBLIC LIBRARY*, 94 N Main St, 57273. (Mail add: PO Box 155, 57273-0155). Tel: 605-947-4748. FAX: 605-947-4748. E-mail: waublibr@midco.net. Web Site: waubay.yoursdlibrary.org. *Co-Librn,* Sandy Himze; *Co-Librn,* Clara Miller
Library Holdings: Bk Vols 7,500
Wireless access
Open Mon-Fri 11-5, Sat 10-2

WEBSTER

P WEBSTER PUBLIC LIBRARY, 800 Main St, 57274. SAN 315-7059. Tel: 605-345-3263. Web Site: webster.yoursdlibrary.org. *Dir,* Teri Ewalt
Founded 1930. Pop 1,956; Circ 17,750
Library Holdings: AV Mats 448; CDs 40; Bk Vols 32,000; Per Subs 59; Talking Bks 402
Special Collections: South Dakota History Coll
Wireless access
Open Mon & Fri 1-6, Tues & Thurs 9-11 & 1-6, Wed 1-5

WESSINGTON

P WESSINGTON PUBLIC LIBRARY*, 240 Wessington St, 57381. (Mail add: PO Box 108, 57381-0108), SAN 315-7067. Tel: 605-458-2596. E-mail: wesspublib@venturecomm.net. *Dir,* Donna Runge
Founded 1937. Pop 800; Circ 4,700
Library Holdings: Bk Titles 6,000; Per Subs 16
Special Collections: South Dakota History; South Dakota Poetry, pamphlets; South Dakota State Laws
Wireless access
Open Wed & Sat 1-5

WESSINGTON SPRINGS

P WESSINGTON SPRINGS CARNEGIE LIBRARY*, 109 W Main St, 57382. SAN 315-7075. Tel: 605-539-1803. E-mail: wscarnegie@venturecomm.net. Web Site: wessingtonsprings.yoursdlibrary.org. *Librn,* Barb Horsley
Founded 1918. Pop 1,203; Circ 8,299
Library Holdings: Bk Titles 18,200; Per Subs 30
Special Collections: Books By or About South Dakotans & South Dakota; Old Newspapers (local)
Wireless access
Open Mon & Thurs 12:30-5:30, Wed 12:30-6:30, Fri 10-11:30 & 12:30-5:30

WHITEWOOD

P WHITEWOOD PUBLIC LIBRARY*, 1201 Ash St, 57793. Tel: 605-269-2616. E-mail: wwdlib@hotmail.com. Web Site: cityofwhitewood.net/whitewood-public-library, whitewoodpublic.yoursdlibrary.org. *Libr Dir,* Position Currently Open; *Librn,* Donn Boyle; *Librn,* Dale O'Dea; *Librn,* Lois Williamson
Founded 1951
Wireless access
Function: Computers for patron use, ILL available, Photocopying/Printing, Scanner, Study rm
Partic in Black Hills Library Consortium
Open Mon, Wed & Fri 9:30-11:30 & 1-5, Tues & Thurs 1-5 & 6:30-8:30, Sat 9:30-11:30

WINNER

P TRIPP COUNTY LIBRARY-GROSSENBURG MEMORIAL*, 442 S Monroe St, 57580. SAN 360-4837. Tel: 605-842-0330. E-mail: tclib@gwtc.net. Web Site: trippcounty.yoursdlibrary.org. *Libr Dir,* Misti Burns
Founded 1921. Pop 6,430; Circ 50,685
Special Collections: Genealogy Coll; South Dakota and Tripp County Historical Coll
Automation Activity & Vendor Info: (Cataloging) Follett Software; (Circulation) Follett Software; (OPAC) Follett Software
Wireless access
Special Services for the Blind - Braille & cassettes; Large print bks; Talking bks & player equip
Open Mon-Wed & Fri 9:30-5:30; Thurs 9:30-7
Friends of the Library Group

WOONSOCKET

P WOONSOCKET CITY LIBRARY*, 101 N Second Ave, 57385. (Mail add: PO Box 428, 57385-0428). SAN 315-7083. Tel: 605-796-1412. E-mail: woonsocket.library@k12.sd.us. Web Site: woonsocket.k12.sd.us/library, www.facebook.com/woonlib. *Librn,* Tracey Steele; E-mail: tracey,steeke@k12.sd.us
Founded 1918. Pop 850; Circ 4,522
Library Holdings: AV Mats 210; Bk Vols 5,274; Per Subs 22
Wireless access
Open Mon-Thurs 7:45-4:15, Fri 7:45-1 (Winter); Mon, Wed & Thurs 10:30-2:30
Friends of the Library Group

YANKTON

C MOUNT MARTY UNIVERSITY*, Mother Jerome Schmitt Library, 1105 W Eighth St, 57078-3725. SAN 315-7091. Tel: 605-668-1555. FAX: 605-668-1357. E-mail: dept.library@mountmarty.edu. Web Site: www.mountmarty.edu/academics/mother-jerome-schmitt-library. *Libr Dir,* Sandra Brown; E-mail: sbrown@mountmarty.edu; *Cat, Circ,* Diane Dvorak; *ILL, Per,* Aimee Huntley; Staff 3 (MLS 1, Non-MLS 2)
Founded 1936. Highest Degree: Master
Subject Interests: Relig studies
Automation Activity & Vendor Info: (Circulation) Ex Libris Group
Wireless access
Partic in Minitex; OCLC Online Computer Library Center, Inc
Open Mon-Thurs 7:30am-10pm, Fri 7:30-5, Sat 11-4, Sun 1-10; Mon-Fri 8-5 (Summer)

P YANKTON COMMUNITY LIBRARY*, 515 Walnut St, 57078. SAN 315-7121. Tel: 605-668-5275. FAX: 605-668-5277. E-mail: library@cityofyankton.org. Web Site: www.cityofyankton.org/departments-services/yankton-community-library. *Libr Dir,* Dana Schmidt; *Asst Dir, Tech Serv,* Linda Dobrovolny; Staff 12 (MLS 1, Non-MLS 11)
Founded 1868. Pop 21,652; Circ 178,344
Library Holdings: Bk Titles 64,000; Bk Vols 72,000; Per Subs 150
Subject Interests: Genealogy, Local hist, SDak hist
Wireless access
Function: 24/7 Electronic res, 24/7 Online cat, Activity rm, Adult bk club, Adult literacy prog, Wheelchair accessible
Open Mon-Thurs 9-8, Fri & Sat 9-5, Sun 1-5 (Fall-Spring); Mon & Tues 9-8, Wed & Thurs 9-6, Fri & Sat 9-5 (Summer)
Friends of the Library Group

TENNESSEE

Date of Statistics: FY 2023-2024
Population, 2020 U.S. Census: 7,126,489
Population Served by Public Libraries: 6,976,008
Total Volumes in Public Libraries: 10,050,092
Volumes Per Capita: 1.47
Total Public Library Circulation: 32,119,076
Circulation Per Capita: 4.70
Digital Resources:
Uses of Electronic Resources: 1,686,122
Total e-books: 864,813
Total audio items (physical & downloadable units): 1,005,609
Total video items (physical & downloadable units): 906,269
Total computers for use by the public: 5,276
Total annual wireless sessions: 5,472,560
Income and Expenditures:
Total Public Library Income: $174,120,741
Income per Capita: $25.49
Source of Income: Mainly public funds; federal, state & local
Expenditures: $172,787,934
Expenditure Per Capita: $25.30
Grants-in-Aid to Public Libraries:
Federal LSTA (2023): 3,689,581; and State 20,326,835
PLEASE NOTE: Tennessee does not give direct state aid to public libraries. Most of the state money flows through the regional library system where a percentage goes to regional salaries and benefits.
Number of County or Multi-county (Regional) Libraries: 9 multi-county, 4 metropolitans
Counties Served: 95
Number of Bookmobiles in State: 7
Information provided courtesy of: Christy M. Chandler, State Data Coordinator; Tennessee State Library & Archives.

ADAMSVILLE

P MCNAIRY COUNTY LIBRARIES*, Irving Meek Jr Memorial Library, 204 W Main St, 38310. (Mail add: PO Box 303, 38310-0303), SAN 315-713X. Tel: 731-632-3572. FAX: 731-632-1391. E-mail: mcnairycountylibrary@gmail.com. Web Site: mcnairylibraries.wordpress.com. *Dir,* Ms Robbie Harris
Founded 1961. Pop 7,050; Circ 33,000
Library Holdings: AV Mats 1,442; Bk Vols 19,993; Per Subs 45
Special Collections: Buford Pusser Memorabilia
Subject Interests: Fossils, Shells
Wireless access
Mem of Hatchie River Regional Library
Open Mon, Tues, Thurs & Fri 10-6, Wed & Sat 10-1
Friends of the Library Group
Branches: 1
JACK MCCONNICO MEMORIAL LIBRARY, 225 Oak Grove Rd, Selmer, 38375, SAN 315-9671. Tel: 731-645-5571. FAX: 731-645-4874. *Dir,* Robbie Harris; *Asst Librn,* Emily Harris; Staff 2 (MLS 1, Non-MLS 1)
Founded 1984. Pop 22,422; Circ 56,861
Library Holdings: AV Mats 1,713; Bk Vols 37,881; Per Subs 44
Special Collections: Historic Old Purdy; Literacy, McNairy Co History; McNairy Co; photo; Vietnam War; Wild Flower Coll
Subject Interests: Genealogy, State hist
Automation Activity & Vendor Info: (Circulation) Follett Software
Function: 24/7 Electronic res, 24/7 Online cat
Publications: Cemetery Records; Early Marriages; McNairy Co History
Open Mon & Fri 9-5:30, Tues & Thurs 9-6, Wed 10-4, Sat 9-1
Friends of the Library Group

ALAMO

P CROCKETT MEMORIAL LIBRARY*, 261 E Church St, 38001-1108. SAN 315-7148. Tel: 731-696-4220. FAX: 731-696-5107. *Dir,* Linda Rice; E-mail: linda.rice.director@gmail.com
Founded 1968
Library Holdings: Bk Vols 20,000
Subject Interests: Local hist
Automation Activity & Vendor Info: (Circulation) Auto-Graphics, Inc; (ILL) Auto-Graphics, Inc
Wireless access
Mem of Obion River Regional Library
Open Mon-Wed & Fri 9-5, Thurs 10-6, Sat 10-3
Friends of the Library Group

ALTAMONT

P ALTAMONT PUBLIC LIBRARY*, 1433 Main St, 37301. (Mail add: PO Box 228, 37301-0228), SAN 315-7156. Tel: 931-692-2457. E-mail: altamontlib@blomand.net. Web Site: www.grundytnlibraries.org/altamont-library. *Libr Dir,* Sonya Rogers; E-mail: apldir19@gmail.com
Library Holdings: Bk Vols 5,000
Wireless access
Open Mon & Thurs 9:30-4, Tues 9-4

ARDMORE

P ARDMORE PUBLIC LIBRARY*, 25836 Main St, 38449. (Mail add: PO Box 517, 38449-0517), SAN 376-7000. Tel: 931-427-4883. FAX: 931-427-3818. E-mail: ardmorelib@ardmore.net. Web Site: www.cityofardmoretn.com/library. *Dir,* Verlin Collins; Staff 3 (Non-MLS 3)
Founded 1977. Pop 2,813; Circ 51,042
Library Holdings: Bk Vols 49,502; Per Subs 21
Automation Activity & Vendor Info: (Cataloging) Auto-Graphics, Inc; (Circulation) Auto-Graphics, Inc
Wireless access
Open Mon-Fri 9-6, Sat 9-1
Friends of the Library Group

ARLINGTON

P SAM T WILSON PUBLIC LIBRARY*, 11968 Walker St, 38002. SAN 378-4452. Tel: 901-867-1954. E-mail: library@townofarlington.org. Web Site: www.townofarlington.org/departments/sam_t_wilson_library. *Head Librn,* Lisa Lance; E-mail: llance@townofarlington.org
Library Holdings: Bk Titles 21,000
Wireless access
Function: Bks on CD
Open Mon 11-7, Tues-Thurs & Sat 10-6
Friends of the Library Group

ARNOLD AFB

A UNITED STATES AIR FORCE*, Arnold Engineering Development Center Technical Library, 100 Kindel Dr, Ste C212, 37389. SAN 360-5078. Tel: 931-454-7220. Interlibrary Loan Service Tel: 931-454-7604. FAX: 931-454-5421. Web Site: www.arnold.af.mil. *Library Contact,* Jean Frantz; Staff 1 (MLS 1)
Founded 1952
Library Holdings: AV Mats 918; e-journals 33; Bk Vols 27,429; Per Subs 273
Special Collections: NACA Technical Reports; NACA Wartime Reports
Subject Interests: Aerospace sci, Astronomy, Chem, Engr, Math, Optics, Physics, Pollution
Automation Activity & Vendor Info: (Acquisitions) SirsiDynix; (Cataloging) SirsiDynix; (Circulation) SirsiDynix; (OPAC) SirsiDynix; (Serials) SirsiDynix
Wireless access
Partic in OCLC Online Computer Library Center, Inc
Restriction: Not open to pub

ASHLAND CITY

P CHEATHAM COUNTY PUBLIC LIBRARY*, 188 County Services Dr, Ste 200, 37015-1726. SAN 315-7172. Tel: 615-792-4828. FAX: 615-792-2054. E-mail: cheathampublic.library@gmail.com. Web Site: sites.google.com/site/cheathamcountylibrary. *Dir,* May Lingner; E-mail: may.lingner@cheathamcountytn.gov; Staff 7 (MLS 1, Non-MLS 6)
Founded 1967. Pop 23,789
Library Holdings: Bk Titles 30,000; Per Subs 55
Special Collections: Oral History
Automation Activity & Vendor Info: (Acquisitions) Book Systems; (Cataloging) Auto-Graphics, Inc; (Course Reserve) Auto-Graphics, Inc; (ILL) Auto-Graphics, Inc
Wireless access
Mem of Red River Regional Library
Special Services for the Blind - Audio mat
Open Mon, Wed & Fri 8:30-5, Tues & Thurs 8:30-8, Sat 8:30-3
Friends of the Library Group

ATHENS

P EDWARD GAUCHE FISHER PUBLIC LIBRARY*, 1289 Ingleside Ave, 37303. SAN 315-7199. Tel: 423-745-7782. FAX: 423-745-1763. Web Site: fisherlibrary.org. *Dir,* Peyton Eastman; E-mail: peytoneastman@fisherlibrary.org; Staff 9 (MLS 1, Non-MLS 8)
Founded 1969. Pop 50,000; Circ 117,414
Library Holdings: Bk Vols 102,000; Per Subs 80; Videos 1,600
Automation Activity & Vendor Info: (Cataloging) SirsiDynix; (Circulation) SirsiDynix; (OPAC) SirsiDynix
Wireless access
Function: 24/7 Electronic res, 24/7 Online cat, Accelerated reader prog, Adult bk club, After school storytime, Art exhibits, Art programs, Audiobks via web, Bk club(s), Bks on CD, Children's prog, Computer training, Computers for patron use, Electronic databases & coll, Family literacy, For res purposes, Free DVD rentals, Games & aids for people with disabilities, Govt ref serv, Health sci info serv, Holiday prog, Homework prog, ILL available, Instruction & testing, Internet access, Life-long learning prog for all ages, Magazines, Makerspace, Meeting rooms, Microfiche/film & reading machines, Movies, Online cat, Online info literacy tutorials on the web & in blackboard, Outreach serv, Photocopying/Printing, Prog for adults, Prog for children & young adult, Ref & res, Ref serv available, Res assist avail, Scanner, Serves people with intellectual disabilities, Spanish lang bks, STEM programs, Story hour, Study rm, Summer & winter reading prog, Summer reading prog, Teen prog, Telephone ref, Visual arts prog, Wheelchair accessible, Workshops, Writing prog
Mem of Ocoee River Regional Library
Open Mon, Tues & Thurs 9:30-8, Wed & Fri 9:30-5:30, Sat 10-5
Friends of the Library Group

P OCOEE RIVER REGIONAL LIBRARY*, 718 George St NW, 37303-2214. SAN 315-7180. Tel: 423-745-5194. Toll Free Tel: 855-692-8186. FAX: 423-649-1501. Web Site: sos.tn.gov/products/tsla/ocoee-river-regional-library. *Dir,* Liz Schreck; *Asst Dir,* Nikki Branam-Snyder; E-mail: Nikki.Branam-Synder@tn.gov; Staff 8 (MLS 2, Non-MLS 6)
Founded 1939. Pop 439,074; Circ 1,886,988
Special Collections: Tennessee Library History Coll (History of Tennessee Regional Service & Public Library Development)
Function: Home delivery & serv to seniorr ctr & nursing homes, Homebound delivery serv, ILL available, Prof lending libr, Workshops
Member Libraries: Audrey Pack Memorial Library; Blount County Public Library; Calhoun Public Library; Cleveland Bradley County Public Library; Clyde W Roddy Library; East Polk Public Library; Edward Gauche Fisher Public Library; Englewood Public Library; Etowah Carnegie Public Library; Graysville Public Library; Greenback Public Library; Harriman Public Library; Kingston Public Library; Lenoir City Public Library; Loudon Public Library; Madisonville Public Library; Meigs County - Decatur Public Library; Niota Public Library; Oliver Springs Public Library; Philadelphia Public Library; Public Library at Tellico Village; Rockwood Public Library; Sweetwater Public Library; Tellico Plains Public Library; Vonore Public Library; West Polk Public Library
Partic in Tenn-Share
Open Mon-Fri 8-4:30

C TENNESSEE WESLEYAN COLLEGE*, Merner-Pfeiffer Library, 23 Coach Farmer Dr, 37303. SAN 315-7202. Tel: 423-746-5250. E-mail: library@tnwesleyan.edu. Web Site: library.tnwesleyan.edu. *Libr Dir,* Julie Adams; Tel: 423-746-5251; *Info Serv Librn,* Alex Sharp; Tel: 423-746-5249, E-mail: asharp@tnwesleyan.edu; Staff 7 (MLS 3, Non-MLS 4)
Founded 1857. Enrl 1,035; Fac 100; Highest Degree: Master
Special Collections: Methodist Church History (Cooke Memorial Coll)
Automation Activity & Vendor Info: (Acquisitions) Innovative Interfaces, Inc; (Cataloging) Innovative Interfaces, Inc; (Circulation) Innovative Interfaces, Inc; (Discovery) EBSCO Discovery Service; (ILL) Innovative Interfaces, Inc; (OPAC) Innovative Interfaces, Inc; (Serials) Innovative Interfaces, Inc
Wireless access
Function: Archival coll, Computers for patron use, Distance learning, Doc delivery serv, E-Reserves, Electronic databases & coll, ILL available, Microfiche/film & reading machines, Music CDs, Online cat, Online ref, Orientations, Photocopying/Printing, Ref & res, Ref serv available, Telephone ref, Wheelchair accessible
Partic in Appalachian College Association; Tenn-Share
Open Mon-Thurs 8am-10pm, Fri 8:30-5, Sun 2-8 (Fall & Winter); Mon-Thurs 8:30-6, Fri 8:30-4 (Summer)
Restriction: Borrowing privileges limited to fac & registered students, Borrowing requests are handled by ILL, In-house use for visitors, Open to fac, students & qualified researchers, Open to pub for ref & circ; with some limitations, Open to staff, students & ancillary prof, Open to students, fac & staff, Pub use on premises

BEAN STATION

P BEAN STATION PUBLIC LIBRARY*, 895 Broadway Dr, 37708. (Mail add: PO Box 100, 37708-0100), SAN 361-011X. Tel: 865-993-3068. FAX: 865-993-3068. E-mail: beanstationlib@gmail.com. *Dir,* Fayrene Miller; Staff 1 (Non-MLS 1)
Library Holdings: Bk Vols 9,242
Wireless access
Mem of Clinch River Regional Library
Open Mon-Fri 9-5

BEERSHEBA SPRINGS

P BEERSHEBA SPRINGS PUBLIC LIBRARY*, Hwy 56, 37305. (Mail add: PO Box 192, 37305-0192), SAN 315-7210. Tel: 931-692-3029. FAX: 931-692-3029. E-mail: beershebalib@blomand.net. Web Site: sites.google.com/view/grundytnlibraries/beersheba-springs-library. *Dir,* Melissa Scruggs
Library Holdings: Bk Vols 3,000
Open Mon-Wed 10-5, Fri 10-4
Friends of the Library Group

BENTON

P WEST POLK PUBLIC LIBRARY*, 126 Polk St, 37307. SAN 315-7229. Tel: 423-338-4536. E-mail: westpolklibrary1@hotmail.com. *Dir,* Lori Cox
Library Holdings: Bk Vols 3,600
Mem of Ocoee River Regional Library
Open Mon, Wed & Fri 11-5, Tues & Thurs 1-7, Sat 10-2

BLAINE

P BLAINE PUBLIC LIBRARY*, 220 Indian Ridge Rd, 37709. (Mail add: PO Box 66, 37709-0066), SAN 370-4394. Tel: 865-933-0845. FAX: 865-933-0845. E-mail: blainepublib@gmail.com. *Dir,* Cindy Chandler
Pop 1,700; Circ 9,081
Library Holdings: CDs 10; DVDs 20; Large Print Bks 150; Bk Vols 6,811; Per Subs 13; Talking Bks 40; Videos 150
Wireless access
Function: CD-ROM, Digital talking bks, Health sci info serv, Homebound delivery serv, ILL available, Internet access, Music CDs, Photocopying/Printing, Prog for children & young adult, Ref serv available, Spoken cassettes & CDs, Spoken cassettes & DVDs, Summer reading prog, Telephone ref, Wheelchair accessible
Mem of Clinch River Regional Library
Special Services for the Blind - Aids for in-house use; Bks on cassette; Bks on CD; Talking bks
Open Mon, Wed & Fri 9-5, Tues 9-3

BLOUNTVILLE

J NORTHEAST STATE COMMUNITY COLLEGE*, Wayne G Basler Library, 2425 Hwy 75, 37617. (Mail add: PO Box 246, 37617-0246), SAN 376-7922. Tel: 423-354-2429. Web Site: library.northeaststate.edu/home. *Dean of Libr,* Chris Demas; E-mail: cddemas@northeaststate.edu; *Librn,* Amy Baghetti; E-mail: acbaghetti@northeaststate.edu; *Librn,* Amy Lippo; E-mail: aslippo@northeaststate.edu; *Librn,* Virginia Salmon; E-mail: vlsalmon@northeaststate.edu; *Librn,* Michelle Wyatt; E-mail: mrwyatt@northeaststate.edu; Staff 11.5 (MLS 7, Non-MLS 4.5)
Founded 1966. Enrl 4,274; Fac 350; Highest Degree: Associate
Library Holdings: Bk Vols 66,473; Per Subs 320
Automation Activity & Vendor Info: (Cataloging) Ex Libris Group; (Circulation) Ex Libris Group; (ILL) OCLC WorldShare Interlibrary Loan; (OPAC) Ex Libris Group
Wireless access

P SULLIVAN COUNTY PUBLIC LIBRARY*, 1655 Blountville Blvd, 37617. (Mail add: PO Box 510, 37617-0510). Tel: 423-279-2714. FAX: 423-279-2836. E-mail: slclibrarydirector@gmail.com. Web Site: wrlibrary.org/sullivan. *Dir,* Megan Hopkins; E-mail: slcmhopkins@gmail.com; *Br Mgr,* Margaret Elsea; Staff 7 (MLS 2, Non-MLS 5)
Founded 1946. Pop 77,290; Circ 160,232
Library Holdings: Bk Vols 108,884; Per Subs 161
Special Collections: Sullivan County History
Subject Interests: Genealogy, Tenn hist
Automation Activity & Vendor Info: (Cataloging) SirsiDynix; (Circulation) SirsiDynix; (OPAC) SirsiDynix
Wireless access
Function: 24/7 Electronic res, Adult bk club, Audiobks via web, Bks on CD, Computer training, Computers for patron use, Electronic databases & coll, Free DVD rentals, ILL available, Internet access, Magazines, Meeting rooms, Music CDs, Notary serv, Online cat, Photocopying/Printing, Printer for laptops & handheld devices, Prog for children & young adult, Scanner, Story hour, Tax forms, Telephone ref, Wheelchair accessible
Mem of Holston River Regional Library
Open Mon-Thurs 9-6, Sat 9-5
Friends of the Library Group
Branches: 4
BLOOMINGDALE BRANCH, 3230 Van Horn St, Kingsport, 37660, SAN 360-5132. Tel: 423-288-1310. FAX: 423-288-1310. *Br Mgr,* Angela Taylor; Staff 2 (Non-MLS 2)
Founded 1962. Pop 87,933; Circ 147,230
Open Mon-Sat 9-5
COLONIAL HEIGHTS BRANCH, 149 Pactolus Rd, Kingsport, 37663, SAN 360-5191. Tel: 423-239-1100. FAX: 423-239-1100. *Br Mgr,* Ms Jo McDavid
Founded 1961
Library Holdings: Bk Vols 15,000
Open Mon-Sat 9-5
Friends of the Library Group
SULLIVAN GARDENS BRANCH, 104 Bluegrass Dr, Kingsport, 37660, SAN 360-5221. Tel: 423-349-5990. FAX: 423-349-5990. *Br Mgr,* Peggy Sutherland
Open Mon-Sat 9-5
Friends of the Library Group
THOMAS MEMORIAL BRANCH, 481 Cedar St, Bluff City, 37618, SAN 360-5167. Tel: 423-538-1980. FAX: 423-538-1980. *Br Mgr,* Angela Taylor; Staff 2 (MLS 1, Non-MLS 1)
Founded 1973
Open Mon-Sat 9-5
Friends of the Library Group

BOLIVAR

P BOLIVAR-HARDEMAN COUNTY LIBRARY, 213 N Washington St, 38008-2020. SAN 315-7237. Tel: 731-658-3436. Administration Tel: 731-658-9045. FAX: 731-658-4660. Web Site: www.bolivarhardemancountylibrary.com, www.cityofbolivar.com/bolivar-hardeman-county-library. *Dir,* Jessica Phillips; E-mail: director.bhcl@gmail.com
Founded 1952. Pop 24,451
Library Holdings: AV Mats 8,374; DVDs 586; Large Print Bks 3,292; Bk Vols 41,522; Per Subs 75; Talking Bks 1,947; Videos 3,588
Special Collections: Civil War (Quinnie Armour Rare Books Coll); Roy Black Coll
Subject Interests: Genealogy, Local hist
Automation Activity & Vendor Info: (Acquisitions) Follett Software; (Cataloging) Follett Software; (Circulation) Follett Software; (ILL) Auto-Graphics, Inc; (OPAC) Auto-Graphics, Inc
Wireless access
Function: 24/7 Online cat, 24/7 wireless access, Activity rm, Adult bk club, Online cat, Outside serv via phone, mail, e-mail & web, OverDrive digital audio bks, Photocopying/Printing, Preschool reading prog, Printer for laptops & handheld devices, Prog for adults, Prog for children & young adult, Scanner, Senior outreach, Serves people with intellectual disabilities, Spanish lang bks, Spoken cassettes & CDs, Spoken cassettes & DVDs, STEM programs, Story hour, Summer reading prog, Teen prog, Wheelchair accessible
Mem of Hatchie River Regional Library
Open Mon-Fri 8-6, Sat 8-12
Friends of the Library Group

BRENTWOOD

P THE JOHN P HOLT BRENTWOOD LIBRARY*, 8109 Concord Rd, 37027. SAN 325-092X. Tel: 615-371-0090. Circulation Tel: 615-371-0090, Ext 8070. Reference Tel: 615-371-0090, Ext 8200. Administration Tel: 615-371-0090, Ext 8000. FAX: 615-371-2238. Reference E-mail: reference@brentwoodtn.gov. Web Site: www.brentwoodtn.gov/departments/library. *Libr Dir,* Susan Earl; Tel: 615-371-0090, Ext 8010, E-mail: susan.earl@brentwoodtn.gov; *Cat Librn, Libr Serv Mgr,* Molly Fulton; Tel: 615-371-0090, Ext 8220, E-mail: molly.fulton@brentwoodtn.gov; *Pub Serv Librn,* Claire Stanton; E-mail: claire.stanton@brentwoodtn.gov; *Ref Librn,* Wonda Damron; Tel: 615-371-0090, Ext 8130, E-mail: wonda.damron@brentwoodtn.gov; *Ref Librn, Spec Coll Librn,* Susannah Choate; Tel: 615-371-0090, Ext 8230, E-mail: susannah.choate@brentwoodtn.gov; *Ch Mgr,* Missy Dillingham; Tel: 615-371-0090, Ext 8410, E-mail: missy.dillingham@brentwoodtn.gov; *Circ Serv Supvr,* Pamela Johnson; Tel: 615-371-0090, Ext 8190, E-mail: pamela.johnson@brentwoodtn.gov; *Coordr, Commun Engagement,* Brigid Day; Tel: 615-371-0090, Ext 8510, E-mail: Brigid.day@brentwoodtn.gov; *ILL Coordr,* Joy Meza; E-mail: joy.meza@brentwoodtn.gov; *Spec Projects Coordr/Vols Coordr,* Elizabeth Johnson; Tel: 615-371-0090, Ext 8860, E-mail: elizabeth.johnson@brentwoodtn.gov; *Children's Serv Team Leader,* Pat Ladnier; E-mail: pat.ladnier@brentwoodtn.gov; *Commun Relations, Libr Tech II,* Sarah Norris; Tel: 615-371-0090, E-mail: sarah.norris@brentwoodtn.gov; *Lead Cataloger,* Robin Walden; E-mail: robin.walden@brentwoodtn.gov. Subject Specialists: *Adult fiction, Children's prog,* Claire Stanton; *Movies,* Wonda Damron; *Non-fiction,* Susannah Choate; *Customer serv,* Pamela Johnson; *Child develop, Children's videos,* Pat Ladnier; *Mkt,* Sarah Norris; Staff 45 (MLS 7, Non-MLS 38)
Founded 1978. Circ 552,041
Jul 2018-Jun 2019 Income $2,604,772, State $11,272, City $2,521,550, County $71,950. Mats Exp $414,850,000, Books $180,000, Per/Ser (Incl. Access Fees) $12,600, AV Mat $90,250, Electronic Ref Mat (Incl. Access Fees) $132,000. Sal $1,057,100
Library Holdings: Audiobooks 12,371; AV Mats 21,159; CDs 12,797; DVDs 21,783; e-books 144,216; e-journals 200; Electronic Media & Resources 107; Large Print Bks 1,000; Microforms 304; Bk Vols 149,610; Per Subs 363
Special Collections: Art Lending Library; Brentwood Local History
Automation Activity & Vendor Info: (Acquisitions) Innovative Interfaces, Inc; (Cataloging) Innovative Interfaces, Inc; (Circulation) Innovative Interfaces, Inc; (ILL) OCLC; (OPAC) Innovative Interfaces, Inc; (Serials) EBSCO Online
Wireless access
Function: 24/7 Electronic res, 24/7 Online cat, 3D Printer, Accelerated reader prog, Activity rm, Adult bk club, After school storytime, Art exhibits, Art programs, Audiobks on Playaways & MP3, Audiobks via web, AV serv, Bk club(s), Bks on CD, Chess club, Children's prog, Computer training, Computers for patron use, Digital talking bks, Distance learning, Electronic databases & coll, Free DVD rentals, Holiday prog, Homework prog, ILL available, Instruction & testing, Internet access, Jazz prog, Learning ctr, Life-long learning prog for all ages, Magazines, Magnifiers for reading, Mail & tel request accepted, Mango lang, Meeting rooms, Microfiche/film & reading machines, Movies, Music CDs, Notary serv, Online cat, Online ref, Outreach serv, OverDrive digital audio bks, Photocopying/Printing, Preschool outreach, Preschool reading prog, Printer for laptops & handheld devices, Prog for adults, Prog for children & young adult, Ref serv available, Res assist avail, Scanner, Senior computer classes, Senior outreach, Spanish lang bks, STEM programs, Story hour, Study rm, Summer & winter reading prog, Tax forms, Teen prog, Telephone ref, Visual arts prog, Wheelchair accessible, Workshops, Writing prog
Publications: Annual Report; The Browser (Monthly newsletter)
Mem of Buffalo River Regional Library
Partic in Nashville Area Libr Alliance; Tenn-Share
Open Mon-Thurs 9-8, Fri 9-6, Sat 10-6, Sun 1-6
Restriction: Circ limited, Circ to mem only, Fee for pub use, Free to mem, In-house use for visitors, Internal use only, Mem only, Non-circulating coll, Non-circulating of rare bks, Non-circulating to the pub, Non-resident fee
Friends of the Library Group

BRICEVILLE

P BRICEVILLE PUBLIC LIBRARY*, 111 Slatestone Rd, 37710. (Mail add: PO Box 61, 37710-0061), SAN 315-7245. Tel: 865-426-6220. FAX: 865-426-6220. E-mail: bricevillepubliclibrary@comcast.net. Web Site: bricevillepubliclibrary.wordpress.com. *Libr Dir,* Daphne L Windham
Library Holdings: Bk Vols 3,000
Automation Activity & Vendor Info: (Cataloging) Auto-Graphics, Inc; (Circulation) Baker & Taylor; (ILL) Auto-Graphics, Inc
Wireless access
Function: ILL available
Mem of Clinch River Regional Library
Open Mon-Fri 12-6
Friends of the Library Group

BRISTOL

P BRISTOL PUBLIC LIBRARY*, Avoca, 1550 Volunteer Pkwy, 37620. SAN 362-7608. Tel: 423-968-9663. FAX: 276-645-8795. E-mail: avoca@bristol-library.org. Web Site: bristol-library.org/avoca-branch-library.

Br Mgr, Brenda G'Fellers; Tel: 423-968-9663, E-mail: bgfellers@bristol-library.org; Staff 4 (MLS 1, Non-MLS 3)
Founded 1974
Library Holdings: Audiobooks 1,000; AV Mats 32; CDs 500; DVDs 4,000; Bk Titles 21,207; Bk Vols 21,640; Per Subs 30
Wireless access
Open Mon-Thurs 9-7, Fri 9-5, Sat 9-Noon
Friends of the Library Group

C KING UNIVERSITY*, King Libraries, 1350 King College Rd, 37620. SAN 315-727X. Tel: 423-652-4716. FAX: 423-652-4871. E-mail: library@king.edu. Web Site: www.king.edu/library. *Univ Librn,* Matt Peltier; Tel: 423-652-4750, E-mail: mspeltie@king.edu; *Electronic Serv Librn,* Keri-Lynn Paulson; Tel: 423-652-4897, E-mail: kpaulson@king.edu; *Instrul Serv Librn,* Emily Krug; Tel: 423-652-6301, E-mail: ekrug@king.edu; *Outreach Serv Librn,* Justin Eastwood; Tel: 865-769-3108, E-mail: jbeastwood@king.edu; *Circ Mgr,* Marika Kimerer; Tel: 423-652-4790, E-mail: hmkimerer@king.edu; Staff 7 (MLS 4.5, Non-MLS 2.5)
Founded 1867. Enrl 1,800; Fac 90; Highest Degree: Doctorate
Library Holdings: Bk Vols 94,080; Per Subs 463
Special Collections: Southern Presbyterian History Coll
Subject Interests: Bus, Classics, Educ, Lit, Missiology, Nursing, Relig studies
Automation Activity & Vendor Info: (Acquisitions) Innovative Interfaces, Inc; (Cataloging) Innovative Interfaces, Inc; (Circulation) Innovative Interfaces, Inc; (Course Reserve) Innovative Interfaces, Inc; (ILL) Innovative Interfaces, Inc; (Media Booking) Innovative Interfaces, Inc; (OPAC) Innovative Interfaces, Inc; (Serials) Innovative Interfaces, Inc
Wireless access
Publications: Accession List; Library Brochure; Library Newsletter; Subject Bibliographies
Partic in Appalachian College Association; Holston Associated Librs Consortium
Open Mon-Thurs 7:30am-9pm, Fri 7:30-5, Sun 4pm-9pm

BROWNSVILLE

P ELMA ROSS PUBLIC LIBRARY*, 1011 E Main St, 38012-2652. SAN 315-7288. Tel: 731-772-9534. FAX: 731-772-5416. E-mail: elmarosslibrary@gmail.com. Web Site: elmarosspubliclibrary.webs.com. *Dir,* Katherine Lee Horn; Staff 2 (MLS 2)
Founded 1910. Pop 19,797; Circ 34,950
Library Holdings: Large Print Bks 500; Bk Vols 27,000; Per Subs 60; Talking Bks 300
Special Collections: Disadvantaged Grant-Core Careers; Literacy Bank for Adults
Subject Interests: Genealogy, W Tenn genealogy
Automation Activity & Vendor Info: (Cataloging) Follett Software; (Circulation) Follett Software; (ILL) Auto-Graphics, Inc
Wireless access
Mem of Hatchie River Regional Library
Partic in Tenn-Share
Open Mon 10-8, Tues-Sat 10-5
Friends of the Library Group

BYRDSTOWN

P PICKETT COUNTY PUBLIC LIBRARY*, 79 Pickett Square Annex, 38549. SAN 315-730X. Tel: 931-864-6281. FAX: 931-864-7078. E-mail: pickettlib@twlakes.net. Web Site: tenv.agverso.com/home?cid=tenv&lid=pickett. *Dir,* Laura Winnigham
Founded 1961. Circ 17,700
Library Holdings: Bk Titles 11,600; Per Subs 10
Automation Activity & Vendor Info: (Circulation) Book Systems
Wireless access
Mem of Falling Water River Regional Library
Open Mon-Fri 8:30-5, Sat 9-2
Friends of the Library Group

CALHOUN

P CALHOUN PUBLIC LIBRARY*, 746 Hwy 163, 37309. (Mail add: PO Box 115, 37309-0115), SAN 315-7318. Tel: 423-336-2348. FAX: 423-336-1527. E-mail: Calhounpubliclibrary@gmail.com. *Dir,* Mary Tickel
Library Holdings: Bk Titles 5,000; Per Subs 12
Automation Activity & Vendor Info: (Acquisitions) LibraryWorld, Inc; (Cataloging) LibraryWorld, Inc; (Circulation) LibraryWorld, Inc
Wireless access
Mem of Ocoee River Regional Library
Open Mon, Wed & Fri 9-5, Tues & Thurs 9-8

CAMDEN

P BENTON COUNTY PUBLIC LIBRARY*, 121 S Forrest Ave, 38320-2055. SAN 315-7326. Tel: 731-584-4772. FAX: 731-584-1098. E-mail: bentoncountypubliclibrary@gmail.com. Web Site: bentoncolibrary.org. *Dir,* Susan Hubbs; *Children/Youth Librn,* Jennifer Thornton; *Computer Lab Librn/Circ,* Jessica Milligan; *Tech/Cat Librn,* Linda Wyatt
Pop 16,000
Special Collections: Benton County Genealogy & History Coll
Automation Activity & Vendor Info: (Cataloging) ComPanion Corp; (Circulation) ComPanion Corp; (OPAC) ComPanion Corp
Wireless access
Mem of Obion River Regional Library
Open Mon, Wed, Fri & Sat 8-6, Tues & Thurs 8-8, Sat 9-5
Friends of the Library Group
Branches: 1
BIG SANDY BRANCH, 12 Front St, Big Sandy, 38221. (Mail add: PO Box 115, Big Sandy, 38221-0115), SAN 377-7464. Tel: 731-593-0225. FAX: 731-593-0226. *Br Mgr,* Elizabeth Cooper
Library Holdings: Bk Vols 5,000
Automation Activity & Vendor Info: (Cataloging) Winnebago Software Co; (Circulation) Winnebago Software Co
Open Mon-Fri 9-5
Friends of the Library Group

CARTHAGE

P SMITH COUNTY PUBLIC LIBRARY*, 215 Main St N, 37030. SAN 360-5345. Tel: 615-735-1326. FAX: 615-735-2317. E-mail: smithpubliclibrary@dtccom.net. Web Site: smithcotn.com/public-library. *Dir,* Amanda Bain; E-mail: scplsdirector@gmail.com
Pop 15,356
Library Holdings: Large Print Bks 500; Bk Vols 22,000; Per Subs 32; Talking Bks 150; Videos 1,000
Subject Interests: Genealogy
Automation Activity & Vendor Info: (Acquisitions) Book Systems; (Cataloging) Book Systems; (Circulation) Book Systems; (OPAC) Book Systems
Wireless access
Mem of Falling Water River Regional Library
Open Mon, Wed & Sat 9-Noon, Tues, Thurs & Fri 9-4:30
Branches: 1
GORDONSVILLE BRANCH, 63 E Main St, Gordonsville, 38563-0217, SAN 360-537X. Tel: 615-683-8063. FAX: 615-683-8063. E-mail: gordonsvillelibrary@dtccom.net. *Br Mgr,* Kay Bennett
Library Holdings: AV Mats 150; Bk Vols 6,000; Per Subs 14
Open Mon, Wed & Fri 9-4:30, Sat 9-Noon

CARYVILLE

P CARYVILLE PUBLIC LIBRARY*, 4839 Old Hwy 63, Ste 2, 37714. SAN 315-7334. Tel: 423-562-1108. FAX: 423-562-4373. E-mail: caryvillepubliclibrary@gmail.com. Web Site: caryvillepubliclib.wixsite.com/caypl. *Libr Asst,* Logan Birdsong
Founded 1966. Pop 2,500; Circ 13,500
Library Holdings: Bk Titles 9,000; Per Subs 16
Automation Activity & Vendor Info: (Acquisitions) Book Systems; (Cataloging) Book Systems; (Circulation) Book Systems; (ILL) Book Systems
Wireless access
Function: Bks on cassette, Bks on CD, Computers for patron use, Free DVD rentals, ILL available, Music CDs, OverDrive digital audio bks, Photocopying/Printing, Prog for children & young adult, Spoken cassettes & CDs, Spoken cassettes & DVDs, Story hour, Summer reading prog, Tax forms, VHS videos, Wheelchair accessible
Mem of Clinch River Regional Library
Partic in Tenn-Share
Special Services for the Deaf - Bks on deafness & sign lang
Special Services for the Blind - Bks on CD
Open Mon-Fri 9-6
Restriction: Borrowing requests are handled by ILL

CELINA

P CLAY COUNTY PUBLIC LIBRARY*, 116 Guffey St, 38551-9802. SAN 315-7342. Tel: 931-243-3442. FAX: 931-243-4876. E-mail: claylibrary@twlakes.net. Web Site: www.claycountypubliclibrarytn.com. *Dir,* Alecia Danielle Burns; E-mail: claylibrary@twlakes.net; *Asst Dir,* Sara Roberson; E-mail: claylibrary@twlakes.net; Staff 2.5 (Non-MLS 2.5)
Pop 7,676; Circ 92,458
Jul 2022-Jun 2023 Income $99,988. Mats Exp $20,203, Books $12,203, AV Mat $8,000. Sal $53,817
Library Holdings: Audiobooks 991; Bks on Deafness & Sign Lang 10; CDs 661; DVDs 7,320; Microforms 293; Bk Titles 26,775; Per Subs 45; Videos 1,959

Automation Activity & Vendor Info: (Cataloging) Book Systems; (Circulation) Book Systems; (ILL) Book Systems
Wireless access
Function: 24/7 Electronic res, 24/7 Online cat, Audiobks on Playaways & MP3, Audiobks via web, Bks on CD, Computers for patron use, Free DVD rentals, ILL available, Internet access, Laminating, Magazines, Magnifiers for reading, Microfiche/film & reading machines, Music CDs, Notary serv, Online cat, Spanish lang bks, Summer reading prog, Tax forms
Mem of Falling Water River Regional Library
Open Mon, Tues, Thurs & Fri 8:30-5:30, Sat 9-2
Restriction: Non-circulating coll, Non-resident fee

CENTERVILLE

P HICKMAN COUNTY PUBLIC LIBRARY*, J B Walker Memorial Library, 120 W Swan St, 37033. SAN 315-7350. Tel: 931-729-5130. FAX: 931-729-4151. E-mail: hclib1@bellsouth.net. Web Site: www.hickmancountylibrary.net. *Dir,* David Dansby; *Asst Dir,* Gayla Bunn
Founded 1935
Library Holdings: Bk Vols 22,000; Per Subs 70
Automation Activity & Vendor Info: (Cataloging) Book Systems; (Circulation) Book Systems; (Course Reserve) Book Systems
Wireless access
Mem of Buffalo River Regional Library
Open Mon 10:30-7, Tues-Thurs 9-5:30, Fri 9-4, Sat 9-2
Branches: 1
EAST HICKMAN PUBLIC LIBRARY, 5009 Hwy 100, Lyles, 37098, SAN 377-7820. Tel: 931-670-5767. FAX: 931-670-1933. *Br Mgr,* Mina Dressler
Open Tues, Wed & Fri 9:30-5, Thurs 11-7, Sat 9-2

CHARLESTON

S OLIN CORP*, Information Resource Center, 1186 Old Lower River Rd, 37310. (Mail add: PO Box 248, 37310), SAN 327-8565. Tel: 423-336-4347. Reference Tel: 423-336-4481. Web Site: olinchloralkali.com. *Supvr,* Connie Upton; *Adminr,* Jennifer Henry; E-mail: jhhenry@olin.com; Staff 2 (Non-MLS 2)
Founded 1976
Library Holdings: Bk Titles 5,000; Per Subs 50
Automation Activity & Vendor Info: (Cataloging) EOS International
Function: Res libr
Restriction: Employees only

CHATTANOOGA

C CHATTANOOGA COLLEGE MEDICAL, DENTAL & TECHNICAL CAREERS*, Library/Electronic Resource Center, 5600 Brainerd Rd, Ste B38, 37411. SAN 375-443X. Tel: 423-305-7781. FAX: 423-305-7786. Web Site: www.chattanoogacollege.edu. *Dir, Libr Serv,* Gayla C Brewer; E-mail: gayla.brewer@chattanoogacollege.edu; Staff 1 (MLS 1)
Founded 1968. Enrl 375; Fac 45; Highest Degree: Associate
Library Holdings: Bk Vols 1,500; Per Subs 10
Subject Interests: Computer sci, Cosmetology, Dental, Electronics, Med, Nursing
Wireless access
Open Mon, Tues & Thurs 8:30am-9:30pm, Wed 8:30-4:30, Fri 8:30-12:30
Restriction: Circ privileges for students & alumni only, Employee & client use only, ID required to use computers (Ltd hrs), Students only, Teacher & adminr only, Use of others with permission of librn

P CHATTANOOGA PUBLIC LIBRARY*, 1001 Broad St, 37402-2652. SAN 360-540X. Tel: 423-643-7700. Circulation Tel: 423-643-7736. E-mail: contact@chattlibrary.org. Web Site: www.chattlibrary.org. *Exec Dir,* Will O'Hearn; E-mail: wohearn@chattanooga.gov; *Interim Asst Dir,* Sheldon Owens; E-mail: sowens@lib.chattanooga.gov; *Chief Admin Officer,* Jason Sullivan; E-mail: jsullivan@lib.chattanooga.gov; *Pub Relations Coordr,* Christina Sacco; Staff 68 (MLS 15, Non-MLS 53)
Founded 1905
Jul 2015-Jun 2016 Income (Main & Associated Libraries) $6,352,914, State $48,700, City $5,815,000, Federal $14,195, Other $475,019. Mats Exp $52,761,130, Books $22,889,597, Per/Ser (Incl. Access Fees) $686,811, AV Equip $2,432,444, AV Mat $8,524,126, Electronic Ref Mat (Incl. Access Fees) $18,216,045, Presv $12,107. Sal $300,536,794
Library Holdings: AV Mats 22,469; Bks on Deafness & Sign Lang 129; Braille Volumes 5; CDs 11,915; DVDs 20,475; e-books 1,245; Electronic Media & Resources 46; Large Print Bks 10,835; Microforms 1,524; Music Scores 81; Bk Titles 189,790; Per Subs 842; Videos 20,475
Special Collections: Genealogy Coll; Interviews Chattanooga & Hamilton County History; Tennesseana (Tennessee Room Coll), bks & microflm. Oral History
Automation Activity & Vendor Info: (Acquisitions) Innovative Interfaces, Inc; (Cataloging) Innovative Interfaces, Inc; (Circulation) Innovative Interfaces, Inc; (OPAC) Innovative Interfaces, Inc; (Serials) Innovative Interfaces, Inc
Wireless access
Function: 24/7 Electronic res, 24/7 Online cat, Activity rm, After school storytime, Archival coll
Publications: A Brief Guide to Genealogical Materials; Bibliographies; Volumes (Bimonthly)
Partic in LYRASIS; National Network of Libraries of Medicine Region 2; OCLC Online Computer Library Center, Inc
Special Services for the Deaf - Bks on deafness & sign lang; Captioned film dep; High interest/low vocabulary bks
Open Mon-Thurs 9-8, Fri & Sat 9-6
Friends of the Library Group
Branches: 3
EASTGATE, 5900 Bldg, 5705 Marlin Rd, Ste 1500, 37411, SAN 360-5434. Tel: 423-643-7770. E-mail: eastgatelibrary@lib.chattanooga.gov. *Exec Dir,* Will O'Hearn; E-mail: wohearn@chattanooga.gov; *Libr Mgr,* Carol Green; Tel: 423-855-2686
Library Holdings: Bk Vols 37,271
Open Mon-Thurs & Sat 9-6
NORTHGATE, 278 Northgate Mall Dr, 37415-6924, SAN 360-5469. Tel: 423-643-7785. Circulation Tel: 423-870-0635. FAX: 423-870-0619. E-mail: northgatelibrary@lib.chattanooga.gov. *Exec Dir,* Will O'Hearn; E-mail: wohearn@chattanooga.gov; *Libr Mgr,* Judy Kelley; Tel: 423-870-0632
Library Holdings: Bk Vols 43,871
Open Mon-Thurs & Sat 9-6
SOUTH CHATTANOOGA, 925 W 39th St, 37410, SAN 360-5493. Tel: 423-643-7780. FAX: 423-825-7239. E-mail: southlibrary@lib.chattanooga.gov. *Exec Dir,* Will O'Hearn; E-mail: wohearn@chattanooga.gov; *Libr Mgr,* Alei Burns
Library Holdings: Bk Vols 19,556
Open Mon-Fri 9-6

J CHATTANOOGA STATE COMMUNITY COLLEGE*, Augusta R Kolwyck Library & Information Commons, 4501 Amnicola Hwy, 37406-1097. SAN 315-7369. Tel: 423-697-4448. Interlibrary Loan Service Tel: 423-697-2584. Reference Tel: 423-697-4436. Administration Tel: 423-697-2457. FAX: 423-697-4409. Web Site: library.chattanoogastate.edu. *Dean,* Susan L Jennings; Tel: 423-697-2576, E-mail: susan.jennings@chattanoogastate.edu; Staff 16 (MLS 10, Non-MLS 6)
Founded 1965. Fac 500; Highest Degree: Associate
Subject Interests: Allied health, Environ sci, Law, Off automation
Automation Activity & Vendor Info: (Acquisitions) Ex Libris Group; (Cataloging) Ex Libris Group; (Circulation) Ex Libris Group; (Course Reserve) Ex Libris Group; (ILL) OCLC; (Media Booking) Ex Libris Group; (OPAC) Ex Libris Group; (Serials) Ex Libris Group
Wireless access
Function: 24/7 Electronic res, 24/7 Online cat
Partic in LYRASIS; TBR Consortium; Tenn-Share
Special Services for the Deaf - ADA equip; Assistive tech; Captioned film dep; Closed caption videos
Special Services for the Blind - Accessible computers; Assistive/Adapted tech devices, equip & products; Bks on CD; PC for people with disabilities; Talking bks; ZoomText magnification & reading software

M ERLANGER HEALTH SYSTEM LIBRARY*, 975 E Third St, 37403. SAN 360-5523. Tel: 423-778-7246. Interlibrary Loan Service Tel: 423-778-6525. FAX: 423-778-7247. E-mail: library@erlanger.org. Web Site: www.erlanger.org. *Mgr,* Rachel Bohannon; E-mail: Rachel.Bohannon@erlanger.org; Staff 4 (MLS 1, Non-MLS 3)
Founded 1940
Library Holdings: Bk Vols 9,000; Per Subs 320
Special Collections: History of Medicine Coll
Subject Interests: Cancer, Hospital admin, Med, Nursing, Orthopedics, Pediatrics, Plastic surgery, Surgery
Automation Activity & Vendor Info: (Cataloging) Follett Software; (Circulation) Follett Software; (OPAC) Follett Software
Wireless access
Publications: LibNews (Newsletter)
Partic in LYRASIS; Tennessee Health Science Library Association
Open Mon-Fri 8-4

S HUNTER MUSEUM OF AMERICAN ART*, Reference Library, Ten Bluff View, 37403. SAN 315-7415. Tel: 423-267-0968. FAX: 423-267-9844. Web Site: huntermuseum.org. *Chief Curator,* Nandini Makrandi; E-mail: nmakrandi@huntermuseum.org
Founded 1959
Library Holdings: Bk Titles 2,093; Bk Vols 2,093; Per Subs 5
Subject Interests: Am art, Antiques, Archit
Wireless access
Restriction: Circulates for staff only, Open to researchers by request, Open to staff only

L MILLER & MARTIN PLLC, Law Library, Volunteer Bldg, Ste 1200, 832 Georgia Ave, 37402-2289. SAN 372-1841. Tel: 423-756-6600. Toll Free Tel: 800-275-7303. FAX: 423-785-8480. Web Site: millermartin.com. *Mgr, Tech Serv,* Donna Williams; Staff 2 (MLS 1, Non-MLS 1)
Library Holdings: Bk Vols 30,000; Per Subs 20; Videos 200
Subject Interests: Corporate, Employment, Labor, Litigation, Real estate
Restriction: Not open to pub

M MOCCASIN BEND MENTAL HEALTH INSTITUTE, Patient Library, 100 Moccasin Bend Rd, 37405. SAN 360-5647. Tel: 423-265-2271. *Dir,* Tyson Keller; E-mail: tyson.keller@tn.gov
Library Holdings: Bk Vols 3,000
Restriction: Not open to pub

CR RICHMONT GRADUATE UNIVERSITY*, Poindexter Library, 1815 McCallie Ave, 37404-3026. Tel: 423-648-2408. FAX: 423-265-7375. Web Site: richmont.edu/library. *Dir of Libr,* Ron Bunger; Tel: 423-648-2410, E-mail: rbunger@richmont.edu; Staff 2 (MLS 1, Non-MLS 1)
Enrl 60; Fac 1; Highest Degree: Master
Library Holdings: AV Mats 4,500; e-books 14,126; e-journals 17,185; Bk Vols 16,657; Per Subs 13; Videos 4,000
Automation Activity & Vendor Info: (Cataloging) Follett Software; (Circulation) Follett Software; (ILL) OCLC Connexion; (Media Booking) Follett Software; (OPAC) Follett Software
Wireless access
Function: Bks on CD, CD-ROM, Computers for patron use, Online ref, Photocopying/Printing, Ref serv available, Spoken cassettes & CDs, Wheelchair accessible
Partic in Georgia Private Acad Librs Consortium
Open Mon-Thurs 9-5:30, Fri 9-4:30
Restriction: Circ to mem only

C UNIVERSITY OF TENNESSEE AT CHATTANOOGA LIBRARY*, UTC Library, 400 Douglas Ave, Dept 6456, 37403-2598. SAN 315-744X. Tel: 423-425-4501. Reference Tel: 423-425-4510. Administration Tel: 423-425-4506. FAX: 423-425-4775. Web Site: www.lib.utc.edu. *Dean,* Theresa Liedtka; Tel: 423-425-4506, E-mail: theresa-liedtka@utc.edu; *Asst Dean,* Michael Bell; E-mail: mike-bell@utc.edu; *Dir, Info Tech,* Brian Rogers; E-mail: brian-rogers@utc.edu; *Dir, Patron Serv,* Sarah Copeland; E-mail: sarah-copeland@utc.edu; *Dir, Res & Instruction Serv,* Lane Wilkinson; E-mail: lane-wilkinson@utc.edu; *Dir, Spec Coll,* Carolyn Runyon; E-mail: carolyn-runyon@utc.edu; *Writing Ctr Dir,* Beth Leahy; E-mail: beth-leahy@utc.edu; *Coll Serv, Dept Head,* Katie Gohn; E-mail: katie-gohn@utc.edu; *Dept Head, Pub Serv, Res,* Bo Baker; E-mail: bo-baker@utc.edu; *Coll Librn,* Rachel Fleming; E-mail: rachel-fleming@utc.edu; *Digital Development Librn,* Andrea Schurr; E-mail: andrea-schurr@utc.edu; *Digital Development Librn,* Steven D Shelton; E-mail: steven-shelton@utc.edu; *Health Sci Librn,* Chapel Cowden; E-mail: chapel-cowden@utc.edu; *Outreach & Assessment Librn,* Chantelle Swaren; E-mail: chantelle-swaren@utc.edu; *Ref & Instruction Librn,* Virginia Cairns; E-mail: virginia-cairns@utc.edu; *Ref & Instruction Librn,* Dunstan McNutt; E-mail: dunstan-mcnutt@utc.edu; *Studio Librarian,* Sarah Kantor; E-mail: sarah-kantor@utc.edu; *Studio Librarian,* Michael Standard; E-mail: michael-standard@utc.edu; *Web Serv Librn,* Brittany Richardson; E-mail: brittany-richardson@utc.edu; *Coordr, Cat,* Valarie Adams; E-mail: valarie-adams@utc.edu; *Coll Spec,* Melanie Dunn; E-mail: melanie-dunn@utc.edu; *Electronic Res,* Charles Remy; E-mail: charles-remy@utc.edu; *Univ Archivist,* Noah Lasley; E-mail: noah-lasley@utc.edu; Staff 39 (MLS 25, Non-MLS 14)
Founded 1872. Enrl 10,781; Fac 403; Highest Degree: Doctorate
Jul 2018-Jun 2019. Mats Exp $4,200,000. Sal $2,400,000
Subject Interests: Civil War, Local hist, Southern lit
Automation Activity & Vendor Info: (Acquisitions) Ex Libris Group; (Cataloging) OCLC Connexion; (Circulation) Ex Libris Group; (Course Reserve) Ex Libris Group; (Discovery) Ex Libris Group; (ILL) OCLC ILLiad; (OPAC) Ex Libris Group; (Serials) Ex Libris Group
Wireless access
Publications: Annual Statistical Report
Partic in LYRASIS; OCLC Online Computer Library Center, Inc; Tenn Acad Libr Collaborative

CLARKSVILLE

C AUSTIN PEAY STATE UNIVERSITY*, Felix G Woodward Library, 601 College St, 37044. (Mail add: PO Box 4595, 37044), SAN 315-7474. Tel: 931-221-7346. Interlibrary Loan Service Tel: 931-221-7679. Reference Tel: 931-221-6186. Toll Free Tel: 800-250-1890. FAX: 931-221-7296. E-mail: librarian@apsu.edu. Web Site: library.apsu.edu. *Dir, Libr Serv,* Position Currently Open; *Bus Librn,* Kristy Cunningham; Tel: 931-221-7017, E-mail: cunninghamk@apsu.edu; *Digital Serv Librn,* Gina J Garber; Tel: 931-221-7028, E-mail: garberg@apsu.edu; *Educ Librn,* Jenny Harris; Tel: 931-221-7914, E-mail: harrisj@apsu.edu; *Electronic Res Librn,* Michael Hooper; Tel: 931-221-7092, E-mail: hooperm@apsu.edu; *Health Sci Librn,* Ross Bowron; Tel: 931-221-7381, E-mail: bowronc@apsu.edu; *Res Mgt Librn,* Nicole Wood; Tel: 931-221-7387, E-mail: woodn@apsu.edu; *Sci Librn,* Ellen Brown; Tel: 931-221-7741, E-mail: browne@apsu.edu; *Soc Sci Librn,* Nancy Gibson; Tel: 931-221-6166, E-mail: gibsonn@apsu.edu; *Syst Librn,* Kebede H Wordofa; Tel: 931-221-7959, E-mail: wordofak@apsu.edu; *Access Serv Coordr,* Elaine W Berg; Tel: 931-221-6405, E-mail: berge@apsu.edu; *Coord, Research & Instruction,* Christina Chester-Fangman; Tel: 931-221-1267, E-mail: chester-fangmanc@apsu.edu; Staff 26 (MLS 12, Non-MLS 14)
Founded 1967. Enrl 10,272; Fac 350; Highest Degree: Doctorate
Special Collections: Clarksville Photograph Coll; Dorothy Dix Coll; Dr Joseph Milton Henry Papers; Robert Penn Warren Coll; The Hillman Papers
Automation Activity & Vendor Info: (Acquisitions) Innovative Interfaces, Inc - Sierra; (Cataloging) Innovative Interfaces, Inc - Sierra; (Circulation) Innovative Interfaces, Inc - Sierra; (Course Reserve) Innovative Interfaces, Inc - Sierra; (ILL) OCLC ILLiad; (OPAC) Innovative Interfaces, Inc - Sierra; (Serials) Innovative Interfaces, Inc - Sierra
Wireless access
Partic in LYRASIS; Nashville Area Libr Alliance; Tenn-Share
Special Services for the Blind - Aids for in-house use
Open Mon-Thurs 7am-midnight, Fri 7-6, Sat 9-5, Sun 1-midnight (Fall & Spring); Mon-Thurs 7am-10pm, Fri 7-6, Sat 9-5, Sun 1-10 (Summer)
Friends of the Library Group

P CLARKSVILLE-MONTGOMERY COUNTY PUBLIC LIBRARY*, 350 Pageant Lane, Ste 501, 37040. SAN 320-2364. Tel: 931-648-8826. FAX: 931-648-8831. Web Site: mcgtn.org/library. *Dir,* Martha Hendricks; E-mail: librarydirector@clarksville.org; *Asst Dir,* Christina Riedel; E-mail: christina@clarksville.org; Staff 20 (MLS 1, Non-MLS 19)
Founded 1894. Pop 214,000; Circ 516,716
Library Holdings: CDs 10,722; DVDs 4,720; Electronic Media & Resources 37; Large Print Bks 4,587; Bk Vols 269,851; Per Subs 128; Videos 12,534
Special Collections: Brown Harvey Genealogy Room; Family & Tennessee History, bks & microfilm
Automation Activity & Vendor Info: (Acquisitions) TLC (The Library Corporation); (Cataloging) TLC (The Library Corporation); (Circulation) TLC (The Library Corporation); (OPAC) TLC (The Library Corporation)
Wireless access
Function: Accelerated reader prog, Art exhibits, Audiobks via web, AV serv, Bilingual assistance for Spanish patrons, Bk reviews (Group), Bks on CD, CD-ROM, Children's prog, Computer training, Computers for patron use, Digital talking bks, E-Reserves, Electronic databases & coll, Free DVD rentals, Genealogy discussion group, Holiday prog, ILL available, Internet access, Mail & tel request accepted, Music CDs, Online cat, Online ref, Orientations, Outside serv via phone, mail, e-mail & web, OverDrive digital audio bks, Photocopying/Printing, Prog for adults, Prog for children & young adult, Ref serv available, Senior computer classes, Spoken cassettes & CDs, Spoken cassettes & DVDs, Tax forms, Teen prog, Telephone ref, VHS videos, Wheelchair accessible
Publications: Friends of the Library (Newsletter)
Mem of Red River Regional Library
Open Mon-Thurs 9-8, Fri & Sat 9-6, Sun 1-5
Restriction: Non-resident fee
Friends of the Library Group

P RED RIVER REGIONAL LIBRARY*, 1753A Alpine Dr, 37040-6729. SAN 315-7482. Tel: 931-645-9531. FAX: 931-905-3030. Web Site: sos.tn.gov/products/tsla/red-river-regional-library. *Dir,* Cecilie Maynor; E-mail: cecilie.maynor@tn.gov; Staff 8 (MLS 2, Non-MLS 6)
Founded 1947. Pop 339,766; Circ 869,320
Library Holdings: Bk Titles 154,006; Per Subs 60
Automation Activity & Vendor Info: (Acquisitions) Book Systems; (Cataloging) Book Systems; (Circulation) Book Systems
Publications: Word from Warioto (Bimonthly); Word from Warioto (Newsletter)
Member Libraries: Cheatham County Public Library; Clarksville-Montgomery County Public Library; Dickson County Public Library; Gallatin Public Library; Houston County Public Library; Humphreys County Public Library; Martin Curtis Hendersonville Public Library; Portland Public Library of Sumner County; South Cheatham Public Library; Stewart County Public Library; Stokes Brown Public Library; Westmoreland Public Library; White House Public Library
Open Mon-Fri 8-4:30

CLEVELAND

P CLEVELAND BRADLEY COUNTY PUBLIC LIBRARY*, 795 Church St NE, 37311-5295. SAN 315-7490. Tel: 423-472-2163. Circulation Tel: 423-472-2163, Ext 119. FAX: 423-339-9791. E-mail: info@clevelandlibrary.org. Web Site: www.clevelandlibrary.org. *Libr Dir,* Andrew Hunt; E-mail: director@clevelandlibrary.org; *Ref Librn,* Wilbertine Scott; E-mail: wscott@clevelandlibrary.org; *Teen Librn,* Shannon Bismark; *Youth Serv Librn,* Parks Keisha; *Circ Mgr,* Rebeckah Coleman; *Coordr, Info Tech,* Robert Knepper; Staff 9 (MLS 4, Non-MLS 5)

Founded 1923. Pop 108,110; Circ 409,484
Library Holdings: Audiobooks 8,386; AV Mats 10,852; e-books 28,501; Electronic Media & Resources 7; Microforms 4,150; Bk Vols 158,202; Per Subs 154
Special Collections: Corn Cherokee Coll; Tennessee Genealogy Coll. Oral History
Subject Interests: Cherokee Indians
Automation Activity & Vendor Info: (Cataloging) TLC (The Library Corporation); (Circulation) Book Systems; (ILL) Auto-Graphics, Inc; (OPAC) Book Systems
Wireless access
Function: Archival coll, Art exhibits, Audio & video playback equip for onsite use, Audiobks via web, AV serv, Bk club(s), Bks on cassette, Bks on CD, Children's prog, Computer training, Computers for patron use, Digital talking bks, Electronic databases & coll, Family literacy, Free DVD rentals, Holiday prog, Homebound delivery serv, ILL available, Mail & tel request accepted, Microfiche/film & reading machines, Music CDs, Outreach serv, OverDrive digital audio bks, Photocopying/Printing, Preschool outreach, Preschool reading prog, Prog for adults, Prog for children & young adult, Ref serv available, Senior computer classes, Spoken cassettes & CDs, Spoken cassettes & DVDs, Story hour, Summer reading prog, Tax forms, Teen prog, Telephone ref, VHS videos, Wheelchair accessible
Publications: Friends of the Library (Newsletter); Genealogical Books
Mem of Ocoee River Regional Library
Special Services for the Deaf - Video & TTY relay via computer
Special Services for the Blind - Bks on cassette; Bks on CD; Closed circuit TV magnifier; Large print bks
Open Mon-Thurs 9-9, Fri & Sat 9-6, Sun 1-5
Restriction: Borrowing requests are handled by ILL, ID required to use computers (Ltd hrs), In-house use for visitors
Friends of the Library Group
Branches: 1
HISTORY BRANCH & ARCHIVES, 833 N Ocoee St, 37311. Tel: 423-479-8367. E-mail: hbranch@clevelandlibrary.org. *Archives Mgr*, Margot Still; Staff 4 (MLS 1, Non-MLS 3)
Library Holdings: Bk Titles 6,500; Per Subs 7
Function: Archival coll, Electronic databases & coll, Ref serv available, Telephone ref
Open Mon-Fri 9-12 & 1-5, Sat 9-2, Sun 1-5
Restriction: Not a lending libr
Bookmobiles: 1. Libr Dir, Andrew Hunt. Bk titles 2,500

J CLEVELAND STATE COMMUNITY COLLEGE LIBRARY*, 3535 Adkisson Dr, 37312-2813. (Mail add: PO Box 3570, 37320-3570), SAN 376-2947. Tel: 423-473-2277, 423-478-6209. Reference Tel: 423-473-2481. E-mail: library@clevelandstatecc.edu. Web Site: www2.clevelandstatecc.edu/library. *Libr Dir*, Gina Cash; E-mail: gcash@clevelandstatecc.edu; *Librn I*, Kathryn Brady; E-mail: kbrady02@clevelandstatecc.edu; *ILL & Circ*, Slade Scoggins; E-mail: sscoggins@clevelandstatecc.edu; Staff 7 (MLS 3, Non-MLS 4)
Founded 1967. Enrl 2,224; Fac 120; Highest Degree: Associate
Library Holdings: e-books 146,012; e-journals 56,101; Bk Vols 53,262; Per Subs 59
Special Collections: Bill Breuer Archives. US Document Depository
Subject Interests: Hist, Legal assisting, Nursing
Automation Activity & Vendor Info: (Cataloging) OCLC Connexion; (Circulation) Ex Libris Group; (Course Reserve) Ex Libris Group; (ILL) OCLC WorldShare Interlibrary Loan; (OPAC) Ex Libris Group; (Serials) Ex Libris Group
Wireless access
Function: Distance learning, For res purposes, Games & aids for people with disabilities, Govt ref serv, ILL available, Large print keyboards, Photocopying/Printing, Ref serv available
Partic in LYRASIS; National Network of Libraries of Medicine Region 2
Special Services for the Blind - Assistive/Adapted tech devices, equip & products
Open Mon-Thurs 7:30am-8pm, Fri 7:30-4:30, Sat 10-2

C LEE UNIVERSITY*, William G Squires Library, 260 11th St NE, 37311. (Mail add: PO Box 3450, 37311), SAN 315-7512. Tel: 423-614-8551. Information Services Tel: 423-614-8562. FAX: 423-614-8555. E-mail: library@leeuniversity.edu. Web Site: www.leeuniversity.edu/library. *Dir, Libr Serv*, Dr Louis F Morgan; *Acq*, Brenda Armstrong; E-mail: barmstrong@leeuniversity.edu; *Pub Serv*, Dawn Bixler; E-mail: dbixler@leeuniversity.edu; Staff 14 (MLS 6.5, Non-MLS 7.5)
Founded 1941. Enrl 4,300; Fac 175; Highest Degree: Master
Library Holdings: Bk Vols 150,000; Per Subs 400
Special Collections: Dixon Pentecostal Research Center Coll
Subject Interests: Educ, Music, Pentecostalism, Relig studies
Automation Activity & Vendor Info: (Acquisitions) Innovative Interfaces, Inc - Millennium; (Cataloging) OCLC; (Circulation) Innovative Interfaces, Inc - Millennium; (Course Reserve) Innovative Interfaces, Inc - Millennium; (ILL) OCLC; (OPAC) Innovative Interfaces, Inc - Millennium; (Serials) Innovative Interfaces, Inc
Wireless access
Publications: Library Newsletter (Online only)
Partic in Appalachian College Association; LYRASIS; OCLC Online Computer Library Center, Inc
Open Mon-Thurs 8am-Midnight, Fri 8-5, Sat 12-8, Sun 1-Midnight

S RED CLAY STATE HISTORIC AREA LIBRARY*, 1140 Red Clay Park Rd SW, 37311. SAN 374-7646. Tel: 423-478-0339. Web Site: tnstateparks.com/parks/about/red-clay. *Mgr*, Erin Medley; E-mail: erin.medley@tn.gov
Library Holdings: Bk Vols 800
Subject Interests: Native Am culture, Native Am hist, Native Am lit
Restriction: Not a lending libr, Open to pub for ref only, Open to pub upon request

CLINTON

P CLINCH RIVER REGIONAL LIBRARY, 130 N Main St, Ste 2, 37716-3693. SAN 315-7539. Tel: 865-220-4000. FAX: 865-425-4468. Web Site: sos.tn.gov/tsla/pages/clinch-river-regional-library. *Dir*, Matthew Jordan; E-mail: matthew.jordan@tn.gov; Staff 5 (MLS 2, Non-MLS 3)
Founded 1946
Automation Activity & Vendor Info: (Cataloging) Auto-Graphics, Inc
Wireless access
Member Libraries: Anna Porter Public Library; Bean Station Public Library; Blaine Public Library; Briceville Public Library; Caryville Public Library; Claiborne County Public Library; Coalfield Public Library; Dandridge Memorial Library; Deer Lodge Public Library; Jacksboro Public Library; Jefferson City Public Library; Jellico Public Library; La Follette Public Library; Luttrell Public Library; Maynardville Public Library; Norris Community Library; Oakdale Public Library; Parrott-Wood Memorial Library; Petros Public Library; Pigeon Forge Public Library; Rocky Top Public Library; Rutledge Public Library; Sevier County Public Library System; Sunbright Public Library; Wartburg Public Library; White Pine Public Library
Open Mon-Fri 8-4:30

P CLINTON PUBLIC LIBRARY*, 118 S Hicks St, 37716. SAN 315-7547. Tel: 865-457-0519. FAX: 865-457-4233. E-mail: questions@clintonpubliclibrary.org. Web Site: clintonpubliclibrary.org. *Dir*, Megan Miria Webb; E-mail: director@clintonpubliclibrary.org; Staff 9 (MLS 2, Non-MLS 7)
Founded 1898. Pop 28,906; Circ 92,162
Library Holdings: Bk Vols 50,001; Per Subs 61
Special Collections: Genealogy Research Coll
Automation Activity & Vendor Info: (Acquisitions) Book Systems; (Cataloging) Book Systems; (Circulation) Book Systems; (Media Booking) Book Systems; (OPAC) Book Systems
Wireless access
Function: 24/7 Electronic res, 24/7 Online cat, Adult bk club, Archival coll, Art programs, Audiobks on Playaways & MP3, Audiobks via web, Bk club(s), Bks on CD, Children's prog, Computer training, Computers for patron use, E-Reserves, Electronic databases & coll, Family literacy, Free DVD rentals, Holiday prog, ILL available, Instruction & testing, Internet access, Large print keyboards, Life-long learning prog for all ages, Magazines, Magnifiers for reading, Meeting rooms, Microfiche/film & reading machines, Online cat, Online ref, OverDrive digital audio bks, Photocopying/Printing, Preschool outreach, Preschool reading prog, Prog for adults, Prog for children & young adult, Ref serv available, Res assist avail, Scanner, Senior computer classes, Senior outreach, Serves people with intellectual disabilities, Spanish lang bks, STEM programs, Story hour, Summer reading prog, Tax forms, Teen prog, Wheelchair accessible, Workshops
Special Services for the Deaf - Adult & family literacy prog; Bks on deafness & sign lang
Special Services for the Blind - Bks on CD; Large print bks; Magnifiers
Open Mon-Fri 9-7, Sat 10-3
Friends of the Library Group

COALFIELD

P COALFIELD PUBLIC LIBRARY*, 112 Jerry Jones Rd, 37719. Tel: 865-435-4275. Toll Free FAX: 888-250-5529. E-mail: coalfieldlibrary@yahoo.com. *Dir*, Evangeline Lauth
Library Holdings: Bk Vols 12,262
Wireless access
Mem of Clinch River Regional Library
Open Mon-Thurs 11-4:30

COALMONT

P COALMONT PUBLIC LIBRARY*, 7426 State Rte 56, 37313-0334. (Mail add: PO Box 334, 37313-0334), SAN 376-6993. Tel: 931-592-9373. FAX: 931-592-9373. E-mail: cmpublib@blomand.net. Web Site:

sites.google.com/site/coalmontpubliclibrary. *Dir,* Brinda Franceine Adams; Staff 1 (Non-MLS 1)
Founded 1960. Pop 2,500; Circ 2,500
Library Holdings: Bk Vols 6,000
Automation Activity & Vendor Info: (Cataloging) Auto-Graphics, Inc; (Circulation) Auto-Graphics, Inc; (ILL) Auto-Graphics, Inc
Wireless access
Function: Accelerated reader prog, After school storytime, Audiobks via web, Bks on CD, Children's prog, Computer training, Computers for patron use, E-Reserves, Electronic databases & coll, Free DVD rentals, ILL available, Internet access, Mail & tel request accepted, Online cat, Online ref, Outside serv via phone, mail, e-mail & web, OverDrive digital audio bks, Photocopying/Printing, Preschool outreach, Ref serv available, Spanish lang bks, Story hour, Summer reading prog, Tax forms, Telephone ref, Wheelchair accessible
Partic in Tenn-Share
Special Services for the Blind - Large print bks
Open Mon 11-5, Wed & Thurs 10-5
Restriction: Authorized patrons

COLLEGEDALE

P COLLEGEDALE PUBLIC LIBRARY*, 9318 Apison Pike, 37363. SAN 372-784X. Tel: 423-396-9300. FAX: 423-396-9334. Web Site: www.collegedalepubliclibrary.org. *Libr Dir,* Natalie Wright; E-mail: natalie.wright@collegedalepubliclibrary.org
Founded 2011
Library Holdings: DVDs 2,200; Bk Vols 45,000
Wireless access
Open Mon-Thurs 10-7, Fri 10-5, Sat & Sun 1-5
Friends of the Library Group

C SOUTHERN ADVENTIST UNIVERSITY*, McKee Library, 4851 Industrial Dr, 37315. (Mail add: PO Box 629, 37315-0629), SAN 360-5671. Tel: 423-236-2788. Interlibrary Loan Service Tel: 423-236-2013. Reference Tel: 423-236-2791. Toll Free Tel: 800-768-8437. FAX: 423-236-1788. Web Site: www.southern.edu/mckee-library. *Dir of Libr,* Deyse Bravo; Tel: 423-236-2789, E-mail: dbravo@southern.edu; *Tutoring Center Dir, Writing Ctr Dir,* Sonja Fordham; Tel: 423-236-2384, E-mail: sfordham@southern.edu; *Digital Res Librn,* Donald Martin; E-mail: dvmartin@southern.edu; *Pub Serv Librn,* Melissa Hortemiller; E-mail: mhortemiller@southern.edu; *Per, Ref Librn,* Seth Shaffer; Tel: 423-236-2792, E-mail: sshaffer@southern.edu; *Research Servs Librn,* Jessica Spears; Tel: 423-236-2009, E-mail: jspears@southern.edu; *Tech Serv Librn,* Stanley Cottrell; Tel: 423-236-2798, E-mail: scottrell@southern.edu; *Cataloger,* Genevieve Cottrell; Tel: 423-236-2795, E-mail: gcottrell@southern.edu; *Circ Mgr,* Carol Harrison; Tel: 423-236-2010, E-mail: charrison@southern.edu; Staff 10 (MLS 7, Non-MLS 3)
Founded 1890. Enrl 2,900; Fac 200; Highest Degree: Doctorate
Library Holdings: Audiobooks 253; Bks on Deafness & Sign Lang 100; e-books 88,000; e-journals 180; Electronic Media & Resources 160; Bk Vols 178,000; Per Subs 495
Special Collections: Abraham Lincoln (Dr Vernon Thomas Memorial Coll), bks, letters, ms, newsp, pamphlets, pictures, maps, paintings & artifacts; Civil War (Dr Vernon Thomas Memorial Coll), bks, letters, ms, newsp, pamphlets, pictures & maps; Duane & Eunice Bietz Coll; Origins & Biology Coll: Books on creationism & evolution; Seventh-day Adventist Church Coll, publs, bks, per, micro & archives; Seventh-day Adventist Heritage & Apocalyptic Studies Coll, bks
Automation Activity & Vendor Info: (Acquisitions) Ex Libris Group; (Cataloging) Ex Libris Group; (Circulation) Ex Libris Group; (Course Reserve) Ex Libris Group; (ILL) OCLC WorldShare Interlibrary Loan; (OPAC) Ex Libris Group; (Serials) Ex Libris Group
Wireless access
Function: 24/7 Electronic res, 24/7 Online cat, Archival coll, Art exhibits, Audio & video playback equip for onsite use, Audiobks on Playaways & MP3, Bilingual assistance for Spanish patrons, Computers for patron use, Doc delivery serv, E-Readers, E-Reserves, Electronic databases & coll, Free DVD rentals, ILL available, Instruction & testing, Meeting rooms, Online cat, Online info literacy tutorials on the web & in blackboard, Online ref, Orientations, Ref & res, Ref serv available, Res assist avail, Res libr, Study rm
Partic in Adventist Librs Info Coop; LYRASIS; OCLC Online Computer Library Center, Inc; Tenn-Share
Open Mon-Thurs 8-Midnight, Fri 8-2, Sun Noon-Midnight (Fall & Winter); Mon-Thurs 9-9, Fri 9-Noon, Sun 2-9 (Summer)
Restriction: Access at librarian's discretion, Authorized patrons, Authorized scholars by appt

COLLIERVILLE

P LUCIUS E & ELSIE C BURCH JR LIBRARY*, Collierville Burch Library, 501 Poplar View Pkwy, 38017. SAN 378-4428. Tel: 901-457-2600. Circulation Tel: 901-457-2602. Reference Tel: 901-457-2601. FAX: 901-854-5893. Web Site: www.colliervilletn.gov/visitors/library-273. *Libr Dir,* Lisa Plath; E-mail: lplath@colliervilletn.gov; *Head, Circ,* Gail Tucci; *Ad,* Mary Grace Berry; *Digital Serv Librn,* Emily Baker; *Youth Serv Librn,* Julia Trumpy; Staff 14.3 (MLS 4.5, Non-MLS 9.8)
Founded 1956. Pop 48,655; Circ 323,768
Automation Activity & Vendor Info: (Acquisitions) Innovative Interfaces, Inc; (Cataloging) Innovative Interfaces, Inc; (Circulation) Innovative Interfaces, Inc; (ILL) Innovative Interfaces, Inc; (OPAC) Innovative Interfaces, Inc
Wireless access
Function: 24/7 Electronic res, Adult bk club, Art exhibits, Audiobks via web, Bk club(s), Bks on CD, Children's prog, Computer training, Computers for patron use, Digital talking bks, Electronic databases & coll, Holiday prog, Homework prog, ILL available, Internet access, Life-long learning prog for all ages, Magazines, Magnifiers for reading, Movies, Museum passes, Music CDs, Online cat, Online ref, Orientations, Outside serv via phone, mail, e-mail & web, OverDrive digital audio bks, Photocopying/Printing, Preschool outreach, Preschool reading prog, Printer for laptops & handheld devices, Prog for adults, Prog for children & young adult, Ref & res, Ref serv available, Senior computer classes, Spoken cassettes & CDs, Story hour, Study rm, Summer reading prog, Tax forms, Teen prog, Telephone ref, Visual arts prog, Wheelchair accessible, Workshops
Special Services for the Blind - Accessible computers; Aids for in-house use; Bks on CD
Open Mon-Thurs 10-8, Fri & Sat 10-6, Sun 1-5
Restriction: Borrowing requests are handled by ILL, ID required to use computers (Ltd hrs), Non-resident fee, Restricted borrowing privileges
Friends of the Library Group

COLUMBIA

P BUFFALO RIVER REGIONAL LIBRARY, 230 E James Campbell Blvd, Ste 108, 38401-3359. SAN 315-7555. Tel: 931-388-9282. FAX: 931-388-1762. *Dir,* Marion K Bryant; Tel: 931-380-2601, E-mail: marion.bryant@tnsos.gov; *Asst Dir,* Anne Reever Osborne; E-mail: anne.osborne@tnsos.gov; *Acq, Cat,* Darlene Young; E-mail: darlene.young@tnsos.gov; Staff 4 (MLS 2, Non-MLS 2)
Founded 1954
Automation Activity & Vendor Info: (ILL) Auto-Graphics, Inc
Wireless access
Member Libraries: Fayetteville-Lincoln County Public Library; Giles County Public Library; Hickman County Public Library; Lewis County Public Library & Archives; Marshall County Memorial Library; Maury County Public Library; Minor Hill Public Library; Spring Hill Public Library; The John P Holt Brentwood Library; Williamson County Public Library
Open Mon-Fri 8-4:30
Restriction: Circ limited

J COLUMBIA STATE COMMUNITY COLLEGE*, Finney Memorial Library, 1665 Hampshire Pike, 38401. SAN 315-7563. Tel: 931-540-2560. FAX: 931-540-2565. E-mail: library@columbiastate.edu. Web Site: columbiastate.edu/library. *Libr Dir,* Anne Scott; E-mail: ascott12@columbiastate.edu; Staff 7 (MLS 3, Non-MLS 4)
Founded 1966. Enrl 5,117
Library Holdings: Audiobooks 50; AV Mats 3,500; e-books 200,000; Bk Vols 69,500; Per Subs 90
Automation Activity & Vendor Info: (Acquisitions) Ex Libris Group; (Cataloging) Ex Libris Group; (Circulation) Ex Libris Group; (Course Reserve) Ex Libris Group; (ILL) OCLC Online; (OPAC) Ex Libris Group; (Serials) Ex Libris Group
Wireless access
Partic in OCLC Online Computer Library Center, Inc; Tenn-Share
Open Mon-Thurs 7:45-7:45, Fri 7:45-4:15; Mon-Thurs 7:45-6, Fri 7:45-4:15 (Summer)

Departmental Libraries:

WILLIAMSON COUNTY CENTER LIBRARY, 104 Claude Yates Dr, Franklin, 37064. Tel: 615-790-4406. *Librn,* Lauren Cole; E-mail: lcole14@columbiastate.edu
Open Mon-Thurs 7:45am-9pm, Fri 7:45-4:15; Mon-Thurs 7:45-6, Fri 7:45-4:15 (Summer)

P MAURY COUNTY PUBLIC LIBRARY*, 211 W Eighth St, 38401. SAN 360-5701. Tel: 931-375-6501. FAX: 931-375-6519. E-mail: maurycountylibrary@maurycounty-tn.gov. Web Site: www.maurycounty-tn.gov/index.aspx?page=72. *Dir,* Zac Fox; E-mail: zfox@maurycounty-tn.gov
Pop 63,888
Library Holdings: Bk Vols 78,808; Per Subs 214
Subject Interests: Genealogy, Local hist, Maury County, Mules, Tenn hist
Wireless access
Mem of Buffalo River Regional Library

Open Mon-Wed 8-8, Thurs-Sat 9-5
Friends of the Library Group
Branches: 1
MOUNT PLEASANT BRANCH, 200 Hay Long Ave, Mount Pleasant, 38474. (Mail add: PO Box 71, Mount Pleasant, 38474-0071), SAN 360-5736. Tel: 931-379-3752. FAX: 931-379-3774. *Dir,* Janice Jones
Pop 6,000
Library Holdings: Bk Vols 10,000
Open Mon & Wed 10-9, Tues & Thurs-Sat 10-5

COOKEVILLE

P FALLING WATER RIVER REGIONAL LIBRARY*, 208 E Minnear St, 38501-3949. SAN 315-7598. Tel: 931-526-4016. Web Site: sos.tn.gov/products/tsla/falling-water-river-regional-library. *Dir,* Matt Kirby; E-mail: matthew.kirby@tn.gov; Staff 9 (MLS 2, Non-MLS 7)
Founded 1946. Pop 162,561; Circ 723,893
Library Holdings: Bk Vols 119,020
Automation Activity & Vendor Info: (Acquisitions) Book Systems; (Cataloging) Book Systems; (Circulation) Book Systems; (Course Reserve) Book Systems; (ILL) Book Systems; (Media Booking) Book Systems; (OPAC) Book Systems; (Serials) Book Systems
Wireless access
Member Libraries: Bledsoe County Public Library; Charles Ralph Holland Memorial Library; Clay County Public Library; DeKalb County Library System; Fentress County Public Library; Millard Oakley Library; Pickett County Public Library; Smith County Public Library
Open Mon-Fri 8-4:30

P PUTNAM COUNTY LIBRARY SYSTEM*, 50 E Broad St, 38501. SAN 315-7571. Tel: 931-526-2416. FAX: 931-372-8517. Web Site: www.pclibrary.org. *Dir,* Kathryn Wisinger; E-mail: kathrynwisinger@pclibrary.org; *IT Dir,* Brian Page; *Ad,* Matt Knieling; *Ch,* Shannon Chaney; Staff 3 (MLS 2, Non-MLS 1)
Founded 1923. Pop 62,315; Circ 355,000
Library Holdings: AV Mats 8,050; Bk Titles 86,374; Per Subs 139; Talking Bks 3,293
Subject Interests: Genealogy
Automation Activity & Vendor Info: (Cataloging) TLC (The Library Corporation); (Circulation) TLC (The Library Corporation)
Wireless access
Special Services for the Deaf - TDD equip
Special Services for the Blind - Bks on cassette; Braille bks
Open Mon-Fri 10-6
Friends of the Library Group
Branches: 3
ALGOOD BRANCH, 125 Fourth Ave, Algood, 38506-5224, SAN 376-7337. Tel: 931-537-3240. FAX: 931-372-8517. E-mail: algood@pclibrary.org. *Br Mgr,* Rochelle Turner
Founded 1980
Library Holdings: Bk Titles 1,390; Bk Vols 4,000
Open Mon-Fri 10:30-4:30
Friends of the Library Group
BAXTER BRANCH, 101 Elmore Tower Rd, Baxter, 38544, SAN 376-8147. Tel: 931-858-1888. E-mail: baxter@pclibrary.org. *Br Mgr,* Matthew Krist
Founded 1958
Library Holdings: Bk Titles 2,781; Bk Vols 5,000
Open Mon-Thurs 11-5, Fri 10-4
Friends of the Library Group
MONTEREY BRANCH, 401 E Commercial Ave, Monterey, 38574, SAN 376-8155. Tel: 931-839-2103. FAX: 931-839-2103. E-mail: mntlib@pclibrary.org. *Br Mgr,* Doylenne Farley
Library Holdings: Bk Titles 4,215
Open Mon & Fri 10-5, Tues-Thurs 10-6
Friends of the Library Group

C TENNESSEE TECHNOLOGICAL UNIVERSITY*, Angelo & Jennette Volpe Library, 1100 N Peachtree Ave, 38505. (Mail add: TTU Campus Box 5066, 38505), SAN 315-758X. Tel: 931-372-3326. FAX: 931-372-6112. Web Site: www.tntech.edu/library. *Dean of Libr,* Kelly McCallister; Tel: 931-372-3884, E-mail: kmccallister@tntech.edu; *Head, Circ,* Charlene McClain; E-mail: cmcclain@tntech.edu; *Metadata Librn,* Mei Hu; E-mail: mhu@tntech.edu; *Archivist,* Megan Atkinson; E-mail: matkinson@tntech.edu; *Electronic Res,* Stephanie Adams; E-mail: sjadams@tntech.edu; Staff 26 (MLS 11, Non-MLS 15)
Founded 1915. Enrl 10,871; Fac 409; Highest Degree: Doctorate
Library Holdings: CDs 3,424; DVDs 4,220; e-books 363,173; e-journals 88,581; Electronic Media & Resources 37; Bk Vols 273,543
Special Collections: Harding Studio Coll; Joe L Evins Coll; Tennessee History Coll; Upper Cumberland History Coll. US Document Depository
Subject Interests: Engr
Automation Activity & Vendor Info: (Acquisitions) Innovative Interfaces, Inc; (Cataloging) Innovative Interfaces, Inc; (Circulation) Innovative Interfaces, Inc; (ILL) OCLC WorldShare Interlibrary Loan; (OPAC) Innovative Interfaces, Inc; (Serials) Innovative Interfaces, Inc
Wireless access
Partic in LYRASIS; OCLC Online Computer Library Center, Inc; Tenn-Share
Special Services for the Blind - ZoomText magnification & reading software
Open Mon-Thurs 7am-10pm, Fri 7-6, Sat 10-6, Sun 1-10 (Fall); Mon-Fri 8-7 (Summer)
Friends of the Library Group

CORDOVA

R MID-AMERICA BAPTIST THEOLOGICAL SEMINARY*, The Ora Byram Allison Memorial Library, 2095 Appling Rd, 38016. SAN 321-4583. Tel: 901-751-3007. Administration Tel: 901-751-8453. Toll Free Tel: 800-968-4508. FAX: 901-259-0398. E-mail: library@mabts.edu. Web Site: www.mabts.edu/academics/library. *Dir, Libr Serv,* Terrence Neal Brown; E-mail: tbrown@mabts.edu; *Head, Circ,* Daphne McCaig; E-mail: library@mabts.edu; Staff 6 (MLS 1, Non-MLS 5)
Founded 1972. Enrl 442; Fac 22; Highest Degree: Doctorate
Library Holdings: Bk Vols 207,000
Subject Interests: Missions, Semitic lang
Wireless access
Partic in LYRASIS; OCLC Online Computer Library Center, Inc
Open Mon-Fri 8-4:30

S NATIONAL COTTON COUNCIL OF AMERICA LIBRARY, 7193 Goodlett Farms Pkwy, 38016. (Mail add: PO Box 2995, 38088-2995), SAN 315-8748. Tel: 901-274-9030. FAX: 901-725-0510. Web Site: www.cotton.org. *Prog Coordr,* Marjorie Walker; E-mail: mwalker@cotton.org
Founded 1950
Library Holdings: Bk Vols 500
Special Collections: History of the National Cotton Council. Oral History
Subject Interests: Agr, Biology, Cotton, Econ, Govt
Publications: Cotton's Week
Restriction: Open by appt only

COSBY

P COSBY COMMUNITY LIBRARY*, 3292 Cosby Hwy, 37722-0052. Tel: 423-487-5885. FAX: 423-487-5885. E-mail: cosbylib@gmail.com. Web Site: sites.google.com/site/cockecountylibraries/cosby-community-library. *Dir,* Amanda Henderson
Library Holdings: Bk Vols 8,000
Automation Activity & Vendor Info: (Cataloging) Follett Software; (Circulation) Follett Software; (OPAC) Follett Software
Wireless access
Mem of Holston River Regional Library
Open Mon, Wed & Fri 12-6
Friends of the Library Group

COVINGTON

P TIPTON COUNTY PUBLIC LIBRARY*, Bldg C, 3149 Hwy 51 S, 38019. SAN 315-761X. Tel: 901-476-8289. FAX: 901-476-0008. E-mail: tiptonpl@tiptonco.com. Web Site: tiptoncountylibrary.com. *Dir,* Stacey Peeler; E-mail: stacey.tcpl@tiptonco.com; Staff 1 (Non-MLS 1)
Founded 1938. Pop 58,000
Library Holdings: DVDs 400; Bk Vols 50,000; Per Subs 30
Subject Interests: County genealogy, State
Wireless access
Function: After school storytime, AV serv, Bks on cassette, Bks on CD, Children's prog, Computer training, Computers for patron use, Free DVD rentals, ILL available, Music CDs, Outreach serv, Photocopying/Printing, Preschool outreach, Prog for children & young adult, Story hour, Summer reading prog, Tax forms, Teen prog, VHS videos, Wheelchair accessible
Mem of Hatchie River Regional Library
Open Mon-Thurs 8-6, Fri 8-5, Sat 9-3
Friends of the Library Group

CROSSVILLE

P ART CIRCLE PUBLIC LIBRARY, Three East St, 38555. SAN 315-7628. Tel: 931-484-6790. FAX: 931-484-2350, 931-707-8956. Web Site: www.artcirclelibrary.info. *Dir,* James S Houston; E-mail: james.houston@artcirclelibrary.info; *Dep Dir,* Kristen Tabor; E-mail: k.tabor@artcirclelibrary.info; *Ad,* Margo L Brown; E-mail: margo.brown@artcirclelibrary.info; *Ch,* Patricia J Dalton; E-mail: patty.dalton@artcirclelibrary.info; *Circ Librn,* Emma Campbell; E-mail: e.campbell@artcirclelibrary.info
Founded 1898
Automation Activity & Vendor Info: (Cataloging) Auto-Graphics, Inc; (Circulation) Book Systems; (ILL) Auto-Graphics, Inc; (OPAC) Book Systems

Wireless access
Function: 24/7 Electronic res, 24/7 Online cat, Archival coll, Art exhibits, Bk club(s), Bks on CD, Children's prog, Computers for patron use, Electronic databases & coll, Free DVD rentals, Genealogy discussion group, ILL available, Internet access, Magazines, Magnifiers for reading, Meeting rooms, Movies, Notary serv, Online cat, Orientations, Outside serv via phone, mail, e-mail & web, OverDrive digital audio bks, Photocopying/Printing, Preschool outreach, Preschool reading prog, Prog for adults, Prog for children & young adult, Ref serv available, Serves people with intellectual disabilities, Spanish lang bks, Story hour, Study rm, Summer reading prog, Tax forms, Teen prog, Telephone ref, Wheelchair accessible, Winter reading prog, Workshops, Writing prog
Open Mon, Tues, Thurs & Fri 8-7, Wed & Sat 8-4
Friends of the Library Group

DANDRIDGE

P DANDRIDGE MEMORIAL LIBRARY*, 1235 Circle Dr, 37725-4750. (Mail add: PO Box 339, 37725-0339), SAN 315-7636. Tel: 865-397-9758. FAX: 865-397-0906. E-mail: danmemlibrary@gmail.com. Web Site: jcpls.org/dandridge-memorial-library. *Dir,* Bethany Jones; *Libr Asst,* Katelyn Boggs; Staff 3 (MLS 1, Non-MLS 2)
Founded 1942. Pop 19,273; Circ 27,407
Library Holdings: Audiobooks 604; Bks on Deafness & Sign Lang 27; Braille Volumes 24; CDs 9; DVDs 1,444; Large Print Bks 483; Microforms 583; Bk Vols 24,366; Per Subs 24; Videos 20
Subject Interests: Genealogy
Automation Activity & Vendor Info: (Cataloging) Auto-Graphics, Inc; (Circulation) Auto-Graphics, Inc; (ILL) Auto-Graphics, Inc
Wireless access
Function: 24/7 Electronic res, 24/7 Online cat, Audiobks on Playaways & MP3, Audiobks via web, Bk club(s), Bks on CD, Computers for patron use, E-Reserves, Electronic databases & coll, Free DVD rentals, ILL available, Internet access, Magazines, Mail & tel request accepted, Microfiche/film & reading machines, Online cat, OverDrive digital audio bks, Photocopying/Printing, Preschool outreach, Preschool reading prog, Printer for laptops & handheld devices, Prog for adults, Prog for children & young adult, Scanner, Story hour, Summer reading prog, Tax forms, Teen prog, Telephone ref
Mem of Clinch River Regional Library
Partic in National Network of Libraries of Medicine Region 2
Open Tues, Wed & Fri 9-6, Thurs 10-7, Sat 9-1
Friends of the Library Group

DAYTON

C BRYAN COLLEGE LIBRARY*, 585 Bryan Dr, 37321. (Mail add: 721 Bryan Dr, No 7793, 37321), SAN 315-7652. Tel: 423-775-7307. FAX: 423-775-7309. E-mail: libdesk@bryan.edu. Web Site: library.bryan.edu/home. *Dir, Libr Serv,* Gary Fitsimmons; Tel: 423-775-7196, E-mail: gary.fitsimmons@bryan.edu; *Literacy Librn, Research Librn,* Kevin Woodruff; Tel: 423-775-7430, E-mail: kevin.woodruff@bryan.edu; *Outreach Serv Librn,* Position Currently Open; *Tech Serv Mgr,* Polly Revis; Fax: 423-775-7229, E-mail: polly.revis@bryan.edu; Staff 4 (MLS 3, Non-MLS 1)
Founded 1930. Enrl 1,209; Fac 160; Highest Degree: Doctorate
Library Holdings: AV Mats 178,453; CDs 44; DVDs 1,244; e-books 574,073; e-journals 89,677; Electronic Media & Resources 774,632; Bk Titles 574,973; Per Subs 16
Special Collections: Audubon Prints Coll; British Literature (Alice Mercer Humanities Coll); Bryan College Archives; Illustrated Shakespeare Plays (Boydell Coll); John Steuart Curry Coll; Rare Book Coll; School, Faculty, and Alumni Publications; Scopes Trial Archives; Stevens Coll (H L Mencken Coll); Tennessee Local History Coll; William Jennings Bryan Coll, Lit, memorabilia
Subject Interests: Humanities
Automation Activity & Vendor Info: (Acquisitions) Innovative Interfaces, Inc - Sierra; (Cataloging) Innovative Interfaces, Inc - Sierra; (Circulation) Innovative Interfaces, Inc - Sierra; (Course Reserve) Innovative Interfaces, Inc - Sierra; (ILL) OCLC WorldShare Interlibrary Loan; (OPAC) Innovative Interfaces, Inc - Sierra; (Serials) Innovative Interfaces, Inc - Sierra
Wireless access
Function: 24/7 Online cat, Archival coll, Audio & video playback equip for onsite use, Computers for patron use, Distance learning, Electronic databases & coll, For res purposes, Free DVD rentals, ILL available, Internet access, Laminating, Learning ctr, Magazines, Mail & tel request accepted, Meeting rooms, Movies, Music CDs, Online cat, Online info literacy tutorials on the web & in blackboard, Orientations, Outreach serv, Outside serv via phone, mail, e-mail & web, Photocopying/Printing, Printer for laptops & handheld devices, Ref & res, Ref serv available, Res assist avail, Scanner, Study rm, Telephone ref, VHS videos, Wheelchair accessible, Workshops
Partic in Appalachian College Association; OCLC Online Computer Library Center, Inc; Tenn-Share
Open Mon-Thurs 7:45am-Midnight, Fri 7:45-5, Sat 1-5, Sun 6pm-Midnight; Mon-Fri 8-4:30 (Summer)
Restriction: Badge access after hrs, Open to pub for ref & circ; with some limitations, Res pass required for non-affiliated visitors

P CLYDE W RODDY LIBRARY*, 371 First Ave, 37321-1499. SAN 315-7644. Tel: 423-775-8406. FAX: 423-775-8422. E-mail: info@clydewroddy.org. Web Site: www.clydewroddy.org. *Dir,* Brittany M West; E-mail: bwest@clydewroddy.org
Library Holdings: Bk Vols 35,000; Per Subs 42
Automation Activity & Vendor Info: (Cataloging) Book Systems; (Circulation) Book Systems; (OPAC) Book Systems
Wireless access
Mem of Ocoee River Regional Library
Open Mon, Wed & Fri 8-4:30, Tues & Thurs 8-8
Friends of the Library Group

DECATUR

P MEIGS COUNTY - DECATUR PUBLIC LIBRARY*, 120 E Memorial Dr, 37322. (Mail add: PO Box 187, 37322-0187), SAN 315-7660. Tel: 423-334-3332. FAX: 423-334-1816. E-mail: meigslibrary@hotmail.com. Web Site: mdpl.blogspot.com. *Dir,* Judith K Reynolds; Staff 2 (Non-MLS 2)
Pop 10,000; Circ 12,000
Library Holdings: Bks on Deafness & Sign Lang 20; Bk Vols 16,000
Automation Activity & Vendor Info: (Cataloging) SirsiDynix; (Circulation) SirsiDynix
Wireless access
Mem of Ocoee River Regional Library
Special Services for the Deaf - TDD equip
Special Services for the Blind - Talking bks
Open Mon & Fri 9-5, Tues & Thurs 9-7, Sat 10-2
Friends of the Library Group

DECATURVILLE

P DECATUR COUNTY LIBRARY*, 20 W Market St, 38329. (Mail add: PO Box 396, 38329-0396), SAN 315-7679. Tel: 731-852-3325. FAX: 731-852-2351. E-mail: dcldsl@tds.net. Web Site: decaturcountytn.org/library. *Dir,* Athalia Boroughs Taylor; *Cat,* Amber Ruth Taylor; *Circ,* Mildred Crawley; *Circ,* Patty Wyatt; Staff 4 (Non-MLS 4)
Founded 1942. Pop 3,111; Circ 39,630
Library Holdings: Bks on Deafness & Sign Lang 15; Large Print Bks 4,000; Bk Titles 23,000; Per Subs 27; Talking Bks 250
Automation Activity & Vendor Info: (Acquisitions) Follett Software; (Cataloging) Auto-Graphics, Inc; (Circulation) Follett Software
Wireless access
Function: Archival coll, Home delivery & serv to seniorr ctr & nursing homes, ILL available, Internet access, Photocopying/Printing, Prog for children & young adult, Summer reading prog, Wheelchair accessible
Mem of Hatchie River Regional Library
Open Mon, Thurs & Fri 10-5, Tues 10-7, Wed 10-2, Sat 9:30-12:30
Friends of the Library Group

DEER LODGE

P DEER LODGE PUBLIC LIBRARY*, 110 Corinne Ave, 37726. (Mail add: PO Box 37, 37726-0037), SAN 376-7558. Tel: 423-965-0101. E-mail: deerlodgepl@highland.net. Web Site: www.galepages.com/tel_p_deerlodge. *Dir,* Katherine Bobinski
Founded 1986. Circ 1,471
Library Holdings: Audiobooks 164; DVDs 480; Bk Vols 7,152
Wireless access
Mem of Clinch River Regional Library
Open Mon 10-2, Thurs 12-4, Fri 2-6

DEL RIO

P MARIE ELLISON MEMORIAL LIBRARY*, 480 S Hwy 107, 37727-9625. SAN 370-6737. Tel: 423-487-5929. FAX: 423-487-5929. E-mail: delriolib@gmail.com. Web Site: tnsos.net/TSLA/PLD/printPage.php?libid=MEL. *Libr Dir,* Lisa Keipp
Founded 1984. Circ 5,890
Library Holdings: Bk Titles 8,000
Automation Activity & Vendor Info: (Cataloging) Follett Software; (Circulation) Follett Software
Wireless access
Open Mon, Wed & Fri 12-6

DICKSON

P DICKSON COUNTY PUBLIC LIBRARY*, 206 Henslee Dr, 37055-2020. SAN 315-7687. Tel: 615-446-8293. FAX: 615-446-9130. Web Site: www2.youseemore.com/dicksonpl. *Dir,* Tamara Hammer; E-mail: dccltamara@comcast.net
Founded 1933. Pop 43,017; Circ 102,991
Library Holdings: CDs 6,732; DVDs 8,086; e-books 3,675; Bk Vols 77,488; Per Subs 110
Subject Interests: Genealogy, Local hist
Automation Activity & Vendor Info: (Acquisitions) Book Systems; (Cataloging) Book Systems; (Circulation) Book Systems; (ILL) Book Systems; (OPAC) Book Systems; (Serials) Book Systems
Wireless access
Mem of Red River Regional Library
Open Mon, Wed, Fri & Sat 9-6, Tues & Thurs 9-8, Sun 2-5
Friends of the Library Group

DOVER

P STEWART COUNTY PUBLIC LIBRARY*, 102 Natcor Dr, 37058. SAN 315-7695. Tel: 931-232-3127. FAX: 931-232-3159. E-mail: stewartcountypubliclibrary@gmail.com. Web Site: stewartcountypubliclibrary.org. *Dir,* Mrs Gracie Armstrong; E-mail: garmstrong@stewartcogov.com; *Asst Dir,* Mrs Barbara Taylor; E-mail: btaylor@stewartcogov.com; *Ch,* Mrs Meagan Blackmon; E-mail: mblackmon@stewartcogov.com; *Outreach Librn,* Mrs Joyce "Petey" Watters; E-mail: jwatters@stewartcogov.com; *Asst Ch,* Mrs Trina Saylor; E-mail: tsaylor@stewartcogov.com; *Tech Coordr,* Mrs Nikki Hardenbrook; E-mail: nhardenbrook@stewartcogov.com; *Circ,* Mrs Cassie Bagwell; E-mail: cbagwell@stewartcogov.com; *Genealogist,* Mrs Norma Loeffler; E-mail: nloeffler@stewartcogov.com; Staff 8 (Non-MLS 8)
Founded 1942
Automation Activity & Vendor Info: (Cataloging) Auto-Graphics, Inc; (Circulation) Auto-Graphics, Inc; (ILL) Auto-Graphics, Inc; (OPAC) Auto-Graphics, Inc
Wireless access
Function: 24/7 Online cat, Accelerated reader prog, Adult bk club, Audiobks via web, Bk club(s), Bk reviews (Group), Bks on CD, Children's prog, Computers for patron use, Electronic databases & coll, Free DVD rentals, Holiday prog, Home delivery & serv to seniorr ctr & nursing homes, Homebound delivery serv, ILL available, Internet access, Magazines, Meeting rooms, Microfiche/film & reading machines, Online cat, Outreach serv, OverDrive digital audio bks, Photocopying/Printing, Preschool outreach, Preschool reading prog, Printer for laptops & handheld devices, Prog for adults, Prog for children & young adult, Ref & res, Scanner, Story hour, Study rm, Summer & winter reading prog, Summer reading prog, Telephone ref
Mem of Red River Regional Library
Partic in Tenn-Share
Open Mon, Tues & Thurs 8-8, Fri 8-4, Sat 8-2
Friends of the Library Group

DRESDEN

P NED R MCWHERTER WEAKLEY COUNTY LIBRARY*, 341 Linden St, 38225-1400. SAN 315-7709. Tel: 731-364-2678. FAX: 731-364-2599. E-mail: weakleycolibrary@frontiernet.com. Web Site: www.weakleycountytn.gov/library.html. *Libr Dir,* Candy McAdams; *Principal Asst Librn,* Carol Tippins; *Asst Librn,* Karen Gertsch. Subject Specialists: *Genealogy,* Carol Tippins; Staff 3 (Non-MLS 3)
Founded 1943. Pop 14,463; Circ 21,377
Library Holdings: Bk Vols 16,000; Per Subs 27
Special Collections: Ned R McWherter Museum
Automation Activity & Vendor Info: (Cataloging) Auto-Graphics, Inc; (Circulation) Auto-Graphics, Inc
Wireless access
Function: 24/7 Online cat, Adult bk club
Mem of Obion River Regional Library
Partic in Tenn-Share
Open Mon-Fri 9-5, Sat 9-2
Friends of the Library Group

DUCKTOWN

P EAST POLK PUBLIC LIBRARY*, 136 Main St, Ste A, 37326. (Mail add: PO Box 40, 37326), SAN 315-7717. Tel: 423-496-4004. E-mail: eastpolklibrary1@hotmail.com. Web Site: sites.google.com/site/eastpolklibrary. *Librn,* Melissa Dillard; *Librn,* Victoria Hill
Pop 3,577; Circ 6,281
Library Holdings: Bk Vols 3,411; Videos 184
Wireless access
Mem of Ocoee River Regional Library
Open Mon, Wed & Fri 11-5, Tues & Thurs 1-7, Sat 10-2

DUNLAP

P SEQUATCHIE COUNTY PUBLIC LIBRARY, 227 Cherry St, 37327. SAN 315-7725. Tel: 423-949-2357. E-mail: info@sequatchiecountylibrary.org, scpl@bledsoe.net. Web Site: www.sequatchiecountylibrary.org. *Dir,* Robin Burgin; *Asst Dir,* Laura Woody
Founded 1959. Pop 17,161; Circ 42,927
Library Holdings: Bk Vols 24,640
Automation Activity & Vendor Info: (Cataloging) Auto-Graphics, Inc; (Circulation) Auto-Graphics, Inc
Wireless access
Function: 24/7 Electronic res, 24/7 Online cat, Adult bk club, Summer reading prog
Open Mon 8-7, Tues & Wed 8-6, Fri 8-5
Restriction: Borrowing requests are handled by ILL
Friends of the Library Group

DYERSBURG

J DYERSBURG STATE COMMUNITY COLLEGE, Learning Resource Center, 1510 Lake Rd, 38024. SAN 315-7733. Tel: 731-286-3283. FAX: 731-286-3228. E-mail: charley@dscc.edu. Web Site: www.dscc.edu/lrc. *Dean of LRC,* Susan J Charley; Tel: 731-286-3361, E-mail: charley@dscc.edu; *Librn I,* Amber Samoussev; Tel: 901-475-3121, E-mail: asamoussev@dscc.edu; *Libr Asst III,* David Tate; Tel: 731-286-3272, E-mail: dctate@dscc.edu; *Libr Asst II,* Crouch Linda; Tel: 731-286-3223, E-mail: crouch@dscc.edu; Staff 4 (MLS 2, Non-MLS 2)
Founded 1969. Enrl 1,762; Highest Degree: Associate
Library Holdings: Audiobooks 79; Braille Volumes 1; CDs 7; DVDs 184; e-books 243; e-journals 9; Electronic Media & Resources 121; Large Print Bks 89; Music Scores 14; Bk Titles 19,973; Per Subs 13
Special Collections: African American Resource Book Coll (AARC); Emmett Kelly Jr Memorabilia; Original Lithographs & Sculptures of Lewis Iselin; Tennessee History Book Coll; Walt Whitman Memorabilia
Automation Activity & Vendor Info: (Cataloging) OCLC CatExpress; (Circulation) Auto-Graphics, Inc; (Course Reserve) Auto-Graphics, Inc; (ILL) OCLC WorldShare Interlibrary Loan; (OPAC) Auto-Graphics, Inc
Wireless access
Partic in LYRASIS; OCLC-LVIS; Tenn-Share; West Tennessee Academic Library Consortium
Special Services for the Deaf - ADA equip; Assistive tech; Bks on deafness & sign lang; Closed caption videos
Special Services for the Blind - Assistive/Adapted tech devices, equip & products; Audio mat; Bks on cassette; Bks on CD; Braille bks; Copier with enlargement capabilities; Dragon Naturally Speaking software; Info on spec aids & appliances; Internet workstation with adaptive software; Large print bks; PC for people with disabilities; Recorded bks; Screen reader software

P MCIVER'S GRANT PUBLIC LIBRARY, 410 W Court St, 38024. SAN 315-7741. Tel: 731-285-5032. FAX: 731-325-5685. Web Site: www.dyersburgdyercolibrary.com. *Dir,* Vanessa Cain; E-mail: vanessa@mciversgrantpubliclibrary.org
Pop 34,663
Library Holdings: AV Mats 1,100; CDs 775; DVDs 375; Bk Vols 38,000; Per Subs 50; Videos 800
Special Collections: Microfilm of State Gazette; Small Genealogy Coll
Automation Activity & Vendor Info: (Cataloging) Auto-Graphics, Inc; (Circulation) Auto-Graphics, Inc
Wireless access
Mem of Obion River Regional Library
Open Mon, Wed & Fri 9-5, Tues & Thurs 9-8, Sat 9-1
Friends of the Library Group

EAST RIDGE

P EAST RIDGE CITY LIBRARY*, 1517 Tombras Ave, 37412-2716. SAN 315-775X. Tel: 423-867-7323. E-mail: library@eastridgetn.gov. Web Site: eastridgetn.gov/Goverment/City-Services/Library.aspx.
Pop 23,000; Circ 40,000
Library Holdings: Bk Vols 20,000; Per Subs 12
Automation Activity & Vendor Info: (Acquisitions) Follett Software; (Cataloging) Follett Software; (Circulation) Follett Software; (Course Reserve) Follett Software; (ILL) Follett Software; (Media Booking) Follett Software; (OPAC) Follett Software; (Serials) Follett Software
Publications: Library Journal; Publisher's Weekly
Open Mon & Wed 10-8, Tues & Thurs-Sat 10-6
Friends of the Library Group

ELIZABETHTON

P ELIZABETHTON-CARTER COUNTY PUBLIC LIBRARY*, 201 N Sycamore St, 37643. SAN 315-7768. Tel: 423-547-6360. FAX: 423-542-1510. E-mail: elizabethtonlibrary@gmail.com. Web Site: owl.ent.sirsi.net/client/en_US/ECCPL. *Libr Dir,* Bernadette Weese; E-mail: bweese@cityofelizabethton.org; *Ch,* Ashlee Williams; E-mail:

awilliams@cityofelizabethton.org; *Teen Librn,* Harley Williams; E-mail: hwilliams@cityofelizabethton.org; *Patron Serv Supvr,* Monica Calhoun; E-mail: mcalhoun@cityofelizabethton.org; Staff 7 (MLS 2, Non-MLS 5)
Founded 1929. Pop 58,622; Circ 126,188
Special Collections: Tennessee History
Wireless access
Mem of Holston River Regional Library
Open Mon & Thurs 9-8, Tues, Wed & Fri 9-6, Sat 9-4
Friends of the Library Group

ENGLEWOOD

P ENGLEWOOD PUBLIC LIBRARY*, 35 Carroll St, 37329. (Mail add: PO Box 150, 37329), SAN 315-7792. Tel: 423-887-7152. E-mail: engpl@comcast.net. Web Site: www.townofenglewood.com/public_library. *Librn,* Madison Webb
Library Holdings: Bk Vols 6,000
Wireless access
Mem of Ocoee River Regional Library
Open Mon-Fri 12-6

ERIN

P HOUSTON COUNTY PUBLIC LIBRARY*, 24 S Spring St, 37061-4073. (Mail add: PO Box 183, 37061-0183), SAN 315-7806. Tel: 931-289-3858. FAX: 931-289-4967. Web Site: sites.google.com/site/houstoncountylibrary. *Dir,* Mrs Robbie Higgins; E-mail: librarydirector@peoplestel.net
Pop 6,871
Library Holdings: Bk Vols 14,500; Per Subs 10
Automation Activity & Vendor Info: (Circulation) Follett Software
Mem of Red River Regional Library
Partic in Tenn Libr Asn
Open Mon-Fri 9-5, Sat 9-12
Friends of the Library Group

ERWIN

P UNICOI COUNTY PUBLIC LIBRARY*, 201 Nolichucky Ave, 37650. SAN 315-7814. Tel: 423-743-6533. FAX: 423-743-0275. Web Site: www.sites.google.com/site/unicoipubliclibrary. *Dir,* Angie Georgeff; E-mail: angiegeorgeff@gmail.com; *Youth Serv Mgr,* Kristy King; *Circ Supvr,* Leanne Dynneson; *Ch Serv,* Cindy Taylor; Staff 5 (MLS 1, Non-MLS 4)
Founded 1921. Pop 17,713; Circ 85,119
Library Holdings: Bk Vols 32,000; Per Subs 10
Special Collections: Unicoi County History Coll
Automation Activity & Vendor Info: (Acquisitions) Innovative Interfaces, Inc; (Cataloging) Innovative Interfaces, Inc; (Circulation) Innovative Interfaces, Inc; (ILL) Innovative Interfaces, Inc; (OPAC) Innovative Interfaces, Inc
Mem of Holston River Regional Library
Special Services for the Blind - Audio mat; Bks on cassette; Bks on CD; Large print bks; Large screen computer & software; Magnifiers
Open Mon-Fri 10-6, Sat 11-3

ETOWAH

P ETOWAH CARNEGIE PUBLIC LIBRARY, 723 Ohio Ave, 37331. SAN 315-7822. Tel: 423-263-9475. FAX: 423-264-2677. E-mail: etowahcarnegielibrary@gmail.com. Web Site: www.etowahlibrary.com. *Libr Dir,* Briana Pagdon; Staff 1 (Non-MLS 1)
Founded 1915. Pop 9,390
Library Holdings: Audiobooks 550; DVDs 1,500; Bk Vols 15,000
Special Collections: Etowah Enterprise Newspaper Coll
Automation Activity & Vendor Info: (ILL) A-G Canada Ltd; (OPAC) Book Systems
Wireless access
Function: 24/7 Electronic res, 24/7 Online cat, 24/7 wireless access, Accelerated reader prog, Art exhibits, Audiobks on Playaways & MP3, Audiobks via web, AV serv, Bk club(s), Bks on CD, Children's prog, Computers for patron use, Electronic databases & coll, Family literacy, Free DVD rentals, Games, Games & aids for people with disabilities, Holiday prog, ILL available, Internet access, Life-long learning prog for all ages, Magazines, Magnifiers for reading, Movies, Notary serv, Online cat, OverDrive digital audio bks, Photocopying/Printing, Preschool reading prog, Prog for adults, Prog for children & young adult, Ref serv available, Res assist avail, Scanner, Senior computer classes, Spanish lang bks, STEM programs, Summer reading prog, Tax forms, Wheelchair accessible
Mem of Ocoee River Regional Library
Open Mon & Sat 10-3, Tues-Fri 10-8
Friends of the Library Group

FAYETTEVILLE

P FAYETTEVILLE-LINCOLN COUNTY PUBLIC LIBRARY*, 306 Elk Ave N, 37334. SAN 315-7830. Tel: 931-433-3286. FAX: 931-433-0063. E-mail: circulation@flcpl.org. Web Site: www.flcpl.org. *Dir,* Meghan Murr; E-mail: director@flcpl.org; Staff 10 (MLS 1, Non-MLS 9)
Founded 1945
Library Holdings: Bk Vols 37,925; Per Subs 67
Automation Activity & Vendor Info: (Acquisitions) Book Systems; (Cataloging) Book Systems; (Circulation) Book Systems; (ILL) Book Systems; (OPAC) Book Systems
Wireless access
Mem of Buffalo River Regional Library
Special Services for the Deaf - Assisted listening device
Open Mon & Wed-Sat 8:30-5, Tues 8:30-7
Friends of the Library Group

FRANKLIN

P WILLIAMSON COUNTY PUBLIC LIBRARY*, 1314 Columbia Ave, 37064. SAN 360-5760. Tel: 615-794-3105. Circulation Tel: 615-595-1277. Reference Tel: 615-595-1243. Administration Tel: 615-595-1250. FAX: 615-595-1245. Reference E-mail: ref@williamson-tn.org. Web Site: lib.williamson-tn.org. *Dir,* Dolores Greenwald; Tel: 615-595-1240, E-mail: dolores.greenwald@williamsoncounty-tn.gov; *Adult Serv Mgr,* Mrs Jeffie Nicholson; Tel: 615-595-1269, E-mail: jnicholson@williamson-tn.org; *Youth Serv Mgr,* Julie Duke; Tel: 615-595-1244, Ext 2, E-mail: jduke@williamson-tn.org; *Tech Serv Mgr,* Marcia Butler; Tel: 615-595-1241, E-mail: mbutler@williamson-tn.org; Staff 27 (MLS 14, Non-MLS 13)
Founded 1927. Pop 106,780; Circ 593,838
Library Holdings: AV Mats 1,653; Bks on Deafness & Sign Lang 236; CDs 555; DVDs 4,536; e-books 7,187; Electronic Media & Resources 14; High Interest/Low Vocabulary Bk Vols 591; Large Print Bks 3,436; Bk Vols 160,598; Per Subs 171; Talking Bks 5,921; Videos 4,813
Special Collections: African-American Genealogy & Photograph Coll; Civil War Coll; Edythe Rucker Whitley Historical & Genealogical Coll; Local Authors Coll; Williamson County Local History & Genealogy
Automation Activity & Vendor Info: (Acquisitions) Innovative Interfaces, Inc; (Cataloging) Innovative Interfaces, Inc; (Circulation) Innovative Interfaces, Inc; (ILL) Auto-Graphics, Inc; (OPAC) Innovative Interfaces, Inc
Wireless access
Function: Adult bk club, Archival coll, Art exhibits, Bi-weekly Writer's Group, Bk club(s), Bks on cassette, Bks on CD, Chess club, Children's prog, Computer training, Computers for patron use, Digital talking bks, Electronic databases & coll, Free DVD rentals, Holiday prog, ILL available, Large print keyboards, Magnifiers for reading, Mail & tel request accepted, Notary serv, Online cat, Online ref, Outside serv via phone, mail, e-mail & web, OverDrive digital audio bks, Photocopying/Printing, Prog for adults, Prog for children & young adult, Ref serv available, Scanner, Spoken cassettes & CDs, Story hour, Summer reading prog, Tax forms, Teen prog, Telephone ref, VHS videos, Wheelchair accessible, Workshops
Publications: Eblast (Online only); WCPLtn Express (Monthly newsletter)
Mem of Buffalo River Regional Library
Open Mon-Thurs 9-8, Fri & Sat 9-5:30, Sun 1-5:30
Restriction: Registered patrons only
Friends of the Library Group
Branches: 5
BETHESDA, 4905 Bethesda Rd, Thompson's Station, 37179-9231, SAN 372-3992. Tel: 615-790-1887. FAX: 615-790-8426. E-mail: bethesda.library@williamsoncounty-tn.gov. *Br Mgr,* Lon Maxwell; E-mail: lon.maxwell@williamsoncounty-tn.gov; Staff 1 (Non-MLS 1)
Library Holdings: Bk Vols 11,172
Open Tues, Wed & Fri 9:30-5:30, Thurs 11-7, Sat 10-2
Friends of the Library Group
COLLEGE GROVE COMMUNITY, 8607 Horton Hwy, College Grove, 37046. Tel: 615-368-3222. E-mail: collegegrovelib@williamson-tn.org. *Br Mgr,* Jennifer Hunsicker
Library Holdings: Bk Vols 2,500
Open Mon & Wed-Fri 9-12 & 12:30-5, Tues 11-4 & 4:30-7
Friends of the Library Group
FAIRVIEW BRANCH, 2240 Fairview Blvd, Fairview, 37062, SAN 360-5825. Tel: 615-224-6087. FAX: 615-799-1399. E-mail: fairview.library@williamsoncounty-tn.gov. *Br Mgr,* Phillip McAndrew; E-mail: pmcandrews@williamsoncounty-tn.gov; Staff 1 (MLS 1)
Library Holdings: Bk Vols 19,778
Function: Satellite serv
Open Mon-Thurs 9-7, Fri 9-5:30, Sat 9-3
Friends of the Library Group
LEIPER'S FORK, 5333 Old Hwy 96, 37064-9357, SAN 370-0011. Tel: 615-794-7019. FAX: 615-591-6976. E-mail: leipersforklib@williamson-tn.org. *Br Mgr,* Emily Anglin; E-mail: eanglin@williamson-tn.org; Staff 1 (Non-MLS 1)
Library Holdings: Bk Vols 12,053

Open Tues & Wed 9-5, Thurs 11-7, Fri 10-6, Sat 10-4
Friends of the Library Group
NOLENSVILLE BRANCH, 915 Oldham Dr, Nolensville, 37135, SAN 328-7181. Tel: 615-776-5490. FAX: 615-776-3626. E-mail: nolensville.library@williamsoncounty-tn.gov. *Br Mgr,* Alexandra Svenpladsen; Staff 1 (Non-MLS 1)
Library Holdings: Bk Vols 15,754
Open Mon, Wed & Fri 9-6, Tues & Thurs 10-7, Sat 9-3
Friends of the Library Group

FRIENDSVILLE

J PELLISSIPPI STATE COMMUNITY COLLEGE*, Blount Harmon Library, 2731 W Lamar Alexander Pkwy, 37737. Tel: 865-981-5325. *Campus Librn,* Will Buck; Tel: 865-981-5326, E-mail: webuck@pstcc.edu
Wireless access
Open Mon-Fri 8-4:30

GAINESBORO

P CHARLES RALPH HOLLAND MEMORIAL LIBRARY*, Jackson County Public Library, 205 W Hull Ave, 38562. (Mail add: PO Box 647, 38562), SAN 315-7849. Tel: 931-268-9190. FAX: 931-268-5706. E-mail: jacksonctylibrary@yahoo.com. Web Site: www.crhmlibrary.com. *Dir,* Penny Pufahl; E-mail: jacksonctylibrary@yahoo.com; *Asst Librn,* Adrianna Scoggins
Founded 1959. Pop 11,211
Library Holdings: Bk Vols 11,000; Per Subs 36
Special Collections: Local History. Oral History
Wireless access
Mem of Falling Water River Regional Library
Open Mon, Tues, Thurs & Fri 10-5, Wed & Sat 10-3

GALLATIN

P GALLATIN PUBLIC LIBRARY*, 123 E Main St, 37066-2509. SAN 315-7857. Tel: 615-452-1722. FAX: 615-451-3319. Web Site: www2.youseemore.com/gallatinPL. *Libr Mgr,* April Mangrum; *Ch Serv Librn,* Sharon Thackson; *Prog Coordr,* Corky Michalski; E-mail: librarian2@ordlibrary.org
Pop 33,400; Circ 67,766
Library Holdings: Bk Vols 60,000; Per Subs 25
Special Collections: Oral History
Automation Activity & Vendor Info: (Cataloging) Book Systems; (Circulation) Book Systems
Wireless access
Function: Summer reading prog
Publications: College for this Community; Daniel Smith; James Winchester
Mem of Red River Regional Library
Open Tues & Thurs 10-8, Wed & Fri 9-6, Sat 9-3
Friends of the Library Group

J VOLUNTEER STATE COMMUNITY COLLEGE LIBRARY*, Thigpin Library, 1480 Nashville Pike, 37066-3188. SAN 324-7783. Tel: 615-230-3400. Circulation Tel: 615-230-3402. Toll Free Tel: 888-335-8722. FAX: 615-230-3410. E-mail: librarian@volstate.edu. Web Site: www.volstate.edu/library. *Dir,* Rebecca Frank; Tel: 615-230-3412, E-mail: rebecca.frank@volstate.edu; *Librn,* Livy I Simpson; Tel: 615-230-3414, E-mail: livy.simpson@volstate.edu; *Libr Serv Coordr,* Lynda Vincent; Tel: 615-230-3415, E-mail: lynda.vincent@volstate.edu; *Librn,* Julie Brown; Tel: 615-230-3438, E-mail: julie.brown@volstate.edu; *Asst Admin,* Donna Warden; Tel: 615-230-3407, E-mail: donna.warden@volstate.edu; *Libr Asst,* Michael Hitzelberger; Tel: 615-452-8600, Ext 2173, E-mail: michael.hitzelberger@volstate.edu; *Libr Asst,* Ann Kirkpatrick; Tel: 615-452-8600, Ext 2750, E-mail: ann.kirkpatrick@volstate.edu; *Libr Assoc,* Marguerite Voorhies; Tel: 615-452-8600, Ext 3404, E-mail: marguerite.voorhies@volstate.edu; Staff 12 (MLS 4, Non-MLS 8)
Founded 1971. Enrl 8,177; Fac 155; Highest Degree: Associate
Library Holdings: AV Mats 2,018; e-books 150,000; Bk Titles 43,837; Per Subs 175
Automation Activity & Vendor Info: (Acquisitions) Innovative Interfaces, Inc - Millennium; (Cataloging) Innovative Interfaces, Inc - Millennium; (Circulation) Innovative Interfaces, Inc - Millennium; (Course Reserve) Innovative Interfaces, Inc - Millennium; (ILL) OCLC FirstSearch; (OPAC) Innovative Interfaces, Inc - Millennium; (Serials) Innovative Interfaces, Inc - Millennium
Wireless access
Function: Audio & video playback equip for onsite use, Bks on CD, Computers for patron use, Distance learning, Doc delivery serv, Electronic databases & coll, ILL available, Instruction & testing, Internet access, Magnifiers for reading, Mail & tel request accepted, Online cat, Online info literacy tutorials on the web & in blackboard, Online ref, Orientations, Outside serv via phone, mail, e-mail & web, Photocopying/Printing, Ref & res, Ref serv available, Scanner, Telephone ref, VHS videos, Wheelchair accessible
Partic in Nashville Area Libr Alliance; Tenn-Share
Special Services for the Deaf - Assistive tech; Bks on deafness & sign lang; Closed caption videos
Special Services for the Blind - Accessible computers; Aids for in-house use; Audio mat; Bks on CD; Cassette playback machines; Computer with voice synthesizer for visually impaired persons; Copier with enlargement capabilities; Internet workstation with adaptive software; Magnifiers; PC for people with disabilities; Screen enlargement software for people with visual disabilities; ZoomText magnification & reading software
Open Mon-Thurs 7:30am-8:30pm, Fri 7:30-4:30, Sat 8-4 (Fall & Spring); Mon-Thurs 7:30am-9pm, Fri 7:30-4:30, Sat 8-Noon (Summer)
Restriction: Borrowing requests are handled by ILL, Non-circulating coll

C WELCH COLLEGE*, Welch Library, 1045 Bison Trail, 37066. SAN 315-9124. Tel: 615-675-5290. Circulation Tel: 615-675-5234. FAX: 615-296-0400. E-mail: library@welch.edu. Web Site: welchlibrary.wordpress.com. *Librn,* Christa Thornsbury; E-mail: cthornsbury@welch.edu; Staff 2 (MLS 1, Non-MLS 1)
Founded 1942. Enrl 419; Highest Degree: Master
Library Holdings: e-books 49,000; Bk Titles 52,000; Bk Vols 70,000; Per Subs 300
Special Collections: Free Will Baptist Historical Coll; Welch College Archive
Subject Interests: Bible, Theol
Automation Activity & Vendor Info: (Acquisitions) EOS International; (Cataloging) EOS International; (Circulation) EOS International; (Course Reserve) EOS International; (Media Booking) EOS International; (OPAC) EOS International; (Serials) EOS International
Wireless access
Publications: Acquisitions (Monthly)
Partic in Christian Libr Network; Nashville Area Libr Alliance; Tenn-Share
Open Mon-Fri 7:45am-11:00pm, Sat 1-11

GATLINBURG

P ANNA PORTER PUBLIC LIBRARY*, 158 Proffitt Rd, 37738. SAN 315-7873. Tel: 865-436-5588. FAX: 865-436-2210. Web Site: www.annaporterpl.org. *Dir,* Kelsey Jones; E-mail: kj@annaporterpl.org; Staff 4 (MLS 1, Non-MLS 3)
Pop 4,000
Library Holdings: Bk Titles 27,000; Per Subs 56
Special Collections: Crafts; Smoky Mountain Region
Automation Activity & Vendor Info: (Cataloging) Follett Software; (Circulation) Follett Software; (OPAC) Follett Software
Mem of Clinch River Regional Library
Open Mon, Fri & Sat 10-5, Tues-Thurs 10-8

GERMANTOWN

P GERMANTOWN COMMUNITY LIBRARY*, 1925 Exeter Rd, 38138. SAN 378-4436. Tel: 901-757-7323. Circulation Tel: 901-757-7323, Ext 7477. FAX: 901-756-9940. Web Site: www.germantown-tn.gov/services/library. *Libr Dir,* Stephen Banister; E-mail: sbanister@germantown-tn.gov; *Asst Dir,* Lisa Marinos; E-mail: lmarinos@germantown-tn.gov; Staff 24 (MLS 5, Non-MLS 19)
Pop 40,977; Circ 289,225
Library Holdings: Audiobooks 2,529; AV Mats 2,639; CDs 978; DVDs 3,327; Electronic Media & Resources 40; Large Print Bks 3,649; Bk Vols 155,506; Per Subs 220; Videos 762
Automation Activity & Vendor Info: (Cataloging) Innovative Interfaces, Inc; (Circulation) Innovative Interfaces, Inc; (Course Reserve) Innovative Interfaces, Inc; (ILL) OCLC; (Serials) Innovative Interfaces, Inc
Wireless access
Special Services for the Blind - Accessible computers; Assistive/Adapted tech devices, equip & products; Bks on CD; Computer with voice synthesizer for visually impaired persons; Large print bks; Magnifiers; Screen enlargement software for people with visual disabilities; Screen reader software
Open Mon-Thurs 9:30-9, Fri & Sat 9:30-6, Sun 1-6
Friends of the Library Group

GLEASON

P GLEASON MEMORIAL LIBRARY*, 105 College St, 38229. (Mail add: 116 N Cedar St, 38229-7228), SAN 315-7881. Tel: 731-648-9020. FAX: 731-648-9020. Web Site: www.gleasononline.com/gleason_library.htm. *Dir,* Michella Wilson; E-mail: director@gleasonlibrary.com
Library Holdings: Bk Titles 2,500; Bk Vols 2,600
Mem of Obion River Regional Library
Open Mon-Fri 1-5

GRAND JUNCTION

P GRAND JUNCTION PUBLIC LIBRARY*, 530 Madison Ave W, 38039. (Mail add: PO Box 751, 38039-0508), SAN 376-7027. Tel: 731-764-2716. FAX: 731-732-1051. E-mail: gjlibrary103@gmail.com. Web Site: grandjunctionpubliclibrary.org. *Dir,* Dianne Callahan
Founded 1982. Pop 306; Circ 3,013
Library Holdings: Bk Vols 7,165
Automation Activity & Vendor Info: (Acquisitions) A-G Canada Ltd
Wireless access
Open Tues & Thurs 12-6, Wed & Fri 12-4
Friends of the Library Group

GRAYSVILLE

P GRAYSVILLE PUBLIC LIBRARY*, 136 Harrison Ave, 37338. (Mail add: PO Box 100, 37338-0100), SAN 315-789X. Tel: 423-775-9242, Ext 4. FAX: 423-775-8137. E-mail: graysvillelib@yahoo.com. Web Site: graysvilletn.org/library. *Dir,* Debbie Pelfrey; *Asst Dir,* Jennifer Mize
Library Holdings: Audiobooks 50; DVDs 300; Bk Vols 4,000
Wireless access
Mem of Ocoee River Regional Library
Open Mon-Fri 9:30-6

GREENBACK

P GREENBACK PUBLIC LIBRARY*, 6889 Morganton Rd, 37742-4143. SAN 315-7903. Tel: 865-856-2841. FAX: 865-856-2841. Web Site: sites.google.com/site/greenbacklibrary. *Dir,* Martha Guldan; E-mail: guldanm@loudoncounty-tn.gov
Pop 1,200; Circ 10,377
Library Holdings: AV Mats 190; CDs 35; DVDs 122; Large Print Bks 1,500; Bk Vols 7,000; Per Subs 15; Talking Bks 20; Videos 255
Wireless access
Function: Audio & video playback equip for onsite use, Computer training, Digital talking bks, E-Reserves, ILL available, Internet access, Online ref, Photocopying/Printing, Preschool outreach, Prog for children & young adult, Senior computer classes, Spoken cassettes & CDs, Spoken cassettes & DVDs, Summer reading prog, Tax forms, Wheelchair accessible
Mem of Ocoee River Regional Library
Open Tues-Thurs 9-5
Friends of the Library Group

GREENEVILLE

P GREENEVILLE GREEN COUNTY PUBLIC LIBRARY*, 210 N Main St, 37745-3816. SAN 315-7911. Tel: 423-638-5034. FAX: 423-638-3841. E-mail: grv.ggcpl@gmail.com. Web Site: www.ggcpl.org. *Dir,* Erin Evans; E-mail: eevans.ggcpl@gmail.com; Staff 1 (MLS 1)
Founded 1908. Pop 54,406; Circ 96,608
Library Holdings: Bk Vols 52,000; Per Subs 50
Automation Activity & Vendor Info: (Acquisitions) SirsiDynix; (Cataloging) SirsiDynix; (Circulation) SirsiDynix; (Course Reserve) SirsiDynix; (ILL) SirsiDynix; (Media Booking) SirsiDynix; (OPAC) SirsiDynix; (Serials) SirsiDynix
Wireless access
Mem of Holston River Regional Library
Open Mon-Thurs 8-6, Fri 9-5, Sat 9-1
Friends of the Library Group
Branches: 1
THE T ELMER COX GENEALOGICAL & HISTORICAL LIBRARY, 229 N Main St, 37745. Tel: 423-638-9866. Web Site: www.telmercoxlibrary.org.
Founded 2000
Special Collections: Historical & Genealogical Coll
Open Wed & Thurs 10-4, Fri & Sat 10-2

G NATIONAL PARK SERVICE, Andrew Johnson National Historic Site Library, 121 Monument Ave, 37743. SAN 325-0911. Tel: 423-638-3551. Web Site: www.nps.gov/anjo. *Adminr,* Kendra Hinkle
Library Holdings: Bk Vols 653
Special Collections: Andrew Johnson Coll; Civil War Coll; National Parks Coll; Presidential History Coll; Tennessee History Coll
Subject Interests: Hist presv, Hist sites, Nat parks, Presidents (US), State hist
Restriction: Staff use only, Use of others with permission of librn

C TUSCULUM UNIVERSITY*, Thomas J Garland Library, 60 Shiloh Rd, 37743. (Mail add: PO Box 5005, 37743-0001), SAN 360-585X. Tel: 423-636-7320. Toll Free Tel: 800-729-0256, Ext 5320. FAX: 423-787-8498. E-mail: library@tusculum.edu. Web Site: garland.tusculum.edu. *Libr Dir,* Kathy Hipps; Tel: 423-636-7320, Ext 5123, E-mail: khipps@tusculum.edu; *Distance Learning Librn, Webmaster,* Crystal Johnson; Tel: 423-636-7320, Ext 5801, E-mail: cjohnson@tusculum.edu; *Circ Serv Coordr,* Lelia Dykes; Tel: 423-636-7320, Ext 5320, E-mail: ldykes@tusculum.edu; Staff 5 (MLS 3, Non-MLS 2)
Founded 1794. Enrl 2,290; Fac 78; Highest Degree: Master
Library Holdings: DVDs 432; e-journals 29,388; Per Subs 206
Special Collections: Childrens Literature; Library Books prior to 1900; Warren W Hobbie Civic Arts Coll
Subject Interests: Bus & mgt, Educ
Automation Activity & Vendor Info: (Cataloging) Innovative Interfaces, Inc; (Circulation) Innovative Interfaces, Inc; (Course Reserve) Innovative Interfaces, Inc; (ILL) Innovative Interfaces, Inc; (Media Booking) Innovative Interfaces, Inc; (OPAC) Innovative Interfaces, Inc; (Serials) Innovative Interfaces, Inc
Wireless access
Publications: Reel'n Page (Newsletter)
Partic in Appalachian College Association; LYRASIS; OCLC Online Computer Library Center, Inc; Tenn-Share
Open Mon-Thurs 8am-Midnight, Fri 8-5, Sun 2pm-Midnight (Fall-Spring); Mon-Thurs 8-6, Fri 8-5 (Summer)

GREENFIELD

P DR NATHAN PORTER MEMORIAL LIBRARY*, 228 N Front St, 38230-9998. SAN 376-3277. Tel: 731-235-9932. FAX: 731-678-0151. E-mail: dnplibrary@gmail.com. Web Site: bit.ly/dnplib. *Dir,* Kathy Watson; E-mail: k.watson@dnplibrary.org
Library Holdings: AV Mats 1,500; Large Print Bks 1,500; Bk Titles 8,000; Per Subs 3
Automation Activity & Vendor Info: (Circulation) Auto-Graphics, Inc
Wireless access
Function: Adult bk club, Electronic databases & coll, ILL available, Photocopying/Printing, Senior computer classes, Spoken cassettes & CDs, Summer reading prog, Tax forms, Wheelchair accessible
Mem of Obion River Regional Library
Partic in Tenn Libr Asn
Open Tues-Fri 9-5, Sat 9-12

HALLS

P HALLS PUBLIC LIBRARY*, 110 N Church St, 38040. (Mail add: PO Box 236, 38040-0236), SAN 321-6330. Tel: 731-836-5302. E-mail: hallspubliclibrary@gmail.com. *Dir,* Ms Robin Meeks
Founded 1980
Library Holdings: Bk Titles 10,000; Per Subs 10
Special Collections: US Tax Cases 1913-current
Wireless access
Mem of Hatchie River Regional Library
Open Mon-Fri 12-5, Sat 9-2

HARRIMAN

P HARRIMAN PUBLIC LIBRARY*, 601 Walden St, 37748-2506. SAN 315-7938. Tel: 865-882-3195. FAX: 865-882-3188. E-mail: info@divilibrary.com. Web Site: harrimanpubliclibrary.org. *Dir,* Tammie Edwards; E-mail: tedwardshpl@comcast.net
Library Holdings: Bk Titles 26,400; Per Subs 40
Automation Activity & Vendor Info: (Cataloging) SirsiDynix; (Circulation) SirsiDynix; (ILL) SirsiDynix; (OPAC) SirsiDynix
Wireless access
Mem of Ocoee River Regional Library
Open Mon-Thurs 9-6, Fri 9-2, Sat 9-1
Friends of the Library Group

J ROANE STATE COMMUNITY COLLEGE LIBRARY*, 276 Patton Lane, 37748-5011. SAN 321-3412. Tel: 865-882-4553. Toll Free Tel: 866-462-7722, Ext 4553. E-mail: librarystaff@roanestate.edu. Web Site: library.roanestate.edu/home. *Interim Libr Dir,* Laura Vaughn; Tel: 865-882-4551, E-mail: vaughnlp@roanestate.edu; *Cat,* Rosemary Bird; Staff 8 (MLS 4, Non-MLS 4)
Founded 1971. Enrl 3,376; Fac 175
Library Holdings: DVDs 1,600; e-books 104,000; Bk Vols 42,000; Per Subs 300; Videos 1,600
Automation Activity & Vendor Info: (Acquisitions) Innovative Interfaces, Inc - Millennium; (Cataloging) Innovative Interfaces, Inc - Millennium; (Circulation) Innovative Interfaces, Inc - Millennium; (Course Reserve) Innovative Interfaces, Inc - Millennium; (ILL) OCLC WorldShare Interlibrary Loan; (OPAC) Innovative Interfaces, Inc - Millennium; (Serials) Innovative Interfaces, Inc - Millennium
Wireless access
Open Mon-Thurs 8am-6:30pm, Fri 8-4:30, Sat 9-1

HARROGATE

C LINCOLN MEMORIAL UNIVERSITY*, Carnegie Vincent Library, 6965 Cumberland Gap Pkwy, 37752. SAN 315-7946. Tel: 423-869-7079. Toll Free Tel: 800-325-0900, Ext 7079. FAX: 423-869-6426. E-mail:

library@lmunet.edu. Web Site: library.lmunet.edu/library. *Libr Dir,* Rhonda Armstrong; Tel: 423-869-6436; *ILL,* Bethany Farmer; *Tech Serv,* Kathy Brunsma; Tel: 423-869-6221, E-mail: kathy.brunsma@lmunet.edu; Staff 15.5 (MLS 12.5, Non-MLS 3)
Founded 1897. Enrl 4,798; Fac 302; Highest Degree: Doctorate
Special Collections: Jesse Stuart Coll; Lincoln Memorial University Authors
Subject Interests: Civil War, Lincolniana
Automation Activity & Vendor Info: (Acquisitions) OCLC; (Cataloging) OCLC; (Circulation) OCLC; (Course Reserve) OCLC; (Discovery) OCLC Worldshare Management Services; (ILL) OCLC ILLiad; (Media Booking) OCLC; (OPAC) OCLC Worldshare Management Services; (Serials) OCLC
Wireless access
Function: For res purposes
Partic in Appalachian College Association; Knoxville Area Health Sciences Library Consortium; LYRASIS; Tenn-Share
Open Mon-Thurs 8am-Midnight, Fri 8-6, Sat 10-6, Sun 2-Midnight

HARTSVILLE

P FRED A VAUGHT MEMORIAL PUBLIC LIBRARY*, 211 White Oak St, 37074. SAN 315-7954. Tel: 615-374-3677. FAX: 615-374-4553. E-mail: favlibrary@gmail.com. Web Site: www.trousdalecountytn.gov/government/county_departments/fred_a_vaught_memorial_library. *Libr Dir,* Megan Lee; E-mail: Megan.Lee@trousdalecountytn.gov
Founded 1961. Pop 7,300; Circ 30,000
Library Holdings: Bk Titles 30,000; Per Subs 25
Automation Activity & Vendor Info: (Cataloging) Book Systems; (Circulation) Book Systems; (ILL) Book Systems; (OPAC) Book Systems
Wireless access
Mem of Stones River Regional Library
Open Mon, Thurs & Fri 9-5, Tues 9-8, Wed & Sat 9-2

HENDERSON

P CHESTER COUNTY PUBLIC LIBRARY*, 1012 E Main St, 38340-0323. SAN 315-7962. Tel: 731-989-4673. FAX: 731-435-1195. E-mail: library@chestercountylibrary.net. Web Site: chestercountylibrarytn.weebly.com. *Libr Dir,* Savannah Gilbert; Staff 6 (MLS 1, Non-MLS 5)
Pop 15,540
Library Holdings: Bk Titles 30,000
Automation Activity & Vendor Info: (Circulation) Follett Software
Wireless access
Function: 24/7 Electronic res, 24/7 Online cat, Adult bk club, Audiobks via web, Bk club(s), Bks on CD, Butterfly Garden, Children's prog, Computer training, Computers for patron use, Holiday prog, Home delivery & serv to seniorr ctr & nursing homes, ILL available, Internet access, Laminating, Life-long learning prog for all ages, Magazines, Makerspace, Meeting rooms, Microfiche/film & reading machines, Movies, Online cat, Online info literacy tutorials on the web & in blackboard, Online ref, OverDrive digital audio bks, Photocopying/Printing, Preschool outreach, Preschool reading prog, Printer for laptops & handheld devices, Prog for adults, Prog for children & young adult, Ref & res, Scanner, Senior computer classes, Spanish lang bks, STEM programs, Story hour, Study rm, Summer & winter reading prog, Summer reading prog, Tax forms, Teen prog, Wheelchair accessible, Writing prog
Mem of Hatchie River Regional Library
Partic in Tenn Libr Asn
Open Mon-Wed & Fri 9:30-5, Thurs Noon-7, Sat 9:30-12:30
Friends of the Library Group

C FREED-HARDEMAN UNIVERSITY*, Loden-Daniel Library, 158 E Main St, 38340-2399. SAN 315-7970. Tel: 731-989-6067. FAX: 731-989-6065. E-mail: library@fhu.edu. Web Site: www.fhu.edu/library. *Libr Dir,* Wade Osburn; E-mail: wosburn@fhu.edu; *Cat, Rare Bks,* Sharon Jennette; *Circ,* Shirley Eaton; *Per,* Teresa Hanger; *Tech Coordr,* John Wilson; Staff 5 (MLS 5)
Founded 1869. Enrl 1,800; Fac 106; Highest Degree: Master
Library Holdings: e-books 14,000; Bk Vols 150,000; Per Subs 1,460
Special Collections: Religion (Restoration Library Coll), bks & tapes. Oral History
Automation Activity & Vendor Info: (Acquisitions) Ex Libris Group; (Cataloging) Ex Libris Group; (Circulation) Ex Libris Group; (Course Reserve) Ex Libris Group; (ILL) Ex Libris Group; (Media Booking) Ex Libris Group; (OPAC) Ex Libris Group; (Serials) Ex Libris Group
Partic in LYRASIS; OCLC Online Computer Library Center, Inc
Open Mon-Thurs 7:30am-11:30pm, Fri 7:30-5:30, Sat 10-5:30, Sun 1-4:30 & 7-11:30

HENDERSONVILLE

P MARTIN CURTIS HENDERSONVILLE PUBLIC LIBRARY*, 140 Saundersville Rd, 37075-3525. SAN 315-7989. Tel: 615-824-0656. FAX: 615-824-3112. E-mail: customerservice@hendersonvillelibrary.org. Web Site: youseemore.com/hendersonville/default.asp. *Interim Dir,* Diane Johnson; E-mail: djohnson@sumnercountytn.gov; Staff 10 (MLS 2, Non-MLS 8)
Founded 1965. Pop 72,505; Circ 189,740
Library Holdings: AV Mats 5,726; Bk Titles 46,000; Per Subs 125
Wireless access
Mem of Red River Regional Library
Open Mon & Thurs 10-8, Tues & Wed 10-6, Sat 10-2
Friends of the Library Group

HOHENWALD

P LEWIS COUNTY PUBLIC LIBRARY & ARCHIVES*, 15 Kyle Ave, 38462-1434. SAN 315-7997. Tel: 931-796-5365. FAX: 931-796-7739. E-mail: lewislibrary@bellsouth.net. Web Site: lewiscountytn.com/public-library. *Libr Dir,* Crystal Nash; Staff 1 (Non-MLS 1)
Founded 1951. Pop 12,363; Circ 41,743
Jul 2020-Jun 2021 Income $128,209. Mats Exp $18,870, Books $14,702, Per/Ser (Incl. Access Fees) $1,572, Manu Arch $1,000, AV Equip $1,326, AV Mat $270. Sal $72,355 (Prof $32,500)
Library Holdings: Audiobooks 222; Bks on Deafness & Sign Lang 33; DVDs 1,096; e-books 672; Large Print Bks 1,353; Microforms 486; Bk Titles 25,603; Per Subs 28
Special Collections: County Archives; Hohenwald, Tennessee History Coll; Lewis County, Tennessee History Coll; Local Newspaper (Lewis County Herald Coll-1915 to present), micro
Subject Interests: County hist, Lewis & Clark expedition, State hist
Automation Activity & Vendor Info: (Acquisitions) Book Systems; (ILL) Auto-Graphics, Inc
Wireless access
Function: 24/7 Electronic res, 24/7 Online cat, Adult literacy prog, Archival coll, Audiobks via web, Bks on CD, Children's prog, Computer training, Computers for patron use, Electronic databases & coll, Family literacy, Free DVD rentals, Govt ref serv, ILL available, Internet access, Large print keyboards, Life-long learning prog for all ages, Magazines, Meeting rooms, Microfiche/film & reading machines, Online cat, Online ref, Orientations, Outreach serv, OverDrive digital audio bks, Photocopying/Printing, Preschool outreach, Preschool reading prog, Printer for laptops & handheld devices, Prog for adults, Prog for children & young adult, Ref serv available, Scanner, Senior computer classes, Spanish lang bks, STEM programs, Story hour, Study rm, Summer reading prog, Teen prog, Telephone ref, Wheelchair accessible
Mem of Buffalo River Regional Library
Special Services for the Deaf - Bks on deafness & sign lang
Special Services for the Blind - Audio mat; Bks available with recordings; Bks on CD; Large print bks
Open Tues, Wed, Fri & Sat 9-5, Thurs 11-7
Restriction: Non-resident fee
Friends of the Library Group

HUMBOLDT

P HUMBOLDT PUBLIC LIBRARY*, 115 S 16th Ave, 38343-3403. SAN 315-8004. Tel: 731-784-2383. FAX: 731-784-0582. Web Site: www.humboldtpublic.org. *Libr Dir,* John A Blankenship; E-mail: john@humboldtpublic.org; *Asst Dir,* Joshua Fisher; E-mail: joshua@humboldtpublic.org; *Children's & Youth Serv,* Sarah Peden; E-mail: sarah@humboldtpublic.org
Pop 13,911; Circ 89,598
Library Holdings: Audiobooks 2,003; Braille Volumes 50; CDs 455; DVDs 2,000; Microforms 113; Bk Vols 33,000; Per Subs 77; Videos 2,004
Special Collections: Music CD's
Automation Activity & Vendor Info: (Acquisitions) Auto-Graphics, Inc; (Cataloging) Auto-Graphics, Inc; (Circulation) Auto-Graphics, Inc; (Course Reserve) Auto-Graphics, Inc; (ILL) Auto-Graphics, Inc; (OPAC) Auto-Graphics, Inc; (Serials) Auto-Graphics, Inc
Wireless access
Function: Home delivery & serv to seniorr ctr & nursing homes
Mem of Obion River Regional Library
Open Mon & Wed-Fri 9-5, Tues 9-7, Sat 10-4
Friends of the Library Group

HUNTINGDON

P CARROLL COUNTY LIBRARY*, 625 High St, Ste 102, 38344-3903. SAN 315-8012. Tel: 731-986-1919. FAX: 731-986-1335. *Dir,* Nikki Cunningham; E-mail: nikki.cunningham@carrollcountylibrary.net; *Circ,* Marcia Mosele; E-mail: marcia.mosele@carrollcountylibrary.net; *Youth Serv,* Kelli Bolen; E-mail: kelli.bolen@carrollcountylibrary.net
Founded 1950. Pop 28,400; Circ 64,683
Library Holdings: Bk Vols 25,000; Per Subs 41
Special Collections: Genealogy, History (Tennessee Coll), Literacy
Automation Activity & Vendor Info: (Acquisitions) Auto-Graphics, Inc; (Cataloging) Auto-Graphics, Inc; (Circulation) Auto-Graphics, Inc; (Course Reserve) Auto-Graphics, Inc; (ILL) Auto-Graphics, Inc; (Media Booking)

Auto-Graphics, Inc; (OPAC) Auto-Graphics, Inc; (Serials) Auto-Graphics, Inc
Wireless access
Mem of Obion River Regional Library
Open Mon-Wed 8-4:30,Thurs 8-5:30, Fri 8-4, Sat 9-12

JACKSBORO

P JACKSBORO PUBLIC LIBRARY*, 585 Main St, Ste 201, 37757. (Mail add: PO Box 460, 37757-0460), SAN 315-8020. Tel: 423-562-3675. FAX: 423-562-9587. E-mail: library@jacksboropubliclibrary.org. Web Site: www.jacksboropubliclibrary.org. *Dir,* Dan Gearing; E-mail: director@jacksboropubliclibrary.org; Staff 3 (Non-MLS 3)
Founded 1976. Pop 7,329; Circ 40,148
Library Holdings: Audiobooks 692; Bks on Deafness & Sign Lang 30; DVDs 2,936; e-books 27,849; Electronic Media & Resources 18; Large Print Bks 818; Bk Titles 12,255; Per Subs 38
Automation Activity & Vendor Info: (Circulation) Follett Software; (ILL) Auto-Graphics, Inc
Mem of Clinch River Regional Library
Partic in National Network of Libraries of Medicine Region 2
Open Mon-Fri 10-6

JACKSON

P HATCHIE RIVER REGIONAL LIBRARY*, 63 Executive Dr, 38305. SAN 315-808X. Tel: 731-668-0710. FAX: 731-668-6663. Web Site: sos.tn.gov/products/tsla/hatchie-river-regional-library. *Regional Dir,* Genny Carter; E-mail: genny.carter@tn.gov; *Asst Dir,* Julie Dahlhauser; E-mail: Julie.Dahlhauser@tn.gov
Founded 1956. Pop 188,198; Circ 586,655
Library Holdings: Bk Vols 115,795
Subject Interests: Tenn
Member Libraries: Bolivar-Hardeman County Library; Chester County Public Library; Decatur County Library; Elma Ross Public Library; Everett Horn Public Library; Halls Public Library; Hardin County Library; Jackson-Madison County Library; Lauderdale County Library; Lee Ola Roberts Public Library; McNairy County Libraries; Middleton Community Library; Munford-Tipton Memorial Library; Parsons Public Library; Somerville-Fayette County Library; Tipton County Public Library
Open Mon-Fri 8-4:30

M JACKSON-MADISON COUNTY GENERAL HOSPITAL*, Learning Center, 620 Skyline Dr, 38301. SAN 320-586X. Tel: 731-541-6023. FAX: 731-541-6983. E-mail: learning.center@wth.org. Web Site: www.wth.org/locations/jackson-madison-co-general. *Coordr, Libr Serv,* Tina Johnson; E-mail: tinag.johnson@wth.org; Staff 1 (Non-MLS 1)
Founded 1972
Library Holdings: Bk Titles 1,500; Per Subs 200
Subject Interests: Hospital admin, Med, Nursing, Nutrition, Pathology, Phys therapy, Radiology, Respiratory therapy, Surgery
Wireless access
Function: Computers for patron use, Online ref, Photocopying/Printing, Ref serv available
Open Mon-Fri 8-4:30
Restriction: Access at librarian's discretion, Badge access after hrs, Borrowing requests are handled by ILL, Lending to staff only, Limited access for the pub, Med & nursing staff, patients & families, Non-circulating to the pub, Not a lending libr, Open to pub for ref only, Open to pub with supv only, Pub use on premises, Ref only to non-staff, Restricted pub use

P JACKSON-MADISON COUNTY LIBRARY*, 433 E Lafayette St, 38301. SAN 315-8039. Tel: 731-425-8600. FAX: 731-425-8609. Web Site: jmclibrary.org. *Dir,* Dinah Harris; E-mail: dharris@madisoncountytn.gov; *Ad,* Jenci Spradlin; E-mail: jspradlin@madisoncountytn.gov; *Spec Coll Librn,* Jack Darrell Wood; E-mail: tnroom.jw@madisoncountytn.gov; *Children's Mgr,* Jennifer Kilbrun; E-mail: jmclkids@gmail.com; *Ref Mgr,* Whitney Norwood; E-mail: wnorwood@madisoncountytn.gov; *Tech Mgr,* Zoe Pride; E-mail: zpride@madisoncountytn.gov; Staff 20 (MLS 3, Non-MLS 17)
Founded 1903. Pop 91,837; Circ 194,720
Library Holdings: AV Mats 11,806; Bk Vols 115,520; Per Subs 211
Special Collections: Genealogy, bks, micro; Jackson Area Business History Coll; Local & State History (Tennessee Room Coll), bks, micro
Automation Activity & Vendor Info: (Cataloging) TLC (The Library Corporation); (Circulation) TLC (The Library Corporation); (OPAC) TLC (The Library Corporation)
Wireless access
Mem of Hatchie River Regional Library
Open Mon-Thurs 9-6, Fri & Sat 9-5
Friends of the Library Group

Branches: 1
NORTH BRANCH, Eight Stonebridge Blvd, Ste F & G, 38305. FAX: 731-300-0370. *Br Mgr,* Brooke Smith; E-mail: bsmith@madisoncountytn.gov; *Tech,* Treavan Mitchell; E-mail: tmitchell@madisoncountytn.gov
Open Tues-Fri 9-6, Sat 9-1

J JACKSON STATE COMMUNITY COLLEGE LIBRARY*, 2046 North Pkwy, 38301. SAN 315-8047. Tel: 731-425-2609. Interlibrary Loan Service Tel: 901-425-2615. Reference Tel: 731-424-3520, Ext 50328. Web Site: www.jscc.edu/library. *Libr Dir,* Scott Cohen; E-mail: scohen@jscc.edu; *Cat/Ref Librn,* Sylvia Rowe; E-mail: srowe1@jscc.edu; *Instruction Librn,* Ruth Slagle; Tel: 731-424-3520, Ext 50572, E-mail: rslagle@jscc.edu. Subject Specialists: *Genealogy,* Sylvia Rowe; *Hist,* Ruth Slagle; Staff 3 (MLS 3)
Founded 1967. Fac 140; Highest Degree: Associate
Jul 2022-Jun 2023 Income $371,000
Library Holdings: AV Mats 965; DVDs 689; e-books 212,000; Per Subs 7
Subject Interests: Careers, Engr tech, Faculty, Health sci, Prof, Tenn hist
Automation Activity & Vendor Info: (Cataloging) Innovative Interfaces, Inc - Sierra; (Circulation) Innovative Interfaces, Inc - Sierra; (OPAC) Innovative Interfaces, Inc - Sierra
Wireless access
Function: 24/7 Electronic res, 24/7 Online cat, Art exhibits, Audio & video playback equip for onsite use, Audiobks via web, Bks on CD, Distance learning, Electronic databases & coll, Free DVD rentals, ILL available, Internet access, Magazines, Magnifiers for reading, Mango lang, Online cat, Online info literacy tutorials on the web & in blackboard, Online ref, Orientations, Outreach serv, Photocopying/Printing, Ref serv available, Res assist avail, Scanner, Tax forms
Partic in West Tennessee Academic Library Consortium
Open Mon-Thurs 7:30am-8pm, Fri 7:30-4:30 (Fall & Spring)

C LANE COLLEGE LIBRARY*, 545 Lane Ave, 38301-4598. SAN 315-8071. Tel: 731-426-7654. FAX: 731-426-7591. Web Site: www.lanecollege.edu/lanepage2.asp?id=080000002. *Head Librn,* Ms Lan Wang; Tel: 731-426-7593, E-mail: lwang@lanecollege.edu; *Assoc Librn,* Janelle Cleaves; Tel: 731-426-7565, E-mail: jcleaves@lanecollege.edu; Staff 5 (MLS 2, Non-MLS 3)
Founded 1882. Enrl 768; Fac 48; Highest Degree: Bachelor
Library Holdings: Bk Vols 84,000; Per Subs 339
Special Collections: Black Studies, AV, bks; Haitian Art; Juvenile, Oral History
Automation Activity & Vendor Info: (Cataloging) LibraryWorld, Inc; (Circulation) LibraryWorld, Inc; (OPAC) LibraryWorld, Inc; (Serials) LibraryWorld, Inc
Wireless access
Publications: Library Usage Manual; Staff Manual
Partic in West Tennessee Academic Library Consortium
Open Mon-Thurs 8am-11pm, Fri 8-5, Sat Noon-4, Sun 6pm-10pm; Mon-Thurs 8-7, Fri 8-5 (Summer)

C UNION UNIVERSITY*, Library at the Logos, 1050 Union University Dr, 38305-3697. SAN 315-8098. Tel: 731-661-5070. Reference Tel: 731-661-6571. Administration Tel: 731-661-5409. FAX: 731-661-5175. E-mail: reference@uu.edu. Web Site: www.uu.edu/library. *Libr Dir,* Melissa Moore; Tel: 731-661-5408, E-mail: mmoore@uu.edu; *Pub Serv Librn,* Savannah Patterson; Tel: 731-661-6544, E-mail: spatterson@uu.edu; *Syst Librn,* Stephen Mount; Tel: 731-661-5419, E-mail: smount@uu.edu; *Tech Serv Librn,* Jeannie Byrd; Tel: 731-661-5339, E-mail: jbyrd@uu.edu; *Circ Assoc,* Tabitha Modisette; E-mail: tmodisette@uu.edu; *Libr Assoc,* Matthew Beyer; Tel: 731-661-5067, E-mail: mbeyer@uu.edu; *Libr Assoc,* Lakreasha Scharcklet; E-mail: lscharcklet@uu.edu; *Circ Mgr,* Olivia Chin; Tel: 731-661-6579, E-mail: ochin@uu.edu; *Evening Circ Supvr,* Rachel Bloomingburg; Tel: 731-661-5418, E-mail: rbloomingburg@uu.edu; *Coll Develop Coordr,* Beth Lynn; Tel: 731-661-5416, E-mail: blynn@uu.edu; *Creative Projects Coordr,* Paul Sorrell; Tel: 731-661-5417, E-mail: psorrell@uu.edu; *Cat,* Susan Kriaski; Tel: 731-661-5426, E-mail: skriaski@uu.edu; *Electronic Res, Ser,* Tara Wingo; Tel: 731-661-5414, E-mail: twingo@uu.edu; Staff 20 (MLS 6, Non-MLS 14)
Founded 1823. Enrl 3,370; Fac 307; Highest Degree: Doctorate
Library Holdings: Audiobooks 315; AV Mats 333,876; CDs 2,006; DVDs 3,691; e-books 200,860; e-journals 42,249; Electronic Media & Resources 19,042; Microforms 74,843; Bk Titles 108,913; Bk Vols 146,368; Per Subs 355
Special Collections: Fonville Neville Coll; R G Lee Coll; West Tennessee Baptist Coll
Automation Activity & Vendor Info: (Cataloging) OCLC; (Circulation) OCLC; (Course Reserve) OCLC; (ILL) OCLC; (OPAC) OCLC; (Serials) OCLC
Wireless access
Function: Online cat
Partic in OCLC Online Computer Library Center, Inc; ProConsort; Tenn-Share; West Tennessee Academic Library Consortium

Open Mon-Thurs 7am-12:30am, Fri 7-5, Sat 11-5, Sun 6pm-12:30am
Restriction: Open to students, fac, staff & alumni
Departmental Libraries:
GERMANTOWN CAMPUS LIBRARY, 2745 Hacks Cross Rd, Germantown, 38138. Tel: 901-959-0029. *Librn,* Shirley Harris; Tel: 901-312-1904, E-mail: sharris@uu.edu; *Libr Asst,* Erica Cole; Tel: 901-312-1948, E-mail: ecole@uu.edu

C UNIVERSITY LIBRARIES, UNIVERSITY OF MEMPHIS, Lambuth Campus Library, 705 Lambuth Blvd, 38301. SAN 315-8063. Tel: 731-425-1918. Web Site: www.memphis.edu/libraries/lambuthlibrary. *Interim Campus Librarian,* Kelly Maust; Tel: 731-425-7351, E-mail: kelly.maust@memphis.edu; *Libr Asst III,* Sara Hand; Tel: 731-425-1983, E-mail: sehand1@memphis.edu; Staff 2 (MLS 1, Non-MLS 1)
Founded 1843. Highest Degree: Doctorate
Library Holdings: AV Mats 160; CDs 75; DVDs 60; Bk Vols 62,000; Per Subs 194,406
Special Collections: Lambuth Archives
Wireless access
Partic in Association of Southeastern Research Libraries
Open Mon-Thurs 8am-9pm, Fri 8-4:30, Sun 4-9 (Fall-Spring); Mon-Fri 8-4:30 (Summer)
Restriction: Open to pub for ref & circ; with some limitations

JAMESTOWN

P FENTRESS COUNTY PUBLIC LIBRARY*, 306 S Main St, 38556-3845. SAN 315-8101. Tel: 931-879-7512. FAX: 931-879-6984. E-mail: fcpublib@twlakes.net. Web Site: fentresscountytn.gov/library. *Dir,* Donna Conatser; *Asst Dir,* Delana Goad; *Ch,* Debra Byrge
Pop 18,878
Library Holdings: Bk Titles 18,000; Per Subs 28
Wireless access
Mem of Falling Water River Regional Library
Open Mon-Thurs 8-6, Fri 8-5, Sat 9-2

JASPER

P JASPER PUBLIC LIBRARY*, 14 W Second St, 37347-3409. SAN 315-811X. Tel: 423-942-3369. FAX: 423-942-6383. Web Site: tenv-verso.auto-graphics.com/mvc. *Dir,* Carolyn Stewart; E-mail: carolynstewart@bellsouth.net; Staff 1 (Non-MLS 1)
Founded 1968. Pop 3,210; Circ 10,878
Library Holdings: AV Mats 5,000; DVDs 301; Bk Vols 26,000; Per Subs 52; Talking Bks 2,000; Videos 3,349
Automation Activity & Vendor Info: (Cataloging) Surpass; (Circulation) Surpass; (OPAC) Surpass
Wireless access
Open Mon 8-8, Tues, Wed & Fri 8-5, Sat 8-2

JEFFERSON CITY

C CARSON-NEWMAN UNIVERSITY*, Stephens-Burnett Memorial Library, 1634 Russell Ave, 37760. (Mail add: Box 70000, 37760), SAN 315-8136. Tel: 865-471-3335. FAX: 865-471-3450. Web Site: cn.libguides.com. *Dean, Libr Serv,* Bruce G Kocour; Tel: 865-471-3336, E-mail: bkocour@cn.edu; *Dir, Media Serv,* Donnie Newman; Tel: 865-471-3220, E-mail: dnewman@cn.edu; *Instrul Serv/Ref Librn,* Jana Redmond; Tel: 865-471-3338, E-mail: jredmond@cn.edu; *Tech Serv Librn,* Lori Thornton; Tel: 865-471-3339, E-mail: lthornton@cn.edu; *Acq,* Sylvia Sawyer; Tel: 865-471-4847, E-mail: ssawyer@cn.edu; *Archivist, Spec Coll,* Albert Lang; Tel: 865-471-3542, E-mail: alang@cn.edu; Staff 7 (MLS 5, Non-MLS 2)
Founded 1851. Enrl 2,200; Fac 120; Highest Degree: Master
Library Holdings: e-books 250,000; Bk Vols 200,000
Special Collections: US Document Depository
Subject Interests: Baptist mat, Family counseling, Marriage
Automation Activity & Vendor Info: (Cataloging) Innovative Interfaces, Inc - Millennium; (Circulation) Innovative Interfaces, Inc - Millennium; (Course Reserve) Innovative Interfaces, Inc - Millennium; (ILL) Innovative Interfaces, Inc - Millennium; (OPAC) Innovative Interfaces, Inc - Millennium
Wireless access
Publications: Carson-Newman Baptist
Partic in Appalachian College Association; Appalachian Libr Info Coop; LYRASIS; OCLC Online Computer Library Center, Inc; Tenn-Share

P JEFFERSON CITY PUBLIC LIBRARY*, 108 City Center Dr, 37760. SAN 315-8128. Tel: 865-475-9094. FAX: 865-475-1253. *Dir,* David Phillips; E-mail: director@jcpls.org; Staff 4 (MLS 1, Non-MLS 3)
Founded 1930. Pop 15,657; Circ 30,748
Jul 2019-Jun 2020 Income $415,468, City $102,837, County $312,631. Mats Exp $16,132, Books $13,132, Per/Ser (Incl. Access Fees) $3,000. Sal $259,400 (Prof $202,600)
Library Holdings: Audiobooks 1,072; DVDs 1,716; Large Print Bks 868; Bk Titles 24,633; Per Subs 11
Automation Activity & Vendor Info: (Cataloging) Auto-Graphics, Inc; (Circulation) Auto-Graphics, Inc; (ILL) Auto-Graphics, Inc; (OPAC) Auto-Graphics, Inc
Wireless access
Function: 24/7 Electronic res, 24/7 Online cat, Activity rm, After school storytime, Audiobks via web, Bilingual assistance for Spanish patrons, Bk club(s), Bks on CD, Children's prog, Computer training, Computers for patron use, E-Reserves, Electronic databases & coll, Free DVD rentals, ILL available, Internet access, Magazines, Meeting rooms, Online cat, Online info literacy tutorials on the web & in blackboard, Online ref, OverDrive digital audio bks, Photocopying/Printing, Preschool outreach, Preschool reading prog, Printer for laptops & handheld devices, Prog for adults, Prog for children & young adult, Scanner, Spanish lang bks, Summer reading prog, Tax forms, Teen prog, Workshops
Mem of Clinch River Regional Library
Partic in National Network of Libraries of Medicine Region 2; Tenn-Share
Special Services for the Deaf - TTY equip
Open Tues-Thurs 9-7, Fri 2-7, Sat 9-2
Friends of the Library Group

JELLICO

P JELLICO PUBLIC LIBRARY*, 104 N Main St, 37762-2004. SAN 315-8144. Tel: 423-784-7488. FAX: 423-784-8745. E-mail: jellicolibrary1@gmail.com. *Dir,* Mark J Tidwell
Library Holdings: Bk Vols 12,000; Per Subs 120
Mem of Clinch River Regional Library
Open Mon-Fri 9:30-5:30

JOHNSON CITY

M BALLAD HEALTH*, Johnson City Medical Center Learning Resources Center, 400 N State of Franklin Rd, 37604-6094. SAN 371-6481. Tel: 423-431-1691. FAX: 423-431-1692. E-mail: medicallibrary@balladhealth.com. Web Site: www.balladhealth.org. *Clinical Librn,* Lanesa Bowman; Staff 4 (MLS 1, Non-MLS 3)
Founded 1981
Library Holdings: Bk Titles 850; Per Subs 25
Subject Interests: Cancer, Med, Nursing, Pediatrics, Surgery
Partic in Med Libr Asn, Southern Chapter; SEND; Tennessee Health Science Library Association
Open Mon-Fri 7:15-4:30

EAST TENNESSEE STATE UNIVERSITY
CM JAMES H QUILLEN COLLEGE OF MEDICINE LIBRARY*, Maple St, Bldg 4, 37614. (Mail add: PO Box 70693, 37614-0693), SAN 360-5949. Tel: 423-439-6252. Circulation Tel: 423-439-6253. Interlibrary Loan Service Tel: 423-439-7032. Reference Tel: 423-439-6246, 423-439-6254. FAX: 423-439-7025. Reference E-mail: medref@etsu.edu. Web Site: com.etsu.edu/medlib. *Dir,* Biddanda (Suresh) P Ponnappa; Tel: 423-439-6355, E-mail: ponnappa@etsu.edu; *Res Mgr,* Martha Whaley; Tel: 423-439-8069, E-mail: whaleym@etsu.edu; *Pub Serv Mgr,* Richard Wallace; Tel: 423-439-8071, E-mail: wallacer@etsu.edu. Subject Specialists: *Hist of med,* Martha Whaley; Staff 15 (MLS 5, Non-MLS 10)
Founded 1975. Fac 4; Highest Degree: Master
Library Holdings: Bk Vols 45,336; Per Subs 618
Special Collections: History of Medicine Coll; Long Coll
Automation Activity & Vendor Info: (Acquisitions) Ex Libris Group; (Cataloging) Ex Libris Group; (Circulation) Ex Libris Group; (Course Reserve) Ex Libris Group; (OPAC) Ex Libris Group; (Serials) Ex Libris Group
Function: Res libr
Partic in National Network of Libraries of Medicine Region 2; Tri-Cities Area Health Sciences Libraries Consortium
Open Mon-Thurs 8am-Midnight, Fri 8-8, Sat 10-6, Sun 1-Midnight

C SHERROD LIBRARY*, Seehorn Dr & Lake St, 37614-0204. (Mail add: PO Box 70665, 37614-1701), SAN 360-5914. Tel: 423-439-4337. Circulation Tel: 423-439-4303. Interlibrary Loan Service Tel: 423-439-6998. Reference Tel: 423-439-4307. Automation Services Tel: 423-439-5227. FAX: 423-439-5090. Reference FAX: 423-439-4720. E-mail: refdesk@etsu.edu. Web Site: sherrod.etsu.edu. *Dean,* David Atkins; E-mail: atkinsdp@etsu.edu; *Dir, Res & Outreach,* Mark Ellis; Tel: 423-439-4715, E-mail: ellism@etsu.edu; *Dir, Tech/Content Serv,* Celia Szarejko; E-mail: szarejko@etsu.edu; *Cat Librn,* Katy Libby; Tel: 423-439-6992, Fax: 423-439-4410, E-mail: libby@etsu.edu; *Distance Educ Librn,* Joanna Anderson; Tel: 423-439-4714, E-mail: andersonjm@etsu.edu; *Grad Serv Librn,* Wendy Doucette; Tel: 423-439-4336, E-mail: doucettew@etsu.edu; *Acq Librn, Res Sharing Librn,* Alison DePollo; Tel: 423-439-6998, E-mail: depollo@etsu.edu; *Pub Relations/Mkt Librn,* Rebecca Tolley-Stokes; Tel: 423-439-4365, E-mail: tolleyst@etsu.edu; *Ref & Instruction Librn,* Kathy Campbell; Tel: 423-439-5629, E-mail: campbeka@etsu.edu; *Student Serv/Outreach*

Librn, Leslie Adebonojo; Tel: 423-439-4308, E-mail: adebonol@etsu.edu; Staff 14 (MLS 10, Non-MLS 4)
Founded 1911. Enrl 14,434; Fac 856; Highest Degree: Doctorate
Library Holdings: AV Mats 4,302; e-books 148,527; Bk Vols 467,559; Per Subs 767
Special Collections: State Document Depository; US Document Depository
Automation Activity & Vendor Info: (Acquisitions) Innovative Interfaces, Inc; (Cataloging) Innovative Interfaces, Inc; (Circulation) Innovative Interfaces, Inc; (Course Reserve) Innovative Interfaces, Inc; (OPAC) Innovative Interfaces, Inc; (Serials) Innovative Interfaces, Inc
Function: ILL available
Partic in Consortium of Southern Biomedical Libraries; LYRASIS; OCLC Online Computer Library Center, Inc; OCLC-LVIS; TBR Consortium; Tenn-Share; Tennessee Health Science Library Association
Special Services for the Deaf - TDD equip
Special Services for the Blind - Reader equip
Friends of the Library Group

R EMMANUEL CHRISTIAN SEMINARY LIBRARY*, One Walker Dr, 37601. SAN 315-8152. Tel: 423-461-1540. FAX: 423-926-6198. E-mail: library@milligan.edu. Web Site: library.milligan.edu. *Librn,* David Kiger; Tel: 423-461-1541, E-mail: dwkiger@milligan.edu; Staff 2 (MLS 2)
Founded 1965. Enrl 150; Fac 10; Highest Degree: Doctorate
Library Holdings: AV Mats 1,415; Bk Vols 100,000; Per Subs 50
Special Collections: Discipliana Coll, Historical Materials Pertaining to the Christian Churches & Churches of Christ
Automation Activity & Vendor Info: (Cataloging) TLC (The Library Corporation); (Circulation) TLC (The Library Corporation); (Course Reserve) TLC (The Library Corporation); (ILL) OCLC; (OPAC) TLC (The Library Corporation); (Serials) TLC (The Library Corporation)
Wireless access
Partic in LYRASIS; Tri-Cities Area Health Sciences Libraries Consortium
Open Mon-Thurs 8am-10pm, Fri 8-5, Sat 11-5, Sun 2-5; Mon-Thurs 8-5, Fri 8-Noon (Summer)

P HOLSTON RIVER REGIONAL LIBRARY*, 2700 S Roan St, Ste 435, 37601-7587. SAN 315-8179. Tel: 423-926-2951. FAX: 423-926-2956. Web Site: sos.tn.gov/tsla/pages/holston-river-regional-library. *Dir,* Jennifer Breuer; E-mail: jennifer.breuer@tn.gov; Staff 6 (MLS 1, Non-MLS 5)
Founded 1942. Pop 415,063
Special Collections: Local History Coll; Professional Resources Coll
Automation Activity & Vendor Info: (Acquisitions) Ex Libris Group; (Cataloging) Ex Libris Group; (Circulation) Ex Libris Group; (ILL) OCLC Online; (OPAC) Ex Libris Group; (Serials) Ex Libris Group
Member Libraries: Cosby Community Library; Elizabethton-Carter County Public Library; Greeneville Green County Public Library; Hancock County Public Library; Johnson City Public Library; Kingsport Public Library & Archives; Morristown-Hamblen Library; Mosheim Public Library; Sullivan County Public Library; Unicoi County Public Library; Washington County Public Library
Special Services for the Blind - Integrated libr/media serv
Open Mon-Fri 8-4:30

P JOHNSON CITY PUBLIC LIBRARY*, 100 W Millard St, 37604. SAN 315-8160. Tel: 423-434-4450. Circulation Tel: 423-434-4455. Reference Tel: 423-434-4454. FAX: 423-434-4469. Web Site: www.jcpl.org. *Dir,* Julia Turpin; Tel: 423-434-4457, E-mail: julia.turpin@jcpl.net; *Asst Dir,* Cathy Griffith; Tel: 423-434-4463, E-mail: cgriffith@jcpl.net; *Adult Serv Mgr,* Holly Russo; Tel: 423-434-4354, E-mail: hrusso@jcpl.net; *Circ Mgr,* Celeste Peck; Tel: 423-434-4472, E-mail: celeste.peck@jcpl.net; *IT Mgr,* Eric Jon Job; Tel: 423-434-4468, E-mail: ejjob@jcpl.net; *Tech Serv Mgr,* David Ownby; Tel: 423-434-4343, E-mail: david.ownby@jcpl.net; *Youth Serv Mgr,* Betty Cobb; Tel: 423-434-4350, E-mail: bcobb@jcpl.net; *Cat Spec,* Juniper Starr; Tel: 423-434-4462, E-mail: juniper.starr@jcpl.net; Staff 38 (MLS 8, Non-MLS 30)
Founded 1895. Pop 71,183; Circ 557,259
Library Holdings: AV Mats 10,475; Microforms 19,045; Bk Vols 130,954; Per Subs 371
Subject Interests: Local hist
Automation Activity & Vendor Info: (Acquisitions) SirsiDynix-WorkFlows; (Cataloging) OCLC; (Circulation) SirsiDynix-WorkFlows; (ILL) OCLC; (OPAC) SirsiDynix-WorkFlows; (Serials) EBSCO Online
Wireless access
Function: 24/7 Electronic res, 24/7 Online cat, Adult bk club, Art exhibits, Audiobks on Playaways & MP3, Bk club(s), Bks on CD, Butterfly Garden, Children's prog, Computer training, Computers for patron use, Digital talking bks, Electronic databases & coll, Free DVD rentals, Holiday prog, Homebound delivery serv, ILL available, Internet access, Life-long learning prog for all ages, Magazines, Magnifiers for reading, Mail & tel request accepted, Makerspace, Mango lang, Meeting rooms, Microfiche/film & reading machines, Movies, Music CDs, Online cat, Outreach serv, OverDrive digital audio bks, Photocopying/Printing, Prog for adults, Prog for children & young adult, Ref & res, Ref serv available, Scanner, Spanish lang bks, Spoken cassettes & CDs, Spoken cassettes & DVDs, STEM programs, Story hour, Study rm, Summer reading prog, Tax forms, Teen prog, Telephone ref, Wheelchair accessible
Mem of Holston River Regional Library
Open Mon-Thurs 9-8, Fri 9-6, Sat 10-6, Sun (Sept-May) Noon-6
Friends of the Library Group

L LEGAL AID OF EAST TENNESSEE LIBRARY*, 311 W Walnut St, 37604. SAN 320-2372. Tel: 423-928-8311. Toll Free Tel: 800-821-1312. FAX: 423-928-9488. Web Site: www.laet.org. *Exec Dir,* Debra House; E-mail: dhouse@laet.org
Founded 1977
Library Holdings: Bk Titles 2,000; Per Subs 37
Open Mon-Fri 8-Noon; Mon-Fri 1-5 (Summer)

JONESBOROUGH

P WASHINGTON COUNTY PUBLIC LIBRARY, Jonesborough Branch, 200 Sabin Dr, 37659. SAN 360-6007. Tel: 423-753-1800. FAX: 423-753-1802. Web Site: wclibrarytn.com. *Dir,* Richard Griffin; E-mail: rgriffin@wclibrarytn.org; *Br Mgr,* Christy Widner; E-mail: cwidner@wclibrarytn.org; Staff 14.3 (MLS 3, Non-MLS 11.3)
Founded 1896. Pop 45,003; Circ 113,042
Library Holdings: AV Mats 6,153; e-books 773; Bk Vols 73,969; Per Subs 72
Special Collections: Railroad Coll
Subject Interests: Genealogy, Local hist
Automation Activity & Vendor Info: (Acquisitions) TLC (The Library Corporation); (Cataloging) TLC (The Library Corporation); (Circulation) TLC (The Library Corporation); (Course Reserve) TLC (The Library Corporation); (Media Booking) TLC (The Library Corporation); (OPAC) TLC (The Library Corporation); (Serials) TLC (The Library Corporation)
Wireless access
Function: Adult literacy prog, ILL available, Photocopying/Printing, Prog for adults, Prog for children & young adult, Ref serv available, Summer reading prog, Tax forms
Mem of Holston River Regional Library
Partic in SouthWest Information Network Group; Tenn-Share
Special Services for the Blind - Audio mat; Bks on cassette; Large print bks; Talking bks
Open Mon & Thurs 9-8, Tues, Wed & Fri 9-6, Sat 9-2
Friends of the Library Group
Branches: 1
GRAY BRANCH, 5026 Bobby Hicks Hwy, Gray, 37615, SAN 360-6031. Tel: 423-477-1550. FAX: 423-477-1553.
Founded 1968
Open Mon & Wed-Fri 9-6, Tues 9-8, Sat 9-2
Friends of the Library Group

KINGSPORT

M BALLAD HEALTH, Holston Valley Medical Center Health Science Library, 130 W Ravine Rd, 37660. SAN 327-1013. Tel: 423-224-6870. E-mail: library@wellmont.org. Web Site: www.balladhealth.org/locations/hospitals/holston-valley. *Library Contact,* Linda Carlson
Library Holdings: Bk Titles 1,000; Bk Vols 1,000; Per Subs 175
Subject Interests: Allied health, Med, Nursing
Partic in National Network of Libraries of Medicine Region 2; SE-Atlantic Regional Med Libr Servs; Tennessee Health Science Library Association; Tri-Cities Area Health Sciences Libraries Consortium

P KINGSPORT PUBLIC LIBRARY & ARCHIVES*, J Fred Johnson Memorial Library, 400 Broad St, 37660-4292. SAN 360-6066. Tel: 423-224-2539. FAX: 423-224-2558. E-mail: referencelibrary@kingsporttn.gov. Web Site: www.kingsportlibrary.org. *Mgr,* Ms Chris Markley; Tel: 423-229-9388, E-mail: chrismarkley@kingsporttn.gov; *Librn,* Jonathan Tallman; E-mail: jonathantallman@kingsporttn.gov; *Archivist,* Brianne Wright; Tel: 423-224-2559, E-mail: briannewright@kingsporttn.gov; Staff 11 (MLS 11)
Founded 1921. Pop 52,962; Circ 264,251
Library Holdings: Bk Vols 101,924; Per Subs 250
Special Collections: Archives of the City of Kingsport; Job & College Info Center; Palmer Regional History Coll
Subject Interests: Local hist
Automation Activity & Vendor Info: (Acquisitions) SirsiDynix; (Cataloging) OCLC; (Circulation) SirsiDynix-WorkFlows; (ILL) OCLC; (OPAC) SirsiDynix-Enterprise; (Serials) Ex Libris Group
Wireless access
Function: 24/7 Electronic res, 24/7 Online cat, Adult bk club, Archival coll, Audio & video playback equip for onsite use, Audiobks on Playaways & MP3, Audiobks via web, Bilingual assistance for Spanish patrons, Bks on cassette, Bks on CD, CD-ROM, Children's prog, Computer training, Computers for patron use, Digital talking bks, E-Reserves, Electronic

databases & coll, Family literacy, For res purposes, Free DVD rentals, Genealogy discussion group, Govt ref serv, Health sci info serv, Holiday prog, Homebound delivery serv, ILL available, Instruction & testing, Internet access, Life-long learning prog for all ages, Magazines, Magnifiers for reading, Mail & tel request accepted, Meeting rooms, Microfiche/film & reading machines, Movies, Online cat, Online ref, Orientations, Outreach serv, Outside serv via phone, mail, e-mail & web, OverDrive digital audio bks, Photocopying/Printing, Preschool outreach, Preschool reading prog, Printer for laptops & handheld devices, Prof lending libr, Prog for adults, Prog for children & young adult, Ref & res, Ref serv available, Scanner, Senior computer classes, Senior outreach, Serves people with intellectual disabilities, Spanish lang bks, Spoken cassettes & CDs, Spoken cassettes & DVDs, Story hour, Study rm, Summer reading prog, Tax forms, Teen prog, Telephone ref, Visual arts prog, Wheelchair accessible, Workshops, Writing prog
Publications: Footnotes (Friends of Library quarterly newsletter); Kingsport Public Library (Monthly newsletter)
Mem of Holston River Regional Library
Partic in Tenn-Share
Special Services for the Deaf - Bks on deafness & sign lang; High interest/low vocabulary bks; Staff with knowledge of sign lang
Special Services for the Blind - Accessible computers; Assistive/Adapted tech devices, equip & products; Bks available with recordings; Bks on cassette; Bks on CD; Digital talking bk; Extensive large print coll; Home delivery serv; Internet workstation with adaptive software; Large print & cassettes; Large print bks; Low vision equip; Magnifiers; Optolec clearview video magnifier; Playaways (bks on MP3); Recorded bks; Ref serv
Open Mon-Thurs 8:30-7, Fri & Sat 8:30-6
Restriction: Circ to mem only, ID required to use computers (Ltd hrs), In-house use for visitors, Non-circulating of rare bks
Friends of the Library Group

KINGSTON

P KINGSTON PUBLIC LIBRARY*, 1004 Bradford Way, 37763. SAN 315-8217. Tel: 865-376-9905. FAX: 865-717-0289. Web Site: www.kingstonpubliclibrarytn.org. *Dir,* Emily Steele; E-mail: directorkpl@comcast.net; *Ch Serv,* Barbara Thorbjornsen
Founded 1947. Pop 15,000; Circ 45,000
Library Holdings: Bk Vols 40,000; Per Subs 35
Special Collections: Oral History
Subject Interests: County genealogy, Hist, Tenn hist
Automation Activity & Vendor Info: (Cataloging) SirsiDynix; (Circulation) SirsiDynix; (ILL) SirsiDynix
Wireless access
Mem of Ocoee River Regional Library
Open Mon-Wed & Fri 9-5:30, Thurs 9-8, Sat 9-Noon
Friends of the Library Group

KINGSTON SPRINGS

P SOUTH CHEATHAM PUBLIC LIBRARY*, 358 N Main St, 37082. (Mail add: PO Box 310, 37082-0310), SAN 373-9317. Tel: 615-952-4752. FAX: 615-952-3803. E-mail: soucpl@comcast.net. Web Site: southcheathamlibrary.com. *Dir,* Janet Walker; Staff 4 (MLS 1, Non-MLS 3)
Founded 1986. Pop 14,948; Circ 32,140
Library Holdings: Large Print Bks 230; Bk Vols 16,400; Per Subs 18; Videos 675
Special Collections: Juvenile Poetry (Brewton/Blackburn Coll). Oral History
Automation Activity & Vendor Info: (Cataloging) Book Systems; (ILL) Auto-Graphics, Inc
Wireless access
Mem of Red River Regional Library
Special Services for the Deaf - High interest/low vocabulary bks; TTY equip
Open Mon, Tues & Thurs 10-8, Wed, Fri & Sat 10-4:30
Friends of the Library Group

KNOXVILLE

CR JOHNSON UNIVERSITY*, Glass Memorial Library, 7902 Eubanks Dr, 37998. (Mail add: 7900 Johnson Dr, 37998). Tel: 865-251-2277. FAX: 865-251-2278. E-mail: library@johnsonu.edu. Web Site: johnsonu.edu/library/tennessee. *Dir,* Carrie Beth Lowe; E-mail: CBLowe@johnsonu.edu; *Ref Librn,* Rick Bower; E-mail: rbower@johnsonu.edu; *Asst Librn,* John Jaeger; Tel: 865-251-2275, E-mail: jjaeger@johnsonu.edu; *Circ,* Heidi Sise; E-mail: hsise@johnsonu.edu; *Per,* Denny Eaton; E-mail: deaton@johnsonu.edu; *Tech Serv,* Jan Christy; E-mail: jchristy@johnsonu.edu; Staff 5.1 (MLS 2.3, Non-MLS 2.8)
Founded 1893. Enrl 1,049; Fac 178; Highest Degree: Doctorate
Library Holdings: AV Mats 15,454; e-books 367,680; e-journals 45,564; Electronic Media & Resources 2,672; Microforms 21,760; Bk Titles 86,442; Bk Vols 121,894; Per Subs 248
Special Collections: Religion (Restoration Movement)
Automation Activity & Vendor Info: (Acquisitions) TLC (The Library Corporation); (Cataloging) TLC (The Library Corporation); (Circulation) TLC (The Library Corporation); (Discovery) EBSCO Discovery Service; (OPAC) TLC (The Library Corporation); (Serials) EBSCO Discovery Service
Wireless access
Function: 24/7 Online cat, Electronic databases & coll, Microfiche/film & reading machines, Online cat, Online ref, Photocopying/Printing, Study rm
Partic in Appalachian College Association; Christian Library Consortium; Tenn-Share
Open Mon-Thurs 7:45am-10:30pm, Fri 7:45-5, Sat 10-5, Sun 5pm-10pm (Fall & Spring); Mon-Fri 8-5 (Summer)

GL KNOX COUNTY GOVERNMENTAL LAW LIBRARY*, Honorable Sharon J Bell Library, M-99 City County Bldg, 400 Main St, 37902. SAN 327-6694. Tel: 865-215-2368. *Law Librn,* Meredith Douglas; E-mail: meredith.douglas@knoxcounty.org
Library Holdings: Bk Vols 60,000
Subject Interests: Legal
Wireless access
Open Mon-Fri 8-5:30
Restriction: Access at librarian's discretion, Authorized patrons, Circ to mem only

P KNOX COUNTY PUBLIC LIBRARY SYSTEM*, Lawson McGhee Library, 500 W Church Ave, 37902. SAN 360-618X. Tel: 865-215-8750. Interlibrary Loan Service Tel: 865-215-8746. Reference Tel: 865-215-8700. FAX: 865-215-8742. Web Site: www.knoxlib.org. *Dir,* Myretta Black; E-mail: mblack@knoxlib.org; *Communications Adminr, Pub Relations,* Mary Pomeroy Claiborne; *Hist Coll Librn,* Steve Cotham; *Archives Mgr, Archivist,* Doris Martinson; *Automation Syst Mgr,* Sally Lodico; Staff 27 (MLS 27)
Founded 1886. Pop 430,019; Circ 406,752
Library Holdings: AV Mats 22,127; e-books 57; Electronic Media & Resources 78; Microforms 39,757; Bk Vols 1,040,078; Per Subs 1,122
Special Collections: History & Genealogy of Tennessee & the Southeast (Calvin M McClung Historical Coll); Knox County Archives. US Document Depository
Automation Activity & Vendor Info: (Cataloging) SirsiDynix; (Circulation) SirsiDynix; (OPAC) SirsiDynix
Wireless access
Function: Adult bk club, After school storytime, Archival coll, Art exhibits, Audiobks via web, AV serv, Bk club(s), Bks on cassette, Bks on CD, Bus archives, Children's prog, Citizenship assistance, Computer training, Computers for patron use, Digital talking bks, E-Reserves, Electronic databases & coll, Genealogy discussion group, Homebound delivery serv, ILL available, Instruction & testing, Internet access, Jazz prog, Mail & tel request accepted, Music CDs, Online cat, Online ref, Outreach serv, OverDrive digital audio bks, Photocopying/Printing, Prog for adults, Prog for children & young adult, Ref & res, Ref serv available, Spoken cassettes & CDs, Spoken cassettes & DVDs, Story hour, Summer reading prog, Teen prog, Telephone ref, VHS videos, Wheelchair accessible, Workshops
Partic in LYRASIS; OCLC Online Computer Library Center, Inc; Tenn-Share
Special Services for the Deaf - TDD equip
Special Services for the Blind - Audio mat; Bks on cassette; Bks on CD; Digital talking bk; Duplicating spec requests; Extensive large print coll; Home delivery serv; Integrated libr/media serv; Large print & cassettes; Large print bks; Magnifiers; PC for people with disabilities; Recorded bks; Sound rec; Talking bk serv referral
Open Mon-Thurs 9-8, Fri 9-5:30, Sat 10-5, Sun 1-5
Restriction: Non-circulating coll, Non-circulating of rare bks
Friends of the Library Group
Branches: 17
BEARDEN BRANCH, 100 Golfclub Rd, 37919, SAN 360-6724. Tel: 865-588-8813. Web Site: www.knoxlib.org/about/hours-and-locations/bearden-branch-library. *Br Mgr,* Susan Poorbaugh; Staff 1 (MLS 1)
Circ 215,909
Library Holdings: Bk Vols 61,824
Open Mon, Tues & Thurs 10-8, Wed, Fri & Sat 10-5:30
Friends of the Library Group
BURLINGTON BRANCH, 4614 Asheville Hwy, 37914, SAN 360-621X. Tel: 865-525-5431. FAX: 865-525-4648. Web Site: www.knoxlib.org/about/hours-and-locations/burlington-branch-library. *Br Mgr,* Jeff Johnston
Circ 63,132
Library Holdings: Bk Vols 19,804
Open Mon & Thurs 10:30-8, Tues & Wed 10:30-5, Fri & Sat 1-5
Friends of the Library Group
CARTER BRANCH, 9036 Asheville Hwy, 37924, SAN 360-6244. Tel: 865-933-5438. FAX: 865-932-1221. Web Site: www.knoxlib.org/about/hours-and-locations/carter-branch-library. *Br Mgr,* Melanie Reseigh

Circ 31,814
Library Holdings: Bk Vols 16,367
Open Mon, Wed & Thurs 10-6, Tues 12-8, Sat 10-5:30
Friends of the Library Group
CEDAR BLUFF BRANCH, 9045 Cross Park Dr, 37923, SAN 377-6522. Tel: 865-470-7033. FAX: 865-470-0927. Web Site: www.knoxlib.org/about/hours-and-locations/cedar-bluff-branch-library. *Br Mgr,* Mr Andy Madson; Staff 1 (MLS 1)
Circ 309,824
Library Holdings: Bk Vols 85,974
Open Mon-Thurs 10-8, Fri & Sat 10-5:30
Friends of the Library Group
CORRYTON BRANCH, 7733 Corryton Rd, Corryton, 37721, SAN 360-6279. Tel: 865-688-1501. FAX: 865-687-7568. Web Site: www.knoxlib.org/about/hours-and-locations/corryton-branch-library. *Br Mgr,* Patricia Sue Walker
Circ 9,920
Library Holdings: Bk Vols 17,079
Open Mon-Fri 1:30-5:30
Friends of the Library Group
FARRAGUT BRANCH, 417 N Campbell Station Rd, Farragut, 37934, SAN 360-6333. Tel: 865-777-1750. FAX: 865-675-7696. Web Site: www.knoxlib.org/about/hours-and-locations/farragut-branch-library. *Br Mgr,* Marilyn Jones; Staff 1 (MLS 1)
Circ 302,942
Library Holdings: Bk Vols 68,619
Open Mon-Thurs 10-8, Fri & Sat 10-5:30
Friends of the Library Group
FOUNTAIN CITY BRANCH, 5300 Stanton Rd, 37918, SAN 360-6368. Tel: 865-689-2681. FAX: 865-689-3481. Web Site: www.knoxlib.org/about/hours-and-locations/fountain-city-branch-library. *Br Mgr,* Elizabeth Nelson; Staff 1 (MLS 1)
Circ 119,967
Library Holdings: Bk Vols 36,291
Open Mon, Tues & Thurs 10-8, Wed, Fri & Sat 10-5:30
Friends of the Library Group
HALLS BRANCH, 4518 E Emory Rd, 37938, SAN 360-6392. Tel: 865-922-2552. FAX: 865-922-6543. Web Site: www.knoxlib.org/about/hours-and-locations/halls-branch-library. *Br Mgr,* Ms Jamie Osborn; Staff 1 (MLS 1)
Circ 136,457
Library Holdings: Bk Vols 41,754
Open Mon, Tues & Thurs 10-8, Wed, Fri & Sat 10-5:30
Friends of the Library Group
KARNS BRANCH, 7516 Oak Ridge Hwy, 37931, SAN 360-6422. Tel: 865-470-8663. FAX: 865-693-7858. Web Site: www.knoxlib.org/about/hours-and-locations/karns-branch-library. *Mgr,* Karen Van Rij
Circ 87,938
Library Holdings: Bk Vols 33,403
Open Mon, Wed & Thurs 10-6, Tues 12-8, Sat 10-5:30
Friends of the Library Group
MASCOT BRANCH, 1927 Library Rd, Mascot, 37806, SAN 360-6457. Tel: 865-933-2620. Web Site: www.knoxlib.org/about/hours-and-locations/mascot-branch-library. *Br Mgr,* Ralph McGhee
Circ 30,227
Library Holdings: Bk Vols 16,553
Open Mon-Fri 2-6
Friends of the Library Group
MURPHY BRANCH, L T Ross Bldg, 2247 Western Ave, 37921, SAN 360-649X. Tel: 865-521-7812. FAX: 865-521-0962. Web Site: www.knoxlib.org/about/hours-and-locations/murphy-branch-library. *Br Mgr,* Heather Willson
Circ 9,469
Library Holdings: Bk Vols 10,928
Open Mon & Thurs 2-6, Tues & Wed 10-5
Friends of the Library Group
NORTH KNOXVILLE BRANCH, 2901 Ocoee Trail, 37917, SAN 360-6511. Tel: 865-525-7036. FAX: 865-525-0796. Web Site: www.knoxlib.org/about/hours-and-locations/north-knoxville-branch-library. *Br Mgr,* Tammie Morgan
Circ 50,397
Library Holdings: Bk Vols 25,355
Open Mon & Tues Noon-8, Wed, Thurs & Sat 9:30-5:30
Friends of the Library Group
NORWOOD BRANCH, 1110 Merchant Dr, 37912, SAN 360-6546. Tel: 865-688-2454. FAX: 865-688-0677. Web Site: www.knoxlib.org/about/hours-and-locations/norwood-branch-library. *Br Mgr,* Laura Honaker
Circ 68,653
Library Holdings: Bk Vols 31,537
Open Mon & Thurs Noon-8, Tues, Wed, Fri & Sat 9:30-5:30
Friends of the Library Group
HOWARD PINKSTON BRANCH, 7732 Martin Mill Pike, 37920. Tel: 865-573-0436. FAX: 865-573-1351. Web Site: www.knoxlib.org/about/hours-and-locations/howard-pinkston-branch-library. *Br Mgr,* Laila Archer
Circ 57,009
Library Holdings: Bk Titles 25,191
Open Mon, Wed & Thurs 9:30-5:30, Tues 12-8, Sat 10-5:30
Friends of the Library Group
POWELL BRANCH, 330 W Emory Rd, 37849, SAN 360-6570. Tel: 865-947-6210. FAX: 865-938-6466. Web Site: www.knoxlib.org/about/hours-and-locations/powell-branch-library. *Br Mgr,* Heather Jennings; Staff 1 (MLS 1)
Circ 151,464
Library Holdings: Bk Vols 43,786
Open Mon, Tues & Thurs 10-8, Wed, Fri & Sat 10-5:30
Friends of the Library Group
SEQUOYAH BRANCH, 1140 Southgate Rd, 37919, SAN 360-6600. Tel: 865-525-1541. FAX: 865-525-3148. Web Site: www.knoxlib.org/about/hours-and-locations/sequoyah-branch-library. *Br Mgr,* Denise Crawhorn
Circ 34,279
Library Holdings: Bk Vols 18,519
Open Mon 12-8, Tues-Thurs & Sat 9:30-5:30
Friends of the Library Group
SOUTH KNOXVILLE BRANCH, 4500 Chapman Hwy, 37920, SAN 360-6635. Tel: 865-573-1772. FAX: 865-579-4912. Web Site: www.knoxlib.org/about/hours-and-locations/south-knoxville-branch-library. *Br Mgr, Ch Serv,* Fredda Williams; Staff 1 (MLS 1)
Circ 88,803
Library Holdings: Bk Vols 32,865
Open Mon, Tues & Thurs 10-8, Wed, Fri & Sat 10-5:30
Friends of the Library Group

G KNOXVILLE-KNOX COUNTY METROPOLITAN PLANNING COMMISSION LIBRARY*, City & County Bldg, Ste 403, 400 Main St, 37902-2476. SAN 326-5684. Tel: 865-215-2500. FAX: 865-215-2068. E-mail: contact@knoxplanning.org. Web Site: www.knoxmpc.org. *Info Serv Mgr,* Terry Gilhula, PhD; Tel: 865-215-3819, E-mail: terry.gilhula@knoxplanning.org; Staff 2 (Non-MLS 2)
Founded 1975
Library Holdings: DVDs 216; Bk Titles 10,000; Per Subs 93; Videos 48
Subject Interests: Urban affairs
Automation Activity & Vendor Info: (Cataloging) New Generation Technologies Inc. (LiBRARYSOFT); (Circulation) New Generation Technologies Inc. (LiBRARYSOFT); (OPAC) New Generation Technologies Inc. (LiBRARYSOFT)
Function: ILL available, Photocopying/Printing, Ref serv available, Telephone ref
Publications: Catalogue of M P C Publications; Monthly Acquisitions
Restriction: Internal circ only, Open to pub for ref only, Pub use on premises

G MUNICIPAL TECHNICAL ADVISORY SERVICE*, 1610 University Ave, 37921-6741. SAN 327-6678. Tel: 865-974-0411. FAX: 865-974-0423. Web Site: www.mtas.tennessee.edu. *Librn,* Frances Adams-O'Brien; Tel: 865-974-9842, E-mail: Frances.Adams-Obrien@tennessee.edu; *Sr Libr Assoc III/Libr Serv,* Dawn McMillen; Tel: 865-974-8970, E-mail: Dawn.Mcmillen@tennessee.edu; Staff 3 (MLS 2, Non-MLS 1)
Founded 1950
Library Holdings: Bk Vols 10,000; Per Subs 120
Special Collections: City Ordinances; Municipal Law
Subject Interests: Municipal
Function: Res libr
Publications: Directory of Tennessee Municipal Officials
Partic in LYRASIS; Tenn-Share
Open Mon-Fri 8:30-5:30
Restriction: Not a lending libr

PELLISSIPPI STATE COMMUNITY COLLEGE
J DIVISION STREET LIBRARY*, 3435 Division St, 37919. Tel: 865-971-5215. *Campus Librn,* Lauren Rider; Tel: 865-971-5254, E-mail: lrider@pstcc.edu
J HARDIN VALLEY LIBRARY*, 10915 Harding Valley Rd, 37933. (Mail add: PO Box 22990, 37933-0990), SAN 327-8050. Tel: 865-694-6516. Reference Tel: 865-539-7107. FAX: 865-694-6625. Web Site: www.pstcc.edu/library. *Dean, Libr Serv,* Mary Ellen Soencer; Tel: 865-694-6517, E-mail: mespencer@pstcc.edu; *Campus Librn,* Lauren Rider; Tel: 865-971-5254, E-mail: lrider@pstcc.edu; *Cat Librn,* Janine Pino; Tel: 865-694-6621, E-mail: jcpino@pstcc.edu; *Circ Librn,* Susan Martel; Tel: 865-539-7047, E-mail: smartel@pstcc.edu; *Ref Librn,* Stephanie Gillespie; Tel: 865-539-7106, E-mail: scgillespie@pstcc.edu; Staff 16 (MLS 9, Non-MLS 7)
Founded 1979. Enrl 6,000; Fac 9; Highest Degree: Associate

Library Holdings: Audiobooks 2,000; AV Mats 2,500; CDs 125; e-books 160,000; e-journals 15,000; Electronic Media & Resources 100; Bk Vols 70,000; Per Subs 200; Videos 2,000
Automation Activity & Vendor Info: (Acquisitions) Ex Libris Group; (Cataloging) Ex Libris Group; (Circulation) Ex Libris Group; (Course Reserve) Ex Libris Group; (Discovery) Ex Libris Group; (ILL) OCLC Online; (OPAC) Ex Libris Group; (Serials) Ex Libris Group
Function: 24/7 Electronic res, 24/7 Online cat, Audiobks via web, Computers for patron use, Distance learning, Electronic databases & coll, ILL available, Internet access, Meeting rooms, Movies, Online cat, Online info literacy tutorials on the web & in blackboard, Online ref, Outside serv via phone, mail, e-mail & web, Photocopying/Printing, Printer for laptops & handheld devices, Ref serv available, Res libr, Scanner, Study rm, Telephone ref, Wheelchair accessible
Partic in LYRASIS; OCLC Online Computer Library Center, Inc; Tenn-Share
Open Mon-Thurs 8-7:30, Fri 8-4:30
Restriction: Open to students, fac & staff

J MAGNOLIA AVENUE LIBRARY*, 1610 E Magnolia Ave, 37917. Tel: 865-329-3110. *Interim Campus Librarian, Ref & Instruction Librn,* Allison Scripa; Tel: 865-539-7237, E-mail: ajscripa@pstcc.edu
Open Mon-Thurs 8-4:30, Fri 8-4

J STRAWBERRY PLAINS ERC*, 7201 Strawberry Plains Pike, 37914. Tel: 865-225-2309. *Campus Librn,* Allison McKittrick; Tel: 865-225-2322, E-mail: almckittrick@pstcc.edu
Open Mon-Fri 8-4

C SOUTH COLLEGE*, Lonas Campus Library, 3904 Lonas Dr, 37909. SAN 328-5758. Tel: 865-251-1832. Reference E-mail: scref@south.edu. Web Site: library.south.edu/lonas. *Dir, Libr Serv,* Anya McKinney; E-mail: amckinney@south.edu; *Cat Librn,* Carl Parham; E-mail: cparham1@south.edu; *Instruction Librn,* James Gill; E-mail: jgill@south.edu; Staff 5 (MLS 4, Non-MLS 1)
Enrl 750; Highest Degree: Master
Library Holdings: CDs 100; DVDs 300; e-books 28,000; e-journals 12,000; Bk Vols 9,700; Per Subs 200; Videos 830
Subject Interests: Allied health, Bus, Law
Automation Activity & Vendor Info: (Cataloging) Follett Software
Wireless access
Function: Electronic databases & coll, Online cat, Orientations
Open Mon-Thurs 8-7, Fri 8-5, Sat 8-1
Restriction: Not open to pub, Open to students, fac & staff

Departmental Libraries:

PARKSIDE CAMPUS LIBRARY, 400 Goody's Lane, Ste 101, 37922. Tel: 865-288-5750. Web Site: library.south.edu/parkside. *Dir, Libr Serv,* Anya McKinney; E-mail: amckinney@south.edu; *Electronic Res Librn,* Jon Hudson; E-mail: jhudson1@south.edu
Open Mon-Thurs 8-7, Fri & Sat 8-5

TENNESSEE VALLEY AUTHORITY

L LEGAL RESEARCH CENTER*, 400 W Summit Hill Dr, 37922, SAN 360-6813. Tel: 865-632-6613. FAX: 865-632-6718. ; Staff 5 (MLS 5)
Founded 1935
Library Holdings: Bk Vols 26,000; Per Subs 13
Subject Interests: Case law, Eminent domain, Energy, Environ, Fed practice, Fed statutory, Procurement, Pub utilities, Water law
Partic in Proquest Dialog; Vutext
Restriction: Not open to pub, Staff use only

G *, WT CC - K, 400 W Summit Hill Dr, 37902, SAN 360-6759. Tel: 865-632-3464. Interlibrary Loan Service Tel: 865-632-7865. E-mail: tvainfo@tva.gov. *Librn,* Nancy Proctor; E-mail: njproctor@tva.gov; Staff 1 (MLS 1)
Founded 1933
Library Holdings: Bk Vols 57,273
Special Collections: TVA History Coll
Subject Interests: Environ, Regional hist
Partic in Federal Library & Information Network; OCLC Online Computer Library Center, Inc
Publications: Current Awareness Lists
Restriction: Open to pub by appt only

CL UNIVERSITY OF TENNESSEE*, Joel A Katz Law Library, Taylor Law Ctr, 1505 W Cumberland Ave, 37996-1800. SAN 360-6937. Tel: 865-974-7419. Reference Tel: 865-974-3771. FAX: 865-974-6595. E-mail: lawref@utk.edu. Web Site: law.utk.edu/library. *Assoc Dean,* Scott Childs; Tel: 865-974-6733; *Head of Research & Instruction Services,* Sibyl Marshall; E-mail: smarshal@utk.edu; *Head, Pub Serv,* Nathan Preuss; Tel: 865-974-6736, E-mail: npreuss@utk.edu; *Head, Tech Serv,* Carol Collins; Tel: 865-974-6552, E-mail: ccollin1@utk.edu; Staff 22 (MLS 9, Non-MLS 13)
Founded 1890. Enrl 478; Fac 35; Highest Degree: Doctorate
Library Holdings: Bk Titles 95,337; Bk Vols 483,372; Per Subs 6,363
Special Collections: US Document Depository
Automation Activity & Vendor Info: (Acquisitions) Innovative Interfaces, Inc; (Cataloging) Innovative Interfaces, Inc; (Circulation) Innovative Interfaces, Inc; (Course Reserve) Innovative Interfaces, Inc; (OPAC) Innovative Interfaces, Inc; (Serials) Innovative Interfaces, Inc
Wireless access
Function: Res libr
Partic in Association of Research Libraries; LYRASIS; Mid-America Law Library Consortium
Open Mon-Thurs 7am-Midnight, Fri 7am-10pm, Sat 8:30am-10pm, Sun 8:30am-Midnight (Winter); Mon-Thurs 8am-10pm, Fri 8-8, Sat Noon-5, Sun Noon-10 (Summer)
Friends of the Library Group

JM UNIVERSITY OF TENNESSEE GRADUATE SCHOOL OF MEDICINE*, Preston Medical Library & Learning Resource Center, 1924 Alcoa Hwy, Box U-111, 37920. SAN 315-8284. Tel: 865-305-9525. FAX: 865-305-9527. E-mail: library@utmck.edu. Web Site: gsm.utmck.edu/library. *Libr Dir,* Martha Earl; Tel: 865-305-6616, E-mail: mearl@utmck.edu; *Asst Dir,* Kelsey Grabeel; Tel: 865-305-5707, E-mail: kgrabeel@utmck.edu; *Head, Coll & Access Serv,* J Michael Lindsay; Tel: 865-305-9528, E-mail: jmlindsay@utmck.edu; *Clinical Librn,* Rebecca Harrington; Tel: 865-305-8776, E-mail: rharrington@mc.utmck.edu; *Libr Supvr,* Jennifer Luhrs; Tel: 865-305-7340, E-mail: jluhrs@utmck.edu; Staff 8 (MLS 4, Non-MLS 4)
Founded 1969. Enrl 180; Highest Degree: Doctorate
Library Holdings: e-books 200; e-journals 4,000; Bk Titles 3,750; Per Subs 150
Subject Interests: Biochem, Cancer, Clinical med, Dentistry, Hematology, Immunology, Perinatology, Trauma
Automation Activity & Vendor Info: (Cataloging) Ex Libris Group; (Circulation) Ex Libris Group; (OPAC) Ex Libris Group; (Serials) EBSCO Online
Wireless access
Function: Workshops
Partic in Knoxville Area Health Sciences Library Consortium; Tenn-Share
Open Mon-Thurs 8:30am-9pm, Fri 8:30-5, Sat 9-5, Sun 1-9
Restriction: Badge access after hrs, Non-circulating to the pub

C UNIVERSITY OF TENNESSEE, KNOXVILLE*, John C Hodges University Libraries, 1015 Volunteer Blvd, 37996-1000. SAN 360-6848. Tel: 865-974-4351. Interlibrary Loan Service Tel: 423-974-4240. Reference Tel: 865-974-4171. Administration Tel: 865-974-6600. FAX: 865-974-4259. Web Site: www.lib.utk.edu. *Dean of Libr,* Steven Smith; E-mail: stevensmith@utk.edu; *Assoc Dean, Res, Coll & Scholarly Communication,* Holly Mercer; E-mail: hollymercer@utk.edu; *Assoc Dean, Res & Learning Serv,* Teresa Walker; E-mail: tbwalker@utk.edu; *Assessment Librn,* Regina Mays; E-mail: rmays@utk.edu; *Marketing & Communications Coord,* Robin A Bedenbaugh; E-mail: rbedenbaugh@utk.edu; Staff 170 (MLS 63, Non-MLS 107)
Founded 1794. Enrl 23,986; Fac 1,477; Highest Degree: Doctorate
Library Holdings: Bk Vols 2,319,379; Per Subs 32,099
Special Collections: Alex Haley Coll; Cherokee Indians; Congressional Papers; Congreve; Early Imprints; Early Voyages & Travel; Nineteenth Century American Fiction; Radiation Biology; Tennessee World War II Veterans. Oral History; State Document Depository; US Document Depository
Automation Activity & Vendor Info: (Acquisitions) Ex Libris Group; (Cataloging) Ex Libris Group; (Circulation) Ex Libris Group; (Course Reserve) Ex Libris Group; (ILL) Ex Libris Group; (Media Booking) Ex Libris Group; (OPAC) Ex Libris Group; (Serials) Ex Libris Group
Wireless access
Publications: Library Development Review (Annual); Library Friends (Newsletter); Mission & Strategic Plan (Annual); The UTK Librarian (Newsletter); The UTK Library Record (Annual report)
Partic in Association of Research Libraries; Center for Research Libraries; Digital Libr Fedn; LYRASIS; OCLC Online Computer Library Center, Inc; OCLC Research Library Partnership
Special Services for the Deaf - TTY equip
Special Services for the Blind - Braille equip
Friends of the Library Group

Departmental Libraries:

ACQUISITIONS & CONTINUING RESOURCES, 1015 Volunteer Blvd, 37996-1000. Tel: 865-974-4236. FAX: 865-974-0551. *Library Contact,* Elyssa Gould
Friends of the Library Group

GEORGE F DEVINE MUSIC LIBRARY, Natalie L Haslam Music Ctr, G04, 1741 Volunteer Blvd, 37996-2600, SAN 360-6961. Tel: 865-974-3474. FAX: 865-974-0564. E-mail: musiclib@utk.edu. Web Site: www.lib.utk.edu/music. *Librn,* Chris Durman; Tel: 865-974-7542, E-mail: cdurman@utk.edu; *Librn,* Nathalie Hristov; Tel: 865-974-9893, E-mail: mhristov@utk.edu; Staff 4 (MLS 2, Non-MLS 2)
Founded 1965
Special Collections: Barry McDonald Music Coll, scores; Canadian Composers' Information File; Opera Libretti, Programs & Ballet Programs (Earl W Quintrell Coll)

Open Mon-Thurs 7:30am-10pm, Fri 7:30-5, Sat 1-5, Sun 2-10 (Fall & Spring); Mon-Thurs 8-7, Fri 8-5 (Summer)
Friends of the Library Group

MAP COLLECTION, James D Hoskins Library, Rms 200 & 219, 1401 Cumberland Ave, 37996, SAN 372-7777. Tel: 865-974-6214. E-mail: closedstacks@utk.edu. Web Site: libguides.utk.edu/map. *Maps Librn,* Jeff French; E-mail: jfrench4@utk.edu; *Maps & Govt Info Librn,* Gregory March; E-mail: gmarch@utk.edu
Open Mon-Fri 8-4
Friends of the Library Group

WEBSTER C PENDERGRASS AGRICULTURE & VETERINARY MEDICINE LIBRARY, A-113 Veterinary Medical Ctr, 2407 River Dr, 37996-4541, SAN 360-6902. Tel: 865-974-7338. FAX: 865-974-4732. E-mail: agvetlib@utk.edu. Web Site: www.lib.utk.edu/agvet. *Agr Librn,* Maggie Albro; E-mail: malbro@utk.edu; *Veterinary Med Librn,* Ann Viera; Tel: 865-974-9015, E-mail: annviera@utk.edu; *Operations Mgr,* Samantha Ward; Tel: 865-974-4728, E-mail: sward22@utk.edu; Staff 7 (MLS 3, Non-MLS 4)
Friends of the Library Group

SPECIAL COLLECTIONS, 121 Hodges Library, 1015 Volunteer Blvd, 37996, SAN 372-7793. Tel: 865-974-4480. E-mail: special@utk.edu. Web Site: www.lib.utk.edu/special. *Dept Head,* Jennifer Benedetto Beals; E-mail: jbeals@utk.edu; *Univ Archivist,* Alesha Shumar; E-mail: ashumar@utk.edu; Staff 5 (Non-MLS 5)
Fac 6
Function: Archival coll
Open Mon-Fri 9-5:30
Restriction: Non-circulating coll
Friends of the Library Group

LA FOLLETTE

P LA FOLLETTE PUBLIC LIBRARY*, 201 S Ninth St, 37766-3606. SAN 315-8330. Tel: 423-562-5154. FAX: 423-566-2468. E-mail: laflib@comcast.net. Web Site: laflib.wordpress.com. *Libr Dir,* Nancy J Green; *Libr Asst,* Norma J Asher; Staff 1 (Non-MLS 1)
Jul 2020-Jun 2021 Income $99,794, City $88,044, Federal $848, County $9,400, Locally Generated Income $1,502. Mats Exp $3,147, Books $2,610, Per/Ser (Incl. Access Fees) $537. Sal $63,795 (Prof $46,265)
Library Holdings: Audiobooks 987; Braille Volumes 1; DVDs 4,350; Large Print Bks 520; Bk Titles 25,460; Per Subs 46; Videos 1,062
Automation Activity & Vendor Info: (Cataloging) Auto-Graphics, Inc; (Circulation) Auto-Graphics, Inc; (OPAC) Auto-Graphics, Inc; (Serials) Auto-Graphics, Inc
Wireless access
Function: 24/7 Online cat, 24/7 wireless access, Adult bk club, AV serv, Bk club(s), Bks on CD, Children's prog, Computers for patron use, Free DVD rentals, Holiday prog, ILL available, Instruction & testing, Internet access, Laminating, Laptop/tablet checkout, Magazines, Mail & tel request accepted, Notary serv, OverDrive digital audio bks, Preschool reading prog, Prof lending libr, Prog for children & young adult, Scanner, Story hour, Summer reading prog, Tax forms, Telephone ref, Wheelchair accessible, Wifi hotspot checkout
Mem of Clinch River Regional Library
Special Services for the Blind - Bks on CD; Free checkout of audio mat; Large print bks; Playaways (bks on MP3)
Open Mon-Fri 8-5
Friends of the Library Group

LA VERGNE

P LA VERGNE PUBLIC LIBRARY*, 5063 Murfreesboro Rd, 37086. SAN 322-7464. Tel: 615-793-7303. FAX: 615-793-7307. E-mail: lavergnelibrary@lavergnetn.gov. Web Site: www.lavergnetn.gov/192/La-Vergne-Public-Library. *Libr Dir,* Donna Bebout; E-mail: dbebout@lavergnetn.gov
Founded 1979. Pop 36,985; Circ 152,991
Library Holdings: Audiobooks 2,116; CDs 574; DVDs 1,492; Large Print Bks 647; Bk Vols 59,881; Per Subs 83; Videos 1,693
Automation Activity & Vendor Info: (Cataloging) Book Systems; (Circulation) Book Systems; (OPAC) Book Systems
Wireless access
Function: Adult bk club, After school storytime, Bks on CD, Children's prog, Computers for patron use, E-Reserves, Electronic databases & coll, Free DVD rentals, Genealogy discussion group, Holiday prog, Instruction & testing, Internet access, Music CDs, Online cat, Outreach serv, Photocopying/Printing, Preschool outreach, Prog for adults, Prog for children & young adult, Spanish lang bks, Story hour, Summer reading prog, Tax forms, Teen prog, VHS videos, Wheelchair accessible
Open Mon, Tues & Thurs 9-8, Wed, Fri & Sat 9-5

LAFAYETTE

P MACON COUNTY PUBLIC LIBRARY*, 311 Church St, 37083. SAN 360-702X. Tel: 615-666-4340. FAX: 615-666-8932. E-mail: maconcountypubliclibrary@gmail.com. Web Site: sites.google.com/site/maconcountypubliclibrarysystem. *Dir,* Dana Richardson
Founded 1957. Pop 22,000; Circ 40,000
Library Holdings: Bk Vols 14,872; Per Subs 46
Automation Activity & Vendor Info: (Circulation) Book Systems
Wireless access
Open Mon-Wed & Fri 9-5:45, Thurs 11-7, Sat 8-1:45
Branches: 1
RED BOILING SPRINGS BRANCH, 335 E Main St, Red Boiling Springs, 37150, SAN 360-7054. Tel: 615-699-3701. FAX: 615-699-3777. *Dir,* Dana Richardson; *Asst Librn,* Amy Copas
Founded 1963
Library Holdings: Bk Vols 6,588
Open Mon-Fri 12-6, Sat 8-2
Friends of the Library Group

LAWRENCEBURG

P LAWRENCE COUNTY PUBLIC LIBRARY*, 519 E Gaines St, 38464-3599. SAN 315-8357. Tel: 931-762-4627. FAX: 931-766-1597. E-mail: libraryinfo@lawcotn.org. Web Site: www.lawcolibrary.org/. *Dir,* Teresa Newton; E-mail: tnewton@lawcotn.org; Staff 1 (Non-MLS 1)
Founded 1941. Pop 42,115; Circ 102,960
Library Holdings: Bk Vols 44,842; Per Subs 127
Special Collections: Oral History
Automation Activity & Vendor Info: (Cataloging) Book Systems; (Circulation) Book Systems; (ILL) Auto-Graphics, Inc; (OPAC) Book Systems
Wireless access
Function: 24/7 Online cat, Adult bk club, Audiobks on Playaways & MP3, Bk club(s), Bks on CD, Children's prog, Computers for patron use, Free DVD rentals, Genealogy discussion group, Holiday prog, ILL available, Internet access, Magazines, Magnifiers for reading, Mail & tel request accepted, Meeting rooms, Microfiche/film & reading machines, Online cat, Online ref, Orientations, OverDrive digital audio bks, Photocopying/Printing, Preschool reading prog, Prog for adults, Prog for children & young adult, Story hour, Summer reading prog, Tax forms, Teen prog, Telephone ref, VHS videos
Publications: The Bookmark (Monthly newsletter)
Special Services for the Deaf - Closed caption videos
Special Services for the Blind - Bks on CD; Large print bks; Magnifiers
Open Mon, Thurs & Fri 9-5:30, Tues & Wed 9-8, Sat 9-2:30
Friends of the Library Group
Branches: 1
LORETTO BRANCH, 102 S Main St, Loretto, 38469-2110. (Mail add: PO Box 338, Loretto, 38469-0338), SAN 377-7847. Tel: 931-853-7323. FAX: 931-853-7324. E-mail: lorettolib@lawcotn.org. *Br Mgr,* Carol Snook; E-mail: lorettolib@lawcotn.org. Subject Specialists: *Children's mat,* Carol Snook
Library Holdings: Bk Vols 6,000; Per Subs 20
Automation Activity & Vendor Info: (Cataloging) Book Systems; (Circulation) Book Systems; (OPAC) Book Systems
Function: 24/7 Electronic res, 24/7 Online cat, Accelerated reader prog, Children's prog, Computers for patron use, Free DVD rentals, ILL available, Internet access, Magazines, Mail & tel request accepted, Online cat, OverDrive digital audio bks, Photocopying/Printing, Preschool outreach, Preschool reading prog, Spanish lang bks, Story hour, Summer reading prog, Tax forms
Open Tues 10-6, Wed & Thurs 12-6, Fri 1-5, Sat 9-3

LEBANON

C CUMBERLAND UNIVERSITY*, Doris & Harry Vise Library, One Cumberland Sq, 37087. SAN 315-8365. Tel: 615-547-1299. Toll Free Tel: 800-467-0562. FAX: 615-444-2569. E-mail: library@cumberland.edu. Web Site: library.cumberland.edu. *Libr Dir,* Bettina Warkentin; Tel: 615-547-1374, E-mail: bwarkentin@cumberland.edu; *Instr Librn,* Jessica Fenn; Tel: 615-547-1302, E-mail: jfenn@cumberland.edu; Staff 3 (MLS 2, Non-MLS 1)
Founded 1842. Enrl 1,270; Fac 61; Highest Degree: Master
Library Holdings: AV Mats 2,131; e-books 269,700; Microforms 1,000; Bk Vols 10,680; Per Subs 350
Special Collections: Childrens Literature Coll; Nobel Laureate Coll; Stockton Archives; Tennessee Room
Subject Interests: Liberal arts, Tenn hist
Automation Activity & Vendor Info: (Cataloging) Surpass; (Circulation) Surpass; (ILL) OCLC FirstSearch; (OPAC) Surpass; (Serials) Surpass
Wireless access
Function: For res purposes
Partic in LYRASIS; Nashville Area Libr Alliance; OCLC Online Computer Library Center, Inc; Tenn-Share
Open Mon-Thurs 7:30am-10pm, Fri 7:30-4:30
Restriction: Non-circulating to the pub

P LEBANON-WILSON COUNTY LIBRARY, 108 S Hatton Ave, 37087-3590. SAN 360-7089. Tel: 615-444-0632. FAX: 615-444-0535. E-mail: director@wilsoncolibrary.org. Web Site: www.youseemore.com/lebanon-wilson/. *Dir,* Alesia Burnley; *Asst Dir,* Dana Bilbrey; E-mail: dana.lb@wilsoncolibrary.org
Founded 1938. Pop 87,849; Circ 283,676
Library Holdings: Audiobooks 3,633; Bk Vols 70,261; Videos 3,470
Automation Activity & Vendor Info: (Cataloging) TLC (The Library Corporation); (Circulation) TLC (The Library Corporation)
Wireless access
Function: 24/7 Online cat, Audiobks on Playaways & MP3, Bks on CD, Children's prog, Computer training, Computers for patron use, Extended outdoor wifi, Free DVD rentals, ILL available, Internet access, Magazines, Movies, Online cat, OverDrive digital audio bks, Photocopying/Printing, Preschool outreach, Printer for laptops & handheld devices, Scanner, Senior computer classes, Senior outreach, Spanish lang bks, Story hour, Study rm, Summer reading prog, Tax forms, Wheelchair accessible, Wifi hotspot checkout
Mem of Stones River Regional Library
Open Mon, Tues & Thurs 8-7, Wed, Fri & Sat 8-5
Restriction: 24-hr pass syst for students only
Friends of the Library Group
Branches: 2
MOUNT JULIET-WILSON COUNTY LIBRARY, 2765 N Mount Juliet Rd, Mount Juliet, 37122, SAN 360-7143. Tel: 615-758-7051. FAX: 615-758-2439. E-mail: mjstaff@wilsoncolibrary.org, mtjuliet@wilsoncolibrary.org. Web Site: www.youseemore.com/mtjuliet/. *Dir,* Alesia Burnley; E-mail: director@wilsoncolibrary.org; *Asst Dir,* Amy Byrum; E-mail: amy.mj@wilsoncolibrary.org; *ILL Librn,* Adrienne Farnan; E-mail: adrienne.mj@wilsoncolibrary.org
Pop 75,825; Circ 427,515
Library Holdings: Audiobooks 1,845; DVDs 5,172; Bk Titles 60,396
Automation Activity & Vendor Info: (Cataloging) TLC (The Library Corporation); (Circulation) TLC (The Library Corporation)
Function: Bk club(s), Bks on CD, Children's prog, Computer training, Computers for patron use, Extended outdoor wifi, Free DVD rentals, ILL available, Internet access, Magazines, Movies, Online cat, Photocopying/Printing, Preschool outreach, Scanner, Story hour, Study rm, Summer reading prog, Tax forms, Wheelchair accessible
Open Mon, Tues & Thurs 8-7, Wed, Fri & Sat 8-5
Friends of the Library Group
WATERTOWN BRANCH, 206 Public Sq, Watertown, 37184-1422, SAN 360-7119. Tel: 615-237-9700. E-mail: watertown@wilsoncolibrary.org. Web Site: www.youseemore.com/Watertown. *Br Mgr,* Ryan Rich
Circ 19,218
Library Holdings: Audiobooks 301; Bk Vols 13,697; Videos 2,633
Function: Bks on CD, Children's prog, Computers for patron use, Movies, Online cat, Photocopying/Printing, Scanner, Story hour, Summer reading prog, Tax forms, Wheelchair accessible
Open Mon & Wed-Sat 9:30-5, Tues 11-7
Friends of the Library Group

LENOIR CITY

P LENOIR CITY PUBLIC LIBRARY*, 100 W Broadway, 37771. SAN 315-8373. Tel: 865-986-3210. Web Site: www.lenoircitypubliclibrary.com. *Dir,* Susan Dorsey; E-mail: dorseys@loudoncounty-tn.gov
Founded 1928
Library Holdings: Bk Vols 25,000; Per Subs 40
Mem of Ocoee River Regional Library
Open Mon 10-6, Tues-Fri 9-6
Friends of the Library Group

LEWISBURG

P MARSHALL COUNTY MEMORIAL LIBRARY*, 310 Old Farmington Rd, 37091. SAN 315-8381. Tel: 931-359-3335. FAX: 931-359-5866. E-mail: mcmlib@bellsouth.net. Web Site: www.marshallcountylibrary.org. *Dir,* Jennifer Pearson
Founded 1944. Pop 26,000; Circ 150,000
Library Holdings: Bk Titles 47,000; Per Subs 90
Subject Interests: Archit, Art, Educ, Genealogy, Hist, Med, Relig studies
Wireless access
Mem of Buffalo River Regional Library
Open Mon-Fri 9-8, Sat 9-5
Friends of the Library Group

LEXINGTON

P EVERETT HORN PUBLIC LIBRARY*, 702 W Church St, 38351-1713. SAN 315-839X. Tel: 731-968-3239. FAX: 731-968-4134. Web Site: www.ehlibrary.com. *Dir,* Crystal Ozier; E-mail: director@ehlibrary.com; Staff 1 (Non-MLS 1)
Founded 1949. Pop 28,049
Library Holdings: Bk Titles 26,342; Per Subs 45
Wireless access
Mem of Hatchie River Regional Library
Open Mon, Wed & Fri 9-5, Tues & Thurs 9-6, Sat 9-3
Friends of the Library Group

LINDEN

P PERRY COUNTY PUBLIC LIBRARY*, 104 College Ave, 37096. SAN 360-7178. Tel: 931-589-5011. FAX: 931-589-6210. E-mail: perrycolib@gmail.com. Web Site: www.perrycountylibrary.info. *Libr Dir,* Nan Garrett; Staff 2 (Non-MLS 2)
Pop 7,915
Library Holdings: Bk Titles 20,000
Automation Activity & Vendor Info: (Cataloging) Auto-Graphics, Inc; (Circulation) Auto-Graphics, Inc; (ILL) Auto-Graphics, Inc
Wireless access
Function: Audiobks via web, Bks on cassette, Bks on CD, Children's prog, Computer training, Computers for patron use, Digital talking bks, Electronic databases & coll, Free DVD rentals, ILL available, Mail & tel request accepted, Microfiche/film & reading machines, Online cat, Online ref, OverDrive digital audio bks, Photocopying/Printing, Preschool outreach, Printer for laptops & handheld devices, Prog for adults, Scanner, Spanish lang bks, Spoken cassettes & CDs, Spoken cassettes & DVDs, Summer reading prog, Tax forms, VHS videos, Wheelchair accessible
Special Services for the Deaf - Staff with knowledge of sign lang
Special Services for the Blind - Large print bks
Open Tues-Thurs 10-6, Fri 10-5, Sat 10-2
Friends of the Library Group
Branches: 1
LOBELVILLE BRANCH, 55 S Main St, Lobelville, 37097, SAN 360-7208. Tel: 931-593-3111. FAX: 931-593-2089. E-mail: lobelvillepubliclibrary@gmail.com. *Br Mgr,* Kathy Gammon; Staff 1.5 (Non-MLS 1.5)
Pop 7,915
Library Holdings: Bk Vols 5,000
Function: After school storytime, Audiobks via web, Bks on cassette, Bks on CD, Children's prog, Computer training, Computers for patron use, Electronic databases & coll, Free DVD rentals, Holiday prog, ILL available, Mail & tel request accepted, Music CDs, Online cat, Outreach serv, Passport agency, Photocopying/Printing, Printer for laptops & handheld devices, Prog for adults, Prog for children & young adult, Scanner, Senior computer classes, Spanish lang bks, Story hour, Summer & winter reading prog, Tax forms, Teen prog, Wheelchair accessible
Special Services for the Blind - Bks on cassette; Bks on CD; Extensive large print coll; Free checkout of audio mat; Large print bks
Open Mon-Fri 10-5
Friends of the Library Group

LIVINGSTON

P MILLARD OAKLEY LIBRARY*, 107 E Main St, 38570. SAN 315-8403. Tel: 931-823-1888. FAX: 931-403-0798. E-mail: overtoncolib@gmail.com. Web Site: www.overtoncolibrary.com. *Libr Dir,* Judith Cutright; Staff 4 (Non-MLS 4)
Founded 1966. Pop 20,566
Library Holdings: Audiobooks 1,034; DVDs 1,972; Bk Vols 26,422; Per Subs 30
Special Collections: Extensive Genealogy Area & Support System; Local Newpapers, Early 1900's to present, microfilm
Automation Activity & Vendor Info: (Circulation) Auto-Graphics, Inc; (ILL) Auto-Graphics, Inc; (OPAC) Auto-Graphics, Inc
Wireless access
Function: 24/7 Electronic res, 24/7 Online cat, 3D Printer, Accelerated reader prog, Adult bk club, Archival coll, Audio & video playback equip for onsite use, Bk club(s), Bks on CD, Children's prog, Computers for patron use, Free DVD rentals, ILL available, Internet access, Jail serv, Laminating, Magazines, Magnifiers for reading, Mail & tel request accepted, Meeting rooms, Microfiche/film & reading machines, Music CDs, Notary serv, Online cat, OverDrive digital audio bks, Photocopying/Printing, Printer for laptops & handheld devices, Prog for adults, Prog for children & young adult, Ref serv available, Res assist avail, Scanner, Story hour, Summer reading prog, Tax forms, Wheelchair accessible
Mem of Falling Water River Regional Library
Open Mon & Thurs 9-6, Tues, Wed & Fri 9-5, Sat 9-2
Restriction: Borrowing requests are handled by ILL, Circ to mem only
Friends of the Library Group

LOUDON

P LOUDON PUBLIC LIBRARY*, 210 River Rd, 37774. SAN 315-842X. Tel: 865-458-3161. FAX: 865-458-3161. E-mail: loudonlibrary@outlook.com. Web Site: loudonlibrary.com. *Dir,* Kate Clabough; E-mail: claboughk@loudoncounty-tn.gov; Staff 2 (Non-MLS 2)
Library Holdings: Bk Vols 10,000; Per Subs 12

Automation Activity & Vendor Info: (Acquisitions) Auto-Graphics, Inc; (Cataloging) Auto-Graphics, Inc; (Circulation) Auto-Graphics, Inc; (ILL) Auto-Graphics, Inc
Wireless access
Mem of Ocoee River Regional Library
Open Mon-Fri 9:30-5:30, Sat 9-2

P PUBLIC LIBRARY AT TELLICO VILLAGE, 300 Irene Lane, 37774. Tel: 865-458-5199. FAX: 865-458-5199. E-mail: tvlibrary.org@gmail.com. Web Site: www.tvlibrary.org. *Libr Mgr,* Gina Mucci Geremia; *Libr Asst,* Cheri Tompkins; Staff 1.5 (MLS 1, Non-MLS 0.5)
Founded 1997
Library Holdings: Audiobooks 300; DVDs 800; Bk Vols 16,000; Per Subs 80
Subject Interests: Astronomy, Consumer health, Local hist, Travel
Automation Activity & Vendor Info: (Cataloging) Auto-Graphics, Inc; (Circulation) Auto-Graphics, Inc; (OPAC) Auto-Graphics, Inc
Wireless access
Function: 24/7 Electronic res, 24/7 Online cat, Adult bk club, Archival coll, Audiobks via web, Bi-weekly Writer's Group, Bks on CD, Children's prog, Computer training, Computers for patron use, Doc delivery serv, Electronic databases & coll, Free DVD rentals, Govt ref serv, Health sci info serv, Home delivery & serv to seniorr ctr & nursing homes, Homebound delivery serv, ILL available, Instruction & testing, Internet access, Life-long learning prog for all ages, Literacy & newcomer serv, Magazines, Mail & tel request accepted, Meeting rooms, Movies, Online cat, Online info literacy tutorials on the web & in blackboard, Outreach serv, OverDrive digital audio bks, Photocopying/Printing, Prog for adults, Ref & res, Scanner, Senior computer classes, Senior outreach, Summer reading prog, Tax forms, VHS videos, Wheelchair accessible
Mem of Ocoee River Regional Library
Special Services for the Deaf - Assisted listening device
Special Services for the Blind - Aids for in-house use
Open Mon, Wed & Fri 9-5, Tues & Thurs 9-6, Sat 9-Noon
Friends of the Library Group

LUTTRELL

P LUTTRELL PUBLIC LIBRARY*, 115 Park Rd, 37779. SAN 315-8438. Tel: 865-992-0208. FAX: 865-992-4354. E-mail: luttrelllibrary@comcast.net. Web Site: facebook.com/luttrelllibrary. *Libr Dir,* Kimberly Todd
Founded 1951
Library Holdings: Bk Titles 5,000
Wireless access
Function: 24/7 Electronic res, 24/7 Online cat, 3D Printer, Activity rm, Adult bk club, Adult literacy prog, After school storytime, Audiobks on Playaways & MP3, Audiobks via web, Bk reviews (Group), Bks on CD, Holiday prog, Home delivery & serv to seniorr ctr & nursing homes, Homework prog, ILL available, Internet access, Laminating, Life-long learning prog for all ages, Magazines, Music CDs, OverDrive digital audio bks, Photocopying/Printing, Preschool reading prog, Printer for laptops & handheld devices, Prog for adults, Prog for children & young adult, Ref & res, Scanner, Senior computer classes, Spanish lang bks, Summer & winter reading prog, Summer reading prog, Visual arts prog, Wheelchair accessible, Writing prog
Mem of Clinch River Regional Library
Open Mon & Wed-Fri 9-6, Sat 9-1
Friends of the Library Group

LYNCHBURG

P MOORE COUNTY PUBLIC LIBRARY*, 17 Majors Blvd, 37352. (Mail add: PO Box 602, 37352-0602). Tel: 931-759-7285. FAX: 931-464-4124. E-mail: mcpl.lynchburg@gmail.com. Web Site: www.moorecountypubliclibrary.com. *Dir,* Lisa Riggs; E-mail: mcldirector@comcast.net; Staff 3 (Non-MLS 3)
Founded 1953. Pop 6,644; Circ 25,331
Library Holdings: Bk Titles 23,280; Per Subs 10
Special Collections: Reagor Motlow Papers Coll
Automation Activity & Vendor Info: (Cataloging) Book Systems; (Circulation) Book Systems; (OPAC) Book Systems
Wireless access
Function: 24/7 Electronic res, 24/7 Online cat, Adult bk club, Children's prog, Computers for patron use, Free DVD rentals, Holiday prog, ILL available, Internet access, Laminating, Magazines, Online cat, OverDrive digital audio bks, Photocopying/Printing, Preschool reading prog, Prog for adults, Ref serv available, Scanner, Story hour, Summer reading prog
Mem of Stones River Regional Library
Special Services for the Deaf - TDD equip
Special Services for the Blind - Bks on cassette
Open Mon, Tues & Fri 9-5:30, Wed 9-6:30

MADISONVILLE

P MADISONVILLE PUBLIC LIBRARY*, 240 Houston St, 37354. SAN 315-8497. Tel: 423-442-4085. FAX: 423-442-8121. Web Site: www.madisonvillelibrary.org. *Dir,* Kim Hicks; E-mail: Kim.Hicks@madisonvillelibrary.org; Staff 6 (Non-MLS 6)
Founded 1915. Pop 15,122; Circ 143,000
Library Holdings: AV Mats 3,000; Bks on Deafness & Sign Lang 10; Large Print Bks 1,000; Bk Titles 28,000; Per Subs 70; Talking Bks 1,200
Special Collections: Genealogy Coll. State Document Depository; US Document Depository
Automation Activity & Vendor Info: (Cataloging) SirsiDynix-WorkFlows; (Circulation) SirsiDynix-Unicorn; (OPAC) SirsiDynix
Wireless access
Function: Archival coll, AV serv, For res purposes, Home delivery & serv to seniorr ctr & nursing homes, Homebound delivery serv, ILL available, Internet access, Large print keyboards, Photocopying/Printing, Prog for children & young adult, Ref serv available, Summer reading prog, Telephone ref, Wheelchair accessible
Mem of Ocoee River Regional Library
Special Services for the Deaf - Bks on deafness & sign lang; Closed caption videos
Special Services for the Blind - Audio mat; Bks available with recordings; Bks on cassette; Bks on CD; Computer with voice synthesizer for visually impaired persons; Copier with enlargement capabilities; Extensive large print coll; Info on spec aids & appliances; Integrated libr/media serv; Large print & cassettes; Large print bks; Large screen computer & software; Magnifiers; Ref serv; Screen enlargement software for people with visual disabilities; Talking bks; Videos on blindness & physical disabilties
Open Tues-Thurs 11-6, Fri 11-4, Sat 11-3
Friends of the Library Group

MANCHESTER

P COFFEE COUNTY-MANCHESTER LIBRARY*, 1005 Hillsboro Hwy, 37355-2099. SAN 376-7310. Tel: 931-723-5143. FAX: 931-723-0713. Web Site: coffeecountylibrary.org. *Dir,* Pauline R Vaughn; E-mail: director@coffeecountylibrary.org
Library Holdings: Bk Titles 51,754; Per Subs 42
Automation Activity & Vendor Info: (Cataloging) SirsiDynix; (Circulation) SirsiDynix; (ILL) Auto-Graphics, Inc; (OPAC) SirsiDynix
Wireless access
Mem of Stones River Regional Library
Open Mon, Tues & Thurs 8-8, Wed, Fri & Sat 9-5
Friends of the Library Group

MARTIN

P MARTIN PUBLIC LIBRARY*, 100 Main St, 38237-2445. SAN 315-8500. Tel: 731-587-3148. FAX: 731-587-4674. E-mail: mpl@martinpubliclibrary.org. Web Site; www.martinpubliclibrary.org. *Dir,* Roberta Peacock; E-mail: rpeacock@martinpubliclibrary.org; Staff 3 (Non-MLS 3)
Founded 1925. Pop 32,896; Circ 60,628
Library Holdings: Bk Vols 45,000
Special Collections: Tennessee Genealogical Colls
Automation Activity & Vendor Info: (Cataloging) Auto-Graphics, Inc; (Circulation) Auto-Graphics, Inc; (OPAC) Auto-Graphics, Inc
Wireless access
Function: Adult bk club, Adult literacy prog, Art exhibits, Audio & video playback equip for onsite use, AV serv, Bk club(s), CD-ROM, Doc delivery serv, Homebound delivery serv, ILL available, Internet access, Magnifiers for reading, Music CDs, Orientations, Photocopying/Printing, Prog for adults, Prog for children & young adult, Ref & res, Ref serv available, Serves people with intellectual disabilities, Spoken cassettes & CDs, Spoken cassettes & DVDs, Summer reading prog, Telephone ref, VHS videos, Wheelchair accessible
Publications: C E Weldon Public Library (Newsletter)
Mem of Obion River Regional Library
Open Mon-Wed & Fri 9:30-5:30, Thurs 9:30-8, Sat 9:30-Noon
Restriction: Authorized patrons
Friends of the Library Group

P OBION RIVER REGIONAL LIBRARY, 542 N Lindell St, 38237. SAN 315-8519. Tel: 731-364-4597. FAX: 731-364-4536. Web Site: sos.tn.gov/tsla/pages/obion-river-regional-library. *Dir,* Jenny Gillihan; E-mail: jenny.gillihan@tnsos.gov; *Asst Dir,* Kathryn McBride; E-mail: kathryn.mcbride@tn.gov; Staff 5 (MLS 3, Non-MLS 2)
Founded 1942. Pop 179,930; Circ 873,558
Library Holdings: Bk Titles 80,000; Bk Vols 120,000
Automation Activity & Vendor Info: (Acquisitions) Follett Software; (Cataloging) Follett Software; (Circulation) Follett Software
Publications: Library Lines (Quarterly)
Member Libraries: Benton County Public Library; Carroll County Library; Crockett Memorial Library; Dr Nathan Porter Memorial Library;

Gibson County Memorial Library; Gleason Memorial Library; Hamilton Parks Public Library; Humboldt Public Library; Martin Public Library; McIver's Grant Public Library; McKenzie Memorial Library; Mildred G Fields Memorial Library; Ned R McWherter Weakley County Library; Newbern City Library; Obion County Public Library; Ridgely Public Library; Sharon Public Library; Tiptonville Public Library; W G Rhea Public Library
Open Mon-Fri 8-4:30

C UNIVERSITY OF TENNESSEE AT MARTIN*, Paul Meek Library, Ten Wayne Fisher Dr, 38238. SAN 315-8527. Tel: 731-881-7065. Interlibrary Loan Service Tel: 731-881-7068. FAX: 731-881-7074. E-mail: library_help@utm.libanswers.com. Web Site: www.utm.edu/library. *Dean,* Erik Nordberg; Tel: 731-881-7070, E-mail: enordber@utm.edu; *Acq Librn,* Bridgette Whitt; Tel: 731-881-7079, E-mail: bwhitt1@utm.edu; *Cat Librn,* Caren Nitcher; Tel: 731-881-7096, E-mail: cnitcher@utm.edu; *Pub Serv Librn,* Heidi Busch; Tel: 731-881-3078, E-mail: hbusch@utm.edu; *Media Ctr Mgr,* Patricia Sanders; Tel: 731-881-7069, E-mail: psander9@utm.edu; *Chief Archivist, Curator,* Sam Richardson; Tel: 731-881-7094, E-mail: richardson@utm.edu; *Spec Coll,* Karen Elmore; Tel: 731-881-7094, E-mail: kelmore@utm.edu; Staff 9 (MLS 8, Non-MLS 1)
Founded 1900. Enrl 6,540; Fac 302; Highest Degree: Master
Library Holdings: CDs 2,849; DVDs 3,029; e-books 92,000; e-journals 350,000; Bk Titles 302,400; Bk Vols 524,119; Per Subs 964; Videos 4,571
Special Collections: Congressman Ed Jones Papers; Governor Ned Ray McWherter Personal & Legislative Papers; Harry Harrison Kroll Coll; Holland McCombs Coll; Weakley County Chancery Records. US Document Depository
Automation Activity & Vendor Info: (Acquisitions) Innovative Interfaces, Inc; (Cataloging) Innovative Interfaces, Inc; (Circulation) Innovative Interfaces, Inc; (Course Reserve) Innovative Interfaces, Inc; (ILL) Innovative Interfaces, Inc; (OPAC) Innovative Interfaces, Inc; (Serials) Innovative Interfaces, Inc
Wireless access
Partic in LYRASIS; OCLC Online Computer Library Center, Inc
Open Mon-Thurs 7:30am-Midnight, Fri 7:30-6, Sat Noon-5, Sun 6pm-Midnight (Fall & Spring)
Friends of the Library Group

MARYVILLE

P BLOUNT COUNTY PUBLIC LIBRARY*, 508 N Cusick St, 37804. SAN 315-8535. Tel: 865-982-0981. FAX: 865-977-1142. Web Site: www.blounttn.org/197/Public-Library. *Dir,* K C Williams; E-mail: bcpl.director@blounttn.org; *Dep Dir,* Anjanae Brueland; E-mail: bcpl.fs@blounttn.org; *Mgr, Patron Serv,* Cynthia Spitler; E-mail: bcplpatronservices@blounttn.org; Staff 13 (MLS 4, Non-MLS 9)
Founded 1919. Pop 113,000; Circ 738,547
Library Holdings: AV Mats 25,739; e-books 3,362; Bk Vols 158,021; Per Subs 411
Subject Interests: Genealogy, Local hist
Automation Activity & Vendor Info: (Cataloging) SirsiDynix; (Circulation) SirsiDynix; (OPAC) SirsiDynix
Wireless access
Function: Art exhibits, Audiobks via web, Bks on cassette, Bks on CD, Children's prog, Computers for patron use, Electronic databases & coll, Free DVD rentals, ILL available, Music CDs, Online cat, Photocopying/Printing, Prog for adults, Prog for children & young adult, Summer reading prog, Tax forms, VHS videos, Wheelchair accessible
Mem of Ocoee River Regional Library
Partic in National Network of Libraries of Medicine Region 2
Special Services for the Deaf - TDD equip
Special Services for the Blind - Scanner for conversion & translation of mats; Videos on blindness & physical disabilties
Open Mon-Thurs 9-7, Fri & Sat 9-5:30
Friends of the Library Group

C MARYVILLE COLLEGE*, Lamar Memorial Library, 502 E Lamar Alexander Pkwy, 37804-5907. SAN 315-8551. Tel: 865-981-8256. Web Site: library.maryvillecollege.edu. *Dir,* Angela Myatt Quick; Tel: 865-981-8038, E-mail: angela.quick@maryvillecollege.edu; *Res & Instruction Librn,* Roger Myers; Tel: 865-981-8259, E-mail: roger.myers@maryvillecollege.edu; *Circ Coordr,* Marina Jaffe; Tel: 865-981-8099, E-mail: marina.jaffe@maryvillecollege.edu; *Evening Supvr,* Matthew O'Connor; Tel: 865-981-8258, E-mail: matthew.oconnor@maryvillecollege.edu
Library Holdings: e-books 340,000; Bk Titles 120,000; Per Subs 153
Automation Activity & Vendor Info: (Cataloging) Innovative Interfaces, Inc
Wireless access
Partic in Appalachian College Association; Tenn-Share
Open Mon-Thurs 7:30am-11pm, Fri 7:30-5, Sat 10-4, Sun 2-11

R NEW PROVIDENCE PRESBYTERIAN CHURCH*, Alexander Smith Library, 703 W Broadway Ave, 37801. SAN 315-856X. Tel: 865-983-0182. FAX: 865-681-0804. E-mail: info@newprovidencepres.org. Web Site: newprovidencepres.org. *Librn,* Linda Dotson; *Librn,* Cynthia Freeman; E-mail: cpfree4@bellsouth.net
Founded 1951
Library Holdings: Bk Titles 7,110
Subject Interests: Children's videos, Church hist, Family, Fine arts, Relig, Travel
Open Mon-Fri 8-5, Sun 7:30am-1pm

MAYNARDVILLE

P MAYNARDVILLE PUBLIC LIBRARY*, 296 Main St, 37807-3400. SAN 315-8578. Tel: 865-992-7106. FAX: 865-992-0202. E-mail: mayna2bk@comcast.net. Web Site: www.maynardvillepubliclibrary.org. *Libr Dir,* Kimberly Todd; Staff 2.5 (Non-MLS 2.5)
Pop 19,076; Circ 63,203
Library Holdings: Bks on Deafness & Sign Lang 10; DVDs 20; Large Print Bks 400; Bk Titles 18,418; Videos 150
Subject Interests: Local hist
Automation Activity & Vendor Info: (Cataloging) Surpass; (Circulation) Surpass; (Course Reserve) Surpass; (ILL) Auto-Graphics, Inc; (OPAC) Auto-Graphics, Inc
Wireless access
Function: 24/7 Electronic res, 24/7 Online cat, 3D Printer, Accelerated reader prog, Audio & video playback equip for onsite use, Audiobks via web, Bk club(s), Bks on CD, Children's prog, Citizenship assistance, Computer training, Computers for patron use, Electronic databases & coll, Free DVD rentals, Health sci info serv, Holiday prog, ILL available, Instruction & testing, Internet access, Life-long learning prog for all ages, Magazines, Magnifiers for reading, Mail & tel request accepted, Movies, Music CDs, Online cat, Orientations, Outreach serv, Outside serv via phone, mail, e-mail & web, OverDrive digital audio bks, Photocopying/Printing, Preschool outreach, Preschool reading prog, Prog for adults, Prog for children & young adult, Ref serv available, Senior computer classes, Senior outreach, Serves people with intellectual disabilities, Story hour, Summer & winter reading prog, Summer reading prog, Teen prog, Wheelchair accessible, Winter reading prog
Mem of Clinch River Regional Library
Open Mon & Wed-Fri 9-6, Sat 9-1
Restriction: Authorized patrons, Borrowing privileges limited to fac & registered students, Borrowing requests are handled by ILL, Circ limited, Circ to mem only, Free to mem
Friends of the Library Group

MCKENZIE

C BETHEL UNIVERSITY, Burroughs Learning Center, 325 Cherry Ave, 38201. SAN 315-8454. Tel: 731-352-4083. E-mail: library@bethelu.edu. Web Site: bethelu.libguides.com/newhome. *Dean of the Library,* Marcie Boutwell; Tel: 731-352-6913, E-mail: boutwellm@bethelu.edu; Staff 1 (MLS 1)
Enrl 650; Fac 32; Highest Degree: Master
Library Holdings: DVDs 1,200; Bk Vols 24,000; Per Subs 30
Automation Activity & Vendor Info: (Cataloging) Koha; (Circulation) Koha; (ILL) OCLC
Wireless access
Partic in West Tennessee Academic Library Consortium

P MCKENZIE MEMORIAL LIBRARY*, 15 Broadway St, 38201. SAN 315-8462. Tel: 731-352-5741. FAX: 731-352-5741. E-mail: mckenzielibrary731@gmail.com. Web Site: mckenzielibrary38201.weebly.com. *Dir,* Jean Alexander
Founded 1957. Pop 5,357; Circ 9,031
Library Holdings: Bk Vols 14,902; Per Subs 10
Subject Interests: Hist
Wireless access
Mem of Obion River Regional Library
Open Mon, Tues, Thurs & Fri 9-5

MCMINNVILLE

P THE W H & EDGAR MAGNESS COMMUNITY HOUSE & LIBRARY*, 118 W Main St, 37110. SAN 315-8470. Tel: 931-473-2428. FAX: 931-473-6778. E-mail: magmain@blomand.net. Web Site: www.magnesslibrary.org. *Dir,* Brad Walker
Founded 1931. Pop 38,296; Circ 68,000
Library Holdings: Bk Vols 41,000
Special Collections: Business & Community Development Coll; Education Coll; Genealogy Coll; Horticulture Coll; Southern Heritage Coll; Tennessee History Coll
Automation Activity & Vendor Info: (Acquisitions) Surpass; (Cataloging) Surpass; (Circulation) Surpass
Wireless access

Function: Adult bk club, After school storytime, Art exhibits, Audio & video playback equip for onsite use, Bk club(s), CD-ROM, Computer training, Genealogy discussion group, ILL available, Mail & tel request accepted, Music CDs, Photocopying/Printing, Preschool outreach, Prof lending libr, Prog for adults, Prog for children & young adult, Ref serv available, Senior computer classes, Serves people with intellectual disabilities, Spoken cassettes & CDs, Spoken cassettes & DVDs, Summer reading prog, Tax forms, Telephone ref, VHS videos, Wheelchair accessible, Workshops
Open Mon & Tues 8-8, Wed-Fri 8-5, Sat 8-3

MEMPHIS

CM BAPTIST HEALTH SCIENCES UNIVERSITY*, Health Sciences Library, 1003 Monroe Ave, 38104. SAN 360-7232. Tel: 901-572-2680. FAX: 901-572-2674. Web Site: baptistu.edu/campus-life/center-academic-excellence/library. *Libr Supvr,* Molly Antoine; E-mail: molly.antoine@baptistu.edu; Staff 2 (Non-MLS 2)
Founded 1991. Enrl 850; Fac 60; Highest Degree: Master
Library Holdings: AV Mats 2,000; Bk Titles 15,000; Per Subs 300
Subject Interests: Allied health, Nursing
Automation Activity & Vendor Info: (Cataloging) EOS International; (Circulation) EOS International; (OPAC) EOS International; (Serials) EOS International
Wireless access
Partic in OCLC Online Computer Library Center, Inc
Open Mon-Thurs 7:30am-10:30pm, Fri & Sat 7:30-6, Sun 1-6

M CAMPBELL FOUNDATION LIBRARY*, 1211 Union Ave, Ste 510, 38104. SAN 325-5085. Tel: 901-759-3271. FAX: 901-759-3278. *Librn,* Tonya Jones Priggel; E-mail: tpriggel@uthsc.edu
Library Holdings: Bk Titles 714; Bk Vols 850; Per Subs 54
Subject Interests: Orthopedics
Wireless access
Partic in SERMLP
Restriction: Residents only, Staff use only

CR CHRISTIAN BROTHERS UNIVERSITY, Plough Library, 650 East Pkwy S, 38104. SAN 315-8616. Tel: 901-321-3432. E-mail: library@cbu.edu. Web Site: www.cbu.edu/library. *Dir,* Kay Cunningham; E-mail: kay.cunningham@cbu.edu; *Acq & Pub Serv Librn,* William Brandon; E-mail: wbrandon@cbu.edu; *Electronic Serv Librn,* Aimee Rankin; E-mail: arankin@cbu.edu; *Instruction & Outreach Librn,* Mark Duncan; E-mail: mduncan6@cbu.edu; *ILL & Evening Circ Coordr,* Melissa Verble; E-mail: mverble@cbu.edu; *Library Asst, Periodicals & Archives,* Maddie Smith; E-mail: msmith98@cbu.edu; Staff 6 (MLS 4, Non-MLS 2)
Founded 1871. Enrl 1,600; Fac 109; Highest Degree: Master
Library Holdings: e-books 357,000; Electronic Media & Resources 250,000; Bk Titles 70,000; Per Subs 64
Special Collections: Bro Leo O'Donnell Archives
Subject Interests: Educ, Engr, Relig
Automation Activity & Vendor Info: (Acquisitions) OCLC Worldshare Management Services; (Cataloging) OCLC Worldshare Management Services; (Circulation) OCLC Worldshare Management Services; (Course Reserve) OCLC Worldshare Management Services; (ILL) OCLC Worldshare Management Services; (OPAC) OCLC Worldshare Management Services; (Serials) OCLC Worldshare Management Services
Wireless access
Function: 24/7 Electronic res, 24/7 Online cat, Art exhibits, Electronic databases & coll, Online cat, Online ref
Partic in LYRASIS; Memphis Area Libr Coun; Tenn-Share; West Tennessee Academic Library Consortium
Open Mon-Thurs 7:30am-10pm, Fri 7:30-4:30, Sun 2-10
Restriction: Circ privileges for students & alumni only, In-house use for visitors, Non-circulating to the pub, Open to pub for ref only

GM DEPARTMENT OF VETERANS AFFAIRS-MEMPHIS*, Medical Library, 1030 Jefferson Ave, 38104-2193. SAN 315-8861. Tel: 901-523-8990, Ext 5883. Interlibrary Loan Service Tel: 901-523-8990, Ext 5881. FAX: 901-577-7338. E-mail: vhamemliblns@va.gov. *Communications Spec,* Pamela Roberson; E-mail: pamela.roberson@va.gov; Staff 2 (MLS 1, Non-MLS 1)
Founded 1941
Library Holdings: AV Mats 1,036; Bk Vols 1,586; Per Subs 305
Subject Interests: Med, Nursing, Patient health educ, Spinal cord injury
Function: Health sci info serv, ILL available, Internet access, Ref serv available
Open Mon-Fri 8-4:30
Restriction: Circulates for staff only, In-house use for visitors, Prof mat only, Restricted borrowing privileges, Restricted loan policy

S DIXON GALLERY & GARDENS LIBRARY*, 4339 Park Ave, 38117. SAN 315-8624. Tel: 901-761-5250. FAX: 901-682-0943. E-mail: info@dixon.org. Web Site: www.dixon.org. *Dir of Educ,* Margarita Sandino
Founded 1976
Library Holdings: AV Mats 200; Bk Vols 5,750; Per Subs 15
Special Collections: Decorative Arts; French & American Impressionist Art; Horticulture; Warda S Stout German Porcelain Coll, bks
Automation Activity & Vendor Info: (Acquisitions) LibraryWorld, Inc; (Cataloging) LibraryWorld, Inc; (Circulation) LibraryWorld, Inc
Function: Archival coll, For res purposes, Photocopying/Printing, Ref serv available
Restriction: Open by appt only

CR HARDING SCHOOL OF THEOLOGY*, L M Graves Memorial Library, 1000 Cherry Rd, 38117. SAN 315-8659. Tel: 901-761-1354. FAX: 901-761-1358. E-mail: hstlib@hst.edu. Web Site: hst.edu/library. *Librn,* Bob Turner; E-mail: rjturner@hst.edu; *Assoc Librn,* Sheila Owen; E-mail: sowen@hst.edu; *Acq Asst, Circ Asst,* Tina Rogers; E-mail: tprogers@hst.edu; Staff 15 (MLS 4, Non-MLS 11)
Founded 1958. Enrl 80
Library Holdings: Bk Vols 126,500; Per Subs 590
Subject Interests: Biblical studies, Christian doctrine, Church hist, Counseling, Missions, Philos, Relig educ
Automation Activity & Vendor Info: (Acquisitions) Ex Libris Group; (Cataloging) Ex Libris Group; (Circulation) Ex Libris Group; (Course Reserve) Ex Libris Group; (ILL) Ex Libris Group; (Media Booking) Ex Libris Group; (OPAC) Ex Libris Group; (Serials) Ex Libris Group
Wireless access
Partic in LYRASIS
Open Mon, Tues & Thurs 8am-9pm, Wed & Fri 8-5, Sat 10-4; Mon, Tues & Thurs 8am-9pm, Wed & Fri 8-5, Sat 10-2 (Summer)

C LEMOYNE-OWEN COLLEGE*, Hollis F Price Library, 807 Walker Ave, 38126. SAN 315-8675. Tel: 901-435-1350. E-mail: library@loc.edu. Web Site: www.loc.edu/academics/library. *Dir, Libr & Info Serv,* Stacey J Smith; Tel: 901-435-1351, E-mail: stacey_smith@loc.edu; Staff 5 (MLS 2, Non-MLS 3)
Founded 1870. Enrl 900; Fac 70; Highest Degree: Bachelor
Library Holdings: Bk Titles 66,000; Bk Vols 120,000; Per Subs 350
Special Collections: Sweeney Coll, bks
Subject Interests: African-Am
Automation Activity & Vendor Info: (Acquisitions) Innovative Interfaces, Inc - Sierra; (Cataloging) Innovative Interfaces, Inc - Sierra; (Circulation) Innovative Interfaces, Inc - Sierra; (Discovery) ProQuest; (OPAC) Innovative Interfaces, Inc - Sierra
Wireless access
Function: 24/7 Electronic res, 24/7 Online cat
Publications: Classified Bibliography of Sweeney Collection (Quarterly newsletter)
Partic in LYRASIS; West Tennessee Academic Library Consortium
Open Mon-Thurs 8-8, Fri 8-5, Sat 9-1
Restriction: Access at librarian's discretion, Borrowing requests are handled by ILL, ID required to use computers (Ltd hrs)

S MEMPHIS BROOKS MUSEUM OF ART LIBRARY*, 1934 Poplar Ave, 38104. SAN 315-8594. Tel: 901-544-6200. FAX: 901-725-4071. E-mail: brooks@brooksmuseum.org. Web Site: www.brooksmuseum.org. *Librn,* Position Currently Open
Founded 1950
Library Holdings: Bk Vols 5,000
Special Collections: Decorative Arts Coll; Dr Louis Levey Coll, prints; Kress Coll; Morrie Moss Coll; The Julie Isenberg Coll
Subject Interests: Am Art 19th-20th Centuries, Art hist
Restriction: Open by appt only

S MEMPHIS MUSEUM OF SCIENCE & HISTORY*, Employee Library, 3050 Central Ave, 38111. SAN 315-8705. Tel: 901-636-2387. FAX: 901-320-6391, 901-636-2320. Web Site: moshmemphis.com. *Dir of Exhibits & Colls,* Raka Nandi; E-mail: raka.nandi@memphistn.gov; *Administrator of Programs,* Alex Eilers; E-mail: alex.eilers@memphistn.gov
Founded 1967
Library Holdings: Bk Titles 5,200
Special Collections: Burge Civil War Coll; Pink Palace Museum Archives
Subject Interests: Archaeology, Botany, Geol, Hist, Zoology
Restriction: Staff use only

P MEMPHIS PUBLIC LIBRARY & INFORMATION CENTER*, Benjamin L Hooks Central Library, 3030 Poplar Ave, 38111. SAN 360-7291. Tel: 901-415-2700. Circulation Tel: 901-415-2702. Interlibrary Loan Service Tel: 901-415-2705. Administration Tel: 901-415-2749. FAX: 901-323-7108. Interlibrary Loan Service FAX: 901-323-7637. Web Site: www.memphislibrary.org. *Dir of Libr,* Keenon McCloy; E-mail: keenon.mccloy@memphistn.gov; *Dep Dir,* Chris Marszalek; E-mail: chris.marszalek@memphistn.gov; *Asst Dir, Libr Communications,* Stephanie Jones; Tel: 901-415-2847, E-mail: stephanie.jones@memphistn.gov; *Asst Dir, Outreach & Spec Projects,* Sue

Schnitzer; Tel: 901-415-2871, E-mail: sue.schnitzer@memphistn.gov; *Asst Dir, Support Serv,* Debby McElroy-Clark; E-mail: debby.mcelroy@memphistn.gov; *Adminr,* Rebecca Stovall; E-mail: rebecca.stovall@memphistn.gov
Founded 1893. Pop 808,113; Circ 2,480,472
Library Holdings: AV Mats 154,217; e-books 16; Electronic Media & Resources 16; Bk Titles 1,398,697; Bk Vols 1,637,596
Special Collections: Afro-American Memphis (Beale Street, WC Handy, J Ashton Hayes, Blair T Hunt, George W Lee, Ethyl Venson Colls); Christian Coll; Commerce & Industry (Rees V Downs, Henry A Montgomery Colls); E H Crump Coll; Family History (Duke-Bedford, Farrow, Price-Davis, Trezevant Colls); Folk History (Morris Solomon, WW Busby, John Ogden Carley, Memphis Historical Society Colls); Health Information Center; Louise Mercer Coll; Mary Love Coll; Maxine Smith Coll; Memphis & Shelby County Archives; Photographs (Poland & Coovert Colls); Politics & Government (Samuel Bates, Robert Cohn, Mayer Henry Loeb, Sen Kennth McKellar, Judge John D Martin, Commissioner James Moore, Page/Lenox, Commissioner Jack W Ramsay, Tennessee Valley Authority Colls); Public Health (Memphis Crippled Childern's Hospital School, Rev George C Harris, Yellow Fever Colls); Religion (Rabbi James A Wax); The Arts (Hugh Higbee Huhn, Sarah B Kennedy, Florence McIntyre, Walter Malone, Music Miscellany, Julia Raine, Searcy Family Colls); War History (William W Goodman, Colton Greene, Memphians During War, Memphis Belle, Gideon J Pillow Colls); William Fowler Coll. Oral History; State Document Depository; US Document Depository
Subject Interests: Archit, Art, Memphis hist
Automation Activity & Vendor Info: (Acquisitions) SirsiDynix; (Cataloging) SirsiDynix; (Circulation) SirsiDynix; (Serials) SirsiDynix
Wireless access
Publications: Friends Newletter; Getting Ready for Summer; InfoDATES; Library Calendar; Library Matters; Staff Newslinc; WYPL Program Guide
Partic in Dow Jones News Retrieval; LYRASIS; National Network of Libraries of Medicine Region 2; Proquest Dialog
Open Mon-Thurs 9-9, Fri & Sat 9-6, Sun 1-5
Friends of the Library Group
Branches: 21

BARTLETT BRANCH, 5884 Stage Rd, Bartlett, 38134, SAN 360-7593. Tel: 901-386-8968. FAX: 901-386-2358. *Regional Mgr,* Gay Cain; E-mail: gay.cain@memphistn.gov; *Br Mgr,* Chip Holiday; E-mail: chip.holiday@memphistn.gov
Pop 40,000; Circ 324,968
Library Holdings: Bk Vols 782,306
Open Mon-Thurs 10-8, Fri & Sat 10-6, Sun 1-5
Friends of the Library Group

BUSINESS/SCIENCES, 3030 Poplar Ave, 38111. Tel: 901-415-2734. *Nonprofit Res Librn, Supvr, Pub Serv,* Jessie W Marshall; E-mail: jessie.marshall@memphistn.gov; *Agency Mgr,* Ruth W Morrison; Tel: 901-415-2736, E-mail: ruth.morrison@memphistn.gov; Staff 7 (MLS 6, Non-MLS 1)
Special Collections: Job & Career Centre; NonProfit Resource Information Center; Personal Finance Coll; Small Business Center. State Document Depository; US Document Depository
Subject Interests: Bus, Govt publ
Open Mon-Thurs 9-9, Fri & Sat 10-5, Sun 1-5
Friends of the Library Group

CHEROKEE BRANCH, 3300 Sharpe, 38111, SAN 360-7623. Tel: 901-415-2762. FAX: 901-743-9030. *Br Mgr,* Deborah Stevens; E-mail: deborah.stevens@memphistn.gov
Circ 23,886
Library Holdings: Bk Vols 28,025
Open Mon-Sat 10-6
Friends of the Library Group

CHILDREN'S DEPARTMENT, 3030 Poplar Ave, 38111. Tel: 901-415-2739. FAX: 901-323-7108. *Coordr, Youth Serv,* Dara Gonzales; E-mail: dara.gonzales@memphistn.gov; Staff 12.5 (MLS 5, Non-MLS 7.5)
Function: Art exhibits, Children's prog, Computers for patron use, Music CDs, Online cat, Online ref, Orientations, Photocopying/Printing, Preschool outreach, Prog for children & young adult, Story hour, Summer reading prog, Wheelchair accessible
Open Mon-Thurs 9-9, Fri & Sat 9-6, Sun 1-5
Friends of the Library Group

CORDOVA BRANCH, 8457 Trinity Rd, Cordova, 38018, SAN 360-7674. Tel: 901-415-2764. FAX: 901-754-6874. *Br Mgr,* Francis Mathews; E-mail: francis.mathews@memphistn.gov
Circ 380,585
Library Holdings: Bk Vols 114,118
Open Mon-Thurs 10-8, Fri & Sat 10-6
Friends of the Library Group

COSSITT BRANCH, 33 S Front St, 38103-2499, SAN 360-7682. Tel: 901-415-2766. FAX: 901-526-0730.
Founded 1888. Circ 14,838
Library Holdings: Bk Vols 10,422
Open Mon-Thurs 10-8, Fri & Sat 10-6
Friends of the Library Group

CORNELIA CRENSHAW MEMORIAL LIBRARY, 531 Vance Ave, 38126-2116, SAN 360-8131. Tel: 901-415-2765. FAX: 901-525-0390. *Br Mgr,* Inger Upchurch; E-mail: inger.upchurch@memphistn.gov
Founded 1939. Circ 12,925
Library Holdings: Bk Vols 22,670
Open Mon-Sat 10-6
Friends of the Library Group

EAST SHELBY BRANCH, 7200 E Shelby Dr, 38125. Tel: 901-415-2767. *Dir,* Kennon McCloy; E-mail: keenon.mccloy@memphistn.gov
Open Mon-Sat 10-6
Friends of the Library Group

FRAYSER BRANCH, 3712 Argonne St, 38127-4414, SAN 360-7712. Tel: 901-415-2768. Web Site: www.memphislibrary.org/about/locations/frayser-library. *Br Mgr,* Shelley Moore; E-mail: shelley.moore@memphistn.gov
Circ 50,330
Library Holdings: Bk Vols 34,026
Open Mon-Sat 10-6
Friends of the Library Group

GASTON PARK BRANCH, 1040 S Third St, 38106-2002, SAN 360-7747. Tel: 901-415-2769. FAX: 901-942-5667. *Br Mgr,* Inger Upchurch
Founded 1978. Circ 11,013
Library Holdings: Bk Vols 12,848
Open Mon-Sat 10-6
Friends of the Library Group

HISTORY, 3030 Poplar Ave, 38111. Tel: 901-415-2742. FAX: 901-323-7981. *Br Mgr,* Thomas Jones
Special Collections: Memphis Coll
Subject Interests: Genealogy, Hist, Travel
Open Mon-Thurs 9-9, Fri & Sat 9-6, Sun 1-5
Friends of the Library Group

HOLLYWOOD BRANCH, 1530 N Hollywood St, 38108, SAN 360-7836. Tel: 901-415-2772. FAX: 901-323-5610. *Commun Outreach Librn,* Courtney Shaw; E-mail: courtney.shaw@memphistn.gov
Circ 18,604
Library Holdings: Bk Vols 24,617
Open Mon-Sat 10-6
Friends of the Library Group

HUMANITIES, 3030 Poplar Ave, 38111. Tel: 901-415-2726. FAX: 901-323-7206. *Mgr,* Chip Holliday; E-mail: elton.holliday@memphistn.gov
Open Mon-Thurs 9-9, Fri & Sat 9-6, Sun 1-5
Friends of the Library Group

LEVI BRANCH, 3676 Hwy 61 S (S 3rd St), 38109-8296, SAN 360-7860. Tel: 901-415-2773. FAX: 901-789-3141. *Br Mgr,* Regina Boone; E-mail: regina.boone@memphistn.gov
Circ 18,408
Library Holdings: Bk Vols 21,099
Open Mon-Sat 10-6
Friends of the Library Group

NORTH BRANCH, 1192 Vollintine Ave, 38107-2899, SAN 360-7925. Tel: 901-415-2775. FAX: 901-726-0731. Web Site: www.memphislibrary.org/. *Br Mgr,* Tamika Parsons; E-mail: tamika.parsons@memphistn.gov
Founded 1961. Circ 20,992
Library Holdings: Bk Vols 25,732
Open Mon-Sat 10-6
Friends of the Library Group

PARKWAY VILLAGE BRANCH, 4655 Knight Arnold Rd, 38118-3234, SAN 360-795X. Tel: 901-415-2776. FAX: 901-794-2344. *Br Mgr,* Deborah Stevens
Founded 1966. Circ 74,654
Library Holdings: Bk Vols 54,980
Open Mon-Sat 10-6
Friends of the Library Group

POPLAR-WHITE STATION BRANCH, 5094 Poplar, 38117-7629, SAN 360-7984. Tel: 901-415-2777. FAX: 901-682-8975. *Br Mgr,* Lisa Ingram; *Youth Serv Librn,* Michelle Allen; E-mail: michelle.allen@memphistn.gov; *Circ Supvr,* Barbara Matthews; E-mail: barbara.matthews@memphistn.gov; Staff 4 (MLS 1, Non-MLS 3)
Circ 149,596
Library Holdings: Bk Vols 52,643
Open Mon-Thurs 10-8, Fri & Sat 10-6
Friends of the Library Group

RALEIGH BRANCH, 3157 Powers Rd, 38128, SAN 360-8018. Tel: 901-415-2778. FAX: 901-371-9495. *Actg Mgr,* Daphney Johnson; E-mail: daphney.johnson@memphistn.gov; *Supvr, Circ,* Mollie Howard; E-mail: mollie.howard@memphistn.gov
Circ 98,716
Library Holdings: Bk Vols 48,985
Open Mon-Thurs 10-8, Fri & Sat 10-6
Friends of the Library Group

RANDOLPH BRANCH, 3752 Given Ave, 38122, SAN 360-8042. Tel: 901-415-2779. FAX: 901-454-9594. *Br Mgr,* Amanda Hill; E-mail: amanda.hill@memphistn.gov; *Br Librn,* Daniel Hodges; E-mail: daniel.hodges@memphistn.gov
Founded 1956. Circ 35,274
Library Holdings: Bk Vols 30,563
Open Mon-Sat 10-6
Friends of the Library Group

SOUTH BRANCH, 1929 S Third St, 38109, SAN 360-8107. Tel: 901-415-2780. FAX: 901-946-1435. *Br Mgr,* Pam Nickleberry-Brooks
Circ 29,631
Library Holdings: Bk Vols 36,608
Open Mon-Sat 10-6
Friends of the Library Group

WHITEHAVEN BRANCH, 4120 Mill Branch Rd, 38116, SAN 360-8166. Tel: 901-415-2781. FAX: 901-332-6150. *Actg Br Mgr, Regional Mgr,* Toni Braswell; E-mail: toni.braswell@memphistn.gov; *Asst Br Mgr,* Patrice Shaw-Brunson
Circ 140,769
Library Holdings: Bk Vols 103,973
Open Mon-Thurs 10-8, Fri & Sat 10-6
Friends of the Library Group

CR MEMPHIS THEOLOGICAL SEMINARY LIBRARY*, 168 E Parkway S, 38104. SAN 315-8713. Tel: 901-334-5858. Circulation Tel: 901-334-5824. Reference Tel: 901-334-5814. FAX: 901-452-4051. E-mail: library@memphisseminary.edu. Web Site: www.memphisseminary.edu/student-resources/mts-library. *Dir, Libr Serv,* Ed Hughes; Tel: 901-334-5614, E-mail: ehughes@memphisseminary.edu; *Libr Asst,* Kimberley Travers; E-mail: kntravers@memphisseminary.edu; Staff 2 (MLS 1, Non-MLS 1)
Founded 1956. Enrl 180; Fac 14; Highest Degree: Doctorate
Aug 2021-Jul 2022 Income $148,000
Library Holdings: AV Mats 1,624; Microforms 1,573; Bk Vols 72,000; Per Subs 5
Special Collections: C S Lewis Coll; Christian Missions (R Pierce Beaver Coll); Cumberland Presbyterian History; Martin Luther King, Jr, papers
Subject Interests: Baptist, Methodism, Presbyterianism
Automation Activity & Vendor Info: (Acquisitions) SirsiDynix; (Cataloging) SirsiDynix; (Circulation) SirsiDynix; (Course Reserve) SirsiDynix; (ILL) OCLC WorldShare Interlibrary Loan; (OPAC) SirsiDynix
Wireless access
Open Mon-Wed 10-6
Restriction: Clients only, Closed stack

A PT BOATS, INC*, WW II PT Boats Museum Archives & Library, 1384 Cordova Cove, Ste 2, 38138-2200. (Mail add: PO Box 38005, Germantown, 38183-0070), SAN 326-1700. Tel: 901-755-8440. E-mail: ptboatsinc@gmail.com. Web Site: www.ptboats.org. *Exec VPres,* Alyce N Guthrie; Staff 2 (Non-MLS 2)
Founded 1946
Library Holdings: CDs 1; DVDs 1; Bk Titles 3,025; Per Subs 5; Spec Interest Per Sub 5; Videos 3
Special Collections: Behney Coll; Two Restored PT Boats
Function: Archival coll, Bks on CD, Mail & tel request accepted, Photocopying/Printing, Ref & res, Res libr, Res performed for a fee
Publications: Knights of the Sea, Mosquito Fleet (Documents); PT Squadrons, Bases, Tenders ALL HANDS (Newsletter)
Restriction: Access at librarian's discretion, External users must contact libr, Fee for pub use, In-house use for visitors, Limited access based on advanced application, Non-circulating, Non-circulating coll, Non-circulating of rare bks, Non-circulating to the pub, Not a lending libr, Open by appt only, Open to fac, students & qualified researchers, Open to qualified scholars, Open to researchers by request, Private libr, Researchers by appt only, Visitors must make appt to use bks in the libr

C RHODES COLLEGE, Paul Barret Jr Library, 2000 North Pkwy, 38112-1694. SAN 315-8810. Tel: 901-843-3890. Information Services Tel: 901-843-3745. Web Site: sites.rhodes.edu/barret. *Dir,* Darlene Brooks; E-mail: brooksd@rhodes.edu; *Assoc Dir, Libr Serv,* William Short; E-mail: short@rhodes.edu; *Asst Dir, User Engagement & Experience,* Steve Brummel; E-mail: brummels@rhodes.edu; *Head, Cataloging & Collection Dev,* Rachel Feinman; E-mail: feinmanr@rhodes.edu; *Head, Circ,* Amanda Ford; E-mail: ford@rhodes.edu; *Electronic Res Librn,* Greg Paraham; E-mail: parahamg@rhodes.edu; *Interlibrary Loan/Info Servs Librn,* Kenan Padgett; E-mail: padgettk@rhodes.edu; *Public, Research & Tech Librn,* Nevenia Hill; E-mail: hilln@rhodes.edu; *Public, Research & Tech Specialist,* Emma Kruse; E-mail: kruse@rhodes.edu. Subject Specialists: *English, Gender studies, Hist,* William Short; *Anthrop, Archaeology, Biochem,* Steve Brummel; *Art hist, Neuroscience, Psychol,* Rachel Feinman; *Africana, Chemistry, Philos,* Greg Paraham; *Acctg, Econ,* Kenan Padgett; *Asian studies, Environ studies, Intl studies,* Nevenia Hill; *Anthrop, Archaeology, Biochem,* Emma Kruse; Staff 9 (MLS 7, Non-MLS 2)
Founded 1848. Enrl 1,936; Fac 160; Highest Degree: Bachelor
Library Holdings: AV Mats 7,000; e-books 64,000; e-journals 4,011; Electronic Media & Resources 8,339; Bk Titles 191,927; Bk Vols 275,000; Talking Bks 417; Videos 6,771
Special Collections: 19th & 20th Century English & American Literature (Walter Armstrong Rare Book Coll), autographed first editions; Art (Clough Hansen Art Memorial for Teaching), paintings, objects d'art
Subject Interests: Liberal arts
Automation Activity & Vendor Info: (Acquisitions) ProQuest; (Cataloging) OCLC Worldshare Management Services; (Circulation) OCLC Worldshare Management Services; (Course Reserve) OCLC Worldshare Management Services; (ILL) OCLC WorldShare Interlibrary Loan; (OPAC) OCLC; (Serials) OCLC Worldshare Management Services
Wireless access
Partic in Associated Colleges of the South; LYRASIS; Oberlin Group; OCLC Online Computer Library Center, Inc; Tenn-Share
Open Mon-Thurs 7:30am-Midnight, Fri 7:30-5, Sat 11-5, Sun 10am-Midnight (Fall & Spring); Mon-Fri 8:30-5 (Summer)
Restriction: Visitor pass required

M SAINT JUDE CHILDREN'S RESEARCH HOSPITAL*, Biomedical Library, 262 Danny Thomas Place, MS 306, 38105-3678. Tel: 901-595-3389. E-mail: library@stjude.org. Web Site: www.stjude.org/library. *Dir,* Robert Britton; E-mail: robert.britton@stjude.org; Staff 5 (MLS 3, Non-MLS 2)
Founded 1962
Library Holdings: e-books 8,000; e-journals 6,000
Subject Interests: Cancer, Immunology, Molecular biol, Pediatrics, Virology
Automation Activity & Vendor Info: (Cataloging) EOS International; (Circulation) EOS International; (OPAC) EOS International; (Serials) EOS International
Wireless access
Partic in National Network of Libraries of Medicine Region 2; OCLC Online Computer Library Center, Inc
Open Mon-Fri 8-5

L SHELBY COUNTY LAW LIBRARY*, 140 Adams Ave, Ste 334, 38103. SAN 315-8691. Tel: 901-527-7041. Administration Tel: 901-527-8498. FAX: 901-522-8935. E-mail: lawlibrary@bellsouth.net. Web Site: www.shelbycountylawlibrary.com. *Dir,* Gary Lynn Johnson; Tel: 901-618-3990, E-mail: gary1391@att.net. Subject Specialists: *English, Hist, Law, Libr sci,* Gary Lynn Johnson; Staff 2 (MLS 1, Non-MLS 1)
Founded 1874
Library Holdings: Bk Vols 51,000
Special Collections: Early English Law Coll; Early Laws of North Carolina Coll; Statutes at Large for First Congress of the United States Coll
Wireless access
Function: 24/7 Electronic res, 24/7 Online cat, Computers for patron use, Online cat, Photocopying/Printing, Scanner
Open Mon-Fri 8-4:30
Restriction: Limited access for the pub, Non-circulating, Non-circulating coll, Non-circulating to the pub, Not a lending libr, Open to pub for ref only, Ref only

CM SOUTHERN COLLEGE OF OPTOMETRY LIBRARY*, 1245 Madison Ave, 38104. SAN 315-8802. Tel: 901-722-3237. FAX: 901-722-3292. E-mail: library@sco.edu. Web Site: www.sco.edu/library. *Mgr, Libr Serv,* Leslie Holland; Tel: 901-722-3238, E-mail: lholland@sco.edu; Staff 2 (MLS 2)
Founded 1938. Enrl 470; Fac 56; Highest Degree: Doctorate
Library Holdings: AV Mats 1,662; Bk Titles 15,000; Bk Vols 15,613; Per Subs 162
Special Collections: Oral History
Subject Interests: Ophthalmology, Optics, Optometry
Automation Activity & Vendor Info: (Acquisitions) Innovative Interfaces, Inc - Millennium; (Cataloging) Innovative Interfaces, Inc - Millennium; (OPAC) Innovative Interfaces, Inc - Millennium; (Serials) Innovative Interfaces, Inc - Millennium
Wireless access
Publications: Visionet (Index to periodicals)
Partic in Association of Vision Science Librarians; Docline; Tennessee Health Science Library Association

J SOUTHWEST TENNESSEE COMMUNITY COLLEGE*, Parrish Library, 737 Union Ave, 38103. SAN 315-8799. Tel: 901-333-5135. FAX: 901-333-5141. Web Site: www.southwest.tn.edu/library. *Exec Dir,* Patrick O'Daniel; Tel: 901-333-5140, E-mail: podaniel@southwest.tn.edu; Staff 20 (MLS 5, Non-MLS 15)
Founded 1972. Enrl 4,000; Fac 200; Highest Degree: Associate
Library Holdings: Music Scores 808; Bk Titles 42,493; Bk Vols 45,917; Per Subs 288; Videos 5,219
Subject Interests: Allied health, Behav sci, Educ, Ethnic studies, Soc sci
Automation Activity & Vendor Info: (Circulation) Innovative Interfaces, Inc - Sierra

Wireless access
Partic in TBR Consortium
Departmental Libraries:
BURT BORNBLUM, 5983 Macon Cove, 38134, SAN 315-8829. Tel: 901-333-4706. Reference Tel: 901-333-4733. FAX: 901-333-4566. *Libr Asst,* LaShonna L Jackson; Tel: 901-333-4105, E-mail: laharris@southwest.tn.edu; *Libr Asst,* Lisa J Lumpkin; Tel: 901-333-4437, E-mail: llumpkin@southwest.tn.edu; Staff 13 (MLS 6, Non-MLS 7)
Founded 2000. Enrl 11,566; Highest Degree: Associate
Library Holdings: CDs 1,866; Music Scores 838; Bk Vols 35,761; Per Subs 147; Talking Bks 1,768; Videos 1,544
Subject Interests: Allied health, Computer, Engr, Paralegal
Automation Activity & Vendor Info: (Cataloging) SirsiDynix; (Circulation) SirsiDynix; (Course Reserve) SirsiDynix; (ILL) SirsiDynix; (OPAC) SirsiDynix; (Serials) SirsiDynix
GILL LIBRARY, 3833 Mountain Terrace, 38127. Tel: 901-333-5979. FAX: 901-333-5980.
Library Holdings: Music Scores 45; Bk Titles 3,254; Per Subs 42; Videos 293
Automation Activity & Vendor Info: (Cataloging) Innovative Interfaces, Inc; (Circulation) Innovative Interfaces, Inc
Friends of the Library Group
MAXINE A SMITH LIBRARY, 8800 E Shelby Dr, 38125. Tel: 901-333-6037. FAX: 901-333-6038.
Library Holdings: Music Scores 92; Bk Titles 2,903; Per Subs 37; Videos 272
Automation Activity & Vendor Info: (Cataloging) Innovative Interfaces, Inc; (Circulation) Innovative Interfaces, Inc
WHITEHAVEN CENTER LIBRARY, 1234 Finley Rd, 38116. Tel: 901-333-6442. FAX: 901-333-6441.
Library Holdings: AV Mats 475; Music Scores 148; Bk Titles 1,681; Per Subs 29; Videos 292
Automation Activity & Vendor Info: (Cataloging) Innovative Interfaces, Inc; (Circulation) Innovative Interfaces, Inc

C UNIVERSITY LIBRARIES, UNIVERSITY OF MEMPHIS*, 3785 Norriswood Ave, 38152. (Mail add: University Libraries, University of Memphis, 126 Ned R McWherter Library, 38152-3250), SAN 360-8190. Circulation Tel: 901-678-2205. Interlibrary Loan Service Tel: 901-678-2262. Reference Tel: 901-678-2208. Administration Tel: 901-678-2201. Automation Services Tel: 901-678-2356. Interlibrary Loan Service FAX: 901-678-2511. Administration FAX: 901-678-8218. E-mail: lib_admin@memphis.edu. Web Site: www.memphis.edu/libraries. *Assoc Dean, Univ Libr, Exec Dir,* Dr John E Evans; E-mail: jevans@memphis.edu; *Head Govt Publ,* Perveen Rustomfram; Tel: 901-678-8203, E-mail: prstmfrm@memphis.edu; *Head, Res & Instrul Serv,* Margaret (Bess) Robinson; Tel: 901-678-8214, E-mail: merobnsn@memphis.edu; *Head, Spec Coll,* Dr Gerald Chaudron; Tel: 901-678-8242, E-mail: gchudron@memphis.edu; *Head, Info Access Serv,* Caitlin Harrington; Tel: 901-678-8226, E-mail: chrrngt4@memphis.edu; *Acq & Coll Develop Librn,* Karen Brunsting; Tel: 901-678-4400, E-mail: kbrnstng@memphis.edu; *Info Syst Librn,* Position Currently Open; *ILL Librn,* Sofiya Dahman; Tel: 901-678-8223, E-mail: spdahman@memphis.edu; *Coordr, Digital Initiatives,* Dr Kenneth Haggerty; Tel: 901-678-4465, E-mail: khggerty@memphis.edu; Staff 85 (MLS 20, Non-MLS 65)
Founded 1914. Enrl 23,000; Fac 1,675; Highest Degree: Doctorate
Library Holdings: Bk Vols 1,311,471; Per Subs 194,406
Special Collections: 90th Bombardment Group Coll; Benjamin Lawson Hooks Papers; Charles P Simonton Family Papers; Church Family Papers; Civil War Coll; Cloar, Carroll & Pat Coll; Commercial Appeal Newspaper Coll; Cordie Lee Majors Papers; Dyer Marion Reynolds Coll; Edmund Orgill Papers; Jefferson Davis-Joel Addison Hayes Jr Family Papers; John S Wilder Papers; Kenneth L Beaudoin Papers; Memphis Press-Scimitar Newspaper Coll; Meriwether Family Papers; OUTMemphis Coll; R B Snowden Family Papers; Sanitation Worker's Strike 1968 (Memphis Search for Meaning Committee Records); Shelby County, Tennessee Coll; T L Crumbaugh Family Papers; Tent City: Fayette & Haywood Counties Civil Rights Coll; Theatre Coll; Tony Conway Coll; Winfield C Dunn Papers. State Document Depository; UN Document Depository; US Document Depository
Automation Activity & Vendor Info: (Acquisitions) Innovative Interfaces, Inc; (Cataloging) Innovative Interfaces, Inc; (Circulation) Innovative Interfaces, Inc; (Course Reserve) EBSCO Discovery Service; (ILL) OCLC ILLiad; (OPAC) Innovative Interfaces, Inc; (Serials) Innovative Interfaces, Inc
Wireless access
Publications: Between the Stacks (Newsletter)
Partic in LYRASIS; Memphis Area Libr Coun; OCLC Online Computer Library Center, Inc; Tenn Acad Libr Collaborative; Tenn-Share
Special Services for the Blind - Reader equip
Open Mon-Thurs 7:30am-Midnight, Fri 7:30-6, Sat 10-6, Sun (Spring-Fall) 1pm-10pm

Restriction: Open to pub for ref & circ; with some limitations
Friends of the Library Group
Departmental Libraries:
BAPTIST MEMORIAL HEALTH CARE LIBRARY, Community Health Bldg, 4055 North Park Loop, 38152-3250. Tel: 901-678-3193. Web Site: www.memphis.edu/libraries/hslibrary. *Health Sci Librn,* Dr Irma Singarella; Tel: 901-678-3829, E-mail: irma.singarella@memphis.edu; Staff 3 (MLS 1, Non-MLS 2)
Library Holdings: Bk Vols 7,000
Subject Interests: Audiology, Nursing, Speech-lang pathology
Open Mon-Thurs 8-6, Fri 8-4:30 (Fall & Spring)
MUSIC LIBRARY, Rudi E Scheidt Music Bldg, Rm 115, 3775 Central Ave, 38152-3250, SAN 360-831X. Tel: 901-678-2330. Web Site: www.memphis.edu/libraries/musiclibrary/index.php. *Head, Br Libr, Music Librn,* Dr Joel Roberts; Tel: 901-678-4412, E-mail: jcrberts@memphis.edu; Staff 3 (MLS 1, Non-MLS 2)
Library Holdings: CDs 12,000; DVDs 450; Music Scores 30,000; Bk Vols 43,092; Per Subs 174
Open Mon-Thurs 8-6, Fri 8-4:30 (Fall & Spring); Mon-Fri 8-4:30 (Summer)
Friends of the Library Group

CL THE UNIVERSITY OF MEMPHIS*, Cecil C Humphreys School of Law Library, One N Front St, 38103. SAN 360-828X. Tel: 901-678-2426. FAX: 901-678-5293. E-mail: lawcirc@memphis.edu. Web Site: www.memphis.edu/law/library. *Dir, Law Libr,* D R Jones; Tel: 901-678-3244, E-mail: drjones@memphis.edu; *Asst Dir, Reference & Access Services,* Blake Beals; Tel: 901-678-5462, E-mail: blbeals@memphis.edu; *Asst Dir, Tech Serv,* Lucinda Valero; Tel: 901-678-2749, E-mail: lvalero@memphis.edu; Staff 7 (MLS 3, Non-MLS 4)
Library Holdings: e-journals 2,420; Bk Vols 247,240; Per Subs 200
Automation Activity & Vendor Info: (Acquisitions) Innovative Interfaces, Inc - Sierra; (Cataloging) Innovative Interfaces, Inc - Sierra; (Circulation) Innovative Interfaces, Inc - Sierra; (Course Reserve) Innovative Interfaces, Inc - Sierra; (ILL) OCLC ILLiad; (OPAC) Innovative Interfaces, Inc - Sierra; (Serials) Innovative Interfaces, Inc - Sierra
Wireless access
Partic in Mid-America Law Library Consortium
Open Mon-Fri 8-4:30

CM UNIVERSITY OF TENNESSEE*, Health Sciences Library & Biocommunications Center, Lamar Alexander Bldg, 877 Madison Ave, 38163. SAN 360-8409. Tel: 901-448-5634. Administration Tel: 901-448-5638. Toll Free Tel: 877-747-0004. FAX: 901-448-7235. E-mail: library@uthsc.edu. Web Site: library.uthsc.edu. *Dir,* Dr Rick Fought; Tel: 901-448-5694, E-mail: rfought1@uthsc.edu; *Assoc Dir,* G Randall Watts; Tel: 901-448-4599, E-mail: gwatts3@uthsc.edu; Staff 27 (MLS 11, Non-MLS 16)
Founded 1913. Enrl 2,600; Fac 790; Highest Degree: Doctorate
Library Holdings: e-journals 2,000; Bk Titles 48,760; Bk Vols 187,000; Per Subs 1,400
Special Collections: History of Medicine; Tennessee Authors (Wallace Memorial Coll)
Subject Interests: Allied health, Dentistry, Med, Nursing, Pharm, Soc work
Automation Activity & Vendor Info: (Acquisitions) Innovative Interfaces, Inc; (Cataloging) Innovative Interfaces, Inc; (Circulation) Innovative Interfaces, Inc; (Course Reserve) Innovative Interfaces, Inc; (ILL) Innovative Interfaces, Inc; (Media Booking) Innovative Interfaces, Inc; (OPAC) Innovative Interfaces, Inc; (Serials) Innovative Interfaces, Inc
Wireless access
Partic in Consortium of Southern Biomedical Libraries; LYRASIS; National Network of Libraries of Medicine Region 2; Proquest Dialog; Southeastern Regional Med Libr Program
Open Mon-Thurs 8am-10pm, Fri & Sat 8-5, Sun 2-10

MIDDLETON

P MIDDLETON COMMUNITY LIBRARY*, 110 Bolton Ave, 38052. (Mail add: PO Box 40, 38052), SAN 376-7035. Tel: 731-376-0680. FAX: 731-376-0680. E-mail: midcomlib@comcast.net. Web Site: cityofmiddleton.org/library.htm. *Dir,* Cynthia Scott
Library Holdings: Bk Titles 5,000; Per Subs 12
Automation Activity & Vendor Info: (Cataloging) Winnebago Software Co; (Circulation) Winnebago Software Co
Wireless access
Mem of Hatchie River Regional Library
Open Tues-Fri 12-5:30, Sat 9-1
Friends of the Library Group

MILAN

P MILDRED G FIELDS MEMORIAL LIBRARY*, 1075-A E Van Hook St, 38358. SAN 315-8888. Tel: 731-686-8268. FAX: 731-686-3207. E-mail: mgflibrary@mgflibrary.net. Web Site: cityofmilantn.com/city-services/library. *Dir,* Missy Blakely; E-mail: missyblakely@mgflibrary.net
Founded 1950. Pop 13,309; Circ 33,425
Library Holdings: Bk Vols 40,000; Per Subs 75
Automation Activity & Vendor Info: (Cataloging) Follett Software; (Circulation) Follett Software; (Serials) Follett Software
Wireless access
Mem of Obion River Regional Library
Open Mon 9-8, Tues 9-6, Wed-Fri 9-5, Sat 9-Noon
Friends of the Library Group

MILLERSVILLE

P MILLERSVILLE PUBLIC LIBRARY OF SUMNER COUNTY*, 1174 Louisville Hwy, 37072. Tel: 615-448-6959. FAX: 615-448-6198. E-mail: mpl@sumnercountytn.gov. Web Site: www1.youseemore.com/millersvillepl. *Libr Dir,* Tess Peters; E-mail: tpeters@sumnercountytn.gov; Staff 3 (MLS 1, Non-MLS 2)
Founded 2015. Pop 10,587; Fac 4
Wireless access
Function: After school storytime, Bks on CD, Children's prog, Computer training, Computers for patron use, Electronic databases & coll, Free DVD rentals, ILL available, Internet access, Movies, Online cat, Photocopying/Printing, Preschool reading prog, Printer for laptops & handheld devices, Prog for adults, Prog for children & young adult, Scanner, Study rm, Teen prog, Wheelchair accessible
Open Mon-Wed 10-7, Fri 10-5, Sat 10-4
Friends of the Library Group

MILLIGAN COLLEGE

C MILLIGAN COLLEGE, P H Welshimer Memorial Library, 200 Blowers Blvd, 37682. (Mail add: PO Box 600, 37682-0600), SAN 315-8896. Tel: 423-461-8703. E-mail: library@milligan.edu. Web Site: library.milligan.edu. *Dir of Libr, Theological Librn,* David Kiger; Tel: 423-461-1541, E-mail: dwkiger@milligan.edu; *Info Res Librn, Univ Archivist,* Katie Banks; Tel: 423-461-8901, E-mail: knbanks@milligan.edu; *Res & Instruction Librn,* Mary Jackson; Tel: 423-461-8697, E-mail: mjackson@milligan.edu; *Student Success Librn,* Janeen Bradley Pennell; Tel: 423-461-8900; *User Serv Librn,* Linda Ray; Tel: 423-461-8495; Staff 5 (MLS 5)
Founded 1881. Enrl 964; Fac 79; Highest Degree: Doctorate
Library Holdings: AV Mats 3,394; CDs 650; DVDs 691; e-books 40,176; e-journals 6,850; Bk Titles 135,253; Bk Vols 142,591; Per Subs 463; Videos 1,336
Special Collections: Restoration History (Restoration of New Testament Christianity)
Subject Interests: Educ, Humanities, Relig studies
Automation Activity & Vendor Info: (Acquisitions) OCLC Worldshare Management Services; (Cataloging) OCLC Worldshare Management Services; (Circulation) OCLC Worldshare Management Services; (Course Reserve) OCLC Worldshare Management Services; (ILL) OCLC Worldshare Management Services; (Media Booking) OCLC Worldshare Management Services; (OPAC) OCLC Worldshare Management Services; (Serials) OCLC Worldshare Management Services
Wireless access
Partic in Appalachian College Association; Holston Assoc Librs, Inc; LYRASIS; OCLC Online Computer Library Center, Inc
Open Mon-Thurs 7:45am-Midnight, Fri 7:45-5, Sat 11-5, Sun 2-Midnight (Fall-Spring); Mon-Thurs 8-5, Fri 8-Noon (Summer)

MILLINGTON

P MILLINGTON PUBLIC LIBRARY*, 4858 Navy Rd, 38053. SAN 378-4444. Tel: 901-872-1585. Web Site: www.millingtonpubliclibrary.org. *Dir,* Stephanie Kinsler; E-mail: stephanie.kinsler@lsslibraries.com; Staff 2 (MLS 1, Non-MLS 1)
Jul 2022-Jun 2023 Income $391,000
Library Holdings: Audiobooks 32,000; DVDs 896; e-books 79,686; Large Print Bks 1,669; Bk Titles 56,764
Wireless access
Function: 24/7 Electronic res, 24/7 Online cat, 24/7 wireless access, Activity rm, Art programs, Audiobks via web, Bks on CD, Children's prog, Computer training, Computers for patron use, Electronic databases & coll, Extended outdoor wifi, Free DVD rentals, Games, Health sci info serv, Holiday prog, ILL available, Internet access, Life-long learning prog for all ages, Mail & tel request accepted, Meeting rooms, Movies, Online cat, OverDrive digital audio bks, Photocopying/Printing, Preschool reading prog, Printer for laptops & handheld devices, Prog for adults, Ref serv available, Res assist avail, Senior computer classes, STEM programs, Story hour, Summer reading prog, Tax forms, Teen prog, Telephone ref, Wheelchair accessible
Special Services for the Blind - Bks available with recordings; Bks on CD; Computer access aids; Large print bks
Open Mon-Thurs 10-6:30, Fri & Sat 10-4
Friends of the Library Group

MINOR HILL

P MINOR HILL PUBLIC LIBRARY, 108 Pickett Dr, 38473. SAN 315-890X. Tel: 931-565-3699. E-mail: minorhilllibrary@gmail.com. *Libr Dir,* Morgan Randolph
Circ 7,028
Library Holdings: Bk Vols 3,500
Wireless access
Mem of Buffalo River Regional Library
Open Mon 10-5, Tues & Fri 10-3, Thurs 10-4

MONTEAGLE

P MAY JUSTUS MEMORIAL LIBRARY*, 24 Dixie Lee Ave, 37356. (Mail add: PO Box 78, 37356), SAN 315-8918. Tel: 931-924-2638. FAX: 931-924-3628. E-mail: mayjustuslib@benlomand.net. Web Site: sites.google.com/site/mayjustusmemoriallibrary. *Dir,* Karen Tittle; Staff 1 (Non-MLS 1)
Founded 1960. Pop 1,500; Circ 18,000
Library Holdings: Bk Titles 14,000; Videos 300
Wireless access
Open Mon 9-5, Tues-Fri 8-4

MORRISTOWN

P MORRISTOWN-HAMBLEN LIBRARY*, 417 W Main St, 37814-4686. SAN 315-8942. Tel: 423-586-6410. FAX: 423-587-6226. E-mail: morristownhamblenlibrary@yahoo.com. Web Site: www.morristownhamblenlibrary.org. *Libr Dir,* Shelly Shropshire; E-mail: shelly.shropshire@morristownhamblenlibrary.org; Staff 10.3 (MLS 2, Non-MLS 8.3)
Founded 1925. Pop 61,026; Circ 257,606
Jul 2018-Jun 2019 Income $706,685, State $6,133, City $278,150, County $278,150, Locally Generated Income $144,252. Mats Exp $61,693, Books $43,696, Per/Ser (Incl. Access Fees) $17,997. Sal $438,751
Library Holdings: CDs 3,907; DVDs 8,061; e-books 214; Microforms 614; Bk Vols 81,867; Per Subs 60
Automation Activity & Vendor Info: (Cataloging) Biblionix; (Circulation) Biblionix; (OPAC) Biblionix
Wireless access
Function: 24/7 Electronic res, 24/7 Online cat, 3D Printer, Adult bk club, Adult literacy prog, Art exhibits, Art programs, Audiobks via web, Bk club(s), Bks on CD, Children's prog, Computer training, Computers for patron use, Electronic databases & coll, Free DVD rentals, ILL available, Internet access, Magazines, Meeting rooms, Microfiche/film & reading machines, Movies, Music CDs, Online cat, Online ref, OverDrive digital audio bks, Photocopying/Printing, Preschool outreach, Preschool reading prog, Printer for laptops & handheld devices, Prog for adults, Prog for children & young adult, Senior computer classes, Spanish lang bks, STEM programs, Story hour, Study rm, Summer reading prog, Teen prog, VHS videos, Wheelchair accessible
Mem of Holston River Regional Library
Partic in National Network of Libraries of Medicine Region 2
Open Mon-Thurs 9-7, Fri 9-6, Sat 9-4
Restriction: Borrowing requests are handled by ILL, Non-resident fee
Friends of the Library Group

J WALTERS STATE COMMUNITY COLLEGE*, R Jack Fishman Library, 500 S Davy Crockett Pkwy, 37813-6899. SAN 315-8969. Tel: 423-585-6903. Reference Tel: 423-585-6946. FAX: 423-585-6959. E-mail: library@ws.edu. Web Site: library.ws.edu. *Dean of Libr,* Jamie Posey; E-mail: Jamie.Posey@ws.edu; Staff 4 (MLS 4)
Founded 1970. Highest Degree: Associate
Library Holdings: Bk Titles 41,570; Bk Vols 47,865; Per Subs 189; Spec Interest Per Sub 189
Automation Activity & Vendor Info: (Acquisitions) TLC (The Library Corporation); (Cataloging) TLC (The Library Corporation); (Circulation) TLC (The Library Corporation); (Course Reserve) TLC (The Library Corporation); (ILL) OCLC; (OPAC) TLC (The Library Corporation)
Wireless access
Partic in LYRASIS
Open Mon-Fri 8-4:15

MOSHEIM

P MOSHEIM PUBLIC LIBRARY, 730 Main St, 37818. SAN 376-2971. Tel: 423-422-7937. FAX: 423-422-6492. E-mail: mostafflib2@gmail.com. Web Site: mosheimlib.org. *Dir,* Denise Duck
Founded 1981. Pop 2,500

Library Holdings: Bk Titles 21,000
Wireless access
Function: Adult bk club, After school storytime, Audiobks via web, Bk club(s), Bks on CD, Children's prog, Computer training, Computers for patron use, Family literacy, Free DVD rentals, Holiday prog, Homework prog, ILL available, Instruction & testing, Internet access, Laminating, Laptop/tablet checkout, Magazines, Online cat, Photocopying/Printing, Printer for laptops & handheld devices, Prof lending libr, Prog for adults, Prog for children & young adult, Scanner, Story hour, Summer reading prog, Tax forms, Wheelchair accessible, Wifi hotspot checkout
Mem of Holston River Regional Library
Special Services for the Blind - Bks on CD
Open Mon-Thurs 11-5, Fri 12-5

MOUNT CARMEL

P MOUNT CARMEL LIBRARY, 100 Main St, 37645-9999. (Mail add: PO Box 1421, 37645-1421), SAN 376-6330. Tel: 423-357-4011. FAX: 423-357-4011. E-mail: mtclibrary.contact@gmail.com. Web Site: www.mountcarmelpubliclibrary.org. *Libr Dir,* Amy Lynn Cross; *Librn,* Alison Christian; *Librn,* Crystal Dockery; *Librn,* Traci Newland
Pop 5,300
Library Holdings: Bk Vols 3,500
Wireless access
Open Mon, Tues & Thurs 10-8, Wed & Fri 10-4, Sat 10-2

MOUNTAIN CITY

P JOHNSON COUNTY PUBLIC LIBRARY*, 219 N Church St, 37683. (Mail add: PO Box 107, 37683-0107), SAN 315-8977. Tel: 423-727-6544. FAX: 423-727-0319. E-mail: johnsoncountypubliclibrarytn@gmail.com. Web Site: www.johnsoncolib.org. *Libr Dir,* Linda Icenhour; E-mail: lindaicenhour25@gmail.com; *Libr Asst,* Luci Cavanaugh; *Libr Asst,* Laura Hayworth
Pop 13,745
Library Holdings: Bk Vols 17,000; Per Subs 20
Automation Activity & Vendor Info: (Cataloging) Ex Libris Group; (Circulation) Ex Libris Group; (OPAC) Ex Libris Group
Wireless access
Partic in Midwest Collaborative for Library Services
Open Mon & Wed-Fri 9-5, Tues 9-8, Sat 9-1
Friends of the Library Group

MUNFORD

P MUNFORD-TIPTON MEMORIAL LIBRARY*, 1476 Munford Ave, 38058. (Mail add: 1397 Munford Ave, 38058), SAN 376-7566. Tel: 901-837-2665. FAX: 901-837-2006. E-mail: library@munford.com. Web Site: munford.com/departments/library. *Dir,* Lindsey Moore; E-mail: lmoore@munford.com; *Asst Libr Dir,* Jennifer Barton
Library Holdings: Bk Vols 1,200
Wireless access
Mem of Hatchie River Regional Library
Open Mon, Wed & Fri 10-5, Tues & Thurs 10-6, Sat 10-1

MURFREESBORO

R FIRST BAPTIST CHURCH LIBRARY*, 200 E Main St, 37130. SAN 315-8993. Tel: 615-893-2514. Web Site: www.fbcmboro.org. *Dir, Media Library,* Juana Cates; E-mail: jlcates3@yahoo.com; Staff 19 (MLS 4, Non-MLS 15)
Founded 1843
Library Holdings: Bk Vols 18,398; Per Subs 31
Special Collections: Children's Coll
Subject Interests: Church curriculum, Relig studies
Open Wed 9-12, Sun 8-11

C MIDDLE TENNESSEE STATE UNIVERSITY*, James E Walker Library, 1611 Alumni Dr, 37132. (Mail add: MTSU, PO Box 13, 37132-0013). Tel: 615-898-2817. Circulation Tel: 615-898-2650. Administration Tel: 615-898-2772. Web Site: library.mtsu.edu. *Dean,* Kathleen L Schmand; Tel: 615-898-2773; *Assoc Dean,* Christy Groves; Tel: 615-898-2652, E-mail: christy.groves@mtsu.edu; *Access Serv Librn,* Jackie Dowdy; Tel: 615-898-5104, E-mail: jacqueline.dowdy@mtsu.edu; *Acq Librn,* Suzanne Mangrum; Tel: 615-904-8517, E-mail: suzanne.mangrum@mtsu.edu; *Cataloging & Metadata Librn,* Linda Turney; Tel: 615-904-8510, E-mail: linda.turney@mtsu.edu; *Collection Assessment Librarian,* Rachel Kirk; Tel: 615-904-8518, E-mail: rachel.kirk@mtsu.edu; *Continuing Resources Librn,* Beverly Geckle; Tel: 615-904-8519, E-mail: beverly.geckle@mtsu.edu; *Spec Coll Librn,* Alan Boehm; Tel: 615-904-8501, E-mail: alan.boehm@mtsu.edu; *Mgr, Libr Tech Serv,* Mike Wheaton; Tel: 615-898-5043, E-mail: michael.wheaton@mtsu.edu; *Chair, Collection Dev & Mgmt,* Susan Martin; Tel: 615-898-2819, E-mail: susan.martin@mysu.edu; *Distance Learning Serv,* Sharon Parente; Tel: 615-898-2549, E-mail: sharon.parente@mtsu.edu; Staff 26 (MLS 26)
Founded 1912. Enrl 22,322; Fac 794; Highest Degree: Doctorate
Library Holdings: Bk Vols 748,888; Per Subs 4,144
Special Collections: Artists Books Coll; Tennesseana. US Document Depository
Subject Interests: Artists bks, Civil War, Tenn hist
Wireless access
Function: Wheelchair accessible
Publications: Library Update (Newsletter)
Partic in LYRASIS; Nashville Area Libr Alliance; OCLC Online Computer Library Center, Inc
Open Mon-Thurs 7am-2am, Fri 7am-8pm, Sat 9-6, Sun 1pm-2am
Departmental Libraries:
CENTER FOR POPULAR MUSIC, John Bragg Media & Entertainment Bldg, Rm 140, 1301 E Main St, 37132. (Mail add: MTSU, PO Box 41, 37132), SAN 323-8199. Tel: 615-898-2449. Reference Tel: 615-898-5513. E-mail: popular.music@mtsu.edu. Web Site: popmusic.mtsu.edu. *Dir,* Dr Gregory Reish; E-mail: gregory.reish@mtsu.edu; *Librn,* Stephanie Bandel; Tel: 615-898-5512, E-mail: stephanie.bandel-koroll@mtsu.edu; *Mgr, Recorded Media Coll,* W Martin Fisher; Tel: 615-898-5509, E-mail: martin.fisher@mtsu.edu; *Archivist,* Rachel Morris; Tel: 615-898-5884, E-mail: rachel.morris@mtsu.edu; Staff 7 (MLS 2, Non-MLS 5)
Founded 1985. Enrl 20,857; Fac 947; Highest Degree: Doctorate
Library Holdings: AV Mats 274,000; CDs 32,000; DVDs 300; Microforms 2,900; Music Scores 115,500; Bk Vols 24,000; Per Subs 200; Spec Interest Per Sub 200; Videos 2,000
Special Collections: 18th & Early 19th Century British Music Imprints (Alfred Moffatt Coll); 19th Century American Songsters & Song Broadsides (Kenneth S Goldstein Coll); Rare Books (Gospel Song Books, Hymnbooks, Instrumental Music Books, Sacred & Secular Oblong Song Books, School Text Hillbilly Song Folios, Text-Only Hymnals); Sheet Music, Late 18th Century to Present; Tennessee Music (John S Mitchell Coll), bks, sheet music, sound recs
Subject Interests: Popular music, Vernacular religious music
Function: Archival coll, Audio & video playback equip for onsite use, Res libr
Open Mon-Fri 8:30-4
Restriction: Closed stack, Non-circulating

P RUTHERFORD COUNTY LIBRARY SYSTEM*, 105 W Vine St, 37130-3673. SAN 360-8581. Tel: 615-893-4131. Circulation Tel: 615-893-4131, Ext 115. Reference Tel: 615-893-4131, Ext 117. Administration Tel: 615-893-4131, Ext 110. FAX: 615-848-5038. Web Site: www.rclstn.org. *Dir of Libr,* Rita Shacklett; Tel: 615-962-7424, E-mail: rshacklett@rclstn,org; *Br Mgr,* Carol Ghattas; Tel: 615-893-4131, Ext 119, E-mail: cghattas@rclstn.org; *Circ Mgr,* Garrett Crowell; Tel: 615-893-4131, Ext 116, E-mail: gcrowell@rclstn.org; *Circ Supvr,* Dave O'Flaherty; *Circ Supvr,* Lisa Ramsay; Tel: 615-893-4131, Ext 123, E-mail: lramsay@rclstn.org; *Coll Develop Coordr,* Valerie Rollins; Tel: 615-962-7424, E-mail: vrollins@rclstn.org; *Youth Serv Coordr,* Laura Loggins; Tel: 615-893-4131, Ext 114, E-mail: lloggins@rclstn.org; Staff 44 (MLS 4, Non-MLS 40)
Founded 1948. Pop 281,440; Circ 1,249,344
Jul 2019-Jun 2020 Income (Main & Associated Libraries) $3,540,733. Mats Exp $392,954, Books $344,375, Per/Ser (Incl. Access Fees) $4,989, Electronic Ref Mat (Incl. Access Fees) $43,590. Sal $1,920,010
Library Holdings: Audiobooks 12,436; DVDs 23,847; e-books 614; Bk Vols 176,070; Per Subs 229
Subject Interests: Genealogy, Local hist
Automation Activity & Vendor Info: (Acquisitions) SirsiDynix-WorkFlows; (Cataloging) SirsiDynix-WorkFlows; (Circulation) SirsiDynix-WorkFlows; (ILL) OCLC; (OPAC) SirsiDynix-iBistro
Wireless access
Function: 24/7 Electronic res, 24/7 Online cat, 3D Printer, Audiobks on Playaways & MP3, Audiobks via web, Bilingual assistance for Spanish patrons, Bk club(s), Bks on CD, Children's prog, Computer training, Computers for patron use, Electronic databases & coll, Free DVD rentals, Genealogy discussion group, Holiday prog, ILL available, Internet access, Learning ctr, Life-long learning prog for all ages, Magazines, Magnifiers for reading, Makerspace, Meeting rooms, Microfiche/film & reading machines, Music CDs, Notary serv, Online cat, Outreach serv, OverDrive digital audio bks, Photocopying/Printing, Preschool outreach, Prog for adults, Prog for children & young adult, Senior computer classes, Spanish lang bks, STEM programs, Story hour, Summer & winter reading prog, Summer reading prog, Tax forms, Teen prog, Wheelchair accessible, Winter reading prog
Open Mon-Thurs 9-9, Fri & Sat 9-5, Sun 1-6
Friends of the Library Group
Branches: 4
EAGLEVILLE BICENTENNIAL BRANCH, 317 Old Hwy 99, Eagleville, 37060, SAN 376-7019. Tel: 615-274-2626. FAX: 615-274-2626. *Br Supvry Clerk,* Donna Jordon; E-mail: djordon@rclstn.org; Staff 2 (Non-MLS 2)
Library Holdings: Bk Vols 12,702
Function: 24/7 Electronic res, Audiobks on Playaways & MP3, Audiobks via web, Bks on CD, Computers for patron use, Free DVD

rentals, Internet access, Music CDs, Online cat, Photocopying/Printing, Story hour, Summer reading prog
Open Mon, Tues & Thurs 1-7, Fri 1-5, Sat 9-4
MYRTLE GLANTON LORD LIBRARY, 521 Mercury Blvd, 37130. Tel: 615-907-3429. FAX: 615-907-7120. *Br Supvr,* Mindy Barrett; E-mail: mbarrett@rclstn.org; Staff 4 (MLS 1, Non-MLS 3)
Circ 20,475
Library Holdings: Bk Vols 10,639
Automation Activity & Vendor Info: (Circulation) SirsiDynix-WorkFlows; (OPAC) SirsiDynix-iBistro
Open Mon-Thurs 9-7, Fri & Sat 9-4
SMYRNA PUBLIC LIBRARY, 400 Enon Springs Rd W, Smyrna, 37167, SAN 360-8611. Tel: 615-459-4884. FAX: 615-459-2370. *Br Mgr,* Ginger Graves; E-mail: ggraves@rclstn.org; *Youth Serv Coordr,* Sandy Kaiser; E-mail: skaiser@rclstn.org; Staff 17 (MLS 1, Non-MLS 16)
Founded 1960. Pop 39,974; Circ 305,186
Library Holdings: Bk Vols 82,754; Per Subs 160
Function: 24/7 Electronic res, 24/7 Online cat, Adult bk club, Audiobks on Playaways & MP3, Audiobks via web, Bk club(s), Bks on CD, Children's prog, Computers for patron use, Electronic databases & coll, Genealogy discussion group, Holiday prog, Internet access, Life-long learning prog for all ages, Magazines, Music CDs, Notary serv, Online cat, Online ref, Photocopying/Printing, Prog for children & young adult, Spanish lang bks, Story hour, Summer reading prog, Teen prog, Winter reading prog
Open Mon-Thurs 9-8, Fri & Sat 9-5
Friends of the Library Group
TECHNOLOGY ENGAGEMENT CENTER, 306 Minerva Dr, 37130. *Br Mgr,* Kathleen Tyree; Tel: 615-225-8312, E-mail: ktyree@rclstn.org; Staff 4 (MLS 1, Non-MLS 3)
Founded 2018
Bookmobiles: 1. Libr Dir, Rita Shacklett. Bk titles 4,814

P STONES RIVER REGIONAL LIBRARY*, 2118 E Main St, 37130-4009. SAN 315-9000. Tel: 615-893-3380. Toll Free Tel: 800-257-7323. FAX: 615-895-6727. Web Site: sos.tn.gov/tsla/pages/stones-river-regional-library. *Dir,* Kate Huddleston; E-mail: kate.huddleston@tn.gov
Founded 1945. Pop 466,511; Circ 2,252,907
Library Holdings: Bk Vols 30,000
Automation Activity & Vendor Info: (Acquisitions) Brodart; (Cataloging) Brodart; (Circulation) Brodart; (Course Reserve) Brodart; (ILL) Brodart; (Media Booking) Brodart; (OPAC) Brodart; (Serials) Brodart
Wireless access
Member Libraries: Cannon County Library System; Coffee County Lannom Memorial Public Library; Coffee County-Manchester Library; Franklin County Library; Fred A Vaught Memorial Public Library; Lebanon-Wilson County Library; Moore County Public Library; Shelbyville-Bedford County Public Library
Open Mon-Fri 8-4:30

NASHVILLE

CR AMERICAN BAPTIST COLLEGE, Susie McClure Library, 1800 Baptist World Center Dr, 37207. SAN 315-9027. Tel: 615-256-1463, 615-687-6899. Reference Tel: 615-687-6935. FAX: 615-226-7855. E-mail: library@abcnash.edu. Web Site: library.abcnash.edu. *Dir, Libr Serv,* Angel Pridgen; Tel: 615-256-1463, Ext 6946, E-mail: apridgen@abcnash.edu
Founded 1953
Library Holdings: Bk Vols 14,000; Per Subs 200
Subject Interests: Ethnic studies, Relig studies
Automation Activity & Vendor Info: (Acquisitions) Book Systems; (Cataloging) TinyCat; (Circulation) Book Systems; (OPAC) TinyCat
Wireless access
Publications: IMPRINTS
Open Mon-Fri 8am-9pm

C BELMONT UNIVERSITY*, Lila D Bunch Library, 1900 Belmont Blvd, 37212-3757. SAN 315-9078. Tel: 615-460-6782. Interlibrary Loan Service Tel: 615-460-5597. Reference Tel: 615-460-5498. Information Services Tel: 615-460-6033. Web Site: library.belmont.edu. *Dir, Libr Serv,* Sue Maszaros; Tel: 615-460-5496, E-mail: sue.maszaros@belmont.edu; Staff 16 (MLS 6, Non-MLS 10)
Founded 1951. Enrl 3,350; Fac 200; Highest Degree: Doctorate
Library Holdings: Bk Vols 242,545; Per Subs 1,106
Subject Interests: Educ, Lit, Music, Natural sci, Nursing, Relig studies, Soc & behav sci
Automation Activity & Vendor Info: (Acquisitions) Ex Libris Group; (Cataloging) Ex Libris Group; (Circulation) Ex Libris Group; (Course Reserve) Ex Libris Group; (ILL) OCLC; (OPAC) Ex Libris Group; (Serials) Ex Libris Group
Wireless access
Partic in OCLC Online Computer Library Center, Inc
Open Mon-Thurs 7:30am-11pm, Fri 7:30-6, Sat 9-6, Sun 2-11 (Winter); Mon-Thurs 7:30am-9pm, Fri 7:30-4:30, Sat 12-4:30, Sun 5-9 (Summer)

S COUNTRY MUSIC HALL OF FAME & MUSEUM*, Frist Library & Archives, 222 Fifth Ave S, 37203. SAN 315-9086. Tel: 615-416-2025. FAX: 615-255-2245. Reference E-mail: reference@countrymusichalloffame.com. Web Site: www.countrymusichalloffame.org/collections. *Library Contact,* Kathleen Campbell; E-mail: kcampbell@countrymusichalloffame.org
Founded 1967
Library Holdings: Bk Titles 100,000; Per Subs 450; Videos 40,000
Special Collections: Country Music & The Music Industry Coll, A-tapes; Nashville Chapter Coll; National Academy of Recording Arts & Sciences; Roy Acuff Coll. Oral History
Subject Interests: Anglo-Am folksong, Commercial popular music in gen, Country music, Culture, Early commercial recording, Folklore, Law, Music copyright, Recorded sound tech, Southern hist
Publications: Journal of Country Music
Restriction: Open by appt only
Friends of the Library Group

C FISK UNIVERSITY*, John Hope & Aurelia E Franklin Library, 1000 17th Ave N, 37208-3051. SAN 315-9116. Tel: 615-329-8730. Circulation Tel: 615-329-8640. Interlibrary Loan Service Tel: 615-329-8734. FAX: 615-329-8761. Web Site: www.fisk.edu/academics/library. *Dean of the Library,* Brandon A Owens, PhD; Tel: 615-668-8731, E-mail: bowens@fisk.edu; *Asst Dir, Libr Serv,* DeLisa Minor Harris; Tel: 615-329-8646, E-mail: dharris@fisk.edu; *Librn Emeritus,* Jessie Carney-Smith, PhD; E-mail: jcsmith@fisk.edu; *Spec Coll Librn,* Diona Layden; E-mail: delayden@fisk.edu; *Night Supvr,* Ester McShepard; E-mail: emcshepa@fisk.edu; *Access Serv, Libr Asst,* Position Currently Open; *Archivist,* Joshua Williams; Tel: 615-329-8838, E-mail: jawilliams@fisk.edu; *Libr Asst, Spec Coll,* Schuyler Carter; E-mail: scarter@fisk.edu; *Libr Asst, Tech Serv,* Paul Springer, Jr; Tel: 615-329-8733, E-mail: pspringer@fisk.edu; Staff 7 (MLS 4, Non-MLS 3)
Founded 1866. Highest Degree: Master
Special Collections: Black Literature (Charles W Chesnutt, James Weldon Johnson, Naomi Madgett, Louise Meriweather); Civil Rights & Politics (Slater King, John Mercer Langston, James Carroll Napier & William L Dawson); Music & Musical Literature (George Gershwin Coll); Music (W C Handy, Scott Joplin, Fisk Jubilee Singers & John W Work); Sociology (WEB DuBois, Marcus Garvey & Charles S Johnson). Oral History; US Document Depository
Subject Interests: African-Am culture, African-Am hist, African-Am lit
Automation Activity & Vendor Info: (Cataloging) Ex Libris Group; (Circulation) Ex Libris Group; (OPAC) Ex Libris Group; (Serials) Ex Libris Group
Wireless access
Function: Archival coll, Art exhibits, Doc delivery serv, Orientations, Photocopying/Printing, Ref serv available, Workshops
Partic in LYRASIS; Nashville Area Libr Alliance; Tenn Acad Libr Collaborative; Tenn-Share
Open Mon-Thurs 7:45am-10pm, Fri 7:45-5, Sat 1-5, Sun 2-10
Restriction: In-house use for visitors

J JOHN A GUPTON COLLEGE*, Memorial Library, 1616 Church St, 37203. SAN 315-9132. Tel: 615-327-3927. FAX: 615-321-4518. Web Site: guptoncollege.edu/resources/library. *Dir & Librn,* William P Bruce; E-mail: pbruce@guptoncollege.edu; Staff 1 (MLS 1)
Founded 1946. Enrl 60; Fac 14; Highest Degree: Associate
Library Holdings: Bk Titles 3,228; Bk Vols 4,050; Per Subs 55
Special Collections: Funeral Service/Grief Psychology
Subject Interests: Mortuary sci
Automation Activity & Vendor Info: (Cataloging) LibraryWorld, Inc; (OPAC) LibraryWorld, Inc
Wireless access
Open Mon & Tues 8:30-8:30, Wed & Thurs 8:30-4:30
Friends of the Library Group

SR VIRGINIA DAVIS LASKEY RESEARCH LIBRARY, 1027 18th Ave S, 37212-2126. E-mail: LaskeyLibrary@scarrittbennett.org. Web Site: ll-sbc.methone.opalsinfo.net/bin/home#0. *Librn,* LaDonna Riddle Weber; E-mail: lweber@scarrittbennett.org; Staff 1 (MLS 1)
Founded 2007
Library Holdings: AV Mats 275; Bk Titles 12,000
Special Collections: Methodist Women's Division Coll; National College & The Kansas City National Training School Records; Scarritt College Archives, cats, col files, newsletters, photog, student rec & yearbooks
Subject Interests: Feminist, Hymnody, Liturgy, Methodist hist, Missionaries, Missions, Multiculturalism, Race relations, Spirituality, Theol, Women's issues
Wireless access
Function: Audio & video playback equip for onsite use, Computers for patron use, ILL available, Photocopying/Printing, Scanner
Restriction: Non-circulating of rare bks, Open to pub for ref & circ; with some limitations, Researchers by appt only
Friends of the Library Group

C LIPSCOMB UNIVERSITY*, Beaman Library, One University Park Dr, 37204-3951. SAN 315-9094. Tel: 615-966-1793. Reference Tel: 615-966-6037. FAX: 615-966-5874. Web Site: library.lipscomb.edu. *Admin Officer,* Morgan Turner; Tel: 615-966-6034, E-mail: morgan.turner@lipscomb.edu; *Electronic Res Librn, Instruction Librn,* Britt Mountford; Tel: 615-966-5803, E-mail: bmountford@lipscomb.edu; *Circ, Ref Librn,* Julie Harston; Tel: 615-966-5717, E-mail: julie.harston@lipscomb.edu; *ILL, Ref Librn,* Eunice F Wells; Tel: 615-966-5836, E-mail: eunice.wells@lipscomb.edu; *Archives, Spec Coll Librn,* Elizabeth Rivera; Tel: 615-966-6083, E-mail: elizabeth.rivera@lipscomb.edu; Staff 10 (MLS 6, Non-MLS 4)
Founded 1891. Enrl 4,300; Fac 300; Highest Degree: Doctorate
Library Holdings: e-books 18,000; Microforms 391,030; Bk Vols 232,907; Per Subs 719
Special Collections: Bailey Hymnology Coll; C E W Dorris Coll; Herald of Truth Videotapes
Subject Interests: Bibliog instruction, Relig
Automation Activity & Vendor Info: (Acquisitions) Innovative Interfaces, Inc; (Cataloging) Innovative Interfaces, Inc; (Circulation) Innovative Interfaces, Inc; (Course Reserve) Innovative Interfaces, Inc; (OPAC) Innovative Interfaces, Inc; (Serials) Innovative Interfaces, Inc
Wireless access
Partic in LYRASIS; Nashville Area Libr Alliance; Tenn-Share
Open Mon-Thurs 7:30am-12:30am, Fri 7:30-5, Sat 10-6, Sun 1-5 & 7:30pm-12:30am (Winter); Mon-Fri 8-5, Sat Noon-5 (Summer)
Friends of the Library Group

CM MEHARRY MEDICAL COLLEGE LIBRARY*, Kresge Learning Resource Center, 2001 Albion St, 37208. SAN 315-9140. Tel: 615-327-5770. Web Site: home.mmc.edu/library. *Exec Dir,* Sandra Parham; E-mail: sparham@mmc.edu; *Ref Librn,* Clare Kimbro; Tel: 615-327-6454, E-mail: ekimbro@mmc.edu; *Ref Librn,* Julia Drew Rather; Tel: 615-327-6465, E-mail: jrather@mmc.edu; *Health Info Coordr,* Vanessa Smith; Tel: 615-327-6463, E-mail: vsmith@mmc.edu; Staff 4 (MLS 3, Non-MLS 1)
Founded 1940
Library Holdings: e-books 9,000; e-journals 7,234; Bk Titles 24,700; Bk Vols 70,500; Per Subs 6,719
Special Collections: Black Medical History
Subject Interests: Biomed sci, Sciences
Automation Activity & Vendor Info: (Cataloging) OCLC; (Circulation) SirsiDynix; (OPAC) SirsiDynix; (Serials) SirsiDynix
Wireless access
Function: Res libr
Partic in Consortium of Southern Biomedical Libraries; OCLC Online Computer Library Center, Inc; SE-Atlantic Regional Med Libr Servs
Open Mon-Fri 7am-1am, Sat & Sun 9am-1am

P NASHVILLE PUBLIC LIBRARY*, 615 Church St, 37219-2314. SAN 360-912X. Tel: 615-862-5800. Reference Tel: 615-862-5793. Web Site: library.nashville.org. *Asst Dir, Admin Serv,* Susan Drye; Tel: 615-880-2614, E-mail: susan.drye@nashville.gov; *Asst Dir, Br Serv,* Terri Luke; Tel: 615-862-5761, E-mail: terri.luke@nashville.gov; *Asst Dir, Colls & Technology,* Felicia Wilson; Tel: 615-862-5805, E-mail: felicia.wilson@nashville.gov; *Asst Direc, Community Engagement & Education,* Elyse Adler; Tel: 615-862-5776, E-mail: elyse.adler@nashville.gov; *Asst Dir, Main Libr,* Jena Schmid; Tel: 615-862-5806, E-mail: jena.schmid@nashville.gov; *Mgr, Ad Serv,* Kyle Barber; Tel: 615-862-5839, E-mail: kyle.barber@nashville.gov; *Mgr, Ch Serv,* Patricia Rua-Bashir; *Coll Develop Mgr,* Noel Rutherford; *Mkt & Communications Mgr,* Andrea Fanta; *Mgr, Spec Coll,* Andrea Blackman; *Teen Serv Mgr,* Luke Herbst; *Adult Literacy Coordr,* Megan Godbey; Tel: 615-880-2264, E-mail: megan.godbey@nashville.gov; *Vols Serv Coordr,* Amy Pierce; Tel: 615-862-5769, E-mail: amy.pierce@nashville.gov; *Archivist,* Ken Fieth; *ILL,* Amanda Dembiec; Tel: 615-862-5780, E-mail: amanda.dembiec@nashville.gov
Founded 1904. Pop 635,475; Circ 4,340,657
Special Collections: Children's International Coll; Deaf Services Coll; Government Archives; Local Genealogy & History (Nashville); Naff (Drama Coll). Oral History; State Document Depository
Subject Interests: Bus, Grants, Tenn hist
Automation Activity & Vendor Info: (Acquisitions) Innovative Interfaces, Inc; (Cataloging) Innovative Interfaces, Inc; (Circulation) Innovative Interfaces, Inc; (OPAC) Innovative Interfaces, Inc; (Serials) Innovative Interfaces, Inc
Wireless access
Partic in LYRASIS; OCLC Online Computer Library Center, Inc
Special Services for the Deaf - ADA equip; Adult & family literacy prog; Am sign lang & deaf culture; Assisted listening device; Assistive tech; Bks on deafness & sign lang; Captioned film dep
Special Services for the Blind - Accessible computers; Aids for in-house use; Assistive/Adapted tech devices, equip & products; Audio mat; Audiovision-a radio reading serv
Open Mon-Fri 9-6, Sat 9-5, Sun 2-5
Friends of the Library Group

Branches: 23
BELLEVUE BRANCH, 720 Baugh Rd, 37221, SAN 360-9146. Tel: 615-862-5854. FAX: 615-862-5758. *Br Mgr,* Katherine Bryant; E-mail: katherine.bryant@nashville.gov
Founded 2015
Library Holdings: Bk Vols 59,142
Open Mon-Thurs 10-8, Fri 10-6, Sat 10-5, Sun 2-5
Friends of the Library Group

BORDEAUX BRANCH, 4000 Clarksville Pike, 37218, SAN 360-9154. Tel: 615-862-5856. FAX: 615-862-5748. *Br Mgr,* Annie Herlocker; E-mail: annie.herlocker@nashville.gov
Founded 1976
Library Holdings: Bk Vols 70,073
Open Mon-Thurs 10-8, Sat 10-5, Sun 2-5
Friends of the Library Group

DONELSON BRANCH, 2315 Lebanon Pike, 37214, SAN 360-9189. Tel: 615-862-5859. FAX: 615-862-5799. *Br Mgr,* Chris Morin; E-mail: chris.morin@nashville.gov
Founded 1966
Library Holdings: Bk Vols 53,485
Open Mon & Wed 9:30-5:30, Tues & Thurs 12-8, Sat 9-5
Friends of the Library Group

EAST BRANCH, 206 Gallatin Ave, 37206, SAN 360-9219. Tel: 615-862-5860. FAX: 615-862-5807. *Br Mgr,* Sara Morse; E-mail: sara.morse@nashville.gov
Library Holdings: Bk Vols 31,880
Open Mon & Wed 9:30-5:30, Tues & Thurs 12-8, Sat 10-5
Friends of the Library Group

EDGEHILL BRANCH, 1409 12th Ave S, 37203, SAN 360-9243. Tel: 615-862-5861. FAX: 615-862-5840. *Br Mgr,* Carlos Shivers; E-mail: carlos.shivers@nashville.gov
Founded 1967
Library Holdings: Bk Vols 18,376
Open Mon-Thurs 10-6, Sat 10-5
Friends of the Library Group

EDMONDSON PIKE BRANCH, 5501 Edmondson Pike, 37211. Tel: 615-880-3957. FAX: 615-880-3961. *Br Mgr,* Linda Harrison; E-mail: linda.harrison@nashville.gov
Library Holdings: Bk Vols 124,905
Open Mon-Thurs 10-8, Sat 10-5, Sun 2-5
Friends of the Library Group

GOODLETTSVILLE BRANCH, 205 Rivergate Pkwy, Goodlettsville, 37072, SAN 360-9278. Tel: 615-862-5862. FAX: 615-862-5798. *Br Mgr,* J D Lovelace; E-mail: john.lovelace@nashville.gov
Founded 2011
Library Holdings: Bk Vols 42,319
Open Mon-Thurs 10-8, Fri 10-6, Sat 10-5
Friends of the Library Group

GREEN HILLS BRANCH, 3701 Benham Ave, 37215, SAN 360-9308. Tel: 615-862-5863. FAX: 615-862-5881. *Br Mgr,* Heidi Berg; E-mail: heidi.berg@nashville.gov
Founded 2000
Library Holdings: Bk Vols 127,747
Open Mon-Thurs 10-8, Fri 10-6, Sat 10-5, Sun 2-5
Friends of the Library Group

HADLEY PARK BRANCH, 1039 28th Ave N, 37208, SAN 360-9332. Tel: 615-862-5865. FAX: 615-862-5887. *Br Mgr,* Lindsay Jensen; E-mail: lindsay.jensen@nashville.gov
Founded 1952
Library Holdings: Bk Vols 26,394
Open Mon-Thurs 10-6, Sat 10-5
Friends of the Library Group

HERMITAGE BRANCH, 3700 James Kay Lane, Hermitage, 37076. Tel: 615-880-3951. FAX: 615-880-3955. *Br Mgr,* Emily Talbot; E-mail: emily.talbot@nashville.gov
Founded 2000
Library Holdings: Bk Vols 120,902
Open Mon-Thurs 10-8, Fri 10-6, Sat 10-5, Sun 2-5
Friends of the Library Group

INGLEWOOD BRANCH, 4312 Gallatin Pike, 37216, SAN 360-9367. Tel: 615-862-5866. FAX: 615-862-5888. *Br Mgr,* Suzanne Robinson; E-mail: suzanne.robinson@nashville.gov
Founded 1969
Library Holdings: Bk Vols 38,056
Open Mon-Thurs 10-8, Fri 10-6 Sat 10-5
Friends of the Library Group

LIBRARY SERVICE FOR THE DEAF & HARD OF HEARING, 615 Church St, 37219-2314, SAN 328-7246. Tel: 615-862-5750. Toll Free Tel: 800-342-3262. FAX: 615-862-5494. E-mail: dhoh@nashville.gov. Web Site: tndeaflibrary.nashville.gov. *Mgr,* Sandy Cohen; E-mail: sandy.cohen@nashville.gov
Founded 1978
Library Holdings: Bk Vols 12,773
Special Services for the Deaf - Bks on deafness & sign lang; TDD equip
Open Mon-Fri 9-5

Z ALEXANDER LOOBY BRANCH, 2301 Rosa L Parks Blvd, 37228, SAN 360-9391. Tel: 615-862-5867. FAX: 615-862-5797. *Br Mgr,* Joanna Roberts; E-mail: joanna.roberts@nashville.gov
Founded 1976
Library Holdings: Bk Vols 27,006
Open Mon-Thurs 10-8, Sat 10-5
Friends of the Library Group

MADISON BRANCH, 610 Gallatin Pike S, Madison, 37115, SAN 360-9421. Tel: 615-862-5868. FAX: 615-862-5889. *Br Mgr,* Jessica Piper; E-mail: jessica.piper@nashville.gov
Founded 2000
Library Holdings: Bk Vols 89,425
Open Mon-Thurs 10-8, Sat 10-5, Sun 2-5
Friends of the Library Group

METROPOLITAN GOVERNMENT ARCHIVES, 615 Church St, 3rd Flr, 37219, SAN 328-7262. Tel: 615-862-5880. Web Site: www.nashville.gov/Metro-Archives. *Archivist,* Kenneth Fieth; E-mail: ken.fieth@nashville.gov
Open Mon-Fri 9:30-6, Sat 9-5, Sun 2-5
Friends of the Library Group

NASHVILLE TALKING LIBRARY, 615 Church St, 37219, SAN 328-722X. Tel: 615-862-5874. FAX: 615-862-5796. E-mail: ntl@nashville.gov. Web Site: library.nashville.org/talking-library. *Mgr,* Michael Wagner; E-mail: michael.wagner@nashville.gov
Special Services for the Blind - Radio reading serv
Open Mon-Fri 9-5
Friends of the Library Group

NORTH BRANCH, 1001 Monroe St, 37208-2543, SAN 360-9162. Tel: 615-862-5858. FAX: 615-862-5749. Web Site: library.nashville.org/locations/north-branch. *Br Mgr,* Cloreace Eppenger; E-mail: cloreace.eppenger@nashville.gov; Staff 4 (MLS 1, Non-MLS 3)
Founded 1915
Library Holdings: Bk Vols 16,060
Function: 24/7 Electronic res, 24/7 Online cat, 24/7 wireless access, Accelerated reader prog, Activity rm, Adult literacy prog
Open Mon-Thurs 10-6, Sat 10-5
Friends of the Library Group

OLD HICKORY BRANCH, 1010 Jones St, Old Hickory, 37138, SAN 360-9456. Tel: 615-862-5869. FAX: 615-862-5896. *Br Mgr,* Chad L'eplattenier; E-mail: chad.leplattenier@nashville.gov
Founded 1964
Library Holdings: Bk Vols 31,299
Open Mon & Wed 10-6, Tues & Thurs Noon-8, Sat 10-5
Friends of the Library Group

MARY & CHARLES W PRUITT BRANCH LIBRARY & LEARNING CENTER, 117 Charles E Davis Blvd, 37210, SAN 375-2941. Tel: 615-862-5985. FAX: 615-862-6745. *Br Mgr,* Raymond Kinzounza; E-mail: raymond.kinzounza@nashville.gov
Founded 1993
Library Holdings: Bk Vols 19,322
Open Mon-Thurs 10-6, Sat 10-5
Friends of the Library Group

RICHLAND PARK BRANCH, 4711 Charlotte Ave, 37209, SAN 360-9480. Tel: 615-862-5870. FAX: 615-862-5897. *Br Mgr,* Annie Herlocker; E-mail: annie.herlocker@nashville.gov
Library Holdings: Bk Vols 51,470
Open Mon-Thurs 10-8, Fri 10-6, Sat 10-5
Friends of the Library Group

SOUTHEAST BRANCH, 5260 Hickory Hollow Pkwy, # 201, Antioch, 37013, SAN 373-1987. Tel: 615-862-5871. FAX: 615-862-5756. *Br Mgr,* Lindsey Patrick; E-mail: lindsey.patrick@nashville.gov
Founded 2014
Library Holdings: Bk Vols 81,455
Open Mon-Thurs 10-8, Fri 10-6, Sat 10-5, Sun 2-5
Friends of the Library Group

THOMPSON LANE BRANCH, 380 Thompson Lane, 37211, SAN 360-9510. Tel: 615-862-5873. FAX: 615-862-5898. *Br Mgr,* Syreeta Butler; E-mail: syreeta.butler@nashville.gov
Founded 1965
Library Holdings: Bk Vols 40,653
Open Mon-Thurs 10-8, Fri 10-6, Sat 10-5
Friends of the Library Group

WATKINS PARK BRANCH, 612 17th Ave N, 37203, SAN 375-295X. Tel: 615-862-5872. FAX: 615-862-6746. *Br Mgr,* Montoya Townsend; E-mail: montoya.townsend@nashville.gov
Founded 1992
Library Holdings: Bk Vols 7,757
Open Mon-Thurs 10-6
Friends of the Library Group

L NASHVILLE SCHOOL OF LAW LIBRARY*, 4013 Armory Oaks Dr, 37204. SAN 321-6144. Tel: 615-256-3684, Ext 7. FAX: 615-244-2383. Web Site: www.nashvilleschooloflaw.net/library.php. *Libr Dir,* Stacey Angello; E-mail: stacey@nashvilleschooloflaw.net; Staff 1 (MLS 1)
Founded 1911
Library Holdings: Bk Titles 165; Bk Vols 16,500; Per Subs 15
Special Collections: Judge Shriver Coll
Wireless access
Publications: Annual Barrister; Annual Catalog
Open Mon-Thurs 8:30am-10:30pm, Fri-Sun 8:30-6

J NASHVILLE STATE TECHNICAL COMMUNITY COLLEGE*, Mayfield Library, 120 White Bridge Rd, 37209-4515. SAN 315-9167. Tel: 615-353-3555. FAX: 615-353-3558. Web Site: www.nscc.edu/library. *Dean, Learning Res,* Margaret Faye Jones; Tel: 615-353-3440, E-mail: faye.jones@nscc.edu; *Instruction Librn,* Emily Bush; Tel: 615-353-3559, E-mail: emily.bush@nscc.edu; *Ref Librn,* Charles May; Tel: 615-353-3554, E-mail: charles.may@nscc.edu; *Cat, Ser,* Sally Robertson; Tel: 615-353-3270, E-mail: sally.robertson@nscc.edu; *Tech Serv,* Faye Vaughn; Tel: 615-353-3560, E-mail: faye.vaughn@nscc.edu; *Libr Asst III,* Jessie Angel; Tel: 615-353-3472, E-mail: jessie.angel@nscc.edu; *Libr Asst III,* Pamela Gadd; Tel: 615-353-3474, E-mail: pamela.gadd@nscc.edu; *Libr Asst II,* Lauren Turner; Tel: 615-353-3552, E-mail: lauren.turner@nscc.edu; Staff 4 (MLS 3, Non-MLS 1)
Founded 1969. Enrl 9,000; Fac 182; Highest Degree: Associate
Automation Activity & Vendor Info: (Acquisitions) SirsiDynix; (Cataloging) SirsiDynix; (Circulation) SirsiDynix; (Course Reserve) SirsiDynix; (ILL) SirsiDynix; (Media Booking) SirsiDynix; (OPAC) SirsiDynix; (Serials) SirsiDynix
Wireless access
Function: Art exhibits, Computers for patron use, Electronic databases & coll, ILL available, Learning ctr, Online cat, Photocopying/Printing
Publications: Annotated AV Lists, Library Guide
Partic in LYRASIS
Open Mon-Thurs 7:30am-8pm, Fri 7:30-4:30, Sat 9-2
Restriction: Co libr

M ST THOMAS HEALTH SERVICES LIBRARY*, Midtown Hospital Medical Library, 2000 Church St, 37236. SAN 315-9051. Tel: 615-222-3051, 615-284-5373. FAX: 615-222-6711. E-mail: medicallibraries@ascension.org. Web Site: sthslibrary.com. *Librn,* Christy Tyson; *Library Contact,* Erin Nunley; Staff 1 (MLS 1)
Founded 1948
Library Holdings: Bk Vols 3,000; Per Subs 160
Special Collections: Internal Medicine emphasis
Subject Interests: Clinical med, Consumer health, Healthcare mgt, Nursing
Publications: Newsletter
Partic in National Network of Libraries of Medicine Region 2; OCLC Online Computer Library Center, Inc
Restriction: Residents only, Staff use only

SR SOUTHERN BAPTIST HISTORICAL LIBRARY & ARCHIVES, 901 Commerce St, Ste 400, 37203-3630. SAN 326-1417. Tel: 615-244-0344. Web Site: sbhla.org. *Archivist, Dir,* Taffey Hall; E-mail: taffey@sbhla.org; *Librn,* Steve Gateley; E-mail: steve@sbhla.org; Staff 4 (MLS 2, Non-MLS 2)
Founded 1938
Library Holdings: AV Mats 4,000; DVDs 500; Electronic Media & Resources 100; Microforms 20,000; Bk Vols 44,000; Per Subs 255
Special Collections: Primitive Baptist Holdings; Southern Baptist Convention Archives Depository; Southern Baptist Convention Leaders' Papers
Subject Interests: Baptist hist
Automation Activity & Vendor Info: (Cataloging) Ex Libris Group; (Circulation) Ex Libris Group; (OPAC) Ex Libris Group; (Serials) Ex Libris Group
Wireless access
Function: Res libr
Partic in OCLC Online Computer Library Center, Inc
Open Mon-Fri 8-4

GL TENNESSEE GENERAL ASSEMBLY, OFFICE OF LEGAL SERVICES*, Legislative Library, 804 Cordell Hull Bldg, 425 Rep John Lewis Way N, 37243. SAN 370-4181. Tel: 615-741-5816. Web Site: www.capitol.tn.gov/joint/staff/legal/library.html. *Legislative Librn,* Eddie Weeks; E-mail: eddie.weeks@capitol.tn.gov; Staff 1 (MLS 1)
Founded 1977
Library Holdings: Bk Vols 6,000; Per Subs 30; Spec Interest Per Sub 25
Special Collections: Acts of the Tennessee Legislature 1827-Present
Subject Interests: Tenn legis mat
Function: Archival coll
Open Mon-Fri 8-4

P TENNESSEE REGIONAL LIBRARY FOR THE BLIND & PHYSICALLY HANDICAPPED*, Tennessee Library for Accessible Books & Media, 403 Seventh Ave N, 37243. SAN 315-9256. Tel: 615-741-3915. Toll Free Tel: 800-342-3308. FAX: 615-532-8856. E-mail:

tlbph.tsla@tn.gov. Web Site: sos.tn.gov/tsla/lbph. *Dir,* Clayton Altom; E-mail: clayton.altom@tn.gov; Staff 6 (MLS 3, Non-MLS 3)
Founded 1970
Library Holdings: Braille Volumes 25,233; Large Print Bks 11,041; Talking Bks 148,570; Videos 564
Wireless access
Publications: Window to the World (Newsletter)
Special Services for the Blind - Accessible computers; Aids for in-house use; Assistive/Adapted tech devices, equip & products; Audio mat; Bks & mags in Braille, on rec, tape & cassette; Bks on cassette; Braille & cassettes; Braille alphabet card; Braille bks; Braille equip; Cassettes; Children's Braille; Copier with enlargement capabilities; Digital talking bk; Newsletter (in large print, Braille or on cassette); Newsline for the Blind; Recorded bks; Ref serv
Open Mon-Fri 8-4:30

P TENNESSEE STATE LIBRARY & ARCHIVES*, 403 Seventh Ave N, 37243-0312. SAN 360-960X. Tel: 615-741-2764. E-mail: reference.tsla@tn.gov. Web Site: sos.tn.gov/tsla. *Archivist, State Librn,* James Ritter; E-mail: jamie.ritter@tn.gov; *Asst State Librn, Admin,* Ashley Bowers; Tel: 615-532-4628, E-mail: ashley.bowers@tn.gov; *Asst State Archivist,* Wayne Moore; Tel: 615-253-3458, E-mail: wayne.moore@tn.gov; *Libr Dir, Tech Serv,* Renee Register; E-mail: renee.register@tn.gov; *Dir of Archival Tech Serv,* Carmack Cathi; Tel: 615-253-3468, E-mail: cathi.carmack@tn.gov; *Dir, Pub Serv,* Gordon Belt; E-mail: gordon.belt@tn.gov; *Dir, Regional Libraries,* Bessie Smith; Tel: 615-532-4629, E-mail: bessie.smith@tn.gov; *Dir, Libr Develop, Dir, Libr Planning,* Jennifer Cowan-Henderson; Tel: 615-741-1923, E-mail: jennifer.cowan-henderson@tn.gov; *Dir, Presv Serv,* Jami Awalt; Tel: 615-253-6446, E-mail: jami.awalt@tn.gov; *Regional Libr Dir,* Marion Bryant; Tel: 931-388-9282, E-mail: marion.bryant@tn.gov; *Regional Libr Dir,* Mary Carpenter; Tel: 731-587-2347; *Regional Libr Dir,* Genny Carter; Tel: 731-668-0710, E-mail: Genny.Carter@tn.gov; *Regional Libr Dir,* BettyJo Jarvis; Tel: 615-893-3380, E-mail: bettyjo.jarvis@tn.gov; *Regional Libr Dir,* Matthew Jordan; Tel: 865-457-0931, E-mail: matthew.jordan@tn.gov; *Regional Libr Dir,* Matthew Kirby; Tel: 931-526-4016, E-mail: matthew.kirby@tn.gov; *Regional Libr Dir,* Cecilie Maynor; E-mail: cecilie.maynor@tn.gov; *Regional Libr Dir,* Nancy Roark; E-mail: nancy.roark@tn.gov; *Regional Libr Dir,* Liz Schreck; Tel: 423-745-8086; Staff 144 (MLS 49, Non-MLS 95)
Founded 1854
Library Holdings: Audiobooks 94,884; Bks-By-Mail 8,402; Braille Volumes 28,276; CDs 34; DVDs 69; e-books 241; e-journals 397; Electronic Media & Resources 386; Large Print Bks 8,425; Microforms 24,574; Music Scores 10; Bk Titles 179,210; Bk Vols 274,915; Per Subs 2,840; Talking Bks 158,127; Videos 1,715
Special Collections: Genealogy Coll; Popular Sheet Music (Rose Music); Southeastern US Maps; Tennessee County & Public Records; Tennessee Newspapers; Tennessee Virtual Archive. Oral History; State Document Depository; US Document Depository
Subject Interests: Genealogy, Local politics, Maps, Southern culture, Southern hist, Tenn hist, Tenn politics
Automation Activity & Vendor Info: (Cataloging) OCLC Connexion; (Circulation) SirsiDynix; (Discovery) EBSCO Discovery Service; (ILL) OCLC; (OPAC) SirsiDynix
Wireless access
Publications: List of Tennessee State Publications (Quarterly); Tennessee Public Library Directory & Statistics (Annual); Tennessee Public Library Trustee Manual; Tennessee Standards for Non-Metropolitan Public Libraries; Tennessee State Library & Archives: Guide to Resources & Services; Tennessee Summer Reading Program (Annual)
Partic in Association for Rural & Small Libraries; Tenn-Share
Special Services for the Blind - Accessible computers; Bks & mags in Braille, on rec, tape & cassette; Braille alphabet card; Braille bks; Children's Braille; Closed circuit TV magnifier; Copier with enlargement capabilities; Large print bks; Newsletter (in large print, Braille or on cassette); Talking bks & player equip
Open Tues-Sat 8-4:30
Friends of the Library Group
Branches: 1
LIBRARY FOR THE BLIND & PHYSICALLY HANDICAPPED
See Separate Entry under Tennessee Regional Library for the Blind & Physically Handicapped

C TENNESSEE STATE UNIVERSITY*, Brown-Daniel Library, 3500 John A Merritt Blvd, 37209. SAN 315-9272. Tel: 615-963-5211. Interlibrary Loan Service Tel: 615-963-5206. FAX: 615-963-5216. Web Site: www.tnstate.edu/library. *Asst Dir, Coll Develop, Interim Exec Dir,* Glenda Alvin; Tel: 615-963-5230, E-mail: galvin@tnstate.edu; *Head, Cat,* Julie Huskey; Tel: 615-963-5236, E-mail: jhuskey@tnstate.edu; *Head, Ref (Info Serv),* Fletcher Moon; Tel: 615-963-5205, E-mail: fmoon@tnstate.edu; *Head, Spec Coll,* Sharon Hull; Tel: 615-963-5219, E-mail: shull@tnstate.edu; *Syst Librn,* Sherry Ge; Tel: 615-963-5237, E-mail: xge@tnstate.edu; *Coordr,* James Scholz; E-mail: jscholz@tnstate.edu; *ILL,* Toccara Porter; E-mail: tporte19@tnstate.edu; *Webmaster,* Phil Yan; Tel: 615-963-5213, E-mail: pyan@tnstate.edu. Subject Specialists: *Info tech,* Phil Yan; Staff 38 (MLS 18, Non-MLS 20)
Founded 1912. Enrl 8,807; Fac 510; Highest Degree: Doctorate
Library Holdings: CDs 379; DVDs 960; e-books 168,866; e-journals 365; Electronic Media & Resources 210; Microforms 101,140; Bk Titles 402,971; Per Subs 1,637; Videos 4,011
Special Collections: Black History Coll; Jazz Recordings; Tennessee History; Tennessee State University History, art objects, bks, micro, pamphlets, per, pictures & newsp files. US Document Depository
Subject Interests: Agr, Art, Astronomy, Biology, Bus, Criminal justice, Educ, Engr, Ethnic studies, Govt affairs, Hist, Music, Nursing, Sociol
Automation Activity & Vendor Info: (Acquisitions) Innovative Interfaces, Inc; (Cataloging) Innovative Interfaces, Inc; (Circulation) Innovative Interfaces, Inc; (Course Reserve) Innovative Interfaces, Inc; (ILL) Innovative Interfaces, Inc; (Media Booking) Innovative Interfaces, Inc; (OPAC) Innovative Interfaces, Inc; (Serials) Innovative Interfaces, Inc
Wireless access
Function: Accelerated reader prog
Publications: Accession List; Annual Report; Newsletter; Student Handbooks
Partic in LYRASIS; NALA; TBR Consortium; Tenn Acad Libr Collaborative; Tenn-Share
Special Services for the Deaf - TDD equip
Special Services for the Blind - Closed circuit TV
Open Mon-Thurs 7:30am-11:45pm, Fri 7:30-4:30, Sat 9:30-6, Sun 2pm-11:45pm
Friends of the Library Group
Departmental Libraries:
AVON WILLIAMS LIBRARY, 330 Tenth Ave N, 37203. Tel: 615-963-7188. FAX: 615-963-7193. Web Site: www.tnstate.edu/library/avonwilliamslibrary. *Libr Coord,* James Scholz; E-mail: jscholz@tnstate.edu; *Circ Librn,* Mitchell Chamberlain; Tel: 615-963-7190, E-mail: mchamberlain@tnstate.edu; *Ser Librn,* Joyce Radcliff; Tel: 615-963-7383, E-mail: radcliff@tnstate.edu; *User Serv Librn,* Christian Langer; Tel: 615-963-7187, E-mail: clanger@tnstate.edu
Open Mon-Thurs 9am-10-pm, Fri & Sat 9-5:30, Sun Noon-8:30; Mon-Fri 9-8, Sat 8am-Midnight (Summer)

C TREVECCA NAZARENE UNIVERSITY*, Waggoner Library, 333 Murfreesboro Rd, 37210. SAN 315-9280. Tel: 615-248-1214. Reference Tel: 615-248-1570. E-mail: library@trevecca.edu. Web Site: library.trevecca.edu. *Dir, Libr Serv, Univ Archivist,* Andrea T Fowler; Tel: 615-248-1798, E-mail: afowler@trevecca.edu; *Coll Serv Librn,* Beth Purtee; Tel: 615-248-1455, E-mail: bpurtee@trevecca.edu; *Electronic Res & Syst Librn,* Sarah Keil; Tel: 615-248-1353, E-mail: skeil@trevecca.edu; *Ref Serv Librn,* Priscilla Speer; Tel: 615-248-1347, E-mail: pspeer@trevecca.edu; Staff 9 (MLS 7, Non-MLS 2)
Founded 2000. Enrl 2,750; Highest Degree: Doctorate
Library Holdings: e-books 200,000; Bk Vols 90,000
Automation Activity & Vendor Info: (Acquisitions) OCLC Worldshare Management Services; (Cataloging) OCLC Worldshare Management Services; (Circulation) OCLC Worldshare Management Services; (Course Reserve) OCLC Worldshare Management Services; (Discovery) OCLC; (ILL) OCLC WorldShare Interlibrary Loan; (Serials) OCLC Worldshare Management Services
Wireless access
Partic in Christian Library Consortium; LYRASIS; Nashville Area Libr Alliance; OCLC Online Computer Library Center, Inc; Tenn-Share
Open Mon-Thurs 8am-Midnight, Fri 8-6, Sat 10-6, Sun 3-Midnight (Fall & Spring); Mon-Thurs 10-8, Fri 10-6, Sat 10-6 (Summer)

C VANDERBILT UNIVERSITY*, Jean & Alexander Heard Libraries, 419 21st Ave S, 37203-2427. SAN 360-8794. Tel: 615-322-2800. Interlibrary Loan Service Tel: 615-322-2408. FAX: 615-343-7276. Web Site: www.library.vanderbilt.edu. *Univ Librn,* Valerie Hotchkiss; Tel: 615-322-4782, E-mail: valerie.hotchkiss@vanderbilt.edu; Staff 154 (MLS 98, Non-MLS 56)
Founded 1873. Enrl 12,721; Fac 3,526; Highest Degree: Doctorate
Library Holdings: e-books 1,857,106; e-journals 124,261; Bk Titles 3,798,548
Special Collections: UN Document Depository; US Document Depository
Automation Activity & Vendor Info: (Acquisitions) Ex Libris Group; (Cataloging) OCLC; (Circulation) Ex Libris Group; (Course Reserve) Ex Libris Group; (Discovery) Ex Libris Group; (ILL) OCLC ILLiad; (OPAC) Ex Libris Group
Wireless access
Partic in Association of Southeastern Research Libraries; Consortium of Southern Biomedical Libraries; LYRASIS; Nashville Area Libr Alliance; OCLC Online Computer Library Center, Inc; Tenn-Share
Friends of the Library Group
Departmental Libraries:
CENTRAL LIBRARY, 419 21st Ave S, 37203-2427. Web Site: www.library.vanderbilt.edu/central. *Dir, Cent Libr,* Kasia Gonnerman; Tel: 615-322-6892, E-mail: kasia.gonnerman@vanderbilt.edu
Founded 1873

Special Collections: 18th Century French Literature (Morris Wachs Coll); 20th Century French Literature (Pascal Pia Coll); 20th Century French Theater (Gilbert Sigaux Coll); WT Bandy Center for Baudelaire & Modern French Studies. UN Document Depository; US Document Depository
Subject Interests: Art, Humanities, Soc sci
Open Mon-Thurs 7:30am-Midnight, Fri 7:30am-9pm, Sat 10-9, Sun 10-6
Friends of the Library Group

CR DIVINITY LIBRARY, 419 21st Ave S, 37203-2427, SAN 360-8913. Tel: 615-322-2865. Web Site: www.library.vanderbilt.edu/divinity. *Interim Dir,* Bobby Smiley; Tel: 615-875-9702, E-mail: bobby.smiley@vanderbilt.edu
Founded 1894. Highest Degree: Doctorate
Special Collections: Judaica Coll; Kelly Miller Smith Coll
Subject Interests: Relig studies, Theol
Partic in OCLC Online Computer Library Center, Inc
Publications: Franz Rosenzweig: His Life & Work; Lectionary Readings for Reference & Reflection; Nahum Glatzer Archives Register; Vanderbilt University Library Brief History of the Judaica Collection
Open Mon-Thurs 7:30am-Midnight, Fri 7:30am-9pm, Sat 10-9, Sun 10-6
Friends of the Library Group

CM ANNETTE & IRWIN ESKIND FAMILY BIOMEDICAL LIBRARY & LEARNING CENTER, 2209 Garland Ave, 37232-8340, SAN 315-9337. Tel: 615-936-1410. Interlibrary Loan Service Tel: 615-936-1405. Web Site: www.library.vanderbilt.edu/biomedical. *Dir,* Philip Walker; Tel: 615-936-2200, E-mail: philip.d.walker@vanderbilt.edu
Founded 1906. Highest Degree: Doctorate
Special Collections: History of Medicine; Hypnotism (Albert Moll Coll); International Neuropsychopharmacology Archives; Nutrition History (Goldberger-Sebrell Coll, Helen Mitchell Coll, Franklin C Bing Coll, Neige Todhunter Culinary Coll, William J Darby Coll, American Society of Nutrition Scientists Archives); VUMC Archives; VUMC History (University of Nashville)
Partic in Nashville Area Libr Alliance; National Network of Libraries of Medicine Region 2; OCLC Online Computer Library Center, Inc
Open Mon-Thurs 7:30am-11pm, Fri 7:30am-8pm, Sat 10-6, Sun Noon-11pm
Friends of the Library Group

CL ALYNE QUEENER MASSEY LAW LIBRARY, 131 21st Ave S, 37203, SAN 315-9345. Tel: 615-343-8731. Administration Tel: 615-322-2187. Web Site: www.library.vanderbilt.edu/law. *Assoc Dean, Dir, Law Libr,* Larry Reeves; Tel: 615-322-0020, E-mail: larry.r.reeves@vanderbilt.edu
Founded 1874
Special Collections: The Nürnberg Krupp Trial Papers of Judge Hu C. Anderson. US Document Depository
Partic in OCLC Online Computer Library Center, Inc
Open Mon-Thurs 7am-Midnight, Fri 7am-10pm, Sat 9am-10pm, Sun 9am-Midnight
Friends of the Library Group

PEABODY LIBRARY, 230 Appleton Pl, PBM 135, 37203, SAN 360-8972. Tel: 615-322-8098. Administration Tel: 615-322-8866. Web Site: www.library.vanderbilt.edu/peabody. *Dir,* Melissa Mallon; Tel: 615-322-3147, E-mail: melissa.mallon@vanderbilt.edu
Founded 1886. Highest Degree: Doctorate
Special Collections: Curriculum Materials Center; Juvenile Literature Coll; Test & Measurement Coll
Subject Interests: Child studies, Educ, Human develop, Leadership, Psychol, Pub policy, Spec educ
Open Mon-Thurs 7:30am-Midnight, Fri 7:30am-9pm, Sat 10-9, Sun 10-Midnight
Friends of the Library Group

SPECIAL COLLECTIONS & UNIVERSITY ARCHIVES, 419 21st Ave S, 37203-2427, SAN 360-9065. Tel: 615-322-2807. Web Site: www.library.vanderbilt.edu/specialcollections. *Dir, Archives, Dir, Spec Coll,* Juanita Murray; E-mail: juanita.g.murray@vanderbilt.edu
Special Collections: 20th Century Film (Delbert Mann Coll); American Literature & Criticism, 1920 to Present (Jesse E Wills Fugitive-Agrarian Coll); Sevier & Rand Coll; Theatre, Music & Dance (Francis Robinson Coll)
Subject Interests: Hist, Performing arts, Politics, Southern lit
Open Mon-Fri 8-4:30
Restriction: Closed stack, Non-circulating, Off-site coll in storage - retrieval as requested, Photo ID required for access
Friends of the Library Group

SARAH SHANNON STEVENSON SCIENCE & ENGINEERING LIBRARY, 419 21st Ave S, 37203-2427, SAN 378-2247. Tel: 615-322-2775. Web Site: www.library.vanderbilt.edu/science. *Libr Dir,* Honora Eskridge; Tel: 615-343-2322, E-mail: honora.eskridge@vanderbilt.edu
Partic in LYRASIS; OCLC Online Computer Library Center, Inc
Friends of the Library Group

WALKER MANAGEMENT LIBRARY, Owen Graduate School of Management, 401 21st Ave S, 37203, SAN 328-9737. Administration Tel: 615-322-2970. Web Site: www.library.vanderbilt.edu/management. *Dir,* Kelly LaVoice; Tel: 615-343-4182; *Libr Serv Coordr,* Benjamin Darling; E-mail: b.darling@vanderbilt.edu
Highest Degree: Doctorate
Open Mon-Thurs 8am-9pm, Fri 8-8, Sat 10-8, Sun 10-9
Friends of the Library Group

ANNE POTTER WILSON MUSIC LIBRARY, Blair School of Music, 2400 Blakemore Ave, 37212, SAN 360-9006. Reference Tel: 615-322-7696. Web Site: www.library.vanderbilt.edu/music. *Dir,* Holling Smith-Borne; Tel: 615-322-5227, E-mail: holling.j.smith-borne@vanderbilt.edu. Subject Specialists: *Music,* Holling Smith-Borne
Founded 1945
Special Collections: Alfred H. Bartles papers; Appalachian Dulcimer Archive & the David Schnaufer papers; Calypso Interviews Coll; Digital Coll of East African Recordings; manuscripts of contemporary composers; Peabody Seminar in Piano Teaching (audio archive of lectures, master classes, recitals, 1970-76)
Open Mon-Thurs 8am-10pm, Fri 8-5, Sun 2-10
Friends of the Library Group

S WATKINS COLLEGE OF ART & DESIGN LIBRARY*, 2298 Rosa L Parks Blvd, 37228. SAN 315-9361. Tel: 615-383-4848. Circulation Tel: 615-277-7427. E-mail: librarian@watkins.edu. Web Site: www.watkins.edu/campus-life/resources-and-services/library. *Dir,* Amy Kammerman
Founded 1885
Library Holdings: AV Mats 3,173; Bk Titles 17,000; Bk Vols 20,000; Per Subs 60; Spec Interest Per Sub 56
Special Collections: Zine Coll
Subject Interests: Art, Film, Graphic design, Interior design, Photog
Automation Activity & Vendor Info: (Cataloging) LibraryWorld, Inc; (Circulation) LibraryWorld, Inc; (Serials) EBSCO Online
Partic in Tenn-Share
Open Mon-Thurs 9-6, Fri 9-4
Friends of the Library Group

R WEST END SYNAGOGUE, 3810 W End Ave, 37205. SAN 360-876X. Tel: 615-269-4592. FAX: 615-269-4695. Web Site: westendsyn.org. *Librn,* Susan Pankowsky; E-mail: spankowsky@westendsyn.org; Staff 1 (MLS 1)
Founded 1874. Pop 500
Library Holdings: Bk Titles 15,000
Subject Interests: Holocaust, Israel, Judaism
Wireless access
Function: 24/7 Online cat
Restriction: Congregants only, Employees & their associates, Limited access for the pub, Open to students, fac & staff, Visitors must make appt to use bks in the libr

NEWBERN

P NEWBERN CITY LIBRARY*, 220 E Main St, 38059-1528. SAN 315-937X. Tel: 731-627-3153. FAX: 731-627-3129. Web Site: www.cityofnewbern.org/departments/library. *Libr Mgr,* Janice Peevyhouse; E-mail: jpeevyhouse@ci.newbern.tn.us
Founded 1969. Pop 3,000; Circ 31,372
Library Holdings: Bk Vols 12,000; Per Subs 47
Automation Activity & Vendor Info: (Cataloging) Follett Software; (Circulation) Follett Software; (ILL) Follett Software
Mem of Obion River Regional Library
Open Mon 11-7, Tues-Sat 11-5

NEWPORT

P STOKELY MEMORIAL LIBRARY*, 383 E Broadway St, 37821-3105. SAN 315-9388. Tel: 423-623-3832. FAX: 423-623-3832. E-mail: stokelyml@gmail.com. Web Site: sites.google.com/site/cockecountylibraries/stokely-memorial-library. *Dir,* Elizabeth Hall
Pop 34,329; Circ 84,632
Library Holdings: Bk Vols 35,000; Per Subs 30
Special Collections: James Stokely Coll
Subject Interests: Genealogy
Automation Activity & Vendor Info: (Acquisitions) Auto-Graphics, Inc; (Cataloging) Auto-Graphics, Inc; (Circulation) Auto-Graphics, Inc
Wireless access
Open Mon-Sat 10-5
Friends of the Library Group

NIOTA

P NIOTA PUBLIC LIBRARY*, 11 E Main St, 37826. (Mail add: PO Box 515, 37826-0515), SAN 315-9396. Tel: 423-568-2613. FAX: 423-568-3026. E-mail: niotalibrary1@tds.net. Web Site: www.cityofniota.org. *Dir,* Sandra Brakebill
Pop 1,303; Circ 19,051
Library Holdings: Bk Vols 5,000; Per Subs 39

Wireless access
Mem of Ocoee River Regional Library
Open Mon, Tues, Thurs & Fri 12:30-5:30

NORRIS

P NORRIS COMMUNITY LIBRARY*, One Norris Sq, 37828. (Mail add: PO Box 1110, 37828-1110), SAN 315-940X. Tel: 865-494-6800. FAX: 865-494-2600. E-mail: questions@norriscommunitylibrary.com. Web Site: norriscommunitylibrary.com. *Libr Dir,* Kimberlee Byrge
Founded 1934. Pop 9,644; Circ 21,871
Library Holdings: Audiobooks 645; DVDs 1,815; Bk Vols 10,912
Wireless access
Function: 24/7 Electronic res, 24/7 Online cat, Activity rm, Adult bk club, After school storytime, Art programs, Audio & video playback equip for onsite use, Audiobks on Playaways & MP3, Audiobks via web, AV serv, Bk club(s), Bks on CD, Children's prog, Citizenship assistance, Computer training, Computers for patron use, Digital talking bks, Electronic databases & coll, Free DVD rentals, Govt ref serv, ILL available, Internet access, Literacy & newcomer serv, Online cat, OverDrive digital audio bks, Photocopying/Printing, Prog for adults, Prog for children & young adult, Ref & res, Ref serv available, Res assist avail, Scanner, Senior outreach, Serves people with intellectual disabilities, STEM programs, Summer reading prog, Wheelchair accessible
Mem of Clinch River Regional Library
Open Mon-Fri 10-6, Sat 10-2
Friends of the Library Group

OAK RIDGE

G ATMOSPHERIC TURBULENCE & DIFFUSION DIVISION LIBRARY, NOAA Air Resources Laboratory, 465 S Illinois Ave, 37830. (Mail add: PO Box 2456, 37831). Tel: 865-576-1233. FAX: 865-576-1327. Web Site: www.arl.noaa.gov/about/arl-divisions/arl-atdd. *Dir,* Dr John Kochendorfer; Tel: 865-220-1740, E-mail: john.kochendorfer@noaa.gov
Partic in NOAA Libraries Network

SR FIRST UNITED METHODIST CHURCH*, Jones Memorial Library, 1350 Oak Ridge Tpk, 37830. SAN 371-6171. Tel: 865-483-4357. E-mail: fumcor.org@jones-memorial-library/. Web Site: www.fumcor.org. *Library Contact,* Jenny Caughman; E-mail: jcaughman@fumcor.org; Staff 1 (MLS 1)
Founded 1967
Library Holdings: Braille Volumes 2; CDs 20; DVDs 173; Large Print Bks 300; Bk Vols 6,354; Spec Interest Per Sub 22; Talking Bks 30
Automation Activity & Vendor Info: (Cataloging) JayWil Software Development, Inc; (OPAC) JayWil Software Development, Inc
Open Mon-Fri 9-5, Sun 9-1
Restriction: External users must contact libr, Open to pub for ref & circ; with some limitations, Use of others with permission of librn
Friends of the Library Group

P OAK RIDGE PUBLIC LIBRARY*, 1401 Oak Ridge Tpk, 37830-6224. (Mail add: PO Box 1, 37831-0001), SAN 315-9469. Tel: 865-425-3455. Reference Tel: 865-425-3465. FAX: 865-425-3429. E-mail: reference@oakridgetn.gov. Web Site: orpl.ent.sirsi.net. *Dir,* Julie Forkner; E-mail: jforkner@oakridgetn.gov; *Tech Serv Librn,* Martha Lux; *Circ,* Virginia Bayne; *ILL,* Teresa Fortney; Staff 15.3 (MLS 4, Non-MLS 11.3)
Founded 1944. Pop 29,303; Circ 130,036
Jul 2016-Jun 2017 Income $1,400,813. Mats Exp $1,400,813, Books $164,610, Other Print Mats $276,606, AV Mat $8,031, Electronic Ref Mat (Incl. Access Fees) $7,901. Sal $943,665
Library Holdings: AV Mats 9,962; DVDs 5,258; e-books 1,890; Electronic Media & Resources 1,511; Microforms 33,522; Bk Vols 114,172; Per Subs 283
Special Collections: Center for Oak Ridge Oral History Coll; Oak Ridge Room. Oral History; State Document Depository
Subject Interests: Local authors, Local hist, Small bus
Automation Activity & Vendor Info: (Acquisitions) SirsiDynix; (Cataloging) SirsiDynix; (Circulation) SirsiDynix; (OPAC) SirsiDynix; (Serials) SirsiDynix
Wireless access
Function: 24/7 Electronic res, Art exhibits, Audiobks via web, AV serv, Bks on CD, CD-ROM, Children's prog, Computer training, Computers for patron use, Digital talking bks, E-Reserves, Electronic databases & coll, Govt ref serv, Home delivery & serv to seniorr ctr & nursing homes, ILL available, Internet access, Magazines, Magnifiers for reading, Microfiche/film & reading machines, Music CDs, Online cat, OverDrive digital audio bks, Photocopying/Printing, Ref serv available, Spoken cassettes & CDs, Story hour, Summer reading prog, Tax forms, Telephone ref, Wheelchair accessible
Publications: Annual report; Orplines (Newsletter)
Partic in Tenn-Share
Open Mon-Thurs 10-9, Fri 10-8, Sat 10-6, Sun 2-6
Friends of the Library Group

G UNITED STATES DEPARTMENT OF ENERGY*, Office of Scientific & Technical Information, PO Box 62, 37831-0062. Tel: 865-576-1188. Toll Free Tel: 800-553-6847. FAX: 865-576-2865. Web Site: www.osti.gov. *Dir,* Brian A Hitson; E-mail: hitsonb@osti.gov; *Librn,* Catherine Pepmiller; E-mail: pepmillerc@osti.gov
Library Holdings: Bk Vols 4,700,000; Per Subs 50
Special Collections: US Department of Energy Research & Development Reports & Monographs
Publications: Radio Active Waste Mgmt

OAKDALE

P OAKDALE PUBLIC LIBRARY*, 212 Queen St, 37829-3137. (Mail add: PO Box 190, 37829-0190), SAN 315-9485. Tel: 423-369-2595. FAX: 423-369-2595. E-mail: oakdalepubliclibrary@gmail.com. Web Site: oakdalepubliclibrary.wordpress.com. *Dir,* Norma A Mathis
Pop 268; Circ 2,686
Library Holdings: Bk Vols 3,042
Wireless access
Mem of Clinch River Regional Library
Open Mon-Wed 5pm-9pm

OLIVER SPRINGS

P OLIVER SPRINGS PUBLIC LIBRARY*, 610 Walker Ave, 37840. SAN 315-9515. Tel: 865-435-2509. E-mail: os_publibrary@comcast.net. Web Site: oliversprings-tn.gov/906/library. *Librn,* Larissa Walker
Pop 3,500; Circ 5,000
Library Holdings: Bk Titles 5,000
Subject Interests: Local hist
Wireless access
Function: ILL available, OverDrive digital audio bks, Photocopying/Printing, Tax forms, Wheelchair accessible
Mem of Ocoee River Regional Library
Open Mon-Fri 9-5
Restriction: Authorized patrons, Circ to mem only, Non-resident fee

ONEIDA

P SCOTT COUNTY PUBLIC LIBRARY*, Oneida Public, 290 S Main St, 37841-2605. SAN 315-9523. Tel: 423-569-8634. FAX: 423-569-3062. E-mail: oneidapl@highland.net. Web Site: www.townofoneida.com/living/library. *Dir,* Dawn Claiborne
Pop 16,618; Circ 17,620
Library Holdings: AV Mats 895; Bk Vols 12,415; Per Subs 38
Open Mon, Wed & Fri 9-5, Tues 10-7, Thurs 1-7, Sat 9-Noon

PALMER

P PALMER PUBLIC LIBRARY*, 2115 Main St, 37365-9999. SAN 315-9531. Tel: 931-779-5292. FAX: 931-779-5292. E-mail: palmerlib@blomand.net. *Dir,* Greta Carrick; E-mail: palmerdirector@gmail.com
Founded 1956. Pop 726
Library Holdings: AV Mats 183; Bk Titles 3,200; Bk Vols 7,589
Automation Activity & Vendor Info: (Cataloging) Book Systems; (Circulation) Book Systems; (OPAC) Book Systems
Wireless access
Open Mon 1-5, Wed 1:30-6, Sat 9:30-12:30

PARIS

P W G RHEA PUBLIC LIBRARY*, 400 W Washington St, 38242-3903. SAN 315-954X. Tel: 731-642-1702. FAX: 731-642-1777. E-mail: Admin@rheapubliclibrary.org. Web Site: www.rheapubliclibrary.org. *Dir,* Kathy Collins; E-mail: kathy.collins@rheapubliclibrary.org
Founded 1960. Pop 31,185; Circ 79,618
Library Holdings: Bks on Deafness & Sign Lang 31; CDs 861; Bk Titles 51,854; Per Subs 100; Talking Bks 2,179
Subject Interests: Genealogy
Automation Activity & Vendor Info: (Circulation) Auto-Graphics, Inc; (OPAC) Auto-Graphics, Inc
Wireless access
Mem of Obion River Regional Library
Open Mon, Wed, Fri & Sat 9-5, Tues & Thurs 9-7
Friends of the Library Group

PARROTTSVILLE

P PARROTTSVILLE COMMUNITY LIBRARY*, 2060 Canary Dr, 37843. Tel: 423-625-8990. FAX: 423-625-8990. E-mail: parrvillelib@gmail.com. Web Site: sites.google.com/site/cockecountylibraries/parrottsville-community-library. *Dir,* Heather Prince
Library Holdings: Bk Vols 25,000

Automation Activity & Vendor Info: (Cataloging) Follett Software; (Circulation) Follett Software; (OPAC) Follett Software
Wireless access
Open Mon, Wed & Fri 12-6
Friends of the Library Group

PARSONS

P PARSONS PUBLIC LIBRARY*, 105 Kentucky Ave S, 38363. SAN 315-9566. Tel: 731-847-6988. FAX: 731-257-1269. *Dir,* Kay Townsend; E-mail: director.parsonslib@gmail.com
Pop 6,500
Library Holdings: Bk Vols 14,000; Per Subs 12
Automation Activity & Vendor Info: (Cataloging) Follett Software; (Circulation) Follett Software; (OPAC) Follett Software
Wireless access
Mem of Hatchie River Regional Library
Open Mon, Tues, Thurs & Fri 9-5, Wed 9-2
Friends of the Library Group

PETROS

P PETROS PUBLIC LIBRARY*, 208 Main St, 37845. (Mail add: PO Box 147, 37845-0147), SAN 315-9574. Tel: 423-324-0101. E-mail: petrospl1@highland.net. Web Site: www.galepages.com/tel_p_ppl. *Libr Dir,* Patricia Conner
Pop 4,676
Library Holdings: Bk Vols 9,111
Wireless access
Mem of Clinch River Regional Library

PHILADELPHIA

P PHILADELPHIA PUBLIC LIBRARY*, 714 Thompson St, 37846. (Mail add: PO Box 117, 37846-0117), SAN 376-2955. Tel: 865-657-9059. *Libr Dir,* Mark Williams; E-mail: williamsm@loudoncounty-tn.gov; Staff 1 (Non-MLS 1)
Pop 650
Library Holdings: Bk Titles 7,375
Wireless access
Function: Internet access, Photocopying/Printing, Summer reading prog
Mem of Ocoee River Regional Library
Open Tues 9-6, Wed & Thurs 9-5, Fri 9-4

PIGEON FORGE

P PIGEON FORGE PUBLIC LIBRARY*, 2449 Library Dr, 37863. Tel: 865-429-7490. FAX: 865-429-7495. E-mail: library@cityofpigeonforgetn.gov. Web Site: www.cityofpigeonforge.com/library.aspx. *Dir,* Marcia Nelson; Staff 10 (MLS 1, Non-MLS 9)
Founded 2001. Pop 6,000
Library Holdings: AV Mats 5,500; Bk Vols 30,000; Per Subs 86
Special Collections: White House Memorabilia (Tennessee Darling Coll). Oral History
Automation Activity & Vendor Info: (Cataloging) Book Systems; (Circulation) Book Systems; (Course Reserve) Book Systems; (ILL) Book Systems; (OPAC) Book Systems
Wireless access
Function: 24/7 Electronic res, 24/7 Online cat, Accelerated reader prog, Adult bk club, Archival coll, Audiobks via web, Bk club(s), Bks on CD, Children's prog, Computer training, Computers for patron use, Electronic databases & coll, Free DVD rentals, Genealogy discussion group, ILL available, Internet access, Magazines, Magnifiers for reading, Mail & tel request accepted, Meeting rooms, Microfiche/film & reading machines, Movies, Music CDs, Notary serv, Online cat, Outside serv via phone, mail, e-mail & web, OverDrive digital audio bks, Passport agency, Photocopying/Printing, Preschool reading prog, Printer for laptops & handheld devices, Prog for adults, Prog for children & young adult, Scanner, Spanish lang bks, Story hour, Summer reading prog, Tax forms, Teen prog, Telephone ref, Wheelchair accessible
Mem of Clinch River Regional Library
Special Services for the Blind - Reader equip
Open Mon 9-6, Tues & Thurs 8-8, Wed & Fri 8-6, Sat 9-5
Friends of the Library Group

PIKEVILLE

P BLEDSOE COUNTY PUBLIC LIBRARY*, 478 Cumberland Ave, 37367. (Mail add: PO Box 465, 37367-0465), SAN 315-9582. Tel: 423-447-2817. FAX: 423-447-3002. Web Site: sites.google.com/view/bledsoelibrary. *Dir,* Carolyne Knight; E-mail: cknightbcpl@bledsoe.net; Staff 2 (Non-MLS 2)
Founded 1952. Pop 12,500; Circ 17,720
Library Holdings: Bk Titles 14,000; Per Subs 16
Automation Activity & Vendor Info: (Acquisitions) Book Systems
Wireless access
Mem of Falling Water River Regional Library
Open Mon, Wed & Thurs 10-6, Tues & Fri 10-5, Sat 9-2

S TENNESSEE DEPARTMENT OF CORRECTIONS, Bledsoe County Correctional Complex Library, 1045 Horsehead Rd, 37367. Tel: 423-881-3251, 423-881-6395. *Library Contact,* Avis Cagle; E-mail: avis.ann.cagle@tn.gov
Library Holdings: Bk Vols 7,000; Per Subs 14
Restriction: Not open to pub

PINEY FLATS

S ROCKY MOUNT HISTORICAL ASSOCIATION LIBRARY*, 200 Hyder Hill Rd, 37686-4630. (Mail add: PO Box 160, 37686-0160), SAN 326-3223. Tel: 423-538-7396. E-mail: info@rockymountmuseum.com. Web Site: www.rockymountmuseum.com. *Exec Dir,* Cody Boring; E-mail: cboring@rockymountmuseum.com
Library Holdings: Bk Vols 3,600
Wireless access
Open Tues-Sat 11-5

PORTLAND

P PORTLAND PUBLIC LIBRARY OF SUMNER COUNTY*, 301 Portland Blvd, 37148-1229. SAN 315-9590. Tel: 615-325-2279. FAX: 615-325-7061. E-mail: ppl.patronservices@gmail.com. Web Site: www.portlandtn.com/library.htm, www1.youseemore.com/portland. *Libr Mgr,* Debra Elledge; E-mail: ppl.delledge@gmail.com; *Asst Mgr,* Alesia Moss; E-mail: ppl.amoss@gmail.com; *Circ Supvr,* Dorothy Long; E-mail: ppl.delong@gmail.com; *Youth Serv,* Linda Ackerman; E-mail: ppl.lackerman@gmail.com; Staff 10 (Non-MLS 10)
Founded 1953. Pop 27,961; Circ 100,494
Library Holdings: Audiobooks 1,298; AV Mats 2,387; Bks on Deafness & Sign Lang 12; e-books 911; Large Print Bks 900; Microforms 76; Bk Titles 39,156; Per Subs 100
Special Collections: Civil War Coll; NASA Coll; Tennessee History Coll
Automation Activity & Vendor Info: (Acquisitions) TLC (The Library Corporation); (Cataloging) TLC (The Library Corporation); (Circulation) TLC (The Library Corporation); (Course Reserve) TLC (The Library Corporation); (ILL) Auto-Graphics, Inc; (OPAC) TLC (The Library Corporation)
Wireless access
Mem of Red River Regional Library
Partic in Tenn-Share
Open Tues & Thurs 10-8, Wed & Fri 10-6, Sat 10-2
Friends of the Library Group

PULASKI

P GILES COUNTY PUBLIC LIBRARY*, 122 S Second St, 38478-3285. SAN 315-9604. Tel: 931-363-2720. FAX: 931-424-7032. E-mail: glibrary@gilescountylibrary.org. Web Site: gilescountylibrary.org. *Dir,* Cindy Nesbitt; *Acq Librn,* Brianna Stephens; *Teen Serv Librn,* Elizabeth Roller; *Acq, Libr Asst,* Kayla Reichardt; Staff 1 (Non-MLS 1)
Founded 1940. Pop 29,036; Circ 85,000
Library Holdings: Bk Titles 40,000; Bk Vols 44,000; Per Subs 90
Special Collections: Census (microfilms); Museum Coll
Subject Interests: Genealogy, Hist, Local hist
Automation Activity & Vendor Info: (Cataloging) Auto-Graphics, Inc; (Circulation) Auto-Graphics, Inc; (ILL) Auto-Graphics, Inc; (OPAC) Auto-Graphics, Inc
Wireless access
Publications: Bulletin (Quarterly)
Mem of Buffalo River Regional Library
Open Mon & Tues 9-7, Wed-Fri 9-5, Sat 10-4, Sun 1-5
Friends of the Library Group
Branches: 2
ELKTON PUBLIC LIBRARY, 168 Main St, Elkton, 38455. (Mail add: PO Box 157, Elkton, 38455-0157), SAN 376-8082. Tel: 931-468-2506. FAX: 931-468-2993. *Br Mgr,* Kasidy Shaw
Library Holdings: Bk Vols 500
Open Mon-Thurs 8-12 & 12:30-4:30
LYNNVILLE BRANCH, 105 Mill St, Lynnville, 38472. Tel: 931-527-0707. *Br Librn,* Lori Edwards
Open Tues-Thurs 10-5

C UNIVERSITY OF TENNESSEE SOUTHERN*, Warden Memorial Library, 433 W Madison St, 38478-2799. SAN 315-9612. Tel: 931-363-9844. Toll Free Tel: 800-467-1273. FAX: 931-363-9844. E-mail: library@utsouthern.edu. Web Site: www.utsouthern.edu/academics/library. *Dir,* Richard Madden; E-mail: rmadden3@utsouthern.edu; *Cat Librn,* Charlotte Brown; E-mail: mbrow257@utsouthern.edu; *Acq Mgr, ILL, Ser,* Chris VanDoran; E-mail: cvandora@utsouthern.edu; *Pub Serv,* Caitlin Augustin; E-mail: caugust6@utsouthern.edu; *Reserves,* Stephen Smith; E-mail: ssmit259@utsouthern.edu; Staff 5 (MLS 2, Non-MLS 3)
Founded 1975. Enrl 780; Fac 55; Highest Degree: Master

Library Holdings: AV Mats 1,300; DVDs 100; e-books 46,000; Bk Titles 80,000; Bk Vols 84,000; Per Subs 670; Videos 700
Special Collections: Glatzer/Zimmerman Judaica; Gregory McDonald Coll, ms; Methodist History Coll; Psychology (William Fitts Coll); Senator Ross Bass Coll
Subject Interests: Local hist, Methodist hist
Automation Activity & Vendor Info: (Acquisitions) Mandarin Library Automation; (Cataloging) Mandarin Library Automation; (Circulation) Mandarin Library Automation; (ILL) OCLC; (Media Booking) Mandarin Library Automation; (OPAC) Mandarin Library Automation; (Serials) Mandarin Library Automation
Wireless access
Function: 24/7 Online cat, Archival coll, ILL available, Instruction & testing, Laminating, Magazines, Online cat, Online info literacy tutorials on the web & in blackboard, Orientations, Ref & res, Ref serv available, Res assist avail, Scanner
Partic in LYRASIS; Tenn-Share
Special Services for the Blind - Braille bks
Open Mon-Thurs 7:30am-10:30pm, Fri 7:30-3:30, Sun 2-10 (Fall & Spring); Mon & Thurs 7:30am-10:30pm, Tues & Wed 7:30-4:30, Fri 7:30-3:30 (Summer)
Restriction: Circ limited, Non-circulating of rare bks, Open to pub for ref & circ; with some limitations

RIDGELY

P RIDGELY PUBLIC LIBRARY*, 134 N Main St, 38080-1316. SAN 315-9620. Tel: 731-264-5809. FAX: 731-264-5809. E-mail: ridgelylibrary58@bellsouth.net. *Dir,* Kristy Choate
Pop 2,213; Circ 7,504
Library Holdings: Bk Vols 14,699
Wireless access
Mem of Obion River Regional Library
Open Mon-Fri 1-5

RIPLEY

P LAUDERDALE COUNTY LIBRARY*, 120 Lafayette St, 38063. SAN 315-9639. Tel: 731-635-1872. FAX: 731-635-8568. *Dir,* Wanda Clark; E-mail: director.lcl38063@gmail.com
Pop 27,000
Library Holdings: Bk Vols 35,000; Per Subs 24
Subject Interests: Genealogy
Automation Activity & Vendor Info: (Cataloging) Follett Software; (Circulation) Follett Software; (Course Reserve) Follett Software; (ILL) Follett Software
Wireless access
Mem of Hatchie River Regional Library
Open Mon-Fri 9-6, Sat 10-3
Friends of the Library Group

ROCKWOOD

P ROCKWOOD PUBLIC LIBRARY*, 117 N Front St, 37854-2320. SAN 315-9647. Tel: 865-354-1281. FAX: 865-354-4302. Web Site: www.rockwoodtn.org/library.asp. *Dir,* Margaret Marrs; E-mail: mmarrs@comcast.net
Library Holdings: Bk Vols 36,000; Per Subs 50
Automation Activity & Vendor Info: (Cataloging) Follett Software; (Circulation) Follett Software
Wireless access
Mem of Ocoee River Regional Library
Open Mon, Wed, Fri & Sat 10-5, Tues & Thurs 10-8

ROCKY TOP

P ROCKY TOP PUBLIC LIBRARY*, 226 N Main St, 37769. (Mail add: PO Box 157, Lake City, 37769-0157), SAN 315-8349. Tel: 865-426-6762. FAX: 865-426-9235. E-mail: info@rockytoppubliclibrary.com. Web Site: rockytoppubliclibrary.com. *Libr Dir,* Norma Day
Library Holdings: Bk Titles 800; Bk Vols 32,000; Per Subs 35
Wireless access
Mem of Clinch River Regional Library
Open Mon, Tues, Thurs & Fri 9:30-6, Sat 9-2
Friends of the Library Group

ROGERSVILLE

P HAWKINS COUNTY LIBRARY SYSTEM*, H B Stamps Memorial Library, 407 E Main St, Ste 1, 37857. SAN 315-9655. Tel: 423-272-8710. FAX: 423-272-9261. Web Site: www.hawkinslibraries.org. *Dir,* Amy-Celeste Quillen; *Br Mgr,* Melissa Montgomery; E-mail: melissa.montgomery@hawkinslibraries.org; Staff 7 (MLS 1, Non-MLS 6)
Founded 1954. Pop 55,851; Circ 56,332
Library Holdings: DVDs 684; Large Print Bks 578; Bk Titles 43,000; Bk Vols 44,902; Per Subs 41; Talking Bks 1,269; Videos 2,106
Special Collections: Hawkins County History & Genealogy (H B Stamps Coll); Juno Altom Genealogy Room; Tennessee Valley Authority
Automation Activity & Vendor Info: (Acquisitions) Book Systems; (Cataloging) Book Systems; (Circulation) Book Systems; (Course Reserve) Book Systems; (ILL) Book Systems; (Media Booking) Book Systems; (OPAC) Book Systems; (Serials) Book Systems
Wireless access
Open Mon, Wed & Fri 9-5, Tues & Thurs 9-8, Sat 9-1
Friends of the Library Group
Branches: 2
CHURCH HILL PUBLIC LIBRARY, 412 E Main Blvd, Church Hill, 37642. (Mail add: PO Box 37, Church Hill, 37642-0037), SAN 315-7458. Tel: 423-357-4591. FAX: 423-357-8396. *Br Mgr,* Dana Parker
Library Holdings: Bk Titles 17,289; Per Subs 42
Open Mon 9:30-7:30, Tues-Fri 9:30-5:30, Sat 10-2
SURGOINSVILLE PUBLIC LIBRARY, 120 Old Stage Rd, Surgoinsville, 37873-3145, SAN 376-754X. Tel: 423-345-4805. FAX: 423-345-4825. *Br Mgr,* Rachel Franklin; E-mail: rachel.franklin@hawkinslibraries.org
Library Holdings: Bk Titles 5,000; Per Subs 15
Open Mon & Wed 9-5, Tues, Thurs & Fri 2-6

RUTLEDGE

P RUTLEDGE PUBLIC LIBRARY*, 8030 Rutledge Pk, 37861. (Mail add: PO Box 100, 37861-9804), SAN 361-008X. Tel: 865-828-4784. FAX: 865-828-4784. E-mail: rutlib@frontiernet.net. Web Site: rutledgepubliclibrary.wordpress.com. *Dir,* Cathy Reynolds
Founded 1946. Pop 16,751
Library Holdings: Bk Vols 35,000; Per Subs 12
Automation Activity & Vendor Info: (Cataloging) Book Systems; (Circulation) Book Systems; (OPAC) Book Systems
Wireless access
Mem of Clinch River Regional Library
Open Mon, Tues, Thurs & Fri 9-12:30 & 1:30-5

SAVANNAH

P HARDIN COUNTY LIBRARY*, 1365 Pickwick St, 38372. SAN 315-9663. Tel: 731-925-4314, 731-925-6848. FAX: 731-925-7132. Web Site: hardincountylibrary.org. *Dir,* Debbie Brannon; E-mail: debbiebrannon@hardincountylibrary.org; *Asst Dir, Ref Serv,* Connie Lewis; E-mail: connielewishcpl@gmail.com; Staff 9 (Non-MLS 9)
Founded 1935. Pop 26,000; Circ 159,191
Library Holdings: Audiobooks 1,295; Bks on Deafness & Sign Lang 10; CDs 348; DVDs 1,253; e-books 1; Microforms 572; Bk Vols 39,158; Per Subs 77; Videos 495
Special Collections: Spanish Language Coll, bks, tapes. Oral History
Subject Interests: Local hist, Tenn hist
Automation Activity & Vendor Info: (Acquisitions) Auto-Graphics, Inc; (Cataloging) MITINET, Inc; (Circulation) Auto-Graphics, Inc; (Course Reserve) Auto-Graphics, Inc; (ILL) Auto-Graphics, Inc
Wireless access
Publications: Hardin County Library Newsletter (Monthly)
Mem of Hatchie River Regional Library
Open Mon, Tues & Thurs 9-8, Wed 9-12, Fri 9-5, Sat 9-1
Friends of the Library Group

SEVIERVILLE

P SEVIER COUNTY PUBLIC LIBRARY SYSTEM*, King Family Library, 408 High St, 37862. SAN 315-968X. Tel: 865-453-3532. FAX: 865-365-1665. Web Site: www.sevierlibrary.org. *Dir,* Rhonda Tippitt; Tel: 865-365-1416, E-mail: rtippitt@sevierlibrary.org; *Asst Dir, Pub Serv,* Robin Cogdill; Tel: 865-365-1417, E-mail: rcogdill@sevierlibrary.org; *Br Mgr,* Vickie Kelly; Staff 19 (MLS 1, Non-MLS 18)
Founded 1922. Pop 66,000; Circ 146,288
Library Holdings: Bk Vols 70,112; Per Subs 177
Subject Interests: Genealogy
Automation Activity & Vendor Info: (Cataloging) Book Systems; (Circulation) Book Systems; (OPAC) Book Systems; (Serials) Book Systems
Wireless access
Function: Homebound delivery serv, ILL available, Photocopying/Printing, Prog for adults, Prog for children & young adult, Ref serv available, Summer reading prog, Workshops
Mem of Clinch River Regional Library
Open Mon-Wed 9-8, Thurs 10-8, Fri 9-6, Sat 9-5
Friends of the Library Group
Branches: 2
KODAK BRANCH, 319 W Dumplin Valley Rd, Kodak, 37764. Tel: 865-933-0078. FAX: 865-933-5888. *Br Mgr,* John Alexander; E-mail: jalexander@sevierlibrary.org; Staff 3 (Non-MLS 3)
Library Holdings: Bk Vols 16,000
Open Mon, Thurs & Fri 10-6, Tues 10-7
Friends of the Library Group

SEYMOUR BRANCH, 137 W Macon Lane, Seymour, 37865. SAN 320-0647. Tel: 865-573-0728. FAX: 865-579-5288. *Br Mgr,* David Phillips; *Children's Prog Coordr,* Spence Perry; E-mail: rperry@sevierlibrary.org
Library Holdings: Bk Titles 18,000
Open Mon, Tues & Fri 10-6, Thurs 10-7
Friends of the Library Group

SEWANEE

C UNIVERSITY OF THE SOUTH*, Jessie Ball DuPont Library, 178 Georgia Ave, 37383-1000. SAN 361-0144. Tel: 931-598-1664. Interlibrary Loan Service Tel: 931-598-1697. Reference Tel: 931-598-3333. Administration Tel: 931-598-1265. Web Site: library.sewanee.edu/library. *Assoc Provost, Info & Tech Serv,* Vicki Sells; Tel: 931-598-3220, E-mail: vsells@sewanee.edu; *Dir of Coll,* Penny Cowan; Tel: 931-598-1573, E-mail: pcowan@sewanee.edu; *Dir, Info Literacy, Dir, Instrul Tech,* Heidi Syler; Tel: 931-598-1709, E-mail: hsyler@sewanee.edu; *Head, Cat, Head, Spec Coll,* Betsy Grant; Tel: 931-598-1663, E-mail: bgrant@sewanee.edu; *Head, Circ,* Courtnay Zeitler; Tel: 931-598-1837, E-mail: mczeitle@sewanee.edu; *Ser Librn,* Joe David McBee; Tel: 931-598-1574, E-mail: dmcbee@sewanee.edu; *Visual Res Curator,* Mary O'Neill; Tel: 931-598-1660, E-mail: moneill@sewanee.edu; Staff 15 (MLS 9, Non-MLS 6)
Founded 1857. Enrl 1,415; Fac 137; Highest Degree: Doctorate
Library Holdings: Bk Vols 709,873; Per Subs 2,531
Special Collections: Allen Tate Coll; Anglican Prayer Book; Anglican Studies; Ayres Architecture; Episcopal Church in Southeast History; Hudson Stuck Coll; Limited Editions Club Publications; Sewaneena; Southern Literature & History; Ward Ritchie Coll. US Document Depository
Subject Interests: Liberal arts, Theol
Automation Activity & Vendor Info: (Acquisitions) Innovative Interfaces, Inc; (Cataloging) Innovative Interfaces, Inc; (Circulation) Innovative Interfaces, Inc; (Course Reserve) Innovative Interfaces, Inc; (ILL) Innovative Interfaces, Inc; (Media Booking) Innovative Interfaces, Inc; (OPAC) Innovative Interfaces, Inc; (Serials) Innovative Interfaces, Inc
Wireless access
Publications: Friends of the Library (Newsletter)
Partic in Appalachian College Association; Asn of Colleges of the South; LYRASIS; OCLC Online Computer Library Center, Inc
Open Mon-Fri 7:45-5, Sat 9-6
Friends of the Library Group

SHARON

P SHARON PUBLIC LIBRARY*, 133 E Main St, 38255. (Mail add: PO Box 235, 38255-0235), SAN 315-9698. Tel: 731-456-2707. FAX: 731-456-2707. E-mail: sharonpubliclibrary@gmail.com. Web Site: sharonpubliclibrary.weebly.com. *Libr Dir,* Deena Smith; Staff 1 (MLS 1)
Library Holdings: Bk Titles 5,000
Wireless access
Mem of Obion River Regional Library
Open Tues-Fri 8:30-12:30 & 1-4:30, Sat 9-12
Friends of the Library Group

SHELBYVILLE

P SHELBYVILLE-BEDFORD COUNTY PUBLIC LIBRARY*, 220 S Jefferson St, 37160. SAN 315-9701. Tel: 931-684-7323. FAX: 931-685-4848. Web Site: www.sbcplibrary.org. *Libr Dir,* Lis Ann Morehart; E-mail: librarianlisann@gmail.com; *Tech Innovation Librn,* Margaret Petty; E-mail: margaret.sbcplibrary@gmail.com; *Coll Develop,* Doris Segroves; E-mail: dorisjs@bellsouth.net; Staff 8 (MLS 1, Non-MLS 7)
Founded 1948. Pop 47,484; Circ 93,656
Library Holdings: Bk Vols 39,796
Special Collections: History (Early Editions of Newspapers in Bedford County), micro
Automation Activity & Vendor Info: (Cataloging) Auto-Graphics, Inc; (Circulation) Auto-Graphics, Inc; (OPAC) Auto-Graphics, Inc
Wireless access
Function: 24/7 Electronic res, 24/7 Online cat, Activity rm, Adult bk club, Archival coll, Audio & video playback equip for onsite use, Audiobks on Playaways & MP3, Audiobks via web, AV serv, Bk club(s), Bks on CD, CD-ROM, Children's prog, Citizenship assistance, Computer training, Computers for patron use, Digital talking bks, E-Reserves, Electronic databases & coll, Family literacy, Free DVD rentals, Holiday prog, Home delivery & serv to seniorr ctr & nursing homes, ILL available, Instruction & testing, Internet access, Laminating, Life-long learning prog for all ages, Magazines, Mail & tel request accepted, Meeting rooms, Microfiche/film & reading machines, Movies, Online cat, Online ref, Outreach serv, Outside serv via phone, mail, e-mail & web, OverDrive digital audio bks, Photocopying/Printing, Preschool outreach, Preschool reading prog, Prog for adults, Prog for children & young adult, Ref & res, Ref serv available, Res assist avail, Res libr, Res performed for a fee, Satellite serv, Scanner, Senior computer classes, Senior outreach, Serves people with intellectual disabilities, Spanish lang bks, Spoken cassettes & DVDs, STEM programs, Story hour, Study rm, Summer & winter reading prog, Summer reading prog, Tax forms, Teen prog, Telephone ref, Wheelchair accessible, Winter reading prog, Workshops
Mem of Stones River Regional Library
Open Mon, Tues & Thurs 9-8, Wed, Fri & Sat 9-5
Friends of the Library Group
Bookmobiles: 1

SHILOH

G NATIONAL PARK SERVICE*, Shiloh National Military Park Study Library, 1055 Pittsburg Landing Rd, 38376. SAN 315-971X. Tel: 731-689-5275. FAX: 731-689-5450. *Chief of Operations,* Stacey Allen; E-mail: stacy_allen@nps.gov
Founded 1895
Library Holdings: Bk Titles 1,752; Bk Vols 2,373
Subject Interests: Civil War
Open Mon-Sun 8-5

SIGNAL MOUNTAIN

P SIGNAL MOUNTAIN PUBLIC LIBRARY*, 1114 James Blvd, 37377-2509. SAN 371-7380. Tel: 423-886-7323. FAX: 423-886-3735. Web Site: www.signalmountainlibrary.com. *Dir,* Karin Glendenning; E-mail: kglendenning@signalmountaintn.gov; *Asst Librn,* John Atkinson; E-mail: jatkinson@signalmountaintn.gov; Staff 5 (MLS 1, Non-MLS 4)
Founded 1970. Pop 8,640; Circ 65,000
Library Holdings: Bk Vols 30,433; Per Subs 20; Videos 1,500
Subject Interests: Local hist
Automation Activity & Vendor Info: (Cataloging) Book Systems; (Circulation) Book Systems; (OPAC) Book Systems
Wireless access
Function: 24/7 Electronic res, 24/7 Online cat, Activity rm, Adult bk club, Archival coll, Art exhibits, Bk club(s), Bks on CD, Chess club, Children's prog, Computers for patron use, Electronic databases & coll, Free DVD rentals, Holiday prog, Internet access, Magazines, Mail & tel request accepted, Meeting rooms, Movies, Online cat, Photocopying/Printing, Preschool reading prog, Printer for laptops & handheld devices, Prog for adults, Prog for children & young adult, Story hour, Study rm, Summer reading prog, Tax forms, Wheelchair accessible
Special Services for the Blind - Home delivery serv
Open Mon & Thurs Noon-8, Tues & Wed 10-6, Sat 10-2
Friends of the Library Group

SMITHVILLE

P DEKALB COUNTY LIBRARY SYSTEM*, Justin Potter Public Library, 101 S First St, 37166-1706. SAN 361-0209. Tel: 615-597-4359. FAX: 615-597-4329. Web Site: dekalblibraries.net. *Dir,* Kathy Hendrixson; E-mail: khend@dtccom.net
Pop 18,694; Circ 54,403
Library Holdings: AV Mats 4,434; Microforms 556; Bk Vols 33,285; Per Subs 99; Videos 2,865
Automation Activity & Vendor Info: (Cataloging) Book Systems; (Circulation) Book Systems; (ILL) Book Systems
Wireless access
Function: Bks on cassette, Bks on CD, Children's prog, Computers for patron use, Holiday prog, ILL available, Music CDs, Notary serv, Photocopying/Printing, Prog for adults, Prog for children & young adult, Story hour, Summer reading prog, Tax forms, Teen prog, VHS videos, Wheelchair accessible
Mem of Falling Water River Regional Library
Open Mon, Wed & Fri 8:30-5, Tues & Thurs 8:30-7, Sat 8:30-Noon
Friends of the Library Group
Branches: 1
ALEXANDRIA BRANCH, 109 Public Sq, Alexandria, 37012-2141. (Mail add: PO Box 7, Alexandria, 37012-0007), SAN 361-0233. Tel: 615-529-4124. FAX: 615-529-4124. E-mail: alexlib@dtccom.net. *Br Mgr,* George K Combs
Open Mon & Fri 11-5, Wed 1-5, Sat 10-2
Friends of the Library Group

SNEEDVILLE

P HANCOCK COUNTY PUBLIC LIBRARY*, 138 Willow St, 37869. SAN 315-9736. Tel: 423-733-2020. E-mail: hancocklibrary@bellsouth.net. Web Site: hancocklibraryblog.wordpress.com. *Dir,* Lois Rosenbaum
Pop 6,887
Library Holdings: Bk Vols 9,000
Automation Activity & Vendor Info: (Cataloging) Book Systems; (Circulation) Book Systems; (OPAC) Book Systems
Wireless access
Mem of Holston River Regional Library

Partic in National Network of Libraries of Medicine Region 2
Open Mon-Fri 9-5:30

SOMERVILLE

P SOMERVILLE-FAYETTE COUNTY LIBRARY*, 216 W Market St, 38068-1592. SAN 315-9744. Tel: 901-465-5248. FAX: 901-465-5271. Web Site: fayettetn.us/departments/fayette-county-library. *Dir,* Laura Winfrey; E-mail: llwinfrey.sfcl@gmail.com; Staff 2 (Non-MLS 2)
Founded 1931. Circ 33,624
Library Holdings: AV Mats 1,064; Bk Titles 30,000; Per Subs 53
Special Collections: Genealogy (Tennessee Coll); Local History (Museum Room)
Automation Activity & Vendor Info: (Circulation) Follett Software
Wireless access
Mem of Hatchie River Regional Library
Open Mon-Wed, Fri & Sat 9-5, Thurs 12-8
Friends of the Library Group

SOUTH PITTSBURG

P BEENE-PEARSON PUBLIC LIBRARY, 208 Elm Ave, 37380-1312. SAN 315-9752. Tel: 423-837-6513. FAX: 423-837-6612. Web Site: www.marioncountytnlibraries.org/beene-pearson-public-library. *Dir,* Kellye Hogan; E-mail: bppldirector@gmail.com; *Asst Dir,* Jaime Parker; E-mail: beeneassist@gmail.com
Founded 1967. Circ 21,967
Library Holdings: Bk Titles 30,000; Per Subs 19
Wireless access
Open Mon, Wed & Fri 8:30-5, Tues 8-6, Sat 9-2

SPARTA

P WHITE COUNTY PUBLIC LIBRARY*, 11 N Church St, 38583. SAN 315-9779. Tel: 931-836-3613. FAX: 931-836-2570. Web Site: www.wtclibrary.org. *Dir,* Cathy M Farley; E-mail: director@wtclibrary.org; Staff 6.8 (MLS 1, Non-MLS 5.8)
Founded 1957. Pop 26,301; Circ 65,000
Library Holdings: Bk Titles 45,800; Per Subs 42
Special Collections: Census for White County, micro 8
Automation Activity & Vendor Info: (Cataloging) Book Systems; (Circulation) Book Systems; (ILL) Auto-Graphics, Inc; (OPAC) Book Systems
Wireless access
Open Mon & Tues 8-8, Wed-Sat 8-5
Friends of the Library Group

SPENCER

P BURRITT MEMORIAL LIBRARY*, 427 College St, 38585. Tel: 931-946-2575. FAX: 931-946-7978. E-mail: burrittlibrary@blomand.net.
Pop 4,994; Circ 12,962
Library Holdings: Bk Vols 9,000; Per Subs 18
Open Mon 8-4, Tues-Fri 10-4

SPRING CITY

P AUDREY PACK MEMORIAL LIBRARY*, 169 W Rhea Ave, 37381. (Mail add: PO Box 382, 37381-0382), SAN 315-9795. Tel: 423-365-9757. FAX: 423-373-1465. E-mail: library@townofspringcitytn.org. Web Site: library54.wixsite.com/audreypack. *Dir,* Cindy Wilkey
Library Holdings: Bk Vols 19,803; Per Subs 21
Automation Activity & Vendor Info: (Acquisitions) Follett Software; (Cataloging) Follett Software; (Circulation) Follett Software; (ILL) Follett Software
Wireless access
Mem of Ocoee River Regional Library
Open Mon-Fri 8-5, Sat 8-12
Friends of the Library Group

SPRING HILL

P SPRING HILL PUBLIC LIBRARY*, 144 Kedron Pkwy, 37174. Tel: 931-486-2932. E-mail: shlibrary@springhilltn.org. Web Site: springhilllibrary.org. *Libr Dir,* Dana Juriew; E-mail: djuriew@springhilltn.org; *Asst Libr Dir,* Amber Halter; E-mail: ahalter@springhilltn.org
Automation Activity & Vendor Info: (Cataloging) TLC (The Library Corporation)
Wireless access
Mem of Buffalo River Regional Library
Open Mon-Thurs 8:30-7:30, Fri & Sat 9-5
Friends of the Library Group

SPRINGFIELD

P STOKES BROWN PUBLIC LIBRARY*, 405 White St, 37172-2340. SAN 315-9809. Tel: 615-384-5123. FAX: 615-384-0106. E-mail: sbplcustomerservice@gmail.com. Web Site: www.youseemore.com/springfieldpl. *Dir,* Michelle Adcock; E-mail: director@gorhampl.org; *Ch Serv,* Patricia Bellar; E-mail: childrenslib@gorhampl.org
Founded 1923. Pop 44,000; Circ 165,000
Library Holdings: High Interest/Low Vocabulary Bk Vols 400; Bk Vols 45,000; Per Subs 64
Special Collections: Joseph Wellington Byrns Coll
Automation Activity & Vendor Info: (Acquisitions) LS 2000; (Cataloging) LS 2000; (Circulation) LS 2000; (OPAC) LS 2000; (Serials) LS 2000
Wireless access
Mem of Red River Regional Library
Open Mon, Wed, Fri & Sat 9-5, Tues & Thurs 9-8, Sun 2:30-5
Friends of the Library Group

STRAWBERRY PLAINS

P PARROTT-WOOD MEMORIAL LIBRARY*, 3133 W Old Andrew Johnson Hwy, 37871. (Mail add: PO Box 399, 37871), SAN 315-9817. Tel: 865-933-1311. FAX: 865-932-3718. *Dir,* Donna Phillips; E-mail: parrodirector@comcast.net
Founded 1955. Pop 4,000; Circ 13,184
Library Holdings: Bk Titles 7,200; Bk Vols 8,500; Per Subs 30; Talking Bks 112
Automation Activity & Vendor Info: (Circulation) Follett Software; (ILL) Auto-Graphics, Inc; (OPAC) Follett Software
Mem of Clinch River Regional Library
Open Mon & Tues Noon-7:30, Wed 9-5:30, Thurs Noon-6:30, Fri 9-2
Friends of the Library Group

SUNBRIGHT

P SUNBRIGHT PUBLIC LIBRARY*, 142 Melton Dr, 37872. (Mail add: PO Box 23, 37872), SAN 315-9825. Tel: 423-628-2439. FAX: 423-628-2439. E-mail: sunbrightlib@highland.net. Web Site: sunbrightlibrary.wordpress.com. *Dir,* Lonetta Beshears; Staff 1 (MLS 1)
Circ 2,597
Library Holdings: AV Mats 158; Large Print Bks 250; Bk Vols 6,972; Talking Bks 50
Subject Interests: Civil War, Environ issues, Tenn hist, World War II
Mem of Clinch River Regional Library
Open Mon-Thurs 4:30-6:30, Sat 9:30-1:30

SWEETWATER

P SWEETWATER PUBLIC LIBRARY*, 210 Mayes Ave, 37874. SAN 315-9833. Tel: 423-337-5274. FAX: 423-337-0552. Web Site: sweetwaterpubliclibrary.org. *Dir,* Tania Rich; E-mail: LibraryDirector.spl@gmail.com
Library Holdings: AV Mats 556; Bk Vols 33,332; Per Subs 18
Subject Interests: Genealogy, Local hist
Wireless access
Mem of Ocoee River Regional Library
Open Mon-Fri 10:30-5:30
Friends of the Library Group

TAZEWELL

P CLAIBORNE COUNTY PUBLIC LIBRARY*, 1304 Old Knoxville Rd, 37879. (Mail add: PO Box 139, 37879-0139), SAN 315-9841. Tel: 423-626-5414. FAX: 423-626-9481. E-mail: claibornelibrary@gmail.com. Web Site: www.claibornelibrary.org. *Dir,* Sandy Rosenbalm; *Asst Dir,* Teresa Noe; *Asst Librn,* Jami Bell; E-mail: cclibrary2012@hotmail.com
Pop 29,820
Library Holdings: Audiobooks 1,100; DVDs 3,720; Bk Vols 27,760; Per Subs 30
Wireless access
Mem of Clinch River Regional Library
Open Mon-Wed 9-5, Thurs & Fri 9-6, Sat 9-2

TELLICO PLAINS

P TELLICO PLAINS PUBLIC LIBRARY*, 209 Hwy 165, 37385. (Mail add: PO Box 658, 37385-0658), SAN 315-985X. Tel: 423-253-7388. FAX: 423-253-6274. E-mail: TPPublicLibrary@gmail.com. *Libr Dir,* Brenda Bertino
Founded 1992. Pop 6,000
Library Holdings: Audiobooks 200; DVDs 1,200; Large Print Bks 6,000; Bk Vols 18,000

Automation Activity & Vendor Info: (Cataloging) Book Systems; (Circulation) Book Systems; (ILL) Auto-Graphics, Inc; (OPAC) Book Systems
Wireless access
Function: Adult literacy prog, Archival coll, Art exhibits, Audiobks via web, AV serv, Bks on CD, Children's prog, Computer training, Computers for patron use, Digital talking bks, E-Reserves, Electronic databases & coll, Family literacy, For res purposes, Free DVD rentals, Games & aids for people with disabilities, Holiday prog, ILL available, Instruction & testing, Internet access, Laminating, Large print keyboards, Learning ctr, Magazines, Magnifiers for reading, Makerspace, Meeting rooms, Movies, Online cat, Online ref, Outreach serv, OverDrive digital audio bks, Photocopying/Printing, Preschool outreach, Preschool reading prog, Prog for adults, Prog for children & young adult, Ref & res, Ref serv available, Res assist avail, Res libr, Scanner, Senior computer classes, Senior outreach, Serves people with intellectual disabilities, STEM programs, Story hour, Study rm, Summer & winter reading prog, Summer reading prog, Teen prog, Telephone ref, Wheelchair accessible, Winter reading prog, Workshops, Writing prog
Mem of Ocoee River Regional Library
Special Services for the Deaf - Adult & family literacy prog; Am sign lang & deaf culture; Bks on deafness & sign lang
Special Services for the Blind - Aids for in-house use
Open Mon & Fri 9-5, Tues-Thurs 10-5, Sat 10-2
Friends of the Library Group

TIPTONVILLE

P TIPTONVILLE PUBLIC LIBRARY*, 126 Tipton St, 38079-1133. SAN 315-9868. Tel: 731-253-7391. FAX: 731-253-7391. E-mail: tipvle@bellsouth.net. *Dir,* Lori Forrest
Founded 1940. Pop 4,800
Library Holdings: DVDs 36; Large Print Bks 448; Bk Vols 11,512; Per Subs 25; Videos 400
Wireless access
Mem of Obion River Regional Library
Open Mon-Fri 11-5
Friends of the Library Group

TOWNSEND

G US NATIONAL PARK SERVICE, Great Smoky Mountains National Park Library & Archives, National Park Services, 8440 State Hwy 73, 37882. SAN 370-2863. Tel: 865-448-2247. Web Site: www.nps.gov/grsm/learn/historyculture. *Librn & Archivist,* Mike Aday
Library Holdings: Bk Vols 7,200
Special Collections: Naturalists Journals. Oral History
Restriction: Open to others by appt, Staff use only

TRACY CITY

P TRACY CITY PUBLIC LIBRARY*, 50 Main St, 37387. Tel: 931-592-9714. FAX: 931-592-9715. E-mail: tcpublib@gmail.com. Web Site: sites.google.com/view/grundytnlibraries/tracy-city-library. *Libr Dir,* Kami Livesay
Library Holdings: Bk Vols 5,490
Wireless access
Open Mon & Wed 10-4:30, Fri 9-4
Friends of the Library Group

TRENTON

P GIBSON COUNTY MEMORIAL LIBRARY*, 303 S High St, 38382-2027. SAN 315-9884. Tel: 731-855-1991. FAX: 731-562-1992. Web Site: sites.google.com/site/gibsontnlibrary. *Dir,* Lindsey Gilles; E-mail: lindsey@gibsoncountylibrary.com; Staff 3 (Non-MLS 3)
Founded 1945. Pop 46,315
Library Holdings: Bk Vols 26,000; Per Subs 80; Talking Bks 600
Special Collections: Original County Records
Subject Interests: Formal educ support, Genealogical res, Popular mat
Automation Activity & Vendor Info: (Acquisitions) Follett Software; (Cataloging) Follett Software; (Circulation) Follett Software; (Course Reserve) Follett Software; (ILL) Follett Software; (Media Booking) Follett Software; (OPAC) Follett Software; (Serials) Follett Software
Wireless access
Mem of Obion River Regional Library
Open Mon 9-6, Tues-Fri 9-5, Sat 9-1
Friends of the Library Group

TRIMBLE

P HAMILTON PARKS PUBLIC LIBRARY*, 74 Parks Plaza, 38259. SAN 376-7752. Tel: 731-297-3601. E-mail: hamiltonparkspubliclibrary@gmail.com. Web Site: hppubliclibrary.org. *Dir,* Lora Milligan
Library Holdings: Bk Vols 17,000
Wireless access
Mem of Obion River Regional Library
Open Tues & Thurs 10-6, Wed 12-6
Friends of the Library Group

TULLAHOMA

P COFFEE COUNTY LANNOM MEMORIAL PUBLIC LIBRARY*, 312 N Collins St, 37388-3229. SAN 315-9906. Tel: 931-455-2460. FAX: 931-454-2300. Web Site: cocl.ent.sirsi.net/client/en_US/lannom. *Dir,* Courtney Mercurio; E-mail: director@lannom.org
Founded 1947. Pop 25,063; Circ 171,061
Library Holdings: Bk Vols 76,143; Per Subs 12
Special Collections: Genealogy Coll
Subject Interests: Local hist
Automation Activity & Vendor Info: (Acquisitions) SirsiDynix; (Cataloging) SirsiDynix; (Circulation) SirsiDynix; (ILL) SirsiDynix; (Media Booking) SirsiDynix; (OPAC) SirsiDynix; (Serials) SirsiDynix
Wireless access
Mem of Stones River Regional Library
Open Mon, Tues & Thurs 9-9, Wed, Fri & Sat 9-5, Sun 1-5

J MOTLOW STATE COMMUNITY COLLEGE LIBRARIES*, Clayton-Glass Library, 6015 Ledford Mill Rd, 37388. (Mail add: PO Box 8500, Lynchburg, 37352-8500), SAN 315-9914. Tel: 931-393-1670. Reference Tel: 931-393-1665. Toll Free Tel: 800-654-4877, Ext 1670. FAX: 931-393-1516. E-mail: librarygroup@mscc.edu. Web Site: www.mscc.edu/library/clayton_glass.aspx. *Dir of Libr,* Sharon Edwards; E-mail: sedwards1@mscc.edu; *ILL, Ref Librn,* Carla Logue; E-mail: clogue@mscc.edu; *Tech Serv Coordr,* Paula Standridge; Tel: 931-393-1669, E-mail: pstandridge@mscc.edu; Staff 4.7 (MLS 2, Non-MLS 2.7)
Founded 1969. Enrl 4,500; Fac 200; Highest Degree: Associate
Library Holdings: Audiobooks 300; CDs 400; DVDs 1,600; e-books 56,000; Microforms 4,700; Bk Vols 70,000; Per Subs 110; Videos 21,000
Special Collections: Oral History
Automation Activity & Vendor Info: (Cataloging) Innovative Interfaces, Inc - Millennium; (Circulation) Innovative Interfaces, Inc - Millennium; (Course Reserve) Innovative Interfaces, Inc - Millennium; (OPAC) Innovative Interfaces, Inc - Millennium; (Serials) Innovative Interfaces, Inc - Millennium
Wireless access
Function: Electronic databases & coll, ILL available, Magazines, Online cat, Orientations, Photocopying/Printing, Scanner
Partic in TBR Consortium; Tenn-Share
Special Services for the Deaf - TDD equip
Open Mon-Thurs 7:30am-9pm, Fri 7:30-4, Sun 1-5 (Fall & Spring); Mon-Thurs 7:30-6:30, Fri 8-4:30 (Summer)

Departmental Libraries:

FAYETTEVILLE CENTER LIBRARY, 1802 Winchester Hwy, Fayetteville, 37334. (Mail add: PO Box 616, Fayetteville, 37334-0618), SAN 373-9201. Tel: 931-438-0028. FAX: 931-438-0619. Web Site: www.mscc.edu/library/fayetteville.aspx. *Br Coordr,* Elizabeth Lamb; E-mail: elamb@mscc.edu; Staff 1 (Non-MLS 1)
Highest Degree: Associate
Library Holdings: Bk Vols 3,500
Open Mon-Thurs 7am-9m, Fri 8-4:30 (Fall-Spring); Mon-Fri 8-4:30 (Summer)

MCMINNVILLE CENTER LIBRARY, 225 Cadillac Lane, McMinnville, 37110, SAN 373-921X. Tel: 913-668-7010, Ext 2113. FAX: 931-668-2172. Web Site: www.mscc.edu/library/mcminnville.aspx. *Br Librn,* Sharon Kay Edwards; E-mail: sedwards1@mscc.edu; Staff 1 (Non-MLS 1)
Library Holdings: Bk Vols 8,000
Open Mon-Thurs 7:30am-9:30pm, Fri 8-4:30 (Fall & Spring); Mon-Thurs 8-4, Fri 8-1:30 (Summer)

SMYRNA CENTER LIBRARY, 5002 Motlow College Blvd, Smyrna, 37167. Tel: 615-220-7815. E-mail: librarygroup@mscc.edu. Web Site: www.mscc.edu/library/smyrna.aspx. *Br Librn,* John Lichtman; E-mail: jlichtman@mscc.edu; Staff 2 (MLS 1, Non-MLS 1)
Founded 2006
Library Holdings: Bk Vols 2,704
Automation Activity & Vendor Info: (ILL) OCLC
Open Mon-Thurs 7:30am-9:30pm, Fri 8-4:30, Sat 8-3:30, Sun 1:30-5:30 (Fall & Spring); Mon-Thurs 8-7, Fri 8-4:30 (Summer)

UNION CITY

P OBION COUNTY PUBLIC LIBRARY*, 1221 E Reelfoot Ave, 38261. SAN 315-9930. Tel: 731-885-7000, 731-885-9411. FAX: 731-885-9638. Web Site: www.oclibrary.org. *Dir,* Carolina Conner; *Asst Dir,* Beth Micke; E-mail: beth.micke@oclibrary.org; *Circ Mgr,* Reba Hudson; E-mail: reba.hudson@oclibrary.org; Staff 2 (Non-MLS 2)
Founded 1939. Pop 33,000; Circ 164,591
Library Holdings: AV Mats 2,642; Bk Titles 81,517; Per Subs 157
Special Collections: Oral History

Wireless access
Function: Ref serv available
Mem of Obion River Regional Library
Open Mon, Tues & Thurs 9-7:30, Wed 9-6, Fri 9-5, Sat 9-3:30
Friends of the Library Group

VONORE

P VONORE PUBLIC LIBRARY*, 611 Church St, 37885. SAN 373-6636. Tel: 423-884-6729. FAX: 423-884-3804. E-mail: vonorepubliclibrary@yahoo.com. Web Site: sites.google.com/view/vonorepubliclibrary. *Dir,* Nicole Wiggins
Founded 1978. Pop 5,000; Circ 10,750
Library Holdings: Bk Titles 9,500; Per Subs 14
Automation Activity & Vendor Info: (Acquisitions) Auto-Graphics, Inc; (Cataloging) Auto-Graphics, Inc; (Circulation) Auto-Graphics, Inc; (ILL) Auto-Graphics, Inc
Wireless access
Mem of Ocoee River Regional Library
Open Mon, Wed & Fri 10-5, Tues & Thurs 9-5, Sat 10-1
Friends of the Library Group

WARTBURG

P WARTBURG PUBLIC LIBRARY*, 514 Spring St, 37887. (Mail add: PO Box 366, 37887-0366). Tel: 423-346-0201. FAX: 423-346-5177. E-mail: wartburgplibrary78@gmail.com. Web Site: galepages.com/tel_p_wartburg. *Libr Dir,* Patricia Conner
Automation Activity & Vendor Info: (Cataloging) Book Systems; (Circulation) Book Systems; (OPAC) Book Systems
Mem of Clinch River Regional Library
Open Mon-Thurs 11-4:30, Fri 10:30-4, Sat 9-2

WASHBURN

P WASHBURN PUBLIC LIBRARY*, 7715 Hwy 131, 37888-9708. (Mail add: PO Box 129, 37888-0129). Tel: 865-497-2506. FAX: 865-497-2506. E-mail: washlib@frontiernet.net. Web Site: washlib.wordpress.com. *Dir,* Amanda Williams
Library Holdings: Bk Vols 5,300; Per Subs 15
Automation Activity & Vendor Info: (Acquisitions) Book Systems; (Cataloging) Book Systems; (Circulation) Book Systems; (Course Reserve) Book Systems
Wireless access
Open Mon, Tues, Thurs & Fri 9-12 & 1-5

WAVERLY

P HUMPHREYS COUNTY PUBLIC LIBRARY*, 201 Pavo St, 37185-1529. SAN 315-9957. Tel: 931-296-2143. E-mail: humphreyslibrary@bellsouth.net. Web Site: www.facebook.com/people/humphreys-county-public-library/100064591097728. *Dir,* Ethel Carmical; E-mail: ethelcarmical@bellsouth.net
Pop 18,500
Library Holdings: Bk Vols 49,000; Per Subs 35
Automation Activity & Vendor Info: (Circulation) Book Systems; (ILL) Auto-Graphics, Inc; (OPAC) Book Systems
Wireless access
Mem of Red River Regional Library
Open Mon, Wed & Fri 9:30-5, Tues 9:30-8, Thurs 9:30-6, Sat 8:30-1 (Winter); Mon-Fri 9:30-5 (Summer)
Friends of the Library Group

WAYNESBORO

P WAYNE COUNTY PUBLIC LIBRARY*, 525A Hwy 64 E, 38485. (Mail add: PO Box 630, 38485-0630), SAN 315-9965. Tel: 931-722-5537. FAX: 931-722-2385. Web Site: sites.google.com/site/waynecountypubliclibrary. *Dir,* Katherine Morris; E-mail: kathymorris@tds.net
Pop 16,300; Circ 56,642
Library Holdings: DVDs 3,400; Large Print Bks 550; Bk Vols 24,000; Talking Bks 285
Automation Activity & Vendor Info: (Acquisitions) Auto-Graphics, Inc; (Cataloging) Auto-Graphics, Inc; (Circulation) Auto-Graphics, Inc
Wireless access
Open Mon-Fri 9-5, Sat 9-1
Branches: 2
CLIFTON BRANCH, 192 Main St, Clifton, 38425. (Mail add: PO Box 186, Clifton, 38425-0186). Tel: 931-676-3678. FAX: 931-676-3678. E-mail: cliftonlibrary@tds.net. *Mgr,* Terri Letson
Library Holdings: Bk Vols 2,000
Open Tues-Fri 10-5, Sat 9-1
COLLINWOOD DEPOT, 101 E Depot St, Collinwood, 38450. (Mail add: PO Box 410, Collinwood, 38450-0410). Tel: 931-724-2498. FAX: 931-724-2498. E-mail: collinwoodlibrary@tds.net. *Br Mgr,* Tammy West
Library Holdings: Bk Vols 6,000; Per Subs 13; Talking Bks 50; Videos 300
Open Mon-Fri 10-5, Sat 9-1

WESTMORELAND

P WESTMORELAND PUBLIC LIBRARY*, 2305 Epperson Springs Rd, 37186. SAN 376-2939. Tel: 615-644-2026. FAX: 615-644-2025. E-mail: westmorelandpubliclibrary@gmail.com. Web Site: youseemore.com/westmoreland. *Dir,* Cynthia Matthews; E-mail: cmatthews@sumnercountytn.gov
Library Holdings: Bk Vols 18,000; Per Subs 15
Automation Activity & Vendor Info: (Cataloging) TLC (The Library Corporation); (Circulation) TLC (The Library Corporation); (OPAC) TLC (The Library Corporation)
Wireless access
Mem of Red River Regional Library
Open Mon-Wed 9-6, Fri 9-5, Sat 10-3
Friends of the Library Group

WHITE HOUSE

P WHITE HOUSE PUBLIC LIBRARY*, 105 B College St, 37188. SAN 376-3110. Tel: 615-672-0239. Web Site: www.youseemore.com/whl. *Libr Dir,* Elizabeth Kozlowski; E-mail: ekozlowski@cityofwhitehouse.com; *Ch Serv,* Courtenay McLaughlin; E-mail: cmclaughlin@cityofwhitehouse.com; Staff 10 (MLS 1, Non-MLS 9)
Founded 1987. Pop 12,667; Circ 54,400
Special Collections: Gardening (Lida Kirby Ragland Memorial Coll); Home Improvement/Renovation (W A Ragland Memorial Coll); Louis L'Amour Coll
Automation Activity & Vendor Info: (Cataloging) Auto-Graphics, Inc; (Circulation) Book Systems; (ILL) Auto-Graphics, Inc; (OPAC) Book Systems
Wireless access
Function: 24/7 Electronic res, 24/7 Online cat, Adult bk club, Audiobks on Playaways & MP3, Audiobks via web, Bk club(s), Bk reviews (Group), Bks on CD, Children's prog, Computer training, Computers for patron use, E-Readers, Free DVD rentals, ILL available, Internet access, Large print keyboards, Magazines, Movies, Music CDs, Online cat, Photocopying/Printing, Preschool outreach, Preschool reading prog, Prog for adults, Prog for children & young adult, Spanish lang bks, Story hour, Study rm, Summer reading prog, Tax forms, Teen prog, Telephone ref, Wheelchair accessible
Mem of Red River Regional Library
Partic in Tenn Libr Asn
Special Services for the Deaf - Bks on deafness & sign lang
Special Services for the Blind - Bks on CD; Large print bks; Talking bks
Open Mon, Tues & Thurs 9-8, Wed 9-5, Sat 9-4
Restriction: Circ to mem only, In-house use for visitors
Friends of the Library Group

WHITE PINE

P WHITE PINE PUBLIC LIBRARY*, 1708 Main St, 37890. SAN 315-9973. Tel: 865-674-6313. FAX: 865-674-8511. *Libr Dir,* Glenda Jones; E-mail: director@wppl.net
Founded 1920. Pop 12,343; Circ 28,367
Library Holdings: Bk Vols 10,500; Per Subs 36
Subject Interests: Local hist
Automation Activity & Vendor Info: (Cataloging) Follett Software; (Circulation) Follett Software; (ILL) Follett Software; (OPAC) Follett Software
Wireless access
Mem of Clinch River Regional Library
Open Mon, Wed & Thurs 8:30-5:30, Fri 9-3
Friends of the Library Group

WHITEVILLE

P LEE OLA ROBERTS PUBLIC LIBRARY*, 140 W Main St, 38075. (Mail add: PO Box 615, 38075-0615), SAN 315-9981. Tel: 731-254-8834. FAX: 731-254-8805. E-mail: lorlibrary1@gmail.com. Web Site: townofwhiteville.com/upcoming_events/lee_ola_roberts_library. *Dir,* Glenda Doyle
Library Holdings: Bk Vols 8,500
Wireless access
Mem of Hatchie River Regional Library
Open Mon-Thurs 9-6, Fri 9-5
Friends of the Library Group

WHITWELL

P ORENA HUMPHREYS PUBLIC LIBRARY, 13535 Tennessee Hwy 28, 37397. (Mail add: PO Box 8, 37397), SAN 315-999X. Tel: 423-658-6134. FAX: 423-658-7726. Web Site: www.marioncountytnlibraries.org. *Libr Dir,* Cathy Black; E-mail: ohpldir@gmail.com; *Asst Dir,* Chase Hardison
Founded 1959. Pop 6,100
Library Holdings: Bk Vols 18,900; Per Subs 57
Automation Activity & Vendor Info: (Acquisitions) Surpass; (Cataloging) Surpass; (Circulation) Surpass
Wireless access
Open Mon 8:30-6:30, Tues, Wed & Fri 8:30-5, Sat 9-1:30
Friends of the Library Group

WINCHESTER

P FRANKLIN COUNTY LIBRARY*, 105 S Porter St, 37398-1546. SAN 361-0268. Tel: 931-967-3706. FAX: 931-962-1477. Web Site: www.franklincountylibrary.org. *Dir,* Tina L Stevens; E-mail: FCLdirector@franklincotn.us
Founded 1925
Library Holdings: Bk Vols 40,000
Subject Interests: Local genealogy, Local hist
Automation Activity & Vendor Info: (Cataloging) Auto-Graphics, Inc; (Circulation) Book Systems; (ILL) Auto-Graphics, Inc
Wireless access
Function: 24/7 Electronic res, 24/7 Online cat, 3D Printer, Accelerated reader prog, Activity rm, Adult bk club, Adult literacy prog, Archival coll, Art exhibits, Art programs, Audio & video playback equip for onsite use, Audiobks on Playaways & MP3, Audiobks via web, AV serv, Bilingual assistance for Spanish patrons, Bk club(s), Bks on CD, Children's prog, Citizenship assistance, Computer training, Computers for patron use, Digital talking bks, E-Reserves, Electronic databases & coll, Free DVD rentals, Games & aids for people with disabilities, Govt ref serv, Health sci info serv, Holiday prog, Homework prog, ILL available, Instruction & testing, Internet access, Life-long learning prog for all ages, Literacy & newcomer serv, Magazines, Magnifiers for reading, Makerspace, Meeting rooms, Microfiche/film & reading machines, Movies, Music CDs, Notary serv, Online cat, Online ref, Outreach serv, OverDrive digital audio bks, Photocopying/Printing, Preschool outreach, Prog for adults, Prog for children & young adult, Ref & res, Ref serv available, Res assist avail, Res libr, Scanner, Senior computer classes, Senior outreach, Serves people with intellectual disabilities, Spanish lang bks, STEM programs, Summer & winter reading prog, Summer reading prog, Tax forms, Teen prog, Telephone ref, Wheelchair accessible, Winter reading prog, Workshops
Mem of Stones River Regional Library
Open Mon-Fri 8-6, Sat 8-1
Friends of the Library Group

WINFIELD

P WINFIELD PUBLIC LIBRARY*, 275 Pine Grove Rd, 37892. SAN 376-6845. Tel: 423-569-9047. FAX: 423-569-9047. E-mail: towlib@highland.net. Web Site: winfieldpubliclibrary.wordpress.com. *Dir,* Missy Chitwood
Library Holdings: Bk Vols 6,000
Wireless access
Open Mon, Tues & Fri 1:30-5:30, Wed 9-2, Sat 9-12
Friends of the Library Group

WOODBURY

P CANNON COUNTY LIBRARY SYSTEM*, Dr & Mrs J F Adams Memorial Library, 212 College St, 37190. SAN 316-0009. Tel: 615-563-5861. FAX: 615-563-2140. E-mail: cannonlib@dtccom.net. Web Site: adamsmemoriallibrary.org. *Dir,* Marsha Petty; Staff 2.7 (MLS 0.8, Non-MLS 1.9)
Founded 1963. Pop 13,900
Library Holdings: Bk Vols 27,000
Subject Interests: County hist, Genealogy, Local hist
Wireless access
Mem of Stones River Regional Library
Special Services for the Deaf - Adult & family literacy prog; Bks on deafness & sign lang; Closed caption videos; High interest/low vocabulary bks; TTY equip
Special Services for the Blind - Magnifiers; Talking bks
Open Mon, Wed & Sat 9-4, Tues 9-7, Thurs 9-6, Fri 9-5
Friends of the Library Group
Branches: 1
ABURNTOWN BRANCH LIBRARY, 73 E Main St, Auburntown, 37016. Tel: 615-464-2622. FAX: 615-464-2623. E-mail: aublib@dtccom.net. *Br Mgr,* Patti Chappell; Staff 1 (Non-MLS 1)
Library Holdings: AV Mats 100; Bk Vols 4,000; Per Subs 10
Open Wed 1-4, Fri 1-4:30

TEXAS

Date of Statistics: FY 2023
Population, 2020 U.S. Census: 30,029,572
Population Served by Public Libraries: 27,221,057
Total Volumes in Public Libraries: 33,516,389
Total Public Library Circulation: 79,397,672
Digital Resources: 65,539,263
Total computers for use by the public: 16,642
Income and Expenditures:
Total Public Library Expenditures: $673,454,193
Expenditures Per Capita: $24.74 (of population served); $22.43 (of total population)

Appropriation for Library Support Services (Library Development and Resource Sharing, FY 2023)
State: $8,799,350
Federal LSTA: $9,635,755
Other: $6,152,901
Number of Counties Served: 231
Number of Counties Unserved: 21
Number of Bookmobiles in State: 21
Information provided courtesy of: Valicia Greenwood, Library Data Coordinator; Texas State Library and Archives Commission.

ABERNATHY

P ABERNATHY PUBLIC LIBRARY*, 811 Ave D, 79311-3400. (Mail add: PO Box 310, 79311-0310), SAN 316-0017. Tel: 806-298-2546, Ext 22. FAX: 806-298-2968. E-mail: lib@cityofabernathy.org. Web Site: abernathy.ploud.net. *Dir,* Jessica Wilbanks
Founded 1951. Pop 3,570
Library Holdings: DVDs 400; Bk Titles 8,807
Automation Activity & Vendor Info: (Cataloging) Koha
Wireless access
Function: Bks on CD, Computers for patron use, Electronic databases & coll, Free DVD rentals, Internet access, Online cat, Photocopying/Printing, Wheelchair accessible
Open Mon-Fri 8-1 & 2-5

ABILENE

C ABILENE CHRISTIAN UNIVERSITY, Margaret & Herman Brown Library, 221 Brown Library, ACU Box 29208, 79699-9208. SAN 361-0322. Tel: 325-674-2316. Interlibrary Loan Service Tel: 325-674-2398. Reference Tel: 325-674-2941. Administration Tel: 325-674-2348. E-mail: ask@acu.libanswers.com. Web Site: www.acu.edu/library. *Assoc Dean, Libr & Info Serv,* Dr Mark McCallon; E-mail: mccallonm@acu.edu; *Dir, Distance & Online Library Services,* Melissa Atkinson; E-mail: melissa.atkinson@acu.edu; *Head, Research Services & Instruction,* Melinda Isbell; E-mail: mgi12a@acu.edu; *Head, Tech Serv & Govt Doc,* Shan Martinez; E-mail: slm05g@acu.edu; *Head, Spec Coll & Archives,* Mac Ice; E-mail: mxi13a@acu.edu; *Assessment & User Experience Librn,* Laura Baker; E-mail: bakerl@acu.edu; *Cat,* Susannah Barrington; E-mail: sfb21a@acu.edu; *ILL,* Kelsey Weems; E-mail: kew11b@acu.edu; Staff 20.5 (MLS 11, Non-MLS 9.5)
Founded 1906. Enrl 4,700; Fac 230; Highest Degree: Doctorate
Library Holdings: AV Mats 65,213; e-books 221,531; e-journals 45,268; Electronic Media & Resources 120; Microforms 1,200,686; Bk Titles 541,309; Bk Vols 567,006; Per Subs 359; Videos 67,026
Special Collections: Austin Taylor Hymn Book Coll; Bibles; Burleson Congressional Papers; Church Historical & Archival Materials; Donner Library of Americanism; Herald of Truth Radio & Television Archives; Robbins Railroad Coll; Sewell Bible Library. Oral History; US Document Depository
Subject Interests: Educ, Humanities, Relig studies
Automation Activity & Vendor Info: (Acquisitions) SirsiDynix; (Cataloging) SirsiDynix; (Circulation) SirsiDynix; (Course Reserve) SirsiDynix; (OPAC) SirsiDynix; (Serials) SirsiDynix
Wireless access
Function: Archival coll, AV serv, Distance learning, Doc delivery serv, Govt ref serv, ILL available, Internet access, Magnifiers for reading, Photocopying/Printing, Ref serv available, Wheelchair accessible
Publications: Library Friends News (Newsletter); Restoration Serials Index (Bibliographies)
Partic in Abilene Library Consortium; Amigos Library Services, Inc; Llano Estacado Info Access Network; OCLC Online Computer Library Center, Inc; Tex Independent Cols & Univ Librs; TexSHARE - Texas State Library & Archives Commission
Special Services for the Blind - Braille equip; Internet workstation with adaptive software; Magnifiers; PC for people with disabilities; Reader equip; Scanner for conversion & translation of mats; ZoomText magnification & reading software
Open Mon-Thurs 8am-Midnight, Fri 7:30-7, Sat 10-7, Sun 2pm-Midnight
Friends of the Library Group

P ABILENE PUBLIC LIBRARY*, 202 Cedar St, 79601-5793. SAN 361-0357. Tel: 325-676-6025. Circulation Tel: 325-677-2474. Interlibrary Loan Service Tel: 325-437-4561. Administration Tel: 325-676-6328. Web Site: abilenetx.gov/city-hall/departments/community-services/library. *Libr Dir,* Lori Grumet; E-mail: lori.grumet@abilenetx.gov; *Head, Info Serv,* Janis Test; Tel: 325-676-6017, E-mail: janis.test@abilenetx.gov; *Head, Tech Serv, ILL,* Janet Bailey; Tel: 352-676-6063, E-mail: janet.bailey@abilenetx.gov; *Customer Serv Mgr,* Marie Noe; Tel: 325-437-4537, E-mail: marie.noe@abilenetx.gov; Staff 24.5 (MLS 10, Non-MLS 14.5)
Founded 1899. Pop 121,885; Circ 803,163
Oct 2017-Sept 2018 Income (Main & Associated Libraries) $2,803,912, City $2,778,520, Federal $16,520, Locally Generated Income $6,902, Other $1,970. Mats Exp $477,365, Books $206,098, AV Mat $54,539, Electronic Ref Mat (Incl. Access Fees) $216,728. Sal $1,297,428
Library Holdings: Audiobooks 10,775; AV Mats 23,239; CDs 13,515; DVDs 9,717; e-books 44,974; Electronic Media & Resources 43,327; Bk Vols 204,986; Per Subs 144
Special Collections: Texas Coll. Oral History
Subject Interests: Genealogy
Automation Activity & Vendor Info: (Acquisitions) SirsiDynix; (Cataloging) OCLC; (Circulation) SirsiDynix-WorkFlows; (Discovery) EBSCO Online; (ILL) OCLC; (OPAC) SirsiDynix-iBistro; (Serials) SirsiDynix-WorkFlows
Wireless access
Function: 24/7 Electronic res, 24/7 Online cat, 3D Printer, Activity rm, Adult bk club, Audiobooks on Playaways & MP3, Audiobks via web, Bilingual assistance for Spanish patrons, Bk club(s), Bks on CD, Chess club, Children's prog, Computer training, Computers for patron use, Digital talking bks, Doc delivery serv, Electronic databases & coll, Free DVD rentals, Holiday prog, Homebound delivery serv, ILL available, Instruction & testing, Internet access, Laminating, Large print keyboards, Life-long learning prog for all ages, Magazines, Magnifiers for reading, Makerspace, Meeting rooms, Microfiche/film & reading machines, Movies, Music CDs, Notary serv, Online cat, Outreach serv, OverDrive digital audio bks, Photocopying/Printing, Preschool outreach, Printer for laptops & handheld devices, Prog for adults, Prog for children & young adult, Ref serv available, Scanner, Serves people with intellectual disabilities, Spanish lang bks, STEM programs, Story hour, Study rm, Summer reading prog, Tax forms, Teen prog, Telephone ref, Wheelchair accessible, Workshops
Partic in Abilene Library Consortium
Special Services for the Blind - Accessible computers; Assistive/Adapted tech devices, equip & products; Bks on CD; Large print bks; Large screen

computer & software; Screen enlargement software for people with visual disabilities
Open Mon, Tues & Thurs 9-9, Wed, Fri & Sat 9-6
Restriction: Non-resident fee
Friends of the Library Group
Branches: 2
MOCKINGBIRD BRANCH, 1326 N Mockingbird, 79603. Tel: 325-437-7323. Administration Tel: 325-437-2665. *Ad,* Tony Redman; E-mail: tony.redman@abilenetx.gov; *Ch,* Darla Casella; E-mail: darla.casella@abilenetx.gov; Staff 9 (MLS 3, Non-MLS 6)
Founded 2009. Circ 101,799
Function: 24/7 Electronic res, 24/7 Online cat, Activity rm, Bk club(s), Bks on CD, Children's prog, Computer training, Computers for patron use, Free DVD rentals, ILL available, Internet access, Large print keyboards, Online cat, OverDrive digital audio bks, Photocopying/Printing, Preschool outreach, Prog for adults, Prog for children & young adult, Story hour, Summer reading prog, Tax forms, Teen prog, Wheelchair accessible
Friends of the Library Group
SOUTH BRANCH LIBRARY, 4310 Buffalo Gap Rd, No 1246, 79606, SAN 371-3024. Tel: 325-698-7565. FAX: 325-698-7621. *Br Mgr,* Alyssa Crow; Tel: 325-698-7378, E-mail: alyssa.crow@abilenetx.gov; *Ch Serv,* Allison Harvey; E-mail: allison.harvey@abilenetx.gov; Staff 10 (MLS 3, Non-MLS 7)
Founded 1998. Circ 241,445
Function: 24/7 Electronic res, 24/7 Online cat, Activity rm, Adult bk club, Bks on CD, CD-ROM, Children's prog, Computers for patron use, Free DVD rentals, Holiday prog, ILL available, Internet access, Magazines, Meeting rooms, Notary serv, Online cat, Outreach serv, OverDrive digital audio bks, Photocopying/Printing, Prog for adults, Prog for children & young adult, Ref serv available, Scanner, Spoken cassettes & CDs, Spoken cassettes & DVDs, Story hour, Study rm, Summer reading prog, Tax forms, Teen prog, Wheelchair accessible
Open Mon, Tues & Thurs 10-9, Wed, Fri & Sat 10-6, Sun 1-6
Restriction: Non-resident fee
Friends of the Library Group

R CRESCENT HEIGHTS BAPTIST CHURCH LIBRARY*, 1902 N Mockingbird Lane, 79603. SAN 316-0041. Tel: 325-677-3749. E-mail: chbc1902@aol.com. Web Site: www.facebook.com/crescentheightsbaptistchurchabilene.
Founded 1959
Library Holdings: Bk Vols 2,460
Open Mon-Thurs 9-12 & 1-4, Fri 9-12, Sun 10:45-12:30

C HARDIN-SIMMONS UNIVERSITY*, Richardson Library, 2200 Hickory St, 79698. (Mail add: PO Box 16195, 79698-6195), SAN 316-0068. Tel: 325-670-1236. Circulation Tel: 325-670-1578. Interlibrary Loan Service Tel: 325-670-1230. Reference Tel: 325-671-2151. FAX: 325-677-8351. Reference E-mail: hsuref@hsutx.edu. Web Site: library.hsutx.edu. *Univ Librn,* Elizabeth Norman; E-mail: enorman@hsutx.edu; *Cat, Coll Develop Librn,* Dr James Floyd; *Pub Serv Librn,* Jeremy Maynard; *Mgr, Spec Coll,* Mary Burke; *Acq, Supvr,* Martha Lovett; *Cat Supvr,* Jennifer Joye; *Admin & Outreach Coordr,* Shannon Maynard; Staff 7 (MLS 3, Non-MLS 4)
Founded 1891. Enrl 2,300; Fac 115; Highest Degree: Doctorate
Library Holdings: CDs 8,193; DVDs 1,848; e-books 41,693; e-journals 67,899; Microforms 1,012; Music Scores 11,001; Bk Titles 322,045; Bk Vols 174,546; Per Subs 183
Special Collections: Barron Faulkner Col; Clayton Coll; Kelley Bible Coll; Local Historical Photography Archives; Printing of Carl Hertzog; Southwest History Coll, bks, micro; Tandy Bible Coll; Texana Coll. Oral History; US Document Depository
Subject Interests: Educ, English, Hist, Music, Theol
Automation Activity & Vendor Info: (Acquisitions) SirsiDynix; (Cataloging) SirsiDynix; (Circulation) SirsiDynix; (Course Reserve) SirsiDynix; (Discovery) EBSCO Discovery Service; (ILL) OCLC WorldShare Interlibrary Loan; (OPAC) SirsiDynix; (Serials) SirsiDynix
Wireless access
Partic in Abilene Library Consortium; Amigos Library Services, Inc; OCLC Online Computer Library Center, Inc; TexSHARE - Texas State Library & Archives Commission
Open Mon-Thurs 7:30am-Midnight, Fri 7:30-5, Sun 3-Midnight

M HENDRICK MEDICAL CENTER*, Sellers Health Sciences Library, 1900 Pine St, 79601. SAN 327-6821. Tel: 325-670-2375. FAX: 325-670-2422. Web Site: www.ehendrick.org. *Library Contact,* Colleen Roberson; E-mail: croberson@ehendrick.org
Library Holdings: AV Mats 1,000; Bk Titles 1,200
Automation Activity & Vendor Info: (Acquisitions) Follett Software; (Cataloging) Follett Software; (Circulation) Follett Software; (Course Reserve) Follett Software; (ILL) Follett Software; (Media Booking) Follett Software; (OPAC) Follett Software; (Serials) Follett Software
Partic in Medical Library Association
Open Mon-Fri 8:30-11:30 & 12:30-4:30

C MCMURRY UNIVERSITY*, Jay-Rollins Library, Bldg 1601 War Hawk Way, One McMurry University # 218, 79697. SAN 316-0084. Tel: 325-793-4692. FAX: 325-793-4930. E-mail: mcmurry.library@mcm.edu. Web Site: library.mcm.edu. *Dir,* Terry S Young; Tel: 325-793-4690, E-mail: youngt@mcm.edu; *Cat Serv Librn,* Amanda Vickers; Tel: 325-793-4684, E-mail: vickers.amanda@mcm.edu; *ILL Librn, Ref,* Keith Waddle, PhD; Tel: 325-793-4678, E-mail: waddle.keith@mcm.edu; *Circ Asst,* Charlie Stanford; Tel: 325-793-4688, E-mail: stanford.charles@mcm.edu; Staff 5 (MLS 3, Non-MLS 2)
Founded 1923. Enrl 1,073; Fac 90; Highest Degree: Master
Library Holdings: Bk Titles 128,602; Bk Vols 151,700; Per Subs 110
Special Collections: E L & A W Yeats Coll; Hunt Library of Texana & Southwest
Subject Interests: 20th Century Am popular culture, 20th Century British, African-Am studies, Am, Relig studies, Spanish-Am lit
Automation Activity & Vendor Info: (Acquisitions) SirsiDynix; (Cataloging) SirsiDynix; (Circulation) SirsiDynix; (Course Reserve) SirsiDynix; (OPAC) SirsiDynix; (Serials) SirsiDynix
Wireless access
Partic in Abilene Library Consortium; Amigos Library Services, Inc
Open Mon-Thurs 7:30am-Midnight, Fri 7:30-5, Sun 2-Midnight
Friends of the Library Group

ALAMO

P SARGEANT FERNANDO DE LA ROSA MEMORIAL LIBRARY*, 416 N Tower Rd, 78516-2795. SAN 322-7529. Tel: 956-787-6160. FAX: 956-787-5154. Web Site: alamolibrary.com. *Libr Dir,* Laura Solis; E-mail: lsolis@alamotexas.org; Staff 1 (Non-MLS 1)
Founded 1980
Library Holdings: Bk Titles 27,000; Bk Vols 28,000; Per Subs 54
Wireless access
Mem of Hidalgo County Library System
Special Services for the Deaf - Bks on deafness & sign lang
Open Mon-Thurs 8-8, Fri 8-5, Sat 10-4
Friends of the Library Group

ALBANY

S THE OLD JAIL ART CENTER, Green Art Research Library, 201 S Second St, 76430. Tel: 325-762-2269. Web Site: theojac.org/green-art-research-library. *Archivist/Librn,* Molly Sauder; E-mail: msauder@theojac.org
Library Holdings: Bk Vols 3,000
Wireless access
Partic in Abilene Library Consortium
Open Tues-Sat 11-5
Restriction: Non-circulating

P SHACKELFORD COUNTY LIBRARY*, 402 N Second St, 76430. (Mail add: PO Box 2167, 76430-8007), SAN 316-0092. Tel: 325-762-2672. FAX: 325-762-2672. E-mail: albanylib@gmail.com. Web Site: albany.ploud.net. *Librn,* Carolyn Waller; *Tech,* Janna Ledbetter
Founded 1956. Pop 3,915
Library Holdings: Bk Vols 8,200; Talking Bks 300
Automation Activity & Vendor Info: (Cataloging) Follett Software; (Circulation) Follett Software
Wireless access
Open Mon, Tues, Thurs & Fri 12-5:30, Wed 10-5

ALEDO

P ALEDO PUBLIC LIBRARY, (Formerly East Parker County Library), 201 FM 1187 N, 76008. SAN 372-5847. Tel: 817-441-6545, 817-769-9313. E-mail: library@aledotx.gov. *Dir,* Beck Gorman; Tel: 817-769-9443, E-mail: librarydirector@aledotx.gov; Staff 7 (MLS 1, Non-MLS 6)
Founded 1988. Pop 13,454
Library Holdings: Bk Titles 1,800
Special Collections: Parker County History Coll
Wireless access
Function: 24/7 Electronic res, 24/7 Online cat, 24/7 wireless access, 3D Printer, Adult bk club, Audiobks via web, Bks on CD, Children's prog, Computer training, Computers for patron use, Electronic databases & coll, Free DVD rentals, Games, Holiday prog, ILL available, Internet access, OverDrive digital audio bks, Photocopying/Printing, Prog for adults, Prog for children & young adult, Ref & res, Scanner, STEM programs, Story hour, Summer reading prog, Teen prog
Open Tues-Fri 10-6, Sat 10-1
Restriction: In-house use for visitors

ALICE

P ALICIA SALINAS CITY OF ALICE PUBLIC LIBRARY*, 401 E Third St, 78332. SAN 361-0446. Tel: 361-664-9506, 361-664-9507. Web Site: youseemore.com/alice. *Dir,* Yolanda Bueno; E-mail: buenoy@cityofalice.org; *Ref Librn,* Jeanine Bertuca

Founded 1932. Pop 25,000; Circ 259,000
Library Holdings: Bk Vols 99,000; Per Subs 175
Subject Interests: Spanish lang, Tex hist
Automation Activity & Vendor Info: (Acquisitions) TLC (The Library Corporation); (Cataloging) TLC (The Library Corporation); (Circulation) TLC (The Library Corporation); (OPAC) TLC (The Library Corporation); (Serials) TLC (The Library Corporation)
Wireless access
Open Mon-Fri 9-6
Friends of the Library Group
Branches: 1
ORANGE GROVE SCHOOL & PUBLIC LIBRARY, 505 S Dibrell St, Orange Grove, 78372, SAN 361-0470. Tel: 361-384-2330, Ext 505, 361-384-2461. *District Librn,* Lisa Jurecek
Library Holdings: Bk Vols 26,000
Open Mon 8-7, Tues-Fri 8-4

ALLEN

P ALLEN PUBLIC LIBRARY*, 300 N Allen Dr, 75013. SAN 316-0106. Tel: 214-509-4900. FAX: 469-342-6672. Web Site: www.cityofallen.org/900/Allen-Public-Library. *Dir,* Jeff Timbs; Tel: 214-509-4902, E-mail: jtimbs@cityofallen.org; *Sr Ref Librn,* Cindy Deboer; Tel: 214-509-4905, E-mail: cdeboer@cityofallen.org; Staff 11 (MLS 11)
Founded 1967. Pop 79,000; Circ 509,400
Library Holdings: AV Mats 11,171; Bk Titles 121,000; Bk Vols 123,600; Per Subs 150
Automation Activity & Vendor Info: (Acquisitions) Innovative Interfaces, Inc; (Cataloging) Innovative Interfaces, Inc; (Circulation) Innovative Interfaces, Inc; (OPAC) Innovative Interfaces, Inc; (Serials) Innovative Interfaces, Inc
Wireless access
Partic in Amigos Library Services, Inc
Open Mon-Thurs 10-9, Fri & Sat 10-6, Sun 1-5
Friends of the Library Group

ALPINE

P ALPINE PUBLIC LIBRARY*, 805 W Ave E, 79830. SAN 361-0535. Tel: 432-837-2621. FAX: 432-837-2501. E-mail: desk@alpinepubliclibrary.org. Web Site: alpinepubliclibrary.org. *Dir,* Don Wetterauer; E-mail: don@alpinepubliclibrary.org; *Ch,* Mary Beth Garrett; E-mail: kids@alpinepubliclibrary.org; Staff 10 (MLS 1, Non-MLS 9)
Founded 1947. Pop 8,129; Circ 83,747
Library Holdings: Audiobooks 850; DVDs 2,114; Bk Titles 26,141; Per Subs 25
Special Collections: Genealogical Coll
Subject Interests: World War II
Wireless access
Function: 24/7 Electronic res, 24/7 Online cat, 3D Printer, Accelerated reader prog, Adult literacy prog, After school storytime
Partic in Partners Library Action Network
Open Mon 9-1, Tues-Fri 9:30-5:30, Sat 9-1
Friends of the Library Group
Branches: 1
MARATHON PUBLIC, 106 N Third St E, Marathon, 79842. (Mail add: PO Box 177, Marathon, 79842-0177), SAN 361-056X. Tel: 432-386-4136. FAX: 432-386-4136. E-mail: marathonpl@sbcglobal.net. *Br Mgr,* Carol Townsend
Library Holdings: Bk Titles 8,000
Automation Activity & Vendor Info: (Cataloging) Biblionix; (Circulation) Biblionix
Open Mon-Fri 11-5
Friends of the Library Group

C SUL ROSS STATE UNIVERSITY*, Bryan Wildenthal Memorial Library, PO Box C-109, 79832. SAN 316-0114. Tel: 432-837-8123. FAX: 432-837-8400. E-mail: SRSUlibrary@sulross.edu. Web Site: library.sulross.edu. *Dean, Libr & Info Tech,* April Aultman Becker; E-mail: april.becker@sulross.edu; *Dir of Access, Instruction & Outreach,* Betsy Evans; E-mail: betsy.evans@sulross.edu; *Coll Develop Librn,* Elizabeth Davis; E-mail: elizabeth.davis@sulross.edu; *Sr Archivist,* Melleta Bell; E-mail: mbell@sulross.edu; Staff 18 (MLS 7, Non-MLS 11)
Founded 1920. Enrl 2,274; Fac 136; Highest Degree: Master
Library Holdings: Bk Vols 221,000; Per Subs 1,245
Special Collections: Archives of the Big Bend. State Document Depository
Subject Interests: Big Bend region of Tex
Automation Activity & Vendor Info: (Acquisitions) SirsiDynix
Wireless access
Partic in Amigos Library Services, Inc; OCLC Online Computer Library Center, Inc; TexSHARE - Texas State Library & Archives Commission
Open Mon-Wed 8am-9pm, Thurs 8-7, Fri 8-5, Sat & Sun 1-5

ALTO

P STELLA HILL MEMORIAL LIBRARY*, 158 W San Antonio St, 75925. (Mail add: PO Box 98, 75925-0098), SAN 316-0122. Tel: 936-858-4343. E-mail: altolibrary@gmail.com. *Dir,* Virginia Singletary
Founded 1957. Pop 1,045; Circ 4,500
Library Holdings: Bk Vols 13,000
Special Collections: Local Hist (incl negatives)
Wireless access
Open Tues & Thurs 2-5, Wed 4-7, Sat 9-12

ALVARADO

P ALVARADO PUBLIC LIBRARY*, 210 N Baugh St, 76009. SAN 370-5064. Tel: 817-783-7323. Web Site: www.alvaradopubliclibrary.org. *Dir,* Precious Moore; E-mail: moorep@cityofalvarado.org; Staff 4 (Non-MLS 4)
Founded 1989. Pop 4,289
Library Holdings: Audiobooks 659; Bks on Deafness & Sign Lang 13; CDs 787; DVDs 3,972; Large Print Bks 176; Microforms 64; Bk Titles 26,648; Bk Vols 26,981; Per Subs 2; Videos 494
Automation Activity & Vendor Info: (Cataloging) Evergreen; (Circulation) Evergreen; (OPAC) Evergreen
Wireless access
Function: 24/7 Online cat, Activity rm, Adult bk club, Art programs, Bilingual assistance for Spanish patrons, Bks on CD, Children's prog, Computer training, Computers for patron use, Electronic databases & coll, Holiday prog, Homebound delivery serv, ILL available, Internet access, Large print keyboards, Magnifiers for reading, Meeting rooms, Microfiche/film & reading machines, Movies, Music CDs, Online cat, Photocopying/Printing, Scanner, Story hour, Teen prog, VHS videos, Wheelchair accessible, Winter reading prog, Workshops
Partic in North Texas Library Consortium
Open Mon-Fri 10-7, Sat 10-1
Restriction: Non-resident fee

ALVIN

J ALVIN COMMUNITY COLLEGE LIBRARY*, 3110 Mustang Rd, 77511. SAN 316-0130. Tel: 281-756-3559. Circulation Tel: 281-756-3562. FAX: 281-756-3854. Web Site: alvincollege.edu/Library. *Head Librn,* Nadia Nazarenko; E-mail: nnazarenko@alvincollege.edu; Staff 2 (MLS 2)
Founded 1948. Enrl 3,800; Fac 102; Highest Degree: Associate
Library Holdings: Bk Titles 12,100; Bk Vols 26,000; Per Subs 43; Spec Interest Per Sub 23
Automation Activity & Vendor Info: (Cataloging) SirsiDynix; (Circulation) SirsiDynix; (Course Reserve) SirsiDynix; (OPAC) SirsiDynix; (Serials) SirsiDynix
Wireless access
Partic in Amigos Library Services, Inc; TexSHARE - Texas State Library & Archives Commission
Special Services for the Deaf - TDD equip
Special Services for the Blind - Computer with voice synthesizer for visually impaired persons
Open Mon-Thurs 7:30am-9pm, Fri 7:30-5, Sun 9-1 (Fall & Spring); Mon-Thurs 7:30am-9pm (Summer)
Restriction: Open to students

ALVORD

P ALVORD PUBLIC LIBRARY, 109 N Wickham St, 76225-5325. (Mail add: PO Box 63, 76225-0323), SAN 376-4699. Tel: 940-427-2842. E-mail: alvordpl@hotmail.com. Web Site: alvord.ploud.net. *Libr Dir,* Pamela AlHusaini; Staff 1 (MLS 1)
Founded 1982. Pop 2,322; Circ 3,725
Library Holdings: Audiobooks 517; AV Mats 1,332; DVDs 615; e-books 50; Bk Vols 15,643; Per Subs 17; Videos 615
Special Collections: Local History & Genealogy Coll
Automation Activity & Vendor Info: (Acquisitions) LRMS, Inc (Library Resource Management Systems); (Cataloging) LRMS, Inc (Library Resource Management Systems); (Circulation) LRMS, Inc (Library Resource Management Systems); (Course Reserve) LRMS, Inc (Library Resource Management Systems); (ILL) LRMS, Inc (Library Resource Management Systems); (Media Booking) LRMS, Inc (Library Resource Management Systems); (OPAC) LRMS, Inc (Library Resource Management Systems); (Serials) LRMS, Inc (Library Resource Management Systems)
Wireless access
Partic in Partners Library Action Network; TexSHARE - Texas State Library & Archives Commission
Open Tues 1-6, Wed-Fri 9-5, Sat 10-1

AMARILLO

J AMARILLO COLLEGE*, Lucille King Lynn Library, 2201 S Washington, 79109. (Mail add: PO Box 447, 79178-0001), SAN 361-0594. Tel: 806-371-5400. Reference Tel: 806-371-5468. Toll Free Tel: 866-371-5468. Web Site: www.actx.edu/library. *Dir,* Emily Gilbert; Tel: 806-371-5403, E-mail: ergilbert@actx.edu; *Asst Dir,* Mindy Weathersbee; Tel: 806-371-5462, E-mail: mlweathersbee@actx.edu; *Librn,* Melissa Eder; Tel: 806-345-5582, E-mail: mseder@actx.edu; *Librn,* Hanna Homfeld; Tel: 806-371-5419, E-mail: h039034@actx.edu; *Circ Supvr,* Jesse Starr; Tel: 806-371-5386, E-mail: jnstarr@actx.edu; Staff 5 (MLS 4, Non-MLS 1)
Founded 1929. Enrl 10,873; Fac 214; Highest Degree: Associate
Library Holdings: e-books 54,668; Bk Titles 20,400; Bk Vols 44,600
Automation Activity & Vendor Info: (Acquisitions) SirsiDynix; (Cataloging) SirsiDynix; (Circulation) SirsiDynix; (Course Reserve) SirsiDynix; (OPAC) SirsiDynix; (Serials) SirsiDynix
Wireless access
Partic in Harrington Library Consortium; TexSHARE - Texas State Library & Archives Commission
Open Mon-Fri 7:30am-9pm, Sun 2-6
Departmental Libraries:
WEST CAMPUS, 6100 W Ninth Ave, 79106. Tel: 806-356-3627. *Campus Librn,* Dee Ann Poynor; E-mail: dee.poyner22@actx.edu
Library Holdings: e-books 24,000

S AMARILLO MUSEUM OF ART LIBRARY*, 2200 S Van Buren St, 79109-2407. SAN 316-0149. Tel: 806-371-5050. E-mail: amoa@actx.edu. Web Site: amoa.org. *Exec Dir,* Kim Mahan; E-mail: kbmahan@actx.edu; *Dir, Mkt,* Claire Ekas; E-mail: claire.ekas@actx.edu
Founded 1972
Library Holdings: Bk Vols 600
Subject Interests: Archit, Art
Wireless access
Open Wed-Sat 11-5, Sun 1-5
Restriction: Open to pub for ref only

P AMARILLO PUBLIC LIBRARY*, 413 E Fourth Ave, 79101. (Mail add: PO Box 2171, 79105-2171), SAN 361-0659. Tel: 806-378-3054. Interlibrary Loan Service Tel: 806-378-3053. FAX: 806-378-9327. TDD: 806-378-9328. Web Site: www.amarillolibrary.org. *Dir,* Amanda Barrera; Tel: 806-378-3050, E-mail: amanda.barrera@amarillolibrary.org; *Asst Dir,* Position Currently Open; *Emerging Tech Librn,* Ben Wilting; E-mail: benjamin.wilting@amarillolibrary.org; *Acq & Cat,* Catherine Urban; E-mail: catherine.urban@amarillolibrary.org; *Circ,* Connie Lomeli; E-mail: connie.lomeli@amarillolibrary.org; *ILL,* Toshia Sanchez; E-mail: toshia.sanchez@amarillolibrary.org; *Literacy Serv,* Lisa White; E-mail: lisa.white@amarillolibrary.org; *Ref,* Sam Jones; E-mail: sam.jones@amarillolibrary.org; *Youth Serv,* Melody Boren; E-mail: melody.boren@amarillolibrary.org; Staff 69 (MLS 8, Non-MLS 61)
Founded 1902. Pop 179,287; Circ 2,030,752
Library Holdings: Audiobooks 16,065; DVDs 45,693; e-books 5,455; Bk Titles 197,492; Bk Vols 385,105; Per Subs 92
Special Collections: Southwestern History (William H Bush & Laurence J Fitzsimon Coll), bks, maps
Subject Interests: Genealogy
Automation Activity & Vendor Info: (Acquisitions) SirsiDynix; (Cataloging) SirsiDynix; (Circulation) SirsiDynix; (ILL) SirsiDynix; (OPAC) SirsiDynix; (Serials) SirsiDynix
Wireless access
Function: 24/7 Electronic res, 24/7 Online cat, Adult bk club, Adult literacy prog, After school storytime, Audiobks via web, AV serv, Bilingual assistance for Spanish patrons, Bk club(s), Bks on CD, Children's prog, Citizenship assistance, Computer training, Computers for patron use, Electronic databases & coll, Family literacy, Free DVD rentals, Genealogy discussion group, Holiday prog, ILL available, Internet access, Life-long learning prog for all ages, Magazines, Mail & tel request accepted, Meeting rooms, Microfiche/film & reading machines, Movies, Music CDs, Online cat, Online ref, Orientations, Outreach serv, Outside serv via phone, mail, e-mail & web, Photocopying/Printing, Preschool outreach, Prog for adults, Prog for children & young adult, Ref serv available, Scanner, Senior outreach, Spanish lang bks, Spoken cassettes & CDs, STEM programs, Story hour, Study rm, Summer & winter reading prog, Summer reading prog, Tax forms, Teen prog, Telephone ref, Wheelchair accessible
Publications: Bibliography of the Bush-FitzSimon-McCarty Southwestern Collections
Partic in Amigos Library Services, Inc; Harrington Library Consortium; OCLC Online Computer Library Center, Inc
Special Services for the Deaf - TTY equip
Open Mon-Thurs 9-9, Fri & Sat 9-6, Sun 2-6
Restriction: Non-resident fee
Friends of the Library Group
Branches: 4
EAST BRANCH, 2232 E 27th St, 79103, SAN 361-0683. Tel: 806-342-1589. FAX: 806-342-1591. *Br Mgr,* Jacob Workman; E-mail: jacob.workman@amarillolibrary.org
Library Holdings: Bk Vols 121,181
Open Mon & Tues Noon-9, Wed-Sat 9-6, Sun 2-6
Friends of the Library Group
NORTH BRANCH, 1500 NE 24th St, 79107, SAN 361-0713. Tel: 806-381-7931. FAX: 806-381-7929. *Br Mgr,* Shaun McDonald; E-mail: shaun.mcdonald@amarillolibrary.org
Library Holdings: Bk Vols 129,811
Open Mon & Tues Noon-9, Wed-Sat 9-6, Sun 2-6
Friends of the Library Group
NORTHWEST BRANCH, 6100 W Ninth, 79106. Tel: 806-359-2035. FAX: 806-359-2037. *Br Mgr,* Jon Barnes; E-mail: jon.barnes@amarillolibrary.org
Library Holdings: Bk Vols 212,000
Open Mon & Tues Noon-9, Wed-Sat 9-6, Sun 2-6
Friends of the Library Group
SOUTHWEST BRANCH, 6801 W 45th St, 79109, SAN 361-0748. Tel: 806-359-2094. FAX: 806-359-2096. *Br Mgr,* Valisa McHugh; E-mail: valisa.mchugh@amarillolibrary.org
Library Holdings: e-books 2,368; Bk Vols 547,646
Open Mon-Thurs 9-9, Fri & Sat 9-6, Sun 2-6
Friends of the Library Group

R ROMAN CATHOLIC DIOCESE OF AMARILLO*, Diocesan Archives, 4512 NE 24th Ave, 79107-8225. (Mail add: PO Box 5644, 79117-5644), SAN 372-9605. Tel: 806-383-2243, Ext 120. Toll Free Tel: 800-658-6643. FAX: 806-383-8452. Web Site: www.amarillodiocese.org/museum-archives. *Archivist,* Susan Garner; E-mail: sgarner@dioama.org
Founded 1926
Library Holdings: Bk Titles 50; Bk Vols 1,107; Spec Interest Per Sub 3
Special Collections: Catholic Church History, Panhandle of Texas; Diocese of Amarillo Bishop's Colls; Genealogy; Official Catholic Directory, 1925-present
Subject Interests: Catholic studies, Relig
Wireless access
Function: Archival coll
Restriction: Open by appt only, Open to researchers by request
Friends of the Library Group

ANAHUAC

P CHAMBERS COUNTY LIBRARY SYSTEM*, 202 Cummings St, 77514. (Mail add: PO Box 520, 77514-0520), SAN 361-0772. Tel: 409-267-2554. FAX: 409-267-5181. E-mail: ccls@chamberstx.gov. Web Site: www.chambers.lib.tx.us. *County Librn,* Valerie Jensen; Tel: 409-267-2550, E-mail: vjensen@chamberstx.gov; *Asst County Librn,* Annie Vass; E-mail: avass@chamberstx.gov; Staff 2 (MLS 2)
Founded 1950. Pop 24,167; Circ 159,768
Library Holdings: Bk Titles 80,145; Bk Vols 103,373; Per Subs 104; Videos 4,177
Subject Interests: Chambers County hist, Texana
Automation Activity & Vendor Info: (Cataloging) Follett Software; (Circulation) Follett Software; (ILL) OCLC ILLiad; (OPAC) Follett Software; (Serials) Follett Software
Wireless access
Open Mon & Thurs 8-7, Tues-Fri 8-5, Sat 9-1
Friends of the Library Group
Branches: 3
CHAMBERS COUNTY LIBRARY, 202 Cummings St, 77514. (Mail add: PO Box 520, 77514-0520). *Br Librn,* Aquilia De La Cruz; E-mail: adelacruz@chamberstx.gov; Staff 13 (MLS 2, Non-MLS 11)
Founded 1950
Automation Activity & Vendor Info: (Cataloging) Auto-Graphics, Inc; (Circulation) Auto-Graphics, Inc; (Course Reserve) Auto-Graphics, Inc
Open Mon & Thurs 10-7, Tues, Wed & Fri 8-5, Sat 9-1
Friends of the Library Group
SAM & CARMENA GOSS MEMORIAL BRANCH, One John Hall Dr, Mont Belvieu, 77580. (Mail add: PO Box 1289, Mont Belvieu, 77580-1289), SAN 361-0829. Tel: 281-576-2245. FAX: 281-576-2496. *Br Librn,* Yolie Belt; E-mail: ybelt@chamberstx.gov; Staff 3 (Non-MLS 3)
Open Mon, Wed & Fri 8-5, Tues & Thurs 8-7, Sat 9-1
Friends of the Library Group
JUANITA HARGRAVES MEMORIAL BRANCH, 924 Hwy 124, Winnie, 77665. (Mail add: PO Box 597, Winnie, 77665-0597), SAN 361-0802. Tel: 409-296-8245. FAX: 409-296-8243. *Br Librn,* Cindy Alegria; E-mail: calegria@chamberstx.gov; Staff 3 (Non-MLS 3)
Open Mon, Wed & Fri 8-5, Tues & Thurs 10-7, Sat 9-1
Friends of the Library Group

ANDREWS

P ANDREWS COUNTY LIBRARY*, 109 NW First St, 79714. SAN 316-0254. Tel: 432-523-9819. FAX: 432-523-4570. Web Site: www.andrews.lib.tx.us. *Dir,* Jessalynn Denison; E-mail: jdenison@andrews.lib.tx.us; Staff 7 (MLS 2, Non-MLS 5)
Founded 1950. Circ 84,550
Library Holdings: Audiobooks 4,664; e-books 408; Bk Vols 83,051; Per Subs 67; Videos 2,458
Automation Activity & Vendor Info: (Acquisitions) Biblionix; (Cataloging) Biblionix; (Circulation) Biblionix; (ILL) OCLC; (OPAC) Biblionix
Wireless access
Function: 24/7 Electronic res, 24/7 Online cat, Activity rm, Adult literacy prog, Audio & video playback equip for onsite use, Audiobks via web, Bilingual assistance for Spanish patrons, Bk club(s), Bks on CD, Children's prog, Computers for patron use, Electronic databases & coll, Free DVD rentals, Home delivery & serv to seniorr ctr & nursing homes, Homebound delivery serv, Homework prog, ILL available, Internet access, Laminating, Large print keyboards, Magazines, Magnifiers for reading, Makerspace, Meeting rooms, Microfiche/film & reading machines, Movies, Online cat, Online info literacy tutorials on the web & in blackboard, Online ref, OverDrive digital audio bks, Photocopying/Printing, Printer for laptops & handheld devices, Prog for adults, Prog for children & young adult, Ref serv available, Scanner, Serves people with intellectual disabilities, Story hour, Study rm, Summer reading prog, Teen prog, Wheelchair accessible
Special Services for the Deaf - Bks on deafness & sign lang
Special Services for the Blind - Bks on CD; Large print bks
Open Mon, Tues & Thurs 9-7, Wed & Fri 9-6, Sat 10-1
Restriction: Borrowing privileges limited to fac & registered students
Friends of the Library Group

ANGLETON

L BRAZORIA COUNTY LAW LIBRARY*, 111 E Locust St, Ste 315-A, 77515. SAN 372-1914. Tel: 979-864-1225. FAX: 979-864-1226. Web Site: www.brazoriacountytx.gov/departments/law-library. *Librn,* Tracy Gonzales; E-mail: tgonzales@brazoriacountytx.gov
Library Holdings: Bk Vols 10,000; Per Subs 20
Wireless access
Open Mon-Fri 8-5

P BRAZORIA COUNTY LIBRARY SYSTEM*, 912 N Velasco, 77515. SAN 361-0837. Tel: 979-864-1505. FAX: 979-864-1298. E-mail: bcls@bcls.lib.tx.us. Web Site: bcls.lib.tx.us. *Libr Dir,* Lisa Loranc; E-mail: lloranc@bcls.lib.tx.us; *Asst Dir, Libr Serv,* Cindy Yell; E-mail: cindyy@bcls.lib.tx.us; *Asst Dir, Pub Serv,* Rachel Orozco; E-mail: rachelo@bcls.lib.tx.us; *Tech Serv Mgr,* Position Currently Open; *Adult Coordr,* Position Currently Open; *Children's Coordr,* Position Currently Open; Staff 38 (MLS 17, Non-MLS 21)
Founded 1941. Pop 335,000; Circ 1,747,809
Oct 2019-Sept 2020 Income (Main & Associated Libraries) $6,079,534, State $57,494, City $555,804, County $5,038,575, Locally Generated Income $427,661. Mats Exp $923,487, Books $855,233, AV Mat $68,254. Sal $4,094,907
Library Holdings: Audiobooks 24,036; AV Mats 179; DVDs 20,901; e-books 388; e-journals 2; Bk Titles 181,363; Bk Vols 527,358; Per Subs 838
Special Collections: Brazoria County History Coll; State History (Texana Coll)
Subject Interests: Genealogy
Automation Activity & Vendor Info: (Acquisitions) Innovative Interfaces, Inc; (Cataloging) Innovative Interfaces, Inc; (Circulation) Innovative Interfaces, Inc; (ILL) Innovative Interfaces, Inc; (OPAC) Innovative Interfaces, Inc; (Serials) Innovative Interfaces, Inc
Wireless access
Function: 24/7 Electronic res, 24/7 Online cat, 3D Printer, Accelerated reader prog, Adult bk club, Art exhibits, Audio & video playback equip for onsite use, Audiobks on Playaways & MP3, Audiobks via web, AV serv, Bilingual assistance for Spanish patrons, Bk club(s), Bks on CD, CD-ROM, Children's prog, Computer training, Computers for patron use, Digital talking bks, Distance learning, Electronic databases & coll, Equip loans & repairs, Free DVD rentals, Holiday prog, Homework prog, ILL available, Internet access, Jail serv, Laminating, Large print keyboards, Life-long learning prog for all ages, Magazines, Makerspace, Microfiche/film & reading machines, Movies, Notary serv, Online cat, Online ref, Outreach serv, Outside serv via phone, mail, e-mail & web, Photocopying/Printing, Preschool outreach, Preschool reading prog, Printer for laptops & handheld devices, Prog for adults, Prog for children & young adult, Ref serv available, Scanner, Senior computer classes, Senior outreach, Spanish lang bks, STEM programs, Story hour, Study rm, Summer & winter reading prog, Summer reading prog, Tax forms, Teen prog, Telephone ref, Wheelchair accessible, Winter reading prog
Publications: Library Newsletter; Union List of Periodicals
Partic in Amigos Library Services, Inc
Friends of the Library Group
Branches: 11
ALVIN BRANCH, 105 S Gordon, Alvin, 77511, SAN 361-0896. Tel: 281-388-4300. FAX: 281-388-4305. E-mail: alvin@bcls.lib.tx.us. *Br Head,* Jennifer Trusty; Tel: 281-388-4301, E-mail: jennifert@bcls.lib.tx.us; Staff 2 (MLS 2)
Open Mon, Wed & Fri 10-6, Tues & Thurs 10-8, Sat 10-5
Friends of the Library Group
ANGLETON BRANCH, 401 E Cedar St, 77515-4652, SAN 361-0861. Tel: 979-864-1519. Information Services Tel: 979-864-1520. FAX: 979-864-1518. E-mail: angleton@bcls.lib.tx.us. *Br Head,* Layna L Lewis; E-mail: layna@bcls.lib.tx.us; *Asst Br Librn, Ref Librn,* Jennifer Hill; Tel: 979-864-1513, E-mail: jenniferh@bcls.lib.tx.us; *Ch Serv,* Geri Swanzy; E-mail: geris@bcls.lib.tx.us; Staff 3 (MLS 3)
Open Mon & Tues 9-8, Wed-Sat 9-6
Friends of the Library Group
BRAZORIA BRANCH, 620 S Brooks, Brazoria, 77422-9022. (Mail add: PO Drawer 1550, Brazoria, 77422-1550), SAN 361-0926. Tel: 979-798-2372. FAX: 979-798-4013. *Br Mgr,* Jo Conway; E-mail: jconway@bcls.lib.tx.us; *Ch Serv,* Natalie Newell; E-mail: natalien@bcls.lib.tx.us; Staff 2 (Non-MLS 2)
Open Mon & Wed 10-6, Tues & Thurs 10-8, Sat 10-5
Friends of the Library Group
CLUTE BRANCH, 215 N Shanks, Clute, 77531-4122, SAN 361-0950. Tel: 979-265-4582. FAX: 979-265-8496. *Br Mgr,* Virginia Koenig; E-mail: ginnyk@bcls.lib.tx.us; Staff 1 (Non-MLS 1)
Open Tues & Thurs 10-8, Wed, Fri & Sat 10-6
Friends of the Library Group
DANBURY BRANCH, 1702 N Main St, Danbury, 77534. (Mail add: PO Box 159, Danbury, 77534-0159). Tel: 979-922-1905. FAX: 979-922-1905. E-mail: danbury@bcls.lib.tx.us. *Br Librn,* Layna Lewis; E-mail: laynal@bcls.lib.tx.us; Staff 1 (Non-MLS 1)
Automation Activity & Vendor Info: (OPAC) Innovative Interfaces, Inc
Open Mon, Wed & Fri 10-6, Tues & Thurs 1-8
Friends of the Library Group
FREEPORT BRANCH, 410 Brazosport Blvd, Freeport, 77541, SAN 361-0985. Tel: 979-233-3622. FAX: 979-233-4300. *Br Librn,* Natalie Newell; E-mail: natalien@bcls.lib.tx.us; *Ch Serv,* Linda Frazee; E-mail: lindaf@bcls.lib.tx.us; Staff 2 (Non-MLS 2)
Open Mon, Wed & Sat 10-6, Tues & Thurs 10-8
Friends of the Library Group
LAKE JACKSON BRANCH, 250 Circle Way, Lake Jackson, 77566, SAN 361-1019. Tel: 979-415-2590. FAX: 979-415-2993. *Br Head,* Grace Heffernan; E-mail: graceh@bcls.lib.tx.us; *Asst Br Librn, Ref Librn,* Karen Detloff; E-mail: karend@bcls.lib.tx.us; *Children's Spec,* Andrea Larsen; E-mail: andel@bcls.lib.tx.us; Staff 3 (MLS 2, Non-MLS 1)
Library Holdings: Bk Vols 96,040
Open Mon, Wed & Thurs 10-8, Tues, Fri & Sat 10-6
Friends of the Library Group
MANVEL BRANCH, 20514B Hwy 6, Manvel, 77578, SAN 361-1027. Tel: 281-489-7596. FAX: 281-489-7596. *Br Mgr,* Carolynn Waites; E-mail: carolynnw@bcls.lib.tx.us; *Ch,* Bayley Aldmon; E-mail: bayleya@bcls.lib.tx.us; Staff 2 (MLS 1, Non-MLS 1)
Open Mon, Wed & Sat 10-6, Tues & Thurs 1-8
Friends of the Library Group
PEARLAND BRANCH, 3522 Liberty Dr, Pearland, 77581, SAN 361-1043. Tel: 281-485-4876. FAX: 281-485-5576. E-mail: pearland@bcls.lib.tx.us. *Br Librn,* Kaitlyn Keever; E-mail: kaitlynk@bcls.lib.tx.us; *Asst Br Librn/Ref,* Kristen Stewart; E-mail: kristens@bcls.lib.tx.us; *Children's Spec,* Angela Lackey; E-mail: angelal@bcls.lib.tx.us; Staff 3 (MLS 2, Non-MLS 1)
Open Mon-Wed 10-9, Thurs-Sat 10-6
Friends of the Library Group
SWEENY BRANCH, 205 W Ashley-Wilson Rd, Sweeny, 77480, SAN 361-1078. Tel: 979-548-2567. FAX: 979-548-2597. E-mail: sweeny@bcls.lib.tx.us. *Br Mgr,* Leslie Smith; E-mail: leslies@bcls.lib.tx.us; Staff 1 (Non-MLS 1)
Friends of the Library Group
WEST COLUMBIA BRANCH, 518 E Brazos, West Columbia, 77486, SAN 361-1108. Tel: 979-345-3394. FAX: 979-345-3652. E-mail: west@bcls.lib.tx.us. *Br Mgr,* Bobby Edge; E-mail: bobbye@bcls.lib.tx.us; Staff 1 (Non-MLS 1)
Open Mon & Wed 10-8, Tues & Thurs 10-6, Sat 10-6
Friends of the Library Group

ANSON

P ANSON PUBLIC LIBRARY*, 1137 12th St, 79501. SAN 316-0262. Tel: 325-823-2711. FAX: 325-823-2711. E-mail: aplibrary@hotmail.com. *Dir,* Debra Lytle
Founded 1962. Pop 2,615; Circ 5,716
Library Holdings: Bk Vols 13,800
Automation Activity & Vendor Info: (Cataloging) Koha; (Circulation) Koha; (OPAC) Koha

Wireless access
Partic in Partners Library Action Network
Open Mon-Thurs 10-5
Friends of the Library Group

ARANSAS PASS

P ED & HAZEL RICHMOND PUBLIC LIBRARY*, 110 N Lamont St, 78336. SAN 316-0270. Tel: 361-758-2350. E-mail: aplibrary@aptx.gov. Web Site: aptx.gov/208/Library. *Librn,* Lillian Villarreal
Founded 1943. Pop 8,800; Circ 24,000
Library Holdings: Bk Titles 17,103; Bk Vols 17,319; Per Subs 9
Subject Interests: Texana
Automation Activity & Vendor Info: (Cataloging) Koha; (Circulation) Koha; (OPAC) Koha
Wireless access
Open Mon-Fri 8:30-5, Sat 10-2

ARCHER CITY

P ARCHER PUBLIC LIBRARY*, 105 N Center St, 76351. (Mail add: PO Box 1574, 76351-1574), SAN 316-0289. Tel: 940-574-4954. Web Site: archer.ploud.net. *Dir,* Gretchen Abernathy-Kuck; E-mail: archerlibrarian@gmail.com
Founded 1968. Pop 8,563; Circ 29,000
Library Holdings: DVDs 3,000; Bk Vols 26,000
Automation Activity & Vendor Info: (Acquisitions) Book Systems; (Cataloging) Book Systems; (Circulation) Book Systems; (Course Reserve) Book Systems; (OPAC) Book Systems; (Serials) Book Systems
Wireless access
Open Mon-Wed & Fri 9-12:30 & 1:30-5:30, Thurs 1-9

ARLINGTON

C ARLINGTON BAPTIST UNIVERSITY*, Earl K Oldham Library, 3001 W Division, 76012. SAN 316-0300. Tel: 817-461-8741, Ext 127. FAX: 817-274-1138. E-mail: helpdesk@arlingtonbaptistcollege.edu. Web Site: www.abu.edu/library. *Dir,* Amy Schaeffer; E-mail: aschaeffer@abu.edu; Staff 3 (MLS 1, Non-MLS 2)
Founded 1939. Enrl 250; Fac 20; Highest Degree: Doctorate
Library Holdings: AV Mats 812; Bk Vols 40,000; Per Subs 280
Subject Interests: Music, Relig studies
Automation Activity & Vendor Info: (Cataloging) Follett Software; (Circulation) Follett Software; (OPAC) Follett Software
Wireless access
Open Mon, Tues & Thurs 7am-9:30pm, Wed & Fri 7-2 (Fall & Spring); Mon-Thurs 7-4, Fri 8-4 (Summer)

P ARLINGTON PUBLIC LIBRARY SYSTEM*, George W Hawkes Downtown Library, 100 S Center St, 76010. SAN 361-1132. Tel: 817-459-6900. FAX: 817-459-6936. Web Site: www.arlingtonlibrary.org. *Dir of Libr,* Norma Zuniga; Tel: 817-459-6914, E-mail: norma.zuniga@arlingtontx.gov; Staff 89 (MLS 14, Non-MLS 75)
Founded 1923. Pop 353,597; Circ 500,689
Library Holdings: AV Mats 46,102; Bks on Deafness & Sign Lang 32; Large Print Bks 8,157; Bk Titles 237,334; Bk Vols 570,029; Per Subs 842; Talking Bks 14,154
Special Collections: US Document Depository
Subject Interests: Careers, Deaf, Foreign lang, Genealogy, Hearing impaired, Texana
Automation Activity & Vendor Info: (Acquisitions) Innovative Interfaces, Inc; (Cataloging) Innovative Interfaces, Inc; (Circulation) Innovative Interfaces, Inc; (OPAC) Innovative Interfaces, Inc
Wireless access
Function: Govt ref serv, ILL available, Large print keyboards, Magnifiers for reading, Photocopying/Printing, Prog for children & young adult, Ref serv available, Res libr, Summer reading prog, Telephone ref, Wheelchair accessible
Partic in TexSHARE - Texas State Library & Archives Commission
Special Services for the Deaf - Assistive tech; Bks on deafness & sign lang; Deaf publ
Special Services for the Blind - Assistive/Adapted tech devices, equip & products; Audio mat; Bks on CD; Closed circuit TV; Closed circuit TV magnifier; Computer with voice synthesizer for visually impaired persons; Large print bks; Large screen computer & software; Magnifiers; PC for people with disabilities; Reader equip; Screen enlargement software for people with visual disabilities; Talking bks; Videos on blindness & physical disabilties
Open Mon-Sat 9-6
Friends of the Library Group
Branches: 6
EAST ARLINGTON, 1817 New York Ave, 76010, SAN 361-1191. Web Site: arlingtonlibrary.org/east-library-and-recreation-center. *Pub Serv Coordr,* Omar Arias-Bautista; E-mail: omar.arias-bautista@arlingtontx.gov; Staff 9 (MLS 3, Non-MLS 6)
Founded 1970
Library Holdings: AV Mats 7,107; Large Print Bks 29; Bk Titles 52,710; Bk Vols 61,856; Per Subs 86
Special Collections: Children's Learning Center Coll; GED/ESL; Multicultural Coll
Function: ILL available, Magnifiers for reading, Photocopying/Printing, Prog for children & young adult, Ref serv available, Summer reading prog, Wheelchair accessible
Open Mon-Thurs 10-8, Fri & Sat 10-5, Sun 2-6
Friends of the Library Group
LAKE ARLINGTON, 4000 W Green Oaks Blvd, 76016, SAN 328-7289. *Pub Serv Coordr,* Derek Perdue; E-mail: derek.perdue@arlingtontx.gov; Staff 11 (MLS 3, Non-MLS 8)
Founded 1986
Library Holdings: AV Mats 7,621; Large Print Bks 287; Bk Titles 58,972; Bk Vols 73,828; Per Subs 88; Talking Bks 2,360
Function: ILL available, Magnifiers for reading, Photocopying/Printing, Prog for children & young adult, Ref serv available, Summer reading prog
Open Mon-Sat 10-6
Friends of the Library Group
NORTHEAST, 1905 Brown Blvd, 76006, SAN 361-1167. *Pub Serv Coordr,* Diana Candelaria; E-mail: diana.candelaria@arlingtontx.gov; Staff 11 (MLS 3, Non-MLS 8)
Founded 1997. Pop 353,597; Circ 500,689
Library Holdings: AV Mats 5,200; Large Print Bks 324; Bk Titles 58,565; Bk Vols 69,591; Per Subs 96
Function: Adult literacy prog, ILL available, Magnifiers for reading, Photocopying/Printing, Prog for children & young adult, Ref serv available, Summer reading prog, Wheelchair accessible
Open Mon-Sat 10-6
Friends of the Library Group
SOUTHEAST, 900 SE Green Oaks Blvd, 76018. *Pub Serv Coordr,* Sandra Williams; E-mail: sandra.williams@arlingtontx.gov; Staff 6 (Non-MLS 6)
Pop 353,597; Circ 500,689
Library Holdings: Bk Vols 25,000
Function: ILL available, Magnifiers for reading, Photocopying/Printing, Prog for children & young adult, Ref serv available, Summer reading prog, Wheelchair accessible
Open Mon-Sat 10-6
Friends of the Library Group
SOUTHWEST, 3311 SW Green Oaks Blvd, 76017. *Pub Serv Coordr,* Samatha Mendez; E-mail: samantha.mendez@arlingtontx.gov
Open Mon-Sat 10-6
Friends of the Library Group
WOODLAND WEST, 2837 W Park Row Dr, 76013, SAN 361-1221. *Pub Serv Coordr,* Robert Linan; E-mail: robert.linan@arlingtontx.gov; Staff 8 (MLS 2, Non-MLS 6)
Founded 1996
Library Holdings: AV Mats 5,038; Large Print Bks 298; Bk Titles 45,267; Bk Vols 50,955; Per Subs 68; Talking Bks 1,988
Function: ILL available, Magnifiers for reading, Photocopying/Printing, Prog for children & young adult, Ref serv available, Summer reading prog, Wheelchair accessible
Open Mon-Sat 10-6
Friends of the Library Group

J TARRANT COUNTY COLLEGE*, Judith J Carrier Library Southeast Campus, Bldg ESED 1200, 2100 Southeast Pkwy, 76018. Tel: 817-515-3082. FAX: 817-515-3183. Web Site: library.tccd.edu. *Dir, Libr Serv,* Jotisa H Klemm; E-mail: jotisa.klemm@tccd.edu; *Asst Libr Dir,* Tracey D Robinson; E-mail: tracey.robinson2@tccd.edu; Staff 5 (MLS 5)
Founded 1996. Enrl 14,780; Fac 350; Highest Degree: Associate
Library Holdings: DVDs 62; e-books 36,000; Bk Titles 47,200; Per Subs 100
Automation Activity & Vendor Info: (Acquisitions) Ex Libris Group; (Cataloging) Ex Libris Group; (Circulation) Ex Libris Group; (Course Reserve) Ex Libris Group; (ILL) Ex Libris Group; (OPAC) Ex Libris Group; (Serials) Ex Libris Group
Wireless access
Partic in Amigos Library Services, Inc
Open Mon-Thurs 7am-10pm, Fri 8-8, Sat 8-5

C UNIVERSITY OF TEXAS AT ARLINGTON LIBRARY, 702 Planetarium Pl, 76019. (Mail add: PO Box 19497, 76019-0497), SAN 316-0343. Tel: 817-272-3000. Circulation Tel: 817-272-3395. Interlibrary Loan Service Tel: 817-272-3344. Administration Tel: 817-272-1413. Web Site: libraries.uta.edu/locations/cen. *Dean of Libr,* John Wang; Tel: 817-272-5318, E-mail: zheng.wang@uta.edu; *Assoc Univ Librn,* Suzanne Byke; Tel: 817-272-9405, E-mail: sbyke@uta.edu; *Assoc Univ Librn,* Katie Musick Peery; Tel: 817-272-1714, E-mail: kapeery@uta.edu; *Assoc Univ Librn,* Peter Zhang; Tel: 817-272-1006, E-mail: pzhang@uta.edu; Staff 47 (MLS 43, Non-MLS 4)
Founded 1895. Enrl 33,239; Fac 1,399; Highest Degree: Doctorate

Library Holdings: CDs 2,333; DVDs 2,602; e-books 432,664; e-journals 39,002; Electronic Media & Resources 17,291; Microforms 123,591; Music Scores 2,738; Bk Titles 934,514; Bk Vols 955,613; Per Subs 81,879; Videos 3,929
Special Collections: Fort Worth Star Telegram Coll; Mexico & MesoAmerica, bks, doc; Organized Labor in Texas & the Southwest, doc; Photographic Archives; Robertson's Colony, doc; Texas & the Mexican War, bks, cartography, doc, maps; Virginia Garrett Cartographic History Library. Oral History; US Document Depository
Automation Activity & Vendor Info: (Acquisitions) Ex Libris Group; (Cataloging) Ex Libris Group; (Circulation) Ex Libris Group; (Course Reserve) Ex Libris Group; (ILL) OCLC ILLiad; (OPAC) Ex Libris Group; (Serials) Ex Libris Group
Wireless access
Publications: Compass Rose (Newsletter)
Partic in Amigos Library Services, Inc; OCLC Online Computer Library Center, Inc; Phoenix Group; TexSHARE - Texas State Library & Archives Commission; UT Sys Electronic Ref Ctr
Special Services for the Deaf - Assistive tech
Special Services for the Blind - Assistive/Adapted tech devices, equip & products
Friends of the Library Group

ASPERMONT

P STONEWALL COUNTY LIBRARY*, 516 S Washington Ave, 79502. (Mail add: PO Box H, 79502-0907), SAN 324-7597. Tel: 940-989-2730. FAX: 940-989-2730. E-mail: stonewall.lib@gmail.com. Web Site: www.stonewall-library.com. *Librn,* Ashlee Sedberry
Founded 1962. Pop 2,340; Circ 18,192
Library Holdings: Bk Titles 11,345; Bk Vols 11,684
Automation Activity & Vendor Info: (Cataloging) LibLime; (Circulation) LibLime
Wireless access
Open Mon-Wed 8-11:30 & 12:30-5
Friends of the Library Group

ATHENS

P HENDERSON COUNTY*, Clint W Murchison Memorial Library, 121 S Prairieville, 75751. SAN 316-0351. Tel: 903-677-7295. FAX: 903-677-7275. E-mail: librarian@henderson-county.com. Web Site: www.hendersoncountylibrary.com. *Dir,* Michelle Zenor; E-mail: mzenor@henderson-county.com; *Asst Dir,* Renotta Mayo; E-mail: renotta.mayo@henderson-county.com; Staff 7 (MLS 2, Non-MLS 5)
Founded 1972. Pop 82,000
Library Holdings: Audiobooks 3,000; DVDs 500; Large Print Bks 10,000; Bk Titles 45,000; Bk Vols 47,000; Per Subs 25
Automation Activity & Vendor Info: (Cataloging) Book Systems; (Circulation) Book Systems
Wireless access
Open Mon-Thurs 10-6:30, Fri 9-5, Sat 9-1
Friends of the Library Group

J TRINITY VALLEY COMMUNITY COLLEGE LIBRARY*, Athens Campus, 100 Cardinal Dr, 75751. SAN 316-036X. Tel: 903-675-6260. Web Site: libguides.tvcc.edu/tvcclibraries, www.tvcc.edu. *Dir,* Dr Karla Bryan; Tel: 903-675-6229, E-mail: kbryan@tvcc.edu; *Ref Librn,* Jaime Mire; E-mail: jmire@tvcc.edu; Staff 2 (MLS 2)
Founded 1946. Highest Degree: Associate
Library Holdings: e-books 29,000; Bk Vols 28,000; Per Subs 150; Videos 2,000
Special Collections: Athens Review, bound vols, microfilm
Automation Activity & Vendor Info: (Acquisitions) SirsiDynix; (Cataloging) SirsiDynix; (Circulation) SirsiDynix; (Course Reserve) SirsiDynix; (ILL) SirsiDynix; (Media Booking) SirsiDynix; (OPAC) SirsiDynix; (Serials) SirsiDynix
Wireless access
Partic in Amigos Library Services, Inc; TexSHARE - Texas State Library & Archives Commission
Open Mon-Thurs 7:45-7:45, Fri 7:45-4:15, Sun 2-5 (Fall & Spring); Mon & Tues 7:45-7:45, Wed & Thurs 7:45-4:45 (Summer)

Departmental Libraries:

PALESTINE CAMPUS, 2970 Hwy 19 N, Palestine, 75803. (Mail add: PO Box 2530, Palestine, 75802-2530), SAN 370-372X. Tel: 903-723-7025. *Dir,* Natalie Ferrell; E-mail: natalie.ferrell@tvcc.edu
Library Holdings: Bk Titles 18,000; Per Subs 131
Open Mon-Thurs 8-5, Fri 8-4:30 (Fall & Spring); Mon-Thurs 8-5 (Summer)

TERRELL CAMPUS, 1200 E I-20, Terrell, 75161, SAN 370-3746. Tel: 972-563-4929. FAX: 972-563-1667. *Dir,* Deanna Thompson Smith; E-mail: thompson@tvcc.edu; Staff 1 (MLS 1)
Library Holdings: Bk Titles 6,200; Per Subs 60
Open Mon-Thurs 7:45am-7pm, Fri 8-Noon (Fall & Spring); Mon-Thurs 8-5 (Summer)

JM TERRELL HSC CAMPUS, 1551 SH 34 S, Terrell, 75160, SAN 370-3738. Tel: 469-416-3805. *Learning Res Spec,* Mark Pratt; E-mail: mark.pratt@tvcc.edu
Library Holdings: Bk Titles 2,013; Per Subs 41
Open Mon-Fri 7:30-4:30 (Fall & Spring); Mon-Thurs 8-5 (Summer)

ATLANTA

P ATLANTA PUBLIC LIBRARY*, 101 W Hiram St, 75551. SAN 376-4451. Tel: 903-796-2112. FAX: 903-799-4067. Web Site: www.atlantalib.com. *Libr Dir,* Kendra Harrell; E-mail: kharrell@atlantatexas.org; Staff 3.6 (MLS 1, Non-MLS 2.6)
Library Holdings: Bk Vols 28,572; Per Subs 20
Wireless access
Open Mon 10-8, Tues-Fri 10-6, Sat 10-2
Friends of the Library Group

AUBREY

P AUBREY AREA LIBRARY*, 226 Countryside Dr, 76227. SAN 376-4672. Tel: 940-365-9162. FAX: 940-365-9411. E-mail: aubreyarealibrary@gmail.com. Web Site: www.aubreytx.gov/pl. *Dir,* Kathy Ramsey; Staff 3 (MLS 1, Non-MLS 2)
Founded 1987. Circ 55,460
Library Holdings: Bk Titles 17,000
Automation Activity & Vendor Info: (Cataloging) Evergreen; (Circulation) Evergreen; (OPAC) Evergreen
Wireless access
Function: 24/7 Electronic res, 24/7 Online cat, Activity rm, Adult bk club, After school storytime
Partic in North Texas Library Consortium; Partners Library Action Network
Friends of the Library Group

AUSTIN

R THE ARCHIVES OF THE EPISCOPAL CHURCH*, 606 Rathervue Pl, 78705. (Mail add: PO Box 2247, 78768-2247), SAN 372-9664. Tel: 512-472-6816. FAX: 512-480-0437. E-mail: research@episcopalarchives.org. Web Site: www.episcopalarchives.org. *Archives Dir,* Mark J Duffy; E-mail: mduffy@episcopalarchives.org; Staff 9 (MLS 5, Non-MLS 4)
Founded 1940
Library Holdings: Bk Vols 12,000; Per Subs 50
Special Collections: Book of Common Prayer. Oral History
Wireless access
Restriction: Closed stack, Open by appt only, Open to pub by appt only, Pub ref by request, Pub use on premises, Researchers by appt only, Restricted access, Restricted loan policy
Friends of the Library Group

J AUSTIN COMMUNITY COLLEGE*, Library Services Administration, 5930 Middle Fiskville Rd, 78752. SAN 316-0386. Tel: 512-223-3084. FAX: 512-223-0903. E-mail: library@austincc.edu. Web Site: library.austincc.edu. *Dean, Libr Serv,* Julie Todaro; Tel: 512-223-7792, E-mail: jtodaro@austincc.edu; *Libr Syst Adminr,* Melissa Airoldi; Tel: 512-223-3464, E-mail: airoldi@austincc.edu; *Head Librn, Tech Serv & Automation,* Linda Barr; Tel: 512-223-3461, E-mail: lbarr@austincc.edu; Staff 9 (MLS 4, Non-MLS 5)
Founded 1973. Enrl 41,988; Fac 2,107; Highest Degree: Associate
Library Holdings: AV Mats 10,006; e-books 37,543; e-journals 76,999; Bk Vols 155,977; Per Subs 1,262
Special Collections: Multicultural Coll
Subject Interests: Health sci
Automation Activity & Vendor Info: (Acquisitions) SirsiDynix; (Cataloging) SirsiDynix; (Circulation) SirsiDynix; (Course Reserve) SirsiDynix; (ILL) SirsiDynix; (Media Booking) SirsiDynix; (OPAC) SirsiDynix; (Serials) SirsiDynix
Wireless access
Publications: Library Instruction; Pathfinders; Study Guides
Partic in Amigos Library Services, Inc; TexSHARE - Texas State Library & Archives Commission
Special Services for the Blind - Computer with voice synthesizer for visually impaired persons
Open Mon-Fri 7am-10pm, Sat 8-5

Departmental Libraries:

CYPRESS CREEK CAMPUS LIBRARY, 1555 Cypress Creek Rd, 1st Flr, Rm 2121, Cedar Park, 78613, SAN 377-5852. Tel: 512-223-2030. Reference Tel: 512-223-2037. FAX: 512-223-2035. *Head Librn,* Terry Barksdale; Tel: 512-223-2135, E-mail: tbarksda@austincc.edu; *Fac Librn,* Jonathan Buckstead; Tel: 512-223-2132, E-mail: jrb@austincc.edu; *Fac Librn,* Linda Clement; Tel: 512-223-2033, E-mail: lclement@austincc.edu; *Fac Librn,* Molly Dahlstrom-Ledbetter; Tel: 512-223-2137, E-mail: mdahlstr@austincc.edu; Staff 8.3 (MLS 4.7, Non-MLS 3.6)
Open Mon-Fri 7:30am-9pm, Sat 8-5

EASTVIEW CAMPUS LIBRARY, 3401 Webberville Rd, 2nd Flr, Rm 2200, 78702, SAN 377-5879. Tel: 512-223-5109. Reference Tel: 512-223-5116. FAX: 512-223-5111. *Head Librn,* Margaret Peloquin; Tel: 512-223-5117, E-mail: peloquin@austincc.edu; *Fac Librn,* Steve Self; Tel: 512-223-5134, E-mail: ses@austincc.edu; *Fac Librn,* Cary Sowell; Tel: 512-223-5232, E-mail: cary@austincc.edu; Staff 9.4 (MLS 4.3, Non-MLS 5.1)
Open Mon-Fri 7:30am-9pm, Sat 8-5

ELGIN CAMPUS LIBRARY, 1501 W US Hwy 290, 3rd Flr, Rm 1376, Elgin, 78621. Tel: 512-223-9434. Reference Tel: 512-223-9435. FAX: 512-223-9593. *Head Librn,* Courtney Mlinar; Tel: 512-223-9433, E-mail: courtney.mlinar@austincc.edu; *Fac Librn,* Mary Havens; Tel: 512-223-9462, E-mail: mary.havens@austincc.edu; Staff 4.7 (MLS 2, Non-MLS 2.7)
Open Mon-Thurs 8am-9pm, Fri 8-5

HAYS CAMPUS LIBRARY, 1200 Kohlers Crossing, 3rd Flr, Rm 1305, Kyle, 78640. Tel: 512-223-1592. Reference Tel: 512-223-1593. FAX: 512-223-1889. *Head Librn,* Keri Moczygemba; Tel: 512-223-1585, E-mail: keri.moczygemba@austincc.edu; *Fac Librn,* Jordan Forbes; Tel: 512-223-1587, E-mail: jordan.forbes@austincc.edu; *Fac Librn,* Barbara Jorge; Tel: 512-223-1586, E-mail: bjorge@austincc.edu; Staff 5.7 (MLS 3, Non-MLS 2.7)
Open Mon-Thurs 7:30am-9pm, Fri 7:30-5

HIGHLAND CAMPUS LIBRARY, 6101 Airport Blvd, 1st Flr, Rm 1325, 78752. Tel: 512-223-7380. Reference Tel: 512-223-7379. FAX: 512-223-7135. *Head Librn,* Carrie Gits; Tel: 512-223-7386, E-mail: carrie.gits@austincc.edu; *Asst Head Librn,* Ashley Carr; Tel: 512-223-7389, E-mail: acarr@austincc.edu; *Fac Librn,* Jon Luckstead; Tel: 512-223-7388, E-mail: jluckste@austincc.edu; *Fac Librn,* Alexander Speetzen; Tel: 512-223-7387, E-mail: alexander.speetzen@austincc.edu; Staff 8 (MLS 4, Non-MLS 4)
Open Mon-Fri 7:30am-9pm, Sat 8-5, Sun 12-6

NORTHRIDGE CAMPUS LIBRARY, 11928 Stone Hollow Dr, 2nd, Rm 1223, 78758, SAN 321-7949. Tel: 512-223-4746. Reference Tel: 512-223-4744. FAX: 512-223-4902. *Head Librn,* Jennifer Weber; Tel: 512-223-4741, E-mail: jweber@austincc.edu; *Fac Librn,* Teresa Ashley; Tel: 512-223-4742, E-mail: tashley@austincc.edu; *Fac Librn,* David Wilson; Tel: 512-223-4743, E-mail: dwilson3@austincc.edu; *Fac Librn,* Betsy Young; Tel: 512-223-4869, E-mail: byoung1@austincc.edu; Staff 8 (MLS 4, Non-MLS 4)
Open Mon-Fri 7:30am-9pm, Sat 8-5, Sun 12-6

RIO GRANDE CAMPUS LIBRARY, 1212 Rio Grande, 78701, SAN 321-7930. Tel: 512-223-3085. Circulation Tel: 512-223-3067. Reference Tel: 512-223-3068. FAX: 512-223-3430. *Head Librn,* Carrie Gits; Tel: 512-223-3066; Staff 1 (MLS 1)

RIVERSIDE CAMPUS LIBRARY, 1020 Grove Blvd, 1st Flr, Rm 1108, 78741, SAN 321-7957. Tel: 512-223-6006. Reference Tel: 512-223-6005. FAX: 512-223-6703. *Head Librn,* Irena Klaic; Tel: 512-223-6603, E-mail: irena.klaic@austincc.edu; *Fac Librn,* Nichole Chagnon; Tel: 512-223-6004, E-mail: nichole.chagnon@austincc.edu; *Fac Librn,* Lynda Infante; Tel: 512-223-6181, E-mail: lynda.infante@austincc.edu; *Fac Librn,* James Loomis; Tel: 512-223-6134, E-mail: james.loomis@austincc.edu; Staff 8.1 (MLS 4, Non-MLS 4.1)
Open Mon-Fri 7:30am-9pm, Sat 8-5, Sun 12-6

ROUND ROCK CAMPUS LIBRARY, 4400 College Park Dr, Round Rock, 78665. Tel: 512-223-0105. Circulation Tel: 512-223-0104. FAX: 512-223-0903. *Head Librn,* Sheila Henderson; Tel: 512-223-0116, E-mail: shender1@austincc.edu; *Asst Head Librn,* Jesse Saunders; Tel: 512-223-0118, E-mail: jesse.saunders@austincc.edu; *Fac Librn,* Kristyn Pittman; Tel: 512-223-0119, E-mail: Kristyn.Pittman@austincc.edu; Staff 7.5 (MLS 3.5, Non-MLS 4)
Open Mon-Fri 7:30am-9pm, Sat 8-5, Sun 12-6

SAN GABRIEL CAMPUS, 449 San Gabriel Campus Dr, 2nd Flr, Rm 1200, Leander, 78641. Tel: 512-223-2565. Reference Tel: 512-223-2566. *Head Librn,* Philip Roche; Tel: 512-223-2564, E-mail: philip.roche@austincc.edu; *Fac Librn,* Lola Cowling Watters; Tel: 512-223-2560, E-mail: lcowling@austincc.edu; Staff 6 (MLS 2, Non-MLS 4)
Open Mon-Thurs 7:30am-8pm, Fri 7:30-5

SOUTH AUSTIN CAMPUS LIBRARY, 1820 W Stassney Lane, 2nd Flr, Rm 1201, 78745. Tel: 512-223-9180. Reference Tel: 512-223-9181. FAX: 512-223-9190. *Head Librn,* Toyya Cisneros; Tel: 512-223-9184, E-mail: toyya.cisneros@austincc.edu; *Fac Librn,* Adrian Graham; Tel: 512-223-9179, E-mail: adrian.graham@austincc.edu; *Fac Librn,* Renee Kuhles; Tel: 512-223-9185, E-mail: marie.kuhles@austincc.edu; Staff 8.1 (MLS 3, Non-MLS 5.1)
Open Mon-Fri 7:30am-9pm, Sat 8-5

CR AUSTIN GRADUATE SCHOOL OF THEOLOGY*, David Worley Library, 7640 Guadalupe St, 78752-1333. SAN 328-3860. Tel: 512-476-2772. FAX: 512-476-3919. E-mail: Library@AustinGrad.edu. Web Site: austingrad.edu/resources. *Dir, Libr Serv,* M Todd Hall; E-mail: THall@AustinGrad.edu; Staff 1 (MLS 1)
Enrl 100; Fac 4; Highest Degree: Master
Library Holdings: Bk Titles 22,500; Bk Vols 25,000; Per Subs 120
Special Collections: Showalter Coll
Subject Interests: Biblical studies
Automation Activity & Vendor Info: (Cataloging) Follett Software; (Circulation) Follett Software
Open Mon 8:30-7, Tues 8:30-5, Wed 8:30-4:30, Thurs 8:30am-10pm, Fri 8:30-3
Friends of the Library Group

CR AUSTIN PRESBYTERIAN THEOLOGICAL SEMINARY*, David L & Jane Stitt Library, 100 E 27th St, 78705-5797. SAN 316-0394. Tel: 512-404-4800. Circulation Tel: 512-404-4879. E-mail: libraryiq@austinseminary.edu. Web Site: www.austinseminary.edu. *Dir,* Timothy D Lincoln; Tel: 512-404-4873, E-mail: tlincoln@austinseminary.edu; *Assoc Dir, Head, Archives & Rec Libr,* Kristy Sorensen; Tel: 512-404-4875, E-mail: ksorensen@austinseminary.edu; *Learning Tech Librn,* Mandy Deen; Tel: 512-404-4874, E-mail: mdeen@austinseminary.edu; *Pub Serv Librn,* Lila Parrish; Tel: 512-404-4878, E-mail: lparrish@austinseminary.edu; Staff 9 (MLS 5, Non-MLS 4)
Founded 1902. Enrl 191; Highest Degree: Doctorate
Library Holdings: Bk Vols 155,000; Per Subs 450
Special Collections: Rumble Communion Token Coll
Subject Interests: Biblical studies
Automation Activity & Vendor Info: (Cataloging) Ex Libris Group; (Circulation) Ex Libris Group; (Course Reserve) Ex Libris Group; (OPAC) Ex Libris Group; (Serials) Ex Libris Group
Wireless access
Partic in Amigos Library Services, Inc
Open Mon-Thurs 8am-10pm, Fri 8-5, Sat 10-5, Sun 3-10

P AUSTIN PUBLIC LIBRARY*, Central Library, 710 W Cesar Chavez St, 78701. (Mail add: PO Box 2287, 78768-2287), SAN 361-1256. Tel: 512-974-7400. Administration Tel: 512-974-7449. Web Site: library.austintexas.gov. *Dir of Libr,* Roosevelt Weeks; E-mail: roosevelt.weeks@austintexas.gov; *Asst Dir, Support Serv,* Dana McBee; E-mail: dana.mcbee@austintexas.gov; Staff 120 (MLS 28, Non-MLS 92)
Founded 1926. Pop 777,559; Circ 4,316,785
Library Holdings: Bk Vols 1,465,765; Per Subs 1,064
Special Collections: Austin History Center. Oral History
Automation Activity & Vendor Info: (Acquisitions) SirsiDynix; (Circulation) SirsiDynix; (ILL) OCLC WorldShare Interlibrary Loan
Wireless access
Partic in Amigos Library Services, Inc; OCLC Online Computer Library Center, Inc; Partners Library Action Network; Proquest Dialog
Special Services for the Deaf - Staff with knowledge of sign lang
Special Services for the Blind - Reader equip
Open Mon-Thurs 10-9, Fri & Sat 10-6, Sun 12-6
Friends of the Library Group

Branches: 21

AUSTIN HISTORY CENTER, 810 Guadalupe St, 78701. (Mail add: PO Box 2287, 78768-2287), SAN 323-9306. Tel: 512-974-7480. FAX: 512-974-7483. Reference E-mail: ahc_reference@austintexas.gov. Web Site: library.austintexas.gov/ahc.
Function: Archival coll
Friends of the Library Group

CARVER, 1161 Angelina St, 78702, SAN 361-1280. Tel: 512-974-1010. FAX: 512-974-1021. Web Site: library.austintexas.gov/carver-branch.

CEPEDA, 651 N Pleasant Valley Rd, 78702, SAN 361-1310. Tel: 512-974-7372. FAX: 512-974-7329. Web Site: library.austintexas.gov/cepeda-branch.
Library Holdings: Bk Vols 18,511

HAMPTON BRANCH AT OAK HILL, 5125 Convict Hill Rd, 78749, SAN 377-7995. Tel: 512-974-9900. FAX: 512-974-9902. Web Site: library.austintexas.gov/hampton-branch-at-oak-hill.

HOWSON, 2500 Exposition Blvd, 78703, SAN 361-1345. Tel: 512-974-8800. FAX: 512-479-8554. Web Site: library.austintexas.gov/howson-branch.

WILLIE MAE KIRK BRANCH, 3101 Oak Springs Dr, 78702, SAN 361-1523. Tel: 512-974-9920. FAX: 512-974-9924. Web Site: library.austintexas.gov/willie-mae-kirk-branch.
Special Collections: Workplace Literary Coll

LITTLE WALNUT CREEK, 835 W Rundberg Lane, 78758, SAN 361-137X. Tel: 512-974-9860. FAX: 512-974-9865. Web Site: library.austintexas.gov/little-walnut-creek-branch.

MANCHACA ROAD, 5500 Manchaca Rd, 78745, SAN 361-140X. Tel: 512-974-8700. FAX: 512-974-8701. Web Site: library.austintexas.gov/manchaca-road-branch.

MILWOOD, 12500 Amherst Dr, 78727, SAN 377-8010. Tel: 512-974-9880. FAX: 512-974-9884. Web Site: library.austintexas.gov/milwood-branch.

NORTH VILLAGE, 2505 Steck Ave, 78757, SAN 361-1493. Tel: 512-974-9960. FAX: 512-974-9965. Web Site: library.austintexas.gov/north-village-branch.

OLD QUARRY, 7051 Village Center Dr, 78731, SAN 361-1558. Tel: 512-974-8860. FAX: 512-794-0459. Web Site: library.austintexas.gov/old-quarry-branch.
PLEASANT HILL, 211 E William Cannon Dr, 78745, SAN 361-1582. Tel: 512-974-3940. FAX: 512-444-6237. Web Site: library.austintexas.gov/pleasant-hill-branch. *Managing Librn,* Steve Reich; E-mail: steve.reich@austintexas.gov
RUIZ BRANCH, 1600 Grove Blvd, 78741, SAN 361-1566. Tel: 512-974-7500. Web Site: library.austintexas.gov/ruiz-branch.
ST JOHN, 7500 Blessing Ave, 78752. Tel: 512-974-7570. FAX: 512-380-7055. Web Site: library.austintexas.gov/st-john-branch.
SOUTHEAST BRANCH, 5803 Nuckols Crossing Rd, 78744, SAN 377-8037. Tel: 512-974-8840. Web Site: library.austintexas.gov/southeast-branch.
SPICEWOOD SPRINGS, 8637 Spicewood Springs Rd, 78759, SAN 326-8454. Tel: 512-974-3800. FAX: 512-974-3801. Web Site: library.austintexas.gov/spicewood-springs-branch.
Special Collections: Chinese (Traditional & Simplified)
Subject Interests: Chinese lang
TERRAZAS, 1105 E Cesar Chavez St, 78702, SAN 361-1612. Tel: 512-974-3625. FAX: 512-974-3628. Web Site: library.austintexas.gov/terrazas-branch.
TWIN OAKS, 1800 S Fifth St, 78704, SAN 361-1647. Tel: 512-974-9980. FAX: 512-974-9988. Web Site: library.austintexas.gov/twin-oaks-branch.
UNIVERSITY HILLS, 4721 Loyola Lane, 78723, SAN 328-9117. Tel: 512-974-9940. FAX: 512-974-9944. Web Site: library.austintexas.gov/university-hills-branch.
WINDSOR PARK, 5833 Westminster Dr, 78723, SAN 361-1671. Tel: 512-974-9840. FAX: 512-974-9844. Web Site: library.austintexas.gov/windsor-park-branch.
YARBOROUGH, 2200 Hancock Dr, 78756, SAN 361-1469. Tel: 512-974-8820. FAX: 512-974-8834. Web Site: library.austintexas.gov/yarborough-branch.
Library Holdings: Bk Vols 30,000
Bookmobiles: 1

SR CATHOLIC ARCHIVES OF TEXAS, Kasner Reference Library, 6225 Hwy 290 E, 78723. SAN 316-0580. Tel: 512-476-6296. FAX: 512-476-3715. Web Site: txcatholic.org/catholic-archives-of-texas. *Exec Dir,* Jennifer Carr Allmon; *Archivist,* Selena Aleman; E-mail: selena@txcatholic.org; Staff 2 (MLS 2)
Founded 1924
Library Holdings: Microforms 7,000; Bk Vols 2,000; Per Subs 12
Special Collections: Catholic Parishes in Texas; Catholic Texas Newspapers (1890 to present); Early Anglo & French Missionaries in Texas; General Information on Texas Catholic Institutions & Organizations; Notre Dame Archives & New Orleans Diocesan Archives, photostats; Spanish Period Documents; Texas Catholic Conference Records, 1964-1990; Texas Coll (Mexican Period); Texas Knights of Columbus Records, 1882-1990; Volunteers for Education & Social Services Records, 1972-2001
Publications: Guide to the Records of Texas Catholic Conference; Guide to the Spanish & Mexican Manuscripts Collection; Our Catholic Heritage in Texas, Journal of Texas Catholic History & Culture; Texas Catholic Historical Society Newsletter
Restriction: Open by appt only

C CONCORDIA UNIVERSITY TEXAS LIBRARY*, CTX Library, 11400 Concordia University Dr, 78726. SAN 316-0432. Tel: 512-313-5050. Administration Tel: 512-313-5051. E-mail: library@concordia.edu. Web Site: www.concordia.edu/library. *Head, Tech Serv,* Marcus Fry; E-mail: marcus.fry@concordia.edu; Staff 3 (MLS 3)
Founded 1926. Enrl 2,500; Fac 70; Highest Degree: Doctorate
Jul 2020-Jun 2021 Income $261,300, Parent Institution $261,300. Mats Exp $188,300, Books $7,000, Per/Ser (Incl. Access Fees) $18,000, AV Equip $500, AV Mat $500, Electronic Ref Mat (Incl. Access Fees) $132,000. Sal $191,000 (Prof $161,000)
Library Holdings: Audiobooks 9; AV Mats 2,883; Bks on Deafness & Sign Lang 25; CDs 122; DVDs 720; e-books 315,000; e-journals 649,030; Electronic Media & Resources 2; Large Print Bks 25; Music Scores 200; Bk Titles 45,030; Bk Vols 48,810; Per Subs 50; Spec Interest Per Sub 5
Automation Activity & Vendor Info: (Cataloging) Ex Libris Group; (Circulation) Ex Libris Group; (Course Reserve) Ex Libris Group; (Discovery) EBSCO Discovery Service; (ILL) OCLC FirstSearch; (OPAC) Ex Libris Group
Wireless access
Function: 24/7 Electronic res, 24/7 Online cat, Archival coll, Art exhibits, Audio & video playback equip for onsite use, Bks on CD, Bus archives, CD-ROM, Computers for patron use, Distance learning, Electronic databases & coll, For res purposes, Free DVD rentals, ILL available, Instruction & testing, Internet access, Learning ctr, Magazines, Magnifiers for reading, Movies, Music CDs, Online cat, Online info literacy tutorials on the web & in blackboard, Online ref, Orientations, Outside serv via phone, mail, e-mail & web, Photocopying/Printing, Ref & res, Ref serv available, Study rm, Telephone ref, Wheelchair accessible
Partic in Amigos Library Services, Inc; Statewide California Electronic Library Consortium; TexSHARE - Texas State Library & Archives Commission
Open Mon-Thurs 7:45am-10pm, Fri 7:45-5, Sat 10-4, Sun 2-10 (Fall & Spring)
Restriction: Access at librarian's discretion, Access for corporate affiliates, Authorized patrons, By permission only, Circ limited, External users must contact libr, In-house use for visitors, Limited access for the pub, Open to authorized patrons, Open to fac, students & qualified researchers, Open to pub for ref & circ; with some limitations, Photo ID required for access, Use of others with permission of librn

R EPISCOPAL THEOLOGICAL SEMINARY OF THE SOUTHWEST*, Booher Library, 501 E 32nd St, 78705. (Mail add: PO Box 2247, 78768-2247), SAN 316-0467. Tel: 512-472-4133, 512-478-5212. FAX: 512-472-4620. Web Site: www.ssw.edu/adacemics/booher-library. *Dir,* Alison Poage; E-mail: alison.poage@ssw.edu; Staff 2 (MLS 2)
Founded 1951. Enrl 125; Fac 9; Highest Degree: Master
Library Holdings: Bk Titles 97,719; Bk Vols 123,347; Per Subs 260
Special Collections: History, Literature & Culture of Latin Culture (Sophie H Winterbotham Coll); Lutheran Seminary Program in the Southwest (LSPS), Seminex Library; Nineteenth Century English Literature-Fine Editions (Charles L Black Coll); Spanish Language Texts
Subject Interests: Biblical studies, Church hist, Cultural studies, Hispanic
Automation Activity & Vendor Info: (Acquisitions) SirsiDynix; (Cataloging) SirsiDynix; (Circulation) SirsiDynix; (Course Reserve) SirsiDynix; (ILL) SirsiDynix; (Media Booking) SirsiDynix; (OPAC) SirsiDynix; (Serials) SirsiDynix
Wireless access
Partic in Amigos Library Services, Inc
Open Mon-Thurs 8am-10pm, Fri 8-6:30, Sat 9-5:30, Sun 2-10 (Winter); Mon-Fri8:15-4:45 (Summer)
Friends of the Library Group

C HUSTON-TILLOTSON UNIVERSITY*, Downs-Jones Library, 900 Chicon St, 78702. SAN 316-0483. Tel: 512-505-3088. Administration Tel: 512-505-3079. E-mail: library@htc.edu. Web Site: htu.edu/academics/library. *Dir, Libr & Media Serv,* Dr Cynthia J Charles; *Syst & Tech Serv Librn,* Katrine Ashton; E-mail: kgashton@htu.edu; Staff 5.3 (MLS 5.3)
Founded 1875. Enrl 1,000; Highest Degree: Master
Library Holdings: Bk Vols 91,375; Per Subs 301
Special Collections: African-American History and Literature; University Archives
Automation Activity & Vendor Info: (Acquisitions) Ex Libris Group; (Cataloging) Ex Libris Group; (Circulation) Ex Libris Group; (OPAC) Ex Libris Group; (Serials) Ex Libris Group
Wireless access
Function: 24/7 Electronic res, Online cat
Publications: Recent Acquisitions List; Student Library Handbook
Partic in TexSHARE - Texas State Library & Archives Commission
Restriction: Authorized patrons, Authorized personnel only, Authorized scholars by appt

L JACKSON WALKER LLP*, Law Library, 100 Congress Ave, Ste 1100, 78701-4099. SAN 327-5426. Tel: 512-236-2000. FAX: 512-236-2002. Web Site: www.jw.com. *Dir, Knowledge Serv,* Greg Lambert; E-mail: glambert@jw.com; Staff 2 (MLS 1, Non-MLS 1)
Founded 1980
Library Holdings: Bk Vols 50,000; Per Subs 200
Automation Activity & Vendor Info: (Acquisitions) EOS International; (Cataloging) EOS International; (OPAC) EOS International; (Serials) EOS International
Wireless access
Function: Res libr
Partic in Proquest Dialog
Restriction: Staff use only

P LAKE TRAVIS COMMUNITY LIBRARY, 1938 Lohmans Crossing, 78734. SAN 376-4737. Tel: 512-263-2885. FAX: 512-535-3044. Web Site: laketravislibrary.org. *Libr Dir,* Morgan McMillian; E-mail: librarian@laketravislibrary.org; Staff 17 (MLS 5, Non-MLS 12)
Founded 1985. Pop 51,475; Circ 400,000
Automation Activity & Vendor Info: (Acquisitions) Biblionix; (Cataloging) Biblionix; (Circulation) Biblionix; (OPAC) Biblionix
Wireless access
Function: 24/7 Electronic res, 24/7 Online cat, 24/7 wireless access, Activity rm, Adult bk club, After school storytime, Art exhibits, Art programs, Audiobks via web, AV serv, Bk club(s), Bks on CD, Butterfly Garden, Chess club, Children's prog, Citizenship assistance, Computer training, Computers for patron use, Digital talking bks, E-Reserves, Electronic databases & coll, Family literacy, Free DVD rentals, Genealogy discussion group, Holiday prog, Home delivery & serv to seniorr ctr & nursing homes, Homebound delivery serv, ILL available, Instruction &

testing, Internet access, Life-long learning prog for all ages, Magazines, Mail & tel request accepted, Mango lang, Meeting rooms, Movies, Music CDs, Notary serv, Online cat, Online Chat, Online ref, Outreach serv, OverDrive digital audio bks, Photocopying/Printing, Preschool outreach, Preschool reading prog, Printer for laptops & handheld devices, Prog for adults, Prog for children & young adult, Ref & res, Ref serv available, Scanner, Senior computer classes, Senior outreach, Serves people with intellectual disabilities, Spanish lang bks, Specialized serv in classical studies, Spoken cassettes & CDs, Spoken cassettes & DVDs, STEM programs, Story hour, Summer & winter reading prog, Summer reading prog, Tax forms, Teen prog, Telephone ref, Wheelchair accessible, Winter reading prog, Workshops, Writing prog
Partic in Partners Library Action Network
Open Mon-Thurs 10-7, Fri & Sat 10-4
Friends of the Library Group
Bookmobiles: Outreach Librn, Karen Ballinger. Bk vols 3,000

L MCGINNIS, LOCHRIDGE*, Law Library, 600 Congress Ave, Ste 2100, 78701. SAN 372-1566. Tel: 512-495-6000. FAX: 512-495-6093. Web Site: www.mcginnislaw.com. *Librn,* Liz Evans; E-mail: eevans@mcginnislaw.com
Library Holdings: Bk Vols 6,500; Per Subs 50
Automation Activity & Vendor Info: (Cataloging) Inmagic, Inc.
Wireless access
Restriction: Staff use only

S NATIONAL ARCHIVES & RECORDS ADMINISTRATION*, Lyndon Baines Johnson Presidential Library, 2313 Red River St, 78705. SAN 361-1760. Tel: 512-721-0200. Administration FAX: 512-721-0170. E-mail: info@lbjlibrary.org. Web Site: www.lbjlibrary.org. *Dir,* Mark Lawrence; Tel: 512-721-0157; *Dep Dir,* Shannon Jarrett; E-mail: shannon.jarrett@nara.gov; Staff 26 (MLS 9, Non-MLS 17)
Founded 1971
Special Collections: President Lyndon B Johnson Coll, fed rec, oral histories, Pre-Presidential, Presidential & Post-Presidential papers. Oral History
Subject Interests: 20th Century Am, Career of Lyndon B Johnson, Econ, Johnson administration, Johnson family, Politics, Presidency, Soc hist, US Presidency, Vietnam War
Wireless access
Publications: Digital List of Holding (Research guide)
Open Mon-Fri 9-5
Friends of the Library Group

G PUBLIC UTILITY COMMISSION OF TEXAS LIBRARY*, 1701 N Congress, 7th Flr, 78701. (Mail add: PO Box 13326, 78711-3326), SAN 327-5582. Tel: 512-936-7075. E-mail: library@puc.state.tx.us. Web Site: www.puc.texas.gov. *Librn,* Carol Maxwell; E-mail: carol.maxwell@puc.texas.gov; Staff 1 (MLS 1)
Founded 1975
Library Holdings: Bk Vols 9,000; Per Subs 10
Subject Interests: Admin law, Electric power, Electric power transmission, Electric utilities, Renewable energy, Telecommunications law, Utility Engineering, Utility Ratemaking, Utility regulation
Automation Activity & Vendor Info: (Cataloging) Biblionix; (OPAC) Biblionix; (Serials) Biblionix
Function: For res purposes
Open Mon-Fri 8-5
Restriction: Non-circulating to the pub

C SAINT EDWARDS UNIVERSITY*, Pat & Bill Munday Library, 3001 S Congress Ave, 78704-6489. SAN 361-1825. Tel: 512-416-5869. Interlibrary Loan Service Tel: 512-448-8471. E-mail: library@stedwards.edu. Web Site: library.stedwards.edu. *Dir,* R Casey Gibbs; E-mail: rgibbs@stedwards.edu; *Archivist & Spec Coll Librn,* Travis Williams; Tel: 512-428-1047, E-mail: twilli17@stedwards.edu; *Research Support Librarian,* Sophie Fahey; Tel: 512-428-1024, E-mail: sfahey@stedwards.edu; *Libr Instruction,* Brittney Johnson; Tel: 512-448-8479, E-mail: bjohnso1@stedwards.edu; Staff 18 (MLS 9, Non-MLS 9)
Founded 1889. Enrl 4,350; Fac 150; Highest Degree: Master
Library Holdings: e-books 700,000; Microforms 6,073; Bk Vols 161,644; Per Subs 1,909; Videos 3,362
Automation Activity & Vendor Info: (Acquisitions) Ex Libris Group; (Cataloging) Ex Libris Group; (Circulation) Ex Libris Group; (Course Reserve) Ex Libris Group; (ILL) OCLC Tipasa; (Media Booking) Ex Libris Group; (OPAC) Ex Libris Group; (Serials) Ex Libris Group
Wireless access
Partic in Amigos Library Services, Inc; OCLC Online Computer Library Center, Inc
Special Services for the Blind - Reader equip
Restriction: Open to researchers by request

G TEXAS COMMISSION ON ENVIRONMENT QUALITY*, Environmental Research Library, Bldg A, Rm 102, 12100 Park 35 Circle, 78753. (Mail add: MC-196, PO Box 13087, 78711-3087), SAN 316-0629. Tel: 512-239-0020. FAX: 512-239-0022. E-mail: library@tceq.texas.gov. Web Site: www.tceq.texas.gov/. *Head Librn,* Vonda K Todd; Tel: 512-239-0024; *Librn,* Jessica Wood; E-mail: jessica.wood@tceq.texas.gov; Staff 2 (MLS 2)
Founded 1964
Library Holdings: Bk Titles 60,000; Bk Vols 66,000; Per Subs 250
Special Collections: Civil Engineering (United States Corps of Engineers Coll); Engineers & United States Bureau of Reclamation Papers; Geology (United States Geological Survey Papers); Water Resources Development (Texas Water Development Board Publications)
Subject Interests: Air, Fields of sci relating to water resources, Geol, Hazardous waste, Hydraulic engr, Land use, Outdoor recreation, Problems, Solid waste, Water quality, Weather modification
Automation Activity & Vendor Info: (Cataloging) SirsiDynix; (Circulation) SirsiDynix; (OPAC) SirsiDynix; (Serials) SirsiDynix
Wireless access
Open Mon-Fri 8-12 & 1-5
Restriction: Open to pub for ref only

GM TEXAS DEPARTMENT OF STATE HEALTH SERVICES*, Library & Information Services Program, 1100 W 49th St, 78756-3199. (Mail add: PO Box 149347, Mailcode 1955, 78714-9347), SAN 316-0696. Tel: 512-776-7559. FAX: 512-776-7474. E-mail: library@dshs.texas.gov. Web Site: www.dshs.texas.gov/library. *Sr Librn,* Anne Tarpey; Tel: 512-776-2882, E-mail: anne.tarpey@dshs.texas.gov; Staff 6 (MLS 4, Non-MLS 2)
Founded 1958
Library Holdings: AV Mats 6,000; Bk Titles 10,400; Bk Vols 15,000; Per Subs 12
Special Collections: Disabilities & Rehabilitation; Early Childhood Intervention; Health & Safety; Texas Health Statistics
Automation Activity & Vendor Info: (Cataloging) EOS International; (Circulation) EOS International; (OPAC) EOS International; (Serials) EOS International
Partic in National Network of Libraries of Medicine Region 3
Open Mon-Fri 7:30-5
Restriction: Circ limited

G TEXAS GENERAL LAND OFFICE, Archives & Records Division, Stephen F Austin Bldg, 1700 N Congress Ave, 78701. SAN 372-9613. Tel: 512-463-5277. Toll Free Tel: 800-998-4456. E-mail: archives@glo.texas.gov. Web Site: www.glo.texas.gov. *Library Contact,* Mark Lambert; Tel: 512-463-5260
Founded 1836
Special Collections: Map Coll; Pub Lands Archives; Spanish Coll
Partic in Amigos Library Services, Inc
Open Mon-Fri 8-5
Restriction: Closed stack, Non-circulating

S TEXAS GRANTS RESOURCE CENTER*, 1191 Navasota St, 78702. SAN 316-0475. Tel: 512-475-7373. E-mail: tgrc@austin.utexas.edu. Web Site: diversity.utexas.edu/tgrc. *Asst Dir,* Amy Loar; Staff 2 (MLS 1, Non-MLS 1)
Founded 1962
Library Holdings: Bk Titles 800; Per Subs 2; Spec Interest Per Sub 2
Subject Interests: Evaluation, Grants, Volunteerism
Open Tues-Fri 9-5
Restriction: Non-circulating

G TEXAS HISTORICAL COMMISSION LIBRARY, 1511 Colorado St, 78701. (Mail add: PO Box 12276, 78711-2276), SAN 326-5323. Tel: 512-463-6100. Administration Tel: 512-936-4323. FAX: 512-936-0237. Web Site: thc.texas.gov/about-us/texas-historical-commission-library. *Admin Serv,* Paige Neumann; E-mail: paige.neumann@thc.texas.gov
Founded 1998
Library Holdings: Bk Titles 3,500; Bk Vols 5,000; Per Subs 30
Special Collections: Archeological Surveys & Reports; National Register in Texas Files; Official Texas Historical Marker Files. Oral History
Subject Interests: Archaeology, Archit
Automation Activity & Vendor Info: (Cataloging) Follett Software
Restriction: Circulates for staff only, Not a lending libr, Staff use, pub by appt

S TEXAS LEGISLATIVE REFERENCE LIBRARY*, State Capitol Bldg, 1100 N Congress Ave, Rm 2N-3, 78701. (Mail add: PO Box 12488, 78711-2488), SAN 316-0513. Tel: 512-463-1252. FAX: 512-475-4626. E-mail: lrl.service@lrl.texas.gov. Web Site: www.lrl.state.tx.us. *Dir,* Mary Camp; E-mail: mary.camp@lrl.texas.gov
Founded 1969
Library Holdings: Bk Vols 50,000
Special Collections: Texas Legislative Bills 1973-Present; Texas State Documents
Subject Interests: Law, Legislation, Polit sci, Pub affairs

Open Mon-Fri 8-5
Restriction: Ref only

M TEXAS MEDICAL ASSOCIATION*, Knowledge Center Library, 401 W 15th St, 78701-1680. SAN 316-0661. Tel: 512-370-1300. Toll Free Tel: 800-880-7955. E-mail: knowledge@texmed.org. Web Site: www.texmed.org. *Dir,* Claire Duncan; Tel: 512-370-1544, E-mail: claire.duncan@texmed.org; *Librn,* Barbara Tims; Tel: 512-370-1548, E-mail: barbara.tims@texmed.org; Staff 8 (MLS 4, Non-MLS 4)
Founded 1922
Library Holdings: Bk Vols 800; Per Subs 80
Special Collections: History of medicine in Texas
Subject Interests: Clinical med
Automation Activity & Vendor Info: (Cataloging) EOS International; (OPAC) EOS International; (Serials) EOS International
Function: Ref serv available, Res libr
Publications: CME Resource Catalog; Library Services Guide for Community Users; Library Services: A Guide for TMA Members
Partic in National Network of Libraries of Medicine Region 3; S Cent Regional Med Libr Program
Restriction: Mem only, Non-circulating
Friends of the Library Group

S TEXAS SCHOOL FOR THE BLIND*, Learning Resource Center Library, 1100 W 45th St, 78756. SAN 326-3819. Tel: 512-454-8631. FAX: 512-206-9450. Web Site: www.tsbvi.edu. *Librn,* Renee Toy; E-mail: toyre@tsbvi.edu; Staff 4 (MLS 1, Non-MLS 3)
Library Holdings: Bk Vols 10,600; Per Subs 50
Special Collections: Special Education for visually handicapped
Automation Activity & Vendor Info: (Cataloging) Follett Software; (Circulation) Follett Software
Restriction: Students only

GL TEXAS STATE LAW LIBRARY*, Tom C Clark Bldg, 205 W 14th St, Rm G01, 78701-1614. (Mail add: PO Box 12367, 78711-2367), SAN 316-0718. Tel: 512-463-1722. FAX: 512-463-1728. Toll Free FAX: 844-829-2843. E-mail: library@sll.texas.gov. Web Site: www.sll.texas.gov. *Dir,* Amy Small; *Asst Dir,* Heather DiChiara-Schilling; Staff 7 (MLS 7)
Founded 1971
Library Holdings: Bk Vols 100,000
Special Collections: US Document Depository
Subject Interests: Law, Legal hist
Wireless access
Open Mon-Fri 8-5

P TEXAS STATE LIBRARY & ARCHIVES COMMISSION*, 1201 Brazos St, 78701. (Mail add: Box 12927, 78711-2927), SAN 361-1914. Tel: 512-463-5474. Reference Tel: 512-463-5455. Administration Tel: 512-463-5460. Toll Free Tel: 800-252-9386 (TX only). E-mail: info@tsl.texas.gov. Web Site: www.tsl.texas.gov. *Dir, State Librn,* Gloria Meraz; E-mail: director.librarian@tsl.texas.gov; *Asst State Librn,* Tim Gleisner; Tel: 512-463-5459, E-mail: tgleisner@tsl.texas.gov; *Chief Fiscal Officer, Chief Operations Officer,* Donna Osborne; Tel: 512-463-5440, Fax: 512-463-3560, E-mail: dosborne@tsl.texas.gov; *Dir, Libr Develop & Networking,* Sarah J Karnes; Tel: 545-651-2463, E-mail: sjacobson@tsl.texas.gov; *State Archivist,* Jelain Chubb; Tel: 512-463-5467, E-mail: jchubb@tsl.texas.gov; *State Rec Mgr,* Craig Kelso; E-mail: ckelso@tsl.texas.gov; Staff 97 (MLS 58, Non-MLS 39)
Founded 1909
Library Holdings: e-books 28,281; Bk Vols 2,000,000; Per Subs 352
Special Collections: Broadside Coll; History Coll, maps, ms; Professional Librarianship Coll; Texas & Federal Government Documents Coll. State Document Depository; US Document Depository
Subject Interests: Fed govt, Genealogy, Pub policy, State govt, Texana
Automation Activity & Vendor Info: (Cataloging) OCLC Connexion; (Circulation) SirsiDynix; (ILL) OCLC WorldShare Interlibrary Loan; (OPAC) SirsiDynix; (Serials) SirsiDynix
Wireless access
Function: Archival coll, Distance learning, Govt ref serv, Homebound delivery serv, ILL available, Internet access, Prof lending libr, Summer reading prog, Workshops
Publications: Instruction Manuals; Library Developments (Online only); Texas Academic Library Statistics
Partic in Amigos Library Services, Inc; Association for Rural & Small Libraries; Western Council of State Libraries, Inc
Special Services for the Blind - Bks & mags in Braille, on rec, tape & cassette; Large print & cassettes; Local mags & bks recorded; Machine repair; Newsletter (in large print, Braille or on cassette); Production of talking bks; Reader equip; Ref serv; Talking bks; Talking bks & player equip; Tel Pioneers equip repair group; Volunteer serv
Open Mon-Fri 9-4
Restriction: Circ limited, Closed stack, Non-circulating coll
Friends of the Library Group

Branches: 1
SAM HOUSTON REGIONAL LIBRARY & RESEARCH CENTER, 650 FM 1011, Liberty, 77575. (Mail add: PO Box 310, Liberty, 77575-0310), SAN 326-4505. Tel: 936-336-8821. FAX: 936-336-7049. E-mail: samhoustoncenter@tsl.state.tx.us. Web Site: www.tsl.state.tx.us/shc/index.html. *Mgr,* Alana Inman; E-mail: ainman@tsl.texas.gov; *Archivist, Curator,* Lisa Meisch; E-mail: lmeisch@tsl.texas.gov
Founded 1977
Library Holdings: Bk Titles 4,500; Per Subs 9
Special Collections: Martin Dies Papers; Price Daniel Papers; Sam Houston Images (Jean Houston Baldwin Coll). Oral History
Function: Archival coll, For res purposes
Open Tues-Fri 8-5, Sat 9-4
Restriction: Non-circulating to the pub
Friends of the Library Group

P TEXAS STATE LIBRARY & ARCHIVES COMMISSION*, Talking Book Program, 1201 Brazos St, 78701. (Mail add: PO Box 12927, 78711-2927), SAN 316-0726. Tel: 512-463-5458. Toll Free Tel: 800-252-9605 (TX only). FAX: 512-936-0685. E-mail: tbp.services@tsl.texas.gov. Web Site: tsl.texas.gov/tbp. *Dir,* Ann Minner; Tel: 512-463-5428, E-mail: aminner@tsl.texas.gov; *Audio Production Admini,* S Miles Lewis; E-mail: slewis@tsl.texas.gov; *Reader Serv Mgr,* Stacey Lewis; E-mail: selewis@tsl.texas.gov; *Operations Supvr,* Guffie Robinson; E-mail: grobinsn@tsl.texas.gov; *Automation Syst Coordr,* Jennifer Ronsen; E-mail: jronsen@tsl.texas.gov; *Disability Info & Referral Coord,* Dina Abramson; E-mail: dabramson@tsl.texas.gov; *Pub Awareness Coordr,* Jaclyn Owusu; Tel: 512-463-5452, E-mail: TBPINFO@tsl.texas.gov; *Vols Serv Coordr,* Stacy Darwin; Tel: 512-475-4605, E-mail: sdarwin@tsl.texas.gov; Staff 37.3 (MLS 12.8, Non-MLS 24.5)
Founded 1931
Library Holdings: Audiobooks 380,386; Braille Volumes 76,543; Large Print Bks 42,754; Bk Titles 33,292
Special Collections: Audio Books; Braille Books; Disability Information; Large Print Books; Realia Coll (board, card & education games); Spanish & Other Languages Coll
Wireless access
Special Services for the Blind - Assistive/Adapted tech devices, equip & products; Audio mat; Bks on flash-memory cartridges; Braille bks; Children's Braille; Digital talking bk; Digital talking bk machines; Disability awareness prog; Extensive large print coll; Free checkout of audio mat; Home delivery serv; Info on spec aids & appliances; Large print bks; Local mags & bks recorded; Machine repair; Mags & bk reproduction/duplication; Newsletter (in large print, Braille or on cassette); Reader equip; Recorded bks; Spanish Braille mags & bks; Talking bk & rec for the blind cat; Talking bks & player equip; Volunteer serv; Web-Braille
Open Mon-Fri 8-5
Friends of the Library Group

L TRAVIS COUNTY LAW LIBRARY*, Ned Granger, 314 W 11th St, Ste 140, 78701. SAN 374-6070. Tel: 512-854-8677. E-mail: referencematerial@traviscountytx.gov. Web Site: lawlibrary.traviscountytx.gov. *Tech Serv Supvr,* Ms Aizul Ortega; Tel: 512-854-9019; *Ref Serv,* Judy Helms; Tel: 512-854-9045, E-mail: judy.helms@traviscountytx.gov; Staff 6 (MLS 2, Non-MLS 4)
Founded 1983
Library Holdings: Bk Titles 360; Bk Vols 12,000; Per Subs 20
Special Collections: Texas & Federal Law Coll
Automation Activity & Vendor Info: (Cataloging) Cuadra Associates, Inc; (OPAC) Cuadra Associates, Inc
Wireless access
Function: For res purposes
Open Mon-Fri 8-5
Restriction: Circ limited, Non-circulating to the pub, Prof mat only

CM UNIVERSITY OF ST AUGUSTINE FOR HEALTH SCIENCES*, Austin Campus Library, 5401 La Crosse Ave, 78739. Tel: 737-202-3229. E-mail: library@usa.edu. Web Site: library.usa.edu. *Librn,* Jessica Cain; E-mail: jcain@usa.edu; *Circ Mgr,* Allison Hradecky; E-mail: ahradecky@usa.edu
Wireless access
Function: ILL available, Photocopying/Printing, Scanner, Study rm
Open Mon-Sun 7am-10pm

C UNIVERSITY OF TEXAS AT AUSTIN*, Center for Transportation Research Library, 3925 W Braker Lane, Ste 4.909, 78759. (Mail add: 3925 W Braker Lane, UT STOP D9300, 78759), SAN 372-9648. Tel: 512-232-3126. E-mail: ctrlib@austin.utexas.edu. Web Site: library.ctr.utexas.edu/catalog. *Mgr, Libr Serv,* Ms Kevyn Barnes-Sanchez; Tel: 512-232-3130; *Libr Assoc/Tech Serv, Ref Librn,* Michael Nugent; *Webmaster,* Geoffrey Potter. Subject Specialists: *Coll mgt & conserv,* Ms Kevyn Barnes-Sanchez; *Cataloging, Data coll, Digitization,* Michael Nugent; *Info mgt,* Geoffrey Potter; Staff 3 (MLS 2, Non-MLS 1)
Founded 1963

Sept 2020-Aug 2021 Income $794,681
Library Holdings: CDs 436; Electronic Media & Resources 22,711; Bk Titles 27,600; Bk Vols 31,900; Spec Interest Per Sub 1; Videos 16
Special Collections: Council of Advanced Transportation Systems; Texas Department of Transportation; Transportation Research Board
Subject Interests: Tex, Transportation engr, Transportation planning, Transportation res, Transportation studies
Automation Activity & Vendor Info: (Cataloging) Inmagic, Inc.; (Circulation) Inmagic, Inc.; (OPAC) Sydney Enterprise
Wireless access
Open Mon-Fri 8-5

C UNIVERSITY OF TEXAS LIBRARIES*, Perry-Castaneda Library, 101 E 21st St, 78705. SAN 361-1973. Tel: 512-495-4300. FAX: 512-495-4296. Web Site: www.lib.utexas.edu/about/locations/pcl. *Vice Provost & Dir,* Dr Lorraine Haricombe; E-mail: ljharic@austin.utexas.edu; *Communications Librn, Syst Librn,* Ronda Rowe; Tel: 512-495-4110, E-mail: ronda@austin.utexas.edu; Staff 138 (MLS 138)
Founded 1883. Enrl 51,426; Fac 2,432; Highest Degree: Doctorate
Library Holdings: Bk Vols 8,482,207; Per Subs 48,096
Special Collections: US Document Depository
Automation Activity & Vendor Info: (Acquisitions) Innovative Interfaces, Inc
Wireless access
Partic in Amigos Library Services, Inc; Association of Research Libraries; Center for Research Libraries; Coun of Libr Info Resources; Digital Libr Fedn; Greater Western Library Alliance; OCLC Online Computer Library Center, Inc; OCLC Research Library Partnership; TexSHARE - Texas State Library & Archives Commission
Friends of the Library Group

Departmental Libraries:

ARCHITECTURE & PLANNING, Battle Hall 200, 302 Inner Campus Dr, S5430, 78712-1413. (Mail add: PO Box P, 78713-8916). Tel: 512-495-4620. Reference Tel: 512-495-4623. E-mail: apl@austin.utexas.edu. Web Site: www.lib.utexas.edu/about/locations/architecture-planning. *Head Librn,* Beth Dodd; E-mail: dodd.beth@austin.utexas.edu; Staff 2 (MLS 2)
Founded 1912
Library Holdings: Bk Vols 100,000; Per Subs 240
Special Collections: Alexander Architectural Archive
Subject Interests: Archit, Archit hist, City planning, Interior design, Landscape archit, Regional planning

NETTIE LEE BENSON LATIN AMERICAN COLLECTION, Sid Richardson Hall, SRH 1108, 2300 Red River St, 78713-8916. (Mail add: Sid Richardson Hall, 1109, 2300 Red River St, Mail Code S5410, 78712-1469), SAN 361-2309. Tel: 512-495-4520. Circulation Tel: 512-495-4522. FAX: 512-495-4568. Web Site: www.lib.utexas.edu/about/locations/benson. *Dir, Librn,* Melissa Guy; E-mail: m.guy@austin.utexas.edu; *Br Supvr,* Linda Gill; E-mail: linda.gill@austin.utexas.edu; *Archivist,* Dylan Joy; E-mail: d.joy@austin.utexas.gov
Library Holdings: Bk Vols 888,670
Special Collections: Afro-Jamaican Folklore (Joseph G Moore Coll); Americo Paredes papers; Brazilian Music (David P Appleby Coll); Central American Materials (Arturo Taracena Flores Coll; Roberto Carpio Nicolle Coll); Cultural History & Literature of Brazil, Chile & the Rio de las Plata Region (Manuel Gondra, Simon Lucuix & Pedro Martinez Reales Colls); Joaquin Fernandez de Lizardi, Alfonso Reyes, Jose Angel Gutierrez, Julian Samora Library, Jose Toribio Medina & Many Literary Figures of Mexico, Argentina, Brazil, Chile & Peru; Jose Cardenas & Intercultural Development Research Association Archives; Julio Cortazar Literary Papers; Letters of Santa Anna & Pancho Villa; Manuscripts from 16th to 20th Century, incl 16th Century Relaciones Geograficas; Martin Fierro Coll; Media Materials of Chile, Bolivia & Peru (Diego Munoz Coll); Mexican Cultural History & Literature (Genaro Garcia, Joaquin Garcia Icazbalceta, Juan Hernandez y Davalos, Sanchez Navarro, Lazaro de la Garza, Pablo Salce Arrendondo & W B Stephens Colls); Papers of Six Mexican Presidents & Other 19th Century Mexican Figures; Presidential Papers of League of United Latin American Citizens; Sor Juana Ines de la Cruz Coll; St John d'el Rey Mining Company Archives
Subject Interests: Latin Am studies
Partic in OCLC Online Computer Library Center, Inc
Publications: Catalog of the Latin American Collection

C BRISCOE CENTER FOR AMERICAN HISTORY, Sid Richard Hall, Unit 2, Rm 2106, 2300 Red River St, 78712-1426. (Mail add: 2300 Red River St, Stop D1100, 78712-1426). Tel: 512-495-4515. Reference Tel: 512-495-4166. Information Services Tel: 512-495-4518. FAX: 512-495-4542. Web Site: briscoecenter.org. *Exec Dir,* Dr Don E Carleton; E-mail: d.carleton@austin.utexas.edu; *Dep Exec Dir,* Erin Purdy; Tel: 512-947-7774, E-mail: erin.purdy@austin.utexas.edu; *Dir of Coll, Res,* Stephanie Malmros; E-mail: smalmros@ustin.utexas.edu; *Dir of Develop,* Lisa Avra; E-mail: l.avra@austin.ugexas.edu; *Spec Project Dir,* Alison M Beck; E-mail: al.beck@austin.utexas.edu
Library Holdings: Bk Vols 150,000; Per Subs 103
Special Collections: American History Coll; Congressional History Coll; Eugene C Barker Texas History Coll; John Nance Garner House & Museum (Uvalde, Texas); Sam Rayburn Library & Museum (Bonham, Texas); The George W Littlefield Southern History Coll; University of Texas Archives; Western Americana Coll; Winedale Historical Center (Round Top, Texas). Oral History
Subject Interests: Archives, Hist of old south, Imprints, Manuscripts, Music, Newsps, Oral hist, Tex
Publications: Newsletter
Open Mon-Fri 8-5

BUREAU OF ECONOMIC GEOLOGY & RESOURCE CENTER, 10100 Burnet Rd, Bldg 131, 78758-4445. (Mail add: University Sta, Box X, 78713-8924). Tel: 512-471-1534, 512-471-7144. FAX: 512-471-0140. Web Site: www.beg.utexas.edu/outreach/resource-center. *Dir,* Scott Tinker; *Info Geologist & Res Ctr Mgr,* Linda Ruiz McCall; E-mail: linda.mccall@beg.utexas.edu; Staff 1 (MLS 1)
Special Collections: Bureau Contract Reports; Historical Geology (Girard Coll); South Texas/Coastal Geology (W Armstrong Price Coll); Unpublished Open-File Documents, letter rpts, maps, theses; Virgil E Barnes Coll, aerial photos, geologic maps
Subject Interests: Gas, Geol, Geophysics, Geoscience, Oil, Tex
Function: Archival coll, Bks on CD, Computers for patron use, Mail & tel request accepted, Online cat, Res libr, Wheelchair accessible
Open Mon-Fri 8-5
Restriction: Circ limited, Circulates for staff only, In-house use for visitors, Non-circulating coll, Not a lending libr

CLASSICS LIBRARY, Waggener Hall, 2210 Speedway, 78712. (Mail add: PO Box P, 78713-8916), SAN 361-2457. Tel: 512-495-4690. Web Site: www.lib.utexas.edu/about/locations/classics. *Br Supvr,* Claudia Fuentes; E-mail: c.fuentes@utexas.edu
Library Holdings: Bk Vols 27,292

EAST ASIAN LIBRARY PROGRAM, Perry-Castaneda Library, 2.302, Mail Code S5431, 101 E 21st St, 78712-1474. Tel: 512-495-4325. *Librn,* Yi Shan; E-mail: yi.shan@austin.utexas.edu; Staff 5 (MLS 2, Non-MLS 3)
Library Holdings: Bk Vols 104,000
Subject Interests: China, Japan, Korea

FINE ARTS LIBRARY, Doty Fine Arts Bldg 3-200, 2306 Trinity St, 78712. (Mail add: 2306 Trinity St, Mail Code S5437, 78712), SAN 361-2511. Tel: 512-495-4481. FAX: 512-495-4490. Web Site: www.lib.utexas.edu/about/locations/fine-arts. *Humanities Liaison Librn,* Mary Rader; Tel: 512-495-4119, E-mail: m.rader@austin.utexas.edu; Staff 30 (MLS 3, Non-MLS 27)
Founded 1979
Library Holdings: AV Mats 50,000; Bk Vols 300,000; Per Subs 600
Special Collections: Historical Music Recordings Coll
Subject Interests: Art, Dance, Music
Function: AV serv, Ref serv available, Res libr
Friends of the Library Group

INTERLIBRARY SERVICES DEPARTMENT, PCL1-343, First Flr Dock, 101 E 21st St, Stop S5463, 78712-1492. Tel: 512-495-4134. Interlibrary Loan Service Tel: 512-495-4131. FAX: 512-495-4283. Web Site: legacy.lib.utexas.edu/services/ils. *Doc Delivery, Librn,* Kristin Walker; E-mail: kristin.walker@austin.utexas.edu
Open Mon-Fri 8-5

KUEHNE PHYSICS-MATHEMATICS-ASTRONOMY LIBRARY, Robert L Moore Hall 4.200, S5441, 2515 Speedway, 78713, SAN 361-2635. Tel: 512-495-4610. E-mail: pma@lib.utexas.edu. Web Site: www.lib.utexas.edu/about/locations/physics-math-astronomy. *Liaison Librn,* Lydia Fletcher; E-mail: l.fletcher@austin.utexas.edu; *Br Supvr,* Britt Wilson; E-mail: britto@austin.utexas.edu
Library Holdings: Bk Vols 118,458

LIFE SCIENCE (BIOLOGY, PHARMACY), Main Bldg, 2400 Inner Campus Dr, 78712, SAN 361-266X. Tel: 512-495-4630. FAX: 512-495-4638. Web Site: www.lib.utexas.edu/about/locations/life-science. *Br Supvr,* Hector Rodriguez; E-mail: h.rodriguez@austin.utexas.edu; *Liaison Librn,* Roxanne Bogucka; E-mail: roxanne.bogucka@austin.utexas.edu
Library Holdings: Bk Vols 220,000; Per Subs 1,800
Subject Interests: Biol sci, Pharm

MALLET CHEMISTRY LIBRARY, Welch Hall 2132, 105 E 24th St, 78713, SAN 361-2422. Tel: 512-495-4600. Web Site: www.lib.utexas.edu/about/locations/chemistry. *Librn,* David Flaxbart; E-mail: flaxbart@austin.utexas.edu; Staff 3 (MLS 1, Non-MLS 2)
Library Holdings: Bk Vols 101,000
Subject Interests: Chem, Chem engr, Food sci

MARINE SCIENCE, Marine Science Institute, 750 Channelview Dr, Port Aransas, 78373-5015, SAN 371-5965. Tel: 361-749-3094. FAX: 361-749-6725. Web Site: www.lib.utexas.edu/about/locations/marine-science. *Liaison Librn,* Liz DeHart; E-mail: l.dehart@austin.utexas.edu; Staff 2 (MLS 1, Non-MLS 1)
Founded 1946. Fac 13; Highest Degree: Doctorate
Library Holdings: Bk Vols 40,000; Per Subs 100

Subject Interests: Ecosystems, Environ toxicology, Marine biosciences, Marine culture systs, Marine sci
Function: Doc delivery serv, For res purposes, ILL available, Internet access, Photocopying/Printing, Ref serv available, Wheelchair accessible
Partic in Association of Research Libraries
Publications: Contributions in Marine Science
Restriction: Circ limited, In-house use for visitors, Internal circ only, Non-circulating to the pub, Open to pub for ref only, Open to students, fac & staff

MCKINNEY ENGINEERING LIBRARY, Engineering Education & Research Center, EER 1706, 2501 Speedway, 78712, SAN 316-0742. Tel: 512-495-4511. FAX: 512-495-4511. E-mail: englib@lib.utexas.edu. Web Site: www.lib.utexas.edu/about/locations/engineering. *Br Supvr,* Adam Hatley; E-mail: arhatley@austin.utexas.edu; *Liaison Librn,* Larayne Dallas; E-mail: ldallas@austin.utexas.edu
Library Holdings: Bk Vols 165,000
Special Collections: Engineering Industry Standards, micro; Master Catalog Service; Patents, micro; US Patents

MIDDLE EASTERN LIBRARY PROGRAM, 2501 Speedway, 78712. (Mail add: PO Box P, 78713-8916). Tel: 512-495-4322. FAX: 512-495-4296. *Librn,* Ms Dale Correa, PhD; E-mail: d.correa@austin.utexas.edu; Staff 5 (MLS 1, Non-MLS 4)
Library Holdings: Bk Vols 319,200
Subject Interests: Islamic world
Publications: Arabic & Persian Periodicals in the Middle East Collection

POPULATION RESEARCH CENTER LIBRARY, 305 E 23rd St, Stop G1800, 78712-1699, SAN 361-2759. Tel: 512-471-5514. FAX: 512-471-4886. Web Site: liberalarts.utexas.edu/prc. *Dir,* Debra Umberson; E-mail: umberson@prc.utexas.edu; *Assoc Dir,* Kelly Raley; E-mail: kelly.raley@mail.utexas.edu; *Asst Dir,* Mary De La Garza; E-mail: marydlg@prc.utexas.edu
Founded 1971
Library Holdings: Bk Vols 35,000
Special Collections: World Fertility Survey, publ depository
Subject Interests: Demography, Domestic demography, Educ, Family life, Human ecology, Latin Am, Relig, Soc policy
Publications: Handbook of National Population Census: Africa & Asia; International Population Census Bibliography: 1965-68; Latin America & the Caribbean, North America, Oceania & Europe; Revision & Update: 1945-1977

HARRY RANSOM CENTER, 300 W 21st St, 78712. (Mail add: University of Texas, PO Box 7219, 78713-7219), SAN 361-2724. Tel: 512-471-8944. Reference Tel: 512-471-9119. E-mail: rvr@hrc.utexas.edu. Web Site: www.hrc.utexas.edu. *Dir,* Stephen Enniss; E-mail: enniss@austin.utexas.edu; *Assoc Dir & Hobby Found Librn,* Jim Kuhn; E-mail: jim.kuhn@austin.utexas.edu; Staff 28 (MLS 17, Non-MLS 11)
Founded 1957
Library Holdings: Bk Titles 800,000; Per Subs 276
Special Collections: 17th & 18th Century First Editions, T J Wise Forgeries (Wrenn Library); 17th-20th Century First Editions; 18th Century First Editions & Source Materials (Aitken Library); A A Knopf Library & Archives; Author Colls of James Agee, Maxwell Anderson, W H Auden, H E Bates, Samuel Beckett, Arnold Bennett, Edmund Blunden, E B & Robert Browning, A Burgess, Byron, J B Cabell, Conrad, Hart Crane, E E Cummings, Edward Dahlberg, J F Dobie, Norman Douglas, A C Doyle, T S Eliot, Faulkner, Fitzgerald, C S Forester, E M Forster, John Fowles, Galsworthy, Goyen, Robert Graves, Graham Greene, D Hare, Lillian Hellman, Hemingway, Hergesheimer, W H Hudson, Huxley, Jacobson, Jeffers, Joyce, Adrienne Kennedy, D H Lawrence, T E Lawrence, Sinclair Lewis, Arthur Machen, Louis MacNeice, E L Masters, Maugham, David Mamet, George Meredith, James Michener, Arthur Miller, Henry Miller, Marianne Moore, Morley, Nabokov, Eugene O'Neill, Poe, Pound, Powys, Priestley, Prokosch, Purdy, Sassoon, Scott, Sexton, G B Shaw, Isaac Bashevis Singer, The Sitwells, C P Snow, Steinbeck, Tom Stoppard, Dylan Thomas, Tennessee Williams, Tutuola, W C Williams, W B Yeats & Louis Zukofsky; Barrie, Eliot, Galsworthy, Shaw, Wilde, Yeats (T E Hanley Library); David O Selznick Archives; Don Delillo Coll; Edward Laroque Tinker Archives; Gernsheim Photography Coll; History of Science Coll; McManus-Young Magic Coll; Norman Mailer Coll; Robert De Niro Coll; Science Fiction (Currey Coll); Southwest Pacificana (Grattan Coll); Terrence McNally Coll; Theatre History & Dramatic Literature (Kemble, Garrick, P T Barnum, Houdini, Norman Bel Geddes Theatre Arts Library); Watergate (Woodward & Bernstein Coll)
Subject Interests: Am lit, British lit, Film, Fr lit, Hist of photog, Performing arts
Restriction: Non-circulating coll
Friends of the Library Group

SERIALS ACQUISITIONS UNIT, PO Box P, 78713-8916. FAX: 512-495-4296. *Assoc Dir, Tech Serv,* Robin Fradenburgh; Tel: 512-495-4159

SOUTH ASIAN LIBRARY PROGRAM, 120 Inner Campus Dr, SG 9300, 78712, SAN 371-4985. Tel: 512-495-4119. FAX: 512-495-4397. Web Site: liberalarts.utexas.edu/asianstudies. *Librn,* Mary Rader; E-mail: m.rader@austin.utexas.edu
Library Holdings: Bk Vols 300,000

WALTER GEOLOGY LIBRARY, Jackson Geological Science Bldg, 4.202, E 23rd St, 78712, SAN 361-2546. Tel: 512-495-4680. FAX: 512-495-4102. Web Site: www.lib.utexas.edu/about/locations/geology. *Br Supvr,* James Galloway; E-mail: j.galloway@austin.utexas.edu
Library Holdings: Bk Vols 134,100
Special Collections: Tobin Geologic Maps Coll

P WELLS BRANCH COMMUNITY LIBRARY*, 15001 Wells Port Dr, 78728. Tel: 512-989-3188. FAX: 512-989-3533. E-mail: staff@wblibrary.org. Web Site: www.wblibrary.org. *Libr Dir,* Donita Ward; E-mail: director@wblibrary.org; Staff 6 (MLS 4, Non-MLS 2)
Founded 1998. Pop 17,800; Circ 170,800
Library Holdings: Audiobooks 1,780; CDs 558; DVDs 6,226; e-books 11,569; Large Print Bks 891; Bk Vols 44,819; Per Subs 50
Wireless access
Function: 24/7 Electronic res, 24/7 Online cat, Activity rm, Adult bk club, After school storytime, Audiobks via web, Bk club(s), Bks on CD, Children's prog, Computer training, Computers for patron use, E-Readers, Electronic databases & coll, Family literacy, Free DVD rentals, Holiday prog, ILL available, Internet access, Life-long learning prog for all ages, Magazines, Mango lang, Movies, Music CDs, Online cat, Outreach serv, OverDrive digital audio bks, Photocopying/Printing, Preschool reading prog, Printer for laptops & handheld devices, Prog for adults, Prog for children & young adult, Scanner, Spanish lang bks, Story hour, Summer & winter reading prog, Summer reading prog, Teen prog, Wheelchair accessible, Winter reading prog, Writing prog
Partic in Central Texas Digital Consortium; Partners Library Action Network; TexSHARE - Texas State Library & Archives Commission
Open Mon-Thurs 10-8, Fri & Sat 10-6, Sun 1-6
Friends of the Library Group

P WESTBANK COMMUNITY LIBRARY DISTRICT*, 1309 Westbank Dr, 78746. SAN 372-6789. Tel: 512-327-3045. Circulation Tel: 512-314-3588. Interlibrary Loan Service Tel: 512-314-3593. Reference Tel: 512-314-3582. Administration Tel: 512-314-3580. FAX: 512-327-3074. Web Site: www.westbanklibrary.com. *Dir,* Mary Jo Finch; E-mail: maryjo@westbanklibrary.com; *Assoc Dir,* Autumn Solomon; E-mail: autumn@westbanklibrary.com; *Admin Coordr, Pub Serv,* Kristi Floyd; E-mail: kristi@westbanklibrary.com; *Cat/Ref Librn,* Donna Woods; E-mail: donna@westbanklibrary.com; *Pub Serv Librn,* Mary Beth Widhalm; E-mail: marybeth@westbanklibrary.com; *Colls Mgr,* Elena Carvajal; E-mail: elena@westbanklibrary.com; *Fac Mgr, Tech Serv Coordr,* Rhonda Kuiper; E-mail: rhonda@westbanklibrary.com; *Tech,* Cesar Martinez; E-mail: cesar@westbanklibrary.com; Staff 7 (MLS 6, Non-MLS 1)
Founded 1984. Pop 29,268; Circ 713,438
Library Holdings: Audiobooks 5,782; CDs 5,782; DVDs 9,696; e-books 440; Electronic Media & Resources 58; Large Print Bks 650; Bk Titles 57,886; Bk Vols 76,415; Per Subs 228; Videos 9,696
Automation Activity & Vendor Info: (Cataloging) Biblionix; (Circulation) Biblionix; (ILL) Biblionix; (OPAC) Biblionix
Wireless access
Function: Adult bk club, After school storytime, Art exhibits, Audiobks via web, Bk club(s), Bks on CD, Chess club, Children's prog, Computers for patron use, E-Reserves, Electronic databases & coll, Free DVD rentals, Genealogy discussion group, Holiday prog, ILL available, Mail & tel request accepted, Online cat, Online info literacy tutorials on the web & in blackboard, Online ref, OverDrive digital audio bks, Photocopying/Printing, Prog for adults, Prog for children & young adult, Ref serv available, Senior outreach, Story hour, Summer reading prog, Tax forms, Telephone ref, Wheelchair accessible
Publications: Annual report; Newflash (Bimonthly); The Dragon's Tale (Bimonthly); The Teen Scene (Bimonthly)
Partic in Partners Library Action Network
Open Mon-Thurs 10-7, Fri-Sun 11-5
Restriction: Non-resident fee
Friends of the Library Group
Branches: 1

LAURA BUSH COMMUNITY LIBRARY, 9411 Bee Cave Rd, 78733. Tel: 512-381-1400. Circulation Tel: 512-381-1401. Interlibrary Loan Service Tel: 512-381-1403. Administration Tel: 512-381-1404. FAX: 512-381-1421.
Founded 2009
Automation Activity & Vendor Info: (Acquisitions) Biblionix; (Cataloging) Biblionix; (Circulation) Biblionix; (Course Reserve) Biblionix; (ILL) Biblionix; (OPAC) Biblionix
Function: Adult bk club, After school storytime, Art exhibits, Bk club(s), Bks on CD, Computer training, Computers for patron use, E-Reserves, Electronic databases & coll, Free DVD rentals, Genealogy discussion group, ILL available, Online cat, Online ref, Orientations, Photocopying/Printing, Prog for adults, Prog for children & young adult,

Ref & res, Ref serv available, Scanner, Spoken cassettes & CDs, Spoken cassettes & DVDs, Story hour, Summer reading prog, Tax forms, Teen prog, Telephone ref, Wheelchair accessible, Writing prog
Open Mon-Thurs 10-7, Fri-Sun 11-5
Restriction: Circ to mem only, Non-resident fee

L WRIGHT & GREENHILL PC, Law Library, 4700 Mueller Blvd, Ste 200, 78723. SAN 375-0221. Tel: 512-866-6681. FAX: 512-476-5382. Web Site: www.wrightgreenhill.com. *Legal Info Librn,* Twyla Tranfaglia; E-mail: ttranfaglia@w-g.com; Staff 2 (MLS 1, Non-MLS 1)
Library Holdings: Bk Vols 5,000; Per Subs 50
Restriction: Staff use only

AZLE

P AZLE MEMORIAL LIBRARY*, 333 W Main St, 76020. SAN 316-0750. Tel: 817-444-7216. FAX: 817-444-7064. E-mail: library@cityofazle.org. Web Site: www.cityofazle.org/index.aspx?NID=203. *Dir,* Curren McLane; Tel: 817-444-7216, Ext 207, E-mail: cmclane@cityofazle.org
Founded 1964. Pop 12,000; Circ 110,744
Library Holdings: AV Mats 10,000; Bk Vols 45,000; Per Subs 100
Subject Interests: Local hist
Automation Activity & Vendor Info: (Cataloging) Innovative Interfaces, Inc; (Circulation) Innovative Interfaces, Inc; (OPAC) Innovative Interfaces, Inc
Wireless access
Open Mon, Wed & Fri 9-6, Tues & Thurs 9-8, Sat 9-2
Friends of the Library Group

BAIRD

P CALLAHAN COUNTY LIBRARY*, Callahan County Courthous, Basement, 100 W Fourth St, B-1, 79504-5305. SAN 316-0769. Tel: 325-854-5875. FAX: 325-854-5841. E-mail: library@callahancounty.org. Web Site: baird.ploud.net. *Librn,* Position Currently Open
Founded 1937. Pop 3,470
Library Holdings: AV Mats 303; Bk Titles 17,000; Bk Vols 34,653; Per Subs 16
Open Mon-Fri 1-5

BALCH SPRINGS

P BALCH SPRINGS LIBRARY-LEARNING CENTER*, 12450 Elam Rd, 75180. SAN 376-4478. Tel: 972-913-3000. FAX: 972-286-8856. E-mail: librarystaff@cityofbalchsprings.com. Web Site: www.balchspringslibrary.org. *Ch,* Stacy Holguin; E-mail: sholguin@cityofbalchsprings.com; *Circulation Specialist Supvr,* Teresa Conley; E-mail: tconley@cityofbalchsprings.com; *Tech Serv,* Kristin Stewart; E-mail: kstewart@cityofbalchsprings.com; Staff 3 (Non-MLS 3)
Founded 1969. Pop 26,000; Circ 40,000
Library Holdings: Bks on Deafness & Sign Lang 15; DVDs 4,500; Bk Titles 31,000; Per Subs 26
Wireless access
Function: 24/7 Electronic res, 24/7 Online cat, Activity rm, Adult bk club, Adult literacy prog, Art exhibits, Art programs, Audiobks on Playaways & MP3, Audiobks via web, AV serv, BA reader (adult literacy), Bilingual assistance for Spanish patrons, Bk club(s), Bks on CD, Children's prog, Citizenship assistance, Computer training, Computers for patron use, Digital talking bks, E-Readers, E-Reserves, Electronic databases & coll, Family literacy, Free DVD rentals, Holiday prog, Homework prog, Large print keyboards, Learning ctr, Magazines, Magnifiers for reading, Mail & tel request accepted, Mail loans to mem, Mango lang, Meeting rooms, Movies, Music CDs, Online cat, Online info literacy tutorials on the web & in blackboard, Online ref, Outreach serv, OverDrive digital audio bks, Photocopying/Printing, Preschool outreach, Preschool reading prog, Printer for laptops & handheld devices, Prof lending libr, Prog for adults, Prog for children & young adult, Ref & res, Res assist avail, Spanish lang bks, Spoken cassettes & CDs, STEM programs, Story hour, Study rm, Summer & winter reading prog, Summer reading prog, Tax forms, Teen prog, Telephone ref, Visual arts prog, Wheelchair accessible, Winter reading prog, Workshops
Special Services for the Blind - Cassettes
Open Mon-Thurs 10-7, Fri 10-6, Sat 10-3
Friends of the Library Group

BALLINGER

P CARNEGIE LIBRARY OF BALLINGER*, 204 N Eighth St, 76821. SAN 316-0777. Tel: 325-365-3616. FAX: 325-365-5004. E-mail: staff@carnegieballinger.org. Web Site: carnegie-ballinger.ploud.net. *Dir,* Carolyn Kraatz; E-mail: carolyn.kraatz@gmail.com; *Ch, Librn,* Amber Self; Tel: 325-365-9315; Staff 2 (Non-MLS 2)
Founded 1909. Pop 6,602; Circ 25,500
Library Holdings: Audiobooks 695; DVDs 1,000; High Interest/Low Vocabulary Bk Vols 500; Large Print Bks 967; Bk Titles 12,000; Per Subs 5
Automation Activity & Vendor Info: (Cataloging) Biblionix; (Circulation) Biblionix; (ILL) OCLC WorldShare Interlibrary Loan
Wireless access
Function: Accelerated reader prog, Activity rm, Audiobks on Playaways & MP3, Audiobks via web, Bks on CD, Children's prog, Computers for patron use, For res purposes, Free DVD rentals, ILL available, Internet access, Life-long learning prog for all ages, Literacy & newcomer serv, Magazines, Meeting rooms, Microfiche/film & reading machines, Movies, Music CDs, Notary serv, Online cat, Online ref, Outside serv via phone, mail, e-mail & web, Photocopying/Printing, Preschool outreach, Preschool reading prog, Prof lending libr, Prog for children & young adult, Scanner, Spanish lang bks, Story hour, Summer reading prog, Wheelchair accessible
Open Mon & Wed-Fri 10-5, Tues 10-6

BALMORHEA

P BALMORHEA PUBLIC LIBRARY, 102 SW Main St, 79718. (Mail add: PO Box 355, 79718-0355), SAN 316-0785. *Head Librn,* Rosa Dominguez; Tel: 432-448-1697, E-mail: rosadominguez55@yahoo.com
Founded 1927. Pop 475
Library Holdings: Bk Vols 4,139
Wireless access
Open Mon-Thurs 9-12 & 1-3, Fri 9-12

BANDERA

P ALBERT & BESSIE MAE KRONKOSKY LIBRARY*, Kronkosky Bandera Public Library, 515 Main St, 78003. (Mail add: PO Box 1568, 78003-1568), SAN 316-0793. Tel: 830-796-4213. FAX: 830-796-3449. E-mail: banderalibrary@gmail.com. Web Site: banderalibrary.org/. *Dir,* Mauri Guillen Fagan; Staff 3 (Non-MLS 3)
Founded 1934. Pop 9,025; Circ 35,000
Library Holdings: Bk Vols 27,393; Per Subs 53
Special Collections: Genealogy; Texana
Automation Activity & Vendor Info: (Cataloging) Biblionix/Apollo; (Circulation) Biblionix/Apollo; (OPAC) Biblionix/Apollo
Wireless access
Function: 24/7 Electronic res, 24/7 Online cat, Activity rm, Adult bk club, After school storytime, Art exhibits, Art programs, Audio & video playback equip for onsite use, Audiobks on Playaways & MP3, Audiobks via web, AV serv, Bilingual assistance for Spanish patrons, Bk club(s), Bks on CD, Children's prog, Computer training, Computers for patron use, Digital talking bks, E-Readers, E-Reserves, Electronic databases & coll, Family literacy, Free DVD rentals, Govt ref serv, Holiday prog, ILL available, Internet access, Laminating, Magazines, Magnifiers for reading, Mail & tel request accepted, Meeting rooms, Microfiche/film & reading machines, Movies, Music CDs, Notary serv, Online cat, OverDrive digital audio bks, Photocopying/Printing, Preschool outreach, Preschool reading prog, Printer for laptops & handheld devices, Prog for adults, Prog for children & young adult, Ref & res, Ref serv available, Res assist avail, Scanner, Spanish lang bks, Summer reading prog, Tax forms, Teen prog, Telephone ref, Wheelchair accessible
Special Services for the Deaf - Videophone (VP)
Special Services for the Blind - Aids for in-house use; Bks on CD; Children's Braille; Large print bks; Large print bks & talking machines; Talking bks
Open Mon-Fri 9-6, Sat 9-1
Friends of the Library Group

BARTLETT

P TEINERT MEMORIAL PUBLIC LIBRARY*, 337 N Dalton St, 76511. (Mail add: PO Box 12, 76511-0012), SAN 316-0815. Tel: 254-527-3208. FAX: 254-527-0217. E-mail: bartlib@sbcglobal.net. *Dir,* Elizabeth Guerra; Staff 1 (Non-MLS 1)
Founded 1976. Pop 1,600; Circ 45,000
Library Holdings: AV Mats 400; Large Print Bks 300; Bk Vols 12,000; Per Subs 40
Special Collections: Texana (Texas History). Oral History
Subject Interests: Local hist
Automation Activity & Vendor Info: (Acquisitions) Follett Software; (Cataloging) Follett Software; (Circulation) Follett Software; (OPAC) Follett Software; (Serials) Follett Software
Wireless access
Open Mon-Fri 9-5

BASTROP

P BASTROP PUBLIC LIBRARY, 1100 Church St, 78602. (Mail add: PO Box 670, 78602-0670), SAN 316-0823. Tel: 512-332-8880. Web Site: www.bastroplibrary.org. *Libr Dir,* Bonnie Pierson; E-mail: bpierson@bastroplibrary.org; *Pub Serv Librn,* Bethany Williams; E-mail: bdietrich@bastroplibrary.org; *Youth Serv Librn,* Eva Bernal; E-mail: ebernal@bastroplibrary.org; *Supvr, Access Serv,* Amie Cuvelier; E-mail: acuvelier@bastroplibrary.org; Staff 11.6 (MLS 3, Non-MLS 8.6)
Founded 1972. Pop 11,189

Library Holdings: Audiobooks 3,246; AV Mats 4,622; e-books 30,758; Bk Vols 39,514
Special Collections: Texana
Subject Interests: Genealogy, Local hist
Automation Activity & Vendor Info: (Cataloging) Biblionix; (Circulation) Biblionix; (ILL) Biblionix; (OPAC) Biblionix
Wireless access
Function: 24/7 Electronic res, 24/7 Online cat, 24/7 wireless access, Activity rm, Adult bk club, Adult literacy prog, Archival coll, Art exhibits, Art programs, Audiobks via web, AV serv, Bilingual assistance for Spanish patrons, Bk club(s), Bks on CD, Butterfly Garden, Chess club, Children's prog, Computer training, Computers for patron use, Digital talking bks, Distance learning, E-Readers, E-Reserves, Electronic databases & coll, Extended outdoor wifi, Family literacy, For res purposes, Free DVD rentals, Games, Genealogy discussion group, Holiday prog, ILL available, Instruction & testing, Internet access, Jail serv, Large print keyboards, Life-long learning prog for all ages, Magazines, Mail & tel request accepted, Mango lang, Meeting rooms, Movies, Music CDs, Online cat, Online info literacy tutorials on the web & in blackboard, Online ref, Outreach serv, OverDrive digital audio bks, Photocopying/Printing, Preschool outreach, Preschool reading prog, Printer for laptops & handheld devices, Prog for adults, Prog for children & young adult, Ref serv available, Scanner, Senior computer classes, Senior outreach, Spanish lang bks, Story hour, Study rm, Summer reading prog, Teen prog, Telephone ref, Wheelchair accessible, Wifi hotspot checkout
Partic in Partners Library Action Network
Open Mon, Wed & Fri 10-6, Tues & Thurs 12-9, Sat 10-4
Restriction: Non-resident fee
Friends of the Library Group

BAY CITY

P BAY CITY PUBLIC LIBRARY*, 1100 Seventh St, 77414. SAN 316-0831. Tel: 979-245-6931. FAX: 979-245-2614. E-mail: library@cityofbaycity.org. Web Site: www.cityofbaycity.org/189/public-library. *Libr Dir,* Samantha Denbow; E-mail: sdenbow@cityofbaycity.org; *Children's Spec,* Pamela Burrell; Staff 9 (MLS 1, Non-MLS 8)
Founded 1913. Pop 26,000
Oct 2017-Sept 2018. Mats Exp $421,750. Sal $192,331 (Prof $55,000)
Library Holdings: Bk Vols 40,000
Subject Interests: Genealogy, Texana
Automation Activity & Vendor Info: (Cataloging) Book Systems; (Circulation) Book Systems; (OPAC) Book Systems
Wireless access
Function: ILL available, Photocopying/Printing, Prog for children & young adult, Ref serv available, Summer reading prog, Telephone ref, Wheelchair accessible
Partic in Amigos Library Services, Inc; Partners Library Action Network
Open Mon-Thurs 9-6, Fri 9-5, Sat 9-3
Friends of the Library Group
Branches: 1
SARGENT BRANCH, 20305 FM 457, Sargent, 77414, SAN 374-4442. Tel: 979-476-1335. *Br Spec,* Adelaide Ellsworth; E-mail: aellsworth@cityofbaycity.org
Founded 1985
Library Holdings: Bk Titles 3,500
Subject Interests: Resorts
Open Tues & Fri 1-6, Wed, Thurs & Sat 9-2
Friends of the Library Group

BAYTOWN

J LEE COLLEGE LIBRARY*, 150 Lee Dr, 77520. (Mail add: 511 S Whiting St, 77520), SAN 316-084X. Tel: 281-425-6379. Reference Tel: 281-425-6584. FAX: 281-425-6557. E-mail: library@lee.edu. Web Site: www.lee.edu/library. *Libr Dir,* Paul A Arrigo; Tel: 281-425-6447, E-mail: parrigo@lee.edu; *Distance Educ, E-Resources Librn,* Will Mayer; Tel: 281-425-4512, E-mail: wmayer@lee.edu; *Instruction Librn,* Samantha Johnson; *Tech Serv Librn,* Sandra Brown; E-mail: sbrown@lee.edu; Staff 5 (MLS 5)
Founded 1935. Enrl 6,087; Fac 198; Highest Degree: Associate
Library Holdings: AV Mats 3,838; e-books 43,017; Bk Vols 96,653; Per Subs 340
Special Collections: Law Library Coll; Lee College Archives. Oral History; US Document Depository
Subject Interests: Film studies, Local hist, Tex gulf coast
Automation Activity & Vendor Info: (Cataloging) Innovative Interfaces, Inc; (Circulation) Innovative Interfaces, Inc; (Course Reserve) Innovative Interfaces, Inc; (ILL) Clio; (OPAC) Innovative Interfaces, Inc; (Serials) Innovative Interfaces, Inc
Wireless access
Partic in Amigos Library Services, Inc; TexSHARE - Texas State Library & Archives Commission
Open Mon-Thurs 7:30am-9pm, Fri 7:30-2, Sat 10-2
Friends of the Library Group

P STERLING MUNICIPAL LIBRARY*, Mary Elizabeth Wilbanks Ave, 77520. SAN 316-0858. Tel: 281-427-7331. E-mail: askLibrary@baytown.org. Web Site: www.baytown.org/206/library. *City Librn,* Jamie Eustace; E-mail: jamie.eustace@baytown.org; *Ch,* Chazley Dotson; E-mail: chazley.dotson@baytown.org; Staff 10 (MLS 10)
Founded 1961. Pop 93,304; Circ 629,000
Library Holdings: Bk Vols 180,000; Per Subs 150
Special Collections: Oral History
Subject Interests: Local hist
Automation Activity & Vendor Info: (Cataloging) Innovative Interfaces, Inc; (Circulation) Innovative Interfaces, Inc; (OPAC) Innovative Interfaces, Inc; (Serials) Innovative Interfaces, Inc
Wireless access
Function: ILL available
Special Services for the Deaf - Bks on deafness & sign lang; Closed caption videos; High interest/low vocabulary bks; TTY equip
Special Services for the Blind - Large print bks
Open Mon-Fri 9-7, Sat 10-5, Sun 1-5
Friends of the Library Group

BEAUMONT

S ART MUSEUM OF SOUTHEAST TEXAS LIBRARY*, 500 Main St, 77701. SAN 316-0874. Tel: 409-832-3432. FAX: 409-832-8508. Web Site: www.amset.org. *Educ Curator,* Christle Feagin; E-mail: cfeagin@amset.org
Founded 1950
Library Holdings: Bk Vols 3,859
Subject Interests: Anthrop, Archaeology, Archit, Art, Cultural hist, Humanities
Wireless access
Open Mon-Fri 9-5, Sat 10-5, Sun 12-5
Restriction: Non-circulating

P BEAUMONT PUBLIC LIBRARY SYSTEM*, 801 Pearl St, 77701. (Mail add: PO Box 3827, 77704), SAN 361-2872. Tel: 409-981-5911. FAX: 409-212-9383. Web Site: beaumonttexas.gov/departments/library. *Libr Adminr,* Paul Eddy; E-mail: paul.eddy@beaumonttexas.gov; *Asst Admin,* Geri Roberts; E-mail: geri.roberts@beaumonttexas.gov; Staff 25 (MLS 7, Non-MLS 18)
Founded 1926. Pop 114,332
Library Holdings: Bk Vols 345,345; Per Subs 126
Automation Activity & Vendor Info: (Acquisitions) SirsiDynix; (Cataloging) SirsiDynix; (Circulation) SirsiDynix; (OPAC) SirsiDynix; (Serials) SirsiDynix
Wireless access
Partic in TexSHARE - Texas State Library & Archives Commission
Open Mon-Fri 10-8
Friends of the Library Group
Branches: 6
BEAUMONT PUBLIC, 801 Pearl St, 77701. (Mail add: PO Box 3827, 77704-3827). Tel: 409-838-6606. Web Site: www.beaumonttexas.gov/263/main-downtown-library. *Br Mgr, Libr Adminr,* Paul Eddy; Tel: 409-981-5911, E-mail: paul.eddy@beaumonttexas.gov; Staff 9 (MLS 1, Non-MLS 8)
Founded 1926
Library Holdings: Bk Vols 35,000
Automation Activity & Vendor Info: (Acquisitions) SirsiDynix; (Cataloging) SirsiDynix; (Circulation) SirsiDynix; (Discovery) SirsiDynix-Enterprise; (OPAC) SirsiDynix
Function: 24/7 Electronic res, 24/7 Online cat, Accelerated reader prog, Activity rm, Adult bk club, Adult literacy prog
Open Mon-Thurs 9-8, Fri 9-6
Restriction: Authorized patrons
Friends of the Library Group
MAUREEN GRAY LITERACY CENTER, 801 Pearl St, 77701. (Mail add: PO Box 3827, 77704-3827), SAN 378-2123. Tel: 409-835-7924. *Br Mgr,* Barbara S Beard; E-mail: barbara.beard@beaumonttexas.gov
Function: Adult literacy prog
Open Mon-Thurs 9-8, Fri 9-5
Friends of the Library Group
THEODORE R JOHNS SR BRANCH LIBRARY, 4255 Fannett Rd, 77705. (Mail add: PO Box 3827, 77704-3827), SAN 375-0159. Tel: 409-842-5233. FAX: 409-838-6838. *Br Mgr,* Amy Albrecht; E-mail: amy.albrecht@beaumonttexas.gov
Open Mon-Sat 9-6
Friends of the Library Group
R C MILLER MEMORIAL, 1605 Dowlen Rd, 77706. (Mail add: PO Box 3827, 77704-3827), SAN 361-2899. Tel: 409-866-9487. FAX: 409-866-3720. *Br Mgr,* Claudia Hairston; E-mail: claudia.hairston@beaumonttexas.gov
Automation Activity & Vendor Info: (Acquisitions) SirsiDynix; (Cataloging) SirsiDynix
Open Mon-Sat 9-6
Friends of the Library Group

TYRRELL HISTORICAL, 695 Pearl St, 77701. (Mail add: PO Box 3827, 77704-3827), SAN 361-2937. Tel: 409-833-2759. *Br Mgr,* William Grace; E-mail: william.grace@beaumonttexas.gov. Subject Specialists: *Archives, Genealogy,* William Grace; Staff 4 (MLS 1, Non-MLS 3)
Library Holdings: Per Subs 44
Special Collections: Archives Coll; Genealogy Coll; Local History Coll
Subject Interests: Genealogy, Texana
Function: Photocopying/Printing
Open Mon-Fri 9-6
Restriction: Closed stack
Friends of the Library Group

ELMO WILLARD BRANCH, 3590 E Lucas Dr, 77708. (Mail add: PO Box 3827, 77704-3827), SAN 378-214X. Tel: 409-892-4988. FAX: 409-898-4088. *Asst Admin, Br Mgr,* Geri Roberts; E-mail: geri.roberts@beaumonttexas.gov
Founded 1998
Library Holdings: Bk Vols 43,000
Automation Activity & Vendor Info: (Cataloging) SirsiDynix; (Circulation) SirsiDynix; (OPAC) SirsiDynix
Open Mon-Sat 9-6
Friends of the Library Group

C LAMAR UNIVERSITY*, Mary & John Gray Library, 4400 Martin Luther King Jr Pkwy, 77705. (Mail add: 211 Red Bird Lane, Box 10021, 77710), SAN 316-0920. Tel: 409-880-7264. Circulation Tel: 409-880-7257. Interlibrary Loan Service Tel: 409-880-8987. Toll Free Tel: 866-375-5565. FAX: 409-880-2309. Web Site: www.lamar.edu/library. *Head, Instructional Service & Assessment, Interim Dean of Libr,* Michael Saar; E-mail: michael.saar@lamar.edu; *Head, Circ,* Kirk Smith; Tel: 409-880-8133, E-mail: kirk.smith@lamar.edu; *Head of Research, Engagement & Learning Services,* Dr Alyse Jordan; Tel: 409-880-8131, E-mail: alyse.jordan@lamar.edu; *Cataloging & Metadata Librn,* Kelly Withrow; Tel: 409-880-7299, E-mail: kwithrow@lamar.edu; *Spec Coll Librn,* Penny Clark; Tel: 409-880-7787, E-mail: penny.clark@lamar.edu; *ILL Supvr,* Severa Norris; E-mail: slnorris@lamar.edu; *Circ, Reserves,* Olivia Rigsby; Tel: 409-880-8980, E-mail: origsby@lamar.edu; Staff 43 (MLS 13, Non-MLS 30)
Founded 1923. Enrl 14,119; Fac 464; Highest Degree: Doctorate
Library Holdings: Bk Titles 395,000; Bk Vols 639,200; Per Subs 1,500
Special Collections: Big Thicket National Preserve Coll; Cookery Coll; Petroleum Refining Coll; Texana Coll. State Document Depository; US Document Depository
Subject Interests: Bus, Computer sci, Deaf educ, Educ, Engr, Nursing
Automation Activity & Vendor Info: (Acquisitions) SirsiDynix; (Cataloging) SirsiDynix; (Circulation) SirsiDynix; (Course Reserve) SirsiDynix; (ILL) OCLC ILLiad; (Media Booking) Dymaxion; (OPAC) SirsiDynix; (Serials) SirsiDynix
Wireless access
Publications: From the Stacks (Library Newsletter)
Partic in Amigos Library Services, Inc; TexSHARE - Texas State Library & Archives Commission
Special Services for the Deaf - Assistive tech; TTY equip
Special Services for the Blind - Accessible computers; Assistive/Adapted tech devices, equip & products; Large screen computer & software; Reader equip
Open Mon-Thurs & Sun 7:30am-2am, Fri 7:30-6, Sat 10-7 (Winter); Mon-Thurs 7:30am-9pm, Fri 7:30-6, Sun 2-9 (Summer)
Friends of the Library Group

SR SAINT MARK'S PARISH LIBRARY*, 680 Calder, 77701. SAN 316-0947. Tel: 409-832-3405. FAX: 409-832-8045. E-mail: info@stmarksbeaumont.org. Web Site: www.stmarksbeaumont.org.
Library Holdings: Bk Vols 1,000
Wireless access
Function: Res libr
Open Mon-Thurs 8-5, Fri 8-1
Restriction: Non-circulating

BEDFORD

P BEDFORD PUBLIC LIBRARY*, 2424 Forest Ridge Dr, 76021. SAN 316-0955. Tel: 817-952-2350. Administration Tel: 817-952-2330. FAX: 817-952-2396. E-mail: bedford.library@bedfordtx.gov. Web Site: www.bedfordlibrary.org. *Dir,* Maria Redburn; E-mail: Maria.Redburn@bedfordtx.gov; *Tech Serv Mgr,* Barbara Glassford Johnson; *Circ Serv Supvr,* Barbara Sparks; Staff 14 (MLS 5, Non-MLS 9)
Founded 1964. Pop 48,000; Circ 393,231
Library Holdings: AV Mats 13,633; Bks on Deafness & Sign Lang 34; e-books 26,048; Large Print Bks 3,208; Bk Titles 75,744; Bk Vols 94,740; Per Subs 239; Spec Interest Per Sub 10; Talking Bks 2,379
Special Collections: Bedford History Coll
Automation Activity & Vendor Info: (Acquisitions) Innovative Interfaces, Inc; (Cataloging) Innovative Interfaces, Inc; (Circulation) Innovative Interfaces, Inc; (OPAC) Innovative Interfaces, Inc; (Serials) Innovative Interfaces, Inc
Wireless access
Function: ILL available
Special Services for the Blind - Low vision equip
Open Mon, Wed & Thurs 10-9, Tues 10-6, Fri & Sat 10-5, Sun 1-5
Friends of the Library Group

CR MESSENGER COLLEGE LIBRARY*, 2701 Brown Trail, Ste 401, 76039. Tel: 817-554-5950. Web Site: www.messengercollege.edu/library. *Dir, Libr Serv,* Mary Thomason; E-mail: mthomason@messengercollege.edu; Staff 1 (MLS 1)
Automation Activity & Vendor Info: (Cataloging) SirsiDynix; (OPAC) SirsiDynix
Function: Res assist avail
Partic in Harrington Library Consortium
Open Mon-Fri 8-5

BEE CAVE

P BEE CAVE PUBLIC LIBRARY*, 4000 Galleria Pkwy, 78738. SAN 378-4398. Tel: 512-767-6620. FAX: 512-767-6629. E-mail: library@beecavetexas.gov. Web Site: www.beecavelibrary.com. *Libr Dir,* Barbara Hathaway; Tel: 512-767-6624, E-mail: bhathaway@beecavetexas.gov; *Asst Libr Dir,* Gretchen Hardin; Tel: 512-767-6634, E-mail: ghardin@beecavetexas.gov; Staff 9 (MLS 3.5, Non-MLS 5.5)
Founded 2005. Pop 7,000; Circ 175,000
Wireless access
Function: 24/7 Electronic res, 24/7 Online cat, Adult bk club, Audiobks on Playaways & MP3, Audiobks via web, Bk club(s), Bks on CD, Chess club, Children's prog, Computers for patron use, Electronic databases & coll, Family literacy, Free DVD rentals, Holiday prog, ILL available, Internet access, Life-long learning prog for all ages, Magazines, Mango lang, Online cat, Outreach serv, OverDrive digital audio bks, Photocopying/Printing, Preschool reading prog, Prog for adults, Prog for children & young adult, Ref serv available, Senior outreach, Story hour, Summer reading prog, Tax forms, Teen prog, Telephone ref, Wheelchair accessible
Partic in Partners Library Action Network
Open Tues & Thurs-Sat 10-5, Wed 10-7
Friends of the Library Group

BEEVILLE

P JOE BARNHART BEE COUNTY PUBLIC LIBRARY*, 110 W Corpus Christi St, 78102-5604. SAN 316-0963. Tel: 361-362-4901. FAX: 361-358-8694. E-mail: support@bclib.org. Web Site: www.bclib.org. *Dir,* Rosie Amaya; E-mail: ramaya@bclib.org; *Libr Mgr,* Patty Alexander; E-mail: patty@bclib.org; *Pub Serv Librn,* Robert Young; E-mail: robert@bclib.org; *Circ Mgr,* Arrial Mendoza; E-mail: arrialam@bclib.org; *Learning Res Spec,* Bobby Henshall; E-mail: bobby@bclib.org; *Tech Serv,* Charles Cook; E-mail: ccook@bclib.org; Staff 6 (MLS 2, Non-MLS 4)
Founded 1939. Pop 25,227; Circ 59,832
Library Holdings: Bk Vols 40,000; Per Subs 100
Automation Activity & Vendor Info: (Cataloging) Biblionix/Apollo; (Circulation) Biblionix/Apollo; (ILL) OCLC CatExpress; (OPAC) Biblionix/Apollo; (Serials) Biblionix/Apollo
Wireless access
Function: 3D Printer, Accelerated reader prog, Adult bk club, Archival coll, Audio & video playback equip for onsite use, Audiobks via web, Bks on CD, Chess club, Children's prog, Computer training, Computers for patron use, Electronic databases & coll, Games & aids for people with disabilities, Health sci info serv, Homework prog, ILL available, Internet access, Life-long learning prog for all ages, Literacy & newcomer serv, Magazines, Magnifiers for reading, Mail & tel request accepted, Meeting rooms, Movies, Music CDs, Notary serv, Online cat, Online info literacy tutorials on the web & in blackboard, Online ref, Outreach serv, Outside serv via phone, mail, e-mail & web, OverDrive digital audio bks, Photocopying/Printing, Printer for laptops & handheld devices, Prog for adults, Prog for children & young adult, Ref & res, Ref serv available, Res assist avail, Scanner, Senior computer classes, Senior outreach, Spanish lang bks, Spoken cassettes & DVDs, Summer reading prog, Tax forms, Teen prog, Telephone ref, Wheelchair accessible
Partic in Amigos Library Services, Inc; Partners Library Action Network
Special Services for the Blind - Braille equip; Computer with voice synthesizer for visually impaired persons
Open Mon-Fri 9-6

J COASTAL BEND COLLEGE, Grady C Hogue Learning Resource Center Library, 3800 Charco Rd, 78102. SAN 316-0971. Tel: 361-354-2737. E-mail: library@coastalbend.edu. Web Site: lrc.coastalbend.edu/about. *Dir, Libr Serv,* Tammy Rands; Tel: 361-354-2741, E-mail: trands@coastalbend.edu; *E-Librn,* Haylee Dobbs; Tel: 361-354-2742, E-mail: hadobbs@coastalbend.edu; *Circ Spec,* Krystal Saldivar; E-mail: klsaldivar@coastalbend.edu; Staff 2 (MLS 1, Non-MLS 1)
Founded 1967. Enrl 4,016; Fac 155

Library Holdings: e-books 23,000; e-journals 723; Large Print Bks 36; Bk Vols 48,000; Per Subs 30
Special Collections: Texana; Teaching Excellence
Automation Activity & Vendor Info: (Acquisitions) EOS International; (Cataloging) EOS International; (Circulation) EOS International; (Discovery) EOS International; (ILL) OCLC; (OPAC) EOS International; (Serials) EOS International
Wireless access
Publications: BookSampler (Monthly newsletter); Recent Titles (Quarterly newsletter)
Partic in Amigos Library Services, Inc; OCLC Online Computer Library Center, Inc; TexSHARE - Texas State Library & Archives Commission
Open Mon-Thurs 8-7, Fri 8-5

BELLAIRE

P BELLAIRE CITY LIBRARY*, 5111 Jessamine, 77401-4498. SAN 316-098X. Tel: 713-662-8160. Web Site: www.bellairetx.gov/657/library. *Dir,* Mary Cohrs; E-mail: mcohrs@bellairetx.gov; *Asst Libr Dir,* Chris Arrowood; Tel: 713-662-8166, E-mail: carrowood@bellairetx.gov; *Youth Serv,* Matthew Amenda; E-mail: mamenda@bellairetx.gov; Staff 7.5 (MLS 3, Non-MLS 4.5)
Founded 1951. Pop 17,206; Circ 190,000
Oct 2023-Sept 2024 Income $880,000, City $870,000, Other $10,000. Mats Exp $81,213, Books $60,300, Per/Ser (Incl. Access Fees) $3,900, AV Mat $2,800, Electronic Ref Mat (Incl. Access Fees) $14,213. Sal $779,700
Library Holdings: Audiobooks 2,079; AV Mats 10,925; DVDs 2,573; e-books 6,298; Bk Titles 74,611; Bk Vols 78,206; Per Subs 67
Subject Interests: Local hist
Automation Activity & Vendor Info: (Acquisitions) SirsiDynix-WorkFlows; (Cataloging) SirsiDynix-WorkFlows; (Circulation) SirsiDynix-WorkFlows; (ILL) Auto-Graphics, Inc; (OPAC) SirsiDynix-Enterprise
Wireless access
Function: 24/7 Electronic res, 24/7 Online cat, Adult bk club, Audio & video playback equip for onsite use, Audiobks on Playaways & MP3, Audiobks via web, Bilingual assistance for Spanish patrons, Bks on CD, Butterfly Garden, Chess club, Children's prog, Computer training, Computers for patron use, Digital talking bks, Electronic databases & coll, Equip loans & repairs, Extended outdoor wifi, Free DVD rentals, Holiday prog, ILL available, Internet access, Life-long learning prog for all ages, Magazines, Mail & tel request accepted, Meeting rooms, Online cat, Outreach serv, OverDrive digital audio bks, Photocopying/Printing, Preschool outreach, Preschool reading prog, Printer for laptops & handheld devices, Prog for adults, Prog for children & young adult, Ref serv available, Scanner, Senior outreach, Spanish lang bks, STEM programs, Story hour, Summer & winter reading prog, Summer reading prog, Tax forms, Teen prog, Telephone ref, Wheelchair accessible, Winter reading prog
Partic in Amigos Library Services, Inc; Houston Area Database Consortium
Open Mon & Tues-Thurs 10-7, Fri 1-5, Sat 9-5
Friends of the Library Group

BELLVILLE

P BELLVILLE PUBLIC LIBRARY*, 12 W Palm St, 77418. SAN 316-0998. Tel: 979-865-3731. FAX: 979-865-2060. E-mail: bellvillelibrary@sbcglobal.net. Web Site: bpltx.org. *Dir,* Aimee Ladewig; *Asst Dir,* Jessica Laas; Staff 5 (Non-MLS 5)
Founded 1968
Library Holdings: Bk Titles 33,018; Bk Vols 33,898; Per Subs 15
Automation Activity & Vendor Info: (Cataloging) Biblionix; (Circulation) Biblionix
Wireless access
Partic in Partners Library Action Network
Open Mon 1:30-5:30, Tues-Fri 9:30-5:30, Sat 9-1

BELTON

P LENA ARMSTRONG PUBLIC LIBRARY, 301 E First Ave, 76513. (Mail add: PO Box 120, 76513-0120), SAN 316-1005. Tel: 254-933-5830. Administration Tel: 254-933-5832. FAX: 254-933-5831. Web Site: www.beltontexas.gov/departments/library. *Dir, Libr Serv,* Kim Adele Kroll; E-mail: kkroll@beltontexas.gov; Staff 5 (MLS 1, Non-MLS 4)
Founded 1899
Oct 2020-Sept 2021. Mats Exp $50,000
Library Holdings: Audiobooks 91; CDs 968; DVDs 1,399; e-books 570; e-journals 30; Large Print Bks 1,455; Microforms 114; Bk Titles 26,102; Bk Vols 27,279; Per Subs 12
Special Collections: Genealogy Coll
Subject Interests: Genealogy, Local hist
Automation Activity & Vendor Info: (Cataloging) Biblionix/Apollo; (Circulation) Biblionix/Apollo
Wireless access
Function: 24/7 Electronic res, 24/7 Online cat, Archival coll, AV serv, Bilingual assistance for Spanish patrons, Bks on CD, Children's prog, Computers for patron use, Digital talking bks, Distance learning, E-Readers, Electronic databases & coll, Free DVD rentals, Holiday prog, Home delivery & serv to seniorr ctr & nursing homes, Homebound delivery serv, ILL available, Internet access, Large print keyboards, Magazines, Mail & tel request accepted, Meeting rooms, Microfiche/film & reading machines, Movies, Music CDs, Online cat, Online info literacy tutorials on the web & in blackboard, Online ref, Outreach serv, Outside serv via phone, mail, e-mail & web, Photocopying/Printing, Preschool outreach, Preschool reading prog, Printer for laptops & handheld devices, Prog for children & young adult, Ref serv available, Scanner, Senior outreach, Spanish lang bks, Story hour, Study rm, Summer reading prog, Tax forms, Telephone ref, Wheelchair accessible, Writing prog
Partic in Partners Library Action Network; TexSHARE - Texas State Library & Archives Commission
Special Services for the Blind - Bks on CD; Large print bks; Large screen computer & software; PC for people with disabilities; Recorded bks; Ref serv
Open Mon-Fri 9:30-6:30, Sat 10-2
Restriction: Non-circulating of rare bks, Open to pub for ref & circ; with some limitations
Friends of the Library Group

CR UNIVERSITY OF MARY HARDIN-BAYLOR*, Townsend Memorial Library, 900 College St, UMHB Sta, Box 8016, 76513-2599. SAN 316-1013. Tel: 254-295-4637. Circulation Tel: 254-295-4637. Interlibrary Loan Service Tel: 254-295-5004. Reference Tel: 254-295-4641. Administration Tel: 254-295-4636. Toll Free Tel: 877-316-3313. E-mail: library@umhb.edu. Web Site: go.umhb.edu/library. *Assoc Dean, Learning Res,* Dr Alan Asher; E-mail: aasher@umhb.edu; *Head, Electronic Serv,* Kathy Harden; Tel: 254-295-4161, E-mail: kharden@umhb.edu; *Head, Pub Serv, Head, Ref,* Anne Price; Tel: 254-295-4639, E-mail: aprice@umhb.edu; *Head, Tech Serv,* Teresa Buck; Tel: 254-295-4640, E-mail: tbuck@umhb.edu; *Cat Librn,* Jennifer Batson; Tel: 254-295-5002, E-mail: jbatson@umhb.edu; Staff 10 (MLS 6, Non-MLS 4)
Founded 1845. Enrl 3,406; Fac 190; Highest Degree: Doctorate
Jun 2020-May 2021. Mats Exp $774,870, Books $153,340, Per/Ser (Incl. Access Fees) $618,132, Presv $3,398
Library Holdings: Audiobooks 884; AV Mats 5,654; Bks on Deafness & Sign Lang 359; Braille Volumes 25; CDs 2,205; DVDs 5,175; e-books 1,046,172; e-journals 357,864; High Interest/Low Vocabulary Bk Vols 189; Large Print Bks 35; Microforms 9,546; Music Scores 1,479; Bk Titles 223,630; Bk Vols 219,218; Per Subs 541
Special Collections: Baptist Coll; Local History Coll; Texas & Mexican History Coll
Subject Interests: Baptist, Baptist women, Educ, Nursing
Automation Activity & Vendor Info: (Acquisitions) Innovative Interfaces, Inc; (Cataloging) Innovative Interfaces, Inc; (Circulation) Innovative Interfaces, Inc; (Course Reserve) Innovative Interfaces, Inc; (ILL) Innovative Interfaces, Inc; (OPAC) Innovative Interfaces, Inc; (Serials) Innovative Interfaces, Inc
Wireless access
Publications: Handbook
Partic in Amigos Library Services, Inc; OCLC Online Computer Library Center, Inc; Texas Council of Academic Libraries; TexSHARE - Texas State Library & Archives Commission
Open Mon-Thurs 7:30am-1am, Fri 7:30-5, Sat 10-6, Sun 2pm-1am

BENBROOK

P BENBROOK PUBLIC LIBRARY*, 1065 Mercedes St, 76126. SAN 378-3693. Tel: 817-249-6632. Automation Services Tel: 817-249-3930. Reference E-mail: reference@benbrooklibrary.org. Web Site: www.benbrooklibrary.org. *Dir,* Steve Clegg; E-mail: steve@benbrooklibrary.org; *Adult Serv,* Cullen Dansby; E-mail: cullen@benbrooklibrary.org; *Youth Serv,* Miranda Bauer; E-mail: miranda@benbrooklibrary.org; Staff 3 (MLS 3)
Founded 1999. Pop 25,000; Circ 80,000
Library Holdings: Bk Titles 24,000; Bk Vols 30,000; Per Subs 100
Automation Activity & Vendor Info: (Acquisitions) Innovative Interfaces, Inc; (Cataloging) Innovative Interfaces, Inc; (Circulation) Innovative Interfaces, Inc; (OPAC) Innovative Interfaces, Inc
Wireless access
Function: ILL available, Photocopying/Printing, Prog for adults, Prog for children & young adult, Ref serv available, Spoken cassettes & CDs, Summer reading prog, Telephone ref, Wheelchair accessible
Partic in MetroShare Libraries
Open Mon-Thurs 8-8, Fri & Sat 10-5
Friends of the Library Group

BIG LAKE

P REAGAN COUNTY LIBRARY, 300 Courthouse Sq, 76932. SAN 316-1021. Tel: 325-884-2854. E-mail: rclibrary@reagancounty.org. Web Site: www.rclibrary.org. *Libr Dir,* Ana Gallegos; Staff 3 (Non-MLS 3)
Founded 1938. Pop 3,796; Circ 7,260
Library Holdings: Bk Titles 19,572
Automation Activity & Vendor Info: (Acquisitions) Biblionix/Apollo; (Cataloging) Biblionix/Apollo; (Circulation) Biblionix/Apollo; (ILL) Biblionix/Apollo; (OPAC) Biblionix/Apollo
Wireless access
Function: 24/7 Electronic res, 24/7 Online cat, Accelerated reader prog, Archival coll, Art exhibits, Audiobks on Playaways & MP3, Audiobks via web, Bilingual assistance for Spanish patrons, Bks on CD, Children's prog, Citizenship assistance, Computer training, Computers for patron use, E-Reserves, Electronic databases & coll, Free DVD rentals, Govt ref serv, Holiday prog, Home delivery & serv to seniorr ctr & nursing homes, ILL available, Internet access, Laminating, Magazines, Mail & tel request accepted, Makerspace, Microfiche/film & reading machines, Online cat, OverDrive digital audio bks, Photocopying/Printing, Prog for children & young adult, Ref serv available, Res assist avail, Scanner, Spanish lang bks, STEM programs, Story hour, Summer reading prog, Wheelchair accessible
Partic in Partners Library Action Network
Open Mon & Wed 8:30-5, Tues & Thurs 8:30-7, Fri 8:30-4

BIG SPRING

J HOWARD COUNTY JUNIOR COLLEGE*, Anthony Hunt Library & Learning Resource Center, 1001 Birdwell Lane, 79720. SAN 316-1056. Tel: 432-264-5090. FAX: 432-264-5094. E-mail: library@howardcollege.edu. Web Site: www.howardcollege.edu/library/big-spring-library. *Dean of Libr,* Mavour Braswell; Tel: 432-264-5025, E-mail: mbraswell@howardcollege.edu; *Sr Libr Spec,* Mina Benavides; E-mail: mbenavides@howardcollege.edu; Staff 3.5 (MLS 1, Non-MLS 2.5)
Founded 1945. Enrl 2,236; Highest Degree: Associate
Library Holdings: Bk Vols 32,000; Per Subs 62
Automation Activity & Vendor Info: (Cataloging) LibLime; (Circulation) LibLime; (OPAC) LibLime
Wireless access
Function: ILL available
Open Mon-Thurs 7:30am-8pm, Fri 8-Noon, Sun 1-5
Departmental Libraries:
SOUTHWEST COLLEGIATE INSTITUTE FOR THE DEAF - LIBRARY, 3200 Ave C, 79720. SAN 328-817X. Tel: 432-218-4056. FAX: 432-264-3726. Web Site: howardcollege.edu/library/swcid-library. *Librn,* Sonia Gonzales; E-mail: sgonzales@howardcollege.edu; Staff 1 (Non-MLS 1)
Founded 1980. Enrl 170; Highest Degree: Associate
Library Holdings: Bks on Deafness & Sign Lang 946; Bk Titles 3,035; Bk Vols 3,262; Per Subs 100
Special Collections: Deafness, AV mat, bks, per. Oral History
Special Services for the Deaf - Staff with knowledge of sign lang
Open Mon-Thurs 7:30-5, Fri 7:30-12

P HOWARD COUNTY LIBRARY*, Dora Roberts Library, 500 Main St, 79720. SAN 316-1064. Tel: 432-264-2260. FAX: 432-264-2263. Reference E-mail: reference@howardcountytx.com. Web Site: howard-county.ploud.net. *Dir,* Ms Mavour Braswell; E-mail: director@howardcountytx.com; *Ref (Info Servs),* Johnny Schafer; Staff 6 (MLS 1, Non-MLS 5)
Founded 1907. Pop 33,200; Circ 161,147
Library Holdings: AV Mats 1,850; Bks on Deafness & Sign Lang 35; DVDs 1,200; Large Print Bks 1,997; Bk Titles 63,831; Bk Vols 70,292; Per Subs 52; Videos 1,257
Special Collections: Texana
Automation Activity & Vendor Info: (Cataloging) Biblionix; (Circulation) Biblionix; (OPAC) Biblionix
Wireless access
Function: Adult bk club, Adult literacy prog, Children's prog, Electronic databases & coll, Genealogy discussion group, ILL available, Mail & tel request accepted, Photocopying/Printing, Summer reading prog, Tax forms, Wheelchair accessible
Partic in Partners Library Action Network
Special Services for the Deaf - Adult & family literacy prog; Bks on deafness & sign lang; High interest/low vocabulary bks
Special Services for the Blind - Bks on CD
Open Mon-Fri 9-6
Friends of the Library Group

BLANCO

P BLANCO COUNTY SOUTH LIBRARY DISTRICT*, James A & Evelyn Williams Memorial Library, 1118 Main St, 78606. Tel: 830-833-4280. FAX: 830-833-2680. E-mail: blancotxlibrary@gmail.com. Web Site: www.blancolib.org. *Libr Dir,* Crystal Spybuck; *Dep Dir,* Brian Fields; *Asst Librn,* Dorothy Trimble; Staff 47 (MLS 1, Non-MLS 46)
Founded 1938. Pop 5,500; Circ 27,000
Automation Activity & Vendor Info: (Cataloging) Follett Software; (Circulation) Follett Software
Wireless access
Function: Adult bk club, Art exhibits, Audio & video playback equip for onsite use, Bks on cassette, Bks on CD, Computer training, Computers for patron use, Electronic databases & coll, Free DVD rentals, ILL available, Mail & tel request accepted, Music CDs, Online cat, OverDrive digital audio bks, Photocopying/Printing, Prog for adults, Scanner, Spoken cassettes & CDs, Story hour, Summer reading prog, Tax forms, VHS videos, Writing prog
Partic in Partners Library Action Network
Special Services for the Blind - Large print bks; Large screen computer & software; Screen enlargement software for people with visual disabilities; Talking bks & player equip
Open Mon-Fri 10-6, Sat 10-2
Restriction: In-house use for visitors, Non-circulating of rare bks, Photo ID required for access
Friends of the Library Group

BOERNE

P BOERNE PUBLIC LIBRARY*, Patrick Heath Public Library, 451 N Main St, Bldg 100, 78006. SAN 316-1102. Tel: 830-249-3053. FAX: 830-249-8410. E-mail: librarian@boernelibrary.org. Web Site: www.boernelibrary.org. *Libr Dir,* Kelly W Skovbjerg; E-mail: skovbjerg@boernelibrary.org; *Asst Libr Dir,* Natalie Morgan; E-mail: morgan@boernelibrary.org; Staff 4 (MLS 4)
Founded 1952. Pop 26,200; Circ 165,600
Library Holdings: AV Mats 4,189; Bk Vols 39,535; Per Subs 68
Subject Interests: German lang, Local hist, Spanish (Lang), Texana
Automation Activity & Vendor Info: (Cataloging) Biblionix; (Circulation) Biblionix; (OPAC) Biblionix
Wireless access
Partic in Partners Library Action Network
Open Mon-Thurs 9-7, Fri 9-6, Sat 10-4
Friends of the Library Group

BONHAM

P BONHAM PUBLIC LIBRARY*, 305 E Fifth St, 75418. SAN 316-1110. Tel: 903-583-3128. FAX: 903-583-8030. E-mail: bonlibstaff@gmail.com. Web Site: www.bonhamlibrary.net. *Libr Dir,* John D Hayden; E-mail: jdhayden@cityofbonham.org; Staff 4.5 (MLS 1, Non-MLS 3.5)
Founded 1901. Pop 10,200; Circ 37,822; Fac 5
Library Holdings: Audiobooks 846; DVDs 1,436; e-books 1,848; Large Print Bks 1,436; Microforms 80; Bk Titles 40,349; Per Subs 24; Videos 60
Special Collections: Oral History
Automation Activity & Vendor Info: (Acquisitions) Book Systems; (Cataloging) Book Systems; (Circulation) Book Systems; (ILL) OCLC WorldShare Interlibrary Loan; (OPAC) Book Systems
Wireless access
Partic in Partners Library Action Network
Special Services for the Blind - Bks on CD; Copier with enlargement capabilities; Large print bks
Open Mon 10-7, Tues-Fri 8-5, Sat 9-1
Restriction: Authorized patrons

S SAM RAYBURN LIBRARY & MUSEUM*, 800 W Sam Rayburn Dr, 75418. (Mail add: PO Box 309, 75418-0309), SAN 316-1129. Tel: 903-583-2455. FAX: 903-583-7394. Web Site: briscoecenter.org/sam-rayburn-museum. *Res Assoc,* Emma Trent; E-mail: e.trent@austin.utexas.edu
Founded 1957
Library Holdings: Bk Vols 20,000
Special Collections: Life & Career of Speaker Sam Rayburn, historical memorabilia, interviews, micro. Oral History
Open Mon-Fri 9-4:30, Sat 10-2
Friends of the Library Group

BORGER

J FRANK PHILLIPS COLLEGE*, James W Dillard Library, 1301 Roosevelt St, 79008. (Mail add: PO Box 5118, 79008-5118), SAN 316-1145. Tel: 806-457-4200, Ext 787. FAX: 806-457-4230. Web Site: www.fpctx.edu/library. *Assoc Dean, Academic Support Servs,* Jason Price; E-mail: jprice@fpctx.edu; Staff 1 (MLS 1)
Founded 1948. Enrl 1,200; Fac 56; Highest Degree: Associate
Library Holdings: AV Mats 1,124; e-books 29,000; Electronic Media & Resources 70; Bk Titles 14,000; Per Subs 25
Special Collections: Rare
Automation Activity & Vendor Info: (Cataloging) SirsiDynix; (Circulation) SirsiDynix; (OPAC) SirsiDynix
Wireless access

Function: AV serv, Homebound delivery serv, ILL available, Internet access, Photocopying/Printing, Ref serv available, Wheelchair accessible
Partic in Harrington Library Consortium
Open Mon-Thurs 8-5, Fri 8-4

P HUTCHINSON COUNTY LIBRARY*, 625 N Weatherly, 79007-3621. SAN 361-302X. Tel: 806-273-0126. FAX: 806-273-0128. E-mail: borgerlibrary@hutchinsoncnty.com. Web Site: www.harringtonlc.org/hutchinson. *Dir,* Carolyn Wilkinson; Staff 7 (Non-MLS 7)
Founded 1938. Pop 22,617; Circ 104,511
Library Holdings: Bk Titles 53,482; Bk Vols 58,894; Per Subs 175
Subject Interests: Genealogy, Tex
Automation Activity & Vendor Info: (Acquisitions) SirsiDynix-DRA
Wireless access
Partic in Harrington Library Consortium
Open Mon-Fri 8-6
Friends of the Library Group
Branches: 2
FRITCH BRANCH, 205 N Cornell, Fritch, 79036. SAN 361-3054. Tel: 806-857-3752. FAX: 806-857-0940. E-mail: fritchlibrary@hutchinsoncnty.com. *Br Mgr,* Delena Burks; Staff 1 (Non-MLS 1)
Library Holdings: Bk Vols 8,895
Open Mon-Thurs 8-12:30 & 1:30-6
Friends of the Library Group
STINNETT BRANCH, Courthouse Basement, 500 S Main St, 79083. Tel: 806-878-4013. FAX: 806-878-4014. E-mail: stinnettlibrary@hutchinsoncnty.com. *Br Mgr,* Cynthia Venzor
Library Holdings: Bk Vols 11,738
Open Mon-Thurs 8-12 & 1-6
Friends of the Library Group

BOWIE

P BOWIE PUBLIC LIBRARY*, Faye Ruth Shaw Memorial Library, 301 Walnut St, 76230. SAN 316-1161. Tel: 940-872-2681. FAX: 940-872-6418. E-mail: bowiepubliclibrary@cityofbowietx.com. Web Site: www.bowiepubliclibrary.com. *Dir,* Beth Hiatt; Staff 5 (Non-MLS 5)
Founded 1926. Pop 6,000; Circ 60,000
Oct 2017-Sept 2018 Income $223,000, City $213,000, Other $10,000. Mats Exp $23,200, Books $20,000, Micro $700, AV Mat $2,500
Library Holdings: Bk Titles 34,000; Per Subs 66
Automation Activity & Vendor Info: (Cataloging) Follett Software; (Circulation) Follett Software; (OPAC) Follett Software
Wireless access
Function: 24/7 Electronic res, 24/7 Online cat, Activity rm, Adult bk club, Archival coll, Art exhibits, Audiobks on Playaways & MP3, Audiobks via web, Bks on CD, CD-ROM, Children's prog, Computer training, Computers for patron use, Digital talking bks, Electronic databases & coll, Free DVD rentals, Genealogy discussion group, Holiday prog, ILL available, Internet access, Laminating, Magazines, Meeting rooms, Microfiche/film & reading machines, Movies, Online cat, Online info literacy tutorials on the web & in blackboard, Online ref, Outreach serv, OverDrive digital audio bks, Photocopying/Printing, Preschool outreach, Preschool reading prog, Printer for laptops & handheld devices, Prog for adults, Prog for children & young adult, Ref & res, Ref serv available, Res assist avail, Scanner, Senior computer classes, Senior outreach, Serves people with intellectual disabilities, STEM programs, Story hour, Study rm, Summer & winter reading prog, Summer reading prog, Teen prog, Wheelchair accessible
Open Mon 10-2, Tues & Thur 10-6, Wed & Fri 9-5, Sat 10-2
Friends of the Library Group

BRACKETTVILLE

P KINNEY COUNTY PUBLIC LIBRARY*, 510 S Ellen St, 78832. (Mail add: PO Box 975, 78832), SAN 324-1270. Tel: 830-563-2884. FAX: 830-563-2312. E-mail: kclibrary4772@gmail.com. *Dir,* Sara Terrazas; Staff 3 (Non-MLS 3)
Founded 1973. Pop 3,413; Circ 18,220
Library Holdings: AV Mats 265; Large Print Bks 325; Bk Titles 9,891; Per Subs 21
Subject Interests: Genealogy, Local hist
Automation Activity & Vendor Info: (Cataloging) Biblionix
Wireless access
Function: Homebound delivery serv, ILL available, Magnifiers for reading, Prog for children & young adult, Ref serv available, Satellite serv, Summer reading prog
Special Services for the Blind - Talking bks
Open Mon-Thurs 9-4, Fri 8-4

BRADY

P MCCULLOCH COUNTY LIBRARY*, 401 E Commerce, 76825. SAN 316-117X. Tel: 325-597-2617. FAX: 325-597-0461. E-mail: mccullochcolib@gmail.com. Web Site: mccullochcountylibrary.ploud.net. *Dir,* Sheridan Hosid; Staff 4 (Non-MLS 4)
Founded 1928. Pop 8,694; Circ 53,823
Library Holdings: AV Mats 49; Bk Titles 20,474; Bk Vols 23,222; Per Subs 13
Automation Activity & Vendor Info: (Cataloging) Follett Software; (Circulation) Follett Software; (OPAC) Follett Software
Function: ILL available, Photocopying/Printing, Ref serv available
Partic in Partners Library Action Network
Open Mon & Wed-Fri 10-5:30, Tues 12-7, Sat 10-1
Friends of the Library Group

BRECKENRIDGE

P BRECKENRIDGE LIBRARY*, 209 N Breckenridge Ave, 76424. SAN 316-1188. Tel: 254-559-5505. FAX: 254-559-5505. E-mail: brecklibrary@att.net. Web Site: www.brecklibrary.org. *Dir,* Heather Schkade; Staff 2 (Non-MLS 2)
Founded 1924. Pop 9,800; Circ 14,640
Library Holdings: CDs 27; High Interest/Low Vocabulary Bk Vols 65; Large Print Bks 1,243; Bk Titles 21,225; Bk Vols 22,250; Per Subs 48; Spec Interest Per Sub 15; Talking Bks 929; Videos 92
Special Collections: Rare & Out-of-Print Books; Texas Coll, 1940-present
Subject Interests: Hist
Automation Activity & Vendor Info: (Cataloging) Winnebago Software Co; (Circulation) Winnebago Software Co
Wireless access
Open Mon-Thurs 10:30-12:30 & 1:30-5:30
Restriction: Residents only
Friends of the Library Group

BREMOND

P BREMOND PUBLIC LIBRARY & VISITORS CENTER*, 115 S Main St, 76629. (Mail add: PO Box 132, 76629-0132). Tel: 254-746-7752. FAX: 254-746-7065. E-mail: bremondpubliclibrary@yahoo.com. Web Site: bremond.ploud.net. *Libr Dir,* Theresa Ann Crawford
Founded 1998. Pop 2,000; Circ 2,911
Library Holdings: Audiobooks 65; Large Print Bks 211; Bk Titles 8,887
Automation Activity & Vendor Info: (Cataloging) Biblionix; (Circulation) Biblionix; (OPAC) Biblionix
Wireless access
Function: Accelerated reader prog, Adult bk club, After school storytime, Art exhibits, Audio & video playback equip for onsite use, Bk club(s), Bk reviews (Group), Bks on cassette, Bks on CD, CD-ROM, Children's prog, Citizenship assistance, Computer training, Computers for patron use, Electronic databases & coll, Family literacy, Holiday prog, Home delivery & serv to seniorr ctr & nursing homes, Homebound delivery serv, Homework prog, ILL available, Internet access, Jail serv, Literacy & newcomer serv, Mail & tel request accepted, Online cat, Outreach serv, Photocopying/Printing, Preschool outreach, Prog for adults, Prog for children & young adult, Ref & res, Scanner, Senior outreach, Story hour, Summer reading prog, Tax forms, Teen prog, Wheelchair accessible, Workshops
Open Mon-Thurs 12-5
Restriction: Registered patrons only
Friends of the Library Group

BRENHAM

J BLINN COLLEGE LIBRARY*, W L Moody Jr Library, 800 Blinn Blvd, 77833. (Mail add: 902 College Ave, 77833), SAN 316-1196. Tel: 979-830-4250. FAX: 979-830-4222. Web Site: www.blinn.edu/library. *Libr Dir,* Linda Gray; E-mail: linda.gray@blinn.edu; *Librn,* Jason Bontrager; E-mail: jason.bontrager@blinn.edu; *Librn,* Robin Chaney; E-mail: rchaney@blinn.edu; *Librn,* Kelly Kingrey-Edwards; E-mail: kelly.kingreyedwards@blinn.edu; Staff 8 (MLS 8)
Founded 1883. Enrl 14,000; Fac 315; Highest Degree: Associate
Library Holdings: AV Mats 10,800; Bk Vols 170,000; Per Subs 2,000
Special Collections: College Archives; Film/Theater Coll; Local History Coll
Subject Interests: Germans in Tex, Local hist
Automation Activity & Vendor Info: (Acquisitions) Innovative Interfaces, Inc; (Cataloging) Innovative Interfaces, Inc; (Circulation) Innovative Interfaces, Inc; (Course Reserve) Innovative Interfaces, Inc; (ILL) OCLC; (OPAC) Innovative Interfaces, Inc; (Serials) Innovative Interfaces, Inc
Wireless access
Partic in Amigos Library Services, Inc
Open Mon-Thurs 7:30am-10pm, Fri 7:45-5, Sat Noon-4, Sun 5:30pm-10:30pm (Fall-Spring); Mon-Thurs 7:30-6, Fri 7:30-5 (Summer)

P NANCY CAROL ROBERTS MEMORIAL LIBRARY*, 100 Martin Luther King Jr Pkwy, 77833. SAN 316-120X. Tel: 979-337-7201. FAX: 979-337-7209. E-mail: library@cityofbrenham.org. Web Site: cityofbrenham.org/library. *Dir,* Kathy Bell; E-mail: kbell@cityofbrenham.org; Staff 1 (MLS 1)
Founded 1901. Pop 30,373; Circ 66,747
Library Holdings: Bk Vols 45,360; Per Subs 66; Talking Bks 2,250
Special Collections: Oral History
Subject Interests: Germans in Tex, Texana
Automation Activity & Vendor Info: (Cataloging) ComPanion Corp; (Circulation) ComPanion Corp
Wireless access
Partic in Partners Library Action Network
Open Mon-Thurs 9-7, Fri 9-5, Sat 9-3

BRIDGE CITY

P BRIDGE CITY PUBLIC LIBRARY*, 101 Parkside Dr, 77611. SAN 376-4079. Tel: 409-735-4242. FAX: 409-738-2127. E-mail: bclib@bridgecitytex.com, bcpl@bridgecitytex.com. Web Site: www.bridgecitypubliclibrary.com. *Dir,* Mary Montgomery; *Ch,* Kelle Miller; Staff 1 (Non-MLS 1)
Founded 1991
Library Holdings: Bk Vols 18,000; Per Subs 40
Automation Activity & Vendor Info: (Cataloging) Biblionix/Apollo; (Circulation) Biblionix/Apollo; (OPAC) Biblionix/Apollo
Wireless access
Partic in Partners Library Action Network
Open Mon-Wed 10-6, Thurs 1-7, Fri 9-2
Friends of the Library Group

BRIDGEPORT

P BRIDGEPORT PUBLIC LIBRARY*, John A & Katherine G Jackson Municipal Library, 2159 Tenth St, 76426. SAN 316-1226. Tel: 940-683-3450. Web Site: www.cityofbridgeport.net/19/Library. *Libr Mgr,* Marisol Cano; E-mail: mcano@cityofbridgeport.net; Staff 4 (MLS 1, Non-MLS 3)
Founded 1960. Pop 16,005; Circ 64,570
Library Holdings: AV Mats 1,400; Bks on Deafness & Sign Lang 10; CDs 580; DVDs 642; Large Print Bks 2,000; Bk Titles 33,000; Bk Vols 33,750; Per Subs 29; Talking Bks 751; Videos 35
Automation Activity & Vendor Info: (Cataloging) Evergreen; (Circulation) Evergreen; (OPAC) EnvisionWare
Wireless access
Open Mon, Wed & Fri 10-6, Tues & Thurs 10-7, Sat 10-2
Friends of the Library Group

BROWNFIELD

P KENDRICK MEMORIAL LIBRARY*, 301 W Tate, 79316-4387. SAN 316-1234. Tel: 806-637-3848. Administration E-mail: kmldirector@yahoo.com. Web Site: brownfield.ploud.net, westtexas.overdrive.com. *Librn, Libr Dir,* Nicole Acevedo
Founded 1957. Pop 12,799; Circ 60,550
Library Holdings: Audiobooks 1,218; Bks on Deafness & Sign Lang 23; e-books 17,647; Bk Titles 38,547; Bk Vols 59,929; Per Subs 44
Automation Activity & Vendor Info: (Cataloging) Koha; (Circulation) ByWater Solutions
Wireless access
Function: 24/7 Online cat, Bks on cassette, Bks on CD, Children's prog, Computers for patron use, Electronic databases & coll, ILL available, Internet access, Magazines, Meeting rooms, Microfiche/film & reading machines, Movies, Online cat, OverDrive digital audio bks, Photocopying/Printing, Preschool reading prog, Spanish lang bks, Story hour, Summer reading prog, VHS videos, Wheelchair accessible
Open Mon, Tues & Thurs 9-5:30, Wed & Fri 9-4:30
Restriction: Circ to mem only, ID required to use computers (Ltd hrs), Lending limited to county residents, Non-circulating of rare bks
Friends of the Library Group

BROWNSVILLE

P BROWNSVILLE PUBLIC LIBRARY SYSTEM*, 2600 Central Blvd, 78520-8824. SAN 375-5541. Tel: 956-548-1055. FAX: 956-548-0684. E-mail: info@bpl.us. Web Site: www.cob.us/709/Brownsville-Public-Library-System. *Dir, Libr Serv,* Juan J Guerra; Tel: 956-548-1055, Ext 2125, E-mail: juan@cob.us; *Head Librn,* Brenda Trevino; Tel: 956-548-1055, Ext 2121, E-mail: brenda.trevino@cob.us; Staff 6 (MLS 5, Non-MLS 1)
Library Holdings: Bk Titles 122,771; Bk Vols 143,755; Per Subs 250
Subject Interests: Genealogy, Local hist, Texana
Automation Activity & Vendor Info: (Acquisitions) TLC (The Library Corporation); (Cataloging) TLC (The Library Corporation); (Circulation) TLC (The Library Corporation)
Wireless access
Partic in Amigos Library Services, Inc
Special Services for the Deaf - TDD equip
Open Mon-Thurs 10-9, Fri & Sat 10-6, Sun 1-8
Friends of the Library Group

C UNIVERSITY OF TEXAS RIO GRANDE VALLEY, Brownsville Campus, One W University Blvd, 78520. SAN 371-4187. Tel: 956-882-8221. Reference Tel: 956-882-7205. Administration Tel: 956-882-7424. Web Site: www.utrgv.edu/library. *Head, Res & Instrul Serv,* Joel Chirinos; Tel: 956-882-7465, E-mail: joel.chirinos@utrgv.edu; *Access Serv Librn,* Carmelita Pecina; Tel: 956-882-7428, E-mail: carmelita.pecina@utrgv.edu; *Coll Develop & Acq Librn,* Raquel Estrada; Tel: 956-882-7267, E-mail: raquel.estrada@utrgv.edu; *Syst Librn,* Ezequiel Melgoza; Tel: 956-882-7591, E-mail: ezequiel.melgoza@utrgv.edu; Staff 9 (MLS 9)
Founded 1926. Enrl 9,308; Highest Degree: Doctorate
Library Holdings: e-books 8,000; e-journals 35,000; Bk Titles 175,000; Per Subs 7,000
Special Collections: Brownsville, Cameron County, Lower Rio Grande Valley & Northeast Mexico History Coll
Subject Interests: Genealogy, Local hist
Automation Activity & Vendor Info: (Acquisitions) Innovative Interfaces, Inc; (Cataloging) Innovative Interfaces, Inc; (Circulation) Innovative Interfaces, Inc; (Course Reserve) Innovative Interfaces, Inc; (ILL) Innovative Interfaces, Inc; (OPAC) Innovative Interfaces, Inc; (Serials) LS 2000
Wireless access
Function: Telephone ref
Publications: Annual Report; Newsletter; Orientation Manuals
Partic in Amigos Library Services, Inc; OCLC Online Computer Library Center, Inc; TexSHARE - Texas State Library & Archives Commission
Open Mon-Thurs 8am-Midnight, Fri & Sat 9-6, Sun 1-10 (Fall-Spring); Mon-Thurs 8am-9pm, Fri 8-5, Sat 9-6, Sun 1-9 (Summer)
Friends of the Library Group

BROWNWOOD

P BROWNWOOD COMMUNITY LIBRARY ASSOCIATION*, Brownwood Library, 600 Carnegie St, 76801-7038. SAN 316-1277. Tel: 325-646-0155. FAX: 325-646-6503. E-mail: staff@brownwoodlibrary.com. Web Site: www.brownwoodlibrary.com. *Dir,* Becky Isbell; E-mail: dir@brownwoodlibrary.com; Staff 5 (MLS 1, Non-MLS 4)
Founded 1904. Pop 38,000
Library Holdings: Bk Vols 78,000; Per Subs 20
Automation Activity & Vendor Info: (Cataloging) Biblionix; (Circulation) Biblionix; (OPAC) Biblionix
Wireless access
Open Mon & Wed-Fri 9-6, Tues 9-8, Sat 9-1
Friends of the Library Group
Branches: 1
GENEALOGY & LOCAL HISTORY, 213 S Broadway, 76801. Tel: 325-646-6006. Web Site: www.brownwoodpubliclibrary.com/genealogy-library.html. *Dir,* Becky Isbell
Founded 2006
Special Collections: 35th District Court Civil Records (1880-1930); Brownwood Bulletin (1894-2008), microfilm; Brownwood City Directories (1909-2007); Brownwood City Maps (1883-1930); Historic Photographs & Rare Books; Military Veterans Information (Civil War, World War I & World War II); Yearbooks for Brownwood High School, Howard Payne University & Daniel Baker College
Subject Interests: Local hist
Function: Scanner
Open Tues-Fri 9-6

C HOWARD PAYNE UNIVERSITY, Walker Memorial Library, 1000 Fisk St, 76801. SAN 316-1285. Tel: 325-649-8602. FAX: 325-649-8904. E-mail: library@hputx.edu. Web Site: www.hputx.edu/library. *Dir of Libr,* Debby Dill; E-mail: ddill@hputx.edu; *Instruction & Outreach Librn,* Wade Kinnin; Tel: 325-649-8095, E-mail: wkinnin@hputx.edu; *Coll, Govt Doc Coordr,* Juanita Sypert; Tel: 325-649-8096, E-mail: jsypert@hputx.edu; Staff 8 (MLS 4, Non-MLS 4)
Founded 1889. Enrl 1,171; Fac 88; Highest Degree: Master
Library Holdings: CDs 1,879; e-books 45,000; Bk Titles 87,000; Bk Vols 121,000; Per Subs 598; Videos 472
Special Collections: US Document Depository
Subject Interests: Bus, Educ, Relig, Sociol
Automation Activity & Vendor Info: (Acquisitions) SirsiDynix; (Cataloging) SirsiDynix; (Circulation) SirsiDynix; (Course Reserve) SirsiDynix; (Discovery) EBSCO Discovery Service; (ILL) OCLC Online; (OPAC) SirsiDynix; (Serials) SirsiDynix
Wireless access
Partic in Abilene Library Consortium; Amigos Library Services, Inc; OCLC Online Computer Library Center, Inc; Tex Independent Cols & Univ Librs; TexSHARE - Texas State Library & Archives Commission

Open Mon-Thurs 7:30am-11pm, Fri 7:30-5, Sun 3-11 (Fall-Spring); Mon-Fri 8-5 (Summer)
Restriction: Authorized patrons

BRYAN

P BRYAN COLLEGE STATION PUBLIC LIBRARY SYSTEM*, 201 E 26th St, 77803-5356. SAN 316-1293. Tel: 979-209-5600. Administration Tel: 979-209-5614. FAX: 979-209-5610. Web Site: www.bcslibrary.org. *Dir, Libr Syst,* Bea Saba; E-mail: bsaba@bryantx.gov; *Supvr, Automation Serv,* Wendell Gragg; Staff 12 (MLS 12)
Founded 1903. Pop 140,000; Circ 731,924
Library Holdings: AV Mats 6,200; Bk Titles 176,084; Bk Vols 235,323; Per Subs 524; Talking Bks 3,600
Subject Interests: Ballet, Genealogy, Humanities, Local hist, Tex, Tex poets
Automation Activity & Vendor Info: (Cataloging) Innovative Interfaces, Inc; (Circulation) Innovative Interfaces, Inc; (OPAC) Innovative Interfaces, Inc
Wireless access
Function: ILL available, Internet access, Music CDs, Photocopying/Printing, Prog for children & young adult, Ref serv available, Spoken cassettes & CDs, Summer reading prog, Telephone ref, Wheelchair accessible
Partic in Partners Library Action Network
Open Mon & Wed 9-5, Tues & Thurs 1-7, Fri 9-1, Sat 1-5
Friends of the Library Group
Branches: 2
CARNEGIE HISTORY CENTER, 111 S Main St, 77803. Tel: 979-209-5630. *Br Mgr,* Rachael Altman; E-mail: raltman@bryantx.gov; Staff 2 (MLS 2)
Library Holdings: Bk Vols 13,428
Subject Interests: Genealogy
Open Mon, Wed & Fri 1-5, Tues & Thurs 10-5
LARRY J RINGER LIBRARY, 1818 Harvey Mitchell Pkwy S, College Station, 77840, SAN 323-7702. Tel: 979-764-3416. FAX: 979-764-6379. *Br Mgr,* Jessica Jones; E-mail: jonesj@bryantx.gov; Staff 7 (MLS 7)
Founded 1987. Pop 140,000; Circ 389,404
Open Mon & Wed 1-7, Tues & Thurs 9-5, Fri 1-5, Sat 9-1
Friends of the Library Group

BUDA

P BUDA PUBLIC LIBRARY*, 405 Loop St, Bldg 100, 78610. SAN 376-4818. Tel: 512-295-5899. FAX: 512-295-6525. Web Site: www.budalibrary.org. *Dir,* Melinda Hodges; E-mail: librarian@budalibrary.org; *Asst Dir, Ch,* Martha Sanders; E-mail: martha@budalibrary.org; Staff 4 (MLS 3, Non-MLS 1)
Founded 1980
Automation Activity & Vendor Info: (Cataloging) Biblionix; (Circulation) Biblionix; (OPAC) Biblionix
Wireless access
Function: AV serv, ILL available, Prog for children & young adult, Summer reading prog, Wheelchair accessible
Partic in Partners Library Action Network
Friends of the Library Group

BUFFALO

P BUFFALO PUBLIC LIBRARY*, 1005 Hill St, 75831. (Mail add: 812 N Buffalo Ave, 75831), SAN 376-4826. Tel: 903-322-4146. FAX: 903-322-3253. E-mail: library@buffalotex.com. Web Site: buffalotex.com/departments/buffalo-public-library.
Founded 1971
Library Holdings: Bk Vols 25,000
Wireless access
Open Mon, Wed & Fri 9-1, Tues & Thurs 12-4, Sat 2-6
Friends of the Library Group

BULLARD

P BULLARD COMMUNITY LIBRARY, 211 W Main, 75757. (Mail add: PO Box 368, 75757-0368). Tel: 903-894-6125. FAX: 903-894-0837. E-mail: director@bullardlibrary.org. Web Site: www.bullardlibrary.org. *Dir,* Carol Olson
Founded 1976. Pop 4,500
Special Collections: Local History Coll
Subject Interests: Genealogy
Automation Activity & Vendor Info: (Cataloging) Book Systems; (Circulation) Book Systems; (ILL) OCLC FirstSearch; (OPAC) Book Systems
Wireless access
Function: 24/7 Electronic res, 24/7 Online cat, Archival coll, Art programs, Audiobks on Playaways & MP3, Audiobks via web, Bk club(s), Bks on CD, Children's prog, Computer training, Computers for patron use, Electronic databases & coll, Family literacy, Free DVD rentals, Holiday prog, ILL available, Instruction & testing, Internet access, Large print keyboards, Magnifiers for reading, Makerspace, Meeting rooms, Microfiche/film & reading machines, Movies, Notary serv, Online cat, Online ref, Outreach serv, OverDrive digital audio bks, Photocopying/Printing, Preschool outreach, Preschool reading prog, Printer for laptops & handheld devices, Prog for adults, Prog for children & young adult, Scanner, Spanish lang bks, Story hour, Study rm, Summer reading prog, Tax forms, Teen prog, Visual arts prog, Workshops
Partic in Northeast Texas Digital Consortium
Open Mon-Thurs 10-5:30
Friends of the Library Group

BULVERDE

P BULVERDE-SPRING BRANCH LIBRARY*, 131 Bulverde Crossing, 78163. SAN 376-4184. Tel: 830-438-4864. FAX: 830-980-3362. E-mail: info@bsblibrary.org. Web Site: www.bsblibrary.org. *Libr Dir,* Susan Herr; *Ad,* Kristin Bowman; *Youth Serv Librn,* Laura Kraus; *Mkt Coordr, Outreach Coordr,* Lacee Sowell; *Adult Programming, Outreach Coordr,* Bethany Corder; *Adult Programming, Outreach Coordr,* Debbie Soelberg; Staff 2 (MLS 2)
Founded 1986. Pop 23,000; Circ 257,579
Library Holdings: AV Mats 8,042; Braille Volumes 75; Large Print Bks 2,054; Bk Titles 44,968; Bk Vols 47,335; Per Subs 63
Automation Activity & Vendor Info: (Acquisitions) Biblionix; (Cataloging) Biblionix; (Circulation) Biblionix; (ILL) OCLC FirstSearch; (OPAC) Follett Software
Wireless access
Function: Adult bk club, Adult literacy prog, Art exhibits, Audiobks via web, Bilingual assistance for Spanish patrons, Bk club(s), Bks on CD, Children's prog, Citizenship assistance, Computer training, Computers for patron use, E-Reserves, Electronic databases & coll, Equip loans & repairs, Free DVD rentals, ILL available, Internet access, Large print keyboards, Magnifiers for reading, Music CDs, Online cat, OverDrive digital audio bks, Photocopying/Printing, Prog for adults, Prog for children & young adult, Ref serv available, Scanner, Spanish lang bks, Story hour, Summer reading prog, Tax forms, Teen prog, Wheelchair accessible
Partic in Partners Library Action Network
Open Mon-Thurs 9-8, Fri 10-6, Sat 10-5, Sun 1-5
Friends of the Library Group

BUNA

P BUNA PUBLIC LIBRARY*, 1042 Hwy 62 S, 77612. (Mail add: PO Box 1571, 77612-1571), SAN 375-555X. Tel: 409-994-5501. FAX: 409-994-4737. E-mail: buna.library@sbcglobal.net. Web Site: www.bunalibrary.org. *Dir,* Lena White; Staff 1 (Non-MLS 1)
Founded 1973. Pop 8,807; Circ 18,352
Library Holdings: AV Mats 1,500; DVDs 1,000; Bk Titles 24,853; Per Subs 6
Wireless access
Special Services for the Deaf - Bks on deafness & sign lang
Open Mon & Tues 10-5:30, Wed 10-4, Thurs 10-4:30, Fri 10-5
Friends of the Library Group

BURKBURNETT

P BURKBURNETT LIBRARY*, 215 E Fourth St, 76354-3446. SAN 316-1315. Tel: 940-569-2991. FAX: 940-569-1620. Web Site: burk.ploud.net. *Libr Dir,* Pamela Miller; E-mail: pmiller@burkburnett.org; *Asst Dir,* Ashlee O'Rourke; E-mail: ashleeorourke@gmail.com; Staff 2 (Non-MLS 2)
Founded 1967. Pop 11,167
Library Holdings: Audiobooks 1,457; DVDs 1,730; e-books 7,726; Bk Titles 20,988; Per Subs 20
Special Collections: Historical Burkburnett Coll; Holiday Book Colls; Spanish Language Materials; Wordless Picture Books
Automation Activity & Vendor Info: (Cataloging) Book Systems; (Circulation) Book Systems; (OPAC) Book Systems
Wireless access
Function: 24/7 Online cat, Adult bk club, Audiobks on Playaways & MP3, Audiobks via web, Bk club(s), Bks on CD, Children's prog, Computers for patron use, Free DVD rentals, Holiday prog, ILL available, Internet access, Magazines, Mail & tel request accepted, Mail loans to mem, Movies, Online cat, Outreach serv, Outside serv via phone, mail, e-mail & web, OverDrive digital audio bks, Photocopying/Printing, Preschool reading prog, Prog for adults, Prog for children & young adult, Scanner, Senior outreach, Spoken cassettes & CDs, Spoken cassettes & DVDs, Story hour, Summer reading prog, Tax forms, Teen prog
Open Tues & Thurs 10-8, Wed & Fri 10-6, Sat 10-2
Friends of the Library Group

BURLESON

P BURLESON PUBLIC LIBRARY, 248 SW Johnson Ave, 76028. SAN 316-1323. Tel: 817-426-9210. E-mail: info@burlesontx.com. Web Site: www.burlesontx.com/library. *Dep Dir,* Sara Miller; E-mail: smiller@burlesontx.com; Staff 14 (MLS 5, Non-MLS 9)
Founded 1971. Pop 55,220; Circ 317,594
Oct 2023-Sept 2024 Income $1,403,845, City $1,401,519, Federal $2,326. Mats Exp $148,510, Books $45,788, AV Mat $11,751, Electronic Ref Mat (Incl. Access Fees) $90,971. Sal $656,184
Library Holdings: Audiobooks 1,192; DVDs 1,020; e-books 43,860; Electronic Media & Resources 73; Bk Vols 48,968
Automation Activity & Vendor Info: (Acquisitions) Brodart; (Cataloging) Koha; (Circulation) Koha; (Discovery) Koha; (ILL) OCLC FirstSearch; (OPAC) Koha
Wireless access
Function: 24/7 Electronic res, 24/7 Online cat, 3D Printer, Accelerated reader prog, Activity rm, Adult bk club, Archival coll, Art programs, Audiobks on Playaways & MP3, Audiobks via web, Bk club(s), Bks on CD, Bus archives, Butterfly Garden, Children's prog, Computers for patron use, Digital talking bks, Doc delivery serv, Electronic databases & coll, Family literacy, For res purposes, Free DVD rentals, Games, Health sci info serv, Holiday prog, Home delivery & serv to seniorr ctr & nursing homes, Homebound delivery serv, Homework prog, ILL available, Instruction & testing, Internet access, Life-long learning prog for all ages, Magazines, Mail & tel request accepted, Meeting rooms, Movies, Museum passes, Online cat, Online info literacy tutorials on the web & in blackboard, Online ref, Outreach serv, Outside serv via phone, mail, e-mail & web, OverDrive digital audio bks, Photocopying/Printing, Preschool reading prog, Printer for laptops & handheld devices, Prog for adults, Prog for children & young adult, Ref & res, Ref serv available, Res assist avail, Scanner, Senior outreach, Serves people with intellectual disabilities, Spanish lang bks, STEM programs, Story hour, Study rm, Summer reading prog, Tax forms, Teen prog, Telephone ref, Wheelchair accessible, Wifi hotspot checkout, Workshops, Writing prog
Partic in MetroShare Libraries
Special Services for the Deaf - Bks on deafness & sign lang
Special Services for the Blind - Bks available with recordings; Bks on CD; Braille bks; Children's Braille; Home delivery serv; Large print bks; Playaways (bks on MP3); Talking bk serv referral
Open Mon-Wed 9-8, Thurs-Sat 9-6
Restriction: Non-resident fee
Friends of the Library Group

BURNET

P BURNET COUNTY LIBRARY SYSTEM*, Herman Brown Free Library, 100 E Washington St, 78611. SAN 361-3208. Tel: 512-715-5228. FAX: 512-715-5249. E-mail: hbfl@burnetcountylibrary.org. Web Site: www.hermanbrownlibrary.org, www2.youseemore.com/burnet/about.asp?p=8. *Dir,* Florence Reeves; E-mail: freeves@burnetcountylibrary.org; *Asst Dir,* Deanne Randle; E-mail: drandle@burnetcountylibrary.org
Founded 1948. Pop 23,000; Circ 180,622
Library Holdings: Bk Titles 65,000; Bk Vols 80,000; Per Subs 250
Special Collections: Oral History
Subject Interests: Genealogy, Texana
Automation Activity & Vendor Info: (Cataloging) TLC (The Library Corporation); (Circulation) TLC (The Library Corporation); (Course Reserve) TLC (The Library Corporation); (ILL) TLC (The Library Corporation); (OPAC) TLC (The Library Corporation); (Serials) TLC (The Library Corporation)
Wireless access
Open Mon-Fri 9-5:30
Friends of the Library Group
Branches: 3
JOANNE COLE-MITTE MEMORIAL LIBRARY, 170 N Gabriel St, Bertram, 78605. SAN 361-3232. Tel: 512-355-2113. FAX: 512-355-3323. *Dir,* Mary Seaman; E-mail: mseaman@burnetcountylibrary.org
Library Holdings: Bk Vols 10,000
Open Mon-Fri 10-6
Friends of the Library Group
MARBLE FALLS PUBLIC LIBRARY, 101 Main St, Marble Falls, 78654. SAN 361-3291. Tel: 830-693-3023. FAX: 830-693-3987. Web Site: marblefallslibrary.org. *Dir,* Amanda Rose; E-mail: arose@burnetcountylibrary.org
Library Holdings: Bk Vols 43,000
Open Mon-Fri 10-6
Friends of the Library Group
OAKALLA PUBLIC LIBRARY, 29011 FM 963, Oakalla, 78608, SAN 376-9496. Tel: 512-556-9085. FAX: 512-556-9085. E-mail: oakallalibrary@yahoo.com. *Librn,* Tricia Pratt
Library Holdings: Bk Vols 9,017
Open Tues 5:30-8:30, Sat 10-1
Friends of the Library Group

CALDWELL

P HARRIE P WOODSON MEMORIAL LIBRARY*, 704 W Hwy 21, 77836-1129. SAN 316-1331. Tel: 979-567-4111. FAX: 979-567-4962. E-mail: library@caldwelltx.gov. Web Site: caldwell.ploud.net. *Librn,* Mary Kuehn
Circ 17,877
Library Holdings: Bk Titles 16,000; Per Subs 15
Automation Activity & Vendor Info: (Cataloging) Biblionix; (Circulation) Biblionix; (OPAC) Biblionix
Wireless access
Partic in Partners Library Action Network
Open Mon-Fri 9-6
Friends of the Library Group

CAMERON

P CAMERON PUBLIC LIBRARY, 304 E Third St, 76520. SAN 316-1358. Tel: 254-697-2401. FAX: 254-605-0851. Web Site: cameron.ploud.net. *Dir, Libr Serv,* Elena Berkes; E-mail: eberkes@camerontexas.net; *Ad,* Heather Zana; *Ch Serv Librn,* Maria Montejano
Founded 1953
Special Collections: DAR Genealogy, mss, vols; Local History Coll; Texas History Coll
Automation Activity & Vendor Info: (Cataloging) Biblionix; (OPAC) Biblionix
Wireless access
Function: 24/7 Electronic res, 24/7 Online cat, 24/7 wireless access, Audiobks via web, Chess club, Children's prog, Computers for patron use, Electronic databases & coll, Extended outdoor wifi, Free DVD rentals, Games, Holiday prog, Home delivery & serv to seniorr ctr & nursing homes, Homebound delivery serv, ILL available, Internet access, Mail & tel request accepted, Online cat, Online ref, Outreach serv, Outside serv via phone, mail, e-mail & web, Photocopying/Printing, Preschool outreach, Preschool reading prog, Prog for children & young adult, Ref & res, Ref serv available, Scanner, Story hour, Summer reading prog, Tax forms
Open Mon-Thurs 10-5
Restriction: Authorized patrons, Open to students
Friends of the Library Group

CAMP WOOD

P CAMP WOOD PUBLIC LIBRARY*, 106 S Nueces, 78833. (Mail add: PO Box 138, 78833-0138), SAN 378-3936. Tel: 830-597-3208. FAX: 830-597-3209. E-mail: campwoodlibrary@gmail.com. Web Site: www.campwoodlibrary.org. *Dir,* Kathy Fulton
Pop 1,706
Library Holdings: AV Mats 200; DVDs 600; Bk Vols 10,143; Videos 300
Automation Activity & Vendor Info: (Cataloging) Biblionix; (Circulation) Biblionix
Wireless access
Partic in Partners Library Action Network; TexSHARE - Texas State Library & Archives Commission
Open Tues-Fri 11-5
Friends of the Library Group

CANADIAN

P HEMPHILL COUNTY LIBRARY*, 500 Main St, 79014. SAN 316-1366. Tel: 806-323-5282. FAX: 806-323-6102. E-mail: library79014@gmail.com. Web Site: harringtonlc.org/canadian. *Dir,* April Dillon; E-mail: aj79014@gmail.com; Staff 1 (MLS 1)
Founded 1927. Pop 3,300
Library Holdings: Bk Titles 39,000; Per Subs 72; Talking Bks 1,379; Videos 729
Special Collections: Local Newspaper since 1887, micro
Subject Interests: Local hist
Automation Activity & Vendor Info: (Cataloging) SirsiDynix; (Circulation) SirsiDynix; (OPAC) SirsiDynix
Wireless access
Partic in Harrington Library Consortium
Open Mon & Thurs 8:30-6, Tues, Wed & Fri 8:30-5, Sat 9-Noon
Friends of the Library Group

CANTON

P VAN ZANDT COUNTY SARAH NORMAN LIBRARY, 317 First Monday Lane, 75103. SAN 320-7498. Tel: 903-567-4276. FAX: 903-567-6981. Web Site: www.vanzandtlibrary.org. *Dir,* Tonja Garten; E-mail: tgarten@vanzandtcounty.org; *Youth Serv Librn,* Jordin Shilling; E-mail: jshilling@vanzandtcounty.org; *Asst Librn,* Kitty White
Pop 21,004
Library Holdings: Bk Vols 38,560; Per Subs 45
Special Collections: Genealogy Coll; Local History Coll; Texas Coll

Automation Activity & Vendor Info: (Cataloging) Book Systems; (Circulation) Book Systems; (ILL) Book Systems; (Media Booking) Book Systems; (OPAC) Book Systems
Wireless access
Function: 24/7 Electronic res, 24/7 Online cat, Accelerated reader prog, Audio & video playback equip for onsite use, Audiobks on Playaways & MP3, Bks on CD, CD-ROM, Children's prog, Computer training, Computers for patron use, Digital talking bks, Doc delivery serv, E-Reserves, Electronic databases & coll, Free DVD rentals, Genealogy discussion group, Home delivery & serv to seniorr ctr & nursing homes, Homework prog, ILL available, Instruction & testing, Internet access, Laminating, Magazines, Magnifiers for reading, Meeting rooms, Microfiche/film & reading machines, Movies, Music CDs, Notary serv, Online cat, Photocopying/Printing, Preschool outreach, Printer for laptops & handheld devices, Prog for adults, Prog for children & young adult, Ref & res, Ref serv available, Scanner, Senior computer classes, Story hour, Summer & winter reading prog, Summer reading prog, Tax forms, Wheelchair accessible
Open Tues, Wed & Fri 9-5, Thurs 11-6
Friends of the Library Group

CANYON

P CANYON AREA LIBRARY*, 1501 Third Ave, 79015. SAN 316-1374. Tel: 806-655-5015. FAX: 806-655-5032. Web Site: www.canyonlibrary.org. *Dir,* Janice Doan; E-mail: jdoan@canyontx.com; *Asst Librn,* Andrea High; E-mail: ahigh@canyontx.com; Staff 10 (MLS 2, Non-MLS 8)
Founded 1928. Pop 36,825; Circ 84,836; Fac 10
Special Collections: Texas Coll
Automation Activity & Vendor Info: (Cataloging) SirsiDynix; (Circulation) SirsiDynix; (ILL) SirsiDynix; (OPAC) SirsiDynix
Wireless access
Function: 24/7 Electronic res, 24/7 Online cat, 3D Printer, Activity rm, Adult bk club, Audiobks on Playaways & MP3, Audiobks via web, Bk club(s), Bks on CD, Children's prog, Computer training, Computers for patron use, Digital talking bks, Electronic databases & coll, ILL available, Internet access, Magazines, Meeting rooms, Movies, Music CDs, Online cat, Photocopying/Printing, Printer for laptops & handheld devices, Prog for adults, Prog for children & young adult, Ref serv available, Scanner, Spanish lang bks, Story hour, Summer reading prog, Tax forms, Teen prog, Wheelchair accessible
Partic in Harrington Library Consortium
Open Mon-Thurs 10-7, Fri 10-5:30, Sat 10-2
Friends of the Library Group

S PANHANDLE-PLAINS HISTORICAL MUSEUM*, Research Center, 2503 Fourth Ave, 79015, (Mail add: WT Box 60967, 79016), SAN 328-6169. Tel: 806-651-2254. Administration FAX: 806-651-2250. Web Site: www.panhandleplains.org. *Dir,* Warren Stricker; E-mail: wstricker@pphm.wtamu.edu; Staff 2 (MLS 1, Non-MLS 1)
Library Holdings: Bk Vols 15,000
Special Collections: Oral History
Subject Interests: Hist of the Tex Panhandle-Plains region, Local hist, Okla Panhandle & Eastern NMex, Petroleum indust, Ranching, State & local govt, SW art & artists
Automation Activity & Vendor Info: (OPAC) Ex Libris Group
Function: 24/7 Online cat, Archival coll, Online cat, Photocopying/Printing, Ref serv available, Res assist avail, Res libr
Open Tue-Fri 10-12 & 1-5 (Fall-Spring); Mon-Fri 10-12 & 1-5 (Summer)
Restriction: Closed stack, Non-circulating

C WEST TEXAS A&M UNIVERSITY*, Cornette Library, 110 26th St, 79016. (Mail add: WTAMU Box 60748, 79016-0001), SAN 316-1382. Tel: 806-651-2230. Circulation Tel: 806-651-2223. FAX: 806-651-2213. Web Site: www.wtamu.edu/library. *Dir,* Shawna Kennedy-Witthar; Tel: 806-651-2227, E-mail: switthar@wtamu.edu; *Head, Acq,* Gonda Stayton; Tel: 806-651-2218, E-mail: gdstayton@wtamu.edu; *Head, Cat,* Mary Rausch; Tel: 806-651-2219, E-mail: mrausch@wtamu.edu; *Head, Circ,* Beth Vizzini; E-mail: bavizzini@wtamu.edu; *Doc Librn,* Carolyn Ottoson; Tel: 806-651-2204, E-mail: cottoson@wtamu.edu; *Ref Librn,* Steve Ely; E-mail: sely@wtamu.edu; *Archives, Spec Coll Librn,* Sidnye Johnson; Tel: 806-651-2209, E-mail: sjohnson@wtamu.edu; Staff 23 (MLS 8, Non-MLS 15)
Founded 1910. Enrl 7,900; Fac 242; Highest Degree: Doctorate
Library Holdings: AV Mats 1,927; Bk Titles 740,579; Bk Vols 1,096,057; Per Subs 19,022
Special Collections: American History (Library of American Civilization), micro; English History (British House of Commons Sessional Papers & Hansard's British Parliamentary Debates), micro; English Literature (Library of English Literature, Parts 1-4), micro; Loula Grace Erdmen Papers; Sheffy Coll, regional hist; Texas Panhandle & Great Plains (Dr L F Sheffy Memorial); Western Americana (Xerox UM Western Americana), micro. Oral History; State Document Depository; US Document Depository
Automation Activity & Vendor Info: (Acquisitions) Ex Libris Group; (Cataloging) Ex Libris Group; (Circulation) Ex Libris Group; (Course Reserve) Ex Libris Group; (ILL) OCLC ILLiad; (Media Booking) Ex Libris Group; (OPAC) Ex Libris Group; (Serials) Ex Libris Group
Wireless access
Publications: Newsletter; Quick Guides
Partic in Amigos Library Services, Inc; Llano Estacado Info Access Network
Special Services for the Blind - VisualTek equip
Open Mon-Thurs 7:45am-Midnight, Fri 7:45-5, Sat 10-5, Sun 2-Midnight
Friends of the Library Group

S WESTERNERS INTERNATIONAL LIBRARY*, c/o Panhandle-Plains Historical Museum, 2503 Fourth Ave, 79015. SAN 328-1310. Tel: 806-654-6920. Toll Free Tel: 800-541-4650. E-mail: westerners@wtamu.edu, wihomeranch@gmail.com. Web Site: www.westerners-international.org. *Chmn,* Bonney MacDonald; E-mail: bmacdonald@wtamu.edu; *Pres,* Tim A Bowman; *Treas,* Janie Rodarte
Library Holdings: Bk Vols 500; Per Subs 10
Wireless access

CANYON LAKE

P TYE PRESTON MEMORIAL LIBRARY*, 16311 S Access Rd, 78133-5301. SAN 324-1238. Tel: 830-964-3744. FAX: 830-964-3126. Web Site: www.tpml.org. *Libr Dir,* Rachel Keeler; E-mail: director@tpml.org; *Pub Serv Coordr,* Jamie Buck; E-mail: jamie@tpml.org; *Youth Serv Coordr,* Betsey Leitko; E-mail: betsey@tpml.org; Staff 8 (MLS 3, Non-MLS 5)
Founded 1977. Pop 30,834; Circ 136,704
Jul 2018-Jun 2019 Income $941,298, Locally Generated Income $851,685, Other $83,839. Mats Exp $80,737, Books $45,360, AV Mat $13,325, Electronic Ref Mat (Incl. Access Fees) $22,052. Sal $293,666 (Prof $44,000)
Library Holdings: Audiobooks 2,285; DVDs 4,437; e-books 8,943; Large Print Bks 4,716; Bk Titles 38,698; Bk Vols 40,732; Per Subs 39
Automation Activity & Vendor Info: (Acquisitions) Biblionix; (Cataloging) Biblionix; (Circulation) Biblionix; (OPAC) Biblionix
Wireless access
Function: Adult bk club, Adult literacy prog, Art exhibits, Audiobks via web, Bi-weekly Writer's Group, Bk club(s), Bks on cassette, Bks on CD, Children's prog, Computer training, Computers for patron use, Electronic databases & coll, Family literacy, Free DVD rentals, Genealogy discussion group, Homebound delivery serv, ILL available, Internet access, Life-long learning prog for all ages, Magazines, Magnifiers for reading, Microfiche/film & reading machines, Movies, Online cat, OverDrive digital audio bks, Photocopying/Printing, Preschool outreach, Preschool reading prog, Printer for laptops & handheld devices, Prog for adults, Prog for children & young adult, Ref serv available, Scanner, Spanish lang bks, Spoken cassettes & CDs, Story hour, Summer reading prog, Tax forms, Teen prog, Telephone ref, Wheelchair accessible, Workshops
Partic in Amigos Library Services, Inc; Partners Library Action Network
Open Mon-Thurs 9-8:30, Fri & Sat 10-5
Friends of the Library Group

CARRIZO SPRINGS

P DIMMIT COUNTY PUBLIC LIBRARY*, 200 N Ninth St, 78834. SAN 376-4141. Tel: 830-876-5788. FAX: 830-876-5788. E-mail: carrizo.librarian@gmail.com. Web Site: www.dimmitlibrary.org. *Libr Dir,* J J Ortiz; Staff 3 (Non-MLS 3)
Founded 1980. Pop 10,460
Library Holdings: Bk Vols 22,539; Per Subs 41
Automation Activity & Vendor Info: (Acquisitions) Biblionix/Apollo; (Cataloging) Biblionix/Apollo; (Circulation) Biblionix/Apollo; (Course Reserve) Biblionix; (ILL) Biblionix/Apollo; (OPAC) Biblionix/Apollo; (Serials) Biblionix/Apollo
Wireless access
Function: Bks on cassette, Bks on CD, CD-ROM, Children's prog, Computers for patron use, Free DVD rentals, Genealogy discussion group, ILL available, Magnifiers for reading, Music CDs, Photocopying/Printing, Summer reading prog, Tax forms, VHS videos, Wheelchair accessible
Open Mon-Fri 9-5
Friends of the Library Group

CARROLLTON

P CARROLLTON PUBLIC LIBRARY*, Josey Ranch Lake Branch, 1700 N Keller Springs Rd, 75006. SAN 319-3268. Tel: 972-466-4800. FAX: 972-466-4265. Web Site: www.cityofcarrollton.com/departments/departments-g-p/library. *Dir,* Jonathan Scheu; Tel: 972-466-3362, E-mail: jonathan.scheu@cityofcarrollton.com; *Access Serv,* Jo Gardner; Tel: 972-466-4812, E-mail: jo.gardner@cityofcarrollton.com; *Acq,* Lana Kelley; Tel: 972-466-4704, E-mail: lana.kelley@cityofcarrollton.com; *Info Serv,* Lynette Jones; Tel: 972-466-4814; E-mail: lynette.jones@cityofcarrollton.com; *Info Serv,* Rachel Young; E-mail: rachel.young@cityofcarrollton.com; *Youth Serv,* Kelly Burns; Tel:

972-466-4717, E-mail: kelly.burns@cityofcarrollton.com; Staff 27.8 (MLS 15, Non-MLS 12.8)
Founded 1963. Pop 121,000; Circ 761,078
Library Holdings: AV Mats 16,035; e-books 1,172; Bk Titles 140,067; Bk Vols 208,000
Special Collections: Genealogy Coll; Local History Coll
Automation Activity & Vendor Info: (Acquisitions) Innovative Interfaces, Inc; (Cataloging) Innovative Interfaces, Inc; (Circulation) Innovative Interfaces, Inc; (ILL) Innovative Interfaces, Inc; (OPAC) Innovative Interfaces, Inc; (Serials) Innovative Interfaces, Inc
Wireless access
Function: ILL available
Open Mon 10-9, Tues, Fri & Sat 10-6, Wed 12-9, Sun 2-6
Friends of the Library Group
Branches: 1
HEBRON & JOSEY BRANCH, 4220 N Josey Lane, 75010. *Br Mgr,* Lynette Jones; E-mail: lynette.jones@cityofcarrollton.com; *Br Mgr,* Lana Kelley; E-mail: lana.kelley@cityofcarrollton.com
Open Mon 10-9, Tues & Thurs 12-9, Wed & Sat 10-6, Sun 2-6
Friends of the Library Group

CARTHAGE

P SAMMY BROWN LIBRARY*, 319 S Market St, 75633. SAN 316-1412. Tel: 903-693-6741. FAX: 903-693-4503. Web Site: www.carthagetexas.us/facilities/sammy-brown-library. *Dir,* Kim Turner; E-mail: kturner@sammybrown.org; Staff 6 (MLS 2, Non-MLS 4)
Founded 1962. Pop 22,350
Sept 2019-Aug 2020 Income $85,850, City $30,000, County $14,850, Locally Generated Income $35,000, Other $6,000. Mats Exp $6,800. Sal $42,300 (Prof $24,000)
Library Holdings: Audiobooks 1,723; DVDs 3,355; Large Print Bks 2,107; Bk Titles 40,531; Per Subs 4
Automation Activity & Vendor Info: (Cataloging) Biblionix/Apollo; (Circulation) Biblionix/Apollo
Wireless access
Function: 24/7 Online cat, Adult bk club, Audio & video playback equip for onsite use, Audiobks via web, Bks on CD, Children's prog, Computers for patron use, Digital talking bks, Electronic databases & coll, Free DVD rentals, Holiday prog, ILL available, Internet access, Magazines, Meeting rooms, Notary serv, Online cat, OverDrive digital audio bks, Photocopying/Printing, Printer for laptops & handheld devices, Prog for adults, Prog for children & young adult, Ref & res, Scanner, Spanish lang bks, STEM programs, Summer reading prog, Tax forms, Teen prog, Telephone ref, Wheelchair accessible
Open Mon-Fri 9-6, Sat 9-1
Friends of the Library Group

J PANOLA COLLEGE*, M P Baker Library, 1109 W Panola St, 75633. SAN 316-1404. Tel: 903-693-2052. Reference Tel: 903-693-1162. FAX: 903-693-1115. Web Site: www.panola.edu/library. *Dir, Libr Serv,* Cristie Ferguson; Tel: 903-693-2091, E-mail: cferguson@panola.edu; *Electronic Res Librn,* Holly Derrick; Tel: 903-693-2013, E-mail: hderrick@panola.edu; *Librn,* Alma Ravenell; Tel: 903-693-1162, E-mail: aravenell@panola.edu; *Instrul Librn,* Veronica Wilkerson; Tel: 903-693-1181, E-mail: vwilkerson@panola.edu; *Circ,* Sharon Hill; Tel: 903-693-1155, E-mail: shill@panola.edu; *Pub Serv Asst,* Shay Joines; E-mail: sjoines@panola.edu; Staff 7 (MLS 4, Non-MLS 3)
Founded 1947. Enrl 2,611; Fac 82; Highest Degree: Associate
Special Collections: East Texas Documents & Genealogies, oral hist
Automation Activity & Vendor Info: (Cataloging) OCLC Worldshare Management Services; (Circulation) OCLC Worldshare Management Services; (Course Reserve) OCLC Worldshare Management Services; (Discovery) OCLC Worldshare Management Services; (ILL) OCLC WorldShare Interlibrary Loan; (Media Booking) OCLC Worldshare Management Services; (OPAC) OCLC Worldshare Management Services; (Serials) OCLC Worldshare Management Services
Wireless access
Function: 24/7 Electronic res, 24/7 Online cat, 3D Printer, Archival coll, Art exhibits, AV serv, Bks on CD, Computers for patron use, Distance learning, Doc delivery serv, Electronic databases & coll, ILL available, Internet access, Magnifiers for reading, Meeting rooms, Online cat, Online info literacy tutorials on the web & in blackboard, Online ref, Orientations, Photocopying/Printing, Printer for laptops & handheld devices, Ref & res, Ref serv available, Scanner, Spoken cassettes & CDs, Spoken cassettes & DVDs, Telephone ref, Wheelchair accessible
Publications: Library Annual Report; M P Baker Library Staff Handbook
Partic in Amigos Library Services, Inc; OCLC Online Computer Library Center, Inc; TexSHARE - Texas State Library & Archives Commission
Special Services for the Deaf - Assistive tech
Special Services for the Blind - Assistive/Adapted tech devices, equip & products
Open Mon-Thurs 7:30am-9pm, Fri 7:30-12:30, Sun 4-9 (Winter); Mon-Thurs 7:30-5, Fri 7:30-12:30 (Summer)
Restriction: Authorized patrons, Open to authorized patrons, Open to students, fac, staff & alumni

CASTROVILLE

P CASTROVILLE PUBLIC LIBRARY*, 802 London St, 78009. SAN 316-1420. Tel: 830-931-4095. FAX: 830-931-9050. E-mail: library@castrovilletx.gov. Web Site: castrovilletx.gov/library. *Libr Mgr,* Angela Alejandro; E-mail: angela.alejandro@castrovilletx.gov; Staff 3 (MLS 1, Non-MLS 2)
Founded 1962. Pop 3,059
Library Holdings: Audiobooks 595; DVDs 1,103; Large Print Bks 1,203; Bk Titles 12,966
Special Collections: Oral History
Subject Interests: Genealogy, Local hist
Automation Activity & Vendor Info: (Cataloging) Biblionix; (Circulation) Biblionix; (ILL) Biblionix
Wireless access
Function: Accelerated reader prog, Adult bk club, Audiobks via web, Bk club(s), Bks on CD, Children's prog, Computer training, Computers for patron use, Distance learning, Family literacy, Free DVD rentals, ILL available, Online cat, OverDrive digital audio bks, Photocopying/Printing, Preschool outreach, Prog for adults, Prog for children & young adult, Ref serv available, Scanner, Senior computer classes, Senior outreach, Story hour, Summer reading prog, Tax forms, Teen prog, Wheelchair accessible
Partic in Partners Library Action Network
Open Mon-Thurs 10-6, Fri 10-5, Sat 10-4
Friends of the Library Group

CEDAR HILL

P ZULA BRYANT WYLIE PUBLIC LIBRARY*, 225 Cedar St, 75104-2655. SAN 361-4107. Tel: 972-291-7323, Ext 1313. Circulation Tel: 972-291-7323, Ext 1315. FAX: 972-291-5361. E-mail: library@cedarhilltx.com. Web Site: www.cedarhilltx.com/676/library. *Mgr, Libr Serv,* Aranda Bell; E-mail: aranda.bell@cedarhilltx.com; *Librn,* Travis Walvoord; E-mail: travis.walvoord@cedarhilltx.com; Staff 12 (MLS 2, Non-MLS 10)
Founded 1948. Pop 43,151; Circ 119,365
Library Holdings: Audiobooks 3,018; Braille Volumes 119; CDs 1,898; DVDs 1,293; e-books 28,281; Large Print Bks 1,913; Microforms 11; Bk Titles 54,254; Bk Vols 55,068; Per Subs 110; Videos 2,860
Special Collections: Spanish Language Coll
Subject Interests: Local hist
Automation Activity & Vendor Info: (Acquisitions) Innovative Interfaces, Inc - Millennium; (Cataloging) Innovative Interfaces, Inc - Millennium; (Circulation) Innovative Interfaces, Inc - Millennium; (OPAC) Innovative Interfaces, Inc - Millennium
Wireless access
Function: Bk club(s), Bks on cassette, Bks on CD, Children's prog, Computers for patron use, Electronic databases & coll, Holiday prog, ILL available, Music CDs, Notary serv, Online cat, Online ref, Photocopying/Printing, Preschool outreach, Prog for adults, Prog for children & young adult, Ref & res, Ref serv available, Story hour, Summer reading prog, Teen prog, Telephone ref, VHS videos
Special Services for the Deaf - Bks on deafness & sign lang; Closed caption videos
Special Services for the Blind - Audio mat; Bks & mags in Braille, on rec, tape & cassette; Bks available with recordings; Bks on cassette; Bks on CD; Braille bks; Large print bks
Open Mon, Tues & Thurs 10-9, Wed & Fri 10-6, Sat 10-5
Friends of the Library Group

CEDAR PARK

P CEDAR PARK PUBLIC LIBRARY*, 550 Discovery Blvd, 78613. SAN 325-5158. Tel: 512-401-5600. FAX: 512-259-5236. E-mail: library@cedarparktexas.gov. Web Site: www.cedarparktexas.gov/departments/library. *Libr Dir,* Julia Mitschke; Tel: 512-401-5630, E-mail: julia.mitschke@cedarparktexas.gov; *Asst Libr Dir,* Catherine E Ingram; Tel: 512-401-5640, E-mail: catherine.ingram@cedarparktexas.gov; Staff 23.6 (MLS 5.3, Non-MLS 18.3)
Founded 1981. Pop 52,058; Circ 573,685
Library Holdings: AV Mats 4,713; CDs 1,744; DVDs 2,468; Large Print Bks 1,239; Bk Titles 91,434; Bk Vols 106,056; Per Subs 217; Talking Bks 5,740; Videos 2,468
Subject Interests: Texana
Automation Activity & Vendor Info: (Cataloging) SirsiDynix; (Circulation) SirsiDynix; (ILL) OCLC FirstSearch; (OPAC) SirsiDynix
Wireless access
Function: Adult bk club, Bks on cassette, Bks on CD, Children's prog, Computers for patron use, Electronic databases & coll, ILL available, Music CDs, Online cat, Photocopying/Printing, Prog for adults, Prog for

children & young adult, Story hour, Summer reading prog, Tax forms, Teen prog
Partic in Partners Library Action Network
Open Mon-Thurs 9-9, Fri & Sat 9-5, Sun 1-6
Friends of the Library Group

CELINA

P CELINA PUBLIC LIBRARY*, 142 N Ohio St, 75009. SAN 376-4494. Tel: 972-382-8655. FAX: 972-382-3736. Web Site: www.celina-tx.gov/379/Library. *Libr Supvr,* Jessica Kanaan; E-mail: jkanaan@celina-tx.gov; Staff 1 (Non-MLS 1)
Founded 1992. Pop 6,222
Library Holdings: Bk Titles 10,900; Bk Vols 11,150; Per Subs 30
Subject Interests: Educ
Automation Activity & Vendor Info: (Acquisitions) Follett Software; (Cataloging) Follett Software; (Circulation) Follett Software; (Course Reserve) Follett Software; (ILL) Follett Software; (OPAC) Follett Software; (Serials) Follett Software
Open Mon & Tues 10-8, Wed & Thurs 10-6, Fri & Sat 10-4

CENTER

P FANNIE BROWN BOOTH MEMORIAL LIBRARY*, 619 Tenaha St, 75935. SAN 316-1439. Tel: 936-598-5522. FAX: 936-598-7854. Web Site: www.centerlibrary.org. *Libr Dir,* Sandra Davis; E-mail: fbbl.sandradavis@yahoo.com; *Asst Librn,* Cassaundra Neal; E-mail: fbbl.cassey@yahoo.com; Staff 2 (Non-MLS 2)
Pop 5,678; Circ 19,458
Library Holdings: Audiobooks 604; Bks-By-Mail 68; Bks on Deafness & Sign Lang 6; Braille Volumes 14; CDs 850; DVDs 903; Large Print Bks 604; Microforms 69; Bk Titles 15,462; Bk Vols 16,059; Per Subs 8; Spec Interest Per Sub 5; Videos 857
Special Collections: Texas History Coll. Municipal Document Depository
Automation Activity & Vendor Info: (Cataloging) Follett Software; (Circulation) Follett Software; (OPAC) Follett Software
Wireless access
Function: Accelerated reader prog
Open Tues-Thurs 10-6, Fri 10-5, Sat 10-2
Friends of the Library Group

CENTERVILLE

P LEON COUNTY LIBRARY*, Elmer P & Jewel Ward Memorial Library, 207 E Saint Mary's, 75833. (Mail add: PO Box 567, 75833-0567). Tel: 903-536-3726. FAX: 903-536-3727. E-mail: wardmemoriallibrary@gmail.com. *Dir,* Christina Gray
Pop 950
Library Holdings: Bk Vols 12,000
Wireless access
Open Tues-Fri 8:30-4

CHANDLER

P CHANDLER PUBLIC LIBRARY*, 900 Hwy 31 E, 75758. (Mail add: PO Box 301, 75758), SAN 323-6994. Tel: 903-849-4122. FAX: 903-849-4122. E-mail: library@chandlertx.com. Web Site: www.chandlertx.com/101/library. *Libr Dir,* Nancy Bertholf; Staff 1 (MLS 1)
Founded 1987. Pop 2,000
Jan 2023-Dec 2023 Income $10,200, Locally Generated Income $1,200, Other $9,000. Mats Exp $2,000
Automation Activity & Vendor Info: (Acquisitions) Biblionix/Apollo; (Cataloging) Biblionix/Apollo; (Circulation) Biblionix/Apollo
Wireless access
Partic in Northeast Texas Digital Consortium
Open Tues-Fri 10-6, Sat 9-1
Friends of the Library Group

CHARLOTTE

P CHARLOTTE PUBLIC LIBRARY*, Eight Couser Blvd, 78011. (Mail add: PO Box 757, 78011), SAN 376-4206. Tel: 830-277-1212. FAX: 830-771-0110. E-mail: charlottelibrary16@gmail.com. *Dir & Librn,* Marianne McGinnis; Staff 1 (Non-MLS 1)
Founded 1984
Library Holdings: Audiobooks 15; Bks on Deafness & Sign Lang 2; DVDs 189; Large Print Bks 178
Wireless access
Function: Activity rm, After school storytime
Open Mon-Fri 8-5
Restriction: Authorized patrons, Free to mem
Friends of the Library Group

CHICO

P CHICO PUBLIC LIBRARY INC*, 106 W Jacksboro St, 76431. (Mail add: PO Box 707, 76431-0707), SAN 376-4648. Tel: 940-644-2330. FAX: 940-644-0004. E-mail: chicopublib1@gmail.com. Web Site: chico.ploud.net. *Dir,* Michelle Slonaker
Founded 1973
Library Holdings: Bk Vols 20,371
Automation Activity & Vendor Info: (Cataloging) Book Systems; (Circulation) Book Systems; (OPAC) Book Systems
Wireless access
Open Mon-Fri 10-6

CHILDRESS

P CHILDRESS PUBLIC LIBRARY*, 117 Ave B NE, 79201-4509. SAN 316-1455. Tel: 940-937-8421. FAX: 940-937-8421. E-mail: childresspubliclibrary@gmail.com. Web Site: childress.harringtonlc.org. *Dir,* Summer Trosper; *Asst Librn,* Sara Burton; Staff 2 (Non-MLS 2)
Founded 1900. Pop 7,532; Circ 14,877
Library Holdings: AV Mats 432; Large Print Bks 200; Bk Vols 18,028; Talking Bks 412
Wireless access
Function: Telephone ref
Partic in Harrington Library Consortium
Open Mon-Thurs 9-5, Fri 9-1
Friends of the Library Group

CISCO

J CISCO COLLEGE*, Maner Memorial Library, 101 College Heights, 76437. SAN 316-1463. Tel: 254-442-5011. Administration Tel: 254-442-5118. FAX: 254-442-5100. E-mail: ciscocollegelibrary@cisco.edu. Web Site: www.cisco.edu/about/cisco-campus. *Dir, Libr Serv,* Donna Clark; Tel: 254-442-5026, E-mail: donna.clark@cisco.edu; *Libr Mgr,* Klarissa Myers; Staff 6 (MLS 2, Non-MLS 4)
Founded 1940. Enrl 3,516; Highest Degree: Associate
Library Holdings: AV Mats 3,000; CDs 153; DVDs 127; e-books 36,398; e-journals 40; Electronic Media & Resources 99; Music Scores 200; Bk Titles 27,127; Per Subs 190
Special Collections: Local History Archives, bks, clippings, local newsp, oral hist, maps; Old West, Native Americans & US Military History (Randy Steffen Coll), bks, per; Texas Coll, bks, per. Oral History
Automation Activity & Vendor Info: (Acquisitions) Book Systems; (Cataloging) Book Systems; (Circulation) Book Systems; (Course Reserve) Book Systems; (Discovery) EBSCO Discovery Service; (ILL) OCLC; (Media Booking) Book Systems; (OPAC) Book Systems; (Serials) Book Systems
Wireless access
Function: 24/7 Electronic res, 24/7 Online cat, Archival coll, Art exhibits, AV serv, Bks on cassette, Bks on CD, Distance learning, Doc delivery serv, E-Reserves, Electronic databases & coll, Equip loans & repairs, Free DVD rentals, ILL available, Internet access, Magazines, Mail & tel request accepted, Microfiche/film & reading machines, Movies, Music CDs, Online cat, Online info literacy tutorials on the web & in blackboard, Online ref, Orientations, Outside serv via phone, mail, e-mail & web, Photocopying/Printing, Ref serv available, Scanner, Summer reading prog, Telephone ref, Wheelchair accessible
Publications: Maner Monthly (Newsletter)
Partic in Amigos Library Services, Inc; TexSHARE - Texas State Library & Archives Commission
Special Services for the Blind - Large screen computer & software; ZoomText magnification & reading software
Open Mon-Thurs 7:30am-9pm, Fri 8-2, Sun 8pm-10pm
Restriction: Lending limited to county residents, Open to pub for ref & circ; with some limitations, Photo ID required for access

Departmental Libraries:

ABILENE EDUCATIONAL CENTER LIBRARY, 717 E Industrial Blvd, Abilene, 79602. Tel: 325-794-4481. *Libr Mgr,* Klarissa Myers; Tel: 325-794-4466, E-mail: klarissa.myers@cisco.edu; Staff 2 (MLS 1, Non-MLS 1)
Founded 2004. Enrl 2,637; Highest Degree: Associate
Automation Activity & Vendor Info: (Circulation) Book Systems; (Discovery) EBSCO Discovery Service; (OPAC) Book Systems
Function: 24/7 Electronic res, 24/7 Online cat, AV serv, E-Reserves, Electronic databases & coll, ILL available, Internet access, Online info literacy tutorials on the web & in blackboard, Orientations, Photocopying/Printing, Ref serv available, Telephone ref
Open Mon 7:30-6:30, Tues 7:30-5, Wed & Thurs 7:30-4, Fri 8-noon

P CISCO PUBLIC LIBRARY*, 600 Ave G, 76437. SAN 316-1471. Tel: 254-442-1020. E-mail: clibrary@txol.net. *Librn,* Janet Hounshell
Circ 4,029
Library Holdings: Bk Vols 20,000
Wireless access
Open Mon, Wed & Fri 12:30-5:30

CLARENDON

P G B BURTON MEMORIAL LIBRARY, 217 S Kearney, 79226. (Mail add: PO Box 783, 79226-0783), SAN 316-148X. Tel: 806-874-3685. FAX: 806-874-9750. Web Site: www.facebook.com/burtonmemoriallibrary. *Librn,* Jerri Shields; E-mail: j.shields@cityofclarendontx.com
Founded 1923. Pop 4,100; Circ 26,393
Library Holdings: Bk Titles 26,000; Per Subs 20
Automation Activity & Vendor Info: (Cataloging) SirsiDynix-DRA; (Circulation) SirsiDynix-DRA; (OPAC) SirsiDynix-DRA
Wireless access
Partic in Harrington Library Consortium
Open Mon-Fri 9-5
Friends of the Library Group

J CLARENDON COLLEGE*, Vera Dial Dickey Library, 1122 College Dr, 79226. (Mail add: PO Box 968, 79226-0968), SAN 316-1498. Tel: 806-874-4815. Toll Free Tel: 800-687-9737, Ext 115, 800-687-9737, Ext 116. FAX: 806-874-5080. Web Site: clarendoncollege.edu/library. *Dir,* Pamela Reed; E-mail: pamela.reed@clarendoncollege.edu; *Librn,* Donna Smith; E-mail: donna.smith@clarendoncollege.edu; Staff 3 (MLS 1, Non-MLS 2)
Founded 1898. Highest Degree: Associate
Library Holdings: e-books 18,000; Bk Titles 22,600; Bk Vols 37,300; Per Subs 78
Special Collections: Clarendon Coll. Oral History
Subject Interests: Tex
Automation Activity & Vendor Info: (Acquisitions) SirsiDynix; (Cataloging) SirsiDynix; (Circulation) SirsiDynix; (Course Reserve) SirsiDynix; (ILL) SirsiDynix; (Media Booking) SirsiDynix; (OPAC) SirsiDynix; (Serials) SirsiDynix
Wireless access
Function: AV serv, Distance learning, Doc delivery serv, Homebound delivery serv, ILL available, Internet access, Magnifiers for reading, Orientations, Outside serv via phone, mail, e-mail & web, Spoken cassettes & CDs, Telephone ref, Wheelchair accessible, Workshops
Publications: Faculty Handbook; Student Handout
Partic in Harrington Library Consortium
Special Services for the Blind - Web-Braille
Open Mon-Thurs 9-8, Fri 9-3 (Fall & Spring); Mon-Thurs 8-5 (Summer)
Restriction: Open to pub for ref & circ; with some limitations

CLARKSVILLE

P RED RIVER COUNTY PUBLIC LIBRARY*, 307 N Walnut St, 75426. (Mail add: PO Box 508, 75426-0508), SAN 316-1501. Tel: 903-427-3991. FAX: 903-427-0088. E-mail: rrlibrary@email.com. Web Site: www.rrlibrary.org. *Dir,* Kathy Peterson
Founded 1961. Pop 12,000
Library Holdings: Audiobooks 500; DVDs 500; Large Print Bks 650; Bk Vols 34,107; Per Subs 15
Automation Activity & Vendor Info: (Cataloging) Book Systems; (Circulation) Book Systems; (OPAC) Book Systems
Wireless access
Partic in Partners Library Action Network
Open Mon & Wed-Fri 12-5, Tues 9-12 & 1-5, Sat 9-12
Friends of the Library Group

CLAUDE

P RICHARD S & LEAH MORRIS MEMORIAL LIBRARY*, 605 High St, 79019. SAN 316-151X. Tel: 806-226-2341. FAX: 806-226-2057. Web Site: harringtonlc.org/claude. *Dir,* Leslie Whitaker; E-mail: leslie.whitaker@claudeisd.net
Founded 1979. Pop 1,895; Circ 2,049
Library Holdings: Bk Vols 9,684
Partic in Harrington Library Consortium
Open Mon-Fri 7:30-12 & 12:30-4 (Winter); Mon-Thurs 7:30-12:30 (Summer)

CLEBURNE

P CLEBURNE PUBLIC LIBRARY*, 302 W Henderson St, 76033. (Mail add: PO Box 677, 76033-0657), SAN 316-1528. Tel: 817-645-0934. FAX: 817-556-8816. E-mail: library@cleburne.net. Web Site: www.cleburne.net/1309/Library. *Librn,* Tina Dunham; Tel: 817-645-0936; Staff 7 (MLS 2, Non-MLS 5)
Founded 1905. Pop 45,000
Library Holdings: AV Mats 1,033; Bks on Deafness & Sign Lang 20; Bk Titles 41,846; Bk Vols 44,067; Per Subs 80; Talking Bks 740
Special Collections: Carnegie Library Coll, rare bks; Genealogy (Cleburne & Johnson County History Coll)
Automation Activity & Vendor Info: (Cataloging) TLC (The Library Corporation); (Circulation) TLC (The Library Corporation)
Wireless access
Function: Homebound delivery serv, ILL available
Publications: Bookbuzz (Newsletter)
Partic in Partners Library Action Network
Special Services for the Deaf - Adult & family literacy prog; Bks on deafness & sign lang; High interest/low vocabulary bks; TTY equip
Special Services for the Blind - Home delivery serv
Open Mon 10-8:30, Tues & Wed 10-6, Thurs 10:30-7, Fri 10-5, Sat 10-3
Friends of the Library Group

S LAYLAND MUSEUM*, Research Library & Archives, 201 N Caddo St, 76031. SAN 370-1689. Tel: 817-645-0940. E-mail: museum@cleburne.net. Web Site: laylandmuseum.com. *Mgr,* Jessica Baber; E-mail: Jessica.Baber@cleburne.net
Founded 1963
Library Holdings: Bk Vols 3,000
Special Collections: Texana (Layland Book Coll)
Subject Interests: North Cent Tex hist
Wireless access
Function: For res purposes
Open Tues-Fri 10-5, Sat 10-4
Friends of the Library Group

CLEVELAND

P AUSTIN MEMORIAL LIBRARY*, 220 S Bonham Ave, 77327-4591. SAN 316-1536. Tel: 281-592-3920. FAX: 281-593-0361. E-mail: aml@austinmemlib.org. Web Site: www.austinmemlib.org. *Libr Dir,* Mary Cohn
Founded 1952. Pop 7,200; Circ 42,000
Library Holdings: Bk Vols 46,000
Subject Interests: Genealogy, Tex
Automation Activity & Vendor Info: (Acquisitions) SirsiDynix; (Cataloging) SirsiDynix; (Circulation) SirsiDynix; (Course Reserve) SirsiDynix; (ILL) SirsiDynix; (OPAC) SirsiDynix; (Serials) SirsiDynix
Wireless access
Partic in TexSHARE - Texas State Library & Archives Commission
Open Mon-Fri 9-6

P TARKINGTON COMMUNITY LIBRARY*, 3032 FM 163, 77327. Tel: 281-592-5136. FAX: 281-592-5136. E-mail: info@tarkingtonlib.org. Web Site: tarkingtonlib.org. *Dir,* Ruth Stetson; *Librn,* Laura Walker; E-mail: laura.walker@tarkingtonlib.org; Staff 2 (MLS 1, Non-MLS 1)
Founded 1996. Pop 9,800
Library Holdings: Audiobooks 134; DVDs 603; Bk Titles 13,000
Automation Activity & Vendor Info: (Acquisitions) Biblionix/Apollo; (Cataloging) Biblionix/Apollo; (Circulation) Biblionix/Apollo
Wireless access
Function: 24/7 Online cat, Children's prog, Computers for patron use, Electronic databases & coll, Free DVD rentals, Holiday prog, Internet access, Online cat, Photocopying/Printing, Preschool outreach, Prog for adults, Prog for children & young adult, Ref & res, Scanner, Senior outreach, STEM programs, Summer reading prog, Teen prog, Wheelchair accessible
Open Mon, Thurs & Fri Noon-5, Wed 9-1
Restriction: Authorized patrons
Friends of the Library Group

CLIFTON

P NELLIE PEDERSON CIVIC LIBRARY*, 406 Live Oak St, 76634. (Mail add: PO Box 231, 76634-0231). Tel: 254-675-6495. FAX: 254-675-3175. E-mail: cliftonlib@cliftontexas.us. Web Site: www.cliftonlib.com. *Libr Dir,* Lewis Stansell; Staff 1 (Non-MLS 1)
Pop 6,700; Circ 10,000
Library Holdings: Bk Vols 11,500
Automation Activity & Vendor Info: (Cataloging) Biblionix/Apollo; (Circulation) Biblionix/Apollo; (OPAC) Biblionix/Apollo
Wireless access
Partic in Partners Library Action Network; TexSHARE - Texas State Library & Archives Commission
Open Mon-Fri 10-5
Friends of the Library Group

CLYDE

P CLYDE PUBLIC LIBRARY*, 125 Oak St, 79510-4702. (Mail add: PO Box 1779, 79510-1779), SAN 324-7457. Tel: 325-893-5315. FAX: 325-893-3866. E-mail: library@clyde-tx.gov. Web Site: https://www.clyde-tx.gov/library. *Libr Dir,* Linda Cavanaugh; E-mail: lcavanaugh@clyde-tx.gov
Founded 1972
Library Holdings: Bk Titles 10,577; Per Subs 6
Special Collections: Texas (Callahan County Coll)
Automation Activity & Vendor Info: (Cataloging) Biblionix/Apollo; (Circulation) Biblionix/Apollo; (OPAC) Biblionix/Apollo
Wireless access

Function: 24/7 Electronic res, 24/7 Online cat, ILL available
Open Tues-Fri 10-5, Sat 10-2
Friends of the Library Group

COLDSPRING

P COLDSPRING AREA PUBLIC LIBRARY*, 14221 State Hwy 150 W, 77331. (Mail add: PO Box 1756, 77331-1756), SAN 329-0891. Tel: 936-653-3104. FAX: 936-653-4628. E-mail: capl@eastex.net. Web Site: www.coldspringpubliclibrary.com. *Co-Dir,* Maggie Moseley; *Co-Dir,* Margaret Welker; *Asst Librn,* Barbara Ponter; Staff 3 (Non-MLS 3)
Founded 1983. Pop 714; Circ 13,684
Library Holdings: AV Mats 92; Bks on Deafness & Sign Lang 12; DVDs 270; Large Print Bks 1,130; Bk Titles 18,883; Per Subs 27; Talking Bks 638; Videos 1,148
Special Collections: Genealogy Coll; Spanish Language Books; Texas Coll
Automation Activity & Vendor Info: (Acquisitions) ComPanion Corp; (Cataloging) ComPanion Corp; (Circulation) ComPanion Corp
Wireless access
Partic in Partners Library Action Network; TexSHARE - Texas State Library & Archives Commission
Special Services for the Deaf - Bks on deafness & sign lang
Special Services for the Blind - Magnifiers
Open Tues-Fri 10-5, Sat 10-1
Friends of the Library Group

COLEMAN

P COLEMAN PUBLIC LIBRARY*, 402 S Commercial Ave, 76834-4202. SAN 316-1544. Tel: 325-625-3043. FAX: 325-625-3629. E-mail: colemanlibrary@yahoo.com, cpl@web-access.net. Web Site: www.cityofcolemantx.us/library. *Dir,* Sue Dossey; *Libr Asst,* Cindy Dempsey; Staff 3 (Non-MLS 3)
Founded 1885. Pop 7,684; Circ 39,500
Oct 2023-Sept 2024. Mats Exp $450
Library Holdings: DVDs 2,312; Electronic Media & Resources 5; Large Print Bks 395; Bk Titles 32,824; Bk Vols 34,560; Per Subs 20
Special Collections: Local History/Genealogy Coll; Mac Woodward Texas Coll; Texana; Walter Gann Coll; World War II Coll
Automation Activity & Vendor Info: (Acquisitions) Biblionix/Apollo; (Cataloging) Biblionix/Apollo; (Circulation) Biblionix/Apollo; (Course Reserve) Biblionix/Apollo; (Discovery) Biblionix/Apollo; (ILL) Biblionix/Apollo; (Media Booking) Biblionix/Apollo; (OPAC) Biblionix/Apollo; (Serials) Biblionix/Apollo
Wireless access
Function: 24/7 Electronic res, 24/7 Online cat, 24/7 wireless access, 3D Printer, Activity rm, Children's prog, Computers for patron use, Electronic databases & coll, Free DVD rentals, Games, Holiday prog, ILL available, Internet access, Laminating, Learning ctr, Magazines, Mail & tel request accepted, Meeting rooms, Online cat, Photocopying/Printing, Preschool outreach, Preschool reading prog, Printer for laptops & handheld devices, Prog for adults, Prog for children & young adult, Ref & res, Scanner, Spanish lang bks, Story hour, Summer & winter reading prog, Summer reading prog, Teen prog, Wheelchair accessible
Partic in Partners Library Action Network; TexSHARE - Texas State Library & Archives Commission
Open Tues & Thurs 10-6, Wed & Fri Noon-6, Sat 9-Noon
Restriction: Borrowing requests are handled by ILL, Circ limited, Non-circulating coll, Non-circulating of rare bks, Non-circulating to the pub
Friends of the Library Group

COLLEGE STATION

S NATIONAL ARCHIVES & RECORDS ADMINISTRATION*, George H W Bush Presidential Library & Museum, 1000 George Bush Dr W, 77845. Tel: 979-691-4000. FAX: 979-691-4050. E-mail: library.bush@nara.gov. Web Site: bush41.org. *Dir,* Dawn Hammatt; E-mail: dawn.hammatt@nara.gov; *Supvry Archivist,* Chris Pembelton; E-mail: chris.pembelton@nara.gov
Wireless access
Open Mon-Sat 9:30-5, Sun 12-5

C TEXAS A&M UNIVERSITY LIBRARIES*, Sterling C Evans Library & Library Annex, 400 Spence St, 77843. Circulation Tel: 979-845-3731. Interlibrary Loan Service Tel: 979-845-5641. Administration Tel: 979-845-8111. FAX: 979-845-6238. Web Site: library.tamu.edu. *Asst Provost, Univ Librn,* Julie Mosbo Ballestro; E-mail: jmosbo@library.tamu.edu; *Asst Dean,* Michael Bolton; Tel: 979-845-5751, E-mail: michael.bolton@library.tamu.edu; *Assoc Dean, User Serv,* Susan Goodwin; Tel: 979-458-0138, E-mail: sgoodwin@library.tamu.edu; *Dir, Doc Delivery,* Lan Yang; Tel: 978-862-1904, E-mail: zyang@library.tamu.edu; *Cat Librn,* Jeanette Ho; E-mail: jaho@library.tamu.edu; *User Serv & Instruction Design Librn,* Elizabeth German; Tel: 979-847-5846, E-mail: egerman@library.tamu.edu. Subject Specialists: *Humanities, Soc sci,* Susan Goodwin; Staff 139 (MLS 80, Non-MLS 59)
Founded 1876. Enrl 49,861; Fac 80; Highest Degree: Doctorate
Library Holdings: Bk Vols 4,088,969; Per Subs 91,580
Special Collections: Maps & GIS. Oral History; State Document Depository; US Document Depository
Automation Activity & Vendor Info: (Acquisitions) Ex Libris Group; (Cataloging) Ex Libris Group
Wireless access
Partic in Amigos Library Services, Inc; Center for Research Libraries; Digital Libr Fedn; Greater Western Library Alliance; Houston Area Research Library Consortium
Friends of the Library Group

Departmental Libraries:

BUSINESS LIBRARY & COLLABORATION COMMONS, 214 Olsen Blvd, 77843. (Mail add: 5001 TAMU, 77843-5001). Tel: 979-845-2111. Circulation Tel: 979-862-1983. FAX: 979-862-2977. Web Site: blcc.library.tamu.edu. *Libr Mgr,* Tonya Carter; E-mail: tcarter89@library.tamu.edu; *Libr Spec III,* Matt Hood; E-mail: mrhood@library.tamu.edu; *Libr Assoc II,* Wade Harris; E-mail: wharris@library.tamu.edu; Staff 4 (MLS 4)
Founded 1994. Enrl 46,000; Highest Degree: Doctorate
Subject Interests: Bus
Function: Bks on CD, Computers for patron use, E-Reserves, Electronic databases & coll, ILL available, Magnifiers for reading, Online cat, Online ref, Photocopying/Printing, Ref serv available, Wheelchair accessible
Restriction: Borrowing privileges limited to fac & registered students, In-house use for visitors, Open to pub for ref & circ; with some limitations
Friends of the Library Group

CUSHING MEMORIAL LIBRARY & ARCHIVES, 400 Spencer St, 77843. Tel: 979-845-1951. FAX: 979-845-1441. E-mail: cushingreference@library.tamu.edu. Web Site: cushing.library.tamu.edu. *Assoc Dean, Dir,* Beth T Kilmarx; E-mail: bkilmarx@library.tamu.edu; *Curator,* Robin Hutchison; E-mail: r.hutchison@library.tamu.edu; *Curator,* Kevin O'Sullivan; E-mail: kmosullivan@library.tamu.edu; *Rare Bk Cataloger,* Felicia Piscitelli; E-mail: f.piscitelli@library.tamu.edu; Staff 8.8 (MLS 4, Non-MLS 4.8)
Founded 1994. Enrl 48,112; Highest Degree: Doctorate
Library Holdings: Bk Vols 180,000
Special Collections: Americana Coll; Illustration, Military History (Ragan Coll); Literary Coll (R Kipling, S Maugham, M Arnold, Sea Fiction, R Fuller, A E Coppard, P G Wodehouse, et al); Local Texas History Coll; Mexican Colonial Coll; Nautical Archaeology/Naval Architecture, Botanicals, Incunables & Fore Edge Paintings (Loran Laughlin Coll); Nineteenth Century Prints (Kelsey Coll); Ornithology (Kincaid Coll); Political Papers of Texans (eg, William Clements Papers); Printing History Coll; Range Livestock (Jeff Dykes Coll); Science Fiction Coll; Texas A&M Coll; Texas Agriculture (TAES/TAEX Archives). Oral History
Function: Archival coll, Art exhibits, Internet access, Mail & tel request accepted, Online cat, Online ref, Ref serv available, Telephone ref, VHS videos, Wheelchair accessible, Workshops
Open Mon-Fri 8-6
Restriction: Non-circulating
Friends of the Library Group

CM MEDICAL SCIENCES, 202 Olsen Blvd, 77843. (Mail add: 4462 TAMU, 77843-4462). Tel: 979-845-7428. FAX: 979-845-7493. E-mail: askMSL@library.tamu.edu. Web Site: msl.library.tamu.edu. *Assoc Dean, Libr Dir,* Stephanie Fulton; Tel: 979-845-7540, E-mail: s-fulton@library.tamu.edu; Staff 25 (MLS 13, Non-MLS 12)
Founded 1940. Enrl 48,039; Highest Degree: Doctorate
Library Holdings: Bk Vols 119,698; Per Subs 1,633
Subject Interests: Biology, Veterinary med
Automation Activity & Vendor Info: (Acquisitions) Ex Libris Group; (Cataloging) Ex Libris Group; (Circulation) Ex Libris Group; (Course Reserve) Docutek; (ILL) OCLC ILLiad; (OPAC) Ex Libris Group; (Serials) Ex Libris Group
Function: Res libr
Partic in SCAMeL; Tex A&M Univ Consortium of Med Librs; TexSHARE - Texas State Library & Archives Commission
Publications: TAMU Medical Sciences Library Newsletter

POLICY SCIENCES & ECONOMICS, Presidential Conference Ctr, Rm 1019, 1002 George Bush Dr W, 77845. (Mail add: 5002 Tamu, 77843-5002). Tel: 979-862-3544. FAX: 979-862-3791. E-mail: pseldesk@library.tamu.edu. Web Site: psel.library.tamu.edu. *Mgr,* Joyce Gribble; E-mail: joycegribble@library.tamu.edu; Staff 3 (MLS 1, Non-MLS 2)
Founded 1997
Library Holdings: Bk Vols 6,000; Per Subs 50; Videos 400
Automation Activity & Vendor Info: (Cataloging) Ex Libris Group; (Circulation) Ex Libris Group; (OPAC) Ex Libris Group
Open Mon-Thurs 8am-9pm, Fri 8-5, Sun 1-9

COLLEYVILLE

P COLLEYVILLE PUBLIC LIBRARY*, 110 Main St, 76034. Tel: 817-503-1150, 817-503-1154 (Youth Serv), 817-503-1155 (Adult Serv). Circulation Tel: 817-503-1161. E-mail: circulation@colleyville.com. Reference E-mail: reference@colleyville.com. Web Site: www.colleyvillelibrary.com. *Libr Dir,* Mary Rodne; E-mail: mrodne@colleyville.com; *Ad,* Kara Teeter; E-mail: kteeter@colleyville.com; *Circ & Info Serv Librn,* Jack Pawlowski; E-mail: jpawlowski@colleyville.com; *Youth Serv Librn,* Arielle Vaverka; E-mail: avaverka@colleyville.com
Wireless access
Function: Chess club, Children's prog
Open Mon & Wed 10-6, Tues & Thurs 10-8, Fri 10-5, Sat 10-3

COLORADO CITY

P MITCHELL COUNTY PUBLIC LIBRARY*, 340 Oak St, 79512. SAN 316-1552. Tel: 325-728-3968. E-mail: mcp.library1@gmail.com. Web Site: www.mitchellcountylibrary.org. *Dir,* Maggie Bootman
Founded 1926. Pop 8,545; Circ 23,981
Library Holdings: AV Mats 573; Bk Titles 35,159; Bk Vols 38,331; Per Subs 23; Talking Bks 1,350
Wireless access
Open Mon-Fri 9-5:30
Friends of the Library Group

COLUMBUS

P NESBITT MEMORIAL LIBRARY*, 529 Washington St, 78934-2326. SAN 316-1560. Tel: 979-732-3392. FAX: 979-732-3392. E-mail: library@columbustexas.net, nesbittlibrary@gmail.com. Web Site: www.columbustexaslibrary.net. *Dir,* Susan Chandler; *Asst Librn,* Susan Archuletta; E-mail: library2@columbustexas.net; *Asst Librn,* Jessica Neath; E-mail: library3@columbustexas.net; Staff 3 (Non-MLS 3)
Founded 1979. Pop 6,629; Circ 44,334
Library Holdings: Bk Titles 41,000; Per Subs 40
Subject Interests: Archit, Art, Hist, Tex hist
Automation Activity & Vendor Info: (Cataloging) Follett Software; (Circulation) Follett Software
Wireless access
Partic in Partners Library Action Network
Open Mon, Wed & Fri 9-6, Tues & Thurs 10-7, Sat 10-2
Friends of the Library Group

COMANCHE

P COMANCHE PUBLIC LIBRARY*, 311 N Austin St, 76442. (Mail add: PO Box 777, 76442-0777), SAN 316-1579. Tel: 325-356-2122. E-mail: comanchepl@verizon.net. Web Site: www.comanchepubliclibrary.org. *Dir,* Deborah Hanson; Tel: 325-356-2122, E-mail: comanchepl@verizon.net; Staff 3 (Non-MLS 3)
Founded 1960. Pop 9,000; Circ 17,600
Oct 2020-Sept 2021 Income $145,000, City $72,500, County $72,500. Mats Exp $19,573, Books $2,123, Electronic Ref Mat (Incl. Access Fees) $96. Sal $76,236 (Prof $33,798)
Library Holdings: Bk Titles 24,980; Bk Vols 26,532; Per Subs 15
Special Collections: Genealogy Coll; State & Local History Coll, bks, maps, microfilm, photographs
Subject Interests: Area hist, Genealogy
Wireless access
Function: 24/7 Online cat, Audiobks via web, Bks on CD, Computers for patron use, Electronic databases & coll, ILL available, Internet access, Magazines, Microfiche/film & reading machines, Online cat, Photocopying/Printing, Ref serv available, Scanner, Summer reading prog, Telephone ref, Wheelchair accessible
Partic in TexSHARE - Texas State Library & Archives Commission
Open Mon & Fri 8-6, Tues 8-8, Wed 9-5, Thurs 12-8, Sat 10-3

COMFORT

P COMFORT PUBLIC LIBRARY*, 701 High St, 78013. (Mail add: PO Box 536, 78013-0036), SAN 316-1587. Tel: 830-995-2398. FAX: 830-995-5574. E-mail: comfort.librarian@gmail.com. Web Site: www.comfortpubliclibrary.org. *Dir,* Kimberli Evans; E-mail: director@comfortpubliclibrary.org; *Asst Dir,* Tracy Ahrens; E-mail: asstdirector@comfortpubliclibrary.org; *Prog Coordr,* Mary Anne Johnson; E-mail: programs@comfortpubliclibrary.org; Staff 4 (Non-MLS 4)
Founded 1956. Pop 7,981; Circ 18,974
Library Holdings: Bk Titles 22,098; Per Subs 58
Subject Interests: Local hist, Texana
Automation Activity & Vendor Info: (Cataloging) Biblionix; (Circulation) Biblionix
Wireless access
Function: 24/7 Electronic res, 24/7 Online cat, Activity rm, Adult bk club, Adult literacy prog, Archival coll, Audiobks via web, Bilingual assistance for Spanish patrons, Bk club(s), Bks on CD, Children's prog, Citizenship assistance, Computer training, Computers for patron use, Doc delivery serv, Electronic databases & coll, Family literacy, Free DVD rentals, Govt ref serv, ILL available, Internet access, Laminating, Learning ctr, Magazines, Magnifiers for reading, Mail & tel request accepted, Meeting rooms, Online cat, Online ref, OverDrive digital audio bks, Photocopying/Printing, Preschool outreach, Preschool reading prog, Printer for laptops & handheld devices, Prog for adults, Prog for children & young adult, Scanner, Senior computer classes, Spanish lang bks, STEM programs, Story hour, Study rm, Summer reading prog, Tax forms, Wheelchair accessible
Open Tues-Fri 10-6, Sat 9-1
Restriction: Borrowing requests are handled by ILL
Friends of the Library Group

COMMERCE

P COMMERCE PUBLIC LIBRARY*, 1210 Park St, 75428. SAN 316-1595. Tel: 903-886-6858. Web Site: www.commercepubliclibrary.org. *Libr Dir,* Nan Clay; E-mail: director@commercepubliclibrary.org; Staff 5 (MLS 1, Non-MLS 4)
Founded 1954. Pop 19,252; Circ 38,234
Library Holdings: Audiobooks 1,435; AV Mats 3,900; Bks on Deafness & Sign Lang 29; CDs 600; DVDs 149; Electronic Media & Resources 50; Large Print Bks 1,811; Microforms 186; Bk Titles 32,847; Per Subs 35; Videos 1,450
Special Collections: Commerce History Coll, bks, maps, newsp, photogs; Texas History Coll
Automation Activity & Vendor Info: (Cataloging) Book Systems; (Circulation) Book Systems; (OPAC) Book Systems
Wireless access
Function: Adult literacy prog, Archival coll, Bks on cassette, Bks on CD, Children's prog, Computer training, Computers for patron use, Electronic databases & coll, ILL available, Internet access, Museum passes, Music CDs, Notary serv, Online cat, Online ref, Photocopying/Printing, Prog for adults, Prog for children & young adult, Senior computer classes, Story hour, Summer reading prog, Tax forms, Telephone ref, VHS videos
Publications: The Pictorial History of Commerce, 1885-2010
Partic in TexSHARE - Texas State Library & Archives Commission
Open Mon-Fri 10-2, Sat 9-12
Friends of the Library Group

C TEXAS A&M UNIVERSITY-COMMERCE, Velma K Waters Library, 2600 S Neal St, 75428. (Mail add: PO Box 3011, 75429-3011), SAN 361-3534. Tel: 903-886-5718. FAX: 903-886-5434. Web Site: www.tamuc.edu/library. *Asst Vice Provost, Dean of Libr,* Lanee Dunlap; Tel: 903-886-5738, E-mail: lanee.dunlap@tamuc.edu; *Assoc Dean, Collections & Discovery,* Sandy Hayes; Tel: 903-886-5137, E-mail: sandy.hayes@tamuc.edu; *Dir, Res & Instruction Serv,* Sarah Northam; Tel: 903-886-5721, E-mail: sarah.northam@tamuc.edu; *Marketing & Communication Librn,* Zephyr Rankin; Tel: 903-468-8661, E-mail: zephyr.rankin@tamuc.edu; *Res & Instruction Librn,* A P Anderson; Tel: 903-886-5713, E-mail: ap.anderson@tamuc.edu; *Res & Instruction Librn,* Emily N Davis; Tel: 903-886-5720, E-mail: emily.davis@tamuc.edu; *Res & Instruction Librn,* Inbar Michael; E-mail: inbar.michael@tamuc.edu; *Systems & Discovery Librn,* Ashlie Hight; Tel: 903-886-5385, E-mail: ashlie.hight@tamuc.edu; *Digital Archivist,* Adam Northam; Tel: 903-886-5463, E-mail: adam.northam@tamuc.edu; *Univ Archivist,* Sawyer Magnus; Tel: 903-886-5433, E-mail: sawyer.magnus@tamuc.edu; Staff 17 (MLS 15, Non-MLS 2)
Founded 1894. Enrl 11,100; Fac 505; Highest Degree: Doctorate
Sept 2017-Aug 2018 Income (Main & Associated Libraries) $3,400,000, Locally Generated Income $1,300,000, Parent Institution $2,100,000. Mats Exp $1,812,300, Books $342,000, Per/Ser (Incl. Access Fees) $530,000, AV Equip $4,300, AV Mat $20,000, Electronic Ref Mat (Incl. Access Fees) $889,000, Presv $27,000. Sal $1,558,141 (Prof $1,073,716)
Library Holdings: CDs 4,322; DVDs 80; e-books 42,836; e-journals 22,000; Electronic Media & Resources 126; Bk Titles 644,413; Bk Vols 1,090,021; Per Subs 1,667; Videos 198
Special Collections: Aviation (Jeana Yeager/Voyager Coll); Foreign Diplomatic Service (Ambassador Fletcher Warren Papers); Jazz (Louise Tobin/Peanuts Hucko Coll); Music (Ruby Allmond Coll); Texas Literature (Elithe Hamilton Kirkland Papers); Texas Poetry (Faye Carr Adams Coll); Texas Political History (A M Aiken, T C Chaddick & Celia M Wright Colls); US Government & Politics (Congressmen Ray Roberts and Ralph Hall Papers). Oral History; US Document Depository
Automation Activity & Vendor Info: (Acquisitions) Ex Libris Group; (Cataloging) Ex Libris Group; (Circulation) Ex Libris Group; (Course Reserve) Ex Libris Group; (ILL) OCLC; (Media Booking) Ex Libris Group; (OPAC) Ex Libris Group; (Serials) Ex Libris Group
Wireless access
Function: Art exhibits, Audio & video playback equip for onsite use, Computers for patron use, Distance learning, Doc delivery serv, Electronic databases & coll, Govt ref serv, ILL available, Large print keyboards, Music CDs, Online cat, Online info literacy tutorials on the web & in

blackboard, Online ref, Photocopying/Printing, Ref serv available, Scanner, Tax forms, Wheelchair accessible
Partic in Amigos Library Services, Inc; OCLC Online Computer Library Center, Inc
Special Services for the Blind - Braille equip; Computer with voice synthesizer for visually impaired persons
Open Mon-Thurs 7:30am-1am, Fri 7:30am-9pm, Sat 9-9, Sun Noon-Midnight
Restriction: Non-circulating of rare bks
Departmental Libraries:
MESQUITE METROPLEX CENTER LIBRARY, 3819 Towne Crossing Blvd, Mesquite, 75150, SAN 361-4913. Tel: 972-613-7591. E-mail: mesquite.metroplex@tamuc.edu. Web Site: www.tamuc.edu/mesquite-metroplex-center. *Admin Coordr,* Dana Toles; E-mail: dana.toles@tamuc.edu; Staff 1 (Non-MLS 1)
Founded 1978. Enrl 1,100; Highest Degree: Doctorate
Library Holdings: Bk Titles 252; Bk Vols 327

CONROE

P MONTGOMERY COUNTY MEMORIAL LIBRARY SYSTEM*, 104 I-45 N, 77301-2720. SAN 361-3593. Tel: 936-788-8377. Circulation Tel: 936-788-8360. Reference Tel: 936-788-8361. FAX: 936-788-8398. Web Site: www.countylibrary.org. *Dir,* Rhea Young; Tel: 936-522-2123, E-mail: rhea.young@countylibrary.org; *Asst Dir,* Sarah Booth; Tel: 936-788-8377, Ext 6236, E-mail: sarah.booth@countylibrary.org; *Bus Mgr,* Lana Beathard; Tel: 936-788-8377, Ext 6238, E-mail: lana.beathard@countylibrary.org; *Tech Serv Mgr,* Elizabeth Sargent; Tel: 936-788-8377, Ext 2118, E-mail: Elizabeth.Sargent@countylibrary.org; *Adult Serv Coordr,* Jenn Wigle; Tel: 936-788-8377, Ext 2122, E-mail: jennifer.wigle@countylibrary.org; *Children's Serv Coordr,* Position Currently Open; *Circ Coordr,* Ruby Chandler; Tel: 936-788-8377, Ext 6244, E-mail: ruby.chandler@countylibrary.org; *Coll Develop Coordr,* Andrea Yang; Tel: 936-522-2102, E-mail: andrea.yang@countylibrary.org; *Mkt Coordr,* Natasha Benway; Tel: 936-522-2137, E-mail: natasha.benway@countylibary.org; Staff 139.5 (MLS 47.5, Non-MLS 92)
Founded 1948. Pop 570,934; Circ 2,547,829
Oct 2018-Sept 2019 Income (Main & Associated Libraries) $9,274,269, State $3,612, County $9,001,866, Locally Generated Income $268,791. Mats Exp $986,697, Books $552,448, Per/Ser (Incl. Access Fees) $74,000, Micro $8,000, AV Mat $185,787, Electronic Ref Mat (Incl. Access Fees) $161,462, Presv $5,000. Sal $4,833,481 (Prof $2,396,904)
Library Holdings: Audiobooks 36,509; AV Mats 31,315; e-books 23,051; Bk Titles 268,814; Bk Vols 618,800; Per Subs 1,082
Subject Interests: Genealogy
Automation Activity & Vendor Info: (Acquisitions) SirsiDynix-WorkFlows; (Cataloging) SirsiDynix-WorkFlows; (Circulation) SirsiDynix-WorkFlows; (Discovery) SirsiDynix-Enterprise; (OPAC) SirsiDynix-WorkFlows
Wireless access
Function: 24/7 Electronic res, 24/7 Online cat, Adult bk club
Open Mon-Thurs 9-9, Fri & Sat 9-5
Friends of the Library Group
Branches: 6
R F MEADOR BRANCH, 709 W Montgomery, Willis, 77378, SAN 371-9820. Tel: 936-442-7740. FAX: 936-856-3360. *Br Mgr,* Michelle Kovacs; E-mail: michelle.kovacs@countylibrary.org; Staff 8.5 (MLS 3, Non-MLS 5.5)
Circ 121,948
Library Holdings: Bk Vols 55,204
Function: 24/7 Electronic res, 24/7 Online cat, Adult bk club
Open Mon-Wed 9-6, Thurs 9-8, Fri & Sat 9-5
Friends of the Library Group
GEORGE & CYNTHIA WOODS MITCHELL LIBRARY, 8125 Ashlane Way, The Woodlands, 77382. Tel: 281-364-4298. Toll Free Tel: 936-442-7728. FAX: 281-362-0772. *Br Mgr,* Donna Dzierlenga; Tel: 936-442-7728, Ext 307, E-mail: donna.dzierlenga@countylibrary.org; Staff 25.5 (MLS 9, Non-MLS 16.5)
Circ 591,882
Library Holdings: Bk Vols 105,496
Automation Activity & Vendor Info: (Acquisitions) SirsiDynix-WorkFlows; (Cataloging) SirsiDynix-WorkFlows; (Circulation) SirsiDynix-WorkFlows; (Discovery) SirsiDynix-Enterprise; (OPAC) SirsiDynix-WorkFlows
Function: 24/7 Electronic res, 24/7 Online cat, Adult bk club
Open Mon-Thurs 9-9, Fri & Sat 9-5
MALCOLM PURVIS LIBRARY, 510 Melton St, Magnolia, 77354, SAN 326-7415. Tel: 936-788-8324. FAX: 936-788-8304. *Br Mgr,* Elaine Taylor; E-mail: elaine.taylor@countylibrary.org; Staff 10 (MLS 3, Non-MLS 7)
Circ 105,182
Library Holdings: Bk Vols 71,001
Function: 24/7 Electronic res, 24/7 Online cat
Open Mon 9-8, Tues-Thurs 9-6, Fri & Sat 10-4
Friends of the Library Group
SOUTH REGIONAL LIBRARY, 2101 Lake Robbins Dr, The Woodlands, 77380, SAN 361-3658. Tel: 281-364-4294. FAX: 936-788-8372. *Br Mgr,* Lynn Garcia; Tel: 936-442-7727, E-mail: lynn.garcia@countylibrary.org; Staff 24 (MLS 8, Non-MLS 16)
Circ 571,415
Library Holdings: Bk Vols 133,552
Function: 24/7 Electronic res, 24/7 Online cat, Adult bk club, Audiobks via web, Bk club(s), Bks on CD, Children's prog, Computer training, Computers for patron use, Electronic databases & coll, ILL available, Internet access, Magazines, Meeting rooms, Music CDs, Photocopying/Printing, Prog for adults, Prog for children & young adult, Ref & res, Scanner, Tax forms
Open Mon-Thurs 9-9, Fri & Sat 9-5
Friends of the Library Group
CHARLES B STEWART - WEST BRANCH, 202 Bessie Price Owen Dr, Montgomery, 77356, SAN 329-630X. Tel: 936-442-7718, 936-788-8314. FAX: 936-788-8349. *Br Mgr,* Mat Wilson; E-mail: matthew.wilson@countylibrary.org; Staff 13.1 (MLS 5, Non-MLS 8.1)
Circ 142,576
Library Holdings: Bk Vols 64,997
Function: 24/7 Electronic res, 24/7 Online cat, Adult bk club
Open Mon, Tues & Thurs 9-8, Wed 9-6, Fri & Sat 9-5
Friends of the Library Group
R B TULLIS BRANCH, 21569 US Hwy 59, New Caney, 77357, SAN 361-3623. Tel: 281-577-8968. FAX: 281-577-8992. *Br Mgr,* Position Currently Open
Circ 237,895
Library Holdings: Bk Vols 80,158
Function: 24/7 Electronic res, 24/7 Online cat, Adult bk club
Open Mon, Tues & Thurs 9-9, Wed 9-6, Fri & Sat 9-5
Friends of the Library Group

CONVERSE

P CONVERSE PUBLIC LIBRARY*, 601 S Seguin Rd, 78109. SAN 376-4192. Tel: 210-659-4160. E-mail: librarian@conversetx.net. Web Site: www.conversetx.net. *Libr Dir,* Sandy Underwood; E-mail: sunderwood@conversetx.net; Staff 4.5 (MLS 1, Non-MLS 3.5)
Founded 1991. Pop 20,323; Circ 28,000
Library Holdings: Audiobooks 415; DVDs 1,319; Large Print Bks 744; Videos 392
Automation Activity & Vendor Info: (Cataloging) Biblionix/Apollo; (Circulation) Biblionix/Apollo; (OPAC) Biblionix/Apollo
Wireless access
Function: 24/7 Electronic res, 24/7 Online cat, Adult bk club, Audiobks via web, Bk club(s), Children's prog, Electronic databases & coll, Free DVD rentals, Holiday prog, ILL available, Laminating, Mango lang, Movies, Online cat, Outreach serv, OverDrive digital audio bks, Photocopying/Printing, Prog for adults, Prog for children & young adult, Ref serv available, Scanner, Spanish lang bks, Summer reading prog, Tax forms, Teen prog, VHS videos
Partic in Amigos Library Services, Inc
Open Mon-Thurs 9-6, Fri 9-5, Sat 10-2

COOPER

P DELTA COUNTY PUBLIC LIBRARY*, 300 W Dallas Ave, 75432-1632. SAN 376-7981. Tel: 903-395-4575. FAX: 903-395-4575. E-mail: deltacountylibrary@gmail.com. *Librn,* Lydia Toon
Founded 1983. Pop 4,600
Library Holdings: Bks on Deafness & Sign Lang 37; Bk Titles 15,000; Per Subs 3
Subject Interests: Genealogy
Automation Activity & Vendor Info: (Cataloging) Book Systems; (Circulation) Book Systems; (OPAC) Book Systems
Wireless access
Function: Adult bk club, Computers for patron use, Free DVD rentals, Internet access, Laminating, Meeting rooms, Microfiche/film & reading machines, Online cat, Photocopying/Printing, Prog for adults, Ref & res, Scanner, Story hour
Special Services for the Blind - Large print bks; Talking bks
Open Tues-Fri 10-4
Restriction: Authorized patrons
Friends of the Library Group

COPPELL

P WILLIAM T COZBY PUBLIC LIBRARY*, 177 N Heartz Rd, 75019. SAN 361-4131. Tel: 972-304-3655. Administration Tel: 972-304-3626. FAX: 972-304-3622. E-mail: library@coppelltx.gov. Web Site: www.coppelltx.gov/residents/public-library. *Dir,* Kent Collins; E-mail: kcollins@coppelltx.gov; *Asst Dir,* Dennis Quinn; Tel: 972-304-3660, E-mail: dquinn@coppelltx.gov; *Librn Supvr,* Kevin Carrothers; Tel: 972-304-7048, E-mail: kcarrothers@coppelltx.gov; *Librn Supvr,* Amy Pittman-Hassett; Tel: 972-304-3656, E-mail: ahassett@coppelltx.gov; Staff 20.5 (MLS 9, Non-MLS 11.5)

Pop 39,224; Circ 575,974
Wireless access
Function: Adult bk club, Audiobks via web, Bk club(s), Bks on CD, Children's prog, Computers for patron use, Electronic databases & coll, Free DVD rentals, Holiday prog, ILL available, Internet access, Magazines, Mango lang, Online cat, Photocopying/Printing, Preschool reading prog, Prog for adults, Prog for children & young adult, Ref serv available, Story hour, Study rm, Summer reading prog, Tax forms, Teen prog, Wheelchair accessible, Workshops
Open Mon-Thurs 10-9, Fri 10-6, Sat 10-5, Sun 1-5
Friends of the Library Group

COPPERAS COVE

P COPPERAS COVE PUBLIC LIBRARY*, 501 S Main St, 76522. SAN 316-1609. Tel: 254-547-3826. FAX: 254-542-7279. Web Site: www.copperascovetx.gov/library. *Dir,* Kevin Marsh; E-mail: kmarsh@copperascovetx.gov; *Libr Supvr,* Valerie Reynolds; E-mail: vreynolds@copperascovetx.gov; Staff 1 (MLS 1)
Founded 1959. Pop 31,300; Circ 127,648
Library Holdings: Bk Titles 66,388; Bk Vols 68,387
Subject Interests: Texana
Automation Activity & Vendor Info: (Cataloging) Biblionix/Apollo; (Circulation) Biblionix/Apollo; (ILL) OCLC WorldShare Interlibrary Loan; (OPAC) Biblionix/Apollo
Wireless access
Partic in Partners Library Action Network; TexSHARE - Texas State Library & Archives Commission
Open Mon-Thurs 9-7, Fri & Sat 10-2
Friends of the Library Group

CORPUS CHRISTI

M CHRISTUS SPOHN HEALTH SYSTEM*, Health Sciences Library, 600 Elizabeth St, 78404. SAN 316-1706. Tel: 361-902-4348. FAX: 361-902-6307. E-mail: library@christushealth.org. *Med Librn,* Leta J Dannelley; Staff 1 (MLS 1)
Founded 1972
Library Holdings: Bk Vols 1,000; Per Subs 45
Subject Interests: Allied health sci, Med, Nursing
Automation Activity & Vendor Info: (Cataloging) SoutronGLOBAL; (Circulation) SoutronGLOBAL; (OPAC) SoutronGLOBAL; (Serials) SoutronGLOBAL
Wireless access
Function: Health sci info serv
Partic in National Network of Libraries of Medicine Region 3
Restriction: Not open to pub

S CORPUS CHRISTI MUSEUM OF SCIENCE & HISTORY*, 1900 N Chaparral St, 78401. SAN 316-1641. Tel: 361-826-4667. E-mail: ccmuseum@cctexas.com. Web Site: www.ccmuseum.com. *Gen Mgr,* Kyle Winston; Staff 1 (Non-MLS 1)
Founded 1957
Library Holdings: Bk Vols 20,000; Per Subs 35
Special Collections: 1930's Pictorial History of Corpus Christi; Children's Fiction (Horatio Alger, Tom Swift & others); Law Coll-19th & 20th Centuries; Library Archival Material (mid 19th century); Museological Coll; Natural History (Netting Periodicals Coll)
Subject Interests: Anthrop, Archaeology, Hist, Museology, Natural hist
Open Mon-Sat 10-5, Sun 12-5

P CORPUS CHRISTI PUBLIC LIBRARIES*, La Retama Central Library, 805 Comanche, 78401. SAN 361-3682. Tel: 361-826-7055. FAX: 361-826-7046. E-mail: library@cctexas.com. Web Site: www.cclibraries.com. *Dir,* Laura Zavala Garcia; E-mail: lauraga@cctexas.com; Staff 17 (MLS 17)
Founded 1909. Pop 280,000; Circ 1,400,000
Library Holdings: AV Mats 7,892; Bk Vols 376,395; Per Subs 622
Special Collections: State Document Depository
Subject Interests: Genealogy, Hispanic genealogy, Local hist
Wireless access
Partic in Amigos Library Services, Inc; Partners Library Action Network; Tex State Libr Communications Network
Open Tues & Wed 10-6, Thurs-Sat 9-6
Friends of the Library Group
Branches: 5
DR CLOTILDE P GARCIA PUBLIC LIBRARY, 5930 Brockhampton, 78414. Tel: 361-826-2360. *Library Contact,* Laura Garcia
Open Mon & Tues 10-8, Wed 10-9, Thurs-Sat 10-6
Friends of the Library Group
JANET F HARTE PUBLIC LIBRARY, 2629 Waldron Rd, 78418, SAN 361-3712. Tel: 361-826-2310. *Library Contact,* Laura Garcia; Staff 1 (MLS 1)
Founded 2000
Library Holdings: Bk Vols 76,000
Open Mon-Wed 10-3:30, Thur 10-8, Fri 10-6:30, Sat 10-6
Friends of the Library Group
OWEN R HOPKINS PUBLIC LIBRARY, 3202 McKinzie Rd, 78410, SAN 361-3763. Tel: 361-826-2350. *Br Mgr,* Daniel Schwartz; E-mail: danielsc@cctexas.com; Staff 7.4 (MLS 2, Non-MLS 5.4)
Pop 27,000
Library Holdings: Audiobooks 1,000; Large Print Bks 400; Bk Vols 54,000; Videos 833
Automation Activity & Vendor Info: (Cataloging) ByWater Solutions; (Circulation) ByWater Solutions; (OPAC) ByWater Solutions
Open Mon-Thurs 9-6, Fri & Sat 9-1
Friends of the Library Group
BEN F MCDONALD BRANCH, 4044 Greenwood Dr, 78416, SAN 361-3747. Tel: 361-826-2356. *Br Mgr,* Dorothea Castanon; E-mail: dorotheac@cctexas.com; Staff 2 (MLS 1, Non-MLS 1)
Library Holdings: Audiobooks 779; CDs 261; DVDs 668; High Interest/Low Vocabulary Bk Vols 53; Large Print Bks 227; Bk Vols 23,035; Per Subs 30
Open Mon 9-8, Tues & Wed 10-8, Thurs-Sat 10-6
Friends of the Library Group
ANITA & W T NEYLAND PUBLIC LIBRARY, 1230 Carmel Pkwy, 78411, SAN 361-3771. Tel: 361-826-2370. *Librn,* Michelle Balis; E-mail: michelleb@cctexas.com
Pop 109,000; Circ 480,000
Open Mon-Wed 10-8, Thurs-Sat 10-6, Sun (Sept-May) Noon-4
Friends of the Library Group

J DEL MAR COLLEGE*, William F White Jr Library, 101 Baldwin Blvd, 78404. SAN 361-3801. Tel: 361-698-1310. Interlibrary Loan Service Tel: 361-698-2136. Reference Tel: 361-698-1311. Administration Tel: 361-698-1308. Automation Services Tel: 361-698-1951. FAX: 361-698-1182. Administration FAX: 361-698-1949. Automation Services FAX: 361-698-2133. TDD: 361-698-1174. Web Site: delmar.edu/library. *Dir, Libr Serv,* Hope Beyer; Tel: 361-698-1382, E-mail: hbeyer@delmar.edu; *Head, Tech Serv,* Merry Bortz; Tel: 361-698-1951, E-mail: mbortz@delmar.edu; *Ref Librn,* Alan Berecka; Tel: 361-698-1933, E-mail: aberecka@delmar.edu; *Reference & Electronic Resources Librn,* Jennifer Jimenez; Tel: 361-698-1977, E-mail: jjimenez14@delmar.edu; Staff 20.3 (MLS 6.3, Non-MLS 14)
Founded 1937. Enrl 11,030; Fac 778; Highest Degree: Associate
Library Holdings: AV Mats 18,038; e-books 34,008; Electronic Media & Resources 100; Microforms 9,476; Bk Vols 178,119; Per Subs 309
Automation Activity & Vendor Info: (Cataloging) SirsiDynix; (Circulation) SirsiDynix; (Course Reserve) SirsiDynix; (ILL) SirsiDynix; (OPAC) SirsiDynix; (Serials) SirsiDynix
Wireless access
Partic in Amigos Library Services, Inc; OCLC Online Computer Library Center, Inc; TexSHARE - Texas State Library & Archives Commission
Special Services for the Deaf - Bks on deafness & sign lang; Closed caption videos; Video & TTY relay via computer
Special Services for the Blind - Internet workstation with adaptive software; Large print bks; Talking bks
Closed for renovation 2022-
Departmental Libraries:
WINDWARD CAMPUS, BARTH LEARNING RESOURCE CENTER, 4101 Old Brownsville Rd, 78405. (Mail add: 101 Baldwin Blvd, 78404). Tel: 361-698-1754. Reference Tel: 361-698-1877. Administration Tel: 361-698-1742. FAX: 361-698-1795. E-mail: refdesk@delmar.edu. *Br Librn,* Lisa Muilenburg; E-mail: lmuilenb1@delmar.edu; *Library Campus Asst,* Garza Marissa; Tel: 361-698-1753, E-mail: mgarza610@delmar.edu; *Libr Asst,* Armando Herrera; Tel: 361-698-1878, E-mail: aherrera@delmar.edu; Staff 3 (MLS 1, Non-MLS 2)
Open Mon-Thurs 7am-9pm, Fri 7:30-2, Sat 9-5, Sun 11-7

M DRISCOLL CHILDREN'S HOSPITAL*, Robert Bell Parrish Medical Library, 3533 S Alameda St, 3rd Flr, 78411-1721. SAN 316-1692. Tel: 361-694-5467. FAX: 361-808-2141. Web Site: www.driscollchildrens.org/professionals/robert-bell-parrish-medical-library. *Libr Dir,* Dr Paula Scott; *Info Spec,* Cindy Munoz; E-mail: cindy.munoz@dchstx.org; Staff 2 (MLS 1, Non-MLS 1)
Library Holdings: e-journals 244; Bk Titles 1,300; Per Subs 80
Subject Interests: Pediatric med
Automation Activity & Vendor Info: (Acquisitions) Innovative Interfaces, Inc; (Cataloging) Innovative Interfaces, Inc; (Circulation) Innovative Interfaces, Inc
Wireless access
Function: Electronic databases & coll, ILL available, Internet access, Online cat, Photocopying/Printing, Prof lending libr, Ref & res, Ref serv available, Scanner
Restriction: Circulates for staff only, Hospital employees & physicians only

TEXAS A&M UNIVERSITY-CORPUS CHRISTI

C ART MUSEUM OF SOUTH TEXAS LIBRARY*, 1902 N Shoreline, 78401-1164, SAN 316-1617. Tel: 361-825-3500. FAX: 361-825-3520. E-mail: artmuseum@tamucc.edu. Web Site: www.artmuseumofsouthtexas.org. *Dir,* Joseph Schenk
Founded 1965
Library Holdings: Bk Titles 1,000; Per Subs 10
Subject Interests: Art hist
Open Tues-Sat 10-5, Sun 1-5
Restriction: Non-circulating to the pub

C MARY & JEFF BELL LIBRARY*, 6300 Ocean Dr, 78412-5501, SAN 316-1676. Tel: 361-825-2643. Interlibrary Loan Service Tel: 361-825-2340. Reference Tel: 361-825-2609. FAX: 361-825-5973. Web Site: rattler.tamucc.edu. *Dir,* Christine Shupala; E-mail: christine.shupala@tamucc.edu; *Assoc Dir,* Edward Kownslar; E-mail: edward.kownslar@tamucc.edu; *Archivist, Spec Coll Librn,* Dr Thomas Kreneck; E-mail: thomas.kreneck@tamucc.edu
Founded 1973. Highest Degree: Doctorate
Library Holdings: Bk Vols 433,185; Per Subs 1,706
Special Collections: 18th, 19th & 20th Century Books (Texas-Southwest Coll); 19th Century Maps & Land Title Papers of South Texas & Northern Mexico (Charles F H Von Blucher Coll); Sarita Kenedy East Estate (Turcotte Coll); South Texas (Dan E Kilgore Coll), bks, mss; South Texas (Dr Hector P Garcia Coll), mss; Southwest & Mexico in Fine Binding (Sanders Key Stroud II Memorial Coll); Texas Legislature (L Dewitt Hale Coll); University History Coll; Veracruz, Mexico Archives (Archivo Notaria de Jalapa, Archivo Paroquial de Cordoba)
Automation Activity & Vendor Info: (Acquisitions) Innovative Interfaces, Inc; (Cataloging) Innovative Interfaces, Inc; (Circulation) Innovative Interfaces, Inc; (Serials) Innovative Interfaces, Inc
Function: Archival coll, Distance learning, Doc delivery serv, For res purposes, Govt ref serv, Health sci info serv, ILL available, Internet access, Photocopying/Printing, Wheelchair accessible
Partic in Amigos Library Services, Inc; OCLC Online Computer Library Center, Inc
Friends of the Library Group

S THE TEXAS STATE MUSEUM OF ASIAN CULTURES & EDUCATIONAL CENTER, 1809 N Chaparral, 78401. SAN 371-2974. Tel: 361-881-8827. E-mail: info@texasasianculturesmuseum.org. Web Site: texasasianculturesmuseum.org. *Dir, Operations,* Richard Hafemeister
Library Holdings: Bk Vols 1,500
Special Collections: Billie Chandler Coll
Wireless access
Function: Ref serv available
Restriction: Non-circulating, Open by appt only

A UNITED STATES NAVY, Naval Air Station Library & Resource Center, Bldg 1872, Midway St, 78419. SAN 361-395X. Tel: 361-961-3574. E-mail: lrcnascc@gmail.com. *Librn,* Laura Garza
Founded 1941
Library Holdings: CDs 9; DVDs 40; Bk Vols 34,000; Per Subs 72; Talking Bks 396; Videos 219
Special Collections: Aviation Coll; Military Coll; World War II Coll
Wireless access
Open Mon-Fri 8-5
Restriction: Mil only

CORRIGAN

P MICKEY REILY PUBLIC LIBRARY*, 604 S Matthews St, 75939. SAN 316-1757. Tel: 936-398-4156. FAX: 936-600-3236. E-mail: mrpl_1986@yahoo.com. Web Site: mickeyreilypubliclibrary.com. *Dir,* Quanah Monique Bookman; *Asst Dir,* Dana Vanya; Staff 2 (Non-MLS 2)
Founded 1970. Pop 1,724; Circ 4,000
Library Holdings: Bk Titles 25,918; Bk Vols 28,160; Per Subs 45
Subject Interests: Local hist
Automation Activity & Vendor Info: (Cataloging) Surpass; (Circulation) Surpass
Wireless access
Open Mon-Fri 10-5:30

CORSICANA

P CORSICANA PUBLIC LIBRARY*, 100 N 12th St, 75110. SAN 316-1765. Tel: 903-654-4810. Administration Tel: 903-654-4813. FAX: 903-654-4814. Web Site: www.cityofcorsicana.com/328/Library. *Libr Dir,* Marianne Wilson; E-mail: mwilson@ci.corsicana.tx.us; Staff 7 (MLS 2, Non-MLS 5)
Founded 1901. Pop 48,000; Circ 112,273
Library Holdings: Bk Titles 55,450; Bk Vols 64,342; Per Subs 5,362
Subject Interests: Genealogy
Automation Activity & Vendor Info: (Cataloging) Book Systems; (Circulation) Book Systems; (Course Reserve) Book Systems; (OPAC) Book Systems
Wireless access
Open Mon & Tues 10-8, Wed-Fri 10-6, Sat 10-4
Restriction: 24-hr pass syst for students only
Friends of the Library Group

J NAVARRO COLLEGE*, Richard M Sanchez Library, 3200 W Seventh Ave, 75110-4899. SAN 316-1773. Tel: 903-875-7442. FAX: 903-875-7449. Web Site: navarrocollege.edu/library. *Dean of Libr,* Tim Kevil; E-mail: tim.kevil@navarrocollege.edu; *Librn,* Chad Freeze; E-mail: chad.freeze@navarrocollege.edu; Staff 3 (MLS 3)
Founded 1946. Enrl 4,360; Fac 86; Highest Degree: Associate
Library Holdings: Bk Vols 60,500; Per Subs 290
Special Collections: Indian Artifacts (R S Reading Coll); Samuels Hobbit Coll. US Document Depository
Subject Interests: Bus admin, Computer sci, Electronics, Fine arts, Law, Law enforcement, Liberal arts, Med lab tech, Nursing, Occupational therapy, Sci, Soc sci
Automation Activity & Vendor Info: (Cataloging) SirsiDynix; (Circulation) SirsiDynix; (OPAC) SirsiDynix
Wireless access
Partic in Amigos Library Services, Inc
Open Mon-Thurs 7:30am-10pm, Fri 7:30-5, Sat 9-1, Sun 6pm-10pm (Winter); Mon-Fri 7:30-5 (Summer)

COTULLA

P ALEXANDER MEMORIAL LIBRARY*, 201 S Center St, 78014-2255. SAN 316-179X. Tel: 830-879-2601. FAX: 830-483-5030. E-mail: librarian@alexandermemorial.com. Web Site: aml9612.wixsite.com/mysite. *Libr Dir,* Nora G Martinez; *Libr Asst,* Bettie Patterson
Founded 1936. Pop 5,000; Circ 16,000
Library Holdings: Audiobooks 50; AV Mats 1,215; Bks on Deafness & Sign Lang 11; DVDs 953; Large Print Bks 450; Bk Titles 17,150; Per Subs 10; Videos 750
Wireless access
Partic in TexSHARE - Texas State Library & Archives Commission
Open Mon 9-4, Tues-Thurs 11:30-5:30, Fri 9-2
Branches: 1
LA SALLE COUNTY LIBRARY - ENCINAL BRANCH, 201 Center St, 78014. E-mail: encinal@alexandermemorial.com. *Libr Asst,* Gracie Chavez; *Libr Asst,* Bettie Patterson; *Libr Asst,* Maria Yanez; Staff 1 (Non-MLS 1)
Function: 24/7 Electronic res, 24/7 Online cat, 24/7 wireless access
Open Mon 9-4, Tues-Thurs 11:30-5:30, Fri 9-2

CRANDALL

P CRANDALL-COMBINE COMMUNITY LIBRARY*, 13385 FM 3039, 75114. (Mail add: PO Box 128, 75114-0128). Tel: 972-427-6120. FAX: 972-427-8171. Web Site: crandall-isdtx.booksys.net/opac/crandall-combine/index.html, crandall.ploud.net. *Dir,* Donna Gillespie; E-mail: dgillespie@crandall-isd.net
Pop 5,526; Circ 6,668
Library Holdings: AV Mats 592; e-books 3; Large Print Bks 210; Bk Titles 21,191; Bk Vols 24,581; Per Subs 25
Automation Activity & Vendor Info: (Cataloging) Book Systems; (Circulation) Book Systems
Wireless access
Partic in TexSHARE - Texas State Library & Archives Commission
Open Mon & Wed 8:30-4:30, Tues & Thurs 8:30-7, Fri 8:30-4, Sat 9-1; Mon-Thurs 8-6 (July-Aug)

CRANE

P CRANE COUNTY LIBRARY*, 701 S Alford St, 79731-2521. SAN 316-1803. Tel: 432-558-1142. FAX: 432-558-1144. E-mail: crncolib@yahoo.com. *Dir,* Kelli Thurman; *Libr Asst,* Roger Gonzalez
Founded 1950. Pop 3,500; Circ 30,000
Oct 2018-Sept 2019 Income $143,000. Mats Exp $27,342, Books $22,000, AV Mat $5,200, Electronic Ref Mat (Incl. Access Fees) $142. Sal $30,000
Library Holdings: AV Mats 600; Bks-By-Mail 100; CDs 60; DVDs 200; Large Print Bks 200; Bk Titles 29,115; Per Subs 86; Talking Bks 600; Videos 500
Special Collections: Christian Fiction Coll; Multicultural & Spanish Coll; Texana; Western Coll
Wireless access
Partic in Partners Library Action Network
Open Mon & Wed-Fri 9-5, Tues 12-8

CROCKETT

P J H WOOTTERS CROCKETT PUBLIC LIBRARY*, 709 E Houston Ave, 75835-2124. SAN 316-1811. Tel: 936-544-3089. FAX: 936-544-4139. E-mail: library@crockettlibrary.com. Web Site: www.crockettlibrary.com. *Dir,* Judy Scott; E-mail: jscott@crockettlibrary.com

Founded 1904. Pop 23,700; Circ 44,119
Library Holdings: Bk Vols 39,000; Per Subs 56
Special Collections: Houston County (Genealogy Coll); Rare Books Coll; Texana Coll; Texas History & Literature Coll
Subject Interests: Genealogy
Automation Activity & Vendor Info: (Cataloging) Biblionix; (Circulation) Biblionix; (OPAC) Biblionix
Wireless access
Open Mon, Tues & Thurs 8:30-7, Wed 8:30-5, Sat 9-1

CROSBYTON

P CROSBY COUNTY LIBRARY*, 114 W Aspen St, 79322. SAN 316-1838. Tel: 806-675-2673. FAX: 806-675-2673. E-mail: crosbycountylibrary@yahoo.com. Web Site: ccl.ploud.net. *Dir,* Janelle Berry
Founded 1960. Pop 6,000; Circ 13,000
Library Holdings: AV Mats 200; Bk Vols 23,210; Per Subs 15
Wireless access
Open Mon-Thurs 9-12 & 1-5
Branches: 2
LORENZO BRANCH, 409 Van Buren, Lorenzo, 79343-2553. (Mail add: PO Box 430, Lorenzo, 79343-0430), SAN 373-9465. Tel: 806-634-5639. FAX: 806-634-5639. E-mail: branchlibrarylorenzo@yahoo.com. *Dir,* Joan Stone
Library Holdings: Bk Vols 6,000; Per Subs 56
Open Mon & Wed 10-12 & 1-5, Thurs 10-12 & 1-4
RALLS BRANCH, 813 Main St, Ralls, 79357. (Mail add: PO Box 608, Ralls, 79357-0608), SAN 373-9473. Tel: 806-253-2755. FAX: 806-253-2755. E-mail: rallslibrary2006@yahoo.com. *Librn,* Eva Lozano; *Asst Librn,* Linda Isbell
Library Holdings: Bk Vols 12,000
Open Mon & Fri 9-3, Tues 9-12 & 1-5, Wed & Thurs 9-5

S CROSBY COUNTY PIONEER MEMORIAL MUSEUM LIBRARY*, 101 W Main, 79322. SAN 316-1846. Tel: 806-675-2331. FAX: 806-675-7012. E-mail: ccpmmuseum@gmail.com. Web Site: www.cityofcrosbyton.org/site/visitors/pioneer-memorial. *Curator,* Melinda Cagle; Staff 3 (MLS 2, Non-MLS 1)
Founded 1958
Library Holdings: Bk Titles 300
Special Collections: Rare Books. Oral History
Subject Interests: Genealogy, Ranch hist, Regional hist, Tex hist, Tex Indians
Publications: A History of Crosby County Tex; Aunt Hanks Rock House Kitchen; Estacado, The Cradle of Culture & Civilization on the Staked Plains of Texas; Gone But Not Forgotten, The Cemetery Survey of Crosby County; History of Black families in Crosby County Tex; McNeill SR Ranch, 100 years in Blanco Canyon; Spikes & Ellis Through the Years; Sun Rising on the West, the Saga of Henry Clay & Elizabeth Smith; Teachers Manuals, 3-5th Grade Level; The Bridwell Site Archaeology in Crosby County; The Bridwell Site Archaeology in Crosby County Tex
Open Tues-Sat 9-12 & 1-5

CROSS PLAINS

P CROSS PLAINS PUBLIC LIBRARY*, 149 N Main St, 76443. (Mail add: PO Box 333, 76443), SAN 376-4028. Tel: 254-725-7722. FAX: 254-725-6629. E-mail: cppubliclibrary79@gmail.com. Web Site: www.crossplainslibrary.com. *Dir,* Debbie Box; Staff 1 (Non-MLS 1)
Library Holdings: Bk Vols 17,668; Per Subs 19
Wireless access
Open Mon-Thurs 12-5

CROWELL

P FOARD COUNTY LIBRARY*, 110 E California St, 79227. SAN 316-1854. Tel: 940-684-1250. FAX: 940-684-1250. E-mail: fclibrary@srcaccess.net. Web Site: foardcounty.ploud.net. *Dir,* Jackie Diggs
Pop 1,500
Library Holdings: Bk Titles 15,000; Bk Vols 16,760; Per Subs 15
Automation Activity & Vendor Info: (Cataloging) Follett Software; (Circulation) Follett Software; (OPAC) Follett Software
Wireless access
Open Mon-Fri 12-5
Friends of the Library Group

CROWLEY

P CROWLEY PUBLIC LIBRARY*, 409 Oak St, 76036. SAN 371-7674. Tel: 817-297-6707. Circulation Tel: 817-297-6707, Ext 2050. Administration Tel: 817-297-6707, Ext 2090. FAX: 817-297-4910. Web Site: ci.crowley.tx.us/90/Library. *Dir,* Cristina Winner; E-mail: cwinner@ci.crowley.tx.us; *Ch,* Teresa Copeland; Tel: 817-297-6707, Ext 2030, E-mail: tcopeland@crowley.tx.us; Staff 4 (MLS 2, Non-MLS 2)
Founded 1989. Pop 14,102; Circ 77,328
Library Holdings: Bks on Deafness & Sign Lang 40; Bk Titles 35,000; Per Subs 72
Special Collections: Deaf Education (Sign Language) Coll
Automation Activity & Vendor Info: (Acquisitions) SirsiDynix-WorkFlows; (Cataloging) SirsiDynix-WorkFlows; (Circulation) SirsiDynix-WorkFlows; (OPAC) SirsiDynix-WorkFlows; (Serials) SirsiDynix-WorkFlows
Wireless access
Function: 24/7 Electronic res, Accelerated reader prog, Adult bk club, Adult literacy prog, Audiobks via web, Bilingual assistance for Spanish patrons, Bks on CD, Children's prog, Computer training, Computers for patron use, E-Reserves, Electronic databases & coll, Free DVD rentals, Holiday prog, Homework prog, ILL available, Internet access, Magazines, Movies, Notary serv, Online cat, OverDrive digital audio bks, Photocopying/Printing, Preschool reading prog, Prog for adults, Prog for children & young adult, Ref serv available, Res libr, Scanner, Senior outreach, Story hour, Study rm, Summer & winter reading prog, Summer reading prog, Tax forms, Teen prog, Telephone ref, Wheelchair accessible, Winter reading prog
Partic in Partners Library Action Network
Special Services for the Deaf - Bks on deafness & sign lang; Videos & decoder
Open Tues-Fri 9-6, Sat 10-3
Restriction: Borrowing requests are handled by ILL
Friends of the Library Group

CRYSTAL CITY

J SOUTHWEST TEXAS JUNIOR COLLEGE*, Crystal City Campus Library, 215 W Zavala St, 78839. Tel: 830-374-2828, Ext 7611. Web Site: library.swtjc.edu. *Librn II,* Melissa Alvarado; E-mail: maalvarado17629@swtjc.edu
Function: ILL available, Photocopying/Printing, Study rm
Open Mon-Thurs 8-7, Fri 8-12

CUERO

P CUERO PUBLIC LIBRARY*, 207 E Main St, 77954. SAN 316-1862. Tel: 361-275-2864. FAX: 361-275-6265. Web Site: tx-cuero.civicplus.com/186/library. *Librn,* Katelynn Meitzen
Pop 6,890; Circ 18,020
Library Holdings: Bk Vols 27,292; Per Subs 17
Automation Activity & Vendor Info: (Cataloging) Book Systems; (Circulation) Book Systems; (OPAC) Book Systems
Wireless access
Partic in Partners Library Action Network
Open Mon-Fri 8:30-5:30, Sat 9-12

DAINGERFIELD

P DAINGERFIELD PUBLIC LIBRARY*, 207 Jefferson St, 75638. SAN 316-1889. Tel: 903-645-2823. FAX: 903-645-7478. E-mail: daingerfieldlibrary@gmail.com. Web Site: daingerfield.ploud.net. *Head Librn,* Earlene Walton; Staff 2 (Non-MLS 2)
Pop 3,000; Circ 19,053
Library Holdings: Bk Vols 20,000; Per Subs 16
Automation Activity & Vendor Info: (Cataloging) LibLime; (Circulation) LibLime
Wireless access
Open Mon-Fri 8-12 & 1-5
Friends of the Library Group

DALHART

P DALLAM-HARTLEY COUNTY LIBRARY*, 420 Denrock Ave, 79022. SAN 316-1897. Tel: 806-244-2761. FAX: 806-244-2761. E-mail: dallamhartleycountylibrary@gmail.com, dhcl@dallam.org. Web Site: harringtonlc.org/dallam. *Dir,* Kinsey Nicholson; Staff 1 (Non-MLS 1)
Founded 1908. Pop 10,200; Circ 35,000
Library Holdings: Bk Vols 28,000
Automation Activity & Vendor Info: (Cataloging) SirsiDynix; (Circulation) SirsiDynix; (OPAC) SirsiDynix
Wireless access
Partic in Harrington Library Consortium
Special Services for the Blind - Bks on CD; Large print bks
Open Mon 10-5, Tues-Thurs 9-5, Fri 9-4
Friends of the Library Group

DALLAS

L AKIN, GUMP, STRAUSS, HAUER & FELD LLP*, Law Library, 1700 Pacific Ave, Ste 4100, 75201-4624. SAN 325-5395. Tel: 214-969-4628. FAX: 214-969-4343. Web Site: www.akingump.com. *Tech Serv Mgr,* Wendy Lyon; E-mail: wlyon@akingump.com
Library Holdings: Bk Vols 30,000; Per Subs 100

Wireless access
Open Mon-Fri 8-5

SR ALL SAINTS CATHOLIC CHURCH, Parish Resource Library, 5231 Meadowcreek at Arapaho, 75248-4046. SAN 329-1383. Tel: 972-778-0327. FAX: 972-233-5401. E-mail: library@allsaintsdallas.org. Web Site: allsaintslibrary.follettdestiny.com, www.allsaintsdallas.org/Get involved/Faith Formation/Parish Resource Library. *Librn,* Maria Isabel Garcia; Staff 1 (MLS 1)
Founded 1979
Jul 2023-Jun 2024 Income $13,865, Locally Generated Income $3,865, Parent Institution $10,000. Mats Exp $3,228, Books $2,140, Per/Ser (Incl. Access Fees) $211, AV Equip $730, AV Mat $147
Library Holdings: Audiobooks 106; AV Mats 7,327; CDs 2,561; DVDs 2,144; Electronic Media & Resources 152; Large Print Bks 31; Bk Titles 13,778; Bk Vols 8,625; Per Subs 15; Spec Interest Per Sub 15; Videos 2,144
Special Collections: Antique Bibles; Antique Books; Bibles in 33 international languages; Parish Archives
Subject Interests: Catholic lit, Christian lit
Automation Activity & Vendor Info: (Acquisitions) Follett Software; (Cataloging) Follett Software; (Circulation) Follett Software; (OPAC) Follett Software
Wireless access
Publications: Acquisitions list; Bibliographies; Newsletter (Bimonthly)
Open Mon & Fri 9:30-12:30, Tues & Thurs 9:30-12:30 & 6:30-8:30, Sat 4:30-7, Sun 8:30-1:30 & 4:30-7
Restriction: Mem only
Friends of the Library Group

C THE ART INSTITUTE OF DALLAS*, Mildred M Kelley Library, Two North Park E, 8080 Park Lane, Ste 100, 75231-5993. SAN 321-4737. Tel: 214-692-8080. Reference Tel: 469-587-1403. FAX: 214-692-8106. E-mail: aidlibrary@aii.edu. *Dir, Libr Serv,* Lisa Casto; Tel: 469-587-1246; Staff 1 (MLS 1)
Founded 1981. Enrl 500; Fac 40; Highest Degree: Master
Library Holdings: Bk Titles 12,000; Bk Vols 14,000; Per Subs 100
Special Collections: Anime Coll; Manga Coll
Subject Interests: Computer art, Culinary arts, Fashion design, Graphic design, Interior design, Video production
Automation Activity & Vendor Info: (Circulation) Ex Libris Group; (OPAC) Ex Libris Group

M BAYLOR HEALTH SCIENCES LIBRARY*, 3302 Gaston Ave, 75246. SAN 316-1935. Tel: 214-820-2377, 214-828-8151. FAX: 214-820-2095. Web Site: bhslibrary.tamhsc.edu. *Dir,* Rosanna Ratliff; E-mail: rratliff@tamu.edu; *Head, Pub Serv,* Mandrell Bufford; E-mail: mbufford@tamu.edu; Staff 12.5 (MLS 4.5, Non-MLS 8)
Subject Interests: Dentistry, Med, Nursing
Automation Activity & Vendor Info: (Acquisitions) Ex Libris Group; (Cataloging) Ex Libris Group; (Circulation) Ex Libris Group; (Course Reserve) Ex Libris Group; (ILL) Ex Libris Group; (OPAC) Ex Libris Group
Wireless access
Partic in Healthline
Open Mon-Thurs 7am-10pm, Fri 7-6, Sat 10-6, Sun 1-10

R CHURCH OF THE INCARNATION*, Marmion Library, 3966 McKinney Ave, 75204. SAN 316-2001. Tel: 214-521-5101, Ext 2025. FAX: 214-528-7209. E-mail: library@incarnation.org. Web Site: incarnation.org/resources/affiliates. *Librn,* Mary Griffith; Staff 2 (Non-MLS 2)
Founded 1955
Library Holdings: Bk Vols 12,500; Per Subs 25
Subject Interests: Adult fiction, Biog, Children's lit, Hist, Relig studies
Open Mon-Thurs 9:30-2:30, Sun 8:30-12:30
Restriction: Mem only

L CLARK HILL PLC LIBRARY*, 901 Main St, Ste 6000, 75202. SAN 373-6555. Tel: 214-651-4300. FAX: 214-651-4330. Web Site: www.clarkhill.com. *Librn,* Donna Bostic; E-mail: dbostic@clarkhill.com
Founded 1939
Library Holdings: Bk Vols 40,000; Per Subs 1,500
Special Collections: Law; Texas Law
Automation Activity & Vendor Info: (Cataloging) Inmagic, Inc.
Wireless access
Restriction: Staff use only

P COCKRELL HILL PUBLIC LIBRARY*, 4125 W Clarendon, 75211. SAN 376-4443. Tel: 214-330-9935. FAX: 214-330-5483. E-mail: library@cockrell-hill.tx.us. Web Site: cityofcockrellhill.us/2170/library, cockrellhill.ploud.net. *Librn,* Jennifer Marks; Staff 2 (MLS 1, Non-MLS 1)
Pop 45,000
Library Holdings: Bk Titles 13,000
Automation Activity & Vendor Info: (Cataloging) Biblionix; (Circulation) Biblionix; (OPAC) Biblionix
Wireless access
Function: Children's prog, Computers for patron use, Free DVD rentals, ILL available, Internet access, Jail serv, Magazines, Online cat, Outreach serv, Photocopying/Printing, Printer for laptops & handheld devices, Ref serv available, Scanner, Spanish lang bks, Summer reading prog, Wheelchair accessible
Open Tues-Thurs 11-6:30, Fri 11-4:30

CR CRISWELL COLLEGE*, Wallace Library, 4010 Gaston Ave, 75246. SAN 320-751X. Tel: 214-818-1378. Toll Free Tel: 800-899-0012, Ext 1378. FAX: 214-818-1310. E-mail: library@criswell.edu. Web Site: www.criswell.edu/academics/wallace-library. *Dir,* Philip Nott; E-mail: pnott@criswell.edu; Staff 3 (MLS 2, Non-MLS 1)
Founded 1976. Enrl 300; Highest Degree: Master
Library Holdings: Bk Vols 70,000; Per Subs 300
Special Collections: Baptist History & Theology
Automation Activity & Vendor Info: (Acquisitions) OCLC; (Cataloging) OCLC; (Circulation) OCLC; (Course Reserve) OCLC; (ILL) OCLC; (OPAC) OCLC; (Serials) OCLC
Wireless access
Partic in OCLC Online Computer Library Center, Inc; TexSHARE - Texas State Library & Archives Commission
Open Mon, Tues & Thurs 7:30am-9pm, Wed & Fri 8-4

CR DALLAS BAPTIST UNIVERSITY*, Vance Memorial Library, 3000 Mountain Creek Pkwy, 75211-9299. SAN 316-2044. Tel: 214-333-5320. Interlibrary Loan Service Tel: 214-333-5389. Reference Tel: 214-333-5221. Toll Free Tel: 800-483-7048. Circulation E-mail: lib_circ@dbu.edu. Reference E-mail: lib_ref@dbu.edu. Web Site: libguides.dbu.edu/library. *Libr Dir, Research Librn,* Scott Jeffries; E-mail: scottj@dbu.edu; *Dir, Distance Learning Library Servs,* John Hong; Tel: 214-333-5225, E-mail: johnh@dbu.edu; *Spec Coll Librn, Univ Archivist,* Traci West; Tel: 214-333-5210, E-mail: traci@dbu.edu; *Tech Serv Librn,* Donna Daniel; Tel: 214-333-5299, E-mail: donnad@dbu.edu; *User Serv Librn,* Sarah Jones; Tel: 214-333-5220, E-mail: sarahj@dbu.edu; *Supvr, Circ,* Marcy Fisher; E-mail: mfisher@dbu.edu; *Supvr, ILL,* Shelby McClenny; E-mail: shelbym@dbu.edu; *Acq & ILL Asst,* Olivia Osborn; Tel: 214-333-5260, E-mail: oliviao@dbu.edu. Subject Specialists: *Hist,* Traci West; Staff 11 (MLS 7.5, Non-MLS 3.5)
Founded 1898. Enrl 5,156; Fac 133; Highest Degree: Doctorate
Jun 2015-May 2016. Mats Exp $263,403, Books $11,250, Per/Ser (Incl. Access Fees) $85,718, Electronic Ref Mat (Incl. Access Fees) $166,435
Library Holdings: AV Mats 7,986; e-books 65,765; e-journals 39,400; Microforms 521,772; Bk Titles 168,169; Bk Vols 237,167; Per Subs 302
Special Collections: Baptist Coll; ERIC, microfiche; Evangelical Coll; Library of American Literature, ultrafiche; Library of English Literature, ultrafiche. US Document Depository
Subject Interests: Bus, Educ, Evangelicalism, Music, Natural sci, Relig
Automation Activity & Vendor Info: (Acquisitions) OCLC Worldshare Management Services; (Cataloging) OCLC Connexion; (Circulation) OCLC Worldshare Management Services; (Course Reserve) OCLC Worldshare Management Services; (ILL) OCLC WorldShare Interlibrary Loan; (OPAC) OCLC Worldshare Management Services; (Serials) OCLC Worldshare Management Services
Wireless access
Function: Archival coll, Audio & video playback equip for onsite use, Computers for patron use, Distance learning, Doc delivery serv, Electronic databases & coll, ILL available, Internet access, Learning ctr, Mail loans to mem, Music CDs, Online cat, Online ref, Photocopying/Printing, Ref & res, Ref serv available, VHS videos, Wheelchair accessible
Partic in Amigos Library Services, Inc; Christian Library Consortium; Llano Estacado Info Access Network; Statewide California Electronic Library Consortium; Tex Independent Cols & Univ Librs; TexSHARE - Texas State Library & Archives Commission
Open Mon-Wed 6:30am-Midnight, Thurs & Fri 6:30am-11pm, Sat 7:30-6, Sun 2:30-Midnight
Restriction: Borrowing privileges limited to fac & registered students, External users must contact libr

CR DALLAS CHRISTIAN COLLEGE, C C Crawford Memorial Library, 2700 Christian Pkwy, 75234. SAN 316-2060. Tel: 214-453-8109. FAX: 972-241-8021. E-mail: library@dallas.edu. Web Site: www.dallas.edu. *Dir, Libr Serv,* Position Currently Open; Staff 2 (MLS 1, Non-MLS 1)
Founded 1950. Enrl 300; Fac 19; Highest Degree: Master
Library Holdings: e-books 2,000,000; e-journals 16,000; Bk Vols 25,000
Special Collections: History & Writings of the Restoration Movement
Subject Interests: Biblical studies, Relig, Theol
Wireless access
Function: Res libr
Partic in Amigos Library Services, Inc; Christian Libr Network; OCLC Online Computer Library Center, Inc
Open Mon-Thurs 8am-9pm, Fri 8-Noon

J DALLAS COLLEGE*, El Centro Campus Library, 801 Main St, 75202-3605. SAN 316-2214. Tel: 214-860-2174. Circulation Tel: 214-860-2175. Web Site: www.dcccd.edu, www.elcentrocollege.edu/library. *Asst Dean,* Dr Norman Howden; Tel: 214-860-2176, E-mail: norman@dcccd.edu; *Librn,* Lela Evans; E-mail: lela.evans@dcccd.edu; *Librn,* Margarette Jones; E-mail: mjones1@dcccd.edu; *Coordr, Access Serv,* Josy Thomas; Staff 9 (MLS 6, Non-MLS 3)
Founded 1966
Library Holdings: Bk Titles 69,471; Bk Vols 76,814
Subject Interests: Allied health, Culinary arts, Ethnic studies, Nursing
Automation Activity & Vendor Info: (Acquisitions) Ex Libris Group; (Cataloging) Ex Libris Group; (Circulation) Ex Libris Group; (OPAC) Ex Libris Group
Wireless access
Function: 24/7 Online cat, Computers for patron use, Electronic databases & coll, Online cat, Online ref, Photocopying/Printing, Scanner, Telephone ref, Wheelchair accessible
Partic in TexSHARE - Texas State Library & Archives Commission
Open Mon-Thurs 7:30am-8:30pm, Fri 8-4:30, Sat 10-2:30
Restriction: Authorized patrons, Authorized scholars by appt, ID required to use computers (Ltd hrs), Open to fac, students & qualified researchers, Use of others with permission of librn

J DALLAS COLLEGE*, Mountain View Campus Library, 4849 W Illinois, 75211-6599. SAN 316-2451. Tel: 214-860-8669. Reference Tel: 214-860-8527. FAX: 214-860-8667. E-mail: MVClibrary@dcccd.edu. Web Site: www.mountainviewcollege.edu/services/academic-support/library. *Lead Librn,* Jean Baker; E-mail: jeanbaker@dcccd.edu; *Librn III,* Margaret Knox; E-mail: mpknox@dcccd.edu; Staff 3 (MLS 3)
Founded 1970. Enrl 6,876; Fac 83; Highest Degree: Associate
Library Holdings: AV Mats 1,706; e-books 28,000; Bk Titles 46,596; Bk Vols 51,118; Per Subs 200
Subject Interests: Aviation
Automation Activity & Vendor Info: (Acquisitions) Innovative Interfaces, Inc; (Cataloging) Innovative Interfaces, Inc; (Circulation) Innovative Interfaces, Inc; (Course Reserve) Innovative Interfaces, Inc; (ILL) Innovative Interfaces, Inc; (Media Booking) Innovative Interfaces, Inc; (OPAC) Innovative Interfaces, Inc; (Serials) Innovative Interfaces, Inc
Wireless access
Function: ILL available, Magnifiers for reading, Photocopying/Printing, Ref serv available, Telephone ref, Wheelchair accessible
Partic in TexSHARE - Texas State Library & Archives Commission
Special Services for the Blind - Closed circuit TV; Computer with voice synthesizer for visually impaired persons
Open Mon-Thurs 7:30am-9pm, Fri 7:30-4:30, Sat 8:30-1:30

J DALLAS COLLEGE*, Richland Campus Library, 12800 Abrams Rd, 75243. SAN 316-2524. Tel: 972-238-6081. Reference Tel: 972-238-6082. E-mail: richlandlibrary@dcccd.edu. Web Site: www.dallascollege.edu/libraries. *Dean, Libr Serv,* Jean Baker; E-mail: jeanbaker@dcccd.edu; *Regional Mgr,* Angela Harris; E-mail: angelaharris@dcccd.edu; *Librn,* Megan Dyer; E-mail: megandyer@dcccd.edu; *Librn,* Laura Gonzales; E-mail: laura.gonzales@dcccd.edu; Staff 15 (MLS 7, Non-MLS 8)
Founded 1972. Highest Degree: Associate
Library Holdings: Bk Titles 78,800; Bk Vols 91,000; Per Subs 210
Automation Activity & Vendor Info: (Acquisitions) Innovative Interfaces, Inc; (Cataloging) Innovative Interfaces, Inc; (Circulation) Innovative Interfaces, Inc; (Course Reserve) Innovative Interfaces, Inc; (ILL) Innovative Interfaces, Inc; (Media Booking) Innovative Interfaces, Inc; (OPAC) Innovative Interfaces, Inc; (Serials) Innovative Interfaces, Inc
Wireless access
Partic in TexSHARE - Texas State Library & Archives Commission
Open Mon-Thurs 8am-9pm, Fri 8-5, Sat Noon-4 (Winter); Mon-Fri 8-5 (Summer)

L DALLAS COUNTY LAW LIBRARY*, George Allen Courts Bldg, 600 Commerce St, Rm 760, 75202-4606. SAN 316-2087. Tel: 214-653-7481. FAX: 214-653-6103. E-mail: lawlibrary@dallascounty.org. Web Site: www.dallascounty.org. *Dir, Law Libr,* David Wilkinson; E-mail: David.Wilkinson@dallascounty.org; *Assoc Dir,* Karen Dibble; Tel: 214-653-6031, E-mail: Karen.Dibble@dallascounty.org; *Ref Librn,* David Bader; Tel: 214-653-6027, E-mail: David.Bader@dallascounty.org; *Web Coordr,* Patricia Altamirano; Tel: 214-653-6947, E-mail: Patricia.Altamirano@dallascounty.org; *Tech Serv,* Jonathan Wells; Tel: 214-653-6013, E-mail: Jonathan.Wells@dallascounty.org; Staff 8 (MLS 4, Non-MLS 4)
Founded 1894
Library Holdings: Bk Vols 5,000
Automation Activity & Vendor Info: (Cataloging) OCLC; (ILL) OCLC
Wireless access
Function: 24/7 Online cat, Bilingual assistance for Spanish patrons, Computers for patron use, Electronic databases & coll, ILL available, Internet access, Meeting rooms, Online cat, Ref serv available, Scanner, Wheelchair accessible
Open Mon-Fri 8-4:30
Restriction: Borrowing requests are handled by ILL, Non-circulating, Open to pub for ref only

S DALLAS HISTORICAL SOCIETY*, G B Dealey Library, Hall of State in Fair Park, 3939 Grand Ave, 75210. (Mail add: PO Box 150038, 75315-0038). Tel: 214-421-4500. FAX: 214-421-7500. Web Site: www.dallashistory.org. *Exec Dir,* Karl Chiao; Tel: 214-421-4500, Ext 102, E-mail: director@dallashistory.org; *Colls Mgr,* Chris Bohannon; Tel: 214-421-4500, Ext 117, E-mail: collections@dallashistory.org; *Archivist,* Kaitlyn Price; E-mail: kaitlyn@dallashistory.org; Staff 1 (Non-MLS 1)
Founded 1922
Library Holdings: Bk Vols 14,807
Special Collections: 1936 Texas Centennial Coll; Maps of Dallas & the Southwest, 1800-2000; P P Martinez Coll, Spanish ms; Personal Papers of Thomas B Love, Joseph W Bailey, Hatton W Sumners, Sarah Horton Cockrell, Ann McClarmonde Chase, Margaret Scruggs Caruth, Jesse Daniel Ames, John M Moore, Elmer Scott, George W Biggs, G B Dealey & Sam Acheson; Photographs of Dallas & Texas, 1870-2000 (J Johnson & C E Arnold Colls); Photos of Historic Sites & Courthouses of Texas ca. 1936-1940 (R M Hayes Coll); Photos of Texas, 1895-1896 (Henry Stark Coll); Social & Urban History of Dallas
Function: Archival coll
Publications: Guide to Fair Park, Dallas; Legacies: A History Journal for Dallas & North Central Texas; When Dallas Became a City: The Letters of John Milton McCoy, 1870-1881
Open Tues-Fri 9-5
Restriction: Non-circulating, Not a lending libr, Photo ID required for access

C DALLAS INTERNATIONAL UNIVERSITY LIBRARY*, 7500 W Camp Wisdom Rd, 75236-5699. SAN 326-6125. Tel: 972-708-7416. FAX: 972-708-7292. E-mail: library@diu.edu, library_director@diu.edu. Web Site: www.diu.edu/library. *Libr Dir,* Position Currently Open; *Interim Libr Dir, Pub Serv Librn,* Wendy Payton; E-mail: wendy_payton@diu.edu; *Pub Serv Librn,* Barbara Thomas; E-mail: barbara_thomas@diu.edu; *Ref Librn,* Dorothy Buice; E-mail: dorothy_buice@diu.edu; *Ref Librn,* Robert Sivigny; E-mail: robert_sivigny@diu.edu; Staff 7 (MLS 4, Non-MLS 3)
Founded 1999. Enrl 220; Fac 70; Highest Degree: Doctorate
Library Holdings: AV Mats 35; e-books 428; e-journals 184; Electronic Media & Resources 1,326; Bk Titles 42,800; Bk Vols 61,125; Per Subs 80
Subject Interests: Linguistics, Literacy, Minority lang, Sociolinguistics, Translation
Automation Activity & Vendor Info: (Cataloging) Follett Software; (Circulation) Follett Software; (ILL) OCLC WorldShare Interlibrary Loan; (OPAC) Follett Software
Wireless access
Partic in Amigos Library Services, Inc; Christian Library Consortium; Southwest Area Theological Library Association
Open Mon-Thurs 9-9, Fri & Sat 9-5
Restriction: Badge access after hrs, In-house use for visitors, Open to fac, students & qualified researchers

S DALLAS MUNICIPAL ARCHIVES*, 1500 Marilla St, Rm L2 D North, 75201. SAN 371-1900. Tel: 214-670-5270. Web Site: dallascityhall.com/government/citysecretary/archives/pages/archives_home.aspx. *Archivist/Librn,* John H Slate; E-mail: john.slate@dallascityhall.com
Library Holdings: Bk Titles 150
Special Collections: Dallas City Government Records Coll
Function: Archival coll
Restriction: Open by appt only

S DALLAS MUSEUM OF ART*, Mildred R & Frederick M Mayer Library, 1717 N Harwood, 75201. SAN 316-2125. Tel: 214-922-1277. FAX: 214-954-0174. E-mail: library@dma.org. Web Site: www.dma.org. *Librn,* Jenny Stone; Staff 5 (MLS 4, Non-MLS 1)
Founded 1938
Library Holdings: Bk Titles 80,000; Bk Vols 106,000; Per Subs 110
Subject Interests: 19th Century French Art, African art, Contemporary art, Gen art hist, Indigenous art
Automation Activity & Vendor Info: (Cataloging) Ex Libris Group; (Circulation) Ex Libris Group; (OPAC) Ex Libris Group
Wireless access
Function: 24/7 Online cat, Ref serv available
Partic in Amigos Library Services, Inc; OCLC Online Computer Library Center, Inc
Restriction: Closed stack, Non-circulating to the pub

P DALLAS PUBLIC LIBRARY*, 1515 Young St, 75201-5415. SAN 361-4379. Tel: 214-670-1400. Circulation Tel: 214-670-1740. Interlibrary Loan Service Tel: 214-670-1741. Administration Tel: 214-670-7809. Information Services Tel: 214-670-1700. E-mail: askalibrarian@dallaslibrary.org. Web Site: dallaslibrary.org. *Dir of Libr,*

Mary Jo Giudice; E-mail: Maryjo.Giudice@dallascityhall.com; *Asst Dir,* Kjerstine Nielsen; E-mail: kjerstine.nielsen@dallascityhall.com; *Asst Dir, Operations,* Clinton Lawrence; E-mail: clinton.lawrence@dallascityhall.com; *Adminr,* Ronnie Jessie; E-mail: ronnie.jessie@dallascityhall.com; *Adminr, Adult Serv,* Heather Lowe; E-mail: heather.lowe@dallascityhall.com; *Adminr, Youth Serv,* Melissa Dease; E-mail: melissa.dease@dallascityhall.com; *Mgr, Technology & Contracts,* Sallie Lockhart; E-mail: sallie.lockhart@dallascityhall.com; Staff 157 (MLS 49, Non-MLS 108)
Founded 1901. Pop 1,306,350; Circ 5,703,875
Library Holdings: Audiobooks 28,860; AV Mats 130,453; Bk Titles 1,755,802; Bk Vols 2,056,540; Per Subs 3,650; Videos 113,477
Special Collections: Automobile Repair Manual Coll; Black Dallas History (Juanita Craft Coll, Dallas Negro Chamber of Commerce Coll); Business Histories; Children's Literature Coll, hist & rare children's bks & per; Classical Literature (Louie N Bromberg Coll); Classical Recordings (Rual Askew Coll); Dallas Black History (John & Ethelyn M Chisum Coll), diaries, ms, photogs; Dallas Theater Center; Dance (Juana De Laban Coll, Jerry Bywaters Coll); Dance (Mary Bywaters Coll), dance progs, mss, pamphlets, per; Fashion (Bergdorf Goodman Coll), bks, clippings, micro, pamphlets, photogs; Genealogy, bks, micro, per; Grants (Cooperating Coll of the Foundation Center), bks, looseleaf, microfiche; History of Printing, early printing, bks; Lakewood Area History, oral hist; Oil & Gas (Hamon Oil & Gas Resource Center), bks, per, databases; Poetry Society of Texas' Coll, bks & chapbooks; Sears Catalog, micro; Standards & Specifications, bks, micro & pamphlets; Texas & Dallas, archives, bks, clippings, maps, micro, per, photogs; Theater (William Ely Hill Coll, Interstate Theatre Coll, Margo Jones Coll), bks, clippings, disc recordings, micro, pamphlets, per, photogs, slides; US Marshal Clinton T Peoples Coll, scrapbks, photogs, correspondence concerning law enforcement in Texas; US Serial Set. Oral History; State Document Depository; US Document Depository
Automation Activity & Vendor Info: (ILL) OCLC; (OPAC) Innovative Interfaces, Inc
Wireless access
Function: Archival coll, Art exhibits, Bus archives, Govt ref serv, ILL available, Prog for adults, Prog for children & young adult, Ref serv available
Publications: Catalog of Large Type Books - Dallas Pub Libr Syst; Dallas Public Library: The First 75 Years; Dallas WPA Guide & History; In Beauty it is Finished, The McDermott Collection of Navajo Blankets; Long Range Plan for Public Library Service: A Self Study; Reminiscences, A Glimpse of Old East Dallas; The Cartoonist's Art: Editorial Cartoons by Ficklen, McClanahan, Taylor & DeOre; The Dallas Public Library: Celebrating a Century of Services, 1901-2001
Partic in Amigos Library Services, Inc; OCLC Online Computer Library Center, Inc; Tex State Libr Communications Network
Special Services for the Deaf - Staff with knowledge of sign lang; TDD equip
Special Services for the Blind - BiFolkal kits; Children's Braille; Closed circuit TV; Reader equip; Talking bks; ZoomText magnification & reading software
Open Mon, Fri & Sat 10-6, Tues-Thurs 10-8, Sun 1-5
Restriction: Non-resident fee
Friends of the Library Group

Branches: 29

ARCADIA PARK, 1302 N Justin Ave, 75211-1142. Tel: 214-670-6446. E-mail: arcadiapark@dallaslibrary.org. Web Site: dallaslibrary2.org/branch/arcadia.php. *Mgr,* Barbara Alvarez; E-mail: barbara.alvarez@dallascityhall.com; Staff 10 (MLS 3, Non-MLS 7)
Automation Activity & Vendor Info: (Acquisitions) Innovative Interfaces, Inc; (Cataloging) Innovative Interfaces, Inc; (Circulation) Innovative Interfaces, Inc; (Course Reserve) Innovative Interfaces, Inc
Open Mon & Tues 7:45am-8pm, Wed-Fri 7:45-5, Sat 10-5

AUDELIA ROAD, 10045 Audelia Rd, 75238-1999, SAN 361-4409. Tel: 214-670-1350. E-mail: audeliaroad@dallaslibrary.org. Web Site: dallaslibrary2.org/branch/audelia.php. *Mgr,* Juli Gonzalez; E-mail: juli.gonzalez@dallascityhall.com; Staff 10.5 (MLS 3, Non-MLS 7.5)
Founded 1964
Automation Activity & Vendor Info: (Acquisitions) Innovative Interfaces, Inc; (Cataloging) Innovative Interfaces, Inc; (Circulation) Innovative Interfaces, Inc; (Course Reserve) Innovative Interfaces, Inc
Open Mon, Fri & Sat 10-6, Tues-Thurs 10-8, Sun 1-5
Friends of the Library Group

BACHMAN LAKE, 9480 Webb Chapel Rd, 75220-4496, SAN 361-4883. Tel: 214-670-6376. E-mail: bachmanlake@dallaslibrary.org. Web Site: dallaslibrary2.org/branch/bachman.php. *Mgr,* Position Currently Open; Staff 9.5 (MLS 3, Non-MLS 6.5)
Founded 1961
Automation Activity & Vendor Info: (Acquisitions) Innovative Interfaces, Inc; (Cataloging) Innovative Interfaces, Inc; (Circulation) Innovative Interfaces, Inc; (Course Reserve) Innovative Interfaces, Inc
Open Mon, Fri & Sat 10-6, Tues-Thurs 10-8, Sun 1-5
Friends of the Library Group

BOOKMARKS-NORTHPARK CENTER, 8687 N Central Expressway, Ste 154, 75225. Tel: 214-671-1381. E-mail: northpark@dallaslibrary.org. *Mgr,* Sandra King; E-mail: sandra.king@dallascityhall.com; Staff 4 (Non-MLS 4)
Automation Activity & Vendor Info: (Acquisitions) Innovative Interfaces, Inc; (Cataloging) Innovative Interfaces, Inc; (Circulation) Innovative Interfaces, Inc; (Course Reserve) Innovative Interfaces, Inc
Open Mon & Wed-Sat 10-6, Sun 12-5

DALLAS WEST, 2332 Singleton Blvd, 75212-3790, SAN 361-4468. Tel: 214-670-6445. E-mail: dallaswest@dallaslibrary.org. Web Site: dallaslibrary2.org/branch/dallaswest.php. *Mgr,* Juan Moa; E-mail: juan.moa@dallascityhall.com; Staff 8.5 (MLS 2, Non-MLS 6.5)
Automation Activity & Vendor Info: (Acquisitions) Innovative Interfaces, Inc; (Cataloging) Innovative Interfaces, Inc; (Circulation) Innovative Interfaces, Inc; (Course Reserve) Innovative Interfaces, Inc
Open Mon, Fri & Sat 10-6, Tues-Thurs 10-8, Sun 1-5

PAUL LAURENCE DUNBAR LANCASTER-KIEST BRANCH, 2008 E Kiest Blvd, 75216-4448, SAN 361-4646. Tel: 214-670-1952. E-mail: lancasterkiest@dallaslibrary.org. Web Site: dallaslibrary2.org/branch/lancaster.php. *Br Mgr,* Tsigereda Teketele; E-mail: tsigereda.teketele@dallas.gov; Staff 9.5 (MLS 2, Non-MLS 7.5)
Open Mon, Fri & Sat 10-6, Tues-Thurs 10-8, Sun 1-5
Friends of the Library Group

FOREST GREEN, 9015 Forest Lane, 75243-4114, SAN 361-4492. Tel: 214-670-1335. E-mail: forestgreen@dallaslibrary.org. Web Site: dallaslibrary2.org/branch/forest.php. *Mgr,* Courtney Lloyd; E-mail: courtney.lloyd@dallas.gov; Staff 8.5 (MLS 2, Non-MLS 6.5)
Automation Activity & Vendor Info: (Acquisitions) Innovative Interfaces, Inc; (Cataloging) Innovative Interfaces, Inc; (Circulation) Innovative Interfaces, Inc; (Course Reserve) Innovative Interfaces, Inc
Open Mon-Wed 10-8, Thurs-Sat 10-6
Friends of the Library Group

FRETZ PARK, 6990 Belt Line Rd, 75254-7963, SAN 361-4522. Tel: 214-670-6421. E-mail: fretzpark@dallaslibrary.org. Web Site: dallaslibrary2.org/branch/fretz.php. *Mgr,* Position Currently Open; Staff 9 (MLS 3, Non-MLS 6)
Automation Activity & Vendor Info: (Acquisitions) Innovative Interfaces, Inc; (Cataloging) Innovative Interfaces, Inc; (Circulation) Innovative Interfaces, Inc; (Course Reserve) Innovative Interfaces, Inc
Open Mon-Wed 10-8, Thurs-Sat 10-6
Friends of the Library Group

HAMPTON-ILLINOIS, 2951 S Hampton Rd, 75224, SAN 361-4557. Tel: 214-670-7646. E-mail: hamptonillinois@dallaslibrary.org. Web Site: dallaslibrary2.org/branch/hampton.php. *Mgr,* Lisa Zinkie; E-mail: lisa.zinkie@dallas.gov; Staff 15 (MLS 3, Non-MLS 12)
Automation Activity & Vendor Info: (Acquisitions) Innovative Interfaces, Inc; (Cataloging) Innovative Interfaces, Inc; (Circulation) Innovative Interfaces, Inc - Millennium; (Course Reserve) Innovative Interfaces, Inc
Open Mon-Wed 7:45am-8pm, Thurs & Fri 7:45-5, Sat 10-5, Sun 1-5
Friends of the Library Group

HIGHLAND HILLS, 6200 Bonnie View Rd, 75241, SAN 361-4565. Tel: 214-670-0987. E-mail: highlandhills@dallaslibrary.org. Web Site: dallaslibrary2.org/branch/highland.php. *Mgr,* Rotina Jones; E-mail: rotina.jones@dallascityhall.com; Staff 8.5 (MLS 2, Non-MLS 6.5)
Automation Activity & Vendor Info: (Acquisitions) Innovative Interfaces, Inc; (Cataloging) Innovative Interfaces, Inc; (Circulation) Inmagic, Inc.; (Course Reserve) Innovative Interfaces, Inc
Open Mon-Wed 10-8, Thurs-Sat 10-6
Friends of the Library Group

MARTIN LUTHER KING JR BRANCH, 2922 Martin Luther King Jr Blvd, 75215-2393, SAN 361-4670. Tel: 214-670-0344. E-mail: martinlutherkingjr@dallaslibrary.org. Web Site: dallaslibrary2.org/branch/martin.php. *Mgr,* Shannon Adams; E-mail: shannon.adams@dallascityhall.com; Staff 9 (MLS 3, Non-MLS 6)
Automation Activity & Vendor Info: (Acquisitions) Innovative Interfaces, Inc; (Cataloging) Innovative Interfaces, Inc; (Circulation) Innovative Interfaces, Inc; (Course Reserve) Innovative Interfaces, Inc
Open Mon-Wed 10-8, Thurs-Sat 10-6
Friends of the Library Group

KLEBERG-RYLIE, 1301 Edd Rd, 75253-4010, SAN 376-947X. Tel: 214-670-8471. E-mail: klebergrylie@dallas.gov. Web Site: dallaslibrary2.org/branch/kleberg.php. *Mgr,* Gayle Gordon; E-mail: gayle.gordon@dallascityhall.com; Staff 5 (MLS 2, Non-MLS 3)
Automation Activity & Vendor Info: (Acquisitions) Innovative Interfaces, Inc; (Cataloging) Innovative Interfaces, Inc; (Circulation) Innovative Interfaces, Inc; (Course Reserve) Innovative Interfaces, Inc
Open Tues & Fri 9-5, Wed & Thurs 10-7, Sat 9-4

LAKEWOOD, 6121 Worth St, 75214-4497, SAN 361-4611. Tel: 214-670-1376. E-mail: lakewood@dallaslibrary.org. Web Site: dallaslibrary2.org/branch/lakewood.php. *Mgr,* Leslie Lake; E-mail: leslie.lake@dallascityhall.com; Staff 8.5 (MLS 2, Non-MLS 6.5)
Automation Activity & Vendor Info: (Acquisitions) Innovative Interfaces, Inc; (Cataloging) Innovative Interfaces, Inc; (Circulation) Innovative Interfaces, Inc; (Course Reserve) Innovative Interfaces, Inc

Open Mon-Wed 10-8, Thurs-Sat 10-6
Friends of the Library Group
LOCHWOOD, 11221 Lochwood Blvd, 75218. Tel: 214-670-8403. E-mail: lochwood@dallascityhall.com. Web Site: dallaslibrary2.org/branch/lochwood.php. *Mgr,* Terrah Carter; E-mail: terrah.carter@dallascityhall.com; Staff 8.5 (MLS 2, Non-MLS 6.5)
Automation Activity & Vendor Info: (Acquisitions) Innovative Interfaces, Inc; (Cataloging) Innovative Interfaces, Inc; (Circulation) Innovative Interfaces, Inc; (Course Reserve) Innovative Interfaces, Inc
Open Mon-Wed 10-8, Thurs-Sat 10-6
Friends of the Library Group
MOUNTAIN CREEK, 6102 Mountain Creek Pkwy, 75249, SAN 374-4477. Tel: 214-670-6704. E-mail: mountaincreek@dallaslibrary.org. Web Site: dallaslibrary2.org/branch/mountain.php. *Mgr,* Matthew Shank; E-mail: matthew.shank@dallascityhall.com; Staff 8.5 (MLS 2, Non-MLS 6.5)
Automation Activity & Vendor Info: (Acquisitions) Innovative Interfaces, Inc; (Cataloging) Innovative Interfaces, Inc; (Circulation) Innovative Interfaces, Inc; (Course Reserve) Innovative Interfaces, Inc
Open Mon-Wed 10-8, Thurs-Sat 10-6
Friends of the Library Group
NORTH OAK CLIFF, 302 W Tenth St, 75208-4617, SAN 361-4581. Tel: 214-670-7555. E-mail: northoakcliff@dallaslibrary.org. Web Site: dallaslibrary2.org/branch/north.php. *Br Mgr,* Juan Moa; E-mail: juan.moa@dallas.gov; Staff 9.5 (MLS 2, Non-MLS 7.5)
Open Mon, Fri & Sat 10-6, Tues-Thurs 10-8, Sun 1-5
Friends of the Library Group
OAK LAWN, 4100 Cedar Springs Rd, 75219-3522, SAN 361-4700. Tel: 214-670-1359. E-mail: oaklawn@dallaslibrary.org. Web Site: dallaslibrary2.org/branch/oaklawn.php. *Mgr,* Position Currently Open; Staff 10.5 (MLS 3, Non-MLS 7.5)
Open Mon, Fri & Sat 10-6, Tues-Thurs 10-8, Sun 1-5
Friends of the Library Group
PARK FOREST, 3421 Forest Lane, 75234-7776, SAN 361-4735. Tel: 214-670-6333. E-mail: parkforest@dallaslibrary.org. Web Site: dallaslibrary2.org/branch/park.php. *Mgr,* Pam Cash; E-mail: pamela.cash@dallascityhall.com; Staff 8.5 (MLS 2, Non-MLS 6.5)
Open Mon-Wed 10-8, Thurs-Sat 10-6
Friends of the Library Group
PLEASANT GROVE, 7310 Lake June Rd, 75217, SAN 361-476X. Tel: 214-670-0965. E-mail: pleasantgrove@dallaslibrary.org. Web Site: dallaslibrary.org/pleasant.htm. *Mgr,* Patrick Reilly; E-mail: patrick.reilly@dallascityhall.com; Staff 9.5 (MLS 3, Non-MLS 6.5)
Open Mon, Fri & Sat 10-6, Tues-Thurs 10-8, Sun 1-5
Friends of the Library Group
POLK-WISDOM, 7151 Library Lane, 75232-3899, SAN 361-4794. Tel: 214-670-1947. E-mail: polkwisdom@dallaslibrary.org. Web Site: dallaslibrary.org/polk.htm. *Br Mgr,* Sandra King; E-mail: sandra.king@dallas.gov; Staff 9.5 (MLS 2, Non-MLS 7.5)
Open Mon, Fri & Sat 10-6, Tues-Thurs 10-8, Sun 1-5
Friends of the Library Group
PRESTON ROYAL BRANCH, 5626 Royal Lane, 75229-5599, SAN 361-4824. Tel: 214-670-7128. E-mail: prestonroyal@dallaslibrary.org. Web Site: dallaslibrary2.org/branch/preston.php. *Mgr,* Connie Maxwell; E-mail: connie.maxwell@dallascityhall.com; Staff 10.5 (MLS 3, Non-MLS 7.5)
Open Mon, Fri & Sat 10-6, Tues-Thurs 10-8, Sun 1-5
Friends of the Library Group
RENNER FRANKFORD BRANCH, 6400 Frankford Rd, 75252-5747, SAN 328-7300. Tel: 214-670-6100. E-mail: rennerfrankford@dallaslibrary.org. Web Site: dallaslibrary.org/renner.htm. *Mgr,* Sara Frymark; E-mail: sara.frymark@dallascityhall.com; Staff 10 (MLS 3, Non-MLS 7)
Open Mon, Fri & Sat 10-6, Tues-Thurs 10-8, Sun 1-5
Friends of the Library Group
SKILLMAN SOUTHWESTERN, 5707 Skillman St, 75206, SAN 376-9488. Tel: 214-670-6078. E-mail: skillmansouthwestern@dallaslibrary.org. Web Site: dallaslibrary2.org/branch/skillman.php. *Mgr,* Lynn Lewis; E-mail: donna.lewis@dallascityhall.com; Staff 8.5 (MLS 1, Non-MLS 7.5)
Open Mon-Wed 10-8, Thurs-Sat 10-6
Friends of the Library Group
SKYLINE, 6006 Everglade Rd, 75227-2799, SAN 361-4859. Tel: 214-670-0938. E-mail: skyline@dallaslibrary.org. Web Site: dallaslibrary.org/skyline.php. *Br Mgr,* Jabari Jones; E-mail: jabari.jones@dallas.gov; Staff 8.5 (MLS 2, Non-MLS 6.5)
Open Mon-Wed 10-8, Thurs-Sat 10-6
Friends of the Library Group
VICKERY PARK, 8333 Park Lane, 75231. Tel: 214-671-2101. E-mail: vickerypark@dallas.gov. Web Site: dallaslibrary2.org/branch/vickerypark.php. *Br Mgr,* Jessica Alvarado; E-mail: jessica.alvarado@dallas.gov
Function: Homework prog
Open Mon 9-6, Tues-Thurs 9-8, Fri 9-5, Sat 9-4, Sun 11-5

CR DALLAS THEOLOGICAL SEMINARY*, Turpin Library, 3909 Swiss Ave, 75204. SAN 316-2168. Tel: 214-887-5280. E-mail: library@dts.edu. Web Site: library.dts.edu. *Dir,* Marvin Hunn; Tel: 214-887-5281, E-mail: mhunn@dts.edu; *Head, Acq, Head, Electronic Res, Head, Metadata Serv,* Jessie Zhong; Tel: 214-887-5289, E-mail: jzhong@dts.edu; *Coll Develop Librn,* Jefferson Webster; Tel: 214-887-5287, E-mail: jwebster@dts.edu; *ILL, Ref,* Debbie Hunn; Tel: 214-887-5284, E-mail: dhunn@dts.edu; *Pub Serv, Spec Coll,* Lolana Thompson; Tel: 214-887-5290, E-mail: lthompson@dts.edu; Staff 5 (MLS 3, Non-MLS 2)
Founded 1924. Highest Degree: Doctorate
Library Holdings: AV Mats 11,707; e-books 11,302; e-journals 2,269; Microforms 56,034; Bk Vols 231,007; Per Subs 632
Automation Activity & Vendor Info: (Cataloging) SirsiDynix; (Circulation) SirsiDynix
Wireless access
Function: Res libr
Partic in TexSHARE - Texas State Library & Archives Commission
Open Mon-Thurs 7:30am-10pm, Fri 7:30-6, Sat 9-6

S DEGOLYER & MACNAUGHTON LIBRARY, 5001 Spring Valley Rd, Ste 800 E, 75244. SAN 316-2184. Tel: 214-368-6391. FAX: 214-369-4061. Web Site: www.demac.com. *Library Contact,* Nicole Hurley
Founded 1939
Library Holdings: Bk Titles 9,000; Per Subs 50
Subject Interests: Econ, Energy minerals, Engr, Geol, Natural gas, Petroleum
Wireless access
Restriction: Staff use only

GM DEPARTMENT OF VETERANS AFFAIRS NORTH TEXAS HEALTH CARE SYSTEM, Library Service, Library Service 142D, 4500 S Lancaster Rd, 75216. SAN 316-2737. Tel: 214-857-1245. Interlibrary Loan Service Tel: 214-857-1248. E-mail: ntxlibrary@va.gov. *Libr Tech,* Penny Greathouse; Staff 4 (MLS 3, Non-MLS 1)
Founded 1940
Wireless access
Open Mon-Fri 8-4

G ENVIRONMENTAL PROTECTION AGENCY*, EPA Region 6 Sunder Ram Library, 1445 Ross Ave, Ste 1200, 75202. SAN 316-2222. Tel: 214-665-6424. FAX: 214-665-8574. E-mail: library_region6@epa.gov. Web Site: www.epa.gov/epalibraries/region-6-library-services. *Librn,* Tanya Slaughter; Staff 1 (MLS 1)
Founded 1971
Library Holdings: Bk Titles 2,600
Special Collections: EPA Documents; Risk Assessment; USDA Soil Surveys for Arkansas, Louisiana, Oklahoma, New Mexico & Texas
Subject Interests: Environ issues
Automation Activity & Vendor Info: (Cataloging) OCLC Online
Function: Govt ref serv, ILL available, Photocopying/Printing, Ref serv available
Partic in OCLC-LVIS
Restriction: Circulates for staff only, In-house use for visitors, Open by appt only, Open to pub for ref & circ; with some limitations, Photo ID required for access

S FEDERAL RESERVE BANK OF DALLAS LIBRARY*, 2200 N Pearl St, 75201. SAN 316-2257. Tel: 214-922-6000, Ext 5182. FAX: 214-922-5222. E-mail: FedHistory@dal.frb.org. Web Site: www.dallasfed.org. *Mgr, Libr Serv,* Fanying Kong; Staff 4 (MLS 4)
Founded 1921
Library Holdings: Bk Titles 19,000; Per Subs 750
Subject Interests: Banking, Econ, Finance, Labor, Petroleum, SW region
Automation Activity & Vendor Info: (Acquisitions) SirsiDynix; (Cataloging) SirsiDynix; (Circulation) SirsiDynix; (ILL) OCLC; (OPAC) SirsiDynix; (Serials) SirsiDynix
Wireless access
Restriction: Open by appt only, Open to pub for ref only

R FIRST BAPTIST CHURCH OF DALLAS*, Truett Memorial Library, 1707 San Jacinto, 75201. SAN 316-2273. Tel: 214-969-2442. E-mail: truettlibrary@firstdallas.org. Web Site: firstdallas.monkpreview2.com/library, www.firstdallas.org/ministries/truett-memorial-library. *Dir,* Ruthe Turner
Founded 1898
Library Holdings: CDs 707; DVDs 1,193; e-books 5,000; Bk Titles 9,000; Bk Vols 18,000
Special Collections: Children's Library; Contemporary Christian Nonfiction; Inspirational Fiction
Subject Interests: Archives, Missions hist, Relig
Automation Activity & Vendor Info: (Cataloging) Book Systems; (Circulation) Book Systems; (OPAC) Book Systems
Wireless access
Open Mon 1-4, Tues & Thurs 9-4, Wed 9-6
Restriction: Staff & mem only

L HAYNES & BOONE LLP*, Law Library, 2323 Victory Ave, Ste 700, 75219. SAN 326-6044. Tel: 214-651-5711. E-mail: library@haynesboone.com. Web Site: www.haynesboone.com. *Libr Mgr,* Lee Bernstein; E-mail: lee.bernstein@haynesboone.com; *Sr Librn,* David P Bader; Tel: 214-651-5709, E-mail: david.bader@haynesboone.com; *Ref Librn,* Riva Laughlin; E-mail: riva.laughlin@haynesboone.com; *Tech Serv Librn,* Jennifer S Stephens; E-mail: jennifer.stephens@haynesboone.com; Staff 6 (MLS 4, Non-MLS 2)
Founded 1970
Library Holdings: Bk Titles 6,900; Bk Vols 60,000; Per Subs 130
Automation Activity & Vendor Info: (Acquisitions) Inmagic, Inc.; (Cataloging) Inmagic, Inc.; (Serials) Inmagic, Inc.
Wireless access
Open Mon-Fri 8:30-5

S HELLMUTH, OBATA & KASSABAUM, INC LIBRARY*, 717 N Harwood St, Ste 2850 LB 8, 75201. SAN 327-5469. Tel: 214-720-6000. FAX: 214-720-6005. E-mail: dallas@hok.com. Web Site: www.hok.com. *Mgr,* Barbara Burr; E-mail: barbara.burr@hok.com
Subject Interests: Archit, Engr, Interior design, Planning
Wireless access
Restriction: Not open to pub

SR HIGHLAND PARK PRESBYTERIAN CHURCH*, Meyercord Library, 3821 University Blvd, 75205. SAN 327-5647. Tel: 214-526-7457. E-mail: meyercordlibrary@hppc.org. Web Site: www.hppc.org. *Libr Consult,* Margaret Lindstrom; Tel: 214-525-4277
Library Holdings: Bk Vols 16,752
Special Collections: Civil War Pioneers (James Spearman Coll); Unique Birds (Marianne Roach Coll)
Subject Interests: Relig
Open Mon-Fri 8-5, Sun 8-1

R HIGHLAND PARK UNITED METHODIST CHURCH LIBRARY*, 3300 Mockingbird Lane, 75205. SAN 316-2354. Tel: 214-521-3111. Web Site: www.hpumc.org/library. *Libr Coord,* Amy Berry; E-mail: berrya@hpumc.org; Staff 1 (Non-MLS 1)
Founded 1950
Library Holdings: Bk Vols 17,000; Per Subs 14
Special Collections: Large Print Books
Subject Interests: Arts, Educ, Hist, Nature, Psychol, Relig, Travel
Open Mon-Wed 11-2, Sun 9-11

L JACKSON WALKER LLP*, Law Library, Bank of America Plaza, 901 Main St, Ste 6000, 75202. SAN 372-1604. Tel: 214-953-6038. FAX: 214-953-5822. Web Site: www.jw.com. *Dir, Libr & Res Serv,* Greg Lambert; E-mail: glambert@jw.com; *Librn,* Ann H Jeter; E-mail: ajeter@jw.com
Library Holdings: Bk Titles 5,000; Bk Vols 35,000; Per Subs 200
Automation Activity & Vendor Info: (Acquisitions) EOS International; (Cataloging) EOS International; (OPAC) EOS International; (Serials) EOS International
Wireless access
Restriction: Not open to pub

L JONES DAY*, Law Library, 2727 N Harwood St, 75201-1515. SAN 316-2435. Tel: 214-969-4823. FAX: 214-969-5100. Web Site: www.jonesday.com. *Mgr, Libr Serv,* Anne Leather; E-mail: aleather@jonesday.com; *Librn,* John L Adams; Staff 3 (MLS 3)
Library Holdings: Bk Vols 60,203
Wireless access
Open Mon-Fri 9-5

L K&L GATES LIBRARY*, 1717 Main St, Ste 2800, 75201. SAN 321-7906. Tel: 214-939-5510. FAX: 214-939-5849. Web Site: www.klgates.com. *Librn,* Mr Walker Chaffin; E-mail: walker.chaffin@klgates.com; Staff 2 (MLS 2)
Library Holdings: Bk Vols 9,920; Per Subs 400
Subject Interests: Law
Wireless access
Partic in IRSC; Pacer; Proquest Dialog
Restriction: Not open to pub

S NATIONAL ARCHIVES & RECORDS ADMINISTRATION, George W Bush Presidential Library, 2943 SMU Blvd, 75205. Tel: 214-346-1557. FAX: 214-346-1699. E-mail: reference.gwbush@nara.gov. Web Site: www.georgewbushlibrary.gov. *Dir,* Dr Pearl T Ponce; E-mail: pearl.ponce@nara.gov; *Supvry Archivist,* Justin Banks; E-mail: justin.banks@nara.gov
Function: Archival coll
Restriction: Not a lending libr, Open by appt only, Open to pub by appt only

SR PARK CITIES BAPTIST CHURCH*, Media Library, 3933 Northwest Pkwy, 75225. (Mail add: PO Box 12068, 75225-0068), SAN 378-1267. Tel: 214-860-1500. FAX: 214-860-1538. E-mail: library@pcbc.org. Web Site: www.pcbc.org/media/library. *Librn,* Linda Wachel; Tel: 214-860-1593, E-mail: lawachel@pcbc.org; Staff 4 (MLS 2, Non-MLS 2)
Founded 1944. Pop 8,000; Circ 18,000
Library Holdings: Bk Vols 20,000; Per Subs 35
Subject Interests: Theol
Automation Activity & Vendor Info: (Cataloging) Follett Software; (Circulation) Follett Software; (OPAC) Follett Software
Open Tues & Thurs 9-2, Wed 9-8, Sun 8:45-12:15; Tues-Thurs 10-2, Sun 8:45-12:15 (Summer)

§C PARKER UNIVERSITY LIBRARY, 2540 Walnut Hill Lane, 75220. Tel: 214-902-2408. E-mail: asklibrary@parker.edu. Web Site: library.parker.edu. *Dir, Libr Serv,* Tina Berumen; Tel: 214-902-3404, E-mail: tinaberumen@parker.edu; *Academic Success Librarian,* Samantha Tran; E-mail: samanthatran@parker.edu; *Digital Ref Librn,* Lydia Obregon; Tel: 972-438-6932, Ext 7517, E-mail: lobregon@parker.edu; *Health Sci Librn,* Amy Ferguson; Tel: 972-438-6932, Ext 1846, E-mail: amyferguson@parker.edu
Library Holdings: e-books 375,000; e-journals 17,000; Bk Vols 3,000; Videos 20,000
Automation Activity & Vendor Info: (OPAC) Ex Libris Group
Wireless access
Function: Online Chat, Study rm
Partic in Amigos Library Services, Inc; Chiropractic Libr Consortium; Healthline; Med Libr Asn, Southern Chapter; OCLC Online Computer Library Center, Inc; TexSHARE - Texas State Library & Archives Commission
Restriction: Borrowing privileges limited to fac & registered students

C PAUL QUINN COLLEGE*, Zale Library, 3837 Simpson Stuart Rd, 75241. SAN 316-8328. Tel: 214-379-5576. Web Site: www.pqc.edu/zale-library. *Dir,* Clarice Weeks; E-mail: cweeks@pqc.edu
Library Holdings: Bk Vols 80,000; Per Subs 163
Special Collections: Afro-American Ethnic & Cultural Coll; AME Church Archives; College Archives
Automation Activity & Vendor Info: (Cataloging) Ex Libris Group; (Circulation) Ex Libris Group; (OPAC) Ex Libris Group
Wireless access
Open Mon-Fri 8:30-5

S PEROT MUSEUM OF NATURE & SCIENCE, E W Mudge Jr Ornithology Library, 2021 Postal Way, 75212. (Mail add: 2201 N Field St, 75201), SAN 372-6940. Tel: 214-428-5555. Web Site: www.perotmuseum.org. *Coll Mgr,* Karen Morton; E-mail: karen.morton@perotmuseum.org
Founded 1985
Library Holdings: Bk Titles 1,510; Bk Vols 2,494
Special Collections: Illustrated Ornithological Works, 1556 to present; Travel Histories, 1600 to present
Restriction: Open by appt only

R PLEASANT GROVE CHRISTIAN CHURCH LIBRARY*, 1324 Pleasant Dr, 75217. SAN 316-2494. Tel: 214-391-3159. FAX: 214-391-3150. E-mail: pgcc1324@sbcglobal.net. *Librn,* Mary Simms
Library Holdings: Bk Vols 4,000
Restriction: Mem only, Not open to pub

SOUTHERN METHODIST UNIVERSITY

CR BRIDWELL LIBRARY-PERKINS SCHOOL OF THEOLOGY*, 6005 Bishop Blvd, 75205. (Mail add: PO Box 750476, 75275-0476), SAN 361-5189. Tel: 214-768-3483. Circulation Tel: 214-768-3441. Interlibrary Loan Service Tel: 214-768-3984. Reference Tel: 214-768-4046. FAX: 214-768-4295. E-mail: bridadmin@smu.edu. Web Site: www.smu.edu/bridwell. *Dir & J S Bridwell Endowed Librn,* Roberta Schaafsma; *Assoc Dir,* James McMillin; *Head, Spec Coll,* Daniel Slive; *Ref Librn,* Jane Elder; *Ref & Digital Librn,* David Schmersal; Staff 20 (MLS 11, Non-MLS 9)
Founded 1915
Library Holdings: Microforms 138,000; Bk Vols 375,200; Per Subs 1,120
Special Collections: 15th Century Printing Coll; Bible Coll; Methodism Coll; Savonarola Coll
Subject Interests: Bibles, Fine binding, Methodist hist, Reformation, Theol
Automation Activity & Vendor Info: (Cataloging) Ex Libris Group; (Circulation) Ex Libris Group; (Course Reserve) Ex Libris Group; (ILL) OCLC ILLiad; (OPAC) Ex Libris Group
Partic in OCLC Online Computer Library Center, Inc; Southwest Area Theological Library Association
Publications: Exhibition Catalogs

Open Mon-Thurs 8am-11pm, Fri 8-6, Sat 10-6, Sun 2-10
Friends of the Library Group

C CENTRAL UNIVERSITY LIBRARIES*, 6414 Robert S Hyer Lane, 75205. (Mail add: PO Box 750135, 75275-0135). Tel: 214-768-2401. Circulation Tel: 214-768-2329. Interlibrary Loan Service Tel: 214-768-2328. Reference Tel: 214-768-2326. Automation Services Tel: 214-768-3229. FAX: 214-768-3815. Reference FAX: 214-768-1842. Web Site: www.smu.edu/cul. *Dean & Dir,* Gillian McCombs; E-mail: gmccombs@smu.edu; *Asst Dean, Scholarly Res & Research Serv,* Mary Hollerich; Tel: 214-768-4960. Subject Specialists: *Illinois,* Mary Hollerich; Staff 82 (MLS 38, Non-MLS 44)
Founded 1915. Enrl 10,929; Fac 1,156; Highest Degree: Doctorate
Library Holdings: CDs 19,869; DVDs 18,329; e-books 983,319; e-journals 71,262; Bk Titles 2,453,431; Bk Vols 3,100,932
Special Collections: State Document Depository; US Document Depository
Subject Interests: Classics, Geol, Texana, Theatre, Transportation, Western Americana
Automation Activity & Vendor Info: (Acquisitions) Ex Libris Group; (Cataloging) Ex Libris Group; (Circulation) Ex Libris Group; (Course Reserve) Ex Libris Group; (ILL) OCLC ILLiad; (OPAC) Ex Libris Group; (Serials) SerialsSolutions
Function: 24/7 Electronic res, Archival coll, Art exhibits, Audio & video playback equip for onsite use, Bks on CD, Computers for patron use, Distance learning, Doc delivery serv, E-Reserves, Electronic databases & coll, Free DVD rentals, ILL available, Internet access, Microfiche/film & reading machines, Movies, Music CDs, Online cat, Online ref, Outreach serv, Photocopying/Printing, Ref & res, Ref serv available, Res libr, Scanner, Spanish lang bks, Spoken cassettes & CDs, Study rm, Telephone ref, VHS videos, Wheelchair accessible, Workshops
Partic in Amigos Library Services, Inc; Greater Western Library Alliance; OCLC Online Computer Library Center, Inc; TexSHARE - Texas State Library & Archives Commission
Restriction: 24-hr pass syst for students only, Badge access after hrs, Open to students, fac, staff & alumni, Pub use on premises
Friends of the Library Group

C DEGOLYER LIBRARY OF SPECIAL COLLECTIONS*, 6404 Robert S Hyer Lane, 75275. (Mail add: PO Box 750396, 75275). Tel: 214-768-3234. FAX: 214-768-1565. E-mail: degolyer@mail.smu.edu. Web Site: www.smu.edu/cul/degolyer. *Dir,* Russell Martin; E-mail: rlmartin@smu.edu; *Cataloger/Ref Librn,* Cynthia Franco; Tel: 214-768-3605, E-mail: cafranco@smu.edu; *Archivist,* Pamalla Anderson; Tel: 214-768-0829, E-mail: andersonp@smu.edu; *Archivist,* Joan Gosnell; Tel: 214-768-2261, E-mail: jgosne@smu.edu; *Curator,* Anne Peterson; Tel: 214-768-2661. Subject Specialists: *Women's hist,* Pamalla Anderson; *Photog,* Anne Peterson; Staff 6 (MLS 3, Non-MLS 3)
Library Holdings: Bk Titles 143,326
Special Collections: Archives of Women of the Southwest; Belo Archives; Budner Theodore Roosevelt Coll; Horton Foote Archive; JC Penney Archives; Modern Authors Coll; Photographs; Railroads (Baldwin Archives); SMU Archives; Stanley Marcus Archive; Texana; Texas Instruments Coll; Trade Catalogs; Transportation Coll; Western Americana Coll
Subject Interests: Bus hist, Travel, Voyages, Western Americana
Partic in OCLC Online Computer Library Center, Inc
Publications: Book Club of Texas; Informal Publications & Guides to the Collections; The DeGolyer Library Publication Series
Restriction: Closed stack, Non-circulating of rare bks

C FONDREN LIBRARY*, 6414 Robert S Hyer Lane, 75205. (Mail add: PO Box 750135, 75275-0135). Tel: 214-768-2401. Circulation Tel: 214-768-2329. Interlibrary Loan Service Tel: 214-768-2328. Reference Tel: 214-768-2326. Automation Services Tel: 214-768-3229. FAX: 214-768-3815. Reference FAX: 214-768-1842. Web Site: www.smu.edu/cul/flc. *Dean & Dir,* Gillian McCombs; E-mail: gmccombs@smu.edu; *Asst Dean, Scholarly Res & Research Serv,* Mary Hollerich; Tel: 214-768-4960. Subject Specialists: *Illinois,* Mary Hollerich
Enrl 10,929; Fac 1,156; Highest Degree: Doctorate
Library Holdings: Bk Vols 1,792,981
Special Collections: State Document Depository; US Document Depository
Subject Interests: Am hist, Anthrop, Classical studies, Contemporary biog & lit, Earth sci, Econ, English lit (18th Century), English lit (19th Century), Humanities, Polit sci, Sciences, Soc sci, Tex hist
Automation Activity & Vendor Info: (Acquisitions) Ex Libris Group

C HAMON ARTS LIBRARY*, 6101 N Bishop Blvd, 75275. (Mail add: PO Box 750356, 75275-0356). Tel: 214-768-1855. Circulation Tel: 214-768-3813. Reference Tel: 214-768-1853. FAX: 214-768-1800. Web Site: www.smu.edu/cul/hamon/index.asp. *Music Dir,* Jolene de Varges; *Film, Theatre & Communications Librn, Head, Jones Film & Video Coll,* Amy Turner; E-mail: aeturner@smu.edu; *Head, Spec Coll,* Sam Ratcliffe; E-mail: sratclif@smu.edu; *Art & Dance Librn,* Beverly Mitchell; E-mail: bmitchel@smu.edu; *Supvr, AV Serv & Coll,* Maristella Feustle; *Curator, Spec Coll,* Ellen Buie Niewyk; E-mail: eniewyk@smu.edu. Subject Specialists: *Music,* Jolene de Varges; *Communications, Theatre,* Amy Turner; *Art, Art hist, Dance,* Beverly Mitchell
Founded 1990
Library Holdings: AV Mats 38,541; Bk Vols 157,726; Per Subs 300
Automation Activity & Vendor Info: (Cataloging) Ex Libris Group; (Circulation) Ex Libris Group

C INSTITUTE FOR STUDY OF EARTH & MAN READING ROOM*, N L Heroy Science Hall, Rm 129, 3225 Daniels Ave, 75275. (Mail add: PO Box 750274, 75275-0274). Tel: 214-768-2430. FAX: 214-768-4289. Web Site: www.smu.edu/cul/isemrr. *Librn,* John Phinney; E-mail: jphinney@smu.edu
Library Holdings: Bk Vols 9,840; Per Subs 30
Automation Activity & Vendor Info: (Cataloging) Ex Libris Group; (Circulation) Ex Libris Group

SR TEMPLE EMANU-EL*, Alex F Weisberg Library, 8500 Hillcrest Rd, 75225. SAN 361-5308. Tel: 214-706-0000, Ext 185. FAX: 214-706-0025. Web Site: www.tedallas.org/learning/libraries. *Dir, Libr & Archives,* Anjelica Ruiz; E-mail: aruiz@tedallas.org; *Early Childhood Librn,* Jeanne Zamutt; E-mail: jzamutt@tedallas.org
Founded 1957
Library Holdings: Braille Volumes 4; DVDs 97; Large Print Bks 12; Bk Vols 20,000; Spec Interest Per Sub 2
Subject Interests: Judaica, Related humanities
Automation Activity & Vendor Info: (Cataloging) Follett Software; (Circulation) Follett Software
Wireless access
Open Mon-Fri 9-5, Sun 9-12
Branches:
WILLIAM P BUDNER YOUTH LIBRARY, 8500 Hillcrest Rd, 75225. *Dir, Libr & Archives,* Anjelica Ruiz; Tel: 214-706-0000, Ext 114, E-mail: aruiz@tedallas.org
Library Holdings: Bk Vols 5,000
Subject Interests: Judaica, Youth

M TEXAS HEALTH PRESBYTERIAN HOSPITAL LIBRARY*, Green Learning Center, 8200 Walnut Hill Lane, 75231. SAN 371-8816. Tel: 214-345-2310. E-mail: planetree@texashealth.org. Web Site: www.texashealth.org/locations/texas-health-dallas.
Founded 1966
Library Holdings: Bk Titles 311; Bk Vols 650; Per Subs 181
Subject Interests: Allied health, Healthcare admin, Med, Nursing
Wireless access
Function: Health sci info serv, Internet access, Ref serv available
Open Mon-Fri 8-5
Restriction: In-house use for visitors, Internal circ only, Med & nursing staff, patients & families, Non-circulating to the pub, Restricted borrowing privileges

M TEXAS SCOTTISH RITE HOSPITAL, Brandon Carrell MD Medical Library, 2222 Welborn St, 75219. SAN 329-1340. Tel: 214-559-5000, 214-559-7573. Web Site: scottishriteforchildren.org/med/education. *Library Contact,* Mary Anne Fernandez; E-mail: maryanne.fernandez@tsrh.org
Founded 1979
Library Holdings: Bk Titles 800; Per Subs 100
Special Collections: History of Pediatric Orthopedics
Subject Interests: Neurology, Orthopedics, Pediatrics
Automation Activity & Vendor Info: (Cataloging) LibraryWorld, Inc; (OPAC) LibraryWorld, Inc; (Serials) EBSCO Online
Wireless access
Function: Computers for patron use, Doc delivery serv, Electronic databases & coll, Health sci info serv, Internet access, Online cat, Orientations, Photocopying/Printing, Wheelchair accessible
Partic in Health Libraries Information Network; National Network of Libraries of Medicine Region 3
Restriction: Employees only, External users must contact libr, In-house use for visitors

CM TEXAS WOMAN'S UNIVERSITY*, Institute of Health Sciences Dallas Library, 5500 Southwestern Medical Ave, 75235-7200. SAN 316-2621. Tel: 214-689-6580. Web Site: www.twu.edu/library. *Libr Mgr,* John Humphrey; E-mail: jhumphrey2@twu.edu; Staff 5 (MLS 3, Non-MLS 2)
Founded 1966. Highest Degree: Doctorate
Library Holdings: Bk Vols 12,000; Per Subs 160
Subject Interests: Health studies, Nursing, Occupational therapy, Phys therapy
Automation Activity & Vendor Info: (Acquisitions) Ex Libris Group; (Cataloging) Ex Libris Group; (Circulation) Ex Libris Group; (Course Reserve) Ex Libris Group; (OPAC) Ex Libris Group; (Serials) Ex Libris Group
Wireless access
Partic in OCLC Online Computer Library Center, Inc
Open Mon-Thurs 7:30am-9pm, Fri 7:30-5, Sat 10-2
Friends of the Library Group

L THOMPSON & KNIGHT*, Law Library, One Arts Plaza, 1722 Routh St, Ste 1500, 75201. SAN 316-263X. Tel: 214-969-1350. FAX: 214-969-1751. E-mail: Libraryr@tklaw.com. Web Site: www.tklaw.com. *Mgr, Libr Res,* Angela Kennedy; E-mail: angela.kennedy@tklaw.com; Staff 8 (MLS 3, Non-MLS 5)
Founded 1914
Library Holdings: Bk Titles 2,500; Bk Vols 40,000
Automation Activity & Vendor Info: (Cataloging) EOS International
Wireless access
Function: ILL available
Restriction: Open to staff only

CM UNIVERSITY OF TEXAS SOUTHWESTERN MEDICAL CENTER*, Health Sciences Digital Library & Learning Center, 5323 Harry Hines Blvd, 75390-9049. SAN 316-2729. Tel: 214-648-2001. FAX: 214-648-2826. Web Site: library.utsouthwestern.edu. *Asst VPres, Libr Serv,* Kelly Gonzalez; Tel: 214-648-2626, E-mail: kelly.gonzalez@utsouthwestern.edu; *Assoc Dir,* Richard Wayne; Tel: 214-645-4957, E-mail: richard.wayne@utsouthwestern.edu; *Mgr, Archives & Spec Coll,* Chianta Dorsey; Tel: 214-648-8991, E-mail: chianta.dorsey@utsouthwestern.edu; *Doc Serv Coordr, Mgr, Libr Admin,* Kristy Reynolds; Tel: 214-648-9070, E-mail: kristy.reynolds@utsouthwestern.edu; Staff 21 (MLS 18, Non-MLS 3)
Founded 1943. Enrl 3,429; Fac 4,056; Highest Degree: Doctorate
Library Holdings: e-journals 90,504; Bk Titles 458,589; Per Subs 24,200
Special Collections: History of Health Sciences Coll
Subject Interests: Biomed sci
Wireless access
Function: Res libr
Partic in National Network of Libraries of Medicine Region 3; OCLC Online Computer Library Center, Inc; South Central Academic Medical Libraries Consortium; UT-System
Restriction: Not a lending libr

DAYTON

P JONES PUBLIC LIBRARY*, 801 South Cleveland, Ste A, 77535. SAN 375-3328. Tel: 936-258-7060. Web Site: www.jonespubliclibrary.org. *Dir,* Sherry Sikes; E-mail: ssikes@daytontx.org
Founded 1980. Pop 20,000; Circ 54,812
Library Holdings: Bk Titles 29,000; Per Subs 66
Wireless access
Open Mon-Thurs 9:30-5:30, Fri & Sat 10-2
Friends of the Library Group

DE LEON

P DE LEON CITY COUNTY LIBRARY*, 125 E Reynosa St, 76444-1862. SAN 316-2788. Tel: 254-893-2417. FAX: 254-893-4915. E-mail: dllib@cctc.net. Web Site: www.cityofdeleon.org/departments/library. *Librn,* Rebecca Hurteau; *Asst Librn,* Mary Young
Pop 4,231
Library Holdings: Bk Vols 10,710
Automation Activity & Vendor Info: (Cataloging) LibLime; (Circulation) LibLime
Wireless access
Partic in TexSHARE - Texas State Library & Archives Commission
Open Mon-Fri 9-5

DECATUR

P DECATUR PUBLIC LIBRARY*, 1700 Hwy 51 S, 76234-9292. SAN 316-2796. Tel: 940-393-0290. FAX: 940-627-6763. Web Site: www.decaturpubliclibrary.com. *Dir,* Dawn Wilbert; E-mail: dwilbert@decaturtx.org; Staff 6 (MLS 2, Non-MLS 4)
Founded 1970. Pop 28,000; Circ 110,428
Oct 2021-Sept 2022 Income $538,907. Mats Exp $54,100, Books $38,000, Per/Ser (Incl. Access Fees) $900, AV Mat $8,000, Electronic Ref Mat (Incl. Access Fees) $4,000. Sal $333,000 (Prof $114,000)
Library Holdings: Bk Titles 52,191; Bk Vols 58,714; Per Subs 26
Special Collections: Texas Coll
Automation Activity & Vendor Info: (Cataloging) Koha; (Circulation) Koha; (OPAC) Koha
Wireless access
Function: 24/7 Electronic res, 24/7 Online cat, Activity rm, Adult bk club, Art exhibits, Audiobks via web, AV serv, Bi-weekly Writer's Group, Bks on CD, Butterfly Garden, Chess club, Children's prog, Computer training, Computers for patron use, Electronic databases & coll, Free DVD rentals, Holiday prog, ILL available, Internet access, Life-long learning prog for all ages, Magazines, Mango lang, Movies, Online cat, Photocopying/Printing, Preschool outreach, Preschool reading prog, Printer for laptops & handheld devices, Prog for adults, Prog for children & young adult, Ref serv available, Scanner, Spanish lang bks, Story hour, Summer reading prog, Teen prog, Wheelchair accessible
Partic in MetroShare Libraries; North Texas Library Consortium; Partners Library Action Network
Open Mon, Wed & Fri 10-6, Tues & Thurs 10-7, Sat 10-2
Friends of the Library Group

DEER PARK

P DEER PARK PUBLIC LIBRARY*, 3009 Center St, 77536. SAN 316-280X. Tel: 281-478-7208. FAX: 281-478-7212. E-mail: library@deerparktx.org. Web Site: www.deerparktx.gov/2054/library. *Libr Serv Dir,* Rebecca Pool; E-mail: rpool@deerparktx.org; *Ch,* Susan Zykorie; E-mail: szykorie@deerparktx.org; *Circ Supvr,* Sonia Guzman; Staff 4 (MLS 2, Non-MLS 2)
Founded 1962. Pop 31,000; Circ 163,567
Library Holdings: AV Mats 2,519; Bk Vols 57,300; Per Subs 250
Special Collections: CAER Coll
Subject Interests: Commun awareness, Emergency response
Automation Activity & Vendor Info: (Cataloging) Innovative Interfaces, Inc; (Circulation) Innovative Interfaces, Inc; (OPAC) Innovative Interfaces, Inc
Wireless access
Open Mon & Wed 10-6, Tues & Thurs 10-8, Fri & Sat 10-5
Friends of the Library Group

DEL RIO

J SOUTHWEST TEXAS JUNIOR COLLEGE*, Del Rio Campus Library, 207 Wildcat Dr, 78840. Tel: 830-703-1563. Web Site: library.swtjc.edu. *Res Tech,* Dora Padilla; E-mail: dzpadila@swtjc.edu; *Res Tech,* Evelio Valiente; E-mail: evaliente17474@swtjc.edu
Wireless access
Function: ILL available, Photocopying/Printing, Study rm
Open Mon-Thurs 7:30am-9pm, Fri 8-4, Sun 1-6

P VAL VERDE COUNTY LIBRARY*, 300 Spring St, 78840. SAN 316-2850. Tel: 830-774-7595. FAX: 830-774-7607. E-mail: library@valverdecounty.texas.gov. Web Site: valverdecounty.texas.gov/181/library. *Asst Admin,* Richard D'Avy; *Librn,* David Bond; E-mail: dbond@valverdecounty.texas.gov; *Ch,* Reba Benavides; *Tech Serv Librn,* Adrian Gonzalez; *Circ Supvr,* Victor Cirilo; Staff 6 (MLS 1, Non-MLS 5)
Founded 1940. Pop 48,000; Circ 90,000
Library Holdings: AV Mats 3,000; e-books 1,500; Electronic Media & Resources 100; Bk Titles 70,000; Bk Vols 100,000; Per Subs 200
Special Collections: John R Brinkley Coll; Local History (Del Rio Coll)
Subject Interests: Local hist, Texana
Automation Activity & Vendor Info: (Cataloging) Follett Software; (Circulation) Follett Software; (ILL) OCLC FirstSearch; (OPAC) Follett Software
Wireless access
Function: Adult bk club, After school storytime, Archival coll, Audio & video playback equip for onsite use, Bilingual assistance for Spanish patrons, Bk reviews (Group), Bks on cassette, Bks on CD, Children's prog, Computer training, Computers for patron use, E-Reserves, Electronic databases & coll, Family literacy, ILL available, Mail & tel request accepted, Music CDs, Online cat, Photocopying/Printing, Preschool outreach, Prog for adults, Prog for children & young adult, Ref serv available, Scanner, Senior computer classes, Summer reading prog, Teen prog, Telephone ref, VHS videos, Wheelchair accessible
Partic in Partners Library Action Network
Open Mon-Thurs 10-7, Fri 10-6, Sat & Sun 1-5
Friends of the Library Group

DEL VALLE

P EAST TRAVIS GATEWAY LIBRARY DISTRICT*, Elroy Community Library, 13512 Fm 812, 78617. Tel: 512-243-1981. E-mail: contact.us@etgld.org. Web Site: www.etgld.org. *Dir,* Joe D Gunter
Library Holdings: Bk Vols 3,150
Wireless access
Partic in Partners Library Action Network
Open Mon & Thurs 11-6, Fri & Sat 11-5
Friends of the Library Group
Branches: 1
GARFIELD LIBRARY, 5121 Albert Brown Dr, 78617. Tel: 512-247-7371. *Br Supvr,* Jennifer Nigoche; E-mail: jnigoche@etgld.org; *Asst Librn,* Brittany Burke
Open Mon-Thurs 10-7, Fri 10-5, Sat 10-3

DELL CITY

P GRACE GREBING PUBLIC LIBRARY, 110 N Main St, 79837. (Mail add: PO Box 37, 79837-0037), SAN 376-4362. Tel: 915-964-2663. FAX: 915-964-2468. Web Site: www.dellcityisd.net.
Library Holdings: Bk Vols 16,346; Per Subs 28

Automation Activity & Vendor Info: (Cataloging) Follett Software; (Circulation) Follett Software; (ILL) Follett Software; (OPAC) Follett Software
Wireless access
Restriction: Not open to pub, Open to students

DENISON

P DENISON PUBLIC LIBRARY*, 300 W Gandy St, 75020-3153. SAN 316-2877. Tel: 903-465-1797. FAX: 903-465-1130. E-mail: library@cityofdenison.com. Web Site: cityofdenison.com/library. *Dir,* Greg Mitchell; E-mail: gmitchell@cityofdenison.com; *Assoc Dir/Librn,* Steve McGowen; E-mail: smcgowen@cityofdenison.com; *Youth Serv Librn,* Deborah Wise; E-mail: dwise@cityofdenison.com; Staff 3 (MLS 3)
Founded 1936. Pop 22,300; Circ 162,151
Library Holdings: Bk Titles 98,097; Per Subs 149
Special Collections: Area History & Books by Area Authors (Texoma Coll), print, bks, pamphlet
Subject Interests: Genealogy
Automation Activity & Vendor Info: (Acquisitions) Biblionix; (Cataloging) Biblionix
Wireless access
Partic in Partners Library Action Network
Open Mon, Wed & Fri 9-6, Tues & Thurs 9-7, Sat 9-5
Friends of the Library Group

J GRAYSON COUNTY COLLEGE LIBRARY*, 6101 Grayson Dr, 75020-8299. SAN 316-2885. Tel: 903-463-8637. FAX: 903-465-4123. E-mail: library@grayson.edu. Web Site: grayson.edu/library. *Libr Dir,* Lisa Hebert; E-mail: lharris@grayson.edu; *Ref Librn,* Roland Commons; E-mail: commonsr@grayson.edu; Staff 4 (MLS 4)
Founded 1965. Enrl 3,843; Fac 126
Library Holdings: Bk Titles 60,000; Per Subs 50
Automation Activity & Vendor Info: (Cataloging) TLC (The Library Corporation); (Circulation) TLC (The Library Corporation); (ILL) OCLC; (OPAC) TLC (The Library Corporation)
Wireless access
Partic in Amigos Library Services, Inc
Open Mon-Thurs 8-6, Fri 8-5, Sun 2-6

DENTON

P DENTON PUBLIC LIBRARY*, Emily Fowler Central Library, 502 Oakland St, 76201. Tel: 940-349-8752. Interlibrary Loan Service Tel: 940-349-8760. Administration Tel: 940-349-8754. Automation Services Tel: 940-349-8772. FAX: 940-349-8101. Administration FAX: 940-349-8123. E-mail: library@cityofdenton.com. Web Site: www.dentonlibrary.com. *Dir of Libr,* Jennifer Bekker; Tel: 940-349-8753, E-mail: Jennifer.Bekker@cityofdenton.com; *Libr Mgr,* Kimberly Wells; E-mail: kimberly.wells@cityofdenton.com; *Mgr, Br,* Stacy Sizemore; Tel: 940-349-8761, E-mail: stacy.sizemore@cityofdenton.com; *Tech Serv Mgr,* Jennifer Reaves; E-mail: jennifer.reaves@cityofdenton.com; *Spec Coll,* Laura Douglas; Tel: 940-349-8749, E-mail: laura.douglas@cityofdenton.com; Staff 46.9 (MLS 19, Non-MLS 27.9)
Founded 1949. Pop 136,268; Circ 1,151,962
Oct 2018-Sept 2019 Income (Main & Associated Libraries) $5,774,503, City $5,742,354, Federal $32,149. Mats Exp $616,433. Sal $2,360,530
Special Collections: Genealogy Coll; Municipal Archive; Texas & Denton History Coll, archives, bks, clippings, maps, micro, pamphlets, photog
Automation Activity & Vendor Info: (Acquisitions) Innovative Interfaces, Inc; (Cataloging) Innovative Interfaces, Inc; (Circulation) Innovative Interfaces, Inc; (ILL) Innovative Interfaces, Inc; (OPAC) Innovative Interfaces, Inc; (Serials) Innovative Interfaces, Inc
Wireless access
Function: 24/7 Electronic res, 24/7 Online cat, 3D Printer, Activity rm, Adult bk club, Adult literacy prog, After school storytime, Archival coll, Art exhibits, Art programs, Audiobks via web, Bilingual assistance for Spanish patrons, Bk club(s), Bks on CD, Chess club, Children's prog, Computer training, Computers for patron use, Electronic databases & coll, Equip loans & repairs, Free DVD rentals, Genealogy discussion group, Holiday prog, Home delivery & serv to seniorr ctr & nursing homes, Homebound delivery serv, ILL available, Internet access, Jail serv, Life-long learning prog for all ages, Magazines, Magnifiers for reading, Makerspace, Meeting rooms, Microfiche/film & reading machines, Movies, Music CDs, Online cat, Outreach serv, OverDrive digital audio bks, Photocopying/Printing, Preschool outreach, Printer for laptops & handheld devices, Prog for adults, Prog for children & young adult, Ref & res, Ref serv available, Scanner, Senior computer classes, Senior outreach, Serves people with intellectual disabilities, Spanish lang bks, Spoken cassettes & CDs, STEM programs, Story hour, Study rm, Summer & winter reading prog, Summer reading prog, Tax forms, Teen prog, Telephone ref, Wheelchair accessible, Winter reading prog, Workshops
Partic in OCLC Online Computer Library Center, Inc
Special Services for the Deaf - Assistive tech
Special Services for the Blind - ZoomText magnification & reading software
Open Mon, Wed, Fri & Sat 9-6, Tues & Thurs 9-9, Sun 1-5
Restriction: Authorized patrons, Circ to mem only, In-house use for visitors, Non-resident fee, Pub use on premises, Registered patrons only, Residents only
Friends of the Library Group
Branches: 2
NORTH BRANCH, 3020 N Locust St, 76209. FAX: 940-387-5367. *Mgr,* Rebecca Ivey; E-mail: rebecca.ivey@cityofdenton.com
Open Mon-Wed 9-9, Thurs-Sat 9-6, Sun 1-5
SOUTH BRANCH, 3228 Teasley Lane, 76210, SAN 376-1452. FAX: 940-349-8383. *Mgr,* Stacy Sizemore; E-mail: stacy.sizemore@cityofdenton.com
Open Mon 12-9, Tues & Thurs-Sat 9-6, Wed 9-9, Sun 1-5
Friends of the Library Group

C UNIVERSITY OF NORTH TEXAS LIBRARIES*, 1155 Union Circle, No 305190, 76203-5017. SAN 361-5510. Tel: 940-565-2413. Administration Tel: 940-565-3025. Circulation E-mail: circ@library.unt.edu. Web Site: www.library.unt.edu. *Dean of Libr,* Diane Bruxvoort; E-mail: diane.bruxvoort@unt.edu; *Assoc Dean Coll Mgt,* Sian Brannon; Tel: 940-891-6945, E-mail: sian.brannon@unt.edu; *Assoc Dean for Special Libraries,* Sue Parks; Tel: 940-369-7249, E-mail: sue.parks@unt.edu; *Assoc Dean for Digital Libraries,* Mark Phillips; Tel: 940-565-2415, E-mail: mark.phillips@unt.edu; *Assoc Dean, Pub Serv,* Mary Ann Venner; Tel: 940-565-2868, E-mail: maryann.venner@unt.edu; *Asst Dean, External Relations,* Dreanna Belden; Tel: 940-369-8740, E-mail: dreanna.belden@unt.edu; *Asst Dean, Finance & Admin,* A K Khan; Tel: 940-369-8165, E-mail: mohammadayub.khan@unt.edu; *Asst Dean, Facilities & Systems,* Scott Jackson; Tel: 940-565-3024, E-mail: scott.jackson@unt.edu; *Head, Learning Serv,* Julie A Leuzinger; Tel: 940-565-3980, E-mail: julie.leuzinger@unt.edu
Founded 1890. Enrl 41,000; Fac 1,200; Highest Degree: Doctorate
Library Holdings: e-books 1,151,032; Microforms 3,877,996; Bk Vols 2,123,159
Special Collections: Jean-Baptiste Lully Coll; Miniature Book Coll; Portal to Texas History Electronic Coll; Weaver Coll. Oral History; State Document Depository; US Document Depository
Automation Activity & Vendor Info: (Acquisitions) Innovative Interfaces, Inc; (Cataloging) Innovative Interfaces, Inc; (Circulation) Innovative Interfaces, Inc; (Course Reserve) Innovative Interfaces, Inc; (ILL) Innovative Interfaces, Inc; (Media Booking) Innovative Interfaces, Inc; (OPAC) Innovative Interfaces, Inc; (Serials) Innovative Interfaces, Inc
Wireless access
Partic in Amigos Library Services, Inc
Departmental Libraries:
DALLAS CAMPUS LIBRARY, 7350 University Hills Blvd, 3rd Flr, Dallas, 75241. Tel: 972-338-1616. E-mail: library@untdallas.edu. Web Site: library.untdallas.edu. *Librn,* Brenda Robertson; Tel: 972-338-1617, E-mail: brenda.robertson@untdallas.edu; *Librn,* Robert Taylor; E-mail: robert.taylor@untdallas.edu; Staff 2 (MLS 2)
Founded 1999
Library Holdings: Bk Titles 756; Videos 132
Open Mon-Thurs 8-8, Fri & Sat 8-5, Sun 12-5

DENVER CITY

P YOAKUM COUNTY / CECIL BICKLEY LIBRARY*, 205 W Fourth St, 79323. SAN 316-2907. Tel: 806-592-2754. FAX: 806-592-2439. E-mail: ycdclib_circ_comments@yahoo.com. *Librn,* Ginger Wilson; E-mail: ycdc_79323@hotmail.com; *Asst Librn,* Maria Cortez
Founded 1957. Pop 8,000; Circ 63,130
Library Holdings: Bk Vols 45,000; Per Subs 70
Automation Activity & Vendor Info: (Cataloging) Biblionix; (Circulation) Biblionix
Wireless access
Open Mon-Fri 9-5:30

DESOTO

P DESOTO PUBLIC LIBRARY*, 211 E Pleasant Run Rd, Ste C, 75115. SAN 370-7423. Tel: 972-230-9656. Circulation Tel: 972-230-9665. Reference Tel: 972-230-9661. Administration Tel: 972-230-9658. Automation Services Tel: 972-230-9660. FAX: 972-230-5797. Web Site: www.desototexas.gov/110/Library. *Managing Dir,* Mr Kerry McGeath; E-mail: kmcgeath@desototexas.gov; *Adult Serv Supvr,* Angela Alford; E-mail: aalford@desototexas.gov; *Supvr, Ch Serv, Supvr, Youth Serv,* Janelle Valera; *Circ Supvr,* Marquenez Runnels; E-mail: mrunnels@desototexas.gov; *Tech Serv Supvr,* Chad Hetterley; Staff 9 (MLS 4, Non-MLS 5)
Founded 1943. Pop 50,000
Library Holdings: Bk Titles 80,000; Per Subs 125

Automation Activity & Vendor Info: (Cataloging) Innovative Interfaces, Inc; (Circulation) Innovative Interfaces, Inc; (OPAC) Innovative Interfaces, Inc
Wireless access
Partic in Partners Library Action Network
Open Mon-Thurs 10-8, Fri 10-6, Sat 9-5
Friends of the Library Group

DEVINE

P DRISCOLL PUBLIC LIBRARY*, 202 E Hondo Ave, 78016. (Mail add: c/o City of Devine, 303 S Teel Dr, 78016), SAN 316-2915. Tel: 830-663-2993. FAX: 830-663-6380. E-mail: driscoll.library@gmail.com. *Head Librn,* Debra DuBose
Founded 1965. Pop 7,362; Circ 15,783
Library Holdings: Bk Titles 19,000; Per Subs 20
Automation Activity & Vendor Info: (Cataloging) Biblionix; (Circulation) Biblionix; (OPAC) Biblionix
Function: 24/7 Electronic res, 24/7 Online cat, Audiobks via web, Bks on CD, Children's prog, Computers for patron use, Electronic databases & coll, Free DVD rentals, ILL available, Laminating, Magazines, Movies, OverDrive digital audio bks, Photocopying/Printing, Preschool reading prog, Prog for children & young adult, Scanner, Spanish lang bks, Story hour, Summer reading prog, Tax forms, Writing prog
Open Mon-Fri 10-6
Friends of the Library Group

DIBOLL

P TLL TEMPLE MEMORIAL LIBRARY*, 300 Park St, 75941. SAN 316-2923. Tel: 936-829-5497. FAX: 936-829-5465. Web Site: www.dibolllibrary.com. *Libr Dir,* Justin Barkley; E-mail: justin@dibolllibrary.com; Staff 7 (MLS 1, Non-MLS 6)
Founded 1961. Pop 5,359; Circ 30,775
Jan 2016-Dec 2016 Income $468,570, City $27,000, Locally Generated Income $345,725, Other $75,844. Mats Exp $15,568, Books $13,943, Per/Ser (Incl. Access Fees) $516, AV Mat $1,109. Sal $142,432 (Prof $110,000)
Library Holdings: Bk Titles 44,948; Bk Vols 47,797; Per Subs 26
Special Collections: Judge John Hannah Coll; Large Print Coll; Texana Material (John S Redditt Texas Coll). Oral History
Automation Activity & Vendor Info: (Acquisitions) Baker & Taylor; (Cataloging) OCLC FirstSearch; (Circulation) Biblionix/Apollo; (ILL) Biblionix/Apollo; (Serials) EBSCO Online
Wireless access
Function: Movies, Outreach serv, Story hour, Summer & winter reading prog, Summer reading prog, Tax forms, Teen prog, Telephone ref, Wheelchair accessible, Workshops
Partic in Partners Library Action Network
Special Services for the Deaf - High interest/low vocabulary bks; Interpreter on staff
Special Services for the Blind - Bks on CD; Extensive large print coll; Free checkout of audio mat; Home delivery serv; Large print bks
Open Mon-Fri 9-5:30
Restriction: Authorized personnel only, Borrowing requests are handled by ILL, Circ to mem only, Free to mem, Lending libr only via mail, Non-circulating coll

DICKINSON

P DICKINSON PUBLIC LIBRARY*, 4411 Hwy 3, 77539. SAN 316-2931. Tel: 281-534-3812. Web Site: dickinsonpubliclibrary.org/?b=g&d=a. *Libr Dir,* Julianne Lane; E-mail: jlane@ci.dickinson.tx.us; *Asst Dir, Ch,* Kathy Soehl; E-mail: ksoehl@ci.dickinson.tx.us; Staff 1 (MLS 1)
Founded 1966. Pop 20,826; Circ 89,839
Library Holdings: Audiobooks 1,132; Bk Titles 35,782; Bk Vols 36,889; Per Subs 79; Videos 1,147
Automation Activity & Vendor Info: (Cataloging) Book Systems; (Circulation) Book Systems; (OPAC) Book Systems
Wireless access
Mem of Galveston County Library System
Partic in Houston Area Research Library Consortium; OCLC Online Computer Library Center, Inc
Open Mon-Fri 10-5
Friends of the Library Group

DILLEY

P DILLEY PUBLIC LIBRARY*, 231 W FM 117, 78017. SAN 378-3960. Tel: 830-965-1951. E-mail: dilley.librarian@gmail.com. Web Site: www.dilleylibrary.org. *Librn,* Norma Herrara; *Asst Librn,* Maria Guana
Pop 3,674; Circ 6,256
Library Holdings: AV Mats 200; Bk Titles 15,000
Automation Activity & Vendor Info: (Cataloging) Follett Software; (Circulation) Follett Software; (OPAC) Follett Software
Wireless access
Partic in Partners Library Action Network; TexSHARE - Texas State Library & Archives Commission
Open Mon-Fri 8-5
Friends of the Library Group

DIMMITT

P RHOADS MEMORIAL LIBRARY*, 103 SW Second St, 79027. SAN 316-294X. Tel: 806-647-3532. FAX: 806-647-1038. E-mail: rhoadsmlibrary@gmail.com. Web Site: dimmitt.harringtonlc.org. *Dir,* Gaye Reily; *Asst Dir,* Sulema Oltivero; Staff 2 (Non-MLS 2)
Founded 1971. Pop 7,396; Circ 14,730
Library Holdings: AV Mats 724; Bk Titles 21,068; Bk Vols 34,029; Per Subs 52; Talking Bks 526
Automation Activity & Vendor Info: (Cataloging) SirsiDynix; (Circulation) SirsiDynix; (OPAC) SirsiDynix
Wireless access
Partic in Harrington Library Consortium
Open Tues-Fri 9-6, Sat 9-12

DONNA

P DONNA PUBLIC LIBRARY*, 301 S Main St, 78537. SAN 316-2958. Tel: 956-464-2221. FAX: 956-464-2172. E-mail: arincon@cityofdonna.org. Web Site: cityofdonna.org/departments/public-library, donnapl.com. *Circ Librn,* Veronica Navarro; E-mail: vnavarro@cityofdonna.org; *Ref Librn,* Albert Chambers; E-mail: achambers@cityofdonna.org
Founded 1938. Pop 17,366; Circ 50,134
Library Holdings: Bk Vols 45,715
Special Collections: Spanish Coll; Texas Coll
Automation Activity & Vendor Info: (Cataloging) TLC (The Library Corporation); (Circulation) TLC (The Library Corporation); (OPAC) TLC (The Library Corporation)
Wireless access
Publications: Monthly Calendar; Newsletter (Quarterly)
Mem of Hidalgo County Library System
Open Mon-Fri 8-8
Friends of the Library Group

DRIPPING SPRINGS

P DRIPPING SPRINGS COMMUNITY LIBRARY*, 501 Sportsplex Dr, 78620. SAN 376-480X. Tel: 512-858-7825. FAX: 512-858-2639. Web Site: www.dscl.org. *Libr Dir,* Marcia Atilano; E-mail: director@dscl.org; *Asst Libr Dir,* Tammy Mierow; E-mail: tammy@dscl.org; *Ch,* Marie Kimbrough; E-mail: marie@dscl.org; Staff 13 (MLS 3, Non-MLS 10)
Founded 1985
Library Holdings: Bk Titles 40,000; Per Subs 69; Talking Bks 990; Videos 910
Subject Interests: Local hist
Automation Activity & Vendor Info: (Acquisitions) Biblionix; (Cataloging) Biblionix; (Circulation) Biblionix; (OPAC) Biblionix/Apollo
Wireless access
Function: 24/7 Electronic res, 24/7 Online cat, Activity rm, Adult bk club, Archival coll, Art programs, Audio & video playback equip for onsite use, Audiobks on Playaways & MP3, Audiobks via web, Bilingual assistance for Spanish patrons, Bk club(s), Bk reviews (Group), Bks on CD, Chess club, Children's prog, Computer training, Computers for patron use, E-Reserves, Electronic databases & coll, Free DVD rentals, Genealogy discussion group, Health sci info serv, Holiday prog, ILL available, Internet access, Jail serv, Jazz prog, Life-long learning prog for all ages, Literacy & newcomer serv, Magazines, Mail & tel request accepted, Mail loans to mem, Makerspace, Mango lang, Meeting rooms, Movies, Music CDs, Notary serv, Online cat, Outreach serv, OverDrive digital audio bks, Photocopying/Printing, Preschool outreach, Preschool reading prog, Printer for laptops & handheld devices, Prof lending libr, Prog for adults, Prog for children & young adult, Ref serv available, Scanner, Serves people with intellectual disabilities, Spanish lang bks, STEM programs, Story hour, Summer & winter reading prog, Summer reading prog, Tax forms, Teen prog, Telephone ref, VHS videos, Wheelchair accessible, Winter reading prog, Workshops, Writing prog
Partic in Partners Library Action Network
Open Mon, Tues & Wed 9-7, Thurs 9-8, Fri 9-6, Sat 10-5
Restriction: Borrowing requests are handled by ILL, Circ to mem only, Non-resident fee
Friends of the Library Group

DUBLIN

P DUBLIN PUBLIC LIBRARY*, 206 W Blackjack St, 76446. (Mail add: PO Box 427, 76446-2204), SAN 316-2966. Tel: 254-445-4141. FAX: 254-445-2176. E-mail: staff@dublinlibrary.org. Web Site: dublinlibrary.org, www.ci.dublin.tx.us/library. *Dir,* Adina Dunn
Founded 1952. Pop 3,887; Circ 10,734
Library Holdings: AV Mats 600; Large Print Bks 200; Bk Titles 17,500; Bk Vols 18,690; Per Subs 30; Talking Bks 200

Special Collections: Erath County Genealogical Society Coll; Local History Archives
Subject Interests: Genealogy
Automation Activity & Vendor Info: (Acquisitions) AmLib Library Management System; (Cataloging) AmLib Library Management System; (OPAC) AmLib Library Management System
Wireless access
Open Tues-Fri 9-6, Sat 9-2

DUMAS

P MOORE COUNTY LIBRARY SYSTEM*, Killgore Memorial Library, 124 S Bliss Ave, 79029-3889. SAN 361-5723. Tel: 806-935-4941. FAX: 806-935-3324. Web Site: www.mocolib.net. *Libr Dir,* Deborah Skinner; E-mail: director@moore-tx.com; *Asst Libr Dir,* Linzi Holt; E-mail: asstdir@moore-tx.com; Staff 5 (Non-MLS 5)
Founded 1936. Pop 14,785; Circ 30,242
Library Holdings: Audiobooks 1,984; Bks on Deafness & Sign Lang 17; Braille Volumes 31; DVDs 4,482; e-books 5,455; Electronic Media & Resources 71; Large Print Bks 1,286; Bk Titles 24,429; Per Subs 40
Special Collections: Genealogy; Spanish; Texas
Wireless access
Function: 24/7 Electronic res, 24/7 Online cat, Activity rm, Audiobks via web, Bks on CD, Children's prog, Computers for patron use, Digital talking bks, E-Readers, Electronic databases & coll, Free DVD rentals, Holiday prog, ILL available, Internet access, Magazines, Mango lang, Microfiche/film & reading machines, Movies, Online cat, Photocopying/Printing, Preschool reading prog, Prog for adults, Prog for children & young adult, Ref serv available, Scanner, Serves people with intellectual disabilities, Spanish lang bks, Story hour, Summer reading prog, Teen prog, Telephone ref, Wheelchair accessible
Partic in Harrington Library Consortium
Open Mon-Fri 9-6
Restriction: Borrowing requests are handled by ILL, Circ limited, Circ to mem only, Co libr, ID required to use computers (Ltd hrs), Non-resident fee, Restricted borrowing privileges
Branches: 2
BRITAIN MEMORIAL LIBRARY, 118 E Fifth St, Sunray, 79086-0180. (Mail add: P O Box 180, Sunray, 79086), SAN 361-5758. Tel: 806-948-5501. FAX: 806-948-5369. E-mail: bml@moore-tx.com. *Br Librn,* Hanna Ivins; E-mail: bml@moore-tx.com; Staff 1 (Non-MLS 1)
Founded 1960. Pop 1,906; Circ 7,422
Library Holdings: Bks on Deafness & Sign Lang 13; DVDs 3,219; e-books 5,455; Electronic Media & Resources 71; Large Print Bks 505; Bk Titles 12,359; Per Subs 16
Subject Interests: Spanish, Tex
Function: 24/7 Electronic res, 24/7 Online cat, Audiobks via web, Children's prog, Computers for patron use, Digital talking bks, E-Readers, Electronic databases & coll, Free DVD rentals, Holiday prog, ILL available, Internet access, Magazines, Mango lang, Movies, Online cat, Photocopying/Printing, Prog for adults, Prog for children & young adult, Spanish lang bks, Story hour, Summer reading prog, Teen prog, Telephone ref, Wheelchair accessible
Open Mon-Fri 10-12 & 1-6
Restriction: Borrowing requests are handled by ILL, Circ limited, Circ to mem only, Co libr, ID required to use computers (Ltd hrs), Non-resident fee, Restricted borrowing privileges
CACTUS BRANCH LIBRARY, 407 Sherri, Cactus, 79013. (Mail add: P O Box 99, Cactus, 79013-0099). Tel: 806-966-3706. FAX: 806-966-3921. E-mail: cbl@moore-tx.com. *Br Librn,* Eloisa Quiroz; E-mail: cbl@moore-tx.com; Staff 1 (Non-MLS 1)
Founded 1999. Pop 3,259; Circ 6,306
Library Holdings: Bks on Deafness & Sign Lang 6; DVDs 3,247; e-books 5,455; Electronic Media & Resources 71; Large Print Bks 47; Bk Titles 6,976; Per Subs 12
Subject Interests: Spanish, Tex
Function: 24/7 Electronic res, 24/7 Online cat, Audiobks via web, Children's prog, Computers for patron use, Digital talking bks, E-Readers, Electronic databases & coll, Free DVD rentals, Holiday prog, ILL available, Internet access, Magazines, Mango lang, Movies, Online cat, Photocopying/Printing, Prog for adults, Prog for children & young adult, Spanish lang bks, Story hour, Summer reading prog, Teen prog, Telephone ref, Wheelchair accessible
Open Mon-Fri 10-12 & 1-6
Restriction: Borrowing requests are handled by ILL, Circ limited, Circ to mem only, Co libr, ID required to use computers (Ltd hrs), Non-resident fee, Restricted borrowing privileges

DUNCANVILLE

P DUNCANVILLE PUBLIC LIBRARY*, 201 James Collins Blvd, 75116. SAN 320-8362. Tel: 972-780-5050. Reference Tel: 972-780-5052. E-mail: slott@ci.duncanville.tx.us. Web Site: www.duncanville.com/departments/library. *Libr Dir,* Julio Velasquez; Tel: 972-780-5053, E-mail: jvelasquez@duncanville.com; *Circ Supvr, Commun Outreach Librn,* Stephanie Lott; *Tech Serv Librn,* Hannah Olsen; *Youth Serv Librn,* Danene Hudson
Founded 1955. Pop 36,000; Circ 125,000
Library Holdings: Bk Titles 97,000; Bk Vols 105,500; Per Subs 141
Special Collections: Texana; Texas Heritage Resource Center. Oral History
Subject Interests: Genealogy
Automation Activity & Vendor Info: (Acquisitions) TLC (The Library Corporation); (Cataloging) TLC (The Library Corporation); (Circulation) TLC (The Library Corporation); (OPAC) TLC (The Library Corporation)
Wireless access
Publications: Duncanville History Videos; Duncanville Treasures Videos
Open Tues-Thurs 10-8, Fri 10-6, Sat 10-5
Friends of the Library Group

EAGLE LAKE

P EULA & DAVID WINTERMANN LIBRARY*, 101 N Walnut Ave, 77434. SAN 316-2974. Tel: 979-234-5411. FAX: 979-234-5442. E-mail: wintermannlibrary@gmail.com. Web Site: www.wintermannlib.org. *Librn,* Vicki L Powers; Staff 1 (Non-MLS 1)
Founded 1975. Pop 5,610; Circ 15,000
Library Holdings: AV Mats 846; Large Print Bks 120; Bk Titles 16,500; Bk Vols 17,000; Per Subs 33; Talking Bks 327
Automation Activity & Vendor Info: (Cataloging) Biblionix; (Circulation) Biblionix
Wireless access
Partic in Partners Library Action Network
Open Mon-Fri 10-6, Sat 10-2
Friends of the Library Group

EAGLE PASS

P EAGLE PASS PUBLIC LIBRARY*, 589 Main St, 78852. SAN 316-2982. Tel: 830-773-7323. FAX: 830-773-4204. E-mail: librarypatron@eaglepasstx.us. Web Site: eaglepasspubliclibrary.org. *Dir,* Cesar Villa; E-mail: Cvilla@eaglepasstx.us; Staff 1 (MLS 1)
Founded 1939. Pop 40,000
Library Holdings: Bk Titles 60,000; Per Subs 75
Special Collections: Spanish Coll; Texana Coll
Wireless access
Partic in Partners Library Action Network
Open Mon & Wed 10-8, Tues & Thurs 10-6, Fri 10-5, Sat 10-3
Friends of the Library Group

J SOUTHWEST TEXAS JUNIOR COLLEGE*, Eagle Pass Campus Library, 3101 Bob Rogers Dr, 78852. Tel: 830-758-4118. Web Site: library.swtjc.edu. *Res Tech,* Gabriela Casarez; E-mail: gacasarezrodriguez@swtjc.edu
Wireless access
Function: ILL available, Photocopying/Printing, Study rm
Open Mon-Thurs 8am-9pm, Fri 8-4, Sun 1-6

EASTLAND

P CENTENNIAL MEMORIAL LIBRARY*, 210 S Lamar St, 76448-2794. SAN 316-2990. Tel: 254-629-2281. E-mail: ecmlibrary01@gmail.com. Web Site: centennial-memorial.ploud.net. *Dir,* Lou Jane Davis
Founded 1904. Pop 10,838
Library Holdings: Bk Titles 13,092; Bk Vols 15,506
Automation Activity & Vendor Info: (Cataloging) Follett Software; (Circulation) Follett Software; (OPAC) Follett Software
Open Tues 12-7, Wed 12-5, Thurs 10-6

GL TEXAS STATE COURT OF APPEALS*, Eleventh Supreme Judicial District Law Library, County Courthouse, 100 W Main St, Ste 300, 76448. SAN 328-6088. Tel: 254-629-2638. FAX: 254-629-2191. Web Site: www.txcourts.gov/11thcoa. *Court Adminr,* Marla Hanks; E-mail: marla.hanks@txcourts.gov
Restriction: Open to staff only

EDEN

P EDEN PUBLIC LIBRARY*, 117 Market St, 76837. (Mail add: PO Box 896, 76837-0896), SAN 376-4931. Tel: 325-869-7761. FAX: 325-869-8212. E-mail: eden.library@verizon.net. Web Site: www.edentexas.com/library. *Librn,* Tanya Garcia; Staff 1 (Non-MLS 1)
Library Holdings: Bk Vols 20,060
Automation Activity & Vendor Info: (Cataloging) LibLime; (Circulation) LibLime; (OPAC) LibLime
Wireless access
Open Mon 10:30-5:30, Wed & Fri 11-5:30
Friends of the Library Group

EDINBURG

L HIDALGO COUNTY LAW LIBRARY*, Courthouse, 100 N Closner, 78539. SAN 328-4743. Tel: 956-318-2155. FAX: 956-381-4269. Web Site: www.hidalgocounty.us/214/Law-Library. *Law Librn,* Angelica Chapa; E-mail: Angie.Chapa@co.hidalgo.tx.us
Library Holdings: Bk Titles 22,000
Open Mon-Fri 8-5

CR RIO GRANDE BIBLE INSTITUTE & LANGUAGE SCHOOL*, Richard Wade & Glen Vyck McKinney Library, 4300 S Business Hwy 281, 78539-9650. SAN 316-3016. Tel: 956-380-8100. Circulation Tel: 956-380-8138. Administration Tel: 956-380-8128. FAX: 956-380-8101. E-mail: biblioteca@riogrande.edu. Web Site: www.riogrande.edu.. *Librn,* Donna Antoniuk; E-mail: drantoniuk@riogrande.edu; Staff 3 (MLS 2, Non-MLS 1)
Founded 1952. Enrl 200; Fac 21; Highest Degree: Master
Library Holdings: AV Mats 986; Bk Titles 15,850; Bk Vols 31,458; Per Subs 88; Videos 1,924
Subject Interests: Christian theol works in the Spanish lang, Missions
Automation Activity & Vendor Info: (Cataloging) Follett Software; (Circulation) Follett Software; (OPAC) Follett Software
Wireless access
Function: Archival coll, Photocopying/Printing, Prof lending libr
Restriction: Open to students, Pub use on premises

P DUSTIN MICHAEL SEKULA MEMORIAL LIBRARY*, 1906 S Closner Blvd, 78539. SAN 316-3008. Tel: 956-383-6246. Interlibrary Loan Service Tel: 956-383-6247. FAX: 956-318-3446. Web Site: www.edinburg.lib.tx.us. *Dir,* Letty Leija; E-mail: letty@edinburglibrary.us; *Asst Dir,* Jose Tamez; E-mail: jose@edinburglibrary.us; *Head, Children's Servx,* Crissy Cruz; E-mail: ccruz@edinburglibrary.us; *Head, Circ,* Jeanette Castillo; E-mail: jcastillo@edinburglibrary.us; *Head, Ref,* Omero Morales; E-mail: omero.morales@edinburglibrary.us. Subject Specialists: *Adult, Mil,* Omero Morales; Staff 10 (MLS 2, Non-MLS 8)
Founded 1967. Pop 64,328; Circ 314,800
Library Holdings: Bk Titles 90,662; Bk Vols 95,000; Per Subs 215
Special Collections: Bilingual-Bicultural (Spanish), bk, flm, per; Literacy & Adult Basis Education, bk, per, videocassettes; Texana, bk, flm, per
Subject Interests: Ethnic studies, Hist, Spanish, Texana
Automation Activity & Vendor Info: (Cataloging) TLC (The Library Corporation); (Circulation) TLC (The Library Corporation); (OPAC) TLC (The Library Corporation)
Wireless access
Mem of Hidalgo County Library System
Open Mon-Thurs 8am-9pm, Fri 8-5, Sat 11-3, Sun 1-5
Friends of the Library Group

C UNIVERSITY OF TEXAS RIO GRANDE VALLEY, Edinburg Campus, 1201 W University Blvd, 78541-2999. SAN 361-5812. Tel: 956-665-2005. Administration Tel: 956-665-2755. Web Site: www.utrgv.edu/library. *Univ Librn,* Paul Sharpe; Tel: 956-665-2344, E-mail: paul.sharpe@utrgv.edu; *Head, Spec Coll & Archives,* Shannon Pensa; Tel: 956-665-5288, E-mail: shannon.pensa@utrgv.edu; *Assoc Univ Librn, Resource Management,* Peter Cortez; Tel: 956-665-2758, E-mail: peter.cortez@utrgv.edu; *Syst Librn,* Daniel McGinnis; Tel: 956-665-2878, E-mail: daniel.mcginnis@utrgv.edu; Staff 58 (MLS 19, Non-MLS 39)
Founded 1927. Enrl 17,337; Fac 884; Highest Degree: Doctorate
Library Holdings: AV Mats 25,174; Bks on Deafness & Sign Lang 710; CDs 1,109; DVDs 212; e-books 45,742; e-journals 33,158; Electronic Media & Resources 1,319; Bk Vols 598,008; Per Subs 1,846; Videos 5,679
Special Collections: De la Gauza papers; Depository for the Texas Regional Historical Resource Depository Program, Cameron, Hidalgo, Jim Hogg, Starr, Webb, Willacy & Zapata Counties; Lower Rio Grande Valley Coll; Rare Books; Shary papers; University Archives. State Document Depository; US Document Depository
Subject Interests: Lower Rio Grande Valley
Automation Activity & Vendor Info: (Acquisitions) Innovative Interfaces, Inc; (Cataloging) Innovative Interfaces, Inc; (Circulation) Innovative Interfaces, Inc; (ILL) Innovative Interfaces, Inc; (OPAC) Innovative Interfaces, Inc; (Serials) Innovative Interfaces, Inc
Wireless access
Publications: Reflections/Reflecciones (Newsletter)
Partic in Amigos Library Services, Inc; OCLC Online Computer Library Center, Inc; Paisano Consortium; TexSHARE - Texas State Library & Archives Commission; UT-System
Special Services for the Deaf - Assisted listening device
Special Services for the Blind - Assistive/Adapted tech devices, equip & products
Open Mon-Thurs 7:30am-Midnight, Fri 7:30-6, Sat 11-6, Sun 1-6 (Winter); Mon-Fri 8-5 (Summer)
Restriction: Borrowing privileges limited to fac & registered students

EDNA

P JACKSON COUNTY MEMORIAL LIBRARY*, 411 N Wells St, Rm 121, 77957-2734. SAN 316-3024. Tel: 361-782-2162. FAX: 361-782-6708. E-mail: jclibrary@jcml-tx.org. Web Site: www.jcml-tx.org. *Dir,* Cherie Robinson; Staff 2 (Non-MLS 2)
Pop 15,000
Library Holdings: Bk Titles 40,000; Per Subs 26
Automation Activity & Vendor Info: (Cataloging) Biblionix/Apollo; (Circulation) Biblionix/Apollo
Wireless access
Open Mon-Wed 9-5, Thurs 9-7, Fri 9-3

EL PASO

J EL PASO COMMUNITY COLLEGE LIBRARY*, Valle Verde Campus Library, 919 Hunter St, Rm C200, 79915. (Mail add: PO Box 20500, 79998). Tel: 915-831-2442. FAX: 915-831-2341. E-mail: askalib@epcc.edu. Web Site: www.epcc.edu/services/libraries. *Head Librn,* Oscar Baeza; E-mail: obaeza1@epcc.edu; *Librn,* Debi Lopez; E-mail: dlope156@epcc.edu; *Librn,* Adrian Morales; E-mail: amoral85@epcc.edu
Library Holdings: AV Mats 2,649; DVDs 1,918; e-books 24,600; Bk Titles 47,443; Bk Vols 56,474
Automation Activity & Vendor Info: (Acquisitions) Innovative Interfaces, Inc; (Cataloging) Innovative Interfaces, Inc; (Circulation) Innovative Interfaces, Inc; (Course Reserve) Innovative Interfaces, Inc; (ILL) Innovative Interfaces, Inc; (OPAC) Innovative Interfaces, Inc; (Serials) Innovative Interfaces, Inc
Wireless access
Partic in Amigos Library Services, Inc; Del Norte Biosciences Library Consortium; OCLC Online Computer Library Center, Inc
Open Mon-Thurs 7am-10pm, Fri 7-4, Sat 9-4, Sun Noon-4 (Winter); Mon-Thurs 8-8, Fri 8-4, Sat 10-3 (Summer)

Departmental Libraries:

LIBRARY TECHNICAL SERVICES, 919 Hunter St, Rm C300M, 79915. (Mail add: PO Box 20500, 79998-0500). Tel: 915-831-2484, 915-831-2671. *Librn,* Ana E Ochoa; E-mail: aochoa5@epcc.edu
Subject Interests: Allied health fields, Mexican-Am mats
Open Mon-Fri 8-5

MISSION DEL PASO CAMPUS LIBRARY, 10700 Gateway E, Rm C-102, 79927. (Mail add: PO Box 20500, 79998-0500). Tel: 915-831-7040. *Head Librn,* Norma Ballenger; Tel: 915-831-7052, E-mail: nkoube@epcc.edu
Library Holdings: AV Mats 1,302; Bk Vols 24,714
Special Services for the Deaf - Sorenson video relay syst
Special Services for the Blind - Accessible computers; Internet workstation with adaptive software; Telesensory - Genie Pro screen enlarger
Open Mon-Thurs (Winter) 7:30am-8pm, Fri 7:30-4, Sat 8:30am-12:30pm; Mon-Thurs (Summer) 8-5, Fri 8-4

RIO GRANDE CAMPUS LIBRARY, 100 W Rio Grande Ave, Rm E100, 79902. (Mail add: PO Box 20500, 79998). Tel: 915-831-4019. E-mail: rglrc@epcc.edu. *Head Librn,* Gale Sanchez; E-mail: gsanc127@epcc.edu; *Pub Serv Librn,* Rebecca Perales; E-mail: rperale4@epcc.edu; *Pub Serv Librn,* Antonio Rodarte; E-mail: arodar37@epcc.edu; Staff 10 (MLS 6, Non-MLS 4)
Founded 1975. Enrl 1,946; Highest Degree: Associate
Library Holdings: DVDs 763; Bk Vols 22,500
Function: 24/7 Electronic res, 24/7 Online cat, Bilingual assistance for Spanish patrons, Computers for patron use, Distance learning, E-Reserves, Electronic databases & coll, For res purposes, ILL available, Internet access, Magazines, Online cat, Online Chat, Online ref, Orientations, Photocopying/Printing, Ref & res, Ref serv available
Open Mon-Thurs 7:30am-8pm, Fri 7:30-5, Sat 8:30-12:30

TRANSMOUNTAIN CAMPUS LIBRARY, 9570 Gateway Blvd N, Rm 1600, 79924. Tel: 915-831-5098. *Head Librn,* Carlos Humphreys; E-mail: chumphr6@epcc.edu; *Librn,* Lourdes Garcia; E-mail: lgarc136@epcc.edu; *Librn,* Manual Herrera; E-mail: mherre66@epcc.edu; Staff 3 (MLS 3)
Library Holdings: AV Mats 3,994; Bk Vols 50,494
Open Mon-Thurs 7:30am-10pm, Fri 7:30-5, Sat 9-5, Sun 12-4

JENNA WELCH & LAURA BUSH COMMUNITY LIBRARY, Northwest Campus, 6701 S Desert Rd, Rm L100, 79932. Tel: 915-831-8889. FAX: 915-831-8816. Web Site: www.epcc.edu/Services/Libraries/Northwest. *Head Librn,* Lorely Ambriz; E-mail: lambriz@epcc.edu; *Librn,* Blake Klimasara; E-mail: bklimasa@epcc.edu
Library Holdings: AV Mats 1,643; Bk Titles 25,000
Open Mon-Thurs 7:30am-8pm, Fri 7:30-4, Sat 10-4 (Fall-Spring); Mon-Thurs 7:30-6, Fri 7:30-4 (Summer)

GL EL PASO COUNTY LAW LIBRARY, The Robert J Galvan Law Library, Court House, 12th Flr, 500 E San Antonio St, Rm 1202, 79901. Tel: 915-273-3699. FAX: 915-546-2250. E-mail: eplawlibrary@epcounty.com. Web Site: www.epcounty.com/lawlibrary. *Dir, Librn,* Lynn E Sanchez;

E-mail: lsanchez@epcounty.com; *Asst Libr Mgr,* Sandra Andrade; E-mail: sandrade@epcounty.com
Library Holdings: Bk Vols 38,000; Per Subs 49
Wireless access
Partic in SW Law Librs
Open Mon-Fri 8-5

S EL PASO MUSEUM OF ART*, Algur H Meadows Maker Space, One Arts Festival Plaza, 79901. SAN 316-3067. Tel: 915-212-3061. FAX: 915-532-1010. E-mail: epmaeducation@elpasotexas.gov. Web Site: www.epma.art/art-school. *Community Engagement Coord,* Josie Jimarez-Howard; *Educ Coordr,* Ivan I Calderon; Staff 12 (Non-MLS 12)
Library Holdings: Bk Vols 1,000
Special Collections: Renaissance & Baroque Artists Coll
Subject Interests: Gen, Modern art
Restriction: Open to pub by appt only

P EL PASO PUBLIC LIBRARY*, 501 N Oregon St, 79901. SAN 361-5901. Tel: 915-212-7323. Circulation Tel: 915-212-3220. Reference Tel: 915-212-0363. Web Site: www.elpasolibrary.org. *Dir,* Norma Martinez; Tel: 915-212-3200, E-mail: martineznp@elpasotexas.gov; Staff 168.6 (MLS 43, Non-MLS 125.6)
Founded 1894
Library Holdings: Bk Vols 931,884; Per Subs 355
Special Collections: Raza Coll. State Document Depository; US Document Depository
Subject Interests: Genealogy, Literacy, Local archit, Local hist, Local photog, Mexican Revolutionary, Spanish
Automation Activity & Vendor Info: (Acquisitions) SirsiDynix; (Cataloging) SirsiDynix; (Circulation) SirsiDynix; (ILL) SirsiDynix; (OPAC) SirsiDynix; (Serials) SirsiDynix
Wireless access
Function: 24/7 Electronic res, 24/7 Online cat, Accelerated reader prog, Adult bk club, Adult literacy prog
Publications: Great Constellations, Tom Lea Bibliography; Henry C Trost, Architect of the Southwest
Partic in TexSHARE - Texas State Library & Archives Commission
Special Services for the Deaf - Assistive tech
Special Services for the Blind - Assistive/Adapted tech devices, equip & products; Children's Braille; Talking bks
Open Mon-Thurs 10-7, Fri 11-6, Sat 10-6, Sun 12-6
Friends of the Library Group
Branches: 11
ESPERANZA ACOSTA MORENO REGIONAL, 12480 Pebble Hills Blvd, 79938. Tel: 915-212-0442. Web Site: www.elpasolibrary.org/locations/esperanza-moreno-branch. *Br Mgr,* Aimee Camp
Open Mon & Sat 10-6, Tues-Thurs 10-7, Fri 1-6
Friends of the Library Group
ARMIJO, 620 E Seventh Ave, 79901, SAN 361-5936. Tel: 915-212-0369. Web Site: www.elpasolibrary.org/locations/armijo-branch. *Br Mgr,* Suzanne Mancillas
Open Mon 10-6, Tues-Thurs 10-7, Fri 1-6, Sat 10-6
Friends of the Library Group
RICHARD BURGES REGIONAL, 9600 Dyer St, Ste C, 79924, SAN 361-5960. Tel: 915-212-0317. Web Site: www.elpasolibrary.org/locations/richard-burges-branch. *Br Mgr,* Ellen Eyberg
Open Mon & Sat 10-6, Tues-Thurs 10-7, Fri 1-6
Friends of the Library Group
JOSE CISNEROS CIELO VISTA, 1300 Hawkins Blvd, 79907-6803, SAN 361-5995. Tel: 915-212-0450. Web Site: www.elpasolibrary.org/locations/jose-cisneros-cielo-vista-branch. *Br Mgr,* Michael Pitterman
Open Mon & Sat 10-6, Tues-Thurs 10-7, Fri 1-6
Friends of the Library Group
CLARDY FOX BRANCH, 5515 Robert Alva Ave, 79905, SAN 361-6029. Tel: 915-212-0456. Web Site: www.elpasolibrary.org/locations/clardy-fox-branch. *Br Mgr,* Martha Holguin
Subject Interests: Spanish lang
Open Mon & Sat 10-6, Tues-Thurs 10-7, Fri 1-6
Friends of the Library Group
JUDGE EDWARD S MARQUEZ MISSION VALLEY BRANCH, 610 N Yarbrough Dr, 79915, SAN 361-6053. Tel: 915-212-0600. Web Site: www.elpasolibrary.org/locations/judge-marquez-lower-valley-branch. *Br Mgr,* Position Currently Open
Subject Interests: Spanish lang
Open Mon & Sat 10-6, Tues-Thurs 10-7, Fri 1-6
Friends of the Library Group
MEMORIAL PARK, 3200 Copper Ave, 79930, SAN 361-6088. Tel: 915-212-0448. Web Site: www.elpasolibrary.org/locations/memorial-park-branch. *Br Mgr,* Martha Andrade
Open Mon & Sat 10-6, Tues-Thurs 10-7, Fri 1-6
Friends of the Library Group
IRVING SCHWARTZ BRANCH, 1865 Dean Martin Dr, 79936. Tel: 915-212-0315. Web Site: www.elpasolibrary.org/locations/irving-schwartz-branch. *Br Mgr,* Position Currently Open
Open Mon & Sat 10-6, Tues-Thurs 10-7, Fri 1-6
Friends of the Library Group
SERGIO TRONCOSO BRANCH, 9321 Alameda Ave, 79907, SAN 361-6142. Tel: 915-212-0453. Web Site: www.elpasolibrary.org/locations/sergio-troncoso-branch. *Br Mgr,* Position Currently Open
Subject Interests: Spanish lang
Open Mon & Sat 10-6, Tues-Thurs 10-7, Fri 1-6
Friends of the Library Group
DORRIS VAN DOREN BRANCH, 551 Redd Rd, 79912. Tel: 915-212-0440. Web Site: www.elpasolibrary.org/locations/dorris-van-doren-branch. *Br Mgr,* Patricia Hernandez
Subject Interests: Spanish lang
Open Mon & Sat 10-6, Tues-Thurs 10-7, Fri 1-6
Friends of the Library Group
WESTSIDE, 125 Belvidere St, 79912, SAN 361-6118. Tel: 915-212-0445. Web Site: www.elpasolibrary.org/locations/westside-branch. *Br Mgr,* Susan Barnum
Open Mon & Sat 10-6, Tues-Thurs 10-7, Fri 1-6
Friends of the Library Group
Bookmobiles: 1. Libr Servs Supvr, Norma Orozco. Bk titles 51,734

R FIRST PRESBYTERIAN CHURCH LIBRARY*, 1340 Murchison St, 79902. SAN 316-3083. Tel: 915-533-7551. FAX: 915-534-7167. E-mail: office@fpcep.org. Web Site: firstpresbyterian.church. *Library Contact,* Rev Neal Locke
Founded 1957
Library Holdings: Bk Titles 3,700
Subject Interests: Hist, Theol
Open Mon-Thurs 8-5, Fri 8-3, Sun 8-Noon

L MOUNCE, GREEN, MEYERS, SAFI, PAXON & GALATZAN*, Law Library, 100 N Stanton, Ste 1000, 79901. SAN 372-1647. Tel: 915-532-2000. FAX: 915-541-1597. Web Site: www.mgmsg.com. *Librn,* Sylvia T Contreras; E-mail: scon@mgmsg.com
Library Holdings: Bk Vols 15,000; Per Subs 15
Restriction: Staff use only

G NATIONAL PARK SERVICE*, Chamizal National Memorial Library, 800 S San Marcial St, 79905-4123. SAN 326-3282. Tel: 915-532-7273, Ext 127. FAX: 915-532-7240. *Library Contact,* Rodney Sauter; E-mail: rodney_sauter@nps.gov
Library Holdings: Bk Titles 1,000; Bk Vols 1,500
Special Collections: Museum Coll. Contains history of the surveying of international boundary, national park service, theater, music and border region
Function: Ref serv available
Open Mon-Fri 8-4:30
Restriction: Non-circulating to the pub

S SCOTTHULSE, PC*, Law Library, One San Jacinto Plaza, 201 E Main Dr, Ste 1100, 79901. (Mail add: PO Box 99123, 79999-9123), SAN 326-4513. Tel: 915-533-2493, Ext 307. FAX: 915-546-8333. Web Site: www.scotthulse.com. *Library Contact,* Danielle Stanfield; E-mail: dsta@scotthulse.com
Subject Interests: Labor
Publications: Acquisitions List
Restriction: Staff use only

CM TEXAS TECH UNIVERSITY HEALTH SCIENCES CENTER EL PASO*, Doris F Eisenberg Library of the Health Sciences, Medical Educ Bldg, Rm 2100, 5001 El Paso Dr, 79905. Tel: 915-215-4306. *Managing Dir,* Lisa Beinhoff; *Mgr,* Andrew Contreras; E-mail: andrew.contreras@ttuhsc.edu
Wireless access
Departmental Libraries:
MONTES-GALLO DELIA LIBRARY, 170 Rick Francis Dr, 79905, SAN 316-3113. Tel: 915-215-4306, 915-215-4681. Web Site: elpaso.ttuhsc.edu/libraries. *Managing Dir,* Dr Lisa Beinhoff; E-mail: lisa.beinhoff@ttuhsc.edu; Staff 7 (MLS 4, Non-MLS 3)
Founded 1976. Highest Degree: Doctorate
Library Holdings: CDs 92; e-books 871,260; e-journals 35,584; Bk Vols 34,910
Special Collections: TTUHSCEP Archive
Subject Interests: Local hist, Med, Pathology
Automation Activity & Vendor Info: (Cataloging) Ex Libris Group; (Circulation) Ex Libris Group; (Discovery) Ex Libris Group; (ILL) OCLC ILLiad; (Media Booking) Springshare, LLC; (OPAC) Ex Libris Group; (Serials) Ex Libris Group

Function: 24/7 Online cat, 3D Printer
Partic in SCAMeL
Restriction: Authorized patrons, Badge access after hrs, Borrowing requests are handled by ILL, Circ privileges for students & alumni only, ID required to use computers (Ltd hrs)

C UNIVERSITY OF TEXAS AT EL PASO LIBRARY*, 500 W University Ave, 79968-0582. SAN 361-6231. Tel: 915-747-5683. Circulation Tel: 915-747-5674. Interlibrary Loan Service Tel: 915-747-5678. Reference Tel: 915-747-5643. FAX: 915-747-5345. E-mail: libraryref@utep.edu. Web Site: libraryweb.utep.edu. *Libr Dir, Assoc VPres for Univ Advan,* Robert Stakes; Tel: 915-747-6710, E-mail: rlstakes@utep.edu; *Assoc Dir, Access Serv, Assoc Dir, Res & Instruction,* Harvey Castellano; Tel: 915-747-6734, E-mail: hcastell@utep.edu; *Asst Dir, Operations,* Bonnie Cardona; Tel: 915-747-5686, E-mail: dcardona@utep.edu; *Asst Dir, Tech Serv,* Kathy Poorman; Tel: 915-747-5394, E-mail: kpoorman@utep.edu; *Head, Cat,* Virginia Rassaei; *Head, Spec Coll,* Claudia Rivers; Tel: 915-747-6725, E-mail: crivers@utep.edu; *Ms & Archives Librn,* Abbie Weiser. Subject Specialists: *Sociol, SW,* Claudia Rivers; Staff 25 (MLS 21, Non-MLS 4)
Founded 1919. Enrl 23,397; Fac 1,334; Highest Degree: Doctorate
Library Holdings: AV Mats 3,465; CDs 2,212; DVDs 238; e-books 253,862; e-journals 183,081; Electronic Media & Resources 140,941; Microforms 54,785; Bk Titles 730,511; Bk Vols 835,283; Per Subs 3,172; Videos 71,875
Special Collections: Mexican History Manuscripts Coll, micro; Military History (SLA Marchall Coll); Onamastics Coll; Printing & Bookmaking (Carl Hertzog Coll), bks & papers. Oral History; State Document Depository; US Document Depository
Subject Interests: Art, Border studies, Chicano studies, Composition, Engr, Environ studies, Geol, Hist, Judaica, Mexico, Psychol, Rare bks, SW, SW anthrop, SW archit, SW region, Western stories
Automation Activity & Vendor Info: (Acquisitions) Innovative Interfaces, Inc; (Cataloging) Innovative Interfaces, Inc; (Circulation) Innovative Interfaces, Inc; (Course Reserve) Innovative Interfaces, Inc; (ILL) Innovative Interfaces, Inc; (Media Booking) Innovative Interfaces, Inc; (OPAC) Innovative Interfaces, Inc; (Serials) Innovative Interfaces, Inc
Wireless access
Publications: Keywords (Newsletter)
Partic in Amigos Library Services, Inc; Association of Research Libraries; Del Norte Biosciences Library Consortium; TexSHARE - Texas State Library & Archives Commission
Special Services for the Blind - Accessible computers; Aids for in-house use; Assistive/Adapted tech devices, equip & products
Open Mon-Thurs 7am-1am, Fri 7am-8pm, Sat 9-6, Sun Noon-1am
Friends of the Library Group

ELDORADO

P SCHLEICHER COUNTY PUBLIC LIBRARY, 201 SW Main St, 76936. (Mail add: PO Box 611, 76936-0611), SAN 376-4036. Tel: 325-853-3767. FAX: 325-853-2963. E-mail: librarian@schleicherlibrary.com. Web Site: schleicherlibrary.weebly.com. *Librn,* Michele Bischoffberger; Staff 1 (Non-MLS 1)
Library Holdings: Bk Vols 10,000
Automation Activity & Vendor Info: (Acquisitions) Biblionix; (Cataloging) Biblionix; (Circulation) Biblionix
Wireless access
Open Mon 12-5:30, Tues, Wed & Fri 9-2, Thurs 12-5

ELECTRA

P ELECTRA PUBLIC LIBRARY*, 401 N Waggoner St, 76360. SAN 316-3148. Tel: 940-495-2208. FAX: 940-495-4143. E-mail: electrapubliclibrary@gmail.com. Web Site: www.electrapubliclibrary.org. *Libr Dir,* Stacy Nelson; *Asst Librn,* Patti Pettiet; Staff 2 (Non-MLS 2)
Founded 1925. Pop 2,700; Circ 34,898
Library Holdings: AV Mats 4,456; Bk Titles 20,005; Bk Vols 20,074; Per Subs 36
Special Collections: Hometown Genealogy
Automation Activity & Vendor Info: (Cataloging) Book Systems; (Circulation) Book Systems; (OPAC) Book Systems
Wireless access
Function: 24/7 Electronic res, 24/7 Online cat, Accelerated reader prog, Activity rm, Audio & video playback equip for onsite use, Audiobks via web, Bks on CD, Children's prog, Computer training, Computers for patron use, Doc delivery serv, Electronic databases & coll, Free DVD rentals, Genealogy discussion group, Holiday prog, Home delivery & serv to seniorr ctr & nursing homes, Homebound delivery serv, ILL available, Internet access, Laminating, Large print keyboards, Magazines, Magnifiers for reading, Mail & tel request accepted, Meeting rooms, Movies, Online cat, Online ref, Outside serv via phone, mail, e-mail & web, OverDrive digital audio bks, Photocopying/Printing, Preschool reading prog, Printer for laptops & handheld devices, Prog for children & young adult, Scanner, Story hour, Study rm, Summer reading prog, Wheelchair accessible
Partic in TexSHARE - Texas State Library & Archives Commission
Special Services for the Blind - Bks on CD; Large print bks
Open Mon-Fri 10-6
Friends of the Library Group

ELGIN

P ELGIN PUBLIC LIBRARY*, 404 N Main St, 78621. SAN 376-4842. Tel: 512-281-5678. FAX: 512-285-3015. E-mail: library@ci.elgin.tx.us. Web Site: www.elginpubliclibrary.org. *Dir,* Brittany Labinger; Staff 2 (MLS 1, Non-MLS 1)
Founded 1986. Pop 10,064
Library Holdings: AV Mats 2,411; CDs 82; Large Print Bks 1,559; Bk Vols 30,172; Per Subs 25; Talking Bks 1,102; Videos 3,185
Automation Activity & Vendor Info: (Cataloging) Book Systems; (Circulation) Book Systems; (OPAC) Book Systems
Wireless access
Partic in Partners Library Action Network
Open Tues & Thurs 9-7, Wed & Fri 9-5, Sat 9-2
Friends of the Library Group

ELSA

P ELSA PUBLIC LIBRARY*, 711 N Hidalgo St, 78543. (Mail add: PO Box 1447, 78543-1447), SAN 316-3156. Tel: 956-262-3061. FAX: 956-262-3066. E-mail: library@elsa.lib.tx.us. Web Site: elsa.ploud.net. *Libr Dir,* Hilda Molina; E-mail: hilda@elsa.lib.tx.us; *Head, Ref,* Blanca Garza; E-mail: blanca@elsa.lib.tx.us; *Prog Coordr,* Amanda Garcia; E-mail: amanda@elsa.lib.tx.us
Founded 1974. Pop 9,500; Circ 38,869
Library Holdings: Bk Titles 27,000; Per Subs 28; Talking Bks 125; Videos 785
Automation Activity & Vendor Info: (Cataloging) TLC (The Library Corporation); (Circulation) TLC (The Library Corporation); (ILL) OCLC WorldShare Interlibrary Loan
Wireless access
Function: 24/7 Online cat, Adult literacy prog, Children's prog, Computers for patron use, Electronic databases & coll, Free DVD rentals, Holiday prog, ILL available, Magazines, Meeting rooms, Movies, Online cat, Photocopying/Printing, Preschool reading prog, Prog for adults, Scanner, Tax forms, Teen prog, Telephone ref
Mem of Hidalgo County Library System
Open Mon-Thurs 9-6, Fri 8-5

EMORY

P RAINS COUNTY PUBLIC LIBRARY*, 150 Doris Briggs Pkwy, 75440-3012. (Mail add: PO Box 189, 75440-0189), SAN 376-4486. Tel: 903-473-5096. FAX: 903-473-5097. Web Site: www.co.rains.tx.us/default.aspx?Rains-County/Library. *Dir,* Wendy Byrd; E-mail: wendy.byrd@co.rains.tx.us
Library Holdings: Bk Vols 17,000; Per Subs 15
Automation Activity & Vendor Info: (Cataloging) Book Systems; (Circulation) Book Systems
Wireless access
Open Mon, Wed & Fri 10-5, Tues & Thurs 10-6, Sat 10-2
Friends of the Library Group

ENNIS

P ENNIS PUBLIC LIBRARY*, 115 W Brown St, 75119. SAN 316-3164. Tel: 972-875-5360. FAX: 972-878-9649. E-mail: library@ennistx.gov. Web Site: www.ennistx.gov/library. *Dir,* Jessica Diaz; *Ref Librn,* Lonnie Berrett; E-mail: reference@ennistx.gov; Staff 7 (MLS 3, Non-MLS 4)
Founded 1939
Library Holdings: Audiobooks 887; Bks on Deafness & Sign Lang 13; DVDs 793; Large Print Bks 2,274; Bk Titles 26,133; Bk Vols 27,105; Per Subs 35
Special Collections: Ennis Historic Archives
Subject Interests: Genealogy, Tex hist
Automation Activity & Vendor Info: (Acquisitions) Baker & Taylor; (Cataloging) Book Systems; (Circulation) Book Systems; (ILL) OCLC WorldShare Interlibrary Loan; (OPAC) Book Systems; (Serials) Readerware
Wireless access
Function: 24/7 Electronic res, 24/7 Online cat, ILL available
Partic in Northeast Texas Digital Consortium; TexSHARE - Texas State Library & Archives Commission
Open Mon-Wed & Fri 10-6, Thurs 10-8, Sat 10-2
Friends of the Library Group

EULESS

P MARY LIB SALEH EULESS PUBLIC LIBRARY*, 201 N Ector Dr, 76039-3595. SAN 316-3172. Tel: 817-685-1480. Circulation Tel: 817-685-1481. Administration Tel: 817-685-1679. FAX: 817-267-1979. E-mail: library@eulesstx.org. Web Site: www.eulesstx.gov/library. *Libr Adminr,* Sherry Knight; Tel: 817-685-1482, E-mail: sknight@eulesstx.gov;

Sr Librn, Adult & YA Serv, Eric Terry; *Sr Librn/Youth Serv,* Angela Jones; *Ref & Ad Serv Librn,* Donna Gooch; *Youth Serv Librn,* Lacey Fliger; Staff 28 (MLS 5, Non-MLS 23)
Founded 1961. Pop 52,000; Circ 375,000
Library Holdings: Bk Titles 80,000; Bk Vols 109,000; Per Subs 290
Automation Activity & Vendor Info: (Cataloging) Innovative Interfaces, Inc; (Circulation) Innovative Interfaces, Inc; (ILL) Innovative Interfaces, Inc; (OPAC) Innovative Interfaces, Inc
Wireless access
Open Mon, Tues & Thurs 10-9, Wed 10-6, Fri & Sat 10-5, Sun 1-5
Friends of the Library Group

FAIRFIELD

P FAIRFIELD LIBRARY ASSOCIATION, INC*, Mary Moody Northern Municipal Library, 350 W Main, 75840. Tel: 903-389-3574. FAX: 903-389-5636. E-mail: fairfieldtxlibrary@gmail.com. Web Site: www.fairfieldtxlibrary.org. *Libr Dir,* Gary Wiggins; *Libr Asst,* Jessica Jones
Founded 1966. Pop 8,800; Circ 17,000
Library Holdings: Bk Titles 24,451; Per Subs 28
Special Collections: Genealogy; Texas
Wireless access
Partic in Partners Library Action Network
Open Tues-Fri 9:30-5:30
Friends of the Library Group

FALFURRIAS

P ED RACHAL MEMORIAL LIBRARY*, 203 S Calixto Mora Ave, 78355. SAN 316-3202. Tel: 361-325-2144. Web Site: co.brooks.tx.us/page/brooks.library. *Libr Supvr,* Mary Beth Munoz; E-mail: m.munoz@co.brooks.tx.us; Staff 1 (Non-MLS 1)
Founded 1960. Pop 6,964; Circ 9,727
Library Holdings: Large Print Bks 600; Microforms 300; Bk Vols 39,791; Per Subs 23
Subject Interests: English, Genealogy, Law, Lit
Automation Activity & Vendor Info: (Cataloging) Follett Software; (Circulation) Follett Software; (OPAC) Follett Software
Wireless access
Open Mon-Fri 8-12 & 1-4:30

FALLS CITY

P FALLS CITY PUBLIC LIBRARY*, 206 N Irvin, 78113. (Mail add: PO Box 220, 78113-0220), SAN 376-4214. Tel: 830-254-3361. FAX: 830-254-3954. E-mail: fcpublib@yahoo.com. *Libr Dir,* Donna Ermis
Founded 1975. Pop 1,091
Library Holdings: AV Mats 850; Bk Titles 13,636; Bk Vols 13,924; Per Subs 38; Talking Bks 113
Automation Activity & Vendor Info: (Acquisitions) Biblionix; (Cataloging) Biblionix; (Circulation) Biblionix
Mem of Karnes County Library System
Open Mon & Wed-Fri 11:30-5:30, Tues 10:30-5:30

P KARNES COUNTY LIBRARY SYSTEM*, Falls City Public Library, 206 N Irvin, 78113. (Mail add: PO Box 220, 78113-0190), SAN 316-5388. Tel: 830-254-3361. FAX: 830-254-3954. E-mail: fcpublib@yahoo.com. *Dir,* Donna Ermis
Founded 1969
Special Collections: Holchak & McClane Coll, scrapbooks; Local History (M S Yeater Coll), biog, papers
Member Libraries: Falls City Public Library; Karnes City Public Library; Kenedy Public Library; Runge Public Library
Open Mon-Fri 11:30-5:30

FARMERS BRANCH

J DALLAS COLLEGE*, Brookhaven Campus Library, Bldg L, 3939 Valley View Lane, 75244-4997. SAN 316-3210. Tel: 972-860-4854. Reference Tel: 972-860-4862. FAX: 972-860-4675. Web Site: www.brookhavencollege.edu/library. *Dean,* Sarah Ferguson; E-mail: sferguson@dcccd.edu; *Librn III,* John Flores; E-mail: JFlores@dcccd.edu; Staff 5 (MLS 5)
Founded 1978. Enrl 4,946; Fac 241
Library Holdings: Bk Titles 55,603; Bk Vols 55,890; Per Subs 119
Special Collections: Plotkin Holocaust Coll
Automation Activity & Vendor Info: (Acquisitions) Innovative Interfaces, Inc; (Cataloging) Innovative Interfaces, Inc; (Circulation) Innovative Interfaces, Inc; (Course Reserve) Innovative Interfaces, Inc; (ILL) Innovative Interfaces, Inc; (Media Booking) Innovative Interfaces, Inc; (OPAC) Innovative Interfaces, Inc; (Serials) Innovative Interfaces, Inc
Wireless access
Open Mon-Thurs 8am-9pm, Fri 8-3:30, Sat 10-2

§P FARMERS BRANCH MANSKE LIBRARY, 13613 Webb Chapel Rd, 75234. Tel: 972-247-2511. Circulation Tel: 972-919-9830. E-mail: library@farmersbranchtx.gov. Web Site: www.farmersbranchtx.gov/192/library. *Libr Dir,* Heather Fuller; Tel: 972-919-9800, E-mail: heather.fuller@farmersbranchtx.gov; *Adult Serv,* Ryann Dekat; Tel: 972-919-9810, E-mail: ryann.dekat@farmersbranchtx.gov; *Circulation/Account Servs,* Caren Khan; Tel: 972-919-9830, E-mail: caren.khan@farmersbranchtx.gov; *Youth Serv,* Dustin Nordt; Tel: 972-919-9813, E-mail: dustin.nordt@farmersbranchtx.gov
Founded 1949
Automation Activity & Vendor Info: (Cataloging) Innovative Interfaces, Inc. - Polaris; (OPAC) Innovative Interfaces, Inc. - Polaris
Wireless access
Function: Computers for patron use, ILL available, Internet access, Meeting rooms
Partic in Amigos Library Services, Inc
Open Mon-Thurs 10-9, Fri & Sat 10-6, Sun 1-5

P MANSKE LIBRARY*, 13613 Webb Chapel, 75234-3756. SAN 316-3229. Tel: 972-247-2511. Reference Tel: 972-919-9810. FAX: 972-919-9844. E-mail: library@farmersbranchtx.gov. Web Site: www.farmersbranchtx.gov/192/library. *Dir,* Trevor Hunter; E-mail: trevor.hunter@farmersbranchtx.gov; *Circ Supvr,* Caren Khan; E-mail: caren.khan@farmersbranchtx.gov
Founded 1961. Pop 35,900; Circ 75,707
Library Holdings: Bk Titles 70,800; Bk Vols 93,710; Per Subs 320
Subject Interests: Tex hist
Automation Activity & Vendor Info: (Cataloging) SirsiDynix; (Circulation) SirsiDynix; (OPAC) SirsiDynix
Wireless access
Partic in Dow Jones News Retrieval; Proquest Dialog
Open Mon-Thurs 10-9, Fri & Sat 10-6, Sun 1-5

FARMERSVILLE

P CHARLES J RIKE MEMORIAL LIBRARY*, 203 Orange St, 75442. SAN 322-8053. Tel: 972-782-6681. FAX: 972-782-7608. E-mail: library@farmersvilletx.com. Web Site: www.rikelibrary.com. *Libr Dir,* Trisha Dowell; E-mail: t.dowell@farmersvilletx.com
Founded 1979. Pop 3,000; Circ 26,557
Library Holdings: Bk Titles 28,000
Automation Activity & Vendor Info: (Cataloging) Biblionix; (Circulation) Biblionix
Wireless access
Open Tues & Thurs 8:30-6, Wed & Fri 8:30-4:30, Sat 9-2

FERRIS

P FERRIS PUBLIC LIBRARY*, 301 E Tenth St, 75125. SAN 316-3237. Tel: 972-544-3696. E-mail: ferrislibrary@ferristexas.gov. Web Site: ferris.ploud.net, www.ferristexas.gov/library. *Libr Dir,* Kathy Harrington; Tel: 972-904-1788, E-mail: kathyharrington@ferristexas.gov
Founded 1971. Pop 2,600; Circ 2,700
Library Holdings: Audiobooks 120; Bk Titles 15,000; Per Subs 35
Special Collections: Judge Grace Campbell Coll; McKnight Genealogy Coll
Subject Interests: Genealogy
Automation Activity & Vendor Info: (Cataloging) Book Systems; (Circulation) Book Systems; (OPAC) Book Systems
Wireless access
Partic in TexSHARE - Texas State Library & Archives Commission
Open Mon-Fri 9-6

FLATONIA

P FLATONIA PUBLIC LIBRARY*, 208 N Main St, 78941. (Mail add: PO Box 656, 78941-0656). Tel: 361-772-2088. E-mail: flatoniapubliclibrary@gmail.com. *Head Librn,* Evelyn C Miller
Founded 1988. Pop 1,397; Circ 2,936
Library Holdings: Large Print Bks 75; Bk Vols 10,000
Wireless access
Open Mon-Fri 3-5

FLORENCE

P FLORENCE PUBLIC LIBRARY*, Eula Hunt Beck Public Library, 207 E Main St, 76527-4048. (Mail add: PO Box 430, 76527-0430), SAN 376-4834. Tel: 254-793-2672. FAX: 254-793-2102. E-mail: library@florencetex.com. Web Site: florencetex.com/departments/eula-hunt-beck-florence-public-library. *Libr Dir,* Jean Flahive
Library Holdings: Bk Vols 12,000
Wireless access
Partic in Partners Library Action Network

Open Mon-Fri 9:30-1 & 1:30-5
Friends of the Library Group

FLORESVILLE

P WILSON COUNTY PUBLIC LIBRARIES*, Sam Fore Jr Public Library (Headquarters), 1103 Fourth St, 78114. SAN 316-3245. Tel: 830-393-7361. Administration Tel: 830-393-7360. FAX: 830-393-7337. E-mail: librarian.wcpl@gmail.com, library@wilsoncountytx.gov, wilsoncolibrary@gmail.com. Web Site: www.wilsoncountylibrary.org. *Dir & Librn,* Nicki Stohr; E-mail: nstohr@wilsoncountytx.gov; *Asst Librn,* Sheri Mantei; E-mail: smantei@wilsoncountytx.gov; *Computer Lab Mgr,* Lesa McCall; E-mail: lmccall@wilsoncountytx.gov; *ILL,* Rebecca Upchurch; E-mail: rupchurch@wilsoncountytx.gov. Subject Specialists: *Genealogy,* Nicki Stohr; Staff 4.5 (MLS 1, Non-MLS 3.5)
Founded 1934. Pop 37,529; Circ 78,036
Library Holdings: AV Mats 3,612; Bk Titles 34,342; Per Subs 37
Special Collections: Texas Reference (local hist & genealogy mat)
Subject Interests: County genealogy, County hist, Texana
Automation Activity & Vendor Info: (Cataloging) Biblionix; (Circulation) Biblionix; (ILL) OCLC FirstSearch
Wireless access
Function: Children's prog, Computers for patron use, ILL available, Music CDs, Photocopying/Printing, Printer for laptops & handheld devices, Summer reading prog, Tax forms, VHS videos, Winter reading prog
Partic in Partners Library Action Network
Open Mon-Wed 9-6, Thurs 9-8, Fri 9-5, Sat 9-1
Friends of the Library Group
Branches: 3
SARAH BAIN CHANDLER PUBLIC LIBRARY, 602 W Main St, Stockdale, 78160. Tel: 830-996-3114. *Libr Mgr,* Nikkii Myrick; E-mail: librarian.sbc@gmail.com
Open Mon-Fri 10-5, Sat 10-2
JANE YELVINGTON MCCALLUM PUBLIC LIBRARY, 112 E Chihuahua, La Vernia, 78121. Tel: 830-542-4010. E-mail: librarian.jym@gmail.com.
Open Tues-Thurs 10-6, Fri 10-5, Sat 11-3
WILSON COUNTY HISTORICAL COMMISSION ARCHIVES, 1144 C St, 78114. E-mail: wchc.tx.archives@gmail.com. *Archives,* Sandra Smith; E-mail: sandra.smith@wilsoncountytx.gov
Open Mon-Thurs 9-12 & 1-5

FLOWER MOUND

P FLOWER MOUND PUBLIC LIBRARY*, 3030 Broadmoor Lane, 75022. SAN 376-4702. Tel: 972-874-6200. Circulation Tel: 972-874-6172. FAX: 972-874-6466. E-mail: fmpl@flower-mound.com. Web Site: www.flower-mound.com/135/library. *Libr Dir,* Sue Ridnour; E-mail: sue.ridnour@flower-mound.com; Staff 23 (MLS 8, Non-MLS 15)
Founded 1984. Pop 64,669; Circ 483,632
Library Holdings: Audiobooks 2,634; AV Mats 12,133; Bks on Deafness & Sign Lang 31; Braille Volumes 1; CDs 1,900; DVDs 6,198; e-books 2,751; Electronic Media & Resources 30,721; Large Print Bks 1,237; Bk Titles 78,208; Bk Vols 91,163; Per Subs 197; Talking Bks 249; Videos 943
Automation Activity & Vendor Info: (Acquisitions) Innovative Interfaces, Inc; (Cataloging) Innovative Interfaces, Inc; (Circulation) Innovative Interfaces, Inc; (OPAC) Innovative Interfaces, Inc
Wireless access
Open Mon-Wed 9-9, Thurs 9-5, Fri & Sat 11-5, Sun 1-5
Friends of the Library Group

FLOYDADA

P FLOYD COUNTY LIBRARY*, 111 S Wall St, 79235. SAN 361-638X. Tel: 806-983-4922. FAX: 806-983-4922. Web Site: fcl.ploud.net. *Head Librn,* Mary Jane Cisneros; Staff 2 (MLS 2)
Pop 10,516; Circ 29,960
Library Holdings: Bk Vols 17,000; Per Subs 20
Automation Activity & Vendor Info: (Cataloging) Follett Software; (Circulation) Follett Software; (OPAC) Follett Software
Wireless access
Open Mon, Wed & Thurs 8-12:45 & 1:15-5:30, Tues 8-4, Fri 8-1
Friends of the Library Group
Branches: 1
LOCKNEY BRANCH, 124 S Main, Lockney, 79241. (Mail add: PO Box 249, Lockney, 79241-0249), SAN 361-641X. Tel: 806-652-3561. *Librn,* Neta Marble
Library Holdings: Bk Titles 14,000; Per Subs 12
Automation Activity & Vendor Info: (Cataloging) LibLime; (Circulation) LibLime; (OPAC) LibLime
Open Mon, Tues, Thurs & Fri 1-5, Wed 2-6
Friends of the Library Group

FOREST HILL

P FOREST HILL PUBLIC LIBRARY*, 6962 Forest Hill Dr, 76140. Tel: 817-551-5354. FAX: 817-551-6368. E-mail: fhplstaff@gmail.com. Web Site: www.foresthilllibrary.org. *Pres of Board,* Dulani Masimini
Founded 2008
Automation Activity & Vendor Info: (Acquisitions) Book Systems; (Cataloging) Book Systems; (Circulation) Book Systems; (OPAC) Book Systems
Wireless access
Partic in MetroShare Libraries
Open Tues-Thurs 11-7, Sat 10-6
Friends of the Library Group

FORNEY

P ELLEN BROOKS WEST MEMORIAL LIBRARY*, Forney Public Library, 1800 College Ave, 75126. SAN 376-4400. Tel: 972-564-7027. E-mail: Forney-Library@edu.forneyisd.net. Web Site: sites.google.com/forneyisd.net/ellenbrookslibrary. *Librn,* Cherise Nichols; E-mail: cherise.nichols@edu.forneyisd.net; Staff 1 (MLS 1)
Function: 24/7 Online cat, Bks on CD, Computers for patron use, Internet access, Scanner, Summer reading prog, Tax forms
Open Mon 8-5, Tues-Thurs 8-7, Fri 8-4, Sat 10-2 (Sept-May); Mon & Wed 10-4, Tues & Thurs Noon-7, Sat 10-2 (June-Aug)
Restriction: Non-resident fee

FORT BLISS

UNITED STATES ARMY
A MICKELSEN COMMUNITY LIBRARY*, Mickelsen Library, Bldg 2E Sheridan Rd, 79916, SAN 361-6444. Tel: 915-568-6156. Administration Tel: 915-568-3089. Information Services Tel: 915-568-1491. FAX: 915-568-5754. Web Site: www.blissmwr.com/library. *Chief Librn,* Michael W McDaniel; E-mail: michael.w.mcdaniel2@us.army.mil; Staff 5 (MLS 1, Non-MLS 4)
Founded 1942
Library Holdings: Bk Titles 34,370; Bk Vols 34,788; Per Subs 65
Subject Interests: Mil hist, SW
Automation Activity & Vendor Info: (Acquisitions) Innovative Interfaces, Inc - Millennium; (Cataloging) Innovative Interfaces, Inc - Millennium; (Circulation) Innovative Interfaces, Inc - Millennium; (Course Reserve) Innovative Interfaces, Inc - Millennium; (ILL) OCLC; (OPAC) Innovative Interfaces, Inc - Millennium
Function: Audio & video playback equip for onsite use, Electronic databases & coll, ILL available, Prog for children & young adult, Spoken cassettes & CDs, Summer reading prog, Tax forms, VHS videos, Wheelchair accessible
Partic in OCLC Online Computer Library Center, Inc; Tralinet
Publications: Library Handbook
Open Mon-Fri 8-6, Sat 9-6
Restriction: Authorized patrons
A SERGEANTS MAJOR ACADEMY LEARNING RESOURCES CENTER*, Commandant USASMA, 11291 SGT E Churchill St, 79918-8002, SAN 361-6568. Tel: 915-744-8176, 915-744-8451. Administration Tel: 915-744-8122. FAX: 915-744-8484. Web Site: usasma.bliss.army.mil. *Supvry Librn,* Angelica Garcia; E-mail: angelica.garcia5.civ@mail.mil; Staff 3 (MLS 1, Non-MLS 2)
Founded 1972
Library Holdings: Bk Titles 29,601; Bk Vols 39,655; Per Subs 249
Special Collections: Army Unit History Coll; Autographed Coll
Subject Interests: Mil hist, Mil sci
Automation Activity & Vendor Info: (Acquisitions) TLC (The Library Corporation); (Cataloging) TLC (The Library Corporation); (Circulation) TLC (The Library Corporation); (ILL) OCLC FirstSearch; (OPAC) TLC (The Library Corporation)
Partic in OCLC Online Computer Library Center, Inc; Tradoc
Publications: LRC Brochure (Research guide); Periodical Holdings (Union list of periodicals)
Open Mon-Thurs 7:30-6, Fri 7:30-4:30
Restriction: Circ limited, Pub use on premises

AM UNITED STATES ARMY, William Beaumont Army Medical Center, Medical Library, 18511 Highlander Medics St, 79918. SAN 361-6177. Tel: 915-569-3277, 915-742-8783. FAX: 915-742-1674. E-mail: usarmy.bliss.medcom-wbamc.other.library@health.mil. *Librn,* Joy Marion; E-mail: joy.b.marion.civ@health.mil; *Libr Tech,* Position Currently Open; Staff 2 (MLS 1, Non-MLS 1)
Founded 1922
Library Holdings: Bk Vols 3,800; Per Subs 165
Subject Interests: Dentistry, Med, Nursing, Orthopedics, Surgery
Automation Activity & Vendor Info: (Cataloging) OCLC; (Circulation) OCLC; (ILL) OCLC Worldshare Management Services; (OPAC) OCLC; (Serials) OCLC

Partic in National Network of Libraries of Medicine Region 3; OCLC Online Computer Library Center, Inc
Restriction: Not open to pub, Staff use only

FORT DAVIS

P JEFF DAVIS COUNTY LIBRARY*, 100 Memorial Sq, 79734. (Mail add: PO Box 1054, 79734-1054), SAN 376-4338. Tel: 432-426-3802. FAX: 432-426-2225. E-mail: library@co.jeff-davis.tx.us. Web Site: jeffdaviscountylibrary.ploud.net. *Librn,* Gwin Grimes; Staff 1 (Non-MLS 1)
Founded 1999. Pop 2,200; Circ 24,000
Library Holdings: Audiobooks 1,192; DVDs 3,237; Large Print Bks 1,365; Bk Titles 11,235; Per Subs 20
Subject Interests: SW
Automation Activity & Vendor Info: (Cataloging) Biblionix/Apollo; (Circulation) Biblionix/Apollo; (ILL) Biblionix/Apollo; (OPAC) Biblionix/Apollo
Wireless access
Function: 24/7 Electronic res, 24/7 Online cat, 3D Printer, Activity rm, Adult bk club, Archival coll, Art exhibits, Art programs, Audio & video playback equip for onsite use, Bilingual assistance for Spanish patrons, Bk club(s), Bks on CD, Butterfly Garden, Children's prog, Citizenship assistance, Computer training, Computers for patron use, Digital talking bks, E-Readers, E-Reserves, Electronic databases & coll, Family literacy, Free DVD rentals, Govt ref serv, Health sci info serv, ILL available, Instruction & testing, Internet access, Laminating, Learning ctr, Life-long learning prog for all ages, Magazines, Mail & tel request accepted, Makerspace, Movies, Notary serv, Online cat, Online info literacy tutorials on the web & in blackboard, Online ref, Orientations, Outreach serv, Outside serv via phone, mail, e-mail & web, Photocopying/Printing, Preschool reading prog, Printer for laptops & handheld devices, Prog for adults, Prog for children & young adult, Ref & res, Ref serv available, Res assist avail, Scanner, Senior computer classes, Senior outreach, Spanish lang bks, STEM programs, Story hour, Summer & winter reading prog, Summer reading prog, Tax forms, Telephone ref, Visual arts prog, Wheelchair accessible, Workshops, Writing prog
Partic in Partners Library Action Network
Open Mon-Fri 10-6, Sat 10-2
Friends of the Library Group

FORT HANCOCK

P FORT HANCOCK ISD/PUBLIC LIBRARY*, 100 School Dr, 79839. (Mail add: PO Box 98, 79839-0098), SAN 376-4354. Tel: 915-769-3811. FAX: 915-769-3940. Web Site: fhisd.ss7.sharpschool.com/departments/library. *Dir,* Gloria Galindo; Tel: 915-769-3811, Ext 1306, E-mail: lgalindo@fhisd.net; Staff 3 (MLS 1, Non-MLS 2)
Founded 1990. Pop 1,200
Library Holdings: Bk Vols 12,500; Per Subs 21
Open Mon-Fri 8-4

FORT HOOD

UNITED STATES ARMY
A CASEY MEMORIAL LIBRARY*, 72nd St & 761st Tank Battalion, Bldg 3202, 76544-5024. Tel: 254-287-0025. Circulation Tel: 254-287-4921. Reference Tel: 254-287-5202. FAX: 254-288-4029. Web Site: www.hoodmwr.com/casey_library.htm. *Dir,* Pamela Shelton; E-mail: pamela.a.shelton.naf@mail.mil; *Syst Librn,* Jane Mohammadi; E-mail: jane.l.mohammadi.naf@mail.mil; *Cataloger,* Lauren K Herring; E-mail: lauren.k.herring.naf@mail.mil; *Pub Serv,* Jennifer Hauschildt; E-mail: jennifer.k.hauschildt.naf@mail.mil; *Ref Serv,* Beth Underwood; E-mail: beth.e.underwood.naf@mail.mil; Staff 18 (MLS 5, Non-MLS 13)
Founded 1942
Library Holdings: CDs 1,200; DVDs 5,000; e-books 5,000; Bk Titles 70,000; Bk Vols 90,000; Per Subs 204
Subject Interests: General reading, Grad, Mil sci, Undergrad studies
Automation Activity & Vendor Info: (Cataloging) Innovative Interfaces, Inc - Millennium; (Circulation) Innovative Interfaces, Inc - Millennium; (ILL) OCLC Connexion; (OPAC) Innovative Interfaces, Inc - Millennium
Function: Audio & video playback equip for onsite use, Bks on cassette, Bks on CD, Computer training, Computers for patron use, Govt ref serv, ILL available, Music CDs, Photocopying/Printing, Prog for adults, Prog for children & young adult, Ref & res, Summer reading prog, Tax forms, Telephone ref
Partic in OCLC Online Computer Library Center, Inc; Worldcat
Open Mon-Thurs 10-8, Fri & Sat 10-6, Sun 12-8

AM MEDICAL LIBRARY*, Bldg 36000, Carl R Darnall Medical Ctr, 76544-5063, SAN 361-6657. Tel: 254-288-8366. FAX: 254-288-8368. *Librn,* Beatrice Nichols; *Asst Librn,* Cathy Newell
Founded 1952
Library Holdings: Bk Vols 8,000; Per Subs 195
Subject Interests: Basic sci, Dentistry, Med, Specialities, Surgical
Automation Activity & Vendor Info: (Cataloging) Ex Libris Group; (Circulation) Ex Libris Group; (OPAC) Ex Libris Group
Partic in National Network of Libraries of Medicine Region 3; OCLC Online Computer Library Center, Inc; Proquest Dialog; S Cent Regional Libr Prog
Restriction: Staff use only

FORT SAM HOUSTON

A JOINT BASE SAN ANTONIO LIBRARIES*, Keith A Campbell Memorial Library, 3011 Harney Path, 78234. SAN 361-6770. Tel: 210-221-4387, 210-221-4702. E-mail: camplibraryftsam@gmail.com. Web Site: www.jbsalibraries.org. *Libr Mgr,* Darrell Hankins; E-mail: darrell.hankins.3@us.af.mil; *Ref Librn,* Susan Weart Artiglia; E-mail: susan.artiglia@us.af.mil; Staff 3 (MLS 3)
Founded 1918
Library Holdings: Bk Titles 82,000; Bk Vols 98,000; Per Subs 25
Subject Interests: Mil hist, Patient educ
Automation Activity & Vendor Info: (Cataloging) Innovative Interfaces, Inc; (Circulation) Innovative Interfaces, Inc; (ILL) OCLC Online; (Media Booking) Baker & Taylor; (OPAC) Innovative Interfaces, Inc - Millennium
Wireless access
Function: Bks on cassette, Bks on CD, Children's prog, Computers for patron use, Electronic databases & coll, Free DVD rentals, ILL available, Internet access, Masonic res mat, Music CDs, Online cat, Orientations, Photocopying/Printing, Preschool outreach, Prog for children & young adult, Ref serv available, Scanner, Spoken cassettes & CDs, Spoken cassettes & DVDs, Story hour, Summer reading prog, Tax forms, Telephone ref, VHS videos, Wheelchair accessible
Partic in OCLC Online Computer Library Center, Inc
Restriction: Authorized personnel only, Borrowing requests are handled by ILL, Circ to mem only, In-house use for visitors

UNITED STATES ARMY
AM INSTITUTE OF SURGICAL RESEARCH LIBRARY*, 3698 Chambers Pass, Bldg 3611, 78234-6315. Tel: 210-539-4559. FAX: 210-539-1460. E-mail: usarmy.jbsa.medcom-aisr.mbx.webmaster@health.mil. *Libr Mgr,* Gerri Trumbo; *Libr Tech,* Frank Hernandez
Library Holdings: e-journals 121; Bk Vols 3,000; Per Subs 125
Subject Interests: Med
Automation Activity & Vendor Info: (Cataloging) Ex Libris Group
Restriction: Staff use only

AM STIMSON LIBRARY*, Medical Department Ctr & School, Bldg 2840, Ste 106, 3630 Stanley Rd, 78234-7697, SAN 361-6746. Tel: 210-221-6900. Interlibrary Loan Service Tel: 210-221-6230. Reference Tel: 210-221-6249. FAX: 210-221-8264. Web Site: www.cs.amedd.army.mil/stimlib. *Ref (Info Servs),* Joan Bares; Staff 11 (MLS 4, Non-MLS 7)
Founded 1932
Library Holdings: e-journals 8,000; Bk Titles 30,000; Bk Vols 60,000; Per Subs 600
Subject Interests: Allied health, Anesthesiology, Healthcare admin, Mil med, Nursing, Pub health
Automation Activity & Vendor Info: (Acquisitions) Ex Libris Group; (Cataloging) Ex Libris Group; (Circulation) Ex Libris Group; (Course Reserve) Ex Libris Group; (ILL) Ex Libris Group; (OPAC) Ex Libris Group; (Serials) Ex Libris Group
Function: ILL available
Partic in Council of Research & Academic Libraries; Health Oriented Libraries of San Antonio
Restriction: Not open to pub

FORT STOCKTON

P FORT STOCKTON PUBLIC LIBRARY*, 500 N Water St, 79735. SAN 316-327X. Tel: 432-336-3374. FAX: 432-336-6648. E-mail: info@fort-stockton.lib.tx.us. Web Site: www.fort-stockton.lib.tx.us. *Dir,* Elva Valadez; E-mail: director@fort-stockton.lib.tx.us; Staff 7 (Non-MLS 7)
Founded 1911. Pop 12,000; Circ 120,000
Library Holdings: AV Mats 1,226; CDs 733; DVDs 754; Large Print Bks 1,064; Music Scores 85; Bk Titles 48,144; Bk Vols 52,218; Per Subs 164; Videos 2,234
Subject Interests: Genealogy, SW
Automation Activity & Vendor Info: (Acquisitions) Book Systems; (Cataloging) Book Systems; (Circulation) Book Systems; (ILL) OCLC; (OPAC) Book Systems
Wireless access
Function: ILL available
Publications: FSPL Monthly News; Young Adult Writers & Artists (Annual)
Partic in Partners Library Action Network
Open Mon-Fri 8-5
Friends of the Library Group

FORT WORTH

S BOTANICAL RESEARCH INSTITUTE OF TEXAS LIBRARY, 1700 University Dr, 76107. SAN 374-6631. Tel: 817-332-4441, 817-463-4102. FAX: 817-332-4112. E-mail: library@fwbg.org. Web Site: fwbg.org/science-conservation. *Dir,* Barney Lipscomb; E-mail: barney@brit.org; *Librn,* Ana Nino; E-mail: anino@brit.org; Staff 1 (MLS 1)
Founded 1987
Library Holdings: Bk Titles 18,000; Bk Vols 125,000; Per Subs 1,100
Special Collections: Botany, Taxonomy (Lloyd Shinners Coll in Systematic Botany)
Wireless access
Function: Adult bk club, Internet access, Ref serv available
Publications: Journal of the Botanical Research Institute of Texas; SIDA Botanical Miscellany
Partic in Cultural District Library Consortium
Restriction: Non-circulating to the pub, Open by appt only, Visitors must make appt to use bks in the libr

S AMON CARTER MUSEUM OF AMERICAN ART*, Research Library, 3501 Camp Bowie Blvd, 76107-2695. SAN 316-3318. Tel: 817-738-1933. Reference Tel: 817-989-5040. FAX: 817-989-5079. E-mail: library@cartermuseum.org. Web Site: www.cartermuseum.org/library. *Exec Dir,* Lynn Castle; E-mail: lcastle@amset.org; *Libr Dir,* Samuel Duncan; *Archivist, Ref Serv Mgr,* Jonathan Frembling; E-mail: jon.frembling@cartermuseum.org; Staff 2 (MLS 1, Non-MLS 1)
Founded 1961
Library Holdings: Microforms 66,000; Bk Titles 50,000; Bk Vols 55,000; Per Subs 120
Special Collections: 19th-century US Newspapers, micro; American Artist & Photographer Coll, bio/ephemera files; American Illustrated Book Coll; Archives of American Art Associated Research Center, unrestricted micro; Auction Catalogs; Eliot Porter Archives; Laura Gilpin Archives; Roman Bronze Works Archives
Subject Interests: Am art, Am photog, Hist of the Am West
Automation Activity & Vendor Info: (Cataloging) Ex Libris Group; (OPAC) Ex Libris Group
Function: Archival coll, Art exhibits, Computers for patron use, Doc delivery serv, Electronic databases & coll, ILL available, Internet access, Microfiche/film & reading machines, Outside serv via phone, mail, e-mail & web, Photocopying/Printing, Ref & res, Ref serv available, Res libr, Scanner
Partic in Cultural District Library Consortium; OCLC Online Computer Library Center, Inc
Open Wed & Fri 11-4, Thurs 11-7
Restriction: Closed stack, Lending to staff only, Non-circulating to the pub, Open to pub with supv only, Pub use on premises, Restricted borrowing privileges

GL THE DELL DEHAY LAW LIBRARY OF TARRANT COUNTY*, Tarrant County Historical Courthouse, 100 W Weatherford St, Rm 420, 76196-0800. SAN 316-3504. Tel: 817-884-1481. E-mail: lawlibrary@tarrantcountytx.gov. Web Site: www.tarrantcountytx.gov/en/law-library.html. *Dir,* Cara Sitton; *Asst Dir,* Amanda Hill; Staff 6 (MLS 3, Non-MLS 3)
Founded 1944
Automation Activity & Vendor Info: (Cataloging) EOS International; (Circulation) EOS International
Wireless access
Function: 24/7 Electronic res, 24/7 Online cat, Bilingual assistance for Spanish patrons, Computers for patron use, Electronic databases & coll, For res purposes, Internet access, Online cat, Photocopying/Printing, Ref serv available
Open Mon-Fri 8-4
Restriction: In-house use for visitors, Non-circulating, Not a lending libr

P FAIRMOUNT COMMUNITY LIBRARY, 1310 W Allen Ave, 76110. Tel: 682-710-3223. E-mail: fairmountcommunitylibraryfw@gmail.com. Web Site: www.fairmountcommunitylibrary.org. *Chmn of Libr Board,* Kat Valentine; E-mail: katvalentinefcl@gmail.com
Founded 2015
Library Holdings: Bk Vols 13,000
Wireless access
Function: 24/7 Online cat, Adult bk club, Art programs, Bk club(s), Children's prog, Computers for patron use, Games, Holiday prog, Internet access, Magazines, Meeting rooms, Online cat, Photocopying/Printing, Printer for laptops & handheld devices, Scanner, Story hour, Teen prog, Workshops, Writing prog
Open Mon-Fri 12-6, Sat 10-2

P FORT WORTH LIBRARY*, Central Library, 500 W Third St, 76102. SAN 361-6800. Tel: 817-392-7323. Interlibrary Loan Service Tel: 817-392-7731. Administration Tel: 817-392-7705. TDD: 817-392-8926. E-mail: LibraryWebMail@fortworthtexas.gov. Web Site: fortworthtexas.gov/library. *Dir,* Manya Shorr; E-mail: manya_shorr@fortworthtexas.gov; *Asst Dir, Operations,* Marilyn Marvin; *Asst Dir, Pub Serv,* Michele Gorman; Staff 209 (MLS 80, Non-MLS 129)
Founded 1901
Library Holdings: Bk Titles 990,293; Bk Vols 2,240,515; Per Subs 1,392
Special Collections: Bookplates; Early Children's Books; Earth Science; Fort Worth History/Archives; Genealogy Coll; Popular Sheet Music; Postcards. Oral History; State Document Depository; US Document Depository
Automation Activity & Vendor Info: (Cataloging) SirsiDynix; (Circulation) SirsiDynix; (OPAC) SirsiDynix; (Serials) SirsiDynix
Wireless access
Special Services for the Deaf - TDD equip
Open Mon 12-8, Tues-Thurs 10-8, Fri & Sat 10-6, Sun 12-6
Restriction: Residents only
Friends of the Library Group
Branches: 15

BOLD (BUTLER OUTREACH LIBRARY DIVISION), 1801 N South Frwy, 76102-5742. (Mail add: 500 W Third St, 76102-7305). Tel: 817-392-5514. *Librn,* Ms L G Swift
Library Holdings: Bk Vols 1,263
Open Tues-Sat 9-5
Friends of the Library Group

COOL (CAVILE OUTREACH OPPORTUNITY LIBRARY), 5060 Ave G, 76105-1906. Tel: 817-392-5512. Web Site: fortworthtexas.gov/library/branches/cool. *Library Contact,* L G Swift
Open Tues-Sat 9-5

DIAMOND HILL/JARVIS BRANCH, 1300 NE 35th St, 76106, SAN 323-8385. Tel: 817-392-6010. *Librn,* Sheila Barnett
Library Holdings: Bk Vols 49,977
Open Mon 12-8, Tues-Thurs 10-8, Fri & Sat 10-6
Friends of the Library Group

EAST BERRY, 4300 E Berry St, 76105, SAN 361-6959. Tel: 817-392-5470. *Mgr,* Osei Baffour; Staff 7 (MLS 2, Non-MLS 5)
Library Holdings: Bk Vols 53,699
Open Mon 12-8, Tues-Thurs 10-8, Fri & Sat 10-6
Friends of the Library Group

EAST REGIONAL, 6301 Bridge St, 76105, SAN 376-9321. Tel: 817-892-5550. *Mgr,* Osei Baffour; Staff 6 (MLS 3, Non-MLS 3)
Founded 1943
Library Holdings: Bk Vols 56,991
Open Mon 12-8, Tues-Thurs 10-8, Fri & Sat 10-6, Sun 12-6
Friends of the Library Group

ESKILLS LIBRARY & JOB CENTER, 2800 Stark St, 76112, SAN 361-6835. Tel: 817-392-6621. *Supvr,* Ms L G Swift
Library Holdings: Bk Vols 67,449
Open Mon 12-8, Tues-Thurs 10-8, Fri & Sat 10-6
Friends of the Library Group

NORTHSIDE, 601 Park St, 76106, SAN 361-686X. Tel: 817-392-6641. *Librn,* Sheila Barnett
Library Holdings: Bk Vols 46,225
Open Mon 12-8, Tues & Thurs 10-8, Fri & Sat 10-6
Friends of the Library Group

NORTHWEST, 6228 Crystal Lake Dr, 76179. Tel: 817-392-5420. *Librn,* Sheila Barnett
Founded 2010. Circ 253,702
Open Mon 12-8, Tues-Thurs 10-8, Fri & Sat 10-6
Friends of the Library Group

RIDGLEA, 3628 Bernie Anderson Ave, 76116-5403, SAN 361-7017. Tel: 817-392-6631. *Librn,* Barbara Henderson
Library Holdings: Bk Vols 95,152
Open Mon 12-8, Tues-Thurs 10-8, Fri & Sat 10-6
Friends of the Library Group

RIVERSIDE, 2913 Yucca Ave, 76111, SAN 361-6894. Tel: 817-392-5560. FAX: 817-392-5403. *Librn,* Sheila Barnett; Staff 3 (MLS 3)
Founded 1966
Library Holdings: Bk Vols 55,413
Special Collections: Spanish Coll; Vietnamese Coll, bks, CDs, DVDs
Function: Adult literacy prog, Audiobks via web, AV serv, Bilingual assistance for Spanish patrons, Bks on CD, Children's prog, Citizenship assistance, Computer training, Computers for patron use, E-Reserves, Electronic databases & coll, Family literacy, ILL available, Literacy & newcomer serv, Magnifiers for reading, Mail & tel request accepted, Museum passes, Music CDs, Online cat, Orientations, OverDrive digital audio bks, Photocopying/Printing, Prog for children & young adult, Ref & res, Ref serv available, Senior computer classes, Spoken cassettes & CDs, Spoken cassettes & DVDs, Story hour, Summer reading prog, Tax forms, Teen prog, Telephone ref, Wheelchair accessible
Open Mon 12-8, Tues-Thurs 10-8, Fri & Sat 10-6
Friends of the Library Group

SEMINARY SOUTH, 501 E Bolt St, 76110, SAN 361-6924. Tel: 817-392-5490. *Librn,* Barbara Henderson; Staff 6 (MLS 2, Non-MLS 4)
Library Holdings: Bk Vols 66,333

Open Mon 12-8, Tues-Thurs 10-8, Fri & Sat 10-6
Friends of the Library Group
ELLA MAE SHAMBLEE, 1062 Evans Ave, 76104-5135, SAN 361-6916. Tel: 817-392-5580. FAX: 817-392-5583. *Librn,* Ms L G Swift
Library Holdings: Bk Vols 32,337
Open Mon 12-8, Tues-Thurs 10-8, Fri & Sat 10-6
Friends of the Library Group
SOUTHWEST REGIONAL, 4001 Library Lane, 76109, SAN 328-7327. Tel: 817-392-5860. *Librn,* Barbara Henderson
Library Holdings: Bk Vols 131,489
Open Mon 12-8, Tues-Thurs 10-8, Fri & Sat 10-6, Sun 12-6
Friends of the Library Group
SUMMERGLEN, 4205 Basswood Blvd, 76137-1402. Tel: 817-392-5970. *Librn,* Osei Baffour
Library Holdings: Bk Vols 43,744
Automation Activity & Vendor Info: (Cataloging) Follett Software; (Circulation) Follett Software; (ILL) Follett Software; (OPAC) Follett Software
Open Mon 12-8, Tues-Thurs 10-8, Fri & Sat 10-6
Friends of the Library Group
WEDGWOOD, 3816 Kimberly Lane, 76133, SAN 361-6983. Tel: 817-392-5480. *Librn,* Barbara Henderson; Staff 4.5 (MLS 4, Non-MLS 0.5)
Founded 1962. Circ 277,105
Library Holdings: Bk Titles 23,400; Bk Vols 35,498; Per Subs 38
Automation Activity & Vendor Info: (Cataloging) Horizon; (Circulation) Horizon; (OPAC) Horizon
Open Mon 12-8, Tues-Thurs 10-8, Fri & Sat 10-6
Friends of the Library Group

S FORT WORTH MUSEUM OF SCIENCE & HISTORY LIBRARY*, 1600 Gendy St, 76107. SAN 316-3369. Tel: 817-255-9305. FAX: 817-255-9595. Web Site: fwmuseum.org. *Dir, Initiatives & Stragegies,* Denise Hamilton; E-mail: dbollinger@fwmsh.org; *Dir, Hist & Archives,* Leigh Ann Naylor; E-mail: archives@fwmsh.org; *Asst Curator,* Leishawn Spotted Bear; Tel: 817-255-9323, E-mail: lspottedbear@fwmsh.org. Subject Specialists: *Hist, Sci,* Leishawn Spotted Bear; Staff 1 (MLS 1)
Founded 1954
Library Holdings: Bk Vols 6,000
Special Collections: Institutional Archives
Subject Interests: Archaeology, Astronomy, Ethnology, Geol, Local hist, Museology, Natural sci, Texana
Function: Archival coll, For res purposes, Photocopying/Printing, Ref serv available, Res libr, Telephone ref
Restriction: Circ limited, Closed stack, In-house use for visitors, Non-circulating to the pub, Open by appt only

P BILLIE HAMILTON MEMORIAL LIBRARY*, 301 S Blue Mound Rd, Blue Mound, 76131. SAN 316-1099. Tel: 817-847-4095. FAX: 817-232-8050. E-mail: bluemoundlib2004@sbcglobal.net. *Librn,* Position Currently Open; *Library Contact,* DeAnn Gage
Pop 2,500; Circ 5,745
Library Holdings: Bk Vols 13,000; Per Subs 10
Automation Activity & Vendor Info: (Cataloging) Follett Software; (Circulation) Follett Software
Wireless access
Open Mon-Thurs 10-5, Fri 10-6, Sat 10-2 (Sept-May); Tues-Thurs 10-5, Fri 10-6, Sat 10-2 (June-Aug)

L KELLY HART & HALLMAN*, Law Library, Wells Fargo Tower, 201 Main St, Ste 2500, 76102. SAN 372-1639. Tel: 817-332-2500. FAX: 817-878-9280. Web Site: www.kellyhart.com. *Librn,* Amy E Yawn; E-mail: amy.yawn@kellyhart.com
Subject Interests: Gen law
Wireless access
Restriction: Staff use only

S KIMBELL ART MUSEUM LIBRARY, 3333 Camp Bowie Blvd, 76107. SAN 316-3415. Tel: 817-332-8451. E-mail: library@kimbellmuseum.org. Web Site: kimbellart.org/about/library. *Librn,* Caroline Clavell
Founded 1967
Library Holdings: Microforms 23,000; Bk Vols 50,000; Per Subs 100
Special Collections: Deloynes Coll; Witt Library Coll
Subject Interests: Ancient to early 20th Century art (excluding Am)
Automation Activity & Vendor Info: (Acquisitions) Ex Libris Group; (Cataloging) OCLC Connexion; (Circulation) Ex Libris Group; (ILL) OCLC WorldShare Interlibrary Loan; (OPAC) Ex Libris Group; (Serials) Ex Libris Group
Wireless access
Partic in Amigos Library Services, Inc; Cultural District Library Consortium; OCLC Online Computer Library Center, Inc
Restriction: Open by appt only

A NAVY GENERAL LIBRARY PROGRAM*, NAS Fort Worth JRB Library, 1802 Doolittle Ave, NAS Fort Worth JRB, 76127. SAN 361-5480. Tel: 817-782-7735. FAX: 817-782-7219. E-mail: cnicseftwonmr-library@us.navy.mil. *Libr Dir,* Patricia Tellman; Staff 3 (MLS 1, Non-MLS 2)
Subject Interests: Mil hist
Automation Activity & Vendor Info: (Cataloging) EOS International; (Circulation) EOS International; (OPAC) EOS International
Wireless access
Restriction: Not open to pub

M JOHN PETER SMITH HOSPITAL*, John S Marietta Memorial Medical Library, John S Marietta Memorial, 1500 S Main St, 76104. SAN 316-3490. Tel: 817-702-5057. E-mail: Medicalibrary@JSPHealth.org. Web Site: jps.hsc.unt.edu. *Libr Mgr,* Tim Kenny; E-mail: tkenny@jpshealth.org; *Clinical Librn,* Kellie Boyd; E-mail: kboyd2@jpshealth.org
Founded 1960
Library Holdings: e-books 10,377; e-journals 10,091; Bk Vols 20,000; Per Subs 300
Subject Interests: Dental surgery, Family practice, Gynecology, Internal med, Nursing, Obstetrics, Pediatrics, Psychiat, Radiology
Wireless access
Partic in Healthline; SCC/MLA
Open Mon-Fri 8-5

R SOUTHWESTERN BAPTIST THEOLOGICAL SEMINARY LIBRARIES*, A Webb Roberts Library, 2001 W Seminary Dr, 76115-2157. (Mail add: PO Box 22490, 76122-0490), SAN 361-7106. Tel: 817-923-1921, Ext 4000. Interlibrary Loan Service Tel: 817-923-1921, Ext 2750. FAX: 817-921-8765. Circulation E-mail: rlcirc@swbts.edu. Web Site: www.swbts.edu/libraries. *Dean of Libr,* Dr Craig Kubic; E-mail: ckubic@swbts.edu; *Archivist & Spec Coll Librn,* Jill Botticelli; *Digital Res Librn,* Robert Burgess; *Music Librn,* Dr Jason Runnels; *Tech Serv Librn,* Heather Hicks; *Pub Serv Mgr,* James McKinney; *Acq,* Dorothy Smith
Founded 1908. Enrl 3,400; Fac 141; Highest Degree: Doctorate
Library Holdings: Bk Vols 464,586; Per Subs 736
Special Collections: Baptist History (James M Carroll, George W Truett & M E Dodd Coll), ms files; Hymnals
Subject Interests: Relig educ, Sacred music, Theol
Automation Activity & Vendor Info: (Acquisitions) Innovative Interfaces, Inc - Sierra; (Cataloging) Innovative Interfaces, Inc - Sierra; (Circulation) Innovative Interfaces, Inc - Sierra; (Course Reserve) Innovative Interfaces, Inc - Sierra; (Discovery) EBSCO Discovery Service; (ILL) OCLC Worldshare Management Services; (OPAC) SirsiDynix; (Serials) SirsiDynix
Function: 24/7 Electronic res, 24/7 Online cat, Activity rm, Archival coll, Computers for patron use, Internet access, Mango lang, Online cat, Orientations, Ref & res, Scanner
Publications: New Titles List
Partic in Amigos Library Services, Inc; OCLC Online Computer Library Center, Inc; TexSHARE - Texas State Library & Archives Commission

Departmental Libraries:

KATHRYN SULLIVAN BOWLD MUSIC LIBRARY, 1809 W Broadus, Rm 113, 76115-2157. Tel: 817-923-1921, Ext 2070. FAX: 817-921-8762. *Librn,* Dr Fang-Lan Hsieh; E-mail: fhsieh@swbts.edu. Subject Specialists: *Church music,* Dr Fang-Lan Hsieh
Library Holdings: Bk Titles 21,546
Special Collections: George Stebbins Memorial; Hymnals
Subject Interests: Church, Relig scores, Sacred music
HOUSTON CAMPUS LIBRARY, 4105 Broadway St, Houston, 77087. Tel: 713-634-0011. FAX: 713-634-0018. *Librn,* Dr Stefana Laing; Tel: 713-634-0011, Ext 225, E-mail: slaing@swbts.edu

TARRANT COUNTY COLLEGE

J NORTHWEST CAMPUS WALSH LIBRARY, 4801 Marine Creek Pkwy, 76179, SAN 361-7254. Tel: 817-515-7725. FAX: 817-515-7720. Web Site: library.tccd.edu. *Dir, Libr Serv,* Alexis (Alex) Potemkin; E-mail: alexis.potemkin@tccd.edu; *Asst Dir,* James Baxter; E-mail: james.baxter@tccd.edu; Staff 11 (MLS 5, Non-MLS 6)
Founded 1975. Enrl 8,100; Fac 90; Highest Degree: Associate
Library Holdings: Bk Vols 41,024; Per Subs 200
Library is temporarily located in Bldg NW 05 1202 until Fall 2026
Open Mon-Thurs 7:30am-9pm, Fri 7:30-5, Sat 10-4 (Fall/Spring); Mon-Thurs 7:30am-9pm (Summer)

J SOUTH CAMPUS JENKINS GARRETT LIBRARY*, 5301 Campus Dr, 76119, SAN 361-7289. Tel: 817-515-4524. FAX: 817-515-4436. Web Site: www.tccd.edu. *Dir, Libr Serv,* Linda Jenson; *Asst Dir,* Erik France; *Circ Mgr,* Jeanne Wright; *Pub Serv,* Lynda De los Santos; *Pub Serv,* Jennifer Jackson; Staff 5 (MLS 5)
Founded 1967. Enrl 7,142; Fac 175
Library Holdings: Bk Vols 65,747; Per Subs 268
Partic in Amigos Library Services, Inc
Open Mon-Thurs 7:45am-10pm, Fri 7:45-3, Sat 9-3

J TRINITY RIVER CAMPUS LIBRARY*, 300 Trinity Campus Circle, 76102. Tel: 817-515-1220. FAX: 817-515-0706. Circulation E-mail: tr.circ@tccd.edu. *Asst Dir,* Danelle Toups; Tel: 817-515-1222, E-mail: danelle.toups@tccd.edu
Partic in Amigos Library Services, Inc
Open Mon-Fri 7am-9pm, Sat 8-5, Sun Noon-5; Mon-Thurs 7am-9pm (Summer)

C TEXAS CHRISTIAN UNIVERSITY*, Mary Couts Burnett Library, 2913 Lowden St, TCU Box 298400, 76129. SAN 361-7319. Tel: 817-257-7106. Circulation Tel: 817-257-7112. Reference Tel: 817-257-7117. FAX: 817-257-7282. TDD: 817-257-7716. E-mail: reference@tcu.edu. Web Site: library.tcu.edu. *Dean,* Tracy Hull; E-mail: t.hull@tcu.edu; *Dir, Admin Serv,* James Lutz; *Dir, Libr Syst,* Kerry Bouchard; *Dir, Spec Coll,* Ann Hodges; *Head of Ref & Instrul Serv,* Linda Chenoweth; *Head, Circ,* Cheryl Sassman; *Head, Tech Serv,* Dennis Odom; *Access Serv Librn,* Kristen Barnes; *Electronic Res Librn,* Leah Hamrick; *Music & Media Librn,* Cari Alexander; *Rare Bk Librn,* Julie Christenson; *Cat,* Sara Dillard; *Cat,* David Hamrick; *Info Tech,* Stephanie Folse; *ILL,* Kay Edmondson; *Sr Archivist,* Mary Saffell; Staff 29 (MLS 26, Non-MLS 3)
Founded 1873. Enrl 10,918; Fac 698; Highest Degree: Doctorate
Jun 2016-May 2017. Mats Exp $6,968,064, Books $1,582,940, Per/Ser (Incl. Access Fees) $5,365,691, Presv $7,460. Sal $2,036,028 (Prof $1,115,880)
Library Holdings: AV Mats 70,423; e-books 1,383,493; e-journals 154,582; Electronic Media & Resources 136,136; Microforms 511,710; Bk Titles 970,323; Bk Vols 1,366,490; Per Subs 166,332
Special Collections: International Piano Competition (Van Cliburn Foundation Archives), AV mat; Juvenile Literature (The Erisman-Odom Coll of Juvenile Literature in Series); Literature (William Luther Lewis Coll); United States History (Amon G Carter Archives); United States History (James C Wright Jr Archives). State Document Depository; US Document Depository
Subject Interests: Chem, English, Hist, Lit, Music, Nursing, Psychol, Theol
Automation Activity & Vendor Info: (Acquisitions) Ex Libris Group; (Cataloging) Ex Libris Group; (Circulation) Ex Libris Group; (Course Reserve) Ex Libris Group; (Discovery) ProQuest; (ILL) OCLC; (OPAC) Ex Libris Group; (Serials) Ex Libris Group
Wireless access
Function: Wheelchair accessible
Publications: Windows
Partic in Amigos Library Services, Inc; LYRASIS; Statewide California Electronic Library Consortium; TexSHARE - Texas State Library & Archives Commission
Special Services for the Blind - Closed circuit TV magnifier
Friends of the Library Group

M TEXAS HEALTH HARRIS METHODIST FORT WORTH HOSPITAL*, 1301 Pennsylvania Ave, 76104. SAN 316-3393. Tel: 817-250-2118. Reference Tel: 817-250-2917. FAX: 817-250-5119. *Dir,* Scarlett Burchfield; Tel: 817-250-2916; *Outreach Serv Librn,* Jamie Furrh Quinn; Tel: 817-250-3191, E-mail: jamiequinn@texashealth.org; Staff 5 (MLS 4, Non-MLS 1)
Founded 1948
Library Holdings: Bk Titles 10,000; Bk Vols 10,400; Per Subs 330
Subject Interests: Internal med, Surgery
Wireless access
Function: Doc delivery serv, For res purposes, Homebound delivery serv, ILL available, Photocopying/Printing
Partic in Healthline; S Cent Regional Med Libr Program; Tarrant County Consortium of Health Sci Libr
Restriction: Co libr, Employees & their associates, In-house use for visitors, Lending to staff only, Med staff only, Open to pub for ref only, Restricted borrowing privileges

C TEXAS WESLEYAN UNIVERSITY*, Eunice & James L West Library, 1201 Wesleyan St, 76105. SAN 316-3512. Tel: 817-531-4800. Reference Tel: 817-531-4802. Administration Tel: 817-531-4821. FAX: 817-531-4806. Web Site: westlibrary.txwes.edu. *Dir,* Elizabeth Howard; E-mail: ehoward@txwes.edu; *Univ Archivist,* Louis Sherwood, Jr; Tel: 817-531-4822, E-mail: lsherwood@txwes.edu; *Ref & Instruction Librn,* Marquel Anteola; Tel: 817-531-4813, E-mail: manteola@txwes.edu; *Per, Syst Librn,* Shelley Almgren; Tel: 817-531-4816, E-mail: salmgren@txwes.edu; *Library Services & Assessment Mgr,* Sheri Parker; E-mail: sparker@txwes.edu; Staff 12 (MLS 6, Non-MLS 6)
Founded 1891. Enrl 1,792; Fac 142; Highest Degree: Master
Library Holdings: AV Mats 5,261; CDs 150; e-books 69,800; Music Scores 8,169; Bk Titles 210,000; Bk Vols 227,215; Per Subs 287
Special Collections: Bobby Bragen Baseball Memorabillia Coll; Joe Brown Theatre Coll, microfiche; Music Scores; Twyla Miranda Juvenile Coll
Subject Interests: Lit
Automation Activity & Vendor Info: (Acquisitions) SirsiDynix; (Cataloging) SirsiDynix; (Circulation) SirsiDynix; (Course Reserve) SirsiDynix; (OPAC) SirsiDynix; (Serials) SirsiDynix
Wireless access
Function: Archival coll, Audio & video playback equip for onsite use, Electronic databases & coll, ILL available, Internet access, Online ref, Orientations, Photocopying/Printing, Ref & res, Telephone ref, VHS videos
Partic in Amigos Library Services, Inc; OCLC Online Computer Library Center, Inc
Open Mon-Thurs 7:30am-10pm, Fri 7:30-5, Sat 8-5, Sun 1-10 (Fall & Winter); Mon-Thurs 7:30-7, Fri 7:30-5, Sat & Sun 12-6 (Summer)
Restriction: Open to students, fac & staff, Photo ID required for access, Private libr

R TRAVIS AVENUE BAPTIST CHURCH LIBRARY*, 800 W Berry St, 76110. SAN 316-3520. Tel: 817-924-4266. FAX: 817-921-9620. E-mail: contactus@travis.org. Web Site: www.travis.org. *Librn,* Judy Smith
Library Holdings: Bk Vols 1,250
Restriction: Mem only

CM UNIVERSITY OF NORTH TEXAS HEALTH SCIENCE CENTER AT FORT WORTH*, Gibson D Lewis Health Science Library, 955 Montgomery St, 76107. SAN 316-3466. Tel: 817-735-2070. Circulation Tel: 817-735-2465. Administration Tel: 817-735-2589. Toll Free Tel: 800-687-5302. Web Site: library.unthsc.edu. *Univ Librn,* Daniel E Burgard; E-mail: daniel.burgard@unthsc.edu; Staff 30 (MLS 16, Non-MLS 14)
Founded 1970. Enrl 2,400; Fac 400; Highest Degree: Doctorate
Special Collections: History of Osteopathic Medicine; Texas Osteopathic Medical Association Archives; William G Sutherland Coll. Oral History
Subject Interests: Allied health prof, Med, Osteopathic med, Pub health
Automation Activity & Vendor Info: (Acquisitions) SirsiDynix; (Cataloging) SirsiDynix; (Circulation) SirsiDynix; (OPAC) SirsiDynix
Wireless access
Function: Audio & video playback equip for onsite use, Computers for patron use, Doc delivery serv, E-Reserves, Electronic databases & coll, Health sci info serv, ILL available, Internet access, Online cat, Online ref, Outreach serv, Photocopying/Printing, Ref serv available, VHS videos
Publications: Acquisition List; Bibliography of Faculty Publications; Collection Catalog; Library Guide; Library Handbook; New Books List (Audio-visual catalog); On-Line Services Guide; Oral History Collection CAT; Research Guide
Partic in Amigos Library Services, Inc; Healthline; National Network of Libraries of Medicine Region 3; South Central Academic Medical Libraries Consortium; TexSHARE - Texas State Library & Archives Commission

FRANKLIN

P ROBERTSON COUNTY CARNEGIE LIBRARY*, 315 E Decherd St, 77856. (Mail add: PO Box 1027, 77856-1027), SAN 316-3547. Tel: 979-828-4331. FAX: 979-828-4331. E-mail: carnegie@valornet.com. Web Site: www.franklincarnegielibrary.net. *Dir,* Melanie Redden
Pop 1,884
Library Holdings: Large Print Bks 1,000; Bk Titles 8,500; Bk Vols 9,000; Per Subs 2; Talking Bks 62
Automation Activity & Vendor Info: (Cataloging) LRMS, Inc (Library Resource Management Systems); (Circulation) LRMS, Inc (Library Resource Management Systems)
Wireless access
Open Mon-Fri 8-12 & 1-5
Friends of the Library Group

FRANKSTON

P FRANKSTON DEPOT LIBRARY*, 159 W Railroad St, 75763. (Mail add: PO Box 639, 75763-0639), SAN 376-4435. Tel: 903-876-4463. E-mail: frankstondepotlibrary@gmail.com. Web Site: www.frankstondepotlibrary.org. *Dir,* Sabrina Carter
Founded 1985
Library Holdings: Bk Vols 16,000; Per Subs 30
Automation Activity & Vendor Info: (Cataloging) Biblionix; (Circulation) Biblionix; (OPAC) Biblionix
Wireless access
Open Tues, Thurs & Sat 9-5
Friends of the Library Group

FREDERICKSBURG

S ADMIRAL NIMITZ NATIONAL MUSEUM OF THE PACIFIC WAR, Nimitz Education & Research Center, 311 E Austin St, 78624. (Mail add: 328 E Main St, 78624), SAN 374-4620. Tel: 830-997-4379, Ext 262. Web Site: www.pacificwarmuseum.org/. *Library Contact,* Nicole Bagley; E-mail: nbagley@nimitzfoundation.org
Founded 1978
Library Holdings: Bk Titles 4,500

Special Collections: Admiral Chester Nimitz Coll, bks, paper, photogs; World War II Pacific Coll, bks, maps, paper, photogs, posters; World War II Vet. Oral History
Restriction: Open by appt only
Friends of the Library Group

P PIONEER MEMORIAL LIBRARY*, 115 W Main St, 78624. SAN 316-3555. Tel: 830-997-6513. FAX: 830-997-6514. E-mail: library@gillespiecounty.org. Web Site: www1.youseemore.com/pioneer. *Libr Dir,* Brian MacWithey; Staff 1 (MLS 1)
Founded 1966. Pop 19,635; Circ 88,693
Library Holdings: Bk Vols 45,000; Per Subs 75
Special Collections: German Coll
Automation Activity & Vendor Info: (Cataloging) TLC (The Library Corporation); (Circulation) TLC (The Library Corporation); (OPAC) TLC (The Library Corporation)
Wireless access
Open Mon, Tues & Thurs 9-6, Wed 9-7, Fri & Sat 9-2
Friends of the Library Group

FRIENDSWOOD

P FRIENDSWOOD PUBLIC LIBRARY*, 416 S Friendswood Dr, 77546-3897. SAN 316-358X. Tel: 281-482-7135. FAX: 281-482-2685. E-mail: frpublib@friendswood.lib.tx.us. Web Site: www.friendswood.lib.tx.us. *Dir,* Matthew Riley; E-mail: mriley@friendswood.com; *Asst Libr Dir,* Karen Hart; E-mail: khart@friendswood.com; *Ref Librn,* Kim Zrubek; E-mail: kzrubek@friendswood.com; *Tech Serv Librn,* Keith Rogers; E-mail: krogers@friendswood.com; *Youth Serv Librn,* Christina Hicks; E-mail: chicks@friendswood.com; Staff 8 (MLS 5, Non-MLS 3)
Founded 1965. Pop 37,000; Circ 320,000
Library Holdings: AV Mats 6,244; DVDs 6,781; e-books 39,314; Bk Titles 72,109; Bk Vols 80,426; Per Subs 57
Automation Activity & Vendor Info: (Cataloging) SirsiDynix; (Circulation) SirsiDynix; (ILL) OCLC Online
Wireless access
Function: Adult bk club, After school storytime, Art exhibits, Bilingual assistance for Spanish patrons, Bk club(s), Bks on CD, Children's prog, Computer training, Computers for patron use, Digital talking bks, E-Reserves, Electronic databases & coll, ILL available, Magazines, Online cat, OverDrive digital audio bks, Photocopying/Printing, Preschool outreach, Prog for adults, Prog for children & young adult, Story hour, Summer reading prog, Tax forms, Teen prog, Telephone ref, Wheelchair accessible
Mem of Galveston County Library System
Partic in Amigos Library Services, Inc
Open Mon-Thurs 10-9, Fri & Sat 10-6
Friends of the Library Group

FRIONA

P FRIONA PUBLIC LIBRARY*, 109 W Seventh St, 79035-2548. SAN 316-3598. Tel: 806-250-3200. FAX: 806-250-2185. E-mail: library@frionatx.us. Web Site: www.frionalibrary.org. *Dir,* Anahi Gomez; *Asst Dir,* Becky Upton
Founded 1963. Pop 4,171
Library Holdings: Bk Vols 43,665; Per Subs 80
Automation Activity & Vendor Info: (Cataloging) SirsiDynix; (Circulation) SirsiDynix; (OPAC) SirsiDynix
Wireless access
Partic in Harrington Library Consortium; OCLC Online Computer Library Center, Inc
Special Services for the Blind - Reader equip
Open Mon-Fri 9-6
Friends of the Library Group

FRISCO

J COLLIN COLLEGE*, Preston Ridge Campus Library, 9700 Wade Blvd, 75035. Tel: 972-377-1560. Reference Tel: 972-377-1571. FAX: 972-377-1511. Web Site: www.collin.edu/library. *Libr Dir,* Vidya Krishnaswamy; Tel: 972-377-1575, E-mail: vkrishnaswamy@collin.edu
Library Holdings: Audiobooks 923; AV Mats 11,216; CDs 1,777; DVDs 8,452; e-books 34,898; e-journals 24,099; Electronic Media & Resources 2,949,229; Bk Titles 74,010; Per Subs 330
Automation Activity & Vendor Info: (Acquisitions) Innovative Interfaces, Inc; (Cataloging) Innovative Interfaces, Inc; (Circulation) Innovative Interfaces, Inc; (Course Reserve) Innovative Interfaces, Inc; (ILL) Innovative Interfaces, Inc; (OPAC) Innovative Interfaces, Inc; (Serials) Innovative Interfaces, Inc
Wireless access
Open Mon 11-4, Tues 9-2, Wed & Thurs 1-6

P FRISCO PUBLIC LIBRARY*, 6101 Frisco Square Blvd, 75034-3000. SAN 378-4606. Tel: 972-292-5669. FAX: 972-292-5699. E-mail: library@friscotexas.gov. Web Site: friscolibrary.com. *Dir, Libr Serv,* Shelley Holley; *Asst Dir, Pub Serv,* Mayra Diaz; E-mail: mdiaz@friscotexas.gov; *Asst Dir, Operations,* Rachel Harris; E-mail: rdharris@friscotexas.gov; *Mgr, Ad Serv,* Thomas Finley; E-mail: tfinley@friscotexas.gov; *Mgr, Circ Serv,* Adela Arteaga; E-mail: arteaga@friscotexas.gov; *Mgr, Mat Serv,* Elizabeth Chase; E-mail: echase@friscotexas.gov; Staff 8 (MLS 8)
Pop 102,000; Circ 1,200,000
Library Holdings: Audiobooks 5,566; AV Mats 27,944; CDs 6,788; DVDs 15,590; e-books 7,344; Large Print Bks 2,437; Bk Titles 89,034; Bk Vols 132,095; Per Subs 74; Talking Bks 5,566; Videos 15,590
Automation Activity & Vendor Info: (Acquisitions) SirsiDynix; (Cataloging) SirsiDynix; (Circulation) SirsiDynix; (OPAC) SirsiDynix
Wireless access
Function: Adult bk club, After school storytime, Audio & video playback equip for onsite use, Audiobks via web, Bilingual assistance for Spanish patrons, Bk club(s), Bk reviews (Group), Bks on cassette, Bks on CD, CD-ROM, Children's prog, Computer training, Computers for patron use, Digital talking bks, Doc delivery serv, E-Reserves, Electronic databases & coll, Free DVD rentals, Homework prog, ILL available, Instruction & testing, Internet access, Mail & tel request accepted, Music CDs, Notary serv, Online cat, Online ref, Orientations, Outreach serv, Outside serv via phone, mail, e-mail & web, OverDrive digital audio bks, Photocopying/Printing, Preschool outreach, Prog for adults, Prog for children & young adult, Ref & res, Ref serv available, Scanner, Senior computer classes, Spoken cassettes & CDs, Spoken cassettes & DVDs, Story hour, Summer reading prog, Tax forms, Teen prog, Telephone ref, Wheelchair accessible, Workshops
Partic in TexSHARE - Texas State Library & Archives Commission
Open Mon-Thurs 9-9, Fri 9-6, Sat 10-6, Sun 1-5
Restriction: In-house use for visitors
Friends of the Library Group

S MUSEUM OF THE AMERICAN RAILROAD LIBRARY, 6455 Page St, 75034. SAN 372-977X. Tel: 214-428-0101. FAX: 214-426-1937. Web Site: www.historictrains.org. *Pres & Chief Exec Officer,* Robert H LaPrelle; *Chief Operating Officer,* Kellie Murphy; E-mail: kmurphy@historictrains.org; Staff 1 (MLS 1)
Library Holdings: Bk Titles 500; Bk Vols 700
Special Collections: Railroad Technical Manuals
Subject Interests: Energy, Railroads
Wireless access
Function: Res libr
Open Wed-Sat 10-5, Sun 1-5
Restriction: Not a lending libr

GAINESVILLE

P COOKE COUNTY LIBRARY*, 200 S Weaver St, 76240-4731. SAN 316-361X. Tel: 940-668-5530. FAX: 940-668-5533. E-mail: cookectylib@gmail.com. Web Site: cookecountylibrary.org. *Dir,* Jennifer Johnson-Spence; E-mail: jjspence@ntin.net; Staff 7 (MLS 1, Non-MLS 6)
Founded 1921. Pop 29,841; Circ 70,353
Library Holdings: Audiobooks 1,146; AV Mats 3,824; Bks on Deafness & Sign Lang 13; CDs 390; DVDs 1,211; Electronic Media & Resources 51; Large Print Bks 513; Microforms 557; Bk Titles 60,268; Bk Vols 69,903; Per Subs 55; Videos 1,467
Special Collections: Local History Coll
Subject Interests: Genealogy, Local hist
Automation Activity & Vendor Info: (Acquisitions) Book Systems; (Cataloging) Book Systems; (Circulation) Book Systems; (OPAC) Book Systems; (Serials) EBSCO Online
Wireless access
Function: Accelerated reader prog, Archival coll, Children's prog, Computers for patron use, Electronic databases & coll, Homework prog, ILL available, Online cat, Photocopying/Printing, Prog for children & young adult, Ref & res, Spoken cassettes & CDs, Spoken cassettes & DVDs, Story hour, Summer reading prog, Tax forms, Telephone ref, VHS videos, Wheelchair accessible
Open Mon & Wed-Fri 9-5:30, Tues 9-7, Sat 10-2
Friends of the Library Group

J NORTH CENTRAL TEXAS COLLEGE LIBRARY*, 1525 W California St, 76240-0815. SAN 316-3601. Tel: 940-668-4283. Web Site: www.nctc.edu/Library.aspx. *Dean of Libr,* Diane Roether; Tel: 940-668-4283, Ext 4338, E-mail: droether@nctc.edu; Staff 6 (MLS 6)
Founded 1924. Enrl 9,500; Fac 150; Highest Degree: Associate
Library Holdings: e-books 15,000; Bk Titles 50,000; Per Subs 30
Automation Activity & Vendor Info: (Cataloging) SirsiDynix; (Circulation) SirsiDynix; (OPAC) SirsiDynix; (Serials) SirsiDynix
Wireless access
Publications: Bibliographies; Faculty Handbook

Partic in Amigos Library Services, Inc
Open Mon-Thurs 7:30am-9pm, Fri 7:30-Noon, Sun 1-5 (Fall & Spring); Mon-Thurs 7:30-5:30 (Summer)

GALVESTON

J GALVESTON COLLEGE*, David Glenn Hunt Memorial Library, 4015 Ave Q, 77550. SAN 316-3636. Tel: 409-944-1240. Reference Tel: 409-944-1242. Administration Tel: 409-944-1285. E-mail: gclibrary@gc.edu. Web Site: library.gc.edu. *Dir, Libr & Learning Res,* Telishia Murray; E-mail: tmurray@gc.edu; *Librn,* Alexandria Trombley; E-mail: atrombley@gc.edu; *Tech Asst,* Amanda Newell; Tel: 409-844-1246, E-mail: anewell@gc.edu; Staff 4 (MLS 3, Non-MLS 1)
Founded 1967. Enrl 2,300; Highest Degree: Associate
Library Holdings: e-books 28,281; Bk Titles 43,000; Per Subs 200
Subject Interests: Educ, Lit, Local hist, Nursing
Automation Activity & Vendor Info: (Cataloging) EOS International; (Circulation) EOS International; (OPAC) EOS International; (Serials) EOS International
Wireless access
Function: ILL available, Internet access, Large print keyboards, Magazines, Magnifiers for reading, Microfiche/film & reading machines, Orientations, Ref & res, Telephone ref, VHS videos
Partic in Amigos Library Services, Inc
Open Mon-Thurs 7:30am-9pm, Fri 8-5, Sat 8-Noon (Winter); Mon-Thurs 7:30-6 (Summer)

P GALVESTON COUNTY LIBRARY SYSTEM*, Rosenberg Library (Headquarters), 2310 Sealy Ave, 77550. SAN 316-3652. Tel: 409-763-8854. Circulation Tel: 409-763-8854, Ext 111. Reference Tel: 409-763-8854, Ext 115. Administration Tel: 409-763-8854, Ext 121. FAX: 409-763-0275. Administration E-mail: admin@rosenberg-library.org. Web Site: www.rosenberg-library.org. *Exec Dir,* John F Augelli; *Head, Children's Servx,* Karen Stanley; Tel: 409-763-8854, Ext 119, E-mail: kstanley@rosenberg-library.org; *Head, Circ,* Carolyn Williams; Tel: 409-763-8854, Ext 141, E-mail: cwilliams@rosenberg-library.org; *Acq Mgr, Adult Serv,* Jesus Moya; Tel: 409-763-8854, Ext 137, E-mail: jmoya@rosenberg-library.org; *Computer Serv Mgr,* Jay Sims; Tel: 409-763-8854, Ext 131, E-mail: jsims@rosenberg-library.org; *Mgr, Spec Coll,* Lauren Martino; Tel: 409-763-8854, Ext 117, E-mail: lmartino@rosenberg-library.org; Staff 12 (MLS 9, Non-MLS 3)
Founded 1904. Pop 56,388; Circ 331,812
Library Holdings: Audiobooks 3,250; CDs 2,590; DVDs 12,550; Electronic Media & Resources 36,940; Large Print Bks 10,400; Bk Titles 95,760; Bk Vols 111,340; Per Subs 255
Special Collections: Early Texas & Galveston (Museum Coll); Galveston & Texas History, archit drawings, hist doc, maps, photogs; Rare Books (Colonel Milo Pitcher Fox & Agness Peel Fox Rare Room), bks, maps, ms
Subject Interests: Early Texas & Galveston hist
Automation Activity & Vendor Info: (Acquisitions) SirsiDynix; (Cataloging) SirsiDynix; (Circulation) SirsiDynix
Wireless access
Function: 24/7 Electronic res, Activity rm, Adult bk club, After school storytime, Archival coll, Art exhibits, Audio & video playback equip for onsite use, Audiobks via web, Bilingual assistance for Spanish patrons, Bk club(s), Bks on CD, CD-ROM, Children's prog, Computer training, Computers for patron use, Digital talking bks, Electronic databases & coll, Free DVD rentals, Games & aids for people with disabilities, Holiday prog, Home delivery & serv to seniorr ctr & nursing homes, Homebound delivery serv, ILL available, Internet access, Magazines, Magnifiers for reading, Mail & tel request accepted, Microfiche/film & reading machines, Movies, Music CDs, Notary serv, Online cat, Online ref, Outreach serv, OverDrive digital audio bks, Photocopying/Printing, Preschool outreach, Preschool reading prog, Printer for laptops & handheld devices, Prog for adults, Prog for children & young adult, Ref & res, Ref serv available, Scanner, Senior computer classes, Spanish lang bks, Spoken cassettes & CDs, Spoken cassettes & DVDs, Story hour, Study rm, Summer reading prog, Tax forms, Teen prog, Telephone ref, Wheelchair accessible, Workshops
Publications: A Descriptive Catalog of the Cartographic Coll of the Rosenberg Library; Fragile Empires: The Texas Correspondence of Samuel Swartwout & James Morgan, 1836-1856; Galveston County Library System Newsletter (Biannually); Julius Stockfleth: Gulf Coast Marine & Landscape Painter; Manuscript Sources in the Rosenberg Library
Member Libraries: Dickinson Public Library; Friendswood Public Library; Genevieve Miller Hitchcock Public Library; Helen Hall Library; La Marque Public Library; Mae S Bruce Library; Moore Memorial Public Library
Partic in Amigos Library Services, Inc; Houston Area Database Consortium; TexSHARE - Texas State Library & Archives Commission
Open Mon-Thurs 9-9, Fri & Sat 9-6
Friends of the Library Group

C TEXAS A&M UNIVERSITY AT GALVESTON*, Jack K Williams Library, Bldg 3010, 200 Seawolf Pkwy, 77554. (Mail add: PO Box 1675, 77553-1675), SAN 316-3644. Tel: 409-740-4560. Interlibrary Loan Service Tel: 409-740-4564. FAX: 409-740-4702. E-mail: library@tamug.edu. Web Site: www.tamug.edu/library. *Dir, Libr Serv,* David Baca, PhD; Tel: 409-740-4568, E-mail: bacad@tamug.edu; *Assoc Dir, Libr Serv,* Amy Caton; Tel: 409-740-4711, E-mail: caton@tamug.edu; *Libr Mgr,* Michael Sweeney; E-mail: sweeneym@tamug.edu; *Coll Serv Librn,* Mary Ellen Vedas; Tel: 409-740-7179, E-mail: mvedas@tamug.edu; Staff 4 (MLS 2, Non-MLS 2)
Founded 1972. Enrl 2,000; Fac 91; Highest Degree: Doctorate
Library Holdings: AV Mats 2,492; DVDs 761; e-journals 10,000; Microforms 54,187; Bk Vols 93,748; Per Subs 400; Spec Interest Per Sub 200
Special Collections: Galveston Bay Information Center
Subject Interests: Marine biol, Maritime, Oceanography, Transportation
Automation Activity & Vendor Info: (Acquisitions) OCLC Worldshare Management Services; (Cataloging) OCLC Worldshare Management Services; (Circulation) OCLC Worldshare Management Services; (Course Reserve) OCLC Worldshare Management Services; (Discovery) OCLC Worldshare Management Services; (ILL) OCLC WorldShare Interlibrary Loan; (Media Booking) Ex Libris Group; (OPAC) OCLC Worldshare Management Services; (Serials) OCLC Worldshare Management Services
Wireless access
Function: 24/7 Electronic res, 24/7 Online cat, Archival coll, Art exhibits, AV serv, Computers for patron use, Doc delivery serv, Electronic databases & coll, Equip loans & repairs, For res purposes, Govt ref serv, ILL available, Instruction & testing, Internet access, Literacy & newcomer serv, Magazines, Meeting rooms, Movies, Online cat, Online info literacy tutorials on the web & in blackboard, Orientations, Outreach serv, Photocopying/Printing, Ref & res, Ref serv available, Res assist avail, Res libr, Scanner, Study rm, Wheelchair accessible, Workshops, Writing prog
Partic in Amigos Library Services, Inc; TexSHARE - Texas State Library & Archives Commission
Open Mon-Thurs 7am-3am, Fri 7am-10pm, Sat 10-8, Sun 10am-3am
Restriction: Borrowing privileges limited to fac & registered students, Borrowing requests are handled by ILL, Fee for pub use, Limited access for the pub, Open to students, fac & staff

CM UNIVERSITY OF TEXAS MEDICAL BRANCH*, Moody Medical Library, 914 Market St, 77555. SAN 316-3687. Tel: 409-772-4164. Circulation Tel: 409-772-2385. Reference Tel: 409-772-2372. FAX: 409-762-9782. Web Site: www.utmb.edu/ar/moody-medical-library. *Assoc VP, Academic Resources,* Patricia Ciejka; E-mail: pciejka@utmb.edu; *Assoc Dir,* Julie Trimble; Tel: 409-772-3642, E-mail: jtrumble@utmb.edu; *Libr Serv Mgr,* Jorja Aularkh; E-mail: jmaulakh@utmb.edu; Staff 49 (MLS 9, Non-MLS 40)
Founded 1891
Library Holdings: Bk Titles 212,535; Bk Vols 201,879; Per Subs 30,598
Special Collections: History of Medicine & Archives
Subject Interests: Allied health sci, Med, Nursing
Automation Activity & Vendor Info: (Acquisitions) Ex Libris Group; (Cataloging) Ex Libris Group; (Circulation) Ex Libris Group; (OPAC) Ex Libris Group; (Serials) Ex Libris Group
Wireless access
Function: Doc delivery serv
Partic in Houston Area Research Library Consortium; National Network of Libraries of Medicine Region 3; Tex Health Sci Libr Consortium; UT Syst Librns
Open Mon-Thurs 7am-Midnight, Fri 7am-9pm, Sat 9-8, Sun Noon-11

GARLAND

C AMBERTON UNIVERSITY*, Library Resource Center, 1700 Eastgate Dr, 75041. Tel: 972-279-6511, Ext 136. FAX: 972-686-5567. E-mail: library@amberton.edu. Web Site: www.amberton.edu/current-students/library. *Dir, Libr Serv,* Jamie Quinn; E-mail: jquinn@amberton.edu; Staff 6 (MLS 2, Non-MLS 4)
Founded 1971. Enrl 1,500; Highest Degree: Master
Library Holdings: e-books 121,001; Bk Vols 15,000; Per Subs 4
Subject Interests: Bus admin, Counseling, Ethics, Human relations
Wireless access
Function: For res purposes
Partic in Amigos Library Services, Inc; TexSHARE - Texas State Library & Archives Commission
Open Mon-Thurs 10-6:30, Fri & Sat 10-1:30

P NICHOLSON MEMORIAL LIBRARY SYSTEM*, Central Library, 625 Austin St, 75040-6365. SAN 361-7467. Tel: 972-205-2500. Circulation Tel: 972-205-2524. Reference Tel: 972-205-2501. FAX: 972-205-2523. Web Site: www.library.garlandtx.gov. *Dir of Libr,* Karen Archibald; Tel: 972-205-2545, E-mail: karchibald@garlandtx.gov; *Libr Coord,* Sabrina Ellis; Tel: 972-205-2547, E-mail: sellis@garlandtx.gov
Founded 1933. Circ 1,549,358

Library Holdings: Audiobooks 8,801; CDs 8,029; DVDs 42,512; e-books 10,586; Large Print Bks 5,405; Microforms 23; Bk Titles 177,850; Bk Vols 348,465; Per Subs 774
Automation Activity & Vendor Info: (Acquisitions) SirsiDynix; (Cataloging) SirsiDynix-WorkFlows; (Circulation) SirsiDynix-WorkFlows; (ILL) OCLC WorldShare Interlibrary Loan; (OPAC) SirsiDynix; (Serials) SirsiDynix
Wireless access
Function: Adult bk club, Bk club(s), Bks on CD, Computer training, Computers for patron use, Electronic databases & coll, Free DVD rentals, ILL available, Microfiche/film & reading machines, Online cat, OverDrive digital audio bks, Photocopying/Printing, Prog for adults, Prog for children & young adult, Ref serv available, Story hour, Summer reading prog, Teen prog
Publications: ACCESS (Newsletter)
Open Mon-Thurs 10-9, Fri & Sat 10-6, Sun 2-6
Friends of the Library Group
Branches: 3
NORTH GARLAND BRANCH, 3845 N Garland Ave, 75040, SAN 372-7920. Tel: 972-205-2803. Circulation Tel: 972-205-2802. *Br Mgr,* Barbara Robinson
Open Tues & Thurs 1-9, Wed, Fri & Sat 10-6
SOUTH GARLAND BRANCH LIBRARY, 4845 Broadway Blvd, 75043. Tel: 972-205-3920. Reference Tel: 972-205-3931. *Br Mgr,* Becky Crow; Staff 11 (MLS 6, Non-MLS 5)
Open Tues & Thurs 1-9, Wed, Fri & Sat 10-6
Friends of the Library Group
WALNUT CREEK BRANCH LIBRARY, 3319 Edgewood Dr, 75042-7118, SAN 361-7521. Tel: 972-205-2587. Circulation Tel: 972-205-2586. *Br Mgr,* Dianne Dupont
Open Tues & Thurs 1-9, Wed, Fri & Sat 10-6

GATESVILLE

P GATESVILLE PUBLIC LIBRARY*, 111 N Eighth St, 76528. SAN 316-375X. Tel: 254-865-5367. FAX: 254-248-0986. Web Site: www.gatesvilletx.com/library. *Libr Dir,* Shea Harp; E-mail: scourtney@gatesvilletx.com; Staff 4 (MLS 1, Non-MLS 3)
Founded 1970. Pop 16,000; Circ 40,975
Library Holdings: Bk Titles 42,170; Bk Vols 48,000; Per Subs 40
Subject Interests: Genealogy, Local hist, Tex
Automation Activity & Vendor Info: (Cataloging) Book Systems; (Circulation) Book Systems; (OPAC) Book Systems
Wireless access
Partic in Partners Library Action Network
Open Mon, Wed & Fri 8:30-6, Tues & Thurs 8:30-8, Sat 8:30-4:30
Friends of the Library Group

GEORGE WEST

P LIVE OAK COUNTY LIBRARY*, George West Branch, 402 N Houston St, 78022. SAN 361-7556. Tel: 361-449-1124. E-mail: librarygw@gmail.com. Web Site: liveoak.biblionix.com/atoz/catalog. *Dir,* Marco Marroquin; Staff 4 (Non-MLS 4)
Special Collections: US Document Depository
Automation Activity & Vendor Info: (Cataloging) Follett Software; (Circulation) Follett Software
Wireless access
Function: Home delivery & serv to seniorr ctr & nursing homes, ILL available, Photocopying/Printing, Spoken cassettes & CDs, Summer reading prog, Tax forms, VHS videos
Open Mon-Thurs 11:30-6, Fri 1-5, Sat 9-1
Restriction: Open to pub for ref & circ; with some limitations
Branches: 1
THREE RIVERS, 102 Leroy St, Three Rivers, 78071, SAN 361-7580. Tel: 361-786-3037. E-mail: librarytr@gmail.com. *Dir,* Marco Marroquin
Open Mon-Thurs 11:30-6, Fri 1-5, Sat 9-1

GEORGETOWN

P GEORGETOWN PUBLIC LIBRARY*, 402 W Eighth St, 78626. SAN 316-3768. Tel: 512-930-3551. Reference Tel: 512-930-3627. FAX: 512-931-7628. E-mail: library@georgetown.org. Web Site: library.georgetown.org. *Libr Dir,* Sally Miculek; E-mail: sally.miculek@georgetown.org; *Ch,* Bethni King; *Fine Arts Librn,* Dana Hendrix; Staff 32 (MLS 9, Non-MLS 23)
Founded 1967. Pop 70,000; Circ 550,000
Library Holdings: CDs 1,500; Large Print Bks 1,789; Bk Vols 80,966; Per Subs 118; Videos 4,400
Subject Interests: Genealogy, Local hist, Tex hist
Automation Activity & Vendor Info: (Cataloging) Biblionix; (Circulation) Biblionix; (OPAC) Biblionix
Wireless access
Function: 24/7 Electronic res, 24/7 Online cat, 3D Printer, ILL available
Partic in Partners Library Action Network
Special Services for the Blind - Bks on cassette; Bks on CD
Open Mon, Tues, Thurs & Fri 9-6, Wed 12-6, Sat 9-5
Restriction: Authorized patrons
Friends of the Library Group
Bookmobiles: 2. Outreach Librn, Sheri Miklaski

C SOUTHWESTERN UNIVERSITY*, A Frank Smith Jr Library Center, 1100 E University Ave, 78626. (Mail add: PO Box 770, 78627-0770), SAN 316-3776. Circulation Tel: 512-863-1563. Interlibrary Loan Service Tel: 512-863-1638. Information Services Tel: 512-863-7333. Web Site: www.southwestern.edu/library-and-it. *Libr Dir,* Alexia Riggs; E-mail: riggsa@southwestern.edu; *Dir, Libr Res,* Amy Anderson; Tel: 512-863-1639, E-mail: andersoa@southwestern.edu; *Archives, Head, Spec Coll,* Megan Firestone; Tel: 512-863-1221, E-mail: firestom@southwestern.edu; *Operations Mgr,* Jean Whewell; Tel: 512-863-1635, E-mail: whewellj@southwestern.edu; Staff 8 (MLS 7, Non-MLS 1)
Founded 1840. Highest Degree: Bachelor
Special Collections: John G Tower Papers; Texana
Automation Activity & Vendor Info: (Acquisitions) OCLC Worldshare Management Services; (Cataloging) OCLC Worldshare Management Services; (Circulation) OCLC Worldshare Management Services; (Discovery) OCLC Worldshare Management Services; (ILL) OCLC ILLiad; (OPAC) OCLC Worldshare Management Services; (Serials) OCLC Worldshare Management Services
Wireless access
Partic in Midwest Libr Consortium; OCLC Online Computer Library Center, Inc; Statewide California Electronic Library Consortium; TexSHARE - Texas State Library & Archives Commission

GIDDINGS

P GIDDINGS PUBLIC LIBRARY & CULTURAL CENTER*, 276 N Orange St, 78942-3317. SAN 316-3784. Tel: 979-542-2716. FAX: 979-542-1879. E-mail: gplacc@hotmail.com. Web Site: www.giddingspubliclibrary.org. *Dir,* Jessi Akin
Founded 1920. Pop 5,105; Circ 33,707
Library Holdings: AV Mats 400; Bks on Deafness & Sign Lang 20; Large Print Bks 606; Bk Titles 35,000; Bk Vols 36,000; Per Subs 54; Talking Bks 789
Special Collections: Baseball Coll; Indian Artifact Display; Large Print Coll, audio cassettes, videos
Subject Interests: Cookery, Gardening, Genealogy, Handicrafts, Local hist, Texana
Automation Activity & Vendor Info: (Cataloging) Follett Software; (Circulation) Follett Software; (ILL) OCLC
Wireless access
Partic in Partners Library Action Network; TexSHARE - Texas State Library & Archives Commission
Open Mon-Fri 10-6, Sat 10-1
Friends of the Library Group

GILMER

P UPSHUR COUNTY LIBRARY*, 702 W Tyler St, 75644. SAN 316-3792. Tel: 903-843-5001. FAX: 903-843-3995. E-mail: upshurcountylibrary@yahoo.com. Web Site: upshur.biblionix.com/catalog. *County Libr Dir,* Cynthia E King; Staff 4 (MLS 1, Non-MLS 3)
Founded 1929. Pop 35,483
Library Holdings: Audiobooks 852; DVDs 2,212; e-books 10,820; Large Print Bks 4,602; Microforms 150; Bk Titles 63,231; Bk Vols 66,588; Per Subs 45
Special Collections: Library of America
Subject Interests: Civil War, Local genealogy, Texana
Automation Activity & Vendor Info: (Cataloging) TLC (The Library Corporation); (Circulation) TLC (The Library Corporation); (OPAC) TLC (The Library Corporation)
Wireless access
Function: 24/7 Electronic res, 24/7 Online cat, After school storytime, Audiobks via web, Bks on cassette, Bks on CD, Children's prog, Computers for patron use, Electronic databases & coll, Family literacy, Free DVD rentals, Holiday prog, ILL available, Internet access, Magazines, Magnifiers for reading, Mail & tel request accepted, Mango lang, Meeting rooms, Microfiche/film & reading machines, Movies, Online cat, Orientations, Outreach serv, OverDrive digital audio bks, Photocopying/Printing, Preschool outreach, Preschool reading prog, Prof lending libr, Prog for adults, Prog for children & young adult, Ref serv available, Spanish lang bks, Story hour, Summer reading prog, Tax forms, Teen prog, Telephone ref, VHS videos, Wheelchair accessible
Special Services for the Deaf - Bks on deafness & sign lang
Special Services for the Blind - Audio mat; Bks on CD; Copier with enlargement capabilities; Free checkout of audio mat; Large print bks; Magnifiers
Open Tues-Thurs 8-6, Fri 8-2, Sat 10-2
Friends of the Library Group

GLADEWATER

P LEE PUBLIC LIBRARY*, Gladewater Public Library, 312 W Pacific, 75647-2135. SAN 316-3806. Tel: 903-845-2640. FAX: 903-845-2648. E-mail: leelibrary@cityofgladewater.com. *Dir,* Judy Hagle-Kiper; Staff 3 (MLS 1, Non-MLS 2)
Founded 1937. Pop 8,950; Circ 31,502
Library Holdings: Bk Titles 31,813; Bk Vols 32,213; Per Subs 15
Special Collections: Texana (John Ben Shepperd Jr Coll)
Automation Activity & Vendor Info: (Cataloging) Follett Software; (Circulation) Follett Software
Open Mon-Fri 10-4
Friends of the Library Group

GLEN ROSE

§P GLEN ROSE PUBLIC LIBRARY, Somervell County Public Library, 108 Allen Dr, 76043. Tel: 254-897-4582. Web Site: www.facebook.com/somervellcountylibrary, www.somervell.co/additional-offices/library. *Dir,* Peggy Oldham
Wireless access
Function: Summer reading prog
Partic in Amigos Library Services, Inc
Open Mon-Wed 10-6, Thurs 11-7, Fri 9-5

P SOMERVELL COUNTY LIBRARY*, 108 Allen Dr, 76043. SAN 376-4583. Tel: 254-897-4582. FAX: 254-897-9882. E-mail: somlib@hotmail.com. Web Site: www.glenrosetexas.org/living/community/library. *Librn,* Peggy Oldham; Staff 4 (Non-MLS 4)
Library Holdings: Audiobooks 903; DVDs 70; Bk Titles 38,243; Per Subs 40
Wireless access
Open Mon-Wed 10-6, Thurs 11-7, Fri 9-5

GOLDTHWAITE

P JENNIE TRENT DEW LIBRARY*, 1113 Fisher St, 76844. (Mail add: PO Box 101, 76844-0101). Tel: 325-648-2447. FAX: 325-648-2447. E-mail: librarian@jtdlibrary.net. Web Site: jtdlibrary.net.
Pop 4,723; Circ 13,763
Library Holdings: Bk Titles 10,079; Bk Vols 11,123
Automation Activity & Vendor Info: (Cataloging) Biblionix; (Circulation) Biblionix
Wireless access
Partic in Central Texas Digital Consortium; Partners Library Action Network
Friends of the Library Group

GOLIAD

P GOLIAD COUNTY LIBRARY*, 320 S Commercial St, 77963. (Mail add: PO Box 1025, 77963-1025), SAN 316-3814. Tel: 361-645-2291. FAX: 361-645-8956. E-mail: library@goliadcountytx.gov. Web Site: www.co.goliad.tx.us/page/goliad.library. *County Librn,* Claudine Janota; E-mail: cjanota@goliadcountytx.gov
Founded 1958. Pop 7,626; Circ 35,077
Library Holdings: AV Mats 284; Bk Vols 53,077; Per Subs 72
Subject Interests: Tex hist
Automation Activity & Vendor Info: (Cataloging) Follett Software; (Circulation) Follett Software; (OPAC) Follett Software
Wireless access
Open Mon-Thurs 7-12 & 1-5:30
Friends of the Library Group

GONZALES

P ROBERT LEE BROTHERS, JR MEMORIAL LIBRARY, 301 St Joseph St, 78629. (Mail add: PO Box 220, 78629-0220), SAN 316-3822. Tel: 830-672-6315. Administration Tel: 830-672-9433. FAX: 830-672-8735. Web Site: www.gonzales.texas.gov/p/departments/library. *Dir,* Caroline C Helms; E-mail: chelms@gonzales.texas.gov; Staff 5 (Non-MLS 5)
Pop 7,471; Circ 27,000
Library Holdings: Audiobooks 744; AV Mats 16; Bks on Deafness & Sign Lang 25; DVDs 1,890; Large Print Bks 531; Bk Titles 28,670; Per Subs 65
Special Collections: Genealogy Coll; Texana Coll
Automation Activity & Vendor Info: (Cataloging) Biblionix/Apollo; (Circulation) Biblionix/Apollo; (ILL) OCLC FirstSearch; (OPAC) Biblionix/Apollo
Wireless access
Partic in Partners Library Action Network
Open Mon 11-7, Tues-Sat 9-5
Friends of the Library Group

GOODFELLOW AFB

A UNITED STATES AIR FORCE*, Goodfellow Base Library FL 3030, 17 FSS/FSDL, 265 W Kearney Blvd, Bldg 316, 76908-4711. SAN 361-7645. Tel: 325-654-3589. Circulation Tel: 325-654-3232. Interlibrary Loan Service Tel: 325-654-3046. FAX: 325-654-1109. E-mail: gafblibrary@suddenlinkmail.com. Web Site: www.gafblibrary.org.
Founded 1942
Library Holdings: Audiobooks 904; AV Mats 1,855; CDs 105; DVDs 3,160; Bk Titles 23,206; Per Subs 98
Automation Activity & Vendor Info: (Cataloging) OCLC Connexion; (Circulation) ComPanion Corp; (ILL) OCLC
Wireless access
Restriction: Not open to pub

GORMAN

P CHARLIE GARRETT MEMORIAL LIBRARY, 103 S Fisher St, 76454. Tel: 254-734-3301. E-mail: gormanpubliclibrary@gmail.com. Web Site: www.facebook.com/gormanpubliclibrary.
Pop 3,580
Library Holdings: Bk Vols 11,443
Wireless access
Open Tues-Thurs 3-5
Friends of the Library Group

GRAHAM

P LIBRARY OF GRAHAM*, 910 Cherry St, 76450-3547. SAN 316-3830. Tel: 940-549-0600. FAX: 940-276-1213. E-mail: library@libraryofgraham.org. Web Site: grahamtexas.net/live/library-of-graham. *Dir,* Sherrie R Gibson; E-mail: sherrie@libraryofgraham.org; *Ch Serv,* Selena Shifflett; Staff 6 (Non-MLS 6)
Founded 1911. Pop 8,716; Circ 111,518
Library Holdings: AV Mats 3,389; Large Print Bks 2,187; Bk Titles 40,946; Bk Vols 43,399; Per Subs 82; Talking Bks 3,000
Special Collections: Texana Coll; Young County Coll. Oral History
Automation Activity & Vendor Info: (Cataloging) Book Systems; (Circulation) Book Systems; (ILL) OCLC; (OPAC) Book Systems
Wireless access
Partic in Partners Library Action Network
Open Mon-Fri 9-5:30
Friends of the Library Group

GRANBURY

P HOOD COUNTY PUBLIC LIBRARY*, 222 N Travis, 76048. SAN 316-3849. Tel: 817-573-3569. FAX: 817-573-3969. Web Site: www.co.hood.tx.us/index.aspx?nid=297, www.hoodcountylibrary.com. *Libr Dir,* Jennifer Logsdon; E-mail: jlogsdon@co.hood.tx.us; *Asst Dir, Youth Serv Librn,* Diana Haun; E-mail: dhaun@co.hood.tx.us; Staff 6 (MLS 2, Non-MLS 4)
Pop 51,182; Circ 108,000
Library Holdings: Bk Titles 39,900; Per Subs 75
Automation Activity & Vendor Info: (Cataloging) TLC (The Library Corporation); (Circulation) TLC (The Library Corporation)
Wireless access
Function: Bks on CD, Children's prog, Computers for patron use, Free DVD rentals, ILL available, Photocopying/Printing, Prog for children & young adult, Spoken cassettes & CDs, Spoken cassettes & DVDs, Summer reading prog, Tax forms, VHS videos
Partic in Partners Library Action Network
Open Mon 10-7, Tues 10-9, Wed-Sat 10-6
Friends of the Library Group

GRAND PRAIRIE

P GRAND PRAIRIE PUBLIC LIBRARY SYSTEM*, 901 Conover Dr, 75051. SAN 316-3857. Tel: 972-237-5700. Administration Tel: 972-237-5702. FAX: 972-237-5750. Web Site: gp.ent.sirsi.net/client/en_US/library, www.gptx.org/city-government/city-departments/library. *Dir,* Amy Sprinkles; E-mail: asprinkles@gptx.org; *Head, Tech Serv,* Jennifer Douglas; E-mail: jdouglas@gptx.org; *ILL Librn,* Rachel Oropeza; E-mail: roropeza@gptx.org; *Libr Serv Mgr,* Jennifer Walker; E-mail: jwalker@gptx.org; *Communications, Advocacy & Outreach Serv Coordr,* Elisabeth McMahon; E-mail: emcmahon@gptx.org; *Ch Serv,* Joette Cook; E-mail: jcook@gptx.org; Staff 34 (MLS 13, Non-MLS 21)
Founded 1937. Pop 181,230; Circ 253,614
Library Holdings: Bk Vols 140,586
Special Collections: Local History, bks, doc, micro, ms, photog, slides, tapes
Automation Activity & Vendor Info: (Acquisitions) SirsiDynix; (Cataloging) SirsiDynix; (Circulation) SirsiDynix; (OPAC) SirsiDynix
Wireless access

Open Mon-Thurs 10-9, Fri & Sat 10-6, Sun 1-5
Friends of the Library Group
Branches: 2
TONY SHOTWELL BRANCH, 2750 Graham St, 75050. Tel: 972-237-7540. *Br Mgr,* Mike Broussard
Library Holdings: Bk Titles 10,000
Automation Activity & Vendor Info: (Cataloging) Horizon; (Circulation) Horizon
Open Mon, Tues & Thurs 2-9, Wed & Sat 10-6
BETTY WARMACK BRANCH LIBRARY, 760 Bardin Rd, 75052. Tel: 972-237-5772. Circulation Tel: 972-237-5770. *Br Mgr,* Laurie Arredondo; E-mail: larredondo@gptx.org
Library Holdings: Bk Vols 35,000; Per Subs 95
Automation Activity & Vendor Info: (Cataloging) Horizon; (Circulation) Horizon; (OPAC) Horizon
Open Mon, Tues & Thurs 1-9, Wed & Sat 9-6, Sun 1-5
Friends of the Library Group

GRAND SALINE

P GRAND SALINE PUBLIC LIBRARY*, 201 E Pacific Ave, 75140. SAN 320-8478. Tel: 903-962-5516. FAX: 903-962-6866. E-mail: grandsalinelibrary@gmail.com. Web Site: www.grandsalinelibrary.com. *Librn,* Kelli Bryant
Founded 1966. Pop 5,000
Library Holdings: Bk Vols 22,000
Automation Activity & Vendor Info: (Cataloging) Biblionix/Apollo; (Circulation) Biblionix/Apollo; (OPAC) Biblionix/Apollo
Wireless access
Open Tues-Fri 9-5
Friends of the Library Group

GRANDVIEW

P GRANDVIEW PUBLIC LIBRARY*, 112 S Third St, 76050. (Mail add: PO Box 694, 76050-0694). Tel: 817-866-3965. FAX: 817-866-2037. E-mail: info@grandviewlibrary.net. Web Site: grandviewlibrary.net. *Dir,* Judy Tidwell
Pop 1,346; Circ 2,003
Library Holdings: Bk Vols 11,000; Talking Bks 400
Automation Activity & Vendor Info: (Cataloging) Book Systems; (Circulation) Book Systems
Wireless access
Open Mon-Thurs 12-5

GRAPELAND

P GRAPELAND PUBLIC LIBRARY, 106 N Oak St, 75844. (Mail add: PO Box 879, 75844-0879). Tel: 936-687-3425. E-mail: info@grapelandlib.org. Web Site: www.grapelandlib.org. *Librn,* Leslie Carroll
Founded 2002. Circ 1,374
Library Holdings: AV Mats 81; CDs 143; DVDs 231; Bk Titles 9,259; Videos 196
Subject Interests: Genealogy, Regional hist
Automation Activity & Vendor Info: (Cataloging) Surpass; (Circulation) Surpass; (OPAC) Surpass
Wireless access
Open Mon-Thurs 10-3

GRAPEVINE

P GRAPEVINE PUBLIC LIBRARY*, 1201 Municipal Way, 76051. SAN 316-3881. Tel: 817-410-3400. FAX: 817-410-3084. E-mail: reference@grapevinetexas.gov. Web Site: grapevinetexas.gov/1240/library. *Libr Dir,* Leigh Kapsos; Tel: 817-410-3405, E-mail: lkapsos@grapevinetexas.gov; *Tech Librn,* Chris Woodward; Tel: 817-410-3407, E-mail: cwoodward@grapevinetexas.gov; *Genealogy Librn II,* Nancy Maxwell; Tel: 817-410-3429, E-mail: nmaxwell@grapevinetexas.gov. Subject Specialists: *3D printing, Robotics,* Chris Woodward; Staff 10 (MLS 10)
Founded 1923. Pop 49,898; Circ 307,662
Oct 2016-Sept 2017 Income $1,708,423. Mats Exp $313,331, Books $169,361, Per/Ser (Incl. Access Fees) $20,000, AV Mat $35,480, Electronic Ref Mat (Incl. Access Fees) $87,490, Presv $1,000. Sal $1,152,861 (Prof $685,684)
Library Holdings: CDs 10,454; DVDs 14,391; e-books 76,689; e-journals 82; Electronic Media & Resources 3,500; Bk Titles 128,795; Bk Vols 151,880; Per Subs 90; Talking Bks 10,508
Special Collections: Oral History
Subject Interests: Genealogy, Tex
Automation Activity & Vendor Info: (Acquisitions) SirsiDynix; (Cataloging) SirsiDynix; (Circulation) SirsiDynix; (OPAC) SirsiDynix
Wireless access
Function: 24/7 Electronic res, 24/7 Online cat, 3D Printer, Adult bk club, After school storytime, Archival coll
Partic in Partners Library Action Network
Open Mon-Thurs 10-9, Fri 10-6, Sat 10-5, Sun 2-6
Friends of the Library Group

GREENVILLE

P W WALWORTH HARRISON PUBLIC LIBRARY*, One Lou Finney Ln, 75401-5988. SAN 316-3903. Tel: 903-457-2992. FAX: 903-457-2961. *Libr Dir,* Olivia Moreno; E-mail: ogriggs@ci.greenville.tx.us; Staff 3 (MLS 3)
Founded 1904. Pop 28,263; Circ 99,000
Library Holdings: AV Mats 1,780; DVDs 3,500; Bk Vols 48,500; Per Subs 6; Talking Bks 1,444
Subject Interests: Genealogy, Local hist
Automation Activity & Vendor Info: (Cataloging) TLC (The Library Corporation); (Circulation) TLC (The Library Corporation); (ILL) OCLC; (OPAC) TLC (The Library Corporation)
Wireless access
Function: 24/7 Electronic res, 24/7 Online cat, Accelerated reader prog, Activity rm, Adult bk club, Archival coll, Audiobks via web, Bilingual assistance for Spanish patrons, Bks on CD, Bus archives, Butterfly Garden, Children's prog, Computer training, Computers for patron use, Digital talking bks, Electronic databases & coll, For res purposes, Free DVD rentals, Genealogy discussion group, Govt ref serv, Holiday prog, ILL available, Internet access, Life-long learning prog for all ages, Magazines, Magnifiers for reading, Meeting rooms, Microfiche/film & reading machines, Movies, Museum passes, Music CDs, Online cat, Outside serv via phone, mail, e-mail & web, OverDrive digital audio bks, Photocopying/Printing, Preschool reading prog, Printer for laptops & handheld devices, Prog for adults, Prog for children & young adult, Ref & res, Ref serv available, Res assist avail, Res performed for a fee, Scanner, Serves people with intellectual disabilities, Spanish lang bks, Spoken cassettes & CDs, Spoken cassettes & DVDs, STEM programs, Story hour, Study rm, Summer & winter reading prog, Tax forms, Teen prog, Wheelchair accessible
Partic in Amigos Library Services, Inc; Northeast Texas Digital Consortium; Partners Library Action Network
Special Services for the Deaf - Bks on deafness & sign lang; Closed caption videos
Special Services for the Blind - Bks on CD; Large print bks; Magnifiers
Open Mon & Tues 10-8, Wed, Fri & Sat 10-6, Thurs Noon-8
Restriction: Open to pub for ref & circ; with some limitations
Friends of the Library Group

L MORGAN & GOTCHER LAW OFFICE LIBRARY, 2610 Stonewall St, 75401. (Mail add: PO Box 556, 75403-0556), SAN 372-9796. Tel: 903-455-3183. FAX: 903-454-4654. Web Site: www.morgan-gotcher.com.
Library Holdings: Bk Vols 5,000; Per Subs 15
Restriction: Staff use only

GROESBECK

P GROESBECK MAFFETT PUBLIC LIBRARY*, 601 W Yeagua St, 76642-1658. SAN 316-392X. Tel: 254-729-3667. FAX: 254-729-2345. E-mail: info@groesbecklibrary.org. Web Site: www.groesbecklibrary.org. *Libr Dir,* Jamie N McLean; E-mail: director@groesbecklibrary.org; Staff 3 (MLS 1, Non-MLS 2)
Founded 1976. Pop 7,500; Circ 12,385
Library Holdings: Bks on Deafness & Sign Lang 10; High Interest/Low Vocabulary Bk Vols 50; Large Print Bks 350; Bk Titles 21,045; Per Subs 66
Special Collections: Limestone County History Coll; Ray A Walter Coll. Oral History
Automation Activity & Vendor Info: (Acquisitions) Baker & Taylor; (Cataloging) Biblionix; (Circulation) Biblionix; (ILL) OCLC WorldShare Interlibrary Loan
Wireless access
Partic in Partners Library Action Network
Special Services for the Deaf - Adult & family literacy prog; Assisted listening device; Assistive tech; Bks on deafness & sign lang; High interest/low vocabulary bks
Special Services for the Blind - Talking bks & player equip; Videos on blindness & physical disabilties
Open Mon-Wed 10:30-5, Thurs 10:30-6, Sat 9-Noon
Friends of the Library Group

GROVES

P GROVES PUBLIC LIBRARY, 5600 W Washington St, 77619. SAN 325-0113. Tel: 409-962-6281. FAX: 409-962-3379. E-mail: groveslibrary5600@gmail.com. Web Site: www.groveslibrary.org. *Dir,* Louella Doucet; *Ch, Circ Desk Mgr, Libr Asst,* Jacqueline Nieves-Goss; E-mail: jnieves-goss@cigrovestx.com
Founded 1930. Pop 17,335; Circ 51,000
Library Holdings: Audiobooks 1,000; DVDs 2,400; Large Print Bks 818; Bk Vols 40,000; Per Subs 52
Automation Activity & Vendor Info: (Cataloging) Follett Software; (Circulation) Follett Software; (OPAC) Follett Software

Wireless access
Function: Adult bk club, Audiobks via web, Bilingual assistance for Spanish patrons, Bk club(s), Bks on CD, Children's prog, Computers for patron use, Extended outdoor wifi, Free DVD rentals, Holiday prog, ILL available, Instruction & testing, Internet access, Magazines, Magnifiers for reading, Meeting rooms, Notary serv, Online cat, OverDrive digital audio bks, Photocopying/Printing, Preschool reading prog, Ref & res, Ref serv available, Scanner, Serves people with intellectual disabilities, Spanish lang bks, STEM programs, Story hour, Summer reading prog, Telephone ref, Wheelchair accessible, Workshops
Partic in Partners Library Action Network; TexSHARE - Texas State Library & Archives Commission
Special Services for the Deaf - Assisted listening device; Bks on deafness & sign lang; High interest/low vocabulary bks; Spec interest per
Special Services for the Blind - Assistive/Adapted tech devices, equip & products; Bks on CD; Magnifiers
Open Mon, Wed & Thurs 8:30-5:50, Tues 12-7:50, Fri 8:30-4:50, Sat 11-2:50

GROVETON

P GROVETON PUBLIC LIBRARY, Ethel Reese Library, 125 W First St, 75845. (Mail add: PO Box 399, 75845-0399), SAN 376-4095. Tel: 936-642-2483. E-mail: grovetonpubliclibrary@gmail.com. Web Site: cityofgroveton.com/library. *Librn,* Cathy Czajkowski
Library Holdings: Large Print Bks 120; Bk Titles 7,500; Videos 130
Automation Activity & Vendor Info: (Cataloging) Follett Software; (Circulation) Follett Software
Open Mon-Fri 1-6

GRUVER

P GRUVER CITY LIBRARY*, 504 King St, 79040. (Mail add: PO Box 701, 79040-0701), SAN 316-3938. Tel: 806-733-2191. FAX: 806-733-2419. E-mail: gruverlibrary@gmail.com. *Dir,* Carolyn Fletcher
Founded 1961. Pop 1,444; Circ 3,036
Library Holdings: Bk Vols 14,097
Wireless access
Open Mon, Wed & Fri 2-6, Tues & Thurs 9-1

HALE CENTER

P HALE CENTER PUBLIC LIBRARY*, 609 Main St, 79041. (Mail add: PO Box 214, 79041-0214), SAN 316-3946. Tel: 806-839-2055. FAX: 806-839-2055. E-mail: halecenterlibrary@gmail.com. *Librn,* Elia Madrigal
Pop 2,000; Circ 5,234
Library Holdings: Bk Vols 20,000
Special Collections: Texas Heritage Resource Center
Automation Activity & Vendor Info: (Cataloging) LibLime; (Circulation) LibLime; (OPAC) LibLime
Wireless access
Open Mon, Wed & Fri 9-12 & 1-5:30
Friends of the Library Group

HALLETTSVILLE

P FRIENCH SIMPSON MEMORIAL LIBRARY*, 705 E Fourth St, 77964-2828. SAN 316-3954. Tel: 361-798-3243. FAX: 361-798-5833. Web Site: www.hallettsvillelibrary.org. *Dir,* Brenda Lincke-Fisseler; E-mail: fsmlib.director@gmail.com; *Asst Dir,* Penny Kristek; E-mail: fsmlib.kristek@gmail.com; *Ch Serv,* Breana Kristek; E-mail: fsmlib.bkristek@gmail.com; Staff 4 (MLS 1, Non-MLS 3)
Founded 1962. Pop 2,550; Circ 45,000
Library Holdings: Bk Titles 23,800; Per Subs 35
Subject Interests: Genealogy, Local hist
Automation Activity & Vendor Info: (Cataloging) Follett Software; (Circulation) Follett Software; (OPAC) Follett Software
Wireless access
Function: 24/7 Electronic res, 24/7 Online cat, Activity rm
Partic in Partners Library Action Network
Open Tues & Thurs 9-5:30, Wed & Fri Noon-5:30, Sat 9-Noon
Friends of the Library Group

HALTOM CITY

P HALTOM CITY PUBLIC LIBRARY*, 4809 Haltom Rd, 76117-3622. SAN 316-3962. Tel: 817-222-7786. Administration Tel: 817-222-7790. FAX: 817-788-1499. E-mail: library@haltomcitytx.com. Web Site: www.haltomcitytx.com/departments/library. *Dir, Libr Serv,* Lesly M Smith; Tel: 817-222-7791, E-mail: lmsmith@haltomcitytx.com; *Asst Libr Dir,* Erica Gill; Tel: 817-222-7792, E-mail: egill@haltomcitytx.com; *Adult Serv, Sr Librn,* Lani Hahn; Tel: 817-222-7770, E-mail: lhahn@haltomcitytx.com; *Ch Serv, Sr Librn,* Kansas Terry; Tel: 817-222-7788, E-mail: kterry@haltomcitytx.com; *Sr Librn, Teen Serv,* Christina Barton; Tel: 817-222-7769, E-mail: cbarton@haltomcitytx.com; *Librn,* Dean Hodges; Tel: 817-222-7758, E-mail: dhodges@haltomcitytx.com; *Librn, Outreach Serv,* Alison Long; Tel: 817-222-7768, E-mail: along@haltomcitytx.com; Staff 18 (MLS 5, Non-MLS 13)
Founded 1961. Pop 40,000
Oct 2020-Sept 2021 Income $1,182,552. Mats Exp $106,645, Books $80,750, Per/Ser (Incl. Access Fees) $4,400, AV Mat $10,000, Electronic Ref Mat (Incl. Access Fees) $4,023. Sal $1,001,683
Library Holdings: Audiobooks 9,663; DVDs 9,295; e-books 11,097; Electronic Media & Resources 69; Bk Titles 87,121; Per Subs 38
Automation Activity & Vendor Info: (Acquisitions) Innovative Interfaces, Inc; (Circulation) Innovative Interfaces, Inc; (OPAC) Innovative Interfaces, Inc
Wireless access
Function: 24/7 Electronic res, 24/7 Online cat, Adult bk club, Adult literacy prog, Art exhibits, Art programs, Audiobks via web, Bilingual assistance for Spanish patrons, Bk club(s), Bks on CD, Children's prog, Computers for patron use, E-Reserves, Electronic databases & coll, Free DVD rentals, Govt ref serv, Health sci info serv, Holiday prog, Home delivery & serv to seniorr ctr & nursing homes, Homebound delivery serv, ILL available, Internet access, Magazines, Mail & tel request accepted, Meeting rooms, Movies, Music CDs, Notary serv, Online cat, Outreach serv, OverDrive digital audio bks, Photocopying/Printing, Preschool outreach, Preschool reading prog, Prog for adults, Prog for children & young adult, Ref serv available, Senior outreach, Spanish lang bks, STEM programs, Story hour, Study rm, Summer reading prog, Tax forms, Teen prog, Telephone ref, Wheelchair accessible, Workshops
Partic in MetrOPAC Consortium; MetroShare Libraries; Partners Library Action Network
Special Services for the Blind - Bks on CD; Home delivery serv; Large print bks
Open Mon-Thurs 10:30-8, Fri 10:30-6, Sat 10:30-5
Friends of the Library Group

HAMILTON

P HAMILTON PUBLIC LIBRARY, 201 N Pecan St, 76531. SAN 376-4796. Tel: 254-386-3474. FAX: 254-386-4447. E-mail: hamiltonpubliclibrary.texas@gmail.com. Web Site: www.hamilton-public-library.org. *Dir,* Nancy Diaz; Staff 3 (Non-MLS 3)
Founded 1966. Pop 8,300; Circ 19,983
Library Holdings: Audiobooks 500; DVDs 900; Large Print Bks 240; Bk Vols 17,300; Per Subs 10; Talking Bks 650; Videos 1,000
Automation Activity & Vendor Info: (Acquisitions) Baker & Taylor; (Cataloging) Biblionix; (Circulation) Biblionix; (ILL) OCLC
Wireless access
Function: 24/7 Electronic res, 24/7 Online cat, 24/7 wireless access, 3D Printer, Accelerated reader prog, Activity rm, Adult bk club, Adult literacy prog, Archival coll, Art programs, Audio & video playback equip for onsite use, Audiobks via web, Bk club(s), Children's prog, Computer training, Computers for patron use, Family literacy, Free DVD rentals, Genealogy discussion group, ILL available, Instruction & testing, Internet access, Laminating, Magazines, Makerspace, Meeting rooms, Online cat, Online Chat, Online ref, OverDrive digital audio bks, Photocopying/Printing, Preschool reading prog, Printer for laptops & handheld devices, Prog for adults, Prog for children & young adult, Res performed for a fee, Scanner, Spanish lang bks, STEM programs, Story hour, Study rm, Summer reading prog, Telephone ref, Wheelchair accessible
Partic in Central Texas Digital Consortium; Partners Library Action Network
Special Services for the Blind - Aids for in-house use
Open Tues-Fri 10-6
Friends of the Library Group

HARKER HEIGHTS

P HARKER HEIGHTS PUBLIC LIBRARY*, 400 Indian Trail, 76548. SAN 376-4788. Tel: 254-259-5491. Circulation E-mail: circulation@ci.harker-heights.tx.us. Web Site: www.ci.harker-heights.tx.us. *Libr Dir,* Lisa D Youngblood; E-mail: lyoungblood@ci.harker-heights.tx.us; Staff 10 (MLS 2, Non-MLS 8)
Pop 18,000
Library Holdings: Bk Titles 53,131; Per Subs 40
Automation Activity & Vendor Info: (Cataloging) Follett Software; (Circulation) Follett Software; (OPAC) Follett Software
Wireless access
Function: Ref serv available
Partic in Partners Library Action Network
Open Mon-Thurs 9-8, Fri & Sat 9-6
Friends of the Library Group

HARLINGEN

P HARLINGEN PUBLIC LIBRARY*, 410 76 Dr, 78550. SAN 316-3997. Tel: 956-216-5800. Circulation Tel: 956-216-5810. Reference Tel: 956-216-5807 (Periodicals), 956-216-5821. FAX: 956-430-6654. E-mail: administration@harlingenlibrary.com. Web Site: harlingenlibrary.org. *Libr*

Dir, Dauna Campbell; Tel: 956-216-5803, E-mail: dcampbell@harlingenlibrary.com; *Asst Libr Dir,* Molly Walter; E-mail: mwalter@harlingenlibrary.com; Staff 16.5 (MLS 3, Non-MLS 13.5)
Founded 1920. Pop 93,435; Circ 177,061
Library Holdings: Audiobooks 8,824; AV Mats 5,251; Electronic Media & Resources 53; Bk Titles 120,601; Bk Vols 153,564; Per Subs 443
Subject Interests: Genealogy, Railroad hist, Spanish, Tex hist
Automation Activity & Vendor Info: (Acquisitions) Biblionix; (Cataloging) Biblionix; (Circulation) Biblionix; (ILL) Biblionix; (OPAC) Biblionix
Wireless access
Function: Archival coll, Art exhibits, Audio & video playback equip for onsite use, Audiobks via web, AV serv, Bks on CD, CD-ROM, Chess club, Computer training, Computers for patron use, E-Reserves, Electronic databases & coll, Free DVD rentals, Genealogy discussion group, Holiday prog, ILL available, Internet access, Magnifiers for reading, Microfiche/film & reading machines, Music CDs, Online cat, Online ref, Orientations, Outreach serv, OverDrive digital audio bks, Photocopying/Printing, Prog for adults, Prog for children & young adult, Ref & res, Ref serv available, Scanner, Spanish lang bks, Story hour, Summer & winter reading prog, Tax forms, Teen prog, Telephone ref, Wheelchair accessible
Special Services for the Deaf - TDD equip
Special Services for the Blind - Reader equip
Open Mon-Thurs 10-8, Fri & Sat 10-5, Sun 1-5
Restriction: Circ to mem only, Non-circulating coll, Open to pub for ref & circ; with some limitations
Friends of the Library Group

J TEXAS STATE TECHNICAL COLLEGE*, J Gilbert Leal Learning Resource Center, 1902 N Loop 499, 78550. SAN 316-4012. Tel: 956-364-4609. Toll Free Tel: 800-852-8784. E-mail: library@harlingen.tstc.edu. Web Site: www.tstc.edu/student_life/learningresource. *Dir,* Nancy Hendricks; Tel: 956-364-4708, E-mail: nlhendricks@tstc.edu; *Tech Serv Librn,* Kelly Withrow; Tel: 956-364-4612, E-mail: kjwithrow@tstc.edu; Staff 6 (MLS 2, Non-MLS 4)
Founded 1969. Enrl 5,800; Fac 150; Highest Degree: Associate
Library Holdings: AV Mats 31; Bks on Deafness & Sign Lang 30; CDs 567; DVDs 142; e-books 53,707; e-journals 10,041; Bk Titles 31,600; Bk Vols 34,720; Per Subs 320; Videos 179
Subject Interests: Allied health
Automation Activity & Vendor Info: (Acquisitions) SirsiDynix-iBistro; (Cataloging) SirsiDynix-iBistro; (Circulation) SirsiDynix-iLink; (ILL) OCLC; (OPAC) SirsiDynix
Wireless access
Function: Online cat, Photocopying/Printing, Wheelchair accessible
Partic in TexSHARE - Texas State Library & Archives Commission
Special Services for the Blind - Reader equip
Open Mon-Thurs 7:30am-8pm, Fri 7:30-5, Sat 12-4

CM UNIVERSITY OF TEXAS RIO GRANDE VALLEY*, Mario E Ramirez, MD Library, School of Medicine, 2102 Treasure Hills Blvd, 78550. Tel: 956-296-1500. E-mail: somlibrary@utrgv.edu. *Assoc Univ Librn,* Kathy Carter; Tel: 956-296-1507, E-mail: kathleen.carter@utrgv.edu
Wireless access
Partic in Amigos Library Services, Inc
Open Mon-Thurs 7:30am-9pm, Fri 7:30-5, Sat 10-6, Sun1-5

HASKELL

P HASKELL COUNTY LIBRARY*, 300 N Ave E, 79521-5706. SAN 316-4020. Tel: 940-864-2747. FAX: 940-864-2747. E-mail: haskell.library@yahoo.com. Web Site: haskell.ploud.net. *Dir,* Marilyn Griffith; *Asst Librn,* Paula Garcia; Staff 1 (Non-MLS 1)
Founded 1902. Pop 6,093; Circ 14,500
Library Holdings: AV Mats 325; Large Print Bks 500; Bk Titles 9,217; Bk Vols 9,840; Per Subs 8; Talking Bks 1,275
Subject Interests: Local county hist, Local genealogy, Local hist
Automation Activity & Vendor Info: (Cataloging) LibLime; (Circulation) LibLime
Wireless access
Open Mon-Thurs 9-5:30, Fri 9-4:30
Friends of the Library Group

HASLET

P HASLET PUBLIC LIBRARY*, 100 Gammill, 76052. Tel: 817-439-4278. Administration Tel: 817-439-4278, Ext 203. FAX: 817-439-3559. E-mail: library@haslet.org. Web Site: www.haslet.org/192/Library. *Dir,* Barbara Thompson; E-mail: bthompson@haslet.org; Staff 3.5 (MLS 2, Non-MLS 1.5)
Library Holdings: Bk Titles 24,233
Function: 24/7 Electronic res, 24/7 Online cat, Adult bk club
Partic in MetroShare Libraries
Open Mon-Thurs 10-7, Fri 12-5, Sat 10-3

HAWKINS

P ALLEN MEMORIAL PUBLIC LIBRARY*, 121 E Blackbourn St, 75765. (Mail add: PO Box 329, 75765-0329), SAN 370-7431. Tel: 903-769-2241. E-mail: hawkins.library@yahoo.com. Web Site: www.hawkinslibrary.org. *Dir,* Norma Hallmark
Founded 1988. Pop 5,936
Library Holdings: Bk Vols 14,921; Per Subs 12
Wireless access
Open Mon-Thurs 10-5, Fri 10-3

C JARVIS CHRISTIAN COLLEGE*, Olin Learning Resource Center, Hwy 80 E, 75765. (Mail add: PO Box 1470, 75765-1470), SAN 316-4039. Tel: 903-730-4890, Ext 2172. FAX: 903-769-5822. Web Site: www.jarvis.edu/current-students/library. *Dir,* Rodney Atkins; Tel: 903-730-4890, Ext 2171, E-mail: ratkins@jarvis.edu; Staff 4 (MLS 2, Non-MLS 2)
Founded 1920. Enrl 500; Fac 53; Highest Degree: Bachelor
Library Holdings: Bk Titles 65,000; Bk Vols 69,000; Per Subs 126
Subject Interests: Bus admin, Educ, Relig
Automation Activity & Vendor Info: (Acquisitions) Innovative Interfaces, Inc; (Cataloging) Innovative Interfaces, Inc; (Circulation) Innovative Interfaces, Inc; (Course Reserve) Innovative Interfaces, Inc; (OPAC) Innovative Interfaces, Inc; (Serials) Innovative Interfaces, Inc
Wireless access
Open Mon-Thurs 8am-11pm, Fri 8-5, Sat 11-3, Sun 6-10

HEARNE

P SMITH-WELCH MEMORIAL LIBRARY*, 105 W Fifth St, 77859. SAN 316-4047. Tel: 979-279-5191. FAX: 979-200-6340. E-mail: info@swmlibrary.com. Web Site: www.swmlibrary.com. *Libr Dir,* Kaitlyn Gonzalez; E-mail: librarydirector@swmlibrary.com; Staff 3 (Non-MLS 3)
Pop 10,738; Circ 21,125
Sept 2019-Aug 2020 Income $182,900, City $179,900, County $3,000. Mats Exp $10,500, Books $10,500. Sal $38,617
Library Holdings: Audiobooks 339; Bks on Deafness & Sign Lang 3; DVDs 1,028; Large Print Bks 764; Bk Titles 1,446; Per Subs 12
Automation Activity & Vendor Info: (Acquisitions) Baker & Taylor; (Cataloging) Biblionix/Apollo; (Circulation) Biblionix/Apollo; (ILL) OCLC WorldShare Interlibrary Loan; (OPAC) Biblionix/Apollo
Wireless access
Function: 24/7 Electronic res, 24/7 Online cat, Adult bk club, After school storytime, Audio & video playback equip for onsite use, Audiobks via web, Bilingual assistance for Spanish patrons, Bk club(s), Bks on CD, Children's prog, Computer training, Computers for patron use, Electronic databases & coll, Free DVD rentals, Homebound delivery serv, ILL available, Instruction & testing, Internet access, Laminating, Large print keyboards, Magazines, Mail loans to mem, Movies, Notary serv, Online cat, Online info literacy tutorials on the web & in blackboard, Online ref, Outside serv via phone, mail, e-mail & web, OverDrive digital audio bks, Photocopying/Printing, Printer for laptops & handheld devices, Prog for adults, Prog for children & young adult, Scanner, Senior computer classes, Spanish lang bks, Spoken cassettes & CDs, Spoken cassettes & DVDs, Story hour, Summer & winter reading prog, Summer reading prog, Tax forms, Teen prog, Wheelchair accessible, Winter reading prog
Partic in Central Texas Digital Consortium; Partners Library Action Network; TexSHARE - Texas State Library & Archives Commission
Open Mon-Fri 8-5

HEBBRONVILLE

P JIM HOGG COUNTY PUBLIC LIBRARY, 210 N Smith Ave, 78361. SAN 316-4055. Tel: 361-527-3421. FAX: 361-235-4097. E-mail: jcguerra@co.jim-hogg.tx.us. Web Site: www.co.jim-hogg.tx.us/page/jim-hogg.public.library. *Asst Librn,* Elena A Guerrero
Pop 5,265; Circ 9,000
Library Holdings: Bk Vols 17,232; Per Subs 42
Automation Activity & Vendor Info: (Cataloging) Follett Software; (Circulation) Follett Software
Wireless access
Open Mon-Fri 9-12 & 1-5

HEMPHILL

P J R HUFFMAN PUBLIC LIBRARY*, 375 Sabine St, 75948. Tel: 409-787-4829. FAX: 409-787-2957. E-mail: huffmanlibrary@yahoo.com. Web Site: www.hemphilltxlibrary.com. *Dir,* JaNelle Trexler
Founded 1994. Pop 1,242; Circ 27,526
Library Holdings: Bk Vols 22,800; Per Subs 20
Special Collections: Forestry, Dr Hiram Arnold Coll; Genealogical Research & Family History Coll
Subject Interests: Local hist, Tex hist, Westerns

Automation Activity & Vendor Info: (Acquisitions) Follett Software; (Cataloging) Follett Software; (Circulation) Follett Software; (OPAC) Follett Software
Partic in TexSHARE - Texas State Library & Archives Commission
Open Mon-Fri 9-4
Friends of the Library Group

HEMPSTEAD

P WALLER COUNTY LIBRARY*, 2331 11th St, 77445-6724. SAN 316-4063. Tel: 979-826-7658. FAX: 979-826-7659. E-mail: wallercountylibrary@gmail.com. Web Site: hempstead.ploud.net. *Libr Dir,* Lynda Fairchild; E-mail: l.fairchild@wallercounty.us; Staff 5 (MLS 1, Non-MLS 4)
Founded 1974. Pop 43,218; Circ 70,000
Jan 2016-Dec 2016 Income (Main & Associated Libraries) $301,000. Mats Exp $35,000. Sal $218,000 (Prof $47,000)
Library Holdings: Large Print Bks 1,200; Bk Titles 30,106; Per Subs 11
Automation Activity & Vendor Info: (Acquisitions) Biblionix/Apollo; (Cataloging) Biblionix/Apollo; (Circulation) Biblionix/Apollo; (Course Reserve) Biblionix/Apollo; (Discovery) Biblionix/Apollo; (ILL) Biblionix/Apollo; (OPAC) Biblionix/Apollo
Wireless access
Partic in Partners Library Action Network
Open Mon-Fri 9-5
Friends of the Library Group
Branches: 1
BROOKSHIRE PATTISON BRANCH, 3815 Sixth St, Brookshire, 77423. Tel: 281-375-5550. FAX: 281-934-3516. E-mail: brookshirepattison@gmail.com. *Libr Dir,* Lynda Fairchild; Tel: 281-375-5550; Staff 4 (Non-MLS 4)
Library Holdings: AV Mats 1,000; Bk Titles 20,000
Open Mon-Fri 9-5
Friends of the Library Group

HENDERSON

P RUSK COUNTY LIBRARY SYSTEM*, Rusk County Library, 106 E Main St, 75652. SAN 361-767X. Tel: 903-657-8557. FAX: 903-657-7637. E-mail: rclstaff7@gmail.com. Web Site: www.youseemore.com/rusk. *Libr Mgr,* Michelle Pollard; Staff 11 (Non-MLS 11)
Founded 1937. Pop 48,887; Circ 318,406
Library Holdings: AV Mats 3,159; DVDs 90; Large Print Bks 2,288; Bk Titles 59,300; Bk Vols 64,679; Per Subs 139
Special Collections: Texas Heritage Resource Center
Subject Interests: Hist, Rusk county genealogy
Automation Activity & Vendor Info: (Acquisitions) TLC (The Library Corporation); (Cataloging) TLC (The Library Corporation); (Circulation) TLC (The Library Corporation); (OPAC) TLC (The Library Corporation)
Wireless access
Function: 24/7 Electronic res, 24/7 Online cat, 3D Printer, Audiobks via web, AV serv, Bks on CD, Children's prog, Computers for patron use, Electronic databases & coll, For res purposes, Free DVD rentals, ILL available, Internet access, Magazines, Meeting rooms, Music CDs, Online cat, Outreach serv, OverDrive digital audio bks, Photocopying/Printing, Printer for laptops & handheld devices, Prog for children & young adult, Ref serv available, Scanner, Spanish lang bks, Story hour, Summer reading prog, Teen prog, Telephone ref, Wheelchair accessible
Open Mon, Wed & Fri 8:30-5:30, Tues & Thurs 8:30-7
Friends of the Library Group
Branches: 3
MCMILLAN MEMORIAL LIBRARY, 401 S Commerce St, Overton, 75684. (Mail add: PO Box 290, Overton, 75684), SAN 361-770X. Tel: 903-834-6318. FAX: 903-834-6937. E-mail: mcmillanmemoriallibrary@gmail.com. *Br Mgr,* Jennifer Freeman; Staff 4 (MLS 1, Non-MLS 3)
Founded 1956
Library Holdings: Audiobooks 398; CDs 77; DVDs 1,434; Large Print Bks 986; Bk Titles 10,810; Per Subs 23
Function: 24/7 Electronic res, 24/7 Online cat, Bk reviews (Group), Bks on cassette, Bks on CD, Children's prog, Computer training, Computers for patron use, Electronic databases & coll, Free DVD rentals, Holiday prog, ILL available, Internet access, Magazines, Meeting rooms, Music CDs, Online cat, Outreach serv, OverDrive digital audio bks, Photocopying/Printing, Preschool outreach, Preschool reading prog, Printer for laptops & handheld devices, Prog for adults, Prog for children & young adult, Ref & res, Ref serv available, Scanner, Senior computer classes, Spoken cassettes & CDs, Summer reading prog, Tax forms, Teen prog, VHS videos, Wheelchair accessible
Open Mon-Wed & Fri 8-5, Thurs 10-7
Friends of the Library Group
MOUNT ENTERPRISE PUBLIC LIBRARY, 201 NW Second St, Mount Enterprise, 75681. (Mail add: PO Box 367, Mount Enterprise, 75681-0367), SAN 361-7734. Tel: 903-822-3532. FAX: 903-822-3296. E-mail: mtentlib@gmail.com. *Br Mgr,* Nell Langford; Staff 4 (MLS 1, Non-MLS 3)
Founded 1960
Library Holdings: AV Mats 1,016; Large Print Bks 646; Bk Titles 13,494; Bk Vols 13,933; Per Subs 25
Function: 24/7 Electronic res, 24/7 Online cat, 3D Printer, Bks on CD, Children's prog, Computer training, Free DVD rentals, ILL available, Internet access, Magazines, Meeting rooms, Music CDs, Online cat, Outreach serv, OverDrive digital audio bks, Photocopying/Printing, Printer for laptops & handheld devices, Prog for adults, Prog for children & young adult, Ref & res, Ref serv available, Res assist avail, Scanner, Summer reading prog, Tax forms, Teen prog, Telephone ref, Wheelchair accessible
Open Mon-Fri 8-5
Friends of the Library Group
TATUM PUBLIC, 335 Hood St, Tatum, 75691. (Mail add: PO Box 1087, Tatum, 75691-1087), SAN 361-7769. Tel: 903-947-2211. FAX: 903-947-3215. E-mail: tatumpubliclib@gmail.com. *Br Mgr,* April Pettigrew; Staff 2.5 (Non-MLS 2.5)
Library Holdings: AV Mats 1,199; Large Print Bks 938; Bk Titles 15,528; Bk Vols 16,109; Per Subs 27
Automation Activity & Vendor Info: (Cataloging) TLC (The Library Corporation); (Circulation) TLC (The Library Corporation); (OPAC) TLC (The Library Corporation); (Serials) TLC (The Library Corporation)
Function: ILL available, Photocopying/Printing, Summer reading prog, Wheelchair accessible
Open Mon-Fri 8-5

HENRIETTA

P EDWARDS PUBLIC LIBRARY, 210 W Gilbert St, 76365-2816. SAN 316-4098. Tel: 940-538-4791. FAX: 940-538-5861. Web Site: www.edwardspl.org. *Libr Dir,* Norma Jean Ruiz-Hearne; E-mail: edwards.pl@claycountytx.net; Staff 2 (MLS 1, Non-MLS 1)
Founded 1932. Pop 10,450; Circ 44,292
Library Holdings: Bk Titles 31,466; Bk Vols 32,356; Per Subs 70
Automation Activity & Vendor Info: (Acquisitions) Baker & Taylor; (Cataloging) Book Systems; (Circulation) Book Systems; (OPAC) Book Systems
Wireless access
Open Mon-Wed & Fri 9-12:30 & 1:30-5, Thurs 9-8

HEREFORD

P DEAF SMITH COUNTY LIBRARY*, 211 E Fourth St, 79045. SAN 316-4101. Tel: 806-364-1206. FAX: 806-363-7063. E-mail: dsclibraryinfo@gmail.com. Web Site: www.deafsmithcolib.org. *Dir,* Linda Perry; *Asst Dir,* Evelyn Taylor; Staff 7 (Non-MLS 7)
Founded 1910. Pop 18,561
Library Holdings: Audiobooks 1,994; CDs 1,994; DVDs 2,309; e-books 5,544; Electronic Media & Resources 80; Bk Vols 50,640; Per Subs 74
Subject Interests: Spanish
Automation Activity & Vendor Info: (Cataloging) SirsiDynix; (Circulation) SirsiDynix; (OPAC) SirsiDynix
Wireless access
Partic in Harrington Library Consortium
Open Mon & Thurs 9-9, Tues, Wed & Fri 9-6, Sat 9-1
Friends of the Library Group

HEWITT

P HEWITT PUBLIC LIBRARY, 200 Patriot Ct, 76643. SAN 376-477X. Tel: 254-666-2442. FAX: 254-666-6025. E-mail: library@cityofhewitt.com. Web Site: www.cityofhewitt.com. *Libr Dir,* Matthew Glaser; E-mail: librarydirector@cityofhewitt.com; *Mgr,* Simon Dulock; E-mail: sdulock@cityofhewitt.com; *Prog Mgr,* Kayla Pecina; E-mail: kpecina@cityofhewitt.com; Staff 3 (MLS 1, Non-MLS 2)
Founded 1984. Pop 25,831
Library Holdings: High Interest/Low Vocabulary Bk Vols 763; Large Print Bks 340; Bk Vols 38,000
Automation Activity & Vendor Info: (Acquisitions) Biblionix/Apollo; (Cataloging) Biblionix/Apollo; (Circulation) Biblionix/Apollo; (ILL) Biblionix/Apollo; (OPAC) Biblionix/Apollo
Wireless access
Function: 24/7 Electronic res, 24/7 Online cat, 24/7 wireless access, 3D Printer, Adult bk club, Art programs, Children's prog, Computers for patron use, Family literacy, Free DVD rentals
Partic in Central Texas Digital Consortium; Partners Library Action Network
Open Mon-Thurs 9:30-8, Fri & Sat 9:30-5:30
Friends of the Library Group

HIDALGO

P HIDALGO PUBLIC LIBRARY, 710 Ramon Ayala Dr, 78557. Tel: 956-843-2093. FAX: 956-843-8841. E-mail: hpl@cityofhidalgo.net. Web Site: cityofhidalgo.net/public-library. *Dir,* Juan Viveros; Staff 3 (Non-MLS 3)
Founded 1998. Pop 18,785
Library Holdings: Bk Titles 13,099; Bk Vols 14,128; Per Subs 15; Talking Bks 116; Videos 375
Automation Activity & Vendor Info: (Acquisitions) TLC (The Library Corporation); (Cataloging) TLC (The Library Corporation); (Circulation) TLC (The Library Corporation); (ILL) TLC (The Library Corporation); (OPAC) TLC (The Library Corporation)
Wireless access
Function: Adult literacy prog, After school storytime, Bilingual assistance for Spanish patrons, Bks on cassette, Bks on CD, CD-ROM, Children's prog, Computer training, Computers for patron use, Distance learning, Electronic databases & coll, Free DVD rentals, Holiday prog, ILL available, Instruction & testing, Internet access, Magnifiers for reading, Mail & tel request accepted, Online cat, Online ref, Photocopying/Printing, Prog for children & young adult, Ref & res, Ref serv available, Scanner, Spoken cassettes & CDs, Story hour, Summer & winter reading prog, Tax forms, Telephone ref, VHS videos, Wheelchair accessible
Mem of Hidalgo County Library System
Open Mon-Thurs 10-8, Fri 10-5, Sat 10-2

HIGGINS

P HIGGINS PUBLIC LIBRARY*, 201 N Main St, 79046. SAN 316-411X. Tel: 806-852-2214. FAX: 806-852-2214. E-mail: readyreader@yahoo.com. Web Site: www.higginslibrary.org. *Dir,* Kelly Cribb; Staff 1 (Non-MLS 1)
Pop 3,486
Library Holdings: Bk Titles 12,000; Bk Vols 12,250; Per Subs 15; Talking Bks 475
Wireless access
Function: Adult bk club, Bks on CD, Children's prog, Free DVD rentals, ILL available, Internet access, Magazines, Makerspace, Photocopying/Printing, Summer reading prog
Special Services for the Blind - Talking bks
Open Mon-Wed 9-12 & 1-5

HIGHLAND PARK

P HIGHLAND PARK LIBRARY*, 4700 Drexel Dr, 75205-3198. SAN 316-1994. Tel: 214-559-9400. FAX: 214-559-9335. E-mail: hplibrary@hplibrary.info. Web Site: tx-highlandpark.civicplus.com/index.aspx?NID=106. *Town Librn,* Kortney Nelson; Tel: 214-559-9404, E-mail: knelson@hplibrary.info; *Ch,* Deadre Henderson; E-mail: chenderson@hplibrary.info; Staff 7 (MLS 2, Non-MLS 5)
Founded 1930. Pop 8,800; Circ 41,000
Library Holdings: AV Mats 1,972; CDs 1,169; DVDs 533; e-books 1,300; Large Print Bks 630; Bk Titles 35,542; Bk Vols 37,115; Per Subs 55; Talking Bks 2,076; Videos 1,656
Automation Activity & Vendor Info: (Cataloging) TLC (The Library Corporation); (Circulation) TLC (The Library Corporation); (OPAC) TLC (The Library Corporation)
Wireless access
Function: Bks on CD, Children's prog, Computers for patron use, Digital talking bks, Electronic databases & coll, Free DVD rentals, Magazines, Movies, Music CDs, Online cat, OverDrive digital audio bks, Photocopying/Printing, Story hour, Summer reading prog, Wheelchair accessible
Partic in Partners Library Action Network
Special Services for the Deaf - Bks on deafness & sign lang; High interest/low vocabulary bks
Special Services for the Blind - Audio mat; Bks on cassette; Bks on CD; Cassettes; Copier with enlargement capabilities; Extensive large print coll; Large print bks; Talking bks; Videos on blindness & physical disabilties
Open Tues-Sat 9:30-5:30
Friends of the Library Group

HILLSBORO

J HILL COLLEGE LIBRARY*, 112 Lamar Dr, 76645. SAN 316-4128. Tel: 254-659-7830. E-mail: library@hillcollege.edu. Web Site: www.hillcollege.edu/campuslife/library. *Librn,* Eve Bowen; Tel: 254-659-7831, E-mail: ebowen@hillcollege.edu; Staff 7 (MLS 4, Non-MLS 3)
Founded 1962. Enrl 1,958; Fac 84
Library Holdings: Bk Titles 48,000; Per Subs 183
Special Collections: Light Crust Doughboys Papers; Texas Heritage Research Center. Oral History
Automation Activity & Vendor Info: (Acquisitions) SirsiDynix; (Cataloging) SirsiDynix; (Circulation) SirsiDynix; (Course Reserve) SirsiDynix; (ILL) SirsiDynix; (Media Booking) SirsiDynix; (OPAC) SirsiDynix; (Serials) SirsiDynix
Wireless access
Partic in Amigos Library Services, Inc
Open Mon-Thurs 7:30am-10pm, Fri 7:30-4, Sun 2-10
Departmental Libraries:
JOHNSON COUNTY CAMPUS, 2112 Mayfield Pkwy, Cleburne, 76033. Tel: 817-760-5830.
Library Holdings: Bk Vols 10,239; Per Subs 65
Open Mon-Thurs 7:30am-8pm, Fri 7:30-4 (Winter)

P HILLSBORO CITY LIBRARY*, 118 S Waco St, 76645. SAN 316-4136. Tel: 254-582-7385. FAX: 254-582-7765. E-mail: hillsborolibrary@hillsborotx.org. Web Site: www.hillsborotx.org/city-departments/library. *Dir,* Susan S Mann; *Asst Librn,* Russell W Keelin
Library Holdings: Bk Titles 48,000; Per Subs 105
Subject Interests: Tex
Automation Activity & Vendor Info: (Cataloging) Biblionix; (Circulation) Biblionix; (OPAC) Biblionix
Wireless access
Partic in Partners Library Action Network; Tex ILL Syst
Open Mon & Thurs 9-7, Tues, Wed & Fri 9-5, Sat 9-Noon
Friends of the Library Group

HITCHCOCK

P GENEVIEVE MILLER HITCHCOCK PUBLIC LIBRARY*, 8005 Barry Ave, 77563. SAN 376-4109. Tel: 409-986-7814. FAX: 409-986-6353. E-mail: hitchpl@comcast.net. Web Site: www.hitchcockpubliclibrary.org. *Dir,* Joyce Kleimann; Staff 5 (MLS 1, Non-MLS 4)
Library Holdings: Audiobooks 437; DVDs 1,613; Bk Vols 32,766; Per Subs 16
Automation Activity & Vendor Info: (Cataloging) Surpass; (Circulation) Surpass
Wireless access
Mem of Galveston County Library System
Partic in Partners Library Action Network
Open Tues, Wed & Fri 10-5, Thurs 10-6, Sat 10-3
Friends of the Library Group

HOLLAND

P B J HILL LIBRARY*, 402 W Travis St, 76534-3015. (Mail add: PO Box 217, 76534-0217). Tel: 254-657-2884. E-mail: bjhilllibrary@gmail.com. Web Site: www.facebook.com/bjhilllibrary. *Dir,* Holly Naizer
Library Holdings: Bk Vols 10,400
Automation Activity & Vendor Info: (Cataloging) Follett Software; (Circulation) Follett Software
Wireless access
Open Mon-Wed 3-6, Sat 9-9
Friends of the Library Group

HOLLY LAKE RANCH

P HOLLY COMMUNITY LIBRARY, 1620 FM 2869, 75765. Tel: 903-769-5142. Web Site: www.hollylakeranch.com.
Pop 3,000
Library Holdings: AV Mats 400; Bk Titles 13,000; Talking Bks 600
Open Tues, Thurs & Fri 10-2

HONDO

P HONDO PUBLIC LIBRARY, 2003 Ave K, 78861-2431. (Mail add: 1600 Ave M, 78861), SAN 324-1289. Tel: 830-426-5333. Web Site: www.hondo-tx.org/251/library. *Libr Dir,* Elsie Purcell; E-mail: epurcell@hondo-tx.org; *Ch, Circ,* Tina Leos; E-mail: cleos@hondo-tx.org; *Circ,* Lareyna Cook; E-mail: lcook@hondo-tx.org; *Circ, ILL,* Barbara Desrosiers; E-mail: bdesrosiers@hondo-tx.org; *Circ, Spec Serv,* Carl Leon; E-mail: cleon@hondo-tx.org; Staff 5.5 (MLS 1, Non-MLS 4.5)
Founded 1967. Pop 8,387; Circ 29,369
Oct 2022-Sept 2023. Mats Exp $20,000, Books $18,000, Per/Ser (Incl. Access Fees) $1,000, AV Mat $1,000
Library Holdings: Audiobooks 953; Braille Volumes 1; DVDs 1,340; Electronic Media & Resources 2; Large Print Bks 1,938; Bk Titles 11,735; Bk Vols 12,483; Per Subs 11
Special Collections: Davis Memorial Coll; Rowland Coll; Texana
Automation Activity & Vendor Info: (Cataloging) Biblionix; (Circulation) Biblionix
Wireless access
Function: 24/7 Online cat, 3D Printer, Activity rm, Adult bk club, Archival coll, Art programs, Audiobks via web, Bilingual assistance for Spanish patrons, Bk club(s), Bks on CD, Children's prog, Computer training, Computers for patron use, Electronic databases & coll, Equip loans & repairs, Free DVD rentals, Games, ILL available, Internet access, Laminating, Laptop/tablet checkout, Life-long learning prog for all ages,

Magazines, Magnifiers for reading, Mail & tel request accepted, Makerspace, Meeting rooms, Movies, Notary serv, Online cat, OverDrive digital audio bks, Photocopying/Printing, Preschool outreach, Preschool reading prog, Printer for laptops & handheld devices, Prog for adults, Prog for children & young adult, Ref serv available, Scanner, Senior computer classes, Senior outreach, Serves people with intellectual disabilities, Spanish lang bks, Spoken cassettes & CDs, STEM programs, Story hour, Study rm, Summer reading prog, Tax forms, Teen prog, Wheelchair accessible, Wifi hotspot checkout
Partic in Amigos Library Services, Inc; Partners Library Action Network
Open Mon, Wed & Thurs 10-6, Tues 10-8, Fri 10-5, Sat 10-3
Restriction: ID required to use computers (Ltd hrs), In-house use for visitors, Non-resident fee

HONEY GROVE

P HONEY GROVE LIBRARY & LEARNING CENTER*, 500 N Sixth St, 75446. (Mail add: PO Box 47, 75446), SAN 316-4144. Tel: 903-378-2206. Web Site: honeygrovelibrary.org. *Libr Dir,* Mitzi Sherwood; E-mail: sherwood@honeygrove.org
Founded 1962. Pop 1,700
Library Holdings: Bk Titles 21,263
Automation Activity & Vendor Info: (Cataloging) Biblionix/Apollo; (Circulation) Biblionix/Apollo; (ILL) OCLC CatExpress; (OPAC) Biblionix/Apollo
Wireless access
Function: 24/7 Online cat, 24/7 wireless access, 3D Printer, Activity rm, Adult bk club, Adult literacy prog, After school storytime, Archival coll, Art exhibits, Art programs, Audiobks via web, AV serv, Bilingual assistance for Spanish patrons, Bk club(s), Children's prog, Computer training, Computers for patron use, Electronic databases & coll, Equip loans & repairs, Extended outdoor wifi, Family literacy, Free DVD rentals, Games, Genealogy discussion group, Holiday prog, ILL available, Internet access, Laminating, Laptop/tablet checkout, Learning ctr, Life-long learning prog for all ages, Literacy & newcomer serv, Meeting rooms, Microfiche/film & reading machines, Movies, Online cat, Orientations, Outreach serv, OverDrive digital audio bks, Photocopying/Printing, Preschool outreach, Preschool reading prog, Printer for laptops & handheld devices, Prog for adults, Prog for children & young adult, Ref serv available, Scanner, Senior computer classes, Serves people with intellectual disabilities, Spanish lang bks, STEM programs, Study rm, Summer reading prog, Teen prog, Visual arts prog, Wheelchair accessible, Workshops
Partic in Association for Rural & Small Libraries; TexSHARE - Texas State Library & Archives Commission
Special Services for the Deaf - ADA equip
Special Services for the Blind - Accessible computers; Aids for in-house use; Bks on CD; Large print bks & talking machines; Low vision equip
Open Tues & Thurs 10-7, Wed & Fri 10-5, Sat 10-2
Friends of the Library Group

HOOKS

P HOOKS PUBLIC LIBRARY*, 108 W First St, 75561. (Mail add: PO Box 1540, 75561-1540), SAN 375-5126. Tel: 903-547-3365. E-mail: hplib@windstream.net. Web Site: hooks.ploud.net. *Dir,* Shannon Heflin; Staff 1 (Non-MLS 1)
Founded 1990. Pop 3,500
Library Holdings: Bk Titles 12,576
Special Collections: Hooks Family Geneaology
Subject Interests: Tex
Automation Activity & Vendor Info: (Cataloging) LibraryWorld, Inc; (Circulation) LibraryWorld, Inc; (OPAC) LibraryWorld, Inc
Wireless access
Function: AV serv, Home delivery & serv to seniorr ctr & nursing homes, ILL available, Photocopying/Printing, Prog for children & young adult, Summer reading prog, Wheelchair accessible
Open Tues & Wed 1-5, Thurs & Fri 12-6
Restriction: Open to pub for ref & circ; with some limitations, Pub use on premises
Friends of the Library Group

HOUSTON

L BAKER & BOTTS LLP, Law Library, One Shell Plaza, 910 Louisiana St, 77002. SAN 316-4160. Tel: 713-229-1643. FAX: 713-229-1522. Web Site: www.bakerbotts.com. *Mgr, Libr Serv,* Robert Downie; *Research Librn,* Cynthia Montalvo
Founded 1872
Library Holdings: Bk Vols 80,000
Special Collections: Corporate Law Coll; Securities Coll; Tax Coll; Utilities Coll
Publications: Library Notes (Monthly); User Location Guide to Baker & Botts Library
Partic in D&B; LivEdgar; Proquest Dialog
Restriction: Staff use only

L CHAMBERLAIN HRDLICKA ATTORNEYS AT LAW*, Law Library, 1200 Smith St, Ste 1400, 77002. SAN 371-6287. Tel: 713-658-1818. Toll Free Tel: 800-342-5829. FAX: 713-658-2553. E-mail: firm@chamberlainlaw.com. Web Site: www.chamberlainlaw.com. *Dir, Knowledge & Res Serv,* Melinda Elder; Staff 2 (MLS 1, Non-MLS 1)
Library Holdings: Bk Vols 20,000; Per Subs 90

SR CHAPELWOOD UNITED METHODIST CHURCH*, Carey B Sayers Memorial Library, 11140 Greenbay St, 77024. SAN 328-4751. Tel: 713-354-4427, 713-465-3467. FAX: 713-365-2808. E-mail: library@chapelwood.org. Web Site: www.chapelwood.org/. *Librn,* Kris Jodon; Tel: 713-465-3467, Ext 127, E-mail: kjodon@chapelwood.org; Staff 2 (MLS 2)
Founded 1955
Library Holdings: Bks on Deafness & Sign Lang 10; Large Print Bks 90; Bk Vols 15,000; Per Subs 5; Talking Bks 75
Special Collections: Vidio & Audio Coll
Subject Interests: Relig
Automation Activity & Vendor Info: (Cataloging) Book Systems
Wireless access
Open Mon-Thurs & Sun 9-4, Fri 9-1

GM DEPARTMENT OF VETERANS AFFAIRS MEDICAL CENTER*, Medical Library, 2002 Holcombe Blvd, 77030. SAN 316-5027. Tel: 713-794-7856. FAX: 713-794-7456. Web Site: www.houston.va.gov. *Librn,* Ferlandez Alando Garmon; Tel: 713-794-1414, Ext 27856, E-mail: FERLANDEZ.GARMON@VA.GOV
Library Holdings: Bk Vols 3,000; Per Subs 500
Automation Activity & Vendor Info: (Cataloging) Inmagic, Inc.; (Circulation) Inmagic, Inc.; (OPAC) Inmagic, Inc.
Open Mon-Fri 7:30-4:30
Restriction: Staff use only

R FIRST PRESBYTERIAN CHURCH*, Adult Library, 5300 Main St, 77004. SAN 316-4365. Tel: 713-620-6500. FAX: 713-620-6550. E-mail: info@fpchouston.org. Web Site: fpchouston.org/resources/facilities. *Librn,* Erin Vernell; E-mail: evarnell@fpchouston.org
Founded 1951
Library Holdings: Bk Titles 3,000; Bk Vols 3,200
Subject Interests: Relig studies
Publications: Christianity Today; Presbyterian Outlook; Presbyterians Today
Restriction: Not open to pub

S H O K, INC*, Resource Library, 3200 SW Freeway, Ste 900, 77027. SAN 316-4241. Tel: 713-407-7700. FAX: 713-407-7809. E-mail: houston@hok.com. Web Site: www.hok.com/about/locations/houston. *Library Contact,* Cindy Fleming
Founded 1968
Library Holdings: Bk Vols 3,000
Subject Interests: Archit, Art, Construction, Engr, Planning
Wireless access
Partic in Proquest Dialog; SDC Search Serv; Vutext
Restriction: Staff use only

S HALLIBURTON ENERGY SERVICES, Houston Technical Library, 3000 N Sam Houston Pkwy E, 77032. SAN 324-1866. Tel: 281-871-2699. E-mail: fdunlibrary@halliburton.com. Web Site: www.halliburton.com. *Tech Librn,* Lina Wang; Staff 1 (Non-MLS 1)
Founded 1979
Library Holdings: Bk Titles 9,000; Bk Vols 11,000; Per Subs 105
Special Collections: Association & Industry Standards; Military Specifications; Society of Petroleum Engineers Coll; United States Patents Coll (1972-present)
Subject Interests: Chem, Electronics, Engr
Automation Activity & Vendor Info: (Cataloging) Inmagic, Inc.; (OPAC) Inmagic, Inc.
Publications: Acquisitions List (Monthly); Brief Guide to the Technical Information Center; Master Serials List
Restriction: Open by appt only

GL HARRIS COUNTY ROBERT W HAINSWORTH LAW LIBRARY*, Congress Plaza, 1019 Congress, 1st Flr, 77002. SAN 316-4454. Tel: 713-755-5183. E-mail: lawlibrary@harriscountytx.gov. Web Site: www.harriscountylawlibrary.org. *Dir,* Joseph Lawson; *Dep Dir,* Lori-Ann Craig; *Assoc Law Librn,* Sara Nouri
Founded 1913
Library Holdings: Bk Vols 100,000
Automation Activity & Vendor Info: (Cataloging) EOS International; (OPAC) EOS International; (Serials) EOS International
Wireless access
Open Mon-Fri 8-4

P HARRIS COUNTY PUBLIC LIBRARY*, 5749 S Loop E, 77033. SAN 361-8129. Tel: 713-274-6600. FAX: 713-749-9090. Web Site: www.hcpl.net. *Dir,* Edward Melton; *Dir, Prog & Partnerships, Div Head,* Linda Stevens; *Admin Serv, Div Dir, Br Serv,* Theodora Muokebe; *Coll, Div Dir, Tech Serv,* Amber Seely; *Div Head, Financial Serv,* Daisy Torres; *Dir, Res & Develop,* Megan LeMaster; *Div Dir, Info Tech,* Ty Beauchamp; *Div Dir, Human Res,* Lori Remington; Staff 121 (MLS 104, Non-MLS 17)
Founded 1921. Pop 2,064,400; Circ 9,518,572
Oct 2022-Sept 2023. Mats Exp $6,490,000, Books $1,621,997, Per/Ser (Incl. Access Fees) $46,173, Other Print Mats $96,903, AV Mat $218,796, Electronic Ref Mat (Incl. Access Fees) $4,325,283, Presv $11,000
Library Holdings: Audiobooks 69,757; AV Mats 168,213; Bks on Deafness & Sign Lang 96,537; Braille Volumes 133; CDs 11,996; DVDs 98,456; e-books 161,762; e-journals 4,311; Electronic Media & Resources 224,300; Large Print Bks 40,496; Bk Titles 775,503; Bk Vols 1,627,759; Per Subs 260; Videos 98,546
Automation Activity & Vendor Info: (Acquisitions) SirsiDynix; (Cataloging) SirsiDynix; (Circulation) SirsiDynix; (Course Reserve) SirsiDynix; (ILL) OCLC; (Media Booking) SirsiDynix; (OPAC) SirsiDynix; (Serials) SirsiDynix
Wireless access
Function: 24/7 Electronic res, 24/7 Online cat, 3D Printer, Adult literacy prog, Audiobks via web, Bilingual assistance for Spanish patrons, Children's prog, Citizenship assistance, Computer training, Computers for patron use, Electronic databases & coll, Family literacy, For res purposes, ILL available, Internet access, Jail serv, Laminating, Learning ctr, Life-long learning prog for all ages, Literacy & newcomer serv, Makerspace, Meeting rooms, Online cat, Online Chat, Online info literacy tutorials on the web & in blackboard, Online ref, Outreach serv, OverDrive digital audio bks, Photocopying/Printing, Preschool outreach, Preschool reading prog, Prog for adults, Prog for children & young adult, Ref & res, Ref serv available, Scanner, Senior computer classes, Senior outreach, Spanish lang bks, STEM programs, Summer reading prog, Teen prog, Wheelchair accessible
Partic in Amigos Library Services, Inc
Special Services for the Deaf - TDD equip
Special Services for the Blind - Low vision equip; Screen reader software
Open Mon-Fri 8-5
Restriction: Authorized personnel only, Limited access for the pub
Friends of the Library Group

Branches: 27

ALDINE BRANCH, 11331 Airline Dr, 77037, SAN 361-8153. Tel: 832-927-5410. E-mail: ald@hcpl.net. Web Site: www.hcpl.net/location/aldine-branch-library. *Br Mgr,* Carl Smith; Staff 13 (MLS 3, Non-MLS 10)
Founded 1974
Function: Adult literacy prog, Citizenship assistance, Computer training, Computers for patron use, Meeting rooms, Passport agency, Photocopying/Printing, Scanner, Study rm
Open Mon 11-6, Tues & Thurs 10-8, Wed 10-6, Fri 1-6, Sat 10-5
Friends of the Library Group

ATASCOCITA BRANCH, 19520 Pinehurst Trail Dr, Humble, 77346, SAN 376-9461. Tel: 832-927-5560. E-mail: ata@hcpl.net. Web Site: www.hcpl.net/location/atascocita-branch-library. *Br Mgr,* Beth Krippel; Staff 10 (MLS 5, Non-MLS 5)
Founded 1996
Function: Audio & video playback equip for onsite use, Computers for patron use, Meeting rooms, Study rm
Open Mon 11-6, Tues & Thurs 10-8, Wed 10-6, Fri 1-6, Sat 10-5
Friends of the Library Group

BALDWIN BOETTCHER BRANCH, 22306 Aldine Westfield Rd, Humble, 77338, SAN 322-5704. Tel: 832-927-5480. E-mail: bb@hcpl.net. Web Site: www.hcpl.net/location/baldwin-boettcher-branch-library-mercer-park. *Interim Br Mgr, Youth Serv,* Victoria Alardin; Staff 5 (MLS 3, Non-MLS 2)
Founded 1986
Function: Adult literacy prog, Children's prog, Citizenship assistance, Family literacy, Outreach serv, Prog for adults, Prog for children & young adult, Teen prog
Special Services for the Deaf - TDD equip
Open Mon-Sat 10-5
Friends of the Library Group

BARBARA BUSH BRANCH AT CYPRESS CREEK, 6817 Cypresswood Dr, Spring, 77379, SAN 361-8242. Tel: 832-927-7800. E-mail: cc@hcpl.net. Web Site: www.hcpl.net/branch/barbara-bush-branch-library-cypress-creek. *Br Mgr,* Clara Maynard; Staff 29 (MLS 9, Non-MLS 20)
Founded 1977
Function: Adult literacy prog, Children's prog, Computer training, Computers for patron use, Prog for adults, Prog for children & young adult, Senior outreach, Teen prog
Special Services for the Blind - Closed circuit TV magnifier; Reader equip
Open Mon-Wed 10-8, Thurs 10-6, Fri 1-6, Sat 10-5
Friends of the Library Group

CLEAR LAKE CITY-COUNTY FREEMAN BRANCH, 16616 Diana Lane, 77062, SAN 361-8307. Tel: 832-927-5420. E-mail: fm@hcpl.net. Web Site: www.hcpl.net/location/clear-lake-city-county-freeman-branch-library. *Br Mgr,* Christina Thompson; Staff 31 (MLS 11, Non-MLS 20)
Founded 1964
Function: Adult literacy prog, Audio & video playback equip for onsite use, Children's prog, Makerspace, Prog for adults, Prog for children & young adult, Teen prog
Open Mon-Wed 10-8, Thurs 10-6, Fri 1-6, Sat 10-5
Friends of the Library Group

CROSBY EDITH FAE COOK COLE BRANCH, 135 Hare Rd, Crosby, 77532, SAN 361-8218. Tel: 832-927-7790. E-mail: cy@hcpl.net. Web Site: www.hcpl.net/branch/crosby-edith-fae-cook-cole-branch-library. *Br Mgr,* Molly McGinty; Staff 6 (MLS 2, Non-MLS 4)
Founded 1921
Function: Adult literacy prog, Children's prog, Computers for patron use, Family literacy, Outreach serv, Photocopying/Printing, Preschool outreach, Prog for adults, Prog for children & young adult, Scanner, Senior outreach, Teen prog
Open Mon 11-8, Tues & Thurs 10-6, Wed 10-8, Fri 1-6, Sat 10-5
Friends of the Library Group

FAIRBANKS BRANCH, 7122 N Gessner, 77040, SAN 361-8277. Tel: 832-927-7890. E-mail: fb@hcpl.net. Web Site: www.hcpl.net/location/fairbanks-branch-library. *Br Mgr,* Suellen Dunn; Staff 8 (MLS 3, Non-MLS 5)
Founded 1922
Function: Bk club(s), Computer training, Computers for patron use, Meeting rooms, Photocopying/Printing, Scanner, STEM programs
Open Mon 11-8, Tues & Thurs 10-6, Wed 10-8, Fri 1-6, Sat 10-5
Friends of the Library Group

OCTAVIA FIELDS MEMORIAL BRANCH, 1503 S Houston Ave, Humble, 77338, SAN 361-8455. Tel: 832-927-5500. E-mail: OF@hcpl.net. Web Site: www.hcpl.net/location/octavia-fields-branch-library. *Br Mgr,* Sara West; Staff 11 (MLS 3, Non-MLS 8)
Circ 183,022
Function: After school storytime, Citizenship assistance, Computer training, Computers for patron use, Meeting rooms, Passport agency, Photocopying/Printing, Scanner, Study rm, Teen prog
Open Mon 11-8, Tues & Thurs 10-6, Wed 10-8, Fri 1-6, Sat 10-5
Friends of the Library Group

GALENA PARK BRANCH, 1500 Keene St, Galena Park, 77547, SAN 361-8331. Tel: 832-927-5470. E-mail: gp@hcpl.net. Web Site: www.hcpl.net/location/galena-park-branch-library. *Br Mgr,* Sisi Medina; Staff 6 (MLS 1, Non-MLS 5)
Founded 1996
Function: Adult literacy prog, Children's prog, Citizenship assistance, Computer training, Computers for patron use, Family literacy, Meeting rooms, Outreach serv, Photocopying/Printing, Preschool outreach, Prog for adults, Prog for children & young adult, Scanner, Teen prog
Open Mon 11-8, Tues & Thurs 10-6, Wed 10-8, Fri 1-6, Sat 10-5
Friends of the Library Group

HIGH MEADOWS BRANCH, 4500 Aldine Mail Rte, 77039, SAN 361-834X. Tel: 832-927-5540. E-mail: hm@hcpl.net. Web Site: www.hcpl.net/branch/high-meadows-branch-library. *Br Mgr,* Position Currently Open; Staff 10 (MLS 3, Non-MLS 7)
Founded 1983. Pop 21,730; Circ 32,253
Function: Adult literacy prog, Citizenship assistance, Prog for adults, Prog for children & young adult, Teen prog
Open Mon 11-8, Tues & Thurs 10-6, Wed 10-8, Fri 1-6, Sat 10-5
Friends of the Library Group

JACINTO CITY BRANCH, 921 Akron, Jacinto City, 77029, SAN 361-8366. Tel: 832-927-5520. E-mail: jc@hcpl.net. Web Site: www.hcpl.net/location/jacinto-city-branch-library. *Br Mgr,* Claudia Hairston; Staff 5 (MLS 1, Non-MLS 4)
Founded 1957
Function: Adult literacy prog, Children's prog, Citizenship assistance, Computers for patron use, Learning ctr, Meeting rooms, Photocopying/Printing, Prog for children & young adult, Scanner, Teen prog
Open Mon 11-6, Tues & Thurs 10-8, Wed 10-6, Fri 1-6, Sat 10-5

KATY BRANCH, 5414 Franz Rd, Katy, 77493, SAN 361-8390. Tel: 281-391-3509. E-mail: kt@hcpl.net. Web Site: www.hcpl.net/branch/katy-branch-library. *Br Mgr,* Elizabeth Boggs; Staff 11 (MLS 3, Non-MLS 8)
Founded 1921. Circ 255,355
Function: Adult literacy prog, Children's prog, Computers for patron use, Family literacy, Meeting rooms, Outreach serv, Photocopying/Printing, Preschool outreach, Prog for adults, Prog for children & young adult, Scanner, Study rm, Teen prog
Open Mon 11-6, Tues & Thurs 10-8, Wed 10-6, Fri 1-6, Sat 10-5
Friends of the Library Group

KINGWOOD BRANCH, 4400 Bens View Lane, Kingwood, 77339, SAN 361-8404. Tel: 832-927-7830. E-mail: kw@hcpl.net. Web Site: www.hcpl.net/branch/kingwood-branch-library. *Br Mgr*, Ryan Fennell; Staff 25 (MLS 11, Non-MLS 14)
Founded 1983
Function: Adult literacy prog, Computer training, Computers for patron use, Makerspace, Meeting rooms, Photocopying/Printing, Ref serv available, Scanner, Study rm
Open Mon-Wed 10-8,Thurs 10-6, Fri 1-6, Sat 10-5
Friends of the Library Group

LA PORTE COMMUNITY LIBRARY, 600 S Broadway, La Porte, 77571, SAN 361-8420. Tel: 281-471-4022. E-mail: lap@hcpl.net. Web Site: www.hcpl.net/location/la-porte-branch-library. *Br Mgr*, Rhiannon Perry; Staff 10 (MLS 4, Non-MLS 6)
Founded 1921. Circ 62,408
Function: Adult literacy prog, Children's prog, Citizenship assistance, Computers for patron use, Photocopying/Printing, Prog for adults, Prog for children & young adult, Scanner, Teen prog
Special Services for the Blind - Accessible computers; Large screen computer & software
Open Mon 11-8, Tues & Thurs 10-6, Wed 10-8, Fri 1-6, Sat 10-5
Friends of the Library Group

LONE STAR COLLEGE-CYFAIR LIBRARY, 9191 Barker Cypress Rd, Cypress, 77429. Tel: 281-290-3210. E-mail: cyf@hcpl.net, cyfairlibrary@lonestar.edu. Web Site: www.hcpl.net/location/cy-fair-college-library. *Br Mgr*, Melanie Wachsmann; Staff 31 (MLS 16, Non-MLS 15)
Founded 2003
Open Mon-Thurs 8-8, Fri 8-5, Sat 10-5, Sun 11-4
Friends of the Library Group

LONE STAR COLLEGE-TOMBALL COMMUNITY LIBRARY, 30555 Tomball Pkwy, Tomball, 77375, SAN 361-8579. Tel: 832-559-4200. E-mail: tb@hcpl.net. Web Site: www.hcpl.net/branch/lone-star-college-tomball-community-library. *Br Mgr*, Janna Hoglund; Staff 32 (MLS 12, Non-MLS 20)
Founded 1972. Enrl 9,000; Circ 684,547; Fac 4; Highest Degree: Bachelor
Function: Adult literacy prog, Bk club(s), Children's prog, Citizenship assistance, Computer training, Computers for patron use, Genealogy discussion group, Makerspace, Notary serv, Passport agency, Prog for adults, Prog for children & young adult, Study rm, Teen prog
Open Mon-Thurs 8-8, Fri 8-6, Sat 10-5
Friends of the Library Group

MAUD SMITH MARKS BRANCH, 1815 Westgreen Blvd, Katy, 77450, SAN 373-529X. Tel: 832-927-7860. E-mail: mm@hcpl.net. Web Site: www.hcpl.net/branch/maud-smith-marks-branch-library. *Br Mgr*, Akhila Bhat; Staff 12 (MLS 4, Non-MLS 8)
Founded 1993
Open Mon 11-8, Tues 9-6, Wed 10-8, Thurs 10-6, Fri 1-6, Sat 10-5
Friends of the Library Group

EVELYN MEADOR BRANCH LIBRARY, 2400 N Meyer Ave, Seabrook, 77586. Tel: 281-474-9142. E-mail: ev@hcpl.net. Web Site: www.hcpl.net/branch/evelyn-meador-branch-library. *Br Mgr*, Milagros Andrada-Tanega; Staff 11 (MLS 3, Non-MLS 8)
Founded 1988
Function: Makerspace
Open Mon 11-6, Tues & Thurs 10-8, Wed 10-6, Fri 1-6, Sat 10-5
Friends of the Library Group

NORTH CHANNEL BRANCH, 15741 Wallisville Rd, 77049, SAN 361-8633. Tel: 832-927-5550. E-mail: nc@hcpl.net. Web Site: www.hcpl.net/location/north-channel-branch-library. *Br Mgr*, Maria Rawls; Staff 13 (MLS 3, Non-MLS 10)
Founded 1994. Circ 135,455
Function: Adult literacy prog, After school storytime, Children's prog, Citizenship assistance, Computer training, Computers for patron use, Outreach serv, Passport agency, Prog for children & young adult, Teen prog
Open Mon 11-6, Tues & Thurs 10-8, Wed 10-6, Fri 1-6, Sat 10-5
Friends of the Library Group

NORTHWEST BRANCH LIBRARY, 11355 Regency Green Dr, Cypress, 77429, SAN 370-0216. Tel: 832-927-5460. E-mail: nw@hcpl.net. Web Site: www.hcpl.net/branch/northwest-branch-library. *Br Mgr*, Jessica Lilly; Staff 10 (MLS 4, Non-MLS 6)
Founded 1983. Circ 390,000
Function: Adult literacy prog, Children's prog, Citizenship assistance, Computers for patron use, Family literacy, Makerspace, Meeting rooms, Photocopying/Printing, Prog for adults, Prog for children & young adult, Scanner, Teen prog
Open Mon 11-8, Tues & Thurs 10-6, Wed 10-8, Fri 1-6, Sat 10-5
Friends of the Library Group

SOUTH HOUSTON BRANCH, 607 Ave A, South Houston, 77587, SAN 361-848X. Tel: 832-927-5530. E-mail: sho@hcpl.net. Web Site: hcpl.net/locations/sho. *Br Mgr*, Clara Lopez; Staff 5 (MLS 1, Non-MLS 4)
Founded 1927
Function: Adult literacy prog, Children's prog, Citizenship assistance, Computer training, Computers for patron use, Prog for adults, Prog for children & young adult, Teen prog
Special Services for the Blind - Scanner for conversion & translation of mats; Screen enlargement software for people with visual disabilities
Open Mon 11-8, Tues & Thurs 10-6, Wed 10-8, Fri 1-6, Sat 10-5
Friends of the Library Group

SPRING BRANCH MEMORIAL BRANCH, 930 Corbindale, 77024, SAN 361-851X. Tel: 832-927-5510. E-mail: SM@hcpl.net. Web Site: www.hcpl.net/branch/spring-branch-memorial-branch-library. *Br Mgr*, Jennifer Finch; Staff 11 (MLS 6, Non-MLS 5)
Founded 1955. Circ 387,287
Function: Adult literacy prog, After school storytime, Bks on CD, Citizenship assistance, Computers for patron use, Magazines, Makerspace, Movies, Music CDs, Online ref, Photocopying/Printing, Ref serv available
Open Mon 11-8, Tues & Thurs 10-8, Wed 10-6, Fri 1-6, Sat 10-5
Friends of the Library Group

STRATFORD LIBRARY HIGHLANDS, 509 Stratford, Highlands, 77562, SAN 361-8544. Tel: 832-927-5400. E-mail: str@hcpl.net. Web Site: www.hcpl.net/branch/stratford-branch-library. *Br Mgr*, Mandy Sheffield; Staff 5 (MLS 2, Non-MLS 3)
Founded 1927
Function: Citizenship assistance, Computers for patron use, Photocopying/Printing
Open Mon 11-6, Tues & Thurs 10-6, Fri 1-6, Sat 10-5
Friends of the Library Group

KATHERINE TYRA BRANCH @ BEAR CREEK, 16719 Clay Rd, 77084, SAN 361-8161. Tel: 832-927-5590. E-mail: bc@hcpl.net. Web Site: www.hcpl.net/location/katherine-tyra-branch-library-bear-creek. *Br Mgr*, Amy Campbell; Staff 13 (MLS 4, Non-MLS 9)
Founded 1983
Open Mon 11-6, Tues & Thurs 10-8, Wed 10-6, Fri 1-6, Sat 10-5
Friends of the Library Group

WEST UNIVERSITY BRANCH, 6108 Auden, 77005, SAN 361-8609. Tel: 832-927-4590. E-mail: wu@hcpl.net. Web Site: www.hcpl.net/branch/west-university-branch-library. *Br Mgr*, John Harbaugh; Staff 6 (MLS 2, Non-MLS 4)
Founded 1963. Circ 188,697
Function: Adult literacy prog, Children's prog, Photocopying/Printing, Prog for adults, Prog for children & young adult, Scanner, Summer reading prog, Teen prog
Special Services for the Blind - Braille & cassettes; Braille bks; Braille equip
Open Mon 11-8, Tues & Thurs 10-6, Wed 10-8, Fri 1-6, Sat 10-5
Friends of the Library Group

PARKER WILLIAMS BRANCH, 10851 Scarsdale Blvd, Ste 510, 77089, SAN 373-5281. Tel: 832-927-7870. E-mail: pw@hcpl.net. Web Site: www.hcpl.net/branch/parker-williams-branch-library. *Br Mgr*, Michael Saperstein; Staff 11 (MLS 3, Non-MLS 8)
Founded 1993
Function: Adult literacy prog, Children's prog, Citizenship assistance, Computer training, Computers for patron use, Passport agency, Prog for adults, Prog for children & young adult, Teen prog
Open Mon 11-8, Tues & Thurs 10-6, Wed 10-8, Fri 1-6, Sat 10-5
Friends of the Library Group

Bookmobiles: 6

M HOUSTON ACADEMY OF MEDICINE, Texas Medical Center Library, 1133 John Freeman Blvd, No 100, 77030. SAN 316-4470. Tel: 713-795-4200. Interlibrary Loan Service Tel: 713-799-7105. Administration Tel: 713-799-7108. Web Site: www.library.tmc.edu. *Exec Dir*, Katie Prentice; E-mail: katie.prentice@library.tmc.edu; *Head, Res & Instruction*, Beatriz Varman; Tel: 713-799-7169, E-mail: beatriz.varman@library.tmc.edu; *Head, Res Mgt*, Joanne Romano; Tel: 713-799-7144, E-mail: joanne.romano@library.tmc.edu; *Circ Supvr*, Jesse Gonzalez; Tel: 713-799-7148, E-mail: jesse.gonzalez@library.tmc.edu; *ILL*, Alisa Hemphill; E-mail: alisa.hemphill@library.tmc.edu; Staff 35 (MLS 15, Non-MLS 20)
Founded 1949. Highest Degree: Doctorate
Library Holdings: e-books 1,000,000; e-journals 77,000; Bk Vols 357,023
Special Collections: John P McGovern Historical Coll & Research Center (Prominent colls include Texas Medical Center, Atomic Bomb Casualty Commission, and Medical World News Photograph Coll). Oral History
Subject Interests: Consumer health, Hist of med, Med res, Nursing, Patient info, Psychiat
Automation Activity & Vendor Info: (Acquisitions) Ex Libris Group; (Cataloging) Ex Libris Group; (Circulation) Ex Libris Group; (ILL) Clio; (OPAC) Ex Libris Group; (Serials) Ex Libris Group
Wireless access
Function: Electronic databases & coll, ILL available, Online cat, Online Chat, Orientations, Prof lending libr, Ref & res, Ref serv available, Res libr
Partic in SCAMeL; Tex Health Sci Libr Consortium; TexSHARE - Texas State Library & Archives Commission
Open Mon-Thurs 7am-10pm, Fri 7-6, Sat 9-6, Sun 1-10

Restriction: Private libr
Friends of the Library Group

CR HOUSTON BAPTIST UNIVERSITY*, Moody Memorial Library, 7502 Fondren Rd, 77074-3298. SAN 316-4497. Tel: 281-649-3304. Interlibrary Loan Service Tel: 281-649-3181. Reference Tel: 281-649-3180. E-mail: reference@hbu.edu. Web Site: hbu.edu/academics/moody-library. *Libr Dir,* Dean Riley; Tel: 281-649-3182, E-mail: driley@hbu.edu; *Asst Systems Manager, Circ Supvr,* Tri Nguyen; *Acq, Cat, Coll Develop,* Bonita Crider; Tel: 281-649-3179, E-mail: bcrider@hbu.edu; *ILL, Ref (Info Servs),* Kristin Fance; E-mail: kfance@hbu.edu; *Ref & Libr Instruction, Ser,* Diane Casebier; Tel: 281-649-3178, E-mail: dcasebier@hbu.edu; Staff 9.8 (MLS 6, Non-MLS 3.8)
Founded 1963. Enrl 2,403; Fac 120; Highest Degree: Master
Library Holdings: AV Mats 9,968; CDs 1,989; DVDs 1,208; e-books 51,064; e-journals 60,147; Bk Vols 237,996; Videos 3,565
Special Collections: Gilbert & Sullivan (Linder Coll); History & Literature (Palmer Bradley Coll); History (Hicks Memorial Coll)
Subject Interests: Baptist hist, SW, Tex, Victorian lit
Automation Activity & Vendor Info: (Acquisitions) SirsiDynix; (Cataloging) SirsiDynix; (Circulation) SirsiDynix; (Course Reserve) SirsiDynix; (ILL) OCLC; (OPAC) SirsiDynix
Wireless access
Function: Audio & video playback equip for onsite use, Computers for patron use, Electronic databases & coll, ILL available, Online cat, Photocopying/Printing, Ref serv available
Partic in Amigos Library Services, Inc
Open Mon-Sun 7am-Midnight
Restriction: Open to pub for ref only, Open to students, fac, staff & alumni

S HOUSTON CHRONICLE LIBRARY*, 4747 Southwest Fwy, 77027. SAN 316-4500. Tel: 713-362-7171. Web Site: www.houstonchronicle.com. *Archivist,* Linda Bias; E-mail: linda.bias@houstonchronicle.com; Staff 2 (MLS 2)
Founded 1961
Library Holdings: Bk Vols 2,000; Per Subs 14
Subject Interests: News files, Texana
Restriction: Co libr, Not open to pub

HOUSTON COMMUNITY COLLEGE-CENTRAL COLLEGE
J CENTRAL CAMPUS LIBRARY*, 1300 Holman, 77004, SAN 316-4519. Tel: 713-718-6133. Information Services Tel: 713-718-6141. FAX: 713-718-6154. E-mail: aska.librarian@hccs.edu. Web Site: library.hccs.edu. *Dir,* Erica Hubbard; E-mail: erica.hubbard@hccs.edu; *Librn,* Marcia Braun; E-mail: marcia.braun@hccs.edu; *Librn,* Leo Cavazos; E-mail: leo.cavazos@hccs.edu; *Librn,* Len Cazares; E-mail: len.cazares@hccs.edu; *Librn,* Stephanie Emesih; E-mail: stephanie.emesih@hccs.edu
Founded 1972. Enrl 70,000; Fac 980
Library Holdings: AV Mats 4,161; e-books 19,000; Bk Vols 56,924; Per Subs 97
Subject Interests: Med
Automation Activity & Vendor Info: (Acquisitions) Innovative Interfaces, Inc; (Cataloging) Innovative Interfaces, Inc; (Circulation) Innovative Interfaces, Inc - Millennium; (Course Reserve) Innovative Interfaces, Inc; (Media Booking) Innovative Interfaces, Inc; (OPAC) Innovative Interfaces, Inc; (Serials) Innovative Interfaces, Inc
Partic in Amigos Library Services, Inc; OCLC Online Computer Library Center, Inc
Open Mon-Thurs 7:30am-9pm, Fri 7:30-4, Sat 9-3 (Fall & Spring)

J COLEMAN CAMPUS LIBRARY*, 1900 Pressler St, 77030. Tel: 713-718-7399. FAX: 713-718-7396.
Highest Degree: Associate
Library Holdings: AV Mats 2,750; e-books 19,000; Bk Vols 9,051; Per Subs 120
Open Mon-Thurs 7:30am-9pm, Fri 7:30-4, Sat 9-1

HOUSTON COMMUNITY COLLEGE - NORTHEAST COLLEGE
J CODWELL CAMPUS LIBRARY*, 555 Community College Dr, 77013-6127. Tel: 713-718-8354. Reference Tel: 713-718-8320. FAX: 713-718-8330. *Dir,* Mildred Joseph; E-mail: mildred.joseph@hccs.edu; *Librn,* Denise Coles; E-mail: denise.coles@hccs.edu; *Librn,* James Smith; E-mail: james.smith@hccs.edu
Highest Degree: Associate
Library Holdings: AV Mats 1,912; e-books 19,000; Bk Vols 16,526; Per Subs 134
Automation Activity & Vendor Info: (Acquisitions) Innovative Interfaces, Inc; (Cataloging) Innovative Interfaces, Inc; (Circulation) Innovative Interfaces, Inc - Millennium; (Course Reserve) Innovative Interfaces, Inc; (ILL) Innovative Interfaces, Inc; (Media Booking) Innovative Interfaces, Inc; (OPAC) Innovative Interfaces, Inc; (Serials) Innovative Interfaces, Inc
Open Mon-Thurs 8am-9pm, Fri 8-4:30, Sat 9-3, Sun 12-4

J NORTH FOREST CAMPUS LIBRARY*, 7525 Tidwell Rd, 77016-4413. Tel: 713-635-0427. *Dir,* Mildred Joseph; E-mail: mildred.joseph@hccs.edu
Automation Activity & Vendor Info: (Acquisitions) Innovative Interfaces, Inc; (Cataloging) Innovative Interfaces, Inc; (Circulation) Innovative Interfaces, Inc - Millennium; (Course Reserve) Innovative Interfaces, Inc; (ILL) Innovative Interfaces, Inc; (Media Booking) Innovative Interfaces, Inc; (OPAC) Innovative Interfaces, Inc; (Serials) Innovative Interfaces, Inc
Open Mon-Thurs 5pm-9pm

J NORTHLINE LIBRARY*, 8001 Fulton St, 77022. Tel: 713-718-8045. Reference Tel: 713-718-8061. FAX: 713-718-8063. *Dir, Libr Serv,* Gwendolyn Richard; E-mail: gwen.richard@hccs.edu; *Librn,* Lawrence Anderson; E-mail: lawrence.anderson@hccs.edu; *Librn,* Jennifer Stidham; E-mail: jennifer.stidham@hccs.edu
Library Holdings: AV Mats 1,079; e-books 19,000; Bk Vols 14,687; Per Subs 74
Automation Activity & Vendor Info: (Acquisitions) Innovative Interfaces, Inc; (Cataloging) Innovative Interfaces, Inc; (Circulation) Innovative Interfaces, Inc - Millennium; (Course Reserve) Innovative Interfaces, Inc; (ILL) Innovative Interfaces, Inc; (Media Booking) Innovative Interfaces, Inc; (OPAC) Innovative Interfaces, Inc; (Serials) Innovative Interfaces, Inc
Open Mon-Thurs 8am-9pm, Fri & Sat 8-4:30, Sun Noon-4 (Winter); Mon-Thurs 8am-9pm, Fri 8-4:30 (Summer)

J PINEMONT CAMPUS LIBRARY*, 1265 Pinemont, 77018-1303. Tel: 713-718-8443. FAX: 713-718-8438. *NE Dir of Libr Serv,* Gwendolyn Richard; E-mail: gwen.richard@hccs.edu; *Librn,* Tolley Reeves; E-mail: tolley.reeves@hccs.edu
Library Holdings: AV Mats 144; e-books 19,000; Bk Vols 1,187; Per Subs 48
Automation Activity & Vendor Info: (Acquisitions) Innovative Interfaces, Inc; (Cataloging) Innovative Interfaces, Inc; (Circulation) Innovative Interfaces, Inc - Millennium; (Course Reserve) Innovative Interfaces, Inc; (ILL) Innovative Interfaces, Inc; (Media Booking) Innovative Interfaces, Inc; (OPAC) Innovative Interfaces, Inc; (Serials) Innovative Interfaces, Inc
Open Mon-Thurs 8am-9pm, Fri 8-4:30

HOUSTON COMMUNITY COLLEGE - NORTHWEST COLLEGE
J KATY CAMPUS LIBRARY*, 1550 Foxlake Dr, 77084-6029. Tel: 713-718-5747. FAX: 281-492-6075. *Librn,* Cynthia Belmar; Tel: 713-718-5849, E-mail: cynthia.belmar@hccs.edu; *Librn,* Daniel Dylla; Staff 3 (MLS 2, Non-MLS 1)
Library Holdings: AV Mats 1,768; e-books 30,000; Bk Vols 16,000; Per Subs 68
Automation Activity & Vendor Info: (Acquisitions) Innovative Interfaces, Inc; (Cataloging) Innovative Interfaces, Inc; (Circulation) Innovative Interfaces, Inc - Millennium; (Course Reserve) Innovative Interfaces, Inc; (ILL) Innovative Interfaces, Inc; (Media Booking) Innovative Interfaces, Inc; (OPAC) Innovative Interfaces, Inc; (Serials) Innovative Interfaces, Inc
Open Mon-Thurs 7:30am-9pm, Fri 7:30-4
Restriction: Open to students, fac & staff, Pub use on premises

J SPRING BRANCH CAMPUS LIBRARY*, 1010 W Sam Houston Pkwy N, 77043-5008. Tel: 713-718-5655. Reference Tel: 713-718-5434, 713-718-7502. Administration Tel: 713-718-5849. FAX: 713-718-5745. *Pub Serv Librn,* Christina Curtin; E-mail: christina.curtin@hccs.edu=; *Librn,* Melba Martin; Tel: 713-718-5656, E-mail: melba.martin@hccs.edu; Staff 5 (MLS 3, Non-MLS 2)
Library Holdings: AV Mats 1,779; e-books 29,000; Bk Vols 16,529; Per Subs 65
Automation Activity & Vendor Info: (Acquisitions) Innovative Interfaces, Inc; (Cataloging) Innovative Interfaces, Inc; (Circulation) Innovative Interfaces, Inc - Millennium; (Course Reserve) Innovative Interfaces, Inc; (ILL) Innovative Interfaces, Inc; (Media Booking) Innovative Interfaces, Inc; (OPAC) Innovative Interfaces, Inc; (Serials) Innovative Interfaces, Inc
Open Mon-Thurs 7:30am-9pm, Fri 7:30-4, Sat (Aug-May) 9-1
Restriction: Open to students, fac & staff, Pub use on premises

HOUSTON COMMUNITY COLLEGE - SOUTHEAST COLLEGE
J EASTSIDE CAMPUS LIBRARY*, 6815 Rustic St, 77087. Tel: 713-718-7050. Reference Tel: 713-718-7084. FAX: 713-718-7551. Web Site: library.hccs.edu. *Chairperson,* Michael Mitchell; E-mail: michael.mitchell@hccs.edu; *Librn,* Henri Achee; E-mail: henri.achee@hccs.edu; *Librn,* Richard Conn; E-mail: richard.conn@hccs.edu; *Librn,* Keitha Robinson; E-mail: keitha.robinson@hccs.edu; Staff 3.9 (MLS 3.9)
Founded 1990. Enrl 7,500; Fac 3; Highest Degree: Associate
Library Holdings: AV Mats 3,200; e-books 28,559; Bk Vols 31,454; Per Subs 162
Automation Activity & Vendor Info: (Acquisitions) Innovative Interfaces, Inc; (Cataloging) Innovative Interfaces, Inc; (Circulation) Innovative Interfaces, Inc - Millennium; (Course Reserve) Innovative

Interfaces, Inc; (ILL) Innovative Interfaces, Inc; (Media Booking) Innovative Interfaces, Inc; (OPAC) Innovative Interfaces, Inc; (Serials) Innovative Interfaces, Inc
Open Mon-Thurs 8-8, Fri 8-4, Sat 10-4

E FELIX FRAGA ERC*, 301 N Drennan St, 77003. Tel: 713-718-6960. *Chairperson,* Michael Mitchell; E-mail: michael.mitchell@hccs.edu
Open Mon-Thurs 9-6

HOUSTON COMMUNITY COLLEGE - SOUTHWEST COLLEGE

E ALIEF CONTINUING EDUCATION CENTER*, 13803 Bissonnet, 77083. Tel: 713-718-5447. *Librn,* Cathy Montoya
Automation Activity & Vendor Info: (Acquisitions) Innovative Interfaces, Inc; (Cataloging) Innovative Interfaces, Inc; (Circulation) Innovative Interfaces, Inc - Millennium; (Course Reserve) Innovative Interfaces, Inc; (ILL) Innovative Interfaces, Inc; (Media Booking) Innovative Interfaces, Inc; (OPAC) Innovative Interfaces, Inc; (Serials) Innovative Interfaces, Inc
Open Mon-Fri 7:30-5 (Sept-May)

E MISSOURI CITY (SIENNA) CAMPUS*, 5855 Sienna Springs Way, Missouri City, 77459. Tel: 713-718-2942. FAX: 713-718-2474. *Librn,* Daphene Keys
Open Mon-Thurs 7:30-9pm, Fri 7:30-1 (Sept-May)

J STAFFORD CAMPUS LIBRARY*, 9910 Cash Rd, Stafford, 77477-4405. Tel: 713-718-7823. Reference Tel: 713-718-7824. FAX: 713-718-6723. *Dir,* Bill Hord; E-mail: bill.hord@hccs.edu; *Librn,* Trudy Cleveland; E-mail: trudy.cleveland@hccs.edu
Library Holdings: AV Mats 608; Bk Vols 18,486; Per Subs 81
Automation Activity & Vendor Info: (Acquisitions) Innovative Interfaces, Inc; (Cataloging) Innovative Interfaces, Inc; (Circulation) Innovative Interfaces, Inc - Millennium; (Course Reserve) Innovative Interfaces, Inc; (ILL) Innovative Interfaces, Inc; (Media Booking) Innovative Interfaces, Inc; (OPAC) Innovative Interfaces, Inc; (Serials) Innovative Interfaces, Inc
Open Mon-Thurs 7:30am-9pm, Fri 7:30-3, Sat (Fall & Spring) 10-2

J WEST LOOP CENTER LIBRARY*, 5601 West Loop S, 77081-2221. Tel: 713-718-7880. FAX: 713-718-7881. *Dir,* Bill Hord; *Librn,* Kathleen Dillon; E-mail: kathleen.dillon@hccs.edu
Library Holdings: AV Mats 472; Bk Vols 18,270; Per Subs 110
Automation Activity & Vendor Info: (Acquisitions) Innovative Interfaces, Inc; (Cataloging) Innovative Interfaces, Inc; (Circulation) Innovative Interfaces, Inc - Millennium; (Course Reserve) Innovative Interfaces, Inc; (ILL) Innovative Interfaces, Inc; (Media Booking) Innovative Interfaces, Inc; (OPAC) Innovative Interfaces, Inc; (Serials) Innovative Interfaces, Inc
Open Mon-Thurs 7:30am-9pm, Fri 7:30-1, Sat 8-1

S HOUSTON MUSEUM OF NATURAL SCIENCE, Curatorial Library, 5555 Hermann Park Dr, 77030-1799. SAN 316-4543. Tel: 713-639-4670. Web Site: www.hmns.org. *VPres, Coll,* Lisa Rebori; E-mail: lrebori@hmns.org; *Colls, Database & Digitization Asst,* Anne Avara; E-mail: aavara@hmns.org; Staff 1 (MLS 1)
Founded 1969
Library Holdings: Bk Titles 12,000; Per Subs 80
Subject Interests: Anthrop, Astronomy, Entomology, Hist, Malacology, Mineralogy, Paleontology, Tech, Vertebrate zool
Function: Archival coll, Res libr
Restriction: Access at librarian's discretion, Authorized personnel only, Authorized scholars by appt, Non-circulating, Open by appt only

P HOUSTON PUBLIC LIBRARY*, 500 McKinney Ave, 77002-2534. SAN 361-8692. Tel: 832-393-1313. Interlibrary Loan Service Tel: 832-393-1447. Administration Tel: 832-393-1300. FAX: 832-393-1324. E-mail: hplemail.reference@houstontx.gov. Web Site: houstonlibrary.org. *Exec Dir,* Dr Rhea Lawson, PhD; E-mail: rhea.lawson@houstontx.gov; *Dep Dir,* Nicole Robinson; Staff 473 (MLS 93, Non-MLS 380)
Founded 1901. Pop 2,231,335; Circ 7,352,410
Library Holdings: Audiobooks 33,249; CDs 100,131; DVDs 92,369; Electronic Media & Resources 51,941; Large Print Bks 18,402; Microforms 23,300; Music Scores 550; Bk Vols 1,560,121; Per Subs 3,755
Special Collections: Architectural Coll; Archives & Manuscripts Department (Houston Metropolitan Research Center) contains 12,000 linear ft of archival material & 1.5 million photographs & negatives related to Houston including manuscript Coll; Bibles, Civil War, Salvation Army, Milsap Coll; Early Houston & Texas Maps; Early Printing & Illuminated Manuscript (Annette Finnigan Coll); Juvenile Literature (Norma Meldrum, Special Coll & Historical Juvenile Coll); Petroleum (Barton, Dumble, & DeWolf Coll); Posters; Sheet Music (Max Hornstein, Adele Margulies, Henry Thayer & Edna Joseph Coll); Texana (Maresh & Blake Coll). Oral History; State Document Depository; US Document Depository
Subject Interests: Archit, Art, Genealogy
Automation Activity & Vendor Info: (Acquisitions) Innovative Interfaces, Inc - Millennium; (Cataloging) Innovative Interfaces, Inc - Millennium; (Circulation) Innovative Interfaces, Inc - Millennium; (OPAC) Innovative Interfaces, Inc - Millennium; (Serials) Innovative Interfaces, Inc - Millennium
Wireless access
Function: Archival coll, Audiobks via web, Bilingual assistance for Spanish patrons, Bk club(s), Bks on CD, Bus archives, Children's prog, Computer training, Computers for patron use, Electronic databases & coll, Genealogy discussion group, ILL available, Internet access, Music CDs, Online cat, Online ref, Prog for adults, Prog for children & young adult, Senior computer classes, Spoken cassettes & CDs, Story hour, Summer reading prog, Tax forms, Teen prog, Telephone ref
Partic in Amigos Library Services, Inc; Northwest Library Federation
Special Services for the Deaf - Captioned film dep; Spec interest per; TTY equip
Special Services for the Blind - Reader equip
Open Mon-Thurs 10-8, Fri & Sat 10-5, Sun 1-5
Friends of the Library Group
Branches: 41

THE AFRICAN AMERICAN LIBRARY AT THE GREGORY SCHOOL, 1300 Victor St, 77019. Tel: 832-393-1440.
Founded 2009
Library Holdings: Bk Vols 5,000
Special Collections: Photographs, manuscripts, oral history, government papers & records
Subject Interests: African-Am hist & culture
Open Tues & Wed 10-6, Thurs 12-8, Fri & Sat 10-5
Restriction: Non-circulating, Researchers only

BRACEWELL NEIGHBORHOOD LIBRARY, 9002 Kingspoint Dr, 77089, SAN 361-9230. Tel: 832-393-2580. FAX: 832-393-2581.
Founded 1970
Open Mon 2-6, Tues & Wed 10-6, Thurs 12-8, Fri & Sat 10-5
Friends of the Library Group

CARNEGIE NEIGHBORHOOD LIBRARY & CENTER FOR LEARNING, 1050 Quitman, 77009. (Mail add: 500 McKinney Ave, 77002), SAN 361-9265. Tel: 832-393-1720. FAX: 832-393-1721.
Founded 1982
Open Mon & Thurs Noon-8, Tues & Wed 10-6, Fri & Sat 1-5
Friends of the Library Group

CLAYTON LIBRARY CENTER FOR GENEALOGICAL RESEARCH, 5300 Caroline, 77004-6896, SAN 361-8846. Tel: 832-393-2600.
Library Holdings: CDs 200; Bk Vols 85,000; Per Subs 2,648
Subject Interests: Genealogy
Partic in OCLC Online Computer Library Center, Inc
Publications: In-house Bibligraphies
Open Tues & Wed 10-6, Thurs 12-8, Fri & Sat 10-5
Restriction: Non-circulating
Friends of the Library Group

COLLIER REGIONAL LIBRARY, 6200 Pinemont, 77092, SAN 326-7563. Tel: 832-393-1740. FAX: 832-393-1741.
Function: Adult bk club
Open Mon & Thurs Noon-8, Tues & Wed 10-6, Fri 1-5, Sat 10-5
Friends of the Library Group

DIXON NEIGHBORHOOD LIBRARY, 8002 Hirsch, 77016, SAN 361-929X. Tel: 832-393-1760.
Open Mon & Thurs Noon-8, Tues & Wed 10-6, Fri 1-5, Sat 10-5
Friends of the Library Group

FLORES NEIGHBORHOOD LIBRARY, 110 N Milby, 77003, SAN 361-9338. Tel: 832-393-1780.
Friends of the Library Group

MORRIS FRANK LIBRARY & HPL EXPRESS LOCATION, Brays Oaks Towers Bldg, 10103 Fondren, 77096, SAN 361-9346. Tel: 832-393-2410.
Founded 1984
Open Mon 2-6, Tues & Wed 10-6, Thurs 12-8, Fri & Sat 1-5
Friends of the Library Group

FREED MONTROSE NEIGHBORHOOD LIBRARY, 4100 Montrose, 77006. Tel: 832-393-1800. FAX: 832-393-1801.
Open Mon 2-6, Tues & Wed 10-6, Thurs 12-8, Fri & Sat 1-5
Friends of the Library Group

HEIGHTS NEIGHBORHOOD LIBRARY, 1302 Heights Blvd, 77008, SAN 361-9354. Tel: 832-393-1810. FAX: 832-393-1811.
Function: Bks on CD, Children's prog, Computer training, Computers for patron use, Free DVD rentals, Holiday prog, Homework prog, Music CDs, Online cat, OverDrive digital audio bks, Photocopying/Printing, Prog for adults, Prog for children & young adult, Ref serv available, Spoken cassettes & CDs, Spoken cassettes & DVDs, Story hour, Summer & winter reading prog, Tax forms, Wheelchair accessible
Open Mon & Thurs Noon-8, Tues & Wed 10-6, Fri & Sat 1-5

HENINGTON ALIEF REGIONAL LIBRARY, 7979 S Kirkwood, 77072, SAN 322-5682. Tel: 832-393-1820.
Open Mon & Thurs Noon-8, Tues & Wed 10-6, Fri 1-5, Sat 10-5
Friends of the Library Group

HILLENDAHL NEIGHBORHOOD LIBRARY, 2436 Gessner Rd, 77080, SAN 361-9419. Tel: 832-393-1940.
Subject Interests: African-Am, Chinese lang, Korean (Lang), Spanish lang, Vietnamese (Lang)
Open Mon 2-6, Tues & Wed 10-6, Thurs 12-8, Fri & Sat 1-5
Friends of the Library Group

HOUSTON METROPOLITAN RESEARCH CENTER, Julia Ideson Bldg, 500 McKinney, 77002, SAN 361-8722. Tel: 832-393-1662.
Founded 1854
Special Collections: Regional Historical Records for Texas State Depository (select records of 5 surrounding counties)
Function: Archival coll, Res libr
Open Tues & Wed 10-6, Thurs 12-8, Fri & Sat 10-5
Restriction: Closed stack, Non-circulating coll
Friends of the Library Group

HPL EXPRESS DISCOVERY GREEN, 1500 McKinney St, R2, 77010. Tel: 832-393-1375.
Friends of the Library Group

HPL EXPRESS SOUTHWEST, 6400 High Star, 77074. Tel: 832-393-2660.
Open Mon 2-6, Tues & Wed 10-6, Thurs 12-8, Fri 1-5, Sat 8-12
Friends of the Library Group

JOHNSON NEIGHBORHOOD LIBRARY, 3517 Reed Rd, 77051, SAN 361-9443. Tel: 832-393-2550.
Open Mon 2-6, Tues & Wed 10-6, Thurs 12-8, Fri & Sat 1-5
Friends of the Library Group

JUNGMAN NEIGHBORHOOD LIBRARY, 5830 Westheimer Rd, 77057, SAN 361-9478. Tel: 832-393-1860.
Open Mon & Thurs Noon-8, Tues & Wed 10-6, Fri & Sat 1-5
Friends of the Library Group

KENDALL NEIGHBORHOOD LIBRARY, 609 N Eldridge, 77079, SAN 361-9532. Tel: 832-393-1880.
Friends of the Library Group

LAKEWOOD NEIGHBORHOOD LIBRARY, Northeast Multi-Service Ctr, 9720 Spaulding St, Rm 122, 77016, SAN 361-9591. Tel: 832-393-2530, 832-395-0504.
Founded 1963
Open Mon-Fri 9:30-1:30
Friends of the Library Group

LOOSCAN NEIGHBORHOOD LIBRARY, 2510 Willowick Rd, 77027, SAN 361-9621. Tel: 832-393-1900.
Open Mon 2-6, Tues & Wed 10-6, Thurs 12-8, Fri & Sat 1-5
Friends of the Library Group

MANCUSO NEIGHBORHOOD LIBRARY, 6767 Bellfort, 77087, SAN 361-963X. Tel: 832-393-1920.
Open Mon 2-6, Tues & Wed 10-6, Thurs 12-8, Fri & Sat 1-5
Friends of the Library Group

MCCRANE-KASHMERE GARDENS NEIGHBORHOOD LIBRARY, Kashmere Multi-Service Center, 4802 Lakewood Dr, 77026, SAN 361-9508. Tel: 832-393-2450.
Founded 1971
Open Tues & Wed 10-6, Thurs 12-8, Fri 1-5, Sat 10-5
Friends of the Library Group

MCGOVERN-STELLA LINK NEIGHBORHOOD LIBRARY, 7405 Stella Link Rd, 77025. Tel: 832-393-2630.
Open Mon & Thurs Noon-8, Tues & Wed 10-6, Fri 1-5, Sat 10-5

MELCHER NEIGHBORHOOD LIBRARY, 7200 Keller St, 77012, SAN 361-9656. Tel: 832-393-2480.
Friends of the Library Group

MOODY NEIGHBORHOOD LIBRARY, 9525 Irvington Blvd, 77076, SAN 361-9710. Tel: 832-393-1950.
Open Mon 2-6, Tues & Wed 10-6, Thurs 12-8, Fri 1-5
Friends of the Library Group

OAK FOREST NEIGHBORHOOD LIBRARY, 1349 W 43rd St, 77018, SAN 361-9745. Tel: 832-393-1960. FAX: 832-393-1961.
Founded 1961
Function: Bk club(s), Children's prog, Computers for patron use, Free DVD rentals, ILL available, Music CDs, Online cat, OverDrive digital audio bks, Photocopying/Printing, Prog for adults, Story hour, Summer reading prog, Tax forms, Teen prog, Wheelchair accessible
Open Mon 2-6, Tues & Wed 10-6, Thurs 12-8, Fri 1-5

PARK PLACE REGIONAL LIBRARY, 8145 Park Place Blvd, 77017, SAN 361-977X. Tel: 832-393-1970.
Open Mon & Thurs Noon-8, Tues & Wed 10-6, Fri 1-5, Sat 10-5
Friends of the Library Group

PLEASANTVILLE NEIGHBORHOOD LIBRARY, 1520 Gellhorn Dr, 77029, SAN 361-980X. Tel: 832-393-2330.
Open Mon 2-6, Tues & Wed 10-6, Thurs 12-8, Fri 1-5
Friends of the Library Group

RING NEIGHBORHOOD LIBRARY, 8835 Long Point Rd, 77055, SAN 361-9834. Tel: 832-393-2000.
Open Mon 2-6, Tues & Wed 10-6, Thurs 12-8, Fri & Sat 1-5
Friends of the Library Group

ROBINSON-WESTCHASE NEIGHBORHOOD LIBRARY, 3223 Wilcrest, 77042, SAN 371-9669. Tel: 832-393-2011.
Open Mon & Thurs Noon-8, Tues & Wed 10-6, Fri & Sat 1-5
Friends of the Library Group

SCENIC WOODS REGIONAL LIBRARY, 10677 Homestead Rd, 77016, SAN 326-758X. Tel: 832-393-2030.
Open Mon & Thurs Noon-8, Tues & Wed 10-6, Fri & Sat 1-5
Friends of the Library Group

SHEPARD–ACRES HOMES NEIGHBORHOOD LIBRARY, 8501 W Montgomery Rd, 77088, SAN 361-9176. Tel: 832-393-1700.
Founded 1976
Open Mon 2-6, Tues & Wed 10-6, Thurs 12-8, Fri & Sat 1-5
Friends of the Library Group

SMITH NEIGHBORHOOD LIBRARY, 3624 Scott St, 77004, SAN 361-9893. Tel: 832-393-2050.
Open Mon-Wed 10-6, Thurs 12-8, Fri & Sat 1-5
Friends of the Library Group

STANAKER NEIGHBORHOOD LIBRARY, 611 S-Sgt Macario Garcia, 77011. Tel: 832-393-2080.
Open Mon 2-6, Tues & Wed 10-6, Thurs 12-8, Fri & Sat 1-5

STIMLEY BLUE RIDGE NEIGHBORHOOD LIBRARY, 7007 W Fuqua, 77489. Tel: 832-393-2370.
Founded 1999
Open Mon 2-6, Tues 12-8, Wed 10-6, Thurs 9:30-6, Fri & Sat 9-4
Friends of the Library Group

TUTTLE NEIGHBORHOOD LIBRARY, 702 Kress, 77020, SAN 361-9958. Tel: 832-393-2100.
Open Mon-Wed 10-6, Thurs 12-8, Fri & Sat 1-5
Friends of the Library Group

VINSON NEIGHBORHOOD LIBRARY, 3810 W Fuqua, 77045, SAN 361-9982. Tel: 832-393-2120.
Open Mon 2-6, Tues & Wed 10-6, Thurs 12-8, Fri 1-5
Friends of the Library Group

WALTER NEIGHBORHOOD LIBRARY, 7660 Clarewood, 77036, SAN 362-0018. Tel: 832-393-2500.
Open Mon 2-6, Tues & Wed 10-6, Thurs 12-8, Fri & Sat 1-5
Friends of the Library Group

YOUNG NEIGHBORHOOD LIBRARY, 5107 Griggs Rd, 77021, SAN 362-0042. Tel: 832-393-2140.
Open Mon & Thurs Noon-8, Tues & Wed 10-6, Fri & Sat 1-5
Friends of the Library Group

R ISLAMIC DA'WAH CENTER LIBRARY*, IDC Library, 201 Travis St, 77002. Tel: 713-223-3311. E-mail: library@islamicdawahcenter.org. Information Services E-mail: info@islamicdawahcenter.org. Web Site: www.islamicdawahcenter.org. *Exec Dir,* Ameer Abuhalimeh
Special Collections: Dr Mohammad Rashad Khalil Coll
Subject Interests: Studies in Islam
Automation Activity & Vendor Info: (Cataloging) ComPanion Corp; (Circulation) ComPanion Corp
Wireless access

L JACKSON WALKER LLP, Law Library, 1401 McKinney, Ste 1900, 77010. SAN 372-1612. Tel: 713-752-4479. FAX: 713-752-4221. *Chief Knowledge Officer,* Greg Lambert; Tel: 713-752-4357; *Research Attorney,* Caren Zentner Luckie; E-mail: cluckie@jw.com; Staff 10 (MLS 3, Non-MLS 7)
Library Holdings: Bk Vols 1,000; Per Subs 30
Automation Activity & Vendor Info: (Cataloging) EOS International; (OPAC) EOS International; (Serials) EOS International
Restriction: Not open to pub

L JONES DAY*, Law Library, 717 Texas St, Ste 3300, 77002. Tel: 832-239-3939. FAX: 832-239-3600. Web Site: www.jonesday.com. *Assoc Dir, Research Servs,* Kimberly Serna; E-mail: ktserna@jonesday.com
Library Holdings: Bk Titles 357; Per Subs 57
Restriction: Staff use only

S LOCKWOOD, ANDREWS & NEWNAM, INC*, Information Resource Center, 2925 Briarpark Dr, Ste 400, 77042. SAN 327-3857. Tel: 713-266-6900. FAX: 713-266-2089. E-mail: info@lan-inc.com. Web Site: www.lan-inc.com. *Adminr,* Position Currently Open
Library Holdings: Bk Vols 1,500; Per Subs 40
Subject Interests: Archit, Engr
Restriction: Staff use only

J LONE STAR COLLEGE SYSTEM*, Library Technical Services, 20515 State Hwy 249, Bldg 11, Rm 11437, 77070-2607. SAN 316-4713. Tel: 281-290-2843. FAX: 281-290-2979. Web Site: www.lonestar.edu/library. *Dir,* Position Currently Open; *Authority Control Librn,* Kathleen Whitsitt; Tel: 281-290-2842, E-mail: kathleen.s.whitsitt@lonestar.edu; Staff 9.5 (MLS 3, Non-MLS 6.5)
Founded 1973
Automation Activity & Vendor Info: (Acquisitions) SirsiDynix; (Cataloging) SirsiDynix; (Circulation) SirsiDynix; (Course Reserve) SirsiDynix; (OPAC) SirsiDynix; (Serials) SirsiDynix
Wireless access
Partic in Amigos Library Services, Inc
Open Mon-Fri 7-5 (Winter); Mon-Thurs 7-5 (Summer)

Departmental Libraries:

CYFAIR LIBRARY, 9191 Barker Cypress Rd, Cypress, 77433. Tel: 281-290-3214, 281-290-3219. E-mail: cyfairlibrary@lonestar.edu. *Libr Dir,* Melanie S Wachsmann; E-mail: melanie.s.wachsmann@lonestar.edu;

Asst Dir, Ch, Melanie Metzger; E-mail: melanie.r.metzger@lonestar.edu; *Ch,* Krissy Conn; E-mail: kristen.s.conn@lonestar.edu; *Ref Librn,* Dorrie Scott; E-mail: dorrie.scott@lonestar.edu
Open Mon-Thurs 7am-10pm, Fri & Sat 8-6, Sun 1-6 (Winter); Mon-Thurs 7am-10pm, Fri 9-5, Sat 10-6, Sun 1-6 (Summer)

KINGWOOD COLLEGE LIBRARY, 20000 Kingwood Dr, Kingwood, 77339, SAN 325-352X. Tel: 281-312-1691. Reference Tel: 281-312-1693. FAX: 281-312-1456. Reference E-mail: Kingwood.LRC-Ref@LoneStar.edu. *Dir,* Anthony McMillan; Tel: 281-290-5997, E-mail: Anthony.J.McMillan@lonestar.edu; *Circ Coordr,* Anne McGittigan; E-mail: Anne.L.McGittigan@LoneStar.edu; Staff 11 (MLS 11)
Founded 1984. Enrl 11,000; Fac 140; Highest Degree: Associate
Library Holdings: e-books 39,000; Bk Vols 40,000; Per Subs 350
Automation Activity & Vendor Info: (Acquisitions) Horizon; (Cataloging) Horizon; (Circulation) Horizon; (Course Reserve) Horizon; (OPAC) Horizon; (Serials) Horizon
Open Mon-Thurs 7am-9pm, Fri 7-4:30, Sat 9-2

MONTGOMERY COLLEGE LIBRARY, 3200 College Park Dr, Conroe, 77384. SAN 376-222X. Tel: 936-273-7388, 936-273-7392. Circulation Tel: 936-273-7387. Reference Tel: 936-273-7390. FAX: 936-273-7395. E-mail: mclr@lonestar.edu. *Dir,* Janice Lucas Peyton, PhD; *Access & Circ Serv Librn,* Norma Medina; Tel: 936-273-7494, E-mail: norma.i.medina@lonestar.edu; *Ref (Info Servs),* Cheryl Mansfield-Egans; Tel: 936-273-7393, E-mail: cheryl.mansfield-egans@lonestar.edu; *Ref Serv,* Deborah Cox; Tel: 936-273-7490, E-mail: debbie.cox@lonestar.edu; *Ref Serv,* Daniel Stevens; Tel: 936-273-7487, E-mail: daniel.stevens@lonestar.edu. Subject Specialists: *Bus,* Cheryl Mansfield-Egans; *English, Humanities,* Deborah Cox; *Liberal arts,* Daniel Stevens; Staff 5 (MLS 5)
Founded 1995. Enrl 11,500; Fac 402; Highest Degree: Associate
Library Holdings: AV Mats 3,016; CDs 87; e-books 41,500; Bk Vols 43,114; Per Subs 462; Talking Bks 96
Special Collections: McKay Everett (Children's Coll)
Function: Art exhibits, Audio & video playback equip for onsite use, Distance learning, For res purposes, ILL available
Open Mon-Thurs 7:30am-9:30pm, Fri 7:30-7:30, Sat 9-4, Sun 1-6
Restriction: Authorized patrons, Fee for pub use, Non-circulating coll

NORTH HARRIS COLLEGE LIBRARY, 2700 W W Thorne Dr, 77073, SAN 323-6943. Tel: 281-618-5491. Reference Tel: 281-618-5707. FAX: 281-618-5695. E-mail: nhc.libweb@lonestar.edu. *Dir,* Pradeep Lele; Tel: 281-618-5497; *Head, Ref,* Dr Carolyn Jacobs; Tel: 281-618-5487; *Doc, Ref Librn,* Virginia Rigby; Tel: 281-618-5490; *Ref & Acq Librn,* Karen Parker; *Ref & Instruction Librn,* Olia Palmer; *Ref & Tech Librn,* Norma Drepaul; Staff 13 (MLS 6, Non-MLS 7)
Founded 1972. Enrl 11,000; Fac 390; Highest Degree: Associate
Library Holdings: AV Mats 11,869; Bk Vols 101,000; Per Subs 1,041
Special Collections: ERIC Junior College Fiche Coll. US Document Depository
Publications: Library Dateline
Open Mon-Thurs 7:30am-9:30pm, Fri 7:30-4:30, Sat 9-5, Sun 1-6

TOMBALL COLLEGE LIBRARY, 30555 Tomball Pkwy, Tomball, 77375-4036, SAN 323-696X. Tel: 832-559-4206. Reference Tel: 832-559-4211. FAX: 832-559-4248. Reference E-mail: tcref@LoneStar.edu. *Dir,* Pam Shafer; Tel: 832-559-4217, E-mail: Pamela.N.Shafer@lonestar.edu; *Ref Librn,* Elizabeth Gault; E-mail: Elizabeth.K.Gault@lonestar.edu; *Circ,* Margaret Dawson
Founded 1988. Enrl 11,000; Fac 209; Highest Degree: Associate
Library Holdings: Bk Titles 24,486; Bk Vols 32,469; Per Subs 486
Open Mon-Thurs 8am-9:30pm, Fri 8-6, Sat 10-5 (Fall & Spring)

THE UNIVERSITY CENTER LIBRARY, 3232 College Park Dr, The Woodlands, 77384. Tel: 281-618-7140, 936-273-7562. FAX: 936-273-7616. Web Site: www.lonestar.edu.
Library Holdings: e-books 42,000
Open Mon-Thurs 8am-9pm, Fri & Sat 8-5

S LUNAR & PLANETARY INSTITUTE LIBRARY, 3600 Bay Area Blvd, 77058-1113. SAN 362-0107. Tel: 281-486-2172. Administration Tel: 281-486-2188. E-mail: library@lpi.usra.edu. Web Site: www.lpi.usra.edu/library. *Mgr, Libr Serv,* Renee Dotson; E-mail: rdotson@lpi.usra.edu; *Library Services, Tech Serv,* Elyssa Jasso; E-mail: ejasso@lpi.usra.edu; Staff 3 (Non-MLS 3)
Founded 1969
Library Holdings: Bk Titles 28,000; Bk Vols 63,000
Special Collections: Planetary Maps & Globes; Regional Planetary Image Facility
Subject Interests: Astronomy, Geol, Planetary sci, Space sci
Automation Activity & Vendor Info: (Cataloging) EOS International; (Circulation) EOS International; (ILL) OCLC; (OPAC) EOS International
Wireless access
Function: Res libr
Partic in Amigos Library Services, Inc
Restriction: Open by appt only

S MENIL FOUNDATION, The Menil Collection Library, 1533 Sul Ross St, 77006. SAN 373-6164. Tel: 713-535-3102. E-mail: library@menil.org. Web Site: www.menil.org. *Assoc Librn,* Donna Torok-Oberholtzer; Staff 1 (MLS 1)
Founded 1987
Library Holdings: Bk Titles 41,891; Bk Vols 43,000; Per Subs 64
Special Collections: Rare Book Room
Subject Interests: Art hist
Automation Activity & Vendor Info: (Cataloging) Koha
Wireless access
Function: Res libr
Partic in Amigos Library Services, Inc
Restriction: Open by appt only

S MUSEUM OF FINE ARTS, HOUSTON*, Hirsch Library, 1001 Bissonnet St, 77005. (Mail add: PO Box 6826, 77265-6826), SAN 316-4683. Tel: 713-639-7325. FAX: 713-639-7795. E-mail: hirsch@mfah.org. Web Site: www.mfah.org/research/hirsch-library. *Archives Chief, Chief Librn,* Jon Evans; *Collections Strategy Librn,* Jason Valdez; *Cat, Managing Librn,* Sarah Stanhope; *Metadata Librn,* Sunyoung Park; *Pub Serv & Instruction Librn,* Rebekah Scoggins; *Libr Asst, Stacks Mgr,* Katie Bogan; *Tech Serv Librn,* Joel Pelanne; *Acq, Libr Asst,* Shannon Huff; *Libr Asst, Ref,* Stephanie Darling; Staff 9.5 (MLS 6, Non-MLS 3.5)
Founded 1926
Library Holdings: Bk Titles 90,000; Bk Vols 175,000; Per Subs 270
Automation Activity & Vendor Info: (Acquisitions) OCLC Worldshare Management Services; (Cataloging) OCLC Worldshare Management Services; (Circulation) OCLC Worldshare Management Services; (ILL) OCLC WorldShare Interlibrary Loan; (OPAC) OCLC Worldshare Management Services; (Serials) OCLC Worldshare Management Services
Wireless access
Partic in OCLC Research Library Partnership
Open Tues, Wed & Fri 10-5, Thurs 10-9, Sat Noon-5

G NASA*, Johnson Space Center Scientific & Technical Information Center, 2101 NASA Pkwy, B30A/1077, 77058. SAN 316-4691. Tel: 281-483-4245. FAX: 281-244-6624. E-mail: jsc-sti-center@mail.nasa.gov. Web Site: www.nasa.gov/content/nasa-scientific-and-technical-information-sti-program. *Libr Supvr,* Janine C Bolton; E-mail: janine.c.bolton@nasa.gov; Staff 11 (MLS 4, Non-MLS 7)
Founded 1962
Library Holdings: e-books 7,000; e-journals 317; Electronic Media & Resources 105; Bk Vols 6,000; Per Subs 120
Special Collections: NASA, JSC & Other Proprietary Government Publications
Subject Interests: Aeronaut, Astronautics, Computer sci, Earth resources, Engr, Guidance, Life sci, Math, Navigation, Physics, Space med, Space sci, Space shuttles, Space sta, Telemetry
Automation Activity & Vendor Info: (Acquisitions) SirsiDynix; (Cataloging) SirsiDynix; (Circulation) SirsiDynix; (ILL) OCLC; (OPAC) SirsiDynix; (Serials) SerialsSolutions
Partic in NASA Library Network; OCLC Online Computer Library Center, Inc
Restriction: Not open to pub

S PIERCE, GOODWIN, ALEXANDER & LINVILLE LIBRARY*, 3131 Briarpark, Ste 200, 77042. SAN 328-4395. Tel: 713-622-1444. FAX: 713-968-9333. Web Site: www.pgal.com. *Library Contact,* Ali Lam; E-mail: htx-interiors@pgal.com
Library Holdings: Bk Vols 580
Subject Interests: Archit
Wireless access
Restriction: Not open to pub

S PLANNING & FORECASTING CONSULTANTS LIBRARY*, PO Box 820228, 77282-0228. SAN 372-9915. Tel: 281-497-2179. *Mgr,* Dale Steffes; E-mail: dalesteffes@comcast.net
Library Holdings: Bk Vols 1,750; Per Subs 38
Subject Interests: Energy, Natural gas
Restriction: Clients only

C RICE UNIVERSITY*, Fondren Library, 6100 Main, MS-44, 77005. (Mail add: PO Box 1892, 77251-1892), SAN 316-506X. Tel: 713-348-5113. Circulation Tel: 713-348-4021. Interlibrary Loan Service Tel: 713-348-2284. Reference Tel: 713-348-5119. Administration Tel: 713-348-5698. FAX: 713-348-5258. Web Site: library.rice.edu. *Vice Provost & Univ Librn,* Sara Lowman; *Exec Dir, Digital Scholarship Serv,* Lisa Spiro; Tel: 713-348-2480, E-mail: lspiro@rice.edu; *Head, Acq,* David Bynog; Tel: 713-348-4811, E-mail: dbynog@rice.edu; *Head, Cat & Metadata Serv,* Position Currently Open; *Head, Spec Coll & Archives,* Amanda Focke; Tel: 713-348-2124, E-mail: afocke@rice.edu; *Asst Univ Librn, Res Serv,* Sandra Edwards; Tel: 713-348-2504, E-mail: edwards@rice.edu; *Asst Univ Librn, Tech Serv,* Denis Galvin; Tel: 713-348-3634, E-mail: dgalvin@rice.edu; *Presv Librn,* Andrew Damico; Tel: 713-348-2602, E-mail: adamico@rice.edu; *Access Serv Mgr,* Susan R

Garrison; Tel: 713-348-2573, E-mail: susan.garrison@rice.edu; *Govt Info Coordr,* Anna Xiong; Tel: 713-348-6212, E-mail: axiong@rice.edu; Staff 65 (MLS 33, Non-MLS 32)
Founded 1912. Enrl 6,351; Fac 641; Highest Degree: Doctorate
Library Holdings: AV Mats 91,047; CDs 1,300; DVDs 2,000; e-books 129,118; e-journals 154,101; Microforms 3,514,034; Bk Titles 2,440,291; Bk Vols 2,881,508; Per Subs 155,658; Videos 1,000
Special Collections: 18th & 19th Century British Maritime & Naval History, ms; 18th Century British Drama (Axson Coll), rare bks; 19th & 20th Century Texas (Judge James L Autry, Gen William Hamman, Mirabeau B Lamar Journal, Harris Masterson, John P Osterhout, Walter B & Estelle B Sharp, J Russell Wait, E O Lovett, Hutcheson Family, Stuart Family, Townsend Family, William W Watkin & Anderson-Greenwood Colls); Americas Coll; Architecture (William Ward Watkin Papers, William Cannady, Anderson Todd, Arthur E Jones & Charles Tapley Architectural Records); Cruikshank Coll; Fine & Performing Arts (Ann Holmes Fine Arts Archive, Ensemble Theater Records, Marion Kessel Performing Arts, Vera Prasilova Scott Portraiture Colls, Arthur Hall & Paul Cooper Papers, Sacred Music Coll); Historical Maps & Atlases; History of Aeronautics (Anderson Coll); History of Science, rare bks; Limited Edition Coll; Local & Texas History (Masterson Coll, Clarence Wharton, Marguerite Johnston Barnes, Tanglewood/William G Farrington, ChampionsGolf Club, South Main Alliance Records); Maximilian & Carlotta Coll; Military Intelligence & Espionage Coll; Modern American Literature (Larry McMurtry, David Westheimer, William Goyen, J P Miller & Thornton Wilder Colls); Oil & Gas (Panhandle Eastern, Merchants & Planters Oil Co, Huffington Pol Co, El Paso Natural Gas); Papermaking Coll; Rice University (Julian S Huxley & Juliette Huxley Papers); Texas Entrepreneurs/Business (Dillingham Family, Walter W & Ella F Fondren, Groce Family, Gus S Wortham, family & business, Merchants & Planters Oil Co, Baker & Botts Historical Archives, William L Clayton Papers, Brown & Root Records); Texas Politics (Oveta Culp Hobby Papers, Billie Carr, Frankie Randolph, Fagan Dickson, Walter Hall, William Clayton & Albert Thomas Coll); US Civil War & Slavery, diaries, doc, imprints, letters, photog; William Martin Religious Right Coll. State Document Depository; US Document Depository
Automation Activity & Vendor Info: (Acquisitions) Ex Libris Group; (Cataloging) Ex Libris Group; (Circulation) Ex Libris Group; (Course Reserve) Ex Libris Group; (Discovery) Ex Libris Group; (ILL) Ex Libris Group; (OPAC) Ex Libris Group; (Serials) Ex Libris Group
Wireless access
Function: 24/7 Electronic res, Archival coll, Art exhibits, Audio & video playback equip for onsite use, Bks on CD, CD-ROM, Computer training, Computers for patron use, Doc delivery serv, E-Reserves, Electronic databases & coll, Free DVD rentals, Govt ref serv, ILL available, Internet access, Microfiche/film & reading machines, Music CDs, Online cat, Online ref, Orientations, Photocopying/Printing, Ref serv available, Scanner, Study rm, Tax forms, Telephone ref, VHS videos, Wheelchair accessible, Workshops
Publications: News from Fondren
Partic in Amigos Library Services, Inc; Association of Research Libraries; Coalition for Networked Information; Coun of Libr Info Resources; Digital Libr Fedn; Greater Western Library Alliance; Inter-University Consortium for Political & Social Research; Scholarly Publ & Acad Resources Coalition; TexSHARE - Texas State Library & Archives Commission
Restriction: Open to pub for ref only
Friends of the Library Group

J SAN JACINTO COLLEGE NORTH*, Dr Edwin E Lehr Library, 5800 Uvalde Rd, 77049-4599. SAN 362-0131. Tel: 281-459-7116. FAX: 281-459-7166. Web Site: www.sjcd.edu/library. *Libr Dir,* Lyn C Garner; E-mail: Lyn.Garner@sjcd.edu; *Ref Librn,* Karyn Jones; Tel: 281-998-6150, Ext 7359, E-mail: Karyn.Jones@sjcd.edu; *Circ, ILL,* Stephanie Trice; Tel: 281-998-6150, Ext 7352, E-mail: Stephanie.Trice@sjcd.edu; Staff 4 (MLS 4)
Founded 1974. Enrl 6,000; Highest Degree: Associate
Library Holdings: High Interest/Low Vocabulary Bk Vols 200; Bk Vols 80,000; Per Subs 17,145
Special Collections: Law Library; Texana Coll
Automation Activity & Vendor Info: (Cataloging) Innovative Interfaces, Inc - Millennium; (Circulation) Innovative Interfaces, Inc - Millennium; (Course Reserve) Innovative Interfaces, Inc - Millennium; (OPAC) Innovative Interfaces, Inc - Millennium; (Serials) Innovative Interfaces, Inc - Millennium
Wireless access
Special Services for the Blind - Reader equip
Open Mon-Thurs 7:30am-9pm, Fri 7:30-3, Sat 11-2; Mon-Thurs 7:30am-9pm, Fri 7:30-Noon, Sat 11-2 (Summer)

J SAN JACINTO COLLEGE SOUTH*, Parker Williams Library, 13735 Beamer Rd, S10, 77089-6099. SAN 362-0166. Tel: 281-998-6150, Ext 3306. FAX: 281-922-3470. Web Site: www.sanjac.edu/library. *Dir,* Richard McKay; Tel: 281-922-3416, E-mail: Richard.McKay@sjcd.edu; *Ref Librn,* Rosalind Clifford; E-mail: Rosalind.Clifford@sjcd.edu; *ILL, Ref Librn,* Lynda delos Santos; E-mail: Lynda.delosSantos@sjcd.edu; Staff 9 (MLS 3, Non-MLS 6)
Founded 1979. Enrl 9,100; Fac 339; Highest Degree: Associate
Library Holdings: Bk Vols 63,000; Per Subs 101
Special Collections: Texana
Subject Interests: Am lit, British lit, Health sci, Texana
Automation Activity & Vendor Info: (Cataloging) OCLC Online; (Circulation) Innovative Interfaces, Inc - Millennium; (ILL) OCLC Online; (OPAC) Innovative Interfaces, Inc - Millennium
Wireless access
Function: For res purposes, ILL available, Photocopying/Printing, Telephone ref, Wheelchair accessible
Partic in TexSHARE - Texas State Library & Archives Commission
Open Mon-Thurs 7:30am-9pm, Fri 7:30-3, Sat 10-1

CL SOUTH TEXAS COLLEGE OF LAW HOUSTON*, The Fred Parks Law Library, 1303 San Jacinto St, 77002-7006. SAN 316-4845. Tel: 713-646-1711. Reference Tel: 713-646-1712. FAX: 713-659-2217. E-mail: askpat@stcl.edu. Web Site: stcl.edu/library. *Dir,* Colleen C Manning; Tel: 713-646-1729; *Assoc Dir, Pub Serv,* Monica Ortale; Tel: 713-646-1721; *Archivist & Spec Coll Librn,* Heather Kushnerick; Tel: 713-646-1720; *Core Operations Librn,* Barbara Szalkowski; Tel: 713-646-1724; *Electronic Serv Librn, Ref,* Karen Kronenberg; Tel: 713-646-1725; Staff 5 (MLS 5)
Founded 1923. Enrl 950; Fac 55; Highest Degree: Doctorate
Library Holdings: Electronic Media & Resources 831; Microforms 345,154; Bk Titles 66,398; Bk Vols 248,570
Special Collections: Law School Archives; Rare Book Coll. US Document Depository
Automation Activity & Vendor Info: (Acquisitions) Innovative Interfaces, Inc; (Cataloging) Innovative Interfaces, Inc; (Circulation) Innovative Interfaces, Inc; (Course Reserve) Innovative Interfaces, Inc; (Discovery) SerialsSolutions; (ILL) OCLC Tipasa; (OPAC) Innovative Interfaces, Inc; (Serials) Innovative Interfaces, Inc
Wireless access
Publications: Accession List (Monthly); Library Guides (Online only)
Partic in Amigos Library Services, Inc; OCLC Online Computer Library Center, Inc
Open Mon-Thurs 6am-Midnight, Fri 6am-10pm, Sat 8:30am-10pm, Sun 8am-10pm

M TEXAS CHILDREN'S HOSPITAL*, Pi Beta Phi Patient/Family Library, West Tower 16th Flr, Rm 16265, 6621 Fannin St, 77030. SAN 316-490X. Tel: 832-826-1619. FAX: 832-826-1601. Web Site: www.texaschildrens.org/departments/child-life/libraries. *Coordr,* Catherine Zdunkewicz; E-mail: cczdunke@texaschildrens.org
Founded 1984
Library Holdings: Bk Vols 5,000
Subject Interests: Bks for all ages, Children's lit, Med, Movies, Parenting
Wireless access
Open Mon-Fri 8-5, Sat 10-3
Friends of the Library Group

C TEXAS SOUTHERN UNIVERSITY*, Library Learning Center, 3100 Cleburne Ave, 77004. SAN 362-0255. Tel: 713-313-7402. Interlibrary Loan Service Tel: 713-313-1082. Administration Tel: 713-313-7785. FAX: 713-313-1080. Web Site: www.tsu.edu/academics/library. *Interim Exec Dir,* Haiying Sarah Li; Tel: 713-313-7169, E-mail: haiying.li@tsu.edu; *Assoc Dir of Tech & Digital Services,* Nicolas O Castellanos; Tel: 713-313-5024, E-mail: nicolas.castellanos@tsu.edu; *Interim Asst Dir, Ser Librn,* Leocadia Hooks; Tel: 713-313-4304, E-mail: leocadia.hooks@tsu.edu; *Evening/Weekend Ref Librn,* Rajeev Mathai; E-mail: rajeev.mathai@tsu.edu; Staff 5 (MLS 5)
Founded 1947. Enrl 8,965; Fac 606; Highest Degree: Doctorate
Library Holdings: Microforms 228; Bk Vols 66,589; Per Subs 2,957
Special Collections: Barbara Jordan Archives; Heartman Coll; Traditional African Art Gallery; University Archives
Automation Activity & Vendor Info: (Acquisitions) OCLC Worldshare Management Services; (Cataloging) OCLC Worldshare Management Services; (Circulation) OCLC Worldshare Management Services; (Course Reserve) OCLC Worldshare Management Services; (ILL) OCLC Worldshare Management Services; (Media Booking) OCLC Worldshare Management Services; (OPAC) OCLC Worldshare Management Services; (Serials) OCLC Worldshare Management Services
Wireless access
Function: Archival coll, Art exhibits, Computers for patron use, Distance learning, Doc delivery serv, Electronic databases & coll, Health sci info serv, ILL available, Internet access, Magazines, Microfiche/film & reading machines, Orientations, Photocopying/Printing
Publications: Catalog of the Traditional African Art Gallery
Partic in Amigos Library Services, Inc; OCLC Online Computer Library Center, Inc; TexSHARE - Texas State Library & Archives Commission
Open Mon-Thurs 7am-Midnight, Fri 7:30am-8pm, Sat 9-6, Sun Noon-Midnight

Departmental Libraries:

CL THURGOOD MARSHALL SCHOOL OF LAW LIBRARY, 3100 Cleburne Ave, 77004, SAN 362-028X. Tel: 713-313-7125. FAX: 713-313-4483. Web Site: www.tsulaw.edu/library. *Actg Dir, Faculty Res Librn,* Tara Long-Taylor; Tel: 713-313-4470, E-mail: tara.long@tmslaw.tsu.edu; *Circ Librn,* Patrina Epperson; Tel: 713-313-1011, E-mail: patrina.epperson@tmslaw.tsu.edu; *Ref Librn,* Nanette Collins; Tel: 713-313-1106, E-mail: nanette.collins@tmslaw.tsu.edu; Staff 3 (MLS 1, Non-MLS 2)
Founded 1948. Enrl 400; Fac 32; Highest Degree: Doctorate
Library Holdings: Bk Titles 350,000; Per Subs 2,500
Automation Activity & Vendor Info: (Acquisitions) OCLC; (Cataloging) OCLC; (Circulation) OCLC; (Course Reserve) OCLC; (ILL) OCLC; (Media Booking) OCLC; (OPAC) OCLC; (Serials) OCLC
Open Mon-Fri 7:30am-9pm, Sat 9-9, Sun Noon-9pm

M TIRR MEMORIAL HERMANN, Rehabilitation & Research Library, 1333 Moursund St, 77030. SAN 316-4934. Tel: 713-797-5947, 713-799-5000 ((Main)). Web Site: www.memorialhermann.org. *Librn,* Brenda Eames
Founded 1969
Library Holdings: Bk Vols 2,500; Per Subs 25
Special Collections: Polio & Post-Polio
Subject Interests: Head injury, Rehabilitation, Spinal cord injury
Wireless access
Function: Res libr, Telephone ref
Restriction: Not open to pub, Ref only to non-staff

L UNITED STATES COURTS LIBRARY*, 515 Rusk Ave, Rm 6311, 77002. SAN 372-1620. Tel: 713-250-5696. FAX: 713-250-5091. E-mail: 5satlib-Houston@ca5.uscourts.gov. Web Site: www.lb5.uscourts.gov. *Librn,* Andrew Jackson; E-mail: Andrew_Jackson@ca5.uscourts.gov
Library Holdings: Bk Vols 50,000; Per Subs 70
Automation Activity & Vendor Info: (Acquisitions) SirsiDynix; (Cataloging) SirsiDynix; (Serials) SirsiDynix
Wireless access
Open Mon-Fri 8-4:45
Restriction: Non-circulating

UNIVERSITY OF HOUSTON

C M D ANDERSON LIBRARY*, 114 University Libraries, 77204-2000. Tel: 713-743-9800. FAX: 713-743-9811. Web Site: libraries.uh.edu. *Dean, Univ Libr,* Athena Jackson; E-mail: anjackson7@uh.edu; *Assoc Dean of Libr,* Linda Thompson; *Assoc Dean, Personnel Planning & Syst,* John Lehner; *Assoc Dean, Pub Serv,* Marilyn Myers; *Prog Dir, Coll,* Miranda Bennett; *ILL Coordr,* Nora Dethloff; Staff 60 (MLS 60)
Founded 1927. Enrl 34,663; Fac 2,953; Highest Degree: Doctorate
Library Holdings: Bk Vols 2,298,433; Per Subs 21,845
Special Collections: American History (Israel Shreve Coll), papers; Architecture (Franzheim Memorial Coll); Bibliography & History of Printing; Botts Coll of LGBT History 1973-2014, Resurrection Metropolitan Community Church docs, photogs, film, flyers, awards & plaques; British & American Authors (A Huxley, Thurber, Jeffers, Patchen, Updike, Lowry & McMurtry Colls); City of Houston (George Fuermann Coll); Creative Writing & Performing Arts Archive; History of Science (Jadish Hehra Coll); James E & Miriam A Ferguson Coll, papers; James V Allred Coll of Texas gubernatorial papers; Texana & Western Americana (W B Bates Coll), bks, mss. State Document Depository; US Document Depository
Subject Interests: Chem, Computer sci, Engr
Automation Activity & Vendor Info: (Acquisitions) Innovative Interfaces, Inc; (Cataloging) Innovative Interfaces, Inc; (Circulation) Innovative Interfaces, Inc; (Course Reserve) Innovative Interfaces, Inc; (ILL) Innovative Interfaces, Inc; (Media Booking) Innovative Interfaces, Inc; (OPAC) Innovative Interfaces, Inc; (Serials) Innovative Interfaces, Inc
Partic in Amigos Library Services, Inc; Association of Research Libraries; Center for Research Libraries; Greater Western Library Alliance; OCLC Research Library Partnership
Publications: Public-Access Computer Systems Review
Open Mon-Thurs 7:45am-10pm, Fri 7:45-5, Sat & Sun 1-6

C WILLIAM R JENKINS ARCHITECTURE & ART LIBRARY*, 122 Architecture Bldg, 77204-4000, SAN 362-0417. Tel: 713-743-2340. Interlibrary Loan Service Tel: 713-743-9720. FAX: 713-743-9917. Web Site: libraries.uh.edu/locations/jenkins. *Sr Librn,* Keith Daniels; E-mail: kadaniels4@uh.edu
Library Holdings: Bk Vols 80,000; Per Subs 225
Subject Interests: Archit, Art, Landscape archit, Urban design
Partic in Amigos Library Services, Inc; Association of Research Libraries; Houston Area Research Library Consortium; Texas Council of Academic Libraries; TexSHARE - Texas State Library & Archives Commission
Open Mon-Fri 7:45am-10pm, Fri 7:45-5, Sat & Sun 1-6

C MUSIC LIBRARY*, 220 Moores School of Music Bldg, 77204-4017. (Mail add: 114 University Libraries, 77204-2000). Tel: 713-743-3197. FAX: 713-743-9918. E-mail: musiclib@uh.edu. Web Site: info.lib.uh.edu/music. *Dir,* Ericka Patillo; Tel: 713-743-3770; *Head Music Libr,* Madelyn Washington; Tel: 713-743-4231, E-mail: mswashington@uh.edu; Staff 4 (MLS 2, Non-MLS 2)
Founded 1968. Highest Degree: Doctorate
Library Holdings: Bk Vols 54,000; Per Subs 195
Automation Activity & Vendor Info: (Acquisitions) Innovative Interfaces, Inc; (Cataloging) Innovative Interfaces, Inc; (Circulation) Innovative Interfaces, Inc; (Course Reserve) Innovative Interfaces, Inc; (ILL) OCLC ILLiad; (Media Booking) Innovative Interfaces, Inc; (OPAC) Innovative Interfaces, Inc; (Serials) Innovative Interfaces, Inc
Function: ILL available, Ref serv available, Wheelchair accessible
Partic in Amigos Library Services, Inc; Association of Research Libraries
Open Mon-Fri 7:45-5

CM OPTOMETRY LIBRARY*, 505 J Davis Armistead Bldg, 77204-2020, SAN 362-0441. Tel: 713-743-1910. FAX: 713-743-2001. Web Site: info.lib.uh.edu/local/optometr.htm. *Librn,* Rachel Helbing; Tel: 713-743-5462, E-mail: rrhelbin@central.uh.edu
Library Holdings: Bk Vols 10,000; Per Subs 137
Subject Interests: Ophthalmology, Optometry, Physiological optics, Vision sci
Partic in Amigos Library Services, Inc; Association of Research Libraries
Open Mon-Fri 7-6

CL THE O'QUINN LAW LIBRARY*, 12 Law Library, 77204-6054. Tel: 713-743-2300. Interlibrary Loan Service Tel: 713-743-2286. Reference Tel: 713-743-2327. Administration Tel: 713-743-2331. FAX: 713-743-2296. Web Site: www.law.uh.edu/libraries. *Dir,* Spencer Simons; *Assoc Dir,* Mon Yin Lung; *Head, Acq & Coll Serv,* Marek Waterstone; *Head, Cat & Ser,* Yuxin Li; *Head, Doc Serv,* Helen E Boyce; *Instrul Serv Librn,* Christopher Dykes; *Ref Serv,* Lauren Schroeder; Staff 12 (MLS 10, Non-MLS 2)
Founded 1947. Enrl 1,100; Fac 46; Highest Degree: Doctorate
Library Holdings: e-books 21,925; Electronic Media & Resources 26; Microforms 1,670,675; Bk Titles 125,251; Bk Vols 569,358; Per Subs 2,598; Videos 175
Special Collections: Congressional Publications (CIS Microfiche Library); Texas Supreme Court Briefs. US Document Depository
Subject Interests: Admiralty law, Energy law, Intellectual property law, Intl trade, Maritime law, Taxes
Automation Activity & Vendor Info: (Acquisitions) Innovative Interfaces, Inc; (Cataloging) Innovative Interfaces, Inc; (Circulation) Innovative Interfaces, Inc; (OPAC) Innovative Interfaces, Inc; (Serials) Innovative Interfaces, Inc
Partic in Amigos Library Services, Inc; Association of Research Libraries
Open Mon-Thurs 7:30am-Midnight, Fri 7:30am-11pm, Sat 9-8, Sun 9am-11pm
Restriction: Pub use on premises

C UNIVERSITY OF HOUSTON - CLEAR LAKE, Alfred R Neumann Library, Bayou Bldg 2402, 2700 Bay Area Blvd, 77058-1002. SAN 362-0468. Tel: 281-283-3900. FAX: 281-283-3937. E-mail: library@uhcl.edu. Web Site: www.uhcl.edu/library. *Exec Dir,* Lee Hilyer; E-mail: hilyer@uhcl.edu; *Assoc Dir, Evaluation Assessment,* Martha Hood; Tel: 281-283-3920, E-mail: hood@uhcl.edu; *Assoc Dir, Res Mgt, Assoc Dir, Tech,* Jingshan Xiao; Tel: 281-283-3912, E-mail: xiao@uhcl.edu; *Univ Archivist,* Roberto Nanes; Tel: 281-283-3933, E-mail: nanes@uhcl.edu; Staff 26 (MLS 14, Non-MLS 12)
Founded 1973. Enrl 7,733; Fac 295; Highest Degree: Doctorate
Special Collections: Johnson Space Center History Coll (Papers of Max Faget & others). US Document Depository
Subject Interests: Acctg, Environ, Software engr
Automation Activity & Vendor Info: (Acquisitions) Ex Libris Group; (Cataloging) Ex Libris Group; (Circulation) Ex Libris Group; (Course Reserve) Ex Libris Group; (ILL) OCLC ILLiad; (OPAC) Ex Libris Group; (Serials) Ex Libris Group
Wireless access
Function: Computers for patron use, Distance learning, Doc delivery serv, Electronic databases & coll, Free DVD rentals, Magnifiers for reading, Online cat, Photocopying/Printing, Ref & res, Ref serv available, Telephone ref, Wheelchair accessible
Partic in Amigos Library Services, Inc; TexSHARE - Texas State Library & Archives Commission
Special Services for the Blind - Computer with voice synthesizer for visually impaired persons; Internet workstation with adaptive software
Open Mon-Thurs 7am-11pm, Fri 7-6, Sat & Sun 10-6
Restriction: Restricted borrowing privileges

C UNIVERSITY OF HOUSTON-DOWNTOWN*, W I Dykes Library, One Main St, 77002. SAN 362-0492. Tel: 713-221-8187. Circulation Tel: 713-221-8186. Administration Tel: 713-221-8011. Automation Services Tel: 713-221-8054. FAX: 713-221-8037. Web Site: www.uhd.edu/library/Pages/library-index.aspx. *Exec Dir, Libr Serv,* lisa Braysen; E-mail: braysenl@uhd.edu; Staff 34 (MLS 16, Non-MLS 18)
Founded 1974. Enrl 14,262; Fac 662; Highest Degree: Master

Library Holdings: Audiobooks 310; AV Mats 818; e-books 573,947; e-journals 141,220; Electronic Media & Resources 81,711; Microforms 5,691; Bk Titles 138,262; Bk Vols 184,835; Per Subs 10,409; Videos 3,343
Special Collections: University Archives
Automation Activity & Vendor Info: (Acquisitions) Innovative Interfaces, Inc - Millennium; (Cataloging) Innovative Interfaces, Inc - Millennium; (Circulation) Innovative Interfaces, Inc - Millennium; (ILL) OCLC; (OPAC) Innovative Interfaces, Inc - Millennium; (Serials) SerialsSolutions
Wireless access
Function: Bks on CD, Computers for patron use, Distance learning, Doc delivery serv, E-Reserves, Electronic databases & coll, Internet access, Magnifiers for reading, Microfiche/film & reading machines, Movies, Music CDs, Online cat, Online info literacy tutorials on the web & in blackboard, Online ref, Orientations, Photocopying/Printing, Printer for laptops & handheld devices, Ref & res, Ref serv available, Scanner, Spoken cassettes & CDs, Spoken cassettes & DVDs, Study rm, Telephone ref, Wheelchair accessible
Partic in Amigos Library Services, Inc; OCLC Online Computer Library Center, Inc; TexSHARE - Texas State Library & Archives Commission
Special Services for the Blind - Bks on CD
Open Mon-Thurs 7am-10pm, Fri 7-6, Sat 9-6, Sun 1-6 (Fall & Spring); Mon-Thurs 7am-9:30pm, Fri 7-5, Sat 1-5 (Summer)
Restriction: Open to pub for ref & circ; with some limitations

C UNIVERSITY OF SAINT THOMAS, Robert Pace & Ada Mary Doherty Library, 3800 Montrose Blvd, 77006. SAN 362-0522. Tel: 713-525-2192. Circulation Tel: 713-525-2180. Reference Tel: 713-525-2188. Automation Services Tel: 713-525-2183. E-mail: circulation@stthom.edu, loans@stthom.edu. Reference E-mail: reference@stthom.edu. Web Site: www.stthom.edu/library-research. *Dean of Libr,* James Piccininni; E-mail: jpicci@stthom.edu; *Head, Circ,* Silvia Coy; E-mail: coys@stthom.edu; *Coll Develop Librn,* Nicholas Kowalski; Tel: 713-525-2182, E-mail: kowalsn@stthom.edu; *Electronic Res Librn,* Kaitlyn Keever; Tel: 713-525-2175, E-mail: kaitlyn.keever@stthom.edu; *Pub Serv Librn,* Position Currently Open; *Tech Serv Librn,* Ashley Delagarza; E-mail: delagaar@stthom.edu; *Circ Supvr,* Azalia Herebia; Staff 8 (MLS 5, Non-MLS 3)
Founded 1972. Enrl 3,237; Fac 153; Highest Degree: Doctorate
Library Holdings: AV Mats 2,141; e-books 225,500; Electronic Media & Resources 200; Microforms 608,337; Bk Vols 270,000; Per Subs 75,000
Special Collections: Business Ethics (Sally S Slick & William T Slick Jr Endowed Coll); Dr Lee Williames & David Theis Coll; Environmental Studies (Peggy Shiffick Endowed Coll); Greenwood Endowment for Children's Literature; Irish Studies Research (McFadden-Moran Coll); Janice Gordon-Kelter Coll; L Tuffly Ellis Coll Endowed Fund; The Albert & Ethel Herzstein Coll; The John O Whitney - Readex Archive of Americana Coll
Automation Activity & Vendor Info: (Acquisitions) SirsiDynix; (Cataloging) SirsiDynix; (Circulation) SirsiDynix; (Course Reserve) SirsiDynix; (OPAC) SirsiDynix; (Serials) EBSCO Online
Wireless access
Function: 24/7 Electronic res, 24/7 Online cat, 3D Printer, Archival coll, Art exhibits, CD-ROM, Computers for patron use, E-Reserves, Electronic databases & coll, ILL available, Instruction & testing, Internet access, Literacy & newcomer serv, Magnifiers for reading, Online cat, Online info literacy tutorials on the web & in blackboard, Online ref, Orientations, Outside serv via phone, mail, e-mail & web, Photocopying/Printing, Ref & res, Ref serv available, Summer reading prog, VHS videos, Workshops
Publications: Folio
Partic in Amigos Library Services, Inc; OCLC Online Computer Library Center, Inc; Tex Independent Cols & Univ Librs
Open Mon-Thurs 7:45am-11pm, Fri 7:45-6, Sat 10-6, Sun 1-11
Restriction: Circ limited, Non-circulating coll, Non-circulating of rare bks, Open to pub for ref & circ; with some limitations, Open to students, fac & staff, Photo ID required for access
Friends of the Library Group

Departmental Libraries:

CARDINAL BERAN LIBRARY AT SAINT MARY'S SEMINARY, 9845 Memorial Dr, 77024-3498, SAN 362-0581. Tel: 713-654-5772. E-mail: beran@smseminary.com. Web Site: www.smseminary.com/library. *Chair,* Amanda Renevier; Tel: 713-654-5771, E-mail: renevia@stthom.edu; *Public & Collection Dev Librarian,* Ashley Pitts; Tel: 713-654-5773, E-mail: pittsa@stthom.edu; *Ser Librn,* Noemi Flores; Tel: 713-654-5774, E-mail: floresnl@stthom.edu; Staff 3.8 (MLS 2.8, Non-MLS 1)
Founded 1954. Fac 8; Highest Degree: Master
Library Holdings: Bk Vols 65,712; Per Subs 169
Special Collections: Catholic Fiction Coll; John Henry Newman Coll; Vatican II Coll
Subject Interests: Relig studies, Theol
Partic in Amigos Library Services, Inc
Open Mon-Wed 9-9, Thurs 9-7, Fri 9-5, Sat & Sun 12-5 (Aug-June)
Restriction: Borrowing privileges limited to fac & registered students, Photo ID required for access
Friends of the Library Group

UNIVERSITY OF TEXAS

CM M D ANDERSON CANCER CENTER RESEARCH MEDICAL LIBRARY*, 1400 Pressler St, 77030-3722, SAN 362-0646. Tel: 713-792-2282. Interlibrary Loan Service Tel: 713-745-4531. FAX: 713-563-3650. Web Site: www3.mdanderson.org/library. *Exec Dir,* Clara Fowler; Tel: 713-745-1538, E-mail: cfowler@mdanderson.org; *Info Syst Mgr,* Wes Browning; Tel: 713-745-1545, E-mail: wbrownin@mdanderson.org; *Colls Librn,* Allen Lopez; Tel: 713-792-2729, E-mail: alopez8@mdanderson.org; *Sr Info Spec,* Greg Pratt; Tel: 713-745-5156, E-mail: gfpratt@mdanderson.org; *Archivist,* Javier F Garza; Tel: 713-792-2285, E-mail: jjgarza@mdanderson.org; *Cat,* Linda Olewine; Tel: 713-745-3086, E-mail: lolewine@mdanderson.org; *Doc Delivery,* Chris Oria; Tel: 713-745-4531, E-mail: mcoria@mdanderson.org; Staff 13 (MLS 10, Non-MLS 3)
Founded 1941
Library Holdings: AV Mats 849; CDs 32; e-books 42,257; e-journals 20,786; Bk Titles 17,496; Bk Vols 20,431; Per Subs 670
Special Collections: Historical Resources Center; Leland Clayton Barbee History of Cancer Coll, early treatises, rare bks. Oral History
Subject Interests: Cancer, Radiology
Automation Activity & Vendor Info: (Acquisitions) Ex Libris Group; (Cataloging) Ex Libris Group; (Circulation) Ex Libris Group; (Course Reserve) Ex Libris Group; (ILL) OCLC ILLiad; (OPAC) Ex Libris Group; (Serials) Ex Libris Group
Function: Archival coll, Distance learning, Doc delivery serv, Health sci info serv, Homebound delivery serv, ILL available, Internet access, Photocopying/Printing, Ref serv available, Res libr
Partic in Tex Health Sci Libr Consortium
Publications: NewsBytes (Newsletter)
Open Mon-Fri 7:30-7

CM HEALTH SCIENCE CENTER AT HOUSTON, DENTAL BRANCH LIBRARY*, 7500 Cambridge St, 77054, SAN 362-0611. Tel: 713-486-4094. Web Site: www.db.uth.tmc.edu/education/library. *Asst Libr Dir,* Janet Peri; Tel: 713-486-4204; Staff 4 (MLS 1, Non-MLS 3)
Founded 1943. Fac 180; Highest Degree: Doctorate
Library Holdings: Bk Titles 14,937; Bk Vols 32,246; Per Subs 204
Special Collections: Dentistry (Historical Coll), first editions & rare bks
Subject Interests: Dentistry
Partic in OCLC Online Computer Library Center, Inc
Open Mon-Fri 8-5

CM SCHOOL OF PUBLIC HEALTH LIBRARY*, 1200 Herman Pressler Blvd, 77030-3900. (Mail add: PO Box 20186, 77225-0186), SAN 316-5019. Tel: 713-500-9121. Interlibrary Loan Service Tel: 713-500-9130. Reference Tel: 713-500-9129. FAX: 713-500-9125. Web Site: sph.uth.edu/current-students/library. *Dir, Ref (Info Servs),* Helena M VonVille; E-mail: helena.m.vonville@uth.tmc.edu; *Acq,* Elaine Wilson; *Tech Serv,* Richard Guinn; *Pub Serv,* Amy Taylor; Staff 4 (MLS 4)
Founded 1969. Enrl 1,500; Fac 145; Highest Degree: Doctorate
Library Holdings: Bk Titles 55,000; Bk Vols 72,000; Per Subs 250
Special Collections: International Census Statistics; Pan American Health Organization; World Health Organization
Subject Interests: Epidemiology, Health econ, Health promotion, HIV-AIDS, Infectious diseases, Nutrition, Pub health
Automation Activity & Vendor Info: (Acquisitions) Ex Libris Group; (Cataloging) Ex Libris Group; (Circulation) Ex Libris Group; (OPAC) Ex Libris Group; (Serials) Ex Libris Group
Partic in National Network of Libraries of Medicine Region 3; OCLC Online Computer Library Center, Inc; S Cent Regional Med Libr Program; Tex Health Sci Libr Consortium; TexSHARE - Texas State Library & Archives Commission; UT Syst Librns
Open Mon-Thurs 8-6, Fri 8-5, Sat 12-6

L VINSON & ELKINS, Law Library, Texas Tower, 845 Texas Ave, Ste 4700, 77002. SAN 316-5035. Tel: 713-758-2222, 713-758-2990. FAX: 713-615-5211. Web Site: www.velaw.com. *Dir, Res,* Michael McHenry; E-mail: mmchenry@vlaw.com; *Operations Mgr,* Kelley Bocell
Founded 1917
Library Holdings: Bk Vols 145,000
Wireless access
Restriction: Staff use only

R WINDWOOD PRESBYTERIAN CHURCH LIBRARY*, 10555 Spring Cypress Rd, 77070. SAN 316-1870. Tel: 281-378-4040. E-mail: windwood@windwoodpc.org. Web Site: www.windwoodpc.org. *Library Contact,* Meredith Ridenour
Founded 1971
Library Holdings: Bk Vols 650
Restriction: Mem only

L WINSTON & STRAWN LIBRARY*, 1111 Louisiana St, 25th Flr, 77002-5242. SAN 320-8737. Tel: 713-651-2600. FAX: 713-787-1440. Web Site: www.winston.com. *Dir, Res,* Gwen Watson; E-mail: gwatson@winston.com
Library Holdings: Bk Vols 9,000; Per Subs 100

Subject Interests: Copyrights, Franchises, Patents, Trademarks, Unfair competition
Restriction: Not open to pub

HOWE

P HOWE COMMUNITY LIBRARY, 315 S Collins Freeway, 75459. SAN 376-4540. Tel: 903-745-4050. Web Site: www.howeisd.net. *Dir, Libr Serv,* Torrey Stricklin; E-mail: stricklin.torrey@howeisd.net; Staff 3 (MLS 1, Non-MLS 2)
Founded 1982. Pop 6,638; Circ 38,637
Library Holdings: Audiobooks 304; Bks on Deafness & Sign Lang 5; DVDs 1,532; e-books 232; High Interest/Low Vocabulary Bk Vols 30; Large Print Bks 50; Bk Titles 18,789; Bk Vols 19,263; Per Subs 89; Videos 1,532
Automation Activity & Vendor Info: (Acquisitions) Book Systems; (Cataloging) Book Systems; (Circulation) Book Systems; (OPAC) Book Systems
Wireless access
Open Mon-Fri 8-5:30, Sat 9-12; Mon-Fri 9-5, Sat 9-12 (Summer)
Friends of the Library Group

HUBBARD

P WILKES MEMORIAL LIBRARY*, 300 NW Sixth St, 76648. Tel: 254-576-2527. E-mail: fsggc@hotmail.com. *Librn,* Linda Jordon; Staff 1 (MLS 1)
Library Holdings: Bk Titles 8,000
Wireless access
Open Wed & Sat 10-4

HUNTINGTON

P MCMULLEN MEMORIAL LIBRARY*, 900 N Main St, 75949. (Mail add: PO Box 849, 75949-0849). Tel: 936-876-4516. FAX: 936-570-9081. Web Site: huntington.ploud.net. *Dir,* Debra Bashaw; E-mail: dbashaw992@gmail.com
Library Holdings: AV Mats 2,000; Bk Vols 25,000; Per Subs 12
Wireless access
Open Mon & Wed-Fri 8-4, Tues 8-8, Sat 10-2

HUNTSVILLE

P HUNTSVILLE PUBLIC LIBRARY*, 1219 13th St, 77340. SAN 316-5094. Tel: 936-291-5472. E-mail: hpl@myhuntsvillelibrary.com. Web Site: huntsvilletx.gov/171/public-library. *Libr Dir,* Rachel McPhail; Tel: 736-291-5470, E-mail: rachel.mcphail@lsslibraries.com; *Dep Libr Dir,* Joshua Sabo; Tel: 936-291-5485, E-mail: joshua.sabo@lsslibraries.com
Founded 1967. Circ 31,060
Library Holdings: Bk Vols 70,300; Per Subs 100
Special Collections: Adult Education; Genealogy; Ornithology
Automation Activity & Vendor Info: (Cataloging) SirsiDynix; (Circulation) SirsiDynix; (OPAC) SirsiDynix
Wireless access
Open Mon-Fri 10-7, Sat 12-4
Friends of the Library Group

C SAM HOUSTON STATE UNIVERSITY*, Newton Gresham Library, 1830 Bobby K Marks Dr, 77340. (Mail add: PO Box 2179, 77341), SAN 316-5108. Tel: 936-294-1614. Administration Tel: 936-294-1613. Toll Free Tel: 866-645-4636. FAX: 936-229-3615. E-mail: library@shsu.edu. Web Site: library.shsu.edu. *Dir, Libr Serv,* Eric Owen; Tel: 936-294-1613; *Head, ILL,* Ann Jerabek; Tel: 936-294-3528; *Head, Ref,* Lisa Shen; Tel: 936-294-3587, E-mail: lshen@shsu.edu; *Head, Tech Serv,* Michael Hanson; Tel: 936-294-1620, E-mail: hansonm@shsu.edu; *Digital Res Librn,* Susan Elkins; Tel: 936-294-1524, E-mail: selkins@shsu.edu; *Music Librn,* Bruce Hall; Tel: 936-294-4800, E-mail: lib_bdh@shsu.edu; *Res & Instruction Librn,* Lisa Connor; Tel: 936-294-3527, E-mail: lconnor@shsu.edu; *Res & Instruction Librn,* Ashley Crane; Tel: 936-294-4686, E-mail: abc064@shsu.edu; *Archivist,* Barbara A Kievit-Mason; Tel: 936-294-3699, E-mail: lib_bak@shsu.edu; Staff 22 (MLS 14, Non-MLS 8)
Founded 1879. Enrl 16,000; Highest Degree: Doctorate
Library Holdings: AV Mats 21,848; e-books 24,310; Bk Vols 1,202,263; Per Subs 4,521
Special Collections: Col John W Thomason Coll; Criminology (Bates, Bennett, Colfield, Eliasburg & McCormick Coll); Gertrude Stein Coll; Mark Twain Coll; Texana & the Southwest (Shettles Coll); Texana Coll; Texas (J L Clark Coll). State Document Depository; US Document Depository
Subject Interests: Criminal justice, Educ, Texana
Automation Activity & Vendor Info: (Acquisitions) SirsiDynix; (Cataloging) SirsiDynix; (Circulation) SirsiDynix; (OPAC) SirsiDynix; (Serials) SirsiDynix
Wireless access
Publications: Newsletter
Partic in Amigos Library Services, Inc
Open Mon-Wed 7:30am-1am, Thurs 7:30am-Midnight, Fri 7:30-6, Sat 10-7, Sun 2pm-1am (Fall & Spring); Mon-Wed 7:30am-11pm, Thurs 7:30am-10pm, Fri 7:30-6, Sat 10-5, Sun 2-11 (Summer)

HURST

P HURST PUBLIC LIBRARY*, 901 Precinct Line Rd, 76053. SAN 316-5124. Tel: 817-788-7300. Administration Tel: 817-788-7351. FAX: 817-590-9515. Web Site: www.hursttx.gov/about-us/departments/library. *Dir,* Jesse Loucks; E-mail: jloucks@hursttx.gov; Staff 23.5 (MLS 10, Non-MLS 13.5)
Founded 1959. Pop 40,000; Circ 329,375
Library Holdings: AV Mats 15,489; e-books 27; Bk Titles 99,067; Bk Vols 109,387; Per Subs 243; Talking Bks 2,249
Special Collections: Oral History
Subject Interests: Local hist
Automation Activity & Vendor Info: (Acquisitions) SirsiDynix; (Cataloging) SirsiDynix; (Circulation) SirsiDynix; (Course Reserve) SirsiDynix; (OPAC) SirsiDynix
Wireless access
Partic in Partners Library Action Network
Open Mon, Wed, Fri & Sat 10-6, Tues & Thurs 10-9
Friends of the Library Group

J TARRANT COUNTY COLLEGE*, J Ardis Bell Library, Northeast Campus, 828 W Harwood Rd, 76054. SAN 361-722X. Tel: 817-515-6627. Reference Tel: 817-515-6629. Administration Tel: 817-515-6477. Web Site: library.tccd.edu/services/ne. *Dir, Libr Serv,* Mark Dolive; Tel: 817-515-6637, E-mail: mark.dolive@tccd.edu; *Asst Dir,* April Martinez; Tel: 817-515-6232, E-mail: april.martinez@tccd.edu; *Pub Serv Librn,* Bonnie Hodges; Tel: 817-515-6626; *Pub Serv Librn,* Twyla Reese-Hornsby; Tel: 817-515-6365, E-mail: twyla.reese-hornsby@tccd.edu; *Circ Mgr,* Priscilla Harrison; Tel: 817-515-6622, E-mail: priscilla.harrison@tccd.edu; *Mgr, Network Serv,* Michael Buccieri; Tel: 817-515-6623, E-mail: michael.buccieri@tccd.edu; *Mgr, Per,* James Ponder; Tel: 817-515-6658, E-mail: james.ponder@tccd.edu. Subject Specialists: *Humanities,* Bonnie Hodges; *Bus, Soc sci,* Twyla Reese-Hornsby; Staff 10 (MLS 7, Non-MLS 3)
Founded 1968. Enrl 15,000; Fac 300; Highest Degree: Associate
Sept 2019-Aug 2020. Mats Exp $140,000. Sal $972,976
Library Holdings: DVDs 380; e-books 74,000; Bk Vols 54,172; Per Subs 145
Subject Interests: Bus, Humanities, Sci tech, Soc sci
Automation Activity & Vendor Info: (Acquisitions) Ex Libris Group; (Cataloging) Ex Libris Group; (Circulation) Ex Libris Group; (Course Reserve) Ex Libris Group; (ILL) Ex Libris Group; (Media Booking) Ex Libris Group; (OPAC) Ex Libris Group; (Serials) Ex Libris Group
Wireless access
Function: Computers for patron use, Distance learning, Electronic databases & coll, Online ref, Photocopying/Printing, Ref & res, Ref serv available
Partic in Amigos Library Services, Inc
Open Mon-Thurs 7:30am-10pm, Fri & Sat 7:30am-9pm, Sun 12-5
Restriction: Non-circulating coll, Open to pub for ref & circ; with some limitations

HUTCHINS

P HUTCHINS-ATWELL PUBLIC LIBRARY*, 300 N Denton St, 75141-9404. (Mail add: PO Box 888, 75141-0888), SAN 361-4042. Tel: 972-225-4711. FAX: 972-225-4593. E-mail: atwelllibrary@cityofhutchins.org. Web Site: cityofhutchins.org/residents/library.html. *Librn,* Cheryl Hawkins; Staff 2 (MLS 2)
Library Holdings: Bk Titles 23,862
Automation Activity & Vendor Info: (Cataloging) LibraryWorld, Inc; (Circulation) LibraryWorld, Inc; (OPAC) LibraryWorld, Inc
Wireless access
Open Mon-Fri 9-6

HUTTO

P HUTTO PUBLIC LIBRARY*, 500 W Live Oak St, 78634. Tel: 512-459-4008. Web Site: www.huttotx.gov/departments/library/index.php. *Libr Mgr,* Lisa Riggs; E-mail: lisa.riggs@huttotx.gov; Staff 4.5 (MLS 1, Non-MLS 3.5)
Founded 2008
Wireless access
Function: 24/7 Online cat, Activity rm, Adult bk club, Adult literacy prog, Art exhibits, Art programs, Audiobks via web, Bilingual assistance for Spanish patrons, Bks on CD, Chess club, Children's prog, Citizenship assistance, Computer training, Computers for patron use, Electronic databases & coll, Free DVD rentals, Genealogy discussion group, Holiday prog, ILL available, Internet access, Magazines, Meeting rooms, Movies,

Music CDs, Online cat, Outreach serv, OverDrive digital audio bks, Photocopying/Printing, Preschool outreach, Preschool reading prog, Prog for adults, Prog for children & young adult, Ref & res, Ref serv available, Res assist avail, Scanner, Spanish lang bks, Story hour, Study rm, Summer & winter reading prog, Summer reading prog, Tax forms, Teen prog, Winter reading prog, Workshops
Partic in Partners Library Action Network
Open Mon, Wed & Fri 10-6, Tues & Thurs 10-8, Sat 10-2
Friends of the Library Group
Bookmobiles: 1

IDALOU

P IDALOU COMMUNITY LIBRARY, 210 Main St, 79329. (Mail add: PO Box 138, 79329-0138), SAN 376-4257. Tel: 806-892-2114. FAX: 806-892-2284. E-mail: library@cityofidalou.com. Web Site: idaloutx.com/departments/library. *Dir,* Ester Espinoza
Library Holdings: Audiobooks 50; AV Mats 4; CDs 50; e-books 3,029; Electronic Media & Resources 9; Large Print Bks 343; Bk Titles 13,201
Automation Activity & Vendor Info: (Cataloging) Follett Software; (Circulation) Follett Software; (OPAC) Follett Software
Open Mon-Fri 12-5

IMPERIAL

P IMPERIAL PUBLIC LIBRARY, 222 W Hwy 11, 79743. (Mail add: PO Box 307, 79743-0307), SAN 376-4370. Tel: 432-536-2236. FAX: 432-536-2211. E-mail: imperialpubliclibrary@yahoo.com. Web Site: imperial.ploud.net. *Dir,* Wanda Lewis
Pop 1,605
Library Holdings: Audiobooks 240; DVDs 1,561; Bk Titles 19,161; Bk Vols 20,962; Per Subs 29
Automation Activity & Vendor Info: (Cataloging) Book Systems; (Circulation) Book Systems; (ILL) OCLC WorldShare Interlibrary Loan; (OPAC) Book Systems
Wireless access
Open Mon-Thurs 8-6

INDUSTRY

P INDUSTRY PUBLIC LIBRARY*, West End Public Library, 1646 N Main St, 78944. (Mail add: PO Box 179, 78944-0179). Tel: 979-357-4434. FAX: 979-357-4470. E-mail: staffwe@industryinet.com. Web Site: industry.ploud.net. *Dir & Librn,* Monika Foltz; *Asst Librn,* Andrea Nesbit
Library Holdings: AV Mats 840; Bk Titles 9,000; Talking Bks 200
Automation Activity & Vendor Info: (Cataloging) Follett Software; (Circulation) Follett Software
Wireless access
Open Mon-Thurs 8-5, Sat 8:30-12:30

INGLESIDE

P INGLESIDE PUBLIC LIBRARY*, 2775 Waco St, 78362. (Mail add: PO Drawer 400, 78362-0400), SAN 316-5159. Tel: 361-776-5355. FAX: 361-776-2264. E-mail: inglesidelibrary@inglesidetx.gov. *Dir, Libr Serv,* Belinda Cassanova; E-mail: bcasanova@inglesidetx.gov; *ILL Coordr,* Irene Rojas; E-mail: iriojas@inglesidetx.gov
Founded 1933. Pop 8,547; Circ 25,868
Library Holdings: Audiobooks 569; Bks on Deafness & Sign Lang 34; Braille Volumes 1; DVDs 4,451; Large Print Bks 399; Bk Titles 31,968; Per Subs 70
Special Collections: Municipal Libr Coll
Subject Interests: Oceanography, Texana
Wireless access
Open Mon & Thurs 8:30-6, Tues & Wed 8:30-7, Fri 8:30-5, Sat 9-4
Friends of the Library Group

IOWA PARK

P TOM BURNETT MEMORIAL LIBRARY*, 400 W Alameda St, 76367. SAN 320-5134. Tel: 940-592-4981. FAX: 940-592-4664. E-mail: library@iowapark.com. Web Site: www.iowapark.com/departments/library. *Dir,* Amie Schultz; E-mail: aschultz@iowapark.com
Founded 1962. Pop 6,535
Library Holdings: AV Mats 333; DVDs 630; Large Print Bks 500; Bk Titles 18,436; Per Subs 3; Videos 1,000
Subject Interests: Genealogy
Automation Activity & Vendor Info: (Cataloging) Book Systems; (Circulation) Book Systems; (OPAC) Book Systems
Wireless access
Open Mon-Thurs 9-8, Fri 9-5, Sat 9-2

IRAAN

P IRAAN PUBLIC LIBRARY*, 120 W Fifth St, 79744. (Mail add: PO Box 638, 79744-0638), SAN 316-5167. Tel: 432-639-2235. FAX: 432-639-2276. E-mail: iraanlibrary@yahoo.com. Web Site: iraan.ploud.net. *Librn,* Minnie Quintero
Founded 1950. Pop 1,500
Library Holdings: Bk Titles 15,900; Per Subs 26
Automation Activity & Vendor Info: (Cataloging) Book Systems; (Circulation) Book Systems; (OPAC) Book Systems
Wireless access
Open Mon-Thurs 9-5, Fri 8-4

IRVING

J DALLAS COLLEGE*, North Lake Campus Library, 5001 N MacArthur Blvd, 75062. SAN 324-2064. Tel: 972-273-3400. Reference Tel: 972-273-3401. FAX: 972-273-3431. E-mail: ncllibrary@dcccd.edu. Web Site: www.northlakecollege.edu/services/academic-support/library. *Head Librn,* Dr Enrique Chamberlain; E-mail: echamberlain@dcccd.edu; *Librn,* Jane Bell; E-mail: janebell@dcccd.edu; *Librn,* Olga Murr; *Librn,* Lina Rinh; E-mail: lrinh@dcccd.edu; *Librn,* Brittany Schick
Library Holdings: Bk Vols 50,000; Per Subs 325
Automation Activity & Vendor Info: (Cataloging) Innovative Interfaces, Inc; (Circulation) Innovative Interfaces, Inc; (OPAC) Innovative Interfaces, Inc
Wireless access
Open Mon-Thurs 8am-9pm, Fri 8-4, Sat 9-1

P IRVING PUBLIC LIBRARY*, Administrative Offices & Archives, 801 W Irving Blvd, 75015. (Mail add: PO Box 152288, 75015-2288), SAN 362-0670. Circulation Tel: 972-721-2440. Interlibrary Loan Service Tel: 972-721-4629. Administration Tel: 972-721-2628. Circulation FAX: 972-721-2491. Interlibrary Loan Service FAX: 972-721-4771. Web Site: www.cityofirving.org/library. *Dir,* Lynette Roberson; E-mail: lroberson@cityofirving.org; *Sr Library Services Mgr; Community & Colls,* Corine Barberena; Tel: 972-721-2439, Fax: 972-721-2329, E-mail: cbarberena@cityofirving.org; *Sr Library Services Mgr; Operations & Customer Service,* Ben Toon; *Sr Archivist,* Kevin Kendro; Tel: 972-721-3729, E-mail: kkendro@cityofirving.org; Staff 81 (MLS 22, Non-MLS 59)
Founded 1961. Pop 201,950; Circ 1,377,286
Library Holdings: AV Mats 343,118; Bk Titles 253,320; Bk Vols 531,380; Per Subs 1,089; Talking Bks 31,808; Videos 36,067
Subject Interests: Genealogy, Local hist
Automation Activity & Vendor Info: (Acquisitions) SirsiDynix; (Cataloging) SirsiDynix; (Circulation) SirsiDynix; (Course Reserve) SirsiDynix; (ILL) OCLC ILLiad; (OPAC) SirsiDynix; (Serials) SirsiDynix
Wireless access
Function: Adult bk club, Adult literacy prog, After school storytime, Archival coll, Bilingual assistance for Spanish patrons, Bks on cassette, Bks on CD, CD-ROM, Children's prog, Computer training, Computers for patron use, Electronic databases & coll, Free DVD rentals, ILL available, Internet access, Music CDs, Online cat, OverDrive digital audio bks, Photocopying/Printing, Prog for adults, Prog for children & young adult, Story hour, Summer reading prog, Tax forms, Teen prog, Telephone ref, VHS videos, Wheelchair accessible
Partic in Amigos Library Services, Inc; OCLC Online Computer Library Center, Inc; Partners Library Action Network; TexSHARE - Texas State Library & Archives Commission
Open Mon-Fri 8-5
Friends of the Library Group
Branches: 4
EAST LIBRARY & LEARNING CENTER, 440 S Nursery Rd, 75060. (Mail add: PO Box 152288, 75015-2288). Tel: 972-721-3722. FAX: 972-721-3724. *Sr Libr Mgr,* Ben Toon; E-mail: btoon@cityofirving.org; Staff 2 (MLS 2)
Circ 61,964
Library Holdings: Bk Vols 21,212
Subject Interests: Mat in Spanish
Open Mon-Thurs 3-7
Friends of the Library Group
SOUTH IRVING LIBRARY, 601 Schulze Dr, 75060. Tel: 972-721-2606. *Br Mgr,* Amanda Hipp; E-mail: ahipp@cityofirving.org
Open Mon-Thurs 10-9, Fri & Sat 10-6
Friends of the Library Group
VALLEY RANCH LIBRARY, 401 Cimmaron Trail, 75063-4680. (Mail add: PO Box 152288, 75015-2288), SAN 376-950X. Tel: 972-721-4669. FAX: 972-831-0672. *Br Mgr,* Roberto Salinas; E-mail: rxsalinas@cityofirving.org; Staff 3 (MLS 3)
Circ 284,643
Library Holdings: Bk Vols 71,788
Open Mon-Thurs 10-9, Fri & Sat 10-6
Friends of the Library Group

WEST IRVING LIBRARY, 4444 W Rochelle Rd, 75062. (Mail add: PO Box 152288, 75015-2288), SAN 362-0700. Tel: 972-721-2691. FAX: 972-721-3637. *Br Mgr,* Roberto Salinas; E-mail: rxsalinas@cityofirving.org; Staff 2 (MLS 2)
Circ 156,232
Library Holdings: Bk Vols 57,042
Open Mon, Wed, Fri & Sat 10-6, Tues & Thurs 12-9, Sun 1-5
Friends of the Library Group
Bookmobiles: 1. Mgr, Deborah Vaden. Bk titles 7,017

CR UNIVERSITY OF DALLAS*, Cowan-Blakley Memorial Library, 1845 E Northgate Dr, 75062-4736. SAN 316-5175. Tel: 972-721-5328. Circulation Tel: 972-721-5329. Interlibrary Loan Service Tel: 972-721-5057. Reference Tel: 972-721-5315. Automation Services Tel: 972-721-5040. FAX: 972-721-4010. Web Site: www.udallas.edu/library. *Dean, Univ Libr, Res,* Cherie Hohertz; E-mail: chohertz@udallas.edu; *Head, Cat,* Lely White; Tel: 972-721-5310, E-mail: lely@udallas.edu; *Head, Ref Serv,* Elizabeth Barksdale; Tel: 972-721-5350, E-mail: ebarksdale@udallas.edu; *Ref Librn,* Susannah Bingham Buck; Tel: 972-721-5075, E-mail: sbuck@udallas.edu; *Cat Librn,* Kristie Powell; Tel: 972-721-4031, E-mail: kpowell@udallas.edu; *Instrul Serv Librn, Outreach Librn,* Lauren Younger; Tel: 972-721-4128, E-mail: lyounger@udallas.edu; *Access Serv, Syst Librn,* Charlotte Vandervoort; Tel: 972-721-5282, E-mail: cvandervoort@udallas.edu; *Acq, Supvr,* Deborah Hathaway; Tel: 972-721-4122, E-mail: dhathaw@udallas.edu; *ILL Coordr,* Elizabeth Belyeu; E-mail: lbelyeu@udallas.edu; *Univ Archivist,* Shelley Gayler-Smith; Tel: 972-721-5397, E-mail: sgayler@udallas.edu; *Ser,* Susan Vaughan; Tel: 972-721-4130, E-mail: svaughan@udallas.edu. Subject Specialists: *Bus, Music,* Cherie Hohertz; *German studies,* Lely White; *English, Spanish,* Elizabeth Barksdale; *Hist,* Susannah Bingham Buck; *Intercultural studies, Sociol,* Lauren Younger; *English,* Charlotte Vandervoort; *Bus, Human relations,* Deborah Hathaway; *Archives, Rare bks, Spec coll,* Shelley Gayler-Smith; *Bus, Hist,* Susan Vaughan; Staff 16 (MLS 10, Non-MLS 6)
Founded 1956. Enrl 2,548; Fac 139; Highest Degree: Doctorate
Jun 2019-May 2020. Mats Exp $737,441, Books $117,535, Per/Ser (Incl. Access Fees) $262,453, Electronic Ref Mat (Incl. Access Fees) $356,387, Presv $1,066. Sal $769,090 (Prof $717,623)
Library Holdings: CDs 1,365; DVDs 273; e-books 226,775; e-journals 105; Electronic Media & Resources 2,865; Microforms 75,404; Bk Titles 177,924; Bk Vols 224,871; Per Subs 472; Videos 881
Special Collections: Index Thomisticus; Jacques Migne; Kendall Memorial Library Coll; Louise & Donald Cowan Coll; Patrologiae Cursus Completus, micro
Subject Interests: Bus mgt, Liberal arts, Philos, Polit sci, Theol
Automation Activity & Vendor Info: (Acquisitions) SirsiDynix; (Cataloging) SirsiDynix; (Circulation) SirsiDynix; (Course Reserve) SirsiDynix; (ILL) OCLC ILLiad; (OPAC) SirsiDynix; (Serials) SirsiDynix
Wireless access
Function: Distance learning, Doc delivery serv, For res purposes, ILL available, Ref serv available, Telephone ref
Partic in Amigos Library Services, Inc; OCLC Online Computer Library Center, Inc; Statewide California Electronic Library Consortium; TexSHARE - Texas State Library & Archives Commission
Open Mon-Thurs 8am-Midnight, Fri 8am-10pm, Sat 9-6, Sun 1-Midnight
Restriction: Open to students, fac & staff

CM UNIVERSITY OF ST AUGUSTINE FOR HEALTH SCIENCES*, Dallas Campus Library, 5010 Riverside Dr, 75039. Tel: 469-498-5705. E-mail: library@usa.edu. Web Site: library.usa.edu. *Librn,* Esther Garcia; E-mail: egarcia2@usa.edu
Wireless access
Function: ILL available, Photocopying/Printing, Scanner
Open Mon-Thurs, Sat & Sun 7am-10pm, Fri 7am-9pm

ITALY

P S M DUNLAP MEMORIAL LIBRARY*, 300 W Main St, 76651. SAN 316-5183. Tel: 972-483-6481. E-mail: dunlaplibrary@hotmail.com. Web Site: ci.italy.tx.us/community/library. *Librn,* Lou Ann Wolaver
Pop 2,400
Library Holdings: Bk Vols 7,200
Automation Activity & Vendor Info: (Cataloging) Biblionix
Wireless access
Open Tues-Sat 9-5

JACKSBORO

P GLADYS JOHNSON RITCHIE PUBLIC LIBRARY*, 626 W College St, 76458-1655. SAN 376-4656. Tel: 940-567-2240. FAX: 940-567-2240. *Librn,* Lanora Joslin; E-mail: ljoslin.gjlib@att.net
Pop 8,981; Circ 57,757
Library Holdings: Bk Vols 25,549; Per Subs 14
Automation Activity & Vendor Info: (Cataloging) Biblionix/Apollo; (Circulation) Biblionix/Apollo; (OPAC) Biblionix/Apollo
Wireless access
Open Mon-Fri 9-6, Sat 9-12
Friends of the Library Group

JACKSONVILLE

R BAPTIST MISSIONARY ASSOCIATION THEOLOGICAL SEMINARY, Kellar Library, 1530 E Pine St, 75766-5407. (Mail add: PO Box 670, 75766-0670), SAN 316-5191. Tel: 903-586-2501, Ext 215, 903-586-2501, Ext 216. Information Services Tel: 903-586-2501. Toll Free Tel: 800-259-5673. FAX: 903-586-0378. E-mail: bmats@bmats.edu. Web Site: www.bmats.edu. *Dir,* Phillip Waddell; E-mail: phillip.waddell@bmats.edu; Staff 2 (MLS 1, Non-MLS 1)
Founded 1957. Enrl 73; Fac 10; Highest Degree: Master
Library Holdings: AV Mats 9,543; CDs 897; DVDs 5,126; e-books 31,000; e-journals 15; Electronic Media & Resources 31,838; Microforms 1,415; Bk Titles 72,900; Bk Vols 88,000; Per Subs 40; Videos 936
Special Collections: Annuals of Baptist Yearly Meetings, bks, micro
Subject Interests: Hist, Relig studies
Wireless access
Function: 24/7 Electronic res, 24/7 Online cat, Archival coll, Computers for patron use, ILL available, Internet access, Laminating, Microfiche/film & reading machines, Notary serv, Photocopying/Printing, Ref & res, Scanner
Partic in American Theological Library Association; Association of Christian Librarians; Christian Library Consortium
Open Mon, Tues & Thurs 7:45am-9pm, Wed & Fri 7:45-4:45, Sat 9-1
Restriction: Fee for pub use, Free to mem, In-house use for visitors

P JACKSONVILLE PUBLIC LIBRARY*, 526 E Commerce St, 75766. SAN 316-5213. Tel: 903-586-7664. Administration Tel: 903-339-3320. E-mail: library@jacksonvilletx.org. Web Site: jacksonvilletx.org/417/jacksonville-public-library. *Libr Dir,* Trina Stidham; E-mail: trina.stidham@jacksonvilletx.org; *Circ Supvr,* Susan LeAnn Blake; E-mail: susan.blake@jacksonvilletx.org; *Coll Coordr,* Jamie Dorsey; E-mail: jamie.dorsey@jacksonvilletx.org; *Ch Serv,* Geraly Turner; E-mail: geraly.turner@jacksonvilletx.org; Staff 4 (Non-MLS 4)
Founded 1913. Pop 13,553; Circ 82,303
Library Holdings: Bk Vols 58,321; Per Subs 105
Special Collections: Cake Pans; The Vanishing Texana Museum, antiquities, curiosities, ephemera
Subject Interests: Cherokee County, Tex
Automation Activity & Vendor Info: (Circulation) Book Systems
Wireless access
Publications: Jacksonville In Sesquicentennial Retrospection 1872-2022 (Local historical information)
Open Mon & Thurs Noon-8, Tues, Wed & Fri 9-6, Sat 10-2, Sun 1-5
Friends of the Library Group

JASPER

P JASPER PUBLIC LIBRARY*, 175 E Water St, 75951. SAN 316-5248. Tel: 409-384-3791. FAX: 409-384-5881. Web Site: www.jaspertx.org/page/library_home. *Dir,* Denise Milton; E-mail: dmilton@jaspertx.org; Staff 5 (MLS 1, Non-MLS 4)
Founded 1936. Pop 7,838
Library Holdings: Bks on Deafness & Sign Lang 10; Large Print Bks 1,008; Bk Titles 32,420; Bk Vols 35,486; Per Subs 69; Talking Bks 1,425
Automation Activity & Vendor Info: (Circulation) ComPanion Corp; (OPAC) ComPanion Corp; (Serials) EBSCO Online
Wireless access
Partic in Partners Library Action Network
Special Services for the Blind - Bks on cassette; Bks on CD
Open Mon-Fri 10-6, Sat 10-5
Friends of the Library Group

JAYTON

P KENT COUNTY LIBRARY*, 156 W Fourth St, 79528. (Mail add: PO Box 28, 79528-0028), SAN 316-5256. Tel: 806-237-3287. FAX: 806-237-2511. E-mail: klibrary@caprock-spur.com. Web Site: kent.ploud.net. *Dir,* Dana Brinkman; Staff 1 (MLS 1)
Founded 1961. Pop 1,110; Circ 5,179
Library Holdings: Bk Vols 25,000
Wireless access
Open Mon-Fri 9-5

JEFFERSON

P JEFFERSON CARNEGIE LIBRARY*, 301 W Lafayette, 75657. SAN 316-5264. Tel: 903-665-8911. FAX: 903-665-8911. E-mail: carnegielibrary@sbcglobal.net. Web Site: www.jeffersoncarnegielibrary.com. *Dir,* Peter Kuchta; Staff 2 (MLS 1, Non-MLS 1)
Founded 1907. Pop 9,000; Circ 12,000

Library Holdings: CDs 88; Large Print Bks 549; Bk Titles 12,116; Per Subs 2; Talking Bks 918; Videos 478
Automation Activity & Vendor Info: (Acquisitions) Book Systems; (Cataloging) Book Systems; (Circulation) Book Systems; (ILL) OCLC FirstSearch; (OPAC) Book Systems
Wireless access
Open Mon-Thurs 10-6, Fri 10-5, Sat 10-3
Friends of the Library Group

JOHNSON CITY

P JOHNSON CITY LIBRARY DISTRICT*, 501 Nugent Ave, 78636. (Mail add: PO Box 332, 78636-0332), SAN 316-5272. Tel: 830-868-4469. E-mail: johnsoncitylibrary@verizon.net. Web Site: www.jclibrarysite.org. *Dir,* Maggie Goodman; Staff 1 (Non-MLS 1)
Founded 1940. Pop 2,500; Circ 9,109
Library Holdings: Bk Titles 14,000; Per Subs 15
Special Collections: L B Johnson Coll; Texana; Texas Authors
Automation Activity & Vendor Info: (Cataloging) Follett Software; (Circulation) Follett Software
Wireless access
Partic in Partners Library Action Network; TexSHARE - Texas State Library & Archives Commission
Open Mon-Fri 9-7, Sat 9-2
Friends of the Library Group

G NATIONAL PARK SERVICE, Lyndon B Johnson National Historical Park, 100 Lady Bird Lane, 78636. (Mail add: PO Box 329, 78636-0329), SAN 316-5280. Tel: 830-868-7128. FAX: 830-868-7863. Web Site: www.nps.gov/lyjo. *Interim Superintendent,* Christine Jacobs
Founded 1975
Library Holdings: Bk Titles 3,000; Per Subs 29
Special Collections: Oral History
Subject Interests: Hill County hist, Life, Natural hist subjects, Tex frontier, Times of Lyndon B Johnson
Restriction: Non-circulating to the pub, Open to pub by appt only, Open to researchers by request

JONESTOWN

P JONESTOWN COMMUNITY LIBRARY*, 18649 FM 1431, Ste 10A, 78645. SAN 376-4850. Tel: 512-267-7511. FAX: 512-267-2013. E-mail: library@jonestown.org. Web Site: www.jonestown.org/library. *Dir,* Galen Hodges; *Libr Asst,* Mary Jo Zabaly; Staff 2 (MLS 1, Non-MLS 1)
Founded 1991. Pop 2,105
Library Holdings: AV Mats 324; High Interest/Low Vocabulary Bk Vols 450; Bk Vols 10,803; Per Subs 10; Videos 324
Automation Activity & Vendor Info: (Cataloging) Biblionix; (Circulation) Biblionix
Wireless access
Partic in Partners Library Action Network
Open Mon, Wed & Fri 9-6, Tues & Thurs 9-8, Sat 9-1
Friends of the Library Group

JOSHUA

P JOSHUA SCHOOL & PUBLIC LIBRARY*, 907 S Broadway, 76058. Tel: 817-202-2547. FAX: 817-202-9134. E-mail: joshualibrary@joshuaisd.org. Web Site: www.joshualibrary.org. *Librn,* Sheila Carter
Circ 19,321
Library Holdings: AV Mats 371; DVDs 1,234; Bk Titles 31,833; Talking Bks 371
Automation Activity & Vendor Info: (Cataloging) ComPanion Corp; (Circulation) ComPanion Corp; (ILL) ComPanion Corp; (OPAC) ComPanion Corp
Wireless access
Open Mon-Fri 10-6, Sat 10-2
Friends of the Library Group

JOURDANTON

P JOURDANTON COMMUNITY LIBRARY*, 1101 Campbell Ave, 78026. SAN 316-5302. Tel: 830-769-3087. E-mail: jourdlib@txun.net. Web Site: jourdanton.ploud.net. *Dir,* Dorothy Manning
Founded 1976
Library Holdings: Bk Vols 25,000; Per Subs 60
Special Collections: Texana
Automation Activity & Vendor Info: (Cataloging) Follett Software; (Circulation) Follett Software
Wireless access
Partic in Partners Library Action Network
Special Services for the Deaf - Bks on deafness & sign lang; Spec interest per
Open Mon-Fri 9-6, Sat 9-1
Friends of the Library Group

JUNCTION

P KIMBLE COUNTY LIBRARY*, 208 N Tenth St, 76849. SAN 316-5310. Tel: 325-446-2342. FAX: 325-446-3615. E-mail: kimblelibrary@gmail.com. Web Site: www.kimblecountylibrary.org. *Dir,* Andrew Helton
Founded 1933. Pop 4,396; Circ 8,031
Library Holdings: Bk Vols 32,551; Per Subs 30
Subject Interests: Tex
Automation Activity & Vendor Info: (Cataloging) LibLime; (Circulation) LibLime
Wireless access
Open Mon, Tues & Thurs 9-6, Wed 9-5, Fri 9-4
Friends of the Library Group

JUSTIN

P JUSTIN COMMUNITY LIBRARY*, 408 Pafford St, 76247-9442. SAN 376-4664. Tel: 940-648-2541, Ext 6. FAX: 940-648-8423. E-mail: library@cityofjustin.com. Web Site: www.cityofjustin.com/165/Library. *Dir,* Lesa Keith
Founded 1986. Pop 4,000; Circ 3,500
Library Holdings: Audiobooks 301; Bks on Deafness & Sign Lang 10; DVDs 696; Large Print Bks 200; Bk Titles 16,200; Videos 1,386
Automation Activity & Vendor Info: (Cataloging) Evergreen; (Circulation) Evergreen
Wireless access
Function: Bks on cassette, Bks on CD, Children's prog, Computers for patron use, Free DVD rentals, ILL available, Photocopying/Printing, Scanner, Story hour, Summer reading prog, Tax forms, VHS videos, Wheelchair accessible
Open Mon-Wed 12-7
Restriction: Non-circulating coll
Friends of the Library Group

KARNES CITY

P KARNES CITY PUBLIC LIBRARY*, 302 S Panna Maria Ave, 78118. SAN 316-5329. Tel: 830-780-2539. E-mail: kclibrary@sbcglobal.net. Web Site: karnes-city.ploud.net. *Dir,* Amy McCarley
Founded 1972. Pop 4,623; Circ 48,655
Library Holdings: Bk Titles 18,540; Per Subs 25
Automation Activity & Vendor Info: (Cataloging) Follett Software; (Circulation) Follett Software
Wireless access
Mem of Karnes County Library System
Open Mon-Fri 9-5:30

KAUFMAN

P KAUFMAN COUNTY LIBRARY*, 3790 S Houston St, 75142. SAN 316-5345. Tel: 972-932-6222. FAX: 972-932-0681. E-mail: library@kaufmancountylibrary.net. Web Site: www.kaufmancountylibrary.net. *Dir,* Yasma Holland; E-mail: yholland@kaufmancountylibrary.net; Staff 3 (MLS 1, Non-MLS 2)
Founded 1970. Pop 12,000; Circ 21,000
Library Holdings: Bk Titles 44,000; Per Subs 22
Automation Activity & Vendor Info: (Cataloging) Brodart; (Circulation) Brodart
Wireless access
Partic in Partners Library Action Network
Open Mon, Tues & Thurs 10-6, Wed 10-5, Fri 10-4, Sat 9-1
Friends of the Library Group

KEENE

CR SOUTHWESTERN ADVENTIST UNIVERSITY*, Chan Shun Centennial Library, 101 W Magnolia St, 76059. SAN 316-5353. Tel: 817-202-6242. FAX: 817-556-4722. Web Site: library.swau.edu. *Libr Dir,* Cristina Thomsen; E-mail: thomsenc@swau.edu; *Pub Serv Librn,* Tony Zbaraschuk; Tel: 817-202-6480, E-mail: tony.z@swau.edu; *Coordr, Tech Serv,* Joseph Alway; Tel: 817-202-6603, E-mail: jalway@swau.edu; Staff 5 (MLS 3, Non-MLS 2)
Founded 1894. Enrl 900; Fac 60; Highest Degree: Master
Library Holdings: AV Mats 1,900; Bk Vols 110,000; Per Subs 460
Special Collections: Seventh-day Adventist Church History
Subject Interests: Bus, Elem educ, Liberal arts, Nursing
Automation Activity & Vendor Info: (Acquisitions) TLC (The Library Corporation); (Cataloging) TLC (The Library Corporation); (Circulation) TLC (The Library Corporation); (Course Reserve) TLC (The Library Corporation); (OPAC) TLC (The Library Corporation); (Serials) EOS International
Wireless access
Partic in Adventist Librs Info Coop; Amigos Library Services, Inc
Open Mon-Thurs 7:30am-10:30pm, Fri 7:30-2, Sun Noon-10:30

KELLER

P KELLER PUBLIC LIBRARY*, 640 Johnson Rd, 76248. SAN 325-1527. Tel: 817-743-4800. FAX: 817-743-4890. Web Site: www.cityofkeller.com/library. *Dir,* Ann Flournoy; E-mail: aflournoy@cityofkeller.com; Staff 19 (MLS 5, Non-MLS 14)
Founded 1972. Pop 47,266; Circ 637,599
Library Holdings: Bk Titles 80,000; Bk Vols 82,000; Per Subs 160
Automation Activity & Vendor Info: (Discovery) Innovative Interfaces, Inc
Wireless access
Function: 24/7 Electronic res, 24/7 Online cat, Activity rm, Adult bk club, Art exhibits, Audiobks on Playaways & MP3, Audiobks via web, Bk club(s), Bks on CD, Children's prog, Computer training, Computers for patron use, E-Reserves, Electronic databases & coll, Free DVD rentals, Holiday prog, ILL available, Internet access, Magazines, Mail & tel request accepted, Meeting rooms, Movies, Music CDs, Online cat, Outside serv via phone, mail, e-mail & web, OverDrive digital audio bks, Photocopying/Printing, Prog for adults, Prog for children & young adult, Ref & res, Ref serv available, Scanner, Senior outreach, STEM programs, Story hour, Study rm, Summer reading prog, Tax forms, Teen prog, Telephone ref, Writing prog
Partic in MetroShare Libraries
Special Services for the Deaf - Bks on deafness & sign lang; Spec interest per
Special Services for the Blind - Bks on CD; Magnifiers
Open Mon-Wed 10-8, Thurs & Fri 10-6, Sat & Sun 12-5
Friends of the Library Group

KENDALIA

P KENDALIA PUBLIC LIBRARY*, 2610-B Hwy 473, 78027. (Mail add: PO Box 399, 78027), SAN 316-5361. Tel: 830-336-2002. FAX: 830-336-2002. E-mail: kendalialibrary@gvtc.com. Web Site: www.kendalialibrary.com. *Dir,* Anya Ludolf; Staff 1 (Non-MLS 1)
Founded 1961. Pop 1,802; Circ 2,695
Library Holdings: Audiobooks 457; DVDs 827; Bk Vols 9,700; Per Subs 5
Automation Activity & Vendor Info: (Cataloging) Follett Software; (Circulation) Follett Software; (OPAC) Follett Software
Wireless access
Function: Res libr
Open Mon 10-5, Wed 9-6, Fri 1-5

KENEDY

P KENEDY PUBLIC LIBRARY*, 303 W Main St, 78119. Tel: 830-583-3313. FAX: 830-583-3270. E-mail: kenedylibrary@sbcglobal.net. Web Site: www.kenedypubliclibrary.org. *Dir,* Sylvia Pena; Staff 1 (MLS 1)
Library Holdings: Bk Vols 19,000; Per Subs 25
Automation Activity & Vendor Info: (Cataloging) Biblionix; (Circulation) Biblionix
Wireless access
Mem of Karnes County Library System
Open Mon-Fri 8-5

KENNEDALE

P KENNEDALE PUBLIC LIBRARY*, 316 W Third St, 76060-2202. Tel: 817-985-2136. FAX: 817-483-0660. Web Site: www.cityofkennedale.com/412/Library. *Libr Dir,* Elizabeth Partridge; E-mail: epartridge@cityofkennedale.com
Pop 7,700
Wireless access
Open Tues-Thurs 10-8, Fri & Sat 10-5
Friends of the Library Group

KERMIT

P WINKLER COUNTY LIBRARY*, 307 S Poplar St, 79745-4300. SAN 362-0824. Tel: 432-586-3841. FAX: 432-586-2462. E-mail: wclib@hotmail.com. Web Site: kermit.ploud.net. *Dir,* Laurie Shropshire
Founded 1929. Pop 8,015
Library Holdings: Bk Vols 62,000; Per Subs 35
Automation Activity & Vendor Info: (Cataloging) LibLime; (Circulation) LibLime
Wireless access
Open Mon-Fri 8-5
Branches: 1
WINK BRANCH, 207 Roy Orbison Dr, Wink, 79789. (Mail add: PO Box 608, Wink, 79789-0608), SAN 362-0859. Tel: 432-527-3691. *Librn,* Pauline Kline
Open Mon, Tues, Thurs & Fri 12-6

KERRVILLE

P BUTT-HOLDSWORTH MEMORIAL LIBRARY*, 505 Water St, 78028. SAN 316-5396. Tel: 830-257-8422. E-mail: library.webmaster@kerrvilletx.gov. Web Site: www.kerrvilletx.gov/92/library. *Libr Dir,* Danielle Brigati; *Asst Libr Dir,* Keith Zengler; *Patron Serv Librn,* Rachael Carruthers; Staff 4 (MLS 3, Non-MLS 1)
Founded 1967. Pop 22,905
Special Collections: Texana Coll. Oral History
Automation Activity & Vendor Info: (Acquisitions) Innovative Interfaces, Inc; (Cataloging) Innovative Interfaces, Inc; (Circulation) Innovative Interfaces, Inc; (OPAC) Innovative Interfaces, Inc
Wireless access
Function: 24/7 Electronic res, 24/7 Online cat, Adult bk club, Audiobks via web, Bks on CD, Children's prog, Computers for patron use, E-Readers, Electronic databases & coll, Free DVD rentals, Holiday prog, ILL available, Internet access, Magazines, Magnifiers for reading, Meeting rooms, Microfiche/film & reading machines, Movies, Online cat, Photocopying/Printing, Preschool reading prog, Prog for adults, Prog for children & young adult, Ref serv available, Spanish lang bks, Story hour, Summer reading prog, Tax forms, Teen prog, Wheelchair accessible
Open Mon-Sat 10-6
Restriction: Non-resident fee
Friends of the Library Group

S MUSEUM OF WESTERN ART*, Research Library, 1550 Bandera Hwy, 78028-9547. SAN 370-7342. Tel: 830-896-2553. FAX: 830-257-5206. Web Site: www.museumofwesternart.com. *Exec Dir,* Darrell G Beauchamp, EdD; E-mail: dbeauchamp@mowatx.com; Staff 1 (MLS 1)
Founded 1983
Library Holdings: Bk Titles 6,000; Per Subs 10
Subject Interests: Hist of the Am West, Western art
Wireless access
Function: Res libr
Publications: Special Indexes Listing Periodical
Open Tues-Sat 10-4

C SCHREINER UNIVERSITY*, W M Logan Library, 2100 Memorial Blvd, 78028-5697. SAN 316-5418. Tel: 830-792-7312. E-mail: library@schreiner.edu. Web Site: library.schreiner.edu. *Dir,* Lisa McCormick; Tel: 830-792-7312, E-mail: LMMcCormick@schreiner.edu; Staff 4 (MLS 4)
Founded 1967. Enrl 1,013; Fac 72; Highest Degree: Master
Library Holdings: Bk Titles 120,000; Bk Vols 160,000; Per Subs 260
Special Collections: Schreiner University Coll; Texas Hill Country Coll
Subject Interests: Liberal arts
Automation Activity & Vendor Info: (Acquisitions) Ex Libris Group; (Cataloging) Ex Libris Group; (Circulation) Ex Libris Group; (Course Reserve) Ex Libris Group; (OPAC) Ex Libris Group; (Serials) Ex Libris Group
Wireless access
Function: Archival coll, Audio & video playback equip for onsite use, Computers for patron use, Electronic databases & coll, Mail & tel request accepted, Online ref, Photocopying/Printing, Ref & res, Scanner, Tax forms, Wheelchair accessible
Partic in Amigos Library Services, Inc; Coun of Res & Acad Librs; OCLC Online Computer Library Center, Inc
Open Mon-Thurs 7:30am-Midnight, Fri 7:30-4, Sat Noon-4, Sun 3-Noon (Fall & Spring); Mon-Thurs 7:30-6, Fri 7:30-4 (Summer)

KILGORE

J KILGORE COLLEGE*, Randolph C Watson Library, 1100 Broadway, 75662. SAN 316-5434. Tel: 903-983-8237. Web Site: library.kilgore.edu. *Dir,* Susan Black; Tel: 903-983-8236, E-mail: sblack@kilgore.edu; *ILL Librn, Pub Serv Librn,* Susan Wilson; Tel: 903-983-8239, E-mail: swilson@kilgore.edu; Staff 5 (MLS 1, Non-MLS 4)
Founded 1935. Enrl 5,780; Fac 336; Highest Degree: Associate
Library Holdings: e-books 107,469; e-journals 76,067; Bk Vols 45,118; Per Subs 48
Special Collections: Habenicht Texana Coll; Hill Texana Coll; Spear Coll (American & English Literature)
Automation Activity & Vendor Info: (Acquisitions) OCLC Worldshare Management Services; (Cataloging) OCLC Worldshare Management Services; (Circulation) OCLC Worldshare Management Services; (Course Reserve) OCLC Worldshare Management Services; (OPAC) OCLC Worldshare Management Services
Wireless access
Partic in Amigos Library Services, Inc; OCLC Online Computer Library Center, Inc
Friends of the Library Group

P KILGORE PUBLIC LIBRARY*, 301 Henderson Blvd, 75662-2799. SAN 362-0883. Tel: 903-984-1529. FAX: 903-218-6893. E-mail: kilgorelibrary@cityofkilgore.com. Web Site: kilgorelibrary.org. *Dir,* Stacey Cole; E-mail: stacey.cole@cityofkilgore.com; Staff 8 (MLS 1, Non-MLS 7)
Founded 1933. Pop 14,037; Circ 65,796
Library Holdings: AV Mats 1,098; Large Print Bks 1,889; Bk Vols 38,923; Per Subs 79; Talking Bks 1,758
Automation Activity & Vendor Info: (Cataloging) Book Systems; (Circulation) Book Systems
Wireless access
Function: 24/7 Online cat, After school storytime, Audiobks on Playaways & MP3, Audiobks via web, Bks on CD, Children's prog, Computers for patron use, E-Readers, Electronic databases & coll, Free DVD rentals, Holiday prog, ILL available, Internet access, Magazines, Mango lang, Online cat, Online ref, Photocopying/Printing, Prog for adults, Prog for children & young adult, Ref & res, Res assist avail, Scanner, Story hour, Study rm, Summer reading prog, Tax forms, Teen prog, Telephone ref, Wheelchair accessible
Partic in TexSHARE - Texas State Library & Archives Commission
Open Mon-Fri 9-6
Friends of the Library Group

KILLEEN

J CENTRAL TEXAS COLLEGE*, Oveta Culp Hobby Memorial Library, Bldg 102, 6200 W Central Texas Expressway, 76549. (Mail add: PO Box 1800, 76540-1800), SAN 316-5469. Tel: 254-526-1237. Circulation Tel: 254-526-1621. Reference Tel: 254-526-1871. Toll Free Tel: 800-223-4760, Ext 1237 (Instate), 800-792-3348, Ext 1237 (Out of state). FAX: 254-526-1878. E-mail: ReferenceRequest@ctcd.edu. Web Site: www.ctcd.edu/academics/library. *Dean & Dir, Libr Serv,* Lori Purser; Tel: 254-526-1486, E-mail: lori.purser@ctcd.edu; *Asst Admin,* Martha Tipton; Tel: 254-526-1474, E-mail: martha.tipton@ctcd.edu; *Outreach Librn, Ref Librn,* Cynthia Oser; Tel: 254-526-1475, E-mail: coser2@ctcd.edu; *Syst Librn,* Ashley Garcia; Tel: 254-616-3310, E-mail: AGarcia2@ctcd.edu; *Virtual Librn,* Margaret Handrow; Tel: 254-526-1619, E-mail: margaret.handrow@ctcd.edu; *Tech Serv Supvr,* Kelly Williams; Tel: 254-616-3307, E-mail: kwilliams3@ctcd.edu; Staff 21 (MLS 5, Non-MLS 16)
Founded 1967. Enrl 5,890; Fac 332; Highest Degree: Associate
Library Holdings: e-books 181,000; Bk Vols 45,000; Per Subs 121
Subject Interests: Educ, Law
Automation Activity & Vendor Info: (Cataloging) OCLC Worldshare Management Services; (Circulation) OCLC Worldshare Management Services; (ILL) OCLC WorldShare Interlibrary Loan; (OPAC) OCLC Worldshare Management Services; (Serials) OCLC Worldshare Management Services
Wireless access
Partic in Amigos Library Services, Inc
Special Services for the Deaf - ADA equip
Special Services for the Blind - Internet workstation with adaptive software; Reader equip; ZoomText magnification & reading software
Open Mon-Thurs 7:30am-10pm, Fri 7:30-7:30, Sat & Sun 12:30-7:30

P KILLEEN PUBLIC LIBRARY*, 205 E Church Ave, 76541. SAN 316-5477. Tel: 254-501-8990. Circulation Tel: 254-501-8996. Interlibrary Loan Service Tel: 254-501-8808. Reference Tel: 254-501-8991. Administration Tel: 254-501-8994. FAX: 254-501-7704. E-mail: library@killeentexas.gov. Web Site: killeentexas.gov/171/libraries, portal.killeentexas.gov. *Dir,* Deanna A Frazee; Tel: 254-501-8995, E-mail: dfrazee@killeentexas.gov; *Cat Librn,* Kenneth Gober; E-mail: kgober@killeentexas.gov; *Ch Serv Librn,* Amy Gibson; E-mail: agibson@killeentexas.gov; *Programming Librn,* Katie Loucks; Tel: 254-501-7882, E-mail: kloucks@killeentexas.gov; *Circ Supvr,* Debbie Eubanks; E-mail: deubanks@killeentexas.gov; *Circ Supvr,* Annie Lowe; E-mail: hlowe@killeentexas.gov; *Libr Spec, Ill & Tech Serv,* Louisa Hassan; E-mail: lhassan@killeentexas.gov; Staff 5 (MLS 5)
Founded 1958
Subject Interests: Automotive repair, Ch, County hist, Genealogy, Local hist, Mechanics, Texana
Automation Activity & Vendor Info: (Cataloging) Evergreen; (Circulation) Evergreen; (OPAC) Evergreen
Wireless access
Function: 24/7 Electronic res, 24/7 Online cat, 3D Printer, Adult bk club, Bks on CD, Children's prog, Computers for patron use, Digital talking bks, Electronic databases & coll, Free DVD rentals, Holiday prog, ILL available, Internet access, Magazines, Makerspace, Online cat, Ref serv available, Spanish lang bks, Story hour, Summer reading prog
Partic in Partners Library Action Network
Open Mon & Wed 9:30-6, Tues & Thurs 9:30-7, Fri & Sat 10-6
Restriction: In-house use for visitors, Non-circulating coll, Open to pub for ref & circ; with some limitations
Friends of the Library Group

C TEXAS A&M UNIVERSITY CENTRAL TEXAS*, Warrior Hall University Library, 1001 Leadership Pl, 76549. SAN 316-5450. Tel: 254-519-5798. Administration Tel: 254-519-5484. FAX: 254-519-5417. E-mail: library@tamuct.edu. Web Site: tamuct.libguides.com/c.php?g=182954. *Dir of the Univ Libr,* Bridgit McCafferty; E-mail: bmccaffe@tamuct.edu; Staff 6 (MLS 2, Non-MLS 4)
Founded 1973. Enrl 1,879; Fac 60; Highest Degree: Master
Library Holdings: AV Mats 1,161; Bk Titles 32,455; Bk Vols 35,666; Per Subs 58
Special Collections: Crime & Juvenile Delinquency, micro; Energy Management (Solar Energy), docs
Automation Activity & Vendor Info: (Acquisitions) SirsiDynix; (Cataloging) SirsiDynix; (Circulation) SirsiDynix; (Course Reserve) SirsiDynix; (ILL) OCLC ILLiad; (Media Booking) SirsiDynix; (OPAC) SirsiDynix; (Serials) SirsiDynix
Wireless access
Function: Archival coll, Art exhibits, Audio & video playback equip for onsite use, AV serv, Bks on cassette, CD-ROM, Computers for patron use, Distance learning, Doc delivery serv, E-Reserves, Electronic databases & coll, Equip loans & repairs, ILL available, Instruction & testing, Internet access, Large print keyboards, Mail & tel request accepted, Mail loans to mem, Music CDs, Online cat, Online info literacy tutorials on the web & in blackboard, Online ref, Orientations, Outside serv via phone, mail, e-mail & web, Photocopying/Printing, Ref & res, Tax forms, Telephone ref, VHS videos, Wheelchair accessible
Partic in Amigos Library Services, Inc
Open Mon-Thurs 7:30am-9:30pm, Fri 7:30-4:30, Sat 11-5, Sun 1-8

KINGSVILLE

J COASTAL BEND COLLEGE, Kingsville Campus Library, 1814 S Brahma Blvd, Rm 135A, 78363. Tel: 361-592-1615, Ext 4084. E-mail: library@coastalbend.edu. Web Site: www.coastalbend.edu/sites/kingsville. *Dir,* Tammy Rands; Tel: 361-354-2741, E-mail: trands@coastalbend.edu; *Libr Asst,* Jo Ann De Leon
Library Holdings: Bk Vols 500
Automation Activity & Vendor Info: (Acquisitions) Koha; (Cataloging) Koha; (Circulation) Koha; (Course Reserve) Koha; (ILL) Koha; (OPAC) Koha; (Serials) Koha
Wireless access
Open Mon-Fri 8-5

P ROBERT J KLEBERG PUBLIC LIBRARY*, 220 N Fourth St, 78363. SAN 316-5493. Tel: 361-592-6381. Web Site: www.kleberglibrary.com. *Dir,* Robert Rodriguez; E-mail: kpldirector@kleberglibrary.com; *Asst Admin,* Ruth Valdez; *Acq,* Hector Vela; *Ch Serv,* Danielle Friend; *Circ,* Andrea Vidaurri; *Ref (Info Servs),* Mary Ann Escamilla; Staff 6 (MLS 1, Non-MLS 5)
Founded 1907. Pop 32,513; Circ 33,697
Library Holdings: AV Mats 554; Bks on Deafness & Sign Lang 22; e-books 1,557; Bk Titles 46,291; Bk Vols 53,596; Per Subs 93; Videos 83
Special Collections: Genealogy Reference; Texas Reference
Automation Activity & Vendor Info: (Cataloging) TLC (The Library Corporation); (Circulation) TLC (The Library Corporation); (OPAC) TLC (The Library Corporation)
Wireless access
Partic in Partners Library Action Network
Open Tues-Fri 8-6, Sat 9-1
Friends of the Library Group

C TEXAS A&M UNIVERSITY-KINGSVILLE, James C Jernigan Library, 1050 University Blvd, MSC 197, 78363. (Mail add: 700 University Blvd, MSC 197, 78363-8202), SAN 316-5507. Tel: 361-593-3319. Circulation Tel: 361-593-3408. Interlibrary Loan Service Tel: 361-593-2109, 361-593-3500. Administration Tel: 361-593-3416. FAX: 361-593-4093. Web Site: lib.tamuk.edu. *Libr Dir,* Christine Radcliff; E-mail: christine.radcliff@tamuk.edu; *Head, Tech Serv,* Samantha Villalobos; E-mail: samantha.villalobos@tamuk.edu; *Admin Coordr,* Sylvia Martinez; Tel: 361-593-4029, E-mail: sylvia.martinez@tamuk.edu
Founded 1925. Enrl 6,130; Fac 225; Highest Degree: Doctorate
Library Holdings: e-journals 13,700; Bk Vols 681,013; Per Subs 1,400
Special Collections: Bilingual Education Coll; Botany (Runyon Coll); Western Americana (McGill Coll). Oral History; State Document Depository; UN Document Depository; US Document Depository
Automation Activity & Vendor Info: (Acquisitions) Innovative Interfaces, Inc; (Cataloging) Innovative Interfaces, Inc; (Circulation) Innovative Interfaces, Inc; (Course Reserve) Innovative Interfaces, Inc; (ILL) Innovative Interfaces, Inc; (Media Booking) Innovative Interfaces, Inc; (OPAC) Innovative Interfaces, Inc; (Serials) Innovative Interfaces, Inc
Wireless access
Partic in Amigos Library Services, Inc; OCLC Online Computer Library Center, Inc
Open Mon-Thurs 7am-1am, Fri 7am-10pm, Sat Noon-6, Sun 1pm-1am (Fall-Winter); Mon-Thurs 7am-10pm, Fri 7-5, Sat Noon-5, Sun 3-10 (Summer)

A UNITED STATES NAVY*, Naval Air Station Library, 601 Nimitz Ave, Bldg 3766, 78363. SAN 362-0948. Tel: 361-516-6449. FAX: 361-516-6971. Web Site: www.navymwrkingsville.com. *Librn,* Patricia Villarreal; E-mail: patricia.i.villarreal.nas@us.navy.mil; *Mgr,* Daniel Callahan
Founded 1943
Library Holdings: Bk Vols 13,000; Per Subs 34
Special Collections: Military History Coll
Automation Activity & Vendor Info: (Cataloging) Bibliovation; (Circulation) Bibliovation
Restriction: Not open to pub, Staff use only

KIRBYVILLE

P KIRBYVILLE PUBLIC LIBRARY*, 210 S Elizabeth St, 75956. (Mail add: PO Box 567, 75956-0567), SAN 316-5515. Tel: 409-423-4653. FAX: 409-423-5545. E-mail: kirbyvillelibrary@sbcglobal.net. Web Site: www.kirbyvillelibrary.org. *Dir,* Sherri Fussell; *Asst Librn,* Melanie Sutton; *Circ Librn,* Sandra Caulkins; *Coll Librn,* Melissa Booker; Staff 4 (Non-MLS 4)
Founded 1937. Pop 4,295; Circ 13,582
Library Holdings: Bk Titles 18,000; Bk Vols 19,000; Per Subs 39
Automation Activity & Vendor Info: (Acquisitions) Surpass; (Cataloging) Surpass; (Circulation) Surpass; (OPAC) Surpass
Wireless access
Function: Accelerated reader prog, Adult literacy prog, Children's prog, Mail loans to mem, Notary serv, Scanner, Serves people with intellectual disabilities, Story hour, Tax forms
Open Tues-Fri 9-6
Restriction: Borrowing requests are handled by ILL, Free to mem
Friends of the Library Group

KOUNTZE

P KOUNTZE PUBLIC LIBRARY*, 800 S Redwood Ave, 77625. SAN 316-5523. Tel: 409-246-2826. FAX: 409-246-4659. Web Site: www.kountzelibrary.org. *Libr Dir,* Tami Winger; E-mail: tami.kountzelib@gmail.com
Pop 10,000; Circ 17,668
Library Holdings: Bk Vols 18,486; Per Subs 20
Automation Activity & Vendor Info: (Cataloging) Follett Software; (Circulation) Follett Software; (OPAC) Follett Software
Wireless access
Partic in Partners Library Action Network
Open Mon 9-6, Tues-Fri 8:30-5:30, Sat 9:30-12:30
Friends of the Library Group

KRUM

P KRUM PUBLIC LIBRARY*, 815 E McCart St, 76249-6823. (Mail add: PO Box 780, 76249-0780), SAN 376-4567. Tel: 940-482-3455. FAX: 940-482-0088. E-mail: librarian@krumlibrary.org. Web Site: www.krumlibrary.org. *Libr Dir,* Donna Pierce; Staff 1 (MLS 1)
Founded 1979. Pop 6,676; Circ 22,390
Oct 2017-Sept 2018 Income $167,177, City $153,577, County $13,600. Mats Exp $9,500, Books $6,700, AV Mat $2,300, Electronic Ref Mat (Incl. Access Fees) $500. Sal $95,962 (Prof $44,344)
Library Holdings: Audiobooks 392; DVDs 1,937; Large Print Bks 2,000; Bk Titles 19,240; Per Subs 5
Automation Activity & Vendor Info: (Cataloging) Evergreen; (Circulation) Evergreen; (OPAC) Evergreen
Wireless access
Function: 24/7 Electronic res, 24/7 Online cat, Activity rm, Adult bk club, Art exhibits, Bk club(s), Bks on CD, Butterfly Garden, Children's prog, Computer training, Computers for patron use, Electronic databases & coll, Free DVD rentals, Holiday prog, ILL available, Internet access, Large print keyboards, Life-long learning prog for all ages, Magazines, Magnifiers for reading, Mail & tel request accepted, Meeting rooms, Online cat, Online info literacy tutorials on the web & in blackboard, Online ref, Photocopying/Printing, Preschool reading prog, Prog for adults, Prog for children & young adult, Ref serv available, Serves people with intellectual disabilities, Spanish lang bks, STEM programs, Story hour, Study rm, Summer reading prog, Teen prog, Telephone ref
Partic in North Texas Library Consortium; Partners Library Action Network
Special Services for the Deaf - Assistive tech
Special Services for the Blind - Assistive/Adapted tech devices, equip & products
Open Tues-Fri 10-7, Sat 10-2
Friends of the Library Group

KYLE

P KYLE PUBLIC LIBRARY*, 550 Scott St, 78640. (Mail add: PO Box 2349, 78640-2349), SAN 316-5531. Tel: 512-268-7411. FAX: 512-268-0021. Circulation E-mail: circulation@cityofkyle.com. Web Site: www.cityofkyle.com/library. *Dir, Libr Serv,* Paul Phelan; E-mail: Pphelan@cityofkyle.com; Staff 11 (MLS 3, Non-MLS 8)
Founded 1958. Pop 41,016; Circ 153,712
Library Holdings: Audiobooks 1,056; DVDs 4,612; e-books 6,928; Large Print Bks 600; Bk Titles 41,230; Bk Vols 46,026; Per Subs 52
Special Collections: Katherine Ann Porter Coll
Automation Activity & Vendor Info: (Acquisitions) Biblionix/Apollo; (Cataloging) Biblionix/Apollo; (Circulation) Biblionix/Apollo; (ILL) Biblionix/Apollo; (OPAC) Biblionix/Apollo
Wireless access
Function: 24/7 Electronic res, Activity rm, Adult bk club, After school storytime, Audiobks via web, Bilingual assistance for Spanish patrons, Bk club(s), Bks on CD, Children's prog, Computer training, Computers for patron use, Electronic databases & coll, Free DVD rentals, Holiday prog, ILL available, Internet access, Magazines, Movies, Online cat, Outreach serv, OverDrive digital audio bks, Photocopying/Printing, Prog for adults, Prog for children & young adult, Ref serv available, Scanner, Spanish lang bks, Spoken cassettes & CDs, Spoken cassettes & DVDs, Story hour, Summer reading prog, Tax forms, Teen prog, Telephone ref, VHS videos, Wheelchair accessible, Workshops
Partic in Partners Library Action Network
Open Mon-Thurs 10-8, Fri 10-6, Sat 10-4
Friends of the Library Group

LA FERIA

P BAILEY H DUNLAP MEMORIAL PUBLIC LIBRARY*, 400 S Main St, 78559. Tel: 956-797-1242. FAX: 956-797-5408. Web Site: cityoflaferia.com/departments/library. *Dir,* Lori Vogt; E-mail: lvogt78559@gmail.com
Pop 8,400; Circ 20,100
Library Holdings: Bk Vols 24,000; Per Subs 40
Automation Activity & Vendor Info: (Cataloging) SirsiDynix; (Circulation) SirsiDynix; (OPAC) SirsiDynix
Wireless access

LA GRANGE

P FAYETTE PUBLIC LIBRARY*, 855 S Jefferson St, 78945. SAN 316-5558. Tel: 979-968-3765. FAX: 979-968-5357. E-mail: library@cityoflg.com. Web Site: www.cityoflg.com/library. *Dir,* Allison MacKenzie; E-mail: amackenzie@cityoflg.com; *Circ Mgr,* Kelly Ceder-Ryba; *Youth Serv Coordr,* Carol Perales; *Archives,* Rox Ann Johnson; E-mail: rjohnson@cityoflg.com; *Archives,* Maria Rocha; E-mail: mrocha@cityoflg.com; Staff 5.5 (Non-MLS 5.5)
Pop 5,500; Circ 83,500
Library Holdings: Audiobooks 438; Bks on Deafness & Sign Lang 10; CDs 902; DVDs 3,503; Large Print Bks 440; Bk Titles 19,856; Bk Vols 20,519; Per Subs 62; Videos 3,350
Special Collections: Texana Coll
Subject Interests: Local hist archives
Automation Activity & Vendor Info: (Cataloging) Book Systems; (Circulation) Book Systems; (ILL) OCLC; (OPAC) Book Systems
Wireless access
Function: Archival coll, Art exhibits, Bks on cassette, Bks on CD, Children's prog, Computers for patron use, Free DVD rentals, ILL available, Microfiche/film & reading machines, Music CDs, Online cat, OverDrive digital audio bks, Photocopying/Printing, Preschool reading prog, Ref serv available, Story hour, Summer reading prog, Tax forms, Telephone ref, VHS videos, Wheelchair accessible
Partic in Partners Library Action Network
Open Tues & Thurs 10-6, Wed & Fri 10-5, Sat 10-1, Sun Noon-4
Friends of the Library Group

LA JOYA

P LA JOYA MUNICIPAL LIBRARY*, 201 Palm Shores Blvd, 78560. Tel: 956-581-4533. FAX: 956-580-7023. E-mail: lajoyalib@yahoo.com. Web Site: www.youseemore.com/lajoya. *Libr Dir,* Susana Villegas
Founded 1999. Pop 5,322
Library Holdings: Bk Vols 11,200; Talking Bks 23
Mem of Hidalgo County Library System
Open Mon-Thurs 9-6, Fri 9-5, Sat 9-1

LA MARQUE

P LA MARQUE PUBLIC LIBRARY*, 1011 Bayou Rd, 77568-4195. SAN 316-5566. Tel: 409-938-9270. FAX: 409-935-1112. Web Site: cityoflamarque.org/216/La-Marque-Public-Library. *Dir,* Amy Miller; E-mail: a.miller@cityoflamarque.org; *Ref Librn, Tech Serv,* Tom Hansen; E-mail: t.hansen@cityoflamarque.org; *Libr Asst,* Brittany Carreon; E-mail: b.karreon@cityoflamarque.org; Staff 4 (MLS 1, Non-MLS 3)
Founded 1946. Pop 23,691
Library Holdings: AV Mats 2,954; Bk Titles 39,962; Per Subs 50
Automation Activity & Vendor Info: (Acquisitions) Biblionix; (Cataloging) Biblionix; (Circulation) Biblionix

Wireless access
Mem of Galveston County Library System
Partic in Partners Library Action Network
Open Tues & Wed 10-6, Thurs 10-7, Fri & Sat 9-4
Friends of the Library Group

LA PORTE

S SAN JACINTO MUSEUM & BATTLEFIELD ASSOCIATION, Albert & Ethel Herzstein Library, One Monument Circle, 77571-9585. SAN 321-8155. Tel: 281-479-2421. FAX: 281-479-2428. E-mail: library@sanjacinto-museum.org. Web Site: www.sanjacinto-museum.org/learn/library. *Libr Dir,* Lisa A Struthers; E-mail: lstruthers@sanjacinto-museum.org; Staff 1 (MLS 1)
Founded 1939
Library Holdings: Bk Vols 19,500; Per Subs 35
Subject Interests: Tex hist
Automation Activity & Vendor Info: (Cataloging) SirsiDynix; (OPAC) SirsiDynix
Wireless access
Function: Archival coll, Online cat, Outside serv via phone, mail, e-mail & web, Photocopying/Printing, Ref serv available
Restriction: Non-circulating, Open to pub by appt only

LACKLAND AFB

A JOINT BASE SAN ANTONIO LIBRARIES, Lackland Library, 1930 George Ave, 78236. SAN 316-5574. Tel: 210-671-3610. E-mail: lacklandlibrary@gmail.com. Web Site: www.jbsalibraries.org. *Supvry Librn,* Ashlee Hickson; E-mail: ashlee.hickson.1@us.af.mil; Staff 10 (MLS 1, Non-MLS 9)
Founded 1967
Library Holdings: Audiobooks 1,231; Bks on Deafness & Sign Lang 10; DVDs 4,741; Electronic Media & Resources 724; Large Print Bks 485; Bk Titles 23,504; Per Subs 19
Special Collections: Test Prep Coll
Automation Activity & Vendor Info: (Acquisitions) Bibliovation; (Cataloging) Bibliovation; (Circulation) Bibliovation; (ILL) OCLC WorldShare Interlibrary Loan; (OPAC) Bibliovation
Wireless access
Function: 24/7 Electronic res, 24/7 Online cat, 24/7 wireless access, 3D Printer, Activity rm, Adult bk club, Adult literacy prog, Art programs, Audiobks on Playaways & MP3, Audiobks via web, Bk club(s), Bks on CD, Children's prog, Computer training, Computers for patron use, Doc delivery serv, E-Readers, Electronic databases & coll, Extended outdoor wifi, Family literacy, For res purposes, Free DVD rentals, Games, Govt ref serv, Health sci info serv, Holiday prog, Homework prog, ILL available, Instruction & testing, Internet access, Life-long learning prog for all ages, Literacy & newcomer serv, Magazines, Makerspace, Mango lang, Meeting rooms, Movies, Online cat, Online ref, Orientations, Outreach serv, Outside serv via phone, mail, e-mail & web, OverDrive digital audio bks, Photocopying/Printing, Preschool outreach, Preschool reading prog, Prof lending libr, Prog for adults, Prog for children & young adult, Ref & res, Ref serv available, Res assist avail, Res libr, Scanner, Senior computer classes, Senior outreach, Serves people with intellectual disabilities, Spanish lang bks, STEM programs, Story hour, Study rm, Summer & winter reading prog, Summer reading prog, Teen prog, Telephone ref, Wheelchair accessible, Winter reading prog, Workshops, Writing prog
Open Mon-Thurs 9-6, Fri & Sat 11-5

M WILFORD HALL MEDICAL CENTER LIBRARY*, Wilford Hall Ambulatory Surgical Ctr, 1100 Wilford Hall Loop, Bldg 4554JBSA, 78236. SAN 362-0972. Tel: 210-292-7204. E-mail: USAF.JBSA.59-MDW.MBX-MEDICALLIBRARY@MAIL.MIL.
Founded 1950
Library Holdings: Bk Titles 9,500; Per Subs 333
Subject Interests: Clinical med, Dentistry, Nursing
Automation Activity & Vendor Info: (Cataloging) SerialsSolutions
Restriction: Mil only, Staff use only

LAGO VISTA

P LAGO VISTA PUBLIC LIBRARY*, 5803 Thunderbird, Ste 40, 78645. Tel: 512-267-3868. FAX: 512-267-4855. E-mail: lvlibrary@austin.rr.com. Web Site: www.lagovista.lib.tx.us. *Dir,* Jan Steele; *Librn,* P J Ellison; Staff 1 (MLS 1)
Pop 6,500; Circ 14,189
Library Holdings: Bk Titles 14,916; Bk Vols 17,200; Per Subs 42
Automation Activity & Vendor Info: (Acquisitions) Biblionix; (Cataloging) Biblionix; (Circulation) Biblionix; (Course Reserve) Biblionix; (ILL) Biblionix
Wireless access
Function: Archival coll, Computers for patron use, ILL available, Music CDs, Online cat, Photocopying/Printing, Prog for adults, Senior computer classes, Story hour, Summer reading prog, Tax forms, Wheelchair accessible, Workshops, Writing prog
Partic in Partners Library Action Network
Open Mon, Wed & Fri 10-6, Tues & Thurs 10-8, Sat 10-2
Friends of the Library Group

LAGUNA VISTA

P LAGUNA VISTA PUBLIC LIBRARY*, 1300 Palm Blvd, 78578. Tel: 956-943-7155. FAX: 956-943-2371. E-mail: library@lvtexas.us. Web Site: www.lvlibrary.org. *Dir,* Pura Mireles; Staff 2 (Non-MLS 2)
Pop 2,024; Circ 2,259
Library Holdings: Bk Vols 15,000; Per Subs 55
Wireless access
Function: Photocopying/Printing, Summer reading prog, Wheelchair accessible
Special Services for the Deaf - Bks on deafness & sign lang
Open Mon-Fri 9-6
Friends of the Library Group

LAKE DALLAS

P LAKE DALLAS PUBLIC LIBRARY*, 302 S Shady Shores Rd, 75065-3609. SAN 376-4559. Tel: 940-497-3566. FAX: 940-497-3567. E-mail: lakedallasstaff@lakedallas.com. Web Site: www.lakedallas.com/387/lake-dallas-public-library. *Dir, Libr Serv,* Rachel Hadidi; Staff 2 (MLS 1, Non-MLS 1)
Founded 1975
Library Holdings: Bk Vols 40,562; Per Subs 30
Automation Activity & Vendor Info: (Cataloging) Evergreen; (Circulation) Evergreen; (OPAC) Evergreen
Wireless access
Function: CD-ROM, Home delivery & serv to seniorr ctr & nursing homes, Homebound delivery serv, ILL available, Internet access, Music CDs, Prog for children & young adult, Spoken cassettes & CDs, Summer reading prog, VHS videos, Wheelchair accessible, Workshops
Partic in North Texas Library Consortium
Open Tues & Thurs 10-1 & 1:30-5, Sat 11-3
Friends of the Library Group

LAKE JACKSON

J BRAZOSPORT COLLEGE LIBRARY*, 500 College Dr, 77566. SAN 316-5582. Tel: 979-230-3310. FAX: 979-230-3185. Web Site: brazosport.edu/library. *Dir, Libr Serv,* Phil Roche; Tel: 979-230-3259, E-mail: phil.roche@brazosport.edu; *Instruction Librn, Research Librn,* Brent Cooper; Tel: 979-230-3366, E-mail: brent.cooper@brazosport.edu; Staff 6 (MLS 4, Non-MLS 2)
Founded 1968. Enrl 4,022; Fac 68; Highest Degree: Bachelor
Library Holdings: e-books 46,000; Bk Titles 60,000; Bk Vols 70,000; Per Subs 350
Special Collections: Children's Coll; New Book Coll; Rare Book Coll; Small Business Development Coll
Automation Activity & Vendor Info: (Cataloging) SirsiDynix; (Circulation) SirsiDynix; (ILL) OCLC; (OPAC) SirsiDynix; (Serials) SirsiDynix
Wireless access
Partic in Amigos Library Services, Inc
Open Mon-Thurs 7:30am-9:30pm, Fri 7:30-Noon

LAKE WORTH

P MARY LOU REDDICK PUBLIC LIBRARY*, 7005 Charbonneau Rd, 76135. SAN 316-5590. Tel: 817-237-9681. FAX: 817-237-9671. Web Site: www.lakeworthtx.org/library. *Dir, Libr & Commun Serv,* Lara Strother; E-mail: laras@lakeworthlib.org
Pop 5,000; Circ 18,684
Library Holdings: Bk Vols 22,000; Per Subs 22
Automation Activity & Vendor Info: (Cataloging) Biblionix; (Circulation) Biblionix; (OPAC) Biblionix
Wireless access
Function: Children's prog, ILL available
Open Tues, Thurs & Fri 9-5, Wed 9-6, Sat 9-1

LAKEHILLS

P LAKEHILLS AREA LIBRARY, 7200 FM 1283, 78063. SAN 378-3952. Tel: 830-510-2777. FAX: 830-510-2777. E-mail: lakehillslibrary@gmail.com. Web Site: lakehillslibrary.org. *Dir,* Dianna Landes; Staff 2 (Non-MLS 2)
Founded 1999
Jan 2024-Dec 2024 Income $91,667
Library Holdings: Audiobooks 542; DVDs 1,448; Large Print Bks 1,223; Bk Titles 17,266
Automation Activity & Vendor Info: (Acquisitions) Biblionix; (Cataloging) Biblionix; (Circulation) Biblionix; (Course Reserve) Biblionix

Wireless access
Function: 24/7 Electronic res, 24/7 Online cat, 24/7 wireless access, Activity rm, Adult bk club, Art exhibits, Art programs, Audiobks via web, Bk club(s), Bks on CD, Children's prog, Computer training, Computers for patron use, Electronic databases & coll, Extended outdoor wifi, Free DVD rentals, Games, Govt ref serv, Health sci info serv, ILL available, Internet access, Laminating, Large print keyboards, Life-long learning prog for all ages, Meeting rooms, Movies, Notary serv, Online cat, Outside serv via phone, mail, e-mail & web, OverDrive digital audio bks, Photocopying/Printing, Preschool reading prog, Printer for laptops & handheld devices, Prog for adults, Prog for children & young adult, Ref serv available, Scanner, Senior computer classes, Spanish lang bks, STEM programs, Story hour, Summer reading prog, Tax forms, Telephone ref, Wheelchair accessible, Writing prog
Special Services for the Blind - Talking bk serv referral
Open Mon, Wed & Fri 10-5, Tues & Thurs 10-6, Sat 10-2

LAMESA

P DAWSON COUNTY LIBRARY*, 511 N Third St, 79331. (Mail add: PO Box 1264, 79331-1264), SAN 316-5604. Tel: 806-872-6502. FAX: 806-872-2435. E-mail: dclib@windstream.net. Web Site: dclib.ploud.net. *Dir,* Debbie Garza
Founded 1933. Pop 14,000; Circ 129,871
Library Holdings: AV Mats 1,722; Bks on Deafness & Sign Lang 10; e-books 19,000; Large Print Bks 1,246; Bk Titles 40,200; Per Subs 75; Talking Bks 2,585
Special Collections: Genealogy, Texas Heritage
Automation Activity & Vendor Info: (Acquisitions) Follett Software; (Cataloging) Follett Software; (Circulation) Follett Software; (OPAC) Follett Software
Wireless access
Open Mon-Fri 9-5:30, Sat 9-12:30

LAMPASAS

P LAMPASAS PUBLIC LIBRARY*, 201 S Main St, 76550. SAN 316-5612. Tel: 512-556-3251. FAX: 512-556-4065. Web Site: www.lampasas.org/252/library. *Dir,* Subia Shanda; E-mail: shanda@cityoflampasas.com; Staff 3 (Non-MLS 3)
Founded 1902. Pop 7,948; Circ 50,358
Library Holdings: Audiobooks 464; Large Print Bks 828; Bk Titles 26,607; Bk Vols 26,996; Per Subs 30; Videos 593
Automation Activity & Vendor Info: (Cataloging) Biblionix; (Circulation) Biblionix; (OPAC) Biblionix
Wireless access
Partic in Partners Library Action Network
Open Mon & Wed 10-6, Tues & Thurs 10-7, Fri 10-5, Sat 10-3

LANCASTER

J DALLAS COLLEGE*, Cedar Valley Campus Library, 3030 N Dallas Ave, 75134-3799. SAN 321-3501. Tel: 972-860-8140. FAX: 972-860-8221. E-mail: cvref-grp@dcccd.edu. Web Site: libguides.cedarvalleycollege.edu. *Dir, Libr Serv,* Vidya Krishnaswamy; E-mail: vkrishnaswamy@dcccd.edu; *Librn,* Amanda Caudill; E-mail: acaudill@dcccd.edu; *Librn,* Jared Saxon; E-mail: jsaxon@dcccd.edu; *Librn,* Ed Stith; E-mail: estith@dcccd.edu; Staff 3 (MLS 3)
Founded 1977. Highest Degree: Associate
Library Holdings: AV Mats 50,000; Bk Titles 47,585; Per Subs 200
Subject Interests: Automotive, Commercial music, Mkt, Veterinary tech
Automation Activity & Vendor Info: (Circulation) Innovative Interfaces, Inc; (OPAC) Innovative Interfaces, Inc
Wireless access
Partic in OCLC Online Computer Library Center, Inc
Open Mon-Thurs 8am-9pm, Fri 8-4:30, Sat 9-Noon
Restriction: In-house use for visitors, Open to students, fac & staff

P LANCASTER VETERANS MEMORIAL LIBRARY*, 1600 Veterans Memorial Pkwy, 75134. SAN 376-4419. Tel: 972-227-1080. FAX: 972-227-5560. Web Site: www.lancaster-tx.com/149/Library-Services. *Libr Mgr,* John Melton; Tel: 972-275-1419, E-mail: jmelton@lancaster-tx.com; *Asst Libr Mgr,* Jimi Davis; Tel: 972-275-1415, E-mail: jdavis@lancaster-tx.com; Staff 8.5 (MLS 2, Non-MLS 6.5)
Founded 1923. Pop 33,550
Library Holdings: High Interest/Low Vocabulary Bk Vols 15,314; Bk Vols 63,000; Per Subs 99
Special Collections: Genealogy Coll
Subject Interests: Local hist
Automation Activity & Vendor Info: (Acquisitions) Innovative Interfaces, Inc; (Cataloging) Innovative Interfaces, Inc; (Circulation) Innovative Interfaces, Inc; (OPAC) Innovative Interfaces, Inc
Wireless access
Open Mon-Thurs 10-8, Fri 10-6, Sat 9-5
Friends of the Library Group

LAREDO

P JOE A GUERRA LAREDO PUBLIC LIBRARY*, 1120 E Calton Rd, 78041. SAN 316-5639. Tel: 956-795-2400. FAX: 956-795-2403. Web Site: laredolibrary.org. *Dir,* Maria G Soliz; E-mail: mgsoliz@laredolibrary.org; *Asst Dir,* Position Currently Open; *Pub Serv Mgr,* Position Currently Open; *Librn III/Ref,* Henry Wang; *Ref Librn II,* Robert Brown; *Spec Coll Librn,* Renee LaPerriere; *Tech Serv Mgr,* Eva Hernandez; Staff 38 (MLS 8, Non-MLS 30)
Founded 1951. Pop 208,754; Circ 472,113
Library Holdings: Audiobooks 5,848; AV Mats 11,037; Bks on Deafness & Sign Lang 3,870; Braille Volumes 13; CDs 6,296; DVDs 12,812; e-books 357; Electronic Media & Resources 80; Large Print Bks 3,056; Microforms 1,052; Bk Vols 26,000; Per Subs 337; Talking Bks 150
Special Collections: Funding Information Library (Foundation Center Cooperating Coll); Laredo Historical Coll, bks, clippings
Subject Interests: Grantsmanship, Local authors, Webb County hist
Automation Activity & Vendor Info: (Acquisitions) SirsiDynix; (Cataloging) SirsiDynix; (Circulation) SirsiDynix; (ILL) OCLC; (OPAC) SirsiDynix; (Serials) EBSCO Online
Wireless access
Function: Archival coll, Art exhibits, BA reader (adult literacy), Bilingual assistance for Spanish patrons, Bk club(s), Bks on cassette, Bks on CD, CD-ROM, Citizenship assistance, Computer training, Computers for patron use, Digital talking bks, Distance learning, E-Reserves, Electronic databases & coll, Equip loans & repairs, Free DVD rentals, Games & aids for people with disabilities, Holiday prog, Homework prog, ILL available, Instruction & testing, Internet access, Magnifiers for reading, Mail & tel request accepted, Music CDs, Online cat, Online info literacy tutorials on the web & in blackboard, Orientations, Outreach serv, Outside serv via phone, mail, e-mail & web, OverDrive digital audio bks, Passport agency, Photocopying/Printing, Preschool outreach, Prog for adults, Prog for children & young adult, Ref & res, Ref serv available, Satellite serv, Senior computer classes, Senior outreach, Serves people with intellectual disabilities, Specialized serv in classical studies, Spoken cassettes & CDs, Spoken cassettes & DVDs, Story hour, Summer reading prog, Tax forms, Teen prog, Telephone ref, VHS videos, Visual arts prog, Wheelchair accessible, Workshops
Publications: Bookletters (Monthly newsletter)
Partic in Amigos Library Services, Inc
Special Services for the Blind - Assistive/Adapted tech devices, equip & products; Bks on cassette; Bks on CD; Computer with voice synthesizer for visually impaired persons; Large print bks; Talking bks
Open Mon, Fri & Sat 9-6, Tues-Thurs 9-8, Sun 1-5
Friends of the Library Group
Branches: 5
BARBARA FASKEN BRANCH LIBRARY, 15201 Cerralvo Dr, 78045. Tel: 956-795-2400, Ext 2600. Web Site: laredolibrary.org/bfaskenbranchlib.html. *Librn II,* Tess Rawls; *Libr Tech I,* Joseph Moser
Open Mon-Fri 10-7
BRUNI PLAZA BRANCH LIBRARY, 1120 San Bernardo Ave, 78040. Tel: 956-795-2400, Ext 2300. Web Site: laredolibrary.org/brunibranchlibra.html. *Circ Supvr,* Jhonnathan Gonzalez
Open Tues-Sat 10-7
SOPHIE CHRISTEN MCKENDRICK, FRANCISCO OCHOA & FERNANDO A SALINAS BRANCH, 1920 Palo Blanco St, 78046. Tel: 956-795-2400, Ext 2403. Web Site: laredolibrary.org/mosbranchlibrary.html. *Librn IV,* Analiza Perez Gomez; *Librn III,* Priscilla Garcia
Open Mon & Thurs-Sat 9-6, Tues & Wed 9-8
SANTA RITA EXPRESS BRANCH LIBRARY, 301 Castro Urdiales Loop, 78046. Tel: 956-568-5952. Web Site: laredolibrary.org/santaritaexpress.html. *Librn IV,* Analiza Perez Gomez
Open Mon-Fri 3-6; Mon-Fri 11-2 (June-Aug)
LAMAR BRUNI VERGARA INNER CITY BRANCH LIBRARY, 202 W Plum St, 78041. Tel: 956-795-2400, Ext 2520. Web Site: laredolibrary.org/lbvinnercitybran.html. *Libr Tech II,* Elizabeth Castañeda
Open Mon-Fri 9-6
Bookmobiles: 2

J LAREDO COLLEGE*, Harold R Yeary Library, West End Washington St, 78040. SAN 316-5620. Tel: 956-721-5275. Interlibrary Loan Service Tel: 956-721-5270. Reference Tel: 956-721-5274. Reference E-mail: reference_desk@laredo.edu. Web Site: library.laredo.edu. *Libr Dir,* Cynthia Y Rodriguez; Tel: 956-721-5845, E-mail: cynthia.rodriguez@laredo.edu; *Info Literacy Librn,* Omelia Arreola; Tel: 956-721-5813, E-mail: omelia.arreola@laredo.edu; *Acq, Supvr,* Ana Velasquez; Tel: 956-721-5271, E-mail: ana.velasquez@laredo.edu; *Circ Supvr,* Rosa Rios; E-mail: rosa.rios@laredo.edu; *Automated Syst Coordr,* Jose Eddie Perez; Tel: 956-721-5282, E-mail: eddiep@laredo.edu; *Cat Spec,* Dinorah Ramon; Tel: 956-721-5272, E-mail: dino.ramon@laredo.edu; *Libr Mat Proc Spec,* Jessica Gonzalez; Tel: 956-721-5279, E-mail: jessica.gonzalez@laredo.edu; *Cat Tech,* Melina Villarreal; Tel: 956-721-5269, E-mail:

melina.ramirez@laredo.edu. Subject Specialists: *Automation, Networking,* Jose Eddie Perez; Staff 5 (MLS 4, Non-MLS 1)
Founded 1947. Enrl 9,453; Fac 175; Highest Degree: Bachelor
Library Holdings: AV Mats 15; Bks on Deafness & Sign Lang 49; Braille Volumes 30; CDs 83; DVDs 540; Electronic Media & Resources 23; Large Print Bks 148; Microforms 11,045; Music Scores 11; Bk Titles 94,313; Bk Vols 113,367; Per Subs 415; Videos 1,214
Special Collections: Laredo Archives; Old Fort MacIntosh Records
Subject Interests: Behav sci, Soc sci, Voc-tech
Automation Activity & Vendor Info: (Acquisitions) SirsiDynix-iBistro; (Cataloging) SirsiDynix-iBistro; (Circulation) SirsiDynix-iBistro; (Course Reserve) SirsiDynix-iBistro; (ILL) OCLC WorldShare Interlibrary Loan; (Media Booking) SirsiDynix-iBistro; (OPAC) SirsiDynix-iBistro; (Serials) SirsiDynix-iBistro
Wireless access
Publications: Library E-News (Online only); Yeary Library Tidings (Newsletter)
Partic in Amigos Library Services, Inc
Special Services for the Blind - Computer with voice synthesizer for visually impaired persons; Reader equip
Open Mon-Thurs 8am-9pm, Fri 8-Noon, Sat 10-2, Sun 1-5
Restriction: Authorized patrons

C TEXAS A&M INTERNATIONAL UNIVERSITY*, Sue & Radcliffe Killam Library, 5201 University Blvd, 78041-1900. SAN 316-5647. Tel: 956-326-2112. Reference Tel: 956-326-2138. Administration Tel: 956-326-2400. FAX: 956-326-2399. E-mail: researchhelp@tamiu.edu. Web Site: www.tamiu.edu/library. *Interim Dir,* Malynda Dalton; Tel: 956-326-2403, E-mail: mdalton@tamiu.edu; *Cat Librn,* Eva Hernandez; Tel: 956-326-2114, E-mail: eva.hernandez@tamiu.edu; *Spec Coll Librn,* Jeanette Hatcher; Tel: 956-326-2404, E-mail: jhatcher@tamiu.edu; Staff 25 (MLS 6, Non-MLS 19)
Founded 1970. Enrl 5,180; Fac 140; Highest Degree: Doctorate
Library Holdings: e-books 634,244; e-journals 69,000; Electronic Media & Resources 303; Bk Titles 256,100; Bk Vols 313,000; Per Subs 2,300
Special Collections: Faculty Authored Book Coll (FAB); Laredo Spanish Archives on MF; Raza Unida Papers. State Document Depository; US Document Depository
Subject Interests: Intl trade, Nursing
Automation Activity & Vendor Info: (Acquisitions) OCLC; (Cataloging) OCLC; (Circulation) OCLC; (Course Reserve) OCLC; (Discovery) OCLC; (ILL) OCLC WorldShare Interlibrary Loan; (OPAC) OCLC; (Serials) OCLC
Wireless access
Partic in Amigos Library Services, Inc; TexSHARE - Texas State Library & Archives Commission
Open Mon-Thurs 7:30am-Midnight, Fri 7:30am-5pm, Sat 10am-6pm, Sun Noon-Midnight

LAROSITA

P STARR COUNTY PUBLIC LIBRARY*, La Rosita Branch, 4192 W Hwy 83, 78582. SAN 376-1045. Tel: 956-849-2606. E-mail: larositalibrarypct2@gmail.com. *Br Mgr,* Marie Pena
Wireless access
Open Mon-Fri 8-5
Friends of the Library Group

LAUGHLIN AFB

A UNITED STATES AIR FORCE, Laughlin Air Force Base Library, 201 Mitchell Blvd, Bldg 223, 78843-5212. SAN 362-1030. Tel: 830-298-5119. Reference Tel: 830-298-4377. Administration Tel: 830-298-5757. E-mail: laughlin.library@us.af.mil. Circulation E-mail: laughlinafblibrary@gmail.com. Web Site: www.laughlinfss.com/library. *Head Librn,* Sue A Blankemeyer; E-mail: sue.blankemeyer@us.af.mil; Staff 5 (MLS 1, Non-MLS 4)
Library Holdings: Audiobooks 1,167; AV Mats 719; CDs 517; DVDs 1,080; Bk Titles 20,895; Per Subs 27
Special Collections: CLEP & DANTES Testing Materials; Exceptional Family Members; Language & Culture Coll; Military, Chief of Staff Coll
Automation Activity & Vendor Info: (Cataloging) Bibliovation; (Circulation) Bibliovation; (ILL) OCLC; (OPAC) Bibliovation; (Serials) Bibliovation
Wireless access
Function: 24/7 Electronic res, 3D Printer, Activity rm, Adult bk club, Audiobks on Playaways & MP3, Audiobks via web, AV serv, Bks on CD, Children's prog, Computers for patron use, Digital talking bks, E-Readers, Electronic databases & coll, Free DVD rentals, Holiday prog, ILL available, Internet access, Magazines, Makerspace, Mango lang, Movies, Music CDs, Online cat, OverDrive digital audio bks, Photocopying/Printing, Prog for adults, Prog for children & young adult, Ref & res, Ref serv available, Scanner, STEM programs, Story hour, Study rm, Summer reading prog, Tax forms
Partic in Amigos Library Services, Inc
Open Tues, Wed & Fri 10-5, Thurs 10-6:30, Sat 10-2
Restriction: Authorized patrons, Mil, family mem, retirees, Civil Serv personnel NAF only

LEAGUE CITY

P HELEN HALL LIBRARY*, 100 W Walker, 77573-3899. SAN 316-5671. Tel: 281-554-1111. Circulation Tel: 281-554-1120. Reference Tel: 281-554-1101. FAX: 281-554-1118. Reference FAX: 281-554-1117. Web Site: leaguecitylibrary.org. *City Librn,* Teresa Potter; E-mail: teresa.potter@leaguecitytx.gov; *Asst City Librn, Pub Serv,* Darla Rance; Tel: 281-554-1102, E-mail: darla.rance@leaguecitytx.gov; *Ad,* Joanne Turner; Tel: 281-554-1103, E-mail: joanne.turner@leaguecitytx.gov; *Ch Serv Librn,* Lisa Socha; Tel: 281-554-1112, E-mail: lisa.socha@leaguecitytx.gov; *Electronic Serv Librn,* Amelia Chau; E-mail: amelia.chau@leaguecitytx.gov; *Local Hist Librn,* Caris Brown; Tel: 281-554-1105, E-mail: caris.brown@leaguecitytx.gov; *Tech Serv, Tech Serv Librn, Webmaster,* Meredith Layton; Tel: 281-554-1127, E-mail: meredith.layton@leaguecitytx.gov; *Teen Serv, Teen Serv Librn,* Sheldon Freeman; Tel: 281-554-1133, E-mail: sheldon.freeman@leaguecitytx.gov; *Circ Serv Supvr,* Kelsea Meza; Tel: 281-554-1123, E-mail: kelsea.meza@leaguecitytx.gov; Staff 10 (MLS 9, Non-MLS 1)
Founded 1972. Pop 83,000; Circ 776,647
Library Holdings: Braille Volumes 91; CDs 6,885; DVDs 15,781; Electronic Media & Resources 1; Large Print Bks 5,161; Microforms 2; Music Scores 111; Bk Titles 139,414; Bk Vols 169,728; Per Subs 268; Talking Bks 3,128
Automation Activity & Vendor Info: (Acquisitions) SirsiDynix; (Cataloging) SirsiDynix; (Circulation) SirsiDynix; (ILL) OCLC; (OPAC) SirsiDynix; (Serials) SirsiDynix
Wireless access
Function: Audiobks via web, Bk club(s), Bk reviews (Group), Bks on cassette, Bks on CD, Children's prog, Computers for patron use, ILL available, Internet access, Mail & tel request accepted, Music CDs, Online cat, Outreach serv, OverDrive digital audio bks, Photocopying/Printing, Preschool outreach, Prog for adults, Prog for children & young adult, Ref serv available, Senior computer classes, Spoken cassettes & CDs, Story hour, Summer reading prog, Tax forms, Teen prog, Telephone ref
Publications: League City: A History from 1913-1924, vol 2
Mem of Galveston County Library System
Partic in Amigos Library Services, Inc
Open Mon-Thurs 10-9, Fri & Sat 10-6, Sun 1-5
Friends of the Library Group

LEAKEY

P REAL COUNTY PUBLIC LIBRARY LEAKEY*, 225 Main St, 78873. (Mail add: PO Box 488, 78873-0488), SAN 376-4125. Tel: 830-232-5199. FAX: 830-232-5913. E-mail: rcplea@gmail.com. *Libr Dir,* Betty Meyer; *Asst Librn,* Martha Tom; Staff 3 (Non-MLS 3)
Founded 1991
Sept 2015-Aug 2016 Income $69,096, County $7,500, Locally Generated Income $60,596, Other $1,000. Mats Exp $3,562, Books $3,124, Per/Ser (Incl. Access Fees) $357, Electronic Ref Mat (Incl. Access Fees) $81. Sal $30,181
Library Holdings: Audiobooks 1,611; Bks on Deafness & Sign Lang 5; CDs 12; DVDs 1,623; e-books 7,138; Electronic Media & Resources 1,611; Large Print Bks 674; Bk Titles 16,895; Bk Vols 17,501; Per Subs 15
Automation Activity & Vendor Info: (Acquisitions) Biblionix/Apollo; (Cataloging) Biblionix/Apollo; (Circulation) Biblionix/Apollo; (ILL) Biblionix/Apollo; (Serials) Biblionix/Apollo
Wireless access
Function: 24/7 Electronic res, 24/7 Online cat, Accelerated reader prog, Activity rm, Adult bk club
Partic in Partners Library Action Network
Special Services for the Deaf - Bks on deafness & sign lang
Special Services for the Blind - Assistive/Adapted tech devices, equip & products; Bks on CD; Large print bks; Low vision equip; Photo duplicator for making large print
Open Mon-Fri 9-5
Friends of the Library Group

LEANDER

P LEANDER PUBLIC LIBRARY*, 1011 S Bagdad Rd, 78641. SAN 375-5118. Tel: 512-259-5259. FAX: 512-528-0434. E-mail: leanderpl@leandertx.gov. Web Site: leandertx.gov/library. *Dir,* Peggy Parrish; Tel: 512-259-5259, Ext 5, E-mail: pparrish@leandertx.gov; Staff 7.2 (MLS 3.8, Non-MLS 3.4)
Founded 1987. Pop 62,608; Circ 175,000
Library Holdings: AV Mats 5,000; Large Print Bks 4,000; Bk Titles 49,000; Bk Vols 51,500; Per Subs 107; Talking Bks 2,000; Videos 4,000
Automation Activity & Vendor Info: (Cataloging) TLC (The Library Corporation); (Circulation) TLC (The Library Corporation)
Wireless access

Partic in Partners Library Action Network
Open Mon-Sat 10:30-6:30

LEON VALLEY

P LEON VALLEY PUBLIC LIBRARY*, 6425 Evers Rd, 78238-1453. SAN 372-5944. Tel: 210-684-0720. FAX: 210-684-2088. Web Site: www.leonvalley.lib.tx.us, *Libr Dir,* Regina Reed; E-mail: r.reed@leonvalleytexas.gov; *Asst Libr Dir,* Theresa Brader; E-mail: t.brader@leonvalleytexas.gov; Staff 4 (MLS 2, Non-MLS 2)
Founded 1977
Library Holdings: Bk Titles 50,000; Per Subs 100
Special Collections: Leon Valley Historical Society. Oral History
Automation Activity & Vendor Info: (Cataloging) Biblionix; (Circulation) Biblionix; (OPAC) Biblionix
Wireless access
Function: 24/7 Electronic res, 24/7 Online cat, 3D Printer, Archival coll, Bks on CD, Children's prog, Computers for patron use, Electronic databases & coll, Family literacy, Free DVD rentals, Genealogy discussion group, Home delivery & serv to seniorr ctr & nursing homes, Homebound delivery serv, ILL available, Internet access, Mail & tel request accepted, Movies, Notary serv, Online cat, Online ref, Outreach serv, Outside serv via phone, mail, e-mail & web, OverDrive digital audio bks, Photocopying/Printing, Prog for adults, Prog for children & young adult, Ref & res, Ref serv available, Scanner, Senior outreach, Spanish lang bks, Spoken cassettes & CDs, Spoken cassettes & DVDs, Story hour, Study rm, Summer reading prog, Teen prog, Telephone ref, Wheelchair accessible, Workshops
Partic in Amigos Library Services, Inc; Partners Library Action Network
Special Services for the Deaf - Bks on deafness & sign lang
Open Mon, Wed & Fri 10-6, Tues & Thurs 10-8, Sat 10-2, Sun 2-6
Restriction: Non-resident fee
Friends of the Library Group

LEONARD

P LEONARD PUBLIC LIBRARY*, 102 S Main St, 75452. (Mail add: PO Box 1188, 75452-1188), SAN 376-6500. Tel: 903-587-2391. FAX: 903-587-0311. E-mail: info@leonardlibrary.net. Web Site: leonard.ploud.net. *Libr Dir,* Sandra Sims; E-mail: Sandra@leonardlibrary.net
Library Holdings: Bk Vols 24,000
Automation Activity & Vendor Info: (Cataloging) Follett Software; (Circulation) Follett Software
Wireless access
Open Tues & Fri 10-7, Wed & Thurs 2-7
Friends of the Library Group

LEVELLAND

P HOCKLEY COUNTY MEMORIAL LIBRARY, 811 Austin St, 79336. (Mail add: 802 Houston St, Ste 108, 79336), SAN 316-568X. Tel: 806-894-6750. E-mail: librarian@hockleycounty.org. Web Site: hockleylvl.biblionix.com/catalog, www.facebook.com/hockleycountylibrary. *Dir,* Amy Cantwell; Staff 2 (MLS 1, Non-MLS 1)
Founded 1946. Pop 24,500; Circ 67,115
Library Holdings: Bk Titles 37,517; Bk Vols 43,479; Per Subs 77
Subject Interests: Tex hist
Automation Activity & Vendor Info: (Cataloging) Biblionix; (Circulation) Biblionix; (OPAC) Biblionix
Wireless access
Function: 24/7 Online cat, Activity rm, Audiobks via web, Bks on CD, Children's prog, Computers for patron use, Electronic databases & coll, Free DVD rentals, ILL available, Internet access, Magazines, Mail & tel request accepted, Movies, Online cat, Photocopying/Printing, Preschool reading prog, Ref serv available, Scanner, Story hour, Study rm, Summer reading prog, Tax forms
Partic in Partners Library Action Network; TexSHARE - Texas State Library & Archives Commission
Open Mon-Wed & Fri 9-5, Thurs 9-7
Friends of the Library Group

J SOUTH PLAINS COLLEGE LIBRARY*, 1401 S College Ave - Box E, 79336. SAN 316-5698. Tel: 806-716-2300, 806-716-2330. Circulation Tel: 806-716-2299. Administration Tel: 806-716-2304. E-mail: ref@southplainscollege.edu. Web Site: library.southplainscollege.edu. *Dir, Libr Serv,* Mark Gottschalk; E-mail: mgottschalk@southplainscollege.edu; *Librn,* Robert Baumle; Tel: 806-716-4888, E-mail: rbaumle@southplainscollege.edu; *Librn,* Tracey Pineda; Tel: 806-716-4694, E-mail: tpineda@southplainscollege.edu; *Pub Serv Librn,* Callie Nations; Tel: 806-716-2298, E-mail: cnations@southplainscollege.edu; Staff 10 (MLS 7, Non-MLS 3)
Founded 1958. Enrl 9,600; Highest Degree: Associate
Sept 2017-Aug 2018 Income $856,058
Library Holdings: Audiobooks 800; AV Mats 3,500; e-books 42,000; Microforms 30,000; Bk Vols 75,000; Per Subs 200
Automation Activity & Vendor Info: (Acquisitions) OCLC; (Cataloging) OCLC; (Circulation) OCLC; (Course Reserve) OCLC; (ILL) OCLC FirstSearch; (OPAC) OCLC; (Serials) OCLC
Wireless access
Function: Archival coll, Art exhibits, Audio & video playback equip for onsite use, Bks on CD, Computer training, Computers for patron use, Electronic databases & coll, Free DVD rentals, ILL available, Mail & tel request accepted, Microfiche/film & reading machines, Online cat, Online info literacy tutorials on the web & in blackboard, Online ref, Orientations, Photocopying/Printing, Printer for laptops & handheld devices, Ref serv available, Scanner, Spoken cassettes & CDs, Spoken cassettes & DVDs, Telephone ref, VHS videos, Wheelchair accessible
Partic in Amigos Library Services, Inc; OCLC Online Computer Library Center, Inc; TexSHARE - Texas State Library & Archives Commission; US National Library of Medicine
Special Services for the Blind - Magnifiers
Open Mon-Wed 7:45am-8pm, Thurs 7:45-6, Fri 7:45-4 (Winter); Mon-Thurs 7:45-4, Fri 7:45-3 (Summer)

LEWISVILLE

S AMERICAN DONKEY & MULE SOCIETY LIBRARY*, 1346 Morningside Ave, 75057. (Mail add: PO Box 1210, 75067), SAN 324-0983. Tel: 972-219-0781. FAX: 972-219-0781. E-mail: lovelongears@hotmail.com. Web Site: www.lovelongears.com/books. *Librn,* Betty Posey. Subject Specialists: *Equine,* Betty Posey
Founded 1967
Library Holdings: Bk Titles 1,000
Special Collections: Breed Association Coll (private); Historical: Studbooks
Subject Interests: Donkeys, Horses, Mules
Restriction: Open by appt only

P LEWISVILLE PUBLIC LIBRARY SYSTEM*, 1197 W Main St, 75067. (Mail add: PO Box 299002, 75029-9002), SAN 920-7058. Tel: 972-219-3570. Circulation Tel: 972-219-3576, 972-219-3578. Reference Tel: 972-219-3779. Administration Tel: 972-219-3571. FAX: 972-219-5094. Web Site: library.cityoflewisville.com. *Dir,* Carolyn Booker; Tel: 972-219-3571, E-mail: cbooker@cityoflewisville.com; *Ref & Adult Serv Supvr,* Kelly Brouillard; Tel: 972-219-3758, E-mail: kbrouillard@cityoflewisville.com; *Youth Serv Supvr,* Renee Kirchner; Tel: 972-219-3691, E-mail; rkirchner@cityoflewisville.com; Staff 8 (MLS 8)
Founded 1968. Pop 98,000; Circ 637,396
Library Holdings: Audiobooks 15,950; AV Mats 27,876; e-books 3,945; Bk Titles 154,242; Bk Vols 173,432; Per Subs 80; Videos 13,783
Special Collections: Oral History
Automation Activity & Vendor Info: (Acquisitions) SirsiDynix; (Cataloging) SirsiDynix; (Circulation) SirsiDynix; (OPAC) SirsiDynix
Wireless access
Function: Adult bk club, Bk club(s), Bks on CD, Children's prog, Computers for patron use, Electronic databases & coll, Free DVD rentals, Holiday prog, ILL available, Life-long learning prog for all ages, Magazines, Mail & tel request accepted, Makerspace, Mango lang, Microfiche/film & reading machines, Movies, Music CDs, Online cat, Photocopying/Printing, Scanner, Story hour, Study rm, Wheelchair accessible
Special Services for the Deaf - ADA equip
Special Services for the Blind - Accessible computers
Open Mon-Wed 9-8, Thurs 9-6, Fri & Sat 11-5
Friends of the Library Group

LIBERTY

P LIBERTY MUNICIPAL LIBRARY*, 1710 Sam Houston Ave, 77575-4741. SAN 316-571X. Tel: 936-336-8901. FAX: 936-336-2414. Web Site: liberty.ploud.net. *Libr Dir,* Amber Ursprung; *Ch,* Katie Edgell; *Circ,* Peggy Carr; Staff 6 (Non-MLS 6)
Founded 1940. Pop 8,173
Library Holdings: Bk Vols 42,000; Per Subs 80
Automation Activity & Vendor Info: (Cataloging) Follett Software; (Circulation) Follett Software
Wireless access
Open Mon-Thurs 10-6, Fri 1-5, Sat 10-4
Friends of the Library Group

LIBERTY HILL

P LIBERTY HILL PUBLIC LIBRARY*, 355 Loop 332, 78642. (Mail add: PO Box 1072, 78642-1072). Tel: 512-778-6400. FAX: 512-778-5822. E-mail: librarian@lhpl.org. Web Site: www.lhpl.org. *Libr Dir,* Angela K Palmer; E-mail: angela.palmer@lhpl.org; Staff 2 (Non-MLS 2)
Founded 2002. Pop 13,000; Circ 64,644
Automation Activity & Vendor Info: (Acquisitions) Biblionix; (Cataloging) Biblionix; (Circulation) Biblionix; (OPAC) Biblionix

Wireless access
Function: 24/7 Electronic res, Adult bk club, After school storytime, Bk club(s), Bks on CD, Children's prog, Computers for patron use, Electronic databases & coll, Free DVD rentals, Holiday prog, Homework prog, ILL available, Instruction & testing, Internet access, Magazines, Mail & tel request accepted, Notary serv, Online cat, Outreach serv, OverDrive digital audio bks, Photocopying/Printing, Preschool outreach, Prog for adults, Prog for children & young adult, Ref serv available, Scanner, Summer reading prog, Wheelchair accessible
Partic in Partners Library Action Network
Open Mon-Fri 10-6, Sat 10-4, Sun 1-6

LINDALE

P LILLIE RUSSELL MEMORIAL LIBRARY, 200 E Hubbard St, 75771-3397. (Mail add: PO Box 1570, 75771-1570). Tel: 903-882-1900. FAX: 903-882-1236. E-mail: patrons.75771@gmail.com. Web Site: www.lillierussellibrary.org. *Dir,* Shannon Reid; E-mail: director@lillierusselllibrary.org
Founded 1993
Library Holdings: Audiobooks 1,500; AV Mats 147; Bks on Deafness & Sign Lang 12; CDs 60; DVDs 2,300; e-books 28,281; Large Print Bks 300; Bk Vols 60,000; Per Subs 10
Automation Activity & Vendor Info: (Cataloging) Book Systems; (Circulation) Book Systems; (ILL) OCLC FirstSearch; (OPAC) Book Systems
Wireless access
Partic in TexSHARE - Texas State Library & Archives Commission
Open Tues-Thurs 10-6, Fri & Sat 10-4
Friends of the Library Group

LITTLE ELM

P LITTLE ELM PUBLIC LIBRARY*, 100 W Eldorado Pkwy, 75068. Tel: 214-975-0430. Administration Tel: 214-975-0435. FAX: 214-618-3582. Reference E-mail: library@littleelm.org. Web Site: www.littleelmlibrary.org. *Libr Mgr,* Lynette Roberson; *Ref/Tech Serv Librn,* Laurie McKee; E-mail: lmckee@littleelm.org; *Youth Serv Librn,* Cherie Pryseski; E-mail: cpryseski@littleelm.org; *Circ Supvr,* Robert Dowdy; E-mail: rdowdy@littleelm.org; Staff 3.8 (MLS 2, Non-MLS 1.8)
Founded 1998. Pop 24,000; Circ 34,857
Automation Activity & Vendor Info: (Cataloging) SirsiDynix; (Circulation) SirsiDynix; (OPAC) SirsiDynix
Wireless access
Function: Adult literacy prog, Art exhibits, Audio & video playback equip for onsite use, Bks on cassette, Bks on CD, CD-ROM, Children's prog, Computer training, Computers for patron use, Distance learning, E-Reserves, Electronic databases & coll, Family literacy, Free DVD rentals, Holiday prog, ILL available, Instruction & testing, Internet access, Music CDs, Online cat, Outreach serv, Outside serv via phone, mail, e-mail & web, Photocopying/Printing, Preschool outreach, Prog for adults, Prog for children & young adult, Ref & res, Ref serv available, Scanner, Senior computer classes, Senior outreach, Spoken cassettes & CDs, Spoken cassettes & DVDs, Story hour, Summer reading prog, Tax forms, Teen prog, Telephone ref, VHS videos, Visual arts prog, Wheelchair accessible, Workshops, Writing prog
Partic in Partners Library Action Network
Special Services for the Blind - Bks on cassette; Bks on CD; Large print bks; Talking bks
Open Mon-Thurs 10-8, Fri 10-5, Sat & Sun 10-3
Friends of the Library Group

LITTLEFIELD

P LAMB COUNTY LIBRARY, 110 E Sixth St, 79339. SAN 316-5728. Tel: 806-385-5223. FAX: 806-385-0030. Web Site: littlefield.ploud.net. *Dir,* Selena Ramirez; E-mail: sramirez@co.lamb.tx.us
Founded 1913. Pop 6,500
Library Holdings: Bk Vols 11,700; Per Subs 28
Automation Activity & Vendor Info: (Cataloging) Biblionix; (Circulation) Biblionix
Wireless access
Partic in Partners Library Action Network
Open Mon-Wed & Fri 8:30-5, Thurs 1-8:30, Sat 9-Noon

LIVINGSTON

P LIVINGSTON MUNICIPAL LIBRARY*, 707 N Tyler Ave, 77351. SAN 316-5736. Tel: 936-327-4252. FAX: 936-327-4162. E-mail: library@livingstonlibrary.net. Web Site: www.livingstonlibrary.net. *Libr Dir,* Priscilla E Emrich; Staff 1 (MLS 1)
Founded 1969. Pop 5,169; Circ 49,848
Library Holdings: AV Mats 1,210; Large Print Bks 1,031; Bk Titles 21,587; Bk Vols 22,560; Per Subs 65; Talking Bks 488
Automation Activity & Vendor Info: (Cataloging) Biblionix; (Circulation) Biblionix; (OPAC) Biblionix
Wireless access
Function: 24/7 Electronic res, 24/7 Online cat, Activity rm, Audiobks via web, Bilingual assistance for Spanish patrons, Bks on CD, Children's prog, Computer training, Computers for patron use, Digital talking bks, Electronic databases & coll, Free DVD rentals, Holiday prog, ILL available, Internet access, Magazines, Meeting rooms, Movies, Music CDs, Online cat, Outside serv via phone, mail, e-mail & web, OverDrive digital audio bks, Photocopying/Printing, Preschool outreach, Prog for adults, Prog for children & young adult, Ref serv available, Senior computer classes, Spanish lang bks, Story hour, Study rm, Summer reading prog, Tax forms, Teen prog, Telephone ref, Wheelchair accessible
Partic in Partners Library Action Network
Open Mon-Fri 10-6, Sat 10-2
Restriction: ID required to use computers (Ltd hrs), Non-circulating of rare bks, Non-resident fee
Friends of the Library Group

LLANO

P LLANO COUNTY LIBRARY SYSTEM*, Llano County Public Library, 102 E Haynie St, 78643. SAN 362-109X. Tel: 325-247-5248. FAX: 325-247-1778. E-mail: llanocountylibrary@yahoo.com. Web Site: www.llano-library-system.net. *Dir,* Tommi Myers; Staff 12 (MLS 1, Non-MLS 11)
Founded 1939. Pop 17,044; Circ 123,998
Library Holdings: Bk Titles 30,149; Bk Vols 49,745; Per Subs 58
Special Collections: Oral History
Subject Interests: Genealogy
Automation Activity & Vendor Info: (Cataloging) Follett Software; (Circulation) Follett Software; (OPAC) Follett Software
Wireless access
Function: 24/7 Electronic res, 24/7 Online cat, Adult bk club, Children's prog, Computer training, Computers for patron use, Electronic databases & coll, Free DVD rentals, ILL available, Internet access, Magazines, Meeting rooms, Movies, Online cat, Preschool outreach, Preschool reading prog, Prog for adults, Prog for children & young adult, Scanner, Story hour, Summer reading prog, Teen prog, Wheelchair accessible
Partic in Partners Library Action Network; TexSHARE - Texas State Library & Archives Commission
Open Mon 9-7, Tues-Fri 9-5:30, Sat 10-1
Friends of the Library Group
Branches: 2
KINGSLAND LIBRARY, 125 W Polk St, Kingsland, 78639, SAN 362-112X. Tel: 325-388-3170. *Dir,* Amber Milum; E-mail: amilum.klib@yahoo.com
Open Mon-Fri 9-5:30, Sat 9-12
Friends of the Library Group
LAKE SHORE LIBRARY, 7346 Ranch Rd 261, Buchanan Dam, 78609, SAN 376-2297. Tel: 325-379-1174. FAX: 325-379-3054. E-mail: lakeshore.library@gmail.com. *Dir,* Melissa Macdougall
Open Mon-Fri 9-5:30
Friends of the Library Group

LOCKHART

P DR EUGENE CLARK LIBRARY, Lockhart Public Library, 217 S Main St, 78644-2742. (Mail add: PO Box 209, 78644-0209), SAN 316-5744. Tel: 512-398-3223. FAX: 512-398-8316. E-mail: clarklibrary@lockhart-tx.org. Web Site: www.clark-library-lockhart.org. *Dir, Libr Serv,* Bertha Martinez; Tel: 512-398-3223, Ext 284, E-mail: bmartinez@lockhart-tx.org; *Asst to the Dir,* Jeanna Trejo
Founded 1900. Pop 13,000; Circ 88,000
Library Holdings: AV Mats 6,406; Bk Vols 37,677; Per Subs 175; Videos 4,001
Special Collections: Dr Eugene Clark Special Coll; Lockhart Post-Register Coll. Oral History
Subject Interests: Tex
Automation Activity & Vendor Info: (Cataloging) Biblionix
Wireless access
Partic in Partners Library Action Network
Open Mon, Wed & Fri 8:30-6, Tues & Thurs 8:30-7, Sat 8:30-3
Friends of the Library Group

LONE OAK

P LONE OAK AREA PUBLIC LIBRARY, 102 Jones St, 75453. (Mail add: PO Box 501, 75453-0501). Tel: 903-662-4565. FAX: 903-662-0955. E-mail: library@cumbytel.com. Web Site: www.loneoaklibrary.org. *Librn,* Susan Bishop
Pop 1,073
Library Holdings: AV Mats 100; Bk Titles 8,000; Talking Bks 200
Automation Activity & Vendor Info: (Acquisitions) Book Systems; (Cataloging) Book Systems; (Circulation) Book Systems; (Course Reserve) Book Systems; (OPAC) Book Systems
Wireless access
Open Tues-Fri 10-5, Sat 10-2

LONGVIEW

M CHRISTUS GOOD SHEPHERD HEALTH SYSTEM*, Medical Library, 700 E Marshall Ave, 75601. SAN 375-7676. Tel: 903-315-2165. FAX: 903-315-2034. E-mail: library@christushealth.org. Web Site: www.christushealth.org/good-shepherd/healthcare-professionals. *Librn,* Meredith Burks; Staff 1 (Non-MLS 1)
Library Holdings: Bk Titles 75
Wireless access
Open Mon-Fri 8-4:30

R FIRST BAPTIST CHURCH*, John L Whorton Media Center Library, 209 E South St, 75601. SAN 316-5779. Tel: 903-758-0681. Web Site: www.fbcl.org/resources/media-center. *Dir, Media Serv,* Donna Hutchison; Tel: 903-212-3309, E-mail: dhutchison@fbcl.org
Founded 1942
Library Holdings: Bk Vols 21,000; Per Subs 14
Subject Interests: Am hist, Biblical, Cookbks, Inspirational, Tex hist, World hist
Automation Activity & Vendor Info: (Cataloging) Library Concepts; (Circulation) Library Concepts; (OPAC) Library Concepts
Wireless access
Open Mon-Wed 9-Noon, Sun 9am-9:30am
Restriction: Mem only

CR LETOURNEAU UNIVERSITY*, Margaret Estes Library, 2100 S Mobberly Ave, 75602-3524. (Mail add: PO Box 7001, 75607-7001), SAN 316-5787. Tel: 903-233-3260. Administration Tel: 903-233-3271. Toll Free Tel: 800-388-5327, Ext 3260. FAX: 903-233-3263. E-mail: library@letu.edu. Web Site: www.letu.edu/library. *Dir, Dir, Archives,* Shelby Ware; E-mail: shelbyware@letu.edu; *Circ Supvr,* Sandy Flinn; Tel: 903-233-3263, E-mail: sandyflinn@letu.edu; Staff 7 (MLS 6, Non-MLS 1)
Founded 1946. Enrl 3,983; Fac 84; Highest Degree: Master
Library Holdings: AV Mats 4,969; e-books 500; e-journals 22,546; Bk Titles 73,852; Bk Vols 94,251; Per Subs 527
Special Collections: Harmon General Hospital Coll, newsp, rpts; Robert G LeTourneau Archives & Museum, bks, flm
Subject Interests: Aviation, Biblical studies, Engr, Humanities
Automation Activity & Vendor Info: (Cataloging) OCLC; (ILL) OCLC
Wireless access
Partic in TexSHARE - Texas State Library & Archives Commission
Open Mon-Thurs 8am-Midnight, Fri 8-8, Sat 12-8, Sun 3-Midnight

P LONGVIEW PUBLIC LIBRARY*, 222 W Cotton St, 75601. SAN 362-1189. Tel: 903-237-1350. Interlibrary Loan Service Tel: 903-237-1349. Administration Tel: 903-237-1341. Web Site: www.longviewtexas.gov/2163/Library. *Dir,* Jennifer Eldridge; E-mail: jeldridge@longviewtexas.gov; *Head, Circ,* Bronwyn Pegues; Staff 23 (MLS 7.5, Non-MLS 15.5)
Founded 1932. Pop 121,730; Circ 278,608
Library Holdings: Bk Titles 139,743; Per Subs 187
Special Collections: East Texas; Oil Field Production Records. US Document Depository
Subject Interests: Genealogy, Texana
Wireless access
Function: ILL available
Partic in Amigos Library Services, Inc; Partners Library Action Network
Open Mon, Wed, Fri & Sat 10-6, Tues & Thurs 10-9, Sun 1-5
Friends of the Library Group
Branches: 1
BROUGHTON BRANCH, Broughton Recreation Ctr, 801 S Martin Luther King Jr Blvd, 75601. Tel: 903-237-1326. Web Site: www.longviewtexas.gov/2892/Broughton-Branch-Library. *Dir,* Jennifer Eldridge
Open Mon-Thurs 2-7

LOS FRESNOS

P ETHEL L WHIPPLE MEMORIAL LIBRARY*, 402 W Ocean Blvd, 78566. SAN 316-5795. Tel: 956-233-5330. FAX: 956-233-3203. Web Site: www.los-fresnos.lib.tx.us. *Dir,* Angie Lugo; E-mail: angie@los-fresnos.lib.tx.us
Pop 26,000
Library Holdings: Bk Titles 27,699; Bk Vols 30,000; Per Subs 25
Automation Activity & Vendor Info: (Acquisitions) TLC (The Library Corporation); (Cataloging) TLC (The Library Corporation); (Circulation) TLC (The Library Corporation); (Course Reserve) TLC (The Library Corporation); (ILL) TLC (The Library Corporation); (OPAC) TLC (The Library Corporation); (Serials) TLC (The Library Corporation)
Open Mon-Thurs 10-6, Fri 9-5
Friends of the Library Group

LUBBOCK

M COVENANT HEALTH SYSTEM, Covenant Medical Library, 3615 19th St, 79410. SAN 316-5825. Tel: 806-725-0602. Web Site: www.covenanthealth.org. *Med Librn,* Alex Ferguson; E-mail: alex.ferguson@providence.org; Staff 1 (MLS 1)
Library Holdings: e-books 7,000; Bk Titles 60
Subject Interests: Allied health, Med, Nursing
Automation Activity & Vendor Info: (Cataloging) CyberTools for Libraries; (Circulation) CyberTools for Libraries; (OPAC) CyberTools for Libraries
Wireless access
Partic in National Network of Libraries of Medicine Region 3
Open Mon-Fri 8-5
Restriction: Open to pub for ref only, Open to staff only

CR LUBBOCK CHRISTIAN UNIVERSITY LIBRARY*, 5601 19th St, 79407-2009. SAN 316-5817. Tel: 806-720-7326. E-mail: libadmin@lcu.edu. Web Site: lib.lcu.edu. *Libr Dir,* Amanda Guthrie; E-mail: amanda.guthrie@lcu.edu; *Electronic Res Librn,* K-Dee Anderson; E-mail: k-dee.anderson@lcu.edu; *Pub Serv Librn,* Karlee Burleson; Tel: 806-720-7331, E-mail: karlee.burleson@lcu.edu; Staff 4 (MLS 4)
Founded 1957. Enrl 2,000; Fac 80; Highest Degree: Master
Library Holdings: Bk Vols 126,000; Per Subs 250
Subject Interests: Relig studies
Automation Activity & Vendor Info: (Acquisitions) SirsiDynix; (Cataloging) SirsiDynix; (Circulation) SirsiDynix; (Course Reserve) SirsiDynix; (OPAC) SirsiDynix; (Serials) SirsiDynix
Wireless access
Partic in Amigos Library Services, Inc; TexSHARE - Texas State Library & Archives Commission
Restriction: In-house use for visitors

P LUBBOCK PUBLIC LIBRARY*, Mahon (Main), 1306 Ninth St, 79401. SAN 362-1278. Tel: 806-775-2834, 806-775-2835. FAX: 806-775-2827. E-mail: LibMahon@mylubbock.us. Web Site: ci.lubbock.tx.us/departments/library. *Interim Dir,* L Thompson; E-mail: LThomason@mylubbock.us; *Mat Mgr,* Janet Henderson; E-mail: jhenderson@mylubbock.us; Staff 53 (MLS 13, Non-MLS 40)
Founded 1966
Library Holdings: Bk Titles 206,336; Bk Vols 417,633; Per Subs 164
Subject Interests: Genealogy
Automation Activity & Vendor Info: (Circulation) SirsiDynix; (OPAC) SirsiDynix; (Serials) SirsiDynix
Wireless access
Publications: Exploring New Worlds
Partic in Amigos Library Services, Inc
Open Mon-Wed 9-9, Thurs-Sat 9-6, Sun 1-5
Friends of the Library Group
Branches: 3
GODEKE, 5034 Frankford Ave, 79424, SAN 362-1308. Tel: 806-775-3362. FAX: 806-767-3762. E-mail: LibGodeke@mylubbock.us. *Br Mgr,* Lorraine Knipstein
Library Holdings: Bk Vols 103,768
Open Mon & Tues 12-9, Wed-Sat 9-6
Friends of the Library Group
GROVES, 5520 19th St, 79407, SAN 377-662X. Tel: 806-767-3733. FAX: 806-795-9641. E-mail: LibGroves@mylubbock.us. *Br Mgr,* Nancy Cammack
Library Holdings: Bk Titles 61,182
Open Mon & Tues 12-9, Wed-Sat 9-6
Friends of the Library Group
PATTERSON BRANCH, 1836 Parkway Dr, 79403. Tel: 806-767-3300. FAX: 806-767-3302. E-mail: LibPatterson@mylubbock.us. *Br Mgr,* Melissa Barber
Library Holdings: Bk Titles 51,018
Open Mon & Tues 10-7, Wed-Sat 9-6
Friends of the Library Group

CL TEXAS TECH UNIVERSITY*, School of Law Library, 3311 18th St, 79409. SAN 362-1456. Tel: 806-742-3957. Reference Tel: 806-742-7155. E-mail: reference.law@ttu.edu. Web Site: depts.ttu.edu/law/lawlibrary. *Assoc Dean, Dir,* Ms Jamie J Baker; E-mail: jamie.baker@ttu.edu
Founded 1967. Highest Degree: Doctorate
Library Holdings: Bk Vols 225,220; Per Subs 2,114
Special Collections: US Document Depository
Subject Interests: Commercial law
Automation Activity & Vendor Info: (Acquisitions) Innovative Interfaces, Inc; (Cataloging) Innovative Interfaces, Inc; (Circulation) Innovative Interfaces, Inc; (Course Reserve) Innovative Interfaces, Inc; (OPAC) Innovative Interfaces, Inc; (Serials) Innovative Interfaces, Inc
Wireless access
Partic in OCLC Online Computer Library Center, Inc
Open Mon-Thurs 7:30am-10pm, Fri 7:30-5, Sat 9-5, Sun 1-10

CM TEXAS TECH UNIVERSITY HEALTH SCIENCES CENTER*, Preston Smith Library of the Health Sciences, 3601 Fourth St, 79430. SAN 321-2432. Tel: 806-743-2200. Administration Tel: 806-743-2203. FAX: 806-743-2218. Web Site: www.ttuhsc.edu/libraries. *Interim Exec Dir,* Andrew Escude; E-mail: andrew.escude@ttuhsc.edu; *Assoc Dir, Pub Serv,* Stephanie Shippey; *Supvr, Ser,* Judy Ford; *Mgr, Patron Serv,* Sharon Beckham; Staff 59 (MLS 19, Non-MLS 40)
Founded 1971. Enrl 1,547; Fac 516; Highest Degree: Doctorate
Library Holdings: Bk Vols 289,736; Per Subs 2,144
Special Collections: Oral History
Subject Interests: Allied health, Med, Nursing
Automation Activity & Vendor Info: (Acquisitions) CyberTools for Libraries; (Cataloging) CyberTools for Libraries; (Circulation) CyberTools for Libraries; (Course Reserve) CyberTools for Libraries; (OPAC) CyberTools for Libraries; (Serials) CyberTools for Libraries
Wireless access
Publications: Newsletter
Partic in Del Norte Biosciences Library Consortium; SCAMeL
Open Mon-Thurs 7:30am-Midnight, Fri 7:30am-10pm, Sat 9am-10pm, Sun 9am-Midnight
Friends of the Library Group

Departmental Libraries:

HARRINGTON LIBRARY, 1400 Wallace Blvd, Amarillo, 79106, SAN 371-6996. Tel: 806-414-9964. FAX: 806-354-5430. *Assoc Dir,* Terri Wilson; *Asst Dir,* Skyla Bryant; E-mail: skyla.bryant@ttuhsc.edu; Staff 6 (MLS 3, Non-MLS 3)
Founded 1977
Library Holdings: AV Mats 3,500; e-journals 24,000; Bk Titles 15,259; Per Subs 40
Partic in US National Library of Medicine
Open Mon-Thurs 7:30am-11pm, Fri 7:30am-8pm, Sat 9-5, Sun 2-10
Friends of the Library Group

ODESSA CAMPUS, 800 W Fourth St, Odessa, 79763, SAN 322-5739. Tel: 432-703-5035. FAX: 432-335-5170. *Regional Libr Dir,* Erik Wilkinson; E-mail: e.wilkinson@ttuhsc.edu; *Asst Dir,* Travis Real; E-mail: travis.real@ttuhsc.edu
Library Holdings: Bk Titles 11,500; Per Subs 200
Open Mon-Fri 8-8, Sat 10-2, Sun 1-5
Friends of the Library Group

C TEXAS TECH UNIVERSITY LIBRARIES, 2802 18th St, 79409. SAN 362-1391. Tel: 806-742-2265. Administration Tel: 806-742-2261. E-mail: libraries.website@ttu.edu. Web Site: www.depts.ttu.edu/library. *Dean of Libr,* Earnstein Dukes; Tel: 806-834-1938, E-mail: earnstein.dukes@ttu.edu; *Assoc Dean, Librn,* Ryan Litsey; Tel: 806-834-1156, E-mail: ryan.litsey@ttu.edu; *Assoc Dean of Libr,* Jennifer Spurrier; Tel: 806-834-2252, E-mail: jenny.spurrier@ttu.edu; *Assoc Librn,* Jayne Sappington; Tel: 806-834-4734, E-mail: jayne.sappington@ttu.edu; Staff 57 (MLS 51, Non-MLS 6)
Founded 1923. Enrl 24,000; Fac 871; Highest Degree: Doctorate
Library Holdings: Bk Vols 1,700,000
Special Collections: Archive of Turkish Oral Narrative; CNN World News Report Archive; Institute for Studies in Pragmatism; Southwest Coll; Vietnam Archive. State Document Depository; US Document Depository
Automation Activity & Vendor Info: (Acquisitions) Ex Libris Group; (Cataloging) Ex Libris Group; (Circulation) Ex Libris Group; (Course Reserve) Ex Libris Group; (OPAC) Ex Libris Group; (Serials) Ex Libris Group
Wireless access
Function: Res libr
Publications: ACCESS (Newsletter); Guides to Library Collections; Library News; Southwest Chronicle (Newsletter); Texas Tech University Library
Partic in Amigos Library Services, Inc

LUFKIN

C ANGELINA COLLEGE LIBRARY*, 3500 S First St, 75904. (Mail add: PO Box 1768, 75902-1768), SAN 316-5841. Tel: 936-633-5220. FAX: 936-633-5442. E-mail: aclibrary@angelina.edu. Web Site: www.angelina.edu/ac-library. *Dir, Learning Res,* Dr Tom McKinney; E-mail: tmckinney@angelina.edu; *Lead Librn,* Christopher Fanning; E-mail: cfanning@angelina.edu; *Librn,* Kimberly England; E-mail: kengland@angelina.edu; Staff 3 (MLS 3)
Founded 1968. Enrl 2,490; Highest Degree: Associate
Sept 2020-Aug 2021 Income $342,519. Mats Exp $352,100
Library Holdings: e-books 85,100; Bk Titles 36,000; Per Subs 69
Automation Activity & Vendor Info: (Acquisitions) SirsiDynix; (Cataloging) SirsiDynix; (Circulation) SirsiDynix; (Course Reserve) SirsiDynix; (OPAC) SirsiDynix; (Serials) SirsiDynix
Wireless access
Function: 24/7 Online cat, Audio & video playback equip for onsite use, Computers for patron use, Electronic databases & coll, For res purposes, Internet access, Magazines, Movies, Online cat, Online ref, Photocopying/Printing, Ref & res, Study rm
Partic in Amigos Library Services, Inc; TexSHARE - Texas State Library & Archives Commission
Open Mon-Thurs 7:30am-9pm, Fri 7:30-5 (Spring); Mon-Thurs 7:30-7 (Summer)

R FIRST UNITED METHODIST CHURCH LIBRARY*, 805 E Denman Ave, 75901. SAN 328-6142. Tel: 936-639-3141. FAX: 936-639-3667. Web Site: lufkinfirst.com. *Ch Serv,* Carolee Brink; Tel: 936-631-3233, E-mail: cbrink@lufkinfirst.com
Library Holdings: Bk Vols 7,000
Subject Interests: Relig
Wireless access
Open Sun 9-12

P KURTH MEMORIAL LIBRARY*, 706 S Raguet St, 75904. SAN 316-585X. Tel: 936-630-0560. FAX: 936-639-2487. Web Site: kurthmemoriallibrary.com. *Libr Dir,* Lorraine Simoneau; E-mail: lsimoneau@cityoflufkin.com; *Asst Dir,* Julie Massey; E-mail: jmassey@cityoflufkin.com; Staff 16 (MLS 3, Non-MLS 13)
Founded 1932. Pop 86,000; Circ 200,000
Library Holdings: Per Subs 54
Subject Interests: Genealogy, Local hist, Spanish lit
Automation Activity & Vendor Info: (Cataloging) SirsiDynix; (Circulation) SirsiDynix; (OPAC) SirsiDynix
Wireless access
Function: Accelerated reader prog, Audiobks via web, Bilingual assistance for Spanish patrons, Bk club(s), Bks on CD, Children's prog, Citizenship assistance, Computer training, Computers for patron use, Digital talking bks, E-Readers, Electronic databases & coll, Family literacy, For res purposes, Free DVD rentals, Genealogy discussion group, Health sci info serv, Holiday prog, Home delivery & serv to seniorr ctr & nursing homes, ILL available, Internet access, Mail & tel request accepted, Microfiche/film & reading machines, Movies, Online cat, Online info literacy tutorials on the web & in blackboard, Online ref, Outreach serv, OverDrive digital audio bks, Photocopying/Printing, Preschool outreach, Preschool reading prog, Prog for adults, Prog for children & young adult, Ref serv available, Senior computer classes, Senior outreach, Spanish lang bks, Spoken cassettes & CDs, Story hour, Study rm, Summer & winter reading prog, Summer reading prog, Tax forms, Teen prog, Telephone ref, Winter reading prog, Workshops
Open Mon-Thurs 10-7, Fri 10-6, Sat 10-2
Friends of the Library Group

LULING

P J B NICKELLS MEMORIAL LIBRARY*, 215 S Pecan Ave, 78648. SAN 316-5892. Tel: 830-875-2813. FAX: 830-875-2038. E-mail: library@cityofluling.net. Web Site: www.cityofluling.net/214/public-library. *Librn,* Mona Harmon; Staff 2 (MLS 1, Non-MLS 1)
Founded 1969. Pop 5,599; Circ 21,996
Library Holdings: AV Mats 312; DVDs 1,313; Large Print Bks 720; Bk Titles 19,218; Per Subs 30; Talking Bks 292; Videos 142
Subject Interests: Tex
Automation Activity & Vendor Info: (Cataloging) Biblionix; (Circulation) Biblionix; (OPAC) Biblionix
Wireless access
Partic in Partners Library Action Network
Open Mon, Wed & Fri 8:30-5, Tues & Thurs 8:30-8, Sat 9-1
Friends of the Library Group

LUMBERTON

P LUMBERTON PUBLIC LIBRARY*, 130 E Chance Rd, 77657-7763. SAN 376-4885. Tel: 409-755-7400. E-mail: lumbertonpubliclibrary@gmail.com. Web Site: www.lumbertonpubliclibrary.org. *Libr Dir,* Amanda Rodriguez; E-mail: director@lumbertonpubliclibrary.org; Staff 6 (Non-MLS 6)
Founded 1994. Pop 16,900; Circ 56,764
Library Holdings: Bk Vols 31,648; Per Subs 46
Special Collections: Texana
Automation Activity & Vendor Info: (Acquisitions) ComPanion Corp; (Cataloging) ComPanion Corp; (Circulation) ComPanion Corp; (OPAC) ComPanion Corp
Wireless access
Function: Audio & video playback equip for onsite use, Bks on cassette, Bks on CD, CD-ROM, Children's prog, Computer training, Computers for patron use, Electronic databases & coll, Equip loans & repairs, Free DVD rentals, Games & aids for people with disabilities, Home delivery & serv to seniorr ctr & nursing homes, ILL available, Internet access, Magnifiers for reading, Music CDs, Online cat, Photocopying/Printing, Ref & res, Ref serv available, Scanner, Senior computer classes, Spoken cassettes & CDs, Spoken cassettes & DVDs, Story hour, Summer reading prog, Tax forms, VHS videos, Workshops
Open Mon-Fri 10-6, Sat 10-1
Friends of the Library Group

LYTLE

P LYTLE PUBLIC LIBRARY*, 19325 W FM Rd, 2790 S, 78052. (Mail add: PO Box 831, 78052-0831), SAN 376-415X. Tel: 830-709-4142. FAX: 830-772-3675. E-mail: lytle_library@sbcglobal.net. Web Site: lytletx.org/index.aspx?nid=115. *Libr Dir,* Cassandra Cortez; Staff 1 (Non-MLS 1)
Founded 1972. Pop 4,500; Circ 19,000
Library Holdings: Bk Vols 21,000
Automation Activity & Vendor Info: (Cataloging) Biblionix; (Circulation) Biblionix
Wireless access
Partic in Partners Library Action Network
Open Mon, Wed & Fri 9:30-5:30, Tues & Thurs 11-7

MABANK

P TRI-COUNTY LIBRARY*, 132 E Market St, 75147. SAN 376-4389. Tel: 903-887-9622. FAX: 903-887-9622. E-mail: info@tricountylibrary.org. Web Site: www.tricountylibrary.org. *Dir,* Melissa Newland; E-mail: melissa@tricountylibrary.org; *Asst Dir,* Sammie Neighbors
Founded 1991. Pop 4,050
Library Holdings: CDs 31; DVDs 48; Large Print Bks 350; Bk Titles 22,000; Bk Vols 25,000; Per Subs 26; Talking Bks 517
Special Collections: Genealogy Coll
Automation Activity & Vendor Info: (Cataloging) Follett Software; (Circulation) Follett Software
Wireless access
Partic in Partners Library Action Network
Open Tues-Thurs 9-5:30, Fri 9-3:30
Friends of the Library Group

MADISONVILLE

P MADISON COUNTY LIBRARY*, 605 S May, 77864. SAN 316-599X. Tel: 936-348-6118. E-mail: mclib@madisoncountytx.org. Web Site: www.madisonlibrarytx.org. *Dir,* Veronica Grooms
Pop 10,000; Circ 25,375
Library Holdings: Bk Vols 25,000; Per Subs 45
Subject Interests: Genealogy
Automation Activity & Vendor Info: (Cataloging) Biblionix; (Circulation) Biblionix
Wireless access
Partic in Partners Library Action Network
Open Mon & Wed-Fri 9-5, Tues 11-7
Friends of the Library Group

MALAKOFF

P RED WALLER COMMUNITY LIBRARY*, 109 Melton St, 75148. (Mail add: PO Box 1177, 75148-1177), SAN 316-6007. Tel: 903-489-1818. FAX: 903-489-2517. Web Site: cityofmalakoff.net/departments/library.html. *Dir,* Charlotte Regester; E-mail: cregester@cityofmalakoff.net; Staff 1.5 (MLS 1, Non-MLS 0.5)
Founded 1972. Pop 7,535
Library Holdings: AV Mats 1,061; Large Print Bks 1,000; Bk Titles 32,062; Bk Vols 32,162; Per Subs 46; Talking Bks 456
Special Collections: Bicentennial Package (American Issues Forum Coll); Malakoff History Coll. Oral History
Automation Activity & Vendor Info: (Cataloging) LibraryWorld, Inc; (Circulation) LibraryWorld, Inc
Function: AV serv, Games & aids for people with disabilities, ILL available, Magnifiers for reading, Photocopying/Printing, Prof lending libr, Prog for children & young adult, Ref serv available, Summer reading prog, Telephone ref, Wheelchair accessible, Workshops
Open Mon 1-5, Tues-Fri 9:30-5
Friends of the Library Group

MANSFIELD

P MANSFIELD PUBLIC LIBRARY*, 104 S Wisteria St, 76063. SAN 316-6015. Tel: 817-728-3690. E-mail: mpl@mansfieldtexas.gov. Web Site: www.mansfieldtexas.gov/154/library. *Dir, Libr Serv,* Yolanda Botello; E-mail: yolanda.botello@mansfieldtexas.gov; *Asst Libr Dir,* Faria Matin; E-mail: faria.matin@mansfieldtexas.gov; Staff 3 (MLS 3)
Pop 69,350
Library Holdings: Audiobooks 2,592; DVDs 6,174; e-books 30,288; Bk Titles 60,588
Automation Activity & Vendor Info: (Cataloging) Follett Software; (Circulation) Follett Software
Wireless access
Function: Accelerated reader prog, Adult bk club, Art exhibits, Audiobks via web, Bk club(s), Bks on cassette, Bks on CD, Children's prog, Computers for patron use, E-Reserves, Electronic databases & coll, Free DVD rentals, ILL available, Music CDs, Outside serv via phone, mail, e-mail & web, Photocopying/Printing, Prog for adults, Prog for children & young adult, Ref serv available, Res libr, Spoken cassettes & CDs, Spoken cassettes & DVDs, Story hour, Summer reading prog, Tax forms, Teen prog, Wheelchair accessible, Workshops
Partic in Partners Library Action Network
Special Services for the Blind - Audio mat; Bks available with recordings; Bks on cassette; Bks on CD; Large print bks; Talking bk & rec for the blind cat; Talking bk serv referral; Talking bks & player equip
Open Mon, Wed & Fri 10-6, Tues & Thurs 10-8, Sat 10-4
Friends of the Library Group

MARATHON

P MARATHON PUBLIC LIBRARY*, 106 E Third St, 79842. (Mail add: PO Box 177, 79842). Tel: 432-386-4136. FAX: 432-386-4136. E-mail: info@marathonpubliclibrary.org. Web Site: www.marathonpubliclibrary.org. *Dir,* Elizabeth Holt
Wireless access
Function: Adult bk club, After school storytime, Chess club, Children's prog, Computers for patron use, Online cat, Scanner, Story hour
Partic in Partners Library Action Network
Open Mon-Fri 2-6
Friends of the Library Group

MARFA

P MARFA PUBLIC LIBRARY*, 115 E Oak St, 79843. (Mail add: PO Drawer U, 79843-0609), SAN 316-6023. Tel: 432-729-4631. FAX: 432-729-3424. Web Site: www.marfapubliclibrary.org. *Dir,* Mandy Roane; E-mail: director@marfapubliclibrary.org; Staff 3 (Non-MLS 3)
Founded 1947. Pop 2,800; Circ 31,306
Library Holdings: Bk Titles 32,148; Per Subs 22
Special Collections: Genealogy & Texana Coll; Junior Historian Files; Local & Border Regional History
Automation Activity & Vendor Info: (Cataloging) Follett Software; (Circulation) Follett Software; (OPAC) Follett Software
Wireless access
Partic in Partners Library Action Network
Open Mon-Fri 9-5, Sat 10-2
Friends of the Library Group

MARLIN

P PAULINE & JANE CHILTON MEMORIAL MARLIN PUBLIC LIBRARY*, Marlin Public Library, 400 Oaks St, 76661. SAN 316-6031. Tel: 254-883-6602. FAX: 254-883-2673. E-mail: reference@marlinpubliclibrary.com. Web Site: marlinpubliclibrary.com. *Libr Dir,* Christopher Harris; *Librn,* Dale Kling; Staff 2 (Non-MLS 2)
Founded 1925. Pop 5,597; Circ 16,000
Library Holdings: Bk Vols 16,000
Wireless access
Partic in Partners Library Action Network
Open Mon & Tues 10-4, Wed & Thurs 1:30-5:30

MARSHALL

CR EAST TEXAS BAPTIST UNIVERSITY*, Mamye Jarrett Library, One Tiger Dr, 75670-1498. SAN 316-6066. Tel: 903-923-2256. Interlibrary Loan Service Tel: 903-923-2260. Reference Tel: 903-923-2262. FAX: 903-935-3447. Web Site: www.etbu.edu/academic-resources/library. *Dean, Libr Serv,* Elizabeth Ponder; Tel: 903-923-2263, E-mail: eponder@etbu.edu; *Head, Access Serv,* Annie Henderson; Tel: 903-923-2264, E-mail: ahenderson@etbu.edu; *Reference & User Services Librn,* Daniel Vaughan; Tel: 903-923-2260; *Electronic Res, Tech Serv Librn,* Chris Altnau; Tel: 903-923-2259; *Library Asst, Acquisitions,* Linda Morey; Tel: 903-923-2261, E-mail: lmorey@etbu.edu; *Library Asst, Digital Projects,* Paula Cottrell; Tel: 903-923-2258; Staff 6.5 (MLS 3, Non-MLS 3.5)
Founded 1917. Enrl 1,116; Fac 75; Highest Degree: Bachelor
Jun 2015-May 2016 Income $687,271, Parent Institution $687,271. Mats Exp $650,141, Books $4,046, Per/Ser (Incl. Access Fees) $10,362, AV Mat $10,083, Electronic Ref Mat (Incl. Access Fees) $221,492. Sal $211,749
Library Holdings: Audiobooks 5,790; AV Mats 304,517; CDs 2,161; DVDs 172; e-books 3,497,007; e-journals 45,000; Electronic Media & Resources 301,674; Microforms 10,000; Music Scores 5,097; Bk Vols 91,467; Per Subs 20; Videos 259
Special Collections: Alumni Coll; Baptist Coll; College of Marshall/East Texas Baptist College/East Texas Baptist University History Coll, doc, newsp, photog, yearbks; Cope Coll of Texana; Dr & Mrs T C Gardner (Gardner Baptist Training Union Coll), memorabilia, papers; East Texas Ante-Bellum History Coll; H L Mencken (Joseph C Goulden Coll); Lance Fenton Rare Bible Coll; Lentz Coll of Texana; Rare Books
Subject Interests: Baptists, Local hist, Texana, Univ hist
Automation Activity & Vendor Info: (Acquisitions) SirsiDynix; (Cataloging) SirsiDynix; (Circulation) SirsiDynix; (Course Reserve) SirsiDynix; (ILL) OCLC; (OPAC) SirsiDynix; (Serials) SirsiDynix
Wireless access

Function: Archival coll, Audio & video playback equip for onsite use, Electronic databases & coll, ILL available, Instruction & testing, Online cat, Online info literacy tutorials on the web & in blackboard, Online ref, Outside serv via phone, mail, e-mail & web, Photocopying/Printing, Prog for adults, Ref & res, Ref serv available, Telephone ref, VHS videos, Wheelchair accessible, Workshops
Publications: Jarrett Library Blog (Online only)
Partic in Amigos Library Services, Inc; Statewide California Electronic Library Consortium; Tex Independent Cols & Univ Librs; Texas Council of Academic Libraries; TexSHARE - Texas State Library & Archives Commission
Open Mon-Thurs 7:30am-Midnight, Fri 7:30-5, Sat Noon-5, Sun 4pm-Midnight
Restriction: Authorized patrons, Borrowing privileges limited to fac & registered students, Circ limited, Limited access for the pub, Open to pub for ref & circ; with some limitations, Open to pub with supv only, Open to qualified scholars, Open to students, fac, staff & alumni, Photo ID required for access, Res pass required for non-affiliated visitors
Friends of the Library Group

S HARRISON COUNTY HISTORICAL MUSEUM*, Inez Hatley Hughes Research Library, 104 E Crockett St, 75670. (Mail add: PO Box 1987, 75671), SAN 327-7992. Tel: 903-938-2680. E-mail: easttexaskin@gmail.com. Web Site: harrisoncountymuseum.org/research. *Research Librn,* Dr Robert Graves
Founded 1965
Library Holdings: Bk Titles 2,500; Bk Vols 3,000
Special Collections: Census Records; High School Yearbooks; Marshall Telephone Books & City Directories; Pictures; Scrapbooks
Subject Interests: Civil War, Genealogy, Hist, Law, Local hist, Med
Wireless access
Function: Archival coll
Publications: Ancestor Issues (Newsletter)
Open Tues-Fri 10-4

P MARSHALL PUBLIC LIBRARY*, 300 S Alamo Blvd, 75670. SAN 316-6082. Tel: 903-935-4465. FAX: 903-935-4463. E-mail: info@marshallpubliclibrary.org. Web Site: www.marshalltexas.net/186/marshall-public-library. *Dir,* Terri Nalls; E-mail: nalls.terri@marshallpubliclibrary.org; Staff 7 (MLS 2, Non-MLS 5)
Founded 1969. Pop 62,462
Library Holdings: Bk Titles 52,432; Bk Vols 56,323; Per Subs 80
Special Collections: Local Newspaper, 1849-present, micro; Texana
Automation Activity & Vendor Info: (Acquisitions) Biblionix/Apollo; (Cataloging) Biblionix/Apollo; (Circulation) Biblionix/Apollo; (OPAC) Biblionix/Apollo
Wireless access
Function: 24/7 Electronic res, 24/7 Online cat, 24/7 wireless access, Activity rm, Adult bk club, Bks on cassette, Bks on CD, Children's prog, Computer training, Computers for patron use, Free DVD rentals, ILL available, Music CDs, Online cat, Photocopying/Printing, Preschool reading prog, Story hour, Summer reading prog, Tax forms, Wheelchair accessible
Partic in Amigos Library Services, Inc
Open Mon, Tues & Thurs 9:30-7:30, Wed & Fri 9:30-5:30, Sat 9:30-3:30
Friends of the Library Group

C WILEY UNIVERSITY*, Thomas Winston Cole, Sr Library, 711 Wiley Ave, 75670. SAN 316-6090. Tel: 903-927-3272. E-mail: reference@wileyc.edu. Web Site: www.wileyc.edu/about/thomas-w-cole-sr-library. *Dir, Libr Serv,* Elizabeth Bradshaw; Tel: 903-927-3275, E-mail: ebradshaw@wileyc.edu; Staff 2 (MLS 1, Non-MLS 1)
Founded 1873. Enrl 608; Fac 42; Highest Degree: Master
Library Holdings: e-books 178,000; e-journals 29,000; Bk Vols 6,395
Special Collections: Black Studies Coll; Thomas W Cole Coll; Wiley University Special Coll & Archives
Automation Activity & Vendor Info: (Cataloging) TLC (The Library Corporation); (Circulation) TLC (The Library Corporation); (Course Reserve) TLC (The Library Corporation); (ILL) OCLC WorldShare Interlibrary Loan; (OPAC) TLC (The Library Corporation)
Wireless access
Partic in Amigos Library Services, Inc
Open Mon-Thurs 8am-10pm, Fri 8-5, Sun 6-10

MART

P NANCY NAIL MEMORIAL LIBRARY*, 124 S Pearl St, 76664-1425. Tel: 254-876-2465. FAX: 254-876-2465. E-mail: nancynaillibrary@att.net. Web Site: www.martlibrary.org. *Dir,* Pat Curry; *Asst Librn,* George Gibbs; Staff 2 (Non-MLS 2)
Pop 3,731; Circ 7,725
Library Holdings: Audiobooks 37; Bks on Deafness & Sign Lang 18; CDs 37; DVDs 157; Large Print Bks 1,444; Bk Titles 19,485; Bk Vols 21,197; Per Subs 1; Videos 618
Wireless access
Partic in Partners Library Action Network
Open Mon-Fri 1-5

MARTINDALE

P MARTINDALE COMMUNITY LIBRARY*, 411 Main St, 78655. (Mail add: PO Box 255, 78655). Tel: 512-357-4492. E-mail: martindalelibrary@gmail.com. *Libr Dir,* Ashley Guerrero; Staff 1 (MLS 1)
Founded 2005. Pop 1,116
Wireless access
Function: 24/7 Electronic res, 24/7 Online cat, Audiobks on Playaways & MP3, Bks on CD, Children's prog, Computer training, Computers for patron use, Electronic databases & coll, Free DVD rentals, Magazines, Movies, Online cat, OverDrive digital audio bks, Photocopying/Printing, Preschool reading prog, Prog for children & young adult, Res assist avail, Scanner, Summer reading prog
Partic in Partners Library Network
Open Wed & Thurs Noon-6, Fri Noon-4, Sat 10-2
Restriction: Free to mem
Friends of the Library Group

MASON

P MASON COUNTY M BEVEN ECKERT MEMORIAL LIBRARY*, 410 Post Hill, 76856. (Mail add: PO Box 1785, 76856-1785), SAN 316-6104. Tel: 325-347-5446. FAX: 325-347-6562. E-mail: masontexaslibrary@gmail.com. Web Site: mason.ploud.net. *Dir, Librn,* Cristi Slocum; Staff 2 (Non-MLS 2)
Pop 4,012; Circ 27,775
Library Holdings: Bk Vols 10,000; Per Subs 14
Automation Activity & Vendor Info: (Cataloging) Biblionix; (Circulation) Biblionix
Wireless access
Function: 24/7 Electronic res, 24/7 Online cat, Activity rm, Adult bk club, Adult literacy prog, Art exhibits, Audio & video playback equip for onsite use, Audiobks via web, Bk club(s), Bks on CD, Children's prog, Computer training, Computers for patron use, E-Readers, Electronic databases & coll, Family literacy, Free DVD rentals, Holiday prog, Homebound delivery serv, ILL available, Internet access, Laminating, Life-long learning prog for all ages, Magazines, Mail & tel request accepted, Movies, Online cat, Outreach serv, OverDrive digital audio bks, Photocopying/Printing, Preschool outreach, Prog for adults, Prog for children & young adult, Scanner, Senior computer classes, Spanish lang bks, Spoken cassettes & CDs, Story hour, Study rm, Summer reading prog, Wheelchair accessible, Workshops, Writing prog
Open Mon-Fri 10-6
Friends of the Library Group

MATADOR

P MOTLEY COUNTY LIBRARY*, 1105 Main St, 79244. (Mail add: PO Box 557, 79244-0557), SAN 325-2922. Tel: 806-347-2717. E-mail: motleycountylibrary@hotmail.com. Web Site: motley.harringtonlc.org. *Libr Dir,* Carla Meador
Founded 1981. Pop 1,200; Circ 4,711
Library Holdings: Bk Titles 9,613; Bk Vols 10,583
Subject Interests: Genealogy, Tex hist
Wireless access
Partic in Harrington Library Consortium
Special Services for the Deaf - Bks on deafness & sign lang; High interest/low vocabulary bks
Open Mon 2-5, Tues-Thurs 1-6, Fri 10-3
Friends of the Library Group

MATHIS

P MATHIS PUBLIC LIBRARY*, 103 Lamar St, 78368. SAN 316-6112. Tel: 361-547-6201. FAX: 361-547-6201. E-mail: mathispubliclibrary@yahoo.com. Web Site: www.cityofmathis.com/index.aspx?NID=275. *Dir,* Norma Ovalle
Pop 7,416; Circ 8,679
Library Holdings: AV Mats 973; DVDs 1,000; Bk Titles 18,000; Bk Vols 19,000; Per Subs 30
Automation Activity & Vendor Info: (Cataloging) Biblionix; (Circulation) Biblionix
Wireless access
Open Mon 2-6, Tues 9-6, Wed & Thurs 11-6, Fri 1-6
Friends of the Library Group

MAUD

P MAUD PUBLIC LIBRARY*, 335 Houston St, 75567-0388. (Mail add: PO Box 100, 75567-0100), SAN 376-4524. Tel: 903-585-2121. FAX: 903-585-2021. E-mail: maudlibrary@gmail.com. Web Site: maud.ploud.net. *Librn,* Savannah Monroe
Pop 1,016; Circ 2,867

Library Holdings: Bk Titles 15,000; Talking Bks 60; Videos 1,000
Automation Activity & Vendor Info: (Acquisitions) Biblionix/Apollo; (Cataloging) Biblionix/Apollo
Wireless access
Function: 24/7 Online cat, Activity rm, Adult bk club, Archival coll
Open Tues-Fri 9-2
Friends of the Library Group

MCALLEN

P HIDALGO COUNTY LIBRARY SYSTEM*, c/o McAllen Memorial Library, 4001 N 3rd St, 78504. SAN 316-5922. Web Site: www.hcls.lib.tx.us. *Pres,* Kate Horan; Tel: 956-681-3008, E-mail: khoran@mcallen.net; *VPres,* Yenni B Espinoza; Tel: 956-583-5656, E-mail: library@cityofpenitas.com; Staff 1 (MLS 1)
Founded 1971. Pop 506,919
Member Libraries: Donna Public Library; Dr Hector P Garcia Memorial Library; Dustin Michael Sekula Memorial Library; Elsa Public Library; Hidalgo Public Library; La Joya Municipal Library; Mayor Joe V Sanchez Public Library; McAllen Public Library; Penitas Public Library; Pharr Memorial Library; San Juan Memorial Library; Sargeant Fernando de la Rosa Memorial Library; Speer Memorial Library
Open Mon-Thurs 9-9, Fri & Sat 9-6, Sun 1-6

P MCALLEN PUBLIC LIBRARY*, 4001 N 23rd St, 78504. SAN 316-5930. Tel: 956-681-3000. Circulation Tel: 956-681-3019. Reference Tel: 956-681-3061. FAX: 956-681-3009. E-mail: referenceLibrarian@mcallen.net. Web Site: www.mcallenlibrary.net. *Libr Dir,* Kate P Horan; E-mail: khoran@mcallen.net; *Asst Dir, Pub Serv,* Alexandria C Eccles; E-mail: aeccles@mcallen.net; *Asst Dir, Support Serv,* Ed Arjona; E-mail: earjona@mcallen.net; *Children's Serv Supvr,* Kristina Corral; E-mail: kgarcia@mcallen.net; *Ref Supvr,* David Rios; E-mail: drios@mcallen.net; *Syst Supvr,* Jorge Gonzalez; E-mail: jorge_gonzalez@mcallen.net; Staff 17.5 (MLS 16, Non-MLS 1.5)
Founded 1932. Pop 168,000; Circ 536,627
Library Holdings: CDs 11,474; DVDs 10,559; e-books 6,000; Bk Vols 320,000; Per Subs 650
Special Collections: Libros en Espanol; Mexican-American Coll; Mexico Coll; Texas Coll
Subject Interests: Genealogy, Mexico, Tex
Automation Activity & Vendor Info: (Acquisitions) TLC (The Library Corporation); (Cataloging) TLC (The Library Corporation); (Circulation) TLC (The Library Corporation); (OPAC) TLC (The Library Corporation); (Serials) TLC (The Library Corporation)
Wireless access
Publications: Beginnings - A First Course in Spanish (Library handbook)
Mem of Hidalgo County Library System
Partic in OCLC Online Computer Library Center, Inc
Special Services for the Deaf - TDD equip
Special Services for the Blind - Bks on cassette; Braille bks; Reader equip
Open Mon-Thurs 9-9, Fri & Sat 9-6, Sun 1-6
Friends of the Library Group
Branches: 2
LARK BRANCH, 2601 Lark Ave, 78504. Tel: 956-681-3100. FAX: 956-688-3346. *Br Mgr,* Edwardo Lopez; Tel: 956-681-3102, E-mail: elopez@mcallen.net; Staff 10 (MLS 1, Non-MLS 9)
Founded 2001
Library Holdings: Bk Vols 7,500
Open Mon-Thurs 10-9, Fri & Sat 10-5, Sun 1-9
Friends of the Library Group
PALM VIEW BRANCH, 3401 Jordan Rd W, 78503. Tel: 956-681-3110. FAX: 956-688-3366. *Br Mgr,* Rolando Ramirez; Tel: 956-681-3113, E-mail: rolando.ramirez@mcallen.net; Staff 3 (MLS 2, Non-MLS 1)
Founded 2001
Library Holdings: Bk Vols 11,000
Open Mon-Thurs 10-9, Fri & Sat 10-5, Sun 1-9

C SOUTH TEXAS COLLEGE LIBRARY, Pecan Campus, 3201 W Pecan Blvd, 78501-6661. SAN 325-0687. Tel: 956-872-8330. Web Site: library.southtexascollege.edu/aboutus/hourscontact/#pecan. *Dean, Libr & Learning Support,* Dr Jesus Campos; Tel: 956-872-2528, E-mail: jhcampos@southtexascollege.edu; *Assoc Dean, Libr Serv,* Elizabeth Hollenbeck; Tel: 956-872-3482, E-mail: ehollenb@southtexascollege.edu; *Acq Librn, Coll Mgt Librn, Librn III,* Patricia Saenz; Tel: 956-872-2323, E-mail: psaenz8@southtexascollege.edu; *Instruction & Outreach Librn, Librn III,* Katie Hernandez; Tel: 956-872-1983, E-mail: kherna58@southtexascollege.edu; *Librn III, Ref & Circ Librn,* Minerva Alvarez; Tel: 956-872-3442, E-mail: malvarez1@southtexascollege.edu; *Mgr,* Becky Owens; Tel: 956-872-6487, E-mail: bhowens@southtexascollege.edu; Staff 73 (MLS 18, Non-MLS 55)
Founded 1984. Highest Degree: Bachelor
Automation Activity & Vendor Info: (Acquisitions) SirsiDynix; (Cataloging) SirsiDynix; (Circulation) SirsiDynix; (Course Reserve) SirsiDynix; (ILL) SirsiDynix; (Media Booking) SirsiDynix; (OPAC) SirsiDynix; (Serials) SirsiDynix
Wireless access
Partic in Amigos Library Services, Inc; TexSHARE - Texas State Library & Archives Commission
Open Mon-Thurs 8-8, Fri 8-5, Sat 10-2, Sun 2-6

MCCAMEY

P UPTON COUNTY PUBLIC LIBRARY*, 212 W Seventh St, 79752. (Mail add: PO Box 1377, 79752-1377), SAN 316-5949. Tel: 432-652-8718. FAX: 432-652-3858. E-mail: mcclb@yahoo.com. Web Site: mccamey.ploud.net. *Libr Dir,* Celia Hooker; Staff 1 (Non-MLS 1)
Founded 1939. Pop 2,650; Circ 22,770
Library Holdings: Bk Vols 16,500; Per Subs 34
Special Collections: Texana Coll
Automation Activity & Vendor Info: (Cataloging) Follett Software; (Circulation) Follett Software
Open Mon-Thurs 8-12 & 1-5, Fri 8-4

MCGREGOR

P MCGINLEY MEMORIAL PUBLIC LIBRARY, 317 S Main St, 76657. SAN 372-7599. Tel: 254-840-3732. FAX: 254-840-2624. E-mail: mcgregorlibrary317@gmail.com. Web Site: mcgregor.ploud.net. *Librn,* Michelle Lenamon; Staff 1 (Non-MLS 1)
Founded 1983. Pop 5,000
Library Holdings: Bk Titles 19,000; Bk Vols 21,000
Automation Activity & Vendor Info: (Cataloging) Biblionix/Apollo; (Circulation) Biblionix/Apollo
Wireless access
Partic in Partners Library Action Network
Open Mon & Wed 9-2, Tues 2-7, Thurs 12-5

MCKINNEY

J COLLIN COLLEGE, McKinney Campus, 2200 W University, 75071. Tel: 972-548-6860, 972-548-6868. Reference Tel: 972-548-6869. FAX: 972-548-6844. Reference E-mail: cpclibrary@collin.edu. Web Site: www.collin.edu/library. *Exec Dir, Libr Dir,* Faye Davis; Tel: 972-548-6866, E-mail: fdavis@collin.edu; Staff 12 (MLS 11, Non-MLS 1)
Founded 1986. Highest Degree: Bachelor
Library Holdings: Bk Vols 55,000
Automation Activity & Vendor Info: (Acquisitions) OCLC Worldshare Management Services; (Cataloging) OCLC Worldshare Management Services; (Circulation) OCLC Worldshare Management Services; (Course Reserve) OCLC Worldshare Management Services; (ILL) OCLC WorldShare Interlibrary Loan; (OPAC) OCLC Worldshare Management Services
Wireless access
Open Mon-Thurs 7:45am-8pm, Fri 7:45-5, Sat 11-4

L CURT B HENDERSON LAW LIBRARY*, Russell A Steindam Courts Bldg, 2100 Bloomdale Rd, 75071. SAN 372-1671. Tel: 972-424-1460, Ext 4255, 972-424-1460, Ext 4260. E-mail: lawlibrary@co.collin.tx.gov. Web Site: www.collincountytx.gov/law_library. *Law Librn,* Bethany Fansler; E-mail: bfansler@co.collin.tx.us; *Asst Law Librn,* Jonathan Sims; E-mail: jsims@co.collin.tx.us; Staff 2 (MLS 2)
Library Holdings: Bk Vols 25,000; Per Subs 15
Wireless access
Open Mon-Fri 8-5

P MCKINNEY MEMORIAL PUBLIC LIBRARY, Roy & Helen Hall Memorial Library, 101 E Hunt St, 75069. SAN 316-5973. Tel: 972-547-7323. FAX: 972-542-0868. E-mail: contact-library@mckinneytexas.org. Web Site: www.mckinneytexas.org/116/library. *Dir of Libr,* Spencer Smith; E-mail: ssmith3@mckinneytexas.org; Staff 55 (MLS 12, Non-MLS 43)
Founded 1928. Pop 172,298; Circ 1,741,330
Library Holdings: Audiobooks 10,334; AV Mats 30,829; Braille Volumes 5; CDs 10,509; DVDs 20,332; e-books 3,846; Bk Titles 121,474; Bk Vols 175,601; Per Subs 110
Subject Interests: Genealogy, Texana
Automation Activity & Vendor Info: (Cataloging) ByWater Solutions; (OPAC) ByWater Solutions
Wireless access
Function: 24/7 Electronic res, 24/7 Online cat, Activity rm, Adult bk club, Adult literacy prog, After school storytime, Archival coll, Art exhibits, Audiobks via web, Bk club(s), Bks on CD, Children's prog, Citizenship assistance, Computer training, Computers for patron use, Doc delivery serv, Electronic databases & coll, Free DVD rentals, Genealogy discussion group, Holiday prog, ILL available, Internet access, Magazines, Magnifiers for reading, Mail & tel request accepted, Meeting rooms, Microfiche/film & reading machines, Movies, Online cat, Online info literacy tutorials on the web & in blackboard, Outreach serv, Outside serv via phone, mail, e-mail & web, Photocopying/Printing, Printer for laptops & handheld devices, Prog for adults, Prog for children & young adult, Ref & res, Ref

serv available, Res assist avail, Scanner, Senior computer classes, Senior outreach, Serves people with intellectual disabilities, Spanish lang bks, Study rm, Summer reading prog, Tax forms, Teen prog, Telephone ref, Wheelchair accessible
Open Mon-Thurs 8-7, Fri-Sun 10-6
Friends of the Library Group
Branches: 1
JOHN & JUDY GAY LIBRARY, 6861 W Eldorado Pkwy, 75070. *Br Mgr,* Helen Talley; E-mail: htalley@mckinneytexas.org
Open Mon-Thurs 10-9, Fri-Sun 10-6
Friends of the Library Group

MCLEAN

P LOVETT MEMORIAL LIBRARY*, 302 N Main St, 79057. (Mail add: PO Box 8, 79057-0008), SAN 316-5981. Tel: 806-779-2851. FAX: 806-779-3241. E-mail: mcleanplib@gmail.com. Web Site: www.lovettlibrarymclean.org. *Dir & Librn,* Sally Bohlar; Staff 1 (Non-MLS 1)
Founded 1957. Pop 1,387; Circ 19,929
Library Holdings: Bk Titles 13,160
Automation Activity & Vendor Info: (Cataloging) SirsiDynix; (Circulation) SirsiDynix; (OPAC) SirsiDynix
Wireless access
Partic in Harrington Library Consortium; TexSHARE - Texas State Library & Archives Commission
Open Mon-Fri 10-5

MEDINA

P MEDINA COMMUNITY LIBRARY*, 13948 State Hwy 16 N, 78055. (Mail add: PO Box 300, 78055-0300), SAN 378-4002. Tel: 830-589-2825. FAX: 830-589-7514. E-mail: medinalib@gmail.com. Web Site: www.medinacommunitylibrary.us. *Libr Dir,* Alison Harbour
Founded 2001
Library Holdings: Bk Titles 11,692; Per Subs 24
Special Collections: Local Plant & Wildlife Coll
Subject Interests: Local hist, Tex
Automation Activity & Vendor Info: (Cataloging) Biblionix; (Circulation) Biblionix; (OPAC) Biblionix
Wireless access
Open Mon & Thurs 10-6, Tues, Wed & Fri 10-5, Sat 10-1

MELISSA

P CITY OF MELISSA PUBLIC LIBRARY*, Melissa Public Library, 3411 Barker Ave, 75454. SAN 376-4532. Tel: 972-837-4540. FAX: 972-837-2006. E-mail: librarian@cityofmelissa.com. Web Site: www.cityofmelissa.com/208/Library. *Libr Dir,* Jennifer Nehls; E-mail: jnehls@cityofmelissa.com; *Libr Asst,* Victoria Villegas; E-mail: vvillegas@cityofmelissa.com; Staff 6 (MLS 3, Non-MLS 3)
Founded 1994
Library Holdings: Audiobooks 677; Bks on Deafness & Sign Lang 10; Braille Volumes 7; CDs 3; DVDs 5,538; e-books 28,516; Large Print Bks 398; Bk Titles 21,858; Bk Vols 23,286; Per Subs 5
Automation Activity & Vendor Info: (Acquisitions) Biblionix/Apollo; (Cataloging) Biblionix/Apollo; (Circulation) Biblionix/Apollo; (ILL) Biblionix/Apollo; (OPAC) Biblionix/Apollo
Wireless access
Function: 24/7 Online cat, Bks on CD, Children's prog, Computers for patron use, E-Readers, Electronic databases & coll, Family literacy, Free DVD rentals, Genealogy discussion group, Holiday prog, ILL available, Internet access, Large print keyboards, Magazines, Movies, Notary serv, Online cat, OverDrive digital audio bks, Photocopying/Printing, Preschool reading prog, Prog for adults, Prog for children & young adult, Ref serv available, Scanner, Story hour, Summer reading prog, Teen prog, Wheelchair accessible, Workshops, Writing prog
Partic in Northeast Texas Digital Consortium
Open Mon 9-6, Tues, Wed & Fri 10-6, Thurs 12-8, Sat 10-3
Restriction: Authorized patrons
Friends of the Library Group

MEMPHIS

P MEMPHIS PUBLIC LIBRARY*, 303 S Eighth St, 79245. SAN 316-6120. Tel: 806-259-2062. FAX: 806-259-2062. E-mail: mempubliclibrary@gmail.com. Web Site: harringtonlc.org/memphis. *Libr Dir,* Jacqulyn Owens; E-mail: jacqulynhorton@hotmail.com
Pop 3,200; Circ 17,500
Library Holdings: Bk Vols 25,300; Per Subs 30
Automation Activity & Vendor Info: (Cataloging) SirsiDynix; (Circulation) SirsiDynix; (OPAC) SirsiDynix
Wireless access
Open Mon & Fri 1-6, Tues & Thurs 9-12 & 1-6, Sat 9-1
Friends of the Library Group

MENARD

P MENARD PUBLIC LIBRARY*, 100 E Mission St, 76859. (Mail add: PO Box 404, 76859-0404), SAN 316-6139. Tel: 325-396-2717. FAX: 325-396-2717. E-mail: menardpl@verizon.net. Web Site: menardlibrary.weebly.com. *Dir,* Position Currently Open; *Librn,* Sandy Kothmann
Pop 2,252; Circ 13,333
Library Holdings: Bk Vols 11,000; Per Subs 12
Automation Activity & Vendor Info: (Cataloging) Follett Software; (Circulation) Follett Software
Wireless access
Open Mon-Thurs 10-5, Fri 10-2
Friends of the Library Group

MERCEDES

P DR HECTOR P GARCIA MEMORIAL LIBRARY, 434 S Ohio St, 78570. SAN 316-6147. Tel: 956-565-2371. FAX: 956-565-9458. Web Site: cityofmercedes.com/library. *Dir,* Marisol Vidales; E-mail: mvidales@cityofmercedes.com; *Asst Librn,* Michelle Muniz; E-mail: mmuniz@cityofmercedes.com; Staff 4 (MLS 2, Non-MLS 2)
Founded 1940. Pop 24,178; Circ 26,451
Oct 2024-Sept 2025. Mats Exp $19,900, Books $16,000, Per/Ser (Incl. Access Fees) $1,500, AV Mat $2,400. Sal $293,125
Library Holdings: Electronic Media & Resources 49; Large Print Bks 1,120; Bk Titles 35,172; Bk Vols 39,258; Per Subs 56
Subject Interests: Spanish lang, Tex hist
Automation Activity & Vendor Info: (Acquisitions) Insignia Software; (Cataloging) Insignia Software; (Circulation) Insignia Software; (ILL) Auto-Graphics, Inc; (OPAC) Insignia Software; (Serials) Insignia Software
Wireless access
Function: 24/7 Online cat, 24/7 wireless access, 3D Printer, Activity rm, Adult bk club, Adult literacy prog, After school storytime, Art exhibits, Art programs, Audiobks on Playaways & MP3, Bilingual assistance for Spanish patrons, Children's prog, Computer training, Computers for patron use, Electronic databases & coll, Extended outdoor wifi, Family literacy, Free DVD rentals, Govt ref serv, Health sci info serv, Holiday prog, ILL available, Internet access, Large print keyboards, Life-long learning prog for all ages, Magazines, Makerspace, Meeting rooms, Movies, Notary serv, Online cat, Online info literacy tutorials on the web & in blackboard, Online ref, Outreach serv, Photocopying/Printing, Printer for laptops & handheld devices, Prog for adults, Prog for children & young adult, Ref & res, Ref serv available, Res assist avail, Scanner, Senior computer classes, Senior outreach, Serves people with intellectual disabilities, Spanish lang bks, STEM programs, Story hour, Study rm, Summer reading prog, Teen prog, Telephone ref, Wheelchair accessible, Wifi hotspot checkout
Mem of Hidalgo County Library System
Partic in TexSHARE - Texas State Library & Archives Commission
Special Services for the Blind - Large print bks; Magnifiers; Playaways (bks on MP3)
Open Mon-Thurs 9-7, Fri 9-5
Friends of the Library Group

MERIDIAN

P MERIDIAN PUBLIC LIBRARY*, 118 N Main St, 76665. (Mail add: PO Box 679, 76665-0679). Tel: 254-435-9100. FAX: 254-435-9800. E-mail: meridianpubliclibrary@hotmail.com. Web Site: meridian.biblionix.com/catalog. *Libr Dir,* Cheryl Niemeier
Founded 2000. Pop 1,490
Library Holdings: Audiobooks 350; Large Print Bks 200; Bk Vols 17,000
Special Collections: Chronicler of Folk Music (J T Lomax Coll)
Subject Interests: Texana
Automation Activity & Vendor Info: (Cataloging) Biblionix; (Circulation) Biblionix
Wireless access
Function: ILL available
Partic in Partners Library Action Network
Open Tues-Fri 11-5:30, Sat 11-1

MERKEL

P MERKEL PUBLIC LIBRARY*, 100 Kent St, 79536. Tel: 325-928-5054. FAX: 325-928-3171. E-mail: merkelpubliclibrary@gmail.com. Web Site: merkel.ploud.net, merkeltexas.com/public-library. *Libr Dir,* Suzy Pack
Pop 2,433
Library Holdings: Bk Vols 9,300
Automation Activity & Vendor Info: (Cataloging) Biblionix/Apollo; (Circulation) Biblionix/Apollo
Wireless access
Function: Bks on CD, Children's prog, Computers for patron use, Free DVD rentals, Internet access, Magazines, Movies, Music CDs, Photocopying/Printing, Prog for children & young adult, Scanner, Story hour, Summer reading prog

Open Mon-Fri 11:30-5:30
Restriction: Circ to mem only, Free to mem

MERTZON

P M B NOELKE JR MEMORIAL LIBRARY*, 101 S Broadway, 76941-0766. (Mail add: PO Box 766, 76941), SAN 376-4044. Tel: 325-835-2704. FAX: 325-835-2047. E-mail: iclib2019@hotmail.com. Web Site: www.librarycounty.com. *Dir,* T Kae Hampton; E-mail: tkaeaeh2014@gmail.com
Pop 1,739
Library Holdings: Bk Vols 9,090; Per Subs 10
Automation Activity & Vendor Info: (Acquisitions) Biblionix; (Cataloging) Biblionix; (Circulation) Biblionix
Wireless access
Open Mon-Fri 1:30-5:30
Friends of the Library Group

MESQUITE

J DALLAS COLLEGE*, Eastfield Campus Library, L Bldg, Rm L200, 3737 Motley Dr, 75150-2033. SAN 316-6163. Tel: 972-860-7168. Reference Tel: 972-860-7174. E-mail: eastfieldlibrary@dcccd.edu. Web Site: www.dallascollege.edu/libraries. *Exec Dean,* Karla Greer; Tel: 972-860-7173; *Coll Develop,* Judith Bildz; Tel: 972-860-7176, E-mail: judywayne@dcccd.edu; Staff 15.5 (MLS 7, Non-MLS 8.5)
Founded 1970. Highest Degree: Associate
Library Holdings: AV Mats 3,672; e-books 30,940; Electronic Media & Resources 121; Bk Titles 40,368; Bk Vols 46,255; Per Subs 119
Automation Activity & Vendor Info: (Acquisitions) Ex Libris Group; (Cataloging) Ex Libris Group; (Circulation) Ex Libris Group; (Course Reserve) Ex Libris Group; (Discovery) Ex Libris Group; (ILL) Ex Libris Group; (OPAC) Ex Libris Group; (Serials) Ex Libris Group
Wireless access
Open Mon-Thurs 8-8, Fri 8-5, Sat 9-2

P MESQUITE PUBLIC LIBRARY*, 300 W Grubb Dr, 75149. SAN 316-6171. Tel: 972-216-6220. FAX: 972-216-6740. E-mail: mainbr@cityofmesquite.com. Web Site: www.library.mesquite.tx.us. *Dir,* Virginia Mundt; *AV Librn,* Cheryl Hollingsworth; *Youth Serv Librn,* Rachel Kubosumi; *Supvr, Pub Serv,* Sandra Silva; *Supvr, Tech Serv,* Jeannette Curtis; Staff 14 (MLS 10, Non-MLS 4)
Founded 1963. Pop 139,824; Circ 300,000
Library Holdings: Bk Titles 162,705; Bk Vols 199,502; Per Subs 273
Subject Interests: Genealogy
Automation Activity & Vendor Info: (Cataloging) SirsiDynix; (Circulation) SirsiDynix; (OPAC) SirsiDynix
Wireless access
Function: Adult bk club, Audiobks via web, Bks on cassette, Bks on CD, CD-ROM, Children's prog, Computer training, Computers for patron use, Electronic databases & coll, Free DVD rentals, Holiday prog, ILL available, Music CDs, Online cat, Photocopying/Printing, Prog for adults, Prog for children & young adult, Ref & res, Spoken cassettes & CDs, Story hour, Summer reading prog, Tax forms, Teen prog, Telephone ref, VHS videos, Wheelchair accessible
Partic in Partners Library Action Network
Open Mon, Tues & Thurs 9-8, Wed, Fri & Sat 9-6
Friends of the Library Group
Branches: 1
NORTH BRANCH, 2600 Oates Dr, 75150, SAN 328-7556. Tel: 972-681-0465. FAX: 972-681-0467. E-mail: northbr@cityofmesquite.com. *Br Mgr,* Angela Bartula; *Ch,* Sarah Dawson
Open Mon 10-6, Tues, Thurs & Sat 12-6, Wed 12-8
Friends of the Library Group

MEXIA

P GIBBS MEMORIAL LIBRARY*, 305 E Rusk St, 76667. SAN 316-618X. Tel: 254-562-3231. FAX: 254-472-0140. Reference E-mail: gibbs.library@cityofmexia.com. Web Site: www.gibbslibrarymexia.org. *Libr Dir,* ShienDee Pullman; Staff 5 (Non-MLS 5)
Founded 1903. Pop 14,852; Circ 43,323
Library Holdings: Audiobooks 1,248; CDs 1,248; DVDs 2,781; Large Print Bks 1,578; Bk Vols 39,681; Per Subs 20
Special Collections: War of the Rebellion
Subject Interests: Genealogy, Local hist
Automation Activity & Vendor Info: (Cataloging) Biblionix; (Circulation) Biblionix; (ILL) OCLC FirstSearch
Wireless access
Function: 24/7 Electronic res, 24/7 Online cat, 3D Printer, After school storytime, Bks on CD, Children's prog, Computers for patron use, Electronic databases & coll, Free DVD rentals, ILL available, Internet access, Magazines, Magnifiers for reading, Meeting rooms, Microfiche/film & reading machines, Notary serv, Online cat, Photocopying/Printing, Scanner, Senior computer classes, Summer reading prog, Tax forms, Wheelchair accessible
Partic in Partners Library Action Network
Open Mon-Fri 10-6, Sat 10-4
Friends of the Library Group

MIAMI

P ROBERTS COUNTY LIBRARY, 122 E Water St, 79059. SAN 316-6198. Tel: 806-278-8147. E-mail: library@co.roberts.tx.us. Web Site: www.facebook.com/robertscountylibrary. *Librn,* Grace Roberson
Pop 2,081; Circ 6,465
Library Holdings: Bk Vols 13,200
Wireless access
Open Tues, Thurs & Fri 2-5 (Winter); Mon-Fri 2-5 (Summer)

MIDLAND

J MIDLAND COLLEGE, Murray Fasken Learning Resource Center/Library, 3600 N Garfield, 79705. SAN 316-621X. Tel: 432-685-4560. FAX: 432-685-6710. Web Site: www.midland.edu/services-resources/library. *Libr Dir,* Marc Kennedy; Tel: 432-685-4558, E-mail: marck@midland.edu; *Automation/Technical Servs Librn,* Brianna Barnard; Tel: 432-685-4557, E-mail: bbarnard@midland.edu; *Electronic Serv,* Georgia Pisklak; Tel: 432-685-4703, E-mail: gpisklak@midland.edu; *Tech Serv,* Stephanie Shedd; Tel: 432-685-4583, E-mail: sshedd@midland.edu; Staff 5 (MLS 2, Non-MLS 3)
Founded 1973. Enrl 6,000; Fac 200; Highest Degree: Bachelor
Library Holdings: e-books 10,890; Bk Titles 49,274; Bk Vols 62,610; Per Subs 311
Automation Activity & Vendor Info: (Acquisitions) SirsiDynix; (Cataloging) SirsiDynix; (Circulation) SirsiDynix; (Course Reserve) SirsiDynix; (ILL) Auto-Graphics, Inc; (Media Booking) SirsiDynix; (OPAC) SirsiDynix; (Serials) SirsiDynix
Wireless access
Function: 24/7 Electronic res, 24/7 Online cat, 3D Printer, Art exhibits, Computers for patron use, Electronic databases & coll, Games, ILL available, Instruction & testing, Internet access, Laptop/tablet checkout, Learning ctr, Magazines, Meeting rooms, Movies, Online cat, Online Chat, Online ref, Orientations, Photocopying/Printing, Ref & res, Ref serv available, Res assist avail, Scanner, Study rm, Telephone ref, Wheelchair accessible
Partic in Amigos Library Services, Inc; OCLC Online Computer Library Center, Inc; TexSHARE - Texas State Library & Archives Commission
Open Mon-Thurs 7:45am-9pm, Fri 7:45-Noon, Sun 3-9 (Fall-Spring); Mon-Thurs 8-5 (Summer)
Restriction: Open to pub with supv only, Open to students, fac & staff

P MIDLAND COUNTY PUBLIC LIBRARY*, Downtown, 301 W Missouri Ave, 79701. SAN 316-6228. Tel: 432-688-4320. Circulation Tel: 432-688-4330. Interlibrary Loan Service Tel: 432-688-4337. FAX: 432-688-4939. Web Site: www.co.midland.tx.us/departments/lib/locations/pages/downtown-library.aspx. *Exec Dir,* Debbie Garza; E-mail: dgarza@mcounty.com; *Asst Dir,* Pat Brashear; Tel: 432-688-4321, E-mail: libcat01@co.midland.tx.us; *Spec Coll Librn,* Sarah Ross Kelliher; E-mail: libsc02@co.midland.tx.us; *Adult Serv Supvr, Per,* Harry Ogg; E-mail: libref01@co.midland.tx.us; *Ch Serv,* Mary Powers; E-mail: mpowers@co.midland.tx.us; *Circ,* Whitney Hyde; E-mail: libcirc02@co.midland.tx.us; *ILL,* Becky Naranjo; E-mail: libsc03@co.midland.tx.us; Staff 41 (MLS 6, Non-MLS 35)
Founded 1903. Pop 116,009; Circ 405,807
Library Holdings: AV Mats 10,634; DVDs 13,500; Bk Vols 120,147; Per Subs 445
Subject Interests: Genealogy, Petroleum
Automation Activity & Vendor Info: (Cataloging) OCLC; (Circulation) TLC (The Library Corporation); (OPAC) TLC (The Library Corporation)
Wireless access
Publications: Friends of the Library Newsletter (Biannually)
Partic in Amigos Library Services, Inc; OCLC Online Computer Library Center, Inc; Partners Library Action Network
Open Mon-Sat 10-7
Branches: 1
MIDLAND CENTENNIAL, 2503 W Loop 250 N, 79705, SAN 370-4998. Tel: 432-742-7400. FAX: 432-688-4955. E-mail: libadm01@co.midland.tx.us. Web Site: www.co.midland.tx.us/departments/lib/locations/Pages/Centennial-Library.aspx. *Dir,* Debbie Garza; E-mail: dgarza@mcounty.com; *Asst Dir,* Alice White
Library Holdings: Bk Vols 70,000
Open Mon-Thurs 9-8, Fri & Sat 9-6

S PETROLEUM MUSEUM LIBRARY & HALL OF FAME*, Archives Center, 1500 Interstate 20 W, 79701. SAN 370-1905. Tel: 432-683-4403. Web Site: petroleummuseum.org/library-and-archives-center, petroleummuseum.org/reference-library. *Exec Dir,* Kathy Shannon; E-mail: kshannon@petroleummuseum.org; *Dir, Libr & Archives,* Tiffany Bradley;

E-mail: tbradley@petroleummuseum.org. Subject Specialists: *Hist, Petroleum,* Tiffany Bradley
Founded 1975
Library Holdings: Bk Titles 2,500; Per Subs 25
Special Collections: Oil & Gas Industry History; Photograph Archive; Samuel Myers Coll, oil industry, county histories, research mat used for writing of The Permian Basin. Oral History
Subject Interests: Local hist
Function: Ref serv available
Publications: Museum Memo (Quarterly)
Open Mon-Fri 10-5

MIDLOTHIAN

P A H MEADOWS LIBRARY*, 921 S Ninth St, 76065-3636. SAN 376-4516. Tel: 972-775-3417. Web Site: a-h-meadows-public-school-library.business.site. *Librn,* Julie Post; E-mail: julie_post@misd.gs; Staff 2 (MLS 2)
Library Holdings: DVDs 1,000; Bk Vols 38,000; Per Subs 50
Automation Activity & Vendor Info: (Acquisitions) Follett Software; (Cataloging) Follett Software; (Circulation) Follett Software; (OPAC) Follett Software
Wireless access
Open Mon-Thurs 8-8, Fri 8-4, Sat 10-4

MINEOLA

P MINEOLA MEMORIAL LIBRARY, INC*, 301 N Pacific St, 75773. SAN 316-6244. Tel: 903-569-2767. FAX: 903-569-6511. E-mail: minmemlib@gmail.com. Web Site: mineola.ploud.net. *Dir,* Mary Hurley; Staff 1 (MLS 1)
Founded 1950. Pop 9,527
Library Holdings: Bk Titles 42,010; Per Subs 36
Automation Activity & Vendor Info: (Cataloging) Biblionix; (Circulation) Biblionix; (OPAC) Biblionix
Wireless access
Open Tues & Thurs 9-6, Wed, Fri & Sat 9-2
Friends of the Library Group

MINERAL WELLS

P BOYCE DITTO PUBLIC LIBRARY*, 2300 Martin Luther King Jr St, 76067. (Mail add: PO Box 460, 76068). Tel: 940-328-7880. FAX: 940-328-7871. E-mail: library@mineralwellstx.gov. Web Site: www.mineralwellstx.gov/98/Library. *Libr Mgr,* Louanne Noel; E-mail: lnoel@mineralwellstx.gov; *Asst Libr Mgr,* Lori Batchelor; E-mail: lbatchelor@mineralwellstx.gov
Partic in Partners Library Action Network; TexSHARE - Texas State Library & Archives Commission
Open Tues & Thurs 10-8, Wed & Fri 10-6, Sat 10-3

MISSION

P SPEER MEMORIAL LIBRARY*, 801 E 12th St, 78572. SAN 316-6260. Tel: 956-580-8750. FAX: 956-580-8756. E-mail: library@missiontexas.us. Web Site: www.mission.lib.tx.us. *Libr Dir,* Mayra Rocha; E-mail: mayra@missiontexas.us
Pop 105,795; Circ 176,638
Library Holdings: Bk Vols 160,000; Per Subs 103
Subject Interests: Bilingual, English lang, Genealogy, Spanish lang, Tex
Automation Activity & Vendor Info: (Cataloging) TLC (The Library Corporation); (Circulation) TLC (The Library Corporation)
Wireless access
Mem of Hidalgo County Library System
Open Mon-Thurs 8am-9pm, Fri & Sat 8-5, Sun 12-5
Friends of the Library Group

MONAHANS

P WARD COUNTY LIBRARY*, 409 S Dwight, 79756. SAN 316-6279. Tel: 432-943-3332. FAX: 432-943-3332. Web Site: wcl.ploud.net. *Dir,* Brenda Kizziar; E-mail: brenda.kizziar@co.ward.tx.us; Staff 3 (Non-MLS 3)
Pop 10,507; Circ 30,264
Library Holdings: AV Mats 3,828; Large Print Bks 1,100; Bk Vols 63,706; Per Subs 25
Automation Activity & Vendor Info: (Circulation) Follett Software
Wireless access
Open Tues-Sat 8-5
Friends of the Library Group
Branches: 2
BARSTOW BRANCH, Community Bldg, Barstow, 79719. Tel: 432-445-5205. E-mail: barcolib@yahoo.com. *Mgr,* Rachel Contreras; *Libr Asst,* Yoland Villalobos; Staff 2 (Non-MLS 2)
Fac 2
Library Holdings: Bk Vols 1,300
Open Mon & Fri 3-6, Tues-Thurs 2-6

GRANDFALLS PUBLIC, 209 Ave D, Grandfalls, 79742. (Mail add: PO Box 262, Grandfalls, 79742-0262). Tel: 432-547-2861. FAX: 432-547-2861. E-mail: grandfallslibrary@yahoo.com. *Mgr,* Sharon Miller; Staff 2 (Non-MLS 2)
Fac 2
Library Holdings: Bk Titles 6,900
Open Mon-Fri 8-5

MOODY

P MOODY COMMUNITY LIBRARY, 612 Ave D, 76557. (Mail add: PO Box 57, 76557-0057). Tel: 254-853-2004. FAX: 254-853-9704. E-mail: moodycommunitylibrary57@gmail.com. Web Site: www.moody.lib.tx.us. *Libr Dir,* Beth Alton; Tel: 254-853-2044; Staff 2 (MLS 1, Non-MLS 1)
Founded 1994. Pop 1,400; Circ 2,500
Library Holdings: Audiobooks 500; DVDs 700; Large Print Bks 300; Bk Vols 15,000; Talking Bks 50; Videos 100
Wireless access
Function: 24/7 Electronic res, 24/7 Online cat, 24/7 wireless access, Activity rm, Adult bk club
Partic in Partners Library Action Network
Open Mon, Wed & Sat 10-2, Tues & Thurs 3-7

MORTON

P COCHRAN COUNTY LOVE MEMORIAL LIBRARY*, 318 S Main St, 79346-3006. SAN 316-6287. Tel: 806-266-5051. FAX: 806-266-8057. E-mail: cochran.library@co.cochran.tx.us. Web Site: www.cochrancountylibrary.com. *Dir,* Dana Heflin; Staff 1 (Non-MLS 1)
Pop 3,952; Circ 7,748
Library Holdings: Bks on Deafness & Sign Lang 5; CDs 327; Bk Vols 14,000; Per Subs 15; Videos 25
Automation Activity & Vendor Info: (Acquisitions) Biblionix; (Cataloging) Biblionix; (Circulation) Biblionix; (Course Reserve) Biblionix; (ILL) Biblionix; (Media Booking) Biblionix; (OPAC) Biblionix; (Serials) Biblionix
Wireless access
Function: Accelerated reader prog, Adult bk club, Archival coll
Open Mon-Fri 9-12 & 1-5
Restriction: Access at librarian's discretion, Authorized patrons

MOUNT CALM

P MOUNT CALM PUBLIC LIBRARY*, 222 Allyn Ave, 76673. (Mail add: PO Box 84, 76673-0084), SAN 376-4745. Tel: 254-993-2761. E-mail: mtcalmlibrary@gmail.com. Web Site: www.mountcalmlibrary.org. *Librn,* Kathleen Franklin
Founded 1977. Pop 317
Library Holdings: Bk Vols 14,000; Per Subs 3
Automation Activity & Vendor Info: (Cataloging) Biblionix; (Circulation) Biblionix
Wireless access
Partic in Partners Library Action Network
Open Mon & Thurs Noon-5:30, Tues 9-5, Sat 10-Noon

MOUNT PLEASANT

P MOUNT PLEASANT PUBLIC LIBRARY*, 601 N Madison, 75455. SAN 316-6295. Tel: 903-575-4180. FAX: 903-577-8000. E-mail: library@mpcity.org. Web Site: mpcity.net/395/Library. *Head Librn,* Helen Thompson; Staff 5 (MLS 1, Non-MLS 4)
Founded 1968. Pop 16,000; Circ 92,986
Library Holdings: Audiobooks 1,580; AV Mats 1,757; Large Print Bks 1,258; Bk Titles 32,500; Per Subs 60; Talking Bks 1,028
Special Collections: Cross Family Indian Artifact Coll; Newspaper Coll (1923-1967), microfilm; Pioneers & Heroes of Titus County, Online Database; Titus County Genealogical Society Coll
Subject Interests: Local hist
Automation Activity & Vendor Info: (Cataloging) Book Systems; (Circulation) Book Systems; (OPAC) Book Systems
Wireless access
Function: 24/7 Electronic res, 24/7 Online cat, AV serv, Home delivery & serv to seniorr ctr & nursing homes, Homebound delivery serv, ILL available, Internet access, Photocopying/Printing, Prog for adults, Prog for children & young adult, Ref serv available, Summer reading prog, Telephone ref, Wheelchair accessible, Workshops
Publications: Pleasant Reading (Newsletter)
Partic in Partners Library Action Network
Special Services for the Blind - Bks on cassette; Bks on CD; Large print bks; Ref serv
Open Mon-Wed 9-6, Thurs 9-8, Sat 9-1
Friends of the Library Group

J NORTHEAST TEXAS COMMUNITY COLLEGE*, Charlie & Helen Hampton Library, 2886 Farm-to-Market Rd 1735, 75456. (Mail add: PO Box 1307, 75456-1307), SAN 328-106X. Tel: 903-434-8100. Circulation

Tel: 903-434-8151. Reference Tel: 903-434-8152. FAX: 903-572-6712. Web Site: www.ntcc.edu/library. *Dir, Libr Serv,* Ronald Bowden; Tel: 903-434-8163, E-mail: rbowden@ntcc.edu; *Librn,* Heather Shaw; E-mail: hshaw@ntcc.edu; *Tech Serv Spec,* Janice Allen; E-mail: jallen@ntcc.edu; Staff 4 (MLS 2, Non-MLS 2)
Founded 1985. Enrl 2,110; Fac 71; Highest Degree: Associate
Library Holdings: Bk Titles 15,000; Per Subs 100
Automation Activity & Vendor Info: (Cataloging) OCLC Worldshare Management Services; (Circulation) OCLC Worldshare Management Services; (ILL) OCLC WorldShare Interlibrary Loan; (OPAC) OCLC Worldshare Management Services
Wireless access
Partic in Amigos Library Services, Inc; TexSHARE - Texas State Library & Archives Commission
Open Mon-Thurs 8-6, Fri 8-12

MOUNT VERNON

P FRANKLIN COUNTY LIBRARY*, 100 Main St, 75457. (Mail add: PO Box 579, 75457-0579), SAN 376-4397. Tel: 903-537-4916. FAX: 903-537-4319. E-mail: library@co.franklin.tx.us. Web Site: www.franklincolibrary.com. *Librn,* Lisa Lawrence; *Asst Librn,* Julie Baxter
Founded 1977
Library Holdings: Bk Vols 30,000; Per Subs 50
Automation Activity & Vendor Info: (Cataloging) Follett Software; (Circulation) Follett Software; (OPAC) Follett Software
Wireless access
Partic in TexSHARE - Texas State Library & Archives Commission
Open Mon 9-6, Tues-Fri 9-5, Sat 9-12
Friends of the Library Group

MUENSTER

P BETTIE M LUKE MUENSTER PUBLIC LIBRARY*, 418 N Elm St, 76252. SAN 316-6309. Tel: 940-759-4291. FAX: 940-759-2091. E-mail: muensterlibrary@ntin.net. Web Site: www.muensterlibrary.org. *Dir,* Jody Thomas
Founded 1965. Pop 3,000; Circ 17,563
Library Holdings: Bk Titles 16,964; Bk Vols 17,417; Per Subs 28
Automation Activity & Vendor Info: (Cataloging) Book Systems; (Circulation) Book Systems
Wireless access
Open Tues & Thurs 10-6:30, Wed 10-5:30, Sat 10-2:30
Friends of the Library Group

MULESHOE

P MULESHOE AREA PUBLIC LIBRARY*, 322 W Second St, 79347. SAN 316-6317. Tel: 806-272-4707. FAX: 806-272-5031. Web Site: mapl.ploud.net. *Libr Dir,* Frances Recio; E-mail: frecio@muleshoetx.org
Founded 1964. Pop 5,158; Circ 41,409
Library Holdings: Bk Vols 27,000; Per Subs 30
Special Collections: Audio-visual Coll; Large Print Coll; Paperback Coll; Southwest Coll; Spanish Coll; Texas Coll
Automation Activity & Vendor Info: (Cataloging) Biblionix; (Circulation) Biblionix
Wireless access
Function: ILL available, Photocopying/Printing, Ref serv available, Telephone ref
Open Mon-Fri 9-6
Friends of the Library Group

MUNDAY

P CITY COUNTY LIBRARY OF MUNDAY*, 131 S Munday Ave, 76371. (Mail add: PO Box 268, 76371-0268), SAN 316-6325. Tel: 940-422-4877. E-mail: mundaylib@yahoo.com. Web Site: mundaylibrary.webs.com. *Librn,* Peggy Urbanczyk
Pop 5,700; Circ 9,900
Library Holdings: Bk Vols 7,080
Automation Activity & Vendor Info: (Cataloging) Follett Software; (Circulation) Follett Software; (OPAC) Follett Software
Wireless access
Open Tues & Thurs 9-1, Wed 1-5
Friends of the Library Group

NACOGDOCHES

P JUDY B MCDONALD PUBLIC LIBRARY, Nacogdoches Public Library, 1112 North St, 75961-4482. SAN 316-6341. Tel: 936-559-2970. Web Site: www.nactx.us/962/library. *Dir,* Mercedes Franks; Tel: 936-559-2945, E-mail: franksm@nactx.us; Staff 7.5 (MLS 2, Non-MLS 5.5)
Founded 1972. Pop 64,000; Circ 197,217
Library Holdings: AV Mats 9,000; CDs 2,622; DVDs 1,160; Electronic Media & Resources 50; Large Print Bks 3,500; Bk Vols 77,000; Per Subs 107; Talking Bks 3,150; Videos 493
Automation Activity & Vendor Info: (Cataloging) SirsiDynix; (Circulation) SirsiDynix; (ILL) OCLC; (Media Booking) Baker & Taylor; (OPAC) SirsiDynix; (Serials) SirsiDynix
Wireless access
Partic in TexSHARE - Texas State Library & Archives Commission
Special Services for the Blind - Audio mat; Bks on cassette; Bks on CD
Open Mon & Thurs 9-9, Tues, Wed & Fri 9-5:30, Sat 9-5
Friends of the Library Group

C STEPHEN F AUSTIN STATE UNIVERSITY*, Ralph W Steen Library, 1936 North St, 75962. (Mail add: PO Box 13055, SFA Sta, 75962-3055), SAN 316-635X. Tel: 936-468-4636. Circulation Tel: 936-468-1497. Interlibrary Loan Service Tel: 936-468-1720. FAX: 936-468-7610. Web Site: library.sfasu.edu. *Dir,* Shirley Dickerson; E-mail: sdickerson@sfasu.edu; *Dir, E Tex Res Ctr,* Linda Reynolds; Tel: 936-468-1562, E-mail: lreynolds@sfasu.edu; *Head, Digital Strategies,* Edward Iglesias; Tel: 936-468-1444, E-mail: iglesiase@sfasu.edu; *Head, Res & Instrul Serv,* Edward Kownslar; Tel: 936-468-1459, E-mail: kownslarej@sfasu.edu; *Research Librn, Sci,* Shannon Bowman; Tel: 936-468-1528, E-mail: bowmans11@sfasu.edu; *Research Librn,* Tina Oswald; Tel: 936-468-1861, E-mail: toswald@sfasu.edu; *Research Librn,* Janie Richardson; Tel: 936-468-1896, E-mail: richardsj13@sfasu.edu; *Scholarly Communications Librn,* Phil Reynolds; Tel: 936-468-1453, E-mail: preynolds@sfasu.edu; *Spec Coll Librn,* Kyle Ainsworth; Tel: 936-468-1590, E-mail: ainswortk@sfasu.edu; *Electronic Res, Libr Assessment Coordr,* Barbara Olds; E-mail: bolds@sfasu.edu; *Univ Archivist,* Alexandra Schutz; Tel: 936-468-1536, E-mail: schutzaa@sfasu.edu; Staff 29 (MLS 18, Non-MLS 11)
Founded 1923. Enrl 12,999; Fac 648; Highest Degree: Doctorate
Library Holdings: Bk Titles 463,133; Bk Vols 549,952; Per Subs 2,458
Special Collections: Business Documents & Papers of Major East Texas Lumber Companies; East Texas History, bk, mss; The Texas Tides Coll. Oral History; State Document Depository; US Document Depository
Subject Interests: Forestry
Automation Activity & Vendor Info: (Acquisitions) SirsiDynix; (Circulation) SirsiDynix; (Serials) SirsiDynix
Wireless access
Publications: Guide to Special Collections
Partic in Amigos Library Services, Inc; Proquest Dialog
Open Mon-Thurs 7am-1am, Fri 7-6, Sat 10-8, Sun Noon-1am

S STERNE-HOYA HOUSE MUSEUM & LIBRARY*, 211 S Lanana St, 75961. SAN 316-6333. Tel: 936-560-5426. FAX: 936-569-9813. Web Site: www.nactx.us/696/sterne-hoya-house-museum-and-library. *Mgr,* Veronica Amoe; E-mail: amoev@nactx.us
Founded 1958
Library Holdings: Bk Vols 5,000
Special Collections: Genealogy Coll; Texas Coll
Subject Interests: Children's lit
Open Wed-Sat 10-4
Restriction: Non-circulating

NAPLES

P NAPLES PUBLIC LIBRARY*, 103 Walnut St, 75568. (Mail add: PO Box 705, 75568-0705). Tel: 903-897-2964. FAX: 903-897-2964. E-mail: naples_public_library@hotmail.com. Web Site: naples.ploud.net. *Librn,* Joyce Charlton
Founded 1998. Pop 1,496; Circ 4,343
Library Holdings: Bk Vols 12,000; Per Subs 10
Wireless access
Open Mon-Fri 12-5
Friends of the Library Group

NAVASOTA

P NAVASOTA PUBLIC LIBRARY*, 1411 E Washington Ave, 77868. SAN 316-6376. Tel: 936-825-6744. FAX: 936-825-4106. E-mail: plibrary@navasotatx.gov. Web Site: www.navasotatx.gov/public-library. *Librn,* Tiffany Sammon; E-mail: tsammon@navasotatx.gov; Staff 3 (Non-MLS 3)
Founded 1954. Pop 7,400; Circ 54,211
Library Holdings: Bk Vols 45,000; Per Subs 20
Special Collections: Texana Coll
Subject Interests: Local genealogy, Local hist
Automation Activity & Vendor Info: (Cataloging) Follett Software; (Circulation) Follett Software; (OPAC) Follett Software
Wireless access
Function: 24/7 Online cat, Adult bk club, Archival coll, Bks on CD, Children's prog, Free DVD rentals, Internet access, Magazines, Microfiche/film & reading machines, Online cat, Photocopying/Printing, Preschool reading prog, Spanish lang bks, Summer reading prog, Tax forms, Wheelchair accessible
Partic in Partners Library Action Network

Open Mon 1-7, Tues-Fri 8:30-5:30
Friends of the Library Group

NEDERLAND

P MARION & ED HUGHES PUBLIC LIBRARY*, 2712 Nederland Ave, 77627. SAN 320-2623. Tel: 409-722-1255. FAX: 409-721-5469. Web Site: www.ned.lib.tx.us. *Dir, Libr Serv,* Molly Hall; E-mail: mhall@ned.lib.tx.us; Staff 1 (MLS 1)
Founded 1930. Pop 17,422
Wireless access
Partic in Partners Library Action Network
Open Mon 1-9, Tues-Fri 10-6, Sat 10:30-2
Friends of the Library Group

NEW BOSTON

P NEW BOSTON PUBLIC LIBRARY*, 127 N Ellis St, 75570-2905. SAN 376-446X. Tel: 903-628-5414. FAX: 903-628-9739. E-mail: nbpl127@yahoo.com. Web Site: www.newbostonlibrary.org. *Dir,* Christine Woodrow
Library Holdings: Bk Vols 15,553; Per Subs 40
Automation Activity & Vendor Info: (Cataloging) Follett Software; (Circulation) Follett Software
Wireless access
Open Mon, Tues & Thurs 10-6, Wed & Fri 9-5, Sat 9-12
Friends of the Library Group

NEW BRAUNFELS

P NEW BRAUNFELS PUBLIC LIBRARY*, 700 E Common St, 78130-5689. SAN 316-6392. Tel: 830-221-4300. Reference Tel: 830-221-4305. Administration Tel: 830-221-4322. FAX: 830-608-2151. Reference E-mail: reference@nbtexas.org. Web Site: www.nbtexas.org/library. *Dir,* Gretchen Pruett; E-mail: gpruett@nbtexas.org; *Asst Dir,* Lynn Thompson; Tel: 830-221-4315, E-mail: lthompson@nbtexas.org; *Outreach Librn,* Jonathan Margheim; Tel: 830-221-4318, E-mail: jmargheim@nbtexas.org; *Commun Br Supvr,* Pamela Carlile; Tel: 830-221-4316, E-mail: pcarlile@newbraunfels.gov; *Adult Serv,* Jodi Brown; Tel: 830-221-4325, E-mail: jbrown@nbtexas.org; *Tech Serv,* Debbie Martin; Tel: 830-221-4313, E-mail: dmartin@nbtexas.org; *Youth Serv,* Jenny Rodriguez; Tel: 830-221-4314, E-mail: jgrodriguez@nbtexas.org; Staff 30.5 (MLS 8, Non-MLS 22.5)
Founded 1928. Pop 80,000; Circ 900,000
Oct 2017-Sept 2018 Income $2,430,984, City $2,370,984, Other $60,000. Mats Exp $194,725, Books $113,431, AV Mat $16,130, Electronic Ref Mat (Incl. Access Fees) $65,164. Sal $1,049,550
Library Holdings: Audiobooks 9,714; DVDs 15,444; e-books 5,361; Microforms 220; Bk Titles 98,208; Bk Vols 105,984; Per Subs 190
Special Collections: Texana Coll
Automation Activity & Vendor Info: (Acquisitions) Biblionix/Apollo; (Cataloging) Biblionix/Apollo; (Circulation) Biblionix/Apollo; (ILL) OCLC Connexion; (OPAC) Biblionix/Apollo
Wireless access
Function: 24/7 Electronic res, 24/7 Online cat, Adult bk club, Adult literacy prog, Archival coll, Art programs, Audiobks via web, Bi-weekly Writer's Group, Bilingual assistance for Spanish patrons, Bk club(s), Bk reviews (Group), Bks on CD, Children's prog, Citizenship assistance, Computer training, Computers for patron use, Digital talking bks, Distance learning, Doc delivery serv, E-Reserves, Electronic databases & coll, Family literacy, Free DVD rentals, Govt ref serv, Holiday prog, Home delivery & serv to seniorr ctr & nursing homes, Homebound delivery serv, Homework prog, ILL available, Instruction & testing, Internet access, Large print keyboards, Life-long learning prog for all ages, Literacy & newcomer serv, Magazines, Magnifiers for reading, Mail & tel request accepted, Meeting rooms, Microfiche/film & reading machines, Movies, Music CDs, Online cat, Online info literacy tutorials on the web & in blackboard, Online ref, Outreach serv, Outside serv via phone, mail, e-mail & web, OverDrive digital audio bks, Photocopying/Printing, Preschool outreach, Preschool reading prog, Printer for laptops & handheld devices, Prog for adults, Prog for children & young adult, Ref & res, Ref serv available, Satellite serv, Scanner, Senior computer classes, Senior outreach, Serves people with intellectual disabilities, Spanish lang bks, STEM programs, Story hour, Study rm, Summer reading prog, Tax forms, Teen prog, Telephone ref, Wheelchair accessible
Partic in Amigos Library Services, Inc; Partners Library Action Network; TexSHARE - Texas State Library & Archives Commission
Open Mon-Thurs 9-9, Fri 9-6, Sat 9-5, Sun 1-5
Friends of the Library Group
Branches: 1
WESTSIDE COMMUNITY CENTER, 2932 S IH 35 Frontage Rd, 78130. Tel: 830-221-4301. *Br Mgr,* Pamela Carlile; E-mail: pcarlile@newbraunfels.gov; *Coordr, Outreach Serv,* Jennifer Hernandez
Bookmobiles: 1. Librn, Jonathan Margheim. Bk vols 2,000

NEW WAVERLY

P NEW WAVERLY PUBLIC LIBRARY*, 9372 State Hwy 75 S, 77358. SAN 376-4117. Tel: 936-344-2198. FAX: 936-344-2198. E-mail: nwpublib@txun.net. Web Site: www.newwaverlypubliclibrary.org. *Librn,* Kameron Sutton
Library Holdings: Bk Vols 8,500; Per Subs 12
Wireless access
Open Mon-Fri 11-6
Friends of the Library Group

NEWARK

P NEWARK PUBLIC LIBRARY*, Godfrey Pegues Public Library, 207 Hudson St, 76071. (Mail add: PO Box 1219, 76071-1219), SAN 376-4729. Tel: 817-489-2224. FAX: 817-489-3472. E-mail: library@newarktexas.com. Web Site: newarktexaspubliclibrary.weebly.com, www.newarktexas.com/library.html. Staff 1 (Non-MLS 1)
Founded 1988. Pop 1,000; Circ 9,000
Library Holdings: Bk Titles 10,100
Automation Activity & Vendor Info: (Acquisitions) Follett Software; (Cataloging) Follett Software; (Circulation) Follett Software; (Course Reserve) Follett Software
Wireless access
Function: Adult bk club, Bks on cassette, Bks on CD, Children's prog, Computer training, Computers for patron use, Electronic databases & coll, Free DVD rentals, Internet access, Magnifiers for reading, Notary serv, Online cat, Photocopying/Printing, Prog for adults, Prog for children & young adult, Ref serv available, Scanner, Senior computer classes, Story hour, Summer reading prog, VHS videos, Wheelchair accessible, Workshops
Open Mon-Fri 10-5

NEWTON

P NEWTON COUNTY PUBLIC LIBRARY*, 212 High St, 75966. (Mail add: PO Box 657, 75966), SAN 375-3727. Tel: 409-379-8300. FAX: 409-379-2798. E-mail: newtonlibrary@hotmail.com. Web Site: www.newtoncountypubliclibrary.org. *Dir,* Stephanie Ducote; Staff 2 (Non-MLS 2)
Founded 1974. Pop 14,946; Circ 24,390
Library Holdings: AV Mats 600; Bk Vols 17,000; Per Subs 15; Videos 894
Automation Activity & Vendor Info: (Cataloging) Biblionix; (Circulation) Biblionix
Wireless access
Function: AV serv, ILL available, Prog for children & young adult, Summer reading prog, Wheelchair accessible
Partic in Partners Library Action Network
Special Services for the Deaf - Bks on deafness & sign lang; High interest/low vocabulary bks
Special Services for the Blind - Talking bks
Open Mon-Fri 8:30-5
Restriction: Open to pub for ref & circ; with some limitations
Friends of the Library Group
Branches: 1
DEWEYVILLE PUBLIC LIBRARY, Sub-Courthouse, 42520 State Hwy 87 S, Orange, 77632. (Mail add: PO Box 801, Deweyville, 77614-0801). Tel: 409-746-0222.
Library Holdings: Bk Titles 6,000
Open Tues-Thurs 8:30-5, Fri 8:30-1

NIXON

P APHNE PATTILLO NIXON PUBLIC LIBRARY*, 401 N Nixon Ave, 78140. SAN 316-6414. Tel: 830-582-1913. FAX: 830-582-1713. E-mail: nixonpubliclibrary@nixon.texas.gov. Web Site: www.facebook.com/Aphne-Pattillo-Nixon-Public-Library-100068563933896. *Librn,* Sally Brassell
Pop 2,008; Circ 8,500
Library Holdings: Audiobooks 58; DVDs 1,003; Bk Titles 9,835; Videos 354
Automation Activity & Vendor Info: (Cataloging) Follett Software; (Circulation) Follett Software; (OPAC) Follett Software
Wireless access
Open Mon-Fri 8-4
Friends of the Library Group

NOCONA

P NOCONA PUBLIC LIBRARY*, Ten Cooke St, 76255. SAN 376-4591. Tel: 940-825-6373. FAX: 940-825-4587. E-mail: library@cityofnocona.com. Web Site: noconapubliclibrary.org. *Dir,* Karen Teague
Founded 1972. Pop 3,198; Circ 15,049
Library Holdings: Bk Vols 22,000; Per Subs 20

Automation Activity & Vendor Info: (Cataloging) Follett Software; (Circulation) Follett Software
Wireless access
Open Mon-Fri 9-5
Friends of the Library Group

NORTH RICHLAND HILLS

P NORTH RICHLAND HILLS PUBLIC LIBRARY*, 9015 Grand Ave, 76180. SAN 316-344X. Tel: 817-427-6800. Reference Tel: 817-427-6814. FAX: 817-427-6808. E-mail: reference@nrhtx.com. Web Site: www.library.nrhtx.com. *Dir, Libr Serv,* Cecilia Barham; E-mail: cbarham@nrhtx.com; *Ch Serv,* Liz Brockman; Tel: 817-427-6818; Staff 9.9 (MLS 9.9)
Founded 1971. Pop 66,100; Circ 764,195
Library Holdings: Bk Vols 194,821; Per Subs 188
Special Collections: Digital Historic Photo Archives
Wireless access
Publications: Off the Shelf (Newsletter)
Partic in Amigos Library Services, Inc
Open Mon-Thurs 10-7, Fri & Sat 10-5

ODEM

P ODEM PUBLIC LIBRARY*, 516 Voss Ave, 78370. SAN 316-6422. Tel: 361-368-7388. FAX: 361-368-7388. E-mail: odempl@stx.rr.com. *Dir,* Donna Hutchins; Staff 1 (Non-MLS 1)
Founded 1934. Pop 3,448
Library Holdings: AV Mats 375; Bk Titles 9,409; Bk Vols 9,759; Per Subs 20
Automation Activity & Vendor Info: (Cataloging) Follett Software; (Circulation) Follett Software
Function: Adult literacy prog, CD-ROM, Digital talking bks, ILL available, Internet access, Magnifiers for reading, Music CDs, Prog for children & young adult, Ref serv available, Spoken cassettes & CDs, Summer reading prog, Telephone ref, VHS videos, Wheelchair accessible
Special Services for the Blind - Aids for in-house use; Audio mat; Bks on cassette; Bks on CD; Cassettes; Large print bks; Magnifiers; Talking bks
Open Mon, Wed & Fri 9-5, Sat 9-12
Friends of the Library Group

ODESSA

P ECTOR COUNTY LIBRARY*, 321 W Fifth St, 79761-5066. SAN 316-6430. Tel: 432-332-0633. Circulation Tel: 432-332-0633, Ext 2105. Reference Tel: 432-332-0633, Ext 2107. FAX: 432-377-6502. E-mail: library@ector.lib.tx.org. Web Site: ector.lib.tx.us. *Dir,* Rebbecca Taylor; E-mail: rtaylor@ector.lib.tx.us; *Ch Serv,* Lynette Nickell; E-mail: lnickell@ector.lib.tx.us; Staff 26 (MLS 4, Non-MLS 22)
Founded 1938. Pop 121,123; Circ 696,820
Library Holdings: Bk Titles 109,370; Bk Vols 128,570; Per Subs 320
Subject Interests: Genealogy, Local hist, SW hist
Automation Activity & Vendor Info: (Cataloging) SirsiDynix; (Circulation) SirsiDynix; (OPAC) SirsiDynix
Wireless access
Partic in Amigos Library Services, Inc; Partners Library Action Network
Special Services for the Deaf - Bks on deafness & sign lang; High interest/low vocabulary bks
Special Services for the Blind - Bks on cassette; Talking bks
Open Mon & Tues 8:30-8:30, Wed-Sat 9-6
Friends of the Library Group

J ODESSA COLLEGE*, Murry H Fly Learning Resources Center, 201 W University Blvd, 79764. SAN 316-6457. Tel: 432-335-6640. Interlibrary Loan Service Tel: 432-335-6639. FAX: 432-335-6610. E-mail: lrc@odessa.edu. Web Site: www.odessa.edu/current-students/Learning-Resources-Center-Library. *Exec Dir,* Tenisha Muhammad; E-mail: tmuhammad@odessa.edu; *Librn, Tech Serv Coordr,* Patricia Quintero; E-mail: pquintero@odessa.edu; Staff 4 (MLS 4)
Founded 1946. Enrl 4,591; Fac 120; Highest Degree: Associate
Library Holdings: AV Mats 5,752; e-books 48,293; Bk Titles 50,000; Bk Vols 58,794; Per Subs 352
Automation Activity & Vendor Info: (Acquisitions) SirsiDynix; (Cataloging) SirsiDynix; (Circulation) SirsiDynix; (Course Reserve) SirsiDynix; (OPAC) SirsiDynix; (Serials) SirsiDynix
Wireless access
Publications: Faculty Handbook; Permian Basin Directory of Library Resources; Student Brochure (Library handbook); Student Handbook
Partic in Leian; TexSHARE - Texas State Library & Archives Commission
Open Mon-Thurs 7:30am-9:30pm, Fri 7:30-1, Sun 2-5

S SHEPPERD LEADERSHIP INSTITUTE, The Presidential Archives/The Leadership Library, 4919 E University Blvd, 79762. (Mail add: 4901 E University Blvd, 79762), SAN 316-6465. Tel: 432-552-2850. E-mail: jbs@utpb.edu. *Exec Dir, Libr Mgr,* Monica Tschauner
Founded 1964
Library Holdings: Bk Titles 6,000
Special Collections: Constitutional Government; Elective Processes
Subject Interests: The Presidency, all aspects
Open Tues-Sun 12-6
Restriction: Non-circulating

C UNIVERSITY OF TEXAS OF THE PERMIAN BASIN*, J Conrad Dunagan Library, 4901 E University Blvd, 79762. SAN 316-6473. Tel: 432-552-2370. Reference Tel: 432-552-2396. FAX: 432-552-2374. E-mail: libraryservices@utpb.edu. Web Site: www.utpb.edu/library. *Dir,* Dr Sophia Kaane; E-mail: kaane_s@utpb.edu; *Syst Adminr,* Nanci Harris; E-mail: hariis_n@utpb.edu; Staff 12 (MLS 4, Non-MLS 8)
Founded 1973. Enrl 7,500; Fac 160; Highest Degree: Master
Library Holdings: DVDs 8,000; e-books 65,831; e-journals 51,074; Microforms 1,487,303; Bk Titles 397,277; Per Subs 437; Videos 15,025
Special Collections: J Frank Dobie Coll, bks & papers; Texana; Texas Writers Coll; UT Permian Basin Archives
Subject Interests: Film
Automation Activity & Vendor Info: (Cataloging) Innovative Interfaces, Inc; (Circulation) Innovative Interfaces, Inc; (Discovery) ProQuest; (ILL) OCLC WorldShare Interlibrary Loan; (OPAC) Innovative Interfaces, Inc
Wireless access
Function: 24/7 Electronic res, 24/7 Online cat
Partic in Amigos Library Services, Inc; TexSHARE - Texas State Library & Archives Commission
Open Mon-Thurs 7:30am-11:45pm, Fri 8am-11:45am, Sat 10-5:45, Sun 4pm-11:45pm

OLNEY

P OLNEY COMMUNITY LIBRARY & ARTS CENTER*, 807 W Hamilton St, 76374. SAN 316-6481. Tel: 940-564-5513. FAX: 940-564-3453. Web Site: www.olneyisd.net. *Dir,* Lori Cox; E-mail: lcox@olneyisd.net; Staff 5 (MLS 1, Non-MLS 4)
Pop 4,082; Circ 55,071
Library Holdings: Bk Vols 34,000; Per Subs 85
Special Collections: Spanish-Bilingual Coll; Texas Coll; World War II Coll. Oral History
Automation Activity & Vendor Info: (Cataloging) Book Systems; (Circulation) Book Systems; (OPAC) Book Systems
Wireless access
Function: 24/7 Electronic res, 24/7 Online cat, Adult bk club, Archival coll, Art exhibits, Audiobks via web, Bks on CD, Children's prog, Computers for patron use, Electronic databases & coll, Free DVD rentals, Holiday prog, ILL available, Instruction & testing, Internet access, Large print keyboards, Magazines, Meeting rooms, Notary serv, Online cat, OverDrive digital audio bks, Photocopying/Printing, Preschool outreach, Printer for laptops & handheld devices, Prog for children & young adult, Scanner, Story hour, Summer reading prog, Telephone ref, Wheelchair accessible
Open Mon-Fri 9-6:30
Restriction: Authorized patrons

OLTON

P OLTON AREA LIBRARY*, 701 Main St, 79064. (Mail add: PO Box 675, 79064), SAN 321-6160. Tel: 806-285-7772. FAX: 806-285-7770. E-mail: oltonlibrary@gmail.com. *Dir,* Jocelyn Mandrell; Staff 2 (Non-MLS 2)
Founded 1982. Pop 2,137
Library Holdings: Bk Vols 9,358
Automation Activity & Vendor Info: (Acquisitions) Biblionix; (Cataloging) Biblionix; (Circulation) Biblionix
Wireless access
Open Mon & Wed-Fri 9-12 & 1-5:30, Tues 1-8
Friends of the Library Group

ONALASKA

P ONALASKA PUBLIC LIBRARY*, 372 South FM 356, 77360. (Mail add: PO Box 880, 77360). Tel: 936-646-2665. FAX: 936-646-2664. E-mail: librarian@cityofonalaska.us. Web Site: www.cityofonalaska.us/public-library.htm. *Libr Dir,* Sherry Brecheen
Founded 2002. Pop 2,500
Library Holdings: CDs 200; DVDs 50; Bk Vols 8,000
Automation Activity & Vendor Info: (Cataloging) Book Systems; (Circulation) Book Systems
Wireless access
Function: 24/7 Electronic res, 24/7 Online cat, After school storytime
Partic in Partners Library Action Network
Open Mon-Fri 7:30-4:30

ORANGE

J LAMAR STATE COLLEGE ORANGE LIBRARY*, Ron E Lewis Library, 410 Front St, 77630-5796. SAN 370-6982. Tel: 409-882-3352. Circulation Tel: 409-882-3982. Interlibrary Loan Service Tel: 409-882-3080. Reference Tel: 409-882-3082. FAX: 409-882-3903. Web Site: library.lsco.edu. *Dir, Libr Serv,* Samantha Smith; Tel: 409-882-3083, E-mail: samantha.smith@lsco.edu; *Pub Serv Librn,* China Burks; Tel: 409-882-3081, E-mail: china.burks@lsco.edu; *Tech Serv Librn,* Aubrey Kapranos; Tel: 409-882-3953, E-mail: aubrey.kapranos@lsco.edu; *Tech Serv Mgr,* Kungwha Kim; Tel: 409-882-3080, E-mail: kungwha.kim@lsco.edu; *Libr Tech II,* Michaela Cowart; Tel: 409-882-3952, E-mail: Michaela.Cowart@lsco.edu; *Libr Tech II,* Lindsey Stevenson; Tel: 409-882-3065, E-mail: Lindsey.Stevenson@lsco.edu; Staff 6.5 (MLS 3, Non-MLS 3.5)
Founded 1969. Enrl 2,175; Fac 56; Highest Degree: Associate
Library Holdings: DVDs 2,100; Bk Titles 44,000
Special Collections: Local History (Orange County Coll)
Automation Activity & Vendor Info: (Acquisitions) SirsiDynix-WorkFlows; (Cataloging) SirsiDynix-WorkFlows; (Circulation) SirsiDynix-WorkFlows; (ILL) OCLC FirstSearch; (OPAC) SirsiDynix-WorkFlows
Wireless access
Partic in Amigos Library Services, Inc; Texas Council of Academic Libraries; TexSHARE - Texas State Library & Archives Commission
Special Services for the Deaf - Closed caption videos; TDD equip
Special Services for the Blind - Accessible computers; Aids for in-house use; Computer access aids; Computer with voice synthesizer for visually impaired persons; Internet workstation with adaptive software; Low vision equip; PC for people with disabilities; Reader equip; Screen enlargement software for people with visual disabilities; Screen reader software
Restriction: Borrowing privileges limited to fac & registered students, Borrowing requests are handled by ILL, Circ privileges for students & alumni only

P ORANGE PUBLIC LIBRARY*, 220 N Fifth St, 77630. SAN 316-6511. Tel: 409-883-1086. Reference Tel: 409-883-1053. FAX: 409-883-1057. Reference E-mail: reference@orangetx.org. Web Site: www.orangetexaslibrary.com. *Dir,* Brenna Manasco; E-mail: bmanasco@orangetx.org; *Ch Serv Librn,* Karen Phares; *Acq,* Pam Williams; Staff 6 (MLS 1, Non-MLS 5)
Founded 1958. Pop 18,381; Circ 276,971
Library Holdings: Bk Vols 76,591
Special Collections: Large Print Children's Books; SE Texas & SW Louisiana Genealogy
Automation Activity & Vendor Info: (Cataloging) SirsiDynix; (Circulation) SirsiDynix; (OPAC) SirsiDynix
Wireless access
Function: Audio & video playback equip for onsite use, Bks on cassette, Bks on CD, Free DVD rentals, Holiday prog, ILL available, Online cat, Photocopying/Printing, Preschool outreach, Prog for children & young adult, Ref serv available, Summer reading prog, Tax forms, Teen prog, Telephone ref, VHS videos, Wheelchair accessible
Partic in OCLC Online Computer Library Center, Inc; Partners Library Action Network
Special Services for the Deaf - Accessible learning ctr; Adult & family literacy prog; Am sign lang & deaf culture; Assisted listening device; Captioned film dep; Closed caption videos; Coll on deaf educ; Deaf publ; Described encaptioned media prog; FullTalk; Interpreter on staff; Lecture on deaf culture; Pocket talkers; Sorenson video relay syst; Spec interest per; Video & TTY relay via computer; Video relay services; Videos & decoder
Open Mon & Wed-Fri 10-5, Tues 10-8, Sat 10-2
Restriction: Circ to mem only, Non-resident fee, Open to pub for ref & circ; with some limitations
Friends of the Library Group

OZONA

P CROCKETT COUNTY PUBLIC LIBRARY*, 1201 Ave G, 76943. (Mail add: PO Box 3030, 76943-3030), SAN 316-652X. Tel: 325-392-3565. FAX: 325-392-2941. Web Site: crockett.ploud.net. *Dir,* Jennifer Holmsley; E-mail: j.holmsley@co.crockett.tx.us; Staff 4 (Non-MLS 4)
Founded 1985. Pop 4,000
Library Holdings: CDs 1,610; e-books 9,337; Electronic Media & Resources 3,174; Large Print Bks 5,000; Bk Titles 20,650; Bk Vols 21,730; Per Subs 10; Videos 9
Automation Activity & Vendor Info: (Cataloging) Koha; (Circulation) Koha
Wireless access
Open Mon, Wed & Thurs 9-6, Tues 9-8, Fri 9-5
Friends of the Library Group

PADUCAH

P BICENTENNIAL CITY-COUNTY PUBLIC LIBRARY*, 809 Richards St, Ste A, 79248. (Mail add: PO Drawer AD, 79248-1197), SAN 372-7440. Tel: 806-492-2006. E-mail: bicentennialcitycountylibrary@yahoo.com. Web Site: www.facebook.com/paducahlibrary. *Dir,* Juanita Canales; Staff 1 (Non-MLS 1)
Founded 1977. Pop 1,189; Circ 10,000
Library Holdings: Bk Vols 18,000
Special Collections: Local History (Cottle Co & Area Coll)
Automation Activity & Vendor Info: (Acquisitions) Book Systems; (Cataloging) Book Systems; (Circulation) Book Systems; (Course Reserve) Book Systems; (ILL) Book Systems; (OPAC) Book Systems; (Serials) Book Systems
Wireless access
Open Mon-Wed 10-3, Thurs 12-5
Friends of the Library Group

PAINT ROCK

P HARRY BENGE CROZIER MEMORIAL LIBRARY, 184 W Moss St, 76866. (Mail add: PO Box 173, 76866-0173), SAN 375-4812. Tel: 325-732-4320. E-mail: lbr968@aol.com. Web Site: www.facebook.com/people/paint-rock-library-harry-benge-crozier-memorial/100064870830702.
Founded 1971. Pop 500; Circ 1,320
Library Holdings: Audiobooks 38; AV Mats 15; Bk Titles 2,900
Wireless access
Open Tues & Thurs 1-5

PALACIOS

P PALACIOS LIBRARY, INC*, 326 Main St, 77465. SAN 316-6538. Tel: 361-972-3234. FAX: 361-972-2142. E-mail: palacioslibrary@gmail.com. Web Site: www.palacioslibrary.org. *Dir,* Vikijane Mosier; E-mail: vikijane.palacioslibrary@gmail.com; *Asst Librn,* Ana Zamora; Staff 3 (Non-MLS 3)
Founded 1910. Pop 10,000
Library Holdings: Bk Titles 34,000; Per Subs 10
Automation Activity & Vendor Info: (Cataloging) Book Systems; (Circulation) Book Systems; (OPAC) Book Systems
Wireless access
Partic in Amigos Library Services, Inc; Partners Library Action Network
Open Mon-Wed 9-6, Thurs & Fri 1-6, Sat 9-2
Friends of the Library Group
Branches: 1
BLESSING BRANCH, 124 Ninth St, Blessing, 77419. Tel: 361-588-7717. FAX: 361-588-7717. E-mail: blessing_branch@palacioslibrary.org. *Librn,* Renee Huff
Founded 1988
Library Holdings: Bk Vols 32,912
Open Mon, Tues, Thurs & Fri 1-6

PALESTINE

P PALESTINE PUBLIC LIBRARY*, 2000 S Loop 256, Ste 42, 75801-5932. SAN 316-6546. Tel: 903-729-4121. FAX: 903-729-4062. Web Site: cityofpalestinetx.com/158/library. *Libr Dir,* Ana Sanchez; E-mail: asanchez@palestine-tx.org; *Ref, Spec Coll,* Karla Lang; E-mail: klang@palestine-tx.org; Staff 9 (MLS 2, Non-MLS 7)
Founded 1882. Pop 38,208; Circ 199,908
Library Holdings: AV Mats 5,417; Bk Vols 77,499; Per Subs 99
Special Collections: Anderson County, Texas Coll; Civil War Coll; Texana Coll
Subject Interests: Genealogy
Automation Activity & Vendor Info: (Cataloging) TLC (The Library Corporation); (Circulation) TLC (The Library Corporation); (OPAC) TLC (The Library Corporation)
Wireless access
Partic in Amigos Library Services, Inc
Open Mon-Wed & Fri 10-6, Thurs Noon-8
Friends of the Library Group

PAMPA

P LOVETT MEMORIAL LIBRARY*, 111 N Houston St, 79065. (Mail add: PO Box 342, 79066-0342), SAN 316-6562. Tel: 806-669-5780. FAX: 806-669-5782. E-mail: lovettmemorialpampa@hotmail.com. Web Site: harringtonlc.org/lovett, www.cityofpampa.org/library. *Dir,* Misty Guy; E-mail: mguy@cityofpampa.org; Staff 11 (MLS 2, Non-MLS 9)
Founded 1954. Pop 17,887; Circ 81,396
Library Holdings: Large Print Bks 1,000; Bk Titles 42,633; Per Subs 69; Talking Bks 2,045
Subject Interests: Local hist, Spanish
Automation Activity & Vendor Info: (Cataloging) SirsiDynix; (Circulation) SirsiDynix; (OPAC) SirsiDynix
Wireless access

Function: ILL available, Photocopying/Printing, Prog for children & young adult, Ref serv available, Summer reading prog, Telephone ref, Wheelchair accessible
Open Mon-Fri 9-7, Sat 1-5
Friends of the Library Group

PANHANDLE

P CARSON COUNTY PUBLIC LIBRARY*, 401 Main, 79068. (Mail add: PO Box 339, 79068-0339), SAN 362-1510. Tel: 806-537-3742. FAX: 806-537-3780. E-mail: ccl79068@gmail.com. Web Site: harringtonlc.org/panhandle. *Libr Dir,* Mary Hare
Founded 1938. Pop 6,157; Circ 25,598
Library Holdings: AV Mats 3,123; Bk Titles 43,075; Bk Vols 51,652; Per Subs 106
Automation Activity & Vendor Info: (Cataloging) SirsiDynix; (ILL) OCLC WorldShare Interlibrary Loan
Wireless access
Function: Adult bk club, Bk club(s), Bks on cassette, Bks on CD, Children's prog, Computer training, Computers for patron use, Digital talking bks, Electronic databases & coll, Home delivery & serv to seniorr ctr & nursing homes, ILL available, Internet access, Magazines, Magnifiers for reading, Movies, Online cat, Online ref, Outside serv via phone, mail, e-mail & web, OverDrive digital audio bks, Photocopying/Printing, Preschool reading prog, Prof lending libr, Prog for adults, Prog for children & young adult, Ref serv available, Scanner, Senior computer classes, Spanish lang bks, Spoken cassettes & CDs, Story hour, Summer reading prog, Tax forms, Telephone ref
Partic in Harrington Library Consortium
Open Mon-Fri 9-5
Restriction: Authorized patrons, Borrowing requests are handled by ILL, Circ to mem only, Co libr, Free to mem, Mem organizations only
Friends of the Library Group
Branches: 3
GROOM BRANCH, 201 Broadway St, Groom, 79039. (Mail add: PO Box 308, Groom, 79039-0308), SAN 362-1545. Tel: 806-248-7353. FAX: 806-248-7353. *Br Libr*n, Tina Painter
Open Mon-Thurs 1-5, Fri 11-3
Friends of the Library Group
SKELLYTOWN BRANCH, 500 Chamberlain, Skellytown, 79080. (Mail add: PO Box 92, Skellytown, 79080-0092), SAN 362-157X. Tel: 806-848-2551. FAX: 806-848-2551. *Br Librn,* Darlene Ledford
Open Mon-Thurs 1-5, Fri 9-1
Friends of the Library Group
WHITE DEER BRANCH, 200 Fourth St, White Deer, 79097. (Mail add: PO Box 85, White Deer, 79097-0085), SAN 362-160X. Tel: 806-883-7121. FAX: 806-883-7121. *Br Librn,* Beverly Warminski
Open Mon, Wed & Thurs 1-5, Tues & Fri 9-1
Friends of the Library Group

PARIS

J PARIS JUNIOR COLLEGE*, Mike Rheusadil Learning Center, 2400 Clarksville St, 75460. SAN 316-6589. Tel: 903-782-0215, 903-782-0415. FAX: 903-782-0356. Web Site: www.parisjc.edu/index.php/pjc2/main/learning-center. *Supvr, Libr Serv,* Shirley Bridges; E-mail: sbridges@parisjc.edu; Staff 8 (MLS 3, Non-MLS 5)
Founded 1924. Enrl 5,513; Fac 260; Highest Degree: Associate
Library Holdings: AV Mats 5,071; e-books 24,229; Microforms 7,623; Bk Titles 91,217; Bk Vols 76,535; Per Subs 181
Special Collections: A M Aikin Archives; Ethnomusicology (Fred & Shirley Steiner Coll); William Owens Coll
Subject Interests: County hist, Genealogy, Local hist
Automation Activity & Vendor Info: (Cataloging) Horizon; (Circulation) Horizon; (Course Reserve) Horizon; (OPAC) Horizon
Wireless access
Partic in Amigos Library Services, Inc; TexSHARE - Texas State Library & Archives Commission
Open Mon-Thurs 7am-10pm, Fri 8-5, Sun 5-9

P PARIS PUBLIC LIBRARY*, 326 S Main St, 75460. SAN 316-6597. Tel: 903-785-8531. FAX: 903-784-6325. Web Site: www.paristexas.gov/89/public-library. *Dir,* Timothy DeGhelder; E-mail: tdeghelder@paristexas.gov; *Libr Supvr,* Ron Hervey; *Ch Serv,* Tracy Clark; Staff 11 (MLS 1, Non-MLS 10)
Founded 1926
Library Holdings: Bk Vols 88,000; Per Subs 50
Automation Activity & Vendor Info: (Cataloging) Innovative Interfaces, Inc; (Circulation) Innovative Interfaces, Inc; (OPAC) Innovative Interfaces, Inc
Wireless access
Function: 24/7 Electronic res, 24/7 Online cat, Art exhibits, Audiobks via web, Bks on CD, Children's prog, Computers for patron use, Electronic databases & coll, Free DVD rentals, ILL available, Internet access, Magazines, Notary serv, Online cat, Photocopying/Printing, Printer for laptops & handheld devices, Ref serv available, Story hour, Telephone ref, VHS videos, Wheelchair accessible
Special Services for the Blind - Accessible computers; Aids for in-house use
Open Mon & Wed-Sat 9-6, Tues 10-8
Friends of the Library Group

PASADENA

P PASADENA PUBLIC LIBRARY*, 1201 Jeff Ginn Memorial Dr, 77506. SAN 362-1634. Tel: 713-477-0276. FAX: 713-475-7005. E-mail: pasadenalibrary@pasadenatx.gov. Web Site: pasadenalibrary.org. *Dir,* Tim McDonald; E-mail: tmcdonald@cityofpasadena.net; *Executive Asst,* Priscilla Lam; E-mail: plam@cityofpasadena.net; *Br Mgr,* Mark Anderson; *Coll Develop Officer,* Lisa Jackson; *ILL,* William Simpson; *Teen Serv,* Lynnea Fink; Staff 36.3 (MLS 9.5, Non-MLS 26.8)
Founded 1953. Pop 146,439; Circ 440,458
Library Holdings: Bk Vols 118,231; Per Subs 295; Talking Bks 3,289; Videos 13,794
Subject Interests: Local hist
Automation Activity & Vendor Info: (Cataloging) SirsiDynix; (Circulation) SirsiDynix; (OPAC) SirsiDynix; (Serials) SirsiDynix
Wireless access
Publications: Booklets, Brochures & Bookmarks; Newsletter (Monthly)
Partic in Partners Library Action Network
Open Mon-Thurs 10-6, Fri 10-5, Sat 1-5
Friends of the Library Group
Branches: 1
FAIRMONT BRANCH LIBRARY, 4330 Fairmont Pkwy, 77504, SAN 372-7068. Tel: 713-848-5345. *Br Mgr,* Joel Bangilan; Tel: 713-848-5346, E-mail: jobangilan@pasadenatx.gov; Staff 10 (MLS 3, Non-MLS 7)
Founded 1992
Open Mon-Thurs 10-8, Fri & Sat 10-5
Friends of the Library Group

J SAN JACINTO COLLEGE*, Lee Davis Library, 8060 Spencer Hwy, 77505. SAN 362-1693. Tel: 281-476-1850. FAX: 281-478-2734. Web Site: www.sanjac.edu/library. *Dir, Libr Serv,* Karen Blankenship; E-mail: Karen.Blankenship@sjcd.edu; *Libr Asst,* Carolyn Riddle; E-mail: Carolyn.Riddle@sjcd.edu; Staff 6 (MLS 6)
Founded 1961. Enrl 7,336; Fac 500; Highest Degree: Associate
Library Holdings: Bk Vols 157,000; Per Subs 300
Special Collections: Pomeroy Archives on Area History
Automation Activity & Vendor Info: (Cataloging) Innovative Interfaces, Inc - Millennium; (Circulation) Innovative Interfaces, Inc - Millennium; (Course Reserve) Innovative Interfaces, Inc - Millennium; (OPAC) Innovative Interfaces, Inc - Millennium; (Serials) Innovative Interfaces, Inc - Millennium
Wireless access
Partic in Amigos Library Services, Inc
Special Services for the Blind - Reader equip
Open Mon-Thurs 7am-9pm, Fri 7-3, Sat 10-2, Sun 1-5

CM TEXAS CHIROPRACTIC COLLEGE*, Mae Hilty Memorial Library, 5912 Spencer Hwy, 77505. SAN 316-6619. Tel: 281-998-6049. Reference Tel: 281-998-6054. Administration Tel: 281-998-6098. E-mail: TCCLibrary@txchiro.edu. Web Site: txchiro.libguides.com/c.php?g=753953. *Dir,* Caroline Webb; *E-Resources Librn,* Jeff Coyle; *Ref & Info Literacy Librn,* Claire Noll; *Circ,* Sherry Mahana; Staff 4 (MLS 3, Non-MLS 1)
Founded 1908. Enrl 1,908; Fac 42; Highest Degree: Doctorate
Library Holdings: Bk Titles 11,500; Bk Vols 14,000; Per Subs 175
Special Collections: Chiropractic Coll, bks
Subject Interests: Chiropractic, Med, Natural sci
Automation Activity & Vendor Info: (Cataloging) EOS International; (Circulation) EOS International; (Course Reserve) EOS International; (OPAC) EOS International
Wireless access
Partic in Amigos Library Services, Inc; Chiropractic Libr Consortium; National Network of Libraries of Medicine Region 3; OCLC Online Computer Library Center, Inc
Open Mon-Thurs 7am-Midnight, Fri 7-4, Sun Noon-8
Friends of the Library Group

PEARSALL

P PEARSALL PUBLIC LIBRARY*, 200 E Trinity St, 78061. SAN 316-6627. Tel: 830-334-2496. FAX: 830-334-9194. Web Site: www.cityofpearsall.org/215/pearsall-public-library. *Libr Dir,* Jennifer Muñiz; E-mail: jmuniz@cityofpearsall.org
Founded 1962. Pop 9,000; Circ 56,214
Library Holdings: Bk Titles 40,000; Bk Vols 65,607; Per Subs 16
Automation Activity & Vendor Info: (Cataloging) Follett Software; (Circulation) Follett Software

Wireless access
Open Mon-Fri 9-5:45

PECOS

P REEVES COUNTY LIBRARY*, 315 S Oak St, 79772-3735. SAN 316-6635. Tel: 432-755-0914. FAX: 432-445-1028. Web Site: reevescountylibrary.com. *Libr Dir,* Emily Baeza; E-mail: ebaeza@reevescounty.org; Staff 3 (MLS 1, Non-MLS 2)
Founded 1937. Pop 11,842; Circ 40,000
Library Holdings: Bks on Deafness & Sign Lang 10; High Interest/Low Vocabulary Bk Vols 2,500; Bk Titles 35,000; Bk Vols 39,060; Per Subs 40; Spec Interest Per Sub 10
Special Collections: State Document Depository
Subject Interests: Educ K-12, Recreational, Spanish, SW, Tex
Automation Activity & Vendor Info: (Cataloging) Book Systems; (Circulation) Book Systems
Wireless access
Special Services for the Deaf - Bks on deafness & sign lang; Videos & decoder
Special Services for the Blind - Audio mat
Open Mon-Thurs 10-7, Fri & Sat 10-5
Friends of the Library Group

PENITAS

P PENITAS PUBLIC LIBRARY*, 1111 S Main St, 78576. (Mail add: PO Box 204, 78576). Tel: 956-583-5656. FAX: 956-583-5658. E-mail: library@cityofpenitas.com. Administration E-mail: library_asst@cityofpenitas.com. Web Site: www.penitaslibrary.com. *Libr Dir,* Yenni Espinoza; *Libr Asst,* Noemi Garcia; *Libr Asst,* Karla Olivares; *Libr Asst,* Eliamar Salgado; Staff 4 (Non-MLS 4)
Founded 2010
Wireless access
Function: Adult bk club, Adult literacy prog, After school storytime, Art programs, Audiobks via web, Bilingual assistance for Spanish patrons, Bk club(s), Children's prog, Computer training, Computers for patron use, Family literacy, Free DVD rentals, Holiday prog, ILL available, Internet access, Magazines, Meeting rooms, Movies, Online cat, Outreach serv, Preschool outreach, Preschool reading prog, Prog for adults, Prog for children & young adult, Scanner, STEM programs, Story hour, Summer reading prog, Teen prog
Mem of Hidalgo County Library System
Open Mon-Thurs 9-7, Fri 9-5, Sat 12-5
Friends of the Library Group

PERRYTON

P PERRY MEMORIAL LIBRARY, 22 SE Fifth Ave, 79070. SAN 316-6643. Tel: 806-435-5801. FAX: 806-435-4266. E-mail: perrytonlibraryill@gmail.com. Web Site: perryton.harringtonlc.org. *Dir,* Sandra Sears; Staff 3 (MLS 1, Non-MLS 2)
Founded 1925. Pop 10,000; Circ 72,966
Library Holdings: Bk Vols 37,500; Per Subs 10
Special Collections: Texas Coll
Subject Interests: Hist
Automation Activity & Vendor Info: (Cataloging) SirsiDynix; (Circulation) SirsiDynix; (OPAC) SirsiDynix
Wireless access
Partic in Harrington Library Consortium
Open Mon & Thurs 9:30-6, Tues, Wed & Fri 9:30-5:30

PETERSBURG

P PETERSBURG PUBLIC LIBRARY, 1614 Main St, 79250. (Mail add: PO Box 65, 79250-0065). Tel: 806-667-3657. Web Site: www.facebook.com/petersburgtxlibrary. *Librn,* Lacy Mayfield
Pop 2,532; Circ 6,048
Library Holdings: Bk Vols 10,000
Open Tues & Thurs 2-6

PFLUGERVILLE

P PFLUGERVILLE PUBLIC LIBRARY*, 1008 W Pfluger, 78660. SAN 372-5685. Tel: 512-990-6375. E-mail: library@pflugervilletx.gov. Web Site: library.pflugervilletx.gov. *Dir,* Jennifer Coffey; *Asst Dir,* Daniel Berra; *Ad,* Bette McDowell; *Youth Serv Librn,* Amanda Cawthon; E-mail: amandac@pflugervilletx.gov; *Youth Serv Librn,* Melissa Grzybowski; Staff 11 (MLS 5, Non-MLS 6)
Founded 1981. Pop 46,936; Circ 283,000
Library Holdings: DVDs 11,000; Bk Vols 74,000
Subject Interests: Texana
Automation Activity & Vendor Info: (Cataloging) Biblionix; (Circulation) Biblionix; (OPAC) Biblionix
Wireless access
Function: Adult bk club, Art exhibits, Audiobks via web, Bilingual assistance for Spanish patrons, Bk club(s), Bks on CD, Children's prog, Computer training, Computers for patron use, E-Reserves, Electronic databases & coll, Free DVD rentals, Genealogy discussion group, Homebound delivery serv, ILL available, Internet access, Mail & tel request accepted, Music CDs, Online cat, Online ref, Outreach serv, OverDrive digital audio bks, Photocopying/Printing, Preschool reading prog, Prog for adults, Prog for children & young adult, Ref serv available, Scanner, Senior computer classes, Senior outreach, Spanish lang bks, Summer reading prog, Tax forms, Teen prog, Telephone ref, Wheelchair accessible, Writing prog
Partic in Partners Library Action Network
Open Mon-Thurs 10-8, Fri 10-6, Sat & Sun 1-6
Friends of the Library Group

PHARR

P PHARR MEMORIAL LIBRARY*, 121 E Cherokee St, 78577-4826. SAN 316-6651. Tel: 956-402-4650. FAX: 956-787-3345. Web Site: pharr-tx.gov/pharr-library. *Dir,* Adolfo Garcia; E-mail: adolfo.garcia@pharr-tx.gov. Subject Specialists: *Mgt,* Adolfo Garcia; Staff 22 (MLS 2, Non-MLS 20)
Founded 1960. Pop 73,000
Library Holdings: Bk Vols 85,000; Per Subs 70
Special Collections: Large Print Coll; Spanish Coll (Spanish language materials); Texas Coll
Automation Activity & Vendor Info: (Acquisitions) TLC (The Library Corporation); (Cataloging) TLC (The Library Corporation); (Circulation) TLC (The Library Corporation); (OPAC) TLC (The Library Corporation)
Wireless access
Function: Computers for patron use, Prog for children & young adult, Ref serv available, Summer reading prog
Mem of Hidalgo County Library System
Open Mon-Thurs 9-9, Fri & Sat 9-6, Sun 1-6
Friends of the Library Group

PILOT POINT

P PILOT POINT COMMUNITY LIBRARY*, 324 S Washington St, 76258. Tel: 940-686-5004. FAX: 940-686-2833. E-mail: library@cityofpilotpoint.org. Web Site: www.pilotpointlibrary.org. *Libr Dir,* Wendy Turner; *Dep Dir,* Erica Salinas; *Libr Tech,* Lynda Tarsetti
Library Holdings: Bk Vols 18,000; Per Subs 25
Automation Activity & Vendor Info: (Cataloging) Follett Software; (Circulation) Follett Software
Wireless access
Function: AV serv, Bks on CD, Children's prog, ILL available, Photocopying/Printing
Partic in Partners Library Action Network
Open Tues-Thurs 9-6, Fri 9-5, Sat 9-2
Friends of the Library Group

PINELAND

P ARTHUR TEMPLE SR MEMORIAL LIBRARY*, 106 Timberland Hwy, 75968-0847. SAN 316-666X. Tel: 409-584-2546. FAX: 409-584-3206. E-mail: atsmlibrary@valornet.com. Web Site: pinelandlibrary.org. *Dir,* Donna Nichols
Founded 1969. Pop 7,200; Circ 33,559
Library Holdings: AV Mats 2,039; Bk Vols 23,000; Per Subs 16; Videos 1,200
Automation Activity & Vendor Info: (Cataloging) Follett Software; (Circulation) Follett Software; (OPAC) Follett Software
Wireless access
Function: 24/7 Electronic res, 24/7 Online cat, Bks on CD, Computers for patron use, Doc delivery serv, Free DVD rentals, ILL available, Internet access, Magazines, Meeting rooms, Notary serv, Online cat, OverDrive digital audio bks, Photocopying/Printing, Summer reading prog, Tax forms, Wheelchair accessible
Partic in Partners Library Action Network
Open Mon & Wed-Fri 9-4, Tues 10-5
Friends of the Library Group

PITTSBURG

P PITTSBURG-CAMP COUNTY PUBLIC LIBRARY*, 613 Quitman St, 75686-1035. SAN 316-6678. Tel: 903-856-3302. FAX: 903-856-0591. E-mail: info@pittsburglibrary.org. Web Site: www.pittsburglibrary.org. *Libr Dir,* Lily Marshall; Staff 1 (Non-MLS 1)
Founded 1973. Pop 12,413; Circ 81,455
Library Holdings: Audiobooks 1,212; CDs 179; DVDs 1,727; Bk Vols 23,406; Per Subs 20
Special Collections: Genealogy Coll
Automation Activity & Vendor Info: (Acquisitions) Book Systems; (Cataloging) Book Systems; (Circulation) Book Systems; (OPAC) Book Systems

Wireless access
Open Mon-Thurs 9-5:30, Fri 9-5, Sat (Oct-May) 9-12:45
Friends of the Library Group

PLAINS

P YOAKUM COUNTY LIBRARY*, 901 Ave E, 79355. SAN 316-6686. Tel: 806-456-8725. FAX: 806-456-7056. E-mail: yclp_79355@hotmail.com. *Librn,* Anne Benson; *Asst Librn,* Vicki Bayer; Staff 6 (MLS 3, Non-MLS 3)
Founded 1957. Pop 3,500
Library Holdings: Bk Vols 38,000; Per Subs 47
Special Collections: Texas History Coll
Automation Activity & Vendor Info: (Cataloging) Biblionix; (Circulation) Biblionix
Wireless access
Publications: Appraisal; Booklist; Publishers Weekly
Open Mon-Fri 9-5:30

PLAINVIEW

P UNGER MEMORIAL LIBRARY, 825 Austin St, 79072-7235. SAN 316-6694. Tel: 806-296-1148. Administration Tel: 806-296-1149. FAX: 806-291-1245. Web Site: www.plainviewtx.org/141/library. *Librn,* Cynthia Lynn Peterson. Subject Specialists: *Archives, Hist, Music,* Cynthia Lynn Peterson; Staff 5 (MLS 1, Non-MLS 4)
Founded 1913
Oct 2022-Sept 2023 Income $524,866, City $512,980, County $9,500. Mats Exp $55,912, Books $42,500, Per/Ser (Incl. Access Fees) $6,400, AV Mat $205, Electronic Ref Mat (Incl. Access Fees) $6,807. Sal $195,600 (Prof $60,000)
Library Holdings: Audiobooks 1,560; CDs 1,560; DVDs 2,960; e-books 18,500; Electronic Media & Resources 4,500; Large Print Bks 888; Bk Titles 57,200; Bk Vols 61,340; Per Subs 100; Videos 2,960
Special Collections: Hale County Cemetery Records, online database; Hi-Plains Genealogical Society Coll; Plainview & Hale County History Coll
Subject Interests: Genealogy, Local hist
Automation Activity & Vendor Info: (Cataloging) Book Systems; (Circulation) Book Systems; (ILL) Auto-Graphics, Inc; (OPAC) Book Systems
Wireless access
Function: 24/7 Electronic res, 24/7 Online cat, Archival coll, Audio & video playback equip for onsite use, Audiobks on Playaways & MP3, Audiobks via web, Bilingual assistance for Spanish patrons, Bk club(s), Bks on CD, Children's prog, Citizenship assistance, Computers for patron use, Digital talking bks, E-Reserves, Electronic databases & coll, Family literacy, Free DVD rentals, Genealogy discussion group, Holiday prog, ILL available, Instruction & testing, Internet access, Laminating, Life-long learning prog for all ages, Literacy & newcomer serv, Magazines, Mail & tel request accepted, Mango lang, Meeting rooms, Movies, Music CDs, Notary serv, Online cat, Online info literacy tutorials on the web & in blackboard, Online ref, Orientations, Outside serv via phone, mail, e-mail & web, OverDrive digital audio bks, Photocopying/Printing, Preschool outreach, Preschool reading prog, Printer for laptops & handheld devices, Prog for adults, Prog for children & young adult, Ref & res, Ref serv available, Res assist avail, Scanner, Spanish lang bks, Spoken cassettes & CDs, Story hour, Summer reading prog, Tax forms, Teen prog, Telephone ref, Wheelchair accessible, Workshops
Partic in TexSHARE - Texas State Library & Archives Commission
Special Services for the Blind - Talking bk serv referral
Open Mon-Wed & Fri 9-6, Thurs 9-8, Sat 9-5 (Fall-Spring); Mon-Wed & Fri 9-6, Thurs 9-8, Sat 10-2 (Summer)
Restriction: Borrowing requests are handled by ILL, Circ to mem only, ID required to use computers (Ltd hrs), In-house use for visitors
Friends of the Library Group

C WAYLAND BAPTIST UNIVERSITY*, Mabee Learning Resources Center, 1900 W Seventh St, 79072-6957. SAN 316-6708. Tel: 806-291-3700. Reference Tel: 806-291-3708. Toll Free Tel: 800-459-8648. FAX: 806-291-1964. E-mail: lrcref@wbu.edu. Web Site: www.wbu.edu/academics/library. *Dir,* Sally Quiroz; Tel: 806-291-3702, E-mail: sally.quiroz@wbu.edu; *Coll Develop Librn,* John Elliott; Tel: 806-291-3704, E-mail: elliottj@wbu.edu; *Reference & Distance Services Librn,* Robert Jensen; E-mail: jensenr@wbu.edu; Staff 5 (MLS 3, Non-MLS 2)
Founded 1910. Enrl 3,408; Fac 133; Highest Degree: Doctorate
Library Holdings: Bk Vols 130,044; Per Subs 466
Automation Activity & Vendor Info: (Cataloging) SirsiDynix; (Circulation) SirsiDynix; (OPAC) SirsiDynix
Wireless access
Partic in Amigos Library Services, Inc; Harrington Library Consortium; OCLC Online Computer Library Center, Inc
Open Mon-Thurs 7:45am-11pm, Fri 7:45-4, Sat 1-5, Sun 2-5 & 7:30-10

PLANO

J COLLIN COLLEGE*, Spring Creek Campus Library, 2800 E Spring Creek Pkwy, 75074. SAN 328-0276. Tel: 972-881-5860. Reference Tel: 972-881-5985. FAX: 972-881-5911. Web Site: www.collin.edu/library. *Exec Dir,* Linda Kyprios; Tel: 972-881-5726, E-mail: lkyprios@collin.edu; Staff 11 (MLS 6, Non-MLS 5)
Founded 1985. Highest Degree: Associate
Library Holdings: Bk Vols 180,000; Per Subs 937
Automation Activity & Vendor Info: (Cataloging) Innovative Interfaces, Inc; (Circulation) Innovative Interfaces, Inc
Wireless access
Function: Art exhibits, Audio & video playback equip for onsite use, Digital talking bks, Distance learning, For res purposes, ILL available, Magnifiers for reading, Music CDs, Orientations, Prog for adults, Ref serv available, Spoken cassettes & CDs, Telephone ref, VHS videos, Wheelchair accessible, Workshops
Partic in OCLC Online Computer Library Center, Inc
Open Mon-Thurs 7:45am-9:45pm, Fri 7:45-5, Sat 8-5, Sun 1-5
Restriction: In-house use for visitors

P PLANO PUBLIC LIBRARY SYSTEM*, Library Administration, 2501 Coit Rd, 75075. SAN 316-6724. Tel: 972-769-4208. FAX: 972-769-4269. Web Site: www.plano.gov/9/Library. *Libr Dir,* Libby Holtmann; E-mail: libbyh@plano.gov; *Tech Serv Mgr,* Janet Cox; Tel: 972-769-4291, E-mail: janetc@plano.gov; *Coordr of Develop,* Kristin Linscott; Tel: 972-769-4211, E-mail: klinscott@plano.gov; Staff 8 (MLS 7, Non-MLS 1)
Founded 1965. Pop 261,350; Circ 3,882,165
Special Collections: Archives; Genealogy Coll; Local History Coll; Texana Coll
Automation Activity & Vendor Info: (Acquisitions) Innovative Interfaces, Inc; (Cataloging) Innovative Interfaces, Inc; (Circulation) Innovative Interfaces, Inc; (OPAC) Innovative Interfaces, Inc; (Serials) Innovative Interfaces, Inc
Wireless access
Publications: Plano, Texas: The Early Years (Local historical information)
Open Mon-Thurs 9-8, Fri 9-5, Sat 10-5, Sun 1-5
Friends of the Library Group
Branches: 5
MARIBELLE M DAVIS LIBRARY, 7501-B Independence Pkwy, 75025, SAN 378-0317. Tel: 972-208-8000. FAX: 972-208-8037. Web Site: www.plano.gov/989/Davis-Library. *Libr Mgr,* Brent Bloechle; E-mail: brentb@plano.gov; Staff 8 (MLS 8)
Founded 1998. Pop 65,000
Open Mon-Thurs 9-8, Fri 9-5, Sat 10-5, Sun 1-5
Friends of the Library Group
W O HAGGARD JR LIBRARY, 2501 Coit Rd, 75075, SAN 370-0003. Tel: 972-769-4250. FAX: 972-769-4256. Web Site: www.plano.gov/998/Haggard-Library. *Libr Mgr,* Cecily Ponce deLeon; E-mail: cecilyp@plano.gov; Staff 8 (MLS 8)
Founded 1989. Pop 65,000
Subject Interests: Consumer health, Sci
Open Mon-Thurs 9-8, Fri 9-5, Sat 10-5, Sun 1-5
Friends of the Library Group
GLADYS HARRINGTON LIBRARY, 1501 18th St, 75074, SAN 321-1401. Tel: 972-941-7175. FAX: 972-941-7292. Web Site: www.plano.gov/1001/Harrington-Library. *Libr Mgr,* Melissa Shadowens; E-mail: melissas@plano.gov; Staff 7.5 (MLS 7.5)
Founded 1969. Pop 43,000
Open Mon-Thurs 9-8, Fri 9-5, Sat 10-5, Sun 1-5
Friends of the Library Group
CHRISTOPHER A PARR LIBRARY, 6200 Windhaven Pkwy, 75093. Tel: 972-769-4300. FAX: 972-769-4304. Web Site: www.plano.gov/1022/Parr-Library. *Libr Mgr,* Nina Martin; E-mail: Ninaz@plano.gov; *Sr Pub Serv Librn,* Jennifer Strange; E-mail: jennifers@plano.gov; Staff 7 (MLS 7)
Founded 2001. Pop 43,000
Open Mon-Thurs 9-8, Fri 9-5, Sat 10-5, Sun 1-5
Friends of the Library Group
L E R SCHIMELPFENIG LIBRARY, 5024 Custer Rd, 75023, SAN 321-141X. Tel: 972-769-4200. FAX: 972-769-4210. Web Site: www.plano.gov/1025/Schimelpfenig-Library. *Libr Mgr,* Anthony Andros; E-mail: anthonya@plano.gov; *Librn,* Julie Conner; E-mail: juliec@plano.gov; Staff 7 (MLS 7)
Founded 1980. Pop 43,000
Subject Interests: Law, Sci
Open Mon-Thurs 9-8, Fri 9-5:30, Sat 10-5:30, Sun 1-4:30
Friends of the Library Group

PLEASANTON

P PLEASANTON LIBRARY & INFORMATION CENTER*, 115 N Main, 78064. SAN 316-6732. Tel: 830-569-5901. FAX: 830-569-5903. Web Site: www.pleasantontx.gov/departments/library. *Libr Dir,* Dorothy Steelman; E-mail: dsteelman@pleasantontx.gov; Staff 4 (MLS 2, Non-MLS 2)

Founded 1950
Library Holdings: Bks on Deafness & Sign Lang 20; Large Print Bks 500; Bk Titles 35,000; Bk Vols 36,500; Per Subs 70; Talking Bks 2,000
Special Collections: Texana
Automation Activity & Vendor Info: (Acquisitions) Biblionix; (Cataloging) Biblionix; (Circulation) Biblionix; (ILL) OCLC ILLiad; (OPAC) Biblionix; (Serials) Biblionix
Wireless access
Function: 24/7 Electronic res, 24/7 Online cat, Bks on CD, Children's prog, Electronic databases & coll, Free DVD rentals, ILL available, Internet access, Magazines, Movies, Online cat, OverDrive digital audio bks, Photocopying/Printing, Scanner, Story hour, Summer reading prog, Tax forms
Partic in Partners Library Action Network
Open Mon-Fri 8-5

PONDER

P BETTY FOSTER PUBLIC LIBRARY*, 405 Shaffner St, 76259. Tel: 940-479-2683. FAX: 940-479-2314. E-mail: bettyfosterpubliclibrary@pondertx.com. Web Site: www.pondertx.com/library. *Head Librn,* Alexandria Mills; *Libr Asst,* Kelly Goudeau; Staff 2 (Non-MLS 2)
Founded 1996. Circ 7,486
Library Holdings: Audiobooks 344; Bk Vols 9,078
Automation Activity & Vendor Info: (Acquisitions) Biblionix/Apollo; (Cataloging) Biblionix/Apollo; (Circulation) Biblionix/Apollo; (ILL) Biblionix/Apollo; (Serials) Biblionix/Apollo
Wireless access
Function: 24/7 Online cat, Adult bk club, Bk club(s), Bks on CD, Children's prog, Computers for patron use, Holiday prog, ILL available, Internet access, Online cat, Outside serv via phone, mail, e-mail & web, Photocopying/Printing, Preschool reading prog, Prog for adults, Prog for children & young adult, Ref serv available, Scanner, Spanish lang bks, Story hour, Summer reading prog, Tax forms, Teen prog
Open Tues-Thurs 1-6, Fri 12-6, Sat 12-4
Friends of the Library Group

PORT ARANSAS

P ELLIS MEMORIAL LIBRARY*, 700 W Ave A, 78373. SAN 376-4303. Tel: 361-749-4116. FAX: 361-749-5679. E-mail: eml@cityofportaransas.org. Web Site: cityofportaransas.org/departments/library/. *Libr Dir,* Sgefanie Bara; E-mail: sbara@cityofportaransas.org; *Asst Libr Dir,* Toby De La Rosa; E-mail: toby@cityofportaransas.org; Staff 4 (MLS 1, Non-MLS 3)
Pop 3,370
Library Holdings: Bk Vols 16,500; Per Subs 80
Partic in Partners Library Action Network

PORT ARTHUR

C LAMAR STATE COLLEGE*, Gates Memorial Library, 317 Stilwell Blvd, 77640. (Mail add: PO Box 310, 77641-0310), SAN 378-0716. Tel: 409-984-6222. Interlibrary Loan Service Tel: 409-984-6218. Reference Tel: 409-984-6220. FAX: 409-984-6008. *Dean, Libr Serv,* Helena S Gawu; Tel: 409-984-6216, E-mail: arthurh@lamarpa.edu; *Access Serv, Ref Coordr,* Yumi Shin; Tel: 409-984-6221, E-mail: shiny@lamarpa.edu; Staff 4 (MLS 2, Non-MLS 2)
Founded 1909. Enrl 3,000; Fac 135; Highest Degree: Associate
Sept 2017-Aug 2018 Income $139,509. Mats Exp $402,685, Books $48,278, Per/Ser (Incl. Access Fees) $59, Electronic Ref Mat (Incl. Access Fees) $90,200. Sal $189,985 (Prof $116,673)
Library Holdings: AV Mats 2,924; Bks on Deafness & Sign Lang 10; CDs 193; DVDs 553; e-books 90,200; e-journals 27,000; Bk Titles 48,278; Bk Vols 54,000; Per Subs 59
Special Collections: Music Heritage (Janis Joplin Coll); Texana Coll
Subject Interests: Criminal justice, Kinesiology, Law, Music, Nursing
Automation Activity & Vendor Info: (Acquisitions) EOS International; (Cataloging) EOS International; (Circulation) EOS International; (Course Reserve) EOS International; (Discovery) EBSCO Discovery Service; (ILL) OCLC FirstSearch; (OPAC) EOS International; (Serials) EOS International
Wireless access
Partic in Amigos Library Services, Inc; TexSHARE - Texas State Library & Archives Commission
Special Services for the Deaf - ADA equip; Assisted listening device; Assistive tech; Bks on deafness & sign lang; Closed caption videos; Interpreter on staff; Pocket talkers; Sign lang interpreter upon request for prog; Staff with knowledge of sign lang; Video & TTY relay via computer
Special Services for the Blind - Accessible computers; Assistive/Adapted tech devices, equip & products; Audio mat; Bks available with recordings; Compressed speech equip; Computer access aids; Computer with voice synthesizer for visually impaired persons; Copier with enlargement capabilities; Digital talking bk; Ednalite Hi-Vision scope; Internet workstation with adaptive software; Magnifiers
Open Mon-Thurs 7:30-7:30, Fri 7:30-5

P PORT ARTHUR PUBLIC LIBRARY*, 4615 Ninth Ave, 77642. SAN 362-1723. Tel: 409-985-8838. Web Site: paplibrary.org. *Dir,* Steven Williams; E-mail: stwillia@paplibrary.org; *Librn II,* Janell Farris; E-mail: jfarris@paplibrary.org; *Ch,* Carolyn Thibodeaux; E-mail: cthibodeaux@paplibrary.org; Staff 18 (MLS 3, Non-MLS 15)
Founded 1918. Pop 56,827
Library Holdings: CDs 1,782; e-books 1,700; Large Print Bks 5,250; Bk Titles 161,230; Bk Vols 182,000; Per Subs 205; Videos 3,860
Special Collections: Port Arthur History Archives (includes historical photos of Port Arthur people & places; information on Arthur Stilwell, John W "Bet-A-Million" Gates, Janis Joplin, Jimmy Johnson, Robert Rauschenberg, Karen Silkwood & other notables who have called Port Arthur home. Oral History
Automation Activity & Vendor Info: (Cataloging) Innovative Interfaces, Inc; (Circulation) Innovative Interfaces, Inc
Wireless access
Publications: Friends (Newsletter)
Special Services for the Blind - Talking bks
Open Mon-Thurs 9-9, Fri 9-6, Sat 9-5, Sun 1-5
Friends of the Library Group

PORT ISABEL

P PORT ISABEL PUBLIC LIBRARY*, 213 Yturria St, 78578. SAN 316-6783. Tel: 956-943-1822. FAX: 956-943-4638. Web Site: portisabel-texas.com/cityhall/departments/port-isabel-public-library. *Dir,* Janie Villarreal; E-mail: librarydirector@copitx.com; *Asst Dir,* Ida Tellez; E-mail: itellez@copitx.com; *Circ,* Vanja Moore; E-mail: vmoore@copitx.com
Pop 20,000; Circ 28,465
Library Holdings: Bk Titles 24,245; Bk Vols 26,057; Per Subs 72
Automation Activity & Vendor Info: (Cataloging) Biblionix; (Circulation) Biblionix
Wireless access
Partic in Partners Library Action Network
Open Mon & Tues 8:30-5:30, Wed 9-6, Thurs 10-7, Fri 10-5, Sat 9-1
Friends of the Library Group

PORT LAVACA

P CALHOUN COUNTY LIBRARY*, 200 W Mahan St, 77979. SAN 362-1782. Tel: 361-552-7323. Reference Tel: 361-552-7250. FAX: 361-552-5218. Web Site: www.cclibrary.org. *Dir,* Noemi Cruz; E-mail: ncruz@cclibrary.org; Staff 1 (Non-MLS 1)
Founded 1962. Pop 21,300; Circ 105,999
Jan 2016-Dec 2016 Income (Main & Associated Libraries) $423,558. Mats Exp $42,000
Library Holdings: Bk Titles 76,749; Bk Vols 111,867; Per Subs 167
Automation Activity & Vendor Info: (Cataloging) Follett Software; (Circulation) Follett Software
Wireless access
Publications: Booklist; Library Journal; Public Libraries
Partic in Partners Library Action Network
Open Tues & Thurs 10-8, Wed & Fri 10-6, Sat 9-1
Friends of the Library Group
Branches: 3
POINT COMFORT BRANCH, One Lamar St, Point Comfort, 77978. (Mail add: PO Box 424, Point Comfort, 77978-0424), SAN 362-1812. Tel: 361-987-2954. FAX: 361-987-2374. *Librn,* Michael Williams; Staff 2 (MLS 1, Non-MLS 1)
Pop 780
Library Holdings: Bk Vols 15,000; Per Subs 30
PORT O'CONNOR BRANCH, 506 W Main St, Port O'Connor, 77982. (Mail add: PO Box 424, Port O'Connor, 77982), SAN 370-4564. Tel: 361-983-4365. FAX: 316-983-2014. *Librn,* Michelle Martin; Staff 1 (Non-MLS 1)
Pop 1,182
Library Holdings: Bk Vols 25,000; Per Subs 8
Open Tues-Fri 10:30-5, Sat 9-1
Friends of the Library Group
SEADRIFT BRANCH, 502 S 4th St, Seadrift, 77983. (Mail add: PO Box 576, Seadrift, 77983), SAN 362-1847. Tel: 361-785-4241. FAX: 361-785-2346. *Librn,* Robbie Bess; Staff 1 (Non-MLS 1)
Pop 1,230
Library Holdings: Bk Vols 12,000
Open Tues-Fri 10:30-5, Sat 9-1
Friends of the Library Group

PORT NECHES

P EFFIE & WILTON HEBERT PUBLIC LIBRARY*, 2025 Merriman St, 77651. SAN 320-5150. Tel: 409-722-4554. FAX: 409-719-4296. E-mail: ptnlib@ptn.lib.tx.us. Web Site: www.ptn.lib.tx.us. *Dir,* Mark Durham; E-mail: mdurham@ptn.lib.tx.us; Staff 1 (MLS 1)
Founded 1934. Pop 13,944

Library Holdings: Bk Vols 60,000; Per Subs 105
Subject Interests: Acadian genealogy, Texana
Automation Activity & Vendor Info: (Acquisitions) SirsiDynix; (Cataloging) SirsiDynix; (Circulation) SirsiDynix; (OPAC) SirsiDynix
Wireless access
Open Mon-Thurs 8:30-8, Fri 9-5, Sun 2-8
Friends of the Library Group

PORTLAND

P BELL-WHITTINGTON PUBLIC LIBRARY*, 2400 Memorial Pkwy, 78374. SAN 316-6805. Tel: 361-777-4560. FAX: 361-777-4561. Web Site: www.portlandtx.com/181/library. *Dir,* Ginny Moses; E-mail: ginny.moses@portlandtx.com; Staff 11 (MLS 4, Non-MLS 7)
Founded 1934. Pop 21,000; Circ 80,000
Library Holdings: Bk Vols 40,000; Per Subs 70
Special Collections: Oral History
Subject Interests: Antique collecting, Archit, Art, Educ, Genealogy
Automation Activity & Vendor Info: (Cataloging) LibLime; (Circulation) LibLime; (OPAC) LibLime
Wireless access
Publications: Annual Report
Partic in Partners Library Action Network
Open Mon-Thurs 9-8, Fri 9-5, Sat 10-2
Friends of the Library Group

POST

P POST PUBLIC LIBRARY*, 105 E Main St, 79356. SAN 316-6813. Tel: 806-990-2149. E-mail: postpubliclibrary@gmail.com. Web Site: pplib.ploud.net. *Dir,* Peggy Ashley; Staff 1.5 (Non-MLS 1.5)
Founded 1966. Pop 5,182; Circ 16,530
Library Holdings: Bk Titles 14,940; Bk Vols 14,983; Per Subs 12
Special Collections: US Document Depository
Subject Interests: Tex
Wireless access
Open Mon & Thurs 9:30-5, Tues, Wed & Fri Noon-5

POTEET

P POTEET PUBLIC LIBRARY*, 126 S Fifth St, 78065. (Mail add: PO Box 378, 78065-0378), SAN 316-6821. Tel: 830-742-8917. FAX: 830-742-3988. E-mail: poteetlib@poteettexas.gov. Web Site: www.poteettx.org/2154/Library. *Dir,* Lisa Burbridge
Pop 3,495
Library Holdings: Bk Titles 9,500; Per Subs 25
Special Collections: Texana Coll
Wireless access
Partic in Partners Library Action Network
Special Services for the Deaf - Bks on deafness & sign lang; Captioned film dep; High interest/low vocabulary bks; Spec interest per
Open Mon-Fri 8-12 & 1-5
Friends of the Library Group

POTTSBORO

P POTTSBORO AREA PUBLIC LIBRARY*, 104 N Main, 75076. (Mail add: PO Box 477, 75076-0477), SAN 376-4427. Tel: 903-786-8274. FAX: 903-786-8274. E-mail: PottsboroLibrary@gmail.com. Web Site: pottsborolibrary.com. *Dir,* Dianne Connery
Founded 1985. Pop 2,000; Circ 4,000
Library Holdings: Bk Vols 15,000; Per Subs 3
Automation Activity & Vendor Info: (Cataloging) Biblionix; (Circulation) Biblionix
Wireless access
Partic in Partners Library Action Network
Open Mon-Fri 1-5, Sun 3-6
Friends of the Library Group

PRAIRIE LEA

P TRI-COMMUNITY LIBRARY, 6910 Hwy 80, 78661. (Mail add: PO Box 44, 78661-0044). Tel: 512-488-2328, Ext 4. FAX: 512-488-9006. Web Site: www.plisd.net. *Libr Coord,* Lulu Ivarra; E-mail: ivarral@plisd.net; Staff 1 (Non-MLS 1)
Library Holdings: Audiobooks 100; Bk Vols 8,000; Per Subs 15
Partic in Partners Library Action Network
Open Mon, Wed & Thurs 8-4, Tues 8-4:30, Fri 8-3 (Winter); Tues & Wed 9-4, Thurs 9-3 (Summer)

PRAIRIE VIEW

C PRAIRIE VIEW A&M UNIVERSITY*, John B Coleman Library, L W Minor St, University Dr, 77446-0519. (Mail add: PO Box 519, MS 1040, 77446), SAN 316-683X. Tel: 936-261-1500. FAX: 936-261-1539. Web Site: www.pvamu.edu/Library. *Dir of Libr,* Dr Musa Olaka; Tel: 936-261-1533, E-mail: mwolaka@pvamu.edu; *Asst Dir, Libr Serv, Tech Serv,* Karl Henson; Tel: 936-261-1504, E-mail: kehenson@pvamu.edu; *Music Librn,* Christine Moore; Tel: 936-261-3322, E-mail: chmoore@pvamu.edu; *Univ Archivist,* Phyllis Earles; Tel: 936-261-1516, E-mail: plearles@pvamu.edu; Staff 29 (MLS 20, Non-MLS 9)
Founded 1878. Enrl 9,516; Fac 506; Highest Degree: Doctorate
Sept 2019-Aug 2020 Income $3,400,000, State $3,400,000
Library Holdings: Bk Vols 333,057; Per Subs 872
Special Collections: Black Heritage of the West Coll; Black Lawless Coll; Blacks in the US Military Coll
Subject Interests: Biology, Bus, Educ, Engr, Nursing
Automation Activity & Vendor Info: (Acquisitions) Innovative Interfaces, Inc - Sierra; (Cataloging) Innovative Interfaces, Inc - Sierra; (Circulation) Innovative Interfaces, Inc - Sierra; (Course Reserve) Ex Libris Group; (Discovery) EBSCO Discovery Service; (ILL) OCLC WorldShare Interlibrary Loan; (OPAC) Innovative Interfaces, Inc - Sierra; (Serials) Innovative Interfaces, Inc - Sierra
Wireless access
Publications: Taste of Freedom (cook book)
Partic in Amigos Library Services, Inc; OCLC Online Computer Library Center, Inc; TexSHARE - Texas State Library & Archives Commission
Special Services for the Blind - Accessible computers
Open Mon-Thurs 7am-Midnight, Fri & Sat 8-5, Sun 1pm-Midnight (Spring & Fall); Mon-Thurs 8am-9pm, Fri & Sat 8-5 (Summer)

PREMONT

PREMONT PUBLIC LIBRARY*, 115 S Agnes St, 78375. (Mail add: PO Box 829, 78375-0829), SAN 361-0500. Tel: 361-348-3815. E-mail: premontpubliclibrary@gmail.com. Web Site: premont.biblionix.com. *Library Contact,* Susan Cherry
Wireless access
Open Mon-Fri 12-5

PRESIDIO

P CITY OF PRESIDIO PUBLIC LIBRARY*, 1200 E O'Reilly St, 79845. (Mail add: PO Box 2440, 79845-2440), SAN 376-432X. Tel: 432-229-3317. FAX: 432-229-4640. E-mail: presidiolibrary@presidiotx.us. Web Site: www.presidiolibrary.com. *Dir,* Carmen Elguezabal; Staff 2 (Non-MLS 2)
Pop 4,205
Library Holdings: Bk Vols 18,736; Per Subs 29
Automation Activity & Vendor Info: (Circulation) Follett Software; (OPAC) Follett Software
Wireless access
Partic in Partners Library Action Network
Open Mon-Fri 9-1 & 2-6

PROSPER

P PROSPER COMMUNITY LIBRARY*, 200 S Main St, 75078. (Mail add: PO Box 307, 75078-0307). Tel: 972-569-1185. FAX: 972-346-9115. E-mail: library@prospertx.gov. Web Site: www.prospertx.gov/residents/library. *Dir, Libr Serv,* Leslie Scott; E-mail: lscott@prospertx.gov; Staff 14 (MLS 2, Non-MLS 12)
Founded 2001
Library Holdings: Audiobooks 100; DVDs 400; e-books 21,000; Large Print Bks 150; Bk Titles 11,000; Bk Vols 12,000; Per Subs 3
Automation Activity & Vendor Info: (Cataloging) ByWater Solutions; (Circulation) ByWater Solutions; (ILL) ByWater Solutions
Wireless access
Function: 24/7 Online cat, 3D Printer, Audiobks on Playaways & MP3, Bks on CD, Children's prog, Computers for patron use, Electronic databases & coll, Family literacy, Free DVD rentals, Holiday prog, ILL available, Internet access, Magazines, Mango lang, Online cat, OverDrive digital audio bks, Photocopying/Printing, Preschool reading prog, Prog for adults, Prog for children & young adult, Spanish lang bks, STEM programs, Story hour, Study rm, Summer & winter reading prog, Summer reading prog, Teen prog
Open Mon-Thurs 9:30-7, Sat 9:30-3
Friends of the Library Group

QUANAH

P THOMPSON-SAWYER PUBLIC LIBRARY, 403 W Third St, 79252. SAN 376-4613. Tel: 940-663-2654. E-mail: libraryquanahtx@gmail.com. Web Site: quanah.ploud.net. *Dir & Librn,* Martha Davidson
Library Holdings: Bk Vols 25,000; Per Subs 12
Automation Activity & Vendor Info: (Cataloging) Book Systems; (Circulation) Book Systems
Wireless access
Open Mon-Fri 2-6

QUEMADO

P QUEMADO PUBLIC LIBRARY*, 19791 N Hwy 277, 78877. (Mail add: PO Box 210, 78877-0210), SAN 376-4168. Tel: 830-757-1313. FAX: 830-757-3322. E-mail: quemado.librarian@gmail.com. Web Site: quemado.ploud.net. *Libr Dir,* Carmen Brosard
Library Holdings: Bk Vols 14,000; Per Subs 15
Automation Activity & Vendor Info: (Cataloging) Follett Software; (Circulation) Follett Software
Wireless access
Open Mon-Fri 12-6

QUITAQUE

P CAPROCK PUBLIC LIBRARY*, 106 N First, 79255. (Mail add: PO Box 487, 79255-0487), SAN 376-6519. Tel: 806-455-1225. FAX: 806-455-1225. E-mail: caprocklibrary90@gmail.com. Web Site: harringtonlc.org/caprockpublic. *Librn,* Desarae Phipps
Library Holdings: Audiobooks 319; AV Mats 820; DVDs 300; e-books 4,592; Large Print Bks 375; Bk Titles 6,976; Bk Vols 7,081
Wireless access
Function: Adult bk club, Bks on CD, Children's prog, Computers for patron use, Electronic databases & coll, Free DVD rentals, ILL available, Internet access, Magazines, Online cat, Photocopying/Printing, Preschool reading prog, Prog for children & young adult, Scanner, Summer reading prog, Wheelchair accessible
Partic in Harrington Library Consortium
Open Mon-Fri 8-5
Friends of the Library Group

QUITMAN

P QUITMAN PUBLIC LIBRARY*, 202 E Goode St, 75783-2533. (Mail add: PO Box 1677, 75783-1677), SAN 320-8486. Tel: 903-763-4191. FAX: 903-763-2532. E-mail: quitmanlibrarian@gmail.com. Web Site: www.quitmanlibrary.org. *Dir, Libr Serv,* Delene H Allen; *Cat,* Susan Lomanto; *Ch Prog,* Anita Nance; *Circ,* Rebekah Yeager; *Spec Coll,* Georgia V Hoffpauir; Staff 5 (MLS 1, Non-MLS 4)
Founded 1975. Pop 2,030; Circ 30,000
Library Holdings: AV Mats 2,500; Bks-By-Mail 75; Bks on Deafness & Sign Lang 25; Braille Volumes 10; DVDs 50; High Interest/Low Vocabulary Bk Vols 2,000; Large Print Bks 980; Bk Titles 28,000; Bk Vols 28,500; Per Subs 20; Talking Bks 1,050; Videos 2,500
Special Collections: Genealogy (Wood County Genealogy Society Coll); Texas Section. Municipal Document Depository
Subject Interests: Genealogy, Texana
Automation Activity & Vendor Info: (Acquisitions) Biblionix; (Cataloging) Biblionix; (Circulation) Biblionix; (Course Reserve) Biblionix; (ILL) OCLC FirstSearch; (Media Booking) OCLC ILLiad; (OPAC) Biblionix; (Serials) Biblionix
Wireless access
Function: 24/7 Electronic res, 24/7 Online cat, Adult bk club, Adult literacy prog, Audiobks via web, AV serv, BA reader (adult literacy), Bi-weekly Writer's Group, Bks on CD, Children's prog, Computers for patron use, Electronic databases & coll, Free DVD rentals, Genealogy discussion group, Home delivery & serv to seniorr ctr & nursing homes, Homebound delivery serv, ILL available, Instruction & testing, Internet access, Magazines, Magnifiers for reading, Mail & tel request accepted, Mail loans to mem, Meeting rooms, Microfiche/film & reading machines, Movies, Notary serv, Online cat, Online ref, Outside serv via phone, mail, e-mail & web, OverDrive digital audio bks, Photocopying/Printing, Prog for children & young adult, Ref & res, Res assist avail, Scanner, Summer reading prog, Tax forms, Wheelchair accessible, Workshops, Writing prog
Special Services for the Deaf - Adult & family literacy prog; Bks on deafness & sign lang; Closed caption videos; Deaf publ; High interest/low vocabulary bks; Spec interest per; Staff with knowledge of sign lang
Special Services for the Blind - Audio mat; Bks on cassette; Bks on CD; Braille bks; Extensive large print coll; Large print bks; Lending of low vision aids; Magnifiers; Talking bks; Videos on blindness & physical disabilties
Open Tues-Fri 10-6
Restriction: Registered patrons only
Friends of the Library Group

RANDOLPH AFB

A JOINT BASE SAN ANTONIO LIBRARIES*, Randolph Library, Bldg 598, Fifth St E, 78150. SAN 362-1901. Tel: 210-652-5578. E-mail: jbsarandolphlibraries@gmail.com. Web Site: www.jbsalibraries.org. *Supvry Librn,* Diana Lisenbee; E-mail: diana.lisenbee@us.af.mil; Staff 5 (MLS 1, Non-MLS 4)
Founded 1933
Library Holdings: DVDs 800; Bk Titles 50,000; Per Subs 140
Special Collections: Air War College; Embry-Riddle Coll; Project Warrior; Texana
Subject Interests: Mil hist, Prof develop, Tex
Automation Activity & Vendor Info: (Acquisitions) Innovative Interfaces, Inc - Sierra; (Cataloging) Innovative Interfaces, Inc - Sierra; (Circulation) Innovative Interfaces, Inc - Sierra; (Course Reserve) Innovative Interfaces, Inc - Sierra; (ILL) OCLC; (OPAC) Innovative Interfaces, Inc - Sierra; (Serials) Innovative Interfaces, Inc - Sierra
Wireless access
Partic in Coun of Res & Acad Librs
Open Mon-Thurs 9-5, Fri & Sat 11-5
Restriction: Circ to mil employees only

RANGER

P RANGER CITY LIBRARY*, 718 Pine St, 76470. Tel: 254-647-1880. FAX: 254-647-3070. E-mail: rcl@txol.net. Web Site: rangercitylibrary.com. *Librn,* Diana McCullough
Pop 3,600
Library Holdings: Bk Vols 12,000; Per Subs 12
Wireless access
Open Mon 10-7:30, Tues-Fri 10-6

J RANGER COLLEGE*, Golemon Library & Learning Resources Center, 1100 College Circle, 76470-3298. SAN 316-6880. Tel: 254-647-1414. E-mail: library@rangercollege.edu. Web Site: library.rangercollege.edu. *Dir, Libr Serv,* Jon Hall; E-mail: jhall@rangercollege.edu; *Asst Librn,* Jeani Vermillion; E-mail: jvermillion@rangercollege.edu; Staff 2 (MLS 1, Non-MLS 1)
Founded 1926. Enrl 1,937; Fac 32; Highest Degree: Associate
Sept 2015-Aug 2016 Income $21,300. Mats Exp $13,224, Books $4,000, Per/Ser (Incl. Access Fees) $8,600, AV Mat $500, Presv $124. Sal $60,000 (Prof $41,000)
Library Holdings: AV Mats 747; CDs 19; DVDs 133; Microforms 389; Bk Vols 24,705; Per Subs 25; Videos 206
Special Collections: Local History Coll, Artifacts, Bks; Ranger College History Coll, Artifacts, Yearbks; Robert E Howard Coll, Bks, Comic Bks
Automation Activity & Vendor Info: (Cataloging) EOS International; (Circulation) EOS International; (OPAC) EOS International
Wireless access
Partic in TexSHARE - Texas State Library & Archives Commission
Open Mon-Thurs 8am-9pm, Fri 8-1, Sun 4-9

RANKIN

P RANKIN PUBLIC LIBRARY, 310 E Tenth St, 79778. (Mail add: PO Box 6, 79778-0006), SAN 316-6899. Tel: 432-693-2881. FAX: 432-693-2667. Web Site: rankin.ploud.net. *Dir,* Celia Hooker; E-mail: rplcelia@yahoo.com
Founded 1950. Pop 777; Circ 15,600
Library Holdings: Bk Vols 16,000; Per Subs 15
Automation Activity & Vendor Info: (Cataloging) Follett Software; (Circulation) Follett Software
Wireless access
Publications: Newsletter
Open Mon-Thurs 8-12 & 1-5, Fri 8-4
Branches: 1
MIDKIFF PUBLIC, 12701 N FM 2401, Midkiff, 79755. (Mail add: PO Box 160, Midkiff, 79755). Tel: 432-535-2311. FAX: 432-535-2312. *Librn,* Teresa Latzel
Pop 100
Open Tues & Thurs 10:30-5:30

RAYMONDVILLE

P REBER MEMORIAL LIBRARY*, 193 N Fourth St, 78580-1994. SAN 316-6902. Tel: 956-689-2930. FAX: 956-689-6476. E-mail: reber.memorial@co.willacy.tx.us. Web Site: raymondville.ploud.net, www.co.willacy.tx.us/page/willacy.ReberMemorialLibrary. *Interim Dir,* Rosa Sanchez; E-mail: rosa.sanchez@co.willacy.tx.us
Pop 21,000; Circ 40,000
Library Holdings: Bk Vols 48,000; Per Subs 22
Automation Activity & Vendor Info: (Cataloging) Follett Software; (Circulation) Follett Software
Wireless access
Open Mon-Fri 9-6; Mon-Fri 8-5 (Summer)
Friends of the Library Group

RED OAK

P RED OAK PUBLIC LIBRARY, 200 Lakeview Pkwy, 75154. SAN 378-4487. Tel: 469-218-1230. FAX: 469-218-1231. E-mail: librarian@redoaktx.org. Web Site: www.redoaktx.org/206/Library. *Libr Dir,* Elise Cook
Founded 2004
Library Holdings: Audiobooks 100; Bk Vols 10,500; Videos 700
Automation Activity & Vendor Info: (Acquisitions) Innovative Interfaces, Inc

Wireless access
Open Mon-Thurs 11-7, Fri & Sat 1-5

REFUGIO

P DENNIS M O'CONNOR PUBLIC LIBRARY*, 815 S Commerce St, 78377. SAN 316-6929. Tel: 361-526-2608. FAX: 361-526-2608. Web Site: dmopl.com. *Libr Dir,* Tina McGuill; E-mail: tina.mcguill@co.refugio.tx.us
Pop 7,980; Circ 23,668
Library Holdings: AV Mats 769; Bk Titles 21,574; Bk Vols 23,635; Per Subs 53
Special Collections: Texas Room
Automation Activity & Vendor Info: (Cataloging) Follett Software; (Circulation) Follett Software
Wireless access
Open Mon-Fri 8-5

RHOME

P RHOME COMMUNITY LIBRARY*, 265 W BC Rhome Ave, 76078. (Mail add: PO Box 427, 76078). Tel: 817-636-2767. E-mail: rhomecommunitylibrary@gmail.com. Web Site: www.rhomelibrary.org. *Libr Dir,* Pamela Kemp; E-mail: rhomecommunitylibrary@gmail.com
Library Holdings: Bk Vols 2,000
Wireless access
Open Tues 11-7, Wed-Fri 11-5, Sat 11-2

RICHARDSON

SR FIRST UNITED METHODIST CHURCH LIBRARY*, 503 N Central Expressway, 75080. SAN 328-5111. Tel: 972-301-0143. Administration Tel: 972-235-4056. FAX: 972-341-0140. E-mail: library@fumcr.com. Web Site: www.fumcr.com/campus_library.
Founded 1959
Library Holdings: Bk Titles 7,000
Wireless access
Open Mon-Thurs 9-1, Sun 9-12:30

P RICHARDSON PUBLIC LIBRARY*, 2360 Campbell Creek Blvd, Ste 500, 75082. SAN 316-6945. Tel: 972-744-4350. Circulation Tel: 972-744-4363. Interlibrary Loan Service Tel: 972-744-4357. Reference Tel: 972-744-4355. FAX: 972-744-5806. E-mail: askrichardsonlibrary@cor.gov. Web Site: www.cor.net/departments/public-library. *Dir, Libr Serv,* Jennifer Davidson; Tel: 972-744-4353, E-mail: jennifer.davidson@cor.gov; *Asst Dir,* Vrena Patrick; Tel: 972-744-4352, E-mail: vrena.patrick@cor.gov; *ILL Librn,* Hannah Chupp; E-mail: hannah.chupp@cor.gov; *Supvr, Ad Serv,* Hanna Jurecki; Tel: 972-744-4377, E-mail: hanna.jerecki@cor.gov; *Supvr, Youth Serv,* Shay Brooks; Tel: 972-744-4383, E-mail: shay.brooks@cor.gov; Staff 68 (MLS 21, Non-MLS 47)
Founded 1959. Pop 122,615; Circ 938,885
Library Holdings: Audiobooks 6,788; AV Mats 31,632; CDs 6,631; DVDs 18,213; e-books 1,950; Large Print Bks 10,000; Bk Titles 175,000; Bk Vols 245,000; Per Subs 275
Special Collections: Richardson Local History Coll, clippings, local govt publs, photog, scrapbks; World Language Materials Coll (Chinese, Korean, Vietnamese, Hindi, Urdu, Spanish, French & Russian)
Automation Activity & Vendor Info: (Acquisitions) SirsiDynix; (Cataloging) SirsiDynix; (Circulation) SirsiDynix; (OPAC) SirsiDynix; (Serials) SirsiDynix
Wireless access
Function: 24/7 Electronic res, 24/7 Online cat, 24/7 wireless access, 3D Printer, Adult bk club, Adult literacy prog, Art exhibits, Audiobks on Playaways & MP3, Audiobks via web, Bilingual assistance for Spanish patrons, Bk club(s), Bks on CD, Children's prog, Computer training, Computers for patron use, Electronic databases & coll, Free DVD rentals, Holiday prog, Homebound delivery serv, ILL available, Laptop/tablet checkout, Movies, Notary serv, Online cat, OverDrive digital audio bks, Photocopying/Printing, Preschool reading prog, Printer for laptops & handheld devices, Prog for adults, Prog for children & young adult, Ref serv available, Res assist avail, Spanish lang bks, STEM programs, Story hour, Summer reading prog, Tax forms, Wheelchair accessible, Wifi hotspot checkout, Writing prog
Publications: Bibliographies
Open Mon-Thurs 9-9, Fri & Sat 10-6, Sun 2-6
Friends of the Library Group

C UNIVERSITY OF TEXAS AT DALLAS*, Eugene McDermott Library, 800 W Campbell Rd, 75080. (Mail add: PO Box 830643, MC33, 75083-0643), SAN 362-1995. Tel: 972-883-2955. Circulation Tel: 972-883-2953. Interlibrary Loan Service Tel: 972-883-2900. Reference Tel: 972-883-2643. Administration Tel: 972-883-2960. FAX: 972-883-2473. Web Site: www.utdallas.edu/library. *Dean of Libr,* Ellen Derey Saffley; Tel: 972-883-2916, E-mail: safley@utdallas.edu; *Assoc Libr Dir, Tech Serv,* Debbie Montgomery; Tel: 972-883-2963, E-mail: debmontg@utdallas.edu; *Assoc Libr Dir, Syst,* Jean Vik; Tel: 972-883-2623, E-mail: jvik@utdallas.edu; *Asst Dir, Pub Serv,* Travis Goode; E-mail: travis.goode@utdallas.edu; *Asst Dir, Scholarly Communications & Coll,* Davin Pate; Tel: 972-883-2908, E-mail: djp130330@utdallas.edu; *Interim Head, Acq,* Natasha Zinsou; Tel: 972-883-2630; *Head, Info Literacy,* Loreen Henry; Tel: 972-883-2126, E-mail: loreen@utdallas.edu; *Head, Metadata Serv,* Mingyu Chen; Tel: 972-883-3534, E-mail: mxc134930@utdallas.edu; *Head, Res Serv,* Chris Edwards; Tel: 972-883-2614, E-mail: chris.edwards@utdallas.edu; *Access Serv Mgr,* Carina Corsiga; Tel: 972-883-2958, E-mail: carina.corsiga@utdallas.edu; *Interlibrary Loan Services Mgr,* Una Scott; E-mail: una.scott@utdallas.edu; *Web Serv Mgr,* Carion Jackson; Tel: 972-883-2923, E-mail: carion.jackson@utdallas.edu. Subject Specialists: *Mgt,* Loreen Henry; *Behav sci,* Chris Edwards; Staff 60 (MLS 26, Non-MLS 34)
Founded 1969. Enrl 26,375; Fac 1,334; Highest Degree: Doctorate
Sept 2021-Aug 2022 Income (Main & Associated Libraries) $10,900,000, State $1,700,000, Parent Institution $9,200,000. Mats Exp $3,437,517, Books $531,907, Per/Ser (Incl. Access Fees) $2,905,610. Sal $4,160,537
Library Holdings: Audiobooks 40; AV Mats 10,364; CDs 2,425; DVDs 10,070; e-books 1,193,031; e-journals 131,335; Electronic Media & Resources 19,786; Music Scores 391; Bk Vols 1,749,550; Per Subs 210
Special Collections: CAT/Air America Archives; Chance Vought Archives; Eugene & Margaret McDermott Coll; General James H Doolittle Military Aviation Library; History of Aviation Coll; History of the Book; Louise B Belsterling Botanical Library; University Archives; Wildenstein Plattner Library Coll; Wineburgh Philatelic Research Library. US Document Depository
Automation Activity & Vendor Info: (Acquisitions) Ex Libris Group; (Cataloging) Ex Libris Group; (Circulation) Ex Libris Group; (Course Reserve) Ex Libris Group; (Discovery) Ex Libris Group; (ILL) OCLC Tipasa; (OPAC) Ex Libris Group; (Serials) Ex Libris Group
Wireless access
Partic in Amigos Library Services, Inc
Restriction: Borrowing requests are handled by ILL
Friends of the Library Group

Departmental Libraries:

CALLIER LIBRARY, 1966 Inwood Rd, Dallas, 75235, SAN 362-2029. Tel: 972-883-3165. E-mail: callierlibrary@utdallas.edu. Web Site: library.utdallas.edu/callier-library. *Sr Librn,* Chris Edwards; E-mail: chris.edwards@utdallas.edu; *Libr Asst IV,* Jocelyn Chebbour; E-mail: jxz151230@utdallas.edu. Subject Specialists: *Communication disorders,* Chris Edwards; Staff 2 (MLS 1, Non-MLS 1)
Highest Degree: Doctorate
Library Holdings: Bk Vols 4,800
Subject Interests: Audiology, Deaf educ, Speech-lang pathology
Function: 24/7 Online cat, Computers for patron use, Doc delivery serv, E-Reserves, Electronic databases & coll, ILL available, Internet access, Online cat, Online Chat, Orientations, Outside serv via phone, mail, e-mail & web, Res libr, Spoken cassettes & CDs, Spoken cassettes & DVDs
Restriction: Access at librarian's discretion, Authorized patrons, Authorized personnel only, Borrowing privileges limited to fac & registered students, Borrowing requests are handled by ILL, External users must contact libr, Limited access for the pub, Not open to pub, Open to fac, students & qualified researchers, Open to students, fac & staff
Friends of the Library Group

RICHLAND HILLS

P RICHLAND HILLS PUBLIC LIBRARY*, 6724 Rena Dr, 76118-6297. SAN 316-3482. Tel: 817-616-3760. FAX: 817-616-3763. Web Site: richlandhills.com/201/library. *Dir,* Chantele Hancock; E-mail: chantele@richlandhills.com; Staff 7 (MLS 2, Non-MLS 5)
Founded 1960. Pop 8,132; Circ 42,290
Library Holdings: Audiobooks 767; Bks on Deafness & Sign Lang 20; CDs 607; DVDs 873; Electronic Media & Resources 52; Large Print Bks 760; Bk Titles 31,746; Bk Vols 32,963; Per Subs 98; Videos 1,020
Special Collections: Large Print Coll
Subject Interests: Local hist
Automation Activity & Vendor Info: (Cataloging) Koha; (Circulation) Koha; (OPAC) Koha
Wireless access
Function: 24/7 Electronic res, 24/7 Online cat, Adult bk club, Audiobks via web, Bks on CD, Children's prog, Computers for patron use, Electronic databases & coll, Free DVD rentals, Games & aids for people with disabilities, Health sci info serv, Holiday prog, Home delivery & serv to seniorr ctr & nursing homes, Homebound delivery serv, ILL available, Internet access, Life-long learning prog for all ages, Magazines, Movies, Music CDs, Online cat, Outreach serv, OverDrive digital audio bks, Photocopying/Printing, Preschool outreach, Preschool reading prog, Prog for adults, Prog for children & young adult, Ref serv available, Senior outreach, Spanish lang bks, STEM programs, Story hour, Summer reading prog, Tax forms, Teen prog, Telephone ref, Wheelchair accessible
Partic in MetroShare Libraries; Partners Library Action Network
Special Services for the Deaf - Closed caption videos

Special Services for the Blind - Bks on CD; Large print bks
Open Tues-Fri 9-8

RICHMOND

P FORT BEND COUNTY LIBRARIES*, George Memorial Library, 1001 Golfview Dr, 77469-5199. SAN 362-2088. Tel: 281-342-4455. Circulation Tel: 281-341-2606. Interlibrary Loan Service Tel: 281-341-2605. FAX: 832-471-2450. E-mail: GMPublic@fortbend.lib.tx.us. Web Site: www.fortbend.lib.tx.us. *Libr Dir,* Clara Russell; Tel: 281-633-4770, E-mail: crussell@fortbend.lib.tx.us; *Asst Dir,* Joanne Downing; Tel: 281-633-4760, E-mail: jdowning@fortbend.lib.tx.us; *Bus Mgr,* Janie Garza; Tel: 281-633-4778, E-mail: SanJuanita.Garza@fortbend.lib.tx.us; *Circ Mgr,* Mary Beth Winograd; Tel: 281-633-4748, E-mail: mwinograd@fortbend.lib.tx.us; *Tech Coordr,* Jill Sumpter; Tel: 281-633-4760, E-mail: jsumpter@fortbend.lib.tx.us; *Coordr, Youth Serv,* Susan King; Tel: 281-633-4762, E-mail: sking@fortbend.lib.tx.us; *Coll Develop, Ad,* Monique Franklin; Tel: 281-633-4764, E-mail: mfranklin@fortbend.lib.tx.us; Staff 87 (MLS 19, Non-MLS 68)
Founded 1947. Pop 548,000; Circ 569,333
Library Holdings: Audiobooks 11,367; AV Mats 23,263; Braille Volumes 165; CDs 9,379; DVDs 7,332; e-books 22,697; Large Print Bks 5,652; Microforms 23; Bk Titles 125,799; Bk Vols 175,523; Per Subs 323; Videos 5,382
Special Collections: Civil War Coll; Genealogy & Local History Coll; Regional Historical Resource Depository of Texas; Restoration (George Carriage Coll); Texana
Automation Activity & Vendor Info: (Acquisitions) SirsiDynix; (Cataloging) SirsiDynix; (Circulation) SirsiDynix; (ILL) SirsiDynix; (OPAC) SirsiDynix; (Serials) SirsiDynix
Wireless access
Publications: Annual Report; Calendar of Library Events (Monthly); Public Newsletter (Quarterly); Staff Newsletter
Partic in Amigos Library Services, Inc
Open Mon-Thurs 9-6, Fri & Sat 9-5
Friends of the Library Group
Branches: 11
CINCO RANCH, 2620 Commercial Center Blvd, Katy, 77494. Tel: 281-395-1311. FAX: 832-471-2453. E-mail: crpublic@fortbend.lib.tx.us. *Br Mgr,* Myra Ponville; E-mail: myra.ponville@fortbend.lib.tx.us; Staff 23 (MLS 5, Non-MLS 18)
Founded 1999. Circ 773,664
Library Holdings: Audiobooks 3,929; AV Mats 12,920; CDs 5,073; DVDs 4,967; Large Print Bks 855; Bk Titles 73,072; Bk Vols 120,000; Per Subs 186; Videos 1,213
Open Mon-Thurs 9-6, Fri & Sat 9-5
Friends of the Library Group
FIRST COLONY, 2121 Austin Pkwy, Sugar Land, 77479-1219, SAN 374-4345. Tel: 281-238-2800. FAX: 882-471-2454. E-mail: fcpublic@fortbend.lib.tx.us. *Br Mgr,* Elizabeth Bullard; E-mail: ebullard@fortbend.lib.tx.us; Staff 26 (MLS 5, Non-MLS 21)
Circ 760,286
Library Holdings: Audiobooks 3,575; AV Mats 11,734; CDs 4,878; DVDs 4,755; Large Print Bks 765; Bk Titles 69,728; Bk Vols 99,312; Per Subs 153; Videos 676
Special Services for the Deaf - TDD equip
Open Mon-Thurs 9-6, Fri & Sat 9-5
Friends of the Library Group
FORT BEND COUNTY LAW LIBRARY, Inside the Justice Center, Rm 20714, 1422 Eugene Heimann Circle, 77469, SAN 370-9205. Tel: 281-341-3718. FAX: 832-471-2455. E-mail: llpublic@fortbend.lib.tx.us. *Br Mgr,* Andrew Bennett; E-mail: abennett@fortbend.lib.tx.us; Staff 1 (MLS 1)
Founded 1989
Library Holdings: Bk Titles 713; Bk Vols 765; Per Subs 16
Open Mon-Fri 8-5
ALBERT GEORGE BRANCH, 9230 Gene St, Needville, 77461-8313, SAN 362-2118. Tel: 281-238-2850. FAX: 832-471-2451. E-mail: agpublic@fortbend.lib.tx.us. *Br Mgr,* Stephanie Murphree; E-mail: stephanie.murphree@fortbend.lib.tx.us; Staff 4 (MLS 1, Non-MLS 3)
Founded 1974. Circ 56,849
Library Holdings: Audiobooks 779; AV Mats 3,888; CDs 1,462; DVDs 1,618; Large Print Bks 206; Bk Titles 62,043; Bk Vols 83,647; Per Subs 81; Videos 371
Special Services for the Deaf - TDD equip
Open Mon-Thurs 9-6, Fri 9-5, Sat 9-1
Friends of the Library Group
MAMIE GEORGE BRANCH, 320 Dulles Ave, Stafford, 77477-4704, SAN 362-2142. Tel: 281-238-2880. FAX: 832-471-2456. E-mail: mgpublic@fortbend.lib.tx.us. *Br Mgr,* Meagan Metgares; E-mail: meagan.metgares@fortbend.lib.tx.us; Staff 4 (MLS 1, Non-MLS 3)
Founded 1974. Circ 114,838
Library Holdings: Audiobooks 1,295; AV Mats 5,143; CDs 1,742; DVDs 2,162; Large Print Bks 404; Bk Titles 27,154; Bk Vols 35,115; Per Subs 50; Videos 757
Subject Interests: Music
Open Mon-Thurs 9-6, Fri 9-5, Sat 9-1
Friends of the Library Group
BOB LUTTS FULSHEAR SIMONTON BRANCH, 8100 FM 359 S, Fulshear, 77441. (Mail add: PO Box 907, Fulshear, 77441-0907), SAN 373-2762. Tel: 281-633-4675. FAX: 832-471-2452. E-mail: fspublic@fortbend.lib.tx.us. *Br Mgr,* Susan Browning; E-mail: sbrowning@fortbend.lib.tx.us; Staff 6 (MLS 1, Non-MLS 5)
Circ 81,976
Library Holdings: Audiobooks 1,436; AV Mats 5,871; CDs 2,144; DVDs 2,431; Large Print Bks 260; Bk Titles 37,512; Bk Vols 45,400; Per Subs 104; Videos 946
Open Mon-Thurs 9-6, Fri 9-5, Sat 9-1
Restriction: Authorized patrons
Friends of the Library Group
MISSION BEND, 8421 Addicks Clodine Rd, Houston, 77083. Tel: 832-471-5900. FAX: 832-471-2457. E-mail: mbpublic@fortbend.lib.tx.us. *Br Mgr,* Janna Raven; E-mail: janna.raven@fortbend.lib.tx.us
Function: 3D Printer, Children's prog, Computers for patron use, Meeting rooms, Photocopying/Printing, Scanner, Study rm
Open Mon-Thurs 9-6, Fri & Sat 9-5
MISSOURI CITY BRANCH, 1530 Texas Pkwy, Missouri City, 77489-2170, SAN 373-2754. Tel: 281-238-2100. FAX: 832-471-2458. E-mail: mcpublic@fortbend.lib.tx.us. *Br Mgr,* Anita Patel; E-mail: anita.patel@fortbend.lib.tx.us; Staff 16 (MLS 4, Non-MLS 12)
Founded 1992. Circ 241,547
Library Holdings: Audiobooks 2,028; AV Mats 9,366; CDs 3,570; DVDs 3,933; Large Print Bks 489; Bk Titles 62,043; Bk Vols 83,647; Per Subs 171; Videos 1,004
Special Services for the Deaf - TDD equip
Open Mon-Thurs 9-6, Fri & Sat 9-5
Restriction: Access at librarian's discretion
Friends of the Library Group
SIENNA BRANCH, 8411 Sienna Springs Blvd, Missouri City, 77459. Tel: 281-238-2900. FAX: 832-471-2459. E-mail: snpublic@fortbend.lib.tx.us. *Br Mgr,* Jeff Taylor; E-mail: jtaylor@fortbend.lib.tx.us; Staff 27 (MLS 8, Non-MLS 19)
Circ 225,679
Library Holdings: Audiobooks 2,603; AV Mats 11,742; CDs 3,734; DVDs 7,277; Large Print Bks 430; Bk Titles 75,350; Bk Vols 105,602; Per Subs 1,415; Videos 11,915
Open Mon-Thurs 9-6, Fri & Sat 9-5
Friends of the Library Group
SUGAR LAND BRANCH, 550 Eldridge Rd, Sugar Land, 77478. Tel: 281-238-2140. FAX: 832-471-2460. E-mail: slpublic@fortbend.lib.tx.us. *Br Mgr,* Tasneem Lateef; E-mail: tlateef@fortbend.lib.tx.us; Staff 20 (MLS 4, Non-MLS 16)
Founded 1999. Circ 563,268
Library Holdings: Audiobooks 3,994; AV Mats 11,348; CDs 4,213; DVDs 3,712; Large Print Bks 373; Bk Titles 75,350; Bk Vols 105,602; Per Subs 154; Videos 3,305
Open Mon-Thurs 9-6, Fri & Sat 9-5
Friends of the Library Group
UNIVERSITY BRANCH, 14010 University Blvd, Sugar Land, 77479. Tel: 281-633-5100. FAX: 832-471-2461. E-mail: ubpublic@fortbend.lib.tx.us. *Br Mgr,* David Lukose; E-mail: dlukose@fortbend.lib.tx.us
Function: Children's prog, Computers for patron use, Meeting rooms, Photocopying/Printing, Ref serv available, Study rm
Open Mon-Thurs 9-6, Fri & Sat 9-5
Friends of the Library Group

RIO GRANDE CITY

P RIO GRANDE CITY PUBLIC LIBRARY*, 591 E Third St, 78582-3588. SAN 372-7580. Tel: 956-487-4389. FAX: 956-487-7390. E-mail: rgclibrary@yahoo.com. Web Site: www.rgclibrary.org. *Dir,* Norma Gomez Fultz; *Asst Br Mgr,* Leticia Guerra; Staff 6 (Non-MLS 6)
Founded 1990. Pop 11,923
Library Holdings: Bk Titles 35,000; Per Subs 55
Automation Activity & Vendor Info: (Cataloging) Biblionix; (Circulation) Biblionix; (OPAC) OCLC
Wireless access
Function: 24/7 Electronic res, 3D Printer, Adult literacy prog, Bilingual assistance for Spanish patrons, Children's prog, Computers for patron use, Electronic databases & coll, Free DVD rentals, ILL available, Internet access, Mango lang, Online cat, Online ref, OverDrive digital audio bks, Photocopying/Printing, Preschool outreach, Prog for adults, Prog for children & young adult, Scanner, Serves people with intellectual disabilities, Spanish lang bks, Spoken cassettes & CDs, STEM programs, Summer & winter reading prog, Summer reading prog, Teen prog, Wheelchair accessible
Publications: Library Update
Partic in Partners Library Action Network
Open Mon-Thurs 8:30-7, Fri 8:30-5:30
Friends of the Library Group

RIO HONDO

P RIO HONDO PUBLIC LIBRARY*, 121 N Arroyo Blvd, 78583. (Mail add: PO Box 740, 78583-0740), SAN 376-4311. Tel: 956-748-3322. FAX: 956-748-3393. E-mail: library@riohondo.us. Web Site: riohondo.us/public-library. *Librn,* Carolyn Dawson; Staff 2 (Non-MLS 2)
Library Holdings: Bk Titles 12,000; Per Subs 31
Automation Activity & Vendor Info: (Cataloging) Biblionix; (Circulation) Biblionix; (OPAC) Biblionix
Wireless access
Open Mon-Fri 1-6, Sat 10-3

RIVER OAKS

P RIVER OAKS PUBLIC LIBRARY*, 4900 River Oaks Blvd, 76114. SAN 316-6961. Tel: 817-624-7344. FAX: 817-624-6214. E-mail: library@riveroakstx.com. Web Site: riveroakslibrary.org. *Libr Dir,* Jennifer Neathery; Staff 7 (Non-MLS 7)
Founded 1959. Pop 6,900; Circ 58,207
Library Holdings: AV Mats 2,100; Bks on Deafness & Sign Lang 125; Large Print Bks 700; Bk Vols 28,292; Per Subs 30; Talking Bks 500
Wireless access
Open Mon 11-5, Wed & Fri 10-5
Restriction: Residents only
Friends of the Library Group

ROANOKE

P ROANOKE PUBLIC LIBRARY*, 308 S Walnut St, 76262. SAN 373-2800. Tel: 817-491-2691. FAX: 817-491-2729. E-mail: library@roanoketexas.com. Web Site: www.roanoketexas.com/166/Library. *Libr Mgr,* Geoff Sams; *Asst City Librn,* Debra Wallace; Staff 4 (MLS 1, Non-MLS 3)
Founded 1979. Pop 8,700; Circ 57,800
Library Holdings: CDs 692; DVDs 476; Large Print Bks 1,595; Bk Titles 39,200; Per Subs 20; Videos 3,198
Special Collections: Texana. Oral History
Automation Activity & Vendor Info: (Acquisitions) Book Systems; (Cataloging) Book Systems; (Circulation) Book Systems; (OPAC) Book Systems
Wireless access
Function: Adult literacy prog, AV serv, CD-ROM, Digital talking bks, Homebound delivery serv, ILL available, Internet access, Music CDs, Prog for adults, Prog for children & young adult, Ref serv available, Serves people with intellectual disabilities, Spoken cassettes & CDs, Summer reading prog, VHS videos, Wheelchair accessible
Partic in MetroShare Libraries; Midwest Collaborative for Library Services; North Texas Library Consortium
Special Services for the Deaf - Bks on deafness & sign lang; High interest/low vocabulary bks
Open Mon-Thurs 10-9, Fri & Sat 10-6
Restriction: Non-resident fee, Residents only
Friends of the Library Group

ROBERT LEE

P COKE COUNTY LIBRARY*, 706 Austin St, 76945. (Mail add: PO Box 637, 76945-0637), SAN 316-697X. Tel: 325-453-2495. E-mail: cokelibrary@gmail.com. Web Site: coke.ploud.net. *Librn,* R J Holland
Pop 3,323; Circ 4,300
Library Holdings: AV Mats 270; Bk Vols 11,426
Wireless access
Function: 24/7 Online cat
Open Tues & Fri 8-Noon, Wed 8-4, Thurs 1-5

ROBSTOWN

P NUECES COUNTY PUBLIC LIBRARIES, Keach Family Library, 100 Terry Shamsie Blvd, 78380. SAN 362-2177. Tel: 361-387-3431. FAX: 361-387-7964. E-mail: keachlibrary@gmail.com. Web Site: www.library.nuecescountytx.gov. *Actg County Librn,* Crystal Drillen; E-mail: crystal.drillen@nuecescountytx.gov; *Commun Outreach Librn,* Veronica Anguiano; *Youth Serv Spec,* Amy Serrata; Staff 13 (MLS 2, Non-MLS 11)
Founded 1976. Pop 31,549; Circ 254,825
Oct 2018-Sept 2019 Income (Main & Associated Libraries) $803,494, Locally Generated Income $393,033, Other $48,000. Mats Exp $60,000, Books $35,000, Per/Ser (Incl. Access Fees) $2,000, Other Print Mats $1,000, AV Equip $2,000, AV Mat $12,000, Electronic Ref Mat (Incl. Access Fees) $8,000. Sal $236,320 (Prof $116,775)
Library Holdings: Audiobooks 426; AV Mats 119; Bks-By-Mail 136; Bks on Deafness & Sign Lang 14; CDs 169; DVDs 1,699; e-journals 7; Large Print Bks 99; Microforms 83; Bk Titles 32,046; Per Subs 49; Spec Interest Per Sub 1; Videos 230
Special Collections: Robstown Record Newspaper Coll, microfilm
Automation Activity & Vendor Info: (Acquisitions) TLC (The Library Corporation); (Cataloging) TLC (The Library Corporation); (Circulation) TLC (The Library Corporation); (ILL) TLC (The Library Corporation); (Media Booking) TLC (The Library Corporation); (OPAC) TLC (The Library Corporation)
Wireless access
Function: 24/7 Electronic res, 24/7 Online cat, 3D Printer, Accelerated reader prog, Activity rm, Adult bk club, Adult literacy prog, After school storytime, Art exhibits, Art programs, Bilingual assistance for Spanish patrons, Bk club(s), Bks on CD, Children's prog, Citizenship assistance, Computer training, Computers for patron use, E-Reserves, Electronic databases & coll, Family literacy, For res purposes, Free DVD rentals, Govt ref serv, Health sci info serv, Holiday prog, ILL available, Instruction & testing, Internet access, Learning ctr, Life-long learning prog for all ages, Magazines, Makerspace, Meeting rooms, Microfiche/film & reading machines, Movies, Online cat, Online info literacy tutorials on the web & in blackboard, Online ref, Orientations, Outreach serv, OverDrive digital audio bks, Photocopying/Printing, Preschool outreach, Prof lending libr, Prog for adults, Prog for children & young adult, Ref & res, Ref serv available, Res assist avail, Res libr, Scanner, Senior computer classes, Senior outreach, Spanish lang bks, STEM programs, Story hour, Study rm, Summer & winter reading prog, Summer reading prog, Tax forms, Teen prog, Telephone ref, Visual arts prog, Wheelchair accessible, Winter reading prog, Workshops
Partic in Partners Library Action Network
Special Services for the Deaf - Bks on deafness & sign lang
Special Services for the Blind - Bks on cassette; Bks on CD
Open Mon-Thurs 9:30-6:30, Fri & Sat 9:30-2:30
Restriction: Access at librarian's discretion, ID required to use computers (Ltd hrs), Ref only
Branches: 1
BISHOP BRANCH, 115 S Ash Ave, Bishop, 78343, SAN 362-2207. Tel: 361-584-2222. ; Staff 1 (Non-MLS 1)
Founded 2002. Pop 3,126
Function: 24/7 Electronic res, 24/7 Online cat, 3D Printer, Accelerated reader prog, Activity rm, After school storytime, Art programs, Audiobks via web, AV serv, Bk club(s), Bks on CD, Children's prog, Computer training, Computers for patron use, Electronic databases & coll, Family literacy, Free DVD rentals, Govt ref serv, Health sci info serv, Holiday prog, Homework prog, ILL available, Internet access, Literacy & newcomer serv, Magazines, Mail & tel request accepted, Makerspace, Meeting rooms, Movies, Online cat, Online info literacy tutorials on the web & in blackboard, Online ref, Outreach serv, Outside serv via phone, mail, e-mail & web, Photocopying/Printing, Preschool outreach, Preschool reading prog, Ref & res, Ref serv available, Res assist avail, STEM programs, Story hour, Study rm, Summer & winter reading prog, Summer reading prog, Tax forms, Teen prog, Telephone ref
Open Mon & Wed 1-5, Tues & Thurs 10-2

ROCKDALE

P LUCY HILL PATTERSON MEMORIAL LIBRARY*, 201 Ackerman St, 76567. SAN 316-7003. Tel: 512-446-3410. FAX: 512-446-5597. E-mail: pattersonlib@rockdalecityhall.com. Web Site: www.rockdalecityhall.com/index.aspx?NID=115. *Librn,* Melanie Todd; Staff 4 (Non-MLS 4)
Founded 1953. Pop 11,906; Circ 32,368
Library Holdings: AV Mats 1,281; Bk Titles 24,824; Bk Vols 33,000; Per Subs 14; Videos 336
Special Collections: Dr George Hill Patterson Coll (First Editions)
Wireless access
Partic in Partners Library Action Network
Open Mon-Wed & Fri 8-5, Thurs 10:30-7:30, Sat 9-1
Friends of the Library Group

ROCKPORT

P ARANSAS COUNTY PUBLIC LIBRARY, 701 E Mimosa St, 78382-4150. SAN 316-7011. Tel: 361-790-0153. FAX: 361-790-0150. Web Site: www.acplibrary.org. *Dir,* Iris Sanchez; E-mail: isanchez@aransascounty.org; Staff 5 (MLS 1, Non-MLS 4)
Founded 1956. Pop 23,860; Circ 45,000
Jan 2024-Dec 2024 Income $263,265. Mats Exp $23,000. Sal $175,513 (Prof $65,265)
Library Holdings: CDs 584; DVDs 445; Large Print Bks 865; Bk Titles 40,780; Per Subs 11
Subject Interests: Local hist
Automation Activity & Vendor Info: (Cataloging) Auto-Graphics, Inc; (Circulation) Auto-Graphics, Inc
Wireless access
Function: 24/7 Online cat, Adult literacy prog, Bks on CD, Children's prog, Computers for patron use, Electronic databases & coll, Free DVD rentals, ILL available, Internet access, Large print keyboards, Magazines, Meeting rooms, Movies, Online cat, OverDrive digital audio bks,

Photocopying/Printing, Prog for children & young adult, Summer reading prog, Tax forms, Teen prog, Telephone ref, Wheelchair accessible
Special Services for the Deaf - Bks on deafness & sign lang
Special Services for the Blind - Bks on CD; Large print bks; Magnifiers
Open Mon-Fri 9-6, Sat 10-2
Friends of the Library Group

ROCKSPRINGS

P CLAUD H GILMER MEMORIAL LIBRARY*, 201 N Hwy 377, 78880. (Mail add: PO Box 157, 78880-0157). Tel: 830-683-8130. FAX: 830-683-8131. Web Site: www.gilmermemoriallibrary.com. *Dir,* Kristen Satterfield; E-mail: kristen.satterfield@rockspringsisd.net; *Librn,* Allison Schnack; E-mail: allison.schnack@rockspringsisd.net; Staff 3 (Non-MLS 3)
Pop 1,500; Circ 37,734
Library Holdings: AV Mats 350; Bk Titles 23,000; Per Subs 62; Talking Bks 55
Automation Activity & Vendor Info: (Cataloging) Follett Software; (Circulation) Follett Software
Wireless access
Function: Distance learning, ILL available, Photocopying/Printing, Prog for children & young adult, Ref serv available, Summer reading prog, Wheelchair accessible
Special Services for the Deaf - Bks on deafness & sign lang; High interest/low vocabulary bks
Open Mon, Tues, Thurs & Fri 9-2, Wed 9-4 (Summer); Mon-Fri 8-6, Sat 9-Noon (Winter)
Restriction: Open to pub for ref & circ; with some limitations, Open to students, fac & staff, Pub use on premises

ROCKWALL

P ROCKWALL COUNTY LIBRARY*, 1215 E Yellowjacket Lane, 75087. SAN 316-7038. Tel: 972-204-7700. FAX: 972-204-7709. E-mail: rocklib@rocklib.com. Web Site: www.rockwallcountytexas.com/library. *Dir,* Marcine McCulley; *Ch Serv Librn,* Doreen Miller; *Generalist Librn,* Lindsey Snelling; *Ref Librn,* Chantal Walvoord; Staff 7 (MLS 6, Non-MLS 1)
Founded 1945. Pop 78,000; Circ 367,316
Library Holdings: Audiobooks 3,720; CDs 1,876; DVDs 3,580; Large Print Bks 1,781; Bk Titles 60,510; Bk Vols 75,000; Per Subs 100
Subject Interests: Genealogy, Texana
Automation Activity & Vendor Info: (Acquisitions) Innovative Interfaces, Inc; (Cataloging) Innovative Interfaces, Inc; (Circulation) Innovative Interfaces, Inc; (OPAC) Innovative Interfaces, Inc
Wireless access
Function: Audiobks via web, Bks on CD, Citizenship assistance, Computer training, Computers for patron use, Electronic databases & coll, ILL available, Literacy & newcomer serv, Magnifiers for reading, Prog for children & young adult, Summer reading prog, Wheelchair accessible
Partic in Partners Library Action Network
Open Mon & Wed 10-6, Tues & Thurs 10-8, Fri 10-5, Sat 10-4
Friends of the Library Group

ROMA

P STARR COUNTY PUBLIC LIBRARY*, Roma Branch, 1705 N Athens St, 78584. SAN 376-1053. Tel: 956-849-0072. E-mail: romapubliclibrary@yahoo.com. *Librn,* Eliamar Cantu
Library Holdings: Bk Vols 9,500
Wireless access
Open Mon-Fri 8-5

ROSEBUD

P D BROWN MEMORIAL LIBRARY*, 203 N Second St, 76570. (Mail add: PO Box 479, 76570-0479), SAN 316-7046. Tel: 254-583-2328. FAX: 254-583-2328. E-mail: citylibrarian@rosebudtexas.us. Web Site: www.dbrownlibrary.org. *Dir,* Kelly Hughes; Staff 1 (Non-MLS 1)
Pop 1,600
Library Holdings: Bk Vols 12,000
Automation Activity & Vendor Info: (Acquisitions) Book Systems; (Cataloging) Book Systems; (Circulation) Book Systems; (Course Reserve) Book Systems; (Discovery) Book Systems; (ILL) OCLC CatExpress; (OPAC) Book Systems
Wireless access
Open Mon-Thurs 10-5

ROTAN

P ROTAN PUBLIC LIBRARY*, 404 E Sammy Baugh Ave, 79546-3820. SAN 320-5169. Tel: 325-735-3362. FAX: 325-735-2229. E-mail: rotan.library@gmail.com. Web Site: rotan.ploud.net. *Dir,* Helen Elkins; Staff 1 (Non-MLS 1)
Founded 1978. Pop 4,719; Circ 8,333
Library Holdings: Bk Titles 10,679; Bk Vols 11,599; Per Subs 4
Special Collections: Genealogy Coll; Local History Coll; Texas Heritage Resource Center (Southwest Coll)
Automation Activity & Vendor Info: (Cataloging) LibLime; (Circulation) LibLime
Wireless access
Function: Homebound delivery serv
Open Tues & Wed 9-5, Thurs 9-1

ROUND ROCK

P ROUND ROCK PUBLIC LIBRARY*, 200 E Liberty Ave, 78664. SAN 316-7054. Tel: 512-218-7000, 512-218-7001. FAX: 512-218-7061. E-mail: rrpls@roundrocktexas.gov. Web Site: roundrocktexas.gov/city-departments/library-home. *Libr Dir,* Michelle Cervantes; Tel: 512-218-7010, E-mail: mcervantes@roundrocktexas.gov; *Asst Dir,* Geeta Halley; Tel: 512-218-7018, E-mail: ghalley@roundrocktexas.gov; *Libr Mgr,* Rhonda Kuiper; E-mail: rkuiper@roundrocktexas.gov; *Youth Serv Mgr,* Theresa Faris; E-mail: tfaris@roundrocktexas.gov; Staff 40 (MLS 16, Non-MLS 24)
Founded 1963
Wireless access
Function: 24/7 Electronic res, 24/7 Online cat, Activity rm, Adult bk club, Adult literacy prog, After school storytime, Archival coll, Art exhibits, Audiobks on Playaways & MP3, Audiobks via web, AV serv, Bilingual assistance for Spanish patrons, Bk club(s), Bks on CD, Children's prog, Computer training, Computers for patron use, Doc delivery serv, Electronic databases & coll, Family literacy, Free DVD rentals, Genealogy discussion group, Govt ref serv, Holiday prog, ILL available, Internet access, Life-long learning prog for all ages, Literacy & newcomer serv, Magazines, Magnifiers for reading, Mail & tel request accepted, Mango lang, Meeting rooms, Microfiche/film & reading machines, Movies, Music CDs, Online cat, Outreach serv, Outside serv via phone, mail, e-mail & web, OverDrive digital audio bks, Photocopying/Printing, Preschool outreach, Prog for adults, Prog for children & young adult, Ref & res, Ref serv available, Scanner, Senior outreach, Serves people with intellectual disabilities, Spanish lang bks, Story hour, Study rm, Summer reading prog, Tax forms, Teen prog, Telephone ref, Wheelchair accessible, Workshops, Writing prog
Partic in Partners Library Action Network
Open Mon-Thurs 9-9, Fri & Sat 9-6, Sun 1-6
Friends of the Library Group

ROUND TOP

P ROUND TOP LIBRARY ASSOCIATION INC*, Round Top Family Library, 206 W Mill St, 78954. (Mail add: PO Box 245, 78954-0245). Tel: 979-249-2700. FAX: 979-249-2563. E-mail: info@ilovetoread.org. Web Site: ilovetoread.org. *Libr Dir,* Barbara Smith; E-mail: barbara@ilovetoread.org
Founded 2000. Pop 1,177
Library Holdings: Audiobooks 3,000; CDs 250; DVDs 1,500; e-books 2,000; Electronic Media & Resources 20; Large Print Bks 100; Bk Titles 15,000; Per Subs 12; Videos 800
Automation Activity & Vendor Info: (Cataloging) Follett Software; (Circulation) Follett Software; (Course Reserve) Follett Software; (ILL) Follett Software; (OPAC) Follett Software
Wireless access
Partic in Partners Library Action Network
Open Mon-Sat 1:30-5:30
Friends of the Library Group

S UNIVERSITY OF TEXAS AT AUSTIN, BRISCOE CENTER*, Winedale, 3738 FM 2714, 78954-4901. (Mail add: PO Box 11, 78954-0011), SAN 327-8530. Tel: 979-278-3530. FAX: 979-278-3531. Web Site: briscoecenter.org/winedale. *Dir,* Dr Don Carleton; E-mail: d.carleton@austin.utexas.edu
Founded 1969
Subject Interests: Antiques, Hist
Open Mon-Fri 10-5
Restriction: Non-circulating to the pub

ROWLETT

P ROWLETT PUBLIC LIBRARY*, 3900 Main St, Ste 200, 75088-5075. SAN 361-4190. Tel: 972-412-6161. FAX: 972-412-6153. Web Site: www.ci.rowlett.tx.us/93/library. *Interim Libr Dir,* Laura Tschoerner; E-mail: ltschoerner@rowlett.com; Staff 8 (MLS 2.5, Non-MLS 5.5)
Pop 54,869
Library Holdings: Bk Titles 102,651
Automation Activity & Vendor Info: (Cataloging) SirsiDynix; (Circulation) SirsiDynix; (OPAC) SirsiDynix
Wireless access
Open Mon-Thurs 9:30-8:30, Fri & Sat 9:30-5:30
Friends of the Library Group

RUNGE

P RUNGE PUBLIC LIBRARY*, 311 N Helena St, 78151. (Mail add: PO Box 37, 78151-0037), SAN 316-7062. Tel: 830-239-4192. FAX: 830-239-4629. E-mail: rungepubliclibrary@yahoo.com. *Dir,* Alesha J Cruz; Staff 1 (Non-MLS 1)
Founded 1966. Pop 1,955
Library Holdings: Bk Titles 14,448; Per Subs 54
Subject Interests: Texana
Automation Activity & Vendor Info: (Cataloging) Biblionix; (Circulation) Biblionix
Wireless access
Mem of Karnes County Library System
Open Mon, Wed & Fri 9:30-5:30, Tues & Thurs 1-5

RUSK

P SINGLETARY MEMORIAL LIBRARY*, 207 E Sixth St, 75785. SAN 316-7089. Tel: 903-683-5916. E-mail: librarian@rusktx.org. Web Site: rusktx.org/pages/singletary-library. *Libr Dir,* Amy Derrington
Founded 1902. Pop 4,633; Circ 17,000
Library Holdings: Bk Vols 20,000; Per Subs 20
Special Collections: Cherokee County Genealogy; Texana
Automation Activity & Vendor Info: (Cataloging) Book Systems; (Circulation) Book Systems
Wireless access
Partic in Partners Library Action Network
Open Mon-Fri 10-5:30
Friends of the Library Group

SABINAL

P SABINAL PUBLIC LIBRARY*, 312 N Center St, 78881. (Mail add: PO Box 245, 78881-0245), SAN 378-3928. Tel: 830-988-2911. FAX: 830-988-2633. E-mail: sabinal.library@gmail.com. Web Site: sabinal.ploud.net. *Dir,* Caroline Habermacher
Founded 1978. Pop 2,076
Library Holdings: Bk Vols 12,000
Automation Activity & Vendor Info: (Cataloging) TLC (The Library Corporation); (Circulation) TLC (The Library Corporation)
Wireless access
Open Mon-Fri 1-5
Friends of the Library Group

SACHSE

P SACHSE PUBLIC LIBRARY*, 3815 Sachse Rd, Ste C, 75048. SAN 361-4220. Tel: 972-530-8966. FAX: 972-495-7682. Web Site: www.cityofsachse.com/130/library. *Mgr, Libr Serv,* Randall Cross; E-mail: rcross@cityofsachse.com; Staff 5.5 (MLS 2, Non-MLS 3.5)
Library Holdings: DVDs 4,156; e-books 5,295; Bk Vols 32,800; Per Subs 15
Automation Activity & Vendor Info: (Cataloging) Brodart; (Circulation) OCLC
Wireless access
Function: 24/7 Electronic res, 24/7 Online cat, Bks on CD, Children's prog, Computers for patron use, Free DVD rentals, Holiday prog, ILL available, Internet access, Online cat, Prog for children & young adult, Summer reading prog, Tax forms, Teen prog
Open Mon, Wed & Fri 10-6, Tues & Thurs 11-8, Sat 10-4
Friends of the Library Group

SAGINAW

P SAGINAW PUBLIC LIBRARY*, The John Ed Keeter Public Library of Saginaw, 355 W McLeroy Blvd, 76179. SAN 316-7097. Tel: 817-232-0300. FAX: 817-232-8662. Web Site: www.ci.saginaw.tx.us/103/library. *Dir,* Ellen Ritchie; E-mail: eritchie@ci.saginaw.tx.us
Founded 1964. Pop 15,857; Circ 126,338
Library Holdings: Bk Vols 53,000; Per Subs 85
Special Collections: Large Print Coll; Local History Coll; Western Coll
Automation Activity & Vendor Info: (Cataloging) Evergreen; (Circulation) Evergreen; (OPAC) Evergreen
Wireless access
Partic in MetroShare Libraries; Partners Library Action Network
Open Tues & Thurs 9-8, Wed, Fri & Sat 9-6
Friends of the Library Group

SALADO

P SALADO PUBLIC LIBRARY, 1151 N Main St, 76571. (Mail add: PO Box 1178, 76571-1178), SAN 376-4761. Tel: 254-947-9191. FAX: 254-947-9146. E-mail: splstaffcal@gmail.com. Web Site: www.saladolibrary.org. *Dir,* Jeanie Lively; E-mail: jeanie.lively@saladolibrary.org; Staff 9 (MLS 4, Non-MLS 5)
Founded 1985. Pop 9,800; Circ 57,000
Automation Activity & Vendor Info: (Cataloging) Biblionix; (Circulation) Biblionix; (OPAC) Biblionix
Wireless access
Function: 24/7 Electronic res, 24/7 Online cat, 24/7 wireless access, Activity rm, Adult bk club, Archival coll, Art exhibits, Art programs, Audiobks via web, Bilingual assistance for Spanish patrons, Bk club(s), Bks on CD, Butterfly Garden, Children's prog, Computer training, Computers for patron use, Digital talking bks, E-Reserves, Electronic databases & coll, Free DVD rentals, Games, Holiday prog, Home delivery & serv to seniorr ctr & nursing homes, ILL available, Internet access, Laptop/tablet checkout, Life-long learning prog for all ages, Magazines, Mail & tel request accepted, Mango lang, Meeting rooms, Movies, Notary serv, Online cat, OverDrive digital audio bks, Photocopying/Printing, Printer for laptops & handheld devices, Prog for adults, Prog for children & young adult, Senior computer classes, Senior outreach, Spanish lang bks, STEM programs, Story hour, Summer & winter reading prog, Teen prog, Telephone ref, Wheelchair accessible, Wifi hotspot checkout
Partic in Association for Rural & Small Libraries; Partners Library Action Network
Open Mon, Wed & Fri 10-6, Thurs 10-7:30, Sat 10-5
Friends of the Library Group

SAN ANGELO

C ANGELO STATE UNIVERSITY LIBRARY*, Porter Henderson Library, 2025 S Johnson, 76904-5079. (Mail add: ASU Sta 11013, 76909-1013), SAN 316-7119. Tel: 325-942-2222. Circulation Tel: 325-486-6523. Interlibrary Loan Service Tel: 325-486-6551. Reference Tel: 325-486-6534. FAX: 325-942-2198. E-mail: library@angelo.edu. Reference E-mail: reference@angelo.edu. Web Site: www.angelo.edu/services/library. *Exec Dir,* Position Currently Open; *Asst Dir, Access Serv,* Angela L Skaggs; Tel: 325-486-6524, E-mail: angela.skaggs@angelo.edu; *Asst Dir, Res & Instrul Serv,* Mark Allan; Tel: 325-486-6535, E-mail: mark.allan@angelo.edu; *Head, Cat,* Cynthia D Belden; Tel: 325-486-6552, E-mail: cbelden@angelo.edu; *Head, Special Colls & Programs,* Shannon L Sturm; Tel: 325-486-6555, E-mail: shannon.sturm@angelo.edu; *Acq Librn,* Janice Hock; Tel: 325-486-6525, E-mail: janice.hock@angelo.edu; *Digital Repository Librn,* Joseph A Pruett; Tel: 325-486-6548, E-mail: jpruett1@angelo.edu; *Multimedia Support Librn,* Antonella Ward; Tel: 325-486-6540, E-mail: antonella.ward@angelo.edu; *Coordr, Info Literacy, Research Librn,* Kimberly Wirth; Tel: 325-486-6527, E-mail: kimberly.wirth@angelo.edu; *Sr Cat Librn,* Position Currently Open; *Rec Mgr, Sr Archivist,* Erin L Johnson; Tel: 325-486-6553, E-mail: erin.johnson@angelo.edu; Staff 11 (MLS 10, Non-MLS 1)
Founded 1928. Enrl 10,387; Fac 433; Highest Degree: Doctorate
Sept 2017-Aug 2018 Income $2,682,151. Mats Exp $1,174,948. Sal $1,052,275 (Prof $666,432)
Library Holdings: AV Mats 18,114; e-books 100,539; e-journals 54,329; Microforms 460,458; Bk Titles 409,877; Bk Vols 614,037; Per Subs 105
Special Collections: State Document Depository; US Document Depository
Subject Interests: SW hist, Tex hist, W Tex
Automation Activity & Vendor Info: (Acquisitions) Ex Libris Group; (Cataloging) Ex Libris Group; (Circulation) Ex Libris Group; (Course Reserve) Ex Libris Group; (ILL) Ex Libris Group; (OPAC) Ex Libris Group; (Serials) Ex Libris Group
Wireless access
Partic in Amigos Library Services, Inc; OCLC Online Computer Library Center, Inc
Friends of the Library Group

S FORT CONCHO NATIONAL HISTORIC LANDMARK*, Research Library & Archives, 630 S Oakes St, 76903. SAN 321-0219. Tel: 325-481-2646. E-mail: hqtrs@fortconcho.com. Web Site: fortconcho.com/home/about/research-library. *Librn,* Eunice Tibay; Tel: 325-657-4442
Founded 1969
Library Holdings: Bk Titles 6,000; Per Subs 20
Special Collections: Architectural Coll (Oscar Ruffini Papers); Boyd Cornick Papers; Fort Concho History; Fort Concho Museum Records; George Gibson Huntt Papers; M C Ragsdale Photograph Coll; Military History; San Angelo Coll; Texas Photographers Coll, prints; William G Wedemeyer Photograph Coll; William S Veck Papers. Oral History
Wireless access
Restriction: Open by appt only

P TOM GREEN COUNTY LIBRARY SYSTEM*, Stephens Central Library, 33 W Beauregard, 76903. SAN 362-2231. Tel: 325-655-7321. FAX: 325-659-4027. E-mail: infodesk.library@co.tom-green.tx.us. Web Site: www.tgclibrary.com. *Libr Dir,* Jill Donegan; E-mail: jill.donegan@co.tom-green.tx.us; *Asst Libr Dir,* Wanda Green; E-mail: wanda.green@co.tom-green.tx.us; *Ch,* Sally Meyers; E-mail: sally.meyers@co.tom-green.tx.us; Staff 32 (MLS 5, Non-MLS 27)
Founded 1923. Pop 120,000; Circ 545,084

Library Holdings: AV Mats 5,980; Large Print Bks 4,096; Bk Titles 172,769; Bk Vols 304,428; Per Subs 368; Talking Bks 3,338
Subject Interests: Local hist
Automation Activity & Vendor Info: (Acquisitions) TLC (The Library Corporation); (Cataloging) TLC (The Library Corporation); (Circulation) TLC (The Library Corporation); (ILL) OCLC Online; (OPAC) TLC (The Library Corporation)
Wireless access
Function: AV serv, Distance learning, Home delivery & serv to seniorr ctr & nursing homes, Homebound delivery serv, ILL available, Outside serv via phone, mail, e-mail & web, Photocopying/Printing, Prog for children & young adult, Ref serv available, Summer reading prog, Telephone ref, Wheelchair accessible
Partic in Partners Library Action Network
Special Services for the Deaf - TDD equip; TTY equip
Open Mon-Thurs 9-8:30, Fri 9-5:30, Sat 9-4:30
Friends of the Library Group
Branches: 2
NORTH BRANCH, 3001 N Chadbourne St, 76903, SAN 362-2290. Tel: 325-653-8412. E-mail: north@co.tom-green.tx.us. *Br Mgr,* Chelsea Preas; E-mail: chelsea.preas@co.tom-green.tx.us; Staff 1 (MLS 1)
Library Holdings: Bk Vols 18,162
Open Tues-Fri 10-6, Sat 10-5
Friends of the Library Group
WEST BRANCH, 3013 Vista del Arroyo, 76904, SAN 362-2266. Tel: 325-659-6436. E-mail: west@co.tom-green.tx.us. *Br Mgr,* Jill Ratcliffe; E-mail: jill.ratcliffe@co.tom-green.tx.us; Staff 1 (Non-MLS 1)
Library Holdings: Bk Vols 43,386
Open Tues-Fri 10-6, Sat 10-5
Friends of the Library Group
Bookmobiles: 1

J HOWARD COLLEGE - SAN ANGELO LIBRARY*, 3501 N US Hwy 67, 76905. Tel: 325-481-8300, Ext 3310. FAX: 325-481-8321. Web Site: www.howardcollege.edu/library/san-angelo-library. *Librn,* Kleo Hidalgo; E-mail: knhidalgo@howardcollege.edu; *Libr Spec,* Lisa Martin; E-mail: lmartin@howardcollege.edu; Staff 1 (MLS 1)
Enrl 944; Highest Degree: Associate
Library Holdings: Bk Titles 2,679; Per Subs 55
Automation Activity & Vendor Info: (Cataloging) LibLime; (Circulation) LibLime
Wireless access
Partic in Amigos Library Services, Inc
Open Mon-Thurs 7:30-6, Fri 8-3 (Fall & Spring); Mon-Thurs 7:30-5 (Summer)

SAN ANTONIO

R ASSUMPTION SEMINARY LIBRARY, 2600 W Woodlawn, 78228. SAN 316-7151. Tel: 210-734-5137. Web Site: assumptionseminary.org. *Library Contact,* Martin Martinez; E-mail: martin.martinez@archsa.org
Founded 1952
Library Holdings: Bk Vols 10,000; Per Subs 50
Function: Ref serv available
Restriction: Not open to pub, Open to students

M BAPTIST HEALTH SYSTEM*, Bruce A Garrett Medical Library, 8400 Datapoint Dr, 78229. SAN 327-8301. Tel: 210-297-7639. FAX: 210-297-0716. Web Site: www.bshp.edu/current-students/library. *Dir, Libr Serv,* Patricia Melia; E-mail: pxmejia@baptisthealthsystem.com; *Distance Learning Librn,* Monika Talaroc; E-mail: mxtalaro@baptisthealthsystem.com; Staff 3 (MLS 2, Non-MLS 1)
Library Holdings: Bk Titles 3,400; Per Subs 80
Subject Interests: Nursing
Wireless access
Open Mon-Thurs 8:30-5:30, Fri 8:30-3

CR BAPTIST UNIVERSITY OF THE AMERICAS*, Learning Resource Center, 7838 Barlite Blvd, 78224-1364. SAN 321-1843. Tel: 210-924-4338, Ext 230. Web Site: www.bua.edu/en/academics/lrc. *Dir, Learning Res,* Teresa Martinez; E-mail: teresa.martinez@bua.edu
Founded 1955
Library Holdings: Bk Titles 16,500; Bk Vols 25,361; Per Subs 207
Special Collections: Neal Coll
Subject Interests: Theol in Spanish
Automation Activity & Vendor Info: (OPAC) Follett Software
Wireless access
Partic in Council of Research & Academic Libraries
Open Mon, Tues & Thurs 7:30am-10pm, Wed 7:30am-9pm, Fri 7:30-5, Sat 10-3

GL BEXAR COUNTY LAW LIBRARY*, Bexar County Courthouse, 5th Flr, 100 Dolorosa, 78205. SAN 316-7178. Tel: 210-335-3189. E-mail: info@sabar.org. Web Site: www.sanantoniobar.org/law-library-bibliotech. *Head Librn,* James M Allison
Library Holdings: Bk Vols 5,000
Wireless access
Open Mon-Fri 8-4:45

M BEXAR COUNTY MEDICAL SOCIETY*, Association Library, 4334 N Loop 1604 W, Ste 200, 78249-3485. (Mail add: PO Box 781145, 78278-9998), SAN 316-7186. Tel: 210-301-4391. FAX: 210-301-2150. E-mail: bcms@bcms.org. Web Site: www.bcms.org. *Chief Operating Officer, Library Contact,* Monica Jones; E-mail: monica.jones@bcms.org
Founded 1912
Wireless access
Publications: San Antonio Medicine (Monthly); Weekly (Newsletter)
Restriction: Not open to pub

M CHRISTUS SANTA ROSA HEALTH CARE*, Harold S Toy MD Memorial Health Science Library, 333 N Santa Rosa St, Ste F5626, 78207. SAN 316-7429. Tel: 210-704-3785. FAX: 210-704-3177. *Dir, Med Health Info,* Jann Harrison; E-mail: jann.harrison@christushealth.org; *Coordr,* Pamela Voorhies; Tel: 210-704-2701, E-mail: pamela.voorhies@christushealth.org
Founded 1949
Library Holdings: Per Subs 117
Special Collections: Clinical Orthopaedics and Related Research: Volume 1 - present
Subject Interests: Orthopedics, Pediatrics
Partic in Docline
Open Mon-Fri 8:30-5

SR CONGREGATION AGUDAS ACHIM, Goldie & Joe Tills Library, 16550 Huebner Rd, 78248. SAN 316-7216. Tel: 210-479-0307. FAX: 210-479-0295. E-mail: info@agudas-achim.org. Web Site: agudas-achim.org.
Library Holdings: Bk Titles 2,529; Bk Vols 2,632
Special Collections: Judaica Coll
Automation Activity & Vendor Info: (Cataloging) Follett Software
Wireless access
Restriction: Open by appt only

S DAUGHTERS OF THE REPUBLIC OF TEXAS LIBRARY, Bexar County Archives Bldg, 126 E Nueva, 78204. SAN 316-7224. Tel: 210-335-3006. E-mail: drtlibrary@drtinfo.org. Web Site: drtinfo.org/members/members/preservation/002drt-library-collections.aspx. *Spec Coll Librn,* Rhonda Davila; E-mail: rhonda.davila@bexar.org. Subject Specialists: *San Antonio, Tex hist, Tex local hist,* Rhonda Davila; Staff 1 (MLS 1)
Founded 1945
Library Holdings: Bk Titles 32,000; Per Subs 134
Special Collections: Photograph Coll; San Antonio through 1950; Viceregal Mexico & Early Texas Manuscript Coll
Subject Interests: Tex hist: Republic period, the Alamo, US Mexican war
Wireless access
Function: Archival coll, Online cat, Photocopying/Printing, Prog for adults, Res libr
Restriction: Non-circulating coll, Open by appt only, Open to pub for ref only, Photo ID required for access

S EXPRESS NEWS CORP*, San Antonio Express-News Library, 301 Ave E, 78205. (Mail add: PO Box 2171, 78297-2171), SAN 316-7364. Tel: 210-250-3276. Web Site: www.expressnews.com, www.mysanantonio.com. *News Res Librn,* Misty Harris; E-mail: mharris@express-news.net; Staff 1 (MLS 1)
Founded 1962
Library Holdings: Bk Vols 1,000
Special Collections: Digital Photo & Clip Archives
Subject Interests: Current events, Local hist
Wireless access
Restriction: Not open to pub

S INTERCULTURAL DEVELOPMENT RESEARCH ASSOCIATION LIBRARY, 5815 Callaghan Rd, Ste 101, 78228. SAN 329-4161. Tel: 210-444-1710. FAX: 210-444-1714. E-mail: contact@idra.org. Web Site: www.idra.org. *Library Contact,* Christie Goodman; E-mail: christie.goodman@idra.org
Library Holdings: Bk Vols 500; Per Subs 4
Subject Interests: Early childhood, Educ
Automation Activity & Vendor Info: (Cataloging) Follett Software; (Circulation) Follett Software
Wireless access
Function: For res purposes
Open Mon-Fri 8-5
Restriction: Not a lending libr

S MCNAY ART MUSEUM LIBRARY*, 6000 N New Braunfels Ave, 78209. (Mail add: PO Box 6069, 78209-0069), SAN 316-7283. Tel: 210-824-5368. E-mail: library@mcnayart.org. Web Site: www.mcnayart.org/library. *Colls Mgr,* Liz Paris; Tel: 210-805-1737, E-mail: liz.paris@mcnayart.org; Staff 2 (MLS 2)
Founded 1954
Library Holdings: Bk Vols 26,000; Per Subs 41
Subject Interests: 19th Century art hist, 20th Century art hist, 21st Century art hist, Theatre arts
Automation Activity & Vendor Info: (Acquisitions) EOS International; (Cataloging) EOS International; (Circulation) EOS International; (OPAC) EOS International; (Serials) EOS International
Wireless access
Restriction: Open by appt only

J NORTHWEST VISTA COLLEGE*, Library/Learning Resource Center, Redbud Learning Ctr, 3535 N Ellison Dr, 78251. SAN 375-4170. Tel: 210-486-4500. Reference Tel: 210-486-4513. FAX: 210-486-9105. E-mail: nvc-library@alamo.edu. Web Site: www.alamo.edu/nvc/academics/library. *Dir, Libr Serv,* Norma Velez-Vendrell; E-mail: nvelez-vendrell@alamo.edu; *Ref Librn, Tech Serv Librn,* Nancy Kaida; Tel: 210-486-4571, E-mail: nkaida@alamo.edu; *Ref Librn,* Linda Reeves; Tel: 210-486-4569, E-mail: lreeves3@alamo.edu; Staff 13 (MLS 9, Non-MLS 4)
Founded 1998. Enrl 14,500; Highest Degree: Associate
Library Holdings: Audiobooks 50; AV Mats 8,500; CDs 1,500; DVDs 2,300; e-books 35,000; Electronic Media & Resources 100; Music Scores 25; Bk Vols 28,000; Per Subs 100; Videos 1,800
Automation Activity & Vendor Info: (Acquisitions) Innovative Interfaces, Inc; (Cataloging) Innovative Interfaces, Inc; (Circulation) Innovative Interfaces, Inc; (ILL) OCLC; (OPAC) Innovative Interfaces, Inc; (Serials) EBSCO Online
Wireless access
Function: Bks on CD, Electronic databases & coll, ILL available, Music CDs, Online cat, Photocopying/Printing, Ref & res, Wheelchair accessible
Partic in Amigos Library Services, Inc; Council of Research & Academic Libraries
Special Services for the Blind - Accessible computers; Assistive/Adapted tech devices, equip & products; Copier with enlargement capabilities; Internet workstation with adaptive software; Screen enlargement software for people with visual disabilities; Talking bks & player equip; ZoomText magnification & reading software
Open Mon-Thurs 7:30am-8:30pm, Fri 7:30-4, Sat 8:30-2:30
Restriction: Open to pub for ref & circ; with some limitations

L NORTON ROSE FULBRIGHT, Law Library, Frost Tower, 111 W Houston St, Ste 1800, 78205. SAN 323-6269. Tel: 210-224-5575. Web Site: www.nortonrosefulbright.com. *Dir, Knowledge Resources,* Saskia Mehlhorn; E-mail: saskia.mehlhorn@nortonfulbright.com; Staff 1 (MLS 1)
Library Holdings: Bk Vols 30,000; Per Subs 60
Restriction: Staff use only

§CR OBLATE SCHOOL OF THEOLOGY, Donald E O'Shaughnessy Library, 285 Oblate Dr, 78216. Tel: 210-341-1366, Ext 311. E-mail: library@ost.edu. Web Site: ost.edu/library. *Libr Dir,* Maria M Garcia; Tel: 210-341-1366, Ext 310, E-mail: magda@ost.edu; *General Services Mgr,* Carmen Rodriguez; *Provincial Archivist, Rare Book Curator,* Mat Martin; Tel: 210-477-0913, E-mail: mmartin@omiusa.org; *Cataloger,* Bea Tovar; *Libr Asst,* Anne Peters
Library Holdings: Per Subs 289
Special Collections: Assumption Seminary Coll; Oblate College Coll; Oblate Lower Rio Grande Coll; Texana (Kenedy Coll)
Partic in Amigos Library Services, Inc; TexSHARE - Texas State Library & Archives Commission
Open Mon, Tues & Fri 7:30-5:30, Wed & Thurs 7:30am-9pm, Sat 11-5

SR DONALD E O'SHAUGHNESSY LIBRARY*, Oblate School of Theology, 285 Oblate Dr, 78216-6693. SAN 316-7305. Tel: 210-341-1368. Administration Tel: 210-341-1366. FAX: 210-979-6520. Administration FAX: 210-341-4519. E-mail: library@ost.edu. Web Site: www.ost.edu. *Libr Dir,* Maria M Garcia; E-mail: magda@ost.edu; Staff 6 (MLS 2, Non-MLS 4)
Founded 1903. Enrl 144; Fac 18; Highest Degree: Doctorate
Library Holdings: AV Mats 215; Bk Vols 85,000; Per Subs 425
Special Collections: Faculty Dissertations; Missions Documents; Rare Books Coll
Subject Interests: Relig studies
Automation Activity & Vendor Info: (Acquisitions) OCLC Worldshare Management Services; (Cataloging) OCLC Worldshare Management Services; (Circulation) OCLC Worldshare Management Services; (Course Reserve) OCLC Worldshare Management Services; (Discovery) OCLC WorldShare Interlibrary Loan; (ILL) OCLC Worldshare Management Services; (OPAC) OCLC Worldshare Management Services; (Serials) OCLC Worldshare Management Services
Wireless access
Function: For res purposes, ILL available, Internet access, Wheelchair accessible
Publications: Offerings (College journal)
Partic in Council of Research & Academic Libraries; OCLC Online Computer Library Center, Inc; TexSHARE - Texas State Library & Archives Commission
Open Mon 7:30am-8pm, Tues-Thurs 7:30am-9:30pm, Fri 7:30-5:30, Sat 11-5
Restriction: Open to pub upon request, Open to students, fac & staff

C OUR LADY OF THE LAKE UNIVERSITY*, Sueltenfuss Library, 411 SW 24th St, 78207-4689. SAN 362-2320. Circulation Tel: 210-434-6711, Ext 2325. Administration Tel: 210-431-4183. Toll Free Tel: 800-846-4085. E-mail: library@ollusa.edu. Web Site: library.ollusa.edu. *Dir of the Univ Libr,* Maria Cabaniss; E-mail: mecabaniss@ollusa.edu. Subject Specialists: *Hist,* Maria Cabaniss; Staff 7 (MLS 6, Non-MLS 1)
Founded 1896. Enrl 4,024; Fac 181; Highest Degree: Doctorate
Special Collections: History of the Southwest (Texana)
Subject Interests: Educ, Leadership, Mexican-Am, Psychol, Soc work
Automation Activity & Vendor Info: (Acquisitions) SirsiDynix; (Cataloging) SirsiDynix; (Circulation) SirsiDynix; (Course Reserve) SirsiDynix; (ILL) SirsiDynix; (OPAC) SirsiDynix; (Serials) SirsiDynix
Wireless access
Partic in Amigos Library Services, Inc; Council of Research & Academic Libraries; OCLC Online Computer Library Center, Inc; Statewide California Electronic Library Consortium; Texas Council of Academic Libraries; TexSHARE - Texas State Library & Archives Commission

J PALO ALTO COLLEGE*, Ozuna Library, 1400 W Villaret St, 78224-2499. SAN 372-4921. Tel: 210-486-3901. Interlibrary Loan Service Tel: 210-486-3555. Reference Tel: 210-486-3557. FAX: 210-486-9184. Interlibrary Loan Service FAX: 210-486-3556. Web Site: www.alamo.edu/pac/library. *Dean, Learning Res,* Tina Mesa; *Lead Res & Instruction Librn,* Cynthia Sanchez; Tel: 210-486-3579, E-mail: csanchez@alamo.edu; *Access Serv Librn,* Tyler Dunn; Tel: 210-486-3560, E-mail: tdunn20@alamo.edu; *Electronic Res Librn,* Tosca Gonsalves; Tel: 210-486-3573, E-mail: tgonsalves@alamo.edu; Staff 7 (MLS 3, Non-MLS 4)
Founded 1985. Enrl 7,822; Highest Degree: Associate
Special Collections: US Document Depository
Automation Activity & Vendor Info: (Acquisitions) OCLC Worldshare Management Services; (Cataloging) OCLC Worldshare Management Services; (Circulation) OCLC WorldShare Interlibrary Loan; (Course Reserve) OCLC Worldshare Management Services; (ILL) OCLC Worldshare Management Services; (Media Booking) OCLC Worldshare Management Services; (OPAC) OCLC Worldshare Management Services; (Serials) OCLC Worldshare Management Services
Wireless access
Partic in Amigos Library Services, Inc; Council of Research & Academic Libraries; TexSHARE - Texas State Library & Archives Commission
Special Services for the Deaf - Bks on deafness & sign lang
Special Services for the Blind - Accessible computers; Aids for in-house use; Computer access aids; Computer with voice synthesizer for visually impaired persons; Magnifiers; Ref serv; Screen enlargement software for people with visual disabilities; Screen reader software; Text reader
Open Mon-Thurs 8am-9pm, Fri 8-5, Sun 1-9

S MINNIE STEVENS PIPER FOUNDATION*, Student Aid Center Library, 1250 NE Loop 410, Ste 810, 78209-1539. SAN 326-5943. Tel: 210-525-8494. FAX: 210-341-6627. E-mail: mspf@mspf.org. Web Site: comptroller.texas.gov/programs/education/msp. *Exec Dir,* Joyce M Ellis
Founded 1961
Library Holdings: Bk Vols 4,000
Special Collections: College/University Catalogs & Reference Books on Scholarships, Careers & Grants
Wireless access
Function: Res libr
Publications: Compendium of Texas College & Financial Aid Calendar (Online only)
Open Mon-Fri 8:30-12 & 1-4:30

SR SAINT MARK'S EPISCOPAL CHURCH, Adult Reading Room, 315 E Pecan St, 78205. SAN 328-5847. Tel: 210-226-2426. FAX: 210-226-2468. E-mail: stmarks@stmarks-sa.org. Web Site: www.stmarks-sa.org.
Library Holdings: Bk Vols 5,600
Special Collections: Jack Kent Coll
Subject Interests: Relig
Wireless access
Restriction: Mem only

SAINT MARY'S UNIVERSITY
C LOUIS J BLUME LIBRARY*, One Camino Santa Maria, 78228-8608, SAN 362-2479. Tel: 210-436-3441. Reference Tel: 210-436-3508. FAX: 210-436-3782. Web Site: lib.stmarytx.edu, www.stmarytx.edu. *Exec Dir,*

Caroline Byrd; *Asst Dir, Tech Serv,* Margaret Sylvia; *Circ Mgr,* Nettie Lucio; *Bibliog Instr, Ref (Info Servs),* Diane Duesterhoeft; *Bibliog Instr, Ref (Info Servs),* Necia Wolff; *Cat,* Jill Crane; *Govt Doc,* Kathy Amen; *Per,* Marcella Lesher; Staff 8 (MLS 8)
Founded 1852. Enrl 4,300; Fac 194; Highest Degree: Doctorate
Library Holdings: AV Mats 17,500; CDs 7,800; DVDs 2,500; e-books 72,000; e-journals 47,000; Bk Titles 252,000; Bk Vols 270,000; Per Subs 1,100
Special Collections: Hilaire Belloc Coll & G K Chesterton Coll (complete sets of 1st editions); Old Spanish Trail Highway; Peninsular Wars Coll; Political Buttons Coll; Spanish Archives of Laredo, Texas. Municipal Document Depository; State Document Depository; US Document Depository
Subject Interests: Ethic studies, Hist, Law
Automation Activity & Vendor Info: (Acquisitions) Innovative Interfaces, Inc - Millennium; (Cataloging) Innovative Interfaces, Inc - Millennium; (Circulation) Innovative Interfaces, Inc - Millennium; (Course Reserve) Innovative Interfaces, Inc - Millennium; (ILL) Innovative Interfaces, Inc - Millennium; (OPAC) Innovative Interfaces, Inc - Millennium; (Serials) Innovative Interfaces, Inc - Millennium
Partic in Amigos Library Services, Inc; Coun of Res & Acad Librs; Council of Research & Academic Libraries; Novanet
Open Mon-Thurs 7:45am-Midnight, Fri 7:45-5, Sat 9-5, Sun 1pm-Midnight (Fall & Spring); Mon-Thurs 8am-9pm, Fri 8-4, Sun 1-9 (Summer)

CL SARITA KENNEDY EAST LAW LIBRARY*, One Camino Santa Maria, 78228-8605, SAN 362-2509, Tel: 210-436-3435. FAX: 210-436-3240. Web Site: www.stmarytx.edu. *Dir,* Robert H Hu; Tel: 210-431-2056, E-mail: rhu@stmarytx.edu; *Cat,* Lee Unterborn; *Ref (Info Servs),* Mike Martinez, Jr; Tel: 210-436-3435, Ext 1374; *Ref (Info Servs),* Garry Stillman; Tel: 210-436-3435, Ext 1366; Staff 8 (MLS 8)
Founded 1927. Enrl 600; Fac 25
Library Holdings: Bk Titles 32,873; Bk Vols 338,904; Per Subs 3,474
Special Collections: Anglo American Law Coll
Automation Activity & Vendor Info: (Cataloging) SirsiDynix; (Circulation) SirsiDynix; (OPAC) SirsiDynix
Open Mon-Fri 7am-Midnight, Sat 9am-10pm, Sun 10am-Midnight (Fall & Winter); Mon-Fri 8am-10pm, Sat 9am-10pm, Sun 10-10 (Summer)
Friends of the Library Group

J ST PHILIP'S COLLEGE*, Learning Resource Center, 1801 Martin Luther King Dr, 78203-2098. SAN 316-7321. Tel: 210-486-2330. Circulation Tel: 210-486-2555. FAX: 210-486-2335. Web Site: alamo.edu/spc/library. *Dir, Libr Serv,* Andrew Rivera; E-mail: arivera322@alamo.edu; Staff 14 (MLS 8, Non-MLS 6)
Founded 1898. Enrl 8,644; Fac 498
Library Holdings: e-journals 1,050; Bk Vols 117,737
Special Collections: African-American Coll
Automation Activity & Vendor Info: (Acquisitions) Innovative Interfaces, Inc; (Cataloging) Innovative Interfaces, Inc; (Circulation) Innovative Interfaces, Inc; (Course Reserve) Innovative Interfaces, Inc; (ILL) Innovative Interfaces, Inc; (Media Booking) Innovative Interfaces, Inc; (OPAC) Innovative Interfaces, Inc; (Serials) Innovative Interfaces, Inc
Wireless access
Publications: Basic Instruction in Word Perfect 7.0; How to Use the NOTIS OPAC; PowerPoint Library Orientation; Templates for CD-ROM Programs
Partic in Amigos Library Services, Inc; Coun of Res & Acad Librs; Council of Research & Academic Libraries; Tex Coun of Commun/Jr Col Librns; TexSHARE - Texas State Library & Archives Commission
Special Services for the Blind - Assistive/Adapted tech devices, equip & products
Open Mon-Thurs 7am-8pm, Fri 7-5, Sat 9-3

S SAN ANTONIO ART LEAGUE & MUSEUM*, Museum Gallery Archives, 130 King William St, 78204. SAN 316-733X. Tel: 210-223-1140. E-mail: saalm@saalm.org. Web Site: www.saalm.org. *Pres,* Claudia Langford; *Archives, Historian,* Ilna Colemere
Founded 1912
Library Holdings: Bk Vols 350
Special Collections: Davis Coll
Subject Interests: Artist's biog, Hist, How-to
Function: Res libr
Open Tues-Sat 10-3

J SAN ANTONIO COLLEGE*, Library Department, 1819 N Main Ave, 78212. SAN 316-7348. Tel: 210-486-0554. Circulation Tel: 210-486-0570. Interlibrary Loan Service Tel: 210-486-0582. Web Site: www.alamo.edu/sac/library. *Dean, Learning Res,* Dr Alice Johnson; *Dir, Libr Serv, Dir, Technology,* Lee LeBlanc; E-mail: lleblanc7@alamo.edu; *Ref Librn,* Tom Bahlinger; E-mail: tbahlinger@alamo.edu; Staff 9.5 (MLS 8.5, Non-MLS 1)
Founded 1926. Enrl 24,313; Fac 972; Highest Degree: Associate
Library Holdings: AV Mats 8,724; Bks on Deafness & Sign Lang 533; CDs 1,726; DVDs 6,998; e-books 35,148; e-journals 25,735; Bk Vols 168,601; Per Subs 121; Talking Bks 739
Special Collections: 18th Century British Literature (Morrison Coll); McAllister Coll; Texana Coll. US Document Depository
Automation Activity & Vendor Info: (Acquisitions) Innovative Interfaces, Inc; (Cataloging) Innovative Interfaces, Inc; (Circulation) Innovative Interfaces, Inc; (Course Reserve) Innovative Interfaces, Inc; (ILL) OCLC; (OPAC) Innovative Interfaces, Inc; (Serials) EBSCO Online
Wireless access
Partic in Amigos Library Services, Inc; Council of Research & Academic Libraries
Special Services for the Blind - Computer with voice synthesizer for visually impaired persons

S SAN ANTONIO CONSERVATION SOCIETY FOUNDATION LIBRARY, 1146 S Alamo St, 78210. SAN 316-7356. Tel: 210-224-6163. FAX: 210-224-6168. Web Site: www.saconservation.org/library-resources. *Librn,* Beth Standifird; Fax: 210-354-0070, E-mail: bstandifird@saconservation.org; Staff 1 (MLS 1)
Founded 1970
Library Holdings: CDs 43; DVDs 20; Microforms 74; Bk Vols 2,347; Per Subs 1; Spec Interest Per Sub 4
Special Collections: Charles Heuermann Papers; Dorothy Matthies Postcards; Ernst Raba Photographs; Restricted Photographs; Robert H H Hugman River Walk Architectural Drawings; Rosemary Son Photographs; San Antonio City Directories; Sanborn Fire Insurance Maps. Oral History
Subject Interests: Archit hist, Hist presv, San Antonio, Tex hist
Wireless access
Function: 24/7 Online cat, Internet access, Microfiche/film & reading machines, Outside serv via phone, mail, e-mail & web, Photocopying/Printing, Res libr, Telephone ref
Open Mon-Thurs 9:30-12 & 1-3:30
Restriction: Circ to mem only, Non-circulating to the pub, Pub use on premises

P SAN ANTONIO PUBLIC LIBRARY*, 600 Soledad, 78205-2786. SAN 362-2533. Tel: 210-207-2500. Administration Tel: 210-207-2644. FAX: 210-207-2603. E-mail: librarywebadmin@sanantonio.gov. Web Site: www.mysapl.org. *Dir,* Ramiro S Salazar; E-mail: ramiro.salazar@sanantonio.gov; *Asst Dir, Pub Serv,* Dale McNeill; Tel: 210-207-2502, E-mail: dale.mcneill@sanantonio.gov; *Asst Dir, Support Serv,* Kathy Donellan; Tel: 210-207-2572, E-mail: kathy.donellan@sanantonio.gov; *Adminr, Pub Serv,* Haley Holmes; Tel: 210-207-2829; *Adminr, Pub Serv,* Cheryl Sheehan; Tel: 210-207-2587, E-mail: cheryl.sheehan@sanantonio.gov; *Pub Relations Mgr,* Caitlin Cowart; Tel: 210-207-2638; *Coordr, Teen Serv,* Jennifer Velasquez; Tel: 210-207-2567, E-mail: jennifer.velasquez@sanantonio.gov; Staff 130 (MLS 124, Non-MLS 6)
Founded 1903. Pop 1,578,000; Circ 6,601,175
Library Holdings: Bk Titles 552,610; Bk Vols 1,687,881; Per Subs 1,000
Special Collections: Latino Special Coll; Texana Coll. State Document Depository; US Document Depository
Automation Activity & Vendor Info: (Acquisitions) Innovative Interfaces, Inc; (Cataloging) OCLC Online; (Circulation) Innovative Interfaces, Inc; (ILL) OCLC Online; (OPAC) Innovative Interfaces, Inc
Wireless access
Publications: Young Pegasus (children's original poetry book)
Special Services for the Deaf - Bks on deafness & sign lang; Captioned film dep; High interest/low vocabulary bks; TTY equip
Open Mon-Thurs 9-9, Fri & Sat 9-5, Sun 11-5
Friends of the Library Group
Branches: 31
BAZAN, 2200 W Commerce St, 78207, SAN 362-2800. Tel: 210-207-9160. Web Site: www.mysapl.org/Visit/Locations/Bazan-Library. *Libr Mgr,* Jimmy Jimenez; Staff 5 (MLS 3, Non-MLS 2)
Founded 1977. Pop 60,000; Circ 74,000
Function: After school storytime, Audiobks via web, Bilingual assistance for Spanish patrons, Bks on cassette, Bks on CD, Children's prog, Citizenship assistance, Computer training, Computers for patron use, Digital talking bks, Electronic databases & coll, Photocopying/Printing
Open Mon & Wed 12-8, Tues & Thurs-Sun 10-6
Restriction: ID required to use computers (Ltd hrs), In-house use for visitors, Non-resident fee, Open to pub for ref & circ; with some limitations
Friends of the Library Group
BROOK HOLLOW, 530 Heimer Rd, 78232, SAN 362-2584. Tel: 210-207-9030. *Libr Mgr,* Heidi Novotny
Open Mon & Wed 12-8, Tues & Thurs-Sun 10-6
CARVER, 3350 E Commerce St, 78220, SAN 362-2835. Tel: 210-207-9180. *Libr Mgr,* D L Grant
Open Mon, Wed & Fri-Sun 10-6, Tues & Thurs 12-8

CHILDREN'S DEPARTMENT, 600 Soledad, 78205-2786. *Interim Coordr,* Crescencia Huff
Open Mon-Thurs 9-9, Fri & Sat 9-5, Sun 11-5
CODY, 11441 Vance Jackson, 78230, SAN 362-2630. Tel: 210-207-9100. *Mgr,* Samantha Gordano
Open Mon, Wed & Fri-Sun 10-6, Tues & Thurs 12-8
COLLINS GARDEN, 200 N Park Blvd, 78204, SAN 322-5542. Tel: 210-207-9120. *Libr Mgr,* Jeannette Davis
Open Mon, Wed & Fri-Sun 10-6, Tues & Thurs 12-8
CORTEZ, 2803 Hunter Blvd, 78224, SAN 362-2843. Tel: 210-207-9130. *Libr Mgr,* Cammie Brantley
Open Mon, Wed & Fri-Sun 10-6, Tues & Thurs 12-8
ENCINO, 2515 E Evans Rd, 78259. Tel: 210-207-9250. *Mgr,* Michelle Ricondo
Open Tues & Thurs-Sun 10-6, Mon & Wed 12-8
FOREST HILLS, 5245 Ingram Rd, 78228, SAN 329-6520. Tel: 210-207-9230. *Libr Mgr,* Mary Naylor
Open Mon & Wed 12-8, Tues & Thurs-Sun 10-6
GREAT NORTHWEST, 9050 Wellwood, 78251, SAN 374-6755. Tel: 210-207-9210. *Libr Mgr,* Catherine Prazak
Open Mon & Wed 12-8, Tues & Thurs-Sun 10-6
GUERRA, 7978 W Military Dr, 78227. Tel: 210-207-9070. *Libr Mgr,* Dexter Katzman
Open Mon, Wed & Fri-Sun 10-6, Tues & Thurs 12-8
IGO, 13330 Kyle Seale Pkwy, 78249. Tel: 210-207-9080. *Libr Mgr,* Timothy Johnson
Open Mon & Wed 12-8, Tues & Thurs-Sun 10-6
JOHNSTON, 6307 Sun Valley, 78237, SAN 362-2851. Tel: 210-207-9240. *Libr Mgr,* Monica Bustillo
Open Mon & Wed 12-8, Tues & Thurs-Sat 10-6
LANDA, 233 Bushnell Ave, 78212, SAN 362-286X. Tel: 210-207-9090. *Libr Mgr,* Kiyana Stephens
Open Mon & Wed 12-8, Tues & Thurs-Sun 10-6
LAS PALMAS, 515 Castroville Rd, 78237, SAN 362-2894. Tel: 210-207-9200. *Libr Mgr,* Jose Ruiz Alvarez
Open Mon & Wed 12-8, Tues & Thurs-Sun 10-6
MAVERICK, 8700 Mystic Park, 78254. Tel: 210-207-9060. *Mgr,* Jef Martin
Open Mon, Wed & Fri-Sun 10-6, Tues & Thurs 12-8
MCCRELESS, 1023 Ada St, 78223, SAN 362-2924. Tel: 210-207-9170. FAX: 210-207-9175. *Interim Mgr,* Troy Lawrence; Staff 3 (MLS 3)
Founded 1966. Circ 18,000
Open Mon & Wed 12-8, Tues & Thurs-Sun 10-6
MEMORIAL, 3222 Culebra Rd, 78228, SAN 362-2932. Tel: 210-207-9140. *Libr Mgr,* Maria Gonzalez
Open Mon, Wed & Fri-Sun 10-6, Tues & Thurs 12-8
MISSION, 3134 Roosevelt Ave, 78214. Tel: 210-207-2704. FAX: 210-207-2704. *Libr Mgr,* Oscar Gonzalez
Open Mon, Wed & Fri-Sun 10-6, Tues & Thurs 12-8
PAN AMERICAN, 1122 W Pyron Ave, 78221, SAN 362-2983. Tel: 210-207-9150. *Libr Mgr,* Steven Barrera
Open Mon & Wed 12-8, Tues & Thurs-Sun 10-6
PARMAN, 20735 Wilderness Oak, 78258. Tel: 210-207-2703. FAX: 210-207-2703. *Libr Mgr,* Barbara Kwiatkowski
Open Mon, Wed & Fri-Sun 10-6, Tues & Thurs 12-8
POTRANCO, 8765 State Hwy 151, Access Rd, 78245. Tel: 210-207-9280. *Interim Mgr,* Morgan Yoshimura
Open Mon, Wed & Fri-Sun 10-6, Tues & Thurs 12-8
MOLLY PRUITT LIBRARY, 5110 Walzem Rd, 78218. Tel: 210-650-1122. FAX: 210-650-1291. *Lead Librn,* Rachel Downen
Open Mon & Fri-Sun 10-6, Tues-Thurs Noon-8
SAN PEDRO, 1315 San Pedro Ave, 78212, SAN 362-3017. Tel: 210-207-9050. *Mgr,* Diane Backhus; Staff 7 (MLS 2, Non-MLS 5)
Open Mon, Wed & Fri-Sun 10-6, Tues & Thurs 12-8
SCHAEFER, 6322 US Hwy 87 E, 78222. Tel: 210-207-9300. *Libr Mgr,* Jorge Chavez
Open Mon & Wed 12-8, Tues & Thurs-Sun 10-6
SEMMES, 15060 Judson Rd, 78247. Tel: 210-207-9110. *Libr Mgr,* Jamie Flowers
Open Mon, Wed & Thurs-Sun 10-6, Tues & Thurs 12-8
TEEN SERVICES, 600 Soledad, 78205-2786. Tel: 210-207-2678. FAX: 210-207-2553. *Teen Serv Coordr,* Jennifer Velasquez; *Teen Serv Librn,* Matthew Loaiza; *Teen Serv Librn,* Shannan Prukop
Open Mon-Thurs 9-9, Fri & Sat 9-5, Sun 11-5
TEXANA & GENEALOGY, 600 Soledad, 78205-2786. Tel: 210-207-2559. *Mgr, Spec Coll,* Heather Ferguson; Staff 6 (MLS 5, Non-MLS 1)
Library Holdings: Bk Vols 108,535; Per Subs 586
Special Collections: Municipal Document Depository; Oral History
Subject Interests: Genealogy, Govt, Hist, Texana
Open Tues & Thurs 12-8, Wed, Fri & Sat 9-5
Friends of the Library Group
THOUSAND OAKS, 4618 Thousand Oaks, 78233, SAN 328-865X. Tel: 210-207-9190. *Librn,* Theresa Garza
Open Mon & Wed 12-8, Tues & Thurs-Sun 10-6
TOBIN, 4134 Harry Wurzbach, 78209, SAN 362-2959. Tel: 210-207-9040. *Libr Mgr,* Tracey Knouse
Open Mon, Wed & Fri-Sun 10-6, Tues & Thurs 12-8
WESTFALL, 6111 Rosedale Ct, 78201, SAN 362-3041. Tel: 210-207-9220. *Libr Mgr,* Nathaniel Laubner
Open Mon & Wed 12-8, Tues & Thurs-Sun 10-6
Bookmobiles: 2

S SAN ANTONIO SCOTTISH RITE LIBRARY, 308 Ave E, 78205-2044. (Mail add: PO Box 2239, 78298-2239). Tel: 210-222-0133. Toll Free Tel: 866-222-9293. FAX: 210-222-0136. E-mail: secretary@sanantonioscottishrite.com. Web Site: www.sanantonioscottishrite.com/library-and-museum.
Library Holdings: Bk Titles 4,000
Wireless access
Open Mon-Fri 8-4
Restriction: Not a lending libr

§C TEXAS A&M UNIVERSITY-SAN ANTONIO, University Library, One University Way, 78224. Tel: 210-784-1500. FAX: 210-784-1549. E-mail: library@tamusa.edu. Web Site: www.tamusa.edu/library. *Exec Dir of Library & Special Colls, Head, Coll Serv,* Pru Morris; Tel: 210-784-1502, E-mail: pru.morris@tamusa.edu; *Head, Archives & Spec Coll,* Leslie Stapleton; Tel: 210-784-1516, E-mail: leslie.stapleton@tamusa.edu; *Head, Pub Serv,* Sarah Timm; Tel: 210-784-1504, E-mail: sarah.timm@tamusa.edu; *Head, Res Serv,* Deirdre McDonald; Tel: 210-784-1503, E-mail: deirdre.mcdonald@tamusa.edu; *Bus Librn,* Rachel Pecotte; Tel: 210-784-1510, E-mail: rachel.pecotte@tamusa.edu; *Educ Librn,* Kimberly Grotewold; Tel: 210-784-1519, E-mail: kimberly.grotewold@tamusa.edu; *First Year Experience Librn,* Bryant Moore; Tel: 210-784-1507, E-mail: bryant.moore@tamusa.edu; *Coll Serv, Libr Assoc II,* Melissa Gamez Herrera; Tel: 210-784-1505, E-mail: melissa.gamez@tamusa.edu; *Libr Assoc I,* Cat Garza; Tel: 210-784-1508, E-mail: catarina.garza@tamusa.edu; *Coll Serv, Libr Assoc I,* Jamey Nail; Tel: 210-784-1521, E-mail: jamey.nail@tamusa.edu; *Libr Assoc I, Pub Serv,* Jessica Burnette; Tel: 210-784-1514, E-mail: jessica.burnette@tamusa.edu; *Admin Coordinator I,* Jeanine Edralin; Tel: 210-784-1525, E-mail: jeanine.edralin@tamusa.edu; *Proc Archivist,* Jeremy Zuni; Tel: 210-784-1518, E-mail: jeremy.zuni@tamusa.edu
Founded 2009. Enrl 7,309; Fac 365; Highest Degree: Master
Library Holdings: e-books 810,747
Special Collections: Humberto "Bert" V Reyes Coll, 1900-2018; J B Wieser Family Papers, 1854-2013; Robert H Thonhaff Coll; Sara R Massey Coll; Sunshine Cottage School for Deaf Children Coll, 1947-2021; Texas Navy Association Coll, 1823-1861
Wireless access
Function: Study rm
Partic in Amigos Library Services, Inc; Council of Research & Academic Libraries
Open Mon-Thurs 9-9, Fri & Sat 9-6, Sun 1-9; Mon-Fri 9-5 (Summer)

S TEXAS BIOMEDICAL RESEARCH INSTITUTE*, Preston G Northrup Memorial Library, 8715 W Military Dr, 78227-5301. (Mail add: PO Box 760549, 78245-0549). Administration Tel: 210-258-9502, 210-258-9593. E-mail: library@txbiomed.org. *Dir, Libr & Info Serv,* Jayson L Felty; E-mail: jfelty@txbiomed.org; *Librn,* Dawn Field; E-mail: dfield@txbiomed.org; Staff 2 (MLS 2)
Founded 1947
Jan 2020-Dec 2020. Mats Exp $550,000. Sal $156,000
Library Holdings: e-books 12,000; e-journals 400; Bk Titles 7,000; Per Subs 115
Subject Interests: Basic biomed sci, Primatology, Res
Automation Activity & Vendor Info: (Acquisitions) Ex Libris Group; (Cataloging) Ex Libris Group; (Circulation) Ex Libris Group; (Discovery) Ex Libris Group; (ILL) OCLC ILLiad; (OPAC) Ex Libris Group; (Serials) Ex Libris Group
Wireless access
Function: Doc delivery serv, Electronic databases & coll, For res purposes, ILL available, Online cat, Ref & res
Partic in National Network of Libraries of Medicine Region 3
Open Mon-Fri 8-5
Restriction: Lending to staff only, Limited access for the pub

C TRINITY UNIVERSITY*, Coates Library, One Trinity Pl, 78212-7200. SAN 362-3130. Tel: 210-999-8126. Circulation Tel: 210-999-8127. Interlibrary Loan Service Tel: 210-999-8473. Reference Tel: 210-999-7213. FAX: 210-999-8182. Interlibrary Loan Service FAX: 210-999-8021. Web Site: lib.trinity.edu. *Univ Librn,* Benjamin Harris; E-mail: bharris@trinity.edu; *Head, Discovery Serv, Head, Res Mgt,* Jane Costanza; Tel: 210-999-7612, E-mail: jcostanz@trinity.edu; *ILL Asst,* Alaynna Martalla; E-mail: amarttal@trinity.edu; Staff 13 (MLS 11, Non-MLS 2)
Founded 1869. Enrl 2,685; Fac 276; Highest Degree: Master
Library Holdings: e-journals 100,761; Bk Titles 625,696; Bk Vols 710,913; Per Subs 2,342

Special Collections: American Literature (Helen Miller Jones Coll); Archives of Monterrey & the State of Nuevo Leon, Mexico, micro; Greek & Roman Art & Architecture (Denman Coll); Latin America (Hilton Coll); Space Exploration (Campbell Coll & Maloney Coll); Texana (Beretta Coll & Nixon Coll); Trinity University Archives. State Document Depository; US Document Depository
Automation Activity & Vendor Info: (Acquisitions) Innovative Interfaces, Inc; (Cataloging) Innovative Interfaces, Inc - Millennium; (Circulation) Innovative Interfaces, Inc - Millennium; (Course Reserve) Docutek; (ILL) OCLC ILLiad; (OPAC) Innovative Interfaces, Inc; (Serials) Innovative Interfaces, Inc - Millennium
Wireless access
Function: Archival coll, Audio & video playback equip for onsite use, AV serv, Computers for patron use, Doc delivery serv, E-Reserves, Electronic databases & coll, Free DVD rentals, Govt ref serv, ILL available, Internet access, Music CDs, Online info literacy tutorials on the web & in blackboard, Photocopying/Printing, Ref serv available, Spoken cassettes & DVDs, Telephone ref, Wheelchair accessible, Writing prog
Partic in Amigos Library Services, Inc; Associated Colleges of the South; Council of Research & Academic Libraries; NITLE; Oberlin Group; Texas Council of Academic Libraries
Open Mon-Thurs 8am-Midnight, Fri 8-6, Sat 10-6, Sun 10am-Midnight
Restriction: 24-hr pass syst for students only, In-house use for visitors, Limited access for the pub, Non-circulating coll, Non-circulating of rare bks, Open to students, fac, staff & alumni, Private libr, Restricted borrowing privileges, Restricted loan policy

C UNIVERSITY OF TEXAS AT SAN ANTONIO LIBRARIES*, One UTSA Circle, 78249-0671. SAN 316-7496. Tel: 210-458-4574, 210-458-7506. Interlibrary Loan Service Tel: 210-458-8340. Reference Tel: 210-458-4573. Administration Tel: 210-458-4889. E-mail: libraryask@utsa.edu. Web Site: lib.utsa.edu. *Vice Provost & Univ Librn,* Dean Hendrix; E-mail: dean.hendrix@utsa.edu; *Asst Vice Provost, Colls & Curriculum Support,* Posie Aagaard; E-mail: posie.aagaard@utsa.edu; *Sr Assoc Vice Provost for Administration,* Carolyn Ellis; Tel: 210-458-6665, E-mail: carolyn.ellis@utsa.edu; *Info Technology Librarian,* Esteban Cantu; Staff 99 (MLS 45, Non-MLS 54)
Founded 1972. Enrl 29,000; Highest Degree: Doctorate
Library Holdings: e-books 2,149,577; Bk Titles 819,304
Special Collections: Texana, especially San Antonio & South Texas. State Document Depository; US Document Depository
Automation Activity & Vendor Info: (Acquisitions) Ex Libris Group; (Cataloging) Ex Libris Group; (Circulation) Ex Libris Group; (Course Reserve) Ex Libris Group; (ILL) Ex Libris Group; (Media Booking) Ex Libris Group; (OPAC) Ex Libris Group; (Serials) Ex Libris Group
Wireless access
Partic in Amigos Library Services, Inc; Council of Research & Academic Libraries; TexSHARE - Texas State Library & Archives Commission
Open Mon-Thurs 7am-Midnight, Fri 7am-9pm, Sat 9-9
Friends of the Library Group

CM UNIVERSITY OF TEXAS HEALTH SCIENCE CENTER AT SAN ANTONIO LIBRARIES*, Dolph Briscoe Jr Library, 7703 Floyd Curl Dr, MSC 7940, 78229-3900. SAN 362-3165. Tel: 210-567-2450. Circulation Tel: 210-567-2440. Interlibrary Loan Service Tel: 210-567-2460. Administration Tel: 210-567-2413. Web Site: library.uthscsa.edu. *Sr Dir, Libr,* Owen Ellard; E-mail: ellard@uthscsa.edu; *Assoc Dir of Outreach & Community Engagement,* Peg Seger; E-mail: segerp@uthscsa.edu; *Assoc Dir, Res Mgt,* Andrea Schorr; E-mail: schorr@uthscsa.edu; *Electronic Res Librn,* Dana Whitmire; E-mail: whitmired@uthscsa.edu; *Liaison Librn,* Rebecca Howe; E-mail: ajtai@uthscsa.edu; *Liaison Librn,* Emme Lopez; E-mail: lopeze13@uthscsa.edu; *Res Sharing Librn,* Kelley Minars; E-mail: minars@uthscsa.edu. Subject Specialists: *Nursing,* Emme Lopez; Staff 25.5 (MLS 12, Non-MLS 13.5)
Founded 1966. Enrl 3,123; Fac 1,722; Highest Degree: Doctorate
Library Holdings: AV Mats 750; e-books 31,056; e-journals 40,500; Bk Titles 250,088
Special Collections: History of Medicine Coll
Subject Interests: Allied health, Dentistry, Med, Nursing
Automation Activity & Vendor Info: (Acquisitions) Koha; (Cataloging) Koha; (Circulation) Koha; (ILL) OCLC ILLiad; (OPAC) Koha; (Serials) Koha
Wireless access
Function: Archival coll, Art exhibits, Audio & video playback equip for onsite use, Bk club(s), Computers for patron use, Distance learning, Doc delivery serv, Electronic databases & coll, Health sci info serv, ILL available, Internet access, Mail & tel request accepted, Online cat, Online ref, Orientations, Outreach serv, Photocopying/Printing, Printer for laptops & handheld devices, Ref serv available, Res libr, Scanner, Telephone ref, Wheelchair accessible
Publications: Annual Report: The Libraries; News from The Libraries (Newsletter); Newsletter of the Friends of the P I Nixon Medical Historical Library (Annual)
Partic in Council of Research & Academic Libraries; National Network of Libraries of Medicine Region 3; OCLC Online Computer Library Center, Inc; TexSHARE - Texas State Library & Archives Commission
Open Mon-Thurs 7am-Midnight, Fri 7am-10pm, Sat 9am-10pm, Sun 10am-Midnight
Restriction: 24-hr pass syst for students only, Badge access after hrs, ID required to use computers (Ltd hrs), In-house use for visitors, Non-circulating of rare bks, Off-site coll in storage - retrieval as requested
Friends of the Library Group

CR UNIVERSITY OF THE INCARNATE WORD*, JE & LE Mabee Library, 4301 Broadway, CPO 297, 78209-6397. SAN 316-7275. Circulation Tel: 210-829-3836. Reference Tel: 210-829-3835. Web Site: my.uiw.edu/library. *Dean of Libr,* Tracey Mendoza; E-mail: temendo2@uiwtx.edu; *Dir, Pub Serv,* Dell Davis; Tel: 210-829-6054, E-mail: dmdavis@uiwtx.edu; *Dir, Tech Serv,* Mary L Jinks; Tel: 210-829-3839, E-mail: marydlg@uiwtx.edu; *AV Librn,* Farhad L Moshiri; Tel: 210-829-3842, E-mail: moshiri@uiwtx.edu; *Cat Librn,* Melissa Rucker; Tel: 210-829-6097, E-mail: melissa@uiwtx.edu; *Information Literacy Coord,* Leslie Todd; Tel: 210-829-3841, E-mail: todd@uiwtx.edu; *Asst to the Dean of Libraries,* Angelica Velasquez; E-mail: anvelasq@uiwtx.edu; Staff 20 (MLS 10, Non-MLS 10)
Founded 1897. Enrl 7,000; Highest Degree: Doctorate
Library Holdings: AV Mats 15,415; Bks on Deafness & Sign Lang 500; e-books 23,754; Bk Titles 272,159; Per Subs 17,018
Special Collections: Unique & Limited Editions, Rare Books
Subject Interests: Ezra Pound, Texana, Women's studies
Automation Activity & Vendor Info: (Acquisitions) Ex Libris Group; (Cataloging) Ex Libris Group; (Circulation) Ex Libris Group; (ILL) Ex Libris Group; (OPAC) Ex Libris Group; (Serials) Ex Libris Group
Wireless access
Partic in Amigos Library Services, Inc; Coun of Res & Acad Libs; Council of Research & Academic Libraries; Phoenix Group; TexSHARE - Texas State Library & Archives Commission
Open Mon-Thurs 7:30am-Midnight, Fri 7:30am-8pm, Sat 8-8, Sun 1-Midnight
Restriction: Open to fac, students & qualified researchers, Photo ID required for access

SAN AUGUSTINE

P SAN AUGUSTINE PUBLIC LIBRARY*, 413 E Columbia St, 75972. SAN 316-7526. Tel: 936-275-5367. FAX: 936-275-5049. E-mail: sauglib@yahoo.com. Web Site: www.salibrary.org. *Dir,* Adrienne Montgomery; Staff 1 (MLS 1)
Founded 1973. Pop 8,086; Circ 19,000
Library Holdings: Bk Vols 19,949; Per Subs 26
Special Collections: Genealogy (Tex Heritage), bk, micro. Oral History
Automation Activity & Vendor Info: (Cataloging) Follett Software; (Circulation) Follett Software
Wireless access
Publications: Caucasian Cemeteries of San Augustine County, Texas, 3 vols; Probate Cases of San Augustine County, Texas (1828-1940)
Open Mon-Fri 8:30-5
Friends of the Library Group

SAN BENITO

P SAN BENITO PUBLIC LIBRARY*, 101 W Rose St, 78586-5169. SAN 316-7534. Tel: 956-361-3860. FAX: 956-361-3867. Web Site: www.cityofsanbenito.com/141/San-Benito-Public-Library. *Libr Dir,* Gerardo Salazar; E-mail: gsalazar@cityofsanbenito.com; Staff 1 (MLS 1)
Founded 1936. Pop 30,000; Circ 73,500
Library Holdings: Bk Titles 32,000; Bk Vols 34,000; Per Subs 110
Automation Activity & Vendor Info: (Acquisitions) Biblionix; (Cataloging) Biblionix; (Circulation) Biblionix; (Course Reserve) Biblionix; (OPAC) Biblionix
Wireless access
Function: Accelerated reader prog
Open Mon-Thurs 10-9, Fri 10-5, Sat 12-4
Friends of the Library Group

SAN DIEGO

P DUVAL COUNTY-SAN DIEGO PUBLIC LIBRARY*, 315 S Dr E E Dunlap St, 78384. (Mail add: PO Box 1062, 78384-1062), SAN 376-429X. Tel: 361-279-6244. FAX: 361-279-8212. Web Site: www.co.duval.tx.us/default.aspx?name=ss.library. *Senior Clerk,* Melly Tanguma; *Library Contact,* Melissa Martinez; E-mail: melsings79@yahoo.com; Staff 1 (Non-MLS 1)
Founded 1994. Pop 12,578
Library Holdings: AV Mats 229; High Interest/Low Vocabulary Bk Vols 5,000; Bk Vols 16,000; Per Subs 26
Automation Activity & Vendor Info: (Cataloging) ComPanion Corp; (Circulation) ComPanion Corp
Wireless access

Function: Bks on cassette, Children's prog, Computers for patron use, Electronic databases & coll, ILL available, Magnifiers for reading, Photocopying/Printing, Preschool outreach, Ref serv available, Summer reading prog, Tax forms, Wheelchair accessible
Open Mon-Fri 12-6
Friends of the Library Group
Branches: 2
BENAVIDES BRANCH, 131 Mesquite St, Benavides, 78341. (Mail add: PO Box R, Benavides, 78341-0918). Tel: 361-256-4646. FAX: 361-256-4646. *Br Mgr,* Janie Saenz; E-mail: j_saenz79@yahoo.com
Library Holdings: Bk Vols 3,500
Open Tues-Fri 4-8, Sat 10-2
Friends of the Library Group
FREER BRANCH, 608 Carolyn St, Freer, 78357. (Mail add: PO Box 1203, Freer, 78357). Tel: 361-394-5350. FAX: 361-394-5350. *Br Mgr,* Lesbia Lopez
Library Holdings: AV Mats 30; Bk Vols 4,000
Open Mon-Fri 3-7
Friends of the Library Group

SAN JUAN

P SAN JUAN MEMORIAL LIBRARY*, 1010 S Standard Ave, 78589. SAN 378-4479. Tel: 956-702-0926. FAX: 956-783-3444. Web Site: www.cityofsanjuantexas.com/cosj2/library, www.sanjuanlibrary.com. *Libr Dir,* Armandina Sesin; E-mail: sesin@sanjuanlibrary.com; *Libr Supvr,* Richard Rodriguez; E-mail: rrodriguez@sanjuanlibrary.com; Staff 7 (MLS 1, Non-MLS 6)
Pop 44,500
Library Holdings: Bk Vols 34,000
Automation Activity & Vendor Info: (Cataloging) TLC (The Library Corporation); (Circulation) TLC (The Library Corporation); (OPAC) TLC (The Library Corporation)
Wireless access
Mem of Hidalgo County Library System
Open Mon-Thurs 9-7, Fri & Sat 9-5, Sun 1-5

SAN MARCOS

P SAN MARCOS PUBLIC LIBRARY*, 625 E Hopkins, 78666. SAN 316-7550. Tel: 512-393-8200. E-mail: smpl@sanmarcostx.gov. Web Site: www.sanmarcostx.gov/library. *Libr Dir,* Diane Insley; E-mail: dinsley@sanmarcostx.gov; *Ad,* Kim Morgan-Benson; E-mail: kmorgan-benson@sanmarcostx.gov; *Ch,* Ashley Schimelman; E-mail: aschimelman@sanmarcostx.gov; *Marketing & Teen Librarian,* Harleigh McGowan; E-mail: hmcgowan@sanmarcostx.gov; *Tech Serv Librn,* Sara Seyl; E-mail: sseyl@sanmarcostx.gov; *Workforce Librarian,* Deborah Carter; E-mail: dcarter@sanmarcostx.gov; *Mgr, Prog & Outreach,* Suzanne Sanders; E-mail: ssanders@sanmarcostx.gov; *Pub Serv Mgr,* Adam Landry; E-mail: alandry@sanmarcostx.gov; *Tech Serv Mgr,* Arro Smith; E-mail: asmith@sanmarcostx.gov; *Shelving Supervisor,* Tristan Bailey; E-mail: tbailey@sanmarcostx.gov; Staff 9 (MLS 9)
Founded 1966. Pop 89,202
Oct 2021-Sept 2022 Income $2,941,638, City $1,829,838, County $85,000, Locally Generated Income $1,026,800
Library Holdings: Audiobooks 4,028; DVDs 14,757; e-books 17,317; e-journals 30; Electronic Media & Resources 72; Large Print Bks 2,189; Bk Vols 199,372; Per Subs 254
Special Collections: Mike Cox Texas Coll; San Marcos-Hays County Coll
Automation Activity & Vendor Info: (Acquisitions) TLC (The Library Corporation); (Cataloging) TLC (The Library Corporation); (Circulation) TLC (The Library Corporation); (OPAC) TLC (The Library Corporation)
Wireless access
Function: 24/7 Electronic res, 24/7 Online cat, Activity rm, Adult bk club, Adult literacy prog, Archival coll, Computer training, Electronic databases & coll, ILL available, Learning ctr, Magnifiers for reading, Photocopying/Printing, Preschool outreach, Prog for adults, Prog for children & young adult, Summer reading prog, Tax forms, Telephone ref, Wheelchair accessible
Publications: Calendar of Events (Monthly)
Partic in Central Texas Digital Consortium; Partners Library Action Network; TexSHARE - Texas State Library & Archives Commission
Open Mon-Thurs 9-9, Fri 9-6, Sat 10-6, Sun 1-6
Friends of the Library Group

C TEXAS STATE UNIVERSITY, Albert B Alkek Library, 601 University Dr, 78666-4684. SAN 362-322X. Tel: 512-245-2686. Administration Tel: 512-245-2133. FAX: 512-245-0392. Administration FAX: 512-245-3002. E-mail: library@txstate.edu. Web Site: www.library.txstate.edu/alkek. *Univ Librn, Vice Provost,* Dr Kelly Visnak; Tel: 512-408-0576, E-mail: kelly.visnak@txstate.edu; *Assoc Univ Librn, Admin & Organizational Devel,* Somaly Kim Wu; Tel: 512-408-4068, E-mail: skimwu@txstate.edu; *Assoc Univ Librn, Digital Scholarship & Research,* Laura Waugh; Tel: 512-408-2351, E-mail: lwaugh@txstate.edu; *Dir, Systems & Tech Strategies,* Andrew Rechnitz; Tel: 512-408-4006, E-mail: anr209@txstate.edu; *Dir, Teaching & Learning Services,* Jess Williams; Tel: 512-408-1812, E-mail: jmw384@txstate.edu; *Head, Round Rock Libr Serv,* Anthony Guardado; Tel: 512-245-4701, E-mail: guardado@txstate.edu; *Lead Systems Admin,* Palvi Rentz; Tel: 512-908-4423, E-mail: pr11@txstate.edu; Staff 46 (MLS 42, Non-MLS 4)
Founded 1899. Enrl 35,568; Fac 1,705; Highest Degree: Doctorate
Library Holdings: Audiobooks 5,737; AV Mats 167,755; Braille Volumes 189; CDs 14,084; DVDs 11,792; e-books 541,906; e-journals 115,306; Electronic Media & Resources 25,875; Microforms 1,984,058; Music Scores 18,452; Bk Titles 809,058; Bk Vols 940,058; Talking Bks 5,737; Videos 47,060
Special Collections: J Frank Dobie, John Graves, Preston Jones, Larry L King, Elithe Hamilton Kirkland (Southwestern Writers Coll); Wittliff Gallery of Southwestern & Mexican Photography. State Document Depository; US Document Depository
Automation Activity & Vendor Info: (Acquisitions) Innovative Interfaces, Inc - Millennium; (Cataloging) Innovative Interfaces, Inc - Millennium; (Circulation) Innovative Interfaces, Inc - Millennium; (Course Reserve) Docutek; (ILL) OCLC ILLiad; (OPAC) Innovative Interfaces, Inc - Millennium; (Serials) Innovative Interfaces, Inc - Millennium
Wireless access
Partic in Coun of Res & Acad Librs; Greater Western Library Alliance; OCLC Online Computer Library Center, Inc; TexSHARE - Texas State Library & Archives Commission
Open Mon-Thurs, Sat & Sun 7:30am-1am, Fri 7:30am-10pm

SAN SABA

P SAN SABA COUNTY LIBRARY*, Rylander Memorial Library, 103 S Live Oak, 76877. SAN 316-7569. Tel: 325-372-3079. FAX: 325-372-3079. Web Site: www.sansabalibrary.org. *Librn,* Samantha Vargas; E-mail: svargas@co.san-saba.tx.us; Staff 1 (Non-MLS 1)
Pop 5,540; Circ 16,055
Library Holdings: Bk Vols 13,000; Per Subs 25
Automation Activity & Vendor Info: (Cataloging) Biblionix; (Circulation) Biblionix
Wireless access
Partic in Central Texas Digital Consortium; Partners Library Action Network
Open Mon-Fri 11-5, Sat 10-2
Friends of the Library Group

SANDERSON

P TERRELL COUNTY PUBLIC LIBRARY*, Courthouse Sq, 109 Hackberry, 79848. (Mail add: PO Drawer 250, 79848-0250), SAN 376-4346. Tel: 432-345-2294. FAX: 432-345-2144. E-mail: county.librarian@co.terrell.tx.us. Web Site: www.co.terrell.tx.us/default.aspx?Terrell_County/County.Library. *Librn,* Susan Krukowski
Library Holdings: Bk Titles 28,000; Per Subs 32
Automation Activity & Vendor Info: (Cataloging) Follett Software; (Circulation) Follett Software
Wireless access
Partic in Partners Library Action Network
Open Tues-Sat 2-6
Friends of the Library Group

SANGER

P SANGER PUBLIC LIBRARY*, 501 Bolivar St, 76266. SAN 370-7350. Tel: 940-458-3257. E-mail: libraryclerk@sangertexas.org. Web Site: www.sangerlibrary.org. *Libr Dir,* Audry Tolle; E-mail: atolle@sangertexas.org; *Tech Serv,* Laura Klenke; E-mail: lklenke@sangertexas.org; Staff 1.5 (MLS 1.5)
Founded 1970. Pop 9,325; Circ 39,200
Library Holdings: Audiobooks 840; CDs 353; DVDs 1,042; Microforms 86; Bk Titles 17,850; Bk Vols 18,034; Per Subs 19; Videos 724
Special Collections: Sanger Courier, microfilm
Subject Interests: Local hist
Automation Activity & Vendor Info: (Cataloging) Evergreen; (Circulation) Evergreen; (OPAC) Evergreen
Wireless access
Function: Adult bk club, Bks on cassette, Bks on CD, Children's prog, Computer training, Computers for patron use, E-Reserves, Free DVD rentals, Homebound delivery serv, ILL available, Magnifiers for reading, Microfiche/film & reading machines, Music CDs, Online cat, Photocopying/Printing, Ref serv available, Scanner, Spanish lang bks, Story hour, Summer reading prog, Tax forms, VHS videos
Partic in North Texas Library Consortium
Open Mon-Thurs 10-6, Fri 10-5, Sat 10-2
Restriction: Authorized scholars by appt
Friends of the Library Group

SANTA FE

P MAE S BRUCE LIBRARY*, 13302 Sixth St, 77510-9148. (Mail add: PO Box 950, 77510-0950), SAN 326-1816. Tel: 409-925-5540. FAX: 409-925-8697. E-mail: reference@maebrucelibrary.org. Web Site: www.ci.santa-fe.tx.us/library. *Librn,* Brenda Cheatham; Staff 3 (MLS 1, Non-MLS 2)
Founded 1973. Pop 13,783; Circ 37,000
Library Holdings: Bk Vols 28,000; Per Subs 18; Talking Bks 700
Automation Activity & Vendor Info: (Cataloging) Follett Software; (Circulation) Follett Software
Wireless access
Mem of Galveston County Library System
Partic in Houston Area Database Consortium; Partners Library Action Network
Open Mon-Wed & Fri 10-6, Thurs 12-8, Sat 10-1:30
Friends of the Library Group

SCHERTZ

P SCHERTZ PUBLIC LIBRARY*, 798 Schertz Pkwy, 78154. SAN 324-1556. Tel: 210-619-1700. FAX: 210-619-1711. E-mail: librarian@schertz.com. Web Site: schertzlibrary.org. *Libr Dir,* Melissa Uhlhorn; *Ad,* Elizabeth Bertoia; *Virtual Serv Librn,* Natalie Shults; *Youth Serv Librn,* April Toman; Staff 18 (MLS 4, Non-MLS 14)
Founded 1978. Circ 450,000
Library Holdings: Bk Titles 80,000; Bk Vols 86,000; Per Subs 150
Subject Interests: Genealogy, Texana
Wireless access
Function: 24/7 Electronic res, 24/7 Online cat, Adult bk club, Adult literacy prog, Children's prog, Computer training, Computers for patron use, Genealogy discussion group, Homework prog, ILL available, Internet access, Notary serv, Photocopying/Printing, Prog for adults, Prog for children & young adult, Ref serv available, Scanner, Study rm, Summer reading prog, Tax forms, Wheelchair accessible, Winter reading prog
Partic in Partners Library Action Network
Special Services for the Blind - Talking bks & player equip
Open Mon-Thurs 10-8, Fri 10-6, Sat & Sun 12-6

SCHULENBURG

P SCHULENBURG PUBLIC LIBRARY*, 310 Simpson St, 78956. SAN 316-7585. Tel: 979-743-3345. E-mail: splo1@yahoo.com. Web Site: www.schulenburglibrary.org. *Librn,* Cindy Lytle; *Asst Librn,* Donna Holub
Pop 2,730; Circ 32,000
Library Holdings: Audiobooks 300; DVDs 2,916; Large Print Bks 300; Bk Vols 50,000; Per Subs 20
Wireless access
Partic in Partners Library Action Network
Open Mon 10-8, Tues-Fri 10-6, Sat 9-12
Friends of the Library Group

SEAGOVILLE

P SEAGOVILLE PUBLIC LIBRARY*, 702 N Hwy 175, 75159-1774. SAN 316-7593. Tel: 972-287-7720. FAX: 972-287-3891. Web Site: seagoville.ploud.net. *Libr Dir,* Elizabeth Gant; E-mail: lgant@seagovillelibrary.org; *Ch Serv,* Itzel Ramirez
Founded 1942
Library Holdings: AV Mats 802; Bks on Deafness & Sign Lang 23; High Interest/Low Vocabulary Bk Vols 100; Large Print Bks 394; Bk Titles 28,822; Bk Vols 30,000; Per Subs 18; Talking Bks 444
Automation Activity & Vendor Info: (Cataloging) Follett Software; (Circulation) Follett Software; (OPAC) Follett Software
Wireless access
Open Mon & Thurs 11-7, Tues & Fri 10-5, Wed 11-6, Sat 9-1
Friends of the Library Group

SEALY

P VIRGIL & JOSEPHINE GORDON MEMORIAL LIBRARY*, 917 N Circle Dr, 77474. SAN 324-2188. Tel: 979-885-7469. FAX: 979-885-7469. E-mail: gordonlib@sbcglobal.net. *Dir,* Joyce Williams; *Asst Librn,* Guadalupe Amaya; Staff 2 (Non-MLS 2)
Pop 9,000; Circ 111,514
Library Holdings: AV Mats 2,420; CDs 66; DVDs 164; Large Print Bks 280; Bk Titles 29,307; Bk Vols 30,767; Per Subs 20; Videos 1,304
Wireless access
Function: Bks on CD, Children's prog, Computers for patron use, Genealogy discussion group, ILL available, Internet access, Laminating, Magazines, Meeting rooms, Photocopying/Printing, Prog for children & young adult, Scanner, Spanish lang bks, Story hour, Summer reading prog, VHS videos, Wheelchair accessible, Workshops
Open Mon-Fri 10-5:30, Sat 9-1
Friends of the Library Group

SEGUIN

P SEGUIN PUBLIC LIBRARY*, 313 W Nolte St, 78155-3217. SAN 316-7615. Tel: 830-401-2422. E-mail: library@seguintexas.gov. Web Site: library.seguintexas.gov. *Libr Dir,* Jacki Gross; Tel: 830-401-2466, E-mail: jgross@seguintexas.gov; *Asst Libr Dir,* Silvia D Christy; Tel: 830-401-2426, E-mail: schristy@seguintexas.gov; Staff 23 (MLS 4, Non-MLS 19)
Founded 1930. Circ 281,529
Oct 2021-Sept 2022 Income $1,831,115, State $24,480, City $1,520,143, County $173,742, Locally Generated Income $112,750
Special Collections: Guadalupe County Land Records, micro; Historic Photographs (Kubala Coll); Old Seguin Newspapers, micro-filmed
Subject Interests: Guadalupe County hist, Local hist
Automation Activity & Vendor Info: (Acquisitions) Biblionix/Apollo; (Cataloging) Biblionix/Apollo; (Circulation) Biblionix/Apollo; (ILL) Biblionix/Apollo; (OPAC) Biblionix/Apollo
Wireless access
Function: 24/7 Electronic res, 24/7 Online cat, 3D Printer, Adult bk club, Adult literacy prog, Art exhibits, Audiobks via web, Bilingual assistance for Spanish patrons, Bk club(s), Bks on CD, Chess club, Children's prog, Computer training, Computers for patron use, Electronic databases & coll, Extended outdoor wifi, Free DVD rentals, ILL available, Internet access, Laptop/tablet checkout, Magazines, Mail & tel request accepted, Mango lang, Meeting rooms, Microfiche/film & reading machines, Online cat, Online Chat, OverDrive digital audio bks, Photocopying/Printing, Preschool outreach, Printer for laptops & handheld devices, Prog for adults, Prog for children & young adult, Ref & res, Ref serv available, Scanner, Spanish lang bks, STEM programs, Story hour, Study rm, Summer reading prog, Tax forms, Teen prog, Wheelchair accessible, Wifi hotspot checkout
Mem of Central Texas Library System (CTLS)
Partic in Amigos Library Services, Inc
Open Mon-Thurs 9-8, Fri 9-6, Sat 9-5, Sun 1-5
Friends of the Library Group

C TEXAS LUTHERAN UNIVERSITY, Blumberg Memorial Library, 1000 W Court St, 78155-5978. SAN 316-7623. Tel: 830-372-8100. E-mail: librarian@tlu.edu. Web Site: bulldogs.tlu.edu/library. *Interim Libr Dir, Interim Univ Librn,* Mark Dibble; Tel: 830-372-8109, E-mail: mdibble@tlu.edu; *Interim Head of Public Services,* Amelia Koford; Tel: 830-372-8138, E-mail: akoford@tlu.edu; *Tech Systems/E-Resources Librn,* Nate Aubin; Tel: 830-372-8102, E-mail: nbaubin@tlu.edu; Staff 5 (MLS 5)
Founded 1891. Enrl 1,473; Fac 64; Highest Degree: Bachelor
Library Holdings: Bk Vols 102,400; Per Subs 597
Special Collections: American Lutheran Church; German Literature & Culture. US Document Depository
Subject Interests: Gen liberal arts, Relig studies, State hist
Automation Activity & Vendor Info: (Acquisitions) Ex Libris Group; (Cataloging) Ex Libris Group; (Circulation) Ex Libris Group; (OPAC) Ex Libris Group; (Serials) Ex Libris Group
Wireless access
Publications: Library guide; Library newsletter
Partic in Amigos Library Services, Inc; Coun of Res & Acad Libra; Council of Research & Academic Libraries; OCLC Online Computer Library Center, Inc
Open Mon-Thurs 7:30am-9pm, Fri 7:30-5, Sun 2-9

SEMINOLE

P GAINES COUNTY LIBRARY, 704 Hobbs Hwy, 79360. SAN 362-3289. Tel: 432-955-1007. FAX: 432-955-1024. E-mail: library@co.gaines.tx.us. Web Site: www.gainescountylibrary.org. *Libr Dir,* Sabra Hall; E-mail: shall@co.gaines.tx.us; Staff 4 (Non-MLS 4)
Founded 1957. Pop 20,478; Circ 77,931
Oct 2023-Sept 2024 Income (Main & Associated Libraries) $427,120. Mats Exp $35,663, Books $28,512, AV Mat $3,037, Electronic Ref Mat (Incl. Access Fees) $4,114. Sal $262,889
Library Holdings: Audiobooks 1,451; DVDs 2,483; e-books 18,679; Electronic Media & Resources 4; Large Print Bks 1,460; Microforms 100; Bk Titles 45,555; Per Subs 56
Subject Interests: Local hist, Mennonites, Spanish lang
Automation Activity & Vendor Info: (Acquisitions) Biblionix/Apollo; (Cataloging) Biblionix/Apollo; (Circulation) Biblionix/Apollo; (Course Reserve) Biblionix/Apollo; (ILL) Biblionix/Apollo; (OPAC) Biblionix/Apollo; (Serials) EBSCO Online
Wireless access
Function: 24/7 Electronic res, 24/7 Online cat, Accelerated reader prog, Activity rm, Adult bk club, Audiobks via web, Bk club(s), Bks on cassette, Bks on CD, Children's prog, Computer training, Computers for patron use, Digital talking bks, Electronic databases & coll, Free DVD rentals, Health sci info serv, Holiday prog, ILL available, Internet access, Laminating, Learning ctr, Life-long learning prog for all ages, Magazines, Magnifiers for reading, Meeting rooms, Microfiche/film & reading machines, Movies, Online cat, Online ref, Outreach serv, Outside serv via phone, mail, e-mail & web, OverDrive digital audio bks, Photocopying/Printing, Preschool

outreach, Preschool reading prog, Printer for laptops & handheld devices, Prog for adults, Prog for children & young adult, Ref serv available, Scanner, Senior outreach, Spanish lang bks, Story hour, Summer & winter reading prog, Tax forms, Teen prog, Telephone ref, VHS videos, Wheelchair accessible, Winter reading prog
Open Mon-Fri 8:30-5:30
Friends of the Library Group
Branches: 1
SEAGRAVES BRANCH, 310 11th St, Seagraves, 79359. (Mail add: PO Box 366, Seagraves, 79359-0366), SAN 362-3319. Tel: 806-546-2480. FAX: 806-546-3053. *Br Mgr,* Toni Polyak; Staff 2 (Non-MLS 2)
Founded 1958
Library Holdings: AV Mats 1,388; e-books 7,605; Electronic Media & Resources 5; Large Print Bks 453; Bk Titles 11,043; Bk Vols 11,242; Per Subs 36
Function: Audiobks via web, AV serv, Bks on cassette, Bks on CD, Computer training, Computers for patron use, Digital talking bks, Electronic databases & coll, Free DVD rentals, Health sci info serv, ILL available, Internet access, Magazines, Movies, Online cat, Outreach serv, Outside serv via phone, mail, e-mail & web, Photocopying/Printing, Preschool outreach, Preschool reading prog, Printer for laptops & handheld devices, Prog for adults, Prog for children & young adult, Scanner, Spanish lang bks, Summer & winter reading prog, Tax forms, Telephone ref
Open Mon-Fri 8:30-12 & 1-5:30
Friends of the Library Group

SEVEN POINTS

P LIBRARY AT CEDAR CREEK LAKE, 410 E Cedar Creek Pkwy, 75143. (Mail add: PO Box 43711, 75143-0711). Tel: 903-432-4185. FAX: 903-432-4108. E-mail: cedarcreeklibrary@embarqmail.com. Web Site: www.cedarcreeklibrary.com. *Dir,* Sondra Price; Staff 4 (MLS 1, Non-MLS 3)
Pop 6,510; Circ 70,000
Library Holdings: Bk Vols 38,000; Per Subs 14
Automation Activity & Vendor Info: (Acquisitions) LibLime; (Cataloging) LibLime; (Circulation) LibLime; (Course Reserve) LibLime; (ILL) LibLime
Wireless access
Function: Adult bk club, Adult literacy prog, BA reader (adult literacy), Bk club(s), Bks on cassette, Children's prog, Distance learning, Electronic databases & coll, Free DVD rentals, Health sci info serv, Homebound delivery serv, ILL available, Internet access, Music CDs, Online info literacy tutorials on the web & in blackboard, Photocopying/Printing, Preschool outreach, Prog for children & young adult, Ref serv available, Senior computer classes, Senior outreach, Summer reading prog, Tax forms, Teen prog, Telephone ref, VHS videos
Partic in Partners Library Action Network
Open Mon, Wed & Fri 9-5, Tues & Thurs 9-7, Sat 9-1
Friends of the Library Group

SHAMROCK

P SHAMROCK COMMUNITY LIBRARY*, 712 N Main St, 79079. SAN 316-764X. Tel: 806-256-3921. FAX: 806-256-3921. *Dir,* Melanie Starr King
Pop 3,000; Circ 12,057
Library Holdings: Bk Vols 22,000; Per Subs 32
Wireless access
Partic in Harrington Library Consortium
Open Mon-Fri 1-5
Friends of the Library Group

SHEPHERD

P SHEPHERD PUBLIC LIBRARY*, 30 N Liberty St, 77371. SAN 376-4087. Tel: 936-628-3515. FAX: 936-628-6608. E-mail: shepherdpl30@gmail.com. Web Site: shepherdlibrary.org. *Dir,* Position Currently Open
Founded 1963. Pop 2,212; Circ 24,787
Library Holdings: Audiobooks 328; DVDs 605; Bk Titles 17,604; Bk Vols 17,614
Wireless access
Open Mon-Fri 9-1 & 2-6
Friends of the Library Group

SHEPPARD AFB

A UNITED STATES AIR FORCE*, Sheppard Air Force Base Library, 425 Third Ave, Bldg 312, 76311. SAN 362-3343. Tel: 940-676-6152. FAX: 940-855-8854. Web Site: 82fss.com/library. *Dir,* Seyfett Fikirndi; E-mail: seyfett.fikirndi.2@us.af.mil
Founded 1949
Library Holdings: DVDs 1,500; Bk Vols 30,000; Per Subs 140
Subject Interests: Gen, Juv, Mil tech
Automation Activity & Vendor Info: (Acquisitions) Softlink America; (Cataloging) Softlink America; (Circulation) Softlink America; (ILL) OCLC WorldShare Interlibrary Loan; (OPAC) Softlink America; (Serials) Softlink America
Wireless access
Restriction: Not open to pub

SHERIDAN

P SHERIDAN MEMORIAL LIBRARY*, 5805 S Logan Park Dr, 77475. (Mail add: PO Box 274, 77475-0274), SAN 372-7335. Tel: 979-234-5154. FAX: 979-234-5154. E-mail: sheridanlib@elc.net, sheridantxlibrary@gmail.com. Web Site: sheridanmemoriallibrary.org. *Dir,* Marjorie Rychlik; Staff 1 (Non-MLS 1)
Founded 1971. Pop 5,811
Library Holdings: AV Mats 600; CDs 207; DVDs 900; High Interest/Low Vocabulary Bk Vols 50; Large Print Bks 150; Bk Titles 8,500; Per Subs 3
Subject Interests: Genealogy, Tex
Automation Activity & Vendor Info: (Cataloging) Follett Software; (Circulation) Follett Software; (OPAC) Follett Software
Wireless access
Function: AV serv
Open Mon-Thurs 12-5
Restriction: Access at librarian's discretion
Friends of the Library Group

SHERMAN

C AUSTIN COLLEGE*, George T & Gladys H Abell Library Center, 900 N Grand Ave, Ste 6L, 75090-4402. SAN 316-7658. Reference Tel: 903-813-2236. Web Site: aclibrary.austincollege.edu. *Col Librn, Dir,* Barbara Cornelius; E-mail: bcornelius@austincollege.edu; *Archivist, Head, Spec Coll,* Justin Banks; Tel: 903-813-2557, E-mail: jbanks@austincollege.edu; *Coordr, Instrul Serv, Research Servs Librn,* Andrew Smith; Tel: 903-813-2470, E-mail: aasmith@austincollege.edu; *Coordr, Bibliog Serv,* LadyJane Hickey; Tel: 903-813-2237, E-mail: lhickey@austincollege.edu; Staff 5 (MLS 5)
Founded 1849. Enrl 1,330; Fac 109; Highest Degree: Master
Library Holdings: AV Mats 6,693; e-books 27,271; e-journals 3,325; Microforms 121,415; Bk Vols 227,019; Per Subs 5,714
Special Collections: Texas & Southwest Studies (Pate Texana, Margaret White Hoard, Rex & Mary Strickland & Lewis F Russell Colls). Oral History
Automation Activity & Vendor Info: (Acquisitions) OCLC; (Cataloging) OCLC; (Circulation) OCLC; (Course Reserve) OCLC; (Discovery) EBSCO Discovery Service; (ILL) Clio; (OPAC) OCLC; (Serials) EBSCO Online
Wireless access
Function: Archival coll, Art exhibits, Audio & video playback equip for onsite use, Computers for patron use, Doc delivery serv, Electronic databases & coll, ILL available, Internet access, Magazines, Microfiche/film & reading machines, Online cat, Online info literacy tutorials on the web & in blackboard, Photocopying/Printing, Printer for laptops & handheld devices, Study rm, Telephone ref, VHS videos, Wheelchair accessible
Partic in Amigos Library Services, Inc; OCLC Online Computer Library Center, Inc; Statewide California Electronic Library Consortium; Tex Independent Cols & Univ Librs; TexSHARE - Texas State Library & Archives Commission
Open Mon-Thurs 7:45am-Midnight, Fri 7:45-6, Sat 9-8, Sun 1-Midnight; Mon-Fri 9-4 (Summer)
Restriction: In-house use for visitors, Non-circulating of rare bks

P SHERMAN PUBLIC LIBRARY*, 421 N Travis St, 75090. SAN 316-7674. Tel: 903-892-7240. FAX: 903-892-7101. Web Site: www.ci.sherman.tx.us/283/Library. *Libr Serv Adminr,* Melissa Eason; E-mail: melissae@ci.sherman.tx.us; *Ch,* Allie Barton; E-mail: allieb@ci.sherman.tx.us; *Pub Serv Librn,* Susan Banner; E-mail: sbanner@grayson.edu; *Ref Librn,* Michael Miller; E-mail: millerm@grayson.edu; Staff 4 (MLS 4)
Founded 1911. Pop 38,407; Circ 225,538
Library Holdings: AV Mats 19,360; Bk Vols 128,907; Per Subs 139
Special Collections: Grayson County Historical Resources for Texas State Library; Hilmer H Flemming Manuscripts; Mattie Davis Lucas Manuscripts. Oral History
Open Mon & Wed 9-6, Tues & Thurs 9-8, Fri 10-6, Sat 11-5
Friends of the Library Group

SHINER

P SHINER PUBLIC LIBRARY*, 115 E Wolters/Second St, 77984. SAN 376-4281. Tel: 361-594-3044. FAX: 361-594-4249. E-mail: library@shinertexas.gov, shinerpl@fbcglobal.net. Web Site: shinerpubliclibrary.org, www.shinertx.com. *Dir,* Paula Sue Pekar
Founded 1994
Library Holdings: AV Mats 1,295; Bk Vols 14,000; Per Subs 54; Talking Bks 200

Automation Activity & Vendor Info: (Cataloging) Follett Software; (Circulation) Follett Software
Wireless access
Open Mon-Thurs 8-5, Fri & Sat 8:30-11
Friends of the Library Group

SILSBEE

P SILSBEE PUBLIC LIBRARY*, 295 N Fourth St, 77656. SAN 316-7682. Tel: 409-385-4831. E-mail: silsbeelibrary@gmail.com. Web Site: silsbeelibrary.org. *Dir,* Cathy Johnson; E-mail: cathy@cityofsilsbee.com
Pop 13,645; Circ 45,328
Library Holdings: Bk Titles 40,892; Bk Vols 60,330; Per Subs 75
Automation Activity & Vendor Info: (Cataloging) Book Systems; (Circulation) Book Systems
Wireless access
Open Mon-Fri 9-6, Sat 9-1
Friends of the Library Group

SINTON

P SINTON PUBLIC LIBRARY*, 100 N Pirate Blvd, 78387. SAN 316-7712. Tel: 361-364-4545. FAX: 361-364-5711. E-mail: sintonpubliclibrary@sintontexas.org. Web Site: www.sintontexas.org/2170/library. *Libr Dir,* Yolanda Bustamante; Staff 3 (Non-MLS 3)
Founded 1927. Pop 7,239; Circ 16,670
Library Holdings: AV Mats 1,450; Bks on Deafness & Sign Lang 7; Bk Titles 18,077; Bk Vols 18,756; Per Subs 43
Special Collections: Texana Coll
Automation Activity & Vendor Info: (Cataloging) Follett Software; (Circulation) Follett Software
Wireless access
Open Mon 9-8, Tues-Fri 9-6, Sat 10-2
Friends of the Library Group

S ROB & BESSIE WELDER WILDLIFE FOUNDATION LIBRARY, 10429 Welder Wildlife, Hwy 77 N, 78387. (Mail add: PO Box 1400, 78387-1400), SAN 316-7720. Tel: 361-364-2643. Web Site: welderwildlife.org/library. *Chief Exec Officer,* Dr Dale James; *Executive Admin Mgr,* Angela Rangel; E-mail: arangel@welderwildlife.org
Founded 1954
Library Holdings: Bk Titles 7,849; Bk Vols 12,005; Per Subs 80; Videos 119
Special Collections: Ornithology (Alexander Wetmore Coll); Rare Book Coll
Subject Interests: Ecology, Environ & conserv, Natural hist, Ornithology, Range mgt, Sci
Wireless access
Publications: Newsletter (Biennial); Student Symposiums
Restriction: Open by appt only

SLATON

P SLATON CITY LIBRARY*, 200 W Lynn St, 79364-4136. SAN 376-4230. Tel: 806-828-2008. FAX: 806-828-2029. E-mail: slatonlibrary@yahoo.com. Web Site: slaton.ploud.net. *Librn,* Cynthia Olivares
Library Holdings: Audiobooks 150; CDs 150; Bk Vols 10,000; Per Subs 30; Videos 150
Wireless access
Open Mon 10-2 & 3-7, Tues & Thurs 9-1 & 2-5:30, Fri 8:30-1 & 2-5

SMILEY

P STELLA ELLIS HART PUBLIC LIBRARY*, 103 FM 108 North, 78159. SAN 316-7739. Tel: 830-587-6101. E-mail: smileylibrary@gvec.net. Web Site: www.smileytx.com/library. *Librn,* Rebecca Mejia; *Librn,* Susy Parker; Staff 1 (Non-MLS 1)
Founded 1938. Pop 861; Circ 1,702
Library Holdings: Audiobooks 200; Large Print Bks 200; Bk Vols 9,000; Videos 25
Wireless access
Open Mon & Wed 2-5

SMITHVILLE

P SMITHVILLE PUBLIC LIBRARY, 507 Main St, 78957. SAN 316-7755. Tel: 512-237-3282, Ext 6. E-mail: splibrarytx1@gmail.com. Web Site: www.smithvillepubliclibrary.org. *Dir,* Judy Bergeron; E-mail: jbergeron@ci.smithville.tx.us; Staff 7 (Non-MLS 7)
Founded 1929. Pop 4,000; Circ 75,000
Library Holdings: AV Mats 100; Bks on Deafness & Sign Lang 20; High Interest/Low Vocabulary Bk Vols 150; Large Print Bks 700; Bk Titles 30,000; Bk Vols 32,000; Per Subs 30
Special Collections: Genealogy Coll; Handmade Quilts; Literacy Coll; Media Library; Texian Coll; Video Coll

Subject Interests: Alaskana
Automation Activity & Vendor Info: (Cataloging) Biblionix; (Circulation) Biblionix
Wireless access
Partic in Partners Library Action Network
Special Services for the Blind - Magnifiers
Open Mon & Wed 10-6, Tues & Thurs 10-7, Fri 10-5, Sat 9-1
Friends of the Library Group

SNYDER

P SCURRY COUNTY LIBRARY, 1916 23rd St, 79549-1910. SAN 316-7763. Tel: 325-573-5572. FAX: 325-573-1060. E-mail: sclibrary@co.scurry.tx.us. Web Site: scurrycountylibrary.org. *Libr Dir,* Amy Hodges; *Asst Libr Dir,* Jessica Carroll; Staff 5 (Non-MLS 5)
Founded 1958. Pop 16,662; Circ 20,642
Library Holdings: Bk Vols 66,394; Per Subs 23
Subject Interests: Genealogy, SW
Automation Activity & Vendor Info: (Cataloging) LibLime; (Circulation) LibLime
Wireless access
Function: 24/7 Online cat, Activity rm, Adult bk club, Art programs, Bks on CD, Computers for patron use, Holiday prog, ILL available, Magazines, Movies, Online cat, OverDrive digital audio bks, Photocopying/Printing, Preschool outreach, Preschool reading prog, Printer for laptops & handheld devices, Prog for adults, Prog for children & young adult, Ref & res, Scanner, Story hour, Summer reading prog, Wheelchair accessible
Partic in Partners Library Action Network; TexSHARE - Texas State Library & Archives Commission
Open Mon & Wed 10-6, Tues & Thurs 10-7, Fri 10-5:30, Sat 10-3
Restriction: Non-circulating
Friends of the Library Group

J WESTERN TEXAS COLLEGE*, Learning Resource Center, 6200 S College Ave, 79549. SAN 316-7771. Tel: 325-574-7678. FAX: 325-573-9321. E-mail: library@wtc.edu. Web Site: www.wtc.edu/lrc.html. *Libr Dir,* Position Currently Open; *Libr Tech,* Teresa Aguilar; E-mail: teresa.aguilar@wtc.edu; Staff 5 (Non-MLS 5)
Founded 1971. Highest Degree: Associate
Library Holdings: e-books 30,161; Bk Vols 31,000; Per Subs 70
Automation Activity & Vendor Info: (Circulation) Auto-Graphics, Inc
Wireless access
Partic in Amigos Library Services, Inc; TexSHARE - Texas State Library & Archives Commission
Open Mon-Thurs 8-5, Fri 8-4
Restriction: Open to students, fac & staff

SONORA

P SUTTON COUNTY PUBLIC LIBRARY*, 306 E Mulberry St, 76950-2603. SAN 376-401X. Tel: 325-387-2111. FAX: 325-387-9044. E-mail: suttoncopubliclibrary@gmail.com. Web Site: sutton.ploud.net. *Libr Dir,* Deborah Brown; Staff 3 (Non-MLS 3)
Pop 2,815
Library Holdings: AV Mats 2,600; Bk Titles 19,421; Per Subs 26
Automation Activity & Vendor Info: (Cataloging) Biblionix/Apollo; (Circulation) Biblionix/Apollo
Wireless access
Function: 24/7 Online cat, Activity rm, Adult bk club, Archival coll, Audio & video playback equip for onsite use, Audiobks via web, AV serv, Bilingual assistance for Spanish patrons, Bk club(s), Bks on CD, Children's prog, Citizenship assistance, Computer training, Computers for patron use, Digital talking bks, Distance learning, Doc delivery serv, Electronic databases & coll, Extended outdoor wifi, Games, Games & aids for people with disabilities, ILL available, Instruction & testing, Internet access, Laminating, Laptop/tablet checkout, Large print keyboards, Magazines, Magnifiers for reading, Mail & tel request accepted, Mail loans to mem, Meeting rooms, Online cat, Online Chat, Outreach serv, OverDrive digital audio bks, Photocopying/Printing, Preschool reading prog, Printer for laptops & handheld devices, Prog for adults, Prog for children & young adult, Ref & res, Ref serv available, Res assist avail, Scanner, Serves people with intellectual disabilities, Spanish lang bks, Story hour, Study rm, Summer & winter reading prog, Summer reading prog, Wheelchair accessible
Open Mon, Tues & Thurs 8-6, Wed 8-5, Fri 8-4:30

SOURLAKE

P ALMA M CARPENTER PUBLIC LIBRARY*, 300 S Ann, 77659. SAN 316-778X. Tel: 409-287-3592. FAX: 409-287-4777. E-mail: amclibrary@nwcable.net. Web Site: sourlake.ploud.net, www.almacarpenterlibrary.com. *Libr Dir,* Leah Gilfillian
Pop 5,000; Circ 10,600
Library Holdings: Bk Titles 17,217; Per Subs 33
Special Collections: Texas Coll

Automation Activity & Vendor Info: (Cataloging) Surpass; (Circulation) Surpass; (OPAC) Surpass
Open Mon-Fri 9-6

SOUTHLAKE

P SOUTHLAKE PUBLIC LIBRARY*, 1400 Main St, Ste 130, 76092-7640. Tel: 817-748-8243. Reference Tel: 817-748-8247. Administration Tel: 817-748-8384. E-mail: southlakelibrary@ci.southlake.tx.us. Web Site: www.cityofsouthlake.com/93/Library. *City Librn,* Cynthia Pfledderer; E-mail: cpfledderer@ci.southlake.tx.us; *Operations Librn,* Jennifer Tucker; E-mail: jtucker@ci.southlake.tx.us; *Youth Librn,* Stacy Wells; E-mail: swells@ci.southlake.tx.us; *Adult Serv,* Maria Cameron; E-mail: mcameron@ci.southlake.tx.us; Staff 9 (MLS 4, Non-MLS 5)
Founded 2001. Pop 30,000; Circ 335,000
Oct 2020-Sept 2021. Mats Exp $105,779, Books $68,747, Per/Ser (Incl. Access Fees) $5,000, AV Mat $14,179, Electronic Ref Mat (Incl. Access Fees) $17,853
Library Holdings: AV Mats 1,800; Electronic Media & Resources 12; Large Print Bks 348; Bk Titles 39,653; Bk Vols 42,950; Per Subs 106; Talking Bks 1,158
Automation Activity & Vendor Info: (Cataloging) Innovative Interfaces, Inc; (Circulation) Innovative Interfaces, Inc; (ILL) OCLC WorldShare Interlibrary Loan; (OPAC) Innovative Interfaces, Inc
Wireless access
Function: 24/7 Electronic res, 24/7 Online cat, Homebound delivery serv, ILL available, Large print keyboards, Magnifiers for reading, Outside serv via phone, mail, e-mail & web, Photocopying/Printing, Prog for adults, Prog for children & young adult, Ref serv available, Summer reading prog, Telephone ref, Wheelchair accessible, Workshops
Open Mon-Thurs 10-8, Fri & Sat 10-6
Friends of the Library Group

SPEARMAN

P HANSFORD COUNTY LIBRARY*, 122 Main St, 79081. SAN 316-7798. Tel: 806-659-2231. FAX: 806-659-5042. E-mail: hansfordcountylibrary@gmail.com. Web Site: www.hansfordcountylibrary.org. *Dir,* Mandi Vargas; Staff 1 (Non-MLS 1)
Founded 1932. Pop 5,279; Circ 20,400
Library Holdings: AV Mats 824; Large Print Bks 395; Bk Titles 20,262; Bk Vols 39,079; Per Subs 45; Talking Bks 947
Special Collections: Oral History
Wireless access
Partic in Harrington Library Consortium
Open Mon-Fri 9:30-5
Friends of the Library Group

SPICEWOOD

P SPICEWOOD COMMUNITY LIBRARY*, 1011 Spur 191, 78669. (Mail add: PO Box 463, 78669). Tel: 830-693-7892. E-mail: spicewoodlibrary@gmail.com. Web Site: www.spicewoodlibrary.org. *Libr Dir,* Kathy Hoover; Staff 1 (Non-MLS 1)
Founded 2007. Circ 6,340
Oct 2018-Sept 2019 Income $70,555, County $19,700, Locally Generated Income $50,855. Mats Exp $5,500, Books $4,000, Electronic Ref Mat (Incl. Access Fees) $1,500. Sal $18,500
Library Holdings: Audiobooks 450; DVDs 743; e-books 10,733; Large Print Bks 80; Bk Titles 8,784
Automation Activity & Vendor Info: (Acquisitions) Book Systems; (Cataloging) Book Systems; (Circulation) Book Systems; (Course Reserve) Book Systems; (Discovery) Book Systems; (ILL) Book Systems; (OPAC) Book Systems
Wireless access
Function: 24/7 Electronic res, 24/7 Online cat, Accelerated reader prog, Adult bk club, Audiobks on Playaways & MP3, Audiobks via web, AV serv, Bk club(s), Bks on CD, Bus archives, Children's prog, Computer training, Computers for patron use, Digital talking bks, E-Reserves, Electronic databases & coll, For res purposes, Free DVD rentals, ILL available, Internet access, Magazines, Mail & tel request accepted, Meeting rooms, Movies, Notary serv, Online cat, OverDrive digital audio bks, Photocopying/Printing, Prog for adults, Prog for children & young adult, Ref & res, Ref serv available, Scanner, Senior computer classes, Spanish lang bks, Spoken cassettes & CDs, Summer reading prog, Tax forms, Wheelchair accessible, Workshops
Partic in Central Texas Digital Consortium; Partners Library Action Network; TexSHARE - Texas State Library & Archives Commission
Special Services for the Blind - Large print bks
Open Tues 10-6, Thurs 2-6, Fri & Sat 10-3
Friends of the Library Group

SPRINGLAKE

P SPRINGLAKE-EARTH COMMUNITY LIBRARY*, 472 Farm Rd 302, 79082. (Mail add: PO Box 259, Earth, 79031-0259). Tel: 806-257-3357. FAX: 806-257-3927. Web Site: www.springlake-earth.org/library/SE_Library.html. *Librn,* Linda Thompson; E-mail: thompson@springlake-earth.org
Pop 1,858; Circ 28,223
Library Holdings: Bk Vols 15,110; Per Subs 32
Automation Activity & Vendor Info: (Cataloging) ComPanion Corp; (Circulation) ComPanion Corp; (OPAC) ComPanion Corp
Open Mon 8-5, Tues & Wed 8-4:30, Thurs & Fri 8-3 (Winter); Mon-Wed 9-5 (Summer)

SPRINGTOWN

P SPRINGTOWN PUBLIC LIBRARY*, 626 N Main St, 76082. (Mail add: PO Box 448, 76082), SAN 376-463X. Tel: 817-523-5862. FAX: 817-523-5922. E-mail: spl@cityofspringtown.com. Web Site: www.springtownlibrary.com. *Libr Dir,* Andie D'Avignon
Library Holdings: Bk Titles 16,875; Bk Vols 16,915; Per Subs 12
Automation Activity & Vendor Info: (Cataloging) Innovative Interfaces, Inc; (Circulation) Innovative Interfaces, Inc
Wireless access
Open Mon & Sat 9-1, Tues 10-7, Wed-Fri 11-6
Friends of the Library Group

SPUR

P DICKENS COUNTY-SPUR PUBLIC LIBRARY*, 412 E Hill St, 79370-2511. (Mail add: PO Box 282, 79370-0282), SAN 376-4222. Tel: 806-271-3714. FAX: 806-271-4341. E-mail: library2@caprock-spur.com. Web Site: spur.ploud.net. *Librn,* Merla Watson
Founded 2015. Pop 1,088
Library Holdings: Bk Vols 15,821; Spec Interest Per Sub 15
Automation Activity & Vendor Info: (Acquisitions) LibLime; (Cataloging) LibLime; (Circulation) LibLime
Wireless access
Function: Art exhibits, Bks on cassette, Bks on CD, Computers for patron use, Distance learning, Electronic databases & coll, Free DVD rentals, Holiday prog, Homebound delivery serv, ILL available, Mail & tel request accepted, Online cat, Photocopying/Printing, Prog for adults, Prog for children & young adult, Ref serv available, Scanner, Spoken cassettes & CDs, Spoken cassettes & DVDs, Summer reading prog, VHS videos, Wheelchair accessible
Open Mon-Thurs 12-5
Friends of the Library Group

STAMFORD

P STAMFORD CARNEGIE LIBRARY*, 600 E McHarg St, 79553. SAN 316-7801. Tel: 325-773-2532. FAX: 325-773-2654. E-mail: stamlib2@sbcglobal.net. *Libr Dir,* Lucile Wedeking; Staff 2 (Non-MLS 2)
Founded 1910. Pop 5,000; Circ 12,180
Library Holdings: Audiobooks 60; CDs 70; DVDs 120; Bk Titles 12,196; Per Subs 14
Automation Activity & Vendor Info: (Cataloging) Biblionix/Apollo; (Circulation) Biblionix/Apollo
Wireless access
Open Mon-Fri 12:30-6

STANTON

P MARTIN COUNTY LIBRARY*, 200 N Saint Mary, 79782. (Mail add: PO Box 1187, 79782-1187), SAN 316-781X. Tel: 432-756-2472. FAX: 432-756-2681. E-mail: mclibstanton@yahoo.com. Web Site: co.martin.tx.us/177/martin-county-library. *Libr Dir,* Jackie A Garza; E-mail: jgarza@co.martin.tx.us; *Asst Librn,* Marla Hagins; E-mail: mhagins@co.martin.tx.us
Founded 1929. Pop 5,000; Circ 19,400
Library Holdings: Audiobooks 1,071; Bks on Deafness & Sign Lang 30; Large Print Bks 300; Bk Titles 23,883
Automation Activity & Vendor Info: (Cataloging) LibLime; (Circulation) LibLime
Wireless access
Open Mon-Fri 8:30-5:30
Friends of the Library Group

STEPHENVILLE

P STEPHENVILLE PUBLIC LIBRARY*, 174 N Columbia, 76401-3492. SAN 316-7828. Tel: 254-918-1240. FAX: 254-918-1208. Web Site: www.stephenvilletx.gov/parks-leisure/page/library. *Dir,* Mary Meredith; E-mail: mmeredith@stephenvilletx.gov
Founded 1903. Pop 18,000; Circ 66,019

Library Holdings: DVDs 5,000; Large Print Bks 2,000; Bk Vols 31,000; Per Subs 30; Talking Bks 750
Automation Activity & Vendor Info: (Cataloging) AmLib Library Management System; (Circulation) AmLib Library Management System
Wireless access
Open Tues, Wed & Fri 10-6, Thurs Noon-8, Sat 8-4
Friends of the Library Group

C TARLETON STATE UNIVERSITY LIBRARY, Dick Smith Library, 201 Saint Felix, 76401. (Mail add: Box T-0450, 76402), SAN 316-7836. Tel: 254-968-9246. Circulation Tel: 254-968-9450. Interlibrary Loan Service Tel: 254-968-9660. Reference Tel: 254-968-9249. Automation Services Tel: 254-968-9030. Information Services Tel: 254-968-9871. Toll Free Tel: 866-339-5555. FAX: 254-968-9467. Reference E-mail: reference@tarleton.edu. Web Site: www.tarleton.edu/library. *Dean, Univ Libr,* Dr Katherine Quinnell; E-mail: quinnell@tarleton.edu; *Assoc Dir, Access & Collection Servs,* Tracy Holtman; Tel: 254-968-9466, E-mail: holtman@tarleton.edu; *Access Serv Mgr, Circ Supvr,* Shelby Monk; E-mail: smonk@tarleton.edu; *Mgr, Cat Serv,* Melissa Cookson; Tel: 254-968-9339, E-mail: cookson@tarleton.edu; *Graduate & Faculty Services Coord,* Adam Keim; E-mail: keim@tarleton.edu; *Undergrad Serv Coordr,* Kim Gragg; E-mail: gragg@tarleton.edu; *Assessment Specialist,* Paul Salie; E-mail: psalie@tarleton.edu; *Business Admin,* Tonya Dobson; Tel: 254-968-9474, E-mail: dobson@tarleton.edu; Staff 24 (MLS 15, Non-MLS 9)
Founded 1899. Enrl 14,513; Fac 797; Highest Degree: Doctorate
Special Collections: Agricultural, Experiment Station Reports; Texana Coll
Subject Interests: Agr, Bus, Econ, Educ, Hist, Mgt, Sci tech
Automation Activity & Vendor Info: (Acquisitions) SirsiDynix; (Cataloging) SirsiDynix; (Circulation) SirsiDynix; (Course Reserve) SirsiDynix; (ILL) OCLC Tipasa; (OPAC) SirsiDynix; (Serials) SirsiDynix
Wireless access
Partic in Amigos Library Services, Inc; TexSHARE - Texas State Library & Archives Commission
Open Mon-Thurs 7am-1am, Fri 7am-8pm, Sat Noon-8, Sun Noon-1am
Friends of the Library Group

STERLING CITY

P STERLING COUNTY PUBLIC LIBRARY*, 301 Main St, 76951. (Mail add: PO Box 1054, 76951-1054). Tel: 325-378-2212. FAX: 325-378-2212. E-mail: sterlingcountypubliclibrary@gmail.com. Web Site: sterling-county.ploud.net. *Libr Dir,* Betty Coleman; *Ch, Co-Dir,* Terrye Ferguson
Pop 1,219; Circ 2,178
Library Holdings: Audiobooks 339; DVDs 11; Bk Titles 10,238; Per Subs 14
Automation Activity & Vendor Info: (Cataloging) Koha; (Circulation) Koha
Wireless access
Function: 24/7 Online cat, Bks on CD, Children's prog, Computers for patron use, Free DVD rentals, Magazines, Movies, Online cat, Photocopying/Printing, Prog for children & young adult, Scanner, Summer reading prog
Partic in Partners Library Action Network
Open Mon-Thurs 9-5, Fri 10:30-1:30

STRATFORD

P SHERMAN COUNTY LIBRARY*, 719 N Main St, 79084. SAN 316-7844. Tel: 806-366-2200. FAX: 806-366-7551. E-mail: lib2200@xit.net. Web Site: harringtonlc.org/sherman. *Dir,* Sandra Baskin; Staff 2 (Non-MLS 2)
Founded 1957. Pop 2,858; Circ 9,208
Library Holdings: Bk Titles 27,000; Per Subs 36
Special Collections: Texas Coll
Automation Activity & Vendor Info: (Cataloging) SirsiDynix; (Circulation) SirsiDynix
Wireless access
Partic in Harrington Library Consortium
Open Mon 9-7, Tues-Thurs 9-6, Fri 9-1
Friends of the Library Group

SULPHUR SPRINGS

P SULPHUR SPRINGS PUBLIC LIBRARY*, 611 N Davis St, 75482. SAN 316-7852. Tel: 903-885-4926. FAX: 903-439-1052. E-mail: sulphurspringslibrary@gmail.com. Web Site: www.sslibrary.org. *Dir,* Hope Cain; Staff 4 (MLS 1, Non-MLS 3)
Pop 35,371; Circ 32,926
Library Holdings: DVDs 2,500; Bk Vols 50,591
Special Collections: St Clair Music Box Coll (Leo St Clair's Coll)
Wireless access
Open Mon-Wed & Fri 9-6, Thurs 11-8, Sat 9-1
Friends of the Library Group

SUNDOWN

G CITY OF SUNDOWN LIBRARY, 201 E Fifth St, 79372. (Mail add: PO Box 1130, 79372), SAN 375-6025. Tel: 806-214-3099. E-mail: sundownlibrary@gmail.com. Web Site: sundown.ploud.net. *Dir, Librn,* A'ndrea McAdams; Staff 1 (Non-MLS 1)
Circ 5,815
Library Holdings: Bk Titles 6,334; Bk Vols 6,627
Automation Activity & Vendor Info: (Acquisitions) Biblionix/Apollo; (Cataloging) Biblionix/Apollo; (Circulation) Biblionix/Apollo
Open Mon-Fri 9-1 & 2-5

SUNNYVALE

P DORIS PADGETT PUBLIC LIBRARY*, 402 Tower Pl, 75182-9278. SAN 361-428X. Tel: 972-226-4491. FAX: 972-203-0310. E-mail: library@townofsunnyvale.org. Web Site: www.sunnyvalepubliclibrary.org. *Libr Dir,* Matthew Kolman; Staff 3 (MLS 1, Non-MLS 2)
Pop 7,600; Circ 47,000
Library Holdings: Audiobooks 91; Bks on Deafness & Sign Lang 12; Braille Volumes 38; DVDs 732; High Interest/Low Vocabulary Bk Vols 15; Large Print Bks 340; Bk Titles 41,800; Bk Vols 42,777; Per Subs 80; Spec Interest Per Sub 4; Videos 2,077
Automation Activity & Vendor Info: (Cataloging) Book Systems; (Circulation) Book Systems
Wireless access
Function: 24/7 Electronic res, 24/7 Online cat, Accelerated reader prog, Adult bk club, Audiobks on Playaways & MP3, Bks on CD, Children's prog, Computers for patron use, Electronic databases & coll, Family literacy, Free DVD rentals, ILL available, Internet access, Magazines, Movies, Online cat, OverDrive digital audio bks, Prog for adults, Prog for children & young adult, Scanner, Wheelchair accessible
Partic in Northeast Texas Digital Consortium
Open Tues-Sat 10-7
Friends of the Library Group

SWEETWATER

P SWEETWATER COUNTY-CITY LIBRARY*, 206 Elm St, 79556. SAN 316-7860. Tel: 325-235-4978. FAX: 325-235-4979. E-mail: swaterlib@sbcglobal.net. Web Site: www.sweetwaterlibrary.org. *Dir,* Erica Caballero
Founded 1907. Pop 16,744; Circ 53,500
Library Holdings: e-books 150; Bk Titles 38,597; Per Subs 30
Automation Activity & Vendor Info: (Cataloging) LibLime; (Circulation) LibLime
Wireless access
Partic in Partners Library Action Network
Open Mon 1-6, Tues-Fri 9-5, Sat 9-1
Friends of the Library Group

J TEXAS STATE TECHNICAL COLLEGE*, Learning Resource Center, 300 Homer K Taylor Dr, 79556. SAN 316-7879. Tel: 325-235-7406. FAX: 325-738-3341. Web Site: www.tstc.edu. *Libr Tech,* Maria Lopez; E-mail: maria.lopez@tstc.edu; Staff 1 (MLS 1)
Library Holdings: e-books 8,100; Bk Titles 11,405; Bk Vols 12,495; Per Subs 22
Subject Interests: Computer maintenance, Computer sci, Electronics, Robotics, Telecommunication
Wireless access
Publications: New Titles List (Monthly)
Open Mon-Fri 8-5

TAFT

P TAFT PUBLIC LIBRARY*, 501 Green Ave, 78390. (Mail add: PO Box 416, 78390-0416), SAN 316-7895. Tel: 361-528-3512. FAX: 361-528-3515. Web Site: taft.ploud.net, www.cityoftaft.us/library. *Librn,* Georgina Silvas; E-mail: gsilvas@cityoftaft.net
Pop 5,117; Circ 13,515
Library Holdings: Bk Vols 15,900; Per Subs 10
Special Collections: Texana-Spanish Coll
Automation Activity & Vendor Info: (Cataloging) Follett Software; (Circulation) Follett Software
Open Mon-Fri 8-12 & 1-5
Friends of the Library Group

TAHOKA

P CITY COUNTY LIBRARY*, 1717 Main St, 79373. (Mail add: PO Box 1018, 79373-1018), SAN 376-4273. Tel: 806-561-4050. FAX: 806-561-4051. E-mail: tahokalibry@yahoo.com. *Dir,* Cissy Webster; Staff 1 (Non-MLS 1)
Pop 5,500; Circ 11,000
Library Holdings: Bk Vols 10,000

Automation Activity & Vendor Info: (Cataloging) LibLime; (Circulation) LibLime
Wireless access
Function: Bks on cassette, Bks on CD, Children's prog, Computer training, Computers for patron use, Electronic databases & coll, Free DVD rentals, Homebound delivery serv, ILL available, Mail & tel request accepted, Notary serv, Online cat, Photocopying/Printing, Preschool reading prog, Ref serv available, Story hour, Summer reading prog, Tax forms, Telephone ref, VHS videos, Wheelchair accessible
Partic in Partners Library Action Network
Open Mon-Thurs 9-12 & 1-6, Fri 9-12 & 1-5

TAYLOR

P TAYLOR PUBLIC LIBRARY*, 801 Vance St, 76574. SAN 316-7909. Tel: 512-352-3434, 512-365-2235. FAX: 512-352-8080. Web Site: tx-taylor4.civicplus.com/25/Library. *Dir,* Karen Ellis; E-mail: karen.ellis@taylortx.gov; Staff 7 (MLS 2, Non-MLS 5)
Founded 1899. Pop 15,014; Circ 91,408
Library Holdings: AV Mats 755; CDs 425; DVDs 661; Bk Vols 46,115; Per Subs 39; Videos 377
Special Collections: Taylor Local History
Automation Activity & Vendor Info: (Cataloging) Biblionix; (Circulation) Biblionix
Wireless access
Function: Archival coll, Children's prog, Computers for patron use, E-Reserves, Electronic databases & coll, Holiday prog, ILL available, Microfiche/film & reading machines, Online cat, Photocopying/Printing, Prog for adults, Prog for children & young adult, Ref serv available, Senior outreach, Spanish lang bks, Spoken cassettes & CDs, Spoken cassettes & DVDs, Story hour, Summer reading prog, Tax forms, Teen prog, VHS videos, Wheelchair accessible
Partic in Partners Library Action Network
Open Mon & Thurs 9-8, Tues, Wed & Fri 9-6, Sat 9-2
Friends of the Library Group

TEAGUE

P TEAGUE PUBLIC LIBRARY*, 400 Main St, 75860. SAN 316-7917. Tel: 254-739-3311. FAX: 254-739-3118. E-mail: librarian@cityofteaguetx.com. Web Site: www.teaguelibrary.org. *Dir,* Melissa Satterwhite; Staff 3 (Non-MLS 3)
Pop 10,086; Circ 52,085
Library Holdings: Bk Titles 26,853; Bk Vols 28,978; Per Subs 30
Special Collections: Texas History Coll
Automation Activity & Vendor Info: (Cataloging) Biblionix; (Circulation) Biblionix
Wireless access
Partic in Partners Library Action Network
Open Mon-Fri 8:30-5:30
Friends of the Library Group

TEMPLE

S CZECH HERITAGE MUSEUM & GENEALOGY CENTER LIBRARY*, 119 W French Ave, 76501. SAN 327-7984. Tel: 254-899-2935. FAX: 254-742-0294. E-mail: czechheritagemuseum@gmail.com. Web Site: czechheritagemuseum.org. *Library Contact,* Kenny Lange
Founded 2000
Library Holdings: Bk Titles 23,000
Special Collections: Czech Language Coll
Subject Interests: Fiction, Genealogy, Geog, Hist
Wireless access
Function: Ref serv available
Open Tues-Sat 10-4
Friends of the Library Group

GM DEPARTMENT OF VETERANS AFFAIRS*, Central Texas Veterans Health Care System Library System, 1901 Veterans Memorial Dr, 14LIB-T, 76504. SAN 362-3556. Tel: 254-743-0607. Circulation Tel: 254-743-0606. Toll Free Tel: 800-423-2111, Ext 40606 (TX only). FAX: 254-743-0183. Web Site: www.centraltexas.va.gov. *Supv Librn,* Roger Hunceker; E-mail: roger.hunceker@va.gov; *Libr Tech,* Terence Ashton; E-mail: terence.ashton@va.gov; *Libr Tech,* Valentino Head; E-mail: valentino.head@va.gov; Staff 3 (Non-MLS 3)
Founded 1942
Library Holdings: e-journals 300; Electronic Media & Resources 10; Large Print Bks 100; Bk Titles 100; Per Subs 35
Special Collections: Local History Coll
Subject Interests: Allied health, Med, Nursing
Automation Activity & Vendor Info: (Cataloging) Ex Libris Group; (Circulation) Ex Libris Group; (OPAC) Ex Libris Group
Wireless access
Function: Electronic databases & coll, Govt ref serv, Health sci info serv, ILL available, Internet access, Learning ctr, Online ref, Orientations, Photocopying/Printing, Res libr, Telephone ref
Publications: New Additions List (Accession list)
Open Mon-Fri 7-4:15
Restriction: Non-circulating to the pub

M SCOTT & WHITE HEALTHCARE*, Richard D Haines Medical Library, 2401 S 31st, MS-AG-302, 76508. SAN 316-7941. Tel: 254-724-2228. FAX: 254-724-4229. E-mail: medicallibrary@bswhealth.org. Web Site: www.bswhealth.med/education/Pages/medical-library.aspx. *Dir,* Julie Bolin; Staff 7 (MLS 5, Non-MLS 2)
Founded 1919
Library Holdings: e-books 55,000; e-journals 30,000; Bk Titles 4,000; Per Subs 300
Special Collections: Nursing (Laura Cole Coll)
Automation Activity & Vendor Info: (Cataloging) Ex Libris Group; (Circulation) Ex Libris Group
Wireless access
Partic in National Network of Libraries of Medicine Region 3; TAMU Consortium of Med Librs
Restriction: Med staff only

J TEMPLE COLLEGE, Hubert M Dawson Library, 2600 S First St, 76504. SAN 316-795X. Tel: 254-298-8426. FAX: 254-298-8430. E-mail: library@templejc.edu. Web Site: www.templejc.edu/resources/library. *Libr Dir,* Brian Kemp; Tel: 254-298-8424, E-mail: brian.kemp@templejc.edu; *Librn,* Mia Wilson; Tel: 254-298-8622, E-mail: mia.wilson@templejc.edu; Staff 5 (MLS 3, Non-MLS 2)
Founded 1926. Enrl 2,500; Fac 152; Highest Degree: Associate
Library Holdings: e-books 515,288; e-journals 190,969; Electronic Media & Resources 381,190; Bk Titles 49,091; Per Subs 7
Automation Activity & Vendor Info: (Acquisitions) OCLC Worldshare Management Services; (Cataloging) OCLC Worldshare Management Services; (Circulation) OCLC Worldshare Management Services; (Course Reserve) OCLC Worldshare Management Services; (ILL) OCLC WorldShare Interlibrary Loan; (OPAC) OCLC Worldshare Management Services; (Serials) OCLC Worldshare Management Services
Wireless access
Partic in Amigos Library Services, Inc
Open Mon-Thurs 7:45am-9pm, Fri 8-4, Sun 2-6 (Fall); Mon & Thurs 7:45-6, Tues & Wed 7am-9pm, Fri 8-4 (Summer)

P TEMPLE PUBLIC LIBRARY*, 100 W Adams Ave, 76501-7641. SAN 316-7968. Tel: 254-298-5555. Circulation Tel: 254-298-5556. Reference Tel: 254-298-5702. FAX: 254-298-5328. Web Site: www.youseemore.com/templepl. *Libr Dir,* Natalie McAdams; *Youth Serv Librn,* Erin Gaines; Tel: 254-298-5557, E-mail: egaines@templetx.us; *Adult Serv Supvr,* Jackie Cundieff; Tel: 254-298-5333, E-mail: jcundieff@templetx.us; *Circ Supvr,* Mary Garza; E-mail: mgarza@temple.tx.us; *Outreach Coordr,* Cassi Duarte; Tel: 254-298-5295, E-mail: ccoates@templetx.us; Staff 28.4 (MLS 4.5, Non-MLS 23.9)
Founded 1900. Pop 60,118; Circ 448,328
Library Holdings: Audiobooks 6,992; Electronic Media & Resources 54; Bk Titles 130,641; Bk Vols 150,546; Per Subs 202; Videos 9,206
Special Collections: Adult Education; Career & Job Information; Genealogy Coll; Large-Print Coll; Local Authors Coll
Subject Interests: Temple hist
Automation Activity & Vendor Info: (Acquisitions) TLC (The Library Corporation); (Cataloging) TLC (The Library Corporation); (Circulation) TLC (The Library Corporation); (OPAC) TLC (The Library Corporation)
Wireless access
Function: Adult bk club, AV serv, Bk reviews (Group), Bks on cassette, Bks on CD, CD-ROM, Children's prog, Computers for patron use, E-Reserves, Electronic databases & coll, Home delivery & serv to seniorr ctr & nursing homes, ILL available, Internet access, Magnifiers for reading, Mail & tel request accepted, Music CDs, Online cat, Outreach serv, Photocopying/Printing, Preschool outreach, Prog for children & young adult, Ref serv available, Senior outreach, Spoken cassettes & CDs, Spoken cassettes & DVDs, Story hour, Summer & winter reading prog, Summer reading prog, Tax forms, Teen prog, Telephone ref, VHS videos, Wheelchair accessible
Partic in Amigos Library Services, Inc; Partners Library Action Network; TexSHARE - Texas State Library & Archives Commission
Special Services for the Deaf - TDD equip
Special Services for the Blind - Audio mat; BiFolkal kits; Bks on cassette; Bks on CD; Computer with voice synthesizer for visually impaired persons; Extensive large print coll; Large print bks; Magnifiers; Recorded bks; Text reader
Open Mon-Thurs 10-9, Fri 10-6, Sat 10-5, Sun 1-9
Friends of the Library Group
Bookmobiles: 1. Librn, Diane Wolfe. Bk titles 3,809

TERRELL

P RITER C HULSEY PUBLIC LIBRARY*, 301 N Rockwall, 75160-2618. SAN 316-7976. Tel: 972-551-6663. FAX: 972-551-6662. E-mail: library@cityofterrell.org. Web Site: www.hulseypubliclibrary.org. *Dir,*

Rebecca Anderson; E-mail: randerson@cityofterrell.org; Staff 3 (MLS 2, Non-MLS 1)
Founded 1904
Library Holdings: Bk Titles 62,481; Bk Vols 69,160; Per Subs 84; Talking Bks 1,945; Videos 2,187
Subject Interests: Genealogy, Kaufman county hist
Automation Activity & Vendor Info: (Cataloging) Innovative Interfaces, Inc; (Circulation) Innovative Interfaces, Inc; (ILL) OCLC; (OPAC) Innovative Interfaces, Inc
Wireless access
Function: Adult bk club, Adult literacy prog, Art exhibits, Art programs, Audio & video playback equip for onsite use, Audiobks on Playaways & MP3, Audiobks via web, Bilingual assistance for Spanish patrons, Bk club(s), Bks on CD, Children's prog, Citizenship assistance, Computer training, Computers for patron use, Digital talking bks, Electronic databases & coll, Free DVD rentals, Holiday prog, Home delivery & serv to seniorr ctr & nursing homes, Homework prog, ILL available, Internet access, Magazines, Mail & tel request accepted, Meeting rooms, Microfiche/film & reading machines, Movies, Online cat, Online info literacy tutorials on the web & in blackboard, Orientations, OverDrive digital audio bks, Photocopying/Printing, Preschool outreach, Printer for laptops & handheld devices, Prog for adults, Prog for children & young adult, Ref & res, Scanner, Senior computer classes, Spanish lang bks, STEM programs, Story hour, Summer & winter reading prog, Summer reading prog, Tax forms, Teen prog, Telephone ref, Wheelchair accessible
Open Mon & Tues 10-8, Wed & Thurs 10-6, Fri 1-5, Sun Noon-4
Friends of the Library Group

C SOUTHWESTERN CHRISTIAN COLLEGE*, Doris Johnson Library, 200 Bowser St, 75160. (Mail add: PO Box 10, 75160-9002), SAN 316-7984. Tel: 972-524-3341, Ext 109. FAX: 972-563-7133. Web Site: www.swcc.edu/library.html.
Founded 1948. Enrl 206; Fac 24; Highest Degree: Doctorate
Library Holdings: AV Mats 5,170; CDs 41; Electronic Media & Resources 1,058; Microforms 31,800; Bk Vols 26,000; Per Subs 190; Talking Bks 6; Videos 141
Special Collections: African-American Studies Coll; Bible & Religious Studies Coll
Subject Interests: African-Am studies, Arts
Automation Activity & Vendor Info: (Acquisitions) SirsiDynix; (Cataloging) SirsiDynix; (Circulation) SirsiDynix; (OPAC) SirsiDynix
Wireless access
Publications: Library Handbook
Partic in TexSHARE - Texas State Library & Archives Commission
Open Mon, Tues, Thurs & Fri 8am-9pm, Wed 8-5

TEXARKANA

J TEXARKANA COLLEGE*, Palmer Memorial Library, 1024 Tucker St, 75501. SAN 316-8018. Tel: 903-832-3215. E-mail: library@texarkanacollege.edu. Web Site: www.texarkanacollege.edu/library. *Dir, Libr Serv,* Dr Tonja Mackey; *Librn,* Emily Ransom; E-mail: emily.ransom@texarkanacollege.edu; Staff 8 (MLS 1, Non-MLS 7)
Founded 1927. Enrl 3,671; Fac 205; Highest Degree: Associate
Library Holdings: Microforms 216,300; Bk Titles 38,837; Bk Vols 50,495; Per Subs 490
Special Collections: Interstate Commerce (Transportation Coll); Rare Books Coll. US Document Depository
Subject Interests: Nursing
Automation Activity & Vendor Info: (Acquisitions) Innovative Interfaces, Inc; (Cataloging) Innovative Interfaces, Inc; (Circulation) Innovative Interfaces, Inc; (Course Reserve) Innovative Interfaces, Inc; (ILL) Innovative Interfaces, Inc; (Media Booking) Innovative Interfaces, Inc; (OPAC) Innovative Interfaces, Inc; (Serials) Innovative Interfaces, Inc
Wireless access
Partic in Amigos Library Services, Inc; OCLC Online Computer Library Center, Inc; Tex State Libr Communications Network; TexSHARE - Texas State Library & Archives Commission
Open Mon-Thurs 7:30am-9pm, Fri 7:30-4, Sun 2-9

S TEXARKANA MUSEUMS SYSTEM*, Wilbur Smith Research Library & Archives, 219 N State Line Ave, 75501. SAN 316-8026. Tel: 903-793-4831. E-mail: boardpresident@texarkanamuseums.org, morh@texarkanamuseums.org. Web Site: texarkanamuseum.org/museum. *Exec Dir,* Emily Tarr
Founded 1971
Library Holdings: Bk Vols 1,400; Per Subs 10
Special Collections: City Directories Coll; Local Architectural Blue Prints Coll; Local Map Coll; Regional Photograph Coll; Wilbur Smith Coll. Oral History
Subject Interests: Antiques, Arkansas, State
Wireless access
Function: Archival coll, Bus archives, Photocopying/Printing, Res libr
Restriction: Non-circulating to the pub, Open by appt only

P TEXARKANA PUBLIC LIBRARY*, 600 W Third St, 75501-5054. SAN 316-8034. Tel: 903-794-2149. FAX: 903-794-2140. E-mail: txarkpublib@txar-publib.org. Web Site: txark.ent.sirsi.net. *Dir,* Jennifer Strayhorn; E-mail: jstrayhorn@txar-publib.org; Staff 12 (MLS 3, Non-MLS 9)
Founded 1925. Pop 62,200; Circ 159,692
Library Holdings: AV Mats 5,394; Bk Titles 74,542; Bk Vols 89,651; Per Subs 139; Videos 6,804
Special Collections: Genealogy Coll
Subject Interests: Genealogy
Automation Activity & Vendor Info: (Acquisitions) SirsiDynix; (Cataloging) SirsiDynix; (Circulation) SirsiDynix; (OPAC) SirsiDynix
Wireless access
Function: AV serv, CD-ROM, Computer training, Equip loans & repairs, ILL available, Learning ctr, Music CDs, Photocopying/Printing
Partic in Amigos Library Services, Inc
Special Services for the Deaf - TTY equip
Special Services for the Blind - Closed circuit TV; Reader equip
Open Mon-Wed 10-8, Thurs & Fri 10-5
Friends of the Library Group

C TEXAS A&M UNIVERSITY-TEXARKANA*, John F Moss Library, 7101 University Ave, 75503. SAN 321-2378. Tel: 903-223-3100. FAX: 903-334-6695. Web Site: www.tamut.edu/library-services. *Dir,* Teri Stover; E-mail: teri.stover@tamut.edu; *Admin Assoc,* Barbara Mackey; Tel: 903-223-3092, E-mail: barbara.mackey@tamut.edu; *Digital Serv Librn, Electronic Serv Librn,* Olivia Garcia; Tel: 903-223-3148, E-mail: olivia.poulton@tamut.edu; *Circ, Libr Assoc I,* Jeanette L Mitchell; E-mail: jeanette.mitchell@tamut.edu; *Cat, Libr Spec II,* Jenny Pool; Tel: 903-334-6696, E-mail: jenny.pool@tamut.edu; Staff 13 (MLS 5, Non-MLS 8)
Founded 1971. Enrl 1,637; Fac 63; Highest Degree: Doctorate
Library Holdings: e-books 70,000; Electronic Media & Resources 150; Microforms 132,220; Bk Titles 130,000; Bk Vols 145,000; Per Subs 404
Special Collections: US Document Depository
Automation Activity & Vendor Info: (Acquisitions) Innovative Interfaces, Inc; (Cataloging) Innovative Interfaces, Inc; (Circulation) Innovative Interfaces, Inc; (Course Reserve) Innovative Interfaces, Inc; (ILL) Innovative Interfaces, Inc; (Media Booking) Innovative Interfaces, Inc; (OPAC) Innovative Interfaces, Inc; (Serials) Innovative Interfaces, Inc
Wireless access
Partic in Amigos Library Services, Inc; OCLC Online Computer Library Center, Inc; Tex State Libr Communications Network; TexSHARE - Texas State Library & Archives Commission
Open Mon-Thurs 7:30am-10pm, Fri 7:30-5, Sat 10-6, Sun 1-9
Friends of the Library Group

TEXAS CITY

J COLLEGE OF THE MAINLAND LIBRARY*, 1200 Amburn Rd, 77591-2499. SAN 316-8042. Tel: 409-938-8471. Interlibrary Loan Service Tel: 409-933-8448. FAX: 409-938-8918. Web Site: libguides.com.edu. *Libr Dir,* Kathryn Park; E-mail: Kpark@com.edu; Staff 2 (MLS 2)
Founded 1967. Enrl 3,700; Highest Degree: Associate
Library Holdings: e-books 44,098; Bk Titles 43,640; Bk Vols 50,615; Per Subs 183
Special Collections: Texana
Automation Activity & Vendor Info: (Acquisitions) Ex Libris Group; (Cataloging) Ex Libris Group; (Circulation) Ex Libris Group; (OPAC) Ex Libris Group
Wireless access
Partic in Amigos Library Services, Inc
Open Mon-Thurs 7:15am-8:15pm, Fri 7:15-5, Sat 9-1

P MOORE MEMORIAL PUBLIC LIBRARY*, 1701 Ninth Ave N, 77590. SAN 316-8069. Tel: 409-643-5977. Circulation Tel: 409-643-5975. FAX: 409-948-1106. E-mail: library@texascitytx.gov. Web Site: www.texascity-library.org. *Dir,* Cheryl Loewen; Tel: 409-643-5974, E-mail: cloewen@texas-city-tx.org; *Ch,* Carol Hill de Santos; Tel: 409-643-5966, E-mail: chill@texas-city-tx.org; *Syst Librn,* Lesley Ragsdale; Tel: 409-643-5964, E-mail: lragsdale@texas-city-tx.org; *YA Librn,* Position Currently Open; Staff 6 (MLS 3, Non-MLS 3)
Founded 1928. Pop 50,565; Circ 212,000
Library Holdings: Bk Vols 140,000; Per Subs 180
Special Collections: Oral History
Subject Interests: Genealogy, Texana
Automation Activity & Vendor Info: (Cataloging) Inlex; (Cataloging) SirsiDynix; (Circulation) Inlex; (Circulation) SirsiDynix; (OPAC) Inlex; (OPAC) SirsiDynix
Wireless access
Mem of Galveston County Library System
Open Mon-Wed 9-9, Thurs & Fri 9-6, Sat 10-4
Friends of the Library Group

TEXLINE

P TEXLINE PUBLIC LIBRARY, 517 S Second St, 79087. (Mail add: PO Box 356, 79087-0356), SAN 323-469X. Tel: 806-362-4849.
Founded 1980. Pop 529; Circ 1,275
Library Holdings: Large Print Bks 48; Bk Titles 1,559; Bk Vols 1,580
Wireless access
Function: Summer reading prog
Open Mon-Fri 8-12 & 1-5

THE COLONY

P THE COLONY PUBLIC LIBRARY*, 6800 Main St, 75056-1133. SAN 376-4605. Tel: 972-625-1900. Circulation Tel: 972-625-1900, Ext 2. Reference Tel: 972-625-1900, Ext 3. Administration Tel: 925-625-1900, Ext 7. FAX: 972-624-2245. E-mail: reference@thecolonypl.org. Web Site: www.thecolonytx.gov/404/Library. *Dir,* Megan Charters; Tel: 972-624-3184, E-mail: mcharters@thecolonypl.org; Staff 6 (MLS 6)
Founded 1982. Pop 47,356; Circ 140,661
Library Holdings: AV Mats 8,081; e-books 5,590; Electronic Media & Resources 3,419; Bk Titles 64,263; Bk Vols 73,588; Per Subs 102
Special Collections: Local History, genealogies of original settlers, bks, maps, photog & doc
Automation Activity & Vendor Info: (Cataloging) Auto-Graphics, Inc; (Circulation) Auto-Graphics, Inc; (OPAC) Auto-Graphics, Inc
Wireless access
Function: Adult bk club, Art exhibits, Audiobks via web, Bilingual assistance for Spanish patrons, Bk club(s), Bks on CD, CD-ROM, Children's prog, Computer training, Computers for patron use, Digital talking bks, Distance learning, E-Reserves, Electronic databases & coll, Family literacy, Free DVD rentals, Holiday prog, Homework prog, ILL available, Internet access, Magazines, Magnifiers for reading, Mail & tel request accepted, Mango lang, Microfiche/film & reading machines, Movies, Music CDs, Online cat, OverDrive digital audio bks, Photocopying/Printing, Preschool outreach, Preschool reading prog, Prog for adults, Prog for children & young adult, Ref serv available, Scanner, Spanish lang bks, Story hour, Study rm, Summer reading prog, Tax forms, Teen prog, Telephone ref, VHS videos, Wheelchair accessible, Workshops
Partic in Partners Library Action Network
Special Services for the Deaf - Bks on deafness & sign lang; High interest/low vocabulary bks
Special Services for the Blind - Bks on CD; Copier with enlargement capabilities; Large print bks; Low vision equip; Magnifiers; Playaways (bks on MP3)
Open Tues & Thurs 10-9, Wed 1-9, Fri & Sat 10-5, Sun 1-5
Friends of the Library Group

THROCKMORTON

P THE DEPOT PUBLIC LIBRARY*, 120 E Chestnut St, 76483. (Mail add: PO Box 6, 76483-0006). Tel: 940-849-3076. FAX: 940-849-0097. E-mail: depotlibrary@yahoo.com. Web Site: depot.ploud.net. *Dir,* Linda Northam
Pop 730; Circ 3,070
Library Holdings: Bk Vols 9,000
Automation Activity & Vendor Info: (Cataloging) Biblionix; (Circulation) Biblionix
Wireless access
Open Mon & Wed 9-1, Tues 9-1 & 3-6, Thurs 8:30-4:30

TRINITY

P BLANCHE K WERNER PUBLIC LIBRARY*, 203 Prospect Dr, 75862. (Mail add: PO Box 1168, 75862-1168), SAN 316-8093. Tel: 936-594-2087. FAX: 936-594-9513. E-mail: plibrary@valornet.com. Web Site: trinity.ploud.net. *Dir,* Sophia L Evans; E-mail: bkwld@valornet.com; *Asst Dir,* Joy Jackson; Staff 2.3 (Non-MLS 2.3)
Founded 1961. Pop 12,966; Circ 26,000
Library Holdings: Large Print Bks 2,605; Bk Titles 25,760; Bk Vols 27,015; Per Subs 12; Talking Bks 800; Videos 1,309
Automation Activity & Vendor Info: (Acquisitions) Follett Software; (Cataloging) Follett Software; (Circulation) Follett Software; (OPAC) Follett Software
Wireless access
Open Mon-Fri 1-6, Sat 10-1
Friends of the Library Group

TROUP

P CAMERON J JARVIS TROUP MUNICIPAL LIBRARY*, 102 S Georgia, 75789-2020. (Mail add: PO Box 721, 75789-0721), SAN 375-5568. Tel: 903-842-3101. FAX: 903-842-2890. E-mail: tlibrary@trouptx.com. Web Site: www.trouplibrary.org. *Dir,* Melanie Brumit; Staff 7 (MLS 1, Non-MLS 6)
Founded 1992. Pop 6,800
Library Holdings: Bk Vols 23,081; Per Subs 10
Automation Activity & Vendor Info: (Cataloging) Book Systems; (Circulation) Book Systems; (OPAC) Book Systems
Wireless access
Open Tues, Wed & Fri 1-5, Thurs 3-7, Sat 9-1
Friends of the Library Group

TULIA

P SWISHER COUNTY LIBRARY*, 127 SW Second St, 79088. SAN 316-8107. Tel: 806-995-3447. FAX: 806-995-2206. E-mail: swishercountylibrary@gmail.com. Web Site: www.swishercolib.org. *Libr Dir,* Terri McCasland; Staff 2 (Non-MLS 2)
Founded 1922. Pop 7,008
Library Holdings: Bk Titles 20,462; Bk Vols 27,597; Per Subs 30
Special Collections: Texana Coll
Automation Activity & Vendor Info: (Cataloging) SirsiDynix; (Circulation) SirsiDynix
Wireless access
Function: Bks on CD, Computers for patron use, Homebound delivery serv, ILL available, Internet access, Magazines, Online cat, Photocopying/Printing, Spanish lang bks
Partic in Harrington Library Consortium
Open Mon 10-7, Tues & Wed 9-6, Thurs & Fri 9-5

TURKEY

P TURKEY PUBLIC LIBRARY*, 602 Lyles Ave, 79261. (Mail add: PO Box 415, 79261-0415). Tel: 806-423-1033. FAX: 806-423-1221. E-mail: cityofturkey@gmail.com. *Library Contact,* Stephanie Hobbs
Pop 400
Library Holdings: Audiobooks 28; Bks on Deafness & Sign Lang 1; Braille Volumes 1; Large Print Bks 25; Bk Vols 7,518; Videos 31
Wireless access
Open Mon-Fri 8-12 & 1-5

TYLER

M EAST TEXAS MEDICAL CENTER*, Bell-Marsh Memorial Library, 1000 S Beckham Ave, 75701. SAN 316-8131. Tel: 903-531-8685. FAX: 903-535-6464. Web Site: uthealtheasttexas.com. *Dir,* Kelsey Goughnour; E-mail: kelsey.goughnour@uthet.com
Founded 1951
Library Holdings: Bk Titles 725; Per Subs 7
Subject Interests: Med
Wireless access
Restriction: Med staff only, Not open to pub

P NOONDAY COMMUNITY LIBRARY*, 16662 CR 196, 75703. Tel: 903-939-0540. FAX: 903-939-0540. E-mail: noondaylibrary@gmail.com. *Librn,* Vicki Malone
Circ 5,266
Library Holdings: AV Mats 300; Bk Titles 12,443; Talking Bks 350
Automation Activity & Vendor Info: (Acquisitions) LibraryWorld, Inc; (Cataloging) LibraryWorld, Inc; (Circulation) LibraryWorld, Inc; (Course Reserve) LibraryWorld, Inc; (ILL) LibraryWorld, Inc; (OPAC) LibraryWorld, Inc
Open Tues-Fri 10-3

C TEXAS COLLEGE*, D R Glass Library, 2404 N Grand Ave, 75702-4500. SAN 316-814X. Tel: 903-593-8311, Ext 2349. FAX: 903-526-4426. Web Site: www.texascollege.edu/office-of-bracademic-affairs/library. *Dir, Libr Serv,* Linda Simmons-Henry; E-mail: lsimmons-henry@texascollege.edu; Staff 2 (MLS 2)
Founded 1894. Enrl 825; Fac 89; Highest Degree: Bachelor
Library Holdings: Bk Titles 200,000; Bk Vols 233,000; Per Subs 150
Subject Interests: African-Am studies
Automation Activity & Vendor Info: (Acquisitions) TLC (The Library Corporation); (Cataloging) TLC (The Library Corporation); (Circulation) TLC (The Library Corporation); (Course Reserve) TLC (The Library Corporation); (ILL) TLC (The Library Corporation); (Media Booking) TLC (The Library Corporation); (OPAC) TLC (The Library Corporation); (Serials) TLC (The Library Corporation)
Wireless access
Partic in TexSHARE - Texas State Library & Archives Commission
Open Mon-Thurs 8am-10pm, Fri 8-5, Sun 3-8

J TYLER JUNIOR COLLEGE*, Vaughn Library, 1327 S Baxter St, 75701. (Mail add: PO Box 9020, 75711-9020), SAN 316-8174. Tel: 903-510-2502, 903-510-2503. Reference Tel: 903-510-3149. Administration Tel: 903-510-2759. Information Services Tel: 903-510-2501. Toll Free Tel: 800-687-5680, Ext 2503. Web Site: www.tjc.edu/library. *Dir, Learning Commons,* Maggie Ruelle; E-mail: mrue@tjc.edu; *Library Systems Admin,* Daniel McKenzie; Tel: 903-510-2501, E-mail: dmck@tjc.edu; *Archives Librn,* Robin Insalaco; Tel: 903-510-2549, E-mail: rins@tjc.edu; *Coll Develop Librn,* Lilly Smith; Tel: 903-510-2645, E-mail: lsmi2@tjc.edu;

Outreach Serv Librn, Madeleine Nittmo; Tel: 903-510-2759, E-mail: madeleine.nittmo@tjc.edu; *Re/Ser Librn,* Leif Pierson; E-mail: lpie@tjc.edu; *Digitization Projects Mgr,* Kerry Johnson; Tel: 903-510-2309, E-mail: kjoh2@tjc.edu; Staff 29 (MLS 5, Non-MLS 24)
Founded 1926. Enrl 12,000; Fac 600; Highest Degree: Bachelor
Library Holdings: Bk Vols 89,000; Per Subs 295
Special Collections: Allied Health Sciences Coll; Graphic Novels; Legal Assistant Coll; Manga; Texas History Coll; Young Adult
Automation Activity & Vendor Info: (Cataloging) SirsiDynix; (Circulation) SirsiDynix; (Course Reserve) SirsiDynix; (ILL) OCLC; (OPAC) SirsiDynix; (Serials) SirsiDynix
Wireless access
Function: 24/7 Electronic res, 24/7 Online cat, Archival coll, Art exhibits, Audio & video playback equip for onsite use, Bks on CD, Computers for patron use, Distance learning, Electronic databases & coll, Health sci info serv, ILL available, Internet access, Learning ctr, Mail & tel request accepted, Online cat, Online info literacy tutorials on the web & in blackboard, Online ref, Orientations, Outreach serv, Photocopying/Printing, Ref serv available, Scanner, Telephone ref, VHS videos, Wheelchair accessible
Partic in Amigos Library Services, Inc; TexSHARE - Texas State Library & Archives Commission
Open Mon-Thurs 7:30am-11:30pm, Fri 7:30-5, Sat 10-2, Sun 1-5
Restriction: 24-hr pass syst for students only, Access at librarian's discretion, ID required to use computers (Ltd hrs), In-house use for visitors, Limited access for the pub, Open to pub for ref & circ; with some limitations, Open to students, fac & staff, Photo ID required for access, Pub use on premises

S TYLER MUSEUM OF ART LIBRARY*, 1300 S Mahon, 75701. SAN 316-8182. Tel: 903-595-1001. FAX: 903-595-1055. E-mail: info@tylermuseum.org. Web Site: tylermuseum.org. *Exec Dir,* Caleb M Bell; E-mail: cbell@tylermuseum.org; *Educ Mgr,* Rachel Anthony; E-mail: ranthony@tylermuseum.org
Founded 1971
Library Holdings: Bk Vols 3,000; Spec Interest Per Sub 3
Subject Interests: Archit, Art, Design
Publications: Catalogs on selected exhibitions organized by Tyler Museum
Open Tues-Sat 10-5, Sun 1-5
Restriction: Non-circulating

P TYLER PUBLIC LIBRARY*, 201 S College Ave, 75702-7381. SAN 316-8115. Tel: 903-593-7323. FAX: 903-531-1329. Web Site: library.cityoftyler.org. *City Librn,* Mary Vernau; E-mail: cchaney@tylertexas.com; *Ref Librn,* Aleya Stone; *Res Serv Librn,* Pauline Eng; *Youth Serv Librn,* Linda Gray; Staff 4 (MLS 4)
Founded 1899. Pop 99,323
Special Collections: Local & Family History Coll
Automation Activity & Vendor Info: (Acquisitions) Innovative Interfaces, Inc; (Cataloging) Innovative Interfaces, Inc; (Circulation) Innovative Interfaces, Inc; (Course Reserve) Innovative Interfaces, Inc; (ILL) OCLC WorldShare Interlibrary Loan; (Media Booking) Innovative Interfaces, Inc; (OPAC) Innovative Interfaces, Inc; (Serials) Innovative Interfaces, Inc
Wireless access
Function: Accelerated reader prog, Adult bk club, Art exhibits, Audiobks via web, AV serv, Bks on cassette, Bks on CD, CD-ROM, Children's prog, Computers for patron use, E-Readers, Electronic databases & coll, Free DVD rentals, Genealogy discussion group, ILL available, Magazines, Magnifiers for reading, Mail & tel request accepted, Microfiche/film & reading machines, Music CDs, Online cat, OverDrive digital audio bks, Photocopying/Printing, Preschool outreach, Preschool reading prog, Prog for adults, Prog for children & young adult, Ref serv available, Spanish lang bks, Spoken cassettes & CDs, Spoken cassettes & DVDs, Story hour, Summer reading prog, Teen prog, Telephone ref, Wheelchair accessible
Publications: Calendar (Bimonthly)
Partic in Northeast Texas Digital Consortium
Special Services for the Blind - Accessible computers; Assistive/Adapted tech devices, equip & products; Bks on CD; Braille bks; Closed circuit TV magnifier; Computer with voice synthesizer for visually impaired persons; Copier with enlargement capabilities; Internet workstation with adaptive software; Large print bks; Playaways (bks on MP3); Talking bk serv referral
Open Mon-Thurs 10-7, Fri 9-6, Sat 10-5, Sun 1-5
Restriction: Non-resident fee
Friends of the Library Group

C UNIVERSITY OF TEXAS AT TYLER LIBRARY*, Robert R Muntz Library, 3900 University Blvd, 75799. SAN 316-8158. Tel: 903-566-7342. Interlibrary Loan Service Tel: 903-566-7396. Reference Tel: 903-566-7343. Administration Tel: 903-566-7161. E-mail: library@uttyler.edu. Web Site: uttyler.edu/library. *Dean of Libr,* Rebecca McKay; E-mail: rejohnson@uttyler.edu; *Head, Electronic Res & Coll Develop,* Margo Duncan; Tel: 903-566-7174, E-mail: mduncan@uttyler.edu; *Univ Archivist,* Terra Gullings; Tel: 903-565-5849, E-mail: tgullings@uttyler.edu; Staff 19 (MLS 9, Non-MLS 10)
Founded 1973. Enrl 8,483; Fac 400; Highest Degree: Doctorate
Special Collections: State Document Depository
Wireless access
Partic in Amigos Library Services, Inc; TexSHARE - Texas State Library & Archives Commission
Open Mon-Thurs 7:30am-2am, Fri 7:30-5, Sat 9-6, Sun 1pm-2am

CM UNIVERSITY OF TEXAS HEALTH SCIENCE CENTER AT TYLER*, Watson W Wise Medical Research Library, 11937 US Hwy 271, 75708-3154. SAN 321-6462. Tel: 903-877-2865. FAX: 903-877-5412. E-mail: library@uthct.edu. Web Site: www.uthct.edu/library. *Dir, Libr Serv,* Thomas B Craig; E-mail: thomas.craig@uthct.edu; Staff 2 (MLS 2)
Founded 1979. Enrl 52; Fac 100; Highest Degree: Master
Library Holdings: AV Mats 40; e-books 3,000; e-journals 5,000; Bk Titles 2,000; Bk Vols 2,101; Spec Interest Per Sub 5,000
Subject Interests: Environ health, Health admin, Occupational health, Primary health care, Pub health, Pulmonary
Automation Activity & Vendor Info: (Acquisitions) Ex Libris Group; (Cataloging) Ex Libris Group; (Circulation) Ex Libris Group; (ILL) OCLC WorldShare Interlibrary Loan; (OPAC) Ex Libris Group; (Serials) Ex Libris Group
Wireless access
Function: 24/7 Online cat, Archival coll, Electronic databases & coll, For res purposes, Health sci info serv, Online cat, Ref serv available
Publications: Acquisitions List (Bimonthly); Newsletter (Bimonthly)
Partic in Amigos Library Services, Inc; National Network of Libraries of Medicine Region 3; TexSHARE - Texas State Library & Archives Commission
Open Mon-Fri 8-5
Restriction: 24-hr pass syst for students only, Prof mat only

UNIVERSAL CITY

§J ALAMO COLLEGES DISTRICT, Northeast Lakeview College Library, 1201 Kitty Hawk Rd, 78148. Tel: 210-486-5387. Reference Tel: 210-486-5388. E-mail: nlc-reference@alamo.edu. Web Site: www.alamo.edu/nlc/academics/academic-resources/library. *Dir, Libr Serv,* Vicky Hart; Tel: 210-486-5461, E-mail: vhart4@alamo.edu; *Access Serv Librn,* Miranda Robbins; Tel: 210-486-5466, E-mail: mrobbins25@alamo.edu; *Info Literacy Librn,* Amy Lewis; Tel: 210-486-5465, E-mail: alewis35@alamo.edu; *Open Educational Resources Librn,* Angela Fondren; Tel: 210-486-5468, E-mail: afondren@alamo.edu; *Librn,* Deb Martilla; Tel: 210-486-5388, E-mail: dmartilla@alamo.edu
Founded 2007. Highest Degree: Associate
Library Holdings: Electronic Media & Resources 21
Wireless access
Function: ILL available, Photocopying/Printing, Study rm
Partic in Amigos Library Services, Inc; Council of Research & Academic Libraries; TexSHARE - Texas State Library & Archives Commission
Open Mon-Thurs 7:30am-9pm, Fri 7:30-5, Sat 9-1 (Fall-Spring); Mon-Thurs 7:30-7, Fri 7:30-5 (Summer)

P UNIVERSAL CITY PUBLIC LIBRARY*, 100 Northview Dr, 78148-4150. SAN 375-3883. Tel: 210-659-7048. FAX: 210-945-9221. E-mail: librarian@UCTX.gov. Web Site: www.universalcitytexas.com/396/Library. *Librn,* Susan Ennis; *Youth Librn,* Jen Whitaker; E-mail: youthlibrarian@uctx.gov. Subject Specialists: *Early literacy,* Jen Whitaker; Staff 5 (MLS 2, Non-MLS 3)
Founded 1985. Pop 21,000; Circ 36,129
Wireless access
Function: 24/7 Electronic res, 24/7 Online cat, Activity rm, Adult bk club, Adult literacy prog, After school storytime, Art exhibits, Art programs, Bk club(s), Bks on CD, Butterfly Garden, Children's prog, Computers for patron use, Electronic databases & coll, Free DVD rentals, Genealogy discussion group, ILL available, Magazines, Mail & tel request accepted, Meeting rooms, Movies, Online cat, Photocopying/Printing, Preschool reading prog, Prog for adults, Prog for children & young adult, Spanish lang bks, Story hour, Summer reading prog, Tax forms, Writing prog
Open Tues & Wed 9-6, Thurs 11-8, Fri 9-5, Sat 9-2
Friends of the Library Group

UTOPIA

P UTOPIA MEMORIAL LIBRARY*, 800 Main St, 78884. (Mail add: PO Box 677, 78884-0677), SAN 378-3944. Tel: 830-966-3448. FAX: 830-966-3412. E-mail: utopiabk@swtexas.net. Web Site: utopia.ploud.net. *Dir,* Connie Lanphier
Founded 1972. Pop 3,233; Circ 4,000
Oct 2020-Sept 2021 Income $15,999, County $10,400, Locally Generated Income $5,599. Mats Exp $2,966, Books $2,687, Other Print Mats $279
Library Holdings: Audiobooks 439; CDs 466; DVDs 1,577; Electronic Media & Resources 68; Bk Titles 16,530; Per Subs 24; Talking Bks 425; Videos 1,577

Automation Activity & Vendor Info: (Cataloging) TLC (The Library Corporation); (Circulation) TLC (The Library Corporation); (ILL) OCLC WorldShare Interlibrary Loan
Wireless access
Open Mon & Thurs 9-12 & 1-5, Tues, Wed & Fri 9-3

UVALDE

P EL PROGRESO MEMORIAL LIBRARY, 301 W Main St, 78801. SAN 362-3610. Tel: 830-278-2017. FAX: 830-278-4940. E-mail: elprogresomemoriallibrary@yahoo.com. Web Site: www.elprogreso.org. *Dir,* Tammie L Sinclair; E-mail: tsinclair@elprogreso.org; *Dir of Develop,* Mendell D Morgan, Jr; E-mail: mmorgan@elprogreso.org; *Archivist, Mus Dir,* Position Currently Open; *Cat,* Lucy Sandoval; *Ch Serv,* Martha Carreon; *Circ,* Leticia Ruiz. Subject Specialists: *Archives,* Tammie L Sinclair; Staff 5.5 (MLS 2, Non-MLS 3.5)
Founded 1903. Circ 76,266
Jul 2024-Jun 2025 Income $550,000, City $122,000, County $132,000, Locally Generated Income $76,000, Other $220,000. Mats Exp $68,700, Books $12,000, Per/Ser (Incl. Access Fees) $3,200, Manu Arch $27,500, AV Equip $3,000, AV Mat $5,000, Electronic Ref Mat (Incl. Access Fees) $6,000, Presv $12,000. Sal $226,000 (Prof $82,000)
Library Holdings: Audiobooks 884; AV Mats 1,674; Bks on Deafness & Sign Lang 12; DVDs 908; e-books 5,000; Large Print Bks 1,101; Bk Titles 57,000; Bk Vols 64,000; Per Subs 90; Talking Bks 1,440; Videos 1,386
Special Collections: Los Angelitos de Robb Coll; Texana (Uvalde Historical Archive)
Subject Interests: County hist, Local hist
Automation Activity & Vendor Info: (Cataloging) TLC (The Library Corporation); (Circulation) TLC (The Library Corporation); (OPAC) TLC (The Library Corporation)
Wireless access
Function: 24/7 Electronic res, 24/7 Online cat, 24/7 wireless access, 3D Printer, Activity rm, Archival coll, Home delivery & serv to seniorr ctr & nursing homes, Homebound delivery serv, Photocopying/Printing, Prog for children & young adult, Summer reading prog, Wheelchair accessible
Partic in Partners Library Action Network
Special Services for the Blind - Bks on cassette; Bks on CD; Home delivery serv; Volunteer serv
Open Mon-Wed 10-6, Thurs 10-8, Fri 10-4, Sat 10-2
Restriction: Authorized patrons, Borrowing requests are handled by ILL, Circ to mem only, Free to mem, ID required to use computers (Ltd hrs), In-house use for visitors, Lending libr only via mail, Non-circulating of rare bks, Residents only
Friends of the Library Group

J SOUTHWEST TEXAS JUNIOR COLLEGE*, Will C Miller Memorial Library, 2401 Garner Field Rd, 78801. SAN 316-8190. Tel: 830-591-7254, 830-591-7367. FAX: 830-591-4186. E-mail: library@swtjc.edu. Web Site: library.swtjc.edu. *Libr Dir,* Brenda M Cantu; E-mail: bmcantu@swtjc.edu; Staff 11 (MLS 3, Non-MLS 8)
Founded 1945. Enrl 5,750; Highest Degree: Associate
Library Holdings: AV Mats 210; e-books 28,000; Bk Titles 42,300; Bk Vols 44,200; Per Subs 355
Subject Interests: Archives, Texana
Automation Activity & Vendor Info: (Cataloging) TLC (The Library Corporation); (Circulation) TLC (The Library Corporation); (OPAC) TLC (The Library Corporation)
Wireless access
Function: 24/7 Electronic res, Archival coll, Computers for patron use, Distance learning, Doc delivery serv, E-Reserves, Electronic databases & coll, ILL available, Internet access, Magazines, Online cat, Online info literacy tutorials on the web & in blackboard, Online ref, Orientations, Outreach serv, Photocopying/Printing, Ref & res, Ref serv available, Study rm
Partic in Amigos Library Services, Inc
Restriction: Authorized patrons, Borrowing privileges limited to fac & registered students, ID required to use computers (Ltd hrs), In-house use for visitors, Limited access for the pub, Open to students, fac & staff

VALLEY MILLS

P VALLEY MILLS PUBLIC LIBRARY*, 405 Fifth St, 76689. (Mail add: PO Box 25, 76689-0025). Tel: 254-932-6370. FAX: 254-932-6372. E-mail: valleymillslibdir@yahoo.com. Web Site: www.valleymillslibrary.org. *Dir & Librn,* Kathleen Hale; E-mail: khalelibrvm@gmail.com
Pop 1,103; Circ 1,653
Library Holdings: e-books 77; Bk Vols 7,800
Automation Activity & Vendor Info: (Cataloging) Follett Software; (Circulation) Follett Software
Wireless access
Partic in Partners Library Action Network
Open Tues-Fri 10-6, Sat 10:30-3:30 (Spring-Summer); Tues-Fri 10-5 (Fall-Winter)
Friends of the Library Group

VAN ALSTYNE

P VAN ALSTYNE PUBLIC LIBRARY, 151 W Cooper St, 75495. (Mail add: PO Box 247, 75495-0247), SAN 375-5576. Tel: 903-482-5991. FAX: 903-482-1316. Web Site: cityofvanalstyne.us/. *Libr Dir,* Judy Kimzey; E-mail: jkimzey@cityofvanalstyne.us; Staff 6 (MLS 1, Non-MLS 5)
Founded 1970
Oct 2022-Sept 2023 Income $373,543, City $366,811, County $2,280, Locally Generated Income $4,452
Library Holdings: Audiobooks 338; DVDs 969; High Interest/Low Vocabulary Bk Vols 23; Large Print Bks 898; Microforms 51
Special Collections: Local History; Local History Coll
Automation Activity & Vendor Info: (Cataloging) Book Systems; (Circulation) Book Systems; (OPAC) Book Systems
Wireless access
Function: 24/7 Electronic res, 24/7 Online cat, 24/7 wireless access, Adult bk club, After school storytime, Archival coll, Audiobks on Playaways & MP3, Audiobks via web, Bk club(s), Bks on CD, Children's prog, Computers for patron use, Digital talking bks, E-Reserves, Electronic databases & coll, Extended outdoor wifi, Family literacy, Free DVD rentals, Games, Holiday prog, ILL available, Internet access, Laminating, Laptop/tablet checkout, Large print keyboards, Life-long learning prog for all ages, Magnifiers for reading, Meeting rooms, Microfiche/film & reading machines, Movies, Online cat, Online info literacy tutorials on the web & in blackboard, Online ref, Outreach serv, OverDrive digital audio bks, Photocopying/Printing, Preschool reading prog, Prog for adults, Prog for children & young adult, Ref & res, Scanner, Spanish lang bks, Story hour, Summer & winter reading prog, Summer reading prog, Tax forms, Telephone ref, Wifi hotspot checkout, Winter reading prog
Partic in Northeast Texas Digital Consortium
Special Services for the Blind - Accessible computers; Bks on CD; Computer with voice synthesizer for visually impaired persons; Digital talking bk; Extensive large print coll; Large print bks; Magnifiers
Open Mon, Wed & Thurs 11-6, Tues 11-7, Sat 10-2
Friends of the Library Group

VAN HORN

P VAN HORN CITY COUNTY LIBRARY*, 410 Crockett St, 79855. (Mail add: PO Box 129, 79855-0129), SAN 316-8204. Tel: 432-283-2855. FAX: 432-283-8316. Web Site: vanhorn.ploud.net. *Librn,* Leticia M Hernandez; E-mail: lettyhernandez@vanhorntexas.org
Library Holdings: Bk Vols 18,000; Per Subs 20
Automation Activity & Vendor Info: (Cataloging) Book Systems; (Circulation) Book Systems
Wireless access
Open Mon-Fri 8:30-5

VEGA

P OLDHAM COUNTY PUBLIC LIBRARY*, 914 Main St, 79092. (Mail add: PO Box 640, 79092-0640), SAN 375-4944. Tel: 806-267-2635. FAX: 806-267-2635. E-mail: oldhamlibrary@amaonline.com. Web Site: harringtonlc.org/vega. *Dir,* Sherrie Borman; Staff 1 (Non-MLS 1)
Founded 1987. Pop 1,100; Circ 1,430
Library Holdings: Large Print Bks 152; Bk Vols 12,600; Per Subs 10; Talking Bks 145; Videos 50
Special Collections: Texas Sesquicentennial
Wireless access
Open Mon, Wed & Fri 12-6
Friends of the Library Group

VERNON

P CARNEGIE CITY-COUNTY LIBRARY*, 2810 Wilbarger St, 76384. SAN 316-8212. Tel: 940-552-2462. FAX: 940-552-6206. E-mail: carnegieccl@hotmail.com. Web Site: www.vernonlibrary.org. *Dir,* Beth Railsback
Founded 1903. Pop 13,711; Circ 53,000
Library Holdings: AV Mats 2,600; Bk Vols 30,000; Per Subs 60
Automation Activity & Vendor Info: (Acquisitions) Book Systems; (Cataloging) Book Systems; (Circulation) Book Systems; (Course Reserve) Book Systems; (ILL) Book Systems; (OPAC) Book Systems; (Serials) Book Systems
Wireless access
Open Tues & Thurs 10-6, Wed & Fri 10-5, Sat 10-1

M NORTH TEXAS STATE HOSPITAL*, Medical Library, 4730 College Dr, 76384. SAN 316-8522. Tel: 940-552-4117. FAX: 940-552-4644. Web Site: www.hhs.texas.gov/services/mental-health-substance-use/state-hospitals/north-texas-state-hospital. *Librn,* Brittney Von Tungeln; E-mail: brittney.vontungeln@hhs.texas.gov
Founded 1961
Library Holdings: Bk Vols 1,000; Per Subs 30

Special Collections: Clinical Neurology (Baker Coll); Harvard Classics; Medical (Ciba Coll); Nobel Prize Library; Pictures (Metropolitan Miniatures), albums; Remotivation Materials; Scientific American Medicine
Subject Interests: Mental health filmstrips, Nursing, Pharmacology, Psychiat, Psychol
Wireless access
Restriction: Med staff only

J VERNON COLLEGE*, Wright Library, 4400 College Dr, 76384. SAN 329-7853. Tel: 940-552-6291, Ext 2222. Administration Tel: 940-552-6291, Ext 2220. FAX: 940-552-0288. E-mail: librarian@vernoncollege.edu. Web Site: www.vernoncollege.edu/library. *Dir, Libr Serv,* Marian Grona; E-mail: mgrona@vernoncollege.edu; *Librn,* Stephen Stafford; E-mail: sstafford@vernoncollege.edu; *Media Spec,* Gene Frommelt; E-mail: gfrommelt@vernoncollege.edu; Staff 7 (MLS 2, Non-MLS 5)
Founded 1972. Enrl 2,109; Fac 76; Highest Degree: Associate
Library Holdings: Bk Vols 28,000; Per Subs 79
Automation Activity & Vendor Info: (Cataloging) TLC (The Library Corporation); (Circulation) TLC (The Library Corporation); (OPAC) TLC (The Library Corporation)
Wireless access
Open Mon-Thurs 7:30am-9:30pm, Fri 7:30am-Noon, Sat 8-2, Sun 1-8; Mon-Thurs 7:30am-9pm (Summer)

VICTORIA

C UNIVERSITY OF HOUSTON, Victoria College Library, 3006 N Ben Wilson St, 77901. SAN 316-8247. Tel: 361-570-4166. Web Site: library.uhv.edu. *Interim Dir,* Tami Wisofsky; Tel: 361-570-4195, E-mail: wisofskyt@uhv.edu; *Cat Librn,* JoAnna McCulley; Staff 24 (MLS 8, Non-MLS 16)
Founded 1925. Enrl 4,050; Fac 166; Highest Degree: Master
Library Holdings: Bk Titles 202,000; Bk Vols 287,000; Per Subs 285
Special Collections: Local History Coll; Texas Coll. State Document Depository
Subject Interests: Behav sci, Computer sci, Soc sci
Automation Activity & Vendor Info: (Acquisitions) Koha; (Cataloging) Koha; (Circulation) Koha; (Course Reserve) Springshare, LLC; (ILL) OCLC WorldShare Interlibrary Loan; (OPAC) Koha
Wireless access
Partic in Amigos Library Services, Inc; OCLC Online Computer Library Center, Inc
Open Mon-Thurs 8am-9pm, Fri 8-5, Sat & Sun 12-6

P VICTORIA PUBLIC LIBRARY*, 302 N Main St, 77901. SAN 991-9651. Tel: 361-485-3302. Circulation Tel: 361-485-3301. Administration Tel: 361-485-3304. Automation Services Tel: 361-572-6660. FAX: 361-485-3295. E-mail: infodesk@victoriatx.gov. Web Site: www.victoriatx.org/departments/library. *Dir,* Jessica Berger; E-mail: jberger@victoriatx.gov; *Asst Dir,* Jessica Berger; E-mail: jberger@victoriatx.gov; *Circ Serv Mgr,* Sandy Thigpen; E-mail: sthigpen@victoriatx.gov; *Mgr, Programming,* Katie Talhelm; E-mail: ktalhelm@victoriatx.gov; *Tech Serv Mgr,* Katrine Villela; E-mail: kvillela@victoriatx.gov; Staff 25 (MLS 6, Non-MLS 19)
Founded 1932. Pop 93,000
Library Holdings: AV Mats 10,500; e-books 2,210; Bk Titles 128,000; Bk Vols 149,000; Per Subs 312
Automation Activity & Vendor Info: (Acquisitions) Biblionix; (Cataloging) Biblionix; (Circulation) Biblionix; (OPAC) Biblionix
Wireless access
Function: 24/7 Online cat, 3D Printer, Activity rm, Adult bk club, Art exhibits, Art programs, Audiobks on Playaways & MP3, Audiobks via web, Bi-weekly Writer's Group, Bilingual assistance for Spanish patrons, Bks on CD, Children's prog, Computers for patron use, Electronic databases & coll, Free DVD rentals, Holiday prog, Home delivery & serv to seniorr ctr & nursing homes, ILL available, Internet access, Life-long learning prog for all ages, Magazines, Magnifiers for reading, Mail & tel request accepted, Meeting rooms, Microfiche/film & reading machines, Music CDs, Online cat, Online ref, OverDrive digital audio bks, Photocopying/Printing, Preschool outreach, Preschool reading prog, Printer for laptops & handheld devices, Prog for adults, Prog for children & young adult, Ref & res, Ref serv available, Spanish lang bks, Story hour, Summer & winter reading prog, Summer reading prog, Tax forms, Teen prog, Winter reading prog, Writing prog
Partic in Partners Library Action Network
Open Mon & Wed 9-7, Tues, Thurs & Fri 9-6, Sat 10-5
Restriction: Circ limited
Friends of the Library Group

VIDOR

P VIDOR PUBLIC LIBRARY*, 440 E Bolivar St, 77662. SAN 316-8263. Tel: 409-769-7148. FAX: 409-769-5782. E-mail: library@cityofvidor.com. Web Site: vidor.ploud.net, www.cityofvidor.com/depts/library. *Dir,* Colette Turner; E-mail: cturner@cityofvidor.com; *Asst Dir,* Lynn Hartfield; E-mail: lhartfield@cityofvidor.com
Founded 1974. Pop 11,440; Circ 46,143
Library Holdings: AV Mats 2,295; Bk Vols 38,000; Per Subs 30; Videos 2,000
Special Collections: Genealogy Coll; Texana, bks. US Document Depository
Automation Activity & Vendor Info: (Cataloging) Biblionix; (Circulation) Biblionix
Wireless access
Partic in Partners Library Action Network
Open Mon-Fri 9-4
Friends of the Library Group

WACO

S THE ART CENTER OF WACO LIBRARY*, 101 S Third St, 76701. (Mail add: PO Box 114, 76703), SAN 320-8753. Tel: 254-752-4371. FAX: 254-752-3506. E-mail: info@artcenterwaco.org. Web Site: www.artcenterwaco.org. *Interim Dir,* Heidi Lindquist; E-mail: heidi@artcenterwaco.org; Staff 2 (MLS 2)
Founded 1972
Library Holdings: Bk Vols 1,500
Subject Interests: Archit, Contemporary art
Open Tues-Sat 10-5, Sun 1-5
Restriction: Open to pub for ref only

SR BAPTIST GENERAL CONVENTION OF TEXAS, Texas Baptist Historical Collection, 209 N Eighth St, 76701. SAN 328-0519. Tel: 254-754-9446. Web Site: www.texasbaptists.org/ministries/texas-baptist-historical-collection. *Dir,* Alan LeFever; E-mail: alan.lefever@txb.org; *Assoc Dir,* Naomi Taplin; E-mail: naomi.taplin@txb.org
Library Holdings: Bk Titles 5,000
Special Collections: Tex Baptist Convention Doc. Oral History
Wireless access
Restriction: Open by appt only

C BAYLOR UNIVERSITY LIBRARIES*, 1312 S Third St, 76798. (Mail add: One Bear Pl, No 97148, 76798-7148), SAN 362-3726. Tel: 254-710-6702. Circulation Tel: 254-710-6702. Interlibrary Loan Service Tel: 254-710-6707. Interlibrary Loan Service FAX: 254-710-1710. E-mail: ask@baylor.libanswers.com. Web Site: www.baylor.edu/library. *Dean, Univ Libr,* Jeffry Archer; Tel: 254-710-3590, E-mail: jeffry_archer@baylor.edu; *Asst to the Dean of Libraries,* Janell Wellbaum; Tel: 254-710-3590, E-mail: janell_wellbaum@baylor.edu; Staff 127 (MLS 20, Non-MLS 107)
Founded 1845. Enrl 20,709; Fac 1,200; Highest Degree: Doctorate
Library Holdings: AV Mats 128,845; e-books 394,559; e-journals 68,607; Microforms 2,213,631; Bk Vols 2,521,216
Special Collections: Armstrong Browning Library (Robert & Elizabeth Barrett Browning Coll), res mats; Baylor Library Digital Coll; The Texas Coll; W.R. Poage Legislative Library, congressional recs, personal papers. Oral History; State Document Depository; UN Document Depository; US Document Depository
Subject Interests: 19th Century, Church-state, Fine arts, Hist, Law, Lit, Music, Relig studies, Sci engr
Automation Activity & Vendor Info: (Acquisitions) Innovative Interfaces, Inc; (Cataloging) Innovative Interfaces, Inc; (Circulation) Innovative Interfaces, Inc; (Course Reserve) Innovative Interfaces, Inc; (ILL) OCLC ILLiad; (OPAC) Innovative Interfaces, Inc; (Serials) Innovative Interfaces, Inc
Wireless access
Partic in Center for Research Libraries; Greater Western Library Alliance; OCLC Online Computer Library Center, Inc
Friends of the Library Group

Departmental Libraries:

ARTS & SPECIAL COLLECTIONS RESEARCH CENTER, Moody Memorial Library, 1312 S Third St, 76798. (Mail add: One Bear Pl, No 97148, 76798-7148), SAN 362-3793. Tel: 254-710-2164. E-mail: arts_research_center@baylor.edu, rarecollections@baylor.edu. *Assoc Librn, Dir,* Beth Farwell; Tel: 254-710-3679, E-mail: beth_farwell@baylor.edu; *Mgr, Spec Coll,* Andrea Turner; Tel: 254-710-4278, E-mail: andrea_r_turner@baylor.edu
Library Holdings: Audiobooks 65,000; Music Scores 75,000; Bk Titles 35,000; Videos 10,000
Special Collections: 18th & 19th Century English Books on Music & Scores; 18th Century Editions of Ensemble Music; Cecil R Porter Organ Music Coll; Contemporary Christian Sound Recordings (Bob Darden Coll); David W Guion Coll, ms; Francis G Spencer Coll of American Printed Music; Manuscripts of Kurt Kiser; Mrs J W Jennings Coll of Medieval Music Manuscripts; Ouseley Library; Travis Johnson Coll
Open Mon-Fri 8-6
Friends of the Library Group

ARMSTRONG BROWNING LIBRARY & MUSEUM, 710 Speight Ave, 76798. (Mail add: One Bear Pl, No 97152, 76798-7152), SAN 362-3734. Tel: 254-710-3566. Web Site: baylor.edu/library/index.php?id=973825. *Assoc Librn, Dir,* Jennifer Borderud; Tel: 254-710-3825, E-mail: jennifer_borderud@baylor.edu; *Assoc Librn, Curator,* Laura French; Tel: 254-710-4959, E-mail: laura_j_french@baylor.edu; *Admin Coordr,* Christi Klempnauer; Tel: 254-710-4968, E-mail: christi_klempnauer@baylor.edu; Staff 6 (MLS 3, Non-MLS 3)
Founded 1918
Library Holdings: Music Scores 1,500; Bk Vols 27,000; Per Subs 22
Special Collections: 19th-Century Theological Pamphlets; A Joseph Armstrong Coll; Browning Contemporaries Coll; Browning Family Coll; Charles Dickens Coll; Edward Dowden Coll; Edward Robert Bulwer Lytton Coll; Elizabeth Barrett Browning Coll; John Forster Coll; John Henry Newman & Francis William Newman Colls; John Ruskin Coll; Joseph Milsand Archive; Matthew Arnold Coll; Ralph Waldo Emerson Coll; Robert Browning Coll; Wilfred Meynell Family Coll
Subject Interests: 19th Century Am lit, 19th Century British lit, 19th Century women poets
Function: Archival coll, Art exhibits, Audio & video playback equip for onsite use, Res libr, Wheelchair accessible
Publications: Armstrong Browning Library (Newsletter); Baylor Browning Interests (Irregular); Studies in Browning and His Circle (Annual)
Open Mon-Fri 9-5
Restriction: Closed stack, Internal use only, Non-circulating, Photo ID required for access
Friends of the Library Group

JESSE H JONES LIBRARY, 1301 S Second St, 76798. (Mail add: One Bear Pl, No 97148, 76798-7148), SAN 372-8455. Web Site: baylor.edu/library/index.php?id=970210. *Doc Librn,* Sinai Wood; Tel: 254-710-4606, E-mail: sinai_wood@baylor.edu
Friends of the Library Group

MOODY MEMORIAL LIBRARY, 1312 S Third St, 76798. (Mail add: One Bear Place, No 97148, 76798-7148), SAN 362-370X. *Director of Baptist Colls & Library Advancement,* Kathy Hillman; Tel: 254-710-6684, E-mail: kathy_hillman@baylor.edu; *Assoc Librn, Dir of Cataloging and Metadata Services,* Bruce Evans; Tel: 254-710-7863, E-mail: bruce_evans@baylor.edu; *Assoc Dir of Arts & Special Collections,* Beth Farwell; Tel: 254-710-3679, E-mail: beth_farwell@baylor.edu
Friends of the Library Group

CM NURSING LEARNING RESOURCE CENTER, Louise Herrington School of Nursing, 333 N Washington Ave, Dallas, 75246-9100, SAN 362-3807. Tel: 972-576-9200. E-mail: nursinglrc@baylor.edu. Web Site: libguides.baylor.edu/nursing. *Dir,* Ms Jamie Quinn; E-mail: jamie_quinn@baylor.edu; Staff 2 (MLS 2)
Enrl 350; Fac 62; Highest Degree: Doctorate
Library Holdings: Bk Vols 5,826; Per Subs 135
Automation Activity & Vendor Info: (Cataloging) Innovative Interfaces, Inc - Millennium; (Circulation) Innovative Interfaces, Inc - Millennium; (Media Booking) Innovative Interfaces, Inc - Millennium; (OPAC) Innovative Interfaces, Inc - Millennium; (Serials) Innovative Interfaces, Inc - Millennium
Open Mon-Fri 8-5
Restriction: Badge access after hrs

W R POAGE LEGISLATIVE LIBRARY, 201 Baylor Ave, 76706. (Mail add: One Bear Pl, No 97153, 76798-7153), SAN 372-8463. Tel: 254-710-3540. E-mail: poage_library@baylor.edu. Web Site: www.baylor.edu/library/index.php?id=973835. *Asst Librn, Dir,* Mary Goolsby; Tel: 254-710-6735, E-mail: mary_goolsby@baylor.edu; *Archivist, Coll Serv,* Amanda Fisher; Tel: 247-710-3774, E-mail: amanda_mylin@baylor.edu; Staff 6 (MLS 3, Non-MLS 3)
Founded 1979
Library Holdings: Bk Titles 21,598; Bk Vols 23,786
Special Collections: Abraham Lincoln (Jack Hightower Coll); Biles Editorial Cartoons Coll, 1965-1985; Campaign Materials, Buttons & Papers (Bob Platt & Ben Guttery Colls); Commodity Futures Trading Commission, 1982-1992 (Fowler West Papers); Congressional Papers (W R Poage 1936-1978, Marvin Leath 1989-1991, W R Smith, Jack E Hightower 1975-1985, Thomas A Pickett, John V Dowdy Sr 1952-1972, Hatton Summers, Alan W Steelman 1972-1976, O C Fisher 1943-1974, Ed Lee Goossett 1944-1952 & Sam B Hall Jr 1975-1985); District Judge Impeachment Papers (O P Carrillo Coll); Extremist Organizations (Tiller Papers); Federal 5th Circuit Court New Orleans Papers, 1978-1998 (Sam Johnson Coll); Kennedy Assassination Papers, 1963-1998 (Penn Jones Jr Coll; Jack White Coll; Bob Platt Coll & Jack Hightower Coll); Personal Papers: Paul Hoch; L N Stewart; Ed Nichols; Meadowbrook Farm; Jack White; Project 9-11 Coll; Signed Editions (Jack Hightower Coll; Bob Poage Coll); Texas Circuit Court (Bob Thomas Papers); Texas Lieutenant Governor, 1991-1999 (Bob Bullock Papers, 1929-2004); Texas State Legislature Papers (Donald G Adams, E Ray Kirkpatrick 1946-1952 & Allen D Place, Jr); Texas State Senate (Chet Edwards Papers & Jack Hightower Coll; Kip Averitt); Texas Supreme Court Papers (Charles W Barrow Coll; Jack Hightower Coll); US Agriculture Committee Papers (Hyde Murray 1958-1978 & John Hogan 1978-1998; Fowler West, 1963-1982)
Subject Interests: 20th Century politics, JFK assassination, Terrorism
Friends of the Library Group

TEXAS COLLECTION & UNIVERSITY ARCHIVES, 1429 S Fifth St, 76706. (Mail add: One Bear Pl, No 97142, 76798-7142), SAN 362-3823. Tel: 254-710-1268. FAX: 254-710-1368. E-mail: txcoll@baylor.edu. Web Site: baylor.edu/library/index.php?id=973374. *Dir,* Jeff Pirtle; *Asst Dir, Proc Archivist,* Paul Fisher; E-mail: paul_fisher@baylor.edu; Staff 3 (MLS 2, Non-MLS 1)
Founded 1923. Fac 3; Highest Degree: Doctorate
Library Holdings: Bk Titles 93,917; Bk Vols 129,000; Per Subs 1,000
Special Collections: Newsfilm Archive, KWTX-TV, Waco; Regional Historical Resource Depository; Texas State Publications & Documents Depository. Oral History; State Document Depository
Function: ILL available, Wheelchair accessible
Open Mon-Fri 8:15-5
Restriction: Authorized scholars by appt, Borrowing privileges limited to fac & registered students, Circ limited, Closed stack, In-house use for visitors, Non-circulating coll, Non-circulating of rare bks
Friends of the Library Group

CL SHERIDAN & JOHN EDDIE WILLIAMS LEGAL RESEARCH & TECHNOLOGY CENTER, 1114 S University Parks Dr, 76706. (Mail add: One Bear Pl, No 97128, 76798-7128), SAN 362-3769. Tel: 254-710-2168. Reference Tel: 254-710-4587. Web Site: www.baylor.edu/law/library. *Dir,* Brandon Quarles; E-mail: brandon_quarles@baylor.edu; *Cataloging & Metadata Librn,* Tabitha Patterson; E-mail: tabitha_rosebaum@baylor.edu; *Ref Librn,* Chris Galeczka; E-mail: christopher_galeczka@baylor.edu
Library Holdings: Bk Titles 26,446; Bk Vols 112,091; Per Subs 2,212
Special Collections: Frank M Wilson Rare Book Coll. US Document Depository
Automation Activity & Vendor Info: (Acquisitions) Innovative Interfaces, Inc; (Cataloging) Innovative Interfaces, Inc; (Circulation) Innovative Interfaces, Inc; (Course Reserve) Innovative Interfaces, Inc; (ILL) Innovative Interfaces, Inc; (OPAC) Innovative Interfaces, Inc; (Serials) Innovative Interfaces, Inc
Partic in Amigos Library Services, Inc; TexSHARE - Texas State Library & Archives Commission
Open Mon-Thurs 7am-Midnight, Fri 7am-10pm, Sat 10-10, Sun 11am-Midnight

GM DEPARTMENT OF VETERANS AFFAIRS, Doris Miller VA Medical Center Library, 4800 Memorial Dr, 76711. SAN 316-8336. Tel: 254-297-3272. Web Site: www.va.gov/central-texas-health-care.
Library Holdings: Bk Vols 2,300; Per Subs 200

S MASONIC GRAND LODGE LIBRARY & MUSEUM OF TEXAS*, 715 Columbus Ave, 76701-1349. (Mail add: PO Box 446, 76703-0446), SAN 316-828X. Tel: 254-753-7395. FAX: 254-753-2944. E-mail: gs@grandsecretaryoftx.org. Web Site: grandlodgeoftexas.org/library-and-museum.
Founded 1873
Library Holdings: Bk Titles 36,000
Subject Interests: Masonry, Tex hist
Open Mon-Fri 8:30-4
Restriction: Mem only, Open to pub for ref only
Friends of the Library Group

J MCLENNAN COMMUNITY COLLEGE LIBRARY*, 1400 College Dr, 76708-1498. SAN 316-8301. Tel: 254-299-8323, 254-299-8398. Circulation Tel: 254-299-8325. FAX: 254-299-6226. Web Site: www.mclennan.edu/library. *Dir,* Dan Martinsen; Tel: 254-299-8333, E-mail: dmartisen@mclennan.edu; *Sr Librn, Ref,* Sharon K Kenan; Tel: 254-299-8343, E-mail: skenan@mclennan.edu; *Coll Librn, Resource Management,* Kevin Lightfoot; Tel: 254-299-8389, E-mail: klightfoot@mclennan.edu; *Instruction Librn,* Gail Woodward; Tel: 254-299-8390, E-mail: gwoodward@mclennan.edu; Staff 15 (MLS 5, Non-MLS 10)
Founded 1968. Enrl 8,500; Fac 200; Highest Degree: Associate
Library Holdings: Bk Vols 82,591; Per Subs 430
Subject Interests: Law
Automation Activity & Vendor Info: (Cataloging) SirsiDynix; (Circulation) SirsiDynix; (Course Reserve) SirsiDynix; (OPAC) SirsiDynix
Wireless access
Partic in Amigos Library Services, Inc
Open Mon-Thurs 7:30am-10pm, Fri 8-5, Sat 9-3, Sun 3-9

GL MCLENNAN COUNTY LAW LIBRARY*, 501 Washington, 76701. SAN 316-831X. Tel: 254-757-5191. Web Site: www.co.mclennan.tx.us. *Library Contact,* Dustin Chapman; E-mail: dustin.chapman@co.mclennan.tx.us
Library Holdings: Bk Vols 8,000
Wireless access
Function: Res libr
Open Mon-Fri 8-5

S TEXAS RANGER HALL OF FAME & MUSEUM, Tobin & Anne Armstrong Texas Ranger Research Center, 100 Texas Ranger Trail, 76706. (Mail add: PO Box 2570, 76702-2570), SAN 362-3971. Tel: 254-750-8631. Toll Free Tel: 877-750-8631. FAX: 254-750-8629. E-mail: info@texasranger.org. Web Site: www.texasranger.org/pages/research-center. *Research Librn,* Jacqui Sweeney; Tel: 254-750-8639; Staff 2 (MLS 2)
Founded 1976
Library Holdings: Bk Vols 6,800
Special Collections: Bonnie & Clyde (Frank Hamer Papers); Ex-Texas Ranger Association Papers; M D "Kelly" Rogers Coll; M T "Lone Wolf" Gonzaullas Papers; Texarkana Phantom Killer. Oral History
Subject Interests: Law enforcement
Wireless access
Function: Res libr
Restriction: Closed stack, Non-circulating, Open by appt only

J TEXAS STATE TECHNICAL COLLEGE*, Learning Resource Center, Airline Dr, 76705. (Mail add: Technology Name, TSTC Waco, 3801 Campus Dr, 76705), SAN 362-3858. Tel: 254-867-4846. FAX: 254-867-2339. Web Site: www.waco.tstc.edu/student_life/learningresource. *Dir,* Lianna Dick; Tel: 254-867-2349, E-mail: lianna.dick@tstc.edu; Staff 9 (MLS 2, Non-MLS 7)
Founded 1967. Enrl 4,688; Fac 250; Highest Degree: Associate
Library Holdings: DVDs 1,200; Bk Vols 62,000; Per Subs 180; Videos 2,500
Special Collections: Eric Documents; FAA Aerospace Coll; Industrial & Safety Standards; Texas College Catalog; Texas Phone Books
Subject Interests: Auto repairs, Aviation piloting, Computer, Electronics, Food serv, Hazardous mat, Laser mechanics, Nuclear tech, Occupational health, Occupational safety
Automation Activity & Vendor Info: (Acquisitions) SirsiDynix; (Cataloging) SirsiDynix; (Circulation) SirsiDynix; (Course Reserve) SirsiDynix; (ILL) SirsiDynix; (Media Booking) SirsiDynix; (OPAC) SirsiDynix; (Serials) SirsiDynix
Wireless access
Publications: Periodicals By Technology
Open Mon-Thurs 8-6, Fri 8-5, Sat 1-5
Restriction: Open to students, fac & staff

P WACO-MCLENNAN COUNTY LIBRARY SYSTEM*, 1717 Austin Ave, 76701-1794. SAN 362-3882. Tel: 254-750-5941. Circulation Tel: 254-750-5943. Interlibrary Loan Service Tel: 254-750-5955. Reference Tel: 254-750-5944. FAX: 254-750-5940. Web Site: www.waco-texas.com/departments/library. *Dir, Libr Serv,* Essy Day; Tel: 254-750-5946, E-mail: EssyD@wacotx.gov; *Br Mgr,* Sarah Freeland; Tel: 254-750-5958, E-mail: SarahF@ci.waco.tx.us; *Circ Supvr,* Robyn White; Tel: 254-750-5947; Staff 57 (MLS 17, Non-MLS 40)
Founded 1898. Pop 211,275; Circ 658,698
Library Holdings: Audiobooks 18,204; DVDs 22,162; e-books 4,065; Bk Vols 283,397; Per Subs 319
Special Collections: Local Newspaper (Waco Tribune-Herald & Predecessors: 1890-Present), microfilm. Municipal Document Depository; Oral History
Subject Interests: Genealogy, Local hist
Automation Activity & Vendor Info: (Acquisitions) TLC (The Library Corporation); (Cataloging) TLC (The Library Corporation); (Circulation) TLC (The Library Corporation); (ILL) OCLC; (OPAC) TLC (The Library Corporation)
Wireless access
Function: 24/7 Electronic res, 24/7 Online cat, Activity rm, Adult bk club, Archival coll, Art programs, Audio & video playback equip for onsite use, Audiobks on Playaways & MP3, Audiobks via web, Bk club(s), Bks on cassette, Bks on CD, Children's prog, Computer training, Computers for patron use, Electronic databases & coll, Free DVD rentals, Genealogy discussion group, Holiday prog, Home delivery & serv to seniorr ctr & nursing homes, ILL available, Internet access, Large print keyboards, Magazines, Magnifiers for reading, Meeting rooms, Microfiche/film & reading machines, Movies, Museum passes, Music CDs, Online cat, Online ref, Outreach serv, Photocopying/Printing, Preschool outreach, Preschool reading prog, Printer for laptops & handheld devices, Prog for adults, Prog for children & young adult, Ref & res, Ref serv available, Res assist avail, Scanner, Senior outreach, Serves people with intellectual disabilities, Spanish lang bks, Spoken cassettes & CDs, STEM programs, Story hour, Study rm, Summer & winter reading prog, Summer reading prog, Tax forms, Teen prog, Telephone ref, Wheelchair accessible
Partic in Amigos Library Services, Inc; Partners Library Action Network
Open Mon-Wed 10-9, Thurs-Sat 10-6, Sun 1-5
Friends of the Library Group
Branches: 3
EAST WACO, 901 Elm Ave, 76704-2659, SAN 362-3912. Tel: 254-750-8620. FAX: 254-750-8413. *Br Mgr,* Alysha Suchaski; Tel: 254-750-8418, E-mail: alyshas@wacotx.gov
Subject Interests: African-Am hist
Open Mon-Wed, Fri & Sat 10-6, Thurs 10-9
Friends of the Library Group
SOUTH WACO, 2737 S 18th St, 76706, SAN 362-403X. Tel: 254-750-8621. FAX: 254-750-8606. *Br Mgr,* Barbara Frank; Tel: 254-750-8411, E-mail: BarbaraF@wacotx.gov; Staff 1 (MLS 1)
Library Holdings: Audiobooks 1,836; CDs 352; DVDs 3,494; Bk Vols 40,650
Open Mon & Wed-Sat 10-6, Tues 10-9
Friends of the Library Group
WEST WACO LIBRARY & GENEALOGY CENTER, 5301 Bosque Blvd, Ste 275, 76710, SAN 362-4005. Tel: 254-745-6018. Reference Tel: 254-745-6026. FAX: 254-745-6019. *Br Mgr,* Allison Scheu; Tel: 254-750-5975, E-mail: allisons@wacotx.gov
Library Holdings: Audiobooks 2,533; DVDs 3,122; Bk Vols 57,052
Open Mon & Thurs 10-9, Tues, Wed, Fri & Sat 10-6
Friends of the Library Group

WAELDER

P WAELDER PUBLIC LIBRARY*, 310 North Ave E, 78959. (Mail add: PO Box 428, 78959-0428), SAN 316-8344. Tel: 830-788-7167. FAX: 830-788-7541. E-mail: waelder-library@gvec.net. *Head Librn,* Doris Burney
Pop 1,071; Circ 6,097
Library Holdings: Bk Vols 9,000
Automation Activity & Vendor Info: (Cataloging) Biblionix; (Circulation) Biblionix
Open Mon-Fri 1-5

WALLER

P MELANEE SMITH MEMORIAL LIBRARY, 2103 Main St, 77484. Tel: 936-372-3961. Web Site: wallertexas.com/library.html. *Librn,* Deborah Shields; E-mail: dshields@wallertexas.com
Library Holdings: Bk Titles 12,000
Wireless access
Open Tues-Fri 9-12 & 1-5, Sat 9-12
Friends of the Library Group

WALLIS

P AUSTIN COUNTY LIBRARY SYSTEM*, Knox Memorial Library, 6730 Railroad St, 77485. SAN 362-4064. Tel: 979-478-6813. FAX: 979-478-6813. E-mail: knoxlib@austincounty.com. Web Site: wallis.ploud.net. *Head Librn,* Lyndsey Martinez; *Asst Librn,* Melissa McFarland
Pop 3,375
Library Holdings: AV Mats 1,198; Bk Vols 15,500; Per Subs 40; Videos 1,806
Wireless access
Function: CD-ROM, ILL available, Music CDs, Photocopying/Printing, Prog for children & young adult
Open Mon-Thurs 8-5, Sat 8:30-12:30

WASHINGTON

S STAR OF THE REPUBLIC MUSEUM LIBRARY*, 23200 Park Rd 12, 77880. (Mail add: PO Box 317, 77880-0317), SAN 326-2448. Tel: 936-878-2461, Ext 234. FAX: 936-878-2462. E-mail: star@blinn.edu. Web Site: www.thc.texas.gov/historic-sites-star-republic-museum. *Dir,* Jonathan Failor; E-mail: jonathan.failor@thc.texas.gov
Founded 1970
Library Holdings: Bk Titles 3,000; Per Subs 20
Open Mon-Sun 10-5
Restriction: Non-circulating

WASKOM

P WASKOM PUBLIC LIBRARY*, 103 Waskom Ave, 75692-9281. (Mail add: PO Box 1187, 75692-1187). Tel: 903-687-3041. E-mail: waskomlibrary@eastex.net. Web Site: www.waskompubliclibrary.org. *Dir,* Terry Slone; E-mail: terryslone53@gmail.com; Staff 1 (Non-MLS 1)
Founded 1998. Pop 5,280
Library Holdings: Audiobooks 700; AV Mats 161; DVDs 292; Bk Titles 6,957
Automation Activity & Vendor Info: (Acquisitions) Book Systems; (Cataloging) Book Systems; (Circulation) Book Systems; (ILL) Book Systems; (OPAC) Book Systems
Wireless access
Open Mon-Fri 12:30-4:30, Sat 9-2
Friends of the Library Group

WATAUGA

P WATAUGA PUBLIC LIBRARY*, 7109 Whitley Rd, 76148-2024. SAN 375-4804. Tel: 817-514-5864. Reference Tel: 817-514-5865. FAX: 817-581-3910. E-mail: library@wataugatx.org. Web Site: www.cowtx.org/898/Library. *Dir,* Lana Ewell; E-mail: lewell@cowtx.org; *Ad,* Dana Harper; *Youth Serv,* Linda Evers; Staff 5 (MLS 4, Non-MLS 1)
Founded 1983. Pop 24,397; Circ 388,000
Library Holdings: DVDs 9,936; Bk Titles 61,848; Per Subs 141
Automation Activity & Vendor Info: (Cataloging) Horizon; (Circulation) Horizon; (OPAC) Horizon
Wireless access
Function: 24/7 Electronic res, Adult bk club, Adult literacy prog, Art exhibits, Audiobks via web, Bilingual assistance for Spanish patrons, Bks on CD, Chess club, Children's prog, Citizenship assistance, Computer training, Computers for patron use, Electronic databases & coll, Family literacy, Free DVD rentals, Holiday prog, ILL available, Internet access, Life-long learning prog for all ages, Magazines, Movies, Music CDs, Notary serv, Online cat, Outreach serv, OverDrive digital audio bks, Photocopying/Printing, Preschool reading prog, Prog for adults, Prog for children & young adult, Ref serv available, Scanner, Spanish lang bks, Spoken cassettes & CDs, Spoken cassettes & DVDs, Study rm, Summer & winter reading prog, Summer reading prog, Tax forms, Teen prog, Telephone ref, Wheelchair accessible, Winter reading prog, Workshops
Publications: Calendar (Monthly)
Partic in MetroShare Libraries; Partners Library Action Network; TexSHARE - Texas State Library & Archives Commission
Special Services for the Deaf - Adult & family literacy prog; Bks on deafness & sign lang; Captioned film dep; Closed caption videos; High interest/low vocabulary bks; Sign lang interpreter upon request for prog
Special Services for the Blind - Bks & mags in Braille, on rec, tape & cassette; Bks available with recordings; Bks on CD; Large print bks; Magnifiers; Recorded bks
Open Mon & Thurs Noon-8, Tues, Wed & Fri 10-6, Sat Noon-4
Restriction: ID required to use computers (Ltd hrs), Non-circulating coll
Friends of the Library Group

WAXAHACHIE

P NICHOLAS P SIMS LIBRARY*, 515 W Main, 75165-3235. SAN 316-8352. Tel: 972-937-2671. FAX: 972-937-4409. E-mail: info@simslib.org. Web Site: www.simslib.org. *Dir,* Barbara Claspell; E-mail: dir@simslib.org; *Ref (Info Servs), Tech Librn,* Heather Lee; E-mail: adult@simslib.org; *YA Librn,* Connie Colston; E-mail: teens@simslib.org; *Circ Supvr,* Jennifer Graf; E-mail: Circ@simslib.org; *Coordr, Prog,* Nicole Matthews; E-mail: kids1@simslib.org. Subject Specialists: *Genealogy,* Heather Lee; Staff 12 (MLS 3, Non-MLS 9)
Founded 1904. Pop 35,000; Circ 200,000
Oct 2015-Sept 2016 Income $1,094,766, City $1,015,283, Other $79,483. Mats Exp $92,465, Books $38,621, Per/Ser (Incl. Access Fees) $3,000, AV Mat $19,699, Electronic Ref Mat (Incl. Access Fees) $31,145. Sal $469,601 (Prof $213,237)
Library Holdings: Audiobooks 5,106; AV Mats 67; CDs 1,469; DVDs 4,729; e-books 4,368; e-journals 9; Electronic Media & Resources 67; Large Print Bks 2,450; Microforms 1,529; Bk Titles 52,373; Bk Vols 56,426; Per Subs 198; Videos 4,319
Subject Interests: Local genealogy
Automation Activity & Vendor Info: (Cataloging) Biblionix/Apollo; (Circulation) Biblionix/Apollo; (OPAC) Biblionix/Apollo
Wireless access
Function: 24/7 Electronic res, 24/7 Online cat, Activity rm, Adult bk club, Adult literacy prog, Archival coll, Art exhibits, Audiobks via web, AV serv, Bi-weekly Writer's Group, Bilingual assistance for Spanish patrons, Bk club(s), Bks on CD, Bus archives, Chess club, Children's prog, Computer training, Computers for patron use, E-Readers, E-Reserves, Electronic databases & coll, Family literacy, For res purposes, Free DVD rentals, Genealogy discussion group, Health sci info serv, Holiday prog, Home delivery & serv to seniorr ctr & nursing homes, Homework prog, ILL available, Instruction & testing, Internet access, Magazines, Mail & tel request accepted, Mango lang, Meeting rooms, Microfiche/film & reading machines, Movies, Music CDs, Notary serv, Online cat, Online ref, Orientations, Outreach serv, Outside serv via phone, mail, e-mail & web, OverDrive digital audio bks, Photocopying/Printing, Preschool outreach, Preschool reading prog, Printer for laptops & handheld devices, Prog for adults, Prog for children & young adult, Ref & res, Ref serv available, Res performed for a fee, Scanner, Senior computer classes, Senior outreach, Spanish lang bks, Spoken cassettes & CDs, Spoken cassettes & DVDs, Story hour, Summer reading prog, Tax forms, Teen prog, Wheelchair accessible
Partic in Northeast Texas Digital Consortium; TexSHARE - Texas State Library & Archives Commission
Open Tues 9:30-8, Wed-Fri 9:30-6, Sat 9:30-2:30
Friends of the Library Group

CR SOUTHWESTERN ASSEMBLIES OF GOD UNIVERSITY*, P C Nelson Memorial Library, 1200 Sycamore St, 75165-2342. SAN 316-8360. Tel: 972-825-4761. FAX: 972-923-0488. E-mail: library@sagu.edu. Web Site: www.sagu.edu/services/nelson-memorial-library. *Dir, Libr Serv,* Radonna Holmes; E-mail: rholmes@sagu.edu; *Asst Dir,* Tiffany Hudson; E-mail: thudson@sagu.edu; *Circ Coordr, Ref Coordr,* Vanessa Washburn; E-mail: vwashburn@sagu.edu; *Coll Develop,* Anisa Martin; E-mail: amartin@sagu.edu
Founded 1927. Highest Degree: Doctorate
Library Holdings: Bk Titles 96,000; Bk Vols 115,000; Per Subs 200
Special Collections: Charismatic Authors, History & Materials (Pentecostal Alcove), bks & per. Oral History
Subject Interests: Educ, Relig studies
Automation Activity & Vendor Info: (Acquisitions) TLC (The Library Corporation); (Cataloging) TLC (The Library Corporation); (Circulation) TLC (The Library Corporation); (Course Reserve) TLC (The Library Corporation); (ILL) OCLC WorldShare Interlibrary Loan; (OPAC) TLC (The Library Corporation)
Wireless access
Partic in Amigos Library Services, Inc
Special Services for the Deaf - Bks on deafness & sign lang
Open Mon-Fri 7:30am-11pm, Sat 11-11 (Fall & Spring); Mon-Fri 8-5 (Summer)

WEATHERFORD

J WEATHERFORD COLLEGE LIBRARY, Speaker Jim Wright Library, 225 College Park Dr, 76086. SAN 316-8379. Tel: 817-598-6251. FAX: 817-598-6369. TDD: 817-598-6254. E-mail: library@wc.edu. Web Site: wc.libguides.com/libraryhome. *Dir,* Valorie Starr; E-mail: vstarr@wc.edu; *Instruction Librn,* Kathy Renken; Staff 4 (MLS 2, Non-MLS 2)
Founded 1869. Highest Degree: Bachelor
Automation Activity & Vendor Info: (Acquisitions) OCLC Worldshare Management Services; (Cataloging) OCLC Worldshare Management Services; (Circulation) OCLC Worldshare Management Services; (Course Reserve) OCLC Worldshare Management Services; (ILL) OCLC WorldShare Interlibrary Loan; (OPAC) OCLC Worldshare Management Services
Wireless access
Partic in Amigos Library Services, Inc
Special Services for the Deaf - TTY equip
Special Services for the Blind - Braille equip; Braille servs; Closed circuit TV
Open Mon-Thurs 7:30-7, Fri & Sat 7:30-4 (Fall & Spring); Mon-Thurs 7:30-5:30 (Summer)

P WEATHERFORD PUBLIC LIBRARY*, 1014 Charles St, 76086. SAN 316-8387. Tel: 817-598-4150. Reference Tel: 817-598-4151. Administration Tel: 817-598-4159. FAX: 817-598-4161. E-mail: libinfo@weatherfordtx.gov. Web Site: weatherfordtx.gov/142/library. *Dir,* Chris Accardo; E-mail: caccardo@weatherfordtx.gov
Founded 1959. Pop 95,821; Circ 332,000
Library Holdings: AV Mats 9,051; Bk Vols 96,000; Per Subs 200; Videos 3,696
Special Collections: Parker County Historical & Genealogical Coll
Automation Activity & Vendor Info: (Cataloging) Innovative Interfaces, Inc; (Circulation) Innovative Interfaces, Inc
Wireless access
Open Mon & Tues 10-8, Wed & Thurs 10-6, Fri & Sat Noon-6
Friends of the Library Group

WEIMAR

P WEIMAR PUBLIC LIBRARY*, One Jackson Sq, 78962-2019. SAN 316-8395. Tel: 979-725-6608. FAX: 979-725-9033. Web Site: www.weimarpubliclibrary.org. *Libr Dir,* Cindy Kahlden; E-mail: cindykahlden@hotmail.com
Founded 1964. Pop 3,146; Circ 13,992
Library Holdings: e-books 50; Bk Vols 20,000; Per Subs 13
Automation Activity & Vendor Info: (Cataloging) Follett Software; (Circulation) Follett Software; (OPAC) Follett Software
Wireless access
Open Mon & Thurs 8-6:30, Tues, Wed & Fri 8-4:30, Sun Noon-3
Friends of the Library Group

WELLINGTON

P COLLINGSWORTH PUBLIC LIBRARY, 711 15th St, 79095. SAN 316-8409. Tel: 806-447-3183. FAX: 806-447-5240. E-mail: library79095@gmail.com. Web Site: www.collingsworthpubliclibrary.info. *Librn,* Vicki Decker; Staff 1 (Non-MLS 1)
Founded 1924. Pop 3,300; Circ 10,480
Library Holdings: Bk Titles 20,850
Automation Activity & Vendor Info: (Cataloging) SirsiDynix; (Circulation) SirsiDynix; (ILL) SirsiDynix; (OPAC) SirsiDynix
Wireless access

Function: 24/7 Electronic res, 24/7 Online cat, 24/7 wireless access, Accelerated reader prog, Activity rm, Adult bk club, Archival coll, Audiobks on Playaways & MP3, Audiobks via web, AV serv, Bk club(s), Bks on CD, Children's prog, Citizenship assistance, Computer training, Computers for patron use, Digital talking bks, Doc delivery serv, E-Readers, Electronic databases & coll, Extended outdoor wifi, Games, Home delivery & serv to seniorr ctr & nursing homes, ILL available, Internet access, Laminating, Laptop/tablet checkout, Magazines, Magnifiers for reading, Meeting rooms, Movies, Music CDs, Online cat, Photocopying/Printing, Preschool reading prog, Printer for laptops & handheld devices, Prog for adults, Prog for children & young adult, Ref serv available, Scanner, Spanish lang bks, Story hour, Summer & winter reading prog, Summer reading prog, Tax forms, Teen prog, Wheelchair accessible, Winter reading prog
Partic in Harrington Library Consortium
Special Services for the Deaf - Spec interest per
Open Mon-Wed & Fri 8-5:30, Thurs 8-8 (Winter); Mon-Wed 9:30-5:30, Thurs 9:30-8 (Summer)

WELLS

P RUBE SESSIONS MEMORIAL LIBRARY*, 298 Rusk Ave, 75976. (Mail add: PO Box 120, 75976-9009). Tel: 936-867-4757. FAX: 936-867-4760. E-mail: rubelib@gmail.com. Web Site: www.sessions.lib.tx.us. *Librn,* Shannon D Flowers; Staff 1 (Non-MLS 1)
Founded 1975. Pop 10,000; Circ 6,000
Library Holdings: Audiobooks 38; AV Mats 265; Bks on Deafness & Sign Lang 3; CDs 23; DVDs 102; Large Print Bks 509; Bk Titles 8,541; Talking Bks 6; Videos 96
Automation Activity & Vendor Info: (Acquisitions) Biblionix; (Cataloging) Biblionix; (Circulation) Biblionix; (Course Reserve) Biblionix
Wireless access
Function: Art exhibits, Bks on cassette, Bks on CD, Children's prog, Computers for patron use, Mail & tel request accepted, Music CDs, Photocopying/Printing, Preschool outreach, Prog for adults, Prog for children & young adult, Ref serv available, Scanner, Spoken cassettes & CDs, Story hour, Summer reading prog, Tax forms, Teen prog, VHS videos, Wheelchair accessible, Workshops
Special Services for the Deaf - Bks on deafness & sign lang; Closed caption videos
Special Services for the Blind - Bks on cassette; Bks on CD; Large print bks
Open Tues-Fri 9-5

WESLACO

P MAYOR JOE V SANCHEZ PUBLIC LIBRARY*, 525 S Kansas Ave, 78596. SAN 316-8425. Tel: 956-968-4533. Administration Tel: 956-973-3144. FAX: 956-968-8922, 956-969-2665. Web Site: www.weslacopl.us. *Dir,* Arnoldo Becho; E-mail: abecho@weslacopl.us; Staff 11 (MLS 1, Non-MLS 10)
Founded 1948. Pop 53,000; Circ 65,104
Library Holdings: AV Mats 2,285; Bk Titles 50,104; Bk Vols 57,196; Per Subs 85
Special Collections: Texana Coll, bk & tape. Oral History
Subject Interests: Hispanic
Automation Activity & Vendor Info: (Circulation) TLC (The Library Corporation)
Wireless access
Mem of Hidalgo County Library System
Partic in Amigos Library Services, Inc
Open Mon-Thurs 8-8, Fri 8-5, Sat 11-3
Friends of the Library Group

WEST

P WEST PUBLIC LIBRARY*, 209 W Tokio Rd, 76691. SAN 375-3484. Tel: 254-826-3070. FAX: 254-826-4473. Web Site: www.westpl.org. *Librn,* Nancy Hykel; E-mail: nancyhykel@aol.com
Founded 1984. Pop 4,279; Circ 136,400
Library Holdings: AV Mats 380; Bks on Deafness & Sign Lang 20; High Interest/Low Vocabulary Bk Vols 2,000; Large Print Bks 400; Bk Vols 37,000; Talking Bks 270
Automation Activity & Vendor Info: (Cataloging) Follett Software; (Circulation) Follett Software
Wireless access
Partic in Partners Library Action Network
Special Services for the Deaf - Bks on deafness & sign lang
Open Mon, Tues & Thurs 3-7, Wed 10-3, Sat 9-12
Friends of the Library Group

WEST TAWAKONI

P TAWAKONI AREA PUBLIC LIBRARY*, 340 W Hwy 276, 75474-2644. SAN 323-6668. Tel: 903-447-3445. FAX: 903-447-3445. E-mail: TAPL42@hotmail.com. Web Site: www.tawakonipubliclibrary.com. *Dir,* Vicki Nix; Staff 2 (Non-MLS 2)
Founded 1982. Pop 4,891; Circ 18,427
Library Holdings: Bk Titles 26,583; Bk Vols 26,803; Per Subs 141
Special Collections: Texas Literature (Texana Coll). Oral History
Automation Activity & Vendor Info: (Acquisitions) LibraryWorld, Inc; (Cataloging) LibraryWorld, Inc; (Circulation) Follett Software
Wireless access
Function: Bks on cassette, Bks on CD, Children's prog, Computers for patron use, Free DVD rentals, Holiday prog, ILL available, Photocopying/Printing, Scanner, Summer reading prog, Tax forms, Wheelchair accessible
Open Wed-Fri 11-5, Sat 10-4
Friends of the Library Group

WHARTON

J WHARTON COUNTY JUNIOR COLLEGE, J M Hodges Library, 911 Boling Hwy, 77488-3298. SAN 316-8441. Tel: 979-532-6953. Interlibrary Loan Service Tel: 979-532-6509. FAX: 979-532-6527. E-mail: wcjclibrary@wcjc.edu. Web Site: www.wcjc.edu/students/library. *Dir, Libr Serv, Tech Serv,* Dr Christy Ruby; E-mail: rubyc@wcjc.edu; *Acq Tech,* Linda Hines; Tel: 979-532-6446, E-mail: hinesl@wcjc.edu; *Cat Tech, Tech Serv Technician,* Mary Muller; Tel: 979-532-6443, E-mail: mullerm@wcjc.edu; *Circ Asst,* Theresa Martinez; E-mail: martinezt@wcjc.edu. Subject Specialists: *Educ,* Dr Christy Ruby; Staff 5 (MLS 1, Non-MLS 4)
Founded 1946. Enrl 7,500; Fac 404; Highest Degree: Associate
Library Holdings: AV Mats 3,000; DVDs 2,000; e-books 27,000; Electronic Media & Resources 66; Bk Titles 52,000; Bk Vols 54,000; Per Subs 110; Videos 2,000
Automation Activity & Vendor Info: (Cataloging) Book Systems; (Circulation) Book Systems; (OPAC) Book Systems
Wireless access
Partic in Amigos Library Services, Inc; TexSHARE - Texas State Library & Archives Commission
Open Mon-Thurs 7:30am-8pm, Fri 7:30-4 (Fall & Spring); Mon-Thurs 7:30-5, Fri 7:30-Noon (Summer)

P WHARTON COUNTY LIBRARY*, 1920 N Fulton St, 77488. SAN 362-4153. Tel: 979-532-8080. FAX: 979-532-2792. Web Site: www.whartonco.lib.tx.us. *County Libr Dir,* Elene Gedevani; E-mail: egedevani@whartonco.lib.tx.us; *Asst Dir, Tech Serv Librn,* Gloria Barrera; E-mail: gbarrera@whartonco.lib.tx.us; *Ch,* Kay Bollom; E-mail: kbollom@whartonco.lib.tx.us; Staff 2 (MLS 2)
Founded 1938. Pop 41,467; Circ 203,978
Library Holdings: Bk Vols 85,790; Per Subs 114
Automation Activity & Vendor Info: (Cataloging) TLC (The Library Corporation); (Circulation) TLC (The Library Corporation); (OPAC) TLC (The Library Corporation)
Wireless access
Partic in Partners Library Action Network
Open Mon & Tues 9:30-8, Wed-Fri 9:30-6, Sat 9:30-3
Friends of the Library Group
Branches: 3
EAST BERNARD BRANCH, 746 Clubside Dr, East Bernard, 77435. Tel: 979-335-6142. *Br Mgr,* Patricia Orsak; E-mail: porsak@whartonco.lib.tx.us; *Ch,* Sandra Briones; E-mail: sbriones@whartonco.lib.tx.us
Circ 14,750
Library Holdings: Bk Vols 9,610
Open Mon & Wed-Fri 1:30-5:30, Tues 10-6, Sat 9-12
Friends of the Library Group
EL CAMPO BRANCH, 200 W Church St, El Campo, 77437. SAN 362-4218. Tel: 979-543-2362. FAX: 979-543-1545. *Br Mgr,* Brigitte Smith-Vaughan; E-mail: bvaughan@whartonco.lib.tx.us; *Ref Librn,* Renee Harrell; E-mail: rharrell@whartonco.lib.tx.us
Circ 92,780
Library Holdings: Bk Vols 35,165
Open Mon 9:30-8, Tues-Fri 9:30-6, Sat 9-1
Friends of the Library Group
LOUISE BRANCH, 803 Third St, Louise, 77455. SAN 362-4242. Tel: 979-648-2018. *Br Mgr,* Jessie Gonzales; E-mail: jgonzalez@whartonco.lib.tx.us
Circ 14,080
Library Holdings: Bk Vols 5,167
Open Tues 9-11:30 & 12:30-4, Wed 2-6, Thurs 2-4
Friends of the Library Group

WHEELER

P WHEELER PUBLIC LIBRARY*, 306 S Canadian St, 79096. (Mail add: PO Box 676, 79096-0676), SAN 316-845X. Tel: 806-826-5977. E-mail: wheelerpubliclibrary@gmail.com. Web Site: facebook.com/wheelerpubliclibrary1933. *Libr Dir,* Vicki L Ferguson; Staff 2 (Non-MLS 2)
Founded 1954. Pop 1,569; Circ 17,900
Library Holdings: Audiobooks 500; CDs 300; DVDs 350; Electronic Media & Resources 50; High Interest/Low Vocabulary Bk Vols 800; Large Print Bks 500; Bk Vols 60,000; Videos 1,000
Special Collections: All Wars since Indian Wars were waged to recent; Area Artist; Birds of Texas; Cowboy & Ranch History; Family Geneology; Generation Books; Government Officals History; Graveyard Directories for Panhandle area; High School Annuals; History of each Community around Wheeler, TX; History of major cities in the TX Panhandle; Indians of the Panhandle; Oil & Gas Stats; Pioneer Families in Wheeler County; Poetry; Quilting Books; Texas History; Wildflower Colls; World Leaders. Municipal Document Depository; State Document Depository; US Document Depository
Subject Interests: Area pioneer hist
Wireless access
Function: Accelerated reader prog, Activity rm, Adult bk club, After school storytime, Archival coll, Bk club(s), Bks on cassette, Bks on CD, Computer training, Computers for patron use, Digital talking bks, Free DVD rentals, Health sci info serv, Holiday prog, Homebound delivery serv, Jail serv, Meeting rooms, Microfiche/film & reading machines, Movies, Music CDs, Photocopying/Printing, Preschool reading prog, Prog for children & young adult, Ref & res, Scanner, Story hour, Study rm, Summer reading prog, Tax forms, Teen prog, VHS videos, Wheelchair accessible
Open Mon-Thurs 11:30-5, Fri 11:30-12:45
Restriction: Access at librarian's discretion, Authorized patrons, Authorized scholars by appt, By permission only, Clients only, Mem only, Non-circulating of rare bks

WHITE SETTLEMENT

P WHITE SETTLEMENT PUBLIC LIBRARY*, 8215 White Settlement Rd, 76108-1604. SAN 376-4710. Tel: 817-367-0166. FAX: 817-246-8184. E-mail: wspubliclibrary@wstx.us. Web Site: www.wstx.us/181/Library. *Mgr,* Sandra Rosas; E-mail: srosas@wstx.us
Library Holdings: Bk Vols 70,000; Per Subs 77
Automation Activity & Vendor Info: (Cataloging) Biblionix/Apollo; (Circulation) Biblionix/Apollo
Wireless access
Partic in Partners Library Action Network
Open Mon & Thurs 10-8, Tues & Wed 10-6, Sat 10-2
Friends of the Library Group

WHITEHOUSE

P WHITEHOUSE COMMUNITY LIBRARY, INC*, 107 Bascom Rd, 75791-3230. SAN 376-4508. Tel: 903-839-2949. FAX: 903-839-2949. E-mail: whitehousetxlibrary@gmail.com. Web Site: www.whitehousecommunitylibrary.com. *Libr Dir,* Meghan Grudza; Staff 1 (Non-MLS 1)
Founded 1983. Pop 7,000; Circ 14,000
Library Holdings: Bk Vols 30,000; Per Subs 30
Automation Activity & Vendor Info: (Acquisitions) Book Systems; (Cataloging) Book Systems; (Circulation) Book Systems; (OPAC) Book Systems
Wireless access
Function: Adult literacy prog, Audio & video playback equip for onsite use, Audiobks via web, Bk club(s), Bks on CD, CD-ROM, Children's prog, Computer training, Computers for patron use, E-Reserves, Electronic databases & coll, Family literacy, Free DVD rentals, Holiday prog, ILL available, Internet access, Laminating, Magazines, Magnifiers for reading, Mail & tel request accepted, Movies, Music CDs, Notary serv, Online cat, Photocopying/Printing, Printer for laptops & handheld devices, Prog for adults, Prog for children & young adult, Ref serv available, Senior computer classes, Spanish lang bks, Spoken cassettes & CDs, Spoken cassettes & DVDs, Story hour, Summer & winter reading prog, Summer reading prog, Tax forms, Teen prog, VHS videos, Wheelchair accessible, Workshops
Special Services for the Deaf - Bks on deafness & sign lang
Special Services for the Blind - Bks on CD; Large print bks; Magnifiers
Open Mon, Tues & Thurs 11-6, Fri 11-5, Sat 11-3
Restriction: Free to mem, ID required to use computers (Ltd hrs), Non-resident fee

WHITESBORO

P WHITESBORO PUBLIC LIBRARY*, 308 W Main, 76273. SAN 316-8468. Tel: 903-564-5432. FAX: 903-564-9594. E-mail: whlibrary@yahoo.com. Web Site: whitesboropl.org. *Dir,* Virginia Garvin
Founded 1969. Pop 3,197; Circ 30,796
Library Holdings: Bk Vols 28,000; Per Subs 12
Special Collections: Genealogy Coll
Automation Activity & Vendor Info: (Cataloging) Follett Software; (Circulation) Follett Software
Open Mon, Wed & Fri 9-5:30, Tues & Thurs 9-8, Sat 9-2
Friends of the Library Group

WHITEWRIGHT

P WHITEWRIGHT PUBLIC LIBRARY*, 200 W Grand St, 75491. (Mail add: PO Box 984, 75491-0984), SAN 316-8476. Tel: 903-364-2955. FAX: 903-364-5680. E-mail: library@whitewright.com. Web Site: www.whitewright.com/whitewright-library.html, www.whitewright.lib.tx.us. *Librn,* Chris Ely
Circ 19,000
Library Holdings: Bk Vols 20,000; Per Subs 12
Automation Activity & Vendor Info: (Cataloging) Follett Software; (Circulation) Follett Software
Open Mon-Wed & Fri 10-12 & 1-5:30, Thurs 10-12 & 1-7

WHITNEY

P LAKE WHITNEY PUBLIC LIBRARY*, 602 E Jefferson Ave, 76692. (Mail add: PO Box 1158, 76692), SAN 376-4753. Tel: 254-694-4639. E-mail: lwplibrary111@gmail.com. Web Site: www.whitneylibrary.org. *Dir,* Denise Carter; Staff 1 (Non-MLS 1)
Library Holdings: Audiobooks 400; Bk Vols 11,000; Videos 600
Wireless access
Partic in Partners Library Action Network
Open Mon, Wed & Fri 10-5, Thurs 10-6, Sat 9-1
Friends of the Library Group

WICHITA FALLS

C MIDWESTERN STATE UNIVERSITY, George Moffett Library, 3410 Taft Blvd, 76308-2099. SAN 316-8492. Tel: 940-397-4204. Circulation Tel: 940-397-4753. Reference Tel: 940-397-4758. Toll Free Tel: 800-259-8518. E-mail: library@msutexas.edu. Web Site: msutexas.edu/library. *Univ Librn,* Cortny Moorehead; Tel: 940-397-4173, E-mail: cortny.moorehead@msutexas.edu; *Assoc Univ Librn,* Ryan Samuelson; Tel: 940-397-4177, E-mail: ryan.samuelson@msutexas.edu; *Assoc Univ Librn,* Ashley Tipton; Tel: 940-397-4175, E-mail: ashley.tipton@msutexas.edu; *Coll Develop Librn, Syst Librn,* Dan Winslow; Tel: 940-397-4169, E-mail: daniel.winslow@msutexas.edu; *Instruction Librn,* Chris Depineda; Tel: 940-397-4172, E-mail: chris.depineda@msutexas.edu; *Instruction Librn,* Joseph C McNeely; Tel: 940-397-4091, E-mail: joseph.mcneely@msutexas.edu; *Spec Coll Librn,* Alissa Russell; Tel: 940-397-4755, E-mail: alissa.russell@msutexas.edu; *Circ Mgr,* Jason Brezina; Tel: 940-397-4176, E-mail: jason.brezina@mwsu.edu; *Night Circulation Mgr,* Zachary Lindquist; Tel: 940-397-4837, E-mail: zachery.lindquest@msutexas.edu; *Cat Spec,* Laura Hiller; Tel: 940-397-4168, E-mail: laura.hiller@msutexas.edu; *ILL Spec,* Amanda Rivera; Tel: 940-397-4757, E-mail: amanda.rivera@msutexas.edu; *ILL Spec,* Alexis Robinson; Tel: 940-397-4171, E-mail: alexis.robinson@msutexas.edu; Staff 15.4 (MLS 9.7, Non-MLS 5.7)
Founded 1922. Enrl 6,200; Fac 221; Highest Degree: Master
Library Holdings: AV Mats 7,842; e-books 487,497; Bk Titles 245,114; Bk Vols 255,867; Per Subs 70
Special Collections: Americana (Library of American Civilization), ultrafiche; English Literature (Library of English Literature to Early 20th Century), ultrafiche; Forrest D Monahen Railroad Coll; Missouri-Kansas-Texas Railroad Map Coll; MSU Archive & Faculty Coll; Nolan A Moore III Heritage of Print Coll; Political Papers; Walter W Dalquest Coll; What the Camera Saw Coll: Photographs by Jim Cochran; Wichita Falls Archive. State Document Depository; US Document Depository
Subject Interests: Educ, Hist, US
Automation Activity & Vendor Info: (Acquisitions) OCLC Worldshare Management Services; (Cataloging) OCLC Worldshare Management Services; (Circulation) OCLC Worldshare Management Services; (Course Reserve) OCLC Worldshare Management Services; (Discovery) OCLC Worldshare Management Services; (ILL) OCLC Worldshare Management Services; (OPAC) OCLC Worldshare Management Services; (Serials) OCLC Worldshare Management Services
Wireless access
Function: For res purposes
Publications: Libra (Newsletter)
Partic in Amigos Library Services, Inc; OCLC Online Computer Library Center, Inc; TexSHARE - Texas State Library & Archives Commission

Special Services for the Deaf - TDD equip; TTY equip; Videos & decoder
Open Mon-Thurs 8am-Midnight, Fri 8-5, Sat 10-6, Sun 2-Midnight (Fall-Spring); Mon-Thurs 8am-10pm, Fri 8-5, Sat Noon-6, Sun 2-10 (Summer)

S OIL INFORMATION LIBRARY OF WICHITA FALLS*, 710 Lamar St, Ste 100, 76301-6877. SAN 316-8549. Tel: 940-322-4241. FAX: 940-322-8695. E-mail: oillibrary@sbcglobal.net. Web Site: oilwf.org. *Exec Dir,* Gail Baldon Phillips; Staff 3 (MLS 1, Non-MLS 2)
Founded 1966
Library Holdings: Bk Vols 1,200
Subject Interests: Gas records, Geol data, Maps, Oil records
Wireless access
Function: Res libr
Open Mon-Fri 8:30-5

P WICHITA FALLS PUBLIC LIBRARY*, 600 11th St, 76301-4604. SAN 316-8484. Tel: 940-767-0868. Circulation Tel: 940-767-0868, Ext 4221. Interlibrary Loan Service Tel: 940-767-0868, Ext 4230. Reference Tel: 940-767-0868, Ext 4234. FAX: 940-720-6672. Web Site: www.wfpl.net. *Libr Adminr,* Jana Hausburg; Tel: 940-767-0868, Ext 4229, E-mail: jana.hausburg@wfpl.net; *Asst Admin, Head, Ref (Info Serv),* Angela Hill; Tel: 940-767-0868, Ext 4233, E-mail: angela.hill@wfpl.net; *Network Adminr,* Janice Bailey; Tel: 940-767-0868, Ext 4246, E-mail: janice.bailey@wfpl.net; *Head, Circ,* Jamie Dollar; Tel: 940-767-0868, Ext 4225, E-mail: jamie.dollar@wfpl.net; *Acq Librn, Head, Coll Develop,* Andrew Jelen; Tel: 940-767-0868, Ext 4228, E-mail: andrew.jelen@wfpl.net; *Acq Librn,* Efrem Sepulveda; Tel: 940-767-0868, Ext 4241, E-mail: efrem.sepulveda@wfpl.net; *Ch,* Celena Bradley; Tel: 940-767-0868, Ext 4244, E-mail: celena.bradley@wfpl.net; *Ref Librn,* Crystal Land; Tel: 940-767-0868, Ext 4232, E-mail: crystal.land@wfpl.net; *Youth Serv Mgr,* Susan Cooper; Tel: 940-767-0868, Ext 4245, E-mail: susan.cooper@wfpl.net; *Cataloger,* Carolyn Haines; Tel: 940-767-0868, Ext 4231, E-mail: carolyn.haines@wfpl.net. Subject Specialists: *Genealogy,* Andrew Jelen; Staff 17 (MLS 10, Non-MLS 7)
Founded 1918. Pop 125,000; Circ 281,349
Library Holdings: Bk Titles 148,000; Bk Vols 154,000; Per Subs 86
Special Collections: Texana & Southwest (Texas Coll)
Subject Interests: Genealogy, Tex hist
Automation Activity & Vendor Info: (Acquisitions) SirsiDynix; (Cataloging) SirsiDynix; (Circulation) SirsiDynix; (OPAC) SirsiDynix
Wireless access
Partic in Partners Library Action Network
Open Mon-Wed 9-8, Thurs-Sat 9-5
Friends of the Library Group

WILMER

P ELVIS MAXINE GILLIAM MEMORIAL PUBLIC LIBRARY*, 205 E Beltline Rd, 75172. SAN 361-4344. Tel: 972-441-3335. FAX: 972-525-3914. E-mail: librarian@cityofwilmer.net. Web Site: www.cityofwilmer.net/303/library-services. *Libr Dir,* Nallely Navarro; E-mail: nnavarro@cityofwilmer.net; Staff 1 (MLS 1)
Founded 1966. Pop 1,800
Library Holdings: AV Mats 1,400; Bk Vols 16,493; Per Subs 10
Automation Activity & Vendor Info: (Cataloging) Book Systems; (Circulation) Book Systems; (OPAC) Book Systems
Wireless access
Function: Bilingual assistance for Spanish patrons, Bks on cassette, Bks on CD, Computer training, Computers for patron use, Free DVD rentals, Genealogy discussion group, ILL available, Online cat, Outside serv via phone, mail, e-mail & web, Photocopying/Printing, Senior computer classes, Spanish lang bks, Summer reading prog, Tax forms, Telephone ref, VHS videos, Wheelchair accessible
Partic in TexSHARE - Texas State Library & Archives Commission
Open Mon-Thurs 10-6, Fri & Sat 10-2
Friends of the Library Group

WIMBERLEY

P WIMBERLEY VILLAGE LIBRARY*, 400 Farm to Market Rd 2325, 78676. (Mail add: PO Box 1240, 78676), SAN 320-264X. Tel: 512-847-2188. FAX: 512-847-3108. E-mail: reference@wimberleylibrary.org. Web Site: wimberleylibrary.org. *Dir,* Carolyn Manning; E-mail: director@wimberleylibrary.org
Founded 1975. Pop 12,666; Circ 18,000
Library Holdings: Bk Titles 20,000; Bk Vols 21,635; Per Subs 55
Special Collections: History (Herrick Arnold Coll)
Wireless access
Publications: Wimberley - A Way of Life, 1985
Partic in Partners Library Action Network
Open Mon & Wed 10-8, Tues & Thurs-Sat 10-6
Friends of the Library Group

WINNSBORO

P GILBREATH MEMORIAL LIBRARY*, 916 N Main St, 75494. SAN 316-8557. Tel: 903-342-6866. E-mail: winnsborogmlibrary@gmail.com. Web Site: winnsboro.ploud.net. *Libr Dir,* Manuel Pasillas, Jr; Staff 3 (Non-MLS 3)
Pop 7,825; Circ 68,764
Library Holdings: AV Mats 1,938; Large Print Bks 938; Bk Titles 29,103; Bk Vols 29,718; Per Subs 45; Talking Bks 1,018
Automation Activity & Vendor Info: (Cataloging) Book Systems; (Circulation) Book Systems
Wireless access
Open Tues-Fri 8:30-5:45, Sat 8:30-11:45
Friends of the Library Group

WINTERS

P WINTERS PUBLIC LIBRARY*, 120 N Main St, 79567. SAN 316-8565. Tel: 325-754-4251. E-mail: winterspubliclibrary@yahoo.com. Web Site: www.winterspubliclibrary.org. *Dir, Libr Serv,* Sally Spill; Staff 1 (Non-MLS 1)
Founded 1954. Pop 4,500; Circ 8,500
Library Holdings: Bk Titles 8,500
Subject Interests: Hist
Wireless access
Publications: Big Country Major Resource News; Forecast
Open Mon 9-3, Tues-Thurs 12-6, Sat 10-Noon

WOLFE CITY

P WOLFE CITY PUBLIC LIBRARY*, 203 E Williams St, 75496. (Mail add: PO Box 109, 75496-0109), SAN 316-8573. Tel: 903-496-7311. FAX: 903-496-7311. E-mail: wfclibrary496@att.net. Web Site: wolfecity.ploud.net. *Dir,* Valerie Cheshier; Staff 1 (Non-MLS 1)
Founded 1966. Pop 3,700
Library Holdings: Bk Titles 17,000
Wireless access
Open Mon 10-5:30, Tues 10-6, Wed 10-4, Thurs & Fri 1-5:30, Sat 10-1
Friends of the Library Group

WOLFFORTH

P CITY OF WOLFFORTH LIBRARY*, 508 E Hwy 62-82, 79382-7001. (Mail add: PO Box 430, 79382-0430), SAN 376-4265. Tel: 806-855-4150. FAX: 806-855-2595. E-mail: library@wolfforthtx.us. Web Site: wolfforthlibrary.org, wolfforthtx.us/residents/wolfforth-library. *Libr Dir,* Kimberly Brantley; Staff 4.5 (MLS 2, Non-MLS 2.5)
Pop 6,726; Circ 29,236
Library Holdings: AV Mats 200; Bk Titles 19,527; Bk Vols 20,062; Per Subs 6
Special Collections: Frenship ISD Digital Yearbook Coll
Automation Activity & Vendor Info: (Acquisitions) Biblionix; (Cataloging) Biblionix; (Circulation) Biblionix
Wireless access
Open Mon-Fri 9-8, Sat 1-5
Friends of the Library Group

WOODVILLE

P ALLAN SHIVERS LIBRARY & MUSEUM*, 302 N Charlton St, 75979. SAN 316-8581. Tel: 409-283-3709. FAX: 409-283-5258. E-mail: ashivers.library@gmail.com. Web Site: www.allanshiverslibrary.com. *Dir,* Kay Timme; Staff 1 (MLS 1)
Founded 1966. Pop 21,591; Circ 24,200
Library Holdings: Audiobooks 2,305; CDs 239; DVDs 2,000; Large Print Bks 5,170; Bk Vols 44,664; Per Subs 53
Automation Activity & Vendor Info: (Acquisitions) SirsiDynix; (Cataloging) SirsiDynix; (Circulation) SirsiDynix
Wireless access
Open Mon-Fri 9-5, Sat 10-2
Friends of the Library Group

WYLIE

P RITA & TRUETT SMITH PUBLIC LIBRARY*, 300 Country Club Rd, Bldg 300, 75098. SAN 316-859X. Tel: 972-516-6250. Administration Tel: 972-516-6251. E-mail: libinfo@wylietexas.gov. Web Site: www.wylietexas.gov/library.php. *Dir,* Rachel Orozco; *Supvr, Pub Serv,* Donna Shirley
Founded 1970. Pop 9,200; Circ 55,105
Library Holdings: Bk Vols 45,000; Per Subs 50
Automation Activity & Vendor Info: (Cataloging) TLC (The Library Corporation); (Circulation) TLC (The Library Corporation); (OPAC) TLC (The Library Corporation)
Wireless access
Publications: Library Notes (Monthly)

Partic in Partners Library Action Network
Open Mon-Thurs 10-8, Fri & Sat 10-5
Friends of the Library Group

YORKTOWN

P YORKTOWN PUBLIC LIBRARY*, 103 W Main, 78164. (Mail add: PO Box 308, 78164), SAN 316-8611. Tel: 361-564-3232. Web Site: yorktownpubliclibrary.org. *Librn,* Jenni Diehl; E-mail: jdiehl@yorktowntx.gov
Founded 1939. Pop 1,810; Circ 5,362
Library Holdings: Audiobooks 360; AV Mats 150; CDs 212; DVDs 312; Large Print Bks 300; Bk Titles 20,089; Per Subs 43; Videos 500
Automation Activity & Vendor Info: (Cataloging) Follett Software; (Circulation) Follett Software; (ILL) Follett Software; (OPAC) Follett Software
Wireless access
Function: Adult bk club, Art exhibits, Audio & video playback equip for onsite use, Bks on CD, CD-ROM, Children's prog, Computers for patron use, Distance learning, Electronic databases & coll, Free DVD rentals, Home delivery & serv to seniorr ctr & nursing homes, Homebound delivery serv, ILL available, Magnifiers for reading, Mail & tel request accepted, Music CDs, Photocopying/Printing, Preschool outreach, Prog for adults, Prog for children & young adult, Ref serv available, Story hour, Summer reading prog, Tax forms, Telephone ref, Wheelchair accessible, Workshops
Partic in Partners Library Action Network
Special Services for the Deaf - Bks on deafness & sign lang; Closed caption videos
Special Services for the Blind - Accessible computers; Audio mat; Bks available with recordings; Bks on cassette; Bks on CD; Cassettes; Home delivery serv; Large print bks; Magnifiers; Ref serv; Sound rec
Open Mon-Wed 10-6, Fri 9-1
Friends of the Library Group

ZAPATA

P OLGA V FIGUEROA - ZAPATA COUNTY PUBLIC LIBRARY*, 901 Kennedy St, 78076. (Mail add: 2806 Stop 28A, 78076), SAN 325-173X. Tel: 956-765-5351. FAX: 956-765-1578. E-mail: zcpl5351@gmail.com. Web Site: www.co.zapata.tx.us/page/zapata.public.library. *Dir,* Amalia Navarro; Staff 3 (Non-MLS 3)
Founded 1983. Pop 12,200
Library Holdings: CDs 500; DVDs 200; Bk Vols 28,000; Per Subs 48; Talking Bks 175; Videos 300
Special Collections: Genealogical Records, microfiche, microfilm; Texas History Coll
Wireless access
Open Mon-Fri 8-5
Friends of the Library Group

UTAH

Date of Statistics: FY 2021
Population, 2020 U.S. Census: 3,271,616
Population Served by Public Libraries: 3,231,053
Total Volumes in Public Libraries (physical books only): 6,008,545
Volumes Per Capita: 1.83
Collection Per Capita: 6.98
Total Public Library Circulation (Physical Items): 19,275,916
Circulation Per Capita: 589
Digital Resources:
Total e-books: 5,472,312
Total audio items: 10,056,818
Total video items: 1,045,326
Total Library Collection: 22,841,102
Income and Expenditures:
Total Public Library Income (not including Grants-in-Aid): $125,511,054
Source of Income: Local government public funds
Expenditure Per Capita: $38.37
Grants-in-Aid to Public Libraries:
Federal: $1,830,269
State Aid: $565,000
Number of County Libraries: 12 County Systems with 64 outlets.
Tribal Libraries: 7
Number of Bookmobiles in State: 5
Information provided courtesy of: Heidi Fendrick, State Data Coordinator; Library Consultant

AMERICAN FORK

P AMERICAN FORK CITY LIBRARY*, 64 S 100 E, 84003. SAN 316-862X. Tel: 801-763-3070. FAX: 801-763-3073. E-mail: aflibrary@afcity.net. Web Site: www.afcity.org/203/library. *Dir,* Casandria Crane; E-mail: ccrane@afcity.net; Staff 20 (MLS 1, Non-MLS 19)
Pop 26,263; Circ 301,750
Library Holdings: Audiobooks 3,009; CDs 893; DVDs 2,401; Large Print Bks 736; Bk Vols 97,080; Per Subs 93; Videos 2,361
Automation Activity & Vendor Info: (Cataloging) SirsiDynix; (Circulation) SirsiDynix; (OPAC) SirsiDynix
Wireless access
Function: Computers for patron use, Electronic databases & coll, Free DVD rentals, Holiday prog, Homework prog, ILL available, Learning ctr, Music CDs, Online cat, OverDrive digital audio bks, Photocopying/Printing, Preschool reading prog, Prog for adults, Prog for children & young adult, Ref & res, Spanish lang bks, Story hour, Summer reading prog, Tax forms, Teen prog, VHS videos, Wheelchair accessible, Winter reading prog
Partic in Beehive Library Consortium; Pioneer
Open Mon-Thurs 9-9, Fri & Sat 10-6
Restriction: Circ to mem only, In-house use for visitors, Non-resident fee
Friends of the Library Group

G NATIONAL PARK SERVICE*, Timpanogos Cave National Monument Library, Alpine Loop, Hwy 92, 84003. (Mail add: 2038 W Alpine Loop Rd, 84003), SAN 321-8376. Tel: 801-756-5239. FAX: 801-756-5661. E-mail: tica_info@nps.gov. *Integrated Resources Prog Mgr,* Cami McKinney; E-mail: cami_mckinney@nps.gov
Founded 1966
Library Holdings: Bk Titles 925
Subject Interests: Cave related subjs, Caves, Natural res, The Environment

BEAVER

P BEAVER PUBLIC LIBRARY*, 55 W Center St, 84713. (Mail add: PO Box 192, 84713), SAN 316-8638. Tel: 435-438-5274. FAX: 435-438-5826. E-mail: bvlibrary@beaverutah.net. Web Site: beaverutah.net/community/library. *Dir,* Angela Edwards; E-mail: aedwards@beaverutah.net; Staff 1 (Non-MLS 1)
Founded 1920. Pop 2,618; Circ 19,016
Library Holdings: AV Mats 413; Large Print Bks 80; Bk Vols 18,394; Per Subs 26; Talking Bks 326
Automation Activity & Vendor Info: (Acquisitions) Follett Software; (Cataloging) Follett Software; (Circulation) Follett Software; (Course Reserve) Follett Software; (OPAC) Follett Software
Wireless access
Partic in Beehive Library Consortium
Open Mon 10-6, Tues-Thurs 11-6, Sat 11-3

BRIGHAM CITY

P BRIGHAM CITY LIBRARY*, 26 E Forest St, 84302. SAN 316-8646. Tel: 435-723-5850. FAX: 435-723-2813. E-mail: brighamlibrary@gmail.com. Web Site: bcpl.lib.ut.us. *Libr Dir,* Susan H Hill; *Ref Librn,* Diana Huffman; *Ch Serv,* Michele Schumann; *Children's/Young Adult Serv,* Connie Edwards; *Circ/Adult Serv,* Elizabeth Schow; Staff 6 (MLS 1, Non-MLS 5)
Founded 1915. Pop 19,182; Circ 272,358
Library Holdings: e-books 21,270; Bk Vols 63,098; Per Subs 62
Special Collections: Box Elder History, books & pamphlets; Church of Jesus Christ of Latter-day Saints (Mormon) History; Church of Jesus Christ of Latter-day Saints (Mormon) Religion
Automation Activity & Vendor Info: (Cataloging) SirsiDynix; (Circulation) SirsiDynix-WorkFlows; (OPAC) SirsiDynix-Enterprise
Wireless access
Function: 24/7 Electronic res, 24/7 Online cat, 3D Printer, Adult bk club, Adult literacy prog, Audiobks on Playaways & MP3, Bk club(s), Bks on CD, Children's prog, Citizenship assistance, Computers for patron use, Electronic databases & coll, Family literacy, Free DVD rentals, Homebound delivery serv, ILL available, Internet access, Magazines, Meeting rooms, Microfiche/film & reading machines, Online cat, OverDrive digital audio bks, Photocopying/Printing, Prog for children & young adult, Ref & res, Ref serv available, Res assist avail, Scanner, Spanish lang bks, Story hour, Study rm, Summer reading prog, Tax forms, Wheelchair accessible, Writing prog
Partic in Beehive Library Consortium
Open Mon-Thurs 10-8:45, Fri & Sat 10-5:45
Restriction: Non-resident fee
Friends of the Library Group

CASTLE DALE

P EMERY COUNTY LIBRARY SYSTEM*, Castle Dale (Main Library), 115 N 100 E, 84513. (Mail add: PO Box 515, 84513-0515), SAN 316-8670. Tel: 435-381-2554. FAX: 435-381-2699. E-mail: cd@lib.emerycounty.com. Web Site: lib.emerycounty.com/castle-dale.html. *Asst Libr Dir, Br Librn,* Roxanne Jensen; *Asst Br Librn,* Camille Thomas
Pop 10,651; Circ 109,268
Library Holdings: Bk Vols 134,130
Automation Activity & Vendor Info: (Acquisitions) Book Systems; (Cataloging) Book Systems; (Circulation) Book Systems; (Course Reserve) Book Systems; (ILL) Book Systems; (OPAC) Book Systems; (Serials) Book Systems
Wireless access
Partic in Beehive Library Consortium; Pioneer
Open Mon-Wed 9:30-5:30, Thurs 9:30-6, Sat 9:30-5
Branches: 7
CLEVELAND BRANCH, 45 W Main, Cleveland, 84518. (Mail add: PO Box 275, Cleveland, 84518-0275). Tel: 435-653-2204. FAX: 435-653-2104. *Librn,* Loyette Holdaway; *Asst Librn,* Tina Bradley
Open Mon-Fri 9:30-5:30

ELMO BRANCH, 15 S 100 East, Elmo, 84521. (Mail add: PO Box 217, Elmo, 84521). Tel: 435-653-2558. FAX: 435-653-2553. *Librn,* Bonnie Day; *Asst Librn,* Marilyn Olsen
Open Mon-Fri 9:30-5:30

EMERY BRANCH, 100 North Ctr, Emery, 84522. (Mail add: PO Box 127, Emery, 84522-0127). Tel: 435-286-2474. FAX: 435-286-2434. *Librn,* Marian Mangum; *Asst Librn,* Denise Allen
Open Mon-Fri 9:30-5:30

FERRON BRANCH, 55 N 200 West, Ferron, 84523. (Mail add: PO Box 850, Ferron, 84523-0850). Tel: 435-384-2637. FAX: 435-384-2876. *Librn,* Colleen Murdock; *Asst Librn,* Becky Jewkes
Open Mon-Fri 9:30-5:30

GREEN RIVER BRANCH, 85 S Long St, Green River, 84525. (Mail add: PO Box 510, Green River, 84525-0510). Tel: 435-564-3349. FAX: 435-564-3399. *Librn,* Cheri Packer; *Asst Librn,* Jolene Dalton
Open Mon-Fri 9:30-5:30

HUNTINGTON BRANCH, 92 S Main, Huntington, 84528. (Mail add: PO Box 794, Huntington, 84528-0794). Tel: 435-687-9590. FAX: 435-687-9510. *Librn,* Flora Motte; *Asst Librn,* Kay Jeffs
Open Mon-Fri 9:30-5:30

ORANGEVILLE BRANCH, 125 S Main, Orangeville, 84537. (Mail add: PO Box 628, Orangeville, 84537-0628). Tel: 435-748-2726. FAX: 435-748-2736. *Br Librn, Dir,* Carole Larsen; *Asst Br Librn,* Hoffman Melodie
Open Mon-Fri 9:30-5:30

CEDAR CITY

P CEDAR CITY PUBLIC LIBRARY IN THE PARK*, 303 N 100 East, 84720. SAN 316-8689. Tel: 435-586-6661. FAX: 435-865-7280. Web Site: cedarcitylibrary.org. *Dir,* Steven D Decker; E-mail: dsteve@cedarcity.org; *Asst Dir, Ch Serv,* Luene Byers; *Tech Serv,* Martin Barrett; Staff 4 (MLS 1, Non-MLS 3)
Founded 1914. Pop 33,000; Circ 269,400
Jul 2018-Jun 2019 Income $612,484, State $10,550, Locally Generated Income $600,934
Library Holdings: Audiobooks 5,722; CDs 257; DVDs 3,619; e-books 78,270; Bk Vols 86,927; Per Subs 5
Special Collections: Local Newspaper Coll, micro; Rare Book Coll. Oral History
Subject Interests: Consumer guides, Hist, Relig studies, Sci
Automation Activity & Vendor Info: (Cataloging) TLC (The Library Corporation); (Circulation) TLC (The Library Corporation); (OPAC) TLC (The Library Corporation)
Function: 24/7 Electronic res, 24/7 Online cat, 3D Printer, Activity rm
Partic in Beehive Library Consortium
Open Mon-Thurs 9-9; Fri & Sat 9-6

C SOUTHERN UTAH UNIVERSITY*, Gerald R Sherratt Library, 351 W University Blvd, 84720. SAN 316-8697. Tel: 435-586-7933, 435-865-8240. Reference Tel: 435-865-8040. Administration Tel: 435-586-7947. FAX: 435-865-8152. E-mail: library@suu.edu. Web Site: www.suu.edu/library. *Coll Develop, Dean, Libr Serv,* Dr Richard L Saunders; E-mail: rsaunders@suu.edu; *Exec Dir,* Matthew Nickerson; Tel: 435-586-1955, E-mail: nickerson@suu.edu; *Network Adminr,* Julie Wood; Tel: 435-586-8052, E-mail: juliewood@suu.edu; *Acad Librn, Asst Prof,* Abigail Lochtefeld; Tel: 435-586-7952, E-mail: abigaillochtefeld@suu.edu; *Libr Media Prog Dir,* Caitlin Kime; Tel: 435-586-1908, E-mail: caitlingerrity@suu.edu; *Assessment Librn, Data Mgt,* Scott W Lanning; Tel: 435-865-8156, E-mail: lanning@suu.edu; *Outreach Librn,* Dr Anne Diekema; Tel: 435-586-5435, E-mail: annediekema@suu.edu; *Spec Coll Librn,* Paula Mitchell; Tel: 435-586-7976, E-mail: mitchellp@suu.edu. Subject Specialists: *Hist, Music,* Dr Richard L Saunders; *Media,* Abigail Lochtefeld; *Anthrop, Geol, Nutrition,* Caitlin Kime; *Bus,* Scott W Lanning; *Fr, German, Spanish,* Dr Anne Diekema; *Law, Polit sci,* Paula Mitchell; Staff 9.3 (MLS 7.3, Non-MLS 2)
Founded 1897. Enrl 9,000; Fac 275; Highest Degree: Master
Jul 2016-Jun 2017. Mats Exp $374,682, Books $159,582, Per/Ser (Incl. Access Fees) $6,188, AV Mat $5,458, Electronic Ref Mat (Incl. Access Fees) $182,205, Presv $21,249. Sal $1,246,040 (Prof $583,214)
Library Holdings: AV Mats 9,039; e-books 189,751; Electronic Media & Resources 218; Microforms 994; Bk Titles 441,219; Bk Vols 442,461; Per Subs 259
Special Collections: Barbara Treheay Matheson Books: By, For and About Women; Dixie National Forest Coll; Grand Staircase-Escalante National Monument Coll; Howard R Driggs Coll; Iron Mining District; Michael O Leavitt Coll; Mountain West Digital Library; Opera Scores & Books of the 19th Century (Victorian Room); Shakespeare Coll; Southern Paiute Indian Coll; Southern Utah History Coll; US Geology Maps; William R Palmer Coll. Oral History; State Document Depository; US Document Depository
Subject Interests: Music, Opera, Shakespeare, Sibelius, Utah hist
Automation Activity & Vendor Info: (Acquisitions) SirsiDynix-WorkFlows; (Cataloging) SirsiDynix; (Circulation) SirsiDynix; (Course Reserve) SirsiDynix; (ILL) OCLC; (OPAC) SirsiDynix; (Serials) SirsiDynix
Wireless access
Function: Art exhibits, Computers for patron use, Doc delivery serv, E-Reserves, Electronic databases & coll, ILL available, Online cat, Photocopying/Printing, Ref serv available, Wheelchair accessible
Publications: Friends of the Library (Newsletter); Gerald R Sherratt Library Annual Report; Journal of the Wooden O (College journal); SUU Departmental Histories (Local historical information)
Partic in Utah Academic Library Consortium
Special Services for the Blind - Accessible computers; Bks on CD; Computer with voice synthesizer for visually impaired persons; Dragon Naturally Speaking software
Open Mon-Thurs 7am-Midnight, Fri 7-7, Sat 11-7, Sun 2-10
Friends of the Library Group

DELTA

P DELTA CITY LIBRARY*, 76 N 200 W, 84624-9424. SAN 316-8727. Tel: 435-864-4945. FAX: 435-864-4313. E-mail: library@delta.utah.gov. Web Site: sites.google.com/site/deltacitylibrary1. *Librn,* Michelle Lovejoy; Staff 1 (Non-MLS 1)
Founded 1920. Pop 3,622; Circ 28,695
Library Holdings: AV Mats 3,490; Bks on Deafness & Sign Lang 15; High Interest/Low Vocabulary Bk Vols 300; Large Print Bks 155; Bk Titles 35,560; Per Subs 41
Automation Activity & Vendor Info: (Cataloging) OCLC Online; (Circulation) Follett Software
Wireless access
Partic in Beehive Library Consortium
Open Mon-Fri 10-7, Sat 12-4

DUCHESNE

P DUCHESNE LIBRARY*, 130 S Center St, 84021. (Mail add: P O Box 169, 84021-0169). Tel: 435-738-2800. FAX: 435-738-2802. Web Site: www.duchesne.utah.gov/your-government-2/county-departments/library/duchesne-library. *County Libr Dir,* Daniel Mauchley; E-mail: dmauchley@duchesne.utah.gov; *Asst Br Mgr,* Jeannie Meacham; E-mail: jeanniem@duchesne.utah.gov; Staff 1 (MLS 1)
Founded 2007. Pop 17,000; Circ 45,000
Wireless access
Partic in Beehive Library Consortium
Open Mon-Thurs 10-6, Fri & Sat 10-5
Branches: 1

ROOSEVELT BRANCH, 70 W Lagoon 44-4, Roosevelt, 84066-2841, SAN 316-9103. Tel: 435-722-4441. FAX: 435-722-3386. *Br Mgr,* Stephen Moon; E-mail: smoon@duchesne.utah.gov; *Asst Br Mgr,* Deborah Haslam
Circ 52,209
Library Holdings: Bk Vols 52,000; Per Subs 45
Automation Activity & Vendor Info: (Acquisitions) Follett Software; (Cataloging) Follett Software; (Circulation) Follett Software; (Course Reserve) Follett Software; (ILL) Follett Software; (Media Booking) Follett Software; (OPAC) Follett Software; (Serials) Follett Software
Partic in Pioneer
Open Mon-Thurs 9-7, Fri 9-5, Sat 10-5

DUGWAY

A UNITED STATES ARMY DUGWAY PROVING GROUND*, Dugway Post Library, 5124 Kister Ave, IMWE-DUG-MWL MS1, 84022-1097. SAN 362-4277. Tel: 435-831-2178. FAX: 435-831-2178. E-mail: usarmy.mwr.library@mail.mil. Web Site: dugway.armymwr.com/programs/library, mylibraryus.armybiznet.com/search~S12. *Librn,* Mike Beier; Staff 3 (MLS 2, Non-MLS 1)
Library Holdings: CDs 475; DVDs 1,400; Electronic Media & Resources 50; Bk Titles 27,000; Bk Vols 28,000; Per Subs 50; Talking Bks 1,100; Videos 750
Special Collections: Utah Coll
Automation Activity & Vendor Info: (Cataloging) Innovative Interfaces, Inc - Millennium; (Circulation) Innovative Interfaces, Inc - Millennium; (ILL) OCLC; (OPAC) Innovative Interfaces, Inc - Millennium; (Serials) Innovative Interfaces, Inc - Millennium
Wireless access
Function: After school storytime, Audio & video playback equip for onsite use, Audiobks via web, Children's prog, Computer training, Computers for patron use, Digital talking bks, Electronic databases & coll, Free DVD rentals, ILL available, Internet access, Music CDs, Online cat, Orientations, OverDrive digital audio bks, Photocopying/Printing, Prog for adults, Prog for children & young adult, Ref & res, Ref serv available, Scanner, Spoken cassettes & CDs, Story hour, Summer reading prog, VHS videos
Open Mon-Thurs 9-7

A UNITED STATES ARMY, DUGWAY PROVING GROUND*, TEDT-DPW-DMA, MS No 4, 84022-5004. SAN 362-4307. Tel: 435-831-5009. FAX: 435-831-3543. *Lead Libn,* Tracy Elizabeth Lay; E-mail: tracy.e.lay.civ@mail.mil; Staff 1 (MLS 1)
Founded 1950
Library Holdings: Bk Titles 65,000
Special Collections: Dugway Documents Coll (Fort Detrick, Tropic Test Center, Deseret Test Center, Dugway Proving Ground, Joint/CINC Operational Testing & Chemical-Biological Data Source Books)
Subject Interests: Biology, Chem, Chem-Biol defense, Engr, Math, Meteorology, Munitions, Statistics, Zoology
Automation Activity & Vendor Info: (Cataloging) SirsiDynix; (Circulation) SirsiDynix; (ILL) OCLC FirstSearch; (OPAC) SirsiDynix
Function: Orientations, Ref serv available, Res libr
Partic in Federal Library & Information Network; OCLC Online Computer Library Center, Inc
Restriction: Authorized personnel only

EAGLE MOUNTAIN

P EAGLE MOUNTAIN LIBRARY*, 1650 E Stagecoach Run, 84005. Tel: 801-789-6623. Administration Tel: 801-789-6622. FAX: 801-789-6653. E-mail: library@emcity.org. Web Site: eaglemountaincity.com/library. *Libr Dir,* Michele Graves; E-mail: mgraves@emcity.org; *Asst Libr Dir,* Kristin Allred; E-mail: kralled@emcity.org; *Asst Libn,* Rochelle Allen; E-mail: rallen@emcity.org; Staff 13 (Non-MLS 13)
Founded 1999. Pop 49,738; Circ 233,360
Jul 2021-Jun 2022. Mats Exp $50,000. Sal $254,596
Library Holdings: Audiobooks 907; AV Mats 843; DVDs 2,156; e-books 112,338; Electronic Media & Resources 224,788; Bk Titles 66,242; Per Subs 8
Automation Activity & Vendor Info: (Acquisitions) SirsiDynix-WorkFlows; (Cataloging) SirsiDynix-WorkFlows; (Circulation) SirsiDynix-WorkFlows; (OPAC) SirsiDynix-iBistro
Wireless access
Function: 24/7 Electronic res, 24/7 Online cat, Adult bk club, Audiobks via web, Bilingual assistance for Spanish patrons, Bk club(s), Bks on CD, Chess club, Children's prog, Citizenship assistance, Computer training, Computers for patron use, Distance learning, E-Readers, Electronic databases & coll, Free DVD rentals, ILL available, Internet access, Learning ctr, Life-long learning prog for all ages, Magazines, Mail & tel request accepted, Meeting rooms, Movies, Online cat, Outside serv via phone, mail, e-mail & web, OverDrive digital audio bks, Photocopying/Printing, Preschool reading prog, Printer for laptops & handheld devices, Prog for adults, Prog for children & young adult, Ref serv available, Scanner, Spanish lang bks, STEM programs, Story hour, Summer & winter reading prog, Summer reading prog, Telephone ref, Wheelchair accessible
Partic in Beehive Library Consortium
Special Services for the Blind - Bks on CD; Digital talking bk
Open Mon-Thurs 9:30-6:30, Fri 9:30-5:30, Sat 9:30-1:30
Restriction: Non-resident fee

ELSINORE

P ELSINORE TOWN LIBRARY*, 15 E 200 N, 84724. Tel: 435-527-4345. E-mail: library@elsinoreut.com. Web Site: www.facebook.com/ElsinoreTownLibrary. *Dir,* Kim LeMmon
Partic in Beehive Library Consortium
Open Tues-Thurs 3:30pm-5:30pm

EPHRAIM

P EPHRAIM PUBLIC LIBRARY*, 30 S Main St, 84627. SAN 316-8735. Tel: 435-283-4544. Web Site: ephraimcity.org/155/Library. *Dir,* Lori Voshall; E-mail: lori.voshall@ephraimcity.org
Pop 5,500; Circ 44,755
Library Holdings: DVDs 1,400; Bk Vols 33,000; Per Subs 48
Automation Activity & Vendor Info: (Acquisitions) Follett Software; (Cataloging) Follett Software; (Circulation) Follett Software; (OPAC) Follett Software
Wireless access
Partic in Beehive Library Consortium; Pioneer; Utah Libr Asn
Open Mon-Fri 10-8, Sat 10-2
Friends of the Library Group

J SNOW COLLEGE*, Karen H Huntsman Library, 141 E Center St, 84627. (Mail add: 150 College Ave, Box 1025, 84627-1550), SAN 316-8743. Tel: 435-283-7363. Reference Tel: 435-283-7361. Administration Tel: 435-283-7365. Automation Services Tel: 435-283-7360. Toll Free Tel: 800-848-3399. E-mail: library@snow.edu. Web Site: snow.edu/library. *Dir of Libr,* Jon Ostler; E-mail: jon.ostler@snow.edu; *Instruction & Outreach Libn,* Carol Kunzler; E-mail: Carol.Kunzler@snow.edu; *Tech Serv Libn,* Lynn Anderson; Tel: 435-283-7366, E-mail: lynn.anderson@snow.edu; Staff 3 (MLS 3)
Founded 1888. Enrl 5,800; Highest Degree: Bachelor
Library Holdings: Bk Titles 50,000; Bk Vols 50,203; Per Subs 264
Special Collections: Childrens Literature (Demont & Arlea Howell Childrens Literature Coll)
Subject Interests: Col hist, Local authors, Local hist
Automation Activity & Vendor Info: (Acquisitions) Koha; (Cataloging) Koha; (Circulation) Koha; (Course Reserve) Koha; (Discovery) EBSCO Discovery Service; (ILL) OCLC; (OPAC) Koha; (Serials) Koha
Wireless access
Function: Art exhibits, Audio & video playback equip for onsite use, Bks on CD, Free DVD rentals, ILL available, Mail & tel request accepted, Microfiche/film & reading machines, Music CDs, Online ref, Photocopying/Printing, Ref serv available, Res libr, Scanner, Telephone ref
Partic in Utah Academic Library Consortium
Open Mon-Thurs 7:30am-Midnight, Fri 7:30-7, Sat Noon-6, Sun 5pm-11pm (Sept-April); Mon-Fri 8-5 (May-Aug)

FARMINGTON

P DAVIS COUNTY LIBRARY*, 133 S Main St, 84025. (Mail add: PO Box 115, 84025-0115), SAN 362-4331. Tel: 801-451-3030. FAX: 801-451-3031. E-mail: library@daviscountyutah.gov. Web Site: www.daviscountyutah.gov/library. *Libr Dir,* Ms Chris Sanford; Tel: 801-451-3051, E-mail: chriss@co.davis.ut.us; *Dep Dir,* Josh Johnson; *Dep Dir,* Lynnette Mills; *Site Mgr,* Shirleen Wiscombe; *Circ Supvr,* Kimberley Matheson; Staff 116 (MLS 6, Non-MLS 110)
Founded 1946. Pop 315,809; Circ 2,805,128
Library Holdings: AV Mats 79,495; Bk Vols 606,290
Automation Activity & Vendor Info: (Acquisitions) SirsiDynix; (Cataloging) SirsiDynix-WorkFlows; (Circulation) SirsiDynix-WorkFlows; (ILL) OCLC; (OPAC) SirsiDynix-iBistro
Wireless access
Function: Computers for patron use, ILL available, Music CDs, Online cat, OverDrive digital audio bks, Prog for adults, Prog for children & young adult, Story hour, Summer reading prog, Tax forms
Partic in OCLC Online Computer Library Center, Inc
Open Mon-Thurs 10-9, Fri & Sat 10-6
Restriction: Lending limited to county residents, Non-resident fee, Open to pub for ref & circ; with some limitations
Branches: 6

BOUNTIFUL/SOUTH BRANCH, 725 S Main St, Bountiful, 84010, SAN 362-4390. Tel: 451-451-1760. Web Site: www.daviscountyutah.gov/library/locations/bountiful-branch. *Br Mgr,* Mary Moore; *Circ Supvr,* Sabra Fisher; *Ref Supvr,* Michele Hollnagel
Founded 1969. Circ 509,052
Open Mon-Thurs 10-9, Fri & Sat 10-6

CENTERVILLE BRANCH, 45 S 400 West, Centerville, 84014. Tel: 801-451-1775. Web Site: www.daviscountyutah.gov/library/locations/centerville-branch. *Br Mgr,* Brenda Lower; *Circ Supvr,* Nancy Barton
Founded 2006. Circ 305,881
Open Mon-Thurs 10-9, Fri & Sat 10-6

CLEARFIELD/NORTH BRANCH, 562 S 1000 East, Clearfield, 84015, SAN 362-4366. Tel: 801-451-1840. Web Site: www.co.davis.ut.us/library/locations/clearfield-branch. *Br Mgr,* Jon Sears; *Circ Supvr,* Ms Chris Davis
Founded 1975. Circ 255,638
Open Mon-Thurs 10-9, Fri & Sat 10-6

KAYSVILLE BRANCH, 215 N Fairfield Rd, Kaysville, 84037, SAN 316-8832. Tel: 801-451-1800. Web Site: www.daviscountyutah.gov/library/locations/kaysville-branch. *Br Mgr,* Carolyn Myers; *Circ Supvr,* Tracie Terry
Founded 1920. Circ 284,770
Open Mon-Thurs 10-9, Fri & Sat 10-6

LAYTON/CENTRAL BRANCH, 155 N Wasatch Dr, Layton, 84041, SAN 329-6342. Tel: 801-451-1820. Web Site: www.daviscountyutah.gov/library/locations/layton-branch. *Br Mgr,* Ellen Peterson; *Circ Supvr,* Isaac Gange
Founded 1988. Circ 436,856
Open Mon-Thurs 10-9, Fri & Sat 10-6

SYRACUSE/NORTHWEST BRANCH, 1875 S 2000 West, Syracuse, 84075. Tel: 801-451-1850. Web Site: www.daviscountyutah.gov/library/locations/syracuse-branch. *Br Mgr,* Meledie Denhalter; *Circ Supvr,* Lori Gardiner
Founded 2003. Circ 401,552
Open Mon-Thurs 10-9, Fri & Sat 10-6

FILLMORE

P PRESIDENT MILLARD FILLMORE LIBRARY*, 25 S 100 West St, 84631. SAN 316-8751. Tel: 435-743-5314. FAX: 435-743-6710. E-mail: fillmorelibraryill@gmail.com. Web Site: fillmorelibrary.org. *Dir,* Stephanie Aleman; E-mail: saleman@fillmorelibrary.org
Pop 2,253; Circ 36,561
Library Holdings: Bk Vols 27,000; Per Subs 14

Automation Activity & Vendor Info: (Cataloging) Auto-Graphics, Inc; (Circulation) Auto-Graphics, Inc; (OPAC) Auto-Graphics, Inc
Wireless access
Partic in Beehive Library Consortium; Pioneer
Open Mon-Thurs 10-6, Fri 10-5, Sat 9-1 (Winter); Mon-Thurs 10-7, Fri 10-6 (Summer)

GARDEN CITY

P GARDEN CITY PUBLIC LIBRARY*, 69 N Paradise Pkwy, Bldg A, 84028. Tel: 435-946-2950. E-mail: librarydirector@cut.net. Web Site: gardencitylibrary.net.
Automation Activity & Vendor Info: (Cataloging) Follett Software; (OPAC) Follett Software
Partic in Beehive Library Consortium
Open Mon & Fri 2-6, Wed 10-6, Sat 10-2
Friends of the Library Group

GARLAND

P GARLAND PUBLIC LIBRARY*, 86 W Factory St, 84312. (Mail add: PO Box 129, 84312-0147), SAN 316-876X. Tel: 435-257-3118, Ext 1005. E-mail: library@garlandutah.org. Web Site: www.garlandlibrary.org. *Dir,* Linda King; E-mail: lindak@garlandlibrary.org
Founded 1914. Pop 2,598
Library Holdings: Bk Vols 8,483; Per Subs 15
Subject Interests: Agr, Hist, Lit
Automation Activity & Vendor Info: (Cataloging) Biblionix/Apollo; (Circulation) Biblionix/Apollo; (ILL) Follett Software; (OPAC) Biblionix/Apollo
Wireless access
Partic in Beehive Library Consortium; Pioneer
Open Mon 10-7, Tues-Thurs 1-7, Fri 1-5
Friends of the Library Group

GRANTSVILLE

P GRANTSVILLE CITY LIBRARY*, 42 N Bowery St, 84029. Tel: 435-884-1670. FAX: 435-884-1680. E-mail: gcl@grantsvilleut.gov. Web Site: www.grantsvilleut.gov/departments/library. *Libr Dir,* John Ingersoll; E-mail: jingersoll@grantsvilleut.gov; *Libr Tech,* Teena Brown; E-mail: tbrown@grantsvilleut.gov; *Libr Tech,* Allie Higley; E-mail: ahigley@grantsvilleut.gov; *Libr Tech,* Claudia Lowder; E-mail: clowder@grantsvilleut.gov; *Libr Tech,* Valerie Warner; E-mail: vwarner@grantsvilleut.gov
Wireless access
Function: Bk club(s), Computers for patron use, ILL available, Meeting rooms, Photocopying/Printing, Scanner
Partic in Beehive Library Consortium
Open Tues, Thurs & Fri 10-5, Wed 10-7, Sat 10-3
Friends of the Library Group

GUNNISON

P GUNNISON CIVIC LIBRARY*, 38 W Center St, 84634. (Mail add: PO Box 790, 84634-0790), SAN 323-939X. Tel: 435-528-3104. FAX: 435-528-3145. E-mail: gunnlibrary@gunnisoncity.org. Web Site: gunnisoncity.org. *Dir,* Carolyn Childs; E-mail: childsc@gunnisoncity.org
Founded 1945. Pop 2,000; Circ 12,074
Library Holdings: Bk Vols 15,000
Automation Activity & Vendor Info: (Cataloging) Follett Software; (Circulation) Follett Software; (OPAC) Follett Software
Open Mon-Wed 1-5, Thurs 3-7, Sat 11-3
Friends of the Library Group

S UTAH DEPARTMENT OF CORRECTIONS*, Central Utah Correctional Facility Library, 255 E 300 N, 84634. Tel: 435-528-6000. FAX: 435-528-6234. Web Site: corrections.utah.gov/central-utah-correctional-facility. *Librn,* Jaron Jensen; E-mail: jaronjensen@utah.gov
Library Holdings: Bk Vols 24,000
Automation Activity & Vendor Info: (Cataloging) ResourceMATE; (Circulation) ResourceMATE

HEBER CITY

P WASATCH COUNTY LIBRARY*, 465 E 1200 S, 84032-3943. SAN 316-8778. Tel: 435-654-1511. FAX: 435-654-6456. E-mail: library@wasatch.utah.gov. Web Site: wasatchlibrary.org. *Libr Dir,* Juan Tomas Lee; E-mail: jlee@wasatch.utah.gov; Staff 118 (MLS 1, Non-MLS 117)
Founded 1919. Pop 36,173; Circ 306,171
Jan 2024-Dec 2024 Income $1,249,670, State $8,250, Federal $16,700, County $1,166,322, Other $58,398. Mats Exp $111,928, Books $74,550, AV Mat $14,827, Electronic Ref Mat (Incl. Access Fees) $22,551. Sal $509,731
Library Holdings: Audiobooks 6,029; DVDs 6,450; e-books 130,776; Electronic Media & Resources 247,001; Bk Vols 53,130
Automation Activity & Vendor Info: (Cataloging) Koha; (Circulation) Koha; (OPAC) Koha
Wireless access
Function: 24/7 Electronic res, 24/7 Online cat, 3D Printer, Activity rm, Adult bk club, Art exhibits, Art programs, Audiobks on Playaways & MP3, Audiobks via web, Bilingual assistance for Spanish patrons, Bk club(s), Bks on CD, Children's prog, Computer training, Computers for patron use, Electronic databases & coll, Extended outdoor wifi, Free DVD rentals, Games, Holiday prog, Home delivery & serv to seniorr ctr & nursing homes, Homebound delivery serv, ILL available, Instruction & testing, Internet access, Life-long learning prog for all ages, Magazines, Mail & tel request accepted, Meeting rooms, Microfiche/film & reading machines, Movies, Music CDs, Online cat, Online info literacy tutorials on the web & in blackboard, Online ref, Outreach serv, OverDrive digital audio bks, Photocopying/Printing, Preschool outreach, Printer for laptops & handheld devices, Prog for adults, Prog for children & young adult, Ref serv available, Scanner, Senior computer classes, Senior outreach, Spanish lang bks, Spoken cassettes & CDs, STEM programs, Story hour, Study rm, Summer reading prog, Tax forms, Teen prog, Telephone ref, Wheelchair accessible, Wifi hotspot checkout
Partic in Beehive Library Consortium
Open Mon-Fri 10-8, Sat 10-2

HELPER

P HELPER CITY LIBRARY*, 19 S Main St, 84526. SAN 325-1861. Tel: 435-472-5601. FAX: 435-472-3064. E-mail: helperlibrary@helpercity.net. Web Site: helpercitylibrary.wordpress.com. *Dir,* Diana Grant; *Libr Asst,* Shirlee Diaz; *Libr Asst,* Barbara Reagan; Staff 1 (Non-MLS 1)
Founded 1935. Pop 2,200
Library Holdings: Audiobooks 381; AV Mats 200; Bks on Deafness & Sign Lang 26; DVDs 2,400; Large Print Bks 92; Bk Titles 24,195; Talking Bks 381
Automation Activity & Vendor Info: (Cataloging) Follett Software; (Circulation) Follett Software; (OPAC) Follett Software
Wireless access
Partic in Beehive Library Consortium; Pioneer
Open Mon-Thurs 10-6, Fri 10-4
Friends of the Library Group

HIGHLAND

P HIGHLAND CITY LIBRARY*, 5400 W Civic Center Dr, Ste 2, 84003. Tel: 801-772-4528. FAX: 801-756-6903. Web Site: highlandcitylibrary.org. *Dir,* Donna L Cardon; Tel: 801-772-4529, E-mail: librarydirector@highlandcity.org; Staff 3 (MLS 1, Non-MLS 2)
Founded 2008. Pop 19,500; Circ 175,000
Jul 2018-Jun 2019 Income $322,873, State $5,200, City $302,673, Locally Generated Income $15,000. Mats Exp $20,600, Books $19,000, AV Mat $1,000, Electronic Ref Mat (Incl. Access Fees) $600. Sal $215,989 (Prof $85,000)
Library Holdings: Audiobooks 587; CDs 155; DVDs 1,432; e-books 55; Electronic Media & Resources 1; Large Print Bks 50; Bk Vols 43,775; Per Subs 25
Subject Interests: Graphic novels
Automation Activity & Vendor Info: (Acquisitions) Innovative Interfaces, Inc; (Cataloging) OCLC CatExpress; (Circulation) Innovative Interfaces, Inc; (OPAC) Innovative Interfaces, Inc; (Serials) Innovative Interfaces, Inc
Wireless access
Function: 24/7 Electronic res, 24/7 Online cat, Audiobks via web, Bks on CD, Children's prog, Computers for patron use, Free DVD rentals, Home delivery & serv to seniorr ctr & nursing homes, ILL available, Internet access, Magazines, Movies, Online cat, OverDrive digital audio bks, Photocopying/Printing, Prog for children & young adult, Ref serv available, Scanner, Spoken cassettes & CDs, Story hour, Study rm, Summer reading prog, Teen prog, Telephone ref, Wheelchair accessible
Partic in Beehive Library Consortium
Open Mon-Thurs 10-8, Fri 10-4, Sat 12-4
Friends of the Library Group

HILL AFB

A UNITED STATES AIR FORCE*, Gerrity Memorial Library, 75 MSG/SVMG, Bldg 440, 7415 Weiner St, 84056-5006. SAN 362-4455. Tel: 801-777-2533, 801-777-3833. FAX: 801-777-6667. E-mail: gerritymemoriallibrary440@gmail.com. Web Site: hillfss.com/library. *Libr Dir,* Micky Smith; E-mail: micky.smith.2@us.af.mil
Founded 1941
Library Holdings: Bk Vols 27,000; Per Subs 28
Subject Interests: Aeronaut, Children's bks, Gen coll recreational for adults, Gen coll tech, Space, Western hist, Young adult bks
Automation Activity & Vendor Info: (Cataloging) Bibliomation Inc; (Circulation) Bibliomation Inc

Wireless access
Restriction: Authorized personnel only, Not open to pub

HYRUM

P HYRUM LIBRARY, 50 W Main, 84319. SAN 316-8794. Tel: 435-245-6411. E-mail: hyrumlibrary@gmail.com. Web Site: www.hyrumcity.gov/library. *Libr Dir,* Emily Coltrin; E-mail: emily.coltrin@hyrumcity.gov; *Asst Libr Dir,* Rosie Johnson; E-mail: rosie.johnson@hyrumcity.gov; *Ch,* Arielle Ballard; E-mail: hyrumlibrarychildren@gmail.com; *Teen Librn,* Deonna Edgar; E-mail: hyrumlibraryteens@gmail.com; *Asst Librn,* Diane Harris; Staff 10 (MLS 1, Non-MLS 9)
Founded 1969. Circ 309,000
Library Holdings: Audiobooks 2,160; CDs 1,128; DVDs 1,083; Large Print Bks 173; Bk Vols 46,248; Per Subs 53; Talking Bks 67; Videos 3,723
Subject Interests: Hist
Automation Activity & Vendor Info: (Cataloging) Follett Software; (Circulation) Follett Software; (Course Reserve) Follett Software; (OPAC) Follett Software
Wireless access
Function: 24/7 Electronic res, 24/7 Online cat, 24/7 wireless access, Activity rm, Adult bk club, Adult literacy prog, Archival coll, Audiobks on Playaways & MP3, Audiobks via web, AV serv, Bk club(s), Bks on CD, Children's prog, Computers for patron use, Free DVD rentals, ILL available, Internet access, Magazines, Meeting rooms, Movies, Music CDs, Online cat, OverDrive digital audio bks, Preschool reading prog, Printer for laptops & handheld devices, Prog for adults, Prog for children & young adult, Scanner, Spanish lang bks, Story hour, Study rm, Summer reading prog, Teen prog
Partic in Beehive Library Consortium
Open Mon 10-7, Tues-Fri 12-7, Sat 10-3

KANAB

P KANAB CITY LIBRARY*, 374 N Main St, 84741-3259. Tel: 435-644-2394. FAX: 435-644-2822. E-mail: library@kanab.utah.gov. Web Site: www.kanablibrary.org. *Libr Dir,* Jana Lee Peay
Library Holdings: AV Mats 660; Bks on Deafness & Sign Lang 12; CDs 263; DVDs 150; Large Print Bks 57; Bk Titles 32,623; Per Subs 47; Talking Bks 1,247; Videos 1,214
Special Collections: Grandstaircase Oral Histories; South West Coll. Oral History
Subject Interests: SW
Automation Activity & Vendor Info: (Acquisitions) Follett Software; (Cataloging) OCLC CatExpress; (Circulation) Follett Software; (Course Reserve) Follett Software; (ILL) OCLC WorldShare Interlibrary Loan; (OPAC) Follett Software
Wireless access
Partic in Beehive Library Consortium
Open Mon & Fri 10-5, Tues-Thurs 10-6, Sat 10-3
Friends of the Library Group

LEHI

P LEHI CITY LIBRARY*, 120 N Center St, 84043. SAN 316-8840. Tel: 385-201-1050. FAX: 801-766-8856. E-mail: library@lehi-ut.gov. Web Site: lehicity.ent.sirsi.net, www.lehi-ut.gov/services/lehi-city-library. *Dir,* Kristi Seely; E-mail: kseely@lehi-ut.gov; Staff 8 (MLS 1, Non-MLS 7)
Founded 1917. Pop 21,000; Circ 180,000
Library Holdings: Bk Vols 71,000; Per Subs 108
Automation Activity & Vendor Info: (Acquisitions) TLC (The Library Corporation); (Cataloging) TLC (The Library Corporation); (Circulation) TLC (The Library Corporation); (OPAC) TLC (The Library Corporation); (Serials) TLC (The Library Corporation)
Wireless access
Partic in Beehive Library Consortium; Pioneer
Open Mon-Thurs 9-8, Fri & Sat 10-4

LEWISTON

P LEWISTON PUBLIC LIBRARY*, 29 S Main St, 84320. (Mail add: PO Box 36, 84320-0036), SAN 316-8859. Tel: 435-258-5515. Web Site: www.lewiston-ut.org/lewiston-library. *Dir,* Beth Anne Creger; E-mail: bethanne.c@lewiston-ut.org
Founded 1936. Pop 3,400; Circ 18,324
Library Holdings: Bk Vols 20,000; Per Subs 30
Wireless access
Function: 24/7 Online cat, Adult bk club, Audiobks on Playaways & MP3, Audiobks via web, Bk club(s), Bks on CD, CD-ROM, Children's prog, Computers for patron use, Digital talking bks, Free DVD rentals, ILL available, Internet access, Laminating, Movies, Music CDs, Online cat, Photocopying/Printing, Preschool reading prog, Summer reading prog, VHS videos
Partic in Beehive Library Consortium
Open Mon & Thurs 10-5, Tues 10-7, Wed 9-1 & 6-9, Fri & Sat 10-3
Restriction: Circ to mem only

LOGAN

P LOGAN LIBRARY*, 255 N Main, 84321-3914. SAN 316-8867. Tel: 435-716-9123. Circulation Tel: 435-716-9121. Interlibrary Loan Service Tel: 435-716-9129. Reference Tel: 435-716-9120. Web Site: library.loganutah.org. *Dir,* Karen Clark; Tel: 435-716-9130, E-mail: karen.clark@loganutah.org; *Asst Dir,* Joseph Anderson; Tel: 435-716-9137, E-mail: joseph.anderson@loganutah.org; *Librn,* Jason Cornelius; Tel: 435-716-9143, E-mail: jason.cornelius@loganutah.org; *Ch Serv,* Becky Smith; *Computer Serv,* Melanie Liechty; Staff 9 (MLS 7, Non-MLS 2)
Founded 1916. Pop 50,000; Circ 776,295
Library Holdings: Bk Vols 179,293; Per Subs 155
Automation Activity & Vendor Info: (Cataloging) SirsiDynix; (Circulation) SirsiDynix; (ILL) OCLC WorldShare Interlibrary Loan; (OPAC) SirsiDynix
Wireless access
Partic in Beehive Library Consortium; OCLC Online Computer Library Center, Inc
Special Services for the Blind - Internet workstation with adaptive software; Magnifiers
Open Mon-Thurs 10-9, Fri & Sat 10-6
Friends of the Library Group

C UTAH STATE UNIVERSITY*, Merrill-Cazier Library, 3000 Old Main Hill, 84322-3000. SAN 362-448X. Tel: 435-797-2633. Interlibrary Loan Service Tel: 435-797-2680. Reference Tel: 435-797-2678. Administration Tel: 435-797-2631. FAX: 435-797-2880. Interlibrary Loan Service FAX: 435-797-2677. Web Site: library.usu.edu. *Dean of Libr,* Brad Cole; Tel: 435-797-2687, E-mail: brad.cole@usu.edu; *Assoc Dean, Coll, Patron Serv,* Jeanne Davidson; E-mail: jeanne.davidson@usu.edu; *Assoc Dean, Cat, Digital Serv, Spec Coll,* Todd Welch; Tel: 435-797-8268, E-mail: todd.welch@usu.edu; *Head, Cat, Head, Metadata Serv,* Liz Woolcott; Tel: 435-797-9458, E-mail: liz.woolcott@usu.edu; *Head, Coll Mgt, Head, Resource Sharing,* Kevin Brewer; Tel: 435-797-3961, E-mail: Kevin.Brewer@usu.edu; *Head, Digital Libr Serv,* Becky Thoms; Tel: 435-797-0816, E-mail: becky.thoms@usu.edu; *Head, Learning Serv,* Kacy Lundstrom; Tel: 435-797-2285, E-mail: kacy.lundstrom@usu.edu; *Head, Patron Serv,* Vicki Read; Tel: 435-797-2914, E-mail: vicki.read@usu.edu; *Head of Doc Delivery, Head, Resource Sharing,* Carol Kochan; Tel: 435-797-2676, E-mail: carol.kochan@usu.edu; *Dir, Info Tech,* Todd Hugie; Tel: 435-797-2638, E-mail: todd.hugie@usu.edu; *Govt Doc Librn,* Jen Kirk; Tel: 435-797-8033, E-mail: Jen.Kirk@usu.edu; Staff 41 (MLS 34, Non-MLS 7)
Founded 1888. Enrl 28,118; Fac 1,081; Highest Degree: Doctorate
Jul 2015-Jun 2016 Income (Main Library Only) $10,324,392. Mats Exp $6,768,285. Sal $3,556,107 (Prof $2,310,493)
Library Holdings: e-books 700,222; e-journals 74,377; Bk Titles 1,921,880; Bk Vols 1,850,384
Special Collections: Archives of Society of American Range Management; Berten Wendell Allred Western Americana Library; Blanche Browning Rich Coll, rec; Briant H Stringham Papers, ms; Compton Photograph Coll; Cowboy Poetry Coll; Czechoslovakia (Masaryk Coll & Spencer Taggart Coll); Daryl Chase Coll; Dolly Sitton Bentley Memorial Coll; Edgar B Brossard Papers, ms; Fife Folklore Coll; Frederick P Champ Papers, ms; Gunn McKay Congressional Papers, ms; Hand Folklore Coll; Jack London Coll; Medical Artifacts & Books (Robert & Mary Ann Simmons McDill Coll); Ridgway Coll; Utah Woolgrowers Association Archives, ms; Utah, Mormons & Southern Idaho; Western American Literature (David & Beatrice C Evans Coll); Yoder Folklore Coll. Oral History; State Document Depository; US Document Depository
Subject Interests: Agr, Environ studies, Natural sci, Space studies, Western Am art
Automation Activity & Vendor Info: (Acquisitions) Innovative Interfaces, Inc; (Cataloging) Innovative Interfaces, Inc; (Circulation) Innovative Interfaces, Inc; (ILL) OCLC ILLiad; (OPAC) Innovative Interfaces, Inc; (Serials) Innovative Interfaces, Inc
Wireless access
Partic in Greater Western Library Alliance; Utah Academic Library Consortium
Friends of the Library Group
Departmental Libraries:
ANN CARROLL MOORE CHILDREN'S LIBRARY, 6700 Old Main Hill, 84322. Tel: 435-797-3093. *Librn,* Vaughn Larson
Library Holdings: Bk Vols 21,501
Open Mon-Thurs 7-Midnight, Fri 7-6, Sat 11-7, Sun 11-Midnight
REGIONAL DEPOSITORY COLLECTION OF US GOVERNMENT DOCUMENTS, 3000 Old Main Hill, 84322-3000. Tel: 435-797-2684. *Head, Doc Serv,* John Walters; Tel: 435-797-2683, E-mail: john.walters@usu.edu; *Librn,* Stephen Weiss; Tel: 435-797-3661, E-mail: steve.weiss@usu.edu
Open Mon-Fri 8-5

YOUNG EDUCATIONAL TECHNOLOGY CENTER, UMC 2845 - 170 EDUC, Utah State University, 84322-2845. Tel: 435-797-3377. *Librn,* Nathan M Smith

MANTI

P MANTI PUBLIC LIBRARY*, Two S Main St, 84642. SAN 316-8883. Tel: 435-835-2201. FAX: 435-835-2202. E-mail: manticitylibraryut@gmail.com. Web Site: manticity.com/publiclibrary. *Libr Dir,* Cynthia Lopez; Staff 2 (MLS 1, Non-MLS 1)
Founded 1910. Pop 3,429; Circ 16,302
Library Holdings: Bk Vols 24,107; Per Subs 21
Subject Interests: Local hist
Automation Activity & Vendor Info: (Cataloging) ComPanion Corp; (Circulation) ComPanion Corp; (Course Reserve) ComPanion Corp; (OPAC) ComPanion Corp
Wireless access
Partic in Beehive Library Consortium; Pioneer
Open Mon-Fri 10-7, Sat 10-3
Friends of the Library Group

MENDON

P MENDON LIBRARY*, 15 N Main St, 84325. Tel: 435-774-2200. E-mail: mendonutahlibrary@mendoncity.org. Web Site: library.mendoncity.org. *Libr Dir,* Heidi Taylor; E-mail: heiditaylorlibrarian@gmail.com; *Libr Asst,* Jessica Martin
Founded 1975
Library Holdings: Bk Vols 10,000
Automation Activity & Vendor Info: (Cataloging) Follett Software; (OPAC) Follett Software
Function: Bk club(s), Computers for patron use, ILL available, Photocopying/Printing, Story hour
Publications: Newsletter (Monthly)
Partic in Beehive Library Consortium
Open Mon-Thurs 12-6, Sat 12-4
Friends of the Library Group

MIDVALE

S UTAH STATE HISTORICAL SOCIETY*, Utah History Research Center Library, 7292 S State St, 84047. SAN 316-9294. Tel: 801-245-7227. E-mail: historyresearch@utah.gov. Web Site: history.utah.gov/library-collections. *Mgr, Res,* Greg Walz; *Colls Mgr, Libr Mgr,* Doug Misner; *Coll Spec, Librn,* Michele Elnicky; Staff 4 (MLS 4)
Founded 1939
Library Holdings: Bk Vols 50,000; Per Subs 205
Subject Interests: Mormon hist, Utah hist, Western hist
Automation Activity & Vendor Info: (Cataloging) SirsiDynix
Function: Res libr
Publications: Guide to the Women's History Holdings at the Utah State Historical Society Library; Guide to Unpublished Materials at the Utah State Historical Society
Partic in Research Libraries Information Network
Restriction: Non-circulating, Open by appt only

MILFORD

P MILFORD PUBLIC LIBRARY*, 100 West 400 S, 84751. (Mail add: PO Box 69, 84751-0069). Tel: 435-387-5039. FAX: 435-387-5027. E-mail: library@milford.utah.gov. Web Site: www.milfordcityutah.com/index.php/1/library. *Libr Dir,* Cynthia Carter
Library Holdings: AV Mats 519; Bk Vols 17,761; Talking Bks 267
Automation Activity & Vendor Info: (Cataloging) Follett Software; (Circulation) Follett Software
Wireless access
Partic in Beehive Library Consortium
Open Mon-Thurs 12-6:30, Fri 12-6

MINERSVILLE

P MINERSVILLE PUBLIC LIBRARY*, 40 W Main St, 84752. (Mail add: PO Box 250, 84752-0250). Tel: 435-386-2267. FAX: 435-386-1813. E-mail: minersvillelibrary@gmail.com. Web Site: townofminersville.municipalimpact.com/library. *Libr Dir,* Shannon Terry
Library Holdings: Bk Vols 10,000; Talking Bks 200
Automation Activity & Vendor Info: (Cataloging) Auto-Graphics, Inc; (Circulation) Auto-Graphics, Inc
Wireless access
Partic in Beehive Library Consortium
Open Mon, Tues & Thurs 1-7, Wed 1-6, Fri 1-5

MOAB

P GRAND COUNTY PUBLIC LIBRARY*, 257 E Center St, 84532. SAN 316-8891. Tel: 435-259-1111. FAX: 435-259-1380. E-mail: info@moablibrary.org. Web Site: www.grandcountyutah.net/286/Library. *Libr Dir,* Carrie Valdes; Tel: 435-355-0930, E-mail: carrie@moablibrary.org; Staff 9 (MLS 3, Non-MLS 6)
Founded 1915. Pop 9,500; Circ 140,000
Library Holdings: Audiobooks 2,070; AV Mats 6,128; Bks on Deafness & Sign Lang 20; CDs 846; DVDs 1,615; Large Print Bks 924; Bk Titles 44,469; Bk Vols 49,465; Per Subs 105; Videos 1,728
Special Collections: Mountaineering (Chouinard Coll)
Subject Interests: Hispanic
Automation Activity & Vendor Info: (Cataloging) ByWater Solutions; (Circulation) ByWater Solutions; (OPAC) ByWater Solutions
Wireless access
Function: 24/7 Electronic res, 24/7 Online cat, Activity rm, Adult bk club, After school storytime, Art exhibits, Audiobks on Playaways & MP3, Bilingual assistance for Spanish patrons, Bk club(s), Bks on CD, Children's prog, Computers for patron use, E-Readers, Electronic databases & coll, Equip loans & repairs, Free DVD rentals, Govt ref serv, ILL available, Internet access, Jail serv, Life-long learning prog for all ages, Magazines, Magnifiers for reading, Mail & tel request accepted, Mango lang, Meeting rooms, Microfiche/film & reading machines, Movies, Music CDs, Online cat, Online ref, Outreach serv, OverDrive digital audio bks, Photocopying/Printing, Preschool outreach, Preschool reading prog, Prog for adults, Prog for children & young adult, Ref serv available, Scanner, Senior outreach, Spanish lang bks, STEM programs, Story hour, Study rm, Summer & winter reading prog, Summer reading prog, Tax forms, Teen prog, Telephone ref
Partic in Beehive Library Consortium
Special Services for the Deaf - Assistive tech
Special Services for the Blind - Assistive/Adapted tech devices, equip & products
Open Mon-Fri 9-8, Sat 9-5
Friends of the Library Group
Branches: 1
CASTLE VALLEY, Castle Valley Community Ctr, Two Castle Valley Dr, 84532. Tel: 435-259-9998. *Libr Asst,* Tom Spruill; E-mail: tom@moablibrary.org; Staff 1 (Non-MLS 1)
Founded 2004
Open Tues 9-1, Wed 9-4, Fri 1-5

MONROE

P MONROE PUBLIC LIBRARY*, 49 N Main St, 84754. (Mail add: PO Box 120, 84754-0120). Tel: 435-527-4019. FAX: 435-527-4622. E-mail: monroecitylibrary@yahoo.com. Web Site: monroecitylibrary.wordpress.com. *Libr Dir,* Shelly Monroe; E-mail: monroedirector@yahoo.com; Staff 3 (Non-MLS 3)
Founded 1928. Pop 2,256; Circ 11,462
Library Holdings: Audiobooks 1,509; DVDs 556; Large Print Bks 624; Bk Vols 12,228
Subject Interests: Local hist
Automation Activity & Vendor Info: (Cataloging) Book Systems; (Circulation) Book Systems; (OPAC) Book Systems
Wireless access
Function: 24/7 Online cat, 24/7 wireless access, Adult bk club, Audiobks on Playaways & MP3, Bks on CD, Children's prog, Computers for patron use, Extended outdoor wifi, Free DVD rentals, Homebound delivery serv, ILL available, Internet access, Laminating, Online cat, OverDrive digital audio bks, Photocopying/Printing, Preschool reading prog, Printer for laptops & handheld devices, STEM programs, Story hour, Summer reading prog, Wheelchair accessible
Partic in Beehive Library Consortium
Open Tues-Sat 1-6

MONTICELLO

P SAN JUAN COUNTY PUBLIC LIBRARY*, Monticello Branch, 80 N Main St, 84535. (Mail add: PO Box 66, 84535-0066), SAN 362-4609. Tel: 435-587-2281. FAX: 435-587-9980. E-mail: mlibrary@sanjuancounty.org. Web Site: www.sanjuancountylibrary.org. *Libr Dir,* Pat Smith
Pop 9,606; Circ 18,800
Library Holdings: Bk Vols 18,603; Per Subs 45
Automation Activity & Vendor Info: (Cataloging) Follett Software; (Circulation) Follett Software
Partic in Beehive Library Consortium
Open Mon-Fri 10-7, Sat 11-3
Branches: 6
BLANDING BRANCH, 25 W 300 South, Blanding, 84511-3829, SAN 362-4633. Tel: 435-678-2335. FAX: 435-678-2335. E-mail: blibrary@sanjuancounty.org. *Dir,* Lana Latham
Library Holdings: Bk Vols 12,500; Per Subs 40
Open Mon-Thurs 12-7, Fri 2-6, Sat 10-2

BLUFF BRANCH, 480 Black Locust Ave, Bluff, 84512. (Mail add: PO Box 99, Bluff, 84512).
Founded 2010. Pop 400
Function: Audiobks via web, Bks on CD, Computers for patron use, Free DVD rentals, ILL available, Internet access, Notary serv, Photocopying/Printing, Summer reading prog, Tax forms, Wheelchair accessible
Open Tues & Thurs 12-6

MONTEZUMA CREEK LIBRARY, Fifth East St, Montezuma Creek, 84534. Tel: 435-651-3309.
Open Mon, Wed & Fri 12-6

MONUMENT VALLEY BRANCH, 100 Cougar Lane, Monument Valley, 84536. Tel: 435-727-3204. E-mail: mvcc@navajohopisolidarity.org. *Dir,* Nicole Perkins; E-mail: nperkins@sanjuancounty.org
Open Mon-Thurs 5:30pm-7pm

NAVAJO MOUNTAIN BRANCH, Navajo Mountain High School, Navajo Mountain Rd, Rte 16, Navajo Mountain, 84510. (Mail add: PO Box 10040, Tonalea, 86044). Tel: 435-678-1287, Ext 2481. FAX: 435-678-1289. *Librn,* Dathine Atene; E-mail: datene@sjsd.org; Staff 1 (MLS 1)
Open Mon-Thurs 3-6

MORGAN

P MORGAN COUNTY LIBRARY*, 50 N 100 West, 84050. (Mail add: PO Box 600, 84050-0600), SAN 316-8905. Tel: 801-829-3481. Web Site: library.morgancountyutah.gov. *Libr Dir,* Erin Bott; E-mail: ebott@morgancountyutah.gov; *Asst Dir,* Alisa Rose; E-mail: arose@morgancountyutah.gov; Staff 4 (Non-MLS 4)
Pop 10,608; Circ 123,037
Library Holdings: Bk Vols 43,873; Per Subs 25
Special Collections: Morgan County Historical Society Coll
Automation Activity & Vendor Info: (Acquisitions) Follett Software; (Cataloging) Follett Software; (Circulation) Follett Software; (OPAC) Follett Software
Wireless access
Partic in Beehive Library Consortium
Open Mon-Thurs 11-7, Fri 11-5, Sat Noon-5
Friends of the Library Group

MOUNT PLEASANT

P MOUNT PLEASANT PUBLIC LIBRARY*, 24 E Main St, 84647-1429. SAN 316-8913. Tel: 435-462-3240. FAX: 435-462-9115. E-mail: library@mtpleasantcity.com. Web Site: mtpleasantlib.org. *Libr Dir,* Dawn Coates; *Librn,* Susan Fullmer; *Librn,* Paul Kelson; *Librn,* Kallei Miller; *Librn,* Alana Miner
Founded 1917. Circ 60,987
Library Holdings: Bk Vols 23,000
Automation Activity & Vendor Info: (Cataloging) Follett Software; (Circulation) Follett Software; (OPAC) Follett Software
Wireless access
Function: After school storytime, Audiobks via web, Bks on cassette, Bks on CD, CD-ROM, Children's prog, Computer training, Computers for patron use, Digital talking bks, Doc delivery serv, Electronic databases & coll, Free DVD rentals, Holiday prog, ILL available, Instruction & testing, Internet access, Mail & tel request accepted, Music CDs, Online cat, Online ref, Outside serv via phone, mail, e-mail & web, OverDrive digital audio bks, Photocopying/Printing, Preschool outreach, Prog for children & young adult, Ref & res, Ref serv available, Scanner, Spoken cassettes & CDs, Spoken cassettes & DVDs, Story hour, Summer reading prog, Tax forms, Teen prog, VHS videos
Partic in Beehive Library Consortium
Open Mon & Fri 11-5, Tues-Thurs 11-7, Sat 11-3
Friends of the Library Group

MURRAY

P MURRAY PUBLIC LIBRARY*, 166 E 5300 South, 84107. SAN 362-4668. Tel: 801-264-2580. Web Site: www.murraylibrary.org. *Libr Dir,* Kim Fong; Tel: 801-264-2585, E-mail: kfong@murray.utah.gov; Staff 15 (MLS 4, Non-MLS 11)
Founded 1910. Pop 47,000; Circ 600,000
Library Holdings: AV Mats 10,000; Bk Titles 60,000; Per Subs 40
Automation Activity & Vendor Info: (Cataloging) TLC (The Library Corporation); (Circulation) TLC (The Library Corporation); (OPAC) TLC (The Library Corporation)
Wireless access
Open Mon-Thurs 10-9, Fri & Sat 10-6
Friends of the Library Group

NEPHI

P NEPHI PUBLIC LIBRARY*, 21 E 100 N, 84648. SAN 316-8921. Tel: 435-623-1312. E-mail: library@nephi.utah.gov. Web Site: www.nephi.utah.gov/151/Public-Library. *Dir,* Ruth Bonzo; E-mail: rbonzo@nephi.utah.gov; Staff 4 (Non-MLS 4)
Founded 1919. Pop 5,045; Circ 60,760
Library Holdings: Bks on Deafness & Sign Lang 10; Large Print Bks 15; Bk Titles 24,030; Talking Bks 1,515; Videos 601
Automation Activity & Vendor Info: (Cataloging) Follett Software; (Circulation) Follett Software
Partic in Beehive Library Consortium
Open Mon-Thurs 11-7, Fri 1-5, Sat (Sept-May) 10-2
Friends of the Library Group

NEWTON

P NEWTON TOWN LIBRARY*, 51 S Center St, 84327. Tel: 435-563-9283. E-mail: newton.library@newtonutah.org. Web Site: www.newtontownlibrary.com. *Libr Dir,* Sarah Rigby
Library Holdings: AV Mats 142; Bk Vols 20,000
Wireless access
Partic in Beehive Library Consortium
Open Mon 3-7, Tues & Thurs 10-1 & 3-6, Wed 3-6, Sat 12-4
Friends of the Library Group

NORTH LOGAN

P NORTH LOGAN CITY LIBRARY, 475 E 2500 N, 84341. Tel: 435-755-7169. FAX: 435-227-0032. E-mail: staff@northloganlibrary.org. Web Site: northloganlibrary.org. *Libr Dir,* Trenton Bateman; *Ch Assoc,* Judi Poorte; Staff 3 (MLS 2, Non-MLS 1)
Pop 9,683; Circ 215,866
Library Holdings: Bk Vols 64,000; Per Subs 78
Automation Activity & Vendor Info: (Cataloging) SirsiDynix; (Circulation) SirsiDynix
Wireless access
Partic in Beehive Library Consortium
Open Mon-Sat 10-7
Friends of the Library Group

OGDEN

C STEVENS HENAGER COLLEGE LIBRARY*, 1890 S 1350 West, 84401. (Mail add: PO Box 9428, 84409-0428), SAN 316-8956. Tel: 801-622-1567. FAX: 866-990-0038. *Admin Dir,* Marjorie Anderson; E-mail: marjorie.anderson@stevenshenager.edu; Staff 1 (Non-MLS 1)
Founded 1891. Enrl 800; Highest Degree: Master
Library Holdings: Audiobooks 25; DVDs 200; e-books 50; High Interest/Low Vocabulary Bk Vols 150; Bk Titles 1,800; Per Subs 110; Talking Bks 15; Videos 450
Subject Interests: Acctg, Bus, Computer sci, Med, Nursing, Web design
Wireless access
Function: Audio & video playback equip for onsite use, Computer training, Distance learning, Homework prog, Internet access, Learning ctr, Online ref, Orientations, Photocopying/Printing, VHS videos, Wheelchair accessible
Partic in Utah Libr Asn
Open Mon-Thurs 8am-10pm, Fri 8-5
Restriction: Open to students, fac & staff

S UTAH SCHOOL FOR THE DEAF & BLIND*, Educational Resource Center, 742 Harrison Blvd, 84404. SAN 323-7281. Tel: 801-629-4817. FAX: 801-629-4896. E-mail: ogdenerc@usdb.org. Web Site: www.usdb.org/resources/erc-library. *Prog Coordr,* Sarah Lovato; E-mail: sarahlo@usdb.org
Library Holdings: Bk Titles 30,000; Bk Vols 37,000; Per Subs 10
Automation Activity & Vendor Info: (Cataloging) Follett Software; (Circulation) Follett Software
Open Mon-Fri 8-4:30
Branches:
EDUCATIONAL RESOURCE CENTER - SALT LAKE EXTENSION, 1655 E 3300 South, Salt Lake City, 84106. Tel: 801-464-2040. Circulation Tel: 801-464-2039. Web Site: usdb.org/resources/erc-library. *Prog Coordr,* Sarah Lovato; Tel: 801-629-4795, E-mail: sarahlo@usdb.org
Library Holdings: Bk Vols 30,000
Automation Activity & Vendor Info: (Cataloging) Follett Software
Open Mon-Fri 8-4:30

P WEBER COUNTY LIBRARY SYSTEM*, 2464 Jefferson Ave, 84401-2464. SAN 362-4722. Tel: 801-337-2617. FAX: 801-337-2615. Web Site: www.weberpl.lib.ut.us. *Dir,* Lynnda Wangsgard; E-mail: lwangsgard@weberpl.lib.ut.us; *Assoc Dir,* Phoebe Carter; *Tech Serv Mgr,* Monyee Yip; Staff 21 (MLS 20, Non-MLS 1)

Founded 1903. Pop 213,247; Circ 1,346,481
Library Holdings: Audiobooks 8,591; AV Mats 40,097; Bks on Deafness & Sign Lang 496; CDs 21,965; DVDs 9,908; High Interest/Low Vocabulary Bk Vols 1,072; Large Print Bks 4,293; Microforms 11,644; Music Scores 405; Bk Titles 169,824; Bk Vols 329,696; Per Subs 998; Talking Bks 8,591; Videos 13,962
Special Collections: Utah & Western History (Ava J Cooper Spec Coll)
Automation Activity & Vendor Info: (Acquisitions) Innovative Interfaces, Inc; (Cataloging) Innovative Interfaces, Inc; (Circulation) Innovative Interfaces, Inc; (ILL) OCLC; (OPAC) Innovative Interfaces, Inc; (Serials) Innovative Interfaces, Inc
Wireless access
Partic in Beehive Library Consortium
Special Services for the Deaf - Bks on deafness & sign lang; TDD equip; TTY equip
Special Services for the Blind - Assistive/Adapted tech devices, equip & products; Closed circuit TV; Radio reading serv
Open Mon-Thurs 10-9, Fri & Sat 10-6, Sun 1-5
Friends of the Library Group
Branches: 3
NORTH BRANCH, 475 E 2600 North, North Ogden, 84414-2833, SAN 362-4765. Tel: 801-782-8800. FAX: 801-782-8801. *Librn,* Ann Booth; Staff 3 (MLS 3)
Pop 44,887; Circ 197,070
Library Holdings: AV Mats 5,428; Bks on Deafness & Sign Lang 120; High Interest/Low Vocabulary Bk Vols 323; Large Print Bks 582; Bk Titles 49,299; Bk Vols 55,562; Per Subs 80; Talking Bks 5,428
Open Mon-Thurs 10-9, Fri & Sat 10-6, Sun 1-5
Friends of the Library Group
OGDEN VALLEY BRANCH, 131 S 7400 East, Huntsville, 84317-9309, SAN 377-0281. Tel: 801-745-2220. FAX: 801-745-2221. *Librn,* Karen Burton; Staff 2 (MLS 2)
Pop 3,609; Circ 73,235
Library Holdings: AV Mats 4,851; Bks on Deafness & Sign Lang 75; High Interest/Low Vocabulary Bk Vols 260; Large Print Bks 286; Bk Titles 43,157; Bk Vols 47,419; Per Subs 110; Talking Bks 1,057
Open Mon-Thurs 10-9, Fri & Sat 10-6, Sun 1-5
Friends of the Library Group
SOUTHWEST BRANCH, 2039 W 4000 S, Roy, 84067, SAN 362-4781. Tel: 801-773-2556. FAX: 801-773-2557. *Librn,* Phoebe Carter; Staff 50 (MLS 7, Non-MLS 43)
Founded 1965. Pop 93,000; Circ 693,557
Library Holdings: AV Mats 6,034; Bks on Deafness & Sign Lang 90; High Interest/Low Vocabulary Bk Vols 113; Large Print Bks 474; Bk Titles 44,985; Bk Vols 50,528; Per Subs 90; Talking Bks 1,199
Function: 24/7 Electronic res, 24/7 Online cat, 3D Printer, Accelerated reader prog, Activity rm, Adult bk club, Adult literacy prog, After school storytime
Open Mon-Thurs 10-9, Fri & Sat 10-6
Friends of the Library Group

C WEBER STATE UNIVERSITY*, Stewart Library, 3921 Central Campus Dr, Dept 2901, 84408-2901. SAN 316-8972. Tel: 801-626-6403. Circulation Tel: 801-626-6545. Interlibrary Loan Service Tel: 801-626-7487. Reference Tel: 801-626-6415. FAX: 801-626-7045. Web Site: library.weber.edu. *Dean of the Library,* Wendy Holliday; E-mail: wendyholliday@weber.edu; *Head, Access Serv, Head, Tech & Syst Serv,* Chris Hauser; Tel: 801-626-6104, E-mail: chauser@weber.edu; *Head, Cat,* Chandler Anderson; Tel: 801-626-6766, E-mail: chandleranderson1@weber.edu; *Head, Circ,* Roxanne Derda; Tel: 801-626-6546, E-mail: roxxannederda@weber.edu; *Head, Univ Archives & Digital Colls,* Jamie Weeks; Tel: 801-626-6486, E-mail: jweeks@weber.edu; *Bus Librn,* Justin Kani; Tel: 801-626-8662, E-mail: justinkani@weber.edu; *Sci Librn,* Miranda Kispert; Tel: 801-626-6093, E-mail: mirandakispert@weber.edu; *Resource Sharing & Course Materials Mgr,* Misty Allen; Tel: 801-626-7820, E-mail: mallen4@weber.edu; Staff 34 (MLS 11, Non-MLS 23)
Founded 1924. Enrl 17,200; Fac 450; Highest Degree: Master
Library Holdings: e-books 479,065; Electronic Media & Resources 1,023,166; Bk Titles 351,044; Per Subs 12,808
Special Collections: Hyrum & Ruby Wheelwright Coll (Mormon Literature); James A Howell Coll (Literature); Utah Construction/Utah International Coll. State Document Depository; US Document Depository
Automation Activity & Vendor Info: (Acquisitions) SirsiDynix; (Cataloging) SirsiDynix; (Circulation) SirsiDynix; (Course Reserve) SirsiDynix; (ILL) OCLC; (Media Booking) SirsiDynix; (OPAC) SirsiDynix; (Serials) SirsiDynix
Wireless access
Publications: Colophon, Friends of the Stewart Library (Newsletter)
Partic in OCLC Online Computer Library Center, Inc; Proquest Dialog; Utah Academic Library Consortium
Open Mon-Thurs 7am-11pm, Fri 7am-8pm, Sat 9-8, Sun 1-9; Mon-Thurs 7:30am-8pm, Fri 7:30-5, Sat & Sun 1-6 (Summer)
Friends of the Library Group
Departmental Libraries:
DAVIS CAMPUS LIBRARY, 2750 University Park Blvd, D2 Rm 212, Layton, 84041-9099. Tel: 801-395-3472. E-mail: davislibrary@weber.edu. Web Site: library.weber.edu/hours/davis. *Circ Supvr,* Mike Middleton; E-mail: michaelmiddleton@weber.edu
Open Mon-Fri 10-2

OREM

P OREM PUBLIC LIBRARY*, 58 N State St, 84057. SAN 316-8980. Tel: 801-229-7050. Reference Tel: 801-229-7175. Administration Tel: 801-229-7448. Web Site: www.oremlibrary.org. *Dir,* Charlene Crozier; E-mail: ccrozier@orem.org; *Cat,* Janet Low; *Cat,* Evelyn Schmidt; *Media Spec,* James Scarborough; Staff 44 (MLS 8, Non-MLS 36)
Founded 1940. Pop 90,000; Circ 1,100,000
Library Holdings: Bk Vols 330,000; Per Subs 255
Subject Interests: Film classics, Relig studies
Automation Activity & Vendor Info: (Acquisitions) SirsiDynix; (Cataloging) SirsiDynix; (Circulation) SirsiDynix; (OPAC) SirsiDynix
Wireless access
Partic in Beehive Library Consortium; Pioneer
Open Mon-Fri 9-9, Sat 9-6
Friends of the Library Group

PANGUITCH

P GARFIELD COUNTY-PANGUITCH CITY LIBRARY*, 25 S 200 East, 84759. (Mail add: PO Box 75, 84759-0075), SAN 377-2780. Tel: 435-676-2431. E-mail: panguitchlibrary@gmail.com. Web Site: panguitchlibrary.org. *Head Librn,* Suzanne Dunham; *Ch,* Verlaine Spencer
Pop 1,500
Library Holdings: Bk Vols 48,000
Automation Activity & Vendor Info: (Circulation) Innovative Interfaces, Inc; (OPAC) Innovative Interfaces, Inc
Wireless access
Partic in Beehive Library Consortium; Pioneer; Utah Libr Asn
Special Services for the Blind - Home delivery serv
Open Mon, Wed & Fri 1-6, Tues & Thurs 1-7
Friends of the Library Group
Branches: 1
ESCALANTE BRANCH, 90 N 100 West, Escalante, 84726. (Mail add: PO Box 75, 84759-0075). *Br Mgr,* Raymond Christian
Library Holdings: Bk Vols 15,000
Open Wed & Thurs 6pm-7pm
Bookmobiles: 1. Librn, Lyle Talbot. Bk vols 6,000

PARK CITY

P PARK CITY LIBRARY*, 1255 Park Ave, 84060. (Mail add: PO Box 668, 84060-0668), SAN 322-6794. Tel: 435-615-5600. Web Site: parkcitylibrary.org. *Libr Dir,* Adriane Herrick Juarez; Tel: 435-615-5605, E-mail: adriane.juarez@parkcity.org; *Ad,* Kate Mapp; Tel: 435-615-5602, E-mail: kate.mapp@parkcity.org; *Youth Serv Librn,* Katrina Kmak; Tel: 415-615-5603, E-mail: katrina.kmak@parkcity.org; Staff 12 (MLS 5, Non-MLS 7)
Founded 1917. Pop 8,396; Circ 90,977
Library Holdings: Bk Vols 61,881; Per Subs 96
Special Collections: Park City History Coll; Skiing Coll
Subject Interests: Local hist
Automation Activity & Vendor Info: (OPAC) TLC (The Library Corporation)
Wireless access
Function: Art exhibits, Audio & video playback equip for onsite use, Audiobks via web, Bks on CD, Children's prog, Computers for patron use, Electronic databases & coll, Free DVD rentals, ILL available, Magnifiers for reading, Music CDs, Online cat, OverDrive digital audio bks, Photocopying/Printing, Prog for adults, Prog for children & young adult, Senior computer classes, Story hour, Summer reading prog, Tax forms, Teen prog, Wheelchair accessible
Partic in Beehive Library Consortium; OCLC Online Computer Library Center, Inc
Open Mon-Thurs 9-8, Fri & Sat 9-5, Sun 1-5
Friends of the Library Group

P SUMMIT COUNTY LIBRARY*, Kimball Junction Branch & Library Administration, 1885 W Ute Blvd, 84098. Tel: 435-615-3900. Web Site: www1.youseemore.com/SummitCounty. *Libr Dir,* Dan Compton; Tel: 435-615-3947, E-mail: dcompton@summitcounty.org; *Tech Serv Librn,* Darlene Marsh; Tel: 435-615-3901, E-mail: dmarsh@summitcounty.org; *Youth Serv Librn,* Kirsten Nilsson; Tel: 435-615-3903, E-mail: knilsson@summitcounty.org
Pop 26,935
Library Holdings: Large Print Bks 125; Bk Titles 47,222; Per Subs 84
Wireless access
Partic in Beehive Library Consortium

Open Mon-Thurs 10-8, Fri & Sat 10-6
Friends of the Library Group
Branches: 2
COALVILLE BRANCH, 82 N 50 E, Coalville, 84017. Tel: 435-336-3070. *Br Mgr,* Susan Murphy; E-mail: smurphy@summitcounty.org; Staff 2.5 (MLS 1, Non-MLS 1.5)
Library Holdings: Per Subs 7
Open Mon-Fri 10-6, Sat 10-2
KAMAS BRANCH, 110 N Main St, Kamas, 84036. Tel: 435-783-3190. *Br Mgr,* Rachel Spohn; Tel: 435-783-3190, E-mail: rspohn@summitcounty.org
Library Holdings: Bk Titles 23,019; Per Subs 43
Open Mon-Thurs 10-7, Fri 10-6, Sat 10-2
Bookmobiles: 1. Outreach Servs Librn, Dennis Willie

PAROWAN

P PAROWAN PUBLIC LIBRARY*, 16 S Main St, 84761. (Mail add: PO Box 427, 84761-0427), SAN 316-8999. Tel: 435-477-3491. FAX: 435-477-8671. E-mail: parowanlibrary@parowan.org. Web Site: www.parowan.org/library. *City Librn,* Cori Adams
Founded 1915. Pop 2,200; Circ 57,208
Library Holdings: AV Mats 498; Bk Titles 25,000; Per Subs 55
Subject Interests: Hist of Parowan
Automation Activity & Vendor Info: (Acquisitions) Follett Software; (Cataloging) Follett Software; (Circulation) Follett Software; (ILL) Follett Software; (Media Booking) Follett Software; (OPAC) Follett Software; (Serials) Follett Software
Wireless access
Partic in Beehive Library Consortium; Pioneer
Open Mon & Wed 9:30-5, Tues & Thurs 9:30-7:30, Fri & Sat 9:30-12

PAYSON

P PAYSON CITY LIBRARY*, 66 S Main St, 84651-2223. SAN 316-9006. Tel: 801-465-5220. FAX: 801-465-5208. Web Site: www.paysonlibrary.org. *Dir,* Dona Gay; E-mail: donag@payson.org; Staff 14 (MLS 2, Non-MLS 12)
Founded 1878. Pop 19,776; Circ 41,413
Library Holdings: Bk Vols 38,580; Per Subs 74
Automation Activity & Vendor Info: (Cataloging) Koha; (Circulation) Koha; (OPAC) Koha
Wireless access
Function: 24/7 Electronic res, 24/7 Online cat, Adult bk club
Partic in Beehive Library Consortium
Open Mon-Thurs 10-8, Fri & Sat 10-5
Friends of the Library Group

PLEASANT GROVE

P PLEASANT GROVE CITY LIBRARY*, 30 E Center St, 84062. SAN 316-9014. Tel: 801-785-3950. E-mail: pgcitylibemails@gmail.com. Web Site: www.plgrove.org/library. *Dir,* Sheri Britsch; E-mail: sbritsch@pgcity.org
Pop 23,000; Circ 35,000
Library Holdings: Bk Vols 85,000; Per Subs 50
Subject Interests: Local hist
Automation Activity & Vendor Info: (Acquisitions) SirsiDynix; (Cataloging) SirsiDynix; (Circulation) SirsiDynix; (OPAC) SirsiDynix; (Serials) SirsiDynix
Wireless access
Partic in Beehive Library Consortium
Open Mon-Thurs 9-9, Fri & Sat 10-6
Friends of the Library Group

PRICE

P PRICE CITY LIBRARY*, 159 E Main St, 84501-3046. SAN 316-9049. Tel: 435-636-3188. FAX: 435-637-2905. E-mail: library@priceutah.net. Web Site: www.pricecityutah.com/library. *Dir,* Tina Rowley; E-mail: tinar@priceutah.net
Founded 1914. Pop 8,216; Circ 50,603
Library Holdings: Bk Vols 41,397; Per Subs 31
Subject Interests: Heritage, Local hist
Automation Activity & Vendor Info: (Cataloging) Follett Software; (Circulation) Follett Software; (OPAC) Follett Software
Wireless access
Partic in Beehive Library Consortium; Pioneer
Open Mon-Thurs 8-7, Fri 8-5, Sat 9-Noon

J UTAH STATE UNIVERSITY EASTERN LIBRARY*, 451 E & 400 N, 84501. SAN 316-9030. Tel: 435-613-5209. FAX: 435-613-5863. E-mail: Library.Help@usu.edu. Web Site: price.lib.usu.edu. *Dir, Statewide Libr Serv,* Michael Harris; E-mail: m.w.harris@usu.edu; *Archive Spec, Cat Librn,* Sherill Shaw; Tel: 435-613-5208, E-mail: sherill.shaw@usu.edu; *Pub Serv Mgr,* Aimee Lauritsen; Tel: 435-613-5646, E-mail: aimee.lauritsen@usu.edu; Staff 6 (MLS 2, Non-MLS 4)
Founded 1938. Enrl 1,250; Fac 70; Highest Degree: Associate
Library Holdings: Bk Vols 50,000; Per Subs 100
Subject Interests: Local hist, Utah hist
Automation Activity & Vendor Info: (Acquisitions) Innovative Interfaces, Inc - Sierra; (Cataloging) Innovative Interfaces, Inc - Sierra; (Circulation) Innovative Interfaces, Inc - Sierra; (Course Reserve) Innovative Interfaces, Inc - Sierra; (OPAC) Innovative Interfaces, Inc - Sierra; (Serials) Innovative Interfaces, Inc - Sierra
Wireless access
Partic in Utah Academic Library Consortium
Special Services for the Deaf - TTY equip
Special Services for the Blind - Reader equip
Open Mon-Thurs 8am-10pm, Fri 8-5, Sat 12-5, Sun 2-10
Friends of the Library Group

PROVO

BRIGHAM YOUNG UNIVERSITY
CL HOWARD W HUNTER LAW LIBRARY*, 256 JRCB, 84602-8000, SAN 362-4846. Tel: 801-422-3593. Interlibrary Loan Service Tel: 801-422-5481. FAX: 801-422-0404. Web Site: www.law2.byu.edu. *Dir,* Kory Staheli; E-mail: stahelik@lawgate.byu.edu; *Dep Dir,* Gary Hill; E-mail: hillg@lawgate.byu.edu; *Assoc Dir, Access Serv,* Laurie Urquiaga; E-mail: urquiagal@lawgate.byu.edu; *Acq,* Bonnie Geldmacher; *Cat,* Curt E Conklin; *Coll Develop,* Kory Staheli; *Govt Doc,* Galen L Fletcher; *Info Tech,* David Armond; *Ref (Info Servs),* Steve Averett; *Ref (Info Servs),* Dennis Sears; *Ser,* Teresa Odam; Staff 11 (MLS 10, Non-MLS 1)
Founded 1972. Enrl 470; Fac 40; Highest Degree: Doctorate
Library Holdings: AV Mats 1,380; e-books 3,027; Bk Titles 125,828; Bk Vols 345,402; Per Subs 4,121
Special Collections: State Document Depository; US Document Depository
Subject Interests: Am Commonwealth law, Biblical law, British Commonwealth law, Comparative law, Constitutional law, Family law, Feminist legal issues, Foreign law, Native Am law
Automation Activity & Vendor Info: (Acquisitions) SirsiDynix; (Cataloging) SirsiDynix; (Circulation) SirsiDynix; (Course Reserve) SirsiDynix; (ILL) SirsiDynix; (OPAC) SirsiDynix; (Serials) SirsiDynix
Partic in Association of Research Libraries; Research Libraries Information Network
Open Mon-Fri 6am-Midnight, Sat 6am-11pm (Winter); Mon-Sat 8-8 (Summer)

C HAROLD B LEE LIBRARY*, 2060 HBLL, 84602. (Mail add: PO Box 26800, 84602-6800), SAN 362-4811. Tel: 801-422-2927. Circulation Tel: 801-422-6061. Interlibrary Loan Service Tel: 801-422-6344. Administration Tel: 801-422-2905. Web Site: lib.byu.edu. *Assoc Univ Librn, Interim Univ Librn,* Brian Rennick; E-mail: brian_rennick@byu.edu; *Assoc Univ Librn,* Jeffrey Belliston; E-mail: jeffrey_belliston@byu.edu; *Assoc Univ Librn for Coll & Tech Serv(s),* Robert Murdoch; E-mail: robert_murdoch@byu.edu; *Assoc Univ Librn for I.T.,* Bill Lund; E-mail: bill_lund@byu.edu; *Assoc Univ Librn, Spec Coll,* Russ Taylor; E-mail: russ_taylor@byu.edu; *Asst Univ Librn, Pub Serv,* J Michael Hunter; E-mail: mike_hunter@byu.edu; Staff 159 (MLS 87, Non-MLS 72)
Enrl 30,243; Fac 1,267; Highest Degree: Doctorate
Library Holdings: Bk Titles 3,702,998; Bk Vols 4,211,239; Per Subs 94,385
Special Collections: Children's Coll; Herman Melville Coll; Literature; Modern Fine Presses Coll; Mormon & Western Americana; Robert Burns Coll; Victorian Literature Coll; Walt Whitman Coll; Welsh Coll; William Wordsworth Coll; Windsor Press Coll. Oral History; State Document Depository; US Document Depository
Automation Activity & Vendor Info: (Acquisitions) SirsiDynix; (Cataloging) SirsiDynix; (Circulation) SirsiDynix; (OPAC) SirsiDynix; (Serials) SirsiDynix
Partic in Association of Research Libraries; Center for Research Libraries; Greater Western Library Alliance; OCLC Research Library Partnership; Research Libraries Information Network; SDC Search Serv; Utah Academic Library Consortium
Open Mon-Fri 7am-Midnight, Sat 8am-Midnight
Friends of the Library Group

P PROVO CITY LIBRARY*, 550 N University Ave, 84601. SAN 316-9057. Tel: 801-852-6650. Circulation Tel: 801-852-6660. FAX: 801-852-6688. E-mail: information@provolibrary.org. Web Site: www.provolibrary.org. *Dir,* Carla Z Gordon; E-mail: carlag@provolibrary.org; Staff 35 (MLS 18, Non-MLS 17)
Founded 1904. Pop 115,000; Circ 1,471,000
Library Holdings: DVDs 9,285; Bk Vols 240,000
Subject Interests: LDS relig, Utah, Utah County hist
Automation Activity & Vendor Info: (Circulation) SirsiDynix
Wireless access

Function: 24/7 Electronic res, 24/7 Online cat, Activity rm, Art exhibits, Children's prog, Computers for patron use, Electronic databases & coll, Free DVD rentals, ILL available, Internet access, Life-long learning prog for all ages, Magazines, Meeting rooms, Online cat, Outreach serv, OverDrive digital audio bks, Photocopying/Printing, Preschool outreach, Prog for adults, Prog for children & young adult, Scanner, Spanish lang bks, Story hour, Study rm
Publications: Calendar (Monthly)
Partic in Beehive Library Consortium
Open Mon-Fri 9-9, Sat 9-6

M UTAH STATE HOSPITAL, Patient Library, 1300 E Center St, 84606-3554. (Mail add: PO Box 270, 84603-0270), SAN 316-9065. Tel: 801-344-4400. Web Site: ush.utah.gov. *Dir,* Janae Wahnschaffe; Tel: 801-344-4264, E-mail: janwahn@utah.gov; Staff 1 (MLS 1)
Library Holdings: Bk Vols 6,500; Per Subs 25
Automation Activity & Vendor Info: (Cataloging) Follett Software; (Circulation) Follett Software
Wireless access
Restriction: Private libr, Staff & patient use

RANDOLPH

P RICH COUNTY LIBRARY*, 55 N Main St, 84064. Tel: 435-793-2122. E-mail: rclib@allwest.net. Web Site: www.richcountyut.org/library. *Libr Dir,* Melanie Limb; *Libr Dir,* Andrea Weston
Function: Bk club(s), Story hour, Summer reading prog
Partic in Beehive Library Consortium
Open Mon & Wed 10-5, Fri 10-2

RICHFIELD

P RICHFIELD PUBLIC LIBRARY*, 83 E Center St, 84701. SAN 316-9081. Tel: 435-896-5169. FAX: 435-896-6512. E-mail: library@richfieldcity.com. Web Site: www.richfieldlibrary.com. *Dir,* Michelle Olsen; Staff 1 (Non-MLS 1)
Founded 1915. Pop 7,500; Circ 56,542
Library Holdings: DVDs 900; High Interest/Low Vocabulary Bk Vols 120; Large Print Bks 358; Bk Vols 35,155; Per Subs 184; Talking Bks 4,700; Videos 50
Wireless access
Partic in Beehive Library Consortium
Open Mon-Fri 11-6:30, Sat 12:30-4
Friends of the Library Group

RICHMOND

P RICHMOND PUBLIC LIBRARY*, 38 W Main St, 84333-1409. (Mail add: PO Box 202, 84333-0202), SAN 316-909X. Tel: 435-258-5525. FAX: 435-258-3617. E-mail: library@richmondutah.org. Web Site: www.richmondutah.org/library. *Libr Dir,* Lora Smith; Staff 5 (Non-MLS 5)
Founded 1914. Pop 2,800; Circ 30,000
Library Holdings: Audiobooks 740; DVDs 996; Bk Titles 14,650; Per Subs 3
Automation Activity & Vendor Info: (Cataloging) Follett Software; (Circulation) Follett Software
Wireless access
Function: 24/7 Electronic res, 24/7 Online cat, Accelerated reader prog, Adult bk club, Audiobks on Playaways & MP3, Audiobks via web, Bks on CD, Children's prog, Computers for patron use, Digital talking bks, Electronic databases & coll, Free DVD rentals, Homebound delivery serv, ILL available, Instruction & testing, Internet access, Magazines, Mail & tel request accepted, Online cat, Outside serv via phone, mail, e-mail & web, OverDrive digital audio bks, Photocopying/Printing, Preschool reading prog, Printer for laptops & handheld devices, Ref serv available, Scanner, Serves people with intellectual disabilities, Spanish lang bks, Spoken cassettes & CDs, Spoken cassettes & DVDs, Story hour, Summer & winter reading prog, Summer reading prog, Telephone ref
Partic in Beehive Library Consortium
Open Mon, Tues, Thurs & Fri 10-12 & 2-6, Wed 6-8, Sat 10-1
Restriction: Restricted pub use

SAINT GEORGE

C DIXIE STATE UNIVERSITY LIBRARY*, 225 S 700 E, 84770. SAN 316-912X. Tel: 435-652-7714. Reference Tel: 435-634-2081. FAX: 435-656-4169. E-mail: library@dixie.edu. Web Site: library.dixie.edu. *Dean of Library & Open Learning Services,* Kelly Peterson-Fairchild; Tel: 435-652-7711, E-mail: kelly.peterson-fairchild@dixie.edu; *Head, Spec Coll & Archives,* Kathleen Broeder; Tel: 435-652-7718, E-mail: kathleen.broeder@dixie.edu; *Head, Tech Serv, Librn,* David Zielke; Tel: 435-652-7716, E-mail: zielke@dixie.edu; *Educ Librn,* Linda Jones; Tel: 435-879-4243, E-mail: ljones@dixie.edu; *Electronic Res Librn,* John Burns; Tel: 435-879-4712, E-mail: burns@dixie.edu; *Syst Librn,* Caleb Ames; Tel: 435-879-4321, E-mail: ames@dixie.edu; Staff 11 (MLS 4, Non-MLS 7)
Founded 1912. Enrl 4,017; Highest Degree: Bachelor
Library Holdings: Bk Vols 100,000; Per Subs 314
Special Collections: Mormon & Southwest History. Oral History
Subject Interests: Allied health prof, Bus, Computer tech, Humanities, Info tech, Soc sci
Automation Activity & Vendor Info: (Acquisitions) SirsiDynix; (Cataloging) SirsiDynix; (Circulation) SirsiDynix; (Course Reserve) SirsiDynix; (OPAC) SirsiDynix; (Serials) SirsiDynix
Partic in Utah Academic Library Consortium
Open Mon-Thurs 6:45am-Midnight, Fri 6:45am-7pm, Sat Noon-7, Sun 2-10

P WASHINGTON COUNTY LIBRARY SYSTEM*, 88 West 100 S, 84770. SAN 316-9138. Tel: 435-634-5737. Administration Tel: 435-256-6326. FAX: 435-634-5741. Web Site: www.washco.lib.ut.us. *Dir,* Joel Tucker; E-mail: joel.tucker@washco.lib.ut.us; *Ch,* Alicia Burgess; E-mail: alicia.burgess@washco.lib.ut.us; Staff 37 (MLS 1, Non-MLS 36)
Founded 1912. Pop 140,000; Circ 1,060,712
Library Holdings: Bk Vols 106,567; Per Subs 250
Special Collections: Local Histories & Diaries (WPA Pioneer Diary Coll), bks & pamphlets
Automation Activity & Vendor Info: (Cataloging) SirsiDynix; (Circulation) SirsiDynix; (OPAC) SirsiDynix
Wireless access
Publications: Newsletter
Partic in Beehive Library Consortium
Open Mon-Thurs 10-8, Fri & Sat 10-6
Friends of the Library Group
Branches: 6
ENTERPRISE BRANCH, 393 S 200 E, Enterprise, 84725. (Mail add: PO Box 160, Enterprise, 84725-0160), SAN 371-3725. Tel: 435-878-2574. FAX: 435-878-2725. *Br Mgr,* Chris Gardner; E-mail: chris.gardner@washco.lib.ut.us
Library Holdings: Bk Vols 12,000
Open Mon & Fri 10-6, Tues-Thurs 10-7, Sat 10-3
HURRICANE BRANCH, 36 S 300 W, Hurricane, 84737, SAN 325-4011. Tel: 435-635-4621. FAX: 435-635-3845. *Br Mgr,* Lauren Stoddard; E-mail: lauren.stoddard@washco.lib.ut.us
Library Holdings: Bk Vols 41,042
Open Mon-Thurs 10-7, Fri & Sat 10-6
NEW HARMONY BRANCH, 34 S 2900 E, New Harmony, 84757. Tel: 435-867-0065. FAX: 435-867-0222. *Br Mgr,* Robin Nielsen; E-mail: robin.nielsen@washco.lib.ut.us
Library Holdings: Bk Titles 5,000
Open Mon-Thurs 10-7, Fri & Sat 10-4
Friends of the Library Group
SANTA CLARA BRANCH, 1099 N Lava Flow Dr, 84770. Tel: 435-986-0432. FAX: 435-986-0436. *Br Mgr,* Abraham King; Tel: 435-256-6327, E-mail: abraham.king@washco.lib.ut.us
Library Holdings: Bk Titles 35,076
Automation Activity & Vendor Info: (OPAC) SirsiDynix
Open Mon-Thurs 10-7, Fri & Sat 10-6
SPRINGDALE BRANCH, 126 Lion Blvd, Springdale, 84767, (Mail add: PO Box 479, Springdale, 84767), SAN 371-3733. Tel: 435-772-3676. FAX: 435-772-3124. *Br Mgr,* Jeff Lewis; E-mail: jeff.lewis@washco.lib.ut.us
Library Holdings: Bk Vols 12,000
Open Mon-Thurs 10-7, Fri 10-5, Sat 12-5
Friends of the Library Group
WASHINGTON BRANCH, 220 N 300 E, Washington City, 84780. Tel: 435-627-2706. FAX: 435-627-2776. *Br Mgr,* Maricarol Darden; E-mail: maricol.darden@washco.lib.ut.us
Open Mon-Thurs 10-7, Fri & Sat 10-6

SALEM

P SALEM CITY LIBRARY*, 59 S Main St, 84653. Tel: 801-423-2622. E-mail: library@salemcity.org. Web Site: library.salemcity.org. *Libr Dir,* Kerry Burnham
Wireless access
Function: Bk club(s), Computers for patron use, ILL available
Partic in Beehive Library Consortium
Open Mon-Thurs 10-7, Fri 10-5, Sat 12-4

SALINA

P SALINA PUBLIC LIBRARY*, 90 W Main St, 84654. SAN 316-9146. Tel: 435-529-7753. FAX: 435-529-1226. E-mail: publiclibrary@salinacity.org. Web Site: www.salinacity.org/library. *Dir,* Rhonda Huntsman; E-mail: rhuntsman@salinacity.org
Pop 4,900; Circ 19,861
Library Holdings: Bk Titles 11,250; Bk Vols 11,500; Per Subs 30
Automation Activity & Vendor Info: (Cataloging) Auto-Graphics, Inc; (Circulation) Auto-Graphics, Inc
Wireless access

Partic in Beehive Library Consortium
Open Mon-Thurs 12-7, Fri 1-5

SALT LAKE CITY

THE CHURCH OF JESUS CHRIST OF LATTER-DAY SAINTS

SR BOCA RATON FAMILY HISTORY CENTER*, 1530 W Camino Real, Boca Raton, 33486. (Mail add: 1199 SW Ninth Ave, Boca Raton, 33486), SAN 375-278X. Tel: 561-395-6644. FAX: 561-395-8957. *Dir,* Brother Donald W Jennings
Founded 1979
Library Holdings: Microforms 4,000; Bk Titles 800; Per Subs 10
Special Collections: New York Death Indexes
Subject Interests: Genealogy
Open Mon & Wed 10-5, Tues 3-9

SR CHURCH HISTORY LIBRARY & ARCHIVES*, 50 E North Temple, 84150, SAN 362-4935. Tel: 801-240-2272. FAX: 801-240-1845. Web Site: www.lds.org/churchhistory. *Dir,* Christine Cox; Tel: 801-240-3603; *Coll Develop,* Matt Heiss; Tel: 801-240-5944. Subject Specialists: *Church hist,* Christine Cox; Staff 180 (MLS 25, Non-MLS 155)
Founded 1830
Library Holdings: AV Mats 41,000; Bk Titles 250,000; Bk Vols 300,000; Per Subs 799
Special Collections: Church of Jesus Christ of Latter-Day Saints, mss, publs, records. Oral History
Subject Interests: Mormon hist, Mormon theol, Utah hist
Automation Activity & Vendor Info: (OPAC) Innovative Interfaces, Inc; (Serials) Innovative Interfaces, Inc
Function: Photocopying/Printing, Telephone ref
Publications: Index to Periodicals of the Church of Jesus Christ of Latter-Day Saints
Restriction: Circulates for staff only

SR FAMILY HISTORY LIBRARY*, 35 N West Temple St, 84150, SAN 362-496X. Toll Free Tel: 866-406-1830. Web Site: www.familysearch.org. *Mgr,* Linda K Gulbrandsen; *Commun Serv Mgr,* Hasleton Helgeson; Staff 200 (MLS 110, Non-MLS 90)
Founded 1894
Library Holdings: Electronic Media & Resources 943; Bk Titles 888,979; Per Subs 4,500
Special Collections: Oral History
Subject Interests: Family hist, Genealogy, Local hist
Publications: Country & State Research Outlines; Family History Centers Address List; Family History Materials List; International Genealogical Index; International Genealogical Index (Micro); Patron Aids
Special Services for the Deaf - Staff with knowledge of sign lang
Open Mon 8-5, Tues-Fri 8am-9pm, Sat 9-5

L FABIAN VANCOTT*, Law Library, 215 S State St, Ste 1200, 84111-2323. SAN 372-1906. Tel: 801-531-8900. FAX: 801-596-2814. Web Site: fabianvancott.com. *Librn,* Stephanie Falcon; E-mail: sfalcon@fabianvancott.com
Library Holdings: Bk Vols 20,000; Per Subs 15
Restriction: Staff use only

S INTERNATIONAL SOCIETY DAUGHTERS OF UTAH PIONEERS*, Museum & Library, 300 N Main St, 84103-1699. SAN 375-7811. Tel: 801-532-6479. FAX: 801-532-4436. E-mail: info@isdup.org. Web Site: isdup.org. *Librn,* Pam Carson; E-mail: pamcarson@gmail.com; Staff 1 (MLS 1)
Library Holdings: Music Scores 10; Bk Titles 2,400; Per Subs 1
Special Collections: Histories of Pioneers to 1869 & Western History
Wireless access
Open Mon-Fri 9-4:30
Restriction: Open to pub for ref only

J LDS BUSINESS COLLEGE LIBRARY*, 95 N 300 West, 84101. SAN 316-9200. Tel: 801-524-8150. FAX: 801-524-1900. E-mail: library@ldsbc.edu. Web Site: library.ldsbc.edu. *Libr Dir,* Susan Sorenson; E-mail: ssorenson@ldsbc.edu
Founded 1975. Enrl 1,300; Fac 18; Highest Degree: Associate
Library Holdings: Bk Vols 7,500; Per Subs 100
Subject Interests: Acctg, Computer, Computer tech, Econ, Interior design, Med asst, Relig studies, Secretarial
Automation Activity & Vendor Info: (Cataloging) SirsiDynix; (Circulation) SirsiDynix; (OPAC) SirsiDynix
Wireless access
Open Mon & Fri 7-6, Tues-Thurs 7am-10pm, Sat 10-5
Restriction: In-house use for visitors

S NATIONAL SOCIETY OF SONS OF UTAH PIONEERS*, Sons of Utah Pioneers Library, 3301 E 2920 South, 84109. SAN 323-7176. Tel: 801-484-4441. E-mail: sup1847@gmail.com. Web Site: www.sup1847.com. *Co-Dir,* Diane Smith; *Co-Dir,* John Smith; E-mail: jdrooftop@msn.com
Founded 1981
Library Holdings: Bk Titles 6,000; Spec Interest Per Sub 25
Special Collections: Western USA Local History Coll, 1600 to date
Subject Interests: Biographies, Family hist, Local hist
Wireless access
Function: Res libr
Publications: Pioneer (Magazine)
Open Wed & Thurs 10-5
Restriction: Non-circulating

M PRIMARY CHILDREN'S HOSPITAL MEDICAL LIBRARY*, 81 N Mario Capecchi Dr, 84113. SAN 323-6617. Tel: 801-662-1000, 801-662-1390. FAX: 801-662-1393. Web Site: intermountainhealthcare.org/locations/primary-childrens-hospital. *Sr Med Librn,* Emily Eresuma; Tel: 801-662-1391, E-mail: emily.eresuma@imail.org; *Asst Med Librn,* Shawn Steidinger; Tel: 801-662-1390. Subject Specialists: *Pediatrics,* Emily Eresuma; Staff 2 (MLS 2)
Library Holdings: Bk Titles 1,500; Per Subs 240
Subject Interests: Pediatrics
Wireless access
Open Mon-Fri 8:30-5

M SAINT MARK'S HOSPITAL*, Medical Library, 1200 E 3900 South, 84124. SAN 326-2367. Tel: 801-268-7111, 801-268-7676. Web Site: mountainstar.com/locations/st-marks-hospital. *Data Spec,* Michelle Myers; Staff 1 (MLS 1)
Library Holdings: Bk Titles 600; Per Subs 75; Videos 40
Subject Interests: Healthcare
Automation Activity & Vendor Info: (OPAC) LibraryWorld, Inc; (Serials) EBSCO Online
Wireless access
Restriction: Not open to pub

P SALT LAKE CITY PUBLIC LIBRARY*, 210 E 400 South, 84111-3280. SAN 362-4994. Tel: 801-524-8200. FAX: 801-322-8194. Web Site: www.slcpl.org. *Interim Exec Dir,* Deborah Ehrman; E-mail: dehrman@slcpl.org; Staff 181.4 (MLS 36, Non-MLS 145.4)
Founded 1898. Pop 186,440; Circ 3,854,418
Library Holdings: AV Mats 185,949; Bk Vols 767,711; Per Subs 2,385
Special Collections: Foundations; Grants; Salt Lake City Coll
Automation Activity & Vendor Info: (Acquisitions) Innovative Interfaces, Inc; (Cataloging) Innovative Interfaces, Inc; (Circulation) Innovative Interfaces, Inc; (ILL) Innovative Interfaces, Inc; (OPAC) BiblioCommons; (Serials) Innovative Interfaces, Inc
Wireless access
Function: Adult bk club, After school storytime, Art exhibits, Audiobks via web, AV serv, Bilingual assistance for Spanish patrons, Bk reviews (Group), Bks on CD, Children's prog, Computer training, Computers for patron use, Electronic databases & coll, Free DVD rentals, Homework prog, ILL available, Internet access, Museum passes, Music CDs, Online cat, Outreach serv, OverDrive digital audio bks, Photocopying/Printing, Preschool outreach, Prog for adults, Prog for children & young adult, Story hour, Summer reading prog, Tax forms, Teen prog, Visual arts prog, Wheelchair accessible, Workshops, Writing prog
Publications: Events Calendar (Monthly)
Partic in OCLC Online Computer Library Center, Inc
Special Services for the Deaf - TDD equip
Open Mon-Thurs 9-9, Fri & Sat 9-6, Sun 1-5
Friends of the Library Group
Branches: 7
GLENDALE, 1375 S Concord, 84104. Tel: 801-594-8660.
Open Mon-Thurs 10-8, Fri & Sat 10-6
ANDERSON-FOOTHILL, 1135 S 2100 East, 84108. (Mail add: 210 E 400 South, 84111), SAN 322-5763. Tel: 801-594-8611.
Founded 1985
Open Mon-Thurs 10-9, Fri & Sat 10-6
Friends of the Library Group
CHAPMAN, 577 S 900 West, 84104-1302. (Mail add: 210 E 400 South, 84111), SAN 362-5028. Tel: 801-594-8623.
Founded 1912
Open Mon-Thurs 11-8, Fri & Sat 10-7
Friends of the Library Group
DAY-RIVERSIDE, 1575 W 1000 North, 84116. (Mail add: 210 E 400 South, 84111), SAN 362-5052. Tel: 801-594-8632.
Founded 1965
Open Mon-Thurs 10-9, Fri & Sat 10-6, Sun 1-5
Friends of the Library Group
MARMALADE, 280 W 500 North, 84103. Tel: 801-594-8680.
Open Mon-Thurs 10-8, Fri & Sat 10-6
SPRAGUE, 2131 S 1100 East, 84106-2806. (Mail add: 210 E 400 South, 84111), SAN 362-5087. Tel: 801-594-8640.
Founded 1914
Friends of the Library Group

CORINNE & JACK SWEET LIBRARY, 455 F St (Ninth Ave), 84103. (Mail add: 210 E 400 South, 84111), SAN 322-5771. Tel: 801-594-8651.
Founded 1985
Open Mon-Thurs 10-9, Fri & Sat 10-6
Friends of the Library Group

GL US COURTS LIBRARY - TENTH CIRCUIT COURT OF APPEALS*, Ronald N Boyce Library, US Court House, Ste 5.200, 351 S West Temple St, 84101. SAN 372-1892. Tel: 801-535-4220. FAX: 801-524-5375. Web Site: www.ca10.uscourts.gov/library/locations. *Librn,* Bob Revas; E-mail: robert_revas@ca10.uscourts.gov
Library Holdings: Bk Vols 9,800
Automation Activity & Vendor Info: (Cataloging) SirsiDynix
Wireless access
Open Mon-Fri 10:30-5
Restriction: Non-circulating to the pub

UNIVERSITY OF UTAH

CM SPENCER S ECCLES HEALTH SCIENCES LIBRARY*, Bldg 589, 10 N 1900 E, 84112-5890, SAN 362-5680. Tel: 801-581-8771. Circulation Tel: 801-581-8772. Interlibrary Loan Service Tel: 801-581-5282. Reference Tel: 801-581-5534. Toll Free Tel: 866-581-5534 (UT only). FAX: 801-581-3632. Web Site: library.med.utah.edu. *Dir,* Catherine Soehner; E-mail: catherine.soehner@utah.edu; *Dep Dir,* Joan Stoddart; E-mail: joans@lib.med.utah.edu; *Asst Librn, Head, Digital Production Servs,* Bryan E Hull; *Mgr, Digital Production Ctr,* Carmin I Smoot; Staff 10 (MLS 10)
Founded 1966
Special Collections: History of Medicine, bks & journals. Oral History; US Document Depository
Subject Interests: Med, Nursing
Automation Activity & Vendor Info: (OPAC) SirsiDynix
Partic in Center for Research Libraries; Greater Western Library Alliance; Utah Academic Library Consortium
Open Mon-Thurs 7am-11pm, Fri 7am-8pm, Sat 9-8, Sun 11-11
Restriction: In-house use for visitors

C J WILLARD MARRIOTT LIBRARY*, 295 S 1500 East, 84112-0860, SAN 362-5532. Tel: 801-581-8558. Circulation Tel: 801-581-8203. Interlibrary Loan Service Tel: 801-581-6010. Reference Tel: 801-581-6273. FAX: 801-585-7185. Web Site: www.lib.utah.edu. *Dean,* Alberta Comer; E-mail: alberta.comer@utah.edu; *Assoc Dean, Budget & Planning,* Ann Marie Breznay; Tel: 801-581-3852, E-mail: annmarie.breznay@utah.edu; *Assoc Dean, Res & Learning Serv,* Catherine Soehner; E-mail: catherine.soehner@utah.edu; *Assoc Dean, Scholarly Res & Coll,* Rick Anderson; Tel: 801-587-9989, E-mail: rick.anderson@utah.edu; *Assoc Dean, Spec Coll,* Gregory C Thompson; Tel: 801-581-8863; *Head, Scholarly Res,* Maria Hunt; Tel: 801-581-7741, E-mail: maria.hunt@utah.edu; *Circ Serv Coordr,* Natalie Polson; E-mail: natalie.polson@utah.edu; *ILL,* Susan Brusik; Fax: 801-585-3464, E-mail: susan.brusik@utah.edu; Staff 184 (MLS 45, Non-MLS 139)
Founded 1850. Enrl 30,819; Fac 1,555; Highest Degree: Doctorate
Library Holdings: Bk Vols 2,992,502; Per Subs 68,225
Special Collections: 2002 Winter Olympics Coll; Manuscripts Coll; Multimedia Archives; University Archives; US Patents; Utah Artists Project. Oral History; State Document Depository; UN Document Depository; US Document Depository
Subject Interests: Fine arts, Math, Rare bks, Western Americana
Automation Activity & Vendor Info: (Acquisitions) Ex Libris Group; (Cataloging) Ex Libris Group; (Circulation) Ex Libris Group; (Course Reserve) Ex Libris Group; (ILL) OCLC ILLiad; (OPAC) Ex Libris Group
Partic in Association of Research Libraries; OCLC Online Computer Library Center, Inc; Pioneer; Utah Libr Asn
Publications: Inspirations (Newsletter); Ski Archives (Newsletter)
Friends of the Library Group

CL S J QUINNEY LAW LIBRARY*, 332 S 1400 East, 84112-0731, SAN 362-5591. Circulation Tel: 801-581-6438. Reference Tel: 801-581-6184. FAX: 801-585-3033. Web Site: www.law.utah.edu/library. *Libr Dir,* Suzanne Darais; Tel: 801-585-3074; *Asst Dir, Head, Coll Develop,* Lee Warthen; Tel: 801-581-5344, E-mail: lee.warthen@law.utah.edu; *Head, Info Serv,* Linda Stephenson; Tel: 801-581-5800, E-mail: linda.stephenson@law.utah.edu; *Access Technologies Librn,* Valeri Craigle; Tel: 801-585-5475; *Circ Supvr,* Maura Fowler; Tel: 801-581-6296, E-mail: maura.fowler@law.utah.edu; *Coordr, ILL & Doc Delivery Serv,* Laura Ngai; Tel: 801-581-3804, E-mail: laura.ngai@law.utah.edu; Staff 19 (MLS 6, Non-MLS 13)
Founded 1923. Enrl 400; Fac 41; Highest Degree: Doctorate
Library Holdings: Bk Titles 84,000; Bk Vols 230,000; Per Subs 2,300
Special Collections: State Document Depository; US Document Depository
Subject Interests: Law
Automation Activity & Vendor Info: (Acquisitions) Ex Libris Group; (Cataloging) Ex Libris Group; (Circulation) Ex Libris Group; (OPAC) Ex Libris Group; (Serials) Ex Libris Group
Publications: Acquisitions List (Monthly); User Guide

S UTAH GEOLOGICAL SURVEY LIBRARY*, 1594 W North Temple, 84114. (Mail add: PO Box 146100, 84114-6100), SAN 372-865X. Tel: 801-537-3333, 801-538-4846. FAX: 801-537-3400. Web Site: geology.utah.gov/library. *Librn,* Suzanne Sawyer; E-mail: ssawyer@utah.gov
Library Holdings: Bk Vols 14,000
Subject Interests: Geol
Automation Activity & Vendor Info: (Cataloging) Innovative Interfaces, Inc
Restriction: Non-circulating to the pub, Open by appt only

S UTAH PRIDE CENTER LIBRARY*, 210 East 400 S, 84111. (Mail add: PO Box 1078, 84110). Tel: 801-539-8800. Web Site: utahpridecenter.org. *Exec Dir,* Stacey Jackson-Roberts; Tel: 801-539-8000, Ext 1010, E-mail: staceyjacksonroberts@utahpridecenter.org; Staff 2 (MLS 1, Non-MLS 1)
Founded 1982
Library Holdings: Bk Titles 3,100
Special Collections: The Utah Pride Center Library Coll is currently housed and circulated through the Salt Lake City Public Library Main Branch
Subject Interests: Bisexual, Gay, Lesbian, Queer, Transgender
Wireless access
Function: Adult bk club, Art exhibits, Computers for patron use, Teen prog
Restriction: Open to pub for ref & circ; with some limitations

GL UTAH STATE LAW LIBRARY*, 450 S State St, W-13, 84111-3101. (Mail add: PO Box 140220, 84114-0220), SAN 316-9308. Tel: 801-238-7990. E-mail: library@utcourts.gov. Web Site: www.utcourts.gov/lawlibrary. *Dir,* Nathanael Player; E-mail: nathanaelp@utcourts.gov; *Research Librn,* Jennifer Hansen; E-mail: jennyhh@utcourts.gov; Staff 5 (MLS 2, Non-MLS 3)
Library Holdings: Bk Titles 3,500; Bk Vols 60,000
Special Collections: State Document Depository; US Document Depository
Subject Interests: Law
Automation Activity & Vendor Info: (Cataloging) SirsiDynix; (Circulation) SirsiDynix; (OPAC) SirsiDynix; (Serials) SirsiDynix
Wireless access
Function: Ref serv available
Open Mon-Fri 8-5
Restriction: Non-circulating to the pub

P UTAH STATE LIBRARY DIVISION*, 250 N 1950 West, Ste A, 84116-7901. SAN 362-5710. Tel: 801-715-6777. Interlibrary Loan Service Tel: 801-715-6738. Administration Tel: 801-715-6741. Toll Free Tel: 800-662-9150. FAX: 801-715-6767. E-mail: usl@utah.gov. Web Site: library.utah.gov. *Dir, Libr Div, State Librn,* Chaundra Johnson; E-mail: crjohns@utah.gov; *Metadata Librn,* Tober Brian; Tel: 801-715-6752, E-mail: btober@utah.gov; *State Data Coordr,* Heidi Hendrick; Tel: 801-715-6762, E-mail: hlfendrick@utah.gov; *Acq Tech,* Hannah Jones; E-mail: hannahjones@utah.gov; *Prog Spec,* Jeri Openshaw; Tel: 801-715-6737, E-mail: jerio@utah.gov; Staff 67 (MLS 13, Non-MLS 54)
Founded 1957. Pop 2,615,129
Library Holdings: Bk Titles 47,654; Per Subs 83
Special Collections: Local Utah History Coll. State Document Depository
Automation Activity & Vendor Info: (Acquisitions) Innovative Interfaces, Inc. - Polaris; (Cataloging) Innovative Interfaces, Inc. - Polaris; (Circulation) Innovative Interfaces, Inc. - Polaris; (ILL) OCLC WorldShare Interlibrary Loan; (OPAC) Innovative Interfaces, Inc. - Polaris; (Serials) Innovative Interfaces, Inc. - Polaris
Wireless access
Publications: Directions for Utah Libraries; Directory of Public Libraries in Utah; Utah Library Laws; Utah Trustee Manual
Partic in Amigos Library Services, Inc; Beehive Library Consortium; OCLC Online Computer Library Center, Inc; Utah Academic Library Consortium; Utah Libr Network; Western Council of State Libraries, Inc
Open Mon-Fri 8-5
Branches: 1

P PROGRAM FOR THE BLIND & DISABLED, 250 N 1950 West, Ste A, 84116-7901, SAN 316-9316. Tel: 801-715-6789. Toll Free Tel: 800-453-4293, 800-662-5540. FAX: 801-715-6767. TDD: 801-715-6721. E-mail: blind@utah.gov. Web Site: blindlibrary.utah.gov. *Libr Prog Mgr,* Lisa Nelson; Staff 18 (MLS 4, Non-MLS 14)
Founded 1957. Pop 13,000; Circ 267,000
Library Holdings: Bks on Deafness & Sign Lang 30; High Interest/Low Vocabulary Bk Vols 1,829; Talking Bks 470,000
Special Collections: Mormon Literature Coll; Western Books Coll
Subject Interests: Mormon lit
Publications: The See Note Newsletter (Quarterly)
Special Services for the Deaf - TDD equip

Special Services for the Blind - Bks & mags in Braille, on rec, tape & cassette; Descriptive video serv (DVS); Large print bks; Radio reading serv; Rec & flexible discs
Open Mon-Fri 8-5
Bookmobiles: 5. Supervisor, Cristina Reyes. Bk vols 20,000

C WESTMINSTER COLLEGE*, Giovale Library, 1840 S 1300 East, 84105-3697. SAN 316-9340. Tel: 801-832-2250. FAX: 801-832-3109. E-mail: library@westminstercollege.edu. Web Site: www.westminstercollege.edu/library. *Libr Dir,* Emily Swanson; E-mail: eswanson@westminstercollege.edu; *Head, Coll & Access Serv,* Reese Julian; E-mail: rjulian@westminstercollege.edu; *Instruction & Assessment Librn,* Zayden Tethong; E-mail: ztethong@westminstercollege.edu; *Syst Librn,* Spencer Devilbliss; E-mail: sdevibliss@westminstercollege.edu; *Circ Mgr,* Madi Jones; E-mail: mjones@westminstercollege.edu; Staff 9 (MLS 5, Non-MLS 4)
Founded 1875. Enrl 2,800; Fac 132; Highest Degree: Master
Library Holdings: AV Mats 6,000; e-books 58,000; Bk Vols 124,000
Special Collections: Archival Material Relating to Early History of the College & Early History of the Presbyterian Church in Utah & Southern Idaho
Subject Interests: Modern poets, Utah landscape
Automation Activity & Vendor Info: (Acquisitions) SirsiDynix; (Cataloging) SirsiDynix; (Circulation) SirsiDynix; (Course Reserve) SirsiDynix; (ILL) OCLC ILLiad; (OPAC) SirsiDynix; (Serials) SirsiDynix
Wireless access
Special Services for the Blind - Assistive/Adapted tech devices, equip & products; Computer with voice synthesizer for visually impaired persons; Magnifiers; Reader equip; Scanner for conversion & translation of mats; Screen reader software
Open Mon-Thurs 7:30am-11pm, Fri 7:30-6, Sat 9-6, Sun 11-11; Mon-Thurs 8am-10pm, Fri 8-6, Sat 11-5, Sun 11-6 (Summer)
Restriction: Open to pub for ref & circ; with some limitations, Open to students, fac, staff & alumni

SANTAQUIN

P SANTAQUIN CITY LIBRARY*, 20 W 100 South, 84655. SAN 322-8606. Tel: 801-754-3030. E-mail: library@santaquin.org. Web Site: www.santaquin.org/departments___services/library. *Libr Dir,* Lyn Oryall; Tel: 801-754-3030, Ext 261; Staff 1 (Non-MLS 1)
Founded 1932. Pop 9,300; Circ 57,000
Library Holdings: Bk Vols 14,600; Per Subs 9
Automation Activity & Vendor Info: (Acquisitions) Follett Software; (Cataloging) Follett Software; (Circulation) Follett Software
Wireless access
Function: Bks on CD, Children's prog, Computers for patron use, Electronic databases & coll, Free DVD rentals, ILL available, Mail & tel request accepted, Online cat, Photocopying/Printing, Ref & res, Spoken cassettes & CDs, Summer reading prog, Tax forms, Telephone ref, VHS videos
Partic in Beehive Library Consortium
Open Mon-Thurs 12-7:45, Fri 12-4:45, Sat 10-1:45
Friends of the Library Group

SARATOGA SPRINGS

P SARATOGA SPRINGS PUBLIC LIBRARY*, 1307 N Commerce Dr, Ste 140, 84045. Tel: 801-766-6513. E-mail: libraryboard@saratogaspringscity.com. Web Site: www.saratogaspringscity.com/1112/library. *Libr Dir,* Melissa Grygla; E-mail: mgrygla@saratogaspringscity.com
Automation Activity & Vendor Info: (Cataloging) Koha; (OPAC) Koha
Function: Computers for patron use, Photocopying/Printing, Story hour
Partic in Beehive Library Consortium
Open Mon-Thurs 9-8, Fri & Sat 10-6
Friends of the Library Group

SMITHFIELD

P SMITHFIELD PUBLIC LIBRARY*, 25 N Main St, 84335-1957. SAN 316-9359. Tel: 435-563-3555. E-mail: library@smithfieldcity.org. Web Site: smithfieldcity.org/library. *Ch Serv, Interim Dir,* Karen Bowling; E-mail: kbowling@smithfieldcity.org; *Cataloger,* Kathy Downs
Pop 13,571; Circ 78,055
Library Holdings: Bk Vols 31,649; Per Subs 40
Automation Activity & Vendor Info: (Cataloging) Follett Software; (Circulation) Follett Software
Wireless access
Partic in Beehive Library Consortium
Open Mon-Thurs 11-7, Fri 2:30-5, Sat 11-3

SOUTH SALT LAKE

S TEI-LIBRARY SERVICES, LLC, 3455 S 500 W, 84115-4234. (Mail add: PO Box 57025, Murray, 84157-0025), SAN 316-9189. Tel: 801-262-2332. E-mail: librarian@tei-libsvcs.com. Web Site: tei-test.com/library-services. *Head Librn,* Alona MacGregor; E-mail: alona@tei-test.com; *Librn,* Ilonna MacGregor; E-mail: librarian@tei-test.com
Founded 1963
Jan 2025-Dec 2025 Income $125,000, Locally Generated Income $15,000, Parent Institution $75,000, Other $35,000. Mats Exp $75,000, Books $5,000, Per/Ser (Incl. Access Fees) $10,000, Other Print Mats $5,000, AV Equip $5,000, Electronic Ref Mat (Incl. Access Fees) $50,000. Sal $45,000
Library Holdings: CDs 150; DVDs 150; Electronic Media & Resources 45,000; Bk Vols 25,000; Per Subs 25; Videos 50
Special Collections: Industry Standards (UL, ASME, ANSI, CSA, BSI, EN, IEEE, IEC, NFPA, etc)
Subject Interests: Manufacturing, Sci ref, Test standards
Function: Bks on CD, Electronic databases & coll, Mail & tel request accepted, Prof lending libr
Restriction: Access at librarian's discretion, By permission only, Circ limited, Fee for pub use, Lending libr only via mail, Private libr
Friends of the Library Group

SPANISH FORK

P SPANISH FORK PUBLIC LIBRARY*, 49 S Main St, 84660-2030. SAN 316-9367. Tel: 801-804-4480. FAX: 801-798-5014. Web Site: www.spanishfork.org/departments/library. *Dir,* Scott Aylett; E-mail: saylett@spanishfork.org; Staff 16.8 (MLS 1, Non-MLS 15.8)
Founded 1920. Pop 45,000; Circ 423,000
Library Holdings: AV Mats 12,165; DVDs 7,415; e-books 95,035; Large Print Bks 1,040; Bk Vols 59,146; Per Subs 91
Automation Activity & Vendor Info: (Circulation) ByWater Solutions; (Discovery) ByWater Solutions; (ILL) OCLC; (OPAC) ByWater Solutions
Wireless access
Function: 24/7 Electronic res, 24/7 Online cat, Activity rm, Adult literacy prog, Art programs, Audio & video playback equip for onsite use, Audiobks on Playaways & MP3, Audiobks via web, Bk club(s), Bks on CD, Chess club, Children's prog, Computers for patron use, Digital talking bks, E-Readers, Electronic databases & coll, Family literacy, Free DVD rentals, Holiday prog, Home delivery & serv to seniorr ctr & nursing homes, ILL available, Internet access, Laminating, Life-long learning prog for all ages, Literacy & newcomer serv, Magazines, Meeting rooms, Movies, Music CDs, Online cat, Online info literacy tutorials on the web & in blackboard, Outreach serv, Outside serv via phone, mail, e-mail & web, OverDrive digital audio bks, Photocopying/Printing, Preschool reading prog, Printer for laptops & handheld devices, Prog for adults, Prog for children & young adult, Ref & res, Scanner, Senior outreach, Spanish lang bks, STEM programs, Story hour, Study rm, Summer reading prog, Tax forms, Teen prog, Wheelchair accessible
Partic in Beehive Library Consortium
Open Mon-Thurs 10-8, Fri 10-6, Sat 10-4
Restriction: Access at librarian's discretion, Free to mem, Limited access for the pub

SPRINGVILLE

P SPRINGVILLE PUBLIC LIBRARY*, 45 S Main St, 84663. SAN 316-9391. Tel: 801-489-2720. E-mail: springvillepubliclibrary@gmail.com. Web Site: www.springville.org/library. *Dir,* Dan Mickelson; E-mail: dmickelson@springville.org; Staff 4 (MLS 2, Non-MLS 2)
Founded 1916. Pop 20,424
Library Holdings: AV Mats 10,108; Large Print Bks 370; Bk Vols 73,267; Per Subs 150
Special Collections: Local History Coll; Springville History Coll
Automation Activity & Vendor Info: (Cataloging) TLC (The Library Corporation); (Circulation) TLC (The Library Corporation); (OPAC) Wil-Tech Software Ltd
Wireless access
Partic in Beehive Library Consortium
Open Mon-Thurs 10-9, Fri 10-6, Sat 10-4
Friends of the Library Group

STANSBURY PARK

P STANSBURY PARK LIBRARY*, One Country Club Dr, 84074. Tel: 435-882-6188. E-mail: library@stansburypark.org. Web Site: stansburypark.org/stansbury-library. *Libr Dir,* Patricia King
Function: Summer reading prog
Partic in Beehive Library Consortium

TAYLORSVILLE

J SALT LAKE COMMUNITY COLLEGE LIBRARIES*, Markosian Library, Taylorsville Redwood Campus, 4600 S Redwood Rd, 84123-3145. SAN 316-9324. Tel: 801-957-4602. Web Site: libweb.slcc.edu. *Dir, Libr*

Serv, Jon Glenn; Tel: 801-957-4905; *Asst Dir,* Zachary Allred; E-mail: zachary.allred@slcc.edu; Staff 34 (MLS 9, Non-MLS 25)
Founded 1948. Enrl 60,000; Fac 314; Highest Degree: Associate
Library Holdings: AV Mats 5,369; Bks on Deafness & Sign Lang 204; e-books 80,000; High Interest/Low Vocabulary Bk Vols 250; Bk Titles 76,315; Bk Vols 91,570; Per Subs 300
Subject Interests: Gen educ, Indust, Nursing, Sci tech
Automation Activity & Vendor Info: (Cataloging) SirsiDynix; (Circulation) SirsiDynix; (Course Reserve) SirsiDynix; (OPAC) SirsiDynix; (Serials) SirsiDynix
Wireless access
Partic in OCLC Online Computer Library Center, Inc; Utah Academic Library Consortium
Open Mon-Thurs 7:30am-Midnight, Fri 7:30-6, Sat 9:30-6
Departmental Libraries:
JORDAN CAMPUS, Health & Science Bldg, JHS 235, 3500 W Wights Fort Rd, West Jordan, 84088. Tel: 801-957-6202. Web Site: libweb.slcc.edu/about/locations/jordan. *Liaison & Instruction Librn,* Michael Toy; Tel: 801-957-6208
Open Mon-Thurs 8-4:30, Fri 8-3:30
MILLER CAMPUS, Miller Free Enterprise Ctr, Rm 123, 9750 S 300 W, Sandy, 84070. Tel: 801-957-5412. Web Site: libweb.slcc.edu/about/locations/miller. *Liaison & Instruction Librn,* Zachary Allred
Open Mon-Thurs 8-4
SOUTH CITY CAMPUS, Main Bldg, Rm 1-022, 1575 S State St, Salt Lake City, 84115. Tel: 801-957-3432. Web Site: libweb.slcc.edu/about/locations/south. *Liaison & Instruction Librn,* Anita Albright; Tel: 801-957-3435
Open Mon-Fri 8-4:30

TOOELE

P TOOELE CITY PUBLIC LIBRARY*, 128 W Vine St, 84074-2059. SAN 316-9405. Tel: 435-882-2182. Web Site: tooelelibrary.org. *Libr Dir,* Chase Randall; Tel: chaser@tooelecity.org
Founded 1910. Pop 37,104; Circ 201,326
Library Holdings: Bk Vols 60,186
Special Collections: State Document Depository
Automation Activity & Vendor Info: (Cataloging) Follett Software; (Circulation) Follett Software; (OPAC) Follett Software
Wireless access
Partic in Beehive Library Consortium
Open Mon-Thurs 10-8, Fri 10-6, Sat 10-2
Friends of the Library Group

TREMONTON

P TREMONTON CITY LIBRARY*, 210 N Tremont St, 84337-1329. SAN 316-9413. Tel: 435-257-9525. FAX: 435-257-9526. E-mail: library@tremontoncity.com. Web Site: tremontonlibrary.org. *Dir,* Kim L Griffiths
Pop 6,380; Circ 59,145
Library Holdings: Bk Titles 23,583; Bk Vols 24,165; Per Subs 57
Automation Activity & Vendor Info: (Acquisitions) Biblionix/Apollo; (Cataloging) Biblionix/Apollo; (Circulation) Biblionix/Apollo; (OPAC) Biblionix/Apollo
Wireless access
Function: Audiobks via web, Bks on CD, Children's prog, Citizenship assistance, Computer training, Computers for patron use, E-Readers, Electronic databases & coll, Family literacy, Free DVD rentals, Holiday prog, Home delivery & serv to seniorr ctr & nursing homes, Homebound delivery serv, Homework prog, ILL available, Life-long learning prog for all ages, Magazines, Mango lang, Movies, Online cat, OverDrive digital audio bks, Photocopying/Printing, Preschool reading prog, Prog for adults, Prog for children & young adult, Scanner, Senior computer classes, Senior outreach, Story hour, Summer reading prog, Tax forms, Teen prog, Telephone ref, Wheelchair accessible
Partic in Beehive Library Consortium
Open Mon-Fri 10-8, Sat 10-3
Friends of the Library Group

VERNAL

P UINTAH COUNTY LIBRARY*, 204 E 100 North, 84078. SAN 316-943X. Tel: 435-789-0091. FAX: 435-789-6822. E-mail: csummarell@uintah.utah.gov. Web Site: www.uintahlibrary.org. *Libr Dir,* Samuel J Passey; E-mail: passey@uintah.utah.gov; Staff 23 (MLS 1, Non-MLS 22)
Founded 1908. Pop 26,155; Circ 302,687
Library Holdings: Audiobooks 10,791; DVDs 18,386; e-books 130,776; Electronic Media & Resources 1,441; High Interest/Low Vocabulary Bk Vols 500; Large Print Bks 1,313; Music Scores 2,386; Bk Vols 97,592; Per Subs 159
Special Collections: Oral History
Subject Interests: Local hist
Automation Activity & Vendor Info: (Cataloging) Koha; (Circulation) Koha; (OPAC) Koha
Wireless access
Publications: A History of Uintah County: Scratching the Surface; Behind Swinging Doors: Colorful History; Blue Mountain Folks: Their Lives & Legends; Outlaw Trail History (Journal); Rivers We Know; Settlements of Uintah County: Digging Deeper
Partic in Beehive Library Consortium
Open Mon-Thurs 9-9, Fri & Sat 9-6

WEST JORDAN

P SALT LAKE COUNTY LIBRARY SERVICES*, Library Administration, 8030 S 1825 W, 84088. SAN 362-5117. Tel: 801-943-4636. FAX: 801-942-6323. Web Site: www.slcolibrary.org. *Dir,* Jim Cooper; Tel: 801-944-7504, E-mail: jamescooper@slcolibrary.org; *Assoc Dir, Finance & Operations,* Leslie Webster; *Assoc Dir, Prog, Outreach & Ref,* Matt McClain; Tel: 801-944-7513; *Assoc Dir, Pub Serv,* Jennifer Fay; *Acq & Coll, Sr Mgr, Tech,* Christa Warren; *Human Res Mgr,* Pamala Park; *Mkt & Commun Relations Mgr,* Position Currently Open; Staff 322 (MLS 90, Non-MLS 232)
Founded 1938. Pop 753,597; Circ 12,749,312
Library Holdings: Bk Vols 2,000,000; Per Subs 7,000
Automation Activity & Vendor Info: (Acquisitions) SirsiDynix; (Cataloging) SirsiDynix; (Circulation) SirsiDynix; (Media Booking) SirsiDynix; (OPAC) SirsiDynix; (Serials) SirsiDynix
Wireless access
Publications: Library Links (Newsletter); Library Links (Quarterly); Staff Matters (Newsletter); Staff Matters (Monthly)
Partic in OCLC Online Computer Library Center, Inc
Special Services for the Deaf - TTY equip
Open Mon-Thurs 10-9, Fri & Sat 10-6
Branches: 19
ALTA READING ROOM, Alta Community Ctr, 10351 E Hwy 210, Alta, 84121, SAN 362-515X. *Mgr,* Trudy Jorgensen-Price
Open Mon-Sat 9-1
BINGHAM CREEK, 4834 W 9000 S, 84081, SAN 377-7413. *Mgr,* Position Currently Open
Circ 1,089,913
Library Holdings: Bk Vols 125,000
Open Mon-Thurs 10-9, Fri & Sat 10-6
COLUMBUS BRANCH, 2530 S 500 E, South Salt Lake, 84106, SAN 362-5419. *Mgr,* Vern Waters; Staff 7 (MLS 2, Non-MLS 5)
Circ 182,742
Library Holdings: Bk Vols 72,000
Open Mon-Thurs 10-9, Fri & Sat 10-6
DRAPER BRANCH, 1136 E Pioneer Rd, Draper, 84020-9628, SAN 362-5168. *Mgr,* Sarah Brinkerhoff; Staff 30 (MLS 5, Non-MLS 25)
Circ 296,271
Library Holdings: Bk Vols 134,000
Open Mon-Thurs 10-9, Fri & Sat 10-6
HERRIMAN BRANCH, 5380 W Herriman Main St, Herriman, 84096. *Mgr,* Leslie Schow
Library Holdings: Bk Vols 108,000
Open Mon-Thurs 10-9, Fri & Sat 10-6
HOLLADAY, 2150 E Murray-Holladay Rd, 4730 S, Salt Lake City, 84117-5241, SAN 362-5230. *Mgr,* Ann Marie Barrett; Staff 13 (MLS 5, Non-MLS 8)
Circ 569,706
Library Holdings: Bk Vols 88,000
Open Mon-Thurs 10-9, Fri & Sat 10-6
HUNTER BRANCH, 4740 W 4100 S, West Valley City, 84120-4948, SAN 374-8138. *Mgr,* Maggie Mills; Staff 18 (MLS 6, Non-MLS 12)
Circ 843,640
Library Holdings: Bk Vols 154,500
Open Mon-Thurs 10-9, Fri & Sat 10-6
KEARNS BRANCH, 5350 S 4220 W, Kearns, 84118-4314, SAN 362-5265. *Mgr,* Position Currently Open
Founded 1965. Circ 579,789
Library Holdings: Bk Vols 75,800
Function: Audiobks via web, Bilingual assistance for Spanish patrons, Bks on CD, Children's prog, Computers for patron use, Electronic databases & coll, Family literacy, Free DVD rentals, Homework prog, ILL available, Internet access, Magnifiers for reading, Music CDs, Online cat, Online ref, Outreach serv, OverDrive digital audio bks, Photocopying/Printing, Preschool outreach, Prog for adults, Prog for children & young adult, Ref serv available, Story hour, Summer reading prog, Tax forms, Teen prog, Wheelchair accessible
MAGNA BRANCH, 2675 S 8950 W, Magna, 84044, SAN 362-529X. *Mgr,* Melissa Wayman; Staff 8 (MLS 3, Non-MLS 5)
Circ 310,598
Library Holdings: Bk Vols 100,000
Open Mon-Thurs 10-9, Fri & Sat 10-6

MILLCREEK COMMUNITY LIBRARY, 2266 E Evergreen Ave, Salt Lake City, 84109-2927, SAN 362-5176. *Mgr,* Suzanne Tronier; Staff 16 (MLS 6, Non-MLS 10)
Circ 577,013
Library Holdings: Bk Vols 135,000
Open Mon-Thurs 10-9, Fri & Sat 10-6

RIVERTON BRANCH, 12877 S 1830 W, Riverton, 84065-3204, SAN 328-7580. *Mgr,* Stephanie Tilt; Staff 17 (MLS 6, Non-MLS 11)
Circ 692,240
Library Holdings: Bk Vols 95,000
Open Mon-Thurs 10-9, Fri & Sat 10-6

SANDY BRANCH, 10100 S Petunia Way, 1450 E, Sandy, 84092-4380, SAN 372-0292. *Mgr,* Darin Butler; Staff 41 (MLS 11, Non-MLS 30)
Circ 1,479,008
Library Holdings: Bk Vols 219,380
Open Mon-Thurs 10-9, Fri & Sat 10-6

CALVIN S SMITH BRANCH, 810 E 3300 S, Salt Lake City, 84106, SAN 362-5354. *Mgr,* Laura Renshaw; Staff 6 (MLS 2, Non-MLS 4)
Circ 247,350
Library Holdings: Bk Vols 28,500
Open Mon-Thurs 10-9, Fri & Sat 10-6

SOUTH JORDAN BRANCH, 10673 S Redwood Rd, South Jordan, 84095-2481, SAN 362-5389. *Mgr,* Position Currently Open
Founded 1974. Pop 55,557; Circ 1,078,999
Library Holdings: Bk Vols 108,000
Function: Bks on CD, Children's prog, Computers for patron use, Digital talking bks, Electronic databases & coll, Free DVD rentals, Homebound delivery serv, ILL available, Music CDs, Online cat, Outreach serv, Photocopying/Printing, Preschool outreach, Preschool reading prog, Prog for children & young adult, Ref serv available, Story hour, Summer reading prog, Teen prog, Telephone ref
Open Mon-Thurs 10-9, Fri & Sat 10-6

TAYLORSVILLE BRANCH, 4870 S 2700 W, Taylorsville, 84129, SAN 372-0284. *Mgr,* Cindy Smiley; Staff 15 (MLS 5, Non-MLS 10)
Founded 1990. Circ 615,767
Library Holdings: Bk Vols 85,000
Open Mon-Thurs 10-9, Fri & Sat 10-6

RUTH VINE TYLER BRANCH, 8041 S Wood St, 55 W, Midvale, 84047-7559, SAN 362-5443. *Mgr,* David Bird; Staff 6 (MLS 2, Non-MLS 4)
Circ 228,670
Library Holdings: Bk Vols 52,000
Open Mon-Thurs 10-9, Fri & Sat 10-6

WEST JORDAN BRANCH, 8030 S 1825 W, 84088, SAN 328-7602. *Mgr,* Darlene Nethery; Staff 13 (MLS 4, Non-MLS 9)
Circ 562,827
Library Holdings: Bk Vols 125,000
Open Mon-Thurs 10-9, Fri & Sat 10-6

WEST VALLEY BRANCH, 2880 W 3650 S, West Valley City, 84119-3743, SAN 362-5206. *Mgr,* Trish Hull; Staff 10 (MLS 4, Non-MLS 6)
Circ 366,529
Library Holdings: Bk Vols 65,000
Open Mon-Thurs 10-9, Fri & Sat 10-6

WHITMORE BRANCH, 2197 E Fort Union Blvd, Salt Lake City, 84121-3139, SAN 362-5478. *Mgr,* Position Currently Open
Circ 1,089,913
Library Holdings: Bk Vols 65,000
Open Mon-Thurs 10-9, Fri & Sat 10-6

VERMONT

Date of Statistics: FY 2024
Population, 2020 U.S. Census: 643,077
Population Served by Public Libraries: 626,651
Total Volumes in Public Libraries: 2,466,905
Volumes Per Capita: 3.93
Total Public Library Circulation: 3,770,647
Circulation Per Capita: 6.01
Digital Resources:
Total audio items (physical & downloadable units): 102,823
Total video items (physical & downloadable units): 217,335
Total computers for use by the public: 716
Total annual wireless sessions: 905,664
Income and Expenditures:
Total Public Library Income (not including Grants-in-Aid): $29,978,452
Source of Income: Public funds plus fundraising
Income Per Capita: $47.84
Federal (Library Services & Technology Act): n/a
Number of Bookmobiles in State: Four. Three in public libraries, one independent bookmobile service.
Information provided courtesy of: Joshua Muse, Consultant for Library Technology; Vermont Department of Libraries

ALBANY

P ALBANY TOWN LIBRARY*, 530 Main St, 05820. (Mail add: PO Box 194, 05820), SAN 376-4915. Tel: 802-755-6107. E-mail: AlbanyPublicLibraryVT@gmail.com. Web Site: www.albanypubliclibraryvt.org. *Librn,* Kristin Urie
Library Holdings: Bk Vols 3,000; Per Subs 10
Wireless access
Open Tues 12-4, Thurs 9-4, Sat 9-11

ALBURG

P ALBURGH PUBLIC LIBRARY*, 128 S Main St, 05440. (Mail add: PO Box 344, 05440), SAN 376-3439. Tel: 802-796-6077. FAX: 802-796-6077. E-mail: alburghpl@gmail.com. Web Site: alburghpl.org. *Dir,* Gina Lewis; Staff 2 (Non-MLS 2)
Founded 1917. Pop 2,010
Library Holdings: Audiobooks 75; DVDs 200; Large Print Bks 400; Bk Vols 12,305; Per Subs 35
Wireless access
Function: Adult bk club, Adult literacy prog, Bk reviews (Group), Bks on cassette, Bks on CD, Children's prog, Computer training, Computers for patron use, Free DVD rentals, Holiday prog, Homebound delivery serv, ILL available, Mail & tel request accepted, Mail loans to mem, Music CDs, Photocopying/Printing, Preschool outreach, Printer for laptops & handheld devices, Prog for adults, Prog for children & young adult, Senior computer classes, Story hour, Summer reading prog, Tax forms, Teen prog, VHS videos, Wheelchair accessible, Workshops
Partic in Collaborative Libraries of Vermont
Open Mon & Wed-Fri 1-6, Tues 9-5, Sat 10-1
Friends of the Library Group

ARLINGTON

P MARTHA CANFIELD MEMORIAL FREE LIBRARY*, 528 E Arlington Rd, 05250. (Mail add: PO Box 267, 05250-0267), SAN 316-9456. Tel: 802-375-6153. E-mail: martha_canfield_lib@hotmail.com. Web Site: www.marthacanfieldlibrary.org. *Dir,* Phyllis Skidmore; *Libr Asst,* Holly Dix; *Curator,* Bill Budde; Tel: 802-753-6229. Subject Specialists: *Genealogy, Local hist,* Bill Budde; Staff 3 (Non-MLS 3)
Founded 1803. Pop 3,700; Circ 19,500
Library Holdings: AV Mats 1,300; Large Print Bks 700; Bk Titles 29,000; Per Subs 12
Special Collections: Vermontiana (Dr George Russell Coll), bks, clipping, ms, photog
Automation Activity & Vendor Info: (Cataloging) Follett Software; (Circulation) Follett Software; (OPAC) Follett Software
Wireless access
Function: Art exhibits, Bks on CD, Computers for patron use, Free DVD rentals, Homebound delivery serv, ILL available, Internet access, Magazines, Mango lang, Meeting rooms, Movies, Music CDs, Online cat, Photocopying/Printing, Prog for adults, Scanner, Story hour, Tax forms, VHS videos, Wheelchair accessible
Partic in Collaborative Libraries of Vermont; OCLC Online Computer Library Center, Inc
Open Tues & Thurs 9-8, Wed 9-5, Fri 2-6, Sat 10-3

ASCUTNEY

P WEATHERSFIELD PROCTOR LIBRARY*, 5181 Rte 5, 05030. (Mail add: PO Box 519, 05030-0519), SAN 362-5869. Tel: 802-674-2863. FAX: 802-674-9876. E-mail: weathersfieldproctorlibrary@gmail.com. Web Site: www.weathersfieldproctorlibrary.org. *Dir,* Mark Richardson; *Asst Librn,* Judy Topolski; *Youth Librn,* Glenna Coleman; Staff 2 (MLS 1, Non-MLS 1)
Founded 1902. Pop 2,788
Library Holdings: AV Mats 288; Bk Vols 6,908; Per Subs 31; Talking Bks 432
Subject Interests: Local hist
Wireless access
Function: 24/7 Online cat, Adult bk club, Audiobks on Playaways & MP3, Audiobks via web, Bk club(s), Bks on CD, Children's prog, Computer training, Computers for patron use, Digital talking bks, E-Readers, Free DVD rentals, Holiday prog, Homebound delivery serv, ILL available, Internet access, Magazines, Movies, Museum passes, Music CDs, Online cat, Online ref, Photocopying/Printing, Prog for adults, Prog for children & young adult, Ref & res, Ref serv available, Story hour, Summer reading prog, Wheelchair accessible
Open Wed 10-8, Thurs & Fri 10-6, Sat 9-3
Friends of the Library Group

BAKERSFIELD

P H F BRIGHAM FREE PUBLIC LIBRARY, 104 Main St, 05441. (Mail add: PO Box 45, 05441-0045), SAN 316-9464. Tel: 802-827-4414. E-mail: hfbrighamlibrary@gmail.com. Web Site: hfbrigham.aspendiscovery.org/home. *Dir,* Hadley Priebe; *Librn,* Mary Schwartz; Staff 3 (MLS 1, Non-MLS 2)
Pop 1,015; Circ 3,692
Library Holdings: Bk Titles 5,850; Per Subs 15
Wireless access
Partic in Catamount Library Network
Open Tues 9-5, Wed 2-6, Thurs 9-12 & 2-6, Fri 3-6, Sat 9-1

BARNARD

P CHARLES B DANFORTH PUBLIC LIBRARY*, 6208 VT Rte 12, 05031. (Mail add: PO Box 204, 05031-0204), SAN 316-9472. Tel: 802-234-9408. E-mail: charlesdanforthlibrary@gmail.com. *Librn,* Margaret Edwards
Pop 947; Circ 1,400
Library Holdings: Bk Vols 5,100
Mem of Midstate Regional Library
Open Tues, 12-2, Wed 3-5, Sat 10-2

BARNET

P BARNET PUBLIC LIBRARY*, 147 Church St, 05821. SAN 316-9480. Tel: 802-633-4436. FAX: 802-633-4436. E-mail: barnetpl@hotmail.com. Web Site: barnetpubliclibrary.com. *Librn,* Dylan Ford; Staff 1 (Non-MLS 1)
Founded 1900. Pop 1,690; Circ 2,596
Library Holdings: AV Mats 125; CDs 25; DVDs 20; Large Print Bks 100; Bk Vols 7,500; Per Subs 12; Talking Bks 150; Videos 50
Special Collections: Large Print Books
Subject Interests: Vt
Wireless access
Function: Home delivery & serv to seniorr ctr & nursing homes, Homebound delivery serv, ILL available, Photocopying/Printing, Prog for children & young adult, Wheelchair accessible
Special Services for the Blind - Large print bks
Open Tues 10-4, Wed 11-3, Thurs 9-12, Sat 10-2

BARRE

P ALDRICH PUBLIC LIBRARY, Six Washington St, 05641. SAN 316-9499. Tel: 802-476-7550. E-mail: info@aldrichpubliclibrary.org. Web Site: www.aldrichpubliclibrary.org. *Libr Dir,* Kristin Baumann; Tel: 802-476-7550, Ext 307, E-mail: director@aldrichpubliclibrary.org; *Asst Libr Dir,* Garrett Grant; E-mail: assistant.director@aldrichpubliclibrary.org; *Ch,* Ian Gauthier; E-mail: childrens.librarian@aldrichpubliclibrary.org; *Circ Librn,* Mary Ellen Boisvert; E-mail: adult.librarian@aldrichpubliclibrary.org; *Outreach Librn,* Karen O'Donnell-Leach; *Ref & ILL Librn,* Lee Aura Bonamico; *Tech Serv Librn,* Cerese Sanborn; *YA Serv,* Juliet Stephens; Staff 12 (MLS 3, Non-MLS 9)
Founded 1908. Pop 16,893; Circ 53,172
Special Collections: Oral History
Subject Interests: Am sculpture, Ethnic hist, European sculpture, Immigration, Indust hist, Labor hist, Political movements
Automation Activity & Vendor Info: (Cataloging) Follett-Destiny; (Circulation) Follett-Destiny; (OPAC) Follett-Destiny
Wireless access
Function: 24/7 Electronic res, 24/7 Online cat, Adult bk club, Archival coll, Art exhibits, Audiobks via web, AV serv, Bks on CD, Children's prog, Computer training, Computers for patron use, Digital talking bks, Distance learning, E-Readers, Electronic databases & coll, Equip loans & repairs, Free DVD rentals, Games & aids for people with disabilities, Genealogy discussion group, Holiday prog, Home delivery & serv to seniorr ctr & nursing homes, Homebound delivery serv, Homework prog, ILL available, Instruction & testing, Internet access, Large print keyboards, Life-long learning prog for all ages, Magazines, Magnifiers for reading, Mail & tel request accepted, Mango lang, Meeting rooms, Microfiche/film & reading machines, Movies, Museum passes, Music CDs, Notary serv, Online cat, Online info literacy tutorials on the web & in blackboard, Online ref, Outreach serv, OverDrive digital audio bks, Photocopying/Printing, Preschool outreach, Preschool reading prog, Prog for adults, Prog for children & young adult, Ref & res, Ref serv available, Res performed for a fee, Scanner, Senior computer classes, Serves people with intellectual disabilities, Story hour, Study rm, Summer reading prog, Tax forms, Teen prog, Telephone ref, Wheelchair accessible, Workshops
Publications: Barre Granite Heritage with Guide to the Cemeteries (1997); Barre in Retrospect 1776-1995 (Community hist); Barre, VT: An Annotated Bibliography (1979); Guide to the Manuscript Holdings of the Archives of Barre History (1997)
Partic in Collaborative Libraries of Vermont; Green Mountain Library Consortium
Special Services for the Blind - Bks on cassette; Bks on CD; Closed circuit TV magnifier; Home delivery serv; Large print bks
Open Mon-Fri 10-6, Sat 10-2
Friends of the Library Group
Branches: 1
YORK BRANCH, 134 Mill St, East Barre, 05649. (Mail add: Six Washington St, 05641). Tel: 802-476-5118.
Library Holdings: Bk Vols 4,000
Open Tues & Thurs 12-4, Sat 10-1
Friends of the Library Group

P STATE OF VERMONT DEPARTMENT OF LIBRARIES*, 60 Washington St, Ste 2, 05641. SAN 322-7774. Tel: 802-636-0040. Web Site: libraries.vermont.gov. *Interim State Librn,* Tom McMurdo; E-mail: thomas.mcmurdo@vermont.gov; *Asst State Librn,* Janette Schaffer; E-mail: janette.schaffer@vermont.gov; *Govt Doc/Ref Librn,* April Shaw; E-mail: april.shaw@vermont.gov; Staff 19 (MLS 10, Non-MLS 9)
Special Collections: Children's Book Exhibit Center; Library Science Coll. US Document Depository
Subject Interests: Vt
Automation Activity & Vendor Info: (Cataloging) SirsiDynix; (Circulation) SirsiDynix; (ILL) OCLC
Wireless access
Publications: Manual for Vermont Library Trustees (Library handbook); Vermont Department of Libraries eNewsletter (Monthly); Vermont Public Library Annual Report
Partic in Green Mountain Library Consortium; Vermont Consortium of Academic Libraries
Special Services for the Blind - Braille bks; Descriptive video serv (DVS); Digital talking bk; Digital talking bk machines; Large print bks; Newsletter (in large print, Braille or on cassette); Talking bks & player equip
Branches: 1
ABLE LIBRARY
See Separate Entry under Vermont Department of Libraries

P VERMONT DEPARTMENT OF LIBRARIES*, ABLE Library, 60 Washington St, Ste 2, 05641. SAN 317-0748. Tel: 802-636-0020. Toll Free Tel: 800-479-1711 (VT only). E-mail: lib.ablelibrary@vermont.gov. Web Site: able.vermont.gov. *Libr Dir,* Karen Gravlin; E-mail: karen.gravlin@vermont.gov; *Asst Librn,* Wendy Clark; E-mail: wendy.clark@vermont.gov; *Libr Asst,* Sara Blow; E-mail: sara.blow@vermont.gov; Staff 2 (Non-MLS 2)
Founded 1976. Pop 1,368; Circ 66,975
Library Holdings: Braille Volumes 214; DVDs 307; Large Print Bks 8,861; Bk Titles 8,643; Talking Bks 32,608; Videos 196
Automation Activity & Vendor Info: (Acquisitions) Keystone Systems, Inc (KLAS); (Cataloging) Keystone Systems, Inc (KLAS); (Circulation) Keystone Systems, Inc (KLAS); (ILL) SirsiDynix; (OPAC) Keystone Systems, Inc (KLAS); (Serials) Keystone Systems, Inc (KLAS)
Wireless access
Special Services for the Blind - BiFolkal kits; Bks on flash-memory cartridges; Children's Braille; Descriptive video serv (DVS); Digital talking bk; Digital talking bk machines; Large print bks; Newsletter (in large print, Braille or on cassette); Newsline for the Blind; Soundproof reading booth; Talking bks; Talking bks & player equip; Volunteer serv
Open Mon-Fri 7:45-4:30

S VERMONT GRAND LODGE LIBRARY*, 49 East Rd - Berlin, 05641-5390. Tel: 802-223-1883. FAX: 802-223-2187. E-mail: glsec@vtfreemasons.org. Web Site: www.vtfreemasons.org. *Library Contact,* Earl Washburn
Library Holdings: Bk Vols 6,000
Open Mon-Thurs 8-4

S VERMONT HISTORICAL SOCIETY*, Howard & Alba Leahy Library, Vermont History Ctr, 60 Washington St, 05641-4209. SAN 317-073X. Tel: 802-479-8509. FAX: 802-479-8510. E-mail: library@vermonthistory.org. Web Site: vermonthistory.org. *Librn,* Steven Picazio; Tel: 802-479-8508, E-mail: librarian@vermonthistory.org; *Asst Librn,* Marjorie Strong; E-mail: marjorie.strong@vermonthistory.org; Staff 2 (MLS 2)
Founded 1838
Library Holdings: Bk Vols 53,000; Per Subs 220
Special Collections: Broadside Coll; Manuscripts Coll; Photograph Coll; Sheet Music Coll
Subject Interests: Genealogy, Lower Can hist, New England, NY hist, Vt
Automation Activity & Vendor Info: (Cataloging) EOS International; (OPAC) EOS International
Wireless access
Partic in OCLC Online Computer Library Center, Inc
Open Tues, Thurs & Fri 9-4, Wed-9-8
Restriction: Non-circulating to the pub

BARTON

P BARTON PUBLIC LIBRARY*, 100 Church St, 05822. (Mail add: PO Box 549, 05822-0549), SAN 316-9510. Tel: 802-525-6524. FAX: 802-525-6524. E-mail: bartonpubliclibrary@yahoo.com. Web Site: bartonpubliclibrary.org. *Dir,* Toni Eubanks
Founded 1914. Pop 3,000
Library Holdings: DVDs 200; Large Print Bks 200; Bk Vols 7,000; Per Subs 1; Talking Bks 300
Wireless access
Function: Homebound delivery serv, ILL available, Prog for adults, Prog for children & young adult, Summer reading prog, Telephone ref
Open Mon 2-6, Tues 10-2, Wed 10-6, Fri 10-5
Friends of the Library Group

BELLOWS FALLS

P ROCKINGHAM FREE PUBLIC LIBRARY*, 65 Westminster St, 05101. SAN 316-9529. Tel: 802-463-4270. FAX: 802-463-1566. E-mail: reference@rockinghamlibrary.org. Web Site: www.rockinghamlibrary.org. *Libr Dir,* Celina Houlne; E-mail: director@rockinghamlibrary.org; Staff 5.4 (MLS 2.3, Non-MLS 3.1)
Founded 1887. Pop 5,100; Circ 36,699
Jul 2017-Jun 2018 Income $389,850, City $347,070, Other $42,780. Mats Exp $22,605, Books $12,727, Per/Ser (Incl. Access Fees) $3,083, Manu

Arch $215, AV Mat $3,100, Electronic Ref Mat (Incl. Access Fees) $3,480. Sal $219,890 (Prof $22,605)
Library Holdings: AV Mats 4,199; Bk Vols 36,934; Per Subs 70
Special Collections: Rockingham Historical Coll
Subject Interests: Genealogy, Local hist
Automation Activity & Vendor Info: (Acquisitions) Baker & Taylor; (Cataloging) Baker & Taylor; (Circulation) Koha; (OPAC) Koha; (Serials) EBSCO Online
Wireless access
Function: 24/7 Electronic res, 24/7 Online cat, Activity rm, Adult bk club, After school storytime, Archival coll, Art exhibits, Art programs, Audiobks on Playaways & MP3, Audiobks via web, Bks on CD, Children's prog, Computer training, Computers for patron use, Electronic databases & coll, Free DVD rentals, Genealogy discussion group, ILL available, Internet access, Life-long learning prog for all ages, Magazines, Meeting rooms, Microfiche/film & reading machines, Movies, Museum passes, Online cat, Online ref, OverDrive digital audio bks, Photocopying/Printing, Preschool outreach, Prog for adults, Prog for children & young adult, Ref & res, Serves people with intellectual disabilities, Spoken cassettes & CDs, Spoken cassettes & DVDs, STEM programs, Story hour, Summer & winter reading prog, Summer reading prog, Tax forms, Teen prog, Telephone ref, Wheelchair accessible, Winter reading prog, Workshops, Writing prog
Partic in Green Mountain Library Consortium
Open Mon, Tues & Wed 10-7, Thurs & Fri 10-5:30, Sat 10-2
Restriction: Non-circulating of rare bks, Non-resident fee
Friends of the Library Group

BELMONT

P MOUNT HOLLY TOWN LIBRARY*, 26 Maple Hill Rd, 05730. (Mail add: PO Box 92, 05730), SAN 320-5177. Tel: 802-259-3707. E-mail: mthollylibrary@gmail.com. Web Site: mounthollytownlibrary.wordpress.com. *Libr Dir,* Joseph Galbraith; Staff 1 (MLS 1)
Founded 1914. Pop 1,350
Library Holdings: Audiobooks 300; Large Print Bks 120; Bk Vols 12,000; Videos 200
Wireless access
Function: 24/7 Online cat, Activity rm, Adult bk club, Art exhibits, Audiobks via web, Bks on CD, Computers for patron use, Holiday prog, ILL available, Internet access, Mail & tel request accepted, Museum passes, Online cat, Res assist avail, Summer reading prog
Partic in Collaborative Libraries of Vermont
Open Mon & Sat 9-1, Tues 1-5, Wed 2-4

BENNINGTON

C BENNINGTON COLLEGE*, Crossett Library, One College Dr, 05201-6001. SAN 362-5923. Tel: 802-440-4610. Interlibrary Loan Service Tel: 802-440-4605. Reference Tel: 802-440-4737. E-mail: library@bennington.edu. Web Site: library.bennington.edu, www.bennington.edu/crossett-library. *Dean of Libr,* Oceana Wilson; E-mail: owilson@bennington.edu; *Dir, Library Access & Research,* Joe Tucker; E-mail: jtucker@bennington.edu; *Dir, Libr Serv,* Jared Della Rocca; E-mail: jdellarocca@bennington.edu; *Coll Serv Librn,* Vanessa Haverkoch; Tel: 802-440-4602, E-mail: vhaver@bennington.edu; Staff 4 (MLS 3, Non-MLS 1)
Founded 1932. Enrl 750; Fac 105; Highest Degree: Master
Library Holdings: AV Mats 3,000; e-books 194,313; e-journals 28,186; Bk Titles 95,205; Per Subs 275
Special Collections: Literary Reviews; Photography
Subject Interests: Art, Dance, Lit
Automation Activity & Vendor Info: (Cataloging) Innovative Interfaces, Inc; (Circulation) Innovative Interfaces, Inc; (ILL) OCLC; (OPAC) Innovative Interfaces, Inc
Wireless access
Partic in LYRASIS
Open Mon-Wed & Sun 8am-Midnight, Thurs-Sat 8am-10pm
Departmental Libraries:
JENNINGS MUSIC LIBRARY, One College Dr, Jennings Music Bldg, 05201, SAN 362-5958. Tel: 802-440-4512. E-mail: musiclibrary@bennington.edu. *Prog Coordr,* Olivia Biro; E-mail: oliviabiro@bennington.edu
Library Holdings: CDs 5,000; DVDs 50; Music Scores 5,791; Bk Titles 600; Per Subs 8; Videos 145
Subject Interests: Contemporary chamber music
Restriction: Not open to pub, Open to students, fac & staff

P BENNINGTON FREE LIBRARY*, 101 Silver St, 05201. SAN 316-9545. Tel: 802-442-9051. Reference E-mail: reference@bfli.org. Web Site: benningtonfreelibrary.org. *Dir,* Lynne Fonteneau-McCann; *Cat Librn, Circ Librn,* Wendy Sharkey; *Ch, YA Librn,* Linda Donigan; *Ch, YA Librn,* Carrie Gutbier; *Ref Librn,* Karson Kiesinger
Founded 1865. Pop 18,500; Circ 95,000
Library Holdings: Bk Titles 56,105; Per Subs 187
Special Collections: Bennington Banner, 1903-present, flm
Subject Interests: Town hist, Vt hist
Wireless access
Partic in Catamount Library Network
Open Mon 10-7, Tues, Wed & Sat 10-5, Thurs 1-7, Fri 1-5
Friends of the Library Group

S BENNINGTON MUSEUM, Research Library, 75 Main St, 05201. SAN 316-9553. Tel: 802-447-1571. FAX: 802-442-8305. E-mail: library@benningtonmuseum.org. Web Site: benningtonmuseum.org. *Colls Mgr,* Callie Raspuzzi; E-mail: collections@benningtonmuseum.org
Founded 1928
Library Holdings: Bk Titles 4,500
Special Collections: Bennington Town Records & Maps; Bennington's Old First Church Records; Early Vital Records for Southern New England States; Essays & Data on Early Families in New England: Cutter, Savage & Others; Hemenway's Six-Volume 19th Century Vermont Gazetteer: Town, County & State Histories for Vermont, New England, New York; Military Rosters & Data for Vermont, Nearby States: Revolution, Civil War; Published Family Histories, New England-Oriented; The Day Papers: 25 Scrapbooks of Discerning News Clips, 1870-1916; The Harwood Diaries: Rich Details of Life Between 1803 & 1837; US Census Indexes, 1790-1850 for New England, New York & Others; Vermont & Bennington Regional Resources: Aldrich Histories & Child Directories of Vermont Counties, circa 1880; Vermont Vital Records to 1941, microfilm
Subject Interests: Genealogy, Regional hist
Wireless access
Function: Res libr
Open Mon, Thurs & Fri 1-4
Restriction: Non-circulating
Friends of the Library Group

M SOUTHWESTERN VERMONT HEALTH CARE*, Health Sciences Library, 100 Hospital Dr, 05201. SAN 362-6016. Tel: 802-447-5120. Web Site: svhealthcare.org. *Educ Adminr,* Jenna McLain; E-mail: jenna.mclain@svhealthcare.org; Staff 1 (MLS 1)
Founded 1969
Library Holdings: Bk Titles 800; Bk Vols 947; Per Subs 37
Subject Interests: Allied health, Basic sci, Biomed sci, Med, Nursing, Surgery
Automation Activity & Vendor Info: (Cataloging) EOS International; (OPAC) EOS International
Publications: Library Newsletter
Partic in Basic Health Sciences Library Network; Health Sciences Libraries of New Hampshire & Vermont; North Atlantic Health Sciences Libraries, Inc
Open Mon-Fri 8-4

G VERMONT VETERANS HOME LIBRARY*, 325 North St, 05201. SAN 321-1037. Tel: 802-442-6353. FAX: 802-447-6466. Web Site: vvh.vermont.gov. *Library Contact,* Michele Burgess; Tel: 802-447-6520, E-mail: michele.burgess@vermont.gov
Founded 1884
Library Holdings: Bk Vols 800; Per Subs 25
Special Collections: Civil War Coll
Restriction: Residents only

BENSON

P BENSON VILLAGE LIBRARY*, 2724 Stage Rd, 05731. SAN 376-3455. Tel: 802-537-4181. E-mail: bplread@shoreham.net. *Librn,* Jacqueline Lussier
Pop 701
Library Holdings: Bk Vols 4,839; Talking Bks 10
Wireless access
Open Tues & Sat 10-1, Wed 4-7

BETHEL

P BETHEL PUBLIC LIBRARY*, 106 Main St, 05032. (Mail add: PO Box 354, 05032-0354), SAN 316-9596. Tel: 802-234-9107. E-mail: bethelpubliclibrary@gmail.com. Web Site: www.bethelpubliclibrary.org. *Librn,* Cathy Day
Founded 1893. Pop 1,980; Circ 10,090
Library Holdings: Bk Vols 12,000; Per Subs 38
Wireless access
Open Mon & Thurs 2-7, Wed 1-7, Sat 9-1

BONDVILLE

P WINHALL MEMORIAL LIBRARY*, Two Lower Tayler Hill Rd, 05340. (Mail add: PO Box 738, 05340-0738), SAN 316-960X. Tel: 802-297-9741. E-mail: winhallmemoriallibrary@gmail.com. Web Site: winhallmemoriallibrary.org. *Librn,* Dawn Santos
Pop 482; Circ 6,400
Library Holdings: Bk Vols 7,000

Special Collections: Cook & needlepoint bks
Wireless access
Open Tues & Thurs 10-5, Sat 9-12

BRADFORD

P BRADFORD PUBLIC LIBRARY*, 21 S Main St, 05033. (Mail add: PO Box 619, 05033-0619), SAN 316-9618. Tel: 802-222-4536. E-mail: bradfordpubliclibrary@gmail.com. Web Site: bradfordvtlibrary.org. *Libr Dir,* Gail Trede; *Circ Asst,* Kathy Davidow; E-mail: bplstaff45@gmail.com; *Circ Asst, ILL,* Holly Young; E-mail: bplil4536@gmail.com
Founded 1796. Pop 2,800; Circ 20,330
Library Holdings: Large Print Bks 70; Bk Titles 12,000; Per Subs 25; Talking Bks 50; Videos 100
Special Collections: Historical (Trotter Coll), bks, logs, artifacts
Special Services for the Blind - Talking bks
Open Tues & Sat 9-2, Wed & Thurs Noon-8, Fri 10-5
Bookmobiles: 1

BRANDON

P BRANDON FREE PUBLIC LIBRARY*, Four Franklin St, 05733. SAN 316-9626. Tel: 802-247-8230. FAX: 802-247-1212. E-mail: info@brandonpubliclibrary.org. Web Site: www.brandonpubliclibrary.org. *Dir,* Molly Kennedy; Staff 1 (Non-MLS 1)
Founded 1901. Pop 3,697; Circ 30,800
Library Holdings: AV Mats 2,000; Large Print Bks 400; Bk Titles 18,000; Per Subs 75; Talking Bks 800
Automation Activity & Vendor Info: (Cataloging) Insignia Software; (Circulation) Insignia Software; (ILL) Auto-Graphics, Inc; (OPAC) Insignia Software
Wireless access
Function: 24/7 Electronic res, 24/7 Online cat, Adult bk club, After school storytime, Archival coll, Art exhibits, Audiobks on Playaways & MP3, Audiobks via web, AV serv, Bk club(s), Bks on CD, Bus archives, CD-ROM, Chess club, Children's prog, Computer training, Computers for patron use, E-Readers, Electronic databases & coll, Family literacy, For res purposes, Free DVD rentals, Govt ref serv, Holiday prog, Home delivery & serv to seniorr ctr & nursing homes, Homebound delivery serv, ILL available, Instruction & testing, Internet access, Life-long learning prog for all ages, Literacy & newcomer serv, Magazines, Mail & tel request accepted, Mail loans to mem, Meeting rooms, Movies, Museum passes, Music CDs, Online cat, Outreach serv, OverDrive digital audio bks, Photocopying/Printing, Preschool reading prog, Printer for laptops & handheld devices, Prog for adults, Prog for children & young adult, Ref & res, Ref serv available, Scanner, Serves people with intellectual disabilities, Story hour, Summer & winter reading prog, Summer reading prog, Tax forms, Teen prog, Visual arts prog, Wheelchair accessible, Winter reading prog, Workshops
Partic in Collaborative Libraries of Vermont
Open Tues 8:30-8, Wed-Fri 8:30-5, Sat 8:30-1 (Winter); Tues & Wed 8:30-8, Thurs & Fri 8:30-5, Sat 8:30-12 (Summer)
Friends of the Library Group

BRATTLEBORO

P BROOKS MEMORIAL LIBRARY*, 224 Main St, 05301. SAN 362-6040. Tel: 802-254-5290. FAX: 802-257-2309. E-mail: info@brookslibraryvt.org. Web Site: brookslibraryvt.org. *Libr Dir,* Starr LaTronica; E-mail: starr@brookslibraryvt.org; *Cat Librn, Tech Serv Librn,* Sara Luttrell; *ILL,* Jen Robb; *Ref (Info Servs),* Jeanne Walsh; Staff 12 (MLS 4, Non-MLS 8)
Founded 1882. Pop 12,031; Circ 162,000
Library Holdings: Audiobooks 3,570; DVDs 2,536; e-books 80; Electronic Media & Resources 38; Bk Vols 73,184; Per Subs 240
Special Collections: Brattleboro & Surrounding Area (Local History Coll), mixed media; Fine Arts Coll (paintings, drawings, bronzes, sculpted marble); Genealogy (Lawson Coll); Gordon Crandall Abenaki Artifacts; Local History (Bratteboro Photo, Porter Thayer Photo & Benjamin Crown Photo Colls); Windam World Affairs Council Archives
Automation Activity & Vendor Info: (Acquisitions) ByWater Solutions; (Cataloging) ByWater Solutions; (Circulation) ByWater Solutions; (OPAC) ByWater Solutions; (Serials) ByWater Solutions
Wireless access
Publications: Friends of the Library (Quarterly); Friends of the Library, The Brooks Readers
Partic in Catamount Library Network
Special Services for the Blind - Extensive large print coll
Open Mon-Wed 10-9, Thurs & Fri 10-6, Sat 10-5
Friends of the Library Group

C SIT GRADUATE INSTITUTE/SIT STUDY ABROAD*, Donald B Watt Library & Information Commons, One Kipling Rd, 05302. (Mail add: PO Box 676, 05302-0676), SAN 316-9677. Tel: 802-258-3354. Toll Free Tel: 800-257-7751. E-mail: library@sit.edu. Web Site: libguides.sit.edu/wattlibrary. *Libr Dir,* Patrick Spurlock; E-mail: patrick.spurlock@sit.edu; *Access Serv Librn,* John Levin; Tel: 802-258-3533, E-mail: john.levin@sit.edu; Staff 3 (MLS 1, Non-MLS 2)
Founded 1967. Enrl 1,250; Fac 35; Highest Degree: Master
Library Holdings: AV Mats 1,600; Bks on Deafness & Sign Lang 69; DVDs 520; e-books 172,085; e-journals 12,000; Bk Titles 30,000; Bk Vols 35,000; Per Subs 12,000
Special Collections: Foreign Language & ESL Learning Materials (Language Coll); Rob Cash Memorial Coll; SIETAR Coll; Student's Master Theses Coll
Subject Interests: Area studies, Bi-cultural studies, Bilingual studies, Educ
Automation Activity & Vendor Info: (Acquisitions) Koha; (Cataloging) LibLime; (Circulation) Ex Libris Group; (ILL) OCLC ILLiad; (OPAC) Koha; (Serials) Ex Libris Group
Wireless access
Function: Electronic databases & coll, Free DVD rentals, ILL available, Internet access, Online cat, Online ref
Partic in ProConsort
Open Mon-Fri 8:30-8, Sun 2-8

BRISTOL

P LAWRENCE MEMORIAL LIBRARY*, 40 North St, 05443. SAN 376-3358. Tel: 802-453-2366. E-mail: lawrencelibrary1911@gmail.com, readmorenow@gmavt.net. Web Site: www.lawrencelibrary.net. *Dir,* Nancy Wilson
Library Holdings: Bk Vols 15,300; Per Subs 30
Automation Activity & Vendor Info: (Cataloging) Koha
Wireless access
Open Mon 10-5, Tues & Thurs 10-7, Wed & Fri 1-5, Sat 9-3

BROOKFIELD

P BROOKFIELD FREE PUBLIC LIBRARY*, 40 Ralph Rd, 05036. SAN 320-2739. Tel: 802-276-3358. FAX: 802-276-3926. E-mail: brookfieldpublic@gmail.com. Web Site: www.brookfieldvt.org/brookfield-free-public-library. *Librn,* Laura Rochat; Staff 1 (Non-MLS 1)
Founded 1791. Pop 1,271; Circ 5,979
Library Holdings: Bk Titles 5,000
Special Collections: Brookfield Historical Society, files
Open Tues & Sat 9-Noon, Wed & Thurs 1-5:30; Tues & Sat 9-Noon, Wed & Thurs 2-6 (Summer)

BROWNINGTON

S ORLEANS COUNTY HISTORICAL SOCIETY, INC*, Old Stone House Library, 109 Old Stone House Rd, 05860. SAN 316-9723. Tel: 802-754-2022. FAX: 802-754-9336. Web Site: www.oldstonehousemuseum.org. *Dir,* Molly Veysey; E-mail: director@oldstonehousemuseum.org; *Librn, Registrar,* Darlene Young; E-mail: registrar@oldstonehousemuseum.org
Founded 1853
Library Holdings: Bk Titles 1,500
Special Collections: 19th Century School Textbooks
Subject Interests: Orleans County hist, Vt hist
Automation Activity & Vendor Info: (Cataloging) TinyCat; (Circulation) TinyCat; (OPAC) TinyCat
Wireless access
Restriction: Non-circulating, Open by appt only

BURLINGTON

C CHAMPLAIN COLLEGE LIBRARY*, Miller Information Commons, 95 Summit St, 05401. (Mail add: PO Box 670, 05401-0670), SAN 316-974X. Tel: 802-860-2717. Web Site: www.champlain.edu/academics/library. *Dir,* Emily Crist; Tel: 802-651-5827, E-mail: ecrist@champlain.edu; *Head, Ref & Instruction,* Susan Adkins; Tel: 802-865-6489, E-mail: sadkins@champlain.edu; *Sr Circ & Reserves Coordr,* Michael Angel; Tel: 802-383-6295, E-mail: mangel@champlain.edu; Staff 12 (MLS 5, Non-MLS 7)
Founded 1878. Enrl 2,678; Fac 96; Highest Degree: Master
Library Holdings: e-books 40,000; Bk Vols 40,477; Per Subs 187
Special Collections: Art Book Coll; Champlain Coll Hist; Coll Archives; Vermontiana
Subject Interests: Bus mgt, Children's lit, Computer sci, Computing, Educ, Travel
Automation Activity & Vendor Info: (Acquisitions) Innovative Interfaces, Inc; (Cataloging) Innovative Interfaces, Inc; (Circulation) Innovative Interfaces, Inc; (Course Reserve) Innovative Interfaces, Inc; (ILL) OCLC; (OPAC) Innovative Interfaces, Inc
Wireless access
Partic in LYRASIS
Open Mon-Thurs 7:30am-Midnight, Fri 7:30am-8pm, Sat 12-7, Sun 10am-Midnight

L DOWNS RACHLIN MARTIN PLLC*, Law Library, 199 Main St, 05401. (Mail add: PO Box 99, Saint Johnsbury, 05819-0099), SAN 372-3321. Tel: 802-846-8345. Web Site: www.drm.com. *Libr Mgr, Mgr, Res,* Alison Alifano; E-mail: aalifano@drm.com; Staff 1.5 (MLS 1, Non-MLS 0.5)
Wireless access
Open Mon-Fri 8:30-5

P FLETCHER FREE LIBRARY*, 235 College St, 05401. SAN 316-9782. Tel: 802-863-3403. Reference Tel: 802-865-7217. FAX: 802-865-7227. Circulation E-mail: circ@burlingtonvt.gov. Reference E-mail: reference@burlingtonvt.gov. Web Site: www.fletcherfree.org. *Dir,* Mary Danko; E-mail: mdanko@burlingtonvt.gov; *Asst Dir,* Emer Pond Feeney; Tel: 802-865-7218, E-mail: efeeney@burlingtonvt.gov; *Outreach Librn,* Julie Skelly; Tel: 802-865-7224, E-mail: jskelly@burlingtonvt.gov; *Youth Serv Librn,* Megan Butterfield; Tel: 802-865-7216, E-mail: mbutterfield@burlingtonvt.gov; *Circ Mgr,* Michelle Lee; E-mail: mmlee@burlingtonvt.gov; *ILL,* Tenzin Dhondup; Tel: 802-865-7223, E-mail: FFLILL@burlingtonvt.gov; Staff 28 (MLS 9, Non-MLS 19)
Founded 1873. Circ 240,000
Library Holdings: AV Mats 10,381; Bk Vols 123,543; Per Subs 281
Subject Interests: Local hist
Automation Activity & Vendor Info: (Acquisitions) ByWater Solutions; (Cataloging) ByWater Solutions; (Circulation) ByWater Solutions; (OPAC) ByWater Solutions
Wireless access
Function: 24/7 Electronic res, 24/7 Online cat, 24/7 wireless access, 3D Printer, Activity rm, Adult bk club, Adult literacy prog, Art exhibits, Art programs, Bk club(s), Bks on CD, Children's prog, E-Readers, Electronic databases & coll, Extended outdoor wifi, Family literacy, Free DVD rentals, Games, Holiday prog, Home delivery & serv to seniorr ctr & nursing homes, ILL available, Internet access, Laptop/tablet checkout, Large print keyboards, Life-long learning prog for all ages, Magazines, Mail & tel request accepted, Meeting rooms, Microfiche/film & reading machines, Movies, Museum passes, Music CDs, Online cat, Outreach serv, OverDrive digital audio bks, Photocopying/Printing, Preschool outreach, Prof lending libr, Prog for adults, Prog for children & young adult, Ref & res, Ref serv available, Scanner, Senior outreach, Serves people with intellectual disabilities, Spanish lang bks, STEM programs, Story hour, Study rm, Summer & winter reading prog, Summer reading prog, Tax forms, Teen prog, Telephone ref, Wheelchair accessible, Wifi hotspot checkout
Publications: BiblioFile (Monthly)
Partic in Green Mountain Library Consortium
Open Mon & Thurs-Sat 10-6, Tues & Wed 10-8, Sun Noon-6
Friends of the Library Group

C UNIVERSITY OF VERMONT LIBRARIES*, David W Howe Memorial Library, 538 Main St, 05405-0036. SAN 362-6105. Tel: 802-656-2023. FAX: 802-656-4038. E-mail: howecirc@uvm.edu. Web Site: library.uvm.edu. *Dean of Libr,* Bryn Geffert; Tel: 802-656-9757, E-mail: bryn.geffert@uvm.edu; *Asst Dean,* Sarah Gordon; Tel: 802-656-3293, E-mail: sarah.m.gordon@uvm.edu; *Coll Mgt Serv Dir,* Laura Gewissler; Tel: 802-656-2024, E-mail: Laura.Gewissler@uvm.edu; *Dir, Info Serv, Dir, Instrul Serv,* Nancy Fawley; Tel: 802-656-0809, E-mail: Nancy.Fawley@uvm.edu; *Dir, Media Serv, Tech & Access Serv Dir,* Paul Philbin; Tel: 802-656-1369, E-mail: Paul.Philbin@uvm.edu; *Dir, Spec Coll,* Jeffrey Marshall; Tel: 802-656-2596, E-mail: Jeffrey.Marshall@uvm.edu; Staff 66 (MLS 22, Non-MLS 44)
Founded 1791. Enrl 11,902; Fac 695; Highest Degree: Doctorate
Special Collections: Canadian & United States Army Map Service; Civil War (Rush-Hawkins Coll); Geography, Foreign Affairs, Linguistics & Ecology (George Perkins Marsh Coll), ms; Literature & Personal Correspondence (Dorothy Canfield Fisher Coll), bks, ms; Politics & Government Coll, ms; U S Army Map Service; Vermont Local History, Stevens Family & Bookselling (Henry Stevens Coll), ms; Vermontiana (Wilbur Coll). Canadian and Provincial; State Document Depository; US Document Depository
Automation Activity & Vendor Info: (Acquisitions) Ex Libris Group; (Cataloging) Ex Libris Group; (Circulation) Ex Libris Group; (Course Reserve) Ex Libris Group; (Media Booking) Ex Libris Group
Wireless access
Publications: A Newsletter for Friends of Special Collections
Partic in Center for Research Libraries; Collaborative Libraries of Vermont; LYRASIS; NERL; OCLC Online Computer Library Center, Inc
Open Mon-Thurs 8am-Midnight, Fri 8am-10pm, Sat 10-10, Sun 10am-Midnight
Friends of the Library Group

Departmental Libraries:

CM DANA MEDICAL LIBRARY, 81 Colchester Ave, 05405, SAN 362-613X. Tel: 802-656-2200. Reference Tel: 802-656-2201. FAX: 802-656-0762. E-mail: dana@uvm.edu. Web Site: library.uvm.edu/dana. *Interim Dir,* Donna O'Malley; Tel: 802-656-4415, E-mail: donna.omalley@uvm.edu; Staff 19 (MLS 8, Non-MLS 11)
Special Collections: Vermont Medical History
Partic in National Network of Libraries of Medicine Region 7; NERL; OCLC Online Computer Library Center, Inc
Publications: Dana Medical Library Newsletter
Open Mon-Fri 7:30am-11pm, Sat 9-8, Sun 9am-11pm

CABOT

P CABOT PUBLIC LIBRARY*, The Willey Bldg, 3084 Main St, 05647. (Mail add: PO Box 6, 05647-0006), SAN 316-9820. Tel: 802-563-2721. E-mail: cabotlibrary@yahoo.com. Web Site: www.cabotlibrary.org. *Dir,* Kathleen Hoyne
Pop 1,343; Circ 11,723
Library Holdings: Bk Vols 8,000; Per Subs 20
Automation Activity & Vendor Info: (Acquisitions) LibraryWorld, Inc; (Cataloging) LibraryWorld, Inc; (Circulation) LibraryWorld, Inc
Wireless access
Partic in Collaborative Libraries of Vermont
Open Mon 3-6, Tues Noon-6, Wed 2-6, Thurs 9-6, Sat 9-Noon
Friends of the Library Group

CANAAN

P ALICE M WARD MEMORIAL LIBRARY*, 27 Park St, 05903. (Mail add: PO Box 134, 05903-0134), SAN 316-9839. Tel: 802-266-7135. FAX: 802-266-7135. E-mail: alice.ward.library@gmail.com. Web Site: www.aliceward.org. *Dir,* Craig Varley
Founded 1930. Pop 972; Circ 6,000
Library Holdings: Large Print Bks 158; Bk Vols 14,800; Per Subs 23; Talking Bks 150
Subject Interests: Educ, Hist
Automation Activity & Vendor Info: (Cataloging) Follett Software; (Circulation) Follett Software; (Course Reserve) Follett Software; (ILL) Follett Software; (Media Booking) Follett Software; (OPAC) Follett Software; (Serials) Follett Software
Wireless access
Special Services for the Blind - Home delivery serv
Open Mon-Thurs 12-5, Fri 12-4, Sat 9-1

CASTLETON

P CASTLETON FREE LIBRARY*, 638 Main St, 05735. (Mail add: PO Box 296, 05735), SAN 316-9847. Tel: 802-468-5574. E-mail: castletonfreelibrary@gmail.com. Web Site: castletonfreelibrary.org. *Ad, Libr Dir,* Mary Kearns; *Children's & YA Librn,* Sharon Lovett-Graff
Pop 3,637; Circ 11,934
Library Holdings: Bk Vols 19,450
Wireless access
Partic in Green Mountain Library Consortium
Open Tues & Wed 2-6, Thurs Noon-8, Fri 10-6, Sat 10-2
Friends of the Library Group

C VERMONT STATE UNIVERSITY - CASTLETON*, Calvin Coolidge Library, (Formerly Castleton University Library), 178 Alumni Dr, 05735. SAN 316-9855. Tel: 802-468-1256. Reference Tel: 802-468-1257. FAX: 802-468-1475. E-mail: reference@castleton.edu. Web Site: www.castleton.edu/library. *Libr Dir,* Beth Bidlack; E-mail: beth.bidlack@castleton.edu; *Circ,* Stephanie Traverse; *Instruction/Ref Serv,* Charlotte Gerstein; *ILL, Ser,* Kim Bailey; *Tech Serv,* Michele Perry; Staff 8 (MLS 3, Non-MLS 5)
Founded 1787. Enrl 1,958; Fac 100; Highest Degree: Master
Library Holdings: Bk Vols 160,000; Per Subs 500
Special Collections: Vermontiana
Automation Activity & Vendor Info: (Acquisitions) Koha; (Cataloging) Koha; (Circulation) Koha; (Course Reserve) Koha; (Discovery) EBSCO Discovery Service; (ILL) OCLC Tipasa; (OPAC) Koha; (Serials) Koha
Wireless access

CHARLOTTE

P CHARLOTTE LIBRARY*, 115 Ferry Rd, 05445. (Mail add: PO Box 120, 05445-0120), SAN 376-4907. Tel: 802-425-3864. E-mail: info@charlottepubliclibrary.org. Web Site: charlottepubliclibrary.org. *Libr Dir,* Margaret Woodruff
Library Holdings: Bk Vols 14,403; Per Subs 58
Wireless access
Open Mon & Wed 10-7, Tues, Thurs & Fri 10-4, Sat 9-2
Friends of the Library Group

CHELSEA

P CHELSEA PUBLIC LIBRARY*, Alden Speare Memorial Library, 296 VT Rte 110, 05038. (Mail add: PO Box 67, 05038-0067), SAN 316-9871. Tel: 802-685-2188. E-mail: chelsealibraryvt@gmail.com. Web Site: www.chelsealibrary.com. *Libr Dir,* Veronica Golden; Staff 1 (Non-MLS 1)
Founded 1841. Pop 1,233; Circ 20,000
Library Holdings: Bk Vols 10,000; Per Subs 32

Wireless access
Function: 24/7 Electronic res, 24/7 Online cat, Adult bk club, Art exhibits, Art programs, Audiobks on Playaways & MP3, Audiobks via web, AV serv, Bk club(s), Bks on CD, Children's prog, Computer training, Computers for patron use, Digital talking bks, Electronic databases & coll, Free DVD rentals, Games & aids for people with disabilities, Holiday prog, ILL available, Internet access, Laminating, Large print keyboards, Magazines, Magnifiers for reading, Mail & tel request accepted, Mango lang, Meeting rooms, Movies, Museum passes, Music CDs, Online cat, OverDrive digital audio bks, Photocopying/Printing, Printer for laptops & handheld devices, Prog for adults, Prog for children & young adult, Ref & res, Ref serv available, Scanner, Serves people with intellectual disabilities, Spoken cassettes & CDs, Spoken cassettes & DVDs, Story hour, Summer reading prog, Tax forms
Partic in Green Mountain Library Consortium; Vermont State Libr Syst
Special Services for the Deaf - Assisted listening device; Bks on deafness & sign lang; Closed caption videos
Special Services for the Blind - Accessible computers; Assistive/Adapted tech devices, equip & products; Bks & mags in Braille, on rec, tape & cassette; Bks on CD; Computer access aids; Copier with enlargement capabilities; Digital talking bk; Digital talking bk machines; Internet workstation with adaptive software; Large print bks; Large print bks & talking machines; Large screen computer & software; Large type calculator; Lending of low vision aids; Magnifiers; Talking bks & player equip

CHESTER

P WHITING LIBRARY*, 117 Main St, 05143. SAN 316-988X. Tel: 802-875-2277. FAX: 802-875-2277. E-mail: whitinglibrary@yahoo.com, whitinglibrary1@gmail.com. Web Site: www.chestervt.gov/library.html, www.whitinglibrary.org. *Dir,* Sharon Tanzer; Staff 3 (MLS 1, Non-MLS 2)
Founded 1892. Pop 3,000; Circ 20,000
Library Holdings: AV Mats 740; Bk Vols 13,850; Per Subs 24; Talking Bks 525
Special Collections: Vermont Coll
Wireless access
Partic in Collaborative Libraries of Vermont
Open Mon, Wed & Fri 10-6, Sat 10-2
Friends of the Library Group

CHITTENDEN

P CHITTENDEN PUBLIC LIBRARY*, Frederic D Barstow Memorial Library, 223 Chittenden Rd, 05737. (Mail add: PO Box 90, 05737-0090), SAN 316-9898. Tel: 802-773-3531. E-mail: chittendenpl@gmail.com. Web Site: chittendenpubliclibrary.com. *Libr Dir,* Nicole Vachon Hanlon
Pop 1,102; Circ 2,080
Library Holdings: Bk Vols 5,400; Per Subs 25
Automation Activity & Vendor Info: (Cataloging) Follett Software; (Circulation) Follett Software
Wireless access
Open Mon, Wed & Thurs 3-6, Sat 9-Noon
Friends of the Library Group

COLCHESTER

P BURNHAM MEMORIAL LIBRARY*, 898 Main St, 05446. SAN 316-9901. Tel: 802-264-5660. FAX: 802-879-5079. E-mail: burnhamlib@colchestervt.gov. Web Site: colchestervt.gov/library. *Libr Dir,* Kelly McCagg; E-mail: kmccagg@colchestervt.gov; *Asst Dir,* Hannah Peacock; E-mail: hpeacock@colchestervt.gov; Staff 8 (MLS 4, Non-MLS 4)
Founded 1902. Pop 17,000; Circ 125,000
Library Holdings: AV Mats 4,650; Bk Vols 50,072; Per Subs 95
Subject Interests: Local hist
Automation Activity & Vendor Info: (Cataloging) LibLime; (Circulation) LibLime; (OPAC) LibLime
Wireless access
Function: Art exhibits, ILL available, Online cat, Photocopying/Printing, Prog for adults, Prog for children & young adult, Scanner, Senior outreach, Wheelchair accessible
Partic in Green Mountain Library Consortium
Open Mon 1-4, Tues & Wed 10-2, Thurs 3-6, Sat 10-3
Restriction: Non-circulating coll
Friends of the Library Group

CONCORD

P CONCORD PUBLIC LIBRARY*, 374 Main St, 05824. (Mail add: PO Box 188, 05824-0188), SAN 316-9928. Tel: 802-695-2220. E-mail: library@concordvt.org. Web Site: www.concordvt.us/community/concord-library. *Librn,* Beth Cliche
Pop 1,224
Library Holdings: Bk Vols 5,000; Per Subs 15
Open Tues & Thurs 4-6, Sat 9-11

CORNWALL

P CORNWALL FREE PUBLIC LIBRARY*, 2629 Rte 30, 05753-9340. SAN 316-9936. Tel: 802-462-3615. FAX: 802-462-2606. E-mail: cornwallvt@shoreham.net. Web Site: cornwallvt.com/library. *Librn,* Susan Johnson
Pop 1,550
Jul 2015-Jun 2016 Income $6,681, City $4,000, Other $2,681. Mats Exp $6,996
Library Holdings: Audiobooks 280; DVDs 570; Large Print Bks 30; Bk Vols 4,207
Subject Interests: Local authors, Local hist
Wireless access
Open Tues-Fri 9-5

CRAFTSBURY COMMON

P CRAFTSBURY PUBLIC LIBRARY*, 12 Church St, 05827. (Mail add: PO Box 74, 05827-0074), SAN 376-3374. Tel: 802-586-9683. FAX: 802-586-9683. E-mail: librarian@craftsburypubliclibrary.org. Web Site: www.craftsburypubliclibrary.org. *Dir,* Susan O'Connell; E-mail: director@craftsburypubliclibrary.org; *Ch,* Jen McKenzie; Staff 2 (Non-MLS 2)
Founded 1898. Pop 1,240; Circ 15,857
Library Holdings: DVDs 150; Large Print Bks 50; Bk Titles 14,000; Per Subs 25; Talking Bks 260; Videos 342
Special Collections: General Coll
Wireless access
Open Mon & Thurs 2-6, Tues, Wed & Fri 10-6, Sat 10-1
Friends of the Library Group

C STERLING COLLEGE*, Brown Library, 1205 N Craftsbury Rd, 05827. (Mail add: PO Box 72, 05827-0072). Tel: 802-586-7711, Ext 129. FAX: 802-586-2596. E-mail: library@sterlingcollege.edu. Web Site: www.sterlingcollege.edu/academics/brown-library. *Librn,* Petra Vogel; E-mail: pvogel@sterlingcollege.edu; Staff 1 (MLS 1)
Founded 1990. Enrl 140; Fac 50; Highest Degree: Bachelor
Library Holdings: AV Mats 730; CDs 95; DVDs 405; e-books 3,050; e-journals 26,310; Bk Vols 12,100; Per Subs 80; Videos 90
Subject Interests: Ecology, Outdoor educ, Sustainable agr
Automation Activity & Vendor Info: (Cataloging) Koha; (Circulation) Koha; (Course Reserve) Koha; (OPAC) Koha
Wireless access
Partic in Vermont Consortium of Academic Libraries

CUTTINGSVILLE

P SHREWSBURY PUBLIC LIBRARY*, 98 Town Hill Rd, 05738. (Mail add: PO Box 396, 05738-0396), SAN 316-9952. Tel: 802-492-3410. FAX: 802-492-3410. E-mail: shrewsburylibrary492@gmail.com. Web Site: www.shrewsburylibrary.org. *Dir,* Donna Swartz
Founded 1975. Pop 1,100; Circ 3,500
Library Holdings: Bk Vols 8,000
Wireless access
Partic in Vt Libr Asn
Open Mon, Fri & Sat 10-Noon, Tues & Thurs 7pm-9pm, Wed 10-5 & 7-9

DANBY

P SILAS L GRIFFITH MEMORIAL LIBRARY, 74 S Main St, 05739. SAN 316-9960. Tel: 802-293-5106. E-mail: slgriffithlibrary6@gmail.com. Web Site: slgriffithlibrary.wordpress.com. *Librn,* Cheryl Colby
Founded 1908. Pop 1,200; Circ 5,706
Library Holdings: Bk Vols 15,610; Per Subs 18; Talking Bks 69; Videos 359
Wireless access
Open Wed 2-5, Sat 9-12

DANVILLE

P BRAINERD MEMORIAL LIBRARY, 4215 Bruce Badger Memorial Hwy, 05828. Tel: 802-424-1403. E-mail: info@brainerdmemoriallibraryvt.org. Web Site: www.brainerdmemoriallibraryvt.org. *Vols Librn,* Elizabeth A Sargent
Founded 1934. Pop 2,289
Library Holdings: DVDs 100; Electronic Media & Resources 3; Large Print Bks 85; Bk Titles 6,500; Per Subs 1
Wireless access
Function: 24/7 Electronic res, 24/7 Online cat, 24/7 wireless access, After school storytime, Audiobks via web, Bks on CD, Children's prog, Computers for patron use, Free DVD rentals, Internet access, Magazines, Movies, Museum passes, Online cat, Photocopying/Printing, Prog for adults, Prog for children & young adult, Story hour, Wheelchair accessible, Workshops
Open Tues & Thurs 10-2, Wed 6-8

P POPE MEMORIAL LIBRARY*, 121 Park St, 05828. (Mail add: PO Box 260, 05828-0260), SAN 316-9979. Tel: 802-684-2256. FAX: 802-684-2250. E-mail: popememoriallibrary@yahoo.com. Web Site: www.popememoriallibrary.org. *Dir,* Deidre Palmer; Staff 3 (MLS 1, Non-MLS 2)
Founded 1890. Pop 2,200; Circ 12,000
Library Holdings: Audiobooks 400; Large Print Bks 300; Bk Titles 11,700; Per Subs 40; Videos 800
Special Collections: Circulating Toy Coll; Vermont Mysteries & Westerns (fiction & nonfiction)
Subject Interests: Genealogical res, Vt hist
Wireless access
Function: 24/7 Electronic res, 24/7 Online cat, Adult bk club, Bk club(s), Bks on cassette, Bks on CD, Children's prog, Computer training, Computers for patron use, E-Readers, Free DVD rentals, Holiday prog, Home delivery & serv to seniorr ctr & nursing homes, Homebound delivery serv, Homework prog, ILL available, Instruction & testing, Internet access, Magazines, Mail & tel request accepted, Mail loans to mem, Meeting rooms, Museum passes, Online cat, Photocopying/Printing, Preschool outreach, Prog for adults, Prog for children & young adult, Ref serv available, Senior outreach, Story hour, Summer reading prog, Tax forms, Teen prog, Telephone ref, VHS videos, Wheelchair accessible, Writing prog
Open Mon & Fri 10-5, Wed 9-7, Sat 9-Noon

DERBY

P DAILEY MEMORIAL LIBRARY, 101 Junior High Dr, 05829. SAN 316-9987. Tel: 802-766-5063. E-mail: daileylibrary@gmail.com. Web Site: www.daileymemoriallibrary.org. *Dir,* Maureen Badger; *Ch,* Julia Winkler; *Asst Librn,* Jennifer Johnson; Staff 3 (Non-MLS 3)
Founded 1957. Pop 3,951; Circ 13,000
Library Holdings: Audiobooks 256; Large Print Bks 200; Bk Titles 8,479; Bk Vols 12,330; Per Subs 22; Videos 743
Special Collections: Children's Coll; Local History Coll
Automation Activity & Vendor Info: (Acquisitions) LibraryWorld, Inc; (Cataloging) LibraryWorld, Inc; (Circulation) LibraryWorld, Inc
Wireless access
Open Tues & Fri 10-6, Wed & Thurs 10-5, Sat 10-3

DERBY LINE

P HASKELL FREE LIBRARY, INC*, 93 Caswell Ave, 05830. (Mail add: PO Box 337, 05830-0337). Tel: 888-626-2060 (Canada). FAX: 802-873-5019. E-mail: library@haskellopera.com. Web Site: www.haskellopera.com. *Dir,* Position Currently Open; Staff 4 (Non-MLS 4)
Founded 1905. Pop 5,000; Circ 44,000
Library Holdings: Bk Vols 20,000; Per Subs 45
Function: Adult bk club, Art exhibits, Audiobks via web, Bks on cassette, Bks on CD, Children's prog, Computers for patron use, Electronic databases & coll, Free DVD rentals, Holiday prog, Online cat, OverDrive digital audio bks, Prog for adults, Story hour, Summer reading prog, Wheelchair accessible
Partic in Collaborative Libraries of Vermont; Green Mountain Library Consortium
Special Services for the Blind - Bks on cassette
Open Tues, Wed, Fri & Sat 10-5, Thurs 10-6, Sat 10-2

DORSET

P DORSET VILLAGE LIBRARY*, Rte 30 & Church St, 05251. (Mail add: PO Box 38, 05251-0038), SAN 317-0004. Tel: 802-867-5774. E-mail: dorsetvillagelibrary@gmail.com. Web Site: www.dorsetvillagelibrary.org. *Libr Dir,* Erica Shott; Tel: 802-867-4085; *Asst Dir,* Stephen Niles; Staff 4 (MLS 1, Non-MLS 3)
Founded 1871. Pop 2,026; Circ 24,000
Library Holdings: DVDs 1,000; Large Print Bks 700; Bk Titles 20,000; Bk Vols 22,000; Per Subs 20; Talking Bks 1,000
Automation Activity & Vendor Info: (Acquisitions) Baker & Taylor; (Cataloging) LibraryWorld, Inc; (Circulation) LibraryWorld, Inc; (OPAC) LibraryWorld, Inc
Wireless access
Function: 24/7 Electronic res, 24/7 Online cat, Adult bk club, ILL available, Photocopying/Printing
Partic in Collaborative Libraries of Vermont
Open Mon-Fri 11-5, Sat 10-3

EAST BURKE

P EAST BURKE COMMUNITY LIBRARY, 368 Rt 114, 05832. (Mail add: PO Box 309, 05832-0309), SAN 317-0047. Tel: 802-626-9823. E-mail: halfpintvt@yahoo.com. Web Site: www.facebook.com/people/east-burke-community-library/100068530211055. *Librn,* Catherine Brooks
Pop 1,700; Circ 2,300
Library Holdings: Bk Vols 4,000
Wireless access
Open Mon & Wed 2-5, Sat 10-1
Friends of the Library Group

EAST CORINTH

P BLAKE MEMORIAL LIBRARY*, 676 Village Rd, 05040. (Mail add: PO Box D, 05040), SAN 317-0063. Tel: 802-439-5338. FAX: 802-439-5338. Web Site: www.blakememorial.org. *Libr Dir,* Jennifer Spanier; E-mail: libdirector@blakememorial.org; *Libr Asst,* Kimberly Hotelling; Staff 1 (Non-MLS 1)
Founded 1901. Pop 2,600; Circ 14,000
Library Holdings: AV Mats 330; CDs 50; DVDs 75; Large Print Bks 70; Bk Vols 20,000; Per Subs 24; Videos 600
Automation Activity & Vendor Info: (OPAC) Koha
Wireless access
Function: Art exhibits, Bk club(s), Bks on CD, Children's prog, Computers for patron use, Electronic databases & coll, Free DVD rentals, Health sci info serv, ILL available, Internet access, Museum passes, Online cat, Online ref, Outside serv via phone, mail, e-mail & web, Photocopying/Printing, Preschool outreach, Prog for adults, Prog for children & young adult, Story hour, Summer reading prog, Wheelchair accessible
Open Mon & Wed 2-6, Thurs & Sat 9-12, Fri 2-6
Friends of the Library Group

EAST CRAFTSBURY

P JOHN WOODRUFF SIMPSON MEMORIAL LIBRARY, 1972 E Craftsbury Rd, 05826. SAN 317-0071. Tel: 802-586-9692. E-mail: jwsimpsonmemorial@gmail.com. Web Site: www.jwsimpsonmemorial.org. *Librn,* Kristin Urie; Staff 1 (Non-MLS 1)
Founded 1921. Pop 1,000; Circ 5,000
Library Holdings: Bk Titles 11,000; Per Subs 10
Wireless access
Open Wed 9-12 & 6-8, Thurs 9-12 & 2-6, Sat 9-12, Sun 12-2
Friends of the Library Group

EAST DOVER

P DOVER FREE LIBRARY*, 22 Hollands Rd, 05341-9617. SAN 317-008X. Tel: 802-348-7488. E-mail: doverfreelibrary1913@yahoo.com. Web Site: www.doverfreelibrary1913.org. *Libr Dir,* John G Flores; E-mail: john@doverfreelibrary1913.org
Founded 1913. Pop 1,410; Circ 17,265
Library Holdings: AV Mats 657; Bk Vols 15,000; Per Subs 68; Talking Bks 600
Special Collections: Oral History
Subject Interests: Cookery, Early childhood educ, New England, Parenting
Partic in Collaborative Libraries of Vermont
Open Mon & Tues 2-8, Wed & Fri 10-6, Sat 10-2

ENOSBURG FALLS

P ENOSBURGH PUBLIC LIBRARY*, 241 Main St, 05450. (Mail add: PO Box 206, 05450-0206), SAN 317-011X. Tel: 802-933-2328. E-mail: enosburghlibrary@gmail.com. Web Site: enosburghlibrary.net. *Libr Dir,* Brenda Stanley; Staff 1 (MLS 1)
Pop 2,535; Circ 20,000
Library Holdings: Bk Titles 15,000; Per Subs 47
Wireless access
Open Mon-Fri 9-7, Sat 9-3

ESSEX

P ESSEX FREE LIBRARY*, One Browns River Rd, 05451. SAN 317-0128. Tel: 802-879-0313. FAX: 802-879-3727. E-mail: essexfreelibrary@essex.org. Web Site: www.essexvt.org/153/Essex-Free-Library. *Asst Dir,* Victoria Tibbits; E-mail: vtibbits@essex.org; *Ch,* Jasmine Hodgett; E-mail: jhodgett@essex.org; Staff 4.6 (MLS 1.5, Non-MLS 3.1)
Founded 1929. Pop 19,065; Circ 107,722
Library Holdings: Bks on Deafness & Sign Lang 14; Bk Titles 31,240; Bk Vols 34,878; Per Subs 72
Automation Activity & Vendor Info: (Acquisitions) Koha; (Cataloging) Koha; (Circulation) Koha; (Media Booking) Koha; (OPAC) Koha; (Serials) Koha
Wireless access
Open Mon, Wed & Fri 9-5, Tues & Thurs 9-8, Sat 9-2
Friends of the Library Group

ESSEX JUNCTION

P BROWNELL LIBRARY*, Six Lincoln St, 05452-3154. SAN 317-0136. Tel: 802-878-6955. Reference Tel: 802-878-6957. Administration Tel: 802-878-6954. E-mail: frontdesk@brownelllibrary.org. Web Site:

www.brownelllibrary.org. *Dir,* Wendy Hysko; E-mail: wendyh@brownelllibrary.org; *Asst Dir,* Hannah Tracy; E-mail: hannah@brownelllibrary.org; *Circ Librn,* Alison Pierce; E-mail: alison@brownelllibrary.org; *ILL Librn,* Susan Pierce; E-mail: susan@brownelllibrary.org; *Asst Youth Librn,* Erna Deutsch; Staff 5 (MLS 3, Non-MLS 2)
Founded 1897. Pop 14,392; Circ 287,414
Library Holdings: Bk Vols 78,111
Special Collections: Vermont Local History Coll
Subject Interests: Essex Area hist
Automation Activity & Vendor Info: (Cataloging) LibLime Koha; (Circulation) LibLime Koha; (OPAC) LibLime Koha
Wireless access
Function: Adult bk club, Adult literacy prog, After school storytime, Art exhibits, Audio & video playback equip for onsite use, Audiobks via web, Bk club(s), Bks on cassette, Bks on CD, Children's prog, Computer training, Computers for patron use, Doc delivery serv, Equip loans & repairs, Free DVD rentals, Games & aids for people with disabilities, Home delivery & serv to seniorr ctr & nursing homes, Homebound delivery serv, ILL available, Instruction & testing, Internet access, Magnifiers for reading, Mail & tel request accepted, Mail loans to mem, Museum passes, Music CDs, Online cat, Online ref, Orientations, Outside serv via phone, mail, e-mail & web, Photocopying/Printing, Prog for adults, Prog for children & young adult, Ref & res, Ref serv available, Senior computer classes, Senior outreach, Serves people with intellectual disabilities, Spoken cassettes & CDs, Spoken cassettes & DVDs, Story hour, Summer reading prog, Tax forms, Teen prog, Telephone ref, VHS videos, Visual arts prog, Wheelchair accessible, Workshops
Publications: Friends of Brownell (Newsletter)
Special Services for the Blind - Aids for in-house use; Audio mat; Bks on CD; Cassette playback machines; Large print bks; Magnifiers; Reader equip; Talking bks
Open Mon, Wed & Fri 9-9, Tues & Thurs 9-5, Sat (Sept-June) 9-5
Friends of the Library Group

FAIR HAVEN

P FAIR HAVEN FREE LIBRARY*, 107 N Main St, 05743. SAN 317-0160. Tel: 802-265-8011. E-mail: fairhavenfreelibrary@gmail.com. Web Site: fairhavenfree.org. *Librn,* Carol Scott; *Asst Librn,* Mary Kay Miller
Founded 1906. Pop 2,936; Circ 16,149
Library Holdings: Bk Vols 17,500; Per Subs 50
Special Collections: Mystery Coll; Vermontiana Coll
Wireless access
Open Mon & Wed 3-7, Tues & Fri 8:30-4:30, Sat 9-1
Friends of the Library Group

FAIRFAX

P FAIRFAX COMMUNITY LIBRARY*, 75 Hunt St, 05454. SAN 317-0179. Tel: 802-849-2420. E-mail: fairfaxlibrarian@gmail.com. Web Site: fairfaxvtlibrary.org. *Libr Dir,* Emily DiGiulio; Staff 2.5 (MLS 1, Non-MLS 1.5)
Founded 1972. Pop 4,285; Circ 35,000
Library Holdings: Bk Titles 24,000; Per Subs 35
Special Collections: Local History (Fairfax Historical Society Coll)
Automation Activity & Vendor Info: (Acquisitions) Follett Software; (Cataloging) Follett Software; (Circulation) Follett Software; (OPAC) Follett Software
Wireless access
Function: 24/7 Electronic res, 24/7 Online cat, Adult bk club, Audio & video playback equip for onsite use, Audiobks on Playaways & MP3, Audiobks via web, Bks on CD, Chess club, Children's prog, Computer training, Computers for patron use, Digital talking bks, E-Reserves, Free DVD rentals, Homebound delivery serv, ILL available, Internet access, Life-long learning prog for all ages, Magazines, Magnifiers for reading, Mail & tel request accepted, Meeting rooms, Movies, Museum passes, Music CDs, Online cat, Orientations, Outside serv via phone, mail, e-mail & web, OverDrive digital audio bks, Photocopying/Printing, Prog for adults, Prog for children & young adult, Ref serv available, Spanish lang bks, Story hour, Study rm, Summer reading prog, Tax forms, Teen prog, Telephone ref, VHS videos, Wheelchair accessible, Workshops
Partic in Collaborative Libraries of Vermont
Open Mon & Wed 10-5:30, Tues & Thurs 9-7, Fri 10-4:15, Sat 9-1

FAIRFIELD

P BENT NORTHROP MEMORIAL LIBRARY*, 164 Park St, 05455. SAN 376-4893. Tel: 802-827-3945. E-mail: bnmllibrarian@gmail.com. Web Site: www.bentnorthrop.org. *Dir,* Sarah Montgomery; *Libr Asst,* Wendy Maquera
Founded 1988. Pop 1,880; Circ 4,000
Library Holdings: High Interest/Low Vocabulary Bk Vols 30; Large Print Bks 60; Bk Vols 10,500; Per Subs 10
Automation Activity & Vendor Info: (Cataloging) Koha; (Circulation) Koha
Wireless access
Open Tues & Thurs 2:30-8, Wed & Fri 9-5, Sat 9-1 (Summer); Mon 2:30-5, Tues & Thurs 2:30-8, Wed & Fri 9-5, Sat 9-1 (Winter)
Friends of the Library Group

FAIRLEE

P FAIRLEE PUBLIC LIBRARY*, 221 US Rte 5 N, 05045-9584. (Mail add: PO Box 125, 05045-0125), SAN 317-0187. Tel: 802-333-4716. FAX: 802-333-4152. E-mail: fairlee.library@gmail.com. Web Site: www.fairleelibrary.com. *Libr Dir,* Samantha Hickman; Staff 1 (MLS 1)
Founded 1898. Pop 1,848; Circ 11,743
Library Holdings: CDs 478; DVDs 511; e-books 1,100; High Interest/Low Vocabulary Bk Vols 21; Large Print Bks 44; Bk Vols 13,911; Per Subs 43
Automation Activity & Vendor Info: (Cataloging) ByWater Solutions; (Circulation) ByWater Solutions
Wireless access
Partic in Green Mountain Library Consortium
Open Tues 9-5, Wed 1-7, Thurs & Fri 1-5, Sat 9-Noon
Friends of the Library Group

FERRISBURG

S ROKEBY MUSEUM*, Special Collections Library, 4334 Rte 7, 05456-9711. SAN 317-0209. Tel: 802-877-3406. E-mail: info@rokeby.org. Web Site: www.rokeby.org. *Interim Dir,* Joan Gorman; E-mail: jgorman@rokeby.org
Founded 1962
Special Collections: Abolition, Religious History, Social History & Vermont Folklore (Robinson & Stevens Family Papers, 1770-1960)
Subject Interests: Anti-slavery, Biog, Farming, Fishing, Hist, Hunting, Popular lit, Quaker writings, Sch texts, Spiritualism
Wireless access
Restriction: Open by appt only

FRANKLIN

P HASTON LIBRARY*, 5167 Main St, 05457. (Mail add: PO Box 83, 05457-0083), SAN 321-0952. Tel: 802-285-6505. FAX: 802-285-2181. E-mail: librarian@franklinhastonlibraryvt.org. Web Site: franklinhastonlibraryvt.org. *Dir,* Josh Worman; *Asst Librn,* Position Currently Open; Staff 1 (Non-MLS 1)
Founded 1907. Pop 1,586; Circ 4,701
Library Holdings: Audiobooks 425; Large Print Bks 70; Bk Vols 7,726; Per Subs 5; Videos 847
Automation Activity & Vendor Info: (Circulation) OpenBiblio
Wireless access
Function: Adult bk club, Bks on cassette, Bks on CD, Children's prog, Computers for patron use, Electronic databases & coll, Free DVD rentals, Homebound delivery serv, ILL available, Internet access, Museum passes, Photocopying/Printing, Prog for adults, Prog for children & young adult, Ref serv available, Story hour, Summer reading prog, Teen prog, Telephone ref, VHS videos, Wheelchair accessible
Open Mon 10-2, Tues 1-6, Thurs 9-6, Fri & Sat 9-1
Bookmobiles: 1

GAYSVILLE

P THE BELCHER MEMORIAL LIBRARY*, 4452 VT Rte 107, 05746-0144. (Mail add: PO Box 144, 05746), SAN 376-4060. Tel: 802-234-6608. E-mail: belcherlibrary@gmail.com. Web Site: belcherlibrary.wordpress.com. *Actg Librn,* Mary Ellen Dorman
Pop 618
Library Holdings: Bk Vols 2,500
Wireless access
Mem of Midstate Regional Library
Open Tues & Thurs 4-6, Wed 3-6, Sat 9-Noon

GEORGIA

P GEORGIA PUBLIC LIBRARY*, 1697 Ethan Allen Hwy, 05454. SAN 376-3382. Tel: 802-524-4643. E-mail: gplvt@yahoo.com. Web Site: www.georgiapubliclibraryvt.org. *Dir,* Bridget Stone
Library Holdings: Bk Titles 10,000; Per Subs 55
Wireless access
Partic in Catamount Library Network
Open Mon & Wed 9-7, Tues & Thurs 11-5, Fri 9-5, Sat 9-1
Friends of the Library Group

GLOVER

P GLOVER PUBLIC LIBRARY, 51 Bean Hill Rd, 05839. SAN 317-0241. Tel: 802-525-4365. E-mail: littlelibraryinglover@gmail.com. Web Site: gloverlibrary.org. *Dir,* Toni Eubanks; E-mail: toni.eubanks@gmail.com; *Libr Asst,* Ruth Rowell
Founded 1909. Pop 1,100

Library Holdings: Bk Vols 3,000
Wireless access
Open Mon 9-12, Tues & Thurs 10-6, Sat 10-12
Friends of the Library Group

GRAFTON

P GRAFTON PUBLIC LIBRARY*, 204 Main St, 05146. (Mail add: PO Box 129, 05146-0129), SAN 317-0268. Tel: 802-843-2404. E-mail: librarian@graftonpubliclibrary.org. Web Site: www.graftonpubliclibrary.org. *Dir,* Michelle Dufort
Founded 1882
Library Holdings: Large Print Bks 12; Bk Titles 7,699; Per Subs 15; Talking Bks 145
Wireless access
Open Mon & Wed 10-1 & 2-5, Tues 10-1 & 2-8, Thurs & Fri 2-5, Sat 9-Noon
Friends of the Library Group

GRAND ISLE

P GRAND ISLE FREE LIBRARY*, Ten Hyde Rd, 05458. SAN 317-0284. Tel: 802-372-4797. E-mail: grandislefreelibrary@gmail.com. Web Site: grandislefreelibraryvt.wordpress.com. *Dir,* Janet Bonneau; Staff 1 (Non-MLS 1)
Library Holdings: Bk Vols 6,000
Automation Activity & Vendor Info: (Acquisitions) Brodart; (Cataloging) Follett Software; (Circulation) Follett Software
Wireless access
Partic in Collaborative Libraries of Vermont
Open Tues 1-8, Wed 9-Noon, Thurs 4-8, Sat 9-3
Friends of the Library Group

GREENSBORO

P GREENSBORO FREE LIBRARY*, 53 Wilson St, 05841. SAN 317-0306. Tel: 802-533-2531. E-mail: greensborofree@gmail.com. Web Site: greensborofreelibrary.org. *Librn,* Paula Davidson; *Asst Librn,* MacKenna Lapierre
Founded 1900. Pop 6,317; Circ 17,348
Library Holdings: Audiobooks 567; CDs 1,034; Large Print Bks 89; Bk Titles 9,000; Per Subs 46; Videos 1,153
Special Collections: Greensboro Authors
Subject Interests: Craft, Gardening
Wireless access
Function: Art exhibits, Audiobks via web, Bks on cassette, Bks on CD, CD-ROM, Children's prog, Computer training, Computers for patron use, Equip loans & repairs, Family literacy, Free DVD rentals, Health sci info serv, Homebound delivery serv, ILL available, Internet access, Music CDs, Online cat, Photocopying/Printing, Preschool outreach, Preschool reading prog, Printer for laptops & handheld devices, Prog for children & young adult, Scanner, Spoken cassettes & CDs, Spoken cassettes & DVDs, Story hour, Summer reading prog, Tax forms, VHS videos, Wheelchair accessible, Workshops
Publications: Greensboro Free Library Newsletter (Quarterly)
Open Tues 10-7, Thurs & Fri 10-5, Sat 10-2, Sun 11:30-1:30
Friends of the Library Group

GROTON

P GROTON FREE PUBLIC LIBRARY*, 1304 Scott Hwy, 05046. SAN 317-0314. Tel: 802-584-3358. E-mail: grotonlibraryvt@gmail.com. Web Site: grotonlibraryvt.org. *Librn,* Jodi Fleurie-Wohlleb
Founded 1886. Pop 876
Library Holdings: AV Mats 131; Bk Vols 5,350
Automation Activity & Vendor Info: (Cataloging) JayWil Software Development, Inc
Wireless access
Open Mon & Fri 2:30-7, Wed 10-4, Sat 10-Noon
Friends of the Library Group

GUILDHALL

P GUILDHALL PUBLIC LIBRARY*, Rt 102 N, 05905. (Mail add: PO Box 9, 05905-0009), SAN 317-0322. Tel: 802-676-3054. Web Site: www.sites.google.com/site/guildhallpubliclibrary/home. *Librn,* Valerie Foy; E-mail: vfoy10@hotmail.com
Library Holdings: AV Mats 83; CDs 10; DVDs 25; Bk Vols 5,000; Per Subs 18; Videos 15
Wireless access
Open Mon 4-8, Wed 7-8 (Winter); Mon & Wed 2-8, Sat 9-1 (Summer)
Friends of the Library Group

GUILFORD

P GUILFORD FREE LIBRARY*, 4024 Guilford Center Rd, 05301. SAN 317-0330. Tel: 802-257-4603. FAX: 802-257-4603. E-mail: staff@guilfordfreelibraryvt.org. Web Site: www.guilfordfreelibraryvt.org. *Librn,* Cathy Wilken; Tel: 802-254-6545
Pop 2,046; Circ 2,150
Library Holdings: Bk Vols 4,500
Special Collections: Guilford, Vermont History & Biography Coll
Subject Interests: Children's prog, Local hist, Sr prog
Wireless access
Function: Homebound delivery serv, ILL available, Prog for adults, Prog for children & young adult, Summer reading prog, Wheelchair accessible
Publications: At the Guilford Free Library (Newsletter)
Partic in Catamount Library Network
Open Tues 9:30-6, Wed 1-8, Thurs 3-6, Sat 9:30-3

HANCOCK

P HANCOCK FREE PUBLIC LIBRARY*, 1027 Rte 100, 05748. SAN 317-0349. Tel: 802-767-4651. E-mail: hancockvtlibrary@gmail.com. *Dir,* Caroline Meagher
Founded 1920. Pop 326; Circ 1,500
Library Holdings: CDs 20; DVDs 470; Bk Titles 3,000; Bk Vols 3,500; Per Subs 8; Talking Bks 50
Wireless access
Open Wed 12:30-5:30, Thurs 12:30-6:30, Sat 9-Noon
Friends of the Library Group

HARDWICK

P JEUDEVINE MEMORIAL LIBRARY*, 93 N Main St, 05843. (Mail add: PO Box 536, 05843-0536), SAN 317-0357. Tel: 802-472-5948. FAX: 802-472-4012. E-mail: jeudevinelibrary@hardwickvt.gov. Web Site: www.jeudevinememoriallibrary.org. *Libr Dir,* Diane Grenkow; *Youth Serv Librn,* Marilyn McDowell; E-mail: jeudevineyouthlibrarian@hardwickvt.gov; Staff 2 (MLS 1, Non-MLS 1)
Founded 1896. Pop 3,010; Circ 15,661
Jul 2016-Jun 2017 Income $5,179, State $100, Federal $79, Locally Generated Income $3,000, Other $2,000. Mats Exp $8,280, Books $6,500, Per/Ser (Incl. Access Fees) $650, AV Mat $600, Electronic Ref Mat (Incl. Access Fees) $530. Sal $68,459 (Prof $64,218)
Library Holdings: Audiobooks 350; Bks-By-Mail 400; Bks on Deafness & Sign Lang 4; CDs 250; DVDs 200; Electronic Media & Resources 12; Large Print Bks 100; Bk Titles 11,436; Per Subs 28; Talking Bks 500; Videos 400
Special Collections: Vermontiana Coll
Automation Activity & Vendor Info: (Cataloging) LibraryWorld, Inc; (Circulation) LibraryWorld, Inc; (ILL) SirsiDynix
Wireless access
Function: 24/7 Electronic res, 24/7 Online cat, Adult bk club, After school storytime, Bk club(s), Bks on CD, Children's prog, Computer training, Computers for patron use, E-Readers, E-Reserves, Electronic databases & coll, Free DVD rentals, Health sci info serv, Holiday prog, Home delivery & serv to seniorr ctr & nursing homes, Homebound delivery serv, ILL available, Internet access, Magazines, Mail & tel request accepted, Movies, Museum passes, Online cat, Online ref, OverDrive digital audio bks, Photocopying/Printing, Preschool outreach, Preschool reading prog, Prog for adults, Prog for children & young adult, Ref & res, Ref serv available, Scanner, Senior computer classes, Spoken cassettes & CDs, Spoken cassettes & DVDs, Story hour, Summer & winter reading prog, Summer reading prog, Telephone ref, Winter reading prog, Workshops
Partic in Collaborative Libraries of Vermont; Vermont Automated Libr Syst
Open Mon & Wed 1-6, Tues, Thurs & Fri 10-5, Sat 10-2
Restriction: Fee for pub use
Friends of the Library Group

HARTFORD

P THE HARTFORD LIBRARY*, 1587 Maple St, 05047. (Mail add: PO Box 512, 05047-0512), SAN 317-0373. Tel: 802-296-2568. FAX: 802-296-7452. E-mail: hartfordvtlibrary@gmail.com. Web Site: www.hartfordvtlibrary.org. *Librn,* Nadine Hodgdon; *Asst Librn,* Deborah Milne
Founded 1893. Pop 4,500
Library Holdings: Bk Vols 23,000; Per Subs 15
Subject Interests: Genealogy, Vt hist
Wireless access
Function: Bks on CD, Children's prog, Computers for patron use, Electronic databases & coll, Free DVD rentals, Home delivery & serv to seniorr ctr & nursing homes, ILL available, Internet access, Mail & tel request accepted, Online cat, Online ref, Outreach serv, OverDrive digital audio bks, Photocopying/Printing, Scanner, Story hour, Summer reading prog, Tax forms, Telephone ref, Wheelchair accessible
Partic in Green Mountain Library Consortium
Open Mon, Tues & Thurs 9-6, Wed & Fri Noon-6, Sat 9-Noon

HARTLAND

P HARTLAND PUBLIC LIBRARY, 153 US Rte 5, 05048. (Mail add: PO Box 137, 05048-0137), SAN 362-6199. Tel: 802-436-2473. FAX: 802-436-2860. Web Site: www.hartlandlibraryvt.org. *Libr Dir,* Traci Joy; E-mail: director@hartlandlibraryvt.org; Staff 4 (MLS 1, Non-MLS 3)
Pop 3,300; Circ 23,000
Library Holdings: Bk Titles 14,115; Per Subs 64
Special Collections: Vermont & Hartland Hist Coll
Automation Activity & Vendor Info: (Cataloging) Koha; (Circulation) Koha
Wireless access
Function: 24/7 Electronic res, 24/7 Online cat, 24/7 wireless access, Activity rm
Partic in Green Mountain Library Consortium
Open Tues-Thurs 10-6, Fri & Sat 10-4
Friends of the Library Group

HIGHGATE CENTER

P HIGHGATE LIBRARY & COMMUNITY CENTER*, 17 Mill Hill Rd, 05459. (Mail add: PO Box 76, 05459), SAN 317-0381. Tel: 802-868-3970. FAX: 802-868-4839. E-mail: librarian@highgatevt.org. Web Site: hlccvt.org. *Libr Dir,* Adah DeRosier; *Libr Asst,* Patti Snyder
Founded 1897
Library Holdings: Bk Vols 6,000
Wireless access
Open Mon-Wed 9-6, Thurs 2-6, Sat 9-12
Friends of the Library Group

HINESBURG

P CARPENTER-CARSE LIBRARY, 69 Ballards Corner Rd, 05461. SAN 317-039X. Tel: 802-482-2878. E-mail: library@carpentercarse.org. Web Site: www.carpentercarse.org. *Adult Ref Librn, Interim Dir,* Jill Andersen; *Asst Dir,* Richard Pritsky; *Circ Supvr,* Judy Curtis; *Adult Prog Coordr,* Alexandra Koncewicz; *Coordr, Youth Serv,* Jen Amsbary; Staff 4 (MLS 1, Non-MLS 3)
Founded 1947. Pop 4,698; Circ 39,000
Library Holdings: Audiobooks 1,000; CDs 500; DVDs 2,065; Large Print Bks 1,031; Bk Vols 26,400; Per Subs 63; Videos 32
Special Collections: Cookbook Coll; Vermont Coll. Oral History
Automation Activity & Vendor Info: (Acquisitions) ByWater Solutions; (Cataloging) ByWater Solutions; (Circulation) ByWater Solutions; (ILL) Auto-Graphics, Inc; (OPAC) ByWater Solutions; (Serials) ByWater Solutions
Wireless access
Function: 24/7 Electronic res, 24/7 Online cat, 24/7 wireless access, Activity rm, Adult bk club, After school storytime, Art exhibits, Audio & video playback equip for onsite use, Audiobks on Playaways & MP3, Audiobks via web, AV serv, Bk club(s), Bks on cassette, Bks on CD, CD-ROM, Children's prog, Computer training, Computers for patron use, Digital talking bks, Doc delivery serv, E-Reserves, Electronic databases & coll, Free DVD rentals, Holiday prog, Home delivery & serv to seniorr ctr & nursing homes, Homebound delivery serv, ILL available, Internet access, Mail & tel request accepted, Museum passes, Music CDs, Online cat, Outreach serv, OverDrive digital audio bks, Photocopying/Printing, Preschool outreach, Prog for adults, Prog for children & young adult, Ref serv available, Scanner, Senior outreach, Spoken cassettes & CDs, Spoken cassettes & DVDs, Story hour, Summer reading prog, Teen prog, VHS videos, Wheelchair accessible, Workshops
Partic in Green Mountain Library Consortium
Open Mon & Sat 10-3, Tues-Fri 10-7
Restriction: Non-resident fee
Friends of the Library Group

HUNTINGTON

P HUNTINGTON PUBLIC LIBRARY*, 2156 Main Rd, 05462. Tel: 802-434-4583. E-mail: hpl@gmavt.net. Web Site: huntingtonlibraryvt.org. *Dir,* Anne Dannenberg
Founded 1976. Pop 1,609; Circ 4,705
Library Holdings: AV Mats 60; High Interest/Low Vocabulary Bk Vols 50; Large Print Bks 50; Bk Titles 10,000; Talking Bks 250; Videos 80
Subject Interests: Vt
Automation Activity & Vendor Info: (Cataloging) Follett Software; (Circulation) Follett Software; (OPAC) Follett Software
Wireless access
Function: ILL available
Special Services for the Blind - Large print bks
Open Mon 10-6, Tues, Thurs & Sun 12-5, Fri 10-5
Friends of the Library Group

HYDE PARK

P LANPHER MEMORIAL LIBRARY*, 141 Main St, 05655. (Mail add: PO Box 196, 05655-0196), SAN 317-0411. Tel: 802-888-4628. E-mail: hydeparklibrary@yahoo.com. Web Site: www.lanpherlibrary.org. *Libr Dir,* Amy Olsen; *Asst Dir,* Ruth Hay; *Circ Librn,* Christi Dussault
Founded 1895. Pop 2,823
Library Holdings: Bk Titles 8,500; Per Subs 35
Special Collections: Art & Artist; Bound Local Newspapers 1863-1930; Vermont History, Life & Literature
Wireless access
Open Mon Noon-7, Tues, Wed & Fri 10-5, Sat 10-1

IRASBURG

P LEACH PUBLIC LIBRARY, 130 Park Ave, 05845. SAN 325-0482. Tel: 802-754-2526. Web Site: www.leachpubliclibrary.org. *Dir,* Trisha Ingalls; *Librn,* Collette Houle; Staff 1 (Non-MLS 1)
Founded 1926. Pop 1,098; Circ 5,670
Library Holdings: DVDs 120; Bk Titles 10,000; Bk Vols 10,900; Per Subs 22; Talking Bks 44; Videos 320
Special Collections: Howard Frank Mosher Coll
Wireless access
Function: Story hour
Partic in Green Mountain Library Consortium
Open Mon 3-8, Wed & Thurs 3-6, Sat 10-3

ISLAND POND

P ISLAND POND PUBLIC LIBRARY, 49 Mill St Extension, 05846. (Mail add: PO Box 422, 05846-0422), SAN 320-5193. Tel: 802-723-6134. FAX: 802-723-6134. E-mail: ippl@comcast.net. Web Site: islandpondpubliclibrary.com. *Dir,* Michelle Wilcox; *Asst Librn,* Katie Mientka
Founded 1897. Pop 1,562
Library Holdings: Bk Vols 15,600; Per Subs 7
Wireless access
Partic in Collaborative Libraries of Vermont
Open Tues, Thurs & Fri 9-4, Wed 11-6, Sat 9-1

ISLE LA MOTTE

P ISLE LA MOTTE LIBRARY*, 2238 Main St, 05463. SAN 317-042X. Tel: 802-928-4113. E-mail: islemott@fairpoint.net. *Librn,* Joyce Tuck
Founded 1904. Pop 519
Library Holdings: Bk Titles 4,200
Subject Interests: Local hist, State hist
Open Fri 3-6

JACKSONVILLE

P WHITINGHAM FREE PUBLIC LIBRARY*, 2948 Vt Rte 100, 05342. (Mail add: PO Box 500, 05342-0500), SAN 317-0438. Tel: 802-368-7506. E-mail: whitinghamvtlibrary@hotmail.com. Web Site: townofwhitingham-vt.org/library. *Librn,* Kristine Sweeter; *Asst Librn,* Lois Lapointe
Founded 1899. Pop 2,100; Circ 10,000
Library Holdings: AV Mats 1,000; Bk Vols 15,000; Per Subs 20
Wireless access
Partic in Collaborative Libraries of Vermont
Open Mon & Thurs 10-4, Wed 2-7, Sat 9-2

JAMAICA

P JAMAICA MEMORIAL LIBRARY, 17 Depot St, 05343. (Mail add: PO Box 266, 05343-0266), SAN 317-0446. Tel: 802-874-4901. E-mail: librarian@jamaicavtlibrary.org. Web Site: www.jamaicavtlibrary.org. *Libr Dir,* Madeline Helser; *Libr Asst,* Lynnea Gordon; E-mail: assistant@jamaicavtlibrary.org; Staff 2 (MLS 1, Non-MLS 1)
Founded 1924. Pop 1,035; Circ 1,532
Library Holdings: Audiobooks 157; DVDs 264; Large Print Bks 626; Bk Vols 4,400; Per Subs 5
Special Collections: Vermont & Jamaica (VT) Histories Coll
Automation Activity & Vendor Info: (Acquisitions) Ingram Library Services; (Cataloging) Biblionix/Apollo; (Circulation) Biblionix/Apollo; (ILL) Auto-Graphics, Inc; (OPAC) Biblionix/Apollo
Wireless access
Function: 24/7 Electronic res, 24/7 Online cat, 24/7 wireless access, Activity rm, Art programs, Audio & video playback equip for onsite use, Audiobks via web, Bks on CD, Children's prog, Computer training, Computers for patron use, E-Readers, Electronic databases & coll, Family literacy, Free DVD rentals, Games, Games & aids for people with disabilities, Holiday prog, Homebound delivery serv, ILL available, Internet access, Magazines, Movies, Museum passes, Online cat, Online ref, Outreach serv, OverDrive digital audio bks, Photocopying/Printing, Preschool outreach, Preschool reading prog, Printer for laptops & handheld

devices, Prog for adults, Prog for children & young adult, Scanner, Story hour, Summer & winter reading prog, Summer reading prog
Partic in Collaborative Libraries of Vermont
Open Tues & Thurs 11-7, Sat 10-1

JEFFERSONVILLE

P VARNUM MEMORIAL LIBRARY*, 194 Main St, 05464. (Mail add: PO Box 198, 05464-0198). Tel: 802-644-2117. E-mail: thevarnum@gmail.com, varnumrequests@gmail.com. Web Site: varnumlibrary.org. *Librn,* Carrie Watson; E-mail: carriewatson.varnum@gmail.com; *Youth Librn,* Karen Hennig; Staff 2 (Non-MLS 2)
Founded 1894. Pop 3,700
Library Holdings: Audiobooks 300; DVDs 25; Bk Vols 10,000; Per Subs 5; Videos 350
Wireless access
Open Tues & Wed 9-6, Thurs 8-6, Fri & Sat 9-3
Friends of the Library Group

JERICHO

P JERICHO TOWN LIBRARY, Seven Jericho Ctr Circle, 05465. (Mail add: PO Box 1055, 05465-1055). Tel: 802-899-4686. E-mail: library@jerichotownlibraryvt.org. Web Site: sites.google.com/jerichotownlibraryvt.org/jerichotownlibraryvt. *Dir,* Catherine Bass; E-mail: catherine@jerichotownlibraryvt.org
Pop 5,010
Library Holdings: AV Mats 200; Bk Vols 7,455; Per Subs 1
Automation Activity & Vendor Info: (Acquisitions) Baker & Taylor; (Cataloging) Koha; (Circulation) Koha; (OPAC) Koha
Wireless access
Partic in Green Mountain Library Consortium
Open Tues 10-7, Wed & Thurs 10-6, Fri 12-6, Sat 9:30-2:30

P DEBORAH RAWSON MEMORIAL LIBRARY*, Eight River Rd, 05465. SAN 329-0964. Tel: 802-899-4962. FAX: 802-899-5257. E-mail: rawsonlibrary@drml.org. Web Site: www.drml.org. *Dir,* Holly Hall; E-mail: director@drml.org; *Youth Librn,* Kristine Caldwell; E-mail: youth_librarian@drml.org; Staff 1 (Non-MLS 1)
Pop 8,000; Circ 55,000
Library Holdings: Bk Vols 25,662; Per Subs 60
Automation Activity & Vendor Info: (Cataloging) Follett Software; (Circulation) Follett Software
Wireless access
Partic in Catamount Library Network
Open Tues & Thurs 12-8, Wed & Fri 10-6, Sat 10-2, Sun 1-4
Friends of the Library Group

JOHNSON

P JOHNSON PUBLIC LIBRARY*, Seven Library Dr, 05656. (Mail add: PO Box 601, 05656-0601), SAN 317-0497. Tel: 802-635-7141. E-mail: johnsonpubliclibraryvt@gmail.com. Web Site: www.johnsonpubliclibrary.org. *Dir,* Jeanne Engel
Pop 3,000; Circ 4,950
Library Holdings: Bk Vols 7,500; Per Subs 10
Wireless access
Open Tues, Thurs & Fri 10-5, Wed 11-6, Sat 10-1

C VERMONT STATE UNIVERSITY - JOHNSON, Willey Library, (Formerly Northern Vermont University), 337 College Hill, 05656. SAN 317-0500. Tel: 802-635-1494. FAX: 802-635-1294. Web Site: www.northernvermont.edu/about/our-people/directory/nvu-johnson-library. *Fac Librn,* Susan Currier; E-mail: susan.currier@vsc.edu; *Circ Coordr,* Jeff Angione; Tel: 802-635-1273, E-mail: jeffrey.angione@vermontstate.edu; *Resource Sharing Coord,* Alice Godin; Tel: 802-635-1277, E-mail: alice.godin@vermontstate.edu; Staff 3 (MLS 1, Non-MLS 2)
Founded 1866. Enrl 1,268; Fac 62; Highest Degree: Master
Library Holdings: AV Mats 8,280; e-books 12,710; e-journals 36,000; Bk Vols 111,972; Per Subs 70
Special Collections: State Document Depository
Subject Interests: Children's lit
Wireless access
Partic in Collaborative Libraries of Vermont
Open Mon-Thurs 8-6, Fri 8-4, Sun 12-6 (Winter); Mon-Fri 8-4 (Summer)

KILLINGTON

P SHERBURNE MEMORIAL LIBRARY*, 2998 River Rd, 05751. SAN 317-0519. Tel: 802-422-4251, 802-422-9765. FAX: 802-422-4323. Web Site: www.sherburnelibrary.org. *Libr Dir,* Jane Ramos; E-mail: director@sherburnelibrary.org; *Circ Librn,* Lynne Herbst; *Circ Librn,* Sharon Van Niel; *Youth Serv Librn,* Melissa Knipes; Staff 2 (Non-MLS 2)
Founded 1913. Pop 1,000; Circ 38,000
Library Holdings: Bk Vols 22,000; Per Subs 63
Special Collections: Rosenblum Scappaticci Large Print Coll; Vermont Coll, local hist
Subject Interests: Town hist, Vt hist
Automation Activity & Vendor Info: (Cataloging) Insignia Software; (Circulation) Insignia Software; (OPAC) Insignia Software
Wireless access
Function: After school storytime, Archival coll, Art exhibits, Audio & video playback equip for onsite use, Audiobks via web, Bks on CD, Bus archives, Children's prog, Computer training, Computers for patron use, Distance learning, Doc delivery serv, E-Reserves, Electronic databases & coll, Free DVD rentals, Govt ref serv, Homework prog, ILL available, Internet access, Mail & tel request accepted, Museum passes, Music CDs, Online cat, OverDrive digital audio bks, Photocopying/Printing, Preschool outreach, Preschool reading prog, Printer for laptops & handheld devices, Prof lending libr, Prog for adults, Prog for children & young adult, Ref & res, Scanner, Senior computer classes, Serves people with intellectual disabilities, Story hour, Summer reading prog, Tax forms, Wheelchair accessible
Partic in Collaborative Libraries of Vermont; Green Mountain Library Consortium; Vermont Automated Libr Syst
Special Services for the Deaf - Closed caption videos; Sign lang interpreter upon request for prog
Open Mon & Fri 10-5:30, Tues & Thurs Noon-5:30, Wed 9-7, Sat 9-1
Friends of the Library Group

LINCOLN

P LINCOLN LIBRARY*, 222 W River Rd, 05443. SAN 317-0535. Tel: 802-453-2665. E-mail: lincolnlibraryvt@gmail.com. Web Site: www.lincolnlibraryvt.com. *Dir,* Wendy McIntosh; *Asst Librn,* Ellen Hanson; Staff 2 (Non-MLS 2)
Pop 1,217
Library Holdings: Bk Titles 16,525; Per Subs 68
Automation Activity & Vendor Info: (Acquisitions) Auto-Graphics, Inc; (Cataloging) Auto-Graphics, Inc; (Circulation) Auto-Graphics, Inc; (ILL) Auto-Graphics, Inc
Wireless access
Function: 24/7 Online cat, Adult bk club, After school storytime, Art exhibits, Audio & video playback equip for onsite use, Bi-weekly Writer's Group, Bk club(s), Bks on cassette, Bks on CD, CD-ROM, Chess club, Children's prog, Computer training, Computers for patron use, Free DVD rentals, Holiday prog, Home delivery & serv to seniorr ctr & nursing homes, ILL available, Internet access, Magazines, Magnifiers for reading, Meeting rooms, Movies, Museum passes, Music CDs, Online cat, OverDrive digital audio bks, Photocopying/Printing, Preschool outreach, Prog for adults, Prog for children & young adult, Scanner, Senior computer classes, Senior outreach, Serves people with intellectual disabilities, Spanish lang bks, Story hour, Summer reading prog, Tax forms, Teen prog, VHS videos, Wheelchair accessible, Workshops, Writing prog
Partic in Vermont State Libr Syst
Open Mon 2-6, Tues 10-3, Wed 10-8, Fri 10-4, Sat 10-1

LOWELL

P LOWELL COMMUNITY LIBRARY, 2170 Vermont Rte 100, 05847. SAN 317-0543. Tel: 802-744-2317. E-mail: library@lowelltown.org. *Librn,* Nancy Allen; Staff 1 (Non-MLS 1)
Founded 1935. Pop 750; Circ 1,200
Library Holdings: Large Print Bks 100; Bk Vols 6,000; Per Subs 1
Wireless access
Open Tues 1-5, Sat 11-3

LOWER WATERFORD

P DAVIES MEMORIAL LIBRARY*, 532 Maple St, 05848. (Mail add: PO Box 56, 05848-0056), SAN 322-8576. Tel: 802-748-4609. E-mail: davieslibraryvt@gmail.com. Web Site: daviesmemoriallibrary.org. *Libr Dir,* Kandis Barrett; Staff 1 (Non-MLS 1)
Founded 1896. Pop 1,210; Circ 1,319
Library Holdings: Bk Vols 3,500; Per Subs 15
Wireless access
Partic in Collaborative Libraries of Vermont
Open Mon-Fri 9-6, Sat 9-12
Friends of the Library Group

LUDLOW

P FLETCHER MEMORIAL LIBRARY*, 88 Main St, 05149. SAN 317-0551. Tel: 802-228-3517, 802-228-8921. E-mail: fmlnews@gmail.com. Web Site: www.fmlnews.org. *Dir,* Jill Tofferi
Founded 1901. Pop 3,000; Circ 17,000
Library Holdings: Audiobooks 900; DVDs 500; Bk Vols 14,000
Subject Interests: Local hist
Automation Activity & Vendor Info: (Acquisitions) Baker & Taylor; (Cataloging) Baker & Taylor; (Circulation) Baker & Taylor; (OPAC) Koha
Wireless access

Partic in Catamount Library Network
Open Mon-Fri 10-5
Friends of the Library Group

LUNENBURG

P ALDEN BALCH MEMORIAL LIBRARY*, 24 E Main St, 05906. (Mail add: PO Box 6, 05906-0006), SAN 317-056X. Tel: 802-892-5365. E-mail: Aldenbalchlibrary@hotmail.com. *Librn,* Theresa A Lewis
Founded 1904. Pop 1,320; Circ 12,517
Library Holdings: AV Mats 200; Bk Vols 8,000; Per Subs 15
Open Tues-Thurs 10-4, Sun 6-8
Friends of the Library Group

LYNDONVILLE

P COBLEIGH PUBLIC LIBRARY*, 14 Depot St, 05851. (Mail add: PO Box 147, 05851-0147), SAN 317-0578. Tel: 802-626-5475. E-mail: info@cobleighlibrary.org. Web Site: cobleighlibrary.org. *Dir,* Bryn Hoffman; E-mail: bryn@cobleighlibrary.org; Staff 4 (Non-MLS 4)
Founded 1906. Pop 9,873; Circ 52,000
Library Holdings: Bk Vols 25,000
Automation Activity & Vendor Info: (Cataloging) TLC (The Library Corporation); (OPAC) TLC (The Library Corporation)
Wireless access
Partic in Collaborative Libraries of Vermont
Open Mon Noon-5, Tues & Thurs Noon-7, Wed & Fri 10-5, Sat 9-1
Friends of the Library Group
Bookmobiles: 1. Librn, Kari Cochran

C VERMONT STATE UNIVERSITY - LYNDON*, Samuel Read Hall Library, (Formerly Northern Vermont University Lyndon Campus), 1001 College Rd, 05851. SAN 317-0586. Interlibrary Loan Service Tel: 802-626-6449. Reference Tel: 802-626-6450. E-mail: reference-lyndon@northernvermont.edu. Web Site: libraries.northernvermont.edu. *Libr Dir,* Sam Boss; Tel: 802-626-6446; *ILL Supvr,* Alice Godin; E-mail: alice.godin@northernvermont.edu; *Coordr, Acq, Per,* Monique Prive; E-mail: monique.prive@northernvermont.edu; *Archives Coordr, Cataloger,* Tara-jean Samora; E-mail: tara-jean.samora@northernvermont.edu; *Circ Coordr,* Jay Bona; E-mail: jay.bona@northernvermont.edu; Staff 6 (MLS 2, Non-MLS 4)
Founded 1911. Enrl 1,200; Fac 83; Highest Degree: Master
Library Holdings: CDs 1,686; DVDs 2,545; e-books 4,572; Microforms 23,413; Bk Vols 87,294; Per Subs 255
Special Collections: Juvenile & Instructional Coll; Vermont Coll
Automation Activity & Vendor Info: (Acquisitions) SirsiDynix; (Cataloging) SirsiDynix; (Circulation) SirsiDynix; (Course Reserve) SirsiDynix; (ILL) SirsiDynix; (Media Booking) SirsiDynix; (OPAC) SirsiDynix; (Serials) SirsiDynix
Wireless access
Publications: Annual Report; Faculty Handbook; General Guide; Pathfinders
Partic in LYRASIS; OCLC Online Computer Library Center, Inc
Open Mon-Thurs 8am-11pm, Fri 8-4, Sat 10-5, Sun 1-11 (Fall-Spring); Mon-Fri 8-4 (Summer)
Friends of the Library Group

MANCHESTER CENTER

P MANCHESTER COMMUNITY LIBRARY*, 138 Cemetery Ave, Rte 7A, 05255. (Mail add: PO Box 1105, 05255), SAN 317-0594. Tel: 802-362-2607. Web Site: mclvt.org. *Exec Dir,* J Violet Gannon; E-mail: jvgannon@mclvt.org; *Youth Serv Dir,* Gizelle Guyette; E-mail: gguyette@mclvt.org; *Adult Prog Coordr,* Cal Workman; E-mail: cworkman@mclvt.org; Staff 11 (MLS 1, Non-MLS 10)
Founded 1897. Pop 4,359; Circ 46,645
Wireless access
Function: Adult bk club, Bks on CD, Children's prog, Computers for patron use, ILL available, Museum passes, Online cat, Photocopying/Printing, Prog for adults, Prog for children & young adult, Story hour, Summer reading prog, Tax forms
Partic in Collaborative Libraries of Vermont
Open Mon-Thurs 10-6, Fri & Sat 10-4

MARSHFIELD

P JAQUITH PUBLIC LIBRARY, Old Schoolhouse Common, 122 School St, Rm 2, 05658. SAN 317-0624. Tel: 802-426-3581. FAX: 802-426-3581. E-mail: jaquithpubliclibrary@gmail.com. Web Site: www.jaquithpubliclibrary.org. *Dir & Librn,* Susan Green; *Youth Librn,* Sasha McGarvey; E-mail: jaquithyouth@gmail.com; *Prog & Vols Coordr,* Anne Miller; E-mail: programs.jaquithpubliclibrary@gmail.com
Founded 1895. Pop 1,588; Circ 16,000
Library Holdings: Bk Vols 8,000; Per Subs 15
Special Collections: Oral History
Subject Interests: Gen, Local hist
Wireless access
Function: 24/7 Electronic res, 24/7 Online cat, 24/7 wireless access, Activity rm, Adult bk club
Partic in Collaborative Libraries of Vermont
Open Mon, Tues, Thurs & Fri 10-1 & 3-6, Wed 10-1 & 3-7, Sat 9-1
Friends of the Library Group

MIDDLEBURY

S HENRY SHELDON MUSEUM OF VERMONT HISTORY*, Stewart-Swift Research Center, One Park St, 05753. SAN 317-0659. Tel: 802-388-2117. Web Site: www.henrysheldonmuseum.org/archives. *Exec Dir,* Coco Moseley; *Archivist,* Eva Garcelon-Hart; E-mail: eghart@henrysheldonmuseum.org; Staff 1 (MLS 1)
Founded 1882
Library Holdings: Bk Vols 4,000
Special Collections: Manuscripts, Maps, Photographs, Ephemera, Music, Scrapbooks & Middlebury Newspapers; Rare books & pamphlets
Subject Interests: Hist of Addison County, Vt hist
Wireless access
Function: Archival coll, Res libr
Publications: Treasures Gathered Here: A Guide to the Manuscript Collection of the Sheldon Museum Research Center
Restriction: Closed stack, Non-circulating, Open by appt only, Open to pub for ref only

P ILSLEY PUBLIC LIBRARY*, 75 Main St, 05753. SAN 317-0632. Tel: 802-388-4095. FAX: 802-388-4367. E-mail: info@ilsleypubliclibrary.org. Web Site: www.ilsleypubliclibrary.org. *Dir,* Dana Hart; Tel: 802-388-4098, E-mail: dana.hart@ilsleypubliclibrary.org; *Ref Librn,* Chris Kirby; E-mail: chris.kirby@ilsleypubliclibrary.org; *Youth Serv Librn,* Tricia Allen; Tel: 802-388-4097, E-mail: t.allen@ilsleypubliclibrary.org; Staff 15 (MLS 3, Non-MLS 12)
Founded 1866. Pop 8,496; Circ 184,010
Library Holdings: Bk Vols 54,500; Per Subs 108
Subject Interests: Local hist
Automation Activity & Vendor Info: (Acquisitions) Innovative Interfaces, Inc - Millennium; (Cataloging) Innovative Interfaces, Inc - Millennium; (Circulation) Innovative Interfaces, Inc - Millennium
Wireless access
Function: Art exhibits, Audio & video playback equip for onsite use, Audiobks via web, Bks on cassette, Bks on CD, Children's prog, Computer training, Computers for patron use, Distance learning, Electronic databases & coll, Equip loans & repairs, Free DVD rentals, Holiday prog, ILL available, Mail & tel request accepted, Microfiche/film & reading machines, Museum passes, Music CDs, Online cat, OverDrive digital audio bks, Photocopying/Printing, Preschool outreach, Prog for adults, Prog for children & young adult, Ref serv available, Scanner, Spoken cassettes & CDs, Story hour, Summer reading prog, Tax forms, Teen prog, Telephone ref, Wheelchair accessible
Publications: Ilsley Inklings
Open Mon-Sat 10-5
Restriction: Non-resident fee
Friends of the Library Group
Branches: 1
SARAH PARTRIDGE COMMUNITY, 431 E Main St, East Middlebury, 05740. (Mail add: PO Box 330, East Middlebury, 05740-0330). Tel: 802-388-7588. E-mail: SarahPartridge@ilsleypubliclibrary.org. *Librn,* Laura Fetterolf
Founded 1924
Library Holdings: Bk Titles 2,300
Open Tues 9-12, Thurs 2-6, Sat 9-2
Friends of the Library Group

C MIDDLEBURY COLLEGE*, Davis Family Library, 110 Storrs Ave, 05753. SAN 362-6318. Tel: 802-443-5494. Interlibrary Loan Service Tel: 802-443-5498. Reference Tel: 802-443-5496. FAX: 802-443-5698. E-mail: library_circulation@middlebury.edu. Web Site: www.middlebury.edu/academics/lib. *Dean,* Michael D Roy; Tel: 802-443-5490, E-mail: mdroy@middlebury.edu; *Dir, Discovery & Access,* Terry Simpkins; Tel: 802-443-5045, E-mail: tsimpkin@middlebury.edu; *Dir, Spec Coll & Archives,* Rebekah Irwin; Tel: 802-443-3028, E-mail: rirwin@middlebury.edu; *Dir, Res & Instruction Serv,* Carrie MacFarlane; Tel: 802-443-5018, E-mail: cmacfarlane@middlebury.edu; Staff 54 (MLS 15, Non-MLS 39)
Founded 1800. Enrl 2,406; Fac 305; Highest Degree: Doctorate
Library Holdings: Bk Vols 710,649; Per Subs 2,908
Special Collections: Abernethy American Literature Coll, bks, ms; Archives of Traditional Music Flanders Ballad Coll, bks, ms, recording; Vermont Coll. US Document Depository
Subject Interests: Anglo-Am ballad, European langs
Automation Activity & Vendor Info: (Acquisitions) Innovative Interfaces, Inc; (Cataloging) Innovative Interfaces, Inc; (Circulation) Innovative Interfaces, Inc; (Course Reserve) Innovative Interfaces, Inc; (OPAC) Innovative Interfaces, Inc; (Serials) Innovative Interfaces, Inc

Wireless access
Publications: Friends of the Library (Newsletter); Myriad News
Partic in Collaborative Libraries of Vermont; LYRASIS; OCLC Online Computer Library Center, Inc; Proquest Dialog
Open Mon-Thurs 7:30am-1am, Fri 7:30am-11pm, Sat 9am-11pm, Sun 9am-1am
Friends of the Library Group
Departmental Libraries:
ARMSTRONG LIBRARY, McCardell Bicentennial Hall, 05753, SAN 362-6377. Tel: 802-443-5449. FAX: 802-443-2016. *Librn,* Carrie M Macfarlane; Tel: 802-443-5018; Staff 3 (MLS 1, Non-MLS 2)
Library Holdings: Bk Vols 108,064
Partic in OCLC Online Computer Library Center, Inc
Open Mon-Thurs 8am-Midnight, Fri 8-6, Sat 10-6, Sun 10-Midnight (Winter); Mon-Fri 9-5 (Summer)
Friends of the Library Group

MIDDLETOWN SPRINGS

P MIDDLETOWN SPRINGS PUBLIC LIBRARY*, 39 West St, 05757-4401. (Mail add: PO Box 1206, 05757), SAN 320-5185. Tel: 802-235-2435. E-mail: middletownspringslibrary@gmail.com. Web Site: middletownsprings.wordpress.com. *Librn,* Kimberly Bushnell; Staff 1 (MLS 1)
Pop 821; Circ 1,774
Library Holdings: Bk Vols 5,472
Wireless access
Partic in Collaborative Libraries of Vermont
Open Mon-Wed 2-7, Fri 10-2, Sat 10-Noon

MILTON

P MILTON PUBLIC LIBRARY*, 39 Bombadier Rd, 05468. SAN 317-0667. Tel: 802-893-4644. E-mail: library@miltonvt.gov. Web Site: miltonlibraryvt.org. *Dir,* Susan Larson; E-mail: slarson@miltonvt.gov; Staff 8 (MLS 1, Non-MLS 7)
Founded 1898. Pop 10,347; Circ 70,000
Wireless access
Function: 24/7 Electronic res, 24/7 Online cat, Activity rm, Adult bk club, Art exhibits, Art programs, Bk club(s), Bks on CD, Children's prog, Computer training, Computers for patron use, Electronic databases & coll, ILL available, Internet access, Magazines, Meeting rooms, Movies, Museum passes, Online cat, OverDrive digital audio bks, Photocopying/Printing, Prog for adults, Prog for children & young adult, Ref & res, Summer reading prog, Tax forms, Teen prog, Telephone ref, Wheelchair accessible
Open Mon-Thurs 9-8, Fri 9-5, Sat 9-4; Mon-Thurs 9-8, Fri 9-5, Sat 9-2 (Summer)
Friends of the Library Group

MONKTON

P RUSSELL MEMORIAL LIBRARY*, 4333 State Prison Hollow Rd, 05469. (Mail add: PO Box 39, 05469-0039), SAN 317-0675. Tel; 802-453-4471. E-mail: russellmemlibrary@gmail.com. Web Site: russelllibraryvt.wordpress.com. *Librn,* Deborah Chamberlain; *Asst Librn,* Kat Cyr. Subject Specialists: *Graphic novels,* Kat Cyr
Pop 1,201; Circ 1,223
Library Holdings: Bk Vols 2,365
Automation Activity & Vendor Info: (OPAC) LibraryWorld, Inc
Wireless access
Mem of Midstate Regional Library
Partic in Collaborative Libraries of Vermont
Open Tues 3-7, Fri & Sat 9-1

MONTGOMERY CENTER

P MONTGOMERY TOWN LIBRARY*, 86 Mountain Rd, 05471. (Mail add: PO Box 448, 05471-0448), SAN 317-0683. Tel: 802-326-3113. E-mail: montgomery.librarian@gmail.com. Web Site: www.montgomerytownlibrary.com. *Libr Dir,* Marlene Hambleton
Pop 1,100; Circ 5,200
Library Holdings: DVDs 1,600; Bk Vols 7,500; Per Subs 3
Wireless access
Function: Art exhibits, Children's prog, Computers for patron use, Electronic databases & coll, Family literacy, Free DVD rentals, ILL available, Mail & tel request accepted, Museum passes, Outreach serv, Photocopying/Printing, Prog for adults, Prog for children & young adult, Ref serv available, Senior computer classes, Story hour, Summer reading prog, Tax forms, Teen prog, Wheelchair accessible
Open Mon & Wed 10-3 & 4-7, Tues & Thurs 10-4, Fri & Sat 10-2, Sun 10-Noon
Friends of the Library Group

MONTPELIER

P KELLOGG-HUBBARD LIBRARY*, 135 Main St, 05602. SAN 317-0691. Tel: 802-223-3338. FAX: 802-223-3338. E-mail: info@kellogghubbard.org. Web Site: www.kellogghubbard.org. *Co-Dir,* Carolyn Brennan; *Co-Dir,* Jessie Lynn; *Head, Circ, Librn,* Steve Picazio; *Children's Librn, Circ Serv,* Nicole Westborn; *Tech Serv Librn,* Carol Minkiewicz; *Coordr of Develop,* Rachael Senechal; *Outreach Coordr,* Rachael Grossman; Staff 10 (MLS 2, Non-MLS 8)
Founded 1894. Pop 14,713; Circ 275,000
Library Holdings: Bk Titles 89,662; Per Subs 89
Automation Activity & Vendor Info: (Cataloging) Follett Software; (Circulation) Follett Software; (ILL) SirsiDynix; (OPAC) Follett Software
Wireless access
Open Mon-Thurs 10-8, Fri & Sat 10-5:30 (Winter); Mon-Thurs 10-8, Fri 10-5:30, Sat 10-1 (Summer)

C VERMONT COLLEGE OF FINE ARTS*, Gary Library, Vermont College of Fine Arts Library, 36 College St, 05602. Tel: 802-828-8512. E-mail: vcfalibrary@vcfa.edu. Web Site: vcfa.edu/library-resources. *Dir, Emeritus,* Jim Nolte; E-mail: Jim.Nolte@vcfa.edu; *Assoc Dir,* Tia McCarthy; E-mail: tia.mccarthy@vcfa.edu; *Libr Operations Mgr,* Juliet Stevens; Staff 5 (MLS 1, Non-MLS 4)
Founded 1935. Enrl 450; Highest Degree: Master
Jul 2021-Jun 2022 Income $100,000
Wireless access
Function: 24/7 Electronic res, 24/7 Online cat, Archival coll, Audiobks via web, Computers for patron use, Doc delivery serv, Electronic databases & coll, ILL available, Internet access, Mail loans to mem, Online cat, Orientations, OverDrive digital audio bks, Printer for laptops & handheld devices, Ref & res, Ref serv available, Res assist avail, Scanner
Restriction: 24-hr pass syst for students only, Free to mem, Open to researchers by request, Open to students, fac, staff & alumni

MORETOWN

P MORETOWN MEMORIAL LIBRARY*, 1147 Rte 100-B, 05660. SAN 317-0756. Tel: 802-496-9728. E-mail: moretownlibrary@gmail.com. Web Site: moretownlibrary.com. *Libr Dir,* Corey Stephenson; *Libr Serv Coordr,* Nicole Melone
Pop 1,700; Circ 5,000
Wireless access
Open Mon, Tues & Thurs 2-6, Fri & Sat 10-2
Friends of the Library Group

MORRISVILLE

P MORRISTOWN CENTENNIAL LIBRARY*, Seven Richmond St, 05661. (Mail add: PO Box 727, 05661-0727), SAN 317-0772. Tel: 802-888-3853. E-mail: info@centenniallibrary.org. Web Site: centenniallibrary.org. *Dir,* Gizelle Guyette; *Asst Librn,* Mary LeMieux; *Circ, ILL,* Linda Hartin; *Youth Serv,* Rachel Funk Booher; Staff 3 (Non-MLS 3)
Founded 1890. Pop 5,138; Circ 36,259
Library Holdings: AV Mats 1,000; Large Print Bks 550; Bk Vols 19,000; Per Subs 60; Talking Bks 975
Special Collections: Cheney Civil War Coll
Automation Activity & Vendor Info: (Cataloging) Follett Software; (Circulation) Follett Software
Wireless access
Partic in Catamount Library Network
Open Tues & Wed 10-7:30, Thurs & Fri 10-5:30, Sat 9-2
Friends of the Library Group

NEW HAVEN

P NEW HAVEN COMMUNITY LIBRARY*, 78 North St, Ste 2, 05472. SAN 317-0780. Tel: 802-453-4015. E-mail: librarian@nhcl.org. Web Site: www.nhcl.org. *Dir,* Katie Male-Riordan; Staff 1 (Non-MLS 1)
Pop 1,600; Circ 15,525
Library Holdings: AV Mats 700; Bk Vols 12,000
Special Collections: Board game Coll; Vermont Coll
Automation Activity & Vendor Info: (Cataloging) Koha; (Circulation) Koha
Wireless access
Mem of Midstate Regional Library
Open Tues 9-4, Wed & Thurs 1-7, Sat 9-1
Friends of the Library Group

NEWBURY

P TENNEY MEMORIAL LIBRARY*, 4886 Main St S, 05051. (Mail add: PO Box 85, 05051-0085), SAN 317-0802. Tel: 802-866-5366. E-mail: tenneylibrary@gmail.com. Web Site: tenneymemoriallibrary.org. *Libr Dir,* Mary Burnham
Founded 1896. Pop 975; Circ 3,118
Library Holdings: Bk Vols 12,700; Per Subs 20

Special Collections: New England Coll; Town History Coll. State Document Depository
Automation Activity & Vendor Info: (Cataloging) Calico's Lion
Wireless access
Open Tues 10-5, Thurs 2-8, Sat 9-4

NEWFANE

P MOORE FREE LIBRARY, 23 West St, 05345. (Mail add: PO Box 208, 05345-0208), SAN 317-0810. Tel: 802-365-7948. E-mail: moorefreelibrary@gmail.com. Web Site: www.moorefreelibrary.org. *Libr Dir,* Beckley Gaudette; Staff 0.8 (Non-MLS 0.8)
Founded 1898. Pop 1,700; Circ 6,500
Library Holdings: DVDs 2,000; Bk Titles 13,500
Special Collections: Art & Humanities (Robert Crowell Coll); Civil War Coll; Memoirs; Vermont Coll
Subject Interests: Local hist
Automation Activity & Vendor Info: (Acquisitions) Baker & Taylor; (Cataloging) Auto-Graphics, Inc; (Circulation) Auto-Graphics, Inc; (Course Reserve) Auto-Graphics, Inc; (ILL) Auto-Graphics, Inc; (Media Booking) Auto-Graphics, Inc; (OPAC) Auto-Graphics, Inc; (Serials) Auto-Graphics, Inc
Wireless access
Function: Prog for children & young adult, Summer reading prog
Partic in Vermont Automated Libr Syst
Friends of the Library Group

NEWPORT

P GOODRICH MEMORIAL LIBRARY*, 202 Main St, 05855. SAN 317-0829. Tel: 802-334-7902. FAX: 802-334-3890. E-mail: reserve@goodrichlibrary.org. Web Site: www.goodrichlibrary.org. *Dir,* Joanne Pariseau; E-mail: director@goodrichlibrary.org; Staff 9 (Non-MLS 9)
Founded 1898. Pop 6,609; Circ 44,600
Library Holdings: AV Mats 900; CDs 400; DVDs 500; High Interest/Low Vocabulary Bk Vols 50; Large Print Bks 500; Bk Vols 25,000; Per Subs 66; Talking Bks 400
Special Collections: Vermont History Coll, bks, photogs. State Document Depository
Automation Activity & Vendor Info: (Acquisitions) Mandarin Library Automation; (Cataloging) Mandarin Library Automation; (Circulation) Mandarin Library Automation; (Course Reserve) Mandarin Library Automation; (ILL) Mandarin Library Automation; (OPAC) Mandarin Library Automation; (Serials) Mandarin Library Automation
Wireless access
Function: Distance learning, For res purposes, Games & aids for people with disabilities, Home delivery & serv to senior ctr & nursing homes, Homebound delivery serv, ILL available, Large print keyboards, Photocopying/Printing, Prog for children & young adult, Ref serv available, Serves people with intellectual disabilities, Summer reading prog, Telephone ref
Special Services for the Deaf - Bks on deafness & sign lang; Captioned film dep; Closed caption videos; High interest/low vocabulary bks; Staff with knowledge of sign lang
Special Services for the Blind - Home delivery serv
Open Mon-Fri 10-6, Sat 10-3
Bookmobiles: 1

NORTH BENNINGTON

P JOHN G MCCULLOUGH FREE LIBRARY*, Two Main St N, 05257. (Mail add: PO Box 339, 05257-0339), SAN 317-0845. Tel: 802-447-7121. E-mail: mclibrary@comcast.net. Web Site: mcculloughlibrary.org. *Libr Dir,* Jennie Rozycki; E-mail: director@mcculloughlibrary.org; *Ch,* Nicole Hall; Staff 6 (MLS 1, Non-MLS 5)
Founded 1920. Pop 3,500
Library Holdings: Bk Vols 20,000; Per Subs 35
Special Collections: Mose Sage Coll
Subject Interests: Vt hist
Automation Activity & Vendor Info: (Acquisitions) Brodart; (Cataloging) Koha; (Circulation) Koha; (ILL) Auto-Graphics, Inc; (OPAC) Koha
Wireless access
Function: 24/7 Electronic res, 24/7 Online cat, Adult bk club, Adult literacy prog, After school storytime, Art exhibits, Art programs, Audiobks on Playaways & MP3, Audiobks via web, Bk club(s), Bks on CD, Children's prog, Computer training, Computers for patron use, Electronic databases & coll, Free DVD rentals, Holiday prog, ILL available, Internet access, Life-long learning prog for all ages, Literacy & newcomer serv, Magazines, Magnifiers for reading, Movies, Museum passes, Online cat, OverDrive digital audio bks, Photocopying/Printing, Preschool outreach, Prog for adults, Prog for children & young adult, STEM programs, Story hour, Summer reading prog, Teen prog, Telephone ref, Workshops, Writing prog
Partic in Catamount Library Network
Open Tues & Wed 1-8, Thurs & Fri 1-6, Sat 10-2
Friends of the Library Group

NORTH CLARENDON

P BAILEY MEMORIAL LIBRARY, 111 Moulton Ave, 05759-9327. (Mail add: PO Box 116, 05759-0116), SAN 376-4869. Tel: 802-747-7743. E-mail: bbaileylibrary@gmail.com. Web Site: baileylibraryvt.wordpress.com. *Dir,* Linda O'Brien; *Asst Librn,* Toni Flanders; Staff 2 (Non-MLS 2)
Pop 2,881
Library Holdings: AV Mats 320; Bk Vols 10,800; Talking Bks 250
Wireless access
Function: Homebound delivery serv
Open Mon 5-7, Tues 11-7, Wed & Thurs 11-4, Sat 10-3

NORTH HERO

P NORTH HERO PUBLIC LIBRARY*, 3195 US Rte 2, 05474. (Mail add: PO Box 187, 05474), SAN 317-0861. Tel: 802-372-5458. E-mail: nhlibrary@comcast.net. Web Site: www.northherolibrary.org. *Librn,* Caroline Korejko
Founded 1913. Pop 850; Circ 3,500
Jul 2020-Jun 2021 Income $36,783, City $32,003, Locally Generated Income $4,730, Other $50. Mats Exp $5,085, Books $3,700, Other Print Mats $90, AV Mat $1,295. Sal $18,312
Library Holdings: Audiobooks 170; CDs 53; DVDs 500; Large Print Bks 34; Bk Vols 4,000; Per Subs 5
Automation Activity & Vendor Info: (Acquisitions) Brodart; (Cataloging) Brodart; (Circulation) LibraryWorld, Inc
Wireless access
Function: After school storytime, Bks on CD, Children's prog, Computers for patron use, Free DVD rentals, Homebound delivery serv, ILL available, Magazines, Music CDs, Online cat, OverDrive digital audio bks, Photocopying/Printing, Prog for adults, Spoken cassettes & CDs, Story hour, Summer reading prog, Wheelchair accessible
Partic in Collaborative Libraries of Vermont
Open Tues 2-7, Thurs 10-3, Sat 9-1
Friends of the Library Group

NORTH TROY

P WILLIAM H & LUCY F RAND MEMORIAL LIBRARY*, 160 Railroad St, Ste 2, 05859-9492. SAN 317-0888. Tel: 802-988-4741. E-mail: randmemorial@gmail.com. Web Site: randmemorial.com. *Libr Dir,* Jennifer Molinski
Founded 1925. Pop 1,600; Circ 3,526
Library Holdings: Bk Vols 8,000; Per Subs 30
Subject Interests: Local hist, Vt
Wireless access
Open Mon & Tues 3-7, Wed 1-5, Thurs & Fri 8-Noon (May-Sept); Mon & Wed 5-8, Thurs & Fri 8-3 (Oct-April)
Friends of the Library Group

NORTHFIELD

P BROWN PUBLIC LIBRARY, 93 S Main St, 05663. SAN 317-0896. Tel: 802-485-4621. FAX: 802-485-4990. E-mail: bpl.library01@gmail.com. Web Site: www.brownpubliclibrary.org. *Libr Dir,* Sherri Brickey; *Asst Librn,* Sonya Rhodes; *Youth Serv Librn,* Rebecca Pearish; Staff 2 (Non-MLS 2)
Founded 1906. Pop 6,000; Circ 21,530
Library Holdings: AV Mats 2,940; Bks on Deafness & Sign Lang 10; High Interest/Low Vocabulary Bk Vols 50; Large Print Bks 200; Bk Vols 23,500; Per Subs 17
Special Collections: Vermont Coll
Automation Activity & Vendor Info: (Cataloging) Ex Libris Group; (Circulation) Ex Libris Group; (OPAC) Ex Libris Group
Wireless access
Function: 24/7 Online cat
Open Mon, Wed & Thurs 10-6, Tues 12-8, Fri 10-5, Sat 10-2
Friends of the Library Group

NORWICH

P NORWICH PUBLIC LIBRARY*, 368 Main St, 05055-9453. (Mail add: PO Box 290, 05055-0290), SAN 317-0918. Tel: 802-649-1184. FAX: 802-649-3470. Circulation E-mail: circulation.desk@norwichlibrary.org. Web Site: www.norwichlibrary.org. *Dir,* Lucinda H Walker; E-mail: lucinda.walker@norwichlibrary.org; *Asst Dir,* Lisa Milchman; *Tech Serv Librn,* Julia Greider; *Youth Serv Librn,* Erin Davison; Staff 7 (MLS 3, Non-MLS 4)
Founded 1880. Pop 3,544; Circ 67,922
Library Holdings: Bk Vols 28,357
Subject Interests: Local hist

Automation Activity & Vendor Info: (Cataloging) ByWater Solutions; (Circulation) ByWater Solutions; (ILL) Auto-Graphics, Inc; (OPAC) ByWater Solutions
Function: 24/7 Electronic res, 24/7 Online cat, 24/7 wireless access, Adult bk club, Art exhibits, Audio & video playback equip for onsite use, Audiobks via web, AV serv, Bk club(s), Bks on CD, Children's prog, Computer training, Computers for patron use, Doc delivery serv, E-Readers, E-Reserves, Electronic databases & coll, Equip loans & repairs, Extended outdoor wifi, Free DVD rentals, Games, Health sci info serv, Holiday prog, Home delivery & serv to seniorr ctr & nursing homes, Homebound delivery serv, ILL available, Instruction & testing, Internet access, Laminating, Life-long learning prog for all ages, Magazines, Magnifiers for reading, Mail & tel request accepted, Mango lang, Meeting rooms, Movies, Museum passes, Music CDs, Online cat, Online ref, Orientations, Outreach serv, OverDrive digital audio bks, Photocopying/Printing, Preschool outreach, Preschool reading prog, Printer for laptops & handheld devices, Prog for adults, Prog for children & young adult, Ref & res, Ref serv available, Scanner, Senior computer classes, Senior outreach, Serves people with intellectual disabilities, Spoken cassettes & CDs, Spoken cassettes & DVDs, STEM programs, Story hour, Study rm, Summer & winter reading prog, Summer reading prog, Tax forms, Teen prog, Telephone ref, Wheelchair accessible, Winter reading prog, Workshops, Writing prog
Publications: Book Mark (Monthly newsletter)
Partic in Green Mountain Library Consortium; Librarians of the Upper Valley Coop
Open Mon 1-5:30, Tues, Wed & Fri 10-5:30, Thurs 10-7, Sat 10-3
Friends of the Library Group

ORLEANS

P JONES MEMORIAL LIBRARY*, One Water St, 05860. SAN 317-0926. Tel: 802-754-6660. FAX: 802-754-6660. E-mail: jonesmemorial@comcast.net. Web Site: jonesmemoriallibrary.wordpress.com. *Dir,* Jeanette Powell; Staff 3 (Non-MLS 3)
Founded 1950. Pop 1,100; Circ 10,000
Library Holdings: Bk Titles 14,000; Per Subs 1
Wireless access
Publications: Library Journals Adult & Children
Partic in Vermont Automated Libr Syst

ORWELL

P ORWELL FREE LIBRARY*, 473 Main St, 05670. (Mail add: PO Box 92, 05670), SAN 376-3463. Tel: 802-948-2041. E-mail: orwellfreelibrary@gmail.com. Web Site: orwellfreelibrary.org. *Librn,* Kate Hunter
Founded 1896. Pop 1,250
Library Holdings: Audiobooks 60; Large Print Bks 200; Bk Vols 8,000; Per Subs 22
Wireless access
Open Tues 11-7, Wed & Thurs 3-6, Fri 11-4, Sat 9-1
Friends of the Library Group

PAWLET

P PAWLET PUBLIC LIBRARY*, 141 School St, 05761. (Mail add: PO Box 98, 05761), SAN 317-0934. Tel: 802-325-3123. E-mail: pawletpub@gmail.com. Web Site: pawlet.vt.gov/community/pawlet-library. *Dir,* Mary Lou Willits
Pop 1,244
Library Holdings: Bk Vols 10,000; Per Subs 12
Special Collections: Pawlet History; Vermont History
Wireless access
Partic in Association for Rural & Small Libraries
Special Services for the Blind - Bks on CD; Large print bks
Open Tues 11-6, Wed & Thurs 10-5, Fri 1-5, Sat 10-1

PEACHAM

P PEACHAM LIBRARY*, 656 Bayley Hazen Rd, 05862. (Mail add: PO Box 253, 05862-0253), SAN 317-0942. Tel: 802-592-3216. E-mail: peachamlib@fairpoint.net. Web Site: peachamlibrary.org. *Libr Dir,* Susan Smolinsky; *Asst Librn,* Barbara Hegenbart; Staff 1.3 (MLS 0.3, Non-MLS 1)
Founded 1810. Pop 740; Circ 4,521
Library Holdings: Bk Vols 8,000; Per Subs 45; Videos 500
Wireless access
Open Mon, Wed, Fri & Sat 10-Noon, Tues & Thurs 1-7
Friends of the Library Group

PITTSFIELD

P ROGER CLARK MEMORIAL LIBRARY*, 40 Village Green, 05762. (Mail add: PO Box 743, 05762-0743), SAN 317-0950. Tel: 802-746-4067. E-mail: pittsfieldvtlibrary@gmail.com. Web Site: www.pittsfieldlibrary.com. *Treas,* Martha Dietz Beyersdorf
Founded 1901. Pop 249; Circ 2,430
Library Holdings: AV Mats 100; Large Print Bks 20; Bk Vols 4,500
Wireless access
Function: 24/7 Online cat, Audiobks via web, Bk club(s), Bks on CD, Children's prog, Computers for patron use, Distance learning, Electronic databases & coll, Free DVD rentals, Holiday prog, Internet access, Meeting rooms, Movies, Museum passes, Online cat, OverDrive digital audio bks, Prog for adults, Prog for children & young adult, Summer reading prog, Wheelchair accessible, Workshops
Mem of Midstate Regional Library
Partic in Collaborative Libraries of Vermont
Open Tues 10-6, Thurs 2-7, Sat 9-12:30

PITTSFORD

P MACLURE LIBRARY*, 840 Arch St, 05763. (Mail add: PO Box 60, 05763-0060), SAN 317-0969. Tel: 802-483-2972. FAX: 802-483-2703. E-mail: contact@maclurelibrary.org. Web Site: maclurelibrary.org. *Dir,* Shelly Williams; E-mail: contact@maclurelibrary.org; Staff 4 (MLS 1, Non-MLS 3)
Founded 1895. Pop 3,000; Circ 18,000
Library Holdings: Audiobooks 422; DVDs 2,000; Large Print Bks 800; Bk Vols 18,000; Per Subs 4
Special Collections: Biography Coll; History Coll
Wireless access
Function: 24/7 Electronic res, 24/7 Online cat, Adult bk club, Children's prog, Computers for patron use, For res purposes, Free DVD rentals, Holiday prog, Homebound delivery serv, Homework prog, ILL available, Internet access, Laminating, Magazines, Magnifiers for reading, Mail & tel request accepted, Mail loans to mem, Meeting rooms, Movies, Museum passes, Online cat, OverDrive digital audio bks, Photocopying/Printing, Preschool reading prog, Prog for adults, Prog for children & young adult, Ref & res, Ref serv available, Res assist avail, Scanner, Serves people with intellectual disabilities, Story hour, Study rm, Summer reading prog, Tax forms, Teen prog, Wheelchair accessible
Special Services for the Blind - Bks on CD; Large print bks
Open Mon-Fri 10-6, Sat 10-2

PLAINFIELD

P CUTLER MEMORIAL LIBRARY, 151 High St, 05667. (Mail add: PO Box 186, 05667-0186), SAN 376-799X. Tel: 802-454-8504. E-mail: info@cutlerlibrary.org. Web Site: www.cutlerlibrary.org. *Librn,* Angela Ogle; Staff 1 (Non-MLS 1)
Founded 1937
Library Holdings: Bk Vols 7,000
Automation Activity & Vendor Info: (Acquisitions) Brodart; (Cataloging) Brodart; (OPAC) LibraryWorld, Inc
Wireless access
Function: Audio & video playback equip for onsite use, Audiobks via web, Bks on cassette, Bks on CD, Computers for patron use, Distance learning, Free DVD rentals, ILL available, Museum passes, Music CDs, Online cat, Outreach serv, OverDrive digital audio bks, Photocopying/Printing, Preschool outreach, Prog for adults, Prog for children & young adult, Spoken cassettes & CDs, Story hour, Summer reading prog, Tax forms, VHS videos, Wheelchair accessible, Workshops
Open Tues & Thurs 10-6, Wed & Fri 2-5, Sat 10-1
Friends of the Library Group

PLYMOUTH

P TYSON LIBRARY, 26 Library Rd, 05056. SAN 376-8023. Tel: 802-228-4017. E-mail: vttysonlibrary@gmail.com. Web Site: tysonlibrary.wordpress.com.
Library Holdings: Bk Vols 3,500
Open Tues-Sat 10-12 (May-Sept)

POULTNEY

P POULTNEY PUBLIC LIBRARY*, 205 Main St, Ste 1, 05764. SAN 317-1000. Tel: 802-287-5556. E-mail: ppl5556@yahoo.com. Web Site: poultneypubliclibrary.com. *Dir,* Rebecca Cook; *Asst Librn,* Racheal Paquette
Pop 3,498; Circ 25,928
Library Holdings: AV Mats 798; Bk Vols 13,240; Per Subs 47
Special Collections: Vermont
Automation Activity & Vendor Info: (Cataloging) Mandarin Library Automation; (Circulation) Mandarin Library Automation
Partic in Collaborative Libraries of Vermont
Open Mon-Thurs 2-8, Fri 10-5, Sat 10-1

POWNAL

P SOLOMON WRIGHT LIBRARY*, 97 Main St, 05261. (Mail add: PO Box 400, 05261-0400), SAN 317-1019. Tel: 802-823-5400. E-mail: pownalpub@gmail.com. Web Site: www.solomonwrightpubliclibrary.org. *Dir,* Damien McCaffery; Staff 1 (Non-MLS 1)
Founded 1966. Pop 3,505
Library Holdings: Bk Vols 15,000; Per Subs 20
Special Collections: Sweeney Indian Arrowhead Coll
Subject Interests: Family, Pownal hist
Automation Activity & Vendor Info: (Cataloging) LibraryWorld, Inc; (Circulation) LibraryWorld, Inc; (OPAC) LibraryWorld, Inc
Wireless access
Function: 24/7 Electronic res, 24/7 Online cat, Adult bk club, Audio & video playback equip for onsite use, Audiobks via web, Bk club(s), Bks on cassette, Bks on CD, CD-ROM, Computers for patron use, Health sci info serv, ILL available, Internet access, Magazines, Mail & tel request accepted, Movies, Museum passes, Photocopying/Printing, Prog for adults, Prog for children & young adult, Ref serv available, Scanner, Spoken cassettes & DVDs, Study rm, Summer reading prog, Tax forms, Telephone ref, Wheelchair accessible
Partic in Collaborative Libraries of Vermont
Special Services for the Blind - Audio mat; Bks on cassette; Bks on CD; Large print bks
Open Mon, Wed & Fri 10-6, Sat 10-Noon

PROCTOR

P PROCTOR FREE LIBRARY*, Four Main St, 05765. SAN 317-1027. Tel: 802-459-3539. FAX: 802-459-3539. E-mail: proctorfree@gmail.com. Web Site: facebook.com/Proctor-Free-Library-111509095556163. *Librn,* Lisa Miser
Founded 1881. Pop 1,998; Circ 12,000
Library Holdings: AV Mats 460; Large Print Bks 62; Bk Titles 16,442; Bk Vols 17,155; Per Subs 20; Talking Bks 398
Special Collections: Realia (Children); Sports Coll; Vermontiana (Papers of Four Governors from Proctor)
Wireless access
Open Mon 10-5, Tues & Thurs 9-4, Wed 9-7, Fri 9-6
Friends of the Library Group

PROCTORSVILLE

P CAVENDISH FLETCHER COMMUNITY LIBRARY, 573 Main St, 05153. (Mail add: PO Box 266, 05153-0266), SAN 376-3366. Tel: 802-226-7503. FAX: 802-226-7858. E-mail: cavendishlibrary573@gmail.com. Web Site: www.cavendishlibrary.org. *Libr Dir,* Amy McMullen; E-mail: amy.mcmullen@trsu.org; Staff 1 (Non-MLS 1)
Founded 1990. Pop 757; Circ 14,000
Library Holdings: Audiobooks 430; DVDs 1,507; e-books 79; Bk Vols 5,000; Per Subs 37
Automation Activity & Vendor Info: (Cataloging) Follett Software; (Circulation) Follett Software; (OPAC) Follett Software
Wireless access
Function: 24/7 Online cat, Activity rm, Adult bk club, After school storytime, Art exhibits, Audiobks via web, Bk club(s), Bks on cassette, Bks on CD, Chess club, Children's prog, Computers for patron use, E-Readers, Electronic databases & coll, Free DVD rentals, Homebound delivery serv, ILL available, Instruction & testing, Internet access, Magazines, Movies, Museum passes, Music CDs, Online cat, Outreach serv, OverDrive digital audio bks, Photocopying/Printing, Preschool outreach, Preschool reading prog, Prog for children & young adult, Scanner, Story hour, Summer reading prog, VHS videos
Partic in Collaborative Libraries of Vermont; Green Mountain Library Consortium
Open Tues, Wed & Fri 9-6
Restriction: Circ to mem only

PUTNEY

C LANDMARK COLLEGE LIBRARY*, 19 River Rd S, 05346. SAN 329-1480. Tel: 802-387-1648. Interlibrary Loan Service Tel: 802-387-6785. FAX: 802-387-6896. E-mail: library@landmark.edu. Web Site: www.landmark.edu/library. *Dir, Libr Serv,* Jennifer Lann; E-mail: jlann@landmark.edu; *Research Servs Librn,* Jamie Harvey; Tel: 802-387-6763, E-mail: jamieharvey@landmark.edu; *Archives Coordr, Research Servs Librn,* Mary Jane MacGuire; Tel: 802-387-6755, E-mail: mmacguire@landmark.edu; *Tech Serv Coordr,* John Kosakowski; E-mail: johnkosakowski@landmark.edu; *Evening Res Serv Libr Spec,* Liz Wood; E-mail: lizwood@landmark.edu; Staff 5 (MLS 3, Non-MLS 2)
Founded 1985. Enrl 450; Fac 79; Highest Degree: Bachelor
Library Holdings: Audiobooks 312; AV Mats 2,319; Bks on Deafness & Sign Lang 58; CDs 174; DVDs 1,833; e-books 200,000; High Interest/Low Vocabulary Bk Vols 1,185; Bk Titles 26,675; Per Subs 150; Spec Interest Per Sub 10
Special Collections: Learning Disabilities, ADHD & ASD Research Coll
Subject Interests: Asperger's & Autism spectrum disorders (in col students and/or adults), Attention deficit disorder, Col teaching & serv, Learning disabilities
Automation Activity & Vendor Info: (Cataloging) TLC (The Library Corporation); (Circulation) TLC (The Library Corporation); (Course Reserve) TLC (The Library Corporation); (Discovery) EBSCO Discovery Service; (ILL) OCLC WorldShare Interlibrary Loan; (OPAC) TLC (The Library Corporation)
Wireless access
Function: Archival coll, Audio & video playback equip for onsite use, AV serv, Bks on cassette, Bks on CD, Computers for patron use, Digital talking bks, Electronic databases & coll, Free DVD rentals, ILL available, Internet access, Music CDs, Online cat, Online ref, Orientations, Outside serv via phone, mail, e-mail & web, Photocopying/Printing, Scanner, Telephone ref, VHS videos
Partic in Asn of Vermont Independent Col; ProConsort; Vermont Consortium of Academic Libraries
Open Mon-Thurs 8:30am-Midnight, Fri 8:30am-10pm, Sat Noon-5, Sun Noon-Midnight
Restriction: Pub use on premises

P PUTNEY PUBLIC LIBRARY*, 55 Main St, 05346. SAN 317-1035. Tel: 802-387-4407. E-mail: request@putneylibrary.org. Web Site: putneylibrary.org. *Libr Dir,* Emily Zervas; E-mail: emily@putneylibrary.org; *Youth Serv Librn,* Julia von Ranson; E-mail: julia@putneylibrary.org
Pop 2,700; Circ 20,000
Library Holdings: Bk Vols 22,000; Per Subs 14
Automation Activity & Vendor Info: (Cataloging) Koha; (Circulation) Koha; (OPAC) Koha
Wireless access
Partic in Catamount Library Network
Open Mon-Fri 10:30-6, Sat 10-1; Mon-Fri 10:30-6, Sat 10-3 (Winter)

QUECHEE

P QUECHEE PUBLIC LIBRARY*, 1957 Quechee Main St, 05059. (Mail add: PO Box 384, 05059-0384), SAN 317-0365. Tel: 802-295-1232. FAX: 802-295-1232. E-mail: info@quecheelibrary.org. Web Site: www.quecheeandwilderlibraries.com. *Libr Dir,* Kate Schaal; E-mail: kate@quecheelibrary.org; Staff 2 (Non-MLS 2)
Founded 1896. Pop 9,000
Jul 2015-Jun 2016 Income $179,700, City $161,700, Locally Generated Income $18,000. Mats Exp $15,700. Sal $104,896
Library Holdings: Large Print Bks 80; Bk Vols 35,000; Per Subs 50
Automation Activity & Vendor Info: (Cataloging) Koha; (Circulation) Koha
Wireless access
Function: 24/7 Electronic res, 24/7 Online cat, Activity rm
Open Mon, Wed & Fri 10-6, Tues & Thurs 2-7, Sat 10-2
Friends of the Library Group

RANDOLPH

P KIMBALL PUBLIC LIBRARY*, 67 N Main St, 05060. SAN 317-1051. Tel: 802-728-5073. FAX: 802-728-6735. E-mail: info@kimballlibrary.org. Web Site: www.kimballlibrary.org. *Dir,* Amy Grasmick; E-mail: amy@kimballlibrary.org; Staff 3 (MLS 2, Non-MLS 1)
Founded 1903. Pop 6,047; Circ 47,112
Library Holdings: AV Mats 1,600; DVDs 1,100; Large Print Bks 500; Bk Vols 19,200; Per Subs 30
Subject Interests: Vt
Automation Activity & Vendor Info: (Cataloging) Koha; (Circulation) Koha; (OPAC) Koha
Wireless access
Function: Homebound delivery serv, ILL available, Photocopying/Printing, Prog for adults, Prog for children & young adult, Summer reading prog, Wheelchair accessible
Open Mon & Thurs 2-8, Tues, Wed & Fri 10-5, Sat 10-1
Friends of the Library Group

RANDOLPH CENTER

C VERMONT STATE UNIVERSITY - RANDOLPH*, Hartness Library, (Formerly Vermont Technical College), Main St, 05061. SAN 317-106X. Tel: 802-728-1237. Toll Free Tel: 800-431-0025. FAX: 802-728-1506. E-mail: hartness@vtc.edu. Web Site: hartness.vsc.edu. *Cat Librn,* Julie Taylor; *Ref Librn,* Kim Hannon-Brobst; *Acq,* Candy Daniels; Staff 9 (MLS 4, Non-MLS 5)
Founded 1866. Enrl 970; Fac 67
Library Holdings: e-books 200,000; e-journals 60,000; Bk Titles 60,000; Per Subs 130; Videos 20,000

Subject Interests: Agr, Archit, Automotive tech, Bus mgt, Civil engr, Computer engr, Construction mgt, Electrical engr, Electronic engr, Engr tech, Hort, Mechanical engr, Nursing
Automation Activity & Vendor Info: (Acquisitions) SirsiDynix; (Cataloging) SirsiDynix; (Circulation) SirsiDynix; (Course Reserve) SirsiDynix; (Discovery) EBSCO Discovery Service; (ILL) SirsiDynix; (Media Booking) SirsiDynix; (OPAC) SirsiDynix; (Serials) SirsiDynix
Wireless access
Partic in OCLC Online Computer Library Center, Inc; Vermont Automated Libr Syst
Open Mon-Fri 8-4

READING

P READING PUBLIC LIBRARY*, 717 Vermont Rte 106, 05062. (Mail add: PO Box 7, 05062-0007), SAN 317-1078. Tel: 802-484-5588. E-mail: reading.public.library@comcast.net. Web Site: readinglibrary.org. *Librn,* Tony Pikramenos
Founded 1899. Pop 712; Circ 3,200
Library Holdings: Bk Vols 7,824
Special Collections: Extensive Coll of Bound Harpers & National Geographic Magazines
Wireless access
Function: Wheelchair accessible
Partic in Catamount Library Network
Open Tues 12-3:30 & 4-7, Thurs 10-1:30 & 2-5, Sat 10-2

READSBORO

P READSBORO COMMUNITY LIBRARY*, 301 Phelps Lane, 05350. SAN 317-1086. Tel: 802-423-5460. FAX: 802-423-9914. E-mail: lovestoread2001@yahoo.com. Web Site: www.readsborocommunitylibrary.org. *Dir,* Cyndi M Candiloro
Founded 1874. Pop 763; Circ 4,794
Library Holdings: Bk Vols 8,200; Per Subs 25
Wireless access
Partic in Collaborative Libraries of Vermont
Open Mon 3-5, Tues-Thurs 3-7

RICHFORD

P ARVIN A BROWN PUBLIC LIBRARY, 88 Main St, 05476. SAN 317-1094. Tel: 802-848-3313. FAX: 802-848-7752. E-mail: arvinabrown@gmail.com. Web Site: www.aabrown.org. *Libr Dir,* Harry Michael Hansen; E-mail: librarydirector@aabrown.org; Staff 1 (Non-MLS 1)
Founded 1895. Pop 3,855; Circ 14,963
Library Holdings: Audiobooks 232; CDs 104; DVDs 1,238; Large Print Bks 266; Bk Titles 10,991; Per Subs 92; Videos 420
Special Collections: Vermont Coll
Automation Activity & Vendor Info: (Cataloging) Koha; (Circulation) Koha; (OPAC) Koha
Wireless access
Function: Bks on cassette, Bks on CD, Children's prog, Computers for patron use, Electronic databases & coll, Free DVD rentals, Holiday prog, Home delivery & serv to seniorr ctr & nursing homes, Homebound delivery serv, ILL available, Internet access, Magnifiers for reading, Mail & tel request accepted, Museum passes, Online cat, Photocopying/Printing, Prog for adults, Prog for children & young adult, Ref serv available, Summer reading prog, Tax forms, VHS videos, Wheelchair accessible, Workshops
Special Services for the Deaf - Bks on deafness & sign lang; Closed caption videos
Special Services for the Blind - Large print bks
Open Mon, Wed & Fri 10-6, Sat 9-1

RICHMOND

P RICHMOND FREE LIBRARY*, 201 Bridge St, 05477. (Mail add: PO Box 997, 05477), SAN 317-1108. Tel: 802-434-3036. FAX: 802-434-3223. E-mail: library@richmondvt.gov. Web Site: richmondfreelibraryvt.org. *Dir,* Rebecca Mueller; *Asst Dir, Youth Serv Librn,* Wendy de Forest; E-mail: rfl@gmavt.net; Staff 4 (MLS 1, Non-MLS 3)
Pop 4,090; Circ 37,600
Library Holdings: Bk Vols 23,684
Automation Activity & Vendor Info: (Cataloging) Koha; (Circulation) Koha; (Course Reserve) Koha; (OPAC) Koha
Wireless access
Partic in Green Mountain Library Consortium
Open Mon & Wed 10-8, Tues & Thurs 1-6, Fri 10-6, Sat 10-2
Friends of the Library Group

ROCHESTER

P ROCHESTER PUBLIC LIBRARY*, 22 S Main St, Rte 100, 05767. (Mail add: PO Box 256, 05767), SAN 317-1124. Tel: 802-767-3927. E-mail: rochesterpubliclibraryvt@gmail.com. Web Site: www.rochestervtpubliclibrary.com. *Dir,* Jeannette Bair
Founded 1801. Pop 1,201; Circ 15,000
Library Holdings: Large Print Bks 25; Bk Vols 18,500; Talking Bks 600
Special Collections: Ecology Material; Vermont Books
Wireless access
Open Tues & Thurs 12:30-7, Sat 9-1

ROXBURY

P ROXBURY FREE LIBRARY*, 1491 Roxbury Rd, 05669. (Mail add: PO Box 95, 05669-0095), SAN 376-3447. Tel: 802-485-6860. FAX: 802-485-4645. E-mail: librarian@roxburyfreelibrary.org. Web Site: roxburyfreelibrary.org. *Libr Dir,* Ryan Zajac; Staff 1 (Non-MLS 1)
Founded 1913. Pop 600; Circ 1,000
Library Holdings: Audiobooks 60; DVDs 30; Large Print Bks 20; Bk Titles 5,000; Talking Bks 100; Videos 50
Wireless access
Mem of Midstate Regional Library
Special Services for the Blind - Large print bks; Large print bks & talking machines
Open Tues 10-6, Wed 8-11, Thurs 2-7, Sat 10-1

RUPERT

P R K KITTAY PUBLIC LIBRARY*, 2827 Hwy 153, 05768. (Mail add: PO Box 53, West Rupert, 05776-0053). Tel: 802-394-2444. FAX: 802-394-2444. E-mail: rupertkittaylibrary@gmail.com. Web Site: www.rupertkittaylibrary.org. *Dir,* Paul Thompson
Founded 1999. Pop 709
Jan 2016-Dec 2016 Income $25,000
Library Holdings: Bk Vols 6,621
Special Collections: Art Coll
Wireless access
Function: Adult bk club, Art exhibits, Audio & video playback equip for onsite use, Bks on cassette, Bks on CD, Children's prog, Computers for patron use, ILL available, Photocopying/Printing, Spoken cassettes & CDs, Spoken cassettes & DVDs, Summer reading prog, VHS videos, Wheelchair accessible
Open Tues & Thurs 4-7, Wed, Fri & Sat 10-1

RUTLAND

P RUTLAND FREE LIBRARY*, Ten Court St, 05701-4058. SAN 317-1167. Tel: 802-773-1860. E-mail: rutlandfree@rutlandfree.org. Web Site: rutlandfree.org. *Dir,* Randal Smathers; E-mail: randal@rutlandfree.org; *Asst Dir,* Amy Williams; E-mail: amy@rutlandfree.org; *Ad,* Janet Clapp; E-mail: janet@rutlandfree.org; *Circ Supvr,* Gabrielle Turney; E-mail: gabrielle@rutlandfree.org; *Ch Serv,* Amanda Begin; E-mail: amanda@rutlandfree.org; Staff 5 (MLS 4, Non-MLS 1)
Founded 1886. Pop 22,900; Circ 160,000
Library Holdings: AV Mats 6,000; Electronic Media & Resources 15; Large Print Bks 2,600; Bk Vols 79,995; Per Subs 40
Special Collections: Vermont & Regional History
Automation Activity & Vendor Info: (Cataloging) Koha; (Circulation) Koha; (OPAC) Koha
Wireless access
Partic in Catamount Library Network
Open Mon, Thurs & Fri 10-5:30, Tues & Wed 10-8:30, Sat 10-5
Friends of the Library Group

M RUTLAND REGIONAL MEDICAL CENTER*, Health Science Library, 160 Allen St, 05701. SAN 317-1175. Tel: 802-747-3777. FAX: 802-747-3955. Web Site: rrmc.libguides.com/HIL. *Librn,* Cristina Muia; E-mail: cmmuia@rrmc.org
Library Holdings: Bk Vols 1,000; Per Subs 90
Subject Interests: Consumer health
Automation Activity & Vendor Info: (Cataloging) CyberTools for Libraries
Partic in Health Sciences Libraries of New Hampshire & Vermont
Open Mon-Fri 11-5

SAINT ALBANS

P SAINT ALBANS FREE LIBRARY*, 11 Maiden Lane, 05478. SAN 317-1248. Tel: 802-524-1507. FAX: 802-524-1514. E-mail: stalbansfreelibrary@gmail.com. Web Site: www.stalbansfreelibrary.org. *Dir,* MaryPat Larrabee; *Asst Dir, YA Librn,* Becky Manahan; *Ad,* Roberta Schmidlen; Staff 4 (MLS 4)
Founded 1900. Pop 12,917; Circ 67,650
Library Holdings: Bk Titles 37,900; Per Subs 120
Special Collections: Vermontiana

Wireless access
Publications: The Bookworm
Open Mon, Wed & Fri 10-6, Tues & Thurs 10-8, Sat 10-3
Friends of the Library Group

SAINT JOHNSBURY

S FAIRBANKS MUSEUM & PLANETARIUM*, Kitchel Center for the Study of the Northeast Kingdom, 1302 Main St, 05819. SAN 317-1256. Tel: 802-748-2372. Web Site: www.fairbanksmuseum.org. *Archivist/Librn,* Pat Swartz; E-mail: pswartz@fairbanksmuseum.org
Library Holdings: Bk Titles 1,001; Bk Vols 2,500
Special Collections: Archives Coll; History of Northeast Kingdom of Vermont (Caledonia, Orleans & Essex Counties); Vermont History Coll
Subject Interests: Local hist, Sci
Function: Res libr
Restriction: Not open to pub, Open to others by appt, Staff use only
Friends of the Library Group

M NORTHEASTERN VERMONT REGIONAL HOSPITAL, Marilyn L Moulton Community Health Resource Center, 1315 Hospital Dr, 05819. SAN 369-4658. Tel: 802-748-7501. FAX: 802-748-7316. Web Site: nvrh.org/Community-health-resource-center. *Health Res Ctr Coordr,* Mary Maurer; E-mail: m.maurer@nvrh.org
Founded 1972
Library Holdings: AV Mats 35; High Interest/Low Vocabulary Bk Vols 100; Bk Titles 800; Per Subs 15; Videos 30
Subject Interests: Allied health, Commun health, Med, Nursing, Substance abuse
Wireless access
Partic in North Atlantic Health Sciences Libraries, Inc

P SAINT JOHNSBURY ATHENAEUM*, 1171 Main St, 05819-2289. Tel: 802-748-8291. E-mail: inform@stjathenaeum.org. Web Site: www.stjathenaeum.org. *Dir,* Robert Joly; Staff 7 (MLS 4, Non-MLS 3)
Founded 1871. Pop 7,556; Circ 69,584
Library Holdings: Audiobooks 1,903; AV Mats 2,022; Large Print Bks 1,000; Bk Vols 44,940; Per Subs 35
Special Collections: Fine Art Hudson River School, 100 wks of art (orgs & reprod, incl 10 statues)
Automation Activity & Vendor Info: (Acquisitions) Koha; (Cataloging) Koha; (Circulation) Koha; (ILL) Koha; (OPAC) Koha; (Serials) EBSCO Online
Wireless access
Function: 24/7 Electronic res, 24/7 Online cat, Archival coll, Art exhibits, Bks on CD, Children's prog, Computer training, Computers for patron use, Digital talking bks, E-Readers, Electronic databases & coll, Free DVD rentals, Holiday prog, ILL available, Magazines, Mail & tel request accepted, Microfiche/film & reading machines, Movies, Museum passes, Music CDs, Online cat, Outreach serv, OverDrive digital audio bks, Photocopying/Printing, Preschool outreach, Preschool reading prog, Printer for laptops & handheld devices, Prog for adults, Prog for children & young adult, Ref & res, Scanner, Serves people with intellectual disabilities, Story hour, Summer & winter reading prog, Tax forms, Teen prog, Visual arts prog, Wheelchair accessible, Workshops
Open Mon, Wed & Fri 10-4, Tues & Thurs 12-4, Sat 10-2
Restriction: Non-circulating of rare bks, Pub use on premises, Ref only
Friends of the Library Group

SHARON

P EDWARD K BAXTER MEMORIAL LIBRARY*, 5114 Rte 14, 05065. (Mail add: PO Box 87, 05065), SAN 317-1329. Tel: 802-763-2875. E-mail: sharonbaxterlibrary@gmail.com. Web Site: sharonvtlibrary.com. *Dir,* Shana Hickman; Staff 1 (Non-MLS 1)
Founded 1928. Pop 1,500; Circ 2,100
Library Holdings: Large Print Bks 15; Bk Titles 6,000; Talking Bks 135
Wireless access
Function: 24/7 Electronic res, 24/7 Online cat, Audiobks via web, AV serv, Bks on CD, Butterfly Garden, Children's prog, Computer training, Computers for patron use, Digital talking bks, Distance learning, Electronic databases & coll, Family literacy, Free DVD rentals, ILL available, Internet access, Laminating, Life-long learning prog for all ages, Literacy & newcomer serv, Mail & tel request accepted, Movies, Museum passes, Online cat, Outside serv via phone, mail, e-mail & web, OverDrive digital audio bks, Photocopying/Printing, Prog for adults, Prog for children & young adult, Ref & res, Ref serv available, Res assist avail, Scanner, Serves people with intellectual disabilities, Summer reading prog, Telephone ref, Wheelchair accessible, Workshops, Writing prog
Open Tues, Thurs & Fri 2-6, Sat 10-Noon

SHELBURNE

P PIERSON LIBRARY*, 5376 Shelburne Rd, 05482. SAN 317-1337. Tel: 802-985-5124. Interlibrary Loan Service Tel: 802-264-5016. E-mail: circulation@shelburnvt.org. Web Site: piersonlibrary.org. *Libr Dir,* Position Currently Open; *Circ,* Lisa McCullough; E-mail: lmccullough@shelburnevt.org; *Tech Serv,* Katie Martin-Woodard; *Youth Serv,* Katie Bosley; Staff 8 (Non-MLS 8)
Founded 1888. Pop 7,100; Circ 97,793
Library Holdings: Bk Titles 27,692; Bk Vols 30,267; Per Subs 95; Talking Bks 832; Videos 629
Automation Activity & Vendor Info: (Acquisitions) Baker & Taylor; (Cataloging) OCLC CatExpress; (Circulation) ByWater Solutions; (OPAC) ByWater Solutions
Wireless access
Function: Adult bk club, Art exhibits, Audiobks via web, Bks on CD, Children's prog, Computer training, Computers for patron use, Digital talking bks, Electronic databases & coll, Free DVD rentals, Holiday prog, Homebound delivery serv, ILL available, Museum passes, Notary serv, Online cat, OverDrive digital audio bks, Photocopying/Printing, Prog for adults, Prog for children & young adult, Story hour, Summer reading prog, Tax forms, Wheelchair accessible
Partic in Green Mountain Library Consortium
Open Mon & Sun Noon-5, Tues 10-7, Wed-Sat 10-5
Friends of the Library Group

S SHELBURNE MUSEUM LIBRARY*, 5555 Shelburne Rd, 05482-7491. (Mail add: PO Box 10, 05482-0010), SAN 317-1345. Tel: 802-985-3346. FAX: 802-985-2331. E-mail: info@shelburnemuseum.org, library@shelburnemuseum.org. Web Site: www.shelburnemuseum.org. *Libr & Archives Mgr,* Allison Gillette; Tel: 802-985-3346, E-mail: agillette@shelburnemuseum.org; Staff 1 (MLS 1)
Founded 1947
Library Holdings: Bk Vols 6,000; Per Subs 25
Subject Interests: Am art, Antiques, Contemporary design, Decorative art, Folk art
Function: Archival coll, Res libr
Restriction: Open by appt only

SHELDON

P SHELDON MUNICIPAL LIBRARY*, 1640 Main St, 05483. SAN 376-8007. Tel: 802-933-2524, 802-933-2524, Ext 7. E-mail: smibrarian@gmail.com. Web Site: www.sheldonlibrary.org. *Librn,* Beth Nye
Pop 2,303; Circ 6,141
Library Holdings: Audiobooks 186; Bk Vols 5,768; Per Subs 26; Videos 70
Wireless access
Partic in Collaborative Libraries of Vermont
Open Tues 8-12 & 1-3, Thurs 1-3 & 6-8, Sat 8-Noon
Friends of the Library Group

SHOREHAM

P PLATT MEMORIAL LIBRARY*, 279 Main St, 05770. SAN 317-1353. Tel: 802-897-2647. E-mail: platt@shoreham.net. Web Site: www.plattlib.org. *Librn,* Abigail Adams; *Asst Librn,* Robin Severy
Founded 1823. Pop 1,300
Library Holdings: Bk Titles 11,730; Per Subs 20; Talking Bks 311; Videos 384
Wireless access
Partic in Vermont Automated Libr Syst
Open Mon & Wed 10-6, Thurs Noon-7, Sat 9-1

SOUTH BURLINGTON

P SOUTH BURLINGTON COMMUNITY LIBRARY*, 180 Market St, 05403. SAN 317-1361. Tel: 802-846-4140. FAX: 802-652-7013. E-mail: sbplinfo@southburlingtonvt.gov. Web Site: southburlingtonlibrary.org. *Libr Dir,* Jennifer Murray; E-mail: jmurray@SouthBurlingtonVT.gov; *Ch,* Kelly Kendall; *Supvr, Circ,* Kathryn Plageman; Staff 4 (MLS 1, Non-MLS 3)
Founded 1972. Pop 19,500; Circ 90,000
Library Holdings: Bk Vols 52,000; Per Subs 123
Automation Activity & Vendor Info: (Cataloging) Auto-Graphics, Inc; (Circulation) Auto-Graphics, Inc; (OPAC) Auto-Graphics, Inc
Wireless access
Partic in Collaborative Libraries of Vermont
Open Mon-Thurs 10-7, Fri 10-5, Sat 10-2
Friends of the Library Group

SOUTH HERO

P WORTHEN LIBRARY*, 28 Community Lane, 05486. SAN 317-137X. Tel: 802-372-6209. FAX: 802-372-5188. E-mail: southherolibrary@gmail.com. Web Site: southherolibrary.org. *Dir,* Keagan Calkins; Staff 2 (MLS 2)
Founded 1974. Pop 1,168; Circ 10,544
Library Holdings: Bk Vols 12,874; Per Subs 12
Wireless access

Open Mon, Tues & Thurs 10-3, Wed 10-8, Fri & Sat 10-2
Friends of the Library Group

SOUTH LONDONDERRY

P SOUTH LONDONDERRY FREE LIBRARY*, 15 Old School St, 05155. (Mail add: PO Box 95, 05155-0095), SAN 317-1388. Tel: 802-824-3371. FAX: 802-824-3371. E-mail: southlondonderryfreelibrary@yahoo.com. Web Site: www.southlondonderryfreelibrary.org. *Dir,* Mary Butera; Staff 1 (Non-MLS 1)
Founded 1892. Pop 1,902; Circ 8,102
Library Holdings: AV Mats 500; CDs 400; DVDs 100; Large Print Bks 300; Bk Vols 17,500; Per Subs 50; Talking Bks 200; Videos 75
Subject Interests: Art, Civil War, Classics, Vt
Wireless access
Partic in Collaborative Libraries of Vermont; Vt Libr Asn
Special Services for the Deaf - Adult & family literacy prog; Bks on deafness & sign lang
Special Services for the Blind - Bks available with recordings
Open Mon, Wed & Fri 10-5, Sat 10-1

SOUTH POMFRET

P ABBOTT MEMORIAL LIBRARY*, 15 Library St, 05067. (Mail add: PO Box 95, 05067-0095), SAN 317-1396. Tel: 802-457-2236. E-mail: abbottlibrary@gmail.com. Web Site: abbottmemoriallibrary.org. *Libr Dir,* Cory Smith; *Asst Librn,* Sue Heston
Pop 994; Circ 3,750
Library Holdings: Bk Vols 6,000
Special Collections: Thomas Ware Primitive Portraits
Automation Activity & Vendor Info: (Cataloging) LibraryWorld, Inc; (Circulation) LibraryWorld, Inc; (OPAC) LibraryWorld, Inc
Wireless access
Open Tues & Thurs 10-6, Sat 10-2

SOUTH ROYALTON

P ROYALTON MEMORIAL LIBRARY*, 23 Alexander Pl, 05068. (Mail add: PO Box 179, 05068-0179), SAN 317-1418. Tel: 802-763-7094. E-mail: librarian@royaltonlibrary.org. Web Site: www.royaltonlibrary.org. *Libr Dir,* Marianne Pysarchyk
Founded 1923. Pop 2,300; Circ 14,643
Library Holdings: Bk Vols 12,000; Per Subs 40
Automation Activity & Vendor Info: (Cataloging) Mandarin Library Automation; (Circulation) Mandarin Library Automation
Wireless access
Function: Adult bk club, After school storytime, Art exhibits, Audio & video playback equip for onsite use, Audiobks via web, Bks on CD, Children's prog, Computers for patron use, Electronic databases & coll, Free DVD rentals, Holiday prog, Home delivery & serv to seniorr ctr & nursing homes, Homebound delivery serv, Museum passes, Online cat, Outreach serv, OverDrive digital audio bks, Photocopying/Printing, Preschool reading prog, Senior outreach, Story hour, Summer reading prog
Mem of Midstate Regional Library
Partic in Catamount Library Network; Vermont Automated Libr Syst
Open Tues-Fri 12-6, Sat 10-1

CL VERMONT LAW SCHOOL*, Julien & Virginia Cornell Library, 164 Chelsea St, 05068. (Mail add: PO Box 96, 05068-0060), SAN 317-1426. Tel: 802-831-1461. Administration Tel: 802-831-1449. FAX: 802-831-1408. E-mail: reference@vermontlaw.edu. Web Site: www.vermontlaw.edu/academics/library. *Asst Prof of Law, Libr Dir,* Jane Woldo; E-mail: jwoldow@vermontlaw.edu; *Librn,* Christine Ryan; Tel: 802-831-1448, E-mail: cryan@vermontlaw.edu; *ILS Adminr,* Lisa Donadio; Tel: 802-831-1442, E-mail: ldonadio@vermontlaw.edu; *Access Serv Librn, ILL Librn,* Michele Dill LaRose; Tel: 802-831-1403, E-mail: mlarose@vermontlaw.edu. Subject Specialists: *Environ law,* Christine Ryan; Staff 10 (MLS 6, Non-MLS 4)
Founded 1973. Enrl 650; Fac 61; Highest Degree: Doctorate
Library Holdings: Bk Vols 248,283; Per Subs 2,420
Special Collections: Environmental & Historic Preservation Coll. US Document Depository
Subject Interests: Law
Automation Activity & Vendor Info: (Acquisitions) Innovative Interfaces, Inc; (Cataloging) Innovative Interfaces, Inc; (Circulation) Innovative Interfaces, Inc; (ILL) OCLC FirstSearch; (OPAC) Innovative Interfaces, Inc; (Serials) Innovative Interfaces, Inc
Wireless access
Function: Accelerated reader prog
Partic in LYRASIS; NELLCO Law Library Consortium, Inc.
Open Mon-Fri 8am-9pm, Sat & Sun 9-9
Friends of the Library Group

SOUTH RYEGATE

P SOUTH RYEGATE PUBLIC LIBRARY, INC, 140 Church St, 05069. SAN 320-5207. Tel: 802-584-3675. *Librn,* Elizabeth Achilles
Founded 1954. Pop 1,150
Subject Interests: Ryegate hist
Wireless access
Open Tues 12-2, Thurs 3-5

SPRINGFIELD

P SPRINGFIELD TOWN LIBRARY*, 43 Main St, 05156. SAN 317-1450. Tel: 802-885-3108. FAX: 802-885-3499. E-mail: springfieldlibrary@hotmail.com, stlib@vermontel.net. Web Site: www.springfieldtownlibrary.org. *Libr Dir,* Sue Dowdell; *Ad,* Tracey Craft; E-mail: stlas@vermontel.net; *Youth Serv Librn,* Michelle Stinson; E-mail: stlys@vermontel.net; *Circ Supvr,* Tammy Gould; E-mail: stlcirc@vermontel.net; *IT Coordr,* Christopher Bloomfield; E-mail: stlit@vermontel.net; *Tech Serv,* Tracy Obremski; E-mail: stlts@vermontel.net; Staff 3 (MLS 1, Non-MLS 2)
Founded 1819. Pop 9,078; Circ 53,983
Library Holdings: Audiobooks 2,879; DVDs 2,091; Electronic Media & Resources 83; Bk Vols 49,087; Per Subs 133
Subject Interests: Alternative tech, Machine tool
Automation Activity & Vendor Info: (Cataloging) OCLC; (Circulation) Koha; (OPAC) Koha
Wireless access
Function: 24/7 Electronic res, 24/7 Online cat, Activity rm, Adult bk club, After school storytime
Publications: FOSTL (Quarterly newsletter)
Partic in Catamount Library Network; Green Mountain Library Consortium
Special Services for the Deaf - Bks on deafness & sign lang; High interest/low vocabulary bks
Special Services for the Blind - Accessible computers; Bks available with recordings; Bks on CD; Copier with enlargement capabilities; Home delivery serv; Large print bks; Magnifiers; Merlin electronic magnifier reader; Talking bk serv referral; ZoomText magnification & reading software
Open Mon-Thurs 9-7, Fri 9-5, Sat 10-1
Friends of the Library Group

STAMFORD

P STAMFORD COMMUNITY LIBRARY*, 986 Main Rd, 05352. SAN 317-1469. Tel: 802-694-1379. FAX: 802-694-1636. E-mail: stamlibrary@gmail.com. Web Site: www.stamfordlibrary.org. *Town Librn,* Danielle Smith; Staff 1 (Non-MLS 1)
Founded 1960. Circ 11,573
Library Holdings: Audiobooks 150; Bks on Deafness & Sign Lang 5; DVDs 150; Large Print Bks 4; Bk Vols 9,143; Per Subs 10
Automation Activity & Vendor Info: (Cataloging) Follett Software; (Circulation) Follett Software; (OPAC) Follett Software
Wireless access
Function: 24/7 Online cat, ILL available, Spoken cassettes & CDs, Summer reading prog, VHS videos
Partic in Collaborative Libraries of Vermont
Open Tues & Thurs 3-8, Fri 9-4, Sat 9-1

STARKSBORO

P STARKSBORO PUBLIC LIBRARY*, 2827 VT Rte 116, 05487. (Mail add: PO Box 124, 05487-0124), SAN 376-3471. Tel: 802-453-3732. E-mail: starksboropl@comcast.net. Web Site: starksborolibrary.wordpress.com. *Librn,* Catherine Goldsmith; *Libr Asst,* Lynn Stewart Parker; Staff 2 (MLS 1, Non-MLS 1)
Pop 1,875
Library Holdings: Bk Vols 4,500; Per Subs 20
Wireless access
Function: ILL available, Photocopying/Printing, Prog for adults, Prog for children & young adult, Wheelchair accessible
Partic in Catamount Library Network
Open Mon 10-6, Thurs 10-5, Sat 9-2

STOWE

P STOWE FREE LIBRARY*, 90 Pond St, 05672. (Mail add: PO Box 1029, 05672-1029), SAN 317-1485. Tel: 802-253-6145. E-mail: library@stowevt.gov. Web Site: www.stowelibrary.org. *Dir,* Cindy Weber; Tel: 802-253-6145, Ext 16; Staff 5 (MLS 3, Non-MLS 2)
Founded 1866. Pop 4,339; Circ 101,837
Library Holdings: AV Mats 3,582; Bk Vols 26,091; Per Subs 103
Special Collections: Vermont & Stowe History Coll
Wireless access
Function: Activity rm, Adult bk club, Bk club(s), Children's prog, Computers for patron use, Family literacy, ILL available, Internet access, Mango lang, Online cat, Photocopying/Printing, Preschool reading prog,

Printer for laptops & handheld devices, Prog for adults, Prog for children & young adult, Ref serv available, Spoken cassettes & CDs, Spoken cassettes & DVDs, Story hour, Summer & winter reading prog, Summer reading prog, Wheelchair accessible
Partic in Green Mountain Library Consortium
Open Mon, Wed & Fri 9:30-5:30, Tues & Thurs 12-7, Sat 10-3
Friends of the Library Group

STRAFFORD

P MORRILL MEMORIAL & HARRIS LIBRARY*, 220 Justin Morrill Memorial Hwy, 05072-9730. (Mail add: PO Box 110, 05072-0110), SAN 317-1493. Tel: 802-765-4037. E-mail: straffordvtlibrary@gmail.com. Web Site: www.straffordlibrary.org. *Dir,* Melissa Strayton
Pop 1,098; Circ 11,100
Library Holdings: Bk Vols 10,000
Special Collections: Senator Justin Smith Morrill Coll
Wireless access
Mem of Midstate Regional Library
Partic in Collaborative Libraries of Vermont
Open Mon 1-8, Wed 2-5, Thurs 10-5, Sat 9-Noon
Friends of the Library Group

SWANTON

S NORTHWEST STATE CORRECTIONAL FACILITY LIBRARY, 3649 Lower Newton Rd, 05488. SAN 317-123X. Tel: 802-524-6771. FAX: 802-527-7534. *Library Contact,* Julie Dickie; E-mail: julie.dickie@vermont.gov
Founded 1967
Library Holdings: Bk Vols 3,500

P SWANTON PUBLIC LIBRARY*, One First St, 05488. SAN 317-1515. Tel: 802-868-7656. Web Site: swantonlibrary.org. *Dir,* Abigael Gaudette; E-mail: director@swantonlibrary.org; *Youth Serv Dir,* Hilarie Santiago; *ILL Coordr,* Darla Blondo; Staff 2 (MLS 1, Non-MLS 1)
Founded 1915. Pop 6,500; Circ 16,707
Library Holdings: Bk Vols 17,000; Per Subs 34
Special Collections: Large Print Books; Local Genealogy Coll; Old Vermont History Coll
Wireless access
Function: 24/7 Electronic res, 24/7 Online cat, Activity rm, Adult bk club, Audiobks via web, Bk club(s), Bks on CD, Children's prog, Computers for patron use, Family literacy, For res purposes, Holiday prog, ILL available, Internet access, Magazines, Mail & tel request accepted, Meeting rooms, Movies, Museum passes, Online cat, Online info literacy tutorials on the web & in blackboard, Online ref, OverDrive digital audio bks, Photocopying/Printing, Prog for adults, Prog for children & young adult, Ref & res, Scanner, Senior outreach, Story hour, Summer reading prog, Tax forms, Teen prog, Wheelchair accessible, Workshops, Writing prog
Special Services for the Blind - Large print bks
Open Mon, Wed & Fri 10-6, Tues Thurs & Sat 10-2

THETFORD

P LATHAM MEMORIAL LIBRARY*, 16 Library Lane, 05074. (Mail add: PO Box 240, 05074-0240), SAN 362-6490. Tel: 802-785-4361. FAX: 802-785-4361. E-mail: librarian@thetfordlibrary.org. Web Site: thetfordlibrary.org. *Dir,* Holly Lague; *Asst Dir,* Emily Zollo; Staff 2 (MLS 2)
Founded 1876. Pop 2,617; Circ 18,626
Library Holdings: AV Mats 137; Bk Vols 11,987; Per Subs 25; Talking Bks 241
Special Collections: Peabody Coll; Thetford Authors; Vermont Coll
Automation Activity & Vendor Info: (Cataloging) OPALS (Open-source Automated Library System); (Circulation) OPALS (Open-source Automated Library System); (OPAC) OPALS (Open-source Automated Library System)
Wireless access
Function: 24/7 Online cat, After school storytime, Art exhibits, Audiobks via web, Bks on CD, Computers for patron use, Digital talking bks, E-Readers, Electronic databases & coll, Free DVD rentals, ILL available, Internet access, Magazines, Meeting rooms, Museum passes, Online cat, OverDrive digital audio bks, Photocopying/Printing, Prog for adults, Prog for children & young adult, Scanner, Story hour, Tax forms, Wheelchair accessible, Winter reading prog
Partic in Librarians of the Upper Valley Coop
Open Mon & Thurs 2-8, Tues 2-5, Wed & Fri 10-5, Sat 10-1

TINMOUTH

P TINMOUTH PUBLIC LIBRARY, Nine MountainView Rd, 05773. SAN 376-4001. Tel: 802-446-2498. FAX: 802-446-2498. E-mail: tinmouthtown@vermontel.net. Web Site: tinmouthvt.org/tinmouth-library. *Librn,* Ruth Drachman
Library Holdings: Bk Vols 4,000
Wireless access
Open Mon & Thurs 9:30-12 & 1-4

TOWNSHEND

P TOWNSHEND PUBLIC LIBRARY*, 1971 Rte 30, 05353. (Mail add: PO Box 252, 05353-0252), SAN 317-1523. Tel: 802-365-4039. E-mail: townshendpubliclibrary@gmail.com. Web Site: www.townshendpubliclibrary.org. *Librn,* Karen LaRue; *Asst Librn,* Beth Etman
Founded 1899. Pop 1,149; Circ 8,500
Library Holdings: Bk Vols 15,000; Per Subs 10
Special Collections: Vermont History Coll; West River Valley History Coll. State Document Depository
Automation Activity & Vendor Info: (Acquisitions) LibraryWorld, Inc; (Cataloging) LibraryWorld, Inc; (Circulation) LibraryWorld, Inc; (OPAC) LibraryWorld, Inc
Wireless access
Publications: Atheneum
Partic in Collaborative Libraries of Vermont
Open Mon 1-5, Tues, Fri & Sat 9-1, Wed 1-7
Friends of the Library Group

TUNBRIDGE

P TUNBRIDGE PUBLIC LIBRARY*, 289 Vt Rte 110, 05077. (Mail add: PO Box 9, 05077-0009), SAN 317-1531. Tel: 802-889-9404. FAX: 802-889-9404. E-mail: tunbridgelibrary@gmail.com. Web Site: www.tunbridgelibrary.org. *Librn,* Jean Wolfe; Staff 1 (Non-MLS 1)
Library Holdings: Audiobooks 664; Bk Vols 9,200; Per Subs 10; Videos 714
Special Collections: Vermont Coll
Wireless access
Open Mon & Wed 3-8, Thurs & Fri 3-6, Sat 9-3
Friends of the Library Group

VERGENNES

P BIXBY MEMORIAL FREE LIBRARY*, 258 Main St, 05491. SAN 317-1558. Tel: 802-877-2211. FAX: 802-877-2411. Web Site: www.bixbylibrary.org. *Dir,* Catharine Hays; E-mail: catharine.hays@bixbylibrary.org; *Ad,* Laksamee Putnam Cave; E-mail: laksamee.putnam@bixbylibrary.org; Staff 6 (MLS 2, Non-MLS 4)
Founded 1912. Pop 7,897; Circ 50,102
Library Holdings: Bks on Deafness & Sign Lang 12; CDs 713; DVDs 896; Large Print Bks 913; Bk Titles 28,520; Per Subs 23
Special Collections: Antiques (Cup Plate Coll); Native American Coll; Paperweight Coll; Stamp Coll; Vermont History Coll
Automation Activity & Vendor Info: (Cataloging) LibraryWorld, Inc; (Circulation) LibraryWorld, Inc; (OPAC) LibraryWorld, Inc
Wireless access
Function: Computers for patron use, Magnifiers for reading, Microfiche/film & reading machines, Museum passes, Online cat, Outreach serv, OverDrive digital audio bks, Photocopying/Printing, Preschool outreach, Preschool reading prog, Prog for adults, Prog for children & young adult, Ref & res, Ref serv available, Scanner, Story hour, Summer & winter reading prog, Summer reading prog, Tax forms, Teen prog, VHS videos, Wheelchair accessible, Workshops
Open Mon 12:30-8, Tues & Fri 12:30-5, Wed & Thurs 10-5, Sat 10-2
Restriction: Non-circulating coll, Non-circulating of rare bks, Non-circulating to the pub, Non-resident fee, Open to others by appt, Open to students, Pub use on premises
Friends of the Library Group

VERNON

P VERNON FREE LIBRARY*, 567 Governor Hunt Rd, 05354. SAN 317-1574. Tel: 802-257-0150. FAX: 802-257-4949. E-mail: vernonfreelibrary@comcast.net. Web Site: www.vernonfreelibrary.org. *Dir,* Jean Carr; *Libr Asst,* Beth Armington
Founded 1905. Pop 2,141; Circ 15,494
Library Holdings: Bk Vols 17,000; Per Subs 52
Automation Activity & Vendor Info: (Cataloging) LibLime; (Circulation) LibLime; (OPAC) LibLime
Wireless access
Function: 24/7 Online cat, Adult bk club, Audiobks via web, Bks on CD, Chess club, Children's prog, Computers for patron use, Electronic databases & coll, Free DVD rentals, Homebound delivery serv, ILL available, Internet access, Magazines, Mail & tel request accepted, Museum passes, Music CDs, Online cat, Online ref, OverDrive digital audio bks, Photocopying/Printing, Prog for children & young adult, Res assist avail, Scanner, Story hour, Summer reading prog, Tax forms, Telephone ref, Wheelchair accessible
Open Mon, Wed & Thurs 1-6, Tues 9-12 & 1-6, Sat 9-Noon

VERSHIRE

P VERSHIRE COMMUNITY LIBRARY*, Church-Orr House, Rte 113, 05079. (Mail add: PO Box 112, 05079-0112). Tel: 802-685-9982. E-mail: library@vershare.org. Web Site: www.vershare.org/library. *Dir,* Andrea Harrington
Founded 2002
Library Holdings: Bk Vols 4,000; Talking Bks 70
Open Wed 10-Noon, Thurs 2-5, Sat 10-1

WAITSFIELD

P JOSLIN MEMORIAL LIBRARY*, 4391 Main St, 05673-6155. (Mail add: PO Box 359, 05673-0359), SAN 317-1590. Tel: 802-496-4205. Web Site: www.joslinmemoriallibrary.com. *Libr Dir,* Jason Butler; E-mail: directorjml@gmavt.net; *Ch,* Anna Church; E-mail: kidsjml@madriver.com; *Prog Coordr,* Shevonne Travers; E-mail: joslinprograms@gmail.com; Staff 4 (MLS 1, Non-MLS 3)
Founded 1913. Pop 2,860; Circ 14,400
Jul 2017-Jun 2018 Income $164,022, State $300, City $72,761, Locally Generated Income $90,961. Mats Exp $9,250, Books $8,300, Per/Ser (Incl. Access Fees) $550, AV Mat $400. Sal $36,608 (Prof $31,200)
Library Holdings: Audiobooks 600; CDs 10; Bk Vols 9,000; Per Subs 35
Special Collections: Vermont Coll
Wireless access
Function: 24/7 Electronic res, 24/7 Online cat, Adult literacy prog, Audiobks via web, Bks on CD, Children's prog, Computer training, Computers for patron use, Digital talking bks, E-Readers, Electronic databases & coll, Equip loans & repairs, Home delivery & serv to seniorr ctr & nursing homes, Homebound delivery serv, ILL available, Internet access, Life-long learning prog for all ages, Magazines, Mail & tel request accepted, Mail loans to mem, Museum passes, Online cat, Outside serv via phone, mail, e-mail & web, OverDrive digital audio bks, Photocopying/Printing, Printer for laptops & handheld devices, Prog for adults, Prog for children & young adult, Scanner, Story hour, Summer & winter reading prog, Tax forms, Telephone ref, Winter reading prog
Partic in Green Mountain Library Consortium; Vermont State Libr Syst
Special Services for the Blind - Large print bks
Open Mon-Thurs 10-5, Sat 10-2
Restriction: Authorized patrons, Circ to mem only, Free to mem, In-house use for visitors, Non-circulating coll, Non-circulating of rare bks, Registered patrons only
Friends of the Library Group

WALLINGFORD

P GILBERT HART LIBRARY*, 14 S Main St, 05773. (Mail add: PO Box 69, 05773-0069), SAN 317-1612. Tel: 802-446-2685. FAX: 802-446-2685. E-mail: ghlib@comcast.net. Web Site: ghlib.wordpress.com. *Librn,* Wendy Savery; *Asst Librn,* Susan Gilbert; Staff 1 (Non-MLS 1)
Founded 1795. Pop 2,300
Library Holdings: DVDs 50; Large Print Bks 128; Bk Vols 19,100; Per Subs 50; Talking Bks 700; Videos 150
Special Collections: Vermontiana Coll
Wireless access
Partic in Green Mountain Library Consortium
Open Mon, Thurs & Fri 10-5, Wed 10-8, Sat 9-Noon
Friends of the Library Group

WARDSBORO

P WARDSBORO FREE PUBLIC LIBRARY*, 170 Main St, 05355. (Mail add: PO Box 157, 05355-0157), SAN 317-1620. Tel: 802-896-6988. E-mail: wardsboropubliclibrary@gmail.com. Web Site: www.wardsboropubliclibrary.org. *Libr Dir,* Lizzie Ingraham
Pop 1,027; Circ 5,862
Library Holdings: Bk Vols 8,000; Talking Bks 200
Wireless access
Partic in Collaborative Libraries of Vermont
Open Tues & Wed 10-4, Thurs 2-7, Sat 9-2
Friends of the Library Group

WARREN

P WARREN PUBLIC LIBRARY*, 413 Main St, 05674. (Mail add: PO Box 287, 05674-0287), SAN 320-5215. Tel: 802-496-3913. FAX: 802-496-2418. Web Site: www.warrenlibrary.com. *Dir,* Marie Schmukal; E-mail: director@warrenlibrary.com; Staff 1.7 (MLS 1, Non-MLS 0.7)
Pop 1,705; Circ 14,444
Library Holdings: Audiobooks 746; DVDs 673; Large Print Bks 10; Bk Vols 8,398; Per Subs 30; Videos 281
Automation Activity & Vendor Info: (Acquisitions) ByWater Solutions; (Cataloging) ByWater Solutions; (Circulation) ByWater Solutions; (OPAC) ByWater Solutions
Wireless access
Function: Adult bk club, Audio & video playback equip for onsite use, Audiobks via web, Bk club(s), Bks on cassette, Bks on CD, Children's prog, Computers for patron use, Distance learning, Electronic databases & coll, Equip loans & repairs, Free DVD rentals, Health sci info serv, Homebound delivery serv, ILL available, Internet access, Museum passes, Music CDs, Online cat, Online ref, OverDrive digital audio bks, Photocopying/Printing, Printer for laptops & handheld devices, Prog for adults, Prog for children & young adult, Ref serv available, Scanner, Spoken cassettes & CDs, Story hour, Summer reading prog, Telephone ref, VHS videos, Wheelchair accessible, Workshops
Partic in Green Mountain Library Consortium; OCLC Online Computer Library Center, Inc
Open Mon & Fri 10-6, Wed 10-7, Sat 10-4; Mon & Fri 10-6, Tues 10-2, Wed 10-7, Sat 10-4 (Summer)
Friends of the Library Group

WASHINGTON

P CALEF MEMORIAL LIBRARY*, 2964 VT Rte 110, 05675. (Mail add: PO Box 141, 05675-0141), SAN 317-1639. Tel: 802-883-2343. E-mail: caleflibrary@gmail.com. Web Site: caleflibrary.com. *Librn,* Bethany N Beebe
Pop 1,092; Circ 3,048
Library Holdings: Bk Vols 5,900; Per Subs 24
Automation Activity & Vendor Info: (OPAC) ByWater Solutions
Wireless access
Function: Adult bk club, Audiobks via web, Bks on cassette, Bks on CD, Children's prog, Computer training, Computers for patron use, Distance learning, Electronic databases & coll, Free DVD rentals, Homebound delivery serv, Homework prog, ILL available, Internet access, Literacy & newcomer serv, Museum passes, Online cat, Orientations, OverDrive digital audio bks, Photocopying/Printing, Prog for children & young adult, Ref serv available, Scanner, Story hour, Summer reading prog, Telephone ref, VHS videos
Mem of Midstate Regional Library
Open Mon 11-4, Tues-Thurs 2-7, Sat 9-1

WATERBURY

P WATERBURY PUBLIC LIBRARY*, 28 N Main St, Ste 2, 05676. SAN 317-1647. Tel: 802-244-7036. Web Site: www.waterburypubliclibrary.com. *Libr Dir,* Almy Landauer; E-mail: almy@waterburypubliclibrary.com
Circ 41,839
Library Holdings: Bk Vols 24,000; Per Subs 60; Talking Bks 704; Videos 857
Special Collections: Vermontiana
Automation Activity & Vendor Info: (Cataloging) TLC (The Library Corporation); (Circulation) TLC (The Library Corporation); (OPAC) TLC (The Library Corporation)
Wireless access
Mem of Midstate Regional Library
Partic in Catamount Library Network
Open Mon-Wed 10-8, Thurs & Fri 10-5, Sat 9-2 (Fall & Winter); Mon-Wed 10-8, Thurs & Fri 10-5, Sat 9-Noon (Spring & Summer)
Friends of the Library Group

WATERVILLE

P WATERVILLE TOWN LIBRARY*, 850 VT Rte 109, 05492. SAN 317-1663. E-mail: librarian@watervillelib.org. Web Site: www.watervillelib.org. *Vice Chair,* Alice Godin
Pop 673
Library Holdings: Bk Vols 3,900
Wireless access
Open Tues 9-12, Sat 9-3

WELLS

P WELLS VILLAGE LIBRARY*, Five E Wells Rd, 05774-9791. (Mail add: PO Box 587, 05774-0587), SAN 317-1671. Tel: 802-645-0611. E-mail: wellsvillagelibraryvt@gmail.com. Web Site: wellslibrary.com. *Dir,* Joy Brewster; *Asst Librn,* Erin Thompson
Founded 1944. Pop 902; Circ 1,942
Library Holdings: Bk Vols 6,827
Subject Interests: Adult fiction, Gen juv
Special Services for the Blind - Bks on cassette; Large print bks
Open Tues, Thurs & Fri 3-5, Wed 10-2, Sat 9-1

WELLS RIVER

P BALDWIN MEMORIAL LIBRARY*, 33 Main St N, 05081. (Mail add: PO Box 337, 05081), SAN 317-168X. Tel: 802-757-2693. E-mail: wells_river@vals.state.vt.us. Web Site: baldwinmemoriallibrary.wordpress.com. *Librn,* Peggy Hewes; Staff 1 (Non-MLS 1)
Pop 1,003; Circ 10,000

Library Holdings: Bk Vols 11,000; Per Subs 12
Special Collections: Non-Traditional Items
Wireless access
Open Mon 10-5, Wed 12-6, Fri 12-7

WEST BURKE

P WEST BURKE PUBLIC LIBRARY*, 123 VT Rte 5A, 05871. (Mail add: PO Box 283, 05871), SAN 317-1698. Tel: 201-519-3633. E-mail: westburkepubliclibrary@gmail.com. Web Site: burkevermont.org/library-west-burke.php, westburkepubliclibrary.wordpress.com. *Librn,* Judy Hishikawa
Pop 353; Circ 1,750
Library Holdings: AV Mats 25; Large Print Bks 76; Bk Vols 5,000; Talking Bks 55
Special Collections: Local and more Poets; Peggy McCoy Cookbook Coll; Vermont and Local Interest (diverse interest new and old)
Open Sat 1-4 (April-Dec); Thurs 2-4, Sat 1-4 (June-Aug)

WEST DANVILLE

P WALDEN COMMUNITY LIBRARY, 135 Cahoon Farm Rd, 05873. SAN 317-1604. Tel: 802-563-2195. E-mail: waldencommunitylibrary@outlook.com. *Librn,* Martha Bissell
Founded 1895. Pop 900; Circ 1,000
Library Holdings: Bk Vols 7,000
Special Collections: Vermont Coll
Wireless access
Open Mon 10-12 & 2-4, Tues 9-5, Wed 11-7, Sat 11-1

WEST DUMMERSTON

P LYDIA TAFT PRATT LIBRARY*, 150 West St, 05357. (Mail add: PO Box 70, 05357-0070), SAN 376-8015. Tel: 802-258-9878. E-mail: dummerstonvtlibrary@gmail.com. Web Site: dummerston.org/boards/library.asp. *Librn,* Dena Marger; Staff 1 (MLS 1)
Pop 1,769
Library Holdings: Audiobooks 99; DVDs 62; Large Print Bks 111; Bk Titles 3,330; Videos 20
Automation Activity & Vendor Info: (Cataloging) LibraryWorld, Inc; (OPAC) LibraryWorld, Inc
Wireless access
Function: 24/7 Electronic res, 24/7 Online cat, Activity rm, Adult bk club
Partic in Collaborative Libraries of Vermont
Open Tues 2:30-7, Thurs 10-5, Sat 9:30-Noon
Friends of the Library Group

WEST FAIRLEE

P WEST FAIRLEE FREE PUBLIC LIBRARY*, 894 Vt Rte 113, Unit 3, 05083-4405. SAN 317-171X. Tel: 802-333-3502. E-mail: westfairleelibrary@hotmail.com. Web Site: westfairleelibrary.wordpress.com. *Librn,* Viola Farrar
Founded 1908. Pop 337; Circ 900
Library Holdings: AV Mats 232; Bk Titles 7,000; Bk Vols 17,297; Videos 202
Wireless access
Open Mon 4pm-6pm, Wed 6pm-8pm, Fri 2:30-5:30

WEST HARTFORD

P WEST HARTFORD LIBRARY*, 5133 Rte 14, 05084. (Mail add: PO Box 26, 05084-0026), SAN 317-1728. Tel: 802-295-7992. FAX: 802-295-7992. E-mail: westhartfordlibraryvt@gmail.com. Web Site: westhartfordlibraryvt.wordpress.com. *Librn,* Sandra Cary; Staff 1 (Non-MLS 1)
Founded 1927. Pop 2,500
Library Holdings: CDs 40; DVDs 88; Large Print Bks 141; Bk Titles 9,879; Per Subs 21; Talking Bks 518; Videos 421
Subject Interests: Local authors, State hist
Wireless access
Function: Bks on cassette, Bks on CD, Computers for patron use, Electronic databases & coll, Free DVD rentals, ILL available, Museum passes, Outreach serv, OverDrive digital audio bks, Photocopying/Printing, Summer reading prog, VHS videos, Wheelchair accessible
Partic in Vermont Automated Libr Syst
Open Mon 2-8, Tues & Thurs 9-12 & 1-6, Wed 10-12 & 1-7, Sat 10-1
Friends of the Library Group

WEST RUTLAND

P WEST RUTLAND FREE LIBRARY*, 595 Main St, 05777. (Mail add: PO Box 66, 05777), SAN 317-1736. Tel: 802-438-2964. E-mail: westrutlandlibrary@yahoo.com. Web Site: www.westrutlandfreelibrary.com. *Librn,* Rene Meyer
Pop 2,448; Circ 7,899
Library Holdings: Audiobooks 21; DVDs 115; Large Print Bks 103; Bk Vols 10,000; Per Subs 22
Wireless access
Mem of Midstate Regional Library
Partic in Catamount Library Network
Open Mon, Wed & Fri 1:30-5, Tues & Thurs 9:30-5

WEST WINDSOR

P MARY L BLOOD MEMORIAL LIBRARY*, 41 Brownsville-Hartland Rd, 05037. (Mail add: PO Box 468, Brownsville, 05037-0468), SAN 316-9731. Tel: 802-484-7205. E-mail: marybloodlibrary@gmail.com. Web Site: marybloodlibrary.wordpress.com. *Librn,* Lynn Esty; *Asst Librn,* Mary Jane Wentworth; Staff 2 (Non-MLS 2)
Founded 1901. Pop 1,089; Circ 5,960
Library Holdings: Bks-By-Mail 476; Bk Vols 5,600; Per Subs 19; Videos 223
Wireless access
Function: Adult bk club, Art exhibits, Bi-weekly Writer's Group, Free DVD rentals, Homebound delivery serv, ILL available, Internet access, Magnifiers for reading, Museum passes, Music CDs, Prog for adults, Prog for children & young adult, Summer reading prog
Open Wed 1:30-5:30, Sat 9-1
Friends of the Library Group

WESTFIELD

P HITCHCOCK MEMORIAL MUSEUM & LIBRARY, 1252 Rte 100, 05874. (Mail add: 38 School St, 05874), SAN 376-3420. Tel: 802-744-8258. E-mail: hitchcockmemorial8258@gmail.com. Web Site: westfield.vt.gov/hitchcock-library. *Libr Dir,* Jennifer Johnson; Staff 1 (Non-MLS 1)
Founded 1899
Special Collections: Historic Coll, Natural History
Wireless access
Function: Bks on CD, Computers for patron use, Electronic databases & coll, Extended outdoor wifi, Free DVD rentals, ILL available, Internet access, Movies, Museum passes, Online cat
Open Tues 10-3, Thurs 2-7, Sun 11-3

WESTFORD

P WESTFORD PUBLIC LIBRARY*, 1717 Vermont Rte 128, 05494. (Mail add: PO Box 86, 05494-0086), SAN 376-8031. Tel: 802-878-5639. E-mail: westfordpubliclibrary@gmail.com. Web Site: westfordpubliclibrary.wordpress.com. *Libr Dir,* Bree Drapa; Staff 1 (Non-MLS 1)
Founded 1844. Pop 1,740; Circ 8,400
Library Holdings: AV Mats 200; Large Print Bks 25; Bk Vols 8,000; Per Subs 23
Subject Interests: Vt
Wireless access
Function: ILL available
Open Wed & Fri 1-7, Thurs 10-7, Sat 10-2

WESTMINSTER

P BUTTERFIELD LIBRARY, 3534 US Rte 5, 05158. (Mail add: PO Box 123, 05158-0123), SAN 317-1744. Tel: 802-722-4891. E-mail: butterfieldlib.05158@gmail.com. *Librn,* Alison Baitz
Founded 1924. Pop 271; Circ 4,583
Library Holdings: Bk Vols 10,000; Per Subs 30
Wireless access
Partic in Collaborative Libraries of Vermont
Open Mon, Tues & Thurs 1-6, Sat 10-1

WESTON

P WILDER MEMORIAL LIBRARY*, 24 Lawrence Hill Rd, 05161. SAN 317-1760. Tel: 802-824-4307. Web Site: wildermemoriallibrary.org. *Libr Dir,* Jessica Clapp; E-mail: director@wildermemoriallibrary.org
Pop 600; Circ 1,400
Library Holdings: Bk Vols 4,000; Per Subs 10
Wireless access
Partic in Collaborative Libraries of Vermont
Open Tues & Fri 10-4, Thurs 10-6, Sat 10-1

WHITE RIVER JUNCTION

GM DEPARTMENT OF VETERANS AFFAIRS*, Medical Library, 215 N Main St, 05009. SAN 362-6644. Tel: 802-295-9363. Web Site: www.whiteriver.va.gov. *Libr Tech,* Heather Smith; E-mail: heather.smith5@va.gov; Staff 1 (MLS 1)
Founded 1940
Library Holdings: Bk Vols 750; Per Subs 65
Wireless access

Function: CD-ROM, Computer training, Doc delivery serv, Electronic databases & coll, Govt ref serv, Health sci info serv, ILL available, Internet access, Online ref, Photocopying/Printing, Prof lending libr, Ref & res, Ref serv available, Res libr, Telephone ref, VHS videos, Wheelchair accessible
Restriction: Open to hospital affiliates only, Restricted access

WILDER

P WILDER LIBRARY, 78 Norwich Ave, 05088. (Mail add: PO Box 1928, 05088-1928). Tel: 802-295-6341. E-mail: wilder@quecheelibrary.org. Web Site: www.quecheelibrary.org. *Dir,* Kate Schaal; E-mail: kate@quecheelibrary.org
Open Tues & Sat 10-1, Wed-Fri 2-6

WILLIAMSTOWN

P AINSWORTH PUBLIC LIBRARY, 2338 VT Rte 14, 05679. (Mail add: PO Box 236, 05679-0236), SAN 322-6700. Tel: 802-433-5887. FAX: 802-433-2161. E-mail: library@williamstownvt.org. Web Site: ainsworthpubliclibrary.org. *Dir,* Sarah Snow
Founded 1911. Pop 3,620; Circ 5,817
Library Holdings: Audiobooks 150; CDs 31; DVDs 396; Large Print Bks 240; Bk Titles 11,500; Per Subs 14
Special Collections: Oral History
Automation Activity & Vendor Info: (Cataloging) Koha; (Circulation) ByWater Solutions; (ILL) ByWater Solutions
Wireless access
Function: Children's prog, Computers for patron use, Home delivery & serv to seniorr ctr & nursing homes, ILL available, Magazines, Online cat, Prog for adults, Prog for children & young adult, Ref serv available, Spoken cassettes & CDs, Story hour, Teen prog, Wheelchair accessible
Partic in Catamount Library Network
Open Mon & Thurs 10-6, Tues 2-6, Wed 10-7, Fri 12-7, Sat 10-2
Friends of the Library Group

WILLISTON

P DOROTHY ALLING MEMORIAL LIBRARY*, 21 Library Lane, 05495. SAN 317-1809. Tel: 802-878-4918. FAX: 802-878-3964. E-mail: daml@damlvt.org. Web Site: damlvt.org. *Dir,* Jane Kearns; *Asst Dir,* Debbie Roderer; *Head, Tech Serv,* Allison Benkwitt; *Program Serv Librn,* Position Currently Open; *Info Tech, ILL, Ref & Instrul Serv Librn,* Kim Peine; *Asst Youth Serv,* Danielle Doucette; *Ch Serv, Youth Serv,* Jessica George; *Circ,* Kristina McSalis; *Outreach Serv, Patron Serv,* Sarah Hibbeler; Staff 8 (MLS 3, Non-MLS 5)
Founded 1905. Pop 9,569; Circ 128,001
Jul 2015-Jun 2016 Income $637,767, City $623,378, Locally Generated Income $4,000, Other $10,389. Mats Exp $67,138, Books $31,928, Per/Ser (Incl. Access Fees) $3,620, AV Mat $18,640, Electronic Ref Mat (Incl. Access Fees) $12,950. Sal $348,855
Library Holdings: Audiobooks 3,777; DVDs 3,026; e-books 7,816; Electronic Media & Resources 69; Bk Vols 31,586; Per Subs 107
Special Collections: Local History (Williston Coll), bks, photog, postal cards, scrapbooks, typescripts, oral history
Automation Activity & Vendor Info: (Acquisitions) Koha; (Cataloging) Koha; (Circulation) Koha; (OPAC) Koha
Wireless access
Function: 24/7 Electronic res, 24/7 Online cat, Activity rm, Adult bk club, Archival coll, Art exhibits, Audio & video playback equip for onsite use, Audiobks on Playaways & MP3, Audiobks via web, Bk club(s), Bks on CD, Children's prog, Computer training, Computers for patron use, Digital talking bks, Electronic databases & coll, Equip loans & repairs, Free DVD rentals, Home delivery & serv to seniorr ctr & nursing homes, Homebound delivery serv, ILL available, Internet access, Life-long learning prog for all ages, Magazines, Mail & tel request accepted, Mango lang, Meeting rooms, Microfiche/film & reading machines, Movies, Museum passes, Music CDs, Online cat, Orientations, Outreach serv, OverDrive digital audio bks, Photocopying/Printing, Preschool outreach, Prog for adults, Prog for children & young adult, Ref serv available, Res libr, Scanner, Senior outreach, Serves people with intellectual disabilities, Story hour, Summer & winter reading prog, Summer reading prog, Tax forms, Teen prog, Wheelchair accessible, Workshops, Writing prog
Partic in Green Mountain Library Consortium; Massachusetts Commonwealth Consortium of Libraries in Public Higher Education Institutions
Special Services for the Deaf - Sign lang interpreter upon request for prog
Special Services for the Blind - Bks on CD; Home delivery serv; Large print bks; Ref serv
Open Mon & Wed 10-8, Tues, Thurs & Fri 10-6, Sat 10-3
Friends of the Library Group
Bookmobiles: 1

C VERMONT STATE UNIVERSITY - WILLISTON*, Hartness Library, 401 Lawrence Pl, Rm 409, 05495. Tel: 802-879-8249. *Ref Librn,* Robin Poland; E-mail: rxp00854@vtc.vsc.edu
Wireless access
Open Mon-Fri 8-4

WILMINGTON

P PETTEE MEMORIAL LIBRARY*, Dennis M Zavinsky Law Library, 16 S Main St, 05363. (Mail add: PO Box 896, 05363), SAN 317-1817. Tel: 802-464-8557. E-mail: petteelibrary@yahoo.com. Web Site: petteelibrary.org. *Libr Dir,* Kyrra Howard; *Asst Librn,* Jennifer Razee; *Circ,* Lynne Cannon; Staff 3 (MLS 1, Non-MLS 2)
Founded 1895. Pop 1,800; Circ 20,000
Library Holdings: Audiobooks 600; DVDs 2,000; Large Print Bks 100; Bk Titles 12,000; Per Subs 20
Special Collections: Vermont Shelf (books)
Automation Activity & Vendor Info: (Acquisitions) Biblionix/Apollo; (Cataloging) Biblionix/Apollo; (Circulation) Biblionix/Apollo
Wireless access
Function: 24/7 Electronic res, 24/7 Online cat, Adult bk club, Audio & video playback equip for onsite use, Audiobks on Playaways & MP3, Audiobks via web, Bk club(s), Bk reviews (Group), Bks on CD, Children's prog, Computer training, Computers for patron use, Digital talking bks, E-Readers, Electronic databases & coll, Equip loans & repairs, For res purposes, Free DVD rentals, Holiday prog, Homebound delivery serv, ILL available, Internet access, Large print keyboards, Life-long learning prog for all ages, Magazines, Meeting rooms, Movies, Museum passes, Online ref, Outreach serv, Outside serv via phone, mail, e-mail & web, Photocopying/Printing, Preschool outreach, Printer for laptops & handheld devices, Prog for adults, Prog for children & young adult, Ref & res, Ref serv available, Res assist avail, Scanner, Senior computer classes, Senior outreach, STEM programs, Story hour, Summer reading prog, Teen prog, Telephone ref, Wheelchair accessible
Partic in Collaborative Libraries of Vermont; Vt Libr Syst
Open Mon-Thurs & Sat 10-4, Fri Noon-6, Sun Noon-2
Friends of the Library Group

WINDHAM

P WINDHAM TOWN LIBRARY*, 7071 Windham Hill Rd, 05359. SAN 376-334X. Tel: 802-875-4874. E-mail: windhamlibrary@gmail.com. Web Site: windhamlibrary.wordpress.com. *Chair,* Beverly Carmichael
Library Holdings: Bk Titles 3,100
Wireless access
Open Wed 3-5

WINDSOR

P WINDSOR PUBLIC LIBRARY*, 43 State St, 05089. SAN 317-1841. Tel: 802-674-2556. FAX: 802-674-5767. E-mail: librarian@windsorlibrary.org. Web Site: windsorlibrary.org. *Libr Dir,* Barbara Ball; *Youth Librn,* Sarah Tufts; E-mail: sarah@windsorlibrary.org; *Libr Asst, ILL,* Melissa Ayres; E-mail: melissa@windsorlibrary.org; Staff 3 (MLS 1, Non-MLS 2)
Founded 1882. Pop 3,400; Circ 23,000
Library Holdings: Bk Vols 18,000; Per Subs 10
Special Collections: Old Vermont Newspaper Coll; Vermont History Coll
Wireless access
Open Mon & Wed 9-7, Thurs & Fri 9-4, Sat 9-1
Friends of the Library Group

WINOOSKI

P WINOOSKI MEMORIAL LIBRARY*, 32E Malletts Bay Ave, 05404. SAN 317-1868. Tel: 802-655-6424. Web Site: winooskilibrary.wordpress.com. *Libr Dir,* Nate Eddy; E-mail: neddy@winooskivt.gov
Founded 1930. Pop 7,240; Circ 23,105
Library Holdings: Bk Vols 13,000; Per Subs 26
Automation Activity & Vendor Info: (Acquisitions) Baker & Taylor; (Cataloging) Auto-Graphics, Inc; (Circulation) Auto-Graphics, Inc; (OPAC) LibraryWorld, Inc
Open Tues-Fri 10-6:30, Sat 10-2
Friends of the Library Group

WOLCOTT

P WOLCOTT PUBLIC LIBRARY, (Formerly Glee Merritt Kelley Community Library), 46 Railroad St, 05680. (Mail add: PO Box 106, 05680-0106), SAN 317-1884. Tel: 802-888-8908. E-mail: wolcottvtpubliclibrary@gmail.com. Web Site: www.wolcottvtpubliclibrary.com. *Librn,* Sally Gardner
Founded 1973. Pop 1,619; Circ 14,400
Library Holdings: Bk Vols 11,500; Per Subs 15
Special Collections: Vermont Coll

Wireless access
Open Mon & Tues 10-4, Wed 11-6, Sat 9-1

WOODBURY

P WOODBURY COMMUNITY LIBRARY*, 69 Valley Lake Rd, 05681. (Mail add: PO Box 329, 05681-0329), SAN 376-4923. Tel: 802-472-5710. E-mail: woodburyvermontlibrary@gmail.com. Web Site: woodburycommunitylibrary.wordpress.com.
Library Holdings: Bk Vols 6,000
Automation Activity & Vendor Info: (Acquisitions) LibraryWorld, Inc; (Cataloging) LibraryWorld, Inc; (Circulation) LibraryWorld, Inc; (OPAC) LibraryWorld, Inc; (Serials) LibraryWorld, Inc
Wireless access
Mem of Midstate Regional Library
Partic in Collaborative Libraries of Vermont
Open Mon & Wed 1-5, Sat 10-12
Friends of the Library Group

WOODSTOCK

P NORMAN WILLIAMS PUBLIC LIBRARY*, Ten The Green, 05091. SAN 317-1906. Tel: 802-457-2295. Circulation Tel: 802-457-2295, Ext 113. Reference Tel: 802-457-2295, Ext 125. FAX: 802-457-5181. E-mail: circulation@normanwilliams.org. Web Site: normanwilliams.org. *Libr Dir,* Clare McFarland; E-mail: clare@normanwilliams.org; *Dir, Adult Serv,* Kathy Beaird; Staff 10 (MLS 1, Non-MLS 9)
Founded 1883. Pop 3,232; Circ 66,000
Library Holdings: AV Mats 1,185; Bk Vols 42,303; Per Subs 112; Talking Bks 1,042
Special Collections: Computer Technology (MJUSA Coll); Vermont Genealogy (New England & Local Genealogical Information); Vermont History Discussion Group (Vermont Civil War History Books). Oral History
Subject Interests: Computers, Genealogy, Local hist, State hist
Automation Activity & Vendor Info: (Cataloging) Mandarin Library Automation; (Circulation) Mandarin Library Automation; (OPAC) Mandarin Library Automation
Wireless access
Function: Art exhibits, Audio & video playback equip for onsite use, AV serv, Bk club(s), Computer training, Digital talking bks, Electronic databases & coll, Home delivery & serv to seniorr ctr & nursing homes, Homebound delivery serv, ILL available, Internet access, Magnifiers for reading, Mail & tel request accepted, Online ref, Photocopying/Printing, Prog for adults, Prog for children & young adult, Ref serv available, Summer reading prog, Telephone ref, VHS videos, Wheelchair accessible
Partic in Catamount Library Network; Vermont Automated Libr Syst
Special Services for the Deaf - Bks on deafness & sign lang
Special Services for the Blind - Bks available with recordings; Bks on cassette; Bks on CD; Braille bks; Copier with enlargement capabilities; Extensive large print coll; Home delivery serv; Internet workstation with adaptive software; Large print bks; Low vision equip; Magnifiers
Open Mon, Wed-Fri 10-6, Tues 10-8, Sat 10-5
Friends of the Library Group

S WOODSTOCK HISTORY CENTER*, John Cotton Dana Research Library & Archives, 26 Elm St, 05091. SAN 327-2621. Tel: 802-457-1822. *Exec Dir,* Matthew Powers; E-mail: director@woodstockhistorycenter.org; *Educ Coordr,* Jennie Shurtleff; E-mail: education@woodstockhistorycenter.org; *Colls Mgr,* Becky Talcott; E-mail: collections@woodstockhistorycenter.org; Staff 3 (Non-MLS 3)
Founded 1943
Library Holdings: Bk Vols 2,000
Special Collections: Institutional Records, Family Papers & Diaries from Woodstock Area; Large Photography Archive. Oral History
Subject Interests: Genealogy, Local hist
Wireless access
Restriction: Not a lending libr, Open by appt only

VIRGINIA

Date of Statistics: FY 2023
Population, 2023 U.S. Census: 8,729,032
Population Served by Public Libraries: 8,536,240
Total Items in Public Libraries: 122,565,260
Items Per Capita: 14.0
Total Public Library Circulation: 55,348,998
Digital Resources:
Total e-books: 41,179,354
Total audio items (physical and downloadable units): 61,890,710
Total video items (physical and downloadable units): 4,677,024
Total computers for use by the public: 7,199
Total annual wireless sessions: 14,002,116
Source of Income: Mainly public funds
Income and Expenditures:
Total Public Library Expenditures (including Grants-in-Aid): $344,307,981
Expenditures Per Capita: $39.44
Grants-in-Aid to Public Libraries:
State Aid: $20,543,514
Formula for Apportionment: Legally established libraries receive grants based on local support, population, square miles and number of government units served
Use of Funds: Grants to public libraries and statewide programs for library development
Number of County or Multi-county Regional Libraries: 69
Counties Served: 95
Number of Independent Cities: 38
Cities Served: 38 cities & 3 towns
Number of Bookmobiles in State: 26
Information provided courtesy of: Kimberley Armentrout, Grants and Data Coordinator; Library of Virginia.

ABINGDON

J VIRGINIA HIGHLANDS COMMUNITY COLLEGE LIBRARY*, Learning Resource Center, 100 VHCC Dr, 24210. (Mail add: PO Box 828, 24212-0828), SAN 317-1930. Tel: 276-739-2542. Reference Tel: 276-739-2472. FAX: 276-739-2593. Web Site: www.vhcc.edu/current-students/student-services/library. *Ref Librn,* Sarah Beth White; E-mail: swhite@vhcc.edu; *Libr Serv Coordr,* Joel Rudy; E-mail: jrudy@vhcc.edu; *Cataloger, Libr Spec,* Diana Corns; E-mail: dcorns@vhcc.edu; Staff 4 (MLS 2, Non-MLS 2)
Founded 1967. Enrl 1,588; Fac 66; Highest Degree: Associate
Library Holdings: Bk Vols 32,500; Per Subs 225
Special Collections: VIVA (Virtual Library of Virginia)
Automation Activity & Vendor Info: (Acquisitions) Ex Libris Group; (Cataloging) Ex Libris Group; (Circulation) Ex Libris Group; (OPAC) Ex Libris Group
Wireless access
Partic in SouthWest Information Network Group; Virginia Commun Coll Syst; Virginia's Academic Library Consortium
Open Mon-Thurs 8am-9pm, Fri 8-5, Sat 11-3, Sun 1-5

P WASHINGTON COUNTY PUBLIC LIBRARY*, 205 Oak Hill St, 24210. SAN 317-1949. Tel: 276-676-6222, 276-676-6233. Administration Tel: 276-676-6383. FAX: 276-676-6235. Web Site: www.wcpl.net. *Dir,* Molly Schock; E-mail: mschock@wcpl.net; *Br Coordr,* Diane Lester; E-mail: dlester@wcpl.net; Staff 22 (MLS 4, Non-MLS 18)
Founded 1954. Pop 50,500; Circ 294,637
Library Holdings: Bk Vols 107,657; Per Subs 240
Automation Activity & Vendor Info: (Acquisitions) Innovative Interfaces, Inc; (Cataloging) Innovative Interfaces, Inc; (Circulation) Innovative Interfaces, Inc; (OPAC) Innovative Interfaces, Inc; (Serials) Innovative Interfaces, Inc
Wireless access
Partic in Holston Associated Librs Consortium
Open Mon-Thurs 9-8, Fri 9-6, Sat 9-5, Sun 1-5
Friends of the Library Group
Branches: 4
DAMASCUS BRANCH, 310 Water St, Damascus, 24236, SAN 329-3211. Tel: 276-475-3820. FAX: 276-218-6739. *Br Mgr,* Melissa Watson; E-mail: mwatson@wcpl.net; Staff 2 (Non-MLS 2)
Library Holdings: Bk Vols 22,313; Per Subs 38
Open Tues-Fri 10-6, Sat 9-5
GLADE SPRING BRANCH, 305 N Glade St, Glade Spring, 24340, SAN 320-9504. Tel: 276-429-5626. FAX: 276-218-6744. *Br Mgr,* Stephanie LaFlamme; E-mail: slaflamme@wcpl.net; Staff 1 (Non-MLS 1)
Library Holdings: Bk Vols 25,000; Per Subs 52
Open Tues-Fri 10-6, Sat 9-5
HAYTERS GAP, 7720 Hayters Gap Rd, 24210, SAN 375-1430. Tel: 276-944-4442. FAX: 276-218-6746. *Br Mgr,* Patty Lamie; E-mail: plamie@wcpl.net; Staff 1 (Non-MLS 1)
Library Holdings: Bk Vols 23,000; Per Subs 49
Open Tues-Fri 10-6, Sat 9-5
MENDOTA BRANCH, 2562 Mendota Rd, Mendota, 24270. (Mail add: PO Box 99, Mendota, 24270-0099), SAN 375-1449. Tel: 276-645-2374. FAX: 276-218-6754. *Br Mgr,* Margie Dian; E-mail: mdian@wcpl.net; Staff 1 (Non-MLS 1)
Library Holdings: Bk Vols 23,000; Per Subs 51
Open Tues-Thurs 10-6, Sat 9-5

ACCOMAC

P EASTERN SHORE PUBLIC LIBRARY*, 23610 Front St, 23301. (Mail add: PO Box 25, Parksley, 23421), SAN 317-1957. Tel: 757-787-3400. FAX: 757-787-2241. Web Site: www.espl.org. *Dir,* Cara Burton; E-mail: cburton@espl.org; *ILL,* Charle Ricci; E-mail: cricci@espl.lib.va.us; Staff 3 (MLS 1, Non-MLS 2)
Founded 1957. Pop 45,200; Circ 164,451
Library Holdings: Bk Vols 128,000; Per Subs 108
Special Collections: Local History (Eastern Shore of Virginia Coll), bks, maps, micro
Automation Activity & Vendor Info: (Cataloging) OCLC Connexion; (Circulation) Evergreen; (ILL) OCLC WorldShare Interlibrary Loan; (OPAC) Evergreen
Wireless access
Partic in OCLC Online Computer Library Center, Inc
Open Mon-Wed & Fri 9-6, Thurs 9-9, Sat 9-1
Friends of the Library Group
Branches: 3
CAPE CHARLES MEMORIAL LIBRARY, 201 Mason Ave, Cape Charles, 23310. Tel: 757-331-1300. E-mail: library@capecharles.org. Web Site: espl.org/cape-charles-memorial-library. *Mgr,* Sharon Silvey; Tel: 757-331-1300, E-mail: sharon.silvey@capecharles.org
Founded 1919
Library Holdings: Bk Vols 21,000
Function: 24/7 Electronic res, 24/7 Online cat, Audiobks via web, Bks on CD, Children's prog, Computers for patron use, Family literacy, Free DVD rentals, Holiday prog, Homebound delivery serv, ILL available, Internet access, Magazines, Mail & tel request accepted, Meeting rooms, Notary serv, Online cat, Outreach serv, Photocopying/Printing, Preschool outreach, Prog for adults, Prog for children & young adult, Scanner, Senior outreach, Spanish lang bks, STEM programs, Story hour, Summer reading prog, Teen prog, Wheelchair accessible
Open Mon & Wed-Fri 10-5, Tues 10-6, Sat 10-2
Friends of the Library Group
ISLAND LIBRARY, 4077 Main St, Chincoteague, 23336. Tel: 757-336-3460. E-mail: chincoteagueislandlibrary@yahoo.com. *Br Mgr,* Harriet Lonergan
Library Holdings: Bk Vols 13,000
Open Mon-Wed & Fri 10-4, Thurs 1-7
NORTHAMPTON FREE LIBRARY, 7745 Seaside Rd, Nassawadox, 23413. (Mail add: PO Box 729, Nassawadox, 23413). Tel: 757-414-0010. FAX: 757-414-0424. E-mail: NFL@espl.org. *Br Mgr,* Position Currently Open

Library Holdings: Bk Vols 20,000
Open Mon-Fri 10-5

ALBERTA

J SOUTHSIDE VIRGINIA COMMUNITY COLLEGE LIBRARIES*, Julian M Howell Library, 109 Campus Dr, 23821. SAN 362-6709. Tel: 434-949-1065. FAX: 434-949-0013. E-mail: lrsC@southside.edu. Web Site: www.southside.edu/learning-resource-center. *Campus Librn,* Marika Peterson; E-mail: marika.peterson@southside.edu; *Ser Spec,* Sylvia P Groves; E-mail: sylvia.groves@southside.edu; *Libr Asst,* Evelyn Fenderson; E-mail: evelyn.fenderson@southside.edu
Founded 1970
Library Holdings: Bk Vols 30,000; Per Subs 270
Automation Activity & Vendor Info: (Acquisitions) Ex Libris Group; (Cataloging) Ex Libris Group; (Course Reserve) Ex Libris Group; (OPAC) Ex Libris Group
Partic in Virginia Commun Coll Syst; Virginia's Academic Library Consortium
Open Mon-Thurs 8am-9pm, Fri 8-4:30

ALEXANDRIA

P ALEXANDRIA LIBRARY*, 5005 Duke St, 22304. SAN 362-6733. Tel: 703-746-1702. Administration Tel: 703-746-1701. Administration FAX: 703-746-1738. TDD: 703-746-1790. Web Site: www.alexlibraryva.org. *Exec Dir,* Rose T Dawson; Tel: 703-746-1777, E-mail: rdawson@alexlibraryva.org; *Communications Officer I,* Anton Murray; E-mail: amurray@alexlibraryva.org; *Librn,* Andrea Castillo; E-mail: acastillo@alexlibraryva.org; *Tech Serv,* Lynda Rudd; Tel: 703-746-1764, E-mail: lrudd@alexlibraryva.org; Staff 30.5 (MLS 30.5)
Founded 1794. Pop 145,011; Circ 1,609,843
Jul 2017-Jun 2018 Income $7,907,045, State $169,278, City $6,933,414, Locally Generated Income $459,589, Other $344,764. Mats Exp $516,413, Books $262,864, Per/Ser (Incl. Access Fees) $11,762, AV Mat $93,185, Electronic Ref Mat (Incl. Access Fees) $148,602. Sal $4,430,665
Library Holdings: Audiobooks 12,726; AV Mats 10,881; CDs 4,846; DVDs 23,582; e-books 43,858; Microforms 9; Bk Vols 376,828; Per Subs 618; Talking Bks 14,910; Videos 108
Special Collections: Oral History
Subject Interests: Civil War hist, Genealogy, Town hist
Automation Activity & Vendor Info: (Acquisitions) SirsiDynix; (Cataloging) SirsiDynix; (Circulation) SirsiDynix; (OPAC) SirsiDynix; (Serials) SirsiDynix
Wireless access
Function: 24/7 Electronic res, 24/7 Online cat, Archival coll, Audiobks on Playaways & MP3, Audiobks via web, AV serv, Bilingual assistance for Spanish patrons, Bk club(s), Bks on CD, Children's prog, Computer training, Computers for patron use, Digital talking bks, Electronic databases & coll, Home delivery & serv to seniorr ctr & nursing homes, Homebound delivery serv, ILL available, Internet access, Life-long learning prog for all ages, Magazines, Magnifiers for reading, Mango lang, Meeting rooms, Microfiche/film & reading machines, Movies, Music CDs, Notary serv, Online cat, Online ref, Outreach serv, OverDrive digital audio bks, Passport agency, Photocopying/Printing, Prog for adults, Prog for children & young adult, Ref serv available, STEM programs, Story hour, Summer & winter reading prog, Tax forms, Teen prog, Telephone ref, Wheelchair accessible
Partic in LYRASIS; Metro Coun of Govts; Urban Libraries Council
Special Services for the Deaf - Assisted listening device; Assistive tech; Bks on deafness & sign lang; Sign lang interpreter upon request for prog; TDD equip
Special Services for the Blind - Assistive/Adapted tech devices, equip & products; Computer with voice synthesizer for visually impaired persons; Descriptive video serv (DVS); Large print bks; Talking bks; ZoomText magnification & reading software
Friends of the Library Group
Branches: 8
KATE WALLER BARRETT BRANCH, 717 Queen St, 22314, SAN 372-8056. Tel: 703-746-1703. FAX: 703-746-1709. Reference FAX: 703-746-1708. *Br Mgr,* James Cahill; E-mail: jcahill@alexlibraryva.org; *Ch Serv,* Elizabeth Springer; E-mail: lspringer@alexlibraryva.org; Staff 4.5 (MLS 4.5)
Circ 213,972
Function: Adult bk club, Audiobks via web, Bks on cassette, Bks on CD, Children's prog, Computers for patron use, Electronic databases & coll, Free DVD rentals, Music CDs, Online cat, OverDrive digital audio bks, Photocopying/Printing, Prog for children & young adult, Story hour, Summer reading prog, Tax forms
Special Services for the Deaf - ADA equip; Sign lang interpreter upon request for prog
Open Mon 1-9, Tues 10-9, Wed & Thurs 10-7, Fri 10-6, Sat 10-5, Sun 1-5
Friends of the Library Group
CHARLES E BEATLEY JR CENTRAL, 5005 Duke St, 22304-2903. Tel: 703-746-1702. Circulation Tel: 703-746-1752. Interlibrary Loan Service Tel: 703-746-1745. Reference Tel: 703-746-1751. Administration Tel: 703-746-1701. Circulation FAX: 703-746-1739. Interlibrary Loan Service FAX: 703-746-1763. Administration FAX: 703-746-1738. TDD: 703-746-1790. *Br Mgr,* Diana Price; E-mail: dprice@alexlibraryva.org; *Ref Serv,* Katie Dow; Tel: 703-746-1746, E-mail: kdow@alexlibraryva.org; *YA Serv,* Isaiah West; Tel: 703-746-1767, E-mail: iwest@alexlibraryva.org; Staff 12.5 (MLS 12.5)
Circ 596,664
Function: Audiobks via web, Bks on CD, Children's prog, Computers for patron use, Electronic databases & coll, Free DVD rentals, Homebound delivery serv, ILL available, Internet access, Music CDs, Online ref, Outreach serv, Photocopying/Printing, Prog for adults, Prog for children & young adult, Summer & winter reading prog, Tax forms, Teen prog, Wheelchair accessible
Special Services for the Deaf - Assistive tech; Bks on deafness & sign lang; TDD equip; TTY equip
Special Services for the Blind - Assistive/Adapted tech devices, equip & products
Open Mon-Thurs 10-9, Fri 10-6, Sat 10-5, Sun 1-5
Friends of the Library Group
ELLEN COOLIDGE BURKE BRANCH, 4701 Seminary Rd, 22304, SAN 362-6792. Tel: 703-746-1704. Circulation Tel: 703-746-1772. Reference Tel: 703-746-1771. FAX: 703-746-1775. *Br Mgr,* Genelle Schuler; Tel: 703-746-1704, E-mail: gschuler@alexlibraryva.org; Staff 3.3 (MLS 3.3)
Circ 125,412
Function: Bks on CD, Children's prog, Computer training, Computers for patron use, Free DVD rentals, Music CDs, Online cat, OverDrive digital audio bks, Photocopying/Printing, Story hour, Summer & winter reading prog, Tax forms
Open Mon 10-9, Tues & Wed 10-7, Thurs 1-9, Fri 10-6, Sat 10-5, Sun 1-5
Friends of the Library Group
JAMES M DUNCAN JR BRANCH, 2501 Commonwealth Ave, 22301, SAN 362-6822. Tel: 703-746-1705. Circulation Tel: 703-746-1782. Reference Tel: 703-746-1781. FAX: 703-746-1785. *Br Mgr,* Brack Stovall; E-mail: bstovall@alexlibraryva.org; *Ch Serv,* Kayla Payne; E-mail: kpayne@alexlibraryva.org; Staff 4.3 (MLS 4.3)
Circ 336,014
Function: Audiobks via web, Bks on CD, Butterfly Garden, Children's prog, Computers for patron use, Electronic databases & coll, Free DVD rentals, Music CDs, OverDrive digital audio bks, Photocopying/Printing, Summer & winter reading prog, Tax forms, Wheelchair accessible
Open Mon 10-9, Tues & Thurs 10-7, Wed 1-9, Fri 10-6, Sat 10-5, Sun 1-5
Friends of the Library Group
LOCAL HISTORY/SPECIAL COLLECTIONS, 717 Queen St, 22314-2420, SAN 362-6857. Tel: 703-746-1706. FAX: 703-746-1720. *Br Mgr,* Patricia Walker; Tel: 703-746-1719, E-mail: pwalker@alexlibraryva.org; Staff 2 (MLS 2)
Circ 7,602
Subject Interests: Civil War, Genealogy, Local hist, State hist
Function: Archival coll, Genealogy discussion group, Photocopying/Printing, Ref serv available, Res libr, Wheelchair accessible
Open Mon 1-9, Tues 2-9, Wed 10-7, Fri 10-6, Sat 10-5
Restriction: Internal circ only, Non-circulating coll, Pub use on premises
Friends of the Library Group
P TALKING BOOKS, 5005 Duke St, 22304-2903, SAN 362-6768. Tel: 703-746-1760. TDD: 703-746-1790. *Mgr,* Kym Robertson; Staff 1 (MLS 1)
Founded 1968. Circ 7,308
Special Collections: Blindness & Other Handicaps Reference Material
Function: Audio & video playback equip for onsite use, Games & aids for people with disabilities, Homebound delivery serv, Magnifiers for reading, Mail loans to mem, Wheelchair accessible
Special Services for the Deaf - Closed caption videos; TDD equip
Special Services for the Blind - Assistive/Adapted tech devices, equip & products; Braille equip; Closed circuit TV; Compressed speech equip; Computer with voice synthesizer for visually impaired persons; Descriptive video serv (DVS); Home delivery serv; Machine repair; Newsline for the Blind; Radio reading serv; Reader equip; Spanish Braille mags & bks; Talking bks & player equip; Web-Braille; ZoomText magnification & reading software
Open Mon-Fri 10-3
Friends of the Library Group
TECHNICAL SERVICES, 5005 Duke St, 22304-2903, SAN 372-8048. *Br Mgr,* Lynda Rudd; Tel: 703-746-1764, Fax: 703-746-1747, E-mail: lrudd@alexandria.lib.va.us; Staff 2 (MLS 2)
Function: Prog for children & young adult
Restriction: Open by appt only

S AMERICAN CORRECTIONAL ASSOCIATION*, Anthony Travisono Library, 206 N Washington St, 22314. SAN 321-8309. Tel: 703-224-0194. Toll Free Tel: 800-222-5646, Ext 0194. FAX: 703-224-0054, 703-224-0059. Web Site: www.aca.org. *Dir, Publications & Communications,* Kirk Raymond
Founded 1975
Library Holdings: Bk Titles 5,000
Special Collections: Photograph Coll
Subject Interests: Archives, Corrections
Open Mon-Fri 9-5
Restriction: Open to pub for ref only

S AMERICAN COUNSELING ASSOCIATION*, Professional Library, 2461 Eisenhower Ave, 22331. SAN 302-5705. Tel: 703-823-9800. Toll Free Tel: 800-347-6647. FAX: 703-823-0252. Toll Free FAX: 800-473-2329. TDD: 703-823-6862. E-mail: membership@counseling.org. Web Site: www.counseling.org. *Library Contact,* Carolyn Baker
Founded 1952
Library Holdings: Bk Vols 125; Per Subs 8
Subject Interests: Counseling
Open Mon-Fri 8-5:30

S AMERICAN GEOLOGICAL INSTITUTE LIBRARY*, 4220 King St, 22302-1502. SAN 317-2716. Tel: 703-379-2480, Ext 239. FAX: 703-379-7563. Web Site: www.americangeosciences.org. *Dir, Info Serv,* Sharon Tahirkheli; E-mail: snt@americangeosciences.org; *Librn,* Lin Rose; E-mail: lnr@agiweb.org
Founded 1967
Library Holdings: Bk Titles 400; Bk Vols 1,600; Per Subs 250
Special Collections: American Geological Institute Publications
Subject Interests: Geol
Wireless access
Restriction: Open by appt only

S AMERICAN PHYSICAL THERAPY ASSOCIATION LIBRARY, 3030 Potomac Ave, Ste 100, 22305. SAN 373-0050. Tel: 703-706-8534. Toll Free Tel: 800-999-2782, Ext 8534. E-mail: inforesources@apta.org. Web Site: www.apta.org. *Archivist/Librn,* Gini Blodgett; E-mail: giniblodgett@apta.org; Staff 1 (MLS 1)
Library Holdings: e-books 6,200; e-journals 5,000; Electronic Media & Resources 20; Videos 3,000
Special Collections: 20th Century Association Journal Coll; Early 20th Century Rehabilitation Journals & Photos. Oral History
Subject Interests: Hist, Phys therapy, Rehabilitation
Automation Activity & Vendor Info: (Discovery) EBSCO Discovery Service; (OPAC) Lucidea; (Serials) Prenax, Inc
Wireless access
Partic in National Network of Libraries of Medicine Region 1
Restriction: By permission only, Free to mem, Not a lending libr, Pub ref by request, Researchers by appt only

R BETH EL HEBREW CONGREGATION MEDIA CENTER*, Solomon Dimond Library & Arnold J Fink Lifelong Learning Center, 3830 Seminary Rd, 22304. SAN 317-1973. Tel: 703-370-9400. FAX: 703-370-7730. E-mail: office@bethelhebrew.org. Web Site: www.bethelhebrew.org/media-center.
Founded 1964
Library Holdings: CDs 50; DVDs 175; Bk Vols 5,000
Wireless access

S FORT WARD MUSEUM, Dorothy C S Starr Civil War Research Library, 4301 W Braddock Rd, 22304. SAN 327-2486. Tel: 703-746-4848. FAX: 703-671-7350. Web Site: www.alexandriava.gov/FortWard. *Dir of Collections & Exhibitions,* Susan Cumbey
Library Holdings: Bk Vols 2,500
Subject Interests: Civil War
Restriction: Open by appt only

S INSTITUTE FOR DEFENSE ANALYSES LIBRARY*, 4850 Mark Center Dr, 22311. SAN 317-218X. Tel: 703-845-2087. FAX: 703-820-7194. E-mail: refdesk@ida.org. *Libr Mgr,* Bradley E Gernand; Staff 13.5 (MLS 4.5, Non-MLS 9)
Founded 1960
Library Holdings: e-books 70,000; e-journals 16,000; Bk Titles 21,000; Per Subs 300
Subject Interests: Aeronaut engr, Chem engr, Econ, Math, Physics, Policy analysis, Polit sci
Automation Activity & Vendor Info: (Acquisitions) SydneyPlus; (Cataloging) SydneyPlus; (Circulation) SydneyPlus; (Discovery) EBSCO Discovery Service; (OPAC) SydneyPlus; (Serials) SydneyPlus
Partic in Statewide California Electronic Library Consortium
Restriction: Co libr

S MPR ASSOCIATES, INC*, Technical Library, 320 King St, Ste 400, 22314. SAN 325-8211. Tel: 703-519-0200. E-mail: library@mpr.com. Web Site: www.mpr.com. *Head Librn,* Danielle Harrison; Tel: 703-519-0567, E-mail: dharrison@mpr.com; Staff 4 (MLS 3, Non-MLS 1)
Library Holdings: AV Mats 89,000; Bk Titles 4,400; Per Subs 120
Automation Activity & Vendor Info: (Acquisitions) Cuadra Associates, Inc; (Cataloging) Cuadra Associates, Inc; (Serials) Cuadra Associates, Inc
Publications: Bulletin (Bimonthly)
Restriction: Not open to pub

L OBLON, SPIVAK*, Law Library, 1940 Duke St, 22314-3454. SAN 374-5961. Tel: 703-413-3000. FAX: 703-413-2220. E-mail: obloncontact@oblon.com. Web Site: www.oblon.com. Staff 1 (MLS 1)
Founded 1968
Restriction: Not open to pub, Staff use only

A UNITED STATES DEPARTMENT OF THE ARMY*, Humphreys Engineer Center Support Activity Library, CEHEC-ZL Casey Bldg, 7701 Telegraph Rd, 22315-3860. SAN 337-1522. Tel: 703-428-6388. FAX: 703-428-6310. E-mail: HECSA.Library@usace.army.mil. Web Site: www.usace.army.mil/Library/Headquarters-Library. *Dir,* Annette Evans; *Eng Librn,* Deborah E Keller; *Electronic Serv,* Phillip Ip; *Ref Serv,* Robin Baird. Subject Specialists: *Legal,* Robin Baird; Staff 7 (MLS 5, Non-MLS 2)
Founded 1942
Library Holdings: Bk Titles 100,324; Bk Vols 152,386; Per Subs 427
Special Collections: Civil & Environmental Engineering; Congressional Materials; Corps of Engineers History & Activities, 1776-present; Management Coll
Automation Activity & Vendor Info: (Cataloging) Auto-Graphics, Inc; (Circulation) Auto-Graphics, Inc; (OPAC) Auto-Graphics, Inc; (Serials) Auto-Graphics, Inc
Function: ILL available

G UNITED STATES PATENT & TRADEMARK OFFICE*, Scientific & Technical Information Center, 400 Dulany St, Rm 1D58, 22314. SAN 317-2287. Tel: 571-272-3547. FAX: 571-273-0048. Web Site: www.uspto.gov/. *Mgr,* Bode Fagbohunka; E-mail: bode.fagbohunka@uspto.gov
Founded 1836
Library Holdings: e-journals 17,000; Bk Vols 129,163; Per Subs 300
Special Collections: Foreign Patents
Subject Interests: Biochem, Chem engr design, Computer sci, Fed law, Foreign patents, Intellectual property law, Mechanical engr design
Automation Activity & Vendor Info: (Cataloging) SirsiDynix; (OPAC) SirsiDynix
Open Mon-Fri 8-5
Restriction: Ref only

GL UNITED STATES PATENT & TRADEMARK OFFICE*, Trademark Law Library, 600 Dulany St, MDE OA50, 22314-5791. Tel: 571-272-9650. FAX: 571-273-0030. E-mail: tm.librarian@uspto.gov. *Libr Dir,* Ann Marie Parsons; Tel: 571-272-9694; Staff 14 (MLS 14)
Founded 1992
Library Holdings: Bk Titles 1,800; Bk Vols 2,700; Per Subs 185
Subject Interests: Intellectual property law
Restriction: Employees only, Not open to pub

R VIRGINIA THEOLOGICAL SEMINARY*, Bishop Payne Library, 3737 Seminary Rd, 22304-5201. SAN 317-2074. Tel: 703-461-1733. E-mail: paynelib@vts.edu. Web Site: www.vts.edu/library. *Head Librn, Prof,* Mitzi J Budde; Tel: 703-461-1756, E-mail: mjbudde@vts.edu. Subject Specialists: *Ecumenism, Relig, Theol,* Mitzi J Budde; Staff 8 (MLS 5, Non-MLS 3)
Founded 1823. Enrl 175; Fac 23; Highest Degree: Doctorate
Library Holdings: e-books 300,000; Microforms 7,000; Music Scores 20,000; Bk Vols 230,000; Per Subs 500
Special Collections: Anglicanism & Episcopal Church in the USA; Archives & Afr Am Episcopal Historical Coll; Rare Book Coll
Subject Interests: Church music, Liturgy, Relig, Theol
Automation Activity & Vendor Info: (Acquisitions) Innovative Interfaces, Inc; (Cataloging) Innovative Interfaces, Inc; (Circulation) Innovative Interfaces, Inc; (Course Reserve) Innovative Interfaces, Inc; (Discovery) EBSCO Discovery Service; (ILL) OCLC; (OPAC) Innovative Interfaces, Inc; (Serials) Innovative Interfaces, Inc
Wireless access
Function: Online cat
Partic in OCLC Online Computer Library Center, Inc; Washington Theological Consortium
Restriction: Open to students, fac & staff

AMELIA

S AMELIA COUNTY HISTORICAL SOCIETY LIBRARY*, Jackson Bldg, 16501 Church St, 23002. (Mail add: PO Box 113, 23002-0113), SAN 370-9817. Tel: 804-561-3180. E-mail: ameliahistoricalsociety@tds.net. Web

Site: va-ameliacounty.civicplus.com/389/historical-society. *Librn,* Sylvia Gray
Library Holdings: Bk Vols 13,500; Per Subs 25
Wireless access
Open Mon & Fri 10-4

P JAMES L HAMNER PUBLIC LIBRARY*, 16351 Dunn St, 23002. SAN 322-6611. Tel: 804-561-4559. FAX: 804-561-3174. Circulation E-mail: circulation@hamnerlibrary.org. Web Site: www.hamnerlibrary.org. *Dir,* Jill Hames; *Tech Serv Librn,* Rebecca Russell; Staff 5 (MLS 1, Non-MLS 4)
Founded 1972. Pop 9,200; Circ 21,793
Library Holdings: Bk Vols 52,000; Per Subs 65
Wireless access
Open Tues 9-8, Wed-Fri 9-5
Friends of the Library Group

AMHERST

P AMHERST COUNTY PUBLIC LIBRARY*, 382 S Main St, 24521. (Mail add: PO Box 370, 24521-0370), SAN 362-6946. Tel: 434-946-9488. FAX: 434-946-9348. Web Site: www.acpl.us. *Dir,* Steve Preston; E-mail: spreston@acpl.us; *Head, Pub Serv,* Judy Spencer; *Ref Serv,* Judy Maxham; *Youth Serv,* Maxine Gasser; Staff 21 (MLS 2, Non-MLS 19)
Founded 1964. Pop 32,000
Special Collections: Virginia History Coll
Automation Activity & Vendor Info: (Cataloging) Horizon; (Circulation) Horizon
Wireless access
Partic in LYRASIS
Open Mon & Wed-Fri 10-6, Tues 10-8, Sat 10-2
Friends of the Library Group
Branches: 1
MADISON HEIGHTS BRANCH, 200 River James Shopping Ctr, Madison Heights, 24572. (Mail add: PO Box 540, Madison Heights, 24572-0540), SAN 362-6970. Tel: 434-846-8171. FAX: 434-846-3102. *Dir,* Steve Preston
Open Mon & Wed 9-9, Tues & Thurs-Sat 9-5:30
Friends of the Library Group

ANNANDALE

J NORTHERN VIRGINIA COMMUNITY COLLEGE LIBRARIES*, Goodwin Bldg, CG206, 8333 Little River Tpk, 22003. SAN 362-7004. Tel: 703-323-3217. FAX: 703-323-4258. Web Site: www.nvcc.edu/library. *Dean, Learning & Tech Res,* Dr Braddlee; Tel: 703-323-3004, E-mail: braddlee@NVCC.edu; Staff 24 (MLS 24)
Founded 1965. Enrl 30,238; Fac 1,037; Highest Degree: Associate
Library Holdings: Audiobooks 1,959; AV Mats 24,495; Bks on Deafness & Sign Lang 225; CDs 1,469; DVDs 17,944; e-books 57,857; e-journals 37,276; Electronic Media & Resources 227; High Interest/Low Vocabulary Bk Vols 3,475; Large Print Bks 143; Music Scores 92; Bk Titles 165,160; Bk Vols 242,882; Per Subs 596
Automation Activity & Vendor Info: (Cataloging) Ex Libris Group; (Circulation) Ex Libris Group; (Course Reserve) Ex Libris Group; (ILL) OCLC WorldShare Interlibrary Loan; (OPAC) Ex Libris Group; (Serials) SerialsSolutions
Wireless access
Partic in LYRASIS; Virginia's Academic Library Consortium
Friends of the Library Group
Departmental Libraries:
ALEXANDRIA CAMPUS, Bisdorf Bldg, Rm 232, 5000 Dawes Ave, Alexandria, 22311, SAN 362-7039. Tel: 703-845-6231. Reference Tel: 703-845-6456. E-mail: library-al@nvcc.edu. Web Site: www.nvcc.edu/library/campus.html. *Assoc Dean, Tech & Learning Res, Libr Dir,* Matt Todd; Tel: 703-845-6033, E-mail: mtodd@nvcc.edu; *Coll Develop Librn,* Paul Chapman; Tel: 703-845-5066, E-mail: pchapman@nvcc.edu; *Instruction Librn,* AnneMarie Anderson; Tel: 703-845-6025, E-mail: aanderson@nvcc.edu; *Instrul Tech Librn, Pub Serv Librn,* Katie Hoskins; Tel: 703-845-6031, E-mail: khoskins@nvcc.edu
Special Collections: ESL Resources
ANNANDALE CAMPUS, Goodwin Bldg (CG), 3rd Flr, 8333 Little River Tpk, 22003. Tel: 703-323-3128. Reference Tel: 703-323-3410. E-mail: ANlibrary@nvcc.edu. *Assoc Libr Dir,* Elizabeth Bryan Dellavedova; Tel: 703-323-3066, E-mail: edellavedova@nvcc.edu; Staff 14 (MLS 5, Non-MLS 9)
Fac 5; Highest Degree: Associate
Special Collections: Women's History (Judy Mann DiStefano Coll)
Subject Interests: Admin of justice, Electronic tech, Fire sci, Hotel, Mkt, Restaurant, Tourism, Travel
EXTENDED LEARNING INSTITUTE, 3922 Pender Dr, Fairfax, 22030. Tel: 703-503-6225. E-mail: ELI-Library@nvcc.edu. *Online Learning Librn,* Heather Blicher; *Libr Spec,* Position Currently Open
LOUDOUN CAMPUS, 21200 Campus Dr, Rm 200, Sterling, 20164-8699, SAN 362-7098. Tel: 703-450-2567. Reference Tel: 703-450-2661. E-mail: LD-Library@nvcc.edu. *Emerging Tech Librn,* Julie Combs; Tel: 703-948-2641, E-mail: jcombs@nvcc.edu; *Coll Develop, Outreach Librn,* Chrystie Greges; Tel: 703-450-2642, E-mail: cgreges@nvcc.edu; *Ref Spec,* Emily Jackson Dunlop; E-mail: ejacksondunlop@nvcc.edu
Subject Interests: Communications, Hort, Interior design, Veterinary tech
Open Mon-Thurs 8am-9pm, Fri 8-4, Sat 9-1
MANASSAS CAMPUS, Colgan Hall, Rm 129, 10950 Campus Dr, Manassas, 20109, SAN 362-7128. Tel: 703-257-6640. E-mail: malibrary@nvcc.edu. *Coll Develop,* Liz Leon; Tel: 703-257-6639, E-mail: ileon@nvcc.edu; *Tech & Instruction Librn,* Nathan Mueller; Tel: 703-257-6564, E-mail: nmueller@nvcc.edu; *Circ Spec, Ref Spec,* Rebekah Leitner-Marshall; Tel: 703-368-1079, E-mail: rleitnermarshall@nvcc.edu; Staff 6 (MLS 3, Non-MLS 3)
Fac 2
Open Mon-Thurs 8am-9pm, Fri 8-5, Sat 9-1 (Winter); Mon-Thurs 8:30am-9pm, Fri 8:30-5 (Summer)
MEDIA PROCESSING SERVICES, 8333 Little River Tpk, 22003-3796. Tel: 703-323-3095. *Librn,* Crystal Boyce; E-mail: cboyce@nvcc.edu; *Acq Mgr,* Patricia Pena; E-mail: ppena@nvcc.edu

JM MEDICAL EDUCATION CAMPUS, 6699 Springfield Center Dr, Rm 341, Springfield, 22150. Tel: 703-822-6684. E-mail: medlib@nvcc.edu. *Lead Med Librn,* Diane Kearney; Tel: 703-822-6681, E-mail: dkearney@nvcc.edu; *User Experience Librn,* Kristin Snawder; Tel: 703-822-6682, E-mail: ksnawder@nvcc.edu; *Coll Mgr, ILL,* Andrea Jensen; Tel: 703-822-6683, E-mail: amcelhenny@nvcc.edu; *Acq, Libr Spec II,* Becky Chen Wu; Tel: 703-822-0014, E-mail: hchenwu@nvcc.edu; *Technology Spec,* Kristen Mentzer; Tel: 703-822-9052, E-mail: kmentzer@nvcc.edu; Staff 6 (MLS 3, Non-MLS 3)
Founded 2003. Enrl 3,475; Fac 3; Highest Degree: Associate
Function: 24/7 Electronic res, Art exhibits, Audio & video playback equip for onsite use, Audiobks via web, CD-ROM, Computer training, Computers for patron use, Distance learning, E-Readers, E-Reserves, Electronic databases & coll, Equip loans & repairs, For res purposes, Health sci info serv, ILL available, Internet access, Learning ctr, Magnifiers for reading, Mail & tel request accepted, Online cat, Online info literacy tutorials on the web & in blackboard, Online ref, Orientations, Outside serv via phone, mail, e-mail & web, Photocopying/Printing, Ref serv available, Study rm, Telephone ref, VHS videos, Wheelchair accessible
Open Mon-Thurs 8am-9pm, Fri 8-5, Sat 9-1
Restriction: Open to pub for ref & circ; with some limitations, Open to students, fac & staff
WOODBRIDGE LIBRARY, Bldg WAS, Rm 230, 15200 Neabsco Mills Rd, Woodbridge, 22191, SAN 362-7152. Tel: 703-878-5733. E-mail: wolibrary@nvcc.edu. Web Site: www.nvcc.edu. *Librn,* Kerry J Cotter; E-mail: kcotter@nvcc.edu; *Libr Spec,* Taslima Khatun; E-mail: tkhatun@nvcc.edu; *Libr Spec,* Stephanie Sharkey; E-mail: ssharkey@nvcc.edu
Library Holdings: AV Mats 5,500; Bk Vols 40,000; Per Subs 250
Open Mon-Thurs 8am-9pm, Fri 8-5, Sat 9-3:30; Mon-Thurs 8am-9pm, Fri 8-5 (Summer)

APPOMATTOX

P J ROBERT JAMERSON MEMORIAL LIBRARY*, 157 Main St, 24522. (Mail add: PO Box 789, 24522-0789). Tel: 434-352-5340. FAX: 434-352-0933. E-mail: info@jrjml.org. Web Site: www.jrjml.org. *Dir,* Diana Harvey; E-mail: director@jrjml.org
Founded 1936. Pop 15,500
Library Holdings: Bk Titles 52,000; Per Subs 40; Talking Bks 900
Automation Activity & Vendor Info: (Circulation) Koha; (OPAC) Koha
Wireless access
Open Mon & Fri 9:30-5, Tues-Thurs 9:30-8, Sat 9:30-1
Friends of the Library Group

G NATIONAL PARK SERVICE*, Appomattox Court House Library, PO Box 218, 24522. SAN 370-2774. Tel: 434-352-8987, Ext 232. FAX: 434-352-8330. Web Site: www.nps.gov/apco. *Historian, Library Contact,* Patrick A Schroeder; E-mail: patrick_schroeder@nps.gov
Library Holdings: Bk Titles 2,500
Open Mon-Sun 9-5

ARLINGTON

P ARLINGTON COUNTY DEPARTMENT OF LIBRARIES*, Arlington Public Library, 1015 N Quincy St, 22201. SAN 362-7217. Tel: 703-228-3348, 703-228-5990. Circulation Tel: 703-228-5940. Reference Tel: 703-228-5959. FAX: 703-228-7720. E-mail: libraries@arlingtonva.us. Web Site: library.arlingtonva.us. *Dir,* Diane Kresh; E-mail: dkresh@arlingtonva.us; *Dep Dir,* Anne Gable; Tel: 703-228-5981, E-mail: agable@arlingtonva.us; *Div Chief, Br Serv,* Gale Koritansky; Tel:

703-228-6334; *Br Mgr, Div Chief, Cent Serv,* LeoNard Thompson; Tel: 703-228-5952; *Div Chief, Mat & Tech Mgt,* Peter Petruski; Tel: 703-228-6339; *Virtual Libr Mgr,* Stacia Aho; Tel: 703-228-5968, E-mail: saho@arlingtonva.us
Founded 1937. Pop 209,300
Library Holdings: Bk Titles 569,913
Special Collections: Children's Illustrators (Francis & Elizabeth Booth Silver Coll); State & Local Data (Virginiana Coll). Oral History
Automation Activity & Vendor Info: (Cataloging) Innovative Interfaces, Inc - Millennium; (Circulation) Innovative Interfaces, Inc - Millennium; (OPAC) Innovative Interfaces, Inc - Millennium
Wireless access
Special Services for the Deaf - Staff with knowledge of sign lang; TDD equip
Special Services for the Blind - Bks on cassette; Computer with voice synthesizer for visually impaired persons; Home delivery serv; Talking bks; Talking bks & player equip
Open Mon-Thurs 10-9, Fri & Sat 10-5, Sun 1-9
Friends of the Library Group
Branches: 9
AURORA HILLS, 735 S 18th St, 22202, SAN 362-7241. Tel: 703-228-5715. FAX: 703-892-9378. *Br Mgr,* Michael Davis, Jr; Tel: 703-228-5716
Founded 1973. Circ 163,477
Library Holdings: Bk Vols 42,207
Open Mon & Thurs 10-9, Tues & Wed 1-9, Fri & Sat 10-5
Friends of the Library Group
CENTRAL LIBRARY, 1015 N Quincy St, 22201, SAN 362-7276. Tel: 703-228-5990. *Br Mgr,* LeoNard Thompson
Founded 1961. Circ 949,761
Library Holdings: Bk Vols 290,470
Special Collections: Children's Illustrators; College (Career Coll); Talking Books; Vietnamese Coll
Subject Interests: Art, Local hist, Spanish, Virginiana
Open Mon-Thurs 10-9, Fri & Sat 10-5, Sun 1-9
Friends of the Library Group
CHERRYDALE, 2190 N Military Rd, 22207, SAN 362-7306. Tel: 703-228-6330. *Br Mgr,* Katherine Regeimbal
Circ 117,995
Library Holdings: Bk Vols 32,816
Open Mon & Thurs 10-9, Tues & Wed 1-9, Fri & Sat 10-5
Friends of the Library Group
COLUMBIA PIKE, 816 S Walter Reed Dr, 22204, SAN 362-7330. Tel: 703-228-5710. FAX: 703-228-5559. *Br Mgr,* Megan Biggins; Tel: 703-228-5711
Circ 193,591
Library Holdings: Bk Vols 51,316
Special Collections: Vocational Coll
Open Mon & Wed 10-9, Tues & Sun 1-9, Thurs 10-6, Fri & Sat 10-5
Friends of the Library Group
GLENCARLYN, 300 S Kensington St, 22204, SAN 362-7365. Tel: 703-228-6548. *Br Mgr,* Steven Carr
Circ 78,426
Library Holdings: Bk Titles 27,860
Open Mon & Thurs 10-9, Tues & Wed 1-9, Fri & Sat 10-5
Friends of the Library Group
PLAZA LIBRARY, 2100 Clarendon Blvd, Lobby, 22201, SAN 329-627X. Tel: 703-228-3352. *Br Mgr,* Kerby Valladares
Founded 1989. Circ 39,722
Library Holdings: Bk Titles 2,149
Function: Computers for patron use, Electronic databases & coll, Govt ref serv, ILL available, Mail & tel request accepted, Notary serv, Online cat, Orientations, Photocopying/Printing, Ref serv available, Wheelchair accessible
Open Mon-Fri 8-5
Friends of the Library Group
SHIRLINGTON, 4200 Campbell Ave, 22206, SAN 362-739X. Tel: 703-228-6545. FAX: 703-933-1059. *Br Mgr,* Genelle Schuler; Tel: 703-228-6546, E-mail: gschuler@arlingtonva.us
Circ 276,971
Library Holdings: Bk Titles 59,156
Open Mon & Wed 10-9, Tues & Sun 1-9, Thurs 10-6, Fri & Sat 10-5
Friends of the Library Group
VIRTUAL BRANCH, 1015 N Quincy St, 22201. Tel: 703-228-5990.
Circ 705,343
Function: 24/7 Electronic res, 24/7 Online cat
WESTOVER, 1644 N McKinley Rd, Ste 3, 22205, SAN 362-742X. Tel: 703-228-5260. FAX: 703-228-0531. *Br Mgr,* Kate Moran; E-mail: kmoran@arlingtonva.us
Circ 320,607
Library Holdings: Bk Titles 63,939
Open Mon & Wed 10-9, Tues 1-9, Thurs 10-6, Fri & Sat 10-5
Friends of the Library Group

S BLOOMBERG INDUSTRY GROUP LIBRARY*, 1801 S Bell St, 22202. SAN 326-9256. Tel: 703-341-3303. Interlibrary Loan Service Tel: 703-341-3303. E-mail: library@bna.com. Web Site: www.bloombergindustry.com. *Libr Dir,* Michael G Bernier; Tel: 703-341-5752, E-mail: mbernier@bloomberglaw.com; *Ref Librn,* Lan Choi; Tel: 703-341-3313, E-mail: lchoi@bloomberglaw.com; *Ref Librn,* Catherine A Kitchell; Tel: 703-341-3311, E-mail: ckitchell@bloomberglaw.com; *Cat,* Matthew Newton; Tel: 703-341-3308, E-mail: mnewton@bloomberglaw.com; *ILL,* Robert Te Tan; Tel: 703-341-3315, E-mail: rtetan@bloomberglaw.com; *Tech Serv,* Clare Bailey; Tel: 703-341-3306, E-mail: cbailey@bloomberglaw.com; Staff 6 (MLS 5, Non-MLS 1)
Special Collections: BNA Publications, non-circulating
Subject Interests: Employment, Environ, Healthcare, Human res, Labor, Law, Tax
Automation Activity & Vendor Info: (Acquisitions) SirsiDynix; (Cataloging) SirsiDynix; (Circulation) SirsiDynix; (Discovery) EBSCO Discovery Service; (OPAC) SirsiDynix; (Serials) SirsiDynix
Wireless access
Function: ILL available

S CENTER FOR NAVAL ANALYSES LIBRARY*, 3003 Washington Blvd, 22201. SAN 317-1981. Tel: 703-824-2003. Web Site: www.cna.org. *Supvr,* Joanna Philpotts; Tel: 703-824-2111, E-mail: philpottsj@cna.org; Staff 3 (MLS 1, Non-MLS 2)
Founded 1962
Library Holdings: Bk Vols 15,000; Per Subs 300
Subject Interests: Econ, Math, Mil sci, Polit sci, Statistics
Automation Activity & Vendor Info: (Cataloging) SirsiDynix; (Circulation) SirsiDynix; (ILL) OCLC; (OPAC) SirsiDynix; (Serials) SirsiDynix
Wireless access
Publications: Acquisitions Bulletin; Items of Interest; List of Journal Holdings
Partic in OCLC Online Computer Library Center, Inc
Open Mon-Fri 8-5

S CONSUMER TECHNOLOGY ASSOCIATION (CTA), Research Library, 1919 S Eads St, 22202. SAN 328-1418. Tel: 703-907-7600. E-mail: info@cta.tech. Web Site: www.cta.tech/resources/research. *Sr Libr Mgr,* Angela Titone; *Sr Res Librn,* Lydia Chevalier; *Sr Res Librn,* Kurt Flick; Staff 3 (MLS 3)
Founded 1984
Library Holdings: Bk Titles 800; Per Subs 20
Special Collections: Consumer Technology Association Research Library & Archives; Consumer Technology Industry News
Wireless access

S FMI-THE FOOD INDUSTRY ASSOCIATION*, Information Service, 2345 Crystal Dr, Ste 800, 22202. SAN 371-0300. Tel: 202-452-8444. E-mail: fmi@fmi.org. Web Site: www.fmi.org. *Library Contact,* Susan C Wilkinson; Staff 1 (MLS 1)
Founded 1948
Library Holdings: Bk Vols 3,000; Per Subs 50
Wireless access

S INSURANCE INSTITUTE FOR HIGHWAY SAFETY LIBRARY*, 1005 N Glebe Rd, Ste 800, 22201. SAN 302-6760. Tel: 703-247-1500. FAX: 703-247-1678. Web Site: www.iihs.org. *Librn,* Ellen Adler; E-mail: eadler@iihs.org; Staff 1 (Non-MLS 1)
Founded 1959
Library Holdings: Bk Titles 20,000; Per Subs 150
Special Collections: US Dept of Transportation Regulatory Docket Materials
Subject Interests: Transportation
Automation Activity & Vendor Info: (Circulation) Inmagic, Inc.
Function: Res libr
Restriction: Circulates for staff only, Co libr, Internal circ only, Not a lending libr, Not open to pub

C MARYMOUNT UNIVERSITY*, Emerson G Reinsch Library, 2807 N Glebe Rd, 22207-4299. SAN 317-2198. Tel: 703-284-1533. Reference Tel: 703-284-1649. Administration Tel: 703-284-1673. FAX: 703-284-1685. Administration FAX: 703-526-6820. Web Site: www.marymount.edu/Academics/Library-Learning-Services. *Univ Librn,* Alison Gregory; E-mail: agregory@marymount.edu; *Librn,* Gwen Vredevoogdi; E-mail: gvredevo@marymount.edu; Staff 13 (MLS 11, Non-MLS 2)
Founded 1950. Enrl 3,609; Fac 350; Highest Degree: Doctorate
Library Holdings: AV Mats 2,295; e-books 295; e-journals 3,990; Electronic Media & Resources 108; Bk Titles 155,058; Bk Vols 203,883; Per Subs 31,082
Special Collections: Economics (Gertrude Hoyt Memorial Coll); John T & Agnes J Gomatos Reading Room; Wilhelmina Boldt Reading Room

Subject Interests: Educ, Fashion design, Graphic design, Human resource mgt, Interior design, Nursing, Philos, Psychol
Automation Activity & Vendor Info: (Acquisitions) Ex Libris Group; (Cataloging) Ex Libris Group; (Circulation) Ex Libris Group; (Course Reserve) Ex Libris Group; (ILL) Ex Libris Group; (OPAC) Ex Libris Group; (Serials) Ex Libris Group
Wireless access
Publications: Connection
Partic in OCLC Online Computer Library Center, Inc; Virginia Independent College & University Library Association; Virginia's Academic Library Consortium; Washington Research Library Consortium

L WALTER T MCCARTHY LAW LIBRARY*, Court House, 1425 N Courthouse Rd, Ste 1700, 22201. SAN 317-2120. Tel: 703-228-7005. FAX: 703-228-7360. E-mail: lawlibrary@arlingtonva.us. Web Site: arlingtonva.us/government/departments/courts/walter-t-mccarthy-law-library. *Dir,* Patricia Petroccione; E-mail: ppetroccione@arlingtonva.us; Staff 1 (MLS 1)
Founded 1977
Library Holdings: Bk Vols 22,000; Per Subs 5
Special Collections: All Regional & Federal Reporters; Form Books; Old Codes & Acts of Assembly, Virginia; Virginia Treatises
Open Mon & Fri 11-4, Wed 12-4

S UNITED STATES DEPARTMENT OF JUSTICE*, Drug Enforcement Administration Library, 700 Army Navy Dr, 22202. (Mail add: 8701 Morrissette Dr, Springfield, 22152), SAN 302-6396. Tel: 202-307-8932. FAX: 202-307-8939. E-mail: dea.library@usdoj.gov. *Librn,* Rosemary Russo; Staff 3 (MLS 2, Non-MLS 1)
Founded 1960
Library Holdings: Bk Vols 15,000; Per Subs 147
Subject Interests: Drug abuse, Drug laws
Automation Activity & Vendor Info: (OPAC) Horizon
Publications: Acquisition List (Monthly)

ASHBURN

S HOWARD HUGHES MEDICAL INSTITUTE*, Janelia Research Campus, 19700 Helix Dr, 20147. SAN 323-7087. Tel: 571-209-4124. E-mail: library@janella.hhmi.org. Web Site: www.janelia.org. *Librn,* Jaime Palay; Staff 1 (MLS 1)
Automation Activity & Vendor Info: (Acquisitions) EOS International; (Cataloging) EOS International; (Circulation) EOS International; (Discovery) EBSCO Discovery Service; (OPAC) EOS International; (Serials) EOS International
Wireless access
Function: ILL available
Restriction: Authorized personnel only, Borrowing requests are handled by ILL, Not open to pub

S NATIONAL RECREATION & PARK ASSOCIATION*, Joseph Lee Memorial Library & Archives, 22377 Belmont Ridge Rd, 20148. SAN 370-6915. Tel: 703-858-2151. Toll Free Tel: 800-626-6772. FAX: 703-858-0794. E-mail: customerservice@nrpa.org. Web Site: www.nrpa.org/about-national-recreation-and-park-association/josephleememoriallibrary. *Sr Res Libr Mgr,* Melissa May; E-mail: mmay@nrpa.org
Founded 1989
Library Holdings: Bk Titles 5,000
Special Collections: American Institute of Park Executives Coll; American Park Secrets Coll; National Conference on State Parks Coll; National Recreation Association Coll; Playground Association of America Coll
Publications: Thesaurus of Park Recreation & Leisure Service Terms
Open Mon-Fri 8:30-4:45
Restriction: Non-circulating

ASHLAND

C RANDOLPH-MACON COLLEGE, McGraw-Page Library, 305 Henry St, 23005. (Mail add: PO Box 5005, 23005-5505), SAN 317-2309. Tel: 804-752-7257. Circulation Tel: 804-752-7388. Reference Tel: 804-752-4718. E-mail: library@rmc.edu. Web Site: library.rmc.edu/library. *Libr Dir,* Nancy Falciani-White; Tel: 804-752-7256, E-mail: nancyfalcianiwhite@rmc.edu; Staff 5 (MLS 4, Non-MLS 1)
Founded 1830. Enrl 1,500; Fac 132; Highest Degree: Master
Library Holdings: Bk Vols 153,515
Special Collections: 18th Century European Culture (Casanova & Goudar Coll); Henry Miller Coll; Intellectual History of the Colonial South Coll; Southern History Coll; Virginia Methodism Coll
Automation Activity & Vendor Info: (Acquisitions) OCLC Worldshare Management Services; (Cataloging) OCLC Worldshare Management Services; (Circulation) OCLC Worldshare Management Services; (Course Reserve) OCLC Worldshare Management Services; (ILL) OCLC Worldshare Management Services; (OPAC) OCLC Worldshare Management Services; (Serials) OCLC Worldshare Management Services
Wireless access
Partic in LYRASIS; Oberlin Group; Richmond Academic Library Consortium; Virginia Independent College & University Library Association; Virginia Library Association

BASSETT

S BASSETT HISTORICAL CENTER, 3964 Fairystone Park Hwy, 24055. Tel: 276-629-9191. FAX: 276-629-9840. E-mail: bhcenter3964@gmail.com. Web Site: www.bassetthistoricalcenter.com. *Dir,* Fran Snead; *Asst Dir,* Anne Copeland
Founded 1939
Library Holdings: CDs 141; Microforms 477; Bk Vols 20,000; Per Subs 263; Videos 49
Subject Interests: Genealogy, Local hist
Wireless access
Function: Res libr
Open Mon, Wed & Thurs 10-5, Tues 12-5, Fri 10-2
Restriction: Non-circulating

BEDFORD

P BEDFORD PUBLIC LIBRARY SYSTEM*, 321 N Bridge St, 24523-1924. SAN 317-2317. Tel: 540-586-8911. FAX: 540-586-8875. Web Site: www.bplsonline.org. *Libr Dir,* Jenny Novalis; Tel: 540-586-8911, Ext 1140, E-mail: jnovalis@bpls.org; *Librn,* Katie Hoffman; Tel: 540-586-8911, Ext 1110, E-mail: khoffman@bpls.org; *Youth Serv Librn,* Cassandra Baldwin; Tel: 540-586-8911, Ext 1130, E-mail: cbaldwin@bpls.org; *Homebound Serv,* Lyn Coppedge; Tel: 540-586-8911, Ext 1114, E-mail: lcoppedge@bpls.org; *ILL,* Indya Page; Tel: 540-586-8911, Ext 1112, E-mail: ipage@bpls.org; Staff 17 (MLS 4, Non-MLS 13)
Founded 1900. Pop 67,800; Circ 471,896
Library Holdings: AV Mats 18,691; Bk Vols 199,186; Per Subs 157
Special Collections: World War II
Subject Interests: Local hist
Automation Activity & Vendor Info: (Acquisitions) TLC (The Library Corporation); (Cataloging) TLC (The Library Corporation); (Circulation) TLC (The Library Corporation); (OPAC) TLC (The Library Corporation)
Wireless access
Function: Adult bk club, Art exhibits, Audio & video playback equip for onsite use, Bks on cassette, Bks on CD, Children's prog, Computer training, Computers for patron use, Digital talking bks, Holiday prog, Homebound delivery serv, ILL available, Large print keyboards, Music CDs, Online cat, Photocopying/Printing, Prog for children & young adult, Story hour, Summer reading prog, Tax forms, Teen prog, Wheelchair accessible
Open Mon, Wed, Fri & Sat 9-5:30, Tues & Thurs 9-8, Sun (Sept-May) 1:30-5:30
Friends of the Library Group
Branches: 5
BIG ISLAND LIBRARY, 1111 Schooldays Rd, Big Island, 24526. Tel: 540-425-7000. FAX: 434-299-6151. Web Site: www.bplsonline.org/bi. *Br Librn,* Dawn Fisher; E-mail: dfisher@bpls.org
Open Mon, Thurs & Fri 10-5, Tues 10-7, Sat 9-12
Friends of the Library Group
FOREST LIBRARY, 15583 Forest Rd, Forest, 24551. Tel: 540-425-7002. FAX: 434-525-9232. Web Site: www.bplsonline.org/fo. *Br Librn,* Lauren Harper; E-mail: lharper@bpls.org
Open Mon, Tues & Thurs 9-9, Wed, Fri & Sat 9-5:30, Sun 1:30-5:30
Friends of the Library Group
MONETA/SMITH MOUNTAIN LAKE LIBRARY, 13641 Moneta Rd, Moneta, 24121. Tel: 540-425-7004. FAX: 540-297-6474. Web Site: www.bplsonline.org/mo. *Br Librn,* Jenifer Golston; E-mail: jgolston@bpls.org
Open Mon, Wed, Fri & Sat 9-5:30, Tues & Thurs 9-8
Friends of the Library Group
MONTVALE LIBRARY, 11575 W Lynchburg-Salem Tpk, Montvale, 24122. (Mail add: PO Box 429, Montvale, 24122). Tel: 540-425-7006. FAX: 540-947-0300. Web Site: www.bplsonline.org/mv. *Br Librn,* Kristin Robertson; E-mail: krobertson@bpls.org
Open Mon & Fri 9-5, Tues & Thurs Noon-8, Sat 10-1
Friends of the Library Group
STEWARTSVILLE LIBRARY, 45 Cascade Dr, Vinton, 24179. Tel: 540-425-7008. FAX: 540-890-4530. Web Site: www.bplsonline.org/sv. *Br Librn,* Nicole Sheppard; E-mail: nsheppard@bpls.org
Open Mon & Fri 10-5, Tues & Thurs 10-7, Sat 9-Noon

BERRYVILLE

SR HOLY CROSS ABBEY LIBRARY*, 901 Cool Spring Lane, 22611-2700. SAN 317-2325. Tel: 540-955-4383. FAX: 540-955-1356. E-mail: information@hcava.org. Staff 1 (MLS 1)
Founded 1950
Library Holdings: Bk Vols 25,000; Per Subs 59

Automation Activity & Vendor Info: (Cataloging) TLC (The Library Corporation)
Restriction: Open by appt only

BIG STONE GAP

J MOUNTAIN EMPIRE COMMUNITY COLLEGE*, Wampler Library, Robb Hall, 2nd Flr, 3441 Mountain Empire Rd, 24219. SAN 317-2333. Tel: 276-523-2400, Ext 468. FAX: 276-523-8220. Web Site: www.mecc.edu/library. *Dir, Libr Serv,* Terence Michael Gilley; Tel: 276-523-2400, Ext 304, E-mail: mgilley@mecc.edu; *Tech Serv,* Makenzie Dickenson; Tel: 276-523-2400, Ext 267, E-mail: mdickenson@mecc.edu; Staff 3 (MLS 1, Non-MLS 2)
Founded 1972. Enrl 2,136; Fac 86; Highest Degree: Associate
Library Holdings: AV Mats 2,195; e-books 21,333; e-journals 20,000; Electronic Media & Resources 7,916; Microforms 8,000; Bk Titles 40,006; Bk Vols 44,136; Per Subs 113
Subject Interests: Criminal justice, Nursing, Respiratory therapy
Automation Activity & Vendor Info: (Acquisitions) Ex Libris Group; (Cataloging) Ex Libris Group; (Circulation) Ex Libris Group; (OPAC) Ex Libris Group
Function: Archival coll, Art exhibits, Audiobks via web, Computers for patron use, Electronic databases & coll, ILL available, Online cat, Online info literacy tutorials on the web & in blackboard, Online ref, OverDrive digital audio bks, Photocopying/Printing, Wheelchair accessible
Partic in SouthWest Information Network Group; Virginia Commun Coll Syst; Virginia's Academic Library Consortium
Open Mon-Thurs 8-7:30, Fri 8-4:30, Sat 10-2

BLACKSBURG

C VIRGINIA POLYTECHNIC INSTITUTE & STATE UNIVERSITY LIBRARIES*, Newman Library, 560 Drillfield Dr, 24061. SAN 362-7454. Tel: 540-231-6170. Circulation Tel: 540-231-6340. Reference Tel: 540-231-9232. FAX: 540-231-3946. Web Site: www.lib.vt.edu. *Chief Strategy Officer,* Zhiwu Xie; Tel: 540-231-4453, E-mail: zhiwuxie@vt.edu; *Dean of Libr,* Tyler Walters; Tel: 540-231-5595, E-mail: tyler.walters@vt.edu; *Asst Dean, Dir, IT,* Bill Ingram; Tel: 540-231-8642, E-mail: waingram@vt.edu; *Asst Dean, Dir, Research Collaboration & Engagement,* Ginny Pannabecker; Tel: 540-231-7980, E-mail: vpannabe@vt.edu; *Director of Engagement, Dir of Organizational Dev,* Eric Glenn; *Dir, Scholarly Communications,* Gail McMillan; Tel: 540-231-9252, E-mail: gailmac@vt.edu; *Dir, Commun & Tech Serv,* Leslie O'Brien; Tel: 540-231-4945, E-mail: lobrien@vt.edu; *Dir, Learning Environment,* Patrick Tomlin; Tel: 540-231-9272, E-mail: tomlin@vt.edu; *Dir, Spec Coll,* Aaron Purcell; Tel: 540-231-9672, E-mail: adp@vt.edu; *Assoc Dir, Coll Mgt,* Edward Lener; Tel: 540-231-9249, E-mail: lener@vt.edu; *Asst Dir, Spec Coll & Archives,* Kira Dietz; Tel: 540-231-3810, E-mail: kadietz@vt.edu; *Syst Adminr,* Soumik Ghosh; Tel: 540-231-7022, E-mail: soumikgh@vt.edu; *Head, Acq,* Beth Anderson; Tel: 540-231-4884, E-mail: bporterf@vt.edu; *Head, ILL,* Sharon Gotkiewicz; Tel: 540-231-9202, E-mail: sgotkiew@vt.edu; Staff 128 (MLS 38, Non-MLS 90)
Founded 1872. Enrl 27,887; Fac 1,371; Highest Degree: Doctorate
Library Holdings: CDs 12,975; DVDs 18,185; e-books 192,483; e-journals 9,302; Microforms 6,329,176; Bk Titles 1,466,099; Bk Vols 2,385,815; Per Subs 22,765
Special Collections: American & British Literature, 1880-1940 (Dayton Kohler Coll); Appalachian History & Folk Culture, incl Patrick County Oral History Coll & Blue Ridge Parkway Folk Life Oral History Coll; Archives of American Aerospace Exploration incl Papers of Melvin N Gough, Samuel Herrick, Christopher C Kraft, Jr & John T Parsons; Heraldry (Harry D Temple Coll); History of Technology Coll; History of Women's Involvement in Architecture (International Archive of Women in Architecture, incl Papers of Hanna Schroeder, Verena Dietrich, Ilse Koci & Elise Sundt); Late 19th Century Children's Literature (John H Barnes Coll); Ornithology (Harold H Bailey Coll); Railroad History Coll; Sherwood Anderson Coll; Southwest Virginia History (Black-Kent-Apperson Family Papers, Preston Family Papers & J Hoge Tyler Papers); Western Americana. State Document Depository; US Document Depository
Subject Interests: Agr, Archit, Art, Behav sci, Biology, Engr, Humanities, Phys sci, Soc sci
Automation Activity & Vendor Info: (Cataloging) Innovative Interfaces, Inc; (Circulation) Innovative Interfaces, Inc; (OPAC) Innovative Interfaces, Inc; (Serials) Innovative Interfaces, Inc
Wireless access
Publications: Off the Shelf
Partic in Consortium for Continuing Higher Educ in Northern Va; National Network of Libraries of Medicine Region 1; OCLC Online Computer Library Center, Inc; OCLC Research Library Partnership; Virginia's Academic Library Consortium

Departmental Libraries:

ART & ARCHITECTURE, Cowgill Hall, Rm 100, 24060. Tel: 540-231-9271. Web Site: lib.vt.edu/about-us/libraries/artarch-library.html. *Librn,* Scott Fralin; Tel: 540-231-3068, E-mail: safralin@vt.edu
Library Holdings: Bk Vols 80,000

NORTHERN VIRGINIA RESOURCE CENTER, 7054 Haycock Rd, Falls Church, 22043-2311, SAN 362-7543. Tel: 703-538-8340. E-mail: nvclibrary@vt.edu. Web Site: lib.vt.edu/about-us/libraries/nvc-resource-center.html. *Librn,* Debbie Cash; Tel: 703-538-8341, E-mail: dcash@vt.edu; Staff 2 (Non-MLS 2)
Enrl 1,000; Highest Degree: Doctorate
Library Holdings: Bk Vols 1,300
Open Mon-Thurs 11-8, Fri 11-6, Sat 9-5

CM VETERINARY MEDICINE, 245 Duck Pond Dr, 24061-0442. Tel: 540-231-6610. FAX: 540-231-7367. E-mail: vetmedlib-g@vt.edu. Web Site: guides.lib.vt.edu/vetmed. *Librn,* Kiri DeBose; Tel: 540-231-0495, E-mail: kdebose@vt.edu
Library Holdings: Bk Vols 11,880
Open Mon-Thurs 7:30am-9pm, Fri 7:30-5, Sat 1-6, Sun 11-9 (Winter); Mon-Fri 9-5 (Summer)

BLAND

P BLAND COUNTY LIBRARY*, 697 Main St, 24315. (Mail add: PO Box 480, 24315-0480), SAN 377-6816. Tel: 276-688-3737. FAX: 276-688-9820. Web Site: www.youseemore.com/bcpl. *Dir, Libr Serv,* Ms Cameron Burton; E-mail: cburton@bland.org; *Br Mgr,* Ms Robin Stover; E-mail: robin.stover@bland.org
Founded 1972. Pop 6,800
Library Holdings: Bk Vols 27,000; Per Subs 35
Automation Activity & Vendor Info: (Circulation) Innovative Interfaces, Inc
Wireless access
Function: 24/7 Electronic res, 24/7 Online cat, Activity rm, Art exhibits, Art programs, Audio & video playback equip for onsite use, Audiobks on Playaways & MP3, Audiobks via web, AV serv, Bks on CD, Children's prog, Computer training, Computers for patron use, E-Reserves, Electronic databases & coll, Equip loans & repairs, Free DVD rentals, Holiday prog, Home delivery & serv to seniorr ctr & nursing homes, Homebound delivery serv, Instruction & testing, Internet access, Laminating, Life-long learning prog for all ages, Magazines, Meeting rooms, Microfiche/film & reading machines, Movies, Music CDs, Online cat, Online ref, Outreach serv, OverDrive digital audio bks, Photocopying/Printing, Preschool outreach, Preschool reading prog, Printer for laptops & handheld devices, Prog for adults, Prog for children & young adult, Ref & res, Ref serv available, Res assist avail, Scanner, Senior computer classes, Senior outreach, STEM programs, Story hour, Summer & winter reading prog, Summer reading prog, Tax forms, Teen prog, Wheelchair accessible
Partic in SouthWest Information Network Group
Special Services for the Deaf - Closed caption videos
Special Services for the Blind - Audio mat; Bks on cassette; Bks on CD; Large print bks
Open Mon, Wed, Fri & Sat 10-4:30, Tues & Thurs 10-7:30
Friends of the Library Group

S VIRGINIA DEPARTMENT OF CORRECTIONS, Bland Correctional Center Library, 256 Bland Farm Rd, 24315. Tel: 276-688-3341, Ext 88721. Web Site: vadoc.virginia.gov/facilities-and-offices. *Librn,* Kelly Shelton
Library Holdings: Bk Vols 12,000; Per Subs 40

BLUEFIELD

C BLUEFIELD UNIVERSITY*, Easley Library, 3000 College Ave, 24605. SAN 317-235X. Tel: 276-326-4267. FAX: 276-326-4288. Web Site: bluefield.edu/academics/easley-library. *Co-Director, Library Services, Sr Asst Librn,* Paula Beasley; Tel: 276-326-4269, E-mail: pbeasley@bluefield.edu; *Co-Director, Library Services, Librn,* Werner Lind; E-mail: wlind@bluefield.edu; *Assoc Librn, Ref/Electronic Res Librn,* Lynnette Bartlett; Tel: 276-326-4237, E-mail: lbartlett@bluefield.edu; Staff 3 (MLS 3)
Founded 1922. Enrl 772; Fac 46; Highest Degree: Master
Library Holdings: Bk Titles 55,000; Bk Vols 56,000; Per Subs 250
Special Collections: McKenzie Memorial Religion Coll
Automation Activity & Vendor Info: (Acquisitions) Innovative Interfaces, Inc; (Cataloging) Innovative Interfaces, Inc; (Circulation) Innovative Interfaces, Inc; (Course Reserve) Innovative Interfaces, Inc; (ILL) Innovative Interfaces, Inc; (Media Booking) Innovative Interfaces, Inc; (OPAC) Innovative Interfaces, Inc; (Serials) Innovative Interfaces, Inc
Wireless access
Function: Ref serv available
Publications: Library Home Pages
Partic in Appalachian College Association; LYRASIS; SouthWest Information Network Group; Virginia Independent College & University Library Association; Virginia's Academic Library Consortium

Open Mon-Thurs 7:45am-10pm, Fri 7:45-5, Sat 10-5:30, Sun 2-10
Restriction: Circ limited

BOYCE

S RAILWAY MAIL SERVICE LIBRARY, INC*, 117 E Main St, 22620-9639. SAN 324-7996. Tel: 540-837-9090. Administration Tel: 571-379-3409. Web Site: www.railwaymailservicelibrary.org. *Curator, Pres,* Dr Frank R Scheer; E-mail: fscheer@railwaymailservicelibrary.org; *VPres, Libr & Info Serv,* William J Keller; Staff 5 (Non-MLS 5)
Founded 1951
Library Holdings: AV Mats 23; Bk Titles 1,600; Bk Vols 1,700
Special Collections: Chip Komoroske Railroad Book Coll; E B Bergman Schedule of Mall Routes Coll; E J Maloney Marking Device Coll; H E Rankin General Scheme Coll; J R Mundy Postal Lock Coll; L Cohen International Postal Insignia Coll; R R Schmidt Marking Device Coll
Subject Interests: En-route distribution, Postal markings, Transportation of mail
Wireless access
Function: Archival coll, For res purposes, ILL available, Photocopying/Printing, Res libr
Publications: The Catcher Pouch (Newsletter)
Restriction: Access at librarian's discretion, Closed stack, Non-circulating to the pub, Open by appt only, Open to employees & special libr, Open to fac, students & qualified researchers, Open to pub with supv only, Private libr, Pub use on premises, Restricted loan policy, Use of others with permission of librn
Friends of the Library Group

BOYDTON

P MECKLENBURG COUNTY PUBLIC LIBRARY*, Boydton Public Library (Headquarters), 1294 Jefferson St, 23917. (Mail add: PO Box 10, 23917-0010), SAN 317-2376. Tel: 434-738-6580. FAX: 434-738-6070. Web Site: www.youseemore.com/mecklib. *Dir,* Robert Rosenthal; E-mail: rrosenthal@mecklib.org; *Br Supvr,* Leah Davis; E-mail: ldavis@mecklib.org; Staff 1 (MLS 1)
Founded 1944. Pop 29,596; Circ 176,676
Library Holdings: Bk Titles 69,688; Bk Vols 130,062; Per Subs 365; Talking Bks 3,245; Videos 1,542
Special Collections: Mecklenburg County Newspapers, late 1800s, micro
Subject Interests: Genealogy
Automation Activity & Vendor Info: (Cataloging) TLC (The Library Corporation); (Circulation) TLC (The Library Corporation); (OPAC) TLC (The Library Corporation)
Wireless access
Open Mon-Fri 9-5
Friends of the Library Group
Branches: 3
R T ARNOLD PUBLIC, 110 E Danville St, South Hill, 23970, SAN 372-7076. Tel: 434-447-8162. FAX: 434-447-4050. Web Site: www1.youseemore.com/mecklib/contentpages.asp?loc=44. *Br Supvr,* Gloria Taylor; E-mail: gtaylor@mecklib.org
Founded 1969
Library Holdings: Bk Vols 25,000
Open Mon-Fri 9-5, Sat 9-12
Friends of the Library Group
BURNETT LIBRARY & LEARNING CENTER, 914 Virginia Ave, Clarksville, 23927. (Mail add: PO Box 1146, Clarksville, 23927-1146), SAN 372-7092. Tel: 434-374-8692. FAX: 434-374-8200. Web Site: www1.youseemore.com/mecklib/contentpages.asp?loc=42. *Br Supvr,* Connie Boyd; E-mail: ceboyd@mecklib.org
Library Holdings: Bk Vols 22,500
Open Mon & Thurs 10-8, Tues, Wed & Fri 10-5, Sat 10-2
Friends of the Library Group
BUTLER MEMORIAL, 515 Marshall St, Chase City, 23924, SAN 372-7084. Tel: 434-372-4286. FAX: 434-372-0303. Web Site: www1.youseemore.com/mecklib/contentpages.asp?loc=41. *Br Supvr,* Joyce Parcell-Greene; E-mail: jpgreene@mecklib.org
Founded 1982
Library Holdings: Bk Vols 24,200
Open Mon & Wed-Fri 10-5, Tues 10-8, Sat 10-1
Friends of the Library Group

BRIDGEWATER

C BRIDGEWATER COLLEGE, Forrer Learning Commons, 402 E College St, 22812. SAN 317-2384. Tel: 540-828-5413. Circulation Tel: 540-515-3782. Reference Tel: 540-828-5642. FAX: 540-828-5482. E-mail: circulation@bridgewater.edu. Web Site: libguides.bridgewater.edu. *Dir,* Andrew Pearson; Tel: 540-828-5410, E-mail: apearson@bridgewater.edu; *Learning Services, Librn,* Position Currently Open; *Metadata Librn,* Matt Yohn; Tel: 540-828-5414, E-mail: myohn@bridgewater.edu; *Syst Librn,* Roberta Lowe; Tel: 540-828-5740, E-mail: rlowe@bridgewater.edu; *Circ Supvr,* Position Currently Open; Staff 6 (MLS 6)
Founded 1880. Enrl 1,337; Fac 95; Highest Degree: Master
Library Holdings: Braille Volumes 5; CDs 1,662; DVDs 3,905; e-books 65,887; e-journals 96,171; Electronic Media & Resources 48,973; Microforms 2,105; Music Scores 139,790; Bk Titles 81,176; Bk Vols 85,438; Per Subs 123; Videos 37
Special Collections: Church of the Brethren Material. US Document Depository
Subject Interests: Genealogy, Local hist
Automation Activity & Vendor Info: (Acquisitions) OCLC Worldshare Management Services; (Cataloging) OCLC Worldshare Management Services; (Circulation) OCLC Worldshare Management Services; (ILL) OCLC Worldshare Management Services; (OPAC) OCLC Worldshare Management Services; (Serials) OCLC Worldshare Management Services
Wireless access
Function: Telephone ref
Partic in LYRASIS; OCLC Online Computer Library Center, Inc; Virginia Independent College & University Library Association; Virginia's Academic Library Consortium
Open Mon-Thurs 7:30am-Midnight, Fri 7:30-5, Sat 9-9, Sun Noon-Midnight (Winter); Mon-Fri 8-4:30 (Summer)

BRISTOL

P BRISTOL PUBLIC LIBRARY*, 701 Goode St, 24201. SAN 362-7578. Tel: 276-645-8780. Circulation Tel: 276-821-6133. Reference Tel: 276-645-8781, 276-821-6196. FAX: 276-669-5593. Administration FAX: 276-591-1606. E-mail: library@bristol-library.org. Web Site: bristol-library.org. *Exec Dir,* Tonia Kestner; Tel: 276-645-8782, E-mail: tonia@bristol-library.org; *YA Librn,* Amanda Anderson; Tel: 276-821-6192, E-mail: amandaa@bristol-library.org; *Acq, Cat,* Judy Moore; Tel: 276-821-6195, E-mail: jmoore@bristol-library.org; *Ch Serv,* Michelle Page; Tel: 276-821-6193, E-mail: mpage@bristol-library.org; *Adult Serv,* Jeanne Powers; E-mail: jpowers@bristol-library.org; Staff 34 (MLS 4, Non-MLS 30)
Founded 1909. Pop 73,000; Circ 252,200
Jul 2015-Jun 2016 Income (Main & Associated Libraries) $2,030,715, State $141,818, City $1,652,242, Federal $59,445, County $15,000, Locally Generated Income $162,210. Mats Exp $111,894, Books $73,667, Per/Ser (Incl. Access Fees) $10,443, Micro $4,488, AV Mat $19,647, Electronic Ref Mat (Incl. Access Fees) $3,649. Sal $817,717 (Prof $281,054)
Library Holdings: AV Mats 123; CDs 2,091; DVDs 8,578; Bk Titles 148,733; Bk Vols 151,768; Per Subs 185; Talking Bks 4,182
Subject Interests: Genealogy, Local hist, Tenn, Va
Automation Activity & Vendor Info: (Acquisitions) SirsiDynix; (Cataloging) SirsiDynix; (Circulation) SirsiDynix; (Serials) SirsiDynix
Wireless access
Partic in Mid-Atlantic Library Alliance
Open Mon-Thurs 9-8, Fri & Sat 9-5, Sun 2-5
Friends of the Library Group

BUENA VISTA

CR SOUTHERN VIRGINIA UNIVERSITY*, Von Canon Library, One University Hill Dr, 24416. SAN 317-2406. Tel: 540-261-4084. Administration Tel: 540-261-4090. FAX: 540-266-3898. E-mail: librarian@svu.edu. Web Site: voncanon.svu.edu. *Archivist, Dir, Libr Serv,* Stephanie Hardy; E-mail: stephanie.hardy@svu.edu; Staff 5 (MLS 3, Non-MLS 2)
Founded 1900. Enrl 750; Fac 50; Highest Degree: Bachelor
Library Holdings: Bk Titles 95,000
Special Collections: Melville Coll; Orson Scott Card; The Church of Jesus Christ of Latter-Day Saints (Mormon)
Automation Activity & Vendor Info: (Cataloging) EOS International; (Circulation) EOS International; (OPAC) EOS International
Wireless access
Function: Archival coll, Audio & video playback equip for onsite use, ILL available, Internet access, Photocopying/Printing, Ref serv available, VHS videos
Partic in Virginia Independent College & University Library Association; Virginia's Academic Library Consortium
Open Mon-Thurs 7:30am-Midnight, Fri 7am-8pm, Sat 10-7 (Fall & Spring); Mon-Fri 9-6 (Summer)

CAPRON

S DEERFIELD CORRECTIONAL CENTER*, DCE Library, 21360 Deerfield Dr, 23829. SAN 375-4979. Tel: 434-658-4368. FAX: 434-658-4371. *Librn,* Virginia Wright; E-mail: virginia.wright@vadoc.va.gov
Founded 1994
Library Holdings: Bk Titles 12,000; Bk Vols 15,000; Per Subs 30
Automation Activity & Vendor Info: (Circulation) Follett Software
Special Services for the Deaf - Bks on deafness & sign lang; High interest/low vocabulary bks
Open Mon-Fri 8-3

CATAWBA

GM CATAWBA HOSPITAL*, Professional Library, 5525 Catawba Hospital Dr, 24070. (Mail add: PO Box 200, 24070-0200), SAN 321-6004. Tel: 540-375-4281. FAX: 540-375-4348. *Actg Dir,* Lauren Carr; E-mail: lauren.carr@dbhds.virginia.gov
Founded 1978
Library Holdings: Bk Titles 420; Bk Vols 431; Per Subs 52
Restriction: Staff use only

CEDAR BLUFF

J SOUTHWEST VIRGINIA COMMUNITY COLLEGE LIBRARY*, Earl E & Dorothy J Dellinger Learning Resources Center, Russell Hall, 599 Community College Rd, 24609. (Mail add: PO Box SVCC, Richlands, 24641), SAN 317-3976. Tel: 276-964-7265. Information Services Tel: 276-964-7617. FAX: 276-964-7259. Web Site: www.sw.edu/library. *Coordr, Libr Serv,* Teresa Yearout; Tel: 276-964-7266, E-mail: Teresa.Yearout@sw.edu; *Educ Spec, Ref & Instruction,* Retta West; E-mail: Retta.West@sw.edu; *Circ & ILL,* Nancey Bonney; E-mail: Nancy.Bonney@sw.edu; Staff 3 (MLS 3)
Founded 1968. Enrl 2,856; Fac 162; Highest Degree: Associate
Library Holdings: AV Mats 1,592; Bks on Deafness & Sign Lang 25; e-books 42,000; Bk Vols 43,000; Per Subs 156; Talking Bks 1,422
Automation Activity & Vendor Info: (Cataloging) Ex Libris Group; (Circulation) Ex Libris Group; (ILL) OCLC; (OPAC) Ex Libris Group; (Serials) Ex Libris Group
Wireless access
Partic in Virginia Commun Coll Syst; Virginia's Academic Library Consortium
Open Mon-Thurs 7:45am-9pm, Fri 7:45-4:30, Sun 1-5

CHARLOTTE COURT HOUSE

P CHARLOTTE COUNTY LIBRARY*, 112-116 Legrande Ave, 23923. (Mail add: PO Box 788, 23923-0788), SAN 317-2414. Tel: 434-542-5247. E-mail: cclibrary@hovac.com. Web Site: www.cclibrary.net. *Librn,* Jim Watkins; E-mail: jcw@hovac.com; Staff 3 (Non-MLS 3)
Founded 1937. Circ 50,455
Library Holdings: Bk Vols 46,000; Per Subs 130
Wireless access
Partic in LYRASIS
Open Mon, Wed & Fri 9-5, Tues & Thurs 9-6, Sat 10-1
Friends of the Library Group
Branches: 3
KEYSVILLE BRANCH, 300 King St, Keysville, 23947. (Mail add: PO Box 805, Keysville, 23947-0805), SAN 373-2940. Tel: 434-736-0083. *Library Contact,* Betty Baughan; Staff 2 (Non-MLS 2)
Library Holdings: AV Mats 600; Bk Vols 18,193; Per Subs 12
Open Mon-Fri 10-6, Sat 10-1
Friends of the Library Group
PHENIX BRANCH, Charlotte St, Phenix, 23959. (Mail add: PO Box 187, Phenix, 23959-0187), SAN 373-2959. Tel: 434-542-4654. *Dir,* Jim Watkins; *Librn,* Linda LaPratt; Staff 1 (Non-MLS 1)
Library Holdings: AV Mats 600; Bk Titles 2,500; Bk Vols 5,000; Per Subs 12
Open Mon & Thurs 9-5, Sat 9-12
Friends of the Library Group
WYLLIESBURG COMMUNITY, Hwy 15, Wylliesburg, 23976, SAN 373-2932. Tel: 434-735-8812. *Librn,* Betty Baughan; Staff 2 (Non-MLS 2)
Library Holdings: AV Mats 600; Bk Vols 21,770; Per Subs 12
Open Mon, Wed & Fri 9-5, Sat 9-12
Friends of the Library Group

CHARLOTTESVILLE

P JEFFERSON-MADISON REGIONAL LIBRARY*, Central Library, 201 E Market St, 22902-5287. SAN 362-7632. Tel: 434-979-7151, Ext 6671. FAX: 434-971-7035. TDD: 434-293-6848. E-mail: central@jmrl.org. Web Site: www.jmrl.org. *Dir,* David Plunkett; E-mail: dplunkett@jmrl.org; *Br Mgr,* Krista Farrell; *Coll Develop,* Meredith Dickens; *Ref (Info Servs),* Sarah Hamfeldt; *YA Serv,* Timothy Carrier
Founded 1921. Pop 198,000; Circ 1,549,700
Library Holdings: Bk Vols 521,832
Special Collections: Charlottesville/Albemarle Historical Coll
Automation Activity & Vendor Info: (Cataloging) Innovative Interfaces, Inc; (Circulation) Innovative Interfaces, Inc
Wireless access
Function: Wheelchair accessible
Publications: E-Newsletter; Friends (Newsletter)
Special Services for the Deaf - TDD equip
Open Mon-Thurs 9-9, Fri & Sat 9-5, Sun 1-5
Friends of the Library Group
Branches: 7
CROZET BRANCH, 2020 Library Ave, Crozet, 22932. (Mail add: PO Box 430, Crozet, 22932-0430), SAN 362-7667. Tel: 434-823-4050. FAX: 434-823-8399. E-mail: crozet@jmrl.org. *Br Mgr,* Hayley Tompkins
Open Mon & Tues 1-9, Wed-Sat 9-5
GORDON AVE, 1500 Gordon Ave, 22903-1997, SAN 362-7691. Tel: 434-296-5544. FAX: 434-295-8737. E-mail: gordon@jmrl.org. *Br Mgr,* Camille Thompson
Open Mon 9-9, Tues 9-6, Wed 12-9, Thurs 10-6, Fri & Sat 10-5
Friends of the Library Group
GREENE COUNTY, 222 Main St, Ste 101, Standardsville, 22973, SAN 362-7721. Tel: 434-985-5227. FAX: 434-985-3315. E-mail: greene@jmrl.org. *Br Mgr,* Ginny Reese
Open Mon 1-8, Tues & Thurs 10-6, Fri 1-5, Sat 12-5
Friends of the Library Group
LOUISA COUNTY, 881 Davis Hwy, Mineral, 23117, SAN 362-7756. Tel: 540-894-5853. FAX: 540-894-9810. E-mail: louisa@jmrl.org. *Br Mgr,* Ophelia Payne
Open Mon & Tues Noon-7, Wed-Fri 10-5, Sat 9:30-4
Friends of the Library Group
NELSON MEMORIAL, 8521 Thomas Nelson Hwy, Lovingston, 22949. (Mail add: PO Box 321, Lovingston, 22949-0321), SAN 362-7780. Tel: 434-263-5904. FAX: 434-263-5988. E-mail: nelson@jmrl.org. *Br Mgr,* Susan Huffman
Open Mon & Tues Noon-8, Wed & Thurs 10-5:30, Fri 10-5, Sat 10-2
Friends of the Library Group
NORTHSIDE, 705 W Rio Rd, 22901-1466, SAN 371-9529. Tel: 434-973-7893. FAX: 434-973-5876. E-mail: northside@jmrl.org. *Br Mgr,* Lindsay Ideson
Open Mon & Tues Noon-9, Wed & Thurs 10-6, Fri & Sat 10-5, Sun 1-5
Friends of the Library Group
SCOTTSVILLE BRANCH, 330 Bird St, Scottsville, 24590, SAN 362-7810. Tel: 434-286-3541. FAX: 434-286-4744. E-mail: scottsville@jmrl.org. *Br Mgr,* Megan England
Open Mon & Tues 1-9, Wed-Sat 9-5
Friends of the Library Group
Bookmobiles: 1. Br Mgr, Marien Ruiz-Villaman. Bk vols 26,980

S NATIONAL RADIO ASTRONOMY OBSERVATORY LIBRARY*, 520 Edgemont Rd, 22903-2475. SAN 317-2430. Tel: 434-296-0254. FAX: 434-296-0278. E-mail: libweb@nrao.edu. Web Site: library.nrao.edu. *Libr Dir, Observatory Librn,* Marsha Bishop; *Database Adminr, Librn,* Lance Utley; Tel: 434-296-0215; *Cataloger,* Kristy Davis. Subject Specialists: *Astronomy, Chem, Engr,* Marsha Bishop; *Astronomy,* Lance Utley; Staff 3 (MLS 3)
Founded 1959
Library Holdings: CDs 422; DVDs 316; e-books 7,350; e-journals 2,295; Bk Titles 20,314; Bk Vols 25,014; Per Subs 110
Special Collections: NRAO Memo Series (all NRAO internal publs); Observatory, Astronomical Institute & Government Agency Coll
Subject Interests: Astronomy, Astrophysics, Computers, Electronics, Engr, Physics
Automation Activity & Vendor Info: (Cataloging) OCLC Connexion; (Circulation) SirsiDynix; (ILL) OCLC WorldShare Interlibrary Loan; (OPAC) SirsiDynix
Wireless access
Function: 24/7 Electronic res, Archival coll, Doc delivery serv, E-Reserves, Electronic databases & coll, ILL available, Internet access, Mail & tel request accepted, Online cat, Online ref, Outside serv via phone, mail, e-mail & web, Ref serv available, Res libr
Publications: New Titles List; Publication Metrics (Annual); Publications List (Annual report); Publications Statistics (Quarterly); Published Papers (Annual report)
Open Mon-Fri 8:30-5
Restriction: Authorized patrons, Authorized personnel only, Authorized scholars by appt, Badge access after hrs, Borrowing requests are handled by ILL, External users must contact libr, In-house use for visitors, Open to authorized patrons, Prof mat only

J PIEDMONT VIRGINIA COMMUNITY COLLEGE*, Betty Sue Jessup Library, 501 College Dr, 22902. SAN 317-2449. Tel: 434-961-5308. Reference Tel: 434-961-5309. FAX: 434-977-6842. Reference E-mail: reference@pvcc.edu. Web Site: www.pvcc.edu/student-services/library. *Dir, Libr Serv,* Crystal Newell; Tel: 434-961-5339, E-mail: cnewell@pvcc.edu; Staff 4 (MLS 3, Non-MLS 1)
Founded 1972. Enrl 4,800; Fac 64; Highest Degree: Associate
Library Holdings: e-books 60,000; Bk Titles 36,950; Per Subs 156; Videos 1,849
Automation Activity & Vendor Info: (Acquisitions) Ex Libris Group; (Cataloging) Ex Libris Group; (Circulation) Ex Libris Group; (Course Reserve) Ex Libris Group; (ILL) OCLC; (OPAC) Ex Libris Group
Wireless access
Publications: Periodical Listing

Partic in LYRASIS; Virginia Commun Coll Syst; Virginia's Academic Library Consortium
Open Mon-Thurs 8am-9:30pm, Fri 8-5, Sat (Fall & Spring) 9-Noon

C UNIVERSITY OF VIRGINIA*, Alderman Library, 160 McCormick Rd, 22903. (Mail add: PO Box 400109, 22904-4109), SAN 362-7845. Tel: 434-924-3021. Interlibrary Loan Service Tel: 434-982-2617. FAX: 434-924-1431. E-mail: library@virginia.edu. Web Site: www.library.virginia.edu. *Dean of Libr, Univ Librn,* John M Unsworth; E-mail: jmu2m@virginia.edu; *Dep Dir,* Carla H Lee; E-mail: cl9eb@virginia.edu; *Exec Dir of Advancement,* Robin Lynn Mitchell; E-mail: rlm4kf@virginia.edu; Staff 231 (MLS 67, Non-MLS 164)
Founded 1819. Enrl 19,383; Fac 1,121; Highest Degree: Doctorate
Library Holdings: Bk Vols 2,538,294
Special Collections: State Document Depository; UN Document Depository; US Document Depository
Automation Activity & Vendor Info: (Acquisitions) SirsiDynix; (Cataloging) SirsiDynix; (Circulation) SirsiDynix; (Course Reserve) SirsiDynix; (ILL) OCLC ILLiad; (OPAC) SirsiDynix; (Serials) SirsiDynix
Wireless access
Partic in Association of Southeastern Research Libraries; LYRASIS; Virginia's Academic Library Consortium
Friends of the Library Group

Departmental Libraries:

ASTRONOMY, Charles L Brown Sci & Eng Library, 264 Astronomy Bldg, 530 McCormick Rd, 22904. (Mail add: PO Box 400124, 22904-4124), SAN 378-1445. Tel: 434-924-7209. *Dir,* Carla H Lee; Tel: 434-243-2390, E-mail: cl9eb@virginia.edu; *Librn,* Beth W Blanton; E-mail: bwb9f@virginia.edu
Library Holdings: Bk Vols 13,796
Restriction: Restricted access

CHARLES L BROWN SCIENCE & ENGINEERING LIBRARY, Clark Hall, 22903-3188. (Mail add: PO Box 400124, 22904-4124), SAN 362-8213. Tel: 434-924-7209. FAX: 434-924-4338. Reference E-mail: sciref@virginia.edu. *Dir of Coll,* Beth W Blanton; E-mail: bwb9f@virginia.edu; *Dep Librn,* Carla Lee; E-mail: cl9eb@virginia.edu
Library Holdings: Bk Vols 224,225

CHEMISTRY, Brown Science & Engineering Library, 291 McCormick Rd, 22903. (Mail add: PO Box 400319, 22904-4319), SAN 362-790X. Tel: 434-924-3159. *Mgr,* Cheryl L Summers; E-mail: cls9b@virginia.edu
Library Holdings: Bk Vols 23,765
Open Mon-Fri 9-5

CLEMONS LIBRARY, 164 McCormick Rd, 22904-4710. Tel: 434-924-3684. *Head of Libr,* Judith Thomas; Tel: 434-924-8814, E-mail: jet3h@virginia.edu
Founded 1982
Library Holdings: Bk Vols 123,820
Subject Interests: Film, Media studies
Special Services for the Blind - Reader equip
Open Mon-Thurs 8am-10pm, Sat & Sun 1-5

DARDEN GRADUATE SCHOOL OF BUSINESS-CAMP LIBRARY, Darden Student Services Bldg, 1st & 2nd Flrs, 100 Darden Blvd, 22903. (Mail add: PO Box 6550, 22906-6550), SAN 362-8027. Tel: 434-924-7321. FAX: 434-924-3533. E-mail: library@darden.virginia.edu. Web Site: www.darden.virginia.edu/current-students/camp-library. *Dir,* Tom Marini; Tel: 434-924-7271, E-mail: marinit@darden.virginia.edu
Founded 1955. Enrl 500; Fac 85; Highest Degree: Doctorate
Library Holdings: Bk Vols 79,664
Subject Interests: Bus, Econ
Open Mon-Thurs 7:30am-10pm, Fri 7:30-5:30, Sat 9-6, Sun 9am-10pm

FISKE KIMBALL FINE ARTS LIBRARY, Bayly Dr, 22903. (Mail add: PO Box 400131, 22904-4131), SAN 362-7993. Tel: 434-924-6938. FAX: 434-982-2678. E-mail: finearts@virginia.edu. *Research Librn,* Lucie Stylianopoulos; Tel: 434-924-6604, E-mail: lws4n@virginia.edu
Library Holdings: Bk Vols 152,005
Subject Interests: Archit, Art, Drama, Urban planning
Open Mon-Thurs 9am-11pm, Fri 9-6, Sat 1-6, Sun 1-11

MATHEMATICS, Deparment of Mathematics, Kerchof Hall. Rm 107, 22903. (Mail add: PO Box 400137, 22904-4137), SAN 362-8116. Tel: 434-924-7806. FAX: 434-924-3084. *Mgr,* Cheryl Summers; E-mail: cls9b@virginia.edu
Library Holdings: Bk Vols 33,792
Open Mon-Fri 1-5

CM CLAUDE MOORE HEALTH SCIENCES LIBRARY, Univ Va Health System, 1350 Jefferson Park Ave, 22908. (Mail add: PO Box 800722, 22908-0722), SAN 362-8140. Tel: 434-924-5444. Interlibrary Loan Service Tel: 434-924-0058. Administration Tel: 434-982-3605. FAX: 434-924-0379. Web Site: guides.hsl.virginia.edu/home. *Dir,* Gretchen Arnold; E-mail: gvn8r@virginia.edu
Founded 1911. Enrl 1,436; Fac 1,256; Highest Degree: Doctorate
Library Holdings: Bk Vols 134,292
Special Collections: American Lung Association of Virginia Archives; Kerr L White Health Care Coll; Philip S Hench Walter Reed/Yellow Fever Coll
Subject Interests: Behav sci, Med, Med hist, Natural sci, Nursing, Nursing hist, Soc sci
Automation Activity & Vendor Info: (Acquisitions) SirsiDynix; (Cataloging) SirsiDynix; (Circulation) SirsiDynix; (ILL) OCLC; (OPAC) SirsiDynix; (Serials) SirsiDynix
Partic in LYRASIS; National Network of Libraries of Medicine Region 1; OCLC Online Computer Library Center, Inc
Publications: The Claude Moore Health Sciences Library (Annual report); The Claude Moore Health Sciences Library Inside Information
Open Mon-Thurs 7am-Midnight, Fri 7-7, Sat 9-7, Sun Noon-Midnight

CL ARTHUR J MORRIS LAW LIBRARY, 580 Massie Rd, 22903-1738, SAN 362-8051. Tel: 434-924-3384. Circulation Tel: 434-924-4058. Interlibrary Loan Service Tel: 434-924-3519. Reference Tel: 434-924-7465. FAX: 434-982-2232. E-mail: comm@law.virginia.edu. Reference E-mail: refdesk@law.virginia.edu. Web Site: www.law.virginia.edu/library. *Dir,* Amy Wharton; Tel: 434-924-1816, E-mail: amywharton@law.virginia.edu; *Asst Dir, Head, Res Serv,* Leslie Ashbrook; Tel: 434-243-2493, E-mail: ashbrook@law.virginia.edu; *Head, Access Serv,* Rebecca Owen; E-mail: rowen@law.virginia.edu; *Head, Digital Preservation & Scholarship,* Loren Moulds; Tel: 434-924-3877, E-mail: moulds@law.virginia.edu; *Head, Legal Data Lab,* Li Zhang; Tel: 434-924-4730, E-mail: lzhang@law.virginia.edu; *Head, Libr Instruction,* Ben Doherty; Tel: 434-924-7726, E-mail: bendoherty@law.virginia.edu; *Head, Spec Coll, Historian,* Randi Flaherty; Tel: 434-924-6355, E-mail: rflaherty@law.virginia.edu; *Admin Serv Librn, Research Librn,* John Roper; Tel: 434-924-4327, E-mail: jroper@law.virginia.edu; *Admin Technologies Librarian,* Gregory Whitmore; Tel: 434-924-4674, E-mail: gwhitmore@law.virginia.edu; *Cat & Acq,* Kip Gobin; Tel: 434-924-3745, E-mail: kgobin@law.virginia.edu; *Foreign, Comparative & Intl Law Librn,* Xinh Luu; Tel: 434-924-3970, E-mail: xluu@law.virginia.edu; *Outreach & Res Serv Librn,* Kathryn Boudouris; Tel: 434-924-2522, E-mail: kboudouris@law.virginia.edu; *Research Librn,* Position Currently Open; *Research Librn,* Daniel Radthorne; Tel: 434-982-5090, E-mail: dradthorne@law.virginia.edu; *Research Librn,* Melissa Scheeren; Tel: 434-924-3495, E-mail: mscheeren@law.virginia.edu; *Research Librn,* Latia Ward; Tel: 434-297-9334, E-mail: lward@law.virginia.edu; *Web Serv Librn,* Sarah New; Tel: 434-924-4988, E-mail: snew@law.virginia.edu; *Archivist,* Daniel Cavanaugh; Tel: 434-924-3460, E-mail: dcavanaugh@law.virginia.edu; Staff 17 (MLS 13, Non-MLS 4)
Founded 1819. Enrl 950; Fac 93; Highest Degree: Doctorate
Special Collections: US Document Depository
Subject Interests: Early American law, English law, Ocean law, Va Law
Partic in LYRASIS; OCLC Online Computer Library Center, Inc
Open Mon-Sun 8am-Midnight

MUSIC, Old Cabell Hall, 22904. (Mail add: PO Box 400175, 22904-4175), SAN 362-8175. Tel: 434-924-7041. FAX: 434-924-6033. Web Site: guides.lib.virginia.edu/musiclib, pages.shanti.virginia.edu/UVA_Music_Library. *Music Librn,* Winston K Barham; E-mail: wkb5j@virginia.edu; *Research Librn,* Abigail Flanigan; E-mail: akf3g@virginia.edu
Founded 1977. Fac 10; Highest Degree: Doctorate
Library Holdings: Bk Vols 135,000
Open Mon-Thurs 9am-11pm, Fri 9-6, Sat 1-6, Sun 1-11

ALBERT & SHIRLEY SMALL SPECIAL COLLECTIONS LIBRARY, 170 McCormick Rd, 22904. (Mail add: PO Box 400110, 22904-4110). Tel: 434-243-1776. FAX: 434-924-4968. E-mail: scpubserv@virginia.edu. Web Site: small.library.virginia.edu. *Curator,* Holly Robertson; E-mail: har8n@virginia.edu; *Curator,* David Whitesell; E-mail: dw8sd@virginia.edu
Library Holdings: Bk Vols 291,930
Open Mon-Thurs 9-7, Fri 9-5, Sat 1-5

S VIRGINIA DEPARTMENT OF TRANSPORTATION (VDOT) RESEARCH LIBRARY*, 530 Edgemont Rd, 22903. SAN 376-1940. Tel: 434-293-1902. E-mail: Library@vdot.virginia.gov. Web Site: library.virginiadot.org. *Assoc Libr Dir,* Ken Winter; Tel: 434-962-8979, E-mail: ken.winter@vdot.virginia.gov; *Librn,* Rebecca Ernest; Tel: 434-293-1959, E-mail: Rebecca.Ernest@vdot.virginia.gov; *Librn,* Gil Kenner; Tel: 434-293-1926, E-mail: Gil.Kenner@vdot.virginia.gov; *Librn,* Barb Neyman; E-mail: Barb.Neyman@vdot.virginia.gov; Staff 4 (MLS 2, Non-MLS 2)
Founded 1954. Pop 7,500
Library Holdings: Audiobooks 80,000; e-journals 100; Bk Vols 60,000; Per Subs 50
Special Collections: Professional Engineer's Exam Study Coll; Publications of the American Association of State Highway and Transportation Officials (AASHTO); Publications of the Transportation Research Board (TRB); Virginia Department of Transportation (VDOT) Publications; Virginia Road & Transportation History
Wireless access
Function: 24/7 Electronic res, 24/7 Online cat, E-Reserves, ILL available, Online cat, Online ref, Ref & res, Ref serv available, Res libr, Telephone ref

Restriction: Authorized patrons, Authorized scholars by appt, Borrowing requests are handled by ILL, Circ limited, In-house use for visitors, Open by appt only, Pub ref by request, Restricted access, Restricted borrowing privileges, Restricted loan policy, Restricted pub use

G VIRGINIA DIVISION OF GEOLOGY & MINERAL RESOURCES LIBRARY*, 900 Natural Resources Dr, Ste 500, 22903-2982. SAN 317-2481. Tel: 434-951-6341. FAX: 434-951-6366. *Library Contact,* David Spears; E-mail: david.spears@dmme.virginia.gov
Library Holdings: Bk Vols 1,200
Subject Interests: Forestry, Geol, Mineral res

CHATHAM

P PITTSYLVANIA COUNTY PUBLIC LIBRARY*, 24 Military Dr, 24531. SAN 362-823X. Tel: 434-432-3271. FAX: 434-432-1405. E-mail: info@pcplib.org. Web Site: www.pcplib.org. *Dir,* Rhonda Griffin; E-mail: rhonda.griffin@pcplib.org; *Syst Librn,* David Kahler; E-mail: david.kahler@pcplib.org; Staff 18 (Non-MLS 18)
Founded 1913. Pop 62,807; Circ 355,815
Automation Activity & Vendor Info: (Cataloging) TLC (The Library Corporation); (Circulation) TLC (The Library Corporation); (OPAC) TLC (The Library Corporation)
Wireless access
Function: 24/7 Electronic res, 24/7 Online cat, After school storytime, Archival coll, Art exhibits, Audiobks on Playaways & MP3, Audiobks via web, Bk reviews (Group), Bks on CD, Children's prog, Computer training, Computers for patron use, Electronic databases & coll, Free DVD rentals, Holiday prog, Home delivery & serv to seniorr ctr & nursing homes, Homebound delivery serv, Homework prog, ILL available, Instruction & testing, Internet access, Life-long learning prog for all ages, Magazines, Meeting rooms, Microfiche/film & reading machines, Movies, Museum passes, Music CDs, Online cat, Outreach serv, OverDrive digital audio bks, Photocopying/Printing, Preschool outreach, Preschool reading prog, Prog for adults, Prog for children & young adult, Ref serv available, Scanner, Senior computer classes, Story hour, Summer & winter reading prog, Teen prog, Wheelchair accessible, Writing prog
Open Mon-Thurs 9-8, Fri 9-5, Sat 10-2
Friends of the Library Group
Branches: 3
BROSVILLE/CASCADE, 11948 Martinsville Hwy, Danville, 24541, SAN 321-9232. Tel: 434-685-1285. FAX: 434-685-3347. *Br Mgr,* Tim Rogers; Staff 2.5 (Non-MLS 2.5)
Founded 1992
Automation Activity & Vendor Info: (Circulation) TLC (The Library Corporation)
Open Mon-Wed & Fri 9:30-6, Thurs 9:30-8
Friends of the Library Group
GRETNA BRANCH LIBRARY, 207 Coffey St, Ste A, Gretna, 24557. Tel: 434-656-2579. FAX: 434-656-9030. *Br Mgr,* Adrian Badgett; Staff 3 (Non-MLS 3)
Open Mon, Tues & Thurs 10-8, Wed & Fri 10-6, Sat 10-12
Friends of the Library Group
MT HERMON BRANCH LIBRARY, 4058 Franklin Tpk, Danville, 24540. Tel: 434-835-0326. FAX: 434-835-0321. *Br Mgr,* Beth Marsh
Open Mon-Thurs 10-8, Fri 10-6, Sat 10-2
Friends of the Library Group
Bookmobiles: 1. Outreach Mgr, Myrna Herndon

CHESAPEAKE

P CHESAPEAKE PUBLIC LIBRARY*, 298 Cedar Rd, 23322-5512. SAN 362-8299. Tel: 757-410-7101, 757-410-7104. Circulation Tel: 757-410-7156. Interlibrary Loan Service Tel: 757-926-5754. Reference Tel: 757-410-7145. Automation Services Tel: 757-410-7170. FAX: 757-410-7112. Circulation FAX: 757-410-7159. Interlibrary Loan Service FAX: 757-410-7122. Web Site: www.infopeake.org. *Dir,* Amanda Jackson; Tel: 757-410-7102, E-mail: ajackson@infopeake.org; *Asst Dir,* Kimberly Knight; Tel: 757-410-7110, E-mail: kbknight@infopeake.org; *Cat Librn,* Jodie Reha; Tel: 757-926-5740, E-mail: jreha@infopeake.org; *Cent Libr Mgr,* Zachary Elder; Tel: 757-410-7110, E-mail: zwelder@infopeake.org; *Info Syst Mgr,* Maiko Medina; Tel: 757-410-7170, E-mail: mmedina@infopeake.org; *Adult Serv Coordr,* Melissa Christakos; Tel: 757-410-7135, E-mail: mchrista@infopeake.org; *Coordr, Circ,* Jennifer Luck; Tel: 757-410-7155, E-mail: jluck@infopeake.org; *Family & Youth Serv Coordr,* Heather Simpson; Tel: 757-410-7127, E-mail: hsimpson@infopeake.org; *Acq,* Donna Blair; Tel: 757-926-5747, E-mail: dblair@infopeake.org; Staff 125.3 (MLS 27, Non-MLS 98.3)
Founded 1961. Pop 235,638; Circ 1,782,003
Jul 2018-Jun 2019 Income (Main & Associated Libraries) $10,554,307, State $186,973, City $9,940,326, Other $427,008. Mats Exp $1,152,827, Books $553,578, Per/Ser (Incl. Access Fees) $34,286, AV Mat $416,403, Electronic Ref Mat (Incl. Access Fees) $148,560. Sal $5,194,083
Library Holdings: e-journals 104; Microforms 124; Per Subs 497
Special Collections: Local History (Wallace Memorial Library Coll), Outreach Services
Subject Interests: Family, Hist, Law
Automation Activity & Vendor Info: (Cataloging) SirsiDynix; (Circulation) SirsiDynix; (OPAC) SirsiDynix
Wireless access
Function: 24/7 Electronic res, 24/7 Online cat, Adult bk club, Art exhibits, Audiobks on Playaways & MP3, Audiobks via web, Bk club(s), Bk reviews (Group), Bks on CD, Children's prog, Computer training, Computers for patron use, Digital talking bks, E-Reserves, Electronic databases & coll, Family literacy, Free DVD rentals, Genealogy discussion group, Holiday prog, ILL available, Internet access, Legal assistance to inmates, Life-long learning prog for all ages, Magazines, Meeting rooms, Movies, Music CDs, Notary serv, Online cat, Online ref, Outreach serv, Outside serv via phone, mail, e-mail & web, OverDrive digital audio bks, Photocopying/Printing, Preschool outreach, Preschool reading prog, Prog for adults, Prog for children & young adult, Ref & res, Ref serv available, Scanner, Senior computer classes, Senior outreach, Serves people with intellectual disabilities, Spanish lang bks, Spoken cassettes & CDs, Spoken cassettes & DVDs, Story hour, Study rm, Summer reading prog, Teen prog, Telephone ref, Wheelchair accessible, Workshops
Special Services for the Blind - Reader equip
Open Mon-Thurs 10-8, Fri 10-6, Sat 10-5, Sun 1-5
Friends of the Library Group
Branches: 6
DR CLARENCE V CUFFEE LIBRARY, 2726 Border Rd, 23324-3760. Tel: 757-410-7034. Circulation Tel: 757-410-7036. FAX: 757-410-7044. *Mgr,* Angela Gaskins; Tel: 757-410-7040, E-mail: agaskins@infopeake.org; *Pub Serv Librn,* Kevin Clement; Tel: 757-410-7046, E-mail: kclement@infopeake.org; *Circ Supvr,* Linda Kleiber; Tel: 757-410-7043, E-mail: lkleiber@infopeake.org
Founded 2007
Open Mon-Thurs 10-8, Fri 10-6, Sat 10-5, Sun 1-5
Friends of the Library Group
GREENBRIER, 1214 Volvo Pkwy, 23320-7600, SAN 371-9553. Tel: 757-410-7058. Circulation Tel: 757-410-7061. Administration Tel: 757-410-7067. FAX: 757-410-7071. *Br Mgr,* Rachel Beerthuis; Tel: 757-410-7068, E-mail: rbeerthuis@cityofchesapeake.net; *Librn, Youth & Family Serv,* Jeri Morton; Tel: 757-410-7069, E-mail: jmorton@infopeake.org; *Pub Serv Librn,* Rachel Beerthuis; E-mail: rbeerthu@infopeake.org; *Circ Supvr,* Sylvia Johnson; Tel: 757-410-7070, E-mail: sjohnson@infopeake.org
Founded 1992
Friends of the Library Group
INDIAN RIVER, 2320 Old Greenbrier Rd, 23325, SAN 362-8353. Tel: 757-410-7001. Circulation Tel: 757-410-7003. FAX: 757-410-7014. *Br Mgr,* Jessica Chatham; Tel: 757-410-7007, E-mail: jchatham@infopeake.org; *Librn, Youth & Family Serv,* Ann Maloney; Tel: 757-410-7009, E-mail: amaloney@infopeake.org; *Pub Serv Librn,* Scott Kurhan; Tel: 757-410-7008, E-mail: skurhan@infopeake.org; *Circ Supvr,* Mattie Davis; Tel: 757-410-7010, E-mail: mdavis@infopeake.org
Founded 1965
Open Mon-Thurs 10-8, Fri 10-6, Sat 10-5, Sun 1-5
Friends of the Library Group
MAJOR HILLARD LIBRARY, 824 Old George Washington Hwy N, 23323-2214, SAN 362-8329. Tel: 757-382-1924. Circulation Tel: 757-382-1923. *Br Mgr,* Clyde Hunter; Tel: 757-382-1942, E-mail: chunter@cityofchesapeake.net; *Librn, Youth & Family Serv,* Hollister Finch; Tel: 757-410-7082, E-mail: hfinch@infopeake.org
Founded 1977
Friends of the Library Group
RUSSELL MEMORIAL, 2808 Taylor Rd, 23321-2210, SAN 362-8388. Tel: 757-410-7020. Reference Tel: 757-410-7016. FAX: 757-410-7029. *Br Mgr,* JoLynn Holcomb; Tel: 757-410-7028, E-mail: jholcomb@infopeake.org; *Librn, Youth & Family Serv,* Jennifer Blalock; Tel: 757-410-7027, E-mail: jblalock@infopeake.org; *Pub Serv Librn,* Rekesha Spellman; E-mail: rspellma@infopeake.org; *Circ Mgr,* Julianna Stinebaugh; Tel: 757-410-7023, E-mail: jstinebau@infopeake.org
Founded 1968
Special Collections: Dave Smith Poetry Coll
Subject Interests: Family
Friends of the Library Group
SOUTH NORFOLK MEMORIAL, 1100 Poindexter St, 23324-2447, SAN 362-8418. Tel: 757-410-7052. FAX: 757-410-7055. *Br Mgr,* Clyde Hunter, Jr; Tel: 757-410-7052, E-mail: chunter@infopeake.org; *Librn, Youth & Family Serv,* Rachael Dent; Tel: 757-926-5757, E-mail: rachdent@infopeake.org; *Pub Serv Librn,* Elizabeth Griffing; Tel: 757-410-7053, E-mail: egriffin@infopeake.org; *Circ Mgr,* Jean Cooper; Tel: 757-410-7048, E-mail: jcooper@infopeake.org
Founded 1958
Subject Interests: Family
Friends of the Library Group

M SENTARA COLLEGE OF HEALTH SCIENCES*, Healthcare Library, 1441 Crossways Blvd, Ste 105, 23320. SAN 317-3704. Tel: 757-388-3693. E-mail: library@sentara.com. Web Site: sentara.edu. *Librn,* Suzanne Duncan; E-mail: sxduncan@sentara.com
Founded 1942
Library Holdings: Bk Vols 5,000; Per Subs 260
Subject Interests: Health admin, Med, Nursing
Automation Activity & Vendor Info: (Cataloging) CyberTools for Libraries; (Circulation) CyberTools for Libraries
Wireless access
Open Mon-Thurs 8-6, Fri 8-12

J TIDEWATER COMMUNITY COLLEGE*, Chesapeake Campus Library, 1428 Cedar Rd, 23322. SAN 362-8442. Circulation Tel: 757-822-5160. Reference Tel: 757-822-5162. Web Site: libguides.tcc.edu/chesapeake-library. *Admin Librn,* Lakesha Skinner; E-mail: lskinner@tcc.edu; *Libr Coord,* Heather Fitzgerald; E-mail: hfitzgerald@tcc.edu; Staff 6 (MLS 2, Non-MLS 4)
Founded 1973. Enrl 2,965; Fac 123
Library Holdings: Bk Vols 43,900; Per Subs 245
Subject Interests: Early childhood, Hort
Automation Activity & Vendor Info: (Acquisitions) Ex Libris Group; (Cataloging) Ex Libris Group; (Circulation) Ex Libris Group; (Course Reserve) Ex Libris Group; (ILL) Ex Libris Group; (OPAC) Ex Libris Group; (Serials) Ex Libris Group
Wireless access
Partic in LYRASIS; OCLC Online Computer Library Center, Inc; Virginia Tidewater Consortium for Higher Education; Virginia's Academic Library Consortium
Open Mon-Thurs 8am-9pm, Fri 8-4:30, Sat 9-1

CHESTER

J BRIGHTPOINT COMMUNITY COLLEGE LIBRARY*, (Formerly John Tyler Community College Library), Moyar Hall, M216, 13101 Rte One, 23831-5316. SAN 317-2503. Tel: 804-706-5195. Reference Tel: 804-706-5198. FAX: 804-796-4238. Web Site: www.brightpoint.edu/library. *Dir, Libr Serv,* Suzanne Sherry; Tel: 804-706-5201, E-mail: ssherry@brightpoint.edu; Staff 7 (MLS 1, Non-MLS 6)
Founded 1967. Enrl 5,415; Highest Degree: Associate
Library Holdings: CDs 193; DVDs 695; Bk Vols 36,156; Per Subs 66; Videos 319
Automation Activity & Vendor Info: (Cataloging) Ex Libris Group; (Circulation) Ex Libris Group; (Course Reserve) Ex Libris Group; (ILL) OCLC; (OPAC) Ex Libris Group
Wireless access
Partic in LYRASIS; Richmond Academic Library Consortium; Virginia Commun Coll Syst
Open Mon-Thurs 8-6, Fri 8-5
Departmental Libraries:
MIDLOTHIAN CAMPUS, Hamel Hall, Rm H202, 800 Charter Colony Pkwy, Midlothian, 23114-4383. Tel: 804-594-1519. Reference Tel: 804-594-1520. FAX: 804-594-1525. *Dir, Libr Serv,* Suzanne Sherry; Tel: 804-594-1523; *E-Learning & Instruction Librn,* Molli Gonzalez; Tel: 804-594-1518, E-mail: mgonzalez@jtcc.edu; Staff 7 (MLS 2, Non-MLS 5)
Library Holdings: CDs 3; DVDs 368; Bk Vols 18,516; Per Subs 55; Videos 10
Open Mon-Thurs 8-6, Fri 8-5

CHESTERFIELD

P CHESTERFIELD COUNTY PUBLIC LIBRARY*, 9501 Lori Rd, 23832. (Mail add: PO Box 297, 23832-0297), SAN 362-8507. Tel: 804-751-2275. FAX: 804-751-4679. Web Site: library.chesterfield.gov. *Libr Dir,* Michael R Mabe; E-mail: mabem@chesterfield.gov; *Asst Dir,* Carolyn Sears; Tel: 804-748-1761, E-mail: searsc@chesterfield.gov; *Admin Serv, Chief,* Jenny Stevens; Tel: 804-751-4998, E-mail: stevensj@chesterfield.gov; Staff 131 (MLS 26, Non-MLS 105)
Founded 1965. Pop 370,688; Circ 1,634,005
Library Holdings: Audiobooks 16,301; AV Mats 69,202; Bks on Deafness & Sign Lang 33; CDs 10,951; DVDs 38,875; e-books 50,125; e-journals 2; Electronic Media & Resources 26; Large Print Bks 8,656; Microforms 2; Bk Titles 226,166; Talking Bks 20,570
Special Collections: Law Library Coll; Local History Coll
Subject Interests: Civil War, Local hist, Va
Automation Activity & Vendor Info: (Acquisitions) SirsiDynix-Enterprise; (Cataloging) SirsiDynix-Enterprise; (Circulation) SirsiDynix-Symphony; (Serials) SirsiDynix-Enterprise
Wireless access
Function: 24/7 Electronic res, 24/7 Online cat, 3D Printer, Activity rm, Adult bk club, Adult literacy prog, Archival coll, Art exhibits, Audiobks via web, Bilingual assistance for Spanish patrons, Bk club(s), Bks on CD, Chess club, Children's prog, Computer training, Computers for patron use, Digital talking bks, E-Reserves, Electronic databases & coll, Free DVD rentals, Health sci info serv, Holiday prog, ILL available, Internet access, Jail serv, Makerspace, Meeting rooms, Microfiche/film & reading machines, Movies, Museum passes, Music CDs, Online cat, Online ref, Orientations, Outreach serv, OverDrive digital audio bks, Photocopying/Printing, Printer for laptops & handheld devices, Prog for adults, Prog for children & young adult, Ref & res, Ref serv available, Res assist avail, Scanner, Spanish lang bks, Story hour, Study rm, Summer & winter reading prog, Summer reading prog, Teen prog, Telephone ref, Wheelchair accessible, Workshops
Publications: CCPL Annual Report; CCPL Program Guide (Monthly newsletter)
Open Mon-Thurs 9-8, Fri & Sat 9-5
Friends of the Library Group
Branches: 10
BON AIR, 9103 Rattlesnake Rd, Richmond, 23235, SAN 362-8531. Tel: 804-751-2275. *Br Mgr,* Margaret Howard; *Asst Br Mgr,* Jesse Dodd
Open Mon-Thurs 9-8, Fri & Sat 9-5
Friends of the Library Group
CENTRAL, 7051 Lucy Corr Blvd, 23832. *Br Mgr,* Jennifer Hayek
Open Mon-Thurs 9-8, Fri & Sat 9-5
CHESTER BRANCH, 11800 Centre St, Chester, 23831, SAN 362-8566. Tel: 804-751-2275. *Br Mgr,* Dana Bomba; *Asst Br Mgr,* Jennifer Abbott
Friends of the Library Group
CLOVER HILL, 6701 Deer Run Rd, Midlothian, 23112, SAN 374-6488. Tel: 804-751-2275. *Br Mgr,* Rose Marie Brintzenhofe; *Asst Br Mgr,* Sara Mueller
Friends of the Library Group
ENON, 1801 Enon Church Rd, Chester, 23836, SAN 374-6496. Tel: 804-751-2275. *Br Mgr,* Jackie Downs; *Asst Br Mgr,* Quettara Drayton
Friends of the Library Group
ETTRICK-MATOACA, 4501 River Rd, Petersburg, 23803, SAN 362-8590. Tel: 804-751-2275. *Br Mgr,* Jackie Downs; *Asst Br Mgr,* Quettara Drayton
Friends of the Library Group
LAPRADE, 9000 Hull St Rd, Richmond, 23236, SAN 362-8620. Tel: 804-751-2275. *Br Mgr,* Barbara Ferrara; *Asst Br Mgr,* Danielle Tarullo
Friends of the Library Group
MEADOWDALE, 4301 Meadowdale Blvd, Richmond, 23234, SAN 373-9074. Tel: 804-751-2275. *Br Mgr,* James Hudson; *Asst Br Mgr,* Pam White
Friends of the Library Group
MIDLOTHIAN BRANCH, 521 Coalfield Rd, Midlothian, 23114, SAN 362-8639. Tel: 804-751-2275. *Br Mgr,* Jess Harshbarger; *Asst Br Mgr,* Leslie Johnson
Friends of the Library Group
NORTH COURTHOUSE ROAD, 325 Courthouse Rd, North Chesterfield, 23236. Tel: 804-751-2275.
Open Mon-Thurs 9-8, Fri & Sat 9-5

CHRISTIANSBURG

P MONTGOMERY-FLOYD REGIONAL LIBRARY SYSTEM*, Christiansburg Library, 125 Sheltman St, 24073. SAN 319-9223. Tel: 540-382-6965. Circulation Tel: 540-382-6965, Ext 15. Administration Tel: 540-382-6969. FAX: 540-382-6964. Web Site: www.mfrl.org. *Dir,* Karim Khan; E-mail: kkhan@mfrl.org; *Br Supvr,* Salena Sullivan; E-mail: ssullivan@mfrl.org; Staff 34 (MLS 2, Non-MLS 32)
Founded 1974. Pop 100,200; Circ 781,608
Subject Interests: Genealogy, Local hist
Automation Activity & Vendor Info: (Acquisitions) SirsiDynix; (Cataloging) SirsiDynix; (Circulation) SirsiDynix; (OPAC) SirsiDynix; (Serials) SirsiDynix
Wireless access
Function: 24/7 Online cat, Adult bk club, Adult literacy prog, Art exhibits, Audiobks on Playaways & MP3, Audiobks via web, Bks on CD, Children's prog, Computer training, Computers for patron use, Electronic databases & coll, Family literacy, Free DVD rentals, Home delivery & serv to seniorr ctr & nursing homes, Homebound delivery serv, ILL available, Internet access, Life-long learning prog for all ages, Literacy & newcomer serv, Magazines, Mail & tel request accepted, Mango lang, Meeting rooms, Microfiche/film & reading machines, Music CDs, Notary serv, Online info literacy tutorials on the web & in blackboard, Online ref, Outreach serv, OverDrive digital audio bks, Passport agency, Photocopying/Printing, Preschool outreach, Preschool reading prog, Prog for adults, Prog for children & young adult, Ref serv available, Senior outreach, Serves people with intellectual disabilities, STEM programs, Story hour, Summer reading prog, Teen prog, Telephone ref, Wheelchair accessible
Partic in New River Public Library Cooperative
Open Mon-Thurs 9-8, Fri & Sat 10-5, Sun (Winter) 1-5
Friends of the Library Group
Branches: 3
BLACKSBURG AREA BRANCH, 200 Miller St, Blacksburg, 24060, SAN 362-868X. Tel: 540-552-8246. FAX: 540-552-8265. *Br Mgr,* Laura Dobbins; E-mail: ldobbins@mfrl.org
Open Mon-Thurs 9-8, Fri & Sat 10-5, Sun (Winter) 1-5
Friends of the Library Group

MEADOWBROOK PUBLIC, 267 Alleghany Springs Rd, Shawsville, 24162. Tel: 540-268-1964. FAX: 540-268-2031. *Br Supvr,* Cindy Minnick; E-mail: cminnick@mfrl.org
Open Mon-Thurs 10-8, Fri & Sat 10-5, Sun (Winter) 1-5
JESSIE PETERMAN MEMORIAL, 321 W Main St, Floyd, 24091, SAN 362-871X. Tel: 540-745-2947. FAX: 540-745-4750. *Br Mgr,* Joann Verostko; E-mail: jverostko@mfrl.org
Open Mon-Thurs 10-7, Fri 10-5, Sat 10-3, Sun (Winter) 1-5
Friends of the Library Group
Bookmobiles: 1

CLIFTON FORGE

S CHESAPEAKE & OHIO HISTORICAL SOCIETY ARCHIVES*, C&O Archival Collection, 312 E Ridgeway St, 24422. (Mail add: PO Box 79, 24422-0079), SAN 329-1936. Tel: 540-862-2210. FAX: 540-863-9159. E-mail: cohs@cohs.org. Web Site: www.cohs.org. *Pres,* Mark Totten
Founded 1969
Library Holdings: Bk Titles 7,000
Special Collections: Chesapeake & Ohio Railway, its predecessors, subsidiaries & successors
Open Mon-Fri 9-5
Restriction: Non-circulating

P CLIFTON FORGE PUBLIC LIBRARY*, 535 Church St, 24422-1134. SAN 317-2511. Tel: 540-863-2519. FAX: 540-863-2520. Web Site: cliftonforgelibrary.org. *Dir,* Mike Barnes; E-mail: mbarnes@cliftonforgeva.gov; Staff 1 (Non-MLS 1)
Founded 1972. Pop 4,200; Circ 38,153
Library Holdings: Bk Vols 45,000; Per Subs 54
Automation Activity & Vendor Info: (Cataloging) Innovative Interfaces, Inc; (Circulation) Innovative Interfaces, Inc; (OPAC) Innovative Interfaces, Inc
Wireless access
Open Mon & Thurs 10-7, Tues, Wed & Fri 10-5, Sat 10-1
Friends of the Library Group

J DABNEY S LANCASTER COMMUNITY COLLEGE LIBRARY-LRC*, 1000 Dabney Dr, 24422. SAN 317-252X. Tel: 540-863-2800. Toll Free Tel: 877-733-7522. Web Site: www.dslcc.edu/student-services/library. *Dir,* Nova Wright; E-mail: nwright@dslcc.edu; Staff 1 (MLS 1)
Founded 1964
Library Holdings: Bk Vols 44,317; Per Subs 250
Subject Interests: Commun col educ, Forestry, Law enforcement, Nursing
Automation Activity & Vendor Info: (Acquisitions) Ex Libris Group; (Circulation) Ex Libris Group; (Course Reserve) Ex Libris Group; (ILL) OCLC; (Media Booking) Ex Libris Group; (OPAC) Ex Libris Group
Wireless access
Partic in LYRASIS; Virginia Commun Coll Syst; Virginia's Academic Library Consortium
Open Mon-Thurs 8am-9pm, Fri 8-5, Sun 2-6

COLONIAL HEIGHTS

P COLONIAL HEIGHTS PUBLIC LIBRARY*, 1000 Yacht Basin Dr, 23834. SAN 317-2538. Tel: 804-520-9384. Web Site: colonialheightsva.gov/211/Library. *Libr Dir,* Bruce N Hansen; E-mail: hansenb@colonialheightsva.gov; Staff 6 (MLS 2, Non-MLS 4)
Founded 1968. Circ 203,710
Library Holdings: AV Mats 211,000; Bk Vols 50,500; Per Subs 409; Talking Bks 1,200; Videos 2,000
Automation Activity & Vendor Info: (Cataloging) Follett Software; (Circulation) Follett Software; (OPAC) Follett Software
Wireless access
Function: 24/7 Electronic res, 24/7 Online cat, Accelerated reader prog, Activity rm, Art exhibits, Audiobks via web, Children's prog, Computers for patron use, Digital talking bks, E-Readers, Electronic databases & coll, ILL available, Internet access, Large print keyboards, Magazines, Mail & tel request accepted, Meeting rooms, Movies, Online cat, Photocopying/Printing, Preschool reading prog, Printer for laptops & handheld devices, Ref serv available, Story hour, Study rm, Summer & winter reading prog, Tax forms, Telephone ref, Wheelchair accessible
Open Mon-Wed 9-7, Thurs & Fri 9-6, Sat 10-4

COURTLAND

P BLACKWATER REGIONAL LIBRARY*, Walter Cecil Rawls Library, 22511 Main St, 23837. SAN 362-8744. Tel: 757-653-2821. Administration Tel: 757-653-0298. FAX: 757-653-9374. Web Site: www.blackwaterlib.org. *Libr Dir,* Ben Neal; E-mail: bneal@blackwaterlib.org; *Asst Libr Dir,* Bonnie Lauver; E-mail: blauver@blackwaterlib.org; *Budget Off Mgr, Finance Mgr,* Debbie Carter; E-mail: dcarter@blackwaterlib.org; *Br Mgr,* Donna Pope; E-mail: dpope@blackwaterlib.org; *Coll Develop Mgr,* Elizabeth Qualls; E-mail: equalls@blackwaterlib.org; Staff 58 (MLS 3, Non-MLS 55)
Founded 1958. Pop 80,500; Circ 407,000
Library Holdings: Bk Titles 121,729; Bk Vols 245,822; Per Subs 326
Special Collections: Cary Close Memorial Coll (Civil War Reference Materials); Nat Turner (Cole Coll)
Subject Interests: Genealogy, Local hist
Automation Activity & Vendor Info: (Acquisitions) TLC (The Library Corporation); (Cataloging) TLC (The Library Corporation); (Circulation) TLC (The Library Corporation); (OPAC) TLC (The Library Corporation)
Wireless access
Function: AV serv, Bk club(s), Electronic databases & coll, Family literacy, Homebound delivery serv, ILL available, Internet access, Learning ctr, Photocopying/Printing, Prof lending libr, Prog for adults, Prog for children & young adult, Ref serv available, Spoken cassettes & CDs, Spoken cassettes & DVDs, Summer reading prog, VHS videos, Wheelchair accessible
Open Tues & Fri 9-5, Wed 9-8, Thurs 12-5, Sat 9-Noon
Friends of the Library Group
Branches: 8
RUTH CAMP CAMPBELL MEMORIAL, 280 N College Dr, Franklin, 23851, SAN 376-1029. Tel: 757-562-4801. FAX: 757-562-0162. Web Site: www.blackwaterlib.org/franklin. *Br Mgr,* Stephanie Sproul; E-mail: ssproul@blackwaterlib.org; Staff 6.5 (MLS 1, Non-MLS 5.5)
Pop 8,500; Circ 116,000
Automation Activity & Vendor Info: (ILL) TLC (The Library Corporation)
Function: Bks on CD, Children's prog, Computer training, Computers for patron use, Electronic databases & coll, Free DVD rentals, Games & aids for people with disabilities, Home delivery & serv to seniorr ctr & nursing homes, ILL available, Jail serv, Large print keyboards, Magnifiers for reading, Mail & tel request accepted, Music CDs, Online cat, Online ref, Outreach serv, Photocopying/Printing, Preschool outreach, Prog for adults, Prog for children & young adult, Ref & res, Senior computer classes, Senior outreach, Spoken cassettes & CDs, Spoken cassettes & DVDs, Story hour, Summer reading prog, Tax forms, Teen prog, Telephone ref, VHS videos, Wheelchair accessible
Open Mon & Wed-Fri 9-5, Tues 12-8
Restriction: In-house use for visitors
Friends of the Library Group
CARROLLTON PUBLIC, 14362 New Towne Haven Lane, Carrollton, 23314, SAN 322-5496. Tel: 757-238-2641. FAX: 757-238-3932. Web Site: www.blackwaterlib.org/carrollton. *Br Mgr,* Megan Wilson; E-mail: mwilson@blackwaterlib.org
Founded 1984. Pop 5,000
Open Mon & Thurs 9-5, Tues Noon-7, Wed & Fri Noon-5, Sat 10-1
Friends of the Library Group
CLAREMONT PUBLIC, 91 Mancha Ave, Claremont, 23899. (Mail add: PO Box 40, Claremont, 23899), SAN 326-8136. Tel: 757-866-8627. Toll Free Tel: 877-866-8627. FAX: 757-866-8628. Web Site: www.blackwaterlib.org/claremont. *Br Mgr,* Kim Sperry; E-mail: ksperry@blackwaterlib.org
Open Mon & Sat 9-1, Thurs 3-7, Fri 1-5
Friends of the Library Group
AGNES TAYLOR GRAY BRANCH, 125 Bank St, Waverly, 23890-3235, SAN 362-8795. Tel: 804-834-2192. FAX: 804-834-8671. Web Site: www.blackwaterlib.org/waverly. *Br Mgr,* Laurie Latham; E-mail: llatham@blackwaterlib.org
Open Mon 9-5, Tues 2-8, Wed 1-8, Thurs 12-5, Fri 9-1, Sat 9-12
Friends of the Library Group
SMITHFIELD BRANCH, 255 James St, Smithfield, 23430, SAN 362-8779. Tel: 757-357-2264. FAX: 757-357-0883. Web Site: www.blackwaterlib.org/smithfield. *Br Mgr,* Terry Andrews; E-mail: tandrews@blackwaterlib.org; Staff 8 (Non-MLS 8)
Subject Interests: Genealogy, Local hist
Open Mon 11-8, Tues, Thurs & Fri 9-5, Wed 9-7, Sat 10-1
Friends of the Library Group
SURRY PUBLIC, 270 Colonial Trail E, Surry, 23883, SAN 322-5488. Tel: 757-294-3949. FAX: 757-294-0803. Web Site: www.blackwaterlib.org/surry. *Br Mgr,* Kim Sperry
Subject Interests: Genealogy
Open Mon, Tues, Thurs & Fri 9-5, Wed 9-8, Sat 9-1
Friends of the Library Group
TROXLER MEMORIAL, 100 Wilson Ave, Wakefield, 23888. (Mail add: PO Box 279, Wakefield, 23888), SAN 329-7578. Tel: 757-899-6500. FAX: 757-899-2400. Web Site: www.blackwaterlib.org/wakefield. *Br Mgr,* Laurie Latham
Open Mon 1-8, Tues 10-5, Wed & Thurs 9-1, Fri 12-5
Friends of the Library Group
WINDSOR PUBLIC, 18 Duke St, Windsor, 23487. (Mail add: PO Box 346, Windsor, 23487-0346), SAN 374-8111. Tel: 757-242-3046. FAX: 757-242-3726. Web Site: www.blackwaterlib.org/windsor. *Br Mgr,* Lauren Lombard; E-mail: llombard@blackwaterlib.org
Open Mon & Thurs 1-7, Tues & Wed 10-5, Fri & Sat 9-1
Friends of the Library Group
Bookmobiles: 1

COVINGTON

P ALLEGANY HIGHLANDS REGIONAL LIBRARY, 406 W Riverside St, 24426. SAN 317-2546. Tel: 540-962-3321. FAX: 540-962-8447. E-mail: library@ahrlib.org. Web Site: ahrlib.org. *Libr Dir,* Lisa Sponaugle; Staff 6 (MLS 1, Non-MLS 5)
Founded 1929. Pop 22,000; Circ 65,000
Library Holdings: Bk Titles 55,000; Per Subs 75
Automation Activity & Vendor Info: (Cataloging) TLC (The Library Corporation); (Circulation) TLC (The Library Corporation); (OPAC) TLC (The Library Corporation)
Wireless access
Function: 24/7 wireless access, Bk club(s), Bks on CD, Children's prog, Computers for patron use, E-Reserves, Electronic databases & coll, ILL available, Internet access, Laminating, Magazines, Mail loans to mem, Mango lang, Meeting rooms, Microfiche/film & reading machines, Movies, Notary serv, Online cat, OverDrive digital audio bks, Photocopying/Printing, Printer for laptops & handheld devices, Prog for adults, Prog for children & young adult, Ref serv available, Scanner, Spanish lang bks, Spoken cassettes & CDs, Story hour, Summer reading prog, Tax forms, Wheelchair accessible
Open Mon, Wed & Fri 9:30-5:30, Tues & Thurs 9:30-7, Sat 9:30-2:30
Friends of the Library Group

CREWE

P NOTTOWAY COUNTY PUBLIC LIBRARIES*, 414 Tyler St, 23930. SAN 363-1532. Tel: 434-645-8688. FAX: 434-645-8688. Web Site: www.nottlib.org. *Dir,* Jacqueline Zataweski; E-mail: jzataweski@nottlib.org; Staff 3 (MLS 1, Non-MLS 2)
Founded 1940. Pop 16,000
Subject Interests: Local hist
Automation Activity & Vendor Info: (Cataloging) TLC (The Library Corporation)
Wireless access
Function: 24/7 Electronic res, 24/7 Online cat, Adult bk club, Adult literacy prog, Audiobks on Playaways & MP3, Audiobks via web, Bk club(s), Bks on CD, Children's prog, Citizenship assistance, Computer training, Computers for patron use, Electronic databases & coll, Free DVD rentals, Health sci info serv, Holiday prog, Internet access, Life-long learning prog for all ages, Magazines, Mail & tel request accepted, Meeting rooms, Movies, Online cat, Outreach serv, OverDrive digital audio bks, Photocopying/Printing, Preschool outreach, Preschool reading prog, Prof lending libr, Scanner, Senior computer classes, Senior outreach, Story hour, Summer & winter reading prog, Summer reading prog, Tax forms, Teen prog, Wheelchair accessible, Winter reading prog
Friends of the Library Group
Branches: 3
BLACKSTONE LIBRARY - LOUIS SPENSER EPES LIBRARY, 415 S Main St, Blackstone, 23824, SAN 363-1567. Tel: 434-292-3587. FAX: 434-292-3587. *Librn,* Demetrius Nelson; E-mail: dnelson@nottlib.org; Staff 1 (Non-MLS 1)
Library Holdings: Bk Vols 13,229; Per Subs 18
Automation Activity & Vendor Info: (Cataloging) TLC (The Library Corporation); (Circulation) TLC (The Library Corporation); (OPAC) TLC (The Library Corporation)
Open Tues-Thurs 12-6, Fri & Sat 10-2
Friends of the Library Group
BURKEVILLE BRANCH, 114 S Agnew, Burkeville, 23922, SAN 363-1575. Tel: 434-767-5555. FAX: 434-767-5555. *Librn,* Agnes McCormick; E-mail: amccormick@nottlib.org
Library Holdings: Bk Vols 6,456
Open Tues & Thurs 9:30-5, Fri 10-2, Sat 9-Noon
Friends of the Library Group
CREWE BRANCH, 414 Tyler St, 23930, SAN 363-1591. Tel: 434-645-8688. FAX: 434-645-8688. *Mgr,* Susan Howe; E-mail: showe@nottlib.org; Staff 1 (Non-MLS 1)
Library Holdings: Audiobooks 673; DVDs 892; Bk Vols 29,615; Per Subs 83
Open Mon & Thurs 10-6, Tues & Wed 10-8, Sat 10-2
Friends of the Library Group

CROZIER

G VIRGINIA DEPARTMENT OF CORRECTIONS*, Academy for Staff Development Library, 1900 River Rd W, 23039. SAN 317-4662. Tel: 804-784-6800, 804-784-6841. FAX: 804-784-6999. E-mail: library@vadoc.virginia.gov. *Librn,* Alice Milner; Staff 1 (MLS 1)
Founded 1976
Library Holdings: AV Mats 1,630; Bk Vols 7,500; Per Subs 43
Subject Interests: Corrections, Inmate recovery prog, K-9 training, Leadership mgt
Wireless access
Publications: A/V Catalog; New Materials List (Quarterly)
Restriction: Open to dept staff only

CUMBERLAND

P CUMBERLAND COUNTY PUBLIC LIBRARY*, 1539 Anderson Hwy, 23040. (Mail add: PO Box 98, 23040-0098), SAN 373-8787. Tel: 804-492-5807. FAX: 804-492-9551. E-mail: cumberlandlibraryva@gmail.com. Web Site: www.cumberlandcountypubliclibrary.org. *Dir,* Lisa Blanton Davis; Staff 4 (Non-MLS 4)
Founded 1967. Pop 9,995; Circ 21,555
Library Holdings: Audiobooks 585; DVDs 1,614; Large Print Bks 421; Bk Titles 27,161; Per Subs 35
Automation Activity & Vendor Info: (Cataloging) Evergreen; (Circulation) Evergreen; (ILL) OCLC WorldShare Interlibrary Loan; (OPAC) Evergreen
Wireless access
Function: 24/7 Electronic res, 24/7 Online cat, Audiobks via web, Bks on CD, Children's prog, Computer training, Computers for patron use, Electronic databases & coll, Free DVD rentals, ILL available, Internet access, Laminating, Life-long learning prog for all ages, Magazines, Mail & tel request accepted, Meeting rooms, Notary serv, Online cat, Online info literacy tutorials on the web & in blackboard, OverDrive digital audio bks, Photocopying/Printing, Printer for laptops & handheld devices, Prog for adults, Prog for children & young adult, Ref & res, Scanner, Senior computer classes, Serves people with intellectual disabilities, Summer reading prog, Wheelchair accessible
Partic in Mid-Atlantic Library Alliance
Special Services for the Blind - Closed circuit TV
Open Mon 9-7, Tues-Fri 9-6, Sat 9-2
Friends of the Library Group

DAHLGREN

A UNITED STATES NAVY, Dahlgren General Library, Naval Surface Warfare Ctr, Bldg 1194, 6090 Jenkins Rd, 22448. SAN 362-8809. Tel: 540-653-7474. FAX: 540-653-0260. *Librn,* Lauren Glaettli
Founded 1954
Library Holdings: Bk Vols 12,000
Wireless access
Open Mon-Thurs 8-6, Fri 8-3

DANVILLE

C AVERETT UNIVERSITY LIBRARY*, Mary B Blount Library, 344 W Main St, 24541-2849. SAN 317-2570. Tel: 434-791-5692. Toll Free Tel: 800-543-9440. FAX: 434-791-5637. E-mail: aclib@averett.edu. Web Site: averett.libguides.com. *Head Librn,* Kevin Harden; E-mail: kevin.harden@averett.edu; *Tech Serv Librn,* Jennifer Robinson; Tel: 434-791-5693, E-mail: jrobinson@averett.edu; *Archivist, Ser,* Patrick Wasley, PhD; E-mail: pwasley@averett.edu; *Access Serv, Ref Serv,* Jim Verdini; Tel: 434-791-5694, E-mail: jverdini@averett.edu. Subject Specialists: *Bus, Soc sci,* Kevin Harden; *Children's lit, Communication studies, Journalism,* Jennifer Robinson; *Art, English lit, Modern lang,* Patrick Wasley, PhD; *Music, Relig, Theatre,* Jim Verdini; Staff 5 (MLS 5)
Founded 1859. Enrl 2,600; Fac 80; Highest Degree: Master
Library Holdings: AV Mats 494; e-books 100,000; e-journals 32,840; Bk Titles 102,736; Bk Vols 116,947; Per Subs 33,098
Special Collections: Averett University Archives; Charles R Hawkins Papers; Dan Daniel Archives; Danville History Coll. Oral History
Subject Interests: Civil rights era, Local hist
Automation Activity & Vendor Info: (Cataloging) Innovative Interfaces, Inc; (Circulation) Innovative Interfaces, Inc; (Course Reserve) Innovative Interfaces, Inc; (ILL) Innovative Interfaces, Inc; (OPAC) Innovative Interfaces, Inc
Wireless access
Function: Archival coll, Art exhibits, CD-ROM, Computers for patron use, Distance learning, E-Reserves, Electronic databases & coll, ILL available, Online cat, Online info literacy tutorials on the web & in blackboard, Online ref, Photocopying/Printing, Ref serv available
Publications: Averett Library News (Newsletter)
Partic in LYRASIS; SouthWest Information Network Group; Virginia Independent College & University Library Association; Virginia's Academic Library Consortium
Open Mon-Thurs 8:30am-10pm, Fri 8:30-4:30
Restriction: In-house use for visitors
Friends of the Library Group

J DANVILLE COMMUNITY COLLEGE*, Whittington W Clement Learning Resources Center, 1008 S Main St, 24541-4004. SAN 317-2597. Tel: 434-797-8453. Toll Free Tel: 800-560-4291 (VA only). Web Site: www.dcc.vccs.edu/lrc/lrc/learningresourcescenter.htm. *Dir,* Chris Ford; Tel: 434-797-8598, E-mail: cford@dcc.vccs.edu; *Librn,* Barbara Grether; Tel: 434-797-8405; Staff 9 (MLS 2, Non-MLS 7)
Founded 1968. Enrl 4,000; Fac 51
Library Holdings: AV Mats 3,330; Bks on Deafness & Sign Lang 63; e-journals 8,000; Bk Titles 46,502; Bk Vols 52,218; Per Subs 175

Subject Interests: Local hist
Automation Activity & Vendor Info: (Cataloging) OCLC; (Circulation) Ex Libris Group; (ILL) OCLC; (OPAC) Ex Libris Group
Wireless access
Partic in LYRASIS; OCLC Online Computer Library Center, Inc; Virginia Commun Coll Syst; Virginia's Academic Library Consortium
Open Mon-Thurs 8-8, Fri 8-Noon, Sun 1-5 (Fall & Spring); Mon-Thurs 7:30-6:30, Fri 8-Noon (Summer)

P DANVILLE PUBLIC LIBRARY*, 511 Patton St, 24541. SAN 317-2600. Tel: 434-799-5195. Administration Tel: 434-799-5195, Ext 2774. FAX: 434-792-5172. Web Site: readdanvilleva.org. *Interim Libr Dir,* Russell Carter; E-mail: carterr@danvilleva.gov; Staff 18 (MLS 2, Non-MLS 16)
Founded 1923. Pop 48,411; Circ 273,642
Library Holdings: AV Mats 7,000; Bk Vols 131,186
Subject Interests: Genealogy, Local hist
Automation Activity & Vendor Info: (Cataloging) TLC (The Library Corporation); (Circulation) TLC (The Library Corporation); (OPAC) TLC (The Library Corporation)
Wireless access
Function: Homebound delivery serv, ILL available, Photocopying/Printing, Prog for children & young adult, Ref serv available, Summer reading prog, Telephone ref, Wheelchair accessible
Open Mon & Tues 10-7, Wed 10-6, Thurs 10-8, Fri 10-5, Sat 9-1
Friends of the Library Group
Branches: 2
LAW, 511 Patton St, 24541. Tel: 434-799-5118. FAX: 434-799-5118. Web Site: readdanvilleva.org/136/law-library. *Law Librn, Supvr,* Rebecca Webb; E-mail: webbrw@ci.danville.va.us; Staff 1 (Non-MLS 1)
Founded 1987. Pop 48,411
Library Holdings: Bk Titles 300; Bk Vols 25,300
Function: Photocopying/Printing, Ref serv available, Res libr, Wheelchair accessible
Open Mon-Fri 10-3
Restriction: Non-circulating to the pub
WESTOVER, 94 Clifton St, 24541, SAN 378-1496. Tel: 434-799-5152. *Info Spec,* Patricia Williams; Staff 2 (Non-MLS 2)
Library Holdings: Bk Vols 8,000
Function: Photocopying/Printing, Prog for children & young adult, Ref serv available, Summer reading prog, Wheelchair accessible
Open Mon-Thurs 9-6, Fri 9-5

DAYTON

S ROCKTOWN HISTORY GENEALOGY & RESEARCH LIBRARY, Harrisonburg-Rockingham Historical Society Library, 382 High St, 22821. (Mail add: PO Box 716, 22821-0716), SAN 327-8719. Tel: 540-879-2681. E-mail: info@rocktownhistory.org. Web Site: www.rocktownhistory.org. *Adminr, Researcher,* Margaret Hotchner
Library Holdings: Bk Vols 2,200
Subject Interests: Genealogy, Local hist
Wireless access
Open Tues-Sat 10-4
Restriction: Non-circulating

DILLWYN

S DILLWYN CORRECTIONAL CENTER LIBRARY, 1522 Prison Rd, 23936. (Mail add: PO Box 670, 23936-0670), SAN 375-3387. Tel: 434-983-4200. FAX: 434-983-1821. *Librn,* Courtney Fenters; E-mail: courtney.fenters@vadoc.virginia.gov; Staff 1 (MLS 1)
Founded 1994
Jul 2024-Jun 2025 Income $8,270
Library Holdings: Bk Titles 14,000
Automation Activity & Vendor Info: (Cataloging) ComPanion Corp
Partic in Mid-Atlantic Library Alliance

DUBLIN

J NEW RIVER COMMUNITY COLLEGE*, Learning Resource Center, 226 Martin Hall, 5255 College Dr, 24084. SAN 317-2627. Tel: 540-674-3627. FAX: 540-676-3626. Web Site: www.nr.edu/library/. *Dir, Libr Serv,* Sandra Smith; Tel: 540-674-3600, Ext 4345, E-mail: ssmith@nr.edu; *Ref & ILL Librn,* Yvonne Maute; Tel: 540-674-3600, Ext 4331, E-mail: ymaute@nr.edu; *Circ Mgr,* Gary Bryant; Tel: 540-674-3600, Ext 4334, E-mail: gbryant@nr.edu; *Cataloger,* Teresa Jones; Tel: 540-674-3600, Ext 4297, E-mail: tmjones@nr.edu; Staff 6 (MLS 3, Non-MLS 3)
Founded 1968. Enrl 2,230; Fac 60
Library Holdings: Bks on Deafness & Sign Lang 250; High Interest/Low Vocabulary Bk Vols 300; Bk Titles 29,185; Bk Vols 34,495; Per Subs 406
Subject Interests: Educ, Hist, Humanities
Automation Activity & Vendor Info: (Acquisitions) Ex Libris Group; (Cataloging) Ex Libris Group; (Circulation) Ex Libris Group; (OPAC) Ex Libris Group
Wireless access
Partic in Virginia's Academic Library Consortium
Special Services for the Deaf - Bks on deafness & sign lang; High interest/low vocabulary bks
Open Mon-Thurs 7:45am-9pm, Fri 7:45-5, Sat 9-1, Sun 1-5; Mon & Thurs 7:30am-9pm, Tues & Wed 7:30-6, Fri 7:30-5, Sun 1-5 (Summer)

EDINBURG

P SHENANDOAH COUNTY LIBRARY*, 514 Stoney Creek Blvd, 22824. SAN 322-662X. Tel: 540-984-8200. FAX: 540-984-8207. Web Site: www.shenandoah.co.lib.va.us. *Dir,* Robert Whitesides; Tel: 540-984-8200, Ext 206, E-mail: swhitesides@countylib.org; *Asst Dir,* Zoe Dellinger; Tel: 540-984-8200, Ext 205, E-mail: zdellinger@countylib.org; *Head Cataloger,* Esther Jayne; E-mail: ejayne@countylib.org; *Ad,* David Robinson; E-mail: drobinson@countylib.org; *Circ Supvr,* Elizabeth Dart; E-mail: edart@countylib.org; *Children's Serv Coordr,* Erica Hepner; E-mail: ehepner@countylib.org; *Tech Serv Coordr,* Dallas Moore; E-mail: dmoore@countylib.org; *Archivist,* Zachary Hottel; E-mail: zhottel@countylib.org; Staff 14 (MLS 2, Non-MLS 12)
Founded 1984. Pop 42,000; Circ 235,000
Library Holdings: Audiobooks 7,301; Bks on Deafness & Sign Lang 25; CDs 1,902; DVDs 6,162; e-books 300; Electronic Media & Resources 20,140; High Interest/Low Vocabulary Bk Vols 30; Large Print Bks 5,567; Microforms 245; Bk Titles 116,436; Bk Vols 121,321; Per Subs 115; Spec Interest Per Sub 12; Videos 2,800
Special Collections: Mid-Atlantic Germanic Society (MAGS) Coll; Shenandoah Room Coll
Subject Interests: Civil War, Maryland, Shenandoah County, Shenandoah Valley, Va, WVa
Automation Activity & Vendor Info: (Acquisitions) The Library Co-Op, Inc; (Cataloging) TLC (The Library Corporation); (Circulation) TLC (The Library Corporation); (OPAC) TLC (The Library Corporation)
Wireless access
Publications: Stoney Creek Current (Newsletter)
Partic in Shenandoah County Libr Syst
Special Services for the Blind - Bks on cassette
Open Mon, Wed & Fri 10-6, Tues & Thurs 10-8, Sat 10-3
Friends of the Library Group
Branches: 5
BASYE-ORKNEY SPRINGS COMMUNITY, 1382 Resort Dr, Basye, 22810. (Mail add: PO Box 251, Basye, 22810-0251). Tel: 540-856-8084. FAX: 540-856-2148. E-mail: basyelib@shentel.net.
Open Mon, Wed, Thurs & Sat 10-2, Tues & Fri 10-2 & 4:30-6:30
FORT VALLEY COMMUNITY, 6190 Woodstock Tower Rd, Fort Valley, 22652. (Mail add: PO Box 120, Fort Valley, 22652-0120). Tel: 540-933-6714. FAX: 540-933-6013. E-mail: ftvallib@shentel.net.
Founded 1998
Open Mon 4-7, Tues, Wed & Sat 9:30-12:30, Thurs 4:30-6:30, Fri 9:30-2
MT JACKSON COMMUNITY, 5901 Main St, Mount Jackson, 22842. Tel: 540-477-3327. FAX: 540-477-2294. E-mail: mtjlib@shentel.net.
Open Mon 6-8, Tues, Wed & Fri 1:30-5:30, Thurs 1:30-8, Sat 12-4
NEW MARKET AREA, 160 E Lee St, New Market, 22844. (Mail add: PO Box 452, New Market, 22844). Tel: 540-740-8650. FAX: 540-740-2956. E-mail: nmlib@shentel.net.
Founded 1974
Library Holdings: Bk Vols 5,000; Talking Bks 50
Special Collections: Local History Coll
Open Mon 9-6:30, Tues, Wed & Fri 1-5, Thurs 1-5 & 7-9, Sat 9:30-1, Sun 2-5
Friends of the Library Group
STRASBURG COMMUNITY, 195 W King St, Strasburg, 22657. Tel: 540-465-8464. FAX: 540-465-2739. E-mail: strasburg@countylib.org. Web Site: countylib.org/strasburg.
Founded 1959. Pop 15,000
Library Holdings: Bk Vols 19,000
Function: Activity rm, Adult bk club, Archival coll, Art exhibits, Audiobks via web, Bks on CD, Children's prog, Computers for patron use, For res purposes, ILL available, Meeting rooms, Online info literacy tutorials on the web & in blackboard, Online ref, OverDrive digital audio bks, Photocopying/Printing, Prog for children & young adult, Ref & res, Ref serv available, Res assist avail, Story hour, Study rm, Summer reading prog, Teen prog, Wheelchair accessible
Open Mon & Tues 11-6, Wed & Thurs 10-3:30, Fri 10-4, Sat 10-Noon

EMORY

C EMORY & HENRY COLLEGE*, E&H Library, 30480 Armbrister Dr, 24327. (Mail add: PO Box 948, 24327-0948), SAN 317-2643. Tel: 276-944-6208. Web Site: www.ehc.edu/library. *Libr Dir,* Ruth Castillo; E-mail: rcastillo@ehc.edu; *Govt Doc Librn, Syst & Electronic Res,* Jody Hanshew; E-mail: jhanshew@ehc.edu; *Health Sci Librn,* Jana Schellinger; E-mail: jlschellinger@ehc.edu; *Pub Serv Librn,* Adam Alley; *Tech Serv Librn,* Rebecca Grantham; E-mail: rgrantham@ehc.edu; Staff 7 (MLS 5, Non-MLS 2)
Founded 1836. Enrl 1,200; Fac 117; Highest Degree: Doctorate

Special Collections: Appalachian Oral History Coll; Methodist Church History (I P Martin Coll); Southwestern Virginiana (Goodrich Wilson Papers). Oral History; US Document Depository
Subject Interests: Liberal arts
Automation Activity & Vendor Info: (Acquisitions) Innovative Interfaces, Inc; (Cataloging) Innovative Interfaces, Inc; (Circulation) Innovative Interfaces, Inc; (Discovery) EBSCO Discovery Service; (ILL) OCLC ILLiad; (Media Booking) Innovative Interfaces, Inc; (OPAC) Innovative Interfaces, Inc; (Serials) Innovative Interfaces, Inc
Wireless access
Partic in Appalachian College Association; Holston Assoc Librs, Inc; LYRASIS; Mid-Atlantic Library Alliance; Virginia Independent College & University Library Association; Virginia's Academic Library Consortium

FAIRFAX

P FAIRFAX COUNTY PUBLIC LIBRARY*, Administrative Offices, 12000 Government Center Pkwy, Ste 324, 22035-0012. SAN 363-3578. Tel: 703-324-3100. Interlibrary Loan Service Tel: 703-222-3136. FAX: 703-324-8365. Interlibrary Loan Service FAX: 703-653-9512. Web Site: www.fairfaxcounty.gov/library. *Dir,* Jessica Hudson; E-mail: jessica.hudson@fairfaxcounty.gov; *Dep Dir,* Christine Jones; *Dir, Libr Tech,* Margaret Kositch; *Dir, Tech Serv,* Dianne Coan; *Div Dir, Admin Serv,* Ted Kavich; *Librn,* Suzanne S LaPierre; *Mkt & Communications Mgr,* Mary Mulrenan; *Br Coordr,* Mohammed Esslami; *Br Coordr,* Nancy Ryan.
Subject Specialists: *Virginiana,* Suzanne S LaPierre
Founded 1939
Library Holdings: Bk Vols 2,601,743
Special Collections: Virginia History Coll
Automation Activity & Vendor Info: (Acquisitions) Innovative Interfaces, Inc; (Cataloging) Innovative Interfaces, Inc; (Circulation) Innovative Interfaces, Inc; (Course Reserve) Innovative Interfaces, Inc; (OPAC) Innovative Interfaces, Inc
Wireless access
Publications: Books & Beyond: Fairfax County Public Library's First Fifty Years; Collection Development; Fairfax County Public Library Board of Trustees Policy Manual; Fairfax County Public Library User Study; Information Services Guidelines; Information Services Profile; Materials Availability Study; Page Training Manual; Problem Behavior Manual; Reference Accuracy at the Fairfax County Public Library; Training Checklist for Circulation Staff; Training Checklist for Information Services Staff
Partic in Metrop Wash Libr Coun
Special Services for the Deaf - Assistive tech; TTY equip
Special Services for the Blind - Recorded bks
Open Mon-Fri 8-4:30
Friends of the Library Group
Branches: 22
BURKE CENTRE LIBRARY, 5935 Freds Oak Rd, Burke, 22015-2599. Tel: 703-249-1520. *Br Mgr,* Jill Johnson
Open Mon & Tues 10-9, Wed & Fri 10-6, Thurs 1-9, Sat 10-5
Friends of the Library Group
RICHARD BYRD BRANCH, 7250 Commerce St, Springfield, 22150-3499, SAN 363-3969. Tel: 703-451-8055. *Br Mgr,* Valerie Suttee
Open Mon & Tues 10-9, Wed & Fri 10-6, Thurs 1-9, Sat 10-5
Friends of the Library Group
CENTREVILLE REGIONAL, 14200 Saint Germain Dr, Centreville, 20121-2299, SAN 363-3667. Tel: 703-830-2223. *Br Mgr,* Position Currently Open; *Asst Br Mgr,* Helen Ignatenko
Open Mon-Thurs 10-9, Fri 10-6, Sat 10-5, Sun 1-5
Friends of the Library Group
CHANTILLY REGIONAL, 4000 Stringfellow Rd, Chantilly, 20151-2628, SAN 374-7255. Tel: 703-502-3883. *Br Mgr,* Ingrid Bowers
Open Mon-Thurs 10-9, Fri 10-6, Sat 10-5, Sun 1-5
Friends of the Library Group
CITY OF FAIRFAX REGIONAL LIBRARY, 10360 North St, 22030-2514, SAN 363-3632. Tel: 703-293-6227. *Br Mgr,* Laura Raymond
Subject Interests: Genealogy, Va hist
Open Mon-Thurs 10-9, Fri 10-6, Sat 10-5, Sun 1-5
Friends of the Library Group
GREAT FALLS BRANCH, 9830 Georgetown Pike, Great Falls, 22066-2634, SAN 363-3764. Tel: 703-757-8560. *Br Mgr,* Andrea Spira
Open Mon & Tues 10-9, Wed & Fri 10-6, Thurs 1-9, Sat 10-5
Friends of the Library Group
PATRICK HENRY BRANCH, 101 Maple Ave E, Vienna, 22180-5794, SAN 363-390X. Tel: 703-938-0405. *Br Mgr,* Charles Webb
Open Mon & Tues 10-9, Wed & Fri 10-6, Thurs 1-9, Sat 10-5
Friends of the Library Group
HERNDON FORTNIGHTLY BRANCH, 768 Center St, Herndon, 20170-4640, SAN 363-3780. Tel: 703-437-8855. *Br Mgr,* Amanda T Post
Open Mon & Tues 10-9, Wed & Fri 10-6, Thurs 1-9, Sat 10-5
Friends of the Library Group
THOMAS JEFFERSON BRANCH, 7415 Arlington Blvd, Falls Church, 22042-7499, SAN 363-4027. Tel: 703-573-1060. *Br Mgr,* Laurel Tacoma
Open Mon & Tues 10-9, Wed & Fri 10-6, Thurs 1-9, Sat 10-5
Friends of the Library Group
KINGS PARK, 9000 Burke Lake Rd, Burke, 22015-1683, SAN 363-3845. Tel: 703-978-5600. *Br Mgr,* Valerie Drummond
Open Mon & Tues 10-9, Wed & Fri 10-6, Thurs 1-9, Sat 10-5
Friends of the Library Group
KINGSTOWNE BRANCH, 6500 Landsdowne Ctr, Alexandria, 22315-5011. Tel: 703-339-4610. *Br Mgr,* Barbara Rice
Open Mon & Tues 10-9, Wed & Fri 10-6, Thurs 1-9, Sat 10-5
Friends of the Library Group
LORTON BRANCH, 9520 Richmond Hwy, Lorton, 22079-2124, SAN 363-3853. Tel: 703-339-7385. *Br Mgr,* Lyn McKinney
Friends of the Library Group
DOLLEY MADISON BRANCH, 1244 Oak Ridge Ave, McLean, 22101-2818, SAN 363-3691. Tel: 703-356-0770. *Br Mgr,* Mary Prisbrey
Open Mon & Tues 10-9, Wed & Fri 10-6, Thurs 1-9, Sat 10-5
Friends of the Library Group
JOHN MARSHALL BRANCH, 6209 Rose Hill Dr, Alexandria, 22310-6299, SAN 363-3810. Tel: 703-971-0010. *Br Mgr,* Ivelisse Figueroa
Open Mon & Tues 10-9, Wed & Fri 10-6, Thurs 1-9, Sat 10-5
Friends of the Library Group
GEORGE MASON REGIONAL, 7001 Little River Tpk, Annandale, 22003-5975, SAN 363-3756. Tel: 703-256-3800. *Br Mgr,* Emily Riley
Open Mon-Thurs 10-9, Fri 10-6, Sat 10-5, Sun 1-5
Friends of the Library Group
OAKTON LIBRARY, 10304 Lynnhaven Pl, Oakton, 22124-1785. Tel: 703-242-4020. *Br Mgr,* Lisa Kern
Open Mon & Tues 10-9, Wed & Fri 10-6, Thurs 1-9, Sat 10-5
Friends of the Library Group
POHICK REGIONAL, 6450 Sydenstricker Rd, Burke, 22015-4274, SAN 328-798X. Tel: 703-644-7333. *Br Mgr,* Andrew Pendergrass
Open Mon-Thurs 10-9, Fri 10-6, Sat 10-5, Sun 1-5
Friends of the Library Group
RESTON REGIONAL, 11925 Bowman Towne Dr, Reston, 20190-3311, SAN 363-3934. Tel: 703-689-2700. *Br Mgr,* Katilyn Miller
Open Mon-Thurs 10-9, Fri 10-6, Sat 10-5, Sun 1-5
Friends of the Library Group
SHERWOOD REGIONAL, 2501 Sherwood Hall Lane, Alexandria, 22306-2799, SAN 363-3993. Tel: 703-765-3645. *Br Mgr,* Linda Schlekau
Open Mon-Thurs 10-9, Fri 10-6, Sat 10-5, Sun 1-5
Friends of the Library Group
TYSONS-PIMMIT REGIONAL, 7584 Leesburg Pike, Falls Church, 22043-2099, SAN 363-4051. Tel: 703-790-8088. *Br Mgr,* Daniela Dixon
Open Mon-Thurs 10-9, Fri 10-6, Sat 10-5, Sun 1-5
Friends of the Library Group
MARTHA WASHINGTON BRANCH, 6614 Fort Hunt Rd, Alexandria, 22307-1799, SAN 363-387X. Tel: 703-768-6700. *Br Mgr,* Cathy Noonan
Open Mon & Tues 10-9, Wed & Fri 10-6, Thurs 1-9, Sat 10-5
Friends of the Library Group
WOODROW WILSON BRANCH, 6101 Knollwood Dr, Falls Church, 22041-1798, SAN 363-4086. Tel: 703-820-8774. *Br Mgr,* Sarah Garcia
Open Mon & Tues 10-9, Wed & Fri 10-6, Thurs 1-9, Sat 10-5
Friends of the Library Group

GL FAIRFAX PUBLIC LAW LIBRARY, 4110 Chain Bridge Rd, Rm 115, 22030. SAN 321-8384. Tel: 703-246-2170. Administration Tel: 703-246-2175. FAX: 703-591-0310. E-mail: liblawlibrary@fairfaxcounty.gov. Web Site: www.fairfaxcounty.gov/topics/public-law-library. *Dir,* Cathryn Butler; Staff 2 (Non-MLS 2)
Founded 1956
Special Collections: District of Columbia Coll; Maryland Coll; Virginia Law Coll (Historical Statutes & Session Laws)
Subject Interests: Law
Automation Activity & Vendor Info: (Acquisitions) LibraryWorld, Inc; (Cataloging) LibraryWorld, Inc; (OPAC) LibraryWorld, Inc; (Serials) LibraryWorld, Inc
Wireless access
Function: CD-ROM, Computers for patron use, Electronic databases & coll, Meeting rooms, Online cat, Photocopying/Printing, Wheelchair accessible
Partic in American Association of Law Libraries
Open Mon-Fri 8-4:30
Restriction: Non-circulating, Not a lending libr

C GEORGE MASON UNIVERSITY LIBRARIES*, Fenwick Library, 4348 Chesapeake River Way, 22030. (Mail add: 4400 University Dr, MSN 2FL, 22030), SAN 362-8833. Tel: 703-993-2240. Interlibrary Loan Service Tel: 703-993-2228. Reference Tel: 703-993-2210. Administration Tel: 703-993-2491. FAX: 703-993-2200. Interlibrary Loan Service FAX: 703-993-2255. Reference FAX: 703-993-2255. TDD: 703-993-3992. E-mail: feninfo@gmu.edu. Web Site: library.gmu.edu. *Dean, Libr & Univ*

Librn, John G Zenelis; E-mail: jzenelis@gmu.edu; *Assoc Univ Librn, Coll Mgt Serv,* John Walsh; Tel: 703-993-3711, E-mail: jwalsh@gmu.edu; *Assoc Univ Librn, Digital Programs, Syst,* Wally Grotophorst; Tel: 703-993-9005, E-mail: wallyg@gmu.edu; *Asst Univ Librn,* Bridget Euliano; Tel: 703-993-2445, E-mail: bmiller5@gmu.edu; Staff 128 (MLS 58, Non-MLS 70)
Founded 1957. Enrl 35,960; Fac 2,551; Highest Degree: Doctorate
Jul 2016-Jun 2017. Mats Exp $10,039,042, Books $1,946,515, Per/Ser (Incl. Access Fees) $4,150,190, AV Mat $121,169, Electronic Ref Mat (Incl. Access Fees) $2,910,206, Presv $44,569. Sal $7,295,530 (Prof $3,901,815)
Library Holdings: AV Mats 57,000; e-books 1,790,000; e-journals 189,000; Electronic Media & Resources 166,000; Music Scores 16,000; Bk Vols 1,245,000
Special Collections: Oral History; State Document Depository; US Document Depository
Subject Interests: Antiquarian Books, Archives, Northern Virginia History, Peace & conflict studies, Performing arts, Politics & govt, Rare bks, Regional hist, Theatre, Transportation planning
Automation Activity & Vendor Info: (Acquisitions) Ex Libris Group; (Cataloging) Ex Libris Group; (Circulation) Ex Libris Group; (Course Reserve) Ex Libris Group; (Discovery) Ex Libris Group; (ILL) OCLC Online; (OPAC) Ex Libris Group; (Serials) Ex Libris Group
Wireless access
Publications: inSight (Newsletter); Research Guides; The Libraries at Mason (Annual)
Partic in Association of Southeastern Research Libraries; Center for Research Libraries; LYRASIS; OCLC Online Computer Library Center, Inc; Virginia's Academic Library Consortium; Washington Research Library Consortium
Special Services for the Deaf - Assisted listening device; Closed caption videos
Special Services for the Blind - Accessible computers; Closed circuit TV magnifier; Inspiration software; Screen reader software; ZoomText magnification & reading software
Open Mon-Thurs 8-Midnight, Fri 8-9, Sat 10-9, Sun Noon-Midnight

Departmental Libraries:

ARLINGTON CAMPUS LIBRARY, 3351 Fairfax Dr, MSN IDI, Founders Hall, Rm 201, Arlington, 22201. Tel: 703-993-8188. Reference Tel: 703-993-8230. FAX: 703-993-8142. TDD: 703-993-4970. Web Site: library.gmu.edu/locations/arlington. *Library Contact,* Liz Bass; E-mail: ebass2@gmu.edu
Special Services for the Deaf - Closed caption videos
Special Services for the Blind - Accessible computers; Closed circuit TV magnifier; Inspiration software; Screen reader software; ZoomText magnification & reading software
Open Mon-Thurs 9-9, Fri 9-6, Sat 10-6, Sun Noon-8

CL LAW LIBRARY, 3301 N Fairfax Dr, Arlington, 22201-4426. SAN 362-8906. Tel: 703-993-8100. Interlibrary Loan Service Tel: 703-993-8147. Reference Tel: 703-993-8076. Administration Tel: 703-993-8106. FAX: 703-993-8113. Web Site: www.law.gmu.edu/library. *Assoc Dean, Libr Tech,* Deborah Keene; Tel: 703-993-8110, E-mail: dkeene@gmu.edu; *Dir, Tech Serv,* Jose Coradin; *Access Serv, Head, Admin Serv,* Ellen Feldman; *Head, Coll Develop, Tech Serv,* Cynthia Myers; *Fac Serv Librn, Ref,* John Scherrer; *Acq Mgr,* Kathleen Stewart; *Cat Mgr,* Rekha Pandya; *Circ Mgr,* Maya Karki; *Res Serv Spec,* Mark Leighton; *Tech,* Carlos Sandoval; *Technology Spec,* Corey Gibson; *Fac Serv Librn, Ref,* Geraldine Kalim; *Research Servs Librn,* Peter Vay; Staff 14 (MLS 7, Non-MLS 7)
Founded 1979. Enrl 448; Highest Degree: Doctorate
Jul 2016-Jun 2017. Mats Exp $692,712, Books $38,542, Per/Ser (Incl. Access Fees) $647,640, Electronic Ref Mat (Incl. Access Fees) $6,530
Library Holdings: AV Mats 964; e-books 540,737; Microforms 112,459; Bk Titles 55,986; Bk Vols 221,989; Per Subs 84
Automation Activity & Vendor Info: (Acquisitions) Ex Libris Group; (Cataloging) Ex Libris Group; (Circulation) Ex Libris Group; (Discovery) Ex Libris Group; (OPAC) Ex Libris Group; (Serials) Ex Libris Group
Partic in LYRASIS
Publications: Law Library Guide (Reference guide); Research Guides
Special Services for the Deaf - Assistive tech
Special Services for the Blind - Accessible computers
Open Mon-Thurs 8am-11pm, Fri 8am-10pm, Sat 10-10, Sun 10am-11pm

MERCER LIBRARY, SCIENCE & TECHNOLOGY CAMPUS, 10900 University Blvd, MSN 4E6, Occoquan Bldg, Rm 104, Manassas, 20110. Tel: 703-993-8340. Reference Tel: 703-993-8342. FAX: 703-993-8349. TDD: 703-993-8365. Web Site: library.gmu.edu/locations/mercer. *Sci & Tech Librn, Team Leader,* Kimberly Hoffman; Tel: 703-993-8344, E-mail: khoffma@gmu.edu
Special Services for the Deaf - Closed caption videos
Special Services for the Blind - Accessible computers; Closed circuit TV magnifier; Inspiration software; Screen reader software; ZoomText magnification & reading software
Open Mon-Thurs 8-10, Fri 8-6, Sat 10-6, Sun Noon-8

FALLS CHURCH

S CENTER FOR HEALTH, ENVIRONMENT & JUSTICE*, 7139 Shreve Rd, 22046. (Mail add: PO Box 6806, 22040-6806), SAN 374-5864. Tel: 703-237-2249. FAX: 703-237-8389. E-mail: chej@chej.org. Web Site: www.chej.org/resource-library. *Tech Serv,* Stephen Lester
Founded 1981
Library Holdings: Bk Titles 5,000; Per Subs 58; Spec Interest Per Sub 400
Special Collections: UN Document Depository
Subject Interests: Environ law, Environ sci, Health, Technologies
Function: Res libr
Publications: Newsletter

M INOVA FAIRFAX HOSPITAL*, Jacob D Zylman Health Sciences Library, 3300 Gallows Rd, 22042. SAN 317-2767. Tel: 703-776-3234. Reference Tel: 703-776-3357. FAX: 703-776-3353. E-mail: library@inova.org. Web Site: www.inova.org/locations/inova-fairfax-medical-campus/health-sciences-library. *Dir,* Lois H Culler; E-mail: lois.culler@inova.org; *Med Librn,* Libby Samuel; Staff 4.5 (MLS 3.5, Non-MLS 1)
Founded 1966
Library Holdings: e-books 6,000; e-journals 3,500; Electronic Media & Resources 45; Bk Vols 3,000
Subject Interests: Healthcare admin, Med, Nursing
Automation Activity & Vendor Info: (Acquisitions) Koha; (Cataloging) Koha; (Circulation) Koha; (Media Booking) Koha; (OPAC) Koha; (Serials) Koha
Wireless access
Partic in National Network of Libraries of Medicine Region 1; Proquest Dialog
Open Mon-Fri 8-8, Sat 9-5

P MARY RILEY STYLES PUBLIC LIBRARY*, 120 N Virginia Ave, 22046. SAN 317-2783. Tel: 703-248-5030. Circulation Tel: 703-248-5031. Administration Tel: 703-248-5032. Information Services Tel: 703-248-5035. FAX: 703-531-3395. Web Site: www.fallschurchva.gov/424/Library. *Actg Libr Dir,* Marshall Webster; E-mail: mwebster@fallschurchva.gov; Staff 18.8 (MLS 8, Non-MLS 10.8)
Founded 1898
Jul 2019-Jun 2020. Mats Exp $321,003, Books $147,681, AV Mat $29,700, Electronic Ref Mat (Incl. Access Fees) $143,622. Sal $1,219,311
Library Holdings: AV Mats 9,930; DVDs 6,559; e-books 15,895; e-journals 90; Large Print Bks 1,242; Bk Vols 75,031; Per Subs 122
Special Collections: Falls Church Local History Coll
Automation Activity & Vendor Info: (Acquisitions) Biblionix/Apollo; (Cataloging) Biblionix/Apollo; (Circulation) Biblionix/Apollo; (OPAC) Biblionix/Apollo; (Serials) Biblionix/Apollo
Wireless access
Function: 24/7 Electronic res, 24/7 Online cat, Adult bk club, Adult literacy prog, Archival coll, Audiobks via web, AV serv, Bk club(s), Bks on CD, Children's prog, Computer training, Computers for patron use, E-Reserves, Electronic databases & coll, Free DVD rentals, Home delivery & serv to seniorr ctr & nursing homes, Homebound delivery serv, ILL available, Internet access, Life-long learning prog for all ages, Magazines, Mail & tel request accepted, Microfiche/film & reading machines, Movies, Online cat, Online ref, Outreach serv, OverDrive digital audio bks, Photocopying/Printing, Preschool outreach, Preschool reading prog, Prog for adults, Prog for children & young adult, Ref serv available, Spoken cassettes & CDs, Spoken cassettes & DVDs, Story hour, Summer & winter reading prog, Summer reading prog, Tax forms, Teen prog, Telephone ref, Wheelchair accessible, Winter reading prog
Open Mon, Tues & Thurs 9-9, Wed 1-9, Fri & Sat 9-5, Sun 1-5

FARMVILLE

P CENTRAL VIRGINIA REGIONAL LIBRARY*, Farmville Library, 1303 W Third St, 23901. SAN 371-6791. Tel: 434-392-6924. FAX: 434-392-9784. Web Site: cvrl.net. *Dir,* Rick Ewing; Tel: 434-603-6523, E-mail: rewing@cvrl.net; Staff 3 (MLS 3)
Founded 1993. Circ 70,500
Library Holdings: Bk Vols 60,000; Per Subs 45
Special Collections: African-American History Coll
Subject Interests: Local hist
Automation Activity & Vendor Info: (Cataloging) SirsiDynix-WorkFlows; (Circulation) SirsiDynix-WorkFlows; (OPAC) SirsiDynix-Symphony
Wireless access
Function: 24/7 Electronic res, 24/7 Online cat, Adult bk club, Audiobks via web, Bk club(s), Bks on CD, Children's prog, Computer training, Computers for patron use, E-Reserves, Electronic databases & coll, Free DVD rentals, ILL available, Internet access, Magazines, Meeting rooms, Music CDs, Notary serv, Online cat, OverDrive digital audio bks, Photocopying/Printing, Printer for laptops & handheld devices, Prog for adults, Prog for children & young adult, Scanner, Story hour, Study rm, Summer reading prog, Tax forms, Teen prog, Wheelchair accessible

Open Mon-Thurs 10-8, Fri 10-6, Sat 10-5, Sun 1-5
Friends of the Library Group
Branches: 1
BUCKINGHAM COUNTY PUBLIC LIBRARY, 16266 N James Madison Hwy, Dillwyn, 23936, SAN 373-7063. Tel: 434-983-3848. *Br Mgr,* Position Currently Open
Founded 1983
Special Collections: Backwoods Coll
Subject Interests: Fishing, Hunting, Self sufficiency
Automation Activity & Vendor Info: (Circulation) SirsiDynix-Symphony
Function: 24/7 Electronic res, 24/7 Online cat, Activity rm, Audiobks via web, Bks on CD, Children's prog, Computer training, Computers for patron use, E-Reserves, Electronic databases & coll, Free DVD rentals, ILL available, Internet access, Magazines, Notary serv, Online cat, OverDrive digital audio bks, Photocopying/Printing, Printer for laptops & handheld devices, Prog for adults, Prog for children & young adult, Story hour, Summer reading prog, Tax forms, Teen prog, Wheelchair accessible
Open Mon-Thurs 9-7, Fri & Sat 9-5
Friends of the Library Group

C LONGWOOD UNIVERSITY*, Janet D Greenwood Library, Redford & Race St, 23909. (Mail add: 201 High St, 23909). SAN 317-283X. Circulation Tel: 434-395-2433. Interlibrary Loan Service Tel: 434-395-2446. Reference Tel: 434-395-2747. Administration Tel: 434-395-2431. FAX: 434-395-2453. E-mail: libweb@longwood.edu. Web Site: libguides.longwood.edu. *Dean of Libr,* Brent Roberts; E-mail: robertsbs2@longwood.edu; *Head, Coll, Head, Info Serv,* Tammy Hines; Tel: 434-395-2444, E-mail: hinestm@longwood.edu; *Digital Serv Librn, Research Librn,* Mark Hamilton; Tel: 434-395-2443, E-mail: hamiltonma@longwood.edu; *Instrul & Res Librn,* Jennifer Beach; Tel: 434-395-2257, E-mail: beachjs@longwood.edu; *Mkt Librn, Outreach Librn, Research Servs Librn,* Vicki Palmer; Tel: 434-395-2442, E-mail: palmervm@longwood.edu; *Research Servs Librn,* Sarah Reynolds; Tel: 434-395-2437, E-mail: reynoldsst@longwood.edu; *Budget Off Mgr,* Cindy Elliott; Tel: 434-395-2440, E-mail: elliotcb@longwood.edu; *Colls Mgr,* Kate Culver; Tel: 434-395-2438, E-mail: culverkh@longwood.edu; *Acq Spec,* Cherri Shideler; Tel: 434-395-2742, E-mail: shidelercm@longwood.edu; *Archive Spec,* Jamie Krogh; Tel: 434-395-2432, E-mail: kroghjl@longwood.edu; *Cat Spec,* Betty Eike; Tel: 434-395-2449, E-mail: eikeba@longwood.edu; *Digital Initiatives, Spec,* Hope D Alwine; Tel: 434-395-2873, E-mail: alwinehd@longwood.edu; *ILL Spec,* Dana Owen; E-mail: owendb@longwood.edu; *Ser Spec,* Mary Fran Bell-Johnson; Tel: 434-395-2450, E-mail: belljohnsonmf@longwood.edu; *Archives Assoc, Info Assoc,* Benedict Chatelain; Tel: 434-395-2448, E-mail: chatelainlog@longwood.edu; *Info Assoc,* Ruth Gowin; Tel: 434-395-2741, E-mail: gowinre@longwood.edu. Subject Specialists: *Rec,* Jamie Krogh
Founded 1839. Enrl 4,800; Fac 210; Highest Degree: Master
Library Holdings: CDs 4,000; DVDs 14,000; e-books 18,000; e-journals 34,000; Bk Titles 275,000; Bk Vols 332,000; Per Subs 35,000
Special Collections: State Document Depository
Automation Activity & Vendor Info: (Cataloging) Innovative Interfaces, Inc; (Circulation) Innovative Interfaces, Inc
Wireless access
Partic in Dow Jones News Retrieval; LYRASIS; OCLC Online Computer Library Center, Inc; Proquest Dialog; Source; Specialnet; Virginia's Academic Library Consortium; Wilsonline
Open Mon-Thurs 7:30am-2am, Fri 7:30-5, Sat 10-5, Sun 1pm-2am
Friends of the Library Group

FERRUM

C FERRUM COLLEGE*, Thomas Stanley Library, 150 Wiley Dr, 24088. (Mail add: PO Box 1000, 24088-1000), SAN 317-2848. Tel: 540-365-4424, 540-365-4426. E-mail: stanleylibrary@ferrum.edu. Web Site: ferrum.edu/stanley-library. *Libr Mgr,* Rachel Walton; E-mail: rewalton@ferrum.edu; *Tech Serv Librn,* Peggie Barker; E-mail: pbarker@ferrum.edu; *ILL Coordr,* Cheryl Hundley; E-mail: chundley@ferrum.edu; Staff 4 (MLS 3, Non-MLS 1)
Founded 1913. Enrl 1,000; Highest Degree: Bachelor
Library Holdings: AV Mats 2,086; e-books 100,000; Bk Vols 115,000; Per Subs 14,600
Special Collections: Archives of Governor & Mrs Thomas B Stanley
Subject Interests: Environ studies, Hist, Relig studies
Automation Activity & Vendor Info: (Acquisitions) Innovative Interfaces, Inc; (Cataloging) Innovative Interfaces, Inc; (Circulation) Innovative Interfaces, Inc; (Course Reserve) Docutek; (ILL) OCLC; (OPAC) Innovative Interfaces, Inc; (Serials) Innovative Interfaces, Inc
Wireless access
Partic in Appalachian College Association; LYRASIS; OCLC Online Computer Library Center, Inc; Virginia Independent College & University Library Association; Virginia's Academic Library Consortium
Open Mon-Thurs 7:45am-Midnight, Fri 7:45-6, Sat 10-6, Sun 2-Midnight

FISHERSVILLE

P AUGUSTA COUNTY LIBRARY*, 1759 Jefferson Hwy, 22939. SAN 317-2856. Tel: 540-885-3961, 540-949-6354. FAX: 540-943-5965. Web Site: www.augustacountylibrary.org. *Dir,* Diantha McCauley; E-mail: diantha@augustacountylibrary.org; *Asst Dir,* Debbie Sweeney; *Adult Serv,* Daza Craig; *Youth Serv,* Hailee Coleman; Staff 27 (MLS 6, Non-MLS 21)
Founded 1977. Pop 73,912
Jul 2018-Jun 2019 Income (Main & Associated Libraries) $1,408,612, State $162,052, Federal $20,854, County $1,225,706. Mats Exp $170,906, Books $100,906, Per/Ser (Incl. Access Fees) $10,000, AV Mat $40,000, Electronic Ref Mat (Incl. Access Fees) $20,000. Sal $717,858
Library Holdings: Audiobooks 8,107; AV Mats 30,523; DVDs 22,416; e-books 315,025; Bk Vols 157,994; Per Subs 125
Automation Activity & Vendor Info: (Cataloging) TLC (The Library Corporation); (Circulation) TLC (The Library Corporation); (OPAC) TLC (The Library Corporation)
Wireless access
Function: 24/7 Electronic res, 24/7 Online cat, Activity rm, Adult bk club
Publications: Newsletter (Quarterly)
Partic in LYRASIS; Mid-Atlantic Library Alliance
Open Mon-Thurs 9-8, Fri & Sat 9-5
Friends of the Library Group
Branches: 5
CHURCHVILLE BRANCH, 3714 Churchville Ave, Churchville, 24421. Tel: 540-245-5287. FAX: 540-245-5290. *Br Mgr,* Rachael Phillips; E-mail: rphillips@augustacountylibrary.org; Staff 3 (MLS 1, Non-MLS 2)
Founded 2002
Library Holdings: Bk Vols 25,000; Per Subs 26
Automation Activity & Vendor Info: (Serials) EBSCO Online
Function: 24/7 Electronic res, Activity rm, Adult bk club, Bk club(s), CD-ROM, E-Reserves, Electronic databases & coll, Magnifiers for reading, Online cat, Photocopying/Printing, Prog for children & young adult, Spoken cassettes & CDs, Summer reading prog, Tax forms, VHS videos, Wheelchair accessible
Special Services for the Deaf - Closed caption videos
Special Services for the Blind - Bks on cassette; Bks on CD; Large print bks
Open Mon & Tues Noon-8, Wed 10-6, Fri & Sat 10-5
Friends of the Library Group
CRAIGSVILLE LIBRARY STATION, 18 Hidy St, Craigsville, 24430. Tel: 540-997-0280.
Open Mon, Tues & Wed 1-6, Sat 11-4
DEERFIELD LIBRARY STATION, 59 Marble Valley Rd, Deerfield, 24432. Tel: 540-939-4123.
Open Tues & Thurs 3-8, Wed 1-5, Sat 10-1
MIDDLEBROOK LIBRARY STATION, 3698 Middlebrook Rd, Middlebrook, 24459. Tel: 540-885-1008.
Open Tues & Thurs 3-7, Wed 11-3, Sat 11-2
STUARTS DRAFT LIBRARY STATION, Broadmoor Plaza, Ste 107, Stuarts Draft, 24477. Tel: 540-569-2683.
Open Tues & Thurs Noon-8, Wed 9-6, Sat 10-2

FORT BELVOIR

G DAVID D ACKER LIBRARY & KNOWLEDGE REPOSITORY*, 9820 Belvoir Rd, Bldg 270, 22060. Tel: 703-805-2293. Reference Tel: 703-805-4463. E-mail: library@dau.mil. Web Site: www.dau.mil/library. *Librn,* Mary Tuke Klemmt; Tel: 703-805-5253, E-mail: mary.klemmt@dau.mil; *ILL, Libr Tech,* Selma Jackson; Staff 8 (MLS 4, Non-MLS 4)
Automation Activity & Vendor Info: (Acquisitions) SirsiDynix; (Cataloging) SirsiDynix
Wireless access
Function: ILL available
Restriction: Borrowing privileges limited to fac & registered students, Borrowing requests are handled by ILL

G DEFENSE TECHNICAL INFORMATION CENTER*, 8725 John J Kingman Rd, 22060-6218. SAN 317-199X. Toll Free Tel: 800-225-3842. Reference E-mail: dtic.belvoir.us.mbx.reference@mail.mil. Web Site: discover.dtic.mil/ www.dtic.mil/.
Founded 1945
Special Collections: DoD scientific and technical reports
Partic in Federal Library & Information Network; OCLC Online Computer Library Center, Inc
Open Mon-Fri 7-5
Restriction: Restricted pub use

UNITED STATES ARMY
A CENTER FOR ARMY ANALYSIS*, Bldg 1839, 6001 Goethals Rd, 22060-5230, SAN 328-8668. Tel: 703-806-5191. FAX: 703-806-5724. *Dir, Res,* Mary Bushey; E-mail: mary.bushey@us.army.mil; Staff 1 (MLS 1)

Library Holdings: Bk Titles 5,400; Per Subs 75
Subject Interests: Computer sci, Mil hist
Automation Activity & Vendor Info: (Cataloging) SirsiDynix; (Circulation) SirsiDynix; (OPAC) SirsiDynix
Function: Doc delivery serv, ILL available
Partic in OCLC Online Computer Library Center, Inc
Open Mon-Fri 7:30-4

A THE INSTITUTE OF HERALDRY LIBRARY*, 9325 Gunston Rd, Ste S113, 22060-5579, SAN 362-6911. Tel: 703-806-4967, 703-806-4975. FAX: 703-656-4964. Web Site: www.tioh.hqda.pentagon.mil. *Res Analyst,* Paul Tuohig
Founded 1961
Library Holdings: Bk Titles 12,000; Bk Vols 26,000; Per Subs 26
Subject Interests: Art, Flags, Heraldry, Insignia, Medallic art, Medals, Mil hist, Seals, Symbolism, Symbols, Uniforms
Restriction: Staff use only

A VAN NOY LIBRARY*, 5966 12th St, Bldg 1024, 22060-5554, SAN 362-8922. Tel: 703-806-3323. Reference Tel: 703-806-3324. Administration Tel: 703-806-0096. Web Site: www.belvoirmwr.com/Facilities/Library/. *Libr Dir,* Daniel Sadowitz; E-mail: daniel.sadowitz@us.army.mil; *Librn,* Donna Ramsey; Tel: 703-806-3238, E-mail: donna.ramsey@us.army.mil; *Coll Mgt Librn,* Stephanie Xander; Tel: 703-806-3273, E-mail: stephanie.xander@us.army.mil; *Tech Serv Librn,* Hyesoon H Kim; Tel: 703-806-0093, E-mail: hyesoon.h.kim@us.army.mil; Staff 4 (MLS 4)
Founded 1939
Library Holdings: DVDs 2,000; Bk Vols 45,614; Per Subs 108; Talking Bks 1,173
Subject Interests: Adult fiction, Adult non-fiction, Children's fiction, Mil hist
Automation Activity & Vendor Info: (Cataloging) Innovative Interfaces, Inc - Millennium; (Circulation) Innovative Interfaces, Inc - Millennium; (ILL) OCLC WorldShare Interlibrary Loan; (OPAC) Innovative Interfaces, Inc - Millennium
Function: Audiobks via web, Bks on CD, Computers for patron use, Electronic databases & coll, Photocopying/Printing, Prog for children & young adult, Summer reading prog, Wheelchair accessible
Restriction: Open to mil & govt employees only

FORT EUSTIS

UNITED STATES ARMY

A AVIATION APPLIED TECHNOLOGY DIRECTORATE, TECHNICAL LIBRARY*, Bldg 401, Rm 100C, 23604-5577, SAN 362-9104. Tel: 757-878-0083. FAX: 757-878-0008. *Tech Info Spec,* George Schultz; E-mail: george.schultz@us.army.mil
Founded 1946
Library Holdings: Bk Vols 5,100; Per Subs 100
Subject Interests: Army aircraft, Aviation safety, Composite structures, Gas turbines, Low-speed aeronaut, Propulsion systs
Partic in OCLC Online Computer Library Center, Inc
Open Tues-Thurs 8-2

A GRONINGER LIBRARY*, Bldg 1313, Army Transportation Ctr, Washington Blvd, 23604-5107, SAN 362-9163. Tel: 757-878-5017, 757-878-5583. FAX: 757-878-1024. Web Site: www.eustismwr.com. *Librn,* Valerie Fashion; E-mail: valerie.fashion@us.army.mil
Library Holdings: Bk Titles 80,200; Per Subs 60
Special Collections: Genealogy Coll; Military Science Coll
Automation Activity & Vendor Info: (Cataloging) Follett Software; (Circulation) Follett Software
Publications: Library Brochure
Open Mon-Wed 10-7, Thurs 12-9, Fri-Sun 10-5

A UNITED STATES ARMY, Training & Doctrine Command (TRADOC) Headquarters Library, 705 Washington Blvd, Rm 56, 23604. Tel: 757-501-7138. Web Site: tradochq.libguides.com/library. *Librn,* Kathleen Nichols; E-mail: kathleen.d.nichols2.civ@army.mil; *Archivist,* Dawn R Jones
Founded 1973
Wireless access
Open Mon-Thurs 7:30-4, alternate Fri 7:30-3:30

A US ARMY TRANSPORTATION MUSEUM LIBRARY*, Besson Hall, 300 Washington Blvd, 23604. SAN 370-2588. Tel: 757-878-1115. FAX: 757-878-5656. Web Site: transportation.army.mil/museum/about/researchlibrary.html. *Dir,* Alisha Hamel; E-mail: alisha.k.hamel@mail.mil; *Curator,* Marc Sammis
Library Holdings: Bk Titles 4,500
Restriction: Open by appt only, Ref only

FORT LEE

A UNITED STATES ARMY*, Army Logistics University Library, 562 Quarters Rd, Bldg 12420, 23801-1705. SAN 362-9317. Tel: 804-765-8170. Reference Tel: 804-765-8177. FAX: 804-765-4660. E-mail: usarmy.lee.tradoc.mbx.army-logistics-library@mail.mil. Web Site: www.alu.army.mil/library. *Dir,* Adria P Olmi; E-mail: adria.p.olmi.civ@mail.mil; *Res Sharing Librn,* Lakisha Hughes; *Tech Serv,* Thomas Moss; Staff 5 (MLS 2, Non-MLS 3)
Founded 1971
Library Holdings: Bk Titles 38,000; Bk Vols 40,000; Per Subs 200
Special Collections: Technical Reports
Subject Interests: Computer sci, Logistics, Petroleum
Automation Activity & Vendor Info: (Cataloging) SirsiDynix; (Circulation) SirsiDynix; (ILL) OCLC; (OPAC) SirsiDynix
Wireless access
Publications: Accessions List (Quarterly); Bibliographies; Library Handbook; Periodical Listing
Partic in OCLC Online Computer Library Center, Inc; Proquest Dialog
Open Mon-Thurs 9-3, Fri 9-1
Friends of the Library Group

FORT MONROE

S CASEMATE MUSEUM LIBRARY*, 20 Bernard Rd, 23651-1004. (Mail add: PO Box 51341, 23651-0341), SAN 327-4047. Tel: 757-788-8064. FAX: 757-788-3886. Web Site: fortmonroe.org/visit/casemate-museum. *Colls Mgr, Operations Mgr,* Veronica Gallardo; E-mail: vgallardo@fortmonroe.ord; Staff 2 (Non-MLS 2)
Founded 1975
Library Holdings: CDs 255; DVDs 131; Microforms 400; Bk Vols 12,600; Per Subs 20; Videos 115
Special Collections: Casemate Newspaper 1965-2011; Coast Artillery School. Oral History
Subject Interests: Local hist, Mil hist
Publications: Casemate Papers (Local historical information); Tales of Old Fort Monroe (Local historical information); The Guns of Fort Monroe (Local historical information)
Open Tues-Fri 9-4, Sat 10-4
Restriction: Non-circulating, Not a lending libr

FORT MYER

A JOINT BASE MYER-HENDERSON HALL LIBRARY*, Bldg 417, Rm 120, 239 Sheridan Ave, 22211. SAN 362-9406. Tel: 703-696-3555. E-mail: usarmy.jbmhh.asa.mbx.library@army.mil. Web Site: jbmhh.armymwr.com/programs/library. *Librn,* Position Currently Open
Library Holdings: Bk Vols 45,000; Per Subs 250
Special Collections: Popular Coll
Subject Interests: Computer sci, Juv, Mil hist, Pub admin
Automation Activity & Vendor Info: (Cataloging) EOS International; (Circulation) EOS International; (Course Reserve) EOS International; (OPAC) EOS International; (Serials) EOS International
Wireless access
Function: Electronic databases & coll, ILL available, Internet access, Photocopying/Printing
Partic in OCLC Online Computer Library Center, Inc
Open Mon-Thurs 9-4

FRANKLIN

J PAUL D CAMP COMMUNITY COLLEGE LIBRARY, Franklin Campus, 100 N College Dr, 23851. SAN 317-2880. Tel: 757-569-6741. Web Site: www.pdc.edu/library. *Librn,* Isabel Ramos-Wing; E-mail: iramoswing@pdc.edu; Staff 1 (MLS 1)
Founded 1971. Enrl 1,547; Fac 24
Library Holdings: Bk Titles 21,127; Bk Vols 29,083; Per Subs 200
Automation Activity & Vendor Info: (Cataloging) Ex Libris Group; (Circulation) Ex Libris Group; (OPAC) Ex Libris Group
Wireless access
Function: For res purposes, ILL available, Photocopying/Printing, Ref serv available
Partic in Virginia Tidewater Consortium for Higher Education
Open Mon-Thurs 8-8, Fri 8-5
Departmental Libraries:
HOBBS SUFFOLK CAMPUS, 271 Kenyon Rd, Suffolk, 23434. Tel: 757-925-6345. *Libr Asst,* Robert Finch; E-mail: rfinch@pdc.edu
Open Mon-Thurs 8-8

FREDERICKSBURG

P CENTRAL RAPPAHANNOCK REGIONAL LIBRARY*, Library Administration Center, 125 Olde Greenwich Dr, Ste 160, 22408. SAN 317-2899. Tel: 540-372-1144. FAX: 540-834-0767. Web Site: www.librarypoint.org. *Dir,* Martha Hutzel; Tel: 540-372-1144, Ext 7003, E-mail: martha.hutzel@crrl.org; *Dep Dir,* Rebecca Purdy; Tel: 540-372-1144, Ext 7004, E-mail: rebecca.purdy@crrl.org; *Asst Dir, Info Tech,* Chris Glover; Tel: 540-372-1144, Ext 7050, E-mail: chris.glover@crrl.org; *Br Serv Coordr,* Joy McIntire; Tel: 540-372-1144, Ext 7005, E-mail: joy.mcintire@crrl.org; Staff 97.5 (MLS 44, Non-MLS 53.5)

Founded 1969
Library Holdings: AV Mats 59,911; Bk Vols 449,772; Per Subs 1,192
Subject Interests: Fredericksburg, Law, Va
Automation Activity & Vendor Info: (Acquisitions) BiblioCommons; (Cataloging) BiblioCommons; (Circulation) BiblioCommons; (Course Reserve) BiblioCommons; (ILL) BiblioCommons; (Media Booking) BiblioCommons; (OPAC) BiblioCommons; (Serials) BiblioCommons
Wireless access
Special Services for the Deaf - TTY equip
Special Services for the Blind - Audio mat; Bks & mags in Braille, on rec, tape & cassette; Digital talking bk
Open Mon-Thurs 9-8, Fri & Sat 9-5:30
Friends of the Library Group
Branches: 10
COOPER BRANCH, 20 Washington Ave, Colonial Beach, 22443-2337, SAN 320-0604. Tel: 804-224-0921. FAX: 804-224-1330. *Br Mgr,* Kitty Norris
Open Mon, Fri & Sat 9-1, Tues & Wed 12-8, Thurs 1-5
Friends of the Library Group
P FREDERICKSBURG SUBREGIONAL FOR THE BLIND-PHYSICALLY HANDICAPPED, 125 Olde Greenwich Dr, Ste 160, 22408. Tel: 540-372-1144, Ext 234, 540-372-1160. Toll Free Tel: 800-628-4807, Ext 234. TDD: 540-371-9165. *Head Librn,* Michele Brown; Staff 2 (MLS 1, Non-MLS 1)
Open Mon-Fri 9-5
BARBARA J FRIED CENTER BRANCH, Germanna Community College, 124 Old Potomac Church Rd, Stafford, 22554. FAX: 540-318-3978. Web Site: www.librarypoint.org/locations/fried.
Open Mon-Thurs 4-8, Sat 9-5
WILLIAM J HOWELL BRANCH, 806 Lyons Blvd, 22406. FAX: 540-899-1707. Web Site: www.librarypoint.org/locations/eng. *Br Mgr,* Mary Buck; Tel: 540-372-1144, Ext 7440, E-mail: mary.buck@crrl.org
Open Mon-Thurs 9-8, Fri & Sat 9-5:30
MONTROSS BRANCH, 56 Polk St, Montross, 22520-0308, SAN 321-4958. Tel: 804-493-8194. FAX: 804-493-0446.
Open Mon & Thurs Noon-8, Tues & Sat 1-5, Wed & Fri 9-1
Friends of the Library Group
NEWTON BRANCH, 22 Coles Point Rd, Hague, 22469, SAN 326-7474. Tel: 804-472-3820. FAX: 804-472-5104. *Br Mgr,* Aimee Dillon; E-mail: adillon@crrl.org
Open Mon 12-8, Tues, Thurs & Sat 9-1, Wed 1-5, Fri 9-5
Friends of the Library Group
PORTER BRANCH, 2001 Parkway Blvd, Stafford, 22554-3972, SAN 320-0590. Tel: 540-659-4909. FAX: 540-659-4359. *Br Mgr,* Jessie Farrow
Open Mon-Thurs 9-8, Fri & Sat 9-5:30
Friends of the Library Group
SALEM CHURCH, 2607 Salem Church Rd, 22407-6451, SAN 374-7247. Tel: 540-785-9267. FAX: 540-785-9443. *Br Mgr,* Pamela Smith
Open Mon & Thurs 9-8, Tues, Wed, Fri & Sat 9-5:30
Friends of the Library Group
SNOW BRANCH, 8740 Courthouse Rd, Spotsylvania, 22553-2513, SAN 324-3087. Tel: 540-507-7565. *Br Mgr,* Chuck Gray
Open Mon & Tues 9-8, Wed-Sat 9-5:30
Friends of the Library Group
SPOTSYLVANIA TOWNE CENTRE BRANCH, 390 Spotsylvania Mall, 22407. FAX: 540-318-3977. Web Site: www.librarypoint.org/locations/townctr. *Br Mgr,* Pamela Smith
Open Mon 10-5:30, Tues-Thurs, 10-8, Fri & Sat 10-5
Bookmobiles: 3

J GERMANNA COMMUNITY COLLEGE*, Fredericksburg Campus Library, Science & Engineering Bldg, 10000 Germanna Point Dr, 22408-9543. Tel: 540-891-3015. FAX: 540-891-3060. E-mail: library@germanna.edu. Web Site: www.germanna.edu. *Coordr, Libr Serv,* Tamara Remhof; Tel: 540-891-3013, E-mail: tremhof@germanna.edu
Library Holdings: Bk Titles 10,000; Per Subs 35
Automation Activity & Vendor Info: (Cataloging) TLC (The Library Corporation); (Circulation) TLC (The Library Corporation); (OPAC) TLC (The Library Corporation)
Wireless access
Partic in Virginia's Academic Library Consortium
Open Mon-Thurs 8-8, Fri 8-4, Sat 9-2
Departmental Libraries:
CULPEPER CAMPUS LIBRARY, 18121 Technology Dr, Culpeper, 22701. Tel: 540-937-2924. *Libr Spec II,* Charlene Nibblins; Tel: 540-937-2923, E-mail: cnibblins@germanna.edu
Open Mon-Thurs 9-5
LOCUST GROVE CAMPUS LIBRARY, 2130 Germanna Hwy, Locust Grove, 22508-2102, SAN 317-3240. Tel: 540-423-9163. Web Site: www.germanna.edu/library. *Libr Serv Coordr,* Tamara Remhof; E-mail: tremhof@germanna.edu; Staff 3 (MLS 3)
Founded 1970. Enrl 5,018; Fac 49; Highest Degree: Associate
Library Holdings: e-books 73,894; e-journals 2,086; Bk Vols 31,216; Per Subs 120
Special Collections: Legacy (Supports Germanna Legacy Lectures)
Subject Interests: Hist, Med, Nursing
Automation Activity & Vendor Info: (Cataloging) OCLC Connexion; (ILL) OCLC FirstSearch; (OPAC) Ex Libris Group
Partic in Virginia Commun Coll Syst
Special Services for the Blind - Low vision equip
Open Mon-Thurs 8-5:30, Fri 8-12
STAFFORD CAMPUS LIBRARY, 124 Old Potomac Church Rd, Stafford, 22554. Tel: 540-891-3010. *Med Librn,* Monica McLean; Tel: 540-891-3015, E-mail: mmclean@germanna.edu
Open Mon-Thurs 9-8, Sat 9-5

C UNIVERSITY OF MARY WASHINGTON, Simpson Library, 1801 College Ave, 22401-5300. SAN 317-2910. Circulation Tel: 540-654-1059. Interlibrary Loan Service Tel: 540-654-1749. Reference Tel: 540-654-1148. FAX: 540-654-1067. E-mail: library@umw.edu. Web Site: library.umw.edu/library. *Univ Librn,* Amy Filiatreau; E-mail: afiliatr@umw.edu; *Head, Access Serv, Outreach Librn,* Trish Greene; Tel: 540-654-1758, E-mail: pgreene@umw.edu; *Head, Archives & Spec Coll,* Angie Kemp; Tel: 540-654-1756, E-mail: awhite4@umw.edu; *Head, Coll Serv,* Cindy Lu; Tel: 540-654-1762, E-mail: slu2@umw.edu; *Head, Reference & Scholarly Comms,* Paul Boger; Tel: 540-654-1148, E-mail: pboger@umw.edu; *Head, Tech Serv,* Morgan Mangold; Tel: 540-654-1740, E-mail: mmangold@umw.edu; *Electronic Res Librn,* Nicole St John; Tel: 540-654-1772, E-mail: nstjohn@umw.edu; *ILL Supvr,* Andrea Meckley; Tel: 540-654-1750, E-mail: aklopsis@umw.edu; *Univ Archivist,* Sarah Appleby; Tel: 540-654-1763; *Govt Doc Asst,* Phyllis Johnson; Tel: 540-654-1759, E-mail: pjohnson@umw.edu; Staff 20 (MLS 12, Non-MLS 8)
Founded 1908. Enrl 3,229; Fac 238; Highest Degree: Master
Library Holdings: e-books 1,157,405; e-journals 154,316; Bk Vols 293,626
Special Collections: Claude Bernard Coll; James Joyce Coll; William Butler Yeats Coll. State Document Depository; US Document Depository
Subject Interests: Archit, Art, Behav sci, Hist, Soc sci
Automation Activity & Vendor Info: (Acquisitions) Ex Libris Group; (Cataloging) Ex Libris Group; (Circulation) Ex Libris Group; (Course Reserve) Ex Libris Group; (Discovery) Ex Libris Group; (ILL) OCLC; (OPAC) Ex Libris Group; (Serials) Ex Libris Group
Wireless access
Function: 24/7 Electronic res, 24/7 Online cat, Bus archives, Computers for patron use, Distance learning, Doc delivery serv, E-Reserves, Electronic databases & coll, Equip loans & repairs, Free DVD rentals, Games, Govt ref serv, Health sci info serv, ILL available, Meeting rooms, Microfiche/film & reading machines, Music CDs, Notary serv, Online cat, Online Chat, Online info literacy tutorials on the web & in blackboard, Online ref, Outreach serv, Outside serv via phone, mail, e-mail & web, Photocopying/Printing, Printer for laptops & handheld devices, Ref & res, Ref serv available, Res assist avail, Res libr, Scanner, Study rm, Telephone ref, Wheelchair accessible
Partic in LYRASIS; Virginia's Academic Library Consortium
Open Mon-Thurs 8am-Midnight, Fri 8-5, Sat 11-5, Sun 1pm-Midnight

S GEORGE WASHINGTON FOUNDATION*, 1201 Washington Ave, 22401. SAN 370-1441. Tel: 540-373-3381. FAX: 540-370-0576. E-mail: learn@gwffoundation.org. Web Site: kenmore.org. *Director, Curatorial Operations,* Gretchen Pendleton; E-mail: pendleton@gwffoundation.org
Library Holdings: Bk Titles 400
Special Collections: George Washington; Lewis Family Coll, 18th Century
Wireless access
Restriction: Open by appt only

M MARY WASHINGTON HOSPITAL*, Medical Library, 1001 Sam Perry Blvd, 22401-4453. SAN 317-2945. Tel: 540-741-1598. FAX: 540-741-1514. Web Site: www.marywashingtonhealthcare.com/Mary-Washington-Hospital.aspx. *Med Librn,* Nancy Matthes; Staff 2 (MLS 1, Non-MLS 1)
Founded 1974
Library Holdings: Bk Titles 1,000; Per Subs 2,000
Subject Interests: Behav sci, Biomed sci, Hist of med, Med mgt, Nursing, Soc sci
Wireless access
Partic in National Network of Libraries of Medicine Region 1
Open Mon-Fri 8-4:30

FRONT ROYAL

C CHRISTENDOM COLLEGE*, St John the Evangelist Library, 263 St Johns Way, 22630. (Mail add: St John the Evangelist Library, 134 Christendom Dr, 22630), SAN 321-6608. Tel: 540-551-9100. FAX: 540-636-6569. E-mail: library@christendom.edu. Web Site: library.christendom.edu/home. *Libr Dir,* Andrew Armstrong; Tel: 540-551-9157, E-mail: andrew.armstrong@christendom.edu; *Assoc Librn,* Steven Pilon; Tel: 540-551-9194, E-mail: spilon@christendom.edu; Staff 6 (MLS 2, Non-MLS 4)

Founded 1977. Enrl 500; Fac 30; Highest Degree: Bachelor
Library Holdings: AV Mats 5,000; Bk Titles 98,000; Bk Vols 130,000; Per Subs 400
Subject Interests: Hagiography, Rare bks
Automation Activity & Vendor Info: (Acquisitions) OCLC Worldshare Management Services; (Cataloging) OCLC Worldshare Management Services; (Circulation) OCLC Worldshare Management Services; (Discovery) OCLC FirstSearch; (ILL) OCLC ILLiad; (OPAC) OCLC; (Serials) OCLC Worldshare Management Services
Wireless access
Partic in LYRASIS; OCLC Online Computer Library Center, Inc; Virginia Independent College & University Library Association
Open Mon-Thurs 8am-Midnight, Fri & Sat 1-8, Sun 1-Midnight

P SAMUELS PUBLIC LIBRARY*, 330 E Criser Rd, 22630. SAN 317-2953. Tel: 540-635-3153. Web Site: www.samuelslibrary.net. *Libr Dir,* Michelle Ross; Tel: 540-635-3153, Ext 110, E-mail: mross@samuelslibrary.net; *Dir, Operations,* Eileen Grady; E-mail: egrady@samuelslibrary.net; *Adult Reference Supervisor,* Erin Rooney; E-mail: erooney@samuelslibrary.net; *Youth Reference Supervisor,* Michael Ashby; E-mail: mashby@samuelslibrary.net; Staff 21 (MLS 3, Non-MLS 18)
Founded 1952. Pop 38,077; Circ 379,708
Jul 2015-Jun 2016 Income (Main Library Only) $4,365,308, County $910,000, Other $3,455,308. Mats Exp $883,932, Books $841,160, Per/Ser (Incl. Access Fees) $7,500, AV Equip $6,071, AV Mat $9,201, Electronic Ref Mat (Incl. Access Fees) $20,000. Sal $696,563 (Prof $133,209)
Library Holdings: Audiobooks 2,337; AV Mats 6,795; Bks on Deafness & Sign Lang 6; Braille Volumes 4; CDs 2,193; DVDs 4,321; e-books 76,212; Electronic Media & Resources 35; Large Print Bks 5,957; Bk Titles 109,538; Bk Vols 180,017; Per Subs 129
Special Collections: Virginia Coll. US Document Depository
Subject Interests: Local hist
Automation Activity & Vendor Info: (Acquisitions) TLC (The Library Corporation); (Cataloging) OCLC; (Circulation) TLC (The Library Corporation); (ILL) OCLC Online; (OPAC) TLC (The Library Corporation); (Serials) TLC (The Library Corporation)
Wireless access
Function: 24/7 Electronic res, 24/7 Online cat, Activity rm, Adult bk club, Adult literacy prog, After school storytime, Archival coll, Art exhibits, Audio & video playback equip for onsite use, Audiobks via web, AV serv, BA reader (adult literacy), Bilingual assistance for Spanish patrons, Bk club(s), Bk reviews (Group), Bks on CD, Butterfly Garden, CD-ROM, Chess club, Children's prog, Citizenship assistance, Computer training, Computers for patron use, Digital talking bks, Distance learning, E-Readers, E-Reserves, Electronic databases & coll, Equip loans & repairs, Family literacy, For res purposes, Free DVD rentals, Games & aids for people with disabilities, Genealogy discussion group, Govt ref serv, Health sci info serv, Holiday prog, Home delivery & serv to seniorr ctr & nursing homes, Homebound delivery serv, ILL available, Instruction & testing, Internet access, Jail serv, Learning ctr, Legal assistance to inmates, Life-long learning prog for all ages, Literacy & newcomer serv, Magazines, Magnifiers for reading, Mail & tel request accepted, Mail loans to mem, Meeting rooms, Microfiche/film & reading machines, Movies, Notary serv, Online cat, Online info literacy tutorials on the web & in blackboard, Online ref, Orientations, Outreach serv, Outside serv via phone, mail, e-mail & web, OverDrive digital audio bks, Photocopying/Printing, Preschool outreach, Preschool reading prog, Printer for laptops & handheld devices, Prof lending libr, Prog for adults, Prog for children & young adult, Ref & res, Ref serv available, Res libr, Scanner, Senior computer classes, Serves people with intellectual disabilities, Spanish lang bks, Spoken cassettes & CDs, Spoken cassettes & DVDs, Story hour, Study rm, Summer & winter reading prog, Summer reading prog, Tax forms, Teen prog, Telephone ref, Visual arts prog, Wheelchair accessible, Winter reading prog, Workshops, Writing prog
Special Services for the Deaf - ADA equip; Adult & family literacy prog; Am sign lang & deaf culture; Bks on deafness & sign lang
Special Services for the Blind - Accessible computers; Assistive/Adapted tech devices, equip & products
Open Mon-Thurs 10-8, Fri & Sat 10-5
Friends of the Library Group

GALAX

P GALAX-CARROLL REGIONAL LIBRARY*, Galax Public Library, 610 W Stuart Dr, 24333. SAN 317-2961. Tel: 276-236-2351. FAX: 276-236-5153. Web Site: galaxcarroll.lib.va.us. *Regional Dir,* Trish Fore; E-mail: tfore@galaxcarroll.lib.va.us; *Asst Regional Dir,* Sarah Largen; E-mail: slargen@galaxcarroll.lib.va.us; *Br Mgr,* Jessi Campbell; E-mail: jcampbell@galaxcarroll.lib.va.us; Staff 1 (MLS 1)
Founded 1938. Pop 37,084; Circ 119,808
Library Holdings: Audiobooks 1,478; Bks on Deafness & Sign Lang 25; DVDs 2,761; e-books 6,647; Bk Vols 64,431; Per Subs 120
Subject Interests: Carroll County hist, Galax City hist, Genealogy
Automation Activity & Vendor Info: (Cataloging) Evergreen; (Circulation) Evergreen; (OPAC) Evergreen
Wireless access
Function: 24/7 Electronic res, 24/7 Online cat, After school storytime, Art exhibits, Audiobks on Playaways & MP3, Audiobks via web, Bk club(s), Bks on CD, Children's prog, Computer training, Computers for patron use, Digital talking bks, Electronic databases & coll, Free DVD rentals, Holiday prog, ILL available, Internet access, Magazines, Magnifiers for reading, Mango lang, Meeting rooms, Movies, Notary serv, Online cat, Online ref, Outreach serv, Outside serv via phone, mail, e-mail & web, OverDrive digital audio bks, Photocopying/Printing, Preschool outreach, Preschool reading prog, Prog for adults, Prog for children & young adult, Ref serv available, Spanish lang bks, Story hour, Summer reading prog, Tax forms, Teen prog, Wheelchair accessible, Workshops, Writing prog
Open Mon, Wed, Fri & Sat 9-5, Tues & Thurs 9-7
Restriction: ID required to use computers (Ltd hrs), In-house use for visitors, Ref only
Branches: 1
CARROLL COUNTY PUBLIC, 101 Beaver Dam Rd, Hillsville, 24343. (Mail add: PO Box 1629, Hillsville, 24343-7629), SAN 321-2696. Tel: 276-728-2228, 276-728-3334. FAX: 276-728-3830. *Br Mgr,* June Pike; E-mail: jhpike@galaxcarroll.lib.va.us
Library Holdings: Bk Titles 37,624
Open Mon 10-8, Tues-Fri 10-6, Sat 10-2

GLENNS

J RAPPAHANNOCK COMMUNITY COLLEGE LIBRARY*, Glenns Campus, 12745 College Dr, 23149. SAN 362-9430. Tel: 804-758-6710. FAX: 804-758-6711. E-mail: library@rappahannock.edu. Web Site: www.rappahannock.edu/library. *Interim Library Coord,* Elizabeth Hadley; E-mail: ehadley@rappahannock.edu; *Libr Asst,* Cheyenne Duncan; E-mail: cduncan@rappahannock.edu; *Libr Asst,* Jane Spencer; E-mail: jspencer@rappahannock.edu; Staff 3 (MLS 1, Non-MLS 2)
Founded 1971. Enrl 1,800; Fac 1; Highest Degree: Associate
Library Holdings: AV Mats 4,000; DVDs 4,000; e-books 120,000; e-journals 30,000; Bk Titles 40,000
Subject Interests: Bus, Computer sci, Environ, Health sci
Automation Activity & Vendor Info: (Acquisitions) Ex Libris Group; (Cataloging) Ex Libris Group; (Circulation) Ex Libris Group; (Course Reserve) Ex Libris Group; (ILL) OCLC; (OPAC) Ex Libris Group
Wireless access
Function: 24/7 Electronic res, Bks on CD, Computers for patron use, Distance learning, Doc delivery serv, Electronic databases & coll, Free DVD rentals, ILL available, Internet access, Online cat, Online ref, Orientations, Outside serv via phone, mail, e-mail & web, Photocopying/Printing, Scanner
Partic in Virginia Commun Coll Syst
Open Mon-Thurs 8:30-8:30, Fri 8:30-3, Sat 10-2
Restriction: Pub use on premises
Friends of the Library Group

GLOUCESTER

P GLOUCESTER COUNTY LIBRARY*, 6920 Main St, 23061. (Mail add: PO Box 2380, 23061-2380), SAN 317-297X. Tel: 804-693-2998. FAX: 804-693-1477. E-mail: Library.Questions@gloucesterva.info. Web Site: www.gloucesterva.info/148/Library. *Dir, Libr Serv,* Diane Rebertus; E-mail: drebertus@gloucesterva.info; Staff 13.5 (MLS 2, Non-MLS 11.5)
Founded 1933. Pop 35,700; Circ 210,797
Library Holdings: Bks on Deafness & Sign Lang 40; Bk Vols 82,000; Per Subs 150
Automation Activity & Vendor Info: (Cataloging) TLC (The Library Corporation); (Circulation) TLC (The Library Corporation); (OPAC) TLC (The Library Corporation)
Wireless access
Function: Adult bk club, Art exhibits, Bk club(s), Bks on cassette, Bks on CD, Chess club, Children's prog, Computer training, Computers for patron use, Electronic databases & coll, ILL available, Music CDs, Online cat, Photocopying/Printing, Preschool outreach, Prog for adults, Prog for children & young adult, Spoken cassettes & CDs, Story hour, Summer reading prog, Tax forms, Teen prog, Telephone ref, VHS videos, Wheelchair accessible
Open Mon-Thurs 10-8, Fri & Sat 10-5, Sun 1-5
Friends of the Library Group
Branches: 1
POINT BRANCH, 2354 York Crossing Dr, 23072. (Mail add: PO Box 889, Hayes, 23072). Tel: 804-642-9790. FAX: 804-642-9853. *Dir, Libr Serv,* Diane Rebertus
Library Holdings: Bk Vols 23,000; Per Subs 20
Function: Computers for patron use, Photocopying/Printing
Open Mon, Wed & Fri 10-5, Tues & Thurs 12-8, Sat 10-3
Bookmobiles: 1

GLOUCESTER POINT

C VIRGINIA INSTITUTE OF MARINE SCIENCE, COLLEGE OF WILLIAM & MARY*, William J Hargis Jr Library, 1208 Greate Rd, 23062. (Mail add: 1370 Greate Rd, 23062), SAN 317-2996. Tel: 804-684-7114. Web Site: www.vims.edu/library. *Dir,* Carol Coughlin; E-mail: coughlin@vims.edu; *Digital Serv Librn,* Lauren Manninen; E-mail: manninen@vims.edu; Staff 4 (MLS 3, Non-MLS 1)
Founded 1940
Library Holdings: Bk Vols 91,000; Per Subs 366
Special Collections: Expeditions, Sport Fishing & Hunting (Ross H Walker Coll)
Subject Interests: Chesapeake Bay, Coastal zone, Environ studies, Estuaries, Fisheries, Geol, Marine biol
Automation Activity & Vendor Info: (Cataloging) OCLC; (Circulation) SirsiDynix; (OPAC) SirsiDynix
Wireless access
Function: Wheelchair accessible
Partic in LYRASIS; OCLC Online Computer Library Center, Inc
Open Mon-Fri 9-5

GRUNDY

CL APPALACHIAN SCHOOL OF LAW LIBRARY*, 1221 Edgewater Dr, 24614-7062. Tel: 276-935-6688, Ext 1308. FAX: 276-935-7138. Web Site: www.asl.edu/library. *Asst Prof, Dir, Law Libr,* Christopher King; E-mail: cking@asl.edu; *Access Serv Librn,* Rebecca Belcher; E-mail: rbelcher@asl.edu; Staff 5 (MLS 5)
Founded 1997
Library Holdings: Bk Titles 43,258; Bk Vols 116,648; Per Subs 628
Special Collections: Appalachian Coll. US Document Depository
Automation Activity & Vendor Info: (Acquisitions) Innovative Interfaces, Inc; (Cataloging) Innovative Interfaces, Inc; (Circulation) Innovative Interfaces, Inc; (Course Reserve) Innovative Interfaces, Inc; (ILL) OCLC Connexion; (OPAC) Innovative Interfaces, Inc; (Serials) Innovative Interfaces, Inc
Wireless access
Partic in Virginia Independent College & University Library Association
Open Mon-Fri 8-5

P BUCHANAN COUNTY PUBLIC LIBRARY*, 1185 Poe Town St, 24614-9613. SAN 317-302X. Tel: 276-935-5721. FAX: 276-935-6292. Web Site: www.bcplnet.org. *Dir,* Sherry Bright; E-mail: sherry@bcplnet.org; Staff 6 (Non-MLS 6)
Founded 1960. Pop 26,000; Circ 100,000
Library Holdings: Bk Vols 90,000; Per Subs 155
Subject Interests: Hist, Local hist
Wireless access
Function: Homebound delivery serv, ILL available, Magnifiers for reading, Photocopying/Printing, Prog for children & young adult, Summer reading prog
Partic in LYRASIS
Open Mon 1-8, Tues, Wed, Fri & Sat 8:30-5, Thurs 8:30-8
Friends of the Library Group

HALIFAX

P HALIFAX COUNTY-SOUTH BOSTON REGIONAL LIBRARY, 177 S Main St, 24558. (Mail add: PO Box 1729, 24558-1729), SAN 362-9465. Tel: 434-476-3357. FAX: 434-830-3500. E-mail: webmaster@halifaxlibrary.org. Web Site: halifaxlibrary.org. *Dir,* Jay Stephens; Staff 11 (MLS 1, Non-MLS 10)
Founded 1961. Pop 37,355; Circ 86,768
Library Holdings: AV Mats 1,682; CDs 161; DVDs 1,000; Large Print Bks 2,568; Bk Titles 86,000; Bk Vols 130,000; Per Subs 151; Talking Bks 5,595; Videos 1,344
Subject Interests: Art, Local hist
Automation Activity & Vendor Info: (Acquisitions) Book Systems; (Cataloging) Book Systems; (Circulation) Book Systems; (OPAC) Book Systems
Wireless access
Partic in OCLC Online Computer Library Center, Inc
Open Mon 11:30-8, Tues-Fri 9:30-6, Sat 9:30-3:30
Friends of the Library Group
Branches: 1
SOUTH BOSTON PUBLIC LIBRARY, 509 Broad St, South Boston, 24592, SAN 362-949X. Tel: 434-575-4228. FAX: 434-575-4228. E-mail: sobolibrary@gmail.com. *Br Mgr,* Jenna Austin
Library Holdings: Bk Vols 50,000
Open Mon, Wed & Fri 9:30-6, Tues & Thurs 11:30-8, Sat 9:30-3:30
Friends of the Library Group
Bookmobiles: 1

HAMPDEN SYDNEY

C HAMPDEN SYDNEY COLLEGE*, Bortz Library, 257 Via Sacra, 23943. (Mail add: PO Box 7, 23943), SAN 317-3038. Tel: 434-223-6190. Circulation Tel: 434-223-7227. Reference Tel: 434-223-6302. FAX: 434-223-6351. Web Site: libguides.hsc.edu/library. *Libr Dir,* Shaunna Hunter; Tel: 434-223-6193, E-mail: shunter@hsc.edu; Staff 5 (MLS 4, Non-MLS 1)
Founded 1776. Enrl 1,100; Fac 100; Highest Degree: Bachelor
Library Holdings: Bk Vols 251,234; Per Subs 180
Special Collections: John Peter Mettauer Coll. US Document Depository
Subject Interests: Humanities, Local hist
Automation Activity & Vendor Info: (Acquisitions) Innovative Interfaces, Inc; (Cataloging) Innovative Interfaces, Inc; (Circulation) Innovative Interfaces, Inc; (Course Reserve) Blackboard Inc; (Discovery) EBSCO Discovery Service; (ILL) OCLC ILLiad; (OPAC) Innovative Interfaces, Inc
Wireless access
Partic in OCLC Online Computer Library Center, Inc; Virginia Independent College & University Library Association; Virginia's Academic Library Consortium
Open Mon-Thurs 8am-1am, Fri 8-6, Sat 9-5, Sun Noon-1am

HAMPTON

GM DEPARTMENT OF VETERANS AFFAIRS MEDICAL CENTER*, Medical Library, 100 Emancipation Dr, 23667. SAN 317-3062. Tel: 757-722-9961, Ext 3657. Web Site: www.hampton.va.gov. *Librn,* Jana Liebermann; E-mail: j.liebermann@va.gov
Founded 1870
Library Holdings: Bk Vols 12,500
Subject Interests: Acute care, Geriatrics, Gerontology, Patient educ mats, Rehabilitation med

P HAMPTON PUBLIC LIBRARY*, 4207 Victoria Blvd, 23669-4243. SAN 362-9589. Tel: 757-727-1154. Administration Tel: 757-727-1153. FAX: 757-727-1152. Web Site: hampton.gov/100/Libraries. *Dir,* Valerie Gardner; E-mail: vgardner@hampton.gov; Staff 62 (MLS 6, Non-MLS 56)
Founded 1926. Pop 134,000
Jul 2016-Jun 2017 Income $2,649,647
Library Holdings: Audiobooks 13,156; DVDs 18,586; Electronic Media & Resources 35; Bk Vols 241,668; Per Subs 457
Subject Interests: Genealogy, Hampton, Va hist
Automation Activity & Vendor Info: (Cataloging) SirsiDynix; (Circulation) SirsiDynix
Wireless access
Function: 24/7 Electronic res, 24/7 Online cat, Activity rm, Adult bk club, Adult literacy prog, Archival coll, Art programs, Audio & video playback equip for onsite use, Audiobks on Playaways & MP3, Audiobks via web, Bk club(s), Bks on CD, Children's prog, Citizenship assistance, Computer training, Computers for patron use, Digital talking bks, Doc delivery serv, Electronic databases & coll, Family literacy, Free DVD rentals, Holiday prog, Home delivery & serv to seniorr ctr & nursing homes, Homebound delivery serv, ILL available, Instruction & testing, Internet access, Life-long learning prog for all ages, Literacy & newcomer serv, Magazines, Magnifiers for reading, Mail & tel request accepted, Mail loans to mem, Meeting rooms, Microfiche/film & reading machines, Movies, Music CDs, Online cat, Online ref, Orientations, Outreach serv, Outside serv via phone, mail, e-mail & web, Photocopying/Printing, Preschool outreach, Preschool reading prog, Prog for adults, Prog for children & young adult, Ref & res, Ref serv available, Res assist avail, Scanner, Senior computer classes, Senior outreach, Serves people with intellectual disabilities, Spanish lang bks, STEM programs, Story hour, Study rm, Summer reading prog, Tax forms, Teen prog, Telephone ref, Visual arts prog, Wheelchair accessible, Workshops, Writing prog
Special Services for the Deaf - TDD equip
Open Mon-Thurs 9-9, Fri & Sat 9-5, Sun 1-5
Friends of the Library Group
Branches: 3
NORTHAMPTON BRANCH, 936 Big Bethel Rd, 23669, SAN 362-9619. Tel: 757-825-4558. FAX: 757-825-4646. *Br Mgr,* Shannon Frescura; E-mail: shannon.frescura@hampton.gov; Staff 3 (MLS 1, Non-MLS 2)
Open Mon-Thurs 9-9, Fri 9-5, Sat 10-5, Sun 1-5
Friends of the Library Group
PHOEBUS BRANCH, One S Mallory St, 23663, SAN 362-9643. Tel: 757-727-1149. *Br Mgr,* Eric Wilson; E-mail: eric.wilson@hampton.gov; Staff 2 (MLS 1, Non-MLS 1)
Special Services for the Deaf - Closed caption videos
Special Services for the Blind - Bks on CD; Copier with enlargement capabilities; Large print bks; Screen enlargement software for people with visual disabilities
Open Mon-Thurs 10-6, Fri 10-5, Sat 1-5
Friends of the Library Group

WILLOW OAKS BRANCH, Willow Oaks Village Sq, 227 Fox Hill Rd, 23669, SAN 362-9708. Tel: 757-850-5114. FAX: 757-850-5239. *Br Mgr,* Reynor Jones; E-mail: reynor.jones@hampton.gov; Staff 3 (MLS 1, Non-MLS 2)
Open Mon-Thurs 9-9, Fri 9-5, Sat 10-5, Sun 1-5
Friends of the Library Group

C HAMPTON UNIVERSITY*, William R & Norma B Harvey Library, 129 William R Harvey Way, 23668. SAN 362-952X. Tel: 757-727-5371. Circulation Tel: 757-727-5372. Interlibrary Loan Service Tel: 757-727-5186. Reference Tel: 757-727-5379. FAX: 757-727-5952. Reference E-mail: ereference@hamptonu.edu. Web Site: home.hamptonu.edu/library. *Dir,* Tina Rollins; Tel: 757-727-5388; *Asst Dir, Tech Serv,* Raeshawn McGuffie; Tel: 757-727-6803, E-mail: raeshawn.mcguffie@hamptonu.edu; *Cat Librn,* Dana Evans; Tel: 757-727-5183, E-mail: dana.evans@hamptonu.edu; *Info Res Librn,* Danita White; Tel: 757-727-5179, E-mail: danita.white@hamptonu.edu; *Peabody Librn,* Gladys Bell; Tel: 757-727-5185, E-mail: gladys.bell@hamptonu.edu; *Presv Mgr,* Randy Smith; Tel: 757-727-5553, E-mail: ramdy.smith@hamptonu.edu; *Ref, ILL & Gov Doc,* Elizabeth Evans; E-mail: elizabeth.evans@hamptonu.edu. Subject Specialists: *Psychol,* Danita White; *African-Am works,* Gladys Bell; *Health, Nursing,* Elizabeth Evans; Staff 27 (MLS 9, Non-MLS 18)
Founded 1868. Enrl 4,500; Highest Degree: Doctorate
Library Holdings: DVDs 1,641; e-books 95,000; Electronic Media & Resources 150; Bk Vols 341,359
Special Collections: George Foster Peabody Coll. US Document Depository
Automation Activity & Vendor Info: (Cataloging) SirsiDynix; (Circulation) SirsiDynix; (Discovery) SerialsSolutions; (ILL) Atlas Systems; (OPAC) SirsiDynix; (Serials) EBSCO Online
Wireless access
Function: 24/7 Electronic res, Computers for patron use, Electronic databases & coll, Govt ref serv, ILL available, Online cat, Online ref, Orientations, Photocopying/Printing, Ref serv available, Scanner, Telephone ref
Partic in LYRASIS; OCLC Online Computer Library Center, Inc; Virginia Independent College & University Library Association; Virginia's Academic Library Consortium
Open Mon-Thurs 8am-Midnight, Fri 8-5, Sat 9-5, Sun 2-Midnight

Departmental Libraries:

ARCHITECTURE, Bemis Laboratory, Rm 208, 23668. Tel: 757-727-5443. *Librn,* Johnny Cook; Tel: 757-727-5443, E-mail: johnny.cook@hamptonu.edu; Staff 1 (MLS 1)
Subject Interests: Archit
Open Mon-Fri 8-5

MUSIC, Armstrong Hall, Dewitt Wing, 129 William R Harvey Way, 23668. Tel: 757-727-5411. *Music Librn,* Eric Reif; E-mail: eric.reif@hamptonu.edu
Open Mon-Fri 8-5

J VIRGINIA PENINSULA COMMUNITY COLLEGE LIBRARY, Hampton Campus, (Formerly Thomas Nelson Community College Library), 227C Kecoughtan Hall, 99 Thomas Nelson Dr, 23666. SAN 317-3054. Tel: 757-825-2877. Web Site: guides.vpcc.edu. *Dir, Libr Serv,* Kady Fortier; Tel: 757-825-2871, E-mail: fortierk@vpcc.edu; *Distance Learning Librn,* Bob Harrison; Tel: 757-825-3829, E-mail: harrisonr@vpcc.edu; *Access Serv Spec,* Courtney Marshall; Tel: 757-825-4064, E-mail: marshallc@vpcc.edu; *Circ Spec,* Haddon Wright; Tel: 757-825-3656, E-mail: wrighth@vpcc.edu; *Tech Learning Specialist,* Donald Carr; Tel: 757-825-6503, E-mail: carrd@vpcc.edu; Staff 12 (MLS 4, Non-MLS 8)
Founded 1968. Enrl 4,300; Fac 103; Highest Degree: Associate
Library Holdings: Bks on Deafness & Sign Lang 15; High Interest/Low Vocabulary Bk Vols 100; Bk Vols 59,000; Per Subs 346
Special Collections: Accelerated Readers; Paperbacks
Subject Interests: Computer tech, English lit, Ethnic studies, Instrul develop, Nursing, Soc problems
Automation Activity & Vendor Info: (Circulation) Ex Libris Group; (OPAC) Ex Libris Group
Wireless access
Partic in LYRASIS; OCLC Online Computer Library Center, Inc; Virginia Commun Coll Syst; Virginia Tidewater Consortium for Higher Education; Virginia's Academic Library Consortium; Wilsonline
Open Mon-Thurs 8-7, Fri 8-4

Departmental Libraries:

HISTORIC TRIANGLE CAMPUS, 4601 Opportunity Way, Williamsburg, 23188. Tel: 725-258-6500.
Open Mon-Thurs 8-5, Fri 8-1

HANOVER

P PAMUNKEY REGIONAL LIBRARY*, 7527 Library Dr, 23069. (Mail add: PO Box 119, 23069-0119), SAN 362-9732. Tel: 804-537-6211. FAX: 804-537-6389. E-mail: ask@pamunkeylibrary.org. Web Site: www.pamunkeylibrary.org. *Libr Dir,* Tom Shepley; E-mail: tshepley@pamunkeylibrary.org; *Supv Librn,* Sherida Bradby; *Supv Librn,* Steven Hartung; *Supv Librn,* Jaime Stoops; *Ref Librn,* Carolyn Garner; *Ref Librn,* Jessica Schelleng; Staff 132 (MLS 7, Non-MLS 125)
Founded 1941. Pop 145,011; Circ 957,828
Library Holdings: Audiobooks 22,707; e-books 3,124; Bk Vols 243,811; Per Subs 888
Special Collections: Virginiana
Automation Activity & Vendor Info: (Circulation) SirsiDynix; (ILL) OCLC FirstSearch; (OPAC) SirsiDynix
Wireless access
Function: AV serv, Homebound delivery serv, ILL available, Photocopying/Printing, Prog for children & young adult, Ref serv available, Summer reading prog, Wheelchair accessible
Partic in Richmond Area Network; VA State Libr
Special Services for the Deaf - Closed caption videos; TDD equip
Special Services for the Blind - BiFolkal kits; Bks on cassette; Bks on CD; Large print bks
Friends of the Library Group

Branches: 10

ATLEE BRANCH, 9161 Atlee Rd, Mechanicsville, 23116, SAN 378-1925. Tel: 804-559-0654. FAX: 804-559-0645. *Br Mgr,* Lisa Morgan; Staff 16 (MLS 1, Non-MLS 15)
Founded 1997. Pop 10,000; Circ 200,776
Library Holdings: Bk Vols 50,000; Per Subs 100
Special Services for the Deaf - Bks on deafness & sign lang; Closed caption videos; TDD equip
Special Services for the Blind - BiFolkal kits; Bks on cassette; Bks on CD; Home delivery serv; Large print bks; Ref serv; ZoomText magnification & reading software
Open Mon-Thurs 10-9, Fri & Sat 10-6
Friends of the Library Group

COCHRANE ROCKVILLE BRANCH, 16600 Pouncey Tract Rd, Rockville, 23146. (Mail add: PO Box 220, Rockville, 23146-0220), SAN 362-9856. Tel: 804-749-3146. FAX: 804-749-3631. *Br Mgr,* Christine Snyder; Staff 10 (Non-MLS 10)
Founded 1985. Pop 4,000; Circ 49,267
Library Holdings: Bk Vols 18,000; Per Subs 55
Function: ILL available, Photocopying/Printing, Prog for children & young adult, Ref serv available, Summer reading prog, Wheelchair accessible
Special Services for the Deaf - Bks on deafness & sign lang; Closed caption videos; High interest/low vocabulary bks; TDD equip
Special Services for the Blind - BiFolkal kits; Bks on cassette; Bks on CD; Large print bks; Videos on blindness & physical disabilties; ZoomText magnification & reading software
Open Mon-Thurs 10-9, Fri & Sat 10-6
Friends of the Library Group

RICHARD S GILLIS JR - ASHLAND BRANCH, 201 S Railroad Ave, Ashland, 23005, SAN 362-9767. Tel: 804-798-4072. FAX: 804-798-6276. *Br Mgr,* Michael Natale; Staff 17 (MLS 1, Non-MLS 16)
Founded 1973. Circ 207,385
Library Holdings: Bk Vols 45,000; Per Subs 100
Function: Homebound delivery serv, ILL available, Photocopying/Printing, Prog for children & young adult, Ref serv available, Summer reading prog, Wheelchair accessible
Special Services for the Deaf - Bks on deafness & sign lang; Closed caption videos; High interest/low vocabulary bks; TDD equip
Special Services for the Blind - BiFolkal kits; Bks on cassette; Bks on CD; Large print bks; Videos on blindness & physical disabilties; ZoomText magnification & reading software
Open Mon-Thurs 10-9, Fri & Sat 10-6

GOOCHLAND BRANCH, 3075 River Rd W, Goochland, 23063, SAN 362-9791. Tel: 804-556-4774. FAX: 804-556-2941. *Br Mgr,* Janet Melton; Staff 12 (Non-MLS 12)
Founded 1977. Pop 10,000; Circ 83,000
Library Holdings: Bk Vols 23,000; Per Subs 80
Special Services for the Deaf - Closed caption videos; TDD equip
Special Services for the Blind - BiFolkal kits; Bks on cassette; Bks on CD; Large print bks; Ref serv; ZoomText magnification & reading software
Open Mon-Thurs 9-8, Fri 9-6, Sat 9-4
Friends of the Library Group

HANOVER BRANCH, 7527 Library Dr, 23069. (Mail add: PO Box 119, 23069-0119), SAN 362-9805. Tel: 804-365-6210. FAX: 804-365-6379. *Br Mgr,* Madhu Nainani; Staff 8 (Non-MLS 8)
Founded 1942. Pop 4,000; Circ 55,200
Library Holdings: Bks on Deafness & Sign Lang 10; CDs 100; Electronic Media & Resources 15; Large Print Bks 150; Bk Vols 25,000; Per Subs 33; Talking Bks 150; Videos 200
Special Collections: Virginiana
Partic in LYRASIS
Special Services for the Deaf - Bks on deafness & sign lang; Closed caption videos; High interest/low vocabulary bks; TDD equip

Special Services for the Blind - BiFolkal kits; Bks on cassette; Bks on CD; Large print bks; Videos on blindness & physical disabilties; ZoomText magnification & reading software
Open Mon-Wed 9-9, Thurs & Fri 9-6, Sat 9-2

LOIS WICKHAM JONES - MONTPELIER BRANCH, 17205 Sycamore Tavern Lane, Montpelier, 23192, SAN 378-1909. Tel: 804-883-7116. FAX: 804-883-5165. *Br Mgr,* Renee Sottong; Staff 10 (MLS 1, Non-MLS 9)
Founded 1996. Pop 5,000; Circ 43,378
Library Holdings: Bk Vols 10,000; Per Subs 44
Special Services for the Deaf - Bks on deafness & sign lang; Closed caption videos; High interest/low vocabulary bks; TDD equip
Special Services for the Blind - BiFolkal kits; Bks on cassette; Bks on CD; Large print bks; Videos on blindness & physical disabilties; ZoomText magnification & reading software
Open Mon-Thurs 9-9, Fri 10-6, Sat 10-2

KING & QUEEN BRANCH, 396 Newtown Rd, Saint Stephens Church, 23148. (Mail add: PO Box 279, Saint Stephens Church, 23148-0279), SAN 374-5252. Tel: 804-769-1623. FAX: 804-769-9286. *Br Mgr,* Susan Ayala Rodriguez; Staff 7 (Non-MLS 7)
Founded 1994. Pop 4,000; Circ 36,210
Library Holdings: Bk Vols 8,000; Per Subs 35
Special Services for the Deaf - Bks on deafness & sign lang; Closed caption videos; High interest/low vocabulary bks; TDD equip
Special Services for the Blind - BiFolkal kits; Bks on cassette; Bks on CD; Large print bks; ZoomText magnification & reading software
Open Mon, Wed & Thurs 10-8, Sat 10-2
Friends of the Library Group

MECHANICSVILLE BRANCH, 7461 Sherwood Crossing Pl, Mechanicsville, 23111, SAN 362-9821. Tel: 804-746-9615. FAX: 804-730-4292. *Br Mgr,* Kate Eminhizer; Staff 17 (MLS 2, Non-MLS 15)
Founded 1983. Pop 9,000; Circ 166,411
Library Holdings: Bk Vols 35,000; Per Subs 120
Special Services for the Deaf - Bks on deafness & sign lang; Closed caption videos; High interest/low vocabulary bks; TDD equip
Special Services for the Blind - BiFolkal kits; Bks on cassette; Bks on CD; Large print bks; Videos on blindness & physical disabilties; ZoomText magnification & reading software
Open Mon-Thurs 10-9, Fri & Sat 10-6
Friends of the Library Group

UPPER KING WILLIAM BRANCH, Sharon Office Park, 694-J Sharon Rd, King William, 23086, SAN 375-6017. Tel: 804-769-3731. FAX: 804-769-1176. *Br Mgr,* Susan Ayala Rodriguez; Staff 8 (MLS 1, Non-MLS 7)
Founded 1995. Pop 4,000; Circ 23,673
Library Holdings: Bk Vols 5,000; Per Subs 44
Function: Homebound delivery serv, ILL available, Photocopying/Printing, Prog for children & young adult, Ref serv available, Summer reading prog, Wheelchair accessible
Special Services for the Deaf - Bks on deafness & sign lang; Closed caption videos; High interest/low vocabulary bks; TDD equip
Special Services for the Blind - BiFolkal kits; Bks on cassette; Bks on CD; Large print bks; Videos on blindness & physical disabilties; ZoomText magnification & reading software
Open Mon-Thurs 10-8, Fri 10-6, Sat 10-2

WEST POINT BRANCH, 721 Main St, West Point, 23181. (Mail add: PO Box 1680, West Point, 23181-1680), SAN 362-9880. Tel: 804-843-3244. FAX: 804-843-4158. *Br Mgr,* Elaine Wood; Staff 9 (Non-MLS 9)
Founded 1989. Pop 2,000; Circ 36,210
Library Holdings: Bk Vols 20,000; Per Subs 30
Function: Homebound delivery serv, ILL available, Photocopying/Printing, Prog for children & young adult, Ref serv available, Summer reading prog, Wheelchair accessible
Special Services for the Deaf - Bks on deafness & sign lang; Closed caption videos; High interest/low vocabulary bks; TDD equip
Special Services for the Blind - BiFolkal kits; Bks on cassette; Bks on CD; Large print bks; Videos on blindness & physical disabilties; ZoomText magnification & reading software
Open Mon-Thurs 10-8, Fri 10-6, Sat 10-2
Friends of the Library Group

HARRISONBURG

C JAMES MADISON UNIVERSITY LIBRARIES*, Carrier Library, 880 Madison Dr, MSC 1704, 22807. SAN 317-3089. Tel: 540-568-6150. Web Site: www.lib.jmu.edu. *Dean of Libr,* Bethany Nowviskie; E-mail: nowvisbp@jmu.edu; *Interim Assoc Dean of Libraries,* Stefanie Warlick; Tel: 540-568-4289, E-mail: warlicse@jmu.edu; *Asst Dean for Learning Innovations & Design,* Andrea Adams; Tel: 540-568-6568, E-mail: adamsah@jmu.edu; *Dir, Communications & Outreach,* Kristen Shuyler; Tel: 540-568-7012, E-mail: shuyleks@jmu.edu; *Dir, Interlibrary Loan & Course Reserve,* Mikki Butcher; Tel: 540-568-6807, E-mail: butcheml@jmu.edu; *Dir, Research & Education Services,* Carolyn Schubert; Tel: 540-568-4264, E-mail: schubecf@jmu.edu; *Head, Libr & Info Serv,* Jeff Campbell; Tel: 540-568-6818, E-mail: campbejj@jmu.edu; *Head, Spec Coll,* Kate Morris; Tel: 540-568-3444, E-mail: morriskn@jmu.edu; *Coord of Organizational Learning & Dev,* Jennifer Keach; Tel: 540-568-8749, E-mail: keachja@jmu.edu
Founded 1908. Highest Degree: Doctorate
Library Holdings: e-books 300,000
Special Collections: State Document Depository; US Document Depository
Subject Interests: Shenandoah Valley hist
Wireless access
Partic in Virginia's Academic Library Consortium
Open Mon-Thurs 7:30am-Midnight, Fri 7:30am-8pm, Sat 10-8, Sun 10am-Midnight

Departmental Libraries:

MUSIC LIBRARY, MSC 7301, 22807. Tel: 540-568-6041, 540-568-6197. FAX: 540-568-7819. E-mail: library-music@jmu.edu. Web Site: www.lib.jmu.edu/music. *Libr Serv Mgr,* Karen Snively; Tel: 540-568-3542, E-mail: snivelkl@jmu.edu; *Librn,* Brian Cockburn; Tel: 540-568-6978, E-mail: briancckbrn@jmu.edu; *Libr Asst,* Zach Sensabaugh; Tel: 540-568-8035, E-mail: sensabzd@jmu.edu; Staff 3 (MLS 1, Non-MLS 2)
Highest Degree: Doctorate
Library Holdings: CDs 12,000; Music Scores 18,000; Bk Vols 1,000
Special Collections: Dr Mariann Perkings String Pedagogy Coll; Gena Branscombe Coll; JMU Performance Coll; Paul Lavalle Coll
Function: ILL available
Open Mon-Thurs 8:30-7, Fri 8:30-3, Sun 3-7 (Winter); Mon-Fri 9-5 (Summer)

P MASSANUTTEN REGIONAL LIBRARY*, 174 S Main St, 22801. SAN 362-9910. Tel: 540-434-4475. FAX: 888-334-5211. E-mail: info@mrlib.org. Web Site: www.mrlib.org. *Libr Dir,* Lois Jones; Tel: 540-434-4475, Ext 128, E-mail: ljones@mrlib.org; *Dir of Develop,* Michael Evans; Tel: 540-434-4475, Ext 135, E-mail: mevans@mrlib.org; *Tech Serv Mgr,* Patty Liskey; Tel: 540-434-4475, Ext 119, E-mail: pliskey@mrlib.org; *Youth Serv Coordr,* Denise Munro; Tel: 540-434-4475, Ext 108, E-mail: dmunro@mrlib.org; *ILL,* Linda Derrer; Tel: 540-434-4475, Ext 110, E-mail: lderrer@mrlib.org; Staff 33.8 (MLS 7, Non-MLS 26.8)
Founded 1928
Library Holdings: Audiobooks 6,376; AV Mats 38,707; Braille Volumes 31; CDs 5,435; DVDs 18,734; e-books 408; e-journals 52; Large Print Bks 11,347; Bk Vols 214,361; Per Subs 284; Videos 7,303
Special Collections: Virginia & Family History (Virginia-Genealogy Coll)
Automation Activity & Vendor Info: (Circulation) SirsiDynix; (OPAC) SirsiDynix
Wireless access
Function: 24/7 Electronic res, 24/7 Online cat, Activity rm, Adult bk club, After school storytime, Archival coll, Art exhibits, Audio & video playback equip for onsite use, Audiobks on Playaways & MP3, Audiobks via web, Bk club(s), Bks on CD, Butterfly Garden, Children's prog, Computers for patron use, Digital talking bks, Doc delivery serv, E-Reserves, Electronic databases & coll, Free DVD rentals, Holiday prog, Home delivery & serv to seniorr ctr & nursing homes, Homebound delivery serv, ILL available, Internet access, Life-long learning prog for all ages, Magazines, Magnifiers for reading, Mail & tel request accepted, Microfiche/film & reading machines, Movies, Music CDs, Notary serv, Online cat, Online ref, Outreach serv, OverDrive digital audio bks, Photocopying/Printing, Preschool outreach, Preschool reading prog, Prof lending libr, Prog for adults, Prog for children & young adult, Ref & res, Ref serv available, Res assist avail, Res performed for a fee, Scanner, Senior outreach, Serves people with intellectual disabilities, Spanish lang bks, Spoken cassettes & CDs, STEM programs, Story hour, Study rm, Summer & winter reading prog, Summer reading prog, Tax forms, Teen prog, Telephone ref, Wheelchair accessible, Winter reading prog, Writing prog
Publications: Massanutten Matters (Online only)
Partic in OCLC Online Computer Library Center, Inc; SouthWest Information Network Group
Open Mon-Thurs 9:30-8:30, Fri & Sat 12-4
Friends of the Library Group

Branches: 6

ELKTON COMMUNITY LIBRARY, 106 N Terrace Ave, Elkton, 22827, SAN 375-5150. Tel: 540-434-4475, Ext 2. FAX: 888-334-5211. *Circ Mgr,* Stephanie Mullins; E-mail: smullins@mrlib.org
Library Holdings: Bk Vols 7,190; Per Subs 14
Open Mon & Wed 11-6, Fri 11-2

GROTTOES BRANCH, 601 Dogwood Ave, Grottoes, 24441. (Mail add: PO Box 146, Grottoes, 24441). Tel: 540-434-4475, Ext 3. FAX: 888-334-5211. *Br Mgr,* Peggy Counts; E-mail: pcounts@mrlib.org
Founded 2000
Library Holdings: Bk Vols 8,934; Per Subs 16
Open Mon-Fri 1-6

NORTH RIVER LIBRARY, 118 Mount Crawford Ave, Bridgewater, 22812, SAN 375-5169. Tel: 540-434-4475, Ext 4. FAX: 888-334-5211. *Br Mgr,* Bly Brown
Library Holdings: Bk Vols 13,440; Per Subs 61

Open Mon-Wed 1-7, Thurs & Fri 10-6, Sat 10-2
Friends of the Library Group
PAGE PUBLIC, 100 Zerkel St, Luray, 22835, SAN 362-9945. Tel: 540-434-4475, Ext 5, 540-743-6867. FAX: 888-334-5211. *Br Mgr,* Cindy Campbell
Library Holdings: Bk Vols 26,450; Per Subs 29
Open Mon-Wed 9:30-5, Thurs 9:30-7, Fri & Sat 11-2
SHENANDOAH COMMUNITY, 418 S Third St, Shenandoah, 22849. Tel: 540-434-4475, Ext 6, 540-652-2665. FAX: 888-334-5211. *Br Mgr,* Ruth Reid; E-mail: rreid@mrlib.org
Library Holdings: Bk Vols 18,808; Per Subs 17
Open Tues & Thurs 11-6, Sat 11-2
VILLAGE LIBRARY, 175 N Main St, Broadway, 22815. (Mail add: PO Box 1045, Broadway, 22815), SAN 372-8005. Tel: 540-434-4475, Ext 7. FAX: 888-334-5211. *Br Mgr,* Barbara Andes; E-mail: bandes@mrlib.org
Library Holdings: Bk Vols 12,431; Per Subs 25
Open Mon 10-5 & 7-8:30, Tues-Fri 10-5, Sat 10-2
Friends of the Library Group

M SENTARA RMH MEDICAL CENTER, Virginia Funkhouser Library, 2010 Health Campus Dr, 22801-3293. SAN 317-3097. Tel: 540-689-1777. FAX: 540-689-1770. E-mail: rmh_rmhlibrary@sentara.com. Web Site: www.sentara.com/harrisonburg. *Librn,* Megan Khamphavong; E-mail: mdkhamph@sentara.com; Staff 1 (MLS 1)
Founded 1912
Special Collections: Consumer Health Coll; Grief Coll-Adult, Children & Teens; Leadership, Governance & Management Coll; Medical Imprints 1792-Early 20th Century (Medical & Nursing Historical Works Coll); Sentara RMH Organizational Archive; Sentara RMH School of Nursing Archive
Subject Interests: Allied health, Bus mgt, Clinical med, Consumer health, Nursing
Automation Activity & Vendor Info: (Acquisitions) LibraryWorld, Inc; (Cataloging) LibraryWorld, Inc; (Circulation) LibraryWorld, Inc; (Discovery) EBSCO Discovery Service; (OPAC) LibraryWorld, Inc; (Serials) LibraryWorld, Inc
Wireless access
Function: Computers for patron use, Doc delivery serv, ILL available, Internet access, Outside serv via phone, mail, e-mail & web, Ref & res, Ref serv available, Res assist avail, Telephone ref, Wheelchair accessible
Partic in National Network of Libraries of Medicine Region 1; OCLC Online Computer Library Center, Inc; Southwestern Virginia Health Information Librarians
Open Mon-Fri 8-4:30
Restriction: Badge access after hrs, Hospital staff & commun

HAYNESVILLE

S HAYNESVILLE CORRECTIONAL CENTER*, Department of Corrections, Division of Education Library, 421 Barnfield Rd, 22472. (Mail add: PO Box 129, 22472-0129). Tel: 804-250-4158, 804-333-3577. FAX: 804-333-1295. *Asst Regional Librn,* Edie Hudgins; Tel: 804-250-4158, E-mail: edith.hudgins@vadoc.virginia.gov
Library Holdings: DVDs 94; Bk Vols 10,011; Per Subs 27; Videos 316
Automation Activity & Vendor Info: (Cataloging) ComPanion Corp; (Circulation) ComPanion Corp
Open Tues-Fri 7-11 & 1-5

HEATHSVILLE

P NORTHUMBERLAND PUBLIC LIBRARY, INC, 7204 Northumberland Hwy, 22473. SAN 309-9164. Tel: 804-580-5051. FAX: 804-580-5202. E-mail: library@nplibraryva.org. Web Site: nplibraryva.org. *Libr Dir,* Jane Blue; E-mail: jblue@nplibraryva.org; *Customer Serv Supvr,* Cate Land; E-mail: cland@nplibraryva.org; *Coordr, Ch & Youth Serv,* Nicole Carrington; E-mail: ncarrington@nplibraryva.org; *Outreach Coordr,* Arthur Newman; E-mail: anewman@nplibraryva.org; Staff 5 (MLS 2, Non-MLS 3)
Founded 1969. Pop 12,190; Circ 26,144
Jul 2023-Jun 2024 Income $507,688, State $104,753, County $260,490, Locally Generated Income $98,284, Other $44,161. Mats Exp $57,417, Books $37,522, Per/Ser (Incl. Access Fees) $3,313, AV Mat $2,968, Electronic Ref Mat (Incl. Access Fees) $13,614. Sal $237,827 (Prof $73,500)
Library Holdings: Audiobooks 16,141; DVDs 2,218; e-books 16,988; Electronic Media & Resources 77; High Interest/Low Vocabulary Bk Vols 100; Large Print Bks 1,301; Bk Titles 23,939; Per Subs 48
Special Collections: Northumberland County & Virginia Coll
Automation Activity & Vendor Info: (Acquisitions) Baker & Taylor; (Cataloging) Book Systems; (Circulation) Book Systems; (Course Reserve) Book Systems; (Discovery) Book Systems; (ILL) OCLC; (OPAC) Book Systems
Wireless access
Function: 24/7 Electronic res, 24/7 Online cat, Accelerated reader prog, Activity rm, Adult bk club, Art exhibits, Audiobks via web, Bk club(s), Bks on CD, Children's prog, Citizenship assistance, Computer training, Computers for patron use, Digital talking bks, E-Readers, E-Reserves, Electronic databases & coll, For res purposes, Free DVD rentals, Games & aids for people with disabilities, Govt ref serv, Health sci info serv, Homework prog, ILL available, Internet access, Laminating, Life-long learning prog for all ages, Magazines, Magnifiers for reading, Mail & tel request accepted, Meeting rooms, Movies, Notary serv, Online cat, Online info literacy tutorials on the web & in blackboard, Online ref, Outreach serv, Outside serv via phone, mail, e-mail & web, OverDrive digital audio bks, Photocopying/Printing, Preschool outreach, Preschool reading prog, Printer for laptops & handheld devices, Prog for adults, Prog for children & young adult, Ref & res, Ref serv available, Res assist avail, Scanner, Senior computer classes, Spanish lang bks, Spoken cassettes & DVDs, Story hour, Summer & winter reading prog, Summer reading prog, Teen prog, Telephone ref, Wheelchair accessible, Winter reading prog, Workshops
Partic in Mid-Atlantic Library Alliance
Open Mon-Thurs 9-7, Fri 9-5:30, Sat 9-3
Restriction: 24-hr pass syst for students only, Authorized patrons, In-house use for visitors
Friends of the Library Group
Bookmobiles: 1. Outreach Coordr, Arthur Newman. Bk vols 735

HENRICO

P HENRICO COUNTY PUBLIC LIBRARY*, 1700 N Parham Rd, 23229. SAN 363-2199. Tel: 804-501-1900. FAX: 804-270-2982. Web Site: www.henricolibrary.org. *Libr Dir,* Barbara Weedman; E-mail: bweedman@henricolibrary.org; *Pub Serv Adminr,* Alicia Ahlvers; E-mail: aahlvers@henricolibrary.org; *Pub Serv Adminr,* Ha Hoang; E-mail: hhoang@henricolibrary.org; *Asst Library Dir, Collections & Systemwide Programs,* Alex Hamby; E-mail: ahamby@henricolibrary.org; *Asst Library Dir for Public Services & Branch Operations,* Angela Bennett; E-mail: abennett@henricolibrary.org; *Asst Dept Director for Operations,* John C Gentry; E-mail: jgentry@henricolibrary.org; *Communications & Media Mgr,* Patty Conway; E-mail: pconway@henricolibrary.org; *Circ Coordr,* Debbie Benson; E-mail: dbenson@henricolibrary.org; *Commun Relations Coordr,* Position Currently Open; *Tech Coordr,* Jennifer Wood; E-mail: jwood@henricolibrary.org; *Youth Serv Coordr,* Rick Samuelson; E-mail: rsamuelson@henricolibrary.org; *Mobile Library Services,* Matthew Phillips; Staff 165 (MLS 59, Non-MLS 106)
Founded 1966
Automation Activity & Vendor Info: (Acquisitions) SirsiDynix; (Cataloging) SirsiDynix; (Circulation) SirsiDynix; (ILL) SirsiDynix; (Media Booking) SirsiDynix; (OPAC) SirsiDynix; (Serials) SirsiDynix
Wireless access
Function: 24/7 Electronic res, Activity rm, Adult bk club, Adult literacy prog, After school storytime, Art exhibits, Audiobks via web, Bk club(s), Bks on cassette, Bks on CD, Children's prog, Computer training, Computers for patron use, Digital talking bks, E-Reserves, Electronic databases & coll, Free DVD rentals, Holiday prog, Home delivery & serv to seniorr ctr & nursing homes, ILL available, Internet access, Jazz prog, Life-long learning prog for all ages, Magazines, Meeting rooms, Microfiche/film & reading machines, Movies, Online cat, Online ref, Orientations, Outreach serv, OverDrive digital audio bks, Photocopying/Printing, Preschool outreach, Preschool reading prog, Printer for laptops & handheld devices, Prog for adults, Prog for children & young adult, Ref & res, Ref serv available, Senior outreach, Spanish lang bks, Story hour, Study rm, Summer & winter reading prog, Summer reading prog, Tax forms, Teen prog, Telephone ref, VHS videos, Wheelchair accessible, Workshops, Writing prog
Partic in LYRASIS
Open Mon-Fri 8-4:30
Restriction: Non-resident fee
Friends of the Library Group
Branches: 9
FAIRFIELD AREA LIBRARY, 1401 N Laburnum Ave, 23223. Tel: 804-501-1930. FAX: 804-643-8772. Web Site: henricolibrary.org/fairfield. *Libr Mgr,* Kristyn Saroff; E-mail: fa_manager@henrico.lib.va.us
Open Mon-Thurs 9-9, Fri & Sat 9-6, Sun 1-5
Friends of the Library Group
GAYTON BRANCH LIBRARY, 10600 Gayton Rd, 23238, SAN 329-6288. Tel: 804-501-1960. Web Site: henricolibrary.org/gayton. *Br Mgr,* Kate Cervarich; E-mail: ga_manager@henrico.lib.va.us
Open Mon-Wed 10-9, Thurs 1-9, Fri & Sat 10-6
Friends of the Library Group
GLEN ALLEN BRANCH LIBRARY, 10501 Staples Mill Rd, Glen Allen, 23060, SAN 375-5754. Tel: 804-501-1950. Web Site: henricolibrary.org/glen-allen. *Br Mgr,* Lisa Kroll; E-mail: gl_manager@henrico.lib.va.us
Open Mon-Wed 10-9, Thurs 1-9, Fri & Sat 10-6
Friends of the Library Group

LIBBIE MILL LIBRARY, 2100 Libbie Lake E St, 23230. Tel: 804-501-1940. Web Site: henricolibrary.org/libbie-mill. *Libr Mgr,* Adrienne Minock; E-mail: lm_manager@henricolibrary.org
Founded 2015
Function: 24/7 Electronic res, 24/7 Online cat, Activity rm, Adult bk club, Bk club(s), Bks on CD, Children's prog, Computers for patron use, Electronic databases & coll, Free DVD rentals, Holiday prog, ILL available, Internet access, Life-long learning prog for all ages, Literacy & newcomer serv, Magazines, Meeting rooms, Movies, Online cat, Online ref, OverDrive digital audio bks, Photocopying/Printing, Preschool outreach, Prog for adults, Prog for children & young adult, Ref & res, Senior computer classes, Study rm, Summer reading prog, Tax forms, Teen prog, Telephone ref, Wheelchair accessible, Workshops, Writing prog
Open Mon-Thurs 9-9, Fri & Sat 9-6, Sun 1-5
Friends of the Library Group

NORTH PARK BRANCH LIBRARY, 8508 Franconia Rd, 23227, SAN 323-813X. Tel: 804-501-1970. Web Site: henricolibrary.org/north-park. *Br Mgr,* Honor Zalewski; E-mail: np_manager@henrico.lib.va.us
Open Mon-Wed 10-9, Thurs 1-9, Fri & Sat 10-6
Friends of the Library Group

SANDSTON BRANCH LIBRARY, 23 E Williamsburg Rd, Sandston, 23150, SAN 363-2318. Tel: 804-501-1990. Web Site: henricolibrary.org/sandston. *Br Mgr,* Anita Tarbox; E-mail: sa_manager@henrico.lib.va.us
Open Mon-Wed 10-9, Thurs 1-9, Fri & Sat 10-6
Friends of the Library Group

TUCKAHOE AREA LIBRARY, 1901 Starling Dr, 23229-4564, SAN 363-2342. Tel: 804-501-1910. Web Site: henricolibrary.org/tuckahoe. *Libr Mgr,* Deborah Lammers; E-mail: tu_manager@henrico.lib.va.us
Founded 2006
Special Collections: Joseph P Rapisarda Jr Law Coll
Function: 24/7 Electronic res, 24/7 Online cat, Activity rm, Adult bk club, Art exhibits, Audiobks on Playaways & MP3, Audiobks via web, Bk club(s), Bks on CD, Children's prog, Computers for patron use, Electronic databases & coll, Free DVD rentals, Holiday prog, ILL available, Internet access, Life-long learning prog for all ages, Magazines, Meeting rooms, Microfiche/film & reading machines, Movies, Online cat, OverDrive digital audio bks, Photocopying/Printing, Preschool outreach, Prog for adults, Prog for children & young adult, Ref & res, Ref serv available, Scanner, Senior computer classes, Spanish lang bks, Study rm, Summer reading prog, Teen prog, Telephone ref, Wheelchair accessible, Workshops
Open Mon-Thurs 9-9, Fri & Sat 9-6
Friends of the Library Group

TWIN HICKORY AREA LIBRARY, 5001 Twin Hickory Rd, Glen Allen, 23059, SAN 373-5265. Tel: 804-501-1920. Web Site: henricolibrary.org/twin-hickory. *Libr Mgr,* Tomeka Berry-Mason; E-mail: tw_manager@henrico.lib.va.us
Open Mon-Thurs 9-9, Fri & Sat 9-6
Friends of the Library Group

VARINA AREA LIBRARY, 1875 New Market Rd, 23231, SAN 363-2377. Tel: 804-501-1980. Web Site: henricolibrary.org/varina. *Libr Mgr,* Kareemah Hamdan; E-mail: va_manager@henrico.lib.va.us
Open Mon-Thurs 9-9, Fri & Sat 9-6
Friends of the Library Group

Bookmobiles: 1

HERNDON

S NATIONAL CONCRETE MASONRY ASSOCIATION LIBRARY*, 13750 Sunrise Valley Dr, 20171. SAN 328-3089. Tel: 703-713-1900. FAX: 703-713-1910. E-mail: info@ncma.org. Web Site: www.ncma.org. *Library Contact, VPres,* Jason Thompson; E-mail: jthompson@ncma.org
Library Holdings: Bk Vols 4,000; Per Subs 80
Function: Ref serv available
Open Mon-Fri 8-5

HOPEWELL

P APPOMATTOX REGIONAL LIBRARY SYSTEM*, Maude Nelson Langhorne Library, 209 E Cawson St, 23860. SAN 317-316X. Tel: 804-458-6329. Web Site: www.arls.org. *Libr Dir,* Brian Manning; Tel: 804-458-6329, Ext 2501, E-mail: bmanning@arls.org; *Admin Serv Mgr,* Briana Terry; Tel: 804-458-6329, Ext 2004, E-mail: bterry@arls.org; *Br Operations Mgr,* Ginger Mauler; Tel: 804-458-6329, Ext 2014, E-mail: gmauler@arls.org; Staff 33 (MLS 6, Non-MLS 27)
Founded 1974. Pop 71,300; Circ 252,405
Library Holdings: AV Mats 7,846; Bk Titles 122,241; Bk Vols 170,817; Per Subs 371; Talking Bks 2,200
Automation Activity & Vendor Info: (Cataloging) TLC (The Library Corporation); (Circulation) TLC (The Library Corporation); (OPAC) TLC (The Library Corporation)
Wireless access
Open Mon-Thurs 10-9, Fri & Sat 10-6
Friends of the Library Group
Branches: 7

BURROWSVILLE, 18701 James River Dr, Disputanta, 23842. Tel: 804-458-6329, Ext 2950. Web Site: www.arls.org/visit/locations/burrowsville.
Open Mon-Wed 3-7, Thurs 10-7, Sat 10-1
Friends of the Library Group

CARSON BRANCH, 16101 Halligan Park Rd, Carson, 23830, SAN 328-9869. Tel: 804-458-6329, Ext 2910. Web Site: www.arls.org/visit/locations/carson.
Special Collections: Local Railroad History Coll (Housed in Railroad Caboose)
Open Mon-Thurs 3-7, Fri 10-6, Sat 10-1

DINWIDDIE BRANCH, 14103 Boydton Plank Rd, Dinwiddie, 23841, SAN 321-7426. Tel: 804-458-6329, Ext 2920. Web Site: www.arls.org/visit/locations/dinwiddie.
Open Mon, Tues & Thurs 3-7, Wed 10-7, Fri 3-6, Sat 10-1
Friends of the Library Group

DISPUTANTA BRANCH, 10010 County Dr, Disputanta, 23842, SAN 324-2927. Tel: 804-458-6329, Ext 2930. Web Site: www.arls.org/visit/locations/disputanta.
Open Mon, Wed & Thurs 3-7, Tues 10-7, Fri 3-6

MCKENNEY BRANCH, 20916 Old School Rd, McKenney, 23872, SAN 328-9885. Tel: 804-458-6329, Ext 2940. Web Site: www.arls.org/visit/locations/mckenney.
Open Mon, Wed & Thurs 3-7, Tues 10-7, Fri 3-6

PRINCE GEORGE BRANCH, 6605 Courts Dr, Prince George, 23875, SAN 328-9907. Tel: 804-458-6329, Ext 2970. Web Site: www.arls.org/visit/locations/princegeorge.
Open Mon-Thurs 10-7, Fri & Sat 10-6
Friends of the Library Group

ROHOIC, 7301 Boydton Plank Rd, Petersburg, 23803, SAN 324-2935. FAX: 804-458-6829, Ext 2960. Web Site: www.arls.org/visit/locations/rohoic-library.
Open Mon-Wed 3-7, Thurs 11-7, Fri 3-6

Bookmobiles: 1

S FEDERAL CORRECTIONAL INSTITUTION, Educational Department Law Library, 1100 River Rd, 23860. (Mail add: PO Box 90026, Petersburg, 23804-9000), SAN 317-381X. Tel: 804-733-7881. FAX: 804-863-1543. *Supvr of Educ,* R Spears; *Asst Supervisor, Education,* N Collins
Library Holdings: Bk Vols 4,000; Per Subs 6
Subject Interests: Vocational educ, Vocational recreation
Restriction: Not open to pub

INDEPENDENCE

P WYTHE-GRAYSON REGIONAL LIBRARY*, Grayson County Public, 147 S Independence Ave, 24348. (Mail add: PO Box 159, 24348-0159), SAN 362-997X. Tel: 276-773-3018. FAX: 276-773-3289. Web Site: wythegrayson.lib.va.us/grayson-county-branch. *Regional Dir,* Mary Thomas; E-mail: mthomas@wgrlib.org; *Regional Supvr,* Janet Cox; E-mail: jcox@wgrlib.org; *Br Mgr,* Phyllis Bobbitt; E-mail: pbobbitt@wgrlib.org; Staff 7 (MLS 1, Non-MLS 6)
Founded 1948
Subject Interests: Civil War, Genealogy
Wireless access
Function: ILL available
Partic in LYRASIS
Open Mon-Thurs 9-6, Fri 9-5, Sat 10-2
Friends of the Library Group
Branches: 4

FRIES PUBLIC, 105 W Main St, Fries, 24330. (Mail add: PO Box 325, Fries, 24330-0325), SAN 377-7669. Tel: 276-744-2225. FAX: 276-227-2035. Web Site: wythegrayson.lib.va.us/fries-library-branch. *Libr Asst,* Jackie Frost; E-mail: jfrost@wgrlib.org; Staff 2 (Non-MLS 2)
Function: ILL available
Open Mon 10-6, Wed & Fri 9-5
Friends of the Library Group

RURAL RETREAT PUBLIC, 119 N Greever St, Rural Retreat, 24368. (Mail add: PO Box 276, Rural Retreat, 24368-0276). Tel: 276-686-8337. FAX: 276-250-2097. Web Site: wythegrayson.lib.va.us/rural-retreat-library-branch. *Br Mgr,* Jennifer Groseclose
Function: ILL available
Open Tues-Fri 9-5
Friends of the Library Group

WHITETOP PUBLIC, 16309 Highlands Pkwy, Whitetop, 24292. (Mail add: PO Box 135, Whitetop, 24292-0135), SAN 377-7685. Tel: 276-388-2873, FAX: 276-227-2030. Web Site: wythegrayson.lib.va.us/whitetop-library-branch. *Br Supvr,* Marlena Phillips; E-mail: mmphillips@wgrlib.org; Staff 2 (Non-MLS 2)
Function: ILL available

Open Mon-Thurs 9-6, Fri 9-1
Friends of the Library Group
WYTHE COUNTY PUBLIC, 300 E Monroe St, Wytheville, 24382, SAN 363-0005. Tel: 276-228-4951. FAX: 276-228-6034. Web Site: wythegrayson.lib.va.us/wythe-county-library-branch. *Br Mgr,* Jennifer Groseclose; E-mail: jgroseclose@wgrlib.org
Subject Interests: Genealogy
Function: ILL available
Open Mon, Wed & Fri 9-6, Tues & Thurs 9-8, Sat 9-2
Friends of the Library Group
Bookmobiles: 1. Outreach Servs, Dexter Edwards

KENBRIDGE

P LUNENBURG COUNTY PUBLIC LIBRARY SYSTEM INC*, Ripberger Public, 117 S Broad St, 23944. (Mail add: PO Box 845, 23974-0845), SAN 372-7106. Tel: 434-676-3456. FAX: 434-676-3211. Web Site: www.lunenburglibraries.org. *Dir,* J B Crenshaw; E-mail: jbcrenshaw.lcpls@gmail.com; Staff 7 (Non-MLS 7)
Library Holdings: CDs 113; DVDs 136; Bk Vols 36,000; Talking Bks 637; Videos 350
Special Collections: 16mm Film Coll; Genealogy Coll; Reader's Digest 1930s-present; United Methodist Women's List Coll. State Document Depository
Wireless access
Open Mon 10-8, Tues & Thurs 10-6, Fri 10-5, Sat 9-Noon
Friends of the Library Group
Branches: 1
VICTORIA PUBLIC, 1417 Seventh St, Victoria, 23974. (Mail add: PO Box 1422, Victoria, 23974-1422), SAN 372-7114. Tel: 434-696-3416. FAX: 434-696-2895. E-mail: lunenburglibrary@outlook.com. *Br Mgr,* Susan Smith
Library Holdings: Bk Vols 20,000
Open Mon, Tues, Thurs & Fri 9-5, Sat 9-Noon

KEYSVILLE

J SOUTHSIDE VIRGINIA COMMUNITY COLLEGE, John H Daniel Campus Library, 200 Daniel Rd, 23947. Tel: 434-736-2045. FAX: 434-736-2079. E-mail: LrsD@southside.edu. Web Site: southside.edu/Keysville-library, southside.edu/learning-resource-center. *Librn,* Marika Peterson; Tel: 434-949-1064, E-mail: marika.peterson@southside.edu
Library Holdings: Bk Vols 34,506; Per Subs 85
Automation Activity & Vendor Info: (Cataloging) Ex Libris Group; (Circulation) Ex Libris Group; (Course Reserve) Ex Libris Group; (OPAC) Ex Libris Group
Wireless access
Partic in Virginia Commun Coll Syst
Open Mon-Thurs 8-8, Fri 8-4:30

KILMARNOCK

P LANCASTER COMMUNITY LIBRARY*, 16 Town Center Dr, 22482-3830. (Mail add: PO Box 850, 22482-0850), SAN 317-3178. Tel: 804-435-1729. FAX: 804-435-0255. E-mail: library@lancasterlibrary.org. Web Site: www.lancasterlibrary.org. *Dir, Libr Serv,* Alice Cooper; E-mail: acooper@lancasterlibrary.org; *Ch,* Tonya Carter; E-mail: tmcarter@lancasterlibrary.org; Staff 7 (MLS 1, Non-MLS 6)
Founded 1961. Pop 11,000; Circ 67,000
Jul 2018-Jun 2019 Income $640,000, State $109,000, City $1,000, County $112,000, Other $418,000
Library Holdings: AV Mats 4,243; Large Print Bks 1,554; Bk Titles 37,000; Bk Vols 40,000
Automation Activity & Vendor Info: (Cataloging) TLC (The Library Corporation); (Circulation) TLC (The Library Corporation); (OPAC) TLC (The Library Corporation)
Wireless access
Function: 24/7 Electronic res, 24/7 Online cat, Adult bk club, Art exhibits, Audiobks on Playaways & MP3, Audiobks via web, AV serv, Bks on CD, Children's prog, Computer training, Computers for patron use, Digital talking bks, E-Readers, E-Reserves, Electronic databases & coll, Free DVD rentals, Holiday prog, ILL available, Internet access, Magazines, Mail & tel request accepted, Meeting rooms, Movies, Museum passes, Notary serv, Online cat, Online ref, Outreach serv, Outside serv via phone, mail, e-mail & web, OverDrive digital audio bks, Photocopying/Printing, Preschool outreach, Preschool reading prog, Printer for laptops & handheld devices, Prog for adults, Prog for children & young adult, Ref & res, Ref serv available, Scanner, Spoken cassettes & CDs, STEM programs, Story hour, Study rm, Summer reading prog, Tax forms, Teen prog, Telephone ref, Wheelchair accessible, Workshops, Writing prog
Open Mon & Wed 9-8, Tues, Thurs & Fri 9-6, Sat 10-4
Friends of the Library Group

KING GEORGE

P LEWIS EGERTON SMOOT MEMORIAL LIBRARY*, 9533 Kings Hwy, 22485. SAN 317-3186. Tel: 540-775-2147. FAX: 540-775-3769. E-mail: reference@smoot.org. Circulation E-mail: circulation@smoot.org. Web Site: www.smoot.org/309/l-e-smoot-memorial-library. *Libr Dir,* Robin Tenney; E-mail: librarydirector@smoot.org; *Ad,* Holly Gaertner; *Youth Serv Librn,* Erica Testani; Staff 11 (MLS 1, Non-MLS 10)
Founded 1969. Pop 25,371; Circ 116,412
Library Holdings: Bk Titles 77,001; Bk Vols 70,465; Per Subs 90
Special Collections: Virginiana
Subject Interests: Va hist
Wireless access
Open Mon-Thurs 10-8, Fri & Sat 10-5
Friends of the Library Group

LANCASTER

S MARY BALL WASHINGTON MUSEUM & LIBRARY, INC*, Genealogy & History Research Center, 8346 Mary Ball Rd, 22503. (Mail add: PO Box 97, 22503-0097), SAN 317-3194. Tel: 804-462-7280. FAX: 804-462-6107. E-mail: library@lancastervahistory.org. Web Site: lancastervahistory.org. *Exec Dir,* Karen Hart
Founded 1958
Library Holdings: Electronic Media & Resources 25; Microforms 50; Bk Titles 8,000; Spec Interest Per Sub 5
Special Collections: Genealogy Papers & Research Materials, indexed by surname
Subject Interests: Lancaster County, US hist, Va genealogy, Va hist
Function: Computers for patron use, Electronic databases & coll, Online cat, Photocopying/Printing, Res performed for a fee
Open Wed-Fri 10-4 (March-Nov)
Restriction: Closed stack, Fee for pub use, Non-circulating, Not a lending libr

LANGLEY AFB

A UNITED STATES AIR FORCE*, Herbert H Bateman Library-Langley Air Force Base Library FL4800, 42 Ash Ave, 23665. SAN 363-0064. Tel: 757-764-2906. FAX: 757-764-3315. E-mail: langleyafblibrary@gmail.com. Web Site: www.langleylibrary.org. *Dir,* Ashley Jellison; Staff 6 (MLS 1, Non-MLS 5)
Founded 1942
Library Holdings: Bk Titles 34,000
Special Collections: Bateman Coll
Subject Interests: Aeronaut, Air Force hist, Mil hist, Mil leadership
Automation Activity & Vendor Info: (Cataloging) Bibliomation Inc; (Circulation) Bibliomation Inc; (OPAC) Bibliomation Inc
Wireless access
Function: Free DVD rentals, Makerspace, Online cat, OverDrive digital audio bks, Summer reading prog, Winter reading prog
Partic in OCLC Online Computer Library Center, Inc
Restriction: Authorized personnel only, Not open to pub

LAWRENCEVILLE

P MEHERRIN REGIONAL LIBRARY*, Brunswick County Library, 133 W Hicks St, 23868. SAN 363-0099. Tel: 434-848-2418, Ext 301. Administration Tel: 434-848-6899, Ext 302. FAX: 434-848-4786. Administration FAX: 434-848-6739. E-mail: mrlsweb@gmail.com. Web Site: meherrinlib.org. *Dir,* Becky S Walker; E-mail: bwalker@meherrinlib.org; Staff 17 (MLS 1, Non-MLS 16)
Founded 1940. Pop 36,000; Circ 140,000
Library Holdings: Bk Vols 80,000; Per Subs 200
Special Collections: Oral History
Automation Activity & Vendor Info: (Circulation) TLC (The Library Corporation); (OPAC) TLC (The Library Corporation)
Wireless access
Partic in OCLC Online Computer Library Center, Inc
Open Mon 10-8, Tues-Fri 9:30-5:30, Sat 9:30-12:30
Friends of the Library Group
Branches: 1
WILLIAM E RICHARDSON JR MEMORIAL LIBRARY, 100 Spring St, Emporia, 23847, SAN 363-0129. Tel: 434-634-2539. FAX: 434-634-5489. E-mail: mrls.richardson@gmail.com. *Dir,* Becky Walker; *Br Mgr,* Allison Blount; E-mail: ablount@meherrinlib.org; Staff 4 (MLS 2, Non-MLS 2)
Founded 1977
Library Holdings: AV Mats 2,946; CDs 247; DVDs 224; Large Print Bks 981; Bk Vols 43,529; Per Subs 81; Talking Bks 667; Videos 1,612
Automation Activity & Vendor Info: (Cataloging) TLC (The Library Corporation); (ILL) OCLC FirstSearch; (Serials) TLC (The Library Corporation)
Function: After school storytime, Art exhibits, Audio & video playback equip for onsite use, AV serv, Digital talking bks, Electronic databases & coll, Family literacy, Genealogy discussion group, ILL available, Mail &

tel request accepted, Music CDs, Online ref, Photocopying/Printing, Prog for adults, Prog for children & young adult, Ref & res, Spoken cassettes & CDs, Summer reading prog, Tax forms, Telephone ref, VHS videos, Wheelchair accessible
Open Mon 10-8, Tues-Fri 9:30-5:30, Sat 9:30-12:30
Restriction: Non-resident fee
Bookmobiles: 1

LEBANON

P RUSSELL COUNTY PUBLIC LIBRARY*, 248 W Main St, 24266. (Mail add: PO Box 247, 24266-0247), SAN 317-3216. Tel: 276-889-8044. FAX: 276-889-8045. Web Site: russell.lib.va.us. *Libr Dir,* Kelly McBride Delph; E-mail: kmcbride@russell.lib.va.us; Staff 5 (MLS 1, Non-MLS 4)
Founded 1959. Pop 28,900; Circ 36,315
Jul 2022-Jun 2023 Income (Main & Associated Libraries) $395,048, State $113,367, City $7,500, Federal $2,267, County $266,414, Locally Generated Income $5,500. Mats Exp $44,500, Books $20,702, Per/Ser (Incl. Access Fees) $3,455, AV Mat $9,634, Electronic Ref Mat (Incl. Access Fees) $10,709. Sal $298,121
Library Holdings: AV Mats 1,051; Bks on Deafness & Sign Lang 4; Braille Volumes 12; CDs 679; DVDs 2,411; Electronic Media & Resources 12; Large Print Bks 4,090; Bk Titles 45,767; Bk Vols 48,590; Per Subs 63
Subject Interests: Genealogy, Local hist
Automation Activity & Vendor Info: (Cataloging) TLC (The Library Corporation); (Circulation) TLC (The Library Corporation); (OPAC) TLC (The Library Corporation)
Wireless access
Function: 24/7 Electronic res, 24/7 Online cat, Activity rm, Adult bk club, Audiobks on Playaways & MP3, Audiobks via web, Bk club(s), Bks on CD, Chess club, Children's prog, Computer training, Computers for patron use, Electronic databases & coll, Free DVD rentals, Holiday prog, Home delivery & serv to seniorr ctr & nursing homes, Homebound delivery serv, Internet access, Laminating, Life-long learning prog for all ages, Magazines, Magnifiers for reading, Meeting rooms, Microfiche/film & reading machines, Movies, Music CDs, Online cat, Orientations, OverDrive digital audio bks, Photocopying/Printing, Preschool reading prog, Prog for adults, Prog for children & young adult, Scanner, STEM programs, Story hour, Summer & winter reading prog, Wheelchair accessible, Writing prog
Partic in Mid-Atlantic Library Alliance
Open Mon, Wed & Fri 10-5:30, Tues & Thurs 10-8, Sat 10-3
Restriction: Open to pub for ref & circ; with some limitations
Friends of the Library Group
Branches: 1
HONAKER COMMUNITY LIBRARY, Ten Library Dr, Honaker, 24260. Tel: 276-873-6600. FAX: 276-873-5800. *Br Mgr,* Belinda Levy; E-mail: blevy@russell.lib.va.us; Staff 1 (Non-MLS 1)
Founded 2001. Pop 7,000
Open Mon 12-7, Wed 2-5:30, Fri 12-5:30, Sun 2-5
Friends of the Library Group

LEESBURG

P LOUDOUN COUNTY PUBLIC LIBRARY*, Admin Offices, 102 North St NW, Ste A, 20176. SAN 363-0153. Tel: 703-777-0368. FAX: 703-771-5238. E-mail: libraries@loudoun.gov. Web Site: library.loudoun.gov. *Dir,* Chang Liu; E-mail: chang.liu@loudoun.gov; *Dep Dir,* Mike Van Campen; E-mail: michael.vancampen@loudoun.gov; Staff 41 (MLS 41)
Founded 1973. Pop 279,293; Circ 3,602,004
Library Holdings: Bks on Deafness & Sign Lang 311; e-books 41,497; Large Print Bks 8,506; Bk Titles 193,979; Bk Vols 487,554; Per Subs 1,114
Special Collections: American Sign Language (ASL) Coll; English as a Second Language (ESL) Coll
Automation Activity & Vendor Info: (Acquisitions) SirsiDynix; (Cataloging) SirsiDynix; (Circulation) SirsiDynix; (ILL) OCLC; (OPAC) SirsiDynix; (Serials) SirsiDynix
Wireless access
Publications: Welcome to Loudoun County, Services for Citizens with Disabilities
Special Services for the Deaf - TTY equip
Friends of the Library Group
Branches: 11
ASHBURN BRANCH, 43316 Hay Rd, Ashburn, 20147. Tel: 703-737-8100. Web Site: library.loudoun.gov/ashburn. *Br Mgr,* Mary Butler; E-mail: mary.butler@loudoun.gov
Founded 2003
Open Mon-Thurs 9:30-9, Fri & Sat 9:30-5, Sun Noon-5
Friends of the Library Group
BRAMBLETON BRANCH, 22850 Brambleton Plaza, Brambleton, 20148. Tel: 571-258-3998. Web Site: library.loudoun.gov/brambleton. *Br Mgr,* Christine Thompson; E-mail: christine.thompson@loudoun.gov
Open Mon-Fri 9:30-9, Sat 9:30-5, Sun Noon-5
Friends of the Library Group
CASCADES BRANCH, 21030 Whitfield Pl, Potomac Falls, 20165, SAN 371-988X. Tel: 703-444-3228. Web Site: library.loudoun.gov/cascades. *Br Mgr,* Belinda Blue; E-mail: belinda.blue@loudoun.gov; Staff 11 (MLS 8, Non-MLS 3)
Founded 1992. Circ 1,271,497
Special Services for the Deaf - TTY equip
Open Mon-Thurs 9:30-9, Fri & Sat 9:30-5, Sun Noon-5
Friends of the Library Group
GUM SPRING LIBRARY, 24600 Millstream Dr, Aldie, 20105. Tel: 571-258-3838. Web Site: library.loudoun.gov/gumspring. *Br Mgr,* Vivy Niotis; E-mail: vivy.niotis@loudoun.gov
Open Mon-Thurs 9:30-9, Fri & Sat 9:30-5, Sun Noon-5
Friends of the Library Group
L LAW LIBRARY, 18 E Market St, 20176. Tel: 703-777-0695. Web Site: library.loudoun.gov/law. *Br Mgr,* Alice Zent; E-mail: alice.zent@loudoun.gov
Open Mon-Fri 8-4
LOVETTSVILLE BRANCH, 12 N Light St, Lovettsville, 20180. (Mail add: PO Box 189, Lovettsville, 20180-0189), SAN 328-7645. Tel: 703-737-8050. Web Site: library.loudoun.gov/lovettsville. *Mgr,* Lillian Newton; E-mail: lillian.newton@loudoun.gov
Special Services for the Deaf - TTY equip
Open Mon-Thurs 9:30-9, Fri & Sat 9:30-5
Friends of the Library Group
MIDDLEBURG BRANCH, 101 Reed St, Middleburg, 20117. (Mail add: PO Box 1823, Middleburg, 20118-1823), SAN 328-7629. Tel: 540-687-5730. Web Site: library.loudoun.gov/middleburg. *Br Mgr,* Tina Reid; E-mail: tina.reid@loudoun.gov; Staff 6 (MLS 2, Non-MLS 4)
Founded 1984
Function: Adult bk club, Art exhibits, Audiobks via web, Bks on CD, Children's prog, Computers for patron use, ILL available, Music CDs, Online ref, Photocopying/Printing, Preschool reading prog, Prog for adults, Scanner, Summer reading prog, Tax forms, Wheelchair accessible
Open Mon-Thurs 9:30-9, Fri & Sat 9:30-5
OUTREACH SERVICES, 380 Old Waterford Rd NW, 20176, SAN 377-6506. Tel: 703-771-5621. Web Site: library.loudoun.gov/outreach-services. *Mgr,* Patricia Pacheco; Tel: 703-771-3107
Circ 11,281
Special Services for the Deaf - TDD equip
Open Mon-Fri 9-5
PURCELLVILLE BRANCH, 220 E Main St, Purcellville, 20132, SAN 363-0218. Tel: 703-737-8490. Web Site: library.loudoun.gov/purcellville. *Br Mgr,* Aaron Duplissey; E-mail: aaron.duplissey@loudoun.gov; Staff 20 (MLS 4, Non-MLS 16)
Special Services for the Deaf - TTY equip
Open Mon-Thurs 9:30-9, Fri & Sat 9:30-5, Sun Noon-5
Friends of the Library Group
RUST BRANCH, 380 Old Waterford Rd NW, 20176, SAN 371-9898. Tel: 703-777-0323. Web Site: library.loudoun.gov/rust. *Br Mgr,* Myisha Fuller; E-mail: myisha.fuller@loudoun.gov; Staff 22.1 (MLS 9.4, Non-MLS 12.7)
Founded 1992. Circ 1,290,153
Special Services for the Deaf - Assisted listening device
Open Mon-Thurs 9:30-9, Fri & Sat 9:30-5, Sun Noon-5
Friends of the Library Group
STERLING BRANCH, 22330 S Sterling Blvd, Ste A117, Sterling, 20164, SAN 363-0242. Tel: 571-258-3309. Web Site: library.loudoun.gov/sterling. *Br Mgr,* Amanda Jones; E-mail: amanda.jones@loudoun.org
Open Mon-Thurs 9:30-9, Fri & Sat 9:30-5, Sun Noon-5
Friends of the Library Group
Bookmobiles: 1

LEXINGTON

S GEORGE C MARSHALL FOUNDATION LIBRARY, 340 VMI Parade, 24450. (Mail add: PO Box 1600, 24450-1600), SAN 317-3224. Tel: 540-463-7103, Ext 122. E-mail: gcmf@marshallfoundation.org. Web Site: library.marshallfoundation.org/portal/default/en-us/search/simplesearch. *Dir, Libr & Archives,* Melissa Davis; Staff 1.5 (MLS 1, Non-MLS 0.5)
Founded 1964
Library Holdings: Bk Titles 25,000
Special Collections: Andrew J Goodpaster Papers; Army Signal Corps Photos; Forrest Pogue Oral History Interviews; Frank McCarthy Papers; George C Marshall Papers, 1900-1959; James Van Fleet Papers; Lucian Truscott Jr Papers; National Archives Project, copied mat & microfilm; William & Elizabeth Smith Friedman Colls; World War I & World War II Colls, maps, posters, Oral History
Wireless access
Function: 24/7 Online cat, Archival coll, Microfiche/film & reading machines, Online cat, Ref & res, Res libr, Res performed for a fee
Publications: The Papers of George Catlett Marshall, vols 1-7

Open Mon-Fri 9-4:30
Restriction: External users must contact libr, Not a lending libr, Open by appt only

P ROCKBRIDGE REGIONAL LIBRARY SYSTEM*, 138 S Main St, 24450-2316. SAN 363-0277. Tel: 540-463-4324. FAX: 540-464-4824. Web Site: www.rrlib.net. *Libr Dir,* Julie Goyette; E-mail: JGoyette@rrlib.net; *Adult Serv Mgr,* Debi Ratliff; E-mail: DRatliff@rrlib.net; *Youth Serv Mgr,* Carol Elizabeth Jones; E-mail: CEJones@rrlib.net; Staff 35 (MLS 4, Non-MLS 31)
Founded 1934. Pop 38,800; Circ 230,137
Library Holdings: CDs 2,380; Bk Vols 160,570; Per Subs 271; Talking Bks 3,391; Videos 5,956
Subject Interests: Local hist
Automation Activity & Vendor Info: (Acquisitions) TLC (The Library Corporation); (Cataloging) TLC (The Library Corporation); (Circulation) TLC (The Library Corporation); (Course Reserve) TLC (The Library Corporation); (ILL) TLC (The Library Corporation); (Media Booking) TLC (The Library Corporation); (OPAC) TLC (The Library Corporation); (Serials) TLC (The Library Corporation)
Wireless access
Function: 24/7 Electronic res, 24/7 Online cat, Adult bk club, After school storytime, Audiobks on Playaways & MP3, Audiobks via web, AV serv, Bk club(s), Bks on CD, Children's prog, Computer training, Computers for patron use, E-Reserves, Electronic databases & coll, Family literacy, Free DVD rentals, Holiday prog, Home delivery & serv to seniorr ctr & nursing homes, Homebound delivery serv, ILL available, Internet access, Magazines, Mail & tel request accepted, Meeting rooms, Microfiche/film & reading machines, Movies, Music CDs, Online cat, Outreach serv, Outside serv via phone, mail, e-mail & web, OverDrive digital audio bks, Photocopying/Printing, Preschool outreach, Prog for adults, Prog for children & young adult, Ref serv available, Scanner, Senior outreach, Story hour, Study rm, Summer reading prog, Tax forms, Telephone ref, Workshops
Partic in LYRASIS; Mid-Atlantic Library Alliance; SouthWest Information Network Group
Special Services for the Blind - Talking bks
Open Mon-Thurs 10-7, Fri 1-5, Sat 10-2
Friends of the Library Group
Branches: 4
BATH PUBLIC, 96 Courthouse Hill Rd, Warm Springs, 24484. (Mail add: PO Box 250, Warm Springs, 24484-0250), SAN 363-0307. Tel: 540-839-7286. *Br Mgr,* Amy Porterfield; E-mail: aporterfield@rrlib.net; Staff 3 (Non-MLS 3)
Library Holdings: Bk Vols 30,000; Per Subs 50
Open Mon, Wed & Thurs 10-5, Tues 10-6, Sat 10-2
Friends of the Library Group
BUENA VISTA PUBLIC, 2110 Magnolia Ave, Buena Vista, 24416, SAN 363-0331. Tel: 540-261-2715. *Br Mgr,* Elaina Skovira; E-mail: ESkovira@rrlib.net; Staff 2 (Non-MLS 2)
Library Holdings: AV Mats 158; Bk Vols 17,373; Per Subs 49
Open Mon, Tues & Thurs 10-6, Sat 10-2
Friends of the Library Group
GLASGOW PUBLIC, 1108 Blue Ridge Rd, Glasgow, 24555, SAN 363-0366. Tel: 540-258-2509. *Br Mgr,* Barbara Slough; E-mail: BSlough2@rrlib.net; Staff 2 (Non-MLS 2)
Library Holdings: Bk Vols 10,726; Per Subs 23
Open Mon 10-6, Tues-Thurs 10-5, Sat 10-2
Friends of the Library Group
GOSHEN PUBLIC, 140 Main St, Goshen, 24439. (Mail add: Goshen Public Library, PO Box 129, Goshen, 24439), SAN 323-5718. Tel: 540-997-0351. *Br Mgr,* Ruth Tolson; E-mail: RTolson@rrlib.net; Staff 2 (Non-MLS 2)
Library Holdings: Bk Vols 6,216
Function: 24/7 Online cat, 24/7 wireless access, Adult bk club, Outreach serv
Special Services for the Deaf - Assisted listening device
Special Services for the Blind - Assistive/Adapted tech devices, equip & products
Open Mon 10-7, Tues & Wed 1-6, Thurs 10-6, Sat 10-2
Friends of the Library Group
Bookmobiles: 1. Outreach Servs Mgr, Bo Cunningham

C VIRGINIA MILITARY INSTITUTE*, J T L Preston Library, 345 Letcher Ave, 24450. SAN 317-3232. Tel: 540-464-7129, 540-464-7228. E-mail: library@vmi.edu. Web Site: www.vmi.edu/academics/library. *Libr Dir,* Sennyey Pongracz; Tel: 540-464-7573, E-mail: sennyeypj@vmi.edu; *Ref Librn,* Janet S Holly; Tel: 540-464-7296, E-mail: hollyjs@vmi.edu; *ILL Mgr,* Tonya Moore; Tel: 540-464-7570, E-mail: mooretl@vmi.edu; Staff 7 (MLS 6, Non-MLS 1)
Founded 1839. Enrl 1,300; Fac 106; Highest Degree: Bachelor
Library Holdings: CDs 1,500; DVDs 395; e-journals 20,426; Bk Vols 216,131; Per Subs 618; Videos 3,360
Special Collections: Civil War; Thomas J (Stonewall) Jackson. US Document Depository
Automation Activity & Vendor Info: (Serials) Innovative Interfaces, Inc
Wireless access
Partic in LYRASIS; Virginia's Academic Library Consortium
Open Mon-Thurs 8am-1am, Fri & Sat 8am-10pm, Sat 8-5, Sun 10am-1am
Friends of the Library Group

WASHINGTON & LEE UNIVERSITY
CL WILBUR C HALL LAW LIBRARY*, Lewis Hall, E Denny Circle, 24450, SAN 363-0455. Tel: 540-458-8540. Interlibrary Loan Service Tel: 540-458-8553. FAX: 540-458-8967. Web Site: law.wlu.edu/library. *Dep Dir,* Andrew Christensen; Tel: 540-458-8554, E-mail: christensena@wlu.edu; *Assoc Librn,* John Doyle; Tel: 540-458-8554, E-mail: doylej@wlu.edu; *Head, Tech Serv,* John P Bissett; Tel: 540-458-8546, E-mail: bissettj@wlu.edu; *Archivist,* John Jacob; Tel: 540-458-8969, E-mail: jacobj@wlu.edu; *Doc/Ref Serv,* Judy Stinson; Tel: 540-458-8544, E-mail: stinsonj@wlu.edu; Staff 5 (MLS 5)
Founded 1849. Enrl 411; Fac 35; Highest Degree: Doctorate
Library Holdings: AV Mats 233,279; Bks on Deafness & Sign Lang 8; CDs 45; DVDs 444; e-books 7,439; e-journals 1,783; Electronic Media & Resources 63; Microforms 228,952; Bk Titles 62,616; Bk Vols 467,829; Per Subs 3,055; Videos 460
Special Collections: Appellate Papers (John W Davis Coll); Bankruptcy (U S Senate Committee on the Judiciary Coll); Early Virginia Legal Materials (Burks Coll); Frank Parker, Civil Rights Activist; Impeachment Papers of President Richard M Nixon (Caldwell Butler); Lewis F Powell Jr Archives; Lewis F Powell Papers; Washington & Lee Law School Archives
Automation Activity & Vendor Info: (Acquisitions) Innovative Interfaces, Inc; (Cataloging) Innovative Interfaces, Inc; (Circulation) Innovative Interfaces, Inc; (Course Reserve) Innovative Interfaces, Inc; (ILL) OCLC; (OPAC) Innovative Interfaces, Inc; (Serials) Innovative Interfaces, Inc
Partic in OCLC Online Computer Library Center, Inc; Virginia Independent College & University Library Association; Virginia's Academic Library Consortium
Publications: Acquisitions List; Current Contents; Law Library Guide; Newsletter
Open Mon-Thurs 8am-9pm, Fri 8-5, Sat 10-5, Sun 1-9
C UNIVERSITY LIBRARY*, 204 W Washington St, 24450-2116. Tel: 540-458-8643. E-mail: library@wlu.edu. Web Site: library.wlu.edu. *Univ Librn,* Dr K T Vaughan; E-mail: kvaughan@wlu.edu; *Assoc Univ Librn, Spec Coll & Archives Librn,* Kim Sims; E-mail: ksims@wlu.edu; *Assoc Univ Librarian, Access & Discovery,* Elizabeth Anne Teaff; E-mail: teaffe@wlu.edu; *Digital Humanities Librn, Head, Digital Culture & Info,* Mackenzie Brooks; E-mail: brooksm@wlu.edu; *Coll Strategist Librn,* Julie Kane; E-mail: kanej@wlu.edu; *Digital Scholarship Librn,* Paula Kiser; E-mail: kiserp@wlu.edu; *Res & Instruction Librn,* Mary Abdoney; E-mail: abdoneym@wlu.edu; *Res & Instruction Librn,* Emily Cook; E-mail: cooke@wlu.edu; *Res & Instruction Librn,* John Tombarge; E-mail: tombargej@wlu.edu; *Res & Instruction Librn,* Amira Walker; E-mail: awalker2@wlu.edu; *Archivist,* Mattie Clear; E-mail: mclear@wlu.edu; *Library Tech Developer,* Jeff Barry; E-mail: barryj@wlu.edu. Subject Specialists: *Phys educ, Sciences,* Mary Abdoney; *Humanities,* Emily Cook; *Bus educ,* John Tombarge; *Soc sci,* Amira Walker; Staff 23 (MLS 12, Non-MLS 11)
Founded 1749. Enrl 2,000; Fac 245; Highest Degree: Bachelor
Special Collections: W & L University & Valley of Virginia Manuscripts. US Document Depository
Automation Activity & Vendor Info: (Acquisitions) ProQuest; (Cataloging) ProQuest; (Circulation) ProQuest; (Discovery) ProQuest; (ILL) OCLC Tipasa; (OPAC) ProQuest
Partic in LYRASIS; OCLC Online Computer Library Center, Inc
Restriction: 24-hr pass syst for students only
Friends of the Library Group

LYNCHBURG

M CENTRA LYNCHBURG GENERAL HOSPITAL*, Health Sciences Library, 1901 Tate Springs Rd, 24501-1167. SAN 327-3792. Tel: 434-200-3147. FAX: 434-200-3104. E-mail: library@centrahealth.com. *Librn,* Jana Liebermann; E-mail: jana.liebermann@centrahealth.com
Library Holdings: Bk Vols 2,000; Per Subs 100
Subject Interests: Med, Nursing
Partic in National Network of Libraries of Medicine Region 1; OCLC Online Computer Library Center, Inc; Southwestern Virginia Health Information Librarians
Restriction: Not open to pub, Staff use only

M CENTRA VIRGINIA BAPTIST HOSPITAL*, Barksdale Medical Library, 3300 Rivermont Ave, 24503. SAN 323-5203. Tel: 434-200-3147. *Health Sci Librn,* Jana Liebermann; E-mail: jana.liebermann@centrahealth.com
Library Holdings: Bk Titles 650; Per Subs 55
Subject Interests: Gynecology, Obstetrics, Oncology, Pediatrics, Psychiat
Wireless access

Partic in National Network of Libraries of Medicine Region 1; OCLC Online Computer Library Center, Inc; Southwestern Virginia Health Information Librarians
Restriction: Not open to pub, Staff use only

J CENTRAL VIRGINIA COMMUNITY COLLEGE LIBRARY*, Bedford Hall, Rm 3100, 3506 Wards Rd, 24502-2498. SAN 317-3283. Tel: 434-832-7750. Information Services Tel: 434-832-7752. FAX: 434-386-4677. E-mail: library@centralvirginia.edu. Web Site: centralvirginia.edu/Student-Support/Library. *Coordr, Libr Serv,* Michael T Fein; Tel: 434-832-7751, E-mail: feinm@centralvirginia.edu; *Info Serv Librn,* Elizabeth Boothe; E-mail: boothee@centralvirginia.edu; Staff 5 (MLS 3, Non-MLS 2)
Founded 1967. Enrl 2,200; Fac 95; Highest Degree: Associate
Library Holdings: Bk Titles 32,500; Per Subs 200
Subject Interests: Lynchburg area hist
Automation Activity & Vendor Info: (Circulation) Ex Libris Group
Wireless access
Publications: Acquisitions List (Quarterly)
Partic in LYRASIS; SouthWest Information Network Group; Virginia Commun Coll Syst; Virginia's Academic Library Consortium
Open Mon-Thurs 8-7:30, Fri 8-5

S FRAMATOME INC*, Technical Library, 3315 Old Forest Rd, 24501. SAN 317-3275. Tel: 434-832-2476. FAX: 434-382-3436. E-mail: library@framatome.com. *Res Libr Adminr,* Ella Carr-Payne; E-mail: ella.carrpayne@framatome.com; Staff 1 (MLS 1)
Founded 1955
Library Holdings: Bk Titles 75,000; Per Subs 60
Subject Interests: Chem, Computer application, Math, Nuclear sci, Nuclear tech
Partic in OCLC Online Computer Library Center, Inc
Restriction: Not open to pub

S JONES MEMORIAL LIBRARY*, Lynchburg Public Library Bldg, 2nd Flr, 2311 Memorial Ave, 24501. SAN 317-3305. Tel: 434-846-0501. E-mail: refdesk@jmlibrary.org. Web Site: www.jmlibrary.org. *Dir,* Deborah Smith; E-mail: director@jmlibrary.org; *Res,* Nancy Jamerson Weiland; E-mail: nweiland@jmlibrary.org. Subject Specialists: *Genealogical res,* Nancy Jamerson Weiland; Staff 1 (MLS 1)
Founded 1908
Library Holdings: Bk Titles 1,700; Per Subs 55
Special Collections: Lynchburg Architectural Archives; Personal Family Papers & Correspondence, Records of Clubs & Organizations, Business Records (Manuscript Coll)
Subject Interests: Genealogy, Local hist
Wireless access
Function: For res purposes, Res libr, Wheelchair accessible
Publications: JML Report (Newsletter)
Partic in Lynchburg Information Online Network; OCLC Online Computer Library Center, Inc
Open Tues Noon-8, Wed-Fri 1-5, Sat 9-5
Restriction: Non-circulating

CR LIBERTY UNIVERSITY*, Jerry Falwell Library, 1971 University Blvd, 24515. (Mail add: 1971 University Blvd, MSC Box 710170, 24515), SAN 317-3313. Tel: 434-582-2220. Interlibrary Loan Service Tel: 434-582-2442. Administration Tel: 434-592-3292. E-mail: research@liberty.edu. Web Site: www.liberty.edu/library. *Dean,* Angela Rice; Tel: 434-592-6327, E-mail: amrice3@liberty.edu; *Assoc Dean, Library Technologies & Collection Servs,* Greg Smith; Tel: 434-592-4892, E-mail: gsmith@liberty.edu; *Assoc Dean, Planning, Administration & Ops,* Rory Patterson; Tel: 434-582-2230, E-mail: rlpatterson2@liberty.edu; *Assoc Dean, Research & Customer Services,* Rorie Fredrich; Tel: 434-582-7572, E-mail: rfredrich1@liberty.edu; Staff 84 (MLS 29, Non-MLS 55)
Founded 1971. Enrl 130,000; Fac 2,500; Highest Degree: Doctorate
Library Holdings: Audiobooks 120; AV Mats 31,879; CDs 1,678; DVDs 7,004; e-books 1,163,017; e-journals 138,204; Electronic Media & Resources 281,057; Microforms 544,149; Music Scores 4,188; Bk Titles 280,790; Bk Vols 326,153; Per Subs 185
Special Collections: Digital Commons; Jerry Falwell Coll
Subject Interests: Relig
Automation Activity & Vendor Info: (Acquisitions) Ex Libris Group; (Cataloging) Ex Libris Group; (Circulation) Ex Libris Group; (Course Reserve) Ex Libris Group; (ILL) OCLC ILLiad; (OPAC) Ex Libris Group; (Serials) EBSCO Online
Wireless access
Function: 24/7 Electronic res, 24/7 Online cat, Activity rm, Archival coll, Art exhibits, Audio & video playback equip for onsite use, Audiobks via web, Bks on cassette, Bks on CD, Computers for patron use, Distance learning, Doc delivery serv, Electronic databases & coll, For res purposes, Free DVD rentals, ILL available, Instruction & testing, Internet access, Learning ctr, Magazines, Magnifiers for reading, Mail & tel request accepted, Microfiche/film & reading machines, Movies, Music CDs, Online cat, Online info literacy tutorials on the web & in blackboard, Online ref, Orientations, Outside serv via phone, mail, e-mail & web, Photocopying/Printing, Printer for laptops & handheld devices, Ref & res, Ref serv available, Res libr, Scanner, Spoken cassettes & CDs, Study rm, Wheelchair accessible, Workshops
Partic in American Theological Library Association; Center for Research Libraries; Christian Library Consortium; LYRASIS; OCLC Online Computer Library Center, Inc; Virginia Independent College & University Library Association; Virginia's Academic Library Consortium
Special Services for the Deaf - Sign lang interpreter upon request for prog
Special Services for the Blind - Low vision equip
Open Mon-Thurs 7:30am-11:45pm, Fri 7:30am-10pm, Sat 9:30am-10pm, Sun 1-11:45
Restriction: In-house use for visitors, Open to pub for ref & circ; with some limitations, Open to students, fac & staff

P LYNCHBURG PUBLIC LIBRARY*, 2315 Memorial Ave, 24501. SAN 317-333X. Tel: 434-455-6300. Circulation Tel: 434-455-6336. Reference Tel: 434-455-6310. Administration Tel: 434-455-6330. Administration FAX: 434-847-1578. Web Site: www.lynchburgpubliclibrary.org. *Libr Dir,* Beverly Blair; E-mail: beverly.blair@lynchburgva.gov; *Br Mgr,* Tracy Letzerich; Tel: 434-455-3817, E-mail: tracy.letzerich@lynchburgva.gov; *Digital Serv Librn,* Stephanie Johnston; Tel: 434-455-6309, E-mail: stephanie.johnston@lynchburgva.gov; *Adult Serv,* Leann Underwood; Tel: 434-455-6311, E-mail: leann.underwood@lynchburgva.gov; *Circ,* Ona Dowdy; Tel: 434-455-6312, E-mail: ona.dowdy@lynchburgva.gov; Staff 8 (MLS 6, Non-MLS 2)
Founded 1966
Automation Activity & Vendor Info: (Acquisitions) TLC (The Library Corporation); (Cataloging) TLC (The Library Corporation); (Circulation) TLC (The Library Corporation); (ILL) OCLC FirstSearch; (OPAC) TLC (The Library Corporation); (Serials) TLC (The Library Corporation)
Wireless access
Function: 24/7 Electronic res, 24/7 Online cat, Accelerated reader prog, Activity rm, Adult bk club, After school storytime, Art programs, Audiobks via web, BA reader (adult literacy), Bks on CD, Chess club, Children's prog, Citizenship assistance, Computer training, Computers for patron use, E-Readers, Electronic databases & coll, Family literacy, Free DVD rentals, Holiday prog, ILL available, Internet access, Life-long learning prog for all ages, Magazines, Magnifiers for reading, Mail & tel request accepted, Meeting rooms, Movies, Music CDs, Online cat, OverDrive digital audio bks, Photocopying/Printing, Preschool outreach, Preschool reading prog, Printer for laptops & handheld devices, Prog for adults, Prog for children & young adult, Ref & res, Ref serv available, Res assist avail, Scanner, Senior computer classes, Serves people with intellectual disabilities, Spoken cassettes & CDs, Spoken cassettes & DVDs, STEM programs, Story hour, Study rm, Summer reading prog, Tax forms, Teen prog, Telephone ref, Visual arts prog, Wheelchair accessible
Open Mon, Wed, Fri & Sat 9:30-5;30, Tues & Thurs 9:30-8
Friends of the Library Group
Branches: 1
DOWNTOWN, 900 Church St, 24504. Tel: 434-455-3820. FAX: 434-847-1403. *Br Mgr,* Tracy Letzerich; Tel: 434-455-3817, E-mail: tracy.letzerich@lynchburgva.gov; Staff 3 (Non-MLS 3)
Founded 1987
Library Holdings: Bk Vols 5,000; Per Subs 125
Special Collections: Lynchburg Public Law Library
Function: 24/7 Electronic res, 24/7 Online cat, Art exhibits, Bk club(s), Bks on CD, Citizenship assistance, Computer training, Computers for patron use, Electronic databases & coll, Free DVD rentals, Govt ref serv, ILL available, Internet access, Jail serv, Magazines, Movies, Online cat, OverDrive digital audio bks, Photocopying/Printing, Printer for laptops & handheld devices, Ref & res, Ref serv available, Scanner, Spoken cassettes & CDs, Spoken cassettes & DVDs, Tax forms, Wheelchair accessible
Open Mon-Fri 9:30-5:30
Friends of the Library Group

C RANDOLPH COLLEGE*, Lipscomb Library, 2500 Rivermont Ave, 24503. SAN 317-3348. Tel: 434-947-8133. E-mail: library@randolphcollege.edu. Web Site: library.randolphcollege.edu. *Dir,* Lisa Lee Broughman; E-mail: llee@randolphcollege.edu; *Archivist, Cat Librn,* Michael W Sechler; E-mail: msechler@randolpheollege.edu; *Res & Instruction Librn,* Kelsey Molseed; E-mail: kmolseed@randolphcollege.edu; *ILL,* Catherine Lotspeich; Staff 7 (MLS 3, Non-MLS 4)
Founded 1891. Enrl 500; Fac 61; Highest Degree: Master
Library Holdings: e-books 40,000; Bk Vols 197,000; Per Subs 21,000
Special Collections: Classical Culture (Lipscomb Coll); Lininger, Children's Literature Coll; Pearl S Buck Coll; Writings by Virginia Women
Automation Activity & Vendor Info: (Acquisitions) SirsiDynix; (Cataloging) SirsiDynix; (Circulation) SirsiDynix; (Course Reserve) SirsiDynix; (ILL) OCLC; (OPAC) SirsiDynix; (Serials) SirsiDynix
Wireless access
Publications: Collections of Writings by Virginia Women; Lipscomb Library Guide; Quick Library Facts Sheet

Partic in Knight-Ridder Info, Inc; Lynchburg Information Online Network; LYRASIS; Virginia Independent College & University Library Association; Virginia's Academic Library Consortium
Open Mon-Thurs 8:30-Midnight, Fri 8:30-5, Sun 4-Midnight

C UNIVERSITY OF LYNCHBURG*, Knight-Capron Library, 1501 Lakeside Dr, 24501-3199. SAN 317-3321. Tel: 434-544-8430. Reference Tel: 434-544-8575. E-mail: refdesk@lynchburg.edu. Web Site: libraryguides.lynchburg.edu/knight-capron-library. *Libr Dir,* Jenny Horton; Tel: 434-544-8432, E-mail: horton.jl@lynchburg.edu; *Electronic Res Librn,* Katie Glaeser; Tel: 434-544-8260, E-mail: glaeser_l@lynchburg.edu; *Syst & Tech Serv Librn,* Megan Wade; Tel: 434-544-8206, E-mail: wade_m1@lynchburg.edu; Staff 9.5 (MLS 6, Non-MLS 3.5)
Founded 1903. Enrl 2,700; Fac 150; Highest Degree: Doctorate
Library Holdings: CDs 2,974; DVDs 1,022; e-books 27,000; Bk Titles 175,000; Bk Vols 228,000; Per Subs 473; Videos 2,600
Special Collections: Iron Industry (Capron); Seventeenth, Eighteenth & Nineteenth Century Maps of North America, particularly Virginia (Capron)
Subject Interests: Educ, Nursing
Automation Activity & Vendor Info: (Acquisitions) Innovative Interfaces, Inc - Millennium; (Cataloging) Innovative Interfaces, Inc; (Circulation) Innovative Interfaces, Inc - Millennium; (Course Reserve) Innovative Interfaces, Inc - Millennium; (Discovery) EBSCO Discovery Service; (ILL) OCLC ILLiad; (Media Booking) Innovative Interfaces, Inc - Millennium; (OPAC) Innovative Interfaces, Inc - Millennium; (Serials) Innovative Interfaces, Inc - Millennium
Wireless access
Partic in OCLC Online Computer Library Center, Inc; Virginia Independent College & University Library Association; Virginia's Academic Library Consortium
Open Mon-Thurs 8am-2am, Fri 8-7, Sat 11-7, Sun 1pm-2am (Fall); Mon-Fri 9-5 (Summer)

C VIRGINIA UNIVERSITY OF LYNCHBURG, Mary Jane Cachelin Library, 2058 Garfield Ave, 24501. SAN 317-3356. Tel: 434-528-5276. Web Site: vul.edu. *Librn,* John Whitted; E-mail: jwhitted@vul.edu
Founded 1887
Library Holdings: Bk Vols 30,000; Per Subs 50

MADISON

P MADISON COUNTY LIBRARY, INC*, 402 N Main St, 22727. (Mail add: PO Box 243, 22727-0243), SAN 317-3445. Tel: 540-948-4720. FAX: 540-948-4919. E-mail: info@madisoncountyvalibrary.org. Web Site: madisoncountyvalibrary.org. *Dir,* Bonnie Utz; E-mail: bonnie@madisoncountyvalibrary.org; Staff 8 (Non-MLS 8)
Founded 1937. Pop 13,000; Circ 46,000
Library Holdings: e-books 11,000; Bk Titles 35,000; Bk Vols 33,000; Per Subs 80
Special Collections: American History (Weaver Coll)
Automation Activity & Vendor Info: (Cataloging) Follett Software; (Circulation) Follett Software
Wireless access
Open Mon, Wed & Fri 10-5, Tues & Thurs 10-8, Sat 10-2
Friends of the Library Group

MANASSAS

S MANASSAS NATIONAL BATTLEFIELD PARK LIBRARY*, 6511 Sudley Rd, 20109-2005. SAN 370-2995. Tel: 703-361-1339. FAX: 703-361-7106. Web Site: www.nps.gov/mana. *Mus Spec,* Jim Burgess; E-mail: jim_burgess@nps.gov
Founded 1940
Subject Interests: Manuscripts
Function: For res purposes, Microfiche/film & reading machines, Photocopying/Printing, Res libr
Restriction: Access at librarian's discretion, Non-circulating coll, Open by appt only, Open to pub for ref only, Staff use, pub by appt

GL PRINCE WILLIAM COUNTY LAW LIBRARY*, Judicial Ctr, Rm 039, 9311 Lee Ave, 20110-5555. SAN 372-3518. Tel: 703-792-6262. FAX: 703-792-5390. E-mail: circuitcourt@pwcgov.org. *Librn,* Jeanine Cali
Founded 1983
Library Holdings: Bk Vols 10,000
Subject Interests: Va Law
Function: Res libr
Open Mon-Fri 8:30-4:30
Restriction: Non-circulating

MARION

P SMYTH COUNTY PUBLIC LIBRARY*, 118 S Sheffey St, 24354. SAN 317-3453. Tel: 276-783-2323. Circulation Tel: 276-783-2323, Ext 221. Interlibrary Loan Service Tel: 276-783-2323, Ext 230. Reference Tel: 276-783-2323, Ext 222. Administration Tel: 276-783-2323, Ext 228, 276-783-2323, Ext 229. Automation Services Tel: 276-783-2323, Ext 231. FAX: 276-783-5279. Web Site: scplva.net. *Libr Dir,* Rose M Likins; E-mail: rosel@scplva.net; *Circ & ILL, Supvr, Pub Serv,* Helen Conley; E-mail: helenc@scplva.net; *Supvr, Youth Serv,* Tracey Reed-Armbrister; Tel: 276-783-2323, Ext 223, E-mail: traceyr@scplva.net; Staff 22 (MLS 1, Non-MLS 21)
Founded 1972. Pop 29,750; Circ 252,646
Library Holdings: AV Mats 15,626; Bk Vols 116,795; Per Subs 252; Videos 9,919
Special Collections: Sherwood Anderson Coll; Southwest Virginia Heritage Library
Subject Interests: Genealogy, SW Va hist
Automation Activity & Vendor Info: (Acquisitions) SirsiDynix-Symphony; (Cataloging) SirsiDynix-Symphony; (Circulation) SirsiDynix-Symphony; (ILL) OCLC FirstSearch; (OPAC) SirsiDynix-Enterprise; (Serials) SirsiDynix-Enterprise
Wireless access
Function: 24/7 Electronic res, 24/7 Online cat, Audiobks via web, Bilingual assistance for Spanish patrons, Bks on CD, Children's prog, Computers for patron use, Electronic databases & coll, Free DVD rentals, ILL available, Internet access, Magazines, Meeting rooms, Microfiche/film & reading machines, Online cat, Outreach serv, OverDrive digital audio bks, Photocopying/Printing, Preschool outreach, Prog for adults, Prog for children & young adult, Ref serv available, Scanner, Senior outreach, Serves people with intellectual disabilities, Spanish lang bks, Spoken cassettes & CDs, Spoken cassettes & DVDs, STEM programs, Story hour, Summer reading prog, Tax forms, Teen prog, Telephone ref, Wheelchair accessible
Partic in SouthWest Information Network Group
Special Services for the Deaf - Closed caption videos
Special Services for the Blind - Audio mat; Bks available with recordings; Bks on cassette; Bks on CD; Extensive large print coll; Home delivery serv; Magnifiers
Open Mon 10-8, Tues-Thurs 10-6, Fri 12-6, Sat 10-4
Friends of the Library Group
Branches: 2
CHILHOWIE PUBLIC, 807 Chilhowie St, Chilhowie, 24319. (Mail add: PO Box 610, Chilhowie, 24319-0610). Tel: 276-646-3404. FAX: 276-646-3406. *Br Supvr,* Heather Carter; E-mail: heatherc@scplva.net
Partic in Holston Associated Librs Consortium
Open Mon, Tues & Thurs 11-6, Fri & Sat 11-2
Friends of the Library Group
SALTVILLE PUBLIC, 111 Palmer Ave, Saltville, 24370. (Mail add: PO Box 1033, Saltville, 24370-1033), SAN 375-4839. Tel: 276-496-5514. FAX: 276-496-4249. *Br Supvr,* Kris Sheets; Staff 2 (Non-MLS 2)
Founded 1985. Pop 5,000; Circ 30,732
Library Holdings: Bk Titles 10,643; Per Subs 32
Open Mon-Wed 10-6, Thurs 10-7, Fri 10-2, Sat 10-3
Friends of the Library Group

MARTINSVILLE

P BLUE RIDGE REGIONAL LIBRARY*, 310 E Church St, 24112-2909. (Mail add: PO Box 5264, 24115-5264), SAN 363-0692. Tel: 276-403-5430. Reference Tel: 276-403-5450. FAX: 276-632-1660. E-mail: martinsville@brrl.lib.va.us. Web Site: www.brrl.lib.va.us. *Dir,* Rick Ward; E-mail: rward@brrl.lib.va.us; *Br Mgr,* Cecil Holland; Staff 27 (MLS 5, Non-MLS 22)
Founded 1923. Pop 86,400; Circ 363,203
Library Holdings: Bk Titles 131,648; Bk Vols 261,699; Per Subs 150; Talking Bks 9,954
Special Collections: Genealogy (Virginia Coll); Realia (toys)
Automation Activity & Vendor Info: (Acquisitions) TLC (The Library Corporation); (Cataloging) TLC (The Library Corporation); (Circulation) TLC (The Library Corporation); (ILL) TLC (The Library Corporation); (OPAC) TLC (The Library Corporation); (Serials) TLC (The Library Corporation)
Wireless access
Function: Adult bk club, Art exhibits, Audiobks via web, Bks on CD, Children's prog, Computer training, Computers for patron use, Free DVD rentals, Govt ref serv, ILL available, Internet access, Life-long learning prog for all ages, Magazines, Magnifiers for reading, Meeting rooms, Microfiche/film & reading machines, Music CDs, Notary serv, Online cat, Outreach serv, OverDrive digital audio bks, Photocopying/Printing, Preschool outreach, Prog for adults, Prog for children & young adult, Ref serv available, Scanner, Senior computer classes, Story hour, Summer & winter reading prog, Tax forms, Telephone ref, Wheelchair accessible, Winter reading prog
Partic in Mid-Atlantic Library Alliance
Open Mon-Wed 10-8, Thurs & Fri 10-5:30, Sat 9:30-2
Restriction: Borrowing requests are handled by ILL
Friends of the Library Group

Branches: 4
BASSETT BRANCH, 3969 Fairystone Park Hwy, Bassett, 24055, SAN 372-7890. Tel: 276-629-2426. FAX: 276-629-3808. E-mail: bassett@brrl.lib.va.us. *Br Mgr,* Karen Barley; Staff 1 (Non-MLS 1)
Library Holdings: Bk Vols 40,000; Per Subs 32
Open Mon & Wed 10-6, Tues 10-8, Thurs-Sat 10-2
Friends of the Library Group
COLLINSVILLE BRANCH, 2540 Virginia Ave, Collinsville, 24078, SAN 363-0722. Tel: 276-647-1112. FAX: 276-647-4574. E-mail: collinsville@brrl.lib.va.us. *Br Mgr,* Kim Martin; Staff 3 (Non-MLS 3)
Library Holdings: Bk Vols 40,000; Per Subs 20
Open Mon & Tues 10-8, Thurs 10-6, Fri 10-5, Sat 10-2
Friends of the Library Group
PATRICK COUNTY, 116 W Blue Ridge St, Stuart, 24171. (Mail add: PO Box 787, Stuart, 24171-0787), SAN 363-0757. Tel: 276-694-3352. FAX: 276-694-6744. E-mail: patrick@brrl.lib.va.us. *Br Mgr,* Garry Clifton; Staff 2 (Non-MLS 2)
Library Holdings: Bk Vols 41,000; Per Subs 58
Open Mon & Wed 10-6, Tues 10-8, Thurs Noon-8, Fri & Sat 10-2
Friends of the Library Group
RIDGEWAY BRANCH, 900 Vista View Lane, Ridgeway, 24148. (Mail add: PO Box 1210, Ridgeway, 24148-1210), SAN 371-2990. Tel: 276-956-1828. FAX: 276-956-4081. E-mail: ridgeway@brrl.lib.va.us. *Br Librn,* Amy Bunn; Staff 1 (MLS 1)
Library Holdings: Bk Vols 20,000; Per Subs 30
Open Mon & Thurs 10-6, Tues Noon-8, Fri 10-5, Sat 10-2
Friends of the Library Group
Bookmobiles: 1. Mgr, Tammy Cope. Bk titles 3,500

J PATRICK HENRY COMMUNITY COLLEGE*, Lester Library, 645 Patriot Ave, 24115. SAN 317-3488. Tel: 276-656-0228. Web Site: www.ph.vccs.edu/library2018. *Cat Serv Librn,* Aileen Martin; Tel: 276-656-0439, E-mail: amartin@patrickhenry.edu; *Tech Serv,* Marcia Seaton-Martin; Tel: 276-656-0276, E-mail: mseaton-martin@patrickhenry.edu; Staff 5 (MLS 2, Non-MLS 3)
Founded 1962. Enrl 1,839; Fac 32
Library Holdings: Bk Titles 32,648; Per Subs 136
Special Collections: Stone Coll (Southern History); Thomas Carter Coll (Literature)
Automation Activity & Vendor Info: (Cataloging) Ex Libris Group; (Circulation) Ex Libris Group; (ILL) OCLC; (OPAC) Ex Libris Group
Partic in Virginia's Academic Library Consortium
Open Mon-Thurs 8-8, Fri 8-5, Sat 9-Noon

MASON NECK

S GUNSTON HALL PLANTATION LIBRARY & ARCHIVES*, 10709 Gunston Rd, 22079-3901. SAN 317-3259. Tel: 703-550-9220. FAX: 703-550-9480. E-mail: library@gunstonhall.org. Web Site: www.gunstonhall.org. *Dir,* Scott Stroh; E-mail: sstroh@gunstonhall.org
Founded 1970
Library Holdings: Bk Titles 6,000; Bk Vols 7,500; Per Subs 20
Special Collections: 18th Century Library Rare Books; Papers/Documents of Mason family
Subject Interests: Decorative art, Genealogy, George Mason, Mason family, Va hist
Function: Ref serv available, Res libr
Restriction: Open by appt only

MATHEWS

P MATHEWS MEMORIAL LIBRARY*, 251 Main St, 23109. (Mail add: PO Box 980, 23109-0980), SAN 317-3496. Tel: 804-725-5747. FAX: 804-725-7668. E-mail: staff@mathewslibrary.org. Web Site: www.mathewslibrary.org. *Dir,* Bette Dillehay; E-mail: bettedillehay@mathewslibrary.org; Staff 4 (MLS 1, Non-MLS 3)
Founded 1930. Pop 8,671; Circ 26,985
Library Holdings: e-books 46,000; Bk Titles 40,000; Per Subs 117
Subject Interests: Maritime
Wireless access
Open Mon-Wed & Fri 9-6, Thurs 9-8, Sat 10-2, Sun 1-3
Friends of the Library Group

MCLEAN

S AIR LINE PILOTS ASSOCIATION INTERNATIONAL, Engineering & Air Safety Resource Center, 7950 Jones Branch Dr, Ste 400-S, 22102. SAN 302-5519. Tel: 703-689-4204. FAX: 703-464-2104. E-mail: easlibrary@alpa.org. Web Site: www.alpa.org. *Spec,* Marvin Ramirez
Library Holdings: Bk Vols 60,000
Special Collections: Federal Aviation Regulations; Jeppesen Flight Charts (worldwide); Videos
Subject Interests: Aviation
Open Mon-Fri 9-5

L PILLSBURY WINTHROP SHAW PITTMAN LLP, Law Library, 7900 Tysons One Pl, Ste 500, 22102. SAN 377-3906. Tel: 703-770-7742. FAX: 703-770-7901. Web Site: www.pillsburylaw.com. *Asst Mgr, Research Services,* Eileen McCarrier; E-mail: eileen.mccarrier@pillsburylaw.com; Staff 2 (MLS 2)
Library Holdings: Bk Vols 4,000; Per Subs 30
Subject Interests: Intellectual property law
Automation Activity & Vendor Info: (Cataloging) Sydney; (Circulation) Sydney; (OPAC) Sydney; (Serials) Sydney
Wireless access
Restriction: Staff use only

L WATT, TIEDER, HOFFAR & FITZGERALD*, 1765 Greensboro Station Pl, Ste 1000, 22102. Tel: 703-749-1019. FAX: 703-893-8029. Web Site: wattieder.com. *Law Librn,* Peggy Groscup; E-mail: pgroscup@wthf.com
Library Holdings: Bk Vols 8,000

MELFA

J EASTERN SHORE COMMUNITY COLLEGE*, Learning Resources Center, 29300 Lankford Hwy, 23410. SAN 317-3518. Tel: 757-789-1721. FAX: 757-789-1739. E-mail: lrc@es.vccs.edu. Web Site: es.vccs.edu/library. *Libr Spec II,* Mirissa Sorensen; E-mail: msorensen@es.vccs.edu; Staff 3 (MLS 1, Non-MLS 2)
Founded 1964. Enrl 550; Fac 19; Highest Degree: Associate
Library Holdings: Audiobooks 150; AV Mats 1,200; e-books 40,000; e-journals 10,000; Electronic Media & Resources 170; Large Print Bks 300; Bk Vols 25,000; Per Subs 100
Automation Activity & Vendor Info: (Cataloging) OCLC Connexion; (Circulation) Ex Libris Group; (Course Reserve) Ex Libris Group; (ILL) OCLC; (OPAC) Ex Libris Group
Wireless access
Partic in Virginia Commun Coll Syst; Virginia Tidewater Consortium for Higher Education; Virginia's Academic Library Consortium
Open Mon-Thurs 8-8, Fri 8-4:30

MIDDLEBURG

S NATIONAL SPORTING LIBRARY & MUSEUM*, 102 The Plains Rd, 20117. (Mail add: PO Box 1335, 20118-1335), SAN 317-3526. Tel: 540-687-6542. FAX: 540-446-0071. E-mail: mguzman@nationalsporting.org. *Exec Dir,* Elizabeth Von Hassell; Tel: 540-687-6542, Ext 30, E-mail: evonhassell@nationalsporting.org; *Head Librn,* Michelle Guzman; Tel: 540-687-6542, Ext 18, E-mail: MGuzman@NationalSporting.org; Staff 1 (MLS 1)
Founded 1954
Library Holdings: Bk Titles 18,500; Bk Vols 26,000; Per Subs 15
Special Collections: 16th-19th Century Books on Horses (Huth-Lonsdale-Arundel & Hunersdorf Colls); Foxhunting Papers (Harry Worcester Smith Coll); Sporting Books (John H & Martha Daniel Coll); Woolums Stud Books
Subject Interests: Am sporting art, Am sporting mag, Breeds of horses, British sporting art, English riding, Equine hist, Field sports, Horse sports
Automation Activity & Vendor Info: (Cataloging) SoutronGLOBAL; (Circulation) SoutronGLOBAL; (Discovery) SoutronGLOBAL; (ILL) OCLC WorldShare Interlibrary Loan; (OPAC) SoutronGLOBAL; (Serials) SoutronGLOBAL
Wireless access
Function: Archival coll, Art exhibits, Electronic databases & coll, For res purposes, ILL available, Magazines, Mail & tel request accepted, Online cat, Photocopying/Printing, Prog for adults, Ref & res, Ref serv available, Res libr, Study rm, Telephone ref, Visual arts prog, Wheelchair accessible
Publications: NSLM Newsletter
Partic in OCLC Online Computer Library Center, Inc
Open Wed-Sun 10-5
Restriction: Borrowing requests are handled by ILL, In-house use for visitors, Non-circulating of rare bks, Not a lending libr, Open to pub for ref only

MIDDLETOWN

J LORD FAIRFAX COMMUNITY COLLEGE*, Paul Wolk Library, 173 Skirmisher Lane, 22645. SAN 317-3534. Tel: 540-868-7170. Toll Free Tel: 800-906-5322. FAX: 540-868-7171. Web Site: lfcc.libguides.com, www.lfcc.edu. *Dir, Learning Res,* David Gray; Tel: 540-868-7154, E-mail: dgray@lfcc.edu; *Librn,* Whitney Nelsen; E-mail: wnelsen@lfcc.edu; Staff 8 (MLS 2, Non-MLS 6)
Founded 1970. Enrl 6,630; Fac 50; Highest Degree: Associate
Library Holdings: Bks on Deafness & Sign Lang 50; Bk Titles 56,500; Bk Vols 58,600; Per Subs 300
Automation Activity & Vendor Info: (Cataloging) Ex Libris Group; (Circulation) Ex Libris Group; (Course Reserve) Ex Libris Group; (ILL) Ex Libris Group; (OPAC) Ex Libris Group; (Serials) Ex Libris Group
Wireless access
Function: ILL available

Partic in LYRASIS; Virginia Commun Coll Syst; Virginia's Academic Library Consortium
Open Mon-Thurs 8am-9pm, Fri 8-4, Sat 9-1
Departmental Libraries:
BOB G SOWDER LIBRARY, 6480 College St, Warrenton, 20187. Tel: 540-541-1596. E-mail: lffqlib@lfcc.edu. *Dir, Learning Res,* David Gray; E-mail: dgray@lfcc.edu
Function: ILL available, Photocopying/Printing
Open Mon-Thurs 8am-9pm, Fri 8-4, Sat 9-1

MILFORD

P CAROLINE LIBRARY, INC*, 17202 Richmond Tpk, 22514. (Mail add: PO Box 9, Bowling Green, 22427). Tel: 804-633-5455. FAX: 804-633-9069. E-mail: carolinelibrary@bealenet.com. Web Site: carolinelibrary.org. *Dir,* Megan Upshaw; E-mail: mupshaw@co.caroline.va.us
Pop 22,121
Library Holdings: AV Mats 2,970; Bk Titles 40,000; Per Subs 34
Automation Activity & Vendor Info: (Cataloging) TLC (The Library Corporation); (Circulation) TLC (The Library Corporation); (OPAC) TLC (The Library Corporation)
Wireless access
Open Mon, Tues, Thurs & Fri 9-6, Wed 9-8
Friends of the Library Group
Branches: 3
DAWN BRANCH, 31046 Richmond Tpk, Hanover, 23069. Tel: 804-632-8341. FAX: 804-280-0074. Web Site: carolinelibrary.org/about-us/directory/dawn-branch. *Br Mgr,* Ann Wade
Library Holdings: Bk Titles 3,000
Open Mon-Fri 9-5
Friends of the Library Group
LADYSMITH BRANCH, 7199 Clara Smith Dr, Ruther Glen, 22546. (Mail add: PO Box 536, Ladysmith, 22501). Tel: 804-448-0357. FAX: 804-448-3124. Web Site: carolinelibrary.org/about-us/directory/ladysmith-branch. *Br Mgr,* Carolyn Wenrich
Library Holdings: Bk Titles 10,000
Open Mon & Thurs 9-8, Tues, Wed & Fri 9-5
Friends of the Library Group
PORT ROYAL BRANCH, 419 King St, Port Royal, 22536. (Mail add: PO Box 86, Port Royal, 22536-0086). Tel: 804-742-5254. FAX: 804-742-5263. Web Site: carolinelibrary.org/about-us/directory/port-royal-branch. *Br Mgr,* Position Currently Open
Library Holdings: Bk Titles 2,500
Open Mon & Tues 9-2, Wed & Thurs Noon-5

MONTEREY

P HIGHLAND COUNTY PUBLIC LIBRARY*, 31 N Water St, 24465. (Mail add: PO Box 519, 24465). Tel: 540-468-2373. FAX: 540-468-2085. E-mail: mail@highlandlibrary.com. Web Site: www.highlandlibrary.com. *Libr Dir,* Tomi Herold; Staff 1 (Non-MLS 1)
Founded 1975. Pop 2,300; Circ 28,439
Library Holdings: Audiobooks 948; Bks on Deafness & Sign Lang 11; CDs 698; DVDs 1,124; Electronic Media & Resources 1; Large Print Bks 801; Microforms 68; Bk Vols 15,671; Per Subs 39; Talking Bks 7; Videos 1,040
Special Collections: Forbes Genealogy Coll
Subject Interests: Local genealogy
Automation Activity & Vendor Info: (Acquisitions) Follett Software; (Cataloging) Follett Software; (Circulation) Follett Software; (ILL) OCLC Online; (OPAC) Follett Software
Wireless access
Function: 24/7 Electronic res, 24/7 Online cat, Accelerated reader prog, Activity rm, Adult bk club, After school storytime, Archival coll, Art exhibits, Art programs, Audio & video playback equip for onsite use, Audiobks on Playaways & MP3, Audiobks via web, AV serv, Bi-weekly Writer's Group, Bk club(s), Bks on CD, Children's prog, Computer training, Computers for patron use, Digital talking bks, E-Readers, Electronic databases & coll, Free DVD rentals, ILL available, Internet access, Laminating, Magazines, Magnifiers for reading, Mail & tel request accepted, Meeting rooms, Microfiche/film & reading machines, Movies, Music CDs, Online cat, Online info literacy tutorials on the web & in blackboard, Outside serv via phone, mail, e-mail & web, Photocopying/Printing, Printer for laptops & handheld devices, Prog for adults, Prog for children & young adult, Ref serv available, Spoken cassettes & CDs, Spoken cassettes & DVDs, STEM programs, Story hour, Summer reading prog, Wheelchair accessible
Special Services for the Blind - Talking bks
Open Mon & Fri 9-5, Tues & Thurs 9-8, Wed & Sat 9-Noon
Friends of the Library Group

NARROWS

P R IRIS BRAMMER PUBLIC LIBRARY*, 109 Mary St, 24124. SAN 317-3569. Tel: 540-726-2884. FAX: 540-726-3050. Web Site: townofnarrows.org/iris-brammer-library. *Dir,* Keshia Pyles; E-mail: kpyles@townofnarrows.org; Staff 1 (Non-MLS 1)
Pop 17,646
Library Holdings: Bk Vols 24,604; Talking Bks 40
Partic in New River Public Library Cooperative
Open Mon-Fri 9-12 & 1-5

NEW KENT

P HERITAGE PUBLIC LIBRARY*, 7791 Invicta Lane, 23124. SAN 324-5780. Tel: 804-966-2480. FAX: 804-966-5982. Web Site: heritagepubliclibrary.org. *Dir,* Chandra McPherson; E-mail: cmcpherson@heritagepubliclibrary.org
Founded 1980. Pop 22,000
Library Holdings: Bk Titles 47,000
Special Collections: Religion (Charles Jeffery Smith Coll)
Automation Activity & Vendor Info: (Cataloging) Follett Software; (Circulation) Follett Software
Wireless access
Partic in Mid-Atlantic Library Alliance
Open Mon & Wed-Fri 10-3, Tues 3-7
Friends of the Library Group

NEWPORT NEWS

C CHRISTOPHER NEWPORT UNIVERSITY*, Paul & Rosemary Trible Library, One Avenue of the Arts, 23606. SAN 317-3577. Tel: 757-594-7130. Circulation Tel: 757-594-7133. Interlibrary Loan Service Tel: 757-594-8818. Reference Tel: 757-594-7132. FAX: 757-594-7717. TDD: 757-594-7938. E-mail: library@cnu.edu. Web Site: cnu.edu/library. *Univ Librn,* Mary Sellen; E-mail: mary.sellen@cnu.edu; *Head, Ref,* Beth Young; Tel: 757-594-7134, E-mail: bethany.young@cnu.edu; *Head of Instruction,* Matt Shelley; Tel: 757-594-7245, E-mail: matt.shelley@cnu.edu; *Cat Librn,* Steven York; Tel: 757-594-8702, E-mail: syork@cnu.edu; *Coll Mgt Librn,* Dr Alicia Willson-Metzger; Tel: 757-594-8948, E-mail: awillson@cnu.edu; *Digital Serv Librn,* Johnnie Gray; Tel: 757-594-7249, E-mail: jngray@cnu.edu; *ILL Librn,* Jesse Spencer; E-mail: jesse.spencer@cnu.edu; Staff 9 (MLS 8, Non-MLS 1)
Founded 1961. Enrl 4,489; Fac 262; Highest Degree: Master
Library Holdings: e-books 360,846; e-journals 63,881; Electronic Media & Resources 14,721; Microforms 199,481; Bk Vols 785,346; Per Subs 741
Special Collections: Josephine Hughes Music Coll; Virginia Authors Coll
Automation Activity & Vendor Info: (Acquisitions) Innovative Interfaces, Inc; (Cataloging) Innovative Interfaces, Inc; (Circulation) Innovative Interfaces, Inc; (Course Reserve) Innovative Interfaces, Inc; (ILL) OCLC ILLiad; (OPAC) Innovative Interfaces, Inc; (Serials) Innovative Interfaces, Inc
Wireless access
Function: Archival coll, Computers for patron use, Electronic databases & coll, ILL available, Microfiche/film & reading machines, Music CDs, Online cat, Photocopying/Printing, Res libr, Scanner, Wheelchair accessible
Partic in Virginia Tidewater Consortium for Higher Education; Virginia's Academic Library Consortium

S THOMAS JEFFERSON NATIONAL ACCELERATOR FACILITY*, Jefferson Lab Library, 12050 Jefferson Ave, ARC 126, 23606. (Mail add: 12000 Jefferson Ave, 23606), SAN 317-3615. Tel: 757-269-7525. FAX: 757-269-7848. Administration FAX: 757-269-6228. E-mail: library@jlab.org. Web Site: www.jlab.org/IR. *Head, Info Res,* Dana Cochran; Tel: 757-269-7244, E-mail: cochran@jlab.org; *Rec Mgr,* Kim Edwards; Tel: 757-269-7805, E-mail: kindrew@jlab.org
Founded 1985
Library Holdings: e-journals 4,000; Bk Titles 11,000
Subject Interests: Electrical engr, Math, Nuclear physics
Automation Activity & Vendor Info: (Acquisitions) Ex Libris Group; (Cataloging) Ex Libris Group; (Circulation) Ex Libris Group; (Course Reserve) Ex Libris Group; (ILL) Ex Libris Group; (Media Booking) Ex Libris Group; (OPAC) Ex Libris Group; (Serials) Ex Libris Group
Partic in LYRASIS
Restriction: Open by appt only, Photo ID required for access

S MARINERS' MUSEUM & PARK LIBRARY*, 100 Museum Dr, 23606-3759. SAN 317-3585. Tel: 757-591-7782. E-mail: library@marinersmuseum.org. Web Site: www.marinersmuseum.org/library. *Archivist/Librn,* Jay Moore; *Tech Serv Librn,* Jennifer Anielski; E-mail: janielski@marinersmuseum.org; *Archivist,* Bill Barker; *Photo Archivist,* Sarah Puckitt; *Spec Coll Archivist,* Rachel Conley; Staff 5 (MLS 2, Non-MLS 3)
Founded 1930
Library Holdings: Bk Titles 90,000; Bk Vols 110,000

Special Collections: Chris Craft Archive; Maritime Vessels, archival items, charts, drawings, maps, photos, ship brochures
Subject Interests: Maritime hist, Naval hist, Navigation, Shipbuilding
Wireless access
Function: Ref serv available
Partic in OCLC Online Computer Library Center, Inc
Open Mon-Fri 9-5
Restriction: Not a lending libr

P NEWPORT NEWS PUBLIC LIBRARY SYSTEM*, 700 Town Center Dr, Ste 300, 23606. SAN 363-0781. Tel: 757-926-1350. FAX: 757-926-1365. E-mail: nnlibrary@nnva.gov. Web Site: library.nnva.gov. *Libr Adminr,* Anita Jennings; E-mail: ajennings@nnva.gov; Staff 91 (MLS 17, Non-MLS 74)
Founded 1891. Pop 183,362; Circ 722,879
Library Holdings: Audiobooks 22,190; AV Mats 45,649; Electronic Media & Resources 85,392; Bk Titles 246,145; Per Subs 132
Special Collections: Martha Woodroof Hiden Virginiana Coll; Old Dominion Land Company Coll. Oral History
Subject Interests: Local genealogy, Local hist
Automation Activity & Vendor Info: (Acquisitions) Innovative Interfaces, Inc; (Cataloging) Innovative Interfaces, Inc; (Circulation) Innovative Interfaces, Inc; (OPAC) Innovative Interfaces, Inc; (Serials) Innovative Interfaces, Inc
Wireless access
Function: 24/7 Electronic res, 24/7 Online cat, 3D Printer, Adult bk club, Adult literacy prog, After school storytime, Archival coll, Art exhibits, Audiobks via web, Bi-weekly Writer's Group, Bilingual assistance for Spanish patrons, Bk club(s), Bks on CD, Children's prog, Computer training, Computers for patron use, Doc delivery serv, E-Reserves, Electronic databases & coll, Family literacy, Free DVD rentals, Holiday prog, Homework prog, ILL available, Internet access, Life-long learning prog for all ages, Literacy & newcomer serv, Magazines, Mail & tel request accepted, Meeting rooms, Microfiche/film & reading machines, Movies, Music CDs, Notary serv, Online cat, Online ref, Outreach serv, Outside serv via phone, mail, e-mail & web, OverDrive digital audio bks, Photocopying/Printing, Preschool outreach, Prof lending libr, Prog for adults, Prog for children & young adult, Ref & res, Ref serv available, Scanner, Senior computer classes, Senior outreach, Serves people with intellectual disabilities, Spanish lang bks, Story hour, Summer reading prog, Tax forms, Teen prog, Telephone ref, Wheelchair accessible, Workshops
Partic in OCLC Online Computer Library Center, Inc
Special Services for the Deaf - TDD equip
Restriction: Non-circulating coll, Non-circulating of rare bks, Non-circulating to the pub
Friends of the Library Group
Branches: 5
PEARL BAILEY BRANCH, 2510 Wickham Ave, 23607, SAN 363-096X. Tel: 757-247-8677. FAX: 757-247-2321. *Librn IV,* Anita N Jennings; E-mail: ajennings@nngov.com; Staff 13.8 (MLS 3, Non-MLS 10.8)
Pop 27,649; Circ 68,607
Library Holdings: AV Mats 9,713; Bk Vols 161,753
Function: ILL available, Photocopying/Printing, Prog for children & young adult, Ref serv available, Summer reading prog, Telephone ref
Special Services for the Deaf - TDD equip; TTY equip
Open Mon-Thurs 9-9, Fri & Sat 9-6
Friends of the Library Group
VIRGIL I GRISSOM BRANCH, 366 DeShazor Dr, 23608, SAN 363-0900. Tel: 757-369-3190. FAX: 757-369-3198. *Sr Librn,* Patricia A Manzella; E-mail: pmanzella@nngov.com; Staff 20.9 (MLS 3, Non-MLS 17.9)
Pop 41,875; Circ 270,575
Library Holdings: AV Mats 9,713; Bk Vols 161,753
Function: ILL available, Photocopying/Printing, Prog for children & young adult, Summer reading prog, Wheelchair accessible
Special Services for the Deaf - TDD equip; TTY equip
Open Mon-Thurs 9-9, Fri & Sat 9-6, Sun 1-5
Friends of the Library Group
LAW LIBRARY, 2501 Washington Ave, 23607, SAN 363-0846. Tel: 757-926-8678. FAX: 757-926-8824. *Dir,* Anita Jennings; E-mail: jenningsan@nnva.gov
Founded 1964
Library Holdings: Bk Vols 13,600
Function: For res purposes, Photocopying/Printing
Open Mon-Fri 8-12 & 1-5
Restriction: Open to pub for ref only
Friends of the Library Group
MAIN STREET, 110 Main St, 23601, SAN 363-0870. Tel: 757-591-4858. FAX: 757-591-7425. *Mgr, Info Tech & Media Serv,* Christian Nocera; E-mail: noceraca@nnva.gov; *Librn,* Gregg Grunow; E-mail: ggrunow@nngov.com; Staff 21 (MLS 3, Non-MLS 18)
Circ 234,935
Library Holdings: AV Mats 12,688; Bk Vols 145,671
Special Collections: Martha Hiden Woodroof Virginiana Coll
Subject Interests: Genealogy, Virginiana
Function: Games & aids for people with disabilities, Home delivery & serv to seniorr ctr & nursing homes, Homebound delivery serv, ILL available, Magnifiers for reading, Photocopying/Printing, Prog for children & young adult, Ref serv available, Summer reading prog, Wheelchair accessible
Special Services for the Deaf - TDD equip; TTY equip
Friends of the Library Group

M RIVERSIDE REGIONAL MEDICAL CENTER*, Health Sciences Library, 500 J Clyde Morris Blvd, 23601. SAN 327-3733. Tel: 757-240-2403. FAX: 757-240-2401. E-mail: library@rivhs.com. *Librn,* Cassandra Moore; Staff 3 (MLS 1, Non-MLS 2)
Founded 1980
Library Holdings: e-journals 3,000; Bk Vols 5,000; Per Subs 200
Special Collections: Historical Medicine & Nursing
Subject Interests: Allied health, Med, Nursing
Wireless access
Open Mon, Wed & Fri 7:30-4, Tues & Thurs 7:30-6

S VIRGINIA WAR MUSEUM*, 9285 Warwick Blvd, 23607. SAN 321-0200. Tel: 757-247-8523. E-mail: virginiawarmuseum@nnva.gov. Web Site: newportnewshistory.org/virginia-war-museum. *Coordr, Libr & Educ Serv,* Chris Garcia; E-mail: garciacm@nnva.gov
Founded 1923
Library Holdings: Bk Titles 25,000
Special Collections: American Military History Coll, 1775-present; German Language Propaganda Publications; World Wars I & II, mags, photogs, scrapbks
Wireless access
Function: Res libr
Restriction: Open to pub by appt only

NORFOLK

S CHRYSLER MUSEUM OF ART*, Jean Outland Chrysler Library, Barry Arts Bldg, Rm 1003, 4600 Monarch Way, 23508. (Mail add: Chrysler Museum of Art, One Memorial Place, 23510), SAN 317-364X. Tel: 757-664-6205. Administration Tel: 757-333-6200. E-mail: library@chrysler.org. Web Site: chrysler.org/library. *Librn,* Elizabeth Weir; E-mail: eweir@chrysler.org; Staff 1 (MLS 1)
Founded 1929
Library Holdings: AV Mats 500; Bk Titles 30,000; Bk Vols 106,000; Per Subs 250
Special Collections: 18th-20th century auction & exhibition catalogs; Architecture (Frank A Vanderlip Jr Coll); Knoedler Library
Subject Interests: Am, Art hist, Art nouveau, Decorative art, Drawing, Glass, Painting, Photog, Sculpture, Textiles, Western European
Automation Activity & Vendor Info: (Cataloging) TLC (The Library Corporation); (ILL) OCLC; (Serials) EBSCO Online
Partic in LYRASIS
Open Wed-Fri 10-5
Restriction: Non-circulating

S FRED HEUTTE HORTICULTURAL LIBRARY, Norfolk Botanical Garden Library, 6700 Azalea Garden Rd, 23518-5337. SAN 317-3690. Tel: 757-441-5830. FAX: 757-441-5828. E-mail: library@nbgs.org. Web Site: norfolkbotanicalgarden.org. *Librn,* Marcia Oubre. Subject Specialists: *Hort,* Marcia Oubre; Staff 1 (Non-MLS 1)
Founded 1960
Library Holdings: Bk Vols 4,000; Per Subs 2
Wireless access
Function: Wheelchair accessible
Restriction: Circ to mem only, Pub use on premises

G JOINT FORCES STAFF COLLEGE*, Ike Skelton Library, 7800 Hampton Blvd, 23511-1702. SAN 317-3623. Tel: 757-443-6400. E-mail: registrar2@ndu.edu. Web Site: www.ndu.edu/libraries. *Chief,* Margaret Harrison
Founded 1947
Special Collections: US Document Depository
Wireless access
Partic in Federal Library & Information Network; OCLC Online Computer Library Center, Inc; Virginia Tidewater Consortium for Higher Education
Restriction: Access at librarian's discretion

S MACARTHUR MEMORIAL LIBRARY & ARCHIVES*, MacArthur Sq, 23510. SAN 317-3674. Tel: 757-441-2965. FAX: 757-441-5389. Web Site: www.macarthurmemorial.org. *Archivist,* James W Zobel; E-mail: james.zobel@norfolk.gov
Founded 1964
Library Holdings: Microforms 1,000; Music Scores 200; Bk Titles 33,000; Videos 500
Special Collections: D Clayton James Interviews (Interviews for his 3 volume work on MacArthur); Papers of Commander Charles Parsons

(Philippine Guerrillas, World War II); Papers of General of the Army Douglas MacArthur (World War II to the Korean War and Private Correspondence); Papers of James Halsema (Filipiniana, Papers, Maps and Books); Papers of LGEN Edward M Almond; Papers of LGEN Richard K Sutherland; Papers of MGEN Charles A Willoughby; Papers of MGEN Courtney Whitney (Philippine Guerrillas, World War II, SCAP and Korean War); Papers of MGEN R J Marshall; Papers of Michael & Elizabeth Norman; Papers of William Bartsch (World War II, Philippine, Java and Guadalcanal campaigns); Photographic Coll (Korean War, Occupation of Japan, Spanish American War, WWI, WWII). Oral History
Subject Interests: Korean War, Occupation of Japan, Philippine Insurrection, World War I, World War II
Function: Archival coll, Res libr
Publications: Douglas MacArthur Archives & Library (Brochure); MacArthur Report
Open Mon-Fri 10-5
Restriction: Not a lending libr

S NORFOLK HISTORICAL SOCIETY*, Fort Norfolk, 810 Front St, 23508. (Mail add: PO Box 6367, 23508-0367). Tel: 757-754-2004. E-mail: info@norfolkhistorical.org. *Adminr, Board Pres,* Peggy McPhillips

P NORFOLK PUBLIC LIBRARY*, Administrative Offices & Service Ctr, 1155 Pineridge Rd, 23502. Circulation Tel: 757-664-7323, Option 2. Interlibrary Loan Service Tel: 757-664-7333. Administration Tel: 757-664-7328. FAX: 757-441-5863. E-mail: npl.comments@norfolk.gov. Circulation E-mail: npl.circ@norfolk.gov. Web Site: www.norfolkpubliclibrary.org. *Dir of Libr,* Sonal Rastogi; E-mail: Sonal.Rastogi@norfolk.gov
Founded 1870. Pop 234,403; Circ 992,217
Library Holdings: Audiobooks 1,908; CDs 3,302; DVDs 4,002; e-books 13,579; Music Scores 9,822; Bk Vols 1,840,139
Special Collections: Virginianna (Sargeant Memorial Room), AV, bk & micro. US Document Depository
Subject Interests: African-Am lit, Juv lit, Literary studies, Local hist
Automation Activity & Vendor Info: (Acquisitions) SirsiDynix; (Cataloging) SirsiDynix; (Circulation) SirsiDynix; (ILL) OCLC Connexion; (OPAC) SirsiDynix
Wireless access
Function: Adult bk club, Art exhibits, Bk club(s), Bks on cassette, Bks on CD, Children's prog, Computer training, Computers for patron use, Electronic databases & coll, Family literacy, Free DVD rentals, Govt ref serv, Holiday prog, Homework prog, ILL available, Internet access, Life-long learning prog for all ages, Magnifiers for reading, Meeting rooms, Microfiche/film & reading machines, Movies, Music CDs, Online cat, OverDrive digital audio bks, Photocopying/Printing, Preschool outreach, Preschool reading prog, Prog for adults, Prog for children & young adult, Ref serv available, Scanner, Senior computer classes, Spanish lang bks, Spoken cassettes & CDs, Spoken cassettes & DVDs, Story hour, Study rm, Summer & winter reading prog, Tax forms, Teen prog, Telephone ref, VHS videos, Wheelchair accessible
Special Services for the Blind - Large print bks
Friends of the Library Group
Branches: 12
BARRON F BLACK BRANCH, 6700 E Tanners Creek Rd, 23513, SAN 363-1028. Tel: 757-441-5806. FAX: 757-441-5891. *Br Mgr,* Sarah Davis
Library Holdings: Audiobooks 230; CDs 408; DVDs 1,301; Bk Vols 22,324
Open Mon-Thurs 10-7, Fri & Sat 10-5
Friends of the Library Group
BLYDEN BRANCH, 879 E Princess Anne Rd, 23504, SAN 363-1117. Tel: 757-441-2852. FAX: 757-441-1452. *Br Mgr,* Karen Salaam
Library Holdings: Audiobooks 63; DVDs 1,294; Bk Vols 12,873
Open Mon-Thurs 10-7, Fri & Sat 10-5
Friends of the Library Group
HORACE C DOWNING BRANCH, 555 E Liberty St, 23523, SAN 363-1052. Tel: 757-441-1968. FAX: 757-441-1994. *Br Mgr,* Phyllis Ray
Library Holdings: Audiobooks 134; DVDs 2,057; Bk Vols 10,122
Open Mon-Thurs 10-7, Fri & Sat 10-5
Friends of the Library Group
JANAF BRANCH, 124 Janaf Shopping Ctr, 5900 E Virginia Beach Blvd, 23502, SAN 363-1176. Tel: 757-441-5660. *Br Mgr,* Jennie Radovsky
Library Holdings: Audiobooks 406; DVDs 1,943; Bk Vols 20,617
Open Mon-Thurs 10-7, Fri & Sat 10-5
Friends of the Library Group
JORDAN-NEWBY BRANCH AT BROAD CREEK, 1425 Norchester Ave, 23504, SAN 363-1141. Tel: 757-664-7323. *Br Mgr,* Jessica Harvey; Staff 1 (MLS 1)
Library Holdings: Audiobooks 426; CDs 165; DVDs 1,586; Bk Vols 18,814
Open Mon-Thurs 9-8, Fri 9-5, Sat 10-5
Friends of the Library Group
LAFAYETTE BRANCH, 1610 Cromwell Rd, 23509, SAN 363-1206. Tel: 757-441-2842. *Br Mgr,* Amy Bateman; Staff 1 (MLS 1)
Library Holdings: Audiobooks 727; DVDs 1,230; Bk Vols 29,470
Open Mon-Thurs 10-7, Fri & Sat 10-5
Friends of the Library Group
LARCHMONT BRANCH, 6525 Hampton Blvd, 23508, SAN 363-1230. Tel: 757-441-5335. *Br Mgr,* Jessica Montfort; Staff 1 (MLS 1)
Library Holdings: Audiobooks 475; CDs 71; DVDs 2,742; Bk Vols 27,451
Open Mon-Thurs 10-7, Fri & Sat 10-5
Friends of the Library Group
LITTLE CREEK BRANCH, 7853 Tarpon Pl, 23518, SAN 363-1265. Tel: 757-441-1751. *Br Mgr,* Melanie Greene; Staff 1 (MLS 1)
Library Holdings: Audiobooks 758; DVDs 2,036; Bk Vols 26,790
Open Mon-Thurs 10-7, Fri & Sat 10-5
Friends of the Library Group
PARK PLACE BRANCH, 620 W 29th St, 23508, SAN 363-1087. Tel: 757-664-7330. FAX: 757-664-7331. *Br Mgr,* Alison Gunther-Blackman
Library Holdings: Audiobooks 112; DVDs 948; Bk Vols 6,131
Open Mon-Thurs 10-7, Fri & Sat 10-5
Friends of the Library Group
MARY D PRETLOW ANCHOR BRANCH LIBRARY, 111 W Ocean View Ave, 23503-1608, SAN 363-129X. Tel: 757-441-1750. *Br Mgr,* Cynthia Seay
Library Holdings: Audiobooks 2,241; CDs 2,130; DVDs 5,856; Bk Vols 53,999
Open Mon-Thurs 10-9, Fri & Sat 10-5, Sun 1-5
Friends of the Library Group
SLOVER LIBRARY, 235 E Plume St, 23510. Tel: 757-431-7491. Web Site: www.sloverlibrary.com. *Coms & Multimedia Engagement Mgr,* Raquel Taylor; E-mail: raquel.taylor@norfolk.gov
Library Holdings: Audiobooks 1,211; CDs 878; DVDs 8,350; Bk Vols 132,486
Special Collections: Sargeant Memorial Coll for local history
Open Mon-Thurs 9-8, Fri 9-5, Sat 10-5, Sun 12-5
Friends of the Library Group
VAN WYCK BRANCH, 1368 DeBree Ave, 23517, SAN 363-132X. Tel: 757-441-2844. *Br Mgr,* Lynn Cox
Library Holdings: Audiobooks 716; DVDs 3,198; Bk Vols 25,598
Open Mon-Thurs 10-7, Fri & Sat 10-5
Friends of the Library Group
Bookmobiles: 1. Supvr, Arica White. Bk vols 10,658

C NORFOLK STATE UNIVERSITY LIBRARY*, Lyman Beecher Brooks Library, 700 Park Ave, 23504-8010. SAN 317-3712. Tel: 757-823-2418. Administration Tel: 757-823-8481. E-mail: Library@nsu.edu. Web Site: library.nsu.edu. *Coordr, Tech Serv, Interim Dean, Libr Serv,* C Lynne Harrison; Tel: 757-823-9153, E-mail: clharrison@nsu.edu; *Coll Develop Librn,* Marlene Ballou; Tel: 757-823-2428, E-mail: mballou@nsu.edu; *Ref Librn,* Ann D Cannon; Tel: 757-823-2417, E-mail: adcannon@nsu.edu; *ILL Supvr,* Manju Majumdar; Tel: 757-823-2426, E-mail: mmajumdar@nsu.edu; *Libr Spec,* Cyanna Rodney-Hill; Tel: 757-823-2224, E-mail: cdrodney-hill@nsu.edu; *Access Serv,* Wilbert Wiggins; Tel: 757-823-2418, E-mail: wwiggins@nsu.edu; Staff 28 (MLS 9, Non-MLS 19)
Founded 1935. Enrl 6,000; Fac 350; Highest Degree: Doctorate
Library Holdings: AV Mats 1,828; CDs 587; DVDs 126; e-books 40,000; e-journals 5,600; Music Scores 177; Bk Titles 288,411; Bk Vols 341,000; Per Subs 1,395; Videos 194
Special Collections: African American Materials (Herbert A Marshall Coll); Local & Regional African American Interest, NSU History (Harrison B Wilson Archives)
Subject Interests: Behav sci, Bus mgt, Chem, Computer sci, Educ, Ethnic studies, Humanities, Mat sci, Optical engr, Physics, Soc sci, Soc work
Automation Activity & Vendor Info: (Acquisitions) Innovative Interfaces, Inc; (Cataloging) Innovative Interfaces, Inc; (Circulation) Innovative Interfaces, Inc; (Course Reserve) Innovative Interfaces, Inc; (ILL) Innovative Interfaces, Inc; (OPAC) Innovative Interfaces, Inc; (Serials) Innovative Interfaces, Inc
Wireless access
Function: Archival coll, Distance learning, Doc delivery serv, E-Reserves, ILL available, Internet access, Photocopying/Printing, Ref serv available, Scanner, Spoken cassettes & CDs, VHS videos, Wheelchair accessible
Publications: Bibliographic Guides & Pathfinders; Bibliographic Instruction (Handbooks)
Partic in LYRASIS; OCLC Online Computer Library Center, Inc; Virginia Tidewater Consortium for Higher Education; Virginia's Academic Library Consortium
Special Services for the Deaf - Assistive tech
Special Services for the Blind - Assistive/Adapted tech devices, equip & products
Open Mon-Thurs 8am-11pm, Fri 8-5, Sat 9-5, Sun 2-10
Restriction: Open to students, fac & staff
Departmental Libraries:
VIRGINIA BEACH HIGHER EDUCATION RESOURCE CENTER, 1881 University Dr, Virginia Beach, 23453-8080. Tel: 757-368-4162. FAX: 757-368-4151. E-mail: vblibrary@nsu.edu. Web Site:

www.nsu.edu/vbhec. *Info Spec,* Karma Gaines-Ra; E-mail: kgaines-ra@nsu.edu
Open Mon-Fri 8am-10pm, Sat 8-5:30, Sun 2-5

C OLD DOMINION UNIVERSITY LIBRARIES*, Patricia W & J Douglas Perry Library, 4427 Hampton Blvd, 23529-0256. SAN 317-3720. Tel: 757-683-4141. Circulation Tel: 757-683-4154. Interlibrary Loan Service Tel: 757-683-4170. Reference Tel: 757-683-4182. Automation Services Tel: 757-683-4546. FAX: 757-683-5767. Interlibrary Loan Service FAX: 757-683-5035. Web Site: www.odu.edu/library. *Univ Librn,* George J Fowler; E-mail: gfowler@odu.edu; *Dep Univ Librn,* Stuart Frazer; Tel: 757-683-4143, E-mail: sfrazer@odu.edu; *Head, Spec Coll & Univ Archives,* Jessica Ritchie; Tel: 757-683-4483, E-mail: jhritchi@odu.edu; *Head, Syst Develop,* Junfang Zhang; Tel: 757-683-5952, E-mail: j4zhang@odu.edu; Staff 68.5 (MLS 24.5, Non-MLS 44)
Founded 1930. Enrl 24,670; Fac 1,224; Highest Degree: Doctorate
Special Collections: Desegregation of Education; Historical Archives; Music; Scottish History Coll; Tidewater History Coll. State Document Depository; US Document Depository
Subject Interests: The arts
Automation Activity & Vendor Info: (Acquisitions) Ex Libris Group; (Cataloging) Ex Libris Group; (Circulation) Ex Libris Group; (Course Reserve) Ex Libris Group; (Discovery) Ex Libris Group; (ILL) OCLC ILLiad; (OPAC) Ex Libris Group; (Serials) Ex Libris Group
Wireless access
Partic in LYRASIS; OCLC Online Computer Library Center, Inc; Virginia Tidewater Consortium for Higher Education; Virginia's Academic Library Consortium
Friends of the Library Group
Departmental Libraries:
F LUDGWIG DIEHN COMPOSERS ROOM, 189 Diehn Fine & Performing Arts Ctr, 1339 49th St, 23529.
ELISE N HOFHEIMER ART LIBRARY, Barry Arts Bldg, Rm 2008, 4600 Monarch Way, 23529. Tel: 757-683-4059. Web Site: www.odu.edu/library/art. *Supvr,* Gay P Acompanado; E-mail: gacompan@odu.edu. Subject Specialists: *Art,* Gay P Acompanado; Staff 1 (Non-MLS 1)
Open Mon-Thurs 8am-9pm, Fri 8-5, Sat 9-5, Sun 1-5 (Spring & Fall); Mon-Fri 8-5 (Summer)

J TIDEWATER COMMUNITY COLLEGE LEARNING RESOURCES CENTER*, Norfolk Campus, 300 Granby St, 23510. SAN 377-8304. Tel: 757-822-1100. Circulation Tel: 757-822-1544. Reference Tel: 757-822-1101. Web Site: libguides.tcc.edu/Norfolk-Library, www.tcc.edu/service-support/libraries. *Coordr,* Mary Hanlin; Tel: 757-822-1772, E-mail: maryhanlin@tcc.edu; *Circ,* Catherine Averett; Tel: 757-822-1124, E-mail: caverett@tcc.edu; *Ref Serv,* Jai Stofocik; Tel: 757-822-1775, E-mail: jstofocik@tcc.edu; Staff 4 (MLS 1, Non-MLS 3)
Founded 1997. Highest Degree: Associate
Library Holdings: Bk Titles 15,000; Per Subs 10
Wireless access
Function: Ref serv available
Partic in Virginia's Academic Library Consortium
Open Mon, Tues, Thurs & Fri 8-4:30, Wed 8-7

A UNITED STATES ARMY CORPS OF ENGINEERS*, Norfolk District Library, 803 Front St, 23510-1096. Tel: 757-201-7219. E-mail: CENAO-Library@usace.army.mil. Web Site: www.nao.usace.army.mil/Library. *Librn,* Linda Towne
Library Holdings: Bk Vols 22,000; Per Subs 90; Videos 224
Subject Interests: Sci, Tech
Wireless access
Restriction: Open to pub by appt only

L UNITED STATES COURTS LIBRARY, Walter E Hoffman US Courthouse, 600 Granby St, Rm 319, 23510. SAN 372-3526. Tel: 757-222-7044. FAX: 757-222-7047. Web Site: www.vaed.uscourts.gov/norfolk. *Librn,* Karen J Johnson
Library Holdings: Bk Vols 12,000
Automation Activity & Vendor Info: (Cataloging) SirsiDynix
Restriction: Not open to pub, Ref only

A UNITED STATES NAVY, JEB Little Creek Library, 1481 D St, Bldg 3016, 23521. SAN 363-1419. Tel: 757-462-7691. FAX: 757-462-4950. *Dir,* Emily Byrd; *Librn,* Chloe Andres
Founded 1942
Library Holdings: Bk Vols 35,000; Per Subs 85
Subject Interests: Naval hist
Wireless access
Open Mon-Sat 9-5

OAKWOOD

S KEEN MOUNTAIN CORRECTIONAL CENTER, Department of Correctional Education Library, 3402 Kennel Gap Rd, 24631. (Mail add: PO Box 860, 24631-0860). SAN 373-6903. Tel: 276-498-7411. FAX: 276-498-7341. *Librn,* Jennifer Bundy
Founded 1990
Library Holdings: Bk Vols 22,000; Per Subs 25
Automation Activity & Vendor Info: (Acquisitions) Follett Software; (Cataloging) Follett Software; (Circulation) Follett Software; (OPAC) Follett Software
Restriction: Not open to pub

ORANGE

P ORANGE COUNTY PUBLIC LIBRARY*, 146A Madison Rd, 22960. SAN 317-3771. Tel: 540-672-3811. FAX: 540-672-5040. Web Site: ocplva.org. *Libr Dir,* Katie Hill; Tel: 540-661-5444, E-mail: khill@orangecountyva.gov; *Tech Serv-Section Head,* Teresa Frick; Staff 5 (MLS 3, Non-MLS 2)
Founded 1903. Pop 34,000; Circ 298,000
Jul 2017-Jun 2018 Income (Main & Associated Libraries) $1,083,887, State $149,741, County $871,410, Locally Generated Income $5,196, Other $57,540. Mats Exp $187,402, Books $115,856, Per/Ser (Incl. Access Fees) $5,023, AV Equip $15,972, AV Mat $33,665, Electronic Ref Mat (Incl. Access Fees) $16,886. Sal $688,617 (Prof $306,232)
Library Holdings: Audiobooks 8,765; CDs 2,552; DVDs 27,865; Large Print Bks 6,189; Microforms 1; Bk Titles 114,214; Per Subs 75
Automation Activity & Vendor Info: (Acquisitions) TLC (The Library Corporation); (Cataloging) TLC (The Library Corporation); (Circulation) TLC (The Library Corporation); (OPAC) TLC (The Library Corporation)
Wireless access
Function: 24/7 Electronic res, 24/7 Online cat, Audiobks via web, Bks on CD, Computers for patron use, Free DVD rentals, ILL available, Internet access, Life-long learning prog for all ages, Magazines, Meeting rooms, Music CDs, Online cat, OverDrive digital audio bks, Photocopying/Printing, Preschool reading prog, Prog for adults, Prog for children & young adult, Ref serv available, Scanner, Spanish lang bks, Story hour, Summer reading prog, Tax forms, Teen prog, Wheelchair accessible
Open Mon-Wed 9:30-8, Thurs & Fri 9:30-5:30, Sat 9:30-1:30
Friends of the Library Group
Branches: 2
GORDONSVILLE BRANCH, 319 N Main St, Gordonsville, 22942, SAN 377-9939. Tel: 540-832-0712. FAX: 540-832-0849. *Br Mgr,* Patricia Keister; Staff 1 (MLS 1)
Founded 1998
Library Holdings: CDs 304; DVDs 1,135; Electronic Media & Resources 247; Large Print Bks 136; Bk Titles 12,400; Bk Vols 19,089; Per Subs 17; Talking Bks 412; Videos 908
Function: 24/7 Electronic res, 24/7 Online cat, Audiobks via web, Bks on CD, Children's prog, Computers for patron use, Electronic databases & coll, Free DVD rentals, ILL available, Internet access, Magazines, Meeting rooms, Music CDs, OverDrive digital audio bks, Photocopying/Printing, Preschool reading prog, Prog for adults, Story hour, Summer reading prog, Tax forms, Teen prog
Open Mon, Thurs & Fri 9:30-5:30, Tues & Wed 9:30-7:30, Sat 9:30-1:30
Friends of the Library Group
WILDERNESS, 6421 Flat Run Rd, Locust Grove, 22508. Tel: 540-854-5310. FAX: 540-854-5402. *Br Librn,* Michele B Beamer; *Asst Br Mgr,* Amy Cryst; Staff 2 (MLS 1, Non-MLS 1)
Founded 1995
Library Holdings: AV Mats 8,450; CDs 923; DVDs 2,098; Electronic Media & Resources 363; Large Print Bks 1,445; Bk Vols 35,211; Per Subs 25; Talking Bks 1,950; Videos 2,453
Subject Interests: Civil War
Function: 24/7 Electronic res, 24/7 Online cat, Audiobks via web, Bks on CD, Children's prog, Computers for patron use, Free DVD rentals, ILL available, Internet access, Magazines, Magnifiers for reading, Meeting rooms, Music CDs, Online cat, Photocopying/Printing, Preschool reading prog, Prog for adults, Prog for children & young adult, Story hour, Study rm, Summer reading prog, Tax forms, Wheelchair accessible
Open Mon & Tues 10-7:30, Wed 12:30-7:30, Thurs & Fri 10-5:30, Sat 10-2
Friends of the Library Group

PALMYRA

P FLUVANNA COUNTY PUBLIC LIBRARY, 214 Commons Blvd, 22963. SAN 317-378X. Tel: 434-589-1400. FAX: 434-589-1400. E-mail: fluvannalibrary@gmail.com. Web Site: www2.youseemore.com/fluvanna. *Dir,* Cyndi Hoffman; E-mail: choffman@fluvannacounty.org; Staff 3 (MLS 1, Non-MLS 2)
Founded 1968. Pop 25,691; Circ 237,000

Library Holdings: Audiobooks 2,659; AV Mats 9,590; CDs 1,021; DVDs 8,267; Large Print Bks 3,315; Bk Titles 55,592; Bk Vols 59,265; Per Subs 98
Special Collections: Fluvanna County Historical Society Coll
Subject Interests: Local hist
Automation Activity & Vendor Info: (Cataloging) TLC (The Library Corporation); (Circulation) TLC (The Library Corporation); (ILL) TLC (The Library Corporation); (OPAC) TLC (The Library Corporation)
Wireless access
Open Mon & Tues 9-6, Wed & Thurs 9-8, Fri 9-5, Sat 9-3
Friends of the Library Group

PEARISBURG

P PEARISBURG PUBLIC LIBRARY*, 209 Fort Branch Rd, 24134. SAN 317-3798. Tel: 540-921-2556. FAX: 540-921-1708. Web Site: pearisburglibrary.org. *Dir,* Allison Long; E-mail: along@pearisburg.org; *Asst Librn,* Lori Porterfield; Staff 2 (MLS 1, Non-MLS 1)
Founded 1963
Library Holdings: Bk Vols 35,777; Per Subs 56
Special Collections: Genealogy, including listings of Giles County cemeteries
Automation Activity & Vendor Info: (Acquisitions) Follett Software; (Cataloging) Follett Software; (Circulation) Follett Software; (Course Reserve) Follett Software; (ILL) Follett Software; (Media Booking) Follett Software; (OPAC) Follett Software; (Serials) Follett Software
Wireless access
Publications: Giles County-Virginia, History-Families
Partic in New River Public Library Cooperative
Open Mon 12-8, Tues 12-5, Wed & Fri 9-5, Thurs 9-8, Sat 9-1
Friends of the Library Group

PETERSBURG

M BON SECOURS - SOUTHSIDE REGIONAL MEDICAL CENTER, Medical Library, (Formerly Southside Regional Medical Center), 200 Medical Park Blvd, 23805. SAN 317-3828. Tel: 804-765-6804. Web Site: www.bonsecours.com/locations/hospitals-medical-centers/richmond/southside-regional-medical-center.
Founded 1956
Library Holdings: Bk Vols 400; Per Subs 30
Subject Interests: Med
Wireless access
Partic in National Network of Libraries of Medicine Region 1

P PETERSBURG PUBLIC LIBRARY*, 201 W Washington St, 23803. SAN 363-1680. Tel: 804-733-2387. FAX: 804-733-7972. Web Site: www.ppls.org. *Dir,* Wayne M Crocker; E-mail: wcrocker@ppls.org; *Tech Librn,* Dana Cragg; E-mail: dcragg@ppls.org; Staff 4 (MLS 4)
Founded 1924. Pop 33,740; Circ 132,886
Library Holdings: AV Mats 1,631; Bk Titles 105,139; Bk Vols 153,336; Per Subs 229; Talking Bks 1,555
Special Collections: Newspapers since 1800, bd vols & microfilm; Virginia History (Rare Virginiana & Genealogy, Civil War History Coll)
Automation Activity & Vendor Info: (Cataloging) TLC (The Library Corporation); (Circulation) TLC (The Library Corporation); (OPAC) TLC (The Library Corporation)
Wireless access
Open Mon-Thurs 10-8, Fri & Sat 10-5
Friends of the Library Group
Branches: 2
A P HILL BRANCH, 1237 Halifax St, 23803, SAN 363-1710. Tel: 804-733-2391. FAX: 804-733-2391. *Librn,* Amanda Briggs
Library Holdings: Bk Titles 3,774; Bk Vols 12,758; Per Subs 41
Open Mon, Tues & Thurs 3-6, Wed & Fri 10-6
Friends of the Library Group
RODOF SHOLOM BRANCH, 1865 S Sycamore St, 23805, SAN 363-1745. Tel: 804-733-2393. FAX: 804-733-2422. *Librn,* Dana Cragg; E-mail: dcragg@ppls.org; Staff 3 (MLS 1, Non-MLS 2)
Library Holdings: Bk Titles 9,390; Bk Vols 29,389; Per Subs 71
Open Mon, Wed & Fri 9-5:30, Tues & Thurs 9-9
Friends of the Library Group

J RICHARD BLAND COLLEGE LIBRARY*, Commons Bldg, 11301 Johnson Rd, 23805. SAN 317-3836. Tel: 804-862-6226. Interlibrary Loan Service Tel: 804-862-6228. Reference Tel: 804-862-6227. Administration Tel: 804-862-6208. FAX: 804-862-6125. E-mail: library@rbc.edu. Web Site: www.rbc.edu/library. *Assoc Dean, Learning Res, Assoc Dean, Acad,* Aimee Joyaux; Tel: 804-862-6150, E-mail: ajoyaux@rbc.edu; *Access & Tech Serv Librn,* Irene Handy; E-mail: ihandy@rbc.edu; *Ref & Instrul Design Librn,* Carly Winfield; E-mail: cwinfield@rbc.edu; *Circ Spec, Outreach Serv Spec, Prog Spec,* Susan Moss; E-mail: smoss@rbc.edu; Staff 3 (MLS 2, Non-MLS 1)
Founded 1960. Enrl 1,634; Fac 33; Highest Degree: Associate
Library Holdings: Audiobooks 18; AV Mats 5,320; CDs 192; DVDs 4,384; e-books 56,829; e-journals 20,000; Electronic Media & Resources 760,000; Microforms 3,854; Bk Titles 57,576; Bk Vols 66,444; Per Subs 98; Videos 863
Special Collections: Southside Virginia Coll
Subject Interests: Geog, Hist, Lit, Music, Philos, Psychol, Relig
Automation Activity & Vendor Info: (Cataloging) SirsiDynix; (Circulation) SirsiDynix; (Course Reserve) SirsiDynix; (ILL) OCLC; (OPAC) SirsiDynix; (Serials) SirsiDynix
Wireless access
Function: Archival coll, AV serv, Computers for patron use, Electronic databases & coll, Free DVD rentals, ILL available, Internet access, Music CDs, Online cat, Online ref, Orientations, Photocopying/Printing, Ref serv available, Res libr, Scanner, VHS videos, Wheelchair accessible
Publications: Library Bookmarks (Newsletter)
Partic in Richmond Academic Library Consortium; Virginia's Academic Library Consortium
Open Mon-Thurs 8am-10pm, Fri 8-5, Sat 12-4
Restriction: Limited access for the pub
Friends of the Library Group

C VIRGINIA STATE UNIVERSITY*, Johnston Memorial Library, One Hayden Dr, 23806. (Mail add: PO Box 9406, 23806-9406), SAN 363-177X. Tel: 804-524-5040. Circulation Tel: 804-524-5043. Interlibrary Loan Service Tel: 804-524-6944. Reference Tel: 804-524-5582. Circulation FAX: 804-524-5482. Web Site: library.vsu.edu. *Dean of Libr,* Tessa Perry; E-mail: tperry@vsu.edu; *Assoc Librn, Pub Serv,* Michael C Walker; Tel: 804-524-6946, E-mail: mcwalker@vsu.edu; *Libr Syst Coordr,* Sherod Moses; Tel: 804-524-5942, E-mail: smoses@vsu.edu; *Acq,* Audrey Jones; Tel: 804-524-1030, E-mail: amjones@vsu.edu; *Coll Develop,* Louveller Luster; Tel: 804-524-6945, E-mail: lluster@vsu.edu; *Ref,* Karen Geter; E-mail: kgeter@vsu.edu; Staff 8 (MLS 6, Non-MLS 2)
Founded 1882. Enrl 5,074; Highest Degree: Doctorate
Library Holdings: CDs 470; DVDs 37; e-books 14,959; e-journals 2,828; Electronic Media & Resources 230; Music Scores 702; Bk Titles 285,353; Bk Vols 310,796; Per Subs 4,437; Videos 1,558
Special Collections: US Document Depository
Subject Interests: African-Am studies, Educ
Automation Activity & Vendor Info: (Acquisitions) Innovative Interfaces, Inc; (Cataloging) Innovative Interfaces, Inc; (Circulation) Innovative Interfaces, Inc; (Course Reserve) Docutek; (ILL) OCLC ILLiad; (OPAC) Innovative Interfaces, Inc; (Serials) Innovative Interfaces, Inc
Wireless access
Function: Res libr
Publications: InfoNavigator (Newsletter)
Partic in Richmond Academic Library Consortium; Virginia's Academic Library Consortium
Special Services for the Deaf - Assistive tech; Bks on deafness & sign lang; Closed caption videos; TDD equip; TTY equip
Special Services for the Blind - Assistive/Adapted tech devices, equip & products; Audio mat; Bks on cassette; Bks on CD; Braille servs; Cassette playback machines; Cassettes; Closed circuit TV; Disability awareness prog; Ednalite Hi-Vision scope; Inspiration software; Internet workstation with adaptive software; Low vision equip; Magnifiers; Reader equip
Open Mon-Thurs 8am-11pm, Fri 8-5, Sat 10-3, Sun 3-11

POQUOSON

P POQUOSON PUBLIC LIBRARY*, 500 City Hall Ave, 23662-1996. SAN 321-0936. Tel: 757-868-3060. FAX: 757-868-3106. E-mail: library@poquoson-va.gov. Web Site: ppll.ent.sirsi.net/client/en_us/default, www.ci.poquoson.va.us/190/library. *Dir,* Jessica Hartley; E-mail: jessica.hartley@poquoson-va.gov; Staff 12 (MLS 4, Non-MLS 8)
Founded 1976. Pop 11,800; Circ 199,739
Library Holdings: Audiobooks 1,472; CDs 621; DVDs 3,972; e-books 3,847; Electronic Media & Resources 9; Microforms 3; Bk Titles 50,506; Bk Vols 51,589; Per Subs 180
Automation Activity & Vendor Info: (Acquisitions) SirsiDynix; (Cataloging) SirsiDynix; (Circulation) SirsiDynix; (Course Reserve) SirsiDynix; (ILL) The Library Co-Op, Inc; (OPAC) SirsiDynix
Wireless access
Function: Accelerated reader prog, Adult bk club, Adult literacy prog, After school storytime, Archival coll, Art exhibits, Audio & video playback equip for onsite use, Audiobks via web, AV serv, BA reader (adult literacy), Bk club(s), Bk reviews (Group), Bks on CD, CD-ROM, Children's prog, Computer training, Computers for patron use, Digital talking bks, E-Reserves, Electronic databases & coll, Equip loans & repairs, Family literacy, Free DVD rentals, Genealogy discussion group, Health sci info serv, Holiday prog, Homework prog, ILL available, Internet access, Microfiche/film & reading machines, Music CDs, Notary serv, Online cat, Online ref, Outreach serv, Outside serv via phone, mail, e-mail & web, OverDrive digital audio bks, Passport agency, Photocopying/Printing, Preschool outreach, Preschool reading prog, Printer for laptops & handheld devices, Prog for adults, Prog for children & young adult, Ref serv available, Scanner, Senior computer classes, Senior

outreach, Spoken cassettes & CDs, Spoken cassettes & DVDs, Story hour, Summer reading prog, Tax forms, Teen prog, Telephone ref, Visual arts prog, Wheelchair accessible, Winter reading prog, Words travel prog
Publications: Annual Report; Book Worms (Newsletter); Bookmarks (Newsletter)
Partic in Mid-Atlantic Library Alliance; Virginia Library Association
Open Mon-Thurs 10-9, Fri & Sat 10-5, Sun 1-5
Restriction: Authorized patrons
Friends of the Library Group

PORTSMOUTH

S PORTSMOUTH NAVAL SHIPYARD MUSEUM*, Marshall W Butt Library, Two High St, 23704. (Mail add: 521 Middle St, 23704-3622), SAN 317-3860. Tel: 757-393-8591. FAX: 757-393-5244. Web Site: portsmouthnavalshipyardmuseum.com. *Curator,* Michael R Hogan; Tel: 757-393-8983, Ext 10, E-mail: hoganm@portsmouthva.gov
Founded 1949
Library Holdings: Bk Titles 8,000
Subject Interests: Local hist, Naval hist
Wireless access
Function: Archival coll, Photocopying/Printing, Res libr
Restriction: Not a lending libr, Open to others by appt
Friends of the Library Group

P PORTSMOUTH PUBLIC LIBRARY*, 601 Court St, 23704. SAN 363-1834. Tel: 757-393-8501. Web Site: www.portsmouthpubliclibrary.org. *Dir,* Todd Elliott; Tel: 757-393-8501, Ext 6517, E-mail: elliottt@portsmouthva.gov; *Mgr,* Ben Neal; Tel: 757-393-8501, Ext 6509, E-mail: nealb@portsmouthva.gov; Staff 8 (MLS 8)
Founded 1914. Pop 95,500; Circ 371,257
Library Holdings: Bks on Deafness & Sign Lang 274; CDs 1,167; DVDs 6,944; e-books 5; Large Print Bks 8,545; Bk Titles 213,768; Bk Vols 338,939; Per Subs 460; Talking Bks 5,430; Videos 7,039
Special Collections: Lighthouses & Lightships; Local History Coll, bks, doc. Oral History
Automation Activity & Vendor Info: (Acquisitions) Horizon; (Cataloging) Horizon; (Circulation) Horizon; (ILL) OCLC FirstSearch; (OPAC) Horizon
Wireless access
Function: AV serv, Bks on cassette, Bks on CD, CD-ROM, Children's prog, Computer training, Computers for patron use, E-Reserves, Electronic databases & coll, ILL available, Internet access, Music CDs, Photocopying/Printing, Prog for adults, Prog for children & young adult, Ref serv available, Spoken cassettes & CDs, Summer reading prog, Telephone ref, VHS videos, Wheelchair accessible
Open Mon-Thurs 10-6, Fri & Sat 10-5
Friends of the Library Group
Branches: 3
CHURCHLAND, 4934 High St W, 23703, SAN 363-1869. Tel: 757-686-2538. *Br Mgr,* Melinda Brown; E-mail: melinda.brown@portsmouthva.gov
Automation Activity & Vendor Info: (Acquisitions) SirsiDynix; (Cataloging) SirsiDynix; (Circulation) SirsiDynix
Open Mon-Wed 10-8, Thurs 10-6, Fri & Sat 10-5
Friends of the Library Group
CRADOCK, 28 Prospect Pkwy, 23702, SAN 363-1893. Tel: 757-393-8759. FAX: 757-393-5103. *Br Mgr,* Tammy Zavinski; E-mail: zavinskit@portsmouthva.gov
Library Holdings: CDs 290; DVDs 1,485; Large Print Bks 857; Bk Vols 45,186; Per Subs 43; Talking Bks 773; Videos 1,274
Automation Activity & Vendor Info: (Acquisitions) SirsiDynix; (Cataloging) SirsiDynix; (Circulation) SirsiDynix
Open Mon-Thurs 10-5:30, Sat 10-3
Friends of the Library Group
MANOR, 1401 Elmhurst Lane, 23701, SAN 363-1923. Tel: 757-465-2916. FAX: 757-465-2916. *Br Mgr,* Mary Goodman; E-mail: goodmanm@portsmouthva.gov; Staff 3 (MLS 1, Non-MLS 2)
Library Holdings: DVDs 1,623; Large Print Bks 1,509; Bk Vols 49,674; Per Subs 36; Talking Bks 1,099; Videos 1,656
Automation Activity & Vendor Info: (Acquisitions) SirsiDynix; (Cataloging) SirsiDynix; (Circulation) SirsiDynix
Special Services for the Deaf - Bks on deafness & sign lang
Open Mon-Thurs 10-6, Sat 10-5
Friends of the Library Group

J TIDEWATER COMMUNITY COLLEGE*, Portsmouth Campus Library, 120 Campus Dr, 23701. SAN 363-1958. Circulation Tel: 757-822-2130. Reference Tel: 757-822-2134. Web Site: libguides.tcc.edu/portsmouth-library. *Libr Coord,* Kendra Hawkins; E-mail: khawkins@tcc.edu; Staff 3 (MLS 3)
Founded 1961. Enrl 3,623; Fac 80; Highest Degree: Associate
Library Holdings: Bk Vols 50,385; Per Subs 125
Automation Activity & Vendor Info: (Cataloging) Ex Libris Group; (Circulation) Ex Libris Group; (Course Reserve) Ex Libris Group; (OPAC) Ex Libris Group
Wireless access
Open Mon-Thurs 7:30am-9pm, Fri 7:30-7, Sat 9-1

AM UNITED STATES NAVY, Naval Medical Center Portsmouth Library, Bldg 1, 4th Flr, 620 John Paul Jones Circle, 23708. SAN 363-2040. Tel: 757-953-5383. Reference Tel: 757-953-5384. FAX: 757-953-7533. E-mail: nmcplibraryservices@gmail.com. Web Site: portsmouth.tricare.mil/about-us/education/library-services. *Dept Head,* Lisa Eblen; Staff 4 (MLS 2, Non-MLS 2)
Library Holdings: Bk Titles 8,858; Bk Vols 32,117; Per Subs 110
Subject Interests: Allied sci, Dentistry, Med, Nursing
Automation Activity & Vendor Info: (Cataloging) LibraryWorld, Inc; (Circulation) LibraryWorld, Inc; (OPAC) LibraryWorld, Inc
Wireless access
Partic in OCLC Online Computer Library Center, Inc
Restriction: Authorized patrons, Open by appt only

POWHATAN

P POWHATAN COUNTY PUBLIC LIBRARY*, 2270 Mann Rd, 23139-5748. SAN 375-8710. Tel: 804-598-5670. FAX: 804-598-5671. E-mail: library@powhatanlibrary.net. Web Site: www.powhatanva.gov/247/Powhatan-County-Public-Library. *Dir,* Whitney Berriman; E-mail: director@powhatanlibrary.net
Founded 1988. Pop 28,000
Library Holdings: Bk Vols 54,000; Per Subs 20
Automation Activity & Vendor Info: (Cataloging) TLC (The Library Corporation); (Circulation) TLC (The Library Corporation); (OPAC) TLC (The Library Corporation)
Wireless access
Open Mon-Thurs & Sat 10-4
Friends of the Library Group

PRINCE WILLIAM

P PRINCE WILLIAM PUBLIC LIBRARIES*, Administrative Support Center, 13083 Chinn Park Dr, 22192. SAN 363-0544. Tel: 703-792-8150. FAX: 703-792-4875. E-mail: librarycommunications@pwcgov.org. Web Site: www.pwcgov.org/library. *Dir,* Deborah Wright; E-mail: dlwright@pwcgov.org; Staff 164 (MLS 47, Non-MLS 117)
Founded 1952. Pop 473,125; Circ 3,635,250
Library Holdings: Bk Vols 746,145
Special Collections: Geneaology & Local History Coll; Management & Government Information Center
Subject Interests: Local govt, Local hist
Automation Activity & Vendor Info: (Circulation) Innovative Interfaces, Inc
Wireless access
Partic in Mid-Atlantic Library Alliance; OCLC Online Computer Library Center, Inc
Special Services for the Deaf - TDD equip
Open Mon-Thurs 10-9, Fri & Sat 10-5
Branches: 12
BULL RUN LIBRARY, 8051 Ashton Ave, Manassas, 20109, SAN 374-6887. Tel: 703-792-4500. TDD: 703-792-4524. *Br Mgr,* Miriam Herrell; E-mail: mherrell@pwcgov.org
Special Services for the Deaf - TDD equip
Open Mon-Thurs 10-7, Fri & Sat 10-5
Friends of the Library Group
CENTRAL LIBRARY, 8601 Mathis Ave, Manassas, 20110, SAN 329-644X. Tel: 703-792-8360. *Br Mgr,* Rebecca Lowe; Tel: 703-792-8385, E-mail: rlowe@pwcgov.org
Special Services for the Deaf - TDD equip
Friends of the Library Group
CHINN PARK LIBRARY, 13065 Chinn Park Dr, 22192, SAN 374-4361. Tel: 703-792-4800.
Special Services for the Deaf - TDD equip
Open Mon-Thurs 10-7, Fri & Sat 10-5
Friends of the Library Group
DALE CITY LIBRARY, 4249 Dale Blvd, Dale City, 22193, SAN 326-8284. Tel: 703-792-5670. *Br Mgr,* Ginger Galaini; E-mail: galaini@pwcgov.org
Open Mon & Wed 10-5, Tues & Thurs Noon-7, Sat 10-2
DUMFRIES LIBRARY, 18115 Triangle Shopping Plaza, Dumfries, 22026, SAN 326-8306. Tel: 703-792-5678. *Br Mgr,* Judith Rodriguez; E-mail: jrodriguez@pwcgov.org
Open Mon & Wed 10-5, Tues & Thurs Noon-7, Sat 10-2
INDEPENDENT HILL LIBRARY, 14418 Bristow Rd, Manassas, 20112, SAN 328-9656. Tel: 703-792-5668. *Br Mgr,* Melanie Erhart; E-mail: MErhart@pwcgov.org
Open Mon & Wed 10-5, Tues & Thurs Noon-7, Sat 10-2

LAKE RIDGE LIBRARY, 2239 Old Bridge Rd, Woodbridge, 22192, SAN 326-8322. Tel: 703-792-5675. *Br Mgr,* Lynn Casey; E-mail: emcasey@pwcgov.org
Open Mon & Wed 10-5,Tues & Thurs Noon-7, Sat 10-2
MONTCLAIR LIBRARY, 5049 Waterway Dr, Dumfries, 22025. Tel: 703-792-8740.
Open Mon-Thurs 10-7, Fri & Sat 10-5
Friends of the Library Group
NOKESVILLE LIBRARY, 12993 Fitzwater Dr, Nokesville, 20181, SAN 326-8349. Tel: 703-792-5665. *Br Mgr,* Ursula Juarez-Wall; E-mail: UJuarez-Wall@pwcgov.org
Open Mon & Wed 10-5, Tues & Thurs Noon-7, Sat 10-2
POTOMAC LIBRARY, 2201 Opitz Blvd, Woodbridge, 22191, SAN 363-0579. Tel: 703-792-8330. *Br Mgr,* Robin Sofge; E-mail: rsofge@pwcgov.org
Open Mon-Thurs 10-7, Fri & Sat 10-5
Friends of the Library Group

PULASKI

P PULASKI COUNTY PUBLIC LIBRARY SYSTEM*, 60 W Third St, 24301. SAN 317-3887. Tel: 540-980-7770. Administration Tel: 540-994-2451. Automation Services Tel: 540-994-2453. FAX: 540-980-7775. Web Site: www.pclibs.org. *Libr Dir,* Sally Warburton; E-mail: swarburton@pclibs.org; *Youth Serv Librn,* Jenafer Coalson; *Pub Serv Coordr,* Justine Farlow; Tel: 540-994-2456, E-mail: jbfarlow@pclibc.org; *Tech Coordr,* Carol Smith; Staff 9 (MLS 3, Non-MLS 6)
Founded 1937. Pop 35,170; Circ 79,489
Subject Interests: Pulaski County local hist
Automation Activity & Vendor Info: (Acquisitions) TLC (The Library Corporation); (Cataloging) TLC (The Library Corporation); (Circulation) TLC (The Library Corporation); (ILL) OCLC; (OPAC) TLC (The Library Corporation)
Wireless access
Function: Art exhibits, Audiobks via web, Bk club(s), Bks on CD, Children's prog, Computers for patron use, E-Reserves, Electronic databases & coll, Family literacy, Free DVD rentals, Holiday prog, Home delivery & serv to seniorr ctr & nursing homes, ILL available, Internet access, Online cat, Online ref, Outreach serv, OverDrive digital audio bks, Photocopying/Printing, Preschool outreach, Preschool reading prog, Prog for adults, Prog for children & young adult, Ref serv available, Scanner, Senior outreach, Story hour, Summer & winter reading prog, Teen prog, Wheelchair accessible
Partic in New River Public Library Cooperative
Open Mon 8-8, Tues-Thurs 8-7, Fri 8-5, Sat 9-2
Restriction: Open to pub for ref & circ; with some limitations
Friends of the Library Group
Branches: 1
CHARLES & ONA B FREE MEMORIAL, 300 Giles Ave, Dublin, 24084, SAN 374-5295. Tel: 540-674-2856. FAX: 540-643-0111. *Br Mgr,* Aaron Jarrells; E-mail: ajarrells@pclibs.org; Staff 1.6 (MLS 0.3, Non-MLS 1.3)
Founded 1989. Pop 2,516
Function: Bks on cassette, Bks on CD, Children's prog, Computers for patron use, Electronic databases & coll, Free DVD rentals, ILL available, Online cat, Photocopying/Printing, Preschool outreach, Ref & res, Spoken cassettes & CDs, Spoken cassettes & DVDs, Summer reading prog, Tax forms, VHS videos
Open Mon & Tues 9-7, Wed-Fri 9-5, Sat 9-2
Restriction: Open to pub for ref & circ; with some limitations
Friends of the Library Group

PURCELLVILLE

CR PATRICK HENRY COLLEGE LIBRARY*, Ten Patrick Henry Circle, 20132. Tel: 540-441-8400. FAX: 540-441-8409. E-mail: library@phc.edu. Web Site: www.phc.edu/library. *Libr Dir,* Sara Pensgard; E-mail: sepensgard@phc.edu; *Pub Serv Librn,* Vickie Thornhill; E-mail: vsthornhill@phc.edu; *Libr Asst,* Jennifer Sillars; E-mail: jesillars@phc.edu
Founded 2000. Highest Degree: Bachelor
Wireless access
Open Mon-Thurs 8:30am-11pm, Fri 8:30-5:30, Sat 10-6 (Winter); Mon-Fri 8:30-5 (Summer)

QUANTICO

A LIBRARY OF THE MARINE CORPS*, Gray Research Ctr, 2040 Broadway St, 22134-5107. Tel: 703-784-4409. Reference Tel: 703-784-4411. FAX: 703-784-4306. Reference E-mail: mcu_grc_reference@usmcu.edu. Web Site: grc-usmcu.libguides.com/gray-research-center. *Dir,* Faith Kanno; *Head, Research Branch,* Greg Cina; E-mail: gregory.cina@usmcu.edu; *Head, Virtual Branch,* Monika K Maslowski; E-mail: monika.maslowski@usmcu.edu
Subject Interests: Intl political relations, Leadership, Marine Corps doctrine, Marine Corps hist, Mil art, Mil sci, Warfighting doctrine
Automation Activity & Vendor Info: (Acquisitions) Ex Libris Group; (Cataloging) Ex Libris Group; (Circulation) Ex Libris Group; (OPAC) Ex Libris Group; (Serials) Ex Libris Group
Wireless access
Partic in Consortium of Naval Libraries; Federal Library & Information Center Committee; Federal Library & Information Network; Military Education Coordination Conference

G UNITED STATES DEPARTMENT OF JUSTICE*, Federal Bureau of Investigation Library, One Range Rd, 22135. SAN 317-3895. Tel: 703-632-3200. FAX: 703-632-3214. E-mail: librarian@ic.fbi.gov. Web Site: www.fbi.gov/services/training-academy. *Head Librn,* Denise Campbell; Tel: 703-632-3443, E-mail: dmcampbell2@fbi.gov; *ILL, Pub Serv,* Cheryl Weidner; Tel: 703-632-3204, E-mail: cweidner@fbiacademy.edu; Staff 4 (MLS 3, Non-MLS 1)
Founded 1972
Library Holdings: AV Mats 2,000; Bk Vols 45,000; Per Subs 327
Special Collections: US Document Depository
Subject Interests: Criminal justice, Law enforcement, Police
Automation Activity & Vendor Info: (Acquisitions) EOS International; (Cataloging) EOS International; (Circulation) EOS International; (Course Reserve) EOS International; (OPAC) EOS International; (Serials) EOS International
Wireless access
Function: Online cat
Publications: Subject Bibliographies
Partic in OCLC Online Computer Library Center, Inc; World Criminal Justice Libr Network
Restriction: 24-hr pass syst for students only, By permission only, Not open to pub, Restricted access

RADFORD

P RADFORD PUBLIC LIBRARY*, 30 W Main St, 24141. SAN 317-3917. Tel: 540-731-3621. FAX: 540-731-4857. E-mail: library@radford.va.us. Web Site: www.radfordva.gov/1187/library. *Libr Dir,* Elizabeth Sensabaugh; E-mail: elizabeth.sensabaugh@radfordva.gov; Staff 7 (MLS 3, Non-MLS 4)
Founded 1941. Pop 15,940; Circ 141,233
Library Holdings: Bk Vols 7,500; Per Subs 65
Special Collections: Adult Low Reading Level Coll
Subject Interests: Genealogy, Local hist
Automation Activity & Vendor Info: (Circulation) TLC (The Library Corporation); (OPAC) TLC (The Library Corporation)
Wireless access
Partic in New River Public Library Cooperative
Open Mon-Thurs 9-8, Fri & Sat 10-5
Friends of the Library Group

C RADFORD UNIVERSITY, John Preston McConnell Library, 925 E Main St, 24142. (Mail add: PO Box 6881, 24142-6881), SAN 317-3909. Tel: 540-831-5471. Circulation Tel: 540-831-5364. Interlibrary Loan Service Tel: 540-831-6126. Reference Tel: 540-831-5696. FAX: 540-831-6138. E-mail: frontdesk@radford.edu. Web Site: www.radford.edu/libraries. *Univ Librn,* Jennifer Resor-Whicker; Tel: 540-831-6624, E-mail: jrwhicker@radford.edu; *Dir of Libr Operations,* Beth Johnson; Tel: 540-831-6648, E-mail: ejohnson82@radford.edu; *Head, Coll & Tech Serv,* Kay Johnson; Tel: 540-831-5703, E-mail: kjohnson497@radford.edu; *Head, Res Serv,* Alyssa Archer; Tel: 540-831-5688, E-mail: aarcher2@radford.edu
Founded 1913. Highest Degree: Doctorate
Automation Activity & Vendor Info: (Acquisitions) OCLC Worldshare Management Services; (Cataloging) OCLC Worldshare Management Services; (Circulation) OCLC Worldshare Management Services; (Course Reserve) OCLC Worldshare Management Services; (ILL) OCLC ILLiad; (Media Booking) OCLC Worldshare Management Services; (OPAC) OCLC Worldshare Management Services; (Serials) OCLC Worldshare Management Services
Wireless access
Partic in Virginia's Academic Library Consortium

RESTON

S METRON INC, Scientific Library, 1818 Library St, Ste 600, 20190. SAN 375-6858. Tel: 703-787-8700. FAX: 703-787-3518. Web Site: www.metsci.com. *Library Contact,* Wendy Wang
Library Holdings: Bk Titles 3,000
Wireless access
Restriction: Not open to pub

L ODIN, FELDMAN & PITTLEMAN LIBRARY*, 1775 Weihle Ave, Ste 400, 20190. SAN 377-3892. Tel: 703-218-2100. FAX: 703-218-2160. *Librn,* Halle Hoffman; Tel: 703-218-2362, E-mail: halle.hoffman@ofplaw.com

Library Holdings: Bk Vols 11,000; Per Subs 30
Partic in VA Law Librs Asn
Open Mon-Fri 8:30-6

G UNITED STATES GEOLOGICAL SURVEY LIBRARY*, Clarence King Library, Mail Stop 150, 12201 Sunrise Valley Dr, 20192. SAN 317-3968. Circulation Tel: 703-648-4301. Interlibrary Loan Service Tel: 703-648-6091. Administration Tel: 703-648-6207. Automation Services Tel: 703-648-6243. Information Services Tel: 703-648-4302. Toll Free Tel: 888-275-8747, Ext 5. FAX: 703-648-6373. E-mail: res_lib@usgs.gov. Web Site: library.usgs.gov/reslib.html. *Br Mgr,* Holly Nickle; *Digital Serv Librn,* Inez Bridgett; *Tech Serv,* Sally Roberts; Tel: 703-648-7182; Staff 11 (MLS 7, Non-MLS 4)
Founded 1882
Library Holdings: AV Mats 500; CDs 1,000; DVDs 5,000; e-books 1,000; e-journals 1,000; Microforms 10,000; Bk Vols 1,000,000; Per Subs 700
Special Collections: Gems & Minerals (George F Kunz Coll); Map Coll
Subject Interests: Cartography, Chem, Environ studies, Geol, Geothermal energy, Mineralogy, Oceanography, Paleontology, Petrology, Physics, Planetary geology, Remote sensing, Surveying, Water res, Zoology
Automation Activity & Vendor Info: (Acquisitions) EBSCO Online; (Cataloging) SirsiDynix; (Circulation) SirsiDynix; (OPAC) SirsiDynix; (Serials) SirsiDynix
Partic in OCLC Online Computer Library Center, Inc; Proquest Dialog

RICHMOND

SR BETH AHABAH MUSEUM & ARCHIVES*, 1109 W Franklin St, 23220. SAN 373-8396. Tel: 804-353-2668. E-mail: bama@bethahabah.org. Web Site: www.bethahabah.org. *Exec Dir,* William Obrochta; *Librn/Educator,* Tracy Herman; *Colls Mgr,* Shelly Berger; Staff 3 (Non-MLS 3)
Founded 1977
Library Holdings: Bk Titles 1,400
Special Collections: Beth Sholom Home; Congregation Beth Ahabah; Congregation Beth Shalome; Genealogy Coll; Hebrew Cemetery of Richmond; Jefferson Lakeside Country Club; Jewish Community Center; Jewish Community Federation of Richmond; Jewish Family Services; National Council of Jewish Women; Rabbi Ariel Goldburg Coll; Rabbi Edward N Calisch Coll
Subject Interests: Genealogy
Publications: Generations (Journal)
Open Mon-Thurs & Sun 10-3
Restriction: Non-circulating

S BRAILLE CIRCULATING LIBRARY FOR THE BLIND INC*, 2700 Stuart Ave, 23220. SAN 317-400X. Tel: 804-359-3743. E-mail: braillecirculatinglibrary@gmail.com. Web Site: braillecirculatinglibrary.org. *Exec Dir,* William Jeffries
Founded 1925
Library Holdings: Bk Titles 1,607
Subject Interests: Relig
Wireless access
Special Services for the Blind - Braille bks
Open Mon-Fri 9-4

C BRYANT & STRATTON COLLEGE LIBRARY*, Richmond Campus, 8141 Hull Street Rd, 23235. SAN 372-5332. Tel: 804-745-2444, Ext 333. FAX: 804-745-6884. Web Site: bryantstratton.libguides.com/richmond. *Librn,* Monica Hunasikatti; E-mail: mshunasikatti@bryantstratton.edu
Library Holdings: Audiobooks 70; e-books 150,000; Bk Titles 2,000; Bk Vols 3,500; Per Subs 45
Automation Activity & Vendor Info: (Cataloging) SirsiDynix-Enterprise; (Circulation) SirsiDynix-Enterprise
Wireless access
Open Mon-Thurs 9am-10pm, Fri 9-4

L CHRISTIAN & BARTON, LLP ATTORNEYS AT LAW*, Law Library, 901 East Cary St, Ste 1800, 23219. SAN 372-350X. Tel: 804-697-4100. FAX: 804-697-6112. Web Site: www.cblaw.com. *Law Librn,* Sarah Drye; E-mail: sdrye@cblaw.com
Library Holdings: e-books 3,500; Bk Vols 6,200; Per Subs 60
Restriction: Not open to pub

GL DIVISION OF LEGISLATIVE SERVICES REFERENCE CENTER*, General Assembly Bldg, 2nd Flr, 910 Capitol St, 23219. SAN 372-3496. Tel: 804-786-3591. FAX: 804-371-0169, 804-692-0625. Web Site: dls.virginia.gov/lrc. *Dir,* Ginny Edwards; E-mail: gedwards@dls.virginia.gov
Library Holdings: Bk Vols 8,000; Per Subs 150
Open Mon-Fri 8-5

S FEDERAL RESERVE BANK OF RICHMOND, Research Library, 701 E Byrd St, 23219. (Mail add: PO Box 27622, 23261-7622), SAN 317-4026. Tel: 804-697-5478, 804-697-8000. Web Site: www.richmondfed.org.
Founded 1920
Library Holdings: Bk Titles 10,000
Subject Interests: Banking, Econ, Finance
Function: ILL available, Telephone ref
Partic in OCLC Online Computer Library Center, Inc
Restriction: Open by appt only

SR FIRST BAPTIST CHURCH LIBRARY*, 2709 Monument Ave, 23220. SAN 370-2367. Tel: 804-355-8637, Ext 120. FAX: 804-359-4000. E-mail: library@fbcrichmond.org. Web Site: www.fbcrichmond.org/church-resources/library. *Chmn,* Barbara Watson; Staff 10 (MLS 1, Non-MLS 9)
Founded 1838
Library Holdings: Large Print Bks 32; Bk Vols 6,000; Per Subs 30
Special Collections: Church Archives
Subject Interests: Authors, Church hist
Automation Activity & Vendor Info: (Cataloging) Book Systems; (Circulation) Book Systems; (OPAC) Book Systems
Special Services for the Deaf - Bks on deafness & sign lang
Open Wed 4-7:30, Sun 8:15am-12:30pm
Restriction: Open to pub for ref & circ; with some limitations
Friends of the Library Group

S GRAND LODGE AF&AM OF VIRGINIA LIBRARY, MUSEUM & HISTORICAL FOUNDATION*, Allen E Roberts Masonic Library, 4115 Nine Mile Rd, 23223-4926. SAN 326-0585. Tel: 804-222-3110, Ext 220. FAX: 804-222-4253. E-mail: library@glova.org, library@grandlodgeofvirginia.org. Web Site: grandlodgeofvirginia.org/library-museum. *Librn,* Marie M Barnett; Tel: 804-222-3110, Ext 220. Subject Specialists: *Masonic hist,* Marie M Barnett; Staff 1 (Non-MLS 1)
Founded 1778
Jan 2022-Dec 2022. Mats Exp $6,923, Books $26, Per/Ser (Incl. Access Fees) $50, Presv $6,900. Sal $16,000
Library Holdings: AV Mats 60; CDs 170; DVDs 400; Microforms 150; Bk Titles 600; Bk Vols 3,500; Spec Interest Per Sub 65; Videos 25
Special Collections: Masonic Archival Materials (hist, transactions, bylaws); Masonic Museum objects
Subject Interests: Freemasonry
Automation Activity & Vendor Info: (Cataloging) Book Systems; (OPAC) Book Systems
Wireless access
Function: Res libr
Publications: The Virginia Masonic Herald, published by the Grand Lodge of Virginia (Quarterly)
Open Mon, Wed & Fri 9-12:30 & 1:30-4
Restriction: Mem only, Open to pub for ref only

L HUNTON ANDREWS KURTH LLP*, Law Library, Riverfront Plaza, E Tower, 951 E Byrd St, 23219-4074. SAN 317-4042. Tel: 804-788-8200. FAX: 804-788-8218. Web Site: www.huntonak.com. *Librn,* Frosty Owen; E-mail: fowen@HuntonAk.com
Founded 1901
Library Holdings: Bk Vols 65,000; Per Subs 150
Special Collections: Law Memoranda; Records & Briefs; Speeches of Henry W Anderson
Subject Interests: Acctg, Antitrust, Environ, Fed law, Labor law, Real estate, Utilities, Va Law
Automation Activity & Vendor Info: (Cataloging) SydneyPlus; (Circulation) SydneyPlus; (OPAC) SydneyPlus; (Serials) SydneyPlus
Partic in Proquest Dialog
Restriction: Staff use only

R INTERNATIONAL MISSION BOARD, SOUTHERN BAPTIST CONVENTION, Jenkins Research Library, 3806 Monument Ave, 23230-3932. SAN 317-4158. Tel: 804-219-1429. E-mail: jenkins.library@imb.org. Staff 2.5 (MLS 1, Non-MLS 1.5)
Founded 1960
Library Holdings: Bk Titles 12,800; Per Subs 40
Special Collections: Southern Baptist Missions History Coll
Subject Interests: Cross-cultural communication, Ethnolinguistic people groups, Hist of missions, Missiology
Automation Activity & Vendor Info: (Cataloging) Sydney Enterprise; (Circulation) Sydney Enterprise; (ILL) OCLC WorldShare Interlibrary Loan; (OPAC) Sydney Enterprise; (Serials) Sydney Enterprise
Partic in LYRASIS; OCLC Online Computer Library Center, Inc
Restriction: Internal use only, Lending to staff only, Researchers by appt only

J J SARGEANT REYNOLDS COMMUNITY COLLEGE LIBRARY DOWNTOWN CAMPUS-LIBRARY & INFORMATION SERVICES*, 700 E Jackson St, 2nd Flr, Rm 231, 23219-1543. (Mail add: PO Box 85622, 23285-5622), SAN 363-2407. Tel: 804-523-5211. Reference Tel: 804-523-5333. FAX: 804-523-5273. Web Site: www.reynolds.edu/library.

Dir, Hong Wu; Tel: 804-523-5324, E-mail: hwu@reynolds.edu; *Coordr,* Dr Loftan Miller; Tel: 804-523-5776, E-mail: lfmiller@reynolds.edu; *Circ,* Neale Foster; E-mail: nfoster@reynolds.edu; *Circ,* Rebekah Goodfellow; E-mail: rgoodfellow@reynolds.edu; *Ref (Info Servs),* Khalil Ahmed; E-mail: kahmed@reynolds.edu; Staff 7 (MLS 3, Non-MLS 4)
Founded 1973. Highest Degree: Associate
Library Holdings: Bks on Deafness & Sign Lang 80; CDs 50; Bk Vols 36,500; Per Subs 190; Spec Interest Per Sub 10; Videos 2,500
Special Collections: Business Administration Coll, AV, bks; Film/Video Coll; Health Science Coll
Automation Activity & Vendor Info: (Acquisitions) Ex Libris Group; (Cataloging) Ex Libris Group; (Circulation) Ex Libris Group; (Course Reserve) Ex Libris Group; (ILL) Ex Libris Group; (OPAC) Ex Libris Group
Partic in Richmond Academic Library Consortium; Virginia Commun Coll Syst; Virginia's Academic Library Consortium
Open Mon-Thurs 7:45am-9pm, Fri 7:45-5, Sat 8-12

J GOOCHLAND CAMPUS-LIBRARY & INFORMATION SERVICES*, 1851 Dickinson Rd, Goochland, 23285. (Mail add: PO Box 85622, 23285-5622), SAN 370-3525. Tel: 804-523-5442. Circulation Tel: 804-523-5419. FAX: 804-556-5750. *Coordr, Tech Serv,* Maureen Hady; E-mail: mhady@reynolds.edu; Staff 1 (MLS 1)
Highest Degree: Associate
Library Holdings: Bk Titles 2,900; Bk Vols 3,500; Per Subs 65
Subject Interests: Automotive, Hort
Automation Activity & Vendor Info: (Acquisitions) Ex Libris Group; (Cataloging) Ex Libris Group; (Circulation) Ex Libris Group; (Course Reserve) Ex Libris Group; (OPAC) Ex Libris Group

J PARHAM CAMPUS-LIBRARY & INFORMATION SERVICES*, Massey LTC, Rm 103, 1651 E Parham Rd, 23228. (Mail add: PO Box 85622, 23285-5622), SAN 363-2466. Tel: 804-523-5220. Reference Tel: 804-523-5329. FAX: 804-523-5102. Web Site: www.reynolds.edu/library. *Dir,* Hong Wu; Tel: 804-523-5324, E-mail: hwu@reynolds.edu; *Ref Librn,* Mary Denise Woetzel; Tel: 804-523-5329, E-mail: dwoetzel@reynolds.edu; *Circ,* Lisa Bishop; E-mail: ldbishop@reynolds.edu; *Circ,* Jill Brown; E-mail: jbbrown@reynolds.edu; Staff 11 (MLS 5, Non-MLS 6)
Founded 1974. Enrl 10,725; Fac 120; Highest Degree: Associate
Library Holdings: Bks on Deafness & Sign Lang 25; High Interest/Low Vocabulary Bk Vols 175; Bk Titles 32,000; Bk Vols 56,000; Per Subs 220; Spec Interest Per Sub 10
Subject Interests: Computer aided design, Electronics, Info syst, Legal assisting, Liberal arts, Semiconductors
Partic in LYRASIS; SouthWest Information Network Group; VA Tech Libr Syst; Virginia Commun Coll Syst
Publications: Off the Shelf
Open Mon-Thurs 7:45am-9pm, Fri 7:45-5, Sat 12-4

P THE LIBRARY OF VIRGINIA*, 800 E Broad St, 23219-8000. SAN 363-3128. Tel: 804-692-3500. Circulation Tel: 804-692-3547. Interlibrary Loan Service Tel: 804-692-3532. Reference Tel: 804-692-3777, 804-692-3888 (Archives). Administration Tel: 804-692-3535. FAX: 804-692-3594. Interlibrary Loan Service FAX: 804-692-3537. Reference FAX: 804-692-3556. E-mail: archdesk@lva.virginia.gov. Web Site: www.lva.virginia.gov, www.virginiamemory.com. *State Librn,* Sandra G Treadway; E-mail: sandra.treadway@lva.virginia.gov; *State Archivist,* Mike Strom; E-mail: mike.strom@lva.virginia.gov; *Dir, Info Tech Serv Div,* Paul Casalaspi; E-mail: paul.casalaspi@lva.virginia.gov; *Dir, Pub Serv & Outreach,* Gregg Kimball; E-mail: gregg.kimball@lva.virginia.gov; *Dep Dir, Coll & Prog,* John D Metz; E-mail: john.metz@lva.virginia.gov. Subject Specialists: *Hist of state libr, Va hist, Women's hist,* Sandra G Treadway; *Cultural & soc hist of South, Hist of South, Va hist,* Gregg Kimball; *Southern agri hist, Vernacular archit,* John D Metz; Staff 103 (MLS 36, Non-MLS 67)
Founded 1823. Pop 8,136,123
Library Holdings: AV Mats 376,312; CDs 1,226; DVDs 202; Electronic Media & Resources 38; Microforms 787,083; Music Scores 5,660; Bk Vols 841,605; Per Subs 636; Spec Interest Per Sub 48; Videos 972
Special Collections: Confederate Imprints; Genealogy Coll; Government & Politics Coll; Virginia & Southern History Coll; Virginia Broadsides; Virginia Maps; Virginia Newspapers; Virginia Picture Coll; Virginia Public Records; Virginia State Documents; Virginia-Related Sheet Music. State Document Depository; US Document Depository
Subject Interests: Archit, Art, Engraving, Govt, Local hist, Politics, Prints, Rare bks, Sheet music, Southern hist
Automation Activity & Vendor Info: (Acquisitions) Ex Libris Group; (Cataloging) Ex Libris Group; (Circulation) Ex Libris Group; (ILL) Ex Libris Group; (OPAC) Ex Libris Group; (Serials) Ex Libris Group
Wireless access
Function: Archival coll, Art exhibits, Computers for patron use, Electronic databases & coll, ILL available, Mail & tel request accepted, Online cat, Ref serv available, Summer & winter reading prog, Telephone ref, Wheelchair accessible
Publications: Bibliographical Resources; Broadside (Quarterly); Documentary Editions & Monographs; Historical & Genealogical Research Notes & Guides; Library Statistics; Newsletters (Monthly)
Partic in Association for Information & Image Management; LYRASIS; OCLC Online Computer Library Center, Inc; Richmond Academic Library Consortium; Virginia's Academic Library Consortium
Special Services for the Deaf - TTY equip
Special Services for the Blind - Low vision equip; Magnifiers; Reader equip; Screen enlargement software for people with visual disabilities; Screen reader software
Open Mon-Sat 9-5
Restriction: Closed stack

M J STEPHEN LINDSEY MEDICAL LIBRARY*, 1602 Skipwith Rd, 23229-5205. SAN 371-6163. Tel: 804-289-4728. FAX: 804-289-4960. *Med Librn,* Sue E Terminella; E-mail: sue.terminella@hcahealthcare.com; Staff 1 (MLS 1)
Founded 1980
Library Holdings: CDs 100; e-books 50; e-journals 20; Bk Titles 350; Bk Vols 500; Per Subs 5
Automation Activity & Vendor Info: (Cataloging) CyberTools for Libraries; (Discovery) OVID Technologies; (OPAC) CyberTools for Libraries; (Serials) Prenax, Inc
Wireless access
Restriction: Staff use only

G NATIONAL PARK SERVICE*, Richmond National Battlefield Park Headquarters Library, 3215 E Broad St, 23223. SAN 317-4077. Tel: 804-226-1981. FAX: 804-771-8522. Web Site: www.nps.gov/rich. *Historian,* Robert Krick; E-mail: bob_krick@nps.gov
Founded 1948
Library Holdings: Bk Vols 1,000
Subject Interests: The Civil War
Special Services for the Deaf - Captioned film dep
Open Mon-Fri 9-5

SR REVEILLE UNITED METHODIST CHURCH*, Reveille Memorial Library, 4200 Cary Street Rd, 23221. SAN 317-4093. Tel: 804-359-6041, Ext 121. FAX: 804-359-6090. Web Site: reveilleumc.org/library. *Librn,* Carol Ann Estes; E-mail: carolann.estes@comcast.net; Staff 3 (MLS 1, Non-MLS 2)
Founded 1960
Library Holdings: Braille Volumes 7; Large Print Bks 49; Bk Vols 9,143; Per Subs 7; Videos 131
Open Mon-Fri 8:30-4:30, Sun 9-11 & 12-12:30

P RICHMOND PUBLIC LIBRARY*, 101 E Franklin St, 23219. SAN 363-261X. Tel: 804-646-4256. Circulation Tel: 804-646-2554. Interlibrary Loan Service Tel: 804-646-4867. Reference Tel: 804-646-7223. Automation Services Tel: 804-646-2559. FAX: 804-646-7685. Web Site: www.richmondpubliclibrary.org. *Libr Dir,* Scott Firestine; E-mail: scott.firestine@richmondgov.com; *Dep Dir,* Clayton D Dishon, Jr; Staff 41 (MLS 11, Non-MLS 30)
Founded 1924. Pop 210,309; Circ 1,033,146
Library Holdings: AV Mats 9,170; e-books 2,592; Bk Vols 482,104; Videos 14,983
Special Collections: Rare Children's Books; Richmond Authors
Automation Activity & Vendor Info: (Acquisitions) SirsiDynix; (Cataloging) SirsiDynix; (Circulation) SirsiDynix; (ILL) SirsiDynix; (Media Booking) Right On Programs; (OPAC) SirsiDynix; (Serials) SirsiDynix
Wireless access
Open Mon-Wed 10-7, Thurs & Fri 10-6, Sat 10-5
Friends of the Library Group
Branches: 9
BELMONT BRANCH, 3100 Ellwood Ave, 23221, SAN 363-2644. Tel: 804-646-1139. FAX: 804-646-1105. E-mail: belmontbranch@richmondgov.com. *Br Mgr,* Barbara Booth; Staff 7 (MLS 2, Non-MLS 5)
Founded 1956. Circ 141,701
Library Holdings: AV Mats 3,277; Bk Vols 31,148
Open Mon & Wed 12-8, Tues, Thurs & Fri 10-6, Sat 10-5
Friends of the Library Group
BROAD ROCK, 4820 Warwick Rd, 23224, SAN 363-2679. Tel: 804-646-8488. FAX: 804-646-7014. E-mail: broadrockbranch@richmondgov.com. *Br Mgr,* Heather Mongomery; Staff 5.5 (MLS 2, Non-MLS 3.5)
Founded 1976. Circ 42,989
Library Holdings: AV Mats 2,132; Bk Vols 21,503
Open Mon & Wed 10-8, Tues, Thurs & Fri 10-6, Sat 10-5, Sun 1-5
Friends of the Library Group
EAST END, 1200 N 25th St, 23223, SAN 363-2709. Tel: 804-646-4474. FAX: 804-646-0104. E-mail: eastendbranch@richmondgov.com. *Br Mgr,* Adam Zimmerli; Staff 5 (MLS 1, Non-MLS 4)
Founded 1965. Circ 41,038

Library Holdings: AV Mats 1,259; Bk Vols 16,157
Open Mon-Fri 10-6, Sat 10-5
Friends of the Library Group

GINTER PARK, 1200 Westbrook Ave, 23227, SAN 363-2733. Tel: 804-646-1236. FAX: 804-646-3865. E-mail: ginterparkbranch@richmondgov.com. *Br Mgr,* Kerry Phillips; Staff 5.5 (MLS 1, Non-MLS 4.5)
Founded 1964. Circ 105,737
Library Holdings: AV Mats 2,047; Bk Vols 26,419
Open Mon & Wed 12-8, Tues, Thurs & Fri 10-6, Sat 10-5
Friends of the Library Group

HULL STREET, 1400 Hull St, 23224, SAN 328-7173. Tel: 804-646-8699. FAX: 804-646-8276. E-mail: hullstreetbranch@richmondgov.com. *Br Mgr,* Jennifer Deuell; Staff 5 (MLS 1, Non-MLS 4)
Founded 1986. Circ 57,125
Library Holdings: AV Mats 1,788; Bk Vols 18,267
Open Mon-Fri 10-6, Sat 10-5
Friends of the Library Group

NORTH AVENUE, 2901 North Ave, 23222, SAN 363-275X. Tel: 804-646-6675. FAX: 804-646-3768. E-mail: northavenuebranch@richmondgov.com. *Br Mgr,* Dianne Wilmore; Staff 5 (MLS 1, Non-MLS 4)
Founded 1983. Circ 69,782
Library Holdings: AV Mats 1,575; Bk Vols 20,495
Open Mon 12-8, Tues-Fri 10-6, Sat 10-5
Friends of the Library Group

PUBLIC LAW, 101 E Franklin St, 23219, SAN 372-3976. Tel: 804-646-6500. E-mail: lawlibrary@richmondgov.com.
Library Holdings: AV Mats 3; Bk Vols 640
Open Mon-Wed 10-7, Thurs & Fri 10-6, Sat 10-5
Friends of the Library Group

WEST END, 5420 Patterson Ave, 23226, SAN 363-2768. Tel: 804-646-1877. FAX: 804-646-3769. E-mail: westendbranch@richmondgov.com. *Br Mgr,* Lisa Crisman; Staff 6.5 (Non-MLS 6.5)
Founded 1978. Circ 186,910
Library Holdings: AV Mats 3,415; Bk Vols 48,606
Open Mon & Wed 10-8, Tues, Thurs & Fri 10-6, Sat 10-5
Friends of the Library Group

WESTOVER HILLS, 1408 Westover Hills Blvd, 23225, SAN 363-2792. Tel: 804-646-8833. FAX: 804-646-8714. E-mail: westoverhillsbranch@richmondgov.com. *Br Mgr,* Tori Nunnally; Staff 5.5 (MLS 1, Non-MLS 4.5)
Founded 1959. Circ 163,593
Library Holdings: AV Mats 3,482; Bk Vols 29,597
Open Mon & Wed 12-8, Tues, Thurs & Fri 10-6, Sat 10-5
Friends of the Library Group

R SAINT PAUL'S EPISCOPAL CHURCH LIBRARY, 815 E Grace St, 23219. SAN 317-414X. Tel: 804-643-3589. E-mail: stpauls@stpaulsrva.org. Web Site: www.stpaulsrva.org/connect-and-learn/adult-learning/st-pauls-library.
Founded 1963
Library Holdings: Bk Vols 2,500
Subject Interests: Relig studies
Restriction: Mem only, Not open to pub

L TROUTMAN SANDERS LLP*, Law Library, 1001 Haxall Point, 15th Flr, 23219. (Mail add: PO Box 1122, 23218-1122), SAN 372-3925. Tel: 804-697-1200. FAX: 804-697-1339. Web Site: www.troutmansanders.com. *Research Librn,* Position Currently Open; *Tech Serv Librn,* Ann James; E-mail: ann.james@troutmansanders.com; Staff 3 (MLS 2, Non-MLS 1)
Automation Activity & Vendor Info: (Cataloging) Sydney; (Circulation) Sydney; (OPAC) Sydney; (Serials) Sydney
Function: ILL available
Restriction: Co libr

R UNION PRESBYTERIAN SEMINARY LIBRARY*, Richmond Campus - William Smith Morton Library, 3401 Brook Rd, 23227. Tel: 804-278-4310. Reference Tel: 804-278-4333. Administration Tel: 804-278-4311. Web Site: library.upsem.edu. *Seminary Librarian,* Dr Christopher K Richardson; E-mail: crichardson@upsem.edu; *Dir, Pub Serv, Dir, Spec Coll & Archives, Electronic Serv,* Ryan Douthat; Tel: 804-278-4217, E-mail: rdouthat@upsem.edu; *Head, Tech Serv,* Irina Topping; Tel: 804-278-4314, E-mail: itopping@upsem.edu; *Instrul Res, Instrul Serv Librn,* Dora Rowe; Tel: 804-278-4324, E-mail: dora.rowe@upsem.edu; *Ref Librn,* Dr Robin McCall; E-mail: rmccall@upsem.edu; *Circ Supvr,* Lisa Janes; Tel: 804-278-4335, E-mail: ljanes@upsem.edu; *Acq Asst, ILL Spec,* Mengistu Lemma; Tel: 804-278-4337, E-mail: mlemma@upsem.edu; Staff 13 (MLS 6, Non-MLS 7)
Founded 1806. Enrl 170; Fac 22; Highest Degree: Doctorate
Library Holdings: AV Mats 59,507; CDs 3,548; DVDs 1,218; e-journals 225; Microforms 10,669; Bk Vols 272,917; Per Subs 724; Videos 3,417
Special Collections: Religion (Records of Synod of Virginia), micro; William Blake (Norfleet). Oral History
Subject Interests: Biblical studies, Christian educ, Christianity
Automation Activity & Vendor Info: (Acquisitions) SirsiDynix-WorkFlows; (Cataloging) SirsiDynix-WorkFlows; (Circulation) SirsiDynix-WorkFlows; (Course Reserve) SirsiDynix-Enterprise; (Discovery) SirsiDynix-Enterprise; (ILL) OCLC WorldShare Interlibrary Loan; (Media Booking) SirsiDynix-WorkFlows; (OPAC) SirsiDynix-Enterprise; (Serials) SirsiDynix-WorkFlows
Wireless access
Function: 24/7 Electronic res, 24/7 Online cat, 3D Printer, Archival coll, Art exhibits, Audiobks via web, Bks on cassette, Bks on CD, CD-ROM, Computer training, Computers for patron use, Distance learning, Doc delivery serv, E-Reserves, Electronic databases & coll, ILL available, Internet access, Magazines, Makerspace, Meeting rooms, Microfiche/film & reading machines, Movies, Music CDs, Online cat, Online info literacy tutorials on the web & in blackboard, Online ref, Orientations, Outside serv via phone, mail, e-mail & web, Photocopying/Printing, Printer for laptops & handheld devices, Ref & res, Ref serv available, Res assist avail, Res libr, Scanner, Spoken cassettes & CDs, Spoken cassettes & DVDs, Study rm, VHS videos, Wheelchair accessible, Workshops
Partic in Richmond Academic Library Consortium
Special Services for the Blind - Assistive/Adapted tech devices, equip & products
Open Mon-Thurs 8am-9pm, Fri 8-6, Sat 1-6
Restriction: Open to students, fac, staff & alumni, Researchers by appt only

S UNITED DAUGHTERS OF THE CONFEDERACY, Caroline Meriwether Goodlett Library, 328 N Arthur Ashe Blvd, 23220-4009. SAN 317-4174. Tel: 804-355-1636. FAX: 804-353-1396. E-mail: hqudc@rcn.com. Web Site: hqudc.org. *Archivist,* Teresa Roane; E-mail: archivist@hqudc.org
Founded 1957
Library Holdings: Bk Vols 2,000
Special Collections: Confederacy Coll, diaries, doc, letters, published bks, unpublished mat
Subject Interests: Civil War, Confederacy
Restriction: Open by appt only

GL UNITED STATES COURT OF APPEALS, Fourth Circuit Library, United States Courthouse, 1000 E Main St, 23219-3517. SAN 317-4182. Tel: 804-916-2319. Web Site: www.ca4.uscourts.gov/about-the-court/offices. *Librn,* Suzanne Corriell; Tel: 804-916-2322
Library Holdings: Bk Vols 100,000; Per Subs 300
Special Collections: US Document Depository
Automation Activity & Vendor Info: (Cataloging) SirsiDynix
Partic in LexisNexis; OCLC Online Computer Library Center, Inc
Open Mon-Fri 8:30-5
Restriction: Restricted access

C UNIVERSITY OF RICHMOND*, Boatwright Memorial Library, 261 Richmond Way, 23173. SAN 363-2946. Tel: 804-289-8876. FAX: 804-289-8757. Web Site: library.richmond.edu. *Univ Librn,* Kevin Butterfield; Tel: 804-289-8456; *Head, General Services,* Travis Smith; Tel: 804-289-8672, E-mail: tsmith3@richmond.edu; *Head Music Librn,* Linda Fairtile; Tel: 804-287-6849, E-mail: lfairtil@richmond.edu; *Librn, Emerging Web Tech,* Andy Morton; Tel: 804-287-6047, E-mail: amorton@richmond.edu; *Libr, Humanities & Soc Sci,* Marcia Whitehead; Tel: 804-289-8823, E-mail: mwhitehe@richmond.edu; *Bus Librn,* Carrie Ludovico; Tel: 804-287-6647, E-mail: cludovic@richmond.edu; *Sci Librn,* Melanie Hillner; Tel: 804-289-8262, E-mail: mhiller@richmond.edu; *Outreach Coordr,* Selah Coleman; E-mail: scoleman@richmond.edu; Staff 22 (MLS 18, Non-MLS 4)
Founded 1830. Enrl 3,983; Fac 347; Highest Degree: Master
Library Holdings: e-books 56,891; e-journals 110,000; Music Scores 16,508; Bk Titles 245,000; Bk Vols 500,000; Per Subs 2,232; Talking Bks 1,836; Videos 8,544
Special Collections: 19th-20th Century American Literature Coll; Virginia Baptists (Virginia Baptist Historical Society Coll); Virginia History Coll. US Document Depository
Subject Interests: Confederacy, Leadership studies, Relig
Automation Activity & Vendor Info: (Acquisitions) Ex Libris Group; (Cataloging) Ex Libris Group; (Circulation) Ex Libris Group; (Course Reserve) Ex Libris Group; (ILL) Ex Libris Group; (Media Booking) Ex Libris Group; (OPAC) Ex Libris Group; (Serials) Ex Libris Group
Wireless access
Partic in LYRASIS; Virginia Independent College & University Library Association; Virginia's Academic Library Consortium
Open Mon-Thurs 7am-1am, Fri 7am-10pm, Sat & Sun 10-10
Friends of the Library Group

Departmental Libraries:

MARY MORTON PARSONS MUSIC LIBRARY, Modlin Ctr for the Arts, 453 Westhampton Way, 23173, SAN 363-3004. Tel: 804-289-8286. FAX: 804-287-6899. Web Site: library.richmond.edu/music. *Head of Libr,* Dr Linda B Fairtile; Tel: 804-287-6849, E-mail: lfairtil@richmond.edu;

Music Libr Assoc, Melanie Armstrong; Tel: 804-287-6894, E-mail: marmstr3@richmond.edu; Staff 2 (MLS 1, Non-MLS 1)
Library Holdings: AV Mats 17,000; CDs 13,000; Music Scores 18,000; Bk Vols 12,000; Per Subs 44
Subject Interests: Ethnomusicology, Jazz, Music hist, Music performance, Music theory, Musicology, Popular music
Function: Audio & video playback equip for onsite use
Open Mon-Thurs 8am-11pm, Fri 8-5, Sat 2-5, Sun 2-11

CL WILLIAM T MUSE LAW LIBRARY, 203 Richmond Way, 23173, SAN 378-4061. Tel: 804-289-8637. Interlibrary Loan Service Tel: 804-287-6555. Reference Tel: 804-289-8685. Administration Tel: 804-289-8225. FAX: 804-289-8683. Administration FAX: 804-287-1845. E-mail: lawrefdesk@richmond.edu. Web Site: law.richmond.edu/library. *Assoc Dean, Info Tech,* Roger V Skalbeck; Tel: 804-289-8218, E-mail: rskalbeck@richmond.edu; *Cat & Syst Librn,* Mei Kiu Lo; Tel: 804-289-8226, E-mail: mlo@richmond.edu; *Computer Serv Librn,* Paul M Birch; Tel: 804-289-8222, E-mail: pbirch@richmond.edu; *Digital Res Librn,* Sam Cabo; Tel: 804-289-8217, E-mail: scabo@richmond.edu; *Access Serv,* Andrew Frank; E-mail: afrank@richmond.edu; Staff 17 (MLS 7, Non-MLS 10)
Founded 1870. Enrl 465; Fac 25; Highest Degree: Doctorate
Library Holdings: Bk Titles 190,000; Bk Vols 430,000; Per Subs 4,573
Special Collections: Judge Blackwell N Shelley (Retired Judge) Bankruptcy Decisions; Robert R Merhige (Retired Federal District Judge) Papers; Tokoyo War Crimes Trials (International Military Tribunal for the Far East Coll). US Document Depository
Automation Activity & Vendor Info: (Acquisitions) Ex Libris Group; (Cataloging) Ex Libris Group; (Circulation) Ex Libris Group; (Course Reserve) Ex Libris Group; (OPAC) Ex Libris Group; (Serials) Ex Libris Group
Function: Res libr
Partic in LYRASIS; Richmond Academic Library Consortium
Publications: Museletter (Newsletter); Research Guides Series
Open Mon-Thurs 7:30am-Midnight, Fri 7:30am-9pm, Sat 9-9, Sun 10am-Midnight

S THE VALENTINE*, 1015 E Clay St, 23219-1590. SAN 317-4212. Tel: 804-649-0711. FAX: 804-643-3510. E-mail: archives@thevalentine.org. Web Site: www.thevalentine.org. *Res Serv Mgr,* Michael Kaliris; Tel: 804-649-0711, Ext 342, E-mail: archives@thevalentine.org; Staff 2 (MLS 1, Non-MLS 1)
Founded 1898
Special Collections: Advertising Art (American Tobacco Co Scrapbooks), lithographs; Architectural Drawings; Art Coll, pen, pencil, watercolor & oil; Engravings (Views of Richmond, Scenic & Historical); Mary Wingfield Scott Photo Coll; Photography (Cook-Lancaster-Scott-Minton-Colonial Studios Coll), negatives, prints
Subject Interests: 19th Century advertising art, Artists, Hist of Richmond, Life of Richmond, Tobacco manufacture
Wireless access
Function: Archival coll, Audio & video playback equip for onsite use, Electronic databases & coll, Internet access, Online cat, Ref & res, Ref serv available, Res performed for a fee
Restriction: Limited access for the pub

SR VIRGINIA BAPTIST HISTORICAL SOCIETY & THE CENTER FOR BAPTIST HERITAGE & STUDIES LIBRARY*, 261 Richmond Way, University of Richmond, 23173. (Mail add: 410 Westhampton Way, UR 34, 23173), SAN 326-5986. Tel: 804-289-8434. FAX: 804-289-8953. E-mail: info@baptistheritage.org. Web Site: www.baptistheritage.org. *Exec Dir,* Dr Nathan L Taylor; *Ref (Info Servs),* Mrs Darlene Herod; *Operations Assoc, Spec,* Robbie Miller
Founded 1876
Library Holdings: Bk Vols 25,000
Special Collections: Oral History
Wireless access
Publications: The Virginia Baptist Register (Annual journal)
Open Mon-Fri 9-12 & 1-4:30
Friends of the Library Group

C VIRGINIA COMMONWEALTH UNIVERSITY LIBRARIES*, James Cabell Library, 901 Park Ave, 23284. (Mail add: PO Box 842033, 23284-2033), SAN 363-3071. Tel: 804-828-1111. Administration Tel: 804-828-1105. Toll Free Tel: 844-352-7399. E-mail: library@vcu.edu. Web Site: www.library.vcu.edu. *Dean of Libr, Univ Librn,* Irene M H Herold; E-mail: heroldi@vcu.edu; *Assoc Dean of Libr, Libr Dir,* Teresa L Knott; Tel: 804-828-0634, E-mail: tlknott@vcu.edu; *Assoc Dean for Colls, Discovery & Budget,* Tammy Sugarman; Tel: 804-827-3624, E-mail: tssugarman@vcu.edu; *Asst Dean for Organizational Dev,* Kathy Bradshaw; Tel: 804-828-1171, E-mail: akbradshaw@vcu.edu; *Dir, Communications, Pub Relations,* Sue Robinson; Tel: 804-828-0129, E-mail: srobinson26@vcu.edu; *Head, Acad Outreach,* Bettina Peacemaker; Tel: 804-828-8960, E-mail: bjpeacemaker@vcu.edu; *Head, Innovative Media,* Eric Johnson; Tel: 804-828-2802, E-mail: edmjohnson@vcu.edu; *Head, Teaching & Learning Serv,* Megan Hodge; Tel: 804-827-3910, E-mail: mlhodge@vcu.edu; *Interim Head, Info Services,* Teresa Doherty; Tel: 804-828-8658, E-mail: mtdoherty@vcu.edu; *Interim Head, University Archives,* Jodi Koste; Tel: 804-828-9898, E-mail: jlkoste@vcu.edu; Staff 59 (MLS 52, Non-MLS 7)
Founded 1838. Fac 59; Highest Degree: Doctorate
Library Holdings: e-books 912,011; e-books 912,011; Bk Vols 2,802,253
Special Collections: Book Art Coll (late 20th and 21st century, Womenï¿½s Studio Workshop repository); Comic Arts Coll (personal papers of Fred O Seibel, Charles Henry "Bill" Sykes, & Billy De Beck, Will Eisner Comic Industry Awards archives repository); Manuscripts (personal papers of 20th century Virginia women, African Americans, & LGBT communities, records of Richmond & Central Virginia businesses & organizations, papers & records of local & national literary figures & organizations, including Tom Robbins, Larry Levis, & Helena Lefroy Caperton); Rare Books (James Branch Cabell coll, Samuel Johnson & James Boswell coll, Betty Tisinger pop-up book coll, Scott Tilley Modern Library coll); University Archives (VCU & Richmond Professional Institute)
Automation Activity & Vendor Info: (Acquisitions) Ex Libris Group; (Cataloging) Ex Libris Group; (Circulation) Ex Libris Group; (Course Reserve) Ex Libris Group; (Discovery) Ex Libris Group; (ILL) OCLC ILLiad; (Serials) Ex Libris Group
Wireless access
Function: Res libr
Partic in Association of Southeastern Research Libraries; Richmond Academic Library Consortium; Virginia's Academic Library Consortium
Friends of the Library Group

Departmental Libraries:

CM TOMPKINS-MCCAW LIBRARY FOR THE HEALTH SCIENCES, Medical College of Virginia Campus, 509 N 12th St, 23298-0582, SAN 363-3098. Tel: 804-828-0636. Interlibrary Loan Service Tel: 804-828-0630. Automation Services Tel: 804-828-0032. Toll Free Tel: 844-352-7399. FAX: 804-828-6089. Web Site: www.library.vcu.edu/spaces-tech/health-sciences-library. *Dep Dir, Head, Research & Education,* Emily J Hurst; Tel: 804-828-0626, E-mail: ejhurst@vcu.edu; *Research & Education Librn,* Eric Brody; Tel: 804-828-2004, E-mail: ebrody@@vcu.edu; *Research & Education Librn,* Roy Brown; Tel: 804-828-1592, E-mail: rebrown@vcu.edu; *Research & Education Librn,* John W Cyrus; E-mail: cyrusjw@vcu.edu; *Research & Education Librn,* Rachel A Koenig; Tel: 804-828-1150, E-mail: rakoenig@vcu.edu
Special Collections: Manuscripts (personal papers of Virginia nurses, physicians, dentists, & other health care practitioners, records of health care professional organizations); Medical Artifacts Coll(19th & 20th century); Rare Books (Confederate medical imprints, Herman J. Flax coll); University Archives (VCU & Medical College of Virginia)
Subject Interests: Allied health, Dentistry, Med, Nursing, Pharm
Automation Activity & Vendor Info: (Acquisitions) Ex Libris Group; (Cataloging) Ex Libris Group; (Circulation) Ex Libris Group; (Course Reserve) Ex Libris Group; (Discovery) Ex Libris Group; (ILL) OCLC ILLiad; (OPAC) Ex Libris Group; (Serials) Ex Libris Group

P VIRGINIA DEPARTMENT FOR THE BLIND & VISION IMPAIRED*, Library & Resource Center, 395 Azalea Ave, 23227-3633. SAN 317-4298. Tel: 804-371-3661. Toll Free Tel: 800-552-7015. FAX: 804-371-3508. Web Site: www.vdbvi.org. *Dir,* Donna Cox; E-mail: donna.cox@dbvi.virginia.gov; Staff 5 (MLS 5)
Founded 1958
Library Holdings: Audiobooks 56,429; Braille Volumes 17,292; Large Print Bks 4,581; Talking Bks 56,429; Videos 572
Special Collections: Print Research Material on Blindness
Special Services for the Blind - Braille bks; Cassette playback machines; Textbks on audio-cassettes
Open Mon-Fri 8:15-5

G VIRGINIA DEPARTMENT OF HISTORIC RESOURCES, Archives-Research Library, 2801 Kensington Ave, 23221. SAN 323-6722. Tel: 804-367-2323, 804-482-6446. FAX: 804-367-2391. Web Site: www.dhr.virginia.gov/programs/dhr-archives. *Archivist,* Quatro Hubbard; Tel: 804-482-6102, E-mail: quatro.hubbard@dhr.virginia.gov. Subject Specialists: *Archaeology, Archit hist, Hist presv,* Quatro Hubbard; Staff 2 (Non-MLS 2)
Founded 1966
Library Holdings: Bk Titles 6,000; Per Subs 30
Special Collections: Ferol Brigg's Scrapbooks; Gilmer Confederate Engineer Maps; Historic Virginia Properties (Architectural Inventory); Wood's Maps of Virginia (1820 Series of Maps)
Subject Interests: Archaeology, Archit hist, Hist presv
Function: Archival coll
Publications: Virginia Unpublished Archaeological Reports
Special Services for the Deaf - TDD equip
Restriction: Non-circulating, Open by appt only

S VIRGINIA HISTORICAL SOCIETY LIBRARY*, 428 North Blvd, 23220. (Mail add: PO Box 7311, 23221-0311), SAN 317-4263. Tel: 804-340-1800. Reference Tel: 804-342-9677. FAX: 804-355-2399. Web Site: www.virginiahistory.org/collections. *Pres & Chief Exec Officer,* Jamie Bosket; *VPres, Coll,* Adam Scher; *Dir, Libr & Res Serv,* John McClure; E-mail: jmcclure@virginiahistory.org; *Dir, Tech Serv,* Paulette Schwarting; E-mail: paulette@virginiahistory.org; *Sr Archivist,* Eileen Parris; E-mail: eparris@virginiahistory.org
Founded 1831
Library Holdings: Bk Titles 70,000; Bk Vols 150,000; Per Subs 350
Special Collections: Confederate Imprints, newsp, sheet music; Maryland Steuart Coll, Confederate Weaponry & Military; Virginia Landscapes; Virginia Portraiture & Museum Objects
Subject Interests: Civil rights, Colonial hist, Confederate hist, Early Am hist, Local hist, Southern hist, State hist, Women's hist
Automation Activity & Vendor Info: (Cataloging) OCLC; (OPAC) Sydney
Wireless access
Publications: Document Monograph Series; Virginia Magazine of History & Biography; Virginia History and Culture
Partic in LYRASIS

S VIRGINIA MUSEUM OF FINE ARTS LIBRARY*, Margaret R & Robert M Freeman Library, 200 N Arthur Ashe Blvd, 23220-4007. SAN 317-428X. Tel: 804-340-1495. FAX: 804-340-1431. E-mail: library@vmfa.museum. Web Site: vmfa.museum/library. *Dir, Dir, Spec Coll,* Lee B Ceperich; Tel: 804-340-1496; *Sr Ref Librn,* Michelle Hevron; *Acq Librn, Programming Librn,* Kristen Alexander; *Ref Librn,* Door Williams; *Digital Serv, Mgr, Libr Syst,* Nick Curotto; Tel: 804-340-5523; *Photo Archivist,* Kate Kaluzny; *Asst Archivist,* Emily Johnson; *Cat, Libr Asst,* Zane Allison. Subject Specialists: *Arts, Design, Illustrated bks,* Lee B Ceperich; Staff 8 (MLS 7, Non-MLS 1)
Founded 1935
Library Holdings: CDs 29; DVDs 7; e-journals 20; Bk Titles 82,500; Bk Vols 143,500; Per Subs 251
Special Collections: American Arts (McGlothlin Coll); Art Deco, Art Nouveau (Lewis Coll & Kreuzer Coll); Arts & Crafts (Carol & Fred Brandt Coll); Contemporary Art (Geldzahler Coll); Decorative Arts (Karin Fellowes Coll); East Asian Art (Maxwell Coll); Everett Fahy Western European Art; Faberge Coll; German Expressionist Art (Fischer Coll); Numismatics (St John Tucker Coll); Oriental Arts (Weedon Coll & Coopersmith Coll); Paul Mellon Pre-1850 British Art Coll; Photography. Oral History; State Document Depository
Subject Interests: 20th Century art, African art, Am decorative arts, Ancient art, E Asian art, European art, Indian arts, Numismatics
Automation Activity & Vendor Info: (Acquisitions) ArchivesSpace; (Cataloging) ArchivesSpace; (Circulation) ArchivesSpace; (Discovery) Ex Libris Group; (ILL) OCLC; (OPAC) ArchivesSpace; (Serials) Ex Libris Group
Function: 24/7 Electronic res, 24/7 Online cat, Archival coll, Art exhibits, Audio & video playback equip for onsite use, Computers for patron use, For res purposes, Internet access, Magazines, Magnifiers for reading, Mail & tel request accepted, Online cat, Online ref, Outreach serv, Outside serv via phone, mail, e-mail & web, Photocopying/Printing, Ref & res, Ref serv available, Res assist avail, Res libr, Scanner, Visual arts prog
Partic in LYRASIS; OCLC Online Computer Library Center, Inc
Restriction: Circulates for staff only, Open by appt only
Friends of the Library Group

GL VIRGINIA STATE LAW LIBRARY, Supreme Court Bldg, 2nd Flr, 100 N Ninth St, 23219-2335. SAN 363-2822. Tel: 804-786-2075. FAX: 804-786-4542. E-mail: lawlibrary@vacourts.gov. Web Site: www.vacourts.gov/courtadmin/library/home. *State Law Librn,* Alexis Fetzer Sharp; *Librn,* J David Knight; *Librn,* Victoria W Levy; *Archivist/Librn,* Ashley N Vavra; *Libr Tech,* Janet E Holland; Staff 6 (MLS 4, Non-MLS 2)
Founded 1857
Library Holdings: Bk Vols 100,000; Per Subs 336
Special Collections: 18th Century Legal Treatises; English Reports (Nominative Reports, Mostly Originals). US Document Depository
Automation Activity & Vendor Info: (Cataloging) EOS International; (Circulation) EOS International; (ILL) OCLC; (OPAC) EOS International; (Serials) EOS International
Wireless access
Function: ILL available
Partic in Legal Information Preservation Alliance; NELLCO Law Library Consortium, Inc.
Special Services for the Deaf - TDD equip
Restriction: Authorized patrons, Borrowing requests are handled by ILL, Non-circulating of rare bks, Not open to pub, Restricted access, Restricted borrowing privileges

C VIRGINIA UNION UNIVERSITY*, L Douglas Wilder Library & Learning Resource Center, 1500 N Lombardy St, 23220. SAN 317-431X. Tel: 804-257-5822. Interlibrary Loan Service Tel: 804-257-5721. Reference Tel: 804-278-4122. Administration Tel: 804-257-5820. Web Site: www.vuu.edu/library. *Libr Dir,* Pamela Foreman; Tel: 804-257-5821, E-mail: pforeman@vuu.edu; *E-Res & Ser Librn,* Shanda Lemon; Tel: 804-278-4120; *Archivist/Librn,* Selicia Allen; Tel: 804-257-4117, E-mail: sngregory@vuu.edu; *Tech Serv Librn,* Sara Marrin; Tel: 804-257-5823, E-mail: semarrin@vuu.edu; *Acq, ILL,* Pearl Adzei-Stonnes; Tel: 804-278-4112; *Circ Asst,* Gary Tyler; Tel: 804-257-5690, E-mail: gatyler@vuu.edu; Staff 12 (MLS 7, Non-MLS 5)
Founded 1865. Enrl 1,318; Fac 84; Highest Degree: Doctorate
Library Holdings: AV Mats 4,379; e-books 67,920; Bk Titles 104,790; Bk Vols 128,804; Per Subs 60
Special Collections: L Douglas Wilder Coll; Sampson Watson Coll; Spencer Coll
Subject Interests: Educ, Journalism, Math, Philos, Psychol, Relig
Automation Activity & Vendor Info: (Acquisitions) SirsiDynix; (Cataloging) SirsiDynix; (Circulation) SirsiDynix; (ILL) SirsiDynix; (Serials) SirsiDynix
Wireless access
Function: Prof lending libr
Publications: The Resource (Newsletter)
Partic in OCLC Online Computer Library Center, Inc; Richmond Academic Library Consortium; Virginia Independent College & University Library Association; Virginia's Academic Library Consortium; Washington Theological Consortium
Open Mon-Thurs 8am-Midnight, Fri 8am-10pm, Sat 8-4, Sun Noon-Midnight

ROANOKE

P BOTETOURT COUNTY LIBRARIES*, 28 Avery Row, 24012. SAN 324-5179. Tel: 540-928-2900. E-mail: bocolibraries@botetourtva.gov. Web Site: www.botetourtva.gov/161/Libraries. *Libr Dir,* Julie Phillips; E-mail: jphillips@botetourtva.gov; Staff 10 (MLS 2, Non-MLS 8)
Founded 1979. Pop 24,270; Circ 183,052
Library Holdings: CDs 1,000; Bk Vols 115,324; Per Subs 220; Talking Bks 4,400; Videos 9,600
Automation Activity & Vendor Info: (Cataloging) OCLC; (Circulation) SirsiDynix; (ILL) OCLC; (OPAC) SirsiDynix
Wireless access
Partic in LYRASIS
Open Mon, Tues & Thurs 9-9, Wed 9-6, Fri 9-5, Sat 9-2
Friends of the Library Group
Branches: 3
BUCHANAN BRANCH, 19795 Main St, Buchanan, 24066. (Mail add: PO Box 799, Buchanan, 24066), SAN 324-6248. Tel: 540-254-2538. FAX: 540-254-1793. *Br Mgr,* Janet Buttram; Staff 2 (Non-MLS 2)
Open Mon & Thurs 9-7, Tues, Wed & Fri 9-5, Sat 9-1
Friends of the Library Group
EAGLE ROCK LIBRARY, 55 Eagles Nest Dr, Eagle Rock, 24085. Tel: 540-928-2800. *Mgr,* Jamie Duvall
Open Mon-Thurs 9-7, Fri 9-5, Sat 9-1
FINCASTLE BRANCH, 11 Academy St, Fincastle, 24090-3316. (Mail add: PO Box 129, Fincastle, 24090-0129), SAN 324-623X. Tel: 540-473-8339. FAX: 540-473-1107. *Br Mgr,* Paige Ware; Staff 2 (Non-MLS 2)
Open Mon & Thurs 9-9, Tues & Wed 9-6, Fri 9-5, Sat 9-1
Friends of the Library Group
Bookmobiles: 1

M CARILION ROANOKE MEMORIAL HOSPITAL*, Health Sciences Library, 1906 Belleview Ave, 24014-1838. SAN 324-6329. Tel: 540-981-8039. *Librn,* Jane Burnette; E-mail: ljburnette@carilionclinic.org
Automation Activity & Vendor Info: (Cataloging) EOS International; (Circulation) EOS International; (Discovery) EBSCO Discovery Service; (OPAC) EOS International
Wireless access
Partic in Medical Library Association; Mid-Atlantic Chapter-Med Libr Asn; National Network of Libraries of Medicine Region 1; Southwestern Virginia Health Information Librarians
Open Mon-Fri 8-4:30
Restriction: Circulates for staff only

S HISTORY MUSEUM OF WESTERN VIRGINIA*, Watts Library Research Center, One Market Sq, 3rd Flr, 24011. (Mail add: PO Box 1904, 24008-1904), SAN 329-093X. Tel: 540-342-5770. FAX: 540-224-1256. Web Site: roanokehistory.org. *Registrar,* Linda Steele; Tel: 540-224-1207, E-mail: registrar@vahistorymuseum.org
Library Holdings: Bk Vols 1,300
Special Collections: Breckinridge, Preston, Trout, Borden, Grant, Tayloe, Deyerle, Campbell, Roanoke Hist, Roanoke Photos, Watts, Eubank
Restriction: Open by appt only

C HOLLINS UNIVERSITY, Wyndham Robertson Library, 7950 E Campus Dr, 24020. (Mail add: PO Box 9000, 24020-1000), SAN 317-3143. Tel: 540-362-7465. Interlibrary Loan Service Tel: 540-362-6239. Administration

Tel: 540-362-6232. FAX: 540-362-6756. E-mail: library@hollins.edu. Web Site: www.hollins.edu/library. *Univ Librn,* Luke Vilelle; E-mail: lvilelle@hollins.edu; *Asst Univ Librn,* Rebecca Seipp; Tel: 540-362-6328, E-mail: seipprl@hollins.edu; *Discovery Librn,* James Miller; Tel: 540-362-6653, E-mail: millerjc@hollins.edu; *Info Literacy & Outreach Librn,* Maryke Barber; Tel: 540-362-6592, E-mail: mbarber@hollins.edu; *Coordr, Cat & Acq, Metadata Librn,* Coleman Holth; Tel: 540-362-6240, E-mail: holthct@hollins.edu; *Archivist, Spec Coll Librn,* Isabel Folck; Tel: 540-362-6237, E-mail: folckil@hollins.edu; *Circ Coordr,* Jessi Hood; Tel: 540-362-6090, E-mail: hoodja@hollins.edu; *Interlibrary Serv Coordr,* Shawna Battle; E-mail: battlesa@hollins.edu; Staff 9.5 (MLS 6, Non-MLS 3.5)
Founded 1842. Enrl 946; Fac 82; Highest Degree: Master
Special Collections: Children's Literature (Margaret Wise Brown Coll); Hollins Authors Coll; Hollins University Archives; Incunabula Coll; Paper-Making Coll; Printing Coll; Private Presses
Subject Interests: Art, Behav sci, Life, Lit, Music, Philos, Relig, Soc sci, Women studies
Automation Activity & Vendor Info: (Acquisitions) Ex Libris Group; (Cataloging) Ex Libris Group; (Circulation) Ex Libris Group; (Course Reserve) Ex Libris Group; (ILL) OCLC ILLiad; (OPAC) Ex Libris Group; (Serials) Ex Libris Group
Wireless access
Partic in LYRASIS; Virginia Independent College & University Library Association; Virginia's Academic Library Consortium

CM RADFORD UNIVERSITY*, Carilion (RUC) Library, 101 Elm Ave SE, 5th Flr, 24013. SAN 327-9146. Tel: 540-831-2272. E-mail: ruclibrary@radford.edu. Web Site: www.radford.edu/content/library/RUC-library.html. *Dean,* Paul Orkiszewski; Tel: 540-831-5471, E-mail: porkiszewski@radford.edu; *Head Librn,* Jamie Price; Tel: 540-831-1661, E-mail: jprice13@radford.edu; *Outreach & Instruction Librn,* Mary Catherine Santoro; Tel: 540-831-1823, E-mail: msantoro@radford.edu; *Circ Coordr,* Rhiannon Cooke; Tel: 540-831-1875, E-mail: recooke@radford.edu; *Tech Serv Assoc,* Crystal Dent; E-mail: cdent1@radford.edu; Staff 5 (MLS 3, Non-MLS 2)
Library Holdings: Bk Titles 3,500; Per Subs 100
Subject Interests: Allied health, Med, Nursing
Wireless access
Open Mon-Thurs 7:30-6, Fri 7:30-5, (Winter); Mon-Fri 8-5 (Summer)

P ROANOKE COUNTY PUBLIC LIBRARY*, 6303 Merriman Rd, 24018-6496. SAN 363-3187. Tel: 540-772-7507. Administration Tel: 540-776-7327. FAX: 540-989-3129. Reference FAX: 540-772-2131. E-mail: circulation@roanokecountyva.gov. Web Site: www.rocolibrary.org. *Dir,* Jim Blanton; E-mail: jblanton@roanokecountyva.gov; *Asst Dir,* Toni Cox; E-mail: trcox@roanokecountyva.gov; *Head, Ref,* David Webb; *Sr Br Librn,* Mike Hibben; E-mail: mhibben@roanokecountyva.gov; *Circ Mgr,* Cheryl Wagner; Staff 14 (MLS 14)
Founded 1945
Library Holdings: e-journals 115; Microforms 559; Per Subs 381
Subject Interests: Local hist, Va
Automation Activity & Vendor Info: (Cataloging) SirsiDynix; (Circulation) SirsiDynix; (ILL) OCLC; (OPAC) SirsiDynix
Wireless access
Function: 24/7 Electronic res, 24/7 Online cat, 3D Printer, Activity rm, Adult bk club, Audiobks via web, Bk club(s), Bks on CD, Children's prog, Computer training, Computers for patron use, E-Readers, Electronic databases & coll, Free DVD rentals, Genealogy discussion group, Holiday prog, Home delivery & serv to seniorr ctr & nursing homes, ILL available, Internet access, Life-long learning prog for all ages, Magazines, Mango lang, Microfiche/film & reading machines, Movies, Online cat, Online ref, Outreach serv, OverDrive digital audio bks, Passport agency, Photocopying/Printing, Preschool outreach, Preschool reading prog, Prog for adults, Prog for children & young adult, Ref & res, Ref serv available, Res assist avail, Scanner, Senior computer classes, Senior outreach, Serves people with intellectual disabilities, Story hour, Study rm, Summer & winter reading prog, Summer reading prog, Tax forms, Teen prog, Wheelchair accessible, Winter reading prog
Open Mon-Thurs 10-8, Fri 10-6, Sat 10-5, Sun 1-5
Friends of the Library Group
Branches: 5
BENT MOUNTAIN BRANCH, 10148 Tinsley Lane, Bent Mountain, 24059. Tel: 540-929-4700. FAX: 540-929-4700. E-mail: bentmtnlib@roanokecountyva.gov. *Sr Libr Asst,* Kelli Murrie; E-mail: kellimurrie@roanokecountyva.gov
Open Mon & Fri 1-5, Tues & Thurs 3-7, Wed 10-5, Sat 10-2
Friends of the Library Group
GLENVAR, 3917 Daugherty Rd, Salem, 24153. SAN 363-3241. Tel: 540-387-6163. FAX: 540-380-3951. E-mail: rcplglenvar@roanokecountyva.gov. *Asst Dir,* Toni Cox; E-mail: trcox@roanokecountyva.gov
Open Mon-Thurs 10-8, Fri & Sat 10-5
Friends of the Library Group
HOLLINS, 6624 Peters Creek Rd, 24019. SAN 363-3276. Tel: 540-561-8024. FAX: 540-563-8902. E-mail: rcplhollins@roanokecountyva.gov. *Br Librn,* John Vest
Open Mon-Thurs 10-8, Fri & Sat 10-5, Sun 1-5
Friends of the Library Group
MOUNT PLEASANT, 2918 JAE Valley Rd, 24014. SAN 326-8292. Tel: 540-777-8760. FAX: 540-427-1030. E-mail: mtpleasantlib@roanokecountyva.gov.
Open Mon 10-6, Tues & Thurs 2-8, Wed 2-6, Fri 1-5, Sat 10-2
Friends of the Library Group
VINTON BRANCH, 300 S Pollard St, Vinton, 24179. SAN 363-3306. Tel: 540-857-5043. FAX: 540-344-3285. E-mail: rcplvinton@roanokecountyva.gov. *Br Librn,* Kimberly Burnette-Dean; E-mail: kburnette@roanokecountyva.gov
Open Mon-Thurs 10-8, Fri & Sat 10-5, Sun 1-5
Friends of the Library Group

C ROANOKE HIGHER EDUCATION CENTER LIBRARY*, 108 N Jefferson St, Ste 216, 24016. Tel: 540-767-6011. FAX: 540-767-6012. E-mail: library@education.edu. Web Site: www.education.edu/student-services/library. *Libr Assoc,* Jessica Yopp; Tel: 540-767-6016, E-mail: jessica.yopp@education.edu; Staff 3 (MLS 1, Non-MLS 2)
Founded 2000. Enrl 3,000; Highest Degree: Doctorate
Library Holdings: Bk Titles 4,500
Subject Interests: Distance educ
Automation Activity & Vendor Info: (Cataloging) OCLC Connexion; (Circulation) Innovative Interfaces, Inc; (ILL) OCLC Tipasa; (OPAC) Innovative Interfaces, Inc; (Serials) SerialsSolutions
Wireless access
Partic in Virginia's Academic Library Consortium
Open Mon-Fri 8-5

P ROANOKE PUBLIC LIBRARIES*, 706 S Jefferson St, 24016-5191. SAN 363-3330. Tel: 540-853-2473. Interlibrary Loan Service Tel: 540-853-2477. FAX: 540-853-1781. TDD: 540-853-2641. E-mail: main.library@roanokeva.gov. Web Site: www.roanokegov.com/library. *Dir,* Sheila Umberger; E-mail: Sheila.Umberger@roanokeva.gov; *Head, Tech Serv,* Lisa Bannister; *Pub Serv Librn,* Nathan Flinchum; *Youth Serv Coordr,* Amber Yopp; Staff 16 (MLS 12, Non-MLS 4)
Founded 1921. Pop 100,600
Library Holdings: Bk Vols 339,685; Per Subs 905
Subject Interests: Civil War, Genealogy, Local hist, Virginiana
Automation Activity & Vendor Info: (Acquisitions) SirsiDynix; (Circulation) SirsiDynix; (Serials) SirsiDynix
Special Services for the Deaf - TDD equip
Open Mon, Tues & Thurs 10-8, Wed 10-6, Fri & Sat 10-5
Friends of the Library Group
Branches: 8
GAINSBORO, 15 Patton Ave NW, 24016. SAN 363-3365. Tel: 540-853-2540. FAX: 540-853-1155. E-mail: gainsborolibrary@gmail.com. *Br Mgr,* Megan Mizak; Staff 3 (MLS 1, Non-MLS 2)
Library Holdings: Bk Vols 25,866
Subject Interests: African-Am hist
Open Mon-Wed 10-6, Thurs 10-8, Fri & Sat 10-5
JACKSON PARK, 1101 Morningside St SE, 24013-2515. SAN 363-339X. Tel: 540-853-2640. FAX: 540-853-1156. *Br Mgr,* Nathan Slinchum; E-mail: nathan.slinchum@roanokeva.gov; Staff 1 (Non-MLS 1)
Library Holdings: Bk Vols 30,248
Open Mon 10-8, Tues & Thurs 10-6, Fri & Sat 10-5
Friends of the Library Group
LAW LIBRARY, City of Roanoke Courthouse, 315 Church Ave SW, Ste B, 24016. SAN 320-2720. Tel: 540-853-2268. FAX: 540-853-5474. *Librn,* Joseph Klein; Staff 1 (MLS 1)
Founded 1925
Library Holdings: Bk Vols 19,195
Open Mon 8-4:30, Tues-Fri 8-12
MELROSE, 2502 Melrose Ave NW, Suite D, 24017. Tel: 540-853-2648. FAX: 540-853-1030. *Librn,* Brown Amanda; Staff 1 (MLS 1)
Library Holdings: Bk Vols 27,500
Open Mon & Tues 10-6, Wed 10-8, Fri & Sat 10-5
RALEIGH COURT, 2112 Grandin Rd SW, 24015. SAN 363-3454. Tel: 540-853-2240. FAX: 540-853-1783. ; Staff 1 (MLS 1)
Library Holdings: Bk Vols 49,989
Open Tues & Thurs 10-8, Wed 10-6
WILLIAMSON ROAD, 3837 Williamson Rd NW, 24012. SAN 363-3489. Tel: 540-853-2340. FAX: 540-853-1065. *Librn,* Antoinette Vinciguerra; E-mail: antoinette.vinciguerra@roanokeva.gov; Staff 1 (MLS 1)
Library Holdings: Bk Vols 41,886
Open Tues & Thurs 10-6, Wed 10-8, Fri & Sat 10-5
Bookmobiles: 1

S TAUBMAN MUSEUM OF ART*, Fine Arts Library, 110 Salem Ave SE, 24011. SAN 317-4352. Tel: 540-342-5760. FAX: 540-342-5798. Web Site: www.taubmanmuseum.org. *Registrar,* Mary D LaGue; E-mail: mlague@taubmanmuseum.org
Founded 1952
Library Holdings: Bk Vols 2,500
Subject Interests: Fine arts

J VIRGINIA WESTERN COMMUNITY COLLEGE*, Brown Library, 3095 Colonial Ave SW, 24015. SAN 317-4379. Tel: 540-857-7303. Circulation Tel: 540-857-6941. FAX: 540-857-6058. E-mail: library@virginiawestern.edu. Web Site: www.virginiawestern.edu/library. *Coll Develop, Educ Res Librn,* Dale Dulaney; Tel: 540-857-7438, E-mail: ddulaney@virginiawestern.edu; *Outreach Serv Librn, Tech Serv,* Marci Myers; Tel: 540-857-6693, E-mail: mmyers@virginiawestern.edu; Staff 5 (MLS 3, Non-MLS 2)
Founded 1966. Enrl 9,000; Highest Degree: Associate
Library Holdings: Bk Vols 80,000; Per Subs 200
Automation Activity & Vendor Info: (Cataloging) Ex Libris Group; (Circulation) Ex Libris Group
Wireless access
Partic in Virginia Commun Coll Syst; Virginia's Academic Library Consortium
Open Mon-Thurs 8-8, Fri 8-5, Sat 9-1

L WOODS ROGERS, PLC, Law Library, (Formerly Wood Rogers Vandeventer Black PLC), Wells Fargo Tower, 10 S Jefferson St, Ste 1800, 24011. SAN 372-333X. Tel: 540-983-7600. FAX: 540-983-7711. E-mail: library@woodsrogers.com. *Library Contact,* Tanya Graybeal; Tel: 540-983-7623; *Support Serv Coordr,* Benson Powell; Staff 2 (MLS 2)
Founded 1892
Library Holdings: Electronic Media & Resources 25; Bk Vols 3,000; Per Subs 50; Spec Interest Per Sub 50; Videos 100
Wireless access

ROCKY MOUNT

P FRANKLIN COUNTY PUBLIC LIBRARY, 355 Franklin St, 24151. SAN 317-4387. Tel: 540-483-3098. FAX: 540-483-6652. Web Site: library.franklincountyva.org. *Dir,* Rebecca Ventola; E-mail: rebecca.ventola@franklincountyva.gov; *Ch, YA Librn,* Dorothy Anderson; E-mail: dorothy.anderson@franklincountyva.gov; *Circ,* May Nickolopoulos; E-mail: may.nick@franklincountyva.gov; *Mobile Media Servs,* Wayne Keith; E-mail: wayne.keith@franklincountyva.gov; Staff 6 (MLS 1, Non-MLS 5)
Founded 1975. Pop 54,480; Circ 190,000
Library Holdings: Audiobooks 4,588; DVDs 10,614; e-books 13,894; Bk Vols 121,140; Per Subs 220
Subject Interests: Local hist
Automation Activity & Vendor Info: (Cataloging) Book Systems; (Circulation) Book Systems; (OPAC) Book Systems
Wireless access
Function: 24/7 Electronic res, 24/7 Online cat, 24/7 wireless access, 3D Printer, Accelerated reader prog, Activity rm, Adult bk club, Art exhibits, Art programs, Audiobks on Playaways & MP3, Audiobks via web, Bks on cassette, Bks on CD, Chess club, Children's prog, Computer training, Computers for patron use, Electronic databases & coll, Extended outdoor wifi, Family literacy, Free DVD rentals, Genealogy discussion group, Holiday prog, Home delivery & serv to seniorr ctr & nursing homes, Homebound delivery serv, ILL available, Internet access, Life-long learning prog for all ages, Magazines, Meeting rooms, Microfiche/film & reading machines, Movies, Museum passes, Music CDs, Notary serv, Online cat, Outreach serv, OverDrive digital audio bks, Photocopying/Printing, Preschool outreach, Prog for adults, Prog for children & young adult, Senior computer classes, Senior outreach, STEM programs, Story hour, Study rm, Summer & winter reading prog, Summer reading prog, Tax forms, Teen prog, Wheelchair accessible, Winter reading prog, Workshops
Open Mon, Wed & Fri 9-5, Tues & Thurs 9-7, Sat 9-1
Friends of the Library Group
Branches: 1
WESTLAKE BRANCH, 84 Westalake Rd, Ste 109, Hardy, 24101. Tel: 540-483-3098, Ext 2, 540-719-2383. Web Site: library.franklincountyva.org/westlake-branch-library. *Circ Desk Mgr,* Leah Broholm; E-mail: leah.broholm@franklincountyva.gov
Open Mon, Wed & Fri 9-5, Tues & Thurs 9-7, Sat 9-1
Bookmobiles: 1

RUSTBURG

P CAMPBELL COUNTY PUBLIC LIBRARY*, 684 Village Hwy, Lower Level, 24588. SAN 317-4409. Tel: 434-332-9560. FAX: 434-332-9697. E-mail: rb@co.campbell.va.us. Web Site: campbellcountylibraries.org. *Libr Dir,* Jordan Welborn; E-mail: ljwelborn@co.campbell.va.us; *Br Mgr,* Lyzzie King; E-mail: edking@co.campbell.va.us; Staff 22 (MLS 4, Non-MLS 18)
Founded 1968. Pop 51,078; Circ 94,510
Library Holdings: CDs 8,630; Bk Titles 87,680; Bk Vols 153,400; Per Subs 285; Talking Bks 3,524; Videos 2,347
Subject Interests: Genealogy
Automation Activity & Vendor Info: (Acquisitions) TLC (The Library Corporation); (Cataloging) TLC (The Library Corporation); (Circulation) TLC (The Library Corporation)
Wireless access
Function: ILL available
Publications: Newsletter (Quarterly)
Partic in LYRASIS; SouthWest Information Network Group
Open Mon & Wed-Fri 9-5:30, Tues 9:30-8, Sat 9:30-1
Friends of the Library Group
Branches: 3
PATRICK HENRY MEMORIAL, 204 Lynchburg Ave, Brookneal, 24528, SAN 377-0540. Tel: 434-376-3363. FAX: 434-376-1111. E-mail: phml@co.campbell.va.us. Web Site: campbellcountylibraries.org/locations/brookneal. *Br Mgr,* Cyndal Nash; E-mail: cwnash@co.campbell.va.us
Founded 1938. Pop 4,000; Circ 16,424
Open Tues 10-7, Wed & Thurs 10-5, Sat 10-2
Friends of the Library Group
STAUNTON RIVER MEMORIAL, 500 Washington St, Altavista, 24517, SAN 328-7343. Tel: 434-369-5140. FAX: 434-369-1723. E-mail: srml@co.campbell.va.us. Web Site: campbellcountylibraries.org/locations/altavista. *Br Mgr,* Tim Blankenship; E-mail: twblankenship@co.campbell.va.us
Founded 1956. Pop 5,000; Circ 59,657
Open Mon-Wed & Fri 9:30-5:30, Thurs 9:30-7, Sat 9:30-1
Friends of the Library Group
TIMBROOK BRANCH, 18891 Leesville Rd, Lynchburg, 24501, SAN 325-3988. Tel: 434-592-9551. FAX: 434-237-6784. E-mail: tbl@co.campbell.va.us. Web Site: campbellcountylibraries.org/locations/timbrook. *Br Mgr,* Cody Cole; E-mail: ctcole@co.campbell.va.us
Founded 1968. Pop 25,000; Circ 70,005
Open Mon, Wed & Fri 9:30-6, Tues & Thurs 9:30-8, Sat 10:30-6
Friends of the Library Group
Bookmobiles: 1

SALEM

C AMERICAN NATIONAL UNIVERSITY*, Roanoke Valley Campus Library, 1813 E Main St, 24153-4598. SAN 317-4344. Tel: 540-444-4189, 540-986-1800, Ext 189. Web Site: library.an.edu. *Dir, Libr Serv,* Dr Brandi Porter; E-mail: bkporter@an.edu; Staff 2 (MLS 1, Non-MLS 1)
Founded 1886. Enrl 360; Fac 40; Highest Degree: Master
Library Holdings: Bk Vols 23,358
Special Collections: National Colleges History Coll
Subject Interests: Acctg, Bus, Computers, Healthcare mgt, Hospitality, Info tech, Med, Paralegal, Travel
Wireless access
Function: Bks on cassette, Bks on CD, Computers for patron use, Free DVD rentals, Music CDs, Photocopying/Printing, Ref & res, Wheelchair accessible
Publications: Newsletter
Open Mon-Fri 8am-10pm, Sat 9-1
Restriction: Borrowing privileges limited to fac & registered students
Departmental Libraries:
CHARLOTTESVILLE CAMPUS LIBRARY, 3926 Seminole Trail, Charlottesville, 22911. Tel: 434-295-0136.
Founded 1886. Enrl 120; Fac 8; Highest Degree: Master
Library Holdings: AV Mats 53; CDs 6; DVDs 86; Bk Titles 3,480
Automation Activity & Vendor Info: (Cataloging) LibraryWorld, Inc; (Circulation) LibraryWorld, Inc; (OPAC) LibraryWorld, Inc
Function: AV serv, Computers for patron use, Distance learning, Electronic databases & coll, Internet access, Magazines, Online cat, Online ref, Orientations, Ref serv available, Wheelchair accessible
Open Mon-Thurs 8am-9pm, Fri 8-5
Restriction: Borrowing privileges limited to fac & registered students

GM DEPARTMENT OF VETERANS AFFAIRS, Salem VA Health Care System Library, 1970 Roanoke Blvd, 24153. SAN 363-3519. Tel: 540-982-2463, Ext 2380. FAX: 540-983-1079. *Med Librn,* Jennifer Blankenship; E-mail: jennifer.blankenship2@va.gov; Staff 1 (MLS 1)
Founded 1946
Open Mon-Fri 8-4:30

C ROANOKE COLLEGE*, Fintel Library, 220 High St, 24153-3794. SAN 317-4417. Tel: 540-375-2295. Circulation Tel: 540-375-2294. Administration Tel: 540-375-2293. Automation Services Tel: 540-375-2575. E-mail: library@roanoke.edu. Web Site: libguides.roanoke.edu/library. *Dir,* Elizabeth G McClenney; Tel: 540-375-2508, E-mail: mcclenney@roanoke.edu; *Access Serv Librn, Lending Serv Librn,* Hany Hosny; E-mail: hosny@roanoke.edu; *Content Serv Librn, Metadata Librn,*

Charles Frith; Tel: 540-375-2292, E-mail: cfrith@roanoke.edu; *Instruction & Res Serv Librn,* Sarah Beth White; E-mail: sbwhite@roanoke.edu; *Tech & Digital Serv Librn,* Dave Wiseman; E-mail: dcwiseman@roanoke.edu; Staff 5 (MLS 5)
Founded 1842. Enrl 1,759; Fac 200; Highest Degree: Master
Library Holdings: CDs 1,760; DVDs 4,884; e-books 368,440; e-journals 148,579; Microforms 134,275; Music Scores 4,359; Bk Vols 169,131; Per Subs 401; Videos 1,583
Special Collections: Henry F Fowler Coll; Roanoke College Coll. US Document Depository
Automation Activity & Vendor Info: (Acquisitions) Ex Libris Group; (Cataloging) Ex Libris Group; (Circulation) Ex Libris Group; (Course Reserve) Ex Libris Group; (Discovery) Ex Libris Group; (ILL) OCLC Tipasa; (Media Booking) Ex Libris Group; (OPAC) Ex Libris Group; (Serials) Ex Libris Group
Wireless access
Partic in LYRASIS; Virginia Independent College & University Library Association; Virginia's Academic Library Consortium

R SALEM BAPTIST CHURCH LIBRARY*, 103 N Broad St, 24153. SAN 317-4425. Tel: 540-387-0416. FAX: 540-375-6412. E-mail: salembaptist@salembc.net. Web Site: www.salembc.net. *Dir,* Pat Hancock
Library Holdings: CDs 13; Bk Vols 4,500; Talking Bks 35; Videos 290
Automation Activity & Vendor Info: (Cataloging) Book Systems; (Circulation) Book Systems

P SALEM PUBLIC LIBRARY*, 28 E Main St, 24153. SAN 317-4433. Tel: 540-375-3089. FAX: 540-389-7054. E-mail: library@salemva.gov. Web Site: www.salemva.gov/Departments/Salem-Public-Library. *Dir,* Ann Tripp; E-mail: atripp@salemva.gov; *Access Serv Mgr,* Carol Glosh; *Ch Mgr,* Emily Metrock; *Customer Serv Mgr,* Benita Van Cleave; *Tech Serv Mgr,* Carly L Hathaway; *YA Mgr,* David Butler; Staff 13.5 (MLS 7, Non-MLS 6.5)
Founded 1969. Pop 24,784; Circ 290,390
Library Holdings: Audiobooks 7,959; CDs 779; DVDs 9,942; e-books 25,704; Electronic Media & Resources 28; Large Print Bks 5,840; Bk Vols 104,077; Per Subs 99; Videos 1,240
Special Collections: Literature for Visually Handicapped (Listening Library), cassettes, phonodiscs
Subject Interests: Literacy Vols of Am reading prog
Automation Activity & Vendor Info: (Acquisitions) SirsiDynix; (Cataloging) SirsiDynix; (Circulation) SirsiDynix; (OPAC) SirsiDynix; (Serials) SirsiDynix
Wireless access
Function: Accelerated reader prog, Adult bk club, Bks on cassette, Bks on CD, Children's prog, Computer training, Computers for patron use, Electronic databases & coll, Free DVD rentals, ILL available, Music CDs, Notary serv, Online cat, Outreach serv, Outside serv via phone, mail, e-mail & web, Photocopying/Printing, Prog for children & young adult, Ref serv available, Senior computer classes, Story hour, Summer reading prog, Tax forms, Teen prog, Telephone ref, VHS videos, Wheelchair accessible
Partic in LYRASIS
Open Mon-Thurs 9-9, Fri & Sat 9-5, Sun 1:30-5
Friends of the Library Group

SPRINGFIELD

G UNITED STATES DEPARTMENT OF DEFENSE, National Geospatial-Intelligence Agency Research Library, 7500 GEOINT Dr, Mail Stop N73, 22150-7500. SAN 321-5830. Tel: 571-557-5400. E-mail: publicaffairs@nga.mil. Web Site: www.nga.mil. *Dir,* MaryLynn Francisco
Special Collections: Bathymetric Surveys; Geodetic Control; Geographic Names
Publications: Map & Chart Accession List
Restriction: Open by appt only

STAUNTON

C MARY BALDWIN UNIVERSITY*, Martha S Grafton Library, 201 E Frederick St, 24401. SAN 317-4506. Tel: 540-887-7085. Circulation Tel: 540-887-7311. FAX: 540-887-7137. Web Site: libguides.marybaldwin.edu/home-new. *Univ Librn,* Carol Creager; Tel: 540-887-7310, E-mail: ccreager@marybaldwin.edu; Staff 6 (MLS 4, Non-MLS 2)
Founded 1842. Enrl 1,500; Fac 113; Highest Degree: Master
Library Holdings: DVDs 3,500; e-books 272,000; e-journals 32,000; Bk Vols 110,000; Videos 26,500
Special Collections: College History; Mary Julia Baldwin Coll
Subject Interests: Women's studies
Automation Activity & Vendor Info: (Acquisitions) OCLC Worldshare Management Services; (Cataloging) OCLC Worldshare Management Services; (Circulation) OCLC Worldshare Management Services; (Course Reserve) OCLC Worldshare Management Services; (Discovery) OCLC; (ILL) OCLC; (OPAC) OCLC; (Serials) OCLC
Wireless access
Partic in LYRASIS; Virginia Independent College & University Library Association; Virginia's Academic Library Consortium

P STAUNTON PUBLIC LIBRARY, One Churchville Ave, 24401. SAN 317-4514. Tel: 540-332-3902. FAX: 540-332-3906. E-mail: library@ci.staunton.va.us. Web Site: www.ci.staunton.va.us/departments/library. *Dir,* Sarah Skrobis; Tel: 540-332-3902, Ext 3904, E-mail: skrobissa@ci.staunton.va.us; *Pub Serv Librn,* Ali McCue; Tel: 540-332-3902, Ext 4229, E-mail: mccueab@ci.staunton.va.us; *Tech Serv Librn,* Carrie Whitlock; Tel: 540-332-3902, Ext 4229, E-mail: whitlockcl@ci.staunton.va.us; *Youth Serv Librn,* Lizzy Hill; Tel: 540-332-3902, Ext 4234, E-mail: hillea@ci.staunton.va.us; Staff 3.5 (MLS 3.5)
Founded 1930. Pop 24,222; Circ 388,678
Library Holdings: Audiobooks 13,230; Microforms 2,139; Bk Vols 147,815; Per Subs 173
Subject Interests: Local genealogy, Local hist
Automation Activity & Vendor Info: (Cataloging) TLC (The Library Corporation); (Circulation) TLC (The Library Corporation); (OPAC) TLC (The Library Corporation)
Wireless access
Function: Adult bk club, After school storytime, Art exhibits, Bks on CD, Children's prog, Computer training, Computers for patron use, Museum passes, Music CDs, Online cat, Photocopying/Printing, Prog for adults, Prog for children & young adult, Summer reading prog, Wheelchair accessible
Partic in Mid-Atlantic Library Alliance
Special Services for the Deaf - Assisted listening device; Bks on deafness & sign lang; Closed caption videos; Sign lang interpreter upon request for prog; TDD equip
Special Services for the Blind - Magnifiers; Talking bks
Open Mon-Thurs 9-9, Fri & Sat 9-5, Sun (Sept-May) 1-5
Friends of the Library Group
Branches: 1
P TALKING BOOK CENTER, One Churchville Ave, 24401-3229, SAN 321-6519. Tel: 540-885-6215. Toll Free Tel: 800-995-6215. FAX: 540-332-3906. E-mail: talkingbooks@ci.staunton.va.us. Web Site: www.ci.staunton.va.us/departments/library/talking-book-center. *Reader Advisor, Supvr, Talking Bk,* Llia Desjardins; *Reader Advisor,* Jenn Kidd
Founded 1982. Pop 162,807
Library Holdings: Talking Bks 200,000; Videos 226
Function: Bks on cassette, Digital talking bks, Wheelchair accessible
Special Services for the Blind - Aids for in-house use; Assistive/Adapted tech devices, equip & products; Audio mat; Bks & mags in Braille, on rec, tape & cassette; Bks on cassette; Braille & cassettes; Braille alphabet card; Braille servs; Cassette playback machines; Cassettes; Copier with enlargement capabilities; Descriptive video serv (DVS); Digital talking bk; Home delivery serv; Info on spec aids & appliances; Local mags & bks recorded; Machine repair; PC for people with disabilities; Recorded bks; Screen enlargement software for people with visual disabilities; Sound rec; Soundproof reading booth; Talking bk serv referral; Talking bks; Talking bks & player equip; Tel Pioneers equip repair group; Videos on blindness & physical disabilties; ZoomText magnification & reading software
Open Mon-Fri 10-5
Friends of the Library Group

S WOODROW WILSON PRESIDENTIAL LIBRARY & MUSEUM*, 20 N Coalter St, 24401-4332. (Mail add: PO Box 24, 24402-0024), SAN 317-4522. Tel: 540-885-0897. FAX: 540-886-9874. Web Site: www.woodrowwilson.org. *Pres & Chief Exec Officer,* Robin von Seldeneck; E-mail: rvonseldeneck@woodrowwilson.org; Staff 1 (MLS 1)
Founded 1938
Library Holdings: Bk Vols 3,000
Special Collections: Cary T Grayson Coll; Edith Bolling Wilson Papers; Emily Smith Papers; George L Harrison Coll; Historic Photograph Coll; McClure Coll; President Woodrow Wilson Coll; US Political History Coll (late 19th century-early 20th century); Wilson Manuscript Coll
Subject Interests: 19th-20th Centuries, Accomplishments of Foundation since 1925, Decorative art, Hist of Foundation since 1925, Intl relations, Political hist of the US
Wireless access
Function: Archival coll
Open Mon-Fri 9-5
Restriction: Non-circulating, Not a lending libr, Researchers by appt only

STRATFORD

S JESSIE BALL DUPONT MEMORIAL LIBRARY*, Stratford Hall, 483 Great House Rd, 22558. SAN 321-4753. Tel: 804-493-1940. FAX: 804-493-8006. Web Site: www.stratfordhall.org. *Dir, Libr & Res Serv,* Judith S Hynson; E-mail: jshynson@stratfordhall.org; Staff 2 (Non-MLS 2)
Founded 1980
Library Holdings: Bk Titles 7,900; Bk Vols 11,150; Per Subs 10

Special Collections: 18th Century America (Shippen Coll), antiquarian bks; 18th Century England (Ditchley Coll), antiquarian bks; Cartes de Visite Coll; Lee Family Manuscripts; Walter Herron Taylor Papers
Subject Interests: Manuscripts, Rare bks
Wireless access
Function: Res libr
Publications: Lee Family Digital Archive (Online only)
Open Mon-Fri 9-5
Restriction: Authorized scholars by appt

SUFFOLK

P SUFFOLK PUBLIC LIBRARY SYSTEM*, Morgan Memorial Library, 443 W Washington St, 23434. SAN 317-4530. Tel: 757-514-7323. FAX: 757-539-7155. Web Site: www.suffolkpubliclibrary.com. *Dir,* Clint Rudy; E-mail: crudy@suffolkva.us; *Ref (Info Servs),* Stephanie Bedell; Staff 14 (MLS 14)
Founded 1959
Jul 2021-Jun 2022 Income (Main & Associated Libraries) $3,544,604. Mats Exp $201,754, Books $90,937, Per/Ser (Incl. Access Fees) $3,184, AV Mat $12,850, Electronic Ref Mat (Incl. Access Fees) $94,783. Sal $283,483 (Prof $1,640,418)
Library Holdings: Audiobooks 16,960; Bks on Deafness & Sign Lang 102; e-books 37,799; e-journals 61; Electronic Media & Resources 40; Microforms 30; Bk Vols 117,017; Per Subs 63; Videos 2,098
Special Collections: Black Arts & Literature (Reid Coll)
Automation Activity & Vendor Info: (Cataloging) Innovative Interfaces, Inc; (Circulation) Innovative Interfaces, Inc; (OPAC) Innovative Interfaces, Inc
Wireless access
Function: 24/7 Electronic res, 24/7 Online cat, Accelerated reader prog, Activity rm, Audiobks via web, AV serv, Bks on CD, Children's prog, Computer training, Computers for patron use, Electronic databases & coll, Free DVD rentals, Genealogy discussion group, Govt ref serv, Homework prog, ILL available, Internet access, Magnifiers for reading, Meeting rooms, Online cat, Online ref, Outreach serv, Photocopying/Printing, Preschool outreach, Preschool reading prog, Prog for adults, Prog for children & young adult, Ref & res, Senior outreach, Serves people with intellectual disabilities, Summer & winter reading prog, Summer reading prog, Teen prog, Wheelchair accessible, Winter reading prog, Writing prog
Open Mon-Thurs 10-8, Fri & Sat 10-5
Friends of the Library Group
Branches: 2
CHUCKATUCK BRANCH, 5881 Godwin Blvd, 23432. (Mail add: PO Box 2278, 23432). Tel: 757-514-7310. *Mgr, Br,* Tiffany Duck
Library Holdings: Bk Vols 14,083
Open Mon 12-8, Tues-Thurs 10-5
Friends of the Library Group
NORTH SUFFOLK LIBRARY, 2000 Bennetts Creek Park Rd, 23435. Tel: 757-514-7150. *Mgr, Br,* Tiffany Duck
Library Holdings: Bk Vols 120,000
Open Mon-Thurs 10-8, Fri & Sat 10-5
Friends of the Library Group
Bookmobiles: 1. Outreach Coordr, Megan Mulvey. Bk titles 1,500

SWEET BRIAR

C SWEET BRIAR COLLEGE*, Mary Helen Cochran Library, 134 Chapel Rd, 24595. (Mail add: PO Box 1200, 24595-1200), SAN 363-4175. Tel: 434-381-6138. Interlibrary Loan Service Tel: 434-381-6307. Reference Tel: 434-381-6315. FAX: 434-381-6173. E-mail: library@sbc.edu. Web Site: library.sbc.edu. *Dir, Libr Serv,* Lore Guilmartin; E-mail: lguilmartin@sbc.edu; *Assoc Dir,* Beth Daniel Lindsay; *Head, Cat,* Betty Evans; E-mail: baevans@sbc.edu; *Tech Serv Mgr,* LaVerne Paige; Tel: 434-381-6135, E-mail: mpaige@sbc.edu; *Circ Supvr,* Megan Harris; Tel: 434-381-6308, E-mail: mharris@sbc.edu; Staff 5 (Non-MLS 5)
Founded 1901. Enrl 350; Pop 350; Fac 49; Highest Degree: Bachelor
Library Holdings: Bk Vols 223,218; Per Subs 982
Special Collections: Evelyn D Mullen T E Lawrence Coll; Fletcher Williams Founders Coll; George Meredith Coll; Incunabula; Kellogg Childrens Coll; Vincent Chinese Coll; Virginia Woolf Coll; Wystan Hugh Auden Coll
Automation Activity & Vendor Info: (Acquisitions) SirsiDynix; (Cataloging) SirsiDynix; (Circulation) SirsiDynix; (Course Reserve) Sydney; (ILL) OCLC ILLiad; (OPAC) SirsiDynix; (Serials) SirsiDynix
Wireless access
Publications: Friends of the Library Gazette
Partic in Lynchburg Information Online Network; Virginia Independent College & University Library Association; Virginia's Academic Library Consortium
Open Mon-Thurs 8am-1am, Fri 8-6, Sat 10-6, Sun 10am-1am
Friends of the Library Group

TAPPAHANNOCK

P ESSEX PUBLIC LIBRARY*, 117 N Church Lane, 22560. Tel: 804-443-4945. FAX: 804-443-6444. Web Site: eplva.org. *Dir,* Dana Smook; E-mail: danasmook@eplva.org
Pop 9,989
Library Holdings: AV Mats 577; Bk Titles 37,000; Per Subs 39; Talking Bks 980
Automation Activity & Vendor Info: (Cataloging) Evergreen; (Circulation) Evergreen; (OPAC) Evergreen
Wireless access
Open Mon & Tues 10-6, Wed & Thurs 10-8, Fri 1-6, Sat 10-4
Friends of the Library Group

TAZEWELL

P TAZEWELL COUNTY PUBLIC LIBRARY*, 129 Main St, 24651. (Mail add: PO Box 929, 24651-0929), SAN 363-4264. Tel: 276-988-2541. FAX: 276-988-5980. E-mail: info@tcplweb.org. Web Site: www.tcplweb.org. *Dir,* Lynne Bartlett; E-mail: lbartlett@tcplweb.org; Staff 20.5 (MLS 3, Non-MLS 17.5)
Founded 1964. Pop 44,216; Circ 133,847
Library Holdings: Audiobooks 4,173; DVDs 4,920; e-books 18,568; Microforms 56; Bk Vols 99,034; Per Subs 151
Special Collections: Photographic Archive
Subject Interests: Genealogy, Local hist
Automation Activity & Vendor Info: (Acquisitions) Innovative Interfaces, Inc; (Cataloging) Innovative Interfaces, Inc; (Circulation) Innovative Interfaces, Inc; (OPAC) Innovative Interfaces, Inc; (Serials) Innovative Interfaces, Inc
Wireless access
Function: Adult bk club, After school storytime, Audiobks via web, Bks on CD, Children's prog, Computers for patron use, Electronic databases & coll, ILL available, OverDrive digital audio bks, Photocopying/Printing, Story hour, Summer & winter reading prog, Tax forms
Publications: Guide to Researching Tazewell County, Virginia Ancestors (Research guide); Tasty Tazewell Traditions: 200 Years of Cooking & History in Tazewell County, Virginia (Local historical information)
Partic in Holston Assoc Librs, Inc; Mid-Atlantic Library Alliance
Open Mon & Thurs 9-8, Tues, Wed, Fri & Sat 9-5:30
Friends of the Library Group
Branches: 2
BLUEFIELD BRANCH, 108 Huffard Dr, Bluefield, 24605, SAN 363-4299. Tel: 276-326-1577. FAX: 276-322-5705. *Br Mgr,* Susan Murphy; Staff 5 (Non-MLS 5)
Open Mon & Wed-Sat 9-5:30, Tues 9-8
Friends of the Library Group
RICHLANDS BRANCH, 102 Suffolk Ave, Richlands, 24641-2435. (Mail add: PO Box 860, Richlands, 24641-0860), SAN 325-3252. Tel: 276-964-5282. FAX: 276-963-1107. *Br Mgr,* Jami McDonald; Staff 5 (Non-MLS 5)
Open Mon 9-8, Tues-Sat 9-5:30

TYSONS CORNER

S LMI LIBRARY*, 7940 Jones Branch Dr, 22102. SAN 328-5561. Tel: 703-917-7214. FAX: 703-917-7474. E-mail: library@lmi.org. *Info Serv, Mgr,* Sara Faulk; *Res,* Laura Tyler; Staff 2 (MLS 2)
Library Holdings: Bk Titles 5,600; Bk Vols 6,250; Per Subs 300
Special Collections: History of Military Logistics; LMI Reports
Subject Interests: Climate change, Healthcare mgt, Info tech, Logistics, Mgt
Automation Activity & Vendor Info: (Cataloging) Inmagic, Inc.; (Circulation) Inmagic, Inc.; (OPAC) Inmagic, Inc.; (Serials) Inmagic, Inc.
Function: ILL available
Partic in OCLC Online Computer Library Center, Inc
Restriction: Borrowing requests are handled by ILL, Employee & client use only

L VENABLE LLP LIBRARY, 1850 Towers Crescent Plaza, Ste 400, 22182. SAN 325-3899. Tel: 703-760-1600. FAX: 703-821-8949. Web Site: www.venable.com/offices/tysons-va. Staff 1 (MLS 1)
Founded 1977
Library Holdings: e-journals 20; Electronic Media & Resources 25; Bk Vols 6,000; Per Subs 15
Subject Interests: Bankruptcy, Corporate law, Employment law, Govt contracts, Labor law, Litigation, Pension & benefit law, Real estate, Securities, Taxation, Transportation
Automation Activity & Vendor Info: (Cataloging) Sydney; (Circulation) Sydney; (Serials) Sydney
Restriction: Staff use only

URBANNA

P MIDDLESEX COUNTY PUBLIC LIBRARY*, 150 Grace St, 23175. (Mail add: PO Box 189, 23175-0189), SAN 317-4557. Tel: 804-758-5717. FAX: 804-758-5910. E-mail: yourmiddlesexlibrary@gmail.com. Web Site: www.yourmiddlesexlibrary.org. *Exec Dir,* Carrie Dos Santos; E-mail: cdossantos0910@gmail.com; Staff 2 (MLS 2)
Founded 1927. Pop 10,000; Circ 50,200
Library Holdings: Audiobooks 2,000; AV Mats 4,525; DVDs 525; Large Print Bks 1,725; Bk Titles 42,000; Bk Vols 49,500; Per Subs 50; Videos 2,000
Special Collections: Chesapeake Bay; Virginia History & Genealogy
Automation Activity & Vendor Info: (Cataloging) Evergreen; (Circulation) Evergreen; (OPAC) Evergreen
Wireless access
Function: Art exhibits, Bks on cassette, Bks on CD, Chess club, Children's prog, Computer training, Computers for patron use, Digital talking bks, Free DVD rentals, Homebound delivery serv, ILL available, Internet access, Jail serv, Literacy & newcomer serv, Magazines, Magnifiers for reading, Meeting rooms, Movies, Online cat, Orientations, Outreach serv, Outside serv via phone, mail, e-mail & web, OverDrive digital audio bks, Photocopying/Printing, Preschool outreach, Preschool reading prog, Prog for adults, Prog for children & young adult, Ref & res, Ref serv available, Senior computer classes, Spoken cassettes & CDs, Spoken cassettes & DVDs, Story hour, Summer reading prog, Tax forms, Telephone ref, Wheelchair accessible
Special Services for the Blind - Large print bks
Open Mon & Wed-Fri 10-5, Tues 10-8, Sat 10-2
Restriction: Non-circulating coll
Friends of the Library Group
Branches: 1
DELTAVILLE BRANCH, 35 Lovers Lane, Deltaville, 23043. Tel: 804-776-7362. FAX: 804-776-7423. *Br Mgr,* Tom Samuel; E-mail: tllsamuel@gmail.com
Special Collections: Chesapeake Bay Room
Open Mon 10-8, Tues-Fri 10-5, Sat 10-2
Friends of the Library Group

VIRGINIA BEACH

S ASSOCIATION FOR RESEARCH & ENLIGHTENMENT*, Edgar Cayce Library, 215 67th St, 23451. SAN 317-459X. Tel: 757-428-3588, Ext 7141. E-mail: library@edgarcayce.org. Web Site: www.edgarcayce.org. *Mgr,* Laura Hoff; Tel: 757-457-7223, E-mail: laura.hoff@edgarcayce.org; Staff 5 (MLS 1, Non-MLS 4)
Founded 1940
Library Holdings: Bk Vols 80,000
Special Collections: Atlantis (Egerton Sykes Coll); Metaphysics (Andrew Jackson Davis Coll); Readings (Edgar Cayce Coll)
Subject Interests: Archaeology, Astrology, Civilization, Death, Holistic health, Metaphysics, Reincarnation, Relig, Theosophy, Transpersonal psychology
Automation Activity & Vendor Info: (Cataloging) Follett Software; (Circulation) Follett Software
Wireless access
Publications: Venture Inward (ARE magazine) (Periodical)
Open Thurs-Sat 10-5, Sun 12-5
Restriction: Restricted borrowing privileges
Friends of the Library Group

C HAMPTON UNIVERSITY, College of Virginia Beach Information Resource Center, 253 Town Center Dr, 23462. Tel: 757-637-2200.
Founded 2003
Library Holdings: Bk Titles 300
Wireless access
Partic in Virginia Tidewater Consortium for Higher Education

S PROVIDENCE PRESBYTERIAN CHURCH LIBRARY, 5497 Providence Rd, 23464. SAN 328-123X. Tel: 757-420-6159. FAX: 757-420-7553. E-mail: office@provpres.org. Web Site: www.provpres.org/resources/church-library.html. *Libr Dir,* Christine Ussery; E-mail: ncussery@outlook.com
Founded 1985
Library Holdings: Bk Titles 1,293

CL REGENT UNIVERSITY*, Law Library, 1000 Regent University Dr, 23464. SAN 329-8108. Tel: 757-352-4450. Reference Tel: 757-352-4145. Administration Tel: 757-352-4185. Toll Free Tel: 800-373-5504. FAX: 757-352-4189. Circulation E-mail: lawcirc@regent.edu. Reference E-mail: lawref@regent.edu. Web Site: www.regent.edu/school-of-law-student-life/law-library. *Dean,* Ester Gillie; E-mail: egille@regent.edu; *Head, Access Serv,* Dorothy Hargett; Tel: 757-352-4152, E-mail: dorohar@regent.edu; *Head, Archives, Head, Digital Initiatives, Head, Spec Coll,* Harold Henkel; Tel: 757-352-4198, E-mail: harohen@regent.edu; *Head, Tech Serv,* Carine Mattix; Tel: 757-352-4824, E-mail: cmattix@regent.edu; Staff 4 (MLS 3, Non-MLS 1)
Founded 1986. Enrl 398; Fac 55; Highest Degree: Doctorate
Library Holdings: e-books 186,806; Microforms 86,809; Bk Titles 64,986; Bk Vols 418,435; Per Subs 186
Special Collections: Early American Political Sermons; First Amendment & Civil Rights Coll; Founders Coll; John Brabner-Smith Library & Papers; Ken North Cannon Law Coll; Ken North Coll; Mary Elizabeth Menefee Law & Film Coll; Ralph Johnson Bunche Coll; Richard Henry Dana, Jr Library
Subject Interests: Constitutional hist, Constitutional law, Environ law, Family law, Intellectual property law, Intl human rights, Intl law, Intl trade law, Legal hist, Legis hist, Nat security law, Va Law
Automation Activity & Vendor Info: (Acquisitions) Innovative Interfaces, Inc - Millennium; (Cataloging) Innovative Interfaces, Inc - Millennium; (Circulation) Innovative Interfaces, Inc - Millennium; (Course Reserve) Innovative Interfaces, Inc - Millennium; (ILL) Innovative Interfaces, Inc - Millennium; (OPAC) Innovative Interfaces, Inc - Millennium; (Serials) Innovative Interfaces, Inc - Millennium
Wireless access
Function: Audio & video playback equip for onsite use, Bks on cassette, Bks on CD, Computers for patron use, Doc delivery serv, Electronic databases & coll, ILL available, Internet access, Microfiche/film & reading machines, Online cat, Online ref, Orientations, Photocopying/Printing, Ref serv available, Res libr, VHS videos, Wheelchair accessible, Workshops
Publications: Law Library Blog (Online only)
Partic in Law Library Microform Consortium; LYRASIS; Virginia Tidewater Consortium for Higher Education; Virginia's Academic Library Consortium
Special Services for the Deaf - Closed caption videos; Staff with knowledge of sign lang
Special Services for the Blind - Audio mat; Bks on cassette; Bks on CD; Cassette playback machines; Copier with enlargement capabilities; Ref serv; Talking bks
Open Mon-Thurs 7:30am-Midnight, Fri 7:30am-8pm, Sat 10-7, Sun 2pm-Midnight
Restriction: Circ limited, Open to pub for ref & circ; with some limitations, Open to students, fac, staff & alumni

C REGENT UNIVERSITY LIBRARY*, 1000 Regent University Dr, 23464-5037. SAN 321-6314. Circulation Tel: 757-352-4150. Interlibrary Loan Service Tel: 757-352-4424. FAX: 757-352-4167. Interlibrary Loan Service FAX: 757-352-4179. E-mail: libraryadmin@regent.edu. Web Site: www.regent.edu/lib. *Dean,* Esther Gillie, PhD; Tel: 757-352-4185, E-mail: egillie@regent.edu; *Head, Pub Serv, Resource Management,* Dorothy Hargett; Tel: 757-352-4152, E-mail: dorohar@regent.edu; *Archives, Digital Initiatives, Head, Spec Coll,* Harold Henkel; Tel: 757-352-4198, E-mail: harohen@regent.edu; *Head, Libr Syst, Tech Serv,* Carine Mattix; Tel: 757-352-4824, E-mail: cmattix@regent.edu; *Head, Res & Instruction,* Meredith Ader; Tel: 757-352-4184, E-mail: mader@regent.edu; *Instruction Librn,* Denise Crews, PhD; Tel: 757-352-4121, E-mail: dcrews@regent.edu. Subject Specialists: *Counseling, Psychol,* Dorothy Hargett; *Bus, Educ,* Harold Henkel; Staff 12 (MLS 6, Non-MLS 6)
Founded 1978. Enrl 13,873; Fac 156; Highest Degree: Doctorate
Jul 2018-Jun 2019 Income $2,474,431. Mats Exp $727,179, Books $61,200, Per/Ser (Incl. Access Fees) $117,000, AV Mat $10,000, Electronic Ref Mat (Incl. Access Fees) $421,506. Sal $892,600
Library Holdings: AV Mats 9,830; Bks on Deafness & Sign Lang 864; DVDs 2,436; e-books 544,753; e-journals 93,220; Electronic Media & Resources 23,977; Microforms 593,318; Bk Titles 241,000; Bk Vols 269,857; Per Subs 985
Special Collections: Animated Films Coll; Christian Education Association International Coll; Christian Films Research Coll; Clark Hymnology Coll; Dennis Bennett Coll; J Rodman Williams Coll; John Wimber Papers; Matthews Coll; O C Baptista Film Coll; Pentecostal Research Coll; Scott Ross Cultural Coll; Vince Synan Papers; Wellington Boone Coll; William S Reed Coll
Subject Interests: Biblical studies, Communications, Counseling, Educ, Govt, Hymnology, Leadership studies, Psychol
Automation Activity & Vendor Info: (Acquisitions) Innovative Interfaces, Inc - Sierra; (Cataloging) Innovative Interfaces, Inc - Sierra; (Circulation) Innovative Interfaces, Inc - Sierra; (Course Reserve) Innovative Interfaces, Inc - Sierra; (ILL) OCLC; (OPAC) Innovative Interfaces, Inc - Sierra; (Serials) SerialsSolutions
Wireless access
Function: Res libr
Publications: Library Link Blog (Online only)
Partic in LYRASIS; Virginia Independent College & University Library Association; Virginia Tidewater Consortium for Higher Education; Virginia's Academic Library Consortium
Special Services for the Blind - Screen enlargement software for people with visual disabilities
Open Mon-Thurs 7:30am-Midnight, Fri 7:30am-8pm, Sat 10-7, Sun 2-Midnight; Mon-Thurs 9am-10pm, Fri 9-8, Sat 10-7 (Summer)

J TIDEWATER COMMUNITY COLLEGE*, Virginia Beach Campus Learning Resources Center, 1700 College Crescent, 23453. SAN 317-4603. Circulation Tel: 757-822-7800. Reference Tel: 757-822-7866. Web Site: libguides.tcc.edu/jul. *Libr Coord*, Brittany Horn; E-mail: bhorn@tcc.edu; Staff 9 (MLS 5, Non-MLS 4)
Founded 1971. Enrl 10,114
Library Holdings: AV Mats 938; Bk Vols 47,803; Per Subs 241
Subject Interests: Allied health, Broadcasting, Computer sci, Fire sci, Hotel, Inst mgt, Phys therapy, Radiological tech, Respiratory therapy, Restaurant mgt
Wireless access
Open Mon-Thurs 7:30am-9pm, Fri 7:30-5, Sat 9-5

A UNITED STATES ARMY*, Joint Expeditionary Base Little Creek - Fort Story Library, 8640 Omaha Beach Rd, 23459. SAN 320-9563. Tel: 757-422-7600. E-mail: jeblcff.library.system@gmail.com. *Br Mgr*, Cloe Andres; Staff 2 (MLS 1, Non-MLS 1)
Library Holdings: Bk Titles 34,000; Per Subs 35
Subject Interests: Mil
Automation Activity & Vendor Info: (Cataloging) Bibliomation Inc; (Circulation) Bibliomation Inc
Wireless access
Partic in Tralinet
Open Mon-Sat 9-7

A UNITED STATES NAVAL SCHOOL OF MUSIC, Library & Media Center, JEB Little Creek, 1420 Gator Blvd, 23459-2617. SAN 370-2812. Tel: 757-462-5734. Web Site: www.netc.navy.mil/nsm. *Chief Librn*, Russ Girsberger; E-mail: russ.girsberger@navy.mil; Staff 1 (MLS 1)
Founded 1935
Library Holdings: AV Mats 8,000; Music Scores 25,000; Bk Vols 8,000; Per Subs 20
Automation Activity & Vendor Info: (Cataloging) LibraryWorld, Inc; (Circulation) LibraryWorld, Inc; (OPAC) LibraryWorld, Inc
Function: Ref serv available
Restriction: Borrowing privileges limited to fac & registered students, By permission only

S VIRGINIA AQUARIUM & MARINE SCIENCE CENTER*, 717 General Booth Blvd, 23451. SAN 328-3631. Tel: 757-385-3474. Web Site: www.virginiaaquarium.com. *Library Contact*, Ms Shawn Reid; E-mail: sreid@virginiaaquarium.com
Library Holdings: Bk Vols 1,000; Per Subs 25

P VIRGINIA BEACH PUBLIC LIBRARY*, Administration Office, Municipal Ctr, Bldg 19, Rm 210, 2416 Courthouse Dr, 23452. SAN 363-4329. Tel: 757-385-8709. Interlibrary Loan Service Tel: 757-385-0167. E-mail: library@vbgov.com. Web Site: libraries.virginiabeach.gov/. *Dir*, Eva Poole; E-mail: epoole@vbgov.com; *Adminr, Support Serv*, Clara Hudson; E-mail: chudson@vbgov.com; *Pub Serv Adminr*, Rachel Kopchick; E-mail: rkopchick@vbgov.com; *Admin Serv Mgr*, Shelby Goldsmith; E-mail: sgoldsmi@vbgov.com; *Mkt & Communications Mgr*, Christine Brantley; E-mail: cbrantle@vbgov.com; Staff 46 (MLS 46)
Founded 1959. Pop 454,448; Circ 1,931,864
Jul 2019-Jun 2020 Income (Main & Associated Libraries) $18,991,464, State $234,169, City $18,376,451, Federal $2,434, Locally Generated Income $378,410. Mats Exp $1,897,481, Books $549,367, Per/Ser (Incl. Access Fees) $64,508, Other Print Mats $4,700, AV Mat $182,932, Electronic Ref Mat (Incl. Access Fees) $1,095,974. Sal $22,317,645 (Prof $6,240,140)
Library Holdings: Audiobooks 27,351; CDs 17,174; DVDs 41,585; Large Print Bks 17,765; Bk Vols 430,656; Per Subs 112
Special Collections: Princess Anne County (Princess Anne Historical Coll), bks, microfilm & microcards. Municipal Document Depository
Automation Activity & Vendor Info: (Acquisitions) SirsiDynix-WorkFlows; (Cataloging) SirsiDynix-WorkFlows; (Circulation) SirsiDynix-WorkFlows; (Discovery) SirsiDynix-Enterprise; (ILL) OCLC WorldShare Interlibrary Loan; (OPAC) SirsiDynix-Enterprise
Wireless access
Function: 24/7 Electronic res, 24/7 Online cat, 3D Printer, Activity rm, Adult bk club, Adult literacy prog, After school storytime, Archival coll, Art exhibits, Art programs, Audiobks via web, AV serv, Bk club(s), Bk reviews (Group), Bks on CD, Bus archives, CD-ROM, Chess club, Children's prog, Citizenship assistance, Computer training, Computers for patron use, Digital talking bks, E-Reserves, Electronic databases & coll, Equip loans & repairs, Family literacy, Free DVD rentals, Games & aids for people with disabilities, Genealogy discussion group, Govt ref serv, Holiday prog, Home delivery & serv to seniorr ctr & nursing homes, Homebound delivery serv, ILL available, Internet access, Jazz prog, Large print keyboards, Life-long learning prog for all ages, Magazines, Magnifiers for reading, Mail & tel request accepted, Meeting rooms, Microfiche/film & reading machines, Movies, Music CDs, Notary serv, Online cat, Online ref, Orientations, Outreach serv, OverDrive digital audio bks, Photocopying/Printing, Preschool outreach, Preschool reading prog, Printer for laptops & handheld devices, Prog for adults, Prog for children & young adult, Ref & res, Ref serv available, Res assist avail, Scanner, Senior computer classes, Senior outreach, Serves people with intellectual disabilities, Spanish lang bks, Spoken cassettes & CDs, Spoken cassettes & DVDs, STEM programs, Story hour, Study rm, Summer & winter reading prog, Summer reading prog, Tax forms, Teen prog, Telephone ref, Visual arts prog, Wheelchair accessible, Winter reading prog, Workshops, Writing prog
Publications: The Beach: A History of Virginia Beach (Local historical information); Update (Newsletter)
Partic in LYRASIS; Mid-Atlantic Library Alliance; OCLC Online Computer Library Center, Inc; SouthWest Information Network Group
Special Services for the Deaf - Sign lang interpreter upon request for prog
Special Services for the Blind - Accessible computers; Assistive/Adapted tech devices, equip & products; Braille bks; Children's Braille; Computer with voice synthesizer for visually impaired persons; Digital talking bk; Digital talking bk machines; Disability awareness prog; Extensive large print coll; Free checkout of audio mat; Home delivery serv; Info on spec aids & appliances; Large print bks; Low vision equip; Magnifiers; Mags & bk reproduction/duplication; Newsletter (in large print, Braille or on cassette); Production of talking bks; Talking bk serv referral; Talking bks; Talking bks & player equip; Text reader; Textbks & bks about music in Braille & large print; Volunteer serv
Restriction: ID required to use computers (Ltd hrs), Non-resident fee
Friends of the Library Group
Branches: 11
BAYSIDE AREA & SPECIAL SERVICES LIBRARY, 936 Independence Blvd, 23455, SAN 363-4590. Tel: 757-385-2680. *Libr Mgr*, Susan Paddock; E-mail: spaddock@vbgov.com; Staff 2 (MLS 2)
Founded 1967. Pop 59,929; Circ 213,251
Function: 24/7 Electronic res, 24/7 Online cat, Activity rm, Adult bk club, After school storytime, Art programs, Audiobks via web, Bk club(s), Bks on CD, Children's prog, Computer training, Computers for patron use, Digital talking bks, Electronic databases & coll, Equip loans & repairs, Free DVD rentals, Games & aids for people with disabilities, Holiday prog, Home delivery & serv to seniorr ctr & nursing homes, ILL available, Internet access, Large print keyboards, Life-long learning prog for all ages, Magazines, Magnifiers for reading, Mail & tel request accepted, Meeting rooms, Movies, Music CDs, Notary serv, Online cat, Outreach serv, OverDrive digital audio bks, Photocopying/Printing, Preschool outreach, Preschool reading prog, Printer for laptops & handheld devices, Prog for adults, Prog for children & young adult, Ref & res, Ref serv available, Scanner, Senior outreach, Serves people with intellectual disabilities, Spanish lang bks, Spoken cassettes & CDs, Spoken cassettes & DVDs, STEM programs, Story hour, Summer & winter reading prog, Summer reading prog, Teen prog, Wheelchair accessible, Winter reading prog
Special Services for the Blind - Accessible computers; Aids for in-house use; Assistive/Adapted tech devices, equip & products; Bks & mags in Braille, on rec, tape & cassette; Bks available with recordings; Bks on CD; Bks on flash-memory cartridges; Braille & cassettes; Braille bks; Braille equip; Club for the blind; Computer with voice synthesizer for visually impaired persons; Digital talking bk; Digital talking bk machines; Extensive large print coll; Free checkout of audio mat; Internet workstation with adaptive software; Large print & cassettes; Large print bks; Large print bks & talking machines; Large screen computer & software; Magnifiers; Networked computers with assistive software; Newsletter (in large print, Braille or on cassette); Recorded bks; Talking bk & rec for the blind cat; Talking bks; Talking bks & player equip
Open Mon-Thurs 10-7, Fri & Sat 10-5
Restriction: Circ to mem only, ID required to use computers (Ltd hrs), In-house use for visitors, Non-resident fee
Friends of the Library Group
GREAT NECK AREA, 1251 Bayne Dr, 23454, SAN 363-4620. Tel: 757-385-2606. *Libr Mgr*, Matthew Lighthart; E-mail: mlightha@vbgov.com; Staff 1 (MLS 1)
Pop 40,033; Circ 210,423
Function: 24/7 Electronic res, 24/7 Online cat, 3D Printer, Activity rm, Adult bk club, Bk club(s), Bks on CD, Children's prog, Computer training, Computers for patron use, Electronic databases & coll, Equip loans & repairs, Free DVD rentals, Genealogy discussion group, Holiday prog, Internet access, Life-long learning prog for all ages, Magazines, Meeting rooms, Movies, Music CDs, Notary serv, Online cat, Outreach serv, OverDrive digital audio bks, Photocopying/Printing, Preschool outreach, Preschool reading prog, Printer for laptops & handheld devices, Prog for adults, Prog for children & young adult, Scanner, Spoken cassettes & CDs, STEM programs, Story hour, Summer & winter reading prog, Wheelchair accessible, Winter reading prog
Open Mon-Thurs 10-7, Fri & Sat 10-5
Restriction: Circ to mem only, ID required to use computers (Ltd hrs), Non-resident fee
Friends of the Library Group

INTERLIBRARY LOAN DIVISION, 4100 Virginia Beach Blvd, 23452, SAN 363-4434. Interlibrary Loan Service FAX: 757-431-3741. *ILL,* Jennifer Thalman; E-mail: jthalman@vbgov.com; Staff 1 (Non-MLS 1)
Function: ILL available
Open Mon-Thurs 10-9, Fri & Sat 10-5, Sun 1-5 (Sept-May)
Restriction: Borrowing requests are handled by ILL, Circ to mem only

JOINT-USE LIBRARY, TCC Campus, Bldg L, 1700 College Crescent, 23453, SAN 363-4418. Tel: 757-822-7800. *Libr Mgr,* Denise Walker; E-mail: dwalker@vbgov.com; Staff 2 (MLS 2)
Pop 52,431; Circ 251,833
Function: 3D Printer, Activity rm, Adult bk club, After school storytime, Art programs, Audiobks via web, AV serv, Bk club(s), Bks on CD, Chess club, Children's prog, Computer training, Computers for patron use, Electronic databases & coll, Free DVD rentals, Holiday prog, Instruction & testing, Internet access, Life-long learning prog for all ages, Magazines, Meeting rooms, Movies, Music CDs, Notary serv, Online cat, Outreach serv, OverDrive digital audio bks, Photocopying/Printing, Preschool outreach, Preschool reading prog, Printer for laptops & handheld devices, Prog for adults, Prog for children & young adult, Ref & res, Ref serv available, Res assist avail, Res libr, Scanner, Spanish lang bks, Spoken cassettes & CDs, STEM programs, Story hour, Study rm, Summer & winter reading prog, Summer reading prog, Teen prog, Wheelchair accessible, Winter reading prog
Open Mon-Thurs 8-7:30, Fri & Sat 9-5
Restriction: Circ to mem only, ID required to use computers (Ltd hrs), Non-resident fee

KEMPSVILLE AREA, 832 Kempsville Rd, 23464-2793, SAN 363-4655. Tel: 757-385-2627. *Libr Mgr,* Position Currently Open
Pop 104,869; Circ 308,494
Function: 24/7 Electronic res, 24/7 Online cat, 3D Printer, Activity rm, Adult bk club, After school storytime, Art programs, Audiobks via web, Bk club(s), Bks on CD, Children's prog, Computer training, Computers for patron use, Electronic databases & coll, Equip loans & repairs, Free DVD rentals, Holiday prog, Internet access, Life-long learning prog for all ages, Magazines, Meeting rooms, Movies, Music CDs, Notary serv, Online cat, Outreach serv, OverDrive digital audio bks, Photocopying/Printing, Preschool outreach, Preschool reading prog, Printer for laptops & handheld devices, Prog for adults, Prog for children & young adult, Scanner, Spanish lang bks, Spoken cassettes & CDs, STEM programs, Story hour, Summer & winter reading prog, Summer reading prog, Teen prog, Visual arts prog, Wheelchair accessible, Winter reading prog
Open Mon-Thurs 10-7, Fri & Sat 10-5, Sun 1-5 (Sept-May)
Restriction: Circ to mem only, Non-resident fee

MEYERA E OBERNDORF CENTRAL LIBRARY, 4100 Virginia Beach Blvd, 23452, SAN 377-0567. Tel: 757-385-0150. FAX: 757-431-3134. *Libr Mgr,* Sasha Matthews; E-mail: smatthew@vbgov.com; Staff 9 (MLS 9)
Pop 62,271; Circ 526,564
Special Collections: Municipal Document Depository
Subject Interests: Genealogy, Local hist
Function: 24/7 Electronic res, 24/7 Online cat, 3D Printer, Activity rm, Adult bk club, Adult literacy prog, After school storytime, Archival coll, Art exhibits, Art programs, Audiobks via web, Bk club(s), Bk reviews (Group), Bks on CD, Children's prog, Computer training, Computers for patron use, Electronic databases & coll, Equip loans & repairs, Free DVD rentals, Genealogy discussion group, Govt ref serv, Holiday prog, Home delivery & serv to seniorr ctr & nursing homes, ILL available, Internet access, Jazz prog, Life-long learning prog for all ages, Magazines, Mail & tel request accepted, Meeting rooms, Microfiche/film & reading machines, Movies, Music CDs, Notary serv, Online cat, Outreach serv, OverDrive digital audio bks, Photocopying/Printing, Preschool outreach, Preschool reading prog, Printer for laptops & handheld devices, Prog for adults, Prog for children & young adult, Ref & res, Ref serv available, Res assist avail, Scanner, Senior computer classes, Senior outreach, Serves people with intellectual disabilities, Spanish lang bks, Spoken cassettes & CDs, STEM programs, Story hour, Study rm, Summer & winter reading prog, Summer reading prog, Tax forms, Teen prog, Telephone ref, Visual arts prog, Wheelchair accessible, Winter reading prog, Workshops, Writing prog
Open Mon-Thurs 10-9, Fri & Sat 10-5, Sun 1-5 (Sept-May)
Restriction: Non-circulating coll, Non-circulating of rare bks, Non-resident fee
Friends of the Library Group

OCEANFRONT AREA, 700 Virginia Beach Blvd, 23451, SAN 363-468X. Tel: 757-385-2640. *Libr Mgr,* Cynthia Hart; E-mail: chart@vbgov.com; Staff 1 (MLS 1)
Pop 32,053; Circ 133,262
Function: 24/7 Electronic res, 24/7 Online cat, Activity rm, After school storytime, Art programs, Audiobks via web, Bk club(s), Bks on CD, Children's prog, Computers for patron use, Electronic databases & coll, Free DVD rentals, Holiday prog, Internet access, Life-long learning prog for all ages, Magazines, Meeting rooms, Movies, Music CDs, Online cat, Outreach serv, OverDrive digital audio bks, Photocopying/Printing, Preschool outreach, Prog for adults, Prog for children & young adult, Scanner, STEM programs, Story hour, Summer & winter reading prog, Summer reading prog, Winter reading prog
Open Mon-Thurs 10-7, Fri & Sat 10-5
Friends of the Library Group

PUNGO-BLACKWATER LIBRARY, 916 Princess Anne Rd, 23457, SAN 370-9426. Tel: 757-385-7790. *Libr Mgr,* Sarah Bell; E-mail: sbell@vbgov.com; Staff 1 (MLS 1)
Pop 3,357; Circ 28,652
Function: 24/7 Electronic res, 24/7 Online cat, Children's prog, Computers for patron use, Electronic databases & coll, Holiday prog, Internet access, Life-long learning prog for all ages, Magazines, Movies, Music CDs, Online cat, Outreach serv, OverDrive digital audio bks, Preschool outreach, Preschool reading prog, Printer for laptops & handheld devices, Prog for adults, Prog for children & young adult, Scanner, Senior outreach, Spoken cassettes & CDs, Story hour, Summer & winter reading prog, Summer reading prog, Winter reading prog
Open Mon-Thurs 10-7, Sat 10-5
Friends of the Library Group

L , 2425 Nimmo Pkwy, Judicial Ctr, Court Support Bldg 10B, 23456, SAN 363-4507. Tel: 757-385-6386. *Libr Mgr,* Kimball Boone; E-mail: kboone@vbgov.com; Staff 3 (MLS 1, Non-MLS 2)
Pop 450,000
Function: 24/7 Electronic res, 24/7 Online cat, 24/7 wireless access, Adult bk club, Bilingual assistance for Spanish patrons, CD-ROM, Computers for patron use, Digital talking bks, Doc delivery serv, Electronic databases & coll, For res purposes, Games & aids for people with disabilities, Internet access, Magnifiers for reading, Mail & tel request accepted, Meeting rooms, Microfiche/film & reading machines, Online cat, Outreach serv, OverDrive digital audio bks, Photocopying/Printing, Prog for adults, Ref & res, Ref serv available, Res assist avail, Res libr, Scanner, Spanish lang bks, Telephone ref, Wheelchair accessible, Wifi hotspot checkout, Workshops
Open Mon-Fri 8:30-4:30
Restriction: Non-circulating coll

WINDSOR WOODS AREA, 3612 S Plaza Trail, 23452, SAN 363-471X. Tel: 757-385-2630. *Libr Mgr,* Tamara Sarg; E-mail: tsarg@vbgov.com; Staff 1 (MLS 1)
Pop 27,479; Circ 103,853
Function: 24/7 Electronic res, 24/7 Online cat, Activity rm, Adult bk club, After school storytime, Art programs, Bk club(s), Bks on CD, Children's prog, Computers for patron use, Electronic databases & coll, Equip loans & repairs, Free DVD rentals, Holiday prog, Internet access, Life-long learning prog for all ages, Magazines, Movies, Music CDs, Notary serv, Online cat, Outreach serv, OverDrive digital audio bks, Photocopying/Printing, Preschool outreach, Preschool reading prog, Printer for laptops & handheld devices, Prog for adults, Prog for children & young adult, Scanner, Spoken cassettes & CDs, STEM programs, Story hour, Summer & winter reading prog, Summer reading prog, Winter reading prog
Open Mon-Thurs 10-7, Fri & Sat 10-5
Restriction: ID required to use computers (Ltd hrs), Non-resident fee

Bookmobiles: 1. Early Literacy Outreach Coordr, Karen Schell

C VIRGINIA WESLEYAN UNIVERSITY*, Henry Clay Hofheimer II Library, 5817 Wesleyan Dr, 23455. SAN 317-3755. Tel: 757-455-3224. E-mail: library@vwu.edu. Web Site: www.vwu.edu/library. *Libr Dir,* Susan Erickson; E-mail: serickson@vwu.edu; Staff 4 (MLS 4)
Founded 1969. Enrl 1,500; Highest Degree: Master
Automation Activity & Vendor Info: (Acquisitions) OCLC Worldshare Management Services; (Cataloging) OCLC Worldshare Management Services; (Circulation) OCLC Worldshare Management Services; (Discovery) OCLC; (ILL) OCLC WorldShare Interlibrary Loan; (OPAC) OCLC; (Serials) OCLC
Wireless access
Function: 24/7 Online cat, Online cat
Partic in LYRASIS; Virginia Independent College & University Library Association; Virginia Tidewater Consortium for Higher Education; Virginia's Academic Library Consortium
Restriction: Limited access for the pub, Open to students, fac & staff

WARRENTON

P FAUQUIER COUNTY PUBLIC LIBRARY*, 11 Winchester St, 20186. SAN 317-462X. Tel: 540-422-8500, Ext 1. FAX: 540-422-8520. E-mail: circulation@fauquiercounty.gov. Web Site: fauquierlibrary.org. *Dir,* Maria Del Rosso; Tel: 540-347-8750, Ext 5327, E-mail: maria.delrosso@fauquiercounty.gov; *Ad,* Vicky Ginther; E-mail: vicky.ginther@fauquiercounty.gov; *Youth Serv Librn,* Jennifer Schultz; E-mail: jennifer.schultz@fauquiercounty.gov; *Coll Mgr,* Fran Burke-Urr; E-mail: fran.burke-urr@fauquiercounty.gov; *Pub Serv Mgr,* Dawn Sowers; E-mail: dawn.sowers@fauquiercounty.gov; *Support Serv Mgr,* Linda Yowell; E-mail: linda.yowell@fauquiercounty.gov; Staff 22.9 (MLS 10, Non-MLS 12.9)
Founded 1922. Pop 60,400; Circ 457,485

Library Holdings: CDs 1,244; DVDs 1,400; e-books 31,614; Large Print Bks 1,467; Bk Titles 106,714; Per Subs 291; Talking Bks 4,991; Videos 1,891
Subject Interests: Genealogy, Local hist, Va
Automation Activity & Vendor Info: (Acquisitions) Innovative Interfaces, Inc; (Cataloging) Innovative Interfaces, Inc; (Circulation) Innovative Interfaces, Inc; (OPAC) Innovative Interfaces, Inc; (Serials) Innovative Interfaces, Inc
Wireless access
Function: 24/7 Electronic res, Adult bk club, Audiobks via web, Bk club(s), Bks on cassette, Bks on CD, Children's prog, Computer training, Computers for patron use, Holiday prog, ILL available, Music CDs, Online cat, Photocopying/Printing, Prog for adults, Prog for children & young adult, Summer reading prog, Teen prog, Telephone ref, Wheelchair accessible
Partic in SouthWest Information Network Group
Open Mon-Wed 10-6, Thurs & Fri 10-5, Sat 10-2
Friends of the Library Group
Branches: 2
BEALETON BRANCH, 10877 Willow Dr N, Bealeton, 22712, SAN 371-9294. Tel: 540-422-8500, Ext 2. FAX: 540-439-9731. *Br Mgr,* Natalie Wheeler; E-mail: natalie.wheeler@fauquiercounty.gov; Staff 3.1 (MLS 2.8, Non-MLS 0.3)
Founded 1991. Circ 94,993
Library Holdings: CDs 752; DVDs 643; e-books 31,614; Large Print Bks 748; Bk Vols 43,774; Per Subs 107; Talking Bks 2,572; Videos 1,072
Function: Audiobks via web, Bk club(s), Bks on cassette, Bks on CD, Children's prog, Computer training, Computers for patron use, Electronic databases & coll, Holiday prog, ILL available, Music CDs, Online cat, Photocopying/Printing, Prog for adults, Prog for children & young adult, Ref serv available, Spoken cassettes & CDs, Summer reading prog, Teen prog, Telephone ref, VHS videos, Wheelchair accessible
Open Mon-Wed 10-6, Thurs & Fri 10-5, Sat 10-2
Friends of the Library Group
JOHN MARSHALL BRANCH, 4133 Rectortown Rd, Marshall, 20115, SAN 375-5487. Tel: 540-422-8500, Ext 5. FAX: 540-364-4911. *Br Mgr,* Deborah Cosby; E-mail: deborah.cosby@fauquiercounty.gov; Staff 1 (MLS 1)
Founded 1996. Circ 40,798
Library Holdings: CDs 143; DVDs 328; e-books 31,614; Large Print Bks 412; Bk Vols 26,151; Per Subs 79; Talking Bks 1,385; Videos 832
Function: Adult bk club, Audiobks via web, Bk club(s), Bks on cassette, Bks on CD, Children's prog, Computers for patron use, Holiday prog, Homebound delivery serv, ILL available, Music CDs, Online cat, Photocopying/Printing, Preschool outreach, Prog for adults, Prog for children & young adult, Ref serv available, Senior outreach, Spoken cassettes & CDs, Summer reading prog, VHS videos, Wheelchair accessible
Open Mon-Wed 10-6, Thurs & Fri 10-5, Sat 10-2
Friends of the Library Group

WARSAW

J RAPPAHANNOCK COMMUNITY COLLEGE*, Learning Resource Center, 52 Campus Dr, 22572. SAN 363-4833. Tel: 804-333-6716. FAX: 804-333-0589. Web Site: www.rappahannock.edu/library. *Coordr,* Dan Ream; E-mail: dream@rappahannock.edu; Staff 12 (MLS 3, Non-MLS 9)
Founded 1973. Enrl 3,100; Fac 29; Highest Degree: Associate
Library Holdings: AV Mats 1,255; e-books 33,000; Large Print Bks 625; Bk Titles 43,000; Bk Vols 49,000; Per Subs 203; Talking Bks 989
Special Collections: Children's Library; Cooperative Law Library; Virginiana Coll
Automation Activity & Vendor Info: (Acquisitions) Ex Libris Group; (Cataloging) OCLC; (Circulation) Ex Libris Group; (Course Reserve) Ex Libris Group; (ILL) OCLC; (Media Booking) Ex Libris Group; (OPAC) Ex Libris Group; (Serials) Ex Libris Group
Wireless access
Function: Distance learning, Doc delivery serv, ILL available, Photocopying/Printing, Wheelchair accessible, Workshops
Publications: Learning Resources News (Newsletter)
Partic in LYRASIS; Virginia Commun Coll Syst; Virginia's Academic Library Consortium
Special Services for the Blind - Aids for in-house use; Bks on cassette; Talking bks
Open Mon-Thurs 8:30-8:30, Fri 9-3, Sat 10-2
Friends of the Library Group

P RICHMOND COUNTY PUBLIC LIBRARY*, Rappahannock Community College Library Ctr, 52 Campus Dr, 22572. Tel: 804-333-6710. FAX: 804-333-0589. E-mail: library@rappahannock.edu. Web Site: rcplva.org. *Dir,* Elizabeth Hadley; E-mail: ehadley@rappahannock.edu; *Circ Mgr,* Linda Taylor; *Acq Spec,* Paulina Johnson; Staff 7 (MLS 1, Non-MLS 6)
Founded 1993. Pop 9,100; Circ 39,909
Library Holdings: AV Mats 1,255; e-books 33,000; Electronic Media & Resources 250; Large Print Bks 303; Bk Titles 43,000; Bk Vols 49,000; Per Subs 110; Talking Bks 550
Special Collections: Virginiana (Virginia History, Local History & Geneaology)
Automation Activity & Vendor Info: (Acquisitions) Ex Libris Group; (Cataloging) Ex Libris Group; (Circulation) Ex Libris Group; (ILL) OCLC Online; (Media Booking) Ex Libris Group; (OPAC) Ex Libris Group; (Serials) Ex Libris Group
Wireless access
Function: 24/7 Electronic res, 24/7 Online cat, Art exhibits, Audiobks via web, Bks on CD, Children's prog, Computers for patron use, Electronic databases & coll, Free DVD rentals, Govt ref serv, Holiday prog, ILL available, Internet access, Magazines, Mail & tel request accepted, Mango lang, Microfiche/film & reading machines, Online cat, Outreach serv, OverDrive digital audio bks, Photocopying/Printing, Preschool outreach, Prog for adults, Prog for children & young adult, Ref serv available, Scanner, Story hour, Summer & winter reading prog, Summer reading prog, Teen prog, Telephone ref, Workshops
Special Services for the Deaf - Bks on deafness & sign lang
Special Services for the Blind - Bks on cassette; Bks on CD; Talking bks
Open Mon, Wed & Thurs 8:30-6, Tues 8:30-8, Fri 8:30-Noon, Sat 10-2
Friends of the Library Group

WASHINGTON

P RAPPAHANNOCK COUNTY LIBRARY*, Four Library Rd, 22747. (Mail add: PO Box 55, 22747-0055), SAN 317-4646. Tel: 540-675-3780. FAX: 540-675-1290. E-mail: rapplibrary@gmail.com. Web Site: www.rappahannocklibrary.org. *Dir,* David Shaffer; Staff 3 (Non-MLS 3)
Founded 1963. Circ 16,783
Library Holdings: Bk Titles 26,000; Bk Vols 30,000; Per Subs 100
Automation Activity & Vendor Info: (Circulation) Follett Software; (OPAC) Follett Software
Open Mon & Wed 10-8, Tues, Thurs & Fri 10-6, Sat 10-2
Friends of the Library Group

WAYNESBORO

P WAYNESBORO PUBLIC LIBRARY*, 600 S Wayne Ave, 22980. SAN 363-4868. Tel: 540-942-6746. FAX: 540-942-6753. Web Site: www.waynesboro.va.us/354/Library. *Dir,* Zahir M Mahmoud; E-mail: mahmoudz@ci.waynesboro.va.us; *Asst Dir,* Elzena Anderson; *Ad,* Rebecca Lamb; *Youth Serv Librn,* Jamie Kollar; *Circ Mgr,* Rhonda B Smith; E-mail: smithrb@ci.waynesboro.va.us; *Adult Serv,* Diane H Devoy; Staff 11 (MLS 2, Non-MLS 9)
Founded 1915. Pop 20,405; Circ 305,435
Library Holdings: Audiobooks 3,322; AV Mats 13,206; Bks on Deafness & Sign Lang 82; Braille Volumes 20; CDs 1,093; DVDs 2,398; Electronic Media & Resources 5; High Interest/Low Vocabulary Bk Vols 21; Large Print Bks 6,132; Microforms 1,689; Music Scores 1,163; Bk Titles 162,008; Bk Vols 178,015; Per Subs 141; Spec Interest Per Sub 10; Talking Bks 20; Videos 6,393
Special Collections: Charles Smith Art Coll; George Speck Art Coll, prints; Waynesboro Local History, bks, micro. Oral History
Subject Interests: Genealogy, Local hist
Automation Activity & Vendor Info: (Acquisitions) TLC (The Library Corporation); (Cataloging) TLC (The Library Corporation); (Circulation) TLC (The Library Corporation); (Course Reserve) TLC (The Library Corporation); (OPAC) TLC (The Library Corporation); (Serials) EBSCO Online
Wireless access
Publications: Bookmark (Newsletter); Calendar of Events (Quarterly); The Bookshelf Edition (Newsletter)
Special Services for the Blind - Aids for in-house use; Assistive/Adapted tech devices, equip & products; Audio mat; Bks on cassette; Bks on CD; Braille & cassettes; Braille bks; Braille equip; Home delivery serv; Internet workstation with adaptive software; Large print & cassettes; Large print bks; Large screen computer & software; Magnifiers; Recorded bks; Talking bks
Open Mon-Fri 9-9, Sat 9-5
Friends of the Library Group

WEYERS CAVE

J BLUE RIDGE COMMUNITY COLLEGE*, Houff Library, One College Lane, 24486. (Mail add: PO Box 80, 24486-0080), SAN 317-4689. Tel: 540-453-2247. E-mail: library@brcc.edu. Web Site: brcc.edu/library. *Instruction & Collection Mgmt Librn,* Avie Thacker; E-mail: thackera@brcc.edu; *Access Services Library Specialist,* Taylor Glenn; E-mail: glennt@brcc.edu; *Libr Spec,* Paul Frankel; E-mail: frankelp@brcc.edu; *Libr Spec,* Logan Hilbert; E-mail: hilbertl@brcc.edu; Staff 5 (MLS 3, Non-MLS 2)
Founded 1967. Enrl 4,131; Fac 277; Highest Degree: Associate

Library Holdings: AV Mats 1,784; Bks on Deafness & Sign Lang 20; DVDs 87; e-books 200,000; e-journals 10,000; Bk Titles 50,000; Bk Vols 50,061; Per Subs 100; Talking Bks 76; Videos 43
Special Collections: Virginia Regional Historical Coll
Subject Interests: Nursing, Veterinary tech
Automation Activity & Vendor Info: (Cataloging) Ex Libris Group; (Circulation) Ex Libris Group; (ILL) OCLC FirstSearch; (OPAC) Ex Libris Group
Wireless access
Function: ILL available
Publications: AV Guide; New Accessions; Periodical Listing
Partic in OCLC Online Computer Library Center, Inc; Virginia Commun Coll Syst; Virginia's Academic Library Consortium
Open Mon-Thurs 8-7, Fri 8-3

WILLIAMSBURG

COLLEGE OF WILLIAM & MARY IN VIRGINIA

C EARL GREGG SWEM LIBRARY*, One Landrum Dr, 23187. (Mail add: PO Box 8794, 23187-8794), SAN 363-4922. Tel: 757-221-3050. Circulation Tel: 757-221-3072. Interlibrary Loan Service Tel: 757-221-3089. Reference Tel: 757-221-3067. FAX: 757-221-2635. Circulation FAX: 757-221-3650. Interlibrary Loan Service FAX: 757-221-3088. Web Site: www.swem.wm.edu. *Dean,* Carrie Lynn Cooper; E-mail: clcooper@wm.edu; *Assoc Dean, Res & Pub Serv,* Lisa T Nickel; Tel: 757-221-1777, Fax: 757-221-2535, E-mail: ltnickel@wm.edu; *Dir, Libr Develop,* Karlene N Jennings; Tel: 757-221-7779; *Dir, Media Serv,* Troy Davis; Tel: 757-221-2643, E-mail: mtdavi@wm.edu; *Dir, Spec Coll,* Gerald Gaidmore; Tel: 757-221-1775, Fax: 757-221-5440, E-mail: gpgaidmore@wm.edu; *Head, Acq,* Stephen D Clark; Tel: 757-221-3107, Fax: 757-221-3645, E-mail: sdclar@wm.edu; *Head, Cat,* Trish Kearns; Tel: 757-221-1940, E-mail: pmkear@wm.edu; *Head, Ref,* Donald J Welsh; Tel: 757-221-3068, E-mail: djwels@wm.edu; *Head, Ser,* Jean Sibley; Tel: 757-221-3103, E-mail: bjsibley@wm.edu; *Br Librn,* James T Deffenbaugh; Tel: 757-221-3057; *Ref Librn,* Mary S Molineux; Tel: 757-221-3076, E-mail: msmoli@wm.edu; *Ref/Govt Doc Librn,* Dr Alan F Zoellner; Tel: 757-221-3065, E-mail: afzoel@wm.edu; *Circ Mgr,* David Morales; *Spec Projects,* Kay Domine; Tel: 757-221-3091, E-mail: kjdomi@wm.edu. Subject Specialists: *Music, Sciences,* James T Deffenbaugh; Staff 67 (MLS 24, Non-MLS 43)
Founded 1693. Enrl 7,684; Fac 567; Highest Degree: Doctorate
Library Holdings: Bk Vols 1,846,385
Special Collections: Books with fore-edge Paintings (Ralph Wark Coll); Dogs (Peter Chapin, Murray & Shirley Horowitz Coll); History of Books & Printing; Seed Catalogs; Tucker-Coleman Papers (Virginia Family), 1675-1956; United States History 17th-19th Centuries (Warren E Burger Coll); Virginia History, 17th-20th Centuries, ms. State Document Depository; US Document Depository
Automation Activity & Vendor Info: (Acquisitions) SirsiDynix; (Cataloging) SirsiDynix; (Circulation) SirsiDynix; (Course Reserve) SirsiDynix; (ILL) SirsiDynix; (OPAC) SirsiDynix; (Serials) SirsiDynix
Partic in LYRASIS; Virginia Tidewater Consortium for Higher Education
Friends of the Library Group

CL THE WOLF LAW LIBRARY*, 613 S Henry St, 23187. (Mail add: PO Box 8795, 23187-8795), SAN 363-504X. Tel: 757-221-3255. Reference Tel: 757-221-3257. FAX: 757-221-3051. Web Site: www.wm.edu/law/lawlibrary. *Dir,* James Heller; Tel: 757-221-3252; *Head, Tech Serv,* Kevin Butterfield; *Instrul Serv Librn, Ref (Info Servs), Res,* Christopher Byrne; *Access Serv,* Martha Rush; *Ref Serv,* Frederick Dingledy; *Ref Serv,* Shelley Dowling; *Ref Serv,* Paul Hellyer; *Ref Serv,* Jennifer Sekula; Staff 7.5 (MLS 7.5)
Founded 1779. Enrl 630; Fac 35; Highest Degree: Doctorate
Library Holdings: Bk Titles 216,000; Bk Vols 406,000; Per Subs 4,000
Special Collections: Thomas Jefferson Law Books. US Document Depository
Subject Interests: Constitutional law, Environ law, Legal hist, Roman law
Automation Activity & Vendor Info: (Acquisitions) SirsiDynix; (Cataloging) SirsiDynix; (Circulation) SirsiDynix; (Course Reserve) SirsiDynix; (ILL) SirsiDynix; (OPAC) SirsiDynix; (Serials) SirsiDynix
Partic in LYRASIS; OCLC Online Computer Library Center, Inc
Open Mon-Thurs 7:30am-10pm, Fri 7:30-6, Sat 9-6, Sun 10-10 (Winter); Mon-Fri 8-6, Sat 10-3 (Summer)

S COLONIAL WILLIAMSBURG FOUNDATION, John D Rockefeller Jr Library, 313 First St, 23185-4306. (Mail add: PO Box 1776, 23187-1776), SAN 363-5139. Tel: 757-220-7249. FAX: 757-565-8508. E-mail: rocklibrary@cwf.org. Reference E-mail: libref@cwf.org. Web Site: www.history.org. *Dir,* Emily Guthrie; *Assoc Librn,* Douglas Mayo; Tel: 757-565-8521, Fax: 757-565-8528, E-mail: dmayo@cwf.org; *AV,* Marianne Martin; Tel: 757-565-8542, E-mail: mmartin@cwf.org; Staff 8 (MLS 5, Non-MLS 3)
Founded 1933
Library Holdings: Microforms 6,000; Bk Titles 60,000; Bk Vols 83,517; Per Subs 400
Special Collections: Manuscript Coll 17th-19th Century, doc; Rare Book Coll; Research Query File, 1927 to present; Research Reports; Visual Resource Coll
Subject Interests: African-Am, Archit, Customs, Decorative art, Early Am periods, Econ, Govt, Hist presv, Mus studies, Music, Soc life
Automation Activity & Vendor Info: (Acquisitions) Ex Libris Group; (Cataloging) Ex Libris Group; (Circulation) Ex Libris Group; (Course Reserve) Ex Libris Group; (ILL) Ex Libris Group; (Media Booking) Ex Libris Group; (OPAC) Ex Libris Group; (Serials) Ex Libris Group
Wireless access
Function: For res purposes, ILL available
Publications: Early American History Research Reports from the Colonial Williamsburg Foundation Library (Microfiche)
Open Mon-Fri 9-5
Restriction: Circ limited, Open to pub for ref only

M EASTERN STATE HOSPITAL*, Library Services, 4601 Ironbound Rd, 23188. SAN 317-4700. Tel: 757-208-7813. Web Site: esh.dbhds.virginia.gov. *Mgr,* Teresa Harper; E-mail: teresa.harper@dbhds.virginia.gov; Staff 2 (MLS 2)
Founded 1843
Library Holdings: Bk Titles 17,000; Bk Vols 17,800; Per Subs 343
Special Collections: Galt Papers, ms
Subject Interests: Nursing, Psychiat, Psychol, Soc work
Automation Activity & Vendor Info: (Cataloging) Follett Software; (Circulation) Follett Software; (OPAC) Follett Software
Function: Outside serv via phone, mail, e-mail & web
Publications: Inflow
Partic in OCLC Online Computer Library Center, Inc; Proquest Dialog; Tidewater Health Sci Librs
Open Mon-Fri 7:30-4

GL NATIONAL CENTER FOR STATE COURTS LIBRARY*, 300 Newport Ave, 23185-4147. SAN 317-4719. Tel: 757-259-1823. Toll Free Tel: 800-616-6164. E-mail: library@ncsc.org. Web Site: www.ncsc.org/publications-and-library/library-services. *Librn,* John Holtzclaw; E-mail: jholtzclaw@ncsc.org; Staff 1 (MLS 1)
Founded 1973
Library Holdings: Bk Titles 18,000; Bk Vols 40,000
Special Collections: Judicial Administration; National Center for State Courts Reports; State Court Annual Reports
Subject Interests: Court improvement, Court mgt, Judicial admin
Automation Activity & Vendor Info: (Acquisitions) SirsiDynix; (Cataloging) SirsiDynix; (Circulation) SirsiDynix; (OPAC) SirsiDynix; (Serials) SirsiDynix
Wireless access
Partic in OCLC Online Computer Library Center, Inc
Restriction: Open by appt only

S OMOHUNDRO INSTITUTE OF EARLY AMERICAN HISTORY & CULTURE*, Kellock Library, Swem Library, 400 Landrum Dr, 23185. (Mail add: PO Box 8781, 23187-8781), SAN 327-8832. Tel: 757-221-1114. FAX: 757-221-1047. E-mail: oieahc@wm.edu. Web Site: oieahc.wm.edu.
Library Holdings: Bk Titles 8,730; Per Subs 31
Wireless access
Restriction: Non-circulating

P WILLIAMSBURG REGIONAL LIBRARY*, 7770 Croaker Rd, 23188-7064. SAN 317-4727. Tel: 757-741-3300. E-mail: wrl@wrl.org. Web Site: www.wrl.org. *Dir,* Sandy Towers; E-mail: stowers@wrl.org; *Dir, Adult Serv,* Melissa Simpson; Tel: 757-741-3355, E-mail: msimpson@wrl.org; *Dir, Finance & Gen Serv,* Carrie Binsfeld; Tel: 757-741-3407, E-mail: cbinsfel@wrl.org; *Asst Dir,* Sandra Towers; Tel: 757-741-3385, E-mail: stowers@wrl.org; *Circ Serv Dir,* Alicia Phinney; Tel: 757-741-3353, E-mail: aphinney@wrl.org; *Dir, Info Tech Serv,* Mark Lutner; Tel: 757-741-3329, E-mail: mlutner@wrl.org; *Prog Serv Dir,* Rob Haas; Tel: 757-741-3371, E-mail: rhaas@mail.wrl.org; *Dir, Tech Serv, Spec Project Dir,* Barry Trott; Tel: 757-741-3330, E-mail: btrott@wrl.org; *Youth Serv Dir,* Ben Strohm; Tel: 757-741-3368, E-mail: bstrohm@mail.wrl.org; Staff 85 (MLS 35, Non-MLS 50)
Founded 1911. Pop 90,126; Circ 972,960
Jul 2019-Jun 2020 Income (Main & Associated Libraries) $7,050,568, State $325,590, City $904,244, County $4,933,357, Locally Generated Income $243,076, Other $644,301. Mats Exp $580,000, Books $251,755, Per/Ser (Incl. Access Fees) $20,250, Micro $500, AV Mat $62,845, Electronic Ref Mat (Incl. Access Fees) $214,450. Sal $3,307,375
Library Holdings: Audiobooks 25,084; DVDs 25,476; e-books 26,902; Microforms 19; Bk Vols 209,603
Special Collections: Local Documents
Automation Activity & Vendor Info: (Acquisitions) SirsiDynix; (Cataloging) SirsiDynix; (Circulation) SirsiDynix; (Discovery) EBSCO Discovery Service; (ILL) OCLC; (OPAC) SirsiDynix; (Serials) SirsiDynix
Wireless access

Function: 24/7 Electronic res, 24/7 Online cat, 3D Printer, Accelerated reader prog, Activity rm, Adult bk club, Art exhibits, Art programs, Audiobks on Playaways & MP3, Audiobks via web, AV serv, Bk club(s), Bks on CD, Chess club, Children's prog, Computer training, Computers for patron use, Digital talking bks, Electronic databases & coll, Family literacy, Free DVD rentals, Govt ref serv, Health sci info serv, Holiday prog, Home delivery & serv to seniorr ctr & nursing homes, Homebound delivery serv, ILL available, Internet access, Large print keyboards, Life-long learning prog for all ages, Literacy & newcomer serv, Magazines, Magnifiers for reading, Mail & tel request accepted, Mango lang, Meeting rooms, Microfiche/film & reading machines, Movies, Music CDs, Online cat, Online info literacy tutorials on the web & in blackboard, Online ref, Outreach serv, Outside serv via phone, mail, e-mail & web, Photocopying/Printing, Preschool outreach, Preschool reading prog, Prog for adults, Prog for children & young adult, Ref & res, Ref serv available, Res assist avail, Scanner, Senior computer classes, Senior outreach, Spanish lang bks, Spoken cassettes & CDs, Spoken cassettes & DVDs, STEM programs, Story hour, Study rm, Summer & winter reading prog, Summer reading prog, Tax forms, Teen prog, Telephone ref, Visual arts prog, Wheelchair accessible, Winter reading prog, Workshops, Writing prog
Publications: Beyond the Shelves (Quarterly); WRL-Info (Online only)
Special Services for the Blind - Audio mat; BiFolkal kits; Bks on CD; Digital talking bk; Large print bks; Large screen computer & software; Low vision equip; Magnifiers; Recorded bks
Open Mon-Thurs 10-9, Fri 10-6, Sat 10-5, Sun 1-5
Friends of the Library Group
Bookmobiles: 4

WINCHESTER

P HANDLEY REGIONAL LIBRARY SYSTEM*, Handley Library, 100 W Piccadilly St, 22601. (Mail add: PO Box 58, 22604), SAN 317-4735. Tel: 540-662-9041. FAX: 540-662-9053. Reference E-mail: info@handleyregional.org. Web Site: handleyregional.org. *Dir,* John Huddy; Tel: 540-662-9041, Ext 14, E-mail: jhuddy@handleyregional.org; *Dep Dir,* Ann White; Tel: 540-662-9041, Ext 25, E-mail: awhite@handleyregional.org; Staff 27 (MLS 7, Non-MLS 20)
Founded 1913. Pop 122,316; Circ 854,933
Jul 2015-Jun 2016 Income (Main & Associated Libraries) $2,306,050, State $360,668, City $419,020, County $862,665, Locally Generated Income $390,902, Other $190,000. Mats Exp $296,002, Books $144,573, Per/Ser (Incl. Access Fees) $15,385, Micro $768, AV Mat $80,129, Electronic Ref Mat (Incl. Access Fees) $55,145. Sal $1,185,299 (Prof $375,308)
Library Holdings: AV Mats 26,000; DVDs 27,234; DVDs 27,234; e-books 82,330; e-books 82,330; Microforms 53; Microforms 53; Bk Vols 259,282; Per Subs 315; Talking Bks 4,969
Special Collections: Civil War Coll; Extensive Archives Coll on local history for 9 County area of Virginia/West Virginia; Rare Local Newspapers; Virginiana Coll
Automation Activity & Vendor Info: (Acquisitions) TLC (The Library Corporation); (Cataloging) TLC (The Library Corporation); (Circulation) TLC (The Library Corporation); (OPAC) TLC (The Library Corporation)
Wireless access
Function: 24/7 Electronic res, 24/7 Online cat, Activity rm, Adult literacy prog, Archival coll, Art exhibits, Audiobks via web, AV serv, Bks on CD, Chess club, Children's prog, Computers for patron use, Digital talking bks, Electronic databases & coll, For res purposes, Free DVD rentals, Health sci info serv, Holiday prog, ILL available, Internet access, Life-long learning prog for all ages, Magazines, Magnifiers for reading, Mail & tel request accepted, Mango lang, Meeting rooms, Microfiche/film & reading machines, Movies, Music CDs, Online cat, Online ref, Outreach serv, Outside serv via phone, mail, e-mail & web, OverDrive digital audio bks, Photocopying/Printing, Preschool outreach, Preschool reading prog, Prog for adults, Prog for children & young adult, Ref & res, Ref serv available, Res performed for a fee, Spanish lang bks, Story hour, Study rm, Summer & winter reading prog, Summer reading prog, Tax forms, Teen prog, Wheelchair accessible, Winter reading prog, Workshops, Writing prog
Publications: The Friend
Member Libraries: Handley Regional Library System
Open Mon-Thurs 10-6, Fri 10-5, Sat 10-2
Friends of the Library Group
Branches: 2
MARY JANE & JAMES L BOWMAN BRANCH, 871 Tasker Rd, Stephens City, 22655. (Mail add: PO Box 1300, Stephens City, 22655-1300). Tel: 540-869-9000. Reference Tel: 540-869-9000, Ext 203. Information Services Tel: 540-869-9000, Ext 201. FAX: 540-869-9001. Reference E-mail: reference@handleyregional.org. *Br Mgr,* Mary Anton; E-mail: manton@handleyregional.org; Staff 4 (MLS 4)
Founded 2001
Publications: Handley Regional Library: The First One Hundred Years (Local historical information)
Mem of Handley Regional Library System
Open Mon-Thurs 10-6, Fri 10-5, Sat 10-2
Friends of the Library Group

CLARKE COUNTY LIBRARY, 101 Chalmers Ct, Ste C, Berryville, 22611, SAN 375-5665. Tel: 540-955-5144. FAX: 540-955-5178. E-mail: ccl@handleyregional.org. *Br Mgr,* Laurine Kennedy; Tel: 540-955-5190, E-mail: lkennedy@handleyregional.org
Mem of Handley Regional Library System
Open Mon-Thurs 10-6, Fri 10-5, Sat 10-2
Friends of the Library Group

C SHENANDOAH UNIVERSITY*, Alson H Smith Jr Library, 1460 University Dr, 22601. SAN 317-4743. Tel: 540-665-5424. Interlibrary Loan Service Tel: 540-545-7318. Reference Tel: 540-665-5421. Toll Free Tel: 877-289-4611. FAX: 540-665-4609. E-mail: library@su.edu. Web Site: www.su.edu/university-libraries. *Dir of Libr,* Christopher A Bean; Tel: 540-665-4553, E-mail: cbean@su.edu; *Electronic Res Librn,* Stacy Baggett; Tel: 540-665-4819, E-mail: sbaggett@su.edu; *Grad Prog Librn,* Rosemary Green; Tel: 540-665-4634, E-mail: rgreen@su.edu; *Health Sci Librn,* Denise Blake; Tel: 540-678-4351, E-mail: dblake@su.edu; *Info Literacy & Ref Librn,* Andrew Kulp; Tel: 540-665-5444, E-mail: akulp@su.edu; *Tech Serv Librn,* Megan Williams; Tel: 540-665-4638, E-mail: mwilliam@su.edu; Staff 15 (MLS 6, Non-MLS 9)
Founded 1875. Enrl 4,000; Fac 250; Highest Degree: Doctorate
Library Holdings: CDs 6,000; DVDs 500; e-books 250,000; e-journals 85,000; Electronic Media & Resources 150,000; Microforms 25,000; Music Scores 17,000; Bk Titles 97,000; Bk Vols 107,000
Special Collections: Religion (Evangelical United Brethren Church Historical Room); Shenandoah University Archives
Subject Interests: Bus, Dance, Music, Nursing, Pharm, Phys therapy
Automation Activity & Vendor Info: (Acquisitions) OCLC Worldshare Management Services; (Cataloging) OCLC Worldshare Management Services; (Circulation) OCLC Worldshare Management Services; (Course Reserve) OCLC Worldshare Management Services; (Discovery) OCLC; (ILL) OCLC WorldShare Interlibrary Loan; (OPAC) OCLC; (Serials) OCLC Worldshare Management Services
Wireless access
Function: 24/7 Electronic res, 24/7 Online cat, Ref serv available, Scanner
Partic in LYRASIS; Virginia Independent College & University Library Association; Virginia's Academic Library Consortium
Open Mon-Thurs 8am-Midnight, Fri 8-8, Sat 10-6, Sun 1-Midnight
Restriction: 24-hr pass syst for students only
Friends of the Library Group

WISE

P LONESOME PINE REGIONAL LIBRARY*, Administrative Office, 124 Library Rd SW, 24293-5907. SAN 363-5287. Tel: 276-328-8325. FAX: 276-328-1739. E-mail: reglib@lprlibrary.org. Web Site: www.lprlibrary.org/about/administration-office/. *Dir,* Shannon Steffey; Tel: 276-328-8325, Ext 103, E-mail: steffey@lprlibrary.org; Staff 48 (MLS 3, Non-MLS 45)
Founded 1958. Pop 101,922; Circ 229,204
Library Holdings: Audiobooks 22,418; AV Mats 21,228; Bk Vols 466,137; Per Subs 223
Subject Interests: Genealogy, SW Va hist
Automation Activity & Vendor Info: (Acquisitions) TLC (The Library Corporation); (Cataloging) TLC (The Library Corporation); (Circulation) TLC (The Library Corporation); (ILL) TLC (The Library Corporation); (OPAC) TLC (The Library Corporation); (Serials) TLC (The Library Corporation)
Wireless access
Function: Audiobks via web, Bks on CD, Children's prog, Computers for patron use, Free DVD rentals, Homebound delivery serv, ILL available, Microfiche/film & reading machines, Music CDs, Online cat, OverDrive digital audio bks, Photocopying/Printing, Preschool reading prog, Prog for adults, Prog for children & young adult, Ref serv available, Story hour, Summer & winter reading prog, Tax forms, Teen prog
Open Mon-Fri 8:30-5
Branches: 9
COEBURN COMMUNITY, 111 Third St, Coeburn, 24230. (Mail add: PO Box 2169, Coeburn, 24230-3523), SAN 363-5317. Tel: 276-395-6152. FAX: 276-395-3563. E-mail: ccllib@lprlibrary.org. *Br Mgr,* Emily Williams; E-mail: ewilliams@lprlibrary.org; Staff 5 (Non-MLS 5)
Founded 1972. Circ 73,796
Library Holdings: AV Mats 3,089; Bk Vols 35,448; Per Subs 47; Talking Bks 891
Open Mon, Wed, Fri 9:30-6, Tues 10:30-7, Sat 1-5, Sun 2-5
Friends of the Library Group
JONNIE B DEEL MEMORIAL, 198 Chase St, Clintwood, 24228. (Mail add: PO Box 650, Clintwood, 24228-0650), SAN 363-5309. Tel: 276-926-6617. FAX: 276-926-6795. E-mail: jbdlib@lprlibrary.org. *Br Mgr,* Kimberley Rose; E-mail: krose@lprlibrary.org; Staff 6 (Non-MLS 6)
Founded 1962. Circ 86,858
Library Holdings: AV Mats 3,367; Bk Vols 64,156; Per Subs 65; Talking Bks 1,358
Open Mon, Wed & Fri 8:30-5, Tues & Thurs 11-7:30, Sat 10-2

HAYSI PUBLIC, 157 O'Quinn St, Haysi, 24256. (Mail add: PO Box CC, Haysi, 24256-0431), SAN 363-5376. Tel: 276-865-4851. FAX: 276-865-5441. E-mail: hpllib@lprlibrary.org. *Br Mgr,* Kimberley Rose; E-mail: krose@lprlibrary.org; Staff 3 (Non-MLS 3)
Founded 1970. Circ 29,705
Library Holdings: AV Mats 1,145; Bk Vols 17,058; Per Subs 36; Talking Bks 655
Open Mon, Wed & Fri 8:30-5, Tues & Thurs 11-7:30, Sat 10-2

LEE COUNTY PUBLIC, 539 Joslyn Ave, Pennington Gap, 24277, SAN 363-5341. Tel: 276-546-1141. FAX: 276-546-5136. E-mail: lcplib@lprlibrary.org. *Br Mgr,* Audrey Evans; E-mail: aevans@lprlibrary.org; Staff 7 (Non-MLS 7)
Founded 1965. Circ 83,893
Library Holdings: AV Mats 3,547; Bk Vols 64,961; Per Subs 66; Talking Bks 1,801
Open Mon, Wed, Fri & Sat 8:30-5, Tues & Thurs 11:30-8, Sun 2-5

J FRED MATTHEWS MEMORIAL LIBRARY, 16552 Wise St, Saint Paul, 24283-3522. (Mail add: PO Box 1976, Saint Paul, 24283-1976), SAN 363-5430. Tel: 276-762-9702. FAX: 276-762-0528. E-mail: spblib@lprlibrary.org. *Br Mgr,* Emily Williams; E-mail: ewilliams@lprlibrary.org; Staff 5 (Non-MLS 5)
Founded 1975. Circ 56,613
Library Holdings: AV Mats 3,147; Bk Vols 29,758; Per Subs 42; Talking Bks 1,122
Open Mon, Thurs & Fri 9:30-6, Tues 10:30-7
Friends of the Library Group

ROSE HILL COMMUNITY, 6463 Dr Thomas Rd, Rose Hill, 24281. (Mail add: PO Box 280, Rose Hill, 24281-0280), SAN 363-5422. Tel: 276-445-5329. FAX: 276-445-5329. E-mail: rhplib@lprlibrary.org. *Br Mgr,* Audrey Evans; E-mail: aevans@lprlibrary.org; Staff 1 (Non-MLS 1)
Founded 1979. Circ 9,875
Library Holdings: AV Mats 828; Bk Vols 6,200; Per Subs 20; Talking Bks 361
Open Mon, Tues Thurs & Fri 1-5

SCOTT COUNTY PUBLIC, 297 W Jackson St, Gate City, 24251, SAN 363-5406. Tel: 276-386-3302. FAX: 276-386-2977. E-mail: scplib@lprlibrary.org. *Br Mgr,* Stephanie Griffin; E-mail: sgriffin@lprlibrary.org; Staff 7 (Non-MLS 7)
Founded 1972. Circ 123,165
Library Holdings: AV Mats 5,627; Bk Vols 79,398; Per Subs 77; Talking Bks 2,318
Open Mon, Wed & Fri 8:30-5, Tues & Thurs 11:30-8, Sat 1-5, Sun 2-5
Friends of the Library Group

C BASCOM SLEMP MEMORIAL LIBRARY, 11 Proctor St N, Big Stone Gap, 24219, SAN 363-549X. Tel: 276-523-1334. FAX: 276-523-5306. E-mail: cbslib@lprlibrary.org. *Br Mgr,* Dakota Mullins; E-mail: dmullins@lprlibrary.org; Staff 6 (Non-MLS 6)
Founded 1974. Circ 71,470
Library Holdings: AV Mats 3,152; Bk Vols 53,931; Per Subs 65; Talking Bks 1,284
Open Mon & Wed-Fri 9-6, Tues 11:30-8, Sat 1-5, Sun 2-5
Friends of the Library Group

WISE COUNTY PUBLIC, 124 Library Rd SW, 24293, SAN 363-552X. Tel: 276-328-8061. FAX: 276-328-3627. E-mail: wcplib@lprlibrary.org. *Br Mgr,* Hazel Jessee; E-mail: hjessee@lprlibrary.org; Staff 10 (MLS 1, Non-MLS 9)
Founded 1958. Circ 145,628
Library Holdings: AV Mats 6,618; Bk Vols 135,430; Per Subs 158; Talking Bks 2,193
Open Mon & Wed-Fri 9:30-6, Tues 11:30-8, Sat 1-5, Sun 2-5
Friends of the Library Group

C UNIVERSITY OF VIRGINIA'S COLLEGE AT WISE*, John Cook Wyllie Library, One College Ave, 24293. SAN 317-4751. Tel: 276-328-0150. Circulation Tel: 276-328-0158. Interlibrary Loan Service Tel: 276-328-0160. FAX: 276-328-0105. E-mail: library@uvawise.edu. Web Site: library.uvawise.edu. *Dir, Libr Serv,* Heather Groves Hannan; E-mail: arg9ct@uvawise.edu; *Asst Dir, Pub Serv,* Andy Johnson; E-mail: vez6ke@uvawise.edu; *Cat Librn,* Amelia C Vangundy; Tel: 276-328-0154, E-mail: acv6d@uvawise.edu; *Ref Librn,* Shannon Steffey; Tel: 276-328-0157, E-mail: sb3h@uvawise.edu; *Circ Supvr,* David Locke; E-mail: dal9n@uvawise.edu; Staff 13 (MLS 5, Non-MLS 8)
Founded 1954. Enrl 2,291; Fac 162; Highest Degree: Bachelor
Library Holdings: CDs 469; DVDs 530; e-books 137,262; e-journals 2,785; Microforms 66,463; Bk Titles 99,095; Bk Vols 145,327; Per Subs 623; Videos 1,299
Special Collections: Archives of Southwest Virginia Folklore Society; Beaty-Flannary Papers; Bruce Crawford Papers; Elihu Jasper Sutherland Papers; Emory L Hamilton Papers; Gladys Stallard Coll; James Taylor Adams Papers; Southwest Virginia (Archives of Southwest Virginia Historical Society; Trigg Floyd Papers; Virginia Coal Operators Coll). State Document Depository; US Document Depository
Subject Interests: Appalachian studies
Automation Activity & Vendor Info: (Acquisitions) SirsiDynix; (Cataloging) SirsiDynix; (Circulation) SirsiDynix; (Course Reserve) SirsiDynix; (ILL) OCLC WorldShare Interlibrary Loan; (OPAC) SirsiDynix; (Serials) SirsiDynix
Wireless access
Publications: Guide to Archives & Special Collections; Information Guides
Partic in LYRASIS; OCLC Online Computer Library Center, Inc
Open Mon-Thurs 8am-10pm, Fri 8-5, Sat 1-5, Sun 1:30-10 (Fall & Spring); Mon-Thurs 8-8, Fri 8-5 (Summer)

WYTHEVILLE

J WYTHEVILLE COMMUNITY COLLEGE LIBRARY*, 1000 E Main St, 24382. SAN 317-476X. Tel: 276-223-4743. Toll Free Tel: 800-468-1195, Ext 564743 (VA only). FAX: 276-223-4745. Web Site: www.wcc.vccs.edu/library. *Coordr, Libr Serv,* George Mattis; Tel: 276-223-4744, E-mail: gmattis@wcc.vccs.edu; *Libr Spec,* Jessica Childers; E-mail: jchilders@wcc.vccs.edu; Staff 2 (MLS 1, Non-MLS 1)
Founded 1963. Enrl 3,702; Fac 37; Highest Degree: Associate
Library Holdings: Bk Titles 26,016; Bk Vols 29,634; Per Subs 236
Special Collections: Local History & Genealogy (F B Kegley Library), bks, maps, ms, pamphlets. Oral History
Automation Activity & Vendor Info: (Cataloging) Ex Libris Group; (Circulation) Ex Libris Group; (OPAC) Ex Libris Group
Wireless access
Partic in Virginia Commun Coll Syst; Virginia's Academic Library Consortium
Open Mon-Thurs 8-7, Fri 8-5

YORKTOWN

G NATIONAL PARK SERVICE, Colonial National Historical Park Library, PO Box 210, 23690-0210. SAN 317-4778. Tel: 757-898-2410. *Library Contact,* Michelle Montanaro
Founded 1930
Library Holdings: Bk Vols 2,500
Subject Interests: Colonial hist, Revolutionary war hist
Restriction: Open by appt only

P YORK COUNTY PUBLIC LIBRARY*, Tabb Library, 100 Long Green Blvd, 23693. SAN 317-3003. Tel: 757-890-5100. Circulation Tel: 757-890-5130. Reference Tel: 757-890-5120. Administration Tel: 757-890-5105. FAX: 757-890-5127. TDD: 757-890-3621. E-mail: library_services@yorkcounty.gov. Web Site: www.yorkcounty.gov/library. *Libr Dir,* Kevin W Smith; Tel: 757-890-5134, E-mail: smithk@yorkcounty.gov; *Head, Circ,* Melissa Gardner; *Head, Coll Develop,* Linda Blanchard; Tel: 757-890-5104, E-mail: linda.blanchard@yorkcounty.org; *Head, Youth Serv,* Michelle Paxton; Staff 33.5 (MLS 6, Non-MLS 27.5)
Founded 1968. Pop 65,000; Circ 576,134
Library Holdings: Bk Vols 156,000; Per Subs 160; Talking Bks 6,435; Videos 13,241
Automation Activity & Vendor Info: (Acquisitions) Horizon; (Cataloging) SirsiDynix; (ILL) OCLC WorldShare Interlibrary Loan; (OPAC) Horizon; (Serials) SirsiDynix
Wireless access
Function: Adult bk club, Art exhibits, Audio & video playback equip for onsite use, AV serv, Bk club(s), Bks on CD, Children's prog, Computer training, Computers for patron use, Digital talking bks, Distance learning, E-Reserves, Electronic databases & coll, Free DVD rentals, Holiday prog, ILL available, Internet access, Jail serv, Magnifiers for reading, Mail & tel request accepted, Music CDs, Notary serv, Online cat, Online ref, Orientations, Outreach serv, Photocopying/Printing, Preschool outreach, Prog for adults, Prog for children & young adult, Ref & res, Ref serv available, Story hour, Summer reading prog, Teen prog, Telephone ref, Wheelchair accessible, Workshops, Writing prog
Open Mon-Thurs 10-7, Fri & Sat 10-5
Branches: 1

YORKTOWN BRANCH, 8500 George Washington Memorial Hwy, 23692. Tel: 757-890-3377. Circulation Tel: 757-890-5209. Reference Tel: 757-890-5207. FAX: 757-890-2956. *Libr Mgr,* Elizabeth Land; Tel: 757-890-3378
Founded 1968
Library Holdings: Bk Vols 60,000; Per Subs 260
Special Collections: Virginia & Local History Coll
Open Mon-Thurs 10-7, Fri & Sat 10-5

WASHINGTON

Date of Statistics: FY 2023
Population, 2022 U.S. Census: 7,951,150
Population Served by Public Libraries: 7,838,269
Unserved: 112,881
Total Volumes in Public Libraries: 24,344,315
Volumes Per Capita: 3.11
Total Public Library Circulation: 81,977,615
Circulation Per Capita: 10.46
Digital Resources:
Total e-books: 6,400,994
Total audio items: 5,400,187: (638,144 physical; 4,762,043 downloadable)
Total video items: 1,991,668: (1,129,200 physical; 862,468 downloadable)
Total Internet computers for use by the public: 5,369
Total annual wireless sessions: 9,573,417
Income and Expenditures:
Total Public Library Income: $593,488,291
Source of Income: 94.0% from Local Jurisdiction
Expenditures Per Capita: $73.55
Number of County or Multi-county (Regional) Libraries: 27
Counties Served: 36
Number of Mobile Units in State: 29
Information provided courtesy of: Evelyn Lindberg, Applications Librarian, Library Development; Washington State Library, Office of the Washington Secretary of State.

ABERDEEN

J GRAYS HARBOR COLLEGE*, John Spellman Library, 1620 Edward P Smith Dr, 98520. SAN 317-4786. Tel: 360-538-4050. Reference Tel: 360-538-4054. Toll Free Tel: 800-562-4830, Ext 4050 (WA only). FAX: 360-538-4294. Reference E-mail: lib-ref@ghc.edu. Web Site: ghc.libguides.com. *Interim Assoc Dean, Libr Serv,* Stanley W Horton; Tel: 360-538-4051, E-mail: stan.horton@ghc.edu; *Librn,* Deborah Bancroft; E-mail: deborah.bancrost@ghc.edu; *Librn,* Chris Springer; E-mail: chris.springer@ghc.edu; *Fac Librn,* Adrienne Roush; Tel: 360-538-4053, E-mail: aroush@ghc.edu; Staff 5 (MLS 2, Non-MLS 3)
Founded 1930. Highest Degree: Associate
Library Holdings: AV Mats 4,000; Bk Titles 33,527; Bk Vols 38,559; Per Subs 241
Special Collections: Pacific Northwest; Small Business; Water/Fisheries
Subject Interests: Careers
Automation Activity & Vendor Info: (Acquisitions) Ex Libris Group; (Cataloging) Ex Libris Group; (Circulation) Ex Libris Group; (OPAC) Ex Libris Group; (Serials) Ex Libris Group
Wireless access
Partic in Washington Community & Technical Colleges Library Consortium; Western Libr Network
Open Mon-Wed 7:30am-8pm, Thurs 7:30-6, Fri 7:30-4:30, Sat 10-3

ANACORTES

P ANACORTES PUBLIC LIBRARY*, 1220 Tenth St, 98221-1988. SAN 317-4794. Tel: 360-293-1910. FAX: 360-293-1929. Web Site: www.anacorteswa.gov/220/Library. *Libr Dir,* Ruth Barefoot; E-mail: ruthb@cityofanacortes.org; *Ad,* Jeff Vogel; Tel: 360-293-8128, E-mail: JeffV@cityofanacortes.org; *Ch Serv Librn,* Leslie Wilson; Tel: 360-293-1910, Ext 27, E-mail: LeslieW@cityofanacortes.org; *Tech Serv Librn,* Jeff Vogel; Tel: 360-293-1910, Ext 33, E-mail: jeffv@cityofanacortes.org; *Teen Serv Librn,* Diana Farnsworth; Tel: 360-293-8067, E-mail: DianaF@cityofanacortes.org; *ILL,* Esther Noyes;. Tel: 360-293-1910, Ext 25, E-mail: esthern@cityofanacortes.org; Staff 5 (MLS 4, Non-MLS 1)
Founded 1911. Pop 16,600; Circ 200,416
Library Holdings: Audiobooks 1,966; AV Mats 16,039; e-books 39,791; Large Print Bks 1,860; Bk Vols 86,358; Per Subs 184
Special Collections: Dominic Manieri Jazz & Swing Coll, bks, CD, DVD, pers; Maritime Coll, bks, chts, DVD, maps, pers
Automation Activity & Vendor Info: (Cataloging) SirsiDynix; (Circulation) SirsiDynix; (Course Reserve) SirsiDynix; (Discovery) EBSCO Discovery Service; (ILL) OCLC; (OPAC) SirsiDynix
Wireless access
Function: 24/7 Electronic res, 24/7 Online cat, Activity rm, Adult bk club, Audiobks via web, Bks on cassette, Bks on CD, Children's prog, Computers for patron use, Digital talking bks, E-Reserves, Electronic databases & coll, Free DVD rentals, ILL available, Internet access, Jazz prog, Large print keyboards, Magazines, Magnifiers for reading, Mail & tel request accepted, Mango lang, Meeting rooms, Movies, Music CDs, Online cat, OverDrive digital audio bks, Passport agency, Photocopying/Printing, Preschool reading prog, Printer for laptops & handheld devices, Prog for adults, Prog for children & young adult, Ref serv available, Spanish lang bks, Spoken cassettes & CDs, Spoken cassettes & DVDs, Story hour, Study rm, Summer & winter reading prog, Summer reading prog, Tax forms, Teen prog, Telephone ref, Wheelchair accessible
Partic in OCLC Online Computer Library Center, Inc; Washington Digital Library Consortium
Open Mon-Fri 11-7, Sat & Sun 11-4
Restriction: Non-resident fee
Friends of the Library Group

AUBURN

C GREEN RIVER COLLEGE*, Holman Library, 12401 SE 320th St, 98092-3699. SAN 317-4824. Tel: 253-833-9111. Circulation Tel: 253-288-3491, Ext 2085. Reference Tel: 253-288-3491, Ext 2091. Administration Tel: 253-833-9111, Ext 2099. FAX: 253-288-3436, 253-288-3491. Web Site: www.greenriver.edu/campus/campus-resources/holman-library/. *Dean of Libr, Media Serv,* Jennifer Dysart; Tel: 253-833-9111, Ext 2094, E-mail: jdysart@greenriver.edu; *Fac Librn,* Amanda Chin; Tel: 253-833-9111, E-mail: achin@greenriver.edu; *Fac Librn,* Katie Cunnion; Tel: 253-833-9111, Ext 2104, E-mail: kcunnion@greenriver.edu; *Fac Librn,* Jennifer Rohan; Tel: 253-833-9111, Ext 2102, E-mail: jrohan@greenriver.edu; *Fac Librn,* Jody Segal; Tel: 253-833-9111, Ext 2103, E-mail: jsegal@greenriver.edu; *Coll Develop, Fac Librn,* Marjorie MacKenzie; Tel: 253-833-9111, Ext 2101, E-mail: mmackenzie@greenriver.edu; *Circ Supvr,* Nadine Pavlov; Tel: 253-833-9111, Ext 2088, E-mail: npavlov@greenriver.edu; *Circ & ILL,* Catherine Rabold; Tel: 253-833-9111, Ext 2093, E-mail: crabold@greenriver.edu; *Tech Serv,* Hannah Micona; Tel: 253-833-9111, Ext 2098, E-mail: hmicona@greenriver.edu; Staff 16.4 (MLS 7.6, Non-MLS 8.8)
Founded 1965. Enrl 9,800; Fac 639; Highest Degree: Bachelor
Library Holdings: Bk Titles 39,600; Bk Vols 53,000; Per Subs 285; Videos 4,250
Automation Activity & Vendor Info: (Cataloging) Ex Libris Group; (Circulation) Ex Libris Group; (Course Reserve) Ex Libris Group; (ILL) OCLC; (OPAC) Ex Libris Group; (Serials) Ex Libris Group
Wireless access
Function: 24/7 Electronic res, 24/7 Online cat, Audio & video playback equip for onsite use, Bks on CD, CD-ROM, Computers for patron use, Distance learning, E-Reserves, Electronic databases & coll, Free DVD rentals, ILL available, Internet access, Magazines, Magnifiers for reading, Movies, Music CDs, Online cat, Online info literacy tutorials on the web & in blackboard, Online ref, Orientations, Outside serv via phone, mail, e-mail & web, Photocopying/Printing, Printer for laptops & handheld devices, Ref & res, Ref serv available, Scanner, Telephone ref, Wheelchair accessible
Partic in Washington Community & Technical Colleges Library Consortium

Special Services for the Blind - Assistive/Adapted tech devices, equip & products; Closed circuit TV; Computer with voice synthesizer for visually impaired persons; Reader equip; ZoomText magnification & reading software
Open Mon-Thurs 7am-9pm, Fri 7-4, Sun 1-7 (Fall-Spring); Mon-Thurs 7:30-7:30, Sun 2-6 (Summer)

S WHITE RIVER VALLEY MUSEUM RESEARCH LIBRARY*, 918 H St SE, 98002. SAN 370-3215. Tel: 253-288-7433. FAX: 253-931-3098. Web Site: www.wrvmuseum.org. *Curator of Coll,* Hilary Pittenger; Tel: 253-288-7438, E-mail: hpittenger@auburnwa.gov; Staff 5.8 (Non-MLS 5.8)
Founded 1959
Library Holdings: CDs 10; DVDs 15; Bk Titles 1,000
Special Collections: Historic Photographs, Auburn & Kent; Newspapers, Auburn & Kent (1893 - 2006); Yearbooks, Auburn & Kent Schools 1912-2016
Subject Interests: Local hist
Wireless access
Open Wed-Sun 12-4
Restriction: Not a lending libr

BELLEVUE

C BELLEVUE COLLEGE, Library Media Center, 3000 Landerholm Circle SE, 98007. SAN 317-4832. Tel: 425-564-2252. Reference Tel: 425-564-6161. E-mail: reference@bellevuecollege.edu. Web Site: www.bellevuecollege.edu/lmc. *Assoc Dean of Libr,* Karen R Diller, PhD; Tel: 425-564-3133, E-mail: karen.diller@bellevuecollege.edu; *Syst Librn,* Nicole Longpre; Tel: 425-564-3071, E-mail: nicole.longpre@bellevuecollege.edu; Staff 13 (MLS 7, Non-MLS 6)
Founded 1966. Enrl 11,000; Highest Degree: Bachelor
Library Holdings: High Interest/Low Vocabulary Bk Vols 200; Bk Vols 36,000; Per Subs 27
Automation Activity & Vendor Info: (Acquisitions) Ex Libris Group; (Cataloging) Ex Libris Group; (Circulation) Ex Libris Group; (ILL) OCLC FirstSearch; (OPAC) Ex Libris Group; (Serials) Ex Libris Group
Wireless access
Partic in ORCA Consortium; Washington Community & Technical Colleges Library Consortium
Special Services for the Blind - Computer access aids
Open Mon-Thurs 8-6, Fri 8-5

BELLINGHAM

P BELLINGHAM PUBLIC LIBRARY*, 210 Central Ave, 98225. SAN 363-5589. Tel: 360-778-7323. Administration Tel: 360-778-7220. Web Site: www.bellinghampubliclibrary.org. *Dir,* Rebecca Judd; Tel: 360-778-7221, E-mail: rejudd@cob.org; *Dep Dir,* Bethany Hoglund; Tel: 360-778-7263, E-mail: bhoglund@cob.org; *Head, Commun Relations,* Annette Bagley; Tel: 360-778-7206, E-mail: ambagley@cob.org; *Head, Libr Operations,* Jennifer VanderPloeg; Tel: 360-778-7233, E-mail: jmvanderploeg@cob.org; *Head, Coll Mgt & Digital Serv,* Jon McConnel; Tel: 360-778-7227, E-mail: jlmcconnel@cob.org; *Head, Pub Serv,* Position Currently Open; *Ad,* Suzanne Carlson-Prandini; Tel: 360-778-7236, E-mail: scarlson-prandini@cob.org; *Ad,* Katie Bray; Tel: 360-778-7230, E-mail: knbray@cob.org; *Ch Serv Librn,* Bernice Chang; Tel: 360-778-7266, E-mail: bchang@cob.org; *Ch Serv Librn,* Ali Kubeny; Tel: 360-778-7241, E-mail: alkubeny@cob.org; *Pub Serv Librn,* Liz Hendershott; Tel: 360-778-7246, E-mail: ekhendershott@cob.org; *Pub Serv Librn,* Rob Werner; Tel: 360-778-7214, E-mail: rowerner@cob.org; *Teen Serv Librn,* Jennifer Lovchik; Tel: 360-778-7231, E-mail: jlovchik@cob.org; *Supvr, Pub Serv,* Michelle Becker; Tel: 360-778-7224, E-mail: mebecker@cob.org; *Operations Supvr,* Alison Kuiken; Tel: 360-778-7238, E-mail: aakuiken@cob.org; Staff 10 (MLS 10)
Founded 1904. Pop 93,910; Circ 1,761,217
Library Holdings: DVDs 16,016; e-books 71,593; Bk Vols 164,662; Per Subs 255
Special Collections: Local History Coll. Municipal Document Depository
Automation Activity & Vendor Info: (Acquisitions) Innovative Interfaces, Inc. - Polaris; (Cataloging) OCLC Connexion; (Circulation) Innovative Interfaces, Inc. - Polaris; (ILL) OCLC WorldShare Interlibrary Loan; (OPAC) Innovative Interfaces, Inc. - Polaris; (Serials) Innovative Interfaces, Inc. - Polaris
Wireless access
Function: 24/7 Electronic res, 24/7 Online cat, Adult bk club, Audiobks via web, Bk club(s), Bks on CD, Children's prog, Computer training, Computers for patron use, Digital talking bks, Electronic databases & coll, Free DVD rentals, ILL available, Internet access, Magazines, Magnifiers for reading, Mango lang, Microfiche/film & reading machines, Movies, Museum passes, Music CDs, Online cat, Online ref, Outreach serv, OverDrive digital audio bks, Photocopying/Printing, Preschool outreach, Preschool reading prog, Prog for adults, Prog for children & young adult, Ref serv available, Senior outreach, Spanish lang bks, Story hour, Study rm, Summer reading prog, Tax forms, Teen prog, Telephone ref, Wheelchair accessible
Partic in OCLC Online Computer Library Center, Inc; Washington Digital Library Consortium
Special Services for the Deaf - Bks on deafness & sign lang; Closed caption videos; High interest/low vocabulary bks; Video relay services
Special Services for the Blind - Accessible computers
Open Mon & Tues 10-7, Wed-Sat 10-6, Sun 1-5
Friends of the Library Group
Branches: 3
BARKLEY, 3111 Newmarket St, Ste 102, 98226. Tel: 360-778-7290.
Founded 2008
Open Mon,Tues & Sat 10-2, Wed-Fri 2-6
BELLIS FAIR, One Bellis Fair Pkwy, Ste 616, 98226. Tel: 360-778-7320.
Open Wed-Fri 2-6, Sat 11-6, Sun 1-5
Friends of the Library Group
FAIRHAVEN, 1117 12th St, 98225. SAN 363-5619. Tel: 360-778-7188. FAX: 360-778-7192.
Library Holdings: Bk Vols 10,000
Open Mon, Tues & Sat 10-2, Wed-Fri 2-6

J BELLINGHAM TECHNICAL COLLEGE LIBRARY, 3028 Lindbergh Ave, 98225-1599. Tel: 360-752-8383. E-mail: library@btc.edu. Web Site: www.btc.edu/academics/library. *Exec Dir of Library, eLearning & Academic Support,* Dawn Hawley; Tel: 360-752-8574, E-mail: dhawley@btc.edu; *Lead Librn,* Traci Taylor; Tel: 360-752-8488, E-mail: ttaylor@btc.edu; *Libr Spec,* Eleanor Bishop; E-mail: ebishop@btc.edu; *Libr Spec,* Jennifer McCool; Tel: 360-752-8382, E-mail: jmccool@btc.edu; Staff 2.3 (MLS 2.3)
Founded 1995. Highest Degree: Associate
Library Holdings: e-books 297,400; e-journals 47,500; Electronic Media & Resources 8,900; Bk Titles 10,104; Bk Vols 11,667; Per Subs 59
Automation Activity & Vendor Info: (Cataloging) Ex Libris Group; (Circulation) Ex Libris Group; (Course Reserve) Ex Libris Group; (ILL) OCLC FirstSearch; (OPAC) Ex Libris Group; (Serials) Ex Libris Group
Wireless access
Partic in Washington Community & Technical Colleges Library Consortium
Special Services for the Blind - Audio mat
Open Mon-Fri 8-5

C NORTHWEST INDIAN COLLEGE, Lummi Library, 2522 Kwina Rd, 98226. Tel: 360-392-4218. Toll Free Tel: 877-676-2772, Ext 4218. FAX: 360-733-3385. E-mail: library@nwic.edu. Web Site: www.nwic.edu/lummi-library. *Libr Dir,* Maureen Stewart; Tel: 360-392-4204, E-mail: mmstewart@nwic.edu
Founded 1983
Library Holdings: Bk Titles 35,000
Wireless access
Partic in American Indian Higher Education Consortium
Open Mon-Thurs 8am-9pm, Fri 8-5, Sun 12-5

C WESTERN WASHINGTON UNIVERSITY, Western Libraries, 516 High St, MS 9103, 98225. SAN 363-5643. Tel: 360-650-3084. Administration Tel: 360-650-3051. FAX: 360-650-3044. Web Site: library.wwu.edu. *Dean of Libr,* John Danneker; E-mail: dannekj@wwu.edu; *Asst Dean, Libr,* Kate Cabe; Tel: 360-650-6740, E-mail: cabek@wwu.edu; *Dir of Coll,* Madeline Kelly; Tel: 360-650-4320, E-mail: madeline.kelly@wwu.edu; *Dir, Archives & Spec Coll,* Elizabeth Joffrion; Tel: 360-650-3283, E-mail: elizabeth.joffrion@wwu.edu; *Head, Hacherl Research & Writing Studio,* J Gabriel Gossett; Tel: 360-650-7555, E-mail: gossetj2@wwu.edu; *Head, Metadata & Cat,* Casey Mullin; Tel: 360-650-7458, E-mail: mullinc3@wwu.edu; *Head Music Libr,* Marian Ritter; Tel: 630-650-3696, E-mail: marian.ritter@wwu.edu; *Librn,* Andrea Peterson; Tel: 360-650-3894, E-mail: petersa@wwu.edu; *Children's & YA Literature Librn,* Sylvia Tag; Tel: 360-650-7992, E-mail: stag@wwu.edu; *Student Success Librn,* Elizabeth Stephan; Tel: 360-650-2061, E-mail: stephae@wwu.edu; *Teaching, Learning & Media Librn,* Jeff Purdue; Tel: 360-650-7750, E-mail: purduej@wwu.edu; *Fac Mgr,* Kate Farmer; Tel: 360-650-4994, E-mail: farmerk3@wwu.edu; *Library Communications Mgr,* Clarissa Mansfield; Tel: 360-650-3052, E-mail: mansfic@wwu.edu; *Univ Archivist & Rec Mgr,* Tony Kurtz; Tel: 360-650-3114, E-mail: kurtza@wwu.edu; *Archivist, Ctr for Pac NW Studies,* Ruth Steele; Tel: 360-650-7747, E-mail: steeler@wwu.edu; *Sr Developer, Digital Initiatives,* David Bass. Subject Specialists: *Music,* Marian Ritter; Staff 58 (MLS 16, Non-MLS 42)
Founded 1899. Enrl 15,000; Fac 16; Highest Degree: Master
Special Collections: Canadian Coll; Children's Literature Coll; Fly Fishing Coll; Mongolia-Russian Far East Coll. Oral History; State Document Depository; US Document Depository
Automation Activity & Vendor Info: (Acquisitions) Ex Libris Group; (Cataloging) Ex Libris Group; (Circulation) Ex Libris Group; (Course Reserve) Ex Libris Group; (ILL) Ex Libris Group; (Media Booking) Ex Libris Group; (OPAC) Ex Libris Group; (Serials) Ex Libris Group
Wireless access
Function: ILL available

Partic in Orbis Cascade Alliance; Wash Coop Libr Project
Open Mon-Thurs 8am-9pm, Fri 8-6, Sat 10-6, Sun 1-9 (Fall-Spring); Mon-Fri 8-5 (Summer)

J WHATCOM COMMUNITY COLLEGE LIBRARY*, Heiner Bldg, 231 W Kellogg Rd, 98226. (Mail add: 237 W Kellogg Rd, 98226), SAN 317-4875. Tel: 360-383-3300. Interlibrary Loan Service Tel: 360-383-3294. Reference Tel: 360-383-3285. Administration Tel: 360-383-3295. E-mail: libref@whatcom.edu. Web Site: library.whatcom.edu. *Libr Dir,* Howard Fuller; E-mail: hfuller@whatcom.edu; *Coll Develop Librn, Fac Librn,* Kiki Tommila; E-mail: ktommila@whatcom.edu; *Copyright Librn,* Ro McKernan; E-mail: rmckernan@whatcom.edu; *Fac Librn, Syst Librn,* Sally Sheedy; E-mail: ssheedy@whatcom.edu; *Ref Librn,* Margaret Bikman; E-mail: mbikman@whatcom.edu; *Ref Librn,* Heather Williams; E-mail: hwilliams@whatcom.com; *Circ,* Brian Funk; E-mail: bfunk@whatcom.edu; *ILL,* Kate Harrison; E-mail: kharrison@whatcom.edu; *Pub Serv,* Linda Compton; E-mail: lcompton@whatcom.edu; *Reserves,* Ara Taylor; E-mail: ataylor@whatcom.edu; *Tech Serv,* Brett Straka; E-mail: bstraka@whatcom.edu; Staff 14 (MLS 5, Non-MLS 9)
Founded 1972. Enrl 4,000; Fac 289; Highest Degree: Associate
Library Holdings: Bk Vols 38,837; Per Subs 72
Automation Activity & Vendor Info: (Acquisitions) Ex Libris Group; (Cataloging) Ex Libris Group; (Circulation) Ex Libris Group; (Course Reserve) Ex Libris Group; (ILL) OCLC FirstSearch; (OPAC) Ex Libris Group
Wireless access
Function: Archival coll, Art exhibits, Audio & video playback equip for onsite use, Audiobks via web, Computers for patron use, Electronic databases & coll, ILL available, Internet access, Music CDs, Online cat, Online ref, Orientations, Photocopying/Printing, Ref & res, VHS videos
Partic in Washington Community & Technical Colleges Library Consortium
Open Mon-Thurs 8am-9pm, Fri 8-5, Sat Noon-4 (Fall-Spring); Mon-Thurs 8-5 (Summer)

GL WHATCOM COUNTY LAW LIBRARY*, Courthouse, Ste B-03, 311 Grand Ave, 98225. Tel: 360-778-5790. E-mail: lawlib@co.whatcom.wa.us. Web Site: www.whatcomcounty.us/306/Law-Library, www.whatcomlawlibrary.org. *Law Librn,* Gayle Isaac
Library Holdings: Bk Vols 14,000
Wireless access
Open Wed-Fri 10-4:30

P WHATCOM COUNTY LIBRARY SYSTEM*, 5205 Northwest Dr, 98226. SAN 363-5732. Tel: 360-305-3600. Web Site: www.wcls.org. *Exec Dir,* Christine Perkins; E-mail: christine.perkins@wcls.org; *Dep Dir,* Michael Cox; *Dir, Admin & Finance,* Jackie Saul; *Coll Serv Mgr,* Lisa Gresham; *Commun Relations Mgr,* Mary Vermillion; *Human Res Mgr,* Beth Andrews; *IT Serv Mgr,* Geoff Fitzpatrick; *Adult Prog Coordr,* Ann McAllen; Staff 82 (MLS 13, Non-MLS 69)
Founded 1945. Circ 1,887,853
Library Holdings: Audiobooks 13,147; AV Mats 50,968; CDs 13,190; DVDs 19,267; Large Print Bks 5,953; Bk Vols 245,425; Per Subs 1,017; Videos 4,200
Automation Activity & Vendor Info: (Circulation) Horizon
Wireless access
Function: 24/7 Electronic res, Activity rm, Adult bk club, Audio & video playback equip for onsite use, Audiobks via web, Bilingual assistance for Spanish patrons, Bks on CD, Children's prog, Citizenship assistance, Computer training, Computers for patron use, Digital talking bks, Electronic databases & coll, Free DVD rentals, Home delivery & serv to seniorr ctr & nursing homes, Homebound delivery serv, ILL available, Jail serv, Life-long learning prog for all ages, Magazines, Mango lang, Movies, Music CDs, Online cat, Online ref, Outreach serv, Outside serv via phone, mail, e-mail & web, OverDrive digital audio bks, Photocopying/Printing, Prog for adults, Prog for children & young adult, Ref & res, Ref serv available, Scanner, Story hour, Summer reading prog, Tax forms, Teen prog, Telephone ref, Wheelchair accessible
Partic in OCLC Online Computer Library Center, Inc; Washington Digital Library Consortium
Friends of the Library Group
Branches: 10
BLAINE BRANCH, 610 Third St, Blaine, 98230, SAN 363-5767. Tel: 360-305-3637. *Br Mgr,* Jonathan Jakobitz
Open Mon-Thurs 10-8, Fri 10-6, Sat 10-5
Friends of the Library Group
DEMING BRANCH, 5044 Mount Baker Hwy, Deming, 98244. (Mail add: PO Box 357, Deming, 98244-0357). Tel: 360-592-2422. *Br Mgr,* Katrina Carabba
Open Mon-Thurs 10-8, Fri 10-6, Sat 10-5
Friends of the Library Group
EVERSON MCBEATH COMMUNITY LIBRARY, 104 Kirsch Dr, Everson, 98247. (Mail add: PO Box 250, Everson, 98247). Tel: 360-966-5100. *Br Mgr,* Paul Fullner
Open Mon-Thurs 10-8, Fri 10-6, Sat 10-5
Friends of the Library Group
FERNDALE BRANCH, 2125 Main St, Ferndale, 98248. (Mail add: PO Box 1209, Ferndale, 98248-1209), SAN 363-5759. Tel: 360-384-3647. *Br Mgr,* Alix Prior
Open Mon-Thurs 9-8, Fri 9-6, Sat 9-5, Sun 1-5
Friends of the Library Group
ISLAND BRANCH, 2144 S Nugent Rd, Lummi Island, 98262. Tel: 360-758-7145. *Br Mgr,* Brooke Pederson
Open Tues 1-7, Thurs & Sat 10-5; Tues 1-7, Thurs-Sat 10-5 (July-Aug)
Friends of the Library Group
LYNDEN BRANCH, 216 Fourth St, Lynden, 98264, SAN 363-5910. Tel: 360-354-4883. *Br Mgr,* Dianne Marrs-Smith
Function: Ref serv available
Open Mon-Thurs 9-8, Fri 9-6, Sat 9-5, Sun 1-5
Friends of the Library Group
NORTH FORK COMMUNITY LIBRARY, 7506 Kendall Rd, Maple Falls, 98266. Tel: 360-599-2020. *Br Mgr,* Katrina Buckman
Open Tues & Thurs 10-8, Wed & Fri 10-6, Sat 10-5
Friends of the Library Group
POINT ROBERTS BRANCH, 1431 Gulf Rd, Point Roberts, 98281. (Mail add: PO Box 970, Point Roberts, 98281), SAN 363-6003. Tel: 360-945-6545. *Br Mgr,* Kris Lomedico
Open Tues 1-7, Wed & Sat 10-5; Tues 1-7, Wed, Fri & Sat 10-5 (July-Aug)
Friends of the Library Group
SUMAS BRANCH, 461 Second St, Sumas, 98295. Tel: 360-988-2501. *Br Mgr,* Paul Fullner
Open Mon & Wed 10-6, Sat 10-5
Friends of the Library Group
Bookmobiles: 1. Mobile Servs Mgr, Sam Wallin

BREMERTON

S KITSAP COUNTY HISTORICAL SOCIETY*, Museum Library, 280 Fourth St, 98337-1813. SAN 327-4292. Tel: 360-479-6226. FAX: 360-415-9294. E-mail: research@kitsapmuseum.org. Web Site: kitsapmuseum.org/research-archives. *Librn,* Bonnie Chrey; *Archivist,* Carolyn McClurkan; Staff 3 (MLS 2, Non-MLS 1)
Founded 1948
Library Holdings: Bk Titles 200
Special Collections: Kitsap County; Washington State. Oral History
Function: Res libr
Restriction: Open to pub by appt only

P KITSAP REGIONAL LIBRARY*, 1301 Sylvan Way, 98310-3498. SAN 363-6097. Interlibrary Loan Service Tel: 360-405-9109. Administration Tel: 360-405-9158. Toll Free Tel: 877-883-9900. FAX: 360-405-9128. Web Site: www.krl.org. *Libr Dir,* Jason Driver; *Exec Dir, Found,* Wendy Kile; Tel: 360-405-9115; *Executive Asst,* Tommy Jefferies; E-mail: tjefferies@krl.org; *Chief Financial Officer,* Dan Baer; Tel: 360-405-9137, E-mail: dbaer@krl.org; *Dir, Commun & Tech Serv,* Kwang Kye; Tel: 360-405-9139, E-mail: kkye@krl.org; *Dir, Human Res,* Monica Houston; Tel: 360-475-9160, E-mail: mhouston@krl.org; Staff 31 (MLS 31)
Founded 1955. Pop 254,633; Circ 2,580,685
Library Holdings: Audiobooks 28,310; AV Mats 24,586; e-books 31,044; Bk Titles 349,315; Per Subs 729
Special Collections: Northwest Coll
Automation Activity & Vendor Info: (Acquisitions) Innovative Interfaces, Inc; (Cataloging) Innovative Interfaces, Inc; (Circulation) Innovative Interfaces, Inc; (ILL) Innovative Interfaces, Inc; (OPAC) Innovative Interfaces, Inc; (Serials) Innovative Interfaces, Inc
Wireless access
Partic in OCLC Online Computer Library Center, Inc
Friends of the Library Group
Branches: 9
BAINBRIDGE ISLAND BRANCH, 1270 Madison Ave N, Bainbridge Island, 98110-2747, SAN 363-6127. Tel: 206-842-4162. FAX: 206-780-5310. *Br Mgr,* Courtney Childress; E-mail: cchildress@krl.org
Founded 1963
Library Holdings: Bk Vols 81,306
Open Mon-Sat 10-4
Friends of the Library Group
DOWNTOWN BREMERTON BRANCH, 612 Fifth St, 98337-1416, SAN 363-6135. Tel: 360-377-3955. FAX: 360-479-8206. *Br Mgr,* Pam Crowe; E-mail: pcrowe@krl.org
Founded 1938
Library Holdings: Bk Vols 20,349
Special Collections: Northwest History Coll
Open Mon-Fri 10-4, Sat 10-1

KINGSTON BRANCH, 26159 Dulay Rd NE, Kingston, 98346, SAN 363-6240. Tel: 360-297-3330. FAX: 360-297-2911. *Br Mgr,* Leigh Ann Winterowd; E-mail: lwinterowd@krl.org
Founded 1945
Library Holdings: Bk Vols 12,034
Open Mon-Fri 10-4, Sat 10-1
Friends of the Library Group

LITTLE BOSTON, 31980 Little Boston Rd NE, Kingston, 98346-9700. (Mail add: 31912 Little Boston Rd NE, Kingston, 98346-9700). Tel: 360-297-2670. FAX: 360-297-2011. *Br Mgr,* Tomi Whalen; E-mail: twhalen@krl.org
Founded 1974
Library Holdings: Bk Vols 13,986
Special Collections: Native American Literature Coll
Open Mon-Fri 10-4, Sat 10-1

MANCHESTER BRANCH, 8067 E Main St, Manchester, 98353. (Mail add: PO Box 128, Manchester, 98353), SAN 363-6275. Tel: 360-871-3921. FAX: 360-871-6152. *Br Mgr,* Kathleen Wilson; E-mail: kwilson@krl.org
Founded 1947
Library Holdings: Bk Vols 12,848
Open Mon-Fri 10-4, Sat 10-1
Friends of the Library Group

PORT ORCHARD BRANCH, 87 Sidney Ave, Port Orchard, 98366-5249, SAN 363-6151. Tel: 360-876-2224. FAX: 360-876-9588. *Br Mgr,* Kathleen Wilson
Founded 1964
Library Holdings: Bk Vols 55,024
Open Mon-Sat 10-4
Friends of the Library Group

POULSBO BRANCH, 700 NE Lincoln Rd, Poulsbo, 98370-7688, SAN 363-6186. Tel: 360-779-2915. FAX: 360-779-1051. *Br Mgr,* Sharon Lee; E-mail: sslee@krl.org
Library Holdings: Bk Vols 61,850
Special Collections: Scandinavian Coll
Open Mon-Sat 10-4
Friends of the Library Group

SILVERDALE BRANCH, 3450 NW Carlton St, Silverdale, 98383-8325, SAN 363-6305. Tel: 360-692-2779. FAX: 360-698-7702. *Br Mgr,* Ashley Oaksmith; E-mail: aoaksmith@krl.org
Founded 1945
Library Holdings: Bk Vols 30,473
Open Mon-Sat 10-4
Friends of the Library Group

SYLVAN WAY BRANCH, 1301 Sylvan Way, 98310-3466. Tel: 360-405-9100. FAX: 360-405-9128. *Br Mgr,* Bert Rinderle; E-mail: brinderle@krl.org
Founded 1978
Library Holdings: Bk Vols 104,553
Open Mon-Sat 10-4
Friends of the Library Group

Bookmobiles: 1. Supvr, Jomichelle Seidl

J OLYMPIC COLLEGE*, Haselwood Library, 1600 Chester Ave, 98337. SAN 317-4891. Tel: 360-475-7250. Interlibrary Loan Service Tel: 360-475-7253. Reference Tel: 360-475-7252. Administration Tel: 360-475-7262. Toll Free Tel: 800-259-6718, Ext 7252. FAX: 360-475-7261. E-mail: librarians@olympic.edu. Web Site: libguides.olympic.edu/index, www.olympic.edu/academics/academic-support-services/olympic-college-libraries. *Dean of Libr,* Erica Coe; E-mail: ecoe@olympic.edu; *ILL,* Constance O'Shea; E-mail: coshea@olympic.edu; *Ref Serv,* Dianne Carey; E-mail: dcarey@olympic.edu; *Ref Serv,* Amy Herman; E-mail: aherman@olympic.edu; Staff 6 (MLS 6)
Founded 1946. Enrl 6,480; Fac 400; Highest Degree: Associate
Library Holdings: Bk Titles 65,052; Bk Vols 70,954; Per Subs 308
Special Collections: Mountaineering & Outdoor Literature (George W Martin Coll)
Automation Activity & Vendor Info: (Acquisitions) Ex Libris Group; (Cataloging) Ex Libris Group; (Circulation) Ex Libris Group; (Course Reserve) Ex Libris Group; (ILL) Ex Libris Group; (OPAC) Ex Libris Group; (Serials) Ex Libris Group
Wireless access
Partic in Washington Community & Technical Colleges Library Consortium
Open Mon-Thurs 7:30am-8pm, Fri 7:30-5, Sun 12-6

Departmental Libraries:

JOHNSON LIBRARY, 937 W Alpine Way, Shelton, 98584-1200. Tel: 360-432-5460. FAX: 360-432-5412. *Library Contact,* Kristie Nolasco; E-mail: knolasco@olympic.edu
Library Holdings: Bk Titles 1,930
Open Mon-Thurs 10-2

POULSBO CAMPUS, 1000 Olympic College Pl NW, Poulsbo, 98370. (Mail add: 1600 Chester Ave, 98337). Tel: 360-394-2720. FAX: 360-394-2721. *Circ,* Cora White; Tel: 360-394-2720, E-mail: cwhite@olympic.edu
Library Holdings: Bk Titles 355
Open Mon-Thurs 11-3:30

UNITED STATES NAVY

A COMMAND LIBRARY*, Puget Sound Naval Shipyard & Intermediate Maintenance Facility, 1400 Farragut Ave, 98314-5001, SAN 363-6399. Tel: 360-476-2767. FAX: 360-476-1730. *Librn,* Amanda Quashnick; E-mail: psns-imf_cmd_library@navy.mil; Staff 1 (Non-MLS 1)
Founded 1936
Library Holdings: Audiobooks 55; AV Mats 567; Bk Titles 8,000; Bk Vols 9,599; Per Subs 20; Videos 500
Subject Interests: Bus, Engr, Leadership, Naval, Sci
Restriction: Not open to pub, Open to mil & govt employees only, Open to staff only

AM NAVAL HOSPITAL LIBRARY*, HP01 One Boone Rd, 98312-1898, SAN 363-6429. Tel: 360-475-4316. FAX: 360-475-4324. E-mail: usn.kitsap.navhospbremertonwa.list.oss-op-screen-efm@health.mil. *Head, Knowledge Mgt,* Greg Patterson; *Libr Tech,* Sheila Tacey; E-mail: sheila.tacey@med.navy.mil; Staff 2 (MLS 1, Non-MLS 1)
Founded 1947
Library Holdings: Audiobooks 300; e-books 250; e-journals 4,000; Microforms 750,000; Bk Titles 1,750; Bk Vols 1,800; Per Subs 220
Special Collections: Medical Coll
Automation Activity & Vendor Info: (Acquisitions) Ex Libris Group; (Cataloging) Ex Libris Group; (Circulation) Ex Libris Group
Partic in Proquest Dialog
Open Mon-Fri 6am-3:30pm
Restriction: 24-hr pass syst for students only

A RESOURCE CENTER*, Naval Sta Bremerton Base-MWR, 120 S Dewey St, Bldg 502, 98314-5000, SAN 363-6364. Tel: 360-476-3178. FAX: 360-476-2908. Web Site: www.navylifepnw.com. *Library Contact,* Lela Wessner; Tel: 360-535-5932
Library Holdings: Bk Vols 5,500; Per Subs 55
Subject Interests: Naval hist
Open Mon-Thurs 10-9, Fri 10am-Midnight, Sat 11am-Midnight, Sun 11-9

BURLINGTON

P BURLINGTON PUBLIC LIBRARY*, 820 E Washington Ave, 98233. SAN 317-4913. Tel: 360-755-0760. FAX: 360-755-0717. E-mail: blibrary@burlingtonwa.gov. Web Site: www.burlingtonwa.gov/93/library. *Dir,* Sarah Ward; *Asst Dir,* Janice Burwash; E-mail: janiceb@burlingtonwa.gov; Staff 4 (MLS 3, Non-MLS 1)
Founded 1910. Pop 8,760; Circ 223,252
Library Holdings: Bk Vols 49,859; Per Subs 101
Subject Interests: NW mat
Automation Activity & Vendor Info: (Cataloging) Evergreen; (Circulation) Evergreen; (OPAC) Evergreen
Wireless access
Function: Adult bk club, Adult literacy prog, Art exhibits, Audio & video playback equip for onsite use, Audiobks via web, Bilingual assistance for Spanish patrons, Bk club(s), Bk reviews (Group), Bks on CD, Children's prog, Citizenship assistance, Computer training, Computers for patron use, Electronic databases & coll, ILL available, Magnifiers for reading, Microfiche/film & reading machines, Music CDs, Online cat, Online ref, OverDrive digital audio bks, Photocopying/Printing, Preschool outreach, Preschool reading prog, Prog for adults, Prog for children & young adult, Ref serv available, Spanish lang bks, Story hour, Summer & winter reading prog, Tax forms, Teen prog, Wheelchair accessible, Workshops
Partic in OCLC Online Computer Library Center, Inc
Special Services for the Deaf - Sorenson video relay syst
Open Mon, Fri & Sat 10-5, Tues-Thurs 10-8
Restriction: Non-resident fee
Friends of the Library Group

CAMAS

P CAMAS PUBLIC LIBRARY*, 625 NE Fourth Ave, 98607. SAN 317-4921. Tel: 360-834-4692. E-mail: library@cityofcamas.us. Web Site: www.cityofcamas.us/library. *Libr Dir,* Connie Urquhart; E-mail: curquhart@cityofcamas.us; *Colls Mgr, Tech Mgr,* Danielle Reynolds; E-mail: dreynolds@cityofcamas.us; *Commun Librn, User Experience Librn,* Leah Burch; E-mail: lburch@cityofcamas.us; *Art Coll Coordr, Outreach Librn,* Elliot Stapleton; E-mail: estapleton@cityofcamas.us; *Programming Librn,* Vanessa Perger; E-mail: vperger@cityofcamas.us. Subject Specialists: *Project mgt,* Danielle Reynolds; Staff 18 (MLS 8, Non-MLS 10)
Founded 1923
Subject Interests: Pacific Northwest
Automation Activity & Vendor Info: (Acquisitions) Innovative Interfaces, Inc. - Polaris; (Cataloging) Innovative Interfaces, Inc. - Polaris; (Circulation) Innovative Interfaces, Inc. - Polaris; (Discovery) Innovative Interfaces, Inc; (OPAC) Innovative Interfaces, Inc
Wireless access

Function: 24/7 Electronic res, 24/7 Online cat, 24/7 wireless access, Activity rm, Adult bk club, Adult literacy prog, After school storytime, Art exhibits, Art programs, Audiobks on Playaways & MP3, Audiobks via web, AV serv, Bk club(s), Bks on CD, Chess club, Children's prog, Computer training, Computers for patron use, Digital talking bks, Electronic databases & coll, Extended outdoor wifi, Free DVD rentals, Games, Holiday prog, ILL available, Instruction & testing, Internet access, Laptop/tablet checkout, Life-long learning prog for all ages, Magazines, Meeting rooms, Movies, Music CDs, Online cat, Online Chat, Online ref, Orientations, Outreach serv, Outside serv via phone, mail, e-mail & web, OverDrive digital audio bks, Photocopying/Printing, Preschool outreach, Preschool reading prog, Printer for laptops & handheld devices, Prog for adults, Prog for children & young adult, Ref & res, Ref serv available, Scanner, Senior outreach, STEM programs, Story hour, Study rm, Summer & winter reading prog, Summer reading prog, Tax forms, Teen prog, Telephone ref, Visual arts prog, Wheelchair accessible, Wifi hotspot checkout, Winter reading prog, Workshops, Writing prog
Partic in Metropolitan Information Exchange
Special Services for the Deaf - Bks on deafness & sign lang
Special Services for the Blind - Bks on cassette; Bks on CD; Descriptive video serv (DVS); Large print bks; Playaways (bks on MP3)
Open Mon-Wed 10-8, Thurs-Sat 10-6
Restriction: Non-resident fee
Friends of the Library Group

CASTLE ROCK

P CASTLE ROCK PUBLIC LIBRARY*, 137 Cowlitz St W, 98611. (Mail add: PO Box 1350, 98611-1350), SAN 317-4948. Tel: 360-274-6961. FAX: 360-274-4876. E-mail: rocklibrary@hotmail.com. Web Site: ci.castle-rock.wa.us/library.htm, crplibrary.com. *Dir,* Vicki Selander; Staff 1 (Non-MLS 1)
Founded 1922. Pop 2,100; Circ 21,000
Library Holdings: DVDs 100; Large Print Bks 600; Bk Vols 18,000; Talking Bks 200; Videos 400
Special Collections: Early Learning
Subject Interests: Genealogy, Local hist
Wireless access
Function: Magnifiers for reading, Photocopying/Printing, Prog for children & young adult, Spoken cassettes & CDs, Summer reading prog, Tax forms, VHS videos
Open Mon, Tues, Thurs & Fri 11-6, Wed & Sat 10-3
Restriction: Non-resident fee
Friends of the Library Group

CATHLAMET

P CATHLAMET PUBLIC LIBRARY*, Blanche Bradley Memorial Library, 115 Columbia St, 98612. (Mail add: 375 Second St, 98612), SAN 321-463X. Tel: 360-795-3254. FAX: 360-795-8500. Web Site: www.cathlamet.lib.wa.us. *Librn,* Carol Blix; E-mail: carol@townofcathlamet.com; Staff 0.5 (MLS 0.5)
Founded 1929. Pop 4,400; Circ 6,609
Jan 2017-Dec 2017 Income $41,680, City $39,880, Locally Generated Income $1,800. Mats Exp $6,600, Books $4,500, AV Mat $1,600, Electronic Ref Mat (Incl. Access Fees) $500. Sal $17,400
Library Holdings: Audiobooks 10,755; Bks on Deafness & Sign Lang 4; DVDs 2,384; e-books 35,477; Large Print Bks 526; Bk Titles 18,092
Special Collections: Northwest Coll
Subject Interests: Hist, Hist Pacific NW
Automation Activity & Vendor Info: (Cataloging) Koha; (Circulation) Koha; (OPAC) Koha
Wireless access
Function: 24/7 Electronic res, 24/7 Online cat, Audiobks via web, Bks on CD, Children's prog, Computer training, Computers for patron use, Electronic databases & coll, Free DVD rentals, Internet access, Online cat, Online ref, OverDrive digital audio bks, Photocopying/Printing, Preschool reading prog, Printer for laptops & handheld devices, Ref & res, Scanner, Summer reading prog, Tax forms, Wheelchair accessible
Open Tues-Sat 2-5
Friends of the Library Group

CENTRALIA

J CENTRALIA COLLEGE*, Kirk Library, 600 Centralia College Blvd, 98531. SAN 317-4956. Tel: 360-623-8956. Reference Tel: 360-623-8852. E-mail: librarian@centralia.edu. Web Site: www.centralia.edu/library. *Libr Dir,* Julie Nurse; Tel: 360-623-8567, E-mail: julie.nurse@centralia.edu; *Librn,* Ryer Banta; Tel: 360-623-8121, E-mail: ryer.banta@centralia.edu; *Librn,* Dale Carroll; Tel: 360-623-8373, E-mail: dale.carroll@centralia.edu; *Fac Librn,* Meredith Tummeti; Tel: 360-623-8722, E-mail: meredith.tummeti@centralia.edu; *Circ Supvr,* Hyesoo Albright; Tel: 360-623-8110, E-mail: hyesoo.albright@centralia.edu; Staff 6 (MLS 4, Non-MLS 2)
Founded 1925. Enrl 2,800; Fac 63; Highest Degree: Bachelor
Library Holdings: CDs 700; DVDs 144; e-books 9,979; Bk Vols 37,235; Per Subs 162; Talking Bks 187; Videos 2,899
Special Collections: Centralia Massacre Coll
Automation Activity & Vendor Info: (Acquisitions) Ex Libris Group; (Cataloging) Ex Libris Group; (Circulation) Ex Libris Group; (Course Reserve) Ex Libris Group; (ILL) OCLC; (OPAC) Ex Libris Group; (Serials) Ex Libris Group
Wireless access
Function: Doc delivery serv
Partic in Washington Community & Technical Colleges Library Consortium
Open Mon-Thurs 8-5, Fri 8-2

CHEHALIS

GL LEWIS COUNTY LAW LIBRARY, Law & Justice Ctr, 345 W Main St, 98532. SAN 317-4964. Tel: 360-740-1333. *Library Contact,* Susie Palmateer; E-mail: susie.palmateer@lewiscountywa.gov
Library Holdings: Bk Titles 600
Subject Interests: Legal publications
Wireless access
Open Mon-Fri 8-5

CHENEY

C EASTERN WASHINGTON UNIVERSITY*, John F Kennedy Memorial Library, 320 Media Lane, 100 LIB, 99004-2453. SAN 363-6453. Tel: 509-359-7888. Reference Tel: 509-359-2263. FAX: 509-359-6456. Web Site: www.ewu.edu/library. *Interim Dean of Libr,* Justin Otto; E-mail: jotto@ewu.edu; *Head, Coll Serv,* Merri Hartse; E-mail: mhartse@ewu.edu; *Bus Mgr,* Rose Knight; Tel: 509-359-2306, E-mail: rknight@mail.ewu.edu; *Coll Develop,* Jaclyn Parrott; Tel: 509-359-7895, E-mail: jparrott@ewu.edu; Staff 17.6 (MLS 13.6, Non-MLS 4)
Founded 1890. Enrl 9,350; Fac 607; Highest Degree: Doctorate
Library Holdings: AV Mats 37,875; Bks on Deafness & Sign Lang 233; CDs 3,671; DVDs 2,198; e-books 2,542; e-journals 9,610; Large Print Bks 27; Music Scores 15,343; Bk Titles 724,260; Bk Vols 795,760; Per Subs 5,653; Videos 6,882
Special Collections: EWU History Coll, archival mats; Northwest History Coll, archival mats, bks, micro. Oral History; State Document Depository; US Document Depository
Subject Interests: Applied sci, Behav sci, Bus educ, Educ, Music, Sci, Soc sci, Soc work
Automation Activity & Vendor Info: (Acquisitions) Innovative Interfaces, Inc; (Cataloging) Innovative Interfaces, Inc; (Circulation) Innovative Interfaces, Inc; (Course Reserve) Innovative Interfaces, Inc; (ILL) OCLC; (Media Booking) Innovative Interfaces, Inc; (OPAC) Innovative Interfaces, Inc; (Serials) Innovative Interfaces, Inc
Wireless access
Partic in Orbis Cascade Alliance; Wash Coop Libr Project
Special Services for the Deaf - Assistive tech; Bks on deafness & sign lang; Closed caption videos; High interest/low vocabulary bks; Staff with knowledge of sign lang
Special Services for the Blind - Assistive/Adapted tech devices, equip & products; Audio mat; Bks on cassette; Bks on CD; Braille Webster's dictionary; Cassette playback machines; Closed caption display syst; Computer with voice synthesizer for visually impaired persons; Dragon Naturally Speaking software; Integrated libr/media serv; Internet workstation with adaptive software; Large screen computer & software; Magnifiers; Reader equip; Rec; Ref serv; Rental typewriters & computers; Scanner for conversion & translation of mats; Screen enlargement software for people with visual disabilities; Screen reader software; Soundproof reading booth; Text reader; Videos on blindness & physical disabilties; ZoomText magnification & reading software
Open Mon-Thurs 7:30am-Midnight, Fri 7:30-6, Sat 10-6, Sun 1-Midnight
Friends of the Library Group

CLARKSTON

P ASOTIN COUNTY LIBRARY*, 417 Sycamore St, 99403-2666. SAN 317-4980. Tel: 509-758-5454. FAX: 509-751-1460. E-mail: yourlibrary@aclib.org. Web Site: www.aclib.org. *Dir,* Jennifer Ashby; Tel: 509-758-5454, Ext 102, E-mail: jashby@aclib.org; *Asst Dir, Youth Serv,* Mary Neuman; Tel: 509-758-5454, Ext 103, E-mail: mneuman@aclib.org; *Ad,* Erin Kolb; Tel: 509-758-5454, Ext 105, E-mail: ekolb@aclib.org; Staff 11 (MLS 3, Non-MLS 8)
Founded 1902
Library Holdings: Bk Titles 50,000; Per Subs 98
Subject Interests: NW hist
Automation Activity & Vendor Info: (Acquisitions) ByWater Solutions; (Cataloging) ByWater Solutions; (Circulation) ByWater Solutions; (ILL) OCLC; (OPAC) ByWater Solutions; (Serials) ByWater Solutions
Wireless access
Function: 24/7 Electronic res, 24/7 Online cat, Activity rm, Adult bk club
Open Mon-Wed 10-8, Thurs-Sat 10-5
Friends of the Library Group

Branches: 1
HEIGHTS BRANCH, 2036 Fourth Ave, 99403-1322. Tel: 509-758-4601. E-mail: hts@valnet.org. *Dir,* Jennifer Ashby
Library Holdings: Bk Titles 5,000
Open Mon & Wed 10-5, Tues 10-7, Thurs-Sat Noon-5

CLE ELUM

P CARPENTER MEMORIAL LIBRARY*, 302 N Pennsylvania Ave, 98922. SAN 317-4999. Tel: 509-674-2313. E-mail: cmlibrary@cleelum.gov. Web Site: www.carpenter.lib.wa.us. *Dir,* Jane Agar; E-mail: jagar@cleelum.gov
Founded 1978. Pop 4,500; Circ 18,400
Library Holdings: Bk Titles 12,500; Per Subs 20
Special Collections: Pacific Northwest History (Northwest Book Coll)
Subject Interests: Health, Nutrition, Wash State facts
Automation Activity & Vendor Info: (Acquisitions) Book Systems; (Cataloging) Book Systems; (Circulation) Book Systems; (Course Reserve) Book Systems; (OPAC) Book Systems; (Serials) Book Systems
Wireless access
Open Mon & Tues 9-1 & 1:30-5, Wed 10-1 & 1:30-6, Thurs & Fri 9-3:30, Sat 9:30-12:30
Friends of the Library Group

COLFAX

P WHITMAN COUNTY RURAL LIBRARY DISTRICT*, Colfax (Main) Branch, 102 S Main St, 99111-1863. SAN 317-5006. Tel: 509-397-4366. Toll Free Tel: 877-733-3375. FAX: 509-397-6156. E-mail: info@whitco.lib.wa.us. Web Site: www.whitco.lib.wa.us. *Dir,* Kristie Kirkpatrick; E-mail: kirkpatr@colfax.com; *Assoc Dir, Youth Serv Mgr,* Sheri Miller; E-mail: sheri@whitco.lib.wa.us; *Br Coordr, Circ,* Catalina Flores; *Computer Syst Adminr,* James Morasch; *Teen Serv,* Nicole Kopp; Staff 6 (MLS 1, Non-MLS 5)
Founded 1945. Pop 15,744; Circ 165,000
Library Holdings: Bk Titles 72,000; Bk Vols 78,000
Subject Interests: Local hist
Automation Activity & Vendor Info: (Cataloging) SirsiDynix; (Circulation) SirsiDynix; (Course Reserve) SirsiDynix; (Media Booking) SirsiDynix; (OPAC) SirsiDynix
Wireless access
Special Services for the Blind - Low vision equip
Open Mon-Wed 10-8, Thurs & Fri 10-6, Sat & Sun 1-5
Friends of the Library Group
Branches: 13
ALBION BRANCH, 310 F St, Albion, 99102. Tel: 509-338-9641. E-mail: albion@whitco.lib.wa.us. *Br Mgr,* Amy Ferguson
Library Holdings: Bk Titles 1,600
Open Tues & Thurs 3:30-6:30, Wed 9-1
COLTON BRANCH, 760 Broadway Ave, Colton, 99113. Tel: 509-229-3887. *Br Mgr,* Holly Meyer; Staff 1 (Non-MLS 1)
Library Holdings: Bk Titles 1,600
Open Mon 10-2:30, Thurs 2:30-6:30
ENDICOTT BRANCH, 324 E St, Endicott, 99125. Tel: 509-657-3429. E-mail: endicott@whitco.lib.wa.us. *Br Mgr,* Nanci Selk
Library Holdings: Bk Titles 2,200
Open Tues 1-5, Fri 9-2
FARMINGTON BRANCH, E 203 Main St, Farmington, 99128. Tel: 509-287-3302. E-mail: farmington@whitcolib.org. *Br Mgr,* Rita Ackerman
Library Holdings: Bk Titles 1,400
Open Tues & Thurs 2:30-6:30
GARFIELD BRANCH, 109 N Third, Garfield, 99130. Tel: 509-635-1490. E-mail: garfield@whitcolib.org. *Br Mgr,* Sarah Anderson
Library Holdings: Bk Titles 2,300
Open Mon 1-6, Wed 10-2:30
LACROSSE BRANCH, 201 S Main, LaCrosse, 99143. Tel: 509-549-3770. FAX: 509-549-3330. E-mail: lacrosse@whitco.lib.wa.us. *Br Mgr,* Tami Schwartz
Library Holdings: Bk Titles 1,500
Open Mon 2-6, Thurs 10-2
OAKESDALE BRANCH, 101 E Steptoe, Oakesdale, 99158. Tel: 509-285-4310. E-mail: oakesdale@whitcolib.org. *Br Mgr,* Sanya Pope
Library Holdings: CDs 20; DVDs 15; Large Print Bks 30; Bk Titles 1,800; Talking Bks 25; Videos 45
Open Mon 1-6, Wed 10:30-2
PALOUSE BRANCH, E 120 Main, Palouse, 99149. Tel: 508-878-1513. E-mail: palouse@whitcolib.org. *Br Mgr,* Beverley Pearce
Open Tues 11-6, Thurs 2-6, Fri Noon-6
ROSALIA BRANCH, 402 S Whitman Ave, Rosalia, 99170. Tel: 509-523-3109. E-mail: rosalia@whitcolib.org. *Br Mgr,* Marcy Campbell
Library Holdings: Bk Titles 2,000
Open Tues 10-2 & 3-5, Thurs 3-7, Sat 10-2
ST JOHN BRANCH, One E Front St, Saint John, 99171. Tel: 509-648-3319. E-mail: stjohn@whitcolib.org. *Br Mgr,* Clancy Pool
Pop 1,000; Circ 16,000
Library Holdings: Audiobooks 400; CDs 200; DVDs 200; e-books 3,000; Large Print Bks 100; Bk Titles 4,500; Per Subs 10; Videos 200
Automation Activity & Vendor Info: (Cataloging) OCLC CatExpress; (ILL) OCLC WorldShare Interlibrary Loan
Function: Adult bk club, After school storytime, Art exhibits, Bks on cassette, Bks on CD, Children's prog, Computers for patron use, Electronic databases & coll, Free DVD rentals, Home delivery & serv to seniorr ctr & nursing homes, ILL available, Mail & tel request accepted, Music CDs, Online cat, Outreach serv, Outside serv via phone, mail, e-mail & web, OverDrive digital audio bks, Photocopying/Printing, Preschool outreach, Prog for adults, Prog for children & young adult, Ref serv available, Story hour, Summer & winter reading prog, Summer reading prog, Telephone ref, VHS videos, Wheelchair accessible
Open Mon & Fri 10-1 & 2-5, Wed 2:30-6:30
TEKOA BRANCH, S 139 Crosby, Tekoa, 99033. Tel: 509-284-3121. E-mail: tekoa@whitcolib.org. *Br Mgr,* Shelly Ausmus
Library Holdings: Bk Titles 3,000
Open Tues & Wed 1:30-6, Thurs 12-6
UNIONTOWN BRANCH, 110 S Montgomery, Uniontown, 99179. Tel: 509-229-3880. E-mail: uniontown@whitcolib.org. *Br Mgr,* Holly Meyer
Library Holdings: Bk Titles 1,500
Open Tues & Wed 1:30-6, Thurs 12-6

COLLEGE PLACE

CR WALLA WALLA UNIVERSITY LIBRARIES*, Peterson Memorial Library, 104 S College Ave, 99324-1159. SAN 317-5014. Tel: 509-527-2134. Circulation Tel: 509-527-2191. Administration Tel: 509-527-2107. FAX: 509-527-2001. E-mail: libcirc@wallawalla.edu, reference@wallawalla.edu. Web Site: wallawalla.edu/academics/libraries. *Dir of Libr,* Carolyn Gaskell; E-mail: carolyn.gaskell@wallawalla.edu; *Coll Mgt & Syst Librn,* Mark Copsey; E-mail: mark.copsey@wallawalla.edu; *Educ Serv Librn,* Christy Scott; E-mail: christy.scott@wallawalla.edu; *Sch of Nursing Librn,* Doug McClay; Tel: 503-527-2124, E-mail: douglas.mcclay@wallawalla.edu; Staff 8.4 (MLS 4.4, Non-MLS 4)
Founded 1892. Enrl 1,626; Fac 122; Highest Degree: Doctorate
Special Collections: Bibles, SDA History
Subject Interests: Nursing
Automation Activity & Vendor Info: (Acquisitions) Ex Libris Group; (Cataloging) Ex Libris Group; (Circulation) Ex Libris Group; (Course Reserve) Ex Libris Group; (ILL) OCLC; (OPAC) Ex Libris Group; (Serials) Ex Libris Group
Wireless access
Publications: Course Guides (Reference guide); Research Guides (Online only)
Partic in Orbis Cascade Alliance
Open Mon-Thurs 8am-11pm, Fri 8-1, Sun Noon-11

CONCRETE

P UPPER SKAGIT LIBRARY*, 45952 Main St, 98237. (Mail add: PO Box 99, 98237-0099). Tel: 360-853-7716. FAX: 360-853-7555. E-mail: info@upperskagitlibrary.org. Web Site: upperskagitlibrary.org. *Libr Dir,* Erica Brown; E-mail: director@upperskagitlibrary.org; Staff 5 (MLS 2, Non-MLS 3)
Founded 2005. Pop 4,800; Circ 38,000
Automation Activity & Vendor Info: (Cataloging) Evergreen; (Circulation) Evergreen; (OPAC) Evergreen
Wireless access
Function: 24/7 Electronic res, 24/7 Online cat, Bks on CD, Computer training, Computers for patron use, Electronic databases & coll, ILL available, Internet access, Laminating, Life-long learning prog for all ages, Magazines, Movies, Music CDs, Outreach serv, OverDrive digital audio bks, Photocopying/Printing, Prog for adults, Prog for children & young adult, Ref serv available, Scanner, Story hour, Summer reading prog, Tax forms
Open Tues-Thurs 10-7, Fri & Sat 10-5
Friends of the Library Group

DAVENPORT

P DAVENPORT PUBLIC LIBRARY*, 505 Seventh St, 99122. (Mail add: PO Box 1169, 99122-1169), SAN 317-5049. Tel: 509-725-4355. E-mail: davreference@live.com. Web Site: www.davenport.lib.wa.us. *Librn,* Zerita Hammond
Founded 1926. Pop 1,735; Circ 4,268
Wireless access
Function: Bks on cassette, Bks on CD, Children's prog, Computers for patron use, E-Readers, Family literacy, Free DVD rentals, ILL available, Magazines, Online cat, OverDrive digital audio bks, Preschool reading prog, Prog for children & young adult, Ref serv available, Story hour, Summer reading prog
Partic in Wheatland Libraries Consortium
Special Services for the Blind - Bks on cassette; Bks on CD; Large print bks; Playaways (bks on MP3)

Open Tues-Thurs 3-7, Sat 10-2
Restriction: Non-resident fee, Open to pub for ref & circ; with some limitations

DAYTON

P COLUMBIA COUNTY RURAL LIBRARY DISTRICT*, 111 S Third St, 99328. (Mail add: PO Box 74, 99328-0074). Tel: 509-382-4131. FAX: 509-382-1059. E-mail: info@ccrld.org. Web Site: www.daytonmemoriallibrary.org. *Dir, Libr Serv,* Todd Vandenbark; E-mail: director@ccrld.org; Staff 2.8 (MLS 1, Non-MLS 1.8)
Founded 1937. Pop 4,100; Circ 26,043
Library Holdings: Audiobooks 1,371; DVDs 632; Bk Titles 22,752; Per Subs 40
Wireless access
Function: Audiobks via web, Bks on cassette, Computer training, Computers for patron use, Electronic databases & coll, Free DVD rentals, Homebound delivery serv, ILL available, Magnifiers for reading, Music CDs, Online cat, Preschool outreach, Ref serv available, Scanner, Senior computer classes, Senior outreach, Serves people with intellectual disabilities, Story hour, Summer reading prog, Tax forms, Telephone ref, VHS videos, Workshops
Open Mon, Wed & Fri 10-5, Tues & Thurs 12-8, Sat 10-2

DES MOINES

C HIGHLINE COLLEGE LIBRARY*, 2400 S 240th St, MS 25-4, 98198. (Mail add: PO Box 98000, 98198-9800), SAN 317-5456. Tel: 206-592-3234. Interlibrary Loan Service Tel: 206-592-3127. Reference Tel: 206-592-3232. TDD: 206-870-4853. Web Site: library.highline.edu. *Libr Dir,* Gerie Ventura; Tel: 206-592-3230, E-mail: gventura@highline.edu; *Ref Librn,* Hara Brook; Tel: 206-592-3248, E-mail: hbrook@highline.edu; *Ref Librn,* Karen Fernandez; Tel: 206-592-3809, E-mail: kfernandez@highline.edu; *Ref Librn,* Jack Harton; Tel: 206-592-3806, E-mail: jharton@highline.edu; *Ref Librn,* Deborah Moore; Tel: 206-592-3518, E-mail: dmoore@highline.edu; *Ref Librn,* Monica Twork; Tel: 206-592-4113, E-mail: mtwork@highline.edu; *Circ Serv Supvr,* Cathy Campbell; E-mail: ccampbell@highline.edu; *Libr Syst Coordr, Tech Serv,* Naoko Yasuda; Tel: 206-592-3726, E-mail: nyasuda@highline.edu; Staff 17 (MLS 11, Non-MLS 6)
Founded 1961. Fac 132; Highest Degree: Bachelor
Library Holdings: Bks on Deafness & Sign Lang 250; e-books 6,100; Electronic Media & Resources 119,000; High Interest/Low Vocabulary Bk Vols 3,100; Large Print Bks 70; Bk Titles 45,000; Per Subs 45; Videos 320
Special Collections: State Document Depository; US Document Depository
Subject Interests: Law
Automation Activity & Vendor Info: (Acquisitions) Ex Libris Group; (Cataloging) Ex Libris Group; (Circulation) Ex Libris Group; (Course Reserve) Ex Libris Group; (OPAC) Ex Libris Group; (Serials) Ex Libris Group
Wireless access
Function: 24/7 Electronic res, 24/7 Online cat, Bilingual assistance for Spanish patrons, Computers for patron use, Electronic databases & coll, For res purposes, ILL available, Internet access, Magazines, Magnifiers for reading, Online cat, Online ref, Photocopying/Printing, Ref & res, Spanish lang bks, Wheelchair accessible
Partic in OCLC Online Computer Library Center, Inc; Washington Community & Technical Colleges Library Consortium
Open Mon-Thurs 8-5
Restriction: Open to pub for ref & circ; with some limitations, Restricted borrowing privileges

EASTSOUND

P ORCAS ISLAND LIBRARY DISTRICT*, 500 Rose St, 98245. Tel: 360-376-4985. FAX: 360-376-5750. Web Site: www.orcaslibrary.org. *Libr Dir,* Ingrid Mattson; E-mail: imattson@orcaslibrary.org; Staff 6 (MLS 3, Non-MLS 3)
Founded 1988. Pop 5,300; Circ 123,229
Library Holdings: Audiobooks 4,723; AV Mats 9,053; CDs 2,713; DVDs 2,454; e-books 1,246; Large Print Bks 450; Microforms 138; Bk Titles 35,974; Bk Vols 37,768; Per Subs 126; Talking Bks 4,723; Videos 120
Special Collections: San Juan Islands Coll
Subject Interests: Local hist, Northwestern US
Automation Activity & Vendor Info: (Acquisitions) TLC (The Library Corporation); (Cataloging) OCLC Online; (Circulation) TLC (The Library Corporation); (ILL) OCLC WorldShare Interlibrary Loan; (OPAC) TLC (The Library Corporation)
Wireless access
Function: 24/7 Electronic res, Accelerated reader prog, Adult bk club, Adult literacy prog, Art exhibits, Audiobks via web, Bk club(s), Bks on CD, Chess club, Children's prog, Computer training, Computers for patron use, Digital talking bks, Distance learning, Doc delivery serv, E-Readers, E-Reserves, Electronic databases & coll, Equip loans & repairs, Free DVD rentals, Holiday prog, Home delivery & serv to seniorr ctr & nursing homes, Homebound delivery serv, ILL available, Internet access, Magazines, Magnifiers for reading, Mail & tel request accepted, Microfiche/film & reading machines, Music CDs, Online cat, Online ref, Orientations, Outreach serv, Outside serv via phone, mail, e-mail & web, OverDrive digital audio bks, Photocopying/Printing, Preschool outreach, Prog for adults, Prog for children & young adult, Ref serv available, Scanner, Senior computer classes, Senior outreach, Spanish lang bks, Spoken cassettes & CDs, Spoken cassettes & DVDs, Story hour, Summer & winter reading prog, Summer reading prog, Tax forms, Teen prog, Telephone ref, VHS videos, Wheelchair accessible, Writing prog
Special Services for the Deaf - Bks on deafness & sign lang; Closed caption videos; High interest/low vocabulary bks
Special Services for the Blind - Audio mat; Bks on CD; Copier with enlargement capabilities; Digital talking bk; Extensive large print coll; Home delivery serv; Large print bks; Large type calculator; Magnifiers; Playaways (bks on MP3); Ref serv; Talking bks
Open Mon-Thurs 10-7, Fri & Sat 10-5, Sun 12-3
Restriction: Non-resident fee
Friends of the Library Group

ELLENSBURG

C CENTRAL WASHINGTON UNIVERSITY, James E Brooks Library, 400 E University Way, 98926-7548. SAN 317-5081. Tel: 509-963-1901. Circulation Tel: 509-963-3682. FAX: 509-963-3684. Web Site: www.lib.cwu.edu. *Dean of Libr,* Sydney Thompson; E-mail: sydney.thompson5@cwu.edu; *Assoc Dean of Libr,* Position Currently Open; *Head, Access Serv,* Joanna Hunt; E-mail: joanna.hunt@cwu.edu; *Archivist,* Julia Stringfellow; E-mail: Julia.Stringfellow@cwu.edu; Staff 23 (MLS 8, Non-MLS 15)
Founded 1891. Enrl 7,836; Fac 450; Highest Degree: Master
Library Holdings: Bk Vols 521,548
Special Collections: State Document Depository; US Document Depository
Automation Activity & Vendor Info: (OPAC) Ex Libris Group
Wireless access
Partic in Orbis Cascade Alliance
Friends of the Library Group

P ELLENSBURG PUBLIC LIBRARY*, 209 N Ruby St, 98926-3397. SAN 317-509X. Tel: 509-962-7250. Circulation Tel: 509-962-7110. Reference Tel: 509-962-7228. Administration Tel: 509-962-7252. FAX: 509-962-7295. E-mail: library@ci.ellensburg.wa.us. Web Site: ci.ellensburg.wa.us/144/library. *Dir,* Josephine Camarillo; Tel: 509-962-7218; *Head, Circ,* Ken Paschen; E-mail: paschenk@ci.ellensburg.wa.us; *Hist Coll Librn, Ref Serv,* Regina Tipton-Llamas; E-mail: tiptonr@ci.ellensburg.wa.us. Subject Specialists: *Local hist,* Regina Tipton-Llamas; Staff 11.7 (MLS 2, Non-MLS 9.7)
Founded 1910. Pop 17,800; Circ 201,742
Library Holdings: Audiobooks 5,013; AV Mats 9,488; DVDs 6,913; e-books 30,089; Electronic Media & Resources 10; Bk Titles 54,699; Per Subs 117
Special Collections: Oral History
Subject Interests: Local hist
Automation Activity & Vendor Info: (Cataloging) Horizon; (Circulation) Horizon; (ILL) OCLC WorldShare Interlibrary Loan; (OPAC) Horizon
Wireless access
Function: Art exhibits, Audio & video playback equip for onsite use, Bilingual assistance for Spanish patrons, Bks on cassette, Bks on CD, CD-ROM, Children's prog, Citizenship assistance, Computer training, Computers for patron use, Digital talking bks, Electronic databases & coll, Free DVD rentals, Holiday prog, Home delivery & serv to seniorr ctr & nursing homes, ILL available, Internet access, Magnifiers for reading, Mail & tel request accepted, Museum passes, Music CDs, Online cat, Online ref, Orientations, Outreach serv, Outside serv via phone, mail, e-mail & web, Photocopying/Printing, Prog for adults, Prog for children & young adult, Ref & res, Ref serv available, Scanner, Spoken cassettes & CDs, Spoken cassettes & DVDs, Story hour, Summer reading prog, Tax forms, Teen prog, Telephone ref, VHS videos, Wheelchair accessible, Workshops
Special Services for the Blind - Bks on cassette; Bks on CD; Closed circuit TV; Home delivery serv; Large print bks; Magnifiers; Screen enlargement software for people with visual disabilities; Talking bks; VisualTek equip
Open Mon-Thurs 10-7, Fri 10-6, Sat & Sun 1-5
Friends of the Library Group

EVERETT

J EVERETT COMMUNITY COLLEGE*, John N Terrey Library - Media Center, 2000 Tower St, 98201-1352. SAN 317-5138. Circulation Tel: 425-388-9353. Interlibrary Loan Service Tel: 425-388-9493. Reference Tel: 425-388-9354. E-mail: library@everettcc.edu. Web Site: everettcc.libguides.com/evcc-library. *Dean, Arts & Learning Res,* Lynn Deeken; Tel: 425-388-9502, E-mail: ldeeken@everettcc.edu; *Acq, Cat, Circ,* Heather Uhl; Tel: 425-388-9139, E-mail: huhl@everettcc.edu; *Circ, Pub Serv,* Robert Bertoldi; Tel: 425-388-9492, E-mail:

rbertoldi@everettcc.edu; *Coll Develop, Pub Serv,* Marianne Le; Tel: 425-388-9351, E-mail: mle@everettcc.edu; *Media Spec,* Jeanie Goodhope; Tel: 425-388-9348, E-mail: jgoodhope@everettcc.edu; Staff 6 (MLS 6)
Founded 1948. Highest Degree: Associate
Library Holdings: AV Mats 6,324; Microforms 7; Bk Titles 61,396; Bk Vols 64,797; Per Subs 124
Automation Activity & Vendor Info: (Acquisitions) Ex Libris Group; (Cataloging) Ex Libris Group; (Circulation) Ex Libris Group; (OPAC) Ex Libris Group
Wireless access
Publications: Bookmarks; Brochure; Search Guides
Partic in OCLC Online Computer Library Center, Inc; Washington Community & Technical Colleges Library Consortium
Special Services for the Blind - Assistive/Adapted tech devices, equip & products
Open Mon & Tues 9-7, Wed & Thurs 9-5, Fri 9-Noon, Sat 10-2

P EVERETT PUBLIC LIBRARY*, 2702 Hoyt Ave, 98201-3556. SAN 317-5162. Circulation Tel: 425-257-8010. Interlibrary Loan Service Tel: 425-257-7615. Reference Tel: 425-257-8000. Automation Services Tel: 425-257-8036. FAX: 425-257-8017. Reference FAX: 425-257-8016. Web Site: www.epls.org. *Libr Dir,* Abigail Cooley; Tel: 425-257-8022, E-mail: acooley@everettwa.gov; *Asst Dir, Head, Adult Serv,* Mindy VanWingen; Tel: 425-257-8021, E-mail: mvanwingen@everettwa.gov; *Head, Youth Serv,* Emily Dagg; Tel: 425-257-7632, E-mail: edagg@everettwa.gov; *Circ Mgr,* Carol Ellison; Tel: 425-257-8034, E-mail: cellison@everettwa.gov; Staff 19 (MLS 16, Non-MLS 3)
Founded 1894. Pop 103,100; Circ 1,056,206
Library Holdings: Audiobooks 23,667; CDs 54,482; DVDs 245,051; e-books 9,649; Large Print Bks 14,097; Bk Vols 691,001
Special Collections: City of Everett; Pacific Northwest (Northwest Coll), bks, photos, rec. Oral History; State Document Depository; US Document Depository
Automation Activity & Vendor Info: (Acquisitions) Innovative Interfaces, Inc; (Cataloging) Innovative Interfaces, Inc; (Circulation) Innovative Interfaces, Inc; (ILL) OCLC; (OPAC) Innovative Interfaces, Inc
Wireless access
Open Mon-Sat 10-6
Friends of the Library Group
Branches: 1
EVERGREEN, 9512 Evergreen Way, 98204, SAN 375-5916. Tel: 425-257-8260. Reference Tel: 425-257-8250. FAX: 425-257-8265. *Libr Dir,* Abigail Cooley
Founded 1985
Open Tues, Thurs & Sat 10-6

GL SNOHOMISH COUNTY LAW LIBRARY*, M/S 703 Basement/Courthouse, 3000 Rockefeller Ave, 98201. SAN 317-5200. Tel: 425-388-3010. *Librn,* Lettice Parker; E-mail: lettice.parker@snoco.org; Staff 1 (MLS 1)
Founded 1919
Subject Interests: Case law, Statute law

FAIRCHILD AFB

A UNITED STATES AIR FORCE*, Fairchild Base Library, Two W Castle St, 99011-8532. SAN 363-6518. Tel: 509-247-5228, 509-247-5556. FAX: 509-247-3365. E-mail: fafblibrary@gmail.com. Web Site: www.fairchildfun.com/library. *Librn,* Eileen Stromberger; Staff 5.3 (MLS 2, Non-MLS 3.3)
Founded 1950
Library Holdings: AV Mats 3,390; Electronic Media & Resources 66; Bk Titles 45,000; Per Subs 100
Subject Interests: Mil hist, Mil sci, Northwest
Automation Activity & Vendor Info: (Cataloging) SirsiDynix-Unicorn; (Circulation) SirsiDynix-Unicorn; (ILL) OCLC; (OPAC) SirsiDynix-Unicorn
Wireless access
Function: Accelerated reader prog, Bks on cassette, Bks on CD, CD-ROM, Children's prog, Computers for patron use, Doc delivery serv, Electronic databases & coll, Internet access, Online cat, Orientations, Photocopying/Printing, Prog for adults, Prog for children & young adult, Ref serv available, Scanner, Summer reading prog, Tax forms, Teen prog, Telephone ref, Wheelchair accessible
Partic in OCLC Online Computer Library Center, Inc
Open Mon-Fri 10-6, Sat 10-5:30
Restriction: Authorized patrons

FEDERAL WAY

S RHODODENDRON SPECIES FOUNDATION & BOTANICAL GARDEN*, Lawrence J Pierce Library, 2525 S 336th St, 98003. (Mail add: PO Box 3798, 98063-3798), SAN 328-087X. Tel: 253-838-4646. FAX: 253-838-4686. E-mail: info@rhodygarden.org. Web Site: rhodygarden.org/cms/lawrence-j-pierce-library. *Curator, Exec Dir,* Steve Hootman; Tel: 253-838-4646, Ext 101
Founded 1964
Library Holdings: Bk Titles 2,000; Per Subs 15
Wireless access
Restriction: Open by appt only

FRIDAY HARBOR

P SAN JUAN ISLAND LIBRARY*, 1010 Guard St, 98250-9612. SAN 317-5243. Tel: 360-378-2798. E-mail: sjlib@sjlib.org. Web Site: www.sjlib.org. *Libr Dir,* Laurie Orton; E-mail: lorton@sjlib.org; *Adult Serv Mgr, Asst Dir,* Rowan Buckton; E-mail: rbuckton@sjlib.org; *Develop Dir,* Amy Saxe-Eyler; E-mail: asaxe-eyler@sjlib.org; *IT Admin,* Floyd Bourne; E-mail: fbourne@sjlib.org; *Cat & Acq,* Jen Fleming; E-mail: jfleming@sjlib.org; *Cat & Coll Librn,* Stephanie Mattox; E-mail: smattox@sjlib.org; *ILL & Collections Librn,* Brenna Normann; E-mail: bnormann@sjlib.org; *Youth Serv Librn,* Elizabeth Griffin; E-mail: egriffin@sjlib.org; *Admin Mgr,* Heidi Kuheim; E-mail: hkuheim@sjlib.org; *Circ Mgr,* Sue Vulgares; E-mail: svulgares@sjlib.org; *Youth Serv Mgr,* Melina Lagios; E-mail: mlagios@sjlib.org; *Outreach & Vols Coordr,* Wendy Waxman Kern; E-mail: wwaxman-kern@sjlib.org; *Adult Programs Assoc,* Sarah Benson; E-mail: sbenson@sjlib.org; *Circ Assoc,* Pat Gislason; E-mail: pgislason@sjlib.org; *Public Services Assoc,* Naomi Boydston; E-mail: nboydston@sjlib.org; *Public Services Assoc,* Kasey Rasmussen; E-mail: krasmussen@sjlib.org. Subject Specialists: *Communications, Mkt, Web develop,* Rowan Buckton; Staff 11.9 (MLS 6.7, Non-MLS 5.2)
Founded 1922. Pop 8,605
Jan 2021-Dec 2021 Income $1,707,046, State $426, Locally Generated Income $1,472,989, Other $233,631. Mats Exp $116,346, Books $63,143, Other Print Mats $9,755, AV Mat $17,450, Electronic Ref Mat (Incl. Access Fees) $25,998. Sal $810,227
Library Holdings: Audiobooks 49,317; DVDs 7,183; e-books 64,590; Electronic Media & Resources 51; Bk Vols 44,572; Per Subs 203
Special Collections: Aids for Better Living; Bat Detectors; Birdwatching Kits; Event Equipment; Local (San Juan Islands); Pacific Northwest; Parent/Teacher; Portable DVD Players; Spanish; WiFi Hotspots
Automation Activity & Vendor Info: (Acquisitions) Innovative Interfaces, Inc; (Cataloging) Innovative Interfaces, Inc; (Circulation) Innovative Interfaces, Inc; (ILL) OCLC WorldShare Interlibrary Loan; (OPAC) Innovative Interfaces, Inc; (Serials) Innovative Interfaces, Inc
Wireless access
Function: 24/7 Electronic res, 24/7 Online cat, 3D Printer, Activity rm, Adult bk club, Adult literacy prog, After school storytime, Art exhibits, Art programs, Audio & video playback equip for onsite use, Audiobks on Playaways & MP3, Audiobks via web, AV serv, Bk club(s), Bks on CD, Children's prog, Citizenship assistance, Computer training, Computers for patron use, Digital talking bks, Electronic databases & coll, Equip loans & repairs, Family literacy, Free DVD rentals, Games & aids for people with disabilities, Health sci info serv, Holiday prog, Home delivery & serv to seniorr ctr & nursing homes, Homebound delivery serv, ILL available, Internet access, Life-long learning prog for all ages, Magazines, Magnifiers for reading, Mail & tel request accepted, Meeting rooms, Microfiche/film & reading machines, Movies, Music CDs, Online cat, Online info literacy tutorials on the web & in blackboard, Outreach serv, Outside serv via phone, mail, e-mail & web, OverDrive digital audio bks, Photocopying/Printing, Preschool outreach, Preschool reading prog, Printer for laptops & handheld devices, Prog for adults, Prog for children & young adult, Ref & res, Ref serv available, Scanner, Senior computer classes, Senior outreach, Serves people with intellectual disabilities, Spanish lang bks, STEM programs, Story hour, Study rm, Summer & winter reading prog, Summer reading prog, Tax forms, Teen prog, Telephone ref, Visual arts prog, Wheelchair accessible, Workshops, Writing prog
Publications: Annual Report; Community Newsletter (Annual); Friends of the Library Newsletter (Annual); Monthly Events eNewsletter (Online only)
Partic in Washington Digital Library Consortium
Special Services for the Deaf - ADA equip; Assisted listening device; Assistive tech; Bks on deafness & sign lang; Closed caption videos; Pocket talkers; TTY equip
Special Services for the Blind - Aids for in-house use; Assistive/Adapted tech devices, equip & products; Bks available with recordings; Bks on CD; Compressed speech equip; Copier with enlargement capabilities; Extensive large print coll; Home delivery serv; Large print bks; Lending of low vision aids; Low vision equip; Magnifiers; Playaways (bks on MP3); Spec cats; Talking bks; Talking machines
Open Mon-Fri 10-6, Sat 10-3
Friends of the Library Group

S THE WHALE MUSEUM LIBRARY*, Manfred C Vernon Library, 62 First St N, 98250-7973. (Mail add: PO Box 945, 98250-0945), SAN 329-3041. Tel: 360-378-4710, Ext 31. FAX: 360-378-5790. Web Site: whalemuseum.org. *Curator,* Rebekah Cousins; E-mail: rebekah@whalemuseum.org; *Curator of Res Serv,* Shawn Larson, PhD; E-mail: shawn@whalemuseum.org

Founded 1979
Library Holdings: Bk Titles 600; Bk Vols 800; Videos 50
Subject Interests: Marine mammals, Pacific Northwest
Restriction: Not a lending libr

GRANDVIEW

P GRANDVIEW LIBRARY*, 500 W Main St, 98930-1398. SAN 317-5251. Tel: 509-882-7034, 509-882-7057. FAX: 509-882-7026. E-mail: library@grandview.wa.us. Web Site: www.grandview.wa.us/departments/library. *Libr Dir,* Elizabeth Jahnke; Tel: 509-882-7036, E-mail: librarydirector@grandview.wa.us; *Libr Assoc,* Sophia Alvarez; Staff 2 (MLS 1, Non-MLS 1)
Founded 1914. Pop 13,117; Circ 34,896
Special Collections: Blanche McLane Cook Art Coll; Local History (Special History of Grandview), bks, pamphlets
Subject Interests: Agr, Spanish
Automation Activity & Vendor Info: (Acquisitions) Innovative Interfaces, Inc; (Cataloging) Innovative Interfaces, Inc; (Circulation) Innovative Interfaces, Inc; (ILL) OCLC; (OPAC) Innovative Interfaces, Inc
Wireless access
Function: 24/7 Electronic res, 24/7 Online cat, Activity rm, Adult bk club, Audiobks via web, Bilingual assistance for Spanish patrons, Bks on CD, Children's prog, Computers for patron use, Digital talking bks, Electronic databases & coll, Free DVD rentals, ILL available, Internet access, Magazines, Mail & tel request accepted, Meeting rooms, Music CDs, Online cat, OverDrive digital audio bks, Photocopying/Printing, Preschool outreach, Preschool reading prog, Prog for adults, Prog for children & young adult, Ref serv available, Scanner, Spanish lang bks, Spoken cassettes & CDs, STEM programs, Story hour, Study rm, Summer reading prog, Tax forms, Telephone ref, VHS videos, Wheelchair accessible
Partic in Washington Digital Library Consortium
Open Mon-Thurs 10-5, Fri 10-12
Restriction: Authorized patrons, Free to mem
Friends of the Library Group

HARRINGTON

P HARRINGTON PUBLIC LIBRARY*, 11 S Third St, 99134. (Mail add: PO Box 496, 99134-0496), SAN 317-5278. Tel: 509-253-4345, Option 5. E-mail: librarian@harrington.city. Web Site: harrington.lib.wa.us. *Librn,* Justina Sliter
Pop 430; Circ 3,366
Library Holdings: Bk Titles 7,431
Wireless access
Open Tues 2-5, Thurs 3-6

ISSAQUAH

P KING COUNTY LIBRARY SYSTEM*, Administrative Offices, 960 Newport Way NW, 98027. SAN 317-6061. Tel: 425-462-9600. Administration Tel: 425-369-3233. FAX: 425-369-3255. Web Site: www.kcls.org. *Exec Dir,* Lisa G Rosenblum; E-mail: lgrosenblum@kcls.org; *Dir of Finance,* Nicholas Lee; E-mail: nelee@kcls.org; *Dep Dir,* Cynthia McNabb; E-mail: cjmcnabb@kcls.org
Founded 1942. Pop 1,800,000; Circ 1,912,200
Library Holdings: Braille Volumes 32; CDs 174,158; DVDs 131,861; Large Print Bks 61,691; Bk Vols 916,585; Per Subs 11,000; Talking Bks 69,626; Videos 76,906
Special Collections: Nonprofit & Philanthropy Resource Center; Northwest Coll; World Languages Coll. State Document Depository
Automation Activity & Vendor Info: (Acquisitions) BiblioCommons; (Cataloging) BiblioCommons; (Circulation) Evergreen; (Course Reserve) BiblioCommons; (ILL) BiblioCommons; (Media Booking) BiblioCommons; (OPAC) BiblioCommons; (Serials) BiblioCommons
Wireless access
Function: Accelerated reader prog, Adult literacy prog, After school storytime, Art exhibits, Audio & video playback equip for onsite use, Audiobks via web, BA reader (adult literacy), Bilingual assistance for Spanish patrons, Bk club(s), Bks on cassette, Bks on CD, Bus archives, CD-ROM, Children's prog, Citizenship assistance, Computer training, Computers for patron use, Digital talking bks, E-Reserves, Electronic databases & coll, Family literacy, For res purposes, Free DVD rentals, Games & aids for people with disabilities, Govt ref serv, Home delivery & serv to seniorr ctr & nursing homes, Homebound delivery serv, Homework prog, ILL available, Internet access, Jail serv, Music CDs, Online cat, Online ref, OverDrive digital audio bks, Photocopying/Printing, Preschool outreach, Prog for adults, Prog for children & young adult, Ref & res, Ref serv available, Senior computer classes, Senior outreach, Serves people with intellectual disabilities, Spoken cassettes & CDs, Spoken cassettes & DVDs, Summer reading prog, Tax forms, Teen prog, Telephone ref, VHS videos, Wheelchair accessible, Workshops
Publications: Inside KCLS (Newsletter)
Special Services for the Blind - Large print bks
Open Mon-Fri 9-5
Friends of the Library Group
Branches: 47
ALGONA-PACIFIC LIBRARY, 255 Ellingson Rd, Pacific, 98047, SAN 328-9567. Tel: 253-833-3554. FAX: 206-296-5019.
Open Mon-Thurs 10-9, Fri 10-6, Sat 10-5
Friends of the Library Group
AUBURN LIBRARY, 1102 Auburn Way S, Auburn, 98002, SAN 317-4816. Tel: 253-931-3018. FAX: 253-735-5005.
Founded 1905
Subject Interests: Local hist, Pac NW hist
Open Mon-Thurs 10-9, Fri 10-6, Sat 10-5, Sun 1-5
Friends of the Library Group
BELLEVUE LIBRARY, 1111 110th Ave NE, Bellevue, 98004, SAN 303-528X. Tel: 425-450-1765. FAX: 425-450-2468.
Open Mon-Thurs 9-9, Fri & Sat 10-6, Sun 11-7
Friends of the Library Group
BLACK DIAMOND LIBRARY, 24707 Roberts Dr, Black Diamond, 98010, SAN 328-9583. Tel: 360-886-1105. FAX: 360-886-8159.
Open Mon-Thurs 10-9, Sat 10-5
Friends of the Library Group
BOTHELL LIBRARY, 18215 98th Ave NE, Bothell, 98011, SAN 328-0837. Tel: 425-486-7811. FAX: 206-296-5043.
Open Mon-Thurs 10-9, Fri 10-6, Sat 10-5, Sun 11-7
Friends of the Library Group
BOULEVARD PARK LIBRARY, 12015 Roseberg Ave S, Seattle, 98168, SAN 322-7138. Tel: 206-242-8662. FAX: 206-296-5044.
Founded 1927
Open Mon-Thurs 10-9, Fri 10-6, Sat 10-5
Friends of the Library Group
BURIEN LIBRARY, 400 SW 152nd St, Burien, 98166, SAN 328-9605. Tel: 206-243-3490. FAX: 206-433-3175.
Open Mon-Thurs 10-9, Fri 10-6, Sat 10-5, Sun 11-7
Friends of the Library Group
CARNATION LIBRARY, 4804 Tolt Ave, Carnation, 98014, SAN 328-9621. Tel: 425-333-4398. FAX: 425-333-4402.
Founded 1924
Open Mon-Thurs 10-9, Fri 10-6, Sat 10-5
Friends of the Library Group
COVINGTON LIBRARY, 27100 164th Ave SE, Covington, 98042, SAN 373-8485. Tel: 253-630-8761. FAX: 206-205-0787.
Open Mon-Thurs 10-9, Fri 10-6, Sat 10-5, Sun 1-5
Friends of the Library Group
CROSSROADS LIBRARY CONNECTION, 15600 NE Eight St, Bellevue, 98008. Tel: 425-644-6203. FAX: 425-644-6205.
Open Mon-Sat 10-9, Sun 11-6
Friends of the Library Group
DES MOINES LIBRARY, 21620 11th Ave S, Des Moines, 98198, SAN 328-9648. Tel: 206-824-6066. FAX: 206-296-5047.
Open Mon-Thurs 10-9, Fri 10-6, Sat 10-5, Sun 1-5
Friends of the Library Group
DUVALL LIBRARY, 15508 Main St NE, Duvall, 98019. (Mail add: PO Box 339, Duvall, 98019), SAN 328-9664. Tel: 425-788-1173. FAX: 206-296-7429.
Open Mon-Thurs 10-9, Fri 10-6, Sat 10-5
Friends of the Library Group
ENUMCLAW PUBLIC LIBRARY, 1700 First St, Enumclaw, 98022, SAN 317-5103. Tel: 360-825-2045.
Founded 1922. Pop 11,500; Circ 165,253
Library Holdings: Bk Titles 56,450; Per Subs 147
Subject Interests: Local hist
Open Mon-Thurs 10-9, Fri 10-6, Sat 10-5, Sun 1-5
Friends of the Library Group
FAIRWOOD LIBRARY, 17009 140th Ave SE, Renton, 98058, SAN 328-9680. Tel: 425-226-0522. FAX: 206-296-8115.
Open Mon-Thurs 10-9, Fri 10-6, Sat 10-5, Sun 11-5
Friends of the Library Group
FALL CITY LIBRARY, 33415 SE 42nd Pl, Fall City, 98024. (Mail add: PO Box 340, Fall City, 98024), SAN 328-9702. Tel: 425-222-5951. FAX: 206-296-5048.
Open Mon-Thurs 10-9, Fri 10-6, Sat 10-5
Friends of the Library Group
FEDERAL WAY LIBRARY, 34200 First Way S, Federal Way, 98003, SAN 372-0306. Tel: 253-838-3668. FAX: 253-661-4770.
Open Mon-Thurs 10-9, Fri 10-6, Sat 10-5, Sun 11-7
Friends of the Library Group
FEDERAL WAY 320TH LIBRARY, 848 S 320th St, Federal Way, 98003, SAN 373-8493. Tel: 253-839-0257. FAX: 206-296-5053.
Open Mon-Thurs 10-9, Fri 10-6, Sat 10-5
Friends of the Library Group
GREENBRIDGE LIBRARY, 9720 Eight Ave SW, Seattle, 98106. Tel: 206-762-1682. FAX: 206-762-1684.
Open Mon-Thurs 10-9, Sat 12-4

ISSAQUAH LIBRARY, Ten W Sunset Way, 98027, SAN 328-7874. Tel: 425-392-5430. FAX: 425-392-1406.
Open Mon-Thurs 10-9, Fri 10-6, Sat 10-5, Sun 1-5
Friends of the Library Group
KENMORE LIBRARY, 6531 NE 181st St, Kenmore, 98028, SAN 328-9230. Tel: 425-486-8747. FAX: 206-296-5056.
Open Mon & Wed 11-9, Thurs & Fri 11-6, Sat 10-5
Friends of the Library Group
KENT LIBRARY, 212 Second Ave N, Kent, 98032, SAN 328-9257. Tel: 253-859-3330. FAX: 253-520-2170.
Open Mon-Thurs 10-9, Fri 10-6, Sat 10-5, Sun 1-5
Friends of the Library Group
KENT PANTHER LAKE LIBRARY, 20500 108th Ave SE, Kent, 98031. Tel: 253-854-0211.
Open Mon-Thurs 10-9, Fri 10-6, Sat 10-5
Friends of the Library Group
KINGSGATE LIBRARY, 12315 NE 143rd St, Kirkland, 98034, SAN 328-9273. Tel: 425-821-7686. FAX: 206-296-5061.
Open Mon-Thurs 10-9, Fri 10-6, Sat 10-5, Sun 1-5
Friends of the Library Group
KIRKLAND LIBRARY, 308 Kirkland Ave, Kirkland, 98033, SAN 328-929X. Tel: 425-822-2459. FAX: 425-822-3624.
Open Mon-Thurs 10-9, Fri 10-6, Sat 10-5, Sun 1-5
Friends of the Library Group
LAKE FOREST PARK LIBRARY, Town Center at Lake Forest, A-134, 17171 Bothell Way NE, Lake Forest Park, 98155, SAN 328-9192. Tel: 206-362-8860. FAX: 206-296-5054.
Open Mon-Thurs 10-9, Fri 10-6, Sat 10-5
Friends of the Library Group
LAKE HILLS LIBRARY, 15590 Lake Hills Blvd, Bellevue, 98007, SAN 328-9311. Tel: 425-747-3350. FAX: 425-643-2478.
Open Mon-Thurs 10-9, Fri 10-6, Sat 10-5, Sun 1-5
Friends of the Library Group
MAPLE VALLEY LIBRARY, 21844 SE 248th St, Maple Valley, 98038, SAN 328-9338. Tel: 425-432-4620. FAX: 425-433-0837.
Open Mon-Thurs 10-9, Fri 10-6, Sat 10-5, Sun 1-5
Friends of the Library Group
MERCER ISLAND LIBRARY, 4400 88th Ave SE, Mercer Island, 98040, SAN 328-9354. Tel: 206-236-3537. FAX: 206-296-5064.
Open Mon-Thurs 10-9, Fri 10-6, Sat 10-5, Sun 1-5
Friends of the Library Group
MUCKLESHOOT LIBRARY, 39917 Auburn-Enumclaw Rd SE, Auburn, 98092, SAN 328-9370. Tel: 253-931-6779. FAX: 206-296-0215.
Open Mon-Thurs 10-9, Fri 10-6, Sat 10-5
Friends of the Library Group
NEWPORT WAY LIBRARY, 14250 SE Newport Way NW, Bellevue, 98006-1507, SAN 328-9397. Tel: 425-747-2390.
Open Mon-Thurs 10-9, Fri 10-6, Sat 10-5, Sun 1-5
Friends of the Library Group
NORTH BEND LIBRARY, 115 E Fourth St, North Bend, 98045, SAN 328-9419. Tel: 425-888-0554. FAX: 206-296-0216.
Open Mon-Thurs 10-9, Fri 10-6, Sat 10-5, Sun 1-5
Friends of the Library Group
REDMOND LIBRARY, 15990 NE 85th St, Redmond, 98052, SAN 328-9451. Tel: 425-885-1861. FAX: 206-296-5067.
Open Mon-Thurs 10-9, Fri 10-6, Sat 10-5, Sun 11-7
Friends of the Library Group
RENTON HIGHLANDS, 2801 NE Tenth St, Renton, 98056, SAN 363-9061. Tel: 425-277-1831.
Library Holdings: Bk Vols 40,000
Open Mon-Thurs 10-9, Fri 10-6, Sat 1-5, Sun 1-5
Friends of the Library Group
RENTON LIBRARY, 100 Mill Ave S, Renton, 98057, SAN 363-9037. Tel: 425-226-6043. FAX: 425-277-7609.
Founded 1903. Pop 80,319; Circ 554,233
Special Collections: Pacific Northwest (Washington State Coll), bks, per
Open Mon-Thurs 10-9, Fri 10-6, Sat 10-5, Sun 1-5
Friends of the Library Group
RICHMOND BEACH LIBRARY, 19601 21st Ave NW, Shoreline, 98177, SAN 328-9478. Tel: 206-546-3522. FAX: 206-546-6820.
Open Mon-Thurs 10-9, Fri 10-6, Sat 10-5
Friends of the Library Group
SAMMAMISH LIBRARY, 825 228th Ave SE, Sammamish, 98075, SAN 375-6041. Tel: 425-392-3130. FAX: 425-391-6707.
Founded 1998
Open Mon-Thurs 10-9, Fri 10-6, Sat 10-5, Sun 1-5
Friends of the Library Group
SHORELINE LIBRARY, 345 NE 175th St, Shoreline, 98155, SAN 328-9494. Tel: 206-362-7550. FAX: 206-296-5069.
Open Mon-Thurs 10-9, Fri 10-6, Sat 10-5, Sun 11-7
Friends of the Library Group
SKYKOMISH LIBRARY, 100 Fifth St, Skykomish, 98288, SAN 328-9516. Tel: 360-677-2660. FAX: 360-677-2096.
Open Tues & Sat 10-5, Thurs 1-7
Friends of the Library Group
SKYWAY LIBRARY, 12601 76th Ave S, Seattle, 98178, SAN 325-1195. Tel: 206-772-5541. FAX: 206-296-5070.
Open Mon-Thurs 10-9, Fri 10-6, Sat 10-5
Friends of the Library Group
SNOQUALMIE LIBRARY, 7824 Center Blvd SE, Snoqualmie, 98065, SAN 328-9532. Tel: 425-888-1223. FAX: 206-296-0218.
Open Mon-Thurs 10-9, Fri 10-6, Sat 10-5
Friends of the Library Group
SOUTHCENTER LIBRARY CONNECTION, 1386 Southcenter Mall, Tukwila, 98188. Tel: 425-226-0522.
Open Mon-Sat 10-9, Sun 11-7
Friends of the Library Group
TUKWILA LIBRARY, 14380 Tukwila International Blvd, Tukwila, 98168, SAN 328-9214. Tel: 206-242-1640.
Open Mon-Thurs 10-9, Fri 10-6, Sat 10-5, Sun 11-6
Friends of the Library Group
VALLEY VIEW LIBRARY, 17850 Military Rd S, SeaTac, 98188, SAN 328-9575. Tel: 206-242-6044. FAX: 206-296-5072.
Open Mon-Thurs 10-9, Fri 10-6, Sat 10-5
Friends of the Library Group
VASHON LIBRARY, 17210 Vashon Hwy SW, Vashon Island, 98070, SAN 328-0853. Tel: 206-463-2069. FAX: 206-296-5073.
Founded 1946
Open Mon-Thurs 10-9, Fri 10-6, Sat 10-5, Sun 11-5
Friends of the Library Group
WHITE CENTER LIBRARY, 1409 SW 107th St, Seattle, 98146, SAN 328-9591. Tel: 206-243-0233. FAX: 206-296-5074.
Open Mon-Thurs 10-9, Fri 10-6, Sat 10-5
Friends of the Library Group
WOODINVILLE LIBRARY, 17105 Avondale Rd NE, Woodinville, 98072, SAN 373-8507. Tel: 425-788-0733. FAX: 425-788-9106.
Open Mon-Thurs 10-9, Fri 10-6, Sat 10-5, Sun 1-5
Friends of the Library Group
WOODMONT LIBRARY, 26809 Pacific Hwy S, Des Moines, 98198. Tel: 253-839-0121. FAX: 253-839-3358.
Open Mon-Thurs 10-9, Fri 10-6, Sat 10-5

JOINT BASE LEWIS MCCHORD

JOINT BASE LEWIS-MCCHORD LIBRARY SYSTEM
A MCCHORD LIBRARY*, 851 Lincoln Blvd, Joint Base Lewis-McChord, 98438, SAN 363-6542. Tel: 253-982-3454. Web Site: jblm.armymwr.com/programs/mcchord-library. *Br Mgr,* Brenda Camren; E-mail: brenda.d.camren.naf@army.mil; Staff 16 (MLS 4, Non-MLS 12)
Founded 1942
Library Holdings: Bk Vols 75,000; Per Subs 150
Special Collections: DVD/Video Coll, children's, documentaries, how-to, movies; Korean, German & Spanish Language Colls, bks, mag, mat; Military Science Coll
Subject Interests: Hist, Mil sci
Automation Activity & Vendor Info: (Acquisitions) Innovative Interfaces, Inc - Millennium; (Cataloging) Innovative Interfaces, Inc - Millennium; (Circulation) Innovative Interfaces, Inc - Millennium; (OPAC) Innovative Interfaces, Inc - Millennium; (Serials) Innovative Interfaces, Inc - Millennium
Partic in Defense Digital Library Research Service; Federal Library & Information Network; Merlin; OCLC Online Computer Library Center, Inc
Open Mon & Tues 9-6, Wed 9-7, Thurs & Fri 9-4, Sat 10-3
A GRANDSTAFF LIBRARY, 2109 N Tenth St & Pendleton Ave, 98433. Tel: 253-967-5889. E-mail: usarmy.jblm.imcom.list.dfmwr-grandstaff-library@army.mil. Web Site: jblm.armymwr.com/programs/grandstaff-library. *Supvry Librn,* Kristi Ramsey; E-mail: kristi.j.ramsey.naf@army.mil; Staff 16 (MLS 3, Non-MLS 13)
Function: 24/7 Electronic res, 24/7 Online cat, 3D Printer, Activity rm, Adult bk club, Audio & video playback equip for onsite use, Audiobks on Playaways & MP3, Audiobks via web, BA reader (adult literacy), Bk club(s), Bks on CD, Chess club, Children's prog, Computer training, Computers for patron use, Digital talking bks, E-Readers, Electronic databases & coll, Equip loans & repairs, Family literacy, Free DVD rentals, Games, Genealogy discussion group, Govt ref serv, Health sci info serv, Holiday prog, Homework prog, Internet access, Jail serv, Laminating, Laptop/tablet checkout, Life-long learning prog for all ages, Literacy & newcomer serv, Magazines, Mail & tel request accepted, Mango lang, Meeting rooms, Movies, Museum passes, Online cat, Online info literacy tutorials on the web & in blackboard, Online ref, Orientations, Outreach serv, OverDrive digital audio bks, Photocopying/Printing, Preschool outreach, Preschool reading prog, Prog for adults, Prog for children & young adult, Ref serv available, Res assist avail, Satellite serv, Scanner, Senior computer classes, Senior outreach, Spanish lang bks, Spoken cassettes & CDs, Spoken cassettes & DVDs, STEM programs, Story hour, Study rm, Summer & winter reading prog, Summer reading prog, Teen prog, Telephone ref, Wheelchair accessible, Wifi hotspot checkout, Winter reading prog, Writing prog

Open Mon & Tues 8:30-7, Wed & Thurs 8:30-6, Fri & Sat 8:30-4
Restriction: Authorized patrons

KALAMA

P KALAMA PUBLIC LIBRARY*, 312 N First St, 98625. (Mail add: PO Box 576, 98625), SAN 317-5286. Tel: 360-673-4568. FAX: 360-673-4560. E-mail: contact@kalamalibrary.com. Web Site: kalamalibrary.com. *Dir,* Elaine Bystrom; *Asst Librn,* Carol Day; Staff 4 (Non-MLS 4)
Founded 1900. Circ 9,823
Library Holdings: Bk Vols 11,000
Special Collections: North West Coll
Subject Interests: Classics
Function: ILL available, Prog for children & young adult, Summer reading prog
Open Mon-Fri 12-5, Sat 9-2
Friends of the Library Group

KELSO

P KELSO PUBLIC LIBRARY*, 351 Three Rivers Dr, Ste 1263, 98626. SAN 317-5294. Tel: 360-423-8110. FAX: 360-425-5195. E-mail: kelsopublib@kelso.gov. Web Site: www.kelso.gov/library. *Libr Mgr,* Natalee Corbett; Tel: 360-577-3390, E-mail: ncorbett@kelso.gov; Staff 8 (MLS 1, Non-MLS 7)
Founded 1916. Pop 11,950; Circ 82,124
Library Holdings: Bk Vols 35,289; Per Subs 108
Automation Activity & Vendor Info: (Cataloging) SirsiDynix; (Circulation) SirsiDynix; (OPAC) SirsiDynix
Open Mon-Fri 10-8, Sat 10-6
Friends of the Library Group

KENMORE

CM BASTYR UNIVERSITY LIBRARY*, 14500 Juanita Dr NE, 98028. SAN 323-7664. Tel: 425-602-3020. FAX: 425-602-3188. E-mail: library@bastyr.edu. Web Site: www.bastyr.edu/library. *Dir, Libr Serv,* Position Currently Open; *Sr Librn,* Zemirah Lee; E-mail: zlee@bastyr.edu; *Libr Asst,* Arlene Gillis; *Libr Asst,* Margaret Holt; Staff 6 (MLS 3, Non-MLS 3)
Founded 1980. Enrl 990; Fac 257; Highest Degree: Doctorate
Library Holdings: CDs 1,500; DVDs 450; e-journals 3,000; Bk Titles 19,000; Bk Vols 23,000; Per Subs 245; Videos 500
Special Collections: Bauervic Coll of Homeopathy; Dr Jesse Mercer Gehman Archive, historic records, journals, prof papers; Dr John Bastyr Archive, historic records, journals, prof papers; Largest natural health coll in the PNW (Complementary & Alternative Medicine (CAM) Coll); Naturopathic Medicine Historical Coll
Subject Interests: Acupuncture, Alternative med, Botanical med, Complementary med, Homeopathy, Natural health, Naturopathic med, Nutrition, Traditional Chinese med
Automation Activity & Vendor Info: (Acquisitions) Insignia Software; (Cataloging) Insignia Software; (Circulation) Insignia Software; (Course Reserve) Insignia Software; (OPAC) Insignia Software; (Serials) SERHOLD
Wireless access
Partic in National Network of Libraries of Medicine Region 5
Friends of the Library Group

KENNEWICK

P MID-COLUMBIA LIBRARIES*, Administrative Offices, 405 S Dayton St, 99336. SAN 363-6577. Administration Tel: 509-737-6356. FAX: 509-737-6349. E-mail: comm@midcolumbialibraries.org, communityengagement@midcolumbialibraries.org. Web Site: www.midcolumbialibraries.org. *Exec Dir,* Kyle Cox; *Dir, Coll & Serv,* Michael Huff; *Human Res Dir,* Celina Bishop; *IT Dir,* Jon Stuckel
Founded 1948. Pop 241,000
Special Collections: State Document Depository
Subject Interests: Bus, Econ, Mexican-Am studies
Automation Activity & Vendor Info: (Acquisitions) Innovative Interfaces, Inc; (Cataloging) Innovative Interfaces, Inc; (Circulation) Innovative Interfaces, Inc; (Course Reserve) Innovative Interfaces, Inc; (ILL) Innovative Interfaces, Inc; (Media Booking) Innovative Interfaces, Inc; (OPAC) Innovative Interfaces, Inc; (Serials) Innovative Interfaces, Inc
Wireless access
Function: Bk club(s), CD-ROM, Digital talking bks, Homebound delivery serv, ILL available, Internet access, Prog for adults, Prog for children & young adult, Ref serv available, Summer reading prog, VHS videos
Partic in OCLC Online Computer Library Center, Inc
Open Mon-Fri 8-5
Friends of the Library Group

Branches: 12
BASIN CITY BRANCH, 50-A N Canal Blvd, Basin City, 99343, SAN 373-5273. Tel: 509-269-4201. FAX: 509-269-4201. Web Site: www.midcolumbialibraries.org/branch/basin-city. *Supvr,* Christina Hart
Founded 1990
Open Tues-Fri 2-7, Sat 10-5
Friends of the Library Group
BENTON CITY BRANCH, 810 Horne Dr, Benton City, 99320, SAN 326-7458. Tel: 509-588-6471. FAX: 509-588-4153. Web Site: www.midcolumbialibraries.org/branch/benton-city. *Supvr,* Stacey Baker
Open Mon-Thurs 11-7, Sat 10-3
Friends of the Library Group
CONNELL BRANCH, 118 N Columbia Ave, Connell, 99326. (Mail add: PO Box 657, Connell, 99326-0657), SAN 363-6631. Tel: 509-234-4971. FAX: 509-234-4902. Web Site: www.midcolumbialibraries.org/branch/connell. *Supvr,* Helen Tobin; E-mail: htobin@midcolumbialibraries.org
Founded 1965
Open Mon-Fri 2-7, Sat 10-4
Friends of the Library Group
KAHLOTUS BRANCH, 225 E Weston St, Kahlotus, 99335, (Mail add: PO Box 147, Kahlotus, 99335-0147). Tel: 509-282-3493. FAX: 509-282-3493. Web Site: www.midcolumbialibraries.org/branch/kahlotus. *Supvr,* Shane Thompson; E-mail: sthompson@midcolumbialibraries.org
Founded 1989
Open Mon, Wed & Fri 2-7, Sat 10-3
Friends of the Library Group
KEEWAYDIN PARK, 405 S Dayton St, 99336. Tel: 509-586-3156. Web Site: www.midcolumbialibraries.org/branch/keewaydin-park. *Supvr,* Tiffany Garcia
Open Mon-Fri 11-7, Sat 10-3
Friends of the Library Group
KENNEWICK BRANCH, 1620 S Union St, 99338, SAN 329-3343. Tel: 509-783-7878. FAX: 509-735-2063. Web Site: www.midcolumbialibraries.org/branch/kennewick. *Br Mgr,* Ms Jessie Tomren; *Supvr,* Richard Pruiett
Founded 1949
Open Mon-Thurs 9-9, Fri 9-7, Sat 9-5, Sun 1-5
Friends of the Library Group
MERRILL'S CORNER, 5240 Eltopia W, Eltopia, 99330, SAN 370-4254. Tel: 509-546-8051. FAX: 509-297-4341. Web Site: www.midcolumbialibraries.org/branch/merrills-corner. *Supvr,* Jana Fox
Founded 1988
Open Mon, Wed & Fri 2-7
Friends of the Library Group
OTHELLO BRANCH, 101 E Main St, Othello, 99344, SAN 374-8170. Tel: 509-488-9683. FAX: 509-488-5321. Web Site: www.midcolumbialibraries.org/branch/othello. *Supvr,* Corinne Field
Founded 1995
Open Mon-Fri 11-7, Sat 10-3
Friends of the Library Group
PASCO BRANCH, 1320 W Hopkins St, Pasco, 99301, SAN 363-6666. Tel: 509-545-1019. FAX: 509-547-5416. Web Site: www.midcolumbialibraries.org/branch/pasco. *Supvr,* Mona Gonzalez
Open Mon-Fri 11-7, Sat 10-3, Sun 1-5
Friends of the Library Group
PROSSER BRANCH, 902 Seventh St, Prosser, 99350, SAN 370-4270. Tel: 509-786-2533. FAX: 509-786-7341. Web Site: www.midcolumbialibraries.org/branch/prosser. *Supvr,* Katy McLaughlin
Founded 1973
Open Mon-Fri 11-7, Sat 10-3
Friends of the Library Group
WEST PASCO BRANCH, 7525 Wrigley Dr, Pasco, 99301. Tel: 509-546-8055. Web Site: www.midcolumbialibraries.org/branch/west-pasco. *Supvr,* Ms Carmen Schaben
Founded 2013
Open Mon-Fri 11-7, Sat 10-3, Sun 1-5
Friends of the Library Group
WEST RICHLAND BRANCH, 3803 W Van Giesen St, West Richland, 99353, SAN 363-6682. Tel: 509-967-3191. FAX: 509-967-1224. Web Site: www.midcolumbialibraries.org/branch/west-richland. *Supvr,* Tom Moak
Open Mon-Fri 11-7, Sat 10-3, Sun 1-5
Friends of the Library Group
Bookmobiles: 1. Supvr, Tiffany Garcia

KIRKLAND

J LAKE WASHINGTON INSTITUTE OF TECHNOLOGY*, Library Learning Commons, Technology Ctr, T215, 11605 132nd Ave NE, 98034. Tel: 425-739-8100, Ext 8320. E-mail: library@lwtech.edu. *Fac Librn,* Katherine Kelley; E-mail: katherine.kelley@lwtech.edu; *Libr Tech II,* Emily Dunster
Library Holdings: Bk Titles 20,000; Per Subs 230

Wireless access
Partic in Washington Community & Technical Colleges Library Consortium
Open Mon-Thurs 7:30am-8pm, Fri 7:30-5, Sat 11-5 (Fall & Spring); Mon-Thurs 7:30am-7pm, Fri 7:30-5 (Summer)

CR NORTHWEST UNIVERSITY*, Hurst Library, 5520 108th Ave NE, 98083. (Mail add: PO Box 579, 98083-0579), SAN 363-6720. Tel: 425-889-5266. FAX: 425-889-7801. E-mail: library@northwestu.edu. Web Site: library.northwestu.edu. *Libr Dir,* Abigail Dour; Tel: 425-889-5201, E-mail: abigail.dour@northwestu.edu; *Digital Serv Librn,* Hannah Co; Tel: 425-889-5207, E-mail: hannah.co@northwestu.edu; *Ref & Instruction Librn,* Travis Pardo; Tel: 425-889-5301, E-mail: travis.pardo@northwestu.edu; *Cat Supvr,* Robin Severson; Tel: 425-889-5264, E-mail: robin.severson@northwestu.edu; *Circ Supvr,* Angelica Runstadler; Tel: 425-889-4205, E-mail: angelica.runstadler@northwestu.edu; *Metadata Librn,* Position Currently Open; Staff 6 (MLS 3, Non-MLS 3)
Founded 1934. Fac 61; Highest Degree: Doctorate
Library Holdings: Bk Titles 75,948; Bk Vols 174,060; Per Subs 914
Special Collections: Messianic Jewish Coll; Pacific Rim; Pentecostal Movement
Subject Interests: Relig studies, Teacher educ
Automation Activity & Vendor Info: (Acquisitions) OCLC; (Cataloging) OCLC; (Circulation) Koha; (Course Reserve) Koha; (Discovery) EBSCO Discovery Service; (ILL) Clio; (OPAC) Koha; (Serials) OCLC
Wireless access
Function: 24/7 Electronic res, 24/7 Online cat, Archival coll, ILL available, Movies
Open Mon-Thurs 7:30am-10:30pm, Fri 7:30-5, Sat 11-5, Sun 3-10:30

LA CONNER

P LA CONNER REGIONAL LIBRARY*, 520 Morris St, 98257. (Mail add: PO Box 370, 98257-0370), SAN 317-5324. Tel: 360-466-3352. FAX: 360-466-9178. E-mail: library@lclib.lib.wa.us. Web Site: www.lclib.lib.wa.us. *Dir,* Jean Markert; E-mail: jmarkert@lclib.lib.wa.us; *Libr Found Dir,* Susan Macek; E-mail: smacek@lclib.lib.wa.us; *Libr Tech,* Mathew Wend; E-mail: mwend@lclib.lib.wa.us; *Youth Serv Spec,* Katryna Barber; E-mail: kbarber@lclib.lib.wa.us; Staff 3.4 (MLS 1, Non-MLS 2.4)
Founded 1927. Pop 4,700; Circ 32,000
Jan 2017-Dec 2017 Income $360,000
Automation Activity & Vendor Info: (Circulation) Evergreen; (ILL) OCLC FirstSearch; (OPAC) Evergreen
Wireless access
Function: 24/7 Online cat, Adult bk club, After school storytime, Audiobks via web, Bk reviews (Group), Bks on CD, CD-ROM, Children's prog, Computer training, Computers for patron use, Digital talking bks, E-Reserves, Electronic databases & coll, Family literacy, Free DVD rentals, Holiday prog, Home delivery & serv to seniorr ctr & nursing homes, ILL available, Internet access, Life-long learning prog for all ages, Magazines, Magnifiers for reading, Mail & tel request accepted, Movies, Music CDs, Online cat, OverDrive digital audio bks, Photocopying/Printing, Preschool outreach, Prog for adults, Prog for children & young adult, Senior computer classes, Senior outreach, Story hour, Summer & winter reading prog, Summer reading prog, Tax forms, Teen prog, Wheelchair accessible, Winter reading prog
Open Mon-Fri 11-6, Sat 10-2
Restriction: Authorized patrons, In-house use for visitors, Non-resident fee
Friends of the Library Group

S SKAGIT COUNTY HISTORICAL MUSEUM*, Research Library, 501 S Fourth St, 98257. (Mail add: PO Box 818, 98257-0818), SAN 317-5332. Tel: 360-466-3365. FAX: 360-466-1611. E-mail: museum@co.skagit.wa.us. Web Site: www.skagitcounty.net/departments/historicalsociety. *Dir,* Jo Wolfe; *Archivist,* Mari Densmore
Library Holdings: Bk Titles 1,528; Bk Vols 1,639
Special Collections: Oral History
Subject Interests: County hist, Genealogy, Local hist
Wireless access
Function: Archival coll
Restriction: Open by appt only

LACEY

S PANORAMA LIBRARY*, The Quinault, 1835 Circle Lane SE, 98503. (Mail add: The Panorama Library, 1751 Circle Lane SE, 98503). Tel: 360-456-0111, Ext 4005. E-mail: library@panorama.org. Web Site: kya.panorama.org/panorama-library-3. *Board Pres,* Deb Creveling; *Librn,* Kathy Forsythe
Library Holdings: Bk Vols 4,000
Automation Activity & Vendor Info: (Cataloging) Biblionix/Apollo; (Circulation) Biblionix/Apollo; (OPAC) Biblionix/Apollo
Wireless access

C SAINT MARTIN'S UNIVERSITY*, O'Grady Library, 5000 Abbey Way SE, 98503. SAN 317-5340. Tel: 360-688-2260. Administration Tel: 360-688-2250. FAX: 360-486-8810. Circulation E-mail: circulation@stmartin.edu. Web Site: www.stmartin.edu/academics/academic-resources/ogrady-library. *Dean of Libr,* Amy Stewart-Mailhiot; E-mail: AStewart-Mailhiot@stmartin.edu; *Access Serv Librn,* Stefanie Gorzelsky; Tel: 360-688-2254, E-mail: sgorzelsky@stmartin.edu; *Info Literacy Librn,* Kael Moffat; Tel: 360-688-2257, E-mail: kmoffat@stmartin.edu; Staff 7.8 (MLS 3.3, Non-MLS 4.5)
Founded 1895. Enrl 1,801; Fac 80; Highest Degree: Master
Subject Interests: Catholic theol, Pac NW hist
Automation Activity & Vendor Info: (Acquisitions) Ex Libris Group; (Cataloging) Ex Libris Group; (Circulation) Ex Libris Group; (Course Reserve) Ex Libris Group; (ILL) OCLC ILLiad; (OPAC) Ex Libris Group; (Serials) Ex Libris Group
Wireless access
Partic in OCLC Online Computer Library Center, Inc; Orbis Cascade Alliance

LAKEWOOD

J CLOVER PARK TECHNICAL COLLEGE LIBRARY*, 4500 Steilacoom Blvd SW, Bldg 15, 98499-4098. SAN 324-5160. Tel: 253-589-5544. FAX: 253-589-5726. E-mail: cptclibrary@cptc.edu. Web Site: www.cptc.edu/library. *Learning Res Ctr Coordr,* Deborah Derylak; E-mail: deborah.derylak@cptc.edu; Staff 2 (MLS 2)
Highest Degree: Associate
Library Holdings: Bk Titles 12,000; Per Subs 320
Special Collections: Technical College Materials
Subject Interests: Vocational educ
Automation Activity & Vendor Info: (Cataloging) Horizon; (Circulation) Horizon; (Course Reserve) Horizon; (ILL) Horizon; (OPAC) Horizon
Wireless access
Partic in Washington Community & Technical Colleges Library Consortium
Open Mon, Tues, Thurs & Fri 8-4:30, Wed 8-8

J PIERCE COLLEGE LIBRARY*, Fort Steilacoom Campus, Fort Steilacoom Campus/Cascade Bldg 4, 9401 Farwest Dr SW, 98498. SAN 317-6835. Tel: 253-964-6547. Interlibrary Loan Service Tel: 253-964-7349. Reference Tel: 253-964-6555. FAX: 253-964-6713. Web Site: www.pierce.ctc.edu/library. *Dean, Libr & Learning Res,* Christie Flynn; Tel: 253-964-6553, E-mail: cflynn@pierce.ctc.edu; *Ref & Instruction Librn,* Laurie Shuster; Tel: 253-964-6305, E-mail: lshuster@pierce.ctc.edu; *Circ Supvr, ILL,* Velvet Marlin; E-mail: vmarlin@pierce.ctc.edu; *Ser Tech,* Kathy Gilbert; Tel: 253-964-6740, E-mail: kgilbert@pierce.ctc.edu; Staff 8 (MLS 5, Non-MLS 3)
Founded 1967. Enrl 13,500; Fac 300; Highest Degree: Associate
Library Holdings: Bk Titles 120,000; Per Subs 525
Automation Activity & Vendor Info: (Acquisitions) Ex Libris Group; (Cataloging) Ex Libris Group; (Circulation) Ex Libris Group; (Course Reserve) Ex Libris Group; (OPAC) Ex Libris Group; (Serials) Ex Libris Group
Wireless access
Function: AV serv, Doc delivery serv, ILL available, Photocopying/Printing, Ref serv available, Telephone ref, Wheelchair accessible
Partic in OCLC Online Computer Library Center, Inc; Washington Community & Technical Colleges Library Consortium; Washington Libr Network
Special Services for the Deaf - TTY equip
Restriction: Open to pub for ref & circ; with some limitations, Open to students, Open to students, fac & staff, Photo ID required for access
Departmental Libraries:
PUYALLUP CAMPUS, 1601 39th Ave SE, Puyallup, 98374. Tel: 253-840-8300. FAX: 253-840-8316. *Circ Supvr,* Lori Broberg; E-mail: lbroberg@pierce.ctc.edu; *Ref & Instruction Librn,* Kathy Swart; Tel: 253-840-8305, E-mail: kswart@pierce.ctc.edu; *Ref & Instruction Librn,* Beth Thoms; Tel: 253-840-8303, E-mail: bthoms@pierce.ctc.edu; *Acq, Syst Tech,* John Jennings; Tel: 253-840-8309, E-mail: jjennings@pierce.ctc.edu; Staff 8 (MLS 5, Non-MLS 3)
Founded 1967. Enrl 6,300; Highest Degree: Associate
Function: AV serv, ILL available, Photocopying/Printing, Ref serv available, Telephone ref
Restriction: Open to pub for ref & circ; with some limitations, Open to students, Open to students, fac & staff, Photo ID required for access

LIBERTY LAKE

P LIBERTY LAKE MUNICIPAL LIBRARY*, 23123 E Mission Ave, 99019-7613. Tel: 509-232-2510. Administration Tel: 509-435-0777. FAX: 509-232-2512. E-mail: library@libertylakewa.gov. Web Site: www.libertylakewa.gov/435/library. *Libr Dir,* Jandy Humble; Tel: 509-435-0777, E-mail: jhumble@libertylakewa.gov; *Teen & Adult Librn,*

Joanne Percy; E-mail: jpercy@libertylakewa.gov; *Ch Assoc,* Erin Smith; E-mail: esmith@libertylakewa.gov; *Circ Supvr,* Georgette Rogers; Tel: 509-435-0778, E-mail: grogers@libertylakewa.gov; Staff 9 (MLS 2, Non-MLS 7)
Founded 2003. Pop 11,000; Circ 132,000
Library Holdings: Audiobooks 1,128; AV Mats 217; CDs 1,174; DVDs 1,694; e-books 99; e-journals 20; Large Print Bks 644; Bk Titles 29,021; Per Subs 15
Automation Activity & Vendor Info: (Cataloging) ByWater Solutions; (Circulation) ByWater Solutions; (ILL) ByWater Solutions; (OPAC) ByWater Solutions
Wireless access
Function: 24/7 Electronic res, Accelerated reader prog, Activity rm, Adult bk club, Audiobks via web, AV serv, Bks on CD, Children's prog, Citizenship assistance, Computer training, Computers for patron use, E-Readers, Electronic databases & coll, Free DVD rentals, Holiday prog, Home delivery & serv to seniorr ctr & nursing homes, Homebound delivery serv, ILL available, Instruction & testing, Internet access, Learning ctr, Life-long learning prog for all ages, Magazines, Movies, Music CDs, Online cat, Online ref, Outreach serv, OverDrive digital audio bks, Photocopying/Printing, Preschool outreach, Preschool reading prog, Prog for adults, Prog for children & young adult, Ref serv available, Scanner, Senior computer classes, Senior outreach, Story hour, Summer & winter reading prog, Teen prog, Telephone ref, Wheelchair accessible
Partic in Cooperative Information Network; Washington Digital Library Consortium
Open Mon-Wed & Fri 10-6, Thurs 10-8, Sat 10-4
Friends of the Library Group

LONGVIEW

P LONGVIEW PUBLIC LIBRARY*, 1600 Louisiana St, 98632-2993. SAN 317-5375. Tel: 360-442-5300. Administration Tel: 360-442-5310. FAX: 360-442-5954. Web Site: www.longviewlibrary.org. *Libr Dir,* Chris Skaugset; Tel: 360-442-5309, E-mail: chris.skaugset@ci.longview.wa.us; *Pub Serv Librn,* Position Currently Open; *Tech Serv Librn,* Jennifer King; Tel: 360-442-5324, E-mail: jennifer.king@ci.longview.wa.us; *Youth Serv Librn,* Becky Standal; Tel: 360-442-5323, E-mail: becky.standal@ci.longview.wa.us; Staff 19 (MLS 4, Non-MLS 15)
Founded 1926. Pop 56,000; Circ 408,552
Jan 2019-Dec 2019 Income $2,003,240
Library Holdings: CDs 2,961; DVDs 9,892; e-books 76,846; Bk Vols 127,872; Per Subs 130
Special Collections: '23 Club Oral History Coll, cassettes; Construction of Longview (Long Bell Files), letters; Early Longview History (S M Morris Coll), pictures; Longview Coll (Longview Room). Oral History
Automation Activity & Vendor Info: (Acquisitions) Innovative Interfaces, Inc; (Cataloging) Innovative Interfaces, Inc; (Circulation) Innovative Interfaces, Inc; (Course Reserve) Innovative Interfaces, Inc; (Media Booking) Innovative Interfaces, Inc; (OPAC) Innovative Interfaces, Inc; (Serials) Innovative Interfaces, Inc
Wireless access
Function: 24/7 Electronic res, 24/7 Online cat, Adult bk club, Adult literacy prog, Archival coll, Art exhibits, Art programs, Audiobks on Playaways & MP3, Audiobks via web, AV serv, BA reader (adult literacy), Bilingual assistance for Spanish patrons, Bk club(s), Bks on cassette, Bks on CD, Children's prog, Citizenship assistance, Computer training, Computers for patron use, Digital talking bks, E-Reserves, Electronic databases & coll, Equip loans & repairs, Family literacy, Free DVD rentals, Holiday prog, Home delivery & serv to seniorr ctr & nursing homes, Homebound delivery serv, Homework prog, Instruction & testing, Internet access, Life-long learning prog for all ages, Literacy & newcomer serv, Magazines, Meeting rooms, Microfiche/film & reading machines, Movies, Music CDs, Online cat, Online ref, Outreach serv, Outside serv via phone, mail, e-mail & web, OverDrive digital audio bks, Photocopying/Printing, Preschool outreach, Preschool reading prog, Printer for laptops & handheld devices, Prog for adults, Prog for children & young adult, Ref & res, Ref serv available, Scanner, Senior computer classes, Senior outreach, Spanish lang bks, STEM programs, Story hour, Summer & winter reading prog, Summer reading prog, Tax forms, Teen prog, Telephone ref, Visual arts prog, Wheelchair accessible, Winter reading prog, Workshops
Publications: Dialogue (Newsletter)
Special Services for the Deaf - Bks on deafness & sign lang; TDD equip
Special Services for the Blind - Bks available with recordings; Bks on CD; Copier with enlargement capabilities; Home delivery serv; Large print bks; Talking bks
Open Mon-Wed 10-8, Thurs-Sat 10-5
Friends of the Library Group

J LOWER COLUMBIA COLLEGE*, Alan Thompson Library, 1600 Maple St, 98632-3907. (Mail add: PO Box 3010, 98632-0310), SAN 317-5383. Tel: 360-442-2660. Reference Tel: 360-442-2665. Toll Free Tel: 800-850-2311. FAX: 360-442-2669. Circulation E-mail: library.circulation@lowercolumbia.edu. Reference E-mail: library.reference@lowercolumbia.edu. Web Site: www.lowercolumbia.edu/library. *Dean of Instruction, Dean, Learning Res,* Melinda Harbaugh; Tel: 360-442-2662, E-mail: mharbaugh@lowercolumbia.edu; *Fac Librn,* Lindsay Keevy; Tel: 360-442-2667, E-mail: lkeevy@lowercolumbia.edu; Staff 7 (MLS 5, Non-MLS 2)
Founded 1934. Enrl 6,859; Fac 70; Highest Degree: Bachelor
Automation Activity & Vendor Info: (Cataloging) Ex Libris Group; (Circulation) Ex Libris Group; (Discovery) Ex Libris Group; (OPAC) Ex Libris Group
Wireless access
Function: 24/7 Electronic res, 24/7 Online cat, Archival coll, Art exhibits, Audio & video playback equip for onsite use, Audiobks via web, Computer training, Computers for patron use, Distance learning, Electronic databases & coll, Equip loans & repairs, For res purposes, Free DVD rentals, ILL available, Internet access, Learning ctr, Magazines, Mail & tel request accepted, Meeting rooms, Movies, Music CDs, Online cat, Online info literacy tutorials on the web & in blackboard, Online ref, Orientations, Photocopying/Printing, Prof lending libr, Ref & res, Ref serv available, Res assist avail, Res libr, Scanner, Serves people with intellectual disabilities, Study rm, Telephone ref, Wheelchair accessible, Workshops
Partic in Washington Community & Technical Colleges Library Consortium
Open Mon-Thurs 7:30-7, Fri 7:30-4, Sat 10-2

LOON LAKE

P THE LIBRARIES OF STEVENS COUNTY*, Administrative Office, 4008 Cedar St, 99148-9676. (Mail add: PO Box 744, 98148-0744), SAN 375-4111. Tel: 509-233-3016, 509-233-9621. FAX: 509-233-9621. Web Site: thelosc.org. *Dir,* Amanda Six; Tel: 509-675-5102, E-mail: amanda@scrld.org; *Bus Mgr,* Janet Eide; E-mail: janet@scrld.org; Staff 10 (MLS 6, Non-MLS 4)
Founded 1998. Pop 43,700
Automation Activity & Vendor Info: (Cataloging) TLC (The Library Corporation); (Circulation) TLC (The Library Corporation)
Wireless access
Open Mon, Tues & Thurs 10-6, Fri 10-5
Friends of the Library Group
Branches: 7
CHEWELAH BRANCH, 311 E Clay Ave, Chewelah, 99109. (Mail add: PO Box 87, Chewelah, 99109-0087), SAN 317-4972. Tel: 509-935-6805. FAX: 509-935-4564. *Br Mgr,* Bryan Tidwell; E-mail: bryan@scrld.org; Staff 4 (Non-MLS 4)
Founded 1916. Pop 6,865; Circ 71,156
Library Holdings: Bk Vols 32,939; Per Subs 63
Subject Interests: State hist
Open Mon-Fri 10-6
Friends of the Library Group
COLVILLE BRANCH, 195 S Oak St, Colville, 99114-2845, SAN 317-5022. Tel: 509-684-6620. *Mgr,* Leah Hammerquist; E-mail: leah@scrld.org; Staff 9 (MLS 2, Non-MLS 7)
Pop 10,000; Circ 77,531
Library Holdings: Bk Titles 36,248
Subject Interests: Genealogy, Northwest
Function: For res purposes, Homebound delivery serv, ILL available, Photocopying/Printing, Prog for children & young adult, Summer reading prog, Telephone ref, Wheelchair accessible
Open Mon-Fri 10-6
Friends of the Library Group
HUNTERS BRANCH, 5014 Columbia River Rd, Bldg No 11, Hunters, 99157. (Mail add: PO Box 500, Kettle Falls, 99141). Tel: 509-722-3877. *Mgr,* Katy Pike; E-mail: pike@scrld.org
Library Holdings: Bk Vols 1,800
Open Wed & Fri 10-4
Friends of the Library Group
KETTLE FALLS BRANCH, 605 Meyers St, Kettle Falls, 99141. (Mail add: PO Box 500, Kettle Falls, 99141), SAN 326-2995. Tel: 509-738-6817. FAX: 509-738-2787. *Mgr,* Katy Pike; E-mail: pike@scrld.org; Staff 4 (MLS 1, Non-MLS 3)
Founded 1950. Pop 2,000; Circ 14,000
Special Collections: Old Kettle Falls Photo Coll
Open Mon-Fri 10-6
Friends of the Library Group
LAKESIDE COMMUNITY LIBRARY, 5919 Hwy 291, Ste 2, Nine Mile Falls, 99026. Tel: 509-315-8339. *Mgr,* Brooke Golden; E-mail: brooke@scrld.org
Library Holdings: Bk Vols 8,000; Per Subs 20
Open Mon-Fri 10-6
Friends of the Library Group
NORTHPORT COMMUNITY LIBRARY, 521 Center Ave, Northport, 99157. (Mail add: PO Box 500, Kettle Falls, 99141). Tel: 509-732-8928. *Mgr,* Katy Pike; E-mail: pike@scrld.org
Open Tues 11-6, Thurs 10-6, Fri 2-6, Sat 10-4

ONION CREEK LIBRARY STATION, 2191 Clugston-Onion Creek Rd, Colville, 99114. (Mail add: PO Box 500, Kettle Falls, 99141). Tel: 509-738-6817. *Mgr,* Katy Pike; E-mail: pike@scrld.org
Open Wed 1-4

LOPEZ ISLAND

P LOPEZ ISLAND LIBRARY*, 2225 Fisherman Bay Rd, 98261. (Mail add: PO Box 770, 98261-0770), SAN 326-7105. Tel: 360-468-2265. FAX: 360-468-3850. E-mail: librarian@lopezlibrary.org. Web Site: www.lopezlibrary.org. *Libr Assoc,* Beth St George; Staff 5 (MLS 2, Non-MLS 3)
Founded 1982. Pop 2,400; Circ 58,600
Library Holdings: Audiobooks 1,666; CDs 594; DVDs 3,495; e-books 153; Large Print Bks 1,500; Bk Titles 23,500; Per Subs 115; Videos 1,460
Subject Interests: Native Am art, Northwest Coast hist
Wireless access
Function: ILL available, Photocopying/Printing, Prog for children & young adult, Scanner, Summer reading prog
Open Mon & Sat 10-5, Tues, Thurs & Fri 10-6, Wed 10-9
Friends of the Library Group

LYNNWOOD

J EDMONDS COLLEGE LIBRARY*, 20000 68th Ave W, 98036. SAN 317-543X. Tel: 425-640-1529. Reference Tel: 425-640-1472. Administration Tel: 425-640-1522. Web Site: www.edmonds.edu/library. *Assoc Dean,* Claire Murata; E-mail: claire.murata@edmonds.edu; *Ref & Instrul Serv Librn,* Haley Benjamins; E-mail: haley.benjamins@edmonds.edu; *Ref & Instruction Librn,* Meryl Geffner; E-mail: meryl.geffner@edmonds.edu; *Ref & Instrul Serv Librn,* Johnetta Moore; E-mail: johnettamoore@edmonds.edu; *Tech Serv Librn,* Dan Moore; E-mail: dan.moore@edmonds.edu; *Admin Serv Mgr,* Position Currently Open; *Circ,* Lurana Culligan; E-mail: lculligan@edmonds.edu; *Tech Serv,* Clare Bryant; E-mail: clare.bryant@edmonds.edu; *Tech Serv,* Betty Croy; E-mail: bcroy@edmonds.edu; Staff 5 (MLS 5)
Founded 1967
Subject Interests: Hort, Legal assisting
Automation Activity & Vendor Info: (Acquisitions) Ex Libris Group; (Cataloging) Ex Libris Group; (Circulation) Ex Libris Group; (Course Reserve) Ex Libris Group; (ILL) OCLC; (OPAC) Ex Libris Group; (Serials) Ex Libris Group
Wireless access
Partic in OCLC Online Computer Library Center, Inc; Washington Community & Technical Colleges Library Consortium

MARYSVILLE

P SNO-ISLE LIBRARIES*, Administrative & Service Center, 7312 35th Ave NE, 98271-7417. SAN 363-681X. Tel: 360-651-7000. Toll Free Tel: 877-766-4753. FAX: 360-651-7151. Web Site: www.sno-isle.org. *Exec Dir,* Lois Langer Thomson; Tel: 360-651-7001; *Communications Dir,* Ken Harvey; Tel: 360-651-7030; Staff 499 (MLS 75, Non-MLS 424)
Founded 1945
Library Holdings: CDs 44,392; Microforms 2,391
Automation Activity & Vendor Info: (Acquisitions) TLC (The Library Corporation); (Cataloging) TLC (The Library Corporation); (Circulation) TLC (The Library Corporation)
Wireless access
Partic in OCLC Online Computer Library Center, Inc
Open Mon-Fri 8-5
Friends of the Library Group
Branches: 23
ARLINGTON LIBRARY, 135 N Washington Ave, Arlington, 98223-1422, SAN 363-6844. Tel: 360-435-3033. FAX: 360-435-3854. *Mgr,* Monica Jackson; Staff 4 (MLS 4)
Founded 1981. Circ 196,342
Open Mon & Tues 9-8, Wed & Thurs 10-8, Fri & Sat 10-6, Sun 1-5
Friends of the Library Group
BRIER LIBRARY, 23303 Brier Rd, Brier, 98036-8247, SAN 363-6860. Tel: 425-483-0888. FAX: 425-487-1880. *Libr Mgr,* Kelley Murdock; Staff 1 (MLS 1)
Founded 1996. Circ 58,438
Open Tues & Wed 11-7, Thurs-Sat 10-6
Friends of the Library Group
CAMANO ISLAND LIBRARY, 848 N Sunrise Blvd, Camano Island, 98282-8770. Tel: 360-387-5150. FAX: 360-387-5170. *Libr Mgr,* Kelli Bragg; Staff 1 (MLS 1)
Circ 126,326
Open Mon, Wed, Fri & Sat 10-6, Tues & Thurs 11-7
Friends of the Library Group
CLINTON LIBRARY, 4781 Deer Lake Rd, Clinton, 98236-0530. Tel: 360-341-4280. FAX: 360-341-2989. *Libr Mgr,* Debby Colfer; Staff 1 (MLS 1)
Founded 2000. Circ 39,911
Open Tues, Fri & Sat 10-6, Wed & Thurs 11-7
Friends of the Library Group
COUPEVILLE LIBRARY, 788 NW Alexander St, Coupeville, 98239, SAN 363-6879. Tel: 360-678-4911. FAX: 360-678-5261. *Libr Mgr,* Leslie Franzen; Staff 1 (MLS 1)
Founded 1988. Circ 112,880
Open Mon & Wed 10-8, Tues & Thurs-Sat 10-6, Sun 1-5
Friends of the Library Group
DARRINGTON LIBRARY, 1005 Cascade St, Darrington, 98241, SAN 363-6909. Tel: 360-436-1600. FAX: 360-436-1659. *Libr Mgr,* Asheley Bryson; Staff 1 (MLS 1)
Founded 1990. Circ 42,784
Open Mon & Wed 11-7, Tues & Thurs-Sat 10-6
Friends of the Library Group
EDMONDS LIBRARY, 650 Main St, Edmonds, 98020-3056, SAN 363-6933. Tel: 425-771-1933. FAX: 425-771-1977. *Mgr,* Richard Suico; Staff 4 (MLS 4)
Founded 1982. Circ 336,338
Library Holdings: Bk Vols 63,132
Open Mon-Thurs 9-8, Fri 9-6, Sat 10-6, Sun 1-5
Friends of the Library Group
FREELAND LIBRARY, 5495 Harbor Ave, Freeland, 98249. (Mail add: PO Box 1357, Freeland, 98249-1357), SAN 363-6968. Tel: 360-331-7323. FAX: 360-331-1572. *Libr Mgr,* Betsy Arand; Staff 2 (MLS 2)
Founded 1994. Circ 140,429
Library Holdings: Bk Vols 15,900
Function: Art exhibits, Audiobks via web, Bk reviews (Group), Bks on CD, Children's prog, Citizenship assistance, Computer training, Computers for patron use, Digital talking bks, E-Reserves, Electronic databases & coll, Family literacy, Free DVD rentals, Homebound delivery serv, ILL available, Internet access, Mail & tel request accepted, Music CDs, Online cat, Online ref, Outreach serv, Outside serv via phone, mail, e-mail & web, OverDrive digital audio bks, Photocopying/Printing, Preschool outreach, Prog for adults, Prog for children & young adult, Ref serv available, Story hour, Summer & winter reading prog, Summer reading prog, Tax forms, Teen prog, Telephone ref, Wheelchair accessible
Open Mon, Wed, Fri & Sat 10-6, Tues & Thurs 10-8, Sun 1-5
Friends of the Library Group
GRANITE FALLS LIBRARY, 815 E Galena St, Granite Falls, 98252-8472, SAN 363-6992. Tel: 360-691-6087. FAX: 360-691-5533. *Libr Mgr,* Michelle Callihan; Staff 1 (MLS 1)
Founded 2001. Circ 113,536
Open Mon, Wed, Fri & Sat 10-6, Tues & Thurs 10-8, Sun 1-5
Friends of the Library Group
LAKE STEVENS LIBRARY, 1804 Main St, Lake Stevens, 98258. (Mail add: PO Box 217, Lake Stevens, 98258-0217), SAN 363-7026. Tel: 425-334-1900. FAX: 425-334-9487. *Libr Mgr,* Lindsay Hanson; Staff 2 (MLS 2)
Founded 1988. Circ 138,845
Library Holdings: Bk Vols 19,338
Open Mon-Thurs 10-8, Fri & Sat 10-6, Sun 1-5
Friends of the Library Group
LAKEWOOD/SMOKEY POINT LIBRARY, 3411 169th Place NE, Suites ABC, Arlington, 98223. Tel: 360-651-0774. FAX: 360-651-2393. *Mgr,* Kaley Costello
LANGLEY LIBRARY, 104 Second St, Langley, 98260. (Mail add: PO Box 365, Langley, 98260-0365), SAN 363-7050. Tel: 360-221-4383. FAX: 360-221-3067. *Libr Mgr,* Vicky Welfare
Founded 1922. Circ 80,685
Open Mon & Wed 11-7, Tues & Thurs-Sat 10-6
Friends of the Library Group
LYNNWOOD LIBRARY, 19200 44th Ave W, Lynnwood, 98036-5617, SAN 363-7085. Tel: 425-778-2148. FAX: 425-774-3434. *Libr Mgr,* Michael Delury; Staff 8 (MLS 8)
Founded 1971. Circ 641,950
Special Services for the Deaf - TTY equip
Open Mon-Thurs 9-9, Fri-Sun 10-6
Friends of the Library Group
MARINER LIBRARY, 520 128th St SW, Ste A9 & A10, Everett, 98204. Tel: 425-423-9017. FAX: 425-423-9075. *Libr Mgr,* Sandra Beck
Founded 2017
Open Mon, Wed, Fri & Sat 10-6, Tues & Thurs 11-7
MARYSVILLE LIBRARY, 6120 Grove St, 98270-4127, SAN 363-7115. Tel: 360-658-5000. FAX: 360-659-5050. *Libr Mgr,* Eric Spencer; Staff 5 (MLS 5)
Founded 1995. Circ 470,483
Open Mon-Thurs 9-8, Fri & Sat 10-6, Sun 1-5
Friends of the Library Group
MILL CREEK LIBRARY, 15429 Bothell Everett Hwy, Mill Creek, 98012-1212, SAN 328-9044. Tel: 425-337-4822. FAX: 425-337-3567. *Libr Mgr,* Darlene Weber; Staff 5 (MLS 5)
Founded 1987. Circ 543,507
Library Holdings: Bk Vols 51,002

Open Mon-Thurs 9-8, Fri & Sat 10-6, Sun 1-5
Friends of the Library Group
MONROE LIBRARY, 1070 Village Way, Monroe, 98272-2035, SAN 363-714X. Tel: 360-794-7851. FAX: 360-794-0292. *Libr Mgr,* Philip Spirito; Staff 4 (MLS 4)
Founded 2002. Circ 252,402
Open Mon-Thurs 9-8, Fri & Sat 10-6, Sun 1-5
Friends of the Library Group
MOUNTLAKE TERRACE LIBRARY, 23300 58th Ave W, Mountlake Terrace, 98043-4630, SAN 363-7174. Tel: 425-776-8722. FAX: 425-776-3411. *Libr Mgr,* Kristin Piepho; Staff 4 (MLS 4)
Founded 1988. Circ 153,496
Library Holdings: Bk Vols 26,824
Open Mon-Thurs 9-8, Fri & Sat 10-6, Sun 1-5
Friends of the Library Group
MUKILTEO LIBRARY, 4675 Harbour Pointe Blvd, Mukilteo, 98275-4725. Tel: 425-493-8202. FAX: 425-493-1601. *Libr Mgr,* Jane Crawford; Staff 4 (MLS 4)
Founded 1998. Circ 333,512
Library Holdings: Bk Vols 61,645
Open Mon-Thurs 9-8, Fri & Sat 10-6, Sun 1-5
Friends of the Library Group
OAK HARBOR LIBRARY, 1000 SE Regatta Dr, Oak Harbor, 98277-3091, SAN 363-7263. Tel: 360-675-5115. FAX: 360-679-3761. *Libr Mgr,* Mary Campbell; Staff 4 (MLS 4)
Circ 302,628
Open Mon-Thurs 9-8, Fri & Sat 10-6, Sun 1-5
Friends of the Library Group
SNOHOMISH COMMUNITY LIBRARY, 311 Maple Ave, Snohomish, 98290-2525, SAN 363-7328. Tel: 360-568-2898. FAX: 360-568-1922. *Libr Mgr,* Jude Anderson; Staff 5 (MLS 5)
Founded 2003. Circ 415,180
Special Collections: Genealogy Coll; Local History Coll
Open Mon-Thurs 9-8, Fri & Sat 10-6, Sun 1-5
Friends of the Library Group
STANWOOD LIBRARY, 9701 271st St NW, Stanwood, 98292-8097, SAN 363-7352. Tel: 360-629-3132. FAX: 360-629-3516. *Libr Mgr,* Charles Pratt; Staff 3 (MLS 3)
Founded 1970. Circ 177,424
Open Mon-Thurs 10-8, Fri & Sat 10-6, Sun 1-5
Friends of the Library Group
SULTAN LIBRARY, 319 Main St, Ste 100, Sultan, 98294. (Mail add: PO Box 580, Sultan, 98294-0580), SAN 363-7417. Tel: 360-793-1695. FAX: 360-793-9634. *Libr Mgr,* Jackie Personeus
Founded 1999. Circ 81,017
Open Mon & Tues 11-7, Wed-Sat 10-6
Friends of the Library Group
Bookmobiles: 2. Mgr, Sonia Gustafson

MONTESANO

GL GRAYS HARBOR COUNTY LAW LIBRARY, 100 W Broadway Ave, 98563. SAN 317-5472. Tel: 360-249-5311, Ext 3. Web Site: www.graysharbor.us/government/superior_court/law_library.php. *Librn,* Josh Sedy
Library Holdings: Bk Vols 5,000
Wireless access
Open Mon-Fri 8-5

MOSES LAKE

J BIG BEND COMMUNITY COLLEGE LIBRARY, Bonaudi Library, 1800 Bldg, 7662 Chanute St NE, 98837. SAN 317-5480. Tel: 509-793-2350. E-mail: librarymail@bigbend.edu. Web Site: libguides.bigbend.edu/home. *Dir, Library Resources & eLearning,* Tim Fuhrman; E-mail: timf@bigbend.edu; *Librn,* Rhonda Kitchens; E-mail: rhondak@bigbend.edu; *Librn/eLearning Coordr,* Geri Hopkins; E-mail: gerih@bigbend.edu; *Prog Coordr, Purchasing,* Alex Lopez; E-mail: alexl@bigbend.edu; *Libr Syst Spec,* Amanda Miller; E-mail: amandam@bigbend.edu; *Cat, Ser,* Teresa Curran Sweeney; E-mail: teresac@bigbend.edu; Staff 6.5 (MLS 3, Non-MLS 3.5)
Founded 1963. Enrl 2,000; Fac 50; Highest Degree: Associate
Subject Interests: Grant County hist, Pacific Northwest
Automation Activity & Vendor Info: (Cataloging) OCLC; (Circulation) Ex Libris Group; (ILL) OCLC; (OPAC) Ex Libris Group
Wireless access
Function: Audio & video playback equip for onsite use, Computers for patron use, Distance learning, Electronic databases & coll, Free DVD rentals, Games, ILL available, Internet access, Magnifiers for reading, Music CDs, Online cat, Online Chat, Photocopying/Printing, Ref & res, Ref serv available, Scanner, Study rm, Wheelchair accessible
Partic in Washington Community & Technical Colleges Library Consortium
Special Services for the Deaf - ADA equip; Assistive tech; Closed caption videos
Special Services for the Blind - Accessible computers; Aids for in-house use; Assistive/Adapted tech devices, equip & products; Copier with enlargement capabilities; Dragon Naturally Speaking software; Internet workstation with adaptive software; Magnifiers; PC for people with disabilities; Photo duplicator for making large print; Screen enlargement software for people with visual disabilities; Screen reader software
Open Mon-Thurs 7:30am-8pm, Fri 7:30-2:30, Sat Noon-5:30 (Fall-Spring); Mon-Thurs 7:30-5, Fri 7:30-2:30 (Summer)
Restriction: Limited access for the pub

MOUNT VERNON

P MOUNT VERNON CITY LIBRARY*, 315 Snoqualmie St, 98273. SAN 317-5499. Tel: 360-336-6209, Ext 2202. FAX: 360-336-6259. E-mail: mvlibrary@mountvernonwa.gov. Web Site: www.mountvernonwa.gov/175/library. *Libr Dir,* Isaac Huffman; E-mail: isaach@mountvernonwa.gov; Staff 7 (MLS 4, Non-MLS 3)
Founded 1908. Pop 30,000; Circ 389,116
Library Holdings: AV Mats 8,964; Large Print Bks 1,559; Bk Vols 68,924; Per Subs 327; Talking Bks 1,419
Special Collections: Literacy & ESL Coll; Spanish Language Coll
Automation Activity & Vendor Info: (Acquisitions) SirsiDynix; (Cataloging) SirsiDynix; (Circulation) SirsiDynix; (OPAC) SirsiDynix
Wireless access
Function: ILL available
Partic in OCLC Online Computer Library Center, Inc
Special Services for the Deaf - Video & TTY relay via computer
Open Mon-Thurs 10-8, Fri & Sat 10-5
Friends of the Library Group

GL SKAGIT COUNTY LAW LIBRARY*, Skagit County Courthouse, 205 W Kincaid, Rm 104, 98273. SAN 375-0337. Tel: 360-416-1290. FAX: 360-416-1292. E-mail: lawlibrary@co.skagit.wa.us. Web Site: www.skagitcounty.net. *Librn,* JoAnne Giesbrecht; E-mail: joanneg@co.skagit.wa.us
Library Holdings: Bk Vols 8,000
Open Mon-Fri 8:30-4:30

J SKAGIT VALLEY COLLEGE*, Norwood Cole Library, 2405 E College Way, 98273-5899. SAN 317-5510. Tel: 360-416-7850. Circulation Tel: 360-416-7837. Interlibrary Loan Service Tel: 360-416-7659. Reference Tel: 360-416-7847. Toll Free Tel: 877-385-5360. FAX: 360-416-7698. E-mail: mv.library@skagit.edu. Web Site: library.skagit.edu. *Dept Chair, Pub Serv Librn,* Margret Mills; Tel: 360-416-7760, E-mail: margret.mills@skagit.edu; *Dean of Instruction,* Gretchen Robertson; E-mail: gretchen.robertson@skagit.edu; *Copyright Officer, Syst & Tech Serv Librn,* Elena Bianco; Tel: 360-416-7624, E-mail: elena.bianco@skagit.edu; *Circ Serv, Media Serv,* Sharon Cherney; E-mail: sharon.cherney@skagit.edu; *Tech Serv,* Stephanie Levesen; E-mail: stephanie.levesen@skagit.edu
Founded 1926. Enrl 4,300; Fac 170; Highest Degree: Bachelor
Library Holdings: e-books 1,500; Bk Titles 50,255; Bk Vols 87,785; Per Subs 222
Subject Interests: Skagit County
Automation Activity & Vendor Info: (Acquisitions) Ex Libris Group; (Cataloging) Ex Libris Group; (Circulation) Ex Libris Group; (Course Reserve) Ex Libris Group; (Discovery) Ex Libris Group; (ILL) OCLC WorldShare Interlibrary Loan; (Media Booking) Ex Libris Group; (OPAC) Ex Libris Group
Wireless access
Partic in Washington Community & Technical Colleges Library Consortium
Special Services for the Blind - Reader equip; Telesensory screen enlarger & speech synthesis interface to the OPAC
Departmental Libraries:
WHIDBEY ISLAND CAMPUS LIBRARY, 1900 SE Pioneer Way, Oak Harbor, 98277-3099, SAN 376-2068. Tel: 360-679-5322. Reference Tel: 360-679-5321. FAX: 360-679-5341. *Librn,* Libby Sullivan; E-mail: libby.sullivan@skagit.edu; *Libr Asst,* Kim Mitchell; E-mail: kim.mitchell@skagit.edu; Staff 1.8 (MLS 0.8, Non-MLS 1)

NESPELEM

S CONFEDERATED TRIBES OF THE COLVILLE RESERVATION*, Colville Tribal Library, 12 Lakes Ave, 99155. (Mail add: 21 Colville St, Tribal Library, 99155-0150), SAN 373-6881. Tel: 509-634-2791. Toll Free Tel: 888-881-7684. FAX: 509-634-2784. Web Site: www.cct-ene.com/library. *Libr Operations Mgr,* Marilynn Turner; Tel: 509-634-2791, E-mail: marilyn.turner.hed@colvilletribes.com; Staff 1 (Non-MLS 1)
Founded 1983. Pop 6,000
Library Holdings: Bk Titles 6,000
Special Collections: Confederated Tribes of the Colville Reservation Special Coll; Construction of Grand Coulee Dam & Chief Joseph Dam, 1938-1978, log, notebooks, res data, surveys

Wireless access
Function: Activity rm, Audiobks on Playaways & MP3, Bks on CD, Children's prog, Computer training, Computers for patron use, For res purposes, Free DVD rentals, Internet access, Music CDs, Outreach serv, Photocopying/Printing, Ref & res, Ref serv available, Res assist avail, Scanner, STEM programs, Summer reading prog, Tax forms, Telephone ref
Open Mon & Wed 7am-8:30pm
Branches:
INCHELIUM LIBRARY, 12 Community Loop Rd, Inchelium, 99138. (Mail add: 21 Colville St, Tribal Library, 99155), SAN 373-8108. Tel: 509-722-7037. *Libr Operations Mgr,* Marilynn Turner; Tel: 509-634-2791, E-mail: marilyn.turner.hed@colvilletribes.com; Staff 1 (Non-MLS 1)
Founded 1983
Library Holdings: Bk Vols 5,200
Function: Activity rm, Audiobks on Playaways & MP3, Bks on CD, Computer training, Computers for patron use, Free DVD rentals, Internet access, Outreach serv, Photocopying/Printing, Ref & res, Ref serv available, Res assist avail, Scanner, Summer reading prog
Open Mon & Wed 10-3, Thurs 7:30-5:30
KELLER LIBRARY, 11673 S Hwy 21, Keller, 99140. (Mail add: 21 Colville St, Tribal Library, 99155), SAN 373-8116. Tel: 509-634-2802. *Libr Operations Mgr,* Marilynn Turner; Tel: 509-634-2791, E-mail: marilyn.turner.hed@colvilletribes.com; Staff 1 (Non-MLS 1)
Library Holdings: Bk Vols 3,200
Function: Activity rm, Audiobks on Playaways & MP3, Computer training, Computers for patron use, Free DVD rentals, Outreach serv, Photocopying/Printing, Ref & res, Ref serv available, Res assist avail, Summer reading prog, Tax forms, Wheelchair accessible
Open Mon & Wed 8-Noon, Tues 7-5:30, Sat 9:30-11

NEWPORT

P PEND OREILLE COUNTY LIBRARY DISTRICT*, 116 S Washington Ave, 99156. SAN 326-1735. Toll Free Tel: 800-366-3654. E-mail: info@pocld.org. Web Site: www.pocld.org. *Dir,* Mandy Walters; E-mail: director@pocld.org; Staff 4 (MLS 2, Non-MLS 2)
Founded 1980. Pop 13,400; Circ 83,056
Library Holdings: Audiobooks 2,573; AV Mats 4,859; CDs 650; Bk Vols 45,808; Per Subs 65; Videos 3,906
Subject Interests: Local hist
Automation Activity & Vendor Info: (Cataloging) OCLC; (Circulation) ByWater Solutions; (ILL) OCLC FirstSearch; (Media Booking) ByWater Solutions; (OPAC) ByWater Solutions
Wireless access
Function: 24/7 Electronic res, 24/7 Online cat, 3D Printer, After school storytime, Art exhibits, Audiobks via web, Bk club(s), Bks on CD, Children's prog, Computer training, Computers for patron use, Electronic databases & coll, Family literacy, Free DVD rentals, Holiday prog, Homebound delivery serv, ILL available, Internet access, Magazines, Mango lang, Microfiche/film & reading machines, Movies, Museum passes, Music CDs, Online cat, Outreach serv, OverDrive digital audio bks, Photocopying/Printing, Preschool outreach, Prog for adults, Prog for children & young adult, Ref serv available, Scanner, STEM programs, Story hour, Summer reading prog, Tax forms, Teen prog
Partic in Cooperative Information Network
Friends of the Library Group
Branches: 4
CALISPEL VALLEY LIBRARY, 107 First Ave, Cusick, 99119. (Mail add: PO Box 227, Cusick, 99119-0227), SAN 326-3754. *Br Mgr,* Maria Town; E-mail: maria@pocld.org; Staff 1 (Non-MLS 1)
Library Holdings: Bk Vols 7,910
Open Tues 10-8, Wed & Thurs 10-6, Fri & Sat 10-5
Friends of the Library Group
IONE PUBLIC LIBRARY, 210 Blackwell, Ste 1, Ione, 99139. (Mail add: PO Box 605, Ione, 99139-0605), SAN 326-3770. FAX: 509-442-3248. *Br Mgr,* Jennifer Hampson; E-mail: jhampson@pocld.org; Staff 1 (Non-MLS 1)
Library Holdings: Bk Vols 10,742
Open Tues-Thurs 10-6, Fri & Sat 10-5
Friends of the Library Group
METALINES COMMUNITY LIBRARY, Cutter Bldg, 302 Park St, Metaline Falls, 99153. (Mail add: PO Box 111, Metaline Falls, 99153-0111), SAN 326-3797. FAX: 509-446-2302. *Br Mgr,* Jennifer Hampson; E-mail: jhampson@pocld.org; Staff 1 (Non-MLS 1)
Library Holdings: Bk Vols 10,627
Open Mon 10-6, Wed 10-8, Fri 10-5
Friends of the Library Group
NEWPORT PUBLIC LIBRARY, 116 S Washington Ave, 99156. *Br Mgr,* Celene Thomas; E-mail: cthomas@pocld.org; Staff 5 (MLS 1, Non-MLS 4)
Open Mon-Thurs 10-8, Fri & Sat 10-5
Friends of the Library Group

OAK HARBOR

A UNITED STATES NAVY*, The Convergence Zone Recreation Center Library, NAS Whidbey Island, 3535 N Princeton St, Bldg 2510, 98278. SAN 363-7476. Tel: 360-257-2432. FAX: 360-257-3963. Web Site: whidbey.navylifepnw.com/recreation. *Library Contact,* Leslie Money; Tel: 360-257-8541, E-mail: leslie.money@navy.mil
Founded 1944
Library Holdings: Bk Titles 1,600; Per Subs 23
Special Collections: Transition Assistance Management Program (TAMP); US Navy Professional Reading Program
Subject Interests: Acad support, Recreational reading
Wireless access
Open Wed-Sun 11-6

OCEAN SHORES

P OCEAN SHORES PUBLIC LIBRARY*, 573 Point Brown Ave NW, 98569. SAN 317-5529. Tel: 360-289-3919. E-mail: oslibrary@osgov.com. Web Site: oslibrary.info. *Dir,* Keitha Owen; E-mail: keitha@osgov.com; Staff 1 (MLS 1)
Founded 1972. Pop 6,300; Circ 76,000
Library Holdings: CDs 780; DVDs 2,007; Large Print Bks 350; Bk Vols 20,415; Per Subs 72; Talking Bks 405; Videos 373
Special Collections: Local History (Pacific Northwest Coll)
Subject Interests: Local hist
Automation Activity & Vendor Info: (Acquisitions) Biblionix/Apollo; (Cataloging) Baker & Taylor; (Circulation) Biblionix/Apollo; (Serials) EBSCO Online
Wireless access
Function: 24/7 Electronic res, 24/7 Online cat, Adult bk club, Art exhibits, Audiobks via web, Bks on CD, Children's prog, Computer training, Computers for patron use, Digital talking bks, E-Readers, Electronic databases & coll, Free DVD rentals, Genealogy discussion group, Holiday prog, ILL available, Internet access, Life-long learning prog for all ages, Magazines, Mail & tel request accepted, Meeting rooms, Movies, Music CDs, Online cat, OverDrive digital audio bks, Photocopying/Printing, Preschool reading prog, Prog for adults, Ref serv available, Spoken cassettes & CDs, Spoken cassettes & DVDs, Story hour, Summer & winter reading prog, Summer reading prog, Tax forms, Teen prog, Telephone ref, Wheelchair accessible, Winter reading prog
Publications: History of Ocean Shores
Open Tues-Sat 11-5
Friends of the Library Group

ODESSA

P ODESSA PUBLIC LIBRARY*, 21 E First Ave, 99159. (Mail add: PO Box 218, 99159-0218), SAN 317-5537. Tel: 509-982-2654. FAX: 509-982-2410. E-mail: odessapublib@odessaoffice.com. Web Site: odessa.lib.wa.us. *Librn,* Julie Jantz; Tel: 509-982-2903
Founded 1940. Pop 950; Circ 3,400
Library Holdings: Bk Titles 15,000
Subject Interests: US hist
Automation Activity & Vendor Info: (Acquisitions) Book Systems; (Cataloging) Book Systems; (Circulation) Book Systems
Wireless access
Partic in Wheatland Libraries Consortium
Open Wed 2-5 & 7-9, Sat 12-5
Friends of the Library Group

OLYMPIA

C EVERGREEN STATE COLLEGE*, Daniel J Evans Library, Library Bldg, Rm 2300, 2700 Evergreen Pkwy NW, 98505-0002. SAN 317-5545. Tel: 360-867-6250. Circulation Tel: 360-867-6580. Interlibrary Loan Service Tel: 360-867-6499. Administration Tel: 360-867-6242. FAX: 360-867-6790. Web Site: www.evergreen.edu/library. *Dean, Libr & Media Serv,* Greg Mullins; E-mail: mullinsg@evergreen.edu; *Assoc Dean, Libr Operations,* Mr Ahniwa Ferrari; Tel: 360-867-6288, E-mail: ferraria@evergreen.edu; Staff 11 (MLS 6, Non-MLS 5)
Founded 1969. Enrl 4,102; Fac 173; Highest Degree: Master
Library Holdings: AV Mats 82,023; e-journals 22,185; Bk Titles 438,736; Bk Vols 466,564; Per Subs 459
Special Collections: Chicano & Latino Art Culture of the Pacific Northwest, archives; Evergreen State Authors Project & Special Microfilm Coll; Nisqually Delta Association Archives; TESC Archives; Washington State Folklife Council Archives; Washington Worm Growers Assoc Archives. US Document Depository
Automation Activity & Vendor Info: (Acquisitions) Innovative Interfaces, Inc; (Cataloging) Innovative Interfaces, Inc; (Circulation) Innovative Interfaces, Inc; (Course Reserve) Innovative Interfaces, Inc; (ILL) Innovative Interfaces, Inc; (Media Booking) Innovative Interfaces, Inc; (OPAC) Innovative Interfaces, Inc; (Serials) Innovative Interfaces, Inc
Wireless access
Partic in Coop Libr in Olympia; Orbis Cascade Alliance

Open Mon-Thurs 8am-10:45pm, Fri 8-6:15, Sat 10:30-6:15, Sun Noon-7:45 (Winter); Mon-Thurs 9-6:45, Fri 9-5 (Summer)
Friends of the Library Group

J SOUTH PUGET SOUND COMMUNITY COLLEGE LIBRARY*, 2011 Mottman Rd SW, 98512. SAN 317-5553. Tel: 360-596-5271. Reference Tel: 360-596-5345. Administration Tel: 360-596-5416. FAX: 360-596-5714. E-mail: library@spscc.edu. Web Site: library.spscc.edu. *Dean, Acad Support,* Position Currently Open; *Ref & Instruction Librn,* Sarah Kaip; E-mail: skaip@spscc.edu; *Ref & Instruction Librn,* Margaret Thomas; E-mail: mthomas@spscc.edu; *Coll Mgr,* Scott Stilson; E-mail: sstilson@spscc.edu; *Cataloger,* Kathy Laurente; E-mail: klaurente@spscc.edu; Staff 6 (MLS 3, Non-MLS 3)
Founded 1972. Enrl 6,000; Fac 250; Highest Degree: Associate
Library Holdings: AV Mats 5,200; e-books 28,000; Bk Titles 35,000; Bk Vols 41,000; Per Subs 25; Talking Bks 50; Videos 5,000
Automation Activity & Vendor Info: (Cataloging) Spydus; (Circulation) Spydus; (Course Reserve) Spydus; (ILL) OCLC FirstSearch; (OPAC) Spydus; (Serials) Spydus
Wireless access
Partic in OCLC Online Computer Library Center, Inc; Washington Community & Technical Colleges Library Consortium
Open Mon-Thurs 7:30am-8pm, Fri 7:30-4:30

G WASHINGTON STATE DEPARTMENT OF NATURAL RESOURCES*, Washington Geological Survey Library, Natural Resources Bldg, Rm 173, 1111 Washington St SE, 98504-7007. SAN 317-5561. Tel: 360-902-1473. FAX: 360-902-1785. Web Site: www.dnr.wa.gov/programs-and-services/geology/washington-geology-library. *Librn,* Stephanie Earls; E-mail: stephanie.earls@dnr.wa.gov; Staff 2 (MLS 1, Non-MLS 1)
Founded 1935
Library Holdings: AV Mats 50; CDs 40; DVDs 15; Bk Titles 50,000
Special Collections: Geologic & Historical Topographic Maps; Historic Coal Mine Maps; Theses Coll
Subject Interests: Geol, Maps, Mining
Wireless access
Function: Archival coll, For res purposes, ILL available, Ref serv available, Telephone ref
Publications: Publications List (Online only)
Open Mon 9-12, Tues & Thurs 9-4
Restriction: Non-circulating
Friends of the Library Group

GL WASHINGTON STATE LAW LIBRARY, 415 12th Ave SW, Temple of Justice, 98501. (Mail add: PO Box 40751, 98504-0751), SAN 317-5588. Tel: 360-357-2136. E-mail: law.library@courts.wa.gov. Web Site: www.courts.wa.gov/library. *Dir,* Rob Mead; Staff 8 (MLS 5, Non-MLS 3)
Founded 1889
Special Collections: Rare Law Books; Washington State Supreme Court History Coll. US Document Depository
Subject Interests: Legal
Automation Activity & Vendor Info: (Acquisitions) Koha; (Cataloging) Koha; (Circulation) Koha; (OPAC) Koha; (Serials) Koha
Wireless access
Function: Archival coll, Electronic databases & coll, ILL available, Online cat, Ref serv available, Telephone ref
Publications: Blog (Online only)
Open Mon-Fri 9-4

PASCO

C COLUMBIA BASIN COLLEGE LIBRARY, 2600 N 20th Ave, 99301. SAN 317-5618. Tel: 509-542-4887. Reference Tel: 509-542-4890. E-mail: library@columbiabasin.edu. Web Site: www.columbiabasin.edu/i-am/current-hawk/library. *Dean of Libr & Instrul Serv,* Keri Lobdell; Tel: 509-544-4422, E-mail: klobdell@columbiabasin.edu; *Dir, Libr Serv,* Sarah E North; Tel: 509-542-4894, E-mail: snorth@columbiabasin.edu; *Med Librn,* Ying Yu; Tel: 509-544-8337, E-mail: yyu@columbiabasin.edu; *Circ Serv,* Mary-Alice Correa; Tel: 509-542-5528; *Tech Serv,* Joshua Westbrook; Tel: 509-544-2263, E-mail: jwestbrook@columbiabasin.edu; Staff 8 (MLS 5, Non-MLS 3)
Founded 1955. Enrl 5,779; Fac 133; Highest Degree: Bachelor
Library Holdings: DVDs 505; e-books 45,989; e-journals 26,555; Bk Vols 47,615; Per Subs 165
Special Collections: Medical Library Coll
Automation Activity & Vendor Info: (Acquisitions) LibLime; (Cataloging) OCLC CatExpress; (Circulation) LibLime; (ILL) OCLC; (OPAC) LibLime
Wireless access
Function: ILL available
Partic in OCLC Online Computer Library Center, Inc; Washington Community & Technical Colleges Library Consortium

Special Services for the Blind - Assistive/Adapted tech devices, equip & products
Open Mon-Thurs 7am-7:30pm, Fri 7-4, Sat 11-4

POMEROY

P DENNY ASHBY MEMORIAL LIBRARY*, Pomeroy Public Library, 856 Arlington St, 99347. (Mail add: PO Box 670, 99347-0670). Tel: 509-843-3710. E-mail: dashbylib@pomeroy.lib.wa.us. Web Site: www.pomeroy.lib.wa.us. *Dir,* Lillian Heytvelt
Library Holdings: Bk Titles 8,000; Per Subs 13
Open Mon 1-5, Tues 9-1, Wed 12-6:30, Thurs 1-7:30
Friends of the Library Group

PORT ANGELES

GL CLALLAM COUNTY LAW LIBRARY, County Courthouse Basement, 223 E Fourth St, Rm 175, 98362. SAN 373-742X. Tel: 360-417-2287. Web Site: www.clallamcountywa.gov/1438/law-library-board. *Libr Asst,* Penny Ruby; E-mail: penny.ruby@clallamcountywa.gov
Library Holdings: Bk Vols 7,500
Wireless access
Open Wed 12-4:30

P NORTH OLYMPIC LIBRARY SYSTEM*, 2210 S Peabody St, 98362-6536. SAN 363-8790. Tel: 360-417-8500. FAX: 360-457-3125. E-mail: director@nols.org. Web Site: www.nols.org. *Dir,* Noah Glaude; Tel: 360-417-8500, Ext 7717, E-mail: nglaude@nols.org; Staff 7 (MLS 7)
Founded 1919. Pop 71,000; Circ 965,698
Library Holdings: Bk Vols 278,424; Per Subs 373
Special Collections: Clallam County History (Bert Kellogg Coll); photog, slides; Pacific Northwest History, bks, maps, oral hist
Automation Activity & Vendor Info: (Acquisitions) Innovative Interfaces, Inc; (Cataloging) Innovative Interfaces, Inc; (Circulation) Innovative Interfaces, Inc
Wireless access
Function: 24/7 Electronic res, 24/7 Online cat, Adult bk club, Archival coll, Art exhibits, Audio & video playback equip for onsite use, Audiobks on Playaways & MP3, Audiobks via web, Bk club(s), Bks on CD, Children's prog, Computer training, Computers for patron use, Digital talking bks, E-Readers, Electronic databases & coll, Equip loans & repairs, Free DVD rentals, Holiday prog, Homebound delivery serv, ILL available, Internet access, Jail serv, Large print keyboards, Life-long learning prog for all ages, Magazines, Meeting rooms, Microfiche/film & reading machines, Music CDs, Online cat, Online ref, OverDrive digital audio bks, Photocopying/Printing, Preschool outreach, Preschool reading prog, Printer for laptops & handheld devices, Prog for adults, Prog for children & young adult, Ref serv available, Scanner, Senior outreach, Spanish lang bks, Story hour, Study rm, Summer reading prog, Tax forms, Teen prog, Telephone ref, Wheelchair accessible
Partic in OCLC Online Computer Library Center, Inc
Open Mon-Thurs 10-8, Fri 10-6, Sat 10-5
Friends of the Library Group
Branches: 3
CLALLAM BAY BRANCH, 16990 Hwy 112, Clallam Bay, 98326. (Mail add: PO Box 106, Clallam Bay, 98326-0106), SAN 363-8812. Tel: 360-963-2414. FAX: 360-963-2260. E-mail: clallambay@nols.org. *Br Mgr,* Troi Gale; Tel: 360-963-2414, Ext 7793; Staff 3 (Non-MLS 3)
Circ 24,790
Library Holdings: Bk Vols 17,448
Function: After school storytime, Bks on CD, Children's prog, Computers for patron use, Electronic databases & coll, Free DVD rentals, Internet access, Music CDs, Online cat, Online ref, OverDrive digital audio bks, Photocopying/Printing, Preschool outreach, Printer for laptops & handheld devices, Prog for adults, Prog for children & young adult, Ref serv available, Summer reading prog, Wheelchair accessible
Open Mon-Wed 11-7, Thurs 10-5
Friends of the Library Group
FORKS BRANCH, 171 Forks Ave S, Forks, 98331, SAN 363-8820. Tel: 360-374-6402. FAX: 360-374-6499. E-mail: forks@nols.org. *Br Mgr,* Troi Gale; Staff 6 (MLS 1, Non-MLS 5)
Founded 1946. Circ 69,272
Library Holdings: Bk Vols 35,044
Function: Bks on CD, Children's prog, Computers for patron use, Electronic databases & coll, Free DVD rentals, ILL available, Internet access, Music CDs, Online cat, Online ref, OverDrive digital audio bks, Photocopying/Printing, Printer for laptops & handheld devices, Prog for adults, Prog for children & young adult, Ref serv available, Spanish lang bks, Story hour, Summer reading prog, Telephone ref, Wheelchair accessible
Open Mon-Thurs 10-7, Fri & Sat 10-6
Friends of the Library Group

SEQUIM BRANCH, 630 N Sequim Ave, Sequim, 98382, SAN 363-888X. Tel: 360-683-1161. FAX: 360-681-7811. E-mail: sequim@nols.org. *Br Mgr,* Emily Sly; Staff 11 (MLS 1, Non-MLS 10)
Circ 423,086
Library Holdings: Bk Vols 61,813
Function: Adult bk club, After school storytime, Art exhibits, Bks on CD, Children's prog, Computer training, Computers for patron use, Electronic databases & coll, Free DVD rentals, Homebound delivery serv, ILL available, Internet access, Music CDs, Online cat, Online ref, OverDrive digital audio bks, Photocopying/Printing, Preschool outreach, Printer for laptops & handheld devices, Prog for adults, Prog for children & young adult, Ref serv available, Story hour, Summer reading prog, Teen prog, Telephone ref, Wheelchair accessible
Open Mon-Thurs 10-8, Fri 10-6, Sat 10-5
Friends of the Library Group

J PENINSULA COLLEGE LIBRARY*, John D Glann Library, 1502 E Lauridsen Blvd, 98362-6698. SAN 317-5669. Tel: 360-417-6280. Circulation Tel: 360-417-6282. Automation Services Tel: 360-417-6275. Toll Free Tel: 877-452-9277 (WA only). FAX: 360-417-6295. E-mail: pclibrary@pencol.edu. Web Site: www.pencol.edu/library. *Libr Supvr,* Nina Pitts; *Ref & Instruction Librn,* Tim Williams; E-mail: twilliams@pencol.edu; Staff 8 (MLS 3, Non-MLS 5)
Founded 1961. Enrl 2,100; Fac 60; Highest Degree: Associate
Library Holdings: CDs 114; Music Scores 750; Bk Titles 33,310; Bk Vols 35,002; Per Subs 170; Videos 1,578
Automation Activity & Vendor Info: (Acquisitions) Ex Libris Group; (Cataloging) Ex Libris Group; (Circulation) Ex Libris Group; (Course Reserve) Ex Libris Group; (Media Booking) Ex Libris Group; (OPAC) Ex Libris Group; (Serials) Ex Libris Group
Wireless access
Function: Audio & video playback equip for onsite use, AV serv, ILL available, Outside serv via phone, mail, e-mail & web, Photocopying/Printing, Ref serv available, Telephone ref
Partic in Washington Community & Technical Colleges Library Consortium
Open Mon-Thurs 8-8, Fri 8-4, Sun 5-8

PORT HADLOCK

P JEFFERSON COUNTY RURAL LIBRARY DISTRICT*, 620 Cedar Ave, 98339. SAN 321-4818. Tel: 360-385-6544. Web Site: www.jclibrary.info. *Dir,* Dr Tamara Meredith; E-mail: tmeredith@jclibrary.info; Staff 22 (MLS 7, Non-MLS 15)
Founded 1980. Pop 21,000; Circ 400,000
Automation Activity & Vendor Info: (Cataloging) OCLC; (ILL) OCLC
Wireless access
Function: 24/7 Electronic res, 24/7 Online cat, 3D Printer, Computer training, Computers for patron use, Homebound delivery serv, ILL available, Internet access, Jail serv, Life-long learning prog for all ages, Summer reading prog, Tax forms
Friends of the Library Group
Bookmobiles: 1

PORT ORCHARD

GL KITSAP COUNTY LAW LIBRARY*, 614 Division St, 98366. SAN 323-6471. Tel: 360-337-5788. Web Site: www.kitsaplawlibrary.com/. *Librn,* Paul Fjelstad; E-mail: paul@fjelstad.com
Library Holdings: Bk Vols 10,000
Open Mon-Fri 8:30-4:30

PORT TOWNSEND

P PORT TOWNSEND PUBLIC LIBRARY*, 1220 Lawrence St, 98368-6527. SAN 317-5677. Tel: 360-385-3181. Circulation Tel: 360-344-3051. Administration Tel: 360-344-3054. FAX: 360-385-5805. E-mail: ptlibrary@cityofpt.us. Web Site: ptpubliclibrary.org. *Dir,* Melody Sky Eisler; E-mail: meisler@cityofpt.us; *Libr Mgr, Pub Serv, Tech Serv,* Keith Darrock; E-mail: kdarrock@cityofpt.us; Staff 9 (MLS 1, Non-MLS 8)
Founded 1898. Pop 8,865; Circ 244,151
Library Holdings: Audiobooks 1,618; CDs 990; DVDs 960; Large Print Bks 585; Bk Vols 43,624; Per Subs 160; Videos 4,125
Special Collections: Maritime Resource Center
Subject Interests: Folklore Jungian psychol, Jungian psychol, Maritime, Mythology, Pac NW hist
Automation Activity & Vendor Info: (Acquisitions) Horizon; (Cataloging) SirsiDynix; (Circulation) SirsiDynix; (OPAC) SirsiDynix
Wireless access
Function: Adult bk club, Audiobks via web, Bk reviews (Group), Bks on cassette, Bks on CD, Children's prog, Computers for patron use, Electronic databases & coll, Free DVD rentals, Holiday prog, Home delivery & serv to seniorr ctr & nursing homes, Homework prog, ILL available, Internet access, Large print keyboards, Mail & tel request accepted, Music CDs, Online cat, Online ref, OverDrive digital audio bks, Photocopying/Printing, Preschool outreach, Prog for adults, Prog for children & young adult, Ref serv available, Story hour, Summer reading prog, Tax forms, Teen prog, Telephone ref, VHS videos, Wheelchair accessible
Open Mon-Thurs 10-7, Fri 10-6, Sat 10-5, Sun 1-5
Friends of the Library Group

PULLMAN

P NEILL PUBLIC LIBRARY*, Pullman Public Library, 210 N Grand Ave, 99163-2693. SAN 317-5693. Tel: 509-334-3595. Administration Tel: 509-338-3251. FAX: 509-334-6051. E-mail: library@neill-lib.org. Web Site: www.pullman-wa.gov/government/departments/neill_public_library. *Dir,* Dan Owens; E-mail: dowens@neill-lib.org; Staff 4 (MLS 3, Non-MLS 1)
Founded 1921. Pop 26,590; Circ 356,836
Special Collections: English as a Second Language Coll; Local History (Palouse Region)
Automation Activity & Vendor Info: (Cataloging) Horizon; (Circulation) Horizon; (OPAC) Horizon
Wireless access
Open Mon-Thurs 10-7, Fri & Sat 10-6
Friends of the Library Group

C WASHINGTON STATE UNIVERSITY LIBRARIES*, 100 Dairy Rd, 99164. (Mail add: PO Box 645610, 99164-5610), SAN 363-891X. Tel: 509-335-9671. Interlibrary Loan Service Tel: 509-335-9672. FAX: 509-335-0934. Web Site: libraries.wsu.edu. *Dean of Libr,* Jay Starratt; E-mail: jstarratt@wsu.edu; *Assoc Dean of Libr,* Beth Blakesley; Tel: 509-335-6134, E-mail: beth.blakesley@wsu.edu; *Assoc Dean, Digital Initiatives, Spec Coll,* Trevor James Bond; Tel: 509-335-6693, E-mail: tjbond@wsu.edu; *Head, Coll Develop,* Joel Cummings; Tel: 509-335-6493, E-mail: jcummings@wsu.edu; *Head, Ref Serv,* Pamela Martin; E-mail: pamela.martin@wsu.edu; *Head, Systems & Technical Ops,* Alex Merrill; Tel: 509-335-5426, E-mail: merrilla@wsu.edu; *Liaison Services, Libr Instruction, Team Leader,* Erica Nicol; Tel: 509-335-8614, E-mail: eacarlson@wsu.edu; Staff 82 (MLS 42, Non-MLS 40)
Founded 1892. Enrl 25,272; Fac 2,212; Highest Degree: Doctorate
Jul 2021-Jun 2022. Mats Exp $6,569,097, Books $681,386, Per/Ser (Incl. Access Fees) $5,887,711. Sal $6,031,821
Library Holdings: e-books 939,190; Electronic Media & Resources 101,734; Microforms 3,971,318; Bk Vols 3,325,757; Per Subs 48,193; Videos 35,167
Special Collections: Angling (Vern & Joan Gallup, Roy Hansberry & James C Quick Colls); Bloomsbury Coll; ERDA Coll; Ethnic History (Germans from Russia Coll); Hispanic Americana Coll; Leonard & Virginia Woolf Library; Moldenhauer Music Archives; Pacific Northwest Publishers Archives; Pierre-Jean Desmet Coll; Sitwells Coll; University Archives; Veterinary History (Smithcors Coll), archival rec, ephemera, journals, monographs & pamphlets, ms; Wildlife & Outdoor Recreation Coll, documentary rec, films, ms, photog & printed texts. Oral History; State Document Depository; UN Document Depository; US Document Depository
Automation Activity & Vendor Info: (Acquisitions) Ex Libris Group; (Cataloging) OCLC; (Circulation) Ex Libris Group; (ILL) OCLC ILLiad; (OPAC) Ex Libris Group
Wireless access
Function: 24/7 Electronic res, Archival coll, Audio & video playback equip for onsite use, Audiobks via web, AV serv, Computers for patron use, Distance learning, Doc delivery serv, E-Reserves, Electronic databases & coll, Health sci info serv, ILL available, Microfiche/film & reading machines, Movies, Online cat, Online ref, Photocopying/Printing, Ref serv available, Wheelchair accessible
Partic in Association of Research Libraries; Greater Western Library Alliance; Orbis Cascade Alliance; Wash Coop Libr Project
Friends of the Library Group

Departmental Libraries:

CM ANIMAL HEALTH LIBRARY, 170 Wegner Hall, 99164. (Mail add: PO Box 646512, 99164-6512), SAN 363-9002. Tel: 509-335-9556. Administration Tel: 509-335-5544. Reference E-mail: vetref@wsu.edu. *Head of Libr,* Suzanne Fricke; E-mail: suzanne.fricke@wsu.edu
Founded 1963. Highest Degree: Doctorate
Subject Interests: Pharmacology, Toxicology, Veterinary med
Function: Res libr
Open Mon-Thurs 7:30am-10pm, Fri 7:30-6, Sat 11-5, Sun 1-10

OWEN SCIENCE & ENGINEERING, PO Box 643200, 99164-3200, SAN 363-8979. Tel: 509-335-2672. Reference E-mail: lib.reference@wsu.edu. Web Site: libraries.wsu.edu/about/owen. *Assoc Dean of Libr,* Beth Blakesley; Tel: 509-335-6134, E-mail: beth.blakesley@wsu.edu; *Library & Archives Paraprofessional V,* R J Hart; Tel: 509-335-2675, E-mail: rjhart@wsu.edu
Highest Degree: Doctorate
Open Mon-Thurs 7:30am-10:45pm, Fri 7:30-5:45, Sat Noon-5:45, Sun Noon-8:45

PUYALLUP

P PUYALLUP PUBLIC LIBRARY, 324 S Meridian, 98371. SAN 317-5707. Tel: 253-841-5454. Interlibrary Loan Service Tel: 253-841-5543. Reference Tel: 253-841-5700. Administration Tel: 253-841-5452. FAX: 253-841-5483. TDD: 253-841-5544. E-mail: puylib@ci.puyallup.wa.us. Web Site: www.puyalluplibrary.org. *Dir,* Nicole Erickson; E-mail: nerickson@puyalluppwa.gov; Staff 6 (MLS 6)
Founded 1912. Pop 39,780; Circ 350,000
Jan 2018-Dec 2018 Income $2,714,460. Mats Exp $243,837, Books $163,640, Per/Ser (Incl. Access Fees) $8,700, AV Mat $10,000, Electronic Ref Mat (Incl. Access Fees) $61,497. Sal $957,840
Subject Interests: Local hist (Puyallup Valley)
Automation Activity & Vendor Info: (Acquisitions) Horizon; (Circulation) Horizon; (ILL) OCLC FirstSearch; (OPAC) SirsiDynix
Wireless access
Function: 24/7 Online cat, Activity rm, Audiobks on Playaways & MP3, Children's prog, Computer training, Computers for patron use, Digital talking bks, Electronic databases & coll, Games, Home delivery & serv to seniorr ctr & nursing homes, Internet access, Life-long learning prog for all ages, Magazines, Mango lang, Meeting rooms, Movies, Museum passes, Online cat, Online ref, Outreach serv, Photocopying/Printing, Preschool outreach, Prog for adults, Prog for children & young adult, Ref serv available, Story hour, Summer reading prog, Tax forms, Teen prog, Telephone ref, Wheelchair accessible, Writing prog
Special Services for the Deaf - ADA equip; Assisted listening device; Captioned film dep; Closed caption videos; TDD equip
Special Services for the Blind - Accessible computers; Closed circuit TV magnifier
Open Mon-Wed 10-8, Thurs-Sat 10-5
Friends of the Library Group

REARDAN

P REARDAN MEMORIAL LIBRARY*, 120 S Oak, 99029. (Mail add: PO Box 227, 99029-0227), SAN 317-5715. Tel: 509-994-9997. E-mail: library@townofreardan.com. Web Site: reardan.lib.wa.us. *Librn,* Suzanne Schulz
Pop 450; Circ 3,395
Library Holdings: Bk Vols 9,700
Wireless access
Partic in Wheatland Libraries Consortium
Open Tues 2-5, Thurs 4-7, Sat 10-2
Friends of the Library Group

RENTON

J RENTON TECHNICAL COLLEGE*, Library, 3000 NE Fourth St, 98056. SAN 373-6318. Tel: 425-235-2331. E-mail: librarian@rtc.edu. Web Site: www.rtc.edu/library. *Assoc Dean of Libr,* Emily Elliott; Tel: 425-235-2352, Ext 5678, E-mail: eelliott@rtc.edu; Staff 6 (MLS 3, Non-MLS 3)
Founded 1991. Enrl 3,901; Fac 178; Highest Degree: Associate
Library Holdings: Bk Vols 37,000; Per Subs 90; Videos 4,000
Special Collections: History & Culinary Education in the Pacific Northwest (Chef Daryl Anderson Culinary Archives)
Subject Interests: Culinary
Automation Activity & Vendor Info: (Acquisitions) Ex Libris Group; (Cataloging) Ex Libris Group; (Circulation) Ex Libris Group; (Course Reserve) Ex Libris Group; (ILL) OCLC; (OPAC) Ex Libris Group; (Serials) Ex Libris Group
Wireless access
Function: Archival coll, Audio & video playback equip for onsite use, Computers for patron use, Electronic databases & coll, ILL available, Internet access, Online cat, Online ref, Orientations, Photocopying/Printing, Ref & res, Ref serv available, Scanner, VHS videos, Workshops
Partic in Washington Community & Technical Colleges Library Consortium
Open Mon-Thurs 7am-8pm, Fri 7-4:30

RICHLAND

S PACIFIC NORTHWEST NATIONAL LABORATORY*, Technical Library, 902 Battelle Blvd, 99354. (Mail add: PO Box 999, 99352), SAN 317-5804. Tel: 509-375-3268. E-mail: pnl.techlib@pnnl.gov. Web Site: www.pnnl.gov.
Founded 1948
Library Holdings: Bk Vols 41,000; Per Subs 9,000
Special Collections: Department of Energy Contractor Reports, technical rpts; DOE Public Reading Room
Subject Interests: Engr, Environ studies, Metallurgy, Nuclear tech
Automation Activity & Vendor Info: (Cataloging) Horizon; (Circulation) Horizon; (ILL) OCLC; (OPAC) Horizon; (Serials) Horizon
Wireless access
Function: Res libr
Restriction: Not open to pub

P RICHLAND PUBLIC LIBRARY*, 955 Northgate Dr, 99352. SAN 317-5839. Tel: 509-942-7454. Administration Tel: 509-942-7451. Web Site: myrichlandlibrary.org. *Libr Mgr,* Christopher Nulph; E-mail: cnulph@ci.richland.wa.us; *Community Engagement Supvr,* Michelle Haffner; Tel: 509-942-7665, E-mail: mhaffner@ci.richland.wa.us; *Tech Serv Supvr,* Theresa Barnaby; Tel: 509-942-7679, E-mail: tbarnaby@ci.richland.wa.us; *User Experience Supvr,* Michael Scarfo; Tel: 50-942-7446, E-mail: mscarfo@ci.richland.wa.us; Staff 20.5 (MLS 7, Non-MLS 13.5)
Founded 1951
Automation Activity & Vendor Info: (Acquisitions) Evergreen; (Cataloging) Evergreen; (Circulation) Evergreen; (OPAC) Evergreen; (Serials) Evergreen
Wireless access
Function: 24/7 Electronic res, 24/7 Online cat, Activity rm, Adult bk club, After school storytime, Art exhibits, Art programs, Bk club(s), Bks on CD, Children's prog, Computers for patron use, Electronic databases & coll, Free DVD rentals, Games, ILL available, Internet access, Life-long learning prog for all ages, Magazines, Mango lang, Meeting rooms, Movies, Museum passes, Online cat, Outreach serv, Prog for adults, Prog for children & young adult, Ref serv available, STEM programs, Story hour, Study rm, Summer reading prog, Teen prog, Wheelchair accessible, Wifi hotspot checkout, Writing prog
Open Mon-Thurs 10-9, Fri 10-6, Sat 10-5, Sun Noon-5
Friends of the Library Group

C WASHINGTON STATE UNIVERSITY TRI-CITIES LIBRARY*, Max E Benitz Memorial Library - Consolidated Information Center, 2770 Crimson Way, 99354. (Mail add: 2710 Crimson Way, 99354-1671), SAN 317-5820. Tel: 509-372-7430. Circulation Tel: 509-372-7303. FAX: 509-372-7281. E-mail: tricities.library@wsu.edu. Web Site: www.tricities.wsu.edu. *Emeritus Faculty Librarian,* Harvey R Gover; E-mail: hgover@wsu.edu; *Circ Supvr,* Steve Bisch; Tel: 509-372-7313, E-mail: sbisch@wsu.edu. Subject Specialists: *Hist,* Harvey R Gover; Staff 1 (MLS 1)
Founded 1958. Enrl 1,250; Fac 80; Highest Degree: Doctorate
Library Holdings: CDs 44; DVDs 329; e-books 804,694; e-journals 133,508; Bk Titles 33,350; Bk Vols 37,021; Per Subs 79
Special Collections: Radiation Research
Subject Interests: Health physics
Automation Activity & Vendor Info: (Cataloging) Ex Libris Group; (Circulation) Ex Libris Group; (Course Reserve) Ex Libris Group; (ILL) OCLC; (Media Booking) Ex Libris Group; (OPAC) Ex Libris Group; (Serials) Ex Libris Group
Wireless access
Partic in OCLC Online Computer Library Center, Inc
Open Mon-Fri 8-5
Friends of the Library Group

RITZVILLE

P EAST ADAMS LIBRARY DISTRICT*, Ritzville Public Library, 302 W Main Ave, 99169. SAN 317-5863. Tel: 509-659-1222. FAX: 509-659-1232. E-mail: ritzvillelibrary@outlook.com. Web Site: www.ritzvillelibrary.com. *Libr Dir,* Vanessa Grimm; E-mail: vanessag@ritzvillelibrary.com; Staff 4 (MLS 1, Non-MLS 3)
Founded 1905. Pop 3,500; Circ 19,000
Library Holdings: AV Mats 208; e-books 278; Large Print Bks 218; Bk Titles 17,283; Per Subs 76
Special Collections: Adams Ritzville Journal, microfilm, newsp; Burt Kendrick Photo Coll. Municipal Document Depository
Subject Interests: Local hist
Automation Activity & Vendor Info: (ILL) OCLC
Wireless access
Function: Home delivery & serv to seniorr ctr & nursing homes, ILL available, Photocopying/Printing, Ref serv available, Summer reading prog
Partic in Wheatland Libraries Consortium
Open Mon-Fri 10-8, Sat 10-2
Friends of the Library Group

ROSLYN

P ROSLYN PUBLIC LIBRARY*, 201 S First, 98941. (Mail add: PO Box 451, 98941-0451), SAN 317-5871. Tel: 509-649-3105, Option 4. E-mail: librarian@ci.roslyn.wa.us. Web Site: roslyn.lib.wa.us. *Librn,* Claudia Guilford
Founded 1898. Pop 1,000; Circ 12,321
Wireless access
Function: Art exhibits, Audiobks via web, Bk club(s), Bks on CD, Children's prog, Computer training, Computers for patron use, Digital talking bks, Electronic databases & coll, Free DVD rentals, ILL available, Online cat, OverDrive digital audio bks, Photocopying/Printing, Preschool outreach, Preschool reading prog, Printer for laptops & handheld devices, Prog for adults, Prog for children & young adult, Ref serv available, Story hour, Summer reading prog, Tax forms, Telephone ref, Wheelchair accessible

Open Tues, Wed & Fri 11-5, Thurs 11-7, Sat 11-3
Friends of the Library Group

SEATTLE

M AMERICAN INSTITUTE FOR BIOSOCIAL & MEDICAL RESEARCH INC LIBRARY*, 2800 E Madison St, Ste 202, 98112. (Mail add: PO Box 1174, Tacoma, 98401-1174), SAN 372-8757. Tel: 253-286-2888. FAX: 253-286-2451. E-mail: info@aibmr.com. Web Site: www.aibmr.com. *Dir, Info Serv,* Jared Brodin; E-mail: jared@aibmr.com
Library Holdings: Bk Vols 5,653; Per Subs 360
Restriction: Staff use only

C ANTIOCH UNIVERSITY LIBRARY*, 2400 Third Ave, Ste 200, 98121. Tel: 206-268-4109, 206-268-4210. FAX: 206-441-3307. E-mail: library.aus@antioch.edu. Web Site: www.antioch.edu/seattle/resources/students/library. *Dir, Libr Serv,* Beverly Stuart; E-mail: bstuart@antioch.edu
Library Holdings: AV Mats 200; Bk Titles 5,500; Per Subs 110
Wireless access
Open Mon-Thurs 10-9, Fri 10-7, Sat & Sun 10-6

L CARNEY BADLEY SPELLMAN*, Law Library, 701 Fifth Ave, Ste 3600, 98104-7010. SAN 372-3313. Tel: 206-607-4149, 206-622-8020. FAX: 206-622-8983. Web Site: www.carneylaw.com. *Law Librn,* Melia Mauer Cossette; E-mail: cossette@carneylaw.com
Library Holdings: Bk Vols 10,000; Per Subs 30
Restriction: Staff use only

C CITY UNIVERSITY OF SEATTLE LIBRARY, 521 Wall St, Ste 100, 98121. SAN 321-7191. Tel: 206-239-4550. Toll Free Tel: 800-526-4269. E-mail: library@cityu.edu. Web Site: library.cityu.edu. Staff 7 (MLS 5, Non-MLS 2)
Founded 1973. Highest Degree: Doctorate
Subject Interests: Bus, Communications, Computer syst, Educ, Psychol
Automation Activity & Vendor Info: (Acquisitions) Ex Libris Group; (Cataloging) Ex Libris Group; (Circulation) Ex Libris Group; (Course Reserve) Ex Libris Group; (ILL) OCLC Tipasa; (OPAC) Ex Libris Group; (Serials) Ex Libris Group
Wireless access

C CORNISH COLLEGE OF THE ARTS LIBRARY, 1000 Lenora St, 98121. SAN 317-5952. Tel: 206-726-5041. Reference Tel: 206-726-5145. Reference E-mail: libraryref@cornish.edu. Web Site: libguides.cornish.edu/library. *Dir, Libr Serv,* Bridget Nowlin; Staff 3 (MLS 3)
Founded 1964. Enrl 650; Fac 140; Highest Degree: Bachelor
Library Holdings: CDs 5,756; DVDs 2,542; e-books 150,700; e-journals 12,392; Electronic Media & Resources 3,402,500; Music Scores 5,428; Bk Titles 29,597; Bk Vols 32,151; Per Subs 160; Videos 103
Special Collections: Cornish Historical Archives; Image Coll
Subject Interests: Art, Dance, Design, Film, Interior archit, Music, Performance production, Theatre
Automation Activity & Vendor Info: (Acquisitions) Koha; (Cataloging) Koha; (Circulation) Koha; (Course Reserve) Koha; (ILL) OCLC WorldShare Interlibrary Loan; (OPAC) Koha; (Serials) Koha
Wireless access
Partic in Association of Independent Colleges of Art & Design
Open Mon-Thurs 8-8, Fri 8-6, Sat & Sun 1-5

L DAVIS WRIGHT TREMAINE LLP*, Law Library, 920 Fifth Ave, Ste 3300, 98104-1610. SAN 372-3631. Tel: 206-622-3150. FAX: 206-757-7700. E-mail: info@dwt.com. Web Site: www.dwt.com. *Mgr, Libr & Res Serv,* Mark Desierto; E-mail: markdesierto@dwt.com
Library Holdings: Bk Vols 40,000
Automation Activity & Vendor Info: (Acquisitions) EOS International; (Cataloging) EOS International; (OPAC) EOS International; (Serials) EOS International
Partic in OCLC Online Computer Library Center, Inc
Restriction: Staff use only

GM DEPARTMENT OF VETERANS AFFAIRS*, Puget Sound Health Care System, Seattle Division Medical Library, 1660 S Columbian Way, Bldg 1, 98108-1597. SAN 317-6525. Tel: 206-764-2075. FAX: 206-764-2816. Web Site: www.va.gov/puget-sound-health-care. *Dir, Libr Serv,* Jason Oleston; E-mail: jason.oleston2@va.gov; Staff 4 (MLS 2, Non-MLS 2)
Founded 1951
Library Holdings: Bk Titles 3,327; Bk Vols 4,400; Per Subs 338
Subject Interests: Alcohol abuse, Clinical med, Drug abuse, Gerontology, Metabolism, Psychol, Spinal cord injury
Automation Activity & Vendor Info: (Cataloging) EOS International; (Circulation) EOS International; (OPAC) EOS International; (Serials) EOS International
Partic in National Network of Libraries of Medicine Region 5
Open Mon-Fri 8-4:30

SR THE EPISCOPAL DIOCESE OF OLYMPIA*, Diocesan Resource Center, 1551 Tenth Ave E, 98102. SAN 326-5277. Tel: 206-325-4200, Ext 2043. Toll Free Tel: 800-488-4978 (WA only). FAX: 206-325-4631. E-mail: resource@ecww.org. Web Site: ecww.org/about-the-diocese-of-olympia/diocesan-resource-center. *Dir,* Sue Tait; Staff 1 (MLS 1)
Library Holdings: DVDs 200; Bk Titles 9,000
Special Collections: Episcopal Church in Western Washington
Subject Interests: Relig educ, Theol
Wireless access
Open Mon-Fri 9-5

L FOSTER GARVEY PC*, Research Center, 1111 Third Ave, Ste 3000, 98101. SAN 327-4314. Tel: 206-447-2811. FAX: 206-447-9700. E-mail: library@foster.com. *Managing Librn,* Barbara Rothwell; Tel: 206-447-2811, E-mail: rothb@foster.com; Staff 2 (MLS 1, Non-MLS 1)
Automation Activity & Vendor Info: (ILL) OCLC; (OPAC) EOS International
Function: Res libr
Restriction: Not open to pub

S FRYE ART MUSEUM CURATORIAL LIBRARY*, 704 Terry Ave, 98104. SAN 317-5995. Tel: 206-432-8228. FAX: 206-223-1707. E-mail: collections@fryemuseum.org. Web Site: www.fryemuseum.org. *Interim Head, Coll Develop,* Teresa Redden; E-mail: tredden@fryemuseum.org; Staff 1 (Non-MLS 1)
Founded 1997
Library Holdings: Bk Vols 2,411
Special Collections: 19th & 20th Century American & German Art
Wireless access
Restriction: External users must contact libr, Lending to staff only, Open to pub by appt only, Open to researchers by request, Staff use, pub by appt

M FRED HUTCHINSON CANCER RESEARCH CENTER*, Arnold Library, 1100 Fairview Ave N, B1-010, 98109. (Mail add: PO Box 19024, B1-010, 98109-1024), SAN 317-6037. Tel: 206-667-4314. E-mail: library@fredhutch.org. *Head Librn,* Beth Levine; Staff 5 (MLS 2, Non-MLS 3)
Founded 1975
Subject Interests: Biochem, Biology, Biostatistics, Epidemiology, Gen med, Genetics, Hematology, Immunology, Molecular biol, Oncology, Pathology, Pharmacology, Pub health, Radiology, Surgery, Virology
Automation Activity & Vendor Info: (Acquisitions) ByWater Solutions; (Cataloging) ByWater Solutions; (Circulation) ByWater Solutions; (ILL) OCLC ILLiad; (OPAC) ByWater Solutions; (Serials) SerialsSolutions
Wireless access
Partic in Docline; LYRASIS; Midwest Collaborative for Library Services; OCLC Online Computer Library Center, Inc
Open Mon-Fri 8-5

G KING COUNTY DEPARTMENT OF NATURAL RESOURCES & PARKS*, Technical Document & Research Center, 201 S Jackson St, Ste 190, 98104. Tel: 206-477-4661. FAX: 206-296-0192. E-mail: research.center@kingcounty.gov. *Research Librn,* Dawn Duddleson; Staff 1 (MLS 1)
Founded 1975
Library Holdings: Bk Titles 15,000; Per Subs 50
Subject Interests: Natural res, Transportation
Automation Activity & Vendor Info: (Cataloging) EOS International; (Circulation) EOS International; (OPAC) EOS International; (Serials) EOS International
Function: For res purposes, Govt ref serv
Restriction: Circ limited, External users must contact libr

G KING COUNTY HAZARDOUS WASTE LIBRARY*, 201 S Jackson St, Ste 5600, 98104. SAN 373-6563. Tel: 206-477-4661. Web Site: kingcountyhazwastewa.gov. *Librn,* Dawn Duddleson; E-mail: dawn.duddleson@kingcounty.gov; Staff 0.3 (MLS 0.3)
Founded 1992
Library Holdings: Bk Titles 3,500
Subject Interests: Environ educ, Hazardous waste mgt, Household hazardous waste, Integrated pest mgt
Automation Activity & Vendor Info: (Cataloging) EOS International; (Circulation) EOS International; (OPAC) EOS International

G MARINE MAMMAL LABORATORY LIBRARY*, Bldg 4, Rm 2030, 7600 Sand Point Way NE, 98115-6349. Tel: 206-526-4013. FAX: 206-526-6615. E-mail: mml.library@noaa.gov. Web Site: www.fisheries.noaa.gov/about/marine-mammal-laboratory. *Librn,* Sonja Kromann; E-mail: sonja.kromann@noaa.gov; Staff 1 (MLS 1)
Library Holdings: Bk Vols 15,000

Special Collections: Northern Fur Seal Archive; International Whaling Commission Archive
Subject Interests: Ecosystems, Marine mammals, Marine pollution
Partic in NOAA Libraries Network
Open Mon-Fri 7:30-4

M VIRGINIA MASON MEDICAL CENTER LIBRARY*, Central Pavillion, 1100 Ninth Ave, H11-JLC, 98101. SAN 371-1331. Tel: 206-223-6733. FAX: 206-223-2376. E-mail: medlib@virginiamason.org. Web Site: www.vmfh.org/resources/for-medical-staff/franciscan-library. *Lead Librn,* Mary Beth McAteer; E-mail: mary.mcateer@virginiamason.org; Staff 3 (MLS 2, Non-MLS 1)
Library Holdings: Bk Titles 1,000; Bk Vols 4,500; Per Subs 150
Special Collections: Virginia Mason Historical Archives
Automation Activity & Vendor Info: (OPAC) EOS International; (Serials) SerialsSolutions
Wireless access
Restriction: Staff use only

L MILLER NASH GRAHAM & DUNN LLP*, Law Library, 2801 Alaskan Way, Ste 300, 98121. SAN 317-6010. Tel: 206-624-8300. Reference Tel: 206-903-4801. FAX: 206-340-9599. E-mail: clientservices@millernash.com. Web Site: www.millernash.com. *Librn,* Doug Hull; E-mail: doug.hull@millernash.com; Staff 2 (MLS 1, Non-MLS 1)
Library Holdings: Bk Vols 10,000
Subject Interests: Banking, Employment law, Hospitality, Immigration, Labor law, Real estate, Securities, Tax law
Automation Activity & Vendor Info: (Cataloging) OCLC CatExpress; (Serials) Inmagic, Inc.
Partic in OCLC Online Computer Library Center, Inc
Open Mon-Fri 8-5:30

S MOUNTAINEERS LIBRARY*, 7700 Sand Point Way NE, 98115. SAN 317-6126. Tel: 206-521-6000. FAX: 206-523-6763. E-mail: info@mountaineers.org. Web Site: www.mountaineers.org. *Chief Exec Officer,* Tom Vogl; E-mail: tomv@mountaineers.org; Staff 1 (Non-MLS 1)
Founded 1915
Library Holdings: AV Mats 300; Bk Vols 8,500
Special Collections: Conservation (Mountaineer Foundation Library)
Subject Interests: Climbing, Environ studies, Exploration mountaineering biog, Exploration mountaineering hist, Natural hist
Automation Activity & Vendor Info: (Cataloging) TLC (The Library Corporation)
Wireless access
Function: Archival coll, Doc delivery serv, Mail loans to mem, Photocopying/Printing, Ref serv available
Restriction: Open by appt only, Open to pub for ref & circ; with some limitations, Restricted loan policy
Friends of the Library Group

S MUSEUM OF FLIGHT*, Harl V Brackin Library, 9404 E Marginal Way S, 98108-4097. SAN 370-6028. Tel: 206-764-5700. FAX: 206-764-5707. Web Site: www.museumofflight.org/exhibits-and-events/collections-and-research/library. *Supvry Librn,* Chris Stanton; E-mail: cstanton@museumofflight.org; *Cat Librn,* Janell Schnackenberg; Staff 2 (MLS 1, Non-MLS 1)
Founded 1985
Library Holdings: Bk Titles 26,000; Bk Vols 40,000; Per Subs 100
Special Collections: Aviation-Aerospace (G S Williams Photographic Coll, Peter Bowers Photo Coll); D D Hatfield Aviation History Coll; E B Jeppesen Aviation History & Navigation Coll; Fighter Aces Association Archives; Lear Archives; Wright Airplane Company Coll
Subject Interests: Aerospace, Aviation
Automation Activity & Vendor Info: (Acquisitions) SirsiDynix; (Cataloging) SirsiDynix; (Circulation) SirsiDynix
Function: Archival coll, Audio & video playback equip for onsite use, For res purposes, Online ref, Photocopying/Printing, Ref & res, Ref serv available, Res libr, Telephone ref
Open Mon-Sun 10-5
Restriction: Non-circulating to the pub, Open to pub for ref only

S MUSEUM OF HISTORY & INDUSTRY*, Sophie Frye Bass Library, 5933 Sixth Ave S, 98108. SAN 317-6363. Tel: 206-324-1126, Ext 102. FAX: 206-767-2249. E-mail: library@mohai.org. Web Site: www.mohai.org. *Library Colls Mgr,* Anna Elam; Tel: 206-324-1126, Ext 137, E-mail: anna.elam@mohai.org; Staff 2 (MLS 2)
Founded 1952
Library Holdings: Bk Titles 10,000
Special Collections: PEMCO Webster & Stevens Photography Coll; Seattle Post-Intelligence Photography Coll; Speaking of Seattle Oral History Coll. Oral History
Subject Interests: Alaska, County hist, Hist, Pacific Northwest, Seattle
Wireless access
Function: Photocopying/Printing, Res libr
Restriction: Non-circulating to the pub, Open by appt only, Open to pub for ref only

G NATIONAL ARCHIVES & RECORDS ADMINISTRATION*, The National Archives at Seattle, 6125 Sand Point Way NE, 98115-7999. Tel: 206-336-5115. FAX: 206-336-5112. E-mail: seattle.archives@nara.gov. Web Site: www.archives.gov/seattle. *Dir,* Susan Karren; Tel: 206-336-5141, E-mail: susan.karren@nara.gov
Special Collections: National Archives Documents from NARA Facilities (Microfilm Coll); Records of Federal Agencies & Federal Courts in Idaho, Oregon & Washington State
Function: Archival coll, Art exhibits, Computers for patron use, Distance learning, Electronic databases & coll, For res purposes, Genealogy discussion group, Govt ref serv, Instruction & testing, Internet access, Mail & tel request accepted, Online cat, Online ref, Orientations, Outreach serv, Photocopying/Printing, Ref & res, Ref serv available, Telephone ref, Wheelchair accessible, Workshops
Open Mon-Fri 9-4
Restriction: Open to pub with supv only

G NOAA SEATTLE REGIONAL LIBRARY*, Bldg 3, 7600 Sand Point Way NE, 98115. SAN 373-8647. Tel: 206-526-6241. FAX: 206-526-4535. E-mail: seattle.library@noaa.gov. Web Site: www.wrclib.noaa.gov. *Libr Dir,* Brian Voss; E-mail: brian.voss@noaa.gov
Library Holdings: Bk Titles 15,000; Per Subs 200
Subject Interests: Meteorology, Oceanography
Automation Activity & Vendor Info: (Cataloging) SirsiDynix; (Circulation) SirsiDynix; (ILL) OCLC; (OPAC) SirsiDynix
Partic in NOAA Libraries Network
Open Mon-Fri 8-4:30

NORDIC HERITAGE MUSEUM

S GORDON EKVALL TRACIE MUSIC LIBRARY*, 2655 Northwest Market St, 98107, SAN 326-4920. Tel: 206-789-5707, Ext 13. FAX: 206-789-3271. E-mail: library@nordicmuseum.org. Web Site: www.nordicmuseum.org.
Founded 1995
Library Holdings: AV Mats 3,000; CDs 200; DVDs 50; Music Scores 4,000; Bk Titles 2,500; Spec Interest Per Sub 40; Videos 100
Special Collections: Gordon Ekvall Tracie History Coll; Nordiska Folkdancers Coll; Skandia Folkdance Society Coll
Subject Interests: Customary life, Folk & traditional dance, Folk & traditional music, Folk art, Folk attire
Function: Archival coll, Electronic databases & coll, For res purposes, Music CDs, VHS videos
Restriction: Non-circulating coll, Not a lending libr, Open by appt only

S WALTER JOHNSON MEMORIAL LIBRARY*, 3014 NW 67th St, 98117. Tel: 206-789-5707. FAX: 206-789-3271. E-mail: nordic@nordicmuseum.org. Web Site: www.nordicmuseum.org. *Chief Curator,* Lizette Graden; *Curator of Coll,* Lisa Hill-Festa; Tel: 206-789-5707, Ext 18; Staff 2 (Non-MLS 2)
Founded 1980
Library Holdings: Bk Vols 3,000
Special Collections: Gordon Tracie Music Library; Oral History Project Colls. Oral History
Subject Interests: Danish (Lang), Finnish (Lang), Icelandic (Lang), Norwegian (Lang), Sound rec, Swedish (Lang)
Function: Ref serv available
Restriction: Fee for pub use, Limited access for the pub, Non-circulating coll, Not a lending libr, Open by appt only

J NORTH SEATTLE COMMUNITY COLLEGE*, Library & Media Services, 9600 College Way N, 98103. SAN 317-6169. Tel: 206-527-3607. E-mail: nscclibrary@seattlecolleges.edu. Web Site: libguides.northseattle.edu/welcome. *Dean, Libr & Learning Res,* Aryana Bates; E-mail: aryana.bates@seattlecolleges.edu; *Librarian, Math & Sciences,* Ana Villar; E-mail: ana.villar@seattlecolleges.edu
Founded 1970. Enrl 9,000
Library Holdings: Bk Vols 54,000; Per Subs 594
Automation Activity & Vendor Info: (Cataloging) Ex Libris Group; (Circulation) Ex Libris Group; (OPAC) Ex Libris Group
Wireless access
Partic in Washington Community & Technical Colleges Library Consortium
Open Mon-Thurs 10-3

L OGDEN MURPHY WALLACE ATTORNEYS*, Law Library, 901 Fifth Ave, Ste 3500, 98164. SAN 323-5785. Tel: 206-447-7000. FAX: 206-447-0215. E-mail: info@omwlaw.com. Web Site: omwlaw.com/locations/seattle. *Librn,* Nathan Marr; E-mail: nmarr@omwlaw.com; Staff 2 (MLS 1, Non-MLS 1)
Library Holdings: Bk Vols 6,000; Per Subs 140
Subject Interests: Real estate

Automation Activity & Vendor Info: (Cataloging) Inmagic, Inc.
Wireless access

R PLYMOUTH CHURCH*, Vida B Varey Library, 1217 Sixth Ave, 98101-3199. SAN 317-6223. Tel: 206-622-4865. FAX: 206-622-8726. E-mail: plymouthlibrary@gmail.com. Web Site: plymouthchurchseattle.org/library. *Librn,* Suzanne Sanderson; Staff 1 (MLS 1)
Founded 1948
Library Holdings: CDs 30; DVDs 80; Bk Titles 4,500
Subject Interests: Relig studies
Automation Activity & Vendor Info: (Cataloging) LibraryWorld, Inc; (Circulation) LibraryWorld, Inc; (OPAC) LibraryWorld, Inc
Wireless access
Open Sun 9-1
Friends of the Library Group

SR PROVIDENCE ARCHIVES*, Mother Joseph Province, 4800 37th Ave SW, 98126. SAN 329-5087. Tel: 206-937-4600. FAX: 206-923-4001. E-mail: archives@providence.org. Web Site: www.providence.org/phs/archives. *Archives Dir,* Loretta Zwolak Greene; Tel: 206-923-4010, E-mail: loretta.greene@providence.org; *Visual Res Archivist,* Peter F Schmid; Tel: 206-923-4012, E-mail: peter.schmid@providence.org; *Assoc Archivist,* Elizabeth Russell; Tel: 206-923-4011, E-mail: elizabeth.russell@providence.org; *Asst Archivist-Tech,* Pamela Hedquist; Tel: 509-474-2319, E-mail: pamela.hedquist@providence.org; *Coll Curator,* Jessica Long; Tel: 509-474-2321, E-mail: jessica.long3@providence.org. Subject Specialists: *Artifacts,* Jessica Long; Staff 5 (MLS 2, Non-MLS 3)
Library Holdings: Bk Titles 1,000; Videos 600
Special Collections: Mother Joseph (Esther Pariseau), a Sister of Providence (1823-1902), represents Washington State in Statuary Hall, Washington, DC
Subject Interests: Catholic Church, Educ, Healthcare, Sisters of Providence, Soc welfare in the NW
Wireless access
Function: Archival coll
Publications: Past Forward (Newsletter)
Restriction: Non-circulating, Open by appt only

L PUBLIC LAW LIBRARY OF KING COUNTY*, King County Courthouse, 516 Third Ave, Ste W621, 98104. SAN 317-6053. Tel: 206-477-1305. FAX: 206-205-2905. E-mail: services@kcll.org. Web Site: kcll.org. *Exec Dir,* Barbara Engstrom; *Asst Dir,* Richard Stroup
Library Holdings: Bk Vols 90,000; Per Subs 140
Wireless access
Open Mon-Fri 8-5

S PUGET SOUND REGIONAL COUNCIL*, Information Center, 1011 Western Ave, Ste 500, 98104. SAN 317-6266. Tel: 206-464-7532. FAX: 206-587-4825. E-mail: info@psrc.org. Web Site: www.psrc.org/contact-center/information-center. *Libr Mgr,* Andi Markley; E-mail: amarkley@psrc.org; Staff 1 (MLS 1)
Founded 1967
Library Holdings: Bk Titles 3,000; Per Subs 60
Special Collections: Census; Small Area Regional Forecasts (population, households, employment)
Subject Interests: Econ develop, Growth mgt, Transportation

L REED MCCLURE ATTORNEYS AT LAW*, Law Library, Financial Ctr, 1215 Fourth Ave, Ste 1700, 98161. SAN 373-6601. Tel: 206-292-4900. FAX: 206-223-0152. E-mail: information@rmlaw.com. Web Site: www.rmlaw.com. *Librn,* Position Currently Open
Library Holdings: Bk Vols 4,000
Restriction: Staff use only

SEATTLE ART MUSEUM

S DOROTHY STIMSON BULLITT LIBRARY*, 1300 First Ave, 98101, SAN 317-6320. Tel: 206-654-3220. FAX: 206-654-3135. Web Site: www.seattleartmuseum.org/learn/library/default.asp. *Librn, Mgr, Libr Serv,* Traci Timmons; E-mail: tracit@seattleartmuseum.org; Staff 1 (MLS 1)
Founded 1991
Library Holdings: Bk Vols 20,000; Per Subs 100
Special Collections: History of the Seattle Art Museum, clippings, ephemera; Northwest Artists Files, clippings
Subject Interests: African art, Contemporary art, Decorative art, European art, Modern art, Photog
Automation Activity & Vendor Info: (Cataloging) EOS International; (Circulation) EOS International; (OPAC) EOS International; (Serials) EOS International
Function: Archival coll, Photocopying/Printing, Res libr, Telephone ref
Partic in OCLC Online Computer Library Center, Inc
Open Tues-Fri 10-5
Restriction: Circulates for staff only

S MCCAW FOUNDATION LIBRARY OF ASIAN ART*, Seattle Asian Art Museum, 1400 E Prospect St, 98112, SAN 375-538X. Tel: 206-654-3202. FAX: 206-654-3191. *Librn,* Yueh-Lin Chen; E-mail: yueh-linc@seattleartmuseum.org; Staff 1 (MLS 1)
Founded 1933
Library Holdings: Bk Vols 15,000; Per Subs 100
Subject Interests: Asian art
Automation Activity & Vendor Info: (Cataloging) EOS International; (Circulation) EOS International; (OPAC) EOS International; (Serials) EOS International
Function: Archival coll, Ref serv available, Res libr, Telephone ref
Partic in OCLC Online Computer Library Center, Inc
Restriction: Non-circulating to the pub, Open by appt only

C SEATTLE CENTRAL COLLEGE, Instructional Resource Services Library, 1701 Broadway, BE Rm 2101, 98122. SAN 317-6339. Tel: 206-934-4050. Reference Tel: 206-934-5421. Administration Tel: 206-934-5420. FAX: 206-934-3878. Web Site: library.seattlecentral.edu/welcome. *Dean,* Lynn Kanne; Tel: 206-934-4072, E-mail: lynn.kanne@seattlecolleges.edu; *Ref Librn,* Katy Dichter; Tel: 206-934-4098, E-mail: katy.dichter@seattlecolleges.edu; *Ref Librn,* Dave Ellenwood; Tel: 206-934-6336, E-mail: dave.ellenwood@seattlecolleges.edu; *Ref Librn,* Alyssa Jocson Porter; Tel: 206-934-4483, E-mail: alyssa.jocsonporter@seattlecolleges.edu; *Ref Librn,* Althea Lazzaro; Tel: 206-934-4071, E-mail: althea.lazzaro@seattlecolleges.edu; *Ref Librn,* Adrianna Martinez; Tel: 206-934-4946, E-mail: adrianna.martinez@seattlecolleges.edu; *Ref Librn,* Sharon Spence-Wilcox; Tel: 206-934-4069, E-mail: sharon.spence-wilcox@seattlecolleges.edu; Staff 7 (MLS 7)
Founded 1966. Enrl 7,886; Fac 174
Library Holdings: Bk Vols 53,358; Per Subs 183
Subject Interests: Archit, Art, Ethnic studies
Automation Activity & Vendor Info: (Acquisitions) Ex Libris Group; (Cataloging) Ex Libris Group; (Circulation) Ex Libris Group; (Course Reserve) Ex Libris Group; (OPAC) Ex Libris Group; (Serials) Ex Libris Group
Wireless access
Partic in Washington Community & Technical Colleges Library Consortium

M SEATTLE CHILDREN'S HOSPITAL, Library & Information Commons, 4800 Sand Point Way NE, OB.8.520, 98105. (Mail add: PO Box 5371, 98145-5005), SAN 317-5944. Tel: 206-987-2098. FAX: 206-987-3838. E-mail: library@seattlechildrens.org. *Libr Mgr,* Cheyenne Roduin; *Librn,* Sue Groshong; *Librn,* Elisabeth Nylander; *Librn,* Julia Paulsen; Staff 3 (MLS 3)
Founded 1946
Library Holdings: e-books 1,300; e-journals 35,000; Bk Titles 3,500; Per Subs 30
Subject Interests: Pediatrics
Automation Activity & Vendor Info: (Acquisitions) Koha; (Cataloging) Koha; (Circulation) Koha; (OPAC) Koha
Wireless access
Open Mon-Fri 9-3
Restriction: Badge access after hrs

S SEATTLE GENEALOGICAL SOCIETY LIBRARY*, 6200 Sand Point Way NE, 98115. (Mail add: PO Box 15329, 98115-0329), SAN 321-1053. Tel: 206-522-8658. E-mail: library@seattlegenealogicalsociety.org. Web Site: seagensoc.org, seattlegenealogicalsociety.org. *Libr Dir,* Sue Schack Jensen. Subject Specialists: *Genealogy,* Sue Schack Jensen
Founded 1923
Library Holdings: CDs 320; Electronic Media & Resources 100; Bk Vols 14,500; Per Subs 10
Special Collections: Family Genealogies Coll; Family History & Genealogical Information Coll, digial holdings; International Coll; King County Circuit Court Index; Maps Coll; Mayflower & Colonial America Colls; New Jersey (George C Kent Coll); Seattle - King County Coll; Seattle City Directories; Washington State School Yearbooks
Subject Interests: Genealogy, Local hist
Wireless access
Function: 24/7 Online cat, Archival coll, Computers for patron use, Electronic databases & coll, For res purposes, Genealogy discussion group, Internet access, Magazines, Microfiche/film & reading machines, Online cat, Online ref, Orientations, Photocopying/Printing, Prog for adults, Ref & res, Res assist avail, Res libr, Res performed for a fee, Scanner, Telephone ref, Wheelchair accessible, Workshops
Publications: eNews! (Online only); Journal (Biannually)
Open Tues-Sat 10-3
Restriction: In-house use for visitors, Non-circulating, Pub use on premises

S THE SEATTLE METAPHYSICAL LIBRARY (AS-YOU-LIKE-IT LIBRARY)*, 3450 40th Ave W, 98199. SAN 326-2049. Tel: 206-329-1794. Web Site: www.seattlemetaphysicallibrary.org. *Pres,*

Margaret Bartley; E-mail: margaret@seattlemetaphysicallibrary.org; *Librn,* Martha Rhoda; Tel: 206-551-8277, E-mail: marth@seattlemetaphysicallibrary.org; Staff 2 (Non-MLS 2)
Founded 1961
Library Holdings: Bk Titles 17,000
Special Collections: Alternative Health; Alternative Science (Body-Mind Research, Tesla W Reich); Astrology, bks & mags; Eastern teachings : Hinuism, Taoism, Buddhism, martial and healing arts; Rudolf Steiner; UFOs; Western Esotericism - Masonic, Rosicrucian, Theosophy, Spiritualism; World Religion, mythology
Subject Interests: Ancient hist, Astrology, Feminism, Holistic health, Occult, Parapsychol, Philos, Reincarnation, Relig, Spiritualism
Function: Archival coll, Bks on cassette, CD-ROM, Mail & tel request accepted, Mail loans to mem, Music CDs, Online cat, Spoken cassettes & CDs, Spoken cassettes & DVDs, VHS videos
Publications: News & Events (Newsletter)
Restriction: Circ to mem only, Fee for pub use, Internal circ only, Non-circulating coll, Non-circulating of rare bks, Open evenings by appt, Open to pub for ref & circ; with some limitations, Private libr, Sub libr

C SEATTLE PACIFIC UNIVERSITY LIBRARY*, 3307 Third Ave W, 98119. SAN 363-9363. Tel: 206-281-2228. Interlibrary Loan Service Tel: 206-281-2154. Reference Tel: 206-281-2419. FAX: 206-281-2936. Web Site: spu.edu/library. *Dean of Libr,* R John Robertson; E-mail: rjr@spu.edu; *Head, Access Serv,* Johanna Staman; Tel: 206-281-2789, E-mail: johanna@spu.edu; *Head, Tech Serv,* Natalee Vick; Tel: 206-281-2735, E-mail: nvick@spu.edu; *Syst Librn,* Carrie Fry; Tel: 206-281-2124, E-mail: cfry@spu.edu; *Info Spec,* Stephen Perisho; Tel: 206-281-2417, E-mail: sperisho@spu.edu; *Info Spec,* Cindy Strong; Tel: 206-281-2074, E-mail: clstrong@spu.edu. Subject Specialists: *Health sci,* Carrie Fry; *Philos, Theol,* Stephen Perisho; *Educ,* Cindy Strong; Staff 10 (MLS 9, Non-MLS 1)
Founded 1891. Enrl 3,728; Fac 190; Highest Degree: Doctorate
Library Holdings: e-books 3,395; Bk Titles 163,959; Bk Vols 191,807; Per Subs 1,230
Special Collections: Free Methodism
Subject Interests: Educ, Nursing, Psychol, Relig
Automation Activity & Vendor Info: (Acquisitions) Innovative Interfaces, Inc; (Cataloging) Innovative Interfaces, Inc; (Circulation) Innovative Interfaces, Inc; (Course Reserve) Innovative Interfaces, Inc; (OPAC) Innovative Interfaces, Inc; (Serials) Innovative Interfaces, Inc
Wireless access
Function: ILL available, Photocopying/Printing, Ref serv available, Telephone ref
Partic in Orbis Cascade Alliance; Puget Sound Acad Independent Librs
Open Mon-Thurs 7:30am-11pm, Fri 7:30am-8pm, Sat Noon-8, Sun 3-11 (Winter); Mon-Thurs 8-8, Fri 8-6, Sat 10-6 (Summer)
Restriction: Pub use on premises

M SEATTLE PSYCHOANALYTIC SOCIETY & INSTITUTE*, Edith Buxbaum Library, 4020 E Madison St, Ste 230, 98112. SAN 373-3025. Tel: 206-328-5315. FAX: 206-328-5879. E-mail: info@spsi.org. Web Site: www.spsi.org. *Adminr,* Zan Christensen
Founded 1996
Library Holdings: e-books 30; e-journals 20; Bk Vols 5,000; Per Subs 10
Open Mon-Fri 10-6

P THE SEATTLE PUBLIC LIBRARY*, Central Library & Administrative Offices, 1000 Fourth Ave, 98104-1109. SAN 363-9398. Tel: 206-386-4636. Circulation Tel: 206-386-4190. Administration Tel: 206-386-4147. Web Site: www.spl.org. *City Librn, Exec Dir,* Marcellus Turner; E-mail: chieflibrarian@spl.org; *Dir, Prog & Serv,* Tom Fay; E-mail: tom.fay@spl.org; *Regional Mgr,* Wei Cai; *Regional Mgr,* Steve DelVecchio; *Regional Mgr,* Darth Nielsen; *Regional Mgr,* Karen Spiel; *Regional Mgr,* Francesca Wainwright
Founded 1890. Pop 608,660; Circ 11,572,778
Library Holdings: Bk Vols 926,197
Special Collections: Oral History; State Document Depository; US Document Depository
Subject Interests: Aviation hist, Genealogy, Seattle hist
Automation Activity & Vendor Info: (Acquisitions) BiblioCommons; (Cataloging) BiblioCommons; (Circulation) BiblioCommons; (OPAC) BiblioCommons
Wireless access
Partic in OCLC Online Computer Library Center, Inc
Special Services for the Deaf - Bks on deafness & sign lang; Deaf publ; Staff with knowledge of sign lang; Video & TTY relay via computer
Special Services for the Blind - Assistive/Adapted tech devices, equip & products; Braille bks; Descriptive video serv (DVS); Large print bks; Reader equip
Open Mon-Thurs 10-8, Fri & Sat 10-6, Sun 12-6
Restriction: Circ limited
Friends of the Library Group

Branches: 27
BALLARD, 5614 22nd Ave NW, 98107, SAN 363-972X. Tel: 206-684-4089.
Founded 1907
Library Holdings: Bk Vols 62,518
Open Mon-Thurs 10-8, Fri & Sat 10-6, Sun 12-5
Friends of the Library Group
BEACON HILL, 2821 Beacon Ave S, 98144, SAN 363-9665. Tel: 206-684-4711.
Founded 1945
Library Holdings: Bk Vols 28,994
Open Mon-Thurs 10-8, Fri & Sat 10-6, Sun 12-5
Friends of the Library Group
BROADVIEW, 12755 Greenwood Ave N, 98133, SAN 363-9754. Tel: 206-684-7519.
Founded 1944
Library Holdings: Bk Vols 45,903
Open Mon & Tues 1-8, Wed & Thurs 10-8, Fri & Sat 10-6, Sun Noon-5
Friends of the Library Group
CAPITOL HILL, 425 Harvard Ave E, 98102, SAN 363-9576. Tel: 206-684-4715.
Founded 1954
Library Holdings: Bk Vols 37,283
Open Mon-Thurs 10-8, Fri & Sat 10-6, Sun 12-5
Friends of the Library Group
COLUMBIA, 4721 Rainier Ave S, 98118, SAN 363-9932. Tel: 206-386-1908.
Founded 1909
Library Holdings: Bk Vols 38,957
Open Mon-Thurs 10-8, Fri & Sat 10-6, Sun 12-5
Friends of the Library Group
DELDRIDGE, 5423 Deldridge Way SW, 98106, SAN 377-7502.
Library Holdings: Bk Vols 15,819
Open Mon & Tues 1-8, Wed, Thurs & Sat 11-6, Sun Noon-5
Friends of the Library Group
DOUGLASS-TRUTH, 2300 E Yesler Way, 98122, SAN 363-9967. Tel: 206-684-4704.
Founded 1914
Library Holdings: Bk Vols 45,231
Open Mon-Thurs 10-8, Fri & Sat 10-6, Sun 12-5
Friends of the Library Group
FREMONT LIBRARY, 731 N 35th St, 98103, SAN 363-9789. Tel: 206-684-4084. FAX: 206-684-4085.
Founded 1902
Open Mon & Tues 1-8, Wed, Thurs & Sat 11-6, Sun Noon-5
Friends of the Library Group
GREEN LAKE, 7364 E Green Lake Dr N, 98115, SAN 363-9541. Tel: 206-684-7547.
Founded 1905
Library Holdings: Bk Vols 32,328
Open Mon & Tues 1-8, Wed, Thurs & Sat 11-6, Sun Noon-5
Friends of the Library Group
GREENWOOD, 8016 Greenwood Ave N, 98103, SAN 363-9819. Tel: 206-684-4086.
Founded 1928
Library Holdings: Bk Vols 42,460
Open Mon-Thurs 10-8, Fri & Sat 10-6, Sun 12-5
Friends of the Library Group
HIGH POINT, 3411 SW Raymond St, 98126, SAN 323-9942. Tel: 206-684-7454.
Founded 1942
Library Holdings: Bk Vols 22,672
Open Mon & Tues 1-8, Wed-Sat 11-6, Sun Noon-5
Friends of the Library Group
INTERNATIONAL DISTRICT/CHINATOWN BRANCH, 713 Eighth Ave S, 98104. Tel: 206-386-1300.
Founded 2005
Library Holdings: Bk Vols 10,047
Open Mon & Tues 1-8, Wed-Sat 11-6, Sun Noon-5
Friends of the Library Group
LAKE CITY, 12501 28th Ave NE, 98125, SAN 363-9606. Tel: 206-684-7518.
Founded 1935
Library Holdings: Bk Vols 54,739
Open Mon-Wed 10-8, Thurs & Sat 10-6, Sun 12-5
Friends of the Library Group
MADRONA-SALLY GOLDMARK BRANCH, 1134 33rd Ave, 98122, SAN 323-9888. Tel: 206-684-4705.
Founded 1971
Library Holdings: Bk Vols 12,623
Open Mon & Tues 1-8, Wed, Thurs & Sat 11-6, Sun Noon-5
Friends of the Library Group
MAGNOLIA, 2801 34th Ave W, 98199, SAN 363-9843. Tel: 206-386-4225.
Founded 1943

Library Holdings: Bk Vols 28,916
Open Mon & Tues 1-8, Wed, Thurs & Sat 11-6, Sun Noon-5
Friends of the Library Group
MONTLAKE, 2401 24th Ave E, 98112, SAN 323-9985. Tel: 206-684-4720.
Founded 1944
Library Holdings: Bk Vols 13,737
Open Mon & Tues 1-8, Wed, Thurs & Sat 11-6, Sun Noon-5
Friends of the Library Group
NEWHOLLY, 7058 32nd Ave S, 98118, SAN 323-9969. Tel: 206-386-1905.
Founded 1943
Library Holdings: Bk Vols 15,793
Open Mon & Tues 1-8, Wed, Thurs & Sat 11-6, Sun Noon-5
Friends of the Library Group
NORTHEAST, 6801 35th Ave NE, 98115, SAN 363-9630. Tel: 206-684-7539.
Founded 1945
Library Holdings: Bk Vols 63,213
Open Mon-Wed 10-8, Thurs-Sat 10-6, Sun 12-5
Friends of the Library Group
NORTHGATE, 10548 Fifth Ave NE, 98125. Tel: 206-386-1980.
Founded 2003
Library Holdings: Bk Vols 25,396
Open Mon-Wed 10-8, Thurs-Sat 10-6, Sun 12-5
Friends of the Library Group
QUEEN ANNE BRANCH, 400 W Garfield St, 98119, SAN 363-9878. Tel: 206-386-4227.
Founded 1914
Library Holdings: Bk Vols 30,202
Open Mon & Tues 1-8, Wed, Thurs & Sat 11-6, Sun Noon-5
Friends of the Library Group
RAINIER BEACH, 9125 Rainier Ave S, 98118, SAN 363-9983. Tel: 206-386-1906.
Founded 1912
Library Holdings: Bk Vols 47,096
Open Mon-Wed 10-8, Thurs-Sat 10-6, Sun 12-5
Friends of the Library Group
SOUTH PARK, 8604 Eighth Ave S, 98108. Tel: 206-615-1688. FAX: 206-615-0539.
Founded 2006
Library Holdings: Bk Vols 18,700
Function: Adult bk club, Bilingual assistance for Spanish patrons, Bks on CD, Children's prog, Computer training, Computers for patron use, Electronic databases & coll, Family literacy, Homework prog, Magnifiers for reading, Music CDs, Online cat, Outreach serv, Outside serv via phone, mail, e-mail & web, OverDrive digital audio bks, Photocopying/Printing, Preschool outreach, Prog for children & young adult, Ref serv available, Story hour, Summer reading prog, Tax forms, Telephone ref, Wheelchair accessible
Open Mon & Tues 1-8, Wed-Sat 11-6, Sun Noon-5
Friends of the Library Group
SOUTHWEST, 9010 35th Ave SW, 98126, SAN 363-9991. Tel: 206-684-7455.
Founded 1945
Library Holdings: Bk Vols 35,235
Open Mon-Wed 10-8, Thurs-Sat 10-6, Sun 12-5
Friends of the Library Group
UNIVERSITY BRANCH, 5009 Roosevelt Way NE, 98105. Tel: 206-684-4063.
Founded 1910
Library Holdings: Bk Vols 35,987
Open Mon & Tues 1-8, Wed-Sat 11-6, Sun Noon-5
Friends of the Library Group
WALLINGFORD, 1501 N 45th St, 98103, SAN 323-9926. Tel: 206-684-4088.
Founded 1948
Library Holdings: Bk Vols 12,067
Open Mon & Tues 1-8, Wed, Thurs & Sat 11-6, Sun Noon-5
Friends of the Library Group
WASHINGTON TALKING BOOK & BRAILLE LIBRARY
See Separate Entry under Washington Talking Book & Braille Library
WEST SEATTLE BRANCH, 2306 42nd Ave SW, 98116, SAN 364-0027. Tel: 206-684-7444.
Founded 1910
Library Holdings: Bk Vols 38,785
Open Mon-Wed 10-8, Thurs-Sat 10-6, Sun 12-5
Friends of the Library Group

SEATTLE UNIVERSITY
C A A LEMIEUX LIBRARY*, 901 12th Ave, 98122-4411. (Mail add: PO Box 222000, 98122-1090), SAN 317-6401. Tel: 206-296-6222. Circulation Tel: 206-296-6233. Interlibrary Loan Service Tel: 206-296-6359. Reference Tel: 206-296-6230. Automation Services Tel: 206-296-6228. FAX: 206-296-2572. Interlibrary Loan Service FAX: 206-296-6224. Web Site: www.seattleu.edu/lemlib. *Univ Librn,* John Popko; Tel: 206-296-6201, E-mail: jpopko@seattleu.edu; *Dir, Instrul & Pub Serv,* Judy Solberg; Tel: 206-296-6274, E-mail: solbergj@seattleu.edu; *Circ Mgr,* Holly Sturgeon; Tel: 206-296-6234, E-mail: sturgeon@seattleu.edu; Staff 11 (MLS 11)
Enrl 4,909; Highest Degree: Doctorate
Library Holdings: Bk Vols 216,677; Per Subs 1,604
Subject Interests: Educ, Relig studies, Software engr
Automation Activity & Vendor Info: (Acquisitions) SirsiDynix
Partic in Association of Jesuit Colleges & Universities; NELLCO Law Library Consortium, Inc.; OCLC Online Computer Library Center, Inc; Orbis Cascade Alliance; Puget Sound Acad Independent Librs
Publications: Serials List
CL SCHOOL OF LAW LIBRARY*, Sullivan Hall, 901 12th Ave, 98122-4411. (Mail add: PO Box 222000, 98122-1090), SAN 364-2429. Tel: 206-398-4221. Interlibrary Loan Service Tel: 206-398-4227. Reference Tel: 206-398-4225. FAX: 206-398-4194. Web Site: law.seattleu.edu/library.xml. *Dir,* Kristin Cheney; *Coll Develop,* Kara Phillips; *Ref (Info Servs),* Tina Ching; *Ref (Info Servs),* Barbara Swatt Engstrom; *Ref (Info Servs),* Kerry Fitz-Gerald; *Ref (Info Servs),* Kelly Kunsch; *Ref (Info Servs),* Bob Menanteaux; *Ref (Info Servs),* Stephanie Wilson; *Tech Serv,* Kent Milunovich; Staff 18 (MLS 9, Non-MLS 9)
Founded 1972. Enrl 896; Fac 60; Highest Degree: Doctorate
Library Holdings: Microforms 109,561; Bk Titles 55,300; Bk Vols 171,896
Special Collections: US Document Depository
Automation Activity & Vendor Info: (Acquisitions) Innovative Interfaces, Inc; (Cataloging) Innovative Interfaces, Inc; (Circulation) Innovative Interfaces, Inc; (OPAC) Innovative Interfaces, Inc; (Serials) Innovative Interfaces, Inc
Partic in OCLC Online Computer Library Center, Inc

S SHANNON & WILSON, INC*, Technical Library, 400 N 34th St, Ste 100, 98103. (Mail add: PO Box 300303, 98103-9703), SAN 317-6428. Tel: 206-695-6821. FAX: 206-695-6777. E-mail: info-seattle@shanwil.com. Web Site: www.shannonwilson.com/seattle. *Coop Librn,* Judith Bloch; Staff 1 (MLS 1)
Founded 1965
Library Holdings: Bk Titles 6,500; Bk Vols 7,000; Per Subs 100
Subject Interests: Environ engr, Geol, Geotech engr, Rock mechanics
Wireless access
Partic in OCLC Online Computer Library Center, Inc
Restriction: Open by appt only

J SOUTH SEATTLE COMMUNITY COLLEGE*, Library & Learning Center, 6000 16th Ave SW, 98106-1499. SAN 317-6444. Tel: 206-764-5395. Reference Tel: 206-768-6408. FAX: 206-763-5155. Web Site: libguides.southseattle.edu. *Dean, Libr & Learning Res,* Lynn Kanne; E-mail: lynn.kanne@SeattleColleges.edu; *Ref (Info Servs),* Randy Nelson; Tel: 206-768-6405, E-mail: rnelson@SeattleColleges.edu; *Ref (Info Servs),* Esther Sunde; Tel: 206-768-6663, E-mail: esunde@SeattleColleges.edu; Staff 4 (MLS 4)
Founded 1971. Enrl 6,000; Fac 170
Library Holdings: Bk Vols 33,081; Per Subs 650
Special Collections: Landscape-Horticulture, bk, flm, micro & pamphlets
Subject Interests: Automotive, Aviation, Secretarial
Automation Activity & Vendor Info: (Acquisitions) Ex Libris Group; (Cataloging) Ex Libris Group; (Circulation) Ex Libris Group; (Course Reserve) Ex Libris Group; (Media Booking) Ex Libris Group; (OPAC) Ex Libris Group; (Serials) Ex Libris Group
Wireless access
Partic in Washington Community & Technical Colleges Library Consortium
Special Services for the Blind - Braille servs; VisualTek equip
Open Mon-Thurs 8-7:30, Fri 8-4

L STOEL RIVES LLP*, Law Library, One Union Sq, 600 University St, Ste 3600, 98101. SAN 372-3615. Tel: 206-386-7502. FAX: 206-386-7500. Web Site: www.stoel.com. *Librn,* Nancy Noble; E-mail: nancy.noble@stoel.com
Library Holdings: Bk Vols 2,000
Restriction: Staff use only

M SWEDISH MEDICAL CENTER LIBRARY*, First Hill Campus, 747 Broadway, 98122-4307. SAN 317-6452. Tel: 206-386-2484. FAX: 206-860-6582. E-mail: library.requests@swedish.org. Web Site: www.swedish.org. *Med Librn,* Mike Scully; Staff 1 (Non-MLS 1)
Founded 1910
Library Holdings: Bk Vols 2,500; Per Subs 375
Subject Interests: Hospital admin, Med, Nursing, Surgery
Wireless access
Open Mon-Fri 8-4:30

SR TEMPLE DE HIRSCH SINAI LIBRARY, 1511 E Pike, 98122. SAN 326-7199. Tel: 206-323-8486. E-mail: info@tdhs-nw.org. Web Site: templedehirschsinai.org/libraries. Staff 2 (MLS 1, Non-MLS 1)
Founded 1908
Library Holdings: Bk Vols 10,000
Special Collections: Benjamin Zukor Children's Library; Historical Coll
Subject Interests: Bible, Cooking, Hist, Holocaust, Judaism, Spirituality
Automation Activity & Vendor Info: (Cataloging) OPALS (Open-source Automated Library System); (Circulation) OPALS (Open-source Automated Library System)
Wireless access
Restriction: Open by appt only
Branches:
BELLEVUE BRANCH, 3850 156th Ave SE, Bellevue, 98006. Tel: 206-323-8486, Ext 7423.
Restriction: Open by appt only

A UNITED STATES ARMY CORPS OF ENGINEERS*, Seattle District Library, 4735 E Marginal Way S, 98134. (Mail add: PO Box 3755, 98124-3755), SAN 364-0051. Tel: 206-316-3728. FAX: 206-766-6444. Web Site: www.nws.usace.army.mil/library. *Librn,* Shelly Trulson; E-mail: shelly.r.trulson@usace.army.mil
Founded 1940
Library Holdings: Bk Titles 12,000; Bk Vols 25,000; Per Subs 300
Subject Interests: Engr, Environ, Law
Automation Activity & Vendor Info: (Cataloging) EOS International; (Circulation) EOS International; (ILL) OCLC; (OPAC) EOS International; (Serials) EOS International
Partic in OCLC Online Computer Library Center, Inc
Open Mon-Fri 7:30-4

GL UNITED STATES COURTS LIBRARY, 700 Stewart St, Rm 19105, 98101. SAN 317-6460. Tel: 206-370-8975. *Librn,* Sarah Griffith; *Asst Librn,* Betty Lim; Staff 2 (MLS 2)
Founded 1939
Library Holdings: Bk Titles 4,000; Per Subs 5
Special Collections: US Document Depository
Subject Interests: Law fed states, Ninth circuit states
Automation Activity & Vendor Info: (Acquisitions) SirsiDynix; (Cataloging) SirsiDynix; (OPAC) SirsiDynix
Wireless access
Function: ILL available
Restriction: Open by appt only

G UNITED STATES ENVIRONMENTAL PROTECTION, Region 10 Library, 1200 Sixth Ave, Ste 155, MSD 1 K-03, 98101. SAN 317-5987. Tel: 206-553-1289. E-mail: library-reg10@epa.gov. Web Site: www.epa.gov/epalibraries/region-10-library-services. *Supvry Librn,* Liz Doyle; Tel: 206-553-2134, E-mail: doyle.liz@epa.gov; Staff 2 (MLS 1, Non-MLS 1)
Library Holdings: Bk Vols 10,000; Per Subs 50
Special Collections: EPA reports, working papers
Subject Interests: Air pollution, Ecosystems, Environ law, Environ mgt, Hazardous mat, Solid waste mgt, Water pollution
Partic in Docline; National Network of Libraries of Medicine Region 5; OCLC Online Computer Library Center, Inc
Open Mon-Fri 9-12 & 1-4

S UNIVERSITY OF WASHINGTON BOTANIC GARDENS*, Elisabeth C Miller Library, 3501 NE 41st St, 98105. (Mail add: University of Washington, Box 354115, 98195-4115), SAN 328-0918. Tel: 206-543-0415. Reference Tel: 206-897-5268. FAX: 206-897-1435. E-mail: hortlib@uw.edu. Web Site: www.millerlibrary.org. *Curator, Libr Mgr,* Brian Thompson; E-mail: bthomp@uw.edu; *IT Librn,* Tracy Mehlin; E-mail: tmehlin@uw.edu; *Mgr, Ch Serv,* Laura Blumhagen; E-mail: lbb@uw.edu; *Mgr, Ref Serv, Tech Serv,* Rebecca Alexander; E-mail: rebalex@uw.edu; *Mgr, Ser,* Jessica Anderson; E-mail: anderjl@uw.edu. Subject Specialists: *Horticultural lit,* Brian Thompson; Staff 3.6 (MLS 3.1, Non-MLS 0.5)
Founded 1985
Jul 2017-Jun 2018 Income $310,000, Locally Generated Income $294,000, Parent Institution $16,000. Mats Exp $19,800, Books $7,000, Per/Ser (Incl. Access Fees) $10,200, Presv $2,600. Sal $195,000 (Prof $115,000)
Library Holdings: Bk Vols 16,000; Per Subs 250
Special Collections: Seed Catalogs
Subject Interests: Botanical hist, Botanical illustration, Gardening, Hort, Landscape design
Automation Activity & Vendor Info: (Cataloging) OCLC; (Circulation) Koha; (OPAC) Koha; (Serials) EBSCO Discovery Service
Wireless access
Function: Archival coll, Children's prog, Online cat, Prof lending libr, Ref serv available, Story hour
Partic in OCLC Online Computer Library Center, Inc
Open Mon 9-8, Tues-Fri 9-5, Sat 9-3; Mon Noon-8, Tues-Fri 9-5 (Summer)

C UNIVERSITY OF WASHINGTON LIBRARIES*, Box 352900, 98195-2900. SAN 364-0086. Tel: 206-543-0242. Interlibrary Loan Service Tel: 206-543-1878. Administration Tel: 206-543-1760. FAX: 206-685-8727. Web Site: www.lib.washington.edu. *Dean, Univ Libr,* Simon Neame; E-mail: sneame@uw.edu; *Assoc Dean, Univ Libr,* Tania Bardyn; Tel: 206-685-3299, E-mail: bardyn@uw.edu; *Dir, Res Serv,* Nancy Huling; Tel: 206-685-2211, E-mail: hulingn@uw.edu; *Access Serv, Head, Circ Serv, Interim Co-Dir,* Kirsten Spillum; Tel: 206-685-3987, Fax: 206-685-6972, E-mail: kirsten@uw.edu; Staff 138 (MLS 138)
Founded 1861. Highest Degree: Doctorate
Library Holdings: Bk Vols 6,000,000; Per Subs 50,245
Special Collections: 19th Century American Literature; Architectural Drawings (Seattle & Puget Sound); Book Arts; Can & European Communities; Early Recorded Vocal Music (Eric Offenbacher Mozart Coll); Hans Christian Anderson; Historical Children's Literature; Historical Photography (particularly western Washington, Alaska & Yukon); Pacific Northwest & Alaska; Pacific Northwest Native Americans; Pacific Northwest Poets; Papers of Richard Hugo, Theodore Roethke, Anna Louise Strong, Mark Tobey, Senator Henry M Jackson, Senator Warren G Magnuson & other 20th Century Senators & Representatives from Washington State; Rowing Books; Seattle Jewish Archives; Seattle Theater Programs; Travel & Exploration; William Blake; William Butler Yeats; Wind Instrument Records (Melvin Harris Coll). Oral History; State Document Depository; UN Document Depository; US Document Depository
Automation Activity & Vendor Info: (Acquisitions) Innovative Interfaces, Inc; (Cataloging) Innovative Interfaces, Inc; (Circulation) Innovative Interfaces, Inc; (Serials) Innovative Interfaces, Inc
Wireless access
Publications: Library Directions
Partic in Association of Research Libraries; OCLC Online Computer Library Center, Inc; OCLC Research Library Partnership; Orbis Cascade Alliance
Open Mon-Fri 8-5
Friends of the Library Group
Departmental Libraries:
ART, Arts Bldg, Rm 101, Box 353440, 98195-3440, SAN 364-0205. Tel: 206-543-0648. Web Site: www.lib.washington.edu/art. *Head of Music, Art & Drama Libraries,* Kathryn Miller; E-mail: kmill81@uw.edu; *Fine & Performing Arts Librn,* Madison Sullivan; E-mail: madds@uw.edu
Library Holdings: Bk Vols 44,000
BOTHELL CAMPUS/CASCADIA COLLEGE LIBRARY, University of Washington Bothell, 18225 Campus Way NE, Box 358550, Bothell, 98011-8245. Tel: 425-352-5340. Reference Tel: 425-352-3146. *Facilities Coordr,* Nermina Halilovic; E-mail: nerminah@uw.edu; *Head, Coll, Head, Support Serv,* Suzan Parker; E-mail: sparkerz@uw.edu; *Head, Libr Tech,* Rob Estes; E-mail: restes@uw.edu; *Head, Pub Serv,* Heather Cyre; E-mail: hcyre@uw.edu; *Head, Teaching & Learning Serv,* Leslie Hurst; E-mail: lhurst@uw.edu; *Access Serv Mgr,* Tami Garrard; E-mail: tgarrard@uw.edu
Partic in Washington Community & Technical Colleges Library Consortium
BUILT ENVIRONMENTS LIBRARY, 334 Gould Hall, Box 355730, 98195-5730, SAN 364-0175. Tel: 206-543-4067. Web Site: www.lib.washington.edu/be. *Head of Libr,* Alan R Michelson; Tel: 206-543-7091, E-mail: alanmich@uw.edu
Library Holdings: Bk Vols 41,357
Subject Interests: Archit, Construction mgt, Landscape archit, Urban design, Urban planning
Open Mon-Thurs 8am-9pm, Fri 8-5, Sat & Sun 1-5 (Fall); Mon-Fri 9-5 (Summer)
Friends of the Library Group
DRAMA, Hutchinson Hall, Rm 145, Box 353950, 98195-3950, SAN 364-0299. Tel: 206-543-5148. FAX: 206-543-8512. Web Site: www.lib.washington.edu/drama. *Head of Music, Art & Drama Libraries,* Kathryn Miller; E-mail: kmill81@uw.edu; *Fine & Performing Arts Librn,* Madison Sullivan; E-mail: madds@uw.edu
Library Holdings: Bk Vols 29,600
Special Collections: Acting Editions of Plays
Friends of the Library Group
ENGINEERING LIBRARY, Engineering Library Bldg, Box 352170, 98195-2170, SAN 364-0353. Tel: 206-543-0740. Circulation Tel: 206-685-8324. Reference Tel: 206-543-0741. FAX: 206-543-3305. E-mail: englib@uw.edu. Web Site: www.lib.washington.edu/engineering. *Head, Eng Libr,* Mel DeSart; Tel: 206-685-8369, E-mail: desart@uw.edu; *Asst Head,* Christina A Byrne; Tel: 206-685-8371, E-mail: cbyrne@uw.edu; *Info Serv Librn,* Julie Cook; E-mail: julesck@uw.edu; *Sci, Tech, Eng & Math Librn,* Kira Wyld; E-mail: kwyld@uw.edu
Library Holdings: Bk Vols 164,536; Per Subs 3,136
Special Collections: ACM Depository Coll; Technical Reports; United States Patent & Depository Library
Open Mon-Thurs 8am-10pm, Fri 8-6, Sat 9-5, Sun 1-10 (Fall); Mon-Thurs 8-7, Fri 8-5, Sat & Sun 1-5 (Summer)
Friends of the Library Group

FISHERIES-OCEANOGRAPHY, Suzzallo Library, Research Services, Box 352900, 98195-2900, SAN 364-0388. Tel: 206-685-2126. FAX: 206-685-1665. Web Site: www.lib.washington.edu/fish. *Sci Librn,* Maureen M Nolan; E-mail: nolan@uw.edu. Subject Specialists: *Environ sci, Marine sci,* Maureen M Nolan
Library Holdings: Bk Vols 66,834
Open Mon-Thurs 8am-9pm, Fri 8-5, Sat & Sun 1-5 (Fall); Mon-Fri 8-5 (Summer)
Friends of the Library Group

FOSTER BUSINESS, Paccar Hall, 1st Flr, Box 353224, 98195-3224, SAN 364-023X. Tel: 206-543-4360. FAX: 206-616-6430. *Br Operations Supvr,* Dan Halligan; E-mail: ten@uw.edu; Staff 8 (MLS 4, Non-MLS 4)
Library Holdings: Bk Vols 76,337

FRIDAY HARBOR LIBRARY, 620 University Rd, Box 351812, Friday Harbor, 98250-2900. Tel: 206-616-0758. FAX: 206-543-1273. Web Site: www.lib.washington.edu/fhl. *Librn,* Maureen D Nolan; Tel: 206-685-2126, E-mail: nolan@uw.edu; Staff 2 (MLS 1, Non-MLS 1)
Library Holdings: Bk Vols 18,000
Function: For res purposes
Open Mon-Thurs 7:30am-10pm, Fri 7:30-6, Sat 9-5, Sun Noon-10 (Fall); Mon-Thurs 8am-10pm, Fri 8-5, Sat & Sun 1-5 (Summer)
Friends of the Library Group

CL GALLAGHER LAW LIBRARY, William H Gates Hall, 4000 15th Ave NE, 98195-3020. (Mail add: Box 353025, 38195-3025), SAN 364-0531. Tel: 206-543-6794. FAX: 206-685-2165. E-mail: lawref@uw.edu. Web Site: lib.law.uw.edu. *Assoc Dean, Libr & Info Serv,* Anna Endter; Tel: 206-685-4084, E-mail: aendter@uw.edu; *Head, Pub Serv,* Alena Wolotira; Tel: 206-685-4812, E-mail: alenaw@uw.edu; *Librn, Digital Initiatives,* Cheryl Nyberg; Tel: 206-685-4924, E-mail: cnyberg@uw.edu; *Pub Serv Librn,* Mary Whisner; Tel: 206-543-7672, E-mail: whisner@uw.edu; *Res Sharing Librn,* Judy Ann Davis; Tel: 206-543-4262, E-mail: davisja@uw.edu; *Coll Develop Coordr,* Peggy Jarrett; Tel: 206-543-1941, E-mail: pjarrett@uw.edu; *Coordr, Tech Serv,* Ann Nez; Tel: 206-221-6114, E-mail: acnez@uw.edu; Staff 32 (MLS 14, Non-MLS 18)
Founded 1899. Enrl 715; Fac 50; Highest Degree: Doctorate
Library Holdings: Bk Titles 179,568; Per Subs 5,273
Special Collections: East Asian Legal Materials; Washington State Legal Materials - Historical & Current. US Document Depository
Subject Interests: Indian law, Librarianship, Water law
Automation Activity & Vendor Info: (Acquisitions) Innovative Interfaces, Inc; (Cataloging) Innovative Interfaces, Inc; (Circulation) Innovative Interfaces, Inc; (OPAC) Innovative Interfaces, Inc; (Serials) Innovative Interfaces, Inc
Function: Art exhibits, Computers for patron use, Doc delivery serv, Electronic databases & coll, ILL available, Internet access, Learning ctr, Magnifiers for reading, Online cat, Online ref, Photocopying/Printing, Ref serv available
Partic in OCLC Online Computer Library Center, Inc
Publications: Current Index to Legal Periodicals; Marian Gould Gallagher Library Publication Series
Open Mon-Thurs 8am-11pm, Fri 8-6, Sat 11-6, Sun 11-11 (Spring-Fall); Mon-Wed 8-7, Thurs & Fri 8-5, Sun 11-6 (Summer)
Restriction: 24-hr pass syst for students only
Friends of the Library Group

CM HEALTH SCIENCES LIBRARY, T-334 Health Sciences Bldg, 1959 NE Pacific St, Box 357155, 98195-7155, SAN 364-0507. Tel: 206-543-3390. Interlibrary Loan Service Tel: 206-543-1878. FAX: 206-543-3389. E-mail: hsl@u.washington.edu. Web Site: healthlinks.washington.edu. *Dir,* Tania P Bardyn; Tel: 206-543-0427, E-mail: bardyn@uw.edu; *Assoc Dir,* Cathy Burroughs; Tel: 206-543-9261, E-mail: cburroug@uw.edu; *Asst Dir,* Emily Patridge; Tel: 206-221-3489, E-mail: ep001@uw.edu; *Asst Dir, Syst,* Adam Garrett; Tel: 206-616-4142, E-mail: garrett@uw.edu. Subject Specialists: *Clinical, Data serv,* Emily Patridge; Staff 28 (MLS 21, Non-MLS 7)
Founded 1949
Special Collections: History of Medicine
Subject Interests: Allied health, Dentistry, Med, Nursing, Pharm, Pub health
Partic in Greater Western Library Alliance; National Network of Libraries of Medicine Region 5; OCLC Online Computer Library Center, Inc
Friends of the Library Group

MAP COLLECTION & CARTOGRAPHIC INFORMATION SERVICES, Suzzallo Library, Ground Flr, Universtiy of Washington, Box 352900, 98195-2900, SAN 329-3556. Tel: 206-543-4164. FAX: 206-685-8049. E-mail: maplib@uw.edu. *Librn,* Matthew Parsons; Tel: 206-543-2725, E-mail: parsonsm@uw.edu
Library Holdings: Bk Vols 3,966
Special Collections: Aerial Photography of Washington State, 1944 to present; US Geological Survey Topographic Maps
Subject Interests: Atlases, Geog info systs

MATHEMATICS RESEARCH LIBRARY, Padelford Hall C-306, Box 354350, 98195-4350, SAN 364-0566. Tel: 206-543-7296. Web Site: www.lib.washington.edu/math. *Head of Libr,* Mel DeSart; E-mail: desart@uw.edu; *Sci, Tech, Eng & Math Librn,* Kira Wyld; Tel: 206-685-1469, E-mail: kwyld@uw.edu; Staff 2 (MLS 1, Non-MLS 1)
Library Holdings: Bk Vols 62,192
Subject Interests: Math, Statistics
Open Mon-Thurs 9-6, Fri 9-5, Sun 1-5 (Winter); Mon-Fri 9-5 (Summer)
Friends of the Library Group

MUSIC, 113 Music Bldg, Box 353450, 98195-3450, SAN 364-0590. Tel: 206-543-1159, 206-543-1168. E-mail: musinfo@uw.edu. Web Site: www.lib.washington.edu/music. *Head of Music, Art & Drama Libraries,* Kathryn Miller; E-mail: kmill81@uw.edu; *Head, Media Serv,* John Vallier; E-mail: vallier@uw.edu; *Art Librn, Humanities Librn,* Dylan Burns; E-mail: dburns5@uw.edu; Staff 2.4 (MLS 2.4)
Library Holdings: Bk Vols 60,437
Special Collections: American Music Coll; Harris Wind Instrument Recordings Coll; Offenbacher Mozart Coll
Subject Interests: Music
Open Mon-Thurs 8-8, Fri 8-5, Sat & Sun 1-5 (Fall); Mon-Fri 8-5 (Summer)
Friends of the Library Group

ODEGAARD UNDERGRADUATE LIBRARY, Box 353080, 98195-3080, SAN 364-0116. Tel: 206-543-2990. Administration Tel: 206-685-3752. FAX: 206-685-8485. E-mail: ougl@uw.edu. Web Site: www.lib.washington.edu/ougl. *Dir,* Gordon Aamot; Tel: 206-616-6431, E-mail: aamot@uw.edu; *Ref Coordr,* Kathleen Collins; Tel: 206-685-2771, E-mail: collinsk@uw.edu
Founded 1972
Library Holdings: Bk Vols 180,118
Open Mon-Thurs 8am-10pm, Fri 8-5, Sat 11-5, Sun 1pm-10pm
Friends of the Library Group

TACOMA LIBRARY, 1900 Commerce St, Box 358460, Tacoma, 98402-3100. Tel: 253-692-4440. Reference Tel: 253-692-4442. FAX: 253-692-4445. E-mail: taclib@uw.edu. Web Site: www.tacoma.uw.edu/library. *Assoc Dean & Dir of Libr Serv,* Annie Downey; Tel: 253-692-4444, E-mail: adowney@uw.edu; *Head, Commun Outreach,* Anna Salyer; Tel: 253-692-4448, E-mail: anna3@uw.edu; *Head, Libr Info Tech,* Timothy Bostelle; Tel: 253-692-4650, E-mail: tbostell@uw.edu; *Head, Ref Serv,* Suzanne Klinger; Tel: 253-692-4443, E-mail: alaura@uw.edu; *Instrul Design Librn,* Marisa Petrich; Tel: 253-692-4651, E-mail: marisp2@uw.edu; *Access Serv Mgr,* Hannah Wilson; Tel: 253-692-4391, E-mail: wilsonhd@uw.edu; *Supvr, Access Serv,* Marcia Monroe; Tel: 253-692-4446, E-mail: marcy@uw.edu; *Libr Tech,* Wade Haddaway; Tel: 253-692-5746, E-mail: wadeh@uw.edu; *Electronic Res Tech,* Megan Gregory; Tel: 253-692-4657, E-mail: meganes0@uw.edu; *Media Tech,* Jamal Gabobe; Tel: 253-692-4643, E-mail: jamali@uw.edu; *Ser/Reserves Tech,* Gwen Kempe; Tel: 253-692-5748, E-mail: glewis@uw.edu
Open Mon-Thurs 7am-Midnight, Fri 7-5, Sat & Sun 9-5 (Winter); Mon-Thurs 8am-9pm, Fri 8-5, Sat 9-5 (Summer)
Friends of the Library Group

TATEUCHI EAST ASIA LIBRARY, 322 Gowen Hall, Box 353527, 98195-3527, SAN 364-0329. Tel: 206-543-4490. FAX: 206-221-5298. E-mail: uwlib-ealcirc@uw.edu. Web Site: www.lib.washington.edu/east-asia. *Interim Dir,* Hyokyoung Yi; Tel: 206-543-6603, E-mail: hkyi@uw.edu; *Circ Supvr,* Button Le; E-mail: lab@uw.edu; Staff 12 (MLS 6, Non-MLS 6)
Founded 1937. Highest Degree: Doctorate
Library Holdings: Bk Vols 450,811; Per Subs 2,728
Open Mon-Thurs 8-8, Fri 8-5, Sat & Sun 1-5 (Fall); Mon-Fri 9-5, Sat & Sun 1-5 (Summer)
Friends of the Library Group

P WASHINGTON TALKING BOOK & BRAILLE LIBRARY*, 2021 Ninth Ave, 98121. SAN 317-655X. Tel: 206-615-0400. Administration Tel: 206-615-1588. Toll Free Tel: 800-542-0866. FAX: 206-615-0437. E-mail: wtbbl@sos.wa.gov. Web Site: www.wtbbl.org. *Regional Libr Dir,* Danielle Miller; E-mail: danielle.miller@sos.wa.gov; *Electronic Serv & Instruction Librn,* Herrick Heitman; E-mail: herrick.heitman@sos.wa.gov; *Youth Serv Librn,* Erin Groth; E-mail: erin.groth@sos.wa.gov; *Mgr, Borrower Serv, Outreach Serv,* Amy Ravenholt; E-mail: amy.ravenholt@sos.wa.gov; Staff 18 (MLS 5, Non-MLS 13)
Founded 1931
Library Holdings: Bk Vols 311,000
Special Collections: Northwest Coll; Reference Materials on Blindness & Other Disabilities; Volunteer Produced Braille & Tapes
Automation Activity & Vendor Info: (Acquisitions) Keystone Systems, Inc (KLAS); (Cataloging) Keystone Systems, Inc (KLAS); (Circulation) Keystone Systems, Inc (KLAS); (OPAC) Keystone Systems, Inc (KLAS)
Publications: Catalog of Locally Produced Titles; Large Print Calendar; Newsletters
Special Services for the Blind - Closed circuit TV; Radio reading serv
Open Mon-Fri 8:30-5

SEDRO-WOOLLEY

P CENTRAL SKAGIT LIBRARY DISTRICT*, Sedro-Woolley Public Library, 110 W State St, 98284-1551. SAN 317-6576. Tel: 360-755-3985. E-mail: admin@centralskagitlibrary.org. Web Site: centralskagitlibrary.org. *Libr Dir,* Jeanne Williams; E-mail: jeanne@centralskagitlibrary.org; *Youth Serv Spec,* Allia Allen; E-mail: allia@centralskagitlibrary.org
Pop 26,000; Circ 85,000
Library Holdings: AV Mats 2,000; Bk Vols 50,000; Per Subs 140
Automation Activity & Vendor Info: (Cataloging) TLC (The Library Corporation); (Circulation) TLC (The Library Corporation); (OPAC) TLC (The Library Corporation)
Wireless access
Function: 24/7 Electronic res, 24/7 Online cat, Art programs, Audiobks via web, Bi-weekly Writer's Group, Bilingual assistance for Spanish patrons, Bk club(s), Bks on CD, Children's prog, Computer training, Computers for patron use, Digital talking bks, Electronic databases & coll, Family literacy, Free DVD rentals, Internet access, Life-long learning prog for all ages, Magazines, Magnifiers for reading, Movies, Online cat, OverDrive digital audio bks, Photocopying/Printing, Preschool outreach, Prog for adults, Prog for children & young adult, Scanner, Spanish lang bks, STEM programs, Story hour, Summer & winter reading prog, Summer reading prog, Tax forms, Teen prog, Telephone ref, Wheelchair accessible, Winter reading prog, Workshops, Writing prog
Open Mon-Thurs 10-8, Fri & Sat 10-5
Friends of the Library Group
Bookmobiles: 1. Bk vols 2,000

SEQUIM

S JAMESTOWN S'KLALLAM TRIBAL LIBRARY*, 1070 Old Blyn Hwy, 98382. (Mail add: 1033 Old Blyn Hwy, 98382). Tel: 360-681-4632. FAX: 360-681-4655. E-mail: library@jamestowntribe.org. Web Site: library.jamestowntribe.org/home, www.jamestowntribe.org/library. *Librn,* Bonnie Roos
Wireless access
Open Mon-Fri 9-5, Sat 9-4
Bookmobiles: 1

SHORELINE

J SHORELINE COMMUNITY COLLEGE, Ray W Howard Library, 16101 Greenwood Ave N, 98133-5696. SAN 317-6436. Tel: 206-533-2548. E-mail: library@shoreline.edu. Web Site: library.shoreline.edu. *Exec Director, Learning Resources,* Dawn Lowe-Wincentsen; E-mail: dlowe-wincentsen@shoreline.edu; *Digital & Electronic Resources Librn,* Caitlan Maxwell; E-mail: cmaxwell@shoreline.edu; *Outreach & Inclusion Librarian,* Allison Fader; E-mail: afader@shoreline.edu; *Professional Technical Librn,* Carolyn Callaghan; E-mail: ccallaghan@shoreline.edu; *Web & Usability Librarian,* Lauren Bryant; E-mail: lbryant@shoreline.edu; *Access Services Lead,* River Zorich; E-mail: rzorich@shoreline.edu; *Technical Services Lead,* Saint Jean Devereux; E-mail: sdevereux@shoreline.edu; Staff 12 (MLS 6, Non-MLS 6)
Founded 1964. Enrl 3,804; Fac 150; Highest Degree: Bachelor
Automation Activity & Vendor Info: (Acquisitions) Ex Libris Group; (Cataloging) Ex Libris Group; (Circulation) Ex Libris Group; (Course Reserve) Ex Libris Group; (ILL) OCLC; (Media Booking) Springshare, LLC; (OPAC) Ex Libris Group; (Serials) Ex Libris Group
Wireless access
Special Services for the Deaf - TTY equip; Videos & decoder
Special Services for the Blind - Copier with enlargement capabilities; Large screen computer & software; Magnifiers; Reader equip; Ref serv; Screen reader software; VisualTek equip; ZoomText magnification & reading software
Open Mon-Thurs 8-7, Fri 8-4:30

SPOKANE

SR CATHOLIC DIOCESAN ARCHIVES*, 525 E Mission Ave, 99202. (Mail add: PO Box 1453, 99201-1453), SAN 328-1450. Tel: 509-358-7336. Web Site: dioceseofspokane.org/archives2. *Archivist,* Mary Cole; *Archivist,* Rev Mike Savelesky; E-mail: msavelesky@dioceseofspokane.org
Library Holdings: Bk Vols 2,000
Special Collections: Church; Eastern Washington Catholic Church History Coll; Western American Coll. Oral History
Restriction: Open by appt only

CM EASTERN WASHINGTON UNIVERSITY*, 600 N Riverpoint Blvd, Rm 230, 99202. (Mail add: 412 E Spokane Falls Blvd, 99202), SAN 324-6183. Tel: 509-358-7930. Administration Tel: 509-368-6973. FAX: 509-358-7928. E-mail: spok.lib@wsu.edu. Web Site: spokane.wsu.edu/library, www.ewu.edu/library/spokane. *Dir,* Ann Dyer; E-mail: ann.dyer@wsu.edu; *Asst Dir,* Jonathan Potter; E-mail: jonathan.potter@wsu.edu; *Head, Res Serv,* Electra Enslow; E-mail: electra.enslow@wsu.edu; *Bus Librn, Health Sci Librn,* Kelly Evans; E-mail: kevans21@wsu.edu; *Acq, Circ, Reserves,* Michelanne Adams; E-mail: madams@wsu.edu. Subject Specialists: *Health sci,* Electra Enslow; Staff 9 (MLS 4, Non-MLS 5)
Founded 1969. Enrl 3,000; Fac 150; Highest Degree: Doctorate
Library Holdings: Bk Titles 10,000; Bk Vols 11,000; Per Subs 190
Subject Interests: Acctg, Bus, Communication disorders, Dental hygiene, Health informatics, Health serv admin, Nursing, Nutrition, Occupational therapy, Phys therapy, Pub admin, Pub health, Urban planning
Automation Activity & Vendor Info: (Acquisitions) Ex Libris Group; (Circulation) Ex Libris Group; (Course Reserve) Docutek; (OPAC) Ex Libris Group; (Serials) Ex Libris Group
Wireless access

C GONZAGA UNIVERSITY*, Foley Center Library, 502 E Boone Ave, 99258-0095. SAN 364-0868. Tel: 509-313-6533. Circulation Tel: 509-313-5803. Reference Tel: 509-313-5931. Toll Free Tel: 800-498-5941. FAX: 509-313-5904. E-mail: refdesk@gonzaga.edu. Web Site: www.gonzaga.edu/academics/libraries/foley-library. *Interim Dean,* Heather James; E-mail: jamesh@gonzaga.edu; *Assoc Dean, Libr Serv,* Brad Matthies; E-mail: matthies@gonzaga.edu; *Cat Librn,* Sydney Chambers; Tel: 509-313-6537, E-mail: chambers@gonzaga.edu; *Engagement Librn, Instruction Librn,* Anthony Tardiff; Tel: 509-313-3844; *Instruction Librn,* Catlin Bagley; Tel: 509-313-6529, E-mail: bagley@gonzaga.edu; *Spec Coll Librn,* Stephanie Plowman; Tel: 509-323-3847, E-mail: plowman@gonzaga.edu; *Supvr, User Serv,* Laura Hutton; Tel: 509-313-3813, E-mail: hutton@gonzaga.edu; *Instruction Coordr,* Kelly O'Brien Jenks; Tel: 509-313-3829, E-mail: jenks@gonzaga.edu; *Ref Coordr,* John Spencer; Tel: 509-313-6110, E-mail: spencer@gonzaga.edu; Staff 30 (MLS 10, Non-MLS 20)
Founded 1992. Enrl 4,800; Fac 340; Highest Degree: Doctorate
Library Holdings: e-books 500; e-journals 18,000; Bk Titles 250,192; Bk Vols 305,517; Per Subs 1,169
Special Collections: Bing Crosby Coll, bks, memorabilia, papers & rec; Jesuitica; Labor Unions (Jay Fox Coll); Pacific Northwest History, bks & mss; Victorian Poetry (Gerard Manley Hopkins Coll)
Subject Interests: Behav sci, Philos, Relig studies, Soc sci
Automation Activity & Vendor Info: (Acquisitions) Ex Libris Group; (Cataloging) Ex Libris Group; (Circulation) Ex Libris Group; (Course Reserve) Ex Libris Group; (ILL) OCLC ILLiad; (OPAC) Ex Libris Group; (Serials) Ex Libris Group
Wireless access
Open Mon-Thurs 7:30am-2am, Fri 7:30am-9pm, Sat 10am-6pm, Sun 10am-2am

CL GONZAGA UNIVERSITY SCHOOL OF LAW*, Chastek Library, 721 N Cincinnati St, 99220. SAN 364-0892. Tel: 509-313-5792. Interlibrary Loan Service Tel: 509-323-3755. Reference Tel: 509-313-3758. Administration Tel: 509-313-3781. Toll Free Tel: 800-986-9585. FAX: 509-313-5733. Interlibrary Loan Service FAX: 509-323-5882. Administration FAX: 509-313-5534. Circulation E-mail: circdesk@gonzaga.edu. Web Site: www.gonzaga.edu/school-of-law/academics/chastek-library. *Dir,* Patrick Charles; Tel: 509-313-3739, E-mail: charles@gonzaga.edu; *Head, ILL,* Carolyn Hood; E-mail: hood@gonzaga.edu; *Head, Pub Serv,* Ashley Sundin; Tel: 509-313-3753, E-mail: sundin@gonzaga.edu; *Head, Tech Serv,* Marilyn Johnson; Tel: 509-313-3761, E-mail: johnsonm3@gonzaga.edu; *Cat Librn,* Kimberly Martin; E-mail: martink@gonzaga.edu; *Pub Serv Librn,* Sharalyn Williams; E-mail: williamss2@gonzaga.edu; Staff 8 (MLS 5, Non-MLS 3)
Founded 1912. Enrl 626; Fac 23; Highest Degree: Doctorate
Library Holdings: Bk Titles 34,845; Bk Vols 153,433; Per Subs 2,585
Special Collections: ABA Archives; American Indian Selected Publications; Canon Law Materials; Federal Legislative Histories; Heins American Law Institution Publications; Hein's Legal Thesis & Dissertations; Karl Llewellyn Papers; Scrapbooks of the Honorable Richard Guy; Selected 19th Century Treatises. US Document Depository
Automation Activity & Vendor Info: (Acquisitions) Ex Libris Group; (Cataloging) Ex Libris Group; (Circulation) Ex Libris Group; (Course Reserve) Ex Libris Group; (ILL) OCLC; (OPAC) Ex Libris Group; (Serials) Ex Libris Group
Wireless access
Function: AV serv, Doc delivery serv, ILL available, Photocopying/Printing, Ref serv available, Res libr, Telephone ref, Wheelchair accessible
Publications: Adjunct Faculty User Guide (Library handbook); Faculty User Guide (Library handbook); On Point (Newsletter); Pathfinders (Research guide); Student User Guide (Library handbook)
Partic in NELLCO Law Library Consortium, Inc.; OCLC Online Computer Library Center, Inc
Open Mon-Thurs 7am-10pm, Fri 7-6, Sat 9-6, Sun Noon-10
Restriction: Circ limited, In-house use for visitors

GM MANN-GRANDSTAFF VA MEDICAL CENTER*, Health Library, 4815 N Assembly St, 99205-2697. SAN 317-6770. Tel: 509-434-7575. FAX: 509-434-7103. E-mail: spolibrary@med.va.gov. Web Site: www.va.gov/spokane-health-care. *Mgr,* Mark Overman; E-mail: mark.overman@va.gov

Founded 1951
Library Holdings: Bk Titles 300
Subject Interests: Med, Mgt develop
Restriction: Open to staff only

S NORTHWEST MUSEUM OF ART & CULTURE-EASTERN WASHINGTON STATE HISTORICAL SOCIETY*, Joel E Ferris Research Library & Archives, 2316 W First Ave, 99201-1099. SAN 317-6665. Tel: 509-363-5313, 509-363-5342. E-mail: archives@northwestmuseum.org. Web Site: www.northwestmuseum.org. *Archives Curator, Curator, Spec Coll,* Anna Harbine; *Ref Archivist,* Alex Fergus; Staff 2 (MLS 1, Non-MLS 1)
Founded 1916
Library Holdings: Bk Titles 12,000; Per Subs 20
Special Collections: Manuscript Coll; Photographic Coll. Oral History
Subject Interests: Archit, Films, Hist of mining, Inland NW hist, Plateau Indian cultures, Plateau Indian hist, Women's hist
Wireless access
Function: Archival coll, For res purposes, Govt ref serv, Internet access, Masonic res mat, Photocopying/Printing, Ref serv available, Res assist avail, Res libr
Publications: Libbys' Spokane: A Visual Retrospect 1980; Nolan: A Guide to the Cutter Collection 1984; Nolan: A Night of Terror, Devastation, & Awful Woe; the Spokane Fire of 1889 (1989); Nolan: Frank Palmer, Scenic Photographer 1987; Nolan: Guide to Manuscript Collection 1987
Partic in Orbis Cascade Alliance
Restriction: Closed stack, In-house use for visitors, Non-circulating coll, Open by appt only, Open to pub for ref only, Researchers by appt only, Visitors must make appt to use bks in the libr

M PROVIDENCE SACRED HEART MEDICAL CENTER*, Sacred Heart Library, 101 W Eighth Ave, 99204. SAN 317-669X. Tel: 509-474-3094. FAX: 509-474-4475. E-mail: librarian@providence.org. Web Site: washington.providence.org. *Librn,* Sandy Keno; *Libr Tech,* Gail Leong; Staff 1 (MLS 1)
Library Holdings: Bk Vols 500
Subject Interests: Admin, Allied health, Med, Nursing
Wireless access
Open Mon-Fri 8-4:30

J SPOKANE COMMUNITY COLLEGE/COMMUNITY COLLEGES OF SPOKANE LIBRARY*, MS 2160, 1810 N Greene St, 99217-5399. SAN 317-6711. Tel: 509-533-7055. Circulation Tel: 509-533-8255. Reference Tel: 509-533-8821. Toll Free Tel: 800-248-5644. Web Site: www.scc.spokane.edu/for-our-students/libraries. *Dean of Extended Learning,* Jaclyn Jacot; E-mail: jaclyn.jacot@scc.spokane.edu; *Librn,* Timothy Aman; Tel: 509-533-7054, E-mail: tim.aman@scc.spokane.edu; *Librn,* Linda Keyes; Tel: 509-533-7653, E-mail: linda.keyes@scc.spokane.edu; *Librn,* Melinda Martin; Tel: 509-533-8822, E-mail: melinda.martin@scc.spokane.edu; *Librn,* Jane Odlevak; Tel: 509-533-7046, E-mail: janine.odlevak@scc.spokane.edu; Staff 7 (MLS 4, Non-MLS 3)
Founded 1963. Enrl 5,982; Fac 245
Library Holdings: AV Mats 1,600; e-books 150,000; e-journals 23,512; Bk Titles 48,000; Per Subs 100
Special Collections: Career Center
Subject Interests: Agr, Health sci, Law, Nursing
Automation Activity & Vendor Info: (Acquisitions) Ex Libris Group; (Cataloging) Ex Libris Group; (Circulation) Ex Libris Group; (Course Reserve) Ex Libris Group; (Discovery) Ex Libris Group; (ILL) OCLC ILLiad; (OPAC) Ex Libris Group
Wireless access
Partic in OCLC Online Computer Library Center, Inc; Washington Community & Technical Colleges Library Consortium
Open Mon-Thurs 7:30-7, Fri 7:30-4, Sat 10-2; Mon-Thurs 8-2, Fri 8-Noon (Summer)

GL SPOKANE COUNTY LAW LIBRARY, Spokane County Courthouse, 2nd Flr, 1116 W Broadway, 99260. SAN 317-6738. Tel: 509-477-3680. Web Site: www.spokanecounty.org/1086/law-library. *Dir, Law Librn,* Cynthia R Lucas; E-mail: clucas@spokanecounty.org. Subject Specialists: *Govt,* Cynthia R Lucas
Founded 1920
Automation Activity & Vendor Info: (Cataloging) LibraryWorld, Inc; (Circulation) LibraryWorld, Inc; (OPAC) LibraryWorld, Inc
Wireless access
Open Mon-Fri 8:30-4

P SPOKANE COUNTY LIBRARY DISTRICT*, Administrative Offices, 4322 N Argonne Rd, 99212. SAN 364-0922. Tel: 509-893-8200. FAX: 509-893-8472. Administration E-mail: admin@scld.org. Web Site: www.scld.org. *Exec Dir,* Patrick Roewe; E-mail: proewe@scld.org; *Dir of Finance,* Rick Knorr; E-mail: rknorr@scld.org; *Human Res Dir,* Toni Costa; E-mail: tcosta@scld.org; *Dir, Coll Serv,* Andrea Sharps; E-mail: asharps@scld.org; *Operations Dir,* Doug Stumbough; E-mail: dstumbough@scld.org; *Communications & Develop Officer,* Jane Baker; E-mail: jbaker@scld.org; Staff 32.5 (MLS 6.8, Non-MLS 25.7)
Founded 1942. Pop 252,230; Circ 2,749,618
Library Holdings: Audiobooks 50,450; CDs 17,748; DVDs 38,590; e-books 22,333; Large Print Bks 14,027; Microforms 4; Bk Titles 133,406; Bk Vols 349,197; Per Subs 1,422; Videos 206
Automation Activity & Vendor Info: (Acquisitions) SirsiDynix; (Cataloging) SirsiDynix; (Circulation) SirsiDynix; (ILL) OCLC; (OPAC) SirsiDynix; (Serials) SirsiDynix
Wireless access
Function: Adult bk club, Art exhibits, Audiobks via web, Bks on cassette, Bks on CD, Children's prog, Computer training, Computers for patron use, Digital talking bks, Electronic databases & coll, Free DVD rentals, ILL available, Internet access, Magnifiers for reading, Music CDs, Online cat, Online ref, Outreach serv, Outside serv via phone, mail, e-mail & web, OverDrive digital audio bks, Photocopying/Printing, Preschool outreach, Prog for adults, Prog for children & young adult, Ref & res, Ref serv available, Senior outreach, Story hour, Summer reading prog, Teen prog, Telephone ref, Wheelchair accessible
Partic in OCLC Online Computer Library Center, Inc
Open Mon-Fri 8-4:30
Friends of the Library Group
Branches: 11
AIRWAY HEIGHTS LIBRARY, 1213 S Lundstrom, Airway Heights, 99001-9000, SAN 370-1026. Tel: 509-893-8250. FAX: 509-893-8473. Circulation E-mail: ahstaff@scld.org. *Libr Supvr,* Crystal Miller; Staff 3 (MLS 1, Non-MLS 2)
Circ 52,225
Open Tues & Thurs 10-8, Wed & Sat 10-6, Sun 1-5
Friends of the Library Group
ARGONNE LIBRARY, 4322 N Argonne Rd, 99212-1868, SAN 364-1074. Tel: 509-893-8260. FAX: 509-893-8474. Circulation E-mail: ahstaff@scld.org. *Libr Supvr,* Pat Davis; Staff 6 (MLS 1, Non-MLS 5)
Circ 146,373
Open Mon-Wed 10-8, Thurs-Sat 10-6
Friends of the Library Group
CHENEY LIBRARY, 610 First St, Cheney, 99004-1688, SAN 364-0957. Tel: 509-893-8280. FAX: 509-893-8475. *Libr Supvr,* Catherine Lowry; Staff 6 (MLS 1, Non-MLS 5)
Circ 153,012
Open Mon-Wed 10-8, Thurs-Sat 10-6, Sun 1-5
Friends of the Library Group
DEER PARK LIBRARY, 208 S Forest, Deer Park, 99006. (Mail add: PO Box 729, Deer Park, 99006-0729), SAN 364-0981. Tel: 509-893-8300. FAX: 509-893-8476. Circulation E-mail: dpcirc@scld.org. *Libr Supvr,* Kris Barnes; E-mail: kbarnes@scld.org; Staff 4.7 (Non-MLS 4.7)
Circ 144,862
Open Mon-Wed 10-8, Thurs-Sat 10-6, Sun 1-5
Friends of the Library Group
FAIRFIELD LIBRARY, 305 E Main, Fairfield, 99012. (Mail add: PO Box 48, Fairfield, 99012-0048), SAN 364-1015. Tel: 509-893-8320. FAX: 509-893-8477. Circulation E-mail: ffcirc@scld.org. *Operations Mgr,* Kristy Bateman; E-mail: kbateman@scld.org; Staff 3 (MLS 1, Non-MLS 2)
Circ 20,303
Open Tues 10-8, Thurs & Sat 10-6
Friends of the Library Group
MEDICAL LAKE LIBRARY, 321 E Herb, Medical Lake, 99022. (Mail add: PO Box 249, Medical Lake, 99022-0249), SAN 364-104X. Tel: 509-893-8330. FAX: 509-893-8479. Circulation E-mail: mlcirc@scld.org. *Libr Supvr,* Cecelia McMullen; E-mail: cmcmullen@scld.org; Staff 3 (MLS 1, Non-MLS 2)
Circ 51,262
Open Mon & Wed 10-8, Sat 10-6
Friends of the Library Group
MORAN PRAIRIE LIBRARY, 6004 S Regal St, 99223-6949. Tel: 509-893-8340. FAX: 509-893-8480. Circulation E-mail: mpcirc@scld.org. *Libr Supvr,* Caitlin Wheeler; E-mail: cwheeler@scld.org; Staff 5.4 (Non-MLS 5.4)
Circ 169,897
Open Mon-Wed 10-8, Thurs-Sat 10-6, Sun 1-5
Friends of the Library Group
NORTH SPOKANE LIBRARY, 44 E Hawthorne Rd, 99218-1597, SAN 364-1104. Tel: 509-893-8350. FAX: 509-893-8481. Circulation E-mail: nscirc@scld.org. *Managing Librn,* Brian Vander Veen; E-mail: bvanderveen@scld.org; Staff 26.5 (MLS 8.1, Non-MLS 18.4)
Circ 514,608
Open Mon-Thurs 10-9, Fri & Sat 10-6, Sun 1-5
Friends of the Library Group
OTIS ORCHARDS LIBRARY, 22324 E Wellesley Ave, Otis Orchards, 99027-9336, SAN 371-9723. Tel: 509-893-8390. FAX: 509-893-8482. Circulation E-mail: otcirc@scld.org. *Libr Supvr,* Caitlin Wheeler; E-mail: cwheeler@scld.org; Staff 5 (MLS 1, Non-MLS 4)

Circ 81,348
Open Tues & Wed 10-8, Thurs & Sat 10-6
Friends of the Library Group
SPOKANE VALLEY LIBRARY, 12004 E Main Ave, Spokane Valley, 99206-5114, SAN 364-1139. Tel: 509-893-8400. FAX: 509-893-8483. *Br Mgr,* Danielle Milton; E-mail: dmilton@scld.org; Staff 31.4 (MLS 9.5, Non-MLS 21.9)
Circ 535,978
Open Mon-Thurs 10-9, Fri & Sat 10-6, Sun 1-5
Friends of the Library Group

J SPOKANE FALLS COMMUNITY COLLEGE LIBRARY*, 3410 W Whistalks Way, 99224-5204. SAN 317-6754. Tel: 509-533-3800. Circulation Tel: 509-533-3805. Reference Tel: 509-533-3834. Toll Free Tel: 800-251-1972. FAX: 509-533-3144. Reference E-mail: refdesk@spokanefalls.edu. Information Services E-mail: sfccinfo@spokanefalls.edu. Web Site: sfcc.spokane.edu/for-our-students/library. *Dean,* Chris Pelchat; E-mail: chris.pelchat@sfcc.spokane.edu; *Librn,* Sharde' Mills; Tel: 509-533-3224, E-mail: sharde.mills@sfcc.spokane.edu; *Librn,* Heather Morgan; Tel: 509-533-3807, E-mail: heather.morgan@sfcc.spokane.edu; *Librn,* Mary Nagel; Tel: 509-533-3174, E-mail: mary.nagel@sfcc.spokane.edu; *Librn,* Ben Ugaldea; Tel: 509-533-3806, E-mail: ben.ugaldea@sfcc.spokane.edu; Staff 7 (MLS 4, Non-MLS 3)
Founded 1967. Enrl 3,800; Fac 150; Highest Degree: Bachelor
Jul 2022-Jun 2023. Mats Exp $104,000, Books $50,000, Per/Ser (Incl. Access Fees) $24,000, AV Mat $10,000, Electronic Ref Mat (Incl. Access Fees) $20,000. Sal $649,000 (Prof $377,000)
Library Holdings: Bk Titles 50,000; Bk Vols 59,000; Per Subs 170
Automation Activity & Vendor Info: (Acquisitions) Ex Libris Group; (Cataloging) Ex Libris Group; (Circulation) Ex Libris Group; (Course Reserve) Ex Libris Group; (Discovery) Ex Libris Group; (ILL) OCLC; (OPAC) Ex Libris Group; (Serials) Ex Libris Group
Wireless access
Function: 24/7 Electronic res, 24/7 Online cat, 3D Printer
Partic in OCLC Online Computer Library Center, Inc; Washington Community & Technical Colleges Library Consortium
Open Mon-Thurs 7:15-7, Fri 7:15-4, Sat 10-2; Mon-Thurs 7:15-2:30 (Summer)

P SPOKANE PUBLIC LIBRARY*, Station Plaza, 2nd Flr, 701 W Riverside Ave, 99201. (Mail add: 906 W Main Ave, 99201-0976), SAN 364-1163. Tel: 509-444-5300. Circulation Tel: 509-444-5333. FAX: 509-444-5365. Web Site: www.spokanelibrary.org. *Exec Dir,* Andrew Chanse; E-mail: director@spokanelibrary.org; *Dep Dir,* Caris O'Malley; Tel: 509-444-5310, E-mail: comalley@spokanelibrary.org; *Dir, Mkt & Communications,* Amanda Donovan; *Br Mgr, Commun Engagement Mgr,* Jason Johnson; Tel: 509-444-5334, E-mail: jjohnson@spokanelibrary.org
Founded 1891. Pop 208,916; Circ 338,023
Library Holdings: Electronic Media & Resources 28; Bk Vols 527,456
Special Collections: Adult Literacy Coll; African-American Coll; Genealogy Coll, bks, clippings, mags, microfilms, microcards; History of the Book Coll; Northwest History Room. Oral History; State Document Depository; US Document Depository
Subject Interests: Genealogy
Automation Activity & Vendor Info: (Acquisitions) SirsiDynix; (Cataloging) SirsiDynix; (Circulation) SirsiDynix; (ILL) OCLC Online; (OPAC) SirsiDynix; (Serials) SirsiDynix
Wireless access
Function: Archival coll, AV serv, Govt ref serv, Health sci info serv, Home delivery & serv to seniorr ctr & nursing homes, Homebound delivery serv, ILL available, Internet access, Magnifiers for reading, Outside serv via phone, mail, e-mail & web, Photocopying/Printing, Prog for adults, Prog for children & young adult, Ref serv available, Summer reading prog, Telephone ref, Wheelchair accessible
Special Services for the Deaf - TDD equip; TTY equip
Special Services for the Blind - Audio mat; Bks on cassette; Bks on CD; Extensive large print coll; Home delivery serv; Large print bks; Magnifiers; Reader equip; Soundproof reading booth; Talking bks
Friends of the Library Group
Branches: 5
EAST SIDE, 524 S Stone Ave, 99202, SAN 364-1228. FAX: 509-444-5369. *Br Mgr,* Ellen Peters; E-mail: epeters@spokanelibrary.org
Founded 1995. Circ 87,333
Function: Prof lending libr
Open Tues 10-8, Wed-Sat 10-6
Friends of the Library Group
HILLYARD, 4005 N Cook Ave, 99207, SAN 364-1252. FAX: 509-444-5370. *Br Mgr,* Paul Chapin; E-mail: pchapin@spokanelibrary.org
Founded 1994. Circ 125,741
Open Tues 12-8, Wed-Sat 10-6
Friends of the Library Group
INDIAN TRAIL, 4909 W Barnes Rd, 99208. FAX: 509-444-5399. *Br Mgr,* Paul Chapin
Founded 1998. Circ 134,119
Open Tues 12-8, Wed-Sat 10-6
Friends of the Library Group
SHADLE, 2111 W Wellesley Ave, 99205, SAN 364-1376. FAX: 509-444-5372.
Founded 1997. Circ 408,606
Friends of the Library Group
SOUTH HILL, 3324 S Perry St, 99203, SAN 364-1317. FAX: 509-444-5371. *Br Mgr,* Ellen Peters
Founded 1996. Circ 432,275
Open Mon & Tues 10-8, Wed-Sat 10-6
Friends of the Library Group

S SPOKESMAN-REVIEW*, Newspaper Reference Library, 999 W Riverside Ave, 99201. (Mail add: PO Box 2160, 99210-2160), SAN 317-6762. Tel: 509-459-5523. Toll Free Tel: 800-789-0029, Ext 5523. FAX: 509-459-5098. E-mail: library@spokesman.com. Web Site: www.spokesman.com. *Newsroom Mgr,* Mary Beth Donelan; E-mail: marybethd@spokesman.com
Founded 1883
Library Holdings: Bk Titles 3,000; Per Subs 15
Special Collections: Newspaper Clipping & Photographs
Wireless access
Restriction: Private libr

C WHITWORTH UNIVERSITY*, Harriet Cheney Cowles Memorial Library, 300 W Hawthorne Rd, 99251-0001. SAN 364-1465. Tel: 509-777-3260. Interlibrary Loan Service Tel: 509-777-4930. Reference Tel: 509-777-4491. Administration Tel: 509-777-4482. FAX: 509-777-3221. Web Site: libguides.whitworth.edu. *Libr Dir,* Amanda Clark; E-mail: amandaclark@whitworth.edu; *Head, Coll Mgt,* Paul Ojennus; Tel: 509-777-4480, E-mail: pojennus@whitworth.edu; *Circ Supvr,* Barbara Carden; Tel: 509-777-3767, E-mail: bcarden@whitworth.edu; *Univ Archivist,* Nancy Bunker; Tel: 509-777-4481, E-mail: nbunker@whitworth.edu; *Acq,* Christina Dolan-Derks; Tel: 509-777-4485, E-mail: cdolan-derks@whitworth.edu; *Bibliog Serv, Spec,* Pam Gilchrist; Tel: 509-777-4226, E-mail: pgilchrist@whitworth.edu; Staff 10.5 (MLS 5.5, Non-MLS 5)
Founded 1890. Enrl 2,886; Fac 180; Highest Degree: Master
Library Holdings: Audiobooks 500; AV Mats 9,250; CDs 3,380; DVDs 1,160; e-books 75,000; e-journals 2,300; Microforms 69,850; Music Scores 6,760; Bk Vols 164,800; Per Subs 480; Videos 1,738
Special Collections: Daniel Photography Coll; Pacific Northwest Protestant History Coll
Subject Interests: Bus, Educ, Liberal arts, Sciences
Automation Activity & Vendor Info: (Acquisitions) Ex Libris Group; (Cataloging) Ex Libris Group; (Circulation) Ex Libris Group; (ILL) Ex Libris Group; (OPAC) Ex Libris Group; (Serials) Ex Libris Group
Wireless access
Function: Archival coll, Audio & video playback equip for onsite use, Audiobks via web, Computers for patron use, Electronic databases & coll, ILL available, Music CDs, Online cat, Photocopying/Printing, Ref & res, Scanner, VHS videos, Wheelchair accessible, Writing prog
Partic in OCLC Online Computer Library Center, Inc; Orbis Cascade Alliance
Open Mon-Thurs 7:45am-Midnight, Fri 7:45-5:30, Sat 9-6, Sun 1-Midnight (Winter); Mon-Thurs 8-8, Fri 8-5, Sat 10-5 (Summer)
Restriction: Circ limited, In-house use for visitors, Non-circulating of rare bks, Open to students, fac & staff, Pub use on premises

SPRAGUE

P SPRAGUE PUBLIC LIBRARY, 119 W Second St, 99032. (Mail add: PO Box 264, 99032-0264). Tel: 509-257-2662. FAX: 509-257-2691. Web Site: sprague.lib.wa.us. *Librn,* Merrin Lawrence; E-mail: deputyclerk@sprague-wa.us
Pop 300
Library Holdings: Bk Vols 2,500
Special Collections: Local History Coll
Automation Activity & Vendor Info: (Cataloging) Koha; (Circulation) Koha; (OPAC) Koha
Wireless access
Function: 24/7 Electronic res, 24/7 Online cat, Computers for patron use, Electronic databases & coll, For res purposes, ILL available, Internet access, Laminating, Notary serv, Online cat, Online info literacy tutorials on the web & in blackboard, Online ref, OverDrive digital audio bks, Photocopying/Printing, Ref & res, Scanner, Summer reading prog, Wheelchair accessible
Partic in Wheatland Libraries Consortium
Open Mon-Fri 10-12 & 1-4

TACOMA

J BATES TECHNICAL COLLEGE LIBRARY*, 2201 S 78th St, E201, 98409-9000. Tel: 253-680-7550. FAX: 253-680-7551. E-mail: sclibrary@batestech.edu. Web Site: library.batestech.edu. *Librn,* Michael Wood; E-mail: mwood@batestech.edu
Library Holdings: Bk Titles 8,200
Wireless access
Partic in Washington Community & Technical Colleges Library Consortium
Open Mon-Thurs 8-5, Fri 10:30-4:30

CR FAITH EVANGELICAL SEMINARY LIBRARY*, 3504 N Pearl St, 98407-2607. SAN 317-6827. Tel: 253-752-2020. Toll Free Tel: 888-777-7675. FAX: 253-759-1790. E-mail: fsinfo@faithseminary.edu. Web Site: faithseminary.edu. *Libr Dir,* Dr Timothy Hyun; Tel: 753-752-2020, Ext 117, E-mail: thyun@faithseminary.edu
Founded 1969. Enrl 400; Fac 15; Highest Degree: Doctorate
Library Holdings: Bk Vols 20,000; Per Subs 90
Wireless access
Partic in Puget Sound Area Libr Tech
Open Mon-Thurs 9-5, Fri 9-1

C PACIFIC LUTHERAN UNIVERSITY*, Robert A L Mortvedt Library, 12180 Park Ave S, 98447-0001. SAN 317-6843. Tel: 253-535-7500. Interlibrary Loan Service Tel: 253-535-7508. Reference Tel: 253-535-7507. FAX: 253-535-7315. Interlibrary Loan Service FAX: 253-536-5110. E-mail: library@plu.edu. Web Site: www.plu.edu/library. *Interim Libr Dir,* Genevieve Williams; Tel: 253-535-7443, E-mail: williagr@plu.edu; *Archivist & Spec Coll Librn,* Lauren Loftis; *Instruction & Ref Librn,* Roberto Arteaga; *Ref Librn,* Julie Babka; *Access Serv Mgr,* Scott Sills; *Digital Preservation Specialist,* Josh Smith; *Emeritus Archivist,* Kerstin Ringdahl; *Virtual Ref,* Holly Senn; Staff 11 (MLS 5, Non-MLS 6)
Founded 1894. Enrl 3,661; Fac 238; Highest Degree: Master
Library Holdings: AV Mats 14,032; Bk Titles 261,291; Bk Vols 345,193; Per Subs 4,474
Special Collections: Scandinavian Immigrant Experience Coll. Oral History
Automation Activity & Vendor Info: (Acquisitions) Ex Libris Group; (Cataloging) Ex Libris Group; (Circulation) Ex Libris Group; (Course Reserve) Ex Libris Group; (ILL) OCLC; (Media Booking) Ex Libris Group; (OPAC) Ex Libris Group; (Serials) Ex Libris Group
Wireless access
Function: Archival coll, Art exhibits, Computers for patron use, Electronic databases & coll, For res purposes, Internet access, Online cat, Online Chat, Online ref, Ref & res, Res assist avail
Partic in Puget Sound Acad Independent Librs
Restriction: Borrowing privileges limited to fac & registered students, Pub use on premises, Restricted borrowing privileges

GL PIERCE COUNTY LAW LIBRARY*, County-City Bldg, 930 Tacoma Ave S, Rm 1A - 105, 98402. SAN 317-6851. Tel: 253-798-2691. FAX: 253-798-2989. Web Site: www.piercecountywa.org/232/law-library. *Dir,* Laurie B Miller; E-mail: laurie.miller@piercecountywa.gov; *Libr Tech,* Lancia Speed; E-mail: lancia.speed@piercecountywa.gov; Staff 3 (MLS 1, Non-MLS 2)
Library Holdings: Bk Vols 70,000
Automation Activity & Vendor Info: (Cataloging) Koha; (Circulation) Koha; (OPAC) Koha; (Serials) Koha
Wireless access
Function: ILL available, Photocopying/Printing
Open Mon-Fri 8:30-4:30
Friends of the Library Group

P PIERCE COUNTY LIBRARY SYSTEM*, 3005 112th St E, 98446-2215. SAN 364-1589. Tel: 253-548-3300. FAX: 253-537-4600. Web Site: www.piercecountylibrary.org. *Exec Dir,* Gretchen Caserotti; E-mail: director@piercecountylibrary.org; *Dir, Mkt & Communications,* Mary Getchell; E-mail: mgetchell@piercecountylibrary.org; *Facilities Dir,* Kristina Cintron; Tel: 253-548-3454, E-mail: kcintron@piercecountylibrary.org; *Finance & Bus Dir,* Clifford Jo; Tel: 253-548-3453, E-mail: cjo@piercecountylibrary.org; *Staff Experience Dir,* Cheree Green; Tel: 253-548-3354, E-mail: cgreen@piercecountylibrary.org; Staff 280 (MLS 56, Non-MLS 224)
Founded 1946. Pop 559,561; Circ 8,738,850
Special Collections: Korean & Spanish. US Document Depository
Automation Activity & Vendor Info: (Circulation) Innovative Interfaces, Inc
Wireless access
Partic in OCLC Online Computer Library Center, Inc
Special Services for the Deaf - TDD equip
Special Services for the Blind - Reader equip
Open Mon-Fri 7:30-5
Friends of the Library Group

Branches: 19
ANDERSON ISLAND LIBRARY, 11319 Yoman Rd, Anderson Island, 98303. Tel: 253-548-3536. *Supv Librn,* Elly Krumwiede; E-mail: ekrumwiede@piercecountylibrary.org
Open Wed 11-3
BONNEY LAKE BRANCH, 18501 90th St E, Bonney Lake, 98391, SAN 364-1643. Tel: 253-548-3308. FAX: 253-863-6016. *Sr Librn,* Erin Muske; E-mail: emuske@piercecountylibrary.org
Open Mon-Wed 10-9, Thurs & Fri 10-6, Sat 10-5, Sun 1-5
Friends of the Library Group
BUCKLEY BRANCH, 123 S River Ave, Buckley, 98321, SAN 364-1708. Tel: 253-548-3310, 360-829-0300. FAX: 360-829-2874. *Supv Librn,* Lynsey Sharp; E-mail: LSharp@piercecountylibrary.org
Founded 1903
Library Holdings: Bk Titles 28,550
Open Mon-Wed 11-8, Thurs & Fri 11-6, Sat 11-5
Friends of the Library Group
DUPONT BRANCH, 1540 Wilmington Dr, DuPont, 98327. Tel: 253-548-3326. FAX: 253-964-4010. *Supv Librn,* Susan McBride
Open Mon-Wed 11-8, Thurs & Fri 11-6, Sat 11-5
Friends of the Library Group
EATONVILLE BRANCH, 205 Center St W, Eatonville, 98328, SAN 364-1732. Tel: 253-548-3311, 360-832-6011. FAX: 360-832-7201. *Supv Librn,* Cindy Dargan; E-mail: cdargan@piercecountylibrary.org
Open Mon-Wed 10-7, Thurs & Fri 10-6, Sat 10-5
Friends of the Library Group
FIFE BRANCH, 6622 20th St E, Fife, 98424. Tel: 253-548-3323. FAX: 253-922-5919. *Regional Mgr, Libr Serv,* Steve Carmody; E-mail: SCarmody@piercecountylibrary.org
Library Holdings: Bk Vols 25,000
Open Mon-Wed 11-8, Thurs & Fri 11-6, Sat 11-5
Friends of the Library Group
GIG HARBOR BRANCH, 4424 Point Fosdick Dr NW, Gig Harbor, 98335, SAN 364-1767. Tel: 253-548-3305. FAX: 253-851-8002. *Sr Librn,* Angie Case; E-mail: ACase@piercecountylibrary.org
Open Mon-Thurs 10-9, Fri 10-6, Sat 10-5, Sun 1-5
Friends of the Library Group
GRAHAM BRANCH, 9202 224th St E, Graham, 98338, SAN 373-5656. Tel: 253-548-3322. FAX: 253-846-5174. *Sr Librn,* Corrine Weatherly; E-mail: CWeatherly@piercecountylibrary.org
Founded 1992
Open Mon-Wed 10-9, Thurs & Fri 10-6, Sat 10-5, Sun 1-5
Friends of the Library Group
KEY CENTER, 8905 Key Peninsula Hwy NW, Lakebay, 98349, SAN 364-1791. Tel: 253-548-3309. FAX: 253-884-9553. *Dep Dir, Operations,* Jessica Widmer; E-mail: JWidmer@piercecountylibrary.org
Founded 1946
Open Mon-Wed 11-8, Thurs & Fri 11-6, Sat 11-5
Friends of the Library Group
LAKEWOOD BRANCH, 10202 Gravelly Lake Dr SW, Lakewood, 98499, SAN 364-197X. Tel: 253-548-3302. FAX: 253-589-7377. *Sr Librn,* Deb Derylak; E-mail: DDerylak@piercecountylibrary.org
Founded 1947
Interim library location opened Sept 2024
Open Mon-Wed 10-7, Thurs & Fri 10-6, Sat 10-5, Sun 1-5
Friends of the Library Group
MILTON/EDGEWOOD BRANCH, 900 Meridian Ave E, Ste 29, Milton, 98354, SAN 317-5464. Tel: 253-548-3325. FAX: 253-927-2581. *Supv Librn,* Genevieve Dettmer; E-mail: GDettmer@piercecountylibrary.org
Open Mon-Wed 11-8, Thurs & Fri 11-6, Sat 11-5
Friends of the Library Group
ORTING BRANCH, 202 Washington Ave S, Orting, 98360, SAN 364-1821. Tel: 253-548-3312. FAX: 360-893-1856. *Supv Librn,* Mejin Turner; E-mail: mturner@piercecountylibrary.org
Founded 1982
Open Mon-Wed 11-8, Thurs & Fri 11-6, Sat 11-5
Friends of the Library Group
PARKLAND-SPANAWAY BRANCH, 13718 Pacific Ave S, 98444, SAN 364-1856. Tel: 253-548-3304. FAX: 253-536-3789. *Sr Librn,* Bijan Nowroozian; E-mail: bnowroozian@piercecountylibrary.org
Open Mon-Thurs 10-9, Fri 10-6, Sat 10-5, Sun 1-5
Friends of the Library Group
SOUTH HILL BRANCH, 15420 Meridian E, Puyallup, 98375, SAN 364-1880. Tel: 253-548-3303. FAX: 253-841-4692. *Sr Librn,* Jill Merritt; E-mail: JMerritt@piercecountylibrary.org
Open Mon-Thurs 10-9, Fri 10-6, Sat 10-5, Sun 1-5
Friends of the Library Group
STEILACOOM BRANCH, 2950 Steilacoom Blvd, Steilacoom, 98388, SAN 364-1910. Tel: 253-548-3313. FAX: 253-589-7095. *Supv Librn,* Misha Hacke; E-mail: MHacke@piercecountylibrary.org
Founded 1858
Open Mon-Wed 11-8, Thurs & Fri 11-6, Sat 11-5
Friends of the Library Group

SUMMIT BRANCH, 5107 112th St E, 98446, SAN 373-9090. Tel: 253-548-3321. FAX: 253-536-6301. *Sr Librn,* Neil Derksen; E-mail: nderksen@piercecountylibrary.org
Open Mon-Wed 10-9, Thurs & Fri 10-6, Sat 10-5, Sun 1-5
Friends of the Library Group

SUMNER BRANCH, 1116 Fryar Ave, Sumner, 98390, SAN 364-1945. Tel: 253-548-3306. FAX: 253-863-0650. *Sr Librn,* Ben Haines; E-mail: bhaines@piercecountylibrary.org
Founded 1925
Open Mon-Thurs 10-9, Fri 10-6, Sat 10-5, Sun 1-5
Friends of the Library Group

TILLICUM BRANCH, 14916 Washington Ave SW, Lakewood, 98498, SAN 364-2003. Tel: 253-548-3314. FAX: 253-584-4107. *Supv Librn,* Liz Athey; E-mail: LAthey@piercecountylibrary.org
Founded 1947
Open Mon-Wed 1-8, Thurs-Sat 11-5

UNIVERSITY PLACE BRANCH, 3609 Market Pl W, Ste 100, University Place, 98466, SAN 364-2038. Tel: 253-548-3307. FAX: 253-565-2913. *Sr Librn,* Bonnie Svitavsky; E-mail: BSvitavsky@piercecountylibrary.org
Open Mon-Thurs 10-9, Fri 10-6, Sat 10-5, Sun 1-5
Friends of the Library Group

J TACOMA COMMUNITY COLLEGE LIBRARY*, Pearl A Wanamaker Library, Bldg 7, 6501 S 19th St, 98466-6100. SAN 317-6894. Tel: 253-566-5087. Reference Tel: 253-566-5134. FAX: 253-566-5398. TDD: 253-566-5130. E-mail: library@tacomacc.edu. Web Site: tacomacc.libguides.com/tcclibrary. *Interim Dean, Library & Learning Innovation,* Dale Coleman; Tel: 253-460-5091, E-mail: dcoleman@tacomacc.edu; *Dept Chair,* Rebekah Williams; Tel: 253-566-6028, E-mail: rwilliams@tacomacc.edu; *Librn,* Melissa Adams; Tel: 253-566-5204, E-mail: madams@tacomacc.edu; *Librn,* Heather Gillanders; Tel: 253-566-5102, E-mail: hgillanders@tacomacc.edu; *Librn,* Jennifer Snoek-Brown; Tel: 253-460-3936, E-mail: jsnoek-brown@tacomacc.edu; Staff 14 (MLS 6, Non-MLS 8)
Founded 1966. Fac 4; Highest Degree: Bachelor
Library Holdings: e-books 147,000; Bk Vols 30,000; Per Subs 37
Automation Activity & Vendor Info: (Acquisitions) SirsiDynix; (Cataloging) SirsiDynix; (Circulation) SirsiDynix; (Course Reserve) SirsiDynix; (ILL) SirsiDynix; (Media Booking) SirsiDynix; (OPAC) SirsiDynix; (Serials) SirsiDynix
Wireless access
Partic in Washington Community & Technical Colleges Library Consortium
Open Mon-Thurs 7:15am-8pm, Fri 7:15-5; Mon-Thurs 8-5:30 (Summer)

S TACOMA FAMILY HISTORY CENTER*, 1102 S Pearl St, 98465. SAN 317-6819. Tel: 253-564-1103. E-mail: wa_tacoma@familyhistorymail.org. Web Site: www.familysearch.org/en/wiki/Tacoma_Washington_FamilySearch_Center (URL won't work without caps). *Co-Dir,* Gaaren Anderson; *Co-Dir,* Mary Anderson
Library Holdings: Microforms 9,400; Bk Vols 3,000
Wireless access
Open Tues 10-12 & 6-8, Wed & Thurs 10-8, Sat 10-1

P TACOMA PUBLIC LIBRARY*, 1102 Tacoma Ave S, 98402. SAN 364-2097. Tel: 253-280-2823. Administration Tel: 253-280-2881. E-mail: info@tacomalibrary.org. Web Site: www.tacomalibrary.org. *Libr Dir,* Kate Larsen; Staff 29 (MLS 11, Non-MLS 18)
Founded 1886. Pop 197,000; Circ 2,038,449
Library Holdings: AV Mats 92,779; Bk Vols 2,123,062; Per Subs 1,638
Special Collections: Geneal Coll; Historic Tacoma photos 1923-1980; Local newspapers, history and government; Northwest history, maps, docs, & bks; World War I bks & posters. Municipal Document Depository; State Document Depository; US Document Depository
Automation Activity & Vendor Info: (Acquisitions) Innovative Interfaces, Inc - Millennium; (Cataloging) Innovative Interfaces, Inc - Millennium; (Circulation) Innovative Interfaces, Inc - Millennium; (ILL) OCLC ILLiad; (OPAC) Innovative Interfaces, Inc - Millennium; (Serials) Innovative Interfaces, Inc - Millennium
Wireless access
Publications: Bibliographies; Pioneer
Partic in OCLC Online Computer Library Center, Inc
Special Services for the Deaf - TTY equip
Open Tues & Wed 11-8, Thurs-Sat 9-6
Friends of the Library Group

Branches: 7

FERN HILL, 765 S 84th St, 98444, SAN 364-2127. Tel: 253-341-4724. Administration E-mail: mfitzgerald@tacomalibrary.org. Web Site: www.tacomalibrary.org/locations/2/. *Br Mgr,* Melissa Fitzgerald; E-mail: mfitzgerald@tacomalibrary.org
Library Holdings: Bk Vols 91,434
Open Tues & Wed 12-8, Thurs-Sat 10-6

KOBETICH, 212 Brown's Point Blvd NE, 98422, SAN 364-2151. Tel: 253-280-2920. *Br Mgr,* Michelle Massero; E-mail: mmassero@tacomalibrary.org
Library Holdings: Bk Vols 50,518
Open Tues & Wed 12-8, Thurs & Fri 10-6

MOORE BRANCH, 215 S 56th St, 98408, SAN 364-2216. Tel: 253-280-2930. *Br Mgr,* M White; E-mail: mwhite@tacomalibrary.org
Library Holdings: Bk Vols 103,615
Open Tues & Wed 12-8, Thurs-Sat 10-6

MOTTET BRANCH, 3523 East G St, 98404, SAN 364-2240. Tel: 253-280-2950. *Br Mgr,* Michelle Massero; E-mail: mmassero@tacomalibrary.org
Library Holdings: Bk Vols 54,715
Open Tues & Wed 12-8, Thurs-Sat 10-6

SOUTH TACOMA, 3411 S 56th St, 98409, SAN 364-2275. Tel: 253-280-2960. *Br Mgr,* Melissa Fitzgerald; E-mail: mfitzgerald@tacomalibrary.org
Library Holdings: Bk Vols 63,508
Open Tues & Wed 12-8, Thurs 10-6

SWASEY BRANCH, 7001 Sixth Ave, 98406, SAN 364-2305. Tel: 253-280-2970. *Br Mgr,* JoLyn Reisdorf; E-mail: jreisdorf@tacomalibrary.org
Library Holdings: Bk Vols 96,906
Open Tues & Wed 12-8, Thurs-Sat 10-6

WHEELOCK BRANCH, 3722 N 26th St, 98407, SAN 364-2186. Tel: 253-280-2980. *Br Mgr,* Maria Shackles; E-mail: mshackles@tacomalibrary.org
Library Holdings: Bk Vols 132,738
Open Tues & Wed 12-8, Thurs-Sat 10-6

AM UNITED STATES ARMY*, Madigan Army Medical Center, Medical Library, Medical Mall, 2nd Flr, 9040 Jackson Ave, 98431. (Mail add: Attn MCHJ-CLE-L Medical Library, 98431-1100), SAN 364-2364. Tel: 253-968-0118. FAX: 253-968-0958. E-mail: usarmy.jblm.medcom-mamc.mbx.medical-library@mail.mil. Web Site: www.mamc.health.mil/education/graduate-medical-education/medical-library. *Library Chief,* Jeffery R Ring; E-mail: jeffery.r.ring.civ@mail.mil; *Med Librn,* Jacqueline M Luizzi; E-mail: jaqueline.m.luizzi.civ@mail.mil; Staff 3 (MLS 1, Non-MLS 2)
Founded 1944
Library Holdings: Bk Titles 9,980; Bk Vols 27,101; Per Subs 450
Subject Interests: Health admin, Med, Nursing
Automation Activity & Vendor Info: (Acquisitions) Ex Libris Group; (Cataloging) Ex Libris Group; (Circulation) Ex Libris Group; (OPAC) Ex Libris Group; (Serials) Ex Libris Group
Wireless access
Publications: Accession List
Partic in OCLC Online Computer Library Center, Inc
Restriction: Med & nursing staff, patients & families, Staff use only

C UNIVERSITY OF PUGET SOUND*, Collins Memorial Library, 1604 N Warner St, Upper Loading Dock, 98416. (Mail add: 1500 N Warner St,CMB-1021, 98416), SAN 364-2399. Tel: 253-879-3669. Interlibrary Loan Service Tel: 253-879-3612. Reference Tel: 253-879-3287. Administration Tel: 253-879-3243. Web Site: www.pugetsound.edu/library. *Libr Dir,* Jane A Carlin; Tel: 253-879-3118, E-mail: jcarlin@pugetsound.edu; *Assoc Dir,* Peggy Firman; Tel: 253-879-3615, E-mail: firman@pugetsound.edu; *Assoc Dir, Pub Serv,* Peggy Burge; Tel: 253-879-3512, E-mail: pburge@pugetsound.edu; *Electronic Res Librn,* Dusty Gorman; Tel: 253-879-3617, E-mail: dgorman@pugetsound.edu; *Discovery Librn, Syst,* Hilary Robbeloth; Tel: 253-879-3677, E-mail: hrobbeloth@pugetsound.edu; *Humanities Librn,* Katy Curtis; Tel: 253-879-3672, E-mail: kcurtis@pugetsound.edu; *Liaison Librn,* Angela Weaver; Tel: 253-879-3229, E-mail: aeweaver@pugetsound.edu; *Digital Projects Librn, Scholarly Communications,* Ben Tucker; Tel: 253-879-3667, E-mail: btucker@pugetsound.edu; *Sci Librn,* Eli Gandour-Rood; Tel: 253-879-3678, E-mail: egandourrood@pugetsound.edu; *Electronic Res Coordr, Soc Sci Librn,* Andrea Klyn; Tel: 253-879-2875, E-mail: aklyn@pugetsound.edu; *Archivist, Spec Coll Librn,* Adriana Flores; Tel: 253-879-2669, E-mail: aflores@pugetsound.edu; *Acq, Electronic Res Mgr,* Carmel Thompson; Tel: 253-879-3240, E-mail: cathompson@pugetsound.edu; *Access Serv Supvr,* Cassandra Palmore; Tel: 253-879-3612, E-mail: cpalmore@pugetsound.edu; *Evening Supvr,* Fran Leskovar; Tel: 253-879-2664, E-mail: fleskovar@pugetsound.edu; *Adminr, Coordr, Spec Projects,* Jamie Lee Spaine; Tel: 253-879-3243, E-mail: jspaine@pugetsound.edu; *Tech Coordr,* Jada Pelger; Tel: 253-879-3287, E-mail: jpelger@pugetsound.edu; *Metadata Specialist,* Willow Berntsen; Tel: 253-879-3107, E-mail: wberntsen@pugetsound.edu; *Asst Archivist,* Laura Edgar; Tel: 253-879-6014, E-mail: ledgar@pugetsound.edu; *Pub Serv Spec,* Nick Triggs; Tel: 253-879-3618, E-mail: ntriggs@pugetsound.edu; *Web Spec,* Jeanne Young; Tel: 253-879-2663, E-mail: jmkyoung@pugetsound.edu; *Volunteer Archivist,* John Finney; Tel: 253-879-6014, E-mail: finney@pugetsound.edu. Subject Specialists: *Digital humanities, Teaching,* Peggy Burge; *Fine arts, Performing arts,* Angela Weaver; *Graphics,* Jeanne Young; Staff 19 (MLS 8, Non-MLS 11)

Founded 1888. Enrl 2,210; Fac 200; Highest Degree: Doctorate
Library Holdings: AV Mats 19,095; e-books 45,346; Electronic Media & Resources 24,687; Bk Titles 385,051; Bk Vols 432,583; Per Subs 797
Special Collections: Music Recordings & Scores Coll
Subject Interests: Bus, Leadership, Liberal arts, Music
Automation Activity & Vendor Info: (Acquisitions) Ex Libris Group; (Cataloging) Ex Libris Group; (Circulation) Ex Libris Group; (Course Reserve) Ex Libris Group; (Discovery) Ex Libris Group; (ILL) OCLC Tipasa; (Media Booking) Ex Libris Group; (Serials) Ex Libris Group
Wireless access
Publications: Acquisition List; Faculty Library Handbook
Partic in Orbis Cascade Alliance
Open Mon-Thurs 7:30am-Midnight, Fri 7:30am-8pm, Sat 1-5,Sun 1pm-Midnight

GM VA PUGET SOUND HEALTH CARE SYSTEM*, Library Service (A-142D), American Lake Div, 9600 Veterans Dr SW, Bldg 71, 98493-5000. SAN 317-6924. Tel: 253-583-1513. E-mail: alvalib@va.gov. Web Site: www.va.gov/puget-sound-health-care. *Chief, Libr Serv,* Jason M Oleston; Tel: 253-583-1510, E-mail: jason.oleston2@va.gov; *Libr Tech,* Arthur James Russell, III; E-mail: arthur.russell@va.gov; Staff 3 (MLS 1, Non-MLS 2)
Founded 1924
Library Holdings: AV Mats 1,000; Large Print Bks 150; Bk Titles 5,000; Per Subs 157; Talking Bks 200
Subject Interests: Addictions, Med, Nursing, Psychiat, Psychol, Substance abuse
Automation Activity & Vendor Info: (Cataloging) EOS International; (Circulation) EOS International; (OPAC) EOS International
Function: Audio & video playback equip for onsite use, Doc delivery serv, Health sci info serv, Photocopying/Printing, Satellite serv
Special Services for the Blind - Bks on cassette; Large print bks; Talking bks
Open Mon-Fri 8-4:15
Restriction: Non-circulating to the pub

M VMFH FRANCISCAN LIBRARY, (Formerly CHI Franciscan Library), St Joseph Medical Ctr, 1717 S J St, 98405. (Mail add: PO Box 2197, 98401-2197), SAN 317-6878. Tel: 253-426-6778. FAX: 253-426-6260. *Librn,* Brynn Beals; E-mail: brynn.beals@commonspirit.org; Staff 1 (MLS 1)
Founded 1920
Subject Interests: Hospitals, Med, Nursing, Related subj
Partic in Pacific NW Regional Health Sci Libr; Washington Libr Network

S WASHINGTON STATE HISTORY RESEARCH CENTER, Special Collections Division, 315 N Stadium Way, 98403. SAN 317-6932. Tel: 253-798-5914. FAX: 253-597-4186. *Head, Spec Coll,* Ed Nolan; E-mail: enolan@wshs.wa.gov; *Res Archivist,* Eileen Price; Tel: 253-798-5916, E-mail: eprice@wshs.wa.gov; Staff 2 (MLS 2)
Founded 1891
Library Holdings: Microforms 1,200; Music Scores 900; Bk Vols 15,700
Special Collections: Washington State Coll, ephemera, ms, maps, photos
Subject Interests: Local hist
Wireless access
Restriction: Open by appt only

TOKELAND

S SHOALWATER BAY TRIBAL COMMUNITY LIBRARY*, 4112 State Rte 105, 98590. (Mail add: PO Box 130, 98590). Tel: 360-267-8190. FAX: 360-267-6778. Web Site: www.shoalwaterbay-nsn.gov. *Libr Mgr,* Mary Johnson; E-mail: mjohnson@shoalwaterbay-nsn.gov
Library Holdings: Bk Titles 6,000
Special Collections: Native American
Open Mon-Fri 8:30-4:30

TOPPENISH

C HERITAGE UNIVERSITY, Donald K C North Library, 3240 Fort Rd, 98948. SAN 324-0541. Tel: 509-865-8522, Ext 5423. Toll Free Tel: 888-706-0348, Ext 5423. FAX: 509-865-4144. E-mail: library@heritage.edu. Web Site: libguides.heritage.edu/librarystart. *Libr Dir, Ref Librn,* Daniel Liestman; Tel: 509-865-8520, Ext 5420, E-mail: liestman_d@heritage.edu; *Systems Access & Data Librarian,* Victoria Castro; Tel: 509-865-8500, Ext 5421, E-mail: castro_v@heritage.edu; *Libr Tech,* Daniel Olney; Tel: 509-865-8610, E-mail: olney_d@heritage.edu; Staff 3 (MLS 2, Non-MLS 1)
Founded 1982. Enrl 1,300; Fac 150; Highest Degree: Master
Library Holdings: e-books 10,000; e-journals 20,000; Bk Titles 40,000; Per Subs 160
Special Collections: Native American Coll, Cultural Diversity Emphasis
Subject Interests: Bilingual educ
Automation Activity & Vendor Info: (Acquisitions) Ex Libris Group; (Cataloging) Ex Libris Group; (Circulation) Ex Libris Group; (Course Reserve) Ex Libris Group; (ILL) OCLC; (OPAC) Ex Libris Group; (Serials) EBSCO Online
Wireless access
Function: Res libr
Open Mon-Thurs 8-8, Fri 8-5

P YAKAMA NATION LIBRARY*, 100 Spiel-Yi Loop, 98948. (Mail add: PO Box 151, 98948-0151), SAN 324-0312. Tel: 509-865-2800, Ext 6. Administration Tel: 509-865-5121, Ext 4747. FAX: 509-865-6101. Web Site: www.yakamamuseum.com/library.php. *Libr Adminr,* Merida Kipp; E-mail: merida_kipp@yakama.com; *Computer Spec,* Melannie Belly; E-mail: melannie_belly@yakama.com; *Libr Tech,* Cathy Miller; E-mail: cathy_miller@yakama.com; *Libr Tech III,* Jolena Tillequots; E-mail: jolena_tillequots@yakama.com; Staff 4 (MLS 1, Non-MLS 3)
Founded 1982. Pop 11,440; Circ 29,720
Library Holdings: Bk Vols 17,894; Per Subs 91; Spec Interest Per Sub 88
Special Collections: American Indian Coll; Dr Helen H Schuster Coll; Strongheart Archives (Nipo Strongheart Coll); Yakama Tribal (Yakama Nation Reference Coll). Oral History
Subject Interests: Native American
Automation Activity & Vendor Info: (Acquisitions) SerialsSolutions; (Cataloging) Follett Software; (Circulation) Follett Software; (Course Reserve) Follett Software; (ILL) OCLC WorldShare Interlibrary Loan
Wireless access
Partic in OCLC Online Computer Library Center, Inc
Open Mon-Fri 8-5
Restriction: Residents only, Use of others with permission of librn

TUMWATER

P TIMBERLAND REGIONAL LIBRARY*, Administrative Service Center, 415 Tumwater Blvd SW, 98501-5799. SAN 363-7506. Tel: 360-943-5001. Reference Tel: 360-704-4636. Toll Free Tel: 877-284-6237. FAX: 360-586-6838. Reference FAX: 360-704-4610. Web Site: www.trlib.org. *Libr Dir,* Cheryl Heywood; E-mail: librarydirector@trl.org; *Dir, Coll Serv,* Andrea Heisel; E-mail: aheisel@trl.org; *Operations Dir,* Brenda Lane; *Dep Dir,* Kendra Jones; *District Libr Mgr,* Trisha Cronin; *District Libr Mgr,* Sarah Ogden; *District Libr Mgr,* Ryan Williams; *Finance Mgr, IT Mgr,* Eric Lowell; Staff 66.5 (MLS 56.1, Non-MLS 10.4)
Founded 1968. Pop 458,975; Circ 4,841,244
Library Holdings: Audiobooks 77,130; AV Mats 195,712; e-books 3,655; Bk Vols 1,063,110; Per Subs 3,602; Talking Bks 147,748
Special Collections: State Document Depository
Subject Interests: Genealogy, Sheet music
Automation Activity & Vendor Info: (Acquisitions) SirsiDynix; (Cataloging) SirsiDynix; (Circulation) SirsiDynix; (OPAC) SirsiDynix
Wireless access
Function: Audio & video playback equip for onsite use, Digital talking bks, Home delivery & serv to seniorr ctr & nursing homes, Homebound delivery serv, ILL available, Internet access, Large print keyboards, Magnifiers for reading, Photocopying/Printing, Prog for adults, Prog for children & young adult, Ref serv available, Summer reading prog, Telephone ref, Wheelchair accessible
Open Mon-Fri 8-5
Friends of the Library Group
Branches: 27

ABERDEEN BRANCH, 121 E Market St, Aberdeen, 98520-5292, SAN 363-7565. Tel: 360-533-2360. FAX: 360-533-9771. *Libr Mgr,* Stephenie Reece; Staff 11 (MLS 4, Non-MLS 7)
Founded 1890. Circ 229,777
Open Mon & Tues 10-7, Wed-Fri 10-6, Sat 10-5
Friends of the Library Group

AMANDA PARK BRANCH, 6118 US Hwy 101, Amanda Park, 98526. (Mail add: PO Drawer 89, Amanda Park, 98526-0089), SAN 363-7573. Tel: 360-288-2725. FAX: 360-288-2376. *Libr Mgr,* Susan Howelette-Leite; Staff 1 (Non-MLS 1)
Founded 1977. Circ 18,806
Open Tues & Thurs 10-5, Wed 1-7, Sat 10-4
Friends of the Library Group

CENTRALIA BRANCH, 110 S Silver St, Centralia, 98531-4218, SAN 363-759X. Tel: 360-736-0183. FAX: 360-330-7530. *Libr Mgr,* Susan Faubion; Staff 11 (MLS 5, Non-MLS 6)
Founded 1913. Circ 345,020
Open Mon & Tues 10-7, Wed-Fri 10-6, Sat 10-5
Friends of the Library Group

CHEHALIS BRANCH, 400 N Market Blvd, Chehalis, 98532. (Mail add: PO Box 419, Chehalis, 98532-0419), SAN 363-762X. Tel: 360-748-3301. FAX: 360-748-2169. *Libr Mgr,* Lily Grant; Staff 5.9 (MLS 1, Non-MLS 4.9)
Founded 1910. Circ 130,714
Open Tues 10-8, Wed & Thurs 10-7, Fri 10-6, Sat 10-5
Friends of the Library Group

ELMA BRANCH, 119 N First St, Elma, 98541. (Mail add: PO Box 3017, Elma, 98541-0547), SAN 363-7689. Tel: 360-482-3737. FAX: 360-482-3047. *Libr Mgr,* Dee Depoe; Staff 3 (MLS 1, Non-MLS 2)
Circ 81,914
Open Tues-Thurs 11-7, Fri & Sat 11-5
Friends of the Library Group

HOODSPORT BRANCH, 40 N Schoolhouse Hill Rd, Hoodsport, 98548. (Mail add: PO Box 847, Hoodsport, 98548-0847), SAN 372-512X. Tel: 360-877-9339. FAX: 360-877-9695. *Libr Mgr,* Annie Bowers; Staff 2 (Non-MLS 2)
Founded 1989. Circ 35,541
Open Tues & Wed 10-5, Thurs 10-6, Sat 10-4
Friends of the Library Group

HOQUIAM BRANCH, 420 Seventh St, Hoquiam, 98550-3616, SAN 363-7719. Tel: 360-532-1710. FAX: 360-538-9608. *Libr Mgr,* Mary Thornton; Staff 4 (MLS 1, Non-MLS 3)
Founded 1909. Circ 92,798
Open Tues-Thurs 10-7, Fri & Sat 10-4
Friends of the Library Group

ILWACO BRANCH, 158 First Ave N, Ilwaco, 98624. (Mail add: PO Box 520, Ilwaco, 98624-0520), SAN 363-7743. Tel: 360-642-3908. FAX: 360-642-8417. *Libr Mgr,* Susan Carney; Staff 2.1 (Non-MLS 2.1)
Circ 44,337
Function: Bks on cassette, Bks on CD, Children's prog, Computers for patron use, Digital talking bks, Electronic databases & coll, Family literacy, Free DVD rentals, Homebound delivery serv, ILL available, Mail & tel request accepted, Museum passes, Music CDs, Photocopying/Printing, Preschool outreach, Prog for adults, Prog for children & young adult, Ref serv available, Story hour, Summer reading prog, Tax forms, Teen prog, Telephone ref, Wheelchair accessible
Open Tues & Thurs 10-6, Wed & Fri 10-5, Sat 10-4
Friends of the Library Group

LACEY BRANCH, 500 College St SE, Lacey, 98503-1240, SAN 363-7778. Tel: 360-491-3860. FAX: 360-459-6714. *Libr Mgr,* Holly Paxson; Staff 21 (MLS 5, Non-MLS 16)
Founded 1966. Pop 46,020; Circ 779,638
Open Mon, Tues & Fri 10-6, Wed & Thurs 10-7, Sat 10-5
Friends of the Library Group

MCCLEARY BRANCH, 121 S Fourth St, McCleary, 98557. (Mail add: PO Box 660, McCleary, 98557-0660), SAN 329-6792. Tel: 360-495-3368. FAX: 360-495-4496. *Libr Mgr,* Karen Kienenberger; Staff 2 (MLS 1, Non-MLS 1)
Founded 1969
Open Mon, Fri & Sun 7am-8pm, Tues & Wed 7am-10am & 5pm-8pm, Thurs 7am-1pm, Sat 7am-10am & 4pm-8pm
Friends of the Library Group

MONTESANO BRANCH, 125 Main St S, Montesano, 98563-3794, SAN 363-7530. Tel: 360-249-4211. FAX: 360-249-4203. *Libr Mgr,* Christopher Springer; Staff 2 (MLS 1, Non-MLS 1)
Founded 1960. Circ 88,363
Open Tues & Wed 10-7, Thurs-Sat 10-5
Friends of the Library Group

MOUNTAIN VIEW BRANCH, 210 Silverbrook Rd, Randle, 98377. (Mail add: PO Box 340, Randle, 98377-0340), SAN 328-7114. Tel: 360-497-2665. FAX: 360-497-7080. *Libr Mgr,* Mary Prophit; Staff 2 (Non-MLS 2)
Founded 1988
Open Tues & Thurs 10-6, Wed 1-7, Sat 10-4
Friends of the Library Group

NASELLE BRANCH, Four Parpala Rd, Naselle, 98638. (Mail add: PO Box 190, Naselle, 98638-0190), SAN 328-7092. Tel: 360-484-3877. *Libr Mgr,* Michelle Zilli; Staff 2 (MLS 1, Non-MLS 1)
Founded 1986. Circ 35,463
Library Holdings: Bk Vols 14,000
Open Tues & Wed 11-8, Fri 11-5, Sat 11-3
Friends of the Library Group

NORTH MASON, 23081 NE State Rte 3, Belfair, 98528-9334. (Mail add: PO Box 1179, Belfair, 98528-1179), SAN 363-7867. Tel: 360-275-3232. FAX: 360-275-6999. *Libr Mgr,* Victoria Rexford; Staff 5 (MLS 2, Non-MLS 3)
Founded 1950. Circ 139,054
Open Tues-Thurs 10-7, Fri & Sat 10-5
Friends of the Library Group

OAKVILLE BRANCH, 204 Main St, Oakville, 98568. (Mail add: PO Box G, Oakville, 98568-0079), SAN 363-7891. Tel: 360-273-5305. FAX: 360-273-7446. *Libr Mgr,* Deborah Baker; Staff 1 (Non-MLS 1)
Circ 17,114
Open Tues & Wed 10-5, Thurs 1-7, Sat 10-4
Friends of the Library Group

OCEAN PARK BRANCH, 1308 256th Pl, Ocean Park, 98640. (Mail add: PO Box 310, Ocean Park, 98640-0310), SAN 363-7905. Tel: 360-665-4184. FAX: 360-665-5983. *Libr Mgr,* Jenny Grenfell; Staff 3 (MLS 1, Non-MLS 2)
Founded 1944. Circ 69,868
Open Tues 10-6, Wed 10-7, Thurs-Sat 10-5
Friends of the Library Group

OLYMPIA BRANCH, 313 Eighth Ave SE, Olympia, 98501-1307, SAN 363-7921. Tel: 360-352-0595. FAX: 360-586-3207. *Libr Mgr,* Morgan Sohl; Staff 21 (MLS 6, Non-MLS 15)
Pop 40,000; Circ 873,603
Subject Interests: Genealogy, Music
Function: Adult bk club, Adult literacy prog, Audiobks via web, Bilingual assistance for Spanish patrons, Bk club(s), Bks on cassette, Bks on CD, Chess club, Children's prog, Computer training, Computers for patron use, Digital talking bks, Distance learning, Electronic databases & coll, Free DVD rentals, Genealogy discussion group, Holiday prog, Home delivery & serv to seniorr ctr & nursing homes, Homework prog, ILL available, Instruction & testing, Music CDs, Online cat, Online ref, Orientations, Outreach serv, Photocopying/Printing, Preschool outreach, Prog for adults, Prog for children & young adult, Ref serv available, Senior computer classes, Senior outreach, Spoken cassettes & CDs, Spoken cassettes & DVDs, Story hour, Summer reading prog, Tax forms, Teen prog, Telephone ref, VHS videos, Wheelchair accessible, Workshops, Writing prog
Open Mon & Tues 11-8, Wed & Thurs 11-7, Fri 10-6, Sat 10-5
Friends of the Library Group

PACKWOOD BRANCH, 109 W Main St, Packwood, 98361. (Mail add: PO Box 589, Packwood, 98361-0589), SAN 363-8103. Tel: 360-494-5111. FAX: 360-494-9237. *Libr Mgr,* Judi Brummett; Staff 2 (Non-MLS 2)
Founded 1973. Circ 32,122
Open Tues 12-7, Wed 10-6, Fri 10-5, Sat 10-4
Friends of the Library Group

RAYMOND BRANCH, 507 Duryea St, Raymond, 98577-1829, SAN 363-7956. Tel: 360-942-2408. Toll Free Tel: 800-562-6022. FAX: 360-942-5670. *Libr Mgr,* Emily Popovich; Staff 4 (MLS 1, Non-MLS 3)
Founded 1913. Pop 10,000; Circ 49,371
Function: Adult bk club, Adult literacy prog, Audiobks via web, Bks on cassette, Bks on CD, CD-ROM, Children's prog, Computer training, Computers for patron use, Digital talking bks, Electronic databases & coll, ILL available, Internet access, Magnifiers for reading, Mail & tel request accepted, Museum passes, Music CDs, Online cat, Online ref, Outreach serv, Outside serv via phone, mail, e-mail & web, OverDrive digital audio bks, Photocopying/Printing, Preschool outreach, Prog for adults, Prog for children & young adult, Ref serv available, Senior computer classes, Story hour, Summer reading prog, Tax forms, Teen prog, Telephone ref, VHS videos, Wheelchair accessible
Open Tues & Thurs 10-7, Wed, Fri & Sat 10-5
Friends of the Library Group

SALKUM BRANCH, 2480 US Hwy 12, Salkum, 98582. (Mail add: PO Box 120, Salkum, 98582-0120), SAN 328-7130. Tel: 360-985-2148. FAX: 360-985-7704. *Libr Mgr,* Devon Bergeron; Staff 2 (MLS 1, Non-MLS 1)
Founded 1986. Circ 70,323
Open Tues, Fri & Sat 10-5, Wed & Thurs 1-8
Friends of the Library Group

SHELTON BRANCH, 710 W Alder St, Shelton, 98584-2571, SAN 363-7972. Tel: 360-426-1362. FAX: 360-427-2025. *Libr Mgr,* Donna Feddern; Staff 12 (MLS 4, Non-MLS 8)
Founded 1974. Circ 308,304
Library Holdings: Bk Titles 100,000; Per Subs 279
Open Mon & Tues 10-7, Wed-Fri 10-6, Sat 10-5
Friends of the Library Group

SOUTH BEND BRANCH, First & Pacific, South Bend, 98586. (Mail add: PO Box 368, South Bend, 98586-0368), SAN 363-7980. Tel: 360-875-5532. FAX: 360-875-6563. *Libr Mgr,* Jenny Penoyer; Staff 1 (Non-MLS 1)
Founded 1913. Circ 23,662
Open Tues & Fri 10-5, Wed 10-7, Sat 10-4
Friends of the Library Group

TENINO BRANCH, 172 Central Ave W, Tenino, 98589. (Mail add: PO Box 4017, Tenino, 98589-4017), SAN 363-8006. Tel: 360-264-2369. FAX: 360-264-6846. *Libr Mgr,* Linda McKinnie; Staff 2 (MLS 1, Non-MLS 1)
Circ 44,976
Open Tues & Wed 10-6, Thurs & Fri 10-5, Sat 10-4
Friends of the Library Group

TUMWATER BRANCH, 7023 New Market St, 98501-6563, SAN 363-8014. Tel: 360-943-7790. FAX: 360-586-9028. *Libr Mgr,* Nicole Thode; Staff 15 (MLS 7, Non-MLS 8)
Circ 482,583
Open Mon & Tues 10-7, Wed-Fri 10-6, Sat 10-5
Friends of the Library Group

WESTPORT BRANCH, 101 E Harms Ave, Westport, 98595. (Mail add: PO Box 1410, Westport, 98595-1410), SAN 363-8049. Tel: 360-268-0521. FAX: 360-268-0558. *Libr Mgr,* Jennifer Finlayson; Staff 2 (Non-MLS 2)
Founded 1963. Circ 41,756

Open Tues 10-6, Wed-Fri 10-5, Sat 10-4
Friends of the Library Group
WINLOCK BRANCH, 322 NE First St, Winlock, 98596. (Mail add: PO Box 428, Winlock, 98596-0428), SAN 363-8073. Tel: 360-785-3461. FAX: 360-785-3800. *Libr Mgr,* Aisha Bayness; Staff 4 (MLS 1, Non-MLS 3)
Circ 95,421
Open Tues 10-7, Wed, Fri & Sat 10-5, Thurs 10-6
Friends of the Library Group
YELM BRANCH, 210 Prairie Park St, Yelm, 98597, SAN 363-8138. Tel: 360-458-3374. FAX: 360-458-5172. *Libr Mgr,* Erica McCaleb; Staff 8 (MLS 2, Non-MLS 6)
Founded 1975. Circ 250,270
Open Tues-Thurs 10-8, Fri 10-6, Sat 10-5
Friends of the Library Group

P WASHINGTON STATE LIBRARY*, Point Plaza East, 6880 Capitol Blvd, 98501. (Mail add: PO Box 42460, Olympia, 98504-2460), SAN 363-8162. Tel: 360-704-5200. Circulation Tel: 360-704-5213. Reference Tel: 360-704-5221. FAX: 360-586-7575. Web Site: www.sos.wa.gov/library. *State Librn,* Sara Jones; E-mail: sara.jones@sos.wa.gov; *Dep State Librn,* Crystal Lentz Rowe; E-mail: crystal.rowe@sos.wa.gov; Staff 74 (MLS 35, Non-MLS 39)
Founded 1853
Library Holdings: Braille Volumes 36,502; Bk Vols 1,600,000; Per Subs 1,984; Talking Bks 108,973
Special Collections: Northwest Historical Territory Colls; Washington Newspapers; Washington State Documents. State Document Depository; US Document Depository
Subject Interests: Behav sci, Ecology, Energy, Environ studies, Health, Local govt, Med, Polit sci, Soc sci, State govt, Transportation
Automation Activity & Vendor Info: (Circulation) Innovative Interfaces, Inc
Wireless access
Function: Ref serv available
Publications: Directory of Washington Libraries; Public Administration Bibliography (Monthly); Washington Public Library Statistics; Washington State Publications (Monthly)
Partic in Amigos Library Services, Inc; Association for Rural & Small Libraries; Western Council of State Libraries, Inc
Special Services for the Deaf - Captioned film dep
Special Services for the Blind - Aids for in-house use; Assistive/Adapted tech devices, equip & products; Audio mat; Bks on cassette; Braille bks; Children's Braille; Digital talking bk; Extensive large print coll; Home delivery serv; Large print bks; Local mags & bks recorded; Machine repair; Mags & bk reproduction/duplication; Production of talking bks; Recorded bks; Sound rec; Soundproof reading booth; Talking bk & rec for the blind cat; Talking bks; Talking bks & player equip; Thermoform Brailon duplicator; Transcribing serv; Volunteer serv; Web-Braille
Open Mon-Fri 8-5
Friends of the Library Group
Branches: 11
AIRWAY HEIGHTS CORRECTIONS CENTER, 11919 W Sprague Ave, Airway Heights, 99001. (Mail add: PO Box 1899, Airway Heights, 99001-1899), SAN 378-2115.
Founded 1995
Open Mon & Tues 12:15-8:45, Wed-Fri 7:30-4
CLALLAM BAY CORRECTION CENTER, 1830 Eagle Crest Way, Clallam Bay, 98326-9775, SAN 328-2287. Tel: 360-203-1500, Ext 31345. FAX: 360-963-3293. E-mail: cbcc@sos.wa.gov.
Open Mon & Tues 12:30-9, Wed-Fri 7:30-4
EASTERN STATE HOSPITAL, Maple St, Medical Lake, 99022. (Mail add: PO Box 800, Medical Lake, 99022-0800). Tel: 509-565-4276. FAX: 509-565-4555. E-mail: esh@sos.wa.gov.
Subject Interests: Mental health
Open Mon-Fri 9-2
MONROE CORRECTIONAL COMPLEX - TWIN RIVERS UNIT LIBRARY, 16550 177th Dr SE, Monroe, 98272. (Mail add: PO Box 888, Monroe, 98272-0888), SAN 363-8553. Tel: 360-794-2445. FAX: 360-794-2417. E-mail: trcc@sos.wa.gov.
Founded 1984
Subject Interests: Popular fiction
Partic in OCLC Online Computer Library Center, Inc; Washington Libr Network
Open Mon & Tues 11:30-8, Wed-Fri 7-3:30
STAFFORD CREEK CORRECTIONAL CENTER BRANCH LIBRARY, 191 Constantine Way, Aberdeen, 98520, SAN 363-8197. Tel: 360-537-2258. FAX: 360-537-2501. E-mail: sccc@sos.wa.gov.
Open Mon & Tues 12:30-9, Wed & Thurs 7:45-4, Fri 7:45-3
WASHINGTON CORRECTIONS CENTER, 2321 W Dayton Airport Rd, Shelton, 98584. Tel: 360-432-1509. E-mail: wcc@sos.wa.gov. *Br Librn,* Laura Richardson; E-mail: laura.richardson@sos.wa.gov; Staff 2 (MLS 1, Non-MLS 1)
Open Mon & Tues 11:15-7:45, Wed-Fri 7-3:30
WASHINGTON CORRECTIONS CENTER FOR WOMEN, 9601 Bujacich Rd NW, Gig Harbor, 98332-8300, SAN 378-2158. Tel: 253-858-4230. FAX: 253-858-4271. E-mail: wccw@sos.wa.gov.
Function: ILL available
Open Mon & Tues 12:30-9, Wed-Fri 8-4:30
WASHINGTON STATE PENITENTIARY BRANCH LIBRARY - MAIN INSTITUTION, 1313 N 13th Ave, Walla Walla, 99362. Tel: 509-525-3610, Ext 5071, 509-525-3610, Ext 5072. E-mail: wsp-wc@sos.wa.gov.
Open Mon & Tues 12:15-8:45, Wed-Fri 7:30-4
WASHINGTON STATE REFORMATORY, 16550 177th Ave SE, Monroe, 98272. (Mail add: PO Box 777, Monroe, 98272-0777), SAN 363-8499. Tel: 360-794-2673, 360-794-2872. FAX: 360-794-2648. E-mail: wsr@sos.wa.gov.
Subject Interests: Corrections, Crime, Penology
Restriction: Not open to pub
Friends of the Library Group
WESTERN STATE HOSPITAL BRANCH, 9601 Steilacoom Blvd SW, W27-19, Lakewood, 98498-7213, SAN 363-8677. Tel: 253-756-2593. FAX: 253-756-3970. E-mail: wsh@sos.wa.gov. Web Site: www.dshs.wa.gov/bha/division-state-hospitals/our-library. ; Staff 1 (Non-MLS 1)
Subject Interests: Consumer health, Dual diagnosis, Mental illness, Psychiat, Psychol, Recovery, Substance abuse
Function: ILL available
Open Mon-Fri 8-4:30

UNION GAP

S YAKIMA VALLEY GENEALOGICAL SOCIETY LIBRARY*, 1901 S 12th Ave, 98903. SAN 326-7830. Tel: 509-248-1328. E-mail: yvgs1901@gmail.com. Web Site: www.yvgs.net/index.cfm?fuseaction=Page.ViewPage&pageId=480. *Head Librn,* Opal Myhres; Staff 5 (MLS 1, Non-MLS 4)
Founded 1967
Library Holdings: Bk Titles 18,000; Per Subs 300
Subject Interests: Genealogy
Wireless access
Publications: Bulletin
Open Mon-Sat 10-4

VANCOUVER

J CLARK COLLEGE*, Lewis D Cannell Library, Mail Stop LIB 112, 1933 Fort Vancouver Way, 98663-3598. SAN 317-6975. Tel: 360-992-2151. Circulation Tel: 360-992-2504. Reference Tel: 360-992-2375. Web Site: library.clark.edu. *Interim Dean of Libr,* Julie Austad; Tel: 360-992-2472, E-mail: jaustad@clark.edu; *Ref Librn (Info Serv),* Laura Nagel; Tel: 360-992-2826, E-mail: lnagel@clark.edu; *Interim Tech Services & Systems Librn,* Zachary Grant; Tel: 360-992-2971, E-mail: zgrant@clark.edu; Staff 16 (MLS 8, Non-MLS 8)
Founded 1933. Enrl 8,000; Fac 615; Highest Degree: Bachelor
Library Holdings: Bk Vols 57,846
Automation Activity & Vendor Info: (Acquisitions) Ex Libris Group; (Cataloging) Ex Libris Group; (Circulation) Ex Libris Group; (Course Reserve) Ex Libris Group; (ILL) Ex Libris Group; (Media Booking) Ex Libris Group; (OPAC) Ex Libris Group; (Serials) Ex Libris Group
Wireless access
Partic in OCLC Online Computer Library Center, Inc; Orbis Cascade Alliance; Washington Community & Technical Colleges Library Consortium
Open Mon-Thurs 9-6, Fri 9-Noon (Fall & Spring)
Departmental Libraries:
INFORMATION COMMONS @ COLUMBIA TECH CENTER, Information Commons - CTC 245, 18700 SE Mill Plain Blvd, 98683. Tel: 360-992-6138. Reference Tel: 360-992-6113.
Founded 2009
Partic in Orbis Cascade Alliance
Temporarily closed 2023-

L CLARK COUNTY LAW LIBRARY*, 1200 Franklin St, 98660. (Mail add: PO Box 5000, 98666-5000), SAN 370-5188. Tel: 564-397-2268. E-mail: lawlibrary@clark.wa.gov. Web Site: www.clark.wa.gov/law-library. *Law Librn,* Maria Sosnowski; E-mail: maria.sosnowski@clark.wa.gov
Pop 520,000
Library Holdings: Bk Titles 500; Bk Vols 19,000
Special Collections: Washington Law
Open Mon-Fri 9-2

P FORT VANCOUVER REGIONAL LIBRARY DISTRICT*, Bldg 1, Ste 100, 16821 SE McGillivray Blvd, 98683. SAN 364-2453. Tel: 360-906-5000. Reference Tel: 360-906-5106. Toll Free Tel: 800-921-6211 (Yale Valley), 888-546-2707 (Area Code 509 only). FAX: 360-693-2681. E-mail: contact@fvrl.org. Web Site: www.fvrl.org. *Interim Exec Dir,* Justin

Keeler; E-mail: jkeeler@fvrl.org; *Dir, Mkt & Communications,* Tak Kendrick; E-mail: tkendrick@fvrl.org; Staff 221 (MLS 45, Non-MLS 176)
Founded 1950. Pop 506,444; Circ 4,400,000
Library Holdings: Bk Vols 725,754
Wireless access
Function: 24/7 Electronic res, 24/7 Online cat, 3D Printer, Adult bk club, Art exhibits, Art programs, Audiobks on Playaways & MP3, Audiobks via web, Bilingual assistance for Spanish patrons, Bk club(s), Bks on CD, Children's prog, Computer training, Computers for patron use, Distance learning, Doc delivery serv, Electronic databases & coll, Free DVD rentals, Genealogy discussion group, Govt ref serv, Holiday prog, Home delivery & serv to seniorr ctr & nursing homes, Homebound delivery serv, ILL available, Internet access, Jail serv, Large print keyboards, Life-long learning prog for all ages, Magazines, Magnifiers for reading, Mail & tel request accepted, Mail loans to mem, Mango lang, Meeting rooms, Microfiche/film & reading machines, Movies, Online cat, Online info literacy tutorials on the web & in blackboard, Online ref, Outreach serv, Outside serv via phone, mail, e-mail & web, OverDrive digital audio bks, Photocopying/Printing, Preschool outreach, Preschool reading prog, Printer for laptops & handheld devices, Prof lending libr, Prog for adults, Prog for children & young adult, Ref & res, Ref serv available, Senior computer classes, Senior outreach, Serves people with intellectual disabilities, Spanish lang bks, STEM programs, Story hour, Study rm, Summer & winter reading prog, Summer reading prog, Tax forms, Teen prog, Telephone ref, Visual arts prog, Wheelchair accessible, Winter reading prog, Workshops, Writing prog
Open Mon-Fri 8-5
Friends of the Library Group
Branches: 14

BATTLE GROUND COMMUNITY LIBRARY, 1207 SE Eighth Way, Battle Ground, 98604, SAN 364-2488. *Br Mgr,* Holland Christie; E-mail: hchristie@fvrl.org
Circ 550,461
Open Mon-Thurs 10-8, Fri & Sat 10-6
Friends of the Library Group

CASCADE PARK COMMUNITY LIBRARY, 600 NE 136th Ave, 98684, SAN 377-0397. FAX: 360-256-7987. *Br Mgr,* Rachael Ries; E-mail: rries@fvrl.org
Circ 725,580
Open Mon-Thurs 9-8, Fri & Sat 9-6
Friends of the Library Group

GOLDENDALE COMMUNITY LIBRARY, 131 W Burgen St, Goldendale, 98620, SAN 364-2518. Tel: 509-773-4487. *Br Mgr,* Terra McLeod; E-mail: tmcleod@fvrl.org
Circ 85,232
Open Mon-Sat 10-6
Friends of the Library Group

LA CENTER COMMUNITY LIBRARY, 1411 NE Lockwood Creek Rd, La Center, 98629. Tel: 360-906-4760. *Br Mgr,* Jurinda Swingruber; E-mail: jswingruber@fvrl.org
Circ 59,764
Open Mon-Wed & Fri 10-6, Thurs 10-8
Friends of the Library Group

NORTH BONNEVILLE COMMUNITY LIBRARY, 214 CBD Mall (Inside City Hall), North Bonneville, 98639, SAN 364-2542. Tel: 509-427-4439. *Commun Librn,* David Wyatt; E-mail: dwyatt@fvrl.org
Circ 7,902
Open Tues-Thurs 1-5

RIDGEFIELD COMMUNITY LIBRARY, 228 Simons St, Ridgefield, 98642, SAN 364-2577. *Br Mgr,* Sean McGill; E-mail: smcgill@fvrl.org
Circ 61,863
Open Mon-Sat 10-5
Friends of the Library Group

STEVENSON COMMUNITY LIBRARY, 120 NW Vancouver Ave, Stevenson, 98648, SAN 364-2607. *Br Mgr,* David Wyatt; E-mail: dwyatt@fvrl.org
Circ 54,378
Open Mon-Fri 9-7, Sat 9-5
Friends of the Library Group

THE MALL LIBRARY CONNECTION, 8700 NE Vancouver Mall Dr, Ste 285, 98662, SAN 364-264X. *Commun Librn,* Brandon Cruz; E-mail: bcruz@fvrl.org
Circ 226,094
Open Mon-Thur 10-7, Fri & Sat 10-6, Sun 1-6
Friends of the Library Group

THREE CREEKS COMMUNITY LIBRARY, 800-C NE Tenney Rd, 98685. Tel: 360-906-5000. *Br Mgr,* Barbara Jorgensen; E-mail: bjorgensen@fvrl.org
Circ 470,379
Open Mon-Thurs 10-8, Fri & Sat 10-6
Friends of the Library Group

VANCOUVER COMMUNITY LIBRARY (MAIN LIBRARY), 901 C St, 98660, SAN 364-2631. *Commun Librn,* Kelly Lamm; E-mail: klamm@fvrl.org
Founded 1877. Circ 882,792
Open Mon-Thurs 9-8, Fri-Sun 10-6
Friends of the Library Group

WASHOUGAL COMMUNITY LIBRARY, 1661 C St, Washougal, 98671, SAN 364-2666. *Br Mgr,* Rachael Ries; E-mail: rries@fvrl.org
Circ 78,323
Open Mon-Sat 10-5
Friends of the Library Group

WHITE SALMON VALLEY COMMUNITY LIBRARY, 77 NE Wauna Ave, White Salmon, 98672, SAN 364-2690. Tel: 509-493-1132. *Commun Librn,* Ruth Schafer; E-mail: rschafer@fvrl.org
Circ 137,522
Open Mon-Sat 10-5
Friends of the Library Group

WOODLAND COMMUNITY LIBRARY, 770 Park St, Woodland, 98674. *Br Mgr,* Jennifer Hauan; E-mail: jhauan@fvrl.org
Circ 60,432
Open Mon-Sat 10-5
Friends of the Library Group

YACOLT LIBRARY EXPRESS, 105 E Yacolt Rd, Yacolt, 98675. *Br Mgr,* Holland Christie; E-mail: hchristie@fvrl.org
Circ 49,911
Open Mon, Thurs & Sat 12-3
Friends of the Library Group

Bookmobiles: 2. Sr Libr Asst, Judy Bane

R GATEWAY SEMINARY*, Pacific Northwest Campus, 3200 NE 109th Ave, 98682-7749. Tel: 360-882-2200. FAX: 360-882-2275. Web Site: library.gs.edu. *Dir, Libr Serv,* Bob Phillips; E-mail: BobPhillips@gs.edu; *Campus Librn,* Ashley Seuell; Tel: 360-882-2179, E-mail: ashleys@nwbaptist.org
Wireless access
Open Mon 9:30-9:30, Tues 8:30-5, Wed-Fri 9-4:30

G US NATIONAL PARK SERVICE, Fort Vancouver National Historic Site Library, 1001 E Fifth St, 98661. SAN 317-6991. Tel: 360-816-6244. Web Site: www.nps.gov/fova. *Curator,* Tessa Langford
Founded 1948
Library Holdings: Bk Vols 1,300; Per Subs 4
Special Collections: Fort Vancouver National Historic Site Archaeological Documents
Subject Interests: Hudson's Bay Co, Pac NW fur trade
Wireless access
Restriction: Open to staff only

S WASHINGTON SCHOOL FOR THE DEAF, McGill Library, 611 Grand Blvd, 98661-4498. SAN 317-7017. Tel: 360-696-6525, Ext 4352. Toll Free Tel: 800-833-6384. FAX: 360-418-0418. Web Site: www.wsd.wa.gov/academics/library. *Librn,* Ginger Speranza
Founded 1886
Library Holdings: Bks on Deafness & Sign Lang 150; Bk Vols 10,978; Per Subs 3
Special Collections: Professional Coll for Educators of the Deaf
Special Services for the Deaf - Bks on deafness & sign lang; Captioned film dep; TTY equip; Videos & decoder
Restriction: Not open to pub

C WASHINGTON STATE UNIVERSITY LIBRARIES, Vancouver Library, 14204 NE Salmon Creek Ave, 98686. Tel: 360-546-9680. Interlibrary Loan Service Tel: 360-546-9683. Reference Tel: 360-546-9686. FAX: 360-546-9039. E-mail: van.library@wsu.edu. Web Site: library.vancouver.wsu.edu. *Libr Dir, Student Success Librn,* Ms Sam Buechler; E-mail: sam.buechler@wsu.edu; *Assoc Libr Dir,* Nicole Campbell; Tel: 360-546-9687, E-mail: nmcampbell@wsu.edu; *Ref & Digital Librn,* Mark Hasse; Tel: 360-546-9275, E-mail: mark.hasse@wsu.edu; *Access Serv Mgr, Circ & Reserves Supvr,* Dena Madrid; E-mail: dena.madrid@wsu.edu; *Tech Serv Supvr,* Kerry Hodge; Tel: 360-546-9684, E-mail: hodge@wsu.edu; *Archivist,* Robert Schimelpfenig; Tel: 360-546-9249, E-mail: schimo@wsu.edu; *ILL Spec,* Christopher Wiley-Smith; Tel: 360-546-9154, E-mail: christopher.w.wiley@wsu.edu; Staff 9 (MLS 5, Non-MLS 4)
Founded 1989
Library Holdings: Bk Titles 31,000; Per Subs 412
Automation Activity & Vendor Info: (ILL) OCLC
Wireless access
Open Mon-Thurs 7:30am-8pm, Fri 7:30-5, Sun 1-7 (Fall-Spring); Mon-Thurs 9-6, Fri 9-4, Sun 1-6 (Summer)

WAITSBURG

P WELLER PUBLIC LIBRARY*, 212 Main St, 99361. (Mail add: PO Box 35, 99361-0035). Tel: 509-337-8149. E-mail: wellerpubliclibrary@yahoo.com. Web Site: wellerpubliclibrary.com. *Dir,* Rosie Warehime; Staff 1 (Non-MLS 1)
Pop 1,210; Circ 3,220

Library Holdings: CDs 50; Large Print Bks 200; Bk Vols 2,000; Talking Bks 100
Wireless access
Function: Prog for children & young adult, Summer reading prog
Open Mon & Thurs 10-5, Sat 10-12
Friends of the Library Group

WALLA WALLA

A UNITED STATES ARMY*, Corps of Engineers, Walla Walla District Technical Library, 201 N Third, 99362-1876. SAN 364-278X. Tel: 509-527-7427. FAX: 509-527-7816. E-mail: cenww-im-sl@usace.army.mil. Web Site: www.nww.usace.army.mil/library. *Tech Serv,* Angie Camarillo
Founded 1948
Library Holdings: Bk Vols 19,000; Per Subs 300
Special Collections: Law Coll
Subject Interests: Army field law libr, Civil works constr, Engr, Fish, Hydrol, Water res, Wildlife

GM JONATHAN M WAINWRIGHT MEMORIAL VA MEDICAL CENTER LIBRARY, Walla Walla VAMC Library, 77 Wainwright Dr, 99362. SAN 317-7041. Tel: 509-525-5200, Ext 26162. *Med Librn,* Michael Harvey; E-mail: michael.harvey3@va.gov
Library Holdings: Audiobooks 300; DVDs 300; Bk Vols 5,300; Videos 400
Subject Interests: Med, Nursing
Partic in National Network of Libraries of Medicine Region 5; Veterans Affairs Library Network
Open Mon-Fri 8:15-4:30

J WALLA WALLA COMMUNITY COLLEGE LIBRARY*, 500 Tausick Way, 99362-9267. SAN 317-705X. Tel: 509-527-4277. FAX: 509-527-4480. E-mail: library@wwcc.edu. Web Site: www.wwcc.edu/library. *Dir, Libr Serv,* Jacquelyn Ray; E-mail: jacquelyn.ray@wwcc.edu; *Fac Librn,* Jana Lu Williams; Tel: 509-527-4292, E-mail: jana.lu.williams@wwcc.edu; *Clarkston Ctr Libr Coordr,* Jackson Vance; Tel: 509-758-1714, E-mail: jackson.vance@wwcc.edu; *Cat,* Janelle Meier; Tel: 509-527-4297, E-mail: janelle.meier@wwcc.edu; *ILL,* Jennifer Taylor; E-mail: jennifer.taylor@wwcc.edu; Staff 5 (MLS 2, Non-MLS 3)
Founded 1967. Enrl 2,000; Fac 1; Highest Degree: Associate
Automation Activity & Vendor Info: (Cataloging) LibLime Koha; (Circulation) LibLime Koha; (Course Reserve) LibLime Koha; (ILL) OCLC; (OPAC) LibLime Koha; (Serials) LibLime Koha
Wireless access
Function: 24/7 Electronic res, 24/7 Online cat
Partic in Washington Community & Technical Colleges Library Consortium
Open Mon-Thurs 7:30-5:30, Fri 7:30-4
Restriction: Open to fac, students & qualified researchers, Open to staff, students & ancillary prof, Open to students, Open to students, fac & staff

GL WALLA WALLA COUNTY LAW LIBRARY, County Courthouse, 315 W Main St, 99362. SAN 317-7068. Tel: 509-524-2796. *Law Librn,* Rachel Taylor; Tel: 509-524-2795, E-mail: rtaylor@co.walla-walla.wa.us
Library Holdings: Bk Vols 14,530
Open Mon-Fri 9-4

P WALLA WALLA COUNTY RURAL LIBRARY DISTRICT*, 37 Jade Ave, 99362. SAN 373-8272. Tel: 509-527-3284. Toll Free Tel: 800-547-7349. FAX: 509-527-3740. Web Site: www.wwrurallibrary.com. *Exec Dir,* Rhonda Gould; E-mail: rhondag@wwrurallibrary.com; *Libr Office Mgr,* Jean Sansom; E-mail: jsansom@wwrurallibrary.com; *Tech Mgr,* Mundy Mulligan; E-mail: mundym@wwrurallibrary.com; Staff 15 (MLS 1, Non-MLS 14)
Founded 1972. Pop 16,000
Automation Activity & Vendor Info: (Cataloging) LibLime; (Circulation) LibLime; (ILL) OCLC
Wireless access
Function: For res purposes, Homebound delivery serv, ILL available, Photocopying/Printing, Prog for children & young adult, Ref serv available, Summer reading prog, Telephone ref, Wheelchair accessible
Partic in Association for Rural & Small Libraries; Walla Walla Area Library Network
Special Services for the Deaf - Bks on deafness & sign lang
Friends of the Library Group
Branches: 5
BURBANK LIBRARY, 875 Lake Rd, Burbank, 99323. Tel: 509-545-6549. FAX: 509-545-3151. E-mail: burbank@wwrurallibrary.com. *Br Mgr,* Amy Schmidt; E-mail: amy@wwcrld.org
Library Holdings: Bk Vols 30,000; Per Subs 32
Function: 24/7 Online cat, Adult bk club, Bilingual assistance for Spanish patrons, Bks on CD, Children's prog, Computers for patron use, E-Readers, Electronic databases & coll, Holiday prog, Homework prog, ILL available, Internet access, Magazines, Mango lang, Meeting rooms, Movies, Online cat, Outreach serv, Photocopying/Printing, Prog for children & young adult, Spanish lang bks, Story hour, Summer reading prog, Tax forms, Teen prog, Wheelchair accessible
Open Mon-Thurs 11-7, Fri 12-5, Sat 9-2
Friends of the Library Group
PLAZA LIBRARY, 1640 Plaza Way, 99362. Tel: 509-525-5161. FAX: 509-876-0076. E-mail: plaza@wwrurallibrary.com. *Br Mgr,* Christopher Eckstadt
Function: 24/7 Online cat, Adult bk club, Bilingual assistance for Spanish patrons, Bks on CD, Children's prog, Computers for patron use, E-Readers, Electronic databases & coll, ILL available, Internet access, Magazines, Mango lang, Meeting rooms, Online cat, Prog for children & young adult, Spanish lang bks, Story hour, Summer reading prog, Tax forms, Wheelchair accessible
Open Mon-Thurs 11-7, Fri 11-5, Sat & Sun 11-4
PRESCOTT LIBRARY, 103 S D St, Prescott, 99348. (Mail add: PO Box 114, Prescott, 99348-0114). Tel: 509-849-2411. FAX: 509-849-2411. E-mail: prescott@wwrurallibrary.com. *Exec Dir,* Ana Romero; E-mail: ana@wwcrld.org
Founded 2003
Library Holdings: AV Mats 400; Bk Titles 8,500; Talking Bks 400
Function: 24/7 Online cat, Bks on CD, Children's prog, Computers for patron use, Electronic databases & coll, Holiday prog, ILL available, Internet access, Magazines, Online cat, Prog for children & young adult, Spanish lang bks, Summer reading prog, Teen prog, Wheelchair accessible
Open Tues & Thurs 11-7, Fri 12-6, Sat 11-4
Friends of the Library Group
TOUCHET COMMUNITY LIBRARY, 161 Hanson Rd, Touchet, 99360. (Mail add: PO Box 166, Touchet, 99360-0166). Tel: 509-394-2329. FAX: 509-394-2329. E-mail: touchet@wwcrld.org. *Libr Mgr,* Rebekah Shaw
Founded 1987. Pop 500; Circ 15,000
Library Holdings: Bk Vols 14,000; Per Subs 15
Function: 24/7 Online cat, Adult bk club, Bk club(s), Bks on CD, Children's prog, Computers for patron use, E-Readers, Electronic databases & coll, Free DVD rentals, Holiday prog, ILL available, Internet access, Magazines, Mango lang, Online cat, Photocopying/Printing, Prog for adults, Prog for children & young adult, Spanish lang bks, Story hour, Summer reading prog, Tax forms, Teen prog, Wheelchair accessible
Open Tues & Fri 12-5, Wed 12-8, Sat 10-2
Friends of the Library Group
VISTA HERMOSA LIBRARY, 76 Sarah Lynne Lane, Prescott, 99348. (Mail add: PO Box 658, Prescott, 99348). Tel: 509-749-2099. FAX: 509-749-2099. E-mail: vista@wwrurallibrary.com. *Br Supvr,* Position Currently Open
Founded 2005
Function: 24/7 Online cat, Bilingual assistance for Spanish patrons, Bks on CD, Children's prog, Computers for patron use, Electronic databases & coll, Holiday prog, ILL available, Internet access, Magazines, Mango lang, Online cat, Prog for children & young adult, Spanish lang bks, Summer reading prog
Open Tues & Thurs 12-8, Wed 1-4 & 6-8

P WALLA WALLA PUBLIC LIBRARY*, 238 E Alder St, 99362. SAN 317-7076. Tel: 509-527-4550. FAX: 509-524-7950. Web Site: wallawallapubliclibrary.org. *Dir, Libr Serv,* Heather Vantassell; Tel: 509-524-4433; *Pub Serv Librn,* Twila Johnson Tate; Tel: 509-524-4443; *Support Serv Librn,* Alexis Rodegerdts; Tel: 509-524-4609; *Young People's Librn,* Elizabeth George; Tel: 509-524-4431, E-mail: egeorge@wallawallawa.gov; Staff 13 (MLS 4, Non-MLS 9)
Founded 1897. Pop 33,390; Circ 302,829
Jan 2016-Dec 2016 Income $190,299, City $110,769, Locally Generated Income $53,480, Other $26,050. Mats Exp $153,900, Books $94,740, Per/Ser (Incl. Access Fees) $6,000, AV Mat $25,260, Electronic Ref Mat (Incl. Access Fees) $27,900. Sal $567,430
Library Holdings: Audiobooks 2,854; CDs 2,320; DVDs 4,407; e-books 28,541; Electronic Media & Resources 19; Large Print Bks 1,323; Bk Vols 84,813; Per Subs 106
Subject Interests: Local hist
Automation Activity & Vendor Info: (Cataloging) ByWater Solutions; (Circulation) ByWater Solutions; (ILL) ByWater Solutions; (OPAC) ByWater Solutions; (Serials) ByWater Solutions
Wireless access
Function: 24/7 Electronic res, 24/7 Online cat, Activity rm, Adult bk club, Archival coll, Audiobks via web, Bilingual assistance for Spanish patrons, Bk club(s), Bks on CD, Children's prog, Computer training, Computers for patron use, Digital talking bks, E-Readers, Electronic databases & coll, Family literacy, For res purposes, Free DVD rentals, ILL available, Internet access, Life-long learning prog for all ages, Magazines, Magnifiers for reading, Mail & tel request accepted, Music CDs, Online cat, OverDrive digital audio bks, Photocopying/Printing, Printer for laptops & handheld devices, Prog for adults, Prog for children & young adult, Ref & res, Ref serv available, Scanner, Spanish lang bks, Story hour, Study rm, Summer

& winter reading prog, Summer reading prog, Telephone ref, Wheelchair accessible, Winter reading prog
Open Mon-Fri 10-7, Sat 10-3
Friends of the Library Group

C WHITMAN COLLEGE*, Penrose Library, 345 Boyer Ave, 99362. SAN 317-7092. Tel: 509-527-5191. Circulation Tel: 509-527-5192. Interlibrary Loan Service Tel: 509-527-5914. FAX: 509-526-4785. E-mail: library@whitman.edu. Web Site: library.whitman.edu. *Col Librn,* Ping Fu; Tel: 509-527-5193, E-mail: fup@whitman.edu; *Archivist, Head, Spec Coll,* Alexis Hickey; Tel: 509-526-4731, E-mail: hickeya@whitman.edu; *Head, User Serv,* Julie Carter; Tel: 509-527-5915, E-mail: carterja@whitman.edu; *Coll Strategist Librn,* Position Currently Open; *Digital Assets Librn, Metadata Librn,* Paige Morfitt; Tel: 509-527-5920, E-mail: morfitbp@whitman.edu; *Libr Syst & Applications Librn,* Tracy Tolf; Tel: 509-527-5916, E-mail: tolft@whitman.edu; *Instruction Coordr, Outreach Librn,* M Emily Pearson; Tel: 509-527-5918, E-mail: pearsome@whitman.edu; *Scholarly Communications Librn,* Amy Blau; Tel: 509-527-4905, E-mail: blauar@whitman.edu; *Student Success & Instruction Librn,* Bridget Scoles; Tel: 509-527-5917, E-mail: scolesb@whitman.edu; *ILL, Mgr, Access Serv,* Ari Kirby; E-mail: kirbyk@whitman.edu; *Assoc Archivist,* River Freemont; Tel: 509-526-4703, E-mail: freemonr@whitman.edu; Staff 10 (MLS 10)
Founded 1882. Enrl 1,537; Fac 175; Highest Degree: Bachelor
Jul 2023-Jun 2024. Mats Exp $1,400,887, Books $59,663, Per/Ser (Incl. Access Fees) $611,686, AV Mat $24,451, Electronic Ref Mat (Incl. Access Fees) $705,087. Sal $1,399,359 (Prof $704,992)
Library Holdings: AV Mats 8,230; DVDs 5,529; e-books 800,188; e-journals 139,712; Electronic Media & Resources 50,579; Microforms 1,786; Music Scores 188; Bk Titles 470,559; Bk Vols 645,808; Videos 81,074
Special Collections: Dogwood Press Coll; Early Illustrated Books (McFarlane Coll); Stuart Napoleon Coll. US Document Depository
Automation Activity & Vendor Info: (Acquisitions) Ex Libris Group; (Cataloging) Ex Libris Group; (Circulation) Ex Libris Group; (Discovery) Ex Libris Group; (ILL) OCLC ILLiad; (OPAC) Ex Libris Group; (Serials) Ex Libris Group
Wireless access
Function: 24/7 Electronic res, Archival coll, Art exhibits, Audio & video playback equip for onsite use, Audiobks via web, Computers for patron use, Doc delivery serv, E-Reserves, Electronic databases & coll, ILL available, Internet access, Magnifiers for reading, Microfiche/film & reading machines, Online cat, Online ref, Photocopying/Printing, Printer for laptops & handheld devices, Ref & res, Ref serv available, Scanner, Study rm
Partic in Oberlin Group; OCLC Online Computer Library Center, Inc; Orbis Cascade Alliance
Open Mon-Thurs 7:20am-1am, Fri 7:30-6, Sat 10-6, Sun 10am-1am
Restriction: 24-hr pass syst for students only, Authorized scholars by appt, Fee for pub use, Non-circulating of rare bks, Open to pub for ref & circ; with some limitations

WENATCHEE

M CONFLUENCE HEALTH - CENTRAL WASHINGTON HOSPITAL*, Heminger Health Library, 1201 S Miller St, 98801. SAN 317-7106. Tel: 509-664-3476. FAX: 509-433-3312. E-mail: library@confluencehealth.org. Web Site: confluencehealth.ovidds.com. *Mgr,* Angela Prater; E-mail: angela.prater@confluencehealth.org; *Library Contact,* Jessica Brooks; E-mail: jessica.brooks@confluencehealth.org; Staff 0.5 (Non-MLS 0.5)
Founded 1972
Library Holdings: Bk Titles 500; Per Subs 100
Subject Interests: Consumer health, Health, Hospital mgt, Hospital serv, Med, Nursing
Automation Activity & Vendor Info: (Acquisitions) Ex Libris Group; (Cataloging) Ex Libris Group; (Circulation) Ex Libris Group; (OPAC) Ex Libris Group; (Serials) Ex Libris Group
Wireless access
Partic in National Network of Libraries of Medicine Region 5
Open Mon-Fri 8-4:30

P NORTH CENTRAL WASHINGTON LIBRARIES*, 16 N Columbia St, 98801. SAN 364-281X. Tel: 509-663-1117. Interlibrary Loan Service Tel: 509-662-5021. Toll Free Tel: 800-426-7323. Administration FAX: 509-662-8554. E-mail: info@ncrl.org. Web Site: www.ncrl.org. *Exec Dir,* Barbara Walters; Tel: 509-663-1117, Ext 129, E-mail: bwalters@ncrl.org; *Dir, Pub Serv,* Angela Morris; Tel: 509-663-1117, Ext 119, E-mail: amorris@ncrl.org; *Asst Dir, Info Tech,* Chad Roseburg; Tel: 509-663-1117, Ext 134, E-mail: croseburg@ncrl.org; Staff 85 (MLS 5, Non-MLS 80)
Founded 1961. Pop 239,695; Circ 1,484,715
Library Holdings: Audiobooks 31,385; AV Mats 52,910; Bk Vols 526,560; Per Subs 898
Special Collections: State Document Depository
Subject Interests: Compact discs, NW hist
Automation Activity & Vendor Info: (Acquisitions) ByWater Solutions; (Cataloging) ByWater Solutions; (Circulation) ByWater Solutions; (ILL) OCLC; (OPAC) ByWater Solutions
Wireless access
Function: Bk club(s), Bks on CD, Homebound delivery serv, ILL available, Jail serv, Outreach serv, OverDrive digital audio bks, Senior outreach, Summer reading prog
Publications: Mail Order Library Catalogs (Quarterly)
Partic in OCLC Online Computer Library Center, Inc
Open Mon-Fri 8-5
Restriction: Registered patrons only
Friends of the Library Group
Branches: 30

BREWSTER PUBLIC LIBRARY, 108 S Third St, Brewster, 98812. (Mail add: PO Box 280, Brewster, 98812-0280), SAN 317-4905. Tel: 509-689-4046. FAX: 509-689-4046. E-mail: brewster@ncrl.org. *Librn,* Rebecca Zion
Circ 24,825
Library Holdings: Bk Vols 9,816; Talking Bks 239; Videos 1,030
Open Tues-Sat 10:30-6:30
Restriction: Registered patrons only

BRIDGEPORT PUBLIC LIBRARY, 1206 Columbia Ave, Bridgeport, 98813. (Mail add: PO Box 220, Bridgeport, 98813-0220). Tel: 509-686-7281. FAX: 509-686-7281. E-mail: bridgeport@ncrl.org. *Librn,* Michelle Orosco
Circ 19,968
Library Holdings: Bk Vols 9,147; Talking Bks 243; Videos 1,475
Open Mon-Sat 9-5
Restriction: Registered patrons only
Friends of the Library Group

CASHMERE PUBLIC LIBRARY, 300 Woodring St, Cashmere, 98815-1061. Tel: 509-782-3314. E-mail: cashmere@ncrl.org. Web Site: www.ncwlibraries.org/locations/cashmere-public-library. *Librn,* Lisa Lawless
Circ 36,835
Library Holdings: Bk Vols 13,782; Talking Bks 291; Videos 1,385
Open Mon-Wed & Fri 9-6, Thurs 11-8, Sat 9-1
Restriction: Registered patrons only
Friends of the Library Group

CHELAN PUBLIC LIBRARY, 216 N Emerson St, Chelan, 98816. (Mail add: PO Box 698, Chelan, 98816-0698). Tel: 509-682-5131. E-mail: chelan@ncrl.org. *Librn,* Deidre Beltran del Rio; *Librn,* Alex Hill
Circ 43,136
Library Holdings: Bk Vols 11,946; Talking Bks 366; Videos 1,360
Open Mon, Wed & Fri 10-6, Tues & Thurs 10-8, Sat 11-4
Restriction: Registered patrons only
Friends of the Library Group

COULEE PUBLIC LIBRARY, 405 W Main St, Coulee City, 99115. (Mail add: PO Box 387, Coulee City, 99115-0387). Tel: 509-632-8751. E-mail: couleecity@ncrl.org. *Librn,* Nancy Miller
Circ 12,403
Library Holdings: Bk Vols 5,400; Talking Bks 154; Videos 932
Open Mon-Wed 11-5, Sat 10-1
Restriction: Registered patrons only

CURLEW PUBLIC LIBRARY, 11 River St, Curlew, 99118. (Mail add: PO Box 25, Curlew, 99118). Tel: 509-779-0321. E-mail: curlew@ncrl.org. *Librn,* Emily Patterson
Open Tues-Fri 10-5, Sat 10-2
Friends of the Library Group

EAST WENATCHEE PUBLIC LIBRARY, 271 Ninth St NE, East Wenatchee, 98802-4438. Tel: 509-886-7404. FAX: 509-886-7404. E-mail: eastwenatchee@ncrl.org. *Librn,* Sandi Purcell
Circ 41,496
Library Holdings: Bk Vols 8,875; Talking Bks 364; Videos 1,274
Open Mon-Fri 9-5
Restriction: Registered patrons only
Friends of the Library Group

ENTIAT PUBLIC LIBRARY, 14138 Kinzel St, Entiat, 98822. (Mail add: PO Box 357, Entiat, 98822-0357). Tel: 509-784-1517. E-mail: entiat@ncrl.org. *Librn,* Suzy Nieto
Circ 11,813
Library Holdings: Bk Vols 6,305; Talking Bks 156; Videos 839
Open Mon & Wed 9-5, Tues & Thurs 11-7
Restriction: Registered patrons only

EPHRATA PUBLIC LIBRARY, 45 Alder NW, Ephrata, 98823-1663, SAN 317-5111. Tel: 509-754-3971. E-mail: ephrata@ncrl.org. *Librn,* Aaron Loeffelbein
Circ 74,419
Library Holdings: Bk Vols 25,901; Talking Bks 375; Videos 1,761
Special Collections: Grant County Genealogical Society
Open Mon-Thurs 9-8, Fri 9-5, Sat 11-4
Restriction: Registered patrons only
Friends of the Library Group

GRAND COULEE PUBLIC LIBRARY, 225 Federal St, Grand Coulee, 99133. (Mail add: PO Box 650, Grand Coulee, 99133-0062). Tel: 509-633-0972. E-mail: grandcoulee@ncrl.org. *Librn,* Lisa Moore
Circ 29,606
Library Holdings: Bk Vols 13,421; Per Subs 28; Talking Bks 239; Videos 1,346
Open Mon & Wed 9:30-6, Tues & Thurs 10:30-7:30, Fri 9:30-5:30, Sat 10-2
Restriction: Registered patrons only
Friends of the Library Group

LEAVENWORTH PUBLIC LIBRARY, 700 Hwy 2, Leavenworth, 98826. (Mail add: PO Box 308, Leavenworth, 98826-0308). Tel: 509-548-7923. E-mail: leavenworth@ncrl.org. *Librn,* Joanne Gembe
Circ 40,901
Library Holdings: Bk Vols 15,400; Talking Bks 293; Videos 1,012
Open Mon-Wed & Fri 9-6, Thurs 9-8
Restriction: Registered patrons only
Friends of the Library Group

MANSON PUBLIC LIBRARY, 80 Wapato Way, Manson, 98831-9210. (Mail add: PO Box L, Manson, 98831-0400). Tel: 509-687-3420. E-mail: manson@ncrl.org. *Librn,* Cindy Simmons
Circ 17,604
Library Holdings: Bk Vols 7,021; Talking Bks 162; Videos 1,012
Open Mon, Wed & Thurs 10:30-5:30, Tues 12:30-7:30, Fri 10-2
Restriction: Registered patrons only

MATTAWA PUBLIC LIBRARY, 101 Manson Lane, Mattawa, 99349. (Mail add: PO Box 967, Mattawa, 99349-0954). Tel: 509-932-5507. E-mail: mattawa@ncrl.org. *Librn,* Courtney Tiffany
Founded 2002. Circ 21,926
Library Holdings: Bk Vols 6,900; Talking Bks 243; Videos 1,147
Open Mon & Wed 1-6, Tues & Thurs 9-4, Fri 12-4
Restriction: Registered patrons only

MOSES LAKE PUBLIC LIBRARY, 418 E Fifth Ave, Moses Lake, 98837-1797. Tel: 509-765-3489. E-mail: moseslake@ncrl.org. *Regional Mgr,* Roxanne Southwood; *Librn,* Connie Baulne; Staff 5 (Non-MLS 5)
Circ 15,687
Open Mon-Thurs 9-8, Fri 9-6, Sat 9-5, Sun 1-5
Restriction: Registered patrons only
Friends of the Library Group

OKANOGAN PUBLIC LIBRARY, 228 Pine St, Okanogan, 98840. (Mail add: PO Box 489, Okanogan, 98840-0489). Tel: 509-422-2609. E-mail: okanogan@ncrl.org. *Librn,* Jann Timm
Circ 15,385
Library Holdings: Bk Vols 10,256; Talking Bks 155; Videos 1,299
Open Tues-Fri 11-6, Sat 11-3
Restriction: Registered patrons only

OMAK PUBLIC LIBRARY, 30 S Ash, Omak, 98841. (Mail add: PO Box J, Omak, 98841-0969). Tel: 509-826-1820. E-mail: omak@ncrl.org. *Communications Mgr,* Amanda Brack; E-mail: abrack@ncwlibraries.org
Circ 79,832
Library Holdings: Bk Vols 25,209; Talking Bks 475; Videos 2,789
Open Mon-Thurs 9-8, Fri & Sat 9-5, Sun 1-5
Restriction: Registered patrons only
Friends of the Library Group

OROVILLE PUBLIC LIBRARY, 1276 Main St, Oroville, 98844. Tel: 509-476-2662. E-mail: oroville@ncwlibraries.org. Web Site: www.ncwlibraries.org/locations/oroville-public-library/. *Librn,* Heather Burnell
Founded 1960. Circ 31,900
Function: 24/7 Electronic res, 24/7 Online cat, 24/7 wireless access, Adult bk club, Bks on CD, Children's prog, Computers for patron use, Digital talking bks, Distance learning, Extended outdoor wifi, Free DVD rentals, ILL available, Life-long learning prog for all ages, Magazines, Mail & tel request accepted, Mail loans to mem, Movies, Museum passes, Music CDs, Online cat, Online Chat, Online info literacy tutorials on the web & in blackboard, Outreach serv, Outside serv via phone, mail, e-mail & web, OverDrive digital audio bks, Photocopying/Printing, Prog for adults, Prog for children & young adult, Scanner, Senior outreach, Spanish lang bks, Story hour, Summer & winter reading prog, Summer reading prog, Tax forms, Wheelchair accessible, Wifi hotspot checkout, Winter reading prog
Open Tues 11:30-7:30, Wed-Sat 9:30-5:30
Restriction: Registered patrons only
Friends of the Library Group

PATEROS PUBLIC LIBRARY, 174 Pateros Mall, Pateros, 98846. (Mail add: PO Box 306, Pateros, 98846-0306). Tel: 509-923-2298. E-mail: pateros@ncrl.org. *Librn,* Shari Houck
Circ 16,569
Library Holdings: Bk Vols 5,886; Talking Bks 149; Videos 837
Open Tues 1-6, Wed & Thurs 11-5, Fri 10-5, Sat 10-2
Restriction: Registered patrons only
Friends of the Library Group

PESHASTIN PUBLIC LIBRARY, 8396 Main St, Peshastin, 98847-9734. (Mail add: PO Box 408, Peshastin, 98847-0408). Tel: 509-548-7821. E-mail: peshastin@ncrl.org. *Librn,* Patricia Reed
Circ 10,756
Library Holdings: Bk Vols 6,092; Talking Bks 199; Videos 770
Open Tues 3-7, Wed-Fri 2-6, Sat 9-6
Restriction: Registered patrons only
Friends of the Library Group

QUINCY PUBLIC LIBRARY, 208 Central Ave S, Quincy, 98848-1203. Tel: 509-787-2359. E-mail: quincy@ncrl.org. *Librn,* Schiree Ybarra
Circ 73,806
Library Holdings: Bk Vols 13,864; Talking Bks 487; Videos 1,946
Open Mon-Thurs 9-8, Fri & Sat 9-6, Sun 1-5
Restriction: Registered patrons only

REPUBLIC PUBLIC LIBRARY, 794 S Clark Ave, Republic, 99166-8823. Tel: 509-775-3328. E-mail: republic@ncrl.org. *Librn,* Gailene Hooper; *Librn,* Pam Metcalf
Circ 47,535
Library Holdings: Bk Vols 10,110; Talking Bks 365; Videos 1,372
Open Mon 9-8, Tues-Fri 9-6, Sat & Sun 12-5
Restriction: Registered patrons only
Friends of the Library Group

ROYAL CITY PUBLIC LIBRARY, 136 Camelia St NW, Royal City, 98357. (Mail add: PO Box 548, Royal City, 99357-0548). Tel: 509-346-9281. E-mail: royalcity@ncrl.org. *Librn,* Tim Hoelscher
Circ 20,010
Library Holdings: Bk Vols 5,916; Talking Bks 240; Videos 882
Open Mon 12-7, Tues-Thurs 10:30-5:30
Restriction: Registered patrons only

SOAP LAKE PUBLIC LIBRARY, 32 E Main St, Soap Lake, 98851. (Mail add: PO Box 86, Soap Lake, 98851-0086). Tel: 509-246-1313. E-mail: soaplake@ncrl.org. *Librn,* Caleb Hermans
Circ 24,251
Library Holdings: Bk Vols 11,610; Talking Bks 236; Videos 990
Open Tues, Wed & Fri 9:30-5, Thurs 11:30-7, Sat 10-2
Restriction: Registered patrons only
Friends of the Library Group

TONASKET PUBLIC LIBRARY, 209 A Whitcomb Ave, Tonasket, 98855-8818. Tel: 509-486-2366. E-mail: tonasket@ncrl.org. *Librn,* Daniel Klayton; *Librn,* Sara McVay
Circ 44,686
Library Holdings: Bk Vols 8,856; Talking Bks 355; Videos 1,044
Open Mon & Wed-Sat 9:30-5:30, Tues 11:30-7:30
Restriction: Registered patrons only

TWISP PUBLIC LIBRARY, 201 N Methow Valley Hwy, Rm 1, Twisp, 98856. (Mail add: PO Box 237, Twisp, 98856-0237). Tel: 509-997-4681. E-mail: twisp@ncrl.org. *Librn,* Dawn Woodruff
Circ 30,157
Library Holdings: Bk Vols 7,769; Talking Bks 193; Videos 715
Open Tues, Wed & Fri 10:30-5:30, Thurs 12-7, Sat 10-2
Restriction: Registered patrons only
Friends of the Library Group

WARDEN PUBLIC LIBRARY, 305 S Main St, Warden, 98857-9680. (Mail add: PO Box 813, Warden, 98857-0813). Tel: 509-349-2226. E-mail: warden@ncrl.org. *Librn,* Jean Frank
Circ 21,978
Library Holdings: Bk Vols 5,736; Talking Bks 152; Videos 806
Open Tues 12-7, Wed-Fri 11-6, Sat 10-5
Restriction: Registered patrons only

WATERVILLE PUBLIC LIBRARY, 107 W Locust St, Waterville, 98858. (Mail add: PO Box 807, Waterville, 98858-0807). Tel: 509-745-8354. E-mail: waterville@ncrl.org. *Librn,* Amy Larsen
Circ 16,691
Library Holdings: Bk Vols 6,758; Talking Bks 161; Videos 979
Open Mon, Wed & Fri 9-6, Tues & Thurs 10-7
Restriction: Registered patrons only
Friends of the Library Group

WENATCHEE PUBLIC LIBRARY, 30 S Wenatchee Ave, 98801. Tel: 509-662-5021. FAX: 509-663-9731. E-mail: wenatchee@ncrl.org. *Librn,* Jessica Murphy; *Librn,* Courtney Tiffany
Circ 320,993
Library Holdings: Bk Vols 83,128; Talking Bks 803; Videos 6,066
Automation Activity & Vendor Info: (Cataloging) Horizon; (Circulation) Horizon
Open Mon-Thurs 9-8, Fri & Sat 9-6, Sun 1-5
Restriction: Registered patrons only
Friends of the Library Group

WINTHROP PUBLIC LIBRARY, 49 State Rte 20, Winthrop, 98862. (Mail add: PO Box 519, Winthrop, 99862-0519). Tel: 509-996-2685. E-mail: winthrop@ncrl.org. *Librn,* Sally Portman
Circ 35,824
Library Holdings: Bk Vols 7,968; Talking Bks 237; Videos 907
Open Mon & Wed-Fri 12:30-6, Tues 10-6, Sat 12-5
Restriction: Registered patrons only

Friends of the Library Group
Bookmobiles: 2. Librn, Luke Ellington

J WENATCHEE VALLEY COLLEGE*, John A Brown Library Media Center, 1300 Fifth St, 98801. SAN 317-7130. Tel: 509-682-6710. FAX: 509-682-6711. E-mail: library@wvc.edu. Web Site: commons.wvc.edu/library/mainpage/Home.aspx. *Dir of Libr,* Andrew Tudor; Tel: 509-682-6715, E-mail: ahersh-tudor@wvc.edu; *Ref Librn,* Barbara Oldham; Tel: 509-682-6714, E-mail: boldham@wvc.edu; *Circ,* Kristen Hughes; E-mail: khughes@wvc.edu; *ILL,* Olivia Drakes; Tel: 509-682-6712, E-mail: odrakes@wvc.edu; *Tech Serv,* Anne Livingston; E-mail: alivingston@wvc.edu; Staff 6 (MLS 3, Non-MLS 3)
Founded 1939. Enrl 7,295; Fac 73; Highest Degree: Bachelor
Library Holdings: CDs 304; DVDs 457; Bk Titles 35,000; Per Subs 114; Videos 3,215
Special Collections: Northwest Indian History Coll; Pacific Northwest History Coll
Subject Interests: Archit, Art, Behav sci, Nursing, Soc sci
Automation Activity & Vendor Info: (Acquisitions) Ex Libris Group; (Cataloging) Ex Libris Group; (Circulation) Ex Libris Group; (Course Reserve) Ex Libris Group; (ILL) OCLC FirstSearch; (OPAC) Ex Libris Group
Wireless access
Function: Art exhibits, Audio & video playback equip for onsite use, Computers for patron use, Distance learning, Electronic databases & coll, ILL available, Internet access, Online ref, Orientations, Scanner, Tax forms, VHS videos, Wheelchair accessible
Partic in Washington Community & Technical Colleges Library Consortium
Open Mon-Fri 7:30am-8pm, Sat 10-2; Mon-Thurs 7:30-6, Fri 8-4 (Summer)

WILBUR

P HESSELTINE PUBLIC LIBRARY*, 14 NW Division, 99185. (Mail add: PO Box 185, 99185-0185), SAN 317-7149. Tel: 509-647-5828. E-mail: hplwilbur@gmail.com. Web Site: www.wilbur.lib.wa.us/homepage. *Dir,* Jenna Archer
Founded 1900. Pop 905; Circ 4,070
Library Holdings: AV Mats 11,042; CDs 10; Bk Vols 11,451; Per Subs 13
Special Collections: Local Newspaper Bound 1924, 1931-32, 1934-2013
Subject Interests: NW hist
Wireless access
Function: Audiobks via web, Bks on CD, Children's prog, Computers for patron use, E-Readers, ILL available, Internet access, Magazines, Music CDs, Prog for children & young adult, Summer reading prog, VHS videos
Partic in Wheatland Libraries Consortium
Open Mon, Wed & Thurs 3-5, Fri 3:30-7:30
Friends of the Library Group

YAKIMA

R GRACE OF CHRIST PRESBYTERIAN CHURCH LIBRARY*, Nine S Eighth Ave, 98902. SAN 317-7181. Tel: 509-248-7940. E-mail: info@yakimagrace.com. Web Site: yakimagrace.com. *Librn,* Rondi Downs
Founded 1927
Library Holdings: Bk Vols 2,000
Special Collections: Cassette tapes of sermons; Video Classes
Subject Interests: Autobiographies, Bible study, Biographies, Christian life
Wireless access
Partic in Pac NW Asn Church Librs
Open Mon-Fri 9-5, Sun 8-1

GL YAKIMA COUNTY LAW LIBRARY*, 18 E Lincoln Ave, 98901. SAN 317-7203. Tel: 509-574-2692. Web Site: www.yakimacounty.us/807/law-library. *Law Librn,* Lumi Loudon; E-mail: lumi.loudon@co.yakima.wa.us
Founded 1923
Library Holdings: Bk Vols 6,000
Wireless access
Open Mon-Fri 7-7, Sat 9-12

J YAKIMA VALLEY COLLEGE*, Raymond Library, S 16th Ave at Nob Hill Blvd, 98902. (Mail add: PO Box 22520, 98907-2520), SAN 317-7211. Tel: 509-574-4991. FAX: 509-574-4989. Reference E-mail: refdesk@yvcc.edu. Web Site: www.yvcc.edu/services/library. *Dir,* Tammy Siebenberg; Tel: 509-574-4984, E-mail: tsiebenberg@yvcc.edu; Staff 9 (MLS 3, Non-MLS 6)
Founded 1929. Enrl 3,500; Fac 106
Library Holdings: AV Mats 4,300; Bk Titles 45,000; Per Subs 40
Automation Activity & Vendor Info: (Cataloging) Ex Libris Group; (Circulation) Ex Libris Group; (Course Reserve) Ex Libris Group; (Discovery) Ex Libris Group; (ILL) OCLC; (OPAC) Ex Libris Group
Wireless access
Partic in OCLC Online Computer Library Center, Inc; Washington Community & Technical Colleges Library Consortium
Open Mon-Thurs 7:30am-9pm, Fri 7:30-4:30, Sun Noon-6

P YAKIMA VALLEY LIBRARIES*, 102 N Third St, 98901. SAN 364-2879. Tel: 509-452-8541. FAX: 509-575-2093. E-mail: reference@yvrl.org. Web Site: www.yvrl.org. *Exec Dir,* Kim Hixson; *Dir, Human Res,* Darline Charbonneau; E-mail: dcharbonneau@yvl.org; *Dir, Pub Libr Serv,* Dr Francisco Garcia-Ortiz; E-mail: fgarciaortiz@yvl.org; *Managing Librn,* Ms Georgia Reitmire; E-mail: greitmire@yvl.org; Staff 18 (MLS 18)
Founded 1951. Pop 247,141; Circ 920,037
Library Holdings: Electronic Media & Resources 24; Bk Vols 397,899; Per Subs 581
Special Collections: Northwest Americans & Indians of Pacific Northwest (Relander Coll), bks, clippings, letters, maps, negatives, photog & prints. State Document Depository
Subject Interests: Agr, Archit, Art, Wash hist
Automation Activity & Vendor Info: (Acquisitions) Innovative Interfaces, Inc; (Cataloging) Innovative Interfaces, Inc; (Circulation) Innovative Interfaces, Inc; (Course Reserve) Innovative Interfaces, Inc; (ILL) Innovative Interfaces, Inc; (Media Booking) Innovative Interfaces, Inc; (OPAC) Innovative Interfaces, Inc; (Serials) Innovative Interfaces, Inc
Wireless access
Function: 24/7 Electronic res, 24/7 Online cat
Publications: Annual Report; Large Print Book Catalogs; Local Bibliography of Yakima Valley History; Relander Collection Index; Washington State Phone Book Index
Open Mon-Wed 9-7, Thurs & Fri 9-6, Sat 10-6, Sun 10-5
Friends of the Library Group
Branches: 16
BUENA LIBRARY, 801 Buena Rd, Buena, 98921. (Mail add: PO Box 304, Buena, 98921-0304). Tel: 509-865-2298. FAX: 509-865-3390. *Supvr,* Juanita Torres
Circ 6,248
Library Holdings: Electronic Media & Resources 24; Bk Vols 6,286; Per Subs 25
Open Tues-Thurs 2-7, Fri 1-6, Sat 9-2
Friends of the Library Group
GRANGER LIBRARY, 508 Sunnyside Ave, Granger, 98932. (Mail add: PO Box 797, Granger, 98932-0797). Tel: 509-854-1446. FAX: 509-854-1446. *Supvr,* Sonia Espinoza
Pop 2,859; Circ 11,008
Library Holdings: Electronic Media & Resources 24; Bk Vols 8,720; Per Subs 21
Open Mon & Wed Noon-6, Tues & Thurs 10-6, Sat 12:30-5
HARRAH LIBRARY, 21 E Pioneer St, Harrah, 98933. (Mail add: PO Box 87, Harrah, 98933-0087). Tel: 509-848-3458. FAX: 509-848-3458. *Supvr,* Avelina Garcia
Pop 506; Circ 1,888
Library Holdings: Electronic Media & Resources 24; Bk Vols 4,924; Per Subs 10
Special Collections: Scrapbooks on Harrah History (dating back to the 1940's)
Open Tues & Thurs 1-6, Sat 9-2
MABTON LIBRARY, 415 B St, Mabton, 98935. (Mail add: PO Box 447, Mabton, 98935-0447). Tel: 509-894-4128. FAX: 509-894-4128. *Supvr,* Janella Guiterrez
Pop 2,047; Circ 5,047
Library Holdings: Electronic Media & Resources 24; Bk Vols 6,994; Per Subs 26
Open Mon-Fri 2-6
Friends of the Library Group
MOXEE LIBRARY, 255 W Seattle Ave, Moxee, 98936. Tel: 509-575-8854. FAX: 509-575-8854. *Librn,* Sarah Frecker
Pop 1,836; Circ 15,208
Library Holdings: Electronic Media & Resources 24; Bk Vols 8,573; Per Subs 30
Open Mon & Wed 10-6, Tues & Thurs Noon-7, Fri 1-6, Sat 1-5
Friends of the Library Group
NACHES LIBRARY, 303 Naches Ave, Naches, 98937. (Mail add: PO Box 310, Naches, 98937-0310). Tel: 509-653-2005. FAX: 509-653-2005. *Supvr,* Katherine Ulmer
Pop 691; Circ 9,490
Library Holdings: Electronic Media & Resources 24; Bk Vols 7,335; Per Subs 28
Open Tues & Thurs 2-7, Wed, Fri & Sat 10-3
Friends of the Library Group
RICHARD E OSTRANDER WEST VALLEY COMMUNITY LIBRARY, 223 S 72nd Ave, 98908, SAN 364-2909. Tel: 509-966-7070. FAX: 509-966-7070. *Librn,* Cathy Rathbone; Staff 3 (MLS 3)
Circ 258,845
Library Holdings: Electronic Media & Resources 24; Bk Vols 40,270; Per Subs 68
Open Mon-Thurs 9-8, Fri & Sat 9-6, Sun 10-5
Friends of the Library Group

SELAH PUBLIC LIBRARY, 106 S Second St, Selah, 98942, SAN 317-6584. Tel: 509-698-7345. FAX: 509-698-7345. *Supvr,* Michael Martin
Pop 6,947; Circ 50,673
Library Holdings: Electronic Media & Resources 24; Bk Vols 23,328; Per Subs 67
Open Mon-Thurs 9-7, Fri 9-6, Sat 10-5
Friends of the Library Group

SOUTHEAST YAKIMA LIBRARY, 1211 S Seventh St, 98901, SAN 373-1413. Tel: 509-576-0723. FAX: 509-576-0723. *Supvr,* Gloria Pearcy
Circ 4,815
Library Holdings: Electronic Media & Resources 24; Bk Vols 4,458; Per Subs 24
Open Mon-Fri 1-5
Friends of the Library Group

SUNNYSIDE LIBRARY, 621 Grant Ave, Sunnyside, 98944. Tel: 509-837-3234. FAX: 509-837-3234. *Supvr,* Marcelina Ortega
Pop 14,828; Circ 82,710
Library Holdings: Electronic Media & Resources 24; Bk Vols 42,789; Per Subs 74
Subject Interests: Bks on cassettes
Function: Photocopying/Printing
Open Mon-Thurs 9-7, Fri 9-6, Sat & Sun 10-5
Friends of the Library Group

TERRACE HEIGHTS LIBRARY, 4011 Commonwealth Dr, 98901. Tel: 509-457-5319. FAX: 509-457-5319. *Supvr,* Katie Ruffcorn
Circ 16,291
Library Holdings: Electronic Media & Resources 24; Bk Vols 6,823; Per Subs 26
Open Mon & Wed Noon-7, Tues & Thurs 10-6, Fri & Sat 10-2

TIETON LIBRARY, 418 Maple St, Tieton, 98947. (Mail add: PO Box 395, Tieton, 98947-0395). Tel: 509-673-2621. FAX: 509-673-2621. *Supvr,* Patricia Fehrer
Pop 1,184; Circ 4,905
Library Holdings: Electronic Media & Resources 24; Bk Vols 3,602; Per Subs 18
Open Mon-Thurs 12-5

TOPPENISH LIBRARY, One S Elm St, Toppenish, 98948. Tel: 509-865-3600. FAX: 509-865-3600. *Supvr,* Tino Godina
Pop 9,186; Circ 25,572
Library Holdings: Electronic Media & Resources 24; Bk Vols 19,338; Per Subs 54
Function: Photocopying/Printing
Open Mon-Thurs 12-7, Fri 12-6, Sat 10-2
Friends of the Library Group

WAPATO LIBRARY, 119 E Third St, Wapato, 98951. Tel: 509-877-2882. FAX: 509-877-2882. *Librn,* Diane Tuffs
Pop 4,608; Circ 25,212
Library Holdings: Electronic Media & Resources 24; Bk Vols 15,181; Per Subs 37
Function: Photocopying/Printing
Open Mon-Thurs 11-7, Fri 11-6, Sat 10-3
Friends of the Library Group

WHITE SWAN LIBRARY, 391 First St, White Swan, 98952. (Mail add: PO Box 151, White Swan, 98952-0151). Tel: 509-874-2060. FAX: 509-874-2060. *Supvr,* Michele Flett
Circ 3,904
Library Holdings: Electronic Media & Resources 24; Bk Vols 5,966; Per Subs 27
Open Mon-Fri 12-5
Friends of the Library Group

ZILLAH LIBRARY, 109 Seventh St, Zillah, 98953. (Mail add: PO Box 448, Zillah, 98953-0448). Tel: 509-829-6707. FAX: 509-829-6707. *Supvr,* Gay Lindemuth
Pop 2,611; Circ 15,136
Library Holdings: Electronic Media & Resources 24; Bk Vols 6,419; Per Subs 24
Open Mon-Thurs 2-7, Sat 2-5
Friends of the Library Group

S YAKIMA VALLEY MUSEUM*, Sundquist Research Library & Archives, 2105 Tieton Dr, 98902. SAN 326-4432. Tel: 509-248-0747. FAX: 509-453-4890. E-mail: info@yvmuseum.org. Web Site: www.yvmuseum.org/our-archives. *Chief Curator of Collections & Archives,* Mike Siebol; E-mail: mike@yvmuseum.org; *Archivist, Dir, Emeritus,* John Baule; E-mail: john@yvmuseum.org
Library Holdings: Bk Vols 10,000
Special Collections: Betty Edmondson, Mayor of Yakima; Japanese Coll; Marjorie Lynch Coll (HEW State Legislator); Martha Wiley, Missionary to China 1900-1946, artifacts, correspondence; William O Douglas Coll, bks, photos, slides, stills, tapes. Oral History
Subject Interests: Local hist
Wireless access
Publications: 100 Years 100 Women - 1889-1989
Restriction: Non-circulating to the pub, Open by appt only

WEST VIRGINIA

Date of Statistics: FY 2022
Population, 2020 U.S. Census: 1,793,716
Population Served by Public Libraries: 1,793,716
Total Volumes in Public Libraries: 4,476,357
Digital Resources:
Total e-books: 21,194,845
Total audio items (physical and downloadable units): 6,080,888
Total video items (physical and downloadable units): 2,259,778
Total computers for use by the public: 1,210
Total annual wireless sessions: 84,928

Income and Expenditures:
Source of Income: Public & Private funds
Local Income: $34,615,410
Federal Income: $995,185
Total Income all Sources: $44,995,675
Total Public Library Expenditures (including Grants-in-Aid): 39,589,045
Expenditure Per Capita: $22.07
Grants-in-Aid to Public Libraries: $9,339,815
Number of Regional & Service Center Libraries: 13
Information provided courtesy of: Susan P. Bailey, State Data Coordinator, West Virginia Library Commission

ALDERSON

P ALDERSON PUBLIC LIBRARY*, 115 Walnut Ave, 24910. SAN 376-7787. Tel: 304-445-7221. FAX: 304-445-7221. Web Site: alderson.lib.wv.us. *Dir,* Rose Spencer; E-mail: rose.spencer@mail.mln.lib.wv.us; Staff 2 (Non-MLS 2)
Library Holdings: Bk Titles 8,000; Bk Vols 9,800; Per Subs 23
Automation Activity & Vendor Info: (Cataloging) Innovative Interfaces, Inc; (Circulation) Innovative Interfaces, Inc; (OPAC) Innovative Interfaces, Inc
Wireless access
Partic in West Virginia Library Network
Open Mon, Wed, Fri & Sat 10-4, Tues & Thurs 11-5
Friends of the Library Group

ATHENS

C CONCORD UNIVERSITY*, J Frank Marsh Library, Vermillion St, 24712. (Mail add: PO Box 1000, 24712-1000), SAN 317-722X. Tel: 304-384-5371. Interlibrary Loan Service Tel: 304-384-5375. Reference Tel: 304-384-5374. Administration Tel: 304-384-5366. FAX: 304-384-7955. E-mail: library@concord.edu. Web Site: www.concord.edu/About/Important-Offices-Centers/Library-(1).aspx. *Dir,* Connie Shumate; E-mail: cshumate@concord.edu; *Libr Assoc,* Jonathan Bolt; E-mail: jbolt@concord.edu; *Info Spec,* Douglas Moore; Tel: 304-384-5372, E-mail: moore@concord.edu; *Tech Serv,* Donna Musick; Tel: 304-384-5369, E-mail: dmusick@concord.edu; Staff 5 (MLS 1, Non-MLS 4)
Founded 1872. Enrl 2,800; Fac 100; Highest Degree: Master
Library Holdings: CDs 1,077; DVDs 1,980; Bk Titles 130,000; Bk Vols 156,184; Per Subs 227; Videos 1,000
Special Collections: Fred J. Lucas Audio Coll; Goodykoontz Autograph Coll; Holographs (F Wells Goodykoontz Holograph Coll), photog; West Virginia Coll. State Document Depository; US Document Depository
Automation Activity & Vendor Info: (Acquisitions) Innovative Interfaces, Inc; (Cataloging) Innovative Interfaces, Inc; (Circulation) Innovative Interfaces, Inc; (OPAC) Innovative Interfaces, Inc; (Serials) Innovative Interfaces, Inc
Wireless access
Function: For res purposes
Partic in LYRASIS; West Virginia Library Network
Open Mon-Thurs 7:45-10, Fri 7:45-4, Sat Noon-4, Sun 12-8 (Spring-Fall); Mon-Fri 8-4 (Summer)

BEAVER

G UNITED STATES DEPARTMENT OF LABOR*, Mine Safety & Health Administration Technical Information Center & Library, 1301 Airport Rd, 25813. SAN 320-1279. Tel: 304-256-3266. FAX: 304-256-3372. E-mail: MSHALibrary@dol.gov. Web Site: www.msha.gov/msha-technical-information-center-and-library. *Tech Info Spec,* Katie Kimbrell; E-mail: kimbrell.katie@dol.gov; Staff 6 (MLS 2, Non-MLS 4)
Founded 1976
Library Holdings: AV Mats 1,000; Bk Titles 14,000; Bk Vols 40,000; Per Subs 40
Special Collections: Bureau of Mines (1910-present); Mine Accident Reports (Middle 1800-present); Mine Disasters
Subject Interests: Earth sci, Indust safety, Mine safety, Occupational diseases
Automation Activity & Vendor Info: (Acquisitions) SirsiDynix; (Cataloging) SirsiDynix; (Circulation) SirsiDynix; (OPAC) SirsiDynix; (Serials) SirsiDynix
Function: Archival coll, Audio & video playback equip for onsite use, Electronic databases & coll, Govt ref serv, ILL available, Photocopying/Printing
Publications: Journal holdings list; New publications; New services
Open Mon-Fri 8-4:30
Restriction: Photo ID required for access

BECKLEY

GM DEPARTMENT OF VETERANS AFFAIRS, Beckley VA Medical Center Library, 200 Veterans Ave, No 124D, 25801. SAN 317-7270. Tel: 304-255-2121, Ext 4342. Web Site: www.va.gov/beckley-health-care. *Librn,* Lois Watson
Founded 1952
Library Holdings: Bk Vols 500
Wireless access

P RALEIGH COUNTY PUBLIC LIBRARY*, 221 N Kanawha St, 25801-4716. SAN 364-2933. Tel: 304-255-0511. FAX: 304-255-9161. Web Site: www.rcplwv.org. *Dir,* Amy Stover; E-mail: stovera@raleigh.lib.wv.us; *Asst Dir,* Position Currently Open; *Head, Children's Dept, Head, Circ,* Position Currently Open; Staff 29 (MLS 2, Non-MLS 27)
Founded 1926. Pop 75,400
Jul 2020-Jun 2021 Income $1,340,726, State $401,726, City $44,000, County $420,000, Locally Generated Income $50,000, Other $425,000
Special Collections: West Virginia Heritage Coll
Automation Activity & Vendor Info: (Circulation) Innovative Interfaces, Inc; (Course Reserve) Innovative Interfaces, Inc; (ILL) Innovative Interfaces, Inc; (Media Booking) Innovative Interfaces, Inc; (OPAC) Innovative Interfaces, Inc; (Serials) Innovative Interfaces, Inc
Wireless access
Partic in West Virginia Library Network
Friends of the Library Group
Branches: 2
SHADY SPRING BRANCH, 440 Flat Top Rd, Shady Spring, 25918, SAN 322-5933. Tel: 304-763-2681. FAX: 304-763-3940. *Br Mgr,* Carolyn Light; E-mail: carolyn.light@raleigh.lib.wv.us; Staff 1 (MLS 1)
Library Holdings: AV Mats 1,627; Bk Titles 20,109; Per Subs 41; Talking Bks 763
Open Mon, Wed & Fri 9-5, Tues & Thurs 10-6, Sat 10-2
Friends of the Library Group

SOPHIA BRANCH, General Delivery, 103 First St, Sophia, 25921, SAN 364-2992. Tel: 304-683-5990. FAX: 304-683-3124. E-mail: sophia@mail.mln.lib.wv.us.
Library Holdings: AV Mats 867; Bk Titles 16,247; Per Subs 27; Talking Bks 222
Open Mon & Wed-Fri 9-5, Tues 10-6, Sat 10-2
Friends of the Library Group
Bookmobiles: 2

BELINGTON

P BELINGTON PUBLIC LIBRARY*, 88 Elliott Ave, 26250. (Mail add: PO Box 878, 26250-0878), SAN 325-0458. Tel: 304-823-1026. FAX: 304-823-1026. Web Site: belington.lib.wv.us. *Dir,* Tamela M Smith; E-mail: tammy.smith@clark.lib.wv.us; Staff 1 (Non-MLS 1)
Founded 1980. Pop 6,612; Circ 9,089
Library Holdings: Bk Titles 15,124
Special Collections: Genealogical Books; Language cassettes; Large Print Books
Automation Activity & Vendor Info: (Cataloging) Innovative Interfaces, Inc; (Circulation) Innovative Interfaces, Inc; (OPAC) Innovative Interfaces, Inc; (Serials) Innovative Interfaces, Inc
Wireless access
Partic in West Virginia Library Network
Special Services for the Deaf - Bks on deafness & sign lang; High interest/low vocabulary bks; Spec interest per
Open Mon 11-7, Tues & Thurs 12-7, Wed 9-7, Fri 12-5

BERKELEY SPRINGS

P MORGAN COUNTY PUBLIC LIBRARY*, 105 Congress St, 25411. SAN 317-7289. Tel: 304-258-3350. FAX: 304-258-3350. Web Site: mocolibrary.com. *Dir,* Sarah Drennan; E-mail: sarah.drennan@martin.lib.wv.us; Staff 3 (Non-MLS 3)
Pop 9,962; Circ 60,000
Library Holdings: Bk Vols 40,000; Per Subs 32
Special Collections: West Virginia Historical & Genealogical Coll
Automation Activity & Vendor Info: (Cataloging) TLC (The Library Corporation); (Circulation) TLC (The Library Corporation); (OPAC) TLC (The Library Corporation)
Wireless access
Open Mon, Tues, Thurs & Fri 9-6, Sat 9-1
Friends of the Library Group

BETHANY

CR BETHANY COLLEGE, MARY CUTLIP CENTER FOR LIBRARY & INFORMATION TECHNOLOGY*, T W Phillips Memorial Library, Phillips Library Number 9, 31 E Campus Dr, 26032. SAN 317-7297. Tel: 304-829-7321. FAX: 304-829-7333. E-mail: library@bethanywv.edu. Web Site: www.bethanywv.edu/library. *The Mary Cutlip Dir of Libr & Learning Res,* Heather Ricciuti; Tel: 304-829-7335, E-mail: hricciuti@bethanywv.edu; *Learning Res Librn,* Anna Cipoletti; E-mail: acipoletti@bethanywv.edu; Staff 3 (MLS 2, Non-MLS 1)
Founded 1841. Fac 55; Highest Degree: Master
Special Collections: Alexander Campbell & Christian Church - Disciples of Christ (Alexander Campbell Archives), bk, ms, per; Hazlett-Cummins Civil War Colls; James Schuyler Poetry Coll; Ornithology (Brooks Bird Club Coll), per; Upper Ohio Valley Coll, bks, ms, per
Automation Activity & Vendor Info: (Acquisitions) OCLC Worldshare Management Services; (Cataloging) OCLC Worldshare Management Services; (Circulation) OCLC Worldshare Management Services; (Course Reserve) OCLC Worldshare Management Services; (Discovery) EBSCO Discovery Service; (ILL) OCLC Worldshare Management Services; (OPAC) OCLC Worldshare Management Services
Wireless access
Function: Archival coll, Computers for patron use, Electronic databases & coll, Free DVD rentals, ILL available, Online cat, Photocopying/Printing, Prog for children & young adult, Ref serv available
Partic in Appalachian College Association; LYRASIS; OCLC Online Computer Library Center, Inc
Open Mon-Thurs 9-9, Fri 9-4, Sat Noon-4, Sun 2-9
Restriction: Open to fac, students & qualified researchers, Open to pub for ref & circ; with some limitations

R DISCIPLES OF CHRIST HISTORICAL SOCIETY*, 7229 Main St, 26032-3002. (Mail add: PO Box D, 26032-1404), SAN 315-9108. Tel: 615-327-1444. E-mail: info@discipleshistory.org. Web Site: www.discipleshistory.org.
Founded 1941
Library Holdings: Bk Titles 37,000
Subject Interests: Christian churches, Churches of Christ, Disciples of Christ, Hist, Related relig groups
Automation Activity & Vendor Info: (Cataloging) OCLC; (OPAC) OCLC; (Serials) OCLC
Wireless access
Function: Archival coll, Res libr
Publications: Journal of Disciplianа (Quarterly)
Partic in OCLC Online Computer Library Center, Inc
Open Mon-Fri 10-4
Restriction: Circ to mem only

BLUEFIELD

C BLUEFIELD STATE UNIVERSITY, William B Robertson Library, (Formerly Bluefield State College), 219 Rock St, 24701. SAN 364-3026. Tel: 304-327-4054. Reference Tel: 304-327-4056. Web Site: bluefieldstate.edu/library. *Dir, Libr Serv,* David McMillan; Tel: 304-327-4050, E-mail: dmcmillan@bluefieldstate.edu; *Librn,* Lissa Clark; Tel: 304-327-4564, E-mail: lclark@bluefieldstate.edu; *Archivist, Librn,* James Leedy; Tel: 304-327-4053, E-mail: jsleedy@bluefieldstate.edu; Staff 3 (MLS 3)
Founded 1895. Enrl 1,339; Fac 76; Highest Degree: Master
Library Holdings: e-journals 23; Microforms 664,020; Bk Vols 79,231; Per Subs 59
Special Collections: BSC Archives. State Document Depository; US Document Depository
Automation Activity & Vendor Info: (Cataloging) Innovative Interfaces, Inc; (Circulation) Innovative Interfaces, Inc; (Course Reserve) Innovative Interfaces, Inc; (OPAC) Innovative Interfaces, Inc; (Serials) Innovative Interfaces, Inc
Wireless access
Function: Archival coll, Govt ref serv, ILL available, Photocopying/Printing, Ref serv available
Partic in LYRASIS; Mountain College Libr Network; OCLC Online Computer Library Center, Inc; West Virginia Library Network
Open Mon-Thurs 8-6, Fri 8-4, Sun 12-6; Mon-Fri 8-4 (Summer)

P CRAFT MEMORIAL LIBRARY*, 600 Commerce St, 24701. SAN 317-7319. Tel: 304-325-3943. FAX: 304-325-3702. E-mail: cml@mail.mln.lib.wv.us. Web Site: craftmemorial.lib.wv.us. *Dir,* Eva McGuire; E-mail: mcguiree@mail.mln.lib.wv.us; *Prog Serv Coordr,* Suzette S Sims; E-mail: simss@mail.mln.lib.wv.us; *Curator,* Becky J Kauffman; E-mail: becky.kauffman@mail.mln.lib.wv.us; Staff 2 (MLS 2)
Founded 1972. Pop 47,538; Circ 104,355
Jul 2022-Jun 2023 Income $375,172, State $250,172, City $70,000, County $25,000, Other $30,000. Mats Exp $67,500, Books $50,000, Per/Ser (Incl. Access Fees) $7,500, Other Print Mats $1,000, AV Mat $4,000, Electronic Ref Mat (Incl. Access Fees) $5,000. Sal $140,944 (Prof $118,212)
Library Holdings: CDs 1,086; DVDs 1,114; e-books 88,323; Electronic Media & Resources 21,235; Bk Vols 50,582; Per Subs 8
Special Collections: Eastern Regional Coal Archives; West Virginia & Virginia History Coll
Subject Interests: Coal mining, Local hist
Automation Activity & Vendor Info: (Cataloging) Innovative Interfaces, Inc - Sierra; (Circulation) Innovative Interfaces, Inc - Sierra; (ILL) Innovative Interfaces, Inc - Sierra; (OPAC) Innovative Interfaces, Inc - Sierra
Wireless access
Function: 24/7 Electronic res, 24/7 Online cat, 3D Printer, Activity rm, Adult bk club, After school storytime, Archival coll, Audiobks via web, Bk club(s), Bks on CD, Children's prog, Computer training, Computers for patron use, Free DVD rentals, Holiday prog, Home delivery & serv to seniorr ctr & nursing homes, ILL available, Internet access, Life-long learning prog for all ages, Magazines, Magnifiers for reading, Mail & tel request accepted, Meeting rooms, Microfiche/film & reading machines, Movies, Online cat, Online ref, Orientations, OverDrive digital audio bks, Photocopying/Printing, Prog for adults, Prog for children & young adult, Ref serv available, Res performed for a fee, Story hour, Summer reading prog, Tax forms, Teen prog, Telephone ref, Wheelchair accessible, Workshops
Partic in West Virginia Library Network
Special Services for the Blind - Bks on CD; Large print bks; Magnifiers
Open Mon-Thurs 9:30-7, Fri & Sat 9:30-5
Friends of the Library Group
Bookmobiles: 1. Bkmobile Assoc, Charles Jones. Bk vols 7,000

BRIDGEPORT

P BRIDGEPORT PUBLIC LIBRARY*, 1200 Johnson Ave, 26330. SAN 317-7335. Tel: 304-842-8248. FAX: 304-842-9387. E-mail: library@bridgeportwv.com. Web Site: bplwv.org. *Libr Dir,* Savanna Draper; E-mail: sdraper@bridgeportwv.com; Staff 14 (MLS 2, Non-MLS 12)
Founded 1956. Pop 8,900; Circ 231,000
Library Holdings: AV Mats 12,117; Electronic Media & Resources 14; Bk Titles 90,000; Bk Vols 97,873; Per Subs 175
Special Collections: Michael Benedum Coll, bks, clippings, memorabilia, per, scrapbks; West Virginia Coll, bk, pamphlets. Oral History

Automation Activity & Vendor Info: (Cataloging) TLC (The Library Corporation); (Circulation) TLC (The Library Corporation); (OPAC) TLC (The Library Corporation)
Wireless access
Function: 24/7 Electronic res, 24/7 Online cat, 3D Printer, Adult bk club, Art programs, Audiobks on Playaways & MP3, Audiobks via web, Bk club(s), Bks on CD, Chess club, Children's prog, Computers for patron use, Electronic databases & coll, Free DVD rentals, Holiday prog, Homebound delivery serv, ILL available, Internet access, Life-long learning prog for all ages, Magazines, Makerspace, Mango lang, Movies, Music CDs, Notary serv, Online cat, Online info literacy tutorials on the web & in blackboard, Outreach serv, OverDrive digital audio bks, Photocopying/Printing, Prog for adults, Prog for children & young adult, Senior computer classes, Senior outreach, STEM programs, Story hour, Summer reading prog, Tax forms, Teen prog, Wheelchair accessible, Winter reading prog, Writing prog
Publications: Bridgeport: The Town & Its People
Open Mon-Fri 11-7, Sat 11-2
Friends of the Library Group

BUCKHANNON

P CHARLES W GIBSON PUBLIC LIBRARY*, 105 E Main St, 26201. SAN 317-7343. Tel: 304-472-2339. FAX: 304-472-2339. E-mail: gibson.library@clark.lib.wv.us. Web Site: charlesgibson.lib.wv.us. *Librn,* Catherine Norko; Staff 2 (Non-MLS 2)
Founded 1942. Circ 28,319
Library Holdings: AV Mats 270; Bk Vols 28,500; Per Subs 15
Partic in West Virginia Library Network
Open Mon & Wed 9-6, Tues, Thurs & Fri 11-6, Sat 10-2

P UPSHUR COUNTY PUBLIC LIBRARY*, 1150 Rte 20 South Rd, 26201. SAN 317-7351. Tel: 304-473-4219. FAX: 304-473-4222. E-mail: help@upshur.wvlibrary.info. Web Site: upshur.wvlibrary.info. *Dir,* Paul Norko; E-mail: paul.norko@upshur.wvlibrary.info; *Asst Dir,* Position Currently Open; Staff 5 (MLS 2, Non-MLS 3)
Founded 1956. Pop 18,615; Circ 58,542
Library Holdings: Audiobooks 2,342; DVDs 3,981; Electronic Media & Resources 23; Bk Vols 54,300
Automation Activity & Vendor Info: (Cataloging) Innovative Interfaces, Inc; (Circulation) Innovative Interfaces, Inc; (OPAC) Innovative Interfaces, Inc
Wireless access
Function: 24/7 Electronic res, 24/7 Online cat, Adult bk club, Art exhibits, Audio & video playback equip for onsite use, Audiobks via web, AV serv, Bks on CD, Children's prog, Computer training, Computers for patron use, Digital talking bks, Electronic databases & coll, For res purposes, Free DVD rentals, Games & aids for people with disabilities, Holiday prog, Home delivery & serv to seniorr ctr & nursing homes, ILL available, Internet access, Laminating, Life-long learning prog for all ages, Magazines, Magnifiers for reading, Mail & tel request accepted, Meeting rooms, Microfiche/film & reading machines, Movies, Notary serv, Online cat, Online ref, Outreach serv, Outside serv via phone, mail, e-mail & web, OverDrive digital audio bks, Photocopying/Printing, Preschool reading prog, Printer for laptops & handheld devices, Prof lending libr, Prog for adults, Prog for children & young adult, Ref & res, Ref serv available, Res performed for a fee, Scanner, Senior outreach, Spoken cassettes & CDs, STEM programs, Story hour, Summer & winter reading prog, Summer reading prog, Tax forms, Teen prog, Telephone ref, Wheelchair accessible
Partic in Mid-Atlantic Library Alliance; West Virginia Library Network
Open Mon-Thurs 9-6:30, Fri 9-5, Sat 9-2
Friends of the Library Group

C WEST VIRGINIA WESLEYAN COLLEGE*, Annie Merner Pfeiffer Library, 59 College Ave, 26201. SAN 317-736X. Tel: 304-473-8013. Interlibrary Loan Service Tel: 304-473-8461. Reference Tel: 304-473-8463. FAX: 304-473-8888. E-mail: librarian@wvwc.edu. Web Site: amplibrary.wvwc.edu. *Archivist, Dir, Libr Serv,* Brett T Miller; E-mail: miller_bt@wvwc.edu; Staff 7 (MLS 4, Non-MLS 3)
Founded 1890. Enrl 1,450; Fac 90; Highest Degree: Doctorate
Library Holdings: AV Mats 11,580; CDs 3,970; DVDs 2,992; e-books 340,700; e-journals 13,644; Music Scores 5,266; Bk Titles 124,900; Bk Vols 128,000
Special Collections: Archives of West Virginia Methodism; Charles Aubrey Jones Abraham Lincoln Coll; West Virginia Wesleyan College Archives. State Document Depository
Subject Interests: Civil War hist, Relig studies, WVa Methodist Hist
Automation Activity & Vendor Info: (Acquisitions) Innovative Interfaces, Inc; (Cataloging) Innovative Interfaces, Inc; (Circulation) Innovative Interfaces, Inc; (Course Reserve) Blackboard Inc; (ILL) OCLC; (Media Booking) Innovative Interfaces, Inc; (OPAC) Innovative Interfaces, Inc; (Serials) Innovative Interfaces, Inc
Wireless access
Function: Archival coll, Art exhibits, Bk club(s), Computers for patron use, Electronic databases & coll, ILL available, Internet access, Magazines, Meeting rooms, Notary serv, Online cat, Outside serv via phone, mail, e-mail & web, Photocopying/Printing, Prog for adults, Ref serv available, Res performed for a fee, Scanner, Study rm, Telephone ref, Workshops
Partic in Appalachian College Association; LYRASIS
Open Mon-Thurs 8am-9pm, Fri 8-4:30, Sun 1:30-9:30
Restriction: Non-circulating of rare bks, Non-resident fee, Open to pub for ref & circ; with some limitations

BURLINGTON

P BURLINGTON PUBLIC LIBRARY, Patterson Creek Rd S, 26710. (Mail add: PO Box 61, 26710-0061), SAN 376-6608. Tel: 304-289-3690. FAX: 304-289-3233. Web Site: burlington.lib.wv.us. *Asst Librn,* Gerilyn Cooper; *Br Mgr,* Cesily Dolly; E-mail: c.dolly@ephlibrary.org; Staff 1 (Non-MLS 1)
Library Holdings: Bk Vols 7,500
Automation Activity & Vendor Info: (Cataloging) TLC (The Library Corporation); (Circulation) TLC (The Library Corporation); (OPAC) TLC (The Library Corporation)
Wireless access
Open Tues & Thurs 12-7, Wed 9-4, Fri 9-2

BURNSVILLE

P BURNSVILLE PUBLIC LIBRARY*, 235 Kanawha Ave, 26335. (Mail add: PO Box 141, 26335), SAN 376-6071. Tel: 304-853-2338. FAX: 304-853-2888. Web Site: burnsville.lib.wv.us. *Dir,* Elizabeth A Anderson; E-mail: beth.anderson@clark.lib.wv.us; *Libr Asst,* Rachelle Pritt; Staff 2 (Non-MLS 2)
Library Holdings: AV Mats 78; Bk Vols 9,000; Per Subs 21
Automation Activity & Vendor Info: (Cataloging) Innovative Interfaces, Inc; (Circulation) Innovative Interfaces, Inc; (OPAC) Innovative Interfaces, Inc
Wireless access
Partic in West Virginia Library Network
Open Mon 10-7, Tues-Fri 10-5, Sat 10-2

CAPON BRIDGE

P CAPON BRIDGE PUBLIC LIBRARY*, 2987 Northwestern Pike, 26711. SAN 317-7378. Tel: 304-856-3777. FAX: 304-856-3777. Web Site: caponbridge.lib.wv.us. *Dir,* Nancy Meade; E-mail: nancy.meade@martin.lib.wv.us; Staff 2 (Non-MLS 2)
Founded 1969. Pop 3,545; Circ 14,200
Library Holdings: AV Mats 210; Bk Titles 20,000; Bk Vols 23,000; Per Subs 15
Automation Activity & Vendor Info: (Circulation) TLC (The Library Corporation)
Wireless access
Function: 24/7 Electronic res, 24/7 Online cat, Activity rm, Adult bk club
Open Mon & Wed-Fri 11-6, Tues 11-8, Sat 9-1
Friends of the Library Group

CHAPMANVILLE

P CHAPMANVILLE PUBLIC LIBRARY*, 740 Crowley Creek Rd, 25508. SAN 321-0057. Tel: 304-855-3405. FAX: 304-855-8590. E-mail: chappl@hotmail.com. Web Site: www.facebook.com/chapmanvillepubliclibrary. *Dir,* Rebecca Brock; *Asst Librn,* Position Currently Open; Staff 2 (Non-MLS 2)
Founded 1977. Circ 23,400
Library Holdings: Bk Titles 33,329; Per Subs 16; Talking Bks 340; Videos 523
Special Collections: AV Coll, bks, vf; Logan County Hist Special Coll
Automation Activity & Vendor Info: (Cataloging) SirsiDynix; (Circulation) SirsiDynix; (OPAC) SirsiDynix
Wireless access
Publications: Library Paper (Newsletter)
Open Mon & Thurs 8-5:30, Tues & Wed 8-4, Fri 8-Noon

CHARLES TOWN

P CHARLES TOWN LIBRARY, INC*, 200 E Washington St, 25414. SAN 317-7386. Tel: 304-725-2208. FAX: 304-725-6618. E-mail: librarian@ctlibrary.org. Web Site: ctlibrary.org. *Dir,* Marcella Genz, PhD; E-mail: octldirector@ctlibrary.org; Staff 4.8 (MLS 1, Non-MLS 3.8)
Founded 1927. Circ 80,000
Library Holdings: Bk Titles 70,000; Per Subs 100
Special Collections: History & Genealogy, Civil War (Perry Coll); History & Genealogy, Local History (Locked Reference Coll); Large Type Coll, Fiction & Non-fiction; Spanish Coll
Automation Activity & Vendor Info: (Cataloging) TLC (The Library Corporation); (Circulation) TLC (The Library Corporation); (OPAC) TLC (The Library Corporation)
Wireless access

Function: 24/7 Electronic res, 24/7 Online cat, Activity rm, Adult bk club, Archival coll, Art exhibits, Art programs, Bi-weekly Writer's Group, Bks on CD, Butterfly Garden, Children's prog, Computer training, Computers for patron use, Electronic databases & coll, For res purposes, Free DVD rentals, Instruction & testing, Internet access, Laminating, Magazines, Mail & tel request accepted, Meeting rooms, Museum passes, Music CDs, Online cat, Online info literacy tutorials on the web & in blackboard, Online ref, Photocopying/Printing, Printer for laptops & handheld devices, Prog for adults, Prog for children & young adult, Ref & res, Ref serv available, Res assist avail, Scanner, Spanish lang bks, Spoken cassettes & DVDs, Story hour, Summer reading prog, Tax forms, Telephone ref, Wheelchair accessible
Open Mon-Wed 9-5, Thurs 9-6, Fri 9-3, Sat 9-1

CHARLESTON

S THE CLAY CENTER FOR THE ARTS & SCIENCES OF WEST VIRGINIA, One Clay Sq, 25301. SAN 376-1886. Tel: 304-561-3570. E-mail: info@theclaycenter.org. Web Site: www.theclaycenter.org. *Educ Dir,* Zack Merritt; E-mail: zmerritt@theclaycenter.org
Library Holdings: Bk Vols 4,000
Restriction: Open by appt only

R FIRST PRESBYTERIAN CHURCH OF CHARLESTON LIBRARY*, 16 Leon Sullivan Way, 25301. SAN 317-7408. Tel: 304-343-8961. E-mail: firstpresby@firstpresby.com. Web Site: www.firstpresby.com. *Librn,* Tom Daugherty; Staff 1 (MLS 1)
Library Holdings: AV Mats 340; Bk Vols 10,600; Talking Bks 90
Subject Interests: Bible, Parenting, Relig
Open Mon-Fri 8-4

L JACKSON KELLY, Law Library, 500 Lee St E, Ste 1600, 25301. (Mail add: PO Box 553, 25322-0553), SAN 317-7416. Tel: 412-434-8055. E-mail: libraryresources@jacksonkelly.com. Web Site: www.jacksonkelly.com. *Librn,* Nicole Turner
Partic in SE Asn of Law Librs

P KANAWHA COUNTY PUBLIC LIBRARY*, 123 Capitol St, 25301. SAN 364-314X. Tel: 304-343-4646. FAX: 304-348-6530. Web Site: kanawhalibrary.org. *Libr Dir,* Erika Connelly; E-mail: erika.connelly@kanawhalibrary.org; *Asst Dir,* Sarah Mitchell; E-mail: sarah.mitchell@kanawhalibrary.org; *Head, Children's Servx,* Terri McDougal; E-mail: terri.mcdougal@kanawhalibrary.org; Staff 23 (MLS 23)
Founded 1909. Pop 182,000; Circ 1,158,763
Special Collections: Local History (West Virginia). Oral History; State Document Depository; US Document Depository
Wireless access
Publications: West Virginia Foundation Directory
Open Mon-Thurs 9-9, Fri & Sat 9-5
Friends of the Library Group
Branches: 10
CLENDENIN, 107 Koontz Ave, Ste 100, Clendenin, 25045, SAN 377-0583. Tel: 304-548-6370. FAX: 304-548-6395. *Br Mgr,* Tammy Parker; E-mail: tammy.parker@kanawhalibrary.org
Open Tues & Thurs 10-8, Wed 12-6, Sat 10-3
CROSS LANES, 5449 Big Tyler Rd, 25313, SAN 364-3204. Tel: 304-776-5999. FAX: 304-776-6005. *Br Mgr,* Brittany Rothausen; E-mail: brittany.rothausen@kanawhalibrary.org
Open Tues & Thurs 10-8, Wed 10-6, Fri 10-5, Sat 10-2
DUNBAR PUBLIC, 301 12th Street Mall, Dunbar, 25064, SAN 364-3239. Tel: 304-766-7161. FAX: 304-766-7242. *Br Mgr,* Ben Ball; E-mail: ben.ball@kanawhalibrary.org
Open Mon, Tues & Thurs 10-9, Wed, Fri & Sat 10-5
ELK VALLEY, 313 The Crossing Mall, Elkview, 25071, SAN 364-3263. Tel: 304-965-3636. FAX: 304-965-3702. *Br Mgr,* Ellie Teaford; E-mail: ellie.teaford@kanawhalibrary.org
Open Mon-Thurs 10-8, Fri & Sat 10-5
GLASGOW BRANCH, 129 Fourth Ave, Glasgow, 25086. (Mail add: PO Box 317, Glasgow, 25086-0317), SAN 364-3298. Tel: 304-595-3131. FAX: 304-595-3148. *Br Mgr,* Gabrielle Cochran; Tel: 304-949-2400
Open Thurs 10:30-6
MARMET BRANCH, 9303 Oregon Ave, Marmet, 25315, SAN 364-3301. Tel: 304-949-6628. FAX: 304-949-6639. *Br Mgr,* Position Currently Open; *Actg Br Mgr, Asst Dir,* Sarah Mitchell; E-mail: sarah.mitchell@kanawhalibrary.org
Open Thurs 10-8, Fri 10-5, Sat 10-3
NITRO PUBLIC, 1700 Park Ave, Nitro, 25143, SAN 317-8110. Tel: 304-755-4432. FAX: 304-755-5130. *Br Mgr,* Lynn Godby; E-mail: lynn.godby@kanawhalibrary.org; Staff 1 (Non-MLS 1)
Founded 1964
Automation Activity & Vendor Info: (Acquisitions) SirsiDynix; (Cataloging) SirsiDynix
Open Mon & Thurs 11-7, Tues, Wed & Fri 10-5
RIVERSIDE, One Warrior Way, Belle, 25015. Tel: 304-949-2400. FAX: 304-949-2509. *Br Mgr,* Position Currently Open; *Actg Br Mgr, Asst Dir,* Sarah Mitchell; E-mail: sarah.mitchell@kanawhalibrary.org
Open Mon 3-8, Tues & Thurs 10-8, Wed & Sat 10-5
SAINT ALBANS BRANCH, 602 Fourth St, Saint Albans, 25177, SAN 364-3328. Tel: 304-722-4244. FAX: 304-722-4276. *Asst Dir,* Sarah Mitchell; E-mail: sarah.mitchell@kanawhalibrary.org
Open Mon, Tues & Thurs 10-8, Wed & Fri 10-6, Sat 10-2
SISSONVILLE, One Tinney Lane, 25312, SAN 364-3336. Tel: 304-984-2244. FAX: 304-984-2251. *Br Mgr,* Cathy Mason; E-mail: cathy.mason@kanawhalibrary.org
Open Mon & Wed 10-5, Tues & Thurs 10-8, Sat 10-3
Bookmobiles: 1. Mgr, Melissa Burchette

C UNIVERSITY OF CHARLESTON*, Schoenbaum Library, 2300 MacCorkle Ave SE, 25304-1099. SAN 317-7440. Tel: 304-357-4780. E-mail: librarian@ucwv.edu. Web Site: www.ucwv.edu/library. *Libr Dir,* John Adkins; Tel: 304-357-4779, E-mail: johnadkins@ucwv.edu; *Health Sci Librn,* Rebecca Newman; Tel: 304-357-4986, E-mail: rebeccanewman@ucwv.edu; *Ref & Instruction Librn,* Position Currently Open; Staff 3 (MLS 3)
Founded 1888. Enrl 3,000; Highest Degree: Doctorate
Library Holdings: AV Mats 850; CDs 50; DVDs 800; e-books 120,000; Bk Titles 89,105; Per Subs 40
Special Collections: Appalachian Culture Coll; Civil War (Gorman Coll); Early American History (John Allen Kinnaman Circulating Coll); James Swann Etchings; Kendall Vintroux Political Cartoons; Presidential Biographies (James David Barber Coll); Rare Book Coll; West Virginia Coll
Subject Interests: Am hist, Archit, Art, Health sci, Interior design, Polit sci, Relig
Automation Activity & Vendor Info: (Cataloging) OCLC Worldshare Management Services; (Circulation) OCLC Worldshare Management Services; (Course Reserve) OCLC Worldshare Management Services; (Discovery) EBSCO Discovery Service; (ILL) OCLC WorldShare Interlibrary Loan; (OPAC) OCLC Worldshare Management Services; (Serials) OCLC Worldshare Management Services
Wireless access
Function: Ref serv available
Partic in Appalachian College Association; LYRASIS
Open Mon-Thurs 8am-9pm, Fri 8-5, Sat Noon-5, Sun 1-9
Restriction: Open to students, fac & staff, Restricted pub use

G WEST VIRGINIA ARCHIVES & HISTORY LIBRARY*, Culture Ctr, 1900 Kanawha Blvd E, 25305-0300. SAN 317-7475. Tel: 304-558-0230. FAX: 304-558-4193. Web Site: wvculture.org/agencies/archives-and-history. *Dir,* Aaron P Parsons; Tel: 304-558-0230, Ext 165, E-mail: aaron.p.parsons@wv.gov; *Asst Dir, Libr Mgr,* Debra Basham; Tel: 304-558-0230, Ext 702, E-mail: debra.a.basham@wv.gov; Staff 13 (MLS 1, Non-MLS 12)
Founded 1905
Library Holdings: Microforms 33,730; Bk Vols 77,926; Per Subs 331
Special Collections: Governors' Papers; Original County Records; State Printed Documents, Manuscripts, Archived County and State Public Records, Microforms, A/V & Photos. State Document Depository
Subject Interests: Appalachia, Civil War, Colonial hist, Genealogy, Maps, Mid-Atlantic region, Ohio Valley, Rare bks, WVa hist
Automation Activity & Vendor Info: (Cataloging) Innovative Interfaces, Inc - Sierra; (OPAC) Innovative Interfaces, Inc - Sierra
Wireless access
Function: 24/7 Electronic res, 24/7 Online cat, Archival coll, Electronic databases & coll, For res purposes, Microfiche/film & reading machines, Online cat, Online ref, Photocopying/Printing, Ref & res, Res libr, Res performed for a fee
Partic in West Virginia Library Network
Open Tues-Sat 9-5
Restriction: Non-circulating
Friends of the Library Group

J WEST VIRGINIA JUNIOR COLLEGE LIBRARY, Charleston Campus, 5514 Big Tyler Rd, Ste 200, 25313. SAN 375-3158. Tel: 304-769-0011. Web Site: www.wvjc.edu. *Dir of Libr,* Helen Snaith; E-mail: hsnaith@wvjc.edu; Staff 1 (MLS 1)
Founded 1992. Fac 20
Library Holdings: Bk Vols 4,260; Per Subs 20
Partic in WVa Network for Educ Telecomputing
Open Mon-Thurs 8am-9pm, Fri 9-4

G WEST VIRGINIA LEGISLATIVE REFERENCE LIBRARY*, Capitol Bldg, Rm MB 27, 1900 Kanawha Blvd E, 25305-0591. SAN 317-7505. Tel: 304-347-4830. FAX: 304-347-4901. Web Site: www.wvlegislature.gov. *Res Mgr,* DeAnnia Spelock; E-mail: dee.spelock@wvlegislature.gov
Library Holdings: Bk Vols 3,150; Per Subs 37
Restriction: Non-circulating, Ref only

P WEST VIRGINIA LIBRARY COMMISSION, Culture Center, Bldg 9, 1900 Kanawha Blvd E, 25305. SAN 364-3417. Tel: 304-558-2041. Interlibrary Loan Service Tel: 304-558-2045, Ext 2072. Reference Tel: 304-558-2045. Toll Free Tel: 800-642-9021 (WV only). FAX: 304-558-2044. E-mail: web_one@wvlc.lib.wv.us. Web Site: librarycommission.wv.gov. *Spec Serv Dir,* Donna Calvert; Tel: 304-558-4061, Fax: 304-558-6016, E-mail: donna.b.calvert@wv.gov; Staff 56 (MLS 12, Non-MLS 44)
Founded 1929. Pop 1,852,994
Library Holdings: Audiobooks 5,043; AV Mats 14,322; CDs 232; DVDs 2,452; e-books 2,011; e-journals 19; Electronic Media & Resources 80; Large Print Bks 11,213; Microforms 235,337; Bk Titles 126,124; Per Subs 289; Talking Bks 88,249; Videos 6,595
Special Collections: 16mm Film Coll; Government Documents
Subject Interests: Appalachia, Libr sci, Polit sci, Pub admin, WVa
Automation Activity & Vendor Info: (Acquisitions) Ex Libris Group; (Cataloging) Ex Libris Group; (Circulation) Ex Libris Group; (ILL) OCLC ILLiad; (OPAC) Ex Libris Group; (Serials) Ex Libris Group
Wireless access
Function: Adult literacy prog, Audio & video playback equip for onsite use, Audiobks via web, AV serv, Computer training, Computers for patron use, Electronic databases & coll, Free DVD rentals, Govt ref serv, ILL available, Online ref, Outside serv via phone, mail, e-mail & web, Photocopying/Printing, Ref serv available, Spoken cassettes & CDs, Tax forms, Telephone ref, VHS videos, Wheelchair accessible, Workshops
Publications: Annual Report; Annual Statistical Report
Partic in LYRASIS; West Virginia Library Network
Special Services for the Blind - Cassette playback machines; Cassettes; Descriptive video serv (DVS); Large print bks; Machine repair; Newsline for the Blind; Ref serv
Open Mon-Fri 8:30-5
Restriction: Open to pub for ref & circ; with some limitations

GL WEST VIRGINIA STATE LAW LIBRARY, Bldg 1, Rm E-404, 1900 Kanawha Blvd E, 25305. SAN 317-7521. Tel: 304-558-2607. FAX: 304-558-3673. Web Site: www.courtswv.gov/public-resources/law-library. *State Law Librn,* Janet Nicholson; E-mail: janetm.nicholson@courtswv.gov; *Dep Dir,* Vanessa Perry; E-mail: vanessa.perry@courtswv.gov; Staff 3 (MLS 2, Non-MLS 1)
Founded 1867
Library Holdings: AV Mats 445; Bk Titles 3,462; Bk Vols 62,563; Per Subs 515
Special Collections: State Document Depository; US Document Depository
Subject Interests: Govt, Law
Automation Activity & Vendor Info: (Acquisitions) EOS International; (Cataloging) EOS International; (Circulation) EOS International; (OPAC) EOS International; (Serials) EOS International
Wireless access
Function: 24/7 Online cat, For res purposes
Open Mon-Fri 8:30-4:30
Restriction: Lending to staff only, Non-circulating to the pub, Open to pub for ref only

CM WEST VIRGINIA UNIVERSITY*, Charleston HSC Library, 3110 MacCorkle Ave SE, 25304. SAN 317-753X. Tel: 304-347-1285. FAX: 304-347-1288. E-mail: libraryloans@hsc.wvu.edu. Web Site: library.wvu.edu/libraries/charleston. *Dir, Health Sci Libr,* Susan Arnold; E-mail: susan.arnold@mail.wvu.edu; Staff 1 (Non-MLS 1)
Founded 1977. Highest Degree: Doctorate
Library Holdings: Bk Titles 22,000; Bk Vols 25,000
Special Collections: Dr Lawrence Frankel's Archival Coll
Subject Interests: Clinical med, Pharmaceuticals
Automation Activity & Vendor Info: (Acquisitions) OCLC; (Cataloging) OCLC; (Circulation) OCLC; (Course Reserve) OCLC; (Discovery) OCLC; (ILL) OCLC; (Media Booking) OCLC; (OPAC) OCLC; (Serials) OCLC
Wireless access
Partic in National Network of Libraries of Medicine Region 1; OCLC Online Computer Library Center, Inc
Open Mon-Fri 8-4

CHESTER

P LYNN MURRAY MEMORIAL LIBRARY*, 625 Railroad St, 26034. SAN 317-7548. Tel: 304-387-1010. FAX: 304-387-1010. Web Site: www.facebook.com/profile.php?id=100064877850581. *Dir,* Connie Doughty; E-mail: connie.doughty@weirton.lib.wv.us; Staff 2 (Non-MLS 2)
Founded 1971. Pop 7,409; Circ 23,380
Library Holdings: Large Print Bks 115; Bk Titles 16,081; Per Subs 42; Talking Bks 130
Wireless access
Partic in West Virginia Library Network
Open Mon-Thurs 10-6, Fri 10-5, Sat 10-2

CLARKSBURG

P CLARKSBURG-HARRISON PUBLIC LIBRARY*, 404 W Pike St, 26301. SAN 317-7556. Tel: 304-627-2236. FAX: 304-627-2239. Reference E-mail: help@clarksburglibrary.org. Web Site: clarksburglibrary.info. *Dir,* Beth Nicholson; E-mail: director@clarksburglibrary.org; *Head, Tech Serv,* Dawn McClain; *Ch,* Erica Perry; E-mail: children.chpl@clark.lib.wv.us; *Ref Librn,* Cathy Clevenger; *Spec Coll Librn,* David Houchin; E-mail: houchin@clark.lib.wv.us; *Bus Mgr,* Bill Ellifritt; *Circ Serv Team Leader,* Julia Todd; E-mail: julia.todd@clark.lib.wv.us. Subject Specialists: *Genealogy, Local hist,* David Houchin; Staff 21 (MLS 3, Non-MLS 18)
Founded 1907. Pop 56,898; Circ 115,513
Library Holdings: Bk Titles 64,181; Bk Vols 72,090
Special Collections: UFO (Gray Barker Coll)
Subject Interests: Genealogy, Local hist
Automation Activity & Vendor Info: (Cataloging) Innovative Interfaces, Inc; (Circulation) Innovative Interfaces, Inc; (OPAC) Innovative Interfaces, Inc
Function: ILL available, Magnifiers for reading, Photocopying/Printing, Prog for children & young adult, Ref serv available, Summer reading prog, Wheelchair accessible
Partic in West Virginia Library Network
Special Services for the Blind - Assistive/Adapted tech devices, equip & products
Open Mon-Fri 9-7, Sat 10-3
Friends of the Library Group

GM DEPARTMENT OF VETERANS AFFAIRS*, Louis A Johnson VA Library Service, One Medical Center Dr, 26301. SAN 317-7580. Tel: 304-623-3461. Web Site: www.va.gov/clarksburg-health-care/locations/louis-a-johnson-veterans-administration-medical-center. *Tech Info Spec,* Annette Webb; E-mail; annette.webb@va.gov
Founded 1950
Library Holdings: AV Mats 240; Bk Vols 805; Per Subs 221
Subject Interests: Dentistry, Med, Nursing, Psychiat, Surgery
Automation Activity & Vendor Info: (Cataloging) Follett Software; (OPAC) Follett Software
Partic in National Network of Libraries of Medicine Region 1
Restriction: Not open to pub

CLAY

P CLAY COUNTY PUBLIC LIBRARY*, 614 Main St, 25043. (Mail add: PO Box 60, 25043), SAN 317-7599. Tel: 304-587-4254. FAX: 304-587-7668. Web Site: clay.lib.wv.us. *Libr Dir,* Sheila Thorne; E-mail: sheila.thorne@park.lib.wv.us; Staff 2 (Non-MLS 2)
Founded 1960. Pop 11,000; Circ 22,173
Library Holdings: AV Mats 1,978; Bk Vols 18,891
Automation Activity & Vendor Info: (Cataloging) Follett Software; (Circulation) Follett Software; (OPAC) Follett Software
Wireless access
Open Tues-Thurs 9-6, Fri 9-5
Friends of the Library Group

COWEN

P COWEN PUBLIC LIBRARY*, 47 Mill St, 26206. (Mail add: PO Box 187, 26206-0187), SAN 376-7795. Tel: 304-226-5332. FAX: 304-226-5332. Web Site: cowen.lib.wv.us. *Libr Dir,* Naomi Hagerman; E-mail: naomi.hagerman@wvlc.lib.wv.us
Founded 1978. Pop 4,747
Library Holdings: Audiobooks 220; Bk Vols 19,557; Per Subs 7
Automation Activity & Vendor Info: (Cataloging) Innovative Interfaces, Inc; (Circulation) Innovative Interfaces, Inc; (OPAC) Innovative Interfaces, Inc
Wireless access
Partic in West Virginia Library Network
Open Mon & Wed 8:30-7, Tues & Thurs 8:30-4

CRAIGSVILLE

P CRAIGSVILLE PUBLIC LIBRARY*, 63 Library Lane, 26205. SAN 376-7809. Tel: 304-742-3532. FAX: 304-742-6904. E-mail: craigsvillepubliclibrary@gmail.com. Web Site: craigsvillepubliclibrary.com. *Dir,* Brooke Neil
Founded 1978. Pop 8,854; Circ 30,691
Library Holdings: AV Mats 149; Bks on Deafness & Sign Lang 12; Bk Vols 27,324
Automation Activity & Vendor Info: (Cataloging) Innovative Interfaces, Inc; (Circulation) Innovative Interfaces, Inc; (OPAC) Innovative Interfaces, Inc
Wireless access
Partic in West Virginia Library Network
Open Wed-Fri 9-5, Sat 9-3

DELBARTON

P MINGO COUNTY LIBRARY*, 1481 Helena Ave, 25670. (Mail add: PO Box 10, 25670-0010), SAN 317-7610. Tel: 304-475-2749. FAX: 304-475-3970. *Librn,* Pam Warden; E-mail: pwarden@cabell.lib.wv.us; Staff 1 (Non-MLS 1)
Founded 1972. Pop 28,296; Circ 62,987
Library Holdings: AV Mats 762; Bk Vols 45,000; Per Subs 45
Automation Activity & Vendor Info: (Cataloging) SirsiDynix; (Circulation) SirsiDynix; (OPAC) SirsiDynix
Open Mon 10-6, Tues-Fri 8:30-4:30
Branches: 3
GILBERT BRANCH, City Hall, Gilbert, 25621. (Mail add: PO Box 266, Gilbert, 25621-0266), SAN 324-2641. Tel: 304-664-8886. FAX: 304-664-8886. *Br Librn,* Angela Miller; Staff 1 (Non-MLS 1)
Library Holdings: Bk Vols 4,200; Per Subs 10
Open Mon-Wed & Fri 8:30-4:30, Thurs 10-6
KERMIT BRANCH, 103 Main St, Kermit, 25674. (Mail add: PO Box 272, Kermit, 25674), SAN 324-265X. Tel: 304-393-4553. FAX: 304-393-4553. *Br Librn,* Bobbi Marcum; Staff 1 (Non-MLS 1)
Library Holdings: Bk Vols 7,000; Per Subs 10
Open Mon & Wed-Fri 9-5, Tues 11-7
MATEWAN BRANCH, Warm Hollow Rd, Matewan, 25678. (Mail add: PO Box 716, Matewan, 25678), SAN 324-2668. Tel: 304-426-6306. FAX: 304-426-6306. *Br Librn,* Christina White; Staff 2 (Non-MLS 2)
Library Holdings: Bk Vols 4,000; Per Subs 10
Open Mon-Wed & Fri 8:30-4:30, Thurs 10-6
Bookmobiles: 1

ELIZABETH

P DORA BEE WOODYARD MEMORIAL LIBRARY*, 411 Mulberry St, 26143. (Mail add: PO Box 340, 26143-0340), SAN 317-7629. Tel: 304-275-4295. FAX: 304-275-0404. Web Site: dorabwoodyard.lib.wv.us. *Dir,* Breanna King; E-mail: breanna.king@k12.wv.us; *Libr Asst,* Jessie Powel; *Libr Asst,* Cathy Watkins
Founded 1962. Pop 5,192; Circ 32,466
Library Holdings: Bk Vols 15,652; Per Subs 52
Special Collections: West Virginia History & Ancestry
Automation Activity & Vendor Info: (Cataloging) Innovative Interfaces, Inc; (Circulation) Innovative Interfaces, Inc; (OPAC) Innovative Interfaces, Inc
Wireless access
Publications: Book News
Partic in West Virginia Library Network
Open Mon-Wed & Fri 8-5, Thurs 8-6

ELKINS

C DAVIS & ELKINS COLLEGE*, Booth Library, 100 Campus Dr, 26241. SAN 317-7637. Tel: 304-637-1200. E-mail: library@dewv.edu. Web Site: library.dewv.edu/welcometobooth. *Dir,* Mary Jo DeJoice; Tel: 304-637-1359, E-mail: dejoicem@dewv.edu; *Evening Coordr,* Position Currently Open; Staff 1 (MLS 1)
Founded 1904. Enrl 850; Fac 65; Highest Degree: Bachelor
Library Holdings: Bk Vols 116,000; Per Subs 459
Special Collections: College History Coll; Jim & Ola Comstock Coll. US Document Depository
Automation Activity & Vendor Info: (Cataloging) Innovative Interfaces, Inc - Sierra; (ILL) OCLC; (OPAC) Innovative Interfaces, Inc - Sierra
Wireless access
Function: 24/7 Online cat, Archival coll, Govt ref serv, Mail & tel request accepted, Photocopying/Printing, Ref serv available
Partic in Appalachian College Association; OCLC Online Computer Library Center, Inc
Open Mon-Thurs 9-8, Fri 9-4, Sun 2-10
Restriction: Badge access after hrs, Open to students, fac & staff

P ELKINS-RANDOLPH COUNTY PUBLIC LIBRARY*, 416 Davis Ave, 26241. SAN 317-7645. Tel: 304-637-0287. FAX: 304-637-0288. Web Site: elkinslibrary.com. *Dir,* Jared Howell; E-mail: experienceerlibrary@gmail.com; Staff 6 (MLS 1, Non-MLS 5)
Founded 1969. Pop 14,097; Circ 48,097
Library Holdings: Audiobooks 1,049; AV Mats 2,303; Bks on Deafness & Sign Lang 6; Braille Volumes 50; CDs 149; DVDs 2,303; e-books 113,079; Large Print Bks 1,049; Microforms 29; Bk Vols 30,937; Per Subs 30; Talking Bks 645
Automation Activity & Vendor Info: (Cataloging) Innovative Interfaces, Inc; (Circulation) Innovative Interfaces, Inc; (OPAC) Innovative Interfaces, Inc
Wireless access
Function: Audiobks via web, Bks on CD, Computers for patron use, Electronic databases & coll, Family literacy, Free DVD rentals, ILL available, Microfiche/film & reading machines, Notary serv, Online cat, Online info literacy tutorials on the web & in blackboard, OverDrive digital audio bks, Photocopying/Printing, Preschool reading prog, Prog for children & young adult, Ref serv available, Spanish lang bks, Story hour, Summer & winter reading prog, Tax forms, Telephone ref, Wheelchair accessible
Partic in West Virginia Library Network
Open Mon-Fri 9-6, Sat 10-5
Restriction: Non-circulating of rare bks
Friends of the Library Group

FAIRMONT

C FAIRMONT STATE UNIVERSITY*, Ruth Ann Musick Library, 1201 Locust Ave, 26554. SAN 317-767X. Tel: 304-367-4733. Interlibrary Loan Service Tel: 304-367-4622. Reference Tel: 304-367-4121. FAX: 304-367-4677. Web Site: library.fairmontstate.edu. *Interim Dir, Ref & ILL Librn,* Sharon Mazure; Tel: 304-367-4622, E-mail: smazure@fairmontstate.edu; *Asst Libr Dir,* Jacquelynn Sherman; Tel: 304-368-3643; *Electronic Serv Librn,* Toru Chiba; Tel: 304-367-4594, E-mail: tchiba@fairmontstate.edu; *Student Success Librn,* Ashley Dover; *Coordr, Ref & Instrul Serv,* Charley Hively; Tel: 304-367-4617, E-mail: hhively@fairmontstate.edu; *Circ,* Teresa Efaw; *Circ,* Ed Nutter; *Circ,* Debbie Renick; *Circ,* Jamie Schultz; *Circ,* Valerie Woofter; Staff 10 (MLS 5, Non-MLS 5)
Founded 1867. Enrl 3,870; Fac 5; Highest Degree: Master
Library Holdings: AV Mats 4,626; e-books 81,550; e-journals 27,816; Bk Vols 317,273; Per Subs 54
Special Collections: US Document Depository
Automation Activity & Vendor Info: (Acquisitions) Innovative Interfaces, Inc; (Cataloging) Innovative Interfaces, Inc; (Circulation) Innovative Interfaces, Inc; (ILL) OCLC ILLiad; (OPAC) Innovative Interfaces, Inc; (Serials) Innovative Interfaces, Inc
Wireless access
Function: Audio & video playback equip for onsite use, E-Reserves, Electronic databases & coll, ILL available, Internet access, Mail & tel request accepted, Online info literacy tutorials on the web & in blackboard, Online ref, Orientations, Photocopying/Printing, Ref & res, Ref serv available, Spoken cassettes & DVDs, Telephone ref, Wheelchair accessible
Partic in LYRASIS; OCLC Online Computer Library Center, Inc
Special Services for the Deaf - TTY equip
Special Services for the Blind - Assistive/Adapted tech devices, equip & products
Open Mon-Thurs 7am-10pm, Fri 8-4, Sun 2-10

P MARION COUNTY PUBLIC LIBRARY*, 321 Monroe St, 26554-2952. SAN 317-7688. Tel: 304-366-1210. FAX: 304-366-4831. E-mail: fairmont@mcpls.org. Web Site: mcpls.org. *Dir,* Erika Reed; E-mail: ereed@mcpls.org; *Asst Libr Dir,* Larissa Dean; E-mail: ldean@mcpls.org; Staff 18 (MLS 1, Non-MLS 17)
Founded 1941. Pop 58,367; Circ 163,000
Library Holdings: AV Mats 3,262; Bk Vols 45,361; Per Subs 115
Special Collections: Genealogy Coll
Automation Activity & Vendor Info: (Acquisitions) Innovative Interfaces, Inc; (Cataloging) Innovative Interfaces, Inc; (Circulation) Innovative Interfaces, Inc; (Course Reserve) Innovative Interfaces, Inc; (OPAC) Innovative Interfaces, Inc; (Serials) Innovative Interfaces, Inc
Wireless access
Open Mon & Tues 9-8, Wed-Fri 9-6, Sat 9-4
Friends of the Library Group
Branches: 2
FAIRVIEW PUBLIC, 500 Main St, Fairview, 26570, SAN 324-4717. Tel: 304-449-1021. FAX: 304-449-1195. E-mail: fairview@mcpls.org. *Br Mgr,* Julie Mike; E-mail: jmike@mcpls.org; Staff 2 (Non-MLS 2)
Library Holdings: Bk Vols 12,344; Per Subs 44
Open Mon, Wed & Thurs 10-5, Tues 10-7, Fri & Sat 9-1
Friends of the Library Group
MANNINGTON PUBLIC, 109 Clarksburg St, Mannington, 26582, SAN 324-4725. Tel: 304-986-2803. FAX: 304-986-3425. E-mail: mannington@mcpls.org. *Br Mgr,* Janet Besedich; E-mail: jbesedich@mcpls.org; Staff 2 (MLS 1, Non-MLS 1)
Founded 1964
Library Holdings: Bk Vols 31,186; Per Subs 56
Open Mon 9-7, Tues-Fri 9-5, Sat 9-1
Friends of the Library Group
Bookmobiles: 1

FRANKLIN

P PENDLETON COUNTY LIBRARY, 256 N Main St, 26807. (Mail add: PO Box 519, 26807-0519), SAN 364-3476. Tel: 304-358-7038. FAX: 304-358-7038. Web Site: pendleton.lib.wv.us. *Librn,* Walt Johnson; E-mail: wjohnson@ephlibrary.org; Staff 1 (Non-MLS 1)
Pop 6,400; Circ 35,045
Library Holdings: Bk Vols 40,000; Per Subs 21

Automation Activity & Vendor Info: (Cataloging) TLC (The Library Corporation); (Circulation) TLC (The Library Corporation); (OPAC) TLC (The Library Corporation)
Wireless access
Open Tues-Fri 10-5, Sat 9-3
Friends of the Library Group

GASSAWAY

P GASSAWAY PUBLIC LIBRARY*, 536 Elk St, 26624. SAN 317-770X. Tel: 304-364-8292. FAX: 304-364-8292. Web Site: gassaway.lib.wv.us. *Dir,* Beverly Cottrill; E-mail: beverly.cottrill@clark.lib.wv.us; Staff 3 (Non-MLS 3)
Founded 1967. Pop 3,500; Circ 26,662
Library Holdings: Bk Vols 15,500; Per Subs 10
Wireless access
Partic in West Virginia Library Network
Open Mon-Fri 10-3

GLENVILLE

P GILMER PUBLIC LIBRARY*, 214 Walnut St, 26351. SAN 320-9822. Tel: 304-462-5620. FAX: 304-462-5620. Web Site: gilmerpublib.org. *Dir,* Lisa Hayes-Minney; E-mail: director@gilmerpublib.org; Staff 3 (Non-MLS 3)
Founded 1979. Pop 8,693; Circ 25,300
Library Holdings: AV Mats 646; Bk Vols 20,900; Per Subs 16
Special Collections: Local History Coll; West Virginia Coll
Automation Activity & Vendor Info: (Cataloging) Innovative Interfaces, Inc; (Circulation) Innovative Interfaces, Inc; (OPAC) Innovative Interfaces, Inc
Wireless access
Partic in West Virginia Library Network
Open Mon, Tues, Thurs & Fri 11-6, Sat 11-4
Friends of the Library Group

C GLENVILLE STATE COLLEGE, Robert F Kidd Library, 100 High St, 26351. SAN 317-7718. Tel: 304-462-6160. Reference Tel: 304-462-6164. FAX: 304-462-4049. E-mail: library@glenville.edu. Web Site: www.glenville.edu/library. *Libr Dir,* Jason Gum; Tel: 304-462-6163, E-mail: jason.gum@glenville.edu; *Libr Assoc,* Joseph Lutsy; Tel: 304-462-6162, E-mail: lutsy.josepht@gsu.glenville.edu; Staff 4.7 (MLS 1, Non-MLS 3.7)
Founded 1930. Enrl 1,194; Fac 66; Highest Degree: Master
Jul 2023-Jun 2024. Mats Exp $76,286, Books $14,392, Per/Ser (Incl. Access Fees) $4,339, Electronic Ref Mat (Incl. Access Fees) $56,898, Presv $657. Sal $152,086 (Prof $51,829)
Library Holdings: AV Mats 1,155; e-books 88,869; e-journals 32,897; Bk Titles 99,158; Bk Vols 112,679; Per Subs 93
Special Collections: Archives & Special Coll; Berlin B Chapman Special Coll Room; WV Veterans Legacy Project. Oral History
Subject Interests: WVa
Automation Activity & Vendor Info: (Cataloging) Innovative Interfaces, Inc; (Circulation) Innovative Interfaces, Inc - Millennium; (ILL) OCLC Online; (OPAC) Innovative Interfaces, Inc - Millennium
Wireless access
Function: 24/7 Electronic res, Archival coll, Audio & video playback equip for onsite use, Audiobks via web, Computers for patron use, Electronic databases & coll, Free DVD rentals, ILL available, Laminating, Magazines, Mango lang, Microfiche/film & reading machines, Music CDs, Online cat, Online ref, Orientations, OverDrive digital audio bks, Photocopying/Printing, Ref & res, Ref serv available, Scanner, Spanish lang bks, Telephone ref, VHS videos, Wheelchair accessible
Partic in West Virginia Library Network
Open Mon-Fri 8-8, Sat & Sun 12-8

GRAFTON

P TAYLOR COUNTY PUBLIC LIBRARY*, 200 Beech St, 26354. SAN 317-7726. Tel: 304-265-6121. FAX: 304-265-6122. E-mail: taylib@clark.lib.wv.us. Web Site: www.taylorcountypubliclibrary.com. *Dir,* Alesha Whitehair; E-mail: alesha.tocco@clark.lib.wv.us; *Circ,* Robin Mayle; Staff 3 (Non-MLS 3)
Founded 1979. Pop 16,089; Circ 117,892
Library Holdings: AV Mats 1,808; Large Print Bks 442; Bk Titles 27,375; Bk Vols 35,804; Per Subs 25; Spec Interest Per Sub 30; Talking Bks 822
Special Collections: Rare West Virginia Coll
Subject Interests: Genealogy, Local hist
Automation Activity & Vendor Info: (Acquisitions) Follett Software; (Cataloging) Follett Software; (Circulation) Follett Software; (Course Reserve) Follett Software; (OPAC) Follett Software; (Serials) Follett Software
Wireless access
Function: Archival coll, AV serv, Home delivery & serv to seniorr ctr & nursing homes, Homebound delivery serv, ILL available, Internet access, Photocopying/Printing, Prog for children & young adult, Ref serv available, Satellite serv, Summer reading prog, Telephone ref, Wheelchair accessible
Partic in West Virginia Library Network
Open Mon & Thurs 9-7:30, Tues, Wed & Fri 9-5, Sat (Winter) 9-Noon
Friends of the Library Group

GRANTSVILLE

P CALHOUN COUNTY PUBLIC LIBRARY*, 250 Mill St N, 26147. (Mail add: PO Box 918, 26147-0918), SAN 317-7734. Tel: 304-354-6300. FAX: 304-354-7702. Web Site: calhoun.lib.wv.us. *Librn,* Amy Norman; E-mail: amyallen@mail.mln.lib.wv.us; Staff 2 (Non-MLS 2)
Pop 7,877; Circ 20,685
Library Holdings: AV Mats 20; Bk Vols 18,900; Per Subs 30
Wireless access
Mem of Parkersburg & Wood County Public Library
Partic in West Virginia Library Network
Open Mon, Wed & Fri 8-3, Tues & Thurs 10-6:30

HAMLIN

P LINCOLN COUNTY LIBRARIES*, Hamlin-Lincoln (Main Library), 7999 Lynn Ave, 25523. SAN 364-3654. Tel: 304-824-5481. FAX: 304-824-7014. Web Site: lincolib.org. *Dir,* Melissa Brown; E-mail: melissa@lincolib.org; Staff 3 (MLS 1, Non-MLS 2)
Founded 1972. Pop 21,382; Circ 56,986
Library Holdings: Bk Titles 30,000; Per Subs 30
Special Collections: Genealogical Coll; West Virginia Historical Coll
Automation Activity & Vendor Info: (Cataloging) SirsiDynix; (Circulation) SirsiDynix; (OPAC) SirsiDynix
Wireless access
Open Mon-Thurs 8-5, Fri & Sat 8-12
Branches: 2
ALUM CREEK PUBLIC LIBRARY, 255 Midway School Rd, Alum Creek, 25003. (Mail add: PO Box 530, Alum Creek, 25003-0530). Tel: 304-756-9211. FAX: 304-756-9212. *Br Mgr,* Kathy Cummings; Staff 1 (Non-MLS 1)
Circ 19,807
Library Holdings: Bk Vols 16,633; Per Subs 19
Special Collections: West Virginia Coll
Open Mon-Fri 9-5
GUYAN RIVER PUBLIC LIBRARY, 5320 McClellan Hwy, Branchland, 25506. (Mail add: PO Box 278, Branchland, 25506-0278). Tel: 304-824-4640. FAX: 304-824-4641. *Br Mgr,* Norma Sutherland; Staff 1 (Non-MLS 1)
Circ 23,065
Library Holdings: Bk Vols 17,000; Per Subs 20
Open Mon-Fri 9-5

HARMAN

P PIONEER MEMORIAL PUBLIC LIBRARY*, Rte 33, 26270. (Mail add: 22526 Allegheny Hwy, 26270), SAN 376-6020. Tel: 304-227-4788. FAX: 304-227-4788. E-mail: help@pioneer.wvlibrary.info. Web Site: pioneer.wvlibrary.info. *Interim Libr Dir,* Judy Bucher; E-mail: judy.bucher@pioneer.wvlibrary.info; Staff 2 (Non-MLS 2)
Founded 1985
Library Holdings: Bks on Deafness & Sign Lang 10; DVDs 200; Bk Titles 28,000
Automation Activity & Vendor Info: (Cataloging) Innovative Interfaces, Inc - Sierra; (Circulation) Innovative Interfaces, Inc - Sierra; (OPAC) Innovative Interfaces, Inc - Sierra
Wireless access
Partic in West Virginia Library Network
Open Tues & Thurs 1-6, Wed & Fri 10-4, Sat 10-2
Friends of the Library Group

HARPERS FERRY

P BOLIVAR-HARPERS FERRY PUBLIC LIBRARY*, 151 Polk St, 25425. SAN 326-3622. Tel: 304-535-2301. FAX: 304-535-2301. E-mail: bhfplibrary@gmail.com. Web Site: bolivarharpersferrylibrary.com. *Dir,* Sara Curley; *Adult Serv,* Edie Offutt; *Cat,* Lisa Fox; *Ch Serv,* Martha Kasmier; Staff 4 (MLS 1, Non-MLS 3)
Founded 1977. Pop 14,063; Circ 42,924
Library Holdings: Audiobooks 1,710; Bk Vols 33,428; Per Subs 16; Videos 473
Special Collections: Harpers Ferry Coll
Automation Activity & Vendor Info: (Cataloging) TLC (The Library Corporation); (Circulation) TLC (The Library Corporation); (OPAC) TLC (The Library Corporation)
Wireless access
Function: Audiobks via web, Bks on cassette, Bks on CD, Children's prog, Computers for patron use, Electronic databases & coll, Free DVD rentals, ILL available, Internet access, Online cat, OverDrive digital audio bks, Photocopying/Printing, Prog for children & young adult, Spoken

cassettes & CDs, Spoken cassettes & DVDs, Story hour, Summer reading prog, Tax forms, VHS videos, Wheelchair accessible
Open Mon, Tues, Fri & Sat 10-5:30, Wed & Thurs 10-8
Restriction: Non-resident fee

HARRISVILLE

P RITCHIE COUNTY PUBLIC LIBRARY*, 608 E Main St, 26362. SAN 317-7750. Tel: 304-643-2717. FAX: 304-643-4019. E-mail: ritchiecountylibrary@gmail.com. Web Site: ritchiecountypubliclibrary.squarespace.com. *Dir,* Emilee Duvall; E-mail: seesee@mail.mln.lib.wv.us; Staff 7 (MLS 1, Non-MLS 6)
Founded 1931. Pop 8,444; Circ 42,000
Library Holdings: AV Mats 7,826; Bks on Deafness & Sign Lang 30; Bk Titles 55,000; Per Subs 45
Special Collections: The Minnie Kendall Lowther Memorial Coll, oral hist; West Virginia History & Ritchie County History Coll, bks, rec, micro, slides, A-tapes. Oral History
Automation Activity & Vendor Info: (Cataloging) Innovative Interfaces, Inc - Sierra; (Circulation) Innovative Interfaces, Inc - Sierra; (OPAC) Innovative Interfaces, Inc - Sierra
Wireless access
Partic in West Virginia Library Network
Open Mon & Thurs 9-8, Tues & Fri 9-4, Sat 9-1
Branches: 1
PENNSBORO BRANCH, 411 Main St, Pennsboro, 26415, SAN 376-897X. Tel: 304-659-2197. FAX: 304-659-3698. *Br Librn,* Connie Frederick; E-mail: connie.frederick@wvlc.lib.wv.us; Staff 1 (Non-MLS 1)
Founded 1984. Pop 4,093; Circ 11,000
Library Holdings: Bk Vols 15,000; Per Subs 28
Open Mon, Wed & Fri 9-4, Tues 11-7, Sat 9-1

HELVETIA

P HELVETIA PUBLIC LIBRARY*, 4901 Pickens Rd, 26224. (Mail add: PO Box 15, 26224-0015), SAN 376-6128. Tel: 304-924-5063. FAX: 304-924-5063. Web Site: helvetia.wvlibrary.info. *Libr Dir,* Gracie Chidester; E-mail: gracie.chidester@helvetia.wvlibrary.info; Staff 1 (Non-MLS 1)
Library Holdings: Bk Titles 4,500; Per Subs 20
Wireless access
Partic in West Virginia Library Network
Open Mon & Wed 10-6, Tues & Thurs 2-8

HILLSBORO

S PEARL S BUCK BIRTHPLACE FOUNDATION*, Historic House Museum Library, 8129 Seneca Trail, Rte 219, 24946. (Mail add: PO Box 126, 24946-0126), SAN 377-5003. Tel: 304-653-4430. E-mail: info@pearlsbuckbirthplace.com. Web Site: www.pearlsbuckbirthplace.com, www.pocahontascountywv.com/pearl-s-buck-birthplace. *Mgr,* Phyllis Lubin-Tyler
Library Holdings: Bk Titles 400
Open Mon, Fri & Sat 10-4, Sun 1-4
Restriction: Non-circulating to the pub

HINTON

P SUMMERS COUNTY PUBLIC LIBRARY*, 201 Temple St, 25951. SAN 329-9384. Tel: 304-466-4490. FAX: 304-466-5260. E-mail: summerscolibrary@gmail.com. Web Site: summers.lib.wv.us. *Dir,* Austin Persinger; E-mail: austin.persinger@mail.mln.lib.wv.us; *Asst Librn,* Sherry Gwinn; Staff 3 (MLS 1, Non-MLS 2)
Founded 1977
Library Holdings: Bk Titles 16,604; Per Subs 29; Talking Bks 797; Videos 1,381
Automation Activity & Vendor Info: (Acquisitions) Innovative Interfaces, Inc; (Cataloging) Innovative Interfaces, Inc; (Circulation) Innovative Interfaces, Inc; (OPAC) Innovative Interfaces, Inc
Wireless access
Partic in West Virginia Library Network
Open Mon-Fri 8:30-6
Friends of the Library Group

HUNDRED

P HUNDRED PUBLIC LIBRARY, Rte 250, 26575. (Mail add: PO Box 453, 26575-0453), SAN 364-4731. Tel: 304-775-5161. FAX: 304-775-5161. E-mail: hundredpubliclibrary@gmail.com. Web Site: www.facebook.com/hundredpubliclibrary. *Librn,* Vicki Himelrick; *Mgr,* Gina Gray; Staff 1 (Non-MLS 1)
Pop 1,590; Circ 20,365
Library Holdings: Bk Vols 10,000
Automation Activity & Vendor Info: (Cataloging) Innovative Interfaces, Inc; (Circulation) Innovative Interfaces, Inc; (OPAC) Innovative Interfaces, Inc
Wireless access
Partic in West Virginia Library Network
Open Mon-Fri 10-5, Sat 9-3

HUNTINGTON

P CABELL COUNTY PUBLIC LIBRARY*, 455 Ninth Street Plaza, 25701. SAN 364-3832. Tel: 304-528-5700. Information Services Tel: 304-528-5660. FAX: 304-528-5701. Circulation FAX: 304-528-5866. TDD: 304-528-5694. E-mail: circulation@cabellcountylib.org. Web Site: cabellcounty.ent.sirsi.net. *Dir,* Breana Bowen; E-mail: breana.bowen@cabellcountylib.org; *Asst Dir,* Sara Ramezani; E-mail: sara.ramezani@cabellcountylib.org; *Asst Dir, Adult Serv,* David Owens; E-mail: david.owens@cabellcountylib.org; *Tech Serv Mgr,* Michelle L Kubiak; E-mail: michelle.kubiak@cabellcountylib.org; *Youth Serv Mgr,* Angela Arthur; E-mail: angela.arthur@cabellcountylib.org; Staff 54 (MLS 11, Non-MLS 43)
Founded 1902. Pop 49,625
Library Holdings: Audiobooks 29,453; AV Mats 19,972; CDs 11,876; DVDs 53,888; Bk Titles 196,895; Bk Vols 387,921; Per Subs 321
Subject Interests: Genealogy, Local hist
Automation Activity & Vendor Info: (Cataloging) SirsiDynix-Enterprise; (Circulation) SirsiDynix-Enterprise; (OPAC) SirsiDynix-Enterprise; (Serials) SirsiDynix-Enterprise
Wireless access
Function: Adult bk club, Adult literacy prog, After school storytime, Art exhibits, Audio & video playback equip for onsite use, Audiobks via web, AV serv, Bk club(s), Chess club, Children's prog, Computer training, Computers for patron use, Digital talking bks, E-Reserves, Electronic databases & coll, Free DVD rentals, Home delivery & serv to seniorr ctr & nursing homes, Homework prog, ILL available, Instruction & testing, Internet access, Meeting rooms, Notary serv, Online cat, Online info literacy tutorials on the web & in blackboard, Orientations, OverDrive digital audio bks, Photocopying/Printing, Preschool outreach, Prog for children & young adult, Ref serv available, Senior computer classes, Story hour, Summer reading prog, Tax forms, Teen prog, Telephone ref, Wheelchair accessible
Publications: Library Connection (Newsletter)
Special Services for the Deaf - Bks on deafness & sign lang; TTY equip
Special Services for the Blind - Assistive/Adapted tech devices, equip & products; Braille bks; Computer with voice synthesizer for visually impaired persons
Open Mon 9-8:30, Tues & Fri 9-6, Sat 9-5
Friends of the Library Group
Branches: 8
BARBOURSVILLE BRANCH, 749 Central Ave, Barboursville, 25504, SAN 364-3867. Tel: 304-736-4621. FAX: 304-736-6240. E-mail: barboursville@cabellcountylib.org. *Mgr,* Linda LaRue; E-mail: linda.larue@cabellcountylib.org
Library Holdings: Bk Titles 24,300; Bk Vols 30,508; Per Subs 98
Open Mon-Fri 9-5:30, Sat 9-1
COX LANDING BRANCH, 793 Cox Landing Rd, Lesage, 25537, SAN 376-6942. Tel: 304-733-3022. FAX: 304-733-7022. E-mail: coxlanding@cabellcountylib.org. *Mgr,* Abigail Kojsza; E-mail: abigail.kojsza@cabellcountylib.org; Staff 1 (Non-MLS 1)
Library Holdings: Bk Titles 5,000; Bk Vols 7,615; Per Subs 30
Open Mon-Fri 9-5:30
Friends of the Library Group
GALLAHER VILLAGE, 368 Norway Ave, 25705, SAN 364-3956. Tel: 304-528-5696. FAX: 304-528-5696. E-mail: gallaher@cabellcountylib.org. *Mgr,* Carl Hamlin; E-mail: carl.hamlin@cabellcountylib.org; Staff 2 (Non-MLS 2)
Library Holdings: AV Mats 1,000; Bk Titles 23,000; Bk Vols 29,430; Per Subs 30
Open Mon-Fri 9-5:30, Sat 9-1
GUYANDOTTE, 203 Richmond St, 25702, SAN 364-3980. Tel: 304-528-5698. FAX: 304-528-5698. E-mail: guyandotte@cabellcountylib.org. *Mgr,* Katie Curry; E-mail: katie.curry@cabellcountylib.org; Staff 1 (Non-MLS 1)
Library Holdings: AV Mats 243; Bk Titles 10,020; Bk Vols 10,930; Per Subs 40
Open Mon-Fri 9-5:30, Sat 9-1
MILTON BRANCH, 1140 Smith St, Milton, 25541, SAN 364-4014. Tel: 304-743-6711. FAX: 304-743-6747. E-mail: milton@cabellcountylib.org. *Mgr,* Lynn McGinnis; E-mail: lynn.mcginnis@cabellcountylib.org; Staff 3 (Non-MLS 3)
Library Holdings: AV Mats 738; Bk Titles 10,471; Bk Vols 35,432; Per Subs 54
Open Mon-Fri 9-5:30, Sat 9-1
SALT ROCK BRANCH, 138 Madison Creek Rd, Salt Rock, 25559, SAN 364-4049. Tel: 304-733-2186. FAX: 304-733-3521. E-mail: saltrock@cabellcountylib.org. *Mgr,* Kim Kirwan; E-mail: kim.kirwan@cabellcountylib.org; Staff 2 (Non-MLS 2)

Library Holdings: AV Mats 140; Bk Titles 2,100; Bk Vols 16,301; Per Subs 40
Open Mon-Fri 9-5:30

P SERVICES FOR THE BLIND & PHYSICALLY HANDICAPPED, 455 Ninth St, 1st Flr, 25701. Tel: 304-528-5700, Ext 118. E-mail: talkingbooks@cabellcountylib.org. *Coordr,* Sandra Philp; Staff 1 (Non-MLS 1)
Library Holdings: Large Print Bks 30,000; Talking Bks 20,000
Open Mon-Fri 9-5
Friends of the Library Group

WEST HUNTINGTON, 901 W 14th St, 25704, SAN 364-4073. Tel: 304-528-5697. FAX: 304-528-5767. E-mail: westhuntington@cabellcountylib.org. *Mgr,* Olivia Picklesimer; E-mail: oliviapicklesimer@cabellcountylib.org; Staff 4 (Non-MLS 4)
Library Holdings: AV Mats 925; Bk Titles 15,000; Bk Vols 16,739; Per Subs 31
Open Mon-Fri 9-5:30, Sat 9-1
Friends of the Library Group

S HUNTINGTON MUSEUM OF ART*, James D Francis Art Library, 2033 McCoy Rd, 25701. SAN 317-7793. Tel: 304-529-2701. FAX: 304-529-7447. Web Site: www.hmoa.org/art/james-d.-francis-art-library. *Librn,* Nat DeBruin; E-mail: ndebruin@hmoa.org; *Sr Curator,* John Farley; E-mail: jfarley@hmoa.org
Library Holdings: Bk Titles 18,006; Bk Vols 21,000; Per Subs 55
Special Collections: Fastoria Glass Catalogs & Price Lists 1897-1980; Fine Arts Coll; Fire Arms History & Manufacture Coll; Glass History & Technology Coll
Subject Interests: Am glass, Antique firearms, Antique to contemporary, Fine arts, Tapestries
Automation Activity & Vendor Info: (Cataloging) Mandarin Library Automation
Restriction: Non-circulating, Open by appt only

C MARSHALL UNIVERSITY LIBRARIES*, One John Marshall Dr, 25755-2060. SAN 317-7815. Tel: 304-696-2320. Circulation Tel: 304-696-2321. Interlibrary Loan Service Tel: 304-696-4011. Reference Tel: 304-696-2334. Administration Tel: 304-696-3095. Toll Free Tel: 800-818-9816. FAX: 304-696-5858. Administration FAX: 304-696-3229. E-mail: library@marshall.edu. Web Site: www.marshall.edu/library. *Dean, Univ Libr,* Dr Monica Garcia Brooks; Tel: 304-696-6474, E-mail: brooks@marshall.edu; *Assoc Dean, Univ Libr,* Dr Kelli Johnson; Tel: 304-696-6567, E-mail: kelli.johnson@marshall.edu; *Head, Archives, Spec Coll,* Lori Thompson; Tel: 304-696-3525, E-mail: thompson39@marshall.edu; *Head, Res & Instruction,* Sabrina Thomas; Tel: 304-696-3627, E-mail: tho4@marshall.edu; *Librn, Research & Instruction Services,* Sarah Mollette; Tel: 304-696-2335, E-mail: sarah.mollette@marshall.edu; *Libr Operations Supvr,* Johnny Bradley; Tel: 304-696-6434, E-mail: bradley39@marshall.edu; *Digital Serv, Head, Tech Serv,* Position Currently Open; *Cat, Digital Serv Librn,* Gretchen Beach; Tel: 304-696-2312, E-mail: beachgr@marshall.edu; *Coll Res Mgt Librn,* Angela Strait; Tel: 304-696-4356, E-mail: strait@marshall.edu; *Archivist, Digital Preservation Librn,* Jessica Lowman; Tel: 304-696-3098, E-mail: lowman@marshall.edu; *Digital Serv Librn,* Stephen Tipler; Tel: 304-696-2907, E-mail: tipler@marshall.edu; *Electronic Serv Librn,* Ron Titus; Tel: 304-696-6575, E-mail: titus@marshall.edu; *Open Education Librn, Scholarly Communications,* Larry Sheret; Tel: 304-696-6577, E-mail: sheret@marshall.edu; *Res & Instruction Librn,* Eryn Roles; Tel: 304-696-2336, E-mail: roles1@marshall.edu; *Research & Student Success Librn,* Kacy Lovelace; Tel: 304-606-6226, E-mail: kacy.lovelace@marshall.edu; *Web/Digital Serv Librn,* Paris E Webb; Tel: 304-696-3511, E-mail: webbp@marshall.edu; *Govt Doc Librn,* Patsy Stephenson; Tel: 304-696-6573, E-mail: stephens@marshall.edu; *Coll Develop, Staff Librn,* Jamie Mathis; E-mail: jamie.mathis@marshall.edu; *Archivist, Rec Mgt Librn,* Lindsey Harper; Tel: 304-696-3174, E-mail: harper166@marshall.edu; *Sr Library Sys Specialist,* Chris Hodge; E-mail: chris.hodge@marshall.edu; *Library Video Operation Specialist,* Andy Earles; E-mail: earles@marshall.edu; *Libr Assoc,* Phyllis White-Sellards; E-mail: whitesel@marshall.edu; *Coll Access, Libr Assoc,* Virginia Holderby; E-mail: holderby@marshall.edu; *Coll Access, Libr Assoc,* Meena Wadhwa; E-mail: wadhwa@marshall.edu; *Libr Assoc,* Rebekkah Brown; E-mail: boltr@marshall.edu; *ILL, Libr Assoc,* Eleanor Anders; E-mail: vickers11@marshall.edu; *ILL, Libr Assoc,* Mary Bowsher; E-mail: curtis@marshall.edu; *Libr Assoc, Tech Serv,* Jacqueline Smith; E-mail: smithjd@marshall.edu; *Archivist, Librn,* Joe Geiger; Tel: 304-696-3097, E-mail: geiger1@marshall.edu; *Info Syst, Library Technologist,* Michelle Alford; E-mail: alford4@marshall.edu; *Cat, Libr Assoc,* Lisa Hughes; E-mail: perry5@marshall.edu; *Cat, Staff Librn,* Skyler Schultz; E-mail: schultz35@marshall.edu; *Scholarly Comms Specialist,* Dr Margaret Sullivan; Tel: 304-696-6780, E-mail: sullivanm@marshall.edu; *Librn,* Gena Chattin; E-mail: chattin2@marshall.edu; *Libr Res Spec,* Kenn Long; Tel: 304-746-8904, E-mail: long94@marshall.edu; *Res & Instruction Librn,* Heather Lauer; Tel: 304-746-8906, E-mail: heather.lauer@marshall.edu; Staff 44.5 (MLS 18.5, Non-MLS 26)
Founded 1929. Enrl 11,410; Fac 720; Highest Degree: Doctorate
Jul 2015-Jun 2016. Mats Exp $1,745,000. Sal $2,489,638 (Prof $1,166,161)
Library Holdings: AV Mats 122,572; e-books 115,843; e-journals 50,182; Electronic Media & Resources 150,516; Bk Vols 394,886; Per Subs 1,987
Special Collections: Chuck Yeager Papers & Artifacts; Civil War Newspapers; Congress of Racial Equality Papers; Former West Virginia Secretary of State Ken Hechler Papers; Historic Literature (Pollard, Redgrave & Wing Books, published in England & Scotland, 1400-1700), microfilm; Hoffman History of Medicine Library; Huntington Women's Club Archives; Nelson Bond Papers; The Rosanna Blake Library of Confederate History. Oral History; State Document Depository; US Document Depository
Subject Interests: Tri-state, WVa
Automation Activity & Vendor Info: (Acquisitions) Innovative Interfaces, Inc; (Cataloging) OCLC WorldShare Interlibrary Loan; (Circulation) Innovative Interfaces, Inc - Millennium; (Course Reserve) Innovative Interfaces, Inc - Millennium; (ILL) OCLC ILLiad; (Media Booking) Innovative Interfaces, Inc - Millennium; (OPAC) Innovative Interfaces, Inc - Millennium; (Serials) SerialsSolutions
Wireless access
Function: Res libr
Publications: Carlton D Weaver Transallegheny Map Collection; Guide to Local History & Genealogy; Guide to the Marshall University Libraries; James E Morrow Library Associates Brochure, Library Connection; Library Information Brochure; Marshall Messenger; WVa: Historical Guide
Partic in LYRASIS; OhioNET; Partnership for Academic Library Collaborative & Innovation
Friends of the Library Group

Departmental Libraries:

CM JOAN C EDWARDS SCHOOL OF MEDICINE HEALTH SCIENCE LIBRARIES, 1600 Medical Center Dr, Ste 2400, 25701-3655, SAN 322-6972. Tel: 304-691-1750. Administration Tel: 304-691-1752. FAX: 304-691-1766. Web Site: jcesom.marshall.edu/library. *Doc Delivery,* Denise Ward; E-mail: wardd@marshall.edu; Staff 2 (Non-MLS 2)
Founded 1976
Library Holdings: e-books 235; e-journals 523; Bk Titles 12,545; Per Subs 251
Automation Activity & Vendor Info: (Circulation) Innovative Interfaces, Inc; (OPAC) Innovative Interfaces, Inc; (Serials) Innovative Interfaces, Inc
Open Mon-Thurs 8am-11pm, Fri 8-5, Sat 10-5, Sun 1-10 (Winter); Mon-Thurs 8-8, Fri 8-5, Sat 10-5, Sun 1-5 (Summer)

MORROW LIBRARY, Third Ave, 25755. Tel: 304-696-2343. Web Site: www.marshall.edu/library/libraries/morrowstacks. *Assoc Univ Librn, Dir,* Dr Majed Khader; Tel: 304-696-3121, E-mail: khader@marshall.edu
Open Mon-Fri 8-5

SOUTH CHARLESTON CAMPUS LIBRARY, 100 Angus E Peyton Dr, South Charleston, 25303-1600, SAN 364-4227. Tel: 304-746-8900. Circulation Tel: 304-746-8910. Reference Tel: 304-746-8911. Toll Free Tel: 800-642-9842. FAX: 304-746-8905. *Libr Coord, Res Spec,* Dr Katherine Murphy; E-mail: kayk@marshall.edu; *Librn,* Gena Chattin; E-mail: Chattin2@marshall.edu; *Librn,* Lynne Edington; Tel: 304-746-8902, E-mail: edington@marshall.edu; *Res & Instruction Librn,* Heather Lauer; Tel: 304-746-8906, E-mail: heather.lauer@marshall.edu; *Libr Res Spec,* Kenn Long; Tel: 304-746-8904, E-mail: long94@marshall.edu; Staff 4.5 (MLS 2.5, Non-MLS 2)
Founded 1972. Enrl 2,194; Highest Degree: Master
Library Holdings: Bk Vols 8,000; Per Subs 260
Subject Interests: Educ, Leadership studies
Automation Activity & Vendor Info: (Cataloging) Innovative Interfaces, Inc; (Circulation) Innovative Interfaces, Inc; (OPAC) Innovative Interfaces, Inc
Partic in OCLC Online Computer Library Center, Inc
Open Mon-Thurs 10-9, Fri 10-5, Sat 9-4

HURRICANE

P PUTNAM COUNTY LIBRARY*, 4219 State Rte 34, 25526. SAN 364-4138. Tel: 304-757-7308. FAX: 304-757-7384. E-mail: putnam@putnamlibrarywv.org. Web Site: putnam.lib.wv.us. *Dir,* Megan Tarbett; Tel: 304-757-9680, E-mail: megan.tarbett@putnamlibrarywv.org; Staff 9 (MLS 1, Non-MLS 8)
Founded 1960. Pop 57,440; Circ 226,452
Library Holdings: Bk Vols 93,800; Per Subs 90
Automation Activity & Vendor Info: (Circulation) SirsiDynix
Wireless access
Open Mon-Thurs 9-7, Fri 9-5, Sat 9-2
Friends of the Library Group

Branches: 4

BUFFALO BRANCH, 19209 Buffalo Rd, Buffalo, 25033, SAN 364-4154. Tel: 304-937-3538. FAX: 304-937-3539. E-mail: buffalo@putnamlibrarywv.org. Web Site: putnam.lib.wv.us/buffalo-branch. *Br Mgr,* Rebecca Harvey; E-mail: rebecca.harvey@putnamlibrarywv.org
Open Mon-Fri 9-12:30 & 1:15-5

ELEANOR BRANCH, 401 Roosevelt Blvd, Eleanor, 25070. (Mail add: PO Box 459, Eleanor, 25070-0459), SAN 364-4162. Tel: 304-586-4295. FAX: 304-586-4501. E-mail: eleanor@putnamlibrarywv.org. Web Site: putnam.lib.wv.us/eleanor-branch. *Br Mgr,* Lisa Reedy; E-mail: lisa.reedy@putnamlibrarywv.org
Open Mon-Fri 9-12:30 & 1:15-5

HURRICANE BRANCH, 410 Midland Trail, 25526, SAN 364-4197. Tel: 304-562-6711. FAX: 304-562-1990. E-mail: hurricane@putnamlibrarywv.org. Web Site: putnam.lib.wv.us/hurricane-branch. *Br Mgr,* Vicki Meek; E-mail: vicki.meek@putnamlibrarywv.org
Open Mon-Fri 9-12:45 & 1:30-5

POCA BRANCH, 2858 Charleston Rd, Poca, 25159, SAN 364-4200. Tel: 304-755-3241. FAX: 304-755-3422. E-mail: poca@putnamlibrarywv.org. Web Site: putnam.lib.wv.us/poca-branch. *Br Mgr,* Teresa King; E-mail: teresa.king@putnamlibrarywv.org
Open Mon-Fri 9-12:15 & 1-5

HUTTONSVILLE

S HUTTONSVILLE CORRECTIONAL CENTER LIBRARY, 109 HCC Blvd, 26273. SAN 317-784X. Tel: 304-335-2291, Ext 12078. FAX: 304-335-4256. Staff 2 (Non-MLS 2)
Founded 1968
Library Holdings: Bks on Deafness & Sign Lang 1; High Interest/Low Vocabulary Bk Vols 25; Large Print Bks 35; Music Scores 15; Bk Titles 10,300; Per Subs 27
Special Collections: ABA Recommended Material; Huttonsville Correctional Center Coll; Law (State & Federal) Coll
Function: Computers for patron use, ILL available, Legal assistance to inmates, Notary serv, Photocopying/Printing
Special Services for the Blind - Large print bks & talking machines
Restriction: Inmate patrons, facility staff & vols direct access. All others through ILL only

INSTITUTE

C WEST VIRGINIA STATE UNIVERSITY*, Drain-Jordan Library, Campus Box L17, 25112. (Mail add: PO Box 1002, 25112-1002), SAN 317-7866. Tel: 304-766-3116. Reference Tel: 304-766-3135. Web Site: library.wvstateu.edu. *Dir,* Dr Willette F Stinson, PhD; E-mail: wstinson@wvstateu.edu; *Archivist, Librn,* Seth Caudill; Tel: 304-766-3023, E-mail: seth.caudill@wvstateu.edu; *Per & Govt Doc Librn,* Rachael Jackson; Tel: 304-766-5222, E-mail: rachel.jackson@wvstateu.edu; *Syst Librn,* Deborah Jean Wells; Tel: 304-766-3150, E-mail: wells@wvstateu.edu; *Assoc Ref Librn,* Edward C Lomax, PhD; Tel: 304-766-3162, E-mail: edward.lomax@wvstateu.edu; *Cat,* Tammy Naylor; E-mail: tnaylor1@wvstateu.edu; Staff 15 (MLS 6, Non-MLS 9)
Founded 1891. Enrl 3,190; Fac 190; Highest Degree: Master
Library Holdings: AV Mats 5,367; CDs 1,187; DVDs 160; e-books 3,252; e-journals 49; Microforms 78,798; Bk Titles 191,434; Bk Vols 201,517; Per Subs 319; Videos 2,062
Special Collections: College Archives, correpondence, photog, rpts; John W Davis Papers. Oral History; US Document Depository
Subject Interests: African-Am hist
Automation Activity & Vendor Info: (Acquisitions) Innovative Interfaces, Inc; (Cataloging) Innovative Interfaces, Inc; (Circulation) Innovative Interfaces, Inc; (Course Reserve) Innovative Interfaces, Inc; (OPAC) Innovative Interfaces, Inc; (Serials) Innovative Interfaces, Inc
Wireless access
Function: Computers for patron use, Online cat, Photocopying/Printing, Scanner, Wheelchair accessible
Publications: Periodical Holding List (Index to periodicals)
Partic in LYRASIS; OCLC Online Computer Library Center, Inc
Special Services for the Blind - Accessible computers; Computer with voice synthesizer for visually impaired persons; Scanner for conversion & translation of mats; ZoomText magnification & reading software
Open Mon-Thurs 8am-10pm, Fri 8-5, Sun 2-8

KENOVA

P WAYNE COUNTY PUBLIC LIBRARY*, Ceredo-Kenova Memorial Public Library, 1200 Oak St, 25530. SAN 317-7882. Tel: 304-453-2462. FAX: 304-453-2462. E-mail: wcpl@waynecountylib.org. Web Site: wcpl.lib.wv.us. *Libr Dir,* Mark Esslinger; E-mail: mark.esslinger@waynecountylib.org; Staff 3 (Non-MLS 3)
Pop 39,000; Circ 110,000
Library Holdings: CDs 300; DVDs 1,000; Bk Titles 34,697; Per Subs 15
Automation Activity & Vendor Info: (Acquisitions) Brodart; (Cataloging) SirsiDynix; (Circulation) SirsiDynix; (OPAC) SirsiDynix; (Serials) EBSCO Online
Wireless access
Function: 24/7 Electronic res, 24/7 Online cat
Special Services for the Blind - Assistive/Adapted tech devices, equip & products
Open Mon-Fri 10-5, Sat 9-1
Friends of the Library Group
Branches: 2

FORT GAY PUBLIC, 80 Rear Broadway, Fort Gay, 25514. (Mail add: PO Box 305, Fort Gay, 25514-0305), SAN 324-2625. Tel: 304-648-5338. FAX: 304-648-5338. Web Site: wcpl.lib.wv.us/fort_gay. *Br Mgr,* Sheila Bowen; Staff 2 (Non-MLS 2)
Circ 27,605
Library Holdings: DVDs 50; Bk Titles 12,000; Per Subs 5
Open Mon 10-4, Tues-Fri 10-5
Friends of the Library Group

WAYNE PUBLIC, 325 Keyser St, Wayne, 25570. (Mail add: PO Box 567, Wayne, 25570-0567), SAN 317-851X. Tel: 304-272-3756. FAX: 304-272-3756. Web Site: wcpl.lib.wv.us/wayne. *Br Mgr,* Lana Smith; Staff 2 (Non-MLS 2)
Library Holdings: DVDs 200; Bk Titles 26,078; Per Subs 40; Videos 890
Open Mon-Fri 9-5
Friends of the Library Group

KEYSER

P KEYSER-MINERAL COUNTY PUBLIC LIBRARY*, 105 N Main St, 26726. SAN 317-7890. Tel: 304-788-3222. FAX: 304-788-3222. E-mail: keysermcpl@gmail.com. Web Site: keyser.lib.wv.us. *Dir,* Heather Haynes; *Asst Dir,* Mary Beth Mowen; Staff 4 (MLS 2, Non-MLS 2)
Founded 1937. Pop 25,661; Circ 38,592
Library Holdings: AV Mats 2,205; Bk Vols 22,264; Per Subs 29; Videos 740
Automation Activity & Vendor Info: (Cataloging) TLC (The Library Corporation); (Circulation) TLC (The Library Corporation); (OPAC) TLC (The Library Corporation)
Wireless access
Open Mon & Wed-Fri 9-6, Tues 9-8, Sat 9-1
Branches: 2

BURLINGTON PUBLIC, Patterson Creek Rd S, Burlington, 26710. (Mail add: PO Box 61, Burlington, 26710-0061). Tel: 304-289-3690. FAX: 304-289-3233. Web Site: burlington.lib.wv.us. *Br Mgr,* Tonya Mongold; *Asst Librn,* Kiki Tolias; Staff 2 (Non-MLS 2)
Founded 1981. Circ 10,288
Library Holdings: Bk Vols 10,164; Per Subs 10
Open Tues 12-7, Wed 10-4, Thurs 10-3, Fri 10-2
Friends of the Library Group

FORT ASHBY PUBLIC, 57 President St, Fort Ashby, 26719. (Mail add: PO Box 74, Fort Ashby, 26719-0064). Tel: 304-298-4493. FAX: 304-298-4014. Web Site: fortashby.lib.wv.us. *Br Mgr,* April DeWitt; *Circ,* Krista Price; Staff 2 (Non-MLS 2)
Founded 1974. Circ 18,114
Library Holdings: AV Mats 173; Bk Vols 18,440; Per Subs 11; Videos 261
Open Mon, Wed & Thurs 9-5, Tues 9-6, Sat 9-1
Friends of the Library Group

C POTOMAC STATE COLLEGE OF WEST VIRGINIA UNIVERSITY*, Mary F Shipper Library, 103 Fort Ave, 26726. SAN 317-7904. Tel: 304-788-6901. Administration Tel: 304-788-6902. FAX: 304-788-6946. Web Site: psc.lib.wvu.edu. *Assoc Univ Librn, Libr Dir,* Seth D Caudill; *Staff Librn,* Nicholas M Gardner; E-mail: ngardner@mail.wvu.edu; *Libr Assoc,* Kathleen S Weber; Tel: 304-788-6907, E-mail: ksweber@mail.wvu.edu; Staff 3 (MLS 2, Non-MLS 1)
Founded 1901. Enrl 1,400; Fac 50; Highest Degree: Bachelor
Library Holdings: Bk Vols 9,500
Subject Interests: Local hist, World War II
Automation Activity & Vendor Info: (Cataloging) OCLC Worldshare Management Services; (Circulation) OCLC Worldshare Management Services; (Course Reserve) OCLC Worldshare Management Services; (Discovery) OCLC Worldshare Management Services; (ILL) OCLC WorldShare Interlibrary Loan; (OPAC) OCLC Worldshare Management Services; (Serials) OCLC Worldshare Management Services
Wireless access
Function: AV serv, Doc delivery serv, ILL available, Photocopying/Printing, Ref serv available, Telephone ref, Wheelchair accessible
Partic in OCLC-LVIS; WVNET
Open Mon-Thurs 8am-9pm, Fri 8-4:30, Sun 1-9; Mon-Fri 8-4:30 (Summer)

KINGWOOD

P KINGWOOD PUBLIC LIBRARY*, 205 W Main St, 26537-1418. SAN 317-7912. Tel: 304-329-1499. FAX: 304-329-1499. E-mail: kingwoodpublic@gmail.com. Web Site: kingwood.lib.wv.us. *Dir,* Aaron Johnson; Tel: 304-329-1499; Staff 1 (MLS 1)
Founded 1941. Pop 30,000
Library Holdings: AV Mats 800; Bks on Deafness & Sign Lang 50; Bk Titles 30,751; Bk Vols 31,327; Per Subs 100

Special Collections: Preston County (Local History Coll); West Virginia Coll
Subject Interests: Relig studies
Wireless access
Publications: Highlights (Monthly newsletter)
Partic in West Virginia Library Network
Special Services for the Deaf - Bks on deafness & sign lang; High interest/low vocabulary bks
Open Mon 9-8, Tues & Thurs 12-5, Wed & Fri 9-5, Sat 10-2
Friends of the Library Group

LEWISBURG

P GREENBRIER COUNTY PUBLIC LIBRARY*, 152 Robert W McCormick Dr, 24901. SAN 317-7939. Tel: 304-647-7568. FAX: 304-647-7569. E-mail: greenbrier.library@mail.mln.lib.wv.us. Web Site: www.greenbriercountylibrary.com. *Dir,* Ann Farr; E-mail: farrann@mail.mln.lib.wv.us; *Asst Librn,* Christy Carver; Staff 5 (MLS 2, Non-MLS 3)
Pop 8,143; Circ 64,000
Library Holdings: Bk Vols 25,000; Per Subs 53
Automation Activity & Vendor Info: (Cataloging) Innovative Interfaces, Inc; (Circulation) Innovative Interfaces, Inc; (OPAC) Innovative Interfaces, Inc
Wireless access
Partic in West Virginia Library Network
Open Mon & Sun 1-5, Tues-Thurs 9-8, Fri 9-7, Sat 11-4
Friends of the Library Group

S GREENBRIER HISTORICAL SOCIETY ARCHIVES & LIBRARY, 814 Washington St W, 24901. SAN 329-0379. Tel: 304-645-3398. E-mail: archives@greenbrierhistorical.org. Web Site: www.greenbrierhistorical.org. *Exec Dir,* Dara Vance; Tel: 304 645 3398, E-mail: director@greenbrierhistorical.org; *Librn,* Jane Hughes; *Archivist,* Karly Watts; Tel: 304-645-3398, E-mail: archivist@greenbrierhistorical.org
Founded 1963
Library Holdings: Bk Titles 998; Bk Vols 1,175
Special Collections: Courthouse Documents (Greenbrier County); Dime Novels (Mrs Alex McVeigh Miller Coll), autobiography, poems, stories; Family Genealogy & History Coll; Marriage Bonds; Militia Appointments; Schools Coll; West Virginia (Mrs Arthur Dayton Coll), original drawings; West Virginia Artists (Ashton Reniers & Naomi Hosterman Colls)
Subject Interests: Local hist
Wireless access
Function: Res assist avail
Publications: Greenbrier Historical Society Newsletter; Journal of the Greenbrier Historical Society (Annual)
Open Mon-Sat 10-4
Restriction: Internal use only, Non-circulating

J NEW RIVER COMMUNITY & TECHNICAL COLLEGE*, New River CTC Library, 129 Courtney Dr, 24901. SAN 317-7920. Tel: 304-647-6575. Web Site: www.newriver.edu/current-students/library-services. *Dir, Libr Serv,* Anne E McMillion; E-mail: amcmillion@newriver.edu
Library Holdings: Bk Titles 14,000; Per Subs 50
Special Collections: West Virginia Coll
Automation Activity & Vendor Info: (Cataloging) Innovative Interfaces, Inc; (Circulation) Innovative Interfaces, Inc; (OPAC) Innovative Interfaces, Inc
Partic in West Virginia Library Network
Open Mon & Wed 9-9, Tues & Thurs 1-9, Fri 9-4:30 (Fall & Spring); Mon-Thurs 9-7 (Summer)

CM WEST VIRGINIA SCHOOL OF OSTEOPATHIC MEDICINE, James R Stookey Library, 400 Lee St N, 24901. SAN 317-7947. Tel: 304-647-6261. FAX: 304-645-4443. E-mail: library@osteo.wvsom.edu. Web Site: www.wvsom.edu/library. *Libr Dir,* Mary Essig; Tel: 304-647-6213, E-mail: messig@osteo.wvsom.edu; *Mgr, Libr Serv,* Rachel McGuire; E-mail: rmcguire@osteo.wvsom.edu; *Tech Asst,* Heather Bladen; E-mail: hbladen@osteo.wvsom.edu; Staff 5 (MLS 2, Non-MLS 3)
Founded 1973. Enrl 800; Fac 60; Highest Degree: Doctorate
Subject Interests: Med
Automation Activity & Vendor Info: (Cataloging) Innovative Interfaces, Inc - Sierra; (Circulation) Innovative Interfaces, Inc - Sierra; (ILL) OCLC; (OPAC) Innovative Interfaces, Inc - Sierra
Wireless access
Function: Doc delivery serv, For res purposes, Health sci info serv, ILL available, Internet access
Special Services for the Deaf - TTY equip
Open Mon-Fri 8am-10pm, Sat & Sun 12-10
Restriction: Circ limited, In-house use for visitors, Non-circulating to the pub, Restricted borrowing privileges

LOGAN

P LOGAN AREA PUBLIC LIBRARY*, 16 Wildcat Way, 25601. Tel: 304-752-6652. FAX: 304-752-2684. Web Site: cabe.ent.sirsi.net/client/en_US/logan, logan.lib.wv.us/contact.html. *Dir,* Cassie Parsons
Pop 16,923
Library Holdings: AV Mats 1,540; Bk Titles 30,000; Per Subs 45; Talking Bks 162
Automation Activity & Vendor Info: (Acquisitions) SirsiDynix; (Cataloging) SirsiDynix; (Circulation) SirsiDynix; (ILL) SirsiDynix
Open Mon-Wed 8-5:30, Thurs 9-6, Fri 9-4

M LOGAN REGIONAL MEDICAL CENTER*, Medical Library, 20 Hospital Dr, 25601. SAN 317-7955. Tel: 304-831-1556. FAX: 304-831-1669. *Educ Dir,* Cindy Fleming; E-mail: cindy.fleming@lpnt.net
Library Holdings: Bk Vols 150; Per Subs 25
Wireless access
Publications: Abridged Index Medicus; Hospital Literature Index & Cumulative Index to Nursing & Allied Health
Restriction: Staff use only

LOST CREEK

P SOUTHERN AREA LIBRARY*, 120 E Main St, 26385. (Mail add: PO Box 282, 26385), SAN 376-7760. Tel: 304-745-4865. FAX: 304-745-4865. Web Site: southernarea.lib.wv.us. *Dir,* Bennett Wilma; E-mail: wilma.bennett@clark.lib.wv.us; Staff 1 (Non-MLS 1)
Founded 1972. Pop 496
Library Holdings: Bk Vols 16,214; Per Subs 20; Talking Bks 207; Videos 233
Automation Activity & Vendor Info: (Cataloging) Innovative Interfaces, Inc; (Circulation) Innovative Interfaces, Inc; (OPAC) Innovative Interfaces, Inc
Wireless access
Function: 24/7 Electronic res, 24/7 Online cat, Activity rm
Special Services for the Blind - Large print bks
Open Mon & Tues Noon-6:30, Wed-Fri Noon-6
Friends of the Library Group

MADISON

P BOONE-MADISON PUBLIC LIBRARY*, 375 Main St, 25130. SAN 364-4286. Tel: 304-369-7842. FAX: 304-369-2950. E-mail: boonemadisonlibrary@gmail.com. Web Site: www.bcplwv.org. *Dir,* Tara Holstein; E-mail: tara.holstein@mail.mln.lib.wv.us; Staff 4 (MLS 1, Non-MLS 3)
Founded 1974. Circ 10,365
Library Holdings: Bk Vols 17,536; Per Subs 60
Special Collections: Genealogy (Boone County & Southern West Virginia Coll)
Subject Interests: County hist
Automation Activity & Vendor Info: (Cataloging) Innovative Interfaces, Inc; (Circulation) Innovative Interfaces, Inc; (OPAC) Innovative Interfaces, Inc
Wireless access
Function: Photocopying/Printing
Partic in West Virginia Library Network
Open Mon, Wed & Fri 8-4:50, Tues & Thurs 9-4:50, Sat 9-Noon
Branches: 3
BARRETT-WHARTON BRANCH, 38487 Pond Fork Rd, Wharton, 25208. (Mail add: PO Box 189, Wharton, 25208-0189). Tel: 304-247-6530. FAX: 304-247-6530.
Library Holdings: Bk Vols 8,276
Open Tues & Thurs 10-4:50, Sat 9-Noon; Tues & Thurs 10-4:50 (Summer)
COAL RIVER, 494 John Slack Circle, Racine, 25165, SAN 364-4324. Tel: 304-837-8437. FAX: 304-834-8437.
Library Holdings: Bk Vols 9,362
Open Tues-Sat 10-4:50 (Winter); Mon-Fri 10-4:50 (Summer)
WHITESVILLE BRANCH, 38175 Coal River Rd, Whitesville, 25209. (Mail add: PO Box 747, Whitesville, 25209-0747), SAN 322-5992. Tel: 304-854-0196. FAX: 304-854-0196.
Library Holdings: Bk Vols 9,266
Function: Photocopying/Printing
Open Tues & Fri 10-4:50, Sat 10-1; Tues & Fri 10-4:50 (Summer)

MAN

P BUFFALO CREEK MEMORIAL LIBRARY*, 511 E McDonald Ave, 25635. SAN 317-7971. Tel: 304-583-7887. FAX: 304-583-0182. E-mail: buffalocreekmemoriallibrary@gmail.com. Web Site: www.facebook.com/buffalocreekmemoriallibrary. *Dir,* Eddie Tackett, II; E-mail: eddie.tackett@cabellcountylib.org; *Libr Asst,* Michele Osborne; Staff 3 (Non-MLS 3)
Founded 1973. Pop 11,525; Circ 21,733

Library Holdings: AV Mats 238; Bk Titles 27,000; Bk Vols 33,500; Per Subs 45
Special Collections: Cookbooks-Coal Mining Towns, photos, diet, exercise, nutrition; West Virginia Code
Subject Interests: Diet, Exercise, Nutrition
Wireless access
Function: Bks on CD, Children's prog, Computers for patron use, Electronic databases & coll, Free DVD rentals, ILL available, Internet access, Music CDs, Notary serv, Photocopying/Printing, Preschool outreach, Prog for children & young adult, Serves people with intellectual disabilities, Story hour, Summer reading prog, Tax forms, Teen prog, Wheelchair accessible
Open Mon 8-6, Tues-Thurs 9-6, Fri 8-3
Restriction: Inmate patrons, facility staff & vols direct access. All others through ILL only
Friends of the Library Group

MARLINTON

P POCAHONTAS COUNTY FREE LIBRARIES*, 500 Eighth St, 24954-1227. SAN 364-3565. Tel: 304-799-6000. FAX: 304-799-3988. E-mail: info@pocahontaslibrary.org. Web Site: www.pocahontaslibrary.org. *Dir,* Cree Lahti; E-mail: director@pocahontaslibrary.org; Staff 4 (MLS 1, Non-MLS 3)
Wireless access
Open Mon-Fri 10-6, Sat 10-4
Branches: 5
DURBIN COMMUNITY LIBRARY, 4715 Stauton-Parkersburg Tpk, Durbin, 26264. (Mail add: PO Box 333, Durbin, 26264-0333), SAN 376-2416. Tel: 304-456-3142. FAX: 304-456-3142. *Librn,* Jessica Walton; Staff 1 (Non-MLS 1)
Library Holdings: Bk Vols 8,350; Per Subs 2
Open Wed-Fri 10-6, Sat 10-4
GREEN BANK PUBLIC LIBRARY, 5683 Potomac Highlands Trail, Green Bank, 24944. (Mail add: PO Box 1, Green Bank, 24944-0001), SAN 376-2424. Tel: 304-456-4507. FAX: 304-456-3382. *Librn,* Hallie Herold; Staff 1 (Non-MLS 1)
Library Holdings: AV Mats 85; Bk Vols 19,029; Per Subs 3
Open Tues-Fri 10-6, Sat 10-4
HILLSBORO PUBLIC LIBRARY, 54 Third St, Hillsboro, 24946, SAN 364-359X. Tel: 304-653-4936. FAX: 304-653-4425. *Librn,* Goldie McClure; Staff 1 (Non-MLS 1)
Circ 4,435
Library Holdings: AV Mats 257; Bk Vols 12,904; Per Subs 2
Open Tues-Fri 10-6, Sat 10-4
Friends of the Library Group
LINWOOD COMMUNITY LIBRARY AT SNOWSHOE, 72 Snowshoe Dr, Slatyfork, 26291. Tel: 304-572-2665. FAX: 304-572-2665. *Librn,* Trisha Barb; Staff 1 (Non-MLS 1)
Library Holdings: Bk Vols 7,928
Open Wed-Fri 10-6, Sat 10-4
MCCLINTIC PUBLIC LIBRARY, 500 Eighth St, 24954-1227, SAN 364-362X. *Librn,* Pamela Johnson; Staff 1 (Non-MLS 1)
Circ 16,121
Library Holdings: AV Mats 1,354; Bk Vols 25,240; Per Subs 34
Automation Activity & Vendor Info: (Cataloging) Innovative Interfaces, Inc; (Circulation) Innovative Interfaces, Inc; (OPAC) Innovative Interfaces, Inc
Partic in West Virginia Library Network
Open Mon-Fri 10-6, Sat 10-4
Friends of the Library Group

MARTINSBURG

M BERKELEY MEDICAL CENTER*, Medical Learning Resource Center, 2500 Hospital Dr, 25401. SAN 317-798X. Tel: 304-264-1246. FAX: 304-264-1340. Web Site: wvumedicine.org/berkeley. *Dir, Strategic Initiatives,* Betsy Gambino; E-mail: betsy.gambino@wvumedicine.org
Library Holdings: Bk Vols 260; Per Subs 55
Open Mon-Fri 8-4:30

GM DEPARTMENT OF VETERANS AFFAIRS, Nursing/Education/Learning Resources Section, 510 Butler Ave, 25405. SAN 317-7998. Tel: 304-263-0811, Ext 3826. *Librn,* Shannon Clever; E-mail: shannon.clever@va.gov; Staff 2 (MLS 1, Non-MLS 1)
Founded 1946
Library Holdings: Bk Vols 3,977; Per Subs 200
Subject Interests: Med, Patient educ
Restriction: Not open to pub

P MARTINSBURG-BERKELEY COUNTY PUBLIC LIBRARY*, Martinsburg Public Library, 101 W King St, 25401. SAN 364-4340. Tel: 304-267-8933. FAX: 304-267-9720. Web Site: www.mbcpl.org. *Dir,* Gretchen Fry; Tel: 304-267-8088, E-mail: gretchen.fry@mbcpl.org; *Asst Dir,* David Porterfield; Tel: 304-267-8933, Ext 4012, E-mail: david.porterfield@mbcpl.org; *Info Serv, Tech Serv Mgr,* Keith Hammersla; Tel: 304-267-8933, Ext 4005, E-mail: keith.hammersla@mbcpl.org
Founded 1926. Pop 96,000; Circ 38,000
Library Holdings: CDs 300; DVDs 500; Large Print Bks 500; Bk Vols 150,000; Per Subs 310; Talking Bks 4,000; Videos 2,000
Automation Activity & Vendor Info: (Cataloging) TLC (The Library Corporation); (Circulation) TLC (The Library Corporation); (OPAC) TLC (The Library Corporation); (Serials) TLC (The Library Corporation)
Wireless access
Open Mon, Tues & Thurs 10-7, Wed, Fri & Sat 10-5
Branches: 3
HEDGESVILLE PUBLIC LIBRARY, 207 N Mary St, Hedgesville, 25427, SAN 364-4375. Tel: 304-754-3949. *Br Mgr,* Dana Phelps; E-mail: dana.phelps@mbcpl.org; Staff 5 (MLS 1, Non-MLS 4)
Founded 1957. Pop 15,000
Library Holdings: AV Mats 150; DVDs 300; e-books 3,000; Large Print Bks 100; Bk Titles 8,500; Per Subs 3
Automation Activity & Vendor Info: (Acquisitions) TLC (The Library Corporation); (Cataloging) TLC (The Library Corporation); (Circulation) TLC (The Library Corporation); (OPAC) TLC (The Library Corporation)
Function: Audio & video playback equip for onsite use, Audiobks via web, Bk club(s), Bks on CD, Children's prog, Computers for patron use, Electronic databases & coll, Free DVD rentals, Holiday prog, ILL available, Internet access, Laminating, Life-long learning prog for all ages, Magazines, Mango lang, Movies, Online cat, Online ref, OverDrive digital audio bks, Photocopying/Printing, Preschool reading prog, Prog for adults, Prog for children & young adult, Scanner, Story hour, Summer reading prog, Tax forms, Teen prog, Wheelchair accessible
Open Mon 10-7, Wed & Fri 10-5, Sat 10-3
Friends of the Library Group
MUSSELMAN-SOUTH BERKELEY COMMUNITY LIBRARY, 126 Excellence Way, Inwood, 25428, SAN 364-443X. Tel: 304-229-2220. *Br Mgr,* David Porterfield; Staff 1 (MLS 1)
Library Holdings: AV Mats 12; Bk Titles 18,000; Bk Vols 19,250; Per Subs 65; Talking Bks 50
Special Collections: Archives Rooms
Open Mon-Thurs 7:30-6, Fri 7:30-2:30, Sun 1-4
NORTH BERKELEY PUBLIC LIBRARY, 125 T J Jackson Dr, Falling Waters, 25419, SAN 364-4405. Tel: 304-274-3443. *Br Mgr,* Dana Phelps
Library Holdings: AV Mats 20; Bk Titles 4,000
Open Tues & Thurs 10-7, Wed-Sat 10-5

MIDDLEBOURNE

P TYLER COUNTY PUBLIC LIBRARY*, 300 Broad St, 26149. (Mail add: PO Box 124, 26149-0124), SAN 317-8005. Tel: 304-758-4304. FAX: 304-758-4304. Web Site: middlebourne.lib.wv.us. *Dir,* Rosanne Eastham; E-mail: rosanne.eastham@mail.nln.lib.wv.us
Pop 814; Circ 11,320
Library Holdings: Bk Vols 10,684
Wireless access
Partic in West Virginia Library Network
Open Mon 11-7, Tues & Thurs 11-5:30, Wed & Fri 11-5, Sat 10-3
Friends of the Library Group

MILL CREEK

P RUSSELL MEMORIAL PUBLIC LIBRARY, 10038 Seneca Trail, 26280. (Mail add: PO Box 517, 26280-0517). Tel: 304-335-6277. FAX: 304-335-6277. E-mail: info@russellmemorial.wvlibrary.info. Web Site: tygart.lib.wv.us. *Dir,* Joanna Rennix; *Asst Dir,* Courtney Samples; E-mail: courtney.samples@russellmemorial.wvlibrary.info; Staff 3 (Non-MLS 3)
Founded 1973. Pop 4,620; Circ 18,000
Library Holdings: AV Mats 530; Bk Titles 15,000; Per Subs 3; Talking Bks 360
Automation Activity & Vendor Info: (Cataloging) Innovative Interfaces, Inc; (Circulation) Innovative Interfaces, Inc; (OPAC) Innovative Interfaces, Inc
Wireless access
Function: 24/7 Electronic res, 24/7 Online cat, Accelerated reader prog, Activity rm, Audiobks via web, AV serv, Bks on cassette, Bks on CD, Children's prog, Computers for patron use, Digital talking bks, Electronic databases & coll, Free DVD rentals, ILL available, Instruction & testing, Internet access, Magazines, Magnifiers for reading, Mail & tel request accepted, Mail loans to mem, Meeting rooms, Movies, Notary serv, Online cat, Online ref, Outside serv via phone, mail, e-mail & web, Photocopying/Printing, Scanner, Study rm, Summer reading prog, Tax forms, Telephone ref, Wheelchair accessible
Partic in West Virginia Library Network
Open Tues-Fri 10-6:30

MONTGOMERY

C WEST VIRGINIA UNIVERSITY INSTITUTE OF TECHNOLOGY*, Vining Library, 405 Fayette Pike, 25136-2436. SAN 317-8013. Tel: 304-442-3230. Circulation Tel: 304-442-3495. Interlibrary Loan Service

Tel: 304-442-3734. Administration Tel: 301-981-6247. FAX: 304-442-3091. Web Site: lib.wvu.edu/wvutech. *Univ Librn,* Mary L Strife; E-mail: mary.strife@mail.wvu.edu; *Libr Dir,* Jewel Connell; E-mail: ajconnell@mail.wvu.edu; *Assoc Librn,* Manju Panta; E-mail: manju.panta@mail.wvu.edu; *Staff Librn,* Mitch Casto; E-mail: mitchael.casto@mail.wvu.edu; Staff 7 (MLS 2, Non-MLS 5)
Founded 1897. Enrl 1,224; Fac 88; Highest Degree: Bachelor
Library Holdings: e-journals 20; Electronic Media & Resources 48; Microforms 111,260; Bk Titles 120,100; Bk Vols 151,131; Per Subs 108
Special Collections: West Virginia Coll. State Document Depository; US Document Depository
Automation Activity & Vendor Info: (Acquisitions) Ex Libris Group; (Cataloging) Ex Libris Group; (Circulation) Ex Libris Group; (Course Reserve) Ex Libris Group; (ILL) OCLC ILLiad; (OPAC) Ex Libris Group; (Serials) Ex Libris Group
Wireless access
Function: Computers for patron use, Doc delivery serv, Electronic databases & coll, ILL available, Instruction & testing, Internet access, Microfiche/film & reading machines, Online cat, Photocopying/Printing, Ref & res
Publications: Periodical Directory; Vining Library Handbook
Partic in OCLC Online Computer Library Center, Inc; WVNET
Open Mon-Thurs 7:30am-9pm, Fri 7:30-4:30, Sun 12:30-9; Mon-Fri 8-4:30 (Summer)
Restriction: Borrowing privileges limited to fac & registered students, Borrowing requests are handled by ILL, Limited access for the pub, Open to pub for ref & circ; with some limitations, Open to students, fac, staff & alumni

MOOREFIELD

P HARDY COUNTY PUBLIC LIBRARY*, 102 N Main St, 26836. SAN 364-4464. Tel: 304-538-6560. FAX: 304-538-2639. E-mail: hardycpl@martin.lib.wv.us. Web Site: hardycounty.martin.lib.wv.us. *Dir,* Carol Koontz; E-mail: c.koontz@ephlibray.org; Staff 2 (Non-MLS 2)
Founded 1939. Pop 14,000; Circ 81,482
Library Holdings: Bk Vols 55,520; Per Subs 75
Subject Interests: Local genealogy, Local hist
Automation Activity & Vendor Info: (Cataloging) TLC (The Library Corporation); (Circulation) TLC (The Library Corporation)
Wireless access
Open Mon-Fri 8:30-5, Sat 8:30-12
Friends of the Library Group

MORGANTOWN

G CENTERS FOR DISEASE CONTROL & PREVENTION, Stephen B Thacker CDC Library-Morgantown Branch, 1095 Willowdale Rd, 26505-2888. (Mail add: 1000 Frederick Lane, M/S L-1055, 26508), SAN 317-8048. Tel: 404-639-1717. Web Site: www.cdc.gov/library/branches.html.
Founded 1972
Library Holdings: e-books 8,025; e-journals 1,485; Microforms 275,000; Bk Titles 12,461; Per Subs 4
Special Collections: NIOSH Publications; NIOSHTIC Microfiche
Subject Interests: Occupational lung diseases, Worker safety
Automation Activity & Vendor Info: (Acquisitions) Ex Libris Group; (Cataloging) Ex Libris Group; (Circulation) Ex Libris Group; (ILL) OCLC ILLiad; (OPAC) Ex Libris Group; (Serials) Ex Libris Group
Wireless access
Partic in OCLC Online Computer Library Center, Inc
Open Mon-Fri 8-4:30
Restriction: Badge access after hrs, In-house use for visitors, Photo ID required for access

P MORGANTOWN PUBLIC LIBRARY SYSTEM*, Morgantown Service Center, 373 Spruce St, 26505. SAN 364-4529. Tel: 304-291-7425. FAX: 304-291-7427. Web Site: mympls.org. *Dir,* Sarah Palfrey; E-mail: sarah.palfrey@clark.lib.wv.us; Staff 25 (MLS 3, Non-MLS 22)
Founded 1929. Pop 81,866; Circ 291,460
Library Holdings: AV Mats 8,500; Bk Vols 103,000; Per Subs 85; Talking Bks 10,000
Subject Interests: WVa hist
Automation Activity & Vendor Info: (Cataloging) Innovative Interfaces, Inc; (Circulation) Innovative Interfaces, Inc; (OPAC) Innovative Interfaces, Inc
Wireless access
Function: 24/7 Online cat, Adult bk club, Audiobks on Playaways & MP3, Audiobks via web, Bk club(s), Bks on CD, Children's prog, Computers for patron use, Electronic databases & coll, Free DVD rentals, ILL available, Internet access, Magazines, Mango lang, Meeting rooms, Music CDs, Online cat, OverDrive digital audio bks, Photocopying/Printing, Prog for children & young adult, Scanner, Story hour, Summer & winter reading prog, Tax forms, Teen prog, Wheelchair accessible
Partic in West Virginia Library Network
Open Mon-Thurs 9-8, Fri & Sat 9-4
Friends of the Library Group
Branches: 4
ARNETTSVILLE PUBLIC LIBRARY, 4120 Fairmont Rd, 26501. Tel: 304-278-2021. E-mail: arnettsville.library@clark.lib.wv.us.
Open Mon & Wed 11:30-6:30, Fri 11:30-3:30
CHEAT AREA, 121 Crosby Rd, 26508, SAN 364-4545. Tel: 304-594-1020. FAX: 304-594-1020. E-mail: cheat@clark.lib.wv.us.
Library Holdings: AV Mats 2,000; Bk Vols 23,741; Per Subs 12; Talking Bks 600; Videos 3,113
Open Mon & Wed 10-7, Tues & Fri 10-5, Thurs 10-4, Sat 9-1
Friends of the Library Group
CLAY-BATTELLE PUBLIC LIBRARY, 6059 Mason Dixon Hwy, Blacksville, 26521. (Mail add: Drawer J, Blacksville, 26521-0060), SAN 364-4561. Tel: 304-432-8531. FAX: 304-432-8288. E-mail: claybat@clark.lib.wv.us.
Library Holdings: Bk Vols 14,200; Per Subs 15
Open Mon 10-5, Tues 10-6, Wed-Fri 10-4, Sat 9-Noon
Friends of the Library Group
CLINTON DISTRICT LIBRARY, 2005 Grafton Rd, 26508, SAN 364-4537. Tel: 304-291-0703. FAX: 304-291-0703. E-mail: clinton@clark.lib.wv.us.
Library Holdings: AV Mats 1,933; Bk Vols 12,839; Per Subs 17
Open Mon 10-5, Tues & Thurs 12-5, Wed 10-7, Fri 10-3, Sat 10-1

G UNITED STATES DEPARTMENT OF ENERGY*, National Energy Technology Laboratory Library, 3610 Collins Ferry Rd, 26507. (Mail add: PO Box 880, 26507-0880), SAN 317-803X. Tel: 304-285-4184. Web Site: netl.doe.gov. *Librn,* Sarah Grant; E-mail: sarah.grant@netl.doe.gov; *Librn,* JoAnn Yuill; E-mail: joann.yuill@smc.netl.doe.gov
Founded 1953
Library Holdings: Bk Titles 30,000; Per Subs 150
Special Collections: DOE Fossil Energy Reports; Energy (US Dept of Energy); Mining (US Bureau of Mines Open File Reports); Mining (US Bureau of Mines, Reports of Investigations, Information Circulars)
Subject Interests: Chem, Environ mgt, Environ remediation, Fossil fuels, Geol, Petroleum
Automation Activity & Vendor Info: (Cataloging) EOS International
Partic in OCLC Online Computer Library Center, Inc; Proquest Dialog
Restriction: Non-circulating, Visitors must make appt to use bks in the libr

C WEST VIRGINIA UNIVERSITY LIBRARIES*, 1549 University Ave, 26506. (Mail add: PO Box 6069, 26506-6069), SAN 364-4588. Tel: 304-293-4040. Circulation Tel: 304-293-0355. Interlibrary Loan Service Tel: 304-293-0368. Reference Tel: 304-293-3640. Administration Tel: 304-293-5040. FAX: 304-293-6638. Web Site: library.wvu.edu. *Dean of Libr,* Karen R Diaz; Tel: 304-293-0304, E-mail: karen.diaz@mail.wvu.edu; *Assoc Dean,* Dennis Smith; E-mail: dennis.smith@mail.wvu.edu; *Dir, Health Sci Libr,* Susan Arnold; *Dir, Knowledge Access & Resource Mgmt,* Angela Maranville; *Dir, Res Sharing, Operations Dir,* Hilary Fredette; *Head, Digital & Web Serv,* Jessica M McMillen; *Head, Libr Syst,* William Rafter; *Head, Res Serv,* Alyssa Wright; *Mgr, Libr Depository,* Robert Bess; *Bus Planning Officer,* Tara McMillen; *Curator,* John Cuthbert; Staff 112 (MLS 37, Non-MLS 75)
Founded 1867. Enrl 26,997; Fac 2,164; Highest Degree: Doctorate
Library Holdings: Bk Vols 1,616,340
Special Collections: Oral History; State Document Depository; US Document Depository
Subject Interests: Appalachia, Coal
Wireless access
Publications: ExLibris (Newsletter)
Partic in Greater Western Library Alliance; LYRASIS; OCLC Online Computer Library Center, Inc; Partnership for Academic Library Collaborative & Innovation
Friends of the Library Group
Departmental Libraries:
EVANSDALE LIBRARY, 1212 Evansdale Dr, 26506. (Mail add: PO Box 6105, 26506-6105). Tel: 304-293-4696. Circulation Tel: 304-293-9759. Interlibrary Loan Service Tel: 304-293-9755. Reference Tel: 304-293-8286. FAX: 304-293-7330. Web Site: library.wvu.edu/evansdale. *Dir,* Martha Yancey
CL GEORGE R FARMER JR COLLEGE OF LAW LIBRARY, One Law Center Dr, 26506. (Mail add: PO Box 6135, 26506-6135), SAN 364-4618. Tel: 304-293-5300. Reference Tel: 304-293-8286. FAX: 304-293-6020. Web Site: www.law.wvu.edu/library. *Dir,* Caroline Osborne; Tel: 304-293-7641, E-mail: caroline.osborne@mail.wvu.edu; Staff 6 (MLS 4, Non-MLS 2)
Enrl 470
Library Holdings: DVDs 8; Electronic Media & Resources 10; Bk Vols 339,675; Per Subs 1,070; Videos 770
Automation Activity & Vendor Info: (Acquisitions) Ex Libris Group; (Cataloging) Ex Libris Group; (Circulation) Ex Libris Group; (Course

Reserve) Ex Libris Group; (ILL) Ex Libris Group; (Media Booking) Ex Libris Group; (OPAC) Ex Libris Group; (Serials) Ex Libris Group
Open Mon-Thurs 7:30am-Midnight, Fri 8am-10pm, Sat 9-8, Sun Noon-11 (Sept-April); Mon-Fri 9-8, Sat 9-6, Sun Noon-6 (May-Aug)

CM HEALTH SCIENCES LIBRARY, Robert C Byrd Health Sciences Center N, One Medical Ctr Dr, 26506. (Mail add: PO Box 9801, HSN 2000, 26506-9801), SAN 364-4642. Tel: 304-293-2113. FAX: 304-293-5995. Web Site: library.wvu.edu/libraries/health-sciences-library. *Dir,* Susan Arnold
Enrl 4; Fac 5

WEST VIRGINIA & REGIONAL HISTORY CENTER, 1549 University Ave, 26506-6069, SAN 328-8609. Tel: 304-293-3536. FAX: 304-293-3981. Web Site: wvrhc.lib.wvu.edu. *Curator,* John Cuthbert; E-mail: jcuthber@wvu.edu
Subject Interests: Archives, Cent Appalachian hist, Coal mining hist, Culture, WVa hist

MOUNDSVILLE

P MOUNDSVILLE-MARSHALL COUNTY PUBLIC LIBRARY*, 700 Fifth St, 26041. SAN 364-4677. Tel: 304-845-6911. FAX: 304-845-6912. E-mail: moundsvillelibrary@yahoo.com. Web Site: moundsville.lib.wv.us. *Dir,* Susan Reilly; *Acq,* Susan Shaw; *Pub Serv,* Kayla Gross; *Tech Serv,* Catherine Feryok; Staff 2 (MLS 2)
Founded 1917. Pop 74,802; Circ 378,473
Library Holdings: Bk Vols 174,989; Per Subs 170
Special Collections: West Virginia Coll
Automation Activity & Vendor Info: (Cataloging) Innovative Interfaces, Inc; (Circulation) Innovative Interfaces, Inc; (OPAC) Innovative Interfaces, Inc
Wireless access
Publications: Newsletter (Bimonthly)
Partic in West Virginia Library Network
Open Mon-Wed 10-8, Thurs & Fri 10-6, Sat 10-5
Branches: 2
BENWOOD-MCMECHEN PUBLIC, 201 Marshall St, McMechen, 26040, SAN 364-4766. Tel: 304-232-9720. FAX: 304-232-9720. *Dir,* Susan Reilly
Open Mon & Tues 1-8, Wed & Thurs 11-6, Fri & Sat 10-4
CAMERON PUBLIC, Benedum Bldg, 44 Main St, Cameron, 26033, SAN 364-4707. Tel: 304-686-2140. FAX: 304-686-2140. *Br Librn,* Laurie Winters
Open Mon & Wed 12-8, Tues 9-5, Fri & Sat 9-2

S NORTHERN REGIONAL JAIL CORRECTIONAL FACILITY*, 112 Northern Regional Correctional Dr, 26041. SAN 317-8056. Tel: 304-843-4067, Ext 106. FAX: 304-843-4089. *Assoc Warden of Prog,* Brandy M Miller; E-mail: brandy.m.miller@wv.gov
Library Holdings: Bk Vols 5,000; Per Subs 37
Restriction: Not open to pub

MOUNT GAY

J SOUTHERN WEST VIRGINIA COMMUNITY & TECHNICAL COLLEGE*, Harless Library, Dempsey Branch Rd, 25637. (Mail add: PO Box 2900, 25637-2900), SAN 364-4251. Tel: 304-896-7378. Administration Tel: 304-896-7345. FAX: 304-752-2837. Web Site: www.southernwv.edu/library-services. *Dir,* Kimberly Maynard; Tel: 304-896-7345, E-mail: kimberly.maynard@southernwv.edu; Staff 1 (MLS 1)
Founded 1971. Enrl 1,609; Fac 30; Highest Degree: Associate
Library Holdings: AV Mats 2,755; CDs 293; Bk Titles 47,277; Per Subs 10; Videos 25
Special Collections: Children's Coll; Local History & Genealogy (West Virginia Coll)
Automation Activity & Vendor Info: (Acquisitions) Book Systems; (Cataloging) Book Systems; (Circulation) Book Systems; (Course Reserve) Book Systems; (ILL) OCLC Connexion; (OPAC) Book Systems
Wireless access
Function: Bks on CD, CD-ROM, Computers for patron use, Doc delivery serv, Electronic databases & coll, For res purposes, Free DVD rentals, ILL available, Instruction & testing, Internet access, Magnifiers for reading, Microfiche/film & reading machines, Music CDs, Notary serv, Online cat, Orientations, Photocopying/Printing, Scanner, Wheelchair accessible
Partic in OCLC Online Computer Library Center, Inc
Special Services for the Deaf - Assisted listening device; Assistive tech; TDD equip
Special Services for the Blind - Computer with voice synthesizer for visually impaired persons; Dragon Naturally Speaking software; Reader equip
Open Mon-Thurs 7am-8pm

MOUNT HOPE

CR JOHN VAN PUFFELEN LIBRARY OF THE APPALACHIAN BIBLE COLLEGE*, 161 College Dr, 25880-1040. (Mail add: PO Box ABC, Bradley, 25818-1353), SAN 317-7327. Tel: 304-877-6428. FAX: 304-877-5983. E-mail: abc@abc.edu. Web Site: www.abc.edu. *Librn,* David Dunkerton; Staff 3 (MLS 1, Non-MLS 2)
Founded 1950. Enrl 280; Fac 18; Highest Degree: Master
Library Holdings: AV Mats 70; Bk Titles 49,000; Bk Vols 50,000; Per Subs 250; Spec Interest Per Sub 175
Special Collections: Archives Reference Coll (books 100 years old or more); Cults & Christian Counterfeits Coll; Judiaca Coll
Subject Interests: Missions, Theol, WVa
Automation Activity & Vendor Info: (Cataloging) Winnebago Software Co; (Circulation) Winnebago Software Co; (OPAC) Winnebago Software Co
Function: Res libr

MOUNT OLIVE

S MOUNT OLIVE CORRECTIONAL COMPLEX LIBRARY, One Mountainside Way, 25185. Tel: 304-442-7213. FAX: 304-442-7225. Web Site: dcr.wv.gov/facilities/pages/prisons-and-jails/moccj.aspx. *Librn,* Clifton Karr
Library Holdings: Bk Vols 5,000; Per Subs 20
Restriction: Not open to pub

NEW CUMBERLAND

P SWANEY MEMORIAL LIBRARY*, 210 S Court St, 26047. (Mail add: PO Box 608, 26047-0608), SAN 317-8064. Tel: 304-564-3471. FAX: 304-564-3474. Web Site: www.facebook.com/Swaney-Memorial-Library-272260506349. *Dir,* Kirsten Pierce; E-mail: kirsten.pierce@mail.nln.lib.wv.us; Staff 2 (Non-MLS 2)
Pop 4,666; Circ 14,098
Library Holdings: Bk Vols 20,000; Per Subs 30
Automation Activity & Vendor Info: (Cataloging) Innovative Interfaces, Inc; (Circulation) Innovative Interfaces, Inc; (OPAC) Innovative Interfaces, Inc
Wireless access
Function: ILL available, Photocopying/Printing, Ref serv available
Partic in West Virginia Library Network
Open Mon, Tues & Thurs 10-6, Wed 11-7, Fri 8-4

NEW MARTINSVILLE

P NEW MARTINSVILLE PUBLIC LIBRARY*, 160 Washington St, 26155. SAN 317-8080. Tel: 304-455-4545. FAX: 304-455-4545. E-mail: nmplibrary@hotmail.com. Web Site: newmartinsville.lib.wv.us. *Dir,* Janet Witten Conn; Staff 5 (MLS 1, Non-MLS 4)
Founded 1946. Pop 8,300
Library Holdings: AV Mats 625; Bk Vols 30,000; Per Subs 40
Special Collections: Genealogy; West Virginia materials
Wireless access
Function: Audiobks via web, Bk reviews (Group), Children's prog, Computers for patron use, ILL available, Mail & tel request accepted, Microfiche/film & reading machines, Music CDs, Online cat, OverDrive digital audio bks, Photocopying/Printing, Preschool reading prog, Scanner, Story hour, Summer reading prog, Tax forms, VHS videos, Wheelchair accessible
Partic in Mid-Atlantic Library Alliance; West Virginia Library Network
Open Mon-Wed 10-8, Fri & Sat 10-5
Friends of the Library Group

NUTTER FORT

P NUTTER FORT LIBRARY*, 1300 Buckhannon Pike, 26301-4406. SAN 376-7779. Tel: 304-622-7563. FAX: 304-622-7563. E-mail: nutter@clark.lib.wv.us. Web Site: nutterfort.lib.wv.us. *Dir,* Dottie White; E-mail: dottie.white@clark.lib.wv.us; Staff 2 (Non-MLS 2)
Library Holdings: Bk Titles 12,000; Bk Vols 25,000; Per Subs 15
Wireless access
Partic in West Virginia Library Network
Open Mon Noon-6, Tues 8-4, Wed & Thurs 8-3, Fri Noon-7; Mon Noon-6, Tues 8-4, Wed & Thurs 8-3, Fri Noon-4 (Summer)
Friends of the Library Group

OAK HILL

P FAYETTE COUNTY PUBLIC LIBRARIES*, 531 Summit St, 25901. SAN 364-4820. Tel: 304-465-0121, 304-465-5664. FAX: 304-465-5306. Web Site: fayette.lib.wv.us. *Dir,* Rebecca Kellum; E-mail: becky.kellum@mail.mln.lib.wv.us; *Extn Serv Librn,* Kim Massey; Staff 6 (MLS 1, Non-MLS 5)
Founded 1959. Pop 47,952; Circ 213,170
Library Holdings: Bk Vols 83,000; Per Subs 26

Special Collections: Books About West Virginia & by West Virginia Authors (West Virginia Room Coll); Books-by-Mail Coll
Automation Activity & Vendor Info: (Cataloging) Innovative Interfaces, Inc; (Circulation) Innovative Interfaces, Inc; (OPAC) Innovative Interfaces, Inc
Wireless access
Partic in West Virginia Library Network
Open Mon-Fri 9-5
Branches: 6
ANSTED PUBLIC, 102 Oak St, Ansted, 25812. (Mail add: PO Box 428, Ansted, 25812-0428), SAN 364-4944. Tel: 304-658-5472. FAX: 304-658-5472. *Br Librn,* Rene Nickell; Staff 2 (Non-MLS 2)
Library Holdings: Bk Titles 9,000; Per Subs 15
Open Tues 2-8, Wed-Fri 9-5, Sat 9-2
FAYETTEVILLE BRANCH, 200 W Maple Ave, Fayetteville, 25840, SAN 364-4855. Tel: 304-574-0070. FAX: 304-574-0070. *Br Librn,* Randall Ballard; Staff 2 (Non-MLS 2)
Library Holdings: Bk Vols 23,318; Per Subs 31
Special Collections: West Virginia Coll
Open Mon 11-7, Tues-Fri 10-5, Sat 9-1
MEADOW BRIDGE BRANCH, 53 Montrado St, Meadow Bridge, 25976, SAN 326-8314. Tel: 304-484-7942. FAX: 304-484-7942. *Br Librn,* April Vaughn; Staff 2 (Non-MLS 2)
Library Holdings: Bk Vols 3,113; Per Subs 11
Open Mon, Wed & Thurs 10-4, Tues 12-7
MONTGOMERY BRANCH, 507 Ferry St, Montgomery, 25136, SAN 364-4979. Tel: 304-442-5665. FAX: 304-442-5665. *Br Librn,* Gordon Kent; Staff 2 (Non-MLS 2)
Library Holdings: Bk Vols 9,506; Per Subs 28
Open Mon, Tues, Thurs & Fri 10-5, Wed 12-7
MT HOPE PUBLIC LIBRARY, 500 Main St, Mount Hope, 25880, SAN 364-488X. Tel: 304-877-3260. FAX: 304-877-3260. *Br Librn,* Pamela Bush; Staff 1 (Non-MLS 1)
Library Holdings: Bk Vols 6,800; Per Subs 19
Open Mon-Wed & Fri 9-4, Thurs 11-6
OAK HILL BRANCH, 611 Main St, 25901, SAN 364-491X. Tel: 304-469-9890. FAX: 304-469-9890. *Br Librn,* Laura Fernett; Staff 4 (Non-MLS 4)
Library Holdings: Bk Vols 17,982; Per Subs 39
Open Mon, Wed & Fri 10-5, Tues & Thurs 10-7, Sat 10-2
Bookmobiles: 1. Driver, Blake Feazell

PADEN CITY

P PADEN CITY PUBLIC LIBRARY*, 114 S Fourth Ave, 26159. SAN 317-8129. Tel: 304-337-9333. FAX: 304-337-9333. Web Site: padencity.lib.wv.us. *Dir,* Joanna Casto; E-mail: joanna.casto@weirton.lib.wv.us; *Asst Librn,* Danielle Ice-Davis; Staff 3 (Non-MLS 3)
Founded 1947. Pop 3,500; Circ 12,252
Library Holdings: CDs 15; DVDs 100; Bk Titles 13,583; Per Subs 41; Videos 20
Automation Activity & Vendor Info: (Cataloging) Innovative Interfaces, Inc - Millennium; (Circulation) Innovative Interfaces, Inc - Millennium; (OPAC) Innovative Interfaces, Inc - Millennium
Wireless access
Partic in West Virginia Library Network
Open Mon, Tues & Thurs 1-8, Wed 10-5, Fri 1-5, Sat 10-1

PARKERSBURG

M CAMDEN-CLARK MEMORIAL CENTER*, Medical Library, 800 Garfield Ave, 26101. SAN 317-8137. Tel: 304-424-2976. FAX: 304-424-2076. *Librn,* Jillian McCutcheon; E-mail: jillian.mccutcheon.m@wvumedicine.org; Staff 1 (Non-MLS 1)
Founded 1900
Library Holdings: Bk Titles 2,700; Per Subs 200
Subject Interests: Allied health, Med, Nursing
Partic in National Network of Libraries of Medicine Region 1
Open Mon-Fri 8-4:30

P PARKERSBURG & WOOD COUNTY PUBLIC LIBRARY*, Wood County Service Center, 3100 Emerson Ave, 26104-2414. SAN 364-5002. Tel: 304-420-4587. Circulation Tel: 304-420-4587, Ext 507. Interlibrary Loan Service Tel: 304-420-4587, Ext 517. Reference Tel: 304-420-4587, Ext 511. Administration Tel: 304-420-4587, Ext 501. FAX: 304-420-4589. E-mail: library@park.lib.wv.us. Web Site: parkersburg.lib.wv.us. *Dir,* Brian E Raitz; E-mail: raitzb@park.lib.wv.us; *Ch Serv,* Brenda Gellner; Tel: 304-420-4587, Ext 510, E-mail: taylorb@park.lib.wv.us; *ILL,* Jeanne Michie; E-mail: parkwoodill@gmail.com; *Media Spec,* Teresa Wilkinson; Tel: 304-420-4587, Ext 508; *Ref (Info Servs),* Jeff Cottrell; E-mail: jeff.cottrell@park.lib.wv.us; *Tech Serv,* Hazel Stewart; Tel: 304-420-4587, Ext 513, E-mail: stewarth@park.lib.wv.us; Staff 9.5 (MLS 3, Non-MLS 6.5)
Founded 1905. Pop 76,207; Circ 311,141
Jul 2018-Jun 2019 Income (Main & Associated Libraries) $2,136,288, State $418,873, City $227,164, County $886,806, Locally Generated Income $452,808, Other $150,287. Mats Exp $247,375, Books $129,403, AV Mat $36,412, Electronic Ref Mat (Incl. Access Fees) $62,356. Sal $1,207,460
Library Holdings: AV Mats 11,955; DVDs 10,838; e-books 37,284; Bk Vols 171,744; Per Subs 143
Special Collections: West Virginia History & Genealogical Coll, bks & microfilm
Automation Activity & Vendor Info: (Acquisitions) Innovative Interfaces, Inc; (Cataloging) Innovative Interfaces, Inc; (Circulation) Innovative Interfaces, Inc; (OPAC) Innovative Interfaces, Inc
Wireless access
Function: Activity rm, Adult bk club, Audiobks via web, AV serv, Bks on CD, Chess club, Computer training, Computers for patron use, Digital talking bks, Electronic databases & coll, For res purposes, Free DVD rentals, Govt ref serv, Homebound delivery serv, ILL available, Internet access, Magazines, Magnifiers for reading, Meeting rooms, Microfiche/film & reading machines, Music CDs, Notary serv, Online cat, Outreach serv, OverDrive digital audio bks, Photocopying/Printing, Prog for adults, Prog for children & young adult, Ref & res, Ref serv available, Res assist avail, Res libr, Res performed for a fee, Satellite serv, Spoken cassettes & CDs, Story hour, Study rm, Summer reading prog, Tax forms, Teen prog, Wheelchair accessible
Member Libraries: Calhoun County Public Library
Partic in West Virginia Library Network
Open Mon-Thurs 9-9, Fri & Sat 9-5
Friends of the Library Group
Branches: 4
P SERVICES FOR THE BLIND & PHYSICALLY HANDICAPPED, 3100 Emerson Ave, 26104. Tel: 304-420-4587, Ext 503. FAX: 304-420-4589. *Spec Serv Dir,* Donna Calvert; E-mail: donna.b.calvert@wv.gov
Founded 1970
Special Services for the Blind - Braille equip; Braille paper; Home delivery serv; Magnifiers; Volunteer serv
Open Mon-Sat 9-5
SOUTH PARKERSBURG, 1807 Blizzard Dr, 26101, SAN 364-5061. Tel: 304-428-7041. FAX: 304-428-7041. *Librn,* Olivia Jones; E-mail: olivia.jones@mail.mln.lib.wv.us; Staff 2 (MLS 1, Non-MLS 1)
Founded 1973
Open Mon-Wed 10-8, Thurs-Sat 10-5
Friends of the Library Group
WAVERLY, 450 Virginia St, Waverly, 26184, SAN 377-8215. Tel: 304-464-5668. FAX: 304-464-5668. E-mail: parkwoodref@parkwoodlib.com. *Br Mgr,* Kristine Tucker
Open Mon-Wed 3:30-7:30
Friends of the Library Group
WILLIAMSTOWN BRANCH, 201 W Fifth St, Williamstown, 26187, SAN 364-5096. Tel: 304-375-6052. FAX: 304-375-6052. *Librn,* Lisa Henthorn; E-mail: lisa.henthorn@parkwoodlib.com
Founded 1977
Library Holdings: Large Print Bks 300; Bk Vols 10,500
Open Mon-Thurs 11-6, Fri 10-5, Sat 10-2
Friends of the Library Group
Bookmobiles: 1. Libr Contact, Amy Sandy. Bk titles 4,751

C WEST VIRGINIA UNIVERSITY, Parkersburg Campus Library, 300 Campus Dr, Rm 1332, 26104-8647. SAN 317-8161. Tel: 304-424-8260. E-mail: wvuplibrary@wvup.edu. Web Site: www.wvup.edu/current-students/library. *Libr Assoc,* Kimberly Hitt; E-mail: kimberly.hitt@wvup.edu; *Libr Assoc,* John Myers; E-mail: john.myers@wvup.edu; Staff 2 (Non-MLS 2)
Founded 1971. Enrl 3,329; Fac 119
Library Holdings: e-books 3,000; Bk Vols 55,000; Per Subs 100
Automation Activity & Vendor Info: (Acquisitions) Innovative Interfaces, Inc - Sierra; (Cataloging) Innovative Interfaces, Inc - Sierra; (Circulation) Innovative Interfaces, Inc - Sierra; (ILL) Innovative Interfaces, Inc - Sierra; (OPAC) Innovative Interfaces, Inc - Sierra; (Serials) Innovative Interfaces, Inc - Sierra
Wireless access
Partic in LYRASIS; OCLC Online Computer Library Center, Inc; West Virginia Library Network
Open Mon-Thurs 8-7, Fri 8-4

PARSONS

P FIVE RIVERS PUBLIC LIBRARY*, 301 Walnut St, 26287. SAN 317-820X. Tel: 304-478-3880. FAX: 304-478-3880. E-mail: parsons@clark.lib.wv.us. Web Site: fiverivers.lib.wv.us. *Dir,* Nancy Moore; *Asst Librn,* Lynnette Adams; *Asst Librn,* Kathy Phillips; E-mail: phillipk@clark.lib.wv.us; *Libr Asst,* Angela Johnson
Founded 1974. Pop 4,136; Circ 12,918
Library Holdings: DVDs 1,525; Bk Vols 17,100; Per Subs 8; Talking Bks 192

Automation Activity & Vendor Info: (Cataloging) Innovative Interfaces, Inc; (Circulation) Innovative Interfaces, Inc; (OPAC) Innovative Interfaces, Inc
Wireless access
Partic in West Virginia Library Network
Open Mon 8:30-6:30, Tues-Fri 8:30-4, Sat 9-Noon

PAW PAW

P PAW PAW PUBLIC LIBRARY*, 250 Moser Ave, 25434-9500. (Mail add: PO Box 9, 25434-0009), SAN 317-8218. Tel: 304-947-7013. FAX: 304-947-5218. Web Site: www.pawpawpubliclibrary.com. *Dir,* Virginia DiFrancesco; E-mail: virginia.difrancesco@martin.lib.wv.us; Staff 1 (Non-MLS 1)
Founded 1971. Pop 4,043; Circ 10,000
Library Holdings: Bk Vols 18,000; Per Subs 31; Talking Bks 300
Automation Activity & Vendor Info: (Cataloging) TLC (The Library Corporation); (Circulation) TLC (The Library Corporation); (OPAC) TLC (The Library Corporation)
Wireless access
Special Services for the Blind - Audio mat; Large print bks
Open Mon-Wed & Fri 10-1 & 2-6, Thurs 10-1 & 2-7
Friends of the Library Group

PETERSBURG

P MOOMAU GRANT COUNTY LIBRARY*, 18 Mountain View St, 26847. SAN 317-8226. Tel: 304-257-4122. FAX: 304-257-4122. Web Site: moomau-grant.lib.wv.us. *Dir,* Barbara Carr; E-mail: carrbara@martin.lib.wv.us; Staff 2 (Non-MLS 2)
Founded 1963. Pop 11,299; Circ 36,988
Library Holdings: Bk Vols 36,000; Per Subs 20; Talking Bks 767
Automation Activity & Vendor Info: (Cataloging) TLC (The Library Corporation); (Circulation) TLC (The Library Corporation); (OPAC) TLC (The Library Corporation)
Wireless access
Open Mon-Fri 8-5
Friends of the Library Group
Branches: 1
ALLEGHENY-MOUNTAIN TOP, 8455 Union Hwy, Mount Storm, 26739. (Mail add: PO Box 161, Mount Storm, 26739-0161). Tel: 304-693-7504. FAX: 304-693-7504. *Br Librn,* Dana Carr; Staff 1 (Non-MLS 1)
Library Holdings: Bk Vols 15,500; Per Subs 20
Open Mon 12-6, Tues-Fri 11-5
Friends of the Library Group

PETERSTOWN

P PETERSTOWN PUBLIC LIBRARY*, 23 College Dr, 24963. (Mail add: PO Box 698, 24963-0698). Tel: 304-753-9568. FAX: 304-753-9684. Web Site: peterstown.lib.wv.us. *Dir,* Jeff Chadwell; E-mail: jeff.chadwell@mail.mln.lib.wv.us
Pop 5,665; Circ 25,200
Library Holdings: AV Mats 330; Bk Titles 28,220; Per Subs 21; Talking Bks 160
Automation Activity & Vendor Info: (Cataloging) Innovative Interfaces, Inc; (Circulation) Innovative Interfaces, Inc; (OPAC) Innovative Interfaces, Inc
Wireless access
Function: Distance learning
Partic in West Virginia Library Network
Open Mon, Thurs & Fri 9-5:30, Wed 9-1, Sat 9-12

PHILIPPI

C ALDERSON-BROADDUS UNIVERSITY*, Pickett Library, 101 College Hill Dr, 26416. SAN 317-8234. Tel: 304-457-6229. FAX: 304-457-6239. Web Site: www.ab.edu/academics/pickett-library. *Dir, Libr Serv,* David E Hoxie; Tel: 304-457-6306, E-mail: hoxiede@ab.edu; Staff 1.5 (MLS 1.5)
Enrl 1,100; Fac 58; Highest Degree: Master
Library Holdings: AV Mats 1,000; e-books 150,000; Electronic Media & Resources 91,000; Bk Vols 40,000; Per Subs 11,000
Special Collections: Baptist Archives Coll; Civil War Coll
Subject Interests: Educ
Automation Activity & Vendor Info: (Cataloging) Innovative Interfaces, Inc; (Circulation) Innovative Interfaces, Inc; (Course Reserve) Innovative Interfaces, Inc; (ILL) OCLC; (OPAC) Innovative Interfaces, Inc
Wireless access
Function: 24/7 Electronic res, 24/7 Online cat
Partic in Appalachian College Association; OCLC Online Computer Library Center, Inc

P PHILIPPI PUBLIC LIBRARY, 91 S Main St, 26416. SAN 317-8242. Tel: 304-457-3495. FAX: 304-457-5569. E-mail: info@philippi.wvlibrary.info. Web Site: philippi.wvlibrary.info. *Dir,* Judy Larry; E-mail: judy.larry@philippi.wvlibrary.info; Staff 1 (Non-MLS 1)
Founded 1966. Pop 9,539; Circ 20,260
Library Holdings: Audiobooks 313; Bks on Deafness & Sign Lang 20; Braille Volumes 3; DVDs 769; Large Print Bks 288; Bk Titles 20,834; Per Subs 46
Special Collections: Civil War Coll; Genealogy Coll; Library of America; Local History Coll; West Virginia Coll
Automation Activity & Vendor Info: (Cataloging) Innovative Interfaces, Inc; (Circulation) Innovative Interfaces, Inc; (OPAC) Innovative Interfaces, Inc
Wireless access
Function: 24/7 Electronic res, 24/7 Online cat, Activity rm, Adult literacy prog, Bks on CD, CD-ROM, Children's prog, Computer training, Computers for patron use, Electronic databases & coll, Genealogy discussion group, ILL available, Notary serv, Online cat, Photocopying/Printing, Prog for children & young adult, Ref & res, Scanner, Story hour, Summer reading prog, Tax forms, Wheelchair accessible
Partic in West Virginia Library Network
Open Mon-Wed 10-6, Thurs 10-4, Fri 10-2, Sat 10-1

PIEDMONT

P PIEDMONT PUBLIC LIBRARY*, One Child Ave, 26750. SAN 317-8250. Tel: 304-355-2757. FAX: 304-355-2757. Web Site: piedmont.lib.wv.us. *Dir & Librn,* Paula Boggs; E-mail: pboggs@martin.lib.wv.us; Staff 1 (Non-MLS 1)
Founded 1960. Pop 1,417; Circ 9,048
Library Holdings: Audiobooks 25; Bk Vols 15,047; Per Subs 7; Videos 212
Wireless access
Function: Accelerated reader prog, Bks on cassette, Computers for patron use, Holiday prog, Home delivery & serv to seniorr ctr & nursing homes, Photocopying/Printing, Summer reading prog, Tax forms, Wheelchair accessible
Open Mon-Fri 12-6, Sat 11-3

PINE GROVE

P PINE GROVE PUBLIC LIBRARY*, One Main St, 26419. (Mail add: PO Box 416, 26419), SAN 317-8269. Tel: 304-889-3288. FAX: 304-889-3398. E-mail: pgpubliclibrary@gmail.com. Web Site: pinegrove.lib.wv.us. *Co-Dir,* Michele Ensinger; *Co-Dir,* Donna Goontz; E-mail: donna.goontz@mail.nln.lib.wv.us; Staff 1 (Non-MLS 1)
Founded 1975. Pop 3,386; Circ 7,607
Library Holdings: AV Mats 50; Bk Vols 3,000; Per Subs 15
Automation Activity & Vendor Info: (Circulation) Innovative Interfaces, Inc; (OPAC) Innovative Interfaces, Inc
Wireless access
Partic in West Virginia Library Network
Open Mon-Wed 12-5, Thurs & Fri 12-6, Sat 10-2

PINEVILLE

P WYOMING COUNTY PUBLIC LIBRARY*, Pineville Public, 19 Park St, 24874. (Mail add: PO Box 130, 24874-0130), SAN 364-5126. Tel: 304-732-6228. FAX: 304-732-6228. Web Site: wyoming.lib.wv.us/index.php/about-us/pineville-public-library. *Dir,* Joyce McKinney; E-mail: jmckinney@mail.mln.lib.wv.us
Founded 1966. Pop 25,000; Circ 75,000
Library Holdings: AV Mats 310; Bks on Deafness & Sign Lang 15; High Interest/Low Vocabulary Bk Vols 425; Bk Titles 63,065; Bk Vols 65,220; Per Subs 50
Special Collections: West Virginia History & Literature; Wyoming County, WV Genealogy & History
Automation Activity & Vendor Info: (Cataloging) Innovative Interfaces, Inc; (Circulation) Innovative Interfaces, Inc
Wireless access
Partic in West Virginia Library Network
Open Mon-Fri 9-5, Sat 9-1
Friends of the Library Group
Branches: 3
HANOVER PUBLIC, 5556 Interstate Hwy, Hanover, 24839. (Mail add: PO Box 9, Hanover, 24839-0009). Tel: 304-664-5580, FAX: 304-664-5580. Web Site: wyoming.lib.wv.us/index.php/about-us/hanover. *Br Mgr,* C Jason Sizemore
Open Mon-Fri 9-5
MULLENS AREA PUBLIC, 102 Fourth St, Mullens, 25882, SAN 364-5215. Tel: 304-294-6687. FAX: 304-294-9236. Web Site: wyoming.lib.wv.us/index.php/about-us/mullens-area-public-library. *Br Mgr,* Betty O'Neal
Open Mon-Fri 9-5
OCEANA PUBLIC, 1519 Cook Pkwy, Oceana, 24870. (Mail add: PO Box 1768, Oceana, 24870-1768). Tel: 304-682-6784. FAX: 304-682-6784. Web Site: wyoming.lib.wv.us/index.php/about-us/oceana-library. *Br Mgr,* Laura Mellon
Open Mon-Fri 9-5, Sat 9-1

POINT PLEASANT

P MASON COUNTY LIBRARY SYSTEM*, 508 Viand St, 25550. SAN 364-524X. Tel: 304-675-0894. FAX: 304-675-0895. E-mail: mcpllib@mail.mln.lib.wv.us. Web Site: masoncounty.lib.wv.us. *Dir,* Pamela Thompson; E-mail: thompsnp@mail.mln.lib.wv.us; Staff 7 (MLS 1, Non-MLS 6)
Founded 1930. Pop 27,000; Circ 151,613
Library Holdings: Bk Vols 52,000; Per Subs 50
Special Collections: Local History Coll
Automation Activity & Vendor Info: (Cataloging) Innovative Interfaces, Inc; (Circulation) Innovative Interfaces, Inc; (OPAC) Innovative Interfaces, Inc
Wireless access
Partic in West Virginia Library Network
Open Mon-Fri 10-6
Friends of the Library Group
Branches: 3
HANNAN, 6760 Ashton-Upland Rd, Ashton, 25503, SAN 326-7539. Tel: 304-743-6200. FAX: 304-743-6200. Web Site: masoncounty.lib.wv.us/hannan. *Librn,* Teresa Perry
Library Holdings: Bk Vols 7,232; Per Subs 10
Open Tues & Wed 9-4, Thurs 9-3 (Winter)
MASON CITY PUBLIC, 502 Brown St, Mason, 25260. (Mail add: PO Box 609, Mason, 25260), SAN 364-5274. Tel: 304-773-5580. FAX: 304-773-5580. Web Site: masoncounty.lib.wv.us/mason_city. *Librn,* April Scott
Library Holdings: Bk Vols 7,926; Per Subs 10
Open Wed & Fri 9:30-5:30, Thurs 9-4
Friends of the Library Group
NEW HAVEN PUBLIC, 106 Main St, New Haven, 25265. (Mail add: PO Box 417, New Haven, 25265), SAN 364-5304. Tel: 304-882-3252. FAX: 304-882-3252. Web Site: masoncounty.lib.wv.us/new_haven. *Librn,* Anita Russell
Library Holdings: Bk Vols 8,410; Per Subs 11
Open Mon 11-4:30, Tues 9-4, Wed 11-6, Thurs 11-4
Friends of the Library Group

PRINCETON

M PRINCETON COMMUNITY HOSPITAL LIBRARY*, 122 12th St, 24740-2352. (Mail add: PO Box 1369, 24740-1369), SAN 317-8277. Tel: 304-487-7000, 304-487-7714. Administration Tel: 304-487-7242. FAX: 304-487-7524. Administration FAX: 304-487-2161. Web Site: www.pchonline.org. *Educ Mgr, Libr Mgr,* Ms Alston Sarver; E-mail: alston.sarver@pchonline.org; Staff 1 (Non-MLS 1)
Founded 1970
Library Holdings: Bk Titles 283; Per Subs 12
Wireless access
Restriction: Not open to pub

P PRINCETON PUBLIC LIBRARY*, 920 Mercer St, 24740-2932. SAN 317-8285. Tel: 304-487-5045. FAX: 304-487-5046. E-mail: princetonlibrarywv@gmail.com. Web Site: princetonlibrarywv.com. *Interim Dir,* Laura Lin Buchanan; E-mail: directorpplwv@gmail.com; Staff 8 (MLS 1, Non-MLS 7)
Founded 1914. Pop 12,459; Circ 223,000
Library Holdings: Bk Titles 99,000; Per Subs 160
Special Collections: Genealogy Coll; Local History Coll; Print Coll; West Virginia Coll
Wireless access
Function: 24/7 Electronic res, 24/7 Online cat, 3D Printer, Adult bk club, Art programs, Audio & video playback equip for onsite use, Audiobks via web, AV serv, Bk club(s), Bks on CD, Chess club, Children's prog, Computers for patron use, E-Readers, E-Reserves, Electronic databases & coll, For res purposes, Free DVD rentals, Games & aids for people with disabilities, Holiday prog, ILL available, Internet access, Laminating, Magazines, Magnifiers for reading, Makerspace, Meeting rooms, Microfiche/film & reading machines, Movies, Notary serv, Online cat, Online ref, OverDrive digital audio bks, Photocopying/Printing, Preschool reading prog, Printer for laptops & handheld devices, Prog for adults, Prog for children & young adult, Ref & res, Res assist avail, Scanner, Spanish lang bks, STEM programs, Story hour, Summer reading prog, Tax forms, Teen prog, Visual arts prog, Wheelchair accessible, Winter reading prog, Workshops, Writing prog
Open Mon, Tues & Thurs 9-8, Wed & Fri 9-5, Sat 10-2
Friends of the Library Group

RAINELLE

P RAINELLE PUBLIC LIBRARY*, 378 Seventh St, 25962. SAN 328-0675. Tel: 304-438-3008. FAX: 304-438-4450. Web Site: rainelle.lib.wv.us. *Librn,* Debra Goddard; E-mail: dgoddard@mail.mln.lib.wv.us; Staff 3 (Non-MLS 3)
Founded 1973. Pop 6,954; Circ 48,083
Library Holdings: Bk Titles 13,002; Per Subs 12
Automation Activity & Vendor Info: (Cataloging) Innovative Interfaces, Inc; (Circulation) Innovative Interfaces, Inc; (OPAC) Innovative Interfaces, Inc
Wireless access
Partic in West Virginia Library Network
Open Mon & Fri 10-5, Tues-Thurs 10-6, Sat 10-2
Friends of the Library Group

RICHWOOD

P RICHWOOD PUBLIC LIBRARY*, Eight White Ave, 26261. SAN 317-8307. Tel: 304-846-6222. FAX: 304-846-9290. E-mail: richwoodlibrary@yahoo.com. Web Site: www.richwoodpubliclibrary.com. *Dir,* Robin A Bartlett; E-mail: bartlettr@mail.mln.lib.wv.us; Staff 5 (Non-MLS 5)
Founded 1942. Circ 40,503
Library Holdings: Bk Vols 35,000; Per Subs 95
Automation Activity & Vendor Info: (Cataloging) Innovative Interfaces, Inc; (Circulation) Innovative Interfaces, Inc; (OPAC) Innovative Interfaces, Inc
Wireless access
Partic in West Virginia Library Network
Open Mon, Tues, Thurs & Fri 10-4, Sat 9-3

RIPLEY

P JACKSON COUNTY PUBLIC LIBRARY*, 208 N Church St, 25271-1204. SAN 364-5339. Tel: 304-372-5343. FAX: 304-372-7935. Web Site: jackson.park.lib.wv.us. *Cat, Dir, Teen Prog,* Carla Young; E-mail: jcpldirector@gmail.com; Staff 1 (MLS 1)
Founded 1949. Pop 25,938; Circ 121,630
Library Holdings: Bk Vols 34,266; Per Subs 65
Subject Interests: Genealogy, Local hist
Automation Activity & Vendor Info: (Cataloging) Innovative Interfaces, Inc; (Circulation) Innovative Interfaces, Inc; (OPAC) Innovative Interfaces, Inc
Wireless access
Partic in West Virginia Library Network
Open Mon-Wed 9-5, Thurs 9-8, Fri 11-5, Sat Noon-3 (Winter); Mon & Thurs 9-5, Tues 9-8, Fri 11-5,Sat Noon-3 (Summer)
Branches: 1
RAVENSWOOD BRANCH, 323 Virginia St, Ravenswood, 26164, SAN 364-5363. Tel: 304-273-5343. FAX: 304-273-5395. *Br Mgr,* Angela Howard; Staff 2 (Non-MLS 2)
Library Holdings: Bk Vols 23,586; Per Subs 40
Open Mon & Thurs 9-5, Tues 9-8, Fri 11-5, Sat Noon-3 (Winter); Mon, Tues & Thurs 9-5, Fri 11-5, Sat Noon-3 (Summer)

ROMNEY

P HAMPSHIRE COUNTY PUBLIC LIBRARY, 153 W Main St, 26757. SAN 317-8315. Tel: 304-822-3185. FAX: 304-822-3955. E-mail: library@hamcopl.org. Web Site: hampshirecopubliclib.com. *Dir,* Anna Poland; *Asst Dir,* Melanie Self
Founded 1942
Library Holdings: Bk Vols 51,709; Per Subs 63
Special Collections: Census of the County 1810-1920, micro; Local History Coll; Local Newspaper Coll (1884-present), micro
Automation Activity & Vendor Info: (Acquisitions) Baker & Taylor; (Cataloging) TLC (The Library Corporation); (Circulation) TLC (The Library Corporation); (ILL) Library Systems & Services (LSSI); (OPAC) TLC (The Library Corporation)
Wireless access
Open Mon & Wed-Fri 9-5, Tues 9-7, Sat 10-4
Friends of the Library Group

S WEST VIRGINIA SCHOOL FOR THE DEAF & BLIND LIBRARY*, 301 E Main St, 26757. SAN 317-8331. Tel: 304-822-4894, 304-822-6656. FAX: 304-822-4896. Web Site: www.wvsdb2.state.k12.wv.us/apps/pages/library. *Librn,* Danielle Emerick-Engle; E-mail: demerick@k12.wv.us; Staff 1 (MLS 1)
Founded 1870
Library Holdings: High Interest/Low Vocabulary Bk Vols 1,000; Bk Vols 10,000; Per Subs 40
Special Collections: Braille, talking bks; Deaf & Deafness; Twin-vision (print with braille overlays)
Subject Interests: Blind, Educ of the deaf, Low vision
Wireless access
Special Services for the Deaf - Captioned film dep; High interest/low vocabulary bks; Staff with knowledge of sign lang; TDD equip
Restriction: Open to students, Ref only to non-staff, Staff & mem only

P WEST VIRGINIA SCHOOLS FOR THE DEAF & THE BLIND LIBRARY*, 301 E Main St, 26757. SAN 317-8323. Tel: 304-822-4894. E-mail: wvsdb@k12.wv.us. Web Site:

www.wvsdb2.state.k12.wv.us/apps/pages/library. *Readers' Advisory,* Barbara Kidwell; E-mail: bkidwell@k12.wv.us
Library Holdings: Bks on Deafness & Sign Lang 490; Braille Volumes 8,000; CDs 105; DVDs 130; Large Print Bks 30; Bk Titles 6,000
Special Collections: Visual Impairment & Blindness Coll
Special Services for the Blind - Large print bks; Talking bks
Open Mon-Fri 8-3:30

RONCEVERTE

P RONCEVERTE PUBLIC LIBRARY*, 500 W Main St, 24970. SAN 376-7345. Tel: 304-647-7400. FAX: 304-647-7651. Web Site: www.roncevertelibrary.org. *Libr Dir,* Cherie Davis; E-mail: davis_cl@mail.mln.lib.wv.us; Staff 2 (Non-MLS 2)
Library Holdings: Bk Vols 22,000
Automation Activity & Vendor Info: (Cataloging) Innovative Interfaces, Inc - Sierra; (Circulation) Innovative Interfaces, Inc - Sierra; (OPAC) Innovative Interfaces, Inc - Sierra
Wireless access
Partic in West Virginia Library Network
Open Mon & Wed-Fri 11-5, Tues 11-7, Sat Noon-4
Friends of the Library Group

RUPERT

P RUPERT PUBLIC LIBRARY*, 124 Greenbrier St, 25984. (Mail add: PO Box 578, 25984-0578), SAN 328-0659. Tel: 304-392-6158. FAX: 304-392-5460. Web Site: rupert.lib.wv.us. *Dir,* Carol McClung; E-mail: mcclung@mail.mln.lib.wv.us; Staff 3 (Non-MLS 3)
Founded 1977. Pop 4,185; Circ 8,113
Library Holdings: AV Mats 229; Large Print Bks 100; Bk Titles 14,740; Per Subs 19; Talking Bks 239
Automation Activity & Vendor Info: (Cataloging) Innovative Interfaces, Inc; (Circulation) Innovative Interfaces, Inc; (OPAC) Innovative Interfaces, Inc
Wireless access
Partic in West Virginia Library Network
Open Tues, Wed & Fri 10-5, Thurs 11-6, Sat 10-3

SAINT MARYS

P PLEASANTS COUNTY PUBLIC LIBRARY, 101 Lafayette St, 26170. SAN 317-834X. Tel: 304-684-7494. FAX: 304-684-7495. E-mail: pleasantslibrary@gmail.com. Web Site: www.pleasantslib.com. *Dir,* Mary Hooper
Founded 1935. Pop 7,514
Library Holdings: AV Mats 75; Bk Vols 26,023; Per Subs 25
Automation Activity & Vendor Info: (Cataloging) Innovative Interfaces, Inc; (Circulation) Innovative Interfaces, Inc; (OPAC) Innovative Interfaces, Inc
Wireless access
Function: Adult literacy prog, AV serv, ILL available, Photocopying/Printing, Prog for adults, Prog for children & young adult, Summer reading prog, VHS videos, Wheelchair accessible
Partic in West Virginia Library Network
Special Services for the Blind - Talking bks
Open Mon-Wed 10-8, Thurs 5-8, Fri 10-5, Sat 10-3

S SAINT MARYS CORRECTIONAL CENTER LIBRARY*, 2880 N Pleasants Hwy, 26170. Tel: 304-684-5500. FAX: 304-684-5506. *Librn,* Karen Townsend; E-mail: karen.c.townsend@wv.gov
Library Holdings: Bk Vols 4,000; Per Subs 14

SALEM

C SALEM UNIVERSITY, Benedum Library, 223 W Main St, 26426. SAN 364-5398. Tel: 304-326-1390. E-mail: library@salemu.edu. Web Site: www.salemu.edu/library. *Dir, Libr Serv,* Dr Phyllis D Freedman; E-mail: pfreedman@salemu.edu; *Asst to the Dir,* James Rogers; E-mail: jrogers@salemu.edu. Subject Specialists: *Govt doc, Sciences,* James Rogers; Staff 2 (MLS 1, Non-MLS 1)
Founded 1888. Enrl 990; Fac 31; Highest Degree: Doctorate
Jul 2024-Jun 2025 Income $111,316. Mats Exp $9,022, Books $1,464, Other Print Mats $57, Electronic Ref Mat (Incl. Access Fees) $7,501. Sal $91,705
Library Holdings: Bk Titles 62,385; Bk Vols 67,392; Per Subs 15; Videos 73
Special Collections: Seventh Day Baptist. US Document Depository
Subject Interests: Educ, Local hist
Automation Activity & Vendor Info: (Cataloging) LibraryWorld, Inc; (Circulation) LibraryWorld, Inc; (ILL) OCLC
Wireless access
Function: Archival coll, Computers for patron use, Electronic databases & coll, Govt ref serv, ILL available, Internet access, Microfiche/film & reading machines, Online cat, Online ref, Photocopying/Printing, Ref serv available, Tax forms, Wheelchair accessible
Partic in OCLC Online Computer Library Center, Inc
Open Mon-Thurs 8-8, Fri 1-5, Sun 4-8
Restriction: Limited access for the pub

SAULSVILLE

J SOUTHERN WEST VIRGINIA COMMUNITY & TECHNICAL COLLEGE*, Wyoming/McDowell Campus, 128 College Dr, 25876. (Mail add: PO Box 638, Pineville, 24874-0638). Tel: 304-294-8346. FAX: 304-294-6426. TDD: 304-294-8520. Web Site: www.southernwv.edu. *Info Syst Tech,* Michael Hunter; Tel: 304-294-2006, E-mail: michael.hunter@southernwv.edu
Highest Degree: Associate
Library Holdings: Bk Vols 350
Automation Activity & Vendor Info: (Cataloging) SirsiDynix; (Circulation) SirsiDynix; (OPAC) SirsiDynix
Open Mon-Thurs 7-5, Fri 7-4:30

SHEPHERDSTOWN

C SHEPHERD UNIVERSITY, Scarborough Library, 301 N King St, 25443. (Mail add: PO Box 5000, 25443-5000), SAN 317-8358. Interlibrary Loan Service Tel: 304-876-5691. Reference Tel: 304-876-5421. Administration Tel: 304-876-5418. FAX: 304-876-0731. Web Site: www.shepherd.edu/library. *Access Serv Librn, Dir,* Theresa Smith; E-mail: tsmith@shepherd.edu; *Archives & Spec Coll Librn,* Frances Marshall; Tel: 304-876-5417, E-mail: fmarshal@shepherd.edu; *Coll Develop Librn,* Tara Carlisle; Tel: 304-876-5302, E-mail: tcarlisl@shepherd.edu; *Ref Serv Librn,* Rhonda Donaldson; Tel: 304-876-5424, E-mail: rdonal01@shepherd.edu; *Interlibrary Loan & Course Reserves Coord,* Patrick Weber; E-mail: pweber@shepherd.edu; *Collection Maintenance Asst,* Denise Kretzmer; Tel: 304-876-5379, E-mail: dkretzme@shepherd.edu; Staff 6.5 (MLS 4, Non-MLS 2.5)
Founded 1871. Enrl 3,274; Fac 232; Highest Degree: Doctorate
Library Holdings: Audiobooks 73; Bks on Deafness & Sign Lang 200; CDs 2,502; DVDs 2,989; Microforms 86,009; Per Subs 48,188
Special Collections: Folk Coll; Rare Book Coll; Shepherd Univ Archives; West Virginia Coll. State Document Depository; US Document Depository
Automation Activity & Vendor Info: (Acquisitions) Ex Libris Group; (Cataloging) Ex Libris Group; (Circulation) Ex Libris Group; (ILL) OCLC WorldShare Interlibrary Loan; (OPAC) Ex Libris Group
Wireless access
Function: 24/7 Electronic res, 24/7 Online cat, 24/7 wireless access
Partic in LYRASIS; OCLC Online Computer Library Center, Inc; OCLC-LVIS
Open Mon-Thurs 8-8, Fri 8-4:30, Sun 12-8
Friends of the Library Group

P SHEPHERDSTOWN PUBLIC LIBRARY*, 100 E German St, 25443. (Mail add: PO Box 278, 25443-0278), SAN 329-7012. Tel: 304-876-2783. FAX: 304-876-6213. Web Site: sheplibrary.org. *Dir,* Hali Taylor; E-mail: hali@sheplibrary.org; *Youth Serv Librn,* Tish Wiggs; E-mail: tish@sheplibrary.org; Staff 4 (MLS 1, Non-MLS 3)
Founded 1922
Library Holdings: Bk Titles 18,000; Per Subs 30
Automation Activity & Vendor Info: (Cataloging) TLC (The Library Corporation); (Circulation) TLC (The Library Corporation); (OPAC) TLC (The Library Corporation)
Partic in WV Libr Comm
Open Mon-Fri 10-6, Sat 10-3
Friends of the Library Group

G UNITED STATES FISH & WILDLIFE SERVICE*, National Conservation Library, 698 Conservation Way, 25443. Tel: 304-876-7304. E-mail: library@fws.gov. Web Site: nctc.fws.gov/resources/knowledge-resources. *Chief, Libr Serv Br,* Sarah Gannon-Nagle; Tel: 304-876-7459, E-mail: sarah_gannonnagle@fws.gov; Staff 5 (MLS 1, Non-MLS 4)
Founded 1997
Library Holdings: e-journals 2,600; Electronic Media & Resources 105; Bk Titles 13,000; Bk Vols 15,000; Per Subs 120; Videos 200
Special Collections: Classic Conservation Coll; Environmental Education Coll; FWS National Digital Library. Oral History
Subject Interests: Ecology, Environ educ, Fisheries, Leadership, Natural res mgt, Training, Wildlife conserv
Automation Activity & Vendor Info: (Acquisitions) Baker & Taylor; (Cataloging) OCLC; (ILL) OCLC; (Media Booking) SirsiDynix; (OPAC) OCLC WorldShare Interlibrary Loan
Publications: Journal of Fish & Wildlife Management (Biannually); North American Fauna (Annual)
Special Services for the Blind - Accessible computers
Open Mon-Fri 8:30-5

SHINNSTON

P LOWE PUBLIC LIBRARY*, 40 Bridge St, 26431. SAN 317-8366. Tel: 304-592-1700. FAX: 304-592-6056. Web Site: lowe.lib.wv.us. *Librn,* Deborah Starkey; E-mail: starkeyd@clark.lib.wv.us; Staff 1 (Non-MLS 1)
Pop 2,850; Circ 20,850
Library Holdings: Bk Vols 32,000; Per Subs 4
Wireless access
Partic in West Virginia Library Network
Open Mon 11:30-7, Tues-Fri 11:30-6, Sat 9-Noon
Friends of the Library Group

SISTERSVILLE

P SISTERSVILLE PUBLIC LIBRARY*, 518 Wells St, 26175. SAN 317-8374. Tel: 304-652-6701. FAX: 304-652-6701. Web Site: cityofsistersville.com/library, sistersville.lib.wv.us. *Dir,* Sabrina Kyle; E-mail: sabrina.kyle@weirton.lib.wv.us; Staff 2 (Non-MLS 2)
Founded 1907. Pop 11,320; Circ 13,101
Library Holdings: Bk Vols 18,000; Per Subs 37
Automation Activity & Vendor Info: (Cataloging) SirsiDynix
Wireless access
Partic in West Virginia Library Network
Open Mon & Fri 1-5, Tues & Thurs 1-8, Wed 10-3, Sat 10-2

SOUTH CHARLESTON

P SOUTH CHARLESTON PUBLIC LIBRARY*, 312 Fourth Ave, 25303. SAN 317-8382. Tel: 304-744-6561. FAX: 304-744-8808. Reference E-mail: reference@scplwv.org. Web Site: scplwv.org. *Libr Dir,* Todd Duncan; E-mail: todd@scplwv.org; *Circ Supvr,* Shawana Camehl; Staff 11 (MLS 2, Non-MLS 9)
Founded 1943. Pop 13,450; Circ 133,377
Jul 2020-Jun 2021 Income $750,000, State $68,516, City $462,000, Locally Generated Income $75,695. Mats Exp $86,528, Books $45,655, AV Mat $18,213. Sal $278,305
Library Holdings: Audiobooks 5,886; DVDs 4,327; e-books 39,485; Electronic Media & Resources 13,809; Bk Vols 80,000; Per Subs 61
Subject Interests: WVa hist
Automation Activity & Vendor Info: (Cataloging) TLC (The Library Corporation); (Circulation) TLC (The Library Corporation); (OPAC) TLC (The Library Corporation)
Wireless access
Function: Activity rm, Adult bk club, Bks on CD, Children's prog, Computers for patron use, Holiday prog, ILL available, Internet access, Life-long learning prog for all ages, Magazines, Movies, Music CDs, Notary serv, Online cat, OverDrive digital audio bks, Passport agency, Photocopying/Printing, Preschool outreach, Preschool reading prog, Prog for adults, Prog for children & young adult, Scanner, Story hour, Study rm, Summer reading prog, Teen prog, Wheelchair accessible, Workshops
Open Mon-Fri 10-6, Sat 10-2

SPENCER

P ROANE COUNTY PUBLIC LIBRARY*, 110 Parking Plaza, 25276. SAN 317-8420. Tel: 304-927-1130. FAX: 304-927-1196. Web Site: roanecountylibrary.org. *Dir,* Sherry Husted; E-mail: sherry.husted@roanewvlib.com; Staff 6 (MLS 2, Non-MLS 4)
Founded 1952. Pop 15,952; Circ 48,968
Library Holdings: Bk Vols 39,000; Per Subs 35
Special Collections: West Virginia History, bks, per, memorabilia
Automation Activity & Vendor Info: (Cataloging) Innovative Interfaces, Inc - Sierra; (Circulation) Innovative Interfaces, Inc - Sierra; (OPAC) Innovative Interfaces, Inc - Sierra
Wireless access
Partic in West Virginia Library Network
Open Mon-Fri 9-4:30, Sat 10-1
Friends of the Library Group
Branches: 2
GEARY LIBRARY-HEALTH CARE FACILITY, One Library Lane, Ste 1, Left Hand, 25251. (Mail add: PO Box 90, Left Hand, 25251-0090). Tel: 304-565-4608. FAX: 304-565-4608. *Br Librn,* Sandra Morton; E-mail: morton39@yahoo.com; Staff 1 (Non-MLS 1)
Founded 1993. Pop 3,000; Circ 8,000
Library Holdings: DVDs 300; e-books 500; Large Print Bks 150; Bk Vols 15,000; Per Subs 10
Function: Children's prog, Computer training, Computers for patron use, ILL available, Notary serv, Online cat, Photocopying/Printing, Prog for children & young adult, Senior computer classes, Summer reading prog
Open Mon-Wed 9-5
Friends of the Library Group
WALTON PUBLIC LIBRARY, Two Cunningham Lane, Walton, 25286, SAN 376-6101. Tel: 304-577-6071. FAX: 304-577-6071. E-mail: waltonwvlibrary@gmail.com. *Br Librn,* Debbie Davis; Staff 1 (MLS 1)
Library Holdings: Bk Vols 15,000; Per Subs 10
Open Tues-Thurs 10-6
Friends of the Library Group

SUMMERSVILLE

P SUMMERSVILLE PUBLIC LIBRARY*, 6201 Webster Rd, 26651. SAN 317-8447. Tel: 304-872-0844. FAX: 304-872-0845. E-mail: spl@mail.mln.lib.wv.us. Web Site: summersvillepubliclibrary.org. *Dir,* Robin Holmes
Pop 8,745; Circ 41,000
Library Holdings: AV Mats 500; Bk Vols 32,000; Per Subs 40; Talking Bks 275
Automation Activity & Vendor Info: (Cataloging) Innovative Interfaces, Inc; (Circulation) Innovative Interfaces, Inc; (OPAC) Innovative Interfaces, Inc
Wireless access
Partic in West Virginia Library Network
Open Mon-Fri 9-7

SUMMIT POINT

P SOUTH JEFFERSON PUBLIC LIBRARY*, 49 Church St, 25446. (Mail add: PO Box 17, 25446-0017), SAN 328-1205. Tel: 304-725-6227. FAX: 304-728-2586. Web Site: www.sojeffersonlibrary.com. *Dir,* Dana S Jenkins; E-mail: jenkinsd@martin.lib.wv.us; Staff 1 (Non-MLS 1)
Founded 1984. Pop 17,833
Library Holdings: Bk Titles 21,000; Per Subs 6
Automation Activity & Vendor Info: (Cataloging) TLC (The Library Corporation); (Circulation) TLC (The Library Corporation); (OPAC) TLC (The Library Corporation)
Wireless access
Open Mon-Thurs 10-7, Sat 10-5, Sun 1-5
Friends of the Library Group

SUTTON

P SUTTON PUBLIC LIBRARY*, 500 Main St, 26601. SAN 317-8455. Tel: 304-765-7224. FAX: 304-765-7349. Web Site: sutton.wvlibrary.info. *Libr Dir,* Samantha Foster; E-mail: samatha.foster@sutton.wvlibrary.info; Staff 2 (Non-MLS 2)
Founded 1968. Pop 5,467; Circ 13,000
Library Holdings: High Interest/Low Vocabulary Bk Vols 50; Bk Vols 15,000; Per Subs 20; Talking Bks 300
Automation Activity & Vendor Info: (Cataloging) Innovative Interfaces, Inc; (Circulation) Innovative Interfaces, Inc; (OPAC) Innovative Interfaces, Inc
Wireless access
Partic in West Virginia Library Network
Open Mon & Fri 8-4, Tues & Thurs 11-7
Friends of the Library Group

TERRA ALTA

P TERRA ALTA PUBLIC LIBRARY, 701-B E State Ave, 26764. SAN 317-8463. Tel: 304-789-2724. FAX: 304-789-2724. Web Site: terraalta.lib.wv.us. *Librn,* Karen Chroussis; E-mail: karen.chroussis@clark.lib.wv.us
Founded 1972. Pop 13,000; Circ 70,000
Library Holdings: AV Mats 250; Bks on Deafness & Sign Lang 8; DVDs 2,000; Large Print Bks 1,000; Bk Vols 80,000; Per Subs 86; Videos 100
Special Collections: Barbour, Marion & Taylor Counties & Census, microfilm; Grafton Sentinel, Preston County Journal, Preston County News & West Virginia Argus, microfilm; Obituaries
Subject Interests: Genealogy, Local hist
Wireless access
Function: Computers for patron use, ILL available, Photocopying/Printing, Ref serv available, Telephone ref
Partic in West Virginia Library Network
Open Mon 4-8, Tues-Fri 8:30-5:30

THOMAS

P MOUNTAINTOP PUBLIC LIBRARY*, 384 Second St, 26292. (Mail add: PO Box 217, 26292-0217), SAN 376-611X. Tel: 304-463-4582. FAX: 304-463-4789. Circulation E-mail: mountaintop.library@clark.lib.wv.us. Web Site: mountaintop.lib.wv.us. *Libr Dir,* Debbie A Williams; E-mail: debbie.williams@clark.lib.wv.us; Staff 2 (MLS 1, Non-MLS 1)
Library Holdings: Bk Vols 7,000; Per Subs 12
Automation Activity & Vendor Info: (Cataloging) Innovative Interfaces, Inc; (Circulation) Innovative Interfaces, Inc
Wireless access
Function: 24/7 Online cat, Adult bk club, Audiobks on Playaways & MP3, Audiobks via web, Bks on CD, Children's prog, Computer training, Computers for patron use, Digital talking bks, E-Readers, Electronic databases & coll, Free DVD rentals, Holiday prog, ILL available, Internet access, Laminating, Magazines, Mail loans to mem, Movies, Online cat,

Online info literacy tutorials on the web & in blackboard, Photocopying/Printing, Ref & res, Ref serv available, Scanner, Story hour, Summer reading prog, Tax forms, Wheelchair accessible
Partic in West Virginia Library Network
Open Mon 9-4, Tues & Thurs 12-7, Wed 8-4, Fri 10-2
Restriction: Access at librarian's discretion, Borrowing requests are handled by ILL
Friends of the Library Group

UNION

P MONROE COUNTY PUBLIC LIBRARY*, 303 South St, 24983. (Mail add: PO Box 558, 24983-0558), SAN 317-8471. Tel: 304-772-3038. FAX: 304-772-4052. Web Site: monroe.lib.wv.us. *Libr Dir,* Paulette Kirby; E-mail: paulette.kirby@mail.mln.lib.wv.us; *Asst Librn,* Caroline Klezli; E-mail: caroline.klezli@mail.mln.lib.wv.us; Staff 2 (Non-MLS 2)
Founded 1947. Pop 11,272; Circ 22,125
Library Holdings: Bk Titles 25,000; Per Subs 16
Automation Activity & Vendor Info: (Cataloging) Innovative Interfaces, Inc; (Circulation) Innovative Interfaces, Inc; (OPAC) Innovative Interfaces, Inc
Wireless access
Partic in West Virginia Library Network
Open Mon-Wed & Fri 9-5:30, Sat 9-1
Friends of the Library Group

VALLEY HEAD

P VALLEY HEAD PUBLIC LIBRARY*, 25369 Seneca Trail, 26294. (Mail add: PO Box 98, 26294-0098), SAN 317-848X. Tel: 304-339-6071. FAX: 304-339-6071. Web Site: valleyhead.wvlibrary.info. *Dir,* Nicole Matthew; E-mail: nicole.matthew@valleyhead.wvlibrary.info; Staff 2 (Non-MLS 2)
Founded 1975. Pop 4,300; Circ 5,987
Library Holdings: Bk Vols 10,000; Per Subs 32
Wireless access
Partic in West Virginia Library Network
Open Mon 1:30-9, Tues & Wed 9:30-5, Thurs 9:30-7

VIENNA

C OHIO VALLEY UNIVERSITY LIBRARY*, One Campus View Dr, 26105-8000. SAN 317-8153. Tel: 304-865-6112, 304-865-6113. FAX: 304-865-6001. Web Site: ovu.edu/library. *Dir, Libr & Info Literacy,* Sonya Hescht; E-mail: sonya.hescht@ovu.edu; Staff 3 (MLS 1, Non-MLS 2)
Founded 1960. Enrl 273; Fac 66; Highest Degree: Master
Library Holdings: AV Mats 6,779; e-books 93,763; Bk Vols 34,000; Per Subs 142
Special Collections: Oral History
Subject Interests: Relig studies
Automation Activity & Vendor Info: (Cataloging) Innovative Interfaces, Inc; (Circulation) Innovative Interfaces, Inc; (ILL) OCLC WorldShare Interlibrary Loan; (OPAC) Innovative Interfaces, Inc
Wireless access
Partic in Appalachian College Association; Christian Col Libr; Midwest Libr Consortium; WV Libr Comm
Open Mon, Tues & Thurs 8am-10pm, Wed 8-5 , Fri 9-5

P VIENNA PUBLIC LIBRARY*, 2300 River Rd, 26105. SAN 317-8498. Tel: 304-295-7771. FAX: 304-295-7776. E-mail: info@viennapubliclibrary.org. Web Site: www.viennapubliclibrary.org. *Dir,* Brenna Call; E-mail: brenna@viennapubliclibrary.org; Staff 4 (MLS 2, Non-MLS 2)
Founded 1959. Pop 10,862; Circ 115,000
Library Holdings: Audiobooks 300; Braille Volumes 10; CDs 1,756; DVDs 1,600; Large Print Bks 17,773; Bk Titles 58,000; Bk Vols 58,295; Per Subs 80; Videos 1,200
Special Collections: West Virginia History Coll
Subject Interests: Local hist
Automation Activity & Vendor Info: (Cataloging) Innovative Interfaces, Inc; (Circulation) Innovative Interfaces, Inc; (OPAC) Innovative Interfaces, Inc; (Serials) Innovative Interfaces, Inc
Wireless access
Function: Online cat
Publications: Check It Out (Newsletter)
Partic in West Virginia Library Network
Open Mon-Thurs 10-8, Fri & Sat 10-5
Friends of the Library Group

WAR

P WAR PUBLIC LIBRARY*, 701 Berwind Lake Rd, 24892. (Mail add: PO Box 68, 24892-0068), SAN 320-4278. Tel: 304-875-4622. FAX: 304-875-4622. Web Site: war.lib.wv.us. *Libr Mgr,* Bridgett Greenwell; E-mail: bridgett.greenwell@mail.mln.lib.wv.us; Staff 2 (Non-MLS 2)
Library Holdings: Bk Vols 34,000
Wireless access
Partic in West Virginia Library Network
Open Tues & Thurs 10-6, Fri 10-3, Sat 12-4

WEBSTER SPRINGS

P WEBSTER-ADDISON PUBLIC LIBRARY*, 331 S Main St, 26288. SAN 317-8528. Tel: 304-847-5764. FAX: 304-404-7122. Web Site: websteraddison.lib.wv.us. *Dir,* Lorene Carpenter; E-mail: lorene.carpenter@clark.lib.wv.us
Founded 1972. Pop 9,000
Library Holdings: Bk Vols 21,000; Per Subs 10
Special Collections: West Virginia Coll
Automation Activity & Vendor Info: (Cataloging) Innovative Interfaces, Inc; (Circulation) Innovative Interfaces, Inc; (OPAC) Innovative Interfaces, Inc
Wireless access
Partic in West Virginia Library Network
Open Tues-Thurs 10-5
Friends of the Library Group

WEIRTON

P MARY H WEIR PUBLIC LIBRARY*, 3442 Main St, 26062. SAN 317-8544. Tel: 304-797-8510. FAX: 304-797-8526. E-mail: refdesk@weirton.lib.wv.us. Web Site: www.weirton.lib.wv.us. *Dir,* Richard G Rekowski; *Asst Dir,* Pat Barnett; Staff 19 (MLS 3, Non-MLS 16)
Founded 1958. Pop 38,000
Library Holdings: Bk Vols 113,012; Per Subs 110
Special Collections: State Document Depository; US Document Depository
Subject Interests: Local hist
Automation Activity & Vendor Info: (Acquisitions) Innovative Interfaces, Inc; (Cataloging) Innovative Interfaces, Inc; (Circulation) Innovative Interfaces, Inc; (OPAC) Innovative Interfaces, Inc
Wireless access
Publications: The Way Toward Literacy
Partic in West Virginia Library Network
Special Services for the Deaf - High interest/low vocabulary bks
Open Mon-Thurs 10-8, Fri & Sat 10-5 (Winter); Mon, Fri & Sat 10-5, Tues-Thurs 10-6 (Summer)
Friends of the Library Group

WELCH

P MCDOWELL PUBLIC LIBRARY*, Welch Library, 90 Howard St, 24801. SAN 364-5517. Tel: 304-436-3070. FAX: 304-436-8079. Web Site: mcdowell.lib.wv.us. *Dir,* Barbara Fields; E-mail: barbara.fields@mail.mln.lib.wv.us; Staff 7 (MLS 1, Non-MLS 6)
Founded 1954. Pop 35,233
Library Holdings: Bk Vols 48,226; Per Subs 57
Special Collections: Medical Coll; Southern Appalachian Culture Coll; West Virginiana Coal Mining Coll
Automation Activity & Vendor Info: (Cataloging) Innovative Interfaces, Inc; (Circulation) Innovative Interfaces, Inc; (OPAC) Innovative Interfaces, Inc
Partic in West Virginia Library Network
Open Mon, Tues, Thurs & Fri 8-5, Wed 8-6
Friends of the Library Group
Branches: 3
BRADSHAW BRANCH, City Hall Bldg, Main St, Bradshaw, 24817. (Mail add: PO Box 498, Bradshaw, 24817-0498), SAN 364-5541. Tel: 304-967-5140. FAX: 304-967-5140. *Br Librn,* Iris Shelton; Staff 2 (Non-MLS 2)
Library Holdings: AV Mats 227; Bk Vols 19,005; Per Subs 16; Videos 149
Open Mon-Fri 9-5
Friends of the Library Group
IAEGER BRANCH, 104 W Virginia Ave, Iaeger, 24844. (Mail add: PO Box 149, Iaeger, 24844). Tel: 304-938-3825. *Br Librn,* Marilyn Fain; Staff 1 (Non-MLS 1)
Library Holdings: AV Mats 50; Bk Vols 15,810; Per Subs 16; Videos 130
Open Mon-Fri 10-5
Friends of the Library Group
NORTHFORK BRANCH, Rte 52, Northfork, 24868. (Mail add: PO Box 229, Northfork, 24868-0229), SAN 364-572X. Tel: 304-862-4541. FAX: 304-862-4541. *Br Librn,* Mari Thompson; Staff 1 (Non-MLS 1)
Library Holdings: AV Mats 63; Bk Vols 11,001; Per Subs 10; Videos 152
Open Mon-Fri 10-5
Friends of the Library Group

WELLSBURG

P BROOKE COUNTY PUBLIC LIBRARY*, 945 Main St, 26070. SAN 364-5754. Tel: 304-737-1551. FAX: 304-737-1010. E-mail: bcpl@weirton.lib.wv.us. Web Site: wellsburg.lib.wv.us. *Dir,* Alexandra L Eberle; E-mail: alex.eberle@weirton.lib.wv.us; Staff 13 (MLS 2, Non-MLS 11)
Founded 1898. Pop 24,000
Special Collections: American Defenders of Bataan & Corregidor POW's, WWII, 1941-1945
Subject Interests: Genealogy, Local hist, Tourism, World War II
Automation Activity & Vendor Info: (Cataloging) Innovative Interfaces, Inc - Sierra; (Circulation) Innovative Interfaces, Inc - Sierra; (OPAC) Innovative Interfaces, Inc - Sierra
Wireless access
Function: 24/7 Electronic res, Adult bk club, Bks on CD, Children's prog, Computer training, Computers for patron use, Electronic databases & coll, Family literacy, Free DVD rentals, Genealogy discussion group, Holiday prog, ILL available, Internet access, Laminating, Magazines, Meeting rooms, Movies, Music CDs, Notary serv, Online cat, Photocopying/Printing, Prog for adults, Prog for children & young adult, Ref serv available, Scanner, Story hour, Summer reading prog, Tax forms, Teen prog, Telephone ref, Wheelchair accessible
Partic in West Virginia Library Network
Open Mon-Thurs 10-7, Fri 10-5, Sat 10-4
Restriction: Non-circulating coll, Non-circulating of rare bks
Friends of the Library Group
Branches: 1
FOLLANSBEE BRANCH, 844 Main St, Follansbee, 26037. (Mail add: PO Box 664, Follansbee, 26037-0664), SAN 364-5789. Tel: 304-527-0860. FAX: 304-527-3039. *Dir,* Alexandra L Schneider
Founded 1995
Function: 24/7 Electronic res, 24/7 Online cat, Activity rm, Adult bk club, Bks on CD, Children's prog, Computer training, Computers for patron use, Digital talking bks, Equip loans & repairs, Family literacy, Free DVD rentals, Games, Internet access, Laminating, Laptop/tablet checkout, Magazines, Meeting rooms, Movies, Online cat, Photocopying/Printing, Prog for adults, Prog for children & young adult, Story hour, Summer reading prog, Tax forms, Teen prog, Telephone ref, Wheelchair accessible
Partic in West Virginia Library Network
Open Mon-Thurs 10-6, Fri 9:30-4
Friends of the Library Group

WEST LIBERTY

C WEST LIBERTY UNIVERSITY*, Paul N Elbin Library, 208 University Dr, 26074. SAN 317-8579. Circulation Tel: 304-336-8369. Interlibrary Loan Service Tel: 304-336-8352. Reference Tel: 304-336-8261. Toll Free Tel: 866-937-8542. FAX: 304-336-8186. Web Site: www.westliberty.edu/library. *Head, Libr Operations,* Stacie Groch; Tel: 304-336-8001, E-mail: sgroch@westliberty.edu; *Head, Learning Resources,* Katy Zane; *Circ Serv,* Ed Wolf; Staff 3 (MLS 1, Non-MLS 2)
Founded 1932. Enrl 2,200; Highest Degree: Master
Library Holdings: Bk Titles 190,000; Bk Vols 195,000; Per Subs 125
Special Collections: Nelle Krise Rare Book Room
Subject Interests: Criminal justice, Educ, Music, Nursing
Automation Activity & Vendor Info: (Cataloging) OCLC; (Circulation) OCLC; (ILL) OCLC; (OPAC) OCLC
Wireless access
Partic in WV Libr Comm
Open Mon-Thurs 8am-9pm, Fri 8-4, Sun 3-9
Friends of the Library Group

WEST UNION

P DODDRIDGE COUNTY PUBLIC LIBRARY*, 170 Marie St, 26456. SAN 364-5819. Tel: 304-873-1941. FAX: 304-873-1324. Web Site: doddridge.lib.wv.us. *Libr Dir,* Victoria Gains; E-mail: victoria.gains@clark.lib.wv.us; *Librn,* Sheila McCutchan; Staff 2 (Non-MLS 2)
Founded 1952. Pop 6,994; Circ 61,678
Library Holdings: Bk Titles 29,818; Per Subs 54
Special Collections: Doddridge County History; Farm Women Reading Coll; Local Genealogy; West Virginia History. Oral History
Wireless access
Publications: Booklines (Newsletter)
Partic in West Virginia Library Network
Open Mon-Thurs 8:30-7, Fri 8:30-5, Sat 9-1
Branches: 1
CENTER POINT OUTPOST PUBLIC LIBRARY, 8871 WV Rte 23, Salem, 26426, SAN 364-5843. Tel: 304-782-2461. FAX: 304-782-2461. *Librn,* Christy Nicholson; Staff 2 (Non-MLS 2)
Founded 1978
Library Holdings: Bk Titles 5,146; Per Subs 10
Open Mon, Tues & Fri 8:30-4, Thurs 12-7, Sat 9-12

WESTON

P LOUIS BENNETT PUBLIC LIBRARY*, 148 Court Ave, 26452. SAN 317-8587. Tel: 304-269-5151. FAX: 304-269-7332. Web Site: louisbennett.lib.wv.us. *Interim Dir,* Katrina Johnson; E-mail: katrina.smith@clark.lib.wv.us
Founded 1923. Pop 17,223; Circ 32,390
Library Holdings: Bk Vols 18,000; Per Subs 26
Special Collections: Bennett Family Archive; West Virginia Coll
Automation Activity & Vendor Info: (Cataloging) Follett Software; (Circulation) Follett Software; (OPAC) Follett Software
Wireless access
Partic in West Virginia Library Network
Open Mon & Tues 10-6, Wed-Fri 10-5, Sat 10-2
Friends of the Library Group

M WILLIAM SHARPE JR HOSPITAL, Patients' Library, 936 Sharpe Hospital Rd, 26452. SAN 317-8595. Tel: 304-269-1210, Ext 37148. FAX: 304-269-6235. *Mgr,* Shelly McHenry; E-mail: shelly.l.mchenry@wv.gov
Founded 1969
Library Holdings: Bk Vols 4,600; Per Subs 25
Restriction: Not open to pub

WHEELING

S THE MUSEUMS OF OGLEBAY INSTITUTE LIBRARY*, Mansion Museum & Glass Museum, Oglebay Institute, The Burton Center, 26003. SAN 317-8617. Tel: 304-242-7272. FAX: 304-242-7287. Web Site: oionline.com. *Dir,* Christin L Byrum; E-mail: cbyrum@oionline.com; *Asst Dir,* Mary Coffman; *Curator,* Holly H McCluskey. Subject Specialists: *Glass,* Holly H McCluskey
Founded 1934
Library Holdings: Bk Titles 750
Special Collections: Brown Coll of Wheeling History, photogs; Wheeling & Belmont Bridge Company Papers; Wheeling City Directories
Subject Interests: Decorative art, Local hist
Wireless access
Function: Archival coll, For res purposes, ILL available, Photocopying/Printing
Restriction: Non-circulating, Not a lending libr, Open by appt only

P OHIO COUNTY PUBLIC LIBRARY*, 52 16th St, 26003. SAN 364-5878. Tel: 304-232-0244. FAX: 304-232-6848. Web Site: www.ohiocountylibrary.org. *Dir,* Amy Kastigar; E-mail: amy.kastigar@ohiocountylibrary.org; *Asst Dir, Head, Adult Serv,* Laura Carroll; E-mail: laura.carroll@ohiocountylibrary.org; *Adult Serv Mgr,* Sean Duffy; *Children's Spec,* LeeAnn Cleary; *Outreach Serv Spec,* Julia Bachmann; *Publicity Coord & Web Mgr,* Kyle Knox; E-mail: kyle.knox@ohiocountylibrary.org; *Archivist,* Laura Carroll; Staff 13 (MLS 2, Non-MLS 11)
Founded 1882. Pop 41,411; Circ 269,630
Library Holdings: Audiobooks 7,524; CDs 1,865; DVDs 9,306; Large Print Bks 8,458
Special Collections: Wheeling-Ohio County History (Wheeling Coll)
Automation Activity & Vendor Info: (Cataloging) TLC (The Library Corporation); (Circulation) TLC (The Library Corporation); (ILL) OCLC; (OPAC) TLC (The Library Corporation)
Wireless access
Function: 24/7 Electronic res, 24/7 Online cat, Adult bk club, Archival coll, Audiobks via web, Bks on CD, Children's prog, Computer training, Computers for patron use, Electronic databases & coll, Free DVD rentals, Home delivery & serv to seniorr ctr & nursing homes, Homebound delivery serv, ILL available, Internet access, Jail serv, Magazines, Mail & tel request accepted, Meeting rooms, Microfiche/film & reading machines, Music CDs, Notary serv, Online cat, Outreach serv, OverDrive digital audio bks, Photocopying/Printing, Printer for laptops & handheld devices, Prog for adults, Prog for children & young adult, Ref & res, Scanner, Senior computer classes, Story hour, Study rm, Summer reading prog, Teen prog, Wheelchair accessible
Open Mon-Thurs 9-9, Fri 10-5, Sat 10-3

J WEST VIRGINIA NORTHERN COMMUNITY COLLEGE LIBRARY*, Library/Learning Resource Center, 1704 Market St, 26003-3699. SAN 364-5932. Tel: 304-214-8954. FAX: 304-232-0965. E-mail: library@wvncc.edu. Web Site: www.wvncc.edu/current-students/librarylearning-resource-center/1159. *Dir, Libr Serv,* Adriana Wolf; Tel: 304-214-8952, E-mail: awolf@wvncc.edu; Staff 3 (MLS 1, Non-MLS 2)
Founded 1972. Enrl 2,209; Fac 53; Highest Degree: Associate
Library Holdings: AV Mats 391; Bk Titles 5,916; Bk Vols 6,516; Per Subs 16
Wireless access
Open Mon-Thurs 8-5, Fri 8:30-4:30 (Fall & Spring); Mon-Thurs 8-5, Fri 8-4 (Summer)

Departmental Libraries:
NEW MARTINSVILLE CAMPUS, 141 Main St, New Martinsville, 26155-1211, SAN 317-8102. Tel: 304-510-8766. FAX: 304-510-8765. *Staff Librn,* Janet Corbitt; Tel: 304-510-8781, E-mail: jcorbitt@wvncc.edu
Library Holdings: AV Mats 151; Bk Titles 3,628; Bk Vols 3,854; Per Subs 8
Open Mon-Thurs 9-5, Fri 8:30-4:30 (Fall & Spring); Mon-Thurs 9-5, Fri 8-4 (Summer)
WEIRTON CAMPUS, 150 Park Ave, Weirton, 26062-2797, SAN 317-8552. Tel: 304-723-7516. FAX: 304-723-7509. *Tech Asst,* Nancy Nosko; Tel: 304-723-2210, Ext 4609
Library Holdings: AV Mats 344; Bk Titles 3,885; Bk Vols 4,512; Per Subs 10
Open Mon-Thurs 9-5, Fri 8:30-4:30 (Fall & Spring); Mon-Thurs 9-5, Fri 8-4 (Summer)

C WHEELING JESUIT UNIVERSITY*, Bishop Hodges Library, 316 Washington Ave, 26003-6295. SAN 317-8641. Tel: 304-243-2226. FAX: 304-243-2466. E-mail: library@wju.edu. Web Site: libguides.wju.edu. *Libr Dir,* Kelly Mummert; *Assoc Librn,* Paula Lestini; E-mail: plestini@wju.edu; *Libr Asst,* Barbara Julian; E-mail: bjulian@wju.edu; Staff 4.3 (MLS 2, Non-MLS 2.3)
Founded 1955. Enrl 1,258; Fac 73; Highest Degree: Doctorate
Library Holdings: AV Mats 830; e-books 144,698; e-journals 25,733; Microforms 133,355; Bk Vols 148,383; Per Subs 311
Subject Interests: Local hist
Automation Activity & Vendor Info: (Acquisitions) Innovative Interfaces, Inc - Millennium; (Cataloging) Innovative Interfaces, Inc - Millennium; (Circulation) SirsiDynix; (Course Reserve) Innovative Interfaces, Inc - Millennium; (ILL) OCLC; (OPAC) Innovative Interfaces, Inc - Millennium; (Serials) Innovative Interfaces, Inc - Millennium
Wireless access
Partic in Appalachian College Association; OCLC Online Computer Library Center, Inc; OhioNET; ProConsort

WHITE SULPHUR SPRINGS

P WHITE SULPHUR SPRINGS PUBLIC LIBRARY*, 344 W Main St, 24986. SAN 317-8676. Tel: 304-536-1171. FAX: 304-536-3801. E-mail: spacitylibrary@yahoo.com. Web Site: www.whitesulphurspringspubliclibrary.com. *Dir,* Joann Hartzell; E-mail: joann.hartzell@mail.mln.lib.wv.us; Staff 1 (MLS 1)
Founded 1917. Pop 6,689; Circ 24,000
Library Holdings: CDs 42; Large Print Bks 85; Bk Titles 18,000; Bk Vols 22,000; Per Subs 44; Talking Bks 100; Videos 80
Automation Activity & Vendor Info: (Cataloging) Innovative Interfaces, Inc; (Circulation) Innovative Interfaces, Inc; (OPAC) Innovative Interfaces, Inc
Wireless access
Function: Photocopying/Printing
Partic in West Virginia Library Network
Open Mon-Fri 10-6, Sat 11-3
Friends of the Library Group

WILLIAMSON

J SOUTHERN WEST VIRGINIA COMMUNITY & TECHNICAL COLLEGE*, Williamson Campus Library, 1601 Armory Dr, 25661. SAN 364-5967. Tel: 304-236-7616. Administration Tel: 304-896-7345. FAX: 304-235-6043. Web Site: www.southernwv.edu/library-services. *Dir of Libr,* Kimberly Maynard; E-mail: kimberly.maynard@southernwv.edu; Staff 5 (MLS 1, Non-MLS 4)
Founded 1971. Enrl 1,224; Fac 72; Highest Degree: Associate
Library Holdings: AV Mats 1,608; DVDs 700; Bk Vols 56,365; Per Subs 50
Special Collections: Appalachian Coll; Children's Coll. State Document Depository
Automation Activity & Vendor Info: (Acquisitions) SirsiDynix; (Cataloging) SirsiDynix; (Circulation) SirsiDynix; (ILL) OCLC Connexion; (OPAC) SirsiDynix
Wireless access
Function: Computers for patron use, Photocopying/Printing
Partic in OCLC Online Computer Library Center, Inc
Special Services for the Deaf - Assisted listening device; Assistive tech
Special Services for the Blind - Accessible computers; Dragon Naturally Speaking software; Networked computers with assistive software; Screen reader software; ZoomText magnification & reading software
Open Mon-Thurs 7am-8pm, Fri 7-4:30, Sat 9-1
Restriction: Open to students, fac & staff

P WILLIAMSON PUBLIC LIBRARY*, 101 Logan St, 25661. SAN 317-8684. Tel: 304-235-6029. FAX: 304-235-6031. E-mail: william@cabell.lib.wv.us. Web Site: williamsonlibrary.lib.wv.us. *Dir,* Larry Brown; *Asst Dir,* Jennifer Hatfield; Tel: 304-235-6029, E-mail: jennifer.ooten@cabell.lib.wv.us; Staff 4 (Non-MLS 4)
Pop 4,558; Circ 27,818
Library Holdings: AV Mats 200; DVDs 200; Large Print Bks 300; Bk Titles 17,000; Bk Vols 26,000; Per Subs 8
Automation Activity & Vendor Info: (Acquisitions) SirsiDynix-DRA; (Cataloging) SirsiDynix-DRA; (Circulation) SirsiDynix-DRA; (Course Reserve) SirsiDynix-DRA; (ILL) SirsiDynix-DRA; (Media Booking) SirsiDynix-DRA; (OPAC) SirsiDynix-DRA; (Serials) SirsiDynix-DRA
Wireless access
Open Mon-Fri 8:30-4:30

WISCONSIN

Date of Statistics: FY 2022
Population, 2020 U.S. Census: 5,893,718
Population, 2020 State Est.: 5,854,594
Book & Serial Volumes Owned: 17,188,867
Digital Resources:
Audio Materials: 1,314,649
Video Materials: 2,308,241
Other Materials: 415,239
Periodical Subscriptions: 23,950
Income and Expenditures:
Total Public Library Income: $316,900,809
Total Operating Expenditures: $320,426,365
Public Library System Members: 381 Administrative Entities*; Branches 78; Bookmobiles 8
* For IMLS reporting we have 381 Administrative Entities, but only 379 Central Libraries.
Information provided courtesy of: Melissa Aro, State Data Coordinator; Division for Libraries and Technology.

ABBOTSFORD

P ABBOTSFORD PUBLIC LIBRARY*, 203 N First St, 54405. (Mail add: PO Box 506, 54405-0506), SAN 317-8692. Tel: 715-223-3920. FAX: 715-223-4979. Web Site: abbotsfordpl.org. *Dir,* Jenny Jochimsen; E-mail: director@abbotsford.lib.wi.us
Founded 1903. Pop 2,400; Circ 15,500
Library Holdings: Bk Vols 12,000; Per Subs 40
Automation Activity & Vendor Info: (Acquisitions) Innovative Interfaces, Inc - Sierra; (Cataloging) Innovative Interfaces, Inc - Sierra; (Circulation) Innovative Interfaces, Inc - Sierra; (OPAC) Innovative Interfaces, Inc - Sierra
Wireless access
Partic in Wisconsin Valley Library Service
Open Mon-Thurs 9-7, Fri 9-5, Sat 9-Noon; Mon-Thurs 9-7, Fri 9-5 (Summer)

ADAMS

P ADAMS COUNTY LIBRARY*, 569 N Cedar St, Ste 1, 53910-9800. SAN 317-8706. Tel: 608-339-4250. FAX: 608-339-4575. Web Site: www.adamscountylibrary.info. *Dir,* Erin Foley; E-mail: efoley@adamscountylibrary.info; *Libr Office Mgr,* Marylu Silka; E-mail: msilka@adamscountylibrary.info; *Programming Serv, Youth Serv,* Stephanie Klopotek; E-mail: stephaniek@adamscountylibrary.info; Staff 1 (MLS 1)
Founded 1974. Pop 18,000; Circ 53,165
Library Holdings: AV Mats 3,078; Large Print Bks 500; Bk Titles 23,400; Bk Vols 23,560; Per Subs 107; Talking Bks 1,150
Automation Activity & Vendor Info: (Cataloging) SirsiDynix; (Circulation) SirsiDynix; (OPAC) SirsiDynix
Wireless access
Mem of South Central Library System
Partic in Wis Libr Consortium
Open Mon-Wed 9-7, Thurs 1-7, Fri 9-5, Sat 10-2 (Winter); Mon, Wed & Fri 9-5, Tues 9-7, Thurs 1-7, Sat 10-2 (Summer)
Friends of the Library Group

ALBANY

P ALBERTSON MEMORIAL LIBRARY*, 200 N Water St, 53502. SAN 317-8714. Tel: 608-862-3491. FAX: 608-862-3561. E-mail: albanypl@tds.net. Web Site: www.albertsonlibrary.org. *Dir,* Carolyn Seaver; Staff 3 (Non-MLS 3)
Founded 1964. Pop 1,360; Circ 33,000
Library Holdings: Audiobooks 423; CDs 707; DVDs 3,939; e-books 164,910; Large Print Bks 425; Bk Vols 20,212; Per Subs 84; Videos 79
Automation Activity & Vendor Info: (Cataloging) Follett Software; (Circulation) Follett Software; (OPAC) Follett Software
Wireless access
Function: Adult bk club, Audiobks via web, Children's prog, Computer training, Computers for patron use, E-Readers, Electronic databases & coll, Free DVD rentals, ILL available, Internet access, Magazines, Mail & tel request accepted, Movies, Music CDs, Online cat, OverDrive digital audio bks, Photocopying/Printing, Preschool reading prog, Prog for adults, Prog for children & young adult, Ref serv available, Scanner, Spanish lang bks, Story hour, Summer reading prog, Tax forms, VHS videos, Wheelchair accessible
Mem of South Central Library System
Open Mon-Fri 1-7, Sat 9-1

ALGOMA

P ALGOMA PUBLIC LIBRARY*, 406 Fremont St, 54201. SAN 317-8722. Tel: 920-487-2295. FAX: 920-487-3941. E-mail: alg@algomapubliclibrary.org. Web Site: www.algomapubliclibrary.org. *Dir,* Cathy Kolbeck; E-mail: ckolbeck@algomapubliclibrary.org; Staff 4 (Non-MLS 4)
Founded 1922. Pop 3,348; Circ 100,145
Library Holdings: AV Mats 6,270; Bk Vols 29,312; Per Subs 98; Videos 4,707
Subject Interests: Local hist
Automation Activity & Vendor Info: (Acquisitions) Infor Library & Information Solutions; (Cataloging) Infor Library & Information Solutions; (Circulation) Infor Library & Information Solutions; (ILL) Infor Library & Information Solutions; (OPAC) Infor Library & Information Solutions
Wireless access
Mem of Nicolet Federated Library System
Partic in NE Wis Intertype Librs, Inc; OWLSnet
Open Mon-Fri 10-7, Sat 10-3
Friends of the Library Group

ALMA

P ALMA PUBLIC LIBRARY*, 312 N Main St, 54610. (Mail add: PO Box 217, 54610), SAN 325-3775. Tel: 608-685-3823. FAX: 608-685-4935. E-mail: almapl@wrlsweb.org. Web Site: www.almalibrary.org. *Dir,* Rita Magno
Pop 896
Library Holdings: Bk Vols 12,000; Per Subs 60
Automation Activity & Vendor Info: (Acquisitions) Follett Software; (Cataloging) Follett Software; (Circulation) Follett Software
Wireless access
Mem of Winding Rivers Library System
Open Mon, Wed & Fri 10:30-7

ALTOONA

P ALTOONA PUBLIC LIBRARY*, 1303 Lynn Ave, 54720-0278. SAN 324-7198. Tel: 715-839-5029. E-mail: altoonapl@altoonapubliclibrary.org. Web Site: www.altoonapubliclibrary.org. *Dir,* Arin Wilken; E-mail: awilken@altoonapubliclibrary.org; Staff 4 (MLS 1, Non-MLS 3)
Pop 8,691; Circ 34,764
Library Holdings: Audiobooks 3,090; DVDs 5,310; Bk Vols 45,000; Per Subs 135
Wireless access
Mem of Inspiring & Facilitating Library Success (IFLS)

Open Mon-Thurs 9-8, Fri 9-6, Sat 9-5
Friends of the Library Group

AMERY

P AMERY AREA PUBLIC LIBRARY*, 255 Scholl Ct, 54001. SAN 376-673X. Tel: 715-268-9340. E-mail: library@amerylibrary.org. Web Site: amerylibrary.org. *Dir,* Amy Stormberg
Library Holdings: Bk Vols 46,000; Per Subs 83
Wireless access
Mem of Inspiring & Facilitating Library Success (IFLS)
Open Mon-Thurs 9-7, Fri 9-6, Sat 9-2
Friends of the Library Group

AMHERST

P LETTIE W JENSEN PUBLIC LIBRARY*, 278 N Main St, 54406-9101. Tel: 715-824-5510. E-mail: amhlibrary@yahoo.com. Web Site: lwjlibrary.info. *Dir,* Kelly Bird; E-mail: director@lwjlibrary.info
Pop 3,025; Circ 12,820
Library Holdings: Audiobooks 400; DVDs 1,554; Large Print Bks 1,000; Bk Titles 12,116; Per Subs 21
Automation Activity & Vendor Info: (Cataloging) LibLime Koha; (Circulation) LibLime Koha; (OPAC) LibLime Koha
Wireless access
Mem of South Central Library System
Open Mon 9-12 & 2-5, Tues & Thurs 2-5, Wed 2-8, Sat 9-1
Friends of the Library Group

ANTIGO

P ANTIGO PUBLIC LIBRARY*, 617 Clermont St, 54409. SAN 317-8749. Tel: 715-623-3724. FAX: 715-627-2317. Web Site: www.antigopl.org. *Dir,* Dominic Frandrup; E-mail: director@antigopl.org; *Asst Dir,* Maria Pregler; E-mail: mpregler@antigopl.org; *ILL,* Elizabeth Merry; E-mail: emerry@antigopl.org; *Outreach Serv,* Elizabeth Simek; E-mail: esimek@antigopl.org; Staff 1 (MLS 1)
Founded 1900. Pop 20,618; Circ 169,420
Library Holdings: Bk Vols 72,000; Per Subs 180
Automation Activity & Vendor Info: (Circulation) Horizon; (Course Reserve) Horizon
Wireless access
Partic in Wisconsin Valley Library Service
Open Mon-Thurs 9-6
Friends of the Library Group
Branches: 2
ELCHO BRANCH, Elcho High School, Hwy 45 N, Elcho, 54428. Tel: 715-275-3225, Ext 1815. E-mail: elcholibrary@antigopl.org. *Br Mgr,* Julie Taylor; E-mail: jtaylor@antigopl.org
Library Holdings: Bk Titles 1,500
Open Mon, Wed & Thurs 11-4
WHITE LAKE BRANCH, White Lake Village Hall, 615 School St, White Lake, 54491. Tel: 715-882-8525. E-mail: whitelakelibrary@antigopl.org. *Br Mgr,* John Listle; E-mail: jlistle@antigopl.org
Library Holdings: Bk Titles 1,500
Open Mon-Thurs 12-4

APPLETON

P APPLETON PUBLIC LIBRARY*, 225 N Oneida St, 54911-4780. SAN 317-8765. Tel: 920-832-6173. Circulation Tel: 920-832-6179. Interlibrary Loan Service Tel: 920-832-6353. Information Services Tel: 920-832-6177. FAX: 920-832-6182. E-mail: askus@apl.org. Web Site: www.apl.org. *Dir,* Colleen T Rortvedt; E-mail: crortvedt@apl.org; *Asst Dir,* Tasha Saecker; E-mail: tsaecker@apl.org; Staff 17 (MLS 17)
Founded 1897. Pop 110,000; Circ 1,387,981
Library Holdings: Bk Titles 307,600; Bk Vols 402,883; Per Subs 600
Special Collections: State Document Depository
Subject Interests: Local hist
Automation Activity & Vendor Info: (Acquisitions) Innovative Interfaces, Inc; (Cataloging) Innovative Interfaces, Inc; (Circulation) Innovative Interfaces, Inc; (ILL) OCLC WorldShare Interlibrary Loan; (OPAC) Innovative Interfaces, Inc
Wireless access
Function: Art exhibits, Audio & video playback equip for onsite use, AV serv, CD-ROM, Digital talking bks, Games & aids for people with disabilities, Govt ref serv, Home delivery & serv to seniorr ctr & nursing homes, Homebound delivery serv, ILL available, Magnifiers for reading, Orientations, Outside serv via phone, mail, e-mail & web, Photocopying/Printing, Prog for adults, Prog for children & young adult, Ref serv available, Serves people with intellectual disabilities, Spoken cassettes & CDs, Summer reading prog, Telephone ref, VHS videos, Wheelchair accessible
Mem of Outagamie Waupaca Library System (OWLS)
Partic in OCLC Online Computer Library Center, Inc; OWLSnet
Special Services for the Deaf - TDD equip; TTY equip
Special Services for the Blind - Aids for in-house use; Assistive/Adapted tech devices, equip & products; Audio mat; Bks & mags in Braille, on rec, tape & cassette; Bks on cassette; Bks on CD; Braille bks; Children's Braille; Computer with voice synthesizer for visually impaired persons; Large print bks; Low vision equip; Magnifiers; Reader equip; Talking bk & rec for the blind cat; Talking bks; Volunteer serv
Open Mon-Thurs 9-9, Fri 9-6, Sat 9-5, Sun Noon-5 (Winter); Mon-Thurs 9-8, Fri 9-6, Sat 9-1 (Summer)
Friends of the Library Group

J FOX VALLEY TECHNICAL COLLEGE*, William M Sirek Educational Resource Center, 1825 N Bluemound Dr, Rm G113, 54912. (Mail add: PO Box 2277, 54912-2277), SAN 317-8773. Tel: 920-735-5653. FAX: 920-735-4870. E-mail: library@fvtc.edu. Web Site: library.fvtc.edu, www.fvtc.edu/library. *Libr Mgr,* Kathryn Johnston; E-mail: kathryn.johnston3910@fvtc.edu; *Libr Spec,* Kim L Arntzen; Tel: 920-735-4836, E-mail: arntzen@fvtc.edu; *Libr Spec,* Val Magno; Tel: 920-735-5771, E-mail: magno@fvtc.edu
Founded 1967. Enrl 4,405; Fac 285
Library Holdings: Bk Vols 50,000; Per Subs 303
Subject Interests: Agr, Environ studies, Med
Automation Activity & Vendor Info: (Acquisitions) Ex Libris Group; (Cataloging) Ex Libris Group; (Circulation) Ex Libris Group; (Course Reserve) Ex Libris Group; (ILL) Ex Libris Group; (Media Booking) Ex Libris Group; (OPAC) Ex Libris Group; (Serials) Ex Libris Group
Wireless access
Partic in Fox River Valley Area Library Consortium; WISPALS Library Consortium
Open Mon-Thurs 7:15am-8pm, Fri 7:30-4:30, Sat 9-1 (Winter); Mon-Thurs 7:30-7, Fri 7:30-1:30 (Summer)

C LAWRENCE UNIVERSITY, Seeley G Mudd Library, 113 S Lawe St, 54911-5683. SAN 364-5991. Circulation Tel: 920-832-6750. Interlibrary Loan Service Tel: 920-832-6758. Reference Tel: 920-832-6752. FAX: 920-832-6967. Reference E-mail: reference@lawrence.edu. Web Site: www.lawrence.edu/library. *Dir,* Position Currently Open; *Dir, Tech Serv,* Jill Thomas; *Learning Tech Librn, Ref Librn,* Angela Vanden Elzen; *Music Librn, Ref Librn,* Antoinette Powell; Tel: 920-832-6995; *Ref Librn,* Gretchen Revie; *Supvr, Circ,* Cynthia Patterson; *Coordr, Digital Coll Serv,* Colette Brautigam; *Univ Archivist,* Claire Cannell; Tel: 920-832-6753, E-mail: claire.cannell@lawrence.edu; Staff 14.5 (MLS 8, Non-MLS 6.5)
Founded 1847. Enrl 1,500; Fac 140; Highest Degree: Bachelor
Library Holdings: Bk Vols 395,032; Per Subs 1,787
Special Collections: Lincoln Coll. State Document Depository; US Document Depository
Automation Activity & Vendor Info: (Acquisitions) Ex Libris Group; (Cataloging) Ex Libris Group; (Circulation) Ex Libris Group; (Course Reserve) Ex Libris Group; (OPAC) Ex Libris Group; (Serials) Ex Libris Group
Wireless access
Partic in OCLC Online Computer Library Center, Inc; WiLS; Wis Asn of Independent Col & Univ

P OUTAGAMIE WAUPACA LIBRARY SYSTEM (OWLS)*, 225 N Oneida, 54911. SAN 317-879X. Tel: 920-832-6190. FAX: 920-832-6422. Web Site: www.owlsweb.org. *Dir,* Bradley Shipps; Tel: 920-832-6368, E-mail: bshipps@owlsweb.org; *Cat Librn,* John Wisneski; Tel: 920-832-6366, E-mail: jwisneski@owlsweb.org; *Computer Network Mgr,* Dave Bacon; Tel: 920-832-6193, E-mail: dbacon@owlsweb.org; *Libr Serv Mgr,* Evan Bend; Tel: 920-832-6192, E-mail: ebend@owlsweb.org; Staff 6 (MLS 4, Non-MLS 2)
Founded 1975
Automation Activity & Vendor Info: (Acquisitions) Innovative Interfaces, Inc; (Cataloging) Innovative Interfaces, Inc; (Circulation) Innovative Interfaces, Inc; (ILL) Innovative Interfaces, Inc; (OPAC) Innovative Interfaces, Inc; (Serials) Innovative Interfaces, Inc
Wireless access
Member Libraries: Appleton Public Library; Black Creek Village Library; Clintonville Public Library; Hortonville Public Library; Iola Village Library; Kaukauna Public Library; Kimberly Public Library; Little Chute Public Library; Marion Public Library; Muehl Public Library; Neuschafer Community Library; New London Public Library; Scandinavia Public Library; Shiocton Public Library; Sturm Memorial Library; Waupaca Area Public Library; Weyauwega Public Library
Partic in OWLSnet; Wisconsin Public Library Consortium
Open Mon-Fri 8-5

M THEDACARE MEDICAL LIBRARY*, DeCock Medical Library, 1818 N Meade, 54911-3434. SAN 318-2789. Tel: 920-831-5089. FAX: 920-738-6389. E-mail: library@thedacare.org. *Med Librn,* Diane Giebink-Skoglind; Staff 1 (MLS 1)
Founded 1970
Library Holdings: Bk Titles 1,300; Bk Vols 1,800; Per Subs 20

Subject Interests: Critical care, Maternal fetal med, Neonatal intensive care, Trauma
Wireless access
Partic in Fox River Valley Area Library Consortium
Open Mon-Fri 8:30-4

ARCADIA

P ARCADIA FREE PUBLIC LIBRARY*, 730 Raider Dr, Ste 3140, 54612. SAN 317-8811. Tel: 608-323-7505. FAX: 608-323-7505. E-mail: rkdpubli@wrlsweb.org. Web Site: arcadialibrary.wrlsweb.org. *Dir,* Carol Daul-Elhindi; E-mail: arcadiadirector@wrlsweb.org; *Tech Serv Assoc,* Arlene Servais; *Circ Asst,* Gaylene Amohror; *Circ Asst,* Pam Beam
Founded 1899. Pop 2,159; Circ 38,035
Library Holdings: Bk Vols 17,000; Per Subs 88
Automation Activity & Vendor Info: (Cataloging) Horizon; (Circulation) Horizon; (OPAC) Horizon
Wireless access
Mem of Winding Rivers Library System
Partic in Wiscat
Open Mon, Tues & Thurs 9-6, Wed & Fri 9-5, Sat (May-Sept) 9-Noon

ARGYLE

P ARGYLE PUBLIC LIBRARY*, 401 E Milwaukee St, 53504. (Mail add: PO Box 250, 53504-0250), SAN 317-882X. Tel: 608-543-3193. E-mail: argylelibrary@swls.org. Web Site: argylepubliclibrary.com, argylewi.org/community.html. *Dir,* Sarah Kyrie; E-mail: skyrie@swls.org
Pop 479; Circ 4,726
Library Holdings: Bk Vols 6,703; Per Subs 20
Special Collections: Argyle Atlas Newspaper Coll (bound issues beginning in 1887)
Wireless access
Mem of Southwest Wisconsin Library System
Open Mon-Wed 2-6, Thurs-Sat 9-1

ARPIN

P LESTER PUBLIC LIBRARY OF ARPIN*, 8091 County Rd E, 54410. SAN 317-8838. Tel: 715-652-2273. E-mail: staff@arpinpl.org. Web Site: www.arpinpl.org. *Libr Dir,* Stacy Kundinger
Founded 1951
Library Holdings: Bk Vols 12,422; Per Subs 20
Wireless access
Mem of South Central Library System
Open Mon & Thurs 3-7, Tues & Fri 9-5, Wed & Sat 9-Noon

ASHLAND

L ASHLAND COUNTY LAW LIBRARY*, Courthouse, Rm 304, 201 W Main St, 54806. Tel: 715-682-7016. FAX: 715-682-7919. E-mail: lawlibrary@ashlandcounty.org. Web Site: co.ashland.wi.us/circuit_court. *Librn,* Sandy Paitl; E-mail: sandy.paitl@wicourts.gov
Library Holdings: Bk Vols 6,500; Per Subs 15
Open Mon-Fri 8-4

P NORTHERN WATERS LIBRARY SERVICE*, 3200 E Lakeshore Dr, 54806-2510. SAN 317-8854. Tel: 715-682-2365. Toll Free Tel: 800-228-5684. FAX: 715-685-2704. Web Site: www.nwls.wislib.org. *Dir,* Sherry Machones; E-mail: smachones@northernwaters.org; *ILS Adminr,* Jackee Johnson; Tel: 715-685-1073, E-mail: jjohnson@northernwaters.org; *Asst Dir,* Anne-Marie Itzin; Tel: 715-685-1072, E-mail: amitzin@northernwaters.org; *Bus Mgr,* Michelle Gostomski; Tel: 715-685-1070, E-mail: mgostomski@northernwaters.org; *Tech Support, Technology Spec,* Tony Kriskovich; Tel: 715-685-1076, E-mail: tkriskovich@northernwaters.org
Founded 1972. Pop 140,000; Circ 65,081
Automation Activity & Vendor Info: (Acquisitions) Innovative Interfaces, Inc - Millennium; (Cataloging) Innovative Interfaces, Inc - Millennium; (Circulation) Innovative Interfaces, Inc - Millennium; (ILL) Innovative Interfaces, Inc - Millennium; (OPAC) Innovative Interfaces, Inc - Millennium; (Serials) Innovative Interfaces, Inc - Millennium
Wireless access
Publications: Streams (Online only)
Member Libraries: Bayfield Carnegie Library; Ben Guthrie Lac Du Flambeau Public Library; Boulder Junction Public Library; Drummond Public Library; Evelyn Goldberg Briggs Memorial Library; Forest Lodge Library; Frank B Koller Memorial Library; Grantsburg Public Library; Hurley Public Library; Lac Courte Oreilles Ojibwa Community College Library; Land O'Lakes Public Library; Larsen Family Public Library; Legion Memorial Library; Madeline Island Public Library; Mercer Public Library; Phelps Public Library; Plum Lake Public Library; Presque Isle Community Library; Shell Lake Public Library; Sherman & Ruth Weiss Community Library; Spooner Memorial Library; Superior Public Library; Vaughn Public Library; Walter E Olson Memorial Library; Washburn Public Library; Winchester Public Library; Winter Public Library
Partic in Wisconsin Public Library Consortium
Open Mon-Fri 8-4

C NORTHLAND COLLEGE*, Dexter Library, 1411 Ellis Ave, 54806-3999. SAN 317-8846. Tel: 715-682-1279. Administration Tel: 715-682-1302. FAX: 715-682-1693. E-mail: library@northland.edu. Web Site: my.northland.edu/library. *Libr Dir,* Julia Waggoner; Tel: 715-682-1302, E-mail: jwaggoner@northland.edu; *Syst & Cat Serv Librn,* Anne-Marie Itzin; Tel: 715-682-1559, E-mail: aitzin@northland.edu; Staff 3 (MLS 2, Non-MLS 1)
Founded 1892. Enrl 600; Fac 54; Highest Degree: Bachelor
Library Holdings: Bk Titles 64,000; Bk Vols 74,000; Per Subs 130; Videos 8,000
Subject Interests: Environ studies, Native Am studies
Automation Activity & Vendor Info: (Acquisitions) Ex Libris Group; (Cataloging) Ex Libris Group; (Circulation) Ex Libris Group; (Course Reserve) Ex Libris Group; (ILL) OCLC; (OPAC) Ex Libris Group; (Serials) Ex Libris Group
Wireless access
Partic in WiLS
Open Mon-Thurs 8am-11pm, Fri 8-5, Sat Noon-4, Sun Noon-11

CM NORTHWOOD TECHNICAL COLLEGE*, Ashland Campus Learning Resource Center, 2100 Beaser Ave, 54806. Tel: 715-682-4591, Ext 3108. Toll Free Tel: 800-243-9482, Ext 3108. FAX: 715-682-8040. Web Site: learningcommons.witc.edu/lrc/Ashland. *Libr Tech,* Rebecca Houle; E-mail: becca.houle@northwoodtech.edu; *Libr Tech,* Spencer Taves; E-mail: spencer.taves@northwoodtech.edu
Library Holdings: AV Mats 2,000; Bk Titles 6,300; Per Subs 20
Automation Activity & Vendor Info: (Cataloging) Innovative Interfaces, Inc - Sierra; (Circulation) Innovative Interfaces, Inc - Sierra; (OPAC) Innovative Interfaces, Inc - Sierra
Wireless access
Open Mon-Thurs 7:30-7, Fri 7:30-4

P VAUGHN PUBLIC LIBRARY*, 502 W Main St, 54806. SAN 317-8862. Tel: 715-682-7060. FAX: 715-682-7185. Web Site: vpl.wislib.org. *Dir,* Sarah Adams; Tel: 715-685-1668, E-mail: sadams@vaughnlibrary.org; Staff 9 (MLS 1, Non-MLS 8)
Founded 1888. Pop 12,623; Circ 144,350
Library Holdings: CDs 3,534; DVDs 3,538; e-books 53,430; Large Print Bks 819; Bk Titles 37,582; Per Subs 141
Automation Activity & Vendor Info: (Cataloging) Innovative Interfaces, Inc; (Circulation) Innovative Interfaces, Inc; (OPAC) Innovative Interfaces, Inc
Wireless access
Function: Adult bk club, Art exhibits, Bks on cassette, Bks on CD, Children's prog, Computer training, Computers for patron use, Equip loans & repairs, Family literacy, Free DVD rentals, Holiday prog, ILL available, Instruction & testing, Magnifiers for reading, Music CDs, Online cat, Outside serv via phone, mail, e-mail & web, OverDrive digital audio bks, Photocopying/Printing, Preschool outreach, Printer for laptops & handheld devices, Prog for adults, Prog for children & young adult, Scanner, Senior outreach, Story hour, Summer reading prog, Tax forms, Teen prog, Wheelchair accessible
Mem of Northern Waters Library Service
Partic in Merlin
Open Mon-Wed 8:30-7, Thurs 9-7, Fri 9-5, Sat 9-1
Friends of the Library Group

AUGUSTA

P AUGUSTA MEMORIAL PUBLIC LIBRARY*, 113 N Stone St, 54722-6000. SAN 326-1204. Tel: 715-286-2070. E-mail: aulib@augustalibrary.org. Web Site: augustalibrary.org. *Dir,* Leslie LaRose; E-mail: larose@augustalibrary.org; Staff 1 (Non-MLS 1)
Pop 1,550; Circ 30,293
Library Holdings: e-books 17,736; Large Print Bks 582; Bk Vols 16,433; Per Subs 101; Talking Bks 976; Videos 1,374
Automation Activity & Vendor Info: (Acquisitions) Innovative Interfaces, Inc; (Cataloging) Innovative Interfaces, Inc; (Circulation) Innovative Interfaces, Inc; (Course Reserve) Innovative Interfaces, Inc; (ILL) Innovative Interfaces, Inc; (Media Booking) Innovative Interfaces, Inc; (OPAC) Innovative Interfaces, Inc; (Serials) Innovative Interfaces, Inc
Wireless access
Mem of Inspiring & Facilitating Library Success (IFLS)
Open Mon & Thurs-Sat 10-5, Tues & Wed 9-7
Friends of the Library Group

BALDWIN

P BALDWIN PUBLIC LIBRARY*, 400 Cedar St, 54002. (Mail add: PO Box 475, 54002-0475), SAN 317-8870. Tel: 715-684-3813. FAX: 715-684-5115. E-mail: baldwinstaff@baldwinlibrary.org. Web Site: www.baldwinlibrary.org. *Dir,* Rita Magno; E-mail:

diector@baldwinlibrary.org; *ILL,* Hope Melander; *Youth Serv,* Molly Haley; Staff 3.3 (MLS 1, Non-MLS 2.3)
Founded 1941. Pop 7,000; Circ 90,000
Library Holdings: Bk Titles 25,000; Per Subs 80
Automation Activity & Vendor Info: (Acquisitions) Innovative Interfaces, Inc; (Cataloging) Innovative Interfaces, Inc; (Circulation) Innovative Interfaces, Inc
Wireless access
Function: Adult bk club, Art exhibits, Audiobks on Playaways & MP3, Audiobks via web, Bilingual assistance for Spanish patrons, Bk club(s), Bks on CD, Children's prog, Computer training, Computers for patron use, Doc delivery serv, E-Readers, Electronic databases & coll, Equip loans & repairs, Free DVD rentals, Games & aids for people with disabilities, Genealogy discussion group, Holiday prog, Home delivery & serv to seniorr ctr & nursing homes, Homebound delivery serv, ILL available, Instruction & testing, Internet access, Laminating, Large print keyboards, Life-long learning prog for all ages, Magazines, Magnifiers for reading, Mail & tel request accepted, Meeting rooms, Microfiche/film & reading machines, Movies, Music CDs, Online cat, Outside serv via phone, mail, e-mail & web, OverDrive digital audio bks, Photocopying/Printing, Preschool outreach, Prof lending libr, Prog for adults, Prog for children & young adult, Ref & res, Ref serv available, Res assist avail, Scanner, Senior outreach, Serves people with intellectual disabilities, Spanish lang bks, STEM programs, Story hour, Study rm, Summer & winter reading prog, Summer reading prog, Tax forms, Teen prog, Telephone ref, VHS videos, Wheelchair accessible, Winter reading prog, Workshops
Mem of Inspiring & Facilitating Library Success (IFLS)
Special Services for the Deaf - Assistive tech; Bks on deafness & sign lang; Closed caption videos; Sign lang interpreter upon request for prog
Special Services for the Blind - Assistive/Adapted tech devices, equip & products; Bks available with recordings; Bks on CD; Braille bks; Cassette playback machines; Cassettes; Computer with voice synthesizer for visually impaired persons; Copier with enlargement capabilities; Large print & cassettes; Large print bks; Large screen computer & software; Magnifiers; PC for people with disabilities; Recorded bks; Screen reader software; ZoomText magnification & reading software
Open Mon, Wed & Fri 11-6, Tues & Thurs 10-8, Sat 9-1
Friends of the Library Group

BALSAM LAKE

P BALSAM LAKE PUBLIC LIBRARY, 404 Main St, 54810. (Mail add: PO Box 340, 54810-0340), SAN 317-8889. Tel: 715-485-3215. E-mail: library@balsamlakepl.org. Web Site: balsamlakepubliclibrary.org. *Libr Dir,* Linda Heimstead; E-mail: library@balsamlakepl.org; *Admin Librn, Ad,* Rebekah Smith; E-mail: rsmith@balsamlakepl.org; *Asst Librn,* Alyssa Brown; E-mail: abrown@balsamlakepl.org; *Youth Serv,* Samuel Linder; E-mail: youthservices@balsamlakepl.org
Founded 1946. Pop 1,000; Circ 12,779
Library Holdings: Bk Vols 18,000; Per Subs 30
Special Collections: Wisconsin Coll
Wireless access
Function: 24/7 Electronic res, 24/7 Online cat, 24/7 wireless access, Children's prog, Computers for patron use, Free DVD rentals, Games, Games & aids for people with disabilities, ILL available, Magazines, Magnifiers for reading, Music CDs, Prog for adults, Prog for children & young adult, Scanner, Summer & winter reading prog, Wifi hotspot checkout
Mem of Inspiring & Facilitating Library Success (IFLS)
Open Mon-Thurs 10-6, Fri 10-4, Sat 10-1
Friends of the Library Group

BARABOO

P CARNEGIE-SCHADDE MEMORIAL PUBLIC LIBRARY*, 230 Fourth Ave, 53913. SAN 317-8897. Tel: 608-356-6166. FAX: 608-355-2779. Web Site: www.csmpl.org. *Dir,* Jessica Bergin; E-mail: jessica@csmpl.org; *Ad, Asst Dir,* Nathan Rybarczyk; E-mail: nathan@csmpl.org; *Youth Serv Librn,* Carey Kipp; E-mail: carey@csmpl.org; *Tech Serv,* Mari Jo Burri; E-mail: mari@csmpl.org; Staff 22 (MLS 4, Non-MLS 18)
Founded 1903. Pop 20,599; Circ 230,625
Library Holdings: AV Mats 2,925; Large Print Bks 1,827; Bk Vols 60,910; Per Subs 198; Talking Bks 2,896
Automation Activity & Vendor Info: (Acquisitions) Koha; (Cataloging) Koha; (Circulation) Koha; (ILL) Koha; (OPAC) Koha; (Serials) Koha
Wireless access
Mem of South Central Library System
Open Mon-Thurs 9-8, Fri 9-6, Sat 9-2
Friends of the Library Group

S CIRCUS WORLD MUSEUM*, Robert L Parkinson Library & Research Center, 415 Lynn St, 53913. (Mail add: 550 Water St, 53913-2597), SAN 317-8900. Tel: 608-356-8341. Toll Free Tel: 800-693-1500. FAX: 608-355-7959. Web Site: www.circusworldbaraboo.org/our-treasures/library-research-center. *Archivist,* Peter Shrake; E-mail: pshrake@circusworldbaraboo.org; Staff 2 (MLS 1, Non-MLS 1)
Founded 1966
Library Holdings: Bk Titles 3,259; Bk Vols 4,834; Per Subs 29
Subject Interests: Circus, Wild West
Function: Archival coll
Publications: Current Circus Activity; Loan Lists for Books, Serials, Films & Videos; USA & Canada List
Restriction: Open by appt only

S INTERNATIONAL CRANE FOUNDATION*, Ron Sauey Memorial Library for Bird Conservation, E-11376 Shady Lane Rd, 53913-9778. (Mail add: PO Box 447, 53913-0447), SAN 321-902X. Tel: 608-356-9462, Ext 124. FAX: 608-356-9465. E-mail: library@savingcranes.org. Web Site: www.savingcranes.org/.
Founded 1973
Library Holdings: Bk Titles 4,000; Per Subs 50
Subject Interests: Biology, Conserv, Ornithology, Wetlands
Restriction: Open by appt only

GL SAUK COUNTY LAW LIBRARY*, 515 Oak St, 53913. SAN 377-9874. Tel: 608-355-3287. FAX: 608-355-3480. *Library Contact,* Carrie A Wastlick; E-mail: cwastlick@co.sauk.wi.us
Library Holdings: Bk Vols 3,000
Open Mon-Fri 8-4:30

C UNIVERSITY OF WISCONSIN-PLATTEVILLE BARABOO SAUK COUNTY*, Baraboo Sauk County Campus, T N Savides Library, 1006 Connie Rd, 53913. SAN 317-8927. Tel: 608-800-6817. Web Site: www.uwplatt.edu. *Sr Acad Librn,* Sara Winger; E-mail: wingersa@uwplatt.edu; Staff 3 (MLS 3)
Founded 1968. Enrl 400; Fac 42; Highest Degree: Bachelor
Library Holdings: Bk Vols 37,357; Per Subs 110
Automation Activity & Vendor Info: (Acquisitions) Ex Libris Group; (Cataloging) Ex Libris Group; (Circulation) Ex Libris Group; (ILL) OCLC ILLiad
Wireless access
Partic in OCLC Online Computer Library Center, Inc; S Cent Libr Syst; WiLS
Open Mon, Tues & Thurs 8:30-7, Wed 8:30-5, Fri 8:30-4

BARNEVELD

P BARNEVELD PUBLIC LIBRARY*, 107 W Orbison St, 53507. SAN 317-8935. Tel: 608-924-3711. Web Site: barneveldpubliclibrary.org. *Dir,* Sharilyn Sailing; E-mail: ssailing@swls.org
Founded 1955. Pop 1,088; Circ 2,856
Library Holdings: AV Mats 543; Bk Vols 7,749; Per Subs 14; Talking Bks 189
Subject Interests: Local hist
Automation Activity & Vendor Info: (OPAC) Horizon
Wireless access
Mem of Southwest Wisconsin Library System
Open Mon-Thurs 10-6, Fri 10-5, Sat 10-1
Friends of the Library Group

BARRON

P BARRON PUBLIC LIBRARY*, Ten N Third St, 54812-1119. SAN 317-8943. Tel: 715-537-3881. E-mail: barronpl@barronpl.org. Web Site: www.barronpubliclibrary.org. *Dir,* Susan Queisar; Staff 7 (MLS 1, Non-MLS 6)
Founded 1909
Library Holdings: Bk Vols 30,000; Per Subs 80
Automation Activity & Vendor Info: (Cataloging) SirsiDynix; (Circulation) SirsiDynix
Wireless access
Mem of Inspiring & Facilitating Library Success (IFLS)
Partic in Barron County Library Services
Open Mon-Thurs 9-7, Fri 9-5, Sat 9-12
Friends of the Library Group

BAYFIELD

P BAYFIELD CARNEGIE LIBRARY, 37 N Broad St, 54814. (Mail add: PO Box 727, 54814-0727), SAN 317-8951. Tel: 715-779-3953. E-mail: bayfieldlibraryrequests@gmail.com. Web Site: www.bayfieldlibrary.org. *Dir,* Teresa Weber; E-mail: director@bayfieldlibrary.org; *Asst Librn,* Susan Edwards; *Asst Librn,* Heidi Goehring; *Asst Librn,* Lindy Howe; *Asst Librn,* Laura Rovi; Staff 4 (MLS 1, Non-MLS 3)
Founded 1903. Circ 26,000
Library Holdings: Bk Vols 19,000; Per Subs 28
Wireless access
Function: 24/7 Electronic res, 24/7 Online cat, Adult bk club, Archival coll, AV serv, Bi-weekly Writer's Group, Bk club(s), Bks on CD, Children's prog, Computer training, Computers for patron use, Distance

learning, Doc delivery serv, E-Readers, Family literacy, Free DVD rentals, Holiday prog, ILL available, Internet access, Life-long learning prog for all ages, Literacy & newcomer serv, Magazines, Meeting rooms, Movies, Music CDs, Online cat, Orientations, Outreach serv, Outside serv via phone, mail, e-mail & web, Photocopying/Printing, Preschool reading prog, Prog for adults, Prog for children & young adult, Ref & res, Scanner, Senior outreach, Serves people with intellectual disabilities, Story hour, Summer reading prog, Tax forms, Teen prog, VHS videos, Wheelchair accessible, Workshops, Writing prog
Mem of Northern Waters Library Service
Open Mon-Fri 10-6, Sat 10-2

G NATIONAL PARK SERVICE*, Apostle Islands National Lakeshore Library, 415 Washington Ave, 54814. (Mail add: PO Box 4, 54814-0004), SAN 328-1779. Tel: 715-779-3397. FAX: 715-779-3049. Web Site: www.nps.gov/apis. *Superintendent,* Lynne Dominy; Tel: 715-779-3398, Ext 1101, E-mail: lynne_dominy@nps.gov
Founded 1975
Library Holdings: Bk Vols 1,500; Per Subs 30
Special Collections: Oral History
Subject Interests: Local hist
Restriction: Staff use only

BEAVER DAM

P BEAVER DAM COMMUNITY LIBRARY*, 311 N Spring St, 53916-2043. SAN 317-8978. Tel: 920-219-4631. FAX: 920-887-4633. E-mail: circdesk@beaverdamlibrary.org. Web Site: www.cityofbeaverdam.com/department/index.php?structureid=26. *Dir,* Susan Mary Mevis; Tel: 920-887-4631, Ext 101, E-mail: smevis@beaverdamlibrary.org; *Youth Serv Librn,* Sarah Cournoyer; Tel: 920-887-4631, Ext 105, E-mail: sarah@beaverdamlibrary.org; Staff 12 (MLS 4, Non-MLS 8)
Founded 1884. Circ 386,000
Library Holdings: Bk Vols 150,000; Per Subs 200
Automation Activity & Vendor Info: (Acquisitions) SirsiDynix; (Cataloging) SirsiDynix; (Circulation) SirsiDynix; (Course Reserve) SirsiDynix; (ILL) SirsiDynix; (Media Booking) SirsiDynix; (OPAC) SirsiDynix; (Serials) SirsiDynix
Wireless access
Mem of Monarch Library System
Open Mon-Fri 9-7, Sat 9-1
Friends of the Library Group

J MORAINE PARK TECHNICAL COLLEGE LIBRARY*, Beaver Dam Campus, 700 Gould St, 53916-1994. SAN 317-896X. Tel: 920-887-4406. FAX: 920-887-4473. Web Site: www.morainepark.edu/services/library. *Learning Res Tech,* Rosemary Froeliger; E-mail: rfroeliger@morainepark.edu; Staff 2 (MLS 2)
Library Holdings: Bk Vols 4,000; Per Subs 15
Automation Activity & Vendor Info: (Acquisitions) Ex Libris Group; (Cataloging) Ex Libris Group; (Circulation) Ex Libris Group; (Course Reserve) Ex Libris Group; (ILL) Ex Libris Group; (Media Booking) Ex Libris Group; (OPAC) Ex Libris Group; (Serials) Ex Libris Group
Wireless access
Partic in WISPALS Library Consortium
Open Mon-Thurs 8-8, Fri 8-4, Sat 8-Noon

BELLEVILLE

P BELLEVILLE PUBLIC LIBRARY*, 130 S Vine St, 53508-9102. (Mail add: PO Box 140, 53508-0140), SAN 317-8986. Tel: 608-424-1812. FAX: 608-424-3545. E-mail: blvcirc@blvpl.org. Web Site: www.bellevillelibrary-wi.org. *Dir,* Bronna Lehmann
Founded 1878
Library Holdings: Bk Vols 22,000; Per Subs 65
Subject Interests: Local hist
Wireless access
Mem of South Central Library System
Open Mon-Thurs 9-7, Fri 9-5, Sat 9-Noon
Friends of the Library Group

BELMONT

P JOHN TURGESON PUBLIC LIBRARY*, Belmont Public, 220 S Mound Ave, 53510. SAN 317-8994. Tel: 608-762-5137. FAX: 608-762-5525. Web Site: belmontwi.com/library. *Librn,* Sylvia Henry; E-mail: shenry@swls.org
Pop 1,335; Circ 5,504
Library Holdings: Bk Vols 18,000
Automation Activity & Vendor Info: (Cataloging) SirsiDynix; (Circulation) SirsiDynix
Wireless access
Mem of Southwest Wisconsin Library System
Open Mon, Wed & Fri 1-6:30, Sat 8:30-Noon (Winter); Mon & Fri 1-6:30, Wed 8:30-Noon & 1-6:30 (Summer)

BELOIT

C BELOIT COLLEGE*, Colonel Robert H Morse Library & Richard Black Information Center, 731 College St, 53511. SAN 364-6238. Tel: 608-363-2483. Circulation Tel: 608-363-2230. Interlibrary Loan Service Tel: 608-363-2567. Reference Tel: 608-363-2544. FAX: 608-363-2487. Web Site: www.beloit.edu/library. *Chief Info Officer, Libr Dir,* Ted Wilder; Tel: 608-363-2470, E-mail: wildert@beloit.edu; *Digital Res Librn,* Josh Hickman; Tel: 608-363-2246, E-mail: hickmanj@beloit.edu; *Pub Serv Librn,* Christine Nelson; E-mail: nelsoncn@beloit.edu; Staff 6 (MLS 5, Non-MLS 1)
Founded 1849. Enrl 1,344; Fac 104
Library Holdings: Bk Titles 239,654; Bk Vols 257,417; Per Subs 1,859
Special Collections: Beloit Poetry Journal Coll; Cullister International Coll; Pacifism & Nonviolence (M L King Coll), mat by & about Presidents F D Roosevelt, Woodrow Wilson, Abraham Lincoln. State Document Depository; US Document Depository
Automation Activity & Vendor Info: (Acquisitions) SirsiDynix; (Cataloging) SirsiDynix; (Circulation) SirsiDynix; (Course Reserve) SirsiDynix; (OPAC) SirsiDynix; (Serials) SirsiDynix
Wireless access
Mem of Prairie Lakes Library System (PLLS)
Partic in OCLC Online Computer Library Center, Inc; The Oberlin Group; WiLS; Wis Asn of Independent Col & Univ
Open Mon-Thurs 8:30am-Midnight, Fri 8:30am-10pm, Sat 11-10, Sun 11am-Midnight (Winter); Mon-Fri 9-5 (Summer)

P BELOIT HISTORICAL SOCIETY*, Luebke Family Memorial Library, Lincoln Ctr, 845 Hackett St, 53511. SAN 371-1641. Tel: 608-365-7835. E-mail: info@beloithistoricalsociety.com. Web Site: beloithistoricalsociety.com. *Exec Dir,* Donna Langford; E-mail: dlangford@beloithistoricalsociety.com
Library Holdings: Bk Vols 500; Per Subs 12
Subject Interests: Local hist, Old books
Wireless access
Restriction: Open by appt only

P BELOIT PUBLIC LIBRARY*, 605 Eclipse Blvd, 53511. SAN 317-9001. Tel: 608-364-2905. Circulation Tel: 608-364-2911. Administration Tel: 608-364-2908. FAX: 608-364-2907. Reference E-mail: pserve@beloitlibrary.org. Web Site: beloitlibrary.org. *Libr Dir,* Nick Dimassis; Tel: 608-364-2917, E-mail: ndimassis@beloitlibrary.org; *Head of Programming & Community Engagement,* Katharine Clark; Tel: 608-364-2897, E-mail: kclark@beloitlibrary.org; *Head, Libr Serv,* Jeni Schomber; Tel: 608-364-5754, E-mail: jschomber@beloitlibrary.org; *Head, Res,* Michael Devries; Tel: 608-364-2909, E-mail: mdevries@beloitlibrary.org; *Bus Mgr,* Jennifer Laatz; E-mail: jlaatz@beloitlibrary.org; *IT Mgr,* Wyatt Ditzler; Tel: 608-364-5755, E-mail: wditzler@beloitlibrary.org; *Marketing & Communications Coord,* Amy Mitchell; Tel: 608-364-5743, E-mail: amitchell@beloitlibrary.org; Staff 16.1 (MLS 4, Non-MLS 12.1)
Founded 1902. Pop 48,000; Circ 529,803
Library Holdings: Bk Titles 110,025; Bk Vols 118,330
Special Collections: LGBTQ + Films; Urban Fiction
Subject Interests: Genealogy, Local hist
Automation Activity & Vendor Info: (Cataloging) SirsiDynix-Symphony; (Circulation) SirsiDynix-Symphony; (OPAC) SirsiDynix-Symphony
Wireless access
Function: Art exhibits, Bks on CD, Children's prog, Computer training, Computers for patron use, E-Reserves, Electronic databases & coll, Free DVD rentals, Genealogy discussion group, Home delivery & serv to seniorr ctr & nursing homes, Homebound delivery serv, ILL available, Large print keyboards, Magnifiers for reading, Mail & tel request accepted, Microfiche/film & reading machines, Music CDs, Online cat, Outreach serv, OverDrive digital audio bks, Photocopying/Printing, Prog for adults, Prog for children & young adult, Ref serv available, Scanner, Serves people with intellectual disabilities, Spanish lang bks, Spoken cassettes & CDs, Story hour, Summer reading prog, Tax forms, Teen prog, Telephone ref, Wheelchair accessible
Mem of Prairie Lakes Library System (PLLS)
Open Mon-Thurs 9:30-9, Fri & Sat 9:30-5:30
Friends of the Library Group

BENTON

P BENTON PUBLIC LIBRARY*, 48 W Main St, 53803. (Mail add: PO Box 26, 53803-0026), SAN 317-9052. Tel: 608-759-2665. *Dir,* Michele K Anderson; E-mail: manderson@swls.org; Staff 1 (MLS 1)
Founded 1922. Pop 1,400; Circ 6,000
Library Holdings: Bk Titles 6,000
Special Collections: Local history
Automation Activity & Vendor Info: (Circulation) SirsiDynix
Wireless access
Function: ILL available

Mem of Southwest Wisconsin Library System
Open Mon 1-8, Tues-Thurs 1-6, Fri 9-12, Sat 9-2

BERLIN

P BERLIN PUBLIC LIBRARY*, 121 W Park Ave, 54923. SAN 317-9060. Tel: 920-361-5420. FAX: 920-361-5424. Web Site: www.berlinlibrary.org. *Libr Dir, Patron Serv,* Ms Chris Kalupa; E-mail: kalupa@berlinlibrary.org; *Children's & Teen Serv,* Nicole Overbeck; E-mail: overbeck@berlinlibrary.org; Staff 3 (Non-MLS 3)
Founded 1903. Pop 9,000; Circ 120,000
Library Holdings: Bks on Deafness & Sign Lang 35; High Interest/Low Vocabulary Bk Vols 500; Bk Vols 50,000; Per Subs 101
Special Collections: Literacy Coll; Spanish Language Materials Coll
Subject Interests: Literacy, Local hist
Automation Activity & Vendor Info: (Cataloging) SirsiDynix; (Circulation) SirsiDynix; (OPAC) SirsiDynix
Wireless access
Mem of Winnefox Library System
Special Services for the Deaf - TTY equip
Special Services for the Blind - Magnifiers
Open Mon-Thurs 9-8, Fri 9-6, Sat 9-5; Mon-Thurs 9-8, Fri 9-6, Sat 9-1 (Summer)
Friends of the Library Group

BIG BEND

P BIG BEND VILLAGE LIBRARY*, W230 S9185 Nevins St, 53103. SAN 324-7880. Tel: 262-662-3571. FAX: 262-662-3751. E-mail: bigbendlibrary@bigbend.lib.wi.us. Web Site: www.bigbend.lib.wi.us. *Dir,* Karla Lang; E-mail: klang@villageofbigbend.com; Staff 4 (MLS 1, Non-MLS 3)
Founded 1964. Pop 1,299; Circ 11,799
Library Holdings: Bk Vols 10,000; Per Subs 29
Subject Interests: Local hist
Wireless access
Mem of Bridges Library System
Open Mon & Thurs 1-8, Tues & Wed 9:30-8, Fri 2-6, Sat 9-1

BLACK CREEK

P BLACK CREEK VILLAGE LIBRARY*, 507 S Maple St, 54106-9304. SAN 317-9087. Tel: 920-984-3094. FAX: 920-984-3559. E-mail: bcl@blackcreeklibrary.org. Web Site: www.blackcreeklibrary.org. *Dir & Head Librn,* Rachel Hitt; E-mail: rhitt@blackcreeklibrary.org; Staff 1 (Non-MLS 1)
Founded 1975. Pop 5,132; Circ 61,483
Automation Activity & Vendor Info: (Acquisitions) TLC (The Library Corporation); (Cataloging) TLC (The Library Corporation); (Circulation) TLC (The Library Corporation); (ILL) OCLC FirstSearch; (OPAC) TLC (The Library Corporation)
Wireless access
Function: 24/7 wireless access, Accelerated reader prog, Archival coll, Audiobks via web, AV serv, Bks on CD, Children's prog, Computer training, Computers for patron use, E-Reserves, Electronic databases & coll, Extended outdoor wifi, Home delivery & serv to seniorr ctr & nursing homes, ILL available, Internet access, Laminating, Laptop/tablet checkout, Magazines, Mail & tel request accepted, Music CDs, Online cat, Photocopying/Printing, Prog for adults, Prog for children & young adult, Summer reading prog, Tax forms, Teen prog, Wifi hotspot checkout
Mem of Outagamie Waupaca Library System (OWLS)
Partic in OWLSnet
Open Mon, Tues & Thurs 10-7, Wed 3-7, Fri 9-5, Sat 9-Noon
Friends of the Library Group

BLACK EARTH

P BLACK EARTH PUBLIC LIBRARY*, 1210 Mills St, 53515. (Mail add: PO Box 347, 53515-0347), SAN 317-9095. Tel: 608-767-4905. FAX: 608-767-2064. Web Site: www.blackearthlibrary.org. *Libr Dir,* Bailey Anderson; E-mail: banderson@blackearthlibrary.org; Staff 10 (MLS 2, Non-MLS 8)
Founded 1938. Pop 1,400; Circ 32,445
Library Holdings: AV Mats 1,663; Bk Titles 16,056; Per Subs 54
Automation Activity & Vendor Info: (Cataloging) LibLime; (Circulation) LibLime; (Discovery) LibLime; (Serials) LibLime
Wireless access
Function: 24/7 Electronic res, 24/7 Online cat, Adult bk club, Art programs, Audiobks on Playaways & MP3, Audiobks via web, Bilingual assistance for Spanish patrons, Bk club(s), Bks on CD, Children's prog, Computers for patron use, Digital talking bks, Electronic databases & coll, Free DVD rentals, Holiday prog, ILL available, Internet access, Life-long learning prog for all ages, Magazines, Movies, Music CDs, Notary serv, Online cat, Outside serv via phone, mail, e-mail & web, OverDrive digital audio bks, Photocopying/Printing, Preschool outreach, Prog for adults, Prog for children & young adult, Ref & res, Ref serv available, Scanner, Serves people with intellectual disabilities, Spanish lang bks, STEM programs, Story hour, Summer reading prog, Tax forms, Teen prog, Telephone ref
Mem of South Central Library System
Open Mon-Thurs 9:30-7, Fri 9:30-5, Sat 10-2
Friends of the Library Group

BLACK RIVER FALLS

P BLACK RIVER FALLS PUBLIC LIBRARY*, 222 Fillmore St, 54615. SAN 364-6386. Tel: 715-284-4112. Web Site: www.blackriverfallslibrary.org. *Libr Dir,* Tammy Peasley; E-mail: t.peasley@wrlsweb.org; *Libr Serv Coordr,* Vicki Fisher; E-mail: v.fisher@wrlsweb.org; *Youth Serv Coordr,* Rhonda Groth; E-mail: r.groth@wrlsweb.org
Founded 1872. Pop 16,000; Circ 83,847
Library Holdings: AV Mats 1,362; Large Print Bks 104; Bk Titles 25,481; Per Subs 71; Talking Bks 1,144
Subject Interests: County hist, Genealogy, Indians, Local hist
Automation Activity & Vendor Info: (Circulation) Horizon; (OPAC) Horizon; (Serials) Horizon
Wireless access
Mem of Winding Rivers Library System
Open Mon-Wed 10-7, Thurs & Fri 10-5, Sat 9-1

BLAIR

P BLAIR-PRESTON PUBLIC LIBRARY, 122 S Urberg Ave, 54616. (Mail add: PO Box 165, 54616-0165), SAN 317-9109. Tel: 608-989-2502. E-mail: blairpl@wrlsweb.org. Web Site: blairlibrary.wrlsweb.org. *Libr Dir,* Sarah Waldera
Founded 1916. Pop 1,800; Circ 15,000
Library Holdings: Bk Vols 8,500
Subject Interests: Rural
Automation Activity & Vendor Info: (Cataloging) Horizon; (Circulation) Horizon; (OPAC) Horizon
Wireless access
Mem of Winding Rivers Library System
Open Mon 12:30-7, Tues 11:30-6, Wed-Fri 12:30-6, Sat 10-12:30

BLANCHARDVILLE

P BLANCHARDVILLE PUBLIC LIBRARY*, 208 Mason St, 53506. SAN 317-9117. Tel: 608-523-2055. FAX: 608-523-4321. E-mail: brpldirector@swls.org. Web Site: blanchardville.com/village-government-2-2/blanchardville-public-library. *Dir,* Gretchen Dieterich; E-mail: gdieterich@swls.org
Pop 806; Circ 8,176
Library Holdings: Bk Vols 10,000; Per Subs 60
Subject Interests: Local hist
Automation Activity & Vendor Info: (Cataloging) Horizon; (Circulation) Horizon; (OPAC) Horizon
Wireless access
Mem of Southwest Wisconsin Library System
Open Mon 9-2 & 4:30-7:30, Wed 9-5, Thurs 12-7:30, Sat 9-12

BLOOMER

P BLOOMER PUBLIC LIBRARY*, G E Bleskacek Family Memorial, 1519 17th Ave, 54724. SAN 317-9125. Tel: 715-568-2384. FAX: 715-568-2387. Web Site: www.bloomerpubliclibrary.org. *Dir,* Megan Taylor; E-mail: taylor@bloomerpubliclibrary.org; Staff 3 (Non-MLS 3)
Founded 1916. Pop 4,711; Circ 44,468
Library Holdings: Bk Titles 18,975; Bk Vols 20,000; Per Subs 32
Automation Activity & Vendor Info: (Cataloging) Innovative Interfaces, Inc - Sierra; (Circulation) Innovative Interfaces, Inc - Sierra
Wireless access
Function: 24/7 Electronic res, 24/7 Online cat, Activity rm, Adult bk club, Children's prog, Computers for patron use, Electronic databases & coll, Home delivery & serv to seniorr ctr & nursing homes, Homebound delivery serv, ILL available, Internet access, Life-long learning prog for all ages, Magazines, Microfiche/film & reading machines, Movies, Music CDs, Online cat, Outreach serv, OverDrive digital audio bks, Photocopying/Printing, Preschool reading prog, Prog for adults, Prog for children & young adult, Ref & res, STEM programs, Story hour, Summer & winter reading prog, Tax forms, Teen prog, Wheelchair accessible
Mem of Inspiring & Facilitating Library Success (IFLS)
Open Mon, Wed & Fri 10-6, Tues & Thurs 10-8, Sat 9-12
Friends of the Library Group

BLOOMINGTON

P BLOOMINGTON PUBLIC LIBRARY*, 453 Canal St, 53804. (Mail add: PO Box 38, 53804-0038), SAN 317-9133. Tel: 608-994-2531. Web Site: swls-verso.auto-graphics.com/MVC. *Dir,* Kathy Atkins; E-mail: katkins@swls.org
Founded 1905. Pop 701; Circ 6,457

Library Holdings: Bk Vols 6,929; Per Subs 10
Automation Activity & Vendor Info: (Acquisitions) SirsiDynix; (Cataloging) SirsiDynix; (Circulation) SirsiDynix
Wireless access
Mem of Southwest Wisconsin Library System
Open Mon 9-1, Wed & Fri 9-5:30, Sat 9-Noon

BOSCOBEL

P HILDEBRAND MEMORIAL LIBRARY*, Boscobel Public Library, 1033 Wisconsin Ave, 53805. SAN 317-9141. Tel: 608-375-5723. E-mail: libraryboscobel@gmail.com. Web Site: boscobelwisconsin.com/community-life/library, boscolibrary.wordpress.com. *Libr Dir,* Janelle Miller; E-mail: bwdirector@swls.org
Founded 1906. Pop 3,047; Circ 30,000
Library Holdings: Bk Vols 21,500; Per Subs 36
Special Collections: Boscobel Dial Newspaper Coll, micro
Automation Activity & Vendor Info: (Circulation) Auto-Graphics, Inc
Wireless access
Mem of Southwest Wisconsin Library System
Partic in OCLC Online Computer Library Center, Inc
Open Mon, Tues & Thurs 9-6, Wed 9-7, Fri 9-5, Sat 10-2

S WISCONSIN SECURE PROGRAM FACILITY LIBRARY*, 1101 Morrison Dr, 53805. (Mail add: PO Box 1000, 53805-1000), SAN 378-3774. Tel: 608-375-5656, Ext 3105. Web Site: doc.wi.gov. *Prog Dir,* Trina Kroening-Skime; E-mail: trina.kroeningskime@wisconsin.gov; Staff 1 (MLS 1)
Library Holdings: High Interest/Low Vocabulary Bk Vols 168; Large Print Bks 3; Bk Titles 17,865; Bk Vols 17,891; Per Subs 10
Automation Activity & Vendor Info: (Circulation) EOS International; (OPAC) EOS International
Restriction: Closed stack, Not open to pub, Restricted access, Secured area only open to authorized personnel, Staff & inmates only

BOULDER JUNCTION

P BOULDER JUNCTION PUBLIC LIBRARY*, 5392 Park St, 54512-9605. (Mail add: PO Box 9, 54512-0009), SAN 324-7414. Tel: 715-385-2050. E-mail: info@boulderjunction.wislib.org. Web Site: boulderjunctionlibrary.org. *Libr Dir,* Cherie Sanderson; E-mail: csanderson@boulderjunction.wislib.org; Staff 2 (Non-MLS 2)
Founded 1976. Pop 975
Wireless access
Function: 24/7 Electronic res, 24/7 Online cat, Adult bk club, Art exhibits, AV serv, Bk club(s), Bks on CD, Children's prog, Computer training, Computers for patron use, Electronic databases & coll, Free DVD rentals, Genealogy discussion group, Govt ref serv, Home delivery & serv to seniorr ctr & nursing homes, ILL available, Internet access, Life-long learning prog for all ages, Magazines, Magnifiers for reading, Mail & tel request accepted, Meeting rooms, Movies, Music CDs, Online cat, Online ref, Outreach serv, OverDrive digital audio bks, Photocopying/Printing, Printer for laptops & handheld devices, Prog for adults, Prog for children & young adult, Ref serv available, Scanner, Senior outreach, Summer reading prog, Tax forms, Visual arts prog, Wheelchair accessible
Mem of Northern Waters Library Service
Open Mon, Wed & Fri 10-1, Tues 2-7, Thurs 10-7, Sat 10-1
Friends of the Library Group

BOYCEVILLE

P BOYCEVILLE PUBLIC LIBRARY*, 903 Main St, 54725-9595. SAN 317-915X. Tel: 715-643-2106. E-mail: boycevillepl@boycevillelibrary.org. Web Site: www.boycevillelibrary.org. *Dir,* Ginny Julson; E-mail: ginnyjulson@boycevillelibrary.org; Staff 4 (Non-MLS 4)
Founded 1900. Pop 2,100; Circ 27,000
Library Holdings: Bk Vols 9,030; Per Subs 34
Automation Activity & Vendor Info: (Circulation) Innovative Interfaces, Inc
Wireless access
Mem of Inspiring & Facilitating Library Success (IFLS)
Open Mon, Tues & Thurs 10-6, Wed & Fri 11-7, Sat 10-12:30
Friends of the Library Group

BRANDON

P BRANDON PUBLIC LIBRARY*, 117 E Main St, 53919. (Mail add: PO Box 208, 53919-0208), SAN 317-9168. Tel: 920-346-2350. FAX: 920-346-5895. Web Site: www.brandonlibrary.net. *Dir,* Christina Ross; E-mail: Ross@brandonlibrary.net; Staff 2 (MLS 1, Non-MLS 1)
Founded 1913. Pop 1,263; Circ 8,975
Library Holdings: AV Mats 429; Bks on Deafness & Sign Lang 13; High Interest/Low Vocabulary Bk Vols 143; Large Print Bks 142; Bk Titles 8,200; Per Subs 68; Talking Bks 353
Automation Activity & Vendor Info: (Circulation) Follett Software; (OPAC) Follett Software
Wireless access
Mem of Winnefox Library System
Open Mon-Thurs 12-6, Fri 12-5, Sat 9-Noon
Friends of the Library Group

BRILLION

P BRILLION PUBLIC LIBRARY*, 326 N Main St, 54110. SAN 317-9176. Tel: 920-756-3215. FAX: 920-756-3874. Reference E-mail: brref@mcls.lib.wi.us. Web Site: www.ci.brillion.wi.us/library. *Dir,* Rachel Hitt
Founded 1928. Pop 3,000; Circ 7,800
Library Holdings: Audiobooks 1,751; DVDs 3,319; e-books 122,211; Electronic Media & Resources 29,410; Bk Titles 31,511; Per Subs 151; Spec Interest Per Sub 112
Automation Activity & Vendor Info: (Cataloging) SirsiDynix; (Circulation) SirsiDynix; (ILL) Auto-Graphics, Inc; (OPAC) SirsiDynix-WorkFlows; (Serials) SirsiDynix
Wireless access
Mem of Manitowoc-Calumet Library System
Special Services for the Blind - Bks on CD
Open Mon 8-8, Tues 9-8, Wed & Thurs Noon-8, Fri Noon-6, Sat 9-Noon (Sept-June); Mon 8-8, Tues & Wed 9-8, Thurs Noon-8, Fri Noon-6 (July-Aug)
Restriction: Access for corporate affiliates
Friends of the Library Group

BRODHEAD

P BRODHEAD MEMORIAL PUBLIC LIBRARY, 1207 25th St, 53520. SAN 317-9184. Tel: 608-897-4070. Web Site: www.brodheadlibrary.org. *Dir,* Stuart Bisbee; E-mail: sbisbee@brodheadlibrary.org; *Asst Dir,* Crystal Willegal; *Outreach & Programming Librn,* Sarah Carpenter
Founded 1909. Pop 3,200; Circ 37,132
Library Holdings: Bk Titles 31,600; Per Subs 67
Wireless access
Mem of South Central Library System
Open Mon-Fri 9-6, Sat 9-12
Friends of the Library Group

BROOKFIELD

P BROOKFIELD PUBLIC LIBRARY*, 1900 N Calhoun Rd, 53005. SAN 317-9192. Tel: 262-782-4140. FAX: 262-796-6670. TDD: 262-796-6714. E-mail: brookfieldpubliclibrary@ci.brookfield.wi.us. Web Site: www.ci.brookfield.wi.us/38/library. *Libr Dir,* Cathy Tuttrup; E-mail: tuttrup@ci.brookfield.wi.us; *Dep Libr Dir,* Betsy Bleck; *Tech Serv Mgr,* Sue Brown; *Circ Supvr,* Kim Sagan; Staff 29.4 (MLS 8.7, Non-MLS 20.7)
Founded 1960. Pop 41,000; Circ 543,095
Library Holdings: AV Mats 27,789; Bk Vols 156,011; Per Subs 226
Special Collections: Frank Urban Coll (Railroad History & Sherlock Holmes). Oral History
Automation Activity & Vendor Info: (Serials) Innovative Interfaces, Inc
Wireless access
Publications: BrookBytes (Newsletter)
Mem of Bridges Library System
Open Mon-Thurs 9-9, Fri & Sat 9-5, Sun (Sept-May) 1-4
Friends of the Library Group

S INTERNATIONAL FOUNDATION OF EMPLOYEE BENEFIT PLANS*, Information Center, 18700 W Bluemound Rd, 53045-2936. SAN 317-9214. Tel: 262-786-6710, Ext 5. Toll Free Tel: 888-334-3327, Ext 5. FAX: 262-786-8780. E-mail: infocenter@ifebp.org. Web Site: www.ifebp.org. *Mgr, Ref Serv, Res Serv,* Jennifer M Lucey; E-mail: jlucey@ifebp.org; Staff 5 (MLS 3, Non-MLS 2)
Founded 1970
Library Holdings: e-journals 50; Bk Vols 4,800; Per Subs 250
Subject Interests: Employee benefits, Ins, Pensions
Automation Activity & Vendor Info: (Acquisitions) Inmagic, Inc.; (Cataloging) Inmagic, Inc.; (Circulation) Inmagic, Inc.; (OPAC) Inmagic, Inc.; (Serials) Inmagic, Inc.
Wireless access
Function: Ref serv available, Res libr
Restriction: Lending to staff only, Mem only, Open to others by appt

S HOWARD C RAETHER LIBRARY*, 13625 Bishop's Dr, 53005. SAN 328-3062. Tel: 262-789-1880. Toll Free Tel: 800-228-6332. FAX: 262-789-6977. E-mail: nfda@nfda.org. Web Site: nfda.org/about-nfda/research-and-information. *Associate Dir of Education,* Sara Moss; E-mail: smoss@nfda.org; *Sr Libr Spec,* Jacklyn Ellis; E-mail: jellis@nfda.org. Subject Specialists: *Educ,* Jacklyn Ellis; Staff 1 (MLS 1)
Founded 1998
Library Holdings: Bk Vols 2,000
Special Collections: Books on Dying, Death & Grief (1400's-1900's)
Subject Interests: Death

Wireless access
Function: Res libr
Restriction: Not a lending libr, Open by appt only

BROWN DEER

P BROWN DEER PUBLIC LIBRARY*, 5600 W Bradley Rd, 53223-3510. SAN 317-9230. Tel: 414-357-0106. Reference E-mail: BDPL.Ref@mcfls.org. Web Site: www.browndeerwi.org/departments/brown-deer-public-library. *Dir,* Dana Andersen; E-mail: dana.andersen@mcfls.org; Staff 4 (MLS 4)
Founded 1969. Pop 14,000; Circ 311,563
Library Holdings: Bk Vols 78,500; Per Subs 200
Automation Activity & Vendor Info: (Acquisitions) Innovative Interfaces, Inc - Millennium; (Cataloging) Innovative Interfaces, Inc - Millennium; (Circulation) Innovative Interfaces, Inc - Millennium; (OPAC) Innovative Interfaces, Inc - Millennium; (Serials) Innovative Interfaces, Inc - Millennium
Wireless access
Mem of Milwaukee County Federated Library System
Open Mon-Thurs 10-7, Fri 10-5, Sat 10-2
Friends of the Library Group

BROWNSVILLE

P BROWNSVILLE PUBLIC LIBRARY*, 379 Main St, 53006. (Mail add: PO Box 248, 53006-0248), SAN 317-9249. Tel: 920-583-4325. FAX: 920-583-4325. E-mail: brownlib@monarchlibraries.org. Web Site: www.brownsville.lib.wi.us. *Dir,* Kristen Mielke; E-mail: kmielke@monarchlibraries.org; Staff 4 (Non-MLS 4)
Founded 1949. Pop 2,046; Circ 21,987
Library Holdings: DVDs 3,244; e-books 166,224; Bk Vols 18,858; Per Subs 34
Automation Activity & Vendor Info: (Cataloging) Innovative Interfaces, Inc; (Circulation) Innovative Interfaces, Inc; (OPAC) Innovative Interfaces, Inc
Wireless access
Function: 24/7 Electronic res, 24/7 Online cat, Activity rm, Adult bk club, Audiobks via web, AV serv, Bk club(s), Bks on CD, CD-ROM, Children's prog, Computers for patron use, Electronic databases & coll, Family literacy, Free DVD rentals, Holiday prog, Homebound delivery serv, ILL available, Internet access, Magazines, Meeting rooms, Movies, Music CDs, Online cat, Online info literacy tutorials on the web & in blackboard, Online ref, OverDrive digital audio bks, Photocopying/Printing, Preschool outreach, Preschool reading prog, Prog for adults, Prog for children & young adult, Ref serv available, Scanner, Senior outreach, Spanish lang bks, Spoken cassettes & CDs, STEM programs, Story hour, Summer reading prog, Tax forms, Teen prog, Wheelchair accessible, Workshops
Mem of Monarch Library System
Open Mon, Tues & Thurs 1-7, Wed & Fri 3-6, Sat (Sept-May) 10-Noon

BRUCE

P BRUCE AREA LIBRARY*, 102 W River St, 54819. (Mail add: PO Box 277, 54819), SAN 376-6721. Tel: 715-868-2005. E-mail: brucepl@bruceal.org. Web Site: bruceal.org. *Dir,* Kathryn Stempf; E-mail: stempf@bruceal.org; Staff 1 (Non-MLS 1)
Founded 1985. Pop 2,700; Circ 8,181
Library Holdings: AV Mats 1,000; Bks on Deafness & Sign Lang 10; Large Print Bks 671; Bk Titles 15,000; Per Subs 20; Talking Bks 357
Automation Activity & Vendor Info: (Cataloging) Horizon; (Circulation) Horizon
Wireless access
Mem of Inspiring & Facilitating Library Success (IFLS)
Open Mon, Wed & Fri 10-2, Tues & Thurs 1-5
Friends of the Library Group

BURLINGTON

P BURLINGTON PUBLIC LIBRARY*, 166 E Jefferson St, 53105. SAN 317-9257. Tel: 262-342-1130. Web Site: www.burlingtonlibrary.org. *Libr Dir,* Joe Davies; E-mail: director@burlington.lib.wi.us; *Adult Serv,* Jen Melchi; E-mail: jmelchi@burlington.lib.wi.us; *Ch Serv,* Emily Laidley; E-mail: elaidley@burlington.lib.wi.us; Staff 4 (MLS 3, Non-MLS 1)
Founded 1908. Pop 18,859; Circ 200,000
Library Holdings: Audiobooks 1,700; CDs 1,300; DVDs 5,700; Large Print Bks 2,500; Bk Vols 62,000; Per Subs 117
Special Collections: Church of the Latter Day Saints - Strangite (Strangite Mormon Newspapers & Chronicles)
Automation Activity & Vendor Info: (Acquisitions) SirsiDynix; (Cataloging) SirsiDynix; (Circulation) SirsiDynix; (OPAC) SirsiDynix; (Serials) SirsiDynix
Wireless access
Mem of Prairie Lakes Library System (PLLS)
Partic in Wiscat
Open Mon-Thurs 9-8, Fri 9-6, Sat 9-4
Friends of the Library Group

BUTLER

P BUTLER PUBLIC LIBRARY*, 12808 W Hampton Ave, 53007. SAN 317-9273. Tel: 262-783-2535. E-mail: referencebutler@gmail.com. Web Site: www.butler.lib.wi.us. *Dir,* Genavieve Danes; E-mail: director@butler.lib.wi.us; *Youth Serv Librn,* Melissa Paap-Young; E-mail: mpaapyoung@butler.lib.wi.us
Founded 1964. Pop 1,800
Library Holdings: Bk Vols 22,000; Per Subs 95
Wireless access
Mem of Bridges Library System
Open Mon, Wed & Fri 11-5, Tues & Thurs 11-7, Sat 11-3
Friends of the Library Group

CABLE

P FOREST LODGE LIBRARY*, 13450 County Hwy M, 54821. (Mail add: PO Box 176, 54821-0176), SAN 317-9281. Tel: 715-798-3189. E-mail: cablelibrary@cable.wislib.org. Web Site: cable.wislib.org. *Dir,* Kristine Lendved; E-mail: klendved@cable.wislib.org
Pop 1,000; Circ 7,500
Library Holdings: Bk Titles 8,000; Per Subs 30
Subject Interests: Local hist, Natural hist
Mem of Northern Waters Library Service
Open Mon-Thurs 10-6, Fri 10-5, Sat 10-3
Friends of the Library Group

CADOTT

P CADOTT COMMUNITY LIBRARY*, 331 N Main St, 54727. (Mail add: PO Box 68, 54727-0068), SAN 317-929X. Tel: 715-289-4950. FAX: 715-289-3149. E-mail: cadottpl@cadottlibrary.org. Web Site: www.cadottlibrary.org. *Dir,* Samantha Johnson; E-mail: johnson@cadottlibrary.org; Staff 1 (Non-MLS 1)
Founded 1955. Pop 3,200; Circ 27,718
Jan 2021-Dec 2021 Income $88,203, City $47,000, County $39,719, Other $1,484. Mats Exp $10,055, Books $7,330, Per/Ser (Incl. Access Fees) $150, AV Mat $2,400. Sal $63,066
Library Holdings: AV Mats 6,345; Bk Vols 17,634; Per Subs 14
Special Collections: Oral History
Automation Activity & Vendor Info: (Acquisitions) Innovative Interfaces, Inc; (Cataloging) Innovative Interfaces, Inc; (Circulation) Innovative Interfaces, Inc; (OPAC) Innovative Interfaces, Inc
Wireless access
Function: Adult bk club, ILL available, Photocopying/Printing, Prog for children & young adult, Summer reading prog
Mem of Inspiring & Facilitating Library Success (IFLS)
Open Mon, Thurs & Fri 12-5, Tues & Wed 10-6, Sat 10-2
Friends of the Library Group

CAMBRIA

P JANE MORGAN MEMORIAL LIBRARY*, 109 W Edgewater St, 53923. (Mail add: PO Box 477, 53923-0477), SAN 324-7902. Tel: 920-348-4030. FAX: 920-348-4030. Web Site: www.JMML.org. *Dir,* Amanda Wakeman; E-mail: awakeman@jmml.org
Pop 2,500
Library Holdings: Bk Vols 9,945; Per Subs 50
Subject Interests: Local community, Welsh
Wireless access
Mem of South Central Library System
Open Mon & Wed 9-1 & 3-8, Tues, Thurs, & Fri 9-1 & 3-5, Sat 9-Noon

CAMBRIDGE

P CAMBRIDGE COMMUNITY LIBRARY*, 101 Spring Water Alley, 53523. (Mail add: PO Box 490, 53523-0490), SAN 325-1934. Tel: 608-423-3900. FAX: 608-423-7330. E-mail: camlibmail@gmail.com. Web Site: www.cambridgelib.org. *Dir,* Samantha Seeman; E-mail: sseeman@cambridgelib.org; Staff 5 (MLS 1, Non-MLS 4)
Founded 1978. Pop 4,800; Circ 50,000
Library Holdings: AV Mats 1,696; Bk Titles 18,795; Per Subs 1,218
Subject Interests: Local hist
Automation Activity & Vendor Info: (Cataloging) LibLime Koha; (Circulation) LibLime Koha; (ILL) LibLime Koha; (Serials) LibLime Koha
Wireless access
Mem of South Central Library System
Partic in Library Interchange Network
Open Mon-Wed 10-6, Thurs 12-8, Fri 10-5, Sat 9-Noon
Friends of the Library Group

CAMERON

P CAMERON AREA PUBLIC LIBRARY*, 506 Main St, 54822. (Mail add: PO Box 343, 54822-0343), SAN 377-9300. Tel: 715-458-2267. FAX: 715-458-2267. E-mail: cameronpl@cameronpl.org. Web Site: cameronpl.org. *Dir,* Dawn Ayers
Pop 1,425; Circ 24,069
Library Holdings: Audiobooks 463; Bks on Deafness & Sign Lang 12; Braille Volumes 33; CDs 84; DVDs 636; e-books 67,555; e-books 67,555; Electronic Media & Resources 372; Electronic Media & Resources 372; Large Print Bks 435; Bk Titles 9,056; Per Subs 24; Videos 600
Automation Activity & Vendor Info: (Acquisitions) Innovative Interfaces, Inc; (Cataloging) Innovative Interfaces, Inc; (Circulation) Innovative Interfaces, Inc; (OPAC) Innovative Interfaces, Inc; (Serials) Innovative Interfaces, Inc
Wireless access
Mem of Inspiring & Facilitating Library Success (IFLS)
Open Mon-Fri 11-6, Sat 10-12
Friends of the Library Group

CAMPBELLSPORT

P CAMPBELLSPORT PUBLIC LIBRARY*, 220 N Helena St, 53010-0405. (Mail add: PO Box 405, 53010-0405), SAN 317-9303. Tel: 920-533-8534. FAX: 920-533-8712. Web Site: www.campbellsportlibrary.org. *Dir,* Stephanie Remillard; E-mail: director@campbellsportlibrary.org
Founded 1929. Pop 1,700; Circ 19,421
Library Holdings: Bk Vols 12,000; Per Subs 30
Wireless access
Mem of Winnefox Library System
Open Mon & Tues 9-7, Wed & Fri 9-6, Sat 9-Noon

CASHTON

P CASHTON MEMORIAL LIBRARY*, 720 Broadway St, 54619. (Mail add: PO Box 234, 54619-0234), SAN 377-9610. Tel: 608-654-5465. E-mail: cashtonlib@wrlsweb.org. Web Site: www.wrlsweb.org/cashton. *Librn,* Jill Bjornstad
Library Holdings: Bk Titles 7,000; Per Subs 15
Automation Activity & Vendor Info: (Cataloging) Follett Software; (Circulation) Follett Software
Wireless access
Mem of Winding Rivers Library System
Open Mon & Fri 10-5:30, Tues & Wed 9-5:30, Sat 9-Noon
Friends of the Library Group

CASSVILLE

P ECKSTEIN MEMORIAL LIBRARY*, 1034 E Dewey St, 53806. (Mail add: PO Box 450, 53806), SAN 317-9311. Tel: 608-725-5838. FAX: 608-725-5152. Web Site: ecksteinmemoriallibrary.wordpress.com. *Dir,* Marie McGinnis; E-mail: mmcginnis@swls.org; *Ch,* Patti Wood; E-mail: pwood@swls.org
Founded 1919. Pop 1,085; Circ 14,275
Library Holdings: Audiobooks 410; DVDs 1,697; Large Print Bks 174; Bk Vols 16,251; Per Subs 39
Automation Activity & Vendor Info: (Cataloging) Auto-Graphics, Inc; (Circulation) Auto-Graphics, Inc; (OPAC) Auto-Graphics, Inc
Wireless access
Function: 24/7 Electronic res, 24/7 Online cat, Adult bk club, Audiobks on Playaways & MP3, Audiobks via web, Bks on CD, Children's prog, Computers for patron use, Free DVD rentals, ILL available, Internet access, Laminating, Magazines, Magnifiers for reading, Mango lang, Meeting rooms, Microfiche/film & reading machines, Movies, Music CDs, Online cat, OverDrive digital audio bks, Photocopying/Printing, Prog for adults, Prog for children & young adult, Scanner, Story hour, Summer reading prog, Tax forms
Mem of Southwest Wisconsin Library System
Open Mon & Thurs 10-5, Wed 11-7, Sat 9-Noon

CEDAR GROVE

P CEDAR GROVE PUBLIC LIBRARY*, 131 Van Altena Ave, 53013. (Mail add: PO Box 287, 53013-0287), SAN 317-932X. Tel: 920-668-6834. FAX: 920-668-8744. Web Site: www.cedargrovelibrary.net. *Dir,* Nicole Lynaugh; E-mail: nlynaugh@monarchlibraries.org; Staff 1 (Non-MLS 1)
Founded 1944
Library Holdings: AV Mats 3,210; Bk Vols 31,199; Per Subs 66; Talking Bks 1,858
Special Collections: Small Dutch Heritage Coll
Automation Activity & Vendor Info: (Cataloging) Innovative Interfaces, Inc; (Circulation) Innovative Interfaces, Inc; (OPAC) Innovative Interfaces, Inc
Wireless access
Mem of Monarch Library System
Open Mon-Thurs 10-8, Fri 10-5, Sat 10-12
Friends of the Library Group

CEDARBURG

P CEDARBURG PUBLIC LIBRARY*, W63 N589 Hanover Ave, 53012. SAN 317-9338. Tel: 262-375-7640. FAX: 262-375-7618. Web Site: www.cedarburglibrary.org. *Dir,* Linda Pierschalla; Tel: 262-375-7640, Ext 202, E-mail: lpierschalla@cedarburglibrary.org; *Asst Dir,* David Nimmer; Tel: 262-375-7640, Ext 201, E-mail: dnimmer@cedarburglibrary.org; Staff 13 (MLS 4, Non-MLS 9)
Founded 1911. Pop 18,000; Circ 205,144
Library Holdings: CDs 1,177; DVDs 1,084; Large Print Bks 1,621; Bk Titles 73,000; Bk Vols 75,872; Per Subs 205; Talking Bks 1,852; Videos 3,594
Subject Interests: Civil War, Popular fiction
Automation Activity & Vendor Info: (Circulation) SirsiDynix; (OPAC) Innovative Interfaces, Inc
Wireless access
Mem of Monarch Library System
Open Mon-Thurs 9:30-8, Fri 9:30-5, Sat 9-4
Friends of the Library Group

CENTURIA

P CENTURIA PUBLIC LIBRARY*, 409 Fourth St, 54824-7468. (Mail add: PO Box 370, 54824-0370), SAN 376-6713. Tel: 715-646-2630. FAX: 715-646-2630. Web Site: www.centurialibrary.org. *Dir,* Anna Griffin; E-mail: director@centurialibrary.org; *Asst Librn,* Melissa Schallenberger; Staff 2 (MLS 1, Non-MLS 1)
Library Holdings: Bk Vols 7,300; Per Subs 20
Wireless access
Mem of Inspiring & Facilitating Library Success (IFLS)
Open Mon, Wed & Fri 12-5, Tues & Thurs 12-7, Sat 10-Noon

CHETEK

P CALHOUN MEMORIAL LIBRARY*, Chetek Library, 321 Moore St, 54728. (Mail add: PO Box 25, 54728-0025), SAN 317-9346. Tel: 715-924-3195. FAX: 715-925-2052. Web Site: www.calhounmemoriallibrary.org. *Dir,* Carol Burnham; E-mail: burnham@calhounmemoriallibrary.org
Founded 1888. Pop 4,000; Circ 39,000
Library Holdings: AV Mats 1,500; Braille Volumes 46; Bk Titles 15,764; Per Subs 40; Talking Bks 1,003
Special Collections: Children's Books in Braille
Automation Activity & Vendor Info: (Acquisitions) Innovative Interfaces, Inc; (Cataloging) Innovative Interfaces, Inc; (ILL) Innovative Interfaces, Inc; (OPAC) Innovative Interfaces, Inc
Open Mon, Wed & Fri 9-6, Tues & Thurs 1-6, Sat 9-Noon
Friends of the Library Group

CHILTON

P CHILTON PUBLIC LIBRARY*, 221 Park St, 53014. SAN 317-9354. Tel: 920-849-4414. FAX: 920-849-2370. E-mail: chiltonpubliclibrary@gmail.com. Web Site: www.chiltonlibrary.org. *Libr Dir,* Glenny Whitcomb; E-mail: director@chiltonlibrary.org; Staff 5.3 (Non-MLS 5.3)
Founded 1933. Pop 6,859; Circ 46,600
Library Holdings: Bk Vols 41,204; Per Subs 170
Special Collections: Board Game Coll; Parent/Teachers Coll; Wis Coll
Automation Activity & Vendor Info: (Cataloging) SirsiDynix; (Circulation) SirsiDynix; (OPAC) SirsiDynix
Wireless access
Mem of Manitowoc-Calumet Library System
Open Mon-Thurs 10-8, Fri 10-6, Sat 10-1
Friends of the Library Group

CHIPPEWA FALLS

P CHIPPEWA FALLS PUBLIC LIBRARY*, 105 W Central St, 54729-2397. SAN 317-9362. Tel: 715-723-1146. Administration E-mail: libraryadmin@mycfpl.org. Information Services E-mail: infoservice@mycfpl.org. Web Site: www.chippewafallslibrary.org. *Dir,* Joe Niese; E-mail: jniese@mycfpl.org; *Children's Serv Coordr,* Jessi Peterson; *Circ Serv Coordr,* Brandi Smith; *Info Serv Coordr,* Howard Rakes; *Tech Serv Coordr,* Jeanne Peterson; Staff 11 (MLS 2, Non-MLS 9)
Founded 1893. Circ 278,925
Library Holdings: AV Mats 7,348; e-books 13,385; High Interest/Low Vocabulary Bk Vols 200; Bk Titles 6,074; Bk Vols 94,558; Per Subs 215; Videos 4,192
Special Collections: Local History Coll; Wisconsin Historical Coll, bks, fs, microfilm
Automation Activity & Vendor Info: (Acquisitions) Innovative Interfaces, Inc; (Cataloging) Innovative Interfaces, Inc; (Circulation) Innovative

Interfaces, Inc; (OPAC) Innovative Interfaces, Inc; (Serials) Innovative Interfaces, Inc
Wireless access
Function: 24/7 Online cat, Adult bk club, Audiobks on Playaways & MP3, Audiobks via web, AV serv, Bk club(s), Bks on CD, Chess club, Children's prog, Computers for patron use, E-Readers, Equip loans & repairs, Free DVD rentals, Holiday prog, Home delivery & serv to seniorr ctr & nursing homes, Homebound delivery serv, ILL available, Internet access, Magazines, Magnifiers for reading, Mail & tel request accepted, Microfiche/film & reading machines, Movies, Music CDs, Online cat, OverDrive digital audio bks, Prog for adults, Prog for children & young adult, Ref & res, Ref serv available, Res libr, Scanner, Story hour, Summer reading prog, Tax forms, Teen prog, Wheelchair accessible
Mem of Inspiring & Facilitating Library Success (IFLS)
Special Services for the Blind - Aids for in-house use
Open Mon-Thurs 9-7, Fri 9-5:30, Sat 9-1
Friends of the Library Group

CLEAR LAKE

P CLEAR LAKE PUBLIC LIBRARY*, 350 Fourth Ave, 54005. (Mail add: PO Box 365, 54005-0365), SAN 376-6705. Tel: 715-263-2802. E-mail: clearlakelib@clearlakelibrary.org. Web Site: www.clearlakelibrary.org. *Dir,* Christine LaFond; E-mail: clafond@clearlakelibrary.org; Staff 3.9 (MLS 2.2, Non-MLS 1.7)
Pop 142,536; Circ 19,906
Jan 2022-Dec 2022 Income $134,712; City $74,313, County $59,632, Locally Generated Income $767. Mats Exp $15,898, Books $10,478, Per/Ser (Incl. Access Fees) $958, Other Print Mats $132, AV Mat $4,330. Sal $54,223 (Prof $37,146)
Library Holdings: Audiobooks 1,649; Bks on Deafness & Sign Lang 10; DVDs 3,539; e-books 176,442; Large Print Bks 1,570; Bk Titles 14,628; Per Subs 40
Special Collections: Puzzles
Automation Activity & Vendor Info: (Acquisitions) Innovative Interfaces, Inc; (Cataloging) Innovative Interfaces, Inc; (Circulation) Innovative Interfaces, Inc; (OPAC) Innovative Interfaces, Inc; (Serials) Innovative Interfaces, Inc
Wireless access
Function: 24/7 Online cat, Bks on CD, Children's prog, Computer training, Computers for patron use, Family literacy, Home delivery & serv to seniorr ctr & nursing homes, Homebound delivery serv, ILL available, Internet access, Magazines, Mail & tel request accepted, Movies, Music CDs, Online cat, OverDrive digital audio bks, Photocopying/Printing, Preschool outreach, Prog for adults, Prog for children & young adult, Ref serv available, Scanner, Story hour, Summer reading prog, Tax forms, Telephone ref, Wheelchair accessible
Mem of Inspiring & Facilitating Library Success (IFLS)
Special Services for the Deaf - Assistive tech; Bks on deafness & sign lang; Closed caption videos; Sign lang interpreter upon request for prog
Special Services for the Blind - Accessible computers; Assistive/Adapted tech devices, equip & products; BiFolkal kits; Bks available with recordings; Bks on CD; Copier with enlargement capabilities; Extensive large print coll; Free checkout of audio mat; Home delivery serv; Internet workstation with adaptive software; Large print bks; Large screen computer & software; Playaways (bks on MP3)
Open Mon & Tues 9-7, Wed 10-7, Thurs & Fri 9-5

CLEVELAND

J LAKESHORE TECHNICAL COLLEGE LIBRARY*, 1290 North Ave, 53015. SAN 317-9389. Tel: 920-693-1130. E-mail: library@gotoltc.edu. Web Site: gotoltc.edu/library. *Library Servs Lead,* Ashley McHose; Tel: 920-693-1311, E-mail: ashley.mchose@gotoltc.edu; Staff 3 (MLS 2, Non-MLS 1)
Founded 1965. Enrl 2,500; Fac 85; Highest Degree: Associate
Library Holdings: e-books 100,000; Bk Titles 5,000; Per Subs 50
Special Collections: Diversity & Multicultural
Subject Interests: Criminal justice, Law enforcement, Nursing
Automation Activity & Vendor Info: (Cataloging) Ex Libris Group; (Circulation) Ex Libris Group; (Course Reserve) Ex Libris Group; (OPAC) Ex Libris Group; (Serials) Ex Libris Group
Wireless access
Function: Computers for patron use, Distance learning, Doc delivery serv, ILL available, Internet access, Learning ctr, Online cat, Online info literacy tutorials on the web & in blackboard, Online ref, Orientations, Outreach serv, Photocopying/Printing, Ref serv available, Scanner
Partic in OCLC Online Computer Library Center, Inc; WiLS; WISPALS Library Consortium
Open Mon-Thurs 7:30-5:30, Fri 7:30-3:30
Restriction: 24-hr pass syst for students only

CLINTON

P CLINTON PUBLIC LIBRARY*, 214 Mill St, 53525-9459. (Mail add: PO Box 487, 53525-0487), SAN 317-9397. Tel: 608-676-5569. FAX: 608-676-5607. Web Site: als.lib.wi.us/CPL. *Interim Dir,* Marybeth Miller; E-mail: miller.maribeth@als.lib.wi.us
Founded 1913
Library Holdings: Bk Vols 29,000; Per Subs 50
Automation Activity & Vendor Info: (Acquisitions) Innovative Interfaces, Inc; (Cataloging) Innovative Interfaces, Inc; (Circulation) Innovative Interfaces, Inc
Wireless access
Mem of Prairie Lakes Library System (PLLS)
Open Mon & Fri 8:30-5, Tues-Thurs 8:30-7:30, Sat 8:30-1
Friends of the Library Group

CLINTONVILLE

P CLINTONVILLE PUBLIC LIBRARY*, 75 Hemlock St, 54929-1461. SAN 317-9400. Tel: 715-823-4563. FAX: 715-823-7134. E-mail: cpl@clintonvillelibrary.org. Web Site: www.clintonvillelibrary.org. *Libr Dir,* Jamison Hein; Tel: 715-823-7132; *Youth Serv Librn,* Delanie Sharpe; Tel: 715-823-7133; Staff 3 (MLS 2, Non-MLS 1)
Founded 1905. Pop 4,543; Circ 125,223
Library Holdings: Audiobooks 3,197; AV Mats 874; e-books 17,194; Electronic Media & Resources 11,139; Bk Vols 63,007; Per Subs 149; Videos 4,960
Automation Activity & Vendor Info: (Cataloging) Innovative Interfaces, Inc - Millennium; (Circulation) Innovative Interfaces, Inc - Millennium; (OPAC) Innovative Interfaces, Inc; (Serials) Innovative Interfaces, Inc - Millennium
Wireless access
Function: Adult bk club, After school storytime, Audio & video playback equip for onsite use, Audiobks via web, Bks on cassette, Bks on CD, Children's prog, Computers for patron use, E-Reserves, Electronic databases & coll, Free DVD rentals, Homebound delivery serv, ILL available, Internet access, Large print keyboards, Magnifiers for reading, Microfiche/film & reading machines, Music CDs, Online cat, OverDrive digital audio bks, Photocopying/Printing, Preschool reading prog, Prog for adults, Prog for children & young adult, Ref & res, Scanner, Spanish lang bks, Spoken cassettes & CDs, Story hour, Summer reading prog, Tax forms, Teen prog, Telephone ref, VHS videos, Wheelchair accessible
Mem of Outagamie Waupaca Library System (OWLS)
Partic in OWLSnet
Open Mon-Thurs 9-8, Fri 9-5, Sat 9-1
Friends of the Library Group

COBB

P COBB PUBLIC LIBRARY*, 109 Mifflin St, 53526. SAN 317-9419. Tel: 608-623-2554. FAX: 608-623-2554. Web Site: cobbplwi.wordpress.com. *Dir,* Linda Gard; E-mail: cobbpldirector@swls.org
Founded 1931. Pop 442; Circ 7,972
Library Holdings: Bk Vols 5,833
Wireless access
Mem of Southwest Wisconsin Library System
Open Mon & Wed 4-7, Tues & Thurs 9:30-5:30, Sat 9:30-12:30

COLBY

P COLBY COMMUNITY LIBRARY, 505 W Spence St, 54421. (Mail add: PO Box 318, 54421-0318), SAN 317-9427. Tel: 715-223-2000. Web Site: colbypubliclibrary.org. *Dir,* Vicky Calmes; E-mail: director@colbypubliclibrary.org; Staff 1 (Non-MLS 1)
Founded 1879. Pop 1,823
Wireless access
Function: 24/7 Online cat, Adult bk club, Bk club(s), Bks on CD, Children's prog, Computers for patron use, Electronic databases & coll, Family literacy, Free DVD rentals, Holiday prog, Home delivery & serv to seniorr ctr & nursing homes, Internet access, Laminating, Magazines, Microfiche/film & reading machines, Movies, Online cat, Photocopying/Printing, Preschool outreach, Preschool reading prog, Prog for adults, Ref & res, Ref serv available, Spanish lang bks, STEM programs, Story hour, Study rm, Summer & winter reading prog, Summer reading prog, Tax forms, Teen prog, Wheelchair accessible
Partic in Wisconsin Valley Library Service
Friends of the Library Group

COLFAX

P COLFAX PUBLIC LIBRARY*, 613 Main St, 54730. (Mail add: PO Box 525, 54730), SAN 317-9435. Tel: 715-962-4334. FAX: 715-962-2221. Web Site: www.colfaxpubliclibrary.org. *Circ Librn, Libr Dir,* Lisa Bragg-Hurlburt; E-mail: hurlburt@colfaxpubliclibrary.org
Founded 1901. Pop 1,166; Circ 34,098
Library Holdings: Bk Vols 12,000; Per Subs 41

Wireless access
Function: 24/7 Electronic res, 24/7 Online cat, Accelerated reader prog, Adult bk club, Audiobks via web, Bk club(s), Bks on CD, Children's prog, Citizenship assistance, Computer training, Computers for patron use, Electronic databases & coll, Free DVD rentals, Holiday prog, Home delivery & serv to seniorr ctr & nursing homes, Homebound delivery serv, ILL available, Internet access, Magazines, Movies, Music CDs, Online cat, OverDrive digital audio bks, Photocopying/Printing, Preschool outreach, Preschool reading prog, Printer for laptops & handheld devices, Prof lending libr, Prog for adults, Prog for children & young adult, Ref serv available, Serves people with intellectual disabilities, Spanish lang bks, Spoken cassettes & CDs, Story hour, Summer & winter reading prog, Summer reading prog, Wheelchair accessible
Mem of Inspiring & Facilitating Library Success (IFLS)
Open Mon & Thurs 1-8, Tues, Wed & Fri 10-5, Sat 10-2

COLOMA

P COLOMA PUBLIC LIBRARY*, 155 Front St, 54930-9670. (Mail add: PO Box 99, 54930-0099). Tel: 715-228-2530. FAX: 715-228-2532. Web Site: www.colomalibrary.org. *Dir,* Preston DeBolt; E-mail: director@colomalibrary.org; Staff 3 (Non-MLS 3)
Pop 1,200; Circ 28,183
Library Holdings: Bk Vols 12,000; Per Subs 50
Mem of Winnefox Library System
Open Mon 10-5, Wed & Fri 10-5, Thurs 10-7, Sat 10-1; Mon 10-5, Tues 10-5, Wed & Fri 10-5, Thurs 10-7, Sat 10-1 (Summer)
Friends of the Library Group

COLUMBUS

P COLUMBUS PUBLIC LIBRARY*, 223 W James St, 53925-1572. SAN 317-9443. Tel: 920-623-5910. FAX: 920-623-5928. E-mail: info@columbuspubliclibrary.info. Web Site: www.columbuspubliclibrary.info. *Dir,* Amanda Wakeman; E-mail: amanda@columbuspubliclibrary.info; Staff 8 (MLS 2, Non-MLS 6)
Founded 1877. Pop 15,000; Circ 104,722
Jan 2016-Dec 2016 Income $383,716, State $1,987, City $263,250, Federal $218, County $104,414, Locally Generated Income $13,847. Mats Exp $44,392, Books $34,849, AV Mat $5,247, Electronic Ref Mat (Incl. Access Fees) $4,296. Sal $204,309 (Prof $94,592)
Library Holdings: AV Mats 5,820; e-books 149,771; e-journals 52; Electronic Media & Resources 36,359; Bk Vols 23,904; Per Subs 57; Videos 3,207
Special Collections: Local History (Richard Stare Coll), articles; Local Newspapers Coll 1850-present, microfilm
Subject Interests: Local hist
Automation Activity & Vendor Info: (Cataloging) OpenAccess Software, Inc; (Circulation) LibLime Koha; (Discovery) LibLime Koha; (ILL) LibLime Koha; (OPAC) LibLime Koha
Wireless access
Function: 24/7 Electronic res, 24/7 Online cat, Activity rm, Adult bk club, Adult literacy prog, After school storytime, Archival coll, Audio & video playback equip for onsite use, Audiobks on Playaways & MP3, Audiobks via web, Bilingual assistance for Spanish patrons, Bk club(s), Bks on CD, CD-ROM, Children's prog, Citizenship assistance, Computer training, Computers for patron use, Digital talking bks, E-Readers, E-Reserves, Electronic databases & coll, Family literacy, Free DVD rentals, Genealogy discussion group, Holiday prog, Home delivery & serv to seniorr ctr & nursing homes, Homebound delivery serv, ILL available, Instruction & testing, Internet access, Life-long learning prog for all ages, Literacy & newcomer serv, Magazines, Magnifiers for reading, Mail & tel request accepted, Mail loans to mem, Meeting rooms, Microfiche/film & reading machines, Movies, Music CDs, Notary serv, Online cat, Online ref, Orientations, Outreach serv, Outside serv via phone, mail, e-mail & web, OverDrive digital audio bks, Photocopying/Printing, Preschool outreach, Preschool reading prog, Printer for laptops & handheld devices, Prog for adults, Prog for children & young adult, Ref & res, Ref serv available, Scanner, Senior computer classes, Senior outreach, Serves people with intellectual disabilities, Spanish lang bks, Story hour, Summer reading prog, Tax forms, Teen prog, Telephone ref, Wheelchair accessible, Workshops, Writing prog
Mem of South Central Library System
Partic in Library Interchange Network
Special Services for the Deaf - Closed caption videos
Special Services for the Blind - Aids for in-house use; Bks available with recordings; Bks on CD; Bks on flash-memory cartridges; Digital talking bk; Digital talking bk machines; Large print bks; Magnifiers; Playaways (bks on MP3); Talking bks
Open Mon-Thurs 9-7, Fri 9-5, Sat 9-1
Friends of the Library Group

COON VALLEY

P KNUTSON MEMORIAL LIBRARY*, 500 Central Ave, 54623. (Mail add: PO Box 99, 54623-0099). Tel: 608-452-3757. E-mail: cvlib@wrlsweb.org. Web Site: coonvalleylibrary.wrlsweb.org. *Dir,* Position Currently Open
Pop 1,727
Library Holdings: Bk Titles 9,000; Per Subs 50
Wireless access
Mem of Winding Rivers Library System
Open Mon & Wed 1-6, Tues 1-8, Fri 10-2, Sat 10-1
Friends of the Library Group

CORNELL

P CORNELL PUBLIC LIBRARY*, 117 N Third St, 54732, (Mail add: PO Box 796, 54732-0796), SAN 317-9451. Tel: 715-239-3709. FAX: 715-239-3704. E-mail: publiclibrary@cornellpl.org. Web Site: cornellpl.org. *Libr Dir,* Sharon Shepard
Founded 1928. Pop 3,500; Circ 28,688
Library Holdings: Audiobooks 382; CDs 962; DVDs 2,777; Large Print Bks 580; Bk Titles 9,979; Per Subs 42
Special Collections: Local History Coll
Automation Activity & Vendor Info: (Circulation) Follett Software
Wireless access
Mem of Inspiring & Facilitating Library Success (IFLS)
Open Mon 1-7, Tues 1-5, Wed 3-8, Thurs 10-5, Fri & Sat 10-2
Friends of the Library Group

CRANDON

P CRANDON PUBLIC LIBRARY*, 110 W Polk St, 54520-1458. SAN 317-946X. Tel: 715-478-3784. FAX: 715-478-3784. Web Site: www.crandonpl.org. *Dir,* Stephanie Schmidt; E-mail: director@crandonpl.org
Founded 1910. Pop 9,044; Circ 18,364
Library Holdings: Bk Vols 17,000; Per Subs 27
Wireless access
Partic in Wisconsin Valley Library Service
Open Mon-Wed & Fri 9-5, Thurs 9-7, Sat 9-Noon
Friends of the Library Group

CROSS PLAINS

P ROSEMARY GARFOOT PUBLIC LIBRARY*, 2107 Julius St, 53528. SAN 317-9478. Tel: 608-798-3881. FAX: 608-798-0196. E-mail: csplib@rgpl.org. Web Site: www.rgpl.org. *Dir,* Pam Bosben; E-mail: pbosben@rgpl.org; *Asst Dir,* Kelly McKewin; E-mail: kmckewin@rgpl.org; *Circ Mgr,* Heather Gallina; E-mail: hgallina@rgpl.org; *Circ Mgr,* Marlina Polk McGiveron; E-mail: mpolkmcgiveron@rgpl.org; *Youth Serv Librn,* Catherine Baer; E-mail: cabaer@rgpl.org
Founded 1964. Pop 4,000
Library Holdings: Bk Titles 25,389; Per Subs 125
Special Collections: State Document Depository
Wireless access
Mem of South Central Library System
Open Mon-Thurs 9-7, Fri 9-5, Sat 10-2
Friends of the Library Group

CUDAHY

P CUDAHY FAMILY LIBRARY*, 3500 Library Dr, 53110. (Mail add: PO Box 100450, 53110-6107), SAN 317-9494. Tel: 414-769-2244. FAX: 414-769-2252. Reference E-mail: cpl.reference@mcfls.org. Web Site: www.cudahyfamilylibrary.org. *Libr Dir,* Rebecca Roepke; E-mail: rebecca.roepke@mcfls.org; Staff 4 (MLS 4)
Founded 1906. Pop 18,429; Circ 239,562
Library Holdings: AV Mats 14,863; Bk Vols 100,000; Per Subs 200
Subject Interests: Local hist
Automation Activity & Vendor Info: (Cataloging) Innovative Interfaces, Inc; (Circulation) Innovative Interfaces, Inc; (OPAC) Innovative Interfaces, Inc; (Serials) Innovative Interfaces, Inc
Wireless access
Mem of Milwaukee County Federated Library System
Open Mon-Thurs 10-8, Fri & Sat 9-5, Sun Noon-4 (Winter); Mon-Thurs 10-8, Fri 9-5, Sat & Sun Noon-4 (Summer)
Friends of the Library Group

CUMBERLAND

P THOMAS ST ANGELO PUBLIC LIBRARY*, 1305 Second Ave, 54829. (Mail add: PO Box 97, 54829), SAN 317-9524. Tel: 715-822-2767. E-mail: cupl@cumberlandpl.org. Web Site: cumberlandpl.org. *Dir,* Rob Ankarlo; *Librn,* Barb Powell; *Adult Serv,* Diana Ostness; *Ch Serv,* Julie Anderson
Founded 1898. Pop 2,000; Circ 45,506
Library Holdings: Bk Vols 21,000; Per Subs 61

Automation Activity & Vendor Info: (Cataloging) SirsiDynix; (Circulation) SirsiDynix; (ILL) SirsiDynix; (OPAC) SirsiDynix
Wireless access
Mem of Inspiring & Facilitating Library Success (IFLS)
Open Mon, Wed & Fri 9-6, Tues & Thurs 9-8, Sat 9-1, Sun 1-4
Friends of the Library Group

DALLAS

P MCINTYRE MEMORIAL LIBRARY*, 208 Dallas St, 54733. (Mail add: PO Box 84, 54733-0084). Tel: 715-837-1186. E-mail: dplibrary@live.com. Web Site: www.dallaswi.com/library.htm. *Librn,* Kathy Guibord; *Librn,* Linda Jacobsen
Founded 1969. Pop 400; Circ 4,200
Library Holdings: Bk Titles 4,937; Bk Vols 5,012
Wireless access
Open Tues & Thurs 3-7, Sat 9-12
Friends of the Library Group

DARIEN

P DARIEN PUBLIC LIBRARY*, 47 Park Ave, 53114-0465. (Mail add: PO Box 490, 53114-0490), SAN 317-9540. Tel: 262-882-5155. FAX: 262-882-5157. Web Site: www.darien.lib.wi.us. *Librn,* Jeannine Heskett; E-mail: heskett@darien.lib.wi.us
Founded 1922. Pop 2,700
Library Holdings: Bk Vols 22,000
Automation Activity & Vendor Info: (Acquisitions) SirsiDynix; (Cataloging) SirsiDynix; (Circulation) SirsiDynix
Wireless access
Mem of Prairie Lakes Library System (PLLS)
Open Mon-Thurs 10-7, Sat 10-2
Friends of the Library Group

DARLINGTON

P JOHNSON PUBLIC LIBRARY*, 131 E Catherine St, 53530. SAN 317-9559. Tel: 608-776-4171. Web Site: www.johnsonpubliclibrary.com. *Libr Dir,* Candi Fitzsimons; E-mail: cfitzsimons@swls.org; *Ch,* Mary Jo Erickson; Staff 1 (MLS 1)
Pop 2,400; Circ 46,600
Library Holdings: Bk Titles 25,000; Bk Vols 30,000; Per Subs 95
Special Collections: Darlington Newspapers (1865-present), micro; Lafayette County Newspaper on micro; Parenting Coll
Automation Activity & Vendor Info: (Acquisitions) SirsiDynix; (Cataloging) SirsiDynix; (Circulation) SirsiDynix; (OPAC) SirsiDynix
Wireless access
Mem of Southwest Wisconsin Library System
Open Mon, Wed & Thurs 10-8, Tues & Fri 10-5:30, Sat 10-4
Friends of the Library Group

DE PERE

SR SAINT NORBERT ABBEY*, Augustine Library, 1016 N Broadway, 54115-2697. SAN 317-9575. Tel: 920-337-4354. *Librn & Archivist,* Karen E Mand; E-mail: karen.mand@norbertines.org; Staff 1 (Non-MLS 1)
Founded 1898
Jul 2021-Jun 2022 Income $7,600. Mats Exp $1,500. Sal $4,100
Library Holdings: Bk Titles 8,000; Bk Vols 11,200
Subject Interests: Archives, Bible, Canon law, Church hist, Monasticism, Philos, Premonstratensian hist, Relig orders, Theol
Automation Activity & Vendor Info: (Cataloging) OCLC Worldshare Management Services; (OPAC) OCLC Worldshare Management Services
Function: Archival coll
Restriction: Open by appt only

CR SAINT NORBERT COLLEGE*, Miriam B & James J Mulva Library, 400 Third St, 54115. (Mail add: 100 Grant St, 54115-2002), SAN 317-9583. Circulation Tel: 920-403-3466. Interlibrary Loan Service Tel: 920-403-3283. Reference Tel: 920-403-3160. Administration Tel: 920-403-3290. FAX: 920-403-4076. E-mail: library@snc.edu. Web Site: www.snc.edu/library. *Libr Dir,* Alaina Morales; E-mail: alaina.morales@snc.edu; *Academic Engagement Librn, Instruction Librn,* Joe Dyal; Tel: 920-403-3271, E-mail: joe.dyal@snc.edu; *Archives & Spec Coll Librn,* Sarah Titus; Tel: 920-403-3282, E-mail: sarah.titus@snc.edu; *Coll Mgt Librn,* Mitchell Scott; Tel: 920-403-3422, E-mail: mitchell.scott@snc.edu; *Circ Serv Coordr,* David Bosco; Tel: 920-403-3293, E-mail: david.bosco@snc.edu; *Acq, Doc Delivery Spec,* Connie Meulemans; E-mail: connie.meulemans@snc.edu; *Metadata Specialist,* Rochelle Van Erem; Tel: 920-403-3270, E-mail: rochelle.vanerem@snc.edu; Staff 6 (MLS 5, Non-MLS 1)
Highest Degree: Master
Wireless access
Partic in North East Wisconsin Intertype Libraries, Inc

DE SOTO

P DE SOTO PUBLIC LIBRARY*, 111 S Houghton St, 54624. SAN 376-6632. Tel: 608-648-3593. E-mail: desotopl@wrlsweb.org. Web Site: desotolibrary.wrlsweb.org. *Dir,* Jacquie Greiner; Staff 1 (Non-MLS 1)
Library Holdings: Bk Vols 12,872; Per Subs 20
Wireless access
Function: Bks on CD, Children's prog, Computers for patron use, Free DVD rentals, ILL available, Large print keyboards, Magazines, Movies, Music CDs, Photocopying/Printing, Preschool outreach, Preschool reading prog, Printer for laptops & handheld devices, Prog for adults, Prog for children & young adult, Scanner, Story hour, Summer reading prog
Mem of Winding Rivers Library System
Open Tues & Wed 2-7, Fri 9-4, Sat 10-1

DEER PARK

P DEER PARK PUBLIC LIBRARY*, 112 Front St W, 54007. SAN 377-9882. Tel: 715-269-5464. FAX: 715-269-5464. E-mail: library@deerparkpl.org. Web Site: www.deerparkpl.org. *Libr Dir,* Barbara Krueger; Tel: 715-269-5464, E-mail: bkrueger@deerparkpl.org; *Librn,* Brianna Zemke; *Librn,* Karen Zemke; Staff 1 (Non-MLS 1)
Founded 1972
Library Holdings: Audiobooks 282; Bk Vols 7,500; Per Subs 30; Videos 1,814
Automation Activity & Vendor Info: (Acquisitions) Innovative Interfaces, Inc - Sierra; (Cataloging) Innovative Interfaces, Inc - Sierra; (Circulation) Innovative Interfaces, Inc - Sierra; (Discovery) Innovative Interfaces, Inc; (OPAC) Innovative Interfaces, Inc; (Serials) Innovative Interfaces, Inc - Sierra
Wireless access
Function: 24/7 Electronic res, 24/7 Online cat, Adult bk club, Audiobks on Playaways & MP3, Bks on CD, Children's prog, Computers for patron use, Free DVD rentals, ILL available, Internet access, Laminating, Life-long learning prog for all ages, Magazines, Mail & tel request accepted, Meeting rooms, Movies, Music CDs, Online cat, OverDrive digital audio bks, Photocopying/Printing, Prog for adults, Prog for children & young adult, Ref serv available, Scanner, Senior computer classes, Story hour, Study rm, Summer reading prog, Tax forms, Wheelchair accessible
Mem of Inspiring & Facilitating Library Success (IFLS)
Open Tues-Thurs 1-6, Fri 10-6, Sat 9-Noon

DEERFIELD

P DEERFIELD PUBLIC LIBRARY*, 12 W Nelson St, 53531-9669. (Mail add: PO Box 408, 53531-0408), SAN 317-9591. Tel: 608-764-8102. Web Site: www.deerfieldpubliclibrary.org. *Dir,* Leah Fritsche; E-mail: leah@deerfieldpl.org; *Asst Dir,* Rachael Page; E-mail: rachael@deerfieldpl.org; *Asst Librn,* Jane Brooks; E-mail: jane@deerfieldpl.org; *Youth Serv Librn,* Gail Moynihan; E-mail: gail@deerfieldpl.org
Founded 1974. Pop 2,073; Circ 59,210
Library Holdings: Bk Vols 19,456; Per Subs 86
Automation Activity & Vendor Info: (Cataloging) SirsiDynix; (Circulation) SirsiDynix
Wireless access
Mem of South Central Library System
Open Mon & Thurs Noon-8, Tues, Wed & Fri 9-5, Sat 9-1
Friends of the Library Group

DEFOREST

P DEFOREST AREA PUBLIC LIBRARY*, 203 Library St, 53532. SAN 317-9567. Tel: 608-846-5482. FAX: 608-846-6875. E-mail: deforestlibrary@deforestlibrary.org. Web Site: www.deforestlibrary.org. *Dir,* Janis Berg; E-mail: jberg@deforestlibrary.org; *Asst Dir,* Gisela Newbegin; E-mail: giselan@deforestlibrary.org; *Ch,* Louise Valdovinos; E-mail: louisev@deforestlibrary.org; *Circ Serv Librn,* Traci Lerum; E-mail: tlerum@deforestlibrary.org; *Tech Serv Librn,* LuAnn Kranz; E-mail: luannk@deforestlibrary.org; *Teen Prog Coordr,* Raechel Schink; E-mail: raechs@deforestlibrary.org; Staff 6 (MLS 2, Non-MLS 4)
Founded 1964. Pop 7,997; Circ 286,760
Library Holdings: AV Mats 11,437; Bk Titles 56,655; Per Subs 183
Subject Interests: Popular mat
Automation Activity & Vendor Info: (Cataloging) SirsiDynix; (Circulation) SirsiDynix; (OPAC) SirsiDynix
Wireless access
Function: Adult bk club, Art exhibits, Audiobks via web, Bk club(s), Bks on cassette, Bks on CD, CD-ROM, Computers for patron use, Digital talking bks, Electronic databases & coll, Equip loans & repairs, Free DVD rentals, Holiday prog, Home delivery & serv to seniorr ctr & nursing homes, ILL available, Notary serv, Online cat, Photocopying/Printing, Prog for adults, Prog for children & young adult, Senior computer classes, Senior outreach, Story hour, Summer & winter reading prog, Tax forms, Teen prog, Winter reading prog, Workshops
Mem of South Central Library System

Open Mon-Thurs 9-8, Fri 9-5:30, Sat 9-5 Sun 1-5
Friends of the Library Group

DELAFIELD

P DELAFIELD PUBLIC LIBRARY*, 500 Genessee St, 53018-1895. SAN 317-9605. Tel: 262-646-6230. FAX: 262-646-6232. Web Site: www.delafieldlibrary.org. *Libr Dir,* Stephanie Ramirez; E-mail: sramirez@delafieldlibrary.org
Founded 1907. Circ 145,000
Library Holdings: Bk Vols 60,000; Per Subs 90
Subject Interests: Art, Cooking, Detective fiction, Needlecrafts, Parenting
Automation Activity & Vendor Info: (Cataloging) Innovative Interfaces, Inc; (Circulation) Innovative Interfaces, Inc; (OPAC) Innovative Interfaces, Inc
Wireless access
Mem of Bridges Library System
Open Mon-Thurs 9:30-8, Fri 9:30-5, Sat 9:30-4, Sun 1-4
Friends of the Library Group

DELAVAN

P ARAM PUBLIC LIBRARY*, 404 E Walworth Ave, 53115-1208. SAN 317-9613. Tel: 262-728-3111. FAX: 262-728-5067. E-mail: aramlibrary@aramlibrary.org. Web Site: www.aramlibrary.org. *Libr Dir,* Michelle Carter; E-mail: director@aramlibrary.org; Staff 12 (MLS 2, Non-MLS 10)
Founded 1908. Pop 5,803; Circ 80,095
Library Holdings: Bk Titles 60,000
Automation Activity & Vendor Info: (Cataloging) SirsiDynix; (Circulation) SirsiDynix; (OPAC) SirsiDynix
Wireless access
Function: 24/7 Electronic res, 24/7 Online cat, Adult bk club, Art exhibits, Audiobks on Playaways & MP3, Audiobks via web, Bilingual assistance for Spanish patrons, Bk club(s), Bks on CD, Children's prog, Computer training, Computers for patron use, Electronic databases & coll, Family literacy, Free DVD rentals, Home delivery & serv to seniorr ctr & nursing homes, ILL available, Internet access, Magazines, Mail & tel request accepted, Microfiche/film & reading machines, Movies, Music CDs, Online cat, OverDrive digital audio bks, Preschool outreach, Preschool reading prog, Prog for adults, Prog for children & young adult, Ref serv available, Scanner, Senior computer classes, Spanish lang bks, Story hour, Summer reading prog, Tax forms, Teen prog, Wheelchair accessible
Mem of Prairie Lakes Library System (PLLS)
Special Services for the Deaf - Bks on deafness & sign lang; Closed caption videos; Deaf publ; Interpreter on staff
Special Services for the Blind - Braille bks
Open Mon-Thurs 10-7, Fri 10-5, Sat 10-2
Friends of the Library Group

S WISCONSIN SCHOOL FOR THE DEAF*, WESP-DHH Educational Resource Library, 309 W Walworth Ave, 53115. SAN 317-9621. Tel: 262-728-7127, Ext 7133. FAX: 262-728-7129. Web Site: wesp-dhh.wi.gov/wsd/library. *Librn,* Nell Fleming; E-mail: nell.fleming@wsd.k12.wi.us; *Libr Asst,* Jonathan Petermon; E-mail: jonathan.petermon@wsd.k12.wi.us; Staff 1 (MLS 1)
Founded 1930
Library Holdings: Bk Vols 11,250
Wireless access
Special Services for the Deaf - Coll on deaf educ; Deaf publ
Open Mon-Fri 7:30-4:30

DICKEYVILLE

P BRICKL MEMORIAL LIBRARY*, 500 East Ave, 53808. Tel: 608-568-3142. E-mail: tpfohl@swls.org. Web Site: www.dickeyville.com/brickl-memorial-library. *Dir,* Tina Pfohl; E-mail: tpfohl@swls.org
Wireless access
Mem of Southwest Wisconsin Library System
Open Mon-Thurs 1-6:30, Sat 9-12
Friends of the Library Group

DODGEVILLE

P DODGEVILLE PUBLIC LIBRARY*, 139 S Iowa St, 53533. SAN 317-963X. Tel: 608-935-3728. FAX: 608-935-9405. Web Site: dodgevillelibrary.com. *Dir,* Vickie Stangel; *Ch Serv,* Carol Gleichauf; E-mail: cgleichauf@swls.org; Staff 7 (MLS 1, Non-MLS 6)
Founded 1900. Pop 4,200; Circ 133,645
Library Holdings: Bk Vols 23,131; Per Subs 56
Automation Activity & Vendor Info: (Cataloging) SirsiDynix; (Circulation) SirsiDynix
Wireless access
Function: Homebound delivery serv, ILL available, Photocopying/Printing, Prog for children & young adult, Summer reading prog, Wheelchair accessible
Mem of Southwest Wisconsin Library System
Open Mon-Thurs 10-7, Fri 10-6, Sat 9-1
Friends of the Library Group

DORCHESTER

P DORCHESTER PUBLIC LIBRARY*, 155 N Second St, 54425. SAN 317-9648. Tel: 715-654-5959. Web Site: www.dorchesterpubliclibrary.org. *Dir,* Sue Bedroske; E-mail: director@dorchesterpubliclibrary.org
Pop 698; Circ 10,671
Library Holdings: Bk Vols 12,000; Per Subs 45
Partic in Wiscat; Wisconsin Valley Library Service
Open Mon 11-7, Tues 1-6, Wed 10-6, Fri 9-5
Friends of the Library Group

DRESSER

P GERALDINE E ANDERSON VILLAGE LIBRARY, Dresser Public Library, 117 S Central Ave, 54009. (Mail add: PO Box 547, 54009-0547), SAN 376-6691. Tel: 715-755-2944. E-mail: dresserpl@dresserpubliclibrary.org. Web Site: dresserpubliclibrary.org. *Dir,* Leann French; E-mail: french@dresserpubliclibrary.org; Staff 1.4 (Non-MLS 1.4)
Founded 1935
Library Holdings: Audiobooks 130; DVDs 1,636; e-books 171,980; Electronic Media & Resources 82; Bk Titles 6,994; Per Subs 4
Automation Activity & Vendor Info: (Acquisitions) Baker & Taylor; (Circulation) Innovative Interfaces, Inc - Sierra; (OPAC) BiblioCommons
Wireless access
Function: 24/7 Electronic res, 24/7 Online cat, Adult bk club, Bks on CD, Computers for patron use, Free DVD rentals, Homebound delivery serv, ILL available, Internet access, Magazines, Music CDs, Online cat, OverDrive digital audio bks, Photocopying/Printing, Preschool reading prog, Printer for laptops & handheld devices, Prog for adults, Ref serv available, Scanner, Story hour, Summer reading prog
Mem of Inspiring & Facilitating Library Success (IFLS)
Open Mon, Wed & Thurs 10-7, Tues & Fri 10-5, Sat 10-1

DRUMMOND

P DRUMMOND PUBLIC LIBRARY*, 14990 Superior St, 54832. (Mail add: PO Box 23, 54832-0023), SAN 317-9656. Tel: 715-739-6290. E-mail: drumlib@drummond.wislib.org. Web Site: www.drummondwilibrary.org. *Dir,* Addie Arens
Library Holdings: Bk Vols 7,200
Wireless access
Mem of Northern Waters Library Service
Open Tues-Fri 10-5, Sat 9-1

DURAND

P DURAND PUBLIC LIBRARY*, 604 Seventh Ave E, 54736. (Mail add: PO Box 190, 54736-0190), SAN 317-9664. Tel: 715-672-8730. *Dir,* Patti Blount; E-mail: pblount@durand.k12.wi.us; *Ch, ILL,* Kathy Westberg; E-mail: kwestberg@durand.k12.wi.us; *Ch,* Linda Taverna
Founded 1886. Circ 40,536
Library Holdings: Bk Vols 47,000; Per Subs 51
Special Collections: Local Newspaper, 1889-present
Subject Interests: Local hist
Automation Activity & Vendor Info: (Cataloging) Follett Software; (Circulation) Follett Software
Wireless access
Mem of Inspiring & Facilitating Library Success (IFLS)
Open Mon-Fri 8-7, Sat 9-Noon (Winter); Tues-Fri 9-6 (Summer)

EAGLE

P ALICE BAKER MEMORIAL PUBLIC LIBRARY*, 820 E Main St, 53119. (Mail add: PO Box 520, 53119-0520), SAN 376-6640. Tel: 262-594-2800. FAX: 262-594-5126. Web Site: www.alicebaker.lib.wi.us. *Dir,* Alli Chase; E-mail: chase@eagle.lib.wi.us
Library Holdings: Bk Titles 17,000; Bk Vols 20,000; Per Subs 80
Wireless access
Mem of Bridges Library System
Open Mon-Thurs 9-8, Fri 9-5, Sat 9-1; Mon-Thurs 9-8, Fri 9-5, Sat 9-Noon (Summer)
Friends of the Library Group

EAGLE RIVER

P WALTER E OLSON MEMORIAL LIBRARY, 203 N Main St, 54521. (Mail add: PO Box 69, 54521-0069), SAN 317-9672. Tel: 715-479-8070. FAX: 715-479-2435. E-mail: olsonlibrary@gmail.com. Web Site: olsonlibrary.org. *Dir,* Sara Klemann; Staff 3 (MLS 1, Non-MLS 2)
Founded 1915. Pop 9,600; Circ 51,385
Library Holdings: Audiobooks 1,706; AV Mats 4,624; CDs 748; DVDs 2,300; e-books 11,545; Large Print Bks 3,044; Bk Titles 37,742; Per Subs 80
Special Collections: Harvard Classics; Library of America; Literacy Coll (GED, High interest/low vocabulary, ESL)
Automation Activity & Vendor Info: (Acquisitions) Innovative Interfaces, Inc; (Cataloging) Innovative Interfaces, Inc; (Circulation) Innovative Interfaces, Inc; (ILL) Innovative Interfaces, Inc; (OPAC) Innovative Interfaces, Inc
Wireless access
Function: 24/7 Electronic res, 24/7 Online cat, Adult bk club, Adult literacy prog, Art exhibits, Audio & video playback equip for onsite use, Audiobks on Playaways & MP3, Audiobks via web, Bk club(s), Bks on CD, Children's prog, Computers for patron use, E-Readers, Electronic databases & coll, Equip loans & repairs, Free DVD rentals, Homebound delivery serv, ILL available, Instruction & testing, Internet access, Laminating, Life-long learning prog for all ages, Magazines, Mail & tel request accepted, Meeting rooms, Movies, Museum passes, Music CDs, Online cat, OverDrive digital audio bks, Photocopying/Printing, Preschool reading prog, Printer for laptops & handheld devices, Prog for adults, Prog for children & young adult, Scanner, Story hour, Study rm, Summer reading prog, Tax forms, Telephone ref, Wheelchair accessible, Winter reading prog
Publications: E-newsletter
Mem of Northern Waters Library Service
Partic in Merlin
Special Services for the Deaf - Bks on deafness & sign lang; High interest/low vocabulary bks
Special Services for the Blind - Aids for in-house use; Assistive/Adapted tech devices, equip & products; Audio mat; Bks available with recordings; Bks on cassette; Bks on CD; Cassette playback machines; Copier with enlargement capabilities; Extensive large print coll; Home delivery serv; Internet workstation with adaptive software; Magnifiers
Open Mon 9-7, Tues-Thurs 9-6, Fri 9-5, Sat 9-3
Restriction: ID required to use computers (Ltd hrs)
Friends of the Library Group

EAST TROY

P EAST TROY LIONS PUBLIC LIBRARY*, 3094 Graydon Ave, 53120. SAN 317-9680. Tel: 262-642-6262. E-mail: et@easttroy.lib.wi.us. Web Site: www.easttroy.lib.wi.us. *Dir,* Tami Bartoli; E-mail: bartoli@easttroy.lib.wi.us; *Librn,* Nancy O'Connell; E-mail: oconnell@easttroy.lib.wi.us
Founded 1895. Pop 3,300; Circ 46,000
Library Holdings: Bk Titles 20,000; Bk Vols 24,000; Per Subs 85
Special Collections: State Document Depository; UN Document Depository; US Document Depository
Automation Activity & Vendor Info: (Acquisitions) SirsiDynix; (Cataloging) SirsiDynix; (Circulation) SirsiDynix; (OPAC) SirsiDynix-iBistro
Wireless access
Mem of Prairie Lakes Library System (PLLS)
Open Mon-Thurs 10-7, Fri 10-5, Sat 10-1
Friends of the Library Group

EAU CLAIRE

S CHIPPEWA VALLEY MUSEUM, INC*, 1204 E Half Moon Dr, 54702. (Mail add: PO Box 1204, 54702-1204), SAN 327-8425. Tel: 715-834-7871. FAX: 715-834-6624. E-mail: info@cvmuseum.com. Web Site: www.cvmuseum.com. *Dir & Curator,* Carrie Ronnander; E-mail: c.ronnander@cvmuseum.com
Library Holdings: Bk Vols 3,000
Open Tues 5-8, Wed-Sat 12-5

J CHIPPEWA VALLEY TECHNICAL COLLEGE LIBRARY*, 620 W Clairemont Ave, 54701-6162. SAN 317-9699. Tel: 715-833-6285. FAX: 715-833-6470. Reference E-mail: reference@cvtc.edu. Web Site: www.cvtc.edu/campus-life/library. *Dir,* Vince Mussehl; E-mail: vmussehl@cvtc.edu; *Tech Serv Librn,* Nic Ashman; Tel: 715-831-7281, E-mail: nashman@cvtc.edu; Staff 3 (MLS 1, Non-MLS 2)
Founded 1965. Enrl 4,500; Fac 230; Highest Degree: Associate
Library Holdings: AV Mats 1,337; e-books 13,807; Bk Titles 15,800; Bk Vols 19,613; Per Subs 395; Videos 4,075
Subject Interests: Allied health, Nursing, Paralegal
Automation Activity & Vendor Info: (Acquisitions) Ex Libris Group; (Cataloging) Ex Libris Group; (Circulation) Ex Libris Group; (Course Reserve) Ex Libris Group; (Media Booking) Ex Libris Group; (OPAC) Ex Libris Group; (Serials) Ex Libris Group
Partic in OCLC Online Computer Library Center, Inc; WiLS; WISPALS Library Consortium
Open Mon-Thurs 7:30am-8:30pm, Fri 7:30-5, Sat 9-3 (Fall-Spring); Mon-Fri 7:30-5 (Summer)

P INSPIRING & FACILITATING LIBRARY SUCCESS (IFLS)*, 1538 Truax Blvd, 54703. SAN 317-9729. Tel: 715-839-5082. Toll Free Tel: 800-321-5427. FAX: 715-839-5151. E-mail: tellus@ifls.lib.wi.us. Web Site: www.iflsweb.org. *Dir,* John Thompson; E-mail: thompson@ifls.lib.wi.us; Staff 9 (MLS 4, Non-MLS 5)
Founded 1978. Pop 437,000
Automation Activity & Vendor Info: (Cataloging) Innovative Interfaces, Inc; (Circulation) Innovative Interfaces, Inc; (ILL) Innovative Interfaces, Inc; (OPAC) Innovative Interfaces, Inc
Function: Doc delivery serv, ILL available, Online ref, Prof lending libr, Ref & res, Workshops
Publications: NewsFlashes (Newsletter)
Member Libraries: Altoona Public Library; Amery Area Public Library; Augusta Memorial Public Library; Baldwin Public Library; Balsam Lake Public Library; Barron Public Library; Bloomer Public Library; Boyceville Public Library; Bruce Area Library; Cadott Community Library; Cameron Area Public Library; Carleton A Friday Memorial Library; Centuria Public Library; Chippewa Falls Public Library; Clarella Hackett Johnson Public Library; Clear Lake Public Library; Colfax Public Library; Cornell Public Library; D R Moon Memorial Library; Deer Park Public Library; Durand Public Library; Ellsworth Public Library; Elmwood Public Library; Fairchild Public Library; Fall Creek Public Library; Frederic Public Library; Geraldine E Anderson Village Library; Glenwood City Public Library; Hammond Community Library; Hawkins Area Library; Hazel Mackin Community Library; Hudson Area Public Library; Luck Public Library; Menomonie Public Library; Milltown Public Library; Ogema Public Library; Osceola Public Library; Park Falls Public Library; Pepin Public Library; Phillips Public Library; Plum City Public Library; Prescott Public Library; Rice Lake Public Library; River Falls Public Library; Rusk County Community Library; Somerset Public Library; Spring Valley Public Library; St Croix Falls Public Library; Thomas St Angelo Public Library; Turtle Lake Public Library; Woodville Community Library
Partic in Wisconsin Public Library Consortium
Restriction: Circulates for staff only, Not open to pub

M MAYO CLINIC HEALTH SYSTEM*, Eau Claire Medical Library, 1221 Whipple St, 54703. SAN 317-9737. Tel: 715-838-3248. FAX: 715-838-3289. E-mail: library.eauclaire@mayo.edu. Web Site: www.mayoclinichealthsystem.org/locations/eau-claire. *Supvr,* Jennifer Schram; Staff 2 (MLS 1, Non-MLS 1)
Founded 1930
Library Holdings: Bk Vols 4,260
Special Collections: Consumer Health Information Center Coll
Subject Interests: Allied health, Hospital admin, Med, Nursing
Automation Activity & Vendor Info: (Cataloging) Innovative Interfaces, Inc; (Circulation) Innovative Interfaces, Inc
Publications: Newsletter
Open Mon-Fri 8-4:30

P L E PHILLIPS MEMORIAL PUBLIC LIBRARY*, 400 Eau Claire St, 54701. SAN 317-9710. Tel: 715-839-1648, 715-839-5004. Circulation Tel: 715-839-5003. Interlibrary Loan Service Tel: 715-839-3877. Administration Tel: 715-839-5002. FAX: 715-839-5310. Administration FAX: 715-839-3822. E-mail: librarian@eauclaire.lib.wi.us, reference@eauclaire.lib.wi.us. Web Site: www.ecpubliclibrary.info. *Dir,* Nancy Kerr; *Dep Dir,* Shelly Collins-Fuerbringer; Tel: 715-839-5063, E-mail: shellyc@eauclaire.lib.wi.us; *Dep Dir,* Kimberly Hennings; Tel: 715-839-6225, E-mail: kimberlyh@eauclaire.lib.wi.us; *Early Literacy Librn, Outreach Librn,* Jerissa Koenig; Tel: 715-839-5016, E-mail: jerissak@eauclaire.lib.wi.us; *Tech Librn, Teen Librn,* Andria Rice; Tel: 715-839-2897, E-mail: andriar@eauclaire.lib.wi.us; *Circ Serv Mgr,* Paula Stanton; Tel: 715-839-5098, E-mail: paulas@eauclaire.lib.wi.us; *Mgr, Communications, Mgr, Programming,* Isa Small; Tel: 715-839-5094, E-mail: isas@eauclaire.lib.wi.us; *Ref Serv Mgr,* Elizabeth Steans; Tel: 715-839-1683, E-mail: elizabeths@eauclaire.lib.wi.us; *Tech Serv Mgr,* Julie Woodruff; Tel: 715-839-1647, E-mail: juliew@eauclaire.lib.wi.us; *Tech Mgr,* Kristin Nickel; Tel: 715-839-1684, E-mail: krisn@eauclaire.lib.wi.us; *Youth Serv Mgr,* Kelly Witt; Tel: 715-839-2898, E-mail: kellyw@eauclaire.lib.wi.us; *Community Resources Specialist,* Libby Richter; Tel: 715-839-5061, E-mail: libbyr@eauclaire.lib.wi.us; Staff 13 (MLS 10, Non-MLS 3)
Founded 1875. Pop 104,646; Circ 799,420
Library Holdings: Audiobooks 5,596; Braille Volumes 38; CDs 5,531; DVDs 16,167; e-books 159,486; Large Print Bks 9,332; Microforms 1,644; Music Scores 353; Bk Titles 139,145; Per Subs 125; Videos 2,364
Special Collections: Municipal Document Depository; State Document Depository

Automation Activity & Vendor Info: (Acquisitions) Innovative Interfaces, Inc; (Cataloging) Innovative Interfaces, Inc; (Circulation) Innovative Interfaces, Inc; (Course Reserve) Innovative Interfaces, Inc; (ILL) Innovative Interfaces, Inc; (Media Booking) Innovative Interfaces, Inc; (OPAC) Innovative Interfaces, Inc; (Serials) Innovative Interfaces, Inc
Wireless access
Function: 24/7 Electronic res, 24/7 Online cat, 3D Printer, Activity rm, Adult bk club, Archival coll, Art exhibits, Art programs, Audiobks on Playaways & MP3, Audiobks via web, Bk club(s), Bk reviews (Group), Bks on CD, CD-ROM, Children's prog, Computer training, Computers for patron use, E-Readers, E-Reserves, Electronic databases & coll, Equip loans & repairs, Family literacy, Free DVD rentals, Games & aids for people with disabilities, Genealogy discussion group, Govt ref serv, Holiday prog, Home delivery & serv to seniorr ctr & nursing homes, Homebound delivery serv, ILL available, Instruction & testing, Internet access, Large print keyboards, Life-long learning prog for all ages, Literacy & newcomer serv, Magazines, Magnifiers for reading, Mail & tel request accepted, Makerspace, Mango lang, Meeting rooms, Microfiche/film & reading machines, Movies, Museum passes, Music CDs, Online cat, Online ref, Outreach serv, OverDrive digital audio bks, Photocopying/Printing, Preschool outreach, Preschool reading prog, Printer for laptops & handheld devices, Prof lending libr, Prog for adults, Prog for children & young adult, Ref & res, Ref serv available, Res assist avail, Res libr, Scanner, Senior outreach, Serves people with intellectual disabilities, Spanish lang bks, STEM programs, Story hour, Study rm, Summer & winter reading prog, Summer reading prog, Tax forms, Teen prog, Telephone ref, Visual arts prog, Wheelchair accessible, Winter reading prog, Workshops, Writing prog
Partic in OCLC Online Computer Library Center, Inc
Special Services for the Deaf - High interest/low vocabulary bks; Spec interest per; TDD equip
Special Services for the Blind - Aids for in-house use; Assistive/Adapted tech devices, equip & products; Bks on CD; Braille equip; Braille paper; Home delivery serv; Large print bks; Merlin electronic magnifier reader
Open Mon-Thurs 10-9, Fri 10-6, Sat 10-5, Sun 1-5
Friends of the Library Group

C UNIVERSITY OF WISCONSIN-EAU CLAIRE*, William D McIntyre Library, 103 Garfield Ave, 54701-4932. (Mail add: 105 Garfield Ave, 54701-4811), SAN 317-9761. Tel: 715-836-3715. Circulation Tel: 715-836-3856. Interlibrary Loan Service Tel: 715-836-5377. Reference Tel: 715-836-3858. FAX: 715-836-2949. E-mail: library.reference@uwec.edu. Web Site: www.uwec.edu/library. *Dir,* Jill Markgraf; Tel: 715-836-4827, E-mail: markgrjs@uwec.edu; *Head, Acq, Head, Electronic Res,* Roxanne Backowski; Tel: 715-836-3508, E-mail: backowrm@uwec.edu; *Head, Communication & Instruction,* Kate Hinnant; Tel: 715-836-5117, E-mail: hinnanks@uwec.edu; *Head, Discovery & Assessment,* Robin Miller; Tel: 715-836-3132, E-mail: millerob@uwec.edu; *Archivist, Head, Spec Coll,* Greg Kocken; Tel: 715-834-3873, E-mail: kockeng@uwec.edu; *Head, User Serv,* Hans Kishel; Tel: 715-836-2959, E-mail: kishelhf@uwec.edu; *Digital Learning Librn,* Liliana LaValle; Tel: 715-836-4897, E-mail: lavallel@uwec.edu; *Educ Librn, Res & Instruction Librn,* Kati Schaller; Tel: 715-836-4522, E-mail: schallke@uwec.edu; *Student Engagement Librn,* Helena Sumbulla; Tel: 715-836-6032, E-mail: sumbullh@uwec.edu; *Libr Syst Coordr, Makerspace Mrg,* Dan Hillis; Tel: 715-836-4961, E-mail: hillisdr@uwec.edu; Staff 29 (MLS 11, Non-MLS 18)
Founded 1916. Enrl 9,794; Fac 342; Highest Degree: Doctorate
Special Collections: Area Research Center; Campus Evolution Records (reflecting change from normal school to university); Chippewa Valley Historical Manuscripts & Local Government Records; Early Settlement, Lumbering, Labor, Genealogy & Politics; John L. Buchholz Jazz Library; LaBelle Miller Southwest Pottery Coll; Schmidt Robert Frost Coll; Uniroyal Management & Labor Union Records; Wood Family Farm Diaries. Oral History; State Document Depository; US Document Depository
Automation Activity & Vendor Info: (Acquisitions) Ex Libris Group; (Cataloging) Ex Libris Group; (Circulation) Ex Libris Group; (Course Reserve) Ex Libris Group; (ILL) OCLC; (Media Booking) Ex Libris Group; (OPAC) Ex Libris Group; (Serials) Ex Libris Group
Wireless access
Publications: Off the Shelf (Newsletter)
Open Mon-Thurs 8am-11pm, Fri 8-6, Sat 11-6, Sun 11-11 (Spring & Fall); Mon-Fri 8-5 (Winter & Summer)

EDGERTON

P EDGERTON PUBLIC LIBRARY*, 101 Albion St, 53534-1836. SAN 317-977X. Tel: 608-884-4511. FAX: 608-884-7575. Web Site: als.lib.wi.us/EPL (website URL requires CAPS). *Dir,* Beth Krebs-Smith; E-mail: smith.beth@edgertonpubliclibrary.org; Staff 6 (MLS 2, Non-MLS 4)
Founded 1866. Pop 8,049; Circ 72,449
Library Holdings: AV Mats 3,040; Large Print Bks 1,410; Bk Titles 26,500; Bk Vols 26,546; Per Subs 100
Subject Interests: Local hist
Automation Activity & Vendor Info: (Circulation) Innovative Interfaces, Inc; (OPAC) Innovative Interfaces, Inc
Wireless access
Function: 24/7 Electronic res, 24/7 Online cat, Adult bk club, Archival coll, Art exhibits, Audiobks on Playaways & MP3, Audiobks via web, Bi-weekly Writer's Group, Bk club(s), Bks on CD, Children's prog, Computer training, Computers for patron use, E-Reserves, Electronic databases & coll, Family literacy, Free DVD rentals, ILL available, Internet access, Life-long learning prog for all ages, Magazines, Magnifiers for reading, Mail & tel request accepted, Meeting rooms, Microfiche/film & reading machines, Music CDs, Online cat, Online ref, Outside serv via phone, mail, e-mail & web, OverDrive digital audio bks, Photocopying/Printing, Preschool outreach, Preschool reading prog, Prog for adults, Prog for children & young adult, Ref serv available, Scanner, Spoken cassettes & CDs, Spoken cassettes & DVDs, Story hour, Study rm, Summer & winter reading prog, Summer reading prog, Tax forms, Teen prog, Telephone ref, Wheelchair accessible, Winter reading prog, Writing prog
Mem of Prairie Lakes Library System (PLLS)
Open Mon-Thurs 9-8, Fri 10-5, Sat 9-3
Friends of the Library Group

ELKHART LAKE

P ELKHART LAKE PUBLIC LIBRARY*, 40 Pine St, 53020. (Mail add: PO Box 387, 53020), SAN 376-6624. Tel: 920-876-2554. Circulation E-mail: elcirc@monarchlibraries.org. Web Site: www.elkhartlakepubliclibrary.org. *Libr Dir,* Rachel Montes; E-mail: rmontes@monarchlibraries.org
Library Holdings: Bk Titles 5,000; Bk Vols 16,626; Per Subs 24
Wireless access
Mem of Monarch Library System
Open Mon-Thurs 9-7, Fri 9-5, Sat 9-2
Friends of the Library Group

ELKHORN

J GATEWAY TECHNICAL COLLEGE*, Elkhorn Campus Library, North Bldg, Rm N226, 400 County Rd H, 53121. SAN 317-9788. Tel: 262-741-8042. FAX: 262-741-8585. E-mail: elkhornlrc@gtc.edu. Web Site: libguides.gtc.edu/c.php?g=36352. *District Libr Mgr,* Gary Flynn; Tel: 262-564-2640, E-mail: flynng@gtc.edu; *Libr Instruction & Ref Spec,* Jason Steagall; Tel: 262-741-8438, E-mail: steagallj@gtc.edu; Staff 2 (MLS 1, Non-MLS 1)
Highest Degree: Associate
Library Holdings: Bks on Deafness & Sign Lang 800; CDs 30; DVDs 30; e-books 1,500; e-journals 1,000; Bk Vols 5,900; Per Subs 35; Videos 150
Special Collections: Interpreter for Deaf, bks, v-tapes
Subject Interests: Acctg, Allied health, Bus, Deaf interpreting, Graphic Communications, Info tech, Nursing
Automation Activity & Vendor Info: (Acquisitions) Ex Libris Group; (Cataloging) Ex Libris Group; (Circulation) Ex Libris Group; (Course Reserve) Ex Libris Group; (ILL) OCLC; (OPAC) Ex Libris Group; (Serials) Ex Libris Group
Wireless access
Function: Internet access, Online ref, Orientations
Partic in WISPALS Library Consortium
Open Mon-Thurs 8-8, Fri 8-4

P MATHESON MEMORIAL LIBRARY*, 101 N Wisconsin, 53121. SAN 317-9818. Tel: 262-723-2678. FAX: 262-723-2870. E-mail: mmlinfo@elkhorn.lib.wi.us. Web Site: www.elkhorn.lib.wi.us. *Dir,* Chad Robinson; E-mail: crobinson@elkhorn.lib.wi.us; *Ad,* Chad Robinson; E-mail: crobinson@elkhorn.lib.wi.us; *Youth Serv Librn,* Jennifer Wharton; E-mail: jwharton@elkhorn.lib.wi.us; *Circ Supvr,* Gail Grice; E-mail: ggrice@elkhorn.lib.wi.us; *Tech Serv Supvr,* Lindsay Barnes; E-mail: lbarnes@elkhorn.lib.wi.us; Staff 5 (MLS 3, Non-MLS 2)
Founded 1901. Pop 25,000; Circ 248,508
Jan 2021-Dec 2021 Income $905,794, City $427,480, County $433,314, Locally Generated Income $28,000, Other $17,000. Mats Exp $119,878, Books $52,778, Per/Ser (Incl. Access Fees) $3,500, AV Mat $19,550, Electronic Ref Mat (Incl. Access Fees) $17,500. Sal $469,893
Library Holdings: Audiobooks 2,700; CDs 1,990; DVDs 9,372; High Interest/Low Vocabulary Bk Vols 400; Large Print Bks 1,200; Bk Titles 63,658; Per Subs 105
Special Collections: Robert Burns (Matheson Coll)
Subject Interests: Cookery
Automation Activity & Vendor Info: (Acquisitions) SirsiDynix; (Cataloging) SirsiDynix; (Circulation) SirsiDynix; (OPAC) SirsiDynix; (Serials) SirsiDynix
Wireless access
Function: Adult bk club, Art exhibits, Audiobks on Playaways & MP3, Audiobks via web, AV serv, Bk club(s), Bks on CD, Butterfly Garden, Children's prog, Computer training, Computers for patron use, Doc delivery serv, Electronic databases & coll, Free DVD rentals, Home delivery & serv to seniorr ctr & nursing homes, Homebound delivery serv,

ILL available, Internet access, Magazines, Meeting rooms, Microfiche/film & reading machines, Movies, Music CDs, Online cat, Outreach serv, OverDrive digital audio bks, Photocopying/Printing, Printer for laptops & handheld devices, Prog for adults, Prog for children & young adult, Ref & res, Scanner, Spanish lang bks, Story hour, Study rm, Summer & winter reading prog, Summer reading prog, Tax forms, Teen prog, Wheelchair accessible
Mem of Prairie Lakes Library System (PLLS)
Open Mon-Thurs 9-8, Fri 9-6, Sat 9-2
Friends of the Library Group

ELLSWORTH

P ELLSWORTH PUBLIC LIBRARY*, 312 W Main St, 54011. SAN 317-9826. Tel: 715-273-3209. FAX: 715-273-3209. Web Site: www.ellsworthlibrary.org. *Libr Dir,* Tiffany Meyer; E-mail: director@ellsworthlibrary.org; Staff 4.4 (MLS 0.8, Non-MLS 3.6)
Founded 1924. Pop 9,239; Circ 70,321
Library Holdings: Audiobooks 1,751; Braille Volumes 23; DVDs 3,360; e-books 158,256; Bk Titles 19,529; Per Subs 57
Special Collections: Regional hist Coll
Automation Activity & Vendor Info: (Acquisitions) Innovative Interfaces, Inc; (Cataloging) Innovative Interfaces, Inc; (Circulation) Innovative Interfaces, Inc; (Course Reserve) Innovative Interfaces, Inc; (Discovery) Innovative Interfaces, Inc; (ILL) Innovative Interfaces, Inc; (Media Booking) Innovative Interfaces, Inc; (OPAC) Innovative Interfaces, Inc; (Serials) Innovative Interfaces, Inc
Wireless access
Mem of Inspiring & Facilitating Library Success (IFLS)
Open Mon & Fri 10-6, Tues-Thurs 10-8, Sat 9-1
Friends of the Library Group

ELM GROVE

P ELM GROVE PUBLIC LIBRARY*, 13600 Juneau Blvd, 53122. SAN 317-9834. Tel: 262-782-6717. FAX: 262-780-4827. E-mail: egill@elmgrove.lib.wi.us. Web Site: elmgrovelibrary.org. *Dir,* Sarah Muench; E-mail: muench@elmgrove.lib.wi.us; *Youth Serv Librn,* Sue Daniels; E-mail: sdaniels@elmgrove.lib.wi.us; Staff 8 (MLS 5, Non-MLS 3)
Founded 1962. Pop 6,261; Circ 110,000
Library Holdings: AV Mats 3,460; Large Print Bks 531; Bk Titles 49,414; Per Subs 115; Talking Bks 1,776
Subject Interests: Gen popular
Automation Activity & Vendor Info: (Circulation) SirsiDynix; (OPAC) SirsiDynix-iBistro
Wireless access
Mem of Bridges Library System
Open Mon-Thurs 10-8:30, Fri & Sat 10-5
Friends of the Library Group

ELMWOOD

P ELMWOOD PUBLIC LIBRARY, 111 N Main St, 54740. (Mail add: PO Box 55, 54740-0055). Tel: 715-639-2615. FAX: 715-639-2615. E-mail: elmwoodpl@elmwoodlibrary.org. Web Site: www.elmwoodlibrary.org. *Dir,* Nick Andrews; E-mail: director@elmwoodlibrary.org
Pop 11,432; Circ 15,593
Library Holdings: Bk Titles 11,349; Per Subs 49
Automation Activity & Vendor Info: (Cataloging) Innovative Interfaces, Inc; (Circulation) Innovative Interfaces, Inc
Wireless access
Mem of Inspiring & Facilitating Library Success (IFLS)
Special Services for the Deaf - Assistive tech
Open Tues & Wed 10-5, Thurs 10-6, Fri 10-2
Friends of the Library Group

ELROY

P ELROY PUBLIC LIBRARY*, 501 Second Main St, 53929. SAN 317-9842. Tel: 608-462-2407. FAX: 608-462-2408. E-mail: elroypl2@wrlsweb.org. Web Site: www.elroylibrary.com.
Founded 1908. Pop 1,400; Circ 27,760
Library Holdings: Bk Vols 20,000; Per Subs 40
Wireless access
Mem of Winding Rivers Library System
Open Mon-Fri 10-6
Friends of the Library Group

ENDEAVOR

P ENDEAVOR PUBLIC LIBRARY*, 400 Church St, 53930. (Mail add: PO Box 80, 53930-0080), SAN 322-8525. Tel: 608-587-2902. FAX: 608-587-2902. Web Site: endeavorlibrary.org. *Interim Dir,* Debbie Thome; E-mail: director@endeavorlibrary.org; Staff 2 (Non-MLS 2)
Founded 1962. Pop 433
Library Holdings: Bk Vols 9,025; Per Subs 12
Automation Activity & Vendor Info: (Cataloging) SirsiDynix; (Circulation) SirsiDynix; (OPAC) SirsiDynix
Wireless access
Mem of Winnefox Library System
Open Mon & Wed Noon-5, Tues 11:30-5, Thurs 11:30-6, Fri Noon-4, Sat 9-11
Friends of the Library Group

ETTRICK

P ETTRICK PUBLIC LIBRARY*, 15570 School St, 54627. (Mail add: PO Box 305, 54627). Tel: 608-525-3408. E-mail: ettrickpl@wrlsweb.org. Web Site: www.wrlsweb.org/ettrick. *Dir,* Jody Hanneman
Founded 1999. Pop 525
Library Holdings: Bk Vols 8,000; Talking Bks 500; Videos 400
Automation Activity & Vendor Info: (Cataloging) Innovative Interfaces, Inc - Sierra; (Circulation) Innovative Interfaces, Inc - Sierra; (OPAC) Innovative Interfaces, Inc
Wireless access
Mem of Winding Rivers Library System
Open Mon & Wed-Fri 1-6, Sat 9-1

EVANSVILLE

P EAGER FREE PUBLIC LIBRARY*, 39 W Main St, 53536. SAN 317-9850. Tel: 608-882-2260, 608-882-2275. FAX: 608-882-2261. E-mail: eagerfree@eagerfreelibrary.org. Web Site: als.lib.wi.us/EFPL (URL needs caps). *Dir,* Megan Kloeckner; *Asst Dir, Head, Youth Serv,* Rebecca Van Dan
Founded 1898. Pop 5,791; Circ 47,308
Library Holdings: Bk Titles 24,364; Per Subs 125
Special Collections: Evansville Historical Materials Coll
Wireless access
Mem of Prairie Lakes Library System (PLLS)
Open Mon-Thurs 9:30-7, Fri 9:30-6, Sat 9:30-1
Friends of the Library Group

FAIRCHILD

P FAIRCHILD PUBLIC LIBRARY*, 208 Huron St, 54741. (Mail add: PO Box 149, 54741-0149), SAN 377-9904. Tel: 715-334-4007. E-mail: fairchildlibrary@centurylink.net. Web Site: fairchildpl.org. *Dir,* Rozanne Traczek
Library Holdings: Bk Vols 11,813; Per Subs 20
Wireless access
Mem of Inspiring & Facilitating Library Success (IFLS)
Open Mon-Thurs 1-5, Fri 10:30-5

FALL CREEK

P FALL CREEK PUBLIC LIBRARY*, 122 E Lincoln Ave, 54742-9425. (Mail add: PO Box 426, 54742-0426), SAN 324-1548. Tel: 715-877-3334. FAX: 715-877-2392. E-mail: fallcreekpl@fallcreekpubliclibrary.org. Web Site: www.fallcreekpubliclibrary.org. *Libr Dir,* Laura Tomcik
Library Holdings: Bk Vols 15,000; Per Subs 21
Automation Activity & Vendor Info: (Acquisitions) Innovative Interfaces, Inc; (Cataloging) Innovative Interfaces, Inc; (Circulation) Innovative Interfaces, Inc
Wireless access
Mem of Inspiring & Facilitating Library Success (IFLS)
Open Mon-Thurs 10-6, Fri 10-4, Sat 10-1
Friends of the Library Group

FENNIMORE

P DWIGHT T PARKER PUBLIC LIBRARY*, 925 Lincoln Ave, 53809-1743. SAN 317-9877. Tel: 608-822-6294. E-mail: parker9@tds.net. Web Site: www.fennimore.com/community-life/public-library. *Dir,* Cathy Smith; *Ch,* Mona Winkers
Pop 2,387; Circ 80,546
Library Holdings: Audiobooks 3,026; Bk Vols 31,000; Videos 6,414
Automation Activity & Vendor Info: (Acquisitions) Follett Software; (Cataloging) Follett Software; (Circulation) Follett Software
Wireless access
Function: Prog for children & young adult, Summer reading prog
Publications: A History of Fennimore
Mem of Southwest Wisconsin Library System
Open Mon-Thurs 9-6, Fri 9-4, Sat 9-12
Friends of the Library Group

P SOUTHWEST WISCONSIN LIBRARY SYSTEM*, 1300 Industrial Dr, Ste 2, 53809. SAN 317-9885. Tel: 608-822-3393. Toll Free Tel: 866-866-3393. FAX: 608-822-6251. E-mail: swls@swls.org. Web Site: www.swls.org. *Dir,* David Kranz; E-mail: dkranz@swls.org; *Cat,* Kim F

Streif; *Circ, ILL,* Peggy S Freymiller; E-mail: pfreymiller@swls.org; *Tech Serv,* Betty Sautter; Staff 8 (MLS 2, Non-MLS 6)
Founded 1959. Pop 123,000
Library Holdings: Bk Titles 3,500; Bk Vols 4,000; Per Subs 15
Subject Interests: Regional hist
Automation Activity & Vendor Info: (Cataloging) SirsiDynix; (Circulation) SirsiDynix
Wireless access
Publications: Stepping Stones, Stepping Stones for Children (Newsletter)
Member Libraries: Allen Dietzman Library; Argyle Public Library; Barneveld Public Library; Benton Public Library; Blanchardville Public Library; Bloomington Public Library; Brewer Public Library; Brickl Memorial Library; Cobb Public Library; Cuba City Public Library; Dodgeville Public Library; Dwight T Parker Public Library; Eckstein Memorial Library; Gays Mills Public Library; Hazel Green Public Library; Hildebrand Memorial Library; John Turgeson Public Library; Johnson Public Library; Lone Rock Community Library; McCoy Public Library; Mineral Point Public Library; Montfort Public Library; Muscoda Public Library; Platteville Public Library; Prairie du Chien Memorial Library; Schreiner Memorial Library; Soldiers Grove Public Library; The Mound Center Library; Viola Public Library
Partic in WiLS; Wisconsin Public Library Consortium
Open Mon-Fri 8-4:30

FITCHBURG

P FITCHBURG PUBLIC LIBRARY*, 5530 Lacy Rd, 53711. Tel: 608-729-1760. Circulation Tel: 608-729-1761. Reference Tel: 608-729-1763. E-mail: library@fitchburgwi.gov. Web Site: www.fitchburgwi.gov/822/Library. *Libr Dir,* Wendy Rawson; Tel: 608-729-1764, E-mail: wendy.rawson@fitchburgwi.gov
Founded 2011. Pop 30,000; Circ 389,153
Library Holdings: Bk Vols 90,000
Wireless access
Mem of South Central Library System
Open Mon-Thurs 9-9, Fri & Sat 10-6, Sun 1-5
Friends of the Library Group

FLORENCE

P FLORENCE COUNTY LIBRARY*, 400 Olive Ave, 54121. (Mail add: PO Box 440, 54121-0440), SAN 376-6616. Tel: 715-528-3094. FAX: 715-528-5338. E-mail: flo@florencecountylibrary.org. Web Site: www.florencecountylibrary.org. *Dir,* Stephanie Weber; E-mail: sweber@florencecountylibrary.org
Library Holdings: e-books 71,574; Bk Vols 11,902; Per Subs 1; Talking Bks 700; Videos 2,053
Automation Activity & Vendor Info: (Cataloging) Innovative Interfaces, Inc; (Circulation) Innovative Interfaces, Inc; (OPAC) Innovative Interfaces, Inc
Wireless access
Mem of Nicolet Federated Library System
Open Tues-Thurs 9-5, Fri & Sat 9-Noon
Friends of the Library Group

FOND DU LAC

GL FOND DU LAC CIRCUIT COURT*, Law Library, 160 S Macy St, 54935. SAN 317-9907. Tel: 920-929-3040. FAX: 920-929-3933. *Library Contact,* Shelly Weber; E-mail: michelle.weber@wicourts.gov
Library Holdings: Bk Vols 1,500
Wireless access
Function: Res libr
Open Mon-Fri 8-4:30

S FOND DU LAC COUNTY HISTORICAL SOCIETY*, Library/Archives, 336 Old Pioneer Rd, 54935-6126. (Mail add: PO Box 1284, 54936-1284), SAN 326-4912. Tel: 920-922-1166. E-mail: library@fdlhistory.com. Web Site: www.fdlhistory.com/library. *Exec Dir,* Mary Patricia Voell; Staff 1 (Non-MLS 1)
Founded 1990
Library Holdings: Bk Vols 10,000
Special Collections: Archival Materials (Fond du Lac County)
Subject Interests: Genealogy, Local hist

P FOND DU LAC PUBLIC LIBRARY*, 32 Sheboygon St, 54935. SAN 317-9915. Tel: 920-929-7080. Reference E-mail: reference@fdlpl.org. Web Site: www.fdlpl.org. *Dir,* Jon-Mark Bolthouse; E-mail: bolthouse@fdlpl.org; Staff 32 (MLS 10, Non-MLS 22)
Founded 1876. Pop 71,541; Circ 859,012
Library Holdings: Bk Vols 175,668; Per Subs 372
Special Collections: Municipal. State Document Depository
Automation Activity & Vendor Info: (Acquisitions) SirsiDynix; (Cataloging) SirsiDynix; (Circulation) SirsiDynix; (OPAC) SirsiDynix
Wireless access
Mem of Winnefox Library System
Partic in WiLS
Open Mon-Thurs 9-8, Fri 9-6, Sat 9-4, Sun Noon-4 (Winter); Mon-Thurs 9-8, Fri 9-6, Sat 9-4 (Summer)
Friends of the Library Group

C MARIAN UNIVERSITY*, Cardinal Meyer Library, 45 S National Ave, 54935-4699. SAN 317-9923. Tel: 920-923-7641. Reference Tel: 920-923-8096. FAX: 920-923-7154. Circulation E-mail: circdesk@marianuniversity.edu. Reference E-mail: refdesk@marianuniversity.edu. Web Site: www.marianuniversity.edu/welcome-to-cardinal-meyer-library. *Dean of Student Success,* Jennifer Farvour; Tel: 920-923-8725, E-mail: jkfarvour37@marianuniversity.edu; *Cat Librn, Ref Archivist,* Sarah Thibodeau; Tel: 920-923-8926, E-mail: srthibodeau64@marianuniversity.edu; *Circ & ILL Coordr,* Michele Keifenheim; E-mail: mjkeifenheim00@marianuniversity.edu; Staff 2 (MLS 1, Non-MLS 1)
Founded 1966. Enrl 1,794; Highest Degree: Doctorate
Library Holdings: Bk Vols 91,000; Per Subs 551
Subject Interests: Bus, Educ, Nursing, Theol
Automation Activity & Vendor Info: (Cataloging) OCLC; (Circulation) OCLC; (OPAC) OCLC
Wireless access
Partic in OCLC Online Computer Library Center, Inc
Open Mon-Thurs 7:30am-9pm, Fri 7:30-4:30, Sun 4pm-9pm; Mon-Fri 8-4:30 (Summer)

J MORAINE PARK TECHNICAL COLLEGE LIBRARY*, 235 N National Ave, 54936. (Mail add: PO Box 1940, 54936-1940), SAN 364-6440. Tel: 920-929-2470. Interlibrary Loan Service Tel: 920-924-3118. FAX: 920-924-3117. Web Site: www.morainepark.edu/experience-mptc/services/library. *Libr Serv Coordr,* Hans Baierl; E-mail: hbaierl@morainepark.edu; *Learning Res Tech,* Erika Lloyd; E-mail: elloyd1@morainepark.edu
Founded 1965. Enrl 3,200; Fac 150
Library Holdings: Bk Titles 22,000; Bk Vols 35,000; Per Subs 436
Automation Activity & Vendor Info: (Acquisitions) Ex Libris Group; (Cataloging) Ex Libris Group; (Circulation) Ex Libris Group; (Course Reserve) Ex Libris Group; (ILL) OCLC; (Media Booking) Ex Libris Group; (OPAC) Ex Libris Group; (Serials) Ex Libris Group
Wireless access
Partic in Fox River Valley Area Library Consortium
Open Mon-Thurs 7:30am-9:30pm, Fri 7:30-4, Sat 8-4

S TAYCHEEDAH CORRECTIONAL INSTITUTION LIBRARY*, 751 County Rd K, 54936-1947. SAN 318-4110. Tel: 920-929-3800, Ext 3897. FAX: 920-929-7899. *Librn,* Kelly Huck; E-mail: kelly.huck@wisconsin.gov
Founded 1967
Library Holdings: Bk Vols 14,000; Per Subs 45
Special Collections: Legal Coll - Women's Issues
Automation Activity & Vendor Info: (Acquisitions) Follett Software; (Cataloging) Follett Software; (Circulation) Follett Software
Restriction: Not open to pub

C UNIVERSITY OF WISCONSIN-FOND DU LAC LIBRARY*, 400 University Dr, 54935-2950. Tel: 920-929-1146. FAX: 920-929-7640. E-mail: fdllibrary@uwosh.edu. Web Site: library.uwosh.edu. *Libr Dir,* Sarah Neises; E-mail: neises@uwosh.edu
Library Holdings: Bk Titles 40,000; Per Subs 80
Wireless access
Open Mon-Thurs 8-7, Fri 8-2

FONTANA

P FONTANA PUBLIC LIBRARY*, 166 Second Ave, 53125. (Mail add: PO Box 437, 53125-0437), SAN 317-9966. Tel: 262-275-5107. FAX: 262-275-2179. E-mail: fontana@fontana.lib.wi.us. Web Site: fontana.lib.wi.us. *Dir,* Walter Burkhalter; E-mail: wburkhalter@fontana.lib.wi.us; Staff 3 (MLS 1, Non-MLS 2)
Founded 1931
Library Holdings: Bk Vols 34,000; Per Subs 50
Automation Activity & Vendor Info: (Cataloging) SirsiDynix; (Circulation) SirsiDynix
Wireless access
Mem of Prairie Lakes Library System (PLLS)
Open Mon-Fri 9-5, Sat 9-1

FORT ATKINSON

P DWIGHT FOSTER PUBLIC LIBRARY*, 209 Merchants Ave, 53538-2049. SAN 317-9974. Tel: 920-563-7790. FAX: 920-563-7774. Web Site: www.fortlibrary.org. *Dir,* Eric Robinson; E-mail: erobinson@fortlibrary.org; *Asst Dir, Ref,* Amy Lutzke; E-mail:

alutzke@fortlibrary.org; *Youth Serv Librn,* Minetta Lippert; E-mail: minetta@fortlibrary.org; Staff 3 (MLS 3)
Founded 1890. Pop 21,568; Circ 204,277
Library Holdings: Audiobooks 4,940; DVDs 6,203; Bk Titles 82,462; Per Subs 140
Special Collections: Local History, bks & clippings; Lorine Niedecker Coll
Automation Activity & Vendor Info: (Cataloging) SirsiDynix-Unicorn; (Circulation) SirsiDynix-Unicorn; (OPAC) SirsiDynix-Unicorn
Wireless access
Mem of Bridges Library System
Open Mon-Thurs 8-8, Fri 8-6, Sat 9-2
Friends of the Library Group

S HOARD HISTORICAL MUSEUM LIBRARY*, 401 Whitewater Ave, 53538. SAN 373-3068. Tel: 920-563-7769. FAX: 920-568-3203. E-mail: info@hoardmuseum.org. Web Site: hoardmuseum.org. *Dir,* Merilee Lee; E-mail: mlee@hoardmuseum.org; *Asst Dir,* Dana Bertelsen; E-mail: dbertelsen@hoardmuseum.org
Library Holdings: Bk Vols 5,000
Subject Interests: Civil War, Local hist
Open Tues-Sat 9:30-4:30
Restriction: Not a lending libr

FOX LAKE

S FOX LAKE CORRECTIONAL INSTITUTION LIBRARY, PO Box 147, 53933-0147. SAN 364-6475. Tel: 920-928-3151, Ext 6240. FAX: 920-928-6929. *Librn,* Angela Cypert; E-mail: angela.cypert@wisconsin.gov; Staff 1 (MLS 1)
Founded 1962
Library Holdings: Bk Vols 14,000; Per Subs 70
Subject Interests: Fiction, Legal
Automation Activity & Vendor Info: (Cataloging) Follett Software; (Circulation) Follett Software; (Course Reserve) Follett Software; (ILL) Follett Software; (Media Booking) Follett Software; (OPAC) Follett Software; (Serials) Follett Software

P FOX LAKE PUBLIC LIBRARY*, 117 W State St, 53933-9505. (Mail add: PO Box 47, 53933-0047), SAN 317-9982. Tel: 920-928-3223. FAX: 920-928-3810. E-mail: foxlakelibrary@monarchlibraries.org. Web Site: www.foxlake.lib.wi.us. *Dir,* Erin Anders; Staff 1 (Non-MLS 1)
Founded 1910. Pop 3,000; Circ 30,000
Library Holdings: Bk Titles 12,000; Per Subs 100
Automation Activity & Vendor Info: (Circulation) SirsiDynix
Wireless access
Function: Adult bk club, Audiobks via web, Bks on CD, Children's prog, Free DVD rentals, ILL available, Internet access, Magazines, Magnifiers for reading, Online cat, Photocopying/Printing, Prog for adults, Prog for children & young adult, Res libr, Scanner, Spanish lang bks, Summer reading prog, Tax forms
Mem of Monarch Library System
Open Mon-Thurs 10-7, Fri 10-5, Sat 10-2
Friends of the Library Group

FRANKLIN

P FRANKLIN PUBLIC LIBRARY*, 9151 W Loomis Rd, 53132. SAN 324-0916. Tel: 414-425-8214. FAX: 414-425-9498. Web Site: www.franklinpubliclibrary.org. *Dir,* Jennifer Loeffel; Tel: 414-427-7545, E-mail: Jennifer.Loeffel@mcfls.org; *Asst Dir,* Keri Whitmore; Tel: 414-427-7548, E-mail: Keri.Miller@mcfls.org; *Circ Supvr,* Maureen Walton; E-mail: Maureen.Walton@mcfls.org; *Ref Serv,* Position Currently Open; *Ref Serv,* Andy Scott; E-mail: Andy.Scott@mcfls.org; *Ref Serv, YA,* Laura Gravander; E-mail: Laura.Gravander@mcfls.org; *Youth Serv,* Briony Beckstrom; E-mail: Briony.Zlomke@mcfls.org; *Youth Serv,* Sarah Bublitz; E-mail: Sarah.Stoecker@mcfls.org; Staff 8 (MLS 7, Non-MLS 1)
Founded 1980. Pop 35,000
Jan 2019-Dec 2019. Mats Exp $104,000, Books $95,000, Per/Ser (Incl. Access Fees) $9,000. Sal $780,829 (Prof $388,143)
Library Holdings: Bk Titles 117,000; Per Subs 180
Automation Activity & Vendor Info: (Acquisitions) Innovative Interfaces, Inc - Millennium; (Cataloging) Innovative Interfaces, Inc - Millennium; (Circulation) Innovative Interfaces, Inc; (OPAC) Innovative Interfaces, Inc - Millennium; (Serials) Innovative Interfaces, Inc - Millennium
Wireless access
Function: 24/7 Electronic res, 24/7 Online cat, 3D Printer, Activity rm, Adult bk club
Mem of Milwaukee County Federated Library System
Open Mon-Thurs 10-8:30, Fri 10-6, Sat 10-5, Sun (Sept-May) 1-4
Friends of the Library Group

R SACRED HEART SEMINARY & SCHOOL OF THEOLOGY*, Leo Dehon Library, 7335 Lovers Lane Rd, 53132. (Mail add: PO Box 429, Hales Corners, 53130-0429), SAN 318-0212. Tel: 414-858-4995. Administration Tel: 414-529-6990. E-mail: library@shsst.edu. Web Site: leodehonlibrary.libguides.com/home. *Director of Library & Academic Support,* Dyan Barbeau; E-mail: dbarbeau@shsst.edu; *Digital Serv Librn,* Ann Owen; Tel: 414-858-4659, E-mail: aowen@shsst.edu; *Res & Educ Serv Librn,* Kathleen Harty; Tel: 414-858-4645, E-mail: kharty@shsst.edu. Subject Specialists: *Theol,* Kathleen Harty; Staff 3.5 (MLS 3, Non-MLS 0.5)
Founded 1932. Enrl 163; Fac 40; Highest Degree: Master
Library Holdings: AV Mats 959; e-books 471,843; e-journals 111,726; Microforms 54; Bk Titles 74,636; Bk Vols 82,966; Per Subs 422
Special Collections: Lux Center for Catholic-Jewish Studies; Religious Americana; Sacred Heart/Dehonian Coll
Subject Interests: Canon law, Church hist, Liturgy, Sacred scripture
Automation Activity & Vendor Info: (Acquisitions) Ex Libris Group; (Cataloging) Ex Libris Group; (Circulation) Ex Libris Group; (Course Reserve) Ex Libris Group; (ILL) OCLC; (OPAC) Ex Libris Group; (Serials) Ex Libris Group
Wireless access
Function: Writing prog
Publications: Introduction to Theological Studies - Seminar (Reference guide); Library Policies & Procedures; New Library Acquisitions
Partic in Southeastern Wisconsin Information Technology Exchange, Inc; WiLS
Special Services for the Blind - Braille equip
Open Mon-Fri 8-4:30
Restriction: 24-hr pass syst for students only, Authorized patrons, Borrowing requests are handled by ILL, Open to pub for ref & circ; with some limitations

FREDERIC

P FREDERIC PUBLIC LIBRARY*, 127 Oak St W, 54837. (Mail add: PO Box 700, 54837-0700), SAN 377-9920. Tel: 715-327-4979. E-mail: library@fredericlibrary.org. Web Site: www.fredericlibrary.org. *Dir,* Kris Surbaugh; E-mail: surbaugh@fredericlibrary.org; *Asst Dir,* Marlene Nelson; E-mail: nelson@fredericlibrary.org
Library Holdings: Bk Vols 15,000; Per Subs 40
Wireless access
Mem of Inspiring & Facilitating Library Success (IFLS)
Open Mon-Fri 9-5, Sat 9-12
Friends of the Library Group

FREMONT

P NEUSCHAFER COMMUNITY LIBRARY*, 317 Wolf River Dr, 54940. (Mail add: PO Box 498, 54940-0498), SAN 375-0469. Tel: 920-446-2474. FAX: 920-446-2480. E-mail: fpl@fremontpl.org. Web Site: www.fremontpl.org. *Dir,* Natalie Snyder; *Asst Librn,* Jill Kocovsky
Pop 735; Circ 1,829
Library Holdings: Bk Vols 4,000; Per Subs 44
Mem of Outagamie Waupaca Library System (OWLS)
Open Mon, Tues & Thurs 10-6, Wed 9-6, Fri 10-2
Friends of the Library Group

GALESVILLE

P GALESVILLE PUBLIC LIBRARY*, 16787 S Main St, 54630. (Mail add: PO Box 697, 54630-0697), SAN 317-9990. Tel: 608-582-2552. E-mail: galepublib@wrlsweb.org. Web Site: galesvillelibrary.wrlsweb.org. *Dir,* Meredith Houge; *Asst Librn,* Cindi Schein; *Circ Asst,* Terry Helgeson; *Youth Serv,* Wina Mortenson; Staff 1.6 (Non-MLS 1.6)
Founded 1911. Pop 1,600; Circ 27,737
Library Holdings: Large Print Bks 1,020; Bk Vols 13,700; Per Subs 45; Videos 563
Special Collections: Arrowhead Coll
Wireless access
Function: Adult bk club, Art exhibits, Audio & video playback equip for onsite use, Audiobks via web, Bks on CD, Children's prog, Computers for patron use, Digital talking bks, Distance learning, Home delivery & serv to seniorr ctr & nursing homes, Homebound delivery serv, ILL available, Large print keyboards, Magnifiers for reading, Music CDs, OverDrive digital audio bks, Photocopying/Printing, Prog for adults, Prog for children & young adult, Story hour, Summer reading prog, Tax forms, Telephone ref, Wheelchair accessible
Mem of Winding Rivers Library System
Open Mon & Wed 10-7, Tues & Thurs 1-7
Friends of the Library Group

GAYS MILLS

P GAYS MILLS PUBLIC LIBRARY*, 16381 State Hwy 131, 54631. SAN 318-000X. Tel: 608-735-4331. Web Site: gaysmillslibrary.org. *Libr Dir,* David Gibbs; E-mail: dgibbs@swls.org; *Libr Asst,* Don Lampert; Staff 0.9 (Non-MLS 0.9)
Founded 1941. Pop 519; Circ 6,829

Library Holdings: Audiobooks 503; DVDs 1,359; Large Print Bks 60; Bk Vols 7,905; Per Subs 31
Wireless access
Function: 24/7 Electronic res, 24/7 Online cat, Adult bk club, Audiobks on Playaways & MP3, Bks on CD, Children's prog, Computers for patron use, Electronic databases & coll, Equip loans & repairs, Free DVD rentals, Games & aids for people with disabilities, Govt ref serv, ILL available, Internet access, Laminating, Magazines, Meeting rooms, Movies, Music CDs, Online cat, OverDrive digital audio bks, Photocopying/Printing, Prog for adults, Prog for children & young adult, Ref serv available, Scanner, Serves people with intellectual disabilities, Spoken cassettes & CDs, Story hour, Summer reading prog, Tax forms, Teen prog, Wheelchair accessible
Mem of Southwest Wisconsin Library System
Open Mon, Tues & Thurs 2-7, Wed 9-2, Fri 1-5, Sat 9-Noon
Friends of the Library Group

GENOA CITY

P GENOA CITY PUBLIC LIBRARY*, 126 Freeman St, 53128-2073. (Mail add: PO Box 727, 53128-0727), SAN 318-0018. Tel: 262-279-6188. FAX: 262-279-3665. E-mail: genoa@genoacity.lib.wi.us. Web Site: www.genoacity.lib.wi.us. *Dir,* Arin Wilken; Staff 1 (Non-MLS 1)
Founded 1900. Pop 5,500; Circ 44,000
Library Holdings: Audiobooks 684; CDs 724; DVDs 2,310; e-books 145,293; Bk Vols 26,500; Per Subs 55
Automation Activity & Vendor Info: (Acquisitions) SirsiDynix; (Cataloging) SirsiDynix; (Circulation) SirsiDynix
Wireless access
Mem of Prairie Lakes Library System (PLLS)
Open Mon & Wed 9-7, Tues, Thurs & Fri 9-5, Sat 9-1
Friends of the Library Group

GERMANTOWN

P GERMANTOWN COMMUNITY LIBRARY*, N112W16957 Mequon Rd, 53022. (Mail add: PO Box 670, 53022-0670), SAN 318-0026. Tel: 262-253-7760. FAX: 262-253-7763. Web Site: www.germantownlibrarywi.org. *Dir,* Trisha Smith; E-mail: smithp@germantownlibrarywi.org; *Ch,* Jackie Molitor; E-mail: jmolitor@germantownlibrarywi.org; Staff 17.4 (MLS 1, Non-MLS 16.4)
Founded 1963. Pop 33,000; Circ 238,000
Library Holdings: AV Mats 15,000; e-books 153,000; Electronic Media & Resources 98,000; Bk Vols 115,000; Per Subs 100
Automation Activity & Vendor Info: (Cataloging) Innovative Interfaces, Inc. - Polaris; (Circulation) Innovative Interfaces, Inc. - Polaris; (OPAC) Innovative Interfaces, Inc. - Polaris
Wireless access
Mem of Monarch Library System
Open Mon-Thurs 9-8, Fri 9-5, Sat 9-4
Friends of the Library Group

GILLETT

P GILLETT PUBLIC LIBRARY*, 200 E Main St, 54124. (Mail add: PO Box 109, 54124-0109), SAN 318-0034. Tel: 920-855-6224. FAX: 920-855-6533. E-mail: gil@gilpubliclibrary.org. Web Site: www.gilpubliclibrary.org. *Libr Dir,* Shannon Nichola Stoner; E-mail: sstoner@gilpubliclibrary.org
Founded 1927. Pop 1,300; Circ 44,500
Library Holdings: Bk Vols 15,000; Per Subs 25
Automation Activity & Vendor Info: (Cataloging) CARL.Solution (TLC); (Circulation) CARL.Solution (TLC)
Wireless access
Mem of Nicolet Federated Library System
Open Mon-Thurs 10-6, Fri 10-5
Friends of the Library Group

GILMAN

P WESTERN TAYLOR COUNTY PUBLIC LIBRARY*, 380 E Main St, 54433. (Mail add: PO Box 87, 54433-0087), SAN 318-0042. Tel: 715-447-5486. FAX: 715-447-8134. Web Site: www.gilman.lib.wi.us. *Dir,* Katie Petranovich; E-mail: director@gilman.lib.wi.us
Library Holdings: Bk Vols 7,800; Per Subs 55
Automation Activity & Vendor Info: (Cataloging) Innovative Interfaces, Inc - Sierra; (Circulation) Innovative Interfaces, Inc - Sierra; (OPAC) Innovative Interfaces, Inc - Sierra
Wireless access
Partic in Wisconsin Valley Library Service
Open Mon 10-5, Wed & Fri 12-6

GLENDALE

P NORTH SHORE LIBRARY*, 6800 N Port Washington Rd, 53217. SAN 324-7201. Tel: 414-351-3461. FAX: 414-351-3528. Web Site: www.mcfls.org/northshorelibrary. *Libr Dir,* Annie Bahringer; *Asst Dir,* Alyssa Pisarski; E-mail: alyssa.pisarski@mcfls.org; *Head, Adult Serv,* Melody Schutz; E-mail: melody.schutz@mcfls.org; *Head, Youth Serv,* Lizzy Lowrey; E-mail: lizzy.lowrey@mcfls.org; Staff 6 (MLS 6)
Founded 1979. Pop 25,600; Circ 350,227
Library Holdings: Audiobooks 5,712; e-books 27,088; Bk Vols 127,000; Per Subs 260; Videos 9,082
Automation Activity & Vendor Info: (Acquisitions) Innovative Interfaces, Inc; (Cataloging) Innovative Interfaces, Inc; (Circulation) Innovative Interfaces, Inc; (Course Reserve) Innovative Interfaces, Inc; (ILL) Innovative Interfaces, Inc; (Media Booking) Innovative Interfaces, Inc; (OPAC) Innovative Interfaces, Inc; (Serials) Innovative Interfaces, Inc
Wireless access
Mem of Milwaukee County Federated Library System
Open Mon-Thurs 10-8, Fri & Sat 10-5, Sun 1-5
Friends of the Library Group

GLENWOOD CITY

P GLENWOOD CITY PUBLIC LIBRARY*, 217 W Oak St, 54013-8554. (Mail add: PO Box 247, 54013-0247), SAN 318-0050. Tel: 715-265-7443. E-mail: gclibrary@glenwoodcitylibrary.org. Web Site: glenwoodcitylibrary.org. *Dir,* Rochel Karlson; Staff 1 (MLS 1)
Founded 1900. Pop 1,301; Circ 12,000
Library Holdings: AV Mats 1,200; e-books 8,805; Large Print Bks 300; Bk Titles 8,259; Per Subs 45
Automation Activity & Vendor Info: (Cataloging) Innovative Interfaces, Inc; (Circulation) Innovative Interfaces, Inc; (OPAC) Innovative Interfaces, Inc
Wireless access
Function: 24/7 Online cat, Adult bk club, Audiobks via web, Bks on CD, Children's prog, Computers for patron use, Electronic databases & coll, Family literacy, Free DVD rentals, Holiday prog, Home delivery & serv to seniorr ctr & nursing homes, ILL available, Internet access, Life-long learning prog for all ages, Magazines, Mail & tel request accepted, Movies, Music CDs, Online cat, Online ref, OverDrive digital audio bks, Photocopying/Printing, Prog for adults, Prog for children & young adult, Ref serv available, Scanner, STEM programs, Story hour, Summer reading prog, Tax forms, Teen prog, VHS videos, Wheelchair accessible
Mem of Inspiring & Facilitating Library Success (IFLS)
Special Services for the Blind - Audio mat; Bks on cassette; Bks on CD; Computer access aids; Internet workstation with adaptive software; Large print bks; ZoomText magnification & reading software
Open Mon Noon-7:30, Tues & Wed 10-6, Thurs 10-7:30, Fri 10-5, Sat 10-1
Restriction: Circ to mem only, Non-circulating coll, Non-circulating of rare bks, Non-resident fee
Friends of the Library Group

GRAFTON

P USS LIBERTY MEMORIAL PUBLIC LIBRARY*, 1620 11th Ave, 53024-2404. SAN 318-0069. Tel: 262-375-5315. FAX: 262-375-5317. E-mail: grafton@monarchlibraries.org. Web Site: www.graftonpubliclibrary.net. *Dir,* John Hanson; E-mail: JHanson@monarchlibraries.org; *Head, Youth Serv,* Judy Jones; E-mail: JJones@monarchlibraries.org; Staff 12 (MLS 3, Non-MLS 9)
Founded 1956. Pop 15,000; Circ 193,000
Jan 2018-Dec 2018 Income $886,640, City $727,404, County $42,843, Locally Generated Income $9,973. Mats Exp $71,293, Books $53,408, AV Mat $12,113, Electronic Ref Mat (Incl. Access Fees) $5,772. Sal $399,147 (Prof $178,123)
Library Holdings: AV Mats 14,225; Bks on Deafness & Sign Lang 20; DVDs 7,472; e-books 151,392; High Interest/Low Vocabulary Bk Vols 60; Large Print Bks 1,500; Bk Vols 63,844; Per Subs 134
Automation Activity & Vendor Info: (Cataloging) Innovative Interfaces, Inc; (Circulation) Innovative Interfaces, Inc; (OPAC) Innovative Interfaces, Inc
Wireless access
Publications: Library Letter (Quarterly)
Mem of Monarch Library System
Open Mon-Thurs 9:30-8, Fri 9:30-5, Sat 9:30-2
Friends of the Library Group

GRANTON

P GRANTON COMMUNITY LIBRARY*, 217 N Main St, 54436. SAN 318-0077. Tel: 715-238-5250. Web Site: villageofgranton.com/departments/library.php. *Libr Dir,* Kay Heiting; E-mail: director@granton.lib.wi.us; *Asst Librn, ILL,* Missy Walz; E-mail: mwalz@wvls.lib.wi.us
Pop 425; Circ 4,772
Library Holdings: Bk Vols 7,542; Per Subs 24
Wireless access
Partic in Wisconsin Valley Library Service
Open Mon, Wed & Fri 8-4, Tues & Thurs 8-7, Sat 9:30-Noon

GRANTSBURG

P GRANTSBURG PUBLIC LIBRARY*, 415 S Robert St, 54840-7423. SAN 318-0085. Tel: 715-463-2244. FAX: 715-463-5555. E-mail: notices@grantsburg.wislib.org. Web Site: grantsburglibrary.org. *Dir,* Kristina Kelley-Johnson; E-mail: kristina@grantsburg.wislib.org; *Librn,* Gail Potvin; E-mail: gail@grantsburg.wislib.org
Pop 1,200; Circ 14,510
Library Holdings: Bk Vols 16,000; Per Subs 37
Subject Interests: Local authors, Local hist
Automation Activity & Vendor Info: (Cataloging) Innovative Interfaces, Inc; (Circulation) Innovative Interfaces, Inc; (OPAC) Innovative Interfaces, Inc
Wireless access
Mem of Northern Waters Library Service
Open Mon-Wed & Fri 10-6, Thurs 12-8, Sat 10-2
Friends of the Library Group

GREEN BAY

CM BELLIN COLLEGE*, Phil & Betsy Hendrickson Library, 3201 Eaton Rd, 54311. SAN 318-0093. Tel: 920-433-6659. FAX: 920-433-1939. E-mail: library@bellincollege.edu. Web Site: www.bellincollege.edu/campus-life/library. *Librn,* Cynthia Reinl; Tel: 920-433-6660, E-mail: cindy.reinl@bellincollege.edu; *Asst Librn,* Christine Smits; E-mail: christine.smits@bellincollege.edu; Staff 2 (MLS 1, Non-MLS 1)
Founded 1910
Library Holdings: Bk Vols 2,800; Per Subs 250
Subject Interests: Allied health, Med, Nursing
Wireless access
Partic in Fox River Valley Area Library Consortium; National Network of Libraries of Medicine Region 6; NE Wis Intertype Librs, Inc
Open Mon-Fri 8-4:30

P BROWN COUNTY LIBRARY*, 515 Pine St, 54301. SAN 364-653X. Tel: 920-448-4400. Circulation Tel: 920-448-5825. Interlibrary Loan Service Tel: 920-448-4410. FAX: 920-448-4376. E-mail: BC_Library@browncountywi.gov. Web Site: www.browncountylibrary.org. *Exec Dir,* Sarah Sugden; Tel: 920-448-5810, E-mail: Sarah.Sugden@browncountywi.gov; *Dep Dir,* Emily Rogers; Tel: 920-448-5808, E-mail: Emily.Rogers@browncountywi.gov; *Finance Mgr,* Linda Chosa; Tel: 920-448-5802, E-mail: Linda.Chosa@browncountywi.gov; *Adult Serv Mgr,* Andrea West; Tel: 920-448-4400, Ext 7, E-mail: Andrea.West@browncountywi.gov; *Cent Libr Mgr,* Sandy Kallunki; Tel: 920-448-5830, E-mail: Sandy.Kallunki@browncountywi.gov; *Circ Mgr,* Ashley McHose; Tel: 920-448-5825, E-mail: Ashley.McHose@browncountywi.gov; *Coll Develop & Tech Serv Mgr,* Clare Kindt; Tel: 920-448-5801, E-mail: Clare.Kindt@browncountywi.gov; *Communications & Libr Prog Mgr,* Susan Lagerman; Tel: 920-448-5806, E-mail: susan.lagerman@browncountywi.gov; *Fac Mgr,* Curt Beyler; Tel: 920-448-5849, E-mail: Curt.Beyler@browncoutywi.gov; *Local Hist/Genealogy, Mgr, Spec Coll,* Mary Jane Herber; Tel: 920-448-5815, E-mail: MaryJane.Herber@browncountywi.gov; *Youth Serv Mgr,* Position Currently Open; Staff 33 (MLS 18, Non-MLS 15)
Founded 1968. Pop 261,863; Circ 1,730,300
Library Holdings: AV Mats 41,281; Bk Vols 468,451; Per Subs 1,128
Special Collections: Brown County History Coll; Wisconsin History Coll
Subject Interests: Genealogy
Automation Activity & Vendor Info: (Acquisitions) SirsiDynix; (Cataloging) SirsiDynix; (Circulation) SirsiDynix; (OPAC) SirsiDynix-Enterprise
Wireless access
Function: Adult bk club, Art exhibits, Audiobks via web, Bilingual assistance for Spanish patrons, Bk club(s), Bks on cassette, Bks on CD, Bus archives, CD-ROM, Children's prog, Computer training, Computers for patron use, E-Reserves, Electronic databases & coll, Free DVD rentals, Holiday prog, Home delivery & serv to seniorr ctr & nursing homes, Homebound delivery serv, ILL available, Internet access, Jail serv, Magnifiers for reading, Mail & tel request accepted, Music CDs, Notary serv, Online cat, Online ref, Orientations, Outreach serv, Outside serv via phone, mail, e-mail & web, OverDrive digital audio bks, Photocopying/Printing, Preschool outreach, Prog for adults, Prog for children & young adult, Ref & res, Ref serv available, Scanner, Senior outreach, Story hour, Summer & winter reading prog, Summer reading prog, Tax forms, Teen prog, Telephone ref, Wheelchair accessible, Workshops
Mem of Nicolet Federated Library System
Partic in NE Wis Intertype Librs, Inc
Special Services for the Deaf - Assisted listening device; Assistive tech; Bks on deafness & sign lang; Closed caption videos; High interest/low vocabulary bks; Spec interest per
Special Services for the Blind - Audio mat; BiFolkal kits; Bks on CD; Copier with enlargement capabilities; Internet workstation with adaptive software; Large print bks; Playaways (bks on MP3); Videos on blindness & physical disabilities
Open Mon-Thurs 9-8, Fri 9-5, Sat 9-4, Sun (Sept-May) Noon-4
Friends of the Library Group
Branches: 8
ASHWAUBENON BRANCH, 1060 Orlando Dr, 54304, SAN 364-6599. Tel: 920-492-4913. FAX: 920-492-4914. E-mail: bc_library_ashwaubenon@browncountywi.gov. *Libr Mgr,* Karla Giraldez
Open Mon-Thurs 10-8, Fri & Sat 10-5 (Winter); Mon-Wed 10-8, Thurs & Fri 10-5, Sat 10-1 (Summer)
Friends of the Library Group
DENMARK BRANCH, 450 N Wall St, Denmark, 54208, SAN 364-6629. Tel: 920-863-6613. FAX: 920-863-3001. E-mail: bc_library_denmark@browncountywi.gov. *Libr Mgr,* Bobbie Kuehn
Open Mon & Wed 3:30-8, Tues & Thurs 3:30-6:30
Friends of the Library Group
EAST BRANCH, 2255 Main St, 54302-3743, SAN 364-6742. Tel: 920-391-4600. FAX: 920-391-4601. E-mail: bc_library_east@browncountywi.gov. *Libr Mgr,* Bobbie Kuehn
Open Mon, Tues & Wed 9-8, Thurs & Fri 9-5, Sat 10-2
Friends of the Library Group
KRESS FAMILY BRANCH, 333 N Broadway, De Pere, 54115, SAN 364-6653. Tel: 920-448-4407. FAX: 920-403-1778. E-mail: bc_library_depere@browncountywi.gov. *Br Mgr,* Molly A Senechal
Open Mon, Tues & Wed 9-8, Thurs & Fri 9-5, Sat 10-4
Friends of the Library Group
PULASKI BRANCH, 222 W Pulaski St, Pulaski, 54162, SAN 364-6777. Tel: 920-822-3220. FAX: 920-822-5589. E-mail: bc_library_pulaski@browncountywi.gov. *Libr Mgr,* Becky J Phillips
Open Mon & Wed 1-8, Tues & Thurs 10-5, Fri 1-5
Friends of the Library Group
SOUTHWEST BRANCH, 974 Ninth St, 54304, SAN 364-6807. Tel: 920-492-4910. FAX: 920-492-4911. E-mail: bc_library_southwest@browncountywi.gov. *Libr Mgr,* Karal Giraldez
Open Mon, Tues & Wed 9-8, Thurs & Fri 9-5, Sat 10-2
Friends of the Library Group
WEYERS-HILLIARD BRANCH, 2680 Riverview Dr, 54313, SAN 364-6718. Tel: 920-448-4405. FAX: 920-662-2149. E-mail: bc_library_howard@browncountywi.gov. *Libr Mgr,* Becky Phillips
Open Mon, Tues & Wed 9-8, Thurs & Fri 9-5, Sat 10-4
Friends of the Library Group
WRIGHTSTOWN BRANCH, 615 Main St, Wrightstown, 54180, SAN 364-6831. Tel: 920-532-4011. FAX: 920-532-4199. E-mail: bc_library@browncountywi.gov. *Libr Mgr,* Molly Senechal
Open Mon & Wed 1-8, Tues & Thurs 10-5
Friends of the Library Group
Bookmobiles: 1. Operator, Jenn Koetz

R FIRST UNITED METHODIST CHURCH LIBRARY*, 501 Howe St, 54301. SAN 318-0107. Tel: 920-437-9252. FAX: 920-437-0991. E-mail: office@fumcgb.org. Web Site: www.fumcgb.org. *Librn,* Mary Barrows; E-mail: mary.barrows@sbcglobal.net
Founded 1959
Library Holdings: Bk Titles 1,500; Bk Vols 1,550; Per Subs 10
Wireless access
Open Mon-Fri 8:30-4, Sun 7-12

S GREEN BAY CORRECTIONAL INSTITUTION LIBRARY*, PO Box 19033, 54307-9033. SAN 318-0115. Tel: 920-432-4877, Ext 3457. FAX: 920-432-5388. *Librn,* Rodney Owens; E-mail: Rodney.Owens@wisconsin.gov
Founded 1898
Library Holdings: Bk Vols 8,000; Per Subs 30
Subject Interests: Law
Restriction: Not open to pub

S NEVILLE PUBLIC MUSEUM OF BROWN COUNTY LIBRARY*, 210 Museum Pl, 54303. SAN 329-2568. Tel: 920-448-4460. FAX: 920-448-4458. Web Site: www.nevillepublicmuseum.org. *Exec Dir,* Beth Kowalski; Tel: 920-448-7848, E-mail: beth.kowalski@browncountywi.gov; Staff 1 (Non-MLS 1)
Founded 1915
Library Holdings: Bk Titles 4,500; Per Subs 20
Subject Interests: Art, Dolls, Local hist, Mus practice, Natural sci, Textiles
Function: Photocopying/Printing
Restriction: Not a lending libr, Open by appt only

P NICOLET FEDERATED LIBRARY SYSTEM*, 1595 Allouez Ave, Ste 4, 54311. SAN 318-0123. Tel: 920-448-4410. FAX: 920-448-4420. Web Site: www.nfls.lib.wi.us. *Dir,* Tracy Vreeke; E-mail: tvreeke@nflsoffice.org; *Libr Office Mgr,* Hannah Good Zima; E-mail: hzima@nflsoffice.org; *ILL & Doc Delivery Coordr,* Holly Handt; E-mail: hhandt@nflsoffice.org; *Educ Spec, Mkt & Communications Spec,* Lori Baumgart; E-mail:

lbaumgart@nflsoffice.org; *IT Coordr,* John Kronenburg; E-mail: jkronenburg@nflsoffice.org; Staff 5 (MLS 1, Non-MLS 4)
Founded 1976. Pop 431,057
Automation Activity & Vendor Info: (Acquisitions) Innovative Interfaces, Inc; (Cataloging) Innovative Interfaces, Inc; (Circulation) Innovative Interfaces, Inc; (Course Reserve) Innovative Interfaces, Inc; (ILL) Innovative Interfaces, Inc; (Media Booking) Innovative Interfaces, Inc; (OPAC) Innovative Interfaces, Inc; (Serials) Innovative Interfaces, Inc
Wireless access
Publications: NicBits (Newsletter)
Member Libraries: Algoma Public Library; Brown County Library; College of Menominee Nation Library; Door County Library; Farnsworth Public Library; Florence County Library; Gillett Public Library; Kewaunee Public Library; Lakes Country Public Library; Lena Public Library; Marinette County Library System; Oconto Falls Community Library; Oneida Community Library; Shawano County Library; Suring Area Public Library
Partic in NE Wis Intertype Libs, Inc; OWLSnet; Wisconsin Public Library Consortium
Open Mon-Fri 8-4:30

S NORTHEAST WISCONSIN MASONIC LIBRARY & MUSEUM*, 1950 Bond St, 54303. Tel: 920-498-1985. Web Site: www.newmasoniccenter.com. *Pres,* Tom Pinney, Jr; Tel: 920-493-3727, E-mail: tompinney@charter.net
Library Holdings: Bk Titles 1,600
Restriction: Open by appt only

J NORTHEAST WISCONSIN TECHNICAL COLLEGE LIBRARY, 2740 W Mason St, 54303-4966. (Mail add: PO Box 19042, 54307-9042), SAN 318-0131. Tel: 920-498-5487. Interlibrary Loan Service Tel: 920-498-5493. Reference Tel: 920-498-5490. Interlibrary Loan Service E-mail: interlibrary.loan@nwtc.edu. Web Site: nwtc.edu/student-experience/library. *Mgr, Res Libr Serv,* Kim LaPlante; E-mail: kim.laplante@nwtc.edu; *Supvr, Libr Instruction,* Julie Chapman; E-mail: julie.chapman@nwtc.edu; *Circ,* Jacquelyn Ornelas; Tel: 920-498-5732, E-mail: jacquelyn.ornelas@nwtc.edu; Staff 8 (MLS 4, Non-MLS 4)
Founded 1966. Enrl 4,928; Highest Degree: Associate
Jul 2021-Jun 2022. Mats Exp $281,221, Books $70,313, Electronic Ref Mat (Incl. Access Fees) $210,908. Sal $402,156 (Prof $234,233)
Library Holdings: DVDs 1,080; e-books 210,857; e-journals 200,056; Bk Titles 12,382; Bk Vols 19,026; Per Subs 68
Special Collections: Developmental Education (Student Study Success Coll); Entertainment DVDs; Job Hunting Coll; Test Preparation Coll
Automation Activity & Vendor Info: (Acquisitions) Innovative Interfaces, Inc - Sierra; (Cataloging) Innovative Interfaces, Inc - Sierra; (Circulation) Innovative Interfaces, Inc - Sierra; (Course Reserve) Innovative Interfaces, Inc - Sierra; (Discovery) EBSCO Discovery Service; (ILL) Auto-Graphics, Inc; (Media Booking) Innovative Interfaces, Inc - Sierra; (OPAC) Innovative Interfaces, Inc - Sierra; (Serials) Innovative Interfaces, Inc - Sierra
Wireless access
Function: 24/7 Electronic res, 24/7 Online cat, Adult bk club, Archival coll, Audiobks via web, Bilingual assistance for Spanish patrons, Bk club(s), Computer training, Computers for patron use, Distance learning, Electronic databases & coll, Equip loans & repairs, Family literacy, Free DVD rentals, Health sci info serv, ILL available, Internet access, Laptop/tablet checkout, Learning ctr, Magazines, Movies, Online cat, Online Chat, Online info literacy tutorials on the web & in blackboard, Online ref, Orientations, Outside serv via phone, mail, e-mail & web, OverDrive digital audio bks, Photocopying/Printing, Printer for laptops & handheld devices, Prof lending libr, Ref & res, Ref serv available, Res assist avail, Scanner, Spanish lang bks, Study rm, Telephone ref, Wheelchair accessible, Wifi hotspot checkout
Publications: Copyright Policy & Handbooks (Documents); Library Guides (Research guide); Online Catalog & Database Instruction Handbook (Reference guide); Wisconsin Technical College ILL Directory (Library handbook)
Partic in Fox River Valley Area Library Consortium; WiLS; WISPALS Library Consortium
Special Services for the Deaf - Closed caption videos
Open Mon-Thurs 7:30am-7pm, Fri 7:30-4, Sat 10-2 ; Mon-Thurs 7:30-4:30, Fri 7:30-4 (Summer)

C UNIVERSITY OF WISCONSIN-GREEN BAY*, David A Cofrin Library, 2420 Nicolet Dr, 54311-7001. SAN 318-0158. Administration Tel: 920-465-2537. Information Services Tel: 920-465-2540. E-mail: refdesk@uwgb.edu. Web Site: www.uwgb.edu/library. *Asst Vice Chancellor, Info Tech, Library Services,* Paula M Ganyard; E-mail: ganyard@uwgb.edu; *Asst Dir, Head, Univ Archives & Area Res Ctr,* Debra Anderson; Tel: 920-465-2539, E-mail: andersod@uwgb.edu; *Asst Dir, Coll Develop & Mgt Librn,* Joan Robb; Tel: 920-465-2384, E-mail: robbj@uwgb.edu; *Asst Dir, Outreach Serv, Asst Dir, Res Serv,* Renee Ettinger; Tel: 920-465-2543, E-mail: ettinger@uwgb.edu; *Cat Librn,* Tony LaLuzerne; Tel: 920-465-2964, E-mail: laluzera@uwgb.edu; *Res & Instruction Librn,* Jodi Pierre; E-mail: pierrej@uwgb.edu; *Syst Librn,* Melissa Platkowski; Tel: 920-465-2764, E-mail: platkowm@uwgb.edu; *Coordr, Cat,* Debra Strelka; Tel: 920-465-2960, E-mail: strelkad@uwgb.edu; *Coordr, Pub Serv,* Erica Grunseth; Tel: 920-465-2304, E-mail: grunsete@uwgb.edu; *Archives Asst,* Hannah Hacker; E-mail: hackerh@uwgb.edu; Staff 16 (MLS 11, Non-MLS 5)
Founded 1967. Enrl 6,600; Fac 168; Highest Degree: Master
Library Holdings: Bk Titles 245,961; Bk Vols 287,330; Per Subs 571
Special Collections: Archives & Area Research Center; Belgian-American Ethnic Coll; Fort Howard Business Archives; Local History (Area Research Center), bks, micro, ms. State Document Depository; US Document Depository
Subject Interests: Environ studies, Humanities, Music, Natural sci
Automation Activity & Vendor Info: (Acquisitions) Ex Libris Group; (Cataloging) Ex Libris Group; (Circulation) Ex Libris Group; (Course Reserve) Ex Libris Group; (ILL) OCLC; (Media Booking) Ex Libris Group; (OPAC) Ex Libris Group; (Serials) Ex Libris Group
Wireless access
Partic in Fox River Valley Area Library Consortium; NE Wis Intertype Libs, Inc; North East Wisconsin Intertype Libraries, Inc; OCLC Online Computer Library Center, Inc; WiLS

Departmental Libraries:

MANITOWOC CAMPUS LIBRARY, 705 Viebahn St, Manitowoc, 54220. Tel: 920-683-4715. E-mail: man-libdesk@uwgb.edu. *Assoc Librn,* Anthony Sigismondi; E-mail: sigismoa@uwgb.edu

MARINETTE CAMPUS LIBRARY, 750 W Bay Shore St, Marinette, 54143-4253, SAN 318-1502. Tel: 715-735-4306. FAX: 715-735-4307. E-mail: mnt-libdesk@uwgb.edu. *Acad Librn,* John Kuhlmann; E-mail: kuhlmanj@uwgb.edu; Staff 1 (MLS 1)
Founded 1965. Enrl 551; Fac 30; Highest Degree: Associate
Library Holdings: Bk Vols 33,000; Per Subs 113
Special Collections: Naval Architecture & Boating (Clinton F DeWitt Coll)
Automation Activity & Vendor Info: (Acquisitions) Ex Libris Group; (Cataloging) Ex Libris Group; (Circulation) Ex Libris Group; (Course Reserve) Ex Libris Group; (OPAC) Ex Libris Group; (Serials) Ex Libris Group
Partic in OCLC Online Computer Library Center, Inc; WiLS
Open Mon-Thurs 8am-9pm, Fri 8-4:30

SHEBOYGAN CAMPUS LIBRARY, One University Dr, Sheboygan, 53081-4789, SAN 318-3858. Tel: 920-459-6625. Interlibrary Loan Service Tel: 920-459-6681. Administration Tel: 920-459-6679. FAX: 920-459-6602. E-mail: shblibrary@uwc.edu. Web Site: sheboygan.uwc.edu/library. *Dir,* Dan A Smith; E-mail: smithd@uwgb.edu; *Libr Asst,* Karen McArdle; E-mail: karen.mcardle@uwc.edu; Staff 3 (MLS 2, Non-MLS 1)
Founded 1965. Enrl 690; Fac 29; Highest Degree: Associate
Library Holdings: AV Mats 2,066; Bk Titles 37,137; Bk Vols 42,136; Per Subs 115
Automation Activity & Vendor Info: (Acquisitions) Ex Libris Group; (Cataloging) Ex Libris Group; (Circulation) Ex Libris Group; (Course Reserve) Ex Libris Group; (ILL) OCLC ILLiad; (OPAC) Ex Libris Group
Partic in OCLC Online Computer Library Center, Inc; WiLS
Open Mon-Thurs 8-7, Fri 8-3

GREEN LAKE

P CAESTECKER PUBLIC LIBRARY*, 518 Hill St, 54941-8828. (Mail add: PO Box 278, 54941-0278), SAN 318-0166. Tel: 920-294-3572. FAX: 920-294-6055. Web Site: www.greenlakelibrary.org. *Libr Dir,* Christina Lyon; E-mail: director@greenlakelibrary.org; Staff 1 (MLS 1)
Pop 2,523; Circ 54,786
Library Holdings: Audiobooks 1,600; DVDs 7,323; Bk Vols 22,422; Per Subs 103
Wireless access
Mem of Winnefox Library System
Open Mon-Thurs 9-7, Fri 9-6, Sat 9-1, Sun 1-4
Friends of the Library Group

GREENDALE

P GREENDALE PUBLIC LIBRARY*, 5647 Broad St, 53129. SAN 318-0174. Tel: 414-423-2136. E-mail: library@greendale.org. Web Site: greendale.org/departments/library. *Libr Dir,* Brian Van Klooster; Tel: 414-423-2136, Ext 225, E-mail: librarydirector@greendale.org
Founded 1938. Pop 15,500; Circ 183,251
Library Holdings: AV Mats 2,500; CDs 2,200; DVDs 1,500; Bk Vols 55,540; Per Subs 80
Subject Interests: Local hist
Automation Activity & Vendor Info: (Acquisitions) Innovative Interfaces, Inc; (Cataloging) Innovative Interfaces, Inc; (Circulation) Innovative Interfaces, Inc
Wireless access

Mem of Milwaukee County Federated Library System
Open Mon-Thurs 9-8, Fri 9-6, Sat 9-2, Sun (Sept-May) 1-4
Friends of the Library Group

GREENFIELD

P GREENFIELD PUBLIC LIBRARY*, 5310 W Layton Ave, 53220. SAN 325-1578. Tel: 414-321-9595. FAX: 414-321-8595. Reference E-mail: greenfield.reference@greenfieldwi.us. Web Site: www.greenfieldlibrary.org. *Libr Dir,* Jennifer Einwalter; Staff 20 (MLS 9, Non-MLS 11)
Circ 204,250
Automation Activity & Vendor Info: (Acquisitions) Innovative Interfaces, Inc; (Cataloging) Innovative Interfaces, Inc; (Circulation) Innovative Interfaces, Inc; (Course Reserve) Innovative Interfaces, Inc; (ILL) Innovative Interfaces, Inc; (Media Booking) Innovative Interfaces, Inc; (OPAC) Innovative Interfaces, Inc; (Serials) Innovative Interfaces, Inc
Wireless access
Function: 24/7 Electronic res, 24/7 Online cat, 24/7 wireless access, Adult bk club, Adult literacy prog, Art exhibits, Audio & video playback equip for onsite use, Bi-weekly Writer's Group, Children's prog, Computer training, Computers for patron use, Doc delivery serv, Electronic databases & coll, Extended outdoor wifi, Family literacy, Free DVD rentals, Games, ILL available, Internet access, Life-long learning prog for all ages, Magazines, Meeting rooms, Movies, Museum passes, Music CDs, Online cat, OverDrive digital audio bks, Photocopying/Printing, Preschool outreach, Preschool reading prog, Printer for laptops & handheld devices, Prog for adults, Prog for children & young adult, Ref serv available, Senior outreach, Serves people with intellectual disabilities, STEM programs, Story hour, Study rm, Summer & winter reading prog, Summer reading prog, Tax forms, Teen prog, Telephone ref, Wheelchair accessible, Wifi hotspot checkout, Winter reading prog, Workshops, Writing prog
Mem of Milwaukee County Federated Library System
Open Mon-Thurs 9-8:30, Fri 9-6, Sat 9-4, Sun (Sept-May) 1-5

GREENWOOD

P GREENWOOD PUBLIC LIBRARY*, 102 N Main St, 54437. (Mail add: PO Box 100, 54437-0100), SAN 318-0190. Tel: 715-267-7103. FAX: 715-267-6636. E-mail: circdesk@greenwoodpubliclibrary.org. Web Site: www.greenwoodpubliclibrary.org. *Dir,* Kim Metzke; E-mail: director@greenwoodpubliclibrary.org
Founded 1913. Pop 3,400; Circ 54,164
Library Holdings: AV Mats 855; Bk Titles 19,682; Per Subs 87; Talking Bks 726
Special Collections: National Geographic, 1916-1987
Subject Interests: Hist
Automation Activity & Vendor Info: (Cataloging) SirsiDynix; (Circulation) SirsiDynix
Wireless access
Publications: Booklist; CCBC
Open Mon 12-8, Tues, Thurs & Fri 10-6, Wed 3-8, Sat 10-Noon

HALES CORNERS

P HALES CORNERS LIBRARY*, 5885 S 116th St, 53130-1707. SAN 318-0204. Tel: 414-529-6150. Web Site: www.halescornerslibrary.org. *Dir,* Patricia Laughlin; Tel: 414-529-6150, Ext 20, E-mail: pat.laughlin@halescornerslibrary.org; *Asst Libr Dir,* Eric Branske; E-mail: eric.branske@halescornerslibrary.org; *Youth Serv Librn,* Jessica Staedter; Tel: 414-529-6150, Ext 17, E-mail: jessica.staedter@halescornerslibrary.org; *Circ Supvr,* Seth Harrison; Tel: 414-529-6150, Ext 13, E-mail: seth.harrison@halescornerslibrary.org; Staff 20 (MLS 3, Non-MLS 17)
Founded 1976. Pop 7,619; Circ 124,178
Library Holdings: Audiobooks 2,315; CDs 2,949; DVDs 5,731; Bk Titles 38,261; Per Subs 113
Special Collections: W Ben Hunt Coll
Automation Activity & Vendor Info: (Acquisitions) Innovative Interfaces, Inc; (Cataloging) Innovative Interfaces, Inc; (Circulation) Innovative Interfaces, Inc; (OPAC) Innovative Interfaces, Inc
Wireless access
Function: 24/7 Electronic res, 24/7 Online cat, Adult bk club, Art exhibits, Audiobks on Playaways & MP3, Bk club(s), Bks on CD, Children's prog, Computer training, Computers for patron use, E-Readers, Electronic databases & coll, Free DVD rentals, Holiday prog, Homebound delivery serv, ILL available, Internet access, Life-long learning prog for all ages, Magazines, Magnifiers for reading, Mango lang, Meeting rooms, Movies, Museum passes, Music CDs, Online cat, Outreach serv, OverDrive digital audio bks, Photocopying/Printing, Preschool reading prog, Prog for adults, Prog for children & young adult, Senior outreach, Story hour, Summer & winter reading prog, Summer reading prog, Tax forms, Teen prog, Telephone ref
Mem of Milwaukee County Federated Library System
Open Mon-Thurs 10-8:30, Fri 10-6, Sat 10-5, Sun (Winter) 1-5
Friends of the Library Group

S LIBRARY OF THE FRIENDS OF BOERNER BOTANICAL GARDENS, Boerner Botanical Library, 9400 Boerner Dr, 53130. Tel: 414-525-5637. E-mail: info@fbbg.org. Web Site: boernerbotanicalgardens.org. *Educ Mgr,* Judi Dee; E-mail: jdee@fbbg.org
Library Holdings: Bk Titles 3,200
Subject Interests: Botany
Automation Activity & Vendor Info: (Cataloging) ResourceMATE; (OPAC) ResourceMATE
Wireless access
Open Tues & Thurs 10-4 (May-Aug)
Restriction: Circ to mem only

HAMMOND

P HAMMOND COMMUNITY LIBRARY*, 850 Davis St, 54015. (Mail add: PO Box 120, 54015-0120), SAN 318-0220. Tel: 715-796-2281. FAX: 715-796-2332. E-mail: hammondpl@ifls.lib.wi.us. Web Site: www.hammondpubliclibrary.org. *Dir,* Michelle Johnson; E-mail: mjohnson@hammondpubliclibrary.org
Founded 1968. Pop 1,800; Circ 55,000
Library Holdings: Bk Vols 15,000; Per Subs 80
Automation Activity & Vendor Info: (Acquisitions) Innovative Interfaces, Inc; (Cataloging) Innovative Interfaces, Inc; (Circulation) Innovative Interfaces, Inc
Wireless access
Mem of Inspiring & Facilitating Library Success (IFLS)
Open Mon-Thurs 9-8, Fri 9-6, Sat 9-1
Friends of the Library Group

HANCOCK

P HANCOCK PUBLIC LIBRARY*, 114 S Main St, 54943. (Mail add: PO Box 217, 54943-0217), SAN 318-0239. Tel: 715-249-5817. E-mail: director@hancocklibrary.org. Web Site: www.hancocklibrary.org. *Dir,* Lisa Eisch; E-mail: eisch@hancocklibrary.org
Pop 1,664; Circ 26,551
Library Holdings: Bk Vols 6,000; Per Subs 50
Special Collections: Census, microfilm; Hancock-Coloma News; Plainfield Sun Newsp; Waushara Argus
Subject Interests: Local hist
Wireless access
Mem of Winnefox Library System
Open Mon, Thurs & Fri 12-6, Wed 10-6, Sat 10-1
Friends of the Library Group

HARTFORD

P JACK RUSSELL MEMORIAL LIBRARY*, 100 Park Ave, 53027-1585. SAN 318-0255. Tel: 262-673-8240. FAX: 262-673-8080. E-mail: hartfordpl@hartfordlibrary.org. Web Site: www.hartfordlibrary.org. *Libr Dir,* Jennifer Einwalter; *Asst Dir, Youth Serv Librn,* Jessica Manogue; Staff 14 (MLS 2, Non-MLS 12)
Founded 1904. Pop 25,000; Circ 226,261
Jan 2019-Dec 2019 Income $1,052,226, City $684,733, County $329,493, Locally Generated Income $38,000. Mats Exp $93,109, Books $64,991, Per/Ser (Incl. Access Fees) $5,000, AV Mat $23,118. Sal $97,893
Library Holdings: AV Mats 6,386; DVDs 8,690; e-books 155,074; Bk Vols 121,914; Per Subs 141
Special Collections: All US Census Records for Wisconsin-Washington & Dodge County, micro; History Room Coll; Local History, micro; Local Papers (1864-2011), micro
Automation Activity & Vendor Info: (OPAC) Innovative Interfaces, Inc
Wireless access
Function: Adult bk club, Audiobks on Playaways & MP3, Bk club(s), Bks on CD, Children's prog, Computers for patron use, Electronic databases & coll, For res purposes, Free DVD rentals, Homebound delivery serv, ILL available, Internet access, Life-long learning prog for all ages, Magazines, Meeting rooms, Microfiche/film & reading machines, Movies, Music CDs, Online cat, Outreach serv, Outside serv via phone, mail, e-mail & web, OverDrive digital audio bks, Photocopying/Printing, Preschool outreach, Preschool reading prog, Printer for laptops & handheld devices, Prog for adults, Prog for children & young adult, Ref & res, Ref serv available, Scanner, Senior outreach, STEM programs, Story hour, Study rm, Summer & winter reading prog, Summer reading prog, Tax forms, Teen prog, Telephone ref, Wheelchair accessible, Winter reading prog, Words travel prog
Mem of Monarch Library System
Open Mon-Thurs 9-8, Fri 9-5:30, Sat 9-2
Friends of the Library Group

HARTLAND

P HARTLAND PUBLIC LIBRARY*, 110 E Park Ave, 53029. SAN 318-0263. Tel: 262-367-3350. FAX: 262-369-2251. E-mail: hplinfo@hartland.lib.wi.us. Web Site: villageofhartland.com/520/library. *Dir,* Laura Gest; E-mail: lgest@hartland.lib.wi.us; *Ad,* Andrew Kristensen;

Ch, Peter Blenski; *Engagement Librn,* Emily Sternemann; *Circ Supvr,* Ryan Wong; Staff 9.5 (MLS 4, Non-MLS 5.5)
Founded 1897. Pop 13,553; Circ 200,000
Jan 2021-Dec 2021. Mats Exp $84,000
Library Holdings: Bk Titles 70,000; Per Subs 75
Subject Interests: City hist
Automation Activity & Vendor Info: (Cataloging) Innovative Interfaces, Inc; (Circulation) Innovative Interfaces, Inc; (OPAC) Innovative Interfaces, Inc
Wireless access
Function: Bk club(s), Electronic databases & coll, ILL available, Online ref, Photocopying/Printing, Prog for children & young adult, Spoken cassettes & CDs, Summer reading prog, Tax forms, Telephone ref, Wheelchair accessible
Mem of Bridges Library System
Open Mon-Thurs 9-8, Fri 9-5, Sat 9-4; Mon-Thurs 9-8, Fri 9-5, Sat 8-Noon (Summer)
Friends of the Library Group

HAWKINS

P HAWKINS AREA LIBRARY*, 709 Main St, 54530-9557. (Mail add: PO Box 17, 54530-0017), SAN 324-1246. Tel: 715-585-2311. FAX: 715-585-2311. E-mail: library@hawkinspl.org. Web Site: hawkinspl.org. *Dir & Librn,* Arlene Mabie
Founded 1979. Pop 800; Circ 5,600
Library Holdings: Audiobooks 97; AV Mats 397; CDs 245; DVDs 300; Electronic Media & Resources 8; Large Print Bks 187; Bk Titles 10,500; Per Subs 12; Videos 400
Automation Activity & Vendor Info: (Circulation) Follett Software
Wireless access
Mem of Inspiring & Facilitating Library Success (IFLS)
Partic in OCLC Online Computer Library Center, Inc
Open Mon-Thurs 9-5, Fri 9-1
Friends of the Library Group

HAYWARD

J LAC COURTE OREILLES OJIBWA COMMUNITY COLLEGE LIBRARY*, 13466 W Trepania Rd, 54843-2181. SAN 377-967X. Tel: 715-634-4790, Ext 108. FAX: 715-634-5049. E-mail: library@lco.edu. Web Site: www.lco.edu/library. *Libr Dir,* Caryl Pfaff; E-mail: pfaff@lco.edu
Founded 1990. Enrl 450; Fac 35; Highest Degree: Associate
Library Holdings: Bk Vols 19,000; Per Subs 100
Special Collections: American Indian Coll, audio bks, bks, videos. State Document Depository
Subject Interests: Native Am
Automation Activity & Vendor Info: (Acquisitions) Follett Software; (Cataloging) Follett Software; (Circulation) Follett Software; (Course Reserve) Follett Software
Function: ILL available
Mem of Northern Waters Library Service
Partic in Am Indian Libr Asn; American Indian Higher Education Consortium; Wis Libr Asn
Open Mon-Thurs 8-5:30, Fri 8-4:30 (Winter); Mon-Fri 8-4:30 (Summer)

P SHERMAN & RUTH WEISS COMMUNITY LIBRARY*, 10788 State Hwy 77 W, 54843. (Mail add: PO Box 917, 54843-0917), SAN 318-0271. Tel: 715-634-2161. FAX: 715-634-5257. E-mail: hlibrary@hayward.wislib.org. Web Site: weisscommunitylibrary.com. *Dir,* Molly Lank-Jones; *Asst Dir,* Ann Larson; Staff 3 (MLS 1, Non-MLS 2)
Founded 1904. Circ 67,723
Library Holdings: Bk Vols 33,496; Per Subs 65
Subject Interests: Wis hist
Automation Activity & Vendor Info: (Acquisitions) Innovative Interfaces, Inc - Sierra; (Cataloging) Innovative Interfaces, Inc - Sierra; (Circulation) Innovative Interfaces, Inc - Sierra
Wireless access
Function: Bk club(s), ILL available, Internet access, Magnifiers for reading, Music CDs, Photocopying/Printing, Prog for children & young adult, Ref serv available, Summer reading prog
Mem of Northern Waters Library Service
Open Mon & Wed-Fri 10-5, Tues 10-7
Friends of the Library Group

HAZEL GREEN

P HAZEL GREEN PUBLIC LIBRARY*, 1610 Fairplay St, 53811. (Mail add: PO Box 367, 53811-0367). Tel: 608-854-2952. E-mail: hazelgreendirector@swls.org. Web Site: hazelgreenpubliclibrary.org. *Dir,* Megan Flatley
Founded 1984. Pop 2,134; Circ 17,699
Library Holdings: Bk Vols 7,943; Per Subs 7
Automation Activity & Vendor Info: (Cataloging) Auto-Graphics, Inc; (Circulation) Auto-Graphics, Inc; (OPAC) Auto-Graphics, Inc
Wireless access
Mem of Southwest Wisconsin Library System
Open Mon & Wed-Fri 10-6, Tues 12-8, Sat 9-1

HILLSBORO

P HILLSBORO PUBLIC LIBRARY*, 819 High Ave, 54634. (Mail add: PO Box 468, 54634-0468), SAN 318-0298. Tel: 608-489-2192. E-mail: hlibrary@wrlsweb.org. Web Site: hillsborolibrary.wrlsweb.org. *Dir,* Jackie Pysarenko; E-mail: jpysarenko@wrlsweb.org; *Libr Asst,* Nancy Kaus; *Library Intern,* Zoe Woods
Founded 1898. Pop 1,419; Circ 35,100
Library Holdings: Bk Vols 24,000; Per Subs 20
Wireless access
Function: 24/7 Electronic res, 24/7 Online cat, Activity rm, Adult literacy prog, Art programs, Audiobks on Playaways & MP3, Audiobks via web, Bks on CD, Children's prog, Distance learning, Electronic databases & coll, Free DVD rentals, Games & aids for people with disabilities, Govt ref serv, Holiday prog, ILL available, Internet access, Laminating, Life-long learning prog for all ages, Magazines, Magnifiers for reading, Meeting rooms, Movies, Music CDs, Online cat, Outreach serv, OverDrive digital audio bks, Photocopying/Printing, Preschool reading prog, Prog for adults, Prog for children & young adult, Ref & res, Res libr, Scanner, Serves people with intellectual disabilities, Spanish lang bks, Study rm, Summer & winter reading prog, Summer reading prog, Winter reading prog, Workshops
Mem of Winding Rivers Library System
Partic in Wis Libr Asn; Wiscat
Open Tues-Fri 10-6, Sat 9-12
Friends of the Library Group

HOLMEN

P LA CROSSE COUNTY LIBRARY*, Administration Ctr, 121 W Legion St, 54636. (Mail add: Administration Ctr, PO Box 220, 54636-0220), SAN 364-7196. Tel: 608-526-4198. Administration Tel: 608-399-3390, FAX: 608-526-3299. E-mail: holmenlibrary@lacrossecounty.org. Web Site: www.lacrossecounty.org/library. *Libr Dir,* Christine McArdle Rojo; E-mail: cmcardlerojo@lacrossecounty.org; Staff 7.5 (MLS 1, Non-MLS 6.5)
Founded 1898. Pop 52,160; Circ 452,460
Library Holdings: AV Mats 2,557; Bk Titles 123,228; Per Subs 291; Videos 9,791
Automation Activity & Vendor Info: (Cataloging) Horizon; (Circulation) Horizon; (OPAC) Horizon; (Serials) Horizon
Wireless access
Mem of Winding Rivers Library System
Open Mon-Fri 7:30-4
Friends of the Library Group
Branches: 5
JOHN BOSSHARD MEMORIAL, 1720 Henry Johns Blvd, Bangor, 54614, SAN 364-7226. Tel: 608-486-4408. FAX: 608-486-4408. E-mail: bangorlibrary@lacrossecounty.org. *Libr Asst,* Shari Axelsen; E-mail: saxelsen@lacrossecounty.org; Staff 1.5 (Non-MLS 1.5)
Open Mon, Wed & Thurs 10-8, Tues 10-6, Fri 10-5, Sat 9-1
Friends of the Library Group
HOLMEN AREA, 121 W Legion St, 54636. (Mail add: PO Box 220, 54636-0220). Reference Tel: 608-526-3311. E-mail: holmenlibrary@lacrossecounty.org. *Br Mgr,* Position Currently Open
Open Mon-Thurs 10-8, Fri 10-5, Sat 9-2
Friends of the Library Group
HAZEL BROWN LEICHT MEMORIAL LIBRARY, 702 Industrial Dr, West Salem, 54669-1328, SAN 364-734X. Tel: 608-786-1505. FAX: 608-786-0036. E-mail: westsalemlibrary@lacrossecounty.org. *Br Mgr,* Ashley Giese; E-mail: agiese@lacrossecounty.org; Staff 1 (Non-MLS 1)
Open Mon-Thurs 10-8, Fri 10-5, Sat 9-2
ONALASKA PUBLIC, 741 Oak Ave S, Onalaska, 54650, SAN 364-7315. Tel: 608-781-9568. FAX: 608-781-9594. E-mail: onalaskalibrary@lacrossecounty.org. *Br Mgr,* Sherri Sinniger; E-mail: ssinniger@lacrossecounty.org; Staff 0.5 (MLS 0.5)
Open Mon-Thurs 9-8, Fri 9-5, Sat 9-2
Friends of the Library Group
F J ROBERS LIBRARY, Campbell Town Hall, 2548 Lakeshore Dr, La Crosse, 54603, SAN 364-7250. Tel: 608-783-0052. E-mail: campbelllibrary@lacrossecounty.org. *Br Mgr,* Shelly Parshall; E-mail: sparshall@lacrossecounty.org; Staff 1 (Non-MLS 1)
Open Mon 10-8, Tues & Thurs 1-8, Wed 10-5, Fri & Sat 9-1
Friends of the Library Group

HORICON

P HORICON PUBLIC LIBRARY*, 404 E Lake St, 53032-1297. SAN 318-0301. Tel: 920-485-3535. FAX: 920-485-3536. Web Site: www.horicon.lib.wi.us. *Dir,* Alex Harvancik; E-mail: alex@monarchlibraries.org; *Ch, Programming Librn,* Kate Kirschner; E-mail: kkirschner@mwfls.org; *Libr Tech, Teen Librn,* Anna McCallum; E-mail: amccallum@monarchlibraries.org; Staff 2 (Non-MLS 2)

Founded 1850. Pop 3,655; Circ 48,973
Automation Activity & Vendor Info: (Cataloging) Innovative Interfaces, Inc; (Circulation) Innovative Interfaces, Inc; (Discovery) Innovative Interfaces, Inc; (ILL) Auto-Graphics, Inc; (OPAC) Innovative Interfaces, Inc; (Serials) Innovative Interfaces, Inc
Wireless access
Function: 24/7 Electronic res, 24/7 Online cat, Activity rm, Adult bk club, Adult literacy prog, After school storytime, Archival coll, Art exhibits, Art programs, Audio & video playback equip for onsite use, Audiobks on Playaways & MP3, Audiobks via web, AV serv, Bk club(s), Bks on CD, CD-ROM, Children's prog, Computer training, Computers for patron use, Digital talking bks, Doc delivery serv, E-Readers, Electronic databases & coll, Free DVD rentals, Games & aids for people with disabilities, Holiday prog, ILL available, Internet access, Life-long learning prog for all ages, Magazines, Magnifiers for reading, Mail & tel request accepted, Meeting rooms, Microfiche/film & reading machines, Movies, Museum passes, Music CDs, Online cat, Online info literacy tutorials on the web & in blackboard, Online ref, Outreach serv, Outside serv via phone, mail, e-mail & web, OverDrive digital audio bks, Photocopying/Printing, Printer for laptops & handheld devices, Prog for adults, Prog for children & young adult, Ref & res, Ref serv available, Scanner, Serves people with intellectual disabilities, Spanish lang bks, Spoken cassettes & CDs, Spoken cassettes & DVDs, STEM programs, Story hour, Summer & winter reading prog, Summer reading prog, Tax forms, Teen prog, Telephone ref, Wheelchair accessible, Winter reading prog
Mem of Monarch Library System
Open Mon-Thurs 10-8, Fri 10-6, Sat 10-3
Restriction: Free to mem, In-house use for visitors, Non-circulating coll, Non-circulating of rare bks, Photo ID required for access
Friends of the Library Group

HORTONVILLE

P HORTONVILLE PUBLIC LIBRARY*, 531 N Nash St, 54944. (Mail add: PO Box 25, 54944-0025), SAN 318-031X. Tel: 920-779-4279. Administration Tel: 929-779-5000. FAX: 920-779-5001. E-mail: hpl@hortonvillelibrary.org. Web Site: www.hortonvillelibrary.org. *Dir,* Allie Krause; Staff 1 (Non-MLS 1)
Founded 1920. Pop 8,351; Circ 53,939
Library Holdings: Bks on Deafness & Sign Lang 50; CDs 235; DVDs 254; e-books 125,699; Large Print Bks 453; Bk Vols 19,931; Per Subs 111; Videos 1,704
Automation Activity & Vendor Info: (Acquisitions) Innovative Interfaces, Inc; (Cataloging) Innovative Interfaces, Inc; (Circulation) Innovative Interfaces, Inc; (OPAC) Innovative Interfaces, Inc
Wireless access
Mem of Outagamie Waupaca Library System (OWLS)
Partic in OWLSnet
Open Mon, Tues & Fri 9-6, Wed & Thurs 9-8
Friends of the Library Group

HUDSON

P HUDSON AREA PUBLIC LIBRARY*, 700 First St, 54016. SAN 318-0336. Tel: 715-386-3101. FAX: 715-381-0468. E-mail: hudsonpl@hudsonpubliclibrary.org. Web Site: www.hudsonpubliclibrary.org. *Libr Dir,* Tina Norris; Staff 3 (MLS 1, Non-MLS 2)
Founded 1904. Pop 29,131
Library Holdings: AV Mats 2,356; Bk Vols 59,680; Per Subs 126; Videos 3,006
Automation Activity & Vendor Info: (Cataloging) Innovative Interfaces, Inc; (Circulation) Innovative Interfaces, Inc; (OPAC) Innovative Interfaces, Inc; (Serials) Innovative Interfaces, Inc
Wireless access
Function: Art exhibits, Audiobks via web, Bk club(s), Bks on CD, Children's prog, Computer training, Computers for patron use, Digital talking bks, ILL available, Online cat, OverDrive digital audio bks, Photocopying/Printing, Story hour, Tax forms, Wheelchair accessible
Mem of Inspiring & Facilitating Library Success (IFLS)
Open Mon-Thurs 10-8, Fri 10-6, Sat 10-3
Restriction: 24-hr pass syst for students only
Friends of the Library Group

HURLEY

P HURLEY PUBLIC LIBRARY*, 405 Fifth Ave N, 54534-1170. SAN 318-0344. Tel: 715-561-5707. FAX: 715-561-3222. E-mail: hurl@hurley.wislib.org. *Dir,* Lynne Pedri
Pop 4,080; Circ 15,800
Library Holdings: Bk Vols 12,000; Per Subs 30
Wireless access
Publications: Booklist
Mem of Northern Waters Library Service
Open Mon-Fri 9-5

HUSTISFORD

P HUSTISFORD COMMUNITY LIBRARY*, 609 W Juneau St, 53034. SAN 370-6591. Tel: 920-349-3463. FAX: 920-349-9009. E-mail: hustipl@monarchlibraries.org. Web Site: www.hustisford.lib.wi.us. *Dir,* Nicole Mszal; Tel: 920-349-4542, E-mail: nmszal@monarchlibraries.org; *Ch Serv, Prog Dir,* Monica Wasemiller; Tel: 920-349-4545, E-mail: monicaw@monarchlibraries.org; Staff 2 (Non-MLS 2)
Founded 1986. Pop 2,512; Circ 40,581
Jan 2016-Dec 2016 Income $168,347, State $1,845, City $102,355, County $38,579, Locally Generated Income $15,671, Other $331. Mats Exp $33,139, Books $21,097, AV Mat $12,042. Sal $73,876 (Prof $41,371)
Library Holdings: Audiobooks 1,675; CDs 375; DVDs 5,313; Large Print Bks 307; Bk Vols 20,949; Per Subs 81
Automation Activity & Vendor Info: (ILL) Auto-Graphics, Inc
Wireless access
Function: 24/7 Electronic res, 24/7 Online cat, Adult bk club, Audiobks on Playaways & MP3, Audiobks via web, AV serv, Bk club(s), Bks on CD, CD-ROM, Children's prog, Computer training, Computers for patron use, E-Readers, Free DVD rentals, Holiday prog, ILL available, Internet access, Magazines, Movies, Music CDs, Online cat, Online ref, OverDrive digital audio bks, Photocopying/Printing, Preschool reading prog, Prog for children & young adult, Scanner, Spoken cassettes & CDs, Spoken cassettes & DVDs, Story hour, Summer reading prog, Tax forms, Telephone ref, Wheelchair accessible
Mem of Monarch Library System
Open Mon-Thurs 10-7, Fri 10-5, Sat 9-1
Friends of the Library Group

INDEPENDENCE

P INDEPENDENCE PUBLIC LIBRARY*, 23688 Adams St, 54747. (Mail add: PO Box 99, 54747-0099), SAN 318-0352. Tel: 715-985-3616. FAX: 715-985-2530. E-mail: independencepl@wrlsweb.org, indplbry@triwest.net. Web Site: www.wrlsweb.org/independence. *Dir,* Kayla Mathson
Founded 1908. Pop 1,244; Circ 12,949
Library Holdings: Bk Vols 14,000; Per Subs 65
Automation Activity & Vendor Info: (Cataloging) Follett Software; (Circulation) Follett Software
Mem of Winding Rivers Library System
Open Mon 11-7, Tues-Thurs 10-6, Fri 10-4:30

IOLA

P IOLA VILLAGE LIBRARY*, 180 S Main St, 54945-9689. (Mail add: PO Box 336, 54945-0336), SAN 324-6965. Tel: 715-445-4330. FAX: 715-445-2917. E-mail: ivl@iolalibrary.org. Web Site: iolalibrary.org. *Dir,* Robyn Grove; E-mail: regrove@iolalibrary.org; *Children's Prog,* Lisa Bauer; E-mail: lbauer@mail.owls.lib.wi.us
Pop 3,540; Circ 47,800
Library Holdings: Bk Vols 20,250; Per Subs 70
Automation Activity & Vendor Info: (Cataloging) Infor Library & Information Solutions; (Circulation) Infor Library & Information Solutions
Wireless access
Mem of Outagamie Waupaca Library System (OWLS)
Open Mon-Fri 9-5
Friends of the Library Group

IRON RIDGE

P IRON RIDGE PUBLIC LIBRARY*, 205 Park St, 53035. (Mail add: PO Box 247, 53035-0247), SAN 364-6114. Tel: 920-387-3637. E-mail: ironridge@monarchlibraries.org. Web Site: ironridge.lib.wi.us. *Dir,* Elizabeth Daniels
Founded 1991. Pop 1,279; Circ 3,067
Jan 2019-Dec 2019 Income $43,724
Library Holdings: Bk Vols 21,847; Per Subs 1
Wireless access
Mem of Monarch Library System
Open Tues & Fri 2-7, Wed 10-4, Thurs 3-7, Sat 10-1

IRON RIVER

P EVELYN GOLDBERG BRIGGS MEMORIAL LIBRARY*, 68235 S Main St, 54847. (Mail add: PO Box 145, 54847-0145). Tel: 715-372-5451. FAX: 715-372-5451. E-mail: ironriverlibrary@gmail.com. Web Site: www.ironriverlibrary.org. *Dir,* Jacqueline Pooler; E-mail: irdirector17@gmail.com; Staff 1 (MLS 1)
Library Holdings: Bk Titles 9,000
Wireless access
Mem of Northern Waters Library Service
Open Mon & Tues 10-7, Wed & Thurs 10-5, Sat 10-2
Friends of the Library Group

JANESVILLE

J BLACKHAWK TECHNICAL COLLEGE LIBRARY, 6004 S County Rd G, 53547. (Mail add: PO Box 5009, 53547-5009), SAN 318-0379. Tel: 608-757-7705. E-mail: library@blackhawk.edu. Web Site: www.blackhawk.edu/student-experience/student-services#academic-resources. *Librn,* Madeleine Pitsch; E-mail: mpitsch1@blackhawk.edu; Staff 1 (MLS 1)
Founded 1966. Enrl 2,232; Fac 312; Highest Degree: Associate
Library Holdings: Bks on Deafness & Sign Lang 2; CDs 5; DVDs 15; e-books 60,000; e-journals 89,000; High Interest/Low Vocabulary Bk Vols 600; Bk Titles 1,200; Per Subs 3
Special Collections: Child Care Coll; High/Low Coll; Professional Coll
Automation Activity & Vendor Info: (Circulation) Innovative Interfaces, Inc - Sierra; (OPAC) Innovative Interfaces, Inc - Sierra
Wireless access
Function: 24/7 Electronic res, 24/7 Online cat, 24/7 wireless access, Bk club(s), Electronic databases & coll, ILL available, Laptop/tablet checkout, Learning ctr, Meeting rooms, Online cat, Online Chat, Online info literacy tutorials on the web & in blackboard, Online ref, Outside serv via phone, mail, e-mail & web, OverDrive digital audio bks, Photocopying/Printing, Ref & res, Ref serv available, Res assist avail, Scanner
Mem of Prairie Lakes Library System (PLLS)
Partic in WiLS; WISPALS Library Consortium
Open Mon-Thurs 8-5:30, Fri 8-4:30 (Fall & Spring); Mon-Thurs 8-5, Fri 8-12 (Summer)

P HEDBERG PUBLIC LIBRARY*, 316 S Main St, 53545. SAN 318-0387. Tel: 608-758-6600. Circulation Tel: 608-758-6582. Interlibrary Loan Service Tel: 608-758-6598. Reference Tel: 608-758-6581. FAX: 608-758-6583. E-mail: questions@hedbergpubliclibrary.org. Web Site: www.hedbergpubliclibrary.org. *Dir,* Bryan J McCormick; Tel: 608-758-6594; *Asst Dir,* Charles Teval; Tel: 608-758-6605, E-mail: cteval@hedbergpubliclibrary.org; *Head, Access Serv,* Michelle Dennis; Tel: 608-758-6610, E-mail: mdennis@hedbergpubliclibrary.org; *Head, Youth Serv,* Elizabeth Matson; Tel: 608-758-6584, E-mail: ematson@hedbergpubliclibrary.org; *Computer Syst Mgr,* Emrick Gunderson; Tel: 608-758-6599, E-mail: egunderson@hedbergpubliclibrary.org; *Mkt Mgr,* Elizabeth Hough; Tel: 608-758-6607, E-mail: ehough@hedbergpubliclibrary.org; Staff 52 (MLS 13, Non-MLS 39)
Founded 1884. Pop 82,411; Circ 1,153,991
Library Holdings: AV Mats 45,812; Bk Vols 228,038; Per Subs 579
Special Collections: Job Resource Center; Local History (Janesville Room)
Automation Activity & Vendor Info: (Acquisitions) Innovative Interfaces, Inc - Millennium; (Cataloging) Innovative Interfaces, Inc - Millennium; (Circulation) Innovative Interfaces, Inc - Millennium; (ILL) Auto-Graphics, Inc; (OPAC) Innovative Interfaces, Inc - Millennium; (Serials) Innovative Interfaces, Inc - Millennium
Wireless access
Publications: Library Matters (Newsletter)
Mem of Prairie Lakes Library System (PLLS)
Partic in OCLC Online Computer Library Center, Inc; WILS
Special Services for the Deaf - TDD equip
Special Services for the Blind - Assistive/Adapted tech devices, equip & products
Open Mon-Thurs 9-9, Fri & Sat 9-5, Sun 1-5
Friends of the Library Group

S ROCK COUNTY HISTORICAL SOCIETY*, Archives & Collections, 426 N Jackson St, 53548. SAN 318-0425. Tel: 608-756-4509. E-mail: operations@rchs.us. Web Site: rchs.us. *Exec Dir,* Timothy Maahs; E-mail: tmaahs@rchs.us; *Archivist, Database Mgr,* Eric Hessler; E-mail: ehessler@rchs.us
Founded 1948
Library Holdings: Bk Titles 8,385; Per Subs 19
Special Collections: Carrie Jacobs Bond Coll; Frances Willard Coll; Historic Materials (Samson Tractor Company), papers; Land Speculation (Tallman Family), papers; Local History, diaries & family papers; Local Organizations Coll; Rock County Industrial Development Coll; Women's Christian Temperance Union Coll
Subject Interests: Archit studies of local hist sites, Hist of Rock county, Survey of all hist sites
Wireless access
Function: Archival coll, Bus archives, Electronic databases & coll, For res purposes, Wheelchair accessible
Restriction: In-house use for visitors, Non-circulating, Not open to pub, Open to staff only, Ref only, Ref only to non-staff, Researchers by appt only, Researchers only

R SEVENTH DAY BAPTIST HISTORICAL LIBRARY & ARCHIVES*, 3120 Kennedy Rd, 53545-0225. (Mail add: PO Box 1678, 53547-1678), SAN 310-4311. Tel: 608-752-5055. FAX: 608-752-7711. Web Site: www.sdbhistory.org, www.seventhdaybaptist.org. *Dir of Educ,* Nicholas J Kersten; E-mail: nkersten@seventhdaybaptist.org; Staff 2 (Non-MLS 2)
Founded 1916
Library Holdings: AV Mats 100; Microforms 300; Bk Titles 1,900; Bk Vols 3,000; Per Subs 15
Special Collections: 17th-20th Century English Seventh Day Baptist Churches (Mill Yard Church & Sabbatarian Literature Coll), bks & ms; Archives of Seventh Day Baptist General Conference, USA & Canada; China Mission Coll, 1847-1945, ms & ephemera; Early African Seventh Day Baptist Missions (Nyasaland Missions Coll), 1895-1914; Ephrata, PA Cloister (Julius F Sachse Coll), bks, ms, ephemera, realia
Subject Interests: Hist of the Sabbath, Seventh Day Baptists
Automation Activity & Vendor Info: (Acquisitions) Cuadra Associates, Inc; (Cataloging) Cuadra Associates, Inc; (OPAC) Cuadra Associates, Inc; (Serials) Cuadra Associates, Inc
Wireless access
Function: Res libr
Publications: Annual Report; Books & Pamphlets on Seventh Day Baptist History; Occasional Newsletter
Restriction: Not a lending libr, Open by appt only
Friends of the Library Group

J UNIVERSITY OF WISCONSIN-ROCK COUNTY LIBRARY*, Gary J Lenox Library, 2909 Kellogg Ave, 53546-5606. SAN 318-0433. Tel: 608-758-6533. FAX: 608-758-6560. Web Site: uww.edu/library. *Sr Acad Librn,* Paul Waelchli; E-mail: waelchlip@uww.edu; *Acad Librn,* Beth Webb; Tel: 608-898-5047, E-mail: webbb@uww.edu; *Circ,* Beth Thiel; Tel: 608-898-6533, E-mail: thieleb@uww.edu; *ILL,* Julie Orvis; Tel: 608-898-5046, E-mail: orvisj@uww.edu; Staff 3 (MLS 2, Non-MLS 1)
Founded 1966. Enrl 990; Fac 50; Highest Degree: Associate
Library Holdings: AV Mats 2,129; Bk Titles 54,886
Special Collections: State Document Depository
Automation Activity & Vendor Info: (Acquisitions) Ex Libris Group; (Cataloging) Ex Libris Group; (Circulation) Ex Libris Group; (Course Reserve) Ex Libris Group; (ILL) Ex Libris Group; (OPAC) Ex Libris Group; (Serials) Ex Libris Group
Wireless access
Partic in OCLC Online Computer Library Center, Inc
Open Mon-Thurs 8-6, Fri 8-4 (Winter); Mon-Thurs 8-4:30, Fri 8-Noon (Summer)

S WISCONSIN CENTER FOR THE BLIND & VISUALLY IMPAIRED*, Wisconsin School for the Visually Handicapped Library, 1700 W State St, 53546-5344. SAN 318-0441. Tel: 608-758-6118. Toll Free Tel: 866-284-1107. Web Site: www.wcbvi.k12.wi.us/outreach/media-center. *Library Contact,* Michelle Rueckert; E-mail: michelle.rueckert@wcbvi.k12.wi.us; Staff 1 (Non-MLS 1)
Library Holdings: Bk Vols 15,000; Per Subs 15
Automation Activity & Vendor Info: (Circulation) SirsiDynix
Wireless access

JEFFERSON

P JEFFERSON PUBLIC LIBRARY*, 321 S Main St, 53549-1772. SAN 324-2161. Tel: 920-674-7733. FAX: 920-674-7735. E-mail: information@jeffersonwilibrary.org. Reference E-mail: reference@mwfls.org. Web Site: www.jeffersonwilibrary.org. *Libr Dir,* Melissa Anderson; E-mail: manderson@jeffersonwilibrary.org; *ILL,* Sue McKechnie; *Ref,* Angie Rosch; Staff 7.3 (MLS 1.9, Non-MLS 5.4)
Founded 1871. Pop 11,647; Circ 102,395
Library Holdings: Audiobooks 1,788; DVDs 2,184; e-books 8,825; Electronic Media & Resources 2,745; Bk Titles 51,699; Per Subs 120
Automation Activity & Vendor Info: (Acquisitions) SirsiDynix; (Cataloging) SirsiDynix; (Circulation) SirsiDynix; (Course Reserve) SirsiDynix; (ILL) SirsiDynix; (Media Booking) SirsiDynix; (OPAC) SirsiDynix; (Serials) SirsiDynix
Wireless access
Function: Accelerated reader prog
Mem of Bridges Library System
Open Mon-Thurs 9-8, Fri 9-5, Sat 10-3 (Winter); Mon-Thurs 9-7, Fri 9-5:30, Sat 10-3 (Summer)
Restriction: Access at librarian's discretion
Friends of the Library Group

JOHNSON CREEK

P JOHNSON CREEK PUBLIC LIBRARY*, 125 Lincoln St, 53038. (Mail add: PO Box 130, 53038-0130), SAN 324-1254. Tel: 920-699-3741. FAX: 920-699-3747. E-mail: request@johnsoncreeklibrary.org. Web Site: www.johnsoncreeklibrary.org. *Dir,* Jodi Kessel Szpiszar; E-mail: kszpiszar@johnsoncreeklibrary.org; Staff 2 (MLS 1, Non-MLS 1)
Founded 1902. Pop 3,402; Circ 36,797
Library Holdings: Bk Titles 23,315; Per Subs 8
Automation Activity & Vendor Info: (Acquisitions) SirsiDynix; (Cataloging) SirsiDynix; (Circulation) SirsiDynix; (OPAC) SirsiDynix

Wireless access
Mem of Bridges Library System
Open Mon-Fri 10-5, Sat 9-12
Friends of the Library Group

JUNEAU

P JUNEAU PUBLIC LIBRARY*, 250 N Fairfield Ave, 53039. SAN 318-045X. Tel: 920-386-4805. FAX: 920-386-4806. E-mail: juneau.monarchlibraries@gmail.com. Web Site: www.juneau.lib.wi.us. *Dir,* Jannette Thrane; E-mail: jthrane@monarchlibraries.org
Founded 1949
Library Holdings: Bk Vols 30,000; Per Subs 51
Automation Activity & Vendor Info: (Acquisitions) SirsiDynix; (Cataloging) SirsiDynix; (Circulation) SirsiDynix
Mem of Monarch Library System
Open Mon-Thurs 11-7, Fri 10-4, Sat 9-Noon
Friends of the Library Group

KAUKAUNA

P KAUKAUNA PUBLIC LIBRARY*, 207 Thilmany Rd, Ste 200, 54130-2436. SAN 318-0468. Tel: 920-766-6340. FAX: 920-766-6343. E-mail: kaulib@kaukauna-wi.org. Web Site: www.kaukaunalibrary.org. *Dir,* Ashley Thiem-Menning; E-mail: ashleyt@kaukauna-wi.org; Staff 14 (MLS 2, Non-MLS 12)
Founded 1899. Pop 21,286; Circ 144,342
Library Holdings: Bk Vols 59,756; Per Subs 200
Special Collections: State Document Depository
Subject Interests: Wis hist
Automation Activity & Vendor Info: (Acquisitions) Innovative Interfaces, Inc; (Cataloging) Innovative Interfaces, Inc; (Circulation) Innovative Interfaces, Inc; (Course Reserve) Innovative Interfaces, Inc; (OPAC) Innovative Interfaces, Inc
Wireless access
Function: 24/7 Electronic res, 24/7 Online cat, Activity rm, Adult bk club, Archival coll, Art programs, Audiobks on Playaways & MP3, Audiobks via web, AV serv, Bks on CD, Butterfly Garden, Children's prog, Computer training, Computers for patron use, Electronic databases & coll, Free DVD rentals, Genealogy discussion group, Homebound delivery serv, ILL available, Internet access, Laminating, Life-long learning prog for all ages, Magazines, Meeting rooms, Microfiche/film & reading machines, Movies, Music CDs, Notary serv, Online cat, Outreach serv, OverDrive digital audio bks, Photocopying/Printing, Preschool outreach, Preschool reading prog, Printer for laptops & handheld devices, Prog for adults, Prog for children & young adult, Ref & res, Ref serv available, Res assist avail, Scanner, Senior computer classes, Senior outreach, Spanish lang bks, STEM programs, Story hour, Study rm, Summer & winter reading prog, Summer reading prog, Tax forms, Teen prog, Telephone ref, Visual arts prog, Wheelchair accessible, Winter reading prog, Writing prog
Mem of Outagamie Waupaca Library System (OWLS)
Partic in OWLSnet
Open Mon-Thurs 9-8, Fri 9-5, Sat 9-1
Friends of the Library Group

KENDALL

P KENDALL PUBLIC LIBRARY*, 110 E S Railroad St, 54638. (Mail add: PO Box 126, 54638-0126), SAN 318-0476. Tel: 608-463-7103. E-mail: klibrary@wrlsweb.org. Web Site: kendallpublibrary.wrlsweb.org. *Libr Dir,* Charissa Finn
Founded 1946. Pop 468
Library Holdings: Bk Vols 10,000; Per Subs 25
Automation Activity & Vendor Info: (Acquisitions) SirsiDynix; (Cataloging) SirsiDynix; (Circulation) SirsiDynix; (OPAC) SirsiDynix
Wireless access
Mem of Winding Rivers Library System
Open Tues & Fri 10-6, Thurs 1-6

KENOSHA

C CARTHAGE COLLEGE*, Hedberg Library, 2001 Alford Park Dr, 53140-1900. SAN 318-0492. Tel: 262-551-5950. Interlibrary Loan Service Tel: 262-551-5770. FAX: 262-551-5904. E-mail: help@carthage.edu. Web Site: www.carthage.edu/academics/library. *Dir, Libr Serv & Instrul Tech,* Carol Sabbar; E-mail: csabbar@carthage.edu; *Dir, Media & End User Services,* Mike Love; E-mail: mlove@carthage.edu; *Head, Pub Serv,* Dennis Unterholzner; *Info Access Librn, Info Mgr,* Richard Hren; E-mail: rhren@carthage.edu; *Instrul Tech Librn,* Chris Grugel; E-mail: cgrugel@cathage.edu; *Asst Cat Librn,* Bobbi-Jean Ludwig; *Info Mgr,* Kathy Myers; E-mail: kmyers@carthage.edu; *Archivist,* Ernestine Eger; E-mail: eeger@carthage.edu; *Network Adminr,* Ryan Ade; E-mail: rade@carthage.edu; Staff 7 (MLS 7)
Founded 1847. Enrl 2,250; Fac 125; Highest Degree: Master
Library Holdings: AV Mats 6,500; e-books 12,000; Bk Titles 125,000; Bk Vols 145,000; Per Subs 415
Special Collections: Center for Children's Literature Coll; Civil War (Palumbo Coll)
Automation Activity & Vendor Info: (Acquisitions) LibLime; (Cataloging) LibLime; (Circulation) LibLime; (Course Reserve) LibLime; (ILL) LibLime; (Media Booking) LibLime; (OPAC) LibLime; (Serials) LibLime
Wireless access
Partic in Coun of Wis Librs, Inc; OCLC Online Computer Library Center, Inc; WiLS; Wis Libr Consortium

C GATEWAY TECHNICAL COLLEGE*, Kenosha Campus Library, Academic Bldg, Rm A103, 3520 30th Ave, 53144-1690. SAN 364-7013. Tel: 262-564-2786. Interlibrary Loan Service Tel: 262-564-2378. FAX: 262-564-2787. E-mail: kenoshalrc@gtc.edu. Web Site: libguides.gtc.edu/c.php?g=36352. *District Libr Mgr,* Gary Flynn; *Libr Tech,* Carla Mattmann; E-mail: mattmannc@gtc.edu; Staff 7 (MLS 2, Non-MLS 5)
Founded 1964. Fac 201
Library Holdings: Bks on Deafness & Sign Lang 417; Bk Titles 35,000; Bk Vols 90,000; Per Subs 365
Subject Interests: Aviation, Computer sci, Hort, Interior design, Law enforcement, Nursing, Phys therapy
Automation Activity & Vendor Info: (Acquisitions) Ex Libris Group; (Cataloging) Ex Libris Group; (Circulation) Ex Libris Group; (Course Reserve) Ex Libris Group; (OPAC) Ex Libris Group; (Serials) Ex Libris Group
Special Services for the Deaf - Videos & decoder
Open Mon-Thurs 7:45am-8:30pm, Fri 7:45-4, Sat 9-Noon

S KENOSHA COUNTY HISTORICAL SOCIETY*, Kenosha History Center Archives, 220 51st Pl, 53140. SAN 318-0530. Tel: 262-654-5770. FAX: 262-654-1730. E-mail: kchs@kenoshahistorycenter.org. Web Site: www.kenoshahistorycenter.org. *Exec Dir,* Chris Allen; *Curator,* Cynthia Nelson; Staff 1 (Non-MLS 1)
Founded 1878
Library Holdings: Bk Titles 3,000
Subject Interests: City of Kenosha, Kenosha county, Local hist, State of Wisc
Function: Archival coll
Restriction: Non-circulating, Open to pub for ref only

P KENOSHA COUNTY LIBRARY SYSTEM*, 7979 38th Ave, 53142. Tel: 262-564-6324. FAX: 262-564-6370. Web Site: www.mykcls.info. *Interim Dir,* Brandi Cummings; Tel: 262-564-6113, E-mail: bcummings@mykpl.info
Member Libraries: Community Library; Kenosha Public Library
Partic in Wisconsin Public Library Consortium

P KENOSHA PUBLIC LIBRARY*, Southwest Library, 7979 38th Ave, 53142. SAN 364-7080. Tel: 262-564-6100. Administration Tel: 262-564-6300. Web Site: mykpl.info. *Interim Dir,* Brandi Cummings; Tel: 262-564-6113, E-mail: bcummings@mykpl.info; *Division Head, Public Services,* Linda Noyce; E-mail: lnoyce@mykpl.info; *Division Head, Support Services,* Robert Nunez; E-mail: mnunez@mykpl.info; *Head, Youth & Family Services,* Heather Thompson; E-mail: hthompson@mykpl.info; *Br Mgr,* Shannon Urban; E-mail: surban@mykpl.info; *Human Res Mgr,* Michelle Tucker; E-mail: mtucker@mkpl.info; Staff 80 (MLS 18, Non-MLS 62)
Founded 1981. Pop 99,286; Circ 645,506
Library Holdings: Bk Vols 224,590
Special Collections: Developmental Coll; Kenosha Author Coll; Kenosha History Coll
Subject Interests: Local hist
Automation Activity & Vendor Info: (Acquisitions) SirsiDynix; (Cataloging) SirsiDynix; (Circulation) SirsiDynix; (OPAC) SirsiDynix
Wireless access
Function: Adult bk club, Art exhibits, Audio & video playback equip for onsite use, Audiobks via web, Bk club(s), Bks on CD, Children's prog, Computer training, Computers for patron use, Digital talking bks, E-Reserves, Electronic databases & coll, Family literacy, Games & aids for people with disabilities, Holiday prog, Home delivery & serv to seniorr ctr & nursing homes, Homebound delivery serv, ILL available, Instruction & testing, Large print keyboards, Magnifiers for reading, Music CDs, Online cat, Online ref, Outreach serv, OverDrive digital audio bks, Photocopying/Printing, Preschool outreach, Preschool reading prog, Prog for adults, Prog for children & young adult, Ref & res, Ref serv available, Serves people with intellectual disabilities, Story hour, Summer reading prog, Teen prog, Telephone ref, Wheelchair accessible, Workshops
Publications: Guide to Genealogy; Job Search Information; Kenosha Organization Directory; Local Historical Resources; Newsnotes
Mem of Kenosha County Library System
Partic in WiLS
Special Services for the Blind - Audio mat; Bks on CD; Descriptive video serv (DVS)

Open Mon-Thurs 9-9, Fri 9-6, Sat 9-5, Sun Noon-4
Friends of the Library Group
Branches: 3
NORTHSIDE LIBRARY, 1500 27th Ave, 53140-4679, SAN 364-7137. *Br Mgr,* Jennifer Kozelou; E-mail: jkozelou@mykpl.info
Founded 1993
Library Holdings: Bk Vols 123,656
Open Mon-Thurs 9-9, Fri 9-6, Sat 9-5
Friends of the Library Group
GILBERT M SIMMONS LIBRARY, 711 59th Pl, 53140-4145, SAN 364-7072. *Br Mgr,* Kahlil Griffin; E-mail: kgriffin@mykpl.info
Founded 1900
Library Holdings: Bk Vols 41,292
Open Mon-Thurs 9-8, Fri 9-6, Sat 9-5
Friends of the Library Group
UPTOWN LIBRARY, 2419 63rd St, 53143-4331, SAN 364-7161. *Br Mgr,* Kahlil Griffin
Founded 1925
Library Holdings: Bk Vols 20,114
Open Mon-Fri 9-6, Sat 10-2
Friends of the Library Group
Bookmobiles: 1. Librn, Marcia Siehr. Bk vols 11,706

S KENOSHA PUBLIC MUSEUM LIBRARY*, 5500 First Ave, 53140. SAN 318-0557. Tel: 262-653-4140, 262-653-4426. FAX: 262-653-4437. Web Site: museums.kenosha.org. *Exec Dir,* Peggy Gregorski; E-mail: pgregorski@kenosha.org; *Mgr of Collections & Exhibitions,* Gina Radandt; E-mail: gradandt@kenosha.org; Staff 6 (Non-MLS 6)
Founded 1936
Library Holdings: AV Mats 300; Bk Vols 10,000; Per Subs 21
Special Collections: Art Reference; Civil War Archives; Natural Sciences Reference
Subject Interests: Anthrop, Art, Civil War, Mus, Paleontology
Restriction: Staff use only

C UNIVERSITY OF WISCONSIN-PARKSIDE LIBRARY*, 900 Wood Rd, 53141. (Mail add: PO Box 2000, 53141-2000), SAN 318-0573. Tel: 262-595-3432. Web Site: www.uwp.edu/learn/library. *Dir,* Anna Stadick; Tel: 262-595-2167, E-mail: anna.stadick@uwp.edu; *Head, Archives,* Melissa Olson; E-mail: olsonm@uwp.edu; *Head, Coll,* Dina Kaye; E-mail: kaye@uwp.edu; *Head, Libr Syst,* Jay Dougherty; E-mail: dougherty@uwp.edu; *Head, Ref & Instruction,* Jennie Callas; E-mail: callas@uwp.edu; *Access Serv Mgr,* David Gehring; E-mail: gehring@uwp.edu; Staff 14 (MLS 9, Non-MLS 5)
Founded 1967. Enrl 4,500; Fac 287; Highest Degree: Master
Special Collections: Aviation (John Sullivan Coll); Aviation History of Racine & Kenosha Counties Coll; Charles Nicholas Johnson Coll, slides; Daniel Klapproth World War II Coll, letters, photog; Dr Lillian Trager Papers; Eugene Walter Leach Digital Coll; Irving Wallace Coll; Kenosha & Racine Historic Photos; Nash & AMC (Vincent F Roffolo Coll); Plat Maps of Racine & Kenosha Counties; Racine Journal Times Obituaries, 1949-1978; Ranger News Digital Coll; Small Press Publishers Coll (including Perishable Press, Mother Courage Press & Black Sparrow Press); Wisconsin Genealogy Index, 1852-1907
Wireless access
Partic in Coun of Univ of Wis Librs; OCLC Online Computer Library Center, Inc; WiLS

KESHENA

J COLLEGE OF MENOMINEE NATION LIBRARY*, S Verna Fowler Academic Library/Menominee Public Library, N 172 Hwy 47/55, 54135. (Mail add: PO Box 1179, 54135-1179). Tel: 715-799-5600, Ext 3003. E-mail: library@menominee.edu. Web Site: menominee.libguides.com/cmnlibrary. *Dir,* Maria Escalante; E-mail: mescalante@menominee.edu; *Librn,* Bethany Huse; E-mail: bhuse@menominee.edu; Staff 4 (MLS 1, Non-MLS 3)
Enrl 503; Fac 33; Highest Degree: Bachelor
Library Holdings: AV Mats 1,814; Bk Titles 16,854; Per Subs 30
Special Collections: Native American Coll, incl Menominee Tribe & Tribal Enterprise
Subject Interests: Computer sci, Natural res, Sustainable develop, Tribal legal studies
Automation Activity & Vendor Info: (Cataloging) LibLime; (Circulation) LibLime; (OPAC) LibLime
Function: Archival coll, Art exhibits, Bks on cassette, Bks on CD, Computers for patron use, Electronic databases & coll, ILL available, Music CDs, Outreach serv, Photocopying/Printing, Prog for adults, Ref & res, Scanner
Mem of Nicolet Federated Library System
Partic in American Indian Higher Education Consortium
Open Mon-Thurs 8-8, Fri 9-4:30

KEWASKUM

P KEWASKUM PUBLIC LIBRARY*, 206 First St, 53040-8929. (Mail add: PO Box 38, 53040-0038), SAN 318-059X. Tel: 262-626-4312. Web Site: www.kewaskum.lib.wi.us. *Dir,* Lori Kreis; E-mail: lkreis@monarchlibraries.org; *Asst Dir, Youth Serv,* Kimberly Kluge; E-mail: kkluge@monarchlibraries.org
Founded 1913. Pop 4,000; Circ 79,000
Library Holdings: Bk Vols 27,000; Per Subs 60
Automation Activity & Vendor Info: (Acquisitions) SirsiDynix; (Cataloging) SirsiDynix; (Circulation) SirsiDynix
Wireless access
Mem of Monarch Library System
Open Mon-Thurs 10-8, Fri 10-5, Sat 10-1

KEWAUNEE

P KEWAUNEE PUBLIC LIBRARY*, 822 Juneau St, 54216-1200. SAN 318-0603. Tel: 920-388-5015. FAX: 920-388-5016. E-mail: kew@kewauneepubliclibrary.org. Web Site: kewauneepubliclibrary.org. *Dir,* Carol Petrina; E-mail: cpetrina@kewauneepubliclibrary.org
Founded 1906. Pop 20,103; Circ 63,931
Library Holdings: Bk Vols 31,000; Per Subs 110
Automation Activity & Vendor Info: (Cataloging) Infor Library & Information Solutions; (Circulation) Infor Library & Information Solutions
Wireless access
Mem of Nicolet Federated Library System
Open Mon-Thurs 10-8, Fri 10-6, Sat 9-1
Friends of the Library Group

KIEL

P KIEL PUBLIC LIBRARY*, 511 Third St, 53042. SAN 318-0611. Tel: 920-894-7122. FAX: 920-894-4023. E-mail: kielpl@mcls.lib.wi.us. Web Site: kiellibrary.org. *Dir,* Julia Davis; E-mail: jdavis@mcls.lib.wi.us; Staff 3 (MLS 1, Non-MLS 2)
Founded 1925. Pop 7,500; Circ 80,000
Library Holdings: Bk Vols 40,000; Per Subs 120
Subject Interests: Career, Wis
Automation Activity & Vendor Info: (Cataloging) SirsiDynix; (Circulation) SirsiDynix; (OPAC) SirsiDynix
Wireless access
Mem of Manitowoc-Calumet Library System
Open Mon-Fri 9-6, Sat 9-1
Friends of the Library Group

KIMBERLY

P KIMBERLY PUBLIC LIBRARY*, James J Siebers Memorial Library, 515 W Kimberly Ave, 54136. SAN 318-062X. Tel: 920-788-7515. FAX: 920-788-7516. E-mail: kim@kimberlypubliclibrary.org. Web Site: kimberlypubliclibrary.org. *Dir,* Holly Selwitschka; E-mail: hselwitschka@kimberlypubliclibrary.org
Founded 1907. Pop 7,000
Automation Activity & Vendor Info: (Cataloging) CARL.Solution (TLC); (Circulation) CARL.Solution (TLC); (OPAC) CARL.Solution (TLC)
Wireless access
Mem of Outagamie Waupaca Library System (OWLS)
Open Mon-Fri 9-6, Sat 9-1
Friends of the Library Group

KINGSTON

P MILL POND PUBLIC LIBRARY*, 140 N South St, 53939. (Mail add: PO Box 98, 53939-0098), SAN 318-0638. Tel: 920-394-3281. FAX: 920-394-3281. Web Site: www.millpondlibrary.org. *Dir,* Sara Wilson; E-mail: wilson@millpondlibrary.org
Founded 1964. Circ 10,531
Library Holdings: Bk Vols 7,900
Automation Activity & Vendor Info: (Cataloging) SirsiDynix; (Circulation) SirsiDynix
Wireless access
Mem of Winnefox Library System
Open Mon, Tues & Thurs 1-6, Wed 9-11 & 1-6, Sat 9-11

KOHLER

P KOHLER PUBLIC LIBRARY, 240 School St, 53044. SAN 318-0646. Tel: 920-459-2923. FAX: 920-459-2930. Web Site: kohlerpubliclibrary.org. *Librn,* Erin Coppersmith; E-mail: ecoppers@monarchlibraries.org; Staff 1 (MLS 1)
Pop 2,000; Circ 35,400
Library Holdings: Bk Vols 10,000; Per Subs 60
Automation Activity & Vendor Info: (Acquisitions) Innovative Interfaces, Inc. - Polaris; (Cataloging) Innovative Interfaces, Inc. - Polaris; (Circulation) Innovative Interfaces, Inc. - Polaris

Wireless access
Mem of Monarch Library System
Open Mon-Thurs 9-7, Fri 9-5, Sun 1-4

S SPACES - SAVING + PRESERVING ARTS + CULTURAL ENVIRONMENTS*, Library & Archives, 725-X Woodlake Rd, 53044. SAN 328-2139. Tel: 920-458-1972, Ext 70419. E-mail: archivist@spacesarchives.org, info@spacesarchives.org. Web Site: www.spacesarchives.org/archives/spaces-library. *Curator,* Annalise Flynn
Founded 1978
Special Collections: Art Environments Coll; Popular Culture Coll; Self-taught Artists
Subject Interests: Archit, Art

LA CROSSE

R ENGLISH LUTHERAN CHURCH LIBRARY, 1509 King St, 54601. SAN 318-0662. Tel: 608-784-9335. E-mail: office@englishlutheran.org. Web Site: www.englishlutheran.org. *Librn,* Nancy Mills
Founded 1953
Library Holdings: Bk Titles 3,500
Subject Interests: Bible ref, Children's relig studies, Christian novels, Relig studies
Wireless access
Partic in La Crosse Libr

M GUNDERSEN LUTHERAN HEALTH SYSTEM*, Adolf Gundersen MD Health Sciences Library, 1900 South Ave, H01-011, 54601-9980. SAN 318-0689. Tel: 608-775-5410. FAX: 608-775-6343. E-mail: library@gundersenhealth.org. Web Site: gundersenhealth.libguides.com. *Dir,* Melinda Orebaugh; Staff 5 (MLS 5)
Founded 1965
Library Holdings: e-books 150; e-journals 5,800; Bk Titles 6,000; Bk Vols 8,000; Per Subs 650
Subject Interests: Consumer health, Hospital health sci, Nursing

P LA CROSSE PUBLIC LIBRARY*, 800 Main St, 54601. SAN 364-7374. Tel: 608-789-7100. Circulation Tel: 608-789-7109. Reference Tel: 608-789-7122. Administration Tel: 608-789-7123. FAX: 608-789-7106. E-mail: circdesk@lacrosselibrary.org. Web Site: www.lacrosselibrary.org. *Dir,* Shanneon Grant; E-mail: sgrant@lacrosselibrary.org; *Adult Serv Mgr,* Rochelle Hartman; Tel: 608-789-8191, E-mail: rochelle@lacrosselibrary.org; *Archives Mgr,* Anita T Doering; Tel: 608-789-7136, E-mail: doering@lacrosselibrary.org; *Circ Mgr,* Cynthia Arauz; Tel: 608-789-4909, E-mail: carauz@lacrosselibrary.org; *Youth Serv Mgr,* Dawn Wacek; Tel: 608-789-8190, E-mail: dwacek@lacrosselibrary.org; Staff 27 (MLS 18.6, Non-MLS 8.4)
Founded 1888. Pop 51,719; Circ 1,171,723
Library Holdings: AV Mats 26,586; DVDs 21,108; e-books 65,370; Electronic Media & Resources 321; Bk Vols 200,492; Per Subs 428
Special Collections: State Document Depository; US Document Depository
Subject Interests: Local hist
Automation Activity & Vendor Info: (Acquisitions) Innovative Interfaces, Inc; (Cataloging) Innovative Interfaces, Inc; (Circulation) Innovative Interfaces, Inc; (Serials) Innovative Interfaces, Inc
Wireless access
Function: Archival coll, Art exhibits, Bks on CD, CD-ROM, Computer training, Computers for patron use, Digital talking bks, Electronic databases & coll, Free DVD rentals, Home delivery & serv to seniorr ctr & nursing homes, Homebound delivery serv, ILL available, Magnifiers for reading, Microfiche/film & reading machines, Music CDs, Online cat, OverDrive digital audio bks, Photocopying/Printing, Preschool outreach, Prof lending libr, Prog for adults, Prog for children & young adult, Ref serv available, Scanner, Story hour, Summer reading prog, Tax forms, Teen prog, Telephone ref, Wheelchair accessible, Winter reading prog
Mem of Winding Rivers Library System
Partic in WILS
Special Services for the Deaf - Assistive tech; Closed caption videos
Special Services for the Blind - Aids for in-house use; Assistive/Adapted tech devices, equip & products; BiFolkal kits; Bks on cassette; Bks on CD; Large print bks; Magnifiers; Reader equip; Screen enlargement software for people with visual disabilities; Talking bks
Open Mon-Thurs 9-8, Fri 9-6, Sat 9-5, Sun 1-5
Friends of the Library Group
Branches: 1
NORTH COMMUNITY, 1552 Kane St, 54603, SAN 364-7404. Tel: 608-789-7102. *Br Supvr,* Cynthia Arauz; Tel: 608-789-7189, E-mail: carauz@lacrosselibrary.org
Open Mon-Wed 12-8, Thurs-Sat 10-5
Friends of the Library Group

S MAYO CLINIC HEALTH SYSTEM*, Health Sciences Library, 700 West Ave S, 54601. SAN 318-0697. Tel: 608-785-0940, Ext 2685. E-mail: library.lacrosse@mayo.edu. Web Site: libraryguides.mayo.edu/lacrosse. *Librn,* Heather Jett; E-mail: jett.heather@mayo.edu
Founded 1945
Library Holdings: Bk Titles 1,280; Per Subs 91
Subject Interests: Dentistry, Med, Nursing
Wireless access
Restriction: Not open to pub

C UNIVERSITY OF WISCONSIN-LA CROSSE*, Murphy Library Resource Center, 1631 Pine St, 54601-3748. SAN 318-0727. Tel: 608-785-8505. Circulation Tel: 608-785-8507. Interlibrary Loan Service Tel: 608-785-8636. FAX: 608-785-8639. E-mail: libraryoffice@uwlax.edu. Web Site: www.uwlax.edu/murphylibrary. *Coll Develop Librn, Interim Dir,* John Jax; Tel: 608-785-8567, E-mail: jjax@uwlax.edu; *Acad Librn, Systems & Metadata Librn,* William Doering; Tel: 608-785-8399, E-mail: wdoering@uwlax.edu; *Govt Info Librn, Ref Librn,* Michael Current; Tel: 608-785-8739, E-mail: mcurrent@uwlax.edu; *Outreach Librn,* Chelsea Wyman; Tel: 608-785-8396, E-mail: cwyman@uwlax.edu; *Spec Coll & Archives Librn,* Laura Godden; Tel: 608-785-8511, E-mail: lgodden@uwlax.edu; *Acq,* Katherine Fish; Tel: 608-785-8395, E-mail: kfish@uwlax.edu; *Circ,* Scott Pfitzinger; Tel: 608-785-8943, E-mail: spfitzinger@uwlax.edu; *Info Literacy,* Elizabeth Humrickhouse; Tel: 608-785-8738, E-mail: ehumrickhouse@uwlax.edu; Staff 24 (MLS 11, Non-MLS 13)
Founded 1909. Enrl 9,975; Fac 443; Highest Degree: Master
Library Holdings: e-books 8,308; Electronic Media & Resources 192; Bk Titles 325,525; Bk Vols 410,736; Per Subs 1,052
Special Collections: Contemporary Poetry; Gothic Literature (Arkham House & Skeeters Coll); Inland River Steamboats, photog; Regional History Coll, photographs; Small Presses Coll. Oral History; State Document Depository; US Document Depository
Subject Interests: Allied health, Educ, Phys educ
Automation Activity & Vendor Info: (Acquisitions) Ex Libris Group; (Cataloging) Ex Libris Group; (Circulation) Ex Libris Group; (Course Reserve) Ex Libris Group; (ILL) OCLC; (OPAC) Ex Libris Group; (Serials) Ex Libris Group
Wireless access
Publications: Fine Print (Newsletter)
Partic in OCLC Online Computer Library Center, Inc; WiLS
Special Services for the Blind - Assistive/Adapted tech devices, equip & products
Open Mon-Thurs 7:30am-1am, Fri 7:30am-8pm, Sat 10-8, Sun 11am-1am
Friends of the Library Group

S UPPER MISSISSIPPI RIVER CONSERVATION COMMITTEE LIBRARY*, Murphy Library, UWLC, 1631 Pine St, 54601. (Mail add: 292 San Diego Rd, Carbondale, 62902), SAN 371-7917. Tel: 608-783-8405, 618-579-3129. FAX: 608-785-8507. E-mail: umrcc@mississippiriver.com. Web Site: www.umrcc.org. *Coordr,* Neal Jackson; E-mail: neal_jackson@fws.gov
Library Holdings: Bk Vols 5,000; Per Subs 100
Wireless access
Restriction: Non-circulating to the pub

G USGS*, Upper Midwest Environmental Sciences Center, 2630 Fanta Reed Rd, 54603-1223. SAN 318-0719. Tel: 608-781-6215. FAX: 608-783-6066. E-mail: library@usgs.gov. Web Site: www.usgs.gov/core-science-systems/usgs-library. *Tech Info Spec,* Lisa Hein; E-mail: lhein@usgs.gov
Founded 1959
Library Holdings: Bk Titles 5,000; Per Subs 60
Special Collections: Bulletin of United States Fish Commission
Subject Interests: Chem, Chem registration, Ecology of large river systs, Fish culture, Limnology
Automation Activity & Vendor Info: (Cataloging) SirsiDynix; (OPAC) SirsiDynix

C VITERBO UNIVERSITY*, Todd Wehr Memorial Library, 900 Viterbo Dr, 54601. SAN 318-0743. Tel: 608-796-3270. FAX: 608-796-3275. Reference E-mail: reference@viterbo.edu. Web Site: www.viterbo.edu/library. *Dir,* Kim Olson-Kopp; Tel: 608-796-3263, E-mail: kmolsonkopp@viterbo.edu; *Asst Dir,* Debra Alexander-Friet; Tel: 608-796-3265, E-mail: dafriet@viterbo.edu; *Ref Librn,* Lisa Christie; Tel: 608-796-3268, E-mail: lmchristie@viterbo.edu; *Acq Librn, Outreach Librn,* Mary Rieder; Tel: 608-796-3266, E-mail: mbrieder@viterbo.edu; *Archives, Syst Librn,* Jason Skoog; Tel: 608-796-3262, E-mail: jaskoog@viterbo.edu; *Info Serv Mgr,* Caitlyn Konze; Tel: 608-796-3267, E-mail: cfkonze@viterbo.edu; Staff 9 (MLS 5, Non-MLS 4)
Founded 1890. Enrl 2,470; Fac 120; Highest Degree: Master
Library Holdings: CDs 1,132; e-books 11,884; Bk Titles 69,384; Per Subs 549; Videos 1,974
Special Collections: Catholic History Coll; Music Scores

Subject Interests: Educ, Fine arts, Liberal arts, Nursing, Relig studies
Automation Activity & Vendor Info: (Acquisitions) Innovative Interfaces, Inc; (Cataloging) Innovative Interfaces, Inc; (Circulation) Innovative Interfaces, Inc; (Course Reserve) Innovative Interfaces, Inc; (ILL) OCLC; (OPAC) Innovative Interfaces, Inc; (Serials) Innovative Interfaces, Inc
Wireless access
Partic in Wis Libr Consortium
Open Mon-Thurs 9am-Midnight, Fri 7:45-5, Sat 10-5, Sun 1-Midnight
Restriction: Open to fac, students & qualified researchers, Open to pub for ref & circ; with some limitations
Friends of the Library Group

J WESTERN TECHNICAL COLLEGE LIBRARY*, 400 Seventh St N, 54601. Tel: 608-785-9142. Reference Tel: 608-785-9406. E-mail: library@westerntc.edu. Web Site: www.westerntc.edu/library. *Learning Commons Mgr,* Kirsten Moffler-Daykin; E-mail: daykink@westerntc.edu; Staff 6 (MLS 2, Non-MLS 4)
Founded 1967. Enrl 3,700; Fac 185; Highest Degree: Associate
Library Holdings: High Interest/Low Vocabulary Bk Vols 600; Bk Titles 33,000; Per Subs 260
Automation Activity & Vendor Info: (Cataloging) Follett Software; (Circulation) Follett Software; (OPAC) Follett Software
Wireless access
Partic in WiLS; WISPALS Library Consortium
Open Mon-Thurs 7:30am-8pm, Fri 7:30-4, Sat 9-1

LA FARGE

P LAWTON MEMORIAL LIBRARY*, 118 N Bird St, 54639. SAN 318-0786. Tel: 608-625-2015. FAX: 608-625-2329. E-mail: lafargepl@wrlsweb.org. Web Site: www.lafargelibrary.org. *Dir,* Rita Wachula-Breckel
Founded 1923. Pop 829; Circ 17,361
Library Holdings: Bk Titles 13,000; Per Subs 53
Special Collections: Arrowheads. Oral History
Automation Activity & Vendor Info: (Cataloging) Horizon; (Circulation) Horizon
Wireless access
Mem of Winding Rivers Library System
Open Mon 1-6, Tues & Fri 10-12 & 12:30-6, Wed 1-8, Sat 9-1
Friends of the Library Group

LA POINTE

P MADELINE ISLAND PUBLIC LIBRARY*, One Library St, 54850. (Mail add: PO Box 65, 54850-0065), SAN 318-0794. Tel: 715-747-3662. FAX: 715-747-3661. Web Site: www.madislandlibrary.org. *Dir,* Lauren Schuppe; E-mail: director@madislandlibrary.org
Founded 1960. Pop 180; Circ 4,636
Library Holdings: Bk Vols 6,500; Per Subs 50
Mem of Northern Waters Library Service
Open Mon & Wed 4-8, Tues, Thurs & Fri 10-5, Sat 10-Noon (Winter); Mon & Wed 10-8, Tues, Thurs & Fri 10-5, Sat 10-Noon (Summer)

LA VALLE

P LA VALLE PUBLIC LIBRARY*, 101 W Main, 53941-9564. (Mail add: PO Box 7, 53941-0007), SAN 318-0808. Tel: 608-985-7323. FAX: 608-985-8382. E-mail: lavallelibrary@mwt.net. Web Site: www.lavallelibrary.org. *Dir,* Cindi Morgan
Pop 360; Circ 13,000
Library Holdings: Bk Vols 10,000
Automation Activity & Vendor Info: (Acquisitions) SirsiDynix; (Cataloging) SirsiDynix; (Circulation) SirsiDynix
Wireless access
Mem of South Central Library System
Open Mon & Thurs 2:30-6:30, Wed 9-2
Friends of the Library Group

LAC DU FLAMBEAU

P BEN GUTHRIE LAC DU FLAMBEAU PUBLIC LIBRARY*, 622 Peace Pipe Rd, 54538. (Mail add: PO Box 729, 54538-0729), SAN 376-6586. Tel: 715-588-7001. FAX: 715-588-7101. Web Site: ldflibrary.org. *Libr Dir,* Jeanne M Wolfe; E-mail: jwolfe@ldftribe.com
Library Holdings: Bk Titles 8,778; Bk Vols 15,000; Per Subs 7
Wireless access
Mem of Northern Waters Library Service
Open Mon-Thurs 9:30-5, Fri 9:30-4:30, Sat 10-2

LADYSMITH

P RUSK COUNTY COMMUNITY LIBRARY, Ladysmith Public Library, 418 Corbett Ave W, 54848-1396. SAN 318-0816. Tel: 715-532-2604. FAX: 715-532-2658. E-mail: ladysmithpl@ladysmithpl.org. Web Site: ladysmithpl.org. *Dir,* Christinna Swearingen; E-mail: swearingen@ladysmithpl.org; *Cat,* Tedi Cammire; E-mail: cammire@ladysmithpl.org; *Youth Serv,* Valerie Spooner; E-mail: spooner@ladysmithpl.org; Staff 9 (MLS 1, Non-MLS 8)
Founded 1906. Pop 12,047
Library Holdings: Per Subs 57
Automation Activity & Vendor Info: (Acquisitions) Innovative Interfaces, Inc; (Cataloging) Innovative Interfaces, Inc; (Circulation) Innovative Interfaces, Inc
Wireless access
Function: 24/7 Electronic res, 24/7 Online cat, 24/7 wireless access, Activity rm, Archival coll, Art exhibits, Art programs, Audio & video playback equip for onsite use, Audiobks via web, Bks on CD, Children's prog, Computers for patron use, Electronic databases & coll, Free DVD rentals, Games, Internet access, Laptop/tablet checkout, Life-long learning prog for all ages, Magazines, Magnifiers for reading, Meeting rooms, Music CDs, Preschool outreach, Preschool reading prog, Prog for adults, Prog for children & young adult, Ref & res, Scanner
Mem of Inspiring & Facilitating Library Success (IFLS)
Open Mon & Wed-Fri 10-6, Tues 10-8, Sat 10-3
Friends of the Library Group

LAKE GENEVA

P LAKE GENEVA PUBLIC LIBRARY*, 918 W Main St, 53147-1890. SAN 318-0840. Tel: 262-249-5299. E-mail: lakegene@lglibrary.org. Web Site: lglibrary.org.
Founded 1895
Library Holdings: Bk Vols 46,356; Per Subs 179
Subject Interests: Local hist
Automation Activity & Vendor Info: (Cataloging) SirsiDynix; (Circulation) SirsiDynix; (OPAC) SirsiDynix
Wireless access
Mem of Prairie Lakes Library System (PLLS)
Friends of the Library Group

LAKE MILLS

P L D FARGO PUBLIC LIBRARY*, 120 E Madison St, 53551-1644. SAN 318-0867. Tel: 920-648-2166. FAX: 920-648-5561. Web Site: www.lakemills.lib.wi.us. *Dir,* Gerard Saylor; E-mail: gerardsaylor@lakemills.lib.wi.us; Staff 7 (MLS 2, Non-MLS 5)
Founded 1902. Pop 10,000; Circ 100,000
Library Holdings: Bk Titles 34,000; Per Subs 111
Special Collections: Aztalan Historical Society (Lake Mills) Print & Picture Coll; Local History (Lake Mills Leader 1902-present)
Automation Activity & Vendor Info: (Circulation) Innovative Interfaces, Inc
Wireless access
Mem of Bridges Library System
Open Mon-Thurs 9-8, Fri 9-5, Sat 9-1
Friends of the Library Group

LAKEWOOD

P LAKES COUNTRY PUBLIC LIBRARY*, 15235 Hwy 32, 54138. (Mail add: PO Box 220, 54138-0220), SAN 377-9947. Tel: 715-276-9020. FAX: 715-276-7151. E-mail: lak@lakescountrylibrary.org. Web Site: www.lakescountrylibrary.org. *Dir,* Katie Essermann; E-mail: kessermann@lakescountrylibrary.org
Founded 1982
Library Holdings: Bk Titles 15,000; Per Subs 60
Automation Activity & Vendor Info: (Cataloging) Infor Library & Information Solutions; (Circulation) Infor Library & Information Solutions
Wireless access
Mem of Nicolet Federated Library System
Open Mon, Tues, Thurs & Fri 9-5, Wed 9-8, Sat 9-2
Friends of the Library Group

LANCASTER

P SCHREINER MEMORIAL LIBRARY*, Lancaster Public Library, 113 W Elm St, 53813-1202. SAN 318-0875. Tel: 608-723-7304. Web Site: schreinermemoriallibrary.org. *Libr Dir,* Christina Swearingen; E-mail: cswearingen@swls.org; Staff 1 (MLS 1)
Founded 1901. Pop 3,868; Circ 87,907
Library Holdings: Audiobooks 719; CDs 1,202; DVDs 1,796; Bk Vols 34,949; Per Subs 114; Videos 210
Automation Activity & Vendor Info: (Circulation) Auto-Graphics, Inc; (OPAC) Auto-Graphics, Inc
Wireless access
Function: Activity rm, Archival coll, Art exhibits, Audiobks on Playaways & MP3, Audiobks via web, Bks on CD, Children's prog, Computer training, Computers for patron use, Digital talking bks, E-Reserves, Electronic databases & coll, Free DVD rentals, Holiday prog, Home delivery & serv to seniorr ctr & nursing homes, Homebound delivery serv, ILL available, Internet access, Life-long learning prog for all ages,

Magazines, Magnifiers for reading, Mango lang, Meeting rooms, Microfiche/film & reading machines, Movies, Music CDs, Online cat, Online ref, Outreach serv, OverDrive digital audio bks, Photocopying/Printing, Preschool reading prog, Prog for adults, Prog for children & young adult, Ref & res, Scanner, Senior computer classes, Spanish lang bks, Study rm, Summer & winter reading prog, Summer reading prog, Tax forms, Teen prog, Wheelchair accessible
Mem of Southwest Wisconsin Library System
Partic in WiLS
Open Mon-Thurs 9-8, Fri 9-5, Sat 9-1
Branches: 1
POTOSI BRANCH, 103 N Main St, Potosi, 53820. (Mail add: PO Box 97, Potosi, 53820-0097). Tel: 608-763-2115. *Libr Asst II,* Judy Schaefer; E-mail: jschaefer@swls.org
Founded 2007. Pop 1,912
Library Holdings: Audiobooks 84; CDs 45; DVDs 335; Bk Vols 4,554; Per Subs 30; Videos 188
Automation Activity & Vendor Info: (Circulation) Auto-Graphics, Inc
Open Tues & Thurs 3-8, Wed 10-1, Sat 9-1

LAND O'LAKES

P LAND O'LAKES PUBLIC LIBRARY*, 4242 County Hwy B, 54540. (Mail add: PO Box 450, 54540-0450), SAN 318-0883. Tel: 715-547-6006. FAX: 715-547-6004. Web Site: landolakeslibrary.org. *Dir,* Julie Zelten; E-mail: director@lol.wislib.org; *Youth Serv,* Karen Weber-Mendham
Pop 794; Circ 3,866
Library Holdings: Bk Vols 17,530
Automation Activity & Vendor Info: (Cataloging) Innovative Interfaces, Inc; (Circulation) Innovative Interfaces, Inc; (OPAC) Innovative Interfaces, Inc
Wireless access
Mem of Northern Waters Library Service
Open Mon-Fri 9-5, Sat 10-1 (Summer); Mon, Tues, Thurs & Fri 10-4, Wed 10-6, Sat 10-1 (Winter)
Friends of the Library Group

LAONA

P EDITH EVANS COMMUNITY LIBRARY*, 5216 Forest Ave, 54541. (Mail add: PO Box 127, 54541-0127), SAN 318-0891. Tel: 715-674-4751. FAX: 715-674-5904. Web Site: www.laonapubliclibrary.com. *Dir,* Cynthia Lemerande; E-mail: director@laonapubliclibrary.com
Founded 1917. Pop 2,000
Library Holdings: Bk Vols 12,000; Per Subs 95
Automation Activity & Vendor Info: (Cataloging) Horizon; (Circulation) Horizon
Wireless access
Partic in Wisconsin Valley Library Service
Open Mon 12-5, Tues-Thurs 8:30-4, Fri 8-12:30

LENA

P LENA PUBLIC LIBRARY*, 200 E Main St, 54139. SAN 377-9963. Tel: 920-829-5335. FAX: 920-829-5335. E-mail: len@lenalibrary.org. Web Site: lenalibrary.org. *Dir,* Amy Peterson; E-mail: apeterson@lenalibrary.org; Staff 1 (Non-MLS 1)
Library Holdings: Bk Titles 10,971
Automation Activity & Vendor Info: (Cataloging) Innovative Interfaces, Inc; (Circulation) Innovative Interfaces, Inc; (OPAC) Innovative Interfaces, Inc
Wireless access
Mem of Nicolet Federated Library System
Open Mon-Thurs 10-6, Fri 10-4
Friends of the Library Group

LITTLE CHUTE

LITTLE CHUTE PUBLIC LIBRARY*, Gerard H Van Hoof Library, 625 Grand Ave, 54140. Tel: 920-788-7825. FAX: 920-788-7827. E-mail: lit@littlechutelibrary.org. Web Site: littlechutelibrary.org. *Libr Dir,* Position Currently Open
Library Holdings: Bk Vols 50,000; Per Subs 50
Wireless access
Mem of Outagamie Waupaca Library System (OWLS)
Open Mon-Thurs 9-7, Fri 9-5, Sat 9-1
Friends of the Library Group

LIVINGSTON

P ALLEN DIETZMAN LIBRARY*, Livingston Public Library, 220 W Barber Ave, 53554. (Mail add: PO Box 216, 53554-0216), SAN 318-0905. Tel: 608-943-6801. Web Site: allendietzmanpubliclibrary.wordpress.com. *Dir,* Betty Schambow; E-mail: bschambow@swls.org
Pop 597; Circ 3,380
Library Holdings: AV Mats 230; Bk Vols 4,462; Per Subs 10; Videos 60
Automation Activity & Vendor Info: (Acquisitions) Horizon; (Cataloging) Horizon; (Circulation) Horizon; (OPAC) Horizon
Wireless access
Mem of Southwest Wisconsin Library System
Open Mon 1-6, Wed 12:30-7:30, Thurs 1-4, Sat 9-12

LODI

P LODI WOMAN'S CLUB PUBLIC LIBRARY*, 130 Lodi St, 53555. SAN 318-0913. Tel: 608-592-4130. FAX: 608-592-2327. Web Site: www.lodipubliclibrary.org. *Dir,* Mr Alex LeClair; E-mail: aleclair@lodipubliclibrary.org
Pop 9,000; Circ 99,455
Library Holdings: e-books 8,277; Bk Vols 26,757; Per Subs 144; Talking Bks 1,580
Automation Activity & Vendor Info: (Acquisitions) Horizon; (Course Reserve) Horizon; (OPAC) Horizon
Wireless access
Mem of South Central Library System
Open Mon 9-7, Tues-Fri 9-6, Sat 9-1
Friends of the Library Group

LOMIRA

P LOMIRA QUADGRAPHICS COMMUNITY LIBRARY*, 427 S Water St, 53048-9581. (Mail add: PO Box 1108, 53048-1108), SAN 318-0921. Tel: 920-269-4115, Ext 3. Web Site: www.lomira.lib.wi.us. *Dir,* Camrin Sullivan; E-mail: csullivan@monarchlibraries.org
Founded 1938. Pop 1,732; Circ 18,996
Library Holdings: Bk Titles 17,255; Bk Vols 17,675; Per Subs 52
Special Collections: Commemorative Stamps Coll, 1972-1988; Local Genealogy Coll, church & cemetary rec; Local Newspaper, micro
Automation Activity & Vendor Info: (Cataloging) SirsiDynix-WorkFlows; (Circulation) SirsiDynix-WorkFlows; (OPAC) SirsiDynix-WorkFlows
Wireless access
Mem of Monarch Library System
Open Mon, Tues & Thurs 1-7, Wed 10-7, Fri 10-5, Sat 9-12
Friends of the Library Group

LONE ROCK

P LONE ROCK COMMUNITY LIBRARY*, 234 N Broadway, 53556. (Mail add: PO Box 5, 53556-0007), SAN 318-093X. Tel: 608-583-2034. FAX: 608-583-2034. E-mail: lonerockcomlibrary@gmail.com. Web Site: lonerocklibrary.wordpress.com. *Libr Dir,* Caitlin Opatik
Founded 1972. Pop 1,074; Circ 4,250
Library Holdings: Bk Vols 8,539; Per Subs 12
Automation Activity & Vendor Info: (Cataloging) Horizon; (Circulation) Horizon; (OPAC) Horizon
Wireless access
Function: 24/7 Electronic res, 24/7 Online cat, Activity rm
Mem of Southwest Wisconsin Library System
Open Mon, Tues & Wed 11-5:30, Thurs 10-2

LOYAL

P LOYAL PUBLIC LIBRARY*, 214 N Main St, 54446. (Mail add: PO Box 337, 54446-0337), SAN 318-0948. Tel: 715-255-8189. FAX: 715-255-8348. Web Site: loyalpubliclibrary.org. *Dir,* Teresa Hall; E-mail: director@loyal.lib.wi.us; *Asst Librn,* Deb Roedel; Staff 2 (Non-MLS 2)
Founded 1901. Pop 4,184; Circ 14,794
Library Holdings: AV Mats 570; Bk Titles 15,700; Per Subs 32; Talking Bks 1,100
Automation Activity & Vendor Info: (Circulation) SirsiDynix
Wireless access
Partic in Wisconsin Valley Library Service
Open Mon, Tues, Thurs & Fri 10-5:30, Wed 10-6

LUCK

P LUCK PUBLIC LIBRARY*, 301 S Main St, 54853. SAN 318-0956. Tel: 715-472-2770. E-mail: luckpl@luckpubliclibrary.org. Web Site: luckpubliclibrary.org. *Dir,* Jill Gover; *Asst Dir,* Colleen Allen; E-mail: allen@luckpubliclibrary.org; Staff 2 (Non-MLS 2)
Founded 1948. Pop 1,025; Circ 21,000
Library Holdings: Bk Titles 9,000; Per Subs 13
Special Collections: Oral History
Subject Interests: County hist, Local hist, Wis
Wireless access
Mem of Inspiring & Facilitating Library Success (IFLS)
Open Mon-Thurs 11-7, Fri 11-5, Sat 10-1
Friends of the Library Group

MADISON

S CAPITAL AREA REGIONAL PLANNING COMMISSION LIBRARY*, 100 State St, Ste 400, 53703. SAN 318-1030. Tel: 608-474-6017. E-mail: info@CapitalAreaRPC.org. Web Site: www.capitalarearpc.org. *Admin Serv Mgr,* Tanya Sime; E-mail: tanyas@capitalarearpc.org
Founded 1968
Library Holdings: Bk Vols 3,900; Per Subs 20
Subject Interests: Census, Environ studies, Housing, Land use planning, Master plans, Pop, Transportation, Water res mgt

L DEWITT LLP, Law Library, 25 W Main St, Ste 800, 53703. SAN 372-3593. Tel: 608-283-5504. FAX: 608-252-9243. Web Site: www.dewittllp.com. *Dir,* Richard D Hendricks; E-mail: rdh@dewittllp.com; Staff 2 (MLS 1, Non-MLS 1)
Library Holdings: Bk Vols 17,000; Per Subs 50
Wireless access
Restriction: Staff use only

C EDGEWOOD COLLEGE LIBRARY*, Oscar Rennebohm Library, 959 Edgewood College Dr, 53711-1997. SAN 364-7463. Tel: 608-663-3300. Circulation Tel: 608-663-3278. Interlibrary Loan Service Tel: 608-663-3302. Administration Tel: 608-663-3306. Automation Services Tel: 608-663-3284. FAX: 608-663-6778. E-mail: libanswers@edgewood.edu. Web Site: library.edgewood.edu. *Libr Dir,* Nathan Dowd; Tel: 608-663-2837, E-mail: ndowd@edgewood.edu; *Head, Digital Initiatives,* Jonathan Bloy; *Automation Syst Librn, Head, Electronic Res,* Bonita Dickman; *Circ Supvr,* Julie Wendt; *Ref & Instruction Coordr,* Elizabeth Tappy; *Archivist,* Sarah Naughton; *Sr Libr Asst/Tech Serv,* Karen Cherone; Staff 6 (MLS 4, Non-MLS 2)
Founded 1941. Enrl 1,935; Fac 223; Highest Degree: Doctorate
Library Holdings: e-books 234,352; Bk Vols 65,530; Per Subs 331
Subject Interests: Bus, Educ, Nursing
Automation Activity & Vendor Info: (Acquisitions) SirsiDynix; (Cataloging) SirsiDynix; (Circulation) SirsiDynix; (ILL) OCLC; (OPAC) SirsiDynix; (Serials) SirsiDynix
Wireless access
Partic in WILS
Open Mon-Thurs 7:30am-10pm, Fri 7:30-5, Sat Noon-4, Sun 4pm-10pm

C HERZING UNIVERSITY LIBRARY, Madison Campus, 5218 E Terrace Dr, 53718. SAN 378-0597. Tel: 608-807-1909. Web Site: www.herzing.edu/about/library-services, www.herzing.edu/madison. Highest Degree: Master

J MADISON AREA TECHNICAL COLLEGE*, Truax Library, 3550 Anderson St, Rm A3000, 53704. (Mail add: 1701 Wright St, Rm A3000, 53704), SAN 318-1073. Tel: 608-246-6640. Reference Tel: 608-243-4264. FAX: 608-246-6644. Web Site: madisoncollege.edu. *Dean, Libr & Acad Support,* Julie Gores; Tel: 608-246-6633, E-mail: jgores@madisoncollege.edu; *Bus Librn, Career Dev, Outreach Librn,* Cristina Springfield; Tel: 608-246-6637, E-mail: springfield@madisoncollege.edu; *Learning Librn,* Mark Perkins; Tel: 608-246-6923, E-mail: mcperkins@madisoncollege.edu; *Res Sharing Librn,* Kelley Minica; Tel: 608-243-4086, E-mail: kminica@madisoncollege.edu; *User Experience Librn,* Donna Marconnet; Tel: 608-243-4085, E-mail: dmarconnet@madisoncollege.edu; *User Serv Librn,* Erika Linzner; Tel: 608-246-6659, E-mail: elinzner@madisoncollege.edu; Staff 32 (MLS 5, Non-MLS 27)
Founded 1965. Enrl 7,600; Fac 360
Library Holdings: Bk Titles 55,000; Bk Vols 62,000; Per Subs 900
Automation Activity & Vendor Info: (Acquisitions) SirsiDynix; (Cataloging) SirsiDynix; (Circulation) SirsiDynix; (Course Reserve) SirsiDynix; (ILL) SirsiDynix; (Media Booking) SirsiDynix; (OPAC) SirsiDynix; (Serials) SirsiDynix
Publications: Bibliographies; Library Guide
Open Mon-Thurs 7:30am-9pm, Fri 7:30-4:30, Sat 9-1 (Fall & Spring); Mon-Thurs 7:30-7, Fri 7:30-4:30 (Summer)

P MADISON PUBLIC LIBRARY*, 201 W Mifflin St, 53703. SAN 364-7617. Tel: 608-266-6300. Circulation Tel: 608-266-6357. Interlibrary Loan Service Tel: 608-266-6302. Reference Tel: 608-266-6350. Administration Tel: 608-266-6363. Toll Free Tel: 888-266-7805. E-mail: madcirc@scls.lib.wi.us. Web Site: www.madisonpubliclibrary.org. *Dir,* Greg Mickells; E-mail: gmickells@madisonpubliclibrary.org; Staff 45 (MLS 42, Non-MLS 3)
Founded 1875. Circ 3,907,688
Library Holdings: Audiobooks 25,406; AV Mats 156,575; Bks on Deafness & Sign Lang 103; Braille Volumes 25; CDs 46,000; DVDs 85,974; e-books 138,839; Electronic Media & Resources 36,582; High Interest/Low Vocabulary Bk Vols 1,669; Large Print Bks 18,370; Music Scores 2,806; Bk Vols 606,796; Per Subs 1,390
Special Collections: Local Materials; Music. US Document Depository
Automation Activity & Vendor Info: (Acquisitions) LibLime Koha; (Cataloging) LibLime Koha; (Circulation) LibLime Koha; (ILL) OCLC ILLiad; (OPAC) LibLime Koha; (Serials) LibLime Koha
Wireless access
Function: 24/7 Electronic res, 24/7 Online cat, Activity rm, Adult bk club, After school storytime, Archival coll
Mem of South Central Library System
Special Services for the Deaf - Bks on deafness & sign lang; Spec interest per; TDD equip
Open Mon-Fri 10-5:30, Sat 12-4:30
Friends of the Library Group
Branches: 8
ALICIA ASHMAN BRANCH, 733 N High Point Rd, 53717. Tel: 608-824-1780. FAX: 608-824-1790. E-mail: aliciaashman@madisonpubliclibrary.org. *Br Supvr,* Marc Gartler; Tel: 608-575-9361, E-mail: mgartler@madisonpubliclibrary.org
Open Mon-Fri 10-6, Sat 12-5
Friends of the Library Group
GOODMAN SOUTH MADISON BRANCH, 2222 S Park St, 53713. SAN 364-7889. Tel: 608-266-6395. E-mail: goodmansouth@madisonpubliclibrary.org. *Br Supvr,* Ching Wong; E-mail: gcwong@madisonpubliclibrary.org
Library Holdings: AV Mats 6,260; High Interest/Low Vocabulary Bk Vols 210; Large Print Bks 369; Bk Titles 25,625; Bk Vols 29,140; Per Subs 103; Talking Bks 1,227
Open Mon-Fri 10-6, Sat 12-5
Friends of the Library Group
HAWTHORNE BRANCH, 2707 E Washington Ave, 53704. SAN 364-7641. Tel: 608-246-4548. FAX: 608-246-4549. E-mail: hawthorne@madisonpubliclibrary.org. *Br Supvr,* Jane Jorgenson; E-mail: jjorgenson@madisonpubliclibrary.org
Open Mon-Fri 10-5:30, Sat 12-4:30
Friends of the Library Group
LAKEVIEW, 2845 N Sherman Ave, 53704, SAN 364-7706. Tel: 608-246-4547. E-mail: lakeview@madisonpubliclibrary.org. *Br Supvr,* Carra Davies; E-mail: cdavies@madisonpubliclibrary.org
Library Holdings: AV Mats 8,352; High Interest/Low Vocabulary Bk Vols 112; Large Print Bks 455; Bk Titles 37,713; Bk Vols 43,723; Per Subs 168; Talking Bks 1,351
Open Mon-Fri 10-8, Sat 12-5
Friends of the Library Group
MEADOWRIDGE, 5726 Raymond Rd, 53711, SAN 364-7730. Tel: 608-288-6160. E-mail: meadowridge@madisonpubliclibrary.org. *Actg Br Supvr,* Yesianne Ramirez; E-mail: yramirez@madisonpubliclibrary.org
Library Holdings: AV Mats 8,716; High Interest/Low Vocabulary Bk Vols 107; Large Print Bks 337; Bk Titles 39,606; Bk Vols 46,901; Per Subs 161; Talking Bks 1,353
Open Mon-Fri 10-6, Sat 12-5
Friends of the Library Group
MONROE, 1705 Monroe St, 53711, SAN 364-7765. Tel: 608-266-6390. E-mail: monroestreet@madisonpubliclibrary.org. *Br Supvr,* Ching Wong
Library Holdings: AV Mats 5,860; High Interest/Low Vocabulary Bk Vols 47; Large Print Bks 274; Bk Titles 18,809; Bk Vols 24,267; Per Subs 97; Talking Bks 948
Open Mon, Tues & Fri 10-6
Friends of the Library Group
PINNEY BRANCH, 516 Cottage Grove Rd, 53716, SAN 364-782X. Tel: 608-224-7100. E-mail: pinney@madisonpubliclibrary.org. *Br Supvr,* Jane Jorgenson
Library Holdings: AV Mats 12,820; Bks on Deafness & Sign Lang 16; CDs 4,434; DVDs 1,905; Electronic Media & Resources 217; High Interest/Low Vocabulary Bk Vols 109; Large Print Bks 435; Music Scores 58; Bk Titles 73,964; Bk Vols 89,709; Per Subs 223; Talking Bks 2,625; Videos 3,610
Open Mon-Fri 10-6, Sat 12-5
Friends of the Library Group
SEQUOYA BRANCH, 4340 Tokay Blvd, 53711, SAN 364-7854. Tel: 608-266-6385. E-mail: sequoya@madisonpubliclibrary.org. *Br Supvr,* Marc Gartler
Library Holdings: AV Mats 18,482; High Interest/Low Vocabulary Bk Vols 148; Large Print Bks 744; Bk Titles 83,099; Bk Vols 109,044; Per Subs 246; Talking Bks 3,798
Open Mon-Fri 9-6, Sat 12-5
Friends of the Library Group

G MENDOTA MENTAL HEALTH INSTITUTE*, Patients Library, 301 Troy Dr, 53704-1599. SAN 318-1146. Tel: 608-301-1196. FAX: 608-301-1169. *Dir,* Gregory Van Rybroek; E-mail: Gregory.VanRybroek@dhs.wisconsin.gov; Staff 1 (MLS 1)
Founded 1955
Library Holdings: Audiobooks 75; AV Mats 2,200; Bks on Deafness & Sign Lang 10; Braille Volumes 10; CDs 1,100; DVDs 125; High Interest/Low Vocabulary Bk Vols 150; Large Print Bks 40; Bk Vols 16,000; Per Subs 30; Videos 600
Subject Interests: Mental health, Organizational hist, Self help

Automation Activity & Vendor Info: (Cataloging) Follett Software; (Circulation) Follett Software
Partic in S Cent Libr Syst; Wiscat
Special Services for the Blind - Audio mat; Bks on cassette; Bks on CD; Braille bks; Free checkout of audio mat; Large print bks
Restriction: Not open to pub

M MERITER HOSPITAL*, Medical Library, 202 S Park St, 53715. SAN 364-7587. Tel: 608-417-6234. E-mail: msn_mellibrary@unitypoint.org. Web Site: www.unitypoint.org/madison/consumer-health-and-medical-library.aspx. *Chief Librn,* Robert Koehler; E-mail: robert.koehler@unitypoint.org
Library Holdings: e-books 1,800; e-journals 7,000; Bk Titles 250
Subject Interests: Dentistry, Hospital admin, Med, Nursing
Wireless access
Partic in Regional Med Libr - Region 3
Open Mon-Fri 7-4:30
Restriction: Non-circulating, Open to staff only

S NORWEGIAN AMERICAN GENEALOGICAL CENTER & NAESETH LIBRARY*, 415 W Main St, 53703-3116. SAN 326-0038. Tel: 608-255-2224. FAX: 608-255-6842. E-mail: genealogy@nagcnl.org. Web Site: www.nagcnl.org. *Exec Dir,* Jeanne Wright; E-mail: jwright@nagcnl.org
Founded 1974
Library Holdings: AV Mats 4,000; Bk Titles 4,810; Bk Vols 4,920
Subject Interests: Genealogy, Norwegian (Lang), Norwegian hist
Wireless access
Function: For res purposes, Internet access, Microfiche/film & reading machines, Res libr
Publications: Norwegian Tracks (Biannually)
Restriction: Fee for pub use, Free to mem, In-house use for visitors, Non-circulating, Open to researchers by request
Friends of the Library Group

M ST MARY'S HOSPITAL MEDICAL LIBRARY*, 700 Brooks St, 53715. SAN 318-1219. Tel: 608-258-6533. FAX: 608-258-6119. E-mail: smhmc.medical.library@ssmhealth.com. Web Site: www.ssmhealth.com/locations/st-marys-hospital-madison.
Founded 1974
Library Holdings: e-books 1,500; e-journals 2,000; Bk Titles 1,200; Per Subs 10
Subject Interests: Hospital admin, Med, Nursing
Wireless access
Partic in Greater Midwest Regional Medical Libr Network; Wis Health Sci Libr Asn
Restriction: Badge access after hrs, Staff use only

P SOUTH CENTRAL LIBRARY SYSTEM*, 4610 S Biltmore Lane, Ste 101, 53718-2153. SAN 364-7919. Tel: 608-246-7970. Toll Free Tel: 855-516-7257. FAX: 608-246-7958. Web Site: www.scls.info. *Dir,* Martha Van Pelt; Tel: 608-246-7975, E-mail: mvanpelt@scls.info; *Consulting Serv Coordr,* Mark Ibach; Tel: 608-246-5612, E-mail: mibach@scls.info; *Delivery Serv Coordr,* Corey Baumann; Tel: 608-266-4695, E-mail: cbaumann@sclsdelivery.info; *Human Res & Finance Coordr,* Kerrie Goeden; Tel: 608-246-7972, E-mail: kgoeden@scls.info; *Tech Serv Coordr,* Victoria Teal Lovely; Tel: 608-242-4713, E-mail: vickiteal@scls.info; Staff 52 (MLS 10, Non-MLS 42)
Founded 1975. Pop 837,000
Jan 2021-Dec 2021 Income $6,562,241
Library Holdings: Audiobooks 20,700; AV Mats 26; e-books 65,673; Bk Vols 1,348; Per Subs 12; Videos 321
Subject Interests: Libr, Librarianship
Automation Activity & Vendor Info: (Acquisitions) LibLime; (Cataloging) LibLime; (Circulation) LibLime; (ILL) LibLime; (OPAC) LibLime; (Serials) LibLime
Wireless access
Member Libraries: Adams County Library; Albertson Memorial Library; Angie Williams Cox Public Library; Belleville Public Library; Black Earth Public Library; Brodhead Memorial Public Library; Cambridge Community Library; Carnegie-Schadde Memorial Public Library; Charles & Joann Lester Library; Columbus Public Library; Deerfield Public Library; DeForest Area Public Library; Everett Roehl Marshfield Public Library; Fitchburg Public Library; George Culver Community Library; Hutchinson Memorial Library; Jane Morgan Memorial Library; Kilbourn Public Library; Kraemer Library & Community Center; La Valle Public Library; Lester Public Library of Arpin; Lester Public Library of Rome; Lester Public Library of Vesper; Lettie W Jensen Public Library; Lodi Woman's Club Public Library; Madison Public Library; Marshall Community Library; Mazomanie Free Library; McFarland Public Library; McMillan Memorial Library; Middleton Public Library; Monona Public Library; Monroe Public Library; Monticello Public Library; Mount Horeb Public Library; New Glarus Public Library; North Freedom Public Library; Oregon Public Library; Pittsville Community Library; Portage County Public Library; Portage Public Library; Poynette Area Public Library; Reedsburg Public Library; Rio Community Library; Rock Springs Public Library; Rosemary Garfoot Public Library; Ruth Culver Community Library; Spring Green Community Library; Stoughton Public Library; Sun Prairie Public Library; Verona Public Library; Waunakee Public Library; Wyocena Public Library
Partic in Wisconsin Public Library Consortium

R TRINITY LUTHERAN CHURCH LIBRARY*, 1904 Winnebago St, 53704. SAN 318-1251. Tel: 608-249-8527. FAX: 608-249-9070. E-mail: tlcmsn@gmail.com. Web Site: tlcmsn.org. *Librn,* Jennifer Dyer
Founded 1944
Library Holdings: Bk Vols 4,500
Subject Interests: Relig studies
Open Mon, Tues & Thurs 8-4:30, Wed 12-4, Sun 8:30am-10:30am

G UNITED STATES FOREST SERVICE, Forest Products Laboratory Library, One Gifford Pinchot Dr, 53726-2398. SAN 318-126X. Tel: 608-231-9200. FAX: 608-231-9311. E-mail: sm.fs.fslib@usda.gov. Web Site: research.fs.usda.gov/fpl/fpl-library. *Cat,* David C Smith; *ILL,* Margaret Durow; Staff 4 (MLS 2, Non-MLS 2)
Founded 1910
Library Holdings: Bk Titles 44,000; Bk Vols 99,000; Per Subs 210
Special Collections: Timber Bridge Coll. Oral History
Subject Interests: Adhesives, Drying, Energy from wood, Fire sci, Mycology, Paint & coatings, Pulp & paper, Recycling, Solid wood products, Tech, Wood engr
Automation Activity & Vendor Info: (Cataloging) OCLC; (OPAC) CyberTools for Libraries
Function: ILL available
Partic in FS-Info; OCLC Online Computer Library Center, Inc; WiLS
Restriction: In-house use for visitors, Non-circulating to the pub, Open to pub by appt only

C UNIVERSITY OF WISCONSIN-MADISON*, General Library System & Memorial Library, 728 State St, 53706. SAN 364-8036. Tel: 608-262-3193. Circulation Tel: 608-263-3343. Interlibrary Loan Service Tel: 608-262-1193. Reference Tel: 608-262-3242. FAX: 608-265-2754. Web Site: www.library.wisc.edu/memorial. *Vice Provost & Univ Librn,* Lisa Carter; Tel: 608-262-2600, E-mail: lisa.carter@wisc.edu; *Assoc Univ Librn, Pub Serv,* Lesley Moyo; E-mail: lesley.moyo@wisc.edu
Founded 1850. Enrl 40,793; Fac 2,054; Highest Degree: Doctorate
Library Holdings: Bk Vols 7,300,000; Per Subs 55,000
Special Collections: 17th & 18th Century European Theology (Chwalibog Coll); 20th Century English & American Literature Coll; Alchemy (Duveen Coll); American Gift Books & Annuals; American Music (Tams-Witmark Coll); Balcanica Coll; Belgian Congo Archival Materials (Deryck Coll); Book Plates; Brazilian Positivism Coll; Brodhead Manuscripts; Buddhism Coll; C S Lewis Letters; Calvinist Theology & Dutch History (Tank Coll); Carol von Linee Coll; Chess (Peter G Toepfer Coll); Children's Literature (Burgess Coll); Civil War Band Books; Classical & 19th Century German Literature (George B Wild Coll); Cossack Coll; Dalton Trumbo Coll; Dutch Pamphlets; Early American Women Authors (William Cairns Coll); English 19th Century Free Thought Coll; English 19th Century Social & Economic Pamphlets; English Grammars (Berry Coll); English Manor Rolls; English Romantic Poetry (Arthur Beatty Coll); English Temperance (Guy Hayler Coll); Eugene O'Neill Coll; European & American Student Publications; European Socialism (Herman Schlueter Library & William English Walling Coll); Ferber Coll; French 18th Century Literature & Culture (Tucker Coll); French Political Pamphlets, 1560-1648; French Protestantism (Montauban Coll); French Revolutionary Pamphlets; French Socialist Congresses Coll; French Student Revolt, 1968; German 18th Century Theater Coll; German Expressionism Coll; German Philology Coll; Grotius Coll; Herald Coll (Leon Srabian Herald, Poet & Philosopher); History of Chemistry (Cole Duveen Coll); History of Science Coll; Icelandic History & Literature Coll; Irish History & Literature Coll; Italian 16th Century Imprints (Giolito Coll); Joseph Priestly Coll; Judaica (Joseph L Baron Coll); Juridical Materials, 15th & 16th Century; Latimer Coll (Matthias Coll of the Letters of Marjorie Latimer); Lithuanian History & Literature (Alfred Senn Coll); Little Magazines (Marvin Sukov Coll); Lutheran Theology (Hoyer Coll); Madras History Sources; Mark Twain (George H Brownell & Norman Bassett Coll); Mazarinades Coll; Medieval History Coll; Medieval Spanish Literature Coll; Mesmer Coll; Mexican Pamphlets; Mottey Coll; National Socialism Coll; Natural History & English Literature (Chester H Thordarson Coll); Norwegian Local History Coll; O Henry Coll; Papyri Coll; Polish Literature & History Coll; Private Press Coll; Renaissance Epic Coll; Robert Boyle Coll; Rousseau Coll; Russian Culture (Romanovskii Coll); Russian Revolutionary Movement (Russian Free Press Coll); Russian Satirical Journals; Saint Simon Coll; Scandinavian Literature & Language (Olson Coll); Scandinavian Literature (Mimers Coll); Social Science Materials Coll; Swift (Teerink Coll); Swiss Literature Romande; The Lost Dauphin (William W Wight Coll); Theater (Thomas H Dickinson Coll); Tibetan Coll; Welsh Theology (Jones-Roberts Coll). UN Document Depository; US Document Depository

Automation Activity & Vendor Info: (Acquisitions) Ex Libris Group; (Cataloging) Ex Libris Group; (Circulation) Ex Libris Group; (Course Reserve) Ex Libris Group; (OPAC) Ex Libris Group; (Serials) Ex Libris Group
Wireless access
Partic in Big Ten Academic Alliance
Friends of the Library Group

Departmental Libraries:

BUSINESS LIBRARY, Grainger Hall, Rm 1320, 975 University Ave, 53706, SAN 364-8184. Tel: 608-262-5935. FAX: 608-262-9001. E-mail: askbusiness@library.wisc.edu. Web Site: www.library.wisc.edu/business. *Dir,* Michael Enyart; Tel: 608-263-3902, E-mail: michael.enyart@wisc.edu; *Ref & Data Librn,* Peggy Smith; Tel: 608-890-1901, E-mail: peggy.smith@library.wisc.edu; *Ref/Tech Serv,* Gail Glaze; Tel: 608-262-4007, E-mail: gail.glaze@library.wisc.edu; Staff 7 (MLS 5, Non-MLS 2)
Library Holdings: Bk Vols 53,000
Open Mon-Wed 7:30am-1am, Thurs 7:30am-11pm, Fri 8-6, Sun Noon-1am

CHEMISTRY LIBRARY, Chemistry Bldg, 1101 University Ave, Rm 2132, 53706, SAN 364-8214. Tel: 608-262-4423. Web Site: www.library.wisc.edu/subjects/chemistry. *Chem Librn,* Ariel Andrea; E-mail: ariel.andrea@wisc.edu; Staff 2 (MLS 2)
Library Holdings: Bk Vols 50,722
Open Mon-Fri 8-5

COLLEGE (UNDERGRADUATE) LIBRARY, Helen C White Hall, 600 N Park St, 53706, SAN 364-8060. Tel: 608-262-3245. FAX: 608-262-4631. E-mail: helenc@library.wisc.edu. Web Site: www.library.wisc.edu/college. *Dir,* Carrie Kruse; E-mail: carrie.kruse@wisc.edu; Staff 12.5 (MLS 12.5)
Library Holdings: Bk Vols 96,565
Open Mon-Sun 10am-11:45pm

COOPERATIVE CHILDREN'S BOOK CENTER, Teacher Education Bldg, Rm 401, 225 N Mills St, 53706, SAN 323-9977. Tel: 608-263-3720. FAX: 608-262-4933. E-mail: ccbcinfo@education.wisc.edu. Web Site: ccbc.education.wisc.edu. *Dir,* Tessa Michaelson Schmidt; E-mail: tessa.schmidt@wisc.edu; Staff 3 (MLS 3)
Founded 1963
Library Holdings: Bk Vols 25,000

CM EBLING LIBRARY, Health Sciences Learning Ctr, 750 Highland Ave, 53705, SAN 364-8540. Tel: 608-262-2020. FAX: 608-262-4732. E-mail: askebling@library.wisc.edu. Web Site: ebling.library.wisc.edu. *Dir,* Christopher Hooper-Lane; E-mail: christopher.hooperlane@wisc.edu; Staff 18 (MLS 18)
Library Holdings: Bk Titles 155,105; Bk Vols 39,883
Special Collections: History of Medicine, especially Anatomical Works
Subject Interests: Allied health, Cancer res, Hospital admin, Neuroscience, Nursing
Function: Archival coll, Doc delivery serv, Health sci info serv, ILL available, Photocopying/Printing
Open Mon-Thurs 8-7, Fri 8-5

GEOGRAPHY, Science Hall, Rm 280-B, 550 N Park St, 53706, SAN 364-8249. Tel: 608-262-1706. Web Site: www.library.wisc.edu/subjects/geography. *Librn,* Karen Dunn; E-mail: karen.dunn@wisc.edu; Staff 1.5 (MLS 1, Non-MLS 0.5)
Library Holdings: Bk Vols 65,000
Open Mon-Thurs 9-8, Fri 9-4:30, Sun 1-5; Mon-Fri 9-4:30 (Summer)

NIEMAN GRANT JOURNALISM READING ROOM, 2130 Vilas Hall, 821 University Ave, 53706, SAN 364-8516. Tel: 608-263-3387. E-mail: jrrlib@library.wisc.edu. Web Site: www.library.wisc.edu/journalism. *Projects Officer,* Andrew McDonnell; E-mail: amcdonnell3@wisc.edu
Library Holdings: Bk Vols 1,000; Per Subs 30
Subject Interests: Journalism, Mass communications

STEPHEN COLE KLEENE MATHEMATICS LIBRARY, B224 Van Vleck Hall, 480 Lincoln Dr, 53706, SAN 364-8486. Tel: 608-262-3596. FAX: 608-263-8891. E-mail: mathlib@library.wisc.edu. Web Site: www.library.wisc.edu/math. *Library Services Asst,* Anastasia Hanson; E-mail: anastasia.hanson@wisc.edu; Staff 1 (MLS 1)
Founded 1963
Library Holdings: Bk Vols 56,000
Subject Interests: Computer sci, Math, Physics, Statistics
Function: Res libr
Open Mon-Thurs 8:30-8, Fri 8:30-5, Sun 3-6 (Winter); Mon-Fri 8:30-5 (Summer)

KOHLER ART LIBRARY, 160 Conrad A Elvehjem Bldg, 800 University Ave, 53706, SAN 364-8338. Tel: 608-263-2258. FAX: 608-263-2255. E-mail: askart@library.wisc.edu. Web Site: www.library.wisc.edu/art. *Head of Libr,* Anna Simon; E-mail: ajsimon2@wisc.edu; Staff 4 (MLS 2, Non-MLS 2)
Library Holdings: Bk Vols 185,000; Per Subs 460
Special Collections: Artists' Books; Frank Lloyd Wright Coll; Illuminated Manuscript Facsimiles; Toy & Movable Books
Subject Interests: African art, Decorative art, German & Austrian art, Medieval art, Photog
Open Mon-Thurs 8am-9:45pm, Fri 8-4:45, Sat & Sun 11-4:45 (Winter); Mon-Fri 9-4:45 (Summer)

CL LAW LIBRARY, 975 Bascom Mall, 53706, SAN 364-8397. Tel: 608-262-1128. Reference Tel: 608-262-3394. FAX: 608-262-2775. E-mail: asklawref@law.wisc.edu. Web Site: library.law.wisc.edu. *Assoc Dean, Dir, Law Libr,* Bonnie Shucha; E-mail: bonnie.shucha@wisc.edu; Staff 24 (MLS 13, Non-MLS 11)
Library Holdings: Bk Titles 168,851; Bk Vols 404,061; Per Subs 6,073
Special Collections: US Document Depository
Partic in Mid-America Law Library Consortium

C K LEITH LIBRARY OF GEOLOGY & GEOPHYSICS, 440 Weeks Hall, 1215 W Dayton St, 53706-1692, SAN 364-8273. Tel: 608-262-8956. FAX: 608-262-0693. E-mail: geolib@library.wisc.edu. Web Site: library.wisc.edu/geology. *Librn,* Marie Dvorzak; E-mail: marie.dvorzak@wisc.edu; Staff 2 (MLS 1, Non-MLS 1)
Founded 1974
Library Holdings: Bk Vols 80,000
Special Collections: Map Coll
Subject Interests: Geol, Geophysics
Open Mon-Thurs 8:30-8, Fri 8:30-5, Sun 1-5 (Fall-Spring); Mon-Fri 8:30-5 (Summer)

MERIT LIBRARY (MEDIA, EDUCATION RESOURCES & INFORMATION TECHNOLOGY), 368 Teacher Education Bldg, 225 N Mills St, 53706, SAN 364-8303. Tel: 608-263-4750. Administration Tel: 608-263-8199. FAX: 608-262-6050. E-mail: askmerit@education.wisc.edu. Web Site: merit.education.wisc.edu. *Instrul Serv, Libr Mgr,* James Jonas; Tel: 608-263-4934, E-mail: james.jonas@wisc.edu; *Pub Serv Librn,* Angie Schiappacasse; Tel: 608-262-9950, E-mail: ashiappacas@wisc.edu; *Reserves Mgr, Tech Serv Asst,* Donna Meicher; Tel: 608-263-5797, E-mail: donna.meicher@wisc.edu; Staff 8 (MLS 4, Non-MLS 4)
Founded 1848. Highest Degree: Doctorate
Library Holdings: Bk Vols 75,000; Per Subs 386
Special Collections: US Document Depository
Subject Interests: Teacher educ
Function: Prof lending libr
Partic in WILS
Open Mon-Fri 9-5

MILLS MUSIC LIBRARY, B162 Memorial Library, 728 State St, 53706, SAN 364-8575. Tel: 608-263-1884. E-mail: askmusic@library.wisc.edu. Web Site: library.wisc.edu/music. *Head of Libr,* Jeanette Casey; Tel: 608-263-2721, E-mail: jeanette.casey@wisc.edu; Staff 3 (MLS 3)
Library Holdings: Bk Titles 250,000
Special Collections: 19th Century American Music Imprints; Civil War Band Books
Open Mon-Thurs 8:30am-9pm, Fri 8:30-5, Sat 12-5, Sun 1-9

PHYSICS LIBRARY, 4220 Chamberlin Hall, 1150 University Ave, 53706, SAN 364-863X. Tel: 608-262-9500. FAX: 608-265-2754. E-mail: physlib@library.wisc.edu. Web Site: www.ibrary.wisc.edu/physics. *Library Services Asst,* Anastasia Hanson; E-mail: anastasia.hanson@wisc.edu; Staff 2 (MLS 1, Non-MLS 1)
Founded 1972
Library Holdings: Bk Vols 56,205
Automation Activity & Vendor Info: (ILL) OCLC ILLiad
Function: Res libr
Partic in Council of Independent Colleges; WILS
Open Mon-Thurs 8-7, Fri 8-5, Sun 1-5

ARTHUR H ROBINSON MAP LIBRARY, 310 Science Hall, 550 N Park St, 53706-1491, SAN 364-8451. Tel: 608-262-1471. FAX: 608-265-3991. Web Site: geography.wisc.edu/maplibrary. *Librn,* Jaime Martindale; E-mail: jmartindale@wisc.edu; Staff 1 (MLS 1)
Library Holdings: Bk Vols 900
Special Collections: Wisconsin Aerial Photographs
Subject Interests: Aerial photog, Maps

SCHOOL OF LIBRARY & INFORMATION STUDIES LIBRARY, 4191 Helen C White Hall, 600 N Park St, 53706, SAN 364-8427. Tel: 608-263-2960. FAX: 608-263-4849. E-mail: slislib@library.wisc.edu. Web Site: www.library.wisc.edu/ischool. *Libr Mgr,* Cassy Leeport; Tel: 608-890-4860, E-mail: cassy.leeport@wisc.edu; Staff 1 (MLS 1)
Highest Degree: Doctorate
Library Holdings: Bk Vols 65,000
Subject Interests: Children's lit, Info sci, Libr
Friends of the Library Group

SCHWERDTFEGER LIBRARY, Space Science & Engineering Ctr, Rm 317, 1225 W Dayton St, 53706, SAN 323-9845. Tel: 608-262-0987. FAX: 608-262-5974. E-mail: library@ssec.wisc.edu. Web Site: library.ssec.wisc.edu. *Dir,* Deborah M Helman; Tel: 608-262-7980, E-mail: deborah.helman@wisc.edu; *Librn,* Katherine Johnson; E-mail: katherine.johnson@ssec.wisc.edu; Staff 2 (MLS 2)
Library Holdings: Bk Vols 40,000
Subject Interests: Atmospheric sci, Space sci
Open Mon-Fri 8:30-5

SOCIAL WORK LIBRARY, 236 School of Social Work, 1350 University Ave, 53706, SAN 364-8753. Tel: 608-263-3283, 608-263-3840. E-mail: socworklib@library.wisc.edu. Web Site: www.library.wisc.edu/socialwork. *Soc Work & Soc Sci Librn,* Tom Durkin; E-mail: thomas.durkin@wisc.edu; Staff 1 (MLS 1)
Library Holdings: Bk Vols 26,000
Subject Interests: Child welfare, Family issues, Gerontology
Open Mon-Thurs 8:30-6:30, Fri 8:30-4:30, Sat & Sun 12:30-4:30

STEENBOCK LIBRARY, 550 Babcock Dr, 53706, SAN 364-8095. Tel: 608-262-1371, 608-262-9635. FAX: 608-263-3221. E-mail: asksteenbock@library.wisc.edu. Web Site: www.library.wisc.edu/steenbock. *Head of Libr,* Renee Croushore; E-mail: renee.croushore@wisc.edu; Staff 12 (MLS 12)
Library Holdings: Bk Vols 225,000
Subject Interests: Agr, Engr, Life sci, Veterinary med

WISCONSIN WATER LIBRARY, 1975 Willow Dr, 2nd Flr, 53706-1177, SAN 321-981X. Tel: 608-262-3069. FAX: 608-262-0591. E-mail: askwater@aqua.wisc.edu. Web Site: waterlibrary.aqua.wisc.edu. *Sr Spec Librn,* Anne Moser; E-mail: akmoser@aqua.wisc.edu
Founded 1966
Library Holdings: Bk Titles 24,000; Bk Vols 30,000; Per Subs 20
Special Collections: Water-Related Children's Books
Subject Interests: Great Lakes, Water, Water res, Wis
Automation Activity & Vendor Info: (Cataloging) Ex Libris Group; (Circulation) Ex Libris Group; (OPAC) Ex Libris Group
Function: Homebound delivery serv, ILL available, Ref serv available
Partic in Univ of Wis Spec Campus Libr Group
Publications: Recent Acquisitions & Web Sites of Interest (Monthly)
Open Mon-Fri 9-4:30

WOODMAN ASTRONOMICAL LIBRARY, 6515 Sterling Hall, 475 N Charter St, 53706, SAN 364-8842. Tel: 608-262-1320. FAX: 608-236-6386. E-mail: astrolib@library.wisc.edu. Web Site: www.library.wisc.edu/astronomy. *Library Services Asst,* Anastasia Hanson; E-mail: anastasia.hanson@wisc.edu; Staff 2 (MLS 1, Non-MLS 1)
Founded 1881
Library Holdings: Bk Vols 18,537

WISCONSIN CENTER FOR FILM & THEATER RESEARCH, 816 State St, 53706, SAN 323-9861. Tel: 608-264-6466. FAX: 608-264-6472. E-mail: wcftr@commarts.wisc.edu. Web Site: wcftr.commarts.wisc.edu, www.wisconsinhistory.org/wcftr. *Dir,* Eric Hoyt; E-mail: ehoyt@wisc.edu; *Asst Dir,* Mary Huelsbeck; E-mail: huelsbeck@wisc.edu
Open Mon-Fri 8-5, Sat 9-4

GL WISCONSIN DEPARTMENT OF JUSTICE*, Law Library, 17 W Main St, 53703. (Mail add: PO Box 7857, 53707-7857), SAN 318-1324. Tel: 608-266-0325. *Law Librn,* Amy J Thornton; Staff 1.5 (MLS 1, Non-MLS 0.5)
Founded 1969
Library Holdings: Bk Titles 16,000; Bk Vols 40,000; Per Subs 30
Special Collections: Wisconsin Attorney General Material
Subject Interests: Wis law
Restriction: Not open to pub, Open to staff only

P WISCONSIN DEPARTMENT OF PUBLIC INSTRUCTION*, Division for Libraries & Technology, 125 S Webster St, 53707. (Mail add: PO Box 7841, 53707-7841), SAN 364-8877. Tel: 608-266-2205. FAX: 608-266-8770. Web Site: dpi.wi.gov/dlt. *State Superintendent,* Jill K Underly; *Asst State Superintendent,* Barbara Van Haren; E-mail: barbara.vanharen@dpi.wi.gov; Staff 1 (Non-MLS 1)
Partic in Minitex
Open Mon-Fri 7:30-4:30
Branches: 2

INSTRUCTIONAL MEDIA & TECHNOLOGY TEAM, 125 S Webster St, 53707. (Mail add: PO Box 7841, 53707-7841), SAN 364-8931. Tel: 608-266-3856. Toll Free Tel: 800-441-4563. Web Site: dpi.wi.gov/imt. *Asst Dir,* Tari Raatz; Tel: 608-267 2920, E-mail: tari.raatz@dpi.wi.gov
Open Mon-Fri 7:30-4:30

RESOURCES FOR LIBRARIES & LIFELONG LEARNING, 2109 S Stoughton Rd, 53716-2899, SAN 364-9059. Tel: 608-224-6167. Toll Free Tel: 888-542-5543 (WI only). FAX: 608-224-6178. Web Site: dpi.wi.gov/rl3. *Dir,* Benjamin Miller; Tel: 608-224-6168, E-mail: benjamin.miller@dpi.wi.gov; *Asst Dir,* Lisa Weichert; Tel: 608-224-6168, E-mail: lisa.weichert@dpi.wi.gov; *BadgerLink Coordr,* David McHugh; Tel: 608-224-5389, E-mail: david.mchugh@dpi.wi.gov; *ILL Coordr,* Christine Barth; Tel: 608-224-6171, E-mail: christine.barth@dpi.wi.gov; *WISCAT User Support,* Vickie Long; Tel: 608-224-5394, E-mail: vickie.long@dpi.wi.gov; *Wis Doc Dep Prog/Wis Digital Archives,* Abby Swanton; Tel: 608-224-6174, E-mail: abbigail.swanton@dpi.wi.gov; Staff 12 (MLS 11, Non-MLS 1)
Library Holdings: Bk Titles 140,000; Bk Vols 151,096; Per Subs 60
Automation Activity & Vendor Info: (Circulation) Evolve; (ILL) Auto-Graphics, Inc; (OPAC) Auto-Graphics, Inc
Function: Internet access, Online ref
Partic in OCLC Online Computer Library Center, Inc; Wis Asn of Independent Col & Univ
Special Services for the Blind - Newsline for the Blind
Open Mon-Fri 8-4

S WISCONSIN DEPARTMENT OF VETERANS AFFAIRS*, Wisconsin Veterans Museum Research Center, 30 W Mifflin St, Ste 300, 53703. SAN 325-4992. Tel: 608-267-1790. FAX: 608-264-7615. E-mail: reference.desk@dva.wisconsin.gov. Web Site: wisvetsmuseum.com. *Dir,* Chris Kolakowski; E-mail: christopher.kolakowski@dva.wisconsin.gov; *Colls Mgr,* Andrea Hoffman; Tel: 608-800-6957, E-mail: andrea.hoffman@dva.wisconsin.gov; *Res Archivist,* Russell P Horton; E-mail: russell.horton@dva.wisconsin.gov; Staff 4 (MLS 4)
Founded 1901
Library Holdings: AV Mats 1,200; Music Scores 60; Bk Titles 15,000; Per Subs 40; Videos 200
Special Collections: Manuscript Coll; Veteran Group Organizational Records; Wisconsin National Guard Coll, photogs, rec; Wisconsin Veterans Oral History Project. Oral History
Subject Interests: Mil hist, Wis hist
Automation Activity & Vendor Info: (Cataloging) OCLC
Function: Archival coll
Partic in Wiscat
Restriction: Non-circulating, Open by appt only
Friends of the Library Group

S WISCONSIN HISTORICAL SOCIETY LIBRARY*, 816 State St, 2nd Flr, 53706. SAN 318-1227. Tel: 608-264-6535. FAX: 608-264-6520. E-mail: askarchives@wisconsinhistory.org, asklibrary@wisconsinhistory.org. Web Site: www.wisconsinhistory.org/records/article/CS15310. *Dir, Coll Mgt,* Katie Latham; E-mail: kat.latham@wisconsinhistory.org; *Director, Public Servs & Ref,* Lisa Saywell; E-mail: lisa.saywell@wisconsinhistory.org; *Circ Librn,* Laura K Hemming; E-mail: laura.hemming@wisconsinhistory.org; *Pub Serv Librn,* Keith W Rabiola; E-mail: keith.rabiola@wisconsinhistory.org; *Sr Reference Archivist,* Lee C Grady; E-mail: lee.grady@wisconsinhistory.org; Staff 34 (MLS 19, Non-MLS 15)
Founded 1847
Library Holdings: Bk Vols 4,100,000
Subject Interests: Ethnic hist, Labor hist, Mil hist, Minority hist, Numismatics, Philately, Reform movements, Relig, Relig hist, Women's hist
Automation Activity & Vendor Info: (Cataloging) Ex Libris Group; (OPAC) Ex Libris Group
Wireless access
Partic in Center for Research Libraries; Coun of Wis Librs, Inc; OCLC Online Computer Library Center, Inc
Special Services for the Deaf - TTY equip
Open Mon-Thurs 8-7, Fri 8-5, Sat 9-4

G WISCONSIN STATE DEPARTMENT OF TRANSPORTATION LIBRARY*, 4822 Madison Yards Way, 9th Flr S, 53705. (Mail add: PO Box 7910, 53705-7910), SAN 364-9296. Tel: 608-264-8142. E-mail: library@dot.wi.gov. Web Site: wisconsindot.gov/Pages/about-wisdot/research. *Head Librn, Webmaster,* John Cherney; E-mail: john.cherney@dot.wi.gov; Staff 1.5 (MLS 1.5)
Founded 1967
Library Holdings: Bk Vols 43,000; Per Subs 350
Special Collections: Regional Planning Commission Reports; Traffic Accident Facts from the 50 States; Transportation (Transportation Research Board)
Subject Interests: Air transportation, Construction, Engr, Evaluation, Hwy transportation, Rail transportation, Transportation
Automation Activity & Vendor Info: (Cataloging) OCLC; (Circulation) EOS International; (ILL) OCLC WorldShare Interlibrary Loan; (OPAC) EOS International; (Serials) EOS International
Wireless access
Partic in OCLC Online Computer Library Center, Inc; Wiscat

GL WISCONSIN STATE LAW LIBRARY*, 120 Martin Luther King Jr Blvd, 2nd Flr, 53703. (Mail add: PO Box 7881, 53707-7881). Tel: 608-266-1600. Reference Tel: 608-267-9696. Toll Free Tel: 800-322-9755. FAX: 608-267-2319. Reference E-mail: wsll.ref@wicourts.gov. Web Site: wilawlibrary.gov. *State Law Librn,* Amy Crowder; Tel: 608-261-2340, E-mail: amy.crowder@wicourts.gov; *Dep Law Librn,* Heidi Yelk; Tel: 608-261-7555, E-mail: heidi.yelk@wicourts.gov; Staff 12.5 (MLS 8, Non-MLS 4.5)
Founded 1836
Library Holdings: e-journals 8,000; Bk Vols 120,000; Per Subs 500
Special Collections: Prose & Cons Legal Fiction Coll; Wisconsin Administrative Code Replaced Pages, 1950-Present; Wisconsin Appendices & Briefs, 1836-Present; Wisconsin Court of Appeals Unpublished Opinions, 1978-Present; Wisconsin Judicial Council Coll. US Document Depository

Subject Interests: Court decisions, Fed govt, Govt doc, Legal per, Legal texts, State govt, Statutes
Automation Activity & Vendor Info: (Acquisitions) Innovative Interfaces, Inc; (Cataloging) Innovative Interfaces, Inc; (Circulation) Innovative Interfaces, Inc; (ILL) OCLC Online; (OPAC) Innovative Interfaces, Inc; (Serials) Innovative Interfaces, Inc
Wireless access
Function: Audio & video playback equip for onsite use, Computer training, Doc delivery serv, ILL available, Internet access, Mail & tel request accepted, Orientations, Ref serv available, Telephone ref
Publications: WSLL @ Your Service (Monthly newsletter)
Partic in OCLC Online Computer Library Center, Inc
Open Mon-Fri 8-5
Restriction: Circ limited
Branches:
DANE COUNTY LAW LIBRARY, Courthouse Rm L1007, 215 S Hamilton St, 53703, SAN 321-9941. Tel: 608-266-6316. FAX: 608-266-5988. Reference E-mail: dclrc.ref@wicourts.gov. Web Site: https://wilawlibrary.gov/about/staff.html. *Ref Librn,* Nate Anderson; E-mail: nate.anderson@wicourts.gov; Staff 1.5 (MLS 1, Non-MLS 0.5)
Function: Electronic databases & coll, Mail & tel request accepted, Photocopying/Printing, Ref serv available, Telephone ref
Publications: Dane County Landlord/Tenant Legal Resource Guide (Reference guide); Directory of Wisconsin Law Libraries Open to the Public (Reference guide); Guide to Low-Cost Legal Assistance in Dane County (Reference guide)
Open Mon-Fri 8:30-4:30
Restriction: Circ limited, Non-circulating to the pub
MILWAUKEE COUNTY LAW LIBRARY, Courthouse, Rm G8, 901 N Ninth St, Milwaukee, 53233. Tel: 414-278-4900. FAX: 414-223-1818. E-mail: wsll.ref@wicourts.gov. *Br Librn, Ref Librn,* Jamie Neuendorf; Staff 2.5 (MLS 1, Non-MLS 1.5)
Function: Mail & tel request accepted, Photocopying/Printing, Ref serv available, Telephone ref, Wheelchair accessible
Open Mon-Fri 8-4:30
Restriction: Circ limited, Non-circulating to the pub

MANAWA

P STURM MEMORIAL LIBRARY*, 130 N Bridge St, 54949-9517. (Mail add: PO Box 20, 54949-0020), SAN 318-1405. Tel: 920-596-2252. FAX: 920-596-2234. E-mail: man@manawalibrary.org. Web Site: www.manawalibrary.org. *Dir,* Ellen L Connor; E-mail: econnor@manawalibrary.org
Founded 1910. Pop 2,582; Circ 29,000
Library Holdings: Bk Vols 22,000; Per Subs 60
Subject Interests: Fishing, Hunting, Rodeos, Wis, World War II
Wireless access
Mem of Outagamie Waupaca Library System (OWLS)
Open Mon, Tues, Thurs & Fri 9:30-5:30, Wed 9:30-7, Sat (Winter) 9-Noon

MANITOWISH WATERS

P FRANK B KOLLER MEMORIAL LIBRARY*, 5761 Hwy 51, 54545. (Mail add: PO Box 100, 54545-0100), SAN 376-6659. Tel: 715-543-2700. FAX: 715-543-2700. Web Site: www.kollerlibrary.org. *Librn,* Janelle M Kohl; *Asst Librn,* Sarah Krembs; E-mail: skrembs@koller.wislib.org
Pop 2,000; Circ 23,079
Library Holdings: AV Mats 3,272; Large Print Bks 130; Bk Vols 24,400; Per Subs 69; Talking Bks 1,384
Subject Interests: Arts & crafts, Cooking, Popular fiction, World War II
Automation Activity & Vendor Info: (Cataloging) Innovative Interfaces, Inc; (Circulation) Innovative Interfaces, Inc; (ILL) Brodart; (OPAC) Innovative Interfaces, Inc
Wireless access
Mem of Northern Waters Library Service
Partic in Merlin
Open Mon, Wed & Fri 9-3, Tues & Thurs 3-7, Sat 9-Noon (Winter); Mon, Wed & Fri 9-3, Tues & Thurs Noon-8, Sat 9-1 (Summer)
Friends of the Library Group

MANITOWOC

P MANITOWOC-CALUMET LIBRARY SYSTEM*, 707 Quay St, 54220. SAN 318-1421. Tel: 920-686-3051. Web Site: www.mclsweb.org/mclsweb. *Dir,* Rebecca Schadrie; E-mail: rschadrie@mcls.lib.wi.us; Staff 1 (MLS 1)
Founded 1977
Automation Activity & Vendor Info: (Circulation) SirsiDynix; (ILL) Auto-Graphics, Inc
Wireless access
Publications: What's New? (Monthly bibliography)
Member Libraries: Brillion Public Library; Chilton Public Library; Kiel Public Library; Lester Public Library; Manitowoc Public Library; New Holstein Public Library
Partic in Wisconsin Public Library Consortium
Open Mon-Fri 8-4:30

P MANITOWOC PUBLIC LIBRARY*, 707 Quay St, 54220. SAN 318-143X. Tel: 920-686-3000. E-mail: mplservice@manitowoc.org. Web Site: www.manitowoclibrary.org. *Libr Dir,* Kristin Stoeger; E-mail: kstoeger@manitowoc.org; *Librn, Mat,* Lisa Pike; E-mail: lpike@manitowoc.org; *Fac Mgr,* Stacey Bialek; E-mail: sbialek@manitowoc.org; *Mat Mgt Mgr,* Amy Eisenschink; E-mail: aeisenschink@manitowoc.org; *Pub Serv Mgr,* Karen Hansen; E-mail: khansen@manitowoc.org; *Youth Serv Mgr,* Julie Lee; E-mail: jlee@manitowoc.org; *Adult Literacy Coordr,* Margo Meyer; E-mail: mmeyer@manitowoc.org; *Marketing Specialist,* Tim Gadzinski; E-mail: tgadzinski@manitowoc.org; *Homebound Serv,* Margo Meyer; E-mail: mmeyer@manitowoc.org; *Teen Serv,* Carrie Bruce; E-mail: cbruce@manitowoc.org; Staff 5 (MLS 5)
Founded 1900. Pop 58,213; Circ 674,092
Library Holdings: Bk Vols 200,185; Per Subs 359
Special Collections: Art & Gardening (Ruth West Library of Beauty); Behnke Historic Photo Coll; World War II Personal Narratives. Oral History; State Document Depository
Subject Interests: Submarines
Automation Activity & Vendor Info: (Acquisitions) SirsiDynix; (Circulation) SirsiDynix; (Serials) SirsiDynix
Wireless access
Publications: Newsletter
Mem of Manitowoc-Calumet Library System
Partic in OCLC Online Computer Library Center, Inc
Open Mon-Thurs 9-8, Fri 9-6, Sat 9-3, Sun 12-4
Friends of the Library Group

S WISCONSIN MARITIME MUSEUM*, Library & Archives, 75 Maritime Dr, 54220. SAN 326-5129. Tel: 920-684-0218. Toll Free Tel: 866-724-2356. FAX: 920-684-0219. E-mail: museum@wisconsinmaritime.org. Web Site: www.wisconsinmaritime.org. *Chief Curator, Dep Dir,* Kevin Cullen; E-mail: kcullen@wisconsinmaritime.org; *Colls Mgr,* Hannah Patten; Tel: 920-684-0218, Ext 112, E-mail: hpatten@wisconsinmaritime.org
Founded 1969
Special Collections: 20th Century Great Lakes Ship Construction (Burger Boat Company Coll), blueprints, ms, photos; Captain Timothy Kelley Family Coll, 1870-1943, diaries; Early Great Lakes Shipping (Carus Section of Henry N Barkhausen Coll), ms, photos; Great Lakes Maritime History (Henry N Barkhausen Coll), art, bks, photos; Great Lakes Ship Logs, 19th-20th Centuries; Kahlenberg Coll, affidavits, cats, photos, sales bulletins; Manitowoc Company Coll, blueprints, ms, photos; Maritime History Rare Book Coll, Early 19th-Early 20th Centuries; Wooden Shipbuilding Coll, art, plans, vessel lists; World War II Ship Construction (Berns Photographic Coll); World War II Submarine USS Cobia Coll, blueprints, manuals, tech guides
Subject Interests: Great Lakes maritime hist
Restriction: Open by appt only

MARINETTE

P MARINETTE COUNTY LIBRARY SYSTEM*, Stephenson Public Library, 1700 Hall Ave, 54143-1799. SAN 318-1480. Tel: 715-732-7570. FAX: 715-732-7575. E-mail: mrt@marinettecountylibraries.org. Web Site: marinettecountylibraries.org.
Pop 42,000; Circ 378,319
Library Holdings: Bk Vols 200,000; Per Subs 550
Special Collections: Marinette history
Automation Activity & Vendor Info: (Cataloging) Innovative Interfaces, Inc; (Circulation) Innovative Interfaces, Inc; (OPAC) Innovative Interfaces, Inc; (Serials) Innovative Interfaces, Inc
Wireless access
Mem of Nicolet Federated Library System
Open Mon-Thurs 9-9, Fri 9-6, Sat 9-5 (Winter); Mon-Wed 9-6, Thurs 9-8, Fri 9-5, Sat 9-Noon (Summer)
Friends of the Library Group
Branches: 6
GOODMAN LIBRARY STATION, One Falcon Crest, Goodman, 54125, SAN 323-5637. Tel: 715-336-2575. FAX: 715-336-2576. Web Site: www.marinettecountylibraries.org/goodman. *Br Librn,* Rebecca Livick; E-mail: rlivick@marinettecountylibraries.org
Open Thurs 3:30-6:30
COLEMAN-POUND LIBRARY, 123 W Main St, Coleman, 54112, SAN 329-6466. Tel: 920-897-2400. FAX: 920-897-2400. Web Site: www.marinettecountylibraries.org/coleman-pound. *Br Librn,* Brooke Smith; E-mail: bsmith@marinettecountylibraries.org
Open Mon, Wed & Fri 9-5:30
Friends of the Library Group
CRIVITZ PUBLIC LIBRARY, 606 Louisa St, Crivitz, 54114, SAN 324-038X. Tel: 715-854-7562. FAX: 715-854-7562. Web Site: www.marinettecountylibraries.org/crivitz. *Br Librn,* Tab Yoder; E-mail: TYoder@marinettecountylibraries.org
Open Mon & Wed-Fri 9-5

NIAGARA PUBLIC LIBRARY, 1029 Roosevelt Rd, Niagara, 54151-1205. (Mail add: PO Box 108, Niagara, 54151-0108), SAN 318-2940. Tel: 715-251-3236. FAX: 715-251-3236. Web Site: www.marinettecountylibraries.org/niagara. *Br Librn,* Rebecca Livick; E-mail: rlivick@marinettecountylibraries.org
Open Mon 11-6, Tues 1-6, Wed 9-12 & 1-5, Fri 1-5
Friends of the Library Group

PESHTIGO PUBLIC LIBRARY, 331 French St, Ste B, Peshtigo, 54157-1219, SAN 318-3203. Tel: 715-582-4905. FAX: 715-582-4905. Web Site: www.marinettecountylibraries.org/peshtigo. *Br Librn,* Kristin Willems; E-mail: kwillems@marinettecountylibraries.org
Open Mon, Wed & Fri 9-6

WAUSAUKEE PUBLIC LIBRARY, 703 Main St, Ste 3, Wausaukee, 54177. (Mail add: PO Box 139, Wausaukee, 54177-0139), SAN 324-0398. Tel: 715-856-5995. Web Site: www.marinettecountylibraries.org/wausaukee. *Br Librn,* Karen Kortbein; E-mail: kkortbein@marinettecountylibraries.org
Open Mon, Wed & Fri 9-6
Friends of the Library Group

MARION

P MARION PUBLIC LIBRARY*, 120 N Main St, 54950. (Mail add: PO Box 267, 54950-0267), SAN 318-1510. Tel: 715-754-5368. FAX: 715-754-4610. E-mail: mar@marionpubliclibrary.info. Web Site: marionpubliclibrary.info. *Dir,* LeAnn Hopp; E-mail: lhopp@marionpubliclibrary.info; *Ad,* Lauren Young; E-mail: lyoung@marionpubliclibrary.info; *Ch,* Kelly Schreiber; E-mail: kschreiber@marionpubliclibrary.info
Founded 1924. Pop 1,300; Circ 30,000
Library Holdings: Bk Titles 23,000; Per Subs 10
Wireless access
Mem of Outagamie Waupaca Library System (OWLS)
Open Mon & Thurs 9-6, Tues, Wed & Fri 9-5
Friends of the Library Group

MARKESAN

P MARKESAN PUBLIC LIBRARY*, 75 N Bridge St, 53946. (Mail add: PO Box 160, 53946-0160), SAN 318-1529. Tel: 920-398-3434. Web Site: www.markesanlibrary.org. *Libr Dir,* Nicole Overbeck; E-mail: director@markesanlibrary.org
Pop 3,000; Circ 44,000
Library Holdings: Bk Vols 14,000; Per Subs 40
Wireless access
Mem of Winnefox Library System
Open Mon & Thurs 10-7, Tues, Wed & Fri 10-6, Sat 9-Noon

MARSHALL

P MARSHALL COMMUNITY LIBRARY*, 605 Waterloo Rd, 53559. SAN 318-1537. Tel: 608-655-3123. E-mail: staff@marlib.org. Web Site: www.marlib.org. *Dir,* Callie Armstrong; *Asst Dir,* Laura Rose; Staff 2 (MLS 1, Non-MLS 1)
Founded 1956. Pop 3,450; Circ 45,000
Library Holdings: Bks on Deafness & Sign Lang 20; Bk Vols 29,000; Per Subs 80
Subject Interests: Local hist
Automation Activity & Vendor Info: (Acquisitions) SirsiDynix; (Cataloging) SirsiDynix; (Circulation) SirsiDynix
Mem of South Central Library System
Open Mon-Wed 9-7, Thurs & Fri 9-5, Sat 9-3
Friends of the Library Group

MARSHFIELD

M MARSHFIELD CLINIC*, George E Magnin Medical Library, 1000 N Oak Ave, 54449. SAN 318-1545. Tel: 715-387-5183. FAX: 715-389-5366. E-mail: mc_library@mcrf.mfldclin.edu. Web Site: www.marshfieldclinic.org/education/library. *Libr Mgr,* Lori Gropp; Tel: 715-389-7676, E-mail: gropp.lori@marshfieldclinic.org; *Ref Librn,* Claudia Noonan; Tel: 715-389-3532, E-mail: noonan.claudia@marshfieldclinic.org; Staff 4 (MLS 2, Non-MLS 2)
Founded 1916
Library Holdings: e-journals 1,500; Bk Vols 20,000; Per Subs 100
Subject Interests: Clinical med, Supporting sci
Wireless access
Partic in National Network of Libraries of Medicine Region 6
Open Mon-Fri 7:30-4:30

J MID-STATE TECHNICAL COLLEGE*, Marshfield Campus Library, 2600 W Fifth St, 54449. SAN 318-1561. Tel: 715-389-7020. Web Site: www.mstc.edu/student-services/link. *Dean, Learning Res,* Amber Stancher; E-mail: amber.stancher@mstc.edu; *Learning Res Spec,* Sara Sikora; E-mail: sara.sikora@mstc.edu
Library Holdings: Bk Titles 11,000; Per Subs 50
Automation Activity & Vendor Info: (Acquisitions) Innovative Interfaces, Inc - Sierra; (Cataloging) Innovative Interfaces, Inc - Sierra; (Circulation) Innovative Interfaces, Inc - Sierra; (ILL) Auto-Graphics, Inc; (OPAC) Innovative Interfaces, Inc - Sierra; (Serials) Innovative Interfaces, Inc - Sierra
Wireless access
Partic in WISPALS Library Consortium
Open Mon-Thurs 9-6, Fri 9-Noon, Sat 9-1

P EVERETT ROEHL MARSHFIELD PUBLIC LIBRARY*, 105 S Maple Ave, 54449. SAN 318-1553. Tel: 715-387-8494. FAX: 715-387-6909. E-mail: busoff@marshfieldlibrary.org. Web Site: www.marshfieldlibrary.org. *Libr Dir,* Jill Porter; E-mail: jporter@marshfieldlibrary.org; *Asst Dir, Head, Tech Serv,* Kathy Baker; Tel: 715-387-8494, Ext 2759, E-mail: kbaker@marshfieldlibrary.org; *Head, Adult Serv,* Mary Adler; Tel: 715-387-8494, Ext 2751, E-mail: madler@marshfieldlibrary.org; *Head, Children's Servx,* Kim Ropson; Tel: 715-387-8494, Ext 2767, E-mail: kropson@marshfieldlibrary.org; *Circ,* Rob Schultz; Tel: 715-387-8494, Ext 2755, E-mail: rschultz@marshfieldlibrary.org; *Info Tech,* Rob Mader; Tel: 715-387-8494, Ext 2763, E-mail: rmader@marshfieldlibrary.org; *ILL,* Patty Steele; Tel: 715-387-8494, Ext 2750, E-mail: psteele@marshfieldlibrary.org; Staff 5 (MLS 4, Non-MLS 1)
Founded 1901. Pop 27,985; Circ 339,595
Jan 2017-Dec 2017 Income $1,619,119, State $1,546, City $1,251,974, County $239,603, Locally Generated Income $35,634, Other $90,362. Mats Exp $176,305, Books $99,954, Per/Ser (Incl. Access Fees) $12,468, AV Mat $33,181, Electronic Ref Mat (Incl. Access Fees) $30,702. Sal $813,982 (Prof $260,353)
Library Holdings: AV Mats 34,464; e-books 164,910; Electronic Media & Resources 58; High Interest/Low Vocabulary Bk Vols 336; Large Print Bks 4,428; Microforms 2,269; Music Scores 349; Bk Vols 101,440; Per Subs 206
Special Collections: Foreign Language (Spanish Coll)
Subject Interests: Genealogy, Local hist
Automation Activity & Vendor Info: (Acquisitions) Innovative Interfaces, Inc; (Cataloging) Innovative Interfaces, Inc; (Circulation) Innovative Interfaces, Inc; (ILL) Innovative Interfaces, Inc; (OPAC) Innovative Interfaces, Inc; (Serials) Innovative Interfaces, Inc
Wireless access
Function: 24/7 Electronic res, 24/7 Online cat, Activity rm, Adult bk club, Art exhibits, Audiobks on Playaways & MP3, Audiobks via web, AV serv, Bk club(s), Bks on CD, CD-ROM, Children's prog, Computer training, Computers for patron use, Digital talking bks, Electronic databases & coll, Equip loans & repairs, Free DVD rentals, Genealogy discussion group, Govt ref serv, Health sci info serv, Homebound delivery serv, ILL available, Internet access, Life-long learning prog for all ages, Magazines, Magnifiers for reading, Mail & tel request accepted, Meeting rooms, Microfiche/film & reading machines, Movies, Music CDs, Online cat, Online ref, Outreach serv, OverDrive digital audio bks, Photocopying/Printing, Preschool outreach, Preschool reading prog, Printer for laptops & handheld devices, Prog for adults, Prog for children & young adult, Ref & res, Ref serv available, Serves people with intellectual disabilities, Spanish lang bks, Spoken cassettes & CDs, Spoken cassettes & DVDs, Story hour, Study rm, Summer & winter reading prog, Summer reading prog, Tax forms, Telephone ref, Wheelchair accessible, Winter reading prog, Workshops
Mem of South Central Library System
Partic in OCLC Online Computer Library Center, Inc; WiLS
Special Services for the Deaf - Assistive tech; Closed caption videos; TTY equip; Videos & decoder
Special Services for the Blind - Assistive/Adapted tech devices, equip & products; Audio mat; Bks on CD; Cassette playback machines; Cassettes; Closed circuit TV magnifier; Copier with enlargement capabilities; Descriptive video serv (DVS); Home delivery serv; Internet workstation with adaptive software; Large print & cassettes; Large print bks; Low vision equip; Magnifiers; Talking bks; Videos on blindness & physical disabilties
Open Mon-Fri 9-8, Sat 9-5
Friends of the Library Group

C UNIVERSITY OF WISCONSIN-STEVENS POINT AT MARSHFIELD*, Hamilton Roddis Memorial Library, 2000 W Fifth St, 54449-3310. SAN 318-1588. Tel: 715-389-6512. FAX: 715-389-6539. Web Site: www.uwsp.edu/library/. *Sr Acad Librn,* Laurie Petri; E-mail: lpetri@uwsp.edu; Staff 1 (MLS 1)
Founded 1964. Enrl 600; Highest Degree: Master
Library Holdings: Bk Titles 29,156; Bk Vols 31,954; Per Subs 145
Automation Activity & Vendor Info: (Acquisitions) Ex Libris Group; (Cataloging) Ex Libris Group; (Circulation) Ex Libris Group; (Course Reserve) Ex Libris Group; (ILL) Ex Libris Group; (Media Booking) Ex Libris Group; (OPAC) Ex Libris Group; (Serials) Ex Libris Group
Wireless access
Partic in OCLC Online Computer Library Center, Inc
Open Mon-Thurs 8-5:30, Fri 8-1

MAUSTON

P HATCH PUBLIC LIBRARY*, 111 W State St, 53948-1344. SAN 318-1596. Tel: 608-847-4454. FAX: 608-847-2306. E-mail: maustonpl@wrlsweb.org. Web Site: www.hatchpubliclibrary.org. *Dir,* Bridget Christenson; Staff 9 (Non-MLS 9)
Founded 1897. Pop 7,000; Circ 108,812
Library Holdings: Bks on Deafness & Sign Lang 25; High Interest/Low Vocabulary Bk Vols 600; Bk Vols 32,000; Per Subs 106
Subject Interests: Juneau County hist
Automation Activity & Vendor Info: (Cataloging) SirsiDynix; (Circulation) SirsiDynix
Wireless access
Mem of Winding Rivers Library System
Open Mon-Thurs 9-8, Fri 9-5, Sat 9-3
Friends of the Library Group

MAYVILLE

P MAYVILLE PUBLIC LIBRARY*, 111 N Main St, 53050. SAN 318-160X. Tel: 920-387-7910. FAX: 920-387-7917. E-mail: maylib@monarchlibraries.org. Web Site: www.mayville.lib.wi.us. *Dir,* Jennifer Stasinopoulos; E-mail: jstasinopoulos@monarchlibraries.org; *Cataloger,* Rhonda Klemme; *Ch Serv, ILL,* Sheila Steger; Staff 6 (MLS 1, Non-MLS 5)
Founded 1904. Pop 5,240; Circ 71,138
Library Holdings: Bk Vols 57,000; Per Subs 120
Special Collections: Mayville News, 1906-Present
Automation Activity & Vendor Info: (Acquisitions) SirsiDynix; (Cataloging) SirsiDynix; (Circulation) SirsiDynix
Wireless access
Function: Homebound delivery serv, ILL available, Music CDs, Photocopying/Printing, Prog for children & young adult, Spoken cassettes & CDs, Summer reading prog, Tax forms
Mem of Monarch Library System
Open Mon-Thurs 11-8, Fri 10-6, Sat 9-3 (Winter); Mon-Thurs 11-8, Fri 10-6 (Summer)
Friends of the Library Group

MAZOMANIE

P MAZOMANIE FREE LIBRARY*, 102 Brodhead St, 53560. (Mail add: PO Box 458, 53560-0458), SAN 318-1618. Tel: 608-795-2104. FAX: 608-795-2102. E-mail: mazlib@mazolibrary.org. Web Site: www.mazolibrary.org. *Dir,* Brian Cole; E-mail: bcole@mazolibrary.org; Staff 3 (MLS 1, Non-MLS 2)
Founded 1899
Library Holdings: Bk Vols 18,000; Per Subs 50
Subject Interests: Genealogy, Local hist
Automation Activity & Vendor Info: (Cataloging) Koha; (Circulation) Koha
Wireless access
Mem of South Central Library System
Open Mon-Thurs 10-12 & 2-7, Fri 10-5, Sat 10-1
Friends of the Library Group

MCFARLAND

P MCFARLAND PUBLIC LIBRARY*, E D Locke Public Library, 5920 Milwaukee St, 53558-8962. SAN 377-9343. Tel: 608-838-9030. E-mail: mcflib@mcfarlandlibrary.org. Web Site: www.mcfarland.wi.us/library. *Dir,* Heidi Cox; E-mail: hcox@mcfarlandlibrary.org
Founded 1997
Library Holdings: Bk Vols 30,900; Per Subs 118
Wireless access
Mem of South Central Library System
Open Mon-Thurs 9:30-8, Fri & Sat 9:30-5:30, Sun 12-4
Friends of the Library Group

MEDFORD

P FRANCES L SIMEK MEMORIAL LIBRARY*, 400 N Main St, 54451. SAN 318-1626. Tel: 715-748-2505. FAX: 715-748-3523. Reference E-mail: reference@medford.lib.wi.us. Web Site: citymedfordwi.com/departments/recreation_and_culture/library.php. *Dir,* Maxx Handel; Tel: 715-748-1161, E-mail: director@medford.lib.wi.us; *Ch,* Marlene Klemm; E-mail: mklemm@medford.lib.wi.us
Founded 1916. Pop 13,900; Circ 85,000
Library Holdings: Bk Titles 43,000; Per Subs 99
Automation Activity & Vendor Info: (Cataloging) Innovative Interfaces, Inc; (Circulation) Innovative Interfaces, Inc
Wireless access
Partic in Wisconsin Valley Library Service
Open Mon-Thurs 8:30-8, Fri 8:30-6, Sat (Winter) 8:30-2:30
Friends of the Library Group

MELLEN

P LEGION MEMORIAL LIBRARY*, 106 Iron St, 54546. (Mail add: PO Box 47, 54546-0047), SAN 318-1642. Tel: 715-274-8331. Web Site: www.legionmemoriallibrary.org. *Dir,* Jennie Thewis; E-mail: jenthewis@mellen.wislib.org
Founded 1929. Pop 2,000; Circ 11,000
Library Holdings: Bk Titles 8,000; Per Subs 40
Automation Activity & Vendor Info: (Cataloging) Innovative Interfaces, Inc; (Circulation) Innovative Interfaces, Inc; (OPAC) Innovative Interfaces, Inc
Wireless access
Mem of Northern Waters Library Service
Partic in Merlin
Open Mon-Thurs 10-6, Fri & Sat 9-12
Friends of the Library Group

MENASHA

P MENASHA PUBLIC LIBRARY*, Elisha D Smith Public Library, 440 First St, 54952-3143. SAN 318-1650. Tel: 920-967-3690. Circulation Tel: 920-967-3680. FAX: 920-967-5159. Reference E-mail: reference@menashalibrary.org. Web Site: www.menashalibrary.org. *Dir,* Brian Kopetsky; E-mail: kopetsky@menashalibrary.org; *Adult Serv Supvr,* Joe Bongers; Tel: 920-967-3696, E-mail: bongers@menashalibrary.org; *Children's Serv Supvr,* Kathy Beson; Tel: 920-967-3671, E-mail: beson@menashalibrary.org; *Tech Serv & Circ Supvr,* Catherine Brandt; Tel: 920-967-3683, E-mail: brandt@menashalibrary.org; Staff 8.5 (MLS 6.5, Non-MLS 2)
Founded 1896
Jan 2018-Dec 2018 Income $1,597,171, City $1,093,658, County $478,513, Other $25,000. Mats Exp $185,000. Sal $849,102 (Prof $529,315)
Library Holdings: AV Mats 27,992; Bks on Deafness & Sign Lang 35; e-books 406,474; High Interest/Low Vocabulary Bk Vols 50; Bk Vols 116,565; Per Subs 255
Subject Interests: Local hist
Automation Activity & Vendor Info: (Acquisitions) SirsiDynix; (Cataloging) SirsiDynix; (Circulation) SirsiDynix; (Course Reserve) SirsiDynix; (ILL) SirsiDynix; (Media Booking) SirsiDynix; (OPAC) SirsiDynix; (Serials) SirsiDynix
Wireless access
Function: 24/7 Electronic res, 24/7 Online cat, Activity rm, Adult bk club, Archival coll
Mem of Winnefox Library System
Open Mon-Thurs 8:30-8:30, Fri 8:30-6, Sat 8:30-4:30, Sun 1-5
Friends of the Library Group

J UNIVERSITY OF WISCONSIN-FOX VALLEY LIBRARY*, 1478 Midway Rd, 54952-1297. SAN 318-1669. Tel: 920-832-2672. Interlibrary Loan Service Tel: 920-832-2673. FAX: 920-832-2874. E-mail: foxlibrary@uwc.edu. Web Site: uwosh.edu/uwfox. *Sr Acad Librn,* Ane Carriveau; E-mail: ane.carriveau@uwc.edu; *Acad Librn,* Kelly Johnson; E-mail: kelly.johnson@uwc.edu; Staff 4 (MLS 2, Non-MLS 2)
Founded 1937. Enrl 1,700; Fac 63; Highest Degree: Associate
Library Holdings: Bks on Deafness & Sign Lang 13; Bk Titles 30,188; Bk Vols 34,716; Per Subs 178
Automation Activity & Vendor Info: (Acquisitions) Ex Libris Group; (Cataloging) Ex Libris Group; (Circulation) Ex Libris Group; (Course Reserve) Ex Libris Group; (ILL) Ex Libris Group; (Media Booking) Ex Libris Group; (OPAC) Ex Libris Group
Wireless access
Partic in OCLC Online Computer Library Center, Inc; WiLS
Special Services for the Blind - Magnifiers
Open Mon-Thurs (Winter) 8am-9pm, Fri 8-4, Sun 5-9 (Winter); Mon-Thurs 8-6, Fri 8-4 (Summer)

MENOMONEE FALLS

P MENOMONEE FALLS PUBLIC LIBRARY*, W156 N8436 Pilgrim Rd, 53051. SAN 318-1677. Tel: 262-532-8900. E-mail: mfpl@menomonee-falls.org. Web Site: www.menomoneefallslibrary.org. *Libr Dir,* Jacqueline Rammer; E-mail: jrammer@menomonee-falls.org; *Adult Serv Mgr,* Scott Kifflie; *ILL,* Maggie Davis; Staff 21 (MLS 6, Non-MLS 15)
Founded 1906. Pop 36,000; Circ 344,279
Library Holdings: Bk Vols 117,648; Per Subs 282
Special Collections: Historical Photograph Coll; Menomonee Falls Local History
Automation Activity & Vendor Info: (Acquisitions) Innovative Interfaces, Inc; (Cataloging) Innovative Interfaces, Inc; (Circulation) Innovative Interfaces, Inc; (Course Reserve) Innovative Interfaces, Inc; (ILL) Innovative Interfaces, Inc; (Media Booking) Innovative Interfaces, Inc; (OPAC) Innovative Interfaces, Inc; (Serials) Innovative Interfaces, Inc
Wireless access
Mem of Bridges Library System
Partic in OCLC Online Computer Library Center, Inc

Open Mon-Thurs 9-9, Fri & Sat 9-5
Friends of the Library Group

MENOMONIE

P MENOMONIE PUBLIC LIBRARY*, 600 Wolske Bay Rd, 54751. SAN 318-1685. Tel: 715-232-2164. FAX: 715-232-2324. E-mail: info@menomonielibrary.org. Web Site: menomonielibrary.org. *Dir,* Joleen Sterk; E-mail: sterkj@menomonielibrary.org; *Bus Mgr,* Lisa Murray; E-mail: murrayl@menomonielibrary.org; Staff 15.5 (MLS 2, Non-MLS 13.5)
Founded 1874. Pop 35,000; Circ 388,000
Library Holdings: Bk Vols 54,000; Per Subs 120
Automation Activity & Vendor Info: (Acquisitions) Innovative Interfaces, Inc - Millennium; (Cataloging) Innovative Interfaces, Inc - Millennium; (Circulation) Innovative Interfaces, Inc - Millennium; (ILL) Innovative Interfaces, Inc - Millennium; (OPAC) Innovative Interfaces, Inc - Millennium; (Serials) Innovative Interfaces, Inc - Millennium
Wireless access
Function: Adult bk club, Adult literacy prog, After school storytime, Audiobks via web, Bk club(s), Bks on CD, Children's prog, Computer training, Computers for patron use, Digital talking bks, E-Reserves, Family literacy, Free DVD rentals, ILL available, Magnifiers for reading, Microfiche/film & reading machines, Music CDs, Online cat, Photocopying/Printing, Prog for adults, Prog for children & young adult, Ref serv available, Senior computer classes, Spoken cassettes & CDs, Spoken cassettes & DVDs, Summer reading prog, Tax forms, Teen prog, Telephone ref, Wheelchair accessible, Workshops
Mem of Inspiring & Facilitating Library Success (IFLS)
Special Services for the Deaf - Adult & family literacy prog; Assisted listening device; Assistive tech; TDD equip
Special Services for the Blind - Bks on CD; Copier with enlargement capabilities; Large print bks & talking machines; Large screen computer & software; Magnifiers; Playaways (bks on MP3); Recorded bks; Ref serv; Talking bks
Open Mon-Fri 10-6
Friends of the Library Group

C UNIVERSITY OF WISCONSIN-STOUT*, Robert S Swanson Library & Learning Center, 315 Tenth Ave, 54751-0790. SAN 318-1693. Tel: 715-232-1215. Administration Tel: 715-232-2392. E-mail: reference@uwstout.edu. Web Site: library.uwstout.edu. *Interim Libr Dir,* Kate Kramschuster; Tel: 715-232-4071, E-mail: kramschusterk@uwstout.edu; *Area Research Director, Univ Archivist,* Heather Stecklein; Tel: 715-232-5418, E-mail: steckleinh@uwstout.edu; *Access Serv, Assoc Dir, Cat,* Susan Lindahl; Tel: 715-232-1184, E-mail: lindahls@uwstout.edu; *Coll Develop Librn,* Cory Mitchell; Tel: 715-232-2363, E-mail: mitchellc@uwstout.edu; *Educ Mat Ctr/Instruction/Ref Librn,* Tanya Gunkel; Tel: 715-232-1892, E-mail: gunkelta@uwstout.edu; *Syst Librn,* Ann Vogl; Tel: 715-232-1553, E-mail: voglan@uwstout.edu; *Tech Coordr,* Bryan Vogh; Tel: 715-232-1892, E-mail: voghb@uwstout.edu; *ILL,* Katie Shay; Tel: 715-232-1112, E-mail: shayka@uwstout.edu; Staff 22 (MLS 11.5, Non-MLS 10.5)
Founded 1891. Enrl 9,339; Fac 470; Highest Degree: Master
Jul 2016-Jun 2017. Mats Exp $588,000, Books $26,600, Per/Ser (Incl. Access Fees) $219,000, AV Mat $20,000, Electronic Ref Mat (Incl. Access Fees) $322,400
Library Holdings: AV Mats 14,533; e-books 203,504; e-journals 100,796; Microforms 1,292,457; Bk Vols 234,344; Per Subs 100
Special Collections: Oral History
Subject Interests: Consumer studies, Early childhood educ, Family studies, Hospitality, Indust tech, Manufacturing engr, Tourism, Vocational rehabilitation
Automation Activity & Vendor Info: (Acquisitions) Ex Libris Group; (Cataloging) Ex Libris Group; (Circulation) Ex Libris Group; (Course Reserve) Ex Libris Group; (ILL) Atlas Systems; (OPAC) Ex Libris Group; (Serials) Ex Libris Group
Wireless access
Function: 24/7 Online cat, Art exhibits, Audio & video playback equip for onsite use, Bks on CD, Computers for patron use, Distance learning, E-Reserves, Electronic databases & coll, Internet access, Large print keyboards, Magnifiers for reading, Mail & tel request accepted, Mail loans to mem, Meeting rooms, Online cat, Online ref, Photocopying/Printing, Ref & res, Ref serv available, Res libr, Scanner, Telephone ref, Wheelchair accessible
Partic in OCLC Online Computer Library Center, Inc
Restriction: ID required to use computers (Ltd hrs), In-house use for visitors, Open to pub for ref & circ; with some limitations, Open to students, fac & staff

MEQUON

CR CONCORDIA UNIVERSITY WISCONSIN*, Rincker Memorial Library, 12800 N Lake Shore Dr, 53097-2402. SAN 318-1901. Tel: 262-243-4330. Circulation Tel: 262-243-4420. FAX: 262-243-4424. Web Site: www.cuw.edu/academics/library. *Libr Dir,* Christian Himsel; Tel: 262-243-4534, E-mail: Christian.Himsel@cuw.edu; *Access Serv, ILL, Ref Serv,* Carol Mittag; E-mail: carol.mittag@cuw.edu; *Libr Instruction, Online Serv,* Elaine Gustafson; Tel: 262-243-4403, E-mail: elaine.gustafson@cuw.edu; *Ref Serv/e-Res, Ser,* Kathy Malland; E-mail: kathy.malland@cuw.edu; Staff 8.3 (MLS 4.8, Non-MLS 3.5)
Founded 1881. Enrl 4,268; Highest Degree: Doctorate
Library Holdings: Bk Vols 114,000; Per Subs 600
Special Collections: 16th & 17th Century Lutheran Theology; German Hymnals
Subject Interests: Church music, Educ, Nursing, Phys therapy, Theol
Automation Activity & Vendor Info: (OPAC) Ex Libris Group
Wireless access
Function: Doc delivery serv, ILL available, Outside serv via phone, mail, e-mail & web, Ref serv available, Telephone ref
Partic in Southeastern Wisconsin Information Technology Exchange, Inc; WiLS; Wis Asn of Independent Col & Univ
Open Mon-Thurs 8am-Midnight, Fri 8-6, Sat 9-5, Sun 12:30-Midnight (Fall & Spring); Mon-Thurs 8-8, Fri 8-4:30, Sat 9-5 (Summer)

J MILWAUKEE AREA TECHNICAL COLLEGE*, Mequon Campus Library, 5555 W Highland Rd, Rm A282, 53092-1199. SAN 318-1707. Tel: 262-238-2209. Web Site: guides.matc.edu/MATC_Libraries/mequonlib. *Campus Librn, ILL,* Kathy Blume; Tel: 262-238-2212, E-mail: blumek@matc.edu; *Ref Librn,* Rachael Fealy-Layer; E-mail: fealeylar@matc.edu; Staff 4 (MLS 3, Non-MLS 1)
Founded 1977
Library Holdings: Bk Titles 16,500; Bk Vols 18,051; Per Subs 175
Subject Interests: Bus, Hort, Interior design, Landscape archit, Nursing, Philos, Sociol
Wireless access
Open Mon-Thurs 7:45am-9pm, Fri 7:45-4
Restriction: Non-circulating to the pub

P FRANK L WEYENBERG LIBRARY OF MEQUON-THIENSVILLE*, 11345 N Cedarburg Rd, 53092-1998. SAN 318-1715. Tel: 262-242-2593. FAX: 262-478-3200. Administration E-mail: admin@flwlib.org. Web Site: www.flwlib.org. *Libr Dir,* Rachel Muchin Young; Tel: 262-242-2593, Ext 331, E-mail: director@flwlib.org; *Access Serv Mgr,* Emily Vosberg; E-mail: evosberg@flwlib.org; *Patron Serv Mgr,* Ashley Pike; E-mail: apike@flwlib.org; Staff 5 (MLS 5)
Founded 1954. Pop 27,000; Circ 260,000
Library Holdings: Bk Vols 140,000; Per Subs 105
Special Collections: Local History of Mequon & Thiensville
Automation Activity & Vendor Info: (Acquisitions) Innovative Interfaces, Inc. - Polaris; (Cataloging) Innovative Interfaces, Inc. - Polaris; (Circulation) Innovative Interfaces, Inc. - Polaris; (OPAC) Innovative Interfaces, Inc. - Polaris; (Serials) Innovative Interfaces, Inc. - Polaris
Wireless access
Function: 24/7 Electronic res, 24/7 Online cat, Activity rm, Adult bk club, Art exhibits, Audiobks via web, Bk club(s), Bks on CD, Butterfly Garden, Children's prog, Computer training, Computers for patron use, E-Readers, E-Reserves, Electronic databases & coll, Free DVD rentals, Genealogy discussion group, ILL available, Internet access, Life-long learning prog for all ages, Magazines, Meeting rooms, Music CDs, Online cat, Online ref, Outreach serv, OverDrive digital audio bks, Photocopying/Printing, Preschool reading prog, Prog for adults, Prog for children & young adult, Ref serv available, Story hour, Summer & winter reading prog, Teen prog, Telephone ref, Wheelchair accessible
Mem of Monarch Library System
Open Mon-Thurs 9-8, Fri 9-6, Sat 9-4
Friends of the Library Group

R WISCONSIN LUTHERAN SEMINARY LIBRARY, 11831 N Seminary Dr, 53092-1546. SAN 318-1723. Tel: 262-242-8113. E-mail: library@wls.edu. Web Site: www.wls.edu/resources/library. *Dir,* Nathan R Ericson; Staff 2 (MLS 1, Non-MLS 1)
Founded 1878. Enrl 160; Fac 19; Highest Degree: Master
Library Holdings: Bk Vols 60,000; Per Subs 200
Subject Interests: Bible, Church hist, Doctrinal, Lutheran Church, Practical theol, Relig studies
Wireless access

MERCER

P MERCER PUBLIC LIBRARY, 2648 W Margaret St, 54547. Tel: 715-476-2366. FAX: 715-476-2366. Web Site: mercerpubliclibrary.org. *Dir,* Julia Pusateri; E-mail: director@mercerpubliclibrary.org; Staff 1.8 (MLS 0.8, Non-MLS 1)
Founded 1940. Pop 1,649; Circ 20,000
Library Holdings: Bk Vols 18,170; Per Subs 20
Wireless access
Mem of Northern Waters Library Service
Partic in Merlin

Open Mon, Wed & Fri 9-5, Tues & Thurs 9-6, Sat 9-12; Mon-Thurs 9-7, Fri 9-5, Sat 9-12 (Summer)
Friends of the Library Group

MERRILL

SR OUR SAVIOUR'S LUTHERAN CHURCH LIBRARY*, 300 Logan St, 54452. SAN 324-7228. Tel: 715-536-5813. E-mail: office@oslcelca.org. Web Site: www.oslcelca.org.
Library Holdings: Bk Titles 753; Bk Vols 763
Restriction: Mem only

P T B SCOTT LIBRARY*, Merrill Public Library, 106 W First St, 54452-2398. SAN 318-174X. Tel: 715-536-7191. FAX: 715-536-1705. Web Site: www.tbscottlibrary.org. *Libr Dir,* Laurie Ollhoff; E-mail: director@tbscottlibrary.org; *Head, Youth Serv,* Carolyn Forde; E-mail: cforde@tbscottlibrary.org; *Circ Coordr, Syst Adminr,* Eleanor Schwartz; E-mail: schwartz@tbscottlibrary.com; Staff 21 (MLS 3, Non-MLS 18)
Founded 1891. Pop 21,000; Circ 297,563
Library Holdings: Audiobooks 2,877; AV Mats 11,863; CDs 2,693; DVDs 1,713; Large Print Bks 4,657; Microforms 765; Bk Vols 95,500; Per Subs 177; Videos 3,939
Special Collections: Wisconsin & Local History
Automation Activity & Vendor Info: (Acquisitions) Horizon; (Circulation) Fretwell-Downing; (ILL) Auto-Graphics, Inc; (OPAC) SirsiDynix
Wireless access
Function: Children's prog, Computer training, Computers for patron use, Digital talking bks, E-Reserves, Electronic databases & coll, Free DVD rentals, Games & aids for people with disabilities, Genealogy discussion group, Holiday prog, Home delivery & serv to seniorr ctr & nursing homes, Homebound delivery serv, ILL available, Internet access, Magnifiers for reading, Music CDs, Online cat, Orientations, Outreach serv, Outside serv via phone, mail, e-mail & web, OverDrive digital audio bks, Photocopying/Printing, Preschool outreach, Prof lending libr, Prog for adults, Prog for children & young adult, Ref serv available, Senior computer classes, Senior outreach, Spoken cassettes & CDs, Spoken cassettes & DVDs, Story hour, Summer reading prog, Tax forms, Teen prog, Telephone ref, VHS videos, Wheelchair accessible
Special Services for the Deaf - ADA equip; Assistive tech; Bks on deafness & sign lang; Closed caption videos; High interest/low vocabulary bks; Sign lang interpreter upon request for prog; TDD equip
Special Services for the Blind - Braille music coll; Copier with enlargement capabilities; Large print bks; Low vision equip; Screen enlargement software for people with visual disabilities; Screen reader software; Talking bk serv referral; ZoomText magnification & reading software
Open Mon-Thurs 9:30-8, Fri 9:30-6, Sat 9:30-4, Sun 12-4
Friends of the Library Group

MIDDLETON

P MIDDLETON PUBLIC LIBRARY*, 7425 Hubbard Ave, 53562-3117. SAN 318-1758. Tel: 608-831-5564. Circulation Tel: 608-827-7401. Interlibrary Loan Service Tel: 608-827-7421. Reference Tel: 608-827-7403. Administration Tel: 608-827-7425. FAX: 608-836-5724. E-mail: info@midlibrary.org. Web Site: www.midlibrary.org. *Dir,* Jocelyne Sansing; E-mail: jsansing@midlibrary.org; *Head, Info Tech,* Patrick Williams; Tel: 608-827-7422, E-mail: williams@midlibrary.org; *Head, Adult Serv,* Liz Zimdars; Tel: 608-827-7423, E-mail: lzimdars@midlibrary.org; *Head, Youth Serv,* Lori Bell; Tel: 608-827-7411, E-mail: lori@midlibrary.org; *Head, Tech Serv,* Sarah Hartman; E-mail: hartman@midlibrary.org; *Commun Engagement Librn,* Amy Perry; Tel: 608-827-7417, E-mail: aperry@midlibrary.org; Staff 18 (MLS 7, Non-MLS 11)
Founded 1926. Pop 26,393; Circ 769,485
Library Holdings: Audiobooks 10,808; AV Mats 18,307; Bks on Deafness & Sign Lang 100; Braille Volumes 45; CDs 4,207; DVDs 14,178; e-books 65,673; Electronic Media & Resources 21,321; High Interest/Low Vocabulary Bk Vols 1,518; Large Print Bks 2,000; Bk Vols 86,778; Per Subs 286
Automation Activity & Vendor Info: (Cataloging) LibLime Koha; (Circulation) LibLime Koha; (ILL) OCLC; (OPAC) LibLime Koha; (Serials) LibLime Koha
Wireless access
Function: AV serv, Homebound delivery serv, ILL available, Internet access, Magnifiers for reading, Outside serv via phone, mail, e-mail & web, Photocopying/Printing, Prog for adults, Prog for children & young adult, Ref serv available, Summer reading prog, Telephone ref, Wheelchair accessible, Workshops
Publications: The Bookworm (Bimonthly)
Mem of South Central Library System
Partic in Library Interchange Network; WiLS
Special Services for the Blind - Large print bks; Lending of low vision aids; Low vision equip; Magnifiers
Open Mon-Thurs 9-8, Fri 9-6, Sat 9-5
Friends of the Library Group

MILLTOWN

P MILLTOWN PUBLIC LIBRARY*, 61 W Main St, 54858. (Mail add: PO Box 69, 54858-0069), SAN 318-1766. Tel: 715-825-2313. FAX: 715-825-4422. E-mail: milltownpl@milltownpubliclibrary.org. Web Site: www.milltownpubliclibrary.org. *Libr Dir,* Bonnie Carl; *Libr Asst,* Stephanie Fransler
Pop 900
Automation Activity & Vendor Info: (Acquisitions) Innovative Interfaces, Inc; (Cataloging) Innovative Interfaces, Inc; (Circulation) Innovative Interfaces, Inc
Wireless access
Mem of Inspiring & Facilitating Library Success (IFLS)
Open Mon, Wed & Fri 10-5, Tues & Thurs 12-7, Sat 10-2
Friends of the Library Group

MILTON

P MILTON PUBLIC LIBRARY*, 430 E High St, 53563. SAN 318-1782. Tel: 608-868-7462. FAX: 608-868-6926. E-mail: mpl@als.lib.wi.us. Web Site: www.als.lib.wi.us/MPL. *Dir, Team Librn,* Ashlee Kunkel; E-mail: kunkel.ashlee@als.lib.wi.us; *Asst Dir,* Jayme Anderson; E-mail: anderson.jayme@als.lib.wi.us; Staff 5 (MLS 1, Non-MLS 4)
Founded 1967. Pop 7,577; Circ 79,948
Library Holdings: AV Mats 3,308; Large Print Bks 179; Bk Titles 28,016; Per Subs 42
Automation Activity & Vendor Info: (Acquisitions) Follett Software; (Cataloging) Follett Software; (Circulation) Follett Software
Wireless access
Mem of Prairie Lakes Library System (PLLS)
Open Mon & Tues 10-8, Wed-Fri 10-6, Sat 10-4, Sun 1-4
Friends of the Library Group

MILWAUKEE

M ADVOCATE AURORA LIBRARY*, 2900 W Oklahoma Ave, 53215-4330. (Mail add: PO Box 2901, 53201-2901), SAN 318-2452. Tel: 414-649-7356. FAX: 414-649-7037. E-mail: aah-library@aah.org. Web Site: www.aurorahealthcare.org/education/advocate-aurora-library-network. *Dir,* Karen Hanus; E-mail: karen.hanus@aah.org
Founded 1967
Automation Activity & Vendor Info: (Cataloging) EOS International; (Circulation) EOS International; (Discovery) ProQuest; (OPAC) EOS International; (Serials) Ex Libris Group

C ALVERNO COLLEGE LIBRARY, 3401 S 39th St, 53215. SAN 318-1820. Tel: 414-382-6433. E-mail: library@alverno.edu. Web Site: www.alverno.edu/library. *Dir,* Larry Duerr; Tel: 414-382-6173, E-mail: larry.duerr@alverno.edu; *Diversity, Equity & Inclusion Librn,* Jac Sinclair; Tel: 414-392-6184, E-mail: jac.sinclair@alverno.edu; *Access Serv, Metadata Librn,* Sebastian Black; Tel: 414-382-6183, E-mail: sebastian.black@alverno.edu; *Col Archivist/Rec Mgr, Ref Librn,* Sara Shutkin; Tel: 414-382-6202, E-mail: sara.shutkin@alverno.edu; Staff 13 (MLS 9, Non-MLS 4)
Founded 1887. Enrl 2,815; Fac 118; Highest Degree: Master
Library Holdings: e-books 75,179; Music Scores 2,465; Bk Titles 71,771; Per Subs 429; Videos 2,474
Special Collections: Children's Literature Coll; Corporate Annual Reports; Fine Arts Coll; Teaching Materials Coll
Subject Interests: Educ, Ethnicity, Music, Nursing, Women studies
Automation Activity & Vendor Info: (Acquisitions) Innovative Interfaces, Inc; (Cataloging) Innovative Interfaces, Inc; (Circulation) Innovative Interfaces, Inc; (Course Reserve) Innovative Interfaces, Inc; (ILL) Innovative Interfaces, Inc; (Media Booking) Innovative Interfaces, Inc; (OPAC) Innovative Interfaces, Inc; (Serials) Innovative Interfaces, Inc
Wireless access
Partic in OCLC Online Computer Library Center, Inc; Southeastern Wisconsin Information Technology Exchange, Inc; WiLS; Wis Asn of Independent Col & Univ
Special Services for the Blind - Reader equip

S AMERICAN SOCIETY FOR QUALITY*, Quality Information Center, 600 N Plankinton Ave, 53203. (Mail add: PO Box 3005, 53203-3005), SAN 328-5944. Tel: 414-272-8575. Toll Free Tel: 800-248-1946. E-mail: knowledgecenter@asq.org. Web Site: asq.org/quality-resources. *Research Librn,* Gretchen Peterson; Staff 1 (MLS 1)
Founded 1994
Library Holdings: Bk Vols 3,700; Per Subs 20; Spec Interest Per Sub 15
Special Collections: ANSI/ISO/ASQ Standards; ASQ & Quality Press Publications
Subject Interests: Auditing, Quality assurance, Quality control, Quality mgt

Automation Activity & Vendor Info: (Cataloging) Inmagic, Inc.; (Circulation) Inmagic, Inc.; (OPAC) Inmagic, Inc.
Wireless access
Function: Res libr
Restriction: Not a lending libr, Staff & mem only

M ASCENSION COLUMBIA-SAINT MARY'S HOSPITAL*, Health Sciences Library, Women's Hospital, 2nd Flr, 2323 N Lake Dr, 53211. SAN 318-2460. Tel: 414-585-1626. FAX: 414-585-1738. Web Site: healthcare.ascension.org. *Mgr,* Kellee Selden; E-mail: kellee.selden@columbia-stmarys.org; Staff 1 (MLS 1)
Founded 1959
Library Holdings: Bk Vols 2,500
Subject Interests: Nursing, Rehabilitation
Wireless access
Function: Res libr
Open Mon-Fri 8-4

C CARDINAL STRITCH UNIVERSITY LIBRARY*, 6801 N Yates Rd, 53217. SAN 364-9326. Tel: 414-410-4263. Interlibrary Loan Service Tel: 414-410-4265. Reference Tel: 414-410-4257. Administration Tel: 414-410-4118. Toll Free Tel: 800-347-8822. Reference E-mail: reference@stritch.edu. Web Site: library.stritch.edu. *Dir,* Dyan Barbeau; E-mail: debarbeau@stritch.edu; *Digital Res Librn, Web Librn,* Neal Bogda; E-mail: npbogda@stritch.edu; *Ser & Electronic Res Librn,* Molly Ostendorf; Tel: 414-410-4265, E-mail: mjostendorf@stritch.edu; Staff 3 (MLS 3)
Founded 1937. Enrl 1,658; Highest Degree: Doctorate
Library Holdings: AV Mats 6,280; e-books 11,750; Microforms 121,312; Bk Titles 99,904; Bk Vols 138,740; Per Subs 4,215
Special Collections: Cianciolo Children's & YA Literature Research Center, bks, rare bks, art work; Franciscan Library, bks, rare bks, pers
Subject Interests: Bus, Educ, Nursing
Automation Activity & Vendor Info: (Cataloging) OCLC Connexion; (Circulation) Ex Libris Group; (Course Reserve) Ex Libris Group; (Discovery) Ex Libris Group; (ILL) OCLC ILLiad; (OPAC) Ex Libris Group; (Serials) EBSCO Online
Wireless access
Function: Art exhibits, Audio & video playback equip for onsite use, Computers for patron use, Distance learning, E-Reserves, Electronic databases & coll, ILL available, Instruction & testing, Online cat, Online ref, Outside serv via phone, mail, e-mail & web, Photocopying/Printing, VHS videos, Wheelchair accessible
Partic in OCLC Online Computer Library Center, Inc; Southeastern Wisconsin Information Technology Exchange, Inc; Wis Asn of Independent Col & Univ
Open Mon-Thurs 7:30am-11pm, Fri 7:30-5, Sat 9:30-5, Sun Noon-11; Mon-Thurs 8am-9pm, Fri 8-4:30, Sun Noon-9 (Summer)

R CONGREGATION EMANU-EL B'NE JESHURUN LIBRARY*, Rabbi Dudley Weinberg Library, 2020 W Brown Deer Rd, 53217. SAN 318-191X. Tel: 414-228-7545. FAX: 414-228-7884. E-mail: librarian@ceebj.org. Web Site: www.ceebj.org/learn/library. *Librn,* Paula Fine
Founded 1929
Library Holdings: Bk Vols 8,500; Per Subs 10
Subject Interests: Judaica
Automation Activity & Vendor Info: (Cataloging) Follett Software; (Circulation) Follett Software
Wireless access

R CONGREGATION SHALOM*, Sherman Pastor Memorial Library, 7630 N Santa Monica Blvd, 53217. SAN 318-1928. Tel: 414-352-9288. FAX: 414-352-9280. Web Site: www.cong-shalom.org. *Exec Dir,* Linda Holifield; E-mail: linda@cong-shalom.org
Founded 1970
Library Holdings: Bk Titles 6,000; Per Subs 10
Subject Interests: Children's fiction, Holocaust, Israel, Jewish fiction, Judaica, Non-fiction
Restriction: Access at librarian's discretion, Mem only
Friends of the Library Group

GM DEPARTMENT OF VETERANS AFFAIRS, Medical Library, VA Medical Ctr, 5000 W National Ave, 53295. SAN 365-0375. Tel: 414-384-2000. Toll Free Tel: 800-827-1000. FAX: 414-382-5334. *Librn,* Anne Sneig; Tel: 414-384-2000, Ext 42341, E-mail: anne.snieg@va.gov; Staff 3 (MLS 1, Non-MLS 2)
Library Holdings: Bk Titles 5,392; Per Subs 428
Subject Interests: Allied health, Dentistry, Med, Nursing, Psychol, Rehabilitation, Surgery
Automation Activity & Vendor Info: (Cataloging) LibraryWorld, Inc; (Circulation) LibraryWorld, Inc; (OPAC) LibraryWorld, Inc; (Serials) LibraryWorld, Inc
Wireless access
Partic in National Network of Libraries of Medicine Region 6
Open Mon-Fri 8-4:30

M ENDOMETRIOSIS ASSOCIATION LIBRARY & READING ROOM*, 8585 N 76th Pl, 53223. SAN 374-5104. Tel: 414-355-2200. Toll Free Tel: 800-992-3636. FAX: 414-355-6065. E-mail: endo@endometriosisassn.org, support@EndometriosisAssn.org. Web Site: endometriosisassn.org. *Asst Dir,* Carol Drury
Library Holdings: Bk Vols 300
Function: Res libr
Open Mon-Fri 8:30-5
Restriction: Circ to mem only, Circulates for staff only, Non-circulating to the pub

L FOLEY & LARDNER*, Law Library, 777 E Wisconsin Ave, 53202-5306. SAN 318-1960. Tel: 414-271-2400. FAX: 414-297-4900. Web Site: www.foley.com. *Info Res Mgr,* Pam Noyd; E-mail: pnoyd@foley.com; *Libr Asst,* Linda Lange; Staff 7 (MLS 2, Non-MLS 5)
Founded 1842
Library Holdings: Bk Vols 32,000; Per Subs 450
Subject Interests: Corporate finance, Employment law, Intellectual property, Securities, Tax
Automation Activity & Vendor Info: (Cataloging) Inmagic, Inc.; (Circulation) Inmagic, Inc.
Restriction: Staff use only

C MARQUETTE UNIVERSITY, Raynor Memorial Libraries, 1355 W Wisconsin Ave, 53233. (Mail add: PO Box 3141, 53233-3141), SAN 364-9652. Tel: 414-288-7556. Circulation Tel: 414-288-7555. Interlibrary Loan Service Tel: 414-288-7257. Reference Tel: 414-288-7256. FAX: 414-288-7813. Web Site: www.marquette.edu/library. *Dean of Libr,* Tara Baillargeon; Tel: 414-288-5213, E-mail: tara.baillargeon@marquette.edu; *Associate Dean, Collection Services,* Brenda Fay; Tel: 414-288-7954, E-mail: brenda.fay@marquette.edu; *Assoc Dean, Research & Engagement,* Joe Hardenbrook; Tel: 414-288-5979, E-mail: joseph.hardenbrook@marquette.edu; *Head, Archival Colls & Institutional Repository,* Amy Cooper Cary; Tel: 414-288-5901, E-mail: amy.cary@marquette.edu; *Head, Cataloging & Metadata,* Elisabeth Kaune; Tel: 414-288-3671, E-mail: elisabeth.kaune@marquette.edu; *Head, Libr Info Tech,* Edward Sanchez; Tel: 414-288-6043, E-mail: edward.sanchez@marquette.edu; *Head, Research, Teaching & Learning,* Alissa Fial; Tel: 414-288-3320, E-mail: alissa.fial@marquette.edu; *Coll Mgt Librn,* Rosemary Del Toro; Tel: 414-288-3944, E-mail: rosemary.deltoro@marquette.edu; Staff 34 (MLS 34)
Founded 1881. Enrl 11,782; Fac 1,200; Highest Degree: Doctorate
Library Holdings: e-books 2,500,000; e-journals 55,300; Electronic Media & Resources 430; Bk Vols 1,535,000
Special Collections: Catholic Social Action (Dorothy Day Catholic Worker Coll); Children's Book Coll; Ciszek Catholic Spirituality Coll, bks & videos; James W Foley Coll; Jean Cuje Milwaukee Music Coll; JRR Tolkien Coll; Manresa Coll; Native America Coll; Rare Books Coll; University Records
Subject Interests: Dentistry, Math, Nursing, Philos, Theol
Automation Activity & Vendor Info: (Acquisitions) Innovative Interfaces, Inc; (Cataloging) Innovative Interfaces, Inc; (Circulation) Innovative Interfaces, Inc; (Course Reserve) Innovative Interfaces, Inc; (ILL) OCLC ILLiad; (Media Booking) Innovative Interfaces, Inc; (OPAC) Innovative Interfaces, Inc; (Serials) Innovative Interfaces, Inc
Wireless access
Publications: Foundations in Wisconsin: A Directory (Annual)
Partic in Association of Jesuit Colleges & Universities; Center for Research Libraries; Midwest Health Sci Libr Network; OCLC Online Computer Library Center, Inc
Restriction: Res pass required for non-affiliated visitors

Departmental Libraries:

CL RAY & KAY ECKSTEIN LAW LIBRARY, 1215 Michigan St, 53201. (Mail add: PO Box 3137, 53201-3137), SAN 364-9687. Tel: 414-288-7092. Reference Tel: 414-288-3837. FAX: 414-288-5914. Web Site: law.marquette.edu/law-library. *Dir,* Elena Olson; E-mail: elana.olson@marquette.edu; *Assoc Law Librn,* Leslie Behroozi; E-mail: leslie.behroozi@marquette.edu; *Ref/Copyright Librn,* James A Mumm; E-mail: jim.mumm@marquette.edu; *Ref & Instrul Serv Librn,* Franky Newcomb; E-mail: franky.newcomb@marquette.edu; *Student Serv Librn,* Deborah Darin; E-mail: deborah.darin@marquette.edu; Staff 17 (MLS 8, Non-MLS 9)
Founded 1908
Library Holdings: Bk Titles 150,134; Bk Vols 308,104; Per Subs 3,231
Special Collections: US Document Depository
Partic in Mid-America Law Library Consortium
Publications: Monthly Acquisitions List; Weekly Contents Pages Service

CM MEDICAL COLLEGE OF WISCONSIN LIBRARIES*, Todd Wehr Library, Health Research Ctr, 3rd Flr, 8701 Watertown Plank Rd, 53226-0509. SAN 320-541X. Tel: 414-955-8302. Circulation Tel:

414-955-8300. Interlibrary Loan Service Tel: 414-955-8310. Administration Tel: 414-955-8323. FAX: 414-955-6532. E-mail: librarytw@mcw.libanswers.com. Web Site: mcw.edu/departments/libraries. *Dir,* Ellen Sayed; Tel: 414-955-4852; *Asst Dir, Scholarly Resource Mgmt,* Kathryn Mlsna; Tel: 414-955-8305, E-mail: kmlsna@mcw.edu; *Ref Librn,* Rita Sieracki; Tel: 414-955-8327, E-mail: rsierack@mcw.edu; *Syst Mgr,* Jeff Hagedorn; Tel: 414-955-8515, E-mail: jhagedor@mcw.edu; Staff 28 (MLS 14, Non-MLS 14)
Founded 1913. Enrl 1,200; Highest Degree: Doctorate
Library Holdings: e-books 6,010; e-journals 10,084; Bk Vols 252,533; Per Subs 10,108
Special Collections: Medical History (Horace Manchester Brown Coll)
Subject Interests: Clinical med, Nursing
Automation Activity & Vendor Info: (OPAC) Innovative Interfaces, Inc
Wireless access
Partic in National Network of Libraries of Medicine Region 6

Departmental Libraries:

CHILDREN'S HOSPITAL OF WISCONSIN LIBRARY, 9000 W Wisconsin Ave, 53226. (Mail add: PO Box 1997, 53226-1997). Tel: 414-266-2340. *Clinical Serv Librn,* Position Currently Open
Library Holdings: Per Subs 10,108
Subject Interests: Pediatrics

FROEDTERT HOSPITAL LIBRARY, Froedtert Specialty Clinics Bldg, 2nd Flr, 9200 W Wisconsin Ave, 53226. SAN 318-2142. Tel: 414-805-4311. *Clinical Serv Librn,* Carly Schanock; E-mail: cschanock@mcw.edu; Staff 1 (MLS 1)
Founded 1958
Library Holdings: Per Subs 10,108
Subject Interests: Clinical med, Consumer health, Hospital admin, Nursing
Partic in OCLC Online Computer Library Center, Inc
Open Mon-Fri 9-4

G METROPOLITAN MILWAUKEE FAIR HOUSING COUNCIL LIBRARY*, 600 E Mason St, Ste 401, 53202. SAN 324-1599. Tel: 414-278-1240. FAX: 414-278-8033. E-mail: mmfhc@aol.com. *Exec VPres,* Carla Wertheim
Founded 1977
Library Holdings: Bk Titles 2,500; Per Subs 32
Subject Interests: Civil rights, Fair housing, Landlord-tenant relations
Publications: Brochures in English & Spanish; Case Study Reports; Fair Housing Keys (Newsletter); Your Move, Your Choice (Milwaukee Neighborhoods)
Open Mon-Fri 8-4:30

L MICHAEL BEST & FRIEDRICH LLP*, Information Services Department, 790 N Water St, Ste 2500, 53202. SAN 318-2088. Tel: 414-271-6560. FAX: 414-277-0656. *Dir, Info Serv,* Candace Hall Slaminski; Tel: 414-277-3441, E-mail: chslaminski@michaelbest.com; Staff 3 (MLS 3)
Founded 1848
Library Holdings: Bk Vols 25,000
Subject Interests: Antitrust law, Copyright law, Corporate law, Labor law, Patent law, Taxation law, Trademark law, Wis law
Automation Activity & Vendor Info: (Acquisitions) Inmagic, Inc.; (Cataloging) Inmagic, Inc.; (OPAC) Inmagic, Inc.; (Serials) Inmagic, Inc.
Wireless access
Restriction: Co libr

M MILWAUKEE ACADEMY OF MEDICINE LIBRARY*, 8701 Watertown Plank Rd, 53226. SAN 327-408X. Tel: 414-456-8249. FAX: 414-456-6537. Web Site: www.milwaukeeacademyofmedicine.org. *Exec Dir,* Angie LaLuzerne; E-mail: angie@milwaukeeacademyofmedicine.org
Library Holdings: Bk Vols 1,500
Restriction: Open by appt only

J MILWAUKEE AREA TECHNICAL COLLEGE*, Downtown Milwaukee Campus Library, 700 W State St, 53233-1443. SAN 364-9717. Tel: 414-297-7030. Web Site: www.matc.edu. *Libr Mgr,* Position Currently Open; *Interim Libr Mgr,* Diane Kercheck; E-mail: kerchecd@matc.edu; Staff 12 (MLS 12)
Founded 1935. Enrl 70,000; Fac 811
Library Holdings: Bk Titles 52,000; Bk Vols 70,000; Per Subs 380
Automation Activity & Vendor Info: (Acquisitions) Innovative Interfaces, Inc - Millennium; (Cataloging) Innovative Interfaces, Inc - Millennium; (Circulation) Innovative Interfaces, Inc - Millennium; (Course Reserve) Innovative Interfaces, Inc - Millennium; (OPAC) Innovative Interfaces, Inc - Millennium; (Serials) Innovative Interfaces, Inc - Millennium
Wireless access
Open Mon-Thurs 7:30am-9pm, Fri 7:30-4, Sat 10-2

S MILWAUKEE ART MUSEUM RESEARCH CENTER*, George Peckham Miller Art Research Library, 1201 N Prospect Ave, 53202. (Mail add: Milwaukee Art Museum-Research Ctr, 700 N Art Museum Dr, 53202), SAN 318-2096. Tel: 414-224-3270. FAX: 414-224-3270. E-mail: library@mam.org. Web Site: mam.org/collection/library.php. *Archivist/Librn,* Anthony Morgano; E-mail: anthony.morgano@mam.org; *Mgr, Digital Assets,* Beret Balestrieri Kohn; Tel: 414-224-3829, E-mail: beret.balestrierikohn@mam.org; Staff 2 (MLS 1, Non-MLS 1)
Founded 1916
Library Holdings: Bk Vols 28,000; Per Subs 115
Subject Interests: Archit
Wireless access
Restriction: Open by appt only

P MILWAUKEE COUNTY FEDERATED LIBRARY SYSTEM*, 709 N Eighth St, 53233-2414. SAN 318-2118. Tel: 414-286-3210. FAX: 414-286-3209. Web Site: www.mcfls.org. *Dir,* Steve Heser; E-mail: steve.heser@mcfls.org; Staff 3 (MLS 2, Non-MLS 1)
Founded 1973. Pop 948,201
Library Holdings: Bk Vols 3,300,404
Automation Activity & Vendor Info: (Acquisitions) Innovative Interfaces, Inc; (Circulation) Innovative Interfaces, Inc; (OPAC) Innovative Interfaces, Inc; (Serials) Innovative Interfaces, Inc
Wireless access
Member Libraries: Brown Deer Public Library; Cudahy Family Library; Franklin Public Library; Greendale Public Library; Greenfield Public Library; Hales Corners Library; Milwaukee Public Library; North Shore Library; Oak Creek Public Library; Shorewood Public Library; South Milwaukee Public Library; St Francis Public Library; Wauwatosa Public Library; West Allis Public Library; Whitefish Bay Public Library
Partic in Wis Libr Consortium; Wisconsin Public Library Consortium
Open Mon-Fri 8-5

S MILWAUKEE COUNTY HISTORICAL SOCIETY*, Harry H Anderson Research Library, 910 N Old World Third St, 53203. SAN 318-2126. Tel: 414-273-7487, 414-273-8288. FAX: 414-273-3268. E-mail: library@milwaukeehistory.net. Web Site: milwaukeehistory.net/research/research-library. *Archivist,* Kevin Abing; E-mail: kabing@milwaukeehistory.net; *Asst Archivist,* Steve Schaffer; E-mail: sschaffer@milwaukeehistory.net; Staff 2 (MLS 2)
Founded 1935
Library Holdings: Bk Vols 12,000
Subject Interests: Ethnic hist, Milwaukee, Socialism, Wis
Open Mon-Sat 9:30-5
Restriction: Non-circulating

C MILWAUKEE INSTITUTE OF ART & DESIGN LIBRARY & LEARNING COMMONS*, 273 E Erie St, 53202-6003. SAN 318-2215. Tel: 414-847-3342. FAX: 414-291-8077. E-mail: library@miad.edu. Web Site: www.miad.edu/college-services/academic-services/library-learning-commons. *Dir, Libr Serv,* Nancy Siker; E-mail: nancysiker@miad.edu; *Circ Coordr,* Hannah Schmidt; E-mail: hannahschmidt@miad.edu; Staff 3 (MLS 1, Non-MLS 2)
Founded 1977. Enrl 925; Highest Degree: Bachelor
Library Holdings: AV Mats 1,000; Bk Titles 23,000; Per Subs 82
Subject Interests: Advertising, Aesthetics, Art hist, Artists' monographs, Decorative art, Graphic design, Interior design, Painting, Photog, Sculpture, Typography
Automation Activity & Vendor Info: (Cataloging) OCLC Connexion; (Circulation) ByWater Solutions; (Course Reserve) ByWater Solutions; (OPAC) ByWater Solutions; (Serials) ByWater Solutions
Wireless access
Partic in Southeastern Wisconsin Information Technology Exchange, Inc
Open Mon-Thurs 8am-9pm, Fri 8-5, Sun 1-5 (Fall & Spring); Mon-Thurs 9-4, Fri 10-1 (Summer)

P MILWAUKEE PUBLIC LIBRARY*, 814 W Wisconsin Ave, 53233-2309. SAN 364-9741. Tel: 414-286-3000. Reference Tel: 414-286-3011. FAX: 414-286-2794. Web Site: www.mpl.org. *Libr Dir,* Joan Johnson; E-mail: jrjohns@milwaukee.gov; *Asst Libr Dir, Info Tech,* Judith Pinger; E-mail: JEPing@milwaukee.gov; *Asst Dir, Operations,* Jennifer Meyer-Stearns; E-mail: jrmeyer@milwaukee.gov; *Mgr, Br, Pub Serv Mgr,* Anne Rasmussen; E-mail: AFRasmu@milwaukee.gov; *Youth Serv Coordr,* Kelly Wochinske; E-mail: KLWochi@milwaukee.gov; Staff 90 (MLS 90)
Founded 1878. Pop 595,598; Circ 2,944,880
Library Holdings: AV Mats 247,358; Bk Vols 2,556,562; Per Subs 8,519
Special Collections: Alexander Mitchell Coll; American Maps; Art & Motion Picture Posters; Charles King Coll; City Archives, bk & pamphlet; Cookery (Breta Greim Coll); Current Trade Books for Children (Historical Reference Coll 1976 to date); Early American Imprints, microfiche; Eastman Fairy Tale Coll; Great Lakes Ships & Shipping (Runge Marine Memorial), pamphlets & photog bk; H G Wells Coll; Historical Popular Children's Literature Coll (1850-1940); Historical Recordings; Literature (Definitive Editions of British & American Writers); Milwaukee Artists; Milwaukee Road Railroad Archives; Rare Bird Prints (Audubon Folio Prints), pictures; Significant Publishers Series; United States, British & Canadian Patents; Wisconsin Architectural Archives. State Document Depository; US Document Depository

Subject Interests: Railroad hist
Wireless access
Publications: Milwaukee Reader; Miscellaneous Booklists & Brochures; Staff News (Staff newsletter); Weekly Accessions List
Mem of Milwaukee County Federated Library System
Partic in HQ-WIS Reg Libr for Blind & Physically Handicapped; OCLC Online Computer Library Center, Inc
Special Services for the Deaf - Staff with knowledge of sign lang; TTY equip
Open Mon Noon-8, Tues 9-8, Wed-Fri 9-6, Sat 9-5, Sun (Oct-April) 1-5
Friends of the Library Group
Branches: 12
ATKINSON, 1960 W Atkinson Ave, 53209, SAN 364-9806. Web Site: www.mpl.org/hours_locations/atkinson.php. *Br Mgr,* Mary Lopez; Staff 6 (MLS 4, Non-MLS 2)
Library Holdings: Bk Vols 73,078
Function: Adult bk club, Art exhibits, Audiobks via web, Bks on cassette, Bks on CD, CD-ROM, Children's prog, Computer training, Computers for patron use, E-Reserves, Electronic databases & coll, Free DVD rentals, Holiday prog, Homework prog, ILL available, Large print keyboards, Magnifiers for reading, Music CDs, Online cat, Online ref, OverDrive digital audio bks, Photocopying/Printing, Preschool outreach, Prog for adults, Prog for children & young adult, Ref & res, Spoken cassettes & CDs, Spoken cassettes & DVDs, Summer reading prog, Tax forms, Teen prog, VHS videos, Wheelchair accessible
Open Mon-Wed 12-8, Thurs & Fri 10-6, Sat 10-5
Friends of the Library Group
BAY VIEW, 2566 S Kinnickinnic Ave, 53207, SAN 373-9244. Web Site: www.mpl.org/hours_locations/bay_view.php. *Br Mgr,* Jennifer Fait
Library Holdings: Bk Vols 76,932
Open Mon 10-8, Tues & Wed 12-8, Thurs & Fri 10-6, Sat 10-5
Friends of the Library Group
CAPITOL, 3969 N 74th St, 53216, SAN 364-9830. Web Site: www.mpl.org/hours_locations/capitol.php. *Br Mgr,* Christine Schabel
Library Holdings: Bk Vols 115,705
Open Mon-Wed Noon-8, Thurs & Fri 10-6, Sat 10-5, Sun (Oct-April) 1-5
Friends of the Library Group
CENTER STREET, 2727 W Fond du Lac Ave, 53210, SAN 364-9865. Web Site: www.mpl.org/hours_locations/center_street.php. *Br Mgr,* Tammy Mays
Library Holdings: Bk Vols 72,926
Open Mon 10-8, Tues & Wed 12-8, Thurs & Fri 10-6, Sat 10-5
Friends of the Library Group
EAST, 2320 N Cramer St, 53211, SAN 364-989X. Web Site: www.mpl.org/hours_locations/east.php. *Br Mgr,* Enid Gruszka
Library Holdings: Bk Vols 100,409
Open Mon 10-8, Tues & Wed 12-8, Thurs & Fri 10-6, Sat 10-5
Friends of the Library Group
MARTIN LUTHER KING BRANCH, 310 W Locust St, 53212, SAN 365-0014. Web Site: www.mpl.org/hours_locations/mlking.php. *Br Mgr,* Brett Rohlwing; Staff 8 (MLS 4, Non-MLS 4)
Library Holdings: Bk Vols 92,833
Open Mon-Wed 12-8, Thurs & Fri 10-6, Sat 10-5
Friends of the Library Group
MILL ROAD, 6431 N 76th St, 53223, SAN 365-0049. Web Site: www.mpl.org/hours_locations/mill_road.php. *Br Mgr,* Amelia Osterud
Library Holdings: Bk Vols 89,644
Open Mon-Wed 12-8, Thurs & Fri 10-6, Sat 10-5
Friends of the Library Group
MITCHELL STREET, 906 W Historic Mitchell St, 53204. Web Site: www.mpl.org/hours_locations/mitchell.php. *Br Mgr,* Anthony Frausto
Open Mon-Wed 12-8, Thurs & Fri 10-6, Sat 10-5
Friends of the Library Group
TIPPECANOE, 3912 S Howell Ave, 53207, SAN 365-0138. Web Site: www.mpl.org/hours_locations/tippecanoe.php. *Br Mgr,* David Sikora
Library Holdings: Bk Vols 93,326
Open Mon-Wed 12-8, Thurs & Fri 10-6, Sat 10-5
Friends of the Library Group
VILLARD SQUARE, 5190 N 35th St, 53209, SAN 365-0073. Web Site: www.mpl.org/hours_locations/villard_square.php. *Br Mgr,* Deborah Stewart
Library Holdings: Bk Vols 77,337
Open Mon 10-8, Tues & Wed 12-8, Thurs & Fri 10-6, Sat 10-5
Friends of the Library Group
WASHINGTON PARK, 2121 N Sherman Blvd, 53208, SAN 364-992X. Web Site: www.mpl.org/hours_locations/washington_park.php. *Br Mgr,* JeTaun Colbert
Library Holdings: Bk Vols 61,151
Open Mon 10-8, Tues & Wed 12-8, Thurs & Fri 10-6, Sat 10-5
Friends of the Library Group
ZABLOCKI, 3501 W Oklahoma Ave, 53215, SAN 365-0103. Web Site: www.mpl.org/hours_locations/zablocki.php. *Br Mgr,* David Sikora
Library Holdings: Bk Vols 78,072
Open Mon 10-8, Tues & Wed Noon-8, Thurs & Fri 10-6, Sat 10-5, Sun (Oct-April) 1-5
Friends of the Library Group

S MILWAUKEE PUBLIC MUSEUM*, Library & Archives, 800 W Wells St, 53233. SAN 318-2193. Tel: 414-278-2728. FAX: 414-278-6100. Web Site: www.mpm.edu/research-collections/collection-support/library. *Dean, Acad Support, VPres,* Dr Jennifer Zaspel; E-mail: zaspelj@mpm.edu; *Librn,* Ruth King; E-mail: ruth@mpm.edu; Staff 0.6 (MLS 0.5, Non-MLS 0.1)
Founded 1883
Library Holdings: Bk Titles 50,000; Bk Vols 200,000
Special Collections: Milwaukee Public Museum Archives
Subject Interests: Anthrop, Archaeology, Botany, Decorative art, Ecology, Geol, Museology, Paleontology, Zoology
Wireless access
Restriction: Open by appt only

C MILWAUKEE SCHOOL OF ENGINEERING, Walter Schroeder Library, 500 E Kilbourn Ave, 53202. SAN 318-2207. Tel: 414-277-7180. E-mail: library@msoe.edu. Web Site: msoe.edu/academics/how-we-teach/library. *Libr Dir,* Elizabeth Jerow; *Cat & Metadata, ILL Librn,* Molly Ostendorf; Staff 6 (MLS 4, Non-MLS 2)
Founded 1903. Enrl 2,956; Fac 188; Highest Degree: Master
Library Holdings: AV Mats 1,518; e-books 25,000; e-journals 70,000; Bk Titles 49,527; Per Subs 389
Subject Interests: Archit engr, Biomed engr, Computer engr, Electrical engr, Fluid power, Indust mgt, Mechanical engr, Nursing
Automation Activity & Vendor Info: (Acquisitions) SirsiDynix; (Cataloging) SirsiDynix; (Circulation) SirsiDynix; (Course Reserve) SirsiDynix; (ILL) Clio; (OPAC) SirsiDynix; (Serials) SirsiDynix
Wireless access
Function: ILL available
Partic in OCLC Online Computer Library Center, Inc; WiLS
Open Mon-Thurs 7:30am-Midnight, Fri 7:30-6, Sat 10-6, Sun 1-Midnight
Restriction: Circ limited, In-house use for visitors, Non-circulating to the pub

GL MMSD LAW LIBRARY*, 260 W Seeboth St, 53204. Tel: 414-225-2098. FAX: 414-225-0167. Web Site: www.mmsd.com. *Paralegal Adminr/Law Librn,* Kimberly Bacik; E-mail: kbacik@mmsd.com; Staff 1 (MLS 1)
Founded 1977
Library Holdings: Bk Vols 10,000
Function: Electronic databases & coll, Govt ref serv
Restriction: Govt use only

R MOUNT CARMEL LUTHERAN CHURCH LIBRARY*, 8424 W Center St, 53222. SAN 318-2231. Tel: 414-771-1270. E-mail: office@mountcarmelchurch.org. Web Site: mountcarmelchurch.org.
Founded 1947
Library Holdings: Bk Vols 4,500; Per Subs 10
Special Collections: Bibles; Norwegian Heritage
Subject Interests: Relig
Wireless access
Open Mon-Fri 9-3, Sun 9am-10am

CR MOUNT MARY UNIVERSITY*, Patrick & Beatrice Haggerty Library, 2900 N Menomonee River Pkwy, 53222-4597. SAN 318-224X. Reference Tel: 414-930-3056. Administration Tel: 414-930-3000. E-mail: mmu-library@mtmary.edu. Web Site: mtmary.libguides.com. *Libr Dir,* Daniel Vinson; E-mail: vinsond@mtmary.edu; Staff 6 (MLS 5, Non-MLS 1)
Founded 1913. Enrl 1,218; Fac 110; Highest Degree: Doctorate
Library Holdings: CDs 200; DVDs 700; e-books 170,000; e-journals 210,000; Bk Titles 69,118; Per Subs 68
Subject Interests: Art, Art therapy, Communication, Dietetics, Educ, Fashion design, Fashion merchandising, Graphic novels, Mental health, Occupational therapy, Soc work, Women
Automation Activity & Vendor Info: (Acquisitions) Ex Libris Group; (Cataloging) Ex Libris Group; (Circulation) Ex Libris Group; (Course Reserve) Ex Libris Group; (Discovery) Ex Libris Group; (ILL) OCLC WorldShare Interlibrary Loan; (OPAC) Ex Libris Group; (Serials) Ex Libris Group
Wireless access
Partic in OCLC Online Computer Library Center, Inc; Southeastern Wisconsin Information Technology Exchange, Inc
Open Mon-Thurs 7:45am-11pm, Fri 7:45-5, Sat Noon-4, Sun 2-9

G MUNICIPAL RESEARCH LIBRARY*, Zeidler Municipal Bldg, Rm B-2, 841 N Broadway, 53202-3567. SAN 318-2177. Tel: 414-286-2297. FAX: 414-286-3004. Web Site: city.milwaukee.gov/cityclerk/library. *Libr Mgr,* Eileen Lipinski; Tel: 414-286-8818, E-mail: elipin@milwaukee.gov; *Librn,* Kathleen Williams; Tel: 414-286-2299, E-mail: kwilli@milwaukee.gov; Staff 4 (MLS 2, Non-MLS 2)
Founded 1908
Library Holdings: Bk Vols 10,500; Per Subs 30

Special Collections: Census Reports; City of Milwaukee, docs; Milwaukee Code of Ordinances. Municipal Document Depository
Subject Interests: Milwaukee, Municipal govt, Urban affairs
Automation Activity & Vendor Info: (Acquisitions) EOS International; (Cataloging) EOS International; (OPAC) EOS International; (Serials) EOS International
Wireless access
Function: Govt ref serv, ILL available, Photocopying/Printing, Res libr, Telephone ref
Open Mon-Fri 8-4:45
Restriction: Circ limited, Closed stack, Lending to staff only, Pub use on premises

S PLANNED PARENTHOOD OF WISCONSIN, INC, Maurice Ritz Resource Center, 302 N Jackson St, 53202. SAN 318-2355. Administration Tel: 414-271-8045. FAX: 414-271-3975. Web Site: www.plannedparenthood.org/planned-parenthood-wisconsin. *Training & Resource Spec,* Anne Brosowsky-Roth; Staff 1 (Non-MLS 1)
Founded 1972
Library Holdings: AV Mats 50; Bks on Deafness & Sign Lang 1; Braille Volumes 1; Bk Titles 3,000; Spec Interest Per Sub 20
Subject Interests: Family planning, Human sexuality, Reproductive health, Sex educ
Automation Activity & Vendor Info: (Cataloging) TinyCat; (OPAC) TinyCat
Function: ILL available, Photocopying/Printing, Prof lending libr, Ref serv available, Res libr, Telephone ref
Publications: Audiovisual Bibliography; Check It Out (Acquisition list); Health News Alert (Newsletter); Literature Bibliography; The Educator's Report (Newsletter)
Partic in Association of Population/Family Planning Libraries & Information Centers-International
Restriction: Open by appt only

G PUBLIC POLICY FORUM*, Researching Community Issues, 633 W Wisconsin Ave, Ste 406, 53203. SAN 326-0445. Tel: 414-276-8240. FAX: 414-276-8240. E-mail: info@publicpolicyforum.org. Web Site: www.publicpolicyforum.org. *Pres,* Ron Henken; E-mail: rhenken@publicpolicyforum.org; Staff 2 (MLS 2)
Founded 1913
Library Holdings: Bk Titles 3,000; Per Subs 100
Publications: Bulletin (Monthly); Special Reports
Restriction: Open by appt only
Friends of the Library Group

L QUARLES & BRADY*, Law Library, 411 E Wisconsin Ave, Ste 2400, 53202-4491. SAN 318-2371. Tel: 414-277-5000. FAX: 414-271-3552. Web Site: www.quarles.com. *Mgr, Libr & Res Serv,* Lynn Dilts-Hill; Staff 7 (MLS 7)
Founded 1910
Library Holdings: Bk Vols 12,700
Subject Interests: Banking, Bankruptcy, Bus law, Dispute resolution, Employee benefits, Employment, Energy, Environ law, Estates, Franchises, Health law, Immigration, Intellectual property law, Labor, Litigation, Product liability, Real estate, Sch law, Securities, Taxation, Trademarks, Trusts, Unfair competition
Automation Activity & Vendor Info: (Cataloging) Softlink America; (Circulation) Softlink America; (OPAC) Softlink America; (Serials) Softlink America
Wireless access
Open Mon-Fri 8-5

L REINHART BOERNER VAN DEUREN SC, Information Resource Center, 1000 N Water St, Ste 1700, 53202. SAN 324-0177. FAX: 414-298-8097. Web Site: www.reinhartlaw.com. *Info Res Mgr,* Carol J Schmitt; Tel: 608-229-2232, E-mail: cschmitt@reinhartlaw.com
Founded 1975
Library Holdings: Bk Titles 6,000; Bk Vols 20,000; Per Subs 460
Subject Interests: Employee benefits
Automation Activity & Vendor Info: (Acquisitions) EOS International; (Cataloging) EOS International; (Circulation) EOS International; (OPAC) EOS International; (Serials) EOS International

GL UNITED STATES COURTS LIBRARY*, 517 E Wisconsin Ave, Rm 516, 53202. SAN 372-364X. Tel: 414-297-1698. FAX: 414-297-1695. Web Site: www.lb7.uscourts.gov/MilwaukeeHome.html. *Librn,* Barbara Fritschel; E-mail: barbara_fritschel@ca7.uscourts.gov; *Libr Tech,* Lucien Jung
Library Holdings: Bk Vols 20,000
Open Mon-Fri 8:30-5

C UNIVERSITY OF WISCONSIN-MILWAUKEE LIBRARIES*, Golda Meir Library, 2311 E Hartford Ave, 53211. (Mail add: PO Box 604, 53201-0604), SAN 365-0227. Tel: 414-229-4785, 414-229-6202. Circulation Tel: 414-229-4132. Interlibrary Loan Service Tel: 414-229-4493. Reference Tel: 414-229-4659. FAX: 414-229-6766. TDD: 800-947-3529. Web Site: uwm.edu/libraries. *Assoc Vice-Provost, Dir of Libr,* Michael Doylen; E-mail: doylenm@uwm.edu; Staff 74 (MLS 40, Non-MLS 34)
Founded 1956. Enrl 24,722; Fac 1,593; Highest Degree: Doctorate
Library Holdings: Bk Titles 1,670,813; Bk Vols 2,213,354; Per Subs 57,270
Special Collections: 17th Century Literature Coll; Area Research Center of the State Historical Society of Wisconsin, bks, ms; Blatz Brewing Company Records; Camus Bibliography Research Coll; Franklin Delano Roosevelt (Jagodzinski Coll); George Hardie Aerospace Coll; Institutional History (University of Wisconsin-Milwaukee Archives), ms; Layton School of Art Library Coll; Little Review Papers, ms; Milwaukee Press Club Records; Social Justice (Fromkin Memorial Coll); Wisconsin Legislation Reference Bureau Clippings File, micro. State Document Depository; US Document Depository
Subject Interests: Archit, Art, Behav sci, Cartography, Econ, Educ, Engr, Geog, Geol sci, Hist, Soc sci, Urban studies
Wireless access
Function: Online Chat
Publications: Annual Report
Partic in National Network of Libraries of Medicine Region 6; OCLC Online Computer Library Center, Inc; Proquest Dialog; SDC Info Servs; WiLS
Special Services for the Deaf - TDD equip
Special Services for the Blind - Assistive/Adapted tech devices, equip & products; Braille bks; Braille Webster's dictionary; Reader equip; ZoomText magnification & reading software

Departmental Libraries:

AMERICAN GEOGRAPHICAL SOCIETY LIBRARY, Golda Meir Library, 2311 E Hartford Ave, 53211. (Mail add: PO Box 399, 53201-0399), SAN 365-0251. Tel: 414-229-3984, 414-229-6282. Toll Free Tel: 800-558-8993. FAX: 414-229-3624. E-mail: agsl@uwm.edu, gisdata@uwn.edu. Web Site: uwm.edu/libraries/agsl. *Curator, Library Assoc Dir for Distinctive Collections,* Marcy Bidney; E-mail: bidney@uwm.edu; *Geospatial Information Librarian,* Stephen Appel; E-mail: srappell@uwm.edu; *Pub Serv Librn,* Georgia Brown; E-mail: browngl@uwm.edu; *Libr Asst,* Olivia Hickner; E-mail: ohickner@uwm.edu; *Cat,* Angie Cope; E-mail: acope@uwm.edu. Subject Specialists: *Cartography,* Angie Cope; Staff 6 (MLS 6)
Founded 1851
Subject Interests: Cartography, Exploration, Geog
Function: Res libr
Publications: AGS Library Special Publications; Current Geographical Publications: Contents (Online only); Online Geographical Bibliography (GEOBIB)
Open Mon-Fri 9-4

C WISCONSIN LUTHERAN COLLEGE LIBRARY, Marvin M Schwan Library, 8800 W Bluemound Rd, 53226. SAN 324-7236. Tel: 414-443-8864. FAX: 414-443-8505. E-mail: library@wlc.edu. Web Site: www.wlc.edu/academics/library.html. *Dir, Libr Serv,* Jenny Baker; *Librn,* Michelle Rekowski; Staff 2 (MLS 2)
Founded 1978. Enrl 1,169; Fac 50; Highest Degree: Master
Subject Interests: Liberal arts, Lutheran theol
Automation Activity & Vendor Info: (Cataloging) OCLC Connexion; (Circulation) Ex Libris Group; (Course Reserve) Ex Libris Group; (ILL) OCLC WorldShare Interlibrary Loan; (OPAC) Ex Libris Group
Wireless access
Partic in OCLC Online Computer Library Center, Inc; Southeastern Wisconsin Information Technology Exchange, Inc

P WISCONSIN TALKING BOOK & BRAILLE LIBRARY*, 813 W Wells St, 53233-1436. SAN 318-2614. Tel: 414-286-3045. Toll Free Tel: 800-242-8822. FAX: 414-286-3102. E-mail: wtbbl@milwaukee.gov. Web Site: dpi.wi.gov/talkingbooks. *Libr Serv Mgr,* Zarina Mohd Shah; E-mail: zmohds@milwaukee.gov; *Outreach Librn,* Catherine (Katie) Saldutte; Tel: 414-286-6918, E-mail: cesaldu@milwaukee.gov; *Ref Librn,* Kimberly Tomlinson; E-mail: kstomli@milwaukee.gov; Staff 10 (MLS 3, Non-MLS 7)
Founded 1960
Library Holdings: Audiobooks 95,719; Braille Volumes 14,821; DVDs 890; Per Subs 70
Special Collections: Wisconsin Subjects & Authors, braille & digital cartridges
Automation Activity & Vendor Info: (Acquisitions) Keystone Systems, Inc (KLAS); (Cataloging) Keystone Systems, Inc (KLAS); (Circulation) Keystone Systems, Inc (KLAS); (Course Reserve) Keystone Systems, Inc (KLAS); (ILL) Keystone Systems, Inc (KLAS); (OPAC) Keystone Systems, Inc (KLAS); (Serials) Keystone Systems, Inc (KLAS)
Wireless access
Function: 24/7 Online cat, Adult bk club, Audiobks via web, Computers for patron use, Digital talking bks, Home delivery & serv to seniorr ctr & nursing homes, Homebound delivery serv, Large print keyboards,

Magnifiers for reading, Mail & tel request accepted, Mail loans to mem, Online cat, Outreach serv, OverDrive digital audio bks, Spoken cassettes & DVDs, Summer reading prog, Wheelchair accessible, Winter reading prog
Publications: Bulletin Board (Newsletter)
Special Services for the Blind - Accessible computers; Bks on flash-memory cartridges; Braille bks; Computer access aids; Digital talking bk; Digital talking bk machines; Free checkout of audio mat; Home delivery serv; Internet workstation with adaptive software; Newsletter (in large print, Braille or on cassette); Newsline for the Blind; Recorded bks; Screen reader software; Soundproof reading booth; Talking bks; Talking bks & player equip; Web-Braille; ZoomText magnification & reading software
Open Mon-Fri 9-5
Restriction: Restricted borrowing privileges

MINERAL POINT

P MINERAL POINT PUBLIC LIBRARY*, 137 High St, Ste 2, 53565. SAN 318-2622. Tel: 608-987-2447. FAX: 608 987-2447. Web Site: mineralpointpubliclibrary.wordpress.com. *Libr Dir,* Diane Palzkill; E-mail: mppldirector@swls.org; *Circ Librn,* Mary Baehler; *Circ Librn,* Kaelyn Martin; *Curator,* Shan Thomas; E-mail: mparchive@swls.org; *Asst Curator,* Joel Gosse; *Asst Librn, Youth Serv Coordr,* Kayla Beck. Subject Specialists: *Local hist,* Shan Thomas; Staff 6 (MLS 1, Non-MLS 5)
Founded 1895. Pop 2,617
Jan 2016-Dec 2016 Income $331,062, City $177,141, Federal $498, County $36,758, Other $116,665. Mats Exp $26,816, Books $17,779, Other Print Mats $1,371, AV Mat $7,020, Electronic Ref Mat (Incl. Access Fees) $646. Sal $84,308 (Prof $11,273)
Library Holdings: AV Mats 1,191; Bks on Deafness & Sign Lang 6; DVDs 2,614; e-books 148,791; Electronic Media & Resources 39,137; Large Print Bks 340; Microforms 232; Bk Titles 18,339; Per Subs 48
Special Collections: Mineral Point Library Archives
Subject Interests: Local hist
Automation Activity & Vendor Info: (Cataloging) Auto-Graphics, Inc; (Circulation) Auto-Graphics, Inc; (ILL) Auto-Graphics, Inc; (OPAC) Auto-Graphics, Inc
Wireless access
Function: 24/7 Electronic res, 24/7 Online cat, 3D Printer, Activity rm, Archival coll, Audio & video playback equip for onsite use, Audiobks on Playaways & MP3, Audiobks via web, Bks on CD, Children's prog, Computer training, Computers for patron use, Digital talking bks, E-Readers, Electronic databases & coll, Equip loans & repairs, Free DVD rentals, Homebound delivery serv, ILL available, Internet access, Magazines, Magnifiers for reading, Mail & tel request accepted, Mango lang, Meeting rooms, Microfiche/film & reading machines, Movies, Music CDs, Online cat, Online info literacy tutorials on the web & in blackboard, OverDrive digital audio bks, Photocopying/Printing, Preschool outreach, Preschool reading prog, Prog for adults, Prog for children & young adult, Ref & res, Ref serv available, Scanner, Senior computer classes, Spanish lang bks, Story hour, Study rm, Summer reading prog, Tax forms, Telephone ref, Wheelchair accessible
Mem of Southwest Wisconsin Library System
Open Mon-Wed & Fri 10-5:30, Thurs 10-8, Sat 10-4

MINOCQUA

P MINOCQUA PUBLIC LIBRARY*, 415 Menominee St, 54548. SAN 318-2630. Tel: 715-356-4437. FAX: 715-358-2873. E-mail: public.library@minocqualibrary.org. Web Site: www.minocqualibrary.org. *Dir,* Peggy O'Connell; E-mail: director@minocqualibrary.org; *Adult Serv Coordr,* Cindy Wendt; E-mail: chultman@minocqualibrary.org
Founded 1933
Library Holdings: Bk Vols 35,000; Per Subs 150
Automation Activity & Vendor Info: (Cataloging) Innovative Interfaces, Inc; (Circulation) Innovative Interfaces, Inc; (OPAC) Innovative Interfaces, Inc
Wireless access
Partic in Wisconsin Valley Library Service
Open Mon-Thurs 10-6
Friends of the Library Group

MONDOVI

P MONDOVI PUBLIC LIBRARY*, 146 W Hudson St, 54755. SAN 318-2649. Tel: 715-926-4403. E-mail: mondovipl@wrlsweb.org. Web Site: www.wrlsweb.org/mondovi. *Dir,* Katelyn Noack; Staff 5 (Non-MLS 5)
Founded 1902. Pop 5,000; Circ 36,000
Library Holdings: AV Mats 825; CDs 172; Large Print Bks 423; Bk Vols 22,825; Per Subs 55; Talking Bks 317; Videos 507
Automation Activity & Vendor Info: (Cataloging) Follett Software; (Circulation) Follett Software; (OPAC) Follett Software
Mem of Winding Rivers Library System
Open Mon & Wed 9-6, Tues & Thurs 2-8, Fri 1-3, Sat 9-12
Friends of the Library Group

MONONA

P MONONA PUBLIC LIBRARY*, 1000 Nichols Rd, 53716. SAN 318-2657. Tel: 608-222-6127. E-mail: ask@mononalibrary.org. Web Site: mymonona.com/131/library. *Libr Dir,* Ryan Claringbole; Tel: 608-216-7458, E-mail: ryan@mononalibrary.org; *Info Serv Coordr,* Toni Streckert; Tel: 608-216-7457, E-mail: tonis@mononalibrary.org; *Youth Serv Coordr,* Karen Wendt; Tel: 608-216-7453, E-mail: karen@mononalibrary.org
Founded 1964. Pop 11,000; Circ 280,100
Library Holdings: Bk Vols 60,672; Per Subs 80
Special Collections: Living History of Historic Blooming Grove. Oral History
Automation Activity & Vendor Info: (Acquisitions) SirsiDynix; (Cataloging) SirsiDynix; (Circulation) SirsiDynix
Wireless access
Mem of South Central Library System
Open Mon-Wed 9-8, Thurs & Fri 9-6, Sat 9-5, Sun 1-5
Friends of the Library Group

MONROE

M MONROE CLINIC*, Medical Library, 515 22nd Ave, 53566. SAN 322-7634. Tel: 608-324-1090. E-mail: library@monroeclinic.org. *Library Contact,* Rhonda Urban; E-mail: rhonda.urban@monroeclinic.org
Founded 1973
Library Holdings: Bk Titles 700; Per Subs 100
Subject Interests: Med, Nursing
Wireless access
Restriction: Non-circulating to the pub

P MONROE PUBLIC LIBRARY*, 925 16th Ave, 53566-1497. SAN 318-2665. Tel: 608-328-7010. FAX: 608-329-4657. E-mail: staff@monroepubliclibrary.org. Web Site: www.monroepubliclibrary.org. *Dir,* Suzann Holland; E-mail: sholland@monroepubliclibrary.org; *Adult Serv,* Laura Schmiedicke; E-mail: aschmiedicke@monroepubliclibrary.org; Staff 1 (MLS 1)
Founded 1904. Pop 18,446; Circ 221,732
Library Holdings: Bk Vols 67,430; Per Subs 90
Subject Interests: Green County, Wis hist
Automation Activity & Vendor Info: (Circulation) SirsiDynix
Wireless access
Mem of South Central Library System
Open Mon-Thurs 9-9, Fri 12-6, Sat 9-4
Friends of the Library Group

MONTELLO

P MONTELLO PUBLIC LIBRARY*, 128 Lake Ct, 53949-9204. (Mail add: PO Box 457, 53949-0457), SAN 325-2892. Tel: 608-297-7544. Web Site: www.montellolibrary.org. *Dir,* Andrea Klapper; E-mail: director@montellolibrary.org; Staff 1 (MLS 1)
Founded 1936. Pop 1,500; Circ 24,591
Library Holdings: Bk Titles 12,000; Per Subs 40
Special Collections: John Muir Coll, bks & magazines
Automation Activity & Vendor Info: (Cataloging) SirsiDynix; (Circulation) SirsiDynix
Wireless access
Mem of Winnefox Library System
Open Mon-Thurs 10-6, Fri 9-5, Sat 9-1
Friends of the Library Group

MONTFORT

P MONTFORT PUBLIC LIBRARY*, 102 E Park St, 53569. SAN 318-2673. Tel: 608-943-6265. FAX: 608-943-6917. E-mail: montfortlibrary@swls.org. Web Site: villageofmontfort.com/community-3/public-library. *Librn,* Marcie Harwick; *Asst Librn,* Jessica Hrubes; *Asst Librn,* Alyssa Trevorrow
Founded 1885. Pop 663; Circ 429,000
Library Holdings: AV Mats 210; Large Print Bks 85; Bk Vols 6,049; Talking Bks 125
Wireless access
Mem of Southwest Wisconsin Library System
Open Mon & Tues Noon-6, Wed & Thurs 9-3, Sat 9-Noon

MONTICELLO

P MONTICELLO PUBLIC LIBRARY*, 512 E Lake Ave, 53570-9658. SAN 377-998X. Tel: 608-938-4011. E-mail: mntpublib.info@gmail.com. Web Site: www.monticellopubliclibrary.org. *Libr Dir,* Katrina Linde-Moriarty; E-mail: mntpublib.director@gmail.com
Library Holdings: Bk Titles 14,000; Per Subs 50
Automation Activity & Vendor Info: (Acquisitions) Baker & Taylor; (Cataloging) Koha; (Circulation) Koha; (ILL) OCLC FirstSearch
Wireless access

Mem of South Central Library System
Open Mon-Fri 10-7, Sat 10-2

MOUNT HOREB

P MOUNT HOREB PUBLIC LIBRARY*, 105 Perimeter Rd, 53572. SAN 318-2711. Tel: 608-437-5021. FAX: 608-437-6264. E-mail: mhpl@mounthorebwi.info. Web Site: mhpl.org. *Dir,* Jessica Williams; Tel: 608-437-9378, E-mail: jessica.williams@mounthorebwi.info; *Circ Supvr,* Emily Noffke; Tel: 608-437-9372, E-mail: emily.noffke@mounthorebwi.info; Staff 18 (MLS 4, Non-MLS 14)
Founded 1877. Pop 7,000; Circ 166,125
Library Holdings: AV Mats 1,993; Bk Vols 32,753; Per Subs 166; Talking Bks 1,552
Special Collections: Girl & Boy Scout Coll; Mount Horeb Mail Newspaper, July 17, 1883-1992
Wireless access
Function: Homebound delivery serv, ILL available, Magnifiers for reading, Photocopying/Printing, Prog for children & young adult, Ref serv available, Summer reading prog, Telephone ref, Wheelchair accessible
Mem of South Central Library System
Partic in Library Interchange Network
Special Services for the Blind - Bks on CD; Digital talking bk; Home delivery serv; Low vision equip; Magnifiers
Open Mon-Thurs 9-8, Fri 9-5:30, Sat 9-5
Friends of the Library Group

MUKWONAGO

P MUKWONAGO COMMUNITY LIBRARY*, 511 Division St, 53149-1204. SAN 318-272X. Tel: 262-363-6411. Toll Free FAX: 866-489-5499. Reference E-mail: mukref@gmail.com. Web Site: www.mukwonagolibrary.org. *Dir,* Angela Zimmermann; Tel: 262-363-6411, Ext 4100, E-mail: azimmermann@mukcom.lib.wi.us; *Libr Office Mgr,* Laura Frisch; Tel: 262-363-6441, Ext 4106, E-mail: lfrisch@mukcom.lib.wi.us
Library Holdings: Bk Vols 69,000; Per Subs 152
Subject Interests: Hist
Automation Activity & Vendor Info: (Cataloging) SirsiDynix; (Circulation) SirsiDynix; (OPAC) SirsiDynix
Wireless access
Mem of Bridges Library System
Open Mon-Thurs 9-8:30, Fri 9-5, Sat 9-4; Mon-Thurs 9-8:30, Fri 9-5, Sat 9-2 (Summer)
Friends of the Library Group

MUSCODA

P MUSCODA PUBLIC LIBRARY*, 400 N Wisconsin Ave, 53573. SAN 318-2738. Tel: 608-739-3510. Web Site: www.muscodapubliclibrary.wordpress.com. *Dir,* Lorna Aigner; *Asst Librn,* Lynn Meister; E-mail: lmeister@swls.org
Founded 1926. Pop 1,453; Circ 15,915
Library Holdings: Bk Titles 8,000; Bk Vols 10,541; Per Subs 25
Subject Interests: Local hist
Automation Activity & Vendor Info: (Cataloging) Auto-Graphics, Inc; (Circulation) Auto-Graphics, Inc; (OPAC) Auto-Graphics, Inc
Wireless access
Mem of Southwest Wisconsin Library System
Open Mon & Fri 10-4, Tues & Thurs Noon-6, Wed 2-8, Sat 9-Noon
Friends of the Library Group

MUSKEGO

P MUSKEGO PUBLIC LIBRARY*, S73 W16663 Janesville Rd, 53150. SAN 318-2746. Tel: 262-971-2100. Circulation Tel: 262-971-2111. Interlibrary Loan Service Tel: 262-971-2112. Reference Tel: 262-971-2101. Administration Tel: 262-971-2119. Automation Services Tel: 262-971-2108. Information Services Tel: 262-971-2105. FAX: 262-971-2115. Circulation E-mail: circulation@cityofmuskego.org. Web Site: www.cityofmuskego.org/library. *Dir,* Brittany Larson; E-mail: blarson@cityofmuskego.org; *Head, Pub Serv,* Elke Saylor; E-mail: esaylor@cityofmuskego.org; *Circ Supvr,* Jane Matusinec; E-mail: jmatusinec@cityofmuskego.org; Staff 8 (MLS 2, Non-MLS 6)
Founded 1960. Pop 26,000; Circ 193,522
Library Holdings: AV Mats 9,016; Bks on Deafness & Sign Lang 50; High Interest/Low Vocabulary Bk Vols 200; Large Print Bks 2,500; Bk Titles 98,000; Bk Vols 110,670; Per Subs 300
Automation Activity & Vendor Info: (Cataloging) Innovative Interfaces, Inc; (Circulation) Innovative Interfaces, Inc; (OPAC) Innovative Interfaces, Inc; (Serials) Innovative Interfaces, Inc
Wireless access
Function: Adult bk club, Bk club(s), Bks on CD, Children's prog, Computer training, Computers for patron use, E-Reserves, Electronic databases & coll, Free DVD rentals, Holiday prog, ILL available, Internet access, Magnifiers for reading, Mail & tel request accepted, Music CDs, Online cat, Online ref, OverDrive digital audio bks, Photocopying/Printing, Preschool outreach, Prof lending libr, Prog for adults, Prog for children & young adult, Ref & res, Ref serv available, Summer reading prog, Tax forms, Teen prog, Telephone ref, Wheelchair accessible, Workshops, Writing prog
Mem of Bridges Library System
Partic in OCLC Online Computer Library Center, Inc; Wiscat
Open Mon-Thurs 9-8:30, Fri & Sat 9-5
Restriction: Authorized patrons
Friends of the Library Group

NASHOTAH

R NASHOTAH HOUSE*, The Frances Donaldson Library, 2777 Mission Rd, 53058-9793. SAN 318-2754. Tel: 262-646-6536. FAX: 262-646-6504. E-mail: circ@nashotah.edu. Web Site: www.nashotah.edu/library. *Libr Dir,* David Sherwood; Tel: 262-646-6534, E-mail: librarian@nashotah.edu; *Electronic Serv Librn,* Craig Reardon; Tel: 262-646-6537, E-mail: eservices@nashotah.edu; *Circ, ILL,* Carolina Johnson; E-mail: cjohnson@nashotah.edu. Subject Specialists: *Theol,* David Sherwood; Staff 4 (MLS 2, Non-MLS 2)
Founded 1842. Enrl 100; Fac 11; Highest Degree: Doctorate
Library Holdings: Bk Vols 125,000; Per Subs 260
Special Collections: Archives of Nashotah House; National Altar Guild Coll; Prayer Books (Underwood Coll)
Subject Interests: Anglicana, Bibles, Bks of common prayer, Pre-1800 imprints
Automation Activity & Vendor Info: (Acquisitions) OCLC Worldshare Management Services; (Cataloging) OCLC Worldshare Management Services; (Circulation) OCLC Worldshare Management Services; (Course Reserve) OCLC Worldshare Management Services; (Discovery) OCLC Worldshare Management Services; (ILL) OCLC Worldshare Management Services; (OPAC) OCLC Worldshare Management Services; (Serials) OCLC Worldshare Management Services
Wireless access
Partic in OCLC Online Computer Library Center, Inc; WiLS
Open Mon-Fri 9-4:20

NECEDAH

P NECEDAH COMMUNITY -SIEGLER MEMORIAL LIBRARY*, 217 Oak Grove Dr, 54646. (Mail add: PO Box 279, 54646-0279), SAN 318-2762. Tel: 608-565-2253. E-mail: necmem@wrlsweb.org. Web Site: necedahlibrary.wrlsweb.org. *Libr Dir,* Autumn Herried-Kuhl; E-mail: necmem@wrlsweb.org; Staff 1 (MLS 1)
Founded 1914. Pop 3,000; Circ 37,393
Library Holdings: Bk Vols 12,398; Per Subs 42
Wireless access
Mem of Winding Rivers Library System
Open Mon-Wed & Fri 11-5, Sat 9-1
Friends of the Library Group

NEENAH

S J J KELLER & ASSOCIATES, INC*, Research & Technical Library, 3003 W Breezewood Lane, 54956-9611. (Mail add: PO Box 368, 54957-0368), SAN 318-2797. Tel: 920-722-2848. FAX: 920-727-7519. Web Site: www.jjkeller.com.
Founded 1953
Subject Interests: Distribution, Hazardous waste, Human resources, Occupational safety, Regulatory law, Safety, Security, Transportation, Trucking
Wireless access
Restriction: Staff use only

P NEENAH PUBLIC LIBRARY*, 240 E Wisconsin Ave, 54956. (Mail add: PO Box 569, 54957-0569), SAN 318-2819. Tel: 920-886-6315. Circulation Tel: 920-886-6320. Interlibrary Loan Service Tel: 920-886-6313. Administration Tel: 920-886-6300. FAX: 920-886-6324. Circulation FAX: 920-886-6323. E-mail: library@neenahlibrary.org. Web Site: www.neenahlibrary.org. *Dir,* Gretchen Raab; Tel: 920-886-6300, E-mail: raab@neenahlibrary.org; *Asst Dir, Head, Adult Serv,* Melissa Kazmer; *Adult Serv,* Nicole Hardina-Wilhelm; *Adult Serv,* Cheryl Kraft; *Adult Serv,* Michael Thomas; Tel: 920-886-6311; *Circ,* Nancy Britten; *Youth Serv,* Katrina Collins; Tel: 920-886-6330; Staff 8 (MLS 8)
Founded 1884. Pop 50,000; Circ 950,000
Library Holdings: Audiobooks 8,000; CDs 12,000; DVDs 25,000; e-books 15,000; Electronic Media & Resources 800; High Interest/Low Vocabulary Bk Vols 300; Large Print Bks 3,000; Bk Vols 200,000; Per Subs 375; Videos 6,000
Subject Interests: Local hist, Naval hist
Automation Activity & Vendor Info: (Acquisitions) SirsiDynix; (Cataloging) SirsiDynix; (Circulation) SirsiDynix; (OPAC) SirsiDynix; (Serials) SirsiDynix
Wireless access

Function: AV serv, Home delivery & serv to seniorr ctr & nursing homes, Homebound delivery serv, ILL available, Internet access, Photocopying/Printing, Prog for adults, Prog for children & young adult, Ref serv available, Serves people with intellectual disabilities, Summer reading prog, Telephone ref, Wheelchair accessible
Publications: Newsletters (Bimonthly)
Mem of Winnefox Library System
Open Mon-Thurs 9-9, Fri 9-6, Sat 10-4, Sun Noon-4 (Winter); Mon-Thurs 9-9, Fri 9-6, Sat 9-1 (Summer)
Friends of the Library Group

NEILLSVILLE

P NEILLSVILLE PUBLIC LIBRARY*, 409 Hewett St, 54456-1923. SAN 318-2827. Tel: 715-743-2558. FAX: 715-743-6213. Web Site: neillsvillepubliclibrary.org. *Dir,* Cara Hart; E-mail: director@neillsville.lib.wi.us; *Ch,* Kathy Wegner; E-mail: kwegner@neillsville.lib.wi.us
Pop 6,900; Circ 79,358
Library Holdings: Bk Vols 28,000; Per Subs 97
Automation Activity & Vendor Info: (Cataloging) Follett Software; (Circulation) Follett Software; (OPAC) Follett Software
Wireless access
Partic in Wisconsin Valley Library Service
Open Mon & Wed 10-8, Tues, Thurs & Fri 9-5, Sat 9-Noon
Friends of the Library Group

NEKOOSA

P CHARLES & JOANN LESTER LIBRARY*, 100 Park St, 54457. SAN 318-2835. Tel: 715-886-7879. FAX: 715-886-7918. E-mail: staff@nekoosalibrary.com. Web Site: www.nekoosalibrary.com. *Dir,* Darla Allen
Founded 1939. Pop 2,794; Circ 48,340
Library Holdings: Bk Vols 40,000; Per Subs 40
Wireless access
Mem of South Central Library System
Open Mon-Thurs 9-7, Fri 9-5, Sat 9-Noon
Friends of the Library Group

P LESTER PUBLIC LIBRARY OF ROME*, 1157 Rome Center Dr, 54457. Tel: 715-325-8990. FAX: 715-325-8993. Web Site: www.romepubliclibrary.org. *Libr Dir,* Renee Daley; E-mail: rdaley@romepubliclibrary.org; *Libr Asst,* Kathy Nelson; *Libr Asst,* Rachel Stascak; *Libr Asst,* Cassi Williams; *Youth Serv,* Coltyn Drollinger
Founded 2001. Pop 2,750
Library Holdings: AV Mats 1,261; DVDs 3,695; Bk Titles 14,028; Per Subs 33
Automation Activity & Vendor Info: (Cataloging) Book Systems; (Circulation) Book Systems
Wireless access
Function: 24/7 Electronic res, 24/7 Online cat, Adult bk club, Audiobks via web, Bks on CD, Children's prog, Computer training, Computers for patron use, E-Reserves, Electronic databases & coll, Free DVD rentals, Homebound delivery serv, ILL available, Instruction & testing, Internet access, Large print keyboards, Magazines, Music CDs, Notary serv, Online cat, Online info literacy tutorials on the web & in blackboard, Online ref, OverDrive digital audio bks, Photocopying/Printing, Preschool reading prog, Printer for laptops & handheld devices, Prog for adults, Prog for children & young adult, Ref & res, Scanner, Senior computer classes, Story hour, Summer reading prog, Teen prog, Telephone ref
Mem of South Central Library System
Open Mon-Thurs 9-6, Fri 9-5, Sat 9-2
Friends of the Library Group

NESHKORO

P NESHKORO PUBLIC LIBRARY, 132 S Main St, 54960. (Mail add: PO Box 196, 54960-0196), SAN 378-0007. Tel: 920-293-4026. FAX: 920-293-4026. Web Site: www.neshkorolibrary.org. *Libr Dir,* Mary G Fowler; E-mail: fowler@neshkorolibrary.org; Staff 2 (Non-MLS 2)
Founded 1975. Pop 484
Library Holdings: Bk Titles 10,000; Per Subs 20
Wireless access
Mem of Winnefox Library System
Open Mon & Wed-Fri 11-4, Tues 11-4 & 5:30-7:30
Friends of the Library Group

NEW BERLIN

P NEW BERLIN PUBLIC LIBRARY*, 15105 Library Lane, 53151. SAN 318-2851. Tel: 262-785-4980. FAX: 262-785-4984. E-mail: nbinfo@newberlinlibrary.org. Web Site: www.newberlinlibrary.org. *Dir,* Natalie Beacom; E-mail: nbeacom@newberlinlibrary.org; *Mgr, Libr Serv,* Michelle Neubauer; *Adult Services Lead,* Kate Kennedy; *Youth Services Lead,* Kate Krause-Blaha; Staff 22 (MLS 9, Non-MLS 13)
Founded 1969. Pop 39,000; Circ 378,000
Library Holdings: Bk Vols 150,000; Per Subs 253
Special Collections: State Document Depository
Subject Interests: Cookery, Hist, Indust
Wireless access
Publications: Annotated Bibliographies for Young Readers & Their Parents; Annotated Bibliographies of Business Resources; Library Info (Brochure)
Mem of Bridges Library System
Open Mon-Thurs 9-9, Fri & Sat 9-5, Sun (Sept-May) 1-4
Friends of the Library Group

NEW GLARUS

P NEW GLARUS PUBLIC LIBRARY*, 319 Second St, 53574. (Mail add: PO Box 35, 53574-0035), SAN 318-286X. Tel: 608-527-2003. FAX: 608-527-5126. E-mail: staff@ngpl.org. Web Site: www.newglaruspubliclibrary.org. *Dir,* Amy Trumble; E-mail: amy@ngpl.org; *Asst Dir,* Erica Leoffelholtz; E-mail: erica@ngpl.org
Founded 1934. Pop 2,100; Circ 71,000
Library Holdings: Bk Vols 22,179; Per Subs 104
Wireless access
Mem of South Central Library System
Open Mon-Fri 10-7, Sat 10-3
Friends of the Library Group

NEW HOLSTEIN

P NEW HOLSTEIN PUBLIC LIBRARY*, 2115 Washington St, 53061-1098. SAN 318-2878. Tel: 920-898-5165. FAX: 920-898-9022. Reference E-mail: nhref@newholsteinlibrary.org. Web Site: newholsteinlibrary.org. *Dir,* D Hankins; E-mail: d@newholsteinlibrary.org; *Chief Librn,* Amy Wolff; *Asst Librn,* Ann Heus; Staff 4.1 (MLS 1, Non-MLS 3.1)
Founded 1929. Pop 6,000; Circ 41,000
Library Holdings: Bk Vols 40,462; Per Subs 111
Automation Activity & Vendor Info: (Cataloging) SirsiDynix; (Circulation) SirsiDynix; (OPAC) SirsiDynix
Wireless access
Mem of Manitowoc-Calumet Library System
Open Mon-Fri 9-6, Sat 9-1

NEW LISBON

S NEW LISBON CORRECTIONAL INSTITUTION LIBRARY, 2000 Progress Rd, 53950. Tel: 608-562-6400. FAX: 608-562-6410. Web Site: doc.wi.gov/Pages/OffenderInformation/AdultInstitutions/NewLisbonCorrectionalInstitution.aspx.
Founded 2003
Library Holdings: Bk Vols 17,000; Per Subs 30
Restriction: Staff & inmates only

P NEW LISBON MEMORIAL LIBRARY*, 115 W Park St, 53950-1250. SAN 318-2886. Tel: 608-562-3213. FAX: 608-562-3213. E-mail: nlploff@wrlsweb.org. Web Site: newlisbonlibrary.org. *Dir,* Deanna Rosier
Founded 1931
Library Holdings: Bk Vols 24,000; Per Subs 97
Special Collections: Indian Artifacts (Harry Mortenson Coll), bks
Automation Activity & Vendor Info: (Acquisitions) Innovative Interfaces, Inc - Sierra; (Cataloging) Innovative Interfaces, Inc - Sierra; (Circulation) Innovative Interfaces, Inc - Sierra
Wireless access
Mem of Winding Rivers Library System
Open Mon 9-7, Tues, Wed & Fri 9-6, Thurs 3-7, Sat 9-Noon

NEW LONDON

P NEW LONDON PUBLIC LIBRARY, 406 S Pearl St, 54961-1441. SAN 318-2908. Tel: 920-982-8519. FAX: 920-982-8617. E-mail: nlp@newlondonlibrary.org. Web Site: newlondonlibrary.org. *Dir,* Ann Hunt; E-mail: ahunt@newlondonlibrary.org; *Ad,* Position Currently Open; *Ch Serv Librn,* Amy Wojnowski; E-mail: awojnowski@newlondonlibrary.org; Staff 7 (MLS 1, Non-MLS 6)
Founded 1895. Pop 12,000
Jan 2021-Dec 2021 Income $539,694. Mats Exp $62,377, Books $38,200, Per/Ser (Incl. Access Fees) $3,100, Other Print Mats $5,000, AV Mat $12,500, Electronic Ref Mat (Incl. Access Fees) $3,577. Sal $303,111 (Prof $208,488)
Library Holdings: Bk Titles 49,900; Bk Vols 54,900; Per Subs 119
Special Collections: Historical Coll; Local Newspaper on microfilm, 1897-present
Automation Activity & Vendor Info: (Acquisitions) CARL.Solution (TLC); (Cataloging) CARL.Solution (TLC); (Circulation) CARL.Solution (TLC); (ILL) Brodart; (OPAC) BiblioCommons
Wireless access
Mem of Outagamie Waupaca Library System (OWLS)
Special Services for the Blind - Braille music coll

Open Mon-Thurs 9-8, Fri 9-6, Sat 9-2
Friends of the Library Group

NEW RICHMOND

P CARLETON A FRIDAY MEMORIAL LIBRARY*, New Richmond Community Library, 155 E First St, 54017. SAN 318-2916. Tel: 715-243-0431. FAX: 715-246-2691. E-mail: info@newrichmondlibrary.org. Web Site: www.newrichmondlibrary.org. *Libr Dir,* Position Currently Open; *Asst Librn,* Nora Allen; E-mail: noraa@newrichmondlibrary.org; *Asst Librn,* Britta Kingwill; E-mail: brittak@newrichmondlibrary.org; *Circ Supvr,* Maureen LeVesque; E-mail: maureenl@newrichmondlibrary.org; *Info Coordr, Ref Coordr,* Jennifer Rickard; E-mail: jenniferr@newrichmondlibrary.org; *Youth Serv Coordr,* Jessica LaPean; E-mail: jessical@newrichmondlibrary.org; Staff 16 (MLS 1, Non-MLS 15)
Founded 1883. Pop 20,000; Circ 197,286
Library Holdings: Audiobooks 2,598; CDs 3,682; DVDs 6,462; e-books 166,979; Electronic Media & Resources 48,025; Large Print Bks 2,077; Bk Vols 39,636; Per Subs 79
Special Collections: New Richmond Historical Coll. Oral History
Automation Activity & Vendor Info: (Acquisitions) Innovative Interfaces, Inc; (Cataloging) Innovative Interfaces, Inc; (Circulation) Innovative Interfaces, Inc; (OPAC) Innovative Interfaces, Inc; (Serials) Innovative Interfaces, Inc
Wireless access
Function: 24/7 Electronic res, 24/7 Online cat, Adult bk club, Bk club(s), Bks on CD, Children's prog, Computers for patron use, Electronic databases & coll, Free DVD rentals, Home delivery & serv to seniorr ctr & nursing homes, ILL available, Internet access, Magazines, Microfiche/film & reading machines, Movies, Music CDs, Online cat, Outreach serv, OverDrive digital audio bks, Photocopying/Printing, Preschool reading prog, Prog for adults, Prog for children & young adult, Scanner, Senior outreach, STEM programs, Story hour, Summer reading prog, Tax forms, Teen prog
Mem of Inspiring & Facilitating Library Success (IFLS)
Open Mon-Thurs 9-8, Fri 9-6, Sat 9-3
Friends of the Library Group

J NORTHWOOD TECHNICAL COLLEGE*, New Richmond Campus Learning Resources Center, 1019 S Knowles Ave, 54017. SAN 318-2924. Tel: 715-246-6561. Toll Free Tel: 800-243-9482. FAX: 715-246-2777. *Classroom Support Technician,* Taylor Goossen; E-mail: taylor.goossen@northwoodtech.edu; Staff 2 (MLS 1, Non-MLS 1)
Founded 1968. Enrl 1,000; Fac 52
Library Holdings: Bk Titles 1,516; Per Subs 160
Subject Interests: Agr, Allied health, Bus, Indust, Nursing, Trade
Wireless access
Partic in WISPALS Library Consortium
Open Mon-Thurs 8-7, Fri 8-4

NORTH FOND DU LAC

P SPILLMAN PUBLIC LIBRARY*, 719 Wisconsin Ave, 54937-1335. SAN 318-2959. Tel: 920-929-3771. FAX: 920-929-3669. Web Site: www.northfonddulaclibrary.org. *Dir,* Heather Wegner; E-mail: director@northfonddulaclibrary.org; *Ch,* Hanna Wetherbee; E-mail: wetherbee@northfonddulaclibrary.org
Library Holdings: Bk Vols 25,000; Per Subs 50
Automation Activity & Vendor Info: (Cataloging) SirsiDynix; (Circulation) SirsiDynix; (OPAC) SirsiDynix
Wireless access
Mem of Winnefox Library System
Open Mon & Thurs 10-8, Tues, Wed & Fri 10-5, Sat 10-1

NORTH FREEDOM

P NORTH FREEDOM PUBLIC LIBRARY*, 105 N Maple St, 53951. SAN 318-2967. Tel: 608-522-4571. E-mail: caboose@northfreedomlibrary.com. Web Site: www.northfreedomlibrary.com. *Dir,* Raina Roloff; *Asst Dir,* Carol Brueggeman
Founded 1898. Pop 701; Circ 18,000
Library Holdings: Bk Titles 4,500; Bk Vols 4,600; Per Subs 30
Subject Interests: Hist, Natural sci
Wireless access
Mem of South Central Library System
Open Mon-Thurs 1-7, Fri & Sat 9-2
Friends of the Library Group

NORTH LAKE

P TOWN HALL LIBRARY*, N 76 W 31429 Hwy VV, 53064. (Mail add: PO Box 158, 53064-0158), SAN 318-2975. Tel: 262-966-2933. FAX: 262-966-0208. Web Site: townhalllibrary.org. *Dir,* Kaushalya Iyengar; E-mail: kiyengar@townhall.lib.wi.us; Staff 1 (MLS 1)
Founded 1966. Pop 8,500
Library Holdings: Audiobooks 1,747; DVDs 6,432; Bk Vols 53,228; Per Subs 110
Special Collections: Art Coll
Subject Interests: Local hist
Automation Activity & Vendor Info: (Cataloging) Innovative Interfaces, Inc. - Polaris; (Circulation) Innovative Interfaces, Inc. - Polaris; (Course Reserve) Innovative Interfaces, Inc. - Polaris; (ILL) Innovative Interfaces, Inc. - Polaris; (Media Booking) Innovative Interfaces, Inc. - Polaris; (OPAC) Innovative Interfaces, Inc. - Polaris; (Serials) Innovative Interfaces, Inc. - Polaris
Wireless access
Function: 24/7 Electronic res, 24/7 Online cat, Activity rm, Adult bk club, Art exhibits, Audiobks on Playaways & MP3, Audiobks via web, Bks on CD, Butterfly Garden, Chess club, Children's prog, Computers for patron use, Electronic databases & coll, ILL available, Internet access, Life-long learning prog for all ages, Magazines, Movies, Music CDs, Photocopying/Printing, Preschool reading prog, Prog for adults, Prog for children & young adult, Ref serv available, Story hour, Study rm, Summer reading prog, Teen prog, Telephone ref, Wheelchair accessible
Mem of Bridges Library System
Open Mon-Thurs 9-8, Fri 9-5, Sat 9-1
Friends of the Library Group

NORWALK

P NORWALK PUBLIC LIBRARY*, 101 Railroad St, 54648. (Mail add: PO Box 132, 54648-0132). Tel: 608-823-7473. E-mail: norwalkpl@wrlsweb.org. Web Site: norwalklibrary.wrlsweb.org. *Dir,* Ken Kittleson; Staff 1 (Non-MLS 1)
Founded 1995. Pop 636; Circ 6,674
Library Holdings: AV Mats 400; Bk Titles 8,000; Per Subs 10; Talking Bks 200
Automation Activity & Vendor Info: (Cataloging) Follett Software; (Circulation) Follett Software
Wireless access
Mem of Winding Rivers Library System
Open Mon & Fri Noon-6, Tues & Thurs 3-7, Wed 10-7, Sat 8-Noon

OAK CREEK

J MILWAUKEE AREA TECHNICAL COLLEGE*, Oak Creek Library, 6665 S Howell Ave, 53154. SAN 318-2991. Circulation Tel: 414-571-4720. Reference Tel: 414-571-4602. FAX: 414-571-4747. Web Site: book.matc.edu. *Campus Librn,* Jenn Medved; Tel: 414-571-4604, E-mail: medvedj@matc.edu; *Ref Librn,* Laura Emanuelson; E-mail: emanulj1@matc.edu; *Ref Librn,* Steve Midthun; E-mail: midthuns@matc.edu; Staff 5 (MLS 3, Non-MLS 2)
Founded 1977. Enrl 9,800; Highest Degree: Associate
Library Holdings: DVDs 6,400; High Interest/Low Vocabulary Bk Vols 1,200; Bk Vols 19,000; Per Subs 72
Special Collections: Adult Literacy
Subject Interests: Air conditioning, Computer sci, Criminology, Culinary arts, Energy conserv, Fire sci, Heating-ventilating, Holocaust mat, Police sci, Refrigeration, Trades, Welding
Automation Activity & Vendor Info: (Acquisitions) Innovative Interfaces, Inc - Sierra; (Cataloging) Innovative Interfaces, Inc - Sierra; (Circulation) Innovative Interfaces, Inc - Sierra; (Course Reserve) Innovative Interfaces, Inc - Sierra; (Discovery) EBSCO Discovery Service; (OPAC) Innovative Interfaces, Inc - Sierra; (Serials) Innovative Interfaces, Inc - Sierra
Wireless access
Open Mon-Thurs 7:30am-8pm, Fri 7:30-4
Restriction: Open to students, fac, staff & alumni, Photo ID required for access, Restricted pub use

P OAK CREEK PUBLIC LIBRARY*, Drexel Town Sq, 8040 S Sixth St, 53154. SAN 318-3009. Tel: 414-766-7900. FAX: 414-766-7942. E-mail: library@oakcreekwi.gov. Web Site: oakcreeklibrary.org. *Libr Dir,* Jill Lininger; E-mail: jlininger@oakcreekwi.gov; *Asst Libr Dir,* Jennifer Davies; E-mail: jenny.davies@mcfls.org; *Circ Supvr,* Laurel Bird Johnson; E-mail: laurel.johnson@mcfls.org; *Tech Librn,* Joanne Ratke; E-mail: joanne.ratke@mcfls.org; *YA Librn,* Sarah Corso; E-mail: sarah.corso@mcfls.org; *Youth Serv Librn,* Jake Bowen; Staff 4.5 (MLS 4.5)
Founded 1972. Pop 32,341; Circ 264,672
Library Holdings: AV Mats 11,467; CDs 4,392; DVDs 2,654; e-books 11,956; Large Print Bks 1,950; Bk Vols 65,112; Per Subs 195; Videos 3,585
Subject Interests: Popular mat
Automation Activity & Vendor Info: (Cataloging) Innovative Interfaces, Inc; (Circulation) Innovative Interfaces, Inc; (Media Booking) Innovative Interfaces, Inc; (OPAC) Innovative Interfaces, Inc; (Serials) Innovative Interfaces, Inc
Wireless access
Publications: Bookmark; Calendar (Monthly)
Mem of Milwaukee County Federated Library System

Open Mon-Fri 9-8, Sat 9-4
Friends of the Library Group

OAKFIELD

P OAKFIELD PUBLIC LIBRARY*, 130 N Main St, 53065-9563. SAN 318-3017. Tel: 920-583-4552. FAX: 920-583-2544. Web Site: www.oakfieldlibrary.org. *Dir,* Linda Alsum-O'Donovan; E-mail: director@oakfieldlibrary.org; Staff 1.1 (Non-MLS 1.1)
Founded 1898. Pop 2,250; Circ 25,476
Jan 2020-Dec 2020 Income $80,991, City $54,000, County $26,991. Mats Exp $14,603
Library Holdings: CDs 709; DVDs 2,140; e-books 158,252; Bk Titles 17,924; Per Subs 38
Automation Activity & Vendor Info: (Cataloging) SirsiDynix; (Circulation) SirsiDynix-WorkFlows; (OPAC) SirsiDynix
Wireless access
Function: Computers for patron use, Internet access, Online cat
Mem of Winnefox Library System
Open Mon, Wed & Thurs 1-7, Tues & Fri 10-5
Friends of the Library Group

OCONOMOWOC

P OCONOMOWOC PUBLIC LIBRARY*, 200 South St, 53066-5213. SAN 318-3033. Tel: 262-569-2193. FAX: 262-569-2176. E-mail: contactus@oconomowoclibrary.org. Web Site: www.oconomowoclibrary.org. *Dir,* Betsy Bleck; E-mail: bbleck@oconomowoclibrary.org; Staff 30 (MLS 3, Non-MLS 27)
Founded 1893. Pop 27,000; Circ 248,907
Library Holdings: Bk Vols 99,920; Per Subs 240
Subject Interests: Art, Biog
Automation Activity & Vendor Info: (Cataloging) Innovative Interfaces, Inc. - Polaris; (Circulation) Innovative Interfaces, Inc. - Polaris; (ILL) Innovative Interfaces, Inc. - Polaris; (OPAC) Innovative Interfaces, Inc. - Polaris
Wireless access
Mem of Bridges Library System
Open Mon-Thurs 9-8, Fri & Sat 9-5, Sun 1-4 (Winter); Mon-Thurs 9-8, Fri 9-5, Sat 9-1 (Summer)
Friends of the Library Group

OCONTO

P FARNSWORTH PUBLIC LIBRARY*, 715 Main St, 54153. SAN 318-3041. Tel: 920-834-7730. E-mail: oco@ocontolibrary.org. Web Site: ocontolibrary.org. *Libr Dir,* Amy Peterson; E-mail: apeterson@ocontolibrary.org; Staff 4.3 (Non-MLS 4.3)
Founded 1903. Pop 4,513; Circ 33,794
Library Holdings: CDs 1,400; e-books 174,398; Bk Vols 20,051; Per Subs 38; Videos 3,978
Subject Interests: Local hist
Automation Activity & Vendor Info: (Cataloging) Innovative Interfaces, Inc; (Circulation) Innovative Interfaces, Inc; (OPAC) Innovative Interfaces, Inc
Wireless access
Mem of Nicolet Federated Library System
Partic in OWLSnet; Wiscat
Open Mon-Thurs 9-6, Fri 9-5
Friends of the Library Group

OCONTO FALLS

P OCONTO FALLS COMMUNITY LIBRARY*, 251 N Main St, 54154. SAN 318-305X. Tel: 920-846-2673. FAX: 920-846-9946. E-mail: ocf@ocontofallslibrary.org. Web Site: www.ocontofallslibrary.org. *Dir,* Rachel Pascoe; E-mail: rpascoe@ocontofallslibrary.org
Pop 4,500; Circ 43,110
Library Holdings: AV Mats 1,874; Bk Vols 14,371; Per Subs 20; Talking Bks 761; Videos 4,400
Automation Activity & Vendor Info: (Cataloging) CARL.Solution (TLC); (Circulation) CARL.Solution (TLC); (OPAC) CARL.Solution (TLC)
Wireless access
Mem of Nicolet Federated Library System
Open Mon-Wed 9-6, Thurs & Fri 9-5, Sat 9-Noon
Friends of the Library Group

ODANAH

P BAD RIVER PUBLIC TRIBAL LIBRARY*, 72682 Maple St, 54861. (Mail add: PO Box 39, 54861), SAN 377-9386. Tel: 715-682-7111, Ext 1530. FAX: 715-682-7118. Web Site: badriver-nsn.gov. *Actg Librn,* Stephanie Julian; E-mail: educationdirector@badriver-nsn.gov
Library Holdings: Audiobooks 112; Bk Titles 13,500
Subject Interests: Native Am
Partic in Wis Libr Asn
Open Mon-Fri 10-6 (Winter); Mon-Thurs 11-6, Fri 11-5 (Summer)

OGEMA

P OGEMA PUBLIC LIBRARY, W 5005 State Rd 86, 54459. (Mail add: PO Box 603, 54459-0603), SAN 322-838X. Tel: 715-767-5130. FAX: 715-767-5130. Web Site: www.ogemalibrary.org. *Dir,* Amy Abele
Founded 1973. Pop 1,000; Circ 10,000
Library Holdings: Bk Titles 16,000
Automation Activity & Vendor Info: (Cataloging) Follett Software; (Circulation) Follett Software
Wireless access
Mem of Inspiring & Facilitating Library Success (IFLS)
Open Tues-Thurs 10-6, Fri 10-1, Sat (Oct-May) 10-1
Friends of the Library Group

OMRO

P CARTER MEMORIAL LIBRARY*, Omro Public Library, 405 E Huron St, 54963-1405. SAN 324-7244. Tel: 920-685-7016. FAX: 920-685-7017. E-mail: director@omrolibrary.org. Web Site: omrolibrary.org. *Dir,* Anna Dinkel; E-mail: dinkel@omrolibrary.org; Staff 2.5 (MLS 1, Non-MLS 1.5)
Pop 7,000; Circ 56,000
Library Holdings: Bk Vols 23,600; Per Subs 20
Special Collections: Local History Coll
Automation Activity & Vendor Info: (Cataloging) SirsiDynix; (Circulation) SirsiDynix; (OPAC) SirsiDynix
Wireless access
Function: 24/7 Electronic res, 24/7 Online cat, 24/7 wireless access, Activity rm, Adult bk club, Art programs, Audiobks on Playaways & MP3, Bk club(s), Bks on CD, Children's prog, Computer training, Computers for patron use, Digital talking bks, Electronic databases & coll, Extended outdoor wifi, Free DVD rentals, Games, Home delivery & serv to seniorr ctr & nursing homes, ILL available, Internet access, Laminating, Life-long learning prog for all ages, Magazines, Meeting rooms, Movies, Online cat, Orientations, Outreach serv, Outside serv via phone, mail, e-mail & web, OverDrive digital audio bks, Photocopying/Printing, Printer for laptops & handheld devices, Prog for adults, Prog for children & young adult, Ref & res, Ref serv available, Res assist avail, Scanner, STEM programs, Story hour, Summer & winter reading prog, Summer reading prog, Tax forms, Teen prog, Telephone ref, Wifi hotspot checkout, Winter reading prog
Mem of Winnefox Library System
Open Mon-Thurs 9-6, Fri 9-5, Sat 9-Noon
Friends of the Library Group

ONEIDA

P ONEIDA COMMUNITY LIBRARY*, 201 Elm St, 54155. (Mail add: PO Box 365, 54155-0365), SAN 324-7791. Tel: 920-869-2210. FAX: 920-869-1299. E-mail: oneidacommunitylibrary@oneidanation.org. Web Site: oneida-nsn.gov/resources/library. *Libr Mgr,* Eliza Skenandore; E-mail: eskenan6@oneidanation.org; *Asst Libr Mgr,* Wanda Boivin; E-mail: wboivin@oneidanation.org
Founded 1968. Pop 4,232; Circ 10,000
Library Holdings: Bk Titles 16,000; Per Subs 42
Special Collections: Iroquois-Oneida Indian Coll, bks, flms; Native American Coll, bks, flms, reels, fiche
Mem of Nicolet Federated Library System
Open Mon-Thurs 9-6, Fri 11-5
Branches: 1
GREEN EARTH BRANCH LIBRARY, W1273 Redtail Dr, De Pere, 54155-9423, SAN 375-4766. Tel: 920-833-7226. *Librn,* Kim Cackowski; E-mail: kcackows@oneidanation.org
Founded 1996. Pop 4,232
Library Holdings: Bk Titles 4,940
Open Mon-Thurs 9-5, Fri 11-5

ONTARIO

P ONTARIO PUBLIC LIBRARY*, 313 Main St, 54651. (Mail add: PO Box 69, 54651-0069), SAN 318-3068. Tel: 608-337-4651. FAX: 608-337-4814. E-mail: ontlibr@wrlsweb.org. Web Site: ontariolibrary.wrlsweb.org. *Dir,* April Arndt
Circ 18,000
Library Holdings: AV Mats 424; Bk Vols 11,843; Per Subs 66; Videos 275
Wireless access
Mem of Winding Rivers Library System
Open Mon & Fri 10-5, Tues Noon-6, Wed 10-6, Sat 9-Noon

OOSTBURG

P OOSTBURG PUBLIC LIBRARY*, 213 N Eighth St, 53070. SAN 318-3076. Tel: 920-564-2934. Reference E-mail: oostburgref@monarchlibraries.org. Web Site: www.oostburglibrary.org. *Dir,*

Jesse Rogers; E-mail: jrogers@monarchlibraries.org; *Cat Librn,* Colleen Swart; E-mail: cswart@monarchlibraries.org; *ILL Librn,* Tricia Oonk; E-mail: toonk@monarchlibraries.org; *Ch Serv,* Lori Walker; E-mail: lwalker@monarchlibraries.org; *Circ,* Vicki Markham; E-mail: vmarkham@monarchlibraries.org; *Circ,* Laurie Schuh; E-mail: lschuh@monarchlibraries.org
Founded 1941. Pop 7,000
Library Holdings: Bk Vols 26,000; Per Subs 50
Automation Activity & Vendor Info: (Acquisitions) Innovative Interfaces, Inc. - Polaris; (Cataloging) Innovative Interfaces, Inc. - Polaris; (Circulation) Innovative Interfaces, Inc. - Polaris; (OPAC) Innovative Interfaces, Inc. - Polaris
Wireless access
Mem of Monarch Library System
Open Mon-Thurs 9-7, Fri 9-5, Sat 10-Noon; Mon-Thurs 9-7, Fri 9-5 (June-Aug)
Friends of the Library Group

OREGON

P OREGON PUBLIC LIBRARY*, 256 Brook St, 53575. SAN 318-3084. Tel: 608-835-3656. E-mail: orelib@oregonlibrary.org. Web Site: www.oregonpubliclibrary.org. *Libr Dir,* Jennifer Endres Way; E-mail: jway@oregonlibrary.org; *Youth Serv Librn,* Kelly Allen; E-mail: kallen@oregonlibrary.org; *Circ Supvr,* Alicia Fischer; E-mail: afischer@oregonlibrary.org; *Tech Serv Supvr,* Laura Dewey; E-mail: ldewey@oregonlibrary.org; Staff 9 (MLS 3, Non-MLS 6)
Library Holdings: AV Mats 10,326; CDs 4,384; DVDs 5,942; e-books 123,095; Bk Titles 51,091; Per Subs 118
Automation Activity & Vendor Info: (Acquisitions) LibLime Koha; (Cataloging) LibLime Koha; (Circulation) LibLime Koha; (ILL) LibLime Koha; (OPAC) LibLime Koha; (Serials) LibLime Koha
Wireless access
Mem of South Central Library System
Open Mon-Thurs 9-8, Fri 9-6, Sat 9-3
Friends of the Library Group

ORFORDVILLE

P ORFORDVILLE PUBLIC LIBRARY*, 519 E Beloit St, 53576. SAN 318-3092. Tel: 608-879-9229. FAX: 608-879-2031. Web Site: www.als.lib.wi.us/OPL. *Dir,* Sarah Strunz; E-mail: strunz.sarah@orfordvillelibrary.org; Staff 2 (Non-MLS 2)
Founded 1905. Pop 1,200; Circ 20,000
Automation Activity & Vendor Info: (Cataloging) SirsiDynix; (Circulation) SirsiDynix; (OPAC) SirsiDynix
Wireless access
Mem of Prairie Lakes Library System (PLLS)
Open Mon-Thurs 11-7, Fri 11-5, Sat 9-Noon
Friends of the Library Group

OSCEOLA

P OSCEOLA PUBLIC LIBRARY*, 102 Chieftain St, 54020. (Mail add: PO Box 816, 54020), SAN 376-608X. Tel: 715-294-2310. FAX: 715-755-3510. E-mail: osceolapl@osceolapubliclibrary.org. Web Site: osceolapubliclibrary.org. *Libr Dir,* Shelby Friendshuh; E-mail: sfriendshuh@osceolapubliclibrary.org
Library Holdings: Bk Vols 19,000; Per Subs 79
Automation Activity & Vendor Info: (Acquisitions) Innovative Interfaces, Inc; (Cataloging) Innovative Interfaces, Inc; (Circulation) Innovative Interfaces, Inc; (Course Reserve) Innovative Interfaces, Inc; (ILL) Innovative Interfaces, Inc; (Media Booking) Innovative Interfaces, Inc; (OPAC) Innovative Interfaces, Inc; (Serials) Innovative Interfaces, Inc
Wireless access
Mem of Inspiring & Facilitating Library Success (IFLS)
Open Mon-Thurs 10-7, Fri 10-5, Sat 10-3
Friends of the Library Group

OSHKOSH

S EAA LIBRARY*, Boeing Aeronautical, 3000 Poberezny Rd, 54904. (Mail add: PO Box 3086, 54903-3086), SAN 324-7252. Tel: 920-426-4800. Toll Free Tel: 800-564-6322. FAX: 920-426-4873. Web Site: www.eaa.org/museum. *Curator,* Chris Henry; E-mail: chenry@eaa.org; Staff 1 (Non-MLS 1)
Founded 1972
Library Holdings: Bk Titles 11,000; Per Subs 30
Special Collections: Don Dwiggins Coll; Max Conrad Coll
Subject Interests: Aircraft, Amateur construction, Aviation, Aviation hist
Restriction: Not a lending libr, Not open to pub

M MERCY MEDICAL CENTER, The Clark Family Health Science Library, 500 S Oakwood Rd, 54904. SAN 318-3106. Tel: 920-223-0342, 920-223-2000. FAX: 920-223-0343. E-mail: wimedlibrary@ascension.org. Web Site: healthcare.ascension.org/locations/wisconsin. *Librn,* Michele Matucheski; Tel: 920-223-0340; Staff 1.5 (MLS 1, Non-MLS 0.5)
Founded 1906
Library Holdings: e-books 300; Bk Vols 5,000; Per Subs 250
Subject Interests: Consumer health, Med, Nursing, Surgery
Automation Activity & Vendor Info: (Cataloging) LibraryWorld, Inc; (OPAC) LibraryWorld, Inc; (Serials) LibraryWorld, Inc
Wireless access
Partic in Fox River Valley Area Library Consortium; National Network of Libraries of Medicine Region 6
Restriction: Open to staff only

S OSHKOSH CORRECTIONAL INSTITUTION LIBRARY, 1730 W Snell Rd, 54903. (Mail add: PO Box 3530, 54903-3530). Tel: 920-231-4010, Ext 2220. FAX: 920-236-2626. Web Site: doc.wi.gov/Pages/OffenderInformation/AdultInstitutions/OshkoshCorrectionalInstitution.aspx.
Library Holdings: Bk Vols 30,000; Per Subs 40

P OSHKOSH PUBLIC LIBRARY*, 106 Washington Ave, 54901-4985. SAN 365-0405. Tel: 920-236-5201, 920-236-5205. Circulation Tel: 920-236-5203. Administration Tel: 920-236-5210. FAX: 920-236-5228. TDD: 920-236-5204. Web Site: www.oshkoshpubliclibrary.org. *Dir,* Jeff Gilderson-Duwe; E-mail: gilderson-duwe@oshkoshpubliclibrary.org; *Asst Dir,* Vicki Vandenberg; Staff 17 (MLS 13, Non-MLS 4)
Founded 1895. Pop 87,358; Circ 1,109,915
Library Holdings: AV Mats 47,471; Bk Vols 270,178; Per Subs 560
Subject Interests: Genealogy, Local hist
Automation Activity & Vendor Info: (Acquisitions) SirsiDynix; (Cataloging) SirsiDynix; (Circulation) SirsiDynix; (OPAC) SirsiDynix
Wireless access
Publications: Library Lines (Newsletter)
Mem of Winnefox Library System
Partic in OCLC Online Computer Library Center, Inc
Special Services for the Deaf - TDD equip
Special Services for the Blind - Assistive/Adapted tech devices, equip & products; BiFolkal kits; Bks on cassette; Bks on CD; Computer with voice synthesizer for visually impaired persons; Large print & cassettes; Large print bks; Talking bks; ZoomText magnification & reading software
Open Mon-Thurs 8-8, Fri 8-6, Sat 9-5, Sun 1-5
Friends of the Library Group

S OSHKOSH PUBLIC MUSEUM LIBRARY*, 1331 Algoma Blvd, 54901-2799. SAN 318-3114. Tel: 920-236-5799. Web Site: www.oshkoshmuseum.org. *Archivist,* Amy Fels; E-mail: afels@ci.oshkosh.wi.us
Founded 1924
Library Holdings: Bk Titles 6,000
Special Collections: Local History (Oshkosh Pioneers), bks, doc, photog. Oral History
Subject Interests: Archaeology, Archit, Art, Local hist, Logging, Lumbering, Meteorites, Natural hist
Wireless access
Function: Archival coll
Restriction: Open by appt only

C UNIVERSITY OF WISCONSIN OSHKOSH*, Polk Library, 801 Elmwood Ave, 54901. Tel: 920-424-4333. Circulation Tel: 920-424-7316. FAX: 920-424-7338. E-mail: infodesk@uwosh.edu. Web Site: www.uwosh.edu/library. *Dir,* Sarah Neises; Tel: 920-424-2147, E-mail: neises@uwosh.edu; *Head, Access Serv,* Crystal Buss; Tel: 920-424-7315, E-mail: buss@uwosh.edu; *Head, Tech Serv,* Ronald Hardy; Tel: 920-424-2097, E-mail: hardyr@uwosh.edu; *Archivist & Communications Librn, Head, Pub Serv,* Joshua Ranger; Tel: 920-424-0828, E-mail: ranger@uwosh.edu; *Acad Librn,* Ane Carriveau; Tel: 920-832-2675, E-mail: carriveaua@uwosh.edu; *Acad Librn,* Kelly Johnson; Tel: 920-832-5337, E-mail: johnsonk@uwosh.edu; *Assoc Librn,* Melissa Motl; Tel: 920-929-1148, E-mail: motlm@uwosh.edu; *Distance Educ Librn,* Erin McArthur; Tel: 920-424-1361, Fax: 920-424-7334, E-mail: mcarthue@uwosh.edu; *Distance Learning Librn, Info Literacy,* Joe Pirillo; Tel: 920-424-7332, E-mail: pirilloj@uwosh.edu; *Educ Mat Ctr Librn,* Jessica Ammons; Tel: 920-424-2320, E-mail: Ammonsj@uwosh.edu; *Electronic Res Librn,* Robert Karels; Tel: 920-424-0371, Fax: 920-424-7734, E-mail: Karelsr@uwosh.edu; *Info Literacy Librn,* Theodore Mulvey; Tel: 920-424-7329, E-mail: mulveyt@uwosh.edu; *Metadata Librn,* Colleen Hallfrisch; Tel: 920-424-7369, E-mail: Hallfrischc@uwosh.edu; *Coordr, Info Literacy,* Marisa Finkey; Tel: 920-424-3436, E-mail: finkey@uwosh.edu; *ILL,* Matthew Reinhardt; Tel: 920-424-3348, E-mail: reinharm@uwosh.edu; Staff 22 (MLS 14, Non-MLS 8)
Founded 1871. Enrl 13,942; Fac 543; Highest Degree: Doctorate
Library Holdings: AV Mats 8,982; CDs 3,512; e-books 209,627; e-journals 20,811; Electronic Media & Resources 78,112; Microforms 28,068; Bk Vols 509,928; Per Subs 183
Special Collections: University Archives Coll; Wisconsin Area Research Center Coll
Subject Interests: Bus, Educ, Nursing, Undergrad studies

Automation Activity & Vendor Info: (Acquisitions) Ex Libris Group; (Cataloging) Ex Libris Group; (Circulation) Ex Libris Group; (Course Reserve) Ex Libris Group; (Discovery) Ex Libris Group; (ILL) OCLC ILLiad; (OPAC) Ex Libris Group; (Serials) Ex Libris Group
Wireless access
Publications: Polk Library News (Newsletter)
Partic in Fox River Valley Area Library Consortium; OCLC Online Computer Library Center, Inc
Open Mon-Thurs 7am-midnight, Fri 7-6, Sat 10-6, Sun 10am-midnight

GL WINNEBAGO COUNTY COURT HOUSE*, Law Library, Court House, 415 Jackson St, 54903-4794. (Mail add: PO Box 2808, 54903-2808), SAN 318-3130. Tel: 920-236-4808. FAX: 920-424-7780. *Library Contact,* Teresa Basiliere
Library Holdings: Bk Vols 6,000
Open Mon-Fri 8-4:30

P WINNEFOX LIBRARY SYSTEM*, 106 Washington Ave, 54901-4985. SAN 318-3149. Tel: 920-236-5220. FAX: 920-236-5228. Web Site: www.winnefox.org. *Exec Dir,* Jeff Gilderson-Duwe; E-mail: gilderson-duwe@winnefox.org; *Asst Dir,* Mark Arend; E-mail: arend@winnefox.org; *ILL Mgr,* Karla Smith; E-mail: smith@winnefox.org; Staff 10 (MLS 4, Non-MLS 6)
Founded 1977. Pop 205,522
Library Holdings: Bk Vols 10,685; Per Subs 31
Publications: Trustee Tales (Newsletter); Winnefox Library System Directory; Winnefox Library System Interlibrary Loan Manual
Member Libraries: Berlin Public Library; Brandon Public Library; Caestecker Public Library; Campbellsport Public Library; Carter Memorial Library; Coloma Public Library; Endeavor Public Library; Fond Du Lac Public Library; Hancock Public Library; Leon-Saxeville Township Library; Markesan Public Library; Menasha Public Library; Mill Pond Public Library; Montello Public Library; Neenah Public Library; Neshkoro Public Library; Oakfield Public Library; Oshkosh Public Library; Oxford Public Library; Packwaukee Public Library; Patterson Memorial Library; Plainfield Public Library; Poy Sippi Public Library; Princeton Public Library; Redgranite Public Library; Ripon Public Library; Spillman Public Library; Wautoma Public Library; Westfield Public Library; Winneconne Public Library
Partic in Wisconsin Public Library Consortium

OSSEO

P HAUGE MEMORIAL LIBRARY*, 50655 Charles St, 54758. (Mail add: PO Box 659, 54758-0659), SAN 318-3157. Tel: 715-597-3444. E-mail: haugeml@triwest.net. Web Site: osseopubliclibrary.com. *Libr Dir,* Gina Waters
Pop 1,500; Circ 27,000
Library Holdings: Bk Vols 16,000; Per Subs 38
Automation Activity & Vendor Info: (Cataloging) Follett Software; (Circulation) Follett Software
Wireless access
Mem of Winding Rivers Library System
Open Mon, Wed & Thurs 9-7, Fri 9-4
Friends of the Library Group

OWEN

P OWEN PUBLIC LIBRARY*, 414 Central Ave, 54460-9777. (Mail add: PO Box 130, 54460-0130), SAN 318-3165. Tel: 715-229-2939. FAX: 715-229-2939. Web Site: www.owenpubliclibrary.org. *Dir,* Loralee Petersen; E-mail: director@owen.lib.wi.us
Pop 1,000; Circ 29,000
Library Holdings: Bk Vols 19,000; Per Subs 45
Automation Activity & Vendor Info: (Acquisitions) SirsiDynix; (Cataloging) SirsiDynix; (Circulation) SirsiDynix; (OPAC) SirsiDynix
Wireless access
Partic in Wisconsin Valley Library Service
Open Mon-Fri 1-8

OXFORD

P OXFORD PUBLIC LIBRARY*, 129 S Franklin St, 53952. (Mail add: PO Box 32, 53952-0032), SAN 376-6594. Tel: 608-586-4458. FAX: 608-586-4459. E-mail: director@oxfordlibrary.org. Web Site: www.oxfordlibrary.org. *Dir,* Julia Metcalf; E-mail: metcalf@oxfordlibrary.org
Library Holdings: AV Mats 1,100; Bk Vols 10,700; Per Subs 30
Wireless access
Mem of Winnefox Library System
Open Mon 10-6, Wed-Fri 10-5

PACKWAUKEE

P PACKWAUKEE PUBLIC LIBRARY*, N3511 State St, 53953. (Mail add: PO Box 406, 53953-0403), SAN 377-9734. Tel: 608-589-5202. FAX: 608-589-5202. E-mail: director@packwaukeelibrary.org. Web Site: packwaukeelibrary.org. *Dir,* Carol Deer; E-mail: deer@packwaukeelibrary.org
Library Holdings: Bk Titles 7,500; Per Subs 30
Wireless access
Mem of Winnefox Library System
Open Mon & Thurs Noon-7, Tues, Wed & Fri Noon-5, Sat 10-2

PALMYRA

P POWERS MEMORIAL LIBRARY*, 115 Main St, 53156. (Mail add: PO Box O, 53156-0922), SAN 318-3173. Tel: 262-495-4605. FAX: 262-495-8617. E-mail: pmlpaquestions@gmail.com. Web Site: www.palmyra.lib.wi.us. *Libr Dir,* Kristine Dexheimer; E-mail: kdexheimer@palmyra.lib.wi.us; Staff 1 (MLS 1)
Founded 1927. Pop 2,500; Circ 44,431
Library Holdings: Bk Vols 27,686; Per Subs 90
Special Collections: Local Newspaper-Palmyra Enterprise, 1874-present, bd vols & micro
Automation Activity & Vendor Info: (Acquisitions) SirsiDynix; (Cataloging) SirsiDynix; (Circulation) SirsiDynix; (ILL) Auto-Graphics, Inc
Wireless access
Mem of Bridges Library System
Open Mon-Thurs 10-7, Fri 10-5, Sat 10-2
Friends of the Library Group

PARDEEVILLE

P ANGIE WILLIAMS COX PUBLIC LIBRARY*, 119 N Main St, 53954. (Mail add: PO Box 370, 53954-0370), SAN 318-3181. Tel: 608-429-2354. FAX: 608-429-4308. E-mail: staff@pardeevillelibrary.com. Web Site: www.pardeevillelibrary.com. *Dir,* Kristie Nielson Corning; E-mail: knielson@pardeevillelibrary.com
Founded 1925
Library Holdings: AV Mats 1,137; Bk Vols 19,293; Per Subs 25; Talking Bks 556
Automation Activity & Vendor Info: (Cataloging) SirsiDynix; (Circulation) SirsiDynix; (OPAC) SirsiDynix; (Serials) SirsiDynix
Wireless access
Function: ILL available, Prog for children & young adult, Summer reading prog, Wheelchair accessible
Mem of South Central Library System
Open Mon & Fri 10-4, Tues-Thurs 10-6, Sat 8-Noon
Friends of the Library Group

PARK FALLS

P PARK FALLS PUBLIC LIBRARY*, 121 N Fourth Ave, 54552. SAN 318-319X. Tel: 715-762-3121. E-mail: pfpl@parkfallslibrary.org. Web Site: www.parkfallslibrary.org. *Libr Dir,* Debra Hyde; *Ad,* Alyssa Woods; *Ch Serv Librn,* Alyssa Cleland; Staff 3 (MLS 3)
Founded 1906. Pop 15,000; Circ 60,080
Library Holdings: Bk Titles 36,000; Per Subs 130
Subject Interests: Local hist, Lumber, Lumbering
Wireless access
Mem of Inspiring & Facilitating Library Success (IFLS)
Open Mon-Fri 10-8, Sat (Fall-Spring) 10-2
Friends of the Library Group

PEPIN

P PEPIN PUBLIC LIBRARY*, 510 Second St, 54759. SAN 374-5465. Tel: 715-442-4932. Web Site: pepinpubliclibrary.org. *Dir,* Christy Rundquist; E-mail: director@pepinpubliclibrary.org; Staff 3 (Non-MLS 3)
Founded 1948. Circ 15,955
Jan 2017-Dec 2017. Mats Exp $6,519, Books $4,003, Per/Ser (Incl. Access Fees) $1,235, AV Mat $459, Electronic Ref Mat (Incl. Access Fees) $822
Library Holdings: Audiobooks 796; DVDs 1,467; e-books 166,979; Bk Titles 12,143; Per Subs 42
Automation Activity & Vendor Info: (Cataloging) Innovative Interfaces, Inc; (Circulation) Innovative Interfaces, Inc; (OPAC) Innovative Interfaces, Inc
Wireless access
Function: 24/7 Electronic res, 24/7 Online cat, Adult bk club, Audiobks via web, Bks on CD, CD-ROM, Children's prog, Computer training, Computers for patron use, Electronic databases & coll, Free DVD rentals, ILL available, Internet access, Magazines, Magnifiers for reading, Mail & tel request accepted, Movies, Music CDs, Online cat, OverDrive digital audio bks, Photocopying/Printing, Prog for adults, Prog for children & young adult, Ref & res, Scanner, Spanish lang bks, Spoken cassettes & CDs, Story hour, Study rm, Summer reading prog, Tax forms, Telephone ref, Wheelchair accessible

Mem of Inspiring & Facilitating Library Success (IFLS)
Open Tues-Thurs 10-7, Sat 9-12
Friends of the Library Group

PEWAUKEE

P PEWAUKEE PUBLIC LIBRARY*, 210 Main St, 53072. SAN 318-3211. Tel: 262-691-5670. FAX: 262-691-5673. E-mail: pwlib@pewaukee.lib.wi.us. Web Site: www.pewaukeelibrary.org. *Dir,* Nan Champe; Tel: 262-691-5670, Ext 920, E-mail: director@pewaukeelibrary.org; Staff 13 (MLS 7, Non-MLS 6)
Founded 2005. Pop 20,000; Circ 344,000
Library Holdings: Audiobooks 3,273; CDs 2,109; DVDs 5,347; e-books 3,024; Bk Vols 92,677; Per Subs 196; Videos 965
Automation Activity & Vendor Info: (Acquisitions) SirsiDynix-WorkFlows; (Cataloging) SirsiDynix-WorkFlows; (Circulation) SirsiDynix-WorkFlows; (ILL) SirsiDynix-WorkFlows; (OPAC) SirsiDynix-iBistro; (Serials) SirsiDynix-WorkFlows
Wireless access
Function: Adult bk club, After school storytime, Archival coll, Art exhibits, Bks on cassette, Bks on CD, Children's prog, Computer training, Computers for patron use, Digital talking bks, E-Reserves, Free DVD rentals, Holiday prog, Home delivery & serv to seniorr ctr & nursing homes, Homebound delivery serv, ILL available, Internet access, Music CDs, Online cat, Online ref, Outreach serv, Outside serv via phone, mail, e-mail & web, OverDrive digital audio bks, Photocopying/Printing, Preschool outreach, Prog for adults, Prog for children & young adult, Ref serv available, Senior computer classes, Senior outreach, Serves people with intellectual disabilities, Spoken cassettes & CDs, Spoken cassettes & DVDs, Story hour, Summer reading prog, Tax forms, Teen prog, Telephone ref, VHS videos, Wheelchair accessible
Mem of Bridges Library System
Open Mon-Thurs 9-8, Fri 9-5, Sat 9-4; Mon-Thurs 9-8, Fri 9-5, Sat 9-1 (Summer)
Friends of the Library Group

J WAUKESHA COUNTY TECHNICAL COLLEGE LIBRARY*, 800 Main St, 53072. SAN 318-322X. Tel: 262-691-5316. Reference Tel: 262-691-5409. Web Site: libguides.wctc.edu. *Dir, Libr Serv,* Amy Manion; E-mail: amanion@wctc.edu; Staff 7.9 (MLS 3.4, Non-MLS 4.5)
Founded 1965. Enrl 3,439; Fac 235; Highest Degree: Associate
Library Holdings: e-books 110,000; Bk Titles 38,738; Per Subs 285
Special Collections: Career Coll; Educational Resources Information Center Coll (ERIC); International Trade
Subject Interests: Electronics, Financial planning, Fire sci, Intl trade, Mkt, Nursing, Police, Printing, Publ, Retail mgt, Sci
Automation Activity & Vendor Info: (Acquisitions) Innovative Interfaces, Inc - Sierra; (Cataloging) Innovative Interfaces, Inc - Sierra; (Circulation) Innovative Interfaces, Inc - Sierra; (Course Reserve) Innovative Interfaces, Inc - Sierra; (OPAC) Innovative Interfaces, Inc - Sierra; (Serials) Innovative Interfaces, Inc - Sierra
Wireless access
Function: Computers for patron use, Distance learning, Doc delivery serv, Electronic databases & coll, Equip loans & repairs, ILL available, Instruction & testing, Magazines, Online info literacy tutorials on the web & in blackboard, Photocopying/Printing, Ref & res
Partic in WiLS; WISPALS Library Consortium
Open Mon-Thurs 7am-8pm, Fri 7-4:30, Sat 9-1
Restriction: Open to pub for ref & circ; with some limitations

PHELPS

P PHELPS PUBLIC LIBRARY*, Eleanor Ellis Public Library, 4495 Town Hall Rd, 54554. SAN 318-3238. Tel: 715-545-2887. FAX: 715-545-2887. Web Site: www.phelpspubliclibrary.org. *Dir,* Cari Hutton; E-mail: director@phelps.wislib.org
Founded 1934
Library Holdings: Bk Vols 10,916; Per Subs 19
Subject Interests: Wis
Automation Activity & Vendor Info: (Cataloging) Innovative Interfaces, Inc; (Circulation) Innovative Interfaces, Inc
Wireless access
Mem of Northern Waters Library Service
Open Mon, Tues, Thurs & Fri 10-4, Sat 10-12

PHILLIPS

P PHILLIPS PUBLIC LIBRARY*, 286 Cherry St, 54555. SAN 374-6046. Tel: 715-339-2868. Web Site: www.phillipspl.org. *Dir,* Rebecca Puhl; E-mail: rebeccas@phillipspl.org; *Cat,* Jessica Wear; *Ch Serv,* Jake Wyrzykowski; *Circ,* Valerie Fraundorf; *Circ,* Susan Freiboth; *Circ, ILL,* Jody Hartmann; Staff 1 (MLS 1)
Founded 1917. Pop 8,500; Circ 93,482
Library Holdings: AV Mats 856; CDs 1,716; DVDs 1,059; e-books 8,805; Large Print Bks 377; Bk Titles 25,000; Per Subs 78; Talking Bks 500; Videos 800
Automation Activity & Vendor Info: (Cataloging) Innovative Interfaces, Inc; (Circulation) Innovative Interfaces, Inc; (ILL) Innovative Interfaces, Inc; (OPAC) Innovative Interfaces, Inc; (Serials) Innovative Interfaces, Inc
Mem of Inspiring & Facilitating Library Success (IFLS)
Open Mon-Fri 9-7:30, Sat 9-1
Friends of the Library Group

PINE RIVER

P LEON-SAXEVILLE TOWNSHIP LIBRARY*, Pine River Public Library, N4715 County Rd E, 54965. (Mail add: PO Box 247, 54965-0247), SAN 318-3246. Tel: 920-987-5110. FAX: 920-987-5110. Web Site: www.pineriverlibrary.org. *Dir,* Collette Ross; E-mail: director@pineriverlibrary.org; Staff 1.2 (Non-MLS 1.2)
Founded 1960. Pop 2,300
Automation Activity & Vendor Info: (Cataloging) SirsiDynix; (Circulation) SirsiDynix; (ILL) OCLC WorldShare Interlibrary Loan
Wireless access
Mem of Winnefox Library System
Open Mon, Tues, Thurs & Fri 2-7, Wed 10-7, Sat 10-1

PITTSVILLE

P PITTSVILLE COMMUNITY LIBRARY*, 5291 Third Ave, 54466-0911. SAN 318-3254. Tel: 715-884-6500. E-mail: pitlib@tds.net. Web Site: www.scls.lib.wi.us/pit/index.html. *Libr Dir,* Barbara Calaway
Founded 1975. Pop 2,000
Library Holdings: Bk Vols 14,000; Per Subs 80
Automation Activity & Vendor Info: (Acquisitions) Follett Software; (Cataloging) Follett Software; (Circulation) Follett Software
Wireless access
Function: 24/7 Electronic res, 24/7 Online cat, Accelerated reader prog, Adult bk club, Bk club(s), Bks on CD, Children's prog, Computers for patron use, Free DVD rentals, ILL available, Internet access, Life-long learning prog for all ages, Magazines, Online cat, Outside serv via phone, mail, e-mail & web, OverDrive digital audio bks, Photocopying/Printing, Preschool reading prog, Prog for adults, Prog for children & young adult, Res assist avail, Story hour, Summer & winter reading prog, Summer reading prog, Tax forms, Wheelchair accessible
Mem of South Central Library System
Open Tues & Fri 9-7, Wed 12-5, Thurs 12-6, Sat 9-2

PLAIN

P KRAEMER LIBRARY & COMMUNITY CENTER*, 910 Main St, 53577. SAN 318-3262. Tel: 608-546-4201. FAX: 608-546-4201. E-mail: askus@kraemerlibrary.org. Web Site: www.kraemerlibrary.org. *Dir,* Nicholas Studnicka; E-mail: nstudnicka@kraemerlibrary.org
Founded 1964. Pop 815
Library Holdings: Bk Vols 10,820; Per Subs 40
Automation Activity & Vendor Info: (Cataloging) SirsiDynix; (Circulation) SirsiDynix
Wireless access
Mem of South Central Library System
Open Mon & Tues 10-7, Wed & Thurs 1-7, Fri 10-6, Sat 10-2

PLAINFIELD

P PLAINFIELD PUBLIC LIBRARY*, 126 S Main St, 54966-0305. (Mail add: PO Box 305, 54966-0305), SAN 318-3270. Tel: 715-335-4523. FAX: 715-335-6712. E-mail: director@plainfieldlibrary.org. Web Site: www.plainfieldlibrary.org. *Dir,* Bernadette Stainbrook; E-mail: stainbrook@plainfieldlibrary.org
Founded 1915. Pop 902; Circ 16,558
Library Holdings: Bk Vols 10,000
Special Collections: Oral History
Subject Interests: Local hist
Wireless access
Mem of Winnefox Library System
Open Mon 12-5, Tues & Fri 10-5, Wed 10-6, Sat 9-Noon
Friends of the Library Group

PLATTEVILLE

P PLATTEVILLE PUBLIC LIBRARY*, 225 W Main St, 53818. SAN 318-3289. Tel: 608-348-7441. Interlibrary Loan Service Tel: 608-348-7441, Ext 4. Reference E-mail: reference@plattevillepubliclibrary.org. Web Site: plattevillepubliclibrary.org. *Dir,* Jessie Lee-Jones; Tel: 608-348-7441, Ext 5, E-mail: director@plattevillepubliclibrary.org; Staff 4 (MLS 1, Non-MLS 3)
Founded 1906. Pop 10,035; Circ 114,009
Library Holdings: Bk Vols 40,000; Per Subs 150
Automation Activity & Vendor Info: (Acquisitions) Horizon; (Cataloging) Horizon; (Circulation) Horizon; (OPAC) Horizon
Wireless access
Function: Homebound delivery serv

Mem of Southwest Wisconsin Library System
Open Mon-Thurs 9-8, Fri 9-6, Sat 9-5

C UNIVERSITY OF WISCONSIN - PLATTEVILLE*, Elton S Karrmann Library, One University Plaza, 53818. SAN 318-3297. Tel: 608-342-1668. Interlibrary Loan Service Tel: 608-342-1648. Administration Tel: 608-342-1688. Automation Services Tel: 608-342-1210. Information Services Tel: 608-342-1421. Toll Free Tel: 888-450-4632. FAX: 608-342-1645. Reference E-mail: reference@uwplatt.edu. Web Site: www.uwplatt.edu/department/karrmann-library. *Head Librn,* Todd Roll; Tel: 608-342-1229, E-mail: rollt@uwplatt.edu; *Head, Circ & Ref,* John Berg; Tel: 608-342-1355, E-mail: bergjo@uwplatt.edu; *Head, Cat, Webmaster,* Jessica Donahoe; Tel: 608-342-1348, E-mail: donahoej@uwplatt.edu; *Head, Instrul Mat Lab,* Regina Pauly; Tel: 608-342-1099, E-mail: paulyr@uwplatt.edu; *Head, Syst,* Jon Musselman; Tel: 608-342-1649, E-mail: musselmj@uwplatt.edu; Staff 9 (MLS 8, Non-MLS 1)
Founded 1866. Enrl 7,124; Fac 365; Highest Degree: Master
Library Holdings: Audiobooks 69; AV Mats 15,555; CDs 784; DVDs 1,887; e-books 13; e-journals 20; Electronic Media & Resources 93; Microforms 1,023,415; Bk Titles 209,239; Bk Vols 240,625; Per Subs 927; Videos 12,060
Special Collections: Archives (Area Research Center), ms; Regional History. State Document Depository; US Document Depository
Subject Interests: Computer sci, Engr, Indust tech mgt, Middle-level educ, Project mgt
Automation Activity & Vendor Info: (Acquisitions) Ex Libris Group; (Cataloging) Ex Libris Group; (Circulation) Ex Libris Group; (ILL) OCLC; (Media Booking) Ex Libris Group; (OPAC) Ex Libris Group; (Serials) Ex Libris Group
Wireless access
Partic in Dubuque Area Library Information Consortium
Open Mon-Thurs 7:45am-Midnight, Fri 7:45am-8pm, Sat 11-8, Sun 1-Midnight

PLUM CITY

P PLUM CITY PUBLIC LIBRARY*, 611 Main St, 54761-9044. (Mail add: PO Box 203, 54761-0203), SAN 378-0023. Tel: 715-647-2373. FAX: 715-647-2373. E-mail: pcbooks@plumcitylibrary.org. Web Site: www.plumcitylibrary.org. *Dir,* Jenna Beyer; E-mail: director@plumcitylibrary.org
Library Holdings: Bk Titles 13,700; Per Subs 48
Subject Interests: Local hist
Wireless access
Mem of Inspiring & Facilitating Library Success (IFLS)
Open Tues, Thurs & Fri 10-5, Wed 10-8, Sat 10-1

PLYMOUTH

S KETTLE MORAINE CORRECTIONAL INSTITUTION LIBRARY*, W9071 Forest Dr, 53073. (Mail add: PO Box 31, 53073-0031), SAN 324-1734. Tel: 920-526-3244, Ext 2309. FAX: 920-526-3989. *Librn,* Sara Hildebrand; E-mail: sara.hildebrand@wisconsin.gov
Library Holdings: Bk Titles 23,000; Per Subs 45
Automation Activity & Vendor Info: (Acquisitions) Follett Software; (Cataloging) Follett Software; (Circulation) Follett Software
Open Mon-Thurs 8-4:30 & 5:30-8:30, Fri 8-4:30

C LAKELAND UNIVERSITY*, John Esch Library, W3718 South Dr, 53073. SAN 318-3807. Tel: 920-565-1038, Ext 2420. *Dir, Libr Serv,* Ann Penke; Tel: 920-565-1038, Ext 2416, E-mail: penkea@lakeland.edu; *Distance Educ Librn,* James Kellner; Tel: 920-565-1038, Ext 2419, E-mail: kellnerja@lakeland.edu; *Engagement Librn, Ref Serv,* Melanie Jones; Tel: 920-565-1038, Ext 2418, E-mail: Jonesmm@lakeland.edu; Staff 3 (MLS 3)
Founded 1940. Enrl 835; Fac 59; Highest Degree: Master
Library Holdings: AV Mats 2,986; CDs 1,490; DVDs 297; e-books 174,535; e-journals 309,057; Microforms 36,879; Music Scores 952; Bk Titles 60,453; Bk Vols 71,104; Per Subs 270; Videos 856
Subject Interests: Jewish holocaust, Modern Am poetry
Automation Activity & Vendor Info: (Cataloging) OCLC Connexion; (Circulation) Innovative Interfaces, Inc; (ILL) OCLC WorldShare Interlibrary Loan; (OPAC) Innovative Interfaces, Inc; (Serials) Innovative Interfaces, Inc
Wireless access
Partic in WiLS
Open Mon-Thurs 7:30am-10pm, Fri 7:30-4:30, Sat Noon-5, Sun Noon-10

P PLYMOUTH PUBLIC LIBRARY*, 130 Division St, 53073. SAN 318-3300. Tel: 920-892-4416. FAX: 920-892-6295. E-mail: plref@monarchlibraries.org. Web Site: www.plymouthpubliclibrary.net. *Dir,* Leslie Jochman; E-mail: ljochman@monarchlibraries.org; *Adult Serv,* Anthony Sigismondi; *Ch Serv,* Samantha Spottek; Staff 2 (MLS 2)
Founded 1909. Pop 12,600; Circ 112,000
Library Holdings: AV Mats 4,000; Bks on Deafness & Sign Lang 100; e-books 7,000; High Interest/Low Vocabulary Bk Vols 50; Large Print Bks 1,500; Bk Vols 71,000; Per Subs 180; Talking Bks 500
Subject Interests: Local city (Plymouth) hist
Automation Activity & Vendor Info: (Cataloging) Innovative Interfaces, Inc; (Circulation) Innovative Interfaces, Inc; (ILL) Innovative Interfaces, Inc; (OPAC) Innovative Interfaces, Inc; (Serials) Innovative Interfaces, Inc
Wireless access
Mem of Monarch Library System
Open Mon-Thurs 9-7, Fri 9-5, Sat 9-1

PORT WASHINGTON

P W J NIEDERKORN LIBRARY*, Port Washington Public, 316 W Grand Ave, 53074-2293. SAN 318-3319. Tel: 262-284-5031. FAX: 262-284-7680. E-mail: infowjnlib@gmail.com. Web Site: wjnlib.org. *Dir,* Tom Carson; E-mail: tcarson@monarchlibraries.org; *Asst Dir,* Rosalia Slawson; E-mail: rslawson@monarchlibraries.org; *Head, Children's Servx,* Cindy Haas; E-mail: chaas@monarchlibraries.org; *Head, Circ,* Dave MacGregor; E-mail: dmacgregor@monarchlibraries.org; *Adult Serv,* Darcie Kileen; E-mail: dkileen@monarchlibraries.org
Pop 10,617; Circ 222,094
Library Holdings: AV Mats 3,478; e-books 7,583; Bk Vols 55,000; Per Subs 202; Talking Bks 2,417
Wireless access
Mem of Monarch Library System
Open Mon-Thurs 9-8, Fri 9-6, Sat 9-1
Friends of the Library Group

PORTAGE

S COLUMBIA CORRECTIONAL INSTITUTION LIBRARY, 2925 Columbia Dr, 53901. (Mail add: PO Box 950, 53901-0950), SAN 370-7407. Tel: 608-742-9100. FAX: 608-742-9111.
Founded 1986
Library Holdings: High Interest/Low Vocabulary Bk Vols 100; Bk Titles 16,500; Bk Vols 20,000; Per Subs 25
Automation Activity & Vendor Info: (Acquisitions) EOS International; (Cataloging) EOS International; (Circulation) EOS International
Function: Legal assistance to inmates, Photocopying/Printing, Tax forms
Special Services for the Blind - Large print bks
Restriction: Circ limited, Internal circ only, Not open to pub

P PORTAGE PUBLIC LIBRARY*, 253 W Edgewater St, 53901. SAN 318-3335. Tel: 608-742-4959. E-mail: info@portagelibrary.us. Web Site: www.portagelibrary.us. *Dir,* Debbie Bird; E-mail: dbird@portagelibrary.us; Staff 6 (MLS 3, Non-MLS 3)
Founded 1901. Pop 10,327; Circ 100,700
Library Holdings: AV Mats 3,365; e-books 173,351; Electronic Media & Resources 71,796; Bk Vols 50,060; Per Subs 105
Special Collections: Zona Gale Coll
Automation Activity & Vendor Info: (Circulation) LibLime
Wireless access
Mem of South Central Library System
Open Mon-Thurs 9-7, Fri 9-6, Sat 9-2
Friends of the Library Group

POY SIPPI

P POY SIPPI PUBLIC LIBRARY*, W2251 Commercial St, 54967-8423. SAN 318-3343. Tel: 920-987-5737. Web Site: www.poysippilibrary.org. *Dir,* Jeanne Williamson; E-mail: director@poysippilibrary.org
Founded 1963. Pop 2,734
Library Holdings: Bks on Deafness & Sign Lang 15; DVDs 86; e-books 7,951; High Interest/Low Vocabulary Bk Vols 72; Large Print Bks 58; Music Scores 72; Bk Titles 10,727; Talking Bks 82; Videos 1,647
Automation Activity & Vendor Info: (Cataloging) SirsiDynix; (Circulation) SirsiDynix; (OPAC) SirsiDynix
Mem of Winnefox Library System
Open Mon 10-7, Wed & Fri 11-7, Sat 10-1
Friends of the Library Group

POYNETTE

P POYNETTE AREA PUBLIC LIBRARY*, 118 N Main St, 53955. (Mail add: PO Box 368, 53955-0368), SAN 318-3351. Tel: 608-635-7577. FAX: 608-635-7577. E-mail: poylib@poynettelibrary.com. Web Site: www.poynettelibrary.com. *Libr Dir,* Ms Jodi Bailey; E-mail: jbailey@poynettelibrary.com
Founded 1941. Pop 5,000; Circ 10,000
Library Holdings: e-books 173,351; Bk Titles 14,711; Per Subs 51
Automation Activity & Vendor Info: (Acquisitions) Bibliomation Inc; (Cataloging) Bibliomation Inc; (Circulation) Bibliomation Inc; (OPAC) Bibliomation Inc
Wireless access
Mem of South Central Library System

Open Mon-Fri 9:30-6:30, Sat 9:30-Noon
Friends of the Library Group

PRAIRIE DU CHIEN

P PRAIRIE DU CHIEN MEMORIAL LIBRARY*, Joseph W & Emma L Wachute Memorial, 125 S Wacouta Ave, 53821-1632. SAN 318-336X. Tel: 608-326-6211. Web Site: www.pdcpubliclibrary.org. *Dir,* Elisabeth Byers; Tel: 608-326-6211, E-mail: pdcdirector@swls.org; Staff 5 (MLS 1, Non-MLS 4)
Founded 1897. Pop 5,487; Circ 64,000
Library Holdings: Bk Vols 32,000; Per Subs 49
Special Collections: Local Newspapers 1864-2001, microfilm
Subject Interests: Local hist, Wis
Automation Activity & Vendor Info: (Cataloging) Horizon; (Circulation) Horizon; (OPAC) Horizon
Function: 24/7 Electronic res, Activity rm, Adult bk club, Art exhibits, Audiobks on Playaways & MP3, Audiobks via web, Bks on CD, Children's prog, Computers for patron use, Electronic databases & coll, Free DVD rentals, ILL available, Internet access, Magazines, Magnifiers for reading, Meeting rooms, Microfiche/film & reading machines, Movies, OverDrive digital audio bks, Photocopying/Printing, Scanner, Study rm, Summer & winter reading prog, Summer reading prog, Tax forms, Teen prog
Mem of Southwest Wisconsin Library System
Open Mon 9-7, Tues-Thurs 9-6, Fri 9-5, Sat 9-Noon
Friends of the Library Group

PRAIRIE DU SAC

P RUTH CULVER COMMUNITY LIBRARY*, 540 Water St, 53578. SAN 318-3378. Tel: 608-643-8318. FAX: 608-643-4897. Web Site: www.pdslibrary.org. *Dir,* Lauren White; E-mail: lwhite@pdslibrary.org; *Asst Dir, Teen & Adult Librn,* Meagan Statz; E-mail: mstatz@pdslibrary.org; *Ch,* Beth Hays; E-mail: bhays@pdslibrary.org
Founded 1900
Library Holdings: Bk Vols 36,000; Per Subs 134
Subject Interests: Local hist
Wireless access
Mem of South Central Library System
Open Mon-Fri 9-8, Sat 9-4
Friends of the Library Group

PRESCOTT

P PRESCOTT PUBLIC LIBRARY*, 800 Borner St N, 54021. SAN 318-3394. Tel: 715-262-5555. FAX: 715-262-4229. E-mail: prescottlib@prescottpubliclibrary.org. Web Site: prescottpubliclibrary.org. *Dir,* Carissa Langer
Founded 1900. Pop 3,900; Circ 51,000
Library Holdings: Bk Vols 22,000; Per Subs 35
Subject Interests: Local hist, Wis hist
Automation Activity & Vendor Info: (Circulation) Innovative Interfaces, Inc
Mem of Inspiring & Facilitating Library Success (IFLS)
Open Mon-Thurs 10-8, Fri 10-6, Sat 10-2

PRESQUE ISLE

P PRESQUE ISLE COMMUNITY LIBRARY, 8306 School Loop Rd, 54557. (Mail add: PO Box 200, 54557-0200), SAN 376-6667. Tel: 715-686-7613. FAX: 715-686-2588. Web Site: www.presqueislelibrary.org. *Dir,* Christal Schermeister-Simons; E-mail: director@presqueisle.wislib.org
Library Holdings: AV Mats 2,500; Bk Vols 12,000; Per Subs 26
Automation Activity & Vendor Info: (Acquisitions) Innovative Interfaces, Inc; (Cataloging) Innovative Interfaces, Inc; (Circulation) Innovative Interfaces, Inc; (OPAC) Innovative Interfaces, Inc
Wireless access
Mem of Northern Waters Library Service
Open Mon & Wed 9-6, Tues, Thurs & Sat 9-12, Fri 9-3
Friends of the Library Group

PRINCETON

P PRINCETON PUBLIC LIBRARY*, 424 W Water St, 54968-9147. (Mail add: PO Box 234, 54968-0234), SAN 318-3416. Tel: 920-295-6777. FAX: 920-295-3303. Web Site: www.princetonpublib.org. *Dir,* Clairellyn Sommersmith; E-mail: director@princetonpublib.org
Founded 1933
Library Holdings: CDs 1,900; DVDs 4,000; Bk Titles 17,000; Per Subs 65
Automation Activity & Vendor Info: (Cataloging) SirsiDynix; (Circulation) SirsiDynix; (Course Reserve) SirsiDynix; (OPAC) SirsiDynix; (Serials) SirsiDynix
Wireless access
Mem of Winnefox Library System
Open Mon 9-6, Tues-Thurs 10-8, Fri 9-5, Sat 9-1
Friends of the Library Group

RACINE

S DEKOVEN FOUNDATION*, DeKoven Center Library, 600 21st St, 53403. SAN 374-6194. Tel: 262-633-6401. FAX: 262-633-6401. E-mail: info@dekovencenter.org. Web Site: www.dekovencenter.org.
Founded 1852
Library Holdings: Bk Vols 5,000
Special Collections: History of Racine & The DeKoven Foundation, 1852-(Walker Archives), docs
Publications: Reflections (Newsletter); To Hear Celestial Harmonies: Essays on James DeKoven & The DeKoven Center (Local historical information)
Open Mon-Fri 9-5

J GATEWAY TECHNICAL COLLEGE*, Learning Resources Center/Library, Lake Bldg, Lower Level, Rm L008, 1001 S Main St, 53403-1582. SAN 324-3362. Tel: 262-619-6220. E-mail: racinelrc@gtc.edu. Web Site: libguides.gtc.edu. *District Libr Mgr,* Gary Flynn; Tel: 262-564-2640, E-mail: flynng@gtc.edu; Staff 3 (MLS 2, Non-MLS 1)
Enrl 2,200; Fac 85; Highest Degree: Associate
Library Holdings: Bk Vols 15,000; Per Subs 150
Subject Interests: Culinary arts, Electronics, Fire sci, Gen educ, Word processing
Automation Activity & Vendor Info: (Acquisitions) Ex Libris Group; (Cataloging) Ex Libris Group; (Circulation) Ex Libris Group; (Course Reserve) Ex Libris Group; (OPAC) Ex Libris Group; (Serials) Ex Libris Group
Wireless access
Function: ILL available, Internet access, Orientations
Open Mon-Thurs 7:45am-8:30pm, Fri 7:45-4, Sat 9-Noon
Restriction: Open to pub for ref & circ; with some limitations, Open to students, fac & staff, Photo ID required for access

S RACINE ART MUSEUM LIBRARY*, 441 Main St, 53403. (Mail add: PO Box 187, 53401-0187), SAN 318-3505. Tel: 262-638-8300. FAX: 262-898-1045. E-mail: raminfo@ramart.org. Web Site: www.ramart.org. *Curator of Coll, Exec Dir,* Bruce W Pepich; Tel: 262-638-8300, Ext 106, E-mail: bpepich@ramart.org
Founded 1941
Library Holdings: Bk Vols 5,000; Per Subs 6
Special Collections: Exhibition Catalogues
Subject Interests: Art, Art hist, Out-of-print
Wireless access
Function: For res purposes
Partic in Tri County Libr Consortium
Restriction: Open by appt only

S RACINE HERITAGE MUSEUM*, Archives-Research Center, 701 S Main St, 53403-1211. SAN 318-3467. Tel: 262-636-3926. FAX: 262-636-3940. E-mail: Inquire@RacineHeritageMuseum.org. Web Site: www.racineheritagemuseum.org. *Archivist,* Mary Nelson; *Curator,* Samantha Machalik; Staff 1 (Non-MLS 1)
Founded 1969
Library Holdings: Bk Titles 500
Special Collections: Racine County Histories, City & County Directories, Photographs, Corporate Historical Documents, Maps & Atlases, Obituaries, Family History Documents & Genealogies, Indexes to Cemeteries, Naturalizations, Censuses, Surnames & Subjects
Subject Interests: Corp hist, Local family hist, Mil hist, Racine Co hist
Function: Res libr
Publications: Newsletter
Open Tues 1-4:30, Sat 10-1
Restriction: Non-circulating

P RACINE PUBLIC LIBRARY*, 75 Seventh St, 53403. SAN 365-0588. Tel: 262-636-9241. Interlibrary Loan Service Tel: 262-636-9299. Reference Tel: 262-636-9217. FAX: 262-636-9260. E-mail: racine_reference@racinelibrary.info. Web Site: www.racinelibrary.info. *Interim Exec Dir,* Nick Demske; E-mail: nick.demske@racinelibrary.info; Staff 16 (MLS 16)
Founded 1897. Pop 142,112; Circ 971,175
Library Holdings: AV Mats 29,279; Bks on Deafness & Sign Lang 211; e-books 8,869; High Interest/Low Vocabulary Bk Vols 160; Large Print Bks 4,637; Bk Titles 198,710; Bk Vols 267,447; Per Subs 465; Spec Interest Per Sub 299; Talking Bks 8,367
Special Collections: Early Childhood Resource Coll; Racine City & County Historical Material, bks, pamphlets & clippings. Oral History; State Document Depository; US Document Depository
Automation Activity & Vendor Info: (Acquisitions) SirsiDynix; (Cataloging) SirsiDynix; (Circulation) SirsiDynix; (Course Reserve)

SirsiDynix; (ILL) SirsiDynix; (Media Booking) SirsiDynix; (OPAC) SirsiDynix; (Serials) SirsiDynix
Wireless access
Mem of Prairie Lakes Library System (PLLS)
Partic in OCLC Online Computer Library Center, Inc
Special Services for the Deaf - Assisted listening device; Bks on deafness & sign lang; Captioned film dep; Closed caption videos; TTY equip
Special Services for the Blind - Accessible computers; Audio mat; Bks & mags in Braille, on rec, tape & cassette; Bks on CD; Computer with voice synthesizer for visually impaired persons; Copier with enlargement capabilities; Descriptive video serv (DVS); Extensive large print coll; Home delivery serv; Internet workstation with adaptive software; Large print bks; Large screen computer & software; Ref serv; Screen enlargement software for people with visual disabilities; Talking bks
Open Mon-Thurs 9-8, Fri & Sat 11-4
Friends of the Library Group
Bookmobiles: 1. Head of Extension/Adult Servs, Jill Hartmann. Bk titles 4,570

WHEATON FRANCISCAN HEALTHCARE - ALL SAINTS
M LIBRARY & COMMUNITY CENTER*, 3801 Spring St, 53405, SAN 328-3429. Tel: 262-687-4300. Web Site: www.mywheaton.org/allsaints. *Dir, Libr Serv,* Carrie Papa
Library Holdings: Bk Titles 575
Subject Interests: Cardiology, Nursing, Orthopedics, Pediatrics, Surgery
Open Mon-Fri 8-4:30

M LIBRARY & COMMUNITY RESOURCE CENTER*, c/o Saint Mary's Medical Ctr, 3801 Spring St, 53405, SAN 318-3483. Tel: 262-636-4300. Founded 1932
Library Holdings: Bk Titles 175; Per Subs 175
Subject Interests: Med, Nursing
Partic in Regional Med Libr - Region 3
Open Mon-Fri 8-4:30

RANDOLPH

P HUTCHINSON MEMORIAL LIBRARY*, Randolph Library, 228 N High St, 53956. SAN 318-3521. Tel: 920-326-4640. FAX: 920-326-4642. Web Site: www.randolphlib.org. *Dir,* Whitney Parrillo; E-mail: whitney.parrillo@randolphlib.org
Founded 1906. Pop 1,869; Circ 32,000
Library Holdings: DVDs 4,825; e-books 123,634; Microforms 200; Bk Titles 24,474; Per Subs 68
Special Collections: Randolph Advance Newspapers (1890-present), micro
Automation Activity & Vendor Info: (Cataloging) SirsiDynix; (Circulation) SirsiDynix; (OPAC) SirsiDynix; (Serials) SirsiDynix
Wireless access
Function: 24/7 Online cat, Adult bk club, Art exhibits, Audiobks on Playaways & MP3, Bks on cassette, Bks on CD, Children's prog, Computers for patron use, E-Reserves, Free DVD rentals, Home delivery & serv to seniorr ctr & nursing homes, Homebound delivery serv, Magazines, Music CDs, OverDrive digital audio bks, Photocopying/Printing, Ref serv available, Spanish lang bks, Story hour, Summer reading prog, Tax forms, Wheelchair accessible
Mem of South Central Library System
Open Mon-Thurs 9-6, Fri 9-2, Sat 9-12
Friends of the Library Group

RANDOM LAKE

P LAKEVIEW COMMUNITY LIBRARY*, 112 Butler St, 53075. SAN 318-353X. Tel: 920-994-4825. FAX: 920-994-2230. Reference E-mail: lakeview@monarchlibraries.org. Web Site: lakeviewcommunitylibrary.org. *Dir,* Camrin Sullivan; Staff 6 (Non-MLS 6)
Founded 1957. Pop 5,000; Circ 59,188
Library Holdings: AV Mats 2,978; Bk Titles 33,377; Per Subs 72
Automation Activity & Vendor Info: (Acquisitions) Innovative Interfaces, Inc. - Polaris; (Cataloging) Innovative Interfaces, Inc. - Polaris; (Circulation) Innovative Interfaces, Inc. - Polaris; (Course Reserve) Innovative Interfaces, Inc. - Polaris; (ILL) Innovative Interfaces, Inc. - Polaris; (Media Booking) Innovative Interfaces, Inc. - Polaris; (OPAC) Innovative Interfaces, Inc. - Polaris; (Serials) Innovative Interfaces, Inc. - Polaris
Wireless access
Mem of Monarch Library System
Open Mon-Thurs 10-7, Fri 10-5, Sat 10-1
Friends of the Library Group

READSTOWN

P READSTOWN PUBLIC LIBRARY*, 129 W Wisconsin, 54652. Tel: 608-629-5465. FAX: 608-629-5465. E-mail: readslib@yahoo.com. Web Site: www.wrlsweb.org/readstown. *Dir.* Claudia Dull
Library Holdings: Bk Titles 18,000; Per Subs 100; Talking Bks 250
Wireless access
Mem of Winding Rivers Library System
Open Mon, Tues, Thurs & Fri 2-6, Wed 9-5, Sat 9-Noon

REDGRANITE

P REDGRANITE PUBLIC LIBRARY*, 135 W Bannerman Ave, 54970. (Mail add: PO Box 291, 54970-0291), SAN 318-3548. Tel: 920-566-0176. E-mail: director@redgranitelibrary.org. Web Site: www.redgranitelibrary.org. *Libr Dir,* Lisa Zwickey; Staff 2 (MLS 1, Non-MLS 1)
Library Holdings: AV Mats 700; Large Print Bks 100; Bk Vols 10,000; Per Subs 30; Talking Bks 50
Special Collections: Local History
Automation Activity & Vendor Info: (Cataloging) SirsiDynix; (Circulation) SirsiDynix; (OPAC) SirsiDynix
Mem of Winnefox Library System
Open Mon, Wed & Fri 10:30-5, Sat 9-Noon
Friends of the Library Group

REEDSBURG

P REEDSBURG PUBLIC LIBRARY*, 370 Vine St, 53959. SAN 318-3556. Tel: 608-768-7323. FAX: 608-524-9024. E-mail: info@reedsburglibrary.org. Web Site: www.reedsburglibrary.org. *Dir,* Sue Ann Kucher; *Asst Dir,* Kris Houtler; E-mail: khoutler@reedsburglibrary.org; *Circ Supvr,* Jo Clark; *Youth Serv,* Tina Peerenboom; Staff 12 (MLS 2, Non-MLS 10)
Founded 1898. Pop 18,000; Circ 289,365
Library Holdings: Bk Titles 70,555; Per Subs 137
Automation Activity & Vendor Info: (Circulation) SirsiDynix; (Serials) SirsiDynix
Wireless access
Mem of South Central Library System
Open Mon-Thurs 8:30-8, Fri 8:30-5, Sat 9-4, Sun Noon-3
Friends of the Library Group

REESEVILLE

P REESEVILLE PUBLIC LIBRARY*, 216 S Main St, 53579. (Mail add: PO Box 279, 53579-0279), SAN 364-6173. Tel: 920-927-7390. FAX: 920-927-7390. E-mail: reesevillelibrary@monarchlibraries.org. Web Site: www.reeseville.lib.wi.us. *Dir,* Kay Kromm; E-mail: kay.kromm@monarchlibraries.org
Founded 1964
Library Holdings: Bk Vols 9,675
Mem of Monarch Library System
Open Mon, Tues & Thurs 11-7, Wed & Fri 3-5, Sat 10-Noon

RHINELANDER

J NICOLET AREA TECHNICAL COLLEGE*, Richard J Brown Library, Lakeside Center, 3rd Flr, 5364 College Dr, 54501. SAN 318-3572. Tel: 715-365-4479. Toll Free Tel: 800-544-3039, Ext 4479. FAX: 715-365-4404. TDD: 715-365-4448. E-mail: LibraryInfo@nicoletcollege.edu. Web Site: nicoletcollege.libguides.com/home. *Mgr, Libr Serv,* Nora Craven; Tel: 715-365-4576, E-mail: ncraven@nicoletcollege.edu; *Cat, Resource Management,* Kathleen Tromp; Tel: 715-365-4479, E-mail: ktromp@nicoletcollege.edu; *Access Serv Spec, Info Serv Spec,* Peggy Klein; Tel: 715-365-4606, E-mail: pklein@nicoletcollege.edu; Staff 4 (MLS 1, Non-MLS 3)
Founded 1969. Enrl 1,500; Fac 75; Highest Degree: Associate
Library Holdings: Bk Vols 45,000; Per Subs 350
Special Collections: State Document Depository
Subject Interests: Art, Native Am, Nursing
Automation Activity & Vendor Info: (Cataloging) Follett Software; (Circulation) Follett Software; (ILL) OCLC WorldShare Interlibrary Loan; (OPAC) Follett Software
Wireless access
Publications: Handbook; Subject Bibliographies & Pathfinders
Partic in OCLC Online Computer Library Center, Inc; WiLS
Open Mon-Thurs 8-8, Fri & Sat 8-4 (Fall & Winter); Mon-Thurs 8-6, Fri 8-4 (Summer)

P RHINELANDER DISTRICT LIBRARY*, 106 N Stevens St, 54501-3193. SAN 318-3580. Tel: 715-365-1070. FAX: 715-365-1076. Web Site: www.rhinelanderlibrary.org. *Exec Dir,* Virginia Roberts; E-mail: director@rhinelanderlibrary.org; *Assoc Dir,* Debbie Valine; E-mail: dvaline@rhinelanderlibrary.org; *Adult Serv,* Cathy Oelrich; E-mail: COelrich@rhinelanderlibrary.org; *Ch Serv,* Denise Chojnacki; E-mail: denise@rhinelanderlibrary.org; Staff 13 (MLS 3, Non-MLS 10)
Founded 1898. Pop 18,511; Circ 190,605
Library Holdings: Bk Vols 80,144; Per Subs 98; Videos 6,430
Special Collections: Art (Ruth Smith Bump Coll)
Subject Interests: Archit, Art, Genealogy, Local hist, State hist

Automation Activity & Vendor Info: (Acquisitions) Innovative Interfaces, Inc; (Cataloging) Innovative Interfaces, Inc; (Circulation) Innovative Interfaces, Inc
Wireless access
Function: 24/7 Electronic res, 24/7 Online cat, Adult bk club, Art programs, Audiobks on Playaways & MP3, Audiobks via web, Bk club(s), Bks on CD, Children's prog, Computers for patron use, Distance learning, Electronic databases & coll, Free DVD rentals, Genealogy discussion group, Home delivery & serv to seniorr ctr & nursing homes, ILL available, Internet access, Magazines, Mail & tel request accepted, Music CDs, Notary serv, Online cat, OverDrive digital audio bks, Photocopying/Printing, Preschool outreach, Preschool reading prog, Printer for laptops & handheld devices, Prog for adults, Prog for children & young adult, Ref serv available, Serves people with intellectual disabilities, Summer reading prog, Tax forms, Teen prog, VHS videos, Wheelchair accessible, Winter reading prog
Partic in Wisconsin Valley Library Service
Open Mon 9-8, Tues-Fri 9-6, Sat 9-1
Friends of the Library Group

RIB LAKE

P RIB LAKE PUBLIC LIBRARY*, 645 Pearl St, 54470. (Mail add: PO Box 188, 54470-0188), SAN 318-3599. Tel: 715-427-5769. FAX: 715-804-2630. Web Site: riblakepl.org. *Dir,* Tammie Blomberg; E-mail: director@riblakepl.org; *Asst Dir,* Krista Blomberg; Staff 5 (Non-MLS 5)
Founded 1900. Pop 2,000; Circ 25,000
Jan 2020-Dec 2020. Mats Exp $14,000. Sal $56,000 (Prof $21,000)
Library Holdings: Audiobooks 200; CDs 100; DVDs 1,200; Large Print Bks 300; Bk Titles 20,000; Per Subs 83
Special Collections: Rib Lake Heralds 1902-1970
Subject Interests: Local hist
Automation Activity & Vendor Info: (Cataloging) Innovative Interfaces, Inc - Sierra; (Circulation) Innovative Interfaces, Inc - Sierra; (Discovery) EBSCO Discovery Service; (OPAC) Innovative Interfaces, Inc - Sierra
Wireless access
Function: 24/7 Electronic res, 24/7 Online cat, Adult bk club, Audiobks on Playaways & MP3, Audiobks via web, Bks on CD, Children's prog, Computers for patron use, Electronic databases & coll, Free DVD rentals, ILL available, Internet access, Laminating, Magazines, Movies, Music CDs, Online cat, Online ref, OverDrive digital audio bks, Photocopying/Printing, Preschool outreach, Preschool reading prog, Prog for adults, Prog for children & young adult, Ref & res, Scanner, Senior outreach, Serves people with intellectual disabilities, Spoken cassettes & CDs, Story hour, Summer reading prog, Tax forms, Teen prog, Wheelchair accessible, Writing prog
Partic in Wiscat; Wisconsin Valley Library Service
Open Mon, Tues, Thurs & Fri 10-6, Wed 12-8

RICE LAKE

J NORTHWOOD TECHNICAL COLLEGE*, Learning Resource Center, 1900 College Dr, 54868. SAN 318-3629. Tel: 715-234-7082. Toll Free Tel: 800-243-9482. Web Site: itlc.northwoodtech.edu/itlc/library. *Classroom Support Technician,* Stephen Anderson; E-mail: stephen.anderson@northwoodtech.edu; *Classroom Support Technician,* Alexander Birkholz; E-mail: alexander.birkholz@northwoodtech.edu
Library Holdings: Bk Titles 747; Per Subs 30
Automation Activity & Vendor Info: (Cataloging) Innovative Interfaces, Inc - Sierra; (Circulation) Innovative Interfaces, Inc - Sierra; (Course Reserve) Innovative Interfaces, Inc - Sierra; (OPAC) Innovative Interfaces, Inc - Sierra
Wireless access
Open Mon-Thurs 8-7, Fri 8-4

P RICE LAKE PUBLIC LIBRARY*, Two E Marshall St, 54868. SAN 318-3602. Tel: 715-234-4861. FAX: 715-234-5026. Web Site: www.rlpl.org. *Dir,* Katherine Elchert; Tel: 715-234-4861, Ext 1111, E-mail: katherineelchert@ricelakegov.org; *Adult & Teen Prog Coordr,* Kerri Ashlin; Tel: 715-234-4861, Ext 1115, E-mail: kerriashlin@ricelakegov.org; *Coordr, ILL,* Kati Schnacky; Tel: 715-234-4861, Ext 1112, E-mail: katischnacky@ricelakegov.org; *Technical Servs & Staff Educ,* Linda Mullin; Tel: 715-234-4861, Ext 1116, E-mail: lindamullin@ricelakegov.org; Staff 14.1 (MLS 3, Non-MLS 11.1)
Founded 1896. Pop 8,580; Circ 204,000
Library Holdings: AV Mats 1,661; DVDs 1,000; e-books 15,845; Bk Vols 40,224; Per Subs 189; Videos 760
Subject Interests: Local hist
Automation Activity & Vendor Info: (Cataloging) Innovative Interfaces, Inc; (Circulation) Innovative Interfaces, Inc; (OPAC) Innovative Interfaces, Inc; (Serials) Innovative Interfaces, Inc
Wireless access
Function: Adult bk club, Audio & video playback equip for onsite use, Audiobks via web, Bi-weekly Writer's Group, Bks on cassette, Bks on CD, Children's prog, Computers for patron use, Home delivery & serv to seniorr ctr & nursing homes, ILL available, Large print keyboards, Magnifiers for reading, Music CDs, Notary serv, Online cat, Online ref, OverDrive digital audio bks, Photocopying/Printing, Prog for adults, Prog for children & young adult, Scanner, Story hour, Summer reading prog, Tax forms, Teen prog, Wheelchair accessible
Mem of Inspiring & Facilitating Library Success (IFLS)
Special Services for the Blind - Assistive/Adapted tech devices, equip & products; Bks on cassette; Bks on CD; Computer with voice synthesizer for visually impaired persons; Large print bks; Open bk software on pub access PC
Open Mon-Fri 9-7, Sat 9-5
Restriction: 24-hr pass syst for students only
Friends of the Library Group

J UNIVERSITY OF WISCONSIN-EAU CLAIRE*, Barron County Campus Library, 1800 College Dr, 54868-2497. SAN 318-3610. Tel: 715-788-6250. E-mail: ecbclibdesk@uwec.edu. Web Site: barron.uwec.edu/library. *Acad Librn,* Cecelia Cole; *Libr Asst,* Linda L Snider; E-mail: sniderll@uwec.edu; Staff 3 (MLS 1, Non-MLS 2)
Founded 1968. Enrl 434; Fac 26; Highest Degree: Associate
Library Holdings: Bk Titles 27,269; Bk Vols 32,168; Per Subs 460
Automation Activity & Vendor Info: (Acquisitions) Ex Libris Group; (Cataloging) Ex Libris Group; (Circulation) Ex Libris Group; (ILL) Ex Libris Group
Wireless access
Function: For res purposes
Open Mon-Thurs 8-6, Fri 8-4

RICHLAND CENTER

P BREWER PUBLIC LIBRARY*, 325 N Central Ave, 53581. SAN 318-3637. Tel: 608-647-6444. E-mail: richlandcenterpl@gmail.com. Web Site: brewerpubliclibrary.org. *Dir,* Martha Bauer; E-mail: mbauer@swls.org
Founded 1969. Pop 5,114; Circ 104,233
Library Holdings: Bk Vols 52,119; Per Subs 111
Special Collections: Richland County History Coll. Oral History
Wireless access
Mem of Southwest Wisconsin Library System
Open Mon-Thurs 9-8, Fri 9-5, Sat 10-2
Friends of the Library Group

C UNIVERSITY OF WISCONSIN-PLATTEVILLE RICHLAND CAMPUS*, Miller Memorial Library, 1200 US Hwy 14 W, 53581. SAN 318-3645. Tel: 608-800-6817. Circulation Tel: 608-800-6803. Web Site: www.uwplatt.edu/department/karrmann-library. *Acad Librn,* Sarah Winger; Tel: 608-800-6817, E-mail: wingersa@uwplatt.edu; Staff 2 (MLS 1, Non-MLS 1)
Founded 1967. Enrl 60; Fac 7; Highest Degree: Associate
Library Holdings: Bk Vols 20,348
Automation Activity & Vendor Info: (Acquisitions) Ex Libris Group; (Cataloging) Ex Libris Group; (Circulation) Ex Libris Group; (Course Reserve) Ex Libris Group; (ILL) Ex Libris Group; (Media Booking) Ex Libris Group; (OPAC) Ex Libris Group; (Serials) Ex Libris Group
Partic in OCLC Online Computer Library Center, Inc; WiLS
Open Mon-Thurs 9-4, Fri 9-3

RIO

P RIO COMMUNITY LIBRARY*, 324 W Lyons St, 53960. (Mail add: PO Box 306, 53960-0306), SAN 318-3653. Tel: 920-992-3206. FAX: 920-992-3983. E-mail: questions@riolibrary.org. Web Site: www.riolibrary.org. *Dir,* Jenna Assmus; E-mail: jassmus@riolibrary.org; *Asst Dir,* Jon Pribbenow; E-mail: jpribbenow@riolibrary.org; Staff 2 (MLS 1, Non-MLS 1)
Founded 1917. Pop 2,683; Circ 35,000
Library Holdings: Audiobooks 639; CDs 657; DVDs 1,610; e-books 65,673; Electronic Media & Resources 321; High Interest/Low Vocabulary Bk Vols 547; Large Print Bks 1,141; Microforms 1; Bk Vols 19,464; Per Subs 60; Videos 1,088
Automation Activity & Vendor Info: (Cataloging) Book Systems; (Circulation) Book Systems; (OPAC) Book Systems
Wireless access
Function: Art exhibits, Bk club(s), Bks on cassette, Bks on CD, Children's prog, Computers for patron use, Electronic databases & coll, Free DVD rentals, Holiday prog, ILL available, Internet access, Mail & tel request accepted, Music CDs, Notary serv, Online cat, Online ref, OverDrive digital audio bks, Photocopying/Printing, Prog for children & young adult, Ref & res, Ref serv available, Spoken cassettes & CDs, Spoken cassettes & DVDs, Story hour, Summer reading prog, Tax forms, Telephone ref, VHS videos, Wheelchair accessible
Mem of South Central Library System
Open Mon & Wed 10-8, Tues, Thurs & Fri 10-5, Sat 10-3
Friends of the Library Group

RIPON

C RIPON COLLEGE*, Lane Library, 300 Seward St, 54971. (Mail add: PO Box 248, 54971-0248), SAN 318-3661. Tel: 920-748-8175. Interlibrary Loan Service Tel: 920-748-8750. FAX: 920-748-7243. E-mail: library@ripon.edu. Web Site: www.ripon.edu/library. *Libr Dir, User Serv Librn,* Andrew R Prellwitz; E-mail: prellwitza@ripon.edu; *Acq, Bus Mgr,* Amy Stephens; E-mail: stephensa@ripon.edu; Staff 3.8 (MLS 2, Non-MLS 1.8)
Founded 1851. Enrl 816; Fac 74; Highest Degree: Bachelor
Library Holdings: Bk Titles 162,802; Bk Vols 190,751; Per Subs 500
Special Collections: ColisLotory; Local History (Pedrick Coll); Wisconsin Authors (Wisconsin's Own Library). State Document Depository; US Document Depository
Subject Interests: Liberal arts
Automation Activity & Vendor Info: (Acquisitions) Innovative Interfaces, Inc; (Cataloging) Innovative Interfaces, Inc; (Circulation) Innovative Interfaces, Inc; (Course Reserve) Innovative Interfaces, Inc; (ILL) Clio; (OPAC) Innovative Interfaces, Inc; (Serials) Innovative Interfaces, Inc
Wireless access
Function: ILL available
Publications: Bibliographic Guides
Partic in OCLC Online Computer Library Center, Inc; WiLS
Open Mon-Thurs 7:30am-Midnight, Fri 7:30am-8pm, Sat 10-8, Sun Noon-Midnight; Mon-Fri 8-5 (Summer)
Friends of the Library Group

P RIPON PUBLIC LIBRARY*, 120 Jefferson St, 54971. SAN 318-367X. Tel: 920-748-6160. Web Site: riponlibrary.org. *Dir,* Desiree M Bongers; E-mail: director@riponlibrary.org; *Ch,* Linda DeCramer; Staff 5 (MLS 2, Non-MLS 3)
Founded 1885. Pop 11,500
Library Holdings: AV Mats 5,772; Bk Titles 56,837; Per Subs 152
Automation Activity & Vendor Info: (Cataloging) SirsiDynix; (Circulation) SirsiDynix; (OPAC) SirsiDynix
Wireless access
Publications: Ripon Public Library (Newsletter)
Mem of Winnefox Library System
Open Mon-Thurs 9:30-8, Fri 9-6, Sat 9-4, Sun 1-4 (Winter); Mon-Thurs 9:30-8, Fri 9-6, Sat 9-1 (Summer)
Friends of the Library Group

RIVER FALLS

P RIVER FALLS PUBLIC LIBRARY*, 140 Union St, 54022. SAN 318-3688. Tel: 715-425-0905. FAX: 715-425-0914. Web Site: www.riverfallspubliclibrary.org. *Libr Dir,* Tanya Misselt; Tel: 715-426-3498, E-mail: tmisselt@riverfallslibrary.org; *Ref Serv,* Kim Kiiskinen; Tel: 715-425-0905, Ext 664, E-mail: kkiiskinen@riverfallspubliclibrary.org; *Tech Serv,* Jon George; Tel: 715-425-0905, Ext 3497, E-mail: jgeorge@riverfallspubliclibrary.org; *Youth Serv,* Monica LaVold; Tel: 715-425-0905, Ext 3484, E-mail: mlavold@riverfallspubliclibrary.org; Staff 14 (MLS 4, Non-MLS 10)
Circ 347,000
Library Holdings: Bk Titles 70,000; Per Subs 200
Subject Interests: Hist of River Falls
Automation Activity & Vendor Info: (Cataloging) Innovative Interfaces, Inc; (Circulation) Innovative Interfaces, Inc; (OPAC) Innovative Interfaces, Inc; (Serials) Innovative Interfaces, Inc
Wireless access
Function: Art exhibits, Audiobks via web, Bk club(s), Bks on cassette, Bks on CD, Computers for patron use, Equip loans & repairs, Home delivery & serv to seniorr ctr & nursing homes, ILL available, Magnifiers for reading, Music CDs, Online cat, Online ref, Outreach serv, Photocopying/Printing, Prog for adults, Prog for children & young adult, Scanner, Senior outreach, Story hour, Summer reading prog, Tax forms, Teen prog, Telephone ref, Wheelchair accessible
Mem of Inspiring & Facilitating Library Success (IFLS)
Special Services for the Deaf - Closed caption videos
Special Services for the Blind - Accessible computers; Bks on cassette; Bks on CD
Open Mon-Thurs 9-8, Fri 9-6, Sat 10-4, Sun (Sept-May) 1-4

C UNIVERSITY OF WISCONSIN-RIVER FALLS*, Chalmer Davee Library, 410 S Third St, 54022. SAN 318-3696. Tel: 715-425-3321. E-mail: refdesk@uwrf.edu. Web Site: www.uwrf.edu/library. *Dir,* Maureen Olle-LaJoie; Tel: 715-425-3799, E-mail: maureen.olle-lajoie@uwrf.edu; *E-Resources & Systems Librn,* Amanda Moeller; Tel: 715-425-3963, E-mail: amanda.moeller@uwrf.edu; *First Year Experience Librn,* Kim Westberry; Tel: 715-425-4918, E-mail: kimberley.westberry@uwrf.edu; *Access Serv Mgr,* Christy Boyer; Tel: 715-425-3542, E-mail: christy.boyer@uwrf.edu; *Textbook Services Mgr,* Daniel Rivera; Tel: 715-425-4721, E-mail: daniel.rivera@uwrf.edu; *Access Serv Asst,* Rachel Nelson; Tel: 715-425-4975, E-mail: rachel.a.nelson@uwrf.edu; *Access Serv Asst,* Stephanie Trinidad; Tel: 715-425-4155, E-mail: stephanie.trinidad@uwrf.edu; *ILL Asst,* Kelly Hood; Tel: 715-425-4325, E-mail: kelly.hood@uwrf.edu; *Tech Serv Asst,* Helen Spasojevich; Tel: 715-425-4628, E-mail: helen.m.spasojevich@uwrf.edu; *Tech Serv Asst,* Anne Tuveson; Tel: 715-425-4887, E-mail: anne.tuveson@uwrf.edu; *Textbook Services Asst,* Jesse Aerlyn-Crook; Tel: 715-425-4003, E-mail: jesse.aerlyncrook@uwrf.edu; *Textbook Services Asst,* Dawn Goenner; Tel: 715-425-4303, E-mail: dawn.goenner@uwrf.edu; *Community Archivist,* Shelby Edwards; Tel: 715-425-4633, E-mail: shelby.edwards@uwrf.edu; *Univ Archivist & Rec Mgr,* Morgan Paavola; Tel: 715-425-3567, E-mail: morgan.paavola@uwrf.edu; Staff 15 (MLS 6, Non-MLS 9)
Founded 1875. Enrl 4,902; Fac 182; Highest Degree: Doctorate
Jul 2020-Jun 2021. Mats Exp $495,685, Books $16,516, Per/Ser (Incl. Access Fees) $295,296, Other Print Mats $238, Micro $24,505, AV Mat $1,343, Electronic Ref Mat (Incl. Access Fees) $157,787. Sal $604,809 (Prof $377,741)
Library Holdings: AV Mats 14,579; e-books 458,684; e-journals 50,725; Electronic Media & Resources 136,449; Microforms 97,000; Music Scores 5,443; Bk Vols 266,008; Per Subs 24
Special Collections: Northwestern Wisconsin History; University History. Oral History; State Document Depository; US Document Depository
Subject Interests: Agr, Educ, Hist
Automation Activity & Vendor Info: (Acquisitions) Ex Libris Group; (Cataloging) Ex Libris Group; (Circulation) Ex Libris Group; (Course Reserve) Ex Libris Group; (Discovery) Ex Libris Group; (ILL) OCLC ILLiad; (OPAC) Ex Libris Group; (Serials) Ex Libris Group
Wireless access
Partic in CUWL; OCLC Online Computer Library Center, Inc; WiLS
Special Services for the Blind - Accessible computers; Magnifiers

ROBERTS

P HAZEL MACKIN COMMUNITY LIBRARY*, 311 W Warren St, 54023. (Mail add: PO Box 88, 54023-0088), SAN 318-370X. Tel: 715-749-3849. E-mail: HMCL@robertspubliclibrary.org. Web Site: www.robertspubliclibrary.org. *Dir,* Tori Schoess; E-mail: schoess@robertspubliclibrary.org; *Adult Programming, Youth Serv,* Brittany Fahrencamp; E-mail: fahrenkamp@robertspubliclibrary.org; Staff 1 (Non-MLS 1)
Founded 1975. Pop 1,500; Circ 21,429
Library Holdings: AV Mats 759; Bks on Deafness & Sign Lang 25; e-books 15,845; Large Print Bks 390; Bk Titles 12,206; Per Subs 47; Talking Bks 670; Videos 740
Automation Activity & Vendor Info: (Cataloging) Innovative Interfaces, Inc; (Circulation) Innovative Interfaces, Inc; (ILL) Innovative Interfaces, Inc; (OPAC) Innovative Interfaces, Inc
Wireless access
Mem of Inspiring & Facilitating Library Success (IFLS)
Open Mon, Wed & Fri 10-6, Tues & Thurs 1-8, Sat 10-1

ROCHESTER

P ROCHESTER PUBLIC LIBRARY*, 208 W Spring St, 53167. (Mail add: PO Box 245, 53167-0245), SAN 318-3718. Tel: 262-534-3533. FAX: 262-534-3531. E-mail: info@rochester.lib.wi.us. Web Site: www.rochester.lib.wi.us. *Dir,* Mary Stapleton; E-mail: stapleto@rochester.lib.wi.us
Founded 1890
Library Holdings: Bk Vols 15,000; Per Subs 56
Automation Activity & Vendor Info: (Acquisitions) SirsiDynix; (Cataloging) SirsiDynix; (Circulation) SirsiDynix; (OPAC) SirsiDynix
Wireless access
Mem of Prairie Lakes Library System (PLLS)
Open Mon-Thurs 9:30-7:30, Sat 9:30-3, Sun 1-4 (Winter); Mon-Thurs 9:30-7:30, Sat 9:30-1 (Summer)
Friends of the Library Group

ROCK SPRINGS

P ROCK SPRINGS PUBLIC LIBRARY*, 251 Railroad St, 53961. (Mail add: PO Box 246, 53961-0246), SAN 318-3726. Tel: 608-737-1063. E-mail: librarian@rockspringslibrary.com. Web Site: www.rockspringslibrary.com. *Libr Dir,* Rebecca Lynn Anderson; E-mail: director@rockspringslibrary.com; *Librn,* Shane Harvey; *Asst Librn,* Mrs Kristine Blauert; *Circ Asst,* Mrs Judy Polkky
Founded 1957. Pop 1,500; Circ 9,300
Library Holdings: Bk Titles 6,638
Subject Interests: Local hist
Automation Activity & Vendor Info: (Cataloging) Bibliovation; (Circulation) Bibliovation; (ILL) Bibliovation
Wireless access
Mem of South Central Library System
Open Mon 10-6, Tues & Thurs 1-5, Wed 10-3
Friends of the Library Group

SAINT CROIX FALLS

P ST CROIX FALLS PUBLIC LIBRARY*, 230 S Washington St, 54024. (Mail add: PO Box 608, 54024-0608), SAN 378-004X. Tel: 715-483-1777. FAX: 715-483-1782. E-mail: scflibrary@scfpl.org. Web Site: stcroixfallslibrary.org. *Libr Dir,* Su Leslie; E-mail: sleslie@scfpl.org; Staff 3 (MLS 1, Non-MLS 2)
Founded 1921. Pop 5,000; Circ 70,000
Library Holdings: Bk Titles 18,000; Per Subs 32
Special Collections: Wisconsin History Coll; Wisconsin Newspapers 1872-
Wireless access
Mem of Inspiring & Facilitating Library Success (IFLS)
Open Mon-Thurs 9:30-6, Fri 9:30-1
Friends of the Library Group

SAINT FRANCIS

P ST FRANCIS PUBLIC LIBRARY*, 4230 S Nicholson Ave, 53235. SAN 323-4738. Tel: 414-481-7323. FAX: 414-481-1413. E-mail: stfrancis@mcfls.org. *Libr Dir,* Amy Krahn; E-mail: amy.krahn@mcfls.org; *Ch Serv,* Jessica Norris; *Circ Serv,* Lisa Liban
Founded 1987. Pop 9,400
Automation Activity & Vendor Info: (Cataloging) Innovative Interfaces, Inc; (Circulation) Innovative Interfaces, Inc
Wireless access
Publications: Annual Report
Mem of Milwaukee County Federated Library System
Special Services for the Deaf - TDD equip
Open Mon-Thurs 9:30-8, Fri 9:30-5, Sat 9:30-4
Friends of the Library Group

R SAINT FRANCIS SEMINARY*, Salzmann Library, 3257 S Lake Dr, 53235-0905. SAN 318-2436. Tel: 414-747-6479. Interlibrary Loan Service Tel: 414-747-6478. Reference Tel: 414-747-6476. Web Site: www.sfs.edu/Salzmann.html. *Dir,* Mark Schrauth; E-mail: mschrauth@sfs.edu; *Libr Asst,* Marijo Zielinski; E-mail: mzielinski@sfs.edu; Staff 4 (MLS 3, Non-MLS 1)
Founded 1845. Enrl 152; Fac 18; Highest Degree: Master
Library Holdings: Bk Titles 80,000; Bk Vols 84,120; Per Subs 508
Special Collections: Rembert G Weakland Coll
Subject Interests: Biblical works, Bioethics, Canon law, Church hist, Milwaukee, Patristics, Scripture, Theol, Wis, Women's studies
Automation Activity & Vendor Info: (Acquisitions) Innovative Interfaces, Inc; (Cataloging) Innovative Interfaces, Inc; (Circulation) Innovative Interfaces, Inc; (Course Reserve) Innovative Interfaces, Inc; (ILL) OCLC Online; (Media Booking) Innovative Interfaces, Inc; (OPAC) Innovative Interfaces, Inc; (Serials) Innovative Interfaces, Inc
Function: ILL available, Photocopying/Printing, Ref serv available, Telephone ref
Partic in OCLC Online Computer Library Center, Inc; Southeastern Wisconsin Information Technology Exchange, Inc; WiLS
Open Tues-Thurs 12-8, Wed, Fri & Sat 10-4
Friends of the Library Group

SALEM

P COMMUNITY LIBRARY*, 24615 89th St, 53168. SAN 377-9521. Tel: 262-843-3348. FAX: 262-843-3144. Web Site: www.communitylib.org. *Dir,* LeeAnn Briese; E-mail: lbriese@communitylib.org; *Head, Pub Serv,* Irene Scherer; E-mail: ischerer@community.lib.wi.us; *Circ Serv Supvr,* Sharon Larson; E-mail: slarson@community.lib.wi.us; *Support Serv Mgr,* Danijela Smitz; E-mail: dsmitz@community.lib.wi.us
Founded 1977
Library Holdings: Bk Titles 48,000; Per Subs 275
Automation Activity & Vendor Info: (Acquisitions) Infor Library & Information Solutions; (Cataloging) Infor Library & Information Solutions; (Circulation) Infor Library & Information Solutions
Wireless access
Mem of Kenosha County Library System
Open Mon-Thurs 9-8, Fri & Sat 9-4
Branches: 1
TWIN LAKES BRANCH, 110 S Lake Ave, Twin Lakes, 53181, SAN 377-9815. Tel: 262-877-4281. FAX: 262-877-2682. *Support Serv Mgr,* Danijela Smitz
Open Mon-Thurs 10-8, Sat 10-4

SAND CREEK

P CLARELLA HACKETT JOHNSON PUBLIC LIBRARY*, E9311 County Rd I, 54765. (Mail add: PO Box 156, 54765-0156), SAN 378-0066. Tel: 715-658-1269. E-mail: sandcreeklib@sandcreekpl.org. Web Site: sandcreekpl.org. *Dir,* Catherine LeFevre
Pop 500
Library Holdings: Bk Titles 8,000; Per Subs 30
Wireless access
Mem of Inspiring & Facilitating Library Success (IFLS)
Open Mon, Wed & Fri 10-5, Sat 9-12
Friends of the Library Group

SAUK CITY

P GEORGE CULVER COMMUNITY LIBRARY*, 615 Phillips Blvd, 53583-1159. SAN 318-3750. Tel: 608-643-8346. E-mail: info@saukcitylibrary.org. Web Site: www.saukcitylibrary.org. *Libr Dir,* Kylee Bear; E-mail: kylee@saukcitylibrary.org
Founded 1924
Library Holdings: Bk Vols 28,000; Per Subs 96
Special Collections: Oral History
Wireless access
Function: Homebound delivery serv
Mem of South Central Library System
Special Services for the Blind - Audio mat; Large print bks
Open Mon-Thurs 9-8, Fri 9-5:30, Sat 9-2
Friends of the Library Group

SAUKVILLE

P OSCAR GRADY PUBLIC LIBRARY*, 151 S Main St, 53080. SAN 324-7988. Tel: 262-284-6022. FAX: 262-284-1933. Web Site: www.oscargradylibrary.org. *Libr Dir,* Emily Laws; E-mail: elaws@village.saukville.wi.us; Staff 10 (MLS 1, Non-MLS 9)
Founded 1972. Pop 4,100; Circ 87,600
Library Holdings: Bk Vols 40,000; Per Subs 100
Special Collections: Saukville History
Automation Activity & Vendor Info: (Cataloging) SirsiDynix; (Circulation) SirsiDynix; (OPAC) SirsiDynix; (Serials) SirsiDynix
Wireless access
Function: Prog for children & young adult, Summer reading prog, Telephone ref
Mem of Monarch Library System
Special Services for the Deaf - Bks on deafness & sign lang
Special Services for the Blind - BiFolkal kits; Bks on CD; Talking bks
Open Mon-Thurs 10-8, Fri 10-5, Sat 10-2
Friends of the Library Group

SAYNER

P PLUM LAKE PUBLIC LIBRARY, 8789 Peterson St, 54560. (Mail add: PO Box 229, 54560-0229), SAN 318-3769. Tel: 715-542-2020. FAX: 715-542-2627. Web Site: plumlakelibrary.org. *Dir,* Emilie Braunel; E-mail: ebraunel@sayner.wislib.org; Staff 1.1 (Non-MLS 1.1)
Founded 1939. Pop 800; Circ 27,475
Library Holdings: AV Mats 4,408; CDs 1,948; DVDs 2,460; e-books 28,240; Large Print Bks 550; Bk Titles 21,174; Bk Vols 21,724; Per Subs 118; Talking Bks 1,056
Special Collections: Memorial Coll
Subject Interests: Local hist
Automation Activity & Vendor Info: (Acquisitions) Innovative Interfaces, Inc; (Cataloging) Innovative Interfaces, Inc; (Circulation) Innovative Interfaces, Inc; (ILL) Brodart; (OPAC) Innovative Interfaces, Inc
Wireless access
Mem of Northern Waters Library Service
Partic in Merlin
Open Mon & Wed 10-6, Tues & Thurs-10-2, Fri 10-4, Sat 10-1
Friends of the Library Group

SCANDINAVIA

P SCANDINAVIA PUBLIC LIBRARY*, 349 N Main St, 54977. (Mail add: PO Box 157, 54977-0157), SAN 377-9750. Tel: 715-467-4636. E-mail: sca@scalib.org. Web Site: www.scandinavialibrary.org. *Dir,* Susan Vater-Olsen; E-mail: svater@scalib.org; Staff 1 (Non-MLS 1)
Pop 642
Library Holdings: AV Mats 1,500; Bk Titles 6,300; Per Subs 3
Wireless access
Mem of Outagamie Waupaca Library System (OWLS)
Partic in OWLSnet
Open Mon, Tues & Fri 2-6, Thurs 9-1 & 2-6, Sat 9-1

SEYMOUR

P MUEHL PUBLIC LIBRARY*, 436 N Main, 54165-1021. SAN 318-3777. Tel: 920-833-2725. FAX: 920-833-9804. E-mail: sey@muehlpubliclibrary.org. Web Site: www.muehlpubliclibrary.org. *Libr Dir, Programmer,* Elizabeth M Timmins; E-mail: etimmins@muehlpubliclibrary.org; Staff 1 (Non-MLS 1)
Founded 1901. Pop 7,000; Circ 70,512
Jan 2018-Dec 2018 Income $235,464, City $133,000, County $89,285, Locally Generated Income $13,179. Mats Exp $44,842, Books $29,585, AV Mat $14,046, Electronic Ref Mat (Incl. Access Fees) $1,211. Sal $124,040 (Prof $51,189)

Library Holdings: Audiobooks 1,503; CDs 96; DVDs 1,790; Large Print Bks 822; Bk Titles 26,759; Per Subs 16; Videos 2,180
Special Collections: Graphic Novels; Playaways
Automation Activity & Vendor Info: (Circulation) Innovative Interfaces, Inc; (OPAC) Innovative Interfaces, Inc
Wireless access
Function: 24/7 Online cat, Activity rm, Adult bk club, Art exhibits, Audiobks on Playaways & MP3, Audiobks via web, Bk club(s), Bks on CD, Children's prog, Computers for patron use, Doc delivery serv, Electronic databases & coll, Family literacy, Free DVD rentals, ILL available, Instruction & testing, Internet access, Laminating, Magnifiers for reading, Mail & tel request accepted, Meeting rooms, Movies, Music CDs, Online cat, Orientations, Outreach serv, Photocopying/Printing, Preschool outreach, Preschool reading prog, Prog for adults, Prog for children & young adult, Ref serv available, Scanner, Story hour, Study rm, Summer reading prog, Teen prog, Telephone ref, Workshops
Mem of Outagamie Waupaca Library System (OWLS)
Partic in OWLSnet
Open Mon-Thurs 10-8, Fri 10-6, Sat 10-2 (Winter); Mon-Thurs 10-8, Fri 10-5 (Summer)
Friends of the Library Group

SHARON

P BRIGHAM MEMORIAL LIBRARY*, 131 Plain St, 53585. SAN 318-3785. Tel: 262-736-4249. FAX: 262-736-3239. E-mail: brigham@sharon.lib.wi.us. Web Site: www.sharon.lib.wi.us. *Dir,* Mollie Hein
Founded 1927. Pop 2,511; Circ 39,300
Library Holdings: Bk Vols 12,948; Per Subs 25
Wireless access
Mem of Prairie Lakes Library System (PLLS)
Open Mon & Thurs 10-6, Tues Noon-8, Wed & Fri 9-5, Sat 9-Noon
Friends of the Library Group

SHAWANO

P SHAWANO COUNTY LIBRARY*, 128 S Sawyer St, 54166. SAN 365-0642. Tel: 715-526-3829. FAX: 715-526-6772. E-mail: sha@shawanolibrary.org. Web Site: www.shawanolibrary.org. *Libr Dir,* Kristie Hauer; E-mail: khauer@shawanolibrary.org; Staff 11.5 (MLS 1, Non-MLS 10.5)
Founded 1899. Pop 42,000; Circ 356,500
Library Holdings: AV Mats 15,466; Electronic Media & Resources 16,553; Bk Vols 131,333; Per Subs 40
Special Collections: Christmas Coll; Native American Coll
Automation Activity & Vendor Info: (Acquisitions) Innovative Interfaces, Inc; (Cataloging) Innovative Interfaces, Inc; (Circulation) Innovative Interfaces, Inc; (ILL) Innovative Interfaces, Inc; (Media Booking) Innovative Interfaces, Inc; (OPAC) Innovative Interfaces, Inc
Wireless access
Function: After school storytime, Audiobks via web, AV serv, Bks on cassette, Bks on CD, Children's prog, Computers for patron use, Digital talking bks, E-Reserves, Electronic databases & coll, Equip loans & repairs, Family literacy, Free DVD rentals, Holiday prog, Home delivery & serv to seniorr ctr & nursing homes, ILL available, Music CDs, Online cat, OverDrive digital audio bks, Photocopying/Printing, Preschool outreach, Prof lending libr, Prog for adults, Prog for children & young adult, Ref serv available, Scanner, Story hour, Summer & winter reading prog, Summer reading prog, Tax forms, Teen prog, Telephone ref, VHS videos, Wheelchair accessible
Mem of Nicolet Federated Library System
Partic in OWLSnet
Open Mon 8-8, Tues-Thurs 8-6, Fri 8-5, Sat 9-1
Friends of the Library Group
Branches: 5
BIRNAMWOOD BRANCH, 337 S Main St, Birnamwood, 54414-9259, SAN 365-0669. Tel: 715-449-3120.
Library Holdings: Bk Vols 25,897
Open Mon & Wed 2-8, Tues & Thurs 10-5, Sat 9-Noon
Friends of the Library Group
BONDUEL BRANCH, 125 N Washington St, Bonduel, 54107. (Mail add: PO Box 687, Bonduel, 54107-0687), SAN 365-0677. Tel: 715-758-2267. FAX: 715-758-6841. *Librn,* Allison Mead Schultz
Library Holdings: Bk Vols 13,963
Open Mon & Wed 3-7, Tues & Thurs 9-5, Sat 9-Noon
Friends of the Library Group
MATTOON BRANCH, 311 Slate Ave, Mattoon, 54450-0266, SAN 329-3505. Tel: 715-489-3333. *Librn,* Catherine Knowles
Library Holdings: Bk Vols 5,971
Open Tues 2-6, Wed 10-2
Friends of the Library Group
TIGERTON BRANCH, 221 Birch St, Tigerton, 54486. (Mail add: PO Box 166, Tigerton, 54486-0166), SAN 365-0707. Tel: 715-535-2194. FAX: 715-535-2666. *Librn,* Caitlin Witter
Library Holdings: Bk Vols 12,570
Open Wed & Thurs 10-6, Fri 2-8, Sat 2-5
Friends of the Library Group
WITTENBERG BRANCH, 302 S Cherry St, Wittenberg, 54499. (Mail add: PO Box 295, Wittenberg, 54499-0295), SAN 365-0715. Tel: 715-253-2936.
Library Holdings: Bk Vols 15,020
Open Mon, Tues & Thurs 2-7, Wed & Fri 10-5, Sat 9-Noon
Friends of the Library Group

SHEBOYGAN

S JOHN MICHAEL KOHLER ARTS CENTER*, Resource Center, 608 New York Ave, 53081-4507. SAN 318-3793. Tel: 920-458-6144. FAX: 920-458-4473. E-mail: rc@jmkac.org. Web Site: www.jmkac.org. *Dir,* Sam Gappmayer; *Syst Mgr,* Lisa Schultz; E-mail: lschultz@jmkac.org; Staff 1 (MLS 1)
Founded 1967
Library Holdings: Bk Titles 4,000; Bk Vols 5,500; Per Subs 65
Subject Interests: Contemporary Am crafts, Contemporary art, Self taught artists
Automation Activity & Vendor Info: (Cataloging) Follett Software; (Circulation) Follett Software; (OPAC) Follett Software
Wireless access
Function: Res libr
Publications: Exhibition Catalogs & Related Publications
Open Mon-Fri 10-5
Restriction: Non-circulating

P MEAD PUBLIC LIBRARY, 710 N Eight St, 53081-4563. SAN 318-3815. Tel: 920-459-3400. Circulation Tel: 920-459-3400, Ext 2075. Interlibrary Loan Service Tel: 920-459-3400, Ext 2048. Reference Tel: 920-459-3400, Ext 2076. Administration Tel: 920-459-3400, Ext 2039. FAX: 920-459-0204. Web Site: www.meadpl.org. *Dir, Libr Serv,* Mr Garrett Erickson; Tel: 920-459-3400, Ext 2041, E-mail: garrett.erickson@meadpl.org; *Dep Dir,* Melissa Prentice; Tel: 920-459-3400, Ext 2033, E-mail: melissa.prentice@meadpl.org; *Support Serv Mgr,* Cheryl Nessman; Tel: 920-459-3400, Ext 2010, E-mail: cheryl.nessman@meadpl.org; *IT Spec,* Chase DeVrou; Tel: 920-459-3400, Ext 2042, E-mail: chase.devrou@meadpl.org; Staff 48 (MLS 11, Non-MLS 37)
Founded 1897
Library Holdings: Audiobooks 16,217; AV Mats 23,471; e-books 65,732; Bk Vols 307,875; Per Subs 419
Special Collections: United States & State Census Coll
Subject Interests: Furniture, Local hist
Automation Activity & Vendor Info: (Acquisitions) Innovative Interfaces, Inc. - Polaris; (Cataloging) Innovative Interfaces, Inc. - Polaris; (Circulation) Innovative Interfaces, Inc. - Polaris; (OPAC) Innovative Interfaces, Inc. - Polaris; (Serials) Innovative Interfaces, Inc. - Polaris
Wireless access
Function: 24/7 Electronic res, 24/7 Online cat, 3D Printer, Activity rm, Adult bk club, Adult literacy prog, Archival coll, Art exhibits, Art programs, Audio & video playback equip for onsite use, Audiobks on Playaways & MP3, Audiobks via web, AV serv, Bilingual assistance for Spanish patrons, Bk club(s), Bks on CD, Bus archives, CD-ROM, Children's prog, Computer training, Computers for patron use, E-Readers, Electronic databases & coll, Equip loans & repairs, Family literacy, For res purposes, Free DVD rentals, Games & aids for people with disabilities, Govt ref serv, Holiday prog, Homebound delivery serv, Homework prog, ILL available, Instruction & testing, Internet access, Life-long learning prog for all ages, Literacy & newcomer serv, Magazines, Magnifiers for reading, Mail & tel request accepted, Makerspace, Meeting rooms, Microfiche/film & reading machines, Movies, Museum passes, Music CDs, Notary serv, Online cat, Online info literacy tutorials on the web & in blackboard, Online ref, Orientations, Outreach serv, Outside serv via phone, mail, e-mail & web, OverDrive digital audio bks, Photocopying/Printing, Preschool outreach, Preschool reading prog, Printer for laptops & handheld devices, Prog for adults, Prog for children & young adult, Ref & res, Ref serv available, Res assist avail, Res libr, Scanner, Senior computer classes, Senior outreach, Serves people with intellectual disabilities, Spanish lang bks, Specialized serv in classical studies, STEM programs, Story hour, Study rm, Summer reading prog, Tax forms, Teen prog, Visual arts prog, Wheelchair accessible, Workshops, Writing prog
Publications: Annual Report; Footnotes (Quarterly)
Mem of Monarch Library System
Open Mon-Thurs 8:30-8, Fri & Sat 8:30-5
Restriction: Badge access after hrs
Friends of the Library Group
Bookmobiles: 1

P MONARCH LIBRARY SYSTEM*, 4632 S Taylor Dr, 53081-1107. SAN 318-3831. Tel: 920-208-4900. FAX: 920-208-4901. Web Site: www.monarchlibraries.org. *Interim Dir,* Jennifer Chamberlain; Tel: 920-208-4900, Ext 312; *Database Mgt Librn,* Alison Hoffman; Tel: 920-208-4900, Ext 314, E-mail: ahoffman@monarchlibraries.org; *Pub Info,* Heather Fischer; E-mail: hfischer@monarchlibraries.org
Founded 1979. Pop 201,092; Circ 80,568
Library Holdings: Audiobooks 449; e-books 12,071; Electronic Media & Resources 4,748; Bk Vols 26,658; Per Subs 56; Videos 1,303
Automation Activity & Vendor Info: (Acquisitions) Innovative Interfaces, Inc; (Cataloging) Innovative Interfaces, Inc; (Circulation) Innovative Interfaces, Inc; (ILL) Auto-Graphics, Inc; (Media Booking) Innovative Interfaces, Inc; (OPAC) Innovative Interfaces, Inc; (Serials) Innovative Interfaces, Inc
Wireless access
Function: Doc delivery serv, Electronic databases & coll, Jail serv, Online cat, Outreach serv, OverDrive digital audio bks, Summer reading prog, Workshops
Publications: The Library Connection (Newsletter)
Member Libraries: Beaver Dam Community Library; Brownsville Public Library; Cedar Grove Public Library; Cedarburg Public Library; Elkhart Lake Public Library; Fox Lake Public Library; Frank L Weyenberg Library of Mequon-Thiensville; Germantown Community Library; Horicon Public Library; Hustisford Community Library; Iron Ridge Public Library; Jack Russell Memorial Library; Juneau Public Library; Kewaskum Public Library; Kohler Public Library; Lakeview Community Library; Lomira QuadGraphics Community Library; Lowell Public Library; Mayville Public Library; Mead Public Library; Oostburg Public Library; Oscar Grady Public Library; Plymouth Public Library; Reeseville Public Library; Sheboygan Falls Memorial Library; Slinger Community Library; Theresa Public Library; USS Liberty Memorial Public Library; W J Niederkorn Library; Waupun Public Library; West Bend Community Memorial Library
Partic in WiLS; Wisconsin Public Library Consortium
Special Services for the Blind - BiFolkal kits
Bookmobiles: 1. Bk titles 24,970

SHEBOYGAN FALLS

S SHEBOYGAN COUNTY HISTORICAL RESEARCH CENTER LIBRARY*, 518 Water St, 53085. SAN 325-5557. Tel: 920-467-4667. Web Site: www.schrc.org. *Exec Dir,* Beth Dippel; *Lead Research Asst,* Kathy Jeske; E-mail: kathyjeske@schrc.org; *Library Contact,* Katie Reilly; E-mail: katie.reilly@schrc.org
Founded 1983
Library Holdings: Bk Vols 5,000
Special Collections: Oral History
Subject Interests: Sheboygan County hist
Publications: The Researcher
Open Tues-Fri 9-4
Friends of the Library Group

P SHEBOYGAN FALLS MEMORIAL LIBRARY*, 330 Buffalo St, 53085-1399. SAN 318-3866. Tel: 920-467-7908. E-mail: SheboyganFallsLibrary@gmail.com. Web Site: www.sheboyganfallslibrary.org. *Dir,* Mark Rozmarynowski
Founded 1924. Pop 13,764; Circ 130,068
Library Holdings: AV Mats 9,600; Bk Vols 46,000; Per Subs 140
Automation Activity & Vendor Info: (Acquisitions) Innovative Interfaces, Inc; (Cataloging) Innovative Interfaces, Inc; (Circulation) Innovative Interfaces, Inc; (OPAC) Innovative Interfaces, Inc
Wireless access
Mem of Monarch Library System
Open Mon-Fri 9-6
Friends of the Library Group

SHELL LAKE

P SHELL LAKE PUBLIC LIBRARY*, 501 First St, 54871. (Mail add: PO Box 318, 54871-0318), SAN 318-3874. Tel: 715-468-2074. FAX: 715-468-7638. E-mail: staffslpibrary@gmail.com. Web Site: shelllakelibrary.org. *Dir,* Christine Seaton
Circ 11,194
Library Holdings: Bk Vols 17,000
Special Collections: Holiday Coll; Hunting Fishing Coll; Wisconsin Coll
Automation Activity & Vendor Info: (Acquisitions) Follett Software; (Cataloging) Follett Software; (Circulation) Follett Software
Wireless access
Mem of Northern Waters Library Service
Open Mon & Wed 10-8, Tues, Thurs & Fri 10-5, Sat 10-1
Friends of the Library Group

G WASHBURN COUNTY LAW LIBRARY*, Courthouse, 10 W Fourth Ave, 2nd Flr, 54871. (Mail add: PO Box 339, 54871-0339), SAN 328-3569. Tel: 715-468-4677. FAX: 715-468-4678. E-mail: washburn.coc@wicounts.gov. *Library Contact,* Shannon Anderson
Library Holdings: Bk Vols 150
Wireless access
Open Mon-Fri 8-4:30

SHIOCTON

P SHIOCTON PUBLIC LIBRARY*, W7740 Pine St, 54170. SAN 378-0082. Tel: 920-986-3933. E-mail: shi@shioctonlibrary.org. Web Site: www.shioctonlibrary.org. *Libr Dir,* Shay Foxenberg
Automation Activity & Vendor Info: (Cataloging) Innovative Interfaces, Inc; (Circulation) Innovative Interfaces, Inc; (OPAC) Innovative Interfaces, Inc
Wireless access
Mem of Outagamie Waupaca Library System (OWLS)
Open Mon & Wed Noon-7, Tues 10-5, Thurs & Fri Noon-5

SHOREWOOD

P SHOREWOOD PUBLIC LIBRARY*, 3920 N Murray Ave, 53211-2385. SAN 318-3882. Tel: 414-847-2670. E-mail: shorewood@mcfls.org. Web Site: www.shorewoodlibrary.org. *Dir,* Jen Gerber; E-mail: jen.gerber@mcfls.org; *Asst Dir,* Emily Vieyra; E-mail: emily.vieyra@mcfls.org; *Adult Serv,* Hayley Johnson; *Ch Serv,* Heide Piehler; *YA Serv,* Lisa Quintero; Staff 5 (MLS 5)
Founded 1903. Pop 13,000; Circ 320,000
Library Holdings: Bk Vols 51,000; Per Subs 110
Automation Activity & Vendor Info: (Acquisitions) Innovative Interfaces, Inc; (Cataloging) Innovative Interfaces, Inc; (Circulation) Innovative Interfaces, Inc; (OPAC) Innovative Interfaces, Inc; (Serials) Innovative Interfaces, Inc
Wireless access
Mem of Milwaukee County Federated Library System
Open Mon-Thurs 9-7, Fri 9-6, Sat 10-3
Friends of the Library Group

SHULLSBURG

P MCCOY PUBLIC LIBRARY*, Shullsburg Public, 190 N Judgement St, 53586. SAN 318-3890. Tel: 608-965-4424, Ext 5. FAX: 608-965-4809. Web Site: mccoypubliclibrary.wordpress.com. *Dir,* Virgina Grossen; E-mail: vgrossen@swls.org
Pop 1,246; Circ 10,144
Library Holdings: Bk Vols 5,740; Per Subs 12
Wireless access
Mem of Southwest Wisconsin Library System
Open Tues & Wed 12-8, Thurs & Fri 10-6, Sat 9-12
Friends of the Library Group
Branches: 1
GRATIOT ANNEX, 5895 Main St, Gratiot, 53541. Tel: 608-922-3803. *Dir,* Jennifer Detra; Tel: 608-965-4424, Ext 5, E-mail: mpldirector@swls.org; Staff 3 (Non-MLS 3)
Founded 2003
Library Holdings: Bk Vols 1,200; Per Subs 10
Function: 24/7 Electronic res, 24/7 Online cat, 24/7 wireless access, Audiobks on Playaways & MP3, Bks on CD, Children's prog, Computers for patron use, Digital talking bks, Electronic databases & coll, Extended outdoor wifi, Family literacy, For res purposes, Free DVD rentals, Games, Holiday prog, ILL available, Internet access, Magazines, Magnifiers for reading, Makerspace, Outreach serv, OverDrive digital audio bks, Prog for adults, Prog for children & young adult, Ref & res, Ref serv available, Spanish lang bks, Summer reading prog, Wheelchair accessible, Wifi hotspot checkout
Mem of Southwest Wisconsin Library System
Open Tues 9am-11am, Wed 1:30-4, Thurs 5-8, Sat 9-Noon
Friends of the Library Group

SLINGER

P SLINGER COMMUNITY LIBRARY*, 220 Slinger Rd, 53086. SAN 378-0104. Tel: 262-644-6171. FAX: 262-644-8061. Web Site: www.slingerlibrary.org. *Libr Dir,* Leslie Schultz; E-mail: lschultz@monarchlibraries.org; Staff 8 (MLS 1, Non-MLS 7)
Pop 12,645; Circ 126,524
Library Holdings: CDs 500; DVDs 2,673; Large Print Bks 1,200; Bk Titles 33,158; Per Subs 60; Talking Bks 1,000
Automation Activity & Vendor Info: (Acquisitions) Innovative Interfaces, Inc; (Cataloging) Innovative Interfaces, Inc; (Circulation) Innovative Interfaces, Inc; (OPAC) Innovative Interfaces, Inc
Wireless access
Mem of Monarch Library System
Partic in Wis Libr Asn
Open Mon, Tues & Thurs 9-8, Wed 9-6, Fri 9-5, Sat 9-12
Friends of the Library Group

SOLDIERS GROVE

P SOLDIERS GROVE PUBLIC LIBRARY*, Solar Town Ctr, 102 Passive Sun Dr, 54655. (Mail add: PO Box 6, Solar Town Ctr, 54655-0006), SAN 318-3912. Tel: 608-624-5815. Web Site: soldiersgrovelibrary.org. *Librn,* Sarah DiPadova; E-mail: sdipadova@swls.org; Staff 2 (MLS 1, Non-MLS 1)
Founded 1971. Pop 653; Circ 14,000
Library Holdings: Bk Vols 12,427
Automation Activity & Vendor Info: (Cataloging) Auto-Graphics, Inc; (Circulation) Auto-Graphics, Inc; (OPAC) Auto-Graphics, Inc
Wireless access
Function: 24/7 Online cat, Bk club(s), Bks on CD, Children's prog, Computers for patron use, Electronic databases & coll, Family literacy, For res purposes, Free DVD rentals, Games & aids for people with disabilities, Magazines, Magnifiers for reading, Movies, OverDrive digital audio bks, Photocopying/Printing, Printer for laptops & handheld devices, Prog for adults, Prog for children & young adult, Ref & res, Story hour
Mem of Southwest Wisconsin Library System
Open Mon & Wed 1:30-5:30, Tues & Thurs 10-7, Fri & Sat 10-1
Restriction: Borrowing requests are handled by ILL

SOMERSET

P SOMERSET PUBLIC LIBRARY*, 208 Hud St, 54025. SAN 318-3920. Tel: 715-247-5228. FAX: 715-247-5146. E-mail: somersetpl@somersetlibrary.org. Web Site: www.somersetlibrary.org. *Dir,* Kristina Kelly-Johnson; E-mail: kristina@somersetlibrary.org
Founded 1974. Pop 8,100; Circ 49,294
Library Holdings: DVDs 3,400; Bk Vols 16,000; Per Subs 45
Special Collections: Somerset History
Automation Activity & Vendor Info: (Cataloging) Innovative Interfaces, Inc; (Circulation) Innovative Interfaces, Inc
Wireless access
Mem of Inspiring & Facilitating Library Success (IFLS)
Open Mon, Wed & Fri 9-6, Tues & Thurs 9-7, Sat 9-1

SOUTH MILWAUKEE

P SOUTH MILWAUKEE PUBLIC LIBRARY*, 1907 Tenth Ave, 53172. SAN 318-3939. Tel: 414-768-8195. Web Site: smlibrary.org. *Libr Dir,* Tristan Boswell; E-mail: tristan.boswell@mcfls.org; *Asst Libr Dir,* Bethany Meyer; E-mail: bethany.meyer@mcfls.org; *Librn,* Shirley Langebartels; E-mail: shirley.langebartels@mcfls.org; *Youth Serv Librn,* Stephanie Jurss; E-mail: stephanie.jurss@mcfls.org; Staff 4 (MLS 3, Non-MLS 1)
Founded 1899. Pop 21,310; Circ 211,013
Library Holdings: Audiobooks 2,986; AV Mats 7,827; CDs 13,049; DVDs 2,804; e-books 361; Large Print Bks 2,144; Bk Vols 127,564; Per Subs 106; Videos 7,273
Special Collections: Cookbooks; Local History-South Milwaukee
Automation Activity & Vendor Info: (Acquisitions) Baker & Taylor; (Cataloging) Innovative Interfaces, Inc; (Circulation) Innovative Interfaces, Inc; (ILL) Innovative Interfaces, Inc; (OPAC) Innovative Interfaces, Inc; (Serials) Innovative Interfaces, Inc
Wireless access
Mem of Milwaukee County Federated Library System
Special Services for the Deaf - Closed caption videos
Special Services for the Blind - Audio mat; Bks on CD; Large print bks
Open Mon & Thurs 11-7, Tues, Wed & Fri 9-5, Sat 10-2
Friends of the Library Group

SPARTA

S MONROE COUNTY LOCAL HISTORY ROOM*, Museum & Library, 200 W Main St, 54656. SAN 326-6192. Tel: 608-269-8680. E-mail: mclhr@centurytel.net. Web Site: www.monroecountyhistory.org/libandgen.php. *Dir,* Jarrod Roll
Library Holdings: Bk Vols 2,000; Per Subs 30
Special Collections: Municipal Document Depository
Open Tues-Sat 9-4

P SPARTA FREE LIBRARY*, 124 W Main St, 54656. SAN 318-3947. Tel: 608-269-2010. E-mail: spartalibrary@wrlsweb.org. Web Site: www.spartalibrary.org. *Dir,* Michelle Tryggestad; Tel: 608-269-2010, Ext 4
Founded 1861. Pop 15,000
Library Holdings: Bks on Deafness & Sign Lang 10; Bk Vols 50,800; Per Subs 150; Spec Interest Per Sub 20
Subject Interests: Best sellers, Bicycles, Bicycling, Local hist
Automation Activity & Vendor Info: (Cataloging) Innovative Interfaces, Inc - Sierra; (Circulation) Innovative Interfaces, Inc - Sierra; (OPAC) Innovative Interfaces, Inc - Sierra
Wireless access
Publications: Sparta Free Library Newsletter
Mem of Winding Rivers Library System
Open Mon-Thurs 9-7, Fri 9-4, Sat 9-1
Friends of the Library Group

SPOONER

P SPOONER MEMORIAL LIBRARY*, 421 High St, 54801. SAN 318-3955. Tel: 715-635-2792. FAX: 715-635-2147. E-mail: spoonerlibrary@gmail.com. Web Site: www.spoonerlibrary.org. *Ch, Dir,* Angela Bodzislaw; E-mail: spoonerlibrarydirector@gmail.com; *Adult Prog Coordr, Tech Serv,* Eva Apelquest; *Acq,* Shar Parish; *ILL,* Jill Fredrickson
Founded 1915. Pop 2,500; Circ 42,640
Library Holdings: Bk Vols 33,000; Per Subs 160
Subject Interests: Archit, Art
Automation Activity & Vendor Info: (Cataloging) Follett Software; (Circulation) Follett Software
Wireless access
Mem of Northern Waters Library Service
Open Mon-Thurs 9-8, Fri 9-5, Sat 9-4

SPRING GREEN

P SPRING GREEN COMMUNITY LIBRARY*, 230 E Monroe St, 53588-8035. SAN 318-3971. Tel: 608-588-2276. Web Site: www.springgreenlibrary.org. *Libr Dir,* Emily Whitmore; E-mail: ewhitmore@springgreenlibrary.org; *Youth Serv Librn,* Christina Makos; E-mail: cmakos@springgreenlibrary.org; *Circ Serv,* Jean Porter; *Circ Serv,* Bridget Roberts
Founded 1905. Pop 3,000; Circ 50,000
Library Holdings: Bks on Deafness & Sign Lang 50; Bk Vols 21,965; Per Subs 91
Special Collections: Frank Lloyd Wright Coll; Wisconsin Authors Coll; Wisconsin History Coll
Automation Activity & Vendor Info: (Acquisitions) Baker & Taylor; (Circulation) LibLime Koha; (OPAC) LibLime Koha
Wireless access
Mem of South Central Library System
Open Mon-Thurs 10-7, Fri 10-5, Sat 9-1
Friends of the Library Group

SPRING VALLEY

P SPRING VALLEY PUBLIC LIBRARY*, E 121 S Second St, 54767. SAN 376-6675. Tel: 715-778-4590. FAX: 715-778-4595. Web Site: springvalleylibrary.org. *Libr Dir,* Katie Schneider; E-mail: kschneider@svlibrary.org
Library Holdings: Bk Titles 14,000; Per Subs 33
Automation Activity & Vendor Info: (Acquisitions) Innovative Interfaces, Inc; (Cataloging) Innovative Interfaces, Inc; (Circulation) Innovative Interfaces, Inc; (Course Reserve) Innovative Interfaces, Inc; (ILL) Innovative Interfaces, Inc; (Media Booking) Innovative Interfaces, Inc; (OPAC) Innovative Interfaces, Inc; (Serials) Innovative Interfaces, Inc
Wireless access
Mem of Inspiring & Facilitating Library Success (IFLS)
Open Mon-Thurs 10-7, Fri 10-5, Sat 10-1
Friends of the Library Group

STANLEY

P D R MOON MEMORIAL LIBRARY*, 154 Fourth Ave, 54768. SAN 318-398X. Tel: 715-644-2004. FAX: 715-644-2941. E-mail: stanleypl@stanleylibrary.org. Web Site: stanleylibrary.org.
Founded 1901. Pop 3,737; Circ 19,672
Library Holdings: Audiobooks 1,412; DVDs 3,364; Bk Vols 13,069; Per Subs 38
Wireless access
Function: 24/7 Electronic res, 24/7 Online cat, Adult bk club, Audiobks via web, Bks on CD, Children's prog, Computer training, Computers for patron use, Free DVD rentals, Holiday prog, Home delivery & serv to seniorr ctr & nursing homes, Homebound delivery serv, ILL available, Internet access, Laminating, Magazines, Music CDs, Photocopying/Printing, Prog for adults, Prog for children & young adult, Ref & res, Scanner, Spanish lang bks, Story hour, Summer reading prog, Tax forms
Mem of Inspiring & Facilitating Library Success (IFLS)
Open Mon-Fri 10-6, Sat 10-12
Friends of the Library Group

S STANLEY CORRECTIONAL INSTITUTION LIBRARY*, 100 Corrections Dr, 54768. Tel: 715-644-2960, Ext 3445. FAX: 715-644-3777. Web Site: doc.wi.gov/pages/offenderinformation/adultinstitutions/stanleycorrectionalinstitution.aspx. *Librn,* Betsy Pribel; E-mail: betsy.pribel@wisconsin.gov
Library Holdings: Bk Vols 14,000; Per Subs 20
Automation Activity & Vendor Info: (Cataloging) Follett Software; (Circulation) Follett Software

STETSONVILLE

P JEAN M THOMSEN MEMORIAL LIBRARY*, 105 N Gershwin St, 54480. (Mail add: PO Box 99, 54480-0099), SAN 318-3998. Tel: 715-678-2892. FAX: 715-678-2892. Web Site: www.jmtmlibrary.com. *Dir,* Carla Huston; E-mail: director@stetsonville.lib.wi.us
Pop 715; Circ 14,850
Library Holdings: AV Mats 1,132; Bk Titles 15,114; Per Subs 53
Subject Interests: Cookery, Handicrafts
Automation Activity & Vendor Info: (Cataloging) SirsiDynix; (Circulation) SirsiDynix; (OPAC) SirsiDynix
Wireless access
Partic in Wisconsin Valley Library Service
Open Mon, Tues, Thurs & Fri 10-6, Wed 10-8

STEVENS POINT

J MID-STATE TECHNICAL COLLEGE*, Stevens Point Campus Library, 1001 Centerpoint Dr, 54481. SAN 318-4005. Tel: 715-342-3129. FAX: 715-342-3134. E-mail: libraryspcampus@mstc.edu. *Librn,* Amber Stancher; E-mail: amber.stancher@mstc.edu
Founded 1914. Highest Degree: Associate
Automation Activity & Vendor Info: (Acquisitions) Innovative Interfaces, Inc - Sierra; (Cataloging) Innovative Interfaces, Inc - Sierra; (Circulation) Innovative Interfaces, Inc - Sierra; (ILL) Auto-Graphics, Inc; (OPAC) Innovative Interfaces, Inc
Wireless access
Open Mon-Thurs 9:30-6, Fri 8-4:30

P PORTAGE COUNTY PUBLIC LIBRARY*, Charles M White Library Bldg, 1001 Main St, 54481-2860. SAN 318-403X. Tel: 715-346-1544. FAX: 715-346-1239. Web Site: www.pocolibrary.org. *Dir,* Larry Oathout; E-mail: loathout@pocolibrary.org; *Br Librn, Mgr, Br,* Laura Fuller; E-mail: lfuller@poplibrary.org; *Ref/Tech Support Librn,* Charles A Danner; *Youth Serv Librn,* Nicole E Ozanich; *Tech Serv Librn,* Victoria A Billings; Staff 46 (MLS 6, Non-MLS 40)
Founded 1895. Pop 70,785; Circ 506,079
Library Holdings: Bk Vols 157,918; Per Subs 391
Automation Activity & Vendor Info: (Acquisitions) Ex Libris Group; (Cataloging) Ex Libris Group; (Circulation) Ex Libris Group; (OPAC) Ex Libris Group; (Serials) Ex Libris Group
Wireless access
Mem of South Central Library System
Open Mon-Fri 10-6
Friends of the Library Group
Branches: 3
ALMOND BRANCH, Village Hall, 122 Main St, Almond, 54909. Tel: 715-366-2151. FAX: 715-366-2151. E-mail: almondlibrary@co.portage.wi.us.
Open Tues 10-1:30 & 2-6, Wed & Thurs 2-6
PLOVER BRANCH, 2151 Roosevelt Dr, Plover, 54467. Tel: 715-341-4007. FAX: 715-346-1601.
Open Tues-Fri 10-6
ROSHOLT BRANCH, Village Hall, 137 N Main St, Rosholt, 54473. Tel: 715-677-4512, FAX: 715-677-4512. Web Site: rosholtlibrary@co.portage.wi.us.
Open Mon, Tues, Thurs & Fri 2-6, Wed 10-6

C UNIVERSITY OF WISCONSIN-STEVENS POINT*, University Library, 900 Reserve St, 54481-1985. SAN 318-4021. Tel: 715-346-2540. Reference Tel: 715-346-2836. E-mail: librefd@uwsp.edu. Web Site: www.uwsp.edu/library. *Libr Dir,* Mindy King; Tel: 715-346-2321, E-mail: mking@uwsp.edu; *Info Syst Librn,* Terri Muraski; Tel: 715-346-3349, E-mail: tmuraski@uwsp.edu; *Ref & ILL Librn,* Troy Espe; Tel: 715-346-4443, E-mail: tespe@uwsp.edu; *Archivist,* Brad Casselberry; Tel: 715-346-2586, E-mail: bcasselb@uwsp.edu; Staff 33 (MLS 15, Non-MLS 18)
Founded 1894. Enrl 8,800; Highest Degree: Master
Library Holdings: Bk Titles 244,441; Bk Vols 321,226; Per Subs 8,470
Special Collections: John F Kennedy Assassination. State Document Depository; US Document Depository
Subject Interests: Censorship, Educ, Environ studies, Ethnic studies, Hist
Automation Activity & Vendor Info: (Acquisitions) Ex Libris Group; (Cataloging) Ex Libris Group; (Circulation) Ex Libris Group; (ILL) Ex Libris Group; (OPAC) Ex Libris Group; (Serials) Ex Libris Group
Wireless access
Partic in WiLS
Open Mon-Wed 7:45am-Midnight, Thurs & Fri 7:45am-9pm, Sat 9-9, Sun Noon-Midnight

STOUGHTON

P STOUGHTON PUBLIC LIBRARY*, 304 S Fourth St, 53589. SAN 318-4048. Tel: 608-873-6281. Reference E-mail: storef@stolib.org. Web Site: www.stoughtonpubliclibrary.org. *Libr Dir,* James Ramsey; E-mail: jramsey@stolib.org; *Adult Serv,* Amanda Bosky; *Ch Serv,* Mary Ostrander; *Circ,* Robin Behringer; *Tech Serv,* Sarah Bukrey; Staff 3 (MLS 3)
Founded 1901
Library Holdings: Bk Vols 69,556; Per Subs 115
Automation Activity & Vendor Info: (Acquisitions) Bibliomation Inc; (Cataloging) Bibliomation Inc; (Circulation) Bibliomation Inc; (OPAC) Bibliomation Inc; (Serials) Bibliomation Inc
Wireless access
Mem of South Central Library System
Special Services for the Blind - Accessible computers; Bks on CD; Computer access aids
Open Mon-Thurs 9-8, Fri 9-6, Sat 9-5
Friends of the Library Group

STRUM

P STRUM PUBLIC LIBRARY*, 114 Fifth Ave S, 54770. (Mail add: PO Box 10, 54770-0010), SAN 318-4056. Tel: 715-695-3848. FAX: 715-695-5225. E-mail: strumpl@wrlsweb.org. Web Site: strumlibrary.weebly.com. *Dir,* Dawn Hering
Pop 6,000; Circ 9,000
Library Holdings: Bk Titles 10,000; Per Subs 24
Automation Activity & Vendor Info: (Acquisitions) Follett Software; (Cataloging) Follett Software; (Circulation) Follett Software
Mem of Winding Rivers Library System
Open Mon & Fri 9-4, Tues & Thurs 9-7:30, Sat 9-Noon
Friends of the Library Group

STURGEON BAY

P DOOR COUNTY LIBRARY*, 107 S Fourth Ave, 54235. SAN 318-4064. Tel: 920-743-6578. FAX: 920-743-6697. Web Site: www.doorcountylibrary.org. *Dir,* Tina Kakuske; E-mail: tkakuske@doorcountylibrary.org; *Head, Circ,* Linda Streyle; Tel: 920-746-5599, E-mail: lstreyle@doorcountylibrary.org; *Ad,* Laura Kayacan; Tel: 920-746-7121, E-mail: lkayacan@mail.nfls.lib.wi.us; *Acq & Cat, Tech Serv,* Rebecca Buchmann; Tel: 920-746-7116, E-mail: rbuchmann@doorcountylibrary.org; *Acq & Cat, Tech Serv,* Rebecca Lin; Tel: 920-746-2491, E-mail: rlin@doorcountylibrary.org; *Commun Relations, Libr Asst,* Morgan Mann; Tel: 920-746-7122, E-mail: mmann@doorcountylibrary.org; *Youth Serv,* Beth Lokken; Tel: 920-746-7119, E-mail: blokken@doorcountylibrary.org; Staff 34 (MLS 8, Non-MLS 26)
Founded 1950. Circ 283,143
Library Holdings: Bk Vols 154,066; Per Subs 466
Special Collections: Door County Authors
Subject Interests: Local hist
Wireless access
Function: 24/7 Electronic res, 24/7 Online cat, Adult bk club, After school storytime, Archival coll, Art exhibits, Audiobks via web, AV serv, Bk club(s), Bks on CD, Children's prog, Computers for patron use, Electronic databases & coll, Free DVD rentals, Holiday prog, Homebound delivery serv, ILL available, Internet access, Life-long learning prog for all ages, Magazines, Magnifiers for reading, Makerspace, Meeting rooms, Microfiche/film & reading machines, Music CDs, Notary serv, Online cat, Outreach serv, OverDrive digital audio bks, Photocopying/Printing, Preschool outreach, Preschool reading prog, Prog for adults, Prog for children & young adult, Ref & res, Ref serv available, Scanner, Senior outreach, Spanish lang bks, STEM programs, Story hour, Summer & winter reading prog, Tax forms
Publications: Friends of Door County Libraries
Mem of Nicolet Federated Library System
Partic in OWLSnet
Open Mon-Thurs 9-9, Fri 9-6, Sat 9-5
Friends of the Library Group
Branches: 8
BAILEYS HARBOR BRANCH, 2392 Hwy F, Baileys Harbor, 54202. (Mail add: PO Box 307, Baileys Harbor, 54202-0307), SAN 324-3095. Tel: 920-839-2210. E-mail: bai@doorcountylibrary.org. *Br Mgr,* Jeanne Majeski
Library Holdings: Bk Vols 9,161
Open Mon & Fri 10-4, Wed 1-7, Sat 9-2
EGG HARBOR BRANCH, 7860 Hwy 42, Egg Harbor, 54209. (Mail add: PO Box 207, Egg Harbor, 54209-0207), SAN 324-3109. Tel: 920-868-2664. E-mail: egg@doorcountylibrary.org. *Br Mgr,* Dixie Jorns
Library Holdings: Bk Vols 8,413
Open Tues 3-6, Wed & Thurs 10-2, Sat 10-Noon (Winter); Tues 1-7, Wed & Thurs 10-4, Sat 10-2 (Summer)
Friends of the Library Group
EPHRAIM BRANCH, 9996 Water St, Ephraim, 54211. (Mail add: PO Box 150, Ephraim, 54211-0150), SAN 324-3117. Tel: 920-854-2014. E-mail: eph@doorcountylibrary.org. *Br Mgr,* Linda Malmgren
Library Holdings: Bk Vols 8,200
Subject Interests: Ephraim hist
Friends of the Library Group

FISH CREEK BRANCH, 4097 Hwy 42, Fish Creek, 54212. (Mail add: PO Box 7, Fish Creek, 54212-0007), SAN 324-3125. Tel: 920-868-3471. FAX: 920-868-3072. E-mail: fis@doorcountylibrary.org. *Br Mgr,* Holly Somerhalder
Library Holdings: Bk Vols 11,261
Friends of the Library Group

FORESTVILLE BRANCH, 123 Hwy 42 S, Forestville, 54213. (Mail add: PO Box 308, Forestville, 54213-0308), SAN 324-3133. Tel: 920-856-6886. E-mail: for@doorcountylibrary.org. *Br Mgr,* Jennifer Bacall
Library Holdings: Bk Vols 10,586
Open Mon & Wed 1-7, Tues 9-2, Fri 9-5
Friends of the Library Group

SISTER BAY-LIBERTY GROVE BRANCH, 301 Mill Rd, Sister Bay, 54234. (Mail add: PO Box 347, Sister Bay, 54234-0347), SAN 324-3141. Tel: 920-854-2721. E-mail: sis@doorcountylibrary.org. *Br Mgr,* Betty Ann Curzon
Library Holdings: Bk Vols 13,715
Open Mon 10-7, Tues 1-7, Wed 10-5, Fri 10-4, Sat 10-2 (Winter); Mon-Wed 10-8, Thurs & Fri 10-5, Sat 10-2 (Summer)
Friends of the Library Group

STURGEON BAY BRANCH, 107 S Fourth Ave, 54235. *Adult Serv,* Laura Kayacan; *Ch Serv, YA Serv,* Beth Lokken; *Circ,* Linda Streyle
Library Holdings: Bk Vols 75,940
Subject Interests: Door County hist, Local hist
Open Mon-Thurs 9-9, Fri 9-6, Sat 9-5
Friends of the Library Group

WASHINGTON ISLAND BRANCH, Main & Lakeview Rds, Washington Island, 54246, SAN 324-315X. Tel: 920-847-2323. E-mail: wsh@doorcountylibrary.org. *Br Mgr,* Marcia Carr
Library Holdings: Bk Vols 15,715
Open Mon & Wed 1-4, Tues 9-1 & 6-8, Thurs 9-1, Fri 1-5

STURTEVANT

S RACINE CORRECTIONAL INSTITUTION LIBRARY, 2019 Wisconsin St, 53177. Tel: 262-886-3214, Ext 3800. FAX: 262-886-3514. Web Site: doc.wi.gov/Pages/OffenderInformation/AdultInstitutions/RacineCorrectionalInstitution.aspx. *Librn,* Emily Clements; E-mail: emily.clements@wisconsin.gov
Library Holdings: Bk Vols 11,900; Per Subs 20
Automation Activity & Vendor Info: (Cataloging) Follett Software; (Circulation) Follett Software
Restriction: Staff & inmates only

SUN PRAIRIE

P SUN PRAIRIE PUBLIC LIBRARY*, 1350 Linnerud Dr, 53590. SAN 318-4072. Tel: 608-825-7323. Information Services Tel: 608-825-0702. FAX: 608-825-3936. E-mail: sunref@sunlib.org. Web Site: www.sunprairiepubliclibrary.org. *Dir,* Svetha Hetzler; E-mail: shetzler@sunlib.org; *Head, Access Serv, Head, Circ,* Steev Baker; *Head, Adult Serv,* Erin Williams Hart; *Head, Tech Serv,* Kate Hull; *Head, Youth Serv,* Lynn Montague; Staff 10 (MLS 7, Non-MLS 3)
Founded 1901
Wireless access
Function: 24/7 Electronic res, 24/7 Online cat, Activity rm, Adult bk club, Adult literacy prog, After school storytime
Mem of South Central Library System
Partic in Library Interchange Network
Special Services for the Blind - Talking bks
Open Mon-Thurs 9-9, Fri & Sat 9-5, Sun 1-5 (Sept-May)
Friends of the Library Group

SR WISCONSIN CONFERENCE UNITED METHODIST CHURCH*, Historical Library, 750 Windsor St, 53590. SAN 323-6358. Tel: 608-837-7328. Toll Free Tel: 888-240-7328. FAX: 608-837-8547. E-mail: archives@wisconsinumc.org. Web Site: www.wisconsinumc.org/ministries/worship-witness/archives-history/the-archives. *Archivist,* Lynn Lubkeman; Tel: 608-837-7320, E-mail: llubkeman@wisconsinumc.org
Library Holdings: Bk Titles 2,000
Special Collections: Diaries of William Ames 1857-98, Michael Benson 1832-1919 & Joseph Austin 1838-85
Restriction: Open by appt only

SUPERIOR

P SUPERIOR PUBLIC LIBRARY*, 1530 Tower Ave, 54880-2532. SAN 365-0731. Tel: 715-394-8860. Circulation Tel: 715-394-8863. Interlibrary Loan Service Tel: 715-394-8875. Administration Tel: 715-394-8877. FAX: 715-394-8870. TDD: 715-394-8878. Web Site: superiorlibrary.org. *Libr Dir,* Susan Heskin; E-mail: heskins@ci.superior.wi.us; *Children & Youth Serv Librn,* Kelly Wiisanen; *Circ Serv,* Kyle Hawley; Staff 4 (MLS 4)
Founded 1888. Pop 27,638; Circ 399,368
Library Holdings: Audiobooks 6,759; AV Mats 10,690; Bk Vols 132,140; Per Subs 234
Special Collections: Art (Anna B Butler Coll), photogs; City of Superior & Douglas County, Wisconsin, archives (State Historical Society of Wisconsin Area Research Center); Learning Disabilities (Burton Ansell Memorial Coll), bks, pamphlets, film; Rare Books (Henry S Butler Coll); Superior, Wisconsin, Newspapers from 1855; Wisconsin History (Henry E Legler Coll), bks, docs, micro, mss, film, photogs, A-tapes, V-tapes, pamphlets. State Document Depository
Subject Interests: Archit, Art, Genealogy, Heraldry, Hist, Labor hist, Music
Automation Activity & Vendor Info: (Cataloging) Innovative Interfaces, Inc; (Circulation) Innovative Interfaces, Inc; (OPAC) Innovative Interfaces, Inc
Wireless access
Publications: "Remembering the Globe" Video (Local historical information)
Mem of Northern Waters Library Service
Partic in Merlin
Special Services for the Blind - Reader equip
Open Mon & Wed-Fri 10-5, Tues 10-7
Friends of the Library Group
Branches: 1

JOAN SALMEN MEMORIAL, Village Hall, 9240 E Main St, Solon Springs, 54873. (Mail add: PO Box 295, Solon Springs, 54873-0295). Tel: 715-378-4452. *Librn,* Kathy McDonald
Library Holdings: Bk Titles 3,000
Open Mon 1-6, Thurs 9:30-2:30

C UNIVERSITY OF WISCONSIN-SUPERIOR*, Jim Dan Hill Library, 907 N 19th St, 54880. (Mail add: Belknap & Catlin, PO Box 2000, 54880-2000), SAN 318-4099. Tel: 715-394-8343. Interlibrary Loan Service Tel: 715-394-8130. FAX: 715-394-8462. Reference E-mail: askref@uwsuper.edu. Web Site: library.uwsuper.edu. *Libr Dir,* Jamie White-Farnham; Tel: 715-394-8201; *Asst Libr Dir,* Stephanie Warden; Tel: 715-394-8342, E-mail: swarden1@uwsuper.edu; Staff 9 (MLS 3, Non-MLS 6)
Founded 1896. Enrl 2,495; Fac 105; Highest Degree: Master
Library Holdings: e-books 2,258; Bk Titles 70,894; Bk Vols 76,464; Per Subs 351
Special Collections: Barton Sutter Coll, lit journals; Lake Superior Marine Museum Association Coll; Literature (John W R Beecroft); Regional History Coll. State Document Depository; US Document Depository
Subject Interests: Educ, Govt, Maritime
Automation Activity & Vendor Info: (Acquisitions) Ex Libris Group; (Cataloging) Ex Libris Group; (Circulation) Ex Libris Group; (Course Reserve) Ex Libris Group; (OPAC) Ex Libris Group; (Serials) Ex Libris Group
Wireless access
Publications: IITC Connections
Partic in Coun of Wis Librs, Inc; ISI; OCLC Online Computer Library Center, Inc; WiLS
Open Mon-Thurs 7:45am-11pm, Fri 7:45am-6pm, Sat Noon-4, Sun 5pm-11pm (Sept-June)

SURING

P SURING AREA PUBLIC LIBRARY*, 604 E Main St, 54174. (Mail add: PO Box 74, 54174-0074). Tel: 920-842-4451. E-mail: sur@suringpubliclibrary.org. Web Site: www.suringpubliclibrary.org. *Libr Dir,* Jill Trochta; E-mail: jtrochta@suringpubliclibrary.org; Staff 1.5 (MLS 1, Non-MLS 0.5)
Founded 1986. Pop 3,000
Library Holdings: Bk Titles 15,000; Per Subs 68
Automation Activity & Vendor Info: (Acquisitions) Innovative Interfaces, Inc; (Cataloging) Innovative Interfaces, Inc; (Circulation) Innovative Interfaces, Inc; (ILL) Innovative Interfaces, Inc; (OPAC) Innovative Interfaces, Inc; (Serials) Innovative Interfaces, Inc
Wireless access
Function: Adult bk club, Audiobks via web, Bk club(s), Bks on cassette, Bks on CD, Children's prog, Computers for patron use, Electronic databases & coll, Holiday prog, Homework prog, ILL available, Music CDs, Online cat, OverDrive digital audio bks, Photocopying/Printing, Prog for adults, Prog for children & young adult, Ref serv available, Serves people with intellectual disabilities, Story hour, Summer reading prog, Tax forms, Teen prog, VHS videos, Wheelchair accessible
Mem of Nicolet Federated Library System
Partic in OWLSnet
Open Mon, Tues & Thurs 9-5, Wed 9-6, Fri 1-5
Friends of the Library Group

SUSSEX

P PAULINE HAASS PUBLIC LIBRARY*, N64 W23820 Main St, 53089-3120. SAN 324-1300. Tel: 262-246-5180. FAX: 262-246-5236. E-mail: phrefsub@phpl.lib.wi.us. Web Site: www.phplonline.org. *Dir,* Kathy Klager; E-mail: phdirect@phpl.lib.wi.us; *Asst Dir,* Adele Loria; Tel: 262-246-5181; *Ch Mgr,* Valerie Johnson; Tel: 262-246-5182, E-mail: phyouth@phpl.lib.wi.us; *Circ Mgr,* Sallie Ratelle; Staff 27 (MLS 8, Non-MLS 19)
Founded 1988. Pop 19,722; Circ 302,000
Library Holdings: Bk Vols 75,857; Per Subs 161
Automation Activity & Vendor Info: (Cataloging) SirsiDynix; (Circulation) SirsiDynix; (OPAC) SirsiDynix
Wireless access
Publications: Checking In: News from the Pauline Haass Public Library (Newsletter)
Mem of Bridges Library System
Open Mon-Thurs 9:30-8, Fri 9:30-5, Sat 9:30-4, Sun 1-4; Mon-Thurs 9:30-8, Fri 9:30-5, Sat 9:30-1, Sun 1-4 (Summer)
Friends of the Library Group

TAYLOR

P TAYLOR MEMORIAL LIBRARY*, 402 Second St, 54659. (Mail add: PO Box 130, 54659-0130). Tel: 715-662-2310. FAX: 715-662-2034. E-mail: taylorlibrary@wrlsweb.org. Web Site: taylorlibrary.wrlsweb.org. *Dir,* Mindy Hess
Founded 1999. Pop 519
Library Holdings: Bk Titles 7,000; Talking Bks 20; Videos 200
Wireless access
Mem of Winding Rivers Library System
Open Mon 10-6, Tues & Thurs 2-6, Fri 10-2 (Winter); Mon & Tues 10-4, Thurs 2-6, Fri 10-2 (Summer)

THERESA

P THERESA PUBLIC LIBRARY*, 290 Mayville St, 53091-0307. SAN 364-6203. Tel: 920-488-2342. FAX: 920-488-2342. E-mail: tpl@monarchlibraries.org. Web Site: www.theresa.lib.wi.us. *Dir,* Mary Alice Bodden; *Asst Librn,* Faye Beck; *Asst Librn,* Donna Geiger; *Asst Librn,* Mary Mekelburg
Pop 2,500
Library Holdings: Bk Titles 23,045; Per Subs 63
Subject Interests: Collectibles, Local hist
Automation Activity & Vendor Info: (Cataloging) SirsiDynix; (Circulation) SirsiDynix
Wireless access
Mem of Monarch Library System
Open Mon-Thurs 12-6:30, Fri 12-5
Friends of the Library Group

THORP

P THORP PUBLIC LIBRARY*, 401 S Conway Dr, 54771. (Mail add: PO Box 407, 54771-0407), SAN 318-4129. Tel: 715-669-5953. FAX: 715-669-7319. Web Site: www.thorppubliclibrary.org. *Libr Dir,* Julie Beloungy; E-mail: director@thorppubliclibrary.org; *Libr Asst,* Ann VanCalcar; E-mail: libassistant@thorppubliclibrary.org
Founded 1898. Pop 1,650; Circ 43,540
Library Holdings: CDs 170; DVDs 545; Large Print Bks 350; Bk Vols 25,000; Per Subs 72; Talking Bks 150; Videos 352
Automation Activity & Vendor Info: (Cataloging) Innovative Interfaces, Inc - Sierra; (Circulation) Innovative Interfaces, Inc - Sierra; (OPAC) Innovative Interfaces, Inc - Sierra
Wireless access
Partic in Wisconsin Valley Library Service
Open Mon & Tues 10-7, Wed & Thurs 10-5, Fri 9-4, Sat 10-Noon
Friends of the Library Group

THREE LAKES

P EDWARD U DEMMER MEMORIAL LIBRARY*, 6961 W School St, 54562. (Mail add: PO Box 760, 54562), SAN 318-4137. Tel: 715-546-3391. FAX: 715-546-3914. E-mail: demmer@demmerlibrary.org. Web Site: www.demmerlibrary.org. *Dir,* Erica Brewster; E-mail: director@demmerlibrary.org; *Asst Dir,* Lyn Pietila; E-mail: lpietila@demmerliabrary.org; *Ch,* Charlotte Horant; *Outreach Coordr,* Carolyn Eaglesham
Founded 1949. Pop 2,500; Circ 33,203
Library Holdings: Audiobooks 1,769; Bk Vols 25,168; Per Subs 75; Videos 1,807
Automation Activity & Vendor Info: (Cataloging) Innovative Interfaces, Inc - Sierra; (Circulation) Innovative Interfaces, Inc - Sierra; (Discovery) EBSCO Discovery Service; (ILL) Innovative Interfaces, Inc - Sierra; (OPAC) Innovative Interfaces, Inc - Sierra
Wireless access
Function: 24/7 Electronic res, 24/7 Online cat, Adult bk club, Art programs, Audio & video playback equip for onsite use, Audiobks via web, Bk club(s), Bks on CD, Children's prog, Computer training, Computers for patron use, E-Reserves, Electronic databases & coll, Free DVD rentals, Genealogy discussion group, Homebound delivery serv, ILL available, Internet access, Large print keyboards, Life-long learning prog for all ages, Magazines, Magnifiers for reading, Mail & tel request accepted, Microfiche/film & reading machines, Museum passes, Music CDs, Online cat, Online info literacy tutorials on the web & in blackboard, Online ref, Outside serv via phone, mail, e-mail & web, OverDrive digital audio bks, Photocopying/Printing, Prog for adults, Prog for children & young adult, Ref serv available, Senior computer classes, Senior outreach, Serves people with intellectual disabilities, Spoken cassettes & CDs, Spoken cassettes & DVDs, STEM programs, Story hour, Study rm, Summer reading prog, Tax forms, Teen prog, Wheelchair accessible, Workshops
Publications: Demmer Library Newsletter (Monthly)
Partic in Wisconsin Valley Library Service
Open Mon & Wed 9-8, Tues, Thurs & Fri 9-5, Sat 9-2

TOMAH

GM DEPARTMENT OF VETERAN AFFAIRS*, VA Medical Center Library, 500 E Veterans St, 54660. SAN 318-4153. Tel: 608-372-3971, Ext 66267. FAX: 608-372-1670. E-mail: tomahlibrarystaff@va.gov. *Health Sci Librn, Libr Mgr,* Deb Friet; *Libr Tech,* Austin Uhing; Staff 2 (MLS 1, Non-MLS 1)
Founded 1947
Library Holdings: AV Mats 5,076; Electronic Media & Resources 60; Bk Titles 56,982; Per Subs 9,580
Subject Interests: Clinical med, Nursing, Patient health educ, Psychiat, Psychol
Automation Activity & Vendor Info: (Cataloging) LibraryWorld, Inc; (Circulation) LibraryWorld, Inc; (OPAC) LibraryWorld, Inc
Wireless access
Partic in Docline; Greater Midwest Regional Medical Libr Network; Wiscat
Open Mon-Fri 8-4

P TOMAH PUBLIC LIBRARY*, 716 Superior Ave, 54660. SAN 318-4145. Tel: 608-374-7470. FAX: 608-374-7471. E-mail: Tomah_public_library@yahoo.com. Web Site: www.tomahpubliclibrary.org. *Dir,* Irma Keller; *Ad,* SinDee Thomas; *Ch,* Dave Deprey; *ILL,* Cindy Gnewikow; Staff 6 (MLS 1, Non-MLS 5)
Founded 1876. Pop 16,547; Circ 116,368
Library Holdings: Bk Vols 50,722
Automation Activity & Vendor Info: (Cataloging) Follett Software; (Circulation) Follett Software; (ILL) Brodart; (OPAC) Follett Software
Wireless access
Function: Ref serv available
Mem of Winding Rivers Library System
Friends of the Library Group

TOMAHAWK

P TOMAHAWK PUBLIC LIBRARY*, 300 W Lincoln Ave, 54487. SAN 318-4161. Tel: 715-453-2455. FAX: 715-453-1630. E-mail: copy@tomahawk.lib.wi.us. Web Site: www.tomahawk.lib.wi.us. *Dir,* Heidi O'Hare; E-mail: director@tomahawk.lib.wi.us; *Asst Dir,* Allison Puestow; E-mail: catalog@tomahawk.lib.wi.us; *Ch,* Annette Miller; E-mail: youth@tomahawk.lib.wi.us; Staff 5 (Non-MLS 5)
Pop 4,261; Circ 40,339
Jan 2020-Dec 2020 Income $423,816, City $185,240, County $177,100, Other $61,476. Mats Exp $62,936. Sal $169,163
Library Holdings: Audiobooks 3,665; Bk Titles 45,307
Automation Activity & Vendor Info: (Acquisitions) Innovative Interfaces, Inc - Sierra; (Cataloging) Innovative Interfaces, Inc - Sierra; (Circulation) Innovative Interfaces, Inc - Sierra; (OPAC) Innovative Interfaces, Inc - Sierra; (Serials) Innovative Interfaces, Inc - Sierra
Wireless access
Function: Activity rm, Telephone ref
Partic in Wisconsin Valley Library Service
Open Mon-Thurs 10-6, Fri 10-3
Friends of the Library Group

TREMPEALEAU

P SHIRLEY M WRIGHT MEMORIAL LIBRARY*, 11455 Fremont St, 54661. SAN 318-417X. Tel: 608-534-6197. FAX: 608-534-5076. Web Site: swmlibrary.org. *Dir,* Jessica Schoonover; E-mail: swmldirector@wrlsweb.org
Founded 1913. Pop 1,519; Circ 28,000
Library Holdings: Bk Vols 16,000; Per Subs 42
Automation Activity & Vendor Info: (Acquisitions) Horizon; (Cataloging) Horizon; (Circulation) Horizon; (OPAC) Horizon
Wireless access
Mem of Winding Rivers Library System

Open Mon Noon-8, Tues & Wed Noon-6, Thurs & Fri 9-6, Sat 9-1
Friends of the Library Group

TURTLE LAKE

P TURTLE LAKE PUBLIC LIBRARY*, 301 Maple St S, 54889. (Mail add: PO Box 272, 54889-0272), SAN 376-6748. Tel: 715-986-4618. E-mail: tlstaff@turtlelakepubliclibrary.org. Web Site: www.turtlelakepubliclibrary.org. *Dir,* Allison Lutz; E-mail: alutz@turtlelakepubliclibrary.org; Staff 1.9 (Non-MLS 1.9)
Founded 1960. Pop 2,409; Circ 26,552
Library Holdings: Audiobooks 200; e-books 5,000; Bk Titles 20,000; Per Subs 25
Automation Activity & Vendor Info: (Cataloging) Innovative Interfaces, Inc - Sierra; (Circulation) Innovative Interfaces, Inc - Sierra; (OPAC) Innovative Interfaces, Inc - Sierra
Wireless access
Mem of Inspiring & Facilitating Library Success (IFLS)
Special Services for the Blind - Braille bks
Open Mon, Wed & Fri 10-4, Tues & Thurs 10-6, Sat 10-Noon
Friends of the Library Group

TWO RIVERS

P LESTER PUBLIC LIBRARY*, 1001 Adams St, 54241. SAN 318-4188. Tel: 920-793-8888. FAX: 920-793-7150. Reference E-mail: lesref@lesterlibrary.org. Web Site: www.lesterlibrary.org. *Libr Dir,* Jeff Dawson; Tel: 920-793-7104, E-mail: jdawson@lesterlibrary.org; *Adult Serv Coordr,* Chris Hamburg; Tel: 920-793-7113, E-mail: chamburg@lesterlibrary.org; *Customer Serv Coordr,* Marie Bonde; Tel: 920-793-7105, E-mail: mbonde@lesterlibrary.org; *Youth Serv Coordr,* Terry Ehle; Tel: 920-793-7118, E-mail: tehle@lesterlibrary.org; Staff 5 (MLS 3, Non-MLS 2)
Founded 1891. Pop 19,045; Circ 186,636
Library Holdings: Bk Vols 80,000; Per Subs 150
Subject Interests: Genealogy, Local hist
Automation Activity & Vendor Info: (Acquisitions) SirsiDynix; (Cataloging) SirsiDynix; (Circulation) SirsiDynix; (Course Reserve) SirsiDynix; (ILL) SirsiDynix; (Media Booking) SirsiDynix; (OPAC) SirsiDynix; (Serials) SirsiDynix
Wireless access
Function: Adult bk club, Audio & video playback equip for onsite use, Audiobks via web, Bk club(s), Bks on CD, Children's prog, Computer training, Computers for patron use, E-Readers, E-Reserves, Electronic databases & coll, Family literacy, For res purposes, Free DVD rentals, Genealogy discussion group, Home delivery & serv to seniorr ctr & nursing homes, Homebound delivery serv, ILL available, Internet access, Life-long learning prog for all ages, Magazines, Mail & tel request accepted, Meeting rooms, Microfiche/film & reading machines, Movies, Music CDs, Online cat, Outreach serv, OverDrive digital audio bks, Photocopying/Printing, Preschool outreach, Preschool reading prog, Prog for adults, Prog for children & young adult, Ref & res, Ref serv available, Scanner, Senior computer classes, Story hour, Study rm, Summer & winter reading prog, Summer reading prog, Tax forms, Teen prog, Telephone ref, Wheelchair accessible, Winter reading prog, Workshops
Mem of Manitowoc-Calumet Library System
Open Mon-Thurs 10-8, Fri 10-5:30, Sat 10-2
Friends of the Library Group

UNION GROVE

P GRAHAM PUBLIC LIBRARY*, 1215 Main St, 53182-1303. SAN 318-4196. Tel: 262-878-2910. FAX: 262-878-0213. Web Site: www.uniongrove.lib.wi.us. *Dir,* Kathryn A Hanson; E-mail: khanson3@uniongrove.lib.wi.us; Staff 2 (Non-MLS 2)
Pop 8,291; Circ 70,092
Library Holdings: CDs 1,258; DVDs 1,012; e-books 8,948; Electronic Media & Resources 4,307; Bk Titles 36,084; Per Subs 102
Subject Interests: Local genealogy, Local hist
Automation Activity & Vendor Info: (Cataloging) SirsiDynix; (Circulation) SirsiDynix; (OPAC) SirsiDynix
Wireless access
Mem of Prairie Lakes Library System (PLLS)
Partic in OCLC Online Computer Library Center, Inc
Open Mon-Thurs 9-8, Fri 9-5, Sat 9-3

VERONA

P VERONA PUBLIC LIBRARY*, 500 Silent St, 53593. SAN 318-4218. Tel: 608-845-7180. FAX: 608-845-8917. E-mail: vpl@veronapubliclibrary.org. Web Site: www.veronapubliclibrary.org. *Dir,* Stacy Burkart; E-mail: sburkart@veronapubliclibrary.org; *Asst Dir, Head, Youth Serv,* Julie Harrison; E-mail: jharrison@ci.verona.wi.us; *Head, Ref Serv,* Emma Cobb; E-mail: ecobb@ci.verona.wi.us; Staff 22 (MLS 5, Non-MLS 17)
Founded 1959. Pop 19,678; Circ 499,380
Library Holdings: Audiobooks 2,480; Bks on Deafness & Sign Lang 39; Braille Volumes 28; CDs 3,543; DVDs 2,899; e-books 8,276; Electronic Media & Resources 2,012; Large Print Bks 1,087; Bk Vols 499,350; Per Subs 139; Videos 2,097
Automation Activity & Vendor Info: (Acquisitions) Baker & Taylor; (Cataloging) SirsiDynix; (Circulation) SirsiDynix; (ILL) ADLiB; (OPAC) SirsiDynix
Wireless access
Function: Adult bk club, Bks on cassette, Bks on CD, Children's prog, Computers for patron use, E-Reserves, Electronic databases & coll, ILL available, Magnifiers for reading, Music CDs, Online cat, Outreach serv, Photocopying/Printing, Preschool outreach, Prog for adults, Prog for children & young adult, Ref serv available, Scanner, Story hour, Summer reading prog, Tax forms, Teen prog, Telephone ref, VHS videos, Wheelchair accessible, Workshops
Mem of South Central Library System
Special Services for the Deaf - Bks on deafness & sign lang; Closed caption videos; Sign lang interpreter upon request for prog
Special Services for the Blind - Assistive/Adapted tech devices, equip & products; Bks on cassette; Bks on CD; Braille bks; Large print bks; Magnifiers; Recorded bks
Open Mon-Thurs 9-9, Fri 9-6, Sat 9-4, Sun 1-5
Friends of the Library Group

VESPER

P LESTER PUBLIC LIBRARY OF VESPER*, 6550 Virginia St, 54489-9493. (Mail add: PO Box 31, 54489-0031), SAN 318-4226. Tel: 715-569-4669. E-mail: vespl@tds.net. *Dir,* Andrea L Halbersma; Staff 1 (Non-MLS 1)
Founded 1950. Circ 10,515
Jan 2018-Dec 2018 Income $46,716, State $700, City $19,000, County $14,428, Other $12,588. Mats Exp $6,796, Books $6,280, AV Mat $255, Electronic Ref Mat (Incl. Access Fees) $261. Sal $23,399 (Prof $15,340)
Library Holdings: Audiobooks 169; CDs 70; DVDs 2,088; e-books 153,050; Electronic Media & Resources 52,575; Bk Vols 14,998; Per Subs 17; Videos 2,088
Special Collections: DIY Kits; Games; IEEE sponsored Science Kits; Inspirational Fiction; Puzzles; Stamp Sets. Municipal Document Depository
Automation Activity & Vendor Info: (Acquisitions) Baker & Taylor; (Circulation) Koha; (ILL) LibLime Koha
Wireless access
Function: 24/7 Electronic res, 24/7 Online cat, Activity rm, Adult literacy prog, Art programs, Audiobks via web, Bks on CD, Butterfly Garden, Children's prog, Computer training, Computers for patron use, E-Readers, Electronic databases & coll, Family literacy, Free DVD rentals, Holiday prog, ILL available, Internet access, Laminating, Learning ctr, Life-long learning prog for all ages, Literacy & newcomer serv, Magazines, Magnifiers for reading, Makerspace, Meeting rooms, Movies, Music CDs, Online cat, Outreach serv, OverDrive digital audio bks, Photocopying/Printing, Preschool outreach, Preschool reading prog, Printer for laptops & handheld devices, Prog for adults, Prog for children & young adult, Res assist avail, Scanner, STEM programs, Story hour, Study rm, Summer reading prog, Teen prog, Wheelchair accessible, Workshops
Mem of South Central Library System
Special Services for the Blind - Bks on CD; Large print bks; Low vision equip
Open Mon & Tues 10-5, Wed & Thurs 2-7, Fri & Sat 9-Noon

VIOLA

P VIOLA PUBLIC LIBRARY*, 137 S Main St, 54664-7037. SAN 318-4234. Tel: 608-627-1850. E-mail: violapubliclibrary@gmail.com. Web Site: violapubliclibrary.wordpress.com. *Dir,* L Owens; Staff 1 (Non-MLS 1)
Founded 1918. Pop 1,919; Circ 9,211
Jan 2016-Dec 2016 Income (Main Library Only) $73,988, City $46,038, County $17,711, Other $10,239. Mats Exp $8,595, Books $6,369, Per/Ser (Incl. Access Fees) $1,192, AV Mat $1,034. Sal $30,942 (Prof $25,740)
Library Holdings: Audiobooks 890; AV Mats 3,822; e-books 148,791; Bk Vols 18,966; Per Subs 87
Special Collections: Issues of Local Newspaper 1891-2005 on microfilm
Automation Activity & Vendor Info: (Acquisitions) Auto-Graphics, Inc; (Cataloging) Auto-Graphics, Inc; (Circulation) Auto-Graphics, Inc; (ILL) Auto-Graphics, Inc; (OPAC) Auto-Graphics, Inc; (Serials) Auto-Graphics, Inc
Wireless access
Function: 24/7 Electronic res, 24/7 Online cat, Audiobks on Playaways & MP3, Audiobks via web, AV serv, Bks on CD, Children's prog, Computers for patron use, Digital talking bks, Electronic databases & coll, For res purposes, Free DVD rentals, Homebound delivery serv, ILL available, Internet access, Magazines, Magnifiers for reading, Mail & tel request accepted, Mail loans to mem, Mango lang, Meeting rooms, Microfiche/film & reading machines, Music CDs, Online cat, OverDrive digital audio bks, Photocopying/Printing, Preschool reading prog, Prog for adults, Prog for

children & young adult, Ref & res, Story hour, Summer & winter reading prog, Summer reading prog, Tax forms, Teen prog, Telephone ref, VHS videos, Wheelchair accessible
Mem of Southwest Wisconsin Library System
Open Tues & Thurs 9:30-12:30 & 1-5, Wed & Fri 2-7, Sat 9:30-12:30

VIROQUA

P MCINTOSH MEMORIAL LIBRARY*, 205 S Rock Ave, 54665. SAN 318-4242. Tel: 608-637-7151. Administration Tel: 608-637-7151, Ext 3. Web Site: mcintoshmemoriallibrary.org. *Libr Dir,* Trina Erickson; E-mail: t.erickson@wrlsweb.org; *Dir, Adult Serv,* Lisa Widner; *Youth Serv Dir,* Laci Sheldon; Staff 5 (MLS 1, Non-MLS 4)
Founded 1898. Pop 10,000; Circ 68,000
Library Holdings: AV Mats 1,361; Bks on Deafness & Sign Lang 12; Large Print Bks 1,200; Bk Titles 35,000; Bk Vols 35,478; Per Subs 100; Talking Bks 789
Automation Activity & Vendor Info: (Circulation) Horizon; (OPAC) Horizon
Wireless access
Function: ILL available, Photocopying/Printing, Prog for children & young adult, Summer reading prog, Telephone ref
Mem of Winding Rivers Library System
Partic in WiLS
Open Mon-Thurs 9-8, Fri 9-6, Sat 9-3
Friends of the Library Group

WABENO

P WABENO PUBLIC LIBRARY*, 4556 N Branch St, 54566. (Mail add: PO Box 340, 54566-0340), SAN 318-4250. Tel: 715-473-4131. FAX: 715-473-4131. *Dir,* Cindy Lemerande; E-mail: director@wabeno.lib.wi.us
Founded 1910. Pop 1,200; Circ 16,799
Library Holdings: Bk Titles 7,150; Per Subs 21
Wireless access
Partic in Wisconsin Valley Library Service
Open Tues & Fri 10-5, Wed & Thurs 12-5, Sat 9-Noon
Friends of the Library Group

WALWORTH

P WALWORTH MEMORIAL LIBRARY*, 525 Kenosha St, 53184. (Mail add: PO Box 280, 53184-0280), SAN 318-4277. Tel: 262-275-6322. FAX: 262-275-5315. E-mail: walworth@walworth.lib.wi.us. Web Site: www.walworth.lib.wi.us. *Dir,* Bobbi Sorrentino; E-mail: sorrenti@walworth.lib.wi.us
Pop 3,405; Circ 45,000
Library Holdings: Bk Vols 14,500; Per Subs 33
Automation Activity & Vendor Info: (Cataloging) SirsiDynix; (Circulation) SirsiDynix
Wireless access
Mem of Prairie Lakes Library System (PLLS)
Open Mon & Wed 10-8, Tues & Thurs-Sat 10-5
Friends of the Library Group

WASHBURN

P WASHBURN PUBLIC LIBRARY*, 307 Washington Ave, 54891-1165. (Mail add: PO Box 248, 54891-0248), SAN 318-4285. Tel: 715-373-6172. FAX: 715-373-6186. Web Site: washburnlibrary.org. *Dir,* Darrell Pendergrass; E-mail: dpendergrass@washburn.wislib.org
Founded 1904. Pop 6,000; Circ 45,000
Library Holdings: Bk Titles 30,000; Per Subs 60
Automation Activity & Vendor Info: (OPAC) Innovative Interfaces, Inc
Wireless access
Function: ILL available
Mem of Northern Waters Library Service
Partic in Merlin
Open Mon-Thurs 10-8, Fri 10-5, Sat 10-2
Friends of the Library Group

WATERFORD

P PRAIRIE LAKES LIBRARY SYSTEM (PLLS)*, 29134 Evergreen Dr, Ste 600, 53185. SAN 318-3459. Tel: 262-514-4500. FAX: 262-514-4544. Web Site: www.prairielakes.info. *Adminr,* Steve Ohs; Tel: 262-514-4500, Ext 68, E-mail: sohs@lakeshores.lib.wi.us; *ILL Spec,* Vicki Keith; Tel: 262-514-4500, Ext 64, E-mail: vkeith@lakeshores.lib.wi.us; *IT Mgr,* Jim Novy; Tel: 262-514-4500, Ext 65; Staff 6 (MLS 3, Non-MLS 3)
Founded 1983. Pop 281,000
Automation Activity & Vendor Info: (Acquisitions) SirsiDynix; (Cataloging) SirsiDynix; (Circulation) SirsiDynix; (ILL) SirsiDynix; (OPAC) SirsiDynix; (Serials) SirsiDynix
Wireless access
Publications: Lake Shore Lines
Member Libraries: Aram Public Library; Barrett Memorial Library; Beloit College; Beloit Public Library; Blackhawk Technical College Library; Brigham Memorial Library; Burlington Public Library; Clinton Public Library; Darien Public Library; Eager Free Public Library; East Troy Lions Public Library; Edgerton Public Library; Fontana Public Library; Genoa City Public Library; Graham Public Library; Hedberg Public Library; Lake Geneva Public Library; Matheson Memorial Library; Milton Public Library; Orfordville Public Library; Racine Public Library; Rochester Public Library; Walworth Memorial Library; Waterford Public Library
Partic in Wisconsin Public Library Consortium

P WATERFORD PUBLIC LIBRARY*, 101 N River St, 53185-4149. SAN 318-4307. Tel: 262-534-3988. Administration Tel: 262-534-3988, Ext 30. FAX: 262-534-9624. Web Site: www.waterford.lib.wi.us. *Dir,* Heather Kinkade; E-mail: hkinkade@waterford.lib.wi.us; *Ch,* Tricia Cox; Tel: 262-534-3988, Ext 13, E-mail: tcox@waterford.lib.wi.us; *Teen Librn,* Julie Fick; Tel: 262-534-3988, Ext 15, E-mail: jfick@waterford.lib.wi.us; *Circ Supvr,* Samantha Public Vogel; Tel: 262-534-3988, Ext 12, E-mail: svogel@waterford.lib.wi.us; *Adult Prog Coordr,* Courtney Blawat; Tel: 262-534-3988, Ext 19, E-mail: cblawat@waterford.lib.wi.us; Staff 8 (MLS 1, Non-MLS 7)
Founded 1967. Pop 25,000; Circ 226,877
Library Holdings: Bk Vols 45,000; Per Subs 192
Automation Activity & Vendor Info: (Cataloging) SirsiDynix; (Circulation) SirsiDynix; (Course Reserve) SirsiDynix; (ILL) SirsiDynix; (Media Booking) SirsiDynix; (OPAC) SirsiDynix; (Serials) SirsiDynix
Mem of Prairie Lakes Library System (PLLS)
Open Mon-Thurs 9-8, Fri 9-5, Sat 9-3
Friends of the Library Group

WATERLOO

P KARL JUNGINGER MEMORIAL LIBRARY, 625 N Monroe St, 53594-1183. SAN 318-4315. Tel: 920-478-3344. FAX: 920-478-2351. Web Site: www.waterloo.lib.wi.us. *Libr Dir,* Kelli Mountford; E-mail: kmountford@waterloo.lib.wi.us; *Asst Dir, Youth Serv Librn,* Amanda Brueckner; E-mail: abrueckner@waterloo.lib.wi.us; *Catalog Tech Services, ILL, Outreach Serv,* Paula Jacob; E-mail: pjacob@waterloo.lib.wi.us; Staff 3 (MLS 2, Non-MLS 1)
Founded 1901. Pop 3,300; Circ 50,000
Library Holdings: CDs 400; DVDs 1,600; Bk Vols 29,000; Talking Bks 1,200
Subject Interests: Children's lit, Genealogy, Local hist
Automation Activity & Vendor Info: (Acquisitions) Innovative Interfaces, Inc. - Polaris; (Cataloging) Innovative Interfaces, Inc. - Polaris; (Circulation) Innovative Interfaces, Inc. - Polaris; (OPAC) Innovative Interfaces, Inc. - Polaris; (Serials) Innovative Interfaces, Inc. - Polaris
Wireless access
Function: 24/7 Online cat, 24/7 wireless access, Adult bk club, Audiobks on Playaways & MP3, Bilingual assistance for Spanish patrons, Bk club(s), Bks on CD, Children's prog, Computers for patron use, Digital talking bks, Family literacy, Free DVD rentals, Games, Holiday prog, Home delivery & serv to seniorr ctr & nursing homes, Homebound delivery serv, ILL available, Internet access, Large print keyboards, Magazines, Magnifiers for reading, Microfiche/film & reading machines, Music CDs, Online cat, OverDrive digital audio bks, Photocopying/Printing, Preschool outreach, Prog for adults, Prog for children & young adult, Ref serv available, Spanish lang bks, STEM programs, Story hour, Summer & winter reading prog, Teen prog, Wifi hotspot checkout
Mem of Bridges Library System
Open Mon-Thurs 9-6, Fri 9-5, Sat 9-1
Friends of the Library Group

WATERTOWN

CR MARANATHA BAPTIST UNIVERSITY*, Cedarholm Library, 745 W Main St, 53094. SAN 370-6206. Tel: 920-206-2375. FAX: 920-261-9109. E-mail: library@mbu.edu. Web Site: www.mbu.edu/library. *Libr Dir,* Mark Hanson. Subject Specialists: *Info ethics,* Mark Hanson; Staff 4.1 (MLS 1, Non-MLS 3.1)
Founded 1968. Enrl 644; Fac 49; Highest Degree: Master
Library Holdings: Bks on Deafness & Sign Lang 90; CDs 1,805; DVDs 775; e-books 118,000; Electronic Media & Resources 3,498; Microforms 228; Music Scores 239; Bk Titles 84,013; Per Subs 298
Special Collections: Weeks Coll
Subject Interests: Baptist hist
Automation Activity & Vendor Info: (Acquisitions) EOS International; (Cataloging) EOS International; (Circulation) EOS International; (OPAC) EOS International; (Serials) EOS International
Wireless access
Function: Archival coll, Audiobks via web, Bks on CD, Computers for patron use, Distance learning, Electronic databases & coll, Free DVD rentals, Instruction & testing, Internet access, Learning ctr, Online cat,

Online ref, Orientations, Outside serv via phone, mail, e-mail & web, Photocopying/Printing, Ref & res, Ref serv available, Scanner
Partic in Association of Christian Librarians; WILS; Wiscat
Open Mon, Tues & Thurs 7am-9:30pm, Wed & Fri 7-5, Sat 9-9 (Winter); Mon-Fri 8-4:30 (Summer)
Restriction: 24-hr pass syst for students only, ID required to use computers (Ltd hrs), In-house use for visitors, Non-circulating of rare bks, Non-resident fee, Open to pub for ref & circ; with some limitations, Open to students, fac & staff, Restricted borrowing privileges

P WATERTOWN PUBLIC LIBRARY*, 100 S Water St, 53094-4320. SAN 318-4331. Tel: 920-262-4090. FAX: 920-261-8943. Web Site: watertownpubliclibrary.org. *Libr Dir,* Peg Checkai; Tel: 920-545-2322, E-mail: pcheckai@watertownpubliclibrary.org; *Head, Adult Serv,* Jamie Hernandez; Tel: 920-545-2326, E-mail: jhernandez@watertownpubliclibrary.org; *Ch,* Tina Peerenboom; Tel: 920-262-2330, E-mail: tpeerenboom@watertownpubliclibrary.org; Staff 4 (MLS 4)
Founded 1907
Library Holdings: Bk Vols 99,000
Subject Interests: Local hist
Wireless access
Mem of Bridges Library System
Open Mon-Thurs 9-8, Fri 9-6, Sat 9-1, Sun 12-4
Friends of the Library Group

WAUKESHA

P BRIDGES LIBRARY SYSTEM*, 741 N Grand Ave, Ste 210, 53186. SAN 321-1061. Tel: 262-896-8080. FAX: 262-896-8060. Web Site: bridgeslibrarysystem.org. *Syst Dir,* Karol Kennedy; E-mail: kkennedy@bridgeslibrarysystem.org; *Asst Dir, Automation Syst Coordr,* Mellanie Mercier; Tel: 262-896-8084, E-mail: mmercier@bridgeslibrarysystem.org; *Libr Develop Coordr,* Laurie Freund; Tel: 262-896-8083, E-mail: ljfreund@bridgeslibrarysystem.org; Staff 5 (MLS 5)
Founded 1981. Pop 373,372
Wireless access
Member Libraries: Alice Baker Memorial Public Library; Big Bend Village Library; Brookfield Public Library; Butler Public Library; Delafield Public Library; Dwight Foster Public Library; Elm Grove Public Library; Hartland Public Library; Irvin L Young Memorial Library; Jefferson Public Library; Johnson Creek Public Library; Karl Junginger Memorial Library; L D Fargo Public Library; Menomonee Falls Public Library; Mukwonago Community Library; Muskego Public Library; New Berlin Public Library; Oconomowoc Public Library; Pauline Haass Public Library; Pewaukee Public Library; Powers Memorial Library; Town Hall Library; Watertown Public Library; Waukesha Public Library
Partic in Wisconsin Public Library Consortium
Special Services for the Deaf - Assisted listening device; Assistive tech; Closed caption videos; High interest/low vocabulary bks; Pocket talkers; Sign lang interpreter upon request for prog; TDD equip
Special Services for the Blind - BiFolkal kits; Bks on CD; Extensive large print coll; Home delivery serv; Large print bks; Low vision equip; Magnifiers; Playaways (bks on MP3); Talking bks
Open Mon-Fri 8-5

CR CARROLL UNIVERSITY*, Todd Wehr Memorial Library, 100 N East Ave, 53186. SAN 318-434X. Circulation Tel: 262-524-7175. Reference Tel: 262-650-4892. Web Site: www.carrollu.edu/library. *Dir, Libr Serv,* Joe Hardenbrook; Tel: 262-951-3022, E-mail: jhardenb@carrollu.edu; *Electronic Res Librn, Syst Librn,* Judith Carter; Tel: 262-650-4886, E-mail: carterj@carrollu.edu; *Health Sci Librn,* Loren Mintz; Tel: 262-524-7674, E-mail: lmintz@carrollu.edu; *Archivist, Pub Serv Librn, Tech Serv,* Sue Riehl; Tel: 262-650-4832, E-mail: sriehl@carrollu.edu; *Teaching & Learning Librn,* Alex Gruentzel; Tel: 262-650-4887, E-mail: agruentz@carrollu.edu; *Bus Mgr,* Rachel Aten; Tel: 262-650-4893, E-mail: raten@carrollu.edu; *Libr Operations Supvr,* Debra Brezovar; Tel: 262-524-7307, E-mail: dbrezova@carrollu.edu; *Libr Operations Supvr,* Sara Mosey; Tel: 262-524-7179, E-mail: smosey@carrollu.edu. Subject Specialists: *English lit, Modern lang, Music,* Joe Hardenbrook; *Biology, Chemistry, Computer sci,* Judith Carter; *Nursing, Occupational therapy, Phys therapy,* Loren Mintz; *Art, Hist, Polit sci,* Sue Riehl; *Educ, Philos, Psychol,* Alex Gruentzel; Staff 9 (MLS 5, Non-MLS 4)
Founded 1846. Enrl 3,459; Fac 94; Highest Degree: Doctorate
Library Holdings: e-books 7,343; e-journals 14,000; Bk Vols 150,000; Per Subs 341
Special Collections: English & Scottish 19th Century Literature Coll; Welsh Literature & Language Coll
Subject Interests: Hist, Relig studies
Automation Activity & Vendor Info: (Acquisitions) Innovative Interfaces, Inc; (Cataloging) Innovative Interfaces, Inc; (Circulation) Innovative Interfaces, Inc; (Course Reserve) Innovative Interfaces, Inc; (ILL) Innovative Interfaces, Inc; (OPAC) Innovative Interfaces, Inc; (Serials) Innovative Interfaces, Inc
Wireless access
Partic in Wis Asn of Independent Col & Univ
Open Mon-Thurs 7:30am-Midnight, Fri 7:30am-8pm, Sat 10-8, Sun 10-Midnight
Restriction: Private libr

R FIRST BAPTIST CHURCH LIBRARY-WAUKESHA*, 247 Wisconsin Ave, 53186. SAN 318-4358. Tel: 262-542-7233. E-mail: office@firstbaptistwaukesha.com. Web Site: www.firstbaptistwaukesha.com. *Mgr,* Glen Lunde; Staff 1 (MLS 1)
Library Holdings: Bk Vols 3,000
Special Collections: Christian Education Materials
Subject Interests: Relig
Wireless access

S KALMBACH MEDIA*, David P Morgan Memorial Library, 21027 Crossroads Circle, 53186. (Mail add: PO Box 1612, 53187-1612), SAN 318-2002. Tel: 262-798-6602. *Librn,* Thomas E Hoffmann; E-mail: thoffmann@kalmbach.com
Founded 1949
Library Holdings: Bk Titles 19,000; Per Subs 140; Videos 500
Special Collections: Digital Photo Library
Subject Interests: Mil hist, Railroads, Sciences, Transportation
Wireless access
Restriction: Open by appt only

S WAUKESHA COUNTY HISTORICAL SOCIETY & MUSEUM*, Huelsman Family Research Center, 101 W Main St, 53186. SAN 318-4390. Tel: 262-521-2859, Ext 225. Web Site: www.waukeshacountymuseum.org/research-center. *Curator, Exec Dir,* Bonnie Byrd; Tel: 262-521-2859, E-mail: bbyrd@wchsm.org; *Volunteer Archivist,* John Schoenknecht; Staff 1 (MLS 1)
Founded 1914
Library Holdings: Bk Titles 4,500; Per Subs 49
Special Collections: Waukesha County Family & Local History Coll
Wireless access
Function: Ref serv available
Publications: Landmark (Quarterly history magazine)
Restriction: Non-circulating, Open by appt only

M WAUKESHA MEMORIAL HOSPITAL*, ProHealth Care Library, 725 American Ave, 53188. SAN 318-4404. Tel: 262-928-2150. Toll Free Tel: 800-326-2011. FAX: 262-928-2514. Web Site: www.prohealthcare.org/locations/profile/hospital-waukesha-memorial. *Med Librn,* Dora Davis; E-mail: dora.davis@phci.org; Staff 1 (MLS 1)
Founded 1959
Library Holdings: e-books 140; e-journals 1,525; Bk Vols 2,036; Per Subs 148
Subject Interests: Hospital admin, Med, Nursing
Wireless access
Function: Doc delivery serv, Electronic databases & coll, Health sci info serv, ILL available, Internet access, Online cat, Orientations, Photocopying/Printing, Scanner
Partic in Midwest Health Sci Libr Network
Open Mon-Fri 8-2
Restriction: Hospital staff & commun, Med & nursing staff, patients & families, Open to pub for ref only, Open to students, fac & staff

P WAUKESHA PUBLIC LIBRARY*, 321 Wisconsin Ave, 53186-4713. SAN 318-4412. Tel: 262-524-3680. Circulation Tel: 262-524-3684. Interlibrary Loan Service Tel: 262-524-3889. Administration Tel: 262-524-3694. FAX: 262-524-3677. Web Site: waukeshapubliclibrary.org. *Dir,* Bruce Gay; Tel: 262-524-3681, E-mail: bgay@waukesha-wi.gov; *Head, Libr Operations,* James LaPaz; Tel: 262-522-7280, E-mail: jlapaz@waukesha-wi.gov; *Colls Mgr, Mat Mgr,* Carolyn Peil; Tel: 262-522-3690, E-mail: cpeil@waukesha-wi.gov; *Commun Engagement Mgr,* Kerry Pinkner; Tel: 262-524-3692, E-mail: kpinkner@waukesha-wi.gov; *Mkt & Communications Mgr,* Kori Hall; Tel: 262-524-3682, E-mail: khall@waukesha-wi.gov; *Pub Serv Mgr,* Therese Lyons; Tel: 262-524-3903, E-mail: tlyons@waukesha-wi.gov; *Tech Mgr,* John Klima; Tel: 262-524-3688, E-mail: jklima@waukesha-wi.gov; Staff 44 (MLS 14, Non-MLS 30)
Founded 1896. Pop 93,237; Circ 1,409,738
Library Holdings: AV Mats 26,517; DVDs 34,256; e-books 29,093; Electronic Media & Resources 9,651; Bk Vols 313,996; Per Subs 402
Special Collections: State Document Depository; US Document Depository
Automation Activity & Vendor Info: (Acquisitions) Innovative Interfaces, Inc; (Cataloging) Innovative Interfaces, Inc; (Circulation) Innovative Interfaces, Inc; (ILL) Innovative Interfaces, Inc; (OPAC) Innovative Interfaces, Inc; (Serials) Innovative Interfaces, Inc
Wireless access
Function: Adult bk club, Adult literacy prog, Art exhibits, Audiobks via web, AV serv, Bk club(s), Bks on cassette, Bks on CD, Bus archives,

CD-ROM, Children's prog, Computer training, Computers for patron use, Digital talking bks, E-Reserves, Electronic databases & coll, Free DVD rentals, Home delivery & serv to seniorr ctr & nursing homes, Homebound delivery serv, ILL available, Internet access, Magnifiers for reading, Music CDs, Online cat, Online ref, Outreach serv, OverDrive digital audio bks, Photocopying/Printing, Prog for adults, Prog for children & young adult, Senior computer classes, Story hour, Summer reading prog, Teen prog, Telephone ref, VHS videos, Wheelchair accessible
Mem of Bridges Library System
Special Services for the Deaf - Sign lang interpreter upon request for prog
Special Services for the Blind - Assistive/Adapted tech devices, equip & products; Bks on cassette; Bks on CD; Copier with enlargement capabilities; Large print & cassettes; Large print bks
Open Mon-Thurs 9-9, Fri 9-5, Sat 9-5; Mon-Thurs 9-9, Fri 9-5, Sat 9-1 (Summer)
Restriction: ID required to use computers (Ltd hrs)
Friends of the Library Group

WAUNAKEE

P WAUNAKEE PUBLIC LIBRARY*, 210 N Madison St, 53597. SAN 318-4420. Tel: 608-849-4217. E-mail: waupl@waupl.org. Web Site: www.waunakeepubliclibrary.org. *Libr Dir,* Erick Plumb; E-mail: eplumb@waupl.org; *Adult Services & Outreach Mgr,* Courtney Cosgriff; *Circ Mgr,* Emily Harkins; *Youth Serv Mgr,* Brittany Gitzlaff; E-mail: bgitzlaff@waupl.org
Pop 12,840; Circ 238,905
Library Holdings: AV Mats 7,963; CDs 4,382; DVDs 3,581; e-books 8,153; Bk Titles 60,578; Per Subs 368; Talking Bks 3,896
Special Collections: Oral History
Automation Activity & Vendor Info: (Acquisitions) Koha; (Cataloging) Koha; (Circulation) Koha; (OPAC) Koha; (Serials) Koha
Wireless access
Mem of South Central Library System
Open Mon-Thurs 9-8, Fri 9-6, Sat 9-4, Sun Noon-4 (Winter); Mon-Thurs 9-8, Fri 9-6, Sat 9-4 (Summer)
Friends of the Library Group

WAUPACA

P WAUPACA AREA PUBLIC LIBRARY*, 107 S Main St, 54981-1521. SAN 318-4447. Tel: 715-258-4414. Reference Tel: 715-258-4416. E-mail: wau@waupacalibrary.orrg. Web Site: www.waupacalibrary.org. *Dir,* Peg Burington; E-mail: pburington@waupacalibrary.org; *Asst Libr Dir, IT Coordr,* Emily Heideman; E-mail: eheideman@waupacalibrary.org; *Ad,* Patsy Servey; E-mail: pservey@waupacalibrary.org; *Teen Librn,* Taylor Wilcox; E-mail: twilcox@waupacalibrary.org; *Youth Serv Librn,* Sue Abrahamson; E-mail: sabrahamson@waupacalibrary.org; Staff 4 (MLS 2, Non-MLS 2)
Founded 1900. Pop 17,000; Circ 240,000
Library Holdings: Audiobooks 1,500; CDs 3,000; DVDs 4,000; Large Print Bks 2,500; Bk Vols 64,000; Per Subs 120
Special Collections: Wisconsin History Coll
Automation Activity & Vendor Info: (Cataloging) Innovative Interfaces, Inc; (Circulation) Innovative Interfaces, Inc
Wireless access
Function: 24/7 Online cat, 3D Printer, Adult bk club
Mem of Outagamie Waupaca Library System (OWLS)
Open Mon-Thurs 9-8, Fri 9-5, Sat 9-2
Friends of the Library Group

WAUPUN

S DODGE CORRECTIONAL INSTITUTION LIBRARY*, One W Lincoln St, 53963. (Mail add: PO Box 661, 53963-0661), SAN 365-0855. Tel: 920-324-5577, Ext 6570. FAX: 920-324-6369. *Librn,* Michael Bernstein; E-mail: michael.bernstein@wisconsin.gov; *Librn,* Tammy DeVries; E-mail: tammy.devries@wisconsin.gov; Staff 8 (MLS 2, Non-MLS 6)
Library Holdings: Bk Titles 8,700; Per Subs 67
Subject Interests: Criminal justice, Law
Automation Activity & Vendor Info: (Cataloging) Follett Software; (Circulation) Follett Software; (OPAC) Follett Software

S WAUPUN CORRECTIONAL INSTITUTION LIBRARY*, 200 S Madison St, 53963-2069. (Mail add: PO Box 351, 53963-0351), SAN 318-4463. Tel: 920-324-5571, Ext 1503. FAX: 920-324-7250. *Librn,* Kathryn Hull; E-mail: kathryn.hull@wisconsin.gov; Staff 2 (Non-MLS 2)
Founded 1890
Library Holdings: Bk Vols 13,000; Per Subs 90
Automation Activity & Vendor Info: (Circulation) Follett Software; (OPAC) Follett Software
Open Mon-Fri 7:45-10:30, 12:30-3:30 & 5:45-8:45

P WAUPUN PUBLIC LIBRARY*, 123 S Forest St, 53963. (Mail add: PO Box 391, 53963-0391), SAN 318-4455. Tel: 920-324-7925. E-mail: wpl@monarchlibraries.org. Web Site: www.cityofwaupun.org/library. *Dir,* Bret Jaeger; E-mail: bret@monarchlibraries.org; *Asst Dir,* Pam Garcia; E-mail: pgarcia@monarchlibraries.org; *Youth Serv Librn,* Tami Lont; E-mail: tami@monarchlibraries.org; *Circ,* Emma Sanders; E-mail: esanders@monarchlibraries.org; *ILL,* Wayne Fix; E-mail: waupunill@monarchlibraries.org; Staff 5 (MLS 2, Non-MLS 3)
Founded 1858. Pop 14,000; Circ 114,746
Jan 2022-Dec 2022 Income $739,619, City $516,150, County $217,469, Locally Generated Income $6,000. Mats Exp $101,852, Books $68,269, Per/Ser (Incl. Access Fees) $6,046, AV Mat $15,916, Electronic Ref Mat (Incl. Access Fees) $11,621. Sal $383,343 (Prof $143,290)
Library Holdings: CDs 6,177; DVDs 7,542; e-books 68,917; Electronic Media & Resources 575; Bk Titles 71,116; Per Subs 76
Subject Interests: Wis hist
Automation Activity & Vendor Info: (Cataloging) Innovative Interfaces, Inc. - Polaris; (Circulation) Innovative Interfaces, Inc. - Polaris; (OPAC) Innovative Interfaces, Inc; (Serials) Innovative Interfaces, Inc
Wireless access
Mem of Monarch Library System
Open Mon-Thurs 9-8, Fri & Sat 9-4:30
Friends of the Library Group

WAUSAU

M ASPIRUS HEALTH, Dr Joseph F Smith Medical Library, 333 Pine Ridge Blvd, 54401. SAN 328-3038. Tel: 715-847-2184. FAX: 715-847-2183. E-mail: library@aspirus.org. Web Site: www.aspirus.org/medical-library. *Dir,* Jan Kraus; E-mail: jan.kraus@aspirus.org; Staff 2 (MLS 1, Non-MLS 1)
Wireless access
Partic in Wis Health Sci Libr Asn
Open Mon-Fri 8-4

S MARATHON COUNTY HISTORICAL SOCIETY*, Research Library, 410 McIndoe St, 54403. SAN 324-1572. Tel: 715-848-0378. FAX: 715-848-0576. E-mail: research@marathoncountyhistory.org. Web Site: marathoncountyhistory.org. *Librn,* Gary Gisselman; Staff 2 (MLS 1, Non-MLS 1)
Founded 1980
Library Holdings: Bk Vols 7,500; Per Subs 20
Special Collections: Marathon County Plat Maps & City Directories
Subject Interests: County hist, Genealogy, Logging
Wireless access
Function: Res libr
Open Tues-Fri 9-3:30

P MARATHON COUNTY PUBLIC LIBRARY*, 300 N First St, 54403-5405. SAN 365-0944. Tel: 715-261-7200. Interlibrary Loan Service Tel: 715-261-7244. Reference Tel: 715-261-7230. Information Services Tel: 715-261-7240. FAX: 715-261-7204. Information Services E-mail: info@mcpl.us. Web Site: www.mcpl.us. *Dir,* Leah Giordano; E-mail: leah.giordano@co.marathon.wi.us
Founded 1907. Pop 134,041; Circ 803,108
Library Holdings: AV Mats 37,627; e-books 77,254; Bk Vols 246,155; Per Subs 484
Special Collections: Old Popular Sheet Music; Wisconsin History. Oral History; State Document Depository; US Document Depository
Wireless access
Partic in OCLC Online Computer Library Center, Inc; Wisconsin Valley Library Service
Open Mon-Thurs 9-8:30, Fri & Sat 9-5, Sun 1-5
Friends of the Library Group
Branches: 8
ATHENS BRANCH, 221 Caroline St, Athens, 54411-0910, SAN 365-0979. Tel: 715-257-7292. *Br Coordr,* Jennifer Triolo; E-mail: jennifer.triolo@co.marathon.wi.us
Founded 1926
Library Holdings: Bk Vols 19,206
Open Mon, Wed & Fri 10-2, Tues & Thurs 1-5
Friends of the Library Group
JOSEPH DESSERT BRANCH, 123 Main St, Mosinee, 54455, SAN 365-1037. Tel: 715-693-2144. FAX: 715-693-2144. *Br Coordr,* Sarah Moscatello; E-mail: sarah.moscatello@co.marathon.wi.us
Founded 1899
Library Holdings: Bk Vols 18,353
Open Mon, Wed & Fri 10-2, Tues 3-7, Thurs 1-5
Friends of the Library Group
EDGAR BRANCH, 224 S Third Ave, Edgar, 54426, SAN 365-1061. Tel: 715-352-3155. FAX: 715-352-3155. *Br Coordr,* Debbie Gauerke; E-mail: deb.gauerke@co.marathon.wi.us
Founded 1928
Library Holdings: Bk Vols 13,351
Open Mon & Wed 1-5, Tues, Thurs & Fri 10-2
Friends of the Library Group

HATLEY BRANCH, 435 Curtis Ave, Hatley, 54440. (Mail add: PO Box 129, Hatley, 54440-0129). Tel: 715-446-3537. FAX: 715-446-3537. *Br Supvr,* Marsha Young; E-mail: marsha.young@co.marathon.wi.us; *Br Asst,* Karen Jacobson; E-mail: karen.jacobson@co.marathon.wi.us
Founded 2005
Open Mon & Wed 1-5, Tues, Thurs & Fri 10-2

MARATHON CITY BRANCH, 515 Washington St, Marathon, 54448, SAN 365-1126. Tel: 715-443-2775. *Br Coordr,* Lisa Haessly; E-mail: lisa.haessly@co.marathon.wi.us
Founded 1954
Library Holdings: Bk Vols 11,406
Open Mon 3-7, Tues, Thurs & Fri 10-2, Wed 1-5
Friends of the Library Group

ROTHSCHILD BRANCH, 211 Grand Ave, Rothschild, 54474-1122, SAN 365-1150. Tel: 715-359-6208. FAX: 715-359-6208. *Br Coordr,* Laura L Headrick; E-mail: laura.headrick@co.marathon.wi.us
Founded 1949
Library Holdings: Bk Vols 29,775
Open Mon, Tues & Thurs 2-7, Wed 10-3, Fri 10-2
Friends of the Library Group

SPENCER BRANCH, 105 Park St, Spencer, 54479. (Mail add: PO Box 398, Spencer, 54479-0398), SAN 365-1215. Tel: 715-659-3996. FAX: 715-659-3996. *Br Coordr,* Audrey Kohlbeck; E-mail: audrey.kohlbeck@co.marathon.wi.us
Founded 1875
Library Holdings: Bk Vols 15,694
Open Mon 3-7, Tues, Thurs & Fri 10-2, Wed 1-5
Friends of the Library Group

STRATFORD BRANCH, 213201 Scholar St, Stratford, 54484. (Mail add: PO Box 74, Stratford, 54484-0074), SAN 365-124X. Tel: 715-687-4420. FAX: 715-687-4420. *Br Coordr,* Mary Jo Netzer; E-mail: maryjo.netzer@co.marathon.wi.us
Founded 1930
Library Holdings: Bk Vols 18,093
Open Mon & Fri 10-2, Tues 3-7, Wed Noon-4, Thurs 1-5
Friends of the Library Group

J NORTHCENTRAL TECHNICAL COLLEGE LIBRARY*, 1000 W Campus Dr, 54401. SAN 318-448X. Tel: 715-803-1115. Administration Tel: 715-803-1216. FAX: 715-675-9776. E-mail: library@ntc.edu. Web Site: www.ntc.edu/library. *Librn,* Nikki Framke; E-mail: framke@ntc.edu; Staff 3.4 (MLS 1.7, Non-MLS 1.7)
Founded 1969. Highest Degree: Associate
Library Holdings: Bks on Deafness & Sign Lang 200; Bk Vols 11,643
Special Collections: American Sign Language
Subject Interests: Criminal justice, Dental hygiene, Info, Nursing, Tech, Trades
Automation Activity & Vendor Info: (Acquisitions) Innovative Interfaces, Inc - Sierra; (Cataloging) Innovative Interfaces, Inc - Sierra; (Circulation) Innovative Interfaces, Inc - Sierra; (Discovery) EBSCO Discovery Service; (OPAC) Innovative Interfaces, Inc - Sierra; (Serials) Innovative Interfaces, Inc - Sierra
Wireless access
Partic in WISPALS Library Consortium
Special Services for the Deaf - Am sign lang & deaf culture; Bks on deafness & sign lang; Closed caption videos; Coll on deaf educ; Video relay services
Special Services for the Blind - Accessible computers; Bks on CD; Copier with enlargement capabilities; Large type calculator; Magnifiers; PC for people with disabilities; ZoomText magnification & reading software
Open Mon-Fri 7:30am-10pm, Sat & Sun 9-3

C UNIVERSITY OF WISCONSIN STEVENS POINT LIBRARY*, 518 S Seventh Ave, 54401-5396. SAN 318-4498. Tel: 715-261-6220. Reference Tel: 715-261-6218. FAX: 715-261-6330. E-mail: mth-reference@uwc.edu. Web Site: uwmc.uwc.edu/library. *Sr Acad Librn,* Renee Sikma Wallin; E-mail: renee.wallin@uwc.edu; Staff 4 (MLS 2, Non-MLS 2)
Founded 1938. Enrl 1,300; Fac 45; Highest Degree: Bachelor
Library Holdings: Bk Titles 40,000; Bk Vols 42,000; Per Subs 101
Automation Activity & Vendor Info: (Cataloging) Ex Libris Group; (Circulation) Ex Libris Group; (Course Reserve) Ex Libris Group; (Media Booking) Ex Libris Group; (OPAC) Ex Libris Group; (Serials) Ex Libris Group
Wireless access
Partic in OCLC Online Computer Library Center, Inc; WiLS
Open Mon-Thurs 7:45-7:30, Fri 7:45-4

S LEIGH YAWKEY WOODSON ART MUSEUM LIBRARY*, 700 N 12th St, 54403-5007. SAN 326-5161. Tel: 715-845-7010. FAX: 715-845-7103. E-mail: museum@lywam.org. Web Site: www.lywam.org. *Curator of Coll, Registrar,* Jane Weinke; E-mail: jweinke@lywam.org
Library Holdings: Bk Titles 1,800; Per Subs 30
Subject Interests: Birds, Decorative art
Restriction: Open by appt only

WAUTOMA

P WAUTOMA PUBLIC LIBRARY*, 410 W Main St, 54982-5415. (Mail add: PO Box 269, 54982-0269), SAN 318-451X. Tel: 920-787-2988. FAX: 920-787-7786. Web Site: www.wautomalibrary.org. *Dir,* Hannah Klusmeyer; E-mail: director@wautomalibrary.org; *Asst Dir,* Susan Younger; E-mail: younger@wautomalibrary.org; *Circ Librn, Ref Librn,* Diane Hughes; E-mail: hughes@wautomalibrary.org; Staff 3.2 (Non-MLS 3.2)
Pop 8,886; Circ 98,300
Library Holdings: Bk Vols 25,110; Per Subs 50
Automation Activity & Vendor Info: (OPAC) SirsiDynix
Wireless access
Mem of Winnefox Library System
Open Mon-Fri 9-6, Sat 9-2
Friends of the Library Group

WAUWATOSA

P WAUWATOSA PUBLIC LIBRARY*, 7635 W North Ave, 53213-1718. SAN 318-4544. Tel: 414-471-8484. Administration Tel: 414-471-8487. FAX: 414-479-8984. Web Site: wauwatosalibrary.org. *Dir,* Pete Loeffel; E-mail: ploeffel@wauwatosalibrary.org; *Asst Dir,* Robert Tronley; E-mail: robert.tronley@mcfls.org; *Ch Serv,* Ann Kissinger; Staff 12 (MLS 9, Non-MLS 3)
Founded 1886. Pop 49,300; Circ 834,000
Library Holdings: AV Mats 22,000; Bk Vols 227,000; Per Subs 302
Special Collections: Oral History
Automation Activity & Vendor Info: (Acquisitions) Innovative Interfaces, Inc; (Cataloging) Innovative Interfaces, Inc; (Circulation) Innovative Interfaces, Inc; (OPAC) Innovative Interfaces, Inc
Wireless access
Function: Homebound delivery serv, Prog for children & young adult, Ref serv available
Mem of Milwaukee County Federated Library System
Partic in WiLS
Open Mon-Thurs 9-9, Fri & Sat 9-5

WEBSTER

P LARSEN FAMILY PUBLIC LIBRARY*, 7401 Main St W, 54893-0510. (Mail add: PO Box 510, 54893-0510), SAN 376-6136. Tel: 715-866-7697. FAX: 715-866-8842. Web Site: webster.wislib.org. *Dir,* Patti Meyer; E-mail: pmeyer@webster.wislib.org; *Librn,* Desiree Steinberg; E-mail: dlsteinberg510@gmail.com; Staff 1 (Non-MLS 1)
Founded 1992. Pop 8,851; Circ 46,062
Library Holdings: Bk Vols 20,193; Per Subs 68
Automation Activity & Vendor Info: (Acquisitions) Innovative Interfaces, Inc - Millennium; (Cataloging) Innovative Interfaces, Inc - Millennium; (Circulation) Innovative Interfaces, Inc - Millennium; (OPAC) Innovative Interfaces, Inc
Wireless access
Function: Adult bk club, Adult literacy prog, Audiobks via web, Bks on CD, Children's prog, Computers for patron use, Doc delivery serv, Free DVD rentals, ILL available, Internet access, Large print keyboards, Magnifiers for reading, Mail & tel request accepted, Music CDs, Online cat, OverDrive digital audio bks, Photocopying/Printing, Preschool reading prog, Ref serv available, Scanner, Summer reading prog, Tax forms, VHS videos, Wheelchair accessible
Mem of Northern Waters Library Service
Open Mon-Thurs 10-7, Fri 9-5, Sat 10-3
Friends of the Library Group

WEST ALLIS

M AURORA WEST ALLIS MEDICAL CENTER*, Ziebert Medical Library, 8901 W Lincoln Ave, 53227-0901. SAN 318-4579. Tel: 414-328-7910. FAX: 414-328-7912. E-mail: ziebert.library@aurora.org. Web Site: www.aurorahealthcare.org. *Lead Librn,* Jennifer Deal; E-mail: jennifer.deal@aah.org; *Libr Asst,* Annie Lipski; Staff 2 (MLS 1, Non-MLS 1)
Library Holdings: Bk Titles 600; Per Subs 100
Wireless access

J MILWAUKEE AREA TECHNICAL COLLEGE*, West Allis Campus Library, 1200 S 71st St, Rm 213, 53214-3110. SAN 318-4560. Tel: 414-456-5393. FAX: 414-456-5413. Web Site: guides.matc.edu/about/westallislib. *Campus Librn,* Shelley Peschel; Tel: 414-456-5392, E-mail: peschels@matc.edu; *Evening Librn,* Jennifer Peterson; E-mail: petersjc@matc.edu; *Archives, Circ,* Melissa Stiglich; E-mail: stiglicm@matc.edu; Staff 3 (MLS 2, Non-MLS 1)
Highest Degree: Associate
Library Holdings: Bk Titles 8,000
Special Collections: Adult Literacy

Subject Interests: Design, Electronic systs, Funeral serv, Hotel, Interior design, Liberal arts, Motel mgt, Sci, Welding
Automation Activity & Vendor Info: (Acquisitions) Innovative Interfaces, Inc - Millennium; (Cataloging) Innovative Interfaces, Inc; (Circulation) Innovative Interfaces, Inc; (Discovery) EBSCO Discovery Service; (OPAC) Innovative Interfaces, Inc
Wireless access
Open Mon-Thurs 7:30am-8pm, Fri 7:30-4
Restriction: Open to students, fac & staff, Restricted pub use

P WEST ALLIS PUBLIC LIBRARY*, 7421 W National Ave, 53214-4699. SAN 365-1304. Tel: 414-302-8503. Reference Tel: 414-302-8500. Administration Tel: 414-302-8501. Web Site: www.westalliswi.gov/index.aspx?NID=330. *Dir,* Michael Koszalka; E-mail: Michael.Koszalka@mcfls.org; Staff 8 (MLS 8)
Founded 1898. Pop 60,607; Circ 747,463
Library Holdings: AV Mats 25,627; Electronic Media & Resources 38; Bk Vols 215,767; Per Subs 372
Automation Activity & Vendor Info: (Acquisitions) Innovative Interfaces, Inc; (Cataloging) Innovative Interfaces, Inc; (Circulation) Innovative Interfaces, Inc; (OPAC) Innovative Interfaces, Inc; (Serials) Innovative Interfaces, Inc
Wireless access
Mem of Milwaukee County Federated Library System
Partic in OCLC Online Computer Library Center, Inc
Special Services for the Deaf - TTY equip
Special Services for the Blind - Assistive/Adapted tech devices, equip & products
Open Mon & Wed 9-9, Tues & Thurs Noon-9, Fri & Sat 9-6, Sun (Oct-April) 1-5
Friends of the Library Group

WEST BEND

J MORAINE PARK TECHNICAL COLLEGE*, West Bend Campus Library, 2151 N Main St, 53090-1598. SAN 318-4587. Tel: 262-335-5760. Web Site: www.morainepark.edu. *Ref Librn,* Richard Huebschman; E-mail: rhuebschman@morainepark.edu
Founded 1969
Library Holdings: Bk Titles 5,000; Bk Vols 12,000; Per Subs 35
Subject Interests: Adult basic educ, Computer sci, Indust, Mkt, Nursing, Trade
Automation Activity & Vendor Info: (Acquisitions) Innovative Interfaces, Inc; (Cataloging) Innovative Interfaces, Inc; (Circulation) Innovative Interfaces, Inc; (Course Reserve) Innovative Interfaces, Inc; (ILL) Innovative Interfaces, Inc; (Media Booking) Innovative Interfaces, Inc; (OPAC) Innovative Interfaces, Inc; (Serials) Innovative Interfaces, Inc
Wireless access
Partic in Fox River Valley Area Library Consortium; Mid-Wis Multi-type Libr; WISPALS Library Consortium
Open Mon-Thurs 8am-9:30pm, Fri & Sat 8-4

J UNIVERSITY OF WISCONSIN*, Washington County Library, 400 University Dr, 53095-3619. SAN 318-4595. Tel: 262-335-5206. Web Site: uwm.edu/libraries/washington. *Dir of Libr,* Michael Doylen; E-mail: doylenm@uwm.edu; *Libr Assoc,* Karen Kleist; Tel: 262-808-4141, E-mail: wsh-caseanswerdesk@uwc.edu; Staff 2 (MLS 2)
Founded 1968. Enrl 900; Fac 29; Highest Degree: Associate
Library Holdings: Bk Titles 43,124; Per Subs 150
Special Collections: Indians of North America Coll; International Folk Music Coll
Automation Activity & Vendor Info: (Acquisitions) Ex Libris Group; (Cataloging) Ex Libris Group; (Circulation) Ex Libris Group; (Course Reserve) Ex Libris Group; (OPAC) Ex Libris Group
Wireless access
Partic in Coun of Univ of Wis Librs; OCLC Online Computer Library Center, Inc
Open Mon-Thurs 8-7, Fri 8-2 (Winter); Mon-Thurs 10-6 (Summer)

P WEST BEND COMMUNITY MEMORIAL LIBRARY*, 630 Poplar St, 53095-3380. SAN 318-4617. Tel: 262-335-5151. Reference Tel: 262-335-5152. FAX: 262-335-5150. Reference FAX: 262-335-5169. Reference E-mail: libref@westbendlibrary.org. Web Site: www.westbendlibrary.org. *Libr Dir,* Steve Thiry; E-mail: sthiry@westbendlibrary.org; Staff 22 (MLS 7, Non-MLS 15)
Founded 1901. Pop 50,000; Circ 514,864
Library Holdings: Bk Titles 103,500; Bk Vols 189,761; Per Subs 360
Special Collections: Cake Pans; STEAM Kits
Automation Activity & Vendor Info: (Cataloging) Innovative Interfaces, Inc. - Polaris; (Circulation) Innovative Interfaces, Inc. - Polaris; (OPAC) Innovative Interfaces, Inc. - Polaris; (Serials) Innovative Interfaces, Inc. - Polaris
Wireless access
Mem of Monarch Library System
Open Mon-Thurs 9-9, Fri 9-6, Sat 9-1

WEST SALEM

P WINDING RIVERS LIBRARY SYSTEM*, 980 W Hwy 16, Ste 1, 54669. SAN 318-0778. Tel: 608-789-7151. FAX: 608-789-7106. Web Site: www.wrlsweb.org. *Dir,* Kristen Anderson; E-mail: kristen@wrlsweb.org; Staff 4 (MLS 3, Non-MLS 1)
Founded 1967. Pop 272,732
Automation Activity & Vendor Info: (Cataloging) Horizon; (Circulation) Horizon; (ILL) Auto-Graphics, Inc; (OPAC) Horizon
Wireless access
Publications: Whirlpools (Newsletter)
Member Libraries: Alma Public Library; Arcadia Free Public Library; Bekkum Memorial Library; Black River Falls Public Library; Blair-Preston Public Library; Cashton Memorial Library; De Soto Public Library; Elroy Public Library; Ettrick Public Library; Galesville Public Library; Hatch Public Library; Hauge Memorial Library; Hillsboro Public Library; Independence Public Library; Kendall Public Library; Knutson Memorial Library; La Crosse County Library; La Crosse Public Library; Lawton Memorial Library; McIntosh Memorial Library; Mondovi Public Library; Necedah Community -Siegler Memorial Library; New Lisbon Memorial Library; Norwalk Public Library; Ontario Public Library; Readstown Public Library; Shirley M Wright Memorial Library; Sparta Free Library; Strum Public Library; Taylor Memorial Library; Tomah Public Library; Whitehall Public Library; Wilton Public Library; Wonewoc Public Library
Partic in Wisconsin Public Library Consortium
Restriction: Limited access for the pub

WESTBORO

P WESTBORO PUBLIC LIBRARY, N8855 Second St, 54490. (Mail add: PO Box 127, 54490-0127), SAN 318-4641. Tel: 715-427-5864. FAX: 715-427-5354. Web Site: westborolibrary.org. *Dir,* Melissa Highfill; E-mail: director@westboro.lib.wi.us
Founded 1947. Pop 900; Circ 13,000
Library Holdings: Bk Titles 7,000; Per Subs 62
Automation Activity & Vendor Info: (Cataloging) Innovative Interfaces, Inc - Sierra; (Circulation) Innovative Interfaces, Inc - Sierra; (OPAC) Innovative Interfaces, Inc - Sierra
Wireless access
Partic in Wisconsin Valley Library Service
Open Tues-Thurs 9-5, Sat 9-12

WESTBY

P BEKKUM MEMORIAL LIBRARY*, 206 N Main St, 54667-1108. SAN 318-465X. Tel: 608-634-4419. E-mail: bekkuml@wrlsweb.org. Web Site: www.wrlsweb.org/westby. *Dir,* Michelle Tryggestad
Pop 5,000; Circ 50,000
Library Holdings: Bk Vols 19,000; Per Subs 80
Automation Activity & Vendor Info: (Cataloging) Innovative Interfaces, Inc - Sierra; (Circulation) Innovative Interfaces, Inc - Sierra
Wireless access
Mem of Winding Rivers Library System
Open Mon-Thurs 11-8, Fri 11-5, Sat 9-3, Sun (Winter) 1-4
Friends of the Library Group

WESTFIELD

P WESTFIELD PUBLIC LIBRARY*, Ethel Everhard Memorial Library, 117 E Third St, 53964-9107. (Mail add: PO Box 355, 53964-0355), SAN 318-4668. Tel: 608-296-2544. FAX: 608-296-2622. Web Site: www.westfieldlibrary.org. *Dir,* Aaron Raschke; E-mail: director@westfieldlibrary.org
Pop 3,948; Circ 25,451
Library Holdings: Bk Vols 13,000; Per Subs 38
Subject Interests: Wis
Automation Activity & Vendor Info: (Cataloging) SirsiDynix; (Circulation) SirsiDynix; (OPAC) SirsiDynix
Wireless access
Mem of Winnefox Library System
Partic in Midwest Collaborative for Library Services
Open Mon-Thurs 9-6, Fri & Sat 9-1
Friends of the Library Group

WEYAUWEGA

P WEYAUWEGA PUBLIC LIBRARY*, 301 S Mill St, 54983. (Mail add: PO Box 6, 54983-0006), SAN 318-4676. Tel: 920-867-3742. FAX: 920-867-3741. E-mail: wey@wegalibrary.org. Web Site: www.wegalibrary.org. *Interim Dir,* Kelly Kneisler; E-mail: kkneisler@wegalibrary.org; *Ch,* Margo Lambert; E-mail: mlambert@wegalibrary.org; Staff 1 (Non-MLS 1)
Founded 1912. Pop 3,500; Circ 53,000
Library Holdings: DVDs 2,500; Bk Vols 23,494; Per Subs 104
Wireless access

Mem of Outagamie Waupaca Library System (OWLS)
Open Mon & Wed 9:30-8, Tues & Thurs 9:30-6, Fri 9:30-5, Sat 9:30-1:30

WHITEFISH BAY

P WHITEFISH BAY PUBLIC LIBRARY*, 5420 N Marlborough Dr, 53217. SAN 318-2568. Tel: 414-964-4380. Reference E-mail: reference@wfblibrary.org. Web Site: www.wfblibrary.org. *Libr Dir,* Nyama Reed; Tel: 414-755-6551, E-mail: n.reed@wfblibrary.org; *Head, Adult Serv,* Scott Lenski; E-mail: s.lenski@wfblibrary.org; *Head, Circ Serv,* Theresa Hoge; E-mail: t.hoge@wfblibrary.org; *Head, Youth Serv,* Katie Kiekhaefer; E-mail: k.kiekhaefer@wfblibrary.org; Staff 11.2 (MLS 5.2, Non-MLS 6)
Founded 1936. Pop 14,905; Circ 275,529
Library Holdings: Bk Vols 75,853; Per Subs 146
Subject Interests: Local hist
Automation Activity & Vendor Info: (Cataloging) Innovative Interfaces, Inc; (Circulation) Innovative Interfaces, Inc; (OPAC) Innovative Interfaces, Inc
Wireless access
Function: 24/7 Online cat, Activity rm, Adult bk club, Archival coll, Bk club(s), Bks on CD, Children's prog, Computers for patron use, Electronic databases & coll, For res purposes, Free DVD rentals, Magazines, Mail & tel request accepted, Mango lang, Meeting rooms, Movies, Music CDs, Online cat, Online ref, OverDrive digital audio bks, Photocopying/Printing, Prog for adults, Prog for children & young adult, Ref & res, Ref serv available, Scanner, Story hour, Study rm, Summer reading prog, Teen prog, Telephone ref, Wheelchair accessible
Publications: Newsletter
Mem of Milwaukee County Federated Library System
Open Mon-Thurs 9:30-8:30, Fri 9:30-5:30, Sat 9:30-4
Friends of the Library Group

WHITEHALL

P WHITEHALL PUBLIC LIBRARY*, 36351 Main St, 54773. (Mail add: PO Box 36, 54773-0036), SAN 318-4684. Tel: 715-538-4107. FAX: 715-538-2301. E-mail: whitehallpubliclibrary@wrlsweb.org. Web Site: whtlpl.org. *Dir,* Amanda Hegge; E-mail: whtlpldirector@wrlsweb.org
Pop 3,415; Circ 14,243
Library Holdings: Bk Vols 15,437
Mem of Winding Rivers Library System
Open Mon-Fri 11-6

WHITEWATER

C UNIVERSITY OF WISCONSIN-WHITEWATER, Andersen Library, 750 W Main St, 53190-1790. (Mail add: PO Box 900, 53190-0900), SAN 365-1398. Tel: 262-472-5511. Reference Tel: 262-472-1032. FAX: 262-472-5727. E-mail: circdesk@uww.edu, libill@uww.edu, refdesk@uww.edu. Web Site: www.uww.edu/llibrary. *Dir,* Paul Waelchli; Tel: 262-472-5516, E-mail: waelchlp@uww.edu; *Head, Access Serv,* Andy Kramer; Tel: 262-472-1022, E-mail: kramera@uww.edu; *Head, Archives,* Jennifer Motszko; Tel: 262-472-5515, E-mail: motszkoj@uww.edu; *Head, Systems & Tech Services,* Patricia Fragola; Tel: 262-472-5673, E-mail: fragolap@uww.edu; *Cat Librn,* Macaela Willadsen; Tel: 262-472-7165, E-mail: willadsm@uww.edu; *Electronic Res Librn,* Nancy Bennett; Tel: 262-472-5517, E-mail: bennetna@uww.edu; *Govt Doc Librn,* Kate Braman; Tel: 262-472-4671, E-mail: davisk@uww.edu; *Ref & Instruction Librn,* Ellen Latorraca; Tel: 262-472-5525, E-mail: latorrae@uww.edu; *Ref & Instruction Librn,* Rebecca Paulraj; Tel: 262-472-5519, E-mail: paulrajr@uww.edu; *Ref & Instruction Librn,* Martha Stephenson; Tel: 262-472-4366, E-mail: stephenm@uww.edu; *User Serv Librn,* Diana Shull; Tel: 262-472-5011, E-mail: shulld@uww.edu. Subject Specialists: *Environ sci, Geog, Geol,* Kate Braman; *Educ, Music,* Ellen Latorraca; *Bus, Econ,* Rebecca Paulraj; *Lit, Philos, Relig studies,* Martha Stephenson; Staff 11.5 (MLS 11.5)
Founded 1868. Enrl 12,000; Fac 502; Highest Degree: Doctorate
Library Holdings: Audiobooks 693; AV Mats 20,098; CDs 5,768; DVDs 5,727; e-books 113,000; e-journals 6,469; Electronic Media & Resources 300; Microforms 439,774; Bk Vols 592,122; Per Subs 6,804; Videos 9,652
Special Collections: George A Custer (Kenneth Hammer Coll); Local History (Area Research Center Coll), bks, ms & archives (records for Rock, Jefferson & Walworth counties); UWW Campus History (Minneiska yearbooks, scrapbooks, Royal Purple, student newspaper). State Document Depository; US Document Depository
Subject Interests: Educ, Finance
Automation Activity & Vendor Info: (Acquisitions) Ex Libris Group; (Cataloging) Ex Libris Group; (Circulation) Ex Libris Group; (Course Reserve) Ex Libris Group; (ILL) OCLC ILLiad; (OPAC) Ex Libris Group; (Serials) Ex Libris Group
Wireless access
Function: Audio & video playback equip for onsite use, Computers for patron use, E-Reserves, Electronic databases & coll, Online cat, Online ref, Wheelchair accessible
Partic in Coun of Wis Librs, Inc; CUWL; WiLS
Special Services for the Blind - Computer with voice synthesizer for visually impaired persons; Reader equip; ZoomText magnification & reading software
Open Mon-Thurs 7:30am-Midnight, Fri 7:30-6, Sat 11-4, Sun 1pm-Midnight (Fall); Mon-Thurs 8-6, Fri 8-4:30 (Summer)
Restriction: Authorized patrons, In-house use for visitors, Open to students, fac & staff

P IRVIN L YOUNG MEMORIAL LIBRARY*, 431 W Center St, 53190. SAN 318-4692. Tel: 262-473-0530. Web Site: whitewaterlibrary.org. *Dir,* Stacey Lunsford; E-mail: slunsford@whitewater-wi.gov; *Adult Serv, Asst Dir, Ref (Info Servs),* Diane Jaroch; E-mail: djaroch@whitewater-wi.gov; *Youth Serv,* Deana Rolfsmeyer; E-mail: drolfsmeyer@whitewater-wi.gov; Staff 3 (MLS 2, Non-MLS 1)
Founded 1899. Pop 19,000; Circ 171,639
Library Holdings: Bks on Deafness & Sign Lang 20; High Interest/Low Vocabulary Bk Vols 100; Bk Titles 63,000; Bk Vols 65,500; Per Subs 287
Special Collections: Achen Photographs; Whitewater history
Subject Interests: Local hist, Spanish
Automation Activity & Vendor Info: (Cataloging) SirsiDynix; (Circulation) SirsiDynix; (OPAC) SirsiDynix
Wireless access
Mem of Bridges Library System
Partic in Association for Rural & Small Libraries
Open Mon-Thurs 9-8:30, Fri 9-5:30, Sat 9-3
Friends of the Library Group

WILD ROSE

P PATTERSON MEMORIAL LIBRARY*, 500 Division St, 54984. (Mail add: PO Box 305, 54984-0305), SAN 318-4706. Tel: 920-622-3835. FAX: 920-622-5140. E-mail: director@wildroselibrary.org. Web Site: www.wildroselibrary.org. *Dir,* Kent A Barnard; E-mail: barnard@wildroselibrary.org. Subject Specialists: *Early literacy,* Kent A Barnard; Staff 4 (MLS 1, Non-MLS 3)
Founded 1930. Pop 3,500; Circ 56,500
Library Holdings: Audiobooks 101; Bks on Deafness & Sign Lang 10; CDs 250; DVDs 1,000; High Interest/Low Vocabulary Bk Vols 200; Bk Titles 15,500; Per Subs 50; Videos 210
Special Collections: Local Oral History on Audio Cassette & CD. Oral History
Automation Activity & Vendor Info: (Cataloging) SirsiDynix; (Circulation) SirsiDynix; (OPAC) SirsiDynix
Wireless access
Function: Accelerated reader prog, Activity rm, Adult bk club, After school storytime, Art exhibits, Audio & video playback equip for onsite use, Audiobks via web, AV serv, Bk club(s), Bks on cassette, Bks on CD, Children's prog, Computer training, Computers for patron use, Digital talking bks, E-Readers, Electronic databases & coll, Equip loans & repairs, Free DVD rentals, Home delivery & serv to seniorr ctr & nursing homes, Homework prog, ILL available, Instruction & testing, Internet access, Magazines, Magnifiers for reading, Movies, Music CDs, Online cat, Online ref, OverDrive digital audio bks, Photocopying/Printing, Printer for laptops & handheld devices, Prog for adults, Prog for children & young adult, Senior computer classes, Spanish lang bks, Spoken cassettes & CDs, Story hour, Summer reading prog, Tax forms, Teen prog, VHS videos, Wheelchair accessible, Workshops
Mem of Winnefox Library System
Open Mon-Fri 10-6, Sat 9-1
Friends of the Library Group

WILLIAMS BAY

P BARRETT MEMORIAL LIBRARY*, 65 W Geneva St, 53191. SAN 318-4714. Tel: 262-245-2709. E-mail: wmsbay@williamsbay.lib.wi.us. Web Site: www.williamsbay.lib.wi.us. *Dir,* Joy Schnupp; E-mail: jschnupp@williamsbay.lib.wi.us; Staff 6 (MLS 2, Non-MLS 4)
Founded 1903. Pop 2,415; Circ 70,210
Library Holdings: Bk Titles 18,006; Bk Vols 18,350; Per Subs 64
Automation Activity & Vendor Info: (Cataloging) SirsiDynix; (Circulation) SirsiDynix; (OPAC) SirsiDynix
Wireless access
Function: 24/7 Electronic res, 24/7 Online cat, Adult bk club, Audiobks on Playaways & MP3, Audiobks via web, Bk club(s), Bks on CD, Children's prog, Computers for patron use, Electronic databases & coll, Holiday prog, Internet access, Magazines, Magnifiers for reading, Museum passes, Music CDs, Online cat, Outside serv via phone, mail, e-mail & web, OverDrive digital audio bks, Photocopying/Printing, Preschool reading prog, Printer for laptops & handheld devices, Prog for adults, Prog for children & young adult, Scanner, STEM programs, Story hour, Study rm, Summer reading prog, Teen prog, Telephone ref, Wheelchair accessible
Mem of Prairie Lakes Library System (PLLS)
Open Mon-Fri 9-6, Sat 9-1
Friends of the Library Group

WILTON

P WILTON PUBLIC LIBRARY*, 400 East St, 54670. (Mail add: PO Box 280, 54670-0280), SAN 318-4730. Tel: 608-435-6710. E-mail: wiltonlibrary@wrlsweb.org. Web Site: www.wrlsweb.org/wilton. *Dir,* Gina Rae
Circ 10,130
Library Holdings: Bk Titles 14,000; Per Subs 55
Automation Activity & Vendor Info: (Cataloging) Horizon; (Circulation) Horizon; (OPAC) Horizon
Wireless access
Mem of Winding Rivers Library System
Partic in Wiscat
Open Mon, Wed & Fri 10-6, Sat 9-11:30

WINCHESTER

P WINCHESTER PUBLIC LIBRARY*, 2117 Lake St, 54557-9104. SAN 370-7008. Tel: 715-686-2926. FAX: 715-686-2926. E-mail: winplibrary@irtc.net. Web Site: www.winchesterpubliclibrary.org. *Libr Dir,* Darlene Smith; Staff 1 (Non-MLS 1)
Founded 1986. Pop 400; Circ 4,392
Library Holdings: AV Mats 1,100; Bks on Deafness & Sign Lang 20; CDs 25; Large Print Bks 550; Bk Titles 13,400; Per Subs 39; Talking Bks 400
Wireless access
Mem of Northern Waters Library Service
Partic in Wiscat
Open Mon-Wed & Fri 10-3, Thurs 10-6, Sat 9-Noon (Summer); Thurs 10-6, Fri 10-3, Sat 10-Noon (Winter)
Friends of the Library Group

WINNECONNE

P WINNECONNE PUBLIC LIBRARY*, 31 S Second St, 54986. (Mail add: PO Box 518, 54986-0518). Tel: 920-582-7091. Web Site: www.winneconnelibrary.org. *Dir,* Holly Selwitschka; E-mail: director@winneconnelibrary.org; *Ch,* Amanda O'Neal; E-mail: o'neal@winneconnelibrary.org; *Customer Serv Spec,* Tracy Aerts; E-mail: aerts@winneconnelibrary.org; *Mkt Coordr,* Kelly Nelson; E-mail: nelson@winneconnelibrary.org; Staff 4 (MLS 1, Non-MLS 3)
Founded 1913. Pop 2,500; Circ 68,000
Library Holdings: AV Mats 1,190; Bks on Deafness & Sign Lang 50; CDs 815; DVDs 1,680; e-books 7,270; Large Print Bks 1,000; Bk Vols 25,740; Per Subs 94; Videos 1,910
Subject Interests: Local hist
Automation Activity & Vendor Info: (Acquisitions) SirsiDynix; (Cataloging) SirsiDynix; (Circulation) SirsiDynix; (ILL) SirsiDynix; (Media Booking) SirsiDynix; (OPAC) SirsiDynix; (Serials) SirsiDynix
Wireless access
Function: 24/7 Electronic res, 24/7 Online cat, Activity rm, Adult bk club, Archival coll, Art exhibits, Audio & video playback equip for onsite use, Audiobks on Playaways & MP3, Audiobks via web, Bk club(s), Bks on CD, Children's prog, Computer training, Computers for patron use, Doc delivery serv, Electronic databases & coll, Family literacy, Free DVD rentals, Holiday prog, ILL available, Internet access, Life-long learning prog for all ages, Magazines, Magnifiers for reading, Makerspace, Meeting rooms, Movies, Music CDs, Online cat, Outreach serv, OverDrive digital audio bks, Photocopying/Printing, Preschool outreach, Printer for laptops & handheld devices, Prog for adults, Prog for children & young adult, Scanner, Story hour, Summer reading prog, Tax forms, Teen prog, Wheelchair accessible
Mem of Winnefox Library System
Open Mon-Wed & Fri 10-6, Thurs 10-7, Sat 10-1; Mon-Wed & Fri 9-6, Thurs 9-7, Sat 9-1 (Summer)
Friends of the Library Group

WINTER

P WINTER PUBLIC LIBRARY*, 5129 N Main St, 54896. (Mail add: PO Box 340, 54896-0340), SAN 318-4757. Tel: 715-266-2144. E-mail: winter.wislib@gmail.com. Web Site: www.winterwislib.org. *Dir,* Donna Knuckey
Pop 2,300; Circ 28,000
Library Holdings: Audiobooks 385; AV Mats 8; DVDs 1,963; e-books 175,000; Bk Vols 14,000; Per Subs 42
Automation Activity & Vendor Info: (Cataloging) Innovative Interfaces, Inc - Sierra; (Circulation) Innovative Interfaces, Inc - Sierra
Wireless access
Mem of Northern Waters Library Service
Open Mon, Tues, Thurs & Fri 10-5, Wed 10-7, Sat 10-2; Mon, Tues, Thurs & Fri 9-5, Wed 9-7, Sat 9-2 (Summer)
Friends of the Library Group

WISCONSIN DELLS

P KILBOURN PUBLIC LIBRARY*, 620 Elm St, 53965. SAN 318-4765. Tel: 608-254-2146. E-mail: staff@dellslibrary.org. Web Site: www.dellslibrary.org. *Dir,* Cathy Jean Borck; E-mail: cathyb@dellslibrary.org; *Youth Serv,* Jody DelaGardelle; E-mail: jodydela@dellslibrary.org; Staff 4 (MLS 1, Non-MLS 3)
Founded 1897. Pop 2,500; Circ 52,463
Library Holdings: Bk Titles 40,000; Per Subs 95
Special Collections: Local Newspapers from 1856 to Date, micro
Subject Interests: Hist
Automation Activity & Vendor Info: (Acquisitions) SirsiDynix; (Cataloging) SirsiDynix; (Circulation) SirsiDynix; (OPAC) SirsiDynix; (Serials) SirsiDynix
Wireless access
Mem of South Central Library System
Partic in S Cent Libr Syst
Open Mon-Thurs 9-8, Fri 9-5, Sat 9-2
Friends of the Library Group
Bookmobiles: 1

WISCONSIN RAPIDS

P MCMILLAN MEMORIAL LIBRARY*, 490 E Grand Ave, 54494-4898. SAN 318-4781. Tel: 715-422-5136. Circulation Tel: 715-422-5133. Administration Tel: 715-422-5129. FAX: 715-423-2665. TDD: 715-422-5138. E-mail: ask@mcmillanlibrary.org. Web Site: www.mcmillanlibrary.org. *Dir,* Andrew Barnett; E-mail: abarnett@mcmillanlibrary.org; *Asst Dir,* JoAnn Ogreenc; Tel: 715-422-5144, E-mail: jogreenc@mcmillanlibrary.org; *Head, Support Serv,* Eric Norton; *Adult Serv Mgr,* Colin McGinnis; Tel: 715-422-5126, E-mail: cmcguiness@mcmillanlibrary.org; *YA Mgr,* Alicia Woodland; E-mail: awoodland@mcmillanlibrary.org; *Youth Serv Mgr,* Kerry Preece; Staff 8 (MLS 6, Non-MLS 2)
Founded 1890
Library Holdings: AV Mats 23,022; Per Subs 227
Subject Interests: Genealogy, Local hist, Paper indust
Automation Activity & Vendor Info: (Acquisitions) LibLime; (Cataloging) LibLime; (Circulation) LibLime; (OPAC) LibLime
Wireless access
Function: 24/7 Electronic res, 24/7 Online cat, 3D Printer, Accelerated reader prog, Activity rm, Adult bk club, Adult literacy prog, After school storytime, Art exhibits, Art programs, Audiobks on Playaways & MP3, Audiobks via web, AV serv, Bi-weekly Writer's Group, Bk club(s), Bks on CD, Butterfly Garden, Children's prog, Computer training, Computers for patron use, Electronic databases & coll, For res purposes, Free DVD rentals, Govt ref serv, Holiday prog, Home delivery & serv to seniorr ctr & nursing homes, Homebound delivery serv, ILL available, Instruction & testing, Internet access, Life-long learning prog for all ages, Magazines, Magnifiers for reading, Mail & tel request accepted, Makerspace, Meeting rooms, Microfiche/film & reading machines, Movies, Music CDs, Online cat, Online ref, Outreach serv, Outside serv via phone, mail, e-mail & web, OverDrive digital audio bks, Photocopying/Printing, Preschool outreach, Preschool reading prog, Printer for laptops & handheld devices, Prog for adults, Prog for children & young adult, Ref & res, Ref serv available, Res assist avail, Scanner, Senior outreach, Spanish lang bks, STEM programs, Story hour, Summer reading prog, Tax forms, Teen prog, Telephone ref, Wheelchair accessible, Writing prog
Mem of South Central Library System
Special Services for the Deaf - TDD equip
Open Mon-Fri 9-6, Sat 9-5

J MID-STATE TECHNICAL COLLEGE*, Wisconsin Rapids Campus Library, 500 32nd St N, 54494. SAN 365-1576. Tel: 715-422-5470. Interlibrary Loan Service Tel: 715-422-5468. Administration Tel: 715-422-5469. FAX: 715-422-5466. E-mail: librarywrcampus@mstc.edu. Web Site: mstc.edu/student-services/link.
Highest Degree: Associate
Subject Interests: Nursing
Automation Activity & Vendor Info: (Acquisitions) Innovative Interfaces, Inc - Sierra; (Cataloging) Innovative Interfaces, Inc - Sierra; (Circulation) Innovative Interfaces, Inc - Sierra; (ILL) Auto-Graphics, Inc; (OPAC) Innovative Interfaces, Inc
Wireless access
Partic in WiLS
Open Mon-Thurs 7:30-6, Fri 7:30-4 (Winter); Mon-Thurs 7:30-5:30 (Summer)

WITHEE

P WITHEE PUBLIC LIBRARY*, 511 Division St, 54498. (Mail add: PO Box 147, 54498-0147), SAN 318-479X. Tel: 715-229-2010. FAX: 715-229-2010. Web Site: www.witheelibrary.org. *Dir,* Justine Paulson; E-mail: director@withee.lib.wi.us; Staff 1.2 (Non-MLS 1.2)
Pop 1,590; Circ 11,000

Library Holdings: AV Mats 1,000; Large Print Bks 50; Bk Titles 9,600; Per Subs 23
Special Collections: Oral History
Partic in Wisconsin Valley Library Service
Open Mon, Tues, Thurs & Fri 10-5, Sat 10-2

WONEWOC

P WONEWOC PUBLIC LIBRARY*, 305 Center St, 53968. SAN 318-4803. Tel: 608-464-7625. E-mail: wonewoc@wrlsweb.org. Web Site: www.wrlsweb.org/wonewoc. *Dir,* Kim Dearth
Founded 1910. Pop 1,500; Circ 24,357
Library Holdings: Bk Titles 15,000; Per Subs 40
Special Collections: Wonewoc Genealogy; Wonewoc History
Automation Activity & Vendor Info: (Cataloging) Horizon; (Circulation) Horizon; (OPAC) Horizon
Wireless access
Mem of Winding Rivers Library System
Open Mon 9-8, Tues-Fri 9-5:30
Friends of the Library Group

WOODVILLE

P WOODVILLE COMMUNITY LIBRARY*, 124 Main St, 54028. (Mail add: PO Box 204, 54028-0204), SAN 318-4811. Tel: 715-698-2430. FAX: 715-698-2441. E-mail: woodpl@woodvillelibrary.org. Web Site: www.woodvillelibrary.org. *Dir,* Karen Furo-Bonnstetter
Founded 1963. Pop 3,000
Library Holdings: Bk Titles 10,000; Per Subs 20
Automation Activity & Vendor Info: (Cataloging) Innovative Interfaces, Inc; (Circulation) Innovative Interfaces, Inc; (OPAC) Innovative Interfaces, Inc
Wireless access
Mem of Inspiring & Facilitating Library Success (IFLS)
Open Mon & Fri 10-5, Tues & Thurs 10-7, Wed Noon-5, Sat 9-Noon

WYOCENA

P WYOCENA PUBLIC LIBRARY*, 165 E Dodge St, 53969. (Mail add: PO Box 913, 53969-0913). Tel: 608-429-4899. Web Site: www.wyocenalibrary.org. *Dir,* Darrell Fehd; Staff 1 (Non-MLS 1)
Founded 2005. Pop 768
Library Holdings: AV Mats 300; CDs 200; Bk Vols 5,000; Per Subs 19
Automation Activity & Vendor Info: (Cataloging) SirsiDynix; (Circulation) SirsiDynix; (OPAC) SirsiDynix
Wireless access
Mem of South Central Library System
Partic in Library Interchange Network
Open Mon 9-5, Tues & Wed 9-12 & 1-5, Thurs 10-3
Friends of the Library Group

WYOMING

Date of Statistics: FY 2021
Population, 2020 U.S. Census: 582,328
Population Served by Public Libraries: 578,851
Total Volumes in Public Libraries: 2,075,842
  Volumes Per Capita: 3.99
Total Public Library Circulation: 3,867,442
  Circulation Per Capita: 6.7
Income and Expenditures:
Source of Income: 91.5% local government, 7.7% Other (fines, fees, donations, etc.) near-zero state and federal
Total Public Library Income: $33,153,929
  Local Public Funds: $30,345,317
  State Funds: $158,500
  Other sources: $2,555,434 (does not include Federal - reported below)
  Federal: $94,253
  Expenditures Per Capita: $53.27
Number of County Libraries: 23
Information provided courtesy of: Conrrado Saldivar, Outreach and Development Librarian; Wyoming State Library

BASIN

P BIG HORN COUNTY LIBRARY*, 430 West C St, 82410. (Mail add: PO Box 231, 82410), SAN 365-1606. Tel: 307-568-2388. FAX: 307-568-2011. E-mail: basin.library@bighorncountywy.gov. Web Site: www.bhcwylibrarysystem.org. *Dir,* Gail Gillard; E-mail: gail.gillard@bighorncountywy.gov; *Br Mgr,* Maria Garay; E-mail: maria.garay@bighorncountywy.gov; Staff 8 (MLS 2, Non-MLS 6)
Founded 1903. Pop 12,301; Circ 71,113
Library Holdings: CDs 57; Large Print Bks 201; Bk Titles 98,304; Bk Vols 99,111; Per Subs 147; Talking Bks 802; Videos 701
Subject Interests: Wyo
Automation Activity & Vendor Info: (Cataloging) SirsiDynix; (Circulation) SirsiDynix; (ILL) SirsiDynix; (Serials) SirsiDynix
Wireless access
Function: Bus archives
Partic in WYLD Network
Open Mon, Wed & Fri 10-5, Tues & Thurs 10-6
Friends of the Library Group
Branches: 4
DEAVER BRANCH, 180 W First St, Deaver, 82421. (Mail add: PO Box 202, Deaver, 82421-0202), SAN 365-169X. Web Site: www.bhcwylibrarysystem.org/deaver-library. *Librn,* Molly Yates; Staff 1 (MLS 1)
Pop 150
Library Holdings: Bk Titles 5,860; Bk Vols 6,000
Open Mon & Wed 3:30-5:30
FRANNIE BRANCH, 305 Fifth St, Frannie, 82423. (Mail add: PO Box 23, Frannie, 82423-0023), SAN 365-172X. Web Site: www.bhcwylibrarysystem.org/frannie-library. *Librn,* Molly Yates; Staff 1 (MLS 1)
Pop 150
Library Holdings: Bk Titles 7,610; Bk Vols 8,000
Open Tues & Thurs 3:30-5:30
GREYBULL BRANCH, 325 Greybull Ave, Greybull, 82426, SAN 365-1754. Tel: 307-765-2551. E-mail: greybull.library@bighorncountywy.gov. Web Site: www.bhcwylibrarysystem.org/greybull-library. *Br Mgr,* Cynthia Garay; *Asst Mgr,* Julie Craft; Staff 2 (Non-MLS 2)
Pop 1,800
Library Holdings: Bk Titles 16,181; Bk Vols 17,012; Per Subs 20
Open Mon, Tues, Thurs & Fri 10-5, Wed 10-6
Friends of the Library Group
LOVELL BRANCH LIBRARY, 300 Oregon Ave, Lovell, 82431. Tel: 307-548-7228. E-mail: lovell.library@bighorncountywy.gov. Web Site: www.bhcwylibrarysystem.org/lovell-library. *Br Mgr,* Cathleen Collins; *Asst Mgr,* Linda Mangus; Staff 2 (Non-MLS 2)
Pop 2,000
Library Holdings: Bk Titles 17,800; Bk Vols 18,900; Per Subs 37
Open Mon, Wed & Fri 10-5, Tues & Thurs 10-6
Friends of the Library Group

BUFFALO

P JOHNSON COUNTY LIBRARY*, 171 N Adams Ave, 82834. SAN 318-4846. Tel: 307-684-5546. FAX: 307-684-7888. Web Site: www.jclwyo.org. *Dir,* Steve Rzasa; E-mail: srzasa@johnsoncountylibraries.org; *Asst Dir, Ch Serv,* Mary Rhoads; E-mail: mrhoads@johnsoncountylibraries.org; Staff 9.9 (MLS 1, Non-MLS 8.9)
Founded 1909. Pop 8,600; Circ 77,993
Library Holdings: AV Mats 5,000; CDs 2,523; DVDs 2,487; e-books 20,000; Large Print Bks 1,000; Bk Vols 63,037; Per Subs 168
Special Collections: Local History Coll; Western History Coll. Oral History
Subject Interests: Wyo hist
Automation Activity & Vendor Info: (Circulation) SirsiDynix; (ILL) SirsiDynix; (OPAC) SirsiDynix; (Serials) SirsiDynix
Wireless access
Partic in WYLD Network; Wyo Libr Database
Open Mon, Tues & Wed 10-8, Thurs 10-6, Fri & Sat 10-5
Friends of the Library Group
Branches: 1
KAYCEE BRANCH, 231 Ritter Ave, Kaycee, 82639. (Mail add: PO Box 226, Kaycee, 82639-0226), SAN 325-3198. Tel: 307-738-2473. FAX: 307-738-2473. Web Site: jclwyo.org/pages/kaycee. *Br Mgr,* Bonnie Ross; E-mail: bross@johnsoncountylibraries.org; *Asst Librn,* Monica Brock
Library Holdings: AV Mats 796; Bk Vols 5,788; Per Subs 26
Open Tues 10-12 & 1-7, Wed 1-5:30, Fri 10-12 & 1-4, Sat 2-5
Friends of the Library Group

CASPER

J CASPER COLLEGE*, Goodstein Foundation Library, 125 College Dr, 82601. SAN 318-4870. Tel: 307-268-2269. Interlibrary Loan Service Tel: 307-268-2275. FAX: 307-268-2682. E-mail: library@caspercollege.edu. Web Site: caspercollege.edu/library. *Dir,* Katrina Brown; E-mail: katrina.brown@caspercollege.edu; *Librn,* Sarah Mailloux; E-mail: smailloux@caspercollege.edu; Staff 10 (MLS 4, Non-MLS 6)
Founded 1945. Enrl 2,806; Fac 169; Highest Degree: Associate
Library Holdings: e-journals 1,200; Bk Vols 70,000; Per Subs 35
Automation Activity & Vendor Info: (Acquisitions) SirsiDynix; (Cataloging) SirsiDynix; (Circulation) SirsiDynix; (Course Reserve) SirsiDynix; (ILL) SirsiDynix; (OPAC) SirsiDynix; (Serials) SirsiDynix
Wireless access
Partic in OCLC Online Computer Library Center, Inc; WYLD Network; Wyo Libr Database
Open Mon-Thurs 7:30am-8:30pm, Fri & Sat 8-4, Sun Noon-8; Mon-Fri 8-4 (Summer)

P NATRONA COUNTY LIBRARY*, 307 E Second St, 82601. SAN 365-1843. Tel: 307-577-7323. FAX: 307-266-3734. Reference E-mail: reference@natronacountylibrary.org. Web Site: www.natronacountylibrary.org. *Exec Dir,* Lisa Scroggins; E-mail:

lscroggins@natronacountylibrary.org; *Asst Dir,* Kate Mutch; E-mail: kmutch@natronacountylibrary.org; *Adult Serv Mgr, Ref Librn,* Betsy O'Neil; E-mail: boneil@natronacountylibrary.org; *Bus Mgr, Human Res Officer,* Greta Lehnerz; *Pub Relations & Mkt Mgr,* Megan Bratton; Staff 34 (MLS 6, Non-MLS 28)
Founded 1910. Pop 69,010; Circ 570,538
Library Holdings: AV Mats 19,923; Bk Vols 129,541; Per Subs 200
Special Collections: Selective Government Documents
Subject Interests: Local hist
Automation Activity & Vendor Info: (Cataloging) SirsiDynix; (Circulation) SirsiDynix; (ILL) SirsiDynix; (OPAC) SirsiDynix; (Serials) SirsiDynix
Wireless access
Function: 24/7 Electronic res, 24/7 Online cat, 3D Printer, Activity rm, Adult bk club, Adult literacy prog, After school storytime, Archival coll, Art programs, Audiobks on Playaways & MP3, Audiobks via web, AV serv, Bi-weekly Writer's Group, Bilingual assistance for Spanish patrons, Bk club(s), Bk reviews (Group), Bks on CD, Bus archives, CD-ROM, Children's prog, Computer training, Computers for patron use, Digital talking bks, Doc delivery serv, E-Readers, E-Reserves, Electronic databases & coll, Family literacy, For res purposes, Free DVD rentals, Games & aids for people with disabilities, Genealogy discussion group, Govt ref serv, Health sci info serv, Holiday prog, Home delivery & serv to seniorr ctr & nursing homes, Homebound delivery serv, Homework prog, ILL available, Instruction & testing, Internet access, Laminating, Life-long learning prog for all ages, Literacy & newcomer serv, Magazines, Magnifiers for reading, Mail & tel request accepted, Makerspace, Mango lang, Meeting rooms, Microfiche/film & reading machines, Movies, Music CDs, Notary serv, Online cat, Outreach serv, Outside serv via phone, mail, e-mail & web, OverDrive digital audio bks, Passport agency, Photocopying/Printing, Preschool outreach, Preschool reading prog, Printer for laptops & handheld devices, Prof lending libr, Prog for adults, Prog for children & young adult, Ref & res, Ref serv available, Res assist avail, Satellite serv, Scanner, Senior computer classes, Senior outreach, Serves people with intellectual disabilities, Spanish lang bks, STEM programs, Story hour, Study rm, Summer reading prog, Tax forms, Teen prog, Telephone ref, Visual arts prog, Wheelchair accessible, Workshops, Writing prog
Publications: Monthly Calendar of Events; Newsletter (Quarterly)
Partic in WYLD Network
Open Mon-Thurs 9-7, Fri & Sat 9-5
Friends of the Library Group
Branches: 1
MARK J DAVIS JR MEMORIAL - EDGERTON BRANCH, 935 Cottonwood, Edgerton, 82635. (Mail add: PO Box 269, Edgerton, 82635), SAN 365-1878. Tel: 307-437-6617. FAX: 307-437-6617. *Librn,* Michelle Butler; Staff 2 (Non-MLS 2)
Pop 708; Circ 2,140
Library Holdings: Bk Vols 6,000; Per Subs 10; Videos 51
Open Mon & Fri 11-5, Wed 1-7
Bookmobiles: 1. Coordr, Lee Tschetter

G WYOMING GAME & FISH DEPARTMENT LIBRARY*, 3030 Energy Lane, 82604. Tel: 307-473-3400. Toll Free Tel: 800-233-8544 (WY only). FAX: 307-473-3433. *Mgr,* Kindra Brown; Tel: 307-473-3402, E-mail: kindra.brown@wyo.gov; Staff 1 (Non-MLS 1)
Library Holdings: Bk Titles 158; Bk Vols 259; Per Subs 40
Special Collections: Wyoming Game & Fish Publications; Wyoming Wildlife Magazine
Subject Interests: Conserv, Fisheries, Wildlife
Function: ILL available
Special Services for the Deaf - Spec interest per
Special Services for the Blind - Bks on cassette
Restriction: Not open to pub

CHEYENNE

GM DEPARTMENT OF VETERANS AFFAIRS*, Learning Resources Service, 2360 E Pershing Blvd, 82001. SAN 318-4927. Tel: 307-772-7728. Web Site: www.cheyenne.va.gov. *Learning Services, Officer,* Kimberly Bennett-Sutton; Tel: 307-778-7550, E-mail: kimberly.bennett-sutton@va.gov; Staff 2 (MLS 1, Non-MLS 1)
Library Holdings: Bk Vols 1,500; Per Subs 216
Automation Activity & Vendor Info: (Circulation) SirsiDynix; (OPAC) SirsiDynix
Open Mon-Fri 8-4:30

S GRAND LODGE OF ANCIENT FREE & ACCEPTED MASONS OF WYOMING LIBRARY*, Masonic Temple, 1820 Capitol Ave, 82001. SAN 327-7690. Tel: 307-630-5933. E-mail: cmdsea@aol.com. *Librn,* Gary D Skillern; Staff 1 (Non-MLS 1)
Founded 1875
Library Holdings: Bk Vols 3,250
Special Collections: American History; Masonic Related Subjects; Masonic Subjects
Function: For res purposes, ILL available, Masonic res mat, Res assist avail
Restriction: Access at librarian's discretion, Open by appt only, Open to pub upon request, Researchers by appt only, Restricted access, Restricted borrowing privileges

J LARAMIE COUNTY COMMUNITY COLLEGE*, Ludden Library, 1400 E College Dr, 82007-3204. SAN 318-4900. Tel: 307-778-1206. Circulation Tel: 307-778-1205. Administration Tel: 307-778-1377. Toll Free Tel: 800-522-2993, Ext 1206. Reference E-mail: libref@lccc.wy.edu. Web Site: www.lccc.wy.edu/library. *Assoc Dean,* Meghan Kelly; Tel: 307-778-1201, E-mail: mkelly@lccc.wy.edu; *Librn,* Jennifer Markus; Tel: 307-778-1204, E-mail: jmarkus@lccc.wy.edu; *Electronic Res Librn,* Maggie Swanger; Tel: 307-778-1283, E-mail: mswanger@lccc.wy.edu; *User Serv Librn,* Paula Badgett; Tel: 307-778-1378, E-mail: pbadgett@lccc.wy.edu; Staff 9 (MLS 6, Non-MLS 3)
Founded 1969. Enrl 3,292; Fac 90
Library Holdings: AV Mats 31,428; e-journals 30; Bk Titles 45,078; Bk Vols 53,075; Per Subs 240
Special Collections: Foundation Center Coll; Higher Education Prof Coll
Subject Interests: Equine, Nursing, Radiography
Automation Activity & Vendor Info: (Acquisitions) SirsiDynix; (Cataloging) SirsiDynix; (Circulation) SirsiDynix; (OPAC) SirsiDynix; (Serials) SirsiDynix
Wireless access
Publications: Wyoming Foundation Directory
Partic in WYLD Network
Open Mon-Fri 9-4; Mon-Thurs 9-5, Fri 9-4 (Summer)
Departmental Libraries:
LARAMIE CAMPUS LIBRARY, 1125 Boulder Dr, Rm 105, Laramie, 82070. Tel: 307-772-4263. Web Site: lccc.wy.edu/library/acc.aspx. *Fac Librn,* Seth Perkins; Tel: 307-772-4285, E-mail: sperkins@lccc.wy.edu
Open Mon-Thurs 7:30am-9pm, Fri 7:30-5

P LARAMIE COUNTY LIBRARY SYSTEM*, 2200 Pioneer Ave, 82001-3610. SAN 365-1908. Tel: 307-634-3561. FAX: 307-634-2082. Interlibrary Loan Service E-mail: ill@lclsonline.org. Web Site: www.laramiecountylibrary.org, www.lclsonline.org. *County Librn, Exec Dir,* Carey D Hartmann; Tel: 307-773-7222, E-mail: chartmann@lclsonline.org; *Dep Dir, Operations,* Laura Block; Tel: 307-773-7223, E-mail: lblock@lclsonline.org; *Dep Dir, Pub Serv,* Jeff Collins; Tel: 307-773-7220, E-mail: jcollins@lclsonline.org; *Outreach Librn,* Melanie Hornbeck; Tel: 307-773-7229, E-mail: mhornbeck@lclsonline.org; *Asst Circ Mgr, Branch Services, Readers' Advisor Librn,* Lori Lewis; Tel: 307-773-7211, E-mail: llewis@lclsonline.org; *Adult Serv, Asst Mgr, Spec Coll Librn,* Elaine Jones Hayes; Tel: 307-773-7232, E-mail: ehayes@lclsonline.org; *Asst Mgr, Youth & Outreach Serv, Youth Librn,* Megan Fox; Tel: 307-773-7226, E-mail: mfox@lclsonline.org; *Mgr, Ad Serv,* Elizabeth Cuckow Thorson; Tel: 307-773-7230, E-mail: ethorson@lclsonline.org; *Mgr, Circ & Br Serv,* Kashawna White; Tel: 307-773-7210, E-mail: kwhite@lclsonline.org; *Mgr, Computer Ctr & Cat Serv,* Cara Nett; Tel: 307-773-7231, E-mail: cnett@lclsonline.org; *Mgr, Info Tech,* Mike Kamber; Tel: 307-773-7234, E-mail: mkamber@lclsonline.org; *Mgr, Youth & Outreach Serv,* Beth Cook; Tel: 307-773-7227, E-mail: bcook@lclsonline.org; *AV Coordr,* Bobby Phillipps; Tel: 307-773-7212, E-mail: bphillipps@lclsonline.org; *Bus Serv Coordr,* Rachael Svoboda; Tel: 307-773-7200, E-mail: rsvoboda@lclsonline.org; *Coll Develop Coordr,* Mary Gilgannon; Tel: 307-773-5139, E-mail: mgilgannon@lclsonline.org; *ILL Spec,* Kim Storey; Tel: 307-773-7233, E-mail: kstorey@lclsonline.org; *Communications Coordr,* Kasey Mossey; Tel: 307-773-7225, E-mail: kmossey@lclsonilne.org; *Outreach Specialist, Sr Serv,* Susan Parkins; Tel: 307-773-7228, E-mail: sparkins@lclsonline.org; *Head, Exhibitions, Supvr,* Jennifer Rife; Tel: 307-773-7218, E-mail: jrife@lclsonline.org; *Early Literacy Specialist, Outreach Specialist,* EvaLyn Flores; Tel: 307-773-7204, E-mail: eflores@lclsonline.org; *Facilities Servs, Superintendent,* Jim VanCise; Tel: 307-773-7213, E-mail: jvancise@lclsonline.org. Subject Specialists: *Fiction,* Mary Gilgannon; *Design,* Jennifer Rife; Staff 37 (MLS 12, Non-MLS 25)
Founded 1886. Pop 98,976; Circ 557,728
Jul 2020-Jun 2021 Income $7,472,150, County $6,637,465, Locally Generated Income $1,731,128, Other $103,558. Mats Exp $6,760,920. Sal $4,100,499
Library Holdings: Audiobooks 14,041; CDs 9,007; DVDs 17,475; Large Print Bks 9,474; Microforms 8,507; Bk Titles 166,213; Bk Vols 228,715; Per Subs 170
Special Collections: Trails Coll; Western Hist Coll; Wyoming Hist Coll
Subject Interests: Genealogy
Automation Activity & Vendor Info: (Acquisitions) SirsiDynix; (Cataloging) SirsiDynix; (Circulation) SirsiDynix; (Course Reserve) SirsiDynix; (Discovery) SirsiDynix; (ILL) OCLC; (Media Booking) DEMCO; (OPAC) SirsiDynix; (Serials) SirsiDynix
Wireless access
Function: 24/7 Electronic res, 24/7 Online cat, 3D Printer, Activity rm, Archival coll, Art exhibits, Art programs, Audiobks on Playaways & MP3,

Audiobks via web, AV serv, Bilingual assistance for Spanish patrons, Bks on CD, Children's prog, Computer training, Computers for patron use, Doc delivery serv, E-Readers, Electronic databases & coll, Family literacy, For res purposes, Genealogy discussion group, Govt ref serv, Health sci info serv, Holiday prog, Home delivery & serv to seniorr ctr & nursing homes, Homebound delivery serv, ILL available, Instruction & testing, Internet access, Laminating, Learning ctr, Life-long learning prog for all ages, Magazines, Magnifiers for reading, Mail & tel request accepted, Makerspace, Mango lang, Meeting rooms, Microfiche/film & reading machines, Movies, Music CDs, Notary serv, Online cat, Online info literacy tutorials on the web & in blackboard, Online ref, Orientations, Outreach serv, Outside serv via phone, mail, e-mail & web, OverDrive digital audio bks, Photocopying/Printing, Preschool outreach, Preschool reading prog, Printer for laptops & handheld devices, Prog for adults, Prog for children & young adult, Ref & res, Ref serv available, Res assist avail, Res libr, Satellite serv, Scanner, Senior outreach, Serves people with intellectual disabilities, Spanish lang bks, STEM programs, Story hour, Study rm, Summer & winter reading prog, Summer reading prog, Tax forms, Teen prog, Telephone ref, Visual arts prog, Wheelchair accessible, Writing prog

Publications: Annual Report; Library Calendar (Monthly); Library eNewsletter

Partic in WYLD Network

Special Services for the Deaf - Assisted listening device; Closed caption videos

Special Services for the Blind - Assistive/Adapted tech devices, equip & products; BiFolkal kits; Computer with voice synthesizer for visually impaired persons; Copier with enlargement capabilities; Large print bks; Low vision equip; Magnifiers; Recorded bks; Screen enlargement software for people with visual disabilities; Sound rec

Open Mon-Thurs 10-9, Fri & Sat 10-6, Sun 1-5

Restriction: In-house use for visitors, Non-circulating coll

Branches: 2

BURNS BRANCH LIBRARY, 112 Main St, Burns, 82053. (Mail add: PO Box 220, Burns, 82053-0220), SAN 365-1932. Tel: 307-547-2249. FAX: 307-547-9253. ; Staff 1 (Non-MLS 1)

Pop 309; Circ 4,213

Library Holdings: Audiobooks 166; DVDs 567; Large Print Bks 3; Bk Titles 7,166; Per Subs 5

Automation Activity & Vendor Info: (Acquisitions) SirsiDynix; (Cataloging) SirsiDynix; (Circulation) SirsiDynix; (Course Reserve) SirsiDynix; (Discovery) SirsiDynix; (ILL) OCLC; (Media Booking) DEMCO; (OPAC) SirsiDynix; (Serials) SirsiDynix

Special Services for the Blind - Assistive/Adapted tech devices, equip & products

Open Mon 1-5, Tues & Fri 10-5, Thurs 10-7, Sat 9-Noon

PINE BLUFFS BRANCH LIBRARY, 110 E Second St, Pine Bluffs, 82082. (Mail add: PO Box 639, Pine Bluffs, 82082-0639), SAN 365-1967. Tel: 307-245-3646. FAX: 307-245-3029. ; Staff 1 (Non-MLS 1)

Pop 1,169; Circ 6,034

Library Holdings: Audiobooks 205; DVDs 794; Large Print Bks 179; Bk Titles 9,518

Automation Activity & Vendor Info: (Acquisitions) SirsiDynix; (Cataloging) SirsiDynix; (Circulation) SirsiDynix; (Course Reserve) SirsiDynix; (Discovery) SirsiDynix; (ILL) OCLC; (Media Booking) DEMCO; (OPAC) SirsiDynix; (Serials) SirsiDynix

Special Services for the Blind - Assistive/Adapted tech devices, equip & products

Open Tues 10-7, Wed & Thurs 10-5, Fri 1-5, Sat 9-Noon

Bookmobiles: Mgr Youth & Outreach Servs, Beth Cook. Bk titles 4,455

GL US COURTS LIBRARY - TENTH CIRCUIT COURT OF APPEALS*, Federal Bldg, Rm 2314, 2120 Capital Ave, 82001. Tel: 307-433-2427. *Circuit Librn,* Diane Bauersfeld; E-mail: diane_bauersfeld@ca10.uscourts.gov

Open Mon-Fri 8-4:30

P WYOMING STATE LIBRARY, 2800 Central Ave, 82002. SAN 365-2084. Tel: 307-777-6333. E-mail: statelibrary@wyo.gov. Web Site: library.wyo.gov. *State Librn,* Abigail Beaver; Tel: 307-777-5913, E-mail: abby.beaver@wyo.gov; *Digital Initiatives Librn,* Katelyn Wittenborn; Tel: 307-777-7282, E-mail: katelyn.wittenborn@wyo.gov; *Fed Doc Librn,* Marci Blaylock; Tel: 307-777-6955, E-mail: marcie.blaylock@wyo.gov; *Legislative Librn,* Vincent Crolla; Tel: 307-777-5914, E-mail: vincent.crolla@wyo.gov; *State Publ Librn,* Anne Kuipers; Tel: 307-777-7281, E-mail: anne.kuipers@wyo.gov; *Bus Mgr,* Melanie Reedy; Tel: 307-777-5917, E-mail: melanie.reedy@wyo.gov; *Info Serv Mgr,* Travis Pollok; Tel: 307-777-8936, E-mail: travis.pollok@wyo.gov; *Libr Develop, Prog Mgr,* Brian Greene; Tel: 307-777-6339, E-mail: brian.greene@wyo.gov; *Marketing Lead,* Greg Mosshammer; Tel: 307-777-6338, E-mail: greg.mosshammer@wyo.gov; *E-Resources & School Library Consultant,* Paige Bredenkamp; Tel: 307-777-6331, E-mail: paige.bredenkamp@wyo.gov; *Research & Statistics Consultant,* Jessica Otto; Tel: 307-777-6330, E-mail: jessica.otto@wyo.gov. Subject Specialists: *Patents, State publications, Trademarks,* Anne Kuipers; Staff 20 (MLS 10, Non-MLS 10)

Founded 1871

Library Holdings: CDs 847; DVDs 1,201; Bk Titles 42,775; Bk Vols 116,691; Per Subs 60

Special Collections: State Document Depository; US Document Depository

Subject Interests: Govt info, Libr sci, Patents, Trademarks, Wyo

Automation Activity & Vendor Info: (Acquisitions) SirsiDynix; (Cataloging) SirsiDynix; (Circulation) SirsiDynix; (Course Reserve) SirsiDynix; (ILL) OCLC; (Media Booking) SirsiDynix; (OPAC) SirsiDynix; (Serials) SirsiDynix

Wireless access

Publications: Outrider (Online only); Wyoming Library Directory (Online only); Wyoming Library Laws

Partic in Amigos Library Services, Inc; Association for Rural & Small Libraries; Western Council of State Libraries, Inc; WYLD Network

Open Mon-Fri 8-5

GL WYOMING SUPREME COURT*, Wyoming State Law Library, Supreme Court Bldg, 2301 Capitol Ave, 82002. SAN 320-4286. Tel: 307-777-7509. FAX: 307-777-7240. E-mail: library@courts.state.wy.us. Web Site: www.courts.state.wy.us/state-law-library. *State Law Librn,* Matt Swift; Staff 4 (MLS 3, Non-MLS 1)

Founded 1871

Library Holdings: Bk Titles 3,000; Bk Vols 113,000; Per Subs 240

Special Collections: US Document Depository

Automation Activity & Vendor Info: (Acquisitions) SirsiDynix; (Cataloging) SirsiDynix; (OPAC) SirsiDynix; (Serials) SirsiDynix

Publications: Quick Index to Wyoming Statutes Annotated

Partic in OCLC Online Computer Library Center, Inc; WYLD Network

CODY

S BUFFALO BILL HISTORICAL CENTER*, McCracken Research Library, 720 Sheridan Ave, 82414. SAN 318-4943. Tel: 307-578-4059. FAX: 307-527-6042. Web Site: centerofthewest.org/research/mccracken-research-library. *Dir,* Mary M Robinson; Tel: 307-578-4063, E-mail: maryr@centerofthewest.org; *Archivist,* Samantha Harper; E-mail: samanthah@centerofthewest.org; Staff 4 (MLS 4)

Founded 1927

Library Holdings: Bk Vols 20,000; Per Subs 96

Special Collections: Archives, photogs; Buffalo Bill Coll, mss; Dude Ranching; W H D Koerner Coll; William F Cody; Winchester Repeating Arms Company Archives; Wyoming Territorial Imprints, 1866-1890; Yellowstone National Park Coll

Subject Interests: Firearms, Mus ref mat, Native Am studies, Western Am natural hist, Western art, Western hist, Western lit

Automation Activity & Vendor Info: (Cataloging) SirsiDynix; (Circulation) SirsiDynix; (ILL) OCLC Online; (OPAC) SirsiDynix

Function: Archival coll, ILL available, Photocopying/Printing, Res libr, Telephone ref

Publications: Annotated Bibliographies

Partic in OCLC Online Computer Library Center, Inc; WYLD Network

Restriction: Closed stack, In-house use for visitors, Internal circ only, Non-circulating coll, Not a lending libr

Friends of the Library Group

P PARK COUNTY LIBRARY SYSTEM*, 1500 Heart Mountain St, 82414. SAN 365-2149. Tel: 307-527-1880. Administration Tel: 307-527-1882. FAX: 307-527-1888. E-mail: cody@parkcountylibrary.org. Web Site: parkcountylibrary.org. *Libr Dir,* Karen Horner; Tel: 307-527-1881, E-mail: khorner@parkcountylibrary.org; *Asst Dir, Br Mgr,* Nicholle Gerharter; E-mail: ngerharter@parkcountylibrary.org; Staff 27 (MLS 4, Non-MLS 23)

Founded 1906. Pop 29,624; Circ 367,735

Jul 2022-Jun 2023 Income (Main & Associated Libraries) $1,969,686. Mats Exp $97,800. Sal $1,763,106

Library Holdings: AV Mats 22,446; Bk Titles 155,085; Per Subs 873

Special Collections: Medical Resource Center; Planetree Health Resource Center. Municipal Document Depository

Subject Interests: County hist, Wyo authors, Yellowstone National Park

Automation Activity & Vendor Info: (Acquisitions) SirsiDynix; (Cataloging) SirsiDynix; (Circulation) SirsiDynix; (ILL) OCLC; (OPAC) SirsiDynix; (Serials) SirsiDynix

Wireless access

Function: Adult bk club, Art exhibits, Audiobks via web, Bk club(s), Bks on CD, Children's prog, Computers for patron use, Digital talking bks, Electronic databases & coll, Family literacy, Free DVD rentals, Govt ref serv, Health sci info serv, Holiday prog, Home delivery & serv to seniorr ctr & nursing homes, Homework prog, ILL available, Instruction & testing, Internet access, Mail & tel request accepted, Meeting rooms, Music CDs, Online cat, Orientations, Outreach serv, Outside serv via phone, mail, e-mail & web, Photocopying/Printing, Preschool outreach, Preschool reading prog, Prof lending libr, Prog for adults, Prog for children & young

adult, Ref & res, Ref serv available, Senior outreach, Spoken cassettes & CDs, Spoken cassettes & DVDs, Story hour, Study rm, Summer reading prog, Tax forms, Teen prog, Telephone ref, Wheelchair accessible, Writing prog
Partic in WYLD Network
Open Mon-Thurs 9-7, Fri & Sat 9-5
Friends of the Library Group
Branches: 2
MEETEETSE BRANCH, 2107 Idaho St, Meeteetse, 82433. (Mail add: PO Box 129, Meeteetse, 82433-0129), SAN 365-2173. Tel: 307-868-2248. FAX: 307-868-2248. E-mail: meeteetse@parkcountylibrary.org. *Br Mgr,* Linda Seaton; Staff 1 (Non-MLS 1)
Founded 1927. Pop 750; Circ 20,000
Function: Audiobks via web, Bks on CD, Children's prog, Citizenship assistance, Computer training, Computers for patron use, Electronic databases & coll, Free DVD rentals, ILL available, Internet access, Music CDs, Photocopying/Printing, Prog for adults, Prog for children & young adult, Story hour, Summer reading prog, Wheelchair accessible
Open Mon-Fri 8-5, Sat 10-2
Friends of the Library Group
POWELL BRANCH, 217 E Third St, Powell, 82435-1903, SAN 365-2203. Tel: 307-754-8828. FAX: 307-754-8824. E-mail: powell@parkcountylibrary.org. *AV, Br Mgr, Outreach Serv,* Rosanne Spiering; E-mail: rspiering@parkcountylibrary.org; *Adult Serv, ILL,* Breanne Thiel; E-mail: bthiel@parkcountylibrary.org; *Ch Serv, Outreach Serv,* Renee Hanlin; E-mail: rhanlin@parkcountylibrary.org; Staff 5 (MLS 1, Non-MLS 4)
Founded 1911. Pop 6,500; Circ 105,356
Automation Activity & Vendor Info: (Acquisitions) OCLC
Function: Art exhibits, AV serv, Children's prog, Computers for patron use, Electronic databases & coll, Home delivery & serv to seniorr ctr & nursing homes, ILL available, Instruction & testing, Internet access, Magazines, Magnifiers for reading, Meeting rooms, Online cat, Online ref, Outreach serv, Photocopying/Printing, Prog for adults, Prog for children & young adult, Ref serv available, Scanner, Senior outreach, Story hour, Summer reading prog, Tax forms, Teen prog, Wheelchair accessible
Special Services for the Deaf - Bks on deafness & sign lang; Sign lang interpreter upon request for prog
Special Services for the Blind - Audio mat; Bks available with recordings; Large print bks; Magnifiers
Open Mon-Thurs 9-6, Fri 9-5, Sat 9-1
Friends of the Library Group

DOUGLAS

P CONVERSE COUNTY LIBRARY*, 300 E Walnut St, 82633. SAN 365-2238. Tel: 307-358-3644. FAX: 307-358-8306. Web Site: www.conversecountylibrary.org, yourccl.org. *Dir,* Cindy Moore; E-mail: director@conversecountylibrary.org; *Asst Dir,* Jes Renz; E-mail: jrenz@conversecountylibrary.org; *Pub Serv Librn, YA Mgr,* Blake Hill; *Bus Mgr,* Crystal Hegglund; *Ch Mgr,* Lindsey Hineman; *Tech Serv Mgr,* Cara Dwyer; Staff 13 (Non-MLS 13)
Founded 1905. Pop 13,578; Circ 88,883
Library Holdings: Audiobooks 4,268; DVDs 3,294; e-books 5,135; Bk Vols 56,218; Per Subs 174
Special Collections: Doris Shannon Garst Coll; Wyoming & Surrounding States (Western American Coll)
Subject Interests: Quilting, Vietnam conflict, Western Americana
Automation Activity & Vendor Info: (Cataloging) SirsiDynix; (Circulation) SirsiDynix; (ILL) SirsiDynix; (OPAC) SirsiDynix; (Serials) SirsiDynix
Wireless access
Function: Adult bk club, Art exhibits, Audiobks via web, Bk club(s), Bks on cassette, Bks on CD, Children's prog, Computers for patron use, Distance learning, Doc delivery serv, E-Reserves, Electronic databases & coll, Free DVD rentals, Holiday prog, Home delivery & serv to seniorr ctr & nursing homes, ILL available, Internet access, Music CDs, Online cat, Online ref, Outreach serv, Photocopying/Printing, Preschool outreach, Prog for adults, Prog for children & young adult, Ref serv available, Scanner, Senior outreach, Spoken cassettes & CDs, Spoken cassettes & DVDs, Story hour, Summer reading prog, Tax forms, Teen prog, Telephone ref, VHS videos, Wheelchair accessible
Publications: Bridges (Newsletter)
Partic in WYLD Network
Open Mon-Wed & Fri 9-6, Thurs 9-8, Sat 10-4
Branches: 1
GLENROCK BRANCH, 506 S Fourth St, Glenrock, 82637. (Mail add: PO Box 1000, Glenrock, 82637-1000), SAN 365-2262. Tel: 307-436-2573. FAX: 307-436-2364. *Br Mgr,* Jennifer Kofoed; E-mail: jkofoed@conversecountylibrary.org; *Ch Serv,* Rita Heath; E-mail: rheath@conversecountylibrary.org; Staff 3 (Non-MLS 3)
Founded 1939. Pop 2,234
Library Holdings: Bk Vols 16,348; Per Subs 55
Function: ILL available
Open Mon-Wed & Fri 9-6, Thurs 9-8, Sat 9-2

ENCAMPMENT

S GRAND ENCAMPMENT MUSEUM, INC LIBRARY*, 807 Barnett Ave, 82325. (Mail add: PO Box 43, 82325-0043), SAN 373-3092. Tel: 307-327-5308. Web Site: gemuseum.com. *Dir,* Tim Nickles; E-mail: gemdirector@gemuseum.com; Staff 19 (MLS 1, Non-MLS 18)
Founded 1964
Library Holdings: Bk Titles 500
Subject Interests: Hist, Wyo
Function: For res purposes, Photocopying/Printing, Res libr
Open Tues-Sat 9-5, Sun 12-4
Restriction: In-house use for visitors, Open to pub for ref only

EVANSTON

P UINTA COUNTY LIBRARY*, 701 Main St, 82930. SAN 365-2297. Tel: 307-783-0481. Reference Tel: 307-783-0484. E-mail: reference@uintalibrary.org. Web Site: uinta.wyldcatalog.org. *Adult Serv, Libr Dir,* Claire Francis; E-mail: cfrancis@uintalibrary.org; *Ch Serv,* Michelle Kallas; Tel: 307-789-1329, E-mail: mkallas@uintalibrary.org; Staff 13 (MLS 2, Non-MLS 11)
Founded 1904. Pop 21,285; Circ 147,488
Library Holdings: Bk Vols 89,536; Per Subs 249
Subject Interests: Nat parks of western US, Western Americana
Automation Activity & Vendor Info: (Cataloging) SirsiDynix; (Circulation) SirsiDynix; (OPAC) SirsiDynix; (Serials) SirsiDynix
Wireless access
Partic in WYLD Network
Open Tues-Thurs 9-6, Fri 9-4, Sat 9-1
Friends of the Library Group
Branches: 2
LYMAN BRANCH, 129 S Franklin St, Lyman, 82937. (Mail add: PO Box 839, Lyman, 82937-0839). Tel: 307-787-6556. FAX: 307-787-6339. E-mail: lyman@uintalibrary.org. *Br Mgr,* Audrey Kemp
Founded 1916. Pop 4,000; Circ 36,470
Library Holdings: Bk Vols 15,583; Per Subs 1
Open Tues & Wed 11-6, Thurs 11-4, Fri 11-2
Friends of the Library Group
MOUNTAIN VIEW BRANCH, 322 W Second St, Mountain View, 82939. (Mail add: PO Box 530, Mountain View, 82939-0530), SAN 365-2351. Tel: 307-782-3161. FAX: 307-782-6640. E-mail: mtview@uintalibrary.org. *Br Mgr,* Melody Bond; Staff 2 (Non-MLS 2)
Founded 1940. Pop 1,800; Circ 44,388
Library Holdings: Bk Vols 16,943; Per Subs 46
Open Mon & Thurs 11-6, Tues & Wed 11-4
Friends of the Library Group

GILLETTE

M CAMPBELL COUNTY HEALTH LIBRARY*, 501 S Burma, 82716-3426. (Mail add: PO Box 3011, 82717-3011), SAN 371-8239. Tel: 307-399-7689, 307-688-6011. *Med Librn,* Michlene D Holwell; E-mail: michlene.holwell@cchwyo.org; Staff 1 (Non-MLS 1)
Library Holdings: Bk Titles 2,000; Per Subs 150
Subject Interests: Mental health
Wireless access
Restriction: Staff use only

P CAMPBELL COUNTY PUBLIC LIBRARY SYSTEM, 2101 S 4-J Rd, 82718. SAN 365-2416. Tel: 307-687-0009. Reference Tel: 307-687-0115. FAX: 307-686-4009. Web Site: www.campbellcountywy.gov/2170/library. *Exec Dir,* John A Jackson; E-mail: john.jackson@campbellcountywy.gov; *Tech Serv,* Lori Kirchoff; E-mail: lori@ccpls.org; Staff 8 (MLS 1, Non-MLS 7)
Founded 1928. Pop 47,000; Circ 35,000
Library Holdings: AV Mats 27,149; Bk Vols 129,247; Per Subs 358
Special Collections: US Geological Survey Map Depository; Western Art. US Document Depository
Automation Activity & Vendor Info: (Acquisitions) SirsiDynix; (Cataloging) SirsiDynix; (Circulation) SirsiDynix; (OPAC) SirsiDynix; (Serials) SirsiDynix
Wireless access
Partic in OCLC Online Computer Library Center, Inc; WYLD Network
Special Services for the Deaf - High interest/low vocabulary bks
Open Mon-Thurs 9-9, Fri & Sat 9-5, Sun (Sept-May) 1-5
Friends of the Library Group
Branches: 1
WRIGHT BRANCH, 305 Wright Blvd, Wright, 82732. (Mail add: PO Box 600, Wright, 82732-0600), SAN 365-2475. Tel: 307-464-0500. FAX: 307-464-0502. Web Site: www.campbellcountywy.gov/472/wright-branch. *Br Mgr,* Sandra Snyder; E-mail: sandra.snyder@campbellcountywy.gov
Founded 1978

Library Holdings: Bk Vols 8,000; Per Subs 30
Open Mon, Tues & Thurs 10-8, Wed & Fri 10-5, Sat 10-2

J NORTHERN WYOMING COMMUNITY COLLEGE DISTRICT - GILLETTE COLLEGE*, Elizabeth Kerns Daly Library, 300 W Sinclair, 82718. Tel: 307-686-6220. E-mail: gclibrary@sheridan.edu. Web Site: libguides.sheridan.edu. *Coordr, Libr Serv,* Samantha Griffis; Tel: 307-681-6221, E-mail: sgriffis@sheridan.edu; Staff 2 (MLS 1, Non-MLS 1)
Library Holdings: Bk Titles 6,500; Per Subs 25
Wireless access
Open Mon-Thurs 8-8, Fri 8-4, Sun Noon-7 (Winter); Mon-Fri 8-4 (Summer)

GREEN RIVER

P SWEETWATER COUNTY LIBRARY SYSTEM*, Sweetwater County Library, 300 N First East, 82935. SAN 365-2505. Tel: 307-875-3615. Administration Tel: 307-872-3200. FAX: 307-872-3203. Administration FAX: 307-872-3249. Web Site: www.sweetwaterlibraries.com. *Libr Dir,* Jason Grubb; Tel: 307-875-3615, Ext 5130, E-mail: jgrubb@sweetwaterlibraries.com; *Asst Dir,* Michelle Krmpotich; E-mail: mkrmpotich@sweetwaterlibraries.com; *Asst Dir, Pub Relations,* Lindsey Travis; Tel: 307-352-6669, E-mail: ltravis@sweetwaterlibraries.com
Founded 1906. Pop 42,000
Subject Interests: Spanish, Western
Automation Activity & Vendor Info: (Acquisitions) SirsiDynix; (Cataloging) SirsiDynix; (Circulation) SirsiDynix; (Serials) SirsiDynix
Wireless access
Publications: The Library Link (Newsletter)
Partic in WYLD Network
Open Mon-Thurs 10-6, Fri 10-5, Sat Noon-4
Branches: 8
BAIROIL BRANCH LIBRARY, 101 Blue Bell St, Bairoil, 82322. (Mail add: PO Box 40, Bairoil, 82322-0040), SAN 365-253X. Tel: 307-328-0239. FAX: 307-328-0239. E-mail: bairoil@sweetwaterlibraries.com. *Br Librn,* Miles Barbara; E-mail: bmiles@sweetwaterlibraries.com
Open Mon-Sat 9-11:30
FARSON BRANCH LIBRARY, Farson Eden School Bldg, 30 Hwy 28, Farson, 82932. (Mail add: PO Box 360, Farson, 82932-0360), SAN 365-2564. Tel: 307-273-9301. E-mail: farson@sweetwaterlibraries.com. *Br Librn,* Anna Smith; E-mail: asmith@sweetwaterlibraries.com
Open Mon-Wed 4pm-8pm
GRANGER BRANCH LIBRARY, 200 First St, Granger, 82934, SAN 365-2572. Tel: 307-875-8038. E-mail: granger@sweetwaterlibraries.com. *Br Librn,* Position Currently Open
Open Mon 1-5, Tues & Fri 2-6
RELIANCE BRANCH LIBRARY, 1329 Main St, Reliance, 82943. (Mail add: PO Box 460, Reliance, 82943-0460), SAN 365-2610. Tel: 307-352-6670. E-mail: reliance@sweetwaterlibraries.com. *Br Librn,* Pat Moreno; E-mail: pmoreno@sweetwaterlibraries.com
Open Mon & Thurs 2-5, Tues & Wed 1:30-5:30
ROCK SPRINGS LIBRARY, 400 C St, Rock Springs, 82901, SAN 365-2629. Tel: 307-352-6667. FAX: 307-352-6657. E-mail: rocksprings@sweetwaterlibraries.com. *Libr Mgr,* Lindsey Travis; E-mail: ltravis@sweetwaterlibraries.com
Founded 1908
Open Mon-Thurs 10-6, Fri 10-5, Sat 12-4
SUPERIOR BRANCH LIBRARY, Three N Main, Superior, 82945. (Mail add: PO Box 99, Superior, 82945-0099), SAN 365-2653. Tel: 307-352-6671. E-mail: superior@sweetwaterlibraries.com. *Br Librn,* Amber George; E-mail: ageorge@sweetwaterlibraries.com
Open Mon-Wed 2-6
WAMSUTTER BRANCH LIBRARY, 230 Tierney, Lot 44, Wamsutter, 82336. (Mail add: PO Box 189, Wamsutter, 82336-0189). Tel: 307-324-9121. E-mail: wamsutter@sweetwaterlibraries.com. *Br Librn,* Bobbie Lenz; E-mail: blenz@sweetwaterlibraries.com
Open Tues-Thurs 12:30-2:30 & 4-6
WHITE MOUNTAIN LIBRARY, 2935 Sweetwater Dr, Rock Springs, 82901, SAN 329-6814. Tel: 307-362-2665. FAX: 307-352-6655. *Libr Mgr,* Michelle Krmpotich; Tel: 307-362-2665, Ext 3120, E-mail: mkrmpotich@sweetwaterlibraries.com
Founded 1987
Open Mon-Thurs 10-6, Fri 10-5, Sat 12-4
Friends of the Library Group

HUDSON

P HUDSON YABLONSKI COMMUNITY LIBRARY, 205 Illinois St, 82515. (Mail add: PO Box 56, 82515-0056). Tel: 307-332-5770. Web Site: library.wyo.gov/directory/hudson-yablonski-community-library. *Libr Mgr,* Mary Ann Robeson
Library Holdings: Bk Titles 7,000
Wireless access
Open Mon 6pm-8pm, Wed & Fri 1-6, Thurs 1-8, alternating Sat 1-6 & 2-5

JACKSON

GM ST JOHN'S MEDICAL CENTER, Medical Library, 625 E Broadway, 83001. (Mail add: PO Box 428, 83001-0428), SAN 323-6145. Tel: 307-739-7370. Web Site: www.stjohns.health. *Library Contact,* Elizabeth Whitaker; E-mail: ewhitaker@tetonhospital.org
Library Holdings: Bk Titles 825; Bk Vols 1,112; Per Subs 101
Partic in National Network of Libraries of Medicine Region 4

P TETON COUNTY LIBRARY*, 125 Virginian Lane, 83001. (Mail add: PO Box 1629, 83001), SAN 365-2688. Tel: 307-733-2164. FAX: 307-733-4568. E-mail: info@tclib.org. Web Site: tclib.org. *Libr Dir,* Kip Roberson; Tel: 307-733-2164, Ext 1300, E-mail: kroberson@tclib.org; *Admin Serv,* Estella Terrazas; Tel: 307-733-2164, Ext 3101, E-mail: eterrazas@tclib.org; *Adult Serv Mgr,* Angela Jordan; Tel: 307-733-2164, Ext 3258, E-mail: ajordan@tclib.org; *Circ Serv Mgr,* Stephanie Franco; Tel: 307-733-2164, Ext 3218, E-mail: sfranco@tclib.org; *Colls Serv Mgr,* Susan Centrella; Tel: 307-733-2164, Ext 3104, E-mail: scentrella@tclib.org; *Youth Serv Mgr,* Jerry Bilek; Tel: 307-733-2164, Ext 3163, E-mail: jbilek@tclib.org; Staff 40 (MLS 8, Non-MLS 32)
Founded 1937. Circ 262,990
Jul 2020-Jun 2021 Income (Main & Associated Libraries) $3,103,439, County $2,822,034, Locally Generated Income $281,405. Mats Exp $203,858. Sal $1,432,544
Library Holdings: AV Mats 10,787; DVDs 9,619; Electronic Media & Resources 5; Bk Titles 62,204; Per Subs 112
Special Collections: Western Americana
Automation Activity & Vendor Info: (Acquisitions) SirsiDynix; (Cataloging) SirsiDynix; (Circulation) SirsiDynix; (Discovery) ByWater Solutions; (OPAC) ByWater Solutions; (Serials) SirsiDynix
Wireless access
Function: 24/7 Electronic res, 24/7 Online cat, Activity rm, Adult bk club, Art exhibits, Art programs, Audio & video playback equip for onsite use, Audiobks on Playaways & MP3, Audiobks via web, Bilingual assistance for Spanish patrons, Bk club(s), Bks on CD, Chess club, Children's prog, Computer training, Computers for patron use, Distance learning, E-Readers, Electronic databases & coll, Family literacy, For res purposes, Free DVD rentals, Genealogy discussion group, Health sci info serv, Holiday prog, Home delivery & serv to seniorr ctr & nursing homes, Homebound delivery serv, ILL available, Internet access, Jail serv, Life-long learning prog for all ages, Literacy & newcomer serv, Magazines, Magnifiers for reading, Mail & tel request accepted, Meeting rooms, Microfiche/film & reading machines, Movies, Music CDs, Notary serv, Online cat, Online info literacy tutorials on the web & in blackboard, Online ref, Outreach serv, Outside serv via phone, mail, e-mail & web, OverDrive digital audio bks, Photocopying/Printing, Preschool outreach, Preschool reading prog, Prog for adults, Prog for children & young adult, Ref & res, Ref serv available, Scanner, Senior outreach, Spanish lang bks, STEM programs, Story hour, Study rm, Summer & winter reading prog, Summer reading prog, Tax forms, Teen prog, Telephone ref, Visual arts prog, Wheelchair accessible, Winter reading prog, Workshops, Writing prog
Partic in WYLD Network
Open Mon-Thurs 9-8, Fri & Sat 9-5, Sun (Sept-May) 1-5
Restriction: Non-circulating coll, Non-resident fee
Friends of the Library Group
Branches: 1
ALTA BRANCH, 50 Alta School Rd, Alta, 83414. Tel: 307-353-2505. FAX: 307-353-2473. E-mail: alta@tclib.org. *Br Mgr,* Eva Dahlgren; Staff 1 (Non-MLS 1)
Founded 1962. Pop 544
Library Holdings: AV Mats 280; CDs 60; DVDs 70; Large Print Bks 10; Bk Titles 4,000; Per Subs 1; Videos 150
Automation Activity & Vendor Info: (Circulation) SirsiDynix; (Discovery) ByWater Solutions; (OPAC) ByWater Solutions
Open Tues & Thurs Noon-6, Wed Noon-7, Fri & Sat 10-4
Friends of the Library Group

KEMMERER

P LINCOLN COUNTY LIBRARY SYSTEM*, Kemmerer Branch, 519 Emerald St, 83101. SAN 365-2742. Tel: 307-877-6961. FAX: 307-877-4147. Web Site: linclib.org. *Dir,* Richard Landreth; *Asst Dir,* Missy Harris; E-mail: mharris@linclib.org; *Ch,* Sarah Humphries; *Tech Serv,* Sheryl Alleman; Staff 18.3 (Non-MLS 18.3)
Founded 1983. Pop 16,383; Circ 192,362
Library Holdings: AV Mats 9,478; Bk Vols 111,473; Per Subs 243
Automation Activity & Vendor Info: (Circulation) SirsiDynix
Wireless access
Function: ILL available
Partic in WYLD Network
Special Services for the Blind - Large print bks
Open Mon-Wed 10-8, Thurs & Fri 10-6, Sat 10-2

Branches: 5
ALPINE BRANCH, 243 River Circle, Alpine, 83128. (Mail add: PO Box 3168, Alpine, 83128). Tel: 307-654-7323. FAX: 307-654-2158. Web Site: linclib.org/alpine-branch. *Br Mgr,* Wendi Walton; E-mail: wwalton@linclib.org; *Ch,* Rachelle Draney; E-mail: rdraney@linclib.org
Open Mon, Wed & Fri 10-6, Tues & Thurs 10-8, Sat 10-2
COKEVILLE BRANCH, 240 E Main St, Cokeville, 83114. (Mail add: PO Box 69, Cokeville, 83114-0069), SAN 365-2807. Tel: 307-279-3213. FAX: 307-279-3263. Web Site: linclib.org/cokeville-branch. *Br Librn,* Gayle Chadwick; E-mail: gchadwick@linclib.org; *Ch,* Tammy Plowman
Open Mon 11-8, Tues-Thurs 11-6, Fri 11-4, Sat 10-2
LABARGE BRANCH, 262 Main St, LaBarge, 83123. (Mail add: PO Box 57, LaBarge, 83123-0057), SAN 365-2815. Tel: 307-386-2571. FAX: 307-386-2569. Web Site: linclib.org/la-barge-branch. *Br Librn, Ch,* Jo Howard; E-mail: jhoward@linclib.org
Founded 1981
Open Mon & Tues 1-8, Wed & Thurs 10-5, Fri 1-6, Sat 10-2
STAR VALLEY BRANCH, 261 Washington, Afton, 83110. (Mail add: PO Box 849, Afton, 83110-0849), SAN 365-2777. Tel: 307-885-3158. FAX: 307-885-9651. Web Site: linclib.org/star-valley-branch. *Br Mgr,* Lizzy Larson; Tel: 307-885-3158, E-mail: llarson@linclib.org; *Ch,* Becky Astle
Open Mon, Wed & Fri 10-6, Tues & Thurs 10-8, Sat 10-2
Friends of the Library Group
THAYNE BRANCH, 250 Van Noy Pkwy, Thayne, 83127. (Mail add: PO Box 660, Thayne, 83127-0660). Tel: 307-883-7323. FAX: 307-883-7324. Web Site: linclib.org/thayne-branch. *Br Mgr,* Kelsey Richards; E-mail: krichards@linclib.org; *Ch,* Rhonda Merritt; E-mail: rmerritt@linclib.org; Staff 5 (MLS 1, Non-MLS 4)
Founded 2008
Library Holdings: Bk Vols 3,000
Open Mon, Wed & Fri 11-6, Tues & Thurs 11-8

LANDER

P FREMONT COUNTY LIBRARY SYSTEM*, Lander Branch & Headquarters, 451 N Second St, 82520. SAN 365-2831. Tel: 307-332-5194. Circulation Tel: 307-332-5194, Ext 303. Administration Tel: 307-332-1600. FAX: 307-332-3909. Administration FAX: 307-332-1504. Web Site: fclsonline.org. *Br Mgr, Libr Dir,* Anita Marple; E-mail: amarple@fclsonline.org; Staff 4 (MLS 1, Non-MLS 3)
Founded 1907. Pop 36,000; Circ 165,677
Library Holdings: AV Mats 14,510; Bk Vols 187,690; Per Subs 228
Special Collections: Western Americana Coll
Subject Interests: Art, Fishing
Automation Activity & Vendor Info: (Acquisitions) SirsiDynix; (Cataloging) SirsiDynix; (Circulation) SirsiDynix; (OPAC) SirsiDynix; (Serials) SirsiDynix
Wireless access
Partic in WYLD Network
Open Mon-Thurs 10-7, Fri & Sat 10-4
Friends of the Library Group
Branches: 2
DUBOIS BRANCH, 202 N First St, Dubois, 82513, SAN 365-2866. Tel: 307-455-2992. FAX: 307-455-2032. Web Site: www.fclsonline.org/dubois-library. *Br Mgr,* Kathy Gettelman; E-mail: kgettelman@fclsonline.org; Staff 5 (Non-MLS 5)
Pop 3,000; Circ 12,000
Library Holdings: AV Mats 1,100; Bk Vols 14,000
Special Collections: Big Horn Sheep Center Coll; Lucius Burch Local History Coll
Open Tues-Thurs 10-7, Fri & Sat 10-5
Friends of the Library Group
RIVERTON BRANCH, 1330 W Park Ave, Riverton, 82501, SAN 365-3048. Tel: 307-856-3556. FAX: 307-857-3722. Web Site: www.fclsonline.org/riverton-library. *Br Mgr,* Shari Haskins; E-mail: shaskins@fclsonline.org
Circ 76,019
Library Holdings: AV Mats 5,000; Bk Vols 74,979; Per Subs 150
Special Collections: Western Americana Coll
Subject Interests: Genealogy, Small bus
Open Mon-Thurs 10-7, Fri & Sat 10-4
Friends of the Library Group

LARAMIE

P ALBANY COUNTY PUBLIC LIBRARY, Laramie Main Library, 310 S Eighth St, 82070-3969. SAN 365-3102. Tel: 307-721-2580. E-mail: info@acplwy.org. Web Site: www.acplwy.org. *Libr Dir,* Rachel Crocker; E-mail: rcrocker@acplwy.org; *Dep Dir,* Darcy Lipp-Accord; E-mail: dlippaccord@acplwy.org; Staff 15 (MLS 4, Non-MLS 11)
Founded 1887. Pop 32,758; Circ 190,042
Subject Interests: County hist, Oral hist, State, Wyo
Automation Activity & Vendor Info: (Acquisitions) SirsiDynix-WorkFlows; (Cataloging) SirsiDynix; (Circulation) SirsiDynix; (ILL) OCLC Connexion; (OPAC) SirsiDynix; (Serials) SirsiDynix
Wireless access
Function: 24/7 Electronic res, 24/7 Online cat, Adult bk club, After school storytime, Audiobks via web, Bk club(s), Bks on CD, Children's prog, Computer training, Computers for patron use, Electronic databases & coll, Family literacy, Free DVD rentals, Games, Home delivery & serv to seniorr ctr & nursing homes, Homebound delivery serv, ILL available, Internet access, Life-long learning prog for all ages, Magazines, Mail & tel request accepted, Meeting rooms, Microfiche/film & reading machines, Movies, Online cat, OverDrive digital audio bks, Photocopying/Printing, Prog for adults, Prog for children & young adult, Ref serv available, Scanner, Story hour, Summer reading prog, Tax forms, Telephone ref
Publications: The Open Book: of the Albany County Public Library Foundation (Newsletter)
Partic in WYLD Network
Special Services for the Deaf - TTY equip
Friends of the Library Group
Branches: 2
CENTENNIAL VALLEY BRANCH, PO Box 188, Centennial, 82055-0188, SAN 365-3137. Tel: 307-745-8393. Web Site: www.centenniallibrary.net/.
Founded 1978
Open Mon-Fri 11-3
Friends of the Library Group
ROCK RIVER BRANCH, 386 Ave D, Rock River, 82083. (Mail add: PO Box 213, Rock River, 82083-0213), SAN 365-3161. *Br Librn,* Shirley Spiegelberg
Pop 202
Library Holdings: AV Mats 315; Large Print Bks 39; Bk Vols 3,889
Automation Activity & Vendor Info: (ILL) Gateway
Function: Adult bk club
Open Wed 9:30-12:30 & 1:30-4:30

S AMERICAN HERITAGE CENTER, Toppan Rare Books Library, Centennial Complex, 2111 Willet Dr, 82071. SAN 377-0591. Tel: 307-766-2565. E-mail: etoppan@uwyo.edu. Web Site: www.uwyo.edu/ahc/toppan. *Rare Book Curator,* Mary Beth Brown; E-mail: mary.brown@uwyo.edu; Staff 1 (MLS 1)
Library Holdings: Bk Titles 30,000
Automation Activity & Vendor Info: (Cataloging) OCLC
Wireless access
Restriction: Open by appt only

S LARAMIE PLAINS MUSEUM ASSOCIATION INC LIBRARY*, 603 Ivinson Ave, 82070-3299. SAN 326-1220. Tel: 307-742-4448. Web Site: www.laramiemuseum.org. *Exec Dir,* Mary Mountain; E-mail: lpmdirector@laramiemuseum.org; *Curator, Registrar,* Konnie Cronk; *Historian, Researcher,* Jerry Hansen
Founded 1972
Library Holdings: Bk Vols 1,000
Special Collections: Oral History
Open Tues-Sat 1-4

CL UNIVERSITY OF WYOMING, George W Hopper Law Library, 1820 E Willett Dr. (Mail add: Dept 3035, 1000 E University Ave, 82071), SAN 365-3374. Tel: 307-766-2210. Reference Tel: 307-766-2210. E-mail: lawref@uwyo.edu. Web Site: www.uwyo.edu/lawlib. *Libr Dir,* Tawnya Plumb; Tel: 307-766-5733, E-mail: tplumb@uwyo.edu; *Head, Pub Serv,* Tracey McCormick; Tel: 307-766-5120, E-mail: tmccorm1@uwyo.edu; *Head, Student Serv,* Meara Hill; Tel: 307-766-5113, E-mail: mhill43@uwyo.edu; *Scholarly Communications Librn,* Shelby Nivitanont; Tel: 307-766-5731, E-mail: snivitan@uwyo.edu; Staff 6 (MLS 5, Non-MLS 1)
Founded 1920. Enrl 235; Highest Degree: Doctorate
Library Holdings: Bk Vols 143,000; Per Subs 1,850; Videos 328
Special Collections: Roman Law (Blume Coll). US Document Depository
Subject Interests: US Law
Automation Activity & Vendor Info: (Acquisitions) Ex Libris Group; (Cataloging) Ex Libris Group; (Circulation) Ex Libris Group; (ILL) OCLC; (OPAC) Ex Libris Group; (Serials) Ex Libris Group
Wireless access
Partic in OCLC Online Computer Library Center, Inc
Open Mon-Fri 8-6, Sat & Sun 12-4

C UNIVERSITY OF WYOMING LIBRARIES*, William Robertson Coe Library, 13th & Ivinson Ave, 1000 E University Ave, 82071. SAN 365-3196. Tel: 307-766-3190. Interlibrary Loan Service Tel: 307-766-5168. FAX: 307-766-2510. Web Site: uwyo.libguides.com/coe. *Dean,* Ivan Gaetz; *Assoc Dean,* Cassandra Kvenild; Tel: 307-766-3859, E-mail: ckvenild@uwyo.edu; *IT Librn,* Stephen Boss; Tel: 307-766-4948, E-mail: sboss@uwyo.edu; *Instrul Design Librn,* Samantha Peter; Staff 91 (MLS 30, Non-MLS 61)
Founded 1887. Enrl 10,538; Fac 624; Highest Degree: Doctorate
Library Holdings: e-books 56,924; Bk Vols 1,483,791; Per Subs 14,006
Special Collections: Grace Raymond Hebard Coll, maps, published mat. US Document Depository

Subject Interests: State hist
Automation Activity & Vendor Info: (Acquisitions) Innovative Interfaces, Inc - Millennium; (Cataloging) Innovative Interfaces, Inc - Millennium; (Circulation) Innovative Interfaces, Inc - Millennium; (Course Reserve) Innovative Interfaces, Inc - Millennium; (ILL) OCLC ILLiad; (Media Booking) Innovative Interfaces, Inc - Millennium; (OPAC) Innovative Interfaces, Inc - Millennium; (Serials) Innovative Interfaces, Inc - Millennium
Wireless access
Function: Archival coll, AV serv, Distance learning, Doc delivery serv, Health sci info serv, ILL available, Internet access, Ref serv available, Wheelchair accessible
Publications: Check It Out (Newsletter); The Library Associate (Quarterly)
Partic in Center for Research Libraries; Colorado Alliance of Research Libraries; Greater Western Library Alliance; LYRASIS; Mid-Continental Regional Med Librs Asn; OCLC Online Computer Library Center, Inc; OCLC Research Library Partnership
Restriction: Open to pub for ref & circ; with some limitations, Open to students, fac & staff
Departmental Libraries:
BRINKERHOFF GEOLOGY LIBRARY (BRINKERHOFF EARTH RESOURCES INFORMATION CENTER), Geology Bldg, Rm 121, 121 SH Knight, 82071. SAN 365-3250. Tel: 307-766-3374. FAX: 307-766-6679. Web Site: uwyo.libguides.com/geologylibrary. *Chair, Res & Instrul Serv, Support Librn,* Larry Schmidt; Tel: 307-766-2844, E-mail: lschmidt@uwyo.edu; *Br Mgr,* Enid Teeter; Tel: 307-766-2633, E-mail: esteeter@uwyo.edu
Subject Interests: Geochemistry, Geol, Geomorphology, Geophysics, Paleontology, Remote sensing, Sedimentology
LEARNING RESOURCE CENTER, Education Bldg 222, N 15th St & Lewis St, 82071, SAN 328-7270. Tel: 307-766-2527. Web Site: uwyo.libguides.com/lrc. *Sr Libr Asst,* Cathy Dodgson; E-mail: cdodgson@uwyo.edu
Special Collections: NASA Regional Teachers Resource Center
Subject Interests: Practical educ
LIBRARY ANNEX, Science Complex, Dept 3254 Basement, 1000 E University Ave, 82071. SAN 365-3285. Tel: 307-766-2070. *Access Serv,* Toni Boughton; Tel: 307-766-6535, E-mail: tlhb@uwyo.edu
ROCKY MOUNTAIN HERBARIUM REFERENCE COLLECTION, Aven Nelson Bldg, 3rd Flr, 1000 E University Ave, 82071, SAN 328-7297. Tel: 307-766-2844. *Research & Instruction Services,* Larry Schmidt; E-mail: lschmidt@uwyo.edu

LUSK

P NIOBRARA COUNTY LIBRARY*, 425 S Main St, 82225. (Mail add: PO Box 510, 82225-0510), SAN 318-4994. Tel: 307-334-3490. FAX: 307-334-3490. E-mail: info@niobraracountylibrary.org. Web Site: niobraracountylibrary.org. *Dir,* Debbie Sturman; E-mail: dsturman@niobraracountylibrary.org; Staff 2.6 (Non-MLS 2.6)
Founded 1913. Pop 2,428; Circ 42,077
Library Holdings: AV Mats 12,000; Bk Titles 50,000; Per Subs 81
Wireless access
Open Mon, Tues, Thurs & Fri 10-6, Wed 12-7
Friends of the Library Group

S WYOMING WOMEN'S CENTER LIBRARY, 1000 W Griffith Blvd, 82225. (Mail add: PO Box 300, 82225-0300), SAN 320-9881. Tel: 307-334-3693. FAX: 307-334-2254. Web Site: library.wyo.gov/directory/wyoming-department-of-corrections-womens-center. *Library Contact,* Sandra Toolen; Staff 1 (Non-MLS 1)
Founded 1980
Library Holdings: Bk Titles 4,121; Bk Vols 4,280; Per Subs 10

NEWCASTLE

S ANNA MILLER MUSEUM LIBRARY*, 401 Delaware Ave, 82701. (Mail add: PO Box 698, 82701), SAN 326-5757. Tel: 307-746-4188. FAX: 307-746-4629. *Dir,* Bobbie Jo Tysdal; E-mail: wcmd@rtconnect.net; Staff 1 (Non-MLS 1)
Library Holdings: Bk Titles 6,120; Bk Vols 6,360; Per Subs 12
Special Collections: Newcastle History; Newsletter Journal, newsp. Oral History
Wireless access
Open Mon-Fri 9-5
Friends of the Library Group

P WESTON COUNTY LIBRARY SYSTEM*, 23 W Main St, 82701. SAN 365-3404. Tel: 307-746-2206. FAX: 307-746-2218. Web Site: www.westongov.com/library. *Dir,* Brenda Mahoney-Ayres; E-mail: bmahoneyayres@westongov.com; *Adult Serv,* Kat Townsend; *Ch Serv,* Amanda Sanford; *Circ Serv,* Lisa Thomas; E-mail: lthomas@westongov.com; Staff 4 (Non-MLS 4)
Founded 1911. Pop 7,236
Jul 2016-Jun 2017 Income (Main & Associated Libraries) $278,174
Library Holdings: Audiobooks 1,964; CDs 190; DVDs 3,781; Bk Vols 42,877
Special Collections: Wyoming Coll
Automation Activity & Vendor Info: (Cataloging) SirsiDynix; (Circulation) SirsiDynix; (ILL) SirsiDynix; (OPAC) SirsiDynix; (Serials) SirsiDynix
Wireless access
Function: 24/7 Electronic res, 24/7 Online cat, Activity rm, Adult bk club, Audio & video playback equip for onsite use, Bks on cassette, Bks on CD, Children's prog, Electronic databases & coll, Free DVD rentals, ILL available, Instruction & testing, Music CDs, Photocopying/Printing, Prog for adults, Prog for children & young adult, Summer reading prog, Tax forms, Telephone ref, VHS videos, Wheelchair accessible
Partic in WYLD Network
Open Mon-Fri 9-6
Restriction: Non-circulating coll
Branches: 1
UPTON BRANCH LIBRARY, 722 Fourth St, Upton, 82730. (Mail add: PO Box 605, Upton, 82730-0605), SAN 365-3439. Tel: 307-468-2324. FAX: 307-468-2324. E-mail: uptnill@westongov.com. Web Site: uptonbranchlibrary.blogspot.com/. *Br Mgr,* Randall Sherri; Staff 1 (Non-MLS 1)
Founded 1968. Pop 900; Circ 10,000
Library Holdings: DVDs 900; Large Print Bks 800; Bk Titles 11,000; Per Subs 3
Automation Activity & Vendor Info: (Cataloging) SirsiDynix-WorkFlows; (Circulation) SirsiDynix-WorkFlows; (ILL) Fretwell-Downing
Open Mon-Fri 12-5

PINEDALE

P SUBLETTE COUNTY LIBRARIES*, Pinedale Library, 155 S Tyler Ave, 82941. (Mail add: PO Box 489, 82941-0489), SAN 318-5001. Tel: 307-367-4114. FAX: 307-367-6722. E-mail: circulation@sublettecountylibrary.org. Web Site: sublettecountylibrary.org. *Exec Dir,* Sukey Hohl; E-mail: shohl@sublettecountylibrary.org; Staff 10 (MLS 1, Non-MLS 9)
Founded 1967. Pop 6,100
Library Holdings: DVDs 6,000; Bk Titles 63,981; Bk Vols 65,710; Per Subs 75
Special Collections: Film books; Rocky Mountain Fur Trade, photogs
Automation Activity & Vendor Info: (Cataloging) SirsiDynix; (Circulation) SirsiDynix
Wireless access
Function: 24/7 Electronic res, 24/7 Online cat, Activity rm, Adult bk club, Art exhibits, Audio & video playback equip for onsite use, Audiobks on Playaways & MP3, Audiobks via web, Bk club(s), Bks on CD, Children's prog, Computer training, Computers for patron use, E-Readers, Free DVD rentals, Holiday prog, Home delivery & serv to seniorr ctr & nursing homes, Homebound delivery serv, ILL available, Instruction & testing, Internet access, Laminating, Life-long learning prog for all ages, Magazines, Magnifiers for reading, Mail & tel request accepted, Meeting rooms, Microfiche/film & reading machines, Music CDs, Notary serv, Online cat, Orientations, Outreach serv, Outside serv via phone, mail, e-mail & web, OverDrive digital audio bks, Photocopying/Printing, Printer for laptops & handheld devices, Prog for adults, Prog for children & young adult, Ref & res, Ref serv available, Scanner, Senior outreach, Spanish lang bks, STEM programs, Story hour, Summer & winter reading prog, Summer reading prog, Tax forms, Teen prog, Wheelchair accessible, Winter reading prog, Writing prog
Partic in WYLD Network
Open Mon-Thurs 10-8, Fri 10-6, Sat 10-5
Restriction: Non-circulating of rare bks
Branches: 1
BIG PINEY LIBRARY, 106 Fish St, Big Piney, 83113. (Mail add: PO Box 768, Big Piney, 83113), SAN 321-7396. Tel: 307-276-3515. FAX: 307-276-3516. E-mail: BPBranch@sublettecountylibrary.org. *Br Mgr,* Tawnya Miller; E-mail: tmiller@sublettecountylibrary.org; Staff 7 (Non-MLS 7)
Library Holdings: CDs 22; Bk Titles 20,879; Bk Vols 22,163; Per Subs 37; Videos 57
Open Mon & Wed 10-5 & 7-9, Tues, Thurs & Fri 10-5, Sat 10-2
Friends of the Library Group

POWELL

J NORTHWEST COLLEGE*, Hinckley Library, 231 W Sixth St, 82435. SAN 318-501X. Tel: 307-754-6207. FAX: 307-754-6010. E-mail: librarian@nwc.edu. Web Site: www.nwc.edu/library. *Libr Dir,* Nancy Miller; E-mail: nancy.miller@nwc.edu; *Interim Librn,* Amanda Hall; E-mail: amanda.hall@nwc.edu; Staff 5 (MLS 3, Non-MLS 2)
Founded 1948. Enrl 1,600; Fac 102; Highest Degree: Associate
Library Holdings: Microforms 18,000; Bk Titles 68,000; Per Subs 385; Videos 121

Special Collections: State Document Depository; US Document Depository
Subject Interests: Country music, Heart Mountain
Wireless access
Partic in WYLD Network; Wyo Libr Database
Open Mon-Thurs 7:45-7, Fri 7:45-5, Sun 3-7

RAWLINS

P CARBON COUNTY LIBRARY SYSTEM*, 215 W Buffalo St, 82301. SAN 365-3463. Tel: 307-328-2618. FAX: 307-328-2615. Web Site: carbonlibraries.org/rawlins. *Exec Dir,* Maria Wenzel; E-mail: director@carbonlibraries.org; *Circ Mgr,* Missi White; Staff 3 (Non-MLS 3)
Founded 1925. Pop 15,690; Circ 19,317
Library Holdings: AV Mats 2,347; CDs 90; Large Print Bks 300; Bk Vols 39,229; Per Subs 10; Videos 5,937
Automation Activity & Vendor Info: (Cataloging) SirsiDynix; (Circulation) SirsiDynix
Wireless access
Partic in WYLD Network
Open Mon-Thurs 10-7, Fri 10-5
Friends of the Library Group
Branches: 7
ELK MOUNTAIN BRANCH, 105 Bridge St, Elk Mountain, 82324. (Mail add: PO Box 156, Elk Mountain, 82324-0156), SAN 365-351X. Tel: 307-348-7421. Web Site: carbonlibraries.org/elk-mountain-library. *Br Mgr,* Jessica Mustard; Staff 2 (Non-MLS 2)
Circ 1,879
Library Holdings: AV Mats 95; Bk Vols 5,226; Per Subs 2; Videos 634
Open Tues & Thurs 12-5
Friends of the Library Group
ENCAMPMENT BRANCH, 202 Rankin St, Encampment, 82325. (Mail add: PO Box 495, Encampment, 82325-0495), SAN 365-3528. Tel: 307-327-5775. Web Site: carbonlibraries.org/encampment-1. *Br Mgr,* Dawna Martin; Staff 1 (Non-MLS 1)
Circ 2,761
Library Holdings: AV Mats 153; Bk Vols 7,231; Per Subs 2; Videos 708
Open Mon & Thurs 11-4, Tues & Wed Noon-5
Friends of the Library Group
HANNA BRANCH, 303 Third St, Hanna, 82327. (Mail add: PO Box 297, Hanna, 82327-0297), SAN 365-3552. Tel: 307-325-9357. Web Site: carbonlibraries.org/hanna. *Br Mgr,* Jo Wohl; Staff 1 (Non-MLS 1)
Circ 1,056
Library Holdings: AV Mats 54; Bk Vols 6,141; Per Subs 4; Videos 572
Open Mon 10-3, Wed 1-6
Friends of the Library Group
LITTLE SNAKE RIVER VALLEY, 105 Second St, Baggs, 82321. (Mail add: PO Box 370, Baggs, 82321-0370), SAN 365-3498. Tel: 307-383-7323. Web Site: carbonlibraries.org/lsrv. *Br Mgr,* Becka Evans; Staff 1 (Non-MLS 1)
Circ 3,577
Library Holdings: AV Mats 301; Bk Vols 9,482; Per Subs 6; Videos 1,389
Open Tues 12-6, Wed & Thurs 9-4
Friends of the Library Group
MEDICINE BOW BRANCH, 314 Sage St, Medicine Bow, 82329. (Mail add: PO Box 279, Medicine Bow, 82329-0279), SAN 365-3587. Tel: 307-379-2888. Web Site: carbonlibraries.org/medicine-bow. *Br Mgr,* Jo Wohl
Circ 1,388
Library Holdings: AV Mats 72; Bk Vols 4,258; Per Subs 2; Videos 427
Open Tues 9-2, Thurs 1-6
Friends of the Library Group
SARATOGA BRANCH, 503 W Elm St, Saratoga, 82331. (Mail add: PO Box 27, Saratoga, 82331-0027), SAN 365-3617. Tel: 307-326-8209. Web Site: carbonlibraries.org/saratoga. *Mgr,* Sue Paddock; Staff 1 (Non-MLS 1)
Circ 11,744
Library Holdings: AV Mats 830; Bk Vols 13,738; Per Subs 3; Videos 2,868
Open Mon 10-6, Tues & Thurs 11-6, Wed & Fri 11-3
Friends of the Library Group
SINCLAIR BRANCH, 604 Lincoln St, Sinclair, 82334. (Mail add: PO Box 178, Sinclair, 82334-0178), SAN 365-3633. Tel: 307-328-5299. FAX: 307-324-6231. Web Site: carbonlibraries.org/sinclair. *Br Mgr,* Missi White
Circ 1,670
Library Holdings: AV Mats 34; Bk Vols 5,845; Per Subs 1; Videos 376
Open Tues & Thurs 3-5:30
Friends of the Library Group

S WYOMING STATE PENITENTIARY LIBRARY*, 2900 S Higley Blvd, 82301. (Mail add: PO Box 400, 82301-0400), SAN 318-5036. Tel: 307-328-1441. *Educ Mgr,* Laurie Heier; E-mail: laurie.heier@wyo.gov; Staff 1 (Non-MLS 1)
Founded 1924
Library Holdings: Bk Titles 5,000; Bk Vols 5,100
Subject Interests: Adventure, Fantasy, Sci fict, Western stories

RIVERTON

J CENTRAL WYOMING COLLEGE LIBRARY*, Library & Academic Resource Center, 2660 Peck Ave, 82501. SAN 318-5044. Tel: 307-855-2141. FAX: 307-855-2094. E-mail: librarian@cwc.edu. Web Site: libguides.cwc.edu/cwc. *Librn,* Rebecca Chavez; E-mail: rchavez@cwc.edu; *Instructional Technologist,* Kristy Hardtke; E-mail: kristy@cwc.edu; Staff 2 (MLS 2)
Founded 1967
Library Holdings: e-books 800,000; Bk Titles 30,000; Per Subs 110; Videos 239
Special Collections: American Indian Coll; Wyoming Coll. Oral History; US Document Depository
Subject Interests: Geol, Wyo
Wireless access
Publications: Specialized Subject Bibliographies
Partic in WYLD Network
Open Mon-Fri 8-5

S WYOMING DEPARTMENT OF CORRECTIONS*, Wyoming Honor Farm Library, 40 Honor Farm Rd, 82501-8400. Tel: 307-856-9578. FAX: 307-856-2505. *Educ Mgr,* Shawn Smith; E-mail: shawn.smith@wyo.gov
Library Holdings: CDs 200; DVDs 150; Bk Vols 5,000; Per Subs 40
Restriction: Not open to pub, Staff & inmates only

ROCK SPRINGS

J WESTERN WYOMING COMMUNITY COLLEGE*, Hay Library, 2500 College Dr, 82902. SAN 318-5079. Tel: 307-382-1700. FAX: 307-382-7665. E-mail: haylibrary@westernwyoming.edu. Web Site: wwcc-wy.libguides.com/hayhome, www.westernwyoming.edu/student-life/campus-amenities/hay-library. *Dir, Libr Serv,* Christopher Murry; Tel: 307-382-1701, E-mail: cmurry@westernwyoming.edu; *Assoc Librn,* Mr Jon Harwood; Tel: 307-382-1702, E-mail: jharwood@westernwyoming.edu; *Ref & Instruction Librn,* Sarah Bryant; E-mail: sbryant@westernwyoming.edu; *Libr Asst, Ser/Circ Coordr,* Linda Halter; Tel: 307-382-1703, E-mail: lhalter@westernwyoming.edu; Staff 4 (MLS 2, Non-MLS 2)
Founded 1959. Enrl 3,147; Fac 250; Highest Degree: Associate
Library Holdings: AV Mats 3,000; e-books 500,000; Bk Vols 60,000; Per Subs 120
Special Collections: Local Newspapers (Rock Springs Rocket & Green River Star), micro. Oral History; State Document Depository; US Document Depository
Automation Activity & Vendor Info: (Acquisitions) Baker & Taylor; (Cataloging) SirsiDynix; (Circulation) SirsiDynix; (ILL) SirsiDynix; (OPAC) SirsiDynix; (Serials) SirsiDynix
Wireless access
Partic in WYLD Network
Open Mon-Thurs 7:30am-10pm, Fri 7:30-5, Sat 1-5, Sun 5-10; Mon-Thurs 7am-8pm (Summer)

SHERIDAN

J NORTHERN WYOMING COMMUNITY COLLEGE DISTRICT - SHERIDAN COLLEGE*, Kooi Library, Griffith Memorial Bldg, One Whitney Way, 82801. SAN 318-5087. Tel: 307-675-0220. E-mail: sclibrary@sheridan.edu. Web Site: sheridan.edu/library. *Dir, Libr Serv,* Michelle Boule; E-mail: mboulesmith@sheridan.edu; *Acad Librn,* Lanelle Richards; E-mail: lrichards@sheridan.edu; *Pub Serv Librn,* Chris Murry; E-mail: cmurry@sheridan.edu; Staff 8 (MLS 3, Non-MLS 5)
Founded 1948. Enrl 3,521; Fac 87; Highest Degree: Associate
Library Holdings: Bk Titles 19,000; Bk Vols 29,000; Per Subs 35
Automation Activity & Vendor Info: (Acquisitions) SirsiDynix-iLink; (Cataloging) SirsiDynix; (Circulation) SirsiDynix; (Course Reserve) SirsiDynix-iLink; (ILL) OCLC; (OPAC) SirsiDynix-iLink; (Serials) SirsiDynix-iLink
Wireless access
Partic in WYLD Network
Special Services for the Blind - Computer with voice synthesizer for visually impaired persons
Open Mon-Thurs 8am-10pm, Fri 8-Noon, Sat 1-5, Sun 1-8; Mon-Fri 8-5 (Summer)

P SHERIDAN COUNTY PUBLIC LIBRARY SYSTEM*, Sheridan County Fulmer Public Library, 335 W Alger St, 82801. SAN 365-3676. Tel: 307-674-8585. Circulation Tel: 307-674-8585, Ext 110. Reference Tel:

307-674-8585, Ext 135. Administration FAX: 307-674-7374. E-mail: scfpl@sheridanwyolibrary.org. Web Site: www.sheridanwyolibrary.org. *Libr Dir,* Cameron Duff; Tel: 307-674-8585, Ext 112, E-mail: cduff@sheridanwyolibrary.org; *Network Adminr,* David Hartschuh; E-mail: dhartschuh@sheridanwyolibrary.org; *Ch,* Michelle Havenga; E-mail: mhavenga@sheridanwyolibrary.org; *Coll Develop Librn,* Marci Mock; E-mail: mmock@sheridanwyolibrary.org; *Info Serv Librn,* Anita Weisheit; E-mail: aweisheit@sheridanwyolibrary.org; *Fac Mgr,* Kip Bethurem; E-mail: kbethurem@sheridanwyolibrary.org; *Prog Coordr, Young Adult Serv Coordr,* Zola Shockley; E-mail: zshockley@sheridanwyolibrary.org; *Homebound Serv,* Denise Gillenwater; E-mail: outreach@sheridanwyolibrary.org; *ILL,* Chris Gonzales; E-mail: cgonzales@sheridanwyolibrary.org; Staff 13 (MLS 3, Non-MLS 10)
Founded 1905. Pop 29,239; Circ 323,238
Library Holdings: AV Mats 15,794; CDs 5,257; DVDs 10,537; Electronic Media & Resources 157; Large Print Bks 5,000; Bk Titles 133,351; Per Subs 191
Special Collections: Folklore & Storytelling (Spell-Spinner Coll). Oral History
Subject Interests: Genealogy, Local hist
Automation Activity & Vendor Info: (Acquisitions) SirsiDynix; (Cataloging) SirsiDynix; (Circulation) SirsiDynix; (ILL) Fretwell-Downing; (OPAC) SirsiDynix; (Serials) SirsiDynix
Function: Bk club(s), Computer training, Digital talking bks, Electronic databases & coll, Home delivery & serv to seniorr ctr & nursing homes, Homebound delivery serv, Homework prog, ILL available, Internet access, Magnifiers for reading, Mail & tel request accepted, Music CDs, Online ref, Orientations, Photocopying/Printing, Preschool outreach, Prog for adults, Prog for children & young adult, Ref serv available, Senior computer classes, Summer reading prog, Tax forms, Telephone ref, VHS videos, Wheelchair accessible
Partic in WYLD Network
Special Services for the Deaf - TTY equip
Open Mon-Fri 9-5, Sat 1-5
Friends of the Library Group
Branches: 3
CLEARMONT BRANCH, 1254 Front St, Clearmont, 82835. (Mail add: PO Box 26, Clearmont, 82835-0026), SAN 365-3706. Tel: 307-758-4331. FAX: 307-758-4331. E-mail: cbl@sheridanwyolibrary.org. Web Site: www.sheridanwyolibrary.org/location-hours/clearmont-branch-library. *Mgr,* Barbara Carlock; Staff 1 (Non-MLS 1)
Library Holdings: AV Mats 916; Bk Titles 8,193; Per Subs 13
Open Mon-Thurs 2-6:30, Fri 9-1
STORY BRANCH, 20 N Piney, Story, 82842. (Mail add: PO Box 188, Story, 82842-0188), SAN 365-3730. Tel: 307-683-2922. FAX: 307-683-3036. E-mail: sbl@sheridanwyolibrary.org. Web Site: www.sheridanwyolibrary.org/location-hours/story-branch. *Mgr,* Stephanie Hutt; Staff 1 (Non-MLS 1)
Library Holdings: AV Mats 868; Bk Titles 9,823
Open Mon-Fri 12:30-5:30, Sat 9-1
TONGUE RIVER BRANCH, 145 Coffeen St, Ranchester, 82839. (Mail add: PO Box 909, Ranchester, 82839-0909), SAN 365-3765. Tel: 307-655-9726. FAX: 307-655-9384. E-mail: trbl@sheridanwyolibrary.org. Web Site: www.sheridanwyolibrary.org/location-hours/tongue-river-branch-library. *Mgr,* Connie Fiedor; Staff 1 (Non-MLS 1)
Pop 2,000; Circ 12,089
Library Holdings: Audiobooks 471; AV Mats 1,296; CDs 889; DVDs 324; e-books 3; Electronic Media & Resources 65; Large Print Bks 284; Bk Titles 13,958; Per Subs 25; Videos 955
Function: Adult bk club, Art exhibits, Computers for patron use, Electronic databases & coll, ILL available, Photocopying/Printing, Prog for children & young adult, Summer reading prog, Tax forms
Special Services for the Blind - Home delivery serv
Open Mon-Fri 10-12 & 1-6

SHOSHONI

P SHOSHONI PUBLIC LIBRARY*, 216 Idaho St, 82649. Tel: 307-876-2777. FAX: 307-876-2525. Web Site: www.shoshoniwyoming.org/2148/Library. *Libr Dir,* Melissa Franklin; E-mail: mfranklin@townofshoshoni.org; Staff 1 (Non-MLS 1)
Fac 1
Jul 2020-Jun 2021 Income $5,000, City $1,000, Locally Generated Income $2,000, Other $2,000
Library Holdings: Audiobooks 385; Bks on Deafness & Sign Lang 3; Braille Volumes 1; DVDs 1,027; Large Print Bks 513; Bk Titles 8,700
Automation Activity & Vendor Info: (Cataloging) JayWil Software Development, Inc; (Circulation) JayWil Software Development, Inc
Wireless access
Function: Audiobks on Playaways & MP3, Bks on CD, Children's prog, Computers for patron use, Free DVD rentals, Holiday prog, Internet access, Makerspace, Photocopying/Printing, Ref & res, Res assist avail, Scanner, Story hour, Study rm, Summer reading prog, Tax forms, Wheelchair accessible
Open Mon, Wed & Fri 10-3, Tues & Thurs 1-6
Restriction: Non-circulating of rare bks, Open to pub for ref & circ; with some limitations
Friends of the Library Group

SUNDANCE

P CROOK COUNTY LIBRARY*, 414 Main St, 82729. (Mail add: PO Box 910, 82729-0910), SAN 365-379X. Tel: 307-283-1006, 307-283-1008. FAX: 307-283-1006. E-mail: crookcountylibrary@rangeweb.net. Web Site: crookcountylib.org. *County Librn,* Jill A Mackey; E-mail: crookcountylib@rangeweb.net; *Br Librn,* Kim Heaster; *Ad,* Carrie Riley; Staff 4 (Non-MLS 4)
Founded 1937. Pop 6,000; Circ 35,890
Library Holdings: Large Print Bks 238; Bk Titles 75,861; Bk Vols 77,490; Per Subs 278; Talking Bks 1,090; Videos 1,816
Special Collections: Wyomingana
Automation Activity & Vendor Info: (Acquisitions) SirsiDynix; (Cataloging) SirsiDynix; (Circulation) SirsiDynix; (ILL) SirsiDynix
Function: Adult bk club, Audio & video playback equip for onsite use, Audiobks via web, AV serv, Bi-weekly Writer's Group, Bks on cassette, Bks on CD, Children's prog, Computers for patron use, E-Reserves, Electronic databases & coll, Free DVD rentals, Govt ref serv, Health sci info serv, Holiday prog, ILL available, Notary serv, Online cat, Outreach serv, Photocopying/Printing, Preschool outreach, Prog for adults, Prog for children & young adult, Spoken cassettes & CDs, Story hour, Summer reading prog, Tax forms, Teen prog, Telephone ref, VHS videos, Wheelchair accessible
Partic in WYLD Network; Wyo Libr Database
Open Mon-Fri 9-5
Friends of the Library Group
Branches: 2
HULETT BRANCH, 401 Sager St, Hulett, 82720. (Mail add: PO Box 219, Hulett, 82720-0219), SAN 365-382X. Tel: 307-467-5676. FAX: 307-467-5250. E-mail: library467@rtconnect.net. Web Site: will.state.wy.us/crook/hulett.htm. *Br Librn,* Nancy Bowles; *Asst Br Librn,* Echo Bohl
Library Holdings: CDs 33; Large Print Bks 60; Bk Titles 31,195; Bk Vols 32,410; Per Subs 57; Videos 90
Open Mon, Tues, Thurs & Fri 9-5, Wed 9-7
Friends of the Library Group
MOORCROFT BRANCH, 105 E Converse, Moorcroft, 82721. (Mail add: PO Box 10, Moorcroft, 82721-0010), SAN 365-3854. Tel: 307-756-3232. FAX: 307-756-3232. *Br Librn,* Maureen Farrier; *Adult Serv,* Pamela Jespersen; *Youth Serv,* Judy Stenbak
Library Holdings: CDs 31; Large Print Bks 57; Bk Titles 27,017; Bk Vols 28,194; Per Subs 63; Videos 88
Open Mon-Fri 10-5:30

THERMOPOLIS

P HOT SPRINGS COUNTY LIBRARY*, 344 Arapahoe St, 82443. (Mail add: PO Box 951, 82443-0951), SAN 318-5109. Tel: 307-864-3104. FAX: 307-864-5416. Web Site: hotspringscountylibrary.wordpress.com. *Dir,* Tracey Kinnaman; E-mail: director@hsclibrary.com; *Youth Serv Librn,* Kailey Dvorak; E-mail: youthservices@hsclibrary.com; Staff 3 (Non-MLS 3)
Founded 1918. Pop 4,665; Circ 35,050
Special Collections: Local Newspapers from 1905, micro; Wyoming History Coll
Automation Activity & Vendor Info: (Cataloging) SirsiDynix; (Circulation) SirsiDynix; (ILL) OCLC Worldshare Management Services; (OPAC) SirsiDynix; (Serials) SirsiDynix
Wireless access
Function: 24/7 Electronic res, Activity rm, Adult bk club, Audiobks on Playaways & MP3, Audiobks via web, AV serv, Bk club(s), Bks on CD, Children's prog, Computers for patron use, E-Reserves, Electronic databases & coll, Equip loans & repairs, Free DVD rentals, Holiday prog, ILL available, Internet access, Laminating, Magazines, Magnifiers for reading, Meeting rooms, Movies, Music CDs, Online cat, Online ref, Photocopying/Printing, Prog for adults, Prog for children & young adult, Ref & res, Ref serv available, Scanner, Spoken cassettes & CDs, Story hour, Study rm, Summer & winter reading prog, Summer reading prog, Tax forms, Teen prog, Telephone ref, Wheelchair accessible, Workshops
Partic in WYLD Network
Open Mon-Fri 9-6, Sat 10-2
Friends of the Library Group

S WYOMING PIONEER HOME LIBRARY, 141 Pioneer Home Dr, 82443. SAN 372-8781. Tel: 307-864-3151. FAX: 307-864-2934. Web Site: health.wyo.gov/aging/pioneerhome. *Librn,* Allison Wrye; E-mail: allison.wrye@wyo.gov
Library Holdings: Bk Vols 1,400; Per Subs 25

Subject Interests: Fiction, Hist
Restriction: Residents only, Staff use only

TORRINGTON

J EASTERN WYOMING COLLEGE LIBRARY*, 3200 West C St, 82240. SAN 318-5117. Tel: 307-532-8210. Web Site: www.ewc.wy.edu/library. *Libr Dir,* Casey Debus; E-mail: casey.debus@ewc.wy.edu; *Libr Tech,* Jessica Anders; E-mail: jessica.anders@ewc.wy.edu; Staff 1 (MLS 1)
Founded 1948. Fac 40; Highest Degree: Associate
Library Holdings: Bk Vols 30,339; Per Subs 86
Special Collections: Oral History
Subject Interests: Agr, Criminal justice, Educ, Hist, Veterinary tech
Wireless access
Partic in WYLD Network
Open Mon-Thurs 8-8, Fri 8-5, Sun 1-4

P GOSHEN COUNTY LIBRARY*, 2001 East A St, 82240-2898. SAN 318-5125. Tel; 307-532-3411. FAX: 307-532-2169. E-mail: read@goshencountylibrary.org. Web Site: goshencountylibrary.org. *Dir,* Joan Brinkley; Staff 5.5 (Non-MLS 5.5)
Founded 1922. Pop 13,249; Circ 67,473
Library Holdings: Electronic Media & Resources 4,047; Bk Vols 42,868; Per Subs 101; Talking Bks 946; Videos 290
Automation Activity & Vendor Info: (Circulation) SirsiDynix; (OPAC) SirsiDynix
Wireless access
Function: ILL available
Partic in WYLD Network; Wyo Libr Database
Open Mon, Tues & Thurs 10-6, Wed 9-6, Fri 10-5, Sat 9-1

WHEATLAND

P PLATTE COUNTY PUBLIC LIBRARY*, 904 Ninth St, 82201. SAN 365-3889. Tel: 307-322-2689. FAX: 307-322-3540. E-mail: pcpl@plattecountylibrary.org. Web Site: plattecountylibrary.org. *Dir,* Julie Henion; E-mail: jhenion@plattecountylibrary.org; *Ch,* Shilo Weber; *Circ Librn,* Angelia Dappen; *Tech Serv,* Lee Miller; E-mail: lmiller@plattecountylibrary.org; Staff 8 (MLS 2, Non-MLS 6)
Founded 1894. Pop 9,012; Circ 73,441
Library Holdings: CDs 110; Bk Titles 61,112; Bk Vols 63,491; Per Subs 94; Videos 542
Special Collections: Oral History
Subject Interests: County hist, Wyo hist
Automation Activity & Vendor Info: (Cataloging) TLC (The Library Corporation); (Circulation) TLC (The Library Corporation)
Wireless access
Partic in WYLD Network
Open Mon-Thurs 10-8, Fri 10-5, Sat 10-2
Friends of the Library Group

Branches: 3
CHUGWATER BRANCH, 301 Second St, Chugwater, 82210. (Mail add: PO Box 215, Chugwater, 82210), SAN 365-3919. Tel: 307-422-3275. *Br Librn,* Darla Teter; Staff 1 (MLS 1)
Pop 244; Circ 908
Library Holdings: Bk Titles 4,031; Bk Vols 5,100; Per Subs 11
Open Mon 1-4, Wed 11-2, Fri 2-5
Friends of the Library Group
GLENDO BRANCH, 204 S Yellowstone, Glendo, 82213. (Mail add: PO Box 122, Glendo, 82213-0122), SAN 365-3943, Tel: 307-735-4480. *Br Librn,* Judy Plazyk
Pop 231; Circ 840
Library Holdings: Large Print Bks 12; Bk Titles 4,062; Bk Vols 5,281; Per Subs 16; Talking Bks 103; Videos 178
Open Tues 11-2:30, Thurs 2-5:30, Sat 10-1
GUERNSEY BRANCH, 108 S Wyoming Ave, Guernsey, 82214. (Mail add: PO Box 607, Guernsey, 82214), SAN 365-3978. Tel: 307-836-2816. *Br Librn,* Becky Bolinger
Pop 1,147; Circ 3,020
Library Holdings: Bk Titles 9,142; Bk Vols 10,111; Per Subs 23
Open Mon-Fri 10-5

WORLAND

P WASHAKIE COUNTY LIBRARY SYSTEM*, 801 Big Horn Ave, Ste 100, 82401. SAN 365-4001. Tel: 307-347-2231. FAX: 307-347-2248. E-mail: worland@washakiecountylibrary.com. Web Site: www.washakiecountylibrary.com. *Dir,* Karen Funk; E-mail: director@washakiecountylibrary.com; Staff 2 (Non-MLS 2)
Founded 1914. Pop 8,290
Library Holdings: Audiobooks 1,427; AV Mats 42; CDs 265; DVDs 3,449; e-books 68,129; e-journals 5,236; Large Print Bks 1,257; Bk Vols 42,157; Per Subs 17
Automation Activity & Vendor Info: (Circulation) SirsiDynix
Wireless access
Partic in WYLD Network
Open Mon, Wed & Fri 9-6, Sat 9-1
Friends of the Library Group
Branches: 1
TEN SLEEP BRANCH, 200 N Fir St, Ten Sleep, 82442. (Mail add: PO Box 107, Ten Sleep, 82442), SAN 365-4036. Tel: 307-366-2348. E-mail: tensleep@washakiecountylibrary.com. *Libr Dir,* Karen Funk
Pop 300
Library Holdings: Audiobooks 274; AV Mats 20; DVDs 1,176; e-books 68,129; e-journals 5,236; Large Print Bks 76; Bk Vols 29,208; Per Subs 21
Function: Free DVD rentals, Games, Holiday prog, Homebound delivery serv, ILL available, Instruction & testing, Internet access, Large print keyboards, Magazines, Magnifiers for reading, Meeting rooms, Online cat, OverDrive digital audio bks, Photocopying/Printing, Preschool reading prog, Prog for adults, Prog for children & young adult, Story hour, Wheelchair accessible, Workshops
Open Mon-Fri 8-5, Sat 9-1
Friends of the Library Group

LIBRARIES IN PUERTO RICO AND REGIONS ADMINISTERED BY THE UNITED STATES

AMERICAN SAMOA

MAPUSAGA

J AMERICAN SAMOA COMMUNITY COLLEGE LIBRARY*, Learning Resource Center, Malaeimi Village, Malaeimi Rd, 96799. (Mail add: PO Box 2609, Pago Pago, 96799-2609), SAN 365-4605. Circulation Tel: 684-699-9155, Ext 418. Reference Tel: 684-699-9155, Ext 419, 684-699-9155, Ext 420. E-mail: info@amsamoa.edu. Web Site: www.amsamoa.edu/institution/lrc.html. *Cat Supvr, Libr Assoc,* Pauline Tuluao; *Libr Assoc,* Mrs Faye Panama; *Libr Assoc,* Robinson Choo; *Libr Assoc,* Ms Diana Pereira; *Libr Assoc,* Sujaniah Reed; Staff 9 (MLS 1, Non-MLS 8)
Founded 1974. Enrl 1,000; Fac 50; Highest Degree: Bachelor
Library Holdings: AV Mats 1,640; Bk Titles 32,861; Bk Vols 35,941; Per Subs 108
Special Collections: Govt & Territory; Pacific & Samoa Coll. US Document Depository
Subject Interests: Anthrop, Archaeology, Creative writing, Ethnography, Forests, Geog, Geol, Indigenous art, Lang, Marine biol, Meteorology, Natural marine resources, Oceanography, Pac lit, Samoan hist
Automation Activity & Vendor Info: (Cataloging) Follett Software; (Circulation) Follett Software; (OPAC) Follett Software
Wireless access
Publications: Library Handbook
Open Mon-Fri 7:30-4

PAGO PAGO

P FELETI BARSTOW PUBLIC LIBRARY*, PO Box 997687, 96799. Tel: 684-633-5816. FAX: 684-633-5823. E-mail: feletibarstow@feletibarstow.info. Web Site: www.feletibarstow.org. *Territorial Librn,* Emma Solaita-Malele
Founded 2000
Library Holdings: Bk Titles 37,195
Automation Activity & Vendor Info: (Cataloging) Follett Software; (Circulation) Follett Software
Wireless access
Open Mon-Fri 9-5, Sat 10-2

HAGATNA

L GUAM LAW LIBRARY*, 141 San Ramon St, 96910-4333. SAN 324-8011. Tel: 671-477-7623. FAX: 671-472-1246. E-mail: gll@guamlawlibrary.org. Web Site: www.guamlawlibrary.org. *Exec Dir/Librn,* Geraldine Amparo Cepeda; E-mail: gcepeda@guamcourts.gov; Staff 3.5 (MLS 1, Non-MLS 2.5)
Founded 1978
Library Holdings: AV Mats 167; Electronic Media & Resources 6; Bk Titles 3,457; Bk Vols 26,747
Special Collections: Guam; Law; Pacific Islands
Automation Activity & Vendor Info: (Cataloging) ResourceMATE; (Circulation) ResourceMATE; (OPAC) ResourceMATE
Wireless access
Function: 24/7 Online cat, Computers for patron use, For res purposes, Internet access, Legal assistance to inmates, Meeting rooms, Orientations, Photocopying/Printing, Ref & res, Res performed for a fee, Scanner, Wheelchair accessible
Open Mon-Fri 8-6, Sat 9-1
Restriction: Circ limited

P GUAM PUBLIC LIBRARY SYSTEM*, Nieves M Flores Memorial Library, 254 Martyr St, 96910. Tel: 671-475-4753, 671-475-4754. FAX: 671-477-9777. E-mail: gpls@gpls.guam.gov. Web Site: gpls.guam.gov. *Dir,* Mr Krishnan Seerengan; E-mail: kris.seerengan@guampls.guam.gov
Library Holdings: AV Mats 1,200; Bk Vols 236,960; Per Subs 100
Special Collections: Guam History; Local Docs; Western Pacific Coll
Subject Interests: Classical lit, Gen ref, Western lit
Automation Activity & Vendor Info: (Acquisitions) Horizon; (Cataloging) Horizon; (Circulation) Horizon
Wireless access
Function: ILL available, Telephone ref
Publications: 1977 Pacific Daily News Index; Guam Newsletter; Index to Vital Statistics; Life of San Vitores; Union Catalog of Guam & Pacific Area Materials; Union List of Serials
Open Mon-Thurs 10-6, Sat 8:30-4:30
Branches: 4
AGAT PUBLIC LIBRARY-MARIA R AGUIGUI MEMORIAL LIBRARY, 165 Follard St, Agat, 96928. (Mail add: 254 Martyr St, 96910). Tel: 671-565-5006.
Open Tues 9-5:30
BARRIGADA PUBLIC LIBRARY, 177 San Rogue Dr, Barrigada, 96913. (Mail add: 254 Martyr St, 96910). Tel: 671-734-5007.
Open Thurs 9-5:30
DEDEDO PUBLIC LIBRARY, 283 W Santa Barbara Ave, Dededo, 96929. (Mail add: 254 Martyr St, 96910). Tel: 671-632-5503.
Open Tues 9:5:30
YONA PUBLIC LIBRARY, 265 Sister Mary Eucharita Dr, Yona, 96915. (Mail add: 254 Martyr St, 96910). Tel: 671-789-5010.
Open Wed 9-5:30
Bookmobiles: 1

MANGILAO

J GUAM COMMUNITY COLLEGE*, Learning Resource Center Library, One Sesame St, 96921. (Mail add: PO Box 23069, Barrigada, 96921). Tel: 671-735-0228, 671-735-0229. E-mail: gcc.library@guamcc.edu. Web Site: www.guamcc.edu/Pages/library.aspx. *Ref & Instruction Librn,* Christine Matson; Tel: 671-735-0231, E-mail: christine.matson@guamcc.edu; Staff 6 (MLS 2, Non-MLS 4)
Founded 1967. Enrl 2,500; Fac 186; Highest Degree: Associate
Library Holdings: Bk Vols 22,000; Per Subs 50
Special Collections: Pacific Coll
Subject Interests: Guam, Micronesia
Automation Activity & Vendor Info: (Cataloging) SirsiDynix; (Circulation) SirsiDynix; (Course Reserve) SirsiDynix; (OPAC) SirsiDynix
Wireless access
Open Mon-Thurs 8-8, Fri 8-4, Sat 9-Noon

C UNIVERSITY OF GUAM*, Richard F Taitano Micronesian Area Research Center, Guam & Micronesia Collection, UOG Sta, 96923. SAN 321-9887. Tel: 671-735-2157, 671-735-2160. Reference Tel: 671-735-2162. Administration Tel: 671-735-2750. FAX: 671-734-7403. Web Site: www.uog.edu/marc. *Assoc Prof, Spanish Doc Coll,* Omaira Brunal-Perry; E-mail: obrunal@triton.uog.edu; *Libr Tech I,* Dora P Herrero; *Libr Tech II,* Carmen F Quintanilla; Tel: 671-735-2161, E-mail: cquintan@uguam.uog.edu; *Ref (Info Servs),* Wai Yi Ma; E-mail: mau@triton.uog.edu; Staff 5 (MLS 2, Non-MLS 3)
Founded 1967. Enrl 4,200; Highest Degree: Master
Library Holdings: Bk Titles 25,000; Bk Vols 40,000
Special Collections: Manuscripts Coll; Reference Coll; Spanish Documents Coll
Subject Interests: Micronesia, Oceania
Automation Activity & Vendor Info: (Cataloging) SirsiDynix; (Circulation) SirsiDynix; (OPAC) SirsiDynix; (Serials) SirsiDynix
Wireless access
Function: For res purposes
Partic in National Network of Libraries of Medicine Region 5
Open Mon-Fri 9-5
Restriction: Non-circulating
Friends of the Library Group

C UNIVERSITY OF GUAM*, Robert F Kennedy Memorial Library, UOG Sta, 96913. SAN 318-5281. Tel: 671-735-2331, 671-735-2332. Interlibrary Loan Service Tel: 671-735-2311. Reference Tel: 671-735-2341. FAX: 671-734-6882. Web Site: www.uog.edu/student-services/rfk-library. *Dean,* Monique Carriveau Storie; Tel: 671-735-2333, E-mail: mstorie@triton.uog.edu; Staff 27 (MLS 9, Non-MLS 18)
Founded 1952. Enrl 3,500; Highest Degree: Master
Library Holdings: AV Mats 7,718; e-books 200,000; e-journals 24,190; Microforms 5,000; Bk Titles 119,000; Bk Vols 213,916; Per Subs 1,379
Special Collections: East Asian Coll; Juvenile Coll; Theses & Special Project Coll. US Document Depository

Subject Interests: Agr, Arts, Educ, Humanities, Libr sci, Lit, Mil sci, Sci, Soc sci
Automation Activity & Vendor Info: (Acquisitions) SirsiDynix; (Cataloging) SirsiDynix; (Circulation) SirsiDynix; (Course Reserve) SirsiDynix; (ILL) SirsiDynix; (Media Booking) SirsiDynix; (OPAC) SirsiDynix; (Serials) SirsiDynix
Wireless access
Partic in Midwest Collaborative for Library Services; National Network of Libraries of Medicine Region 5; OCLC Online Computer Library Center, Inc
Special Services for the Deaf - Adult & family literacy prog
Open Mon-Thurs 7:30-7:30, Fri 9-5, Sat 8-Noon; Mon-Thurs 7:30-5, Fri 9-5 (Spring)
Friends of the Library Group

YIGO

A UNITED STATES AIR FORCE*, Andersen Air Force Base Library, Bldg 25005, Hansell Ave, 96915. SAN 365-4575. Tel: 671-366-4291. FAX: 671-366-4978. E-mail: library3@us.af.mil. Web Site: www.militarymwrguam.com/programs/3dbae2d0-e397-409c-bad4-dabc17271575. *Libr Tech,* Cami Farrales; Staff 2 (MLS 1, Non-MLS 1)
Library Holdings: Bk Vols 33,500; Per Subs 125
Subject Interests: Air War College, Micronesia, Project warrior, SE Asia, The Pacific
Wireless access
Partic in Guam Libr Asn
Open Mon, Wed & Thurs 10-6, Tues 10-7, Fri & Sat 10-3

NORTHERN MARIANA ISLANDS

SAIPAN

P JOETEN-KIYU PUBLIC LIBRARY*, 2745 Insatto St, 96950. (Mail add: PO Box 501092, 96950-1092), SAN 377-0419. Tel: 670-235-7322, 670-235-7323. Administration Tel: 670-235-7316. FAX: 670-235-7350. E-mail: cnmistatelibrary@gmail.com. Web Site: cnmilib.org. *Libr Dir,* Erlinda C Naputi; E-mail: ecnaputi@gmail.com; Staff 9 (MLS 1, Non-MLS 8)
Founded 1992. Pop 78,252
Library Holdings: AV Mats 3,088; Bk Titles 36,735; Bk Vols 40,540; Per Subs 101; Talking Bks 100
Special Collections: Pacific Area & World War II Pacific (Pacific Reference Coll); Saipan, Tinian & Rota History, 1972-1994
Automation Activity & Vendor Info: (Cataloging) SirsiDynix; (Circulation) SirsiDynix
Wireless access
Function: AV serv, Homebound delivery serv, Internet access, Prog for adults, Prog for children & young adult, Summer reading prog, Wheelchair accessible, Workshops
Open Tues-Fri 10-6, Sat 9-4; Tues-Thurs 9-5, Fri 9-6, Sat 10-4 (Summer)
Friends of the Library Group
Branches: 2
ANTONIO C ATALIG MEMORIAL PUBLIC LIBRARY (ROTA PUBLIC), PO Box 537, Rota, 96951, SAN 376-835X. Tel: 670-532-7328. FAX: 670-532-7328. Web Site: www.cnmilib.org/branch-libraries/antonio-c-atalig-memorial-library. *Asst Librn,* Bergitt Maratita; E-mail: bertagirl_8002@yahoo.com
Open Mon-Fri 8:30-4:30, Sat 8-12
TINIAN PUBLIC, PO Box 520704, Tinian, 96952, SAN 376-8368. Tel: 670-433-0504. FAX: 670-433-0450. E-mail: tinianpubliclibrary@gmail.com. Web Site: www.cnmilib.org/branch-libraries/tinian-public-library. *Asst Librn,* Marvieluz Syed; Staff 1 (MLS 1)
Library Holdings: Bk Vols 3,200; Per Subs 10
Open Mon-Fri 8-5
Bookmobiles: 1. Outreach Asst, Xerxes W Mangarero. Bk titles 15,000

J NORTHERN MARIANAS COLLEGE*, Olympio T Borja Memorial Library, Fina Sisu Lane, Bldg O, 96950. (Mail add: PO Box 501250, 96950), SAN 378-0848. Tel: 670-237-6799. Administration Tel: 670-237-6820. FAX: 670-234-0759. Web Site: www.marianas.edu/library. *Dir,* Matthew Pastula; E-mail: matthew.pastula@marianas.edu; Staff 8 (MLS 4, Non-MLS 4)
Founded 1981. Enrl 1,239; Fac 91; Highest Degree: Bachelor
Library Holdings: AV Mats 850; Bk Titles 30,000; Bk Vols 44,000; Per Subs 520
Wireless access
Open Mon-Thurs 8-5, Fri 8-12
Departmental Libraries:
CNMI ARCHIVES & PACIFIC COLLECTION, PO Box 501250, 96950, SAN 378-1860. Tel: 670-237-6795. FAX: 670-234-0759. *Archivist Tech,* Position Currently Open
Library Holdings: Bk Vols 7,500; Per Subs 350
Open Mon-Fri 8-5

PUERTO RICO

AGUADILLA

C INTER-AMERICAN UNIVERSITY OF PUERTO RICO*, Aguadilla Campus Library, Carretera 459, Int 463 Barrio Corrales, Sector Calero, 00605. (Mail add: PO Box 20000, 00605), SAN 318-5346. Tel: 787-891-0925. Circulation Tel: 787-891-0925, Ext 2253. Reference Tel: 787-891-0925, Ext 2255. FAX: 787-882-3020. E-mail: cai@aguadilla.inter.edu. Web Site: www.aguadilla.inter.edu/elcai. *Libr Dir,* Lizzie Colon; E-mail: lcolon@aguadilla.inter.edu; *Coll Develop Librn,* Maria Vazquez; E-mail: mvazquez@aguadilla.inter.edu; Staff 11 (MLS 2, Non-MLS 9)
Founded 1968. Enrl 3,517; Fac 199; Highest Degree: Master
Library Holdings: AV Mats 7,579; DVDs 1,063; e-books 668; e-journals 42; Electronic Media & Resources 69; Bk Vols 61,996; Per Subs 1,063
Special Collections: Manuel Mendez Ballister Coll
Subject Interests: Lit
Wireless access
Publications: Faculty catalog; Periodical catalog; Student catalog
Open Mon-Thurs 8am-8:30pm, Fri 8-5, Sat 8-1

ARECIBO

C INTER-AMERICAN UNIVERSITY OF PUERTO RICO*, Biblioteca Rene Marques, Barrio San Daniel, Carretera 2, km 80.4, 00614. (Mail add: PO Box 4050, 00614-4050), SAN 318-5362. Tel: 787-878-5475, Ext 2321. FAX: 787-880-1624. Web Site: www.arecibo.inter.edu/cai. *Dir,* Sara Abreu; E-mail: sabreu@arecibo.inter.edu; Staff 14 (MLS 2, Non-MLS 12)
Founded 1958. Enrl 3,500; Fac 100; Highest Degree: Master
Library Holdings: Bk Titles 57,389; Bk Vols 67,960; Per Subs 315
Subject Interests: Anesthesia, Biology, Census, Criminal justice, Doc, Educ, Microbiology, Nursing
Automation Activity & Vendor Info: (Acquisitions) SirsiDynix; (Cataloging) SirsiDynix; (Circulation) SirsiDynix; (Course Reserve) SirsiDynix; (ILL) SirsiDynix; (Media Booking) SirsiDynix; (OPAC) SirsiDynix; (Serials) SirsiDynix

C PONTIFICIA CATHOLIC UNIVERSITY OF PUERTO RICO, ARECIBO, Monseñor Iñaki Mallona Library, PO Box 144045, 00614-4045. SAN 318-5354. Tel: 787-881-1212, Ext 6028. Web Site: arecibo.pucpr.edu/vida-estudiantil/bibliotecas.
Founded 1973. Enrl 1,300
Library Holdings: Bk Titles 42,000; Bk Vols 50,000; Per Subs 642
Special Collections: Puerto Rican Coll, bks & printed mat
Automation Activity & Vendor Info: (Acquisitions) Koha; (Cataloging) Koha; (Circulation) Koha; (Course Reserve) Koha; (ILL) Koha; (Media Booking) Koha; (OPAC) Koha; (Serials) Koha
Wireless access
Open Mon-Thurs 8am-10pm, Fri 8am-9pm, Sat 8-4

C UNIVERSITY OF PUERTO RICO*, Arecibo University College Library, Sector Las Dunas, Carr 653 Km 0.8, 00612. (Mail add: PO Box 4010, 00614-4010), SAN 318-5370. Tel: 787-815-0000, Ext 3150. Circulation Tel: 787-815-0000, Ext 3155. Interlibrary Loan Service Tel: 787-815-0000, Ext 3172. Reference Tel: 787-815-0000, Ext 3175. Administration Tel: 787-815-0000, Ext 5000. Automation Services Tel: 787-815-0000, Ext 3153. FAX: 787-878-9363. Web Site: www.upr.edu/biblioteca-upra/. *Dir,* Victor Maldonado; E-mail: victor.maldonado1@upr.edu; *Bibliog Instr,* Jadira Maldonado; *Coll Develop,* Leon Santos; Tel: 787-815-0000, Ext 3161, E-mail: leon.santos@upr.edu; *Media Spec,* Marinilda Fuentes; *Ref (Info Servs),* Angel Corchado; Tel: 787-815-0000, Ext 3175, E-mail: angel.corchado@upr.edu; Staff 6 (MLS 6)
Founded 1967. Enrl 3,445; Fac 225; Highest Degree: Bachelor
Library Holdings: Bk Titles 62,906; Bk Vols 79,845; Per Subs 2,460
Special Collections: Arecibo Region Historical Coll; Francisco Matos Paoli Private Library; Juvenile Coll
Subject Interests: Biology, Computer sci, Educ, Nursing
Open Mon 7am-8:50pm, Tues-Thurs 7am-9:50pm, Fri 7-4:20, Sat 8-4:20

BARRANQUITAS

C INTER-AMERICAN UNIVERSITY OF PUERTO RICO*, Barranquitas Campus Library, Bo Helechal, Carr 156 Intersiccion 719, 00794. (Mail add: PO Box 517, 00794), SAN 318-5389. Tel: 787-857-2585, 787-857-3600, Ext 2013. Reference Tel: 787-857-3600, Ext 2022, 787-857-3600, Ext 2075. FAX: 787-857-2244. Web Site: www.br.inter.edu. *Libr Dir,* Eleane Rosado; E-mail: erosado@br.inter.edu; Staff 3 (MLS 3)
Founded 1959. Enrl 1,250; Highest Degree: Doctorate
Jul 2022-Jun 2023. Mats Exp $79,000, Books $15,000, Per/Ser (Incl. Access Fees) $15,000, Other Print Mats $1,000, AV Mat $1,000, Electronic Ref Mat (Incl. Access Fees) $47,000. Sal $149,616 (Prof $2,400)
Library Holdings: Braille Volumes 4; CDs 542; DVDs 1,085; e-books 371,816; e-journals 33,468; Electronic Media & Resources 156,334; Large Print Bks 2; Bk Titles 35,771; Bk Vols 40,622; Per Subs 30; Talking Bks 13; Videos 243
Automation Activity & Vendor Info: (Acquisitions) SirsiDynix; (Cataloging) OCLC; (Circulation) SirsiDynix; (Course Reserve) SirsiDynix; (OPAC) SirsiDynix
Wireless access
Function: 24/7 Electronic res, 24/7 Online cat, 3D Printer, Audio & video playback equip for onsite use, Audiobks via web, Bks on cassette, CD-ROM, Computer training, Computers for patron use, Distance learning, Electronic databases & coll, ILL available, Internet access, Large print keyboards, Magazines, Magnifiers for reading, Mail & tel request accepted, Meeting rooms, Movies, Museum passes, Online cat, Outside serv via phone, mail, e-mail & web, Photocopying/Printing, Ref serv available, Res assist avail, Res libr, Scanner, Spanish lang bks, Study rm, Telephone ref, VHS videos
Partic in OCLC Online Computer Library Center, Inc
Special Services for the Blind - Accessible computers; Aids for in-house use; Assistive/Adapted tech devices, equip & products
Open Mon-Thurs 7am-9pm, Fri 7-5, Sat 7-4

Restriction: 24-hr pass syst for students only, Access at librarian's discretion, Authorized personnel only, Circ limited, External users must contact libr, ID required to use computers (Ltd hrs), In-house use for visitors, Non-circulating of rare bks, Non-circulating to the pub

BAYAMON

C INTER-AMERICAN UNIVERSITY OF PUERTO RICO*, Recinto de Bayamon, 500 Carretera Dr, John Will Harris, 00957-6257. SAN 318-5400. Tel: 787-279-1912, Ext 2174. Circulation Tel: 787-279-1912, Ext 2259. FAX: 787-279-2205. E-mail: cai@bayamon.inter.edu. Web Site: bayamonweb.azurewebsites.net/cai. *Dir,* Sandra Rosa Gomez; Tel: 787-279-7312, Ext 2149, E-mail: srosa@bayamon.inter.edu; *Librn I,* Norma E Vazquez Figueroa; Tel: 787-279-7312, Ext 2176, E-mail: nvazquez@baymon.inter.edu; Staff 4 (MLS 4)
Founded 1967. Enrl 4,701
Library Holdings: Bk Vols 57,880; Per Subs 1,228
Special Collections: Interamerican Press; Puerto Rico
Subject Interests: Sci
Wireless access
Partic in National Network of Libraries of Medicine Region 2
Open Mon-Thurs 7am-9pm, Fri 7-5, Sat 7-4

§C UNIVERSIDAD CENTRAL DE BAYAMON, Biblioteca CRAAI, PO Box 1725, 00960-1725. Tel: 787-786-3030, Ext 2136. Web Site: ucb.edu.pr/biblioteca-craai. *Dir,* Yanit Delgado Ramos; Tel: 787-786-3030, Ext 2135, E-mail: ydelgado@ucb.edu.pr
Founded 1978
Special Collections: Dr Cesareo Rosa Nieves Coll; Dr Manuel Zeno Gandia Coll; Isabel Gutierrez de Arroyo Coll; Puerto Rican Coll; UCB Historical Archive
Automation Activity & Vendor Info: (Cataloging) Mandarin Library Automation; (OPAC) Mandarin Library Automation
Function: Internet access, Photocopying/Printing
Special Services for the Blind - Accessible computers; Magnifiers
Open Mon-Thurs 8-8, Fri & Sat 8-5

CM UNIVERSIDAD CENTRAL DEL CARIBE*, Biblioteca Arturo L Carrion Pacheco, Avenida Laurel, Santa Juanita, 00956. (Mail add: PO Box 60327, 00960-6032), SAN 370-7288. Tel: 787-785-6039, 787-798-3001, Ext 2304. Information Services Tel: 787-798-3001, Ext 2309. FAX: 787-785-3425. E-mail: ucc@uccaribe.edu. Web Site: www.uccaribe.edu/library. *Dir, Med Libr,* Mildred I Rivera; Tel: 787-798-3001, Ext 2305, E-mail: mildred.rivera@uccaribe.edu; *Per Librn, Ser Librn,* David Saldaña; Tel: 787-798-3001, Ext 2344, E-mail: david.saldana@uccaribe.edu; *Tech Serv Librn,* Jammilah Soto; Tel: 787-798-3001, Ext 2306, E-mail: jammilah.soto@uccaribe.edu; *Libr Asst,* Rafael Santos; E-mail: rafael.santos@uccaribe.edu; *Libr Asst,* Position Currently Open; Staff 5 (MLS 3, Non-MLS 2)
Founded 1976. Fac 115; Highest Degree: Doctorate
Library Holdings: DVDs 114; e-books 1,471; e-journals 5,753; Electronic Media & Resources 40; Bk Titles 4,651; Per Subs 197
Special Collections: Health Sciences Coll
Subject Interests: Anatomy, Biochem, Cell biol, Chiropractic, Imaging, Microbiology, Molecular biol, Neuroscience, Pharmacology, Physiology, Substance abuse
Automation Activity & Vendor Info: (Cataloging) EOS International; (Circulation) EOS International; (OPAC) EOS International; (Serials) EOS International
Wireless access
Function: 24/7 Electronic res, 24/7 Online cat, 3D Printer, Activity rm, AV serv, Doc delivery serv, Health sci info serv, ILL available, Internet access, Photocopying/Printing, Res libr
Partic in National Network of Libraries of Medicine Region 2
Open Mon-Thurs 7am-10pm, Fri 7-6, Sat & Sun 12-8:30
Restriction: 24-hr pass syst for students only, Authorized patrons, Authorized personnel only, Badge access after hrs, Open to pub for ref & circ; with some limitations, Photo ID required for access, Prof mat only

CAROLINA

C UNIVERSIDAD ANA G MENDEZ*, Biblioteca Carolina, Calle 190, Esquina 220 Bo Sabana Abajo, 00983. (Mail add: PO Box 2010, 00984-2010), SAN 320-0515. Tel: 787-257-7373, Ext 2504. Circulation Tel: 787-257-7373, Ext 2507. Reference Tel: 787-257-7373. FAX: 787-257-8790. E-mail: biblioteca_car@uagm.edu. Web Site: myuagm.uagm.edu/web/une-servicios-al-estudiante/biblioteca1. *Dir,* Carmen T Perez Gonzalez; Tel: 787-257-7373, Ext 2550, E-mail: ctperez@uagm.edu; *Librn,* Johana Martinez Rodriguez; E-mail: jomartinez@uagm.edu; Staff 28 (MLS 13, Non-MLS 15)
Founded 1949. Enrl 9,300; Fac 96; Highest Degree: Master
Library Holdings: Bk Titles 50,133; Bk Vols 80,132; Per Subs 370
Special Collections: Ana G Mendez; Jesus T Pinero Numismatica
Subject Interests: Bus admin, Computers, Criminal justice, Educ, Radiology, Sciences
Automation Activity & Vendor Info: (Acquisitions) Ex Libris Group; (Cataloging) Ex Libris Group; (Circulation) Ex Libris Group; (OPAC) Ex Libris Group; (Serials) Ex Libris Group
Wireless access
Function: AV serv, Photocopying/Printing, Ref serv available
Publications: Biblio-Notas; La Revista Informa; Lista de nuevas Adquisiciones (Acquisition list); Manual del CRA para la Facultad; Manual del CRA para los Estudiantes
Partic in LYRASIS
Open Mon-Thurs 7am-8pm, Fri & Sat 8-5

CAYEY

C UNIVERSITY OF PUERTO RICO LIBRARY, CAYEY CAMPUS, Biblioteca Victor M Pons Gil, 205 Ave Antonio R Barcelo, Ste 205, 00736. (Mail add: PO Box 372230, 00737-2230), SAN 318-5443. Tel: 787-738-2161, Ext 2021. Administration Tel: 787-738-5651. Web Site: www.upr.edu/biblioteca-uprcy. *Interim Dir, Spec Coll Librn,* Aixa Leon Nogueras; Tel: 787-738-2161, Ext 2226, E-mail: aixa.leon@upr.edu; *Spec Coll Librn,* Gustavo Salvarrey Iranzo; Tel: 787-738-2161, Ext 2026, E-mail: gustavo.salvarrey@upr.edu; *Ref Librn,* Sonia Davila Cosme; Tel: 787-738-2161, Ext 2131, E-mail: sonia.davila@upr.edu; Staff 28 (MLS 7, Non-MLS 21)
Founded 1967. Enrl 3,202; Fac 240; Highest Degree: Bachelor
Library Holdings: Bk Vols 192,757; Per Subs 1,706
Special Collections: Education & Children's/Young Adult Literature (Joan Miller Room); Hector Campos Parsi Coll; Miguel Melendez Munoz Historical Archive; Music & Media Coll; Puerto Rican Coll; Women & Gender (Luisa Capetillo Room)
Subject Interests: Bus admin, Educ, Humanities, Natural sci, Soc sci, Women
Automation Activity & Vendor Info: (Cataloging) SirsiDynix; (OPAC) SirsiDynix; (Serials) EBSCO Online
Wireless access
Publications: Acquisition List; Bibliographies
Special Services for the Deaf - Assistive tech
Special Services for the Blind - Assistive/Adapted tech devices, equip & products
Open Mon-Thurs 8am-9pm, Fri 8-4:30

FAJARDO

C INTER-AMERICAN UNIVERSITY OF PUERTO RICO - FAJARDO CAMPUS*, Emilio S Belaval Information Access Center, Calle Union, Batey Central, Carretera 195, 00738. (Mail add: Call Box 70003, 00738-7003), SAN 365-4966. Tel: 787-863-2390. Interlibrary Loan Service Tel: 787-863-2390, Ext 2226. FAX: 787-860-3470. Web Site: fajardo.inter.edu. *Dir,* Angie E Colon; Tel: 787-863-2390, Ext 2213, E-mail: angie.colon@fajardo.inter.edu; *Librn,* Yolianna Leon Santos; Tel: 787-863-2390, Ext 2322, E-mail: Yolianna.leon@fajardo.inter.edu; Staff 9 (MLS 3, Non-MLS 6)
Founded 1961. Enrl 1,860; Fac 35; Highest Degree: Bachelor
Library Holdings: Bk Titles 27,000; Bk Vols 34,000; Per Subs 675
Special Collections: Puerto Rico Data Census Center
Subject Interests: Recycling
Wireless access
Open Mon-Thurs 7am-10pm, Fri 7-5, Sat 7:30-5

FORT BUCHANAN

A UNITED STATES ARMY*, Fort Buchanan Post Library, Post Library, Bldg 518, 518 Depot Rd, 00965. SAN 365-5024. Tel: 787-707-3208. Administration Tel: 787-707-3812. FAX: 787-707-3480. Web Site: buchanan.armymwr.com/programs/library. *Supvry Librn,* Eva Cabanas-Malave; E-mail: eva.j.cabanas-malave.naf@mail.mil; Staff 6 (MLS 2, Non-MLS 4)
Library Holdings: Bk Titles 28,787; Bk Vols 29,888; Per Subs 200
Special Collections: Children's Coll
Wireless access
Partic in OCLC Online Computer Library Center, Inc
Open Tues-Fri 10-8, Sat 10-5

GUAYAMA

C INTER-AMERICAN UNIVERSITY OF PUERTO RICO*, Guayama Campus Library, Bo Machete, Carr 744, 00784. SAN 318-5478. Tel: 787-864-2222. FAX: 787-864-8232. Web Site: www.guayama.inter.edu. *Dir,* Edny Santiago; E-mail: edsantiago@guayama.inter.edu; *Librn,* Mrs Wilma Gual Ocasio; E-mail: wilma.gual@guayama.inter.edu; Staff 10 (MLS 3, Non-MLS 7)
Founded 1958. Fac 35
Library Holdings: AV Mats 1,998; e-books 500,000; e-journals 150; Electronic Media & Resources 32; Bk Vols 29,500; Per Subs 75
Special Collections: Afro-antillian Poetry Coll; Luis Palis Matos Coll
Subject Interests: Educ, Humanities, Nursing, Sci

Automation Activity & Vendor Info: (Cataloging) SirsiDynix; (Circulation) SirsiDynix
Publications: Infocai Bulletin
Friends of the Library Group

GURABO

C UNIVERSIDAD DEL TURABO*, Learning Center, Rd 189 Km 3.3, 00778. SAN 321-611X. Tel: 787-743-7979, Ext 4501. Circulation Tel: 787-743-7979, Ext 4522. Reference Tel: 787-743-7979, Ext 4515. FAX: 787-743-7924. E-mail: biiblioteca@uagm.edu. Web Site: ut.suagm.edu. *Vice Chancellor of Info Serv,* Sarai Lastra; *Interim Libr Dir,* Melva L Rivera Caraballos; *Dir, Info Tech,* Luis A Arroyo; *Director, IT & Telecom,* Jose Medina; E-mail: ut_jmedina@suagm.edu; *Librn, Cat,* Myriam Martinez; *Asst Librn,* Marlene Galafa; *Asst Librn, Circ,* Lydia E Martinez; Staff 17 (MLS 7, Non-MLS 10)
Founded 1969. Enrl 15,000; Highest Degree: Master
Library Holdings: e-books 6,000; e-journals 30,000; Bk Titles 94,000; Bk Vols 150,000; Per Subs 450
Automation Activity & Vendor Info: (Acquisitions) Ex Libris Group; (Cataloging) Ex Libris Group; (Circulation) Ex Libris Group; (Course Reserve) Ex Libris Group; (OPAC) Ex Libris Group; (Serials) Ex Libris Group
Wireless access
Publications: Acquisitions List
Open Mon-Thurs 8am-9pm, Fri 8-6, Sat 8-5

HATO REY

CL INTER-AMERICAN UNIVERSITY OF PUERTO RICO*, School of Law Library, PO Box 70351, 00936. SAN 318-5818. Tel: 787-751-1912. Circulation Tel: 787-751-1912, Ext 2075. Interlibrary Loan Service Tel: 787-751-1912, Ext 2027. Reference Tel: 787-751-1912, Ext 2029. Administration Tel: 787-751-1912, Ext 2042. Automation Services Tel: 787-751-1912, Ext 2066. Web Site: www.inter.edu. *Asst Prof, Libr Dir,* Hector Ruben Sanchez; E-mail: hrsanchez@juris.inter.edu; *Librn III,* Dr Ivonne Quintero; Tel: 787-751-1912, Ext 2160, E-mail: ivquintero@juris.inter.edu; *Librn III, Ref Serv,* Maria Estrada; Tel: 787-751-1912, Ext 2098, E-mail: mestrada@juris.inter.edu; *Librn III,* Luz D Pizarro; E-mail: lpizarro@juris.inter.edu; *Librn III,* Delia Cruz; Tel: 787-751-1912, Ext 2031, E-mail: dcruz@juris.inter.edu; *Law Librn, Per Librn,* Jose Manuel Estrada; Tel: 787-751-1912, Ext 2064, E-mail: jestrada@juris.inter.edu; *Spec Coll Librn,* Lillian E Santiago; Tel: 787-751-1912, Ext 2300, E-mail: lsantiago@juris.inter.edu; Staff 18 (MLS 7, Non-MLS 11)
Founded 1961. Enrl 800; Fac 30; Highest Degree: Doctorate
Library Holdings: Per Subs 350
Special Collections: Domingo Toledo Alamo Coll; Fernos Coll; Jose Echeverria Coll
Subject Interests: Civil law
Automation Activity & Vendor Info: (Acquisitions) SirsiDynix; (Cataloging) SirsiDynix; (Circulation) SirsiDynix; (Course Reserve) SirsiDynix; (Media Booking) SirsiDynix; (OPAC) SirsiDynix; (Serials) SirsiDynix
Wireless access
Publications: Acquisitions List; Bibliographies
Open Mon-Thurs 8am-11pm, Fri 8am-10pm, Sat 8-8, Sun 11-8

L MCCONNELL VALDES*, 270 Munoz Rivera Ave, 00918. (Mail add: PO Box 364225, San Juan, 00936-4225), SAN 371-9316. Tel: 787-759-9292. FAX: 787-759-9225. *Library Contact,* Aileen Vias; E-mail: avc@mcvpr.com; Staff 5 (MLS 1, Non-MLS 4)
Founded 1947
Library Holdings: Bk Titles 40,000; Bk Vols 58,000; Per Subs 124
Subject Interests: Corporate law, Taxes
Automation Activity & Vendor Info: (Cataloging) Follett Software; (OPAC) Follett Software; (Serials) Follett Software
Partic in Proquest Dialog
Restriction: Staff use only

L UNITED STATES COURT OF APPEALS*, First Circuit Satellite Library, Federico Degetau Federal Bldg, Rm 121, 150 Carlos Chardon St, 00918. SAN 372-3585. Tel: 787-772-3097. Web Site: www.prd.uscourts.gov. *Satellite Librn,* Jose Luis Garcia; E-mail: jose_garcia@ca1.uscourts.gov; *Libr Tech,* Ana Maria Espinosa Cancel; E-mail: ana_espinosacancel@ca1.uscourts.gov
Library Holdings: Bk Vols 30,000; Per Subs 50
Wireless access
Partic in Lexis, OCLC Online Computer Libr Ctr, Inc
Restriction: Not open to pub

MAYAGUEZ

C PONTIFICAL CATHOLIC UNIVERSITY OF PUERTO RICO*, Mayaguez Branch Library, Ramon Emeterio Betances St 482, 00680. (Mail add: PO Box 1326, 00681-1326), SAN 318-5540. Tel: 787-834-5151, Ext 5008, 787-834-5151, Ext 5051. Information Services Tel: 787-834-5151, Ext 5011. FAX: 787-831-7155. E-mail: bibliotecam@pucpr.edu, edramos@pucpr.edu. Web Site: mayaguez.pucpr.edu/vida-estudiantil/biblioteca-beato-carlos-manuel. *Libr Dir,* Edwin Ramos Caban; *Ref Serv,* Edwin Camacho; Tel: 787-834-5151, Ext 5012, E-mail: edramos@pucpr.edu; *Ref Librn,* Mrs Omayra Irizarry Oliveras; Tel: 787-834-5151, Ext 5010, E-mail: omayra_irizarry@pucpr.edu; Staff 5 (MLS 3, Non-MLS 2)
Enrl 1,800; Fac 100; Highest Degree: Master
Library Holdings: AV Mats 1,150; DVDs 45; e-books 47,000; Bk Titles 35,774; Bk Vols 37,987; Per Subs 78; Videos 889
Subject Interests: Gen (encyclopedias), Relig, Sci
Automation Activity & Vendor Info: (Acquisitions) Horizon; (Cataloging) Horizon; (Circulation) Horizon; (ILL) Horizon; (Media Booking) Horizon; (OPAC) Horizon; (Serials) Horizon
Wireless access
Open Mon-Thurs 7:30am-9pm, Fri 8-4, Sat 9-1

C UNIVERSIDAD ADVENTISTA DE LAS ANTILLAS*, Biblioteca Dennis Soto, Carr 106 Km 2.2, Bo La Quinta, 00680. (Mail add: PO Box 118, 00681). Tel: 787-834-9595, Ext 2216, 787-834-9595, Ext 2993. FAX: 787-834-9597. E-mail: library@uaa.edu. Web Site: www.uaa.edu/biblioteca-dennis-soto. *Dir,* Aixa Vega; Tel: 787-834-9595, Ext 2216, E-mail: avega@uaa.edu; Staff 6 (MLS 3, Non-MLS 3)
Founded 1961. Enrl 767; Fac 72; Highest Degree: Master
Library Holdings: e-books 7,000; e-journals 7,000; Bk Vols 87,706; Per Subs 353
Special Collections: Puerto Rico Coll
Subject Interests: Theol
Automation Activity & Vendor Info: (Cataloging) Mandarin Library Automation; (OPAC) Mandarin Library Automation
Open Mon-Thurs 7:30am-8:30pm, Fri 7:30-1, Sun 3-8

C UNIVERSITY OF PUERTO RICO*, Mayaguez Campus General Library, Alfonso Valdes Ave, 259 Blvd, 00681. (Mail add: PO Box 9000, 00681), SAN 365-5172. Tel: 787-265-3810, 787-832-4040, Ext 2151, 787-832-4040, Ext 2155. Circulation Tel: 787-832-4040, Ext 2159. Interlibrary Loan Service Tel: 787-832-4040, Ext 2205, 787-832-4040, Ext 3752. Reference Tel: 787-832-4040, Ext 2023, 787-832-4040, Ext 2259. FAX: 787-265-5483. E-mail: library@uprm.edu. Web Site: www.upr.edu/biblioteca-rum. *Dir,* Dr Anidza Valentin; E-mail: anidza.valentin@upr.edu; Staff 68 (MLS 25, Non-MLS 43)
Founded 1911. Enrl 12,311; Fac 1,100; Highest Degree: Doctorate
Library Holdings: CDs 2,036; DVDs 132; e-books 5,294; e-journals 38,875; Microforms 284,007; Music Scores 422; Bk Titles 164,303; Bk Vols 215,861; Per Subs 1,046; Videos 4,729
Special Collections: Marine Sciences Coll; Sala Manuel Maria Sama (Puerto Rican Coll). State Document Depository; US Document Depository
Subject Interests: Applied tech, Bus, Census data, Chem engr, Civil engr, Computer engr, Electrical engr, Electronic res, Indust engr, Marine sci, Mechanical engr, Natural sci, Patents trademarks, Soc sci, Visually impaired
Automation Activity & Vendor Info: (Acquisitions) SirsiDynix; (Cataloging) SirsiDynix; (Circulation) SirsiDynix; (OPAC) SirsiDynix; (Serials) SirsiDynix
Wireless access
Function: Art exhibits, Audio & video playback equip for onsite use, AV serv, Computers for patron use, E-Reserves, Electronic databases & coll, Govt ref serv, ILL available, Instruction & testing, Internet access, Large print keyboards, Literacy & newcomer serv, Magnifiers for reading, Mail & tel request accepted, Music CDs, Online cat, Online info literacy tutorials on the web & in blackboard, Online ref, Orientations, Outside serv via phone, mail, e-mail & web, Photocopying/Printing, Ref & res, Ref serv available, Telephone ref, VHS videos, Workshops
Partic in Associated Colleges of the Midwest; LYRASIS; OCLC Online Computer Library Center, Inc
Special Services for the Deaf - Assistive tech
Special Services for the Blind - Accessible computers; Assistive/Adapted tech devices, equip & products; Compressed speech equip; Computer with voice synthesizer for visually impaired persons; Internet workstation with adaptive software; Large screen computer & software; Magnifiers; Networked computers with assistive software
Open Mon-Thurs 6am-2am, Fri 6-4:30, Sat 12-5, Sun 2-Midnight
Restriction: Non-circulating of rare bks
Departmental Libraries:
MARINE SCIENCE, PO Box 9022, 00681-9022. Tel: 787-832-4040, Ext 2513. *Library Contact,* Deixter Mendez; Staff 2 (MLS 1, Non-MLS 1)
Library Holdings: Bk Titles 4,741; Bk Vols 5,449; Per Subs 42
Subject Interests: Aquaculture, Chem oceanography, Fisheries biol, Marine biol
Open Mon-Fri 7:30-4

MERCEDITA

C INTER-AMERICAN UNIVERSITY OF PUERTO RICO*, Ponce Campus Library, 104 Parque Industrial Turpeaux, Rd 1, 00715-1602. SAN 318-5575. Tel: 787-284-1912. Interlibrary Loan Service Tel: 787-284-1912, Ext 2119. FAX: 787-841-0103. E-mail: webcai@ponce.inter.edu. Web Site: ponce.inter.edu/cai. *Info Access Ctr Dir,* Maria Silvestrini; E-mail: msilvest@ponce.inter.edu; *Cataloger, Librn,* Ana Rosa Matos; Tel: 787-284-1912, Ext 2520, E-mail: amatos@ponce.inter.edu; *Coll Develop, Librn,* Jeannette Caban-Padilla; Tel: 787-284-1912, Ext 2125, E-mail: jcaban@ponce.inter.edu; *Librn, Literacy Serv,* Marie Eleane Melendez; Tel: 787-284-1912, Ext 2114, E-mail: mmelende@ponce.inter.edu; *Circ, Libr Asst,* Reinaldo Cintron; Tel: 787-284-1912, Ext 2287, E-mail: rcintron@ponce.inter.edu; *Libr Asst, Ser,* Lucila Jorge; Tel: 787-284-1912, Ext 2170, E-mail: ljorge@ponce.inter.edu; *Webmaster,* Walberto Rodriguez; Tel: 787-284-1912, Ext 2128, E-mail: warodri@ponce.inter.edu; Staff 8 (MLS 4, Non-MLS 4)
Founded 1966. Enrl 4,500; Fac 103; Highest Degree: Doctorate
Library Holdings: AV Mats 2,247; CDs 219; DVDs 691; e-books 262,489; Bk Titles 56,990; Bk Vols 65,030; Per Subs 160
Special Collections: Maria Teresa Babin Coll
Subject Interests: Applied sci, Computers, Econ, Educ
Automation Activity & Vendor Info: (Acquisitions) SirsiDynix-WorkFlows; (Cataloging) SirsiDynix-WorkFlows; (Circulation) SirsiDynix-WorkFlows; (Course Reserve) SirsiDynix-WorkFlows; (Discovery) SirsiDynix-WorkFlows; (ILL) SirsiDynix-WorkFlows; (Media Booking) SirsiDynix-WorkFlows; (OPAC) SirsiDynix-WorkFlows
Wireless access
Function: Ref serv available
Restriction: Not open to pub, Open to students

PONCE

CM PONCE HEALTH SCIENCES UNIVERSITY LIBRARY, 395 Zona Industrial Reparada 2, Calle Dr Luis F Sala, 00716-2348. (Mail add: PO Box 7004, 00732), SAN 371-425X. Tel: 787-840-2575. Circulation Tel: 787-840-2575, Ext 4825. Interlibrary Loan Service Tel: 787-840-2575, Ext 4828. Reference Tel: 787-840-2575, Ext 4823. E-mail: library@psm.edu. Web Site: www.psm.edu/library. *Dir,* Carmen G Malavet; E-mail: cmalavet@psm.edu; Staff 9 (MLS 3, Non-MLS 6)
Founded 1977. Enrl 2,138; Fac 941; Highest Degree: Doctorate
Jul 2023-Jun 2024 Income $822,000. Mats Exp $184,088, Books $4,613, Per/Ser (Incl. Access Fees) $97,107, AV Mat $23,796, Electronic Ref Mat (Incl. Access Fees) $58,572. Sal $225,447 (Prof $270,542)
Library Holdings: AV Mats 631; CDs 302; DVDs 85; e-books 53,937; e-journals 58,572; Electronic Media & Resources 3; Bk Titles 7,045; Per Subs 59; Videos 134
Special Collections: Puerto Rican Coll, bks, journals
Automation Activity & Vendor Info: (Cataloging) TLC (The Library Corporation); (Circulation) TLC (The Library Corporation); (OPAC) TLC (The Library Corporation); (Serials) TLC (The Library Corporation)
Wireless access
Function: 24/7 Electronic res, 24/7 Online cat, AV serv, Bks on CD, CD-ROM, Computer training, Computers for patron use, Doc delivery serv, E-Reserves, Electronic databases & coll, Health sci info serv, Holiday prog, ILL available, Internet access, Large print keyboards, Learning ctr, Magazines, Magnifiers for reading, Mail & tel request accepted, Meeting rooms, Movies, Online cat, Online info literacy tutorials on the web & in blackboard, Online ref, Orientations, Outside serv via phone, mail, e-mail & web, Photocopying/Printing, Ref & res, Ref serv available, Res libr, Scanner, Spanish lang bks, Study rm, Telephone ref, Wheelchair accessible, Workshops
Partic in National Network of Libraries of Medicine Region 2
Special Services for the Deaf - ADA equip
Special Services for the Blind - Accessible computers; Aids for in-house use; Assistive/Adapted tech devices, equip & products; Low vision equip; Magnifiers
Open Mon-Fri 7am-11:30pm, Sat 12-8:30, Sun 3-11:30
Restriction: 24-hr pass syst for students only, Access for corporate affiliates, Authorized patrons, Borrowing privileges limited to fac & registered students, Borrowing requests are handled by ILL, In-house use for visitors

C PONTIFICAL CATHOLIC UNIVERSITY OF PUERTO RICO ENCARNACION VALDES LIBRARY*, 2250 Avenida Las Americas, Ste 509, 00717-0777, SAN 365-5261. Tel: 787-841-2000, Ext 1801, 787-841-2000, Ext 1802. Circulation Tel: 787-841-2000, Ext 1810. Interlibrary Loan Service Tel: 787-841-2000, Ext 1815. Reference Tel: 787-841-2000, Ext 1818. FAX: 787-284-0235. Web Site: www.pucpr.edu. *Dir,* Juanita Peña Nicolau; E-mail: jpena@pucpr.edu; *Asst Librn,* Arleyn D Jusino; Staff 23 (MLS 12, Non-MLS 11)
Founded 1950. Enrl 10,045; Fac 311; Highest Degree: Doctorate
Library Holdings: CDs 4,668; e-books 23,525; e-journals 24,163; Bk Vols 270,453; Per Subs 12,798
Special Collections: Education (ERIC Documents); Monsignor Vincent Murga Coll; Puerto Rican Coll; Strategic Publications Center of the PAHO. US Document Depository
Subject Interests: Bus, Educ, Nursing, Relig, Sciences
Automation Activity & Vendor Info: (Acquisitions) SirsiDynix; (Cataloging) SirsiDynix; (Circulation) SirsiDynix; (Course Reserve) SirsiDynix; (OPAC) SirsiDynix; (Serials) SirsiDynix
Function: For res purposes
Partic in OCLC Online Computer Library Center, Inc
Publications: Annual Report; Faculty handbook; Student handbook
Special Services for the Deaf - Assistive tech
Special Services for the Blind - Computer with voice synthesizer for visually impaired persons
Open Mon-Thurs 7:30am-10pm, Fri 7:30-4, Sat 8-8

CL MONSIGNOR FREMIOT TORRES OLIVER LAW LIBRARY*, 2250 Blvd Luis A Ferre Aguayo, Ste 544, 00717-9997, SAN 365-5296. Tel: 787-841-2000, Ext 1850, 787-841-2000, Ext 1851. Reference Tel: 787-841-2000, Ext 1853. FAX: 787-841-5354. E-mail: bib_derecho@pucpr.edu. Web Site: www.pucpr.edu. *Dir,* Noelia Padua; Tel: 787-841-2000, Ext 1852, E-mail: npadua@pucpr.edu; *Automation Syst Coordr, Cat,* Tammy Martinez; Tel: 787-841-2000, Ext 1858, E-mail: tmartinez@pucpr.edu; *Acq,* Maria del C Gonzalez; Tel: 787-841-2000, Ext 1856, E-mail: mcgonzalez@pucpr.edu; *Circ, Ref (Info Servs),* Miguel Alvarez; E-mail: malvarez@pucpr.edu; *Circ, Ref (Info Servs),* Teresita Guillemard; E-mail: tguillemard@pucpr.edu; Staff 10 (MLS 5, Non-MLS 5)
Founded 1961. Enrl 706; Fac 51
Library Holdings: Bk Titles 31,456; Bk Vols 255,035; Per Subs 2,506
Special Collections: Puerto Rico Coll; Rare Books. UN Document Depository; US Document Depository
Subject Interests: Civil, Constitutional, Criminal, Law, Roman
Function: Electronic databases & coll, Photocopying/Printing, Ref serv available
Partic in LYRASIS; OCLC Online Computer Library Center, Inc
Open Mon-Thurs 7:30am-Midnight, Fri 7:30am-11pm, Sat 9-8, Sun 1-9

SAN GERMAN

C INTER-AMERICAN UNIVERSITY OF PUERTO RICO*, Juan Cancio Ortiz Library, San German Campus, Ave Inter-American University, Rd 102, K 30 6, 00683-9801. (Mail add: PO Box 5100, 00683-9801), SAN 318-5648. Tel: 787-264-1912, Ext 7521. Circulation Tel: 787-264-1912, Ext 7534. Reference Tel: 787-264-1912, Ext 7535. Administration Tel: 787-264-1912, Ext 7520. FAX: 787-264-2544. Web Site: cai.sg.inter.edu. *Libr Dir,* Mayra Rodriguez; E-mail: mayra_rodriguez@sangerman.inter.edu; *Puerto Rican Coll Librn,* María Juárez-Ponce; Tel: 787-264-1912, Ext 7536, E-mail: maria_juarez@alpha.sg.inter.edu; *Ref Librn,* Magdalena Torres-Aveillez; E-mail: magtorres@sg.inter.edu; *Ser Librn,* Jenny Salazar-Mallorquin; Tel: 787-264-1912, Ext 7537, E-mail: jsmallor@sg.inter.edu; Staff 19 (MLS 5, Non-MLS 14)
Founded 1923. Enrl 5,389; Fac 326; Highest Degree: Doctorate
Library Holdings: AV Mats 23,670; Braille Volumes 12; CDs 3,849; DVDs 469; e-books 21,686; e-journals 118; Large Print Bks 17; Microforms 571,242; Music Scores 1,205; Bk Titles 124,052; Bk Vols 159,118; Per Subs 2,294; Videos 2,214
Special Collections: Centro de Documentación Histórica Arturo Morales Carrión, personal docs, bks, pamphlets, periodicals; Museo y Archivo Histórico Interamerican University of Puerto Rico 912 to present, bks, ms, rare bks, pamphlets, pers & photog; Sala de Puerto Rico Angel R González, bks, pamphlets, CDs
Subject Interests: Applied sci, Art, Biology, Bus, Chem, Educ, Environ sci, Liberal arts, Linguistics, Lit, Math, Med tech, Music, Nursing, Phys educ, Psychol, Radiology, Recreation, Soc sci
Automation Activity & Vendor Info: (Acquisitions) SirsiDynix; (Cataloging) SirsiDynix; (Circulation) SirsiDynix; (Media Booking) SirsiDynix; (Serials) SirsiDynix
Wireless access
Function: Art exhibits, AV serv, Computers for patron use, Doc delivery serv, Electronic databases & coll, ILL available, Internet access, Mail & tel request accepted, Microfiche/film & reading machines, Online cat, Online info literacy tutorials on the web & in blackboard, Online ref, Orientations, Outside serv via phone, mail, e-mail & web, Photocopying/Printing, Ref & res, Ref serv available, Telephone ref, VHS videos, Wheelchair accessible
Publications: Bibliographic Instruction Series (Online only); Clases de Informes; Informes Orales; Análisis crítico de un artículo, Informe de investigación o tesis; Propuesta de investigación por C. García (Reference guide); Cómo acceder remotamente a las bases de datos (Reference guide); Cómo renovar libros desde su hogar (Reference guide); Derechos de autor por Rurrego (Reference guide); Guides (Online only); Listado de revistas en el CAI (Online only); Recent Acquisitions Lists (Online only); Recorrido Virtual (Online only)
Partic in LYRASIS
Special Services for the Blind - Accessible computers; Assistive/Adapted tech devices, equip & products; Braille equip; Computer with voice

synthesizer for visually impaired persons; PC for people with disabilities; Text reader; ZoomText magnification & reading software
Open Mon-Thurs 7:30am-10pm, Fri 7:30-5, Sat 8-5, Sun 1-10
Restriction: Non-circulating of rare bks

SAN JUAN

C CARLOS ALBIZU MIRANDA LIBRARY*, San Francisco Corner, 151 Tanca St, 00902. (Mail add: PO Box 9023711, 00902-3711). Tel: 787-725-6500, Ext 1525, 787-725-6500, Ext 1567. Web Site: www.albizu.edu/library. *Dir,* Yolanda Rosario; Tel: 787-725-6500, Ext 1568, E-mail: yrosario@albizu.edu; Staff 5 (MLS 2, Non-MLS 3)
Founded 1966. Fac 200; Highest Degree: Doctorate
Library Holdings: e-books 22,425; e-journals 49,830; Per Subs 194
Special Collections: Dissertations
Subject Interests: Autism, Counseling psychol, Indust/organizational psychol, Lang, Psychol, Speech
Automation Activity & Vendor Info: (Acquisitions) DEMCO; (Cataloging) OCLC Connexion; (Circulation) SirsiDynix; (Course Reserve) SirsiDynix; (Discovery) EBSCO Discovery Service; (ILL) OCLC WorldShare Interlibrary Loan; (OPAC) SirsiDynix-WorkFlows; (Serials) SirsiDynix
Wireless access
Open Mon-Thurs 8am-9pm, Fri 8-4, Sat 8-5

C AMAURY VERAY MUSIC LIBRARY*, 951 Ave Ponce de Leon, 00907-3373. SAN 318-5672. Tel: 787-751-0160, Ext 256. FAX: 787-724-0110. E-mail: biblioteca@cmpr.pr.gov. Web Site: cmpr.edu/biblioteca. *Dir,* María del Carmen Maldonado Bárcenas; Tel: 787-751-0160, Ext 262, E-mail: mcmaldon@cmpr.pr.gov; *Librn,* Carmen Jiménez; Tel: 787 751-0160, Ext 284, E-mail: cjimenez@cmpr.pr.gov; *Lbrn & Info Serv Coordr,* Position Currently Open; *Electronic Res Librn, Info Syst Librn,* Rafael Sustache; Tel: 787-751-0160, Ext 238, E-mail: rsustache@cmpr.pr.gov; *Info Serv Librn,* Samuel Gonzalez; E-mail: sgonzalez@cmpr.pr.gov; *Acq, Asst Librn,* Orlando Toro; Tel: 787-751-0160, Ext 225, E-mail: otoro@cmpr.pr.gov; *Digitization Coordr, Tech Coordr,* Sigfredo López; Tel: 787-751-0160, Ext 279, E-mail: slopez@cmpr.pr.gov; Staff 5 (MLS 4, Non-MLS 1)
Founded 1962. Enrl 416; Fac 79; Highest Degree: Master
Library Holdings: AV Mats 139; Braille Volumes 17; CDs 3,300; DVDs 2,044; e-books 93,499; e-journals 80,064; Electronic Media & Resources 93,051; Music Scores 42,162; Bk Titles 6,735; Bk Vols 8,794; Spec Interest Per Sub 54; Videos 650
Special Collections: Music (Puerto Rican & Latin American Composers)
Subject Interests: Music
Automation Activity & Vendor Info: (Acquisitions) Ex Libris Group; (Cataloging) Ex Libris Group; (Circulation) Ex Libris Group; (Course Reserve) Ex Libris Group; (OPAC) Ex Libris Group; (Serials) Ex Libris Group
Wireless access
Open Mon-Thurs 7:30am-8:30pm, Fri 7:30-5:30, Sat 10-3

GM DEPARTMENT OF VETERANS AFFAIRS*, Library Service, Library Service 142D, Ten Calle Casia, 00921-3201. SAN 318-5745. Tel: 787-641-7582, Ext 12276, 787-641-7582, Ext 31905. Reference Tel: 787-641-7582, Ext 12165, 787-641-7582, Ext 12236. Administration Tel: 787-641-7582, Ext 12227. FAX: 787-641-4550. *Chief Librn,* Carmen J Sierra; E-mail: carmen.sierra-ramirez@va.gov; *Admin Serv, Libr Tech,* Carmen I Santiago-Canchani; E-mail: carmen.santiago-canchani@va.gov; *Libr Tech,* Normary Bermudez-Lopez; E-mail: normary.bermudez-lopez@va.gov; Staff 5 (MLS 2, Non-MLS 3)
Founded 1946
Library Holdings: Audiobooks 69; AV Mats 690; Braille Volumes 125; e-journals 607; Large Print Bks 110; Bk Titles 10,205; Bk Vols 13,942; Per Subs 161; Talking Bks 250
Subject Interests: Allied health, Dentistry, Med, Nursing, Patient educ
Automation Activity & Vendor Info: (Circulation) Mandarin Library Automation; (Discovery) EBSCO Discovery Service; (OPAC) Mandarin Library Automation; (Serials) Electronic Scriptorium
Wireless access
Function: 24/7 Electronic res, 24/7 Online cat, Health sci info serv, ILL available, Internet access, Orientations, Ref serv available, Res libr, Satellite serv, Wheelchair accessible
Partic in National Network of Libraries of Medicine Region 2
Special Services for the Blind - Large print bks
Restriction: Authorized personnel only, Borrowing privileges limited to fac & registered students, Borrowing requests are handled by ILL, Circulates for staff only, Clients only, Employee & client use only, External users must contact libr, Hospital staff & commun, ID required to use computers (Ltd hrs), Lending limited to county residents, Lending to staff only, Limited access based on advanced application, Med & health res only, Med & nursing staff, patients & families, Med staff & students, Open to authorized patrons, Staff & patient use

R EVANGELICAL SEMINARY OF PUERTO RICO*, Juan de Valdes Library, 776 Ponce de Leon Ave, 00925-9907. SAN 328-5162. Tel: 787-763-6700, Ext 233. Web Site: www.se-pr.edu/biblioteca. *Libr Dir,* Milka Vigo-Verestin; E-mail: mvigo@se-pr.edu; *Auxiliary Librarian,* Juliemar Rivera González; Tel: 787-763-6700, E-mail: juliemar.rivera@se-pr.edu; Staff 2 (MLS 1, Non-MLS 1)
Founded 1919. Enrl 126; Fac 6; Highest Degree: Doctorate
Library Holdings: Bk Titles 76,587; Bk Vols 82,842
Special Collections: Historical Archive of Protestantism in Puerto Rico; Old & Rare Books; Puerto Rican Protestantism Coll; Spanish Reformers
Subject Interests: Relig, Theol
Automation Activity & Vendor Info: (Acquisitions) Mandarin Library Automation; (Cataloging) Mandarin Library Automation; (Circulation) Mandarin Library Automation; (Course Reserve) Mandarin Library Automation; (ILL) Mandarin Library Automation; (Media Booking) Mandarin Library Automation; (OPAC) Mandarin Library Automation; (Serials) Mandarin Library Automation
Wireless access
Open Mon-Thurs 9-9

C INTER-AMERICAN UNIVERSITY OF PUERTO RICO*, Information Access Center, 100 Calle Francisco Sein, 00919. (Mail add: PO Box 191293, 00919-1293). SAN 365-5059. Tel: 787-250-1912, Ext 2160, 787-250-1912, Ext 2514. Circulation Tel: 787-250-1912, Ext 2295. Interlibrary Loan Service Tel: 787-250-1913, Ext 2309. FAX: 787-751-3915. Web Site: www.metro.inter.edu/servacad/cai. *Dir,* Maria de Lourdes Resto Ortiz; E-mail: mresto@metro.inter.edu; *ILL,* Pilar Ortiz Del Valle; E-mail: portiz@metro.inter.edu; Staff 16 (MLS 5, Non-MLS 11)
Founded 1961. Enrl 10,500; Fac 693; Highest Degree: Doctorate
Library Holdings: Bk Vols 113,200; Per Subs 2,771
Special Collections: Juvenile Coll; Puerto Rican Coll. Oral History
Subject Interests: Criminal justice, Educ, Liberal arts, Med tech, Nursing, Psychol, Sci tech, Theol
Automation Activity & Vendor Info: (Acquisitions) SirsiDynix; (Cataloging) SirsiDynix; (Circulation) SirsiDynix; (Course Reserve) SirsiDynix; (ILL) SirsiDynix; (Media Booking) SirsiDynix; (OPAC) SirsiDynix; (Serials) SirsiDynix
Wireless access
Function: Govt ref serv, ILL available, Internet access, Large print keyboards, Orientations, Photocopying/Printing, Ref serv available, VHS videos, Wheelchair accessible, Workshops
Special Services for the Deaf - Assistive tech; Staff with knowledge of sign lang
Special Services for the Blind - Assistive/Adapted tech devices, equip & products; Computer with voice synthesizer for visually impaired persons; Scanner for conversion & translation of mats
Open Mon-Thurs 7am-11pm, Fri 7am-8pm, Sat 8-5, Sun 12:30-4:30
Restriction: Open to pub for ref only, Open to students, fac & staff, Photo ID required for access, Restricted pub use

P PUERTO RICO REGIONAL LIBRARY FOR THE BLIND & PHYSICALLY HANDICAPPED*, Biblioteca Regional para Ciegos y Fisicamente Impedidos de Puerto Rico, 705 Hoare Calle, 00907. SAN 320-4294. Tel: 787-721-7170, 787-723-2519. Toll Free Tel: 800-981-8008. E-mail: de33797@miescuela.pr. Web Site: bibliotecapersonasconimpedimentos.wordpress.com. *Dir,* Evelyn Torres; Staff 8 (MLS 1, Non-MLS 7)
Founded 1975. Pop 2,500; Circ 71,128
Library Holdings: Talking Bks 40,100
Special Collections: Braille Books & Magazines in Spanish; Cassette Books & Magazines in English & Spanish
Subject Interests: Braille mat in Spanish incl rec, Cassettes
Function: Equip loans & repairs, ILL available, Mail & tel request accepted, Mail loans to mem, Orientations, Spoken cassettes & CDs, Wheelchair accessible
Publications: Carta Informativa (Bimonthly)
Special Services for the Blind - Bks & mags in Braille, on rec, tape & cassette; Braille alphabet card; Braille equip; Braille servs; Cassette playback machines; Computer with voice synthesizer for visually impaired persons; Internet workstation with adaptive software; Large print bks & talking machines; Multimedia ref serv (large print, Braille using CD-ROM tech); Musical scores in Braille & large print; Newsletter (in large print, Braille or on cassette); Newsline for the Blind; PC for people with disabilities; Reader equip; Scanner for conversion & translation of mats; Spanish Braille mags & bks; Talking machines; Text reader; Transcribing serv; Variable speed audiotape players; VisualTek equip; Web-Braille
Open Mon-Fri 8-4:30
Restriction: Registered patrons only
Friends of the Library Group

GL SUPREME COURT LIBRARY OF PUERTO RICO*, Ave Munoz Rivera Parada 8 1/2 Puerta de Tierra, Parque Munoz Rivera, 00902. (Mail add: PO Box 9022392, 00902-2392). SAN 365-5806. Circulation Tel: 787-723-6033, Ext 2153, 787-723-6033, Ext 2155. Web Site: www.ramajudicial.pr/sistema/supremo/biblioteca.htm. *Dir,* Ivette

Torres-Alvarez; *Circ, Head, Pub Serv,* Evelyn N Ortiz-Hernandez; E-mail: evelyn.ortiz@ramajudicial.pr; *Cat,* Luis Bonilla-Madrigal; Tel: 787-723-6033, Ext 2163, E-mail: luis.bonilla@ramajudicial.pr. Subject Specialists: *Puerto Rican law,* Evelyn N Ortiz-Hernandez; Staff 7 (MLS 3, Non-MLS 4)
Founded 1832
Library Holdings: Per Subs 300
Special Collections: Rare Books Coll
Subject Interests: Civil law, Common law
Automation Activity & Vendor Info: (Cataloging) Ex Libris Group; (Circulation) Ex Libris Group; (OPAC) Ex Libris Group
Wireless access
Function: Activity rm, For res purposes, Govt ref serv, ILL available, Photocopying/Printing
Publications: InfoJuris (Monthly bulletin)
Restriction: Access at librarian's discretion, Authorized patrons, Authorized personnel only, By permission only, Circ to mil employees only, Closed stack, External users must contact libr, Open to pub for ref only, Pub use on premises, Restricted borrowing privileges, Restricted loan policy

UNIVERSITY OF PUERTO RICO

CM CONRADO F ASENJO LIBRARY*, Medical Sciences Campus, Main Bldg, Unit C, 00935. (Mail add: PO Box 365067, 00936-5067), SAN 318-5737. Tel: 787-751-8199, 787-758-2525, Ext 1200. Circulation Tel: 787-758-2526. Interlibrary Loan Service Tel: 787-758-2525, Ext 2923. Reference Tel: 787-758-2525, Ext 1369. Administration Tel: 787-758-2525, Ext 2083. FAX: 787-759-6713. Web Site: www.rcm-library.rcm.upr.edu. *Dir,* Dr Irma Quinones-Mauras; E-mail: irma.quinones1@upr.edu; *Dir, Tech Serv,* Nilca Parrilla; Tel: 787-758-2525, Ext 1346; *Head, Ref,* Margarita Gonzalez; *Spec Coll Librn,* Carmen Santos; Tel: 787-758-2525, Ext 1224; Staff 39 (MLS 12, Non-MLS 27)
Founded 1950. Enrl 2,480; Highest Degree: Doctorate
Library Holdings: AV Mats 2,207; Electronic Media & Resources 20; Bk Titles 42,906; Bk Vols 46,304; Per Subs 1,162
Special Collections: Dr Bailey K Ashford; History of Medicine; Puerto Rican Coll
Subject Interests: Health sci professions
Function: AV serv, ILL available, Internet access, Prof lending libr, Ref serv available, Wheelchair accessible, Workshops
Partic in Consortium of Southern Biomedical Libraries; Greater NE Regional Med Libr Program; National Network of Libraries of Medicine Region 2; SE-Atlantic Regional Med Libr Servs
Open Mon-Thurs 7am-11pm, Sat 8am-10pm, Sun 9am-10pm
Restriction: Non-circulating coll

CL LAW SCHOOL LIBRARY*, Avenidas Ponce de Leon & Gandara, 00931. (Mail add: PO Box 23310, 00931-3310), SAN 365-5474. Tel: 787-999-9684, 787-999-9702. Circulation Tel: 787-999-9702. Interlibrary Loan Service Tel: 787-999-9690. Reference Tel: 787-999-9687, 787-999-9688. Administration Tel: 787-999-9683, 787-999-9685. Information Services Tel: 787-999-9698. FAX: 787-999-9680. Web Site: www.law.upr.edu/biblioteca. *Dir,* Maria M Otero; E-mail: motero@law.upr.edu; *Head, Acq,* Lizette Lopez; Tel: 787-999-9703, E-mail: llopez@law.upr.edu; *Head, Cat,* Esther Villarino; Tel: 787-999-9709, E-mail: evillarino@law.upr.edu; *Head, Circ,* Samuel Serrano; Tel: 787-999-9898, E-mail: sserrano@law.upr.edu; *Head, Ser,* Josefina Ortiz; Tel: 787-999-9691, E-mail: jortiz@law.upr.edu; Staff 36 (MLS 8, Non-MLS 28)
Founded 1913. Enrl 710
Library Holdings: Per Subs 4,800
Special Collections: US Document Depository
Subject Interests: Rare bks
Automation Activity & Vendor Info: (Cataloging) Horizon; (Circulation) Horizon; (OPAC) Horizon; (Serials) Horizon
Partic in LYRASIS; OCLC Online Computer Library Center, Inc
Special Services for the Blind - Computer with voice synthesizer for visually impaired persons

C UNIVERSITY OF PUERTO RICO LIBRARY SYSTEM*, Rio Piedras Campus, 00931. (Mail add: PO Box 23302, 00931-3302), SAN 365-5385. Tel: 787-764-0000, Ext 5085, 787-764-0000, Ext 5086, 787-764-0000, Ext 5087. FAX: 787-772-1479. Web Site: www.upr.edu/biblioteca-rrp. *Interim Dir,* Dr Noraida Dominguez Flores; E-mail: noraida.dominguez@upr.edu; *Interim Asst Dir,* Mariam Feliciano Garcia; E-mail: mariam.feliciano3@upr.edu; Staff 113 (MLS 40, Non-MLS 73)
Founded 1903. Highest Degree: Doctorate
Library Holdings: e-books 35; e-journals 3,000; Bk Titles 4,076,000; Per Subs 3,012
Special Collections: Arts & Dance (Arts Coll); Caribbean & Latin American Studies Coll; El Mundo Newspaper Photographs; History, Literature & Social Science (Puerto Rican Coll); Josefina del Toro Fulladosa Coll, rare bks; Services for the Blind Coll; Zenobia & Juan Ramon Jimenez Literature Coll. Oral History; UN Document Depository; US Document Depository
Automation Activity & Vendor Info: (Acquisitions) Horizon; (Circulation) Horizon
Wireless access
Publications: Al Dia (Newsletter); Collections Description (Brochure); Lumbre (Newsletter); Perspectiva (Journal); Services Description (Brochure); Subject Bibliographies
Partic in OCLC Online Computer Library Center, Inc
Special Services for the Deaf - Assistive tech; Coll on deaf educ; Deaf publ; FullTalk; Spec interest per; Staff with knowledge of sign lang; Video & TTY relay via computer
Special Services for the Blind - Assistive/Adapted tech devices, equip & products; Audio mat; Braille equip; Braille servs; Computer with voice synthesizer for visually impaired persons; Talking bks
Restriction: Open to pub with supv only

Departmental Libraries:

ANGEL QUINTERO ALFARO LIBRARY, Rio Piedras Campus, Faculta de Estudio Generales, 00931. (Mail add: PO Box 23302, 00931-3302), SAN 365-5490. Tel: 787-764-0000. FAX: 787-773-1729. *Chief Librn,* Aurea Maisonet; Tel: 787-764-0000, Ext 85947, E-mail: aurea.maisonet1@upr.edu; Staff 6 (MLS 2, Non-MLS 4)
Founded 1971. Enrl 3,096; Fac 260; Highest Degree: Bachelor
Library Holdings: AV Mats 215; Bk Titles 9,783; Per Subs 19

ARTS COLLECTION, Rio Piedras Campus, Jose M Lazaro Bldg, 2nd Flr, 00931. (Mail add: PO Box 23302, 00931-3302), SAN 327-9871. Tel: 787-764-0000, Ext 85535, 787-764-0000, Ext 85539. E-mail: artes.sb@upr.edu. *Chief Librn,* Dr Iris D Rodriguez-Parrilla; E-mail: iris.rodriguez2@upr.edu; Staff 4 (MLS 1, Non-MLS 3)
Founded 1953
Library Holdings: Bk Vols 34,667
Special Collections: Artist Illustrated Books; Arts Exhibition Catalogs; Catalogos de Expos de Arte Sebastian Gonzalez Garcia; Dance Archives Coll; Rare Art Books
Subject Interests: Graphic, Visual arts
Function: Res libr
Publications: Lista anotada de recursos de la Coleccion de las Artes, Serie: indices; Manual de Instruccion Bibliotecaria: Las artes sus recursos y serv ARTES (Information sheet of organized exhibitions)

BUSINESS ADMINISTRATION LIBRARY, Rio Piedras Campus, Juan Jose Osuno Bldg, 00931. (Mail add: PO Box 23302, 00931-3302), SAN 365-5466. Tel: 787-764-0000, Ext 85866, 787-764-0000, Ext 85867. FAX: 787-772-1479. Web Site: baeuprrp.com. *Chief Librn,* Lourdes Cadiz Ocasio; E-mail: lourdes.cadiz1@upr.edu
Enrl 2,862
Library Holdings: AV Mats 89; Bk Vols 33,777
Subject Interests: Acctg, Computer sci, Finance, Human resources, Mgt, Mkt, Statistics

CARIBBEAN & LATIN AMERICAN STUDIES COLLECTION, Rio Piedras Campus, Jose M Lazaro Bldg, 2nd Flr, 00931. (Mail add: PO Box 23302, 00931-3302), SAN 327-9855. Tel: 787-764-0000, Ext 85855. Web Site: uprrp.libguides.com/brcel. *Chief Librn,* Almaluces Figueroa-Ortiz; E-mail: almaluces.figueroa1@upr.edu
Library Holdings: Bk Vols 142,004
Special Collections: Latin American Pamphlets from the Yale University Library Coll; Peron's Documents Coll; Rare Books and Carribean Organizations Documents; The Latin American Documents Project A & B
Subject Interests: Caribbean-demography, Econ, Educ, Statistics, Tourism, Trade
Publications: ACURIL (Newsletter)

CIRCULATION & RESERVE COLLECTION, Rio Piedras Campus, Jose M Lazaro Bldg, 2nd Flr, 00931. (Mail add: PO Box 23302, 00931-3302), SAN 376-2327. Tel: 787-764-0000, Ext 85540. *Chief Librn,* Manuel Martinez Nazario; E-mail: manuel.martinez8@upr.edu
Library Holdings: Bk Titles 278,686; Bk Vols 391,954
Subject Interests: Humanities, Soc sci

JOSEFINA DEL TORO FULLADOSA COLLECTION, RARE BOOKS & MANUSCRIPTS, Rio Piedras Campus, Jose M Lazaro Bldg, 00931. (Mail add: PO Box 23302, 00931-3302), SAN 327-9898. Administration Tel: 787-764-0000, Ext 85734. *Chief Librn, Rare Bks,* Aura Diaz Lopez; E-mail: aura.diaz1@upr.edu. Subject Specialists: *Latin Am studies, Rare bks,* Aura Diaz Lopez; Staff 1 (MLS 1)
Highest Degree: Doctorate
Library Holdings: Bk Vols 9,594
Special Collections: Genaro Cautino Coll; Nemours Coll, (Haiti)
Subject Interests: Hist (Americana), Lit, Relig
Function: Archival coll, Art exhibits, Computers for patron use, Electronic databases & coll, ILL available, Ref serv available, Wheelchair accessible
Restriction: Closed stack, Internal use only, Non-circulating of rare bks

DOCUMENTS & MAPS COLLECTION, Rio Piedras Campus, Jose M Lazaro Bldg, 2nd Flr, 00931. (Mail add: PO Box 23302, 00931-3302), SAN 376-2335. Tel: 787-764-0000, Ext 85725. FAX: 787-772-1485. Web Site: uprrp.libguides.com/documentosymapas, *Chief Librn,* Manuel Martinez Nazario; E-mail: manuel.martinez8@upr.edu

Library Holdings: AV Mats 125; CDs 509; Microforms 800,553; Bk Vols 896; Per Subs 618
Special Collections: UN Document Depository; US Document Depository
Subject Interests: Caribbean area, Econ, Latin area

ZENOBIA & JUAN RAMON JIMENEZ ROOM, Rio Piedras Campus, Edif Jose M Lazaro, 00931. (Mail add: PO Box 23302, 00931-3302), SAN 327-9936. Tel: 787-764-0000, Ext 85785, 787-764-0000, Ext 85786, 787-764-0000, Ext 85789. *Chief Librn,* Aura Diaz Lopez; Tel: 787-764-0000, Ext 85734, E-mail: aura.diaz1@upr.edu
Library Holdings: Bk Vols 104,937
Special Collections: Bernardo G Candamo Coll; Juan Guerrero Ruiz Personal Library; Rafael Cansinos Assens Coll; Zenobia & Juan R Jimenez Personal Library & Documents
Subject Interests: Spanish lit
Open Mon-Thurs 7:45am-9:45pm, Fri 7:45-4:15, Sat 8:45-4:15

LIBRARY & INFORMATION SCIENCES, Rio Piedras Campus, Jose M Lazaro Bldg, 3rd Flr, 00931. (Mail add: PO Box 23302, 00931-3302), SAN 365-5504. Tel: 787-764-0000, Ext 85980. *Chief Librn,* Ketty Rodriguez; E-mail: ketty.rodriguez@upr.edu
Enrl 131; Highest Degree: Master
Library Holdings: Bk Vols 111,553
Special Collections: Juvenile Coll
Subject Interests: Info, Libr sci
Publications: Egebiana (Journal); Servicio de alerta

LIBRARY SERVICES FOR PERSONS WITH DISABILITIES, Rio Piedras Campus, Jose M Lazaro Bldg, 00931. (Mail add: PO Box 23302, 00931-3302), SAN 327-9790. Tel: 787-764-0000, Ext 85840, 787-764-0000, Ext 85849. TDD: 787-523-7746. *Chief Librn,* Jose Pagan Martinez; E-mail: jose.pagan9@upr.edu
Library Holdings: AV Mats 28; Bk Titles 590; Per Subs 21
Special Collections: Books in Braille; Large Print; Talking Books
Subject Interests: Blind-educ, Hist, Lang, Lit, Printing, Rehabilitation, Writing systs
Special Services for the Blind - Assistive/Adapted tech devices, equip & products
Open Mon-Thurs 8am-9pm, Fri 8-4:30, Sat 8-4

MONSERRATE SANTANA DE PALES LIBRARY, Rio Piedras Campus, Graduate School of Social Work, Beatriz Lassalle Bldg, 2nd Flr, 00931. (Mail add: PO Box 23302, 00931-3302), SAN 365-5652. Tel: 787-764-0000, Ext 85910. *Chief Librn,* Ada Myriam Felicie; E-mail: adamyriam15@hotmail.com
Enrl 595; Highest Degree: Doctorate
Library Holdings: AV Mats 16; Bk Titles 12,265; Bk Vols 13,235; Per Subs 202
Subject Interests: Child abuse, Counseling, Family relations, Med soc work, Psychopathology, Rehabilitation, Soc serv, Soc work
Open Mon-Thurs 10am-11:30pm, Fri 8-4:30, Sat 8-12 & 1-5

MUSIC LIBRARY, Rio Piedras Campus, Agustin Stahl Bldg, 00931. (Mail add: PO Box 23302, Estacion Universidad, 00931-3302), SAN 327-9812. Tel: 787-764-0000, Ext 85930, 787-764-0000, Ext 85933. *Head Librn,* Juana Cabello; E-mail: juana.cabello1@upr.edu
Founded 1953. Enrl 109
Library Holdings: AV Mats 23,839; Music Scores 8,543; Bk Titles 9,250; Bk Vols 12,420; Per Subs 231

PLANNING LIBRARY, Rio Piedras Campus, Plaza Universitaria, 6th Flr, 00931. (Mail add: PO Box 23302, 00931-3302), SAN 365-5563. Tel: 787-764-0000, Ext 85504. FAX: 787-763-5605. *Chief Librn,* Lourdes Ramirez; Tel: 787-764-0000, Ext 85524, E-mail: lourdes.ramirez2@upr.edu
Enrl 118
Library Holdings: AV Mats 89; Bk Titles 17,274; Bk Vols 19,088; Per Subs 360
Subject Interests: Environ, Planning econ, Regional, Soc urban

PUBLIC ADMINISTRATION & PERIODICALS LIBRARY, Rio Piedras Campus, Carmen Rivera de Alvarado Bldg, 2nd Flr, 00931. (Mail add: PO Box 23302, 00931-3302), SAN 365-5598. Tel: 787-764-0000, Ext 85903, 787-764-0000, Ext 85904. *Chief Librn,* Mariam Feliciano; E-mail: mariam.feliciano3@upr.edu
Enrl 189
Library Holdings: AV Mats 154; Bk Vols 29,908
Subject Interests: Admin law, Labor legislation, Organization theory, Personnel admin
Open Mon-Thurs 10-7, Fri 8-4:30, Sat 9-5

PUERTO RICAN COLLECTION, Rio Piedras Campus, Jose M Lazaro Bldg, 2nd Flr, 00931. (Mail add: PO Box 23302, Estacion Universidad, 00931-3302), SAN 327-991X. Tel: 787-764-0000, Ext 85735, 787-764-0000, Ext 85736. *Chief Librn,* Maria E Ordonez-Mercado; E-mail: maria.ordones@upr.edu
Library Holdings: Bk Titles 40,624; Bk Vols 1,147,000; Per Subs 4,665
Special Collections: Antonio S Pedreira Coll; Emilio J Pasarell Coll; Gerardo Selles Sola Coll; Miguel Guerra Mondragon Coll; Sociedad Economica de Amigos del Pais
Subject Interests: Puerto Ricans, Puerto Rico

REFERENCE COLLECTION, Rio Piedras Campus, Jose M Lazaro Bldg, 1st Flr, 00931. (Mail add: PO Box 23302, Estacion Universidad, 00931-3302), SAN 376-2351. Tel: 787-764-0000, Ext 85750, 787-764-0000, Ext 85757, 787-764-0000, Ext 85764. *Chief Librn,* Sylvia Sola-Fernandez; E-mail: sylvia.sola1@upr.edu
Library Holdings: Microforms 681,688; Bk Titles 93,929; Bk Vols 120,559
Subject Interests: Humanities, Soc sci

GERARDO SELLES SOLA LIBRARY, Rio Piedras Campus, Eugenio Maria de Hostos Bldg, Rm 211, 00931. (Mail add: UPR Sta, PO Box 23302, 00931-3302), SAN 365-5482. Tel: 787-764-0000, Ext 85921. Web Site: educacion.uprrp.edu/biblioteca-gerardo-selles-sola. *Chief Librn,* Marisol Gutierrez; Tel: 787-764-0000, Ext 85929, E-mail: marisol.gutierrez1@upr.edu; Staff 7 (MLS 3, Non-MLS 4)
Founded 1946. Fac 230; Highest Degree: Doctorate
Library Holdings: AV Mats 733; Bk Titles 34,333; Bk Vols 40,665; Per Subs 224
Special Collections: Theses & Dissertations
Subject Interests: Counseling, Curric, Educ, Educ philos, Educ sociol, Guidance, Juv, Psychol
Function: Res libr
Special Services for the Blind - Computer with voice synthesizer for visually impaired persons
Open Mon-Thurs 8am-9pm, Fri 8-4:30, Sat 8-4
Restriction: Secured area only open to authorized personnel

C UNIVERSITY OF PUERTO RICO RP COLLEGE OF NATURAL SCIENCES LIBRARY, Nestor M Rodriguez Rivera Library, 17 Ave Universidad, Ste 1701, 00925-2537. SAN 365-5539. Tel: 787-764-0000, Ext 88370. Web Site: www.upr.edu/biblioteca-uprrp-cn. *Actg Dir,* Nivea Santiago-Vazquez; Tel: 787-764-0000, Ext 88399, E-mail: nivea.santiago1@upr.edu; *Librn III,* Purisima C Centeno-Alayon; Tel: 787-764-0000, Ext 88387, E-mail: purisima.centeno1@upr.edu; *Info Spec, Librn,* Sylvia Figueroa-Rodriguez; Tel: 787-764-0000, Ext 88395, E-mail: sylvia.figueroa@upr.edu; *ILL & Reserves Asst,* Jose H Garcia-Rivera; Tel: 787-764-0000, Ext 88379, E-mail: jose.garcia3@upr.edu; Staff 7 (MLS 4, Non-MLS 3)
Founded 1954. Highest Degree: Doctorate
Library Holdings: Bk Titles 40,000
Special Collections: Puerto Rico Science Coll
Subject Interests: Astronomy, Biology, Botany, Chem, Geol, Math, Physics, Pure sci, Zoology
Automation Activity & Vendor Info: (Cataloging) Horizon; (Circulation) Horizon; (Serials) EBSCO Discovery Service
Wireless access
Function: 24/7 Electronic res, Computers for patron use, E-Reserves, Electronic databases & coll, ILL available, Internet access, Online cat, Online Chat, Online ref, Photocopying/Printing, Ref serv available, Res libr, Workshops
Open Mon-Fri 8-6
Restriction: Borrowing privileges limited to fac & registered students, ID required to use computers (Ltd hrs), In-house use for visitors

G USDA FOREST SERVICE*, International Institute of Tropical Forestry Library, Jardin Botanico Sur, 1201 Calle Ceiba, 00926-1119. SAN 322-7944. Tel: 787-764-7859. FAX: 787-766-6302. E-mail: iitf.library@usda.gov. Web Site: www.fs.usda.gov/detailfull/iitf/home/?cid=fseprd602695&width=full. *Libr Dir,* Yariliz R Quiles Martinez; Tel: 787-764-7257, E-mail: yariliz.quiles-martinez@usda.gov; *Libr Tech,* Evelyn Pagán; Tel: 787-764-2250, E-mail: epagan@usda.gov; Staff 4 (MLS 1, Non-MLS 3)
Founded 1939
Library Holdings: Bk Titles 6,000; Per Subs 50
Special Collections: Tropical Forestry
Subject Interests: Tropical ecology, Tropical forestry
Publications: General Technical Reports; IITF Annual Letter; Research Papers; Resource Bulletins
Open Tues & Thurs 8am-11am

SANTURCE

CR UNIVERSITY OF THE SACRED HEART*, Madre Maria Teresa Guevara Library, Rosales St, PO Box 12383, 00914-0383. SAN 318-5788. Tel: 787-728-1515, Ext 4353. E-mail: bmmtg@sagrado.edu. Web Site: biblioteca.sagrado.edu. *Dir,* Alejandro Escobar Nieves; Tel: 787-728-1515, Ext 4354, E-mail: alejandro.escobar@sagrado.edu; *Lead Librn, Tech Serv,* Arleen Garcia Rodriquez; Tel: 787-728-1515, Ext 4364, E-mail: arleen.garcia@sagrado.edu; *Librn II,* Limarie Colls; Tel: 787-728-1515, Ext 2695, E-mail: limarie.colls@sagrado.edu; *Librn II,* Francisco Solis Ortiz; Tel: 787-728-1515, Ext 4357, E-mail: francisco.solis@sagrado.edu; *Info Res Spec,* Jose Carrillo Irizarry; Tel: 787-728-1515, Ext 4357; Staff 15.5 (MLS 6.5, Non-MLS 9)
Founded 1936. Enrl 5,000; Fac 417; Highest Degree: Master
Library Holdings: Bk Titles 120,563; Bk Vols 204,296; Per Subs 1,500
Special Collections: Historical Archives of the Institution

Automation Activity & Vendor Info: (Cataloging) SirsiDynix; (Circulation) SirsiDynix; (Course Reserve) SirsiDynix; (OPAC) SirsiDynix; (Serials) SirsiDynix
Wireless access
Publications: Delfilinea (Quarterly); Guia para la presentacion y aprobacionde una Tesis de Grado; Library Guides; Manual para la Preparacion de un Trabajo de Investigacion; Tapia Ayer y Hoy
Open Mon-Thurs 7am-9pm, Fri 7-6, Sat 8-5
Friends of the Library Group

VIRGIN ISLANDS

CHRISTIANSTED

P VIRGIN ISLANDS DIVISION OF LIBRARIES, ARCHIVES & MUSEUMS*, Regional Library for the Blind & Physically Handicapped, Vitraco Mall, 3012 Golden Rock, 00820. SAN 365-5989. Tel: 340-718-2250. FAX: 340-718-3545. E-mail: regional.library@dpnr.vi.gov. Web Site: usvipubliclibraries.com/libraryregional. *Supvr,* Lisa Lubrin; Staff 4 (MLS 1, Non-MLS 3)
Founded 1968. Pop 200
Library Holdings: Audiobooks 39,000; Talking Bks 39,000
Wireless access
Publications: Regional Newsletter (Biannually)
Special Services for the Deaf - Assistive tech
Special Services for the Blind - Accessible computers; Assistive/Adapted tech devices, equip & products; Bks & mags in Braille, on rec, tape & cassette; Bks on cassette; Bks on flash-memory cartridges; Braille alphabet card; Braille music coll; Cassette playback machines; Cassettes; Computer access aids; Computer with voice synthesizer for visually impaired persons; Digital talking bk; Digital talking bk machines; Disability awareness prog; Home delivery serv; Internet workstation with adaptive software; Musical scores in Braille & large print; Networked computers with assistive software; Newsletter (in large print, Braille or on cassette); PC for people with disabilities
Open Mon-Fri 8-5
Restriction: Authorized patrons
Friends of the Library Group

KINGSHILL

C UNIVERSITY OF THE VIRGIN ISLANDS*, Saint Croix Campus Library-Melvin H Evans Center for Learning, RR 2, Box 10000, 00850-9781. SAN 318-5842. Tel: 340-692-4130. FAX: 340-692-4135. Web Site: www.uvi.edu/academics/libraries. *Libr Mgr,* Celia P Prince-Richard; Tel: 340-692-4134, E-mail: cprince@uvi.edu; Staff 8 (MLS 4, Non-MLS 4)
Founded 1969. Enrl 1,200; Fac 85; Highest Degree: Master
Library Holdings: AV Mats 799; Bk Vols 55,809; Per Subs 171
Special Collections: Caribbean materials; VI documents
Automation Activity & Vendor Info: (Cataloging) SirsiDynix; (Circulation) SirsiDynix; (Course Reserve) SirsiDynix; (OPAC) SirsiDynix
Function: For res purposes, ILL available, Photocopying/Printing
Publications: Acquisitions List; Library Handbook; Library Newsletter
Partic in LYRASIS; National Network of Libraries of Medicine Region 2; Virgin Islands Libr & Info Network
Open Mon-Thurs 8am-9pm, Fri 8-6, Sat & Sun 1-8
Restriction: Open to pub for ref & circ; with some limitations

SAINT CROIX

P FLORENCE A WILLIAMS PUBLIC LIBRARY, 1122 King St Christiansted, 00820. SAN 318-5885. Tel: 340-773-5715. FAX: 340-773-5327. Web Site: www.usvipubliclibraries.com/florence-augusta-williams.
Founded 1920
Library Holdings: Bk Titles 22,180; Bk Vols 24,690; Per Subs 27
Special Collections: Virgin Islands & Caribbean Materials. State Document Depository; US Document Depository
Subject Interests: Hist
Wireless access
Open Tues-Sat 9-6
Friends of the Library Group

SAINT JOHN

P ELAINE IONE SPRAUVE LIBRARY*, Enighed Estate, Cruz Bay, 00831. (Mail add: PO Box 30, 00831), SAN 318-5893. Tel: 340-776-6359. FAX: 340-776-6901. Web Site: www.virginislandspubliclibraries.org. *Actg Dir,* Arlene Pinney-Benjamin; E-mail: arlene.benjamin@dpnr.vi.gov; Staff 2 (MLS 1, Non-MLS 1)
Founded 1959. Pop 5,000
Library Holdings: DVDs 900; Large Print Bks 5; Bk Titles 16,400; Bk Vols 17,900; Per Subs 15
Special Collections: West Indies. State Document Depository
Automation Activity & Vendor Info: (Cataloging) SirsiDynix; (Circulation) SirsiDynix
Open Mon-Fri 9-5
Friends of the Library Group

SAINT THOMAS

C UNIVERSITY OF THE VIRGIN ISLANDS, Ralph M Paiewonsky Library, Two John Brewers Bay, 00802. SAN 365-6012. Tel: 340-693-1367. FAX: 340-693-1365. E-mail: library@uvi.edu. Web Site: www.uvi.edu/library/stthomas-info.html. *Libr Dir,* Mark-Jeffery Deans; Tel: 340-693-1181, E-mail: markjeffery.deans@uvi.edu; Staff 10 (MLS 5, Non-MLS 5)
Founded 1963. Enrl 2,719; Fac 89; Highest Degree: Master
Library Holdings: AV Mats 1,240; Bk Titles 93,450; Bk Vols 96,810; Per Subs 717; Videos 390
Special Collections: Caribbean Area Coll, VF; Melchior Center for Recent Virgin Islands History. US Document Depository
Subject Interests: Caribbean hist, Caribbean lit, Caribbean politics, Govt
Automation Activity & Vendor Info: (Cataloging) SirsiDynix; (Circulation) SirsiDynix; (ILL) SirsiDynix; (OPAC) SirsiDynix
Wireless access
Publications: Acquisitions List; Library Handbooks; Periodical List
Partic in LYRASIS; Virgin Islands Libr & Info Network
Open Mon-Thurs 8-8, Fri 8-4, Sat 12-5, Sun 1-6

P VIRGIN ISLANDS DIVISION OF LIBRARIES, ARCHIVES & MUSEUMS*, Charles Wesley Turnbull Regional Public Library, 4607 Tutu Park Mall, 00802. SAN 365-592X. Tel: 340-774-0630. Web Site: www.virginislandspubliclibraries.org. *Librn,* Symra Chinnery; Staff 41 (MLS 3, Non-MLS 38)
Founded 1920. Pop 40,000; Circ 156,915
Library Holdings: AV Mats 2,117; Large Print Bks 190; Bk Vols 168,724; Per Subs 180; Videos 310

Special Collections: Virgin Islands; Von Scholten Coll, Founded 1920: Danish West Indies, Virgin Islands & Caribbean, bks, doc, local newsp, ms, maps, pamphlets, per, photogs, VF. UN Document Depository
Wireless access
Publications: Annual Report; Caribbeana: Recent Acquisitions of Caribbean Materials in Virgin Islands Libraries; Checklist of Virgin Islands Government Documents; Information (Newsletter); Occasional Papers Series; Union Catalog of 16mm Motion Pictures; Union List of Periodicals & Newspapers; Virgin Islands Govt Blou bks; Virgin Islands Govt Calendar for 1985; Virgin Islands Newspaper Index
Special Services for the Deaf - ADA equip; Assisted listening device; Assistive tech
Special Services for the Blind - Accessible computers; Aids for in-house use
Open Mon-Fri 9-5:45
Friends of the Library Group
Branches: 2
ELAINE IONE SPRAUVE LIBRARY
See Separate Entry in Saint John
FLORENCE A WILLIAMS PUBLIC LIBRARY
See Separate Entry in Saint Croix

LIBRARIES IN CANADA

ALBERTA

Date of Statistics: Not provided.

ACADIA VALLEY

P ACADIA MUNICIPAL LIBRARY*, Warren Peers School, 103 First Ave N, T0J 0A0. (Mail add: PO Box 6, T0J 0A0). Tel: 403-972-3744. FAX: 403-972-2000. E-mail: aavalibrary@marigold.ab.ca. Web Site: www.acadialibrary.ca. *Mgr,* Susan Grudecki
Wireless access
Mem of Marigold Library System
Open Mon, Wed & Thurs 4-8, Tues 1-5
Friends of the Library Group

ACME

P ACME MUNICIPAL LIBRARY*, 610 Walsh Ave, T0M 0A0. (Mail add: PO Box 326, T0M 0A0), SAN 318-5915. Tel: 403-546-3879. FAX: 403-546-2248. E-mail: aamlibrary@marigold.ab.ca. Web Site: www.acmelibrary.ca. *Mgr,* Jonquil Thiessen
Founded 1955. Pop 648; Circ 11,798
Library Holdings: Bk Vols 12,000; Per Subs 40
Special Collections: Can & Prov
Wireless access
Mem of Marigold Library System
Open Tues & Thurs 5-9, Wed 9-12 & 12:30-4

AIRDRIE

P AIRDRIE PUBLIC LIBRARY*, 111-304 Main St SE, T4B 3C3. SAN 325-1993. Tel: 403-948-0600. FAX: 403-912-4002. E-mail: info@airdriepubliclibrary.ca. Web Site: www.airdriepubliclibrary.ca. *Dir,* Deb Cryderman
Founded 1971. Pop 42,000; Circ 200,000
Library Holdings: Bk Vols 55,000; Per Subs 100
Subject Interests: Airdrie hist, District hist
Mem of Marigold Library System
Partic in The Alberta Library
Open Mon-Fri 9-8:30, Sat 10-5
Friends of the Library Group

ALBERTA BEACH

P ALBERTA BEACH MUNICIPAL LIBRARY*, 4815 50 Ave, T0E 0A0. (Mail add: PO Box 186, T0E 0A0). Tel: 780-924-3491. E-mail: ablibrary@yrl.ab.ca. Web Site: www.albertabeachlibrary.ca. *Libr Mgr,* Cathy Brennan
Pop 1,000
Library Holdings: Bk Titles 10,000; Per Subs 10
Automation Activity & Vendor Info: (Acquisitions) SirsiDynix; (Cataloging) Innovative Interfaces, Inc. - Polaris
Wireless access
Function: Laminating, Meeting rooms, Photocopying/Printing, Scanner
Mem of Yellowhead Regional Library
Open Tues & Thurs 2:30-8, Wed 9:30-4:30, Sat 11-3; Tues & Thurs 2:30-8, Wed 9:30-4:30, Fri 10-2, Sat 11-3 (Summer)
Friends of the Library Group

ALDER FLATS

P ALDER FLATS/BUCK LAKE PUBLIC LIBRARY*, PO Box 148, T0C 0A0. Tel: 780-388-3881. FAX: 780-388-3887. E-mail: alderflatslibrary@yrl.ab.ca. Web Site: www.alderflatslibrary.ab.ca. *Libr Mgr,* Orti Weich
Founded 1973
Library Holdings: Bk Titles 10,000
Automation Activity & Vendor Info: (Acquisitions) SirsiDynix
Mem of Yellowhead Regional Library
Open Tues 2-4, Thurs 7pm-9pm; Tues 1-5, Thurs 7pm-9pm (Summer)

ALIX

P ALIX PUBLIC LIBRARY*, 4928 50th St, T0C 0B0. (Mail add: PO Box 69, T0C 0B0). Tel: 403-747-3233. E-mail: alixpublic@prl.ab.ca. Web Site: alixpublic.prl.ab.ca. *Libr Mgr,* Sue Duncan
Pop 900
Library Holdings: Bk Titles 10,000; Per Subs 12
Wireless access
Mem of Parkland Regional Library-Alberta
Open Tues & Thurs 10-6, Sat 10-4

ALLIANCE

P ALLIANCE PUBLIC LIBRARY, 101 First Ave E, T0B 0A0. (Mail add: PO Box 185, T0B 0A0). Tel: 780-879-3733. E-mail: alliancelibrary@prl.ab.ca. Web Site: prl.ab.ca/alliance. *Libr Mgr,* Lisa Neraasen
Pop 210
Library Holdings: Audiobooks 100; DVDs 500; Large Print Bks 200; Bk Titles 6,000; Per Subs 2
Automation Activity & Vendor Info: (Acquisitions) Horizon; (Cataloging) Horizon; (Circulation) Horizon; (ILL) Horizon; (Media Booking) Horizon; (OPAC) Horizon; (Serials) Horizon
Wireless access
Function: 24/7 Electronic res, 24/7 Online cat, Adult bk club, Art exhibits, Audiobks on Playaways & MP3, Audiobks via web, Bks on CD, Children's prog, Computer training, Computers for patron use, Electronic databases & coll, Extended outdoor wifi, Family literacy, Free DVD rentals, Games, Holiday prog, ILL available, Instruction & testing, Internet access, Movies, Online cat, OverDrive digital audio bks, Photocopying/Printing, Prog for adults, Prog for children & young adult, Scanner, Senior computer classes, Summer reading prog, Teen prog, Workshops
Mem of Parkland Regional Library-Alberta
Open Tues & Thurs 10-4 (Summer); Tues 12-6, Thurs 10-4 (Winter)
Friends of the Library Group

AMISK

P AMISK PUBLIC LIBRARY*, 5005 50 St, T0B 0B0. (Mail add: Box 71, T0B 0B0). Tel: 780-628-5457. E-mail: amiskpubliclibrary@prl.ab.ca. Web Site: amisklibrary.prl.ab.ca. *Libr Mgr,* Jacquie Chastellaine; Staff 1 (MLS 1)
Founded 1923. Pop 204
Library Holdings: Bk Titles 7,200
Wireless access
Mem of Parkland Regional Library-Alberta
Open Tues & Wed 12-5, Thurs 12-8

ANDREW

P ANDREW MUNICIPAL PUBLIC LIBRARY*, Village of Andrew Multiplex, 5021-50 St, T0B 0C0. Tel: 587-957-2130. FAX: 780-365-3734. E-mail: librarian@andrewpubliclibrary.ca. Web Site: www.andrewpubliclibrary.ca. *Librn,* Roseann Weleschuk
Founded 1950. Pop 490
Library Holdings: Bk Titles 15,000; Per Subs 20
Automation Activity & Vendor Info: (Acquisitions) Follett Software; (Cataloging) Follett Software; (Circulation) Follett Software; (Media Booking) Follett Software; (OPAC) Follett Software; (Serials) Follett Software
Mem of Northern Lights Library System
Open Mon, Wed & Fri 8:45-3:15, Tues & Thurs 8:45-3:15 & 6:30-9:30

ARROWWOOD

P ARROWWOOD MUNICIPAL LIBRARY*, 22 Centre St, T0L 0B0. (Mail add: PO Box 88, T0L 0B0). Tel: 403-534-3932. FAX: 403-534-3932. E-mail: help@arrowwoodlibrary.ca. Web Site: www.arrowwoodlibrary.ca. *Libr Mgr,* Sherry Malmberg
Pop 230
Library Holdings: Bk Titles 12,000; Per Subs 32
Automation Activity & Vendor Info: (Cataloging) BiblioCommons
Wireless access
Mem of Chinook Arch Regional Library System
Open Tues & Wed 12-5, Thurs 10-5

ASHMONT

P ASHMONT PUBLIC LIBRARY*, Box 330 Main St, T0A 0C0. SAN 329-255X. Tel: 780-726-3777. FAX: 780-726-3818. E-mail: info@ashmontlibrary.ab.ca. Web Site: ashmontlibrary.ab.ca. *Librn,* Tonya Sams
Founded 1984. Pop 746; Circ 21,656
Library Holdings: Bk Titles 16,000; Per Subs 31
Mem of Northern Lights Library System
Special Services for the Deaf - Bks on deafness & sign lang; High interest/low vocabulary bks
Open Tues & Thurs 10-2, Wed 10-1

ATHABASCA

P ATHABASCA MUNICIPAL LIBRARY*, Alice B Donahue Library & Archives, 4716 48th St, T9S 2B6. Tel: 780-675-2735. FAX: 780-675-2735. E-mail: librarian@athabascalibrary.ab.ca. *Librn,* Cynthia Graefe
Pop 29,000; Circ 40,000
Library Holdings: Audiobooks 200; AV Mats 100; DVDs 500; Large Print Bks 481; Bk Vols 23,000; Per Subs 38
Special Collections: Local History Archive Coll
Wireless access
Mem of Northern Lights Library System
Open Tues, Wed & Fri 10-5:30, Thurs 10-8, Sat 10-4

C ATHABASCA UNIVERSITY, Library & Scholarly Resources, One University Dr, T9S 3A3. SAN 321-3781. Tel: 780-675-6254. Toll Free Tel: 800-788-9041, Ext 6254. FAX: 780-675-6477. E-mail: library@athabascau.ca. Web Site: www.athabascau.ca/library. *Dir, Libr & Scholarly Resources,* Elaine Fabbro; E-mail: elainef@athabascau.ca; *Assoc University Librarian, Colls,* Shauna Bryce; E-mail: sbryce@athabascau.ca; *Acting Mgr, Info Services, Circ Supvr,* Joanna Nemeth; E-mail: jnemeth@athabascau.ca; Staff 15 (MLS 7, Non-MLS 8)
Founded 1970. Enrl 7,200; Highest Degree: Doctorate
Library Holdings: e-books 185,000; e-journals 60,000; Bk Titles 155,000; Per Subs 500
Special Collections: Can; Distance Education (Reverend Edward Checkland Coll)
Automation Activity & Vendor Info: (Acquisitions) Innovative Interfaces, Inc; (Cataloging) Innovative Interfaces, Inc; (Circulation) Innovative Interfaces, Inc; (Course Reserve) Innovative Interfaces, Inc; (ILL) Innovative Interfaces, Inc; (OPAC) Innovative Interfaces, Inc; (Serials) Innovative Interfaces, Inc
Partic in The Alberta Library
Open Mon-Fri 8:30-4:30

BANFF

S BANFF CENTRE*, Paul D Fleck Library & Archives, 107 Tunnel Mountain Dr, T1L 1H5. (Mail add: PO Box 1020, Stn 43, T1L 1H5), SAN 320-8826. Tel: 403-762-6265. FAX: 403-762-6266. E-mail: archives@banffcentre.ca, library@banffcentre.ca. Web Site: www.banffcentre.ca/library-and-archives. *Mgr,* Mark Black; Tel: 403-762-6255; *Music Librn,* Keely Burkholder; Staff 3 (MLS 3)
Founded 1979
Library Holdings: DVDs 300; Music Scores 22,000; Bk Vols 40,000; Per Subs 120; Videos 2,000
Special Collections: Artist Book Coll
Subject Interests: Mgt arts, Performing arts, Visual arts
Automation Activity & Vendor Info: (Cataloging) SirsiDynix; (Circulation) SirsiDynix; (OPAC) SirsiDynix
Wireless access
Partic in The Alberta Library
Open Mon-Thurs 9-8, Fri 9-6, Sun 11-7

P BANFF PUBLIC LIBRARY*, 101 Bear St, T1L 1H3. (Mail add: PO Box 996, T1H 1H3), SAN 318-5931. Tel: 403-762-2661. E-mail: info@banfflibrary.ab.ca. Web Site: www.banfflibrary.ab.ca. *Libr Dir,* Sarah McCormack; Staff 10 (MLS 3, Non-MLS 7)
Pop 8,352; Circ 100,000
Library Holdings: Bk Vols 42,000
Subject Interests: Mountaineering
Wireless access
Mem of Marigold Library System
Open Mon-Thurs 10-8, Fri 10-6, Sat & Sun 11-6

S WHYTE MUSEUM OF THE CANADIAN ROCKIES*, Archives & Library, 111 Bear St, T1L 1A3. (Mail add: PO Box 160, T1L 1A3), SAN 318-594X. Tel: 403-762-2291, Ext 335. FAX: 403-762-2339. E-mail: archives@whyte.org. Web Site: www.whyte.org. *Head, Archives & Spec Coll,* Elizabeth Kundert-Cameron; *Archivist,* Nicole Ensing; Staff 3 (MLS 2, Non-MLS 1)
Founded 1967
Library Holdings: Bk Titles 5,000; Bk Vols 6,500; Per Subs 128
Special Collections: Local Newspaper, 1900 to present, micro to 1983; Map Coll
Subject Interests: Can Rocky Mountains, Environ, Hist of Can Rockies, Hist of Western Can
Publications: The Cairn (Newsletter)
Open Mon-Fri 10-5
Restriction: Closed stack, In-house use for visitors, Non-circulating coll, Not a lending libr

BARNWELL

P BARNWELL PUBLIC LIBRARY*, 320 Heritage Rd, T0K 0B0. (Mail add: PO Box 261, T0K 0B0). Tel: 403-223-2902. E-mail: help@barnwelllibrary.ca. Web Site: www.barnwelllibrary.ca. *Libr Mgr,* Kim Shimbashi; E-mail: kshimbashi@barnwelllibrary.ca
Pop 900
Library Holdings: Bk Titles 11,000; Per Subs 15
Wireless access
Open Tues, Wed & Fri 1-5, Thurs 10:30-5

BARRHEAD

P BARRHEAD PUBLIC LIBRARY*, 5103 53 Ave, T7N 1N9. SAN 318-5958. Tel: 780-674-8519. FAX: 780-674-8520. E-mail: library@barrheadpubliclibrary.ca. Web Site: www.barrheadpubliclibrary.ca. *Dir,* Elaine Dickie; Staff 6 (MLS 1, Non-MLS 5)
Founded 1950. Pop 10,967; Circ 218,272
Library Holdings: Bk Titles 46,000; Bk Vols 51,000; Per Subs 135
Subject Interests: Local hist
Wireless access
Mem of Yellowhead Regional Library
Open Mon-Wed & Fri 10-5:30, Thurs 10-7, Sat 12-4
Friends of the Library Group

BASHAW

P BASHAW PUBLIC LIBRARY*, 5020 52 St, T0B 0H0. (Mail add: PO Box 669, T0B 0H0). Tel: 780-372-4055. FAX: 780-372-4055. E-mail: bashawlibrary@prl.ab.ca. Web Site: bashawlibrary.prl.ab.ca. *Libr Mgr,* Cindy Hunter
Pop 850; Circ 9,300
Library Holdings: Large Print Bks 9,150; Bk Titles 13,400; Per Subs 3
Automation Activity & Vendor Info: (Acquisitions) SirsiDynix; (Cataloging) SirsiDynix
Wireless access
Mem of Parkland Regional Library-Alberta
Open Tues 11-5, Wed 10-6, Thurs 10-5, Fri 10-12:30 & 1:30-4:30

BASSANO

P BASSANO MEMORIAL LIBRARY*, 522 Second Ave, T0J 0B0. (Mail add: PO Box 658, T0J 0B0). Tel: 403-641-4065. FAX: 403-641-4065. Web Site: bassano.shortgrass.ca. *Chief Librn,* Bonnie Bennett; E-mail: bonnie@shortgrass.ca
Founded 1960. Pop 3,000; Circ 15,000
Library Holdings: Bk Titles 17,000
Special Collections: Prov
Wireless access
Mem of Shortgrass Library System
Open Tues 10-8, Thurs 2-9, Sat 10-5

BAWLF

P BAWLF PUBLIC LIBRARY*, David Knipe Memorial Library, 203 Hanson St, Box 116, T0B 0J0. Tel: 780-373-3882. FAX: 780-373-3882. E-mail: bawlflibrary@prl.ab.ca. Web Site: www.bawlflibrary.prl.ab.ca. *Libr Mgr,* Fern Reinke; *Asst Libr Mgr,* Betty Crow
Pop 1,500
Library Holdings: DVDs 315; Microforms 7; Bk Titles 5,334
Wireless access
Mem of Parkland Regional Library-Alberta
Open Mon, Wed & Fri 10-5, Thurs 3-7
Friends of the Library Group

BEAR CANYON

P BEAR POINT COMMUNITY LIBRARY*, PO Box 43, T0H 0B0. SAN 372-719X. Tel: 780-595-3771. E-mail: librarian@bearpointlibrary.ab.ca. Web Site: www.bearpointlibrary.ab.ca. *Libr Mgr,* Twila Clay
Founded 1979. Pop 300
Library Holdings: Bk Titles 5,000; Bk Vols 5,200
Automation Activity & Vendor Info: (Cataloging) SirsiDynix; (OPAC) SirsiDynix
Mem of Peace Library System
Open Mon-Fri 10:30-2
Friends of the Library Group

BEAUMONT

P BIBLIOTHEQUE DE BEAUMONT LIBRARY*, 5700 49 St, T4X 1S7. Tel: 780-929-2665. FAX: 780-929-1291. E-mail: library@beaumontlibrary.com. Web Site: www.beaumontlibrary.com. *Dir,* Laura Winton; E-mail: laura@beaumontlibrary.com
Founded 1978. Pop 13,287; Circ 87,064
Library Holdings: AV Mats 2,893; Large Print Bks 300; Bk Vols 26,272
Special Collections: French Reading Materials
Subject Interests: Early literacy, Graphic novels, Parenting
Automation Activity & Vendor Info: (Acquisitions) Innovative Interfaces, Inc; (Cataloging) Innovative Interfaces, Inc; (Circulation) Innovative Interfaces, Inc; (ILL) Innovative Interfaces, Inc; (OPAC) Innovative Interfaces, Inc
Wireless access
Mem of Yellowhead Regional Library
Partic in The Regional Automation Consortium
Open Mon-Thurs 9-8, Fri 9-4, Sat 10-4

BEAVERLODGE

P BEAVERLODGE PUBLIC LIBRARY*, 406 Tenth St, T0H 0C0. (Mail add: PO Box 119, T0H 0C0), SAN 318-5974. Tel: 780-354-2569. FAX: 780-354-3078. E-mail: librarian@beaverlodgelibrary.ab.ca. Web Site: www.beaverlodgelibrary.ab.ca. *Librn,* Ms Tracy Deets; Staff 5 (Non-MLS 5)
Founded 1945. Pop 5,800; Circ 40,000
Library Holdings: Bk Titles 28,000; Per Subs 40
Wireless access
Mem of Peace Library System
Partic in The Regional Automation Consortium
Open Mon-Fri 9-5
Friends of the Library Group

BEISEKER

P BEISEKER MUNICIPAL LIBRARY*, 401 Fifth St, T0M 0G0. (Mail add: PO Box 8, T0M 0G0). Tel: 403-947-3230. FAX: 403-947-3230. E-mail: abemlibrary@marigold.ab.ca. Web Site: www.beisekerlibrary.ca. *Libr Mgr,* Shawna Fox
Pop 930
Library Holdings: Bk Titles 6,500
Subject Interests: Local hist
Automation Activity & Vendor Info: (Acquisitions) SirsiDynix; (Cataloging) SirsiDynix; (Circulation) SirsiDynix; (ILL) SirsiDynix; (Serials) SirsiDynix
Wireless access
Mem of Marigold Library System
Partic in The Regional Automation Consortium
Open Tues & Fri 9-5, Wed & Thurs 2-8

BENTLEY

P BENTLEY MUNICIPAL LIBRARY*, 5014 - 49 Ave, T0C 0J0. (Mail add: Box 361, T0C 0J0). Tel: 403-748-4626. E-mail: bentleylibrary@prl.ab.ca. Web Site: bentleylibrary.prl.ab.ca. *Co-Mgr,* Vera Boettger; *Co-Mgr,* Tammy Izquierdo
Founded 1949. Pop 1,134
Library Holdings: Bk Titles 10,000; Talking Bks 114; Videos 99
Automation Activity & Vendor Info: (Acquisitions) SirsiDynix
Wireless access
Function: 24/7 Online cat, Adult bk club, Bk club(s), Bks on CD, Children's prog, Computers for patron use, Laminating, Magazines, Mail loans to mem, Movies, Music CDs, Online cat, Photocopying/Printing, Prog for adults, Prog for children & young adult, Scanner, Summer reading prog, Teen prog
Mem of Parkland Regional Library-Alberta
Open Tues, Wed & Fri 10-5:30, Sat 11-3
Friends of the Library Group

BERWYN

P BERWYN MUNICIPAL LIBRARY*, 5105 51st St, T0H 0E0. SAN 318-5990. Tel: 780-338-3616. FAX: 780-338-3616. E-mail: librarian@berwynlibrary.ab.ca. Web Site: www.berwynlibrary.ab.ca. Pop 546
Library Holdings: Large Print Bks 150; Bk Titles 8,200
Special Collections: Children's Circle Video Coll
Automation Activity & Vendor Info: (Cataloging) Innovative Interfaces, Inc. - Polaris
Wireless access
Mem of Peace Library System
Partic in The Regional Automation Consortium
Open Mon 10-5, Thurs 1-6, Sat 11-4

BIG VALLEY

P BIG VALLEY MUNICIPAL LIBRARY*, 29 First Ave S, T0J 0G0. (Mail add: PO Box 205, T0J 0G0). Tel: 403-876-2642. FAX: 403-876-2401. E-mail: bigvalleylibrary@prl.ab.ca. Web Site: www.bvlibrary.prl.ab.ca. *Libr Mgr,* Cordelle Rotvik
Pop 365; Circ 1,200
Library Holdings: Bk Titles 12,600; Per Subs 12
Automation Activity & Vendor Info: (Cataloging) Innovative Interfaces, Inc. - Polaris
Wireless access
Function: Homebound delivery serv, ILL available, Mail loans to mem, Outreach serv, Photocopying/Printing
Mem of Parkland Regional Library-Alberta
Open Tues-Thurs 10-1 & 3-6, Fri 10-1

BLACKFALDS

P BLACKFALDS PUBLIC LIBRARY*, 5302 Broadway Ave, T0M 0J0. (Mail add: PO Box 70, T0M 0J0). Tel: 403-885-2343. E-mail: library@blackfaldslibrary.ca. Web Site: www.blackfaldslibrary.ca. *Libr Mgr,* Carley Binder
Library Holdings: Per Subs 40; Talking Bks 500; Videos 1,800
Automation Activity & Vendor Info: (Acquisitions) Innovative Interfaces, Inc. - Polaris; (Cataloging) Innovative Interfaces, Inc. - Polaris; (Circulation) Innovative Interfaces, Inc. - Polaris
Wireless access
Function: 24/7 Electronic res, 24/7 Online cat, Adult bk club, After school storytime, Art exhibits, Art programs, Bk club(s), Free DVD rentals, Homebound delivery serv, ILL available, Mail loans to mem, Photocopying/Printing, Prog for adults, Prog for children & young adult, Ref serv available, Summer reading prog, Wheelchair accessible
Mem of Parkland Regional Library-Alberta
Open Mon & Wed 10-8, Tues, Thurs & Fri 10-6, Sat 10-5, Sun 1-5
Friends of the Library Group

BLAIRMORE

P CROWSNEST PASS MUNICIPAL LIBRARY*, 2114 127 St, T0K 0E0. (Mail add: PO Box 1177, T0K 0E0). Tel: 403-562-8393. FAX: 403-562-8397. E-mail: help@crowsnestpasslibrary.ca. Web Site: crowsnestpasslibrary.ca. *Libr Mgr,* Diane DeLauw
Pop 5,600; Circ 35,000
Library Holdings: Bk Vols 25,000
Wireless access
Function: 24/7 Electronic res, 24/7 Online cat, Children's prog, Free DVD rentals, Magazines, Mango lang, Meeting rooms, Museum passes, Photocopying/Printing, Preschool reading prog, Prog for adults, Scanner,

Senior outreach, Serves people with intellectual disabilities, Spoken cassettes & CDs, Story hour, Study rm, Summer reading prog
Mem of Chinook Arch Regional Library System
Open Mon & Sat 12-4, Tues-Fri 9-7

BLUE RIDGE

P BLUE RIDGE COMMUNITY LIBRARY*, 117 Second Ave, T0E 0B0. (Mail add: PO Box 264, T0E 0B0). Tel: 780-648-3991. E-mail: blueridgelibrary@yrl.ab.ca. Web Site: blueridgelibrary.ab.ca. *Libr Mgr,* Tracy Mindus
Library Holdings: DVDs 2,000; Bk Titles 8,000; Per Subs 18; Talking Bks 75
Automation Activity & Vendor Info: (Acquisitions) SirsiDynix
Wireless access
Mem of Yellowhead Regional Library
Open Tues 12-8, Wed-Fri 12-6, Sat 12-4
Friends of the Library Group

BON ACCORD

P BON ACCORD PUBLIC LIBRARY*, 5025 50th Ave, T0A 0K0. (Mail add: PO Box 749, T0A 0K0), SAN 372-7947. Tel: 780-921-2540. FAX: 780-921-2580. E-mail: librarian@bonaccordlibrary.ab.ca. Web Site: www.bonaccordlibrary.ab.ca. *Libr Mgr,* Joyce Curtis-Bonardi; *ILL,* Shannon Loehr; Staff 1 (Non-MLS 1)
Founded 1982. Pop 1,532; Circ 32,000
Wireless access
Function: 24/7 Electronic res
Mem of Northern Lights Library System
Open Mon & Fri 10-3:30, Tues & Thurs 10-7, Wed 10-6
Friends of the Library Group

BONANZA

P BONANZA MUNICIPAL LIBRARY*, PO Box 53, T0H 0K0. Tel: 780-353-3067. E-mail: librarian@bonanzalibrary.ca. Web Site: www.bonanzalibrary.ca. *Libr Mgr,* Michelle Kettles
Wireless access
Mem of Peace Library System
Open Tues & Thurs 3-6, Sat 10-1

BONNYVILLE

P BONNYVILLE MUNICIPAL LIBRARY*, 4804 49th Ave, T9N 2J3. (Mail add: PO Box 8058, T9N 2J3), SAN 318-6016. Tel: 780-826-3071. FAX: 780-826-2058. E-mail: librarian@bonnyvillelibrary.ab.ca. Web Site: www.bonnyvillelibrary.ab.ca. *Chairperson,* Brian Wood; *Dir,* Ina Smith; *Asst Librn,* Linda Smiley; Staff 1 (MLS 1)
Pop 12,168; Circ 60,000
Library Holdings: Bk Vols 24,000
Special Collections: Audio Books Coll; French Easy Read Coll; Large Print Book Coll
Automation Activity & Vendor Info: (Acquisitions) Innovative Interfaces, Inc; (Cataloging) Innovative Interfaces, Inc; (Circulation) Innovative Interfaces, Inc; (OPAC) Innovative Interfaces, Inc; (Serials) Innovative Interfaces, Inc
Wireless access
Function: Adult bk club, Children's prog, Computers for patron use, Home delivery & serv to seniorr ctr & nursing homes, ILL available, Internet access, Online cat, Online ref, Photocopying/Printing, Scanner
Mem of Northern Lights Library System
Partic in The Regional Automation Consortium
Special Services for the Deaf - Assistive tech
Special Services for the Blind - Accessible computers; Assistive/Adapted tech devices, equip & products; Audio mat; Bks on cassette; Bks on CD; Large print bks
Open Mon-Thurs 9-8, Fri 9-5, Sat 11-5

BOW ISLAND

P BOW ISLAND MUNICIPAL LIBRARY*, Susan Andersen Library, 510 Centre St, T0K 0G0. (Mail add: PO Box 608, T0K 0G0). Tel: 403-545-2828. FAX: 403-545-6642. E-mail: bowlib@shortgrass.ca. Web Site: bowisland.shortgrass.ca. *Libr Mgr,* Kathryn Van Dorp; Staff 1 (Non-MLS 1)
Founded 1975. Pop 1,704; Circ 40,000
Library Holdings: AV Mats 2,000; Bk Vols 18,000; Per Subs 50
Wireless access
Mem of Shortgrass Library System
Open Tues & Wed 10-8, Thurs & Fri 10-5, Sat 10-1
Friends of the Library Group

BOWDEN

P BOWDEN PUBLIC LIBRARY, 2101 20th Ave, Bay # 2, T0M 0K0. (Mail add: Box 218, T0M 0K0). Tel: 403-224-3688. E-mail: bowdenlibrary@prl.ab.ca. Web Site: prl.ab.ca/Bowden. *Libr Mgr,* Julie Hamblin
Library Holdings: Bk Vols 17,000; Per Subs 20
Wireless access
Mem of Parkland Regional Library-Alberta
Open Tues-Thurs 10-6, Sat 10-4

BOYLE

P BOYLE PUBLIC LIBRARY, 4800 Third St S, T0A 0M0. (Mail add: PO Box 450, T0A 0M0). Tel: 780-689-4161. FAX: 780-689-5660. E-mail: info@boylelibrary.ca. Web Site: www.boylelibrary.ca. *Chmn,* Mellisa Gardner; *Libr Mgr,* Kathy Bulmer
Founded 1980. Pop 862
Library Holdings: Bk Titles 10,000
Wireless access
Function: 24/7 Electronic res, 24/7 Online cat, Bks on CD, Children's prog, Computers for patron use, Digital talking bks, Electronic databases & coll, ILL available, Internet access, Magazines, Mail & tel request accepted, Photocopying/Printing, Preschool reading prog, Prog for children & young adult, Story hour, Summer & winter reading prog, Summer reading prog, Wheelchair accessible, Winter reading prog
Mem of Northern Lights Library System
Partic in The Regional Automation Consortium
Special Services for the Blind - Daisy reader; Talking bks
Open Tues, Thurs & Fri 10:30-4:30, Wed Noon-8
Friends of the Library Group

BRETON

P BRETON MUNICIPAL LIBRARY*, 4916-50 Ave, T0C 0P0. (Mail add: PO Box 447, T0C 0P0). Tel: 780-696-3740. FAX: 780-696-3590. E-mail: bretonlibrary@yrl.ab.ca. Web Site: www.bretonlibrary.ab.ca. *Libr Dir,* Diane Shave; Staff 3 (Non-MLS 3)
Founded 1972. Pop 573
Library Holdings: AV Mats 191; Large Print Bks 135; Bk Titles 8,000; Talking Bks 70
Automation Activity & Vendor Info: (Acquisitions) Innovative Interfaces, Inc; (Cataloging) Innovative Interfaces, Inc; (Circulation) Innovative Interfaces, Inc; (ILL) Innovative Interfaces, Inc; (OPAC) Innovative Interfaces, Inc
Wireless access
Function: Bks on cassette, Bks on CD, Computer training, Computers for patron use, Electronic databases & coll, Free DVD rentals, ILL available, Large print keyboards, Music CDs, Online cat, OverDrive digital audio bks, Ref & res, Scanner, Spoken cassettes & CDs, Story hour, Summer reading prog, Telephone ref, VHS videos, Wheelchair accessible
Mem of Yellowhead Regional Library
Open Mon-Thurs 10-5, Fri 10-8, Sat 9-2

BROOKS

P BROOKS PUBLIC LIBRARY*, JBS Canada Recreation Centre, 323 First St E, T1R 1C5. (Mail add: PO Box 1149, T1R 1B9), SAN 318-6024. Tel: 403-362-2947. FAX: 403-362-8111. E-mail: brolib@shortgrass.ca. Web Site: brooks.shortgrass.ca. *Mgr,* Lisa Crosby; Staff 9 (MLS 1, Non-MLS 8)
Founded 1951. Pop 13,000; Circ 130,000
Library Holdings: Audiobooks 1,052; Bks on Deafness & Sign Lang 20; High Interest/Low Vocabulary Bk Vols 2,000; Bk Titles 44,000; Per Subs 197
Special Collections: Scammell (Wild Life & Hunting Coll)
Subject Interests: Gardening, Genealogical, Local hist
Automation Activity & Vendor Info: (Acquisitions) SirsiDynix; (Cataloging) SirsiDynix; (Circulation) SirsiDynix; (OPAC) SirsiDynix; (Serials) SirsiDynix
Wireless access
Mem of Shortgrass Library System
Special Services for the Blind - Bks on cassette; Bks on CD; Braille bks; Reader equip
Open Mon, Fri & Sat 9:30-5, Tues-Thurs 9:30-8, Sun 1-5
Friends of the Library Group

S EASTERN IRRIGATION DISTRICT*, Archives & Library, 550 Industrial Rd W, T1R 1B2. (Mail add: PO Box 128, T1R 1B2), SAN 373-675X. Tel: 403-362-1400. FAX: 403-362-6206. E-mail: archive@eid.ca. Web Site: www.eid.ca. *Librn,* Crystal Lintott
Library Holdings: Bk Titles 1,200
Special Collections: Irrigation (CPR Eastern Section Coll), bks, linens, ms, maps
Automation Activity & Vendor Info: (Acquisitions) Inmagic, Inc.
Restriction: Open by appt only

BROWNFIELD

P BROWNFIELD COMMUNITY LIBRARY*, 5001 Main St, T0C 0R0. (Mail add: PO Box 63, T0C 0R0). Tel: 403-578-2247. FAX: 403-578-4208. E-mail: brownfieldlibrary@prl.ab.ca. Web Site: prl.ab.ca/brownfield. *Libr Mgr,* Darvy Gilbertson
Founded 1992. Pop 200
Library Holdings: Bk Titles 29,000; Videos 250
Automation Activity & Vendor Info: (Acquisitions) Horizon; (Cataloging) Horizon; (Circulation) Horizon; (Course Reserve) Horizon; (ILL) Horizon; (Media Booking) Horizon; (OPAC) Horizon; (Serials) Horizon
Wireless access
Function: 24/7 Electronic res, 24/7 Online cat, 24/7 wireless access, Adult bk club, Audiobks via web, Bk club(s), Children's prog, Computer training, Computers for patron use, Electronic databases & coll, Free DVD rentals, Games, Holiday prog, ILL available, Internet access, Magazines, Mail & tel request accepted, Mail loans to mem, Movies, Online cat, Online ref, Outside serv via phone, mail, e-mail & web, OverDrive digital audio bks, Photocopying/Printing, Prog for adults, Prog for children & young adult, Ref & res, Res libr, Scanner, Summer reading prog, Teen prog, Workshops
Mem of Parkland Regional Library-Alberta
Open Tues 11-5, Thurs 11-4; Thurs 9-3 (Summer)
Friends of the Library Group

BRUDERHEIM

P METRO KALYN COMMUNITY LIBRARY, 5017-49 St, Bag 250, T0B 0S0. Tel: 780-796-3032. FAX: 780-796-3032. E-mail: librarian@bruderheimpl.ab.ca. Web Site: www.bruderheimpl.ab.ca. *Libr Mgr,* Diana Mack
Pop 1,202
Automation Activity & Vendor Info: (Acquisitions) Innovative Interfaces, Inc
Wireless access
Mem of Northern Lights Library System
Open Tues & Thurs 4-7, Wed 12-3

CADOGAN

P CADOGAN PUBLIC LIBRARY*, 112 Second St, T0B 0T0. (Mail add: PO Box 10, T0B 0T0). Tel: 780-753-6933. E-mail: cadoganlibrary@prl.ab.ca. Web Site: cadoganlibrary.prl.ab.ca. *Libr Mgr,* Rochelle Scammell
Wireless access
Mem of Parkland Regional Library-Alberta
Open Mon & Wed 4-7, Tues 12:30-8, Thurs 9-Noon

CALGARY

CR ALBERTA BIBLE COLLEGE LIBRARY*, 635 Northmount Dr NW, T2K 3J6. SAN 326-5005. Tel: 403-282-2994. FAX: 403-282-3084. E-mail: library@abccampus.ca. Web Site: www.abccampus.ca/current-students/library. *Librn,* Marissa Moore; E-mail: mmoore@abccampus.ca; Staff 1.5 (Non-MLS 1.5)
Founded 1937. Enrl 52; Fac 4; Highest Degree: Bachelor
Library Holdings: Bks on Deafness & Sign Lang 2; CDs 10; DVDs 23; e-books 378; e-journals 4; Bk Titles 32,000; Per Subs 245; Spec Interest Per Sub 3; Videos 47
Special Collections: Churches of Christ & Christian Churches in Western Canada
Subject Interests: Biblical studies, Restoration hist
Wireless access
Function: Archival coll, Audiobks via web, Bus archives, CD-ROM, Computers for patron use, Doc delivery serv, E-Reserves, Electronic databases & coll, Free DVD rentals, ILL available, Internet access, Mail & tel request accepted, Mail loans to mem, Online cat, Online ref, Orientations, Outside serv via phone, mail, e-mail & web, Photocopying/Printing, Printer for laptops & handheld devices, Prof lending libr, Ref & res, Ref serv available, Spoken cassettes & CDs, Telephone ref, VHS videos, Wheelchair accessible, Workshops
Partic in Asn of Christian Librs; Can Libr Asn; Christian Library Consortium
Special Services for the Deaf - Bks on deafness & sign lang; Staff with knowledge of sign lang
Special Services for the Blind - Cassettes; Copier with enlargement capabilities; Free checkout of audio mat
Open Mon-Thurs 9-9, Fri 9-5, Sat 10-2
Restriction: Free to mem, Non-circulating of rare bks, Open to fac, students & qualified researchers, Open to pub for ref & circ; with some limitations, Open to staff, students & ancillary prof, Open to students, Open to students, fac & staff, Open to students, fac, staff & alumni

M ALBERTA CHILDREN'S HOSPITAL KNOWLEDGE CENTRE*, 28 Oki Dr NW, A2-908, 2nd Flr, T3B 6A8. SAN 322-7766. Tel: 403-955-7077. FAX: 403-955-2799. E-mail: krs@ahs.ca. Web Site: krs.libguides.com. *Librn,* Rachel Zhao; E-mail: xurongrachel.zhao@albertahealthservices.ca; Staff 3 (MLS 1, Non-MLS 2)
Founded 1982
Library Holdings: Bk Titles 3,000; Bk Vols 4,000; Per Subs 220
Automation Activity & Vendor Info: (Cataloging) SirsiDynix
Open Mon-Fri 8-4

C ALBERTA COLLEGE OF ARTS*, Luke Lindoe Library, 1407 14th Ave NW, T2N 4R3. SAN 320-2798. Tel: 403-284-7667. FAX: 403-289-6682. E-mail: library@auarts.ca. Web Site: auarts.ca/our-campus/library. *Librn,* Andrea Johnston; E-mail: andrea.johnston@auarts.ca; Staff 7 (MLS 2, Non-MLS 5)
Founded 1926. Enrl 999; Fac 97; Highest Degree: Bachelor
Library Holdings: AV Mats 40,000; DVDs 1,052; e-books 67,000; Electronic Media & Resources 32; Bk Titles 40,000; Per Subs 150
Special Collections: Visual Art Images
Automation Activity & Vendor Info: (Acquisitions) SirsiDynix; (Cataloging) SirsiDynix; (Circulation) SirsiDynix; (Course Reserve) SirsiDynix; (OPAC) SirsiDynix
Wireless access
Function: Doc delivery serv, ILL available, Internet access, Photocopying/Printing, Res libr, Telephone ref
Publications: Film Holdings List; Periodical Holdings List
Special Services for the Deaf - Closed caption videos
Restriction: Open to pub for ref & circ; with some limitations, Open to students, fac & staff

ALBERTA LAW LIBRARIES

GL LRTC CALGARY*, Calgary Court Ctr, Ste 501-N, 601 Fifth St SW, T2P 5P7, SAN 318-6032. Tel: 403-297-6148. Toll Free Tel: 866-448-6148. FAX: 403-297-5171. E-mail: lawlibrary@just.gov.ab.ca. Web Site: www.lawlibrary.ab.ca. *Dir,* Sonia Poulin; Tel: 780-422-1011; Staff 6 (MLS 2, Non-MLS 4)
Founded 1905
Library Holdings: Bk Vols 50,000; Per Subs 400
Special Collections: Alberta Legal Archives Program; Historical Index & Biographical File to Superior Court Judges of Southern Alberta (1883-present); Unreported Decisions for Supreme Court, Federal Court & All Levels of Courts of Alberta
Subject Interests: Computer law, Energy law, Law off mgt, Pacific Rim
Automation Activity & Vendor Info: (Cataloging) Ex Libris Group; (Circulation) Ex Libris Group; (OPAC) Ex Libris Group; (Serials) Ex Libris Group
Publications: A Selected Checklist of Legal Publications for the Alberta Practitioner; Energy Law Bibliography; Sample Jury Charges
Open Mon-Fri 8:15-4:30

GL JUDICIAL*, Calgary Courts Ctr, 601-Five St SW, Ste 501N, T2P 5P7. Tel: 403-297-3118. FAX: 403-297-2981. E-mail: judicial-south.libraries@gov.ab.ca. *Law Librn,* Rachel Appleby; Tel: 403-592-4796, E-mail: rachel.appleby@gov.ab.ca; *Law Librn,* Lyn Beattie; Tel: 403-297-8234, E-mail: lyn.beattie@gov.ab.ca; *Law Librn,* Lola Salami; Tel: 403-297-3231, E-mail: lola.salami@gov.ab.ca; Staff 2 (MLS 2)
Library Holdings: Bk Vols 9,200
Subject Interests: Civil, Criminal, Family law, Youth law
Function: For res purposes
Restriction: Not open to pub

S ALBERTA WILDERNESS ASSOCIATION*, Alberta Wilderness Resource Centre, 455 12th St NW, T2N 1Y9. SAN 323-830X. Tel: 403-283-2025. FAX: 403-270-2743. E-mail: awa@abwild.ca. Web Site: www.albertawilderness.ca. *Exec Dir,* Debborah Donnelly
Library Holdings: Bk Titles 15,000; Per Subs 50
Subject Interests: Conserv
Wireless access
Restriction: Open by appt only, Open to pub for ref only

C AMBROSE LIBRARY*, 150 Ambrose Circle SW, T3H 0L5. SAN 320-7870. Tel: 403-410-2000, 403-410-2946. FAX: 403-571-2556. E-mail: library@ambrose.edu. Web Site: www.ambrose.edu/library. *Dir, Libr Serv,* Sandy Ayer; Tel: 403-410-2947, E-mail: sayer@ambrose.edu; Staff 2 (MLS 1, Non-MLS 1)
Founded 1925. Enrl 800; Fac 39; Highest Degree: Master
Library Holdings: CDs 1,651; DVDs 628; e-journals 61,567; Electronic Media & Resources 50; Microforms 28,833; Bk Titles 93,360; Bk Vols 125,000; Per Subs 200; Videos 560
Special Collections: Christian & Missionary Alliance
Subject Interests: Christian studies, Hist, Music
Automation Activity & Vendor Info: (Acquisitions) SirsiDynix; (Cataloging) SirsiDynix; (Circulation) SirsiDynix; (Course Reserve) SirsiDynix; (OPAC) SirsiDynix; (Serials) SirsiDynix
Wireless access
Function: Res libr

Partic in The Alberta Library
Open Mon-Fri 8:30-4:30

S ARUSHA CENTRE*, Community Development Resource Centre, c/o The Old Y Bldg, 233-12 Ave SW, No 106, T2R 0G9. SAN 371-0483. Tel: 403-270-3200. FAX: 403-270-8832. Web Site: www.arusha.org. *Library Contact,* Gerald Wheatley; E-mail: gerald@arusha.org
Library Holdings: DVDs 200; Bk Vols 1,000
Subject Interests: Educ, Intl develop, Multicultural educ, Race relations
Open Tues-Thurs 10:30-3:30

L BENNETT JONES LLP LIBRARY, 4500 Bankers Hall E, 855 Second St SW, T2P 4K7. SAN 327-5000. Tel: 403-298-3165. FAX: 403-265-7219. Web Site: www.bennettjones.com. *Sr Dir, Libr & Info Serv,* Christy MacKinnon; E-mail: mackinnonc@bennettjones.com; Staff 9.2 (MLS 5, Non-MLS 4.2)
Subject Interests: Law
Automation Activity & Vendor Info: (Acquisitions) SirsiDynix; (Cataloging) SirsiDynix; (Circulation) SirsiDynix; (OPAC) SirsiDynix; (Serials) SirsiDynix
Wireless access
Restriction: Staff use only

L BURNET, DUCKWORTH & PALMER, LLP, Information & Research Services, 2400, 525-Eighth Ave SW, T2P 1G1. SAN 327-7623. Tel: 403-260-0100. FAX: 403-260-0332. Web Site: www.bdplaw.com. *Legal Research Specialist,* Joanne McKenzie-Hicks; Staff 1 (MLS 1)
Library Holdings: Bk Vols 10,000
Subject Interests: Law
Wireless access
Restriction: Open to staff only

M CALGARY HEALTH REGION*, Rockyview General Hospital Knowledge Centre, Fisher Bldg, Rm 4EE11, 7007 14th St SW, T2V 1P9. SAN 373-6512. Tel: 403-943-3373. FAX: 403-943-3486. E-mail: krs@ahs.ca. Web Site: krs.libguides.com/aboutus/rgh. *Librn,* Ashley Jane Leonard; E-mail: ashleyjane.leonard@ahs.ca; Staff 3 (MLS 1, Non-MLS 2)
Founded 1986
Library Holdings: e-journals 8,000; Electronic Media & Resources 2,000; Bk Titles 4,000; Per Subs 3
Subject Interests: Allied health, Consumer health, Med, Nursing
Open Mon-Fri 8-4:15

P CALGARY PUBLIC LIBRARY*, 800 Third St SE, Level 4, T2G 2E7. SAN 365-6047. Tel: 403-260-2600. Web Site: www.calgarylibrary.ca. *Chief Exec Officer,* Sarah Meilleur; E-mail: sarah.meilleur@calgarylibrary.ca; Staff 80 (MLS 80)
Founded 1912. Pop 1,042,000; Circ 14,310,227
Library Holdings: Bk Vols 3,029,921; Per Subs 5,208
Special Collections: Canada Coll; Government Documents; Telephone Directories. Canadian and Provincial; Municipal Document Depository
Subject Interests: Directories, Law, Maps, Multilingual
Automation Activity & Vendor Info: (Acquisitions) SirsiDynix; (Cataloging) SirsiDynix; (Circulation) SirsiDynix; (ILL) SirsiDynix; (OPAC) SirsiDynix
Wireless access
Function: Adult bk club, Adult literacy prog, After school storytime, Archival coll, Art exhibits, Audio & video playback equip for onsite use, Audiobks via web, AV serv, Bilingual assistance for Spanish patrons, Bk club(s), Bks on CD, Bus archives, CD-ROM, Children's prog, Citizenship assistance, Computer training, Computers for patron use, Digital talking bks, Doc delivery serv, E-Reserves, Electronic databases & coll, Equip loans & repairs, Family literacy, Free DVD rentals, Games & aids for people with disabilities, Genealogy discussion group, Govt ref serv, Health sci info serv, Holiday prog, Home delivery & serv to seniorr ctr & nursing homes, Homebound delivery serv, Homework prog, ILL available, Internet access, Jail serv, Large print keyboards, Learning ctr, Literacy & newcomer serv, Magnifiers for reading, Mail & tel request accepted, Music CDs, Online cat, Online ref, Orientations, Outreach serv, Photocopying/Printing, Preschool outreach, Prog for adults, Prog for children & young adult, Ref & res, Ref serv available, Res libr, Res performed for a fee, Scanner, Senior computer classes, Senior outreach, Serves people with intellectual disabilities, Spoken cassettes & CDs, Spoken cassettes & DVDs, Story hour, Summer reading prog, Teen prog, Telephone ref, Wheelchair accessible, Workshops, Writing prog
Publications: At Your Library (Quarterly)
Partic in Utlas
Special Services for the Deaf - Adult & family literacy prog; Assisted listening device; Assistive tech; Bks on deafness & sign lang; Closed caption videos; TDD equip; TTY equip
Special Services for the Blind - Accessible computers; Aids for in-house use; Assistive/Adapted tech devices, equip & products; Audio mat; Bks & mags in Braille, on rec, tape & cassette; Bks available with recordings; Bks on cassette; Bks on CD; Braille bks; Computer access aids; Daisy reader; Descriptive video serv (DVS); Digital talking bk; Dragon Naturally Speaking software; Extensive large print coll; Home delivery serv; Large print & cassettes; Large print bks; Large print bks & talking machines; Magnifiers; PC for people with disabilities; Reader equip; Recorded bks; Talking bks; Volunteer serv
Open Mon-Thurs 9-8, Fri 9-5, Sat 10-5, Sun 12-5
Restriction: Circ to mem only, Fee for pub use, Non-circulating coll, Non-circulating to the pub, Non-resident fee, Open to pub for ref & circ; with some limitations, Open to students, Pub ref by request, Pub use on premises, Restricted loan policy
Branches: 21
BOWNESS, 6532 Bowness Rd NW, T3B 0E9, SAN 365-6071. Web Site: calgarylibrary.ca/your-library/locations/bow. *Mgr,* Jean Ludlam
Founded 1979. Pop 14,128; Circ 144,644
Library Holdings: CDs 3,521; Bk Vols 32,748; Per Subs 1,592; Talking Bks 1,670; Videos 1,530
Special Collections: Travelling Coll in Spanish & Dutch
Automation Activity & Vendor Info: (Acquisitions) ARIS-Atlantic Rim Information Systems
Special Services for the Deaf - Adult & family literacy prog; Assistive tech; Bks on deafness & sign lang; Closed caption videos; TDD equip; TTY equip
Special Services for the Blind - Accessible computers; Aids for in-house use; Assistive/Adapted tech devices, equip & products; Audio mat; Bks on cassette; Bks on CD; Braille bks
Open Mon-Wed 10-8, Thurs & Sat 10-5, Fri 10-6, Sun (Fall-Spring) Noon-5
W R CASTELL CENTRAL LIBRARY, 800 Third St SE, T2G 2E7, SAN 365-6055. Web Site: calgarylibrary.ca/your-library/locations/cent. *Cent Libr Mgr,* Allison Thomson
Founded 1963. Pop 51,624; Circ 928,333
Library Holdings: CDs 41,665; DVDs 12,339; Bk Vols 454,656; Per Subs 8,430; Talking Bks 22,461
Special Collections: Archival Coll; Local History Coll. Canadian and Provincial
Special Services for the Deaf - Adult & family literacy prog; Assisted listening device; Bks on deafness & sign lang; Closed caption videos; TDD equip; TTY equip
Special Services for the Blind - Accessible computers; Assistive/Adapted tech devices, equip & products; Bks available with recordings; Bks on CD; Braille bks; Daisy reader; Digital talking bk; Extensive large print coll; Home delivery serv; Large print bks; PC for people with disabilities; Talking bks; Volunteer serv
Open Mon-Thurs 9-8, Fri 9-6, Sat 10-5, Sun 12-5
Restriction: Circ to mem only, Non-circulating coll, Non-circulating of rare bks, Non-resident fee
COUNTRY HILLS, 11950 Country Village Link NE, T3K 6E3. Web Site: calgarylibrary.ca/your-library/locations/chill. *Mgr,* Chelsea Murray
Founded 2004. Pop 60,788; Circ 832,048
Library Holdings: Audiobooks 3,863; CDs 14,363; DVDs 6,272; Bk Vols 104,025; Per Subs 3,996; Talking Bks 3,863
Open Mon-Thurs 9-9, Fri 9-6, Sat 9-5, Sun 12-5
Restriction: Circ to mem only, Non-circulating coll, Non-resident fee
CROWFOOT, 8665 Nose Hill Dr NW, T3G 5T3. Web Site: calgarylibrary.ca/your-library/locations/crow. *Mgr,* Jean Ludlam
Founded 2003. Pop 104,492; Circ 1,442,474
Library Holdings: Audiobooks 7,383; CDs 22,960; DVDs 9,662; Bk Vols 171,614; Per Subs 6,592; Talking Bks 7,383
Special Services for the Deaf - Assistive tech; Bks on deafness & sign lang; Captioned film dep; Closed caption videos; TDD equip; TTY equip
Special Services for the Blind - Accessible computers; Assistive/Adapted tech devices, equip & products; Audio mat; Bks available with recordings; Bks on CD
Open Mon-Thurs 9-9, Fri 9-6, Sat 9-5, Sun 12-5
Restriction: Circ to mem only, Non-resident fee
FISH CREEK, 11161 Bonaventure Dr SE, T2J 6S1, SAN 365-6225. Web Site: calgarylibrary.ca/your-library/locations/fish. *Mgr,* Sara House
Founded 1985. Pop 98,383; Circ 1,059,232
Library Holdings: CDs 23,369; DVDs 6,431; Bk Titles 285,158; Per Subs 7,729; Talking Bks 6,121
Subject Interests: Literacy, Multilingual
Special Services for the Deaf - Adult & family literacy prog; Assistive tech; Bks on deafness & sign lang; TDD equip; TTY equip
Special Services for the Blind - Accessible computers; Aids for in-house use; Assistive/Adapted tech devices, equip & products; Bks available with recordings; Bks on CD; Braille bks; Daisy reader; Digital talking bk; Large print bks; PC for people with disabilities; Recorded bks; Talking bks
Open Mon-Thurs 9-9, Fri 9-6, Sat 9-5, Sun 12-5
Restriction: Circ to mem only, In-house use for visitors, Mem only, Non-circulating coll, Non-resident fee
FOREST LAWN, 4807 Eighth Ave SE, T2A 4M1, SAN 365-6195. Web Site: calgarylibrary.ca/your-library/locations/flawn. *Mgr,* Shannon Slater
Pop 63,849; Circ 455,855

Library Holdings: CDs 7,545; DVDs 3,792; Bk Titles 64,471; Per Subs 3,404; Talking Bks 3,295
Special Collections: Multi-languages Coll
Special Services for the Deaf - Adult & family literacy prog; Assistive tech; Closed caption videos; TDD equip; TTY equip
Special Services for the Blind - Accessible computers; Aids for in-house use; Assistive/Adapted tech devices, equip & products; Bks available with recordings; Bks on cassette; Bks on CD; Braille bks; Computer access aids; Computer with voice synthesizer for visually impaired persons; Daisy reader; Digital talking bk; Extensive large print coll; Home delivery serv; Large print bks; PC for people with disabilities; Recorded bks; Talking bks
Open Mon-Thurs 10-9, Fri 10-6, Sat 10-5, Sun (Fall-Spring) Noon-5
Restriction: Non-resident fee

GIUFFRE FAMILY LIBRARY, 3223 14th St SW, T2T 3V8, SAN 365-6101. Web Site: calgarylibrary.ca/your-library/locations/giuffre. *Mgr,* Donna Bedry
Founded 1954. Pop 37,744; Circ 423,840
Library Holdings: CDs 8,218; DVDs 2,365; Bk Vols 70,546; Per Subs 2,561; Talking Bks 3,074
Special Services for the Deaf - Assistive tech
Special Services for the Blind - Assistive/Adapted tech devices, equip & products; Bks on cassette; Bks on CD
Open Mon-Thurs 10-9, Fri 10-6, Sat 10-5, Sun (Fall-Spring) Noon-5
Restriction: Non-resident fee

MEMORIAL PARK, 1221 Second St SW, T2R 0W5, SAN 365-625X. Web Site: calgarylibrary.ca/your-library/locations/mpark. *Mgr,* Donna Bedry
Founded 1912. Pop 11,217; Circ 144,856
Library Holdings: CDs 4,405; DVDs 1,601; Bk Vols 20,996; Per Subs 1,190; Talking Bks 2,141
Subject Interests: Multilingual
Special Services for the Deaf - Adult & family literacy prog; Assisted listening device; Assistive tech; Closed caption videos; TDD equip; TTY equip
Special Services for the Blind - Aids for in-house use; Assistive/Adapted tech devices, equip & products; Bks on cassette; Bks on CD; Daisy reader; Large print bks; PC for people with disabilities; Recorded bks; Talking bks
Open Mon-Thurs 10-8, Fri 10-6, Sat 10-5, Sun 12-5
Restriction: Circ to mem only, In-house use for visitors, Non-resident fee

NICHOLLS FAMILY LIBRARY, 1421 33rd St SW, T3C 1P2. Web Site: calgarylibrary.ca/your-library/locations/nicholls. *Mgr,* Allison Thomson
Open Mon-Thurs 9-9, Fri 9-6, Sat 10-5, Sun 12-5

NOSE HILL, 1530 Northmount Dr NW, T2L 0G6, SAN 365-6438. Web Site: calgarylibrary.ca/your-library/locations/nose. *Mgr,* Evette Berry
Founded 1976. Pop 46,959; Circ 866,877
Library Holdings: CDs 15,949; DVDs 6,388; Bk Vols 115,474; Per Subs 6,088; Talking Bks 4,667
Special Collections: Multi-languages Coll
Special Services for the Deaf - Accessible learning ctr; Adult & family literacy prog; Assisted listening device; Assistive tech; Deaf publ; TDD equip; TTY equip
Special Services for the Blind - Accessible computers; Aids for in-house use; Assistive/Adapted tech devices, equip & products; Audio mat; Bks available with recordings; Bks on CD; Braille bks; Daisy reader; Digital talking bk; Extensive large print coll; Large print bks; PC for people with disabilities; Talking bks
Open Mon-Thurs 9-9, Fri 9-6, Sat 9-5, Sun (Fall-Spring) Noon-5
Restriction: Circ to mem only, In-house use for visitors, Non-resident fee

QUARRY PARK, 108 Quarry Park Rd SE, T2C 5R1. Web Site: calgarylibrary.ca/your-library/locations/quarry. *Mgr,* Sara House
Open Mon-Thurs 9-9, Fri 9-6, Sat 9-5, Sun 12-5

LOUISE RILEY BRANCH, 1904 14th Ave NW, T2N 1M5, SAN 365-6284. Web Site: calgarylibrary.ca/your-library/locations/riley. *Mgr,* Donna Bedry
Founded 1959. Pop 45,927; Circ 602,120
Library Holdings: CDs 12,206; DVDs 5,202; Bk Vols 79,345; Per Subs 4,530; Talking Bks 4,690
Special Collections: French & Vientamese bks; Travelling Coll of Adult & Children's Chinese & Spanish Books
Special Services for the Deaf - Accessible learning ctr; Adult & family literacy prog; Assisted listening device; Assistive tech; Bks on deafness & sign lang; TDD equip; TTY equip
Special Services for the Blind - Accessible computers; Aids for in-house use; Assistive/Adapted tech devices, equip & products; Audio mat; Bks on CD; Braille bks; Daisy reader; Digital talking bk; Home delivery serv; Large print & cassettes; Large print bks; PC for people with disabilities; Talking bks; Volunteer serv
Open Mon-Thurs 10-9, Fri 10-6, Sat 10-5, Sun 12-5
Restriction: Circ to mem only, In-house use for visitors, Non-resident fee

ROCKY RIDGE, 11300 Rocky Ridge Rd NW, T3G 5H3. Web Site: calgarylibrary.ca/your-library/locations/rocky. *Mgr,* Jean Ludlam
Open Mon-Fri 5:30am-10:30pm, Sat & Sun 7am-8:30pm

SADDLETOWNE LIBRARY, 150 7555 Falconridge Blvd NE, T3J 0C9. Web Site: calgarylibrary.ca/your-library/locations/saddle. *Mgr,* Shannon Slater
Open Mon-Thurs 9-9, Fri 9-6, Sat 9-5, Sun 12-5

SAGE HILL, 19 Sage Hill Passage NW, T3R 0J6. Web Site: calgarylibrary.ca/your-library/locations/sage. *Mgr,* Chelsea Murray
Open Mon-Thurs 10-8, Fri 10-6, Sat 10-5, Sun Noon-5

SETON, 4995 Market St SE, T3M 2P9. Web Site: calgarylibrary.ca/your-library/locations/seton. *Mgr,* Jessie Campbell
Open Mon-Thurs 9-9, Fri 9-6, Sat 9-5, Sun Noon-5

SHAWNESSY, South Fish Creek Complex, 333 Shawville Blvd SE, T2Y 4H3, SAN 328-8048. Web Site: calgarylibrary.ca/your-library/locations/shaw. *Mgr,* Jessie Campbell
Founded 2001. Pop 96,936; Circ 941,836
Library Holdings: CDs 13,248; DVDs 6,355; Bk Vols 119,940; Per Subs 3,661; Talking Bks 5,153
Special Services for the Deaf - Adult & family literacy prog; Assisted listening device; Assistive tech; TDD equip; TTY equip
Special Services for the Blind - Accessible computers; Aids for in-house use; Bks on CD; Braille bks; Daisy reader; Digital talking bk; Home delivery serv; Large print bks; PC for people with disabilities; Recorded bks; Talking bks
Open Mon-Thurs 9-9, Fri 9-6, Sat 9-5, Sun 12-5
Restriction: Circ to mem only, In-house use for visitors, Non-resident fee

SIGNAL HILL, 5994 Signal Hill Centre SW, T3H 3P8, SAN 378-1658. Web Site: calgarylibrary.ca/your-library/locations/sig. *Mgr,* Evette Berry
Founded 1998. Pop 77,053; Circ 812,236
Library Holdings: CDs 10,469; DVDs 4,697; Bk Vols 84,579; Per Subs 3,676; Talking Bks 4,007
Special Services for the Deaf - Adult & family literacy prog; Assistive tech; TDD equip; TTY equip
Special Services for the Blind - Accessible computers; Aids for in-house use; Assistive/Adapted tech devices, equip & products; Audio mat; Bks on CD; Braille bks; Daisy reader; Large print bks; Talking bks; Volunteer serv
Open Mon-Thurs 9-9, Fri 9-6, Sat 9-5, Sun 12-5
Restriction: Circ to mem only, Non-resident fee

SOUTHWOOD, 924 Southland Dr SW, T2W 0J9, SAN 365-6349. Web Site: calgarylibrary.ca/your-library/locations/south. *Mgr,* Sara House
Founded 1966. Pop 49,153; Circ 472,879
Library Holdings: CDs 7,850; DVDs 2,274; Bk Vols 64,351; Per Subs 2,864; Talking Bks 2,935
Special Services for the Deaf - Assisted listening device; Assistive tech; TDD equip; TTY equip
Special Services for the Blind - Accessible computers; Aids for in-house use; Bks on CD; Digital talking bk; Large print bks; Talking bks
Open Mon-Thurs 10-9, Fri 10-6, Sat 10-5, Sun (Fall-Spring) Noon-5
Restriction: Circ to mem only, Non-resident fee

JUDITH UMBACH, 6617 Centre St N, T2K 4Y5, SAN 365-6403. Web Site: calgarylibrary.ca/your-library/locations/umbach. *Mgr,* Chelsea Murray
Founded 1974. Pop 47,299; Circ 544,636
Library Holdings: CDs 7,488; DVDs 4,013; Bk Vols 66,924; Per Subs 3,519; Talking Bks 3,361
Special Collections: Travelling Deposit Colls in Chinese, Vietnamese & Spanish
Open Mon-Thurs 10-9, Fri 10-6, Sat 10-5, Sun (Fall-Spring) Noon-5
Restriction: Circ to mem only, Non-resident fee

VILLAGE SQUARE, 2623 56th St NE, T1Y 6E7, SAN 365-6276. Web Site: calgarylibrary.ca/your-library/locations/vilsq. *Mgr,* Shannon Slater
Founded 1983. Pop 137,000; Circ 1,003,493
Library Holdings: CDs 14,694; DVDs 5,613; Bk Vols 131,121; Per Subs 8,678; Talking Bks 5,703
Open Mon-Thurs 9-9, Fri 9-6, Sat 9-5, Sun 12-5
Restriction: Circ to mem only, Non-resident fee

G CANADA ENERGY REGULATOR LIBRARY*, 210-517 Tenth Ave SW, T2R 0A8. SAN 368-0134. Tel: 403-292-4800. Toll Free Tel: 800-899-1265. FAX: 403-292-5503. Toll Free FAX: 877-288-8803. E-mail: library@cer-rec.gc.ca. Web Site: www.cer-rec.gc.ca.
Founded 1959
Library Holdings: CDs 291; DVDs 72; Microforms 1,264; Bk Titles 18,065; Per Subs 132; Videos 154
Special Collections: CER/NEB Hearing Materials. Canadian and Provincial
Subject Interests: Electricity, Energy, Natural gas, Oil, Petroleum indust, Trade
Wireless access
Partic in Council of Federal Libraries Consortium
Restriction: Open by appt only

S CANLEARN SOCIETY*, 100-1117 Macleod Trail SE, T2G 2M8. SAN 326-7857. Tel: 403-686-9300, Ext 126. Toll Free Tel: 877-686-9300. FAX: 403-686-0627. E-mail: library@canlearnsociety.ca. Web Site: learninglinkslibrary.ca, www.canlearnsociety.ca. *Librn,* Laura Godfrey; Staff 2 (Non-MLS 2)
Founded 1984
Library Holdings: Bk Titles 7,000
Subject Interests: ADHD (Attention deficit hyperactivity disorder), Adult literacy, Attention deficit disorder, Family literacy, Learning difficulties, Spec educ
Open Mon-Fri 8:30-4:30

G CENTRE FOR SUICIDE PREVENTION*, SIEC Library, 105 12 Ave SE, Ste 320, T2G 1A1. SAN 326-5390. Tel: 403-245-3900, Ext 227. FAX: 403-245-0299. Web Site: www.suicideinfo.ca. *Librn,* Robert Olson; E-mail: robert@suicideinfo.ca; Staff 2 (MLS 2)
Founded 1982
Library Holdings: Bk Titles 43,000
Special Collections: Suicide Database (SIEC Coll)
Subject Interests: Suicide
Wireless access
Publications: Facing the Facts: Suicide in Canada; Info Exchange (Bimonthly); Information Kits; Suicide Attempts; Youth Suicide & You
Open Mon-Fri 9-4:30

GL CITY OF CALGARY LAW DEPARTMENT LIBRARY*, 800 Mecleod Trail SE, 12th Flr, No 8053, T2P 2M5. SAN 371-6775. Tel: 403-268-2441. FAX: 403-268-4634. Web Site: www.calgary.ca/CA/law/Pages/Contacts.aspx. *Library Contact,* Elda Figueira; E-mail: elda.figueira@calgary.ca; Staff 1 (MLS 1)
Library Holdings: Bk Titles 1,100; Bk Vols 6,500; Per Subs 125
Wireless access
Restriction: Staff use only

S CNOOC PETROLEUM LIBRARY*, 500 Centre St SE, Ste 2300, T2G 1A6. SAN 371-8956. Tel: 403-699-4000. E-mail: info@intl.cnoocltd.com, library@nexencnoocltd.com. Web Site: cnoocinternational.com.
Library Holdings: Bk Titles 4,000; Bk Vols 6,000; Per Subs 200
Subject Interests: Gas, Oil
Automation Activity & Vendor Info: (Cataloging) Inmagic, Inc.
Restriction: Staff use only

S GLENBOW MUSEUM LIBRARY*, 130 Ninth Ave SE, T2G 0P3. SAN 318-613X. Tel: 403-268-4197. FAX: 403-232-6569. E-mail: library@glenbow.org. Web Site: www.glenbow.org/collections/library. *Ref Librn,* Jennifer Hanblin; Staff 1 (MLS 1)
Founded 1956
Library Holdings: Bk Vols 100,000; Per Subs 80
Special Collections: Equestrian
Subject Interests: Arctic Can, Art exhibits catalogs, Can art, Museology, NW Coast Indians, Plains Indians, Western Can
Publications: Canadian West Discovered
Open Tues-Thurs 8-4:30
Restriction: Non-circulating

S THE HANGAR FLIGHT MUSEUM*, Library & Archives, 4629 McCall Way NE, T2E 8A5. SAN 327-5027. Tel: 403-250-3752. FAX: 403-250-8399. E-mail: info@thehangarmuseum.ca. Web Site: www.thehangarmuseum.ca. *Exec Dir,* Brian Desjardins; E-mail: execdir@thehangarmuseum.ca
Library Holdings: Bk Vols 15,000; Per Subs 25
Special Collections: Original Aviation Log Books
Subject Interests: Hist of aircraft, Hist of aviation
Function: For res purposes
Restriction: Open to pub by appt only

S HATCH LTD*, Knowlege & Information Research Centre, 840 Seventh Ave SW, Ste 400, T2P 3G2. SAN 328-0357. Tel: 403-920-3101. FAX: 403-266-5730. *Librn,* Anneliese Dalmoro; E-mail: anneliese.dalmoro@hatch.ca
Founded 1981
Library Holdings: Bk Titles 1,600; Per Subs 60
Subject Interests: Civil engr
Restriction: Staff use only

S MATRIX SOLUTIONS LIBRARY*, 214-11 Ave SW, T2R 0K1. SAN 371-7526. Tel: 403-237-0606. FAX: 403-263-2493. E-mail: info@matrix-solutions.com. Web Site: www.matrix-solutions.com. *Library Contact,* Linda Blahey
Founded 1984
Library Holdings: Bk Titles 800; Per Subs 15
Special Collections: Soil Science & Reclamation, bks, papers, proceedings; Sulphur & the Environment (Sour Gas Effects Coll), bks, papers, proceedings
Restriction: Not open to pub, Staff use only

L MCCARTHY TETRAULT LLP LIBRARY*, 421 Seventh Ave SW, Ste 4000, T2P 4K9. SAN 372-882X. Tel: 403-260-3500. FAX: 403-260-3501. *Researcher,* Jason Wong; Tel: 403-260-3697, E-mail: jwong@mccarthy.ca; Staff 1 (MLS 1)
Library Holdings: Bk Titles 2,300; Bk Vols 30,000; Per Subs 125
Subject Interests: Law
Automation Activity & Vendor Info: (Acquisitions) SydneyPlus; (Cataloging) SydneyPlus; (Circulation) SydneyPlus; (OPAC) SydneyPlus; (Serials) SydneyPlus
Wireless access
Function: ILL available
Restriction: Staff use only

L MILES DAVISON LIBRARY*, 517 Teath Ave SW, Ste 900, T2R 0A8. SAN 321-5539. Tel: 403-298-0325. E-mail: thefirm@milesdavison.com. Web Site: www.milesdavison.com. *Librn,* Michelle Johnston
Library Holdings: Bk Titles 12,300; Per Subs 62
Subject Interests: Bankruptcy, Insolvency, Law, Native law
Automation Activity & Vendor Info: (Acquisitions) Inmagic, Inc.; (Cataloging) Inmagic, Inc.; (Serials) Inmagic, Inc.
Restriction: Staff use only
Friends of the Library Group

C MOUNT ROYAL UNIVERSITY LIBRARY*, 4825 Mount Royal Gate SW, T3E 6K6. SAN 318-6180. Tel: 403-440-6111. Circulation Tel: 403-440-6019. Interlibrary Loan Service Tel: 403-440-6133. Administration Tel: 403-440-6124. Information Services Tel: 403-440-6088. FAX: 403-440-6758. Web Site: library.mtroyal.ca. *Dean,* Meagan Bowler; Tel: 403-440-6086, E-mail: mbowler@mtroyal.ca; *Assoc Dean, Collections & Metadata,* Francine May; Tel: 403-440-6128, E-mail: fmay@mtroyal.ca; *Assoc Dean, Pub Serv,* Katharine Barrette; Tel: 403-440-6126, E-mail: kbarrette@mtroyal.ca; *Dir, Libr Tech,* Justin Anders; Tel: 403-440-6132, E-mail: janders@mtroyal.ca; *Head, Collections & Content,* Marc d'Avernas; Tel: 403-440-6287, E-mail: mdavernas@mtroyal.ca; *Librn,* Cari Merkley; Tel: 403-440-5068, E-mail: cmerkley@mtroyal.ca; *Librn,* Geoff Owens; Tel: 403-440-7737, E-mail: gowens@mtroyal.ca. Subject Specialists: *Midwifery, Nursing,* Cari Merkley; *Aviation, Bus, Design,* Geoff Owens; Staff 64 (MLS 16, Non-MLS 48)
Highest Degree: Bachelor
Library Holdings: Bk Vols 185,000; Per Subs 8,000
Automation Activity & Vendor Info: (Acquisitions) Ex Libris Group; (Cataloging) Ex Libris Group; (Circulation) Ex Libris Group; (Course Reserve) Ex Libris Group; (ILL) Relais International; (Media Booking) Ex Libris Group; (OPAC) Ex Libris Group; (Serials) Ex Libris Group
Publications: Faculty & Staff Guide; Library Film & Video; Library Handbook; Policy Handbooks; Student Guide
Partic in The Alberta Library
Open Mon-Thurs 7:30am-10pm, Fri 7:30am-8pm, Sat & Sun 10-8

G NATURAL RESOURCES CANADA LIBRARY*, Geological Survey of Canada Calgary Library, 3303 33rd St NW, 2nd Flr, T2L 2A7. SAN 318-6121. Tel: 403-292-7165. Web Site: science-libraries.canada.ca/eng/natural-resources. *Librn,* Ms Yongtao Lin; E-mail: yongtao.lin@canada.ca; Staff 2 (MLS 1, Non-MLS 1)
Library Holdings: Bk Vols 100,000; Per Subs 150
Subject Interests: Can arctic, Energy, Gas, Geol, Oil, Paleontology, Sedimentary geol
Automation Activity & Vendor Info: (Cataloging) Evergreen; (Circulation) Evergreen; (OPAC) Evergreen
Open Mon-Fri 8:30-4:30

L NORTON ROSE FULBRIGHT*, Law Library, Devon Tower, 400 Third Ave SW, Ste 3700, T2P 4H2. SAN 372-395X. Tel: 403-267-9466. FAX: 403-264-5973. Web Site: www.nortonrose.com. *Libr Serv Dir,* Judy Harvie; Tel: 403-921-6607, E-mail: judy.harvie@nortonrosefulbright.com
Library Holdings: Bk Vols 10,000
Automation Activity & Vendor Info: (Cataloging) SirsiDynix
Wireless access

S REPSOL OIL & GAS INC*, Information & Research Centre, 2000, 888 Third St SW, T2P 5C5. SAN 323-8717. Tel: 403-237-1429. E-mail: infocanada@repsol.com. Web Site: www.repsol.ca. *Media Intelligence Analyst,* Barb Miller; *Media Intelligence Analyst,* Margo Price; Tel: 403-231-6176; Staff 2 (MLS 1, Non-MLS 1)
Subject Interests: Bus pub, Engr, Petroleum geol
Automation Activity & Vendor Info: (Acquisitions) Inmagic, Inc.; (Cataloging) Inmagic, Inc.; (Circulation) Inmagic, Inc.; (OPAC) Inmagic, Inc.; (Serials) Inmagic, Inc.

Function: 24/7 Electronic res, Doc delivery serv, Electronic databases & coll, ILL available, Internet access, Online cat, Online ref, Ref & res, Res libr
Open Mon-Fri 7:30-5

S ST VOLODYMYR'S CULTURAL CENTRE*, Mykola Woron Library & Archives, 404 Meredith Rd NE, T2E 5A6. SAN 326-4750. Tel: 403-264-3437. FAX: 403-264-3438. E-mail: woronlibrary@gmail.com. *Librn,* Lesia Savedchuk; *Head of Libr,* Arkadij Chumak
Founded 1958
Library Holdings: Bk Titles 13,000; Per Subs 2,000; Videos 357
Special Collections: Children & Youth Coll; Periodicals; Theatrical Coll; Ukrainian Events in Canada & Abroad, progs
Restriction: Access at librarian's discretion

J SOUTHERN ALBERTA INSTITUTE OF TECHNOLOGY LIBRARY*, 1301 16th Ave NW, T2M 0L4. SAN 318-6229. Tel: 403-210-4477. Interlibrary Loan Service Tel: 403-284-8411. FAX: 403-284-8619. E-mail: library@sait.ca. Web Site: www.sait.ca. *Libr Mgr,* Jessie Campbell; E-mail: jessie.campbell@sait.ca; Staff 20 (MLS 6, Non-MLS 14)
Founded 1921. Enrl 12,780; Fac 575
Library Holdings: e-books 123,000; Bk Vols 99,000; Per Subs 430
Subject Interests: Bus admin, Culinary, Electronics, Info tech, Petroleum, Trades & apprentices
Automation Activity & Vendor Info: (Acquisitions) SirsiDynix; (Cataloging) SirsiDynix; (OPAC) SirsiDynix
Wireless access
Partic in The Alberta Library

C UNIVERSITY OF CALGARY LIBRARY*, 2500 University Dr NW, T2N 1N4. SAN 365-6705. Tel: 403-220-8895. Interlibrary Loan Service Tel: 403-220-5967. Web Site: library.ucalgary.ca. *Vice Provost & Univ Librn,* Mary-Jo Romaniuk; Tel: 403-220-3765, E-mail: maryjo.romaniuk@ucalgary.ca; *Archives & Spec Coll Librn, Assoc Univ Librn,* Annie Murray; Tel: 403-210-9521, E-mail: amurr@ucalgary.ca; *Assoc Univ Librn, Res & Learning,* Claudette Cloutier; Tel: 403-220-3447, E-mail: ccloutie@ucalgary.ca; *Assoc Univ Librn, Digital & Discovery Serv, Tech,* Susan Powelson; Tel: 403-220-5930, E-mail: spowelso@ucalgary.ca; *Assoc University Librarian, Colls,* Heather D'Amour; Tel: 403-220-3591, E-mail: damour@ucalgary.ca; Staff 49 (MLS 43, Non-MLS 6)
Founded 1964. Enrl 28,306; Fac 2,209; Highest Degree: Doctorate
Library Holdings: Bk Titles 1,595,184; Bk Vols 2,535,714; Per Subs 24,928
Special Collections: Arctic Institute of North America Coll; Books & the Book Arts (Evelyn de Mille Coll); Canadian Architectural Archive Coll; Canadian Literature Coll, bks & authors' ms; Canadian Prairies & Arctic (Margaret Hess Coll), bks & govt publications; Contemporary British Poets (Eric W White Coll); Music Archives; Recreational Mathematics (Strens)
Subject Interests: Archit, Educ, Engr, Environ design, Geol, Humanities, Kinesiology, Law, Med, Nursing, Soc work
Automation Activity & Vendor Info: (Acquisitions) SirsiDynix; (Cataloging) SirsiDynix; (Circulation) SirsiDynix; (Course Reserve) SirsiDynix; (ILL) Relais International; (OPAC) SirsiDynix; (Serials) SirsiDynix
Wireless access
Function: Archival coll, Doc delivery serv, ILL available, Photocopying/Printing, Ref serv available, Res libr, Telephone ref
Partic in Canadian Association of Research Libraries; Council of Prairie & Pacific University Libraries; OCLC Research Library Partnership; The Alberta Library
Special Services for the Blind - Large screen computer & software; Magnifiers

Departmental Libraries:

BUSINESS LIBRARY, Haskayne School of Business, 2500 University Dr NW, Scurfield Hall 301, T2N 1N4, SAN 376-995X. Tel: 403-220-6113. E-mail: library@haskayne.ucalgary.ca. Web Site: library.ucalgary.ca/business. *Bus Librn,* Rhiannon Jones; Tel: 403-220-4410, E-mail: rhiannon.jones@ucalgary.ca; Staff 6 (MLS 3, Non-MLS 3)
Enrl 3,000; Fac 90; Highest Degree: Doctorate
Library Holdings: e-journals 4,677; Bk Vols 87,899; Per Subs 250
Subject Interests: Bus, Energy, Mgt

DOUCETTE LIBRARY OF TEACHING RESOURCES, 370 Education Block, 2500 University Dr NW, T2N 1N4. Tel: 403-220-5637. E-mail: doucinfo@ucalgary.ca. Web Site: library.ucalgary.ca/doucette. *Asst Librn,* Bartlomie Lenart; E-mail: bartlomiej.lenart@ucalgary.ca; *Info Spec,* Savannah Sillito; Tel: 403-220-3984, E-mail: savannah.lee@ucalgary.ca; Staff 10 (MLS 1, Non-MLS 9)
Enrl 1,000; Highest Degree: Bachelor
Library Holdings: AV Mats 12,000; Bk Titles 60,000; Per Subs 45
Subject Interests: Curric, Educ
Open Mon-Thurs 8:30-6, Fri 8:30-4:30

GALLAGHER LIBRARY, 170 Earth Sciences, 2500 University Dr NW, T2N 1N4, SAN 365-673X. Reference Tel: 403-220-6042. E-mail: gallagher.library@ucalgary.ca. Web Site: library.ucalgary.ca/gallagher. *Dir,* Diane Lorenzetti; Tel: 403-220-6858, E-mail: dllorenz@ucalgary.ca; *Librn,* Heather Ganshorn; Tel: 403-220-2611, E-mail: heather.ganshorn@ucalgary.ca; *Librn,* Jennifer Lee; Tel: 403-220-3726, E-mail: jennifer.lee@ucalgary.ca; *Librn,* Caitlin McClurg; Tel: 403-220-5319, E-mail: csmcclur@ucalgary.ca; *Asst Librn,* James Murphy; Tel: 403-220-3740, E-mail: james.murphy2@ucalgary.ca. Subject Specialists: *Biol sci, Environ sci, Veterinary med,* Heather Ganshorn; *Chemistry, Med sci, Sci,* Jennifer Lee; *Archit, Engr, Geog,* James Murphy
Founded 1973
Open Mon-Thurs 8:30-6, Fri 8:30-4:30, Sun Noon-4

CM HEALTH SCIENCES LIBRARY, 1450 Health Sci Ctr, 3330 Hospital Dr NW, T2N 4N1, SAN 365-6799. Tel: 403-220-6855. E-mail: hslibr@ucalgary.ca. Web Site: library.ucalgary.ca/hsl. *Dir,* Diane Lorenzetti; Tel: 403-220-6858, E-mail: dllorenz@ucalgary.ca; *Health Librarian,* Nicole Dunnewold; Tel: 403-220-7370, E-mail: nicole.dunnewold@ucalgary.ca; Staff 28.5 (MLS 11, Non-MLS 17.5)
Founded 1968. Highest Degree: Doctorate
Special Collections: Dr E P Scarlett Coll; Dr Frank LeBlanc Coll; Dr Peter J E Cruse Coll; Mackie Family History of Neuroscience Coll
Subject Interests: Med, Med hist, Nursing, Veterinary med
Open Mon-Fri 8:30-6, Sat 12-4

CL BENNETT JONES LAW LIBRARY, Murray Fraser Hall 2340, 2500 University Dr NW, T2N 1N4, SAN 365-6764. Tel: 403-220-3727. Reference Tel: 403-220-7224. E-mail: lawlib@ucalgary.ca. Web Site: library.ucalgary.ca/law. *Dir,* Kim Clarke; Tel: 403-220-6702, E-mail: kim.clarke@ucalgary.ca; *Law Librn,* Nadine Hoffman; Tel: 403-220-8392, E-mail: nadine.hoffman@ucalgary.ca. Subject Specialists: *Can studies, Environ law, Hist,* Nadine Hoffman; Staff 7 (MLS 2, Non-MLS 5)
Founded 1976
Special Collections: 18th-19th Century English Coll; Canadian Parliamentary Guide, 1905-1995; Ernest S Watkins Rare Book Coll; Pre 1900 Canadian Coll
Subject Interests: Environ law, Natural res
Automation Activity & Vendor Info: (OPAC) SirsiDynix
Open Mon-Thurs 8-6, Fri 8-4:30, Sun 12-8

CALLING LAKE

P CALLING LAKE PUBLIC LIBRARY*, 2824 Central Dr, T0G 0K0. (Mail add: PO Box 129, T0G 0K0). Tel: 780-331-3027. FAX: 780-331-3029. E-mail: librarian@callinglakelibrary.ab.ca. Web Site: www.callinglakelibrary.ab.ca. *Libr Mgr,* Diane Collyer
Library Holdings: Bk Vols 2,000
Wireless access
Mem of Peace Library System
Open Mon-Fri 10-4

CALMAR

P CALMAR PUBLIC LIBRARY*, 4705 50th Ave, T0C 0V0. (Mail add: PO Box 328, T0C 0V0), SAN 318-6245. Tel: 780-985-3472. FAX: 780-985-2859. E-mail: circulation@calmarpubliclibrary.ca. Web Site: www.calmarpubliclibrary.ca. *Libr Dir,* Susan Parkinson; E-mail: sparkinson@calmarpubliclibrary.ca; *Circ,* Holly Hughes; *Circ,* Trudy Joosse; *Circ,* Nancy Martin; *Circ,* Katelyn Smith; Staff 5 (MLS 1, Non-MLS 4)
Pop 2,400
Library Holdings: Bk Vols 19,000; Per Subs 32
Wireless access
Function: 24/7 Electronic res, 24/7 Online cat, 24/7 wireless access, Accelerated reader prog, Activity rm, Adult bk club, Art exhibits, Audiobks via web, Bks on cassette, Bks on CD, Children's prog, Computer training, Computers for patron use, Extended outdoor wifi, Family literacy, Free DVD rentals, Games, Holiday prog, Home delivery & serv to seniorr ctr & nursing homes, ILL available, Internet access, Laminating, Life-long learning prog for all ages, Magazines, Mail & tel request accepted, Mango lang, Meeting rooms, Movies, Online cat, Online ref, Orientations, OverDrive digital audio bks, Photocopying/Printing, Preschool reading prog, Prog for adults, Prog for children & young adult, Ref serv available, Senior computer classes, Senior outreach, Summer reading prog, Teen prog, Wheelchair accessible
Mem of Yellowhead Regional Library
Open Mon & Wed 11-8, Tues, Thurs & Fri 11-5, Sat 11-3

CAMROSE

P CAMROSE PUBLIC LIBRARY*, 4710-50th Ave, T4V 0R8. SAN 318-6253. Tel: 780-672-4214. FAX: 780-672-9165. E-mail: cpl@prl.ab.ca. Web Site: cpl.prl.ab.ca. *Libr Dir,* Jennifer McDevitt; E-mail: jmcdevitt@prl.ab.ca
Founded 1919. Pop 17,000; Circ 192,000
Library Holdings: Bk Vols 45,000; Per Subs 65
Subject Interests: Recreational reading

Automation Activity & Vendor Info: (Acquisitions) Innovative Interfaces, Inc. - Polaris; (Cataloging) Innovative Interfaces, Inc. - Polaris; (Circulation) Innovative Interfaces, Inc. - Polaris; (ILL) Innovative Interfaces, Inc. - Polaris; (OPAC) Innovative Interfaces, Inc. - Polaris
Wireless access
Publications: By the Book (Quarterly)
Mem of Parkland Regional Library-Alberta
Open Mon-Fri 10-7, Sat 10-4
Friends of the Library Group

SR CANADIAN LUTHERAN BIBLE INSTITUTE LIBRARY*, 4837 52A St, T4V 1W5. SAN 375-0256. Tel: 780-672-4454. FAX: 780-672-4455. E-mail: info@clbi.edu. Web Site: clbi.edu. *Librn,* Ms Jaime Ocampos
Founded 1932
Library Holdings: Bk Vols 11,000; Per Subs 21
Open Mon-Sun 7:30am-11pm

C UNIVERSITY OF ALBERTA, Augustana Campus Library, 4901 46th Ave, T4V 2R3. SAN 320-281X. Tel: 780-679-1156. E-mail: augustana.library@ualberta.ca. Web Site: guides.library.ualberta.ca/augustana/subject-guides. *Diversity, Equity & Inclusion Librn,* Nancy Goebel; E-mail: nancy.goebel@ualberta.ca; *Librn,* Kara Blizzard; E-mail: kara.blizzard@ualberta.ca; Staff 4 (MLS 2, Non-MLS 2)
Founded 1911. Enrl 1,000; Fac 65
Library Holdings: Bk Titles 150,000; Per Subs 300
Special Collections: Scandinavia, artifacts, bks
Subject Interests: English, Lang, Music, Relig studies, Soc sci
Automation Activity & Vendor Info: (Acquisitions) SirsiDynix; (Cataloging) SirsiDynix; (Circulation) SirsiDynix; (Course Reserve) SirsiDynix; (ILL) Relais International; (OPAC) SirsiDynix; (Serials) SirsiDynix
Wireless access
Partic in Canadian Association of Research Libraries; Canadian Research Knowledge Network; Council of Prairie & Pacific University Libraries; NEOS Library Consortium; The Alberta Library
Open Mon-Thurs 8:30am-9pm, Fri 8:30-5, Sat 1-5, Sun 2-9 (Sept-April); Mon-Fri 9-Noon (May-Aug)

CANMORE

P CANMORE PUBLIC LIBRARY*, 101-700 Railway Ave, T1W 1P4. SAN 321-0642. Tel: 403-678-2468. FAX: 403-678-2165. E-mail: info@canmorelibrary.ab.ca. Web Site: canmorelibrary.ab.ca. *Libr Dir,* Michelle Preston; E-mail: mpreston@canmorelibrary.ab.ca; *Asst Librn,* Audra Hiller; Staff 12 (MLS 2, Non-MLS 10)
Founded 1971. Pop 12,000; Circ 181,079
Library Holdings: Bk Titles 57,145; Per Subs 123
Automation Activity & Vendor Info: (Circulation) SirsiDynix; (OPAC) SirsiDynix
Wireless access
Mem of Marigold Library System
Open Mon-Fri 10-8, Sat & Sun 10-5
Friends of the Library Group

CARBON

P CARBON MUNICIPAL LIBRARY*, 310 Bruce Ave, T0M 0L0. (Mail add: PO Box 70, T0M 0L0), SAN 322-8312. Tel: 403-572-3440. E-mail: acarmlibrary@marigold.ab.ca. Web Site: www.carbonlibrary.ca. *Mgr,* Jay-Lynn Boutin
Founded 1981. Pop 538
Library Holdings: Bk Titles 8,500; Per Subs 10
Automation Activity & Vendor Info: (Acquisitions) SirsiDynix
Wireless access
Mem of Marigold Library System
Special Services for the Deaf - Assisted listening device
Special Services for the Blind - Bks on CD
Open Tues 3-8, Thurs & Fri 1-5, Sat 9-3
Friends of the Library Group

CARDSTON

P JIM & MARY KEARL LIBRARY OF CARDSTON*, 25 Third Ave W, T0K 0K0. SAN 318-6261. Tel: 403-653-4775. FAX: 403-653-4716. E-mail: help@cardstonlibrary.ca. Web Site: www.cardstonlibrary.ca. *Libr Mgr,* Donna Beazer; Staff 7 (Non-MLS 7)
Founded 1931. Pop 3,475; Circ 90,000
Library Holdings: CDs 860; DVDs 800; Bk Vols 29,000; Per Subs 65; Talking Bks 805; Videos 300
Subject Interests: Biographies, LDS fiction & non-fiction, Local hist
Automation Activity & Vendor Info: (Cataloging) SirsiDynix; (Circulation) SirsiDynix; (OPAC) SirsiDynix
Wireless access
Function: After school storytime, CD-ROM, Electronic databases & coll, ILL available, Internet access, Magnifiers for reading, Photocopying/Printing, Prog for children & young adult, Summer reading prog, VHS videos, Wheelchair accessible
Mem of Chinook Arch Regional Library System
Special Services for the Blind - Audio mat; Bks on CD; Extensive large print coll
Open Mon, Wed & Fri 10-6, Thurs 10-8, Sat 12-5

CARMANGAY

P CARMANGAY & DISTRICT MUNICIPAL LIBRARY*, 416 Grand Ave, T0L 0N0. (Mail add: PO Box 11, T0L 0N0). Tel: 403-643-3777. FAX: 403-643-3777. E-mail: help@carmangaylibrary.ca. Web Site: www.carmangaylibrary.ca. *Libr Mgr,* Kelsey Chic
Founded 1981. Pop 250
Library Holdings: Bk Titles 9,560
Automation Activity & Vendor Info: (Acquisitions) BiblioCommons; (Cataloging) BiblioCommons
Wireless access
Mem of Chinook Arch Regional Library System
Open Mon & Wed 5:30pm-8:30pm, Tues 2-6, Thurs 2-6:30, Fri & Sat 9-Noon

CAROLINE

P CAROLINE MUNICIPAL LIBRARY*, 5023 50th Ave, T0M 0M0. (Mail add: PO Box 339, T0M 0M0). Tel: 403-722-4060. FAX: 403-722-4070. E-mail: carolinelibrary@prl.ab.ca. Web Site: carolinelibrary.prl.ab.ca. *Libr Mgr,* Amanda Archibald; *Libr Mgr,* Allison Farr
Library Holdings: Bk Vols 16,000; Per Subs 25
Wireless access
Mem of Parkland Regional Library-Alberta
Open Tues, Thurs & Fri 10-6, Wed 12-7, Sat 11-4
Friends of the Library Group

CARSELAND

P CARSELAND COMMUNITY LIBRARY*, Carseland Community Hall, 330 Railway Ave W, T0J 0M0. Tel: 403-934-6007. E-mail: acarselibrary@marigold.ab.ca. Web Site: www.carselandlibrary.ca.
Library Holdings: Bk Vols 5,000
Automation Activity & Vendor Info: (Cataloging) SirsiDynix; (Circulation) SirsiDynix; (OPAC) SirsiDynix
Wireless access
Mem of Marigold Library System
Open Tues & Thurs 2-4:30 & 7-9, Sat 9:30-12:30

CARSTAIRS

P CARSTAIRS PUBLIC LIBRARY*, 1402 Scarlett Ranch Blvd, T0M 0N0. (Mail add: PO Box 941, T0M 0N0). Tel: 403-337-3943. FAX: 403-337-3943. E-mail: carstairs@prl.ab.ca. Web Site: carstairspublic.prl.ab.ca. *Libr Mgr,* Megan Ginther; E-mail: mginther@prl.ab.ca; *Asst Head Librn,* Marg Reid; Staff 3.5 (MLS 1, Non-MLS 2.5)
Founded 1952. Pop 5,000; Circ 38,470
Library Holdings: Audiobooks 449; DVDs 816; Music Scores 64; Bk Vols 15,597; Per Subs 25
Automation Activity & Vendor Info: (Acquisitions) SirsiDynix; (Cataloging) SirsiDynix; (Circulation) SirsiDynix; (ILL) SirsiDynix
Wireless access
Function: 24/7 Electronic res, 24/7 Online cat, Activity rm, Adult bk club, After school storytime, Art exhibits, Audio & video playback equip for onsite use, Audiobks via web, BA reader (adult literacy), Bk club(s), Bk reviews (Group), Bks on CD, Children's prog, Computer training, Computers for patron use, Digital talking bks, Distance learning, E-Readers, Family literacy, Free DVD rentals, Home delivery & serv to seniorr ctr & nursing homes, Homebound delivery serv, ILL available, Internet access, Life-long learning prog for all ages, Literacy & newcomer serv, Magazines, Mail loans to mem, Mango lang, Meeting rooms, Movies, Music CDs, Online cat, Outreach serv, Photocopying/Printing, Preschool outreach, Preschool reading prog, Prog for adults, Prog for children & young adult, Senior computer classes, Senior outreach, Serves people with intellectual disabilities, Story hour, Summer reading prog, Wheelchair accessible
Mem of Parkland Regional Library-Alberta
Open Tues 9-6, Wed & Thurs 9-8, Fri & Sat 9-5
Restriction: Free to mem
Friends of the Library Group

CASTOR

P CASTOR MUNICIPAL LIBRARY*, 4905 50 Ave, T0C 0X0. (Mail add: PO Box 699, T0C 0X0), SAN 318-627X. Tel: 403-882-3999. FAX: 403-882-3915. E-mail: castorlibrary@prl.ab.ca. Web Site: castorlibrary.prl.ab.ca. *Libr Mgr,* Tess Griebel
Pop 1,000; Circ 8,806
Library Holdings: DVDs 400; Bk Titles 7,000
Automation Activity & Vendor Info: (Cataloging) Innovative Interfaces, Inc. - Polaris; (Circulation) Innovative Interfaces, Inc. - Polaris; (Course Reserve) Innovative Interfaces, Inc. - Polaris; (ILL) Relais International; (OPAC) Innovative Interfaces, Inc. - Polaris
Wireless access
Mem of Parkland Regional Library-Alberta
Open Mon & Fri 2-5, Wed 10-12 & 2-5

CESSFORD

P BERRY CREEK COMMUNITY LIBRARY*, 116 First Ave, T0J 0P0. (Mail add: Berry Creek Community School, General Delivery, T0J 0P0). Toll Free Tel: 844-566-3743. E-mail: bccslibrary@plrd.ab.ca. Web Site: www.berrycreeklibrary.ca. *Librn,* Susan Conners
Library Holdings: Large Print Bks 70; Bk Titles 14,000; Bk Vols 20,000; Talking Bks 60
Automation Activity & Vendor Info: (Cataloging) Insignia Software; (Circulation) Insignia Software; (ILL) Insignia Software; (OPAC) Insignia Software
Wireless access
Mem of Marigold Library System
Open Mon-Thurs 9-4

CHAMPION

P CHAMPION MUNICIPAL LIBRARY*, 132A Second St S, T0L 0R0. (Mail add: PO Box 177, T0L 0R0). Tel: 403-897-3099. FAX: 403-897-3098. E-mail: help@championlibrary.ca. Web Site: www.championlibrary.ca. *Librn,* Patty Abel
Founded 1951. Pop 378
Library Holdings: Bk Vols 10,000
Wireless access
Mem of Chinook Arch Regional Library System
Open Mon 10-12, Tues & Thurs 10-5, Wed 10-12 & 5-8, Fri 10-2
Friends of the Library Group

CHAUVIN

P CHAUVIN MUNICIPAL LIBRARY, 5200 Fourth Ave N, T0B 0V0. (Mail add: PO Box 129, T0B 0V0). Tel: 780-858-3746. FAX: 780-858-2392. Web Site: www.chauvinmunicipallibrary.ab.ca. *Libr Mgr,* Jennifer Waters; E-mail: jwaters@chauvinmunicipallibrary.ab.ca
Pop 378
Library Holdings: Audiobooks 10; Bks on Deafness & Sign Lang 2; Braille Volumes 5; DVDs 104; Bk Vols 12,000
Wireless access
Mem of Northern Lights Library System
Open Mon & Thurs 3:30-6:30

CHESTERMERE

P CHESTERMERE PUBLIC LIBRARY, Chestermere Town Hall, 105B Marina Rd, T1X 1V7. Tel: 403-272-9025. FAX: 403-272-9036. E-mail: info@chestermerepubliclibrary.com. Web Site: www.chestermerepubliclibrary.com. *Libr Mgr,* Miranda Johnson
Founded 2007. Pop 17,203
Library Holdings: AV Mats 1,204; Bk Vols 34,257; Per Subs 120; Talking Bks 1,058
Wireless access
Mem of Marigold Library System
Partic in The Regional Automation Consortium
Open Mon-Thurs 10-7, Fri & Sat 10-5, Sun 12-4
Friends of the Library Group

CLARESHOLM

P CLARESHOLM PUBLIC LIBRARY, 211 49th Ave W, T0L 0T0. (Mail add: PO Box 548, T0L 0T0), SAN 318-6296. Tel: 403-625-4168. E-mail: help@claresholmlibrary.ca. Web Site: www.claresholmlibrary.ca. *Libr Mgr,* Jay Sawatzky; E-mail: jsawatzky@claresholmlibrary.ca; Staff 6 (Non-MLS 6)
Founded 1938. Pop 5,000; Circ 53,000
Library Holdings: Audiobooks 1,282; Bks on Deafness & Sign Lang 10; CDs 328; DVDs 641; Large Print Bks 607; Bk Vols 27,252; Per Subs 70; Videos 2,000
Special Collections: Multilingual Book Coll; Newspaper Coll (1907-present), microfilm
Automation Activity & Vendor Info: (Acquisitions) SirsiDynix-WorkFlows; (Cataloging) SirsiDynix-WorkFlows; (Circulation) SirsiDynix-WorkFlows; (Course Reserve) SirsiDynix-WorkFlows; (Media Booking) SirsiDynix-WorkFlows; (OPAC) SirsiDynix-WorkFlows; (Serials) SirsiDynix-WorkFlows
Wireless access
Function: ILL available, Photocopying/Printing
Mem of Chinook Arch Regional Library System
Special Services for the Blind - Assistive/Adapted tech devices, equip & products; Audio mat; Bks on CD; Computer access aids; Computer with voice synthesizer for visually impaired persons; Copier with enlargement capabilities; Daisy reader; Large print bks; Large print bks & talking machines; Large screen computer & software; Low vision equip; Magnifiers
Open Mon-Wed & Fri 10-5:30, Thurs 10-8, Sat 10-3
Friends of the Library Group

CLEARDALE

P MENNO-SIMONS COMMUNITY LIBRARY*, 521 Cleardale Dr, T0H 3Y0. (Mail add: Bag 100, T0H 3Y0). Tel: 780-685-2340. FAX: 780-685-3665. E-mail: librarian@mennosimonslibrary.ca. Web Site: www.mennosimonslibrary.ca. *Libr Mgr,* Bettina Worrall; E-mail: worrallb@prsd.ab.ca
Wireless access
Mem of Peace Library System
Open Mon & Tues Noon-5, Wed Noon-9, Thurs & Fri Noon-4

CLIVE

P CLIVE PUBLIC LIBRARY*, 5107 50th St, T0C 0Y0. (Mail add: PO Box 209, T0C 0Y0). Tel: 403-784-3131. FAX: 403-784-3131. E-mail: clivelibrary@prl.ab.ca. Web Site: clivepublib.prl.ab.ca. *Libr Mgr,* Melanie Ash
Pop 675
Library Holdings: CDs 30; DVDs 400; Bk Titles 7,000
Automation Activity & Vendor Info: (Acquisitions) SirsiDynix; (Cataloging) Innovative Interfaces, Inc. - Polaris
Wireless access
Mem of Parkland Regional Library-Alberta
Open Tues & Wed 10-5, Thurs 11-6, Fri 12-5

COALDALE

P COALDALE PUBLIC LIBRARY*, 2014 18th St, T1M 1N1. (Mail add: PO Box 1207, T1M 1N1), SAN 318-630X. Tel: 403-345-1340. FAX: 403-345-1342. E-mail: help@coaldalelibrary.ca. Web Site: www.coaldalelibrary.ca. *Head Librn,* Dothlyn McFarlane
Founded 1945. Pop 8,600; Circ 90,000
Library Holdings: Bk Vols 32,000; Per Subs 20
Wireless access
Publications: Newsletter (Monthly)
Mem of Chinook Arch Regional Library System
Open Mon-Thurs 9:30-9, Fri & Sat 11-5
Friends of the Library Group

COCHRANE

P COCHRANE PUBLIC LIBRARY*, Nan Boothby Memorial Library, 405 Railway St W, T4C 2E2. SAN 318-6318. Tel: 403-932-4353. E-mail: info@cochranepubliclibrary.ca. Web Site: www.cochranepubliclibrary.ca. *Asst Dir,* Jessie Pepin; E-mail: jessie.pepin@cochranepubliclibrary.ca; Staff 25 (MLS 2, Non-MLS 23)
Founded 1950. Pop 34,000
Library Holdings: Bk Vols 40,000; Per Subs 93
Automation Activity & Vendor Info: (Circulation) Follett Software; (OPAC) Follett Software
Wireless access
Mem of Marigold Library System
Open Mon-Thurs 10-8, Fri & Sat 10-6
Friends of the Library Group

S STOCKMEN'S MEMORIAL FOUNDATION LIBRARY, Bert Sheppard Library & Archives, 101 RancheHouse Rd, T4C 2K8. SAN 372-5499. Tel: 403-932-3782. E-mail: library@stockmen.ca. Web Site: stockmen.ca. *Exec Dir,* Scott Grattidge; E-mail: scott.grattidge@stockmen.ca; Staff 2 (Non-MLS 2)
Founded 1980
Library Holdings: Bk Vols 13,000; Spec Interest Per Sub 40
Special Collections: Cattle Ranching History Coll, bks, doc; Oral-Video History, v-tapes. Oral History
Automation Activity & Vendor Info: (Cataloging) Inmagic, Inc.
Wireless access
Open Tues-Fri 9-3, Sat & Sun (Summer) 10-4

COLD LAKE

P COLD LAKE PUBLIC LIBRARY*, South Branch, 5513-B 48th Ave, T9M 1X9. SAN 320-5231. Tel: 780-594-5101. Interlibrary Loan Service Tel: 780-594-7425. FAX: 780-594-7787. Web Site: www.coldlakelibrary.ca. *Dir,* Leslie Price; E-mail: lprice@coldlakelibrary.ca; *Asst Dir,* Tanya Boudreau; Tel: 780-639-3967, E-mail: tboudreau@coldlakelibrary.ca; Staff 14 (MLS 1, Non-MLS 13)
Founded 1975. Pop 14,000; Circ 21,600
Library Holdings: AV Mats 3,219; Bk Titles 24,367; Per Subs 49
Wireless access
Function: 24/7 Electronic res, 24/7 Online cat, 3D Printer, Activity rm, Adult bk club
Mem of Northern Lights Library System
Open Mon & Wed 9-6, Tues & Thurs 9-8, Fri 9-5, Sat 9-4
Branches: 1
HARBOR VIEW, 1301 Eighth Ave, T9M 1J7. (Mail add: 5513B 48 Ave, T9M 1X9). Tel: 780-639-3967. FAX: 780-639-3963. *Librn,* Tanya Boudreau; E-mail: asst_director@library.coldlake.ab.ca
Library Holdings: AV Mats 2,585; Bk Titles 24,934; Per Subs 47
Open Mon & Wed 12-8, Tues & Thurs 10-6, Fri 10-5, Sat 10-3

CONSORT

P CONSORT MUNICIPAL LIBRARY*, 5215 50th St, T0C 1B0. (Mail add: PO Box 456, T0C 1B0), SAN 318-6342. Tel: 403-577-2501. E-mail: aconmlibrary@marigold.ab.ca. Web Site: www.consortlibrary.ca. *Libr Mgr,* Pamela Deagle
Pop 729; Circ 17,706
Library Holdings: Bk Vols 20,300
Wireless access
Mem of Marigold Library System
Open Mon-Thurs 3:30-8:30

CORONATION

P CORONATION MEMORIAL LIBRARY*, 5001 Royal St, T0C 1C0. (Mail add: PO Box 453, T0C 1C0), SAN 318-6350. Tel: 403-578-3445. E-mail: coronationlibrary@prl.ab.ca. Web Site: coronationlib.prl.ab.ca. *Libr Mgr,* Jordan Stonehouse; *Asst Librn,* Azusa Watson
Pop 1,074; Circ 9,329
Library Holdings: Audiobooks 50; CDs 60; DVDs 200; Large Print Bks 500; Bk Titles 9,000; Per Subs 10; Talking Bks 20
Wireless access
Mem of Parkland Regional Library-Alberta
Open Mon & Fri Noon-5:30, Tues-Thurs 9-4:30
Friends of the Library Group

COUTTS

P COUTTS MUNICIPAL LIBRARY*, 218 First Ave S, T0K 0N0. (Mail add: Box 216, T0K 0N0). Tel: 403-344-3804. E-mail: libcou@chinookarch.ab.ca. Web Site: couttslibrary.ca/. *Librn,* Sharon Wollersheim; E-mail: sharon.wollersheim@gmail.com
Pop 364
Library Holdings: Bk Titles 7,500
Wireless access
Mem of Chinook Arch Regional Library System
Open Tues 2:30-8:30, Wed 9:30-1:30, Thurs 9:30-1:30 & 6:30-8:30
Friends of the Library Group

CREMONA

P CREMONA MUNICIPAL LIBRARY*, 205 First St E, T0M 0R0. (Mail add: General Delivery, T0M 0R0). Tel: 403-637-3100. FAX: 403-637-2101. E-mail: cremonalibrary@prl.ab.ca. Web Site: cremonalibrary.prl.ab.ca. *Libr Mgr,* Sandra Herbert
Library Holdings: Bk Titles 5,000
Automation Activity & Vendor Info: (Acquisitions) SirsiDynix
Wireless access
Mem of Parkland Regional Library-Alberta
Open Mon 9:30-Noon, Tues 4-8, Wed 11-4:30, Thurs 6pm-8:30pm, Fri 1:30-4:30

CROSSFIELD

P CROSSFIELD MUNICIPAL LIBRARY*, 1210 Railway St, T0M 0S0. (Mail add: PO Box 40, T0M 0S0), SAN 318-6377. Tel: 403-946-4232. FAX: 403-946-4212. Administration E-mail: admin@crossfieldlibrary.ca. Web Site: crossfieldlibrary.ca. *Mgr,* Rianne Rayment; Staff 5 (MLS 1, Non-MLS 4)
Founded 1953. Pop 3,557
Library Holdings: Bk Vols 25,000; Per Subs 54
Wireless access
Function: 24/7 Electronic res, 24/7 Online cat, Art programs, Audiobks via web, Bk club(s), Bks on CD, Children's prog, Computer training, Computers for patron use, Electronic databases & coll, For res purposes, Free DVD rentals, ILL available, Life-long learning prog for all ages, Magazines, Movies, Online cat, OverDrive digital audio bks, Photocopying/Printing, Prog for adults, Prog for children & young adult, Ref & res, Scanner, Story hour, Summer reading prog, Teen prog, Telephone ref, Wheelchair accessible
Mem of Marigold Library System
Partic in The Regional Automation Consortium
Open Mon-Thurs 10-8, Fri 10-6, Sat 10-1
Friends of the Library Group

CZAR

P CZAR MUNICIPAL LIBRARY*, 5005 49th Ave, T0B 0Z0. (Mail add: PO Box 127, T0B 0Z0). Tel: 780-857-3740. FAX: 780-857-2223. E-mail: czarlibrary@prl.ab.ca. Web Site: czarlibrary.prl.ab.ca. *Libr Mgr,* Jackie Almberg
Pop 190
Library Holdings: Bk Titles 3,750
Automation Activity & Vendor Info: (Cataloging) Innovative Interfaces, Inc. - Polaris
Wireless access
Function: ILL available, Photocopying/Printing, Summer reading prog
Mem of Parkland Regional Library-Alberta
Open Mon-Fri 11-5

DARWELL

P DARWELL PUBLIC LIBRARY*, 54-225B Hwy 765, T0E 0L0. (Mail add: PO Box 206, T0E 0L0). Tel: 780-892-3746. FAX: 780-892-3743. E-mail: adarlibrary@yrl.ab.ca. Web Site: darwellpubliclibrary.ab.ca. *Libr Mgr,* Sandra Stepaniuk
Founded 1985. Pop 1,685
Library Holdings: Bk Vols 7,300
Wireless access
Mem of Yellowhead Regional Library
Open Mon, Tues & Thurs 11-4, Wed & Fri 5-8
Friends of the Library Group

DAYSLAND

P DAYSLAND PUBLIC LIBRARY*, 5128 50th St, T0B 1A0. (Mail add: PO Box 700, T0B 1A0). Tel: 780-781-0005. E-mail: dayslandlibrary@prl.ab.ca. Web Site: dayslandlibrary.prl.ab.ca. *Libr Mgr,* Christi Elley; *Libr Asst,* Charlene Zacharias
Pop 820
Library Holdings: Bk Vols 8,000
Wireless access
Mem of Parkland Regional Library-Alberta
Open Tues-Thurs 10-5, Fri 3-6
Friends of the Library Group

DEBOLT

P DEBOLT PUBLIC LIBRARY*, PO Box 480, T0H 1B0. Tel: 780-957-3770. E-mail: librarian@deboltlibrary.ab.ca. Web Site: www.deboltlibrary.ab.ca. *Libr Mgr,* Rachel Stoesz
Library Holdings: Bk Vols 12,000; Per Subs 12
Automation Activity & Vendor Info: (Acquisitions) Innovative Interfaces, Inc; (Cataloging) Innovative Interfaces, Inc; (Circulation) Innovative Interfaces, Inc
Wireless access
Mem of Peace Library System
Open Mon 3-9, Thurs & Sat 10-5

DELBURNE

P DELBURNE MUNICIPAL LIBRARY*, 2210 20th St, T0M 0V0. (Mail add: PO Box 405, T0M 0V0), SAN 321-5792. Tel: 403-749-3848. FAX: 403-749-3847. E-mail: delburnelibrary@prl.ab.ca. Web Site: delburnelibrary.prl.ab.ca. *Libr Mgr,* Judy Nicklom; Staff 1 (MLS 1)
Founded 1928. Pop 896; Circ 5,049
Library Holdings: Bk Vols 6,709
Automation Activity & Vendor Info: (Acquisitions) SirsiDynix; (Cataloging) SirsiDynix; (Circulation) SirsiDynix; (ILL) SirsiDynix; (Serials) SirsiDynix
Wireless access
Mem of Parkland Regional Library-Alberta
Open Tues, Thurs & Fri 11-5, Wed 2-8, Sat 11-3
Friends of the Library Group

DELIA

P DELIA MUNICIPAL LIBRARY, 205 Third Ave N, T0J 0W0. (Mail add: PO Box 236, T0J 0W0). Tel: 403-364-3777. E-mail: delia@delialibrary.ca. Web Site: www.delialibrary.ca. *Libr Mgr,* Teresa Scott; Staff 1 (Non-MLS 1)
Pop 232; Circ 17,644
Library Holdings: Bk Vols 20,016; Per Subs 43
Wireless access
Function: 24/7 Electronic res, 24/7 Online cat, 24/7 wireless access, 3D Printer
Mem of Marigold Library System
Open Mon 2:30-5:30, Tues 4-5, Wed 3:30-7:30, Thurs 3:30-4:30, Fri 11-3
Friends of the Library Group

DEVON

P DEVON PUBLIC LIBRARY*, 101, 17 Athabasca Ave, T9G 1G5. SAN 318-6407. Tel: 780-987-3720. E-mail: devon@devonpubliclibrary.ca. Web Site: devonpubliclibrary.ca. *Dir,* Stephanie Johnson; E-mail: stephanie@devonpubliclibrary.ca; Staff 11 (MLS 1, Non-MLS 10)
Founded 1955. Pop 6,534; Circ 69,177
Library Holdings: Audiobooks 1,413; DVDs 1,497; Bk Vols 26,418; Per Subs 52
Wireless access
Function: 24/7 Electronic res, 24/7 Online cat, Adult bk club, Adult literacy prog, Art exhibits, Art programs, Audiobks via web, AV serv, Bk club(s), Bks on CD, Children's prog, Citizenship assistance, Computer training, Computers for patron use, E-Readers, Electronic databases & coll, Equip loans & repairs, Family literacy, Free DVD rentals, Holiday prog, Home delivery & serv to seniorr ctr & nursing homes, ILL available, Internet access, Life-long learning prog for all ages, Literacy & newcomer serv, Magazines, Meeting rooms, Movies, Online cat, Outreach serv, OverDrive digital audio bks, Photocopying/Printing, Prog for adults, Prog for children & young adult, Ref & res, Scanner, Senior computer classes, Senior outreach, Serves people with intellectual disabilities, Spanish lang bks, STEM programs, Study rm, Summer reading prog, Wheelchair accessible
Mem of Yellowhead Regional Library
Open Mon-Thurs 9-8, Fri 9-6, Sat 10-4
Friends of the Library Group

DIAMOND VALLEY

P SHEEP RIVER LIBRARY*, 129 Main St NW, T0L 2A0. (Mail add: PO Bag 10, T0L 2A0), SAN 325-2485. Tel: 403-933-3278. FAX: 403-933-3298. E-mail: abdsrclibrary@marigold.ab.ca. Web Site: www.sheepriverlibrary.ca. *Libr Mgr,* Jan Burney; *Libr Tech,* Gita Grahame; Staff 4 (Non-MLS 4)
Founded 1981. Pop 4,500; Circ 38,554
Library Holdings: CDs 222; DVDs 683; Large Print Bks 500; Bk Titles 18,532; Per Subs 69; Talking Bks 808
Wireless access
Function: Adult bk club, Bk club(s), ILL available, Photocopying/Printing, Prog for adults, Prog for children & young adult, Scanner, Wheelchair accessible
Mem of Marigold Library System
Partic in The Alberta Library; The Regional Automation Consortium
Open Mon, Fri & Sat 10-5, Tues-Thurs 10-8
Friends of the Library Group

DIDSBURY

P DIDSBURY MUNICIPAL LIBRARY*, 2033 19th Ave, T0M 0W0. (Mail add: PO Box 10, T0M 0W0). Tel: 403-335-3142. FAX: 403-335-3141. E-mail: didsburylibrary@prl.ab.ca. Web Site: dml.prl.ab.ca. *Libr Mgr,* Monique Fiedler; Staff 2 (MLS 1, Non-MLS 1)
Founded 1908. Pop 5,000; Circ 70,000
Jan 2018-Dec 2018 Income (CAN) $358,000, Provincial (CAN) $50,100, City (CAN) $248,700, Federal (CAN) $6,900, County (CAN) $37,300, Other (CAN) $15,000
Library Holdings: Bk Titles 27,000
Wireless access
Function: 24/7 Electronic res, 24/7 Online cat, 3D Printer, Adult bk club, Adult literacy prog, Audio & video playback equip for onsite use, Audiobks via web, AV serv, Bk club(s), Bks on CD, Children's prog, Citizenship assistance, Computer training, Computers for patron use, Digital talking bks, Distance learning, Doc delivery serv, E-Readers, Electronic databases & coll, Equip loans & repairs, Family literacy, Free DVD rentals, Games & aids for people with disabilities, Genealogy discussion group, Govt ref serv, Holiday prog, Home delivery & serv to seniorr ctr & nursing homes, Homebound delivery serv, ILL available, Instruction & testing, Internet access, Laminating, Learning ctr, Life-long learning prog for all ages, Literacy & newcomer serv, Magazines, Magnifiers for reading, Mail & tel request accepted, Mail loans to mem, Meeting rooms, Microfiche/film & reading machines, Movies, Music CDs, Online cat, Online info literacy tutorials on the web & in blackboard, Online ref, Outreach serv, Outside serv via phone, mail, e-mail & web, Photocopying/Printing, Preschool outreach, Preschool reading prog, Prog for adults, Prog for children & young adult, Ref & res, Scanner, Senior computer classes, Senior outreach, Serves people with intellectual disabilities, Spanish lang bks, STEM programs, Story hour, Study rm, Summer & winter reading prog, Summer reading prog, Teen prog, Telephone ref, Visual arts prog, Wheelchair accessible, Winter reading prog, Workshops, Writing prog
Mem of Parkland Regional Library-Alberta
Open Mon, Tues, Fri & Sat 9-5, Wed & Thurs 9-8
Friends of the Library Group

DIXONVILLE

P DIXONVILLE COMMUNITY LIBRARY*, PO Box 206, T0H 1E0. Tel: 780-971-2593. FAX: 780-971-2048. E-mail: librarian@dixonvillelibrary.ab.ca. Web Site: www.dixonvillelibrary.ab.ca. *Libr Mgr,* Cayley Russell; *Asst Librn,* Judy Black; *Asst Librn,* Allie Ramer
Founded 2010
Wireless access
Mem of Peace Library System
Open Tues & Thurs 3:30-6:30, Sat 10-4
Friends of the Library Group

DONALDA

P DONALDA PUBLIC LIBRARY*, 5001 Main St, T0B 1H0. (Mail add: PO Box 40, T0B 1H0). Tel: 403-430-2665. FAX: 403-883-2022. E-mail: donaldalibrary@prl.ab.ca. Web Site: donaldalibrary.prl.ab.ca. *Libr Mgr,* Naomi LaBelle
Library Holdings: Bk Vols 4,000
Automation Activity & Vendor Info: (Cataloging) Horizon; (Circulation) Horizon; (OPAC) Horizon
Wireless access
Mem of Parkland Regional Library-Alberta
Open Mon 2-6, Tues 2-5, Wed 3-6, Thurs 11-4

DRAYTON VALLEY

P DRAYTON VALLEY MUNICIPAL LIBRARY*, 5120 52nd St, T7A 1R7. (Mail add: PO Box 6240, T7A 1R7). Tel: 780-514-2722. FAX: 780-514-2790. E-mail: dvml@draytonvalley.ca. Web Site: www.draytonvalleylibrary.ca. *Libr Dir,* Doug Whistance-Smith; E-mail: dwhistancesmith@draytonvalleylibrary.ca; *Libr Operations Mgr,* Rebecca Wepryk; Staff 7.7 (MLS 1, Non-MLS 6.7)
Founded 1957. Pop 13,000; Circ 66,000
Library Holdings: Audiobooks 1,000; CDs 1,200; DVDs 2,100; Large Print Bks 430; Bk Titles 31,000; Per Subs 32
Automation Activity & Vendor Info: (Circulation) Innovative Interfaces, Inc. - Polaris; (OPAC) Innovative Interfaces, Inc. - Polaris
Wireless access
Function: 24/7 Electronic res, 24/7 Online cat, Audiobks via web, Bk club(s), Bks on CD, Children's prog, Computers for patron use, Digital talking bks, E-Reserves, Electronic databases & coll, Free DVD rentals, Genealogy discussion group, Holiday prog, ILL available, Internet access, Life-long learning prog for all ages, Magazines, Mango lang, Movies, Music CDs, Online cat, Outreach serv, OverDrive digital audio bks, Photocopying/Printing, Preschool reading prog, Prog for adults, Prog for children & young adult, Ref & res, Senior outreach, Story hour, Summer reading prog, Wheelchair accessible
Mem of Yellowhead Regional Library
Partic in The Regional Automation Consortium
Special Services for the Blind - Bks on CD; Digital talking bk; Large print bks; Talking bks
Open Mon & Fri 9-5, Tues-Thurs 9-8, Sat 9-3
Restriction: Non-resident fee
Friends of the Library Group
Bookmobiles: 1. Outreach, Leah Sanderson

DRUMHELLER

P DRUMHELLER PUBLIC LIBRARY*, 80 Veterans Way, T0J 0Y4. (Mail add: PO Box 1599, T0J 0Y0), SAN 318-6423. Tel: 403-823-1371. FAX: 403-823-1374. E-mail: librarystaff@drumhellerlibrary.ca. Web Site: www.drumhellerlibrary.ca. *Dir, Libr Serv,* Emily Hollingshead; E-mail: director@drumhellerlibrary.ca; *Asst Dir,* Robin Locke; E-mail: assistantdirector@drumhellerlibrary.ca
Founded 1922. Pop 8,223
Library Holdings: Audiobooks 908; DVDs 1,738; High Interest/Low Vocabulary Bk Vols 25; Large Print Bks 555; Bk Vols 27,581; Per Subs 76
Special Collections: Area Newspapers from 1914, microfilm; Early Drumheller Records; Family Resource Library; Literacy & ESL
Subject Interests: Dinosauria, Local area hist bks

Automation Activity & Vendor Info: (Cataloging) Innovative Interfaces, Inc; (Circulation) Innovative Interfaces, Inc; (OPAC) Innovative Interfaces, Inc
Wireless access
Function: 24/7 Electronic res, Activity rm, After school storytime, Archival coll, Art exhibits, Audio & video playback equip for onsite use, Audiobks via web, Bks on CD, Children's prog, Computer training, Computers for patron use, Digital talking bks, Electronic databases & coll, Free DVD rentals, Games & aids for people with disabilities, ILL available, Internet access, Life-long learning prog for all ages, Magazines, Magnifiers for reading, Microfiche/film & reading machines, Movies, Online cat, OverDrive digital audio bks, Photocopying/Printing, Preschool outreach, Prog for adults, Prog for children & young adult, Ref serv available, Scanner, Spanish lang bks, Story hour, Summer reading prog, Teen prog, Telephone ref, Visual arts prog, Wheelchair accessible
Publications: Library Information Pamphlets; Weekly Newspaper Column
Mem of Marigold Library System
Partic in The Regional Automation Consortium
Open Mon, Tues, Thurs & Fri 9-5, Wed 9-8, Sat 12-4
Restriction: Circ to mem only, In-house use for visitors, Non-resident fee
Friends of the Library Group

S ROYAL TYRRELL MUSEUM OF PALAEONTOLOGY LIBRARY*, Midland Provincial Park, Hwy 838 N Dinosaur Trail, Box 7500, T0J 0Y0. SAN 371-750X. Tel: 403-823-7707. FAX: 403-823-7131. E-mail: tyrrell.library@gov.ab.ca. Web Site: tyrrellmuseum.com. *Dir, Presv Serv,* Craig Scott; E-mail: craig.scott@gov.ab.ca
Founded 1985
Library Holdings: Bk Titles 20,000; Bk Vols 60,000; Per Subs 100
Subject Interests: Geol, Museology, Paleontology
Restriction: Not open to pub

DUCHESS

P DUCHESS & DISTRICT PUBLIC LIBRARY*, 256A Louise Ave, T0J 0Z0. (Mail add: PO Box 88, T0J 0Z0). Tel: 403-378-4369. FAX: 403-378-4369. E-mail: duclib@shortgrass.ca. Web Site: duchess.shortgrass.ca, www.livenewell.com/profile.asp?bPageID=1126. *Libr Mgr,* Daryl Kimura
Founded 1977. Pop 836
Library Holdings: Bk Vols 6,000
Wireless access
Mem of Shortgrass Library System
Open Tues & Thurs 10-4, Wed 3-8, Fri 1-5, Sat 10-1

DUFFIELD

P DUFFIELD PUBLIC LIBRARY*, One Main St, T0E 0N0. Tel: 780-892-2644. FAX: 780-892-3344. E-mail: duffieldlibrary@pclibraries.ca. Web Site: pclibraries.ca. *Commun Serv Librn,* Alexandra Daum; Tel: 780-718-9493, E-mail: adaum@pclibraries.ca; *Mgr,* Kathy Gardiner; Tel: 780-962-2003, Ext 270, E-mail: kgardiner@pclibraries.ca
Library Holdings: Bk Vols 13,000
Wireless access
Mem of Yellowhead Regional Library
Open Mon & Thurs 9-5, Wed 11-7

P KEEPHILLS PUBLIC LIBRARY, 15 51515 Range Rd 32A, T0E 0N0. (Mail add: Comp 32 Site 1 RR 1, T0E 0N0). Tel: 780-731-0000. E-mail: keephillslibrary@pclibraries.ca. Web Site: pclibraries.ca/about-us/keephills-public-library. *Libr Dir,* Kathy Gardiner; Tel: 780-731-3725, E-mail: kgardiner@pclibraries.ca; *Libr Mgr,* Charllotte Smelski
Library Holdings: Bk Vols 7,000
Wireless access
Mem of Yellowhead Regional Library
Open Tues 8:30-4:30, Wed 12-8, Fri 10-6

EAGLESHAM

P EAGLESHAM PUBLIC LIBRARY*, 4902 53rd Ave, T0H 1H0. SAN 320-9873. Tel: 780-359-3792. E-mail: librarian@eagleshamlibrary.ab.ca. Web Site: www.eagleshamlibrary.ab.ca. *Libr Mgr,* Norma Bolster; E-mail: normabolster@pwsd76.ab.ca
Pop 250; Circ 2,000
Library Holdings: Bk Titles 5,000; Per Subs 10
Wireless access
Mem of Peace Library System
Open Tues-Thurs 12:30-4:30

ECKVILLE

P ECKVILLE MUNICIPAL LIBRARY*, 4855 51 Ave, T0M 0X0. (Mail add: PO Box 492, T0M 0X0). Tel: 403-746-3240. FAX: 403-746-5348. E-mail: eckvillelibrary@prl.ab.ca. Web Site: eckvillelibrary.prl.ab.ca. *Libr Mgr,* Patti Skocdopole
Pop 1,019
Library Holdings: Bk Vols 7,500
Wireless access
Mem of Parkland Regional Library-Alberta
Open Tues, Wed & Fri 10-6, Thurs 10-8
Friends of the Library Group

EDBERG

P EDBERG PUBLIC LIBRARY*, 48 First Ave W, T0B 1J0. (Mail add: PO Box 93, T0B 1J0). Tel: 780-678-5606. FAX: 780-877-2562. E-mail: edberglibrary@prl.ab.ca. Web Site: edberglibrary.prl.ab.ca. *Libr Mgr,* Pam Fankhanel
Pop 150
Library Holdings: Bk Vols 4,500
Automation Activity & Vendor Info: (Circulation) Horizon
Wireless access
Mem of Parkland Regional Library-Alberta
Special Services for the Blind - Bks on CD; Daisy reader; Large print bks
Open Mon 1-4, Tues-Thurs 7pm-9pm, Fri 4-6

EDGERTON

P EDGERTON PUBLIC LIBRARY*, 5037-50 Ave, T0B 1K0. (Mail add: PO Box 180, T0B 1K0). Tel: 780-755-3933, Ext 7. FAX: 780-755-3750. E-mail: librarian@edgertonlibrary.ab.ca. Web Site: edgertonlibrary.ab.ca. *Libr Mgr,* Mary Ann Sparks; Staff 4 (Non-MLS 4)
Pop 403
Library Holdings: Bk Vols 10,500
Automation Activity & Vendor Info: (Acquisitions) Library Systems & Services (LSSI); (Cataloging) Library Systems & Services (LSSI); (Circulation) Library Systems & Services (LSSI); (ILL) Library Systems & Services (LSSI)
Wireless access
Function: 24/7 Electronic res, 24/7 Online cat, Adult bk club
Mem of Northern Lights Library System
Open Mon & Wed-Fri 4-6, Tues 10-12 & 4:30-8; Mon & Wed-Fri 9:30-12 & 12:30-4:30, Tues 1:30-8:30 (Summer)
Restriction: Access at librarian's discretion, Authorized personnel only

EDMONTON

S ACUREN GROUP, INC LIBRARY, 7450 18th St, T6P 1N8. SAN 326-3843. Tel: 780-490-2438. FAX: 780-440-1167. Web Site: www.acuren.com. *Library Contact,* Eric Dowdle; E-mail: eric.dowdle@acuren.com
Founded 1978
Library Holdings: Bk Titles 2,500; Per Subs 50
Subject Interests: Corrosion, Failure analysis, Metallurgy, Non-destructive testing, Ultrasonic flaw detection, Visual inspection, Welding
Wireless access
Open Mon-Fri 8-5
Restriction: Internal circ only

S ALBERTA GENEALOGICAL SOCIETY LIBRARY & RESEARCH CENTRE, No 162-14315-118 Ave, T5L 4S6. SAN 373-8949. Tel: 780-424-4429. E-mail: agsoffice@abgenealogy.ca. Web Site: www.abgenealogy.ca/ags-library-research-centre, www.edmontongenealogy.ca/library. *Pres,* Kurt Paterson; *Libr Dir,* Virginia Crawford
Founded 1982
Library Holdings: Bk Titles 4,000; Per Subs 20
Special Collections: Research & Genealogy Coll
Publications: Relatively Speaking (Quarterly)
Open Tues-Thurs 10-3

G ALBERTA GOVERNMENT LIBRARY*, Capital Blvd, 11th Flr, 10044 - 108 St, T5J 5E6. SAN 365-6977. Tel: 780-427-2985. FAX: 780-427-5927. E-mail: Library.AGL@gov.ab.ca. Web Site: www.servicealberta.ca/alberta-government-library.cfm. *Dir, Libr Serv,* Valerie Footz; *Colls Librn,* Nancy Gerhart; E-mail: aganetha.gerhart@gov.ab.ca; *Digital Serv Librn,* Paul Pype; E-mail: paul.pype@gov.ab.ca; *Open Info Team Lead,* Gary Weber; E-mail: gary.weber@gov.ab.ca; *Open Info Analyst,* Ikram Cheikhi; E-mail: ikram.cheikhi@gov.ab.ca; *Digital Serv, Libr Tech,* Penny Chu; E-mail: penny.chu@gov.ab.ca; *Cat/Metadata Tech,* Yvonne Chan; E-mail: yvonne.s.chan@gov.ab.ca; *Cat/Metadata Tech,* Lisa Drysdale; E-mail: lisa.drysdale@gov.ab.ca; *Circ Tech,* Carol Johnson; E-mail: carol.m.johnson@gov.ab.ca; *ILL,* Blanka Kaiser; E-mail: blanka.kaiser@gov.ab.ca; *Ser & Acq Tech,* Rhonda Dawson; E-mail: rhonda.dawson@gov.ab.ca; Staff 11 (MLS 5, Non-MLS 6)
Founded 1940
Library Holdings: Bk Titles 46,000; Per Subs 300
Special Collections: Archival Annual Reports of all Government of Alberta Ministries; Environmental Impact Assessments for Alberta;

Government of Alberta Publications; Legislation for the Province of Alberta
Automation Activity & Vendor Info: (Acquisitions) SirsiDynix; (Cataloging) SirsiDynix; (Circulation) SirsiDynix; (ILL) A-G Canada Ltd; (OPAC) SirsiDynix; (Serials) SirsiDynix
Wireless access
Function: Ref serv available
Partic in NEOS Library Consortium; The Alberta Library
Open Mon-Fri 8:15-4:30
Restriction: Circ limited

S ALBERTA HISTORICAL RESOURCES FOUNDATION LIBRARY*, 8820 112th St, T6G 2P8. SAN 327-4969. Tel: 780-431-2305. FAX: 780-427-5598. *Library Contact,* Carina Naranjilla; E-mail: carina.naranjilla@gov.ab.ca
Library Holdings: Bk Titles 9,000; Bk Vols 12,000
Special Collections: Alberta History; Archaeology
Open Mon-Fri 8:15-12 & 1-4:30

S ALBERTA INNOVATES*, Library & Information Centre, 250 Karl Clark Rd, T6N 1E4. SAN 365-7035. Tel: 780-450-5229. FAX: 780-450-8996. E-mail: millwoods_library@albertainnovates.ca. Web Site: www.albertatechfutures.ca. *Librn,* Renee Morrissey; E-mail: renee.morrissey@albertainnovates.ca; *Acq of New Ser/Per, Circ, Ref (Info Servs),* Lucy Heintz; Tel: 780-450-5064, E-mail: heintz@albertainnovates.ca; *ILL,* Roberto Pellegrino; Tel: 780-450-5057, E-mail: pellegrino@albertainnovates.ca; Staff 3 (MLS 1, Non-MLS 2)
Founded 1950
Library Holdings: Bk Titles 40,000; Per Subs 300
Subject Interests: Chem, Chem engr, Environ engr, Environ res, Forest res, Heavy oil, Indust engr, Manufacturing tech, Oil sands, Pharmaceuticals, Pulp & paper
Partic in NEOS Library Consortium
Open Mon-Fri 8:30-12 & 1-4:30

Branches:

VEGREVILLE BRANCH, Hwy 16A 75th St, Vegreville, T9C 1T4. (Mail add: PO Box 4000, Vegreville, T9C 1T4), SAN 378-1453. Tel: 780-632-8417. Interlibrary Loan Service Tel: 780-632-8419. FAX: 780-632-8300. *Libr Asst,* Audrey Lyons
Founded 1979
Subject Interests: Air emissions, Environ health, Environ tech, Land reclamation econ, Plant ecology, Solid waste mgt, Toxicology, Waste water treatment, Weed control, Wildlife
Automation Activity & Vendor Info: (Cataloging) SirsiDynix-WorkFlows; (Circulation) SirsiDynix-WorkFlows; (ILL) SirsiDynix-WorkFlows; (OPAC) SirsiDynix-Unicorn; (Serials) SirsiDynix-WorkFlows
Open Mon-Fri 8:15-12 & 1-4:30

ALBERTA LAW LIBRARIES

GL DEPARTMENTAL LIBRARY*, 400A Bowker Bldg, North, 9833 - 109 St, T5K 2E8, SAN 318-6474. Tel: 780-422-6264. Information Services Tel: 780-422-4946. FAX: 780-422-5912. *Librn,* Ana San Miguel; E-mail: ana.sanmiguel@gov.ab.ca; Staff 1 (MLS 1)
Founded 1912
Library Holdings: Bk Vols 23,350
Special Collections: Classical English, Canadian & American Texts (16th-19th Centuries)
Subject Interests: Can civil law, Constitutional law, Crim law, Intl law
Restriction: Not open to pub

GL EDMONTON*, Law Courts Bldg, 2nd Flr S, 1A Sir Winston Churchill Sq, T5J 0R2, SAN 372-3569. Tel: 780-422-2342. Toll Free Tel: 866-230-8068. FAX: 780-427-0397. E-mail: all.edm@gov.ab.ca. *Libr Dir,* Dale Barrie; E-mail: dale.barrie@gov.ab.ca; *Info, Res & Access Mgr,* Linda Harmata; Tel: 780-427-3284; *IT Serv Mgr,* Sophie Song; Tel: 780-415-8580, Fax: 780-427-0481, E-mail: sophie.song@gov.ab.ca; Staff 9 (MLS 4, Non-MLS 5)
Library Holdings: Bk Vols 58,000; Per Subs 200
Automation Activity & Vendor Info: (Acquisitions) Ex Libris Group; (Cataloging) Ex Libris Group; (Circulation) Ex Libris Group; (OPAC) Ex Libris Group; (Serials) Ex Libris Group
Open Mon-Fri 8:15-4:30

GL NORTH LIBRARY*, Law Courts North, 5th Flr, 1A Sir Winston Churchill Sq, T5J 0R2, SAN 321-3641. Tel: 780-427-3327. FAX: 780-427-0481. E-mail: judicial-north.libraries@gov.ab.ca. *Dir,* Dale Barrie; E-mail: dale.barrie@gov.ab.ca; *Info, Res & Access Mgr,* Linda Harmata; Tel: 780-427-3284, Fax: 780-427-0397, E-mail: linda.harmata@gov.ab.ca; *IT Serv Mgr,* Sophie Song; Staff 3 (MLS 3)
Founded 1976
Library Holdings: Bk Vols 15,000
Subject Interests: Civil, Criminal, Family law, Youth law
Automation Activity & Vendor Info: (Acquisitions) Ex Libris Group; (Cataloging) Ex Libris Group; (Circulation) Ex Libris Group; (ILL) Ex Libris Group; (OPAC) Ex Libris Group; (Serials) Ex Libris Group

Function: For res purposes
Publications: Alberta Provincial Court Decisions (Annual)
Restriction: Not open to pub

G ALBERTA LEGISLATURE LIBRARY*, 216 Legislature Bldg, 10800-97 Ave NW, T5K 2B6. SAN 318-6679. Tel: 780-427-2473. FAX: 780-427-6016. E-mail: library.requests@assembly.ab.ca. Web Site: www.assembly.ab.ca. *Dir, Libr Serv,* Heather Close; Tel: 780-427-0204, E-mail: heather.close@assembly.ab.ca; *Bibliog Serv Librn,* Vivianne Fagnan; Tel: 780-427-5893, E-mail: vivianne.fagan@assembly.ab.ca; *Govt Doc Librn,* Louise England; Tel: 780-415-4502, E-mail: louise.england@assembly.ab.ca; *Ref Librn,* Jennifer Goodwin; Tel: 780-427-0208, E-mail: jennifer.goodwin@assembly.ab.ca; *Res & Presv Librn,* Leanne Thompson; Tel: 780-422-9316, E-mail: leanne.thompson@assembly.ab.ca; *Ser Librn,* Warren Maynes; Tel: 780-427-0201, E-mail: warren.maynes@assembly.ab.ca; *Syst Librn,* Adrianne Baker; Tel: 780-415-2904, E-mail: adrianne.baker@assembly.ab.ca; Staff 20 (MLS 9, Non-MLS 11)
Founded 1906
Library Holdings: Bk Vols 450,000; Per Subs 258
Special Collections: Government Publication Coll; Provincial Weekly Newspaper Coll. Canadian and Provincial
Subject Interests: Can hist, Law, Polit sci, Pub admin, Soc
Automation Activity & Vendor Info: (Acquisitions) SirsiDynix-WorkFlows; (Cataloging) SirsiDynix-WorkFlows; (Circulation) SirsiDynix-WorkFlows; (Discovery) SirsiDynix; (OPAC) SirsiDynix; (Serials) SirsiDynix-WorkFlows
Wireless access
Partic in The Alberta Library
Open Mon-Fri 8:15-4:30

S ALBERTA SCHOOL FOR THE DEAF LIBRARY, Edmonton Public School Division, 6240 113 St NW, T6H 3L2. SAN 324-5241. Tel: 780-436-0465. FAX: 780-436-5863. Web Site: asd.epsb.ca. *Librn,* Antonia Gisler; *Asst Librn,* Chrissy Steele
Founded 1966
Library Holdings: Bk Titles 16,000; Per Subs 10
Special Collections: Alberta Curriculum
Subject Interests: Deaf, Spec educ
Special Services for the Deaf - Bks on deafness & sign lang; Captioned film dep; High interest/low vocabulary bks; Spec interest per; Staff with knowledge of sign lang; TTY equip
Restriction: Not open to pub

S ALBERTA TEACHERS' ASSOCIATION LIBRARY*, 11010 142 St, T5N 2R1. SAN 318-6547. Tel: 780-447-9400. FAX: 780-455-6481. E-mail: library@ata.ab.ca. Web Site: library.teachers.ab.ca. *Librn,* Sandra Anderson; *Cataloger,* Sheeba Kamran; Staff 3 (MLS 2, Non-MLS 1)
Founded 1939. Pop 47,000
Library Holdings: e-books 100; e-journals 500; Bk Vols 25,000; Per Subs 50; Videos 500
Special Collections: Canadian Teachers Associations Publications; Gaming Coll; Maker Tech Lending Coll
Subject Interests: Inclusive Education, Indigenous Education, Innovation in Education, Literacy, Maker Technology, Numeracy, Primary educ, Secondary educ, Teacher Retention, Teaching, Truth & Reconciliation
Wireless access
Function: AV serv, Computers for patron use, Electronic databases & coll, For res purposes, Internet access, Online cat, Photocopying/Printing, Ref & res, Ref serv available, Res assist avail, Telephone ref
Open Mon-Fri 8-5 (Winter); Mon-Fri 8-4:30 (Summer)
Restriction: Open to students, Staff & mem only

L BISHOP & MCKENZIE LLP, Barristers & Solicitors Library, 10180 101st St NW, Ste 2300, T5J 1V3. SAN 371-0262. Tel: 780-426-5550. FAX: 780-426-1305. Web Site: bmllp.ca. *Mgr, Libr & Res Serv,* Judy Oberg; E-mail: joberg@bmllp.ca; Staff 1 (MLS 1)
Library Holdings: Bk Titles 1,600; Per Subs 212
Automation Activity & Vendor Info: (Cataloging) Inmagic, Inc.
Restriction: Not open to pub

S CAMERON SCIENCE & TECHNOLOGY LIBRARY*, University of Alberta, Science & Technology Library (Cameron), T6G 2J8. Tel: 780-492-8440. Web Site: library.ualberta.ca/locations/cameron. *Head of Libr,* Tim Klassen; Tel: 780-492-7918, E-mail: tim.klassen@ualberta.ca
Founded 1960
Special Collections: Circumpolar Studies Coll; William C Wonders Map Coll
Automation Activity & Vendor Info: (Cataloging) SirsiDynix
Wireless access
Function: ILL available, Ref serv available

GL CANADA DEPARTMENT OF JUSTICE*, Law Library, EPCOR Tower, 300 10423 101 St, T5H 0E7. SAN 371-7828. Tel: 780-495-2973. Interlibrary Loan Service Tel: 780-495-5539. FAX: 780-495-2854. E-mail:

edmlawlib@justice.gc.ca. *Info Res Mgr,* Cathy Woodside; Staff 5 (MLS 2, Non-MLS 3)
Library Holdings: Bk Titles 2,500; Bk Vols 14,000; Per Subs 75
Subject Interests: Aboriginal law, Can law, Constitutional, Crim law, Litigation, Tax law
Automation Activity & Vendor Info: (Cataloging) SirsiDynix; (Circulation) SirsiDynix; (OPAC) SirsiDynix; (Serials) SirsiDynix
Wireless access
Function: ILL available, Photocopying/Printing
Restriction: Open to staff only

C CONCORDIA UNIVERSITY OF EDMONTON, Arnold Guebert Library, 7128 Ada Blvd, T5B 4E4. SAN 318-658X. Tel: 780-479-9338. Administration Tel: 780-479-9324. FAX: 780-477-1033. E-mail: library@concordia.ab.ca. Web Site: concordia.ab.ca/library. *Asst Libr Dir,* Lynette Toews-Neufeldt; Tel: 780-479-9339, E-mail: lynette.toews-neufeldt@concordia.ab.ca; Staff 7.8 (MLS 3.8, Non-MLS 4)
Founded 1921. Enrl 2,168; Fac 71; Highest Degree: Doctorate
Library Holdings: Bk Vols 54,400
Wireless access
Partic in NEOS Library Consortium
Open Mon-Thurs 8am-10pm, Fri 8-6, Sun 11-5 (Fall-Spring); Mon-Fri 8:30-4:30 (Summer)

M COVENANT HEALTH GREY NUNS COMMUNITY HOSPITAL, Health Sciences Library, 1100 Youville Dr W, Rm 0634, T6L 5X8. SAN 318-6601. Tel: 780-306-7618. FAX: 780-735-7202. E-mail: covenantlibrary@covenanthealth.ca. *Mgr, Libr Serv,* Sharna Polard; E-mail: sharna.polard@covenanthealth.ca; Staff 3 (MLS 1, Non-MLS 2)
Founded 1986
Library Holdings: e-books 1,700; e-journals 5,000; Bk Titles 1,000; Per Subs 3
Subject Interests: Allied health, Med, Nursing, Palliative care
Automation Activity & Vendor Info: (Cataloging) Koha; (Circulation) Koha; (OPAC) Koha
Wireless access
Function: Doc delivery serv, ILL available
Open Mon-Fri 7:30-3:45
Restriction: Non-circulating to the pub

M COVENANT HEALTH MISERICORDIA COMMUNITY HOSPITAL*, Weinlos Library, 16940 87 Ave NW, T5R 4H5. SAN 318-6687. Tel: 780-735-2708. FAX: 780-735-2509. E-mail: CovenantLibrary@covenanthealth.ca. Web Site: medicalstaff.covenanthealth.ca/corporate-services/library-services. *Mgr, Libr Serv,* Sharna Polard; Tel: 780-735-9329, E-mail: sharna.polard@covenanthealth.ca; Staff 3 (MLS 1, Non-MLS 2)
Founded 1971
Library Holdings: e-books 150; e-journals 800; Bk Titles 1,400; Per Subs 21
Subject Interests: Allied health, Med, Nursing
Automation Activity & Vendor Info: (Cataloging) SirsiDynix; (Circulation) SirsiDynix; (OPAC) SirsiDynix; (Serials) SirsiDynix
Wireless access
Function: Doc delivery serv, ILL available
Partic in NEOS Library Consortium
Open Mon-Fri 7:30-3:45
Restriction: Non-circulating to the pub

P EDMONTON PUBLIC LIBRARY*, Stanley A Milner (Downtown) Library, Seven Sir Winston Churchill Sq, T5J 2V4. SAN 365-7159. Tel: 780-496-7000. FAX: 780-496-1885, 780-496-7097. Web Site: www.epl.ca. *Chief Exec Officer,* Pilar Martinez; Tel: 780-496-7050, E-mail: pmartinez@epl.ca; *Chief Financial Officer,* Deborah Rhodes; *Exec Direc, Strategy & Innovation,* Tina Thomas; Tel: 780-496-7046, E-mail: tthomas@epl.ca; *Dir, Human Res,* Mike Lewis; Tel: 780-496-7066, E-mail: mlewis@epl.ca
Founded 1913. Pop 899,447; Circ 12,005,336
Special Collections: CD Coll; Children's Coll; DVD Coll; Heritage Coll; Indigenous Coll; Video Game Coll; World Language Coll - English Language Learning; World Languages Coll. Canadian and Provincial
Automation Activity & Vendor Info: (Acquisitions) BiblioCommons; (Cataloging) BiblioCommons; (Circulation) BiblioCommons
Wireless access
Function: 24/7 Electronic res, 24/7 Online cat, Adult bk club, Adult literacy prog, After school storytime, Art exhibits, Audiobks on Playaways & MP3, Audiobks via web, Bk club(s), Bks on CD, Children's prog, Computer training, Computers for patron use, Digital talking bks, Electronic databases & coll, Family literacy, Free DVD rentals, Holiday prog, Home delivery & serv to seniorr ctr & nursing homes, Homebound delivery serv, Homework prog, ILL available, Internet access, Life-long learning prog for all ages, Literacy & newcomer serv, Magazines, Magnifiers for reading, Mango lang, Meeting rooms, Microfiche/film & reading machines, Movies, Music CDs, Online cat, Outreach serv, OverDrive digital audio bks, Photocopying/Printing, Preschool outreach, Prog for adults, Prog for children & young adult, Satellite serv, Scanner, Senior computer classes, Senior outreach, Spanish lang bks, Story hour, Summer reading prog, Teen prog, Visual arts prog, Wheelchair accessible, Writing prog
Partic in The Alberta Library
Special Services for the Deaf - Bks on deafness & sign lang; Closed caption videos; High interest/low vocabulary bks; Staff with knowledge of sign lang
Special Services for the Blind - Accessible computers; Assistive/Adapted tech devices, equip & products; Bks available with recordings; Bks on CD; Closed circuit TV magnifier; Club for the blind; Computer access aids; Computer with voice synthesizer for visually impaired persons; Copier with enlargement capabilities; Daisy reader; Descriptive video serv (DVS); Digital talking bk; Digital talking bk machines; Extensive large print coll; Free checkout of audio mat; Home delivery serv; Internet workstation with adaptive software; Large print bks; Large screen computer & software; Magnifiers; Networked computers with assistive software; PC for people with disabilities; Scanner for conversion & translation of mats; Screen enlargement software for people with visual disabilities; Screen reader software; Sound rec; Talking bks; Talking bks & player equip; Talking machines; Text reader; Volunteer serv
Open Mon-Fri 9-9, Sat 9-6, Sun 1-5
Friends of the Library Group
Branches: 20
ABBOTTSFIELD-PENNY MCKEE BRANCH, 160-3210 118 Ave NW, T5W 0Z4, SAN 377-8045. Tel: 780-496-7839. FAX: 780-496-8397. *Mgr,* Miranda Koshelek; Tel: 780-496-6298; *Libr Serv Coordr,* Kristy Higgins; Tel: 780-496-7980
Open Mon-Thurs 10-9, Fri & Sat 10-6, Sun 1-5
Friends of the Library Group
CALDER, 12710 131 Ave NW, T5L 2Z6, SAN 365-7183. Tel: 780-496-7090. FAX: 780-496-1453. *Mgr,* Kyle Marshall; Tel: 780-496-6285; *Libr Serv Coordr,* Ana Castilla; Tel: 780-496-7093
Open Mon-Thurs 10-9, Fri & Sat 10-6, Sun 1-5
Friends of the Library Group
CAPILANO, 9915 67 St NW, T6A 0H2, SAN 365-7213. Tel: 780-496-1802. FAX: 780-496-7009. *Mgr,* Caroline Land; Tel: 780-496-7022; *Libr Serv Coordr,* Hayley Redpath; Tel: 780-496-8426
Open Mon-Thurs 10-9, Fri & Sat 10-6, Sun 1-5
Friends of the Library Group
CASTLE DOWNS, 106 Lakeside Landing, 15379 Castle Downs Rd, T5X 3Y7, SAN 365-7221. Tel: 780-496-1804. FAX: 780-496-7005. *Mgr,* Vicky Varga; Tel: 780-496-2708; *Libr Serv Coordr,* Nicole Auriat; Tel: 780-496-2738
Open Mon-Thurs 10-9, Fri & Sat 10-6, Sun 1-5
Friends of the Library Group
CLAREVIEW, 3808 139 Ave, T5Y 3G4. Tel: 780-442-7471. *Mgr,* Jody Crilly; Tel: 780-495-1930; *Libr Serv Coordr,* Mike Eaton; Tel: 780-496-4038
Open Mon-Thurs 10-9, Fri & Sat 10-6, Sun 1-5
Friends of the Library Group
HERITAGE VALLEY, 2755 119A St SW, T6W 3R3. Tel: 708-496-4834. *Mgr,* Leanne Drury Melsness; Tel: 780-496-8348; *Assoc Mgr,* Jessica Niemi; Tel: 780-442-6861; *Libr Serv Coordr,* Christalene Lay; Tel: 780-496-8338
Open Mon-Thurs 10-9, Fri & Sat 10-6, Sun 1-5
HIGHLANDS, 6710 118 Ave NW, T5B 0P3, SAN 365-7272. Tel: 780-496-1806. FAX: 780-496-7012. *Mgr,* Susan Mikytyshyn; Tel: 780-496-4299; *Libr Serv Coordr,* Neil Jackson; Tel: 780-495-9872
Open Mon-Thurs 10-9, Fri & Sat 10-6, Sun 1-5
Friends of the Library Group
LOIS HOLE LIBRARY, 17650 69 Ave NW, T5T 3X9, SAN 376-9534. Tel: 780-442-0888. FAX: 780-442-0887. *Mgr,* Mary Jane Bilsland; Tel: 780-442-0880; *Assoc Mgr,* Margaret Walsh; Tel: 780-442-0879; *Libr Serv Coordr,* Tina Perreault; Tel: 780-442-0882
Open Mon-Thurs 10-9, Fri & Sat 10-6, Sun 1-5
Friends of the Library Group
IDYLWYLDE, 8310 88 Ave NW, T6C 1L1, SAN 365-7302. Tel: 780-496-1808. FAX: 780-496-7092. *Mgr,* Connie Hargreaves; Tel: 780-496-8347; *Libr Serv Coordr,* Taryn Hunchak; Tel: 780-496-7279
Open Mon-Thurs 10-9, Fri & Sat 10-6, Sun 1-5
JASPER PLACE, 9010 156 St, T5R 5X7, SAN 365-7337. Tel: 780-496-1810. FAX: 780-496-7004. *Mgr,* Madeline Gormley; Tel: 780-496-8362; *Libr Serv Coordr,* Erin Hardie-Belair; Tel: 780-496-8359
Open Mon-Thurs 10-9, Fri & Sat 10-6, Sun 1-5
Friends of the Library Group
LONDONDERRY, Londonderry Mall, Ste 166, 137 Ave 66 St NW, T5C 3C8, SAN 365-7248. Tel: 780-496-1814. FAX: 780-496-1452. *Mgr,* Andrew Halberstadt; *Libr Serv Coordr,* Jennifer De Pasquale; Tel: 780-496-6584; Staff 24 (MLS 3, Non-MLS 21)
Founded 1979
Open Mon-Thurs 10-9, Fri 10-6, Sat 9:30-5:30, Sun 1-5
Friends of the Library Group

MILL WOODS, 2610 Hewes Way, T6L 0A9, SAN 365-7345. Tel: 780-496-1818. FAX: 780-496-1450. *Mgr,* Angelica Thompson; Tel: 780-496-7077; *Assoc Mgr,* Jennifer Schell; Tel: 780-496-7842; *Libr Serv Coordr,* Gerry O'Riordan; Tel: 780-496-1821
Open Mon-Thurs 10-9, Fri & Sat 10-6, Sun 1-5
Friends of the Library Group

RIVERBEND, 460 Riverbend Sq, Rabbit Hill Rd & Terwillegar Dr, T6R 2X2. Tel: 780-944-5311. FAX: 780-944-5327. *Mgr,* Virginia Clevette; Tel: 780-944-5320; *Libr Serv Coordr,* Heather Chartier; Tel: 780-944-5323
Open Mon-Thurs 10-9, Fri & Sat 10-6, Sun 1-5
Friends of the Library Group

SPRUCEWOOD, 11555 95 St, T5G 1L5, SAN 365-7396. Tel: 780-496-7099. FAX: 780-496-7010. *Mgr,* Katherine Gibson; Tel: 780-496-1054; *Libr Serv Coordr,* Bernice Linkewich; Tel: 780-496-7043
Open Mon-Thurs 10-9, Fri & Sat 10-6, Sun 1-5
Friends of the Library Group

STRATHCONA, 8331 104 St, T6E 4E9, SAN 365-7426. Tel: 780-496-1828. FAX: 780-496-1451. *Mgr,* Katie Turzansky; Tel: 780-496-3461; *Libr Serv Coordr,* Ashley Dotto; Tel: 780-496-3953
Open Mon-Thurs 10-9, Fri & Sat 10-6, Sun 1-5
Friends of the Library Group

WHITEMUD CROSSING, 145 Whitemud Crossing Shopping Ctr, 4211 106 St, T6J 6L7, SAN 365-7361. Tel: 780-496-1822. FAX: 780-496-7007. *Mgr,* Leanne Drury Melsness; Tel: 780-496-8348; *Assoc Mgr,* Jessica Niemi; Tel: 780-442-6861; *Libr Serv Coordr,* Christalene Lay; Tel: 780-496-8338
Open Mon-Thurs 10-9, Fri & Sat 10-6, Sun 1-5
Friends of the Library Group

WOODCROFT, 13420 114 Ave NW, T5M 2Y5, SAN 365-7450. Tel: 780-496-1830. FAX: 780-496-7089. *Mgr,* Margo Till-Rogers; Tel: 780-496-6894; *Libr Serv Coordr,* Rob Henderson; Tel: 780-496-6891
Founded 1956
Open Mon-Thurs 10-9, Fri & Sat 10-6, Sun 1-5
Friends of the Library Group

Bookmobiles: 4

M GLENROSE REHABILITATION HOSPITAL*, Knowledge Resource Service, 10230 111 Ave NW, T5G 0B7. SAN 320-7722. Tel: 780-735-8823. FAX: 780-735-8863. E-mail: krs@ahs.ca. Web Site: krs.ahs.ca.
Library Holdings: Bk Vols 8,000; Per Subs 25
Subject Interests: Geriatrics, Psychol, Rehabilitation
Wireless access
Partic in NEOS Library Consortium

S INCLUSION ALBERTA, Reg Peters Resource Centre, 11724 Kingsway Ave, T5G 0X5. SAN 374-8936. Tel: 780-451-3055, Ext 225. Toll Free Tel: 800-252-7556 (Canada only). FAX: 780-453-5779. E-mail: library@inclusionalberta.org. Web Site: inclusionalberta.org/resources/reg-peter-s-library. *Librn,* Linda Cook; E-mail: lcook@inclusionalberta.org; Staff 1 (Non-MLS 1)
Library Holdings: AV Mats 100; DVDs 32; Bk Titles 3,700; Per Subs 30; Videos 100
Subject Interests: Deinstitutionalization, Integrated educ
Automation Activity & Vendor Info: (Acquisitions) Follett-Destiny; (Cataloging) Follett-Destiny; (Circulation) Follett-Destiny; (Course Reserve) Follett-Destiny; (ILL) Follett-Destiny; (Media Booking) Follett-Destiny; (OPAC) Follett-Destiny; (Serials) Follett Software
Wireless access
Open Mon-Fri 8:30-4:30

C THE KING'S UNIVERSITY, Simona Maaskant Library, 9125 50th St, T6B 2H3. SAN 325-2345. Tel: 780-465-8304. E-mail: library@kingsu.ca. Web Site: www.kingsu.ca/library. *Mgr,* Bonita Schalk Bjornson; E-mail: bonita.bjornson@kingsu.ca; Staff 3 (MLS 1, Non-MLS 2)
Founded 1979. Enrl 930; Pop 1,500; Fac 90; Highest Degree: Bachelor
Library Holdings: Music Scores 500
Subject Interests: Curric, Liberal arts
Automation Activity & Vendor Info: (Acquisitions) SirsiDynix; (Cataloging) SirsiDynix; (Circulation) SirsiDynix; (OPAC) SirsiDynix
Wireless access
Function: 24/7 Online cat, Computers for patron use, Electronic databases & coll, Online cat, Photocopying/Printing, Study rm, Wheelchair accessible
Partic in Canadian Research Knowledge Network; NEOS Library Consortium; The Alberta Library
Open Mon-Fri 8-4; Mon-Fri 9-3 (Intersession)
Restriction: Authorized patrons, Pub use on premises

C MACEWAN UNIVERSITY LIBRARY, John L Haar Library, 10700 104th Ave, T5J 4S2. (Mail add: PO Box 1796, T5J 2P2), SAN 320-0787. Tel: 780-497-5850. E-mail: library@macewan.ca. Web Site: library.macewan.ca. *Interim Dean,* Eva Revitt; E-mail: revitte@macewan.ca; *Mgr, Libr Operations,* Lily Dane; E-mail: danel@macewan.ca; Staff 17 (MLS 17)
Founded 1971. Fac 551
Library Holdings: AV Mats 53,210; e-books 160,193; e-journals 35,981; Bk Vols 314,538; Per Subs 1,200
Subject Interests: Commun studies, Fine arts, Health, Univ transfer
Wireless access
Function: Telephone ref
Partic in NEOS Library Consortium; The Alberta Library
Open Mon-Thurs 7:30am-11pm, Fri 7:30am-8pm, Sat & Sun 10-8

C NEWMAN THEOLOGICAL COLLEGE LIBRARY*, 10012 84 St NW, T6A 0B2. SAN 373-2851. Tel: 780-392-2450. Toll Free Tel: 844-392-2450. FAX: 780-462-4013. Web Site: www.newman.edu/Library. *Libr Dir,* Jim Derksen; E-mail: jim.derksen@newman.edu; Staff 3 (MLS 1, Non-MLS 2)
Founded 1917. Enrl 100; Fac 20; Highest Degree: Master
Library Holdings: Bk Titles 36,000; Per Subs 230
Automation Activity & Vendor Info: (Cataloging) SirsiDynix; (Circulation) SirsiDynix; (Course Reserve) SirsiDynix; (OPAC) SirsiDynix
Partic in NEOS Library Consortium
Open Mon-Fri 9-4

J NORQUEST COLLEGE*, Learner Center - Library, 10215-108th St, 5th Flr, T5J 1L6. SAN 371-0491. Tel: 708-644-6070. E-mail: library@norquest.ca. Web Site: library.norquest.ca. *Head Librn,* Eve Poirier; E-mail: Eve.Poirier@norquest.ca; *Coordr, Libr Instruction,* Liz Fulton-Lyne; E-mail: Liz.Fulton-Lyne@norquest.ca; *Tech Serv, Tech,* Kathy Zarft; E-mail: Kathy.Zarft@norquest.ca; Staff 11 (MLS 2, Non-MLS 9)
Founded 1965. Enrl 4,023; Fac 255
Library Holdings: AV Mats 5,725; e-books 40,000; Bk Titles 42,460; Per Subs 250
Subject Interests: Acad upgrading, Career educ, English as a second lang
Wireless access
Partic in The Alberta Library
Open Mon-Fri 7:30-7, Sat 8-4

S NORTHERN ALBERTA INSTITUTE OF TECHNOLOGY*, McNally Library, 11762 106 St NW, T5G 2R1. SAN 318-6709. Tel: 780-471-8777. Toll Free Tel: 877-222-1722. E-mail: library@nait.ca. Web Site: library.nait.ca. *Mgr, Libr Serv,* Carmen Reems; E-mail: carmenr@nait.ca
Founded 1963
Library Holdings: Bk Titles 53,000; Per Subs 250
Special Collections: Automotive Manuals; Small Business
Subject Interests: Applied arts, Computer tech, Engr tech, Paramedical, Trades
Automation Activity & Vendor Info: (Acquisitions) Ex Libris Group; (Cataloging) Ex Libris Group; (Circulation) Ex Libris Group; (Course Reserve) Ex Libris Group; (Media Booking) Ex Libris Group; (OPAC) Ex Libris Group; (Serials) Ex Libris Group
Publications: Staff Handbook; Student Brochure
Partic in The Alberta Library
Open Mon-Thurs 7:45am-9pm, Fri 7:45-5, Sat & Sun 12-5

G PROVINCIAL ARCHIVES OF ALBERTA, REFERENCE LIBRARY*, Sandra Thomson Reading Room, 8555 Roper Rd, T6E 5W1. SAN 365-6853. Tel: 780-427-1750. Reference Tel: 780-427-1056. E-mail: paa@gov.ab.ca. Web Site: provincialarchives.alberta.ca. *Exec Dir,* Leslie Latta; *Dir, Access Serv, Dir, Conserv Serv,* Susan Stanton
Founded 1967
Library Holdings: Bk Vols 15,000
Special Collections: Alberta Local History; Alberta Pioneer Railway Association; Archives & Record Management; Government of Alberta (annual reports)
Subject Interests: Alberta hist, Conserv, Local hist, Western Canadiana
Wireless access
Function: Archival coll, Computers for patron use, Online cat, Photocopying/Printing, Ref serv available
Open Tues-Fri 9-4:30
Restriction: Closed stack, Non-circulating, Non-circulating of rare bks, Not a lending libr, Pub use on premises, Registered patrons only

UNIVERSITY OF ALBERTA

C ARCHIVES*, Books & Records Depository, 100 8170 50th St, T6B 1E6. Tel: 780-492-4174. FAX: 780-466-5210. E-mail: archives@ualberta.ca. Web Site: library.ualberta.ca/archives. *Univ Archivist,* Anna Gibson Hollow; Tel: 780-492-9942, E-mail: amg1@ualberta.ca; *Assoc Univ Archivist,* James Franks; Tel: 780-248-1304, E-mail: james.franks@ualberta.ca; Staff 4 (MLS 1, Non-MLS 3)
Founded 1968
Library Holdings: AV Mats 300,000; Bk Vols 100; Per Subs 10
Open Mon-Fri 8:30-4:30

C BIBLIOTHEQUE SAINT-JEAN*, 8406 rue Marie-Anne Gaboury (91 St), T6C 4G9, SAN 365-7876. Tel: 780-465-8711. FAX: 780-468-2550. Reference E-mail: bsjref@library.ualberta.ca. Web Site: www.library.ualberta.ca/francais. *Librn,* Yann Kabore; E-mail: pengdwen@ualberta.ca; Staff 8 (MLS 3, Non-MLS 5)

Founded 1910. Enrl 680; Highest Degree: Master
Library Holdings: Bk Vols 200,000; Per Subs 400
Special Collections: Canadiana, particularly French Canadian & Western Canadian Literature & History Coll; Eduq Microfiche; French Federal Documents
Subject Interests: Arts, Educ, Soc sci
Automation Activity & Vendor Info: (Cataloging) SirsiDynix; (Circulation) SirsiDynix; (Course Reserve) SirsiDynix; (OPAC) SirsiDynix
Function: 24/7 Electronic res, Computers for patron use, Electronic databases & coll, Free DVD rentals, ILL available, Microfiche/film & reading machines, Music CDs, Online cat, Online info literacy tutorials on the web & in blackboard, Orientations, Outside serv via phone, mail, e-mail & web, Photocopying/Printing, Ref serv available, Scanner
Partic in Association of Research Libraries
Publications: Library Guides & Bibliographies in the French Language

C HERBERT T COUTTS EDUCATION & PHYSICAL EDUCATION LIBRARY*, Educations Bldg, T6G 2G5, SAN 365-7663. Tel: 780-492-3770. Circulation Tel: 780-492-4566. Toll Free Tel: 800-207-0172. FAX: 780-492-8367. Reference E-mail: educref@library.ualberta.ca. Web Site: www.library.ualberta.ca. *Head of Libr,* Katherine Koch; Tel: 780-492-1460; Staff 28 (MLS 6, Non-MLS 22)
Founded 1948. Enrl 5,000; Highest Degree: Doctorate
Library Holdings: Bk Titles 250,000; Per Subs 800
Special Collections: Children's Literature (Historical Coll), curriculum mats, textbks; Research Coll on Reading (William S Gray Coll)
Subject Interests: Curric, Educ, Health promotion
Partic in Association of Research Libraries; Spires; Utlas

CL HEALTH LAW INSTITUTE LIBRARY*, Law Ctr, T6G 2H5, SAN 326-7644. E-mail: hliadmin@ualberta.ca. Web Site: www.hli.ualberta.ca. *Exec Dir,* Robyn Hyde-Lay; E-mail: rhydelay@ualberta.ca
Library Holdings: Bk Titles 100; Per Subs 30
Special Collections: Canadian Reported & Unreported Cases Dealing with Health Law, 1950 to present; Canadian, Commonwealth & American Journals & Articles on Medical Legal Issues; English & Commonwealth Health Law Cases, 1975 to present; Law Reform Commission of Canada Reports; Selected United States Health Law Court Cases
Open Mon-Fri 8-4

C RUTHERFORD HUMANITIES & SOCIAL SCIENCES LIBRARY*, 1-01 Rutherford South, T6G 2J8, SAN 365-7698. Tel: 780-492-5791. E-mail: rutherfordhelp@ualberta.ca. Web Site: www.library.ualberta.ca/locations/rutherford. *Head of Libr,* Dr Christine Brown; Tel: 780-492-1405, E-mail: christine.brown@ualberta.ca; *Pub Serv Mgr,* Lindsay Johnston; Tel: 780-492-0598. Subject Specialists: *Slavic studies,* Lindsay Johnston; Staff 22 (MLS 9, Non-MLS 13)
Founded 1973. Fac 3,976; Highest Degree: Doctorate
Library Holdings: Bk Vols 2,100,000; Per Subs 5,000
Special Collections: Bunyan Coll; Milton Coll; Romanticism Coll. Canadian and Provincial
Automation Activity & Vendor Info: (Acquisitions) SirsiDynix; (Cataloging) SirsiDynix; (Circulation) SirsiDynix; (Course Reserve) Talis Aspire; (Discovery) EBSCO Discovery Service; (ILL) Relais International; (OPAC) SirsiDynix; (Serials) SirsiDynix
Function: 24/7 Electronic res, 24/7 Online cat, Audio & video playback equip for onsite use, Computers for patron use, Doc delivery serv, Govt ref serv, ILL available, Internet access, Microfiche/film & reading machines, Music CDs, Online cat, Online info literacy tutorials on the web & in blackboard, Online ref, Orientations, Photocopying/Printing, Ref & res, Ref serv available, Res libr, Scanner, Wheelchair accessible
Partic in Bureau de cooperation Interuniversitaire; Council of Atlantic Academic Libraries (CAAL)
Special Services for the Deaf - Assistive tech
Special Services for the Blind - Assistive/Adapted tech devices, equip & products; Reader equip; Ref serv

CR SAINT JOSEPH'S COLLEGE LIBRARY*, 11325 89th Ave NW, T6G 2J5, SAN 318-6717. Tel: 780-492-7681, Ext 238. FAX: 780-492-8145. Web Site: www.library.ualberta.ca/aboutus/stjosephs. *Dir, Libr Serv,* Donna Meen; E-mail: donna.meen@ualberta.ca; Staff 3 (MLS 1, Non-MLS 2)
Founded 1964. Enrl 1,700; Fac 13
Library Holdings: AV Mats 150; Bk Vols 45,000; Per Subs 75
Special Collections: St Joseph's Ethics Library
Subject Interests: Bible studies, Catholic Church, Ethics, Philos, Theol
Open Mon-Fri 9-4:30

C SCIENCE & TECHNOLOGY LIBRARY*, Cameron Library, T6G 2J8, SAN 365-7728. Tel: 780-492-7912, 780-492-8440. FAX: 780-492-2721. Reference E-mail: sciref@ualberta.ca. Web Site: www.library.ualberta.ca. *Actg Head Librn,* Tim Klassen; Tel: 780-492-7918, E-mail: tim.klassen@ualberta.ca
Highest Degree: Doctorate
Special Collections: Canadian and Provincial
Subject Interests: Agr, Engr, Forestry, Human ecology, Maps, Northern studies

CM JOHN W SCOTT HEALTH SCIENCES LIBRARY*, Walter C Mackenzie Health Sciences Ctr 2K3 28, T6G 2R7, SAN 365-7752. Tel: 780-492-3899. Reference Tel: 780-492-7947. FAX: 780-492-6960. E-mail: jwsinfo@library.ualberta.ca. Web Site: www.library.ualberta.ca. *Head of Libr,* Marlene Dorgan; Tel: 780-492-7945, E-mail: marlene.dorgan@ualberta.ca; *Colls Mgr,* Trish Chatterley; Tel: 780-492-7933, E-mail: trish.chatterley@ualberta.ca; *Pub Serv Mgr,* Linda Slater; Tel: 780-492-7948, E-mail: linda.slater@ualberta.ca; Staff 10 (MLS 10)
Founded 1925. Enrl 47,000; Fac 468; Highest Degree: Doctorate
Special Collections: Historical (Rawlinson)
Subject Interests: Dentistry, Med, Nursing, Pharmaceutical sci, Rehabilitation med
Automation Activity & Vendor Info: (Acquisitions) SirsiDynix; (Cataloging) SirsiDynix; (Circulation) SirsiDynix; (Course Reserve) SirsiDynix; (OPAC) SirsiDynix; (Serials) SirsiDynix
Partic in Association of Research Libraries
Open Mon-Thurs 8am-10pm, Fri 8-6, Sat 11-6, Sun 11-10 (Fall & Winter); Mon-Thurs 8-7, Fri 8-5, Sat & Sun 11-6 (Spring & Summer)

C UNIVERSITY LIBRARY*, 5-02 Cameron Libr, T6G 2J8, SAN 365-7604. Tel: 780-492-3790. FAX: 780-492-8302. *Vice Provost & Chief Librn,* Gerald Beasley; *Assoc Univ Librn,* Kathleen DeLong; Staff 85 (MLS 85)
Founded 1909. Enrl 36,562; Fac 2,055; Highest Degree: Doctorate
Library Holdings: Bk Vols 6,720,775; Per Subs 45,110
Special Collections: Alberta Folklore Coll; Canadian Fine Printing Coll; Contemporary Bookworks Coll; Literature (Bunyan, Milton, Yeats, Lawrence, Cuala Press, Curwen Press, Grabhorn Press & Wordsworth Colls), Javitch Coll of South & North American Indian Material; Salzburg Coll (Theology & Canon Law); Victorian Book Arts, Rutherford Coll of Western Canadiana. Canadian and Provincial; UN Document Depository
Subject Interests: Agr, Legal, Med, Sci, Sociol, Sports
Automation Activity & Vendor Info: (Circulation) SirsiDynix
Partic in Association of Research Libraries

CL JOHN ALEXANDER WEIR MEMORIAL LAW LIBRARY*, Law Ctr, 111 St & 89 Ave, T6G 2H5, SAN 365-7787. Tel: 780-492-3371. FAX: 780-492-7546. Reference E-mail: lawref@library.ualberta.ca. Web Site: guides.library.ualberta.ca. *Librn,* Kim Bates; E-mail: kabates@ualberta.ca; *Circ,* Shelley Brown; Tel: 780-492-1445, E-mail: shelley.brown@ualberta.ca; *Pub Serv,* Grant Kayler; Staff 6.8 (MLS 1.8, Non-MLS 5)
Founded 1951
Library Holdings: Bk Vols 375,000; Per Subs 4,900
Subject Interests: Common law, Health, Tax
Partic in Association of Research Libraries; Proquest Dialog
Publications: Courtroom Decorum; Law Library Guides; Legal Bibliography & Research Manual
Open Mon-Thurs 8am-10pm, Fri 8-6, Sat & Sun 11-10 (Winter); Mon-Fri 9-5 (Summer)

C WILLIAM C WONDERS MAP COLLECTION*, 1-55 Cameron Library, T6G 2J8, SAN 365-7841. Tel: 780-492-8440. FAX: 780-492-2721. Web Site: guides.library.ualberta.ca/maps. *Librn,* Virginia Pow; Tel: 780-492-7919, E-mail: virginia.pow@ualberta.ca; *Cataloger,* David L Jones; Tel: 780-492-3433, E-mail: david.jones@ualberta.ca; Staff 2 (MLS 1, Non-MLS 1)
Founded 1967. Enrl 34,000; Highest Degree: Doctorate
Library Holdings: Bk Vols 6,000; Per Subs 15
Special Collections: Map Sheets & Air Photographs
Subject Interests: Cartography, Exploration, Geog, Geol, Topography
Automation Activity & Vendor Info: (Cataloging) SirsiDynix; (Circulation) SirsiDynix; (OPAC) SirsiDynix
Publications: Maps in the Service of Administration

CR VANGUARD COLLEGE LIBRARY*, Schalm Memorial Collection, 12140 103 St NW, T5G 2J9. SAN 320-3018. Tel: 780-452-0808. Circulation Tel: 780-452-0801, Ext 122. FAX: 780-452-5803. E-mail: library@vanguardcollege.com. Web Site: www.vanguardcollege.com/current-students/library. *Libr Dir,* Karina Dunn; E-mail: karina.dunn@vanguardcollege.com; Staff 2 (MLS 1, Non-MLS 1)
Founded 1947. Enrl 180; Highest Degree: Bachelor
Library Holdings: Bk Titles 55,000; Per Subs 85
Subject Interests: Biblical studies, Christian educ, Counseling, Pastoral theol, Relig studies
Automation Activity & Vendor Info: (Cataloging) SirsiDynix; (Circulation) SirsiDynix-WorkFlows; (Course Reserve) SirsiDynix-WorkFlows
Wireless access
Partic in NEOS Library Consortium

S WOOD*, 5681-70 St, T6B 3P6. SAN 372-8846. Tel: 780-436-2152. FAX: 780-435-8425. Web Site: www.woodplc.com. *Library Contact,* Harley Pankratz; Tel: 204-488-2997, E-mail: harley.pankratz@woodplc.com
Founded 1950
Library Holdings: Bk Vols 1,500; Per Subs 18
Restriction: Staff use only

EDSON

P EDSON & DISTRICT PUBLIC LIBRARY, 4726-8 Ave, T7E 1E3. SAN 318-6741. Tel: 780-723-6691. E-mail: info@edsonlibrary.ca. Web Site: www.edsonlibrary.ca. *Libr Mgr,* Sarah Tonowski; E-mail: stonowski@edsonlibrary.ca
Founded 1940. Pop 13,000; Circ 65,000
Library Holdings: Bk Vols 34,000; Per Subs 39
Special Collections: Can & Prov; Edson Newspapers (Edson Archives)
Automation Activity & Vendor Info: (Cataloging) Innovative Interfaces, Inc; (Circulation) Innovative Interfaces, Inc; (OPAC) Innovative Interfaces, Inc
Wireless access
Mem of Yellowhead Regional Library
Open Mon-Fri 10-8, Sat 12-5
Friends of the Library Group

ELK POINT

P ELK POINT MUNICIPAL LIBRARY*, PO Box 750, T0A 1A0. SAN 318-675X. Tel: 780-724-3737. FAX: 780-724-3739. E-mail: info@elkpointlibrary.ab.ca. Web Site: www.elkpointlibrary.ab.ca. *Libr Mgr,* Daphne Schnurer
Founded 1950. Pop 1,440; Circ 24,685
Library Holdings: Bk Titles 13,000; Bk Vols 14,000; Per Subs 30
Wireless access
Mem of Northern Lights Library System
Open Tues-Thurs 10-5
Friends of the Library Group

P NORTHERN LIGHTS LIBRARY SYSTEM*, 5615-48 St, T0A 1A0. (Mail add: Postal Bag 8, T0A 1A0). Tel: 780-724-2596. Toll Free Tel: 800-561-0387. FAX: 780-724-2597. E-mail: info@nlls.ab.ca. Web Site: www.nlls.ab.ca. *Exec Dir,* Julie Walker; Tel: 780-724-2596, Ext 2112, E-mail: jwalker@nlls.ab.ca
Library Holdings: Bk Titles 12,500
Wireless access
Member Libraries: Alice Melnyk Public Library; Andrew Municipal Public Library; Anne Chorney Public Library; Ashmont Public Library; Athabasca Municipal Library; Bibliotheque Mallaig Library; Bon Accord Public Library; Bonnyville Municipal Library; Boyle Public Library; Chauvin Municipal Library; Cold Lake Public Library; Edgerton Public Library; Edmonton Garrison Community Library; Elk Point Municipal Library; Gibbons Municipal Library; Grassland Public Library; Holden Municipal Library; Innisfree Public Library; Kitscoty Public Library; Lac La Biche County Libraries; Lamont Public Library; Mannville Centennial Public Library; Marwayne Public Library; McPherson Municipal Library; Metro Kalyn Community Library; Morinville Community Library; Mundare Municipal Public Library; Myrnam Community Library; Newbrook Public Library; Phyllis Craig Legacy Library; Radway Public Library; Redwater Public Library; Rochester Municipal Library; Saint Paul Municipal Library; Smoky Lake Municipal Library; Thorhild Library; Three Cities Public Library; Tofield Municipal Library; Vegreville Centennial Library; Vermilion Public Library; Viking Municipal Library; Vilna Municipal Library; Wainwright Public Library; Wandering River Public Library
Open Mon-Fri 8:30-4:30

ELMWORTH

P ELMWORTH COMMUNITY LIBRARY*, 113036 Hwy 722, T0H 1J0. (Mail add: Box 23, T0H 1J0). Tel: 780-354-2930. FAX: 780-354-2930. E-mail: librarian@elmworthlibrary.ab.ca. Web Site: elmworthlibrary.ab.ca. *Libr Mgr,* Michelle Gillis
Library Holdings: Bk Vols 9,000; Per Subs 12
Wireless access
Mem of Peace Library System
Open Tues-Thurs 2-8, Fri & Sat 11-4

ELNORA

P ELNORA PUBLIC LIBRARY*, 210 Main St, T0M 0Y0. Tel: 403-773-3966. FAX: 403-773-3922. E-mail: elnoralibrary@prl.ab.ca. Web Site: elnoralibrary.prl.ab.ca. *Chairperson,* Tony Silbernagel; *Libr Mgr,* Wanda Strandquist
Pop 274
Library Holdings: Bk Vols 1,200
Wireless access
Mem of Parkland Regional Library-Alberta
Open Mon 9-12, Wed 1-5, Thurs 7pm-10pm

EMPRESS

P EMPRESS MUNICIPAL LIBRARY*, Six Third Ave, T0J 1E0. (Mail add: PO Box 188, T0J 1E0). Tel: 403-565-3936. E-mail: aemlibrary@marigold.ab.ca. Web Site: www.empresslibrary.ca. *Libr Mgr,* Dayna Van Dam
Pop 181
Wireless access
Mem of Marigold Library System
Open Tues-Fri 1-5

ENCHANT

P ENCHANT COMMUNITY LIBRARY*, 116 Center St, T0K 0V0. (Mail add: PO Box 3000, T0K 0V0). Tel: 403-739-3835. E-mail: help@enchantlibrary.ca. Web Site: www.enchantlibrary.ca. *Librn/Mgr,* Sharon Hagen
Library Holdings: Bk Vols 10,000
Mem of Chinook Arch Regional Library System
Open Tues & Thurs 9-5

ENTWISTLE

P ENTWISTLE PUBLIC LIBRARY*, 5232 - 50 St, T0E 0S0. (Mail add: PO Box 128, T0E 0S0). Tel: 780-727-3811. FAX: 780-727-2440. E-mail: entwistlelibrary@pclibraries.ca. Web Site: pclibraries.ca/about-us/libraries/entwistle-public-library. *Libr Mgr,* Kathy Gardiner; E-mail: kgardiner@pclibraries.ca; *Commun Serv Librn,* Alexandria Daum; E-mail: adaum@pclibraries.ca
Library Holdings: Bk Vols 10,000
Wireless access
Mem of Yellowhead Regional Library
Open Mon & Tues 11-5, Wed & Thurs 11-7, Sat 11-2

EVANSBURG

P EVANSBURG PUBLIC LIBRARY*, 4707 46th Ave, T0E 0T0. Tel: 780-727-2030, 780-727-3925. FAX: 780-727-2060. Web Site: www.evansburglibrary.ab.ca. *Libr Mgr,* Melissa Ronayne; E-mail: melirona@gypsd.ca
Library Holdings: DVDs 1,000; Bk Vols 10,000; Per Subs 26
Mem of Yellowhead Regional Library
Open Mon 9-12, Tues-Thurs 9-8, Fri 12-8

EXSHAW

P BIGHORN LIBRARY*, Two Heart Mountain Dr, T0L 2C0. (Mail add: PO Box 157, T0L 2C0). Tel: 403-673-3571. FAX: 403-673-3571. E-mail: aexclibrary@marigold.ab.ca. Web Site: www.bighornlibrary.ca. *Libr Mgr,* Jen Smith
Library Holdings: Audiobooks 96; DVDs 404; Bk Vols 8,907; Per Subs 16; Talking Bks 8
Automation Activity & Vendor Info: (Cataloging) Innovative Interfaces, Inc
Wireless access
Mem of Marigold Library System
Special Services for the Blind - Daisy reader
Open Mon 9-3, Tues 9-3 & 6:30-9, Wed 3-5 & 6:30-9, Thurs 3-9, Fri 1-6, Sat 10-1
Friends of the Library Group

FAIRVIEW

P FAIRVIEW PUBLIC LIBRARY*, 10209 109th St, T0H 1L0. (Mail add: PO Box 248, T0H 1L0), SAN 318-6768. Tel: 780-835-2613. FAX: 780-835-2613. E-mail: librarian@fairviewlibrary.ab.ca. Web Site: www.fairviewlibrary.ab.ca. *Libr Mgr,* Chris Burkholder
Founded 1938. Pop 5,100; Circ 31,000
Library Holdings: Bk Titles 25,000; Per Subs 55
Automation Activity & Vendor Info: (ILL) OCLC
Wireless access
Mem of Peace Library System
Open Mon-Fri 9:30-5:30, Sat 10-4

FALHER

P BIBLIOTHEQUE DENTINGER*, Falher Library, 27 Central Ave SE, T0H 1M0. (Mail add: PO Box 60, T0H 1M0), SAN 373-8531. Tel: 780-837-2776. FAX: 780-837-8755. E-mail: librarian@falherlibrary.ab.ca. Web Site: www.falherlibrary.ab.ca. *Libr Mgr,* Doreen Horvath; E-mail: crc@falherlibrary.ab.ca; *Asst Mgr,* Maegan Morin
Pop 4,041
Library Holdings: Bk Titles 13,157
Special Collections: French Coll, bks
Wireless access
Mem of Peace Library System

Open Tues & Fri 8:30-12 & 1-4:30, Wed 1-6, Thurs 1-4:30
Friends of the Library Group

FLATBUSH

P FLATBUSH COMMUNITY LIBRARY*, General Delivery, T0G 0Z0. Tel: 780-681-3756. E-mail: librarian@flatbushlibrary.ab.ca. Web Site: www.flatbushlibrary.ab.ca. *Librn,* Rose Herdman
Library Holdings: Audiobooks 15; AV Mats 150; Bks on Deafness & Sign Lang 5; CDs 10; Bk Vols 6,000; Spec Interest Per Sub 6
Wireless access
Mem of Peace Library System
Open Tues 10-2 & 5-9, Thurs 10-1, Sat 10-3

FOREMOST

P FOREMOST MUNICIPAL LIBRARY*, 103 First Ave E, T0K 0X0. (Mail add: Box 397, T0K 0X0). Tel: 403-867-3855. E-mail: forlib@shortgrass.ca. Web Site: foremost.shortgrass.ca. *Mgr,* Joan Beutler; Staff 2 (Non-MLS 2)
Founded 1987. Pop 2,332
Library Holdings: Bk Vols 12,000; Per Subs 25; Talking Bks 150; Videos 300
Automation Activity & Vendor Info: (Acquisitions) SirsiDynix
Wireless access
Function: 24/7 Electronic res, 24/7 Online cat, Adult bk club, Art exhibits, Audiobks via web, Bks on CD, Children's prog, Computers for patron use, Digital talking bks, Electronic databases & coll, Equip loans & repairs, ILL available, Internet access, Laminating, Magazines, Music CDs, Online cat, OverDrive digital audio bks, Photocopying/Printing, Preschool reading prog, Prog for children & young adult, Res assist avail, Scanner, Serves people with intellectual disabilities, Spoken cassettes & CDs, Story hour, Summer reading prog, Wheelchair accessible
Mem of Shortgrass Library System
Open Tues & Wed 10:30-5:30, Thurs 10:30-7, Fri 10:30-4:30
Friends of the Library Group

FORESTBURG

P FORESTBURG PUBLIC LIBRARY*, 4905 50th St, T0B 1N0. (Mail add: PO Box 579, T0B 1N0), SAN 318-6784. Tel: 780-582-4110. E-mail: forestburglibrary@prl.ab.ca. Web Site: forestburglibrary.prl.ab.ca. *Libr Mgr,* Sarah Tonowski; Staff 1 (MLS 1)
Founded 1955. Pop 900; Circ 10,000
Library Holdings: Bk Titles 9,000
Wireless access
Mem of Parkland Regional Library-Alberta
Open Tues-Fri 10-5
Friends of the Library Group

FORT ASSINIBOINE

P FORT ASSINIBOINE PUBLIC LIBRARY*, 20 First St, T0G 1A0. Tel: 780-584-2227. FAX: 780-674-8575. E-mail: fortassiniboinelibrary@yrl.ab.ca. Web Site: fortassiniboinelibrary.ab.ca. *Libr Mgr,* Megan Petryshen
Pop 4,100
Library Holdings: Bk Vols 17,500
Automation Activity & Vendor Info: (Acquisitions) Innovative Interfaces, Inc; (Cataloging) Innovative Interfaces, Inc; (Circulation) Innovative Interfaces, Inc; (ILL) Innovative Interfaces, Inc
Wireless access
Mem of Yellowhead Regional Library
Open Mon & Wed-Fri 8:30-12:30 & 1-4, Tues 8:30-12:30, 1-4 & 7-9

FORT MACLEOD

P THE TOWN OF FORT MACLEOD LIBRARY*, 264 24th St, T0L 0Z0. SAN 321-0022. Tel: 403-553-3880. E-mail: help@fortmacleodlibrary.ca. Web Site: www.fortmacleodlibrary.ca. *Libr Mgr,* Darlene Hofer; E-mail: headlibrarian@fortmacleod.com
Pop 3,072; Circ 36,000
Library Holdings: Bk Titles 29,000; Bk Vols 32,000; Per Subs 43
Automation Activity & Vendor Info: (Acquisitions) SirsiDynix; (Cataloging) SirsiDynix; (Circulation) SirsiDynix; (OPAC) SirsiDynix
Wireless access
Mem of Chinook Arch Regional Library System
Open Mon & Tues 9-5, Wed Noon-8, Thurs 1-8, Fri 10-2

FORT MCMURRAY

J KEYANO COLLEGE LIBRARY*, 8115 Franklin Ave, T9H 2H7. SAN 321-3986. Tel: 780-791-4917. Toll Free Tel: 800-251-1408. Web Site: www.keyano.ca/library. *Chair, Libr Serv, Res & Instruction Librn,* Sarah Schmidt; Tel: 780-791-8911, E-mail: sarah.schmidt@keyano.ca; *Cat,* Linda White; Tel: 780-791-4916, E-mail: linda.white@keyano.ca; Staff 6 (MLS 2, Non-MLS 4)
Founded 1965. Enrl 1,300; Fac 129
Library Holdings: Bk Titles 36,743; Per Subs 260
Subject Interests: Art, Educ, Local hist, Tech educ, Trades
Automation Activity & Vendor Info: (Acquisitions) SirsiDynix; (Cataloging) SirsiDynix; (Circulation) SirsiDynix; (Course Reserve) SirsiDynix; (OPAC) SirsiDynix; (Serials) SirsiDynix
Wireless access
Publications: Annual Report; Serials Holding List; Staff Handbook; Student Handbook
Open Mon-Thurs 8:30-7, Fri 8:30-5:30, Sat Noon-4; Mon-Fri 8:30-4:30 (Summer)

P WOOD BUFFALO REGIONAL LIBRARY*, One CA Knight Way, T9H 5C5. SAN 318-6792. Tel: 780-743-7800. FAX: 780-743-7938. E-mail: administration@wbrl.ca. Web Site: www.wbrl.ca. *Dir,* Melissa Flett; E-mail: melissa.flett@wbrl.ca; *Mgr, Circ Serv,* Angela Gallant; E-mail: angela.gallant@wbrl.ca; *Coll Develop & Tech Serv Mgr,* Regina Callahan; E-mail: regina.callahan@wbrl.ca; *Commun Serv Mgr,* Sheri Anthony; E-mail: sheri.anthony@wbrl.ca; *Mgr, Info Tech,* Mark Anthony; E-mail: mark.anthony@wbrl.ca; Staff 10 (MLS 4, Non-MLS 6)
Founded 1965. Pop 95,000; Circ 212,000
Subject Interests: Local hist
Automation Activity & Vendor Info: (Acquisitions) SirsiDynix; (Cataloging) SirsiDynix; (Circulation) SirsiDynix; (ILL) SirsiDynix; (OPAC) SirsiDynix
Wireless access
Open Mon-Fri 9-9, Sat 9-5, Sun 12-5

FORT SASKATCHEWAN

P FORT SASKATCHEWAN PUBLIC LIBRARY*, 10011 102nd St, T8L 2C5. SAN 325-2450. Tel: 780-998-4275. FAX: 780-992-3255. Web Site: www.fspl.ca. *Libr Dir,* Michele Fedyk; Tel: 780-998-4288, E-mail: mfedyk@fspl.ca; Staff 25 (MLS 2, Non-MLS 23)
Founded 1953. Circ 215,000
Library Holdings: Bk Vols 100,854
Wireless access
Function: 24/7 Electronic res, 24/7 Online cat, 3D Printer, Activity rm, Adult bk club, Adult literacy prog, After school storytime
Open Mon-Thurs 10-9, Fri 10-6, Sat & Sun 10-5

FORT VERMILION

P FORT VERMILION COMMUNITY LIBRARY*, 5103 River Rd, T0H 1N0. (Mail add: Box 700, T0H 1N0), SAN 318-6806. Tel: 780-927-4279. FAX: 780-927-4746. E-mail: afvclibrary@incentre.net. Web Site: www.fvclibrary.com. *Librn/Mgr,* Debbie Bueckert
Pop 3,000; Circ 5,000
Library Holdings: Bk Vols 20,000; Per Subs 10
Wireless access
Open Tues & Thurs 12:30-8, Fri & Sat 12:30-5:30

FOX CREEK

P FOX CREEK MUNICIPAL LIBRARY*, 501 Eighth St, T0H 1P0. (Mail add: PO Box 1078, T0H 1P0). Tel: 780-622-2343. FAX: 780-622-4160. E-mail: foxcreeklibrary@yahoo.com. Web Site: www.foxcreeklibrary.ca. *Libr Mgr,* Leslie Ann Sharkey
Pop 2,400
Library Holdings: Bk Vols 22,000
Automation Activity & Vendor Info: (Acquisitions) Innovative Interfaces, Inc; (Cataloging) Innovative Interfaces, Inc; (Circulation) Innovative Interfaces, Inc; (ILL) Innovative Interfaces, Inc; (Media Booking) Innovative Interfaces, Inc; (OPAC) Innovative Interfaces, Inc; (Serials) Innovative Interfaces, Inc
Wireless access
Mem of Peace Library System
Open Mon, Wed & Fri 8:15-4, Tues & Thurs 8:15-4 & 6-9, Sat 11-1 (Winter); Tues & Thurs 6-9, Wed 1-4, Sat 11-1 (Summer)

GEM

P GEM JUBILEE LIBRARY*, 125 Center St, T0J 1M0. (Mail add: PO Box 6, T0J 1M0). Tel: 403-641-3245. FAX: 403-641-3245. E-mail: gem.manager@shortgrass.ca. Web Site: gem.shortgrass.ca. *Libr Mgr,* Kim Biette
Founded 1914
Library Holdings: Bk Vols 8,000
Automation Activity & Vendor Info: (Cataloging) BiblioCommons; (OPAC) BiblioCommons
Mem of Shortgrass Library System
Open Mon 10-Noon, Wed 7pm-9pm, Fri 2-4:30

GIBBONS

P GIBBONS MUNICIPAL LIBRARY*, 5111 51 St, T0A 1N0. (Mail add: PO Box 510, T0A 1N0), SAN 372-7734. Tel: 780-923-2004. FAX: 780-923-2015. E-mail: librarian@gibbonslibrary.ab.ca. Web Site: www.gibbonslibrary.ab.ca. *Libr Mgr,* Ryan Edmonds; Staff 3 (MLS 1, Non-MLS 2)
Founded 1973. Pop 3,159; Circ 15,523
Library Holdings: Bk Titles 12,200; Per Subs 20
Automation Activity & Vendor Info: (Acquisitions) Innovative Interfaces, Inc; (Cataloging) Innovative Interfaces, Inc; (Circulation) Innovative Interfaces, Inc; (ILL) Innovative Interfaces, Inc
Wireless access
Function: 24/7 Electronic res, 24/7 Online cat, Audiobks via web, Bk club(s), Bks on CD, Children's prog, Electronic databases & coll, Free DVD rentals, ILL available, Internet access, Magazines, Movies, Outreach serv, Photocopying/Printing, Scanner, Summer & winter reading prog
Mem of Northern Lights Library System
Open Mon-Fri 10-5

GLEICHEN

P GLEICHEN & DISTRICT LIBRARY*, 404 Main St, T0J 1N0. (Mail add: PO Box 160, T0J 1N0), SAN 322-7685. Tel: 403-734-2390. FAX: 403-734-2390. E-mail: agmlibrary@marigold.ab.ca. Web Site: gleichenlibrary.ca. *Libr Mgr,* Morrigan Flebotte
Founded 1979. Pop 400; Circ 1,500
Library Holdings: Bk Vols 10,000
Wireless access
Mem of Marigold Library System
Open Tues & Thurs 10-5:30

GLENWOOD

P GLENWOOD MUNICIPAL LIBRARY*, 59 Main Ave, T0K 2R0. Tel: 403-942-8033. E-mail: help@glenwoodlibrary.ca. Web Site: glenwoodlibrary.ca. *Libr Mgr,* Nikki Francis
Pop 500; Circ 32,000
Library Holdings: DVDs 1,500; Large Print Bks 126; Bk Titles 22,000; Per Subs 20; Talking Bks 200
Wireless access
Mem of Chinook Arch Regional Library System
Open Mon 12-4, Tues 12-7, Wed 1-5, Thurs 3-7, Fri 11-3

GRANDE CACHE

P GRANDE CACHE MUNICIPAL LIBRARY*, 10601 Shand Ave, T0E 0Y0. (Mail add: PO Box 809, T0E 0Y0), SAN 325-0342. Tel: 780-827-2081. FAX: 780-827-3112. E-mail: grandecachelibrary@gmail.com. Web Site: www.grandecachelibrary.ab.ca. *Dir,* Laurel A Kelsch; Staff 5 (Non-MLS 5)
Founded 1970. Pop 3,500; Circ 22,000
Library Holdings: Bk Vols 20,000
Wireless access
Function: 24/7 Electronic res, 24/7 Online cat, 3D Printer, Adult bk club, After school storytime, Art exhibits, Audiobks on Playaways & MP3, Audiobks via web, Bks on CD, Children's prog, Computers for patron use, Digital talking bks, E-Readers, Electronic databases & coll, Free DVD rentals, Games & aids for people with disabilities, Holiday prog, Home delivery & serv to seniorr ctr & nursing homes, Homebound delivery serv, ILL available, Internet access, Laminating, Life-long learning prog for all ages, Magazines, Makerspace, Meeting rooms, Movies, Music CDs, Online cat, Online ref, OverDrive digital audio bks, Photocopying/Printing, Preschool reading prog, Prog for adults, Prog for children & young adult, Ref & res, Scanner, Serves people with intellectual disabilities, STEM programs, Study rm, Summer & winter reading prog, Summer reading prog, Wheelchair accessible, Workshops
Mem of Peace Library System
Open Mon-Thurs 9-8, Fri 9-4, Sat & Sun 11-3

GRANDE PRAIRIE

P GRANDE PRAIRIE PUBLIC LIBRARY*, 101-9839 103 Ave, T8V 6M7. SAN 318-6814. Tel: 780-532-3580. Reference Tel: 780-357-7455. FAX: 780-538-4983. E-mail: info@gppl.ca. Web Site: www.gppl.ca. *Dir,* Deb Cryderman; E-mail: dcryderman@gppl.ca; *Head, Adult Serv,* Hailey McCullough; Tel: 780-357-7474, E-mail: hmccullough@gppl.ca; *Head, Children's Servx,* Bailey Randolph; Tel: 780-357-7477, E-mail: brandolph@gppl.ca; *Head, Customer Serv,* Fran Bartolotta; Tel: 780-357-7470, E-mail: fbartolotta@gppl.ca; Staff 41 (MLS 6, Non-MLS 35)
Founded 1939. Pop 70,000; Circ 500,000
Library Holdings: Bk Vols 120,000; Per Subs 50
Special Collections: Hauge Coll; Isabel Campbell Photo Coll; Peace Country Histories
Subject Interests: Genealogy, Local hist
Automation Activity & Vendor Info: (Circulation) Innovative Interfaces, Inc; (ILL) Innovative Interfaces, Inc; (OPAC) Innovative Interfaces, Inc
Wireless access
Publications: In Touch (eNewsletter)
Mem of Peace Library System
Partic in The Alberta Library; The Regional Automation Consortium
Open Mon-Thurs 10-8, Fri 10-6, Sat 10-5, Sun 1-5

J GRANDE PRAIRIE REGIONAL COLLEGE*, Library & Media Services, 10726 106th Ave, T8V 4C4. SAN 318-6822. Tel: 780-539-2911. Reference Tel: 780-539-2939. Toll Free Tel: 888-539-4772. FAX: 780-539-2832. E-mail: library@gprc.ab.ca. Web Site: www.gprc.ab.ca/library. *Chair, Librn,* Kieren Bailey; Tel: 780-539-2202, E-mail: kbailey@gprc.ab.ca; Staff 16 (MLS 2, Non-MLS 14)
Founded 1966
Library Holdings: Bk Vols 87,422; Per Subs 350
Automation Activity & Vendor Info: (Circulation) SirsiDynix
Wireless access
Function: Archival coll
Partic in NEOS Library Consortium
Open Mon-Fri 8am-9pm, Sat & Sun Noon-6 (Sept-April); Mon-Fri 8:30-4:30 (May-Aug)

P PEACE LIBRARY SYSTEM*, 8301 110 St, T8W 6T2. SAN 373-8221. Tel: 780-538-4656. Toll Free Tel: 800-422-6875. FAX: 780-539-5285. E-mail: peacelib@peacelibrarysystem.ab.ca. Web Site: www.peacelibrarysystem.ab.ca. *Chief Exec Officer,* Louisa Robison; E-mail: lrobison@peacelibrarysystem.ab.ca; *Dep Chief Exec Officer,* Katherine Wiebe; Tel: 780-539-5285, Ext 103, E-mail: kwiebe@peacelibrarysystem.ab.ca; Staff 19 (MLS 6, Non-MLS 13)
Founded 1986. Pop 124,000
Library Holdings: Bk Vols 32,275; Per Subs 10
Automation Activity & Vendor Info: (Acquisitions) Innovative Interfaces, Inc; (Cataloging) Innovative Interfaces, Inc; (Circulation) Innovative Interfaces, Inc; (ILL) Innovative Interfaces, Inc; (OPAC) Innovative Interfaces, Inc
Wireless access
Publications: Peace Library System News 'n' Notes (Newsletter)
Member Libraries: Bear Point Community Library; Beaverlodge Public Library; Berwyn Municipal Library; Bibliotheque de St Isidore; Bibliotheque Dentinger; Bonanza Municipal Library; Brownvale Community Library; Calling Lake Public Library; DeBolt Public Library; Dixonville Community Library; Eaglesham Public Library; Elmworth Community Library; Fairview Public Library; Flatbush Community Library; Fox Creek Municipal Library; Grande Cache Municipal Library; Grande Prairie Public Library; Grimshaw Municipal Library; High Level Municipal Library; High Prairie Municipal Library; Hines Creek Municipal Library; Hythe Municipal Library; Keg River Community Library; Kinuso Municipal Library; La Glace Community Library; Manning Municipal & District Library; McLennan Municipal Library; Menno-Simons Community Library; Nampa Municipal Library; Paddle Prairie Public Library; Peace River Municipal Library; Rainbow Lake Municipal Library; Red Earth Public Library; Rotary Club of Slave Lake Public Library; Rycroft Municipal Library; Savanna Municipal Library; Shannon Municipal Library; Smith Community Library; Spirit River Municipal Library; Tangent Community Library; Valhalla Community Library; Valleyview Municipal Library; Wabasca Public Library; Wembley Public Library; Woking Municipal Library; Worsley & District Public Library
Partic in The Alberta Library
Open Mon-Fri 8-4:30
Friends of the Library Group

GRANUM

P GRANUM PUBLIC LIBRARY*, 310 Railway Ave, T0L 1A0. SAN 318-6830. Tel: 403-687-3912. E-mail: help@granumlibrary.ca. Web Site: www.granumlibrary.ca. *Libr Mgr,* Lisa Wilson
Founded 1953. Pop 420; Circ 6,000
Library Holdings: Bk Vols 9,000
Wireless access
Mem of Chinook Arch Regional Library System
Open Tues, Wed & Fri 11-4, Thurs 2-7

GRASSLAND

P GRASSLAND PUBLIC LIBRARY*, Hwy 63, Box 150, T0A 1V0. Tel: 780-525-3733. FAX: 780-525-3750. E-mail: librarian@grasslandlibrary.ab.ca. Web Site: www.grasslandlibrary.ab.ca. *Librn,* Barb Cholach; *Libr Asst,* Jordan Heatherington; *Libr Asst,* Jalisa Shapka
Library Holdings: Bk Vols 10,000; Per Subs 40
Wireless access
Function: Computers for patron use, Photocopying/Printing, Summer reading prog

Mem of Northern Lights Library System
Open Mon, Wed & Fri 12-3, Tues & Thurs 12-6:30

GRASSY LAKE

P GRASSY LAKE COMMUNITY LIBRARY*, 600 Third St S, T0K 0Z0. Tel: 403-655-2232. FAX: 403-655-2259. E-mail: help@grassylakelibrary.ca. Web Site: www.grassylakelibrary.ca. *Libr Mgr,* Nancy Nelson; E-mail: nancy.nelson@horizon.ab.ca
Library Holdings: Bk Vols 6,000
Wireless access
Open Mon-Thurs 8:30-3:40

GRIMSHAW

P BROWNVALE COMMUNITY LIBRARY*, Box 407, T0H 1W0. Tel: 780-618-6216. E-mail: brownvalelibrary@wispernet.ca. *Libr Mgr,* Bonnie Landaker
Mem of Peace Library System

P GRIMSHAW MUNICIPAL LIBRARY, 4412A 50 St, T0H 1W0. (Mail add: PO Box 588, T0H 1W0), SAN 318-6849. Tel: 780-332-4553. FAX: 780-332-1687. E-mail: read@grimshawlibrary.ab.ca. Web Site: www.grimshawlibrary.ab.ca. *Libr Mgr,* Vivianne Gayton; E-mail: read@grimshawlibrary.ab.ca; Staff 8 (Non-MLS 8)
Founded 1953. Pop 2,620; Circ 304,032
Jan 2019-Dec 2019 Income (CAN) $227,229, Provincial (CAN) $16,650, City (CAN) $81,903, County (CAN) $9,044, Locally Generated Income (CAN) $6,000, Other (CAN) $7,000
Library Holdings: Audiobooks 650; DVDs 875; Large Print Bks 925; Bk Titles 32,000
Automation Activity & Vendor Info: (Acquisitions) BiblioCommons; (Cataloging) Main Library Systems; (Circulation) Baker & Taylor
Wireless access
Function: 24/7 Electronic res, 24/7 Online cat, Adult literacy prog, After school storytime, Art exhibits, Bks on CD, Children's prog, Computer training, Computers for patron use, Family literacy, Holiday prog, ILL available, Internet access, Laminating, Large print keyboards, Life-long learning prog for all ages, Literacy & newcomer serv, Mail & tel request accepted, Meeting rooms, Movies, Online cat, Outside serv via phone, mail, e-mail & web, OverDrive digital audio bks, Photocopying/Printing, Preschool reading prog, Prog for adults, Prog for children & young adult, Ref & res, Res assist avail, Scanner, Story hour, Summer & winter reading prog, Summer reading prog, Teen prog, Telephone ref, Winter reading prog
Mem of Peace Library System
Open Mon-Sat 10-4:30
Restriction: Circ privileges for students & alumni only, Circ to mem only, In-house use for visitors
Friends of the Library Group

GROUARD

C NORTHERN LAKES COLLEGE LIBRARY*, Grouard Campus Library, 64 Mission St, T0G 1C0. SAN 323-8164. Tel: 780-751-3275. Toll Free Tel: 866-652-3475, Ext 3275. FAX: 780-849-2570. E-mail: nlclibrary@northernlakescollege.ca. Web Site: www.nlclibrary.ca. *Library Tech Support Specialist,* Rachel Martins; E-mail: martinsr@northernlakescollege.ca; Staff 1 (MLS 1)
Founded 1975. Enrl 1,000
Library Holdings: Audiobooks 900; Bks on Deafness & Sign Lang 37; CDs 300; DVDs 1,000; e-books 1,500; e-journals 900; Bk Vols 59,370; Per Subs 150; Talking Bks 4,139
Subject Interests: Native Can people
Automation Activity & Vendor Info: (Acquisitions) SirsiDynix; (Cataloging) SirsiDynix; (Circulation) SirsiDynix; (Course Reserve) SirsiDynix; (Media Booking) SirsiDynix; (OPAC) SirsiDynix; (Serials) SirsiDynix
Wireless access
Partic in The Alberta Library
Open Mon-Fri 8:15-4:30

GUNN

P RICH VALLEY PUBLIC LIBRARY*, RR 1, T0E 1A0. Tel: 780-967-3525. E-mail: rvpublib@yrl.ab.ca. Web Site: www.richvalleylibrary.ab.ca. *Libr Mgr,* Betty Ann Laporte
Library Holdings: Bk Vols 10,000
Wireless access
Mem of Yellowhead Regional Library
Open Tues 5-8, Wed 10-2:30, Thurs 2-6:30

HANNA

P HANNA MUNICIPAL LIBRARY*, 202 First St W, T0J 1P0. SAN 318-6865. Tel: 403-854-3865. E-mail: library@hanna.ca. Web Site: www.hannalibrary.ca. *Dir,* Position Currently Open; *ILL,* Jenn Steinbrecker
Founded 1953. Pop 3,003; Circ 31,000
Library Holdings: Bk Vols 26,000
Subject Interests: Local hist
Automation Activity & Vendor Info: (Circulation) SirsiDynix
Wireless access
Mem of Marigold Library System
Partic in Jefferson County Library Cooperative Inc; The Regional Automation Consortium
Special Services for the Blind - VISTA low vision equip loan prog
Open Mon-Wed & Fri 9-5, Thurs 9-8, Sat 2-4

HARDISTY

P HARDISTY PUBLIC LIBRARY*, 5027 - 50 St, T0B 1V0. (Mail add: Box 539, T0B 1V0). Tel: 780-888-3947. FAX: 780-888-3947. E-mail: hardistylibrary@prl.ab.ca. Web Site: hardistylib.prl.ab.ca. *Libr Mgr,* Kelly McDowell; Staff 2 (Non-MLS 2)
Founded 1982. Pop 630
Library Holdings: Bk Vols 10,000
Wireless access
Function: ILL available, Mail loans to mem, Photocopying/Printing, Summer reading prog, Wheelchair accessible
Mem of Parkland Regional Library-Alberta
Open Tues & Thurs 11-5, Wed 1-8, Fri & Sat 1-5
Friends of the Library Group

HAY LAKES

P HAY LAKES MUNICIPAL LIBRARY*, 110 Main St, T0B 1W0. (Mail add: PO Box 69, T0B 1W0), SAN 318-6873. Tel: 780-878-2665. E-mail: haylakeslibrary@prl.ab.ca. Web Site: haylakeslibrary.prl.ab.ca. *Libr Mgr,* Beth Schultz
Founded 1956. Pop 2,000; Circ 5,500
Library Holdings: Bk Titles 6,000; Per Subs 12
Special Collections: Enbridge Environmental Coll
Subject Interests: Alternative agr, Alternative health, Children's fiction, Local hist
Wireless access
Mem of Parkland Regional Library-Alberta
Partic in The Alberta Library
Open Tues & Thurs 10-3
Friends of the Library Group

HAYS

P HAYS PUBLIC LIBRARY*, 210 Second Ave, T0K 1B0. (Mail add: PO Box 36, T0K 1B0). Tel: 403-725-3744. FAX: 403-725-3744. E-mail: help@hayslibrary.ca. Web Site: www.hayslibrary.ca. *Libr Mgr,* Diane Wickenheiser
Library Holdings: Bk Vols 11,000
Wireless access
Mem of Chinook Arch Regional Library System
Open Mon 2-5:30, Tues 9-6, Wed 12-7:30, Thurs 10-6

HEISLER

P HEISLER MUNICIPAL LIBRARY*, 100 Haultain Ave, T0B 2A0. (Mail add: Box 111, T0B 2A0). Tel: 780-889-3925. FAX: 780-889-3925. E-mail: heislerlibrary@prl.ab.ca. Web Site: heislerlibrary.prl.ab.ca. *Libr Mgr,* Dixie Wolbeck
Founded 1992. Pop 151
Library Holdings: Bk Vols 9,000
Wireless access
Mem of Parkland Regional Library-Alberta
Open Wed 9-12 & 1-6

HIGH LEVEL

P HIGH LEVEL MUNICIPAL LIBRARY*, 10601 103 St, T0H 1Z0. Tel: 780-926-2097. E-mail: librarian@highlevellibrary.ab.ca. Web Site: www.highlevellibrary.ab.ca. *Libr Mgr,* Amanda Ebert; Staff 4 (Non-MLS 4)
Founded 1981. Pop 3,887
Library Holdings: Bk Vols 15,586; Per Subs 32
Automation Activity & Vendor Info: (Acquisitions) Innovative Interfaces, Inc; (Cataloging) Innovative Interfaces, Inc; (Circulation) Innovative Interfaces, Inc; (ILL) Innovative Interfaces, Inc; (OPAC) Innovative Interfaces, Inc; (Serials) Innovative Interfaces, Inc
Wireless access
Mem of Peace Library System
Open Tues & Thurs 11-7, Wed & Fri 11-5, Sat 12-4
Friends of the Library Group

HIGH PRAIRIE

P HIGH PRAIRIE MUNICIPAL LIBRARY*, 4723 53rd Ave, T0G 1E0. (Mail add: PO Box 890, T0G 1E0), SAN 318-6881. Tel: 780-523-3838. FAX: 780-523-2537. E-mail: librarian@highprairielibrary.ab.ca. Web Site: www.highprairielibrary.ab.ca. *Libr Mgr,* Tracy Ireland; Staff 1 (Non-MLS 1)
Founded 1953. Pop 2,820; Circ 28,189
Library Holdings: Bk Titles 22,496; Per Subs 124
Wireless access
Mem of Peace Library System
Partic in The Regional Automation Consortium
Open Mon 1-9, Tues & Fri 9:30-5:30, Wed & Thurs 9:30-9, Sat 10:30-5, Sun 1-5

HIGH RIVER

P HIGH RIVER LIBRARY*, 909 First St SW, T1V 1A5. SAN 318-689X. Tel: 403-652-2917. Web Site: www.highriverlibrary.ca. *Dir,* Mary Zazelenchuk; E-mail: director@highriverlibrary.ca; *Asst Dir,* Cheryl Taylor-Smith; Staff 9 (MLS 1, Non-MLS 8)
Founded 1939. Pop 13,420; Circ 101,380
Library Holdings: Bk Vols 34,000; Per Subs 110
Special Collections: High River Times, micro; Local Alberta History Coll. Canadian and Provincial
Wireless access
Function: 24/7 Electronic res, 24/7 Online cat, 3D Printer, Activity rm, Adult bk club, Adult literacy prog, Art exhibits, Audio & video playback equip for onsite use, Audiobks on Playaways & MP3, Audiobks via web, Bilingual assistance for Spanish patrons, Bks on CD, Children's prog, Citizenship assistance, Computer training, Computers for patron use, Digital talking bks, Distance learning, E-Reserves, Electronic databases & coll, Equip loans & repairs, Family literacy, Free DVD rentals, Health sci info serv, Holiday prog, Home delivery & serv to seniorr ctr & nursing homes, Homebound delivery serv, Homework prog, ILL available, Instruction & testing, Internet access, Life-long learning prog for all ages, Literacy & newcomer serv, Magazines, Magnifiers for reading, Mail & tel request accepted, Mango lang, Meeting rooms, Microfiche/film & reading machines, Movies, Music CDs, Online cat, Orientations, Outreach serv, OverDrive digital audio bks, Photocopying/Printing, Preschool reading prog, Prog for adults, Prog for children & young adult, Ref serv available, Scanner, Senior computer classes, Senior outreach, Serves people with intellectual disabilities, Spanish lang bks, Spoken cassettes & CDs, STEM programs, Story hour, Summer reading prog, Teen prog, Telephone ref, Wheelchair accessible, Workshops, Writing prog
Mem of Marigold Library System
Partic in The Regional Automation Consortium
Special Services for the Blind - Assistive/Adapted tech devices, equip & products; Bks on CD; Digital talking bk; Extensive large print coll; Large print bks; Visunet prog (Canada)
Friends of the Library Group

HINES CREEK

P HINES CREEK MUNICIPAL LIBRARY*, 212-10 St, T0H 2A0. (Mail add: PO Box 750, T0H 2A0). Tel: 780-494-3879. FAX: 780-494-3605. E-mail: librarian@hinescreeklibrary.ab.ca. Web Site: www.hinescreeklibrary.ab.ca. *Libr Mgr,* Stacey Noel Obrigewitch; E-mail: librarian@hinescreeklibrary.ab.ca
Pop 396
Library Holdings: Bk Titles 8,500
Wireless access
Mem of Peace Library System
Open Tues-Thurs 10-6

HINTON

P HINTON MUNICIPAL LIBRARY, 803 Switzer Dr, T7V 1V1. SAN 318-6903. Tel: 780-865-2363. Administration Tel: 780-865-6051. FAX: 780-865-4292. Web Site: www.hintonlibrary.org. *Libr Mgr,* Shannen Shott; E-mail: sshott@hintonlibrary.org; *Asst Mgr, Libr Serv,* Lindsey Bennett; Tel: 780-865-6052, E-mail: lbennett@hintonlibrary.org; Staff 9 (MLS 2, Non-MLS 7)
Founded 1969. Pop 10,000; Circ 50,000
Library Holdings: Bk Titles 30,000; Per Subs 70
Special Collections: Hinton Coal Branch Archives
Automation Activity & Vendor Info: (Circulation) SirsiDynix; (OPAC) SirsiDynix
Wireless access
Function: 24/7 Electronic res, 24/7 Online cat, Activity rm, Adult bk club, Archival coll, Art exhibits, Art programs, Audiobks on Playaways & MP3, Audiobks via web, Bk club(s), Bk reviews (Group), Bks on cassette, Bks on CD, Chess club, Children's prog, Computer training, Computers for patron use, Digital talking bks, E-Readers, Electronic databases & coll, Equip loans & repairs, Extended outdoor wifi, Family literacy, For res purposes, Free DVD rentals, Games, Genealogy discussion group, Holiday prog, ILL available, Internet access, Laminating, Laptop/tablet checkout, Life-long learning prog for all ages, Magazines, Magnifiers for reading, Makerspace, Mango lang, Meeting rooms, Microfiche/film & reading machines, Movies, Online cat, Outreach serv, OverDrive digital audio bks, Photocopying/Printing, Preschool outreach, Preschool reading prog, Printer for laptops & handheld devices, Prog for adults, Prog for children & young adult, Ref serv available, Res assist avail, Scanner, Senior outreach, Serves people with intellectual disabilities, STEM programs, Story hour, Study rm, Summer & winter reading prog, Summer reading prog, Teen prog, Wheelchair accessible, Workshops, Writing prog
Mem of Yellowhead Regional Library
Partic in The Regional Automation Consortium
Open Mon-Fri 10-8, Sat & Sun 12-4
Friends of the Library Group

HOLDEN

P HOLDEN MUNICIPAL LIBRARY*, 4912-50 St, T0B 2C0. (Mail add: PO Box 26, T0B 2C0). Tel: 780-688-3838. FAX: 780-688-3838. E-mail: librarian@holdenlibrary.ab.ca. Web Site: www.holdenlibrary.ab.ca. *Librn,* Annette Chrystian
Pop 374
Library Holdings: Bk Vols 2,000
Wireless access
Mem of Northern Lights Library System
Partic in The Alberta Library; The Regional Automation Consortium
Open Tues 10-6, Thurs 4-8, Sat 9-Noon (Winter); Mon Noon-5, Tues 10-6, Wed & Fri 10-5, Thurs Noon-8, Sat 9-Noon (Summer)

HUGHENDEN

P HUGHENDEN PUBLIC LIBRARY*, Seven McKenzie Ave, T0B 2E0. (Mail add: PO Box 36, T0B 2E0). Tel: 780-856-2435. FAX: 780-856-2435. E-mail: hughendenlibrary@prl.ab.ca. Web Site: hughendenlibrary.prl.ab.ca. *Libr Mgr,* Lindsey Damberger
Library Holdings: Bk Vols 8,000
Automation Activity & Vendor Info: (OPAC) Horizon
Wireless access
Mem of Parkland Regional Library-Alberta
Open Tues, Wed & Sat 11-4, Thurs 11-6
Friends of the Library Group

HYTHE

P HYTHE MUNICIPAL LIBRARY*, 10013 100 St, T0H 2C0. (Mail add: PO Box 601, T0H 2C0). Tel: 780-356-3014. FAX: 780-356-3014. E-mail: manager@hythelibrary.ab.ca. Web Site: www.hythelibrary.ab.ca. *Libr Mgr,* Chelsea de Ruiter
Founded 1984
Library Holdings: Bk Vols 14,900
Automation Activity & Vendor Info: (Cataloging) Innovative Interfaces, Inc. - Polaris
Wireless access
Mem of Peace Library System
Partic in The Regional Automation Consortium
Open Wed-Fri 12-4, Sat 10-2

INNISFAIL

P INNISFAIL PUBLIC LIBRARY, 5300A 55th St Close, T4G 1R6. SAN 377-4740. Tel: 403-227-4407. FAX: 403-227-3122. E-mail: innisfail@prl.ab.ca. Web Site: ipl.prl.ab.ca/innisfail. *Libr Mgr,* Amy Ramsay; E-mail: aramsay@prl.ab.ca
Pop 8,500
Library Holdings: Bk Titles 18,000; Bk Vols 52,000
Wireless access
Mem of Parkland Regional Library-Alberta
Open Mon & Fri 10-5:30, Tues-Thurs 10-8, Sat 10-3
Friends of the Library Group

INNISFREE

P INNISFREE PUBLIC LIBRARY, 5317-48 Ave, T0B 2G0. (Mail add: Box 121, T0B 2G0). Tel: 780-592-2122. E-mail: librarian@innisfreelibrary.ca. Web Site: www.innisfreelibrary.ca. *Mgr,* Marilyn Newton; E-mail: mnewton@innisfreelibrary.ca
Wireless access
Mem of Northern Lights Library System
Open Tues 12-4, Wed 1-7, Thurs 12-7, Fri 10-3, Sat 10-2

IRMA

P PHYLLIS CRAIG LEGACY LIBRARY*, 5011 53rd Ave, T0B 2H0. (Mail add: PO Box 250, T0B 2H0). Tel: 780-754-3746. E-mail: librarian@irmalibrary.ca. Web Site: www.irmalibrary.ca. *Libr Mgr,* Krista Gulbraa
Pop 435

Library Holdings: Audiobooks 150; DVDs 300; Bk Titles 10,000
Wireless access
Mem of Northern Lights Library System
Open Mon, Tues, Thurs & Fri 9-3:30, Wed 9-3:30 & 6-8

IRRICANA

P IRRICANA & RURAL MUNICIPAL LIBRARY*, 226 Second St, T0M 1B0. (Mail add: PO Box 299, T0M 1B0). Tel: 403-935-4818. FAX: 403-935-4818. E-mail: aimanager@marigold.ab.ca. Web Site: www.irricanalibrary.ca. *Libr Mgr,* Papari Borthakur
Pop 1,162
Library Holdings: Bk Vols 12,000
Wireless access
Mem of Marigold Library System
Partic in The Alberta Library; The Regional Automation Consortium
Open Tues, Thurs & Fri 11-6, Wed 11-7, Sat 11-3
Friends of the Library Group

IRVINE

P IRVINE COMMUNITY LIBRARY, Irvine Commuity Library, 45 Ross St, T0J 1V0. (Mail add: PO Box 67, T0J 1V0). Tel: 403-834-3437. Web Site: irvine.shortgrass.ca. *Libr Mgr,* Joan Cote; E-mail: irvine.manager@shortgrass.ca
Wireless access
Mem of Shortgrass Library System
Open Mon, Wed & Fri 10-5, Tues & Thurs 12-8

JASPER

P JASPER MUNICIPAL LIBRARY*, 500 Robson St, T0E 1E0. Tel: 780-852-3652. FAX: 780-852-5841. E-mail: jasperlibrary@town.jasper.ab.ca. Web Site: jasperlibrary.ab.ca. *Dir,* Angie Thom; Staff 4 (Non-MLS 4)
Founded 1942. Pop 5,200; Circ 43,000
Library Holdings: AV Mats 5,000; Bk Vols 18,000; Per Subs 24
Automation Activity & Vendor Info: (Acquisitions) Innovative Interfaces, Inc; (Cataloging) Innovative Interfaces, Inc; (Circulation) Innovative Interfaces, Inc; (Course Reserve) Innovative Interfaces, Inc; (ILL) Innovative Interfaces, Inc; (Media Booking) Innovative Interfaces, Inc; (OPAC) Innovative Interfaces, Inc; (Serials) Innovative Interfaces, Inc
Wireless access
Function: ILL available
Mem of Yellowhead Regional Library
Open Wed & Thurs 10-6, Fri & Sat 10-5
Friends of the Library Group

KEG RIVER

P KEG RIVER COMMUNITY LIBRARY*, A-243009 Township Rd 1014, T0H 2M0. Tel: 780-538-4656. E-mail: librarian@kegriverlibrary.ab.ca. *Libr Mgr,* Susan MacDougall
Founded 1967. Pop 100; Circ 1,000
Library Holdings: Audiobooks 177; CDs 31; DVDs 300; Large Print Bks 25; Bk Titles 14,000; Per Subs 17; Videos 1,000
Mem of Peace Library System
Partic in The Regional Automation Consortium
Open Tues 2:30pm-4:30pm

KILLAM

P KILLAM MUNICIPAL LIBRARY*, 5017 49th Ave, T0B 2L0. (Mail add: PO Box 329, T0B 2L0). Tel: 780-385-3032. E-mail: killamlibrary@prl.ab.ca. Web Site: killamlibrary.prl.ab.ca. *Libr Mgr,* Barb Cox; Staff 1 (Non-MLS 1)
Founded 1938. Pop 1,019
Library Holdings: DVDs 350; Large Print Bks 5; Bk Vols 5,853; Per Subs 14; Talking Bks 5
Automation Activity & Vendor Info: (Acquisitions) Horizon; (Cataloging) Horizon; (Circulation) Horizon; (Course Reserve) Horizon; (ILL) Horizon; (Media Booking) Horizon; (OPAC) Horizon; (Serials) Horizon
Wireless access
Mem of Parkland Regional Library-Alberta
Open Mon & Wed 12-5 & 6-8, Fri 8:30-12 & 1-4:30
Friends of the Library Group

KINUSO

P KINUSO MUNICIPAL LIBRARY, PO Box 60, T0G 1K0. Tel: 780-775-3694. FAX: 780-775-3560. E-mail: librarian@kinusolibrary.ab.ca. Web Site: kinusolibrary.ab.ca. *Libr Mgr,* Delaine Labby
Pop 280
Library Holdings: Bk Titles 7,800
Automation Activity & Vendor Info: (Cataloging) Innovative Interfaces, Inc. - Polaris
Wireless access
Mem of Peace Library System
Partic in The Alberta Library; The Regional Automation Consortium
Open Mon, Wed & Fri 8:45-3:22, Tues & Thurs 8:45-5:15

KITSCOTY

P KITSCOTY PUBLIC LIBRARY*, 4910 51 St, T0B 2P0. (Mail add: PO Box 39, T0B 2P0), SAN 326-6451. Tel: 780-846-2822. FAX: 780-846-2215. E-mail: info@kitscotypubliclibrary.ab.ca. Web Site: www.kitscotypubliclibrary.ab.ca. *Librn,* Colleen Tabish; E-mail: librarian@kitscotypubliclibrary.ab.ca
Pop 980
Library Holdings: Bk Titles 10,000
Automation Activity & Vendor Info: (Cataloging) Innovative Interfaces, Inc; (Circulation) Innovative Interfaces, Inc
Wireless access
Mem of Northern Lights Library System
Partic in The Regional Automation Consortium
Open Tues-Thurs 10-7 (July-Aug); Mon & Fri 1-4, Tues-Thurs 1-7:30 (Sept-June)

LA CRETE

P LA CRETE COMMUNITY LIBRARY*, 10102 100 Ave, T0H 2H0. (Mail add: PO Box 609, T0H 2H0), SAN 318-692X. Tel: 780-928-3166. *Head Librn,* Tammy Schellenberg; E-mail: tammys@lacretelibrary.com; Staff 1 (Non-MLS 1)
Pop 9,000
Library Holdings: Audiobooks 870; DVDs 3,000; Large Print Bks 240; Bk Titles 25,000; Per Subs 28
Automation Activity & Vendor Info: (Cataloging) Insignia Software; (Circulation) Insignia Software
Wireless access
Open Tues-Thurs 10-8, Fri 10-4, Sat 12-4

LA GLACE

P LA GLACE COMMUNITY LIBRARY*, 9924 97 Ave, T0H 2J0. (Mail add: PO Box 209, T0H 2J0). Tel: 780-568-4696. FAX: 780-568-4707. E-mail: librarian@laglacelibrary.ab.ca. Web Site: www.laglacelibrary.ab.ca. *Libr Mgr,* Wanda Penner; *Libr Asst,* Lovella Soles
Library Holdings: Bk Vols 18,000
Automation Activity & Vendor Info: (Acquisitions) Innovative Interfaces, Inc. - Polaris; (Cataloging) Innovative Interfaces, Inc. - Polaris; (Circulation) Innovative Interfaces, Inc. - Polaris; (ILL) Innovative Interfaces, Inc. - Polaris; (Serials) Innovative Interfaces, Inc. - Polaris
Wireless access
Mem of Peace Library System
Partic in The Regional Automation Consortium
Open Mon-Wed 11-5, Thurs 11-7, Sat 10-Noon
Friends of the Library Group

LAC LA BICHE

P LAC LA BICHE COUNTY LIBRARIES*, Stuart MacPherson Public Library, 8702 91st Ave, T0A 2C0. (Mail add: Box 2039, T0A 2C0), SAN 325-2914. Tel: 780-623-7467. FAX: 780-623-7497. E-mail: info@llbcl.ca. Web Site: www.llbcl.ca. *Libr Dir,* Maureen Penn; Staff 9 (MLS 1, Non-MLS 8)
Founded 1967. Pop 9,531; Highest Degree: Master
Wireless access
Function: 24/7 Electronic res, 24/7 Online cat, 3D Printer, Activity rm, Art exhibits, Audiobks on Playaways & MP3, Audiobks via web, Bks on CD, Children's prog, Computer training, Computers for patron use, Digital talking bks, Electronic databases & coll, Equip loans & repairs, Family literacy, Free DVD rentals, Games & aids for people with disabilities, Home delivery & serv to seniorr ctr & nursing homes, Homebound delivery serv, Homework prog, ILL available, Internet access, Life-long learning prog for all ages, Literacy & newcomer serv, Magazines, Magnifiers for reading, Mail & tel request accepted, Makerspace, Meeting rooms, Movies, Online cat, Online info literacy tutorials on the web & in blackboard, Orientations, Outreach serv, Outside serv via phone, mail, e-mail & web, OverDrive digital audio bks, Photocopying/Printing, Preschool outreach, Preschool reading prog, Printer for laptops & handheld devices, Prog for adults, Prog for children & young adult, Ref serv available, Scanner, STEM programs, Study rm, Summer & winter reading prog, Teen prog, Wheelchair accessible, Winter reading prog, Workshops
Mem of Northern Lights Library System
Partic in The Regional Automation Consortium
Special Services for the Blind - Playaways (bks on MP3); Talking bks
Open Mon-Thurs 9-8, Fri 9-6, Sat (Sept-June) 9-4
Friends of the Library Group

Branches: 1
PLAMONDON MUNICIPAL LIBRARY, Ecole Plamondon, 9814 100 St, Plamondon, T0A 2T0. (Mail add: Box 2039, T0A 2T0). Tel: 780-798-3852. E-mail: info@llbcl.ca. *Libr Dir,* Maureen Penn; Tel: 780-623-7467
Founded 1959
Special Collections: Russian Materials
Partic in The Regional Automation Consortium
Special Services for the Blind - Large print bks; Talking bks
Open Mon, Tues, Thurs & Fri 8:30-3:30, Wed 8:30-8
Friends of the Library Group

C PORTAGE COLLEGE LIBRARY*, 9531 94th Ave, T0A 2C0. (Mail add: PO Box 417, T0A 2C0). Tel: 780-623-5650. Administration Tel: 780-623-5514. Toll Free Tel: 866-623-5551. FAX: 780-623-5656. E-mail: library@portagecollege.ca. Web Site: www.portagecollege.ca/library. *Libr Serv Coordr,* Christina Wac; Tel: 780 623-5755, E-mail: christina.wac@portagecollege.ca; *Library Services Asst,* Riya Abougoush; E-mail: riya.abougoush@portagecollege.ca; Staff 4 (MLS 1, Non-MLS 3)
Founded 1977. Enrl 874; Fac 80
Library Holdings: AV Mats 1,391; e-books 130,882; Bk Vols 12,531; Per Subs 42
Subject Interests: Col, Col educ
Automation Activity & Vendor Info: (Acquisitions) OCLC Worldshare Management Services; (Cataloging) OCLC Connexion; (Circulation) OCLC Worldshare Management Services; (Discovery) OCLC; (ILL) OCLC WorldShare Interlibrary Loan; (OPAC) OCLC
Wireless access
Function: Computers for patron use, Electronic databases & coll, ILL available, Instruction & testing, Orientations, Photocopying/Printing, Ref serv available, Scanner, VHS videos, Wheelchair accessible
Partic in The Alberta Library
Open Mon-Thurs 8:15am-8:30pm, Fri 8:15-4:30
Restriction: Borrowing privileges limited to fac & registered students, Borrowing requests are handled by ILL, ID required to use computers (Ltd hrs), In-house use for visitors, Open to pub for ref & circ; with some limitations, Open to students, fac & staff

LACOMBE

CR BURMAN UNIVERSITY LIBRARY*, 5410 Ramona Ave, T4L 2B7. SAN 318-6334. Tel: 403-782-3381, Ext 4101. Interlibrary Loan Service Tel: 403-782-3381, Ext 4102. Toll Free Tel: 866-930-4928. E-mail: library@cauc.ca. Web Site: www.burmanu.ca/library. *Librn, Pub Serv,* Sheila Clark; E-mail: sclark@burmanu.ca; *Libr Tech,* Wilmer Tenerife; Tel: 403-782-3381, Ext 4104, E-mail: wtenerife@burmanu.ca; Staff 5 (MLS 2, Non-MLS 3)
Founded 1907. Enrl 500; Fac 37; Highest Degree: Bachelor
Library Holdings: AV Mats 2,406; e-books 1,000; e-journals 9,759; Bk Vols 68,705; Per Subs 200
Special Collections: Seventh-day Adventist Church in Canada
Subject Interests: Liberal arts
Automation Activity & Vendor Info: (Acquisitions) SirsiDynix; (Cataloging) SirsiDynix; (Circulation) SirsiDynix; (Course Reserve) SirsiDynix; (ILL) SirsiDynix; (OPAC) SirsiDynix; (Serials) SirsiDynix
Wireless access
Publications: Framework of Learning Resources (1988)
Partic in NEOS Library Consortium
Open Mon-Thurs 8am-Midnight, Fri 8-3, Sun 10am-Midnight

P LACOMBE PUBLIC LIBRARY*, Mary C Moore Public Library, 101-5214 50 Ave, T4L 0B6. Tel: 403-782-3433. *Head Librn,* Christina Petrisor; E-mail: christinap@prl.ab.ca; Staff 4.5 (MLS 1, Non-MLS 3.5)
Founded 1931. Pop 11,733; Circ 129,273
Jan 2019-Dec 2019 Income (CAN) $860,473, Provincial (CAN) $70,640, City (CAN) $618,429, County (CAN) $17,316, Locally Generated Income (CAN) $83,448, Other (CAN) $70,640. Mats Exp (CAN) $49,104, Books (CAN) $28,908, Per/Ser (Incl. Access Fees) (CAN) $11,000, AV Mat (CAN) $2,000. Sal (CAN) $275,321 (Prof (CAN) $69,888)
Library Holdings: Audiobooks 1,011; CDs 610; DVDs 5,171; e-books 32; Music Scores 1,000; Bk Titles 45,584; Bk Vols 52,416; Per Subs 81; Talking Bks 160
Automation Activity & Vendor Info: (Acquisitions) Innovative Interfaces, Inc; (Cataloging) Innovative Interfaces, Inc; (Circulation) Innovative Interfaces, Inc; (Course Reserve) Innovative Interfaces, Inc; (ILL) Innovative Interfaces, Inc; (Media Booking) Innovative Interfaces, Inc; (OPAC) Innovative Interfaces, Inc; (Serials) Innovative Interfaces, Inc
Wireless access
Function: 24/7 Electronic res, 24/7 Online cat, Activity rm, Adult bk club, After school storytime, Art programs, Audio & video playback equip for onsite use, Audiobks on Playaways & MP3, Audiobks via web, AV serv, Bk club(s), Bk reviews (Group), Bks on CD, CD-ROM, Children's prog, Computers for patron use, Digital talking bks, Distance learning, Doc delivery serv, E-Reserves, Electronic databases & coll, Equip loans & repairs, Family literacy, For res purposes, Free DVD rentals, Genealogy discussion group, Holiday prog, Home delivery & serv to seniorr ctr & nursing homes, Homebound delivery serv, ILL available, Instruction & testing, Internet access, Life-long learning prog for all ages, Magazines, Mail & tel request accepted, Mail loans to mem, Meeting rooms, Movies, Music CDs, Online cat, Online info literacy tutorials on the web & in blackboard, Outreach serv, Outside serv via phone, mail, e-mail & web, Photocopying/Printing, Preschool reading prog, Prog for adults, Prog for children & young adult, Ref & res, Ref serv available, Res assist avail, Scanner, Senior outreach, Serves people with intellectual disabilities, Spoken cassettes & CDs, Spoken cassettes & DVDs, STEM programs, Story hour, Study rm, Summer & winter reading prog, Summer reading prog, Teen prog, Telephone ref, Visual arts prog, Wheelchair accessible, Winter reading prog, Workshops, Writing prog
Mem of Parkland Regional Library-Alberta
Partic in The Alberta Library
Special Services for the Blind - Bks & mags in Braille, on rec, tape & cassette; Bks available with recordings; Bks on CD; Braille bks; Daisy reader; Digital talking bk; Digital talking bk machines; Home delivery serv; Info on spec aids & appliances; Recorded bks; Talking bks & player equip
Open Mon-Thurs 10-8, Fri & Sat 10-5
Restriction: Access at librarian's discretion, By permission only
Friends of the Library Group

P PARKLAND REGIONAL LIBRARY-ALBERTA*, 5404 56th Ave, T4L 1G1. SAN 318-6946. Tel: 403-782-3850. Toll Free Tel: 800-567-9024. Web Site: www.prl.ab.ca. *Dir,* Ronald Sheppard; E-mail: rsheppard@prl.ab.ca; *Mgr,* Colleen Schalm; *Tech Serv,* Karyn Goodwillie; Staff 5 (MLS 5)
Founded 1959
Special Collections: Can
Wireless access
Publications: Annual Report
Member Libraries: Alix Public Library; Alliance Public Library; Amisk Public Library; Bashaw Public Library; Bawlf Public Library; Bentley Municipal Library; Big Valley Municipal Library; Blackfalds Public Library; Bodo Public Library; Bowden Public Library; Brownfield Community Library; Cadogan Public Library; Camrose Public Library; Caroline Municipal Library; Carstairs Public Library; Castor Municipal Library; Clive Public Library; Coronation Memorial Library; Cremona Municipal Library; Czar Municipal Library; Daysland Public Library; Delburne Municipal Library; Didsbury Municipal Library; Donalda Public Library; Eckville Municipal Library; Edberg Public Library; Elnora Public Library; Forestburg Public Library; Hardisty Public Library; Hay Lakes Municipal Library; Heisler Municipal Library; Hughenden Public Library; Innisfail Public Library; Killam Municipal Library; Lacombe Public Library; Lougheed Public Library; Nordegg Public Library; Olds Municipal Library; Penhold & District Public Library; Ponoka Jubilee Library; Provost Municipal Library; Rimbey Municipal Library; Rocky Mountain House Public Library; Sedgewick & District Municipal Library; Spruce View Community Library; Stettler Public Library; Sundre Municipal Library; Sylvan Lake Municipal Library; Water Valley Public Library
Open Mon-Fri 8:30-4:30

LAMONT

P LAMONT PUBLIC LIBRARY*, Lamont High School, 4811 50 Ave, T0B 2R0. (Mail add: PO Box 180, T0B 2R0), SAN 318-6954. Tel: 780-895-2299. FAX: 780-895-2600. E-mail: info@lamontpubliclibrary.ca. Web Site: www.lamontpubliclibrary.ca. *Librn,* Angela Wendorff; E-mail: librarian@lamontpubliclibrary.ca; *Libr Tech,* Rebecca Nice; Staff 1 (Non-MLS 1)
Founded 1955. Pop 1,800; Circ 5,000
Library Holdings: Bk Titles 16,000
Wireless access
Mem of Northern Lights Library System
Open Mon & Fri 8:30-3:30, Tues & Thurs 8:30-3:30 & 5-8, Wed 8:30-3:30 & 4-7

LANCASTER PARK

P EDMONTON GARRISON COMMUNITY LIBRARY*, Bldg 161, Rm 32, Mons Ave & Range Rd 244, T0A 2H0. (Mail add: PO Box 462, T0A 2H0). Tel: 780-973-4011, Ext 6345. E-mail: librarian@garrisonlibrary.ab.ca. Web Site: www.garrisonlibrary.ab.ca. *Head Librn,* Melanie Pole
Founded 1999
Wireless access
Mem of Northern Lights Library System
Open Tues 10-1 & 5-8, Wed & Fri 10-3, Thurs 10-12 & 5-8, Sat 12-3

LEDUC

P LEDUC PUBLIC LIBRARY*, Two Alexandra Park, T9E 4C4. SAN 318-6962. Tel: 780-986-2637. Administration Tel: 780-986-2638. FAX: 780-986-3462. E-mail: help@leducLibrary.ca. Web Site: www.leduclibrary.ca. *Libr Dir,* Carla Frybort; E-mail:

cfrybort@leduclibrary.ca; *Pub Serv Coordr,* Sharon McAmmond; *Adult Prog & Serv,* Holly Lim-Lovatt; Staff 15 (MLS 2, Non-MLS 13)
Pop 33,000; Circ 140,000
Jan 2020-Dec 2020 Income (CAN) $904,025, Provincial (CAN) $67,053, City (CAN) $802,140, County (CAN) $9,838, Locally Generated Income (CAN) $18,718, Other (CAN) $6,276. Mats Exp (CAN) $136,539, Books (CAN) $112,239, Per/Ser (Incl. Access Fees) (CAN) $5,000, AV Mat (CAN) $18,400, Electronic Ref Mat (Incl. Access Fees) (CAN) $900. Sal (CAN) $524,921
Library Holdings: AV Mats 1,093; CDs 2,211; DVDs 670; Electronic Media & Resources 43; Large Print Bks 776; Bk Vols 47,852; Per Subs 102; Videos 1,233
Special Collections: Local Newspaper 1907-1988, microfilm
Automation Activity & Vendor Info: (Cataloging) Innovative Interfaces, Inc
Wireless access
Function: Adult bk club, Adult literacy prog, After school storytime, Art exhibits, Audio & video playback equip for onsite use, AV serv, Bk club(s), Bks on CD, Computer training, Digital talking bks, Electronic databases & coll, Family literacy, ILL available, Large print keyboards, Music CDs, Online cat, Outside serv via phone, mail, e-mail & web, Photocopying/Printing, Preschool outreach, Prog for adults, Prog for children & young adult, Ref serv available, Scanner, Senior computer classes, Spoken cassettes & DVDs, Summer reading prog, Telephone ref, VHS videos, Wheelchair accessible, Workshops
Mem of Yellowhead Regional Library
Partic in The Regional Automation Consortium
Open Mon-Thurs 10-8, Fri 10-5, Sat 12-4
Friends of the Library Group

LETHBRIDGE

GL ALBERTA LAW LIBRARIES - LETHBRIDGE*, Courthouse, 320-Four St S, T1J 1Z8. SAN 320-7757. Tel: 403-381-5639. FAX: 403-381-5703. Web Site: www.lawlibrary.ab.ca. *Dir,* Dale Barrie; E-mail: dale.barrie@gov.ab.ca; *Coordr,* Grant Janzen; Tel: 403-381-5161, E-mail: grant.janzen@gov.ab.ca
Library Holdings: Bk Titles 16,000
Open Mon-Fri 9:15-12 & 1-3:30

P CHINOOK ARCH REGIONAL LIBRARY SYSTEM*, 2902 Seventh Ave N, T1H 5C6. Tel: 403-380-1500. Toll Free Tel: 888-458-1500. FAX: 403-380-3550. E-mail: arch@chinookarch.ca. Web Site: www.chinookarch.ca. *Chief Exec Officer,* Robin Hepher; Tel: 403-380-1505, E-mail: rhepher@chinookarch.ca; *Mgr, Community Dev,* Lisa Weekes; E-mail: lweekes@chinookarch.ca
Library Holdings: e-journals 20,000; Bk Vols 900,000
Wireless access
Member Libraries: Arrowwood Municipal Library; Carmangay & District Municipal Library; Champion Municipal Library; Claresholm Public Library; Coaldale Public Library; Coutts Municipal Library; Crowsnest Pass Municipal Library; Enchant Community Library; Glenwood Municipal Library; Granum Public Library; Hays Public Library; Jim & Mary Kearl Library of Cardston; Lethbridge Public Library; Lomond Community Library; Magrath Public Library; Milk River Municipal Library; Milo Municipal Library; Picture Butte Municipal Library; Pincher Creek & District Municipal Library; Raymond Public Library; Stavely Municipal Library; Stirling Theodore Brandley Municipal Library; Taber Public Library; The Town of Fort Macleod Library; Thelma Fanning Memorial Library; Vauxhall Public Library; Vulcan Municipal Library; Warner Memorial Library; Wrentham Public Library
Open Mon-Fri 8:30-4:30

J LETHBRIDGE COLLEGE*, Buchanan Library, 3000 College Dr S, T1K 1L6. SAN 318-6989. Tel: 403-320-3352. Information Services Tel: 403-320-3355. E-mail: buchanan.library@lethbridgecollege.ca, library.infodesk@lethbridgecollege.ca. Web Site: www.lethbridgecollege.ca/departments/buchanan-library. *Libr Coord,* Darel Bennedbeak; *Info Serv Spec,* Helen Fulara; Staff 2 (MLS 2)
Founded 1967
Library Holdings: Bk Vols 65,000; Per Subs 200
Special Collections: Buchanan Art Coll
Subject Interests: Criminal justice, Environ studies, Nursing
Automation Activity & Vendor Info: (Acquisitions) OCLC; (Cataloging) OCLC; (Circulation) OCLC; (Course Reserve) OCLC; (Media Booking) OCLC; (OPAC) OCLC; (Serials) OCLC
Wireless access
Publications: Buchanan Resource Center Pathfinders; Canadian Perspectives; Library Guide; Library of Congress Classification System Brochure; Student Library Handbook
Partic in OCLC Online Computer Library Center, Inc; The Alberta Library
Open Mon-Thurs 7:30am-9:30pm, Fri 7:30-5, Sat Noon-6 (Winter); Mon-Fri 8:30-4:30 (Summer & Spring)

P LETHBRIDGE PUBLIC LIBRARY*, 810 Fifth Ave S, T1J 4C4. SAN 318-6997. Tel: 403-380-7310. FAX: 403-329-1478. E-mail: questions@lethlib.ca. Web Site: www.lethlib.ca. *Chief Exec Officer,* Terra Plato; Tel: 403-380-7341, E-mail: terra.plato@lethlib.ca; *Assoc Dir, Serv Develop,* Elisabeth Hegerat; Tel: 403-320-4187, E-mail: elisabeth.hegerat@lethlib.ca; *Customer Serv Coordr,* Barbara Longair; Tel: 403-380-7318, E-mail: barbara.longair@lethlib.ca; *Coordr, Youth Serv,* Bonnie Mikalson-Andron; Tel: 403-320-3026; Staff 13 (MLS 10, Non-MLS 3)
Founded 1919. Pop 106,550; Circ 675,050
Special Collections: Southern Alberta History (Senator Buchanan Coll). Canadian and Provincial
Wireless access
Function: Art exhibits, Audiobks via web, Bk club(s), Bks on CD, Computers for patron use, Electronic databases & coll, Home delivery & serv to seniorr ctr & nursing homes, Homebound delivery serv, ILL available, Magnifiers for reading, Museum passes, Music CDs, Online cat, OverDrive digital audio bks, Photocopying/Printing, Prog for adults, Prog for children & young adult, Ref serv available, Story hour, Summer reading prog, Telephone ref
Publications: Annual Report; Happening (Brochure)
Mem of Chinook Arch Regional Library System
Open Mon-Wed & Sat 10-5:30, Thurs & Fri 10-8, Sun 1-5
Friends of the Library Group
Bookmobiles: 1

S SIR ALEXANDER GALT MUSEUM & ARCHIVES*, 502 First St S, T1J 1Y4. SAN 327-442X. Tel: 403-329-7302. FAX: 403-329-4958. E-mail: archives@galtmuseum.com. Web Site: www.galtmuseum.com. *Archivist,* Andrew Chernevych; E-mail: andrew.chernevych@galtmuseum.com; *Asst Archivist,* Ms Bobbie Fox; E-mail: bobbie.fox@galtmuseum.com
Library Holdings: Bk Titles 575; Bk Vols 800
Special Collections: Lethbridge News 1901-1906 & Lethbridge Herald 1905-1918: A Subject & Biographical Index (1987)
Open Mon-Fri 8-4
Friends of the Library Group

S SOUTHERN ALBERTA ART GALLERY LIBRARY*, Turcotte Library, 601 Third Ave S, T1J 0H4. SAN 321-6225. Tel: 403-327-8770. FAX: 403-328-3913. E-mail: info@saag.ca. Web Site: saag.ca. *Exec Dir,* Su Ying Strang; Tel: 403-327-8770, Ext 26, E-mail: systrang@saag.ca; *Operations Mgr,* Meghan Visser; Tel: 403-327-8770, Ext 27, E-mail: mvisser@saag.ca; *Actg Curator, Library Contact,* Adam Whitford; Tel: 403-327-8770, Ext 23, E-mail: awhitford@saag.ca
Founded 1975
Library Holdings: Bk Titles 6,000; Per Subs 17
Special Collections: Artists' Films, Videos & Slides
Wireless access
Open Tues-Sat 10-5, Sun 1-5

C UNIVERSITY OF LETHBRIDGE LIBRARY*, 4401 University Dr, T1K 3M4. SAN 318-7004. Tel: 403-329-2261, 403-329-2263. FAX: 403-329-2234. E-mail: gsdlibrary@uleth.ca. Web Site: www.uleth.ca/lib. *Interim Univ Librn,* Harold Jansen; E-mail: harold.jansen@uleth.ca; Staff 47 (MLS 14, Non-MLS 33)
Founded 1967. Enrl 8,380; Fac 483; Highest Degree: Doctorate
Library Holdings: Bk Vols 533,154; Per Subs 1,296
Special Collections: Can; Canadiana (Woodworth Coll); University Archives
Subject Interests: Educ, Fine arts, Humanities, Native Am studies, Nursing
Automation Activity & Vendor Info: (Acquisitions) Innovative Interfaces, Inc; (Cataloging) Innovative Interfaces, Inc; (Circulation) Innovative Interfaces, Inc; (Course Reserve) Innovative Interfaces, Inc; (ILL) Relais International; (Media Booking) Innovative Interfaces, Inc; (OPAC) Innovative Interfaces, Inc; (Serials) Innovative Interfaces, Inc
Wireless access
Open Mon-Thurs 8am-11pm, Fri 8-6, Sat 10-6, Sun 1-9 (Winter); Mon-Thurs 8am-9pm, Fri 8-4:30, Sat Noon-5, Sun 1-5 (Summer)

LINDEN

P LINDEN MUNICIPAL LIBRARY*, 215 First St SE, T0M 1J0. (Mail add: PO Box 120, T0M 1J0). Tel: 403-546-3757. E-mail: almlibrary@marigold.ab.ca. Web Site: www.lindenlibrary.ca. *Managing Dir,* Jessica Pierson; Staff 1 (Non-MLS 1)
Pop 741
Library Holdings: Bk Vols 8,900
Wireless access
Mem of Marigold Library System
Open Tues & Thurs 4-8, Wed 12-8

LLOYDMINSTER

P LLOYDMINSTER PUBLIC LIBRARY*, 5010 - 49 St, T9V 0K2. SAN 319-9509. Tel: 780-875-0850. Reference Tel: 780-875-0877. FAX: 780-875-6523. Interlibrary Loan Service E-mail: ill@lloydminster.info. Information Services E-mail: info@lloydminster.info. Web Site: lloydminster.info. *Dir,* Darrell Yates; E-mail: director@lakeland.lib.sk.ca; *Head Librn,* Ron Gillies; E-mail: hlib@lloydminster.info; *Ref Librn,* Michele Duczek; E-mail: mduczek@lloydminster.info; Staff 11 (MLS 2, Non-MLS 9)
Pop 31,483; Circ 160,000
Library Holdings: Large Print Bks 2,200; Bk Titles 72,156; Bk Vols 79,155; Per Subs 186; Talking Bks 966; Videos 1,927
Subject Interests: Local hist
Automation Activity & Vendor Info: (Cataloging) Mandarin Library Automation; (Circulation) Mandarin Library Automation; (ILL) Innovative Interfaces, Inc - Millennium; (OPAC) Mandarin Library Automation; (Serials) Mandarin Library Automation
Wireless access
Function: Home delivery & serv to seniorr ctr & nursing homes, Homebound delivery serv, ILL available, Magnifiers for reading, Prog for children & young adult, Ref serv available, Summer reading prog, Telephone ref, Wheelchair accessible
Open Mon-Thurs 10-9, Fri 10-6, Sat 10-5
Friends of the Library Group

LOMOND

P LOMOND COMMUNITY LIBRARY, Two Railway Ave N, T0L 1G0. Tel: 403-792-3934. E-mail: help@lomondlibrary.ca. Web Site: lomondlibrary.ca. *Libr Mgr,* Kate Koch; Staff 1 (Non-MLS 1)
Pop 171
Library Holdings: Bk Vols 11,973
Wireless access
Mem of Chinook Arch Regional Library System
Special Services for the Blind - Bks on cassette
Open Mon 5-8, Tues 10-5, Wed 10-2, Thurs 9-5
Friends of the Library Group

LONGVIEW

P LONGVIEW MUNICIPAL LIBRARY*, 128 Morrison Rd, T0L 1H0. (Mail add: PO Box 189, T0L 1H0). Tel: 403-558-3927. FAX: 403-558-3927. E-mail: alomlibrary@marigold.ab.ca. Web Site: www.longviewlibrary.ca. *Libr Mgr,* Lynda Winfield; Staff 2 (Non-MLS 2)
Pop 400
Library Holdings: Bk Titles 5,471
Wireless access
Mem of Marigold Library System
Open Tues-Thurs 10-5

LOUGHEED

P LOUGHEED PUBLIC LIBRARY*, 5004 50 St, T0B 2V0. (Mail add: PO Box 179, T0B 2V0). Tel: 780-386-2498. FAX: 780-386-2136. E-mail: lougheedlibrary@prl.ab.ca. Web Site: lougheedlibrary.prl.ab.ca. *Libr Mgr,* Barb McConnell
Pop 450
Library Holdings: Audiobooks 10; AV Mats 400; CDs 100; Large Print Bks 45; Bk Titles 9,000; Talking Bks 110; Videos 200
Wireless access
Function: Homebound delivery serv, ILL available, Mail loans to mem, Photocopying/Printing
Mem of Parkland Regional Library-Alberta
Open Mon, Wed & Fri 1-5
Friends of the Library Group

MAGRATH

P MAGRATH PUBLIC LIBRARY*, 27 S Center St, T0K 1J0. SAN 318-7012. Tel: 403-758-6498. E-mail: help@magrathlibrary.ca. Web Site: www.magrathlibrary.ca. *Libr Mgr,* Stephanie Humphreys
Founded 1937. Pop 2,081; Circ 32,173
Library Holdings: Bk Vols 31,521
Wireless access
Mem of Chinook Arch Regional Library System
Open Mon Noon-8, Tues & Thurs 10-5, Wed & Fri Noon-5
Friends of the Library Group

MALLAIG

P BIBLIOTHEQUE MALLAIG LIBRARY*, Mallaig Public Library, 3110 First St E, T0A 2K0. (Mail add: PO Box 90, T0A 2K0). Tel: 780-635-3858. FAX: 780-635-3938. Web Site: www.mallaiglibrary.ab.ca. *Librn,* Pauline Dechaine; E-mail: dechpaul@sperd.ca; Staff 1.1 (Non-MLS 1.1)
Library Holdings: Bk Vols 15,000
Wireless access
Mem of Northern Lights Library System
Open Mon & Fri 8-3:30, Tues & Thurs 8-6:30, Wed 8am-8:30pm

MA-ME-O BEACH

P PIGEON LAKE PUBLIC LIBRARY*, 603 Second Ave, T0C 1X0. SAN 325-2272. Tel: 780-586-3778. E-mail: pigeonlakelibrary@yrl.ab.ca. Web Site: www.pigeonlakepubliclibrary.ab.ca. *Libr Mgr,* Cheryl McKerrall; Staff 1 (Non-MLS 1)
Founded 1967. Pop 5,800
Library Holdings: Videos 550
Wireless access
Function: Activity rm, Adult bk club
Mem of Yellowhead Regional Library
Open Mon, Wed & Thurs 10-6, Sat 10-1

MANNING

P MANNING MUNICIPAL & DISTRICT LIBRARY, 407 Main St, T0H 2M0. (Mail add: PO Box 810, T0H 2M0). Tel: 780-836-3054. FAX: 780-836-0071. E-mail: librarian@manninglibrary.ab.ca. Web Site: manninglibrary.ab.ca. *Libr Mgr,* Ally Johnson
Library Holdings: Bk Vols 12,131
Wireless access
Function: Adult bk club, Art exhibits, Audiobks on Playaways & MP3, Audiobks via web, Bks on CD, Free DVD rentals, Games, Home delivery & serv to seniorr ctr & nursing homes, ILL available, Internet access, Magazines, Mail & tel request accepted, Meeting rooms, Movies, Online cat, OverDrive digital audio bks, Photocopying/Printing, Prog for adults, Prog for children & young adult, Scanner, Wheelchair accessible
Mem of Peace Library System
Special Services for the Deaf - Adult & family literacy prog; Bks on deafness & sign lang; High interest/low vocabulary bks
Special Services for the Blind - Audio mat; Bks available with recordings; Bks on CD; Copier with enlargement capabilities; Large print bks
Open Mon-Fri 10-6, Sat 11-4
Friends of the Library Group
Bookmobiles: 1

MANNVILLE

P MANNVILLE CENTENNIAL PUBLIC LIBRARY*, 5029 50 St, T0B 2W0. (Mail add: PO Box 186, T0B 2W0), SAN 318-7020. Tel: 780-763-3611. FAX: 780-763-3688. E-mail: info@mannvillelibrary.ab.ca. Web Site: www.mannvillelibrary.ab.ca. *Libr Mgr,* Jacqie Carek; E-mail: librarian@mannvillelibrary.ab.ca
Pop 850; Circ 10,000
Subject Interests: Local hist
Automation Activity & Vendor Info: (Cataloging) SirsiDynix; (Circulation) SirsiDynix; (ILL) SirsiDynix
Wireless access
Mem of Northern Lights Library System
Open Tues, Wed & Fri 10-5, Thurs 10-7
Friends of the Library Group

MARWAYNE

P MARWAYNE PUBLIC LIBRARY, PO Box 174, T0B 2X0. Tel: 780-847-3930. E-mail: librarian@marwaynelibrary.ab.ca. Web Site: www.marwaynelibrary.ab.ca. *Libr Mgr,* Carmen Smart
Founded 1972
Automation Activity & Vendor Info: (Cataloging) Innovative Interfaces, Inc. - Polaris; (OPAC) Innovative Interfaces, Inc. - Polaris
Wireless access
Mem of Northern Lights Library System
Open Mon & Thurs 9-3:30, Tues & Wed 9-7, Fri 9-5

MAYERTHORPE

P MAYERTHORPE PUBLIC LIBRARY*, 4601 52nd St, T0E 1N0. (Mail add: PO Box 810, T0E 1N0), SAN 318-7039. Tel: 780-786-2404. E-mail: mayerthorpepl@yrl.ab.ca. Web Site: www.mayerthorpelibrary.ab.ca. *Libr Mgr,* Gloria Wilson; *Libr Asst,* Jessica Farrer; *Libr Asst,* Darsi Hall; Staff 1 (Non-MLS 1)
Founded 1972. Pop 3,000; Circ 20,000
Library Holdings: Bk Vols 10,000
Subject Interests: Local hist
Automation Activity & Vendor Info: (Circulation) Innovative Interfaces, Inc. - Polaris
Wireless access
Mem of Yellowhead Regional Library
Open Tues, Thurs & Fri 10-5, Wed 10-7
Friends of the Library Group

MCLENNAN

P MCLENNAN MUNICIPAL LIBRARY*, 19 First Ave NW, T0H 2L0. (Mail add: Box 298, T0H 2L0). Tel: 780-324-3767. FAX: 780-324-2288. E-mail: librarian@mclennanlibrary.ab.ca. Web Site: mclennanlibrary.ab.ca.
Pop 900
Library Holdings: Audiobooks 81; Braille Volumes 5; CDs 12; DVDs 550; Bk Titles 13,500; Per Subs 35
Automation Activity & Vendor Info: (Acquisitions) Innovative Interfaces, Inc; (Cataloging) Innovative Interfaces, Inc; (Circulation) Innovative Interfaces, Inc; (ILL) Innovative Interfaces, Inc
Wireless access
Mem of Peace Library System
Open Mon-Fri 1-5

MEDICINE HAT

C MEDICINE HAT COLLEGE LIBRARY*, Vera Braken Library, 299 College Dr SE, T1A 3Y6. SAN 318-7047. Tel: 403-529-3867. FAX: 403-504-3634. E-mail: Reference@mhc.ab.ca. Web Site: www.mhc.ab.ca/library. *Exec Dir,* Chuck Payne; Tel: 403-529-3870, E-mail: payne@mhc.ab.ca; Staff 20 (MLS 3, Non-MLS 17)
Founded 1965. Enrl 3,000; Fac 170; Highest Degree: Bachelor
Library Holdings: AV Mats 9,000; e-books 85,000; Music Scores 4,000; Bk Vols 95,000; Per Subs 550
Automation Activity & Vendor Info: (Acquisitions) Innovative Interfaces, Inc; (Cataloging) Innovative Interfaces, Inc; (Circulation) Innovative Interfaces, Inc; (Course Reserve) Innovative Interfaces, Inc; (ILL) Relais International; (Media Booking) Innovative Interfaces, Inc; (OPAC) Innovative Interfaces, Inc; (Serials) Innovative Interfaces, Inc
Wireless access
Partic in The Alberta Library
Open Mon-Thurs 7:30am-10pm, Fri 7:30-6, Sat 10-6, Sun 1-8

P MEDICINE HAT PUBLIC LIBRARY, 414 First St SE, T1A 0A8. SAN 318-7055. Tel: 403-502-8527. Circulation Tel: 403-502-8525. Reference Tel: 403-502-8538. FAX: 403-502-8529. E-mail: mhploffice@shortgraff.ca. Web Site: mhpl.shortgrass.ca. *Chief Librn,* Ken Feser; Tel: 403-502-8528; *Head of Mkt, Head, Community Engagement,* Chris Brown; Tel: 403-502-8536; *Head, Adult Serv,* Keith McLean; Tel: 403-502-8531; *Head, Support Serv,* Annette Ziegler; Tel: 403-502-8539; *Head, Youth Serv,* Carol Ann Cross-Roen; Tel: 403-502-8532; Staff 42 (MLS 4, Non-MLS 38)
Founded 1915. Pop 61,097; Circ 523,538
Library Holdings: Bk Titles 143,826; Per Subs 324
Special Collections: Can
Wireless access
Publications: Library Connection
Mem of Shortgrass Library System
Partic in The Alberta Library
Open Mon, Fri & Sat 10-5, Tues-Thurs 10-8
Friends of the Library Group

P SHORTGRASS LIBRARY SYSTEM*, 2375-Tenth Ave SW, T1A 8G2. Toll Free Tel: 866-529-0550. FAX: 403-528-2473. Web Site: www.shortgrass.ca. *Chief Exec Officer,* Petra Mauerhoff; Tel: 403-529-0550, Ext 101, E-mail: Petra@shortgrass.ca; Staff 3 (MLS 3)
Member Libraries: Alcoma Community Library; Bassano Memorial Library; Bow Island Municipal Library; Brooks Public Library; Duchess & District Public Library; Foremost Municipal Library; Gem Jubilee Library; Graham Community Library; Irvine Community Library; Medicine Hat Public Library; Redcliff Public Library; Rolling Hills Public Library; Rosemary Community Library; Tilley District & Public Library

MILK RIVER

P MILK RIVER MUNICIPAL LIBRARY*, 321 Third Ave NE, T0K 1M0. Tel: 403-647-3793. E-mail: help@milkriverlibrary.ca. Web Site: www.milkriverlibrary.ca. *Libr Mgr,* Peter Denmark
Pop 568
Library Holdings: Bk Vols 10,000; Videos 900
Wireless access
Mem of Chinook Arch Regional Library System
Open Tues 11-7, Wed & Thurs 11-5, Fri 10-3
Friends of the Library Group

MILLARVILLE

P MILLARVILLE COMMUNITY LIBRARY*, 130 Millarville Rd, T0L 1K0. SAN 326-7776. Tel: 403-931-3919. FAX: 403-931-2475. E-mail: amclibrary@marigold.ab.ca. Web Site: www.millarvillelibrary.ca. *Librn,* Natasha Grusendorf
Pop 1,500; Circ 8,341
Library Holdings: Bk Vols 7,613; Talking Bks 220; Videos 2,000
Wireless access
Mem of Marigold Library System
Partic in The Alberta Library; The Regional Automation Consortium
Open Tues 9-12, Wed 10-7:30

MILLET

P MILLET PUBLIC LIBRARY*, 5031 49th Ave, T0C 1Z0. (Mail add: PO Box 30, T0C 1Z0). Tel: 780-387-5222. E-mail: millet@yrl.ab.ca. Web Site: milletlibrary.ca. *Libr Mgr,* Margaret Blackstock
Pop 2,125
Library Holdings: Bk Vols 14,207
Mem of Yellowhead Regional Library
Open Tues-Thurs 10-8, Fri 10-5, Sat 10-3
Friends of the Library Group

MILO

P MILO MUNICIPAL LIBRARY*, Milo Library, 116 Center St, T0L 1L0. (Mail add: PO Box 30, T0L 1L0). Tel: 403-599-3850. FAX: 403-599-3924. E-mail: help@milolibrary.ca, libmil@milolibrary.ca. Web Site: www.milolibrary.ca. *Libr & Archives Mgr,* Joanne Monner
Founded 1983. Pop 350
Library Holdings: Audiobooks 205; Bks on Deafness & Sign Lang 15; Braille Volumes 4; CDs 40; DVDs 1,940; e-books 9,000; Large Print Bks 200; Music Scores 75; Bk Vols 16,000; Per Subs 12
Wireless access
Function: 24/7 Electronic res, 24/7 Online cat, Activity rm, Adult bk club, Adult literacy prog, Archival coll, Art exhibits, Audiobks on Playaways & MP3, Bk club(s), Bk reviews (Group), Bks on CD, Bus archives, Children's prog, Citizenship assistance, Computer training, Computers for patron use, Digital talking bks, Doc delivery serv, E-Readers, Electronic databases & coll, Equip loans & repairs, Family literacy, For res purposes, Free DVD rentals, Govt ref serv, ILL available, Internet access, Life-long learning prog for all ages, Literacy & newcomer serv, Magazines, Magnifiers for reading, Mail & tel request accepted, Mango lang, Meeting rooms, Movies, Museum passes, Music CDs, Online cat, Online info literacy tutorials on the web & in blackboard, Online ref, Outside serv via phone, mail, e-mail & web, OverDrive digital audio bks, Photocopying/Printing, Preschool reading prog, Printer for laptops & handheld devices, Prog for adults, Prog for children & young adult, Ref & res, Ref serv available, Res assist avail, Scanner, Senior computer classes, Spanish lang bks, Spoken cassettes & CDs, Spoken cassettes & DVDs, Story hour, Summer & winter reading prog, Summer reading prog, Wheelchair accessible, Workshops
Mem of Chinook Arch Regional Library System
Open Tues 10-5 & 6-8, Thurs & Fri 10-5
Friends of the Library Group

MORINVILLE

P MORINVILLE COMMUNITY LIBRARY*, 10125 100th Ave, T8R 1P8. SAN 325-1586. Tel: 780-939-3292. FAX: 780-939-2757. E-mail: info@morinvillelibrary.ca. Web Site: www.morinvillelibrary.ca. *Libr Mgr,* Isabelle Cramp; E-mail: director@morinvillelibrary.ca
Pop 9,890; Circ 75,000
Library Holdings: Bk Vols 28,724
Wireless access
Mem of Northern Lights Library System
Open Mon Noon-8, Tues-Thurs 10-8, Fri 10-4, Sat & Sun Noon-4
Friends of the Library Group

MORRIN

P MORRIN MUNICIPAL LIBRARY*, 113 Main St, T0J 2B0. (Mail add: PO Box 284, T0J 2B0). Tel: 403-772-3922. FAX: 403-772-3707. E-mail: amomlibrary@marigold.ab.ca. Web Site: www.morrinlibrary.ca.
Founded 1983. Pop 500
Automation Activity & Vendor Info: (Cataloging) Innovative Interfaces, Inc; (Circulation) Innovative Interfaces, Inc; (ILL) Innovative Interfaces, Inc; (OPAC) Innovative Interfaces, Inc
Wireless access
Mem of Marigold Library System
Open Tues-Thurs 12:30-4:30
Friends of the Library Group

MUNDARE

P MUNDARE MUNICIPAL PUBLIC LIBRARY*, 5128 50th St, T0B 3H0. (Mail add: PO Box 3, T0B 3H0). Tel: 780-764-3929. FAX: 780-764-2003. E-mail: librarian@mundarelibrary.ab.ca. Web Site: www.mundarelibrary.ab.ca. *Libr Mgr,* Evelyn Henke
Pop 855
Library Holdings: Bk Vols 7,200
Wireless access
Mem of Northern Lights Library System
Open Mon & Tues 12-6, Thurs 10-5

MYRNAM

P MYRNAM COMMUNITY LIBRARY*, New Myrnam School, 5105-50 St, T0B 3K0. (Mail add: Box 160, T0B 3K0). Tel: 780-366-3801. FAX: 780-366-2332. Web Site: www.myrnamlibrary.ab.ca. *Libr Mgr,* Ms D'Arcy Evans; E-mail: devans@myrnamlibrary.ab.ca; Staff 1 (Non-MLS 1)
Library Holdings: Bk Vols 4,000
Automation Activity & Vendor Info: (Cataloging) Innovative Interfaces, Inc; (Circulation) Innovative Interfaces, Inc; (OPAC) Innovative Interfaces, Inc
Wireless access
Function: 24/7 Electronic res, 24/7 Online cat, Accelerated reader prog
Mem of Northern Lights Library System
Partic in The Regional Automation Consortium
Open Mon, Wed & Fri 9-3:30, Tues & Thurs 9-7:30

NAMPA

P NAMPA MUNICIPAL LIBRARY*, 10203 99th Ave, T0H 2R0. (Mail add: PO Box 509, T0H 2R0). SAN 318-7063. Tel: 780-322-3805. FAX: 780-322-3955. E-mail: nlibrary@nampalibrary.ab.ca. Web Site: www.nampalibrary.ab.ca. *Libr Mgr,* Cathy Armstrong
Founded 1963. Pop 1,535; Circ 3,948
Library Holdings: Bk Vols 18,200; Per Subs 1
Subject Interests: Area hist
Wireless access
Mem of Peace Library System
Open Tues-Fri 10-12 & 1-5

NANTON

P THELMA FANNING MEMORIAL LIBRARY*, 1907 21 Ave, T0L 1R0. (Mail add: PO Box 310, T0L 1R0). SAN 318-7071. Tel: 403-646-5535. E-mail: help@nantonlibrary.ca. Web Site: www.nantonlibrary.ca. *Libr Mgr,* Gloria McGowan; E-mail: gmcgowan@nantonlibrary.ca
Founded 1908. Pop 2,132; Circ 14,323
Library Holdings: Bk Vols 14,107; Per Subs 26
Wireless access
Function: Homebound delivery serv
Mem of Chinook Arch Regional Library System
Special Services for the Blind - Audio mat; Bks on cassette; Bks on CD
Open Tues-Fri 10-5, Sat 11-4

NEERLANDIA

P NEERLANDIA PUBLIC LIBRARY*, 4918 50th St, T0G 1R0. SAN 318-708X. Tel: 780-674-5384. FAX: 780-674-2927. Web Site: neerlandialibrary.ab.ca. *Librn,* Ms Dagmar Visser; E-mail: dagmar.visser@pembinahills.ca
Founded 1973. Pop 1,000; Circ 28,000
Library Holdings: Bk Vols 12,865; Per Subs 33
Special Collections: Historical Books
Wireless access
Mem of Yellowhead Regional Library
Open Mon-Thurs 9-4:30

NEW SAREPTA

P NEW SAREPTA PUBLIC LIBRARY*, 5150 Centre St, T0B 3M0. (Mail add: PO Box 279, T0B 3M0). Tel: 780-975-7513. FAX: 780-941-2224. E-mail: newsareptalibrary@yrl.ab.ca. Web Site: www.newsareptalibrary.ca. *Libr Dir,* Angie Guderian
Founded 1976. Pop 3,500
Library Holdings: Bk Vols 9,280
Automation Activity & Vendor Info: (Acquisitions) Innovative Interfaces, Inc; (Cataloging) Innovative Interfaces, Inc; (Circulation) Innovative Interfaces, Inc; (ILL) Innovative Interfaces, Inc; (OPAC) Innovative Interfaces, Inc; (Serials) Innovative Interfaces, Inc
Wireless access
Mem of Yellowhead Regional Library
Partic in The Alberta Library; The Regional Automation Consortium
Special Services for the Blind - Daisy reader
Open Tues & Thurs 4-9, Sat 11-5
Friends of the Library Group

NEWBROOK

P NEWBROOK PUBLIC LIBRARY*, 4805 50th St, T0A 2P0. SAN 318-7098. Tel: 780-576-3772. E-mail: librarian@newbrooklibrary.ab.ca. Web Site: www.newbrooklibrary.ab.ca. *Libr Mgr,* Tracy Woloshyniuk; E-mail: twoloshyniuk@newbrooklibrary.ab.ca
Pop 750; Circ 7,000
Library Holdings: Bk Vols 9,500
Wireless access
Mem of Northern Lights Library System
Open Mon, Tues & Thurs 9:30-5, Wed 9:30-1:30

NITON JUNCTION

P NITON LIBRARY*, 5307 50th St, T7E 5A1. Tel: 780-795-2474. Web Site: www.yclibraries.ca/about-us/niton-library. *Libr Dir,* Robert McClure; E-mail: mcclureyclb@yrl.ab.ca; *Libr Mgr,* Toni Smigelski; E-mail: toniice@gypsd.ca
Wireless access
Mem of Yellowhead Regional Library
Open Mon-Wed 10-4:30, Thurs 12:30-8, Fri 10-2

NORDEGG

P NORDEGG PUBLIC LIBRARY*, General Delivery, T0M 2H0. Tel: 403-800-3667. FAX: 403-721-3930. E-mail: nordegglibrary@prl.ab.ca. Web Site: nordegglibrary.prl.ab.ca. *Libr Mgr,* Heather Clement
Circ 1,384
Library Holdings: Audiobooks 14; AV Mats 370; CDs 8; DVDs 25; High Interest/Low Vocabulary Bk Vols 100; Large Print Bks 12; Bk Titles 3,990; Bk Vols 4,000; Per Subs 6; Talking Bks 50; Videos 300
Special Collections: 120 ANF Canadiana Books; Agatha Christie Coll;; Board Books;. Canadian and Provincial
Subject Interests: Classics
Automation Activity & Vendor Info: (Acquisitions) Innovative Interfaces, Inc. - Polaris; (Cataloging) Innovative Interfaces, Inc. - Polaris; (Circulation) Innovative Interfaces, Inc. - Polaris; (Course Reserve) Innovative Interfaces, Inc. - Polaris; (Discovery) Innovative Interfaces, Inc. - Polaris; (ILL) Innovative Interfaces, Inc. - Polaris; (Media Booking) Innovative Interfaces, Inc. - Polaris; (OPAC) Innovative Interfaces, Inc. - Polaris; (Serials) Innovative Interfaces, Inc. - Polaris
Wireless access
Function: 24/7 Electronic res, 24/7 Online cat
Mem of Parkland Regional Library-Alberta
Open Mon 1-4, Tues 2-4, Wed 7pm-9pm, Thurs 12-3, Sun 2-4

OKOTOKS

P OKOTOKS PUBLIC LIBRARY*, 23 Riverside Dr W, T1S 1A6. (Mail add: PO Box 310 Stn Main, T1S 1A6), SAN 372-7130. Tel: 403-938-2220. E-mail: info@okotokslibrary.ca. Web Site: www.okotokslibrary.ca. *Dir,* Sarah Gillie; E-mail: librarian@okotokslibrary.ca; Staff 17 (MLS 3, Non-MLS 14)
Founded 1979. Pop 31,959; Circ 325,000
Library Holdings: Audiobooks 1,831; AV Mats 1,001; DVDs 6,339; Large Print Bks 990; Bk Vols 55,612; Per Subs 114
Automation Activity & Vendor Info: (Acquisitions) Innovative Interfaces, Inc; (Cataloging) Innovative Interfaces, Inc; (Circulation) Innovative Interfaces, Inc; (OPAC) Innovative Interfaces, Inc; (Serials) Innovative Interfaces, Inc
Wireless access
Mem of Marigold Library System
Open Mon-Thurs 10-9, Fri & Sat 10-5
Friends of the Library Group

OLDS

J OLDS COLLEGE LIBRARY*, 4500 50th St, T4H 1R6. SAN 318-7101. Tel: 403-507-7777. E-mail: library@oldscollege.ca. Web Site: www.oldscollege.ca/student-life/learning-commons. *Dir, Libr Serv,* Gordon Gilchrist
Founded 1968. Enrl 1,200; Fac 126
Library Holdings: Bk Vols 60,000; Per Subs 275
Special Collections: Canadian and Provincial
Subject Interests: Agr, Agr bus, Environ, Hort
Automation Activity & Vendor Info: (Acquisitions) SirsiDynix; (Cataloging) SirsiDynix; (Circulation) SirsiDynix; (OPAC) SirsiDynix
Wireless access
Partic in NEOS Library Consortium
Open Mon-Thurs 7:45am-11pm, Fri 7:45-6, Sat 11-5, Sun 2-10

P OLDS MUNICIPAL LIBRARY*, 5217 52nd St, T4H 1H7. SAN 372-686X. Tel: 403-556-6460. FAX: 403-556-6692. E-mail: oml@prl.ab.ca. Web Site: oml.prl.ab.ca. *Libr Mgr,* Lesley Winfield
Pop 8,200; Circ 93,000
Library Holdings: Audiobooks 3,000; AV Mats 6,000; CDs 1,000; DVDs 2,000; Large Print Bks 1,500; Bk Titles 38,000; Per Subs 60
Wireless access
Function: Adult bk club, Adult literacy prog, After school storytime, Art exhibits, Audio & video playback equip for onsite use, Bk club(s), Bks on CD, Children's prog, Citizenship assistance, Computer training, Computers for patron use, Electronic databases & coll, Equip loans & repairs, Family literacy, Genealogy discussion group, Holiday prog, Home delivery & serv to seniorr ctr & nursing homes, Homework prog, Music CDs, Photocopying/Printing, Preschool reading prog, Ref serv available, Scanner, Senior computer classes, Senior outreach, Serves people with intellectual disabilities, Spanish lang bks, Story hour, Summer & winter reading prog,

Tax forms, Teen prog, Telephone ref, Wheelchair accessible, Workshops, Writing prog
Mem of Parkland Regional Library-Alberta
Open Mon-Fri 9-6, Sat 12-5
Friends of the Library Group

ONOWAY

P ONOWAY PUBLIC LIBRARY*, 4708 Lac St Anne Trail, T0E 1V0. (Mail add: Box 484, T0E 1V0). Tel: 780-967-2445. FAX: 888-467-1309. E-mail: onowaylibrary@yrl.ab.ca. Web Site: www.onowaylibrary.ab.ca. *Libr Mgr,* Kelly L Huxley
Pop 1,036
Library Holdings: Bk Vols 15,127
Automation Activity & Vendor Info: (Acquisitions) Innovative Interfaces, Inc; (Cataloging) Innovative Interfaces, Inc; (Circulation) Innovative Interfaces, Inc; (ILL) Innovative Interfaces, Inc
Mem of Yellowhead Regional Library
Open Tues 1:30-7:30, Wed-Sat 10:30-4:30

OYEN

P OYEN MUNICIPAL LIBRARY*, 105 Third Ave W, T0J 2J0. (Mail add: Box 328, T0J 2J0), SAN 318-711X. Tel: 403-664-3644, Ext 2727. FAX: 403-664-2520. E-mail: aoymlibrary@marigold.ab.ca. Web Site: www.oyenlibrary.ca. *Libr Mgr,* Trish Fischbuch; *Librn,* Lois Bedwell
Pop 1,101; Circ 4,337
Library Holdings: Bk Vols 11,525; Per Subs 25
Wireless access
Mem of Marigold Library System
Partic in Marigold Regional Libr
Open Mon, Wed & Thurs 12-5, Tues 3-8
Friends of the Library Group

PADDLE PRAIRIE

P PADDLE PRAIRIE PUBLIC LIBRARY*, Box 58, T0H 2W0. Tel: 780-981-3100. FAX: 780-981-3737. E-mail: librarian@paddleprairielibrary.ab.ca. Web Site: www.paddleprairielibrary.ab.ca. *Libr Mgr,* Dawn Cardinal
Wireless access
Mem of Peace Library System

PARADISE VALLEY

P THREE CITIES PUBLIC LIBRARY*, Corner of Phillippe Ave & Park Ave, Box 89, T0B 3R0. Tel: 780-745-2277. FAX: 780-745-2641. E-mail: librarian@paradisevalleylibrary.ab.ca. Web Site: www.paradisevalleylibrary.ab.ca. *Libr Mgr,* Julie Brundage
Pop 152
Library Holdings: Bk Vols 10,000
Wireless access
Mem of Northern Lights Library System
Partic in The Alberta Library; The Regional Automation Consortium
Open Mon & Wed-Fri 9-3:30, Tues 9-8

PEACE RIVER

GL ALBERTA LAW LIBRARIES - PEACE RIVER, Courthouse, 9905 97 Ave, T8S 1S4. (Mail add: Bag 900-34, T8S 1S4), SAN 372-8862. Tel: 780-624-6418. Web Site: lawlibrary.ab.ca/our-libraries/peace-river. *Libr Coord,* Sandra Willing
Library Holdings: Bk Vols 10,500; Per Subs 50
Automation Activity & Vendor Info: (Acquisitions) Ex Libris Group; (Cataloging) Ex Libris Group; (Circulation) Ex Libris Group; (ILL) Ex Libris Group; (OPAC) Ex Libris Group; (Serials) Ex Libris Group
Function: ILL available
Open Mon & Tues 8:30-12 & 12:30-4, Wed 8:30am-11:50am
Restriction: Non-circulating to the pub

P PEACE RIVER MUNICIPAL LIBRARY*, 9807 97th Ave, T8S 1H6. SAN 318-7128. Tel: 780-624-4076. FAX: 780-624-4086. E-mail: info@prmlibrary.ab.ca. Web Site: www.prmlibrary.ab.ca. *Dir,* Channing Stenhouse; E-mail: director@prmlibrary.ab.ca
Pop 7,000; Circ 41,000
Library Holdings: Bk Vols 35,000
Wireless access
Mem of Peace Library System
Open Tues, Fri & Sat 10-5, Wed & Thurs 10-8
Friends of the Library Group

S PEACE RIVER MUSEUM, ARCHIVES & MACKENZIE CENTRE*, 10302 99th St, T8S 1K1. SAN 374-8847. Tel: 780-624-4261. E-mail: museum@peaceriver.ca. Web Site: peaceriver.ca/community-services/museum. *Archivist,* Emily Harris; E-mail: eharris@peaceriver.ca; Staff 2 (Non-MLS 2)
Founded 1967
Library Holdings: Bk Titles 500
Open Mon-Sat 10-5
Friends of the Library Group

PENHOLD

P PENHOLD & DISTRICT PUBLIC LIBRARY, Penhold Regional Multiplex, One Waskasoo Ave, T0M 1R0. (Mail add: PO Box 675, T0M 1R0), SAN 324-3788. Tel: 403-886-2636. FAX: 403-886-2638. E-mail: penholdlibrary@prl.ab.ca. Web Site: prl.ab.ca/penhold. *Libr Mgr,* Myra Binnendyk; Staff 5 (Non-MLS 5)
Founded 1981
Jan 2024-Dec 2024 Income (Main Library Only) (CAN) $248,989, Provincial (CAN) $28,953, City (CAN) $178,137, Federal (CAN) $4,042, County (CAN) $30,321, Locally Generated Income (CAN) $7,536
Wireless access
Function: 24/7 Electronic res, 24/7 Online cat, 3D Printer, Adult bk club, Art programs, Children's prog, Games, ILL available, Internet access, Movies, Photocopying/Printing, Prog for adults, Prog for children & young adult
Mem of Parkland Regional Library-Alberta
Open Tues, Thurs & Fri 10-5, Wed 10-8, Sat 10-3
Friends of the Library Group

PICTURE BUTTE

P PICTURE BUTTE MUNICIPAL LIBRARY, 120 Fourth St, T0K 1V0. (Mail add: PO Box 1130, T0K 1V0), SAN 318-7136. Tel: 403-732-4141. E-mail: help@picturebuttelibrary.ca. Web Site: www.picturebuttelibrary.ca.
Founded 1962. Pop 1,850; Circ 40,000
Library Holdings: Bk Vols 26,000
Special Collections: Dutch Book Coll
Wireless access
Mem of Chinook Arch Regional Library System
Open Tues & Thurs-Sat 10-5, Wed 10-7
Friends of the Library Group

PINCHER CREEK

P PINCHER CREEK & DISTRICT MUNICIPAL LIBRARY*, 899 Main St, Box 2020, T0K 1W0. SAN 318-7144. Tel: 403-627-3813. E-mail: help@pinchercreeklibrary.ca. Web Site: www.pinchercreeklibrary.ca. *Libr Mgr,* Kayla Lorenzen; Staff 1 (Non-MLS 1)
Pop 7,000; Circ 47,556
Library Holdings: Bk Vols 25,000; Per Subs 25
Wireless access
Mem of Chinook Arch Regional Library System
Special Services for the Blind - Audio mat; Bks available with recordings; Bks on CD; Talking bks
Open Mon & Fri 10-6, Tues-Thurs 10-8, Sat Noon-4
Friends of the Library Group

PONOKA

P PONOKA JUBILEE LIBRARY*, 5604 50 St, T4J 1G7. Tel: 403-783-3843. E-mail: ponokalibrary@prl.ab.ca. Web Site: ponokalibrary.com. *Libr Mgr,* Dan Galway
Library Holdings: Bk Vols 30,000
Wireless access
Mem of Parkland Regional Library-Alberta
Open Mon-Thurs 10-8, Fri 10-6, Sat 12-4

PROVOST

P PROVOST MUNICIPAL LIBRARY*, 5035 49th St, T0B 3S0. SAN 318-7160. Tel: 780-753-2801. FAX: 780-753-2801. E-mail: provostlibrary@prl.ab.ca. Web Site: provostlibrary.prl.ab.ca. *Libr Mgr,* Donna Engel
Founded 1950. Pop 1,800; Circ 7,072
Library Holdings: Bk Vols 8,473
Wireless access
Mem of Parkland Regional Library-Alberta
Open Mon, Wed & Thurs 12-6, Tues 1-7, Fri 10-5

RADWAY

P RADWAY PUBLIC LIBRARY, 4915 50th St, T0A 2V0. (Mail add: PO Box 220, T0A 2V0). Tel: 780-736-3548. E-mail: librarian@radwaylibrary.ab.ca. Web Site: www.radwaylibrary.ab.ca. *Libr Mgr,* Sandra Moschansky
Founded 1943
Library Holdings: Bk Vols 12,000
Wireless access
Mem of Northern Lights Library System
Special Services for the Deaf - Bks on deafness & sign lang

Special Services for the Blind - Accessible computers; Bks on CD; Computer access aids; Daisy reader; Large print bks
Open Tues & Thurs 11-6, Wed 9:30-5
Friends of the Library Group

RAINBOW LAKE

P RAINBOW LAKE MUNICIPAL LIBRARY, One Atco Rd, T0H 2Y0. (Mail add: PO Box 266, T0H 2Y0). Tel: 780-956-3656. FAX: 780-956-3858. E-mail: librarian@rainbowlakelibrary.ab.ca. Web Site: www.rainbowlakelibrary.ab.ca. *Librn,* Maria Fajardo; *Librn,* Suzanne Pankiw
Library Holdings: Bk Vols 11,000
Automation Activity & Vendor Info: (Acquisitions) Innovative Interfaces, Inc; (Cataloging) Innovative Interfaces, Inc; (Circulation) Innovative Interfaces, Inc; (ILL) Innovative Interfaces, Inc
Wireless access
Mem of Peace Library System
Open Mon-Thurs 10-5

RAINER

P ALCOMA COMMUNITY LIBRARY, Alcoma School, T0J 2M0. (Mail add: PO Box 120, T0J 2M0). Tel: 403-362-3741. Web Site: alcoma.shortgrass.ca. *Libr Mgr,* Janet Wagner; E-mail: alcoma.manager@shortgrass.ca
Wireless access
Mem of Shortgrass Library System
Open Mon-Wed & Fri 10-3, Thurs 10-3 & 6:30-8

RALSTON

P GRAHAM COMMUNITY LIBRARY*, Ralston Community Ctr, R35 Dugway Dr, T0J 2N0. (Mail add: PO Box 40, T0J 2N0), SAN 318-7187. Tel: 403-544-3670. FAX: 403-544-3814. E-mail: gracirc@shortgrass.ca. Web Site: graham.shortgrass.ca. *Libr Mgr,* Stefanie Schranz; E-mail: graham.manager@shortgrass.ca; Staff 2 (Non-MLS 2)
Founded 1954. Pop 7,500; Circ 15,000
Library Holdings: Bk Vols 20,000; Per Subs 10
Special Collections: Military History Coll
Subject Interests: British authors
Wireless access
Function: 24/7 Electronic res, 24/7 Online cat, After school storytime, ILL available, Internet access, Laminating, Magazines, Mail loans to mem, Mango lang, Movies, Online cat, Online info literacy tutorials on the web & in blackboard, Online ref, Orientations, Outreach serv, Outside serv via phone, mail, e-mail & web, OverDrive digital audio bks, Photocopying/Printing, Preschool outreach, Preschool reading prog, Prof lending libr, Prog for children & young adult, Ref & res, Ref serv available, Scanner, Senior outreach, Teen prog, Writing prog
Mem of Shortgrass Library System
Open Mon, Wed & Fri 10-4, Tues & Thurs 10-7, Sat 10-3

RAYMOND

P RAYMOND PUBLIC LIBRARY*, 15 Broadway S, T0K 2S0. (Mail add: PO Box 258, T0K 2S0). Tel: 403-752-4785. FAX: 587-271-4710. E-mail: help@raymondlibrary.ca. Web Site: www.raymondlibrary.ca. *Libr Mgr,* Faye Geddes; E-mail: fgeddes@raymondlibrary.ca
Founded 1931. Pop 3,200; Circ 17,894
Library Holdings: Bk Vols 26,000
Wireless access
Mem of Chinook Arch Regional Library System
Special Services for the Blind - Reader equip
Open Mon 10-12 & 1-5, Tues-Fri 10-12 & 1-6, Sat 9-Noon
Friends of the Library Group

RED DEER

M ALBERTA HEALTH SERVICES*, Red Deer Regional Hospital Centre Knowledge Resource Services, 3942 50A Ave, T4N 4E7. SAN 324-4121. Tel: 403-343-4557. FAX: 403-343-4910. E-mail: krs@ahs.ca. Web Site: krs.libguides.com/library_card. *Dir,* Morgan Truax; E-mail: morgan.truax@albertahealthservices.ca
Founded 1980
Library Holdings: AV Mats 244; Bk Titles 863; Bk Vols 4,701; Per Subs 355
Special Collections: Consumer Health Coll; Personal Resource Coll
Subject Interests: Allied health, Med, Nursing
Wireless access
Open Mon-Fri 8-4:15
Friends of the Library Group

GL ALBERTA LAW LIBRARIES - RED DEER*, Courthouse, 4909 - 48 Ave, T4N 3T5. SAN 375-0329. Tel: 403-340-5499. E-mail: lawlibrary@just.gov.ab.ca. Web Site: www.lawlibrary.ab.ca/our-libraries/red-deer. *Dir,* Dale Barrie; E-mail: dale.barrie@gov.ab.ca; Staff 2 (Non-MLS 2)
Automation Activity & Vendor Info: (Acquisitions) Ex Libris Group; (Cataloging) Ex Libris Group; (Circulation) Ex Libris Group; (ILL) Ex Libris Group; (OPAC) Ex Libris Group; (Serials) Ex Libris Group
Open Mon-Fri 8:30-4:30

G RED DEER & DISTRICT ARCHIVES*, 4525 47 A Ave, T4N 3T4. (Mail add: PO Box 5008, T4N 3T4), SAN 373-8280. Tel: 403-309-8403. FAX: 403-340-8728. E-mail: archives@reddeer.ca. Web Site: www.reddeer.ca/about-red-deer/history/archives. *Archivist,* Jillian Staniec; Staff 4 (Non-MLS 4)
Founded 1964
Library Holdings: Bk Titles 2,000; Per Subs 10
Special Collections: Alberta Genealogical Society; City of Red Deer Coll. Oral History
Subject Interests: Genealogy, Local hist
Open Mon-Fri 9-4:30

J RED DEER COLLEGE LIBRARY*, 100 College Blvd, T4N 5H5. (Mail add: PO Box 5005, T4N 5H5), SAN 318-7209. Tel: 403-342-3344. FAX: 403-346-8500. E-mail: rdclibrary@gmail.com. Web Site: rdc.ab.ca/current-students/library. *Dir, Libr Serv,* Kristine Plastow; Tel: 403-342-3578; *Librn,* Michelle Edwards Thomson; Tel: 403-342-3346, E-mail: michelle.edwards.thomson@rdc.ab.ca; *Librn,* Yvonne Phillips; Tel: 403-342-4855, E-mail: yvonne.phillips@rdc.ab.ca; *Librn,* Teneil Vuori; Tel: 403-342-3478, E-mail: teneil.vuori@rdc.ab.ca; *Coordr, Learning Commons,* Barb Mahoney; Tel: 403-342-3575, E-mail: barbara.mahoney@rdc.ab.ca; *Tech Coordr,* Lillian Teh-Frenette; Tel: 403-342-3353, E-mail: lillian.tehfrenette@rdc.ab.ca; Staff 30 (MLS 11, Non-MLS 19)
Founded 1964. Enrl 3,570; Fac 210
Library Holdings: Bk Vols 150,000
Automation Activity & Vendor Info: (OPAC) Bibliomation Inc
Wireless access
Partic in NEOS Library Consortium; The Alberta Library
Open Mon-Thurs 7:45am-9pm, Fri 7:45-5, Sat 9-5, Sun Noon-8 (Fall & Winter); Mon-Fri 7:45-5 (Summer)

P RED DEER PUBLIC LIBRARY, 4818 49th St, T4N 1T9. SAN 318-7217. Tel: 403-346-4576. FAX: 403-341-3110. Web Site: www.rdpl.org. *Chief Exec Officer,* Shelley Ross; E-mail: sross@rdpl.org; Staff 9 (MLS 7, Non-MLS 2)
Founded 1914. Pop 97,000; Circ 813,000
Library Holdings: Bk Titles 139,000; Bk Vols 185,000; Per Subs 180
Automation Activity & Vendor Info: (Acquisitions) SirsiDynix-WorkFlows; (Cataloging) SirsiDynix-WorkFlows; (Circulation) SirsiDynix-WorkFlows; (OPAC) BiblioCommons; (Serials) SirsiDynix-WorkFlows
Wireless access
Function: Adult bk club, Adult literacy prog, Art exhibits, Audiobks via web, Bk club(s), Chess club, Children's prog, Computers for patron use, Electronic databases & coll, Family literacy, Free DVD rentals, Homebound delivery serv, ILL available, Microfiche/film & reading machines, Music CDs, Online cat, OverDrive digital audio bks, Photocopying/Printing, Preschool outreach, Preschool reading prog, Prog for adults, Prog for children & young adult, Ref serv available, Story hour, Summer & winter reading prog, Teen prog, Telephone ref, Wheelchair accessible
Publications: LINK
Special Services for the Blind - PC for people with disabilities
Open Mon-Thurs 9:30-8:30, Fri & Sat 9:30-5:30, Sun 1:30-5
Friends of the Library Group
Branches: 2
DAWE BRANCH, 56 Holt St, T4N 6A6. Tel: 403-341-3822. FAX: 403-343-2120. *Librn,* Tatyana Tilly
Library Holdings: Bk Vols 50,000
Automation Activity & Vendor Info: (Acquisitions) BiblioCommons; (Cataloging) BiblioCommons; (Circulation) BiblioCommons; (Serials) BiblioCommons
Open Mon-Thurs 9:30-8:30, Fri 9:30-5:30, Sat 12-4
TIMBERLANDS BRANCH, 300 Timothy Dr, T4P 0L1. *Librn,* Candice Putnam
Open Mon-Thurs 9-8:30, Fri 9-5, Sat 12-5

RED EARTH CREEK

P RED EARTH PUBLIC LIBRARY*, 115 Sandy Lane, T0G 1X0. (Mail add: PO Box 390, T0G 1X0). Tel: 780-649-3898. FAX: 780-694-3860. E-mail: librarian@redearthlibrary.ab.ca. Web Site: www.redearthlibrary.ab.ca. *Libr Mgr,* Lisa Deering
Wireless access
Mem of Peace Library System
Open Mon, Wed & Fri 8:30-4:30

REDCLIFF

P REDCLIFF PUBLIC LIBRARY*, 131 Main St S, T0J 2P0. (Mail add: PO Box 280, T0J 2P0), SAN 320-5258. Tel: 403-548-3335. FAX: 403-548-6295. E-mail: redcliff.manager@shortgrass.ca. Web Site: redcliff.shortgrass.ca. *Libr Mgr,* Tracy Laturnus
Founded 1967. Pop 5,500; Circ 48,865
Library Holdings: CDs 529; DVDs 1,248; e-books 828; Electronic Media & Resources 236; Bk Vols 16,601; Per Subs 85; Talking Bks 676
Wireless access
Mem of Shortgrass Library System
Special Services for the Deaf - Bks on deafness & sign lang; Closed caption videos
Special Services for the Blind - Bks on CD; Braille bks; Daisy reader; Large print bks; Talking bks
Open Mon-Thurs 10-8, Fri & Sat 10-6
Friends of the Library Group

REDWATER

P REDWATER PUBLIC LIBRARY*, 4915 48th St, T0A 2W0. (Mail add: PO Box 384, T0A 2W0), SAN 318-7225. Tel: 780-942-3464. Web Site: www.redwaterlibrary.ab.ca. *Library Services, Mgr,* Alicea Paszek; E-mail: director@redwaterlibrary.ab.ca
Pop 2,172; Circ 40,000
Automation Activity & Vendor Info: (Acquisitions) Innovative Interfaces, Inc; (Cataloging) Innovative Interfaces, Inc; (Circulation) Innovative Interfaces, Inc; (ILL) Innovative Interfaces, Inc; (OPAC) Innovative Interfaces, Inc; (Serials) Innovative Interfaces, Inc
Wireless access
Mem of Northern Lights Library System
Special Services for the Blind - Accessible computers; Assistive/Adapted tech devices, equip & products; Bks on cassette; Bks on CD; Daisy reader; Large print bks; Mags & bk reproduction/duplication; Talking bks
Open Tues-Thurs 11-7, Fri 10-6, Sat 10-4
Friends of the Library Group

RIMBEY

P RIMBEY MUNICIPAL LIBRARY*, 4938 50th Ave, T0C 2J0. (Mail add: Box 1130, T0C 2J0). Tel: 403-843-2841. E-mail: rimbeylibrarian@prl.ab.ca. Web Site: rimbeylibrary.prl.ab.ca. *Libr Mgr,* Jean Keetch
Pop 2,496
Library Holdings: Bk Vols 20,765
Wireless access
Mem of Parkland Regional Library-Alberta
Open Tues-Sat 10-5
Friends of the Library Group

ROCHESTER

P ROCHESTER MUNICIPAL LIBRARY*, 5202-47 St, T0G 1Z0. (Mail add: PO Box 309, T0G 1Z0). Tel: 780-698-3970. FAX: 780-698-2290. E-mail: librarian@rochesterlibrary.ab.ca. Web Site: www.rochesterlibrary.ab.ca. *Libr Mgr,* Tammy Morey
Founded 1986. Pop 600
Library Holdings: AV Mats 300; Bks on Deafness & Sign Lang 50; High Interest/Low Vocabulary Bk Vols 300; Large Print Bks 60; Bk Titles 13,000; Per Subs 12; Talking Bks 20
Special Collections: Local History. Oral History
Wireless access
Publications: Rochester Library Newsletter (Monthly)
Mem of Northern Lights Library System
Open Mon 12-4, Wed 4-7:30, Thurs 11-7
Friends of the Library Group

ROCKY MOUNTAIN HOUSE

P ROCKY MOUNTAIN HOUSE PUBLIC LIBRARY*, 4922 52nd St, T4T 1B1. (Mail add: Box 1497, T4T 1B1). Tel: 403-845-2042. FAX: 403-845-5633. E-mail: armh@prl.ab.ca. Web Site: rmhlibrary.prl.ab.ca. *Libr Mgr,* Ben Worth
Pop 8,000; Circ 87,028
Library Holdings: Large Print Bks 40; Bk Vols 38,400; Per Subs 50; Talking Bks 70
Automation Activity & Vendor Info: (Acquisitions) Horizon; (Cataloging) Horizon; (Circulation) Horizon; (ILL) Horizon; (Serials) Horizon
Wireless access
Function: Homebound delivery serv, ILL available, Mail loans to mem, Photocopying/Printing
Mem of Parkland Regional Library-Alberta
Special Services for the Blind - Braille bks; Large print bks
Open Mon, Wed & Fri 10-6, Tues & Thurs 10-8, Sat 11-5
Friends of the Library Group

ROCKYFORD

P ROCKYFORD MUNICIPAL LIBRARY*, Community Ctr, 412 Serviceberry Trail, T0J 2R0. (Mail add: PO Box 277, T0J 2R0), SAN 321-0162. Tel: 403-533-3964. E-mail: armlibrary@marigold.ab.ca. Web Site: www.rockyfordlibrary.ca. *Libr Mgr,* Jocelyne Kisko; Staff 2 (Non-MLS 2)
Founded 1963. Pop 316
Library Holdings: Audiobooks 80; DVDs 350; Large Print Bks 100; Bk Titles 4,700; Per Subs 7
Subject Interests: Local hist
Wireless access
Function: 24/7 Electronic res, 24/7 Online cat, Activity rm, Adult bk club, Art exhibits, Audiobks via web, Bk club(s), Bks on CD, Children's prog, Computers for patron use, Electronic databases & coll, Free DVD rentals, Holiday prog, ILL available, Internet access, Life-long learning prog for all ages, Magazines, Mail & tel request accepted, Movies, OverDrive digital audio bks, Photocopying/Printing, Printer for laptops & handheld devices, Prog for adults, Prog for children & young adult, Scanner
Mem of Marigold Library System
Special Services for the Blind - Daisy reader
Open Tues 12-6, Wed & Thurs 2-8
Restriction: Circ to mem only, In-house use for visitors

ROLLING HILLS

P ROLLING HILLS PUBLIC LIBRARY*, 322 Fourth St, T0J 2S0. (Mail add: Box 40, T0J 2S0). Tel: 403-964-2186. E-mail: rolcirc@shortgrass.ca. Web Site: rollinghills.shortgrass.ca. *Libr Mgr,* Johnene Amulung
Library Holdings: Bk Vols 23,000
Automation Activity & Vendor Info: (Cataloging) BiblioCommons; (Circulation) BiblioCommons
Wireless access
Mem of Shortgrass Library System
Open Mon 7pm-9pm, Wed 9-3 & 7-9

ROSEMARY

P ROSEMARY COMMUNITY LIBRARY*, Rosemary School, 622 Dahlia St, T0J 2W0. (Mail add: PO Box 210, T0J 2W0), SAN 318-7233. Tel: 403-378-4493, Ext 150. FAX: 403-378-4388. Web Site: rosemary.shortgrass.ca. *Libr Mgr,* Vanessa Plett; E-mail: vanessa@shortgrass.ca
Pop 366; Circ 7,000
Library Holdings: Bk Vols 11,000
Wireless access
Mem of Shortgrass Library System
Open Mon, Wed & Fri 9-3, Tues & Thurs 9-8; Thurs (Summer) 10-6

RUMSEY

P RUMSEY COMMUNITY LIBRARY*, 229 Main St, T0J 2Y0. (Mail add: PO Box 113, T0J 2Y0). Tel: 403-368-3939. E-mail: arumlibrary@marigold.ab.ca. Web Site: www.rumseylibrary.ca. *Libr Mgr,* Patty Steen
Founded 1978. Pop 300
Library Holdings: Audiobooks 150; AV Mats 50; DVDs 50; Large Print Bks 15; Bk Titles 4,734; Bk Vols 5,000; Per Subs 10
Subject Interests: Gardening
Wireless access
Mem of Marigold Library System
Open Tues & Wed 11-6

RYCROFT

P RYCROFT MUNICIPAL LIBRARY*, 4732-50 St, T0H 3A0. (Mail add: PO Box 248, T0H 3A0). Tel: 780-765-3973. E-mail: librarian@rycroftlibrary.ab.ca. Web Site: www.rycroftlibrary.ab.ca. *Libr Mgr,* Amy Verquin
Pop 609
Library Holdings: Bk Vols 7,000
Wireless access
Mem of Peace Library System
Open Wed 12-7, Thurs 10-5, Sat 12-4

RYLEY

P MCPHERSON MUNICIPAL LIBRARY*, 5113 50 St, T0B 4A0. (Mail add: PO Box 139, T0B 4A0). Tel: 780-663-3999. FAX: 780-663-3909. E-mail: librarian@mcphersonlibrary.ab.ca. Web Site: www.mcphersonlibrary.ab.ca. *Libr Mgr,* Kimberly Murphy; Staff 1 (Non-MLS 1)
Pop 480
Library Holdings: Bk Vols 10,000
Wireless access
Function: Photocopying/Printing, Prog for children & young adult

Mem of Northern Lights Library System
Special Services for the Blind - Large print bks; Reader equip
Open Mon & Thurs 3-6, Tues & Fri 11-6, Wed 1-4, Sat Noon-3
Friends of the Library Group

SANGUDO

P SANGUDO PUBLIC LIBRARY*, 5028 50 Ave, T0E 2A0. (Mail add: PO Box 524, T0E 2A0), SAN 318-725X. Tel: 780-785-2955. FAX: 780-785-2955. E-mail: sangudolibrary@yrl.ab.ca. Web Site: www.sangudolibrary.ca. *Libr Mgr,* Sandra Stepaniuk; *Libr Asst,* Mary Lynn Phillips
Pop 1,308; Circ 2,363
Library Holdings: DVDs 1,084; Large Print Bks 200; Bk Titles 6,595; Bk Vols 8,384; Talking Bks 165
Wireless access
Mem of Yellowhead Regional Library
Open Tues & Thurs 3-8, Fri 11-4
Friends of the Library Group

SEBA BEACH

P SEBA BEACH PUBLIC LIBRARY*, 140 Third St, T0E 2B0. (Mail add: PO Box 159, Tomahawk, T0E 2B0). Tel: 780-797-3940. FAX: 780-797-3800. E-mail: sebabeachlibrary@yrl.ab.ca. Web Site: www.sebabeachlibrary.ab.ca. *Libr Mgr,* Cheryl Taillieu
Pop 137
Library Holdings: Bk Vols 11,000
Special Collections: Movies that Won the Academy Award for Best Picture
Automation Activity & Vendor Info: (Acquisitions) SirsiDynix; (Cataloging) SirsiDynix; (Circulation) SirsiDynix; (Course Reserve) SirsiDynix; (ILL) SirsiDynix; (Media Booking) SirsiDynix; (OPAC) SirsiDynix; (Serials) SirsiDynix
Wireless access
Mem of Yellowhead Regional Library
Partic in The Regional Automation Consortium
Open Tues-Sat 10-5 (Summer)

SEDGEWICK

P SEDGEWICK & DISTRICT MUNICIPAL LIBRARY*, 5011 51st Ave, T0B 4C0. (Mail add: PO Box 569, T0B 4C0). Tel: 780-384-3003. FAX: 780-384-3003. E-mail: sedgewicklibrary@prl.ab.ca. Web Site: sedgpublib.prl.ab.ca. *Libr Mgr,* Barb McConnell
Pop 867
Library Holdings: Bk Vols 11,250
Wireless access
Mem of Parkland Regional Library-Alberta
Open Mon & Wed 5:30pm-8:30pm, Tues & Thurs 12-5:30, Sat 10-1
Friends of the Library Group

SEXSMITH

CR PEACE RIVER BIBLE INSTITUTE LIBRARY*, 9601 100th St, T0H 3C0. (Mail add: Box 99, T0H 3C0), SAN 323-7648. Tel: 780-568-3962. FAX: 780-568-4431. E-mail: library@prbi.edu. Web Site: prbi.daphnis.opalsinfo.net, www.prbi.edu. *Librn,* Scott Butler
Founded 1933. Fac 15; Highest Degree: Bachelor
Library Holdings: Bk Vols 33,000
Subject Interests: Theol
Automation Activity & Vendor Info: (Acquisitions) OPALS (Open-source Automated Library System); (Cataloging) OPALS (Open-source Automated Library System); (Circulation) OPALS (Open-source Automated Library System)
Wireless access
Open Mon 3-5,Tues & Wed 1-5 & 7-9, Thurs 1-2 & 4-5, Fri 1-5, Sat Noon-5
Restriction: Non-circulating

P SHANNON MUNICIPAL LIBRARY, Sexsmith Civic Centre, 9917 99th Ave, T0H 3C0. (Mail add: PO Box 266, T0H 3C0), SAN 318-7268. Tel: 780-568-4333. FAX: 780-568-7249. E-mail: librarian@shannonlibrary.ab.ca. Web Site: www.shannonlibrary.ab.ca. *Libr Dir,* Sheryl Pelletier
Founded 1946. Pop 2,620; Circ 40,000
Library Holdings: CDs 550; DVDs 800; Bk Vols 18,553; Per Subs 22
Automation Activity & Vendor Info: (Cataloging) Innovative Interfaces, Inc; (Circulation) Innovative Interfaces, Inc; (Course Reserve) Innovative Interfaces, Inc; (OPAC) Innovative Interfaces, Inc
Wireless access
Function: 24/7 Online cat, Audiobks via web, Bk club(s), Bks on CD, Children's prog, Electronic databases & coll, Free DVD rentals, ILL available, Instruction & testing, Internet access, Laminating, Magazines, OverDrive digital audio bks, Photocopying/Printing, Printer for laptops & handheld devices, Prog for children & young adult, Ref serv available, Summer reading prog
Mem of Peace Library System
Partic in The Alberta Library; The Regional Automation Consortium
Open Tues & Fri 10-5:30, Wed & Thurs 10-7, Sat 12-4
Friends of the Library Group

SHERWOOD PARK

P STRATHCONA COUNTY LIBRARY, 401 Festival Lane, T8A 5P7. SAN 318-7276. Tel: 780-410-8600. Administration Tel: 780-410-8606. E-mail: info@sclibrary.ca. Web Site: www.sclibrary.ca. *Chief Exec Officer,* Sharon Siga; E-mail: ssiga@sclibrary.ca; *Adult Serv Mgr,* Mark McHale; E-mail: mmchale@sclibrary.ca; *Youth Serv Mgr,* Kerry Vandenhengel; E-mail: kvandenhengel@sclibrary.ca; Staff 100 (MLS 27, Non-MLS 73)
Founded 1977. Pop 103,829; Circ 1,377,269
Jan 2024-Dec 2024 Income (CAN) $12,396,223, Provincial (CAN) $559,934, County (CAN) $11,073,279, Locally Generated Income (CAN) $763,010. Mats Exp (CAN) $1,005,069, Books (CAN) $463,598, Per/Ser (Incl. Access Fees) (CAN) $24,381, AV Mat (CAN) $75,100, Electronic Ref Mat (Incl. Access Fees) (CAN) $441,990. Sal (CAN) $5,952,794 (Prof (CAN) $1,273,779)
Library Holdings: Audiobooks 4,199; CDs 7,357; DVDs 21,554; e-books 46,673; e-journals 5,714; Large Print Bks 4,310; Microforms 544; Bk Titles 152,647; Bk Vols 201,930; Per Subs 234
Subject Interests: Local hist
Automation Activity & Vendor Info: (Acquisitions) SirsiDynix; (Cataloging) SirsiDynix; (Circulation) SirsiDynix; (Discovery) BiblioCommons; (ILL) Relais International; (OPAC) BiblioCommons
Wireless access
Function: 24/7 Electronic res, 24/7 Online cat, 24/7 wireless access, Adult bk club, Adult literacy prog, Audio & video playback equip for onsite use, Audiobks on Playaways & MP3, Audiobks via web, AV serv, Bk club(s), Bks on CD, Chess club, Children's prog, Citizenship assistance, Computer training, Computers for patron use, Digital talking bks, E-Readers, Electronic databases & coll, Extended outdoor wifi, Family literacy, Free DVD rentals, Games & aids for people with disabilities, Genealogy discussion group, Holiday prog, Home delivery & serv to seniorr ctr & nursing homes, Homebound delivery serv, Homework prog, ILL available, Instruction & testing, Internet access, Laptop/tablet checkout, Large print keyboards, Life-long learning prog for all ages, Literacy & newcomer serv, Magazines, Magnifiers for reading, Mail & tel request accepted, Meeting rooms, Microfiche/film & reading machines, Movies, Music CDs, Online cat, Online info literacy tutorials on the web & in blackboard, Online ref, Orientations, Outreach serv, Outside serv via phone, mail, e-mail & web, OverDrive digital audio bks, Photocopying/Printing, Preschool outreach, Preschool reading prog, Printer for laptops & handheld devices, Prog for adults, Prog for children & young adult, Ref & res, Ref serv available, Res assist avail, Satellite serv, Scanner, Senior computer classes, Senior outreach, Serves people with intellectual disabilities, Spoken cassettes & CDs, Spoken cassettes & DVDs, STEM programs, Story hour, Study rm, Summer & winter reading prog, Tax forms, Teen prog, Telephone ref, Visual arts prog, Wheelchair accessible, Winter reading prog, Workshops, Writing prog
Publications: Strathcona County Library Program Guide (Quarterly)
Partic in The Alberta Library
Special Services for the Deaf - Assisted listening device; Assistive tech; Bks on deafness & sign lang; Captioned film dep; High interest/low vocabulary bks
Special Services for the Blind - Accessible computers; Aids for in-house use; Assistive/Adapted tech devices, equip & products; Audio mat; Bks & mags in Braille, on rec, tape & cassette; Bks available with recordings; Bks on CD; Braille bks; Children's Braille; Computer access aids; Computer with voice synthesizer for visually impaired persons; Copier with enlargement capabilities; Daisy reader; Digital talking bk; Digital talking bk machines; Extensive large print coll; Free checkout of audio mat; Home delivery serv; Internet workstation with adaptive software; Large print bks; Large print bks & talking machines; Large screen computer & software; Low vision equip; Magnifiers; Micro-computer access & training; PC for people with disabilities; Playaways (bks on MP3); Premier adaptive tech software; Reader equip; Reading & writing aids; Recorded bks; Screen enlargement software for people with visual disabilities; Screen reader software; Talking bks; Talking bks & player equip; ZoomText magnification & reading software
Open Mon-Fri 9:30-9, Sat 9:30-5, Sun 1-5
Friends of the Library Group
Bookmobiles: 1. Mgr, Diana Balbar. Bk titles 18,000

SILVER VALLEY

P SAVANNA MUNICIPAL LIBRARY*, Box 49, T0H 3E0. Tel: 780-351-3771. FAX: 780-864-1623. Web Site: www.savannalibrary.ca. *Libr Mgr,* Alison Wiebe; E-mail: librarian@savannalibrary.ca
Mem of Peace Library System
Open Mon & Wed 3-6, Sat 10-1

SLAVE LAKE

J NORTHERN LAKES COLLEGE LIBRARY*, 1201 Main St SE, T0G 2A3. SAN 370-6613. Tel: 780-849-8670. Toll Free Tel: 866-652-3456, Ext 8670. FAX: 780-849-2570. Web Site: www.nlclibrary.ca. *Dir, Libr Serv,* Shiloa Thomas; *Libr Asst,* Kaitlin Kirk; Staff 3 (MLS 2, Non-MLS 1)
Founded 1989. Enrl 1,000; Fac 104
Library Holdings: AV Mats 4,000; Bk Vols 37,500; Per Subs 300
Special Collections: Native Canadians Coll
Automation Activity & Vendor Info: (Acquisitions) SirsiDynix; (Cataloging) SirsiDynix; (Circulation) SirsiDynix; (Course Reserve) SirsiDynix; (Media Booking) SirsiDynix; (OPAC) SirsiDynix; (Serials) SirsiDynix
Wireless access
Open Mon-Fri 8:15-4:30

P ROTARY CLUB OF SLAVE LAKE PUBLIC LIBRARY*, 50 Main St SW, T0G 2A0. (Mail add: PO Box 540, T0G 2A0). SAN 372-669X. Tel: 780-849-5250. FAX: 780-849-3275. E-mail: librarian@slavelakelibrary.ab.ca. Web Site: www.slavelakelibrary.ab.ca. *Libr Mgr,* Kendra McRee; *Asst Librn,* Megan Spaner; *Outreach & Prog Coordr,* Suzanne Wilson; *Archivist,* Lyndsey Carmichael; Staff 7 (MLS 1, Non-MLS 6)
Founded 1972. Pop 10,000; Circ 36,000
Library Holdings: Bk Titles 25,000; Per Subs 25
Wireless access
Mem of Peace Library System
Partic in The Regional Automation Consortium
Open Mon-Fri 10-4

SMITH

P SMITH COMMUNITY LIBRARY*, 1005 Ninth St, T0G 2B0. (Mail add: PO Box 134, T0G 2B0). Tel: 780-829-2389. FAX: 780-829-2389. E-mail: librarian@smithlibrary.ab.ca. Web Site: www.smithlibrary.ab.ca. *Regional Libr Mgr,* Kendra McRee; Tel: 780-849-5250
Library Holdings: Bk Vols 25,000; Per Subs 10
Wireless access
Mem of Peace Library System
Partic in The Regional Automation Consortium
Open Tues 12-7, Wed 12:30-3:30, Thurs 12-6

SMOKY LAKE

P SMOKY LAKE MUNICIPAL LIBRARY*, 5010-50 St, T0A 3C0. (Mail add: PO Box 490, T0A 3C0). SAN 318-7284. Tel: 780-656-4212. FAX: 780-656-4212. E-mail: librarian@smokylakelibrary.ab.ca. Web Site: www.smokylakelibrary.ab.ca. *Libr Mgr,* Lise van der Vaart; Staff 1 (Non-MLS 1)
Founded 1941. Pop 1,000
Library Holdings: DVDs 620; Bk Vols 12,140; Per Subs 16; Talking Bks 50
Wireless access
Function: 24/7 Electronic res, 24/7 Online cat, Adult bk club, After school storytime, Audiobks via web, Bks on CD, Children's prog, Electronic databases & coll, Free DVD rentals, ILL available, Internet access, Magazines, Online cat, Photocopying/Printing, Preschool reading prog, Scanner, Summer reading prog
Mem of Northern Lights Library System
Open Mon 3-7, Tues & Wed 10-12 & 2-6, Thurs 2-6, Fri 2-5

SPIRIT RIVER

P SPIRIT RIVER MUNICIPAL LIBRARY, 4816 44th Ave, T0H 3G0. (Mail add: Box 490, T0H 3G0). SAN 318-7292. Tel: 780-864-4038. Web Site: spiritriverlibrary.ab.ca. *Librn,* Tracy Skoworodko; E-mail: librarian@spiritriverlibrary.ab.ca
Pop 1,104; Circ 5,504
Library Holdings: Bk Vols 9,800
Wireless access
Mem of Peace Library System
Open Tues 10-6, Thurs 1-8, Sat 12-5

SPRUCE GROVE

P SPRUCE GROVE PUBLIC LIBRARY*, 35 Fifth Ave, T7X 2C5. SAN 318-7306. Tel: 780-962-4423. FAX: 780-962-4826. E-mail: library@sgpl.ca. Web Site: www.sgpl.ca. *Dir, Libr Serv,* Leanne Myggland-Carter; E-mail: leanne@sgpl.ca; *Executive Asst,* Tiffany Gamboa; E-mail: tiffany@sgpl.ca; Staff 27 (MLS 4, Non-MLS 23)
Founded 1961
Library Holdings: Audiobooks 2,659; Braille Volumes 7; CDs 3,822; DVDs 8,997; Large Print Bks 1,061; Bk Vols 54,306; Per Subs 30
Special Collections: Bibliotherapy Kits; Board Games; Doll Kits; Literacy Backpacks; TransAlta Tri Leisure Centre Family Passes; Video Games
Automation Activity & Vendor Info: (Cataloging) OCLC Connexion; (OPAC) Innovative Interfaces, Inc; (Serials) EBSCO Online
Wireless access
Function: 24/7 Electronic res, 24/7 Online cat, Activity rm, Adult bk club, Adult literacy prog, Art exhibits, Audio & video playback equip for onsite use, Audiobks on Playaways & MP3, Audiobks via web, AV serv, BA reader (adult literacy), Bi-weekly Writer's Group, Bilingual assistance for Spanish patrons, Bk club(s), Bks on CD, Chess club, Children's prog, Computers for patron use, Digital talking bks, Distance learning, E-Readers, Electronic databases & coll, Family literacy, Free DVD rentals, Games & aids for people with disabilities, Govt ref serv, Health sci info serv, Holiday prog, Homebound delivery serv, ILL available, Instruction & testing, Internet access, Life-long learning prog for all ages, Magazines, Magnifiers for reading, Mango lang, Meeting rooms, Movies, Music CDs, Online cat, Online info literacy tutorials on the web & in blackboard, Online ref, Orientations, Outreach serv, Outside serv via phone, mail, e-mail & web, OverDrive digital audio bks, Photocopying/Printing, Preschool reading prog, Printer for laptops & handheld devices, Prof lending libr, Prog for adults, Prog for children & young adult, Ref & res, Ref serv available, Scanner, Senior outreach, Serves people with intellectual disabilities, Spanish lang bks, Spoken cassettes & CDs, Story hour, Study rm, Summer reading prog, Teen prog, Telephone ref, Wheelchair accessible, Workshops, Writing prog
Mem of Yellowhead Regional Library
Partic in The Alberta Library; The Regional Automation Consortium
Open Tues-Sat 10-6, Sun 12-6
Restriction: Authorized patrons, In-house use for visitors, Non-resident fee, Photo ID required for access
Friends of the Library Group

P YELLOWHEAD REGIONAL LIBRARY*, 433 King St, T7X 3B4. (Mail add: Box 4270, T7X 3B4), SAN 318-7314. Tel: 780-962-2003. Administration Tel: 780-962-2003, Ext 221. Toll Free Tel: 877-962-2003. FAX: 780-962-2770. Toll Free FAX: 888-962-2770. E-mail: info@yrl.ab.ca. Web Site: www.yrl.ab.ca. *Dir,* Karla Palichuk; Tel: 780-962-2003, Ext 226, E-mail: kpalichuk@yrl.ab.ca; *Asst Dir, Mgr, Bibliog Serv,* Wendy Sears Ilnicki; Tel: 780-962-2003, Ext 225, E-mail: wsears@yrl.ab.ca; *Client Serv Mgr,* Stephanie Thero; Tel: 780-962-2003, Ext 224, E-mail: sthero@yrl.ab.ca; Staff 22 (MLS 6, Non-MLS 16)
Founded 1971
Automation Activity & Vendor Info: (Acquisitions) Innovative Interfaces, Inc; (Cataloging) Innovative Interfaces, Inc; (Circulation) Innovative Interfaces, Inc; (ILL) Innovative Interfaces, Inc; (OPAC) Innovative Interfaces, Inc
Publications: Kits (Brochure); YRL Annual Report
Member Libraries: Alberta Beach Municipal Library; Alder Flats/Buck Lake Public Library; Barrhead Public Library; Bibliotheque de Beaumont Library; Blue Ridge Community Library; Breton Municipal Library; Calmar Public Library; Darwell Public Library; Devon Public Library; Drayton Valley Municipal Library; Duffield Public Library; Edson & District Public Library; Entwistle Public Library; Evansburg Public Library; Fort Assiniboine Public Library; Hinton Municipal Library; Jasper Municipal Library; Keephills Public Library; Leduc Public Library; Mayerthorpe Public Library; Millet Public Library; Neerlandia Public Library; New Sarepta Public Library; Niton Library; Onoway Public Library; Pigeon Lake Public Library; Rich Valley Public Library; Sangudo Public Library; Seba Beach Public Library; Spruce Grove Public Library; Stony Plain Public Library; Swan Hills Municipal Library; Thorsby Municipal Library; Tomahawk Public Library; Wabamun Public Library; Warburg Public Library; Wetaskiwin Public Library; Whitecourt & District Public Library; Wildwood Public Library; Winfield Community Library
Partic in The Regional Automation Consortium
Open Mon-Fri 8:30-4:30

SPRUCE VIEW

P SPRUCE VIEW COMMUNITY LIBRARY*, Hwy 54, T0M 1V0. (Mail add: PO Box 130, T0M 1V0). Tel: 403-728-0012. FAX: 403-728-3155. E-mail: svlibrary@prl.ab.ca. Web Site: svlibrary.prl.ab.ca. *Libr Mgr,* Ms Paddy Birkeland
Library Holdings: Bk Vols 22,000
Wireless access
Mem of Parkland Regional Library-Alberta
Open Mon, Tues & Thurs 11-4, Wed 11-8

ST. ALBERT

S MUSEE HERITAGE MUSEUM*, Museum & Archives, Five Saint Anne St, T8N 3Z9. SAN 373-6245. Tel: 780-459-1528. FAX: 780-459-1232. E-mail: museum@artsandheritage.ca. Web Site: museeheritage.ca/archives-collections. *Exec Dir,* Ann Ramsden; E-mail: annr@artsandheritage.ca
Founded 1984
Library Holdings: Bk Titles 1,000
Special Collections: Oral History

Subject Interests: Museology
Function: Res libr
Open Tues-Sat 10-5, Sun 1-5
Restriction: Not a lending libr

P ST ALBERT PUBLIC LIBRARY*, Five Saint Anne St, T8N 3Z9. SAN 321-5784. Tel: 780-459-1530. FAX: 780-458-5772. E-mail: sapl@sapl.ca. Web Site: www.sapl.ca. *Chief Exec Officer,* Peter Bailey; E-mail: pbailey@sapl.ca; *Mgr, Customer Serv,* Kathleen Troppmann; *Pub Serv Mgr,* Stephanie Formsky; *Children's Serv Coordr,* Ashley King; *Communications Coordr,* Leslie Greentree; Tel: 780-459-1750; Staff 32.5 (MLS 5, Non-MLS 27.5)
Founded 1961. Pop 60,994; Circ 885,363
Library Holdings: Audiobooks 5,096; AV Mats 24,526; Bks on Deafness & Sign Lang 208; Braille Volumes 11; CDs 8,491; DVDs 9,670; e-books 15,199; e-journals 36,000; High Interest/Low Vocabulary Bk Vols 84; Large Print Bks 3,929; Microforms 171; Bk Titles 151,845; Bk Vols 155,349; Per Subs 375
Special Collections: Can
Automation Activity & Vendor Info: (Acquisitions) SirsiDynix; (Cataloging) SirsiDynix; (Circulation) SirsiDynix; (ILL) SirsiDynix; (OPAC) BiblioCommons
Wireless access
Partic in The Alberta Library
Open Mon-Thurs 10-9, Fri 10-6, Sat 10-5, Sun 1-5
Friends of the Library Group

ST. ISIDORE

P BIBLIOTHEQUE DE ST ISIDORE*, PO Box 1168, T0H 3B0. Tel: 780-624-8192. FAX: 780-624-8192. E-mail: librarian@bibliothequestisidore.ab.ca. Web Site: www.bibliothequestisidore.ab.ca. *Libr Mgr,* Anick Dechene
Library Holdings: Bk Vols 3,000
Wireless access
Mem of Peace Library System
Open Mon 9-12, Tues 10-4, Wed & Thurs 9-4

ST. PAUL

P SAINT PAUL MUNICIPAL LIBRARY*, 4802-53 St, T0A 3A0. SAN 318-7241. Tel: 780-645-4904. FAX: 780-645-5198. E-mail: librarian@stpaullibrary.ab.ca. Web Site: www.stpaullibrary.ab.ca. *Libr Mgr,* Eunhye Cho; Staff 4 (MLS 0.9, Non-MLS 3.1)
Founded 1935. Pop 5,827; Circ 37,000
Library Holdings: Audiobooks 693; CDs 262; DVDs 1,228; Bk Titles 21,449; Per Subs 20
Special Collections: Board game Coll
Wireless access
Function: Computers for patron use, Homebound delivery serv, ILL available, Internet access, Meeting rooms, Music CDs, Orientations, Photocopying/Printing, Prog for adults, Prog for children & young adult, Serves people with intellectual disabilities, Summer reading prog, Telephone ref, Wheelchair accessible, Workshops
Mem of Northern Lights Library System
Open Tues-Thurs 10-8, Fri & Sat 10-5 (Sept-June); Mon & Fri 10-5, Tues-Thurs 10-8 (July-Aug)
Friends of the Library Group

STANDARD

P STANDARD MUNICIPAL LIBRARY*, 822 The Broadway St, T0J 3G0. (Mail add: PO Box 305, T0J 3G0), SAN 324-0401. Tel: 403-644-3995. E-mail: astmlibrary@marigold.ab.ca. Web Site: www.standardlibrary.ca. *Libr Mgr,* Adreena Duffala
Founded 1982. Pop 375; Circ 2,275
Library Holdings: Bk Titles 10,000; Per Subs 15
Wireless access
Mem of Marigold Library System
Open Mon & Tues 2-6, Wed & Thurs 10-2
Friends of the Library Group

STAVELY

P STAVELY MUNICIPAL LIBRARY*, 4823 49th St, T0L 1Z0. (Mail add: PO Box 100, T0L 1Z0). Tel: 403-549-2190. FAX: 403-549-2190. E-mail: help@stavelylibrary.ca. Web Site: stavelylibrary.ca. *Librn,* Bev Olsen
Pop 455
Library Holdings: Bk Vols 5,000
Automation Activity & Vendor Info: (Acquisitions) SirsiDynix; (Cataloging) SirsiDynix; (Circulation) SirsiDynix; (ILL) SirsiDynix
Wireless access
Mem of Chinook Arch Regional Library System
Open Mon 1:30-6, Tues 9-5, Wed 1:30-7, Thurs 1:30-5

STETTLER

P STETTLER PUBLIC LIBRARY, 6202 44th Ave, 2nd Flr, T0C 2L1. SAN 318-7322. Tel: 403-742-2292. FAX: 403-742-5481. E-mail: spl@prl.ab.ca. Web Site: prl.ab.ca/stettler. *Libr Mgr,* Rhonda O'Neil; *Asst Libr Mgr,* Crystal Friars; Staff 4 (MLS 1, Non-MLS 3)
Pop 11,478; Circ 86,878
Wireless access
Function: 24/7 Electronic res, 24/7 Online cat, 24/7 wireless access
Mem of Parkland Regional Library-Alberta
Open Mon, Fri & Sat 10-6, Tues-Thurs 10-8
Friends of the Library Group

STIRLING

P STIRLING THEODORE BRANDLEY MUNICIPAL LIBRARY*, 409 Second St, T0K 2E0. (Mail add: PO Box 100, T0K 2E0). Tel: 403-756-3665. FAX: 403-756-3665. E-mail: help@stirlinglibrary.ca. Web Site: www.stirlinglibrary.ca. *Libr Mgr,* Laura Quinton
Pop 1,147
Library Holdings: Bk Titles 10,000; Bk Vols 13,000
Automation Activity & Vendor Info: (Acquisitions) BiblioCommons; (Cataloging) BiblioCommons; (Circulation) BiblioCommons; (Course Reserve) BiblioCommons; (ILL) BiblioCommons; (Media Booking) BiblioCommons; (OPAC) BiblioCommons; (Serials) BiblioCommons
Wireless access
Mem of Chinook Arch Regional Library System
Open Mon, Tues & Thurs 3-6, Wed 2-9, Fri 1-6

STONY PLAIN

P STONY PLAIN PUBLIC LIBRARY*, 5216 50 St, T7Z 0N5. SAN 373-7268. Tel: 780-963-5440. FAX: 780-963-1746. E-mail: info@mysppl.ca. Web Site: www.mysppl.ca. *Dir,* Robert McClure; E-mail: robertm@mysppl.ca; Staff 7 (Non-MLS 7)
Founded 1945. Pop 25,000; Circ 200,000
Library Holdings: Audiobooks 1,450; CDs 1,300; DVDs 3,800; Large Print Bks 680; Bk Titles 45,000; Per Subs 94; Talking Bks 1,025
Special Collections: Parkland Adult Literacy Coll
Subject Interests: Parenting
Automation Activity & Vendor Info: (Acquisitions) Innovative Interfaces, Inc. - Polaris; (Cataloging) Innovative Interfaces, Inc. - Polaris; (Circulation) Innovative Interfaces, Inc. - Polaris; (Course Reserve) Innovative Interfaces, Inc. - Polaris; (ILL) Innovative Interfaces, Inc. - Polaris; (Media Booking) Innovative Interfaces, Inc. - Polaris; (OPAC) Innovative Interfaces, Inc. - Polaris; (Serials) Innovative Interfaces, Inc. - Polaris
Wireless access
Mem of Yellowhead Regional Library
Open Mon-Fri 10-8, Sat 11-4
Friends of the Library Group

STRATHMORE

P MARIGOLD LIBRARY SYSTEM*, 710 Second St, T1P 1K4. SAN 321-3447. Tel: 403-934-5334. Toll Free Tel: 855-934-5334. FAX: 403-934-5331. Administration E-mail: admin@marigold.ab.ca. Web Site: www.marigold.ab.ca. *Exec Dir, CEO,* Lynne Price; E-mail: lynne@marigold.ab.ca; *Dep Chief Exec Officer,* Laura Taylor; Tel: 403-934-5334, Ext 242, E-mail: laura@marigold.ab.ca; *Mgr, Bibliog Serv,* Jessie Bach; Tel: 403-934-5334, Ext 258, E-mail: jessie@marigold.ab.ca; *Human Res Coordr,* Nora Ott; Tel: 403-934-5334, Ext 222, E-mail: nora@marigold.ab.ca; Staff 9 (MLS 7, Non-MLS 2)
Founded 1981. Pop 290,263; Circ 1,047,084
Library Holdings: Electronic Media & Resources 43; Bk Vols 496,494; Per Subs 15
Special Collections: Complementary & Alternative Medicine Coll; Professional Literature Coll
Wireless access
Publications: Advocacy!@your Library (Bimonthly); Annual Report; Marigold Report (Monthly); Member Library Newsletter (Monthly)
Member Libraries: Acadia Municipal Library; Acme Municipal Library; Airdrie Public Library; Banff Public Library; Beiseker Municipal Library; Berry Creek Community Library; Bighorn Library; Canmore Public Library; Carbon Municipal Library; Carseland Community Library; Cereal Municipal Library; Chestermere Public Library; Cochrane Public Library; Consort Municipal Library; Crossfield Municipal Library; Delia Municipal Library; Drumheller Public Library; Empress Municipal Library; Gleichen & District Library; Hanna Municipal Library; High River Library; Hussar Municipal Library; Irricana & Rural Municipal Library; Linden Municipal Library; Longview Municipal Library; Millarville Community Library; Morrin Municipal Library; Okotoks Public Library; Oyen Municipal Library; Rockyford Municipal Library; Rumsey Community Library; Sheep River Library; Standard Municipal Library; Strathmore Municipal Library; Three Hills Municipal Library; Trochu Municipal Library; Youngstown Municipal Library

Partic in The Alberta Library; The Regional Automation Consortium
Special Services for the Blind - Daisy reader
Open Mon-Fri 8:30-5

P STRATHMORE MUNICIPAL LIBRARY*, 85 Lakeside Blvd, T1P 1A1. SAN 318-7330. Tel: 403-934-5440. FAX: 403-934-1908. E-mail: info@strathmorelibrary.ca. Web Site: www.strathmorelibrary.ca. *Dir, Libr Serv,* Mr Anayo Ugboma; E-mail: director@strathmorelibrary.ca; Staff 6 (MLS 1, Non-MLS 5)
Pop 12,139; Circ 101,000
Library Holdings: Bk Vols 36,000; Per Subs 35
Wireless access
Mem of Marigold Library System
Open Mon-Thurs 10-7, Fri & Sat 10-4

SUNDRE

P SUNDRE MUNICIPAL LIBRARY*, 96-2 Ave NW, No 2, T0M 1X0. (Mail add: Box 539, T0M 1X0). Tel: 403-638-4000. E-mail: sundrelibrary@prl.ab.ca. Web Site: sundre.prl.ab.ca. *Libr Mgr,* Joy Wiillihnganz; E-mail: jwillihnganz@prl.ab.ca; *Libr Asst,* Sandra Huchala; E-mail: shuchala@prl.ab.ca; *Libr Asst,* Jodi Janz; *Libr Asst,* Joy Willihnganz; E-mail: sundrestaff@sundre.prl.ab.ca; *Syst Programmer,* Karen Tubb; E-mail: ktubb@prl.ab.ca. Subject Specialists: *Early childhood literacy & learning,* Karen Tubb; Staff 3 (Non-MLS 3)
Founded 1947. Pop 6,000
Library Holdings: Bk Vols 25,000
Automation Activity & Vendor Info: (Acquisitions) SirsiDynix; (Cataloging) SirsiDynix; (Circulation) SirsiDynix; (Serials) SirsiDynix
Wireless access
Function: 24/7 Electronic res, 24/7 Online cat, 3D Printer, Activity rm, Adult bk club, Adult literacy prog, After school storytime, Art exhibits, Audio & video playback equip for onsite use, Audiobks on Playaways & MP3, Audiobks via web, AV serv, Bi-weekly Writer's Group, Bk club(s), Bks on CD, CD-ROM, Children's prog, Computer training, Computers for patron use, Digital talking bks, E-Readers, Electronic databases & coll, Family literacy, Free DVD rentals, Home delivery & serv to seniorr ctr & nursing homes, ILL available, Instruction & testing, Internet access, Laminating, Life-long learning prog for all ages, Literacy & newcomer serv, Magazines, Mail & tel request accepted, Mail loans to mem, Makerspace, Mango lang, Meeting rooms, Movies, Museum passes, Music CDs, Online cat, Online ref, Orientations, Outreach serv, Outside serv via phone, mail, e-mail & web, Photocopying/Printing, Preschool reading prog, Prog for adults, Prog for children & young adult, Scanner, Senior computer classes, Senior outreach, Serves people with intellectual disabilities, Spoken cassettes & CDs, Spoken cassettes & DVDs, Story hour, Summer & winter reading prog, Summer reading prog, Teen prog, Telephone ref, Visual arts prog, Wheelchair accessible, Winter reading prog, Workshops, Writing prog
Mem of Parkland Regional Library-Alberta
Partic in The Alberta Library
Special Services for the Blind - Daisy reader
Open Tues & Fri 12-5, Wed 12-8, Thurs 9-5, Sat 11-3
Friends of the Library Group

SWAN HILLS

P SWAN HILLS MUNICIPAL LIBRARY*, 5536 Main St, T0G 2C0. (Mail add: PO Box 386, T0G 2C0), SAN 325-240X. Tel: 780-333-4505. FAX: 780-333-4551. Web Site: swanhillslibrary.ab.ca. *Librn,* April Wharton; E-mail: awharton.swanhillslibrary@yrl.ab.ca
Founded 1970. Pop 1,807; Circ 15,097
Library Holdings: AV Mats 500; Bk Titles 14,216; Per Subs 21; Talking Bks 100
Wireless access
Mem of Yellowhead Regional Library
Partic in The Alberta Library; The Regional Automation Consortium
Open Mon & Wed 10-5, Tues & Thurs 1-8, Fri 1-5, Sat Noon-4
Friends of the Library Group

SYLVAN LAKE

P SYLVAN LAKE MUNICIPAL LIBRARY*, 4715-50 Ave, T4S 1A2. Tel: 403-887-2130. E-mail: sylvan.library@prl.ab.ca. Web Site: sylvanlibrary.prl.ab.ca. *Dir,* Caroline Vandriel; Staff 5 (MLS 1, Non-MLS 4)
Founded 1946. Pop 14,816
Library Holdings: Audiobooks 914; CDs 1,279; DVDs 3,215; Large Print Bks 373; Bk Titles 29,354; Per Subs 86
Wireless access
Function: 24/7 Electronic res, 24/7 Online cat, Adult bk club, Art programs, Audiobks via web, BA reader (adult literacy), Bk club(s), Bks on CD, Children's prog, Computer training, Computers for patron use, Digital talking bks, E-Readers, Electronic databases & coll, Equip loans & repairs, Family literacy, Free DVD rentals, Holiday prog, Home delivery & serv to seniorr ctr & nursing homes, Homebound delivery serv, ILL available, Instruction & testing, Internet access, Magazines, Mail loans to mem, Mango lang, Meeting rooms, Movies, Music CDs, Online cat, Outreach serv, Photocopying/Printing, Preschool reading prog, Prog for adults, Prog for children & young adult, Ref serv available, Scanner, Senior computer classes, Senior outreach, Story hour, Summer & winter reading prog, Summer reading prog, Teen prog, Telephone ref, Visual arts prog, Wheelchair accessible, Winter reading prog, Writing prog
Mem of Parkland Regional Library-Alberta
Special Services for the Blind - Aids for in-house use; Bks on CD; Copier with enlargement capabilities; Daisy reader; Extensive large print coll; Home delivery serv; Large print bks; Playaways (bks on MP3)
Open Mon 1-8, Tues-Thurs 10-8, Fri & Sat 10-5, Sun 1-5
Friends of the Library Group

TABER

P TABER PUBLIC LIBRARY*, 5415 50 Ave, T1G 1V2. SAN 318-7349. Tel: 403-223-4343. FAX: 403-223-4314. E-mail: help@taberlibrary.ca. Web Site: www.taberlibrary.ca. *Libr Mgr,* Ms Chris Vowles; E-mail: cvowles@taberlibrary.ca; Staff 6 (MLS 1, Non-MLS 5)
Pop 8,428; Circ 75,873
Library Holdings: Bk Vols 40,000; Per Subs 51
Wireless access
Function: 24/7 Electronic res, 24/7 Online cat, Activity rm, Adult bk club, Art exhibits, Audiobks on Playaways & MP3, Audiobks via web, Bks on CD, CD-ROM, Children's prog, Computer training, Computers for patron use, Digital talking bks, Electronic databases & coll, Free DVD rentals, Holiday prog, ILL available, Instruction & testing, Internet access, Laminating, Life-long learning prog for all ages, Literacy & newcomer serv, Magazines, Mango lang, Meeting rooms, Movies, Museum passes, Music CDs, Online cat, Photocopying/Printing, Prog for adults, Prog for children & young adult, Wheelchair accessible, Workshops, Writing prog
Publications: Newsletter (Monthly)
Mem of Chinook Arch Regional Library System
Open Mon, Thurs & Fri 10-6, Wed 10-7, Sat 10-4

TANGENT

P TANGENT COMMUNITY LIBRARY*, West Entrance, 1009 Railway Ave, T0H 3J0. (Mail add: PO Box 63, T0H 3J0). Tel: 780-359-2666. E-mail: librarian@tangentlibrary.ab.ca. Web Site: www.tangentlibrary.ab.ca. *Libr Mgr,* Pat Boettcher
Library Holdings: Bk Vols 7,750
Wireless access
Mem of Peace Library System
Partic in The Alberta Library; The Regional Automation Consortium
Open Tues 11-3, Thurs 4:30-7:30, Sun 11-2

THORHILD

P THORHILD LIBRARY*, 210 Seventh Ave, T0A 3J0. (Mail add: PO Box 658, T0A 3J0). Tel: 780-398-3502. FAX: 780-398-3504. E-mail: librarian@thorhildlibrary.ab.ca. Web Site: www.thorhildlibrary.ab.ca. *Libr Mgr,* Rose Alexander
Library Holdings: Audiobooks 200; CDs 500; DVDs 450; Bk Vols 10,000; Per Subs 20; Talking Bks 100; Videos 500
Automation Activity & Vendor Info: (Acquisitions) Innovative Interfaces, Inc; (Cataloging) Innovative Interfaces, Inc; (Circulation) Innovative Interfaces, Inc
Wireless access
Mem of Northern Lights Library System
Open Tues-Thurs 10-1 & 2-7, Fri & Sat 10-1 (Winter); Mon & Fri 8:30-4:30, Tues-Thurs 9-7, Sat 9-1 (Summer)
Friends of the Library Group

THORSBY

P THORSBY MUNICIPAL LIBRARY*, 4901 - 48 Ave, T0C 2P0. (Mail add: Box 680, T0C 2P0). Tel: 780-789-3808. FAX: 780-789-3805. E-mail: thorsbypublib@yrl.ab.ca. Web Site: thorsbymunicipallibrary.ab.ca. *Libr Mgr,* Susannah Kotyk
Pop 799
Library Holdings: Bk Vols 8,000
Automation Activity & Vendor Info: (Acquisitions) SirsiDynix; (Cataloging) SirsiDynix; (Circulation) SirsiDynix; (ILL) SirsiDynix
Mem of Yellowhead Regional Library
Open Tues & Wed Noon-7, Thurs & Fri 10-5, Sat (Sept-May) 11-2

THREE HILLS

CR PRAIRIE COLLEGE*, T S Rendall Library, 330 Fourth Ave N, T0M 2N0. (Mail add: Box 4000, T0M 2N0), SAN 320-3050. Tel: 403-443-5511, Ext 3347. FAX: 403-443-5540. E-mail: library@prairie.edu. Web Site: prairie.edu/current-students/library. *Libr Dir,* Emily Kroeker; Tel:

403-443-5511, Ext 553, E-mail: emily.kroeker@prairie.edu; Staff 1.5 (MLS 1, Non-MLS 0.5)
Founded 1922. Enrl 260; Fac 2; Highest Degree: Master
Library Holdings: AV Mats 1,707; CDs 961; DVDs 85; Microforms 12,668; Music Scores 5,212; Bk Titles 58,954; Bk Vols 67,690; Per Subs 93; Videos 10
Subject Interests: Relig studies
Automation Activity & Vendor Info: (Acquisitions) SirsiDynix; (Cataloging) SirsiDynix; (Circulation) SirsiDynix; (Course Reserve) SirsiDynix; (OPAC) SirsiDynix; (Serials) SirsiDynix
Wireless access
Function: Photocopying/Printing, Ref & res, Ref serv available, Res assist avail
Partic in Christian Library Consortium; The Alberta Library
Open Mon-Fri 8am-10pm, Sat 11-9; Mon-Fri 8-5 (Summer)

P THREE HILLS MUNICIPAL LIBRARY*, 135 Third Ave S, T0M 2A0. (Mail add: PO Box 207, T0M 2A0), SAN 318-7357. Tel: 403-443-2360. E-mail: athmlibrary@marigold.ab.ca. Web Site: www.3hillslibrary.com. *Libr Mgr,* Karen Nickel; *Asst Librn, ILL,* Nikki Honecker; *Asst Librn, Programming,* Position Currently Open; *Children's Prog,* Susan Habermahl
Pop 3,322; Circ 48,237
Library Holdings: Audiobooks 365; CDs 72; DVDs 1,856; Bk Vols 14,530; Per Subs 47
Automation Activity & Vendor Info: (Acquisitions) Innovative Interfaces, Inc; (Cataloging) Innovative Interfaces, Inc; (Circulation) Innovative Interfaces, Inc; (Course Reserve) Innovative Interfaces, Inc; (ILL) Innovative Interfaces, Inc; (Media Booking) Innovative Interfaces, Inc; (OPAC) Innovative Interfaces, Inc; (Serials) Innovative Interfaces, Inc
Wireless access
Mem of Marigold Library System
Special Services for the Blind - Talking bks
Open Tues-Fri 10-8, Sat 10-3

TILLEY

P TILLEY DISTRICT & PUBLIC LIBRARY*, 148 First Ave E, T0J 3K0. (Mail add: PO Box 177, T0J 3K0). Tel: 403-377-2233, Ext 150. E-mail: tillib@shortgrass.ca. Web Site: tilley.shortgrass.ca. *Libr Mgr,* Anita Chappell
Pop 422
Library Holdings: Bk Vols 11,000
Wireless access
Mem of Shortgrass Library System
Open Mon 7pm-9pm, Wed 9-11 & 7-9, Sat 10-Noon (Sept-June)

TOFIELD

P TOFIELD MUNICIPAL LIBRARY, 5407 50 St, T0B 4J0. (Mail add: PO Box 479, T0B 4J0), SAN 318-7365. Tel: 780-662-3838. FAX: 780-662-3929. E-mail: librarian@tofieldlibrary.ca. Web Site: www.tofieldlibrary.ca. *Librn,* Sydney Baxter
Founded 1936. Pop 1,720; Circ 31,500
Library Holdings: CDs 281; Large Print Bks 368; Bk Vols 20,700; Per Subs 54; Talking Bks 316; Videos 512
Mem of Northern Lights Library System
Partic in The Regional Automation Consortium
Open Tues-Fri 10-5, Sat 10-12 & 1-5

TOMAHAWK

P TOMAHAWK PUBLIC LIBRARY, 6119 Township Rd 512, Box 69, T0E 2H0. Tel: 780-339-3935. FAX: 780-339-2121. E-mail: tomahawklibrary@pclibraries.ca. Web Site: pclibraries.ca/About-Us/Tomahawk-Public-Library. *Libr Mgr,* Chris Goerz
Library Holdings: Bk Vols 5,000; Per Subs 25
Automation Activity & Vendor Info: (Acquisitions) SirsiDynix; (Cataloging) SirsiDynix; (Circulation) SirsiDynix; (Course Reserve) SirsiDynix; (ILL) SirsiDynix; (Media Booking) SirsiDynix; (OPAC) SirsiDynix
Wireless access
Mem of Yellowhead Regional Library
Open Mon, Tues & Thurs 10-4, Wed 10:30-6:30

TROCHU

P TROCHU MUNICIPAL LIBRARY*, 317 Main St, T0M 2C0. (Mail add: PO Box 396, T0M 2C0), SAN 372-6657. Tel: 403-442-2458. FAX: 403-442-2458. E-mail: atrmlibrary@marigold.ab.ca. Web Site: www.trochulibrary.ca. *Libr Mgr,* Sherie Campbell; Staff 1 (Non-MLS 1)
Founded 1958. Pop 1,072; Circ 5,073
Library Holdings: Bk Titles 10,000; Per Subs 10
Subject Interests: Local hist, Music
Automation Activity & Vendor Info: (Cataloging) Innovative Interfaces, Inc
Wireless access
Mem of Marigold Library System
Open Wed-Fri 10:30-5:30, Sat 9-4

TWO HILLS

P ALICE MELNYK PUBLIC LIBRARY*, 5009 Diefenbaker (50th) Ave, T0B 4K0. (Mail add: PO Box 460, T0B 4K0), SAN 318-7373. Tel: 780-657-3553. FAX: 780-657-3553. E-mail: librarian@twohillslibrary.ab.ca. Web Site: www.twohillslibrary.ab.ca. *Libr Mgr,* Elizabeth Laing-Kobe
Founded 1954. Pop 1,250; Circ 14,000
Library Holdings: Audiobooks 107; CDs 310; DVDs 3,354; Large Print Bks 241; Bk Titles 14,856; Per Subs 40
Automation Activity & Vendor Info: (Circulation) Innovative Interfaces, Inc; (ILL) Innovative Interfaces, Inc
Wireless access
Function: Adult bk club, Art exhibits, Audiobks on Playaways & MP3, Audiobks via web, AV serv, Bi-weekly Writer's Group, Bk club(s), Bks on CD, Children's prog, Computers for patron use, Electronic databases & coll, Family literacy, ILL available, Internet access, Laminating, Meeting rooms, Movies, Music CDs, Online cat, Outreach serv, OverDrive digital audio bks, Photocopying/Printing, Prog for children & young adult, Story hour, Summer & winter reading prog, Summer reading prog, Teen prog, Wheelchair accessible, Winter reading prog
Mem of Northern Lights Library System
Partic in The Regional Automation Consortium
Open Mon-Wed 10-5, Thurs & Fri 10-5:30

VALHALLA CENTRE

P VALHALLA COMMUNITY LIBRARY*, PO Box 68, T0H 3M0. Tel: 780-356-3834. FAX: 780-356-3834. E-mail: librarian@valhallalibrary.ab.ca. Web Site: www.valhallalibrary.ab.ca. *Libr Mgr,* Gail Perry
Library Holdings: Bk Vols 8,000
Automation Activity & Vendor Info: (Circulation) Innovative Interfaces, Inc; (OPAC) Innovative Interfaces, Inc
Mem of Peace Library System
Open Mon 10-4, Tues & Thurs 10-5, Wed 10-8

VALLEYVIEW

P VALLEYVIEW MUNICIPAL LIBRARY*, 4804 50th Ave, T0H 3N0. (Mail add: PO Box 897, T0H 3N0), SAN 321-3595. Tel: 780-524-3033. FAX: 780-524-4563. E-mail: librarian@valleyviewlibrary.ab.ca. Web Site: www.valleyviewlibrary.ab.ca. *Libr Mgr,* Kerri Danner; Staff 1 (Non-MLS 1)
Founded 1970. Pop 7,000; Circ 28,000
Library Holdings: Bks on Deafness & Sign Lang 10; CDs 150; DVDs 500; Bk Titles 27,000; Per Subs 40; Videos 450
Special Collections: Art Gallery Featuring Local Exhibitors; Pictorial History of Valleyview & District
Automation Activity & Vendor Info: (Cataloging) Innovative Interfaces, Inc; (Circulation) Innovative Interfaces, Inc; (OPAC) Innovative Interfaces, Inc
Wireless access
Function: Adult bk club, Adult literacy prog, Art exhibits, Bks on cassette, Bks on CD, CD-ROM, Chess club, Computers for patron use, Family literacy, Govt ref serv, ILL available, Internet access, Music CDs, Online cat, Online info literacy tutorials on the web & in blackboard, Photocopying/Printing, Prog for children & young adult, Scanner, Spoken cassettes & CDs, Summer reading prog, VHS videos, Wheelchair accessible
Mem of Peace Library System
Partic in The Regional Automation Consortium
Special Services for the Deaf - Bks on deafness & sign lang; Closed caption videos
Special Services for the Blind - Bks on cassette; Bks on CD; Daisy reader; Large print bks; Recorded bks; Talking bk serv referral; Talking bks
Open Tues-Fri 11-6
Friends of the Library Group

VAUXHALL

P VAUXHALL PUBLIC LIBRARY, 504 Second Ave N, T0K 2K0. (Mail add: PO Box 265, T0K 2K0). Tel: 403-654-2370. FAX: 403-654-2192. E-mail: help@vauxhalllibrary.ca. Web Site: www.vauxhalllibrary.ca. *Libr Mgr,* Maria Dyck; E-mail: mdyck@vauxhalllibrary.ca
Founded 1948. Pop 1,112
Library Holdings: Bk Vols 1,100
Mem of Chinook Arch Regional Library System
Open Mon, Tues, Thurs & Fri 9-1 & 2-5, Wed 10-1 & 2-6
Friends of the Library Group

VEGREVILLE

P VEGREVILLE CENTENNIAL LIBRARY*, 4709-50 St, T9C 1R1. SAN 318-7381. Tel: 780-632-3491. E-mail: library@vegreville.com. Web Site: www.vegrevillelibrary.ab.ca. *Libr Mgr,* Kira Chalupa; E-mail: kchalupa@vegreville.com; Staff 10 (MLS 1, Non-MLS 9)
Founded 1920. Pop 6,000
Library Holdings: Bk Vols 40,000; Per Subs 50
Wireless access
Function: Adult bk club, Art exhibits, Bks on cassette, Bks on CD, Children's prog, Computers for patron use, E-Reserves, Free DVD rentals, Home delivery & serv to seniorr ctr & nursing homes, Homebound delivery serv, ILL available, Music CDs, Online cat, Photocopying/Printing, Prog for children & young adult, Ref serv available, Serves people with intellectual disabilities, Story hour, Summer reading prog
Mem of Northern Lights Library System
Partic in The Alberta Library
Special Services for the Blind - Bks on cassette; Bks on CD; Large print bks; Talking bks
Open Mon-Thurs 10-8, Fri 10-6, Sat Noon-4 (Winter); Mon, Wed & Fri 10-6, Tues & Thurs 10-8, Sat Noon-4 (Summer)

VERMILION

C LAKELAND COLLEGE LIBRARY*, 5707 College Dr, T9X 1K5. SAN 320-3115. Tel: 780-853-8463. FAX: 780-853-8662. E-mail: library@lakelandcollege.ca. Web Site: www.lakelandcollege.ca/current-students/libraries. *Pub Serv Librn,* Ben Harrison; Tel: 780-871-5797, E-mail: ben.harrison@lakelandcollege.ca; *Pub Serv Librn,* Wanjiku Kaai; Tel: 780-853-8731, E-mail: wanjiku.kaai@lakelandcollege.ca; *Circ, Libr Tech,* Blessing Nzediegwu; E-mail: blessing.nzediegwu@lakelandcollege.ca; *Libr Tech,* Lia Kim; Tel: 780-853-8465, E-mail: lia.kim@lakelandcollege.ca; *Libr Tech,* Kathy Williams; Tel: 780-871-7509, E-mail: kathy.williams@lakelandcollege.ca. Subject Specialists: *Gen,* Blessing Nzediegwu; Staff 6 (MLS 2, Non-MLS 4)
Founded 1913. Enrl 2,100; Fac 120; Highest Degree: Bachelor
Library Holdings: e-books 231,416; Bk Vols 18,000
Subject Interests: Agr, Arts, Environ, Life sci, Soc sci
Wireless access
Partic in NEOS Library Consortium
Open Mon-Fri 8:15-8, Sat & Sun 10-5

P VERMILION PUBLIC LIBRARY*, 5001 49th Ave, T9X 1B8. SAN 318-739X. Tel: 780-853-4288. FAX: 833-792-7170. Administration E-mail: info@vplibrary.ca. Web Site: www.vermilionpubliclibrary.ca. *Libr Mgr,* Stuart Pauls; E-mail: librarian@vermilionpubliclibrary.ca; Staff 6 (Non-MLS 6)
Founded 1932. Pop 4,435; Circ 58,000
Special Collections: Local Newspaper 1900-present, micro
Subject Interests: Bus, Local hist
Wireless access
Function: 24/7 Electronic res, 24/7 Online cat, Activity rm, Adult bk club, Art exhibits, Audiobks via web, AV serv, Bk club(s), Bk reviews (Group), Bks on CD, Children's prog, Computer training, Computers for patron use, E-Readers, Electronic databases & coll, Equip loans & repairs, Family literacy, Free DVD rentals, Games & aids for people with disabilities, Home delivery & serv to seniorr ctr & nursing homes, ILL available, Instruction & testing, Internet access, Life-long learning prog for all ages, Magazines, Magnifiers for reading, Meeting rooms, Microfiche/film & reading machines, Movies, Online cat, Online ref, Outreach serv, OverDrive digital audio bks, Photocopying/Printing, Preschool reading prog, Prog for adults, Prog for children & young adult, Ref serv available, Res assist avail, Scanner, Serves people with intellectual disabilities, Spoken cassettes & CDs, Study rm, Summer & winter reading prog, Summer reading prog, Wheelchair accessible, Winter reading prog, Workshops
Mem of Northern Lights Library System
Partic in The Regional Automation Consortium
Open Mon-Thurs 10-7, Fri 10-5, Sat 10-3
Friends of the Library Group

VETERAN

P VETERAN MUNICIPAL LIBRARY*, 201 Lucknow St, T0C 2S0. (Mail add: Box 527, T0C 2S0). Tel: 403-575-3915. *Librn,* Chricinda Devereux; E-mail: chricinda.devereux@plrd.ab.ca
Pop 300
Library Holdings: Bk Vols 12,000
Wireless access
Open Mon, Wed & Fri 8:30-3:30, Tues & Thurs 8:30-3:30 & 7-9; Tues & Thurs 7pm-9pm (Summer)

VIKING

P VIKING MUNICIPAL LIBRARY*, 5120 45 St, T0B 4N0. (Mail add: PO Box 300, T0B 4N0), SAN 318-7403. Tel: 780-336-4992. FAX: 780-336-4992. E-mail: librarian@vikinglibrary.ab.ca. Web Site: www.vikinglibrary.ab.ca. *Libr Mgr,* Barb Chrystian
Pop 1,100; Circ 8,336
Library Holdings: Bk Vols 8,813
Wireless access
Mem of Northern Lights Library System
Partic in Northern Lights Library Network
Open Mon & Wed 10-5, Tues & Thurs 10-8
Friends of the Library Group

VILNA

P VILNA MUNICIPAL LIBRARY*, 5431-50th St, T0A 3L0. (Mail add: PO Box 119, T0A 3L0). Tel: 780-636-2077. FAX: 780-636-3243. Web Site: www.vilnapubliclibrary.ab.ca. *Libr Mgr,* Rebecca Harakal; E-mail: rharakal@vilnapubliclibrary.ab.ca
Library Holdings: Bk Vols 10,000
Automation Activity & Vendor Info: (Cataloging) SirsiDynix; (Circulation) SirsiDynix; (OPAC) SirsiDynix
Wireless access
Mem of Northern Lights Library System
Open Tues & Thurs 3:30-7:30, Sat Noon-4

VULCAN

P VULCAN MUNICIPAL LIBRARY*, 303 Centre St, T0L 2B0. (Mail add: PO Box 1120, T0L 2B0), SAN 318-7411. Tel: 403-485-2571. FAX: 403-485-5013. E-mail: help@vulcanlibrary.ca. Web Site: www.vulcanlibrary.ca. *Mgr,* Connie Clement
Pop 1,800; Circ 20,000
Library Holdings: Audiobooks 321; CDs 150; DVDs 200; Bk Titles 13,314; Per Subs 4; Videos 800
Automation Activity & Vendor Info: (Cataloging) SirsiDynix; (Circulation) SirsiDynix; (OPAC) SirsiDynix
Wireless access
Function: Adult bk club, Art exhibits, Audio & video playback equip for onsite use, Bks on cassette, Bks on CD, Children's prog, Computer training, Computers for patron use, Electronic databases & coll, Free DVD rentals, Home delivery & serv to seniorr ctr & nursing homes, ILL available, Music CDs, Online cat, Online ref, Photocopying/Printing, Prog for children & young adult, Story hour, Summer reading prog, Wheelchair accessible
Mem of Chinook Arch Regional Library System
Open Mon-Fri 10-5, Sat 11-3
Friends of the Library Group

WABAMUN

P WABAMUN PUBLIC LIBRARY*, 5132 53rd Ave, T0E 2K0. (Mail add: PO Box 89, T0E 2K0). Tel: 780-892-2713. FAX: 780-892-7294. Web Site: www.wabamunlibrary.ca. *Libr Mgr,* James Bryl; E-mail: jamesb@wabamunlibrary.ca
Founded 1960. Pop 664
Library Holdings: AV Mats 1,500; Bk Vols 15,000; Per Subs 45; Talking Bks 172
Automation Activity & Vendor Info: (Cataloging) Innovative Interfaces, Inc; (Circulation) Innovative Interfaces, Inc; (OPAC) Innovative Interfaces, Inc
Mem of Yellowhead Regional Library
Open Tues & Wed 11-7, Thurs & Fri 11-5, Sat 11-2
Friends of the Library Group

WABASCA

P WABASCA PUBLIC LIBRARY*, 2853 Alook Dr, T0G 2K0. (Mail add: PO Box 638, T0G 2K0). Tel: 780-891-2203. FAX: 780-891-2402. E-mail: librarian@wabascalibrary.ab.ca. Web Site: www.wabascalibrary.ab.ca. *Libr Mgr,* Diane Collyer
Founded 2003
Library Holdings: Bk Vols 20,000
Automation Activity & Vendor Info: (Cataloging) Innovative Interfaces, Inc; (Circulation) Innovative Interfaces, Inc; (OPAC) Innovative Interfaces, Inc
Wireless access
Mem of Peace Library System
Open Mon-Fri 11:30-7:30

WAINWRIGHT

P WAINWRIGHT PUBLIC LIBRARY, 921 Third Ave, T9W 1C5. SAN 325-2051. Tel: 780-842-2673. FAX: 780-842-2340. E-mail: librarian@wainwrightlibrary.ab.ca. Web Site: www.wainwrightlibrary.ab.ca. *Libr Mgr,* Jodi Dahlgren; *Asst Librn,* Ginette Crandall
Founded 1935. Pop 6,289; Circ 51,000
Library Holdings: Audiobooks 900; CDs 100; DVDs 2,500; Large Print Bks 1,800; Bk Titles 33,200; Per Subs 70
Automation Activity & Vendor Info: (Cataloging) Innovative Interfaces, Inc; (Circulation) Innovative Interfaces, Inc; (OPAC) Innovative Interfaces, Inc
Wireless access
Function: 24/7 Electronic res, 24/7 Online cat, After school storytime, Art exhibits, Bks on CD, Children's prog, Computers for patron use, Digital talking bks, Electronic databases & coll, Family literacy, Free DVD rentals, Holiday prog, ILL available, Internet access, Laminating, Magazines, Magnifiers for reading, Movies, Music CDs, Online cat, Outreach serv, OverDrive digital audio bks, Photocopying/Printing, Preschool reading prog, Prog for adults, Prog for children & young adult, Scanner, Senior outreach, STEM programs, Story hour, Summer & winter reading prog, Teen prog, Wheelchair accessible, Workshops
Mem of Northern Lights Library System
Special Services for the Blind - Aids for in-house use; Assistive/Adapted tech devices, equip & products
Open Mon, Wed & Fri 10-6, Tues & Thurs 10-8, Sat (Sept-June) Noon-4

WANDERING RIVER

P WANDERING RIVER PUBLIC LIBRARY, Main St, T0A 3M0. (Mail add: PO Box 8, T0A 3M0). Tel: 780-771-3939. FAX: 780-771-2117. E-mail: librarian@wanderingriverlibrary.ab.ca. Web Site: www.wanderingriverlibrary.ab.ca. *Libr Mgr,* Leann Thompson
Founded 1965
Mem of Northern Lights Library System
Open Wed 3:30-5:30, Sat 9-1

WARBURG

P WARBURG PUBLIC LIBRARY*, 5212 50 Ave, T0C 2T0. (Mail add: PO Box 299, T0C 2T0). Tel: 780-848-2391. FAX: 780-848-2296. E-mail: warburglibrary@yrl.ab.ca. Web Site: warburglibrary.ab.ca. *Dir,* Gail O'Neil
Pop 721
Library Holdings: Bk Vols 9,000; Per Subs 15
Automation Activity & Vendor Info: (Acquisitions) Innovative Interfaces, Inc; (Cataloging) Innovative Interfaces, Inc; (Circulation) Innovative Interfaces, Inc; (ILL) Innovative Interfaces, Inc; (Serials) Innovative Interfaces, Inc
Wireless access
Mem of Yellowhead Regional Library
Open Tues-Thurs 10-6, Sat 12-4

WARNER

P WARNER MEMORIAL LIBRARY*, 206 Third Ave, T0K 2L0. SAN 318-7438. Tel: 403-642-3988. E-mail: help@warnerlibrary.ca. Web Site: www.warnerlibrary.ca. *Librn,* Andrea Tapp
Pop 379; Circ 3,576
Library Holdings: Bk Vols 18,000; Per Subs 10
Automation Activity & Vendor Info: (Cataloging) SirsiDynix; (Circulation) SirsiDynix
Wireless access
Mem of Chinook Arch Regional Library System
Open Tues & Thurs 11-6, Wed 2-8

WASKATENAU

P ANNE CHORNEY PUBLIC LIBRARY*, 5111 52 Ave, T0A 3P0. (Mail add: PO Box 130, T0A 3P0). Tel: 780-358-2777. FAX: 780-358-2777. E-mail: librarian@waskatenaulibrary.ab.ca. Web Site: www.waskatenaulibrary.ab.ca. *Libr Mgr,* Tracy Wilhelm
Pop 255
Wireless access
Mem of Northern Lights Library System
Open Tues & Fri 12-7, Thurs 12-3

WATER VALLEY

P WATER VALLEY PUBLIC LIBRARY, PO Box 250, T0M 2E0. Tel: 403-637-3899. E-mail: watervalleylibrary@prl.ab.ca. Web Site: watervalleylibrary.prl.ab.ca. *Libr Mgr,* Jill Maier
Founded 1950
Library Holdings: Bk Vols 8,000
Wireless access
Function: Children's prog, ILL available, Photocopying/Printing
Mem of Parkland Regional Library-Alberta
Open Tues 5pm-8pm, Wed 9-1, Fri 10-2, Sat 9-1

WEMBLEY

P WEMBLEY PUBLIC LIBRARY*, 9719-99 Ave, T0H 3S0. (Mail add: PO Box 926, T0H 3S0). Tel: 780-766-3553. FAX: 780-766-3543. E-mail: librarian@wembleypubliclibrary.ab.ca. Web Site: www.wembleypubliclibrary.ab.ca. *Libr Mgr,* Anna Underwood
Wireless access
Mem of Peace Library System
Partic in The Regional Automation Consortium
Open Wed-Fri 3:30-7:30, Sat 10-3

WESTLOCK

P WESTLOCK MUNICIPAL LIBRARY*, Heritage Bldg No 1, 10007 100 Ave, T7P 2H5. SAN 318-7446. Tel: 780-349-3060. FAX: 780-349-5291. E-mail: info@westlocklibrary.ca. Web Site: www.westlocklibrary.ca. *Dir,* Lisa Old; E-mail: LOld@westlocklibrary.ca
Founded 1945. Pop 17,000; Circ 75,000
Library Holdings: Per Subs 52
Automation Activity & Vendor Info: (Cataloging) Innovative Interfaces, Inc; (Circulation) Innovative Interfaces, Inc; (OPAC) Innovative Interfaces, Inc
Wireless access
Partic in The Regional Automation Consortium
Special Services for the Blind - Talking bks
Open Mon-Fri 9-12 & 1-4
Friends of the Library Group
Branches: 2
M ALICE FROSE LIBRARY, Fawcett Community Hall, Fawcett, T0G 0Y0. (Mail add: PO Box 150, Fawcett, T0G 0y0), SAN 318-6776. Tel: 780-809-2244. FAX: 780-954-3934. *Librn,* Marie Meyn
Founded 1963. Pop 500; Circ 10,000
Library Holdings: Bk Vols 9,000; Per Subs 60
Open Wed 10-2, Thurs 4-7
JARVIE PUBLIC LIBRARY, Jarvie Community Ctr, Jarvie, T0G 1H0. (Mail add: PO Box 193, Jarvie, T0G 1H0). Tel: 780-350-8160. *Librn,* Cheryl Houle
Library Holdings: Bk Vols 9,000
Automation Activity & Vendor Info: (Acquisitions) SirsiDynix; (Cataloging) SirsiDynix; (Circulation) SirsiDynix; (Course Reserve) SirsiDynix; (ILL) SirsiDynix; (Media Booking) SirsiDynix; (OPAC) SirsiDynix; (Serials) SirsiDynix
Open Tues 10-2 & 4-7

WETASKIWIN

S REYNOLDS-ALBERTA MUSEUM REFERENCE CENTRE*, 6426 40th Ave, T9A 2G1. (Mail add: PO Box 6360 Stn Main, T9A 2G1), SAN 318-7454. Tel: 780-312-2080. Web Site: reynoldsmuseum.ca. *Dir,* Noel Ratch; E-mail: Noel.ratch@gov.ab.ca; *Coordr, Coll Serv,* Kathleen Wall; *Curator,* Justin Cuffe; E-mail: justin.cuffe@gov.ab.ca; *Curator,* Brian Manning; E-mail: brian.manning@gov.ab.ca; Staff 4 (MLS 1, Non-MLS 3)
Founded 1992
Library Holdings: Bk Titles 3,000; Per Subs 60; Spec Interest Per Sub 50
Special Collections: Original Trade Publications, manuals, sales literature, subject & advertising files
Subject Interests: Agr, Aviation, Hist of transportation, Indust, Motor vehicles
Automation Activity & Vendor Info: (Cataloging) SirsiDynix
Open Tues & Thurs 10-4
Restriction: Non-circulating

P WETASKIWIN PUBLIC LIBRARY*, 5002 51st Ave, T9A 0V1. SAN 318-7462. Tel: 780-361-4446. FAX: 780-352-3266. E-mail: library@wetaskiwin.ca. Web Site: www.wetaskiwinpubliclibrary.ab.ca. *Mgr, Libr Serv,* Rachelle Kuzyk; *Info Serv Coordr,* Svea Beson; Staff 7 (MLS 1, Non-MLS 6)
Founded 1928. Pop 12,000; Circ 150,000
Library Holdings: Bk Titles 37,000; Per Subs 115
Special Collections: International Fiction Coll
Automation Activity & Vendor Info: (Cataloging) Innovative Interfaces, Inc; (Circulation) Innovative Interfaces, Inc
Mem of Yellowhead Regional Library
Partic in The Regional Automation Consortium
Open Mon-Thurs 10-8, Fri & Sat 10-5
Friends of the Library Group

WHITECOURT

P WHITECOURT & DISTRICT PUBLIC LIBRARY*, 5201 49th St, T7S 1N3. (Mail add: PO Box 150, T7S 1N3). Tel: 780-778-2900. E-mail: info@whitecourtlibrary.ab.ca. Web Site: www.whitecourtlibrary.ab.ca. *Dir,* Joseph Kubelka; Staff 6 (MLS 1, Non-MLS 5)

Founded 1963. Pop 11,000; Circ 62,000
Jan 2020-Dec 2020 Income (CAN) $432,686, Provincial (CAN) $58,686, City (CAN) $307,000, County (CAN) $50,000, Locally Generated Income (CAN) $4,000, Other (CAN) $13,000. Mats Exp (CAN) $27,200, Books (CAN) $12,600, Per/Ser (Incl. Access Fees) (CAN) $2,000, AV Mat (CAN) $12,600. Sal (CAN) $399,000
Library Holdings: Bk Vols 34,000; Per Subs 55
Automation Activity & Vendor Info: (Cataloging) SirsiDynix; (Circulation) SirsiDynix; (OPAC) SirsiDynix
Wireless access
Function: 24/7 Electronic res, 24/7 Online cat, Adult bk club, Art exhibits, Audiobks on Playaways & MP3, AV serv, Bks on CD, Children's prog, Computers for patron use, E-Readers, E-Reserves, Electronic databases & coll, Free DVD rentals, Home delivery & serv to seniorr ctr & nursing homes, ILL available, Instruction & testing, Internet access, Large print keyboards, Mail & tel request accepted, Music CDs, OverDrive digital audio bks, Photocopying/Printing, Prog for adults, Prog for children & young adult, Scanner, Story hour, Summer reading prog, Teen prog, Telephone ref, Wheelchair accessible
Mem of Yellowhead Regional Library
Special Services for the Deaf - Bks on deafness & sign lang
Special Services for the Blind - Bks & mags in Braille, on rec, tape & cassette; Bks on CD; Bks on flash-memory cartridges; Braille bks
Open Mon & Fri 10-6, Tues-Thurs 12-8

WILDWOOD

P WILDWOOD PUBLIC LIBRARY, 5215-50th St, T0E 2M0. (Mail add: PO Box 118, T0E 2M0). Tel: 780-325-3882. FAX: 780-325-3880. Web Site: www.wildwoodlibrary.ab.ca. *Actg Mgr,* Melissa Ronayne; E-mail: melirona@gypsd.ca
Library Holdings: Bk Vols 18,000; Per Subs 52
Automation Activity & Vendor Info: (Acquisitions) Innovative Interfaces, Inc; (Cataloging) Innovative Interfaces, Inc; (Circulation) Innovative Interfaces, Inc; (Course Reserve) Innovative Interfaces, Inc; (ILL) Innovative Interfaces, Inc; (Media Booking) Innovative Interfaces, Inc; (OPAC) Innovative Interfaces, Inc
Wireless access
Mem of Yellowhead Regional Library
Special Services for the Deaf - Bks on deafness & sign lang
Special Services for the Blind - Accessible computers; Assistive/Adapted tech devices, equip & products; Bks & mags in Braille, on rec, tape & cassette; Bks available with recordings
Open Mon, Wed & Fri 10-5, Tues & Thurs 1-8
Friends of the Library Group

WINFIELD

P WINFIELD COMMUNITY LIBRARY*, 401-Fourth Ave E, T0C 2X0. (Mail add: PO Box 360, T0C 2X0). Tel: 780-682-2498. FAX: 780-682-2490. E-mail: winfieldlibrary@yrl.ab.ca. Web Site: www.winfieldlibrary.ab.ca. *Libr Mgr,* Joyce Brown
Library Holdings: Audiobooks 39; Bk Vols 10,689; Per Subs 95; Videos 339
Wireless access
Mem of Yellowhead Regional Library
Partic in The Alberta Library; The Regional Automation Consortium
Open Tues 9-1, Wed & Fri 5-8, Sat 10-3

WOKING

P WOKING MUNICIPAL LIBRARY*, 5245 51st St, No 10, T0H 3V0. Tel: 780-774-3932. E-mail: librarian@wokinglibrary.ca. Web Site: www.wokinglibrary.ca. *Libr Mgr,* Bevonna Livingston
Wireless access
Mem of Peace Library System
Open Mon & Wed 3-6:30, Sat 10-1

WORSLEY

P WORSLEY & DISTRICT PUBLIC LIBRARY*, Worsley Central School, 216 Alberta Ave, T0H 3W0. (Mail add: PO Box 246, T0H 3W0). Tel: 780-685-3842. FAX: 780-685-3766. E-mail: awdlib@hotmail.com. Web Site: www.worsleylibrary.ab.ca. *Libr Mgr,* Melissa Kamphuis
Library Holdings: Bk Titles 3,000; Per Subs 15
Automation Activity & Vendor Info: (Acquisitions) SirsiDynix
Mem of Peace Library System
Open Tues & Fri 8-4 (Sept-July); Wed & Thurs 10-3 (Aug)

WRENTHAM

P WRENTHAM PUBLIC LIBRARY*, 101 Carrigan Ave, T0K 2P0. Tel: 403-222-2485. FAX: 403-222-2101. E-mail: help@wrenthamlibrary.ca. Web Site: www.wrenthamlibrary.ca. *Libr Mgr,* Trudy Fehr
Library Holdings: Bk Vols 3,500
Wireless access
Mem of Chinook Arch Regional Library System
Open Mon-Fri 9-1
Friends of the Library Group

YOUNGSTOWN

P YOUNGSTOWN MUNICIPAL LIBRARY*, 218 Main St, T0J 3P0. (Mail add: PO Box 39, T0J 0R0). Tel: 403-779-3864. FAX: 403-779-3864. E-mail: aymlibrary@marigold.ab.ca. Web Site: www.youngstownlibrary.ca. *Libr Mgr,* Annette Lupuliak
Pop 178
Library Holdings: Bk Vols 8,733
Automation Activity & Vendor Info: (Acquisitions) SirsiDynix; (Cataloging) SirsiDynix; (Circulation) SirsiDynix; (Course Reserve) SirsiDynix; (ILL) SirsiDynix
Wireless access
Mem of Marigold Library System
Partic in The Alberta Library; The Regional Automation Consortium
Open Mon & Wed 10-4:30, Tues 12-7
Friends of the Library Group

ZAMA CITY

P ZAMA CITY COMMUNITY LIBRARY, Zama Cornerstone Bldg, 1025 Aspen Dr, T0H 4E0. (Mail add: PO Box 14, T0H 4E0). Tel: 780-683-2888. Web Site: mclboard.com/municipal-libraries/zama-library. *Library Contact,* Lisa Wardley; E-mail: lisa@mackenziecounty.com
Founded 1974
Library Holdings: Bk Vols 300,000
Wireless access
Open Tues-Thurs 6:30pm-8:30pm
Friends of the Library Group

BRITISH COLUMBIA

Date of Statistics: Calendar Year 2020
Population, 2016 B.C. Census: 4,648,055
Population Served by Public Libraries: 4,603,762
Total Materials, Volumes Held: 41,993,784
Total Public Library Circulation of All Materials: 35,889,323
Income and Expenditures:
Total Public Library Income: $254,120,071
Total Library Materials Expenditure (physical & electronic): $24,010,240
Information provided courtesy of: Aidan Fortier, Research Analyst, Public Libraries Branch; BC Ministry of Municipal Affairs (Victoria)

ABBOTSFORD

CR COLUMBIA BIBLE COLLEGE LIBRARY*, 2940 Clearbrook Rd, V2T 2Z8. SAN 328-0489. Tel: 604-853-3567. FAX: 604-853-3063. E-mail: cbclibrary@columbiabc.edu. Web Site: www.columbiabc.edu/library. *Libr Dir,* Dorothy Gebert; Tel: 604-853-3567, Ext 334, E-mail: dorothy.gebert@columbiabc.edu; Staff 3 (MLS 1, Non-MLS 2)
Enrl 325; Fac 17; Highest Degree: Bachelor
May 2019-Apr 2020. Mats Exp (CAN) $6,209. Sal (CAN) $84,901 (Prof (CAN) $58,006)
Library Holdings: CDs 626; DVDs 816; e-journals 18,335; Microforms 1,178; Bk Titles 33,970; Bk Vols 36,189; Per Subs 67; Videos 390
Subject Interests: Anabaptists, Biblical studies, Church hist, Mennonite, Theol
Automation Activity & Vendor Info: (Acquisitions) Evergreen; (Cataloging) Evergreen; (Circulation) Evergreen; (Course Reserve) Evergreen; (OPAC) Evergreen; (Serials) Evergreen
Wireless access
Partic in BC Libraries Cooperative; British Columbia Electronic Library Network; Electronic Health Library of British Columbia
Open Mon-Thurs 8:15am-9pm, Fri 8:45-4:45, Sat 11-4:45

P FRASER VALLEY REGIONAL LIBRARY*, Administrative Centre, 34589 Delair Rd, V2S 5Y1. SAN 318-7500. Tel: 604-859-7141. Toll Free Tel: 888-668-4141 (BC only). FAX: 604-859-5701. Web Site: www.fvrl.bc.ca. *Chief Exec Officer,* Scott Hargrove; *Customer Experience Dir,* Heather Scoular; E-mail: heather.scoular@fvrl.bc.ca; *Mgr, Info Tech,* Devan Mitchell; *Mgr, Support Serv,* Dean Kelly; E-mail: dean.kelly@fvrl.bc.ca; Staff 336 (MLS 31, Non-MLS 305)
Founded 1930. Pop 600,000
Library Holdings: Bk Vols 973,453
Special Collections: British Columbiana
Automation Activity & Vendor Info: (Circulation) Innovative Interfaces, Inc; (ILL) Innovative Interfaces, Inc; (OPAC) Innovative Interfaces, Inc
Wireless access
Publications: Annual Report, brochures, booklists
Partic in Public Library InterLINK
Friends of the Library Group
Branches: 25
ABBOTSFORD COMMUNITY LIBRARY, 33355 Bevan Ave, V2S 3M1, SAN 321-1908. Tel: 604-853-1753. FAX: 604-853-7861. *Libr Mgr,* Hillary Russell; Tel: 604-859-7814, E-mail: hilary.russell@fvrl.bc.ca
Open Mon-Thurs 10-9, Fri & Sat 10-5, Sun 1-5
AGASSIZ LIBRARY, 7140 Cheam Ave, Agassiz, V0M 1A0. (Mail add: PO Box 7, Agassiz, V0M 1A0), SAN 321-1916. Tel: 604-796-9510. FAX: 604-796-9517. *Libr Mgr,* Nicole Glentworth; Tel: 604-792-1941, E-mail: nicole.glentworth@fvrl.bc.ca
Open Tues-Thurs 10-8, Wed, Fri & Sat 10-5
Friends of the Library Group
ALDERGROVE LIBRARY, 26770 29th Ave, Aldergrove, V4W 3B8, SAN 321-1924. Tel: 604-856-6415. FAX: 604-856-6816. *Libr Mgr,* David Thiessen; E-mail: david.thiessen@fvrl.bc.ca
Open Mon-Thurs 10-9, Fri & Sat 10-5
MURIEL ARNASON LIBRARY, Township of Langley Civic Ctr, 130 - 20338 65th Ave, Langley, V2Y 2X3. Tel: 604-532-3590. FAX: 604-534-3141. *Libr Mgr,* David Thiessen
Open Mon-Thurs 10-9, Fri & Sat 10-5, Sun 1-5
BOSTON BAR LIBRARY, 47643 Old Boston Bar Rd, Boston Bar, V0K 1C0, SAN 321-1932. Tel: 604-867-8847. FAX: 604-867-9549. *Libr Mgr,* Nicole Glentworth; E-mail: nicole.glentworth@fvrl.bc.ca
Open Tues & Thurs 1-5 & 5:30-7:30
BROOKSWOOD LIBRARY, 20045 40th Ave, Langley, V3A 2W2, SAN 321-1940. Tel: 604-534-7055. FAX: 604-532-7432. *Libr Mgr,* David Thiessen
Open Tues & Wed 10-8, Thurs-Sat 10-5
CHILLIWACK LIBRARY, 45860 First Ave, Chilliwack, V2P 7K1, SAN 321-1959. Tel: 604-792-1941. FAX: 604-532-7483. *Libr Mgr,* Nicole Glentworth
Open Mon-Thurs 10-9, Fri 10-6, Sat 10-5, Sun 1-5
Friends of the Library Group
CITY OF LANGLEY LIBRARY, 20399 Douglas Crescent, Langley, V3A 4B3, SAN 321-2033. Tel: 604-514-2850. FAX: 604-534-2985.
Open Mon-Thurs 9-9, Fri 9-5, Sat 10-5, Sun 1-5
Friends of the Library Group
CLEARBROOK LIBRARY, 32320 George Ferguson Way, V2T 6N4, SAN 321-1967. Tel: 604-859-7814. FAX: 604-859-7329. *Libr Mgr,* Hilary Russell
Open Mon-Thurs 10-9, Fri-Sun 10-5
Friends of the Library Group
FORT LANGLEY LIBRARY, 9167 Glover Rd, Fort Langley, V1M 2R6, SAN 321-1991. Tel: 604-888-0722. FAX: 604-882-0729. *Libr Mgr,* David Thiessen
Open Tues & Wed 1-8, Thurs-Sat 10-12:30 & 1-5
TERRY FOX LIBRARY, 2470 Mary Hill Rd, Port Coquitlam, V3C 3B1, SAN 321-2106. Tel: 604-927-7999. FAX: 604-941-8365. E-mail: terry.fox.library@fvrl.bc.ca. *Libr Mgr,* Sarwan Randhawa; E-mail: sarwan.randhawa@fvrl.bc.ca
Open Mon-Thurs 10-9, Fri & Sat 10-5, Sun 1-5
Friends of the Library Group
HOPE LIBRARY, 1005A Sixth Ave, Hope, V0X 1L4, SAN 321-2025. Tel: 604-869-2313. FAX: 604-869-2472. *Libr Mgr,* Nicole Glentworth
Open Tues 10-8, Wed 1-8, Thurs & Fri 10-5, Sat & Sun 1-5
Friends of the Library Group
LADNER PIONEER LIBRARY, 4683 - 51st St, Delta, V4K 2V8, SAN 321-1983. Tel: 604-946-6215. FAX: 604-946-7821. *Libr Mgr,* Courtney Robinson
Open Mon-Thurs 10-9, Fri & Sat 10-5, Sun 11-5
Friends of the Library Group

GEORGE MACKIE LIBRARY, 8440 112th St, Delta, V4C 4W9, SAN 321-2009. Tel: 604-594-8155. FAX: 604-594-9364. *Libr Mgr,* Courtney Robinson; E-mail: courtney.robinson@fvrl.bc.ca
Open Mon-Thurs 10-9, Fri & Sat 10-5, Sun 11-5

MAPLE RIDGE PUBLIC LIBRARY, 130 - 22470 Dewdney Trunk Rd, Maple Ridge, V2X 5Z6, SAN 321-2017. Tel: 604-467-7417. FAX: 604-467-7404. *Interim Libr Mgr,* Heather Scoular; E-mail: heather.scoular@fvrl.bc.ca; Staff 14 (MLS 1, Non-MLS 13)
Pop 60,000; Circ 450,000
Open Mon-Fri 10-9, Sat 10-5, Sun 1-5
Friends of the Library Group

MISSION LIBRARY, 33247 Second Ave, Mission, V2V 1J9, SAN 321-205X. Tel: 604-826-6610. FAX: 604-826-6614. *Libr Mgr,* Deborah Kendze; Tel: 604-841-1261, E-mail: deborah.kendze@fvrl.bc.ca
Open Mon-Thurs 10-9, Fri & Sat 10-5, Sun 1-5
Friends of the Library Group

MOUNT LEHMAN LIBRARY, 5875 Mount Lehman Rd, V4X 1V5, SAN 321-2068. Tel: 604-856-4988. FAX: 604-856-4908. *Libr Mgr,* Hillary Russell
Open Tues-Fri 1:30-5:30

MURRAYVILLE LIBRARY, Unit 100 - 22071 48th Ave, Langley, V3A 3N1. Tel: 604-533-0339. FAX: 604-514-7260. *Libr Mgr,* David Thiessen
Open Mon-Thurs 10-9, Fri & Sat 10-5, Sun 1-5

PITT MEADOWS PUBLIC LIBRARY, 200-12099 Harris Rd, Pitt Meadows, V3Y 0E5, SAN 321-2092. Tel: 604-465-4113. FAX: 604-465-9732. *Interim Libr Mgr,* Heather Scoular; E-mail: heather.scoular@fvrl.bc.ca
Open Mon-Thurs 10-9, Fri & Sat 10-5, Sun 1-5
Friends of the Library Group

SARDIS LIBRAY, 5819 Tyson Rd, Chilliwack, V2R 3R6. Tel: 604-858-5503. FAX: 604-858-5504. *Libr Mgr,* Nicole Glentworth; E-mail: nicole.glentworth@fvrl.bc.ca
Open Mon-Thurs 10-9, Fri 10-6, Sat 10-5, Sun 1-5

TSAWWASSEN LIBRARY, 1321A 56th St, Delta, V4L 2A6, SAN 321-2122. Tel: 604-943-2271. FAX: 604-943-6941. *Libr Mgr,* Courtney Robinson; Staff 8 (MLS 1, Non-MLS 7)
Open Mon-Thurs 10-9, Fri & Sat 10-5, Sun 11-5
Friends of the Library Group

WALNUT GROVE LIBRARY, Walnut Grove Community Ctr, 8889 Walnut Grove Dr, Langley, V1M 2N7, SAN 375-2917. Tel: 604-882-0410. FAX: 604-882-3754. *Libr Mgr,* David Thiessen
Open Mon-Fri 10-9, Sat 10-5, Sun 1-5

WHITE ROCK LIBRARY, 15342 Buena Vista Ave, White Rock, V4B 1Y6, SAN 321-2157. Tel: 604-541-2201. FAX: 604-541-2209. *Libr Mgr,* David Thiessen
Open Mon-Wed 10-9, Thurs-Sat 10-5, Sun 1-5
Friends of the Library Group

YALE LIBRARY, 65050 Albert St, Yale, V0K 2S0, SAN 321-2165. Tel: 604-863-2279. FAX: 604-863-0138. *Libr Mgr,* Nicole Glentworth
Open Wed & Sat 1-5 & 5:30-7:30

YARROW LIBRARY, 4670 Community St, Yarrow, V2R 5E1, SAN 324-2730. Tel: 604-823-4664. FAX: 604-823-4686. *Libr Mgr,* Nicole Glentworth
Open Tues 10-8, Wed 10-4:30, Thurs 1:30-8, Sat 10-3

S PACIFIC INSTITUTION/REGIONAL TREATMENT CENTRE LIBRARY, 33344 King Rd, V2S 4P4. (Mail add: PO Box 3000, V2S 4P4), SAN 370-6303. Tel: 604-870-7700. FAX: 604-870-7630. Web Site: sigles-symbols.bac-lac.gc.ca/eng/search/details?id=3708, www.csc-scc.gc.ca/correctional-service/corporate/facilities-security/institutional-profiles. *Librn,* Jennifer Joslin; E-mail: jennifer.joslin@csc-scc.gc.ca
Library Holdings: Bk Titles 12,000
Restriction: Not open to pub

CR SUMMIT PACIFIC COLLEGE*, Lorne Philip Hudson Memorial Library, 35235 Straiton Rd, V2S 7Z1. (Mail add: PO Box 1700, V2S 7E7), SAN 320-3069. Tel: 604-851-7230. FAX: 604-853-8951. E-mail: librarian@summitpacific.ca. Web Site: library.summitpacific.ca. *Librn,* Kimberly Poleshuk; *Library Technologist,* Les Penner; E-mail: lpenner@summitpacific.ca; Staff 1.8 (MLS 1, Non-MLS 0.8)
Founded 1941. Enrl 196; Highest Degree: Bachelor
Library Holdings: AV Mats 682; Bks on Deafness & Sign Lang 15; Braille Volumes 3; CDs 111; DVDs 28; e-journals 550; Microforms 2,059; Music Scores 112; Bk Titles 56,545; Bk Vols 66,000; Per Subs 40; Videos 248
Special Collections: Pentecostal Church History (The Pentecostal Testimony Coll), per
Subject Interests: Relig studies
Automation Activity & Vendor Info: (Acquisitions) LibraryWorld, Inc; (Cataloging) LibraryWorld, Inc; (Circulation) LibraryWorld, Inc; (OPAC) LibraryWorld, Inc; (Serials) LibraryWorld, Inc
Wireless access
Function: Archival coll, Audio & video playback equip for onsite use, CD-ROM, Computers for patron use, ILL available, Mail loans to mem, Music CDs, Online cat, Photocopying/Printing, Ref & res, Res libr, Scanner, VHS videos
Open Mon, Tues & Thurs 8am-9pm, Wed & Fri 8-5, Sat 9-3
Restriction: Authorized patrons, Borrowing privileges limited to fac & registered students, Borrowing requests are handled by ILL, External users must contact libr, In-house use for visitors, Open to pub upon request, Open to students, fac & staff, Restricted borrowing privileges, Secured area only open to authorized personnel

C UNIVERSITY OF THE FRASER VALLEY, Abbotsford Campus Library, 33844 King Rd, Bldg G, V2S 7M8. SAN 318-7497. Tel: 604-854-4545. Circulation Tel: 604-504-7441, Ext 4344. Interlibrary Loan Service Tel: 604-864-4678. Reference Tel: 604-504-7441, Ext 4221. Administration Tel: 604-864-4696. FAX: 604-853-0795. E-mail: circabb@ufv.ca, refabby@ufv.ca. Web Site: library.ufv.ca. *Univ Librn,* Camille Callison; E-mail: camille.callison@ufv.ca; *Archivist, Assoc Univ Librn,* Kendra Long; Tel: 604-504-7441, Ext 4243, E-mail: kendra.long@ufv.ca; *Assessment Librn,* Colleen Bell; Tel: 604-504-7441, Ext 4396, E-mail: colleen.bell@ufv.ca; *Cat & Syst Librn,* Hongfei Li; Tel: 604-504-7441, Ext 4268, E-mail: hongfei.li@ufv.ca; *Colls Librn,* Martin Warkentin; Tel: 604-504-7441, Ext 4460, E-mail: martin.warkentin@ufv.ca; Staff 25 (MLS 10, Non-MLS 15)
Founded 1974. Enrl 14,600; Fac 718; Highest Degree: Master
Special Collections: Fraser Valley Heritage Coll
Wireless access
Partic in British Columbia Electronic Library Network; Canadian Research Knowledge Network; Centre for Accessible Post-Secondary Education Resources; Council of Prairie & Pacific University Libraries; Electronic Health Library of British Columbia
Open Mon-Thurs 8am-10pm, Fri 8-6, Sat 10-6, Sun 12-6

Departmental Libraries:

CHILLIWACK CAMPUS, 45190 Caen Ave, Bldg A, Chilliwack, V2R 0N3. Tel: 604-795-2824. E-mail: circchil@ufv.ca. *Access Services Team Leader,* Dan de Groot; Tel: 604-504-7441, Ext 2468, E-mail: daniel.degroot@ufv.ca; *Ref & Instruction Librn,* Diane Cruickshank; Tel: 604-504-7441, Ext 2268, E-mail: diane.cruikshank@ufv.ca; *Library Tech, Circulation,* Korina Gratton; Tel: 604-504-7441, Ext 2431, E-mail: korina.gratton@ufv.ca; *Library Tech, Circulation,* Maecyn Klassen; Tel: 604-504-7441, Ext 2472, E-mail: maecyn.klassen@ufv.ca; *Library Tech, Reserves & Circulation,* Lisa Morry; Tel: 604-504-7441, Ext 2471, E-mail: lisa.morry@ufv.ca
Subject Interests: Agr, Health sci, Trades
Open Mon-Thurs 8am-8:30pm, Fri 8-4:30, Sat 10-4

AGASSIZ

G CORRECTIONAL SERVICE OF CANADA-PACIFIC REGION*, Kent Institution Library, 4732 Cemetery Rd, V0M 1A0. (Mail add: PO Box 1500, V0M 1A0), SAN 375-4820. Tel: 604-796-2121, Ext 4329. FAX: 604-796-4500. *Librn,* Charles Bolding; E-mail: charles.bolding@csc-scc.gc.ca; Staff 1 (Non-MLS 1)
Library Holdings: Bk Titles 12,000

ALERT BAY

P ALERT BAY PUBLIC LIBRARY & MUSEUM*, 116 Fir St, V0N 1A0. (Mail add: PO Box 440, V0N 1A0). Tel: 250-974-5721. E-mail: abplb@shaw.ca. Web Site: alertbay.bc.libraries.coop. *Commun Librn, Libr Dir,* Joyce Wilby
Founded 1959
Library Holdings: Audiobooks 17; CDs 10; DVDs 28; Large Print Bks 171; Bk Titles 9,110; Bk Vols 9,197; Per Subs 1
Special Services for the Blind - Bks on CD; Daisy reader; Large print bks; Playaways (bks on MP3)
Open Tues, Wed, Fri & Sat 1-4

BAMFIELD

C WESTERN CANADIAN UNIVERSITIES MARINE SCIENCES SOCIETY*, Bamfield Marine Sciences Centre Library, 100 Pachena Rd, V0R 1B0. SAN 322-8665. Tel: 250-728-3301, Ext 213. FAX: 250-728-3452. E-mail: library@bamfieldmsc.com. Web Site: www.bamfieldmsc.com/resource/library. *Librn,* Beth Rogers; Staff 1 (Non-MLS 1)
Founded 1972
Library Holdings: Bk Titles 4,350; Per Subs 54
Subject Interests: Marine & coastal sci
Automation Activity & Vendor Info: (OPAC) Inmagic, Inc.
Wireless access
Function: Archival coll, Audio & video playback equip for onsite use, AV serv, Doc delivery serv, For res purposes, ILL available, Photocopying/Printing, Ref serv available, Res libr, Wheelchair accessible
Open Mon-Fri 8:30-4:30
Restriction: Circ limited, Not a lending libr

BARKERVILLE

S BARKERVILLE HISTORIC TOWN LIBRARY & ARCHIVES*, 14301 Hwy 26 E, V0K 1B0. (Mail add: Box 19, V0K 1B0), SAN 326-1360. Tel: 250-994-3332. Toll Free Tel: 888-994-3332. FAX: 250-994-3435. E-mail: barkerville@barkerville.ca. Web Site: www.barkerville.ca. *Curator,* M Kilsby; Tel: 250-994-3332, Ext 35; *Archivist, Research Librn,* C Zinz; Tel: 888-994-3332, Ext 26
Library Holdings: Bk Vols 15,000
Special Collections: Barkerville & Cariboo Records; Chinese Coll, doc, photog; Euro-Canadian Records; Photographs Cross Indexed Database
Subject Interests: Genealogy, Mining
Wireless access
Function: Archival coll, Audio & video playback equip for onsite use, Bus archives, Electronic databases & coll, For res purposes, Internet access, Microfiche/film & reading machines, Online cat, Photocopying/Printing, Ref & res, Res libr, Res performed for a fee
Restriction: Access at librarian's discretion, Non-circulating coll, Open by appt only, Open to pub for ref only, Open to pub upon request, Open to researchers by request

BOWEN ISLAND

P BOWEN ISLAND PUBLIC LIBRARY*, 430 Bowen Island Trunk Rd, V0N 1G0. (Mail add: PO Box 10, V0N 1G0). Tel: 604-947-9788. E-mail: info@bowenlibrary.ca. Web Site: bowenlibrary.ca. *Chief Librn,* Tina Nielsen; Staff 3.8 (MLS 1, Non-MLS 2.8)
Founded 1981. Pop 4,256; Circ 48,651
Library Holdings: Audiobooks 139; DVDs 855; e-books 74,877; Bk Titles 12,694; Bk Vols 13,022; Per Subs 17
Automation Activity & Vendor Info: (Cataloging) Evergreen; (Circulation) Evergreen; (ILL) Auto-Graphics, Inc; (OPAC) Evergreen
Wireless access
Function: 24/7 Electronic res, 24/7 Online cat, Bks on CD, Children's prog, Computer training, Computers for patron use, Digital talking bks, E-Readers, E-Reserves, Electronic databases & coll, Equip loans & repairs, Family literacy, Free DVD rentals, Govt ref serv, ILL available, Internet access, Life-long learning prog for all ages, Magazines, Mail & tel request accepted, Meeting rooms, Online ref, OverDrive digital audio bks, Photocopying/Printing, Preschool outreach, Preschool reading prog, Prog for adults, Prog for children & young adult, Ref serv available, Scanner, Story hour, Study rm, Summer reading prog, Telephone ref, Wheelchair accessible, Workshops
Partic in Public Library InterLINK
Open Tues & Wed 10-5, Thurs 10-7, Fri & Sat 10-4, Sun Noon-4
Restriction: Circulates for staff only, Staff use only
Friends of the Library Group

BURNABY

C ALEXANDER COLLEGE*, Burnaby Campus Library, 4805 Kingsway, V5H 4T6. Tel: 604-558-7369. FAX: 604-435-5895. E-mail: library@alexandercollege.ca. Web Site: alexandercollege.ca/student-success/library. *Librn,* Emily Gunn; E-mail: e.gunn@alexandercollege.ca
Automation Activity & Vendor Info: (Cataloging) L4U Library Software; (OPAC) L4U Library Software
Wireless access
Function: Computers for patron use, Study rm
Partic in Electronic Health Library of British Columbia
Open Mon-Thurs 8am-9pm, Fri 8-6
Departmental Libraries:
VANCOUVER CAMPUS LIBRARY, 100-602 W Hastings St, Vancouver, V6B 1P2. Tel: 604-681-5815.

C BRITISH COLUMBIA INSTITUTE OF TECHNOLOGY LIBRARY*, 3700 Willingdon Ave, SE14, V5G 3H2. SAN 318-7519. Tel: 604-432-8370. Interlibrary Loan Service Tel: 604-432-8619. Administration Tel: 604-432-8827. Interlibrary Loan Service FAX: 604-435-9641. Administration FAX: 604-434-1585. Circulation E-mail: libcirc@bcit.ca. Web Site: www.bcit.ca/library. *Dir, Libr Serv,* Alison Nussbaumer; E-mail: anussbaumer@bcit.ca; Staff 35 (MLS 10, Non-MLS 25)
Founded 1964. Enrl 47,969; Fac 1,590; Highest Degree: Master
Library Holdings: AV Mats 4,567; e-books 9,269; e-journals 369; Electronic Media & Resources 102,179; Bk Titles 186,820; Per Subs 978
Special Collections: ANSI Standards; Census; Company Annual Reports; CSA Standards; Government and law; Micro Software; NTIS Reports; SAE Reports; Statistics Canada publications
Subject Interests: Computer sci, Engr, Forestry
Wireless access
Function: Archival coll, AV serv, Bus archives, Distance learning, Doc delivery serv, For res purposes, Govt ref serv, Health sci info serv, ILL available, Internet access, Outside serv via phone, mail, e-mail & web, Photocopying/Printing, Ref serv available, Res libr, Satellite serv, Wheelchair accessible
Partic in British Columbia Electronic Library Network; Centre for Accessible Post-Secondary Education Resources; Electronic Health Library of British Columbia
Special Services for the Deaf - TTY equip
Open Mon-Thurs 8-8, Fri 8-5, Sat 9:30-5
Restriction: Open to pub upon request, Open to students, fac & staff

P BURNABY PUBLIC LIBRARY*, 6100 Willingdon Ave, V5H 4N5. SAN 365-7965. Tel: 604-436-5427. FAX: 604-436-2961. E-mail: eref@bpl.bc.ca. Web Site: www.bpl.bc.ca. *Chief Librn,* Beth Davies; Tel: 604-436-5431, E-mail: beth.davies@bpl.bc.ca; Staff 134.5 (MLS 31.9, Non-MLS 102.6)
Founded 1954. Pop 229,464; Circ 3,517,009
Library Holdings: Bk Titles 400,918; Bk Vols 687,284; Per Subs 992
Automation Activity & Vendor Info: (Acquisitions) SirsiDynix; (Cataloging) SirsiDynix; (Circulation) SirsiDynix; (OPAC) SirsiDynix; (Serials) SirsiDynix
Wireless access
Partic in Public Library InterLINK
Open Mon & Fri 10-5, Tues-Thurs 10-7, Sat 10-4, Sun Noon-4
Branches: 4
CAMERON BRANCH, 9523 Cameron St, V3J 1L6, SAN 365-7973. Tel: 604-421-5454. *Br Mgr,* Jamie McCarthy; Tel: 604-297-4445, E-mail: jamie.mccarthy@bpl.bc.ca; Staff 11.6 (MLS 2.9, Non-MLS 8.7)
Circ 501,245
Open Mon & Fri 10-5 Tues-Thurs 10-7, Sat 10-4, Sun Noon-4
TOMMY DOUGLAS BRANCH, 7311 Kingsway, V5E 1G8, SAN 365-8023. Tel: 604-522-3971. *Br Mgr,* Linton Harrison; Tel: 604-297-4824, E-mail: linton.harrison@bpl.bc.ca; Staff 18.8 (MLS 4.6, Non-MLS 14.2)
Circ 636,644
Open Mon & Fri 10-5, Tues-Thurs 10-7, Sat 10-4, Sun Noon-4
MCGILL BRANCH, 4595 Albert St, V5C 2G6, SAN 365-8058. Tel: 604-299-8955. FAX: 604-299-7000. *Br Mgr,* Jessica Lee; Tel: 604-297-4813, E-mail: jessica.lee@bpl.bc.ca; Staff 22.8 (MLS 6.4, Non-MLS 16.4)
Circ 912,561
Open Mon & Fri 10-5, Tues-Thurs 10-7, Sat 10-4, Sun Noon-4
BOB PRITTIE METROTOWN BRANCH, 6100 Willingdon Ave, V5H 4N5, SAN 372-5170. Tel: 604-436-5400. FAX: 604-436-9087. *Br Mgr,* Elizabeth Davies; Tel: 604-436-5403; Staff 81.2 (MLS 17.9, Non-MLS 63.3)
Circ 1,466,559
Special Collections: British Columbia Coll
Open Mon & Fri 10-5, Tues-Thurs 10-7, Sat 10-4, Sun Noon-4
Bookmobiles: 1

M FRASER HEALTH AUTHORITY*, Burnaby Hospital Library, 3935 Kincaid St, V5G 2X6. SAN 324-4431. Tel: 604-412-6255. Web Site: www.fraserhealth.ca/find-us/hospitals/burnaby-hospital. *Librn,* Julie Mason; E-mail: julie.mason@fraserhealth.ca
Founded 1960
Library Holdings: e-journals 250; Bk Titles 800; Per Subs 45
Subject Interests: Healthcare, Med, Nursing
Partic in Electronic Health Library of British Columbia
Open Mon-Thurs 6-6

G METRO VANCOUVER LIBRARY*, 4515 Central Blvd, Mailroom 11th Flr, V5H 0C6. SAN 321-4591. Tel: 604-432-6335. E-mail: library@metrovancouver.org. Web Site: www.metrovancouver.org/about/library/Pages/default.aspx. *Coop Librn,* Suzanne McBeath; Staff 3 (MLS 2, Non-MLS 1)
Founded 1970
Library Holdings: Bk Titles 10,000; Per Subs 50
Special Collections: Greater Vancouver Regional District Reports; Metro Vancouver Regional District Reports
Subject Interests: Air quality, Drinking water, Engr, Housing, Planning, Pollution control, Recreation, Waste mgt, Wastewater
Automation Activity & Vendor Info: (Acquisitions) SydneyPlus; (Cataloging) SydneyPlus; (Circulation) SydneyPlus; (OPAC) SydneyPlus; (Serials) SydneyPlus
Partic in International Environment Library Consortium
Open Mon-Fri 8-4:30

C SIMON FRASER UNIVERSITY - BURNABY CAMPUS*, W A C Bennett Library, 8888 University Dr, V5A 1S6. SAN 318-7578. Tel: 778-782-4084. Circulation Tel: 778-782-4345. Interlibrary Loan Service Tel: 778-782-3625. Reference Tel: 778-782-5735. FAX: 778-782-3023. Interlibrary Loan Service FAX: 778-782-4908. Reference FAX: 778-782-6926. E-mail: libask@sfu.ca. Web Site: www.lib.sfu.ca. *Dean of Libr,* Gohar Ashoughian; E-mail: gashough@sfu.ca; *Assoc Univ Librn, Admin Serv,* Natalie Gick; Tel: 778-782-3266, E-mail: ngick@sfu.ca; *Assoc Univ Librn, Coll & Scholarly Communication,* Patty Gallilee; E-mail: plg@sfu.ca; *Assoc Univ Librn, Digital Strat,* Mark Jordan; Tel: 778-782-5753, E-mail: mjordan@sfu.ca; *Assoc Univ Librn, Learning & Res Serv,* Karen Munro; Tel: 778-782-3252, E-mail: kemunro@sfu.ca; *Head,*

Access Serv, Mark Christensen; Tel: 778-782-4081, E-mail: Mark_Christensen@sfu.ca; *Head, Resource Acquisition, Metadata & Mgmt,* Gordon Coleman; Tel: 778-782-3916, E-mail: gcoleman@sfu.ca; *Spec Coll Librn,* Melissa Salrin; Tel: 778-782-4626, E-mail: msalrin@sfu.ca; Staff 68 (MLS 48, Non-MLS 20)
Founded 1965. Enrl 26,670; Highest Degree: Doctorate
Library Holdings: AV Mats 983,117; e-books 405,222; e-journals 41,898; Bk Vols 2,369,049; Per Subs 48,558; Videos 9,250
Special Collections: Aldus Pius Manutius (Aldine Coll); Canadian Newspaper Editorial Cartoons, 1952-present (Len Norris, Roy Peterson, Graham Harrop, Bob Krieger & Dan Murphy); Contemporary Literature (20th Century Avant Garde & Innovative Literature Coll); Harrison Brown Coll, photogs; History of Canada & Western Canada (CCF Holdings, Labour & Doukhobor Materials); Special Manuscripts Coll (Bill Bissett, Anne Cameron, Betty Lambert, Ezra Pound, Papers of "Open Letter" magazine, Papers of BP Nichol & Archival Material from Talonbooks); Wordsworth Coll
Automation Activity & Vendor Info: (Acquisitions) Ex Libris Group; (Cataloging) Ex Libris Group; (Circulation) Ex Libris Group; (Course Reserve) Ex Libris Group; (ILL) Relais International; (OPAC) Ex Libris Group; (Serials) Ex Libris Group
Wireless access
Function: Audio & video playback equip for onsite use, Distance learning, Doc delivery serv, For res purposes, ILL available, Makerspace, Photocopying/Printing, Ref serv available, Res libr, Telephone ref, Wheelchair accessible, Workshops
Partic in British Columbia Electronic Library Network; Canadian Research Knowledge Network; Council of Prairie & Pacific University Libraries; Electronic Health Library of British Columbia
Special Services for the Blind - Assistive/Adapted tech devices, equip & products; Talking bks; ZoomText magnification & reading software
Open Mon-Thurs 8am-11:45pm, Fri 8-8, Sat & Sun 10-10
Friends of the Library Group

BURNS LAKE

P BURNS LAKE PUBLIC LIBRARY*, 585 Government St, V0J 1E0. (Mail add: PO Box 449, V0J 1E0), SAN 810-0152. Tel: 250-692-3192. FAX: 250-692-7488. E-mail: libraryn@burnslakelibrary.com. Interlibrary Loan Service E-mail: ill@burnslakelibrary.com. Web Site: burnslake.bc.libraries.coop. *Libr Dir,* Monika Willner; *Asst Dir,* Roberta McKenzie; E-mail: roberta@burnslakelibrary.com; *Ch,* Bonny Remple; E-mail: bonny@burnslakelibrary.com
Founded 1944. Pop 7,000; Circ 56,648
Library Holdings: CDs 106; DVDs 30; Large Print Bks 300; Bk Titles 30,251; Per Subs 45; Talking Bks 500; Videos 204
Automation Activity & Vendor Info: (Cataloging) Follett Software; (Circulation) Follett Software; (ILL) Auto-Graphics, Inc; (OPAC) Follett Software
Function: Adult bk club, CD-ROM, Home delivery & serv to seniorr ctr & nursing homes, Homebound delivery serv, ILL available, Internet access, Music CDs, Photocopying/Printing, Prog for children & young adult, Serves people with intellectual disabilities, Spoken cassettes & CDs, Spoken cassettes & DVDs, Summer reading prog, VHS videos, Wheelchair accessible
Partic in N Cent Libr Asn
Open Mon & Sat Noon-4, Tues-Thurs 9:30-7, Fri 9:30-5

CAMPBELL RIVER

S CAMPBELL RIVER MUSEUM & ARCHIVES*, Reference Library, 470 Island Hwy, V9W 2B7. SAN 323-5246. Tel: 250-287-3103. FAX: 250-286-0109. E-mail: general.inquiries@crmuseum.ca. Web Site: www.crmuseum.ca. *Exec Dir,* Sandra Parrish; *Colls Mgr,* Megan Purcell; E-mail: megan.purcell@crmuseum.ca
Library Holdings: CDs 4; DVDs 34; Bk Vols 1,956; Videos 19
Subject Interests: BC hist, Ethnology, First Nations, Fishing, Logging
Wireless access
Open Tues-Fri 1-4

J NORTH ISLAND COLLEGE*, Campbell River Campus Library, 1685 S Dogwood St, V9W 8C1. Tel: 250-923-9785. Web Site: library.nic.bc.ca. *Libr Supvr,* Katherine Percival; Tel: 250-923-9787, E-mail: katherine.percival@nic.bc.ca; *Coordr, Libr Serv,* Lynette Gallant; E-mail: lynette.gallant@nic.bc.ca
Library Holdings: Bk Titles 8,000
Automation Activity & Vendor Info: (Acquisitions) SirsiDynix; (Cataloging) SirsiDynix; (Circulation) SirsiDynix; (Course Reserve) SirsiDynix; (OPAC) SirsiDynix
Wireless access
Open Mon-Fri 8-4

CASTLEGAR

P CASTLEGAR & DISTRICT PUBLIC LIBRARY*, 1005 Third St, V1N 2A2. SAN 365-8112. Tel: 250-365-6611. FAX: 250-365-7765. E-mail: info@castlegarlibrary.com. Web Site: castlegar.bc.libraries.coop. *Dir,* Kimberly Partanen; Tel: 250-365-7751, E-mail: director@castlegarlibrary.com; Staff 5 (MLS 1, Non-MLS 4)
Founded 1947. Pop 13,427
Library Holdings: Bk Titles 60,000; Per Subs 110
Automation Activity & Vendor Info: (Acquisitions) Evergreen; (Cataloging) Evergreen; (Circulation) Evergreen; (OPAC) Evergreen
Wireless access
Function: ILL available
Mem of Kootenay Library Federation
Special Services for the Blind - Bks on cassette
Open Mon-Thurs 9-6, Fri 9-5, Sat 10-5
Friends of the Library Group

P KOOTENAY LIBRARY FEDERATION, PO Box 3125, V1N 3H4. Tel: 250-608-4490. Web Site: klf.bc.libraries.coop. *Chair,* Mary Kierons; *Exec Dir,* Melanie Reaveley; E-mail: director@klf.bclibrary.ca
Wireless access
Member Libraries: Beaver Valley Public Library; Castlegar & District Public Library; Cranbrook Public Library; Creston Valley Public Library; Elkford Public Library; Fernie Heritage Library; Grand Forks & District Public Library; Greenwood Public Library; Invermere Public Library; Kaslo & District Public Library; Kimberley Public Library; Midway Public Library; Nakusp Public Library Association; Nelson Public Library; Penticton Public Library; Radium Hot Springs Public Library; Rossland Public Library Association; Salmo Valley Public Library; Sparwood Public Library; Trail & District Public Library

J SELKIRK COLLEGE LIBRARY*, 301 Frank Beinder Way, V1N 4L3. SAN 318-7594. Tel: 250-365-1229. FAX: 250-365-7259. E-mail: reference@selkirk.ca. Web Site: library.selkirk.ca/library_home. *Col Librn,* Gregg Currie; Tel: 250-365-1263; *Librn,* Sian Landis; Tel: 250-365-1339; *Instrul Serv Librn,* Ken Laing; Tel: 250-365-1382; Staff 11 (MLS 3, Non-MLS 8)
Founded 1966
Library Holdings: Bk Vols 76,000; Per Subs 500
Special Collections: Kootenay Materials
Automation Activity & Vendor Info: (Circulation) SirsiDynix; (OPAC) SirsiDynix-iLink
Wireless access
Function: ILL available
Publications: Kootenaiana
Partic in British Columbia Electronic Library Network; Centre for Accessible Post-Secondary Education Resources; Electronic Health Library of British Columbia
Open Mon & Fri 7:30-5, Tues-Thurs 7:30-7, Sat 10-4

Departmental Libraries:

SILVER CAMPUS, 2001 Silver King Rd, Nelson, V1L 1C8. Tel: 250-354-3249. Toll Free Tel: 866-301-6601, Ext 13249. *Library Contact,* Anne Verkerk
Open Mon-Thurs 8:30-1:30

TENTH STREET CAMPUS, 820 Tenth St, Nelson, V1l 3C7. Tel: 250-505-1359. Toll Free Tel: 866-301-6601, Ext 11359. *Library Contact,* Jason Asbell
Open Mon-Thurs 8:30-1:30

CHETWYND

P CHETWYND PUBLIC LIBRARY*, 5012 46th St, V0C 1J0. (Mail add: PO Box 1420, V0C 1J0), SAN 318-7608. Tel: 250-788-2559. FAX: 250-788-2186. E-mail: cpl@chetwynd.bclibrary.ca. Web Site: chetwynd.bc.libraries.coop. *Dir,* Melissa Millsap; E-mail: librarydirector@chetwynd.bclibrary.ca; *Asst Libr Dir,* Kayla MacDonald; E-mail: assistantdirector@chetwynd.bclibrary.ca
Founded 1967. Pop 7,000; Circ 44,355
Library Holdings: Bk Vols 22,000; Per Subs 35
Automation Activity & Vendor Info: (Cataloging) Mandarin Library Automation; (Circulation) Mandarin Library Automation; (OPAC) Mandarin Library Automation
Wireless access
Partic in North East Library Federation
Open Mon & Wed 9-6, Tues & Thurs 9-8, Sat Noon-4
Friends of the Library Group

CHILLIWACK

S CHILLIWACK MUSEUM & HISTORICAL SOCIETY*, 9291 Corbould St, V2P 4A6. SAN 326-5218. Tel: 604-795-5210. FAX: 604-795-9255. E-mail: info@chilliwackmuseum.ca. Web Site: www.chilliwackmuseum.ca. *Exec Dir,* Shawna Dwyer; Tel: 604-795-5210, Ext 101, E-mail: shawna@chilliwackmuseum.ca; *Archivist,* Tristan Evans; Tel:

604-795-5210, Ext 104, E-mail: tristan@chilliwackmuseum.ca; *Curator,* Kate Feltren; Tel: 604-795-5210, Ext 105, E-mail: kate@chilliwackmuseum.ca
Library Holdings: Bk Titles 2,000; Per Subs 12
Special Collections: Local municipal govt
Wireless access
Partic in Can Museums Asn
Open Mon-Fri 9-4:30

COQUITLAM

P COQUITLAM PUBLIC LIBRARY*, Poirier Branch, 575 Poirier St, V3J 6A9. SAN 365-8171. Circulation Tel: 604-937-4141. Reference Tel: 604-937-4144. Administration Tel: 604-937-4130. FAX: 604-931-6739. E-mail: askalibrarian@coqlibrary.ca. Web Site: www.coqlibrary.ca. *Exec Dir,* Todd Gnissios; Tel: 604-937-4132, E-mail: tgnissios@coqlibrary.ca; *Dep Dir, Dir, Technology,* Silvana Harwood; Tel: 604-937-4131, E-mail: sharwood@coqlibrary.ca; *Dir, Commun Engagement,* Anthea Goffe; Tel: 604-554-7347, E-mail: agoffe@coqlibrary.ca; *Dir Customer Experience, Main,* Maryn Ashdown; Tel: 604-554-7324, E-mail: mashdown@coqlibrary.ca; *Commun Connections Librn, Mgr, Programming,* Barbara Weston; Tel: 604-937-4143, E-mail: bweston@coqlibrary.ca; *Mgr, Tech Innovation Librn,* Rory Weston; Tel: 604-937-4251, E-mail: rweston@coqlibrary.ca; *Mgr, Mkt, Communications & Develop,* Jay Peters; Tel: 604-937-4147, E-mail: jpeters@coqlibrary.ca; *Customer Experience Mgr, Facilities Servs,* Sharmini Manoharan; Tel: 604-554-7332, E-mail: smanoharan@coqlibrary.ca; *Supvr, Tech Serv,* Melani Williams; Tel: 604-937-4149, E-mail: mwilliams@coqlibrary.ca
Founded 1978. Pop 127,000; Circ 998,216
Library Holdings: Bk Titles 122,000; Per Subs 417
Special Collections: National Film Board of Canada, video
Subject Interests: Auto manuals, Local hist
Wireless access
Partic in Public Library InterLINK
Open Mon-Thurs 9-9, Fri 9-5, Sat 10-5, Sun 12-5
Friends of the Library Group
Branches: 1
CITY CENTRE BRANCH, 1169 Pinetree Way, V3B 0Y1, SAN 365-8228. Tel: 604-554-7323. *Dir, Commun Engagement,* Anthea Goffe; Tel: 604-554-7347, E-mail: agoffe@coqlibrary.ca; *Customer Experience Dir,* Maryn Ashdown; Tel: 604-554-7324, E-mail: mashdown@coqlibrary.ca; *Customer Experience Mgr, Facilities Servs,* Sharmini Manoharan; Tel: 604-554-7332, E-mail: smanoharan@coqlibrary.ca
Open Mon-Thurs 9-9, Fri 9-5, Sat 10-5, Sun 12-5
Friends of the Library Group

S INTERTEK TESTING SERVICES*, Warnock Hersey Library, 1500 Brigantine Dr, V3K 7C1. SAN 374-6208. Tel: 604-520-3321. FAX: 604-524-9186. Web Site: www.intertek.com. *Mgr,* Simon Knight; *Mgr,* Kal Kooner; E-mail: kal.kooner@intertek.com
Library Holdings: Bk Titles 600; Bk Vols 800; Per Subs 500
Open Mon-Fri 7:30-5

COURTENAY

J NORTH ISLAND COLLEGE*, Comox Valley Campus Library, 2300 Ryan Rd, V9N 8N6. Tel: 250-334-5037. FAX: 250-334-5291. Web Site: library.nic.bc.ca. *Info Serv Librn,* Jennifer Evans; E-mail: jennifer.evans@nic.bc.ca; *Coll Develop,* Lynette Gallant; Tel: 250-334-5097, E-mail: lynette.gallant@nic.bc.ca
Library Holdings: Bk Titles 30,000
Automation Activity & Vendor Info: (Acquisitions) SirsiDynix; (Cataloging) SirsiDynix; (Circulation) SirsiDynix; (Course Reserve) SirsiDynix; (OPAC) SirsiDynix
Wireless access
Partic in Centre for Accessible Post-Secondary Education Resources; Electronic Health Library of British Columbia
Open Mon-Thurs 8am-9pm, Fri 8-4

CRANBROOK

P CRANBROOK PUBLIC LIBRARY*, 1212 Second St N, V1C 4T6. SAN 318-7616. Tel: 250-426-4063. FAX: 250-426-2098. E-mail: staff@cranbrookpubliclibrary.ca. Web Site: www.cranbrookpubliclibrary.ca. *Chief Librn,* Ursula Brigl; E-mail: ubrigl@cranbrookpubliclibrary.ca; Staff 11.6 (MLS 1.4, Non-MLS 10.2)
Founded 1925. Pop 26,000; Circ 224,000
Jan 2018-Dec 2018 Income (CAN) $964,490, Provincial (CAN) $100,838, City (CAN) $607,784, County (CAN) $151,946, Locally Generated Income (CAN) $103,922. Mats Exp (CAN) $88,570, Books (CAN) $49,900, Per/Ser (Incl. Access Fees) (CAN) $9,100, AV Mat (CAN) $15,170, Electronic Ref Mat (Incl. Access Fees) (CAN) $14,400. Sal (CAN) $561,617
Library Holdings: Audiobooks 1,781; Bks on Deafness & Sign Lang 40; CDs 1,960; DVDs 4,747; e-books 11,000; e-journals 200; Electronic Media & Resources 26; High Interest/Low Vocabulary Bk Vols 35; Large Print Bks 999; Music Scores 300; Bk Titles 58,642; Bk Vols 60,667; Per Subs 180
Automation Activity & Vendor Info: (Acquisitions) Horizon; (Cataloging) Horizon; (Circulation) Horizon; (Discovery) SirsiDynix-Enterprise; (ILL) Auto-Graphics, Inc; (Media Booking) EnvisionWare; (OPAC) SirsiDynix-Enterprise; (Serials) Horizon
Wireless access
Function: 24/7 Electronic res, 24/7 Online cat, Adult bk club, Adult literacy prog, After school storytime, Audio & video playback equip for onsite use, Audiobks on Playaways & MP3, Audiobks via web, AV serv, Bk club(s), Bks on CD, CD-ROM, Children's prog, Computer training, Computers for patron use, Digital talking bks, E-Readers, E-Reserves, Electronic databases & coll, Equip loans & repairs, Family literacy, Free DVD rentals, Holiday prog, Home delivery & serv to seniorr ctr & nursing homes, Homebound delivery serv, Homework prog, ILL available, Internet access, Large print keyboards, Life-long learning prog for all ages, Magazines, Mail & tel request accepted, Meeting rooms, Movies, Music CDs, Online cat, Online ref, Outreach serv, Outside serv via phone, mail, e-mail & web, OverDrive digital audio bks, Photocopying/Printing, Preschool outreach, Preschool reading prog, Prog for adults, Prog for children & young adult, Ref serv available, Scanner, Senior outreach, Spoken cassettes & CDs, Spoken cassettes & DVDs, STEM programs, Story hour, Summer & winter reading prog, Summer reading prog, Teen prog, Wheelchair accessible, Winter reading prog, Workshops
Publications: Annual Report; Inhouse Publications (Documents)
Mem of Kootenay Library Federation
Special Services for the Blind - Bks on CD; Copier with enlargement capabilities; Daisy reader; Home delivery serv; Large print bks; PC for people with disabilities
Open Mon-Fri 9-8, Sat 9-5, Sun 12-5
Restriction: Non-resident fee
Friends of the Library Group

CRESTON

P CRESTON VALLEY PUBLIC LIBRARY*, 531-16th Ave S, V0B 1G5. SAN 318-7632. Tel: 250-428-4141. FAX: 250-428-4703. E-mail: info@crestonlibrary.com. Web Site: crestonlibrary.com. *Libr Dir,* Saara Itkonen; Staff 1 (MLS 1)
Founded 1921. Pop 11,574; Circ 229,282
Library Holdings: AV Mats 2,748; Large Print Bks 152; Bk Titles 35,039; Bk Vols 38,581; Per Subs 65; Talking Bks 112
Automation Activity & Vendor Info: (Cataloging) Mandarin Library Automation; (Circulation) Mandarin Library Automation; (OPAC) Mandarin Library Automation
Wireless access
Mem of Kootenay Library Federation
Special Services for the Blind - Home delivery serv; Large print bks; Talking bks
Open Tues-Sat 10-6
Friends of the Library Group

DAWSON CREEK

P DAWSON CREEK MUNICIPAL PUBLIC LIBRARY*, 1001 McKellar Ave, V1G 4W7. SAN 318-7640. Tel: 250-782-4661. E-mail: dclib@pris.ca. Web Site: dawsoncreek.bc.libraries.coop. *Libr Mgr,* Pamela Morris; *Ch,* Laurie Youb; Staff 6 (Non-MLS 6)
Founded 1948. Pop 18,326; Circ 121,907
Library Holdings: DVDs 1,000; Large Print Bks 1,575; Bk Vols 72,715; Per Subs 96; Talking Bks 1,291; Videos 1,091
Special Collections: Peace River History (Dorthea Calverley Coll)
Automation Activity & Vendor Info: (Acquisitions) Evergreen; (Cataloging) Evergreen; (Circulation) Evergreen; (ILL) Evergreen; (Media Booking) Evergreen; (OPAC) Evergreen; (Serials) Evergreen
Wireless access
Partic in Sitka
Special Services for the Blind - Home delivery serv
Open Tues-Thurs 9:30-7:30, Fri 9:30-5, Sat 1:30-5
Friends of the Library Group

J NORTHERN LIGHTS COLLEGE LIBRARY*, Dawson Creek Campus Library, 11401 Eighth St, V1G 4G2. SAN 324-2129. Tel: 250-784-7533. Toll Free Tel: 866-463-6652, Ext 7533. FAX: 250-784-7567. E-mail: dc-lib@nlc.bc.ca. Web Site: www.nlc.bc.ca/services/library. *Regional Librn,* Dawna Turcotte; E-mail: dturcotte@nlc.bc.ca; Staff 2 (MLS 2)
Founded 1975. Enrl 1,319; Fac 100; Highest Degree: Associate
Library Holdings: e-books 104,469; Bk Vols 22,988; Per Subs 90
Automation Activity & Vendor Info: (Acquisitions) SirsiDynix; (Cataloging) SirsiDynix; (Circulation) SirsiDynix; (OPAC) SirsiDynix; (Serials) SirsiDynix
Wireless access

Partic in Centre for Accessible Post-Secondary Education Resources; Electronic Health Library of British Columbia
Open Mon-Thurs 9-9, Fri 9-5, Sat 11-5, Sun 10-9

ELKFORD

P ELKFORD PUBLIC LIBRARY*, 816 Michel Rd, Bldg C, V0B 1H0. (Mail add: Box 280, V0B 1H0), SAN 318-7659. Tel: 250-865-2912. FAX: 250-865-2460. E-mail: info@elkfordlibrary.org. Web Site: elkford.bc.libraries.coop. *Dir,* Alexandra Faucher
Founded 1974. Pop 2,741; Circ 12,465
Library Holdings: Bk Vols 28,029
Wireless access
Mem of Kootenay Library Federation
Partic in BC Libraries Cooperative
Open Tues & Wed 10:30-5, Thurs & Fri 11:30-6, Sat 12:30-5

FERNIE

P FERNIE HERITAGE LIBRARY*, 492 Third Ave, V0B 1M0. (Mail add: PO Box 448, V0B 1M0), SAN 318-7667. Tel: 250-423-4458. Administration Tel: 250-423-7135. FAX: 250-423-7906. E-mail: information@ferniheritagelibrary.com. Web Site: fernie.bc.libraries.coop. *Dir,* Emma Dressler; *Asst Librn,* Marilyn Razzo
Founded 1920. Pop 7,909; Circ 54,328
Library Holdings: Bk Titles 30,000
Special Collections: Foreign/Independent Films; Language Learning, cassettes. Oral History
Automation Activity & Vendor Info: (Cataloging) Mandarin Library Automation; (Circulation) Mandarin Library Automation; (OPAC) Mandarin Library Automation
Wireless access
Mem of Kootenay Library Federation
Open Tues, Wed & Fri 11-6, Thurs 11-8, Sat 1-5

FORT NELSON

P FORT NELSON PUBLIC LIBRARY*, Municipal Sq, 5315-50th Ave S, V0C 1R0. (Mail add: PO Box 330, V0C 1R0), SAN 318-7675. Tel: 250-774-6777. FAX: 250-774-6777. E-mail: fnpl@fortnelson.bclibrary.ca. Web Site: fortnelson.bc.libraries.coop. *Libr Dir,* Danika Andrews; *Children & Youth Serv Librn,* Shannon Chabot; *ILL,* Hannah Waughtal; E-mail: ill@fortnelson.bclibrary.ca; *Programmer,* Julia Stidolph; E-mail: librarian@fortnelson.bclibrary.ca
Pop 5,000; Circ 26,809
Library Holdings: Bk Vols 30,000
Wireless access
Partic in North East Library Federation
Open Mon & Fri 10-4, Tues-Thurs 11-8, Sat & Sun Noon-4

FORT SAINT JOHN

P FORT ST JOHN PUBLIC LIBRARY ASSOCIATION*, 10015-100th Ave, V1J 1Y7. SAN 318-7691. Tel: 250-785-3731. FAX: 250-785-7982. E-mail: circ@fsjpl.ca. Web Site: www.fsjpl.ca. *Libr Dir,* Karlene Duncan; Staff 7 (Non-MLS 7)
Founded 1950. Pop 28,000
Library Holdings: Bk Vols 60,000
Automation Activity & Vendor Info: (Acquisitions) Mandarin Library Automation
Wireless access
Partic in North East Library Federation
Open Tues-Fri 10-7, Sat 10-6
Friends of the Library Group

C NORTHERN LIGHTS COLLEGE, Fort St John Campus Library, 9820 120 Ave, V1J 8C3. SAN 324-2137. Tel: 250-787-6213. Toll Free Tel: 866-463-6652, Ext 6213. E-mail: fsj-lib@nlc.bc.ca. Web Site: www.nlc.bc.ca/library. *Regional Librn,* Dawna Turcotte; E-mail: librarian@nlc.bc.ca; Staff 6 (MLS 1, Non-MLS 5)
Founded 1975. Enrl 1,491; Fac 82; Highest Degree: Associate
Library Holdings: DVDs 1,947; e-books 181,461; e-journals 57,369; Electronic Media & Resources 17,270; Bk Titles 25,799; Per Subs 32
Special Collections: Streaming Video Coll
Automation Activity & Vendor Info: (Circulation) Evergreen
Wireless access
Function: 24/7 Electronic res, 24/7 Online cat, Computers for patron use, Distance learning, Doc delivery serv, Electronic databases & coll, ILL available, Internet access, Online cat, Online ref, Orientations, Ref serv available, VHS videos
Partic in British Columbia Electronic Library Network
Open Mon-Thurs 8-7, Fri 8-4 (Sept-April); Mon-Fri 8-4 (July-Aug)

FORT ST. JAMES

P FORT ST JAMES PUBLIC LIBRARY*, Fort St James Bicentennial Library, 425 Manson St, V0J 1P0. (Mail add: PO Box 729, V0J 1P0), SAN 318-7683. Tel: 250-996-7431. FAX: 250-996-7484. E-mail: library@fortstjames.bclibrary.ca. Web Site: fortstjames.bc.libraries.coop. *Libr Dir,* Karli Fisher; Staff 5 (MLS 1, Non-MLS 4)
Pop 4,068; Circ 20,094
Library Holdings: Audiobooks 18; DVDs 2,291; Large Print Bks 206; Bk Titles 13,066; Bk Vols 13,299; Per Subs 27
Wireless access
Function: Adult bk club, Bk club(s), Bks on cassette, Children's prog, Computer training, Computers for patron use, Digital talking bks, Electronic databases & coll, Family literacy, Games & aids for people with disabilities, Holiday prog, Home delivery & serv to seniorr ctr & nursing homes, Homebound delivery serv, ILL available, Instruction & testing, Large print keyboards, Magnifiers for reading, Orientations, Outreach serv, OverDrive digital audio bks, Photocopying/Printing, Preschool outreach, Prog for children & young adult, Ref & res, Ref serv available, Senior computer classes, Senior outreach, Spoken cassettes & CDs, Story hour, Summer reading prog, Teen prog, Telephone ref, Wheelchair accessible
Partic in BC Libraries Cooperative
Open Tues & Fri 11:30-8, Wed & Thurs 11:30-4:30, Sat 11-3

FRASER LAKE

P FRASER LAKE PUBLIC LIBRARY*, 228 Endako Ave, V0J 1S0. (Mail add: PO Box 520, V0J 1S0), SAN 377-2128. Tel: 250-699-8888. FAX: 250-699-8899. E-mail: fllibrarian@bcgroup.net. Web Site: fraserlake.bc.libraries.coop. *Chief Librn,* Audrey Fennema; E-mail: afennema@fraserlake.ca; Staff 3 (Non-MLS 3)
Library Holdings: Bk Vols 17,214; Per Subs 72; Talking Bks 150
Automation Activity & Vendor Info: (Acquisitions) Follett Software; (Cataloging) Follett Software; (Circulation) Follett Software; (ILL) Follett Software; (OPAC) Follett Software
Wireless access
Open Tues & Fri 10-4, Wed & Thurs 12-6, Sat 10-2
Friends of the Library Group

FRUITVALE

P BEAVER VALLEY PUBLIC LIBRARY*, 1847 First St, V0G 1L0. (Mail add: PO Box 429, V0G 1L0), SAN 324-1742. Tel: 250-367-7114. FAX: 250-367-7130. E-mail: bvpublic@telus.net. Web Site: beavervalley.bc.libraries.coop. *Head Librn,* Marie Onyett
Founded 1960
Automation Activity & Vendor Info: (Cataloging) Evergreen
Wireless access
Mem of Kootenay Library Federation
Open Mon-Wed 10-7, Thurs & Fri 10-5, Sat 10-2
Friends of the Library Group

GIBSONS

P GIBSONS & DISTRICT PUBLIC LIBRARY*, 470 S Fletcher Rd, V0N 1V0. (Mail add: PO Box 109, V0N 1V0), SAN 318-7705. Tel: 604-886-2130. FAX: 604-886-2689. E-mail: gdplinfo@gibsons.bclibrary.ca. Web Site: gibsons.bc.libraries.coop. *Libr Dir,* Heather Evans-Cullen; E-mail: hecullen@gibsons.bclibrary.ca; Staff 8 (MLS 4, Non-MLS 4)
Founded 1914. Pop 9,302
Library Holdings: Large Print Bks 500; Bk Vols 40,000; Per Subs 80; Talking Bks 600
Automation Activity & Vendor Info: (Acquisitions) Evergreen; (Cataloging) Evergreen; (Media Booking) Evergreen; (OPAC) Evergreen
Wireless access
Function: Govt ref serv, Home delivery & serv to seniorr ctr & nursing homes, ILL available, Prog for children & young adult, Ref serv available, Summer reading prog, Wheelchair accessible
Open Mon-Sat 10-5
Friends of the Library Group

GRAND FORKS

P GRAND FORKS & DISTRICT PUBLIC LIBRARY*, 7342 Fifth St, V0H 1H0. (Mail add: PO Box 1539, V0H 1H0), SAN 377-063X. Tel: 250-442-3944. FAX: 250-442-2645. E-mail: library@gfpl.ca. Web Site: grandforks.bc.libraries.coop. *Libr Dir,* Cari Lynn Gawletz; E-mail: director@gfpl.ca; Staff 1 (MLS 1)
Pop 9,000
Library Holdings: Bk Titles 33,000; Per Subs 103; Talking Bks 1,004
Automation Activity & Vendor Info: (Cataloging) Mandarin Library Automation; (Circulation) Mandarin Library Automation; (OPAC) Mandarin Library Automation
Wireless access
Mem of Kootenay Library Federation

Open Tues, Wed, Fri & Sat 10-5, Thurs 10-8
Friends of the Library Group

GRANISLE

P GRANISLE PUBLIC LIBRARY*, Two Village Sq, McDonald Ave, V0J 1W0. (Mail add: PO Box 550, V0J 1W0), SAN 377-2241. Tel: 250-697-2713. E-mail: granislelibrary@outlook.com. Web Site: granisle.bc.libraries.coop. *Chief Librn,* Lisa Rees; *Asst Librn,* Ruth Crossley
Pop 600
Library Holdings: Bk Titles 9,200; Bk Vols 9,500; Per Subs 40; Talking Bks 270
Partic in N Cent Libr Asn
Open Mon 3-6, Tues, Thurs & Fri 12-4, Wed 10-12 & 3-6
Friends of the Library Group

GREENWOOD

P GREENWOOD PUBLIC LIBRARY*, 346 S Copper Ave, V0H 1J0. (Mail add: PO Box 279, V0H 1J0), SAN 324-1181. Tel: 250-445-6111. FAX: 250-445-6111. E-mail: greenlib@shaw.ca. Web Site: greenwood.bc.libraries.coop. *Libr Dir,* Yelena Churchill; *Asst Librn,* Leslie Smith; Staff 2 (Non-MLS 2)
Founded 1945. Pop 912; Circ 5,084
Library Holdings: Bk Titles 8,833; Bk Vols 9,165; Per Subs 20
Wireless access
Function: 24/7 Electronic res, 24/7 Online cat, Bks on CD, Children's prog, Computers for patron use, Electronic databases & coll, ILL available, Internet access, Magazines, Magnifiers for reading, Online cat, OverDrive digital audio bks, Photocopying/Printing, Ref serv available, Scanner, Summer reading prog
Mem of Kootenay Library Federation
Open Mon & Fri Noon-5, Wed Noon-7:30, Sat Noon-3

HAZELTON

P HAZELTON DISTRICT PUBLIC LIBRARY*, 4255 Government St, V0J 1Y0. (Mail add: PO Box 323, V0J 1Y0), SAN 318-7721. Tel: 250-842-5961. FAX: 250-842-2176. E-mail: hazlib@citywest.ca. Web Site: hazelton.bc.libraries.coop. *Head Librn,* Brian Butler
Founded 1948. Pop 6,537; Circ 24,321
Library Holdings: Bk Titles 27,439; Bk Vols 28,854; Per Subs 92
Subject Interests: Local hist
Automation Activity & Vendor Info: (Circulation) Follett Software
Wireless access
Partic in Northwest Library Federation
Open Tues 11-6, Wed 11-9, Thurs & Fri 11-5, Sat 1-4

HOUSTON

P HOUSTON PUBLIC LIBRARY*, 3150 14th St, V0J 1Z0. (Mail add: PO Box 840, V0J 1Z0). Tel: 250-845-2256. FAX: 250-845-2088. Administration E-mail: admin@houstonlibrary.ca. Web Site: houston.bc.libraries.coop/. *Libr Dir,* Sara Lewis; *Asst Librn,* Fatima McKilligan; Staff 4 (Non-MLS 4)
Founded 1964. Pop 3,800; Circ 40,000
Library Holdings: Bk Vols 24,692; Per Subs 40
Automation Activity & Vendor Info: (Acquisitions) Follett Software; (Cataloging) Follett Software; (Circulation) Follett Software; (ILL) Auto-Graphics, Inc; (OPAC) Follett Software
Function: ILL available, Photocopying/Printing, Prog for children & young adult, Summer reading prog, Telephone ref, Wheelchair accessible
Open Tues & Thurs 12-7, Wed & Fri 10-5, Sat 12-4

HUDSON'S HOPE

P HUDSON'S HOPE PUBLIC LIBRARY*, 9905 Dudley Dr, V0C 1V0. (Mail add: PO Box 269, V0C 1V0), SAN 318-773X. Tel: 250-783-9414. FAX: 250-783-5272. Web Site: hudsonshope.bc.libraries.coop. *Dir,* Amber Norton; E-mail: director.hhpl@pris.ca
Pop 1,100
Library Holdings: Bk Titles 16,000; Bk Vols 18,000; Per Subs 40
Wireless access
Function: Homebound delivery serv, ILL available, Photocopying/Printing, Ref serv available
Partic in DRAL Libr; North East Library Federation
Open Tues 10-3, Wed 12-5, Thurs 1-6, Fri 11-6
Friends of the Library Group

INVERMERE

P INVERMERE PUBLIC LIBRARY*, 646 Fourth St, V0A 1K0. (Mail add: PO Box 989, V0A 1K0), SAN 318-7748. Tel: 250-342-6416. FAX: 250-342-6461. E-mail: publiclibrary@invermere.net. Web Site: invermere.bc.libraries.coop. *Libr Dir,* Nicole Pawlak; *Librn,* Virginia Walker
Founded 1963. Pop 9,000; Circ 35,000
Library Holdings: Bk Titles 15,000; Bk Vols 15,500; Per Subs 50
Wireless access
Function: ILL available
Mem of Kootenay Library Federation
Open Tues & Thurs-Sat 10-5, Wed 10-8
Friends of the Library Group

KAMLOOPS

M INTERIOR HEALTH LIBRARY*, Royal Inland Hospital Library, 311 Columbia St, V2C 2T1. SAN 375-4855. Tel: 250-314-2234. FAX: 250-314-2189. E-mail: library@interiorhealth.ca. Web Site: www.interiorhealth.ca. *Librn,* Lisa D Gysel; E-mail: lisa.gysel@interiorhealth.ca; *Libr Tech,* Paula Hardy; Tel: 250-314-2342, E-mail: paula.hardy@interiorhealth.ca; Staff 2 (MLS 1, Non-MLS 1)
Library Holdings: Bk Titles 4,300; Per Subs 12,000
Automation Activity & Vendor Info: (Cataloging) SoutronGLOBAL; (Discovery) EBSCO Discovery Service
Wireless access
Partic in Electronic Health Library of British Columbia

P THOMPSON-NICOLA REGIONAL DISTRICT LIBRARY SYSTEM*, 300-465 Victoria St, V2C 2A9. SAN 365-8503. Tel: 250-377-8673. Toll Free Tel: 877-377-8673. FAX: 250-374-8355. Web Site: tnrl.ca. *Chief Librn,* Judy Moore; E-mail: jmoore@tnrd.ca
Founded 1974. Pop 160,000; Circ 1,007,624
Library Holdings: Bk Vols 303,357; Per Subs 200
Special Collections: Canadiana. Canadian and Provincial
Wireless access
Special Services for the Blind - Daisy reader
Open Mon-Fri 8:30-4
Branches: 13
ASHCROFT BRANCH, 201 Brink St, Ashcroft, V0K 1A0. (Mail add: PO Box 789, Ashcroft, V0K 1A0). Tel: 250-453-9042. *Br Head,* Deanna Porter
Open Tues & Sat 10-3, Wed & Thurs 1-6, Fri 12-6
BARRIERE BRANCH, 4511 Barriere Town Rd, Barriere, V0E 1E0. (Mail add: PO Box 100, Barriere, V0E 1E0), SAN 325-2612. Tel: 250-672-5811. FAX: 250-672-5811. *Br Head,* Pam Rudd
Founded 1974. Pop 5,000
Library Holdings: Bk Titles 7,592; Bk Vols 12,000; Per Subs 19
Special Collections: Local History (Barriere District Coll), notes, files, newsp clippings. Oral History
Open Tues, Wed & Fri 10:30-4:30, Thurs 3-7, Sat 10:30-2:30
BLUE RIVER BRANCH, 829 Cedar St, Blue River, V0E 1J0. (Mail add: PO Box 47, Blue River, V0E 1J0). Tel: 250-673-8235. FAX: 250-673-8235. *Br Head,* Rebecca Beaton
Open Tues & Sat 1-5, Wed 10-2, Thurs 3-7
CACHE CREEK BRANCH, 1025 Trans-Canada Hwy, Cache Creek, V0K 1H0. (Mail add: PO Box 429, Cache Creek, V0K 1H0). Tel: 250-457-9953. *Br Head,* Adrienne Teague
Open Tues & Sat 10-2, Wed 1-5, Thurs 3-7
CHASE BRANCH, 614 Shuswap Ave, Chase, V0E 1M0. (Mail add: PO Box 590, Chase, V0E 1M0). Tel: 250-679-3331. *Br Head,* Andrea Finnen
Open Tues, Wed, Fri & Sat 10-4, Thurs 1-7
CLEARWATER BRANCH, 422 Murtle Crescent, Clearwater, V0E 1N1. Tel: 250-674-2543. FAX: 250-674-2543. *Br Head,* Kaylea Prime
Open Tues-Thurs & Sat 10-4, Fri 12-6
CLINTON BRANCH, 1506 Tingley St, Clinton, V0K 1K0. (Mail add: PO Box 550, Clinton, V0K 1K0). Tel: 250-459-7752. FAX: 250-459-7752. *Br Head,* Kat Chatten
Open Tues 12;30-7, Thurs 1:30-7, Sat 10-2
KAMLOOPS BRANCH, 100-465 Victoria St, V2C 2A9. Tel: 250-372-5145. *Br Head,* Margo Schiller
Open Mon, Fri & Sat 10-5, Tues-Thurs 10-8, Sun (Oct-Apr) Noon-4
LOGAN LAKE BRANCH, 130 Chartrand Ave, Logan Lake, V0K 1W0. (Mail add: PO Box 310, Logan Lake, V0K 1W0). Tel: 250-523-6745. FAX: 250-523-6745. *Br Head,* Vesta Giles
Open Tues 1-7, Wed-Sat 10-4
LYTTON BRANCH, 121 Fourth St, Lytton, V0K 1Z0. (Mail add: PO Box 220, Lytton, V0K 1Z0). Tel: 250-455-2521. FAX: 250-455-2521. *Br Head,* Kristi Wiebe
Open Tues & Thurs 3-7, Wed & Fri 10-2
MERRITT BRANCH, 1691 Garcia St, Merritt, V1K 1B8. (Mail add: PO Box 1510, Merritt, V1K 1B8). Tel: 250-378-4737. *Br Head,* Megan Gregory
Open Tues & Wed 10-8, Thurs-Sat 10-5
Friends of the Library Group
NORTH KAMLOOPS BRANCH, 693 Tranquille Rd, V2B 3H7. Tel: 250-554-1124. FAX: 250-376-3825. *Br Head,* Margo Schiller
Open Mon, Fri & Sat 10-5, Tues-Thurs 10-8

SAVONA BRANCH, 60 Savona St, Savona, V0K 2J0. (Mail add: PO Box 169, Savona, V0K 2J0). Tel: 250-373-2666. *Br Head,* Adrienne Teague
Open Wed 12-4, Thurs 3-7, Fri & Sat 10-2
Bookmobiles: 1. Br Head, Michael Brown

C THOMPSON RIVERS UNIVERSITY*, Kamloops Campus Library, 900 McGill Rd, V2C 5N3. (Mail add: Box 3010, V2C 5N3), SAN 328-7815. Tel: 250-828-5000. FAX: 250-828-5313. Web Site: www.tru.ca/library. *Assoc Univ Librn,* Tania Gottschalk; E-mail: tgottschalk@tru.ca; *Acq Librn,* Penny Haggarty; *Distance Learning Librn, Doc Delivery,* Brenda Smith; *Instruction Librn, Outreach Librn,* Elizabeth Rennie; E-mail: erennie@tru.ca; *Syst Librn,* Michael Purcell
Library Holdings: Bk Vols 200,000
Function: ILL available
Partic in British Columbia Electronic Library Network; Centre for Accessible Post-Secondary Education Resources; Electronic Health Library of British Columbia
Open Mon-Thurs 8am-9pm, Fri 8-5, Sat 9-5, Sun 9-9

KASLO

P KASLO & DISTRICT PUBLIC LIBRARY*, 413 Fourth St, V0G 1M0. (Mail add: PO Box 760, V0G 1M0). Tel: 250-353-2942. FAX: 250-353-2943. E-mail: info@kaslo.bclibrary.ca. Web Site: kaslo.bc.libraries.coop. *Libr Dir,* Eva Kelemen; *Prog Coordr,* Angela Bennett
Founded 1920. Pop 1,750; Circ 16,762
Library Holdings: Bk Titles 13,800; Per Subs 22
Wireless access
Mem of Kootenay Library Federation
Open Tues, Wed & Sat 10-4, Thurs 10-8

KELOWNA

C OKANAGAN COLLEGE LIBRARY*, 1000 KLO Rd, V1Y 4X8. SAN 365-9739. Administration Tel: 250-862-5477. Administration FAX: 250-862-5609. E-mail: circklo@okanagan.bc.ca. Web Site: www.okanagan.bc.ca/library. *Dir, Libr Serv,* Ross Tyner; Tel: 250-762-5445, Ext 4665, E-mail: rhtyner@okanagan.bc.ca; *Campus Librn,* Michelle Ward; Tel: 250-762-5445, Ext 4749, E-mail: mward@okanagan.bc.ca; *Bus Liaison Librn, Pub Serv Librn,* Lindsay Willson; Tel: 250-762-5445, Ext 4624, E-mail: lwillson@okanagan.bc.ca; *Cat & Coll Librn,* Greg Hutton; Tel: 250-762-5445, Ext 4490, E-mail: ghutton@okanagan.bc.ca; *Learning Services, Librn,* Jillian Sinotte; Tel: 250-762-5445, Ext 4257, E-mail: jsinotte@okanagan.bc.ca; *Syst Librn,* Gilbert Bede; Tel: 250-762-5445, Ext 4751, E-mail: gbede@okanagan.bc.ca; *Web Serv Librn,* Roën Janyk; Tel: 250-762-5445, Ext 4660, E-mail: rjanyk@okanagan.bc.ca; Staff 28 (MLS 10, Non-MLS 18)
Founded 2005. Enrl 9,000; Fac 460; Highest Degree: Bachelor
Automation Activity & Vendor Info: (Acquisitions) Ex Libris Group; (Cataloging) Ex Libris Group; (Circulation) Ex Libris Group; (Discovery) EBSCO Discovery Service; (OPAC) Ex Libris Group; (Serials) Ex Libris Group
Wireless access
Partic in British Columbia Electronic Library Network; Centre for Accessible Post-Secondary Education Resources; Council of Prairie & Pacific University Libraries; Electronic Health Library of British Columbia
Open Mon-Thurs 7:45am-10pm, Fri 7:45-6, Sat & Sun 9:30-5; Mon-Thurs 8-6, Fri 8-5 (Summer)
Departmental Libraries:
PENTICTON CAMPUS, 583 Duncan Ave W, Penticton, V2A 8E1. Tel: 250-490-3951. *Campus Librn,* Eva Gavaris; E-mail: egavaris@okanagan.bc.ca; Staff 3.5 (MLS 1, Non-MLS 2.5)
Open Mon-Thurs 7:45am-9pm, Fri 7:45-5:30, Sat 9:30-5:30, Sun Noon-4; Mon-Fri 8-4 (Summer)
SALMON ARM CAMPUS, 2552 Tenth Ave NE (THC), Salmon Arm, V1E 2S4. Tel: 250-804-8851. *Campus Librn,* Taryn Schmid; Tel: 250-804-8851, Ext 8253, E-mail: tschmid@okanagan.bc.ca
Open Mon-Thurs 8am-9pm, Fri 8-4:30, Sat 8:30-4, Sun 12-4
VERNON CAMPUS, 7000 College Way, Vernon, V1B 2N5. Tel: 250-545-7291. *Campus Librn,* Jennifer Finlay; Tel: 250-545-7291, Ext 2249, E-mail: jfinlay@okanagan.bc.ca
Open Mon-Thurs 7:45am-9pm, Fri 7:45-5:30, Sat 10-4, Sun 12-4

P OKANAGAN REGIONAL LIBRARY*, 1430 KLO Rd, V1W 3P6. SAN 365-9763. Tel: 250-860-4033. FAX: 250-861-8696. Web Site: www.orl.bc.ca. *Actg Chief Exec Officer,* Jeremy Feddersen; Tel: 250-860-4033, Ext 2471, E-mail: jfeddersen@orl.bc.ca; *Head, Coll Develop,* James Laitinen; E-mail: jlaitinen@orl.bc.ca; *Head, Youth Serv,* Ashley Machum; E-mail: amachum@orl.bc.ca; Staff 21 (MLS 18, Non-MLS 3)
Founded 1936. Pop 359,952
Library Holdings: Microforms 3,113; Bk Titles 173,322; Bk Vols 725,129; Per Subs 1,816; Talking Bks 5,544; Videos 24,423
Automation Activity & Vendor Info: (Acquisitions) SirsiDynix; (Cataloging) SirsiDynix; (Circulation) SirsiDynix; (OPAC) SirsiDynix; (Serials) SirsiDynix
Wireless access
Publications: Annual report
Open Mon-Fri 8-4:30
Friends of the Library Group
Branches: 29
ARMSTRONG BRANCH, 1-3305 Smith Dr, Armstrong, V0E 1B1. Tel: 250-546-8311.
Open Tues, Thurs & Sat 10-5, Wed 1-5, Fri 10-8
Friends of the Library Group
CHERRYVILLE BRANCH, 1114 Hwy 6, Cherryville, V0E 2G3. Tel: 250-547-9776.
Open Wed 4-8, Thurs 11-2
ENDERBY BRANCH, 514 Cliff Ave, Enderby, V0E 1V0. (Mail add: PO Box 226, Enderby, V0E 1V0). Tel: 250-838-6488.
Founded 1865
Open Tues & Wed 10-5, Fri 10-8, Sat 10-4
Friends of the Library Group
FALKLAND BRANCH, 5771 Hwy 97, Falkland, V0E 1W0. (Mail add: PO Box 33, Falkland, V0E 1W0). Tel: 250-379-2705, Ext 1811. E-mail: falkland@orl.bc.ca. *Commun Librn,* Diana McCarthy
Open Tues 2-5 & 6-8, Wed & Thurs 1-6
GOLDEN BRANCH, 819 Park Ave, Golden, V0A 1H0. (Mail add: PO Box 750, Golden, V0A 1H0). Tel: 250-344-6516.
Open Tues, Fri & Sat 10-5, Thurs 10-8
HEDLEY BRANCH, Old Age Pensioner's Hall, Corner of Scott St & Irene, Hedley, V0X 1K0. (Mail add: PO Box 190, Hedley, V0X 1K0). Tel: 250-292-8209.
Open Thurs 2-7
KALEDEN BRANCH, Kaleden Community Hall, 101 Linden Ave, Kaleden, V0H 1K0. (Mail add: PO Box 370, Kaleden, V0H 1K0). Tel: 250-497-8066.
Open Tues 1-8, Thurs & Sat 1-5
KELOWNA BRANCH, 1380 Ellis St, V1Y 2A2. Tel: 250-762-2800.
Open Mon-Thurs 10-8, Fri 10-5:30, Sat 10-5, Sun 11-4
Friends of the Library Group
KEREMEOS BRANCH, 638 Seventh Ave, Keremeos, V0X 1N3. (Mail add: PO Box 330, Keremeos, V0X 1N0). Tel: 250-499-2313.
Open Tues 10-4, Wed 1-7, Fri 1-5, Sat 10-2
Friends of the Library Group
LAKE COUNTRY BRANCH, 2-10150 Bottom Wood Lake Rd, Lake Country, V4V 2M1. Tel: 250-766-3141.
Open Tues & Thurs 10-6, Wed 10-8, Fri & Sat 10-5
Friends of the Library Group
LUMBY BRANCH, 2250 Shields Ave, Lumby, V0E 2G0. (Mail add: PO Box 116, Lumby, V0E 2G0). Tel: 250-547-9528. *Br Head,* Mitzi Fortin
Open Tues, Wed, Fri & Sat 10-3, Thurs 10-7
MISSION, Capital News Ctr, 4105 Gordon Dr, V1W 4Z1. Tel: 250-764-2254.
Open Mon, Fri & Sat 10-5, Tues-Thurs 10-8
Friends of the Library Group
NARAMATA BRANCH, Community Hall, 3580 Third St, Naramata, V0H 1N0. (Mail add: PO Box 190, Naramata, V0H 1N0). Tel: 250-496-5679.
Open Tues & Fri 1-5, Thurs 3-8
Friends of the Library Group
NORTH SHUSWAP, 3867 Squilax Anglemont Hwy, Scotch Creek, V0E 1M5. Tel: 250-955-8198. E-mail: NorthShuswap@orl.bc.ca.
Open Tues 12-5, Wed, Fri & Sun 11-4
OKANAGAN FALLS BRANCH, 101-850 Railway Lane, Okanagan Falls, V0H 1R4. Tel: 250-497-5886. E-mail: OkanaganFalls@orl.bc.ca.
Open Tues 12-8, Wed 10-4, Fri 10-5, Sat 10-2
Friends of the Library Group
OLIVER BRANCH, 1400-5955 Main St, Oliver, V0H 1T0. (Mail add: PO Box 758, Oliver, V0H 1T0). Tel: 250-498-2242.
Open Tues, Thurs & Fri 10-5, Wed 12-7, Sat 9:30-4:30
Friends of the Library Group
OSOYOOS BRANCH, Sonora Ctr, 8505 68th Ave, Osoyoos, V0H 1V7. (Mail add: PO Box 1038, Osoyoos, V0H 1V0). Tel: 250-495-7637.
Open Tues 12-8, Wed & Thurs 12-5, Fri 10-5, Sat 10-3
Friends of the Library Group
OYAMA BRANCH, 15718 Oyama Rd, Oyama, V4V 2E1. Tel: 250-548-3377.
Open Tues & Thurs 3-7
PEACHLAND BRANCH, Peachland Village Mall, 40-5500 Clements Crescent, Peachland, V0H 1X5. Tel: 250-767-9111.
Open Tues 12-6, Wed-Fri 12-5, Sat 11-4
Friends of the Library Group
PRINCETON BRANCH, 107 Vermilion Ave, Princeton, V0X 1W0. (Mail add: PO Box 958, Princeton, V0X 1W0). Tel: 250-295-6495.
Open Tues 12-5, Thurs 12-8, Fri 12-4, Sat 10-1

REVELSTOKE BRANCH, Recreation Ctr, 605 Campbell Ave, Revelstoke, V0E 2S0. (Mail add: PO Box 1289, Revelstoke, V0E 2S0). Tel: 250-837-5095.
Open Tues & Wed 1-8, Thurs-Sat 10-5
RUTLAND, Plaza 33 Mall, 20-301 Hwy 33 West, V1X 1X8. Tel: 250-765-8165.
Open Mon & Thurs-Sat 10-5, Tues & Wed 10-8
Friends of the Library Group
SALMON ARM BRANCH, 285 Piccadilly Place Mall, 1151 Tenth Ave SW, Salmon Arm, V1E 1T3. Tel: 250-832-6161.
Open Mon, Wed, Thurs & Sat 10-5, Tues & Fri 10-8
Friends of the Library Group
SICAMOUS BRANCH, 2-446 Main St, Sicamous, V0E 2V1. (Mail add: PO Box 15, Sicamous, V0E 2V0). Tel: 250-836-4845.
Open Tues & Sat 10-5, Wed 12-4, Fri 12-7
SILVER CREEK, 921 Salmon River Rd, Salmon Arm, V1E 3G3. Tel: 250-832-4719.
Open Tues & Thurs 2-6
SOUTH SHUSWAP BRANCH, 1-2425 Golf Course Dr, Blind Bay, V0E 1H2. Tel: 250-675-4818. E-mail: southshuswap@orl.bc.ca.
Open Tues 10-6, Wed, Fri & Sat 10-5, Thurs 10-3
Friends of the Library Group
SUMMERLAND BRANCH, 9533 Main St, Summerland, V0H 1Z0. (Mail add: Box 1198, Summerland, V0H 1Z0). Tel: 250-494-5591.
Open Tues 10-8, Wed & Thurs 10-6, Fri & Sat 10-5
Friends of the Library Group
VERNON BRANCH, 2800 30th Ave, Vernon, V1T 8S3. Tel: 250-542-7610.
Open Mon, Fri & Sat 10-5:30, Tues-Thurs 10-9, Sun (Oct-Dec) Noon-4
Friends of the Library Group
WESTBANK BRANCH, Westridge Mall, 31-2484 Main St, Hwy 97S, West Kelowna, V4T 2G2. Tel: 250-768-4369.
Open Mon, Tues, Thurs & Fri 10-6, Wed 10-8, Sat 10-5
Friends of the Library Group

KIMBERLEY

P KIMBERLEY PUBLIC LIBRARY*, 115 Spokane St, V1A 2E5. Tel: 250-427-3112. FAX: 250-427-7157. E-mail: staff@kimberleylibrary.ca. Web Site: kimberley.bc.libraries.coop/. *Dir,* Karin von Wittgenstein
Pop 7,000
Library Holdings: AV Mats 850; Large Print Bks 220; Bk Titles 39,500; Per Subs 88; Talking Bks 900
Automation Activity & Vendor Info: (Acquisitions) Evergreen; (Cataloging) Evergreen; (Circulation) Evergreen; (Course Reserve) Evergreen; (ILL) Evergreen; (Media Booking) Evergreen; (OPAC) Evergreen; (Serials) Evergreen
Wireless access
Function: Homebound delivery serv
Mem of Kootenay Library Federation
Partic in BC Libraries Cooperative
Special Services for the Blind - Aids for in-house use; Bks on CD; Daisy reader; Digital talking bk; Home delivery serv; Large print bks; Lending of low vision aids; Magnifiers
Open Tues, Wed, Fri & Sat 10:30-4, Thurs 1:30-7
Friends of the Library Group

KITIMAT

S KITIMAT MUSEUM & ARCHIVES*, 293 City Ctr, V8C 1T6. SAN 329-2193. Tel: 250-632-8950. FAX: 250-632-7429. E-mail: info@kitimatmuseum.ca. Web Site: www.kitimatmuseum.ca. *Exec Dir,* Louise Avery; E-mail: lavery@kitimatmuseum.ca
Founded 1969
Library Holdings: Bk Titles 400
Special Collections: Alcan Coll (1950s); Northern Sentinel Press Ltd Coll. Oral History
Subject Interests: NW native studies
Wireless access
Open Mon-Sat 10-5 (June-Aug); Mon-Fri 10-4, Sat Noon-4 (Sept-May)

P KITIMAT PUBLIC LIBRARY ASSOCIATION*, 940 Wakashan Ave, V8C 2G3. SAN 318-7780. Tel: 250-632-8985. FAX: 250-632-2630. E-mail: ask@kitimatlibrary.ca. Web Site: kitimatlibrary.ca. *Libr Dir,* Samantha Anderson; Staff 7 (MLS 1, Non-MLS 6)
Founded 1955. Pop 8,564; Circ 22,818
Library Holdings: Bk Vols 60,293
Special Collections: Large Print Coll; Multilingual Coll
Subject Interests: Local hist
Wireless access
Partic in Northwest Library Federation
Open Mon, Wed & Fri 10-7, Tues & Thurs 10-5:30, Sat & Sun Noon-4
Restriction: Non-resident fee
Friends of the Library Group

LANGLEY

C TRINITY WESTERN UNIVERSITY*, Norma Marion Alloway Library, 22500 University Dr, V2Y 1Y1. SAN 320-3077. Tel: 604-513-2023. Interlibrary Loan Service Tel: 604-513-2121, Ext 3914. Reference Tel: 604-513-2121, Ext 3903. Administration Tel: 604-513-2121, Ext 3902. FAX: 604-513-2063. E-mail: library@twu.ca. Web Site: www.twu.ca/library. *Univ Librn,* Darcy Gullacher; Tel: 604-513-2121, Ext 3905, E-mail: darcy.gullacher@twu.ca; *Assoc Librn,* William Badke; E-mail: badke@twu.ca; Staff 15 (MLS 7, Non-MLS 8)
Founded 1962. Enrl 2,350; Fac 150; Highest Degree: Master
Library Holdings: CDs 1,182; DVDs 1,000; e-books 11,402; e-journals 12,929; Microforms 333,489; Bk Vols 225,000; Per Subs 813; Videos 3,000
Special Collections: Mel Smith Papers; Robert N Thompson Papers
Automation Activity & Vendor Info: (Acquisitions) SirsiDynix; (Cataloging) SirsiDynix; (Circulation) SirsiDynix; (Course Reserve) SirsiDynix; (Discovery) EBSCO Discovery Service; (ILL) Relais International; (OPAC) SirsiDynix
Wireless access
Partic in British Columbia Electronic Library Network; Canadian Research Knowledge Network; Council of Prairie & Pacific University Libraries; Electronic Health Library of British Columbia
Open Mon & Thurs 7:45am-11pm, Fri 7:45-6, Sat 6-6, Sun 1:30-5

LILLOOET

P LILLOOET AREA LIBRARY ASSOCIATION*, Lillooet Public Library, 930 Main St, V0K 1V0. (Mail add: PO Box 939, V0K 1V0). Tel: 250-256-7944. E-mail: lala@lillooet.bclibrary.ca. Web Site: lillooet.bc.libraries.coop. *Libr Dir,* Toby Mueller; Staff 2 (Non-MLS 2)
Library Holdings: Bk Titles 12,000; Per Subs 25
Automation Activity & Vendor Info: (Acquisitions) Evergreen; (Circulation) Evergreen; (OPAC) Evergreen
Wireless access
Function: Adult literacy prog, Audiobks via web, Bks on cassette, Bks on CD, Children's prog, Computer training, Computers for patron use, Digital talking bks, Electronic databases & coll, Family literacy, Free DVD rentals, Home delivery & serv to seniorr ctr & nursing homes, Homebound delivery serv, ILL available, Internet access, Music CDs, Online cat, Online ref, OverDrive digital audio bks, Photocopying/Printing, Preschool outreach, Ref serv available, Story hour, Summer reading prog, VHS videos, Wheelchair accessible
Open Tues-Thurs 11-6, Fri 11-2
Branches: 2
BRIDGE RIVER BRANCH, 41 Bridge River Town Site, Shalaith, V0N 3C0. Tel: 250-259-8242. E-mail: bridgeriver@lillooet.bclibrary.ca. *Librn,* Vanessa Blake
Library Holdings: Bk Titles 6,000
Open Wed 11-6
GOLD BRIDGE BRANCH, 40 Hurley St, Gold Bridge, V0K 1P0. Tel: 250-238-2521. *Librn,* Jean Shaw; E-mail: jean@lillooet.bclibrary.ca
Library Holdings: Bk Titles 4,698
Open Mon & Thurs 1-5, Sat 11-1
Friends of the Library Group

MACKENZIE

P MACKENZIE PUBLIC LIBRARY*, 400 Skeena Dr, V0J 2C0. (Mail add: Box 750, V0J 2C0). Tel: 250-997-6343. FAX: 250-997-5792. E-mail: mackenziepubliclibrary@gmail.com. Web Site: mackenzie.bc.libraries.coop. *Libr Dir,* Alice Pek; *Asst Librn,* Jenny LeBlanc; E-mail: jenny.leblanc@mackenzie.bc.libraries.coop
Library Holdings: Bk Titles 40,000; Per Subs 93
Automation Activity & Vendor Info: (Cataloging) Evergreen
Wireless access
Function: Bk club(s), Computer training, Photocopying/Printing, Scanner, Summer reading prog
Partic in BC Libraries Cooperative
Open Mon-Fri 10-6, Sat 10-4

MCBRIDE

P MCBRIDE & DISTRICT PUBLIC LIBRARY*, 521 Main St, V0J 2E0. (Mail add: PO Box 489, V0J 2E0). Tel: 250-569-2411. FAX: 250-569-0000. E-mail: library@mcbridebc.org. Web Site: mcbride.bc.libraries.coop. *Libr Dir,* Naomi Balla-Boudreau
Library Holdings: Bk Titles 25,000
Automation Activity & Vendor Info: (Circulation) Evergreen; (OPAC) Evergreen
Wireless access
Open Tues 10-5 & 7-9, Wed & Thurs 10-5, Fri 2-9, Sat 2-5

MERRITT

J NICOLA VALLEY INSTITUTE OF TECHNOLOGY LIBRARY*, 4155 Belshaw St, V1K 1R1. Tel: 250-378-3303. Administration Tel: 250-378-3345. Toll Free Tel: 877-682-3300 (BC only). FAX: 250-378-3332. Web Site: www.nvit.bc.ca/library/index_new.htm. *Librn,* Rita Cavaliere; E-mail: rcavaliere@nvit.bc.ca; *Coordr,* David Leggett
Library Holdings: AV Mats 683; Bk Titles 14,000; Per Subs 150
Automation Activity & Vendor Info: (Cataloging) LEX Systems Inc; (Circulation) LEX Systems Inc; (Course Reserve) LEX Systems Inc; (OPAC) LEX Systems Inc
Partic in Centre for Accessible Post-Secondary Education Resources; Electronic Health Library of British Columbia
Open Mon-Thurs 8:30-8:30, Fri 8:30-4:30, Sat Noon-6, Sun Noon-4 (Sept-April); Mon-Fri 8:30-4:30 (May-Aug)

MIDWAY

P MIDWAY PUBLIC LIBRARY*, 612 Sixth Ave, V0H 1M0. (Mail add: PO Box 268, V0H 1M0). Tel: 250-449-2620. FAX: 250-449-2389. E-mail: midwaypubliclibrary@gmail.com, mplpatrons@gmail.com. Web Site: midway.bc.libraries.coop. *Actg Dir,* Chelsey Boersma-Scott; Staff 1 (Non-MLS 1)
Circ 1,000
Library Holdings: Bk Titles 10,000; Per Subs 12
Automation Activity & Vendor Info: (Acquisitions) L4U Library Software; (Cataloging) L4U Library Software; (Circulation) L4U Library Software; (Course Reserve) L4U Library Software; (ILL) L4U Library Software; (Media Booking) L4U Library Software; (OPAC) L4U Library Software; (Serials) L4U Library Software
Function: Home delivery & serv to seniorr ctr & nursing homes, Homebound delivery serv, ILL available, Internet access, Photocopying/Printing, Prog for children & young adult, Ref & res, Ref serv available, Serves people with intellectual disabilities, Spoken cassettes & CDs, Spoken cassettes & DVDs, Summer reading prog, VHS videos, Wheelchair accessible
Mem of Kootenay Library Federation
Open Tues 2-6, Wed & Thurs 11-5

MISSION

S MISSION COMMUNITY ARCHIVES*, 33215 Second Ave, V2V 4L1. (Mail add: PO Box 3522, V2V 4L1), SAN 328-462X. Tel: 604-820-2621. E-mail: mca@missionarchives.com. Web Site: missionarchives.com. *Archives & Rec Mgr,* Valerie Billesberger; E-mail: manager@missionarchives.com
Library Holdings: Bk Titles 300
Special Collections: Reference Coll
Subject Interests: Genealogy, Local hist
Restriction: Open by appt only

R WESTMINSTER ABBEY LIBRARY, SEMINARY OF CHRIST THE KING*, Library of Westminster Abbey, 34224 Dewdney Trunk Rd, V2V 6Y5. (Mail add: PO Box 3310, V2V 4J5), SAN 324-0460. Tel: 604-826-8975. FAX: 604-826-8725. E-mail: library@westminsterabbey.ca. Web Site: www.westminsterabbey.ca. *Librn,* Fr Leo Barker
Founded 1939. Enrl 60; Fac 20; Highest Degree: Master
Library Holdings: Bk Vols 69,104; Per Subs 60
Subject Interests: Bible, Canon law, Church hist, Liturgy, Philos, Theol

NAKUSP

P NAKUSP PUBLIC LIBRARY ASSOCIATION*, 92 Sixth Ave NW, V0G 1R0. (Mail add: PO Box 297, V0G 1R0), SAN 318-7802. Tel: 250-265-3363. E-mail: contact@nakusplibrary.ca. Web Site: nakusplibrary.ca. *Libr Dir,* Claire Paradis; E-mail: director@nakusplibrary.ca; *Asst Librn,* Susan Rogers; *Asst Librn,* Sandy Watt
Founded 1920. Pop 2,750; Circ 33,500
Library Holdings: Bk Titles 22,865; Bk Vols 22,917; Per Subs 54; Talking Bks 413
Special Collections: Computer Disk Coll; Equip Coll; Literacy Coll
Automation Activity & Vendor Info: (Acquisitions) Evergreen; (Cataloging) Evergreen; (ILL) Evergreen; (OPAC) Evergreen
Wireless access
Mem of Kootenay Library Federation
Special Services for the Blind - Talking bks
Open Tues & Thurs-Sat 12-4
Friends of the Library Group

NANAIMO

P VANCOUVER ISLAND REGIONAL LIBRARY*, 6250 Hammond Bay Rd, V9T 6M9. (Mail add: PO Box 3333, V9R 5N3), SAN 366-0729. Tel: 250-758-4697. Toll Free Tel: 877-415-8475. FAX: 250-758-2482. Information Services E-mail: info@virl.bc.ca. Web Site: www.virl.bc.ca. *Exec Dir,* Rosemary Bonanno; Tel: 250-729-2313, E-mail: executivedirector@virl.bc.ca; *Dir of Finance,* Joel Adams; Tel: 250-729-2312, E-mail: jadams@virl.bc.ca; *Dir, Human Res,* Lisa House; Tel: 250-729-2335, E-mail: lhouse@virl.bc.ca; *Dir, Libr Serv,* Melissa Legacy; Tel: 250-753-1154, Ext 240, E-mail: mjlegacy@virl.bc.ca; Staff 180 (MLS 34, Non-MLS 146)
Founded 1936. Pop 430,000; Circ 4,533,001
Library Holdings: AV Mats 89,413; Bk Titles 246,407; Bk Vols 1,394,347; Per Subs 3,099; Talking Bks 24,628; Videos 48,090
Special Collections: British Columbia History (British Columbia & Northwest Coll)
Automation Activity & Vendor Info: (Acquisitions) SirsiDynix; (Cataloging) SirsiDynix; (Circulation) SirsiDynix; (OPAC) SirsiDynix; (Serials) SirsiDynix
Wireless access
Function: Accelerated reader prog
Publications: NewsBrief
Open Mon-Fri 9-5
Friends of the Library Group
Branches: 39
BELLA COOLA BRANCH, 450 MacKenzie St, Bella Coola, V0T 1C0, SAN 366-0745. Tel: 250-799-5330. FAX: 250-799-5330. E-mail: BellaCoola@virl.bc.ca. Web Site: virl.bc.ca/branches/bella-coola. *Libr Mgr,* Monica Finn
Library Holdings: Bk Vols 17,875
Open Wed 10-1:30, Thurs-Sat 10-1 & 2-5
BOWSER BRANCH, 111-6996 W Island Hwy, Bowser, V0R 1G0. (Mail add: Box 181, Bowser, V0R 1G0). Tel: 250-757-9570. E-mail: Bowser@virl.bc.ca. Web Site: virl.bc.ca/branches/bowser. *Actg Libr Mgr,* Stephani Pettigrew
Founded 2008
Open Tues 10-12 & 1-5, Thurs 1-4 & 5-8, Fri 1-5, Sat 10-2
CAMPBELL RIVER BRANCH, 1240 Shoppers Row, Campbell River, V9W 2C8, SAN 366-0788. Tel: 250-287-3655. FAX: 250-287-2119. E-mail: CampbellRiver@virl.bc.ca. Web Site: virl.bc.ca/branches/campbell-river. *Actg Libr Mgr,* Matt Mukai
Library Holdings: Bk Vols 84,678
Open Mon-Thurs 10-8, Fri & Sat 10-5, Sun 12:30-4
CHEMAINUS BRANCH, 2592 Legion St, Chemainus, V0R 1K0. (Mail add: PO Box 72, Chemainus, V0R 1K0), SAN 366-0818. Tel: 250-246-9471. FAX: 250-246-9411. E-mail: Chemainus@virl.bc.ca. Web Site: virl.bc.ca/branches/chemainus. *Libr Mgr,* Stephen Warren
Library Holdings: Bk Vols 22,745
Open Mon, Wed, Fri & Sat 10-12 & 1-5, Tues 12-4 & 5-8, Thurs 1-4 & 5-8
COMOX BRANCH, 101-1729 Comox Ave, Comox, V9M 1R7, SAN 366-0877. Tel: 250-339-2971. FAX: 250-339-2940. E-mail: Comox@virl.bc.ca. Web Site: virl.bc.ca/branches/comox. *Libr Mgr,* Colleen Nelson
Library Holdings: Bk Vols 30,637
Open Mon, Fri & Sat 10-5, Tues-Thurs 10-8
CORTES ISLAND, Linnaea Farm, 1255 Seaford Rd, Mansons Landing, V0P 1K0. Tel: 250-935-6566. FAX: 250-935-6522. E-mail: CortesIsland@virl.bc.ca. Web Site: virl.bc.ca/branches/cortes-island. *Libr Mgr,* Stephanie Pettigrew
Library Holdings: Bk Vols 9,424
Open Tues 10-12 & 1-5, Wed 1-4 & 5-8, Fri 1-5, Sat 10-2
COURTENAY BRANCH, 300 Sixth St, Courtenay, V9N 9V9, SAN 366-0907. Tel: 250-334-3369. FAX: 250-334-0910. E-mail: Courtenay@virl.bc.ca. Web Site: virl.bc.ca/branches/courtenay. *Libr Mgr,* Greg Gulas
Library Holdings: Bk Vols 103,324
Open Mon-Thurs 10-8, Fri & Sat 10-5, Sun 12:30-4
COWICHAN, 2687 James St, Duncan, V9L 2X5, SAN 366-0966. Tel: 250-746-7661. FAX: 250-746-5595. E-mail: Cowichan@virl.bc.ca. Web Site: virl.bc.ca/branches/cowichan. *Libr Mgr,* Annette Van Koevering
Library Holdings: Bk Vols 97,800
Open Mon-Thurs 10-8, Fri & Sat 10-5, Sun 12:30-4
COWICHAN LAKE, 69 Renfrew Ave, Lake Cowichan, V0R 2G0. (Mail add: PO Box 918, Lake Cowichan, V0R 2G0), SAN 366-1059. Tel: 250-749-3431. E-mail: CowichanLake@virl.bc.ca. Web Site: virl.bc.ca/branches/cowichan-lake. *Libr Mgr,* Annette Van Koevering
Library Holdings: Bk Vols 29,000
Open Tues-Thurs 10-8, Fri & Sat 10-5
CUMBERLAND BRANCH, 2746 Dunsmuir Ave, Cumberland, V0R 1S0. (Mail add: PO Box 378, Cumberland, V0R 1S0), SAN 366-0931. Tel: 250-336-8121. E-mail: Cumberland@virl.bc.ca. Web Site: virl.bc.ca/branches/cumberland. *Libr Mgr,* Colleen Nelson
Library Holdings: Bk Vols 24,039
Open Tues, Fri & Sat 10-5, Wed & Thurs 1-8
GABRIOLA ISLAND BRANCH, Folklife Village, 5-575 North Rd, Gabriola Island, V0R 1X3. Tel: 250-247-7878. FAX: 250-247-7892. E-mail: GabriolaIsland@virl.bc.ca. Web Site: virl.bc.ca/branches/gabriola-island. *Libr Mgr,* Anthony Martin
Circ 59,884

Library Holdings: Bk Vols 22,251
Open Tues-Thurs 10-7, Fri & Sat 10-5
GOLD RIVER BRANCH, 396 Nimpkish Dr, Gold River, V0P 1G0. (Mail add: PO Box 309, Gold River, V0P 1G0), SAN 366-0990. Tel: 250-283-2502. FAX: 250-283-2552. E-mail: GoldRiver@virl.bc.ca. Web Site: virl.bc.ca/branches/gold-river. *Libr Mgr,* Stephanie Pettigrew
Library Holdings: Bk Vols 15,579
Open Tues & Wed 1-5 & 6:30-8:30, Fri 3:30-8, Sat 1-5
HORNBY ISLAND BRANCH, New Horizons Ctr, 1765 Sollans Rd, Hornby Island, V0R 1Z0. (Mail add: PO Box 37, Hornby Island, V0R 1Z0), SAN 329-5990. Tel: 250-335-0044. FAX: 250-335-0134. E-mail: HornbyIsland@virl.bc.ca. Web Site: virl.bc.ca/branches/hornby-island. *Libr Mgr,* Colleen Nelson
Library Holdings: Bk Vols 11,888
Open Tues, Thurs & Sat 10-12 & 1-5, Fri 1-5
LADYSMITH BRANCH, 3-740 First Ave, Ladysmith, V9G 1A3. (Mail add: PO Box 389, Ladysmith, V9G 1A3), SAN 366-1024. Tel: 250-245-2322. FAX: 250-245-2393. E-mail: LadySmith@virl.bc.ca. Web Site: virl.bc.ca/branches/ladysmith. *Libr Mgr,* Stephen Warren
Library Holdings: Bk Vols 55,718
Open Mon, Fri & Sat 10-5, Tues-Thurs 10-8
MASSET BRANCH, 2123 Collison Ave, Masset, V0T 1M0. (Mail add: PO Box 710, Masset, V0T 1M0), SAN 366-1105. Tel: 250-626-3663. FAX: 250-626-3663. E-mail: Masset@virl.bc.ca. Web Site: virl.bc.ca/branches/masset. *Libr Mgr,* Patrick Siebold
Library Holdings: Bk Vols 14,114
Open Tues 10-12 & 1-5, Thurs 1-4 & 5-8, Fri 1-5, Sat 10-2
NANAIMO HARBOURFRONT BRANCH, 90 Commercial St, V9R 5G4, SAN 366-1113. Tel: 250-753-1154. FAX: 250-754-1483. E-mail: NanaimoHarbourfront@virl.bc.ca. Web Site: virl.bc.ca/branches/nanaimo-harbourfront. *Libr Mgr,* Anthony Martin
Library Holdings: Bk Vols 117,242
Open Mon-Thurs 10-8, Fri & Sat 10-5, Sun 12:30-4
NANAIMO NORTH, 6250 Hammond Bay Rd, V9T 5M4. Tel: 250-933-2665. E-mail: NanaimoNorth@virl.bc.ca. Web Site: virl.bc.ca/braches/nanaimo-north. *Libr Mgr,* Jennifer Seper
Open Mon-Thurs 10-8, Fri & Sat 10-5, Sun 12:30-4
NANAIMO WELLINGTON, 3200 N Island Hwy, V9T 1W1, SAN 366-1571. Tel: 250-758-5544. FAX: 250-758-7513. E-mail: nanaimowellington@virl.bc.ca. Web Site: virl.bc.ca/branches/nanaimo-wellington. *Libr Mgr,* Jennifer Seper
Library Holdings: Bk Vols 69,494
Open Mon-Thurs 10-8, Fri & Sat 10-5, Sun 12:30-4
PARKSVILLE BRANCH, 100 Jensen Ave E, Parksville, V9P 1K3. (Mail add: PO Box 508, Parksville, V9P 2G6), SAN 366-1148. Tel: 250-248-3841. FAX: 250-248-0170. E-mail: Parksville@virl.bc.ca. Web Site: virl.bc.ca/branches/parksville. *Libr Mgr,* Stephanie Pettigrew
Library Holdings: Bk Vols 62,981
Open Mon-Thurs 10-8, Fri & Sat 10-5, Sun 12:30-4
PORT ALBERNI BRANCH, 4245 Wallace St, Unit B, Port Alberni, V9Y 3Y6, SAN 366-1172. Tel: 250-723-9511. FAX: 250-723-5366. E-mail: PortAlberni@virl.bc.ca. Web Site: virl.bc.ca/branches/Port-Alberni. *Libr Mgr,* Michael de Leur; Staff 7 (MLS 1, Non-MLS 6)
Founded 1936
Library Holdings: Bk Vols 50,612
Open Mon-Thurs 10-8, Fri & Sat 10-5
PORT ALICE BRANCH, 951 Marine Dr, Port Alice, V0N 2N0. (Mail add: PO Box 190, Port Alice, V0N 2N0), SAN 366-1202. Tel: 250-284-3554. FAX: 250-284-3557. E-mail: PortAlice@virl.bc.ca. Web Site: virl.bc.ca/branches/port-alice. *Libr Mgr,* Louise Broadley
Library Holdings: Bk Vols 15,886
Open Tues 10-12 & 1-5, Thurs 1-4 & 5-8, Fri 1-5, Sat 10-2
PORT CLEMENTS BRANCH, 35 Cedar Ave W, Port Clements, V0T 1R0. (Mail add: PO Box 283, Port Clements, V0T 1R0), SAN 366-1180. Tel: 250-557-4402. FAX: 250-557-4402. E-mail: PortClements@virl.bc.ca. Web Site: virl.bc.ca/branches/port-clements. *Libr Mgr,* Patrick Siebold
Library Holdings: Bk Vols 8,882
Open Tues-Thurs 3-8, Sat 10-12 & 1-5
PORT HARDY BRANCH, 7110 Market St, Port Hardy, V0N 2P0. (Mail add: PO Box 251, Port Hardy, V0N 2P0), SAN 366-1237. Tel: 250-949-6661. FAX: 250-949-6600. E-mail: PortHardy@virl.bc.ca. Web Site: virl.bc.ca/branches/port-hardy. *Libr Mgr,* Louise Broadley
Library Holdings: Bk Vols 21,454
Open Tues, Wed & Sat 10-12 & 1-5, Thurs 1-4 & 5-8, Fri 12-5
PORT MCNEILL BRANCH, 4-1584 Broughton Blvd, Port McNeill, V0N 2R0. (Mail add: PO Box 786, Port McNeill, V0N 2R0), SAN 366-1261. Tel: 250-956-3669. FAX: 250-956-3669. E-mail: PortMcneill@virl.bc.ca. Web Site: virl.bc.ca/branches/port-mcneill. *Libr Mgr,* Louise Broadley
Library Holdings: Bk Vols 20,804
Open Tues & Thurs 10-12 & 1-5, Wed 1-5 & 6-8, Fri 10-3
PORT RENFREW BRANCH, 6638 Deering Rd, Port Renfrew, V0S 1K0, SAN 366-1296. Tel: 250-647-5423. FAX: 250-647-5400. E-mail: PortRenfrew@virl.bc.ca. Web Site: virl.bc.ca/branches/port-renfrew. *Libr Mgr,* Peter Maguire
Library Holdings: Bk Vols 7,379
Open Wed & Thurs 2-5 & 6-8, Fri 12-5, Sat 10-2
QUADRA ISLAND, 654 Harper Rd, Quathiaski Cove, V0P 1N0. (Mail add: PO Box 310, Heriot Bay, V0P 1H0), SAN 329-6016. Tel: 250-285-2216. FAX: 250-285-2248. E-mail: QuadraIsland@virl.bc.ca. Web Site: virl.bc.ca/branches/quadra-island. *Libr Mgr,* Stephanie Pettigrew
Library Holdings: Bk Vols 13,543
Open Tues, Fri & Sat 10-5, Wed & Thurs 1-8
QUALICUM BEACH BRANCH, 101-660 Primrose St, Qualicum Beach, V9K 2R5, SAN 366-1326. Tel: 250-752-6121. FAX: 250-752-6630. E-mail: QualicumBeach@virl.bc.ca. Web Site: virl.bc.ca/branches/qualicum-beach. *Libr Mgr,* Stephanie Pettigrew
Library Holdings: Bk Vols 43,841
Open Mon-Thurs 10-8, Fri & Sat 10-5
QUEEN CHARLOTTE CITY BRANCH, Community Hall, 138 Bay, Queen Charlotte, V0T 1S0. (Mail add: PO Box 339, Queen Charlotte, V0T 1S0), SAN 366-1334. Tel: 250-559-4518. FAX: 250-559-4518. E-mail: QueenCharlotte@virl.bc.ca. Web Site: virl.bc.ca/branches/queen-charlotte. *Libr Mgr,* Patrick Siebold
Library Holdings: Bk Vols 18,780
Open Tues & Sat 10-12 & 1-5, Wed 1-4 & 5-8, Fri 12:30-5
SANDSPIT BRANCH, Seabreeze Plaza, Beach Rd, Sandspit, V0T 1T0. (Mail add: PO Box 228, Sandspit, V0T 1T0), SAN 326-5714. Tel: 250-637-2247. FAX: 250-637-2247. E-mail: Sandspit@virl.bc.ca. Web Site: virl.bc.ca/branches/sandspit. *Libr Mgr,* Patrick Siebold
Library Holdings: Bk Vols 8,914
Open Tues 10-12 & 1-5, Thurs 1-4 & 5-8, Sat 10-2
SAYWARD BRANCH, A-652 H'Kusam Way, Sayward, V0P 1R0. (Mail add: PO Box 310, Sayward, V0P 1R0), SAN 366-1350. Tel: 250-282-5551. FAX: 250-282-5533. E-mail: Sayward@virl.bc.ca. Web Site: virl.bc.ca/branches/sayward. *Libr Mgr,* Stephanie Pettigrew
Library Holdings: Bk Vols 10,988
Open Tues 10-12 & 1-5, Wed & Sat 10-2, Thurs 1-4 & 5-8
SIDNEY/NORTH SAANICH BRANCH, 10091 Resthaven Dr, Sidney, V8L 3G3, SAN 366-1415. Tel: 250-656-0944. FAX: 250-656-6400. E-mail: Sidney@virl.bc.ca. Web Site: virl.bc.ca/branches/sidney-north-saanich. *Libr Mgr,* Sharon Walker
Library Holdings: Bk Vols 72,376
Open Mon-Thurs 10-8, Fri & Sat 10-5, Sun 12:30-4
SOINTULA BRANCH, 280 First St, Sointula, V0N 3E0. (Mail add: PO Box 187, Sointula, V0N 3E0), SAN 371-9863. Tel: 250-973-6493. FAX: 250-973-6493. E-mail: Sointula@virl.bc.ca. Web Site: virl.bc.ca/branches/sointula. *Libr Mgr,* Louise Broadley
Library Holdings: Bk Vols 13,442
Open Tues & Thurs 1-4 & 5-8, Wed 10-12 & 1-3, Sat 10-2
SOOKE BRANCH, 6671 Wadams Way, Sooke, V9Z 0A4. (Mail add: PO Box 468, Sooke, V0S 1N0), SAN 366-144X. Tel: 250-642-3022. FAX: 250-642-3994. E-mail: sooke@virl.bc.ca. Web Site: virl.bc.ca/branches/sooke. *Libr Mgr,* Peter Maguire
Library Holdings: Bk Vols 38,712
Open Mon 1-5, Tues & Wed 10-8, Thurs-Sat 10-5
SOUTH COWICHAN, 310-2720 Mill Bay Rd, Mill Bay, V0R 2P0. (Mail add: PO Box 118, Mill Bay, V0R 2P0), SAN 366-1385. Tel: 250-743-5436. FAX: 250-743-5506. E-mail: SouthCowichan@virl.bc.ca. Web Site: virl.bc.ca/branches/south-cowichan. *Libr Mgr,* Monica Finn
Library Holdings: Bk Vols 38,745
Open Mon, Tues, Fri & Sat 10-5, Wed & Thurs 10-8
TAHSIS BRANCH, 977 Maquinna Dr S, Tahsis, V0P 1X0. (Mail add: PO Box 458, Tahsis, V0P 1X0), SAN 366-1474. Tel: 250-934-6621. FAX: 250-934-6621. E-mail: Tahsis@virl.bc.ca. Web Site: virl.bc.ca/branches/tahsis. *Libr Mgr,* Stephanie Pettigrew
Library Holdings: Bk Vols 11,216
Open Tues 10-12 & 1-5, Wed 1-5, Thurs 1-4 & 5-8, Sat 10-2
TOFINO BRANCH, 331 Main St, Tofino, V0R 2Z0. (Mail add: PO Box 97, Tofino, V0R 2Z0), SAN 366-1504. Tel: 250-725-3713. FAX: 250-725-3743. E-mail: Tofino@virl.bc.ca. Web Site: virl.bc.ca/branches/tofino. *Libr Mgr,* Michael de Leur
Library Holdings: Bk Vols 9,197
Open Tues 10-12 & 1-5, Thurs 1-4 & 5-8, Fri 1-5, Sat 10-2
UCLUELET BRANCH, 500 Matterson Dr, Ucluelet, V0R 3A0. (Mail add: PO Box 247, Ucluelet, V0R 3A0), SAN 366-1563. Tel: 250-726-4642. FAX: 250-726-4622. E-mail: Ucluelet@virl.bc.ca. Web Site: virl.bc.ca/branches/ucluelet. *Libr Mgr,* Michael de Leur
Library Holdings: Bk Vols 14,651
Open Tues 10-12 & 1-5, Thurs 1-4 & 5-8, Fri 1-5, Sat 10-2
UNION BAY BRANCH, 5527 Island Hwy S, Union Bay, V0R 3B0. (Mail add: PO Box 81, Union Bay, V0R 3B0), SAN 366-1539. Tel: 250-335-2433. FAX: 250-335-2492. E-mail: UnionBay@virl.bc.ca. Web Site: virl.bc.ca/branches/union-bay. *Libr Mgr,* Greg Gulas
Library Holdings: Bk Vols 7,965
Open Tues & Fri 10-12 & 1-5, Sat 10-2

WOSS BRANCH, 4503B Railway Ave, Woss, V0N 3P0, SAN 366-158X. Tel: 250-281-2263. FAX: 250-281-2273. E-mail: Woss@virl.bc.ca. Web Site: virl.bc.ca/branches/woss. *Libr Mgr,* Louise Broadley
Library Holdings: Bk Vols 5,896
Open Tues 10-12 & 1-5, Thurs 1-4 & 5-8, Fri 1-5, Sat 10-2

J VANCOUVER ISLAND UNIVERSITY LIBRARY*, 900 Fifth St, V9R 5S5. SAN 318-7829. Tel: 250-753-3245. Circulation Tel: 250-740-6330. FAX: 250-740-6473. E-mail: research.help@viu.ca. Web Site: library.viu.ca. *Univ Librn,* David Alexander; E-mail: david.alexander@viu.ca; *Librn, Spec Coll Coordr,* Andie Tomlinson; E-mail: andie.tomlinson@viu.ca; *Coordr, Coll Serv,* Jean Blackburn; E-mail: jean.blackburn@viu.ca
Founded 1969
Special Collections: Oral History
Automation Activity & Vendor Info: (Acquisitions) SirsiDynix; (Cataloging) SirsiDynix; (Circulation) SirsiDynix; (Course Reserve) SirsiDynix; (Media Booking) SirsiDynix; (OPAC) SirsiDynix; (Serials) SirsiDynix
Wireless access
Partic in British Columbia Electronic Library Network; Centre for Accessible Post-Secondary Education Resources; Electronic Health Library of British Columbia
Open Mon-Thurs 9-9, Fri 9-5, Sat 11-5, Sun 10-9

NELSON

P NELSON PUBLIC LIBRARY*, 602 Stanley St, V1L 1N4. SAN 318-7845. Tel: 250-352-6333. E-mail: library@nelson.ca. Web Site: nelsonlibrary.ca. *Chief Librn,* Tracey Therrien; E-mail: ttherrien@nelson.ca; Staff 9 (MLS 2, Non-MLS 7)
Founded 1920. Pop 21,112; Circ 168,491
Library Holdings: Bk Vols 67,269
Special Collections: Kootenay Archives
Automation Activity & Vendor Info: (Acquisitions) Evergreen; (Cataloging) Evergreen; (Circulation) Evergreen; (OPAC) Evergreen; (Serials) Evergreen
Wireless access
Mem of Kootenay Library Federation
Partic in BC Libraries Cooperative
Open Mon, Wed, Fri & Sat 10-6, Tues & Thurs 10-7
Friends of the Library Group

NEW WESTMINSTER

C DOUGLAS COLLEGE LIBRARY & LEARNING CENTRE, New Westminster Campus, 700 Royal Ave, Rm N2100, V3M 5Z5. SAN 320-7781. Tel: 604-527-5568. Circulation Tel: 604-527-5539. Reference Tel: 604-527-5176. E-mail: library@douglascollege.ca, researchhelp@douglascollege.ca. Web Site: library.douglascollege.ca. *Dir, Learning Resources & Records Mgmt,* Trish Rosseel; Tel: 604-527-5182, E-mail: rosseelt@douglascollege.ca; *Admin Officer, Learning Resources,* Lisa Sim; Tel: 604-527-5180, E-mail: siml@douglascollege.ca; *Head, Ref Serv,* Shannon Moist; Tel: 604-527-5189, E-mail: moists@douglascollege.ca; *Media & Electronic Resources Librn,* Christian Guillou; Tel: 604-527-5184, E-mail: guillouc@douglascollege.ca; *Open Education Librn,* Debra Flewelling; Tel: 604-527-5190, E-mail: flewellingd@douglascollege.ca; Staff 34 (MLS 12, Non-MLS 22)
Founded 1970. Enrl 5,700; Fac 375
Library Holdings: e-books 392,000; e-journals 84,000; Bk Vols 120,000; Per Subs 100; Videos 10,000
Automation Activity & Vendor Info: (Acquisitions) Innovative Interfaces, Inc; (Cataloging) Innovative Interfaces, Inc; (Circulation) Innovative Interfaces, Inc; (Course Reserve) Innovative Interfaces, Inc; (Media Booking) Innovative Interfaces, Inc; (OPAC) Innovative Interfaces, Inc; (Serials) Innovative Interfaces, Inc
Wireless access
Partic in British Columbia Electronic Library Network; Centre for Accessible Post-Secondary Education Resources; Electronic Health Library of British Columbia
Open Mon-Fri 8am-9pm, Sat 9-5 (Winter); Mon-Thurs 8am-9pm, Fri 8-5 (Summer)

Departmental Libraries:

COQUITLAM CAMPUS, 1250 Pinetree Way, Rm A1040, Coquitlam, V3B 7X3. Tel: 604-777-6130. Circulation Tel: 604-777-6139. Reference Tel: 604-777-6131. FAX: 604-777-6138. E-mail: library@douglascollege.ca. *Libr Operations Supvr,* Ann Kuo; Tel: 604-777-6136, E-mail: kuoa@douglascollege.edu
Open Mon-Thurs 8am-9pm, Fri 8-6, Sat 9-5 (Winter); Mon-Fri 8-4 (Summer)

C JUSTICE INSTITUTE OF BRITISH COLUMBIA LIBRARY*, 715 McBride Blvd, V3L 5T4. SAN 318-8299. Tel: 604-528-5599. FAX: 604-528-5593. E-mail: library@jibc.ca. Web Site: www.jibc.ca/library. *Dir, Libr Serv,* April Haddad; Tel: 604-528-5594, E-mail: ahaddad@jibc.ca; *E-Resources & Systems Librn,* Crystal Yin; Tel: 604-528-5597, E-mail: cyin@jibc.ca; *Librarian, Metadata & Collections,* Suyu Dong; Tel: 604-528-5595, E-mail: sdong@jibc.ca; *Ref & Instruction Librn,* Darcye Lovsin; Tel: 604-528-5592, E-mail: dlovsin@jibc.ca; *Libr Asst,* Elizabeth Fletcher; Tel: 604-528-5596, E-mail: efletcher@jibc.ca; *Circ, ILL,* Michael Caparas; Tel: 604-528-5598, E-mail: mcaparas@jibc.ca; *Ser & Acq Tech,* Yvonne Lam; E-mail: ylam@jibc.ca; Staff 7.5 (MLS 4, Non-MLS 3.5)
Founded 1978. Enrl 2,400; Highest Degree: Bachelor
Library Holdings: Audiobooks 160; DVDs 2,452; Per Subs 74
Special Collections: Scholarly publications & institutional history (The Vault)
Subject Interests: Adult educ, Criminology, Disaster planning, Emergency med, Firefighting, Forensic sci, Law mgt, Psychol
Automation Activity & Vendor Info: (Acquisitions) SirsiDynix; (Cataloging) SirsiDynix; (Circulation) SirsiDynix; (Course Reserve) SirsiDynix; (Discovery) EBSCO Discovery Service; (ILL) Auto-Graphics, Inc; (Media Booking) SirsiDynix; (OPAC) SirsiDynix; (Serials) SirsiDynix
Wireless access
Publications: Bibliographies
Partic in British Columbia Electronic Library Network; Centre for Accessible Post-Secondary Education Resources; Council of Prairie & Pacific University Libraries; Electronic Health Library of British Columbia
Open Mon-Thurs 8-8, Fri 8-5, Sat 9-4; Mon-Fri 8-5 (May-Aug)

P NEW WESTMINSTER PUBLIC LIBRARY*, 716 Sixth Ave, V3M 2B3. SAN 318-787X. Tel: 604-527-4660. Circulation Tel: 604-527-4667. Reference Tel: 604-527-4665. E-mail: askus@nwpl.ca. Web Site: www.nwpl.ca. *Actg Chief Librn,* Susan Buss; Tel: 604-527-4669, E-mail: sbuss@nwpl.ca; Staff 55 (MLS 19, Non-MLS 36)
Founded 1865. Pop 57,602; Circ 762,663
Library Holdings: AV Mats 23,880; Bk Titles 191,736; Per Subs 574
Subject Interests: Local hist
Automation Activity & Vendor Info: (Cataloging) SirsiDynix; (Circulation) SirsiDynix; (OPAC) SirsiDynix
Wireless access
Function: Photocopying/Printing
Partic in Public Library InterLINK
Special Services for the Deaf - Closed caption videos; TDD equip
Special Services for the Blind - Closed circuit TV magnifier; Large print bks
Open Mon & Fri 10-6, Tues-Thurs 10-8, Sat & Sun 10-5

Branches: 1

QUEENSBOROUGH, 920 Ewen Ave, V3M 5C8. Tel: 604-636-4450. *Supvr,* Sundeet Chohan
Open Mon-Thurs 10-6, Fri 10-5, Sat 10-4

M ROYAL COLUMBIAN HOSPITAL*, Fraser Health Authority, 330 E Columbia St, V3L 3W7. SAN 324-4628. Tel: 604-520-4755. FAX: 604-520-4804. *Mgr, Libr Serv,* Brooke Scott; E-mail: brooke.scott@fraserhealth.ca
Library Holdings: Bk Titles 5,500; Per Subs 130
Subject Interests: Allied health, Med, Nursing
Restriction: Staff use only

NORTH VANCOUVER

C CAPILANO COLLEGE LIBRARY*, 2055 Purcell Way, V7J 3H5. SAN 318-7888. Tel: 604-984-4944. Reference Tel: 604-984-1769. FAX: 604-984-1728. E-mail: library@capilanou.ca. Web Site: library.capilanou.ca. *Univ Librn,* Dr Christina Neigel; E-mail: christinaneigel@capilanou.ca; Staff 26 (MLS 6, Non-MLS 20)
Founded 1968. Enrl 5,350; Fac 367
Library Holdings: AV Mats 4,825; e-books 800; Bk Vols 113,044; Per Subs 440
Special Collections: Can
Subject Interests: Arts, Asia-Pacific progs, Legal careers, Tech careers
Automation Activity & Vendor Info: (Acquisitions) Innovative Interfaces, Inc; (Cataloging) Innovative Interfaces, Inc; (Circulation) Innovative Interfaces, Inc; (Course Reserve) Innovative Interfaces, Inc; (ILL) Innovative Interfaces, Inc; (Media Booking) Innovative Interfaces, Inc; (OPAC) Innovative Interfaces, Inc; (Serials) Innovative Interfaces, Inc
Wireless access
Partic in British Columbia Electronic Library Network; Centre for Accessible Post-Secondary Education Resources; Electronic Health Library of British Columbia
Open Mon-Thurs 8am-9:30pm, Fri 8-4:30, Sat & Sun 1-5

P NORTH VANCOUVER CITY LIBRARY*, 120 W 14th St, V7M 1N9. SAN 318-790X. Tel: 604-998-3450. Reference Tel: 604-998-3490. FAX: 604-983-3624. E-mail: nvcl@cnv.org. Web Site: www.nvcl.ca. *Chief Librn,* Deb Hutchison Koep; E-mail: dkoep@cnv.org; Staff 40 (MLS 10, Non-MLS 30)
Founded 1924. Pop 52,898; Circ 660,256
Library Holdings: Audiobooks 8,740; AV Mats 17,920; Bks on Deafness & Sign Lang 149; CDs 5,242; DVDs 12,851; e-books 4,565; e-journals

1,889; Electronic Media & Resources 4,439; Large Print Bks 5,478; Microforms 8; Bk Titles 98,303; Bk Vols 117,150; Per Subs 217; Talking Bks 2,396
Automation Activity & Vendor Info: (Acquisitions) SirsiDynix; (Cataloging) SirsiDynix; (Circulation) SirsiDynix; (Discovery) SirsiDynix; (ILL) A-G Canada Ltd; (OPAC) SirsiDynix
Wireless access
Function: 24/7 Electronic res, 24/7 Online cat, Activity rm, Adult bk club, Adult literacy prog
Partic in Public Library InterLINK
Special Services for the Deaf - Staff with knowledge of sign lang
Special Services for the Blind - Assistive/Adapted tech devices, equip & products; Bks on cassette; Bks on CD; Daisy reader; Home delivery serv; Large print bks
Open Mon-Fri 9-9, Sat 9-5, Sun 1-5
Friends of the Library Group

P NORTH VANCOUVER DISTRICT PUBLIC LIBRARY*, Lynn Valley Main, 1277 Lynn Valley Rd, V7J 0A2. SAN 366-1652. Tel: 604-984-0286, 604-990-5800. FAX: 604-984-7600. Web Site: www.nvdpl.ca. *Dir, Libr Serv,* Jacqueline van Dyk; E-mail: jvandyk@nvdpl.ca; *Bus Mgr,* Deborah Hudson; E-mail: hudsond@nvdpl.ca; *Commun Engagement Mgr,* Allison Campbell; E-mail: alicam@nvdpl.ca; *Mgr Fac,* Corinne McConchie; E-mail: McConchieC@nvdpl.ca; *Br Coordr,* Tara Foreman; Staff 21.3 (MLS 9, Non-MLS 12.3)
Founded 1964. Circ 1,538,708
Library Holdings: AV Mats 54,259; Bk Vols 231,367
Automation Activity & Vendor Info: (Acquisitions) BiblioCommons; (Cataloging) BiblioCommons; (Circulation) BiblioCommons; (Course Reserve) BiblioCommons; (ILL) BiblioCommons; (Media Booking) BiblioCommons; (OPAC) BiblioCommons; (Serials) BiblioCommons
Wireless access
Partic in Public Library InterLINK
Special Services for the Blind - Bks on cassette; Bks on CD
Open Mon-Fri 9-9, Sat 9-5, Sun 12-5
Friends of the Library Group
Branches: 2
CAPILANO, 3045 Highland Blvd, V7R 2X4, SAN 366-1687. Tel: 604-987-4471. FAX: 604-987-0956. *Br Coordr,* Carys Brown; E-mail: brownc@nvdpl.ca; Staff 13.3 (MLS 3.8, Non-MLS 9.5)
Founded 1964
Open Mon-Fri 10-9, Sat 10-5, Sun 12-5
Friends of the Library Group
PARKGATE, 3675 Banff Ct, V7H 2Z8, SAN 366-1717. Tel: 604-929-3727. FAX: 604-929-0758. *Br Coordr,* Claire Westlake; Staff 13.4 (MLS 4, Non-MLS 9.4)
Open Mon-Fri 10-9, Sat 10-5, Sun 12-5
Friends of the Library Group

M VANCOUVER COASTAL HEALTH*, Lions Gate Hospital Library, 231 E 15th St, V7L 2L7. SAN 318-7896. Tel: 604-984-5844, 604-988-3131. FAX: 604-984-5823. E-mail: vchlibraryservices@vch.ca. Web Site: www.vch.ca/for-health-professionals/library. *Librn,* Chantalle Jack
Founded 1961
Library Holdings: Bk Titles 750; Per Subs 66
Open Mon-Fri 8-4

PEMBERTON

P PEMBERTON & DISTRICT PUBLIC LIBRARY*, 7390A Cottonwood St, V0N 2L0. Tel: 604-894-6916. E-mail: library@pemberton.bclibrary.ca. Web Site: pemberton.bc.libraries.coop. *Libr Dir,* Emma Gillis; E-mail: egillis@pembertonlibrary.ca; *Sr Libr Asst,* Marilyn Marinus; E-mail: mmarinus@pemberton.bclibrary.ca; *Libr Asst,* Valerie Fowler; E-mail: vfowler@pemberton.bclibrary.ca; Staff 6 (MLS 1, Non-MLS 5)
Founded 1979
Library Holdings: Bk Titles 12,000; Per Subs 20
Automation Activity & Vendor Info: (Acquisitions) Follett Software; (Cataloging) Follett Software; (Circulation) Follett Software; (Course Reserve) Follett Software; (ILL) Follett Software; (Media Booking) Follett Software; (OPAC) Follett Software; (Serials) Follett Software
Wireless access
Function: 24/7 Electronic res, 24/7 Online cat, Adult bk club, Bks on CD, Chess club, Children's prog, Computer training, Computers for patron use, E-Readers, Electronic databases & coll, Family literacy, Free DVD rentals, Holiday prog, ILL available, Internet access, Laminating, Magazines, Movies, Online ref, OverDrive digital audio bks, Photocopying/Printing, Preschool reading prog, Prog for adults, Prog for children & young adult, Scanner, Wheelchair accessible
Open Mon-Fri 10-6, Sat 11-4, Sun 11-2
Friends of the Library Group

PENDER ISLAND

P SOUTHERN GULF ISLANDS COMMUNITY LIBRARIES*, Pender Island Public Library, 4407 Bedwell Harbour Rd, V0N 2M1. (Mail add: PO Box 12, V0N 2M1). Tel: 250-629-3722. E-mail: penderislandlibrary@crd.bc.ca. Web Site: sgicl.bc.libraries.coop. *Libr Dir,* Carmen Oleskevich; E-mail: coleskevich@crd.bc.ca
Library Holdings: Bk Vols 19,500; Per Subs 23
Wireless access
Function: Computers for patron use
Open Tues & Thurs-Sat 10-3
Branches: 4
GALIANO ISLAND COMMUNITY LIBRARY, Two 1290 Sturdies Bay Rd, Galiano Island, V0N 1P0. Tel: 250-539-2141. E-mail: galinolibrary@gmail.com.
Open Wed 11-5, Sun 11-2
MAYNE ISLAND COMMUNITY LIBRARY, 411 Naylor Rd, Mayne Island, V0N 2J0. Tel: 250-539-2597. E-mail: mipl@shaw.ca.
Open Wed, Fri & Sat 11-3
PIERS ISLAND COMMUNITY LIBRARY, Community Fire Hall, C/O Box 2223, Sidney, V8L 3S8. Tel: 250-655-4812, 250-656-3694. E-mail: libraryonpiers@gmail.com.
Open Mon-Fri 9-5
SATURNA ISLAND COMMUNITY LIBRARY, 140 E Point Rd, Saturna Island, VON 2Y0. Tel: 250-539-5312. E-mail: ermlsaturna@gmail.com.
Open Wed & Sat 10-1

PENTICTON

SR BIBLE HOLINESS MOVEMENT LIBRARY*, 311 Falcon Pl, V2A 8K6, (Mail add: PO Box 223, Postal Sta A, Vancouver, V6C 2M3), SAN 374-4264. Tel: 250-492-3376. E-mail: bibleholinessmovement@outlook.com. *Pres,* Wesley H Wakefield
Founded 1949
Library Holdings: AV Mats 80; CDs 14; DVDs 16; Bk Titles 4,160; Bk Vols 4,264; Spec Interest Per Sub 9; Videos 42
Special Collections: Salvationist/Holiness History (mission directories, multi-lang copies of the Bible & original hymn composites); Wesleyan Christian Theology (Wesley's Works Coll)
Subject Interests: Anti-slavery, Evangelism, Missions & missionaries, Substance abuse
Restriction: Open by appt only

P PENTICTON PUBLIC LIBRARY*, 785 Main St, V2A 5E3. SAN 318-7926. Tel: 250-770-7781. Reference Tel: 250-770-7782. Administration Tel: 250-770-7784. E-mail: info@pentictonlibrary.ca. Web Site: www.pentictonlibrary.ca. *Chief Librn,* Heather Buzzell; E-mail: hbuzzell@pentictonlibrary.ca; *Pub Serv Librn,* Stephanie James; Tel: 250-770-7786, E-mail: sjames@pentictonlibrary.ca; *Syst Librn,* Dan Lerch; Tel: 250-770-7785, E-mail: dlerch@pentictonlibrary.ca; *Youth Serv Librn,* Julia Cox; Tel: 250-770-7783, E-mail: jcox@pentictonlibrary.ca; Staff 22 (MLS 4, Non-MLS 18)
Founded 1909. Pop 34,014; Circ 317,978
Library Holdings: CDs 952; DVDs 1,100; Large Print Bks 2,500; Bk Titles 130,000; Per Subs 221; Talking Bks 1,830
Subject Interests: Agr, Local hist, Wine
Automation Activity & Vendor Info: (Cataloging) Koha; (Circulation) Koha; (OPAC) Koha
Wireless access
Mem of Kootenay Library Federation
Special Services for the Blind - Audio mat
Open Mon, Wed, Fri & Sat 9:30-5, Tues & Thurs 9:30-8:30

PORT ALBERNI

J NORTH ISLAND COLLEGE*, Port Alberni Campus Library, 3699 Roger St, V9Y 8E3. Tel: 250-724-8733. FAX: 250-724-8780. Web Site: library.nic.bc.ca. *Libr Tech II,* Sherry Kropninski; Tel: 250-724-8717, E-mail: sherry.kropninski@nic.bc.ca; *Libr Tech I,* Aileen Selbee; Tel: 250-724-8760, E-mail: aileen.selbee@nic.ba.ca; Staff 2 (Non-MLS 2)
Library Holdings: Bk Titles 8,000
Automation Activity & Vendor Info: (Acquisitions) SirsiDynix; (Cataloging) SirsiDynix; (Circulation) SirsiDynix; (Course Reserve) SirsiDynix; (ILL) SirsiDynix; (Media Booking) SirsiDynix; (OPAC) SirsiDynix; (Serials) SirsiDynix
Wireless access
Function: CD-ROM, Electronic databases & coll, ILL available, Online ref, Orientations, Photocopying/Printing, Ref serv available, VHS videos
Partic in British Columbia Electronic Library Network
Special Services for the Deaf - High interest/low vocabulary bks
Special Services for the Blind - Closed circuit TV
Open Mon & Tues 8-4:30, Wed & Thurs 8-6, Fri 8-4
Restriction: In-house use for visitors, Open to students, fac & staff, Pub use on premises

PORT HARDY

J NORTH ISLAND COLLEGE*, Mixalakwila Campus Library, 140-8950 Granville St, V0N 2P0. (Mail add: PO Box 901, V0N 2P0). Tel: 250-949-7912. E-mail: library.research@nic.bc.ca. Web Site: library.nic.bc.ca. *Libr Asst,* Kathy Crawford
Automation Activity & Vendor Info: (Cataloging) SirsiDynix; (OPAC) SirsiDynix
Wireless access
Function: ILL available, Photocopying/Printing, Res assist avail, Scanner, Study rm
Partic in Centre for Accessible Post-Secondary Education Resources
Restriction: Open by appt only

PORT MOODY

P PORT MOODY PUBLIC LIBRARY*, 100 Newport Dr, V3H 5C3. SAN 318-7950. Tel: 604-469-4575. Information Services Tel: 604-469-4577. FAX: 604-469-4576. Web Site: www.portmoodylibrary.ca. *Dir, Libr Serv,* Marc Saunders; E-mail: msaunders@portmoody.ca; *Dep Dir,* Heather Hadley; E-mail: hhadley@portmoody.ca; Staff 15 (MLS 7, Non-MLS 8)
Founded 1943. Pop 34,500; Circ 660,000
Library Holdings: AV Mats 10,259; Bk Titles 96,182; Per Subs 160
Automation Activity & Vendor Info: (Acquisitions) Horizon; (Cataloging) Horizon; (Circulation) Horizon; (Discovery) BiblioCommons; (ILL) A-G Canada Ltd; (OPAC) BiblioCommons
Wireless access
Partic in Public Library InterLINK
Open Mon-Fri 9-9, Sat 9-5, Sun 1-5

POUCE COUPE

P POUCE COUPE PUBLIC LIBRARY*, 5010-52 Ave, V0C 2C0. (Mail add: PO Box 75, V0C 2C0), SAN 318-7969. Tel: 250-786-5765. FAX: 250-786-5761. E-mail: bpoc.ill@pris.bc.ca. Web Site: poucecoupe.bc.libraries.coop. *Libr Dir,* Courtenay Johnston; *Asst Librn,* Dominic St Pierre
Founded 1940. Pop 813; Circ 11,000
Library Holdings: Bk Vols 15,000
Wireless access
Partic in North East Library Federation
Open Mon-Fri 2-8, Sat 9-4; Mon, Tues & Thurs 2-7, Wed, Fri & Sat 10-4 (Summer)
Friends of the Library Group

POWELL RIVER

P POWELL RIVER PUBLIC LIBRARY*, 100-6975 Alberni St, V8A 2B8. SAN 366-1776. Tel: 604-485-4796. Toll Free FAX: 866-489-5778. E-mail: info@prpl.ca. Web Site: prpl.ca. *Chief Librn,* Rebecca Burbank; E-mail: rburbank@prpl.ca; Staff 11 (MLS 2, Non-MLS 9)
Founded 1973. Pop 20,952; Circ 176,000
Library Holdings: AV Mats 5,290; Large Print Bks 1,340; Bk Titles 45,538; Bk Vols 53,305; Per Subs 110; Talking Bks 1,605
Automation Activity & Vendor Info: (Acquisitions) SirsiDynix; (Cataloging) SirsiDynix; (Circulation) SirsiDynix; (Discovery) SirsiDynix; (ILL) Auto-Graphics, Inc; (OPAC) SirsiDynix
Wireless access
Function: Bk club(s), Children's prog, Computer training, Computers for patron use, Digital talking bks, Electronic databases & coll, Free DVD rentals, Homebound delivery serv, ILL available, Online cat, Online ref, Outreach serv, OverDrive digital audio bks, Photocopying/Printing, Preschool outreach, Prof lending libr, Ref & res, Ref serv available, Scanner, Story hour, Summer reading prog, Wheelchair accessible
Open Mon & Thurs 10-6, Tues, Wed & Fri 10-8:30, Sat 10-5, Sun 1-5
Friends of the Library Group

PRINCE GEORGE

L BRITISH COLUMBIA COURTHOUSE LIBRARY SOCIETY*, Court House, 250 George St, V2L 5S2. SAN 328-249X. Tel: 250-614-2763, 800-665-2570. FAX: 250-614-2788. E-mail: librarian@courthouselibrary.ca, princegeorge@courthouselibrary.ca. Web Site: www.courthouselibrary.ca. *Manager of Regional Libraries,* Liz Blackburn; E-mail: lblackburn@courthouselibrary.ca
Library Holdings: Bk Vols 15,000
Wireless access
Open Mon-Fri 8:30-4:30

J COLLEGE OF NEW CALEDONIA LIBRARY*, 3330 22nd Ave, V2N 1P8. SAN 318-7977. Tel: 250-561-5811, 250-562-2131, Ext 5298. Toll Free Tel: 800-371-8111, Ext 5811. FAX: 250-561-5845. E-mail: cnclibrary@cnc.bc.ca, reference@cnc.bc.ca. Web Site: www.cnc.bc.ca/services/library. *Dir,* Katherine Plett; *Bibliog Instr,* James Lovitt; *Pub Serv,* Jennifer Sauve; *Tech Serv,* B Yee; Staff 12 (MLS 4, Non-MLS 8)
Founded 1969. Enrl 3,125; Fac 232; Highest Degree: Associate
Library Holdings: AV Mats 1,500; e-books 9,900; Bk Titles 150,000; Per Subs 311
Special Collections: Canadian and Provincial
Automation Activity & Vendor Info: (Acquisitions) SirsiDynix; (Cataloging) SirsiDynix; (Circulation) SirsiDynix; (Course Reserve) SirsiDynix; (ILL) SirsiDynix; (OPAC) SirsiDynix
Wireless access
Partic in British Columbia Electronic Library Network; Centre for Accessible Post-Secondary Education Resources; Electronic Health Library of British Columbia
Open Mon-Fri 8am-10pm, Sat & Sun 12-4

P PRINCE GEORGE PUBLIC LIBRARY, Bob Harkins Branch, 888 Canada Games Way, V2L 5T6. SAN 318-8000. Tel: 250-563-9251. E-mail: ask@pgpl.ca. Web Site: www.pgpl.ca. *Libr Dir,* Paul Burry; Tel: 250-563-9251, Ext 130, E-mail: pburry@pgpl.ca; *Customer Experience Mgr, Mgr, Serv Delivery,* Sheila Littler; Tel: 250-563-9251, Ext 143, E-mail: slittler@pgpl.ca; *Mgr, Collections & Technology,* Chris Field; Tel: 250-563-9251, Ext 158, E-mail: cfield@pgpl.ca; Staff 19 (MLS 8, Non-MLS 11)
Founded 1955. Pop 88,054; Circ 758,139
Library Holdings: Audiobooks 2,808; CDs 4,168; DVDs 3,033; Bk Titles 129,208; Bk Vols 151,880; Per Subs 303
Special Collections: Local History Coll
Automation Activity & Vendor Info: (Acquisitions) SirsiDynix-Enterprise; (Cataloging) SirsiDynix-Enterprise; (Circulation) SirsiDynix-Enterprise; (OPAC) SirsiDynix-Enterprise
Wireless access
Function: Adult bk club, Art exhibits, Audiobks via web, Bk club(s), Bks on CD, Children's prog, Computer training, Computers for patron use, Electronic databases & coll, Family literacy, Free DVD rentals, ILL available, Music CDs, Online cat, Online ref, Outreach serv, OverDrive digital audio bks, Photocopying/Printing, Prog for adults, Senior outreach, Teen prog, Telephone ref, Wheelchair accessible
Open Mon & Fri 10-6, Tues-Thurs 10-8, Sat 10-5, Sun 12-4
Friends of the Library Group
Branches: 1
NECHAKO BRANCH, 6547 Hart Hwy, V2K 3A4, SAN 321-7434. Tel: 250-563-9251, Ext 300. *Br Coordr,* Leslie Hilder; Tel: 250-563-9251, Ext 401, E-mail: lhilder@pgpl.ca; Staff 1 (Non-MLS 1)
Founded 1980
Library Holdings: Audiobooks 284; CDs 1,258; DVDs 876; Bk Titles 21,818; Bk Vols 27,569; Per Subs 33
Open Mon-Wed & Fri 10-6, Thurs 10-8, Sat 10-5
Friends of the Library Group

M UNIVERSITY HOSPITAL OF NORTHERN BRITISH COLUMBIA*, Northern Health Library Services - Medical Library, Learning & Development Ctr, 1475 Edmonton St, V2M 1S2. SAN 323-8202. Tel: 250-565-2219. FAX: 250-565-2787. *Regional Mgr, Libr Serv,* Julie Creaser; E-mail: julie.creaser@northernhealth.ca
Library Holdings: Bk Titles 1,200; Per Subs 400
Subject Interests: Allied health, Med
Open Mon-Fri 8-4
Restriction: Staff use only

C UNIVERSITY OF NORTHERN BRITISH COLUMBIA LIBRARY*, Geoffrey R Weller Library, 333 University Way, V2N 4Z9. Tel: 250-960-6612. Circulation Tel: 250-960-6613. Reference Tel: 250-960-6475. Toll Free Tel: 888-440-3440 (BC Only). FAX: 250-960-6610. E-mail: library@unbc.ca. Web Site: www.library.unbc.ca. *Univ Librn,* Kevin Stranack; E-mail: kevin.stranack@unbc.ca; *Head, Archives & Spec Coll,* Erica Hernandez-Read; Tel: 250-960-6603, E-mail: erica.hernandez-read@unbc.ca; *Acq Librn,* Heather Empey; Tel: 250-960-6468, E-mail: heather.empey@unbc.ca
Founded 1989
Library Holdings: e-books 70,000; e-journals 50,000; Bk Vols 350,000
Wireless access
Function: Computers for patron use
Partic in British Columbia Electronic Library Network; Electronic Health Library of British Columbia

PRINCE RUPERT

P PRINCE RUPERT LIBRARY*, 101 Sixth Ave W, V8J 1Y9. SAN 318-8019. Tel: 250-627-1345. FAX: 250-627-7743. E-mail: info@princerupertlibrary.ca. Web Site: www.princerupertlibrary.ca. *Chief Librn,* Joe Zelwietro; E-mail: chieflib@citytel.net; *Dep Librn,* Kathleen Larkin; Staff 6 (MLS 2, Non-MLS 4)
Pop 15,500; Circ 80,000
Library Holdings: Bk Vols 70,000
Special Collections: Northwest History Coll
Subject Interests: Boating, Fisheries

Automation Activity & Vendor Info: (Cataloging) Evergreen; (Circulation) Evergreen; (OPAC) Evergreen
Wireless access
Publications: Annual Report
Partic in Northwest Library Federation
Special Services for the Blind - Home delivery serv
Open Mon & Fri 10-5, Tues-Thurs 10-9, Sat & Sun 1-5
Friends of the Library Group

RADIUM HOT SPRINGS

P RADIUM HOT SPRINGS PUBLIC LIBRARY*, 4863 Stanley St, V0A 1M0. (Mail add: PO Box 293, V0A 1M0). Tel: 250-347-2434. FAX: 250-347-2434. E-mail: info@radium.bclibrary.ca. Web Site: radium.bc.libraries.coop. *Dir,* Jane Jones
Library Holdings: Bk Vols 10,000
Wireless access
Mem of Kootenay Library Federation
Open Tues-Fri 11-5, Sat 10-4

RICHMOND

S AIDE CANADA LIBRARY*, 3688 Cessna Dr, V7B 1C7. SAN 372-6975. Tel: 604-207-1980, Ext 2006. E-mail: library@aidecanada.ca. Web Site: library.aidecanada.ca. *Mgr, Library Servs & Resource Discovery,* Allison Hill; E-mail: ahill@aidecanada.ca. Subject Specialists: *Autism,* Allison Hill; Staff 2 (MLS 1, Non-MLS 1)
Founded 2020
Subject Interests: Autism, Educ, Intellectual disability, Mental health
Wireless access
Function: 24/7 Electronic res, 24/7 Online cat, Games & aids for people with disabilities, Health sci info serv, Mail & tel request accepted, Mail loans to mem, Online cat, Online Chat, Online ref, OverDrive digital audio bks, Ref serv available, Res assist avail, Serves people with intellectual disabilities, Wheelchair accessible

P RICHMOND PUBLIC LIBRARY*, Brighouse, 100-7700 Minoru Gate, V6Y 1R9. SAN 318-8035. Tel: 604-231-6422. Circulation Tel: 604-231-6404. Reference Tel: 604-231-6413. FAX: 604-273-0459. Web Site: rpl.yourlibrary.ca. *Chief Librn,* Susan Walters; E-mail: susan.walters@yourlibrary.ca; Staff 23 (MLS 23)
Founded 1976. Pop 172,714; Circ 3,580,000
Library Holdings: Bk Titles 165,692; Bk Vols 421,867
Automation Activity & Vendor Info: (Circulation) Innovative Interfaces, Inc; (OPAC) Innovative Interfaces, Inc
Wireless access
Publications: Annual Report
Open Mon-Fri 9am-9:30pm, Sat & Sun 10-5
Friends of the Library Group
Branches: 3
CAMBIE BRANCH, 150-11590 Cambie Rd, V6X 3Z5. Tel: 604-231-6462.
Founded 1976
Open Mon-Fri 10-9, Sat & Sun 10-5
Friends of the Library Group
IRONWOOD BRANCH, Ironwood Plaza, 8200-11688 Steveston Hwy, V7A 1N6. Tel: 604-231-6468. FAX: 604-274-0454.
Library Holdings: Bk Titles 75,000
Open Mon-Fri 9-9, Sat & Sun 10-5
Friends of the Library Group
STEVESTON BRANCH, 4111 Moncton St, V7E 3A8. Tel: 604-231-6424.
Library Holdings: Bk Titles 6,000
Open Mon-Fri 10-9, Sat & Sun 10-5
Friends of the Library Group

§C VANCOUVER PREMIER COLLEGE, Learning Resource Center, 103-5300 No 3 Rd, V6X 2X9. Tel: 604-730-1628. FAX: 604-730-1633. E-mail: library@vpcollege.com. Web Site: vpcollege.com/learning-resource-center. *Librn,* Iwona Mandera; E-mail: iwonam@vpcollege.edu
Founded 1998
Automation Activity & Vendor Info: (Cataloging) TinyCat; (OPAC) TinyCat
Wireless access
Partic in British Columbia Electronic Library Network
Open Mon-Sat 9-5
Restriction: Open to students, fac & staff

ROSSLAND

P ROSSLAND PUBLIC LIBRARY ASSOCIATION*, 2180 Columbia Ave, V0G 1Y0. (Mail add: PO Box 190, V0G 1Y0), SAN 318-8043. Tel: 250-362-7611. E-mail: info@rossland.bclibrary.ca. Web Site: rossland.bc.libraries.coop. *Dir,* Stacey Boden; E-mail: director@rossland.bclibrary.ca; Staff 6 (Non-MLS 6)
Pop 4,429; Circ 33,093
Library Holdings: Bk Vols 14,517; Per Subs 35
Automation Activity & Vendor Info: (Acquisitions) Evergreen; (Cataloging) Evergreen; (Circulation) Evergreen; (ILL) Auto-Graphics, Inc; (OPAC) Evergreen
Wireless access
Function: 24/7 Electronic res, 24/7 Online cat, Activity rm, Adult literacy prog, Art programs, Bk club(s), Bks on CD, Children's prog, Computers for patron use, Distance learning, E-Readers, Electronic databases & coll, Equip loans & repairs, Family literacy, Free DVD rentals, Holiday prog, Home delivery & serv to seniorr ctr & nursing homes, ILL available, Internet access, Meeting rooms, Movies, Printer for laptops & handheld devices, Prog for adults, Prog for children & young adult, Story hour, Study rm, Wheelchair accessible
Mem of Kootenay Library Federation
Partic in BC Libraries Cooperative
Open Tues-Thurs 10-6, Fri & Sat 10-4

SALMO

P SALMO VALLEY PUBLIC LIBRARY, 104 Fourth St, V0G 1Z0. (Mail add: PO Box 458, V0G 1Z0). Tel: 250-357-2312. FAX: 250-357-2312. E-mail: salmolibrary@salmo.bc.libraries.coop. Web Site: salmo.bc.libraries.coop. *Libr Dir,* Ms Taylor Caron; *Asst Librn, Ch Serv,* Marianne Hanson; E-mail: mhansen@salmo.bc.libraries.coop
Pop 2,600; Circ 24,789
Library Holdings: AV Mats 2,000; Bk Vols 14,121
Automation Activity & Vendor Info: (Cataloging) Mandarin Library Automation; (Circulation) Mandarin Library Automation; (OPAC) Mandarin Library Automation
Wireless access
Mem of Kootenay Library Federation
Open Mon & Fri 10-5, Tues & Thurs 3-8, Sat 10-2

SALT SPRING ISLAND

P SALT SPRING ISLAND PUBLIC LIBRARY*, 129 McPhillips Ave, V8K 2T6. Tel: 250-537-4666. E-mail: info@saltspringlibrary.com. Web Site: saltspring.bc.libraries.coop. *Libr Dir,* Karen Hudson; E-mail: librarian@saltspringlibrary.com; *Asst Dir,* Julia Wagner; *Librn,* Julia Wagner; Staff 4 (MLS 2, Non-MLS 2)
Founded 1960. Pop 10,500; Circ 178,200
Library Holdings: Audiobooks 1,555; CDs 2,664; DVDs 3,481; Electronic Media & Resources 44,236; Large Print Bks 750; Bk Titles 60,000; Per Subs 65
Automation Activity & Vendor Info: (Cataloging) Evergreen; (Circulation) Evergreen; (ILL) Evergreen; (OPAC) Evergreen; (Serials) EBSCO Online
Wireless access
Function: 24/7 Electronic res, 24/7 Online cat, Activity rm, Adult bk club, Archival coll, Art exhibits, Art programs, Audiobks on Playaways & MP3, Audiobks via web, BA reader (adult literacy), Bi-weekly Writer's Group, Bk club(s), Bk reviews (Group), Bks on CD, Children's prog, Citizenship assistance, Computer training, Computers for patron use, Digital talking bks, Doc delivery serv, E-Reserves, Electronic databases & coll, Equip loans & repairs, Family literacy, Free DVD rentals, Genealogy discussion group, Holiday prog, Home delivery & serv to seniorr ctr & nursing homes, Homebound delivery serv, ILL available, Internet access, Large print keyboards, Life-long learning prog for all ages, Literacy & newcomer serv, Magazines, Magnifiers for reading, Mail & tel request accepted, Meeting rooms, Movies, Museum passes, Music CDs, Online cat, Online ref, Orientations, Outreach serv, OverDrive digital audio bks, Photocopying/Printing, Preschool outreach, Preschool reading prog, Prog for adults, Prog for children & young adult, Ref & res, Ref serv available, Res assist avail, Scanner, Senior computer classes, Senior outreach, Serves people with intellectual disabilities, Spoken cassettes & CDs, Spoken cassettes & DVDs, STEM programs, Story hour, Study rm, Summer reading prog, Tax forms, Teen prog, Telephone ref, Visual arts prog, Wheelchair accessible, Workshops, Writing prog
Partic in BC Libraries Cooperative
Special Services for the Deaf - Bks on deafness & sign lang; Closed caption videos
Special Services for the Blind - Bks on CD; Daisy reader; Free checkout of audio mat; Home delivery serv; Large print bks; Lending of low vision aids; Magnifiers; Production of talking bks; Recorded bks; Talking bks
Open Mon-Fri 10-5, Sat 10-3

SECHELT

P SECHELT PUBLIC LIBRARY*, 5797 Cowrie St, V0N 3A0. (Mail add: PO Box 2104, V0N 3A0), SAN 760-4912. Tel: 604-885-3260. FAX: 604-885-5183. E-mail: info@sechelt.bclibrary.ca. Web Site: sechelt.bc.libraries.coop. *Libr Dir,* Leianne Emery; E-mail: leianne.emery@secheltlibrary.ca; Staff 8 (MLS 2, Non-MLS 6)
Founded 1981
Library Holdings: Bk Vols 40,000; Per Subs 107

Automation Activity & Vendor Info: (Acquisitions) Horizon; (Cataloging) Horizon; (Circulation) Horizon; (OPAC) Horizon
Wireless access
Function: Archival coll, ILL available, Internet access, Photocopying/Printing, Prog for children & young adult, Ref serv available, Summer reading prog, Telephone ref, Wheelchair accessible
Open Mon, Tues, Thurs & Fri 10-5, Wed 10-6, Sat 10-4
Friends of the Library Group

SIDNEY

S BRITISH COLUMBIA LAND SURVEYORS FOUNDATION*, Anna Papove Memorial Library, No 301-2400 Bevan Ave, V8L 1W1. SAN 375-832X. Tel: 250-655-7222. FAX: 250-655-7223. E-mail: office@abcls.ca. Web Site: abcls.ca/about-abcls/about-foundation/abcls-library-index. *Chief Admin Officer,* Kelly Stofer; E-mail: kstofer@abcls.ca
Founded 1989
Library Holdings: Bk Titles 1,200
Special Collections: BC Land Surveyors Annual Reports, 1914-2005
Open Mon-Fri 8:30-4

G FISHERIES & OCEANS CANADA*, Institute of Ocean Sciences Library, 9860 W Saanich Rd, V8L 4B2. (Mail add: PO Box 6000, V8L 4B2), SAN 327-2818. FAX: 250-363-6749. E-mail: west.XENT@dfo-mpo.gc.ca. Information Services E-mail: info@dfo-mpo.gc.ca. Web Site: science-libraries.canada.ca/eng/fisheries-oceans. *Head of Libr, Head, Res Serv,* Pamela Wilkins; E-mail: pamela.wilkins@dfo-mpo.gc.ca; Staff 3 (MLS 2, Non-MLS 1)
Restriction: Open by appt only

SMITHERS

P SMITHERS PUBLIC LIBRARY*, 3817 Alfred Ave, V0J 2N0. (Mail add: PO Box 55, V0J 2N0), SAN 318-8078. Tel: 250-847-3043. FAX: 250-847-1533. E-mail: contact@smitherslibrary.ca. Web Site: smithers.bc.libraries.coop. *Dir,* Wendy Wright; E-mail: director@smitherslibrary.ca; *Children's & Youth Serv,* Sandra Schuffert; *ILL, Pub Relations,* Melissa Sawatsky; E-mail: msawatsky@smitherslibrary.ca; *ILL,* Kathy Wilford; *Libr Asst,* Lynnda McDougall; Staff 2 (MLS 1, Non-MLS 1)
Pop 9,069; Circ 86,000
Library Holdings: Bk Vols 30,000; Per Subs 65
Subject Interests: Forestry, Local hist, Mining
Automation Activity & Vendor Info: (Cataloging) Evergreen; (OPAC) Follett Software
Wireless access
Function: ILL available, Photocopying/Printing, Ref serv available, Telephone ref
Partic in Northwest Library Federation
Open Mon, Wed & Fri 12-5, Tues & Thurs 12-9, Sat 10:30-5
Friends of the Library Group

SPARWOOD

P SPARWOOD PUBLIC LIBRARY*, 110 Pine Ave, V0B 2G0. (Mail add: PO Box 1060, V0B 2G0), SAN 318-8086. Tel: 250-425-2299. FAX: 250-425-0229. Web Site: sparwood.bc.libraries.coop. *Head Librn,* James Bertoia; E-mail: jb@sparwoodlibrary.ca; *Libr Asst,* Joanne Plesman; Staff 1 (Non-MLS 1)
Founded 1974. Pop 5,000; Circ 22,213
Library Holdings: AV Mats 300; Bks on Deafness & Sign Lang 10; CDs 200; DVDs 50; Large Print Bks 300; Bk Titles 30,000; Bk Vols 32,000; Per Subs 50; Talking Bks 300; Videos 600
Subject Interests: Local hist
Automation Activity & Vendor Info: (Cataloging) Evergreen; (Circulation) Evergreen; (ILL) Auto-Graphics, Inc; (OPAC) Evergreen
Wireless access
Mem of Kootenay Library Federation

SQUAMISH

P SQUAMISH PUBLIC LIBRARY*, 37907 Second Ave, V8B 0A7. (Mail add: PO Box 1039, V8B 0A7), SAN 318-8094. Tel: 604-892-3110. FAX: 604-892-9376. E-mail: library@squamish.ca. Web Site: squamishlibrary.ca. *Dir, Libr Serv,* Hilary Bloom; E-mail: librarydirector@squamish.ca; Staff 7.7 (MLS 1, Non-MLS 6.7)
Founded 1956. Pop 16,417; Circ 120,582
Library Holdings: Audiobooks 2,176; DVDs 4,451; Bk Vols 66,124; Per Subs 203
Special Collections: Oral Coll; Squasm Area Historical Files (part 1) Basic History & (part 2) Historical Photographs
Automation Activity & Vendor Info: (Acquisitions) Horizon; (Cataloging) Horizon; (Circulation) Horizon; (OPAC) Horizon; (Serials) Horizon
Wireless access
Partic in Public Library InterLINK
Open Mon, Fri & Sat 10-5, Tues-Thurs 10-7
Friends of the Library Group

STEWART

P STEWART PUBLIC LIBRARY, 322 Fifth Ave, V0T 1W0. (Mail add: PO Box 546, V0T 1W0). Tel: 236-749-2003. FAX: 239-749-2003. E-mail: stewartpubliclibrary@gmail.com. Web Site: stewart.bc.libraries.coop. *Libr Dir,* Rebecca Mitchell; *Libr Asst,* Michelle Day
Library Holdings: Bk Vols 16,000; Per Subs 36
Automation Activity & Vendor Info: (Cataloging) Evergreen; (Circulation) Evergreen
Open Mon, Tues, Thurs & Fri 1-6, Wed 4-9

SUMMERLAND

G SUMMERLAND RESEARCH & DEVELOPMENT CENTRE*, 4200 Hwy 97, V0H 1Z0. (Mail add: PO Box 5000, V0H 1Z0), SAN 318-8108. Tel: 250-494-2100. E-mail: aafc.summerlandrdc-crdsummerland.aac@agr.gc.ca. Web Site: profils-profiles.science.gc.ca/en/research-centre/summerland-research-and-development-centre. *Managing Librn,* Dawn Bassett; E-mail: dawn.bassett@agr.gc.ca
Subject Interests: Agr engr, Entomology, Food sci, Fruit processing, Microbiology, Plant pathology, Pomology, Soil sci, Viticulture, Wine chem
Restriction: Open by appt only

SURREY

S BRITISH COLUMBIA GENEALOGICAL SOCIETY*, Resource Centre, 12837 76th Ave, No 211, V3W 2V3. (Mail add: Lansdowne Mall, PO Box 88054, Richmond, V6X 3T6), SAN 328-011X. Tel: 604-502-9119. E-mail: library@bcgs.ca. Web Site: www.bcgs.ca/library. *Libr Adminr,* Ann Buchanan; Staff 30 (Non-MLS 30)
Founded 1979
Library Holdings: Bk Titles 18,000
Special Collections: British Columbia Cemetery Recordings; British Columbia Research Master Card File & Clipping File; Canadian Census Films; United Empire Loyalist
Subject Interests: Genealogy
Wireless access
Function: Res libr
Publications: Catalogue
Open Tues, Thurs & Sat 10-3

C KWANTLEN POLYTECHNIC UNIVERSITY LIBRARY*, Coast Capital Savings Library, 12666 72nd Ave, V3W 2M8. SAN 321-3714. Circulation Tel: 604-599-2103. Interlibrary Loan Service Tel: 604-599-2959. Reference Tel: 604-599-3434. FAX: 604-599-2106. Reference FAX: 604-599-2532. Web Site: www.kpu.ca/library. *Univ Librn,* Todd Mundle; Tel: 604-599-3400, E-mail: todd.mundle@kpu.ca; *Archives & Design Liaison Librn,* Denise Dale; Tel: 604-599-2999, E-mail: denise.dale@kpu.ca; *Bus Liaison Librn,* Andre Iwanchuk; Tel: 604-599-3486, E-mail: andre.iwanchuk@kpu.ca; *Commun Outreach Librn,* Kelsey Chaban; Tel: 604-599-3236, E-mail: kelsey.chaban@kpu.ca; *Data & Criminology Liaison Librn,* Chris Burns; Tel: 604-599-3198, E-mail: chris.burns@kpu.ca; *Electronic Res Librn,* Allison Richardson; Tel: 604-598-6026, E-mail: allison.richardson@kpu.ca; *Liaison Librn,* Sigrid Kargut; Tel: 604-599-2378, E-mail: sigrid.kargut@kpu.ca; *Outreach Librn,* Lisa Hubick; Tel: 604-599-3404, E-mail: lisa.hubick@kpu.ca; *Pub Serv Librn,* Mirela Djokic; Tel: 604-599-3389, E-mail: mirela.djokic@kpu.ca; *Pub Serv Librn,* Ulrike Kestler; Tel: 604-599-3199, E-mail: ulrike.kestler@kpu.ca; *Scholarly Communications Librn,* Karen Meijer-Kline; Tel: 604-599-2978, E-mail: karen.meijer-kline@kpu.ca; *Sci Librn,* Celia Brinkerhoff; Tel: 604-599-3235, E-mail: celia.brinkerhoff@kpu.ca; *Ser Librn, Tech Serv Librn,* Linda Woodcock; Tel: 604-599-2450, E-mail: linda.woodcock@kpu.ca; *Trades, Tech & Physical Sciences Librn,* Angela Ryan; Tel: 604-598-6040, E-mail: angela.ryan@kpu.ca; *Syst, Web & ILL Librn,* Caroline Daniels; Tel: 604-599-3036, E-mail: caroline.daniels@kpu.ca; *Mgr, Libr Res,* Ann McBurnie; Tel: 604-599-3415, E-mail: ann.mcburnie@kpu.ca. Subject Specialists: *Fashion, Graphic design, Interior design,* Denise Dale; *Bus, Entrepreneurship, Pub relations,* Andre Iwanchuk; *Criminology, Govt doc,* Chris Burns; *Music,* Allison Richardson; *Acad & career advanc, Journalism, Polit sci, Sociol,* Sigrid Kargut; *Fine arts,* Mirela Djokic; *Counseling, Cultural studies, Modern lang,* Ulrike Kestler; *Copyright,* Karen Meijer-Kline; *Biology, Chemistry, Environ protection,* Celia Brinkerhoff; *Astronomy, Math, Physics,* Angela Ryan; Staff 55.6 (MLS 16.3, Non-MLS 39.3)
Founded 1981. Enrl 19,757; Fac 706; Highest Degree: Bachelor
Apr 2015-Mar 2016 Income (CAN) $4,580,400. Mats Exp (CAN) $1,075,372, Books (CAN) $267,236, Per/Ser (Incl. Access Fees) (CAN) $109,666, Micro (CAN) $6,388, AV Equip (CAN) $6,000, AV Mat (CAN) $43,628, Electronic Ref Mat (Incl. Access Fees) (CAN) $642,454. Sal (CAN) $3,028,588 (Prof (CAN) $3,009,736)

Library Holdings: AV Mats 30,088; e-books 160,380; e-journals 60,000; Electronic Media & Resources 250,000; Bk Titles 387,530; Bk Vols 848,025; Per Subs 500; Videos 4,785
Special Collections: Langley Advance Newspaper 1931-1977, micro; Richmond Review Newspaper 1932-1986, micro; Surrey Leader Newspaper 1929-2006, micro
Automation Activity & Vendor Info: (Acquisitions) SirsiDynix; (Cataloging) SirsiDynix; (Circulation) SirsiDynix; (Course Reserve) SirsiDynix; (ILL) Relais International; (Media Booking) SirsiDynix; (OPAC) SirsiDynix; (Serials) SirsiDynix
Wireless access
Partic in British Columbia Electronic Library Network; Canadian Research Knowledge Network; Centre for Accessible Post-Secondary Education Resources; Council of Prairie & Pacific University Libraries; Electronic Health Library of British Columbia
Special Services for the Deaf - Bks on deafness & sign lang; Closed caption videos; High interest/low vocabulary bks
Special Services for the Blind - Accessible computers; BC CILS; Telesensory screen enlarger; ZoomText magnification & reading software
Open Mon-Thurs 7:30-11, Fri 7:30-7, Sat 10-4, Sun 12-7

C SIMON FRASER UNIVERSITY - FRASER CAMPUS*, Fraser Library, Central City, Podium 3, 250-13450 102 Ave, V3T 0A3. Tel: 778-782-7411. FAX: 778-782-7420. E-mail: lib-surrey@sfu.edu. Web Site: www.lib.sfu.ca/about/branches-depts/fraser/contact-us. *Head Librn,* Leanna Jantzi; Tel: 778-782-7417, E-mail: ljantzi@sfu.ca; *Educ Librn,* Melissa Smith; Tel: 778-782-7419
Wireless access

P SURREY LIBRARIES*, 10350 University Dr, V3T 4B8. SAN 324-3486. Tel: 604-598-7300. Interlibrary Loan Service Tel: 604-598-7380. Reference Tel: 604-598-7418. FAX: 604-598-7310. Interlibrary Loan Service FAX: 604-598-7361. E-mail: libraryinfo@surrey.ca. Web Site: surreylibraries.ca. *Chief Librn,* Surinder Bhogal; E-mail: sbhogal@surrey.ca; *Dir, Admin Serv,* Michael Ho; E-mail: mho@surrey.ca; *Dir, Coll & Tech,* Niki Penz; E-mail: NPenz@surrey.ca; *Dir, Mkt & Communications,* Seline Kutan; E-mail: seline.kutan@surrey.ca; *Dir, Prog & Partnerships,* Jenny Fry; E-mail: JJFry@surrey.ca; *Pub Serv Dir,* Kristen Andrews; E-mail: ktandrews@surrey.ca
Founded 1983
Special Collections: Automotive & Genealogy (Surrey Genealogical Coll), bks, fiche, flm, pamphlets. Canadian and Provincial
Automation Activity & Vendor Info: (Acquisitions) Horizon; (Cataloging) Horizon; (Circulation) Horizon; (OPAC) Horizon; (Serials) Horizon
Wireless access
Publications: Canadian Genealogical Handbook (Research guide); Planning a Genealogy Trip to the Vancouver Area (Union list of serials)
Special Services for the Blind - Closed circuit TV; Home delivery serv; Large print bks; Screen enlargement software for people with visual disabilities; Talking bks
Branches: 10
CITY CENTRE, 10350 University Dr, V3T 4B8, SAN 324-475X. Tel: 604-598-7420. *Mgr, Strategic Initiatives,* Tanya Thiessen; Tel: 604-598-7430, E-mail: TDThiessen@surrey.ca
CLAYTON LIBRARY, 7155 187A St, V4N 6L9. Tel: 604-592-2727. *Br Mgr,* Sara Church; Tel: 236-598-3087, E-mail: SJChurch@surrey.ca
Founded 1983. Pop 518,000
Function: 24/7 Electronic res, 24/7 Online cat, Activity rm, Adult bk club, Adult literacy prog, After school storytime
CLOVERDALE, 5642 176A St, V3S 4G9, SAN 324-4784. Tel: 604-598-7320. *Br Mgr,* Julie Balenzano; Tel: 604-598-7330, E-mail: JNBalenzano@surrey.ca
FLEETWOOD, 15996 84th Ave, V3S 2N7, SAN 376-1177. Tel: 604-598-7340. *Br Mgr,* Julie Balenzano; Tel: 604-598-7330, E-mail: JNBalenzano@surrey.ca
GUILDFORD, 15105 105th Ave, V3R 7G8, SAN 324-4741. Tel: 604-598-7360. *Br Mgr,* Meghan Savage; Tel: 604-598-7374, E-mail: MSavage@surrey.ca
NEWTON, 13795 70th Ave, V3W 0E1, SAN 324-4768. Tel: 604-598-7400. *Br Mgr,* Harjinder Thind; Tel: 604-598-7410, E-mail: HSThind@surrey.ca
OCEAN PARK, 12854 17th Ave, V4A 1T5, SAN 324-4776. Tel: 604-502-6304. *Br Mgr,* Sara Grant; Tel: 604-592-6911, E-mail: scgrant@surrey.ca
PORT KELLS, 18885 88th Ave, V4N 5T1, SAN 324-4792. Tel: 604-598-7440. *Br Mgr,* Meghan Savage; Tel: 604-598-7374, E-mail: MSavage@surrey.ca
SEMIAHMOO LIBRARY, 1815-152 St, V4A 9Y9. Tel: 604-592-6900. *Br Mgr,* Sara Grant; Tel: 604-592-6911, E-mail: scgrant@surrey.ca
STRAWBERRY HILL, 7399-122nd St, V3W 5J2. Tel: 604-501-5836. *Br Mgr,* Harjinder Thind; Tel: 604-598-7410, E-mail: HSThind@surrey.ca

M SURREY MEMORIAL HOSPITAL*, Bohdan Lesack Memorial Library, 13750 96th Ave, V3V 1Z2. SAN 373-6628. Tel: 604-585-5666, Ext 774510. FAX: 604-953-4760. E-mail: library@fraserhealth.ca. *Librn,* Sarah Gleeson Noyes; E-mail: sarah.gleesonnoyes@fraserhealth.ca. Subject Specialists: *Allied health, Clinical med, Nursing,* Sarah Gleeson Noyes; Staff 2 (MLS 1, Non-MLS 1)
Founded 1987
Library Holdings: DVDs 50; e-books 25; e-journals 5,000; Bk Titles 1,200; Per Subs 37; Videos 100
Subject Interests: Allied health, Health serv admin, Med, Nursing
Automation Activity & Vendor Info: (Cataloging) Inmagic, Inc.; (OPAC) Inmagic, Inc.
Function: For res purposes
Publications: Journal Watches on Select Subject Areas (Current awareness service); Library RX (Monthly newsletter)
Partic in Health Library Association of British Columbia; US National Library of Medicine

TERRACE

J COAST MOUNTAIN COLLEGE LIBRARY*, 5331 McConnell Ave, V8G 4X2. SAN 322-8487. Tel: 250-638-5407. FAX: 250-635-1594. Interlibrary Loan Service E-mail: library@coastmountaincollege.ca. Web Site: www.coastmountaincollege.ca/student-services/library. *Dean,* Collin Elliott; E-mail: celliott@coastmountaincollege.ca; *Campus Librn,* Luba Kasum; E-mail: lkasum@coastmountaincollege.ca; *Libr Coord,* Michele Cook; E-mail: mcook@coastmountaincollege.ca; Staff 8 (MLS 5, Non-MLS 3)
Founded 1975. Enrl 1,800; Fac 300; Highest Degree: Associate
Library Holdings: Bk Titles 68,000; Per Subs 200; Videos 7,000
Special Collections: Local History (Archives of Northwest BC Coll)
Subject Interests: Arts, Culinary arts, Early childhood educ, Natural res, Nursing, Sciences, Tourism, Trades
Wireless access
Partic in British Columbia Electronic Library Network; Centre for Accessible Post-Secondary Education Resources; Electronic Health Library of British Columbia; Northwest Library Federation
Special Services for the Deaf - High interest/low vocabulary bks; Spec interest per
Open Mon-Thurs 8-8, Fri 8-5

P TERRACE PUBLIC LIBRARY*, 4610 Park Ave, V8G 1V6. SAN 318-8116. Tel: 250-638-8177. FAX: 250-635-6207. E-mail: library@terracelibrary.ca. Web Site: www.terracelibrary.ca. *Ch Serv,* Melanie Wilke; Staff 14 (MLS 1, Non-MLS 13)
Founded 1929. Pop 19,917; Circ 213,716
Library Holdings: AV Mats 6,581; Bk Titles 69,352; Bk Vols 70,551; Per Subs 202
Special Collections: Felber Coll, photog; History of the Northwest of British Columbia; Indian Culture of Northwest British Columbia; Terrace Coll. Oral History
Wireless access
Publications: History of Terrace
Partic in Northwest Library Federation
Open Mon 1-5, Tues-Sat 10-5

TRAIL

P TRAIL & DISTRICT PUBLIC LIBRARY*, 1505 Bay Ave, V1R 4B2. SAN 810-1728. Tel: 250-364-1731. E-mail: info@traillibrary.com. Web Site: www.traillibrary.com. *Libr Dir,* Samantha Murphy; E-mail: smurphy@trail.ca; *Ad,* Sam King; Staff 6 (MLS 2, Non-MLS 4)
Pop 9,110; Circ 54,442
Library Holdings: Audiobooks 911; Bks on Deafness & Sign Lang 10; CDs 780; DVDs 2,940; Bk Titles 42,700; Bk Vols 42,700; Per Subs 63
Special Collections: Local History
Automation Activity & Vendor Info: (Acquisitions) L4U Library Software; (Cataloging) L4U Library Software; (Circulation) L4U Library Software; (ILL) Auto-Graphics, Inc; (OPAC) L4U Library Software; (Serials) L4U Library Software
Wireless access
Function: 24/7 Electronic res, 24/7 Online cat, Adult bk club, After school storytime, Audiobks via web, Bk club(s), Bks on CD, Children's prog, Computer training, Computers for patron use, Digital talking bks, E-Readers, Electronic databases & coll, For res purposes, Free DVD rentals, Govt ref serv, Holiday prog, Home delivery & serv to seniorr ctr & nursing homes, Homebound delivery serv, ILL available, Internet access, Magazines, Mail & tel request accepted, Mango lang, Music CDs, Online cat, Outreach serv, OverDrive digital audio bks, Photocopying/Printing, Preschool reading prog, Prog for adults, Prog for children & young adult, Ref serv available, Scanner, Summer & winter reading prog
Mem of Kootenay Library Federation
Open Mon & Fri 9:30-5, Tues-Thurs 9:30-7, Sat 9:30-4
Friends of the Library Group

TUMBLER RIDGE

P TUMBLER RIDGE PUBLIC LIBRARY*, 340 Front St, V0C 2W0. (Mail add: PO Box 70, V0C 2W0), SAN 760-4394. Tel: 250-242-4778. FAX: 250-242-4707. E-mail: info@trlibrary.org. Web Site: tumblerridgelibrary.org. *Head Librn,* Paula Coutts; E-mail: pcoutts@trlibrary.org; *Ch,* Mr Chris Norbury; Staff 4 (Non-MLS 4)
Pop 4,000; Circ 20,375
Library Holdings: Audiobooks 26; CDs 253; DVDs 208; Large Print Bks 317; Bk Titles 33,790; Per Subs 40; Videos 1,324
Automation Activity & Vendor Info: (Acquisitions) Mandarin Library Automation; (Cataloging) Mandarin Library Automation; (Circulation) Mandarin Library Automation; (ILL) A-G Canada Ltd; (OPAC) Mandarin Library Automation; (Serials) Mandarin Library Automation
Wireless access
Function: Adult bk club, After school storytime, Art exhibits, Bk club(s), Bks on cassette, Bks on CD, Children's prog, Computer training, Computers for patron use, Distance learning, E-Reserves, Electronic databases & coll, Equip loans & repairs, Free DVD rentals, Govt ref serv, Holiday prog, Homebound delivery serv, ILL available, Internet access, Literacy & newcomer serv, Music CDs, Online cat, Online ref, Orientations, Outreach serv, OverDrive digital audio bks, Photocopying/Printing, Prog for adults, Prog for children & young adult, Ref & res, Ref serv available, Scanner, Story hour, Summer reading prog, VHS videos, Wheelchair accessible
Partic in North East Library Federation
Open Mon-Thurs 10-8, Fri & Sat 10-5, Sun 1-5

VALEMOUNT

P VALEMOUNT PUBLIC LIBRARY*, 1090A Main St, V0E 2Z0. (Mail add: PO Box 368, V0E 2Z0), SAN 318-8140. Tel: 250-566-4367. FAX: 250-566-4278. E-mail: library@valemount.ca. Web Site: valemount.bc.libraries.coop. *Chief Librn,* Wendy Cinnamon; *Children's Programmer,* Kacie Harray; *Technology & Interlibrary Loan,* Hollie Blanchette
Founded 1964. Pop 1,796; Circ 18,480
Library Holdings: Bk Vols 17,325; Per Subs 38
Wireless access
Partic in BC Libraries Cooperative
Open Tues, Thurs & Fri 11-5, Wed 11-9, Sat 11-3

VANCOUVER

M BC CANCER LIBRARY*, 675 W Tenth Ave, V5Z 1L3. SAN 318-8213. Tel: 604-675-8001. FAX: 604-675-8009. E-mail: library@bccancer.bc.ca. Web Site: libraries.phsa.ca/bcca (Catalog), www.bccancer.bc.ca/our-services/services/library. *Prov Libr Leader,* Chantalle Jack; Tel: 604-675-8004, E-mail: chantalle.jack@bccancer.bc.ca; Staff 7.1 (MLS 5.1, Non-MLS 2)
Founded 1975
Library Holdings: e-books 1,000; e-journals 3,500; Electronic Media & Resources 17; Bk Titles 8,800; Per Subs 13; Videos 1,200
Special Collections: Patient Cancer Library, AV, bks
Subject Interests: Cancer nursing, Cancer treatment, Oncology, Palliative care, Psychol of cancer, Radiation biol, Support serv
Automation Activity & Vendor Info: (Acquisitions) Inmagic, Inc.; (Cataloging) Inmagic, Inc.; (Circulation) Inmagic, Inc.; (OPAC) Inmagic, Inc.; (Serials) EBSCO Discovery Service
Wireless access
Open Mon-Fri 8:30-4:30

M BRITISH COLUMBIA COLLEGE OF NURSES & MIDWIVES*, Regulatory Library, 900 - 200 Granville St, V6C 1S4. SAN 320-3107. Tel: 604-742-6244. E-mail: library@bccnm.ca. *Copyright Librn, Research Librn,* Carol MacFarlane; E-mail: carol.macfarlane@bccnm.ca; Staff 1.3 (MLS 0.8, Non-MLS 0.5)
Founded 1966
Library Holdings: Bks-By-Mail 2,000; DVDs 144; e-books 100; e-journals 850; Bk Titles 2,100; Per Subs 30
Subject Interests: Health, Midwifery, Nursing
Wireless access
Partic in Electronic Health Library of British Columbia; Health Library Association of British Columbia

S BRITISH COLUMBIA SECURITIES COMMISSION*, Knowledge Centre, 701 W Georgia St, V7Y 1L2. (Mail add: Pacific Ctr, PO Box 10142, V7Y 1L2), SAN 370-9663. Tel: 604-899-6500. Toll Free Tel: 800-373-6393. FAX: 604-899-6506. E-mail: knowledgecentre@bcsc.bc.ca. Web Site: www.bcsc.bc.ca.
Library Holdings: Bk Vols 1,500; Per Subs 100
Subject Interests: Securities
Automation Activity & Vendor Info: (Acquisitions) Inmagic, Inc.; (Cataloging) Inmagic, Inc.; (OPAC) Inmagic, Inc.; (Serials) Inmagic, Inc.
Restriction: Open by appt only

M COLLEGE OF PHYSICIANS & SURGEONS*, Medical Library Service, 300-669 Howe St, V6C 0B4. SAN 318-8221. Tel: 604-733-6671. FAX: 604-737-8582. E-mail: medlib@cpsbc.ca. Web Site: www.cpsbc.ca/library. *Dir,* Dr Karen MacDonnell; Staff 12 (MLS 4, Non-MLS 8)
Founded 1906
Subject Interests: Med
Wireless access
Publications: Recent & Recommended Books for Hospital Medical Libraries (annual)
Partic in Electronic Health Library of British Columbia; Medlars
Restriction: Not open to pub

J COLUMBIA COLLEGE LIBRARY*, 438 Terminal Ave, V6A 0C1. SAN 318-823X. Tel: 604-683-8360, Ext 253. FAX: 604-682-7191. E-mail: library@columbiacollege.ca. Administration E-mail: admin@columbiacollege.ca. Web Site: www.columbiacollege.ca/library. *Libr Dir,* Faith Jones; E-mail: fjones@columbiacollege.ca; *Librn,* Joe Haigh; E-mail: jhaigh@columbiacollege.ca; Staff 2 (MLS 2)
Founded 1965. Enrl 600; Fac 70
Library Holdings: e-books 500,000; Bk Titles 10,000
Subject Interests: Acad
Automation Activity & Vendor Info: (Acquisitions) Follett Software; (Cataloging) TLC (The Library Corporation); (Circulation) Follett Software; (Course Reserve) Follett Software; (ILL) Follett Software; (Media Booking) Follett Software; (OPAC) Follett Software; (Serials) Follett Software
Wireless access
Partic in British Columbia Electronic Library Network
Open Mon-Thurs 8:30-7, Fri & Sat 8:30-5

L DLA PIPER (CANADA) LLP*, Law Library, 666 Burrard St, Ste 2800, V6C 2Z7. SAN 327-5515. Tel: 604-643-6432. Web Site: www.dlapiper.com/en/canada. *Mgr, Libr Serv,* Susannah Tredwell; E-mail: susannah.tredwell@dlapiper.com; Staff 3 (MLS 2, Non-MLS 1)
Library Holdings: Bk Vols 14,000
Automation Activity & Vendor Info: (Acquisitions) Sydney Enterprise; (Cataloging) Sydney Enterprise; (Circulation) Sydney Enterprise; (OPAC) Sydney Enterprise
Open Mon-Fri 8-5
Restriction: Internal use only

C EMILY CARR UNIVERSITY OF ART & DESIGN, Ron Burnett Library & Learning Commons, 520 E First Ave, V5T 0H2. SAN 318-8256. Tel: 604-844-3840. E-mail: library@ecuad.ca. Web Site: www.ecuad.ca/library. *Univ Librn,* D Vanessa Kam; E-mail: dvkam@ecuad.ca; *Libr Operations Coordr,* Emma Somers; E-mail: esomers@ecuad.ca
Founded 1927
Library Holdings: AV Mats 2,700; Bk Titles 60,000; Per Subs 200
Subject Interests: Art, Design
Automation Activity & Vendor Info: (Acquisitions) Evergreen; (Cataloging) Evergreen; (Circulation) Evergreen; (Course Reserve) Evergreen; (OPAC) Evergreen; (Serials) Evergreen
Wireless access
Partic in British Columbia Electronic Library Network; Centre for Accessible Post-Secondary Education Resources
Open Mon-Thurs 8-8, Fri 8-6, Sat & Sun 1-5 (Fall-Spring); Mon-Fri 9-5 (Summer)

S FASKEN MARTINEAU DUMOULIN LLP LIBRARY*, 2900-550 Burrard St, V6C 0A3. SAN 321-9038. Tel: 604-631-3131. Reference Tel: 604-631-4716. FAX: 604-631-3232. Reference FAX: 604-632-4716. Reference E-mail: ref@fasken.com. *Dir, Knowledge Serv,* Teresa Gleave; Tel: 604-631-4804, E-mail: tgleave@fasken.com; *Knowledge Services Librn,* Marnie Bailey. Subject Specialists: *Bus, Can law,* Teresa Gleave; *Bus, Can law,* Marnie Bailey; Staff 3 (MLS 2, Non-MLS 1)
Library Holdings: Bk Vols 5,000
Special Collections: Canadian & British law; Canadian Labour Law; Limited American Material
Automation Activity & Vendor Info: (Acquisitions) Inmagic, Inc.; (Cataloging) Inmagic, Inc.; (Circulation) Inmagic, Inc.; (Serials) Inmagic, Inc.
Wireless access
Restriction: Staff use only

S GOLDER ASSOCIATES, LTD*, 2920 Virtual Way, V5M 0C4. SAN 323-8245. Tel: 604-298-6623, Ext 2697. Web Site: www.golder.com. *Librn,* Greg Krewski; E-mail: gkrewski@golder.com
Library Holdings: Bk Titles 3,700; Per Subs 100
Special Collections: Oil Sands
Restriction: Restricted pub use

L HARPER GREY LLP LIBRARY*, 3200-650 W Georgia St, V6B 4P7. Tel: 604-895-2861. FAX: 604-669-9385. Web Site: www.harpergrey.com. *Librn,* Danielle Brosseau; E-mail: dbrosseau@harpergrey.com; *Libr Asst,*

Taryn Gunter; E-mail: tgunter@harpergrey.com; Staff 2 (MLS 1, Non-MLS 1)
Library Holdings: Bk Titles 2,000; Bk Vols 8,000; Per Subs 175
Subject Interests: Law
Automation Activity & Vendor Info: (Cataloging) Inmagic, Inc.
Restriction: Staff use only

S AUDREY & HARRY HAWTHORN LIBRARY & ARCHIVES AT THE UBC MUSEUM OF ANTHROPOLOGY, 6393 NW Marine Dr, V6T 1Z2. SAN 373-7624. Tel: 604-822-4834. FAX: 604-822-2974. E-mail: library@moa.ubc.ca. Web Site: www.moa.ubc.ca/library-archives. *Mgr, Oral History Language Lab,* Gerry Lawson; *Mgr, Res,* Alissa Cherry; *Museum & Digital Asset Archivist,* Katie Ferrante; *Libr & Archives Asst,* Philip Yu; Staff 4 (MLS 2, Non-MLS 2)
Founded 1990
Library Holdings: Bk Titles 12,000; Per Subs 15
Subject Interests: Art, Culture, Mat culture, Mus studies, Northwest Coast hist
Wireless access
Function: Archival coll, Computers for patron use, Electronic databases & coll, Online cat, Photocopying/Printing, Ref serv available
Open Tues-Fri 10-4
Restriction: Circulates for staff only

S KLOHN CRIPPEN BERGER LTD, Library & Records Centre, 500 2955 Virtual Way, V5M 4X6. Tel: 604-669-3800. FAX: 604-669-3835. E-mail: library@klohn.com. Web Site: klohn.com. *Librn,* Ana Rosa Blue; Staff 1 (MLS 1)
Restriction: Open to staff only

C LANGARA COLLEGE LIBRARY, 100 W 49th Ave, V5Y 2Z6. Tel: 604-323-5462. Interlibrary Loan Service Tel: 604-323-5458. Reference Tel: 604-323-5388. Interlibrary Loan Service FAX: 604-323-5512. Reference E-mail: libref@langara.ca. Web Site: langara.ca/library. *Dir, Libr Serv,* Suzanne Rackover; Tel: 604-323-5243, E-mail: srackover@langara.ca; *Librn,* Alison Curtis; Tel; 604-232-5465, E-mail: acurtis@langara.ca; *Librn,* Vivien Feng; E-mail: vfeng@langara.ca; *Coordr, Coll Serv, E-Res & Journals,* Emma Lawson; Tel: 604-232-5464, E-mail: elawson@langara.ca; *ILL,* Richard Birkenes; E-mail: rbirkenes@langara.ca
Library Holdings: Bk Titles 157,350
Wireless access
Partic in British Columbia Electronic Library Network; Centre for Accessible Post-Secondary Education Resources; Electronic Health Library of British Columbia
Open Mon-Thurs 8am-9pm, Fri 8-6, Sat & Sun 11-6 (Winter); Mon-Thurs 8-7:30, Fri 8-6 (Summer)

S LDS - LEARN. DEVELOP. SUCCEED. (LEARNING DISABILITIES SOCIETY), Resource Centre, 3292 E Broadway, V5M 1Z8. SAN 377-2543. Tel: 604-873-8139. E-mail: info@ldsociety.ca. Web Site: ldsociety.ca. *Exec Dir,* Rachel Forbes; E-mail: ed@ldsociety.ca
Founded 1970
Wireless access
Open Mon-Sat 9-6

L MCCARTHY TETRAULT LLP LIBRARY*, 2400-745 Thurlow St, V6E 0C5. SAN 323-9810. Tel: 604-643-7100. FAX: 604-643-7900. Web Site: www.mccarthy.ca. *Res Spec,* Susan Caird; Tel: 604-643-7178; *Res Spec,* Jason Wong; Tel: 604-643-7979, E-mail: jwong@mccarthy.ca. Subject Specialists: *Legal,* Susan Caird; *Legal,* Jason Wong; Staff 2 (MLS 2)
Library Holdings: Bk Vols 14,000
Automation Activity & Vendor Info: (OPAC) EOS International
Wireless access
Restriction: Private libr

G MINISTRY OF THE ATTORNEY GENERAL*, Judge's Library, Superior Law Courts, 800 Smithe St, V6Z 2E1. SAN 366-1954. Tel: 604-660-2799. FAX: 604-660-2382. Web Site: www.courts.gov.bc.ca. *Librn,* Diane Lemieux; *Libr Tech,* Connie Kang; E-mail: connie.kang@courts.gov.ba.ca
Founded 1945
Library Holdings: Bk Titles 2,000; Bk Vols 15,000; Per Subs 20
Partic in Can Libr Asn
Restriction: Staff use only

G NATURAL RESOURCES CANADA LIBRARY*, Geological Survey of Canada, 605 Robson St, Ste 1500, V6B 5J3. SAN 320-779X. Tel: 604-666-1147. Administration Tel: 604-666-3812. FAX: 604-666-1124. E-mail: library-bibliotheque@nrcan-rncan.gc.ca. Web Site: science-libraries.canada.ca/eng/natural-resources. *Libr Mgr,* Warren Wulff; E-mail: warren.wulff@nrcan-rncan.gc.ca; *Libr Tech,* Nina Takahashi; E-mail: nina.takahashi@nrcan-rncan.gc.ca; Staff 2 (MLS 1, Non-MLS 1)
Founded 1918
Library Holdings: e-journals 7,000; Microforms 1,000; Bk Vols 125,000; Per Subs 5,000
Special Collections: Cordilleran & Pacific Continental Shelf Geology. Canadian and Provincial
Subject Interests: BC hist, Biostratigraphy, Coal mining hist, Earth sci, Geohazards, Geol, Geophysics, Indigenous studies, Land use, Marine geol, Micropaleontology, Natural hazards, Paleontology, Urban geol
Wireless access
Function: 24/7 Electronic res, 24/7 Online cat, CD-ROM, Computers for patron use, Doc delivery serv, Electronic databases & coll, For res purposes, Govt ref serv, ILL available, Internet access, Learning ctr, Mail & tel request accepted, Mail loans to mem, Meeting rooms, Microfiche/film & reading machines, Online cat, Online ref, Orientations, Outreach serv, Outside serv via phone, mail, e-mail & web, Photocopying/Printing, Prof lending libr, Ref & res, Ref serv available, Res assist avail, Res libr, Scanner, Study rm, Telephone ref
Open Mon-Fri 8:30-4:30
Restriction: Circ limited, Circ to mem only, Closed stack, In-house use for visitors, Internal circ only, Non-circulating of rare bks, Non-circulating to the pub, Open to pub for ref only, Pub use on premises, Restricted borrowing privileges, Restricted loan policy, Restricted pub use

L NORTON ROSE FULBRIGHT LIBRARY*, 1800-510 W Georgia St, V6B 0M3. SAN 327-2753. Tel: 604-687-6575. FAX: 604-646-2535. E-mail: canvanlibraryservices@nortonrosefulbright.com. Web Site: www.nortonrosefulbright.com. *Mgr, Libr Serv,* Carolyn Petrie; E-mail: carolyn.petrie@nortonrosefulbright.com; Staff 3 (MLS 2, Non-MLS 1)
Library Holdings: Bk Titles 20,000
Restriction: Staff use only

S PACIFIC SALMON COMMISSION LIBRARY*, 1155 Robson St, Ste 600, V6E 1B5. SAN 318-7861. Tel: 604-684-8081. FAX: 604-666-8707. E-mail: library@psc.org. Web Site: www.psc.org.
Library Holdings: Bk Vols 13,000; Per Subs 500
Special Collections: Salmon Fishery Coll, ms, data rpt
Subject Interests: Fish biol, Fish pop dynamics, Fishery mgt, Salmon biol
Automation Activity & Vendor Info: (Cataloging) Inmagic, Inc.
Publications: Annual Report; Annual Report of Fraser River Sockeye Fishing Season; News release; Technical report

CR REGENT COLLEGE*, John Richard Allison Library, 5800 University Blvd, V6T 2E4. Tel: 604-221-3340. Toll Free Tel: 800-663-8664. FAX: 604-224-3097. E-mail: library@regent-college.edu. Web Site: allisonlibrary.regent-college.edu. *Libr Dir,* Dr Cindy Aalders; E-mail: caalders@regent-college.edu; *Circ Coordr,* Mr Alex Strohschein; E-mail: astrohschein@regent-college.edu; *Tech Serv Coordr,* Dannaya Wall; E-mail: dwall@regent-college.edu
Library Holdings: AV Mats 10,191; Bk Vols 163,287; Per Subs 357; Videos 621
Special Collections: 19th Century Pamphlets on Religious, Cultural & Political Topics (Wilberforce Coll); Holocaust Nazi Germany (John S Conway Research Coll); Jacques Ellul Coll; Puritan & Anglican Colls, rare bks
Automation Activity & Vendor Info: (Acquisitions) Innovative Interfaces, Inc; (Cataloging) Innovative Interfaces, Inc; (Circulation) Innovative Interfaces, Inc; (OPAC) Innovative Interfaces, Inc; (Serials) Innovative Interfaces, Inc
Wireless access
Open Mon-Thurs 8am-10pm, Fri 8-5, Sat 9-5

C SIMON FRASER UNIVERSITY - VANCOUVER CAMPUS, Samuel & Frances Belzberg Library, 515 W Hastings St, V6B 5K3. Tel: 778-782-5050. Reference Tel: 778-782-5051. FAX: 778-782-5052. E-mail: belzcirc@sfu.ca. Web Site: www.lib.sfu.ca/about/branches-depts/belzberg. *Head Librn,* Jorge Cardenas; E-mail: jorge_cardenas@sfu.ca; *Liaison Librn,* Ms Moninder Lalli; E-mail: moninder_lalli@sfu.edu; *Liaison Librn,* Sylvia Roberts; E-mail: sroberts@sfu.ca; *Liaison Librn,* Nina Smart; E-mail: nsmart@sfu.ca. Subject Specialists: *Anthrop, Bus admin, Sociol,* Ms Moninder Lalli; *Contemporary art,* Sylvia Roberts; *Gerontology, Publ,* Nina Smart
Library Holdings: Bk Vols 35,000; Per Subs 85
Wireless access
Open Mon-Fri 9-7, Sat 10-5 (Fall-Spring); Mon-Fri 9-7 (Summer)

S TECK RESOURCES LIMITED, Corporate Library, 3300-550 Burrard St, V6C 0B3. SAN 326-4971. Tel: 604-699-4263. Interlibrary Loan Service Tel: 604-697-3539. FAX: 604-699-4711. Web Site: www.teck.com. *Supvr,* Keith Low; E-mail: keith.low@teck.com; Staff 2 (MLS 1, Non-MLS 1)
Library Holdings: Per Subs 200
Special Collections: Resource Company Annual Reports
Subject Interests: Bus, Coal, Geol, Metals, Mgt, Mining
Automation Activity & Vendor Info: (Cataloging) Inmagic, Inc.; (OPAC) Inmagic, Inc.
Open Mon-Fri 8:30-5:30
Restriction: Access at librarian's discretion

S UNION OF BRITISH COLUMBIA INDIAN CHIEFS*, Library and Archives, 312 Main St, V6A 2T2. SAN 373-6644. Tel: 604-684-0231. FAX: 604-684-5726. E-mail: library@ubcic.bc.ca. Web Site: www.ubcic.bc.ca/library. *Librn & Archivist,* Melissa Adams; Staff 1 (MLS 1)
Founded 1972
Library Holdings: Bk Vols 15,000; Per Subs 25
Special Collections: Ecological Knowledge & Environmental Stewardship; First Nations Law in British Columbia (Louise Mandell Legal Research Coll), related mats; UBCIC Archives
Subject Interests: Aboriginal title & rights, Ecological knowledge, First Nations law, Indigenous governance
Automation Activity & Vendor Info: (Cataloging) Evergreen; (OPAC) Evergreen
Wireless access
Function: Archival coll, Art exhibits, Audio & video playback equip for onsite use, Computers for patron use, Doc delivery serv, Electronic databases & coll, ILL available, Microfiche/film & reading machines, Photocopying/Printing, Ref serv available, Res libr, Res performed for a fee, Telephone ref
Publications: Newsletter
Partic in Archives Association of British Columbia; British Columbia Electronic Library Network
Restriction: Access at librarian's discretion, Circ limited, Non-circulating to the pub, Open by appt only, Registered patrons only, Restricted borrowing privileges, Restricted pub use

§C UNIVERSITY CANADA WEST, Vancouver House Campus Library, 1461 Granville St, V6Z 0E5. Toll Free Tel: 877-431-6887. E-mail: ucw.librarian@myucwest.ca, ucwlibrary@ucanwest.ca. Web Site: www.ucanwest.ca/students/current-students/library. *Univ Librn,* Brenda Mathenia; E-mail: brenda.mathenia@ucanwest.ca; *Electronic Resources & Assessment Librn,* Rio Picollo; E-mail: rio.picollo@ucanwest.ca; *Scholarly Comms & Copyright Librn,* Kailey Fukushima; E-mail: kailey.fukushima@ucanwest.ca; *Student Success Librn,* Shannon Murray; E-mail: shannon.murray@ucanwest.ca; *Manager, Library & Learning Commons,* Nicoletta Romano
Founded 2020
Library Holdings: e-books 200,000
Subject Interests: Bus, Econ, Finance, Mkt
Wireless access
Partic in British Columbia Electronic Library Network
Open Mon-Fri 8am-9pm, Sat & Sun 9-5

C UNIVERSITY OF BRITISH COLUMBIA LIBRARY*, 1961 East Mall, V6T 1Z1. SAN 366-1989. Tel: 604-827-3434. Interlibrary Loan Service Tel: 604-822-6596. FAX: 604-822-3893. Web Site: www.library.ubc.ca. *Univ Librn,* Susan Parker; E-mail: susan.parker@ubc.ca; *Assoc Univ Librn, Coll,* Sheldon Armstrong; Tel: 604-822-5300, E-mail: sheldon.armstrong@ubc.ca; *Assoc Univ Librn, Res Serv,* Lea Starr; Tel: 604-822-2826, E-mail: lea.starr@ubc.ca; Staff 285 (MLS 86, Non-MLS 199)
Founded 1915. Enrl 54,677; Fac 2,678; Highest Degree: Doctorate
Library Holdings: Bk Vols 6,478,708
Special Collections: A J T Taylor Coll; A M Donaldson Burns Coll; Chung Coll; Dictionaries & Related Works (H Rocke Robertson Coll); Douglas Coupland Archives; Doukhobor Coll; Early & Historical Children's Literature (Arkley Coll); Harry Hawthorne Angling Coll; History of Medicine & Science; Howay-Reid Coll; Japanese Maps of the Edo Period (George H Beans Coll); Malcolm Lowry Coll; Norman Colbeck Coll; Philip J Thomas Popular Song Coll; P'u-pan Coll; Stockett Thomas J Wise Coll; Stravinsky Coll; Thomas Murray Coll; University Archives. Canadian and Provincial; Municipal Document Depository; UN Document Depository
Automation Activity & Vendor Info: (Acquisitions) Ex Libris Group; (Cataloging) Ex Libris Group; (Circulation) Ex Libris Group; (Course Reserve) Ex Libris Group; (Media Booking) Ex Libris Group; (OPAC) Ex Libris Group; (Serials) Ex Libris Group
Wireless access
Function: Res libr
Publications: Connects (Irving K Barber Learning Centre); Friends of the Library; Guide for Students; Insight (Newsletter); Report to the Senate
Partic in Canadian Association of Research Libraries; Electronic Health Library of British Columbia
Friends of the Library Group

Departmental Libraries:

ASIAN, Asian Ctr, 1871 West Mall, V6T 1Z2, SAN 366-1997. Tel: 604-822-2427. Reference Tel: 604-822-2023. FAX: 604-822-0650. E-mail: asian.library@ubc.ca. Web Site: asian.library.ubc.ca. *Head Librn,* Shirin Eshghi Furuzawa; Tel: 604-822-5905, E-mail: shirin.eshghi@ubc.ca
Founded 1960
Special Collections: Canadian-Japanese Studies; Chinese-Canadian Settlement in British Columbia, Canada; Ching-I Chai Coll; Illegal Chinese Immigrants Virtual Photo Coll; Japanese Government Publications; Pearl Delta Area Research Materials; P'u-pan Coll; Sung Hsueh-Peng Coll; Swann Coll
Subject Interests: Arts, Chinese hist, Culture, Econ, Indonesia, Japanese culture, Korea, Lit, Politics, Relig, S Asia
Partic in Coun on East Asian Librs

IRVING K BARBER LEARNING CENTRE, 1961 East Mall, V6T 1Z1. Tel: 604-822-3310, 604-822-8149. FAX: 604-822-3242. E-mail: barber.library@ubc.ca. Web Site: ikblc.ubc.ca. *Interim Assoc Univ Librn & Dir, Serv,* Sandra Wilkins; Tel: 604-822-3096, E-mail: sandra.wilkins@ubc.ca; *Asst Dir,* Julie Mitchell; Tel: 604-827-4307, E-mail: julie.mitchell@ubc.ca

CM BIOMEDICAL, Gordon & Leslie Diamond Health Care Ctr, 2775 Laurel St, 2nd Flr, V5Z 1M9. (Mail add: Woodward Library, 2198 Health Sciences Mall, V6T 1Z3), SAN 366-2349. Tel: 604-875-4505. FAX: 604-875-4689. E-mail: bmb.library@ubc.ca. Web Site: woodward.library.ubc.ca/bmb, woodward.library.ubc.ca/services-at-hospital/bmb. *Head of Libr,* Aleteia Greenwood; Tel: 604-822-0689, E-mail: aleteia.greenwood@ubc.ca; *Ref Librn,* Dean Guistini; Tel: 604-875-4111, Ext 62392, E-mail: dean.giustini@ubc.ca
Friends of the Library Group

EDUCATION, 2125 Main Mall, V6T 1Z4, SAN 366-2136. Tel: 604-822-5381. Reference Tel: 604-822-3767. FAX: 604-822-5378. E-mail: ed.lib.@ubc.ca. Web Site: education.library.ubc.ca. *Head of Libr,* Wendy Traas; E-mail: wendy.traas@ubc.ca; *Educ Librn,* Emily Fornwald; E-mail: emily.fornwald@ubc.ca

HUMANITIES & SOCIAL SCIENCES, KOERNER LIBRARY, 1958 Main Mall, V6T 1Z2, SAN 366-2012. Tel: 604-822-6363. Reference Tel: 604-822-2725. FAX: 604-822-9122. E-mail: hssd.library@ubc.ca. Web Site: koerner.library.ubc.ca. *Head of Libr,* Anne Olsen; Tel: 604-822-3018, E-mail: anne.olsen@ubc.ca

DAVID LAM MANAGEMENT RESEARCH LIBRARY, UBC Sauder School of Business, 2033 Main Mall, V6T 1Z2, SAN 374-7492. Tel: 604-822-9400. FAX: 604-822-9398. Web Site: lam.library.ubc.ca. *Head Librn,* Christina Sylka; Tel: 604-822-9390, E-mail: christina.sylka@ubc.ca
Founded 1985. Highest Degree: Doctorate
Subject Interests: Bus admin, Commerce

CL LAW, Allard Hall, 1822 Main Mall, V6T 1Z1, SAN 366-2160. Tel: 604-822-4238. Interlibrary Loan Service Tel: 604-822-6432. Reference Tel: 604-822-9379. FAX: 604-822-6864. E-mail: law.library@ubc.ca. Web Site: law.library.ubc.ca. *Head of Libr,* Sandra Wilkins; Tel: 604-822-2396, E-mail: sandra.wilkins@ubc.ca; *Actg Head, Libr,* George Tsiakos; Tel: 604-822-0093, E-mail: george.tsiakos@ubc.ca

MUSIC, ART, ARCHITECTURE & PLANNING, Irving K Barber Learning Ctr, 1961 East Mall, V6T 1Z1, SAN 320-104X. Tel: 604-822-3943. Circulation Tel: 604-288-8149. FAX: 604-822-3779. E-mail: maa.library@ubc.ca. Web Site: barber.library.ubc.ca. *Actg Head Librn, Music Librn,* Kevin Madill; Tel: 604-827-2197, E-mail: kevin.madill@ubc.ca
Special Collections: Rare Book Coll
Subject Interests: Can art
Open Mon-Thurs 9-7, Fri 9-5, Sat 10-5

OKANAGAN LIBRARY, 3333 University Way, Kelowna, V1V 1V7. Tel: 250-807-9107. Reference Tel: 250-807-9128. FAX: 250-807-8057. Web Site: library.ok.ubc.ca. *Interim Chief Librn,* Robert Janke; E-mail: robert.janke@ubc.ca

RARE BOOKS & SPECIAL COLLECTIONS, Irving K Barber Learning Ctr, 1961 East Mall, V6T 1Z1, SAN 376-9208. Tel: 604-822-2521. FAX: 604-822-9587. E-mail: rare.books@ubc.ca. Web Site: rbsc.library.ubc.ca. *Head Librn,* Katherine Kalsbeek; Tel: 604-822-2819, E-mail: katherine.kalsbeek@ubc.ca

UNIVERSITY ARCHIVES, Irving K Barber Learning Ctr, 1961 East Mall, V6T 1Z1. Tel: 604-822-5877. Web Site: archives.library.ubc.ca. *Univ Archivist,* Erwin Wodarczak; Tel: 604-827-3954, E-mail: erwin.wodarczak@ubc.ca; Staff 6 (MLS 4, Non-MLS 2)
Founded 1970

WOODWARD LIBRARY, 2198 Health Sciences Mall, V6T 1Z3, SAN 376-9194. Tel: 604-822-2883. FAX: 604-822-5596. E-mail: wd.ref@ubc.ca. Web Site: woodward.library.ubc.ca. *Biomedical Librn, Head of Libr,* Aleteia Greenwood; Tel: 604-822-0689, E-mail: aleteia.greenwood@ubc.ca

XWI7XWA LIBRARY-FIRST NATIONS HOUSE OF LEARNING, 1985 West Mall, V6T 1Z2. Tel: 604-822-8738. FAX: 604-822-8944. Web Site: xwi7xwa.library.ubc.ca. *Actg Head,* Adolfo Tarango; Tel: 604-822-9615, E-mail: adolfo.tarango@ubc.ca

S VANCOUVER ART GALLERY LIBRARY*, 750 Hornby St, 2nd Flr, V6Z 2H7. SAN 318-8388. Tel: 604-662-4709. FAX: 604-682-1086. E-mail: library@vanartgallery.bc.ca. Web Site: vanartgallerylibrary.wordpress.com, www.vanartgallery.bc.ca/library-and-archives. *Chief Librn,* Jane Devine Mejia; Staff 1 (MLS 0.6, Non-MLS 0.4)
Founded 1931
Library Holdings: Bk Vols 50,000; Per Subs 30
Special Collections: Artistic Biographical Files

Subject Interests: Can fine art, Related subj
Automation Activity & Vendor Info: (Cataloging) LibraryWorld, Inc
Wireless access
Function: 24/7 Online cat, For res purposes, Online cat, Outside serv via phone, mail, e-mail & web, Ref & res, Ref serv available, Res assist avail, Res libr
Restriction: Circulates for staff only, External users must contact libr, Lending to staff only, Non-circulating to the pub, Open by appt only, Open to pub by appt only

J VANCOUVER COMMUNITY COLLEGE*, Broadway & Downtown Campus Libraries, 250 W Pender St, V6B 1S9. Tel: 604-871-7000. Circulation Tel: 604-871-7000, Ext 7323, 604-871-7000, Ext 8340. E-mail: LibraryHelp@vcc.ca. Web Site: library.vcc.ca. *Dean, Library, Teaching & Learning Servs,* Shirley Lew; Tel: 608-871-7000, Ext 7007, E-mail: slew@vcc.ca; *Head, Pub Serv,* Mari Paz Vera; Tel: 604-871-7000, Ext 7319, E-mail: mavera@vcc.ca; *Supvr, Pub Serv,* Melanie Primeau; Tel: 604-871-7000, Ext 8342, E-mail: mprimeau@vcc.ca; *Coordr, Coll Serv, E-Res Coordr,* Elena Kuzmina; Tel: 604-871-7000, Ext 8346, E-mail: ekuzmina@vcc.ca; Staff 33.9 (MLS 9.1, Non-MLS 24.8)
Founded 1971. Enrl 7,969; Fac 451; Highest Degree: Associate
Library Holdings: AV Mats 13,000; e-books 200,000; Bk Vols 82,000; Per Subs 210
Subject Interests: Adult educ, Bus, Computer sci, Health sci, Hospitality, Vocational training
Automation Activity & Vendor Info: (Acquisitions) Innovative Interfaces, Inc; (Cataloging) Innovative Interfaces, Inc; (Circulation) Innovative Interfaces, Inc; (Course Reserve) Innovative Interfaces, Inc; (Media Booking) Innovative Interfaces, Inc; (OPAC) Innovative Interfaces, Inc; (Serials) Innovative Interfaces, Inc
Wireless access
Function: Doc delivery serv, Electronic databases & coll, ILL available, Learning ctr, Music CDs, Online ref, Photocopying/Printing, Wheelchair accessible
Publications: English as a Second Language Bibliographic (Reference guide)
Partic in British Columbia Electronic Library Network; Centre for Accessible Post-Secondary Education Resources; Electronic Health Library of British Columbia; NET
Special Services for the Deaf - TDD equip; TTY equip; Videos & decoder
Special Services for the Blind - Closed circuit TV magnifier; Computer with voice synthesizer for visually impaired persons; Low vision equip
Open Mon-Thurs 9-9, Fri 9-5, Sat 11-5, Sun 10-9
Restriction: Circ to mem only, In-house use for visitors, Open to students, fac & staff, Photo ID required for access, Registered patrons only

S VANCOUVER HOLOCAUST EDUCATION CENTRE*, 50-950 W 41st Ave, V5Z 2N7. SAN 373-7934. Tel: 604-264-0499. E-mail: collections@vhec.org. Web Site: www.vhec.org. *Librn,* Jill Pineau; *Archivist,* S Seller; *Registrar,* C Donaldson; Staff 2.6 (MLS 0.6, Non-MLS 2)
Founded 1988
Library Holdings: DVDs 80; Bk Titles 3,500
Special Collections: Holocaust Studies Coll, archival, audio, AV, bks. Oral History
Wireless access
Function: 24/7 Online cat, Archival coll, Art exhibits, Audio & video playback equip for onsite use, Internet access, Movies, Music CDs, Online cat, Ref & res, Ref serv available, Res assist avail, Res libr, Wheelchair accessible
Restriction: Circ to mem only, Non-circulating of rare bks, Open to pub for ref only

P VANCOUVER PUBLIC LIBRARY*, 350 W Georgia St, V6B 6B1. SAN 366-2527. Tel: 604-331-3603. E-mail: info@vpl.ca. Web Site: www.vpl.ca. *Chief Librn/CEO,* Christina de Castell; E-mail: christina.decastell@vpl.ca; *Chief Financial Officer, Dir, Corporate Serv,* Julia Morrison; E-mail: julia.morrison@vpl.ca; *Dir, Planning & Communication,* Carol Nelson; E-mail: carol.nelson@vpl.ca; *Director, Central Library & Public Services,* Dawn Ibey; E-mail: dawn.ibey@vpl.ca; *Dir, Human Res,* Balwinder Rai; E-mail: balwinder.rai@vpl.ca; *Dir, Information Technology & Collections,* Kay Cahill; E-mail: kay.cahill@vpl.ca; *Dir, Neighborhood & Youth Services,* Maryn Ashdown; E-mail: maryn.ashdown@vpl.ca
Founded 1887. Pop 587,891; Circ 10,115,900
Library Holdings: AV Mats 164,416; Bk Titles 991,191; Bk Vols 2,491,206; Per Subs 11,662; Talking Bks 11,267
Special Collections: Early Children's Books (Marion Thompson Coll); Historical Photographs; North West History
Subject Interests: Econ, Fine arts, Govt, Hist, Lang, Lit, Multicultural, Multilingual, Sci, Soc sci, Sports
Automation Activity & Vendor Info: (Acquisitions) SirsiDynix; (Cataloging) SirsiDynix; (Circulation) SirsiDynix; (ILL) SirsiDynix; (OPAC) SirsiDynix; (Serials) SirsiDynix
Wireless access
Partic in Public Library InterLINK
Open Mon-Thurs 9:30-8:30, Fri 9:30-6, Sat 10-6, Sun 11-6
Friends of the Library Group
Branches: 21
ACCESSIBLE SERVICES, 350 W Georgia St, Level 3, V6B 6B1. Tel: 604-331-4100. E-mail: accessible@vpl.ca. Web Site: www.vpl.ca/accessible-services. *Coordr,* Jennifer Streckmann; Staff 6 (MLS 1, Non-MLS 5)
Open Mon-Fri 9:30-5:30
Friends of the Library Group
BRITANNIA BRANCH, 1661 Napier St, V5L 4X4, SAN 366-2551. Tel: 604-665-2222. Web Site: www.vpl.ca/location/britannia-branch. *Br Head,* Randy Gatley; E-mail: randy.gatley@vpl.ca
Open Mon-Wed 9:30-8, Thurs & Fri 9:30-6, Sat & Sun 9:30-5
Friends of the Library Group
CARNEGIE BRANCH, 401 Main St, V6A 2T7, SAN 366-256X. Tel: 604-665-3010. Web Site: www.vpl.ca/location/carnegie-branch. *Br Head,* Danielle LaFrance; E-mail: danielle.lafrance@vpl.ca
Open Mon-Fri 9:30-9, Sat & Sun 9:30-5
Friends of the Library Group
CHAMPLAIN HEIGHTS BRANCH, 7110 Kerr St, V5S 4W2, SAN 366-2578. Tel: 604-665-3955. Web Site: www.vpl.ca/location/champlain-heights-branch. *Br Head,* Gillian Guilmant-Smith; E-mail: gillian.guilmant-smith@vpl.ca
Open Tues & Thurs 9:30-8, Wed & Fri 9:30-6, Sat & Sun 9:30-5
Friends of the Library Group
COLLINGWOOD BRANCH, 2985 Kingsway, V5R 5J4, SAN 366-2586. Tel: 604-665-3953. Web Site: www.vpl.ca/location/collingwood-branch. *Br Head,* Gillian Guilmant-Smith
Open Tues & Wed 9:30-8, Thurs & Fri 9:30-6, Sat & Sun 9:30-5
Friends of the Library Group
DUNBAR BRANCH, 4515 Dunbar St, V6S 2G7, SAN 366-2616. Tel: 604-665-3968. Web Site: www.vpl.ca/location/dunbar-branch. *Br Head,* Samantha Mills; E-mail: samantha.mills@vpl.ca
Open Tues & Wed 9:30-8, Thurs & Fri 9:30-6, Sat & Sun 9:30-5
Friends of the Library Group
FIREHALL BRANCH, 1455 W Tenth Ave, V6H 1J8, SAN 366-2918. Tel: 604-665-3970. Web Site: www.vpl.ca/location/firehall-branch. *Br Head,* Els Kushner; E-mail: els.kushner@vpl.ca
Open Tues & Wed 9:30-8, Thurs & Fri 9:30-6, Sat & Sun 9:30-5
Friends of the Library Group
FRASERVIEW BRANCH, 1950 Argyle Dr, V5P 2A8, SAN 366-2640. Tel: 604-665-3957. Web Site: www.vpl.ca/location/fraserview-branch. *Br Head,* Katherine Parker; E-mail: katherine.parker@vpl.ca
Open Tues & Wed 9:30-8, Thurs & Fri 9:30-6, Sat & Sun 9:30-5
Friends of the Library Group
HASTINGS BRANCH, 2674 E Hastings St, V5K 1Z6, SAN 366-2675. Tel: 604-665-3959. Web Site: www.vpl.ca/location/hastings-branch. *Br Head,* Julie Douglas; E-mail: julie.douglas@vpl.ca
Open Tues & Wed 9:30-8, Thurs & Fri 9:30-6, Sat & Sun 9:30-5
Friends of the Library Group
JOE FORTES BRANCH, 870 Denman St, V6G 2L8, SAN 366-2705. Tel: 604-665-3972. Web Site: www.vpl.ca/location/joe-fortes-branch. *Br Head,* Mark MacKichan; E-mail: mark.mackichan@vpl.ca
Open Mon & Fri 9:30-6, Tues-Thurs 9:30-8, Sat & Sun 9:30-5
Friends of the Library Group
KENSINGTON BRANCH, 1428 Cedar Cottage Mews, V5N 5Z1, SAN 366-2721. Tel: 604-665-3961. Web Site: www.vpl.ca/location/kensington-branch. *Br Head,* Karen Liebel; E-mail: karen.liebel@vpl.ca
Open Tues & Fri 9:30-6, Wed & Thurs 9:30-8, Sat & Sun 9:30-5
Friends of the Library Group
KERRISDALE BRANCH, 2112 W 42nd Ave, V6M 2B6, SAN 366-273X. Tel: 604-665-3974. Web Site: www.vpl.ca/location/kerrisdale-branch. *Br Head,* Tim McMillan; E-mail: tim.mcmillan@vpl.ca; Staff 2 (MLS 2)
Founded 1943
Open Tues & Thurs 9:30-8, Wed & Fri 9:30-6, Sat & Sun 9:30-5
Friends of the Library Group
KITSILANO BRANCH, 2425 MacDonald St, V6K 3Y9, SAN 366-2799. Tel: 604-665-3976. Web Site: www.vpl.ca/location/kitsilano-branch. *Br Head,* Mark Koep; E-mail: mark.koep@vpl.ca
Open Mon-Thurs 9:30-8, Fri 9:30-6, Sat & Sun 9:30-5
Friends of the Library Group
MARPOLE BRANCH, 8386 Granville St, V6P 4Z7, SAN 366-2888. Tel: 604-665-3978. Web Site: www.vpl.ca/location/marpole-branch. *Br Head,* Shumin Wang; E-mail: shumin.wang@vpl.ca
Open Tues & Wed 9:30-8, Thurs & Fri 9:30-6, Sat & Sun 9:30-5
Friends of the Library Group
MOUNT PLEASANT BRANCH, One Kingsway, V5T 3H7, SAN 366-2829. Tel: 604-665-3962. Web Site: www.vpl.ca/location/mount-pleasant-branch. *Br Head,* Alexis Greenwood; E-mail: alexis.greenwood@vpl.ca
Open Mon-Fri 9:30-8, Sat & Sun 9:30-5
Friends of the Library Group

NECA?MAT CT STRATHCONA, 730 E Hastings St, V6A 1V5, SAN 366-2977. Tel: 604-665-3967. *Br Head,* Randy Gatley
Open Mon-Thurs 9:30-9, Fri-Sun 9:30-5
Friends of the Library Group

OAKRIDGE BRANCH, 6184 Ash St, V5Z 3G9, SAN 366-2853. Tel: 604-665-3980. Web Site: www.vpl.ca/location/oakridge-branch. *Br Head,* Christopher Kevlahan; E-mail: christopher.kevlahan@vpl.ca
Open Mon, Wed & Thurs 9:30-8, Tues & Fri 9:30-6, Sat & Sun 9:30-5
Friends of the Library Group

RENFREW BRANCH, 2969 E 22nd Ave, V5M 2Y3, SAN 374-8146. Tel: 604-257-8705. Web Site: www.vpl.ca/location/renfrew-branch. *Br Head,* Jan Fu; E-mail: jan.fu@vpl.ca
Library Holdings: Bk Vols 52,000
Open Mon-Thurs 9:30-8, Fri 9:30-6, Sat & Sun 9:30-5
Friends of the Library Group

TERRY SALMAN BRANCH, 4575 Clancy Loranger Way, V5Y 2M4. Tel: 604-665-3964. Web Site: www.vpl.ca/location/terry-salman-branch. *Br Head,* Stephanie Kripps; E-mail: stephanie.kripps@vpl.ca
Open Mon-Fri 9:30-8, Sat & Sun 9:30-5
Friends of the Library Group

SOUTH HILL BRANCH, 6076 Fraser St, V5W 2Z7, SAN 366-2942. Tel: 604-665-3965. Web Site: www.vpl.ca/location/south-hill-branch. *Br Head,* Eleonore Shaffer; E-mail: eleonore.shaffer@vpl.ca
Open Tues & Thurs 9:30-8, Wed & Fri 9:30-6, Sat & Sun 9:30-5
Friends of the Library Group

WEST POINT GREY BRANCH, 4566 W Tenth Ave, V6R 2J1, SAN 366-2993. Tel: 604-665-3982. Web Site: www.vpl.ca/location/west-point-grey-branch. *Br Head,* Gladys Chen; E-mail: gladys.chen@vpl.ca
Open Tues & Thurs 9:30-8, Wed & Fri 9:30-6, Sat & Sun 9:30-5
Friends of the Library Group

R VANCOUVER SCHOOL OF THEOLOGY*, H R MacMillan Library, 6015 Walter Gage Rd, V6T 1Z1. SAN 318-840X. Tel: 604-822-9382. FAX: 604-822-9212. Circulation E-mail: circ@vst.edu. Web Site: www.vst.edu/library. *Head, Tech Serv, Libr Coord,* Daniel Baek; E-mail: dbaek@vst.edu; *Pub Serv Coordr,* Faye Chisholm; E-mail: fchisholm@vst.edu; Staff 2.5 (MLS 1.5, Non-MLS 1)
Founded 1971. Enrl 250; Highest Degree: Master
Library Holdings: e-books 350; Bk Vols 35,000; Per Subs 330
Special Collections: Thomas Merton Coll
Subject Interests: Anglican Church, Church hist, Methodist histl mat, Presbyterian churches, Theol
Automation Activity & Vendor Info: (Cataloging) Innovative Interfaces, Inc; (Circulation) Innovative Interfaces, Inc; (Course Reserve) Innovative Interfaces, Inc; (ILL) Innovative Interfaces, Inc; (Media Booking) Innovative Interfaces, Inc; (OPAC) Innovative Interfaces, Inc; (Serials) Innovative Interfaces, Inc
Wireless access
Function: Res libr
Publications: Accessions List
Open Mon-Thurs 8:30-6, Fri 8:30-5, Sat Noon-5 (Sept-April); Mon-Fri 8:30-4:30 (May-Aug)

S YOSEF WOSK LIBRARY & RESOURCE CENTRE*, VanDusen Gardens Library, 5151 Oak St, V6M 4H1. SAN 326-5021. Tel: 604-257-8668. FAX: 604-257-8679. E-mail: library@vandusen.org. Web Site: vandusengarden.org/learn/library. *Libr Coord,* Marina Princz; Staff 1 (MLS 1)
Founded 1977
Library Holdings: Bk Titles 5,800; Per Subs 50
Special Collections: Gardening (Special Collecting Area: Plant Exploration); Horticulture & Botany
Subject Interests: Botany, Hort
Restriction: Circ to mem only

VANDERHOOF

P VANDERHOOF PUBLIC LIBRARY*, 230 Stewart St E, V0J 3A0. (Mail add: Bag 6000, V0J 3A0), SAN 318-8434. Tel: 250-567-4060. E-mail: info@vanderhooflibrary.com. Web Site: www.vanderhooflibrary.com. *Chief Librn,* Jennifer Barg; E-mail: jennifer@vanderhooflibrary.com; *Ch,* Sara Hara; E-mail: sara@vanderhooflibrary.com; *Libr Asst,* Kaimi Giesbrecht; E-mail: kaimi@vanderhooflibrary.com; Staff 3 (Non-MLS 3)
Pop 3,906; Circ 43,000
Library Holdings: Bk Titles 14,909; Bk Vols 14,952
Wireless access
Function: Homebound delivery serv, ILL available, Meeting rooms, Photocopying/Printing
Open Tues & Thurs 9-5, Wed 9-7, Fri 9-6, Sat 10-5
Friends of the Library Group

VICTORIA

GL BRITISH COLUMBIA LEGISLATIVE LIBRARY*, Parliament Bldgs, V8V 1X4. SAN 318-8450. Tel: 250-387-6510. FAX: 250-356-1373. E-mail: llbc.ref@leg.bc.ca. Web Site: www.leg.bc.ca/learn-about-us/legislative-library. *Dir,* Peter Gourlay; Tel: 250-387-6500, E-mail: peter.gourlay@leg.bc.ca; *Mgr, Tech Serv,* Charles Hogg; Tel: 250-387-6505, E-mail: charles.hogg@leg.bc.ca; Staff 15 (MLS 15)
Founded 1863
Library Holdings: Per Subs 708
Special Collections: British Columbia & Canadian Government Publications
Subject Interests: Hist, Law, Parliamentary procedure, Polit sci
Automation Activity & Vendor Info: (Acquisitions) SirsiDynix; (Cataloging) SirsiDynix; (Circulation) SirsiDynix; (OPAC) SirsiDynix; (Serials) SirsiDynix
Wireless access
Open Mon-Fri 8:30-5

G BRITISH COLUMBIA MINISTRY OF EDUCATION*, Libraries & Literacy, 620 Superior St, 5th Flr, V8V 1V2. (Mail add: PO Box 9831, Stn Prov Govt, V8W 9T1), SAN 366-3213. Tel: 250-356-1791. E-mail: llb@gov.bc.ca. Web Site: www2.gov.bc.ca/gov/content/sports-culture/arts-culture/public-libraries. *Dir,* Mari Martin; E-mail: mari.martin@gov.bc.ca
Publications: British Columbia Public Libraries: Statistics

J CAMOSUN COLLEGE*, Alan Batey Library & Learning Commons, Landsdowne Campus, 3100 Foul Bay Rd, V8P 5J2. SAN 318-8477. Tel: 250-370-3619. FAX: 250-370-3624. E-mail: library@camosun.ca. Web Site: www.camosun.bc.ca/library. *Dir, Learning Serv,* Mary Burgess; Tel: 250-370-3604, E-mail: burgessm@camosun.ca; Staff 18 (MLS 5, Non-MLS 13)
Founded 1971. Enrl 7,500; Fac 519; Highest Degree: Associate
Library Holdings: Bk Titles 50,256; Per Subs 164
Automation Activity & Vendor Info: (Acquisitions) Evergreen; (Cataloging) Evergreen; (Circulation) Evergreen; (Course Reserve) Evergreen; (Discovery) EBSCO Discovery Service; (Media Booking) Evergreen; (OPAC) Evergreen; (Serials) Evergreen
Wireless access
Function: 24/7 Electronic res, 24/7 Online cat, Res libr
Partic in British Columbia Electronic Library Network; Centre for Accessible Post-Secondary Education Resources; Electronic Health Library of British Columbia

Departmental Libraries:

LIZ ASHTON CAMPUS CENTRE LIBRARY, 4461 Inteurban Rd, 3rd Flr, V9E 2C1. Tel: 250-370-3828. FAX: 250-370-3652. E-mail: library@camosun.ca. *Dir, Learning Serv,* Erin Howard; Tel: 250-370-3604, E-mail: howarde@camosun.ca; *Librn,* Ally Flynn; Tel: 250-370-4994, E-mail: flynna@camosun.ca; *Acq Librn,* Margie Clarke; Tel: 250-370-4533, E-mail: clarkem@camosun.ca; *Supvr, Access Serv,* Debbie Webb; Tel: 250-370-4531, E-mail: webbd@camosun.ca
Open Mon-Fri 8-5

G J T FYLES NATURAL RESOURCES LIBRARY, 1810 Blanshard St, V8W 9N3. (Mail add: PO Box 9321, Stn Provincial Government, V8W 9N3), SAN 318-8485. Tel: 250-952-0564. FAX: 250-952-0581. Web Site: www2.gov.bc.ca/gov/content/environment/research-monitoring-reporting. *Libr Adminr,* Jennifer Lu; E-mail: jennifer.lu@gov.bc.ca; *Head, Knowledge Resources,* Adrienne Canty; E-mail: adrienne.canty@gov.bc.ca; *Libr Tech,* Kelsey Bishop; E-mail: kelsey.bishop@gov.bc.ca; *Libr Tech,* Kevin Day; E-mail: kevin.day@gov.bc.ca; Staff 4 (MLS 1, Non-MLS 3)
Founded 1896
Library Holdings: CDs 50; DVDs 25; Bk Vols 80,700; Per Subs 70
Subject Interests: Agr, Alternative energy, Botany, Climate change, Ecosystems, Energy, Engr, Entomology, Fisheries, Forestry, Forests, Gas, Geol, Hist, Law, Mining, Oil, Resource mgt, Soils, Wildlife
Automation Activity & Vendor Info: (Cataloging) SirsiDynix; (Circulation) SirsiDynix; (ILL) OCLC WorldShare Interlibrary Loan; (OPAC) SirsiDynix-WorkFlows
Wireless access

P GREATER VICTORIA PUBLIC LIBRARY*, 735 Broughton St, V8W 3H2. SAN 366-306X. Tel: 250-940-4875. Circulation Tel: 250-413-0361. Administration Tel: 250-413-0356. FAX: 250-382-7125. Web Site: www.gvpl.ca. *Chief Exec Officer,* Maureen Sawa; Tel: 250-940-1193, E-mail: msawa@gvpl.ca; *District Coord,* Andrea Brimmell; Tel: 250-940-4875, Ext 237, E-mail: abrimmell@gvpl.ca; Staff 38 (MLS 37, Non-MLS 1)
Founded 1864. Pop 294,773; Circ 4,872,496
Library Holdings: AV Mats 88,646; Bk Titles 314,483; Bk Vols 838,096; Per Subs 2,269; Talking Bks 23,436
Subject Interests: Local hist

Automation Activity & Vendor Info: (Acquisitions) BiblioCommons; (Cataloging) BiblioCommons; (Circulation) BiblioCommons; (OPAC) BiblioCommons; (Serials) BiblioCommons
Wireless access
Publications: Check it Out at the Library
Friends of the Library Group
Branches: 11
EMILY CARR BRANCH, 101-3521 Blanshard St, V8Z 0B9, SAN 366-3183. Tel: 250-940-4875, Ext 744. *Br Supvr,* Darina Perfenova; E-mail: dperfenova@gvpl.ca
Friends of the Library Group
CENTRAL SAANICH, 1209 Clarke Rd, V8M 1P8. Tel: 250-940-4875, Ext 724. *Br Supvr,* Tina Lowery; E-mail: tlowery@gvpl.ca
Open Mon-Sat 12-5
ESQUIMALT, 1231 Esquimalt Rd, V9A 3P1, SAN 366-3094. Tel: 250-940-4875, Ext 764. *Br Supvr,* Emilia Penkova; E-mail: epenkova@gvpl.ca
Friends of the Library Group
GOUDY BRANCH, 119-755 Goldstream Ave, V9B 0H9. Tel: 250-940-4875, Ext 784. *Br Supvr,* Tina Lowery; E-mail: tlowery@gvpl.ca
Function: Computers for patron use
Open Mon-Sat 11-5
BRUCE HUTCHISON BRANCH, 4636 Elk Lake Dr, V8Z 7K2, SAN 374-5228. Tel: 250-940-4875, Ext 704. *Br Supvr,* Veneta Petkova; E-mail: vpetkova@gvpl.ca
Open Mon, Fri & Sat 10-6, Tues-Thurs 10-9
Friends of the Library Group
JAMES BAY BRANCH, 385 Menzies St, V8V 0C2. Tel: 250-940-4875, Ext 684. *Br Supvr,* Martin Brooks; E-mail: mbrooks@gvpl.ca
Open Mon-Wed, Fri & Sat 11-6, Thurs 11-7
JUAN DE FUCA BRANCH, 1759 Island Hwy, V9B 1J1, SAN 376-2238. Tel: 250-940-4875, Ext 804. *Br Supvr,* Natha Pagan; E-mail: npagan@gvpl.ca
Friends of the Library Group
LANGFORD HERITAGE BRANCH, 102-1314 Lakepoint Way, V9B 0S2. Tel: 250-940-4875, Ext 884. *Br Supvr,* Tina Lowery
NELLIE MCCLUNG BRANCH, 3950 Cedar Hill Rd, V8P 3Z9, SAN 366-3124. Tel: 250-940-4875, Ext 824. *Br Supvr,* Becky Lee; E-mail: blee@gvpl.ca
Open Mon, Wed, Fri & Sat 12-6, Tues & Thurs 12-7
Friends of the Library Group
OAK BAY, 1442 Monterey Ave, V8S 4W1, SAN 366-3159. Tel: 250-940-4875, Ext 844. *Br Supvr,* Catherine Cardiff; E-mail: ccardiff@gvpl.ca
Library Holdings: Bk Vols 89,745
Open Mon-Wed & Sat 10-6, Thurs & Fri 10-9
Friends of the Library Group
SAANICH CENTENNIAL BRANCH, G R Pearkes Recreation Ctr, 3110 Tillicum Rd, V9A 6T2. Tel: 250-940-4875, Ext 864. *Br Supvr,* Karen Wong; E-mail: kwong@gvpl.ca
Open Mon, Wed, Fri & Sat 11-6, Tues & Thurs 11-7

GM HEALTH & HUMAN SERVICES LIBRARY, BRITISH COLUMBIA MINISTRY OF HEALTH*, 1515 Blanshard St, Main Flr, V8W 3C8. (Mail add: Box 9637 Stn, V8W 9P1), SAN 366-3000. Tel: 250-952-2196. FAX: 250-952-2180. E-mail: hlth.library@gov.bc.ca. Web Site: www2.gov.bc.ca.
Founded 2002
Library Holdings: Bk Titles 22,000; Per Subs 500; Videos 2,000
Subject Interests: Aboriginal issues, Alcohol abuse, Child welfare, Dentistry, Drug abuse, Epidemiology, Gerontology, Health educ, Hospital admin, Learning disorders, Long term care, Mental health, Nursing, Pub health admin, Pub health inspection, Pub sector mgt, Soc work, Speech disorders
Automation Activity & Vendor Info: (Cataloging) SirsiDynix-Unicorn; (Circulation) SirsiDynix-Unicorn; (Media Booking) SirsiDynix-Unicorn; (OPAC) SirsiDynix-iLink; (Serials) SirsiDynix-Unicorn
Partic in Electronic Health Library of British Columbia; Govt Libr Asn of BC; Health Library Association of British Columbia
Open Mon-Fri 8-4

C LESTER B PEARSON COLLEGE OF THE PACIFIC*, Norman McKee Lang Library, 650 Pearson College Dr, V9C 4H7. SAN 328-1825. Tel: 250-391-2411. Web Site: www.pearsoncollege.ca. *Librn,* Sherry Crowther; E-mail: scrowther@pearsoncollege.ca; Staff 1 (MLS 1)
Founded 1974. Enrl 200; Fac 25
Library Holdings: DVDs 240; Electronic Media & Resources 30; Bk Vols 18,000; Per Subs 90; Videos 400
Special Collections: International Affairs (Giovanni Costigan Lectures Coll); Lester B Pearson Bk Coll; Pearson College Archive
Wireless access
Open Mon-Fri 8:30am-Midnight, Sat & Sun 9am-Midnight

S MARITIME MUSEUM OF BRITISH COLUMBIA LIBRARY*, 634 Humboldt St, Unit 100, V8W 1A4. SAN 322-7073. Tel: 250-385-4222, Ext 116. FAX: 250-382-2869. E-mail: librarian@mmbc.bc.ca. Web Site: www.mmbc.bc.ca. *Librn,* Judy Thompson; Staff 2 (MLS 2)
Founded 1954
Library Holdings: AV Mats 100; CDs 25; DVDs 20; Bk Titles 8,000; Per Subs 25; Videos 10
Special Collections: Maritime Hist (NW Coast & British Columbia)
Automation Activity & Vendor Info: (Acquisitions) PALS
Wireless access
Function: 24/7 Online cat
Open Tues-Sat 10-5
Restriction: Access at librarian's discretion, Authorized scholars by appt, Not a lending libr

C ROYAL ROADS UNIVERSITY LIBRARY*, 2005 Sooke Rd, V9B 5Y2. Tel: 250-391-2575. Toll Free Tel: 800-788-8028. Web Site: library.royalroads.ca. *Univ Librn,* Rosie Croft; Tel: 250-391-2699, E-mail: rosie.croft@royalroads.ca; *Admin Coordr,* Billi-Jo Cavanaugh; Tel: 250-391-2595, E-mail: billijo.cavanaugh@royalroads.ca
Library Holdings: Audiobooks 235; e-books 338,000; Large Print Bks 6; Bk Vols 30,000
Wireless access
Function: Computers for patron use, ILL available, Res assist avail, Study rm, Wheelchair accessible
Partic in Electronic Health Library of British Columbia
Open Mon-Thurs 8am-9pm, Fri 8-6, Sat 10-6, Sun 10-9

UNIVERSITY OF VICTORIA LIBRARIES
C MCPHERSON LIBRARY*, PO Box 1800, V8W 3H5, SAN 366-3450. Tel: 250-721-8211. Circulation Tel: 250-721-6673. Interlibrary Loan Service Tel: 250-721-8236. Reference Tel: 250-721-8274. FAX: 250-721-8215. Interlibrary Loan Service FAX: 250-721-8243. Reference FAX: 250-721-8235. Web Site: gateway.uvic.ca. *Dir, Spec Coll, Univ Archivist,* Lara Wilson; Tel: 250-472-4480, E-mail: ljwilson@uvic.ca; *Asst Univ Librn,* Wendie McHenry; E-mail: wmchenry@uvic.ca; *Dir, Pub Serv,* Shailoo Bedi; E-mail: shailoo@uvic.ca; *Assoc Univ Librn, Coll & Serv, Assoc Univ Librn, Info Serv,* Joanne Henning; E-mail: jhenning@uvic.ca; *Assoc Univ Librn, Info Tech, Assoc Univ Librn, Tech Serv,* Ken Cooley; E-mail: kcooley@uvic.ca; *Spec Coll Librn,* Chris Petter; E-mail: cpetter@uvic.ca; *Coordr, Cat,* Sam Aquila; E-mail: saquila@uvic.ca; *Coordr, Ser,* Elena Romaniuk; E-mail: eromaniu@uvic.ca; *Develop Officer,* Jane Buzza; E-mail: jbuzza@uvic.ca; *Coordr, ILL,* Nancy Stuart; E-mail: nstuart@uvic.ca; *Univ Archivist,* Jane Turner; E-mail: jturner@uvic.ca; Staff 40 (MLS 31, Non-MLS 9)
Founded 1902. Highest Degree: Doctorate
Library Holdings: CDs 64,515; e-journals 11,000; Music Scores 34,704; Bk Vols 1,856,987; Per Subs 14,473; Videos 7,904
Special Collections: English Literature (Anglo-Irish Renaissance); English Literature (John Betjeman Coll), bks, mss; English Literature (Robert Graves Coll), bks & mss; Literature, Art History (Herbert Read Coll), bks, mss. Canadian and Provincial
Subject Interests: Behav sci, Econ, Educ, Environ studies, Hist, Lang, Law, Lit, Music, Natural sci, Soc sci
Automation Activity & Vendor Info: (Acquisitions) Ex Libris Group; (Cataloging) Ex Libris Group; (Circulation) Ex Libris Group; (OPAC) Ex Libris Group
Partic in AG Canada; British Columbia Electronic Library Network; Canadian Association of Research Libraries; Council of Prairie & Pacific University Libraries; Electronic Health Library of British Columbia; OCLC Online Computer Library Center, Inc
Friends of the Library Group
CL DIANA M PRIESTLY LAW LIBRARY*, PO Box 2300, STN CSC, V8W 3B1, SAN 366-3485. Tel: 250-721-8565. FAX: 250-472-4174. *Assoc Prof, Assoc Univ Librn,* Neil A Campbell; *Acq,* I Godfrey
Founded 1974
Library Holdings: Bk Vols 413,000; Per Subs 1,935
Special Collections: Common Law; English Language
Partic in AG Canada; OCLC Online Computer Library Center, Inc
Publications: Constitution Act, 1982 - Canadian Charter of Rights & Freedoms; Law Library Occasional Paper No 1: Judges of British Columbia to 1957; Law Reporting in BC - Out of The West; The Writings of D M Gordon, Esq, QC - A List

S VICTORIA CONSERVATORY OF MUSIC LIBRARY*, 900 Johnson St, Rm 113, V8V 3N4. SAN 323-441X. Tel: 250-386-5311, Ext 5001. E-mail: library@vcm.bc.ca. Web Site: www.vcm.bc.ca. *Head Librn,* Robin Belcher
Library Holdings: Bk Titles 60,000; Per Subs 15
Open Mon-Fri 10-6

S VIEW ROYAL READING CENTRE*, 266 Island Hwy, V9B 1G5. Tel: 250-479-2723. FAX: 250-479-2723. E-mail: vivr.ill@shaw.ca. *Library Contact,* Christine Jackman
Founded 1971. Pop 9,300

Library Holdings: Bk Vols 16,500
Wireless access
Function: Family literacy
Open Mon-Sat 10-4, Sun 1-4
Restriction: Circ to mem only

WEST VANCOUVER

P WEST VANCOUVER MEMORIAL LIBRARY*, 1950 Marine Dr, V7V 1J8. SAN 318-8582. Tel: 604-925-7400. Reference Tel: 604-925-7403. FAX: 604-925-5933. E-mail: info@westvanlibrary.ca. Web Site: www.westvanlibrary.ca. *Dir,* Stephanie Hall; E-mail: shall@westvanlibrary.ca
Founded 1950. Pop 48,340; Circ 700,040
Library Holdings: AV Mats 32,181; Bk Vols 210,705; Per Subs 204
Special Collections: History & Literature of Persia (Persian Language Coll)
Subject Interests: Fine arts, Music
Automation Activity & Vendor Info: (Acquisitions) Innovative Interfaces, Inc; (Cataloging) Innovative Interfaces, Inc; (Circulation) Innovative Interfaces, Inc; (OPAC) Innovative Interfaces, Inc; (Serials) Innovative Interfaces, Inc
Wireless access
Function: Art exhibits, Audio & video playback equip for onsite use, Computer training, Home delivery & serv to seniorr ctr & nursing homes, Homebound delivery serv, ILL available, Prog for adults, Prog for children & young adult, Summer reading prog, Wheelchair accessible
Publications: Annual Report; Fulfilling a Dream: West Vancouver Memorial Library, 1919-1990; Inquiring Mind (Newsletter)
Partic in Public Library InterLINK
Special Services for the Blind - Large print bks & talking machines; Magnifiers
Open Mon-Thurs 10-8, Fri-Sun 10-6
Friends of the Library Group
Bookmobiles: 1

WHISTLER

P WHISTLER PUBLIC LIBRARY*, 4329 Main St, V8E 1B2. Tel: 604-935-8433. FAX: 604-935-8434. E-mail: info@whistlerlibrary.ca. Web Site: www.whistlerlibrary.ca. *Dir,* Elizabeth Tracy; E-mail: etracy@whistlerlibrary.ca; *Pub Serv Librn,* Nadine White; E-mail: nwhite@whistlerlibrary.ca; *Support Serv Librn, Tech Librn,* Chelsea Jordan-Makely; E-mail: cjordan-makley@whistlerlibrary.ca; *Youth Serv Librn,* Kaley O'Brien; E-mail: kobrien@whistlerlibrary.ca; Staff 4 (MLS 4)
Founded 1986. Circ 140,000
Library Holdings: Bk Titles 45,000; Per Subs 129
Automation Activity & Vendor Info: (Cataloging) OCLC CatExpress; (Circulation) Evergreen; (OPAC) Evergreen
Wireless access
Function: 24/7 Electronic res, 24/7 Online cat, Adult literacy prog, Art exhibits, AV serv, Bks on CD, CD-ROM, Children's prog, Citizenship assistance, Computer training, Computers for patron use, Electronic databases & coll, Family literacy, Free DVD rentals
Partic in BC Libraries Cooperative; Public Library InterLINK
Open Mon-Sat 11-7, Sun 11-4
Friends of the Library Group

WILLIAMS LAKE

P CARIBOO REGIONAL DISTRICT LIBRARY*, 180 N Third Ave, Ste A, V2G 2A4. SAN 318-8590. Tel: 250-305-2182, 250-392-3630. E-mail: wlake@cariboord.bc.ca. Web Site: www.cln.bc.ca. *Mgr, Libr Serv,* Anton Dounts; Tel: 250-392-3351, E-mail: adounts@cariboord.bc.ca; *Area Librn,* Jennifer Coupe; Staff 4 (MLS 3, Non-MLS 1)
Founded 1976
Wireless access
Open Tues-Thurs 10-8, Fri & Sat 10-5
Friends of the Library Group
Branches: 14
ALEXIS CREEK BRANCH, 7651 Yells Rd, Alexis Creek, V0L 1A0. (Mail add: PO Box 229, Alexis Creek, V0L 1A0). Tel: 250-394-4346. E-mail: alexis@cariboord.bc.ca. *Commun Librn,* Darlyne Brecknock
Open Tues & Thurs 3-7
ANAHIM LAKE BRANCH, 2409 Whispering Pines Trailer Court, Unit 1, Hwy 20, Anahim Lake, V0l 1C0. (Mail add: General Delivery, Anahim Lake, V0L 1C0). Tel: 250-742-2056. E-mail: anahim@cariboord.bc.ca. *Commun Librn,* Janice Biggin-Pound
Open Tues & Wed 2-6
BIG LAKE BRANCH, 4056 Lakeview Rd, Big Lake, V0L 1G0. (Mail add: PO Box 47, Big Lake, V0L 1G0). Tel: 250-243-2355. E-mail: biglake@cariboord.bc.ca. *Commun Librn,* Esther Kreis
Open Mon 10-4, Thurs 12-6
FOREST GROVE BRANCH, 4485 Eagle Creek Rd, Forest Grove, V0K 1M0. Tel: 250-397-2927. E-mail: forestgrove@cariboord.bc.ca. *Commun Librn,* Susan Burlingham
Open Tues 3-8, Thurs 10-3
HORSEFLY BRANCH, 5779 Walters Dr, Horsefly, V0L 1L0. (Mail add: PO Box 400, Horsefly, V0L 1L0). Tel: 250-620-3345. E-mail: horsefly@cariboord.bc.ca. *Commun Librn,* Shirley Janzen
Open Tues, Thurs & Sat 2-6
INTERLAKES BRANCH, 7170 Levick Circle, Lone Butte, V0K 1X1. Tel: 250-593-4545. E-mail: interlakeslib@cariboord.bc.ca. *Commun Librn,* Brenda Tillyer
Open Wed, Thurs & Sat 2-6
LAC LA HACHE BRANCH, 4787 Clark Ave, Lac la Hache, V0K 1T0. (Mail add: PO Box 246, Lac la Hache, V0K 1T0). Tel: 250-396-7642. E-mail: laclahache@cariboord.bc.ca. *Commun Librn,* Yvette Brown
Open Wed 3-7, Sat 10-3
LIKELY BRANCH, 6163 Keithly Creek Rd, Likely, V0L 1N0. (Mail add: PO Box 86, Likely, V0L 1N0). Tel: 250-790-2234. E-mail: likely@cariboord.bc.ca. *Commun Librn,* Vicki Schill
Open Tues & Wed 1-5
MCLEESE LAKE BRANCH, 6749 Hwy 97 N, McLeese Lake, V0L 1P0. (Mail add: PO Box 100, McLeese Lake, V0L 1P0). Tel: 250-297-6533. E-mail: mcleese@cariboord.bc.ca. *Commun Librn,* Marion Watson
Open Tues 4-8, Sat 12-6
NAZKO BRANCH, 1351 Palmer Rd, Nazko, V2J 3H9. Tel: 250-249-5289. E-mail: nazko@cariboord.bc.ca. *Commun Librn,* Marlene Cline
Open Wed 3-7, Fri 12-4
100 MILE HOUSE BRANCH, 449 S Birch Ave, 100 Mile House, V0K 2E0. Tel: 250-395-2332. E-mail: ohmlib@cariboord.bc.ca. *Area Librn,* Roxy Barnes
Open Tues-Thurs 10-8, Fri & Sat 10-5
QUESNEL BRANCH, 101 410 Kinchant St, Quesnel, V2J 7J5, SAN 325-2140. Tel: 250-992-7912. FAX: 250-992-9882. E-mail: quesnelib@cariboord.bc.ca. *Area Librn,* Heather Lee; Staff 2 (MLS 1, Non-MLS 1)
Founded 1926. Pop 21,000; Circ 120,000
Library Holdings: High Interest/Low Vocabulary Bk Vols 100; Bk Titles 45,000; Per Subs 100
Special Services for the Deaf - Bks on deafness & sign lang; High interest/low vocabulary bks; Staff with knowledge of sign lang
Special Services for the Blind - Talking bks
Open Tues-Thurs 10-8, Fri & Sat 10-5
TATLA LAKE BRANCH, 16451 Chilcotin Hwy, Tatla Lake, V0L 1V0. (Mail add: PO Box 42, Tatla Lake, V0L 1V0). Tel: 250-476-1242. E-mail: tatla@cariboord.bc.ca. *Commun Librn,* Annett Wittwer
Open Mon & Wed 11-5
WELLS BRANCH, 4269 Saunders Ave, Wells, V0K 2R0. (Mail add: PO Box 160, Wells, V0K 2R0). Tel: 250-994-3424. E-mail: wells@cariboord.ca. *Commun Librn,* Kathy Landry
Open Mon & Tues 6:30pm-9pm, Wed & Sat 1-4:30

C THOMPSON RIVERS UNIVERSITY*, Williams Lake Campus Library, 1250 Western Ave, V2G 1H7. Tel: 250-392-8030. FAX: 250-392-4984. E-mail: wlmain@tru.ca. Web Site: www.tru.ca/williamslake. *Librn,* Melissa Svendsen; E-mail: msvendsen@tru.ca
Library Holdings: AV Mats 800; Bk Vols 10,000
Automation Activity & Vendor Info: (Acquisitions) SirsiDynix; (Cataloging) SirsiDynix; (Circulation) SirsiDynix; (Course Reserve) SirsiDynix; (ILL) SirsiDynix; (Media Booking) SirsiDynix; (OPAC) SirsiDynix; (Serials) SirsiDynix

MANITOBA

Date of Statistics: Not provided.

BALDUR

P RURAL MUNICIPALITY OF ARGYLE PUBLIC LIBRARY*, 627 Elizabeth Ave, Hwy 23, R0K 0B0. (Mail add: PO Box 10, R0K 0B0), SAN 378-0120. Tel: 204-535-2314. FAX: 204-535-2242. E-mail: rmargyle@gmail.com. Web Site: rmargyle.wixsite.com/rmargyle. *Chairperson,* Marilynne Pantel; *Librn,* April Hoblyak
Founded 1982. Pop 1,200
Library Holdings: Bk Titles 12,000; Per Subs 15
Wireless access
Partic in Manitoba Public Library Services
Special Services for the Blind - Audio mat; Large print bks
Open Tues & Wed 6pm-8pm; Tues 10-4, Wed 3-9 (Summer)
Friends of the Library Group

BEAUSEJOUR

P BROKENHEAD RIVER REGIONAL LIBRARY*, 427 Park Ave, R0E 0C0. (Mail add: PO Box 1087, R0E 0C0), SAN 377-9831. Tel: 204-268-7570. FAX: 204-268-7570. Web Site: www.brrlibrary.ca. *Dir, Libr Serv, Head Librn,* Debbie Winnicki; E-mail: debbiewinnickibrrl@mts.net
Founded 1981. Pop 6,763
Library Holdings: Bk Titles 30,998; Per Subs 80
Wireless access
Function: ILL available
Partic in Can Libr Asn; Manitoba Libr Trustees Asn; Manitoba Library Association; Manitoba Public Library Services
Open Tues & Thurs 9-5, Wed 11-8, Fri 9-8, Sat (Sept-June) 11-3

BOISSEVAIN

P BOISSEVAIN-MORTON LIBRARY & ARCHIVES*, 409 S Railway, R0K 0E0. (Mail add: PO Box 340, R0K 0E0), SAN 318-8612. Tel: 204-534-6478. E-mail: mail@bmlibrary.ca. Web Site: www.bmlibrary.ca. *Head Librn,* Michelle Scott
Founded 1959. Pop 2,800; Circ 39,000
Library Holdings: Bk Titles 24,000; Per Subs 40
Special Collections: Local History (Boissevain Community Archives), ms, photog. Oral History
Wireless access
Publications: Annual Report
Partic in Manitoba Public Library Services
Open Tues, Thurs & Fri 9:30-4, Wed 9:30-6

BRANDON

J ASSINIBOINE COMMUNITY COLLEGE LIBRARY*, 1430 Victoria Ave E, R7A 2A9. SAN 320-7811. Tel: 204-725-8727. Toll Free Tel: 800-862-6307, Ext 6638. FAX: 204-725-8740. E-mail: library@assiniboine.net. Web Site: assiniboine.net/library. *Mgr, Libr Serv,* Position Currently Open
Founded 1968
Special Collections: Distance Education Coll; ELDERS Coll; Teaching & Learning Coll
Automation Activity & Vendor Info: (Cataloging) Insignia Software; (Circulation) Insignia Software; (Media Booking) Insignia Software; (OPAC) Insignia Software; (Serials) Insignia Software
Wireless access
Partic in BC Libraries Cooperative; Manitoba Library Association; Manitoba Library Consortium, Inc
Open Mon-Thurs 8-7:30, Fri 8-4:30, Sat 10-2
Departmental Libraries:
THE LEARNING HUB, 1035 First St N, R7A 2Y1. Tel: 204-725-8700, Ext 6624. FAX: 204-725-8740.
Automation Activity & Vendor Info: (Cataloging) Insignia Software; (Circulation) Insignia Software; (Course Reserve) Insignia Software; (Media Booking) Insignia Software; (OPAC) Insignia Software; (Serials) Insignia Software

M BRANDON REGIONAL HEALTH AUTHORITY*, Health Resource Center, 150 McTavish Ave E, R7A 2B3. SAN 320-782X. Tel: 204-578-4080. Interlibrary Loan Service Tel: 204-578-4081. FAX: 204-578-4984. E-mail: library@pmh-mb.ca. Web Site: www.prairiemountainhealth.ca/index.php/health-resource-centre. *Mgr, Libr Serv,* Wendy Wareham; Staff 4 (Non-MLS 4)
Founded 1950
Library Holdings: Bk Vols 6,000; Per Subs 150
Special Collections: Consumer Health; Hospital Administrative Archives
Partic in Manitoba Health Libr Asn
Open Mon-Fri 8-4

C BRANDON UNIVERSITY*, John E Robbins Library, 270 18th St, R7A 6A9. SAN 318-8639. Circulation Tel: 204-727-9646. Interlibrary Loan Service Tel: 204-727-7316. Reference Tel: 204-727-9702. Administration Tel: 204-727-9767. Administration FAX: 204-727-8571. Web Site: www.brandonu.ca/library. *Interim Univ Librn,* Rainer Schira; E-mail: schirar@brandonu.ca; *Cat, Metadata Librn,* Stacey Lee; Tel: 204-727-7384, E-mail: lees@brandonu.ca; *Scholarly Communications Librn,* Carmen Kazakoff-Lane; Tel: 204-727-7483, E-mail: kazakoff@brandonu.ca; *Syst Librn,* Chris Hurst; Tel: 204-727-9687, E-mail: hurst@brandonu.ca; *Archivist,* Christy Henry; E-mail: henryc@brandonu.ca; Staff 23 (MLS 5, Non-MLS 18)
Founded 1899. Enrl 2,700; Fac 186; Highest Degree: Master
Library Holdings: Bk Titles 350,000; Bk Vols 450,000; Per Subs 800
Special Collections: Aboriginal Literature Coll; Great Plains Coll; Musical Theatre Coll
Subject Interests: Music, Native studies
Automation Activity & Vendor Info: (Cataloging) Ex Libris Group; (Circulation) Ex Libris Group; (Course Reserve) Ex Libris Group; (OPAC) Ex Libris Group; (Serials) Ex Libris Group
Wireless access
Partic in Canadian Research Knowledge Network; Council of Prairie & Pacific University Libraries; Manitoba Library Consortium, Inc

G MANITOBA CULTURE, HERITAGE & TOURISM*, Public Library Services Branch, B10 - 340 9th St, R7A 6C2. SAN 318-9082. Tel: 204-726-6590. FAX: 204-726-6868. E-mail: pls@gov.mb.ca. Web Site: www.gov.mb.ca/chc/pls. *Dir,* Trevor Surgenor; E-mail: trevor.surgenor@gov.mb.ca
Founded 1972
Library Holdings: Bk Vols 6,000; Per Subs 60
Automation Activity & Vendor Info: (Acquisitions) Evergreen; (Cataloging) Evergreen; (Circulation) Evergreen; (Course Reserve) Evergreen; (ILL) Evergreen; (Media Booking) Evergreen; (OPAC) Evergreen; (Serials) Evergreen
Publications: Manitoba Public Library Statistics; Newsletter
Open Mon-Fri 8:30-4:30

P WESTERN MANITOBA REGIONAL LIBRARY*, 710 Rosser Ave, Unit 1, R7A 0K9. SAN 366-354X. Tel: 204-727-6648. E-mail: info@wmrl.ca. Web Site: www.wmrl.ca. *Dir, Libr Serv,* Erika Martin; E-mail: erika@wmrl.ca; *Asst Librn,* Danielle Hubbard; Staff 2 (MLS 2)
Founded 1967. Pop 56,304; Circ 213,976
Library Holdings: Audiobooks 1,391; DVDs 2,318; Microforms 1,036; Bk Vols 129,235; Per Subs 318
Automation Activity & Vendor Info: (Cataloging) SirsiDynix; (Circulation) SirsiDynix; (OPAC) SirsiDynix
Wireless access
Partic in Manitoba Library Consortium, Inc; Manitoba Public Library Services
Open Mon & Thurs 10-9, Tues, Wed, Fri & Sat 10-6
Branches: 5
BRANDON BRANCH, 710 Rosser Ave, Unit 1, R7A 0K9, SAN 366-3566. Tel: 204-727-6648.
Pop 39,716; Circ 204,605
Library Holdings: AV Mats 4,354; Bk Vols 89,705; Per Subs 178; Talking Bks 628; Videos 1,665
Special Collections: Oral History
Open Mon & Thurs 10-9, Tues, Wed, Fri & Sat 10-6
CARBERRY-NORTH CYPRESS BRANCH, 115 Main St, Carberry, R0K 0H0. (Mail add: PO Box 382, Carberry, R0K 0H0), SAN 366-3574. Tel: 204-834-3043. E-mail: carberry@wmrl..ca. *Br Supvr,* Diane Gawel
Founded 1967. Pop 3,529
Library Holdings: AV Mats 644; Bk Vols 14,349; Per Subs 49; Talking Bks 33
Special Collections: School District Records
Open Tues-Sat 9-5
Friends of the Library Group
GLENBORO/SOUTH CYPRESS LIBRARY BRANCH, 105 Broadway St, Glenboro, R0K 0X0. (Mail add: PO Box 429, Glenboro, R0K 0X0), SAN 366-3582. Tel: 204-827-2874. E-mail: glenboro@wmrl.ca. *Br Supvr,* Kelly Tirschman; E-mail: kelly@wmrl.ca
Pop 1,477
Library Holdings: Audiobooks 15; AV Mats 329; Bks-By-Mail 50; Bks on Deafness & Sign Lang 3; CDs 11; DVDs 178; e-books 500; e-journals 3; Electronic Media & Resources 3; High Interest/Low Vocabulary Bk Vols 42; Large Print Bks 101; Microforms 48; Bk Titles 10,158; Per Subs 39
Special Collections: Local Archives
Automation Activity & Vendor Info: (Acquisitions) Horizon; (Cataloging) Horizon; (Circulation) Horizon
Open Tues-Fri 9-5
HARTNEY/CAMERON BRANCH, 209 Airdrie St, Hartney, R0M 0X0. (Mail add: PO Box 121, Hartney, R0M 0X0). Tel: 204-858-2102. E-mail: hartney@wmrl.ca. *Br Supvr,* Helen Weitman
Pop 942
Open Tues 3-7, Wed-Fri 1-5
Friends of the Library Group
NEEPAWA BRANCH, 280 Davidson St, Neepawa, R0J 1H0. (Mail add: PO Box 759, Neepawa, R0J 1H0), SAN 366-3604. Tel: 204-476-5648. E-mail: neepawa@wmrl.ca. *Br Supvr,* Debra Unger
Pop 4,109
Library Holdings: AV Mats 344; Bk Vols 17,892; Per Subs 49; Videos 217
Open Mon-Wed & Fri 9:30-5:30, Thurs 11-7
Friends of the Library Group

CARMAN

P BOYNE REGIONAL LIBRARY*, 15 First St SW, R0G 0J0. (Mail add: PO Box 788, R0G 0J0), SAN 318-8647. Tel: 204-745-3504. E-mail: boyneregionallibrary@outlook.com. Web Site: boyneregionallibrary.com. *Head Librn,* Sandra Yeo; *Asst Librn,* Diane Cohoe
Founded 1969. Pop 5,599
Library Holdings: Bk Vols 30,000
Wireless access
Partic in Manitoba Public Library Services
Open Tues & Thurs 8:30am-9pm, Wed & Fri 8:30-5, Sat 10-5

CHURCHILL

P CHURCHILL PUBLIC LIBRARY*, Town Centre Complex, 180 Laverendrye Ave, R0B 0E0. (Mail add: PO Box 730, R0B 0E0), SAN 320-989X. Tel: 204-675-2731. E-mail: mchlibrary@yahoo.ca. Web Site: churchill.ca/p/public-library. *Librn,* Bonnie Allen
Founded 1975. Pop 899; Circ 4,581
Library Holdings: Audiobooks 28; Bks on Deafness & Sign Lang 18; CDs 50; DVDs 1,100; Bk Titles 2,400; Per Subs 20
Special Collections: Canada North Coll
Automation Activity & Vendor Info: (Cataloging) LS 2000; (Circulation) LS 2000; (OPAC) LS 2000
Wireless access
Function: 24/7 Electronic res, 24/7 Online cat
Partic in Manitoba Library Association; Manitoba Public Library Services
Open Mon, Thurs-Sat 1-4:45, Tues & Wed 4-7:45

DAUPHIN

P PARKLAND REGIONAL LIBRARY-MANITOBA*, Headquarters, 504 Main St N, R7N 1C9. SAN 318-8663. Tel: 204-638-6410. Toll Free Tel: 866-638-6410. E-mail: prlhq@parklandlib.mb.ca. Web Site: www.parklandlib.mb.ca. *Dir,* Alison Moss; E-mail: amoss@parklandlib.mb.ca; Staff 1 (MLS 1)
Founded 1976. Pop 36,919; Circ 89,472
Library Holdings: AV Mats 5,686; Large Print Bks 6,262; Bk Vols 71,921; Per Subs 134
Automation Activity & Vendor Info: (Acquisitions) Evergreen; (Cataloging) Evergreen; (Circulation) Evergreen; (OPAC) Evergreen
Wireless access
Function: ILL available
Open Mon-Thurs 9:30-7, Fri 9:30-5:30, Sat 12-5
Branches: 23
BIRCH RIVER & DISTRICT LIBRARY, 116 Third St E, Birch River, R0L 0E0. (Mail add: PO Box 245, Birch River, R0L 0E0). Tel: 204-236-4419. E-mail: briver@mymts.net. *Head Librn,* Gwenda Wotton
Open Mon 1:30-4:30, Wed 10-12 & 1:30-4:30, Fri 1:30-4:30
BIRTLE BRANCH, 907 Main St, Birtle, R0M 0C0. (Mail add: PO Box 207, Birtle, R0M 0C0). Tel: 204-842-3418. E-mail: birtlib@outlook.com. *Head Librn,* Christopher Bentley
Open Tues & Thurs Noon-5:30, Sat 10:30-2:30
BOWSMAN BRANCH, 105 Patti's Way, Bowsman, R0L 2H0. (Mail add: PO Box 209, Bowsman, R0L 2H0). Tel: 204-238-4615. E-mail: bows18@mymts.net. *Head Librn,* Fern DeGroot
Open Tues 10-1 & 2-6, Thurs 2-6
DAUPHIN BRANCH, 504 Main St N, R7N 1C9. Tel: 204-638-6410. Circulation Tel: 204-638-6410, Ext 227. Toll Free Tel: 1-866-638-6410. E-mail: dauphinlibrary@parklandlib.mb.ca. *Supvr,* Glenn Irvine; E-mail: girvine@parklandlib.mb.ca; Staff 3 (Non-MLS 3)
Founded 1958
Special Collections: Local Histories
Open Mon-Thurs 9:30-7, Fri 9:30-5:30, Sat Noon-5
ERICKSON BRANCH, 20 Main St W, Erickson, R0J 0P0. (Mail add: PO Box 385, Erickson, R0J 0P0). Tel: 204-636-2325. E-mail: library@ericksonmb.ca. *Head Librn,* Mary Hutchings
Open Tues Noon-4:30, Wed 3:30-6, Thurs Noon-5:30
ERIKSDALE PUBLIC LIBRARY, Nine Main St, Eriksdale, R0C 0W0. (Mail add: PO Box 219, Eriksdale, R0C 0W0), SAN 377-8991. Tel: 204-739-2668. E-mail: epl1@mymts.net. *Head Librn,* Linda Lee
Founded 1997
Partic in Manitoba Library Association; Manitoba Public Library Services
Open Tues & Thurs 11-5, Sat 10-1
FOXWARREN BRANCH, 312 Webster Ave, Foxwarren, R0J 0R0. (Mail add: PO Box 204, Foxwarren, R0J 0R0). Tel: 204-847-2080. E-mail: foxwarrenlibrary@outlook.com. *Head Librn,* Stephanie Parkinson
Open Tues 9-12:30, Wed 9-12 & 12:30-4
GILBERT PLAINS BRANCH, 113 Main St N, Gilbert Plains, R0L 0X0. (Mail add: PO Box 700, Gilbert Plains, R0L 0X0). Tel: 204-548-2733. E-mail: gilbertplainslib@outlook.com. *Head Librn,* Sudesh Malik
Open Tues & Sat 1-5, Thurs 10-12 & 1-5
GLADSTONE BRANCH, 42 Morris Ave N, Gladstone, R0J 0T0. (Mail add: PO Box 720, Gladstone, R0J 0T0). Tel: 204-385-2641. E-mail: gladstonelibrary@outlook.com. *Head Librn,* Shelley Ray
Open Tues, Wed & Fri 11:30-4:30, Sat 10-2
GRANDVIEW BRANCH, 408 Main St, Grandview, R0L 0Y0. (Mail add: PO Box 700, Grandview, R0L 0Y0). Tel: 204-546-5257. E-mail: grandvw@mymts.net. *Head Librn,* Sherry Morran
Open Tues & Thurs 10-12 & 1-4:30, Sat 10-12 & 1-3
HAMIOTA BRANCH, 43 Maple Ave E, Hamiota, R0M 0T0. (Mail add: PO Box 609, Hamiota, R0M 0T0). Tel: 204-764-2680. E-mail: hamiotalibrary@outlook.com. *Head Librn,* Gwen Argue
Open Tues-Fri 10-1 & 2-5

LANGRUTH BRANCH, 402 Main St, Langruth, R0H 0N0. (Mail add: PO Box 154, Langruth, R0H 0N0). Tel: 204-445-2295. E-mail: langlib@mymts.net. *Head Librn,* Tristyn Evenson
Open Mon-Fri 9:30-5

MCCREARY BRANCH, 615 Burrows Rd, McCreary, R0J 1B0. (Mail add: PO Box 297, McCreary, R0J 1B0). Tel: 204-835-2629. E-mail: mccreary@parklandlib.mb.ca. *Head Librn,* Melissa Strynadka
Open Mon & Fri 12:30-4:30, Wed 2-8

MINITONAS BRANCH, 307 Main St, Minitonas, R0L 1G0. (Mail add: PO Box 496, Minitonas, R0L 1G0). Tel: 204-525-3002. E-mail: minitons@wcgwave.ca. *Head Librn,* Perla Turner
Open Tues 2-5, Wed 10-12 & 1-5, Thurs 1-6

OCHRE RIVER BRANCH, 203 Mann St, Ochre River, R0L 1K0. (Mail add: PO Box 219, Ochre River, R0L 1K0). Tel: 204-733-2293. E-mail: orlibrary@outlook.com. *Head Librn,* Jenine Norman
Open Mon & Fri 2-5, Wed 2-6

ROBLIN BRANCH, 123 First Ave NW, Roblin, R0L 1P0. (Mail add: PO Box 1342, Roblin, R0L 1P0). Tel: 204-937-2443. E-mail: library@roblin.ca. *Head Librn,* Myrtle Chase
Open Tues 10-12 & 1-5, Wed 1-6:30, Thurs & Fri 1-5, Sat 10:15-1

ROSSBURN REGIONAL LIBRARY, 53 Main St N, Rossburn, R0J 1V0. (Mail add: PO Box 87, Rossburn, R0J 1V0), SAN 321-1797. Tel: 204-859-2687. E-mail: rossburnlibrary@outlook.com. *Head Librn,* Alicia Grassinger
Founded 1975
Open Tues & Fri 10:30-5, Wed 12:30-7

ST LAZARE BRANCH, 240 Main St, St. Lazare, R0M 1Y0. (Mail add: PO Box 201, St. Lazare, R0M 1Y0). Tel: 204-683-2246. E-mail: lazarelib@mymts.net. *Head Librn,* Darlene Hayden
Open Tues & Thurs 10-12 & 1-5, Wed 1-5, Sat 10-Noon

SHOAL LAKE BRANCH, 418 The Drive, Shoal Lake, R0J 1Z0. (Mail add: PO Box 428, Shoal Lake, R0J 1Z0). Tel: 204-759-2242. E-mail: sholklib@outlook.com. *Head Librn,* Donna Charney
Open Tues & Fri 1-5, Wed 10-12 & 2-5, Thurs 1-7, Sat 10-2

SIGLUNES BRANCH, 3-61 Main St, Ashern, R0C 0E0. (Mail add: PO Box 368, Ashern, R0C 0E0). Tel: 204-768-2048. E-mail: siglun15@mymts.net. *Head Librn,* Judith McCudden
Open Mon Noon-5, Tues & Wed 11-4, Fri 1-6

STE ROSE REGIONAL LIBRARY, 580 Central Ave, Ste Rose du Lac, R0L 1S0, SAN 318-8787. Tel: 204-447-2527. E-mail: steroselibrary@hotmail.com. *Head Librn,* Jessica Labelle
Founded 1962
Open Tues-Fri 12-4:30

STRATHCLAIR BRANCH, 50 Main St, Strathclair, R0J 2C0. (Mail add: PO Box 303, Strathclair, R0J 2C0). Tel: 204-365-2539. E-mail: stratlibrary@outlook.com. *Head Librn,* Deb Summerscales
Open Mon-Sat 8:30-4

WINNIPEGOSIS BRANCH, 130 Second St, Winnipegosis, R0L 2G0. (Mail add: PO Box 10, Winnipegosis, R0L 2G0). Tel: 204-656-4876. E-mail: wpgosis@mymts.net. *Head Librn,* Deborah Falk
Open Tues 10-2, Thurs & Fri 2-6

Bookmobiles: 1

DELORAINE

P BREN DEL WIN CENTENNIAL LIBRARY*, 211 N Railway W, R0M 0M0. (Mail add: PO Box 584, R0M 0M0), SAN 321-351X. Tel: 204-747-2415. E-mail: bdwlib@gmail.com. *Librn,* Lorraine Stovin; Staff 1 (MLS 1)
Founded 1979. Pop 2,392
Library Holdings: Bk Vols 13,800; Per Subs 35
Wireless access
Partic in Manitoba Public Library Services
Open Tues-Sat 9-5

FLIN FLON

P FLIN FLON PUBLIC LIBRARY, 58 Main St, R8A 1J8. SAN 318-8671. Toll Free Tel: 833-960-3519. Toll Free FAX: 888-293-4370. E-mail: ffpl@shaw.ca. Web Site: www.flinflonpubliclibrary.ca. *Libr Adminr,* Lisa Slugoski; *Asst Admin,* Saxanee-Rae Hynes Pelletier
Founded 1958
Wireless access
Partic in Manitoba Public Library Services
Open Tues-Sat 11-5

GILLAM

P BETTE WINNER PUBLIC LIBRARY*, 235 Mattonnabee Ave, R0B 0L0. (Mail add: PO Box 400, R0B 0L0), SAN 321-1789. Tel: 204-652-2617. FAX: 204-652-2617. E-mail: library@townofgillam.com. Web Site: townofgillam.com/p/bette-winner-public-library-. *Head Librn,* Dawna Gray McDonald; *Asst Librn,* Jade Oliver
Pop 1,200
Library Holdings: Bk Titles 7,315; Bk Vols 7,458; Per Subs 8
Automation Activity & Vendor Info: (Cataloging) Insignia Software; (Circulation) Insignia Software
Wireless access
Partic in Manitoba Public Library Services
Open Mon 9:30-1, Tues-Thurs 11:30-7, Sat 11:30-3:30 (Sept-May); Tues & Wed 10-3, Sat 11:30-3:30 (June-Aug)

GIMLI

P EVERGREEN REGIONAL LIBRARY*, 65 First Ave, R0C 1B0. (Mail add: PO Box 1140, R0C 1B0), SAN 366-3639. Tel: 204-642-7912. FAX: 204-642-8319. Web Site: erlibrary.ca. *Head Librn,* Sandra Reykdal; E-mail: exec@mymts.net
Founded 1965. Pop 10,097; Circ 72,615
Library Holdings: AV Mats 1,582; Bks on Deafness & Sign Lang 51; Bk Titles 67,241; Per Subs 86; Talking Bks 779
Special Collections: French, German, Icelandic, Norwegian, Polish & Ukrainian Books
Subject Interests: Icelandic local hist, Ukrainian local hist
Wireless access
Partic in Manitoba Public Library Services
Special Services for the Blind - Braille bks; Talking bks
Open Tues, Thurs & Fri 9-5, Wed 9-8, Sat 10-5
Branches: 2

ARBORG BRANCH, 292 Main St, Arborg, R0C 0A0. (Mail add: Box 4053, Arborg, R0C 0A0), SAN 366-3663. Tel: 204-376-5388. *Br Librn,* Rachel Plett
Library Holdings: Bk Titles 17,500
Open Mon & Thurs 11-5, Tues 1-8, Wed Noon-5

RIVERTON BRANCH, 56 Laura Ave, Riverton, R0C 2R0. (Mail add: Box 310, Riverton, R0C 2R0), SAN 366-3698. Tel: 204-378-2988. E-mail: rlibrary@mymts.net. *Br Librn,* Andrea Bonkowski
Library Holdings: Bk Titles 18,000
Open Tues & Wed 11-5, Thurs 11-7, Fri 10-5

HEADINGLEY

P HEADINGLEY MUNICIPAL LIBRARY*, 49 Alboro St, R4J 1A3. SAN 377-9408. Tel: 204-888-5410. E-mail: hml@headingleylibrary.ca. Web Site: headingleylibrary.ca. *Head Librn,* Alison Au; E-mail: alisonau@shaw.ca; *Ch,* Jessica Major; *Asst Librn,* Mary Carreiro
Library Holdings: Bk Titles 10,000; Per Subs 25
Wireless access
Partic in Manitoba Libr Trustees Asn; Manitoba Library Association; Manitoba Public Library Services
Open Mon-Fri 10-6, Sat 11-3

HOLLAND

P VICTORIA MUNICIPAL LIBRARY*, 102 Stewart Ave, R0G 0X0. (Mail add: PO Box 371, R0G 0X0), SAN 378-0228. Tel: 204-526-2011. E-mail: victorialibrary@rmofvictoria.com. Web Site: victorialibrary.insigniails.com/Library/Home. *Head Librn,* Jo-Ann Verniest
Library Holdings: Bk Titles 8,000; Bk Vols 12,000
Partic in Manitoba Library Association; Manitoba Public Library Services
Open Tues-Fri 10-2 & 4-5:30, Sat 10-2

KILLARNEY

P LAKELAND REGIONAL LIBRARY*, 318 Williams Ave, R0K 1G0. SAN 366-3728. Tel: 204-523-4949. FAX: 204-523-7460. E-mail: info@lakelandregionallibrary.ca, lrl@mymts.net. Web Site: lakelandregionallibrary.ca. *Libr Adminr,* Krista Law
Founded 1959. Pop 5,600; Circ 85,500
Library Holdings: Bk Titles 29,000; Per Subs 60
Wireless access
Partic in Manitoba Public Library Services
Open Tues, Thurs & Fri 9-5, Wed 9-9, Sat 9-4
Branches: 1

CARTWRIGHT BRANCH, 483 Veteran Dr, Cartwright, R0K 0L0, SAN 366-3752. Tel: 204-529-2261. E-mail: cartwright@lakelandregionallibrary.ca. *Librn,* Gloria Kinley
Open Tues-Fri 11:30-5

LA BROQUERIE

P BIBLIOTHEQUE SAINT-JOACHIM LIBRARY*, 29 Normandeau Bay, R0A 0W0. (Mail add: PO Box 39, R0A 0W0), SAN 377-8819. Tel: 204-424-9533. FAX: 204-424-5610. E-mail: bsjl@bsjl.ca. Web Site: www.bsjl.ca. *Librn,* Position Currently Open
Pop 3,659; Circ 30,605
Library Holdings: CDs 917; DVDs 703; Bk Titles 17,913; Per Subs 60; Videos 710
Wireless access

Partic in Manitoba Libr Trustees Asn; Manitoba Library Association; Manitoba Public Library Services
Open Mon-Fri 3:30-8:30 (Fall & Winter); Mon & Tues 1-8, Wed-Fri 10-5 (Summer)

LAC DU BONNET

P LAC DU BONNET REGIONAL LIBRARY*, 84 Third St, R0E 1A0. (Mail add: PO Box 216, R0E 1A0), SAN 377-8835. Tel: 204-345-2653. FAX: 204-345-6827. E-mail: mldb@mymts.net. Web Site: www.lacdubonnetlibrary.ca. *Head Librn,* Jennifer Hudson Stewart; Staff 6 (Non-MLS 6)
Founded 1980. Pop 4,210
Library Holdings: Bk Titles 35,000; Per Subs 21
Wireless access
Function: 24/7 Electronic res, 24/7 Online cat
Partic in BC Libraries Cooperative; Manitoba Libr Trustees Asn; Manitoba Library Consortium, Inc; Manitoba Public Library Services
Open Tues & Thurs 10:30-7, Wed & Fri 10:30-5, Sat 10:30-2:30

LEAF RAPIDS

P LEAF RAPIDS PUBLIC LIBRARY*, 20 Town Ctr Complex, R0B 1W0. (Mail add: Box 190, R0B 1W0), SAN 321-3544. Tel: 204-473-2742. E-mail: leafrapidslibrary@gmail.com. *Librn,* Joan Seddon
Founded 1972. Pop 550; Circ 2,500
Library Holdings: Bk Vols 23,600
Wireless access
Function: ILL available
Partic in Manitoba Libr Trustees Asn; Manitoba Public Library Services
Open Tues-Fri 12-3

LUNDAR

P PAULINE JOHNSON LIBRARY*, 23 Main St, R0C 1Y0. (Mail add: PO Box 698, R0C 1Y0), SAN 377-9424. Tel: 204-762-5367. FAX: 204-762-5367. E-mail: mlpj@mymts.net. Web Site: www.lundar.ca/main.asp?fxoid=FMenu,8&cat_ID=19&sub_ID=286. *Librn,* Laurie Arnason
Founded 1996. Pop 1,339
Library Holdings: Bk Titles 12,500; Per Subs 14
Wireless access
Partic in Can Libr Asn; Manitoba Public Library Services
Open Tues & Thurs 10-6, Wed & Fri 10-5, Sat 10-2

LYNN LAKE

P LYNN LAKE LIBRARY, 503 Sherritt Ave, R0B 0W0. (Mail add: PO Box 1127, R0B 0W0), SAN 377-8959. Tel: 204-356-2418, Ext 5. E-mail: lynnlakelibrary@outlook.com. *Head Librn,* Jamaica Hiebert
Pop 494
Library Holdings: Bk Titles 8,700
Wireless access
Partic in Manitoba Public Library Services
Open Mon-Thurs 1-7, Fri 1-5

MACGREGOR

P NORTH NORFOLK MACGREGOR REGIONAL LIBRARY*, 35 Hampton St E, R0H 0R0. (Mail add: PO Box 760, R0H 0R0), SAN 377-9629. Tel: 204-685-2796. FAX: 204-685-2478. E-mail: maclib@mts.net. Web Site: www.nnmrl.net. *Librn,* Antoinette Blankvoort; Staff 2 (Non-MLS 2)
Founded 1992. Pop 3,900; Circ 20,000
Library Holdings: Bk Vols 12,000; Per Subs 70
Wireless access
Partic in Manitoba Libr Trustees Asn; Manitoba Library Association; Manitoba Public Library Services
Open Tues 10-8, Wed & Fri 10-5, Sat 10-3

MELITA

P SOUTHWESTERN MANITOBA REGIONAL LIBRARY*, Melita Library, 149 Main St, R0M 1L0. (Mail add: PO Box 670, R0M 1L0), SAN 318-868X. Tel: 204-522-3923. FAX: 204-522-3923. E-mail: swmblib@wcgwave.ca. Web Site: southwestern.mb.libraries.coop. *Librn,* Elissa Greenlay; *Asst Librn,* Heather Jones; Staff 2 (Non-MLS 2)
Founded 1959. Pop 3,100; Circ 21,673
Library Holdings: Bk Vols 30,000; Per Subs 53
Automation Activity & Vendor Info: (Cataloging) Insignia Software; (Circulation) Insignia Software; (ILL) Insignia Software
Wireless access
Function: ILL available
Partic in Manitoba Public Library Services
Open Tues-Fri 10-12:30 & 1:30-5
Branches: 2
NAPINKA BRANCH, 57 Souris St, Napinka, R0M 1N0. (Mail add: Box 275, R0M 1L0). E-mail: swmrlnaoinka@outlook.com. *Librn,* Jackie Leforte
Open Wed 9-12 & 7-9
PIERSON LIBRARY, 64 Railway Ave, Pierson, R0M 1S0. (Mail add: Box 39, Pierson, R0M 1S0), SAN 320-0523. Tel: 204-634-2215. E-mail: pcilibrary@outlook.com. *Dir & Librn,* Mary-Anne Minshull; *Asst Librn,* Deb Forsyth
Founded 1978
Library Holdings: Bk Vols 12,000; Per Subs 20
Open Mon, Wed & Fri 10-12 & 1-5

MINNEDOSA

P MINNEDOSA REGIONAL LIBRARY*, 45 First Ave SE, R0J 1E0. (Mail add: Box 1226, R0J 1E0), SAN 318-8698. Tel: 204-867-2585. FAX: 204-867-6140. E-mail: mmr@mymts.net. Web Site: www.minnedosaregionallibrary.com. *Head Librn,* Lisa Bilcowski; *Asst Librn,* Kim Woychyshyn
Founded 1976. Pop 3,657; Circ 46,166
Library Holdings: AV Mats 881; Large Print Bks 637; Bk Vols 19,600; Per Subs 25; Talking Bks 106
Wireless access
Function: 24/7 Electronic res, 24/7 Online cat, 24/7 wireless access, Activity rm, After school storytime, Art exhibits, Bks on CD, Children's prog, Computers for patron use, Digital talking bks, Equip loans & repairs, Family literacy, Free DVD rentals, Games, Games & aids for people with disabilities, Holiday prog, Home delivery & serv to seniorr ctr & nursing homes, Homebound delivery serv, ILL available, Instruction & testing, Internet access, Laminating, Magazines, Magnifiers for reading, Meeting rooms, Microfiche/film & reading machines, Movies, Online cat, Photocopying/Printing, Preschool reading prog, Prog for adults, Prog for children & young adult, Ref serv available, Res assist avail, Scanner, Serves people with intellectual disabilities, Story hour, Study rm, Summer & winter reading prog, Summer reading prog, Teen prog, Wheelchair accessible
Partic in Manitoba Public Library Services
Open Tues 9:30-8, Wed-Sat 9:30-5:30

MORRIS

P VALLEY REGIONAL LIBRARY*, 141 Main St S, R0G 1K0. (Mail add: PO Box 397, R0G 1K0), SAN 377-9548. Tel: 204-746-2136. FAX: 204-746-6953. E-mail: valleyregionallibrary@gmail.com. Web Site: valley.mb.libraries.coop. *Head Librn,* Diane Ali; Staff 3 (Non-MLS 3)
Founded 1993
Library Holdings: Bk Titles 16,828; Per Subs 10
Wireless access
Partic in Can Libr Asn; Manitoba Library Association; Manitoba Public Library Services
Open Tues-Thurs 11-8, Sat 11-3
Friends of the Library Group

NOTRE DAME DE LOURDES

P BIBLIOTHEQUE PERE CHAMPAGNE*, 44 Rue Rogers, R0G 1M0. SAN 377-9890. Tel: 204-248-2386. E-mail: bpcndlib@gmail.com. Web Site: bpcl.fbmb.ca. *Dir,* Gisele Comte
Founded 1988. Pop 620
Library Holdings: Per Subs 12; Videos 500
Wireless access
Function: ILL available
Partic in Manitoba Library Association; Manitoba Public Library Services
Open Tues-Fri 9:30-12:30 & 1:30-4:30
Bookmobiles: 1

OTTERBURNE

CR PROVIDENCE UNIVERSITY COLLEGE & SEMINARY, William Falk Library, (Formerly Providence University College & Seminary Library), Ten College Crescent, R0A 1G0. SAN 318-8701. Tel: 204-433-7488. FAX: 204-433-7158. Web Site: www.prov.ca/campus-life/william-falk-library. *Dir, Libr Serv,* Hannah Loewen; Staff 4 (MLS 2, Non-MLS 2)
Founded 1925. Enrl 400; Fac 50; Highest Degree: Doctorate
Library Holdings: AV Mats 3,300; Bk Vols 88,000; Per Subs 200
Special Collections: Contemporary Religious Movements, VF; Rare Books
Subject Interests: Bible, Counsel, English as a second lang, Missions, Theol
Automation Activity & Vendor Info: (Acquisitions) Ex Libris Group; (Cataloging) Ex Libris Group; (Circulation) Ex Libris Group; (Course Reserve) Ex Libris Group; (OPAC) Ex Libris Group; (Serials) Ex Libris Group
Wireless access

Partic in American Theological Library Association; Association of Christian Librarians; Manitoba Library Consortium, Inc; OCLC Online Computer Library Center, Inc
Open Mon-Fri 8:30-4:30

PINAWA

P PINAWA PUBLIC LIBRARY*, Vanier Rd, R0E 1L0. (Mail add: General Delivery, R0E 1L0), SAN 318-8736. Tel: 204-753-2496. FAX: 204-753-2770. E-mail: email@pinawapubliclibrary.com. Web Site: pinawapubliclibrary.com. *Head Librn,* Lois Bernardin; *Asst Librn,* Cheryl Michaluk; *Asst Librn,* Nikki O'Connor; *Libr Asst,* Denise Van Den Bussche
Founded 1966. Pop 1,485; Circ 17,193
Library Holdings: Audiobooks 148; Bks on Deafness & Sign Lang 5; DVDs 963; Large Print Bks 74; Bk Titles 24,960; Per Subs 57
Automation Activity & Vendor Info: (Cataloging) Insignia Software; (Circulation) Insignia Software; (OPAC) Insignia Software
Wireless access
Function: Audiobks via web, Bks on CD, Computers for patron use, E-Reserves, Electronic databases & coll, Equip loans & repairs, Free DVD rentals, Home delivery & serv to seniorr ctr & nursing homes, Homebound delivery serv, ILL available, Online cat, OverDrive digital audio bks, Photocopying/Printing, Printer for laptops & handheld devices, Scanner, Story hour, Wheelchair accessible
Partic in Manitoba Public Library Services
Open Mon 6:30pm-9pm, Tues-Fri 1:30-4:30 & 6:30-9, Sat 1-3
Friends of the Library Group

PORTAGE LA PRAIRIE

G MANITOBA AGRICULTURE, FOOD & RURAL INITIATIVES*, Food Development Centre Library, 810 Phillips St, R1N 3J9. (Mail add: PO Box 1240, R1N 3J9), SAN 322-7960. Tel: 204-239-3150. Toll Free Tel: 800-870-1044 (CAN only). FAX: 204-239-3180. E-mail: FDCinfo@gov.mb.ca. Web Site: www.manitoba.ca/fdc. *Info Officer,* Ms Shawn Kuharski; E-mail: shawn.kuharski@gov.mb.ca; Staff 1 (MLS 1)
Founded 1978
Library Holdings: AV Mats 100; Bk Titles 2,775; Bk Vols 2,900; Per Subs 80
Special Collections: HACCP Coll; Nutraceuticals & Functional Foods Coll
Subject Interests: Food chem, Food safety, Food sci, Food tech
Wireless access
Function: Doc delivery serv, For res purposes, Govt ref serv, Homebound delivery serv, ILL available, Internet access, Photocopying/Printing, Prof lending libr, Ref serv available, Res libr, Telephone ref, Wheelchair accessible
Restriction: Open to pub by appt only

M MANITOBA DEVELOPMENTAL CENTRE MEMORIAL LIBRARY*, 840 Third St NE, R1N 3C6. (Mail add: PO Box 1190, R1N 3C6), SAN 327-8670. Tel: 204-856-4230. FAX: 204-856-4221. Web Site: www.gov.mb.ca/fs/mdc. *Staff Develop Coordr,* Karen Guth; E-mail: karen.guth@gov.mb.ca; Staff 1 (Non-MLS 1)
Library Holdings: Bk Vols 2,500
Open Mon-Fri 9-4

P PORTAGE LA PRAIRIE REGIONAL LIBRARY*, 40-B Royal Rd N, R1N 1V1. SAN 318-8752. Tel: 204-857-4271. E-mail: library@portagelibrary.com. Web Site: www.portagelibrary.com. *Dir,* Jen Kendall; E-mail: director@portagelibrary.com; Staff 20 (MLS 1, Non-MLS 19)
Founded 1969. Pop 21,000; Circ 107,882
Jan 2019-Dec 2019 Income (CAN) $591,237, Provincial (CAN) $178,439, City (CAN) $264,219, County (CAN) $87,500. Mats Exp (CAN) $65,395, Books (CAN) $53,923, Per/Ser (Incl. Access Fees) (CAN) $4,008, AV Mat (CAN) $7,464
Library Holdings: AV Mats 7,621; CDs 1,510; DVDs 6,111; Bk Titles 71,407; Per Subs 81; Talking Bks 1,510
Subject Interests: Local hist, Native studies
Automation Activity & Vendor Info: (Cataloging) Evergreen; (Circulation) Evergreen; (ILL) Evergreen; (OPAC) Evergreen
Wireless access
Function: 24/7 Electronic res, 24/7 Online cat, Adult bk club, Adult literacy prog, Archival coll, Audiobks via web, Bk club(s), Bks on CD, Children's prog, Computers for patron use, Digital talking bks, E-Reserves, Electronic databases & coll, For res purposes, Home delivery & serv to seniorr ctr & nursing homes, Homebound delivery serv, ILL available, Instruction & testing, Internet access, Large print keyboards, Life-long learning prog for all ages, Literacy & newcomer serv, Magazines, Mail & tel request accepted, Meeting rooms, Microfiche/film & reading machines, Movies, Online cat, Online ref, Outreach serv, Outside serv via phone, mail, e-mail & web, OverDrive digital audio bks, Photocopying/Printing, Prog for adults, Prog for children & young adult, Ref & res, Ref serv available, Res assist avail, Scanner, Serves people with intellectual disabilities, Summer & winter reading prog, Telephone ref, Wheelchair accessible
Partic in Manitoba Public Library Services
Open Tues-Fri 10-8, Sat 9:30-5:30
Restriction: Free to mem, In-house use for visitors, Non-resident fee

RAPID CITY

P RAPID CITY REGIONAL LIBRARY*, 425 Third Ave, R0K 1W0. SAN 321-3552. Tel: 204-826-2732. E-mail: rclib@wcgwave.ca. Web Site: www.rclibrary.ca. *Librn,* Shirley Martin
Founded 1974. Pop 1,283
Library Holdings: Bk Vols 15,018; Per Subs 27
Partic in Manitoba Public Library Services
Open Mon 7pm-9pm, Tues & Thurs 2-5 & 7-9, Fri 2-5, Sat (Sept-June) 9-Noon
Friends of the Library Group

RESTON

P RESTON & DISTRICT LIBRARY, 220 Fourth St, R0M 1X0. (Mail add: PO Box 340, R0M 1X0), SAN 321-3560. Tel: 204-877-3673. E-mail: restonlb2@gmail.com. Web Site: restondistrictlibrary.ca. *Librn,* Terri Vandenberghe
Founded 1975. Pop 2,200; Circ 17,500
Library Holdings: Bk Vols 11,800; Per Subs 734
Automation Activity & Vendor Info: (Acquisitions) Auto-Graphics, Inc; (Cataloging) Auto-Graphics, Inc; (Circulation) Auto-Graphics, Inc; (Course Reserve) Auto-Graphics, Inc; (ILL) Auto-Graphics, Inc
Wireless access
Partic in Manitoba Public Library Services
Open Tues-Fri 9:30-5:30, Sat 9:30-5

RIVERS

P PRAIRIE CROCUS REGIONAL LIBRARY*, 137 Main St, R0K 1X0. (Mail add: PO Box 609, R0K 1X0), SAN 318-8779. Tel: 204-328-7613. E-mail: pclibrary@wcgwave.ca. Web Site: riverslibrary.ca. *Librn,* Sherri Dziver; *Asst Librn,* Michelle Willows
Founded 1971. Pop 2,034
Library Holdings: Bk Vols 15,000
Wireless access
Partic in Manitoba Public Library Services
Open Wed 2-8, Thurs 1-4, Fri 9:30-4:30, Sat 10-2; Wed 2-8, Thurs 1-4, Fri 9:30-4:30 (Summer)

RUSSELL

P RUSSELL & DISTRICT REGIONAL LIBRARY*, 339 Main St, R0J 1W0. (Mail add: PO Box 340, R0J 1W0), SAN 366-3906. Tel: 204-773-3127. FAX: 204-773-3127. E-mail: ruslib@mymts.net. Web Site: russell.mb.libraries.coop. *Mgr,* Christine Podollan; *Librn,* Lisa Clement
Founded 1958. Pop 3,188; Circ 27,450
Library Holdings: Bk Vols 15,000
Automation Activity & Vendor Info: (Cataloging) Evergreen; (Circulation) Evergreen; (OPAC) Evergreen
Wireless access
Function: ILL available
Partic in Manitoba Public Library Services
Open Mon 10-3, Tues, Thurs & Fri 10-5, Wed 10-8, Sat 11-3
Friends of the Library Group
Branches: 1
BINSCARTH BRANCH, 106 Russell St, Binscarth, R0J 0G0. (Mail add: PO Box 379, Binscarth, R0J 0G0), SAN 366-3930. Tel: 204-532-2447. E-mail: binslb@mymts.net. *Librn,* Rayla Buss
Library Holdings: Bk Vols 1,000
Open Tues & Thurs 12-5
Friends of the Library Group

SAINT BONIFACE

S LA SOCIETE HISTORIQUE DE SAINT-BONIFACE BIBLIOTHEQUE*, Centre du patrimoine, 340 Provencher Blvd, R2H 0G7. SAN 329-2282. Tel: 204-233-4888. FAX: 204-231-2562. E-mail: shsb@shsb.mb.ca. Web Site: shsb.mb.ca/apercu-recherche-archives. *Exec Dir,* Janet LaFrance; E-mail: jlafrance@shsb.mb.ca; *Archivist,* Julie Reid; E-mail: jreid@shsb.mb.ca
Founded 1902
Library Holdings: Bk Titles 40,000; Per Subs 40
Special Collections: Oral History
Wireless access
Open Mon-Thurs 9-1 & 2-4:30
Restriction: Non-circulating

SAINT CLAUDE

P BIBLIOTHEQUE SAINT CLAUDE LIBRARY*, 50 First St, R0G 1Z0. (Mail add: PO Box 203, R0G 1Z0), SAN 377-9912. Tel: 204-379-2524. E-mail: stclaudelibrary@gmail.com. Web Site: stclaude.mb.libraries.coop/en/explore/home. *Librn*, Jan Joyal
Pop 2,648
Library Holdings: Bk Titles 10,364; Per Subs 4
Wireless access
Function: ILL available
Partic in Manitoba Public Library Services
Open Tues & Wed 1-5, Thurs 12-6

SAINT GEORGES

P BIBLIOTHEQUE ALLARD REGIONAL LIBRARY, 104086 PTH 11, R0E 1V0. (Mail add: PO Box 157, R0E 1V0), SAN 377-9661. Tel: 204-367-8443. FAX: 204-367-1780. E-mail: info@allardlibrary.com. Web Site: allardlibrary.com. *Head Librn*, Shelley Penziwol; *Asst Librn*, Jen Kemball; Staff 6 (MLS 1, Non-MLS 5)
Founded 1983. Pop 2,600
Library Holdings: Bk Titles 20,600; Per Subs 60
Automation Activity & Vendor Info: (Cataloging) Evergreen; (Circulation) Evergreen
Wireless access
Partic in Manitoba Public Library Services
Open Tues & Fri 11-5, Wed & Thurs 11-7, Sat 11-4
Branches: 1
VICTORIA BEACH BRANCH, East Beaches Senior Scene, Lower Level, Three Atech Rd, Victoria Beach, R0E 2C0. (Mail add: PO Box 279, Victoria Beach, R0E 2C0). Tel: 204-756-2043. E-mail: victoriabeachbranch@allardlibrary.com.
Open Wed & Fri 10-2, Sat 10-3

SAINT PIERRE JOLYS

P JOLYS REGIONAL LIBRARY, 505 Herbert Ave N, R0A 1V0. (Mail add: PO Box 118, R0A 1V0), SAN 366-3965. Tel: 204-433-7729. E-mail: stplibrary@jrlibrary.mb.ca. Web Site: jrlibrary.mb.ca. *Libr Adminr*, Krista Maynard
Founded 1962. Pop 4,300
Library Holdings: AV Mats 500; Bk Titles 36,719; Per Subs 21; Talking Bks 114
Wireless access
Partic in Manitoba Public Library Services
Open Mon-Thurs 4-8, Sat 9-1

SAINTE ANNE

P BIBLIOTHEQUE STE-ANNE*, 16 rue de L'Eglise, R5H 1H8. SAN 377-9440. Tel: 204-422-9958. E-mail: library@steanne.ca. Web Site: bibliothequesteannelibrary.ca. *Libr Dir*, Veronique Ewen
Founded 1990
Library Holdings: Audiobooks 64; CDs 81; DVDs 81; Large Print Bks 287; Bk Titles 21,500; Per Subs 29; Talking Bks 50
Wireless access
Partic in Manitoba Public Library Services
Open Tues-Thurs 10-7, Fri 10-4, Sat 10-1

SAINT-JEAN-BAPTISTE

P BIBLIOTHEQUE MONTCALM LIBRARY, 113, 2e Ave, R0G 2B0. (Mail add: PO Box 345, R0G 2B0), SAN 377-9564. Tel: 204-758-3137. E-mail: bibliomontcalm@hotmail.ca. Web Site: bml.fbmb.ca/en. *Librn*, Francoise Sabourin
Founded 1995. Pop 1,600
Library Holdings: Bk Vols 20,000; Per Subs 5
Wireless access
Function: ILL available
Partic in Manitoba Public Library Services
Open Tues-Thurs 4-8

SELKIRK

P GAYNOR FAMILY REGIONAL LIBRARY*, 806 Manitoba Ave, R1A 2H4. SAN 321-3587. Tel: 204-482-3522. FAX: 204-482-6166. E-mail: library@gfrl.org. Web Site: gfrl.org. *Librn*, Ken Kuryliw; E-mail: kkuryliw@gfrl.org
Founded 1976. Pop 30,000
Library Holdings: Braille Volumes 15; DVDs 4,000; Large Print Bks 2,000; Bk Titles 59,000; Bk Vols 61,000; Per Subs 150; Talking Bks 1,500
Automation Activity & Vendor Info: (Cataloging) Follett Software; (Circulation) Follett Software; (ILL) Follett Software; (OPAC) Follett Software
Wireless access
Partic in Manitoba Public Library Services
Open Tues & Wed 9:30-9, Thurs & Fri 9:30-6, Sat 11-5

SHILO

S ROYAL CANADIAN ARTILLERY MUSEUM LIBRARY*, CFB Shilo, R0K 2A0. (Mail add: PO Box 5000 Stn Main, R0K 2A0), SAN 327-5418. Tel: 204-765-3000, Ext 3076. Web Site: www.artillery.net, www.rcamuseum.com. *Colls Mgr*, Clive Prothero-Brooks; E-mail: prothero-brooks.cc@forces.gc.ca
Library Holdings: Bk Vols 15,000; Per Subs 10
Open Mon-Fri 10-4
Restriction: Closed stack

S SHILO COMMUNITY LIBRARY*, Bldg T114, Notre Dame Ave, R0K 2A0. (Mail add: PO Box 177, R0K 2K0), SAN 318-8809. Tel: 204-765-3000, Ext 3664. E-mail: shilolibrary@gmail.com. *Librn*, Patricia Wells; *Asst Librn*, Emilee De Sommer-Dennis
Library Holdings: Audiobooks 178; DVDs 300; Bk Titles 19,000
Automation Activity & Vendor Info: (Cataloging) Evergreen; (Circulation) Evergreen; (ILL) Evergreen; (OPAC) Evergreen
Wireless access
Open Mon 6pm-8:30pm, Tues & Thurs 9:30-4:30 & 6-8:30, Wed 9:30-4:30

SNOW LAKE

P SNOW LAKE COMMUNITY LIBRARY*, 101 Poplar Ave, R0B 1M0. (Mail add: PO Box 760, R0B 1M0), SAN 377-9688. Tel: 204-358-2322. FAX: 204-358-2116. E-mail: dslibrary@hotmail.com. *Head Librn*, Vivian Bennett
Library Holdings: Bk Titles 19,280
Automation Activity & Vendor Info: (Cataloging) TLC (The Library Corporation); (Circulation) TLC (The Library Corporation); (OPAC) TLC (The Library Corporation)
Wireless access
Partic in Manitoba Libr Trustees Asn; Manitoba Library Association
Open Tues & Thurs 1-4 & 6:30-8:30, Sat 1-4

SOMERSET

P BIBLIOTHEQUE SOMERSET LIBRARY*, 289 Carlton Ave, R0G 2L0. (Mail add: PO Box 279, R0G 2L0), SAN 377-9580. Tel: 204-744-2170. FAX: 204-744-2170. E-mail: bibliosomlibrary@gmail.com. *Head Librn*, Aranda Adams
Library Holdings: Bk Titles 9,500; Per Subs 30
Automation Activity & Vendor Info: (Circulation) Evergreen
Partic in Manitoba Library Association; Manitoba Public Library Services

SOURIS

P GLENWOOD & SOURIS REGIONAL LIBRARY*, 18-114 Second St S, R0K 2C0. (Mail add: PO Box 760, R0K 2C0), SAN 318-8817. Tel: 204-483-2757. FAX: 204-709-0120. E-mail: frontdesk@sourislibrary.mb.ca. Web Site: www.sourislibrary.mb.ca. *Head Librn*, Connie Bradshaw; E-mail: headlib@sourislibrary.mb.ca; *Asst Librn*, Debra Wright
Founded 1958. Pop 2,572; Circ 18,745
Library Holdings: Bk Vols 18,543; Per Subs 40
Wireless access
Partic in Manitoba Public Library Services
Open Tues 12-5 & 7-9, Wed-Sat 12-5
Friends of the Library Group

STEINBACH

P JAKE EPP LIBRARY*, 255 Elmdale Dr, R5G 1N6. SAN 318-8825. Tel: 204-326-6841. E-mail: librarian@jakeepplibrary.com. Web Site: www.jakeepplibrary.com. *Libr Dir*, Chrystie Kroeker Boggs; *Asst Dir*, Aubrey Walker
Founded 1973. Pop 10,000
Library Holdings: Bk Titles 79,000; Per Subs 125
Automation Activity & Vendor Info: (Circulation) Insignia Software
Wireless access
Partic in Manitoba Library Association; Manitoba Public Library Services
Open Mon-Fri 10-9, Sat 10-5
Friends of the Library Group

CR STEINBACH BIBLE COLLEGE LIBRARY*, 50 PTH 12 N, R5G 1T4. SAN 324-4636. Tel: 204-326-6451, Ext 238. FAX: 204-326-6908. E-mail: library@sbcollege.ca. Web Site: www.sbcollege.ca/resources/library. *Dir, Libr Serv*, Sarah Barkman; E-mail: sbarkman@sbcollege.ca; *Asst Librn*, Regina Engel; Staff 1 (MLS 1)
Founded 1937. Enrl 125; Fac 13; Highest Degree: Bachelor
Library Holdings: CDs 200; DVDs 500; Bk Titles 32,000; Bk Vols 37,500; Per Subs 97
Subject Interests: Biblical studies, Hist, Mennonites, Theol

Automation Activity & Vendor Info: (Cataloging) Follett Software; (Circulation) Follett Software; (OPAC) Follett Software
Wireless access
Function: ILL available
Open Mon-Fri 8:30-12 & 1-4:30

STONEWALL

S INSTITUTE FOR WETLAND & WATERFOWL RESEARCH LIBRARY*, Ducks Unlimited Canada Library, One Mallard Bay at Hwy 220, R0C 2Z0. (Mail add: PO Box 1160, R0C 2Z0), SAN 327-4365. Tel: 204-467-3276. Toll Free Tel: 800-665-3825. FAX: 204-467-9028. E-mail: library@ducks.ca. Web Site: iwwr.ducks.ca/our-research/library. *Research Librn,* Ian Glass; E-mail: i_glass@ducks.ca; Staff 1 (MLS 1)
Library Holdings: e-journals 250; Bk Titles 6,000; Per Subs 10
Subject Interests: Biology, Conserv, Ecology, Sustainable agr, Waterfowl, Wetlands, Wildlife biol
Automation Activity & Vendor Info: (Cataloging) Koha; (Circulation) Koha; (OPAC) Koha
Wireless access
Function: ILL available
Partic in International Environment Library Consortium
Restriction: Open to pub by appt only

P SOUTH INTERLAKE REGIONAL LIBRARY*, Stonewall Public Library-Headquarters, 419 Main St, R0C 2Z0. SAN 318-8833. Tel: 204-467-8415. FAX: 204-467-9809. E-mail: stonewall@sirlibrary.com. Web Site: sirlibrary.com. *Libr Dir,* Clint Curle; Tel: 204-467-5767, E-mail: ccurle@sirlibrary.com; *Br Librn,* Joan Ransom
Founded 1967. Circ 178,211
Library Holdings: Bk Titles 55,000; Per Subs 20
Subject Interests: Agr, Econ, Natural sci
Wireless access
Partic in Manitoba Public Library Services
Open Tues 10-7:30, Wed 10-5:30, Thurs 2-7:30, Fri & Sat 10-4 (Fall & Spring); Tues & Wed 10-5:30, Thurs 2-7, Fri & Sat 10-4 (Summer)
Friends of the Library Group
Branches: 1
TEULON BRANCH, 19 Beach Rd E, Teulon, R0C 3B0. (Mail add: PO Box 68, Teulon, R0C 3B0), SAN 372-4980. Tel: 204-886-3648. FAX: 204-886-3661. E-mail: teulon@sirlibrary.com. *Br Librn,* June Makowski
Library Holdings: Bk Vols 8,000
Open Tues 10-8, Wed & Fri 10-5:30, Thurs Noon-8, Sat 10-1
Friends of the Library Group
Bookmobiles: 1. Librn, Pam Palcat

SWAN RIVER

P NORTH-WEST REGIONAL LIBRARY*, 610 First St N, R0L 1Z0. (Mail add: PO Box 999, R0L 1Z0), SAN 366-4023. Tel: 204-734-3880. FAX: 204-734-3880. E-mail: email@swanriverlibrary.com. Web Site: www.swanriverlibrary.ca. *Head Librn,* Kathy Sterma
Founded 1966. Pop 7,291; Circ 84,235
Library Holdings: Bk Titles 21,810; Per Subs 25
Wireless access
Partic in Manitoba Public Library Services
Special Services for the Blind - Bks available with recordings; Bks on cassette; Bks on CD; Cassettes; Daisy reader; Large print bks; Visunet prog (Canada)
Open Mon-Fri 10-5, Sat 10:30-5
Branches: 1
BENITO BRANCH, 140 Main St, Benito, R0L 0C0. (Mail add: PO Box 220, Benito, R0L 0C0), SAN 366-4058. Tel: 204-539-2446. FAX: 204-539-2446. E-mail: email@benitolibrary.ca. Web Site: benitolibrary.ca. *Librn,* Sandra Jankovic
Founded 1965
Library Holdings: Bk Titles 9,355; Per Subs 19; Talking Bks 29
Open Tues 1-5, Thurs 1-7, Fri 12-5, Sat 10-5
Friends of the Library Group

THE PAS

P THE PAS REGIONAL LIBRARY*, 53 Edwards Ave, R9A 1R2. (Mail add: PO Box 4100, R9A 1R2), SAN 318-871X. Tel: 204-623-2023. FAX: 204-623-4594. E-mail: library@mymts.net. Web Site: www.thepasregionallibrary.com. *Adminr,* Lauren Wadelius
Founded 1961. Pop 8,315
Library Holdings: Bk Vols 33,500; Per Subs 90
Special Collections: Northern Canada History Coll
Automation Activity & Vendor Info: (Acquisitions) L4U Library Software; (Cataloging) L4U Library Software; (Circulation) L4U Library Software; (Course Reserve) L4U Library Software; (ILL) L4U Library Software; (Media Booking) L4U Library Software; (OPAC) L4U Library Software; (Serials) L4U Library Software
Wireless access
Function: Adult bk club, BA reader (adult literacy), Digital talking bks, Homebound delivery serv, ILL available, Orientations, Photocopying/Printing, Prog for children & young adult, Ref serv available, Spoken cassettes & CDs, Spoken cassettes & DVDs, Summer reading prog, VHS videos, Wheelchair accessible
Partic in Manitoba Public Library Services
Open Mon-Fri 10-6
Restriction: Circ to mem only, Non-resident fee

C UNIVERSITY COLLEGE OF THE NORTH LIBRARIES*, Oscar Lathlin Research Library, 436 Seventh St E, R9A 1M7. (Mail add: PO Box 3000, R9A 1M7), SAN 320-7838. Tel: 204-627-8561. FAX: 204-623-4597. E-mail: library@ucn.ca. Web Site: www.ucn.ca/sites/library. *Librn/Coll Develop/Info Literacy,* Heather Smith; E-mail: hsmith@ucn.ca; Staff 8 (MLS 3, Non-MLS 5)
Founded 1968. Enrl 900; Highest Degree: Bachelor
Library Holdings: Bk Vols 36,000; Per Subs 120
Special Collections: Aboriginal Languages & Research Coll
Subject Interests: Bus admin, Dentistry, Med nursing, Trades
Automation Activity & Vendor Info: (Cataloging) SirsiDynix-WorkFlows; (OPAC) SirsiDynix-WorkFlows
Wireless access
Function: Art exhibits, Audio & video playback equip for onsite use, CD-ROM, Computers for patron use, Electronic databases & coll, Equip loans & repairs, Govt ref serv, ILL available, Music CDs, Online cat, Orientations, Photocopying/Printing, Res libr, Scanner, VHS videos, Workshops
Partic in Manitoba Library Consortium, Inc
Open Mon-Thurs 8am-10pm, Fri 8-5, Sat 12-5, Sun 5-10
Restriction: Circ privileges for students & alumni only
Departmental Libraries:
NORWAY HOUSE PUBLIC LIBRARY, Box 880, Norway House, R0B 1B0, SAN 377-9645. Tel: 204-359-6296, Ext 2446. FAX: 204-359-6262. *Librn,* Fiona Godwin; E-mail: fgodwin@ucn.ca
Library Holdings: DVDs 280; Large Print Bks 40; Bk Titles 10,000; Talking Bks 35; Videos 50
Function: ILL available
Partic in Manitoba Public Library Services
Open Mon 8:30-12 & 1-4:30, Tues-Fri 8:30-8, Sat 9-12 & 1-5
WELLINGTON & MADELEINE SPENCE MEMORIAL LIBRARY, 55 UCN Dr, Thompson, R8N 1L7, SAN 377-8851. Tel: 204-677-6408. E-mail: libraryth@ucn.ca. *Library Contact,* Position Currently Open
Library Holdings: Bk Vols 3,000; Per Subs 10
Partic in Manitoba Library Association
Open Mon-Thurs 8:30am-10pm, Fri 8:30-5, Sat 1-5, Sun 5pm-10pm

S SAM WALLER MUSEUM LIBRARY, 306 Fischer Ave, R9A 1K4. (Mail add: PO Box 185, R9A 1K4), SAN 377-9726. Tel: 204-623-3802. FAX: 204-623-5506. E-mail: samwallermuseum@mts.net. Web Site: www.samwallermuseum.ca. *Dir,* Jaxon Baker; *Archivist, Curator,* Position Currently Open
Library Holdings: Bk Titles 800; Per Subs 3
Function: Ref serv available
Partic in Asn of Manitoba Museums; Can Museums Asn; Manitoba Hist Soc
Open Mon-Fri 1-5; Mon-Sat 10-5, Sun 12-5 (June-Aug)
Restriction: Not a lending libr
Friends of the Library Group

THOMPSON

P THOMPSON PUBLIC LIBRARY*, 81 Thompson Dr N, R8N 0C3. SAN 318-8841. Tel: 204-677-3717. FAX: 204-778-5844. E-mail: info@thompsonlibrary.com. Web Site: www.thompsonlibrary.com. *Adminr,* Cheryl Davies
Founded 1967. Pop 15,000
Library Holdings: Audiobooks 764; CDs 1,047; DVDs 2,123; e-books 10,015; Large Print Bks 660; Bk Vols 40,237; Per Subs 50
Special Collections: Inter-Universities (North); Native People (The North)
Subject Interests: Native issues, Northern issues
Automation Activity & Vendor Info: (Acquisitions) Insignia Software; (Cataloging) Insignia Software; (Circulation) Insignia Software; (Course Reserve) Insignia Software; (ILL) Insignia Software; (Media Booking) Insignia Software; (OPAC) Insignia Software; (Serials) Insignia Software
Wireless access
Function: Art exhibits, Audiobks via web, Bks on CD, Children's prog, Computers for patron use, Electronic databases & coll, Free DVD rentals, ILL available, Music CDs, OverDrive digital audio bks, Photocopying/Printing, Senior outreach, Spoken cassettes & CDs, Spoken cassettes & DVDs, Story hour, Summer reading prog
Partic in Manitoba Public Library Services
Open Tues & Wed 11-7, Thurs & Fri 11-5, Sat 10-6
Restriction: Circ to mem only, Open to pub for ref & circ; with some limitations
Friends of the Library Group

C UNIVERSITY OF MANITOBA FACULTY OF SOCIAL WORK*, Ann Charter Resource Centre, Three Station Rd, R8N 0N3. Tel: 204-677-1462. FAX: 204-677-4110. Web Site: umanitoba.ca/faculties/social_work/staff/forms/624.html. *Libr Asst,* Eleanor Welton; E-mail: eleanor.welton@umanitoba.ca
Library Holdings: DVDs 500; Bk Titles 2,800; Per Subs 10
Wireless access
Function: ILL available
Open Mon-Fri 8:30-4:30

VIRDEN

P BORDER REGIONAL LIBRARY*, Virden Branch, 312 Seventh Ave, R0M 2C0. (Mail add: PO Box 970, R0M 2C0). Tel: 204-748-3862. FAX: 204-748-3862. E-mail: borderregionallibrary@rfnow.com. Web Site: www.borderregionallibrary.ca. *Coordr,* Mary Anne Lamy; E-mail: brlcoord@rfnow.com; Staff 3 (Non-MLS 3)
Founded 1959. Pop 5,346; Circ 32,500
Library Holdings: Bk Titles 35,000; Per Subs 42
Special Collections: Canadian and Provincial
Subject Interests: Local hist
Wireless access
Function: ILL available, Prog for adults, Prog for children & young adult, Spoken cassettes & CDs, Summer reading prog, VHS videos, Wheelchair accessible
Partic in Manitoba Public Library Services
Special Services for the Deaf - Assistive tech
Special Services for the Blind - Assistive/Adapted tech devices, equip & products; Talking bks
Open Tues, Wed, Fri & Sat 10-5:30, Thurs 10-8
Branches: 2
ELKHORN BRANCH, 110 Richhill Ave E, Elkhorn, R0M 0N0. (Mail add: PO Box 370, Elkhorn, R0M 0N0), SAN 366-4112. Tel: 204-845-2292. E-mail: Elkhornbrl@rfnow.com.
Founded 1959. Pop 1,000; Circ 12,000
Library Holdings: Bk Vols 10,979
Special Collections: Elkhorn Mercury Newspaper Coll
Function: Art exhibits, Home delivery & serv to seniorr ctr & nursing homes, ILL available, Prog for children & young adult, Summer reading prog, VHS videos, Wheelchair accessible
Open Tues, Thurs & Sat 9-5, Wed 6-9
MCAULEY BRANCH, 207 Qu'Appelle St, McAuley, R0M 1H0. (Mail add: PO Box 234, McAuley, R0M 1H0), SAN 370-5781. Tel: 204-722-2221.
Founded 1990. Pop 325; Circ 5,000
Library Holdings: Bk Vols 5,135
Function: Art exhibits, ILL available, Summer reading prog, VHS videos
Open Tues & Fri 9-12 & 1-5

WINKLER

P SOUTH CENTRAL REGIONAL LIBRARY*, 160 Main St, R6W 4B4. SAN 366-3817. Tel: 204-325-5864. E-mail: scrlibraryoffice@gmail.com. Web Site: scrl.mb.libraries.coop. *Dir, Libr Serv,* Cathy Ching; E-mail: scrldirector@gmail.com; Staff 5 (Non-MLS 5)
Founded 1965. Pop 32,481
Library Holdings: Bk Vols 80,000; Per Subs 102
Wireless access
Partic in Manitoba Public Library Services
Open Tues & Thurs 10-8:30, Wed & Fri 10-5:30, Sat 10-4
Branches: 5
ALTONA BRANCH, 113-125 Centre Ave, Altona, R0G 0B0, SAN 370-4599. Tel: 204-324-1503. E-mail: scrlalibrarian@gmail.com. *Br Librn,* Rachael Friesen
Open Tues & Thurs 10-8:30, Wed & Fri 10-5:30, Sat 10-4
MANITOU BRANCH, 418 Main St, Manitou, R0G 1G0. (Mail add: PO Box 432, Manitou, R0G 1G0), SAN 378-0244. Tel: 204-242-3134. FAX: 204-242-3184. E-mail: manitoulib@gmail.com. *Br Supvr,* Angela Lovell; Staff 2 (Non-MLS 2)
Pop 2,500
Library Holdings: AV Mats 463; DVDs 16; Large Print Bks 50; Music Scores 500; Bk Titles 10,833; Per Subs 10; Talking Bks 69; Videos 378
Special Collections: Nellie McClung Coll
Open Tues 10-5:30, Wed 10-8:30, Thurs 1-8:30, Fri 10-12:30 & 1-5:30, Sat 10-12:30 & 1-4
MIAMI BRANCH, 530 Norton Ave, Miami, R0G 1H0. (Mail add: PO Box 431, Miami, R0G 1H0). Tel: 204-435-2032. E-mail: miamilibrary5@gmail.com. *Br Assoc,* Cherie Debruiel
Open Tues & Wed 10-12 & 1-5, Thurs 2-6 & 6:30-8:30, Fri 1:30-4:30, Sat 10-12:30 & 1-4
Friends of the Library Group
MORDEN BRANCH, 514 Stephen St, Morden, R6M 1T7, SAN 373-7020. Tel: 204-822-4092. E-mail: mordenlib@gmail.com. *Br Librn,* Kim Van Vliet
Open Tues & Thurs 10-8:30, Wed & Fri 10-5:30, Sat 10-4
WINKLER BRANCH, 160 Main St, R6W 0M3, SAN 366-3841. Tel: 204-325-7174. E-mail: winklerlib@gmail.com. *Br Librn,* Randall Klassen
Open Tues & Thurs 10-8:30, Wed & Fri 10-5:30, Sat 10-4

WINNIPEG

L AIKINS LAW*, 360 Main St, 30th Flr, R3C 4G1. SAN 323-6056. Tel: 204-957-0050. FAX: 204-957-0840. Web Site: www.aikins.com. *Libr Mgr,* Amanda Linden; E-mail: alinden@mltaikins.com
Founded 1973
Library Holdings: Bk Titles 4,000; Bk Vols 10,000; Per Subs 400
Automation Activity & Vendor Info: (Acquisitions) Inmagic, Inc.; (Cataloging) Inmagic, Inc.; (ILL) Inmagic, Inc.; (OPAC) Inmagic, Inc.; (Serials) Inmagic, Inc.
Restriction: Staff use only

CR BOOTH UNIVERSITY COLLEGE*, John Fairbank Memorial Library, 300-290 Vaughan St, R3B 2L9. SAN 324-2900. Tel: 204-924-4858. Toll Free Tel: 877-924-6684. FAX: 204-924-4873. E-mail: library@boothuc.ca. Web Site: www.boothuc.ca/library. *Dir, Libr Serv,* Meagan Morash; Tel: 204-924-4857, E-mail: Meagan_Morash@BoothUC.ca; Staff 3 (MLS 1, Non-MLS 2)
Founded 1982. Enrl 254; Fac 11; Highest Degree: Bachelor
Library Holdings: AV Mats 1,500; e-books 118,000; Bk Titles 45,000; Bk Vols 55,000; Per Subs 150
Special Collections: Salvation Army Publications
Subject Interests: Ethics, Soc work, Theol
Automation Activity & Vendor Info: (Cataloging) Innovative Interfaces, Inc; (Circulation) Innovative Interfaces, Inc; (Course Reserve) Innovative Interfaces, Inc; (OPAC) Innovative Interfaces, Inc
Wireless access
Function: Archival coll, Audio & video playback equip for onsite use, Computers for patron use, Distance learning, Doc delivery serv, Electronic databases & coll, For res purposes, ILL available, Mail & tel request accepted, Microfiche/film & reading machines, Online cat, Online ref, Photocopying/Printing, Ref serv available, Telephone ref
Partic in Can Libr Asn; Manitoba Library Association; Manitoba Library Consortium, Inc
Open Mon-Thurs 8am-9pm, Fri 8-6, Sat 10-5 (Winter & Spring); Mon-Fri 8-4 (Summer)

SR CANADIAN CONFERENCE OF MENNONITE BRETHREN CHURCHES*, John A Toews Library, 1310 Taylor Ave, R3M 3Z6. SAN R3M 3Z6. Tel: 204-669-6575, Ext 695. Toll Free Tel: 888-669-6575. FAX: 204-654-1865. E-mail: cmbs@mbchurches.ca. Web Site: cmbs.mennonitebrethren.ca, www.mennonitebrethren.ca. *Dir,* Jon Isaak; E-mail: jon.isaak@mbchurches.ca
Founded 1979
Library Holdings: Bk Titles 3,000; Bk Vols 4,000; Per Subs 300
Special Collections: Mennonite (JA Toews Coll). Oral History
Automation Activity & Vendor Info: (Acquisitions) Innovative Interfaces, Inc - Millennium; (Cataloging) Innovative Interfaces, Inc - Millennium; (Circulation) Innovative Interfaces, Inc - Millennium; (ILL) Innovative Interfaces, Inc - Millennium; (Media Booking) Innovative Interfaces, Inc - Millennium; (OPAC) Innovative Interfaces, Inc - Millennium; (Serials) Innovative Interfaces, Inc - Millennium
Wireless access
Open Mon-Fri 8:30-4:30

G CANADIAN GRAIN COMMISSION LIBRARY*, 801-303 Main St, R3C 3G8. SAN 366-4171. Tel: 431-337-6271. E-mail: library-bibliotheque@grainscanada.gc.ca. Web Site: www.grainscanada.gc.ca. *Sr Libr Tech,* Tomaz Booth; Staff 2 (MLS 1, Non-MLS 1)
Founded 1913
Library Holdings: AV Mats 25; e-books 1,200; e-journals 175; Bk Titles 7,500; Per Subs 250
Special Collections: Canadian International Grains Institute - Bound Series of Lectures
Subject Interests: Cereal & oilseed chem, Grain handling
Automation Activity & Vendor Info: (Cataloging) EOS International; (Circulation) EOS International; (OPAC) EOS International; (Serials) EOS International
Function: Res libr
Partic in Can Agr Libr Network; Council of Federal Libraries Consortium
Restriction: Staff use only

CR CANADIAN MENNONITE UNIVERSITY LIBRARY*, 2299 Grant Ave, R3P 2N2. (Mail add: 500 Shaftesbury Blvd, R3P 2N2), SAN 320-7862. Tel: 204-487-3300. Interlibrary Loan Service Tel: 204-487-3300, Ext 394.

Reference Tel: 204-594-0514. FAX: 204-837-7415. E-mail: library@cmu.ca. Web Site: www.cmu.ca/library. *Libr Dir,* Vic Froese, PhD; Tel: 204-487-3300, Ext 393, E-mail: vfroese@cmu.ca; *Assoc Librn,* Paul Friesen; Tel: 204-487-3300, Ext 319, E-mail: pfriesen@cmu.ca. Subject Specialists: *Theol,* Vic Froese, PhD; *Mennonite,* Paul Friesen; Staff 5 (MLS 2, Non-MLS 3)
Founded 2000. Enrl 540; Fac 42; Highest Degree: Master
Library Holdings: AV Mats 3,884; Bks on Deafness & Sign Lang 37; CDs 2,272; DVDs 343; e-books 135,000; e-journals 210,000; Music Scores 709; Bk Titles 122,373; Bk Vols 163,512; Per Subs 240; Videos 261
Special Collections: Mennonite Historical Library
Subject Interests: Arts, Mennonitica, Music, Relig studies
Automation Activity & Vendor Info: (Acquisitions) Innovative Interfaces, Inc; (Cataloging) Innovative Interfaces, Inc; (Circulation) Innovative Interfaces, Inc; (Course Reserve) Innovative Interfaces, Inc; (Media Booking) Innovative Interfaces, Inc - Millennium; (OPAC) Innovative Interfaces, Inc; (Serials) Innovative Interfaces, Inc
Wireless access
Function: Audio & video playback equip for onsite use, Computers for patron use, Doc delivery serv, Electronic databases & coll, Free DVD rentals, ILL available, Music CDs, Online cat, Online ref, Photocopying/Printing, Ref & res, Ref serv available, Telephone ref, VHS videos, Wheelchair accessible
Partic in Council of Prairie & Pacific University Libraries; Manitoba Library Consortium, Inc
Open Mon-Thurs 8am-9pm, Fri 8-5, Sat 11-5 (Fall & Winter); Mon-Fri 8:30-5 (Summer)

M CANCERCARE MANITOBA, Patient & Family Resource Center, 675 McDermot Ave, Rm 1016, R3E 0V9. SAN 320-7900. Tel: 204-787-4357. FAX: 204-787-4761. E-mail: library@cancercare.mb.ca, patientlibrary@cancercare.mb.ca. Web Site: www.cancercare.mb.ca/Patient-Family/support-services/resource-centre/index.html. *Coordr,* Kathleen Helgason; Tel: 204-787-4279, E-mail: khelgason2@cancercare.mb.ca
Founded 1962
Library Holdings: Bk Titles 500; Per Subs 100
Automation Activity & Vendor Info: (Cataloging) Surpass; (OPAC) Surpass
Publications: Annual Report
Restriction: Staff use only

CR CENTRE FOR CHRISTIAN STUDIES LIBRARY*, Woodsworth House, 60 Maryland St, R3G 1K7. SAN 326-4238. Tel: 204-783-4490, Ext 26. FAX: 204-786-3012. E-mail: info@ccsonline.ca. Web Site: ccsonline.ca/resources/library. *Library Contact,* Scott Douglas; E-mail: sdouglas@ccsonline.ca
Founded 1892. Enrl 50
Library Holdings: Bk Vols 4,000; Per Subs 8
Special Collections: Diaconal History Coll
Automation Activity & Vendor Info: (Cataloging) Innovative Interfaces, Inc; (Circulation) Innovative Interfaces, Inc; (OPAC) Innovative Interfaces, Inc
Wireless access
Function: Distance learning, Doc delivery serv, ILL available, Mail loans to mem, Online cat, Outside serv via phone, mail, e-mail & web
Restriction: In-house use for visitors, Open to fac, students & qualified researchers, Open to students, fac & staff

L FILLMORE RILEY LLP*, Law Library, 1700-360 Main St, R3C 3Z3. SAN 328-0616. Tel: 204-956-2970. FAX: 204-957-0516. E-mail: frinfo@fillmoreriley.com. Web Site: www.fillmoreriley.com. *Law Librn,* Allan Chan; Tel: 204-957-8389, E-mail: achan@fillmoreriley.com; Staff 2 (MLS 1, Non-MLS 1)
Library Holdings: Bk Titles 6,000; Bk Vols 10,000; Per Subs 30
Wireless access
Restriction: Staff use only

S GRAND LODGE OF MANITOBA*, Masonic Resource Centre, 420 Corydon Ave, R3L 0N8. SAN 318-9066. Tel: 204-453-7410. Toll Free Tel: 800-665-2712. FAX: 204-284-3527. E-mail: mrc@grandlodge.mb.ca. Web Site: www.glmb.ca/masonic-resource-centre. *Librn,* Brother Brian Rountree; Staff 2 (MLS 1, Non-MLS 1)
Founded 1878
Library Holdings: AV Mats 150; Electronic Media & Resources 15; Music Scores 6; Bk Vols 2,700; Spec Interest Per Sub 7; Videos 50
Subject Interests: Freemasonry
Automation Activity & Vendor Info: (Acquisitions) LibraryWorld, Inc; (Cataloging) LibraryWorld, Inc; (Circulation) LibraryWorld, Inc; (OPAC) LibraryWorld, Inc
Wireless access
Open Tues & Wed 10-1
Restriction: Circ to mem only

S HERITAGE WINNIPEG CORP LIBRARY, 63 Albert St, Ste 509, R3B 1G4. SAN 374-8316. Tel: 204-942-2663. FAX: 204-942-2094. E-mail: info@heritagewinnipeg.com. Web Site: heritagewinnipeg.com. *Exec Dir,* Cindy Tugwell; E-mail: cindy@heritagewinnipeg.com
Library Holdings: Bk Vols 1,200; Per Subs 3
Wireless access
Restriction: Open by appt only

S MANITOBA ASSOCIATION OF PLAYWRIGHTS*, Sydney & Margaret Jarvis Playwrights Resource Centre, Artspace Bldg, 6th Flr, Rm 602, 100 Arthur St, R3B 1H3. SAN 327-487X. Tel: 204-942-8941. E-mail: mbplay@mymts.net, mbplayoutreach@gmail.com. Web Site: mbplays.ca/services/sidney-margaret-jarvis-playwrights-resource-centre. *Exec Dir,* Brian Drader
Library Holdings: Bk Vols 4,000
Special Collections: Manitoba Plays; Theater Archives
Restriction: Open by appt only

S MANITOBA CRAFTS MUSEUM & LIBRARY*, 1-329 Cumberland Ave, R3B 1T2. SAN 327-4349. Tel: 204-615-3951. FAX: 204-615-3951. E-mail: mcml@c2centreforcraft.ca. Web Site: c2centreforcraft.ca/about-mcml. *Curator,* Andrea Reichert
Founded 1932
Library Holdings: Bk Titles 3,500
Special Collections: Rare Books
Open Wed-Sat 12-4

G MANITOBA DEPARTMENT OF SPORT, CULTURE & HERITAGE*, Legislative Library, 200 Vaughan St, Rm 100, R3C 1T5. SAN 318-8965. Tel: 204-945-4330. Toll Free Tel: 800-282-8069, Ext 4330 (Manitoba only). E-mail: legislative_library@gov.mb.ca. Web Site: www.gov.mb.ca/chc/leg-lib. *Head, Ref Serv,* Stuart Hay; Tel: 204-945-8244
Founded 1870
Library Holdings: Bk Titles 300,000
Special Collections: Manitoba Government Publications; Manitoba Newspapers Coll; Provincial Legal Deposit Coll; Rare Books Coll, Canadian and Provincial
Subject Interests: Law & legislation, Political & soc sci, Politics & govt, Pub policy & admin, Western Can hist
Automation Activity & Vendor Info: (Acquisitions) Evergreen; (Cataloging) Evergreen; (Circulation) Evergreen; (ILL) Evergreen; (OPAC) Evergreen
Wireless access
Function: Archival coll, Art exhibits, Computers for patron use, E-Reserves, Electronic databases & coll, Govt ref serv, ILL available, Mail & tel request accepted, Microfiche/film & reading machines, Online cat, Photocopying/Printing, Ref serv available, Wheelchair accessible
Publications: Manitoba Government Publications Checklist (Monthly); Selected New Titles (Monthly)
Partic in Asn of Parliamentary Libraries in Canada; Manitoba Library Consortium, Inc
Open Mon-Fri 10-5
Restriction: Closed stack, Free to mem, In-house use for visitors, Non-circulating of rare bks, Non-circulating to the pub, Photo ID required for access, Pub ref by request, Pub use on premises
Branches:
LEGISLATIVE READING ROOM, 450 Broadway Ave, Rm 260, R3C 0V8, SAN 377-3078. Tel: 204-945-4243. E-mail: reading@leg.gov.mb.ca. *Mem Serv Librn,* Mirabelle Boily-Bernal
Library Holdings: Bk Titles 57,500
Automation Activity & Vendor Info: (Acquisitions) Evergreen; (Cataloging) Evergreen; (Circulation) Evergreen; (Course Reserve) Evergreen; (ILL) Evergreen; (Media Booking) Evergreen; (OPAC) Evergreen; (Serials) Evergreen
Open Mon-Fri 8:30-4:30

S MANITOBA GENEALOGICAL SOCIETY INC LIBRARY*, 1045 St James St, Unit E, R3H 1B1. SAN 328-1728. Tel: 204-783-9139. E-mail: contact@mbgenealogy.com, library@mbgenealogy.com. Web Site: www.mbgenealogy.com/what-we-offer/mgs-library-resource-centre. *Chair,* Mary Bole
Founded 1976
Library Holdings: AV Mats 600; Bk Titles 10,000; Spec Interest Per Sub 120
Special Collections: Manitoba Records, incl Cemetery Transcriptions, Church Records, Newspaper Indexes & Local History Books
Subject Interests: Genealogy, Local family hist
Wireless access

S MANITOBA HYDRO LIBRARY, 360 Portage Ave, 2nd Flr, R3C 0G8. SAN 318-9031. Tel: 204-360-4708. E-mail: docdel@hydro.mb.ca. Web Site: www.hydro.mb.ca. *Libr Tech,* Nancy Voth; Staff 2 (Non-MLS 2)
Subject Interests: Energy, Engr, Manitoba hydro hist

Automation Activity & Vendor Info: (Acquisitions) SydneyPlus; (Cataloging) SydneyPlus; (Circulation) SydneyPlus; (Course Reserve) SydneyPlus; (ILL) SydneyPlus; (Media Booking) SydneyPlus; (OPAC) SydneyPlus; (Serials) SydneyPlus

S MANITOBA INDIGENOUS CULTURE-EDUCATIONAL CENTER*, Peoples Library, 119 Sutherland Ave, R2W 3C9. SAN 327-4381. Tel: 204-942-0228. FAX: 204-947-6564. E-mail: library@micec.com. Web Site: www.micec.com/peoples_library. *Libr Mgr,* Anna Parenteau; *Libr Tech,* Noah Malazdrewicz
Library Holdings: Bk Vols 14,000; Per Subs 250
Wireless access
Open Mon-Fri 8:30-4:30

S THE MANITOBA MUSEUM*, Library & Archives, 190 Rupert Ave, R3B 0N2. SAN 318-904X. Tel: 204-988-0692. FAX: 204-942-3679. E-mail: library@manitobamuseum.ca. Web Site: manitobamuseum.ca/collections-research/collections/information-services. *Library Contact,* Nancy Anderson; Staff 4.1 (MLS 4, Non-MLS 0.1)
Founded 1967
Library Holdings: Bk Titles 22,000; Bk Vols 30,000; Per Subs 100
Special Collections: Oral History
Subject Interests: Applied arts, Astronomy, Fundraising, Human hist, Museology, Natural hist
Wireless access
Restriction: Open by appt only, Open to pub for ref only

S MANITOBA SCHOOL FOR THE DEAF MULTIMEDIA CENTER*, 242 Stradford St, R2Y 2C9. SAN 327-4322. Tel: 204-945-8392. FAX: 204-945-1767. Web Site: www.msd.ca. *Library Contact,* Liana Price; Tel: 204-995-5943, E-mail: lprice@msd.ca
Library Holdings: Bk Vols 10,000
Automation Activity & Vendor Info: (Acquisitions) Koha; (Cataloging) Koha; (Circulation) Koha; (Course Reserve) Koha; (ILL) Koha; (Media Booking) Koha; (OPAC) Koha; (Serials) Koha
Open Mon-Fri 8:30-4:30
Restriction: Open to students, fac & staff

S MFL OCCUPATIONAL HEALTH CENTRE*, Resource Centre, 167 Sherbrook St, R3C 2B7. SAN 328-0632. Tel: 204-949-0811. FAX: 204-956-0848. E-mail: info@ohcmb.ca. Web Site: ohcmb.ca/community-resources/resource-centre. *Coordr,* Tiffany Pau; Tel: 204-926-7909, E-mail: tiffany.pau@ohcmb.ca
Library Holdings: Bk Titles 1,000; Per Subs 20
Special Collections: NIOSH
Wireless access
Open Mon-Fri 9-5
Restriction: Circulates for staff only, Non-circulating to the pub

L MYERS, WEINBERG LLP*, Law Library, 724-240 Graham Ave, R3C 0J7. SAN 324-1912. Tel: 204-942-0501. FAX: 204-956-0625.
Library Holdings: Bk Titles 520; Bk Vols 600; Per Subs 40
Subject Interests: Admin law, Civil litigation, Crim law, Family law, Labor law
Wireless access
Open Mon-Fri 8:30-5

L PITBLADO LAW LIBRARY*, 2500-360 Main St, R3C 4H6. SAN 370-7202. Tel: 204-956-0560, Ext 373. FAX: 204-957-0227. Web Site: www.pitblado.com. *Law Librn,* Christina Lopez; E-mail: lopez@pitblado.com
Library Holdings: Bk Titles 800; Per Subs 20
Wireless access
Restriction: Not open to pub

S RAINBOW RESOURCE CENTRE LIBRARY*, 545 Broadway, R3C 0W3. SAN 326-2278. Tel: 204-474-0212. Toll Free Tel: 855-437-8523. FAX: 204-478-1160. E-mail: library@rainbowresourcecentre.org. Web Site: rainbowresourcecentre.org/programs/library. *Coordr,* Jonah Wilde
Founded 1973
Library Holdings: Bk Titles 1,750
Special Collections: Oral History
Subject Interests: Gay & lesbian, Sexuality
Wireless access
Function: Orientations, Photocopying/Printing, Prog for adults, Prog for children & young adult, Ref serv available
Open Mon-Thurs 10-5
Restriction: Mem only, Open to pub for ref & circ; with some limitations, Open to researchers by request, Pub use on premises

C RED RIVER COLLEGE POLYTECHNIC LIBRARY, 2055 Notre Dame Ave, R3H 0J9. SAN 318-9090. Tel: 204-632-2233. Toll Free Tel: 888-445-0312. FAX: 204-697-4791. E-mail: illmwrr@rrc.ca, library@rrc.mb.ca. Web Site: library.rrc.ca/home. *Actg Dir,* Shifa Hassaun; Tel: 204-632-2528; Staff 23 (MLS 3, Non-MLS 20)
Founded 1963. Enrl 10,000; Fac 800
Library Holdings: Bk Vols 69,856; Per Subs 567
Subject Interests: Applied arts, Educ, Health
Automation Activity & Vendor Info: (Acquisitions) Ex Libris Group; (Cataloging) Ex Libris Group; (Circulation) Ex Libris Group; (Course Reserve) Ex Libris Group; (Media Booking) Ex Libris Group; (OPAC) Ex Libris Group; (Serials) Ex Libris Group
Wireless access
Function: ILL available
Partic in Consortia Canada; Manitoba Library Consortium, Inc
Open Mon-Wed 7:45am-8pm, Thurs & Fri 7:45-5
Departmental Libraries:
JOHN & BONNIE BUHLER LIBRARY, Exchange District Campus, P214-160 Princess St, R3B 1K9. Tel: 204-949-8371, Reference E-mail: pscref@rrc.ca. Web Site: library.rrc.ca/usethelibrary/edc.
Library Holdings: DVDs 600; e-books 2,300; Bk Vols 7,600; Per Subs 112
Open Mon-Fri 7:45-5

S ROYAL AVIATION MUSEUM OF WESTERN CANADA LIBRARY-ARCHIVES*, 2088 Wellington Ave, R3H 1C5. SAN 328-3747. Tel: 204-786-5503. E-mail: info@royalaviationmuseum.com. Web Site: royalaviationmuseum.com/collections-archives-2. *Curator, Pres & Chief Exec Officer,* Terry Slobodian; *Colls Mgr,* Position Currently Open
Library Holdings: Bk Vols 9,000
Special Collections: Aeronautical maps; Aircraft Blueprints; TCA Engineering & Overhaul Dept Records; Technical & Overhaul Manuals
Subject Interests: Metallurgy
Wireless access
Open Mon & Wed 9-2

C UNIVERSITE DE SAINT-BONIFACE, Direction des Ressources Educatives Francaises, 0140-200 Ave de la Cathedrale, R2H 0H7. SAN 320-7846. Tel: 204-945-8594. Toll Free Tel: 800-667-2950. Reference E-mail: dref@gov.mb.ca. Web Site: dref.mb.ca. *Dir,* Carole Michalik; Tel: 204-945-1342, E-mail: carole.michalik@gov.mb.ca; *Chief Librn,* Oxana Chervonnaya; Tel: 204-945-4813, E-mail: oxana.chervonnaya@gov.mb.ca; *Acq Librn,* Marie Shewdeen; E-mail: marie.shewdeen@gov.mb.ca; *Ref Librn,* Diane Carriere; Tel: 204-945-4782, E-mail: diane.carriere@gov.mb.ca
Library Holdings: Audiobooks 300; CDs 337; DVDs 877; Bk Titles 40,000; Bk Vols 60,000; Per Subs 44
Subject Interests: Educ curricula, Interest ctr
Automation Activity & Vendor Info: (Acquisitions) BiblioMondo; (Cataloging) BiblioMondo; (Circulation) BiblioMondo; (Course Reserve) BiblioMondo; (ILL) BiblioMondo; (OPAC) BiblioMondo; (Serials) BiblioMondo
Wireless access
Publications: Newsletter
Open Mon-Fri 8:30-5, Sat 9-4

C UNIVERSITE DE SAINT-BONIFACE, Bibliothèque Alfred-Monnin, 200, ave de la Cathedrale, R2H 0H7. SAN 318-8892. Tel: 204-235-4403. Interlibrary Loan Service Tel: 204-237-1818, Ext 340. Reference Tel: 204-237-1818, Ext 208. Toll Free Tel: 888-233-5112, Ext 403. E-mail: biblio@ustboniface.ca. Web Site: ustboniface.ca/biblio. *Head Librn,* Lise Brin; E-mail: lbrin@ustboniface.ca; *Head, Coll,* Daniel Beaulieu; E-mail: dbeaulieu@ustboniface.ca; Staff 7 (MLS 3, Non-MLS 4)
Founded 1818. Enrl 1,400; Fac 155; Highest Degree: Master
Library Holdings: Bk Titles 96,000; Bk Vols 133,000; Per Subs 492
Special Collections: French & French Canadian Literature Coll
Subject Interests: Arts, Bus admin, Can studies, Educ, Fr Can studies, Humanities, Sci, Translation
Automation Activity & Vendor Info: (Acquisitions) Ex Libris Group; (Cataloging) Ex Libris Group; (Circulation) Ex Libris Group; (Course Reserve) Ex Libris Group; (Discovery) Ex Libris Group; (OPAC) Ex Libris Group; (Serials) Ex Libris Group
Wireless access
Function: Ref serv available
Partic in Manitoba Library Consortium, Inc
Open Mon-Thurs 8am-9:30pm, Fri 8-6, Sat 10-6, Sun 1-5 (Fall & Winter); Mon-Fri 8:30-4:30 (Spring & Summer)

UNIVERSITY OF MANITOBA
C ST ANDREW'S COLLEGE LIBRARY*, 29 Dysart Rd, R3T 2M7, SAN 322-7324. Tel: 204-474-8901. FAX: 204-474-7624. *Librn,* Halia Teterenko; Staff 2 (Non-MLS 2)
Founded 1946. Enrl 80; Fac 8; Highest Degree: Master
Library Holdings: Bk Vols 37,000; Per Subs 20; Spec Interest Per Sub 12
Special Collections: Old Cyrillic Manuscripts & Printed Books
Subject Interests: Eastern Christianity, Soviet studies, Theol, Ukrainian Church, Ukrainian culture, Ukrainian hist, Ukrainian lit

Function: Ref serv available
Publications: Selected Guide to the Rare Book Collection of St Andrew's College Library; Ukranian Serials: A Checklist of Ukranian Periodicals & Newspapers at St Andrew's College
Open Mon-Fri 8:30-4:30

M SEVEN OAKS GENERAL HOSPITAL LIBRARY*, 2300 McPhillips St, R2V 3M3, SAN 324-119X. Tel: 204-632-3107. Circulation Tel: 204-632-3124. FAX: 204-694-8240. E-mail: soghlibrary@umanitoba.ca. *Librn,* Kerry Macdonald; E-mail: kerry.macdonald@umanitoba.ca; Staff 1 (MLS 1)
Founded 1980
Library Holdings: Bk Titles 1,500; Per Subs 70
Subject Interests: Educ, Med, Nursing
Automation Activity & Vendor Info: (Acquisitions) SirsiDynix; (Cataloging) SirsiDynix; (Circulation) SirsiDynix; (Course Reserve) SirsiDynix; (ILL) SirsiDynix; (OPAC) SirsiDynix; (Serials) SirsiDynix
Open Mon-Fri 8:30-4:30

M SISTER ST ODILON LIBRARY, MISERICORDIA HEALTH CENTRE*, Education & Resource Bldg, 691 Wolseley Ave, 1st Flr, R3G 1C3. (Mail add: 99 Cornish Ave, R3C 1A2), SAN 326-3428. Tel: 204-788-8109. FAX: 204-889-4174. E-mail: mhclibrary@umanitoba.ca. Web Site: libguides.lib.umanitoba.ca/misericordia. *Librn,* Laurie Blanchard; Tel: 204-788-8108, E-mail: Laurie_blanchard@umanitoba.ca; *Libr Tech,* Kathy Finlayson; E-mail: Kathy_finlayson@umanitoba.ca; Staff 2 (Non-MLS 2)
Library Holdings: Bk Titles 3,000; Per Subs 10
Subject Interests: Med, Nursing, Ophthalmology
Function: Res libr
Open Mon-Fri 8:30-4:30
Restriction: Non-circulating

C UNIVERSITY OF MANITOBA LIBRARIES*, Elizabeth Dafoe Library, Rm 156, 25 Chancellors Circle, R3T 2N2. SAN 366-435X. Tel: 204-474-9881. FAX: 204-474-7583. Web Site: www.umanitoba.ca/libraries. *Univ Librn,* Lisa O'Hara; Tel: 204-474-8749, E-mail: lisa.ohara@umanitoba.ca; Staff 62 (MLS 62)
Founded 1885. Enrl 29,000; Fac 4,096; Highest Degree: Doctorate
Library Holdings: e-books 199,390; e-journals 36,906; Bk Vols 2,000,000; Per Subs 6,876
Special Collections: Andrew Suknaski Coll, ms, typescripts; Bertram Brooker Coll, bks, ms, typescripts; Canadiana (H Gerald Wade Coll), bks, ms; Catalogues of Archival Coll; Charles M Gordon (Ralph Connor) Coll, ms, typescripts; Dorothy Livesay Coll, bks, ms, typescripts; Dysart Coll, rare bks & ms; Eli Mandel Coll, ms, typescripts; Food & Agriculture Organization Document Depository; Frederick Philip Grove Coll, ms, typescripts; Henry Kreisel Coll, ms, typescripts; History & Religion (Vatican Letters & Documents Concerning North America, 1688-1908), micro, photocopy; Icelandic & Slavic Coll, bks, journals; J W Dafoe Coll, ms, typescripts; John Newlove Coll, ms, typescripts; M Charles Cohen Coll, bks, ms; Marshall J Gauvin Coll; Medicine (Ross Mitchell Coll), classic & rare bks, journals; Oscar Brand Coll, ms, music scores; P H T Thorlakson Coll, ms, speeches, typescripts; Papers of Charles William Gordon; Rt Hon Edward Schreyer Papers; T G Hamilton Coll, affidavits, ms, photogs; The Papers of Dorothy Livesay, For God, King, Pen & Country; University Archives; Winnipeg Tribune, archives, photogs. Canadian and Provincial; UN Document Depository
Subject Interests: Agr, Archit, Dentistry, Educ, Engr, Humanities, Law, Med, Mus, Sci, Soc sci
Automation Activity & Vendor Info: (Acquisitions) SirsiDynix; (Cataloging) SirsiDynix; (Circulation) SirsiDynix; (Course Reserve) SirsiDynix; (ILL) SirsiDynix; (Media Booking) SirsiDynix; (OPAC) SirsiDynix; (Serials) SirsiDynix
Wireless access
Partic in Association of Research Libraries; Can-Ole; Canadian Association of Research Libraries; IDRC; Info-globe; Knowledge Index; OCLC Research Library Partnership; Proquest Dialog; SDC Info Servs
Open Mon-Thurs 8am-11pm, Fri 8am-9pm, Sat 9-5, Sun Noon-8

Departmental Libraries:

ARCHITECTURE & FINE ARTS LIBRARY, 206 Russell Bldg, 84 Curry Pl, R3T 2N2. Tel: 204-474-9216. FAX: 204-474-7539. E-mail: archfalibrary@umanitoba.ca. Web Site: umanitoba.ca/libraries/architecture-fine-arts-library. *Art Librn,* Liv Valmestad; Tel: 204-474-9217, E-mail: liv.valmestad@umanitoba.ca; *Libr Supvr,* Ginette Croteau; Tel: 204-474-6567; *Libr Asst,* Sherri-Lynn Galaschuk; Tel: 204-474-6440, E-mail: sherri-lynn.galaschuk@umanitoba.ca
Library Holdings: Per Subs 475
Subject Interests: Archit, City planning, Design, Environ studies, Fine arts, Interior design, Landscape archit, Regional planning
Open Mon-Fri 8:30-4:30

ALBERT D COHEN MANAGEMENT LIBRARY, 206 Drake Ctr, 181 Freedman Crescent, R3T 5V4. Tel: 204-474-8440. FAX: 204-474-7542. E-mail: managementlibrary@umanitoba.ca. Web Site: umanitoba.ca/libraries/management-library. *Libr Supvr,* Ginette Croteau; Tel: 204-474-6567, E-mail: ginette.croteau@umanitoba.ca
Library Holdings: Per Subs 450
Subject Interests: Acctg, Bus admin, Finance, Mkt
Open Mon-Thurs 8:30-6, Fri 8:30-4:30

DONALD W CRAIK ENGINEERING LIBRARY, E3-361 Engineering Information & Technology Ctr, 75B Chancellors Circle, R3T 5V6. Tel: 204-474-6360. Reference Tel: 204-474-6850. FAX: 204-474-7520. E-mail: sciencelibrary@umanitoba.ca. *Assoc Librn,* Marie Speare; Tel: 204-474-9445, E-mail: marie.speare@umanitoba.ca
Subject Interests: Agr, Civil, Electrical, Geol engr, Mechanical engr
Open Mon-Fri 8am-11pm, Sat & Sun 10-6

ELIZABETH DAFOE LIBRARY, 25 Chancellor's Circle, R3T 2N2. Tel: 204-474-9844. E-mail: dafoe@umanitoba.ca. Web Site: umanitoba.ca/libraries/elizabeth-dafoe-library. *Head, Archives & Spec Coll,* Heather Bidzinski; Tel: 204-474-6350, E-mail: heather.bidzinski@umanitoba.ca; *Languages Librarian,* Emma Popowich; Tel: 204-474-6211, E-mail: emma.popowich@umanitoba.ca; *Archives, Spec Coll,* James Kominowski; Tel: 204-474-9681, E-mail: james.kominowski@umanitoba.ca. Subject Specialists: *German studies, Slavic studies,* James Kominowski
Special Collections: Icelandic & Slavic Coll, archives, ms, rare bks
Subject Interests: Human ecology, Humanities, Nursing
Open Mon-Fri 8am-11pm, Sat & Sun 10-6

ECKHARDT-GRAMATTE MUSIC LIBRARY, T257 Taché Arts Complex, 136 Dafoe Rd, R3T 2N2. Tel: 204-474-9567. E-mail: musiclibrary@umanitoba.ca. Web Site: www.umanitoba.ca/libraries/music-library. *Music Librn,* Katherine Penner; E-mail: k.penner@umanitoba.ca; Staff 4 (MLS 1, Non-MLS 3)
Enrl 300; Highest Degree: Master
Library Holdings: AV Mats 8,000; CDs 6,000; DVDs 128; e-journals 300; Music Scores 21,000; Bk Vols 13,000; Per Subs 145; Videos 350
Open Mon-Fri 8:30-4:30

FATHER HAROLD DRAKE LIBRARY - ST PAUL'S COLLEGE, 70 Dysart Rd, Rm 119, R3T 2M6, SAN 366-4686. Tel: 204-474-8585. FAX: 204-474-7615. E-mail: stpref@umanitoba.edu. Web Site: umanitoba.ca/libraries/st-pauls-college-library. *Circ Supvr,* Bill Wsiaki; E-mail: bill.wsiaki@umanitoba.ca
Library Holdings: Bk Titles 75,000; Per Subs 240
Subject Interests: Catholic studies, Peace & conflict studies
Open Mon-Fri 8:30-4:30

CM NEIL JOHN MACLEAN HEALTH SCIENCES LIBRARY, Brodie Center Atrium, Mezzanine Level, 2nd Flr, 727 McDermot Ave, R3E 3P5, SAN 366-4597. Tel: 204-789-3342. FAX: 204-789-3922. Automation Services FAX: 204-789-3923. E-mail: healthlibrary@umanitoba.ca. Web Site: www.umanitoba.ca/libraries/health-sciences-library. *Actg Head, Health Sci Libr,* Mê-Linh Lê; Tel: 204-228-6775, E-mail: me-linh.le@umanitoba.ca; *Health Sci Librn,* Carol Cooke; E-mail: carol.cooke@umanitoba.ca; *Health Sci Librn,* Caroline Monnin; E-mail: caroline.monnin@umanitoba.ca; *Health Sci Librn,* Christine Neilson; E-mail: christine.neilson@umanitoba.ca; *Liaison Librn,* Janice Linton; E-mail: janice.linton@umanitoba.ca; *Supervisor, Client Services,* Daisy Santos; Tel: 204-789-3462, E-mail: daisy.santos@umanitoba.ca. Subject Specialists: *Med,* Carol Cooke; *Dental hygiene, Dentistry, Physicians assistance studies,* Caroline Monnin; *Nursing,* Christine Neilson; *Indigenous health,* Janice Linton; Staff 12 (MLS 6, Non-MLS 6)
Highest Degree: Doctorate
Library Holdings: AV Mats 5,657; e-books 144,768; e-journals 4,500; Bk Titles 103,977; Per Subs 130
Special Collections: Aboriginal Health Coll; Consumer Health Coll; History of Medicine Coll; Manitoba Authors (Medical Field); Rare Book Coll
Subject Interests: Allied health, Dental, Dental hygiene, Med, Nursing, Occupational therapy, Pediatrics, Phys therapy
Automation Activity & Vendor Info: (Acquisitions) SirsiDynix; (Cataloging) SirsiDynix; (Circulation) SirsiDynix; (Course Reserve) SirsiDynix; (ILL) Relais International; (Media Booking) SirsiDynix; (OPAC) SirsiDynix; (Serials) SirsiDynix
Function: 24/7 Electronic res, 24/7 Online cat, 24/7 wireless access, Archival coll, Art exhibits, Computer training, Computers for patron use, Doc delivery serv, Electronic databases & coll, For res purposes, Health sci info serv, ILL available, Internet access, Magnifiers for reading, Meeting rooms, Online cat, Online Chat, Online info literacy tutorials on the web & in blackboard, Online ref, Orientations, Outreach serv, Photocopying/Printing, Printer for laptops & handheld devices, Ref & res, Ref serv available, Res assist avail, Res libr, Satellite serv, Scanner, Study rm, Wheelchair accessible
Partic in Association of Faculties of Medicine of Canada
Open Mon-Fri 8am-11pm, Sat & Sun 10-6

WILLIAM R NEWMAN LIBRARY (AGRICULTURE), 232 Agriculture Bldg, 66 Dafoe Rd, R3T 2N2. Tel: 204-474-8382. FAX: 204-474-7527. Reference E-mail: agriculturelibrary@umanitoba.ca.
Function: ILL available, Photocopying/Printing
Open Mon-Fri 8:30-4:30
Restriction: Staff use only

ST JOHN'S COLLEGE LIBRARY, 92 Dysart Rd, R3T 2M5, SAN 366-4651. Tel: 204-474-8542. FAX: 204-474-7614. Web Site: umanitoba.ca/libraries/st-johns-college-library.
Special Collections: Dead Sea Scrolls; King James Bible
Subject Interests: Biblical studies, Can studies, Early Christianity, English lit, Fr lit, Hist, Relig
Open Mon-Thurs 8:30-6, Fri 8:30-4:30

SCIENCES & TECHNOLOGY LIBRARY, 211 Machray Hall, 186 Dysart Rd, R3T 2N2. Tel: 204-474-9281. FAX: 204-474-7627. E-mail: sciencelibrary@umanitoba.ca. Web Site: umanitoba.ca/libraries/sciences-technology-libraries. *Actg Head, Libr,* Marie Speare; Tel: 204-789-7063, E-mail: marie.speare@umanitoba.ca
Library Holdings: Bk Vols 220,000; Per Subs 1,900
Subject Interests: Agr, Engr
Open Mon-Fri 8-am-11pm, Sat & Sun 10-6
Friends of the Library Group

CL E K WILLIAMS LAW LIBRARY, 401 Robson Hall, 224 Dysart Rd, R3T 2N2. Tel: 204-474-9997. FAX: 204-474-7582. E-mail: ekwll@umanitoba.ca. *Liaison Librn,* Matthew Renaud; Tel: 204-474-6371, E-mail: matthew.renaud@umanitoba.ca; *Liaison Librn,* Donna Sikorsky; Tel: 204-474-6372, E-mail: donna.sikorsky@umanitoba.ca
Partic in Manitoba Library Consortium, Inc
Open Mon-Fri 8am-11pm, Sat & Sun 10-6

C UNIVERSITY OF WINNIPEG LIBRARY, 515 Portage Ave, R3B 2E9. SAN 318-9171. Tel: 204-786-9801. Circulation Tel: 204-786-9808. Interlibrary Loan Service Tel: 204-786-9814. Reference Tel: 204-786-9815. Toll Free Tel: 888-393-1830. Circulation E-mail: circulation@uwinnipeg.ca. Reference E-mail: reference@uwinnipeg.ca. Web Site: library.uwinnipeg.ca. *Dean, Univ Libr,* Gabrielle Prefontaine; Tel: 204-786-9488, E-mail: g.prefontaine@uwinnipeg.ca; *Assoc Dean,* Emma Hill Kepron; Tel: 204-786-9445, E-mail: e.kepron@uwinnipeg.ca; *Head, Access Serv,* Lauren McGaw; *Head, Coll,* Michael Hohner; E-mail: m.hohner@uwinnipeg.ca; *Head, Ref & Instruction,* Ian Fraser; Tel: 786-204-9813, E-mail: i.fraser@uwinnipeg.ca; *Accessibility Librarian, Int'l Extended Services Librn,* Michael Dudley; Tel: 204-982-1145, E-mail: m.dudley@uwinnipeg.ca; *E-Resources Librn,* Christine Hoeppner; Tel: 204-786-9759, E-mail: c.hoeppner@uwinnipeg.ca; *Pub Serv Mgr,* Allison DaSilva; E-mail: al.dasilva@uwinnipeg.ca; *Digital Coll Curator, Univ Archivist,* Brett Lougheed; E-mail: b.lougheed@uwinnipeg.ca; Staff 38 (MLS 8, Non-MLS 30)
Founded 1871. Enrl 9,800; Fac 325; Highest Degree: Master
Library Holdings: AV Mats 3,934; DVDs 200; e-books 1,081; Bk Titles 406,067; Bk Vols 509,106; Per Subs 1,541
Special Collections: Bhai Kahan Singh Nabha Coll; Children's Picture Book Coll; Dramatic Works Coll; Eastern European Genealogical Society Coll; Rare Book Coll; University of Winnipeg Archives; Wilhelm Wanka Coll
Subject Interests: Liberal arts
Automation Activity & Vendor Info: (Acquisitions) Innovative Interfaces, Inc; (Cataloging) Innovative Interfaces, Inc; (Circulation) Innovative Interfaces, Inc; (Course Reserve) Innovative Interfaces, Inc; (Media Booking) Innovative Interfaces, Inc; (OPAC) Innovative Interfaces, Inc; (Serials) Innovative Interfaces, Inc
Wireless access
Partic in Canadian Research Knowledge Network; Council of Prairie & Pacific University Libraries; MLC
Special Services for the Deaf - Assistive tech
Special Services for the Blind - Closed circuit TV; Computer with voice synthesizer for visually impaired persons; ZoomText magnification & reading software
Open Mon-Thurs 8am-8:45pm, Fri 8-4:45, Sat 9-4:45

S WINNIPEG ART GALLERY LIBRARY*, Clara Lander Library, 300 Memorial Blvd, R3C 1V1. SAN 318-9198. Tel: 204-786-6641. FAX: 204-788-4998. E-mail: librarian@wag.ca. Web Site: www.wag.ca. Staff 1 (MLS 1)
Founded 1950
Library Holdings: Bk Vols 30,000; Per Subs 30
Special Collections: Institutional Archives; Inuit Art Coll
Subject Interests: Can art
Automation Activity & Vendor Info: (Cataloging) Follett Software; (OPAC) Follett Software
Wireless access
Restriction: Open by appt only, Open to pub for ref only

P WINNIPEG PUBLIC LIBRARY*, 251 Donald St, R3C 3P5. SAN 366-4740. Tel: 204-986-6462. FAX: 204-942-5671. Web Site: wpl.winnipeg.ca/library. *Mgr, Libr Serv,* Karin Borland; E-mail: kborland@winnipeg.ca
Founded 1885. Circ 5,723,951
Library Holdings: Bk Vols 1,558,909; Per Subs 1,484
Automation Activity & Vendor Info: (Acquisitions) SirsiDynix; (Cataloging) SirsiDynix; (Circulation) SirsiDynix; (Course Reserve) SirsiDynix; (ILL) SirsiDynix; (Media Booking) SirsiDynix; (OPAC) SirsiDynix; (Serials) SirsiDynix
Wireless access
Partic in Manitoba Public Library Services
Open Mon-Thurs 10-9, Fri & Sat 10-6
Friends of the Library Group
Branches: 20

CHARLESWOOD, 6-4910 Roblin Blvd, R3R 0G7, SAN 366-4775. Tel: 204-986-3072. Circulation Tel: 201-986-3069. FAX: 204-986-3545. *Br Head,* Nadine McCaughan; Tel: 204-806-1119
Open Mon, Tues & Thurs 10-8:30, Fri 10-5
Friends of the Library Group

CORNISH, 20 West Gate, R3C 2E1, SAN 366-4791. Tel: 204-986-4679. FAX: 204-986-7126. *Br Head,* Rick Watkins; Tel: 202-986-4680
Friends of the Library Group

FORT GARRY, 1360 Pembina Hwy, R3T 2B4, SAN 366-483X. Tel: 204-986-4918. FAX: 204-986-3399. *Br Head,* Erica Ball; Tel: 204-986-4917
Open Mon, Tues & Thurs 10-8:30, Wed & Fri 10-5
Friends of the Library Group

HENDERSON, 1-1050 Henderson Hwy, R2K 2M5, SAN 366-4848. Tel: 204-986-4314. FAX: 204-986-3065. *Br Head,* Andrew McCulloch; Tel: 204-986-4318
Open Mon, Tues & Thurs 10-8:30, Wed & Fri 10-5
Friends of the Library Group

MILLENNIUM, 251 Donald St, R3C 3P5, SAN 328-7386. Tel: 204-986-6440. Information Services Tel: 204-986-6450. FAX: 204-942-5671. *Admin Coordr, Cent Libr Serv,* Theresa Lomas
Open Mon-Thurs 10-9, Fri & Sat 10-6
Friends of the Library Group

MUNROE, 489 London St, R2K 2Z4, SAN 366-4880. Tel: 204-986-3736. FAX: 204-986-7125. *Br Head,* Randy Plant; Tel: 204-986-3738
Open Mon, Tues & Thurs 1-8:30, Fri 10-5
Friends of the Library Group

OSBORNE, 625 Osborne St, R3L 2B3, SAN 366-4899. Tel: 204-986-4775. FAX: 204-986-7124. *Br Head,* Carole Reeve; Tel: 204-986-4776
Open Mon, Tues & Thurs 1-8:30, Fri 10-5
Friends of the Library Group

PEMBINA TRAIL, 2724 Pembina Hwy, R3T 2H7, SAN 328-9095. Tel: 204-986-4369. FAX: 204-986-3290. *Br Head,* Kamini Madansingh; Tel: 204-986-4378; Staff 12 (MLS 1, Non-MLS 11)
Open Mon, Tues & Thurs 10-8:30, Fri 10-5
Friends of the Library Group

LOUIS RIEL BRANCH, 1168 Dakota St, R2N 3T8, SAN 370-4556. Tel: 204-986-4568. FAX: 204-986-3274. *Br Head,* Trevor Lockhart; Tel: 204-986-4571
Open Mon, Tues & Thurs 10-8:30, Fri 10-5
Friends of the Library Group

RIVER HEIGHTS, 1520 Corydon Ave, R3N 0J6, SAN 366-4953. Tel: 204-986-4934. FAX: 204-986-3544. *Br Head,* Angela Mehmel; Tel: 204-986-5450
Open Mon, Tues & Thurs 10-8:30, Fri 10-5
Friends of the Library Group

ST BONIFACE, 100-131 Provencher Blvd, R2H 0G2, SAN 366-4929. Tel: 204-986-4331. FAX: 204-986-6827. *Br Head,* Danielle Robidoux; Tel: 204-986-4272
Open Mon-Thurs 10-9, Fri 10-5
Friends of the Library Group

ST JAMES-ASSINIBOIA, 1910 Portage Ave, R3J 0J2, SAN 366-497X. Tel: 204-986-5583. FAX: 204-986-3798. *Br Head,* Stephanie George; Tel: 204-806-1072
Open Mon, Tues & Thurs 10-8:30, Wed & Fri 10-5
Friends of the Library Group

ST JOHN'S, 500 Salter St, R2W 4M5, SAN 366-4988. Tel: 204-986-4689. FAX: 204-986-7123. *Br Head,* Kim Parry; Tel: 204-226-1047
Open Mon, Tues & Thurs 1-8:30, Fri 10-5
Friends of the Library Group

ST VITAL, Six Fermor Ave, R2M 0Y2, SAN 366-4996. Tel: 204-986-5625. FAX: 204-986-3173. *Br Head,* Stephanie Graham; Tel: 204-806-1250
Open Mon, Tues & Thurs 10-8:30, Wed & Fri & 10-5
Friends of the Library Group

SIR WILLIAM STEPHENSON, 765 Keewatin St, R2X 3B9, SAN 377-8061. Tel: 204-986-7070. FAX: 204-986-7201. *Br Head,* Rick Watkins
Open Tues-Thurs 10-9, Fri & Sat 10-5
Friends of the Library Group

HARVEY SMITH LIBRARY - WEST END, 999 Sargent Ave, R3E 3K6, SAN 366-5011. Tel: 204-986-4677. FAX: 204-986-7129. *Br Head,* Kirsten Wurmann; Tel: 204-806-1078
Open Mon 10-5, Tues-Thurs 1-8:30, Fri 10-6
Friends of the Library Group

TRANSCONA, One Transcona Blvd, R2C 5R6, SAN 366-5003. Tel: 204-986-3950. FAX: 204-986-3172. *Br Head,* Alan Chorney; Tel: 204-330-4716
Open Mon, Tues & Thurs 10-8:30, Fri 10-5
Friends of the Library Group

WEST KILDONAN, 365 Jefferson Ave, R2V 0N3, SAN 366-502X. Tel: 204-986-4384. FAX: 204-986-3373. *Br Head,* Evelyn Piush; Tel: 204-986-4387
Open Mon, Tues & Thurs 10-8:30, Wed & Fri 10-5
Friends of the Library Group

WESTWOOD, 66 Allard Ave, R3K 0T3, SAN 366-5038. Tel: 204-986-4742. FAX: 204-986-3799. *Br Head,* Kelsey Middleton; Tel: 204-805-0109
Open Mon, Tues & Thurs 10-8:30, Fri 10-5
Friends of the Library Group

WINDSOR PARK, 1195 Archibald St, R2J 0Y9, SAN 366-5046. Tel: 204-986-4945. FAX: 204-986-7122. *Br Head,* Clark Rempel; Tel: 204-619-4152
Open Mon, Tues & Thurs 1-8:30, Fri 10-5
Friends of the Library Group

NEW BRUNSWICK

Date of Statistics: FY 2023-2024
Population, 2021 Canadian Census: 775,610
Population Served by Regional Libraries: 601,551
Total Volumes in Public Libraries: 1,814,218*
Total Public Library Circulation: 3,199,869*
Digital Resources:
Total downloadable units: 73,603 (60,848 e-books + 12,755 eAudiobooks)
Total downloadable unit circulation: 533,230 (355,422 e-books + 177,808 eAudiobooks)
Traffic (Patron visits): 1,654,051
Total computers for use by the public: 227
Total unique wireless users: 134,458
Income and Expenditures:
Total Public Library Income: $19,355,529
Provincial Grant: $18,738,000
Municipal Funding: $5,597,005
Provincial & Municipal: $24,335,005
Number of Bookmobiles in Province: 0
***Includes physical materials as well as electronic materials available for download through eBook lending platforms.**
Information provided courtesy of: Kate Thompson, Head of Public Services Development; New Brunswick Public Library Service

BATHURST

M CHALEUR REGIONAL HOSPITAL*, Dr D A Thompson Memorial Library, 1750 Sunset Dr, E2A 4L7. SAN 324-394X. Tel: 506-544-2446. *Med Librn,* Mr Araya-Yohannes Bekele; E-mail: araya-yohannes.bekele@vitalitenb.ca
Library Holdings: Bk Titles 1,488; Per Subs 100
Open Mon-Fri 8-4
Restriction: Staff & patient use

CAMPBELLTON

P CHALEUR LIBRARY REGION*, 113A Roseberry St, E3N 2G6. SAN 366-5070. Tel: 506-789-6599. FAX: 506-789-7318. E-mail: NBPLSChaleurAdministrativeStaff@gnb.ca. Web Site: www1.gnb.ca/0003/pages/en/biblio-e.asp?CODE=cr. *Regional Dir,* Georgette Lavail; E-mail: Georgette.Lavail@gnb.ca; Staff 40 (MLS 11, Non-MLS 29)
Founded 1964. Pop 92,947; Circ 334,517
Library Holdings: Bk Vols 255,345; Per Subs 281
Open Mon-Fri 8-5
Branches: 11
BATHURST PUBLIC LIBRARY, 150 St George St , Ste 1, Bathurst, E2A 1B5. Tel: 506-548-0706. FAX: 506-548-0708. E-mail: bibliocn@gnb.ca. *Actg Libr Dir,* Laura Little; E-mail: laura.little@gnb.ca; Staff 5 (MLS 4, Non-MLS 1)
Open Tues & Thurs 10-8, Wed, Fri & Sat 10-5
CAMPBELLTON CENTENNIAL LIBRARY, 19 Aberdeen St, Ste 100, E3N 2J6, SAN 366-5135. Tel: 506-753-5253. FAX: 506-753-3803. E-mail: bibliocc@gnb.ca. *Libr Dir,* Stephane Dupuy; E-mail: stephane.dupuy@gnb.ca; Staff 8.5 (MLS 4, Non-MLS 4.5)
Founded 1966
Open Mon, Tues, Fri-Sun 10-5, Wed & Thurs 10-9
DALHOUSIE CENTENNIAL LIBRARY, 403 rue Adelaïde, Dalhousie, E8C 1B6, SAN 372-0179. Tel: 506-684-7370. FAX: 506-684-7374. E-mail: bibliocd@gnb.ca. *Actg Libr Mgr,* Joanie Tanguay; E-mail: joanie.tanguay@gnb.ca; Staff 2.5 (Non-MLS 2.5)
Founded 1967
Open Tues & Thurs-Sat 10-12 & 1-5, Wed 1-5 & 6-8:30
RAYMOND LAGACE PUBLIC LIBRARY, 275 rue Notre-Dame, Atholville, E3N 4T1, SAN 372-0160. Tel: 506-789-2914. FAX: 506-789-2056. E-mail: biblioda@gnb.ca. *Libr Mgr,* Kevin Soussana; E-mail: Kevin.Soussana@gnb.ca; Staff 1 (Non-MLS 1)
Founded 1967
Open Tues, Wed, Fri & Sat 10-12 & 1-5, Thurs 1-5 & 6-8:30
LAMEQUE PUBLIC LIBRARY, 46 du Pêcheur N St, Lameque, E8T 1J3, SAN 366-516X. Tel: 506-344-3262. FAX: 506-344-3263. E-mail: bibliopl@gnb.ca. *Libr Mgr,* Lison Gaudet; E-mail: Lison.Gaudet@gnb.ca; Staff 1.5 (Non-MLS 1.5)
Founded 1989
Open Tues 1-5 & 6-8:30, Wed-Sat 9:30-12 & 1-5
LAVAL-GOUPIL PUBLIC LIBRARY, 128 Mgr Chiasson St, Shippagan, E8S 1X7, SAN 366-5240. Tel: 506-336-3920. FAX: 506-336-3921. E-mail: bibliops@gnb.ca. *Libr Mgr,* Nadine Robichaud; E-mail: nadine.robichaud@gnb.ca; Staff 2 (Non-MLS 2)
Founded 1980
Open Tues 1-5 & 6-8:30, Wed-Sat 9:30-12 & 1-5
CLAUDE LEBOUTHILLIER PUBLIC LIBRARY, 8185-2 rue Saint Paul, Bas-Caraquet, E1W 6C4, SAN 366-5100. Tel: 506-726-2775. FAX: 506-726-2770. E-mail: bibliobc@gnb.ca. *Libr Mgr,* Mylene May Gionet; E-mail: mylenemay.gionet@gnb.ca; Staff 1.5 (Non-MLS 1.5)
Founded 1989
Open Tues 1-5 & 6-8:30, Wed-Sat 9:30-12 & 1-5
MONSEIGNEUR PAQUET PUBLIC LIBRARY, 10A du Colisée St, Caraquet, E1W 1A5, SAN 366-5224. Tel: 506-726-2681. FAX: 506-726-2685. E-mail: bibliock@gnb.ca. *Libr Dir,* Irene Guraliuc; E-mail: irene.guraliuc@gnb.ca; Staff 2 (Non-MLS 2)
Founded 1973
Open Tues 1-5 & 6pm-8:30pm, Wed-Sat 9:30-12 & 1-5
MONSEIGNEUR ROBICHAUD PUBLIC LIBRARY, 855 Principale St, Local 3, Beresford, E8K 1T3, SAN 372-0187. Tel: 506-542-2704. FAX: 506-542-2714. E-mail: bibliomr@gnb.ca. *Actg Libr Dir,* Julia Maury; E-mail: julia.maury@gnb.ca; Staff 2 (MLS 1, Non-MLS 1)
Founded 1983
Open Tues & Thurs 1-5 & 6-8:30, Wed, Fri & Sat 9:30-12 & 1-5
PETIT-ROCHER PUBLIC LIBRARY, 702 Principale St, Office 110, Petit-Rocher, E8J 1V1, SAN 366-5119. Tel: 506-542-2744. FAX: 506-542-2745. E-mail: bibliopr@gnb.ca. *Libr Mgr,* Sonia Godin; E-mail: Sonia.Godin@gnb.ca; Staff 2 (Non-MLS 2)
Founded 1987
Open Tues & Thurs-Sat 9:30-12 & 1-5, Wed 1-5 & 6-8:30
Friends of the Library Group
PERE ZOEL SAULNIER PUBLIC LIBRARY, PO Box 3654, Tracadie-Sheila, E1X 1G5. (Mail add: CP 3654, Main Postal Office, Tracadie-Sheila, E1X 1G5), SAN 366-5259. Tel: 506-394-4005. FAX: 506-394-4009. E-mail: bibliots@gnb.ca. *Libr Dir,* Marie-Claude Gagnon; E-mail: marie-claude.gagnon@gnb.ca; Staff 2 (MLS 1, Non-MLS 1)
Founded 1975
Open Tues 1:30-5 & 6-8:30, Wed-Sat 9:30-12:30 & 1:30-5

DORCHESTER

S CORRECTIONAL SERVICES OF CANADA, Westmoreland Institution Library, 4902 A Main St, E4K 2Y9. SAN 329-2363. Tel: 506-379-2471.
Founded 1984
Library Holdings: Bk Vols 6,000; Per Subs 40
Subject Interests: Art
Publications: Hill-Top Journal
Restriction: Staff & inmates only
Friends of the Library Group

EDMUNDSTON

P HAUT-SAINT-JEAN REGIONAL LIBRARY*, Region de Bibliotheques du Haut-Saint-Jean, 15 rue de l'Eglise St, Ste 102, E3V 1J3. SAN 366-5283. Tel: 506-735-2074. FAX: 506-735-2193. E-mail: NBPLSHSJAdministrativeStaff@gnb.ca. Web Site: www1.gnb.ca/0003/pages/en/Biblio-e.asp?CODE=HR. *Regional Dir,* Patrick Provencher; E-mail: Patrick.Provencher@gnb.ca; *Asst Regional Dir,* Edith Routhier; E-mail: edith.routhier@gnb.ca; *Coll Mgt Librn,* Alexandra Ferguson; *Pub Serv Librn,* Amy Sutherland; Staff 4 (MLS 4)
Founded 1971
Library Holdings: Bk Vols 339,758
Special Collections: Professional Coll (libr sci)
Wireless access
Publications: Bulletin du Haut-Saint-Jean; Jalons historiques: la Bibliotheque Regionale du Haut-Saint-Jean au nord-ouest du Nouveau-Brunswick
Special Services for the Blind - Accessible computers; Daisy reader; Dep for Braille Inst; Home delivery serv; Internet workstation with adaptive software; Large print bks; Playaways (bks on MP3); Screen enlargement software for people with visual disabilities; Screen reader software; Talking bks
Open Mon-Fri 8:30-5
Friends of the Library Group
Branches: 12
DR WALTER CHESTNUT PUBLIC LIBRARY, 395 Main St, Unit 1, Hartland, E7P 2N3. Tel: 506-375-4876. FAX: 506-375-6816. E-mail: Hartlandl@gnb.ca. *Libr Mgr,* Marsha MacDonald-Nason; E-mail: marsha.macdonald-nason@gnb.ca
Library Holdings: Bk Vols 20,733; Per Subs 23
Open Tues, Wed, Fri & Sat 10-5, Thurs 1-8
L P FISHER PUBLIC LIBRARY, 679 Main St, Woodstock, E7M 2E1. Tel: 506-325-4777. FAX: 506-325-4811. E-mail: LPFisher.Library@gnb.ca. *Libr Dir,* Jennifer Carson; E-mail: jennifer.carson@gnb.ca
Library Holdings: Bk Vols 35,055; Per Subs 40
Open Tues & Thurs 10-8, Wed, Fri & Sat 10-5
GRAND FALLS PUBLIC LIBRARY, 131 rue Pleasant, Ste 201, Grand Sault, E3Z 1G6, SAN 366-5348. Tel: 506-475-7781. FAX: 506-475-7783. E-mail: gfplib@gnb.ca. *Actg Libr Dir,* Patrick Provencher
Founded 1972
Library Holdings: Bk Vols 34,132; Per Subs 16
Subject Interests: Genealogy
Open Tues & Thurs-Sat 10-12 & 1-5, Wed 12-5 & 6-8
LA MOISSON PUBLIC, 206 Canada St, Saint Quentin, E8A 1H1, SAN 366-5380. Tel: 506-235-1955. FAX: 506-235-1957. E-mail: bibliolm@gnb.ca. *Libr Mgr,* Helene DuRepos Theriault; E-mail: helene.durepos-theriault@gnb.ca
Founded 1969
Library Holdings: Bk Vols 26,362; Per Subs 20
Open Tues 1-5 & 6:30-8:30, Wed-Sat 10-12 & 1-5
ANDREW & LAURA MCCAIN PUBLIC LIBRARY, Eight McCain St, Florenceville-Bristol, E7L 3H6. Tel: 506-392-5294. FAX: 506-392-8108. E-mail: Florenpl@gnb.ca. *Libr Mgr,* Julie Craig; E-mail: julie.craig@gnb.ca
Library Holdings: Bk Vols 29,674; Per Subs 24
Open Tues, Wed, Fri & Sat 10:30-5, Thurs 12-8
MONSEIGNEUR PLOURDE PUBLIC, 15 Bellevue St, Saint Francois, E7A 1A4, SAN 366-5364. Tel: 506-992-6052. FAX: 506-992-6047. E-mail: stfplib@gnb.ca. *Libr Mgr,* Tania St-Onge; E-mail: tania.st-onge@gnb.ca
Founded 1983
Library Holdings: Bk Vols 19,309; Per Subs 18
Open Tues 1-5 & 6-8, Wed-Sat 10-12 & 1-5
MONSEIGNEUR W J CONWAY PUBLIC, 33 rue Irene, E3V 1B7, SAN 366-5313. Tel: 506-735-4713. FAX: 506-737-6848. E-mail: biblioed@gnb.ca. *Libr Dir,* Marc Cool; E-mail: marc.cool@gnb.ca
Founded 1972
Library Holdings: Bk Vols 58,972; Per Subs 44
Open Mon, Tues & Fri-Sun 10-5, Wed & Fri 10-9
NACKAWIC PUBLIC-SCHOOL LIBRARY, 30 Landegger Dr, Nackawic, E6G 1E9. Tel: 506-575-2136. FAX: 506-575-2336. E-mail: nackawic.library@gnb.ca. *Libr Mgr,* Paulette Tonner; E-mail: paulette.toner@gnb.ca
Library Holdings: Bk Vols 20,379; Per Subs 11
Open Mon-Wed & Fri 9-1 & 2-5, Thurs 12-5 & 6-8
PERTH-ANDOVER PUBLIC LIBRARY, 642 E Riverside Dr, Perth-Andover, E7H 1Z6. Tel: 506-273-2843. FAX: 506-273-1913. E-mail: biblioperth-andoverlib@gnb.ca. *Libr Mgr,* Tammie Wright; E-mail: tammie.wright@gnb.ca
Library Holdings: Bk Vols 23,015; Per Subs 12
Open Tues, Wed, Fri & Sat 10-12:30 & 1:30-5, Thurs 1-4 & 5-8
PLASTER ROCK PUBLIC-SCHOOL LIBRARY, 290A Main St, Plaster Rock, E7G 2C6. Tel: 506-356-6018. FAX: 506-356-6019. E-mail: Prplib@gnb.ca. *Libr Mgr,* Patricia Corey; E-mail: patricia.corey@gnb.ca
Library Holdings: Bk Vols 20,062; Per Subs 17
Open Mon-Wed & Fri 9:30-12:30 & 1:30-5, Thurs 12-5 & 6-8
DR LORNE J VIOLETTE PUBLIC LIBRARY, 180 rue St-Jean, Saint Leonard, E7E 2B9, SAN 366-5372. Tel: 506-423-3025. FAX: 506-423-3026. E-mail: stlplib@gnb.ca. *Libr Mgr,* Sophie-Michele Cyr; E-mail: sophie-michele.cyr@gnb.ca
Founded 1972
Library Holdings: Bk Vols 23,177; Per Subs 23
Open Tues 12-5 & 6-8, Wed-Sat 10-12 & 1-5

C UNIVERSITY DE MONCTON, Bibliotheque Rhea-Larose, 165 Hebert Blvd, E3V 2S8. SAN 318-9228. Tel: 506-737-5058. FAX: 506-737-5373. E-mail: brl-ce@umoncton.ca. Web Site: www.umoncton.ca/umce-bibliotheque. *Dir,* Emilie Lefrancois; Tel: 506-737-5266, E-mail: Emilie.Lefrancois@umoncton.ca; Staff 4 (MLS 1, Non-MLS 3)
Founded 1972. Enrl 600; Highest Degree: Master
Library Holdings: Bk Vols 50,000; Per Subs 50
Special Collections: State Document Depository
Subject Interests: Forestry sci, Local hist
Automation Activity & Vendor Info: (Acquisitions) Infor Library & Information Solutions; (Cataloging) Infor Library & Information Solutions; (Circulation) Infor Library & Information Solutions; (OPAC) Infor Library & Information Solutions
Publications: Bibliographies
Partic in Council of Atlantic Academic Libraries (CAAL)
Open Mon-Thurs 8:30am-9pm, Fri 8:30-5, Sat & Sun 12-5

FREDERICTON

S BEAVERBROOK ART GALLERY LIBRARY*, 703 Queen St, E3B 1C4. (Mail add: PO Box 605, E3B 5A6), SAN 371-7569. Tel: 506-458-2028. E-mail: info@beaverbrookartgallery.org. Web Site: www.beaverbrookartgallery.org. *Dir/Chief Exec Officer,* Thomas Smart; Tel: 506-458-2030, E-mail: tsmart@beaverbrookartgallery.org; *Mgr of Collections & Exhibitions,* John Leroux; E-mail: jleroux@beaverbrookartgallery.org
Founded 1959
Library Holdings: DVDs 40; Bk Titles 3,000; Videos 20
Special Collections: Contemporary & Historic Art of Atlantic Canada; Early to mid 20th Century British Painting; European Paintings, Drawings & Sculptures; Modern & Historic Canadian Art; Victorian Painting
Wireless access
Restriction: Open by appt only

G CANADIAN AGRICULTURE LIBRARY-FREDERICTON*, Agriculture & Agri-Food Canada, 850 Lincoln Rd, E3B 4Z7. (Mail add: PO Box 20280, E3B 4Z7), SAN 318-9244. Tel: 506-460-4446. FAX: 506-460-4377. Web Site: www.agr.gc.ca/eng. *Sr Info Spec,* André Gionet; E-mail: andre.gionet@canada.ca; Staff 1 (MLS 1)
Founded 1952
Library Holdings: Bk Titles 4,200; Per Subs 30
Subject Interests: Agr, Entomology, Plant breeding, Plant pathology, Potatoes, Soil sci
Restriction: Staff use only

M DR EVERETT CHALMERS HOSPITAL*, Dr G Moffatt Health Sciences Library, 700 Priestman St, E3B 5N5. (Mail add: PO Box 9000, E3B 5N5), SAN 327-4055. Tel: 506-452-5432. FAX: 506-452-5585. E-mail: library@horizonnb.ca.
Library Holdings: Bk Vols 5,000; Per Subs 5
Special Collections: Classics of Medicine Series
Subject Interests: Allied health, Med, Nursing
Wireless access
Publications: Access
Open Mon-Fri 8-4:30

SR DIOCESAN SYNOD OF FREDERICTON, Anglican Diocesan Archives & Medley Library, 23 Dineen Dr, E3B 5H1. SAN 327-3024. Tel: 506-453-2122. FAX: 506-453-3288. E-mail: archivesnb@gnb.ca. *Dir,* Joanna Aiton Kerr; Tel: 506-429-2450
Founded 1963
Library Holdings: Bk Vols 4,000
Subject Interests: Church hist, Music, Theol
Wireless access
Open Mon-Sat 9-5

L LAW SOCIETY OF NEW BRUNSWICK LIBRARY*, Justice Bldg, Rm 305, 427 Queen St, E3B 1B6. (Mail add: PO Box 6000, E3B 5H1), SAN 318-9252. Tel: 506-453-2500. FAX: 506-453-9438. E-mail: biblio@bellaliant.com, lawlibrarynb@bellaliant.com. Web Site:

lawsociety-barreau.nb.ca/en/public/law-libraries. *Law Librn,* Tanya Davis; *Asst Librn,* Judy Lane; E-mail: biblio@bellaliant.com; Staff 1 (MLS 1)
Founded 1846
Library Holdings: Electronic Media & Resources 15; Bk Vols 25,000
Restriction: Not open to pub, Staff & mem only

G LEGISLATIVE LIBRARY OF NEW BRUNSWICK*, Legislative Assembly Bldg, Centre Block, 706 Queen St, E3B 5H1. (Mail add: PO Box 6000, E3B 5H1), SAN 318-9295. Tel: 506-453-2338. FAX: 506-444-5889. E-mail: library.biblio-info@gnb.ca. Web Site: www1.gnb.ca/leglibbib/en/home.aspx/index. *Govt Doc Librn,* Kelly Dickson; E-mail: kelly.dickson@gnb.ca; *Legislative Librn,* Kenda Clark-Gorey; E-mail: kenda.clark.gorey@gnb.ca; *Outreach Librn,* Kathleen Gaudet; E-mail: kathleen.gaudet@gnb.ca; *Automation Spec,* Anthony Lovesey; E-mail: anthony.lovesey@gnb.ca; Staff 7 (MLS 2, Non-MLS 5)
Founded 1841
Library Holdings: Bk Vols 40,000; Per Subs 300
Special Collections: Government Documents; New Brunswickana. Canadian and Provincial
Subject Interests: Behav sci, Soc sci
Automation Activity & Vendor Info: (Cataloging) Horizon; (Circulation) Horizon; (OPAC) Horizon
Publications: New Brunswick Government Documents (Annual); Periodical Contents; Selected Accessions List (Quarterly)
Open Mon-Fri 8:15-4:30
Restriction: Circ limited

G NATURAL RESOURCES CANADA LIBRARY*, Hugh John Flemming Forestry Ctr, 1350 Regent St S, Rm 1-112, E3B 5P7. (Mail add: PO Box 4000, E3B 5P7), SAN 318-9260. Tel: 506-452-3541. FAX: 506-452-3525. E-mail: nrclibrary@canada.ca. *Libr Mgr,* Emmanuel Aregbesola; *Libr Tech,* Kelly Dickson; E-mail: kelly.dickson@canada.ca
Founded 1921
Library Holdings: Bk Vols 15,000; Per Subs 100
Special Collections: Canadian Provincial Forestry Publications
Subject Interests: Bio-diversity, Ecology, Entomology, Forestry incl develop, Genetics, Pathology, Silviculture, Theses
Automation Activity & Vendor Info: (Cataloging) Innovative Interfaces, Inc - Sierra; (Circulation) Innovative Interfaces, Inc - Sierra; (OPAC) Innovative Interfaces, Inc - Sierra
Open Mon-Fri 8:30-4:30

C NEW BRUNSWICK COLLEGE OF CRAFT & DESIGN LIBRARY*, 457 Queen St, E3B 5H1. SAN 374-5775. Tel: 506-453-5938. FAX: 506-457-7352. E-mail: nbcraftlib@gnb.ca. Web Site: www.nbccd.ca/happening-here/nb-library-of-craft-design. *Coordr, Libr Serv,* Julieta Lumbria McDonald; E-mail: julie.mcdonald@gnb.ca; Staff 1 (Non-MLS 1)
Founded 1987. Enrl 230; Fac 65
Library Holdings: AV Mats 11; CDs 10; DVDs 948; Bk Titles 10,584; Per Subs 110; Videos 445
Automation Activity & Vendor Info: (Acquisitions) SirsiDynix-Enterprise; (Cataloging) SirsiDynix-Enterprise; (Circulation) SirsiDynix-Enterprise; (Course Reserve) SirsiDynix-Enterprise; (ILL) SirsiDynix-Enterprise; (Media Booking) SirsiDynix-Enterprise; (OPAC) SirsiDynix-Enterprise
Wireless access
Function: Electronic databases & coll, Instruction & testing, Internet access, Orientations, Photocopying/Printing, Ref serv available
Open Mon-Wed & Fri 9:30-5, Thurs Noon-8; Mon-Wed & Fri 9:30-1, Thurs 4-8 (Summer)
Restriction: Open to students, fac, staff & alumni
Friends of the Library Group

P NEW BRUNSWICK PUBLIC LIBRARY SERVICE (NBPLS)*, Service des bibliothèques publiques du Nouveau-Brunswick (SBPNB), 570 Two Nations Crossing, Ste 2, E3A 0X9. SAN 318-9309. Tel: 506-453-2354. FAX: 506-444-4064. E-mail: nbpls-sbpnb@gnb.ca. Web Site: www.gnb.ca/publiclibraries. *Exec Dir,* Sylvie Nadeau; E-mail: sylvie.nadeau@gnb.ca; *Dir, Client Serv, Operations Dir,* Ella Nason; E-mail: ella.nason@gnb.ca; *Dir, Libr Planning, Res Libr Dir,* Teresa Johnson; E-mail: teresa.johnson@gnb.ca; *Head, Coll Mgt,* Emanuel Actarian; E-mail: emanuel.actarian@gnb.ca; *Access Serv, Head, Circ,* Lorraine Morehouse; E-mail: lorraine.morehouse@gnb.ca; *Develop, Head, Pub Serv,* Kate Thompson; E-mail: kate.thompson@gnb.ca; Staff 14 (MLS 7, Non-MLS 7)
Founded 1954
Subject Interests: Libr sci, Mgt
Automation Activity & Vendor Info: (Acquisitions) SirsiDynix; (Cataloging) SirsiDynix; (Circulation) SirsiDynix; (Discovery) SirsiDynix-Enterprise; (ILL) Relais International; (OPAC) SirsiDynix; (Serials) SirsiDynix
Wireless access
Function: 24/7 Electronic res, 24/7 Online cat, Activity rm, Audiobks on Playaways & MP3, Audiobks via web, Bk club(s), Bks on CD, Children's prog, Computer training, Computers for patron use, Digital talking bks, Electronic databases & coll, Free DVD rentals, Holiday prog, Home delivery & serv to seniorr ctr & nursing homes, Homebound delivery serv, ILL available, Internet access, Life-long learning prog for all ages, Literacy & newcomer serv, Magazines, Magnifiers for reading, Makerspace, Meeting rooms, Microfiche/film & reading machines, Movies, Museum passes, Music CDs, Online ref, Orientations, Outreach serv, OverDrive digital audio bks, Photocopying/Printing, Prof lending libr, Prog for adults, Prog for children & young adult, Ref serv available, Scanner, Senior computer classes, Senior outreach, STEM programs, Story hour, Study rm, Summer reading prog, Teen prog, Wheelchair accessible, Workshops
Publications: New Brunswick Public Library Service Statistics (Annual report)
Special Services for the Blind - Accessible computers; Assistive/Adapted tech devices, equip & products; Audio mat; Bks on CD; Braille bks; Children's Braille; Closed circuit TV magnifier; Computer with voice synthesizer for visually impaired persons; Daisy reader; Digital talking bk; Dragon Naturally Speaking software; Home delivery serv; Internet workstation with adaptive software; Large print bks; Merlin electronic magnifier reader; Playaways (bks on MP3); Scanner for conversion & translation of mats; Screen enlargement software for people with visual disabilities; Screen reader software; ZoomText magnification & reading software
Restriction: In-house use for visitors
Friends of the Library Group

G THE OMBUDSMAN LIBRARY*, 548 York St, E3B 3R2. (Mail add: PO Box 6000, E3B 5H1), SAN 373-4919. Tel: 506-453-2789. FAX: 506-453-5599. E-mail: ombud@gnb.ca. Web Site: ombudnb.ca. *Library Contact,* Julie Dickison; E-mail: julie.dickison@gnb.ca
Library Holdings: Bk Vols 100
Open Mon-Fri 8:30-4:30

S PROVINCIAL ARCHIVES OF NEW BRUNSWICK*, 23 Dineen Dr, E3B 5A3. (Mail add: PO Box 6000, E3B 5H1), SAN 318-9317. Tel: 506-453-2122. FAX: 506-453-3288. E-mail: archivesnb@gnb.ca. Web Site: archives.gnb.ca/archives. *Dir,* Joanna Aiton Kerr; E-mail: joanna.aitonkerr@gnb.ca; *Mgr,* Dean Lund; E-mail: dean.lund@gnb.ca; *Archivist,* Monica Smart; E-mail: monica.smart@gnb.ca; Staff 37 (MLS 2, Non-MLS 35)
Founded 1968
Library Holdings: Bk Vols 4,820
Special Collections: New Brunswick, broadcast rec, bus & family papers, flm & videos, govt rec, maps, photogs, plans
Wireless access
Publications: County Census (Archives guide)
Open Mon-Sat 9-5
Friends of the Library Group

C UNIVERSITY OF NEW BRUNSWICK LIBRARIES*, Harriet Irving Library, Five Macaulay Lane, E3B 5H5. (Mail add: PO Box 7500, E3B 5H5), SAN 366-5402. Tel: 506-453-4740. Circulation Tel: 506-453-4756. Reference Tel: 506-453-3546. E-mail: circhi@unb.ca. Web Site: lib.unb.ca. *Dean of Libr,* Lesley Balcom; Tel: 506-458-7056, E-mail: lbalcom@unb.ca; *Dir, Scholarly Technologies,* James MacKenzie; Tel: 506-259-2774, E-mail: jmackenz@unb.ca; *Head, Archives & Spec Coll,* Christine Lovelace; Tel: 506-447-3263, E-mail: christine.lovelace@unb.ca; *Head, Tech Serv, Librn,* Merle Steeves; Tel: 506-453-5043, E-mail: mas@unb.ca; *Librn,* Erik Moore; Tel: 506-452-6202, E-mail: ecmoore@unb.ca; *Librn,* Mike Nason; Tel: 506-452-6325, E-mail: mnason@unb.ca; *Librn,* Linda Roulston; Tel: 506-451-6879, E-mail: linda.roulston@unb.ca; *Librn,* Richelle Witherspoon; Tel: 506-453-4602, E-mail: r.witherspoon@unb.ca; *History/Special Colls Librn,* Agnieszka Sliwka; Tel: 506-453-5017, E-mail: asliwka@unb.ca; *Ref Librn,* Marc Bragdon; Tel: 506-458-7741, E-mail: mbragdon@unb.ca; Staff 24 (MLS 22, Non-MLS 2)
Founded 1829. Enrl 8,333; Fac 460; Highest Degree: Doctorate
Library Holdings: Bk Vols 1,185,417; Per Subs 3,011
Special Collections: Beaverbrook Rare Books Coll; Canadian Literature (Rufus Hathaway Coll); Historical & Literary Private Papers, R B Bennett, Lord Beaverbrook, Winslow Family, Saunders Family, Robert Hazen, H H Stuart, Lilian Maxwell & E Tappan Adney; King's College Book Coll; Marguerite Vaughan Coll; Maritime Provinces Archives Book Coll; Rare Book Coll; UNB Theses Coll, dissertations, reports theses. Oral History; State Document Depository; UN Document Depository; US Document Depository
Automation Activity & Vendor Info: (Acquisitions) SirsiDynix; (Cataloging) SirsiDynix; (Circulation) SirsiDynix; (Course Reserve) SirsiDynix; (ILL) Relais International; (OPAC) SirsiDynix; (Serials) SirsiDynix
Wireless access
Publications: Maritime Pamphlets Coll annotated list; Quest Users Guide

Partic in Canadian Association of Research Libraries; Canadian Research Knowledge Network; Consortia Canada; Council of Atlantic Academic Libraries (CAAL)
Special Services for the Deaf - Accessible learning ctr; Assistive tech
Special Services for the Blind - Accessible computers; Aids for in-house use; Assistive/Adapted tech devices, equip & products; Bks on CD; Computer with voice synthesizer for visually impaired persons
Open Mon-Thurs 7am-11pm, Fri 7am-9pm, Sat & Sun 9-8

Departmental Libraries:

ENGINEERING & COMPUTER SCIENCE, Sir Edmund Head Hall, Rm C-15, 15 Dineen Dr, E3B 5H5. (Mail add: PO Box 7500, E3B 5H5). Tel: 506-453-4747. E-mail: englib@unb.ca. Web Site: lib.unb.ca/about/engineering-computer-science-library. *Head, Eng Libr,* Saran Croos; Tel: 506-458-7959, E-mail: saran.croos@unb.ca
Library Holdings: Bk Vols 47,000; Per Subs 600

GERARD V LA FOREST LAW LIBRARY, Law School, 2nd Flr, 41 Dineen Dr, E3B 5A3. (Mail add: Bag Service No 44999, E3B 6C9), SAN 366-5526. Tel: 506-453-4734. Circulation Tel: 506-458-7983. FAX: 506-451-6948. E-mail: lawlib@unb.ca. Web Site: www.unb.ca/fredericton/law/library. *Dean,* Michael Marin; Tel: 506-453-4627, E-mail: michael.marin@unb.ca; *Assoc Dean,* Catherine Cotter; Tel: 506-477-3265, E-mail: cacotter@unb.ca; *Ref & Instruction Librn,* Nikki Tanner; Tel: 506-447-3266, E-mail: nikki.tanner@unb.ca; *Tech Serv Librn,* Susan Jones; Tel: 506-447-3267, E-mail: susan.jones@unb.ca; *Circulation & Serials Mgmt,* Heather Doherty; Tel: 506-458-7982, E-mail: hdoherty@unb.ca; *Acq, Cat, ILL/Doc Delivery Serv,* Nicole Lyons-MacFarlane; Tel: 506-458-7978, E-mail: nicole.lyons-macfarlane@unb.ca; *Cat, Reserves,* Janice Stockall; Tel: 506-458-7979, E-mail: janice.stockall@unb.ca; Staff 6.5 (MLS 3, Non-MLS 3.5)
Founded 1892
Special Collections: La Forest Rare Books Reading Room; New Brunswick Legal Heritage (C Anne Crocker Coll)
Subject Interests: Common law
Restriction: Not open to pub, Open to students, fac & staff

SCIENCE & FORESTRY, Four Bailey Dr, E3B 5H5. (Mail add: PO Box 7500, E3B 5H5). Tel: 506-453-4601. E-mail: scilib@unb.ca. Web Site: www.lib.unb.ca/about/science-forestry-library.

P YORK LIBRARY REGION*, 570 Two Nations Crossing, Ste 1, E3A 0X9. SAN 366-5550. Tel: 506-453-5380. FAX: 506-457-4878. E-mail: NBPLSYorkAdministrativeStaff@gnb.ca. Web Site: www1.gnb.ca/0003/pages/en/biblio-e.asp?code=yr. *Regional Dir,* Sarah Kilfoil; Tel: 506-444-2601, E-mail: sarah.kilfoil@gnb.ca; *Asst Regional Dir,* Tyler Griffin; *Pub Serv Librn,* Jessica Larocque; Staff 58 (MLS 14, Non-MLS 44)
Founded 1958. Pop 154,953; Circ 788,100
Library Holdings: AV Mats 49,216; DVDs 1,420; Bk Vols 452,317; Per Subs 453; Talking Bks 3,050; Videos 12,295
Special Collections: New Brunswick Local History Coll; Talking Book Coll. Canadian and Provincial; Oral History
Automation Activity & Vendor Info: (Acquisitions) SirsiDynix; (Cataloging) SirsiDynix; (Circulation) SirsiDynix; (ILL) Anacortes Software Inc; (OPAC) SirsiDynix
Wireless access
Special Services for the Blind - Talking bks
Open Mon-Fri 8-5
Restriction: Not a lending libr

Branches: 14

BIBLIOTHEQUE CARREFOUR BEAUSOLEIL LIBRARY, 300 Chemin Beaverbrook, Miramichi, E1V 1A1, SAN 328-7785. Tel: 506-627-4084. FAX: 506-627-4592. E-mail: bibliobeausoleillib@gnb.ca. Web Site: www1.gnb.ca/0003/pages/en/biblio-e.asp?code=yp. *Libr Dir,* Geneviève Thériault McGraw; E-mail: genevieve.theriault-mcgraw@gnb.ca; Staff 2 (MLS 1, Non-MLS 1)
Founded 1986. Pop 18,508; Circ 20,132
Library Holdings: AV Mats 1,421; DVDs 42; Bk Vols 18,267; Per Subs 23; Videos 464
Open Mon, Tues, Thurs & Fri 9-1 & 2-4:30, Wed 12-5 & 6-8

BIBLIOTHEQUE DRE-MARGUERITE-MICHAUD, 715 Priestman St, E3B 5W7, SAN 366-5585. Tel: 506-453-7100. FAX: 506-453-3958. E-mail: bibliodmm@gnb.ca. *Libr Dir,* Olena Bedoieva; E-mail: olena.bedoieva@gnb.ca; Staff 3 (MLS 1, Non-MLS 2)
Founded 1978. Pop 47,560; Circ 76,204
Library Holdings: AV Mats 4,125; DVDs 173; Bk Vols 32,955; Per Subs 50; Videos 1,582
Open Mon, Wed & Fri 9-5, Tues & Thurs 9-8, Sat 1-5

CHATHAM PUBLIC LIBRARY, 24 King St, Miramichi, E1N 2N1, SAN 366-5615. Tel: 506-773-6274. FAX: 506-773-6963. E-mail: chathmpl@gnb.ca. *Libr Dir,* Jennifer Wilcox; E-mail: jennifer.wilcox@gnb.ca; Staff 2 (MLS 1, Non-MLS 1)
Founded 1975. Pop 18,508; Circ 41,077
Library Holdings: AV Mats 727; Bk Vols 20,025; Per Subs 27; Videos 880
Open Tues & Thurs 1-5 & 6-8, Wed, Fri & Sat 10-12:30 & 1:30-5

CHIPMAN BRANCH, Eight King St, Chipman, E4A 2H3, SAN 366-564X. Tel: 506-339-5852. FAX: 506-339-9804. E-mail: chipman.publiclibrary@gnb.ca. *Libr Mgr,* Krista Blyth; E-mail: krista.blyth@gnb.ca; Staff 1.5 (Non-MLS 1.5)
Founded 1975. Pop 1,432; Circ 18,730
Library Holdings: AV Mats 527; Bk Vols 15,495; Per Subs 20; Videos 391
Open Tues, Thurs & Fri 9-12 & 1-5, Wed 1-5 & 6-8:30, Sat 10-12 & 1-5
Friends of the Library Group

DOAKTOWN COMMUNITY-SCHOOL LIBRARY, 430 Main St, Doaktown, E9C 1E8, SAN 370-131X. Tel: 506-365-2018. FAX: 506-365-2054. E-mail: dtcslib@gnb.ca. *Libr Mgr,* Belva Brown; E-mail: belva.brown@gnb.ca; Staff 2 (Non-MLS 2)
Founded 1986. Pop 955; Circ 23,495
Library Holdings: AV Mats 1,010; Bk Vols 18,863; Per Subs 33; Videos 826
Open Mon, Wed & Fri 9-12:30 & 1:30-5, Tues & Thurs 12-5 & 6-8

FREDERICTON PUBLIC LIBRARY, 12 Carleton St, E3B 5P4, SAN 366-5739. Tel: 506-460-2800. Reference Tel: 506-460-2812. FAX: 506-460-2801. E-mail: ftonpub@gnb.ca. Web Site: www1.gnb.ca/0003/pages/en/biblio-e.asp?code=yf. *Libr Dir,* Julia Stewart; E-mail: julia.stewart@gnb.ca; *Head of Adult & Young Adult Services,* Sarah Aaen; E-mail: sarah.aaen@gnb.ca; *Head, Children's Servx,* Jessica Larocque; E-mail: jessica.larocque@gnb.ca; *Regional Resource Librarian,* Stephanie Furrow; E-mail: stephanie.furrow@gnb.ca; *Circ Supvr,* Kim Bent; E-mail: kim.bent@gnb.ca; Staff 15 (MLS 5, Non-MLS 10)
Founded 1955. Pop 50,000; Circ 342,282
Library Holdings: AV Mats 26,396; DVDs 598; Bk Titles 126,119; Per Subs 103; Talking Bks 3,049; Videos 4,257
Special Services for the Blind - Accessible computers; Bks on CD
Open Mon, Tues & Fri-Sun 10-5, Wed & Thurs 10-9
Friends of the Library Group

FREDERICTON PUBLIC LIBRARY - NASHWAAKSIS, 324 Fulton Ave, E3A 5J4, SAN 373-5109. Tel: 506-453-3241. FAX: 506-444-4129. E-mail: nashwaaksis.library@gnb.ca. *Libr Dir,* Candace Hare; E-mail: candace.hare@gnb.ca; Staff 4 (MLS 1, Non-MLS 3)
Founded 1963. Circ 37,951
Library Holdings: AV Mats 1,023; Bk Vols 31,964; Per Subs 42; Videos 810
Open Mon, Wed, Fri & Sat 10-5, Tues & Thurs 10-9
Friends of the Library Group

HARVEY COMMUNITY LIBRARY, 2055 Rte 3, Harvey Station, E6K 1L1, SAN 370-1328. Tel: 506-366-2206. FAX: 506-366-2210. E-mail: harvey.library@gnb.ca. *Libr Mgr,* Josiane Jolin; E-mail: josiane.jolin@gnb.ca; Staff 1 (Non-MLS 1)
Founded 1986. Enrl 350; Pop 349; Circ 19,014
Library Holdings: AV Mats 132; Braille Volumes 3; CDs 50; DVDs 425; Large Print Bks 130; Bk Vols 14,532; Per Subs 35; Videos 220
Open Mon, Wed & Fri 10-12:30 & 1:30-4:30, Tues & Thurs 12-5 & 6-8

MCADAM PUBLIC LIBRARY, 146 Saunders Rd, McAdam, E6J 1L2, SAN 366-5763. Tel: 506-784-1403. FAX: 506-784-1402. E-mail: mcadam.library@gnb.ca. *Libr Mgr,* Julian Christie; E-mail: julian.christie@gnb.ca; Staff 2 (Non-MLS 2)
Founded 1962. Pop 1,513; Circ 9,234
Library Holdings: AV Mats 733; DVDs 70; Bk Vols 14,532; Videos 354
Open Tues & Thurs 12-5 & 6-8, Wed, Fri & Sat 9-12 & 1-5

MINTO PUBLIC LIBRARY, 420 Pleasant Dr, Unit 2, Minto, E4B 2T3, SAN 373-5095. Tel: 506-327-3220. FAX: 506-327-3041. E-mail: minto.publiclibrary@gnb.ca. *Libr Mgr,* Mary Lambropoulos; E-mail: mary.lambropoulos@gnb.ca; Staff 2 (Non-MLS 2)
Founded 1992. Pop 2,776; Circ 10,270
Open Tues & Thurs-Sat 10-12 & 1-5, Wed 12-4:30 & 5:30-8

NEWCASTLE PUBLIC LIBRARY, 100 Fountain Head Lane, Miramichi, E1V 4A1, SAN 370-1336. Tel: 506-623-2450. FAX: 506-623-2335. E-mail: npublib@gnb.ca. *Libr Dir,* Maureen Wallace; E-mail: maureen.wallace@gnb.ca; Staff 2 (MLS 1, Non-MLS 1)
Founded 1989. Pop 18,508; Circ 48,778
Library Holdings: AV Mats 1,126; Bk Vols 34,021; Per Subs 14; Videos 819
Open Tues & Wed 1-8, Thurs-Sat 10-5

STANLEY COMMUNITY LIBRARY, 28 Bridge St, Unit 2, Stanley, E6B 1B2, SAN 366-5976. Tel: 506-367-2492. FAX: 506-367-2764. E-mail: stanley.library@gnb.ca. *Libr Mgr,* Tim Sarty; E-mail: timothy.sarty@gnb.ca; Staff 1 (Non-MLS 1)
Founded 1968. Pop 460; Circ 13,474
Library Holdings: AV Mats 565; DVDs 30; Bk Vols 13,660; Videos 404
Open Mon-Wed & Fri 9:30-12:30 & 1:30-4:30, Thurs 12-5 & 6-8

FAY TIDD PUBLIC LIBRARY, 54 Miramichi Rd, Oromocto, E2V 1S2, SAN 366-5887. Tel: 506-357-3329. FAX: 506-357-5161. E-mail: faytidd.publiclibrary@gnb.ca. *Libr Dir,* Christin Sheridan; E-mail: christin.sheridan@gnb.ca; Staff 5 (MLS 1, Non-MLS 4)

Founded 1960. Pop 8,843; Circ 68,715
Library Holdings: AV Mats 1,488; Bk Vols 70,212; Per Subs 27; Videos 1,203
Open Mon & Thurs-Sat 10-5, Tues & Wed 10-9
UPPER MIRAMICHI COMMUNITY LIBRARY, Central New Brunswick Academy Bldg, 7263 Rte 8, Unit 1, New Bandon, E9C 2A7, SAN 372-5278. Tel: 506-365-2096. FAX: 506-365-2052. E-mail: uppermiramichi.communitylibrary@gnb.ca. *Libr Mgr,* Gail Ross; E-mail: gail.ross@gnb.ca; Staff 2 (Non-MLS 2)
Founded 1990. Pop 906; Circ 16,296
Library Holdings: AV Mats 606; Bk Titles 13,492; Per Subs 12; Videos 519
Open Mon, Thurs & Fri 9-12:30 & 1:30-5, Tues & Wed 12-5 & 6-8
Bookmobiles: 1. Supvr, Maria Whitlock

MONCTON

P ALBERT-WESTMORLAND-KENT REGIONAL LIBRARY*, 644 Main St, Ste 201, E1C 1E2. SAN 366-600X. Tel: 506-869-6032. FAX: 506-869-6022. E-mail: NBPLSAWKAdministrativeStaff@gnb.ca. Web Site: www1.gnb.ca/0003/pages/en/biblio-e.asp?code=ar. *Regional Dir,* Nadine Goguen; Tel: 506-869-6030, E-mail: nadine.goguen2@gnb.ca; *Asst Regional Dir,* Laura Mason; E-mail: NBPLS-SPBNB@gnb.ca; *Pub Serv Librn,* Robin Illsley; E-mail: robin.illsley@gnb.ca; Staff 6 (MLS 6)
Founded 1957. Pop 187,768
Library Holdings: Bk Titles 154,503; Bk Vols 387,037; Per Subs 372
Subject Interests: Culture, Local hist
Automation Activity & Vendor Info: (Acquisitions) Inlex; (Cataloging) Inlex; (Circulation) Inlex; (ILL) Inlex; (OPAC) Inlex
Wireless access
Publications: Panorama (Newsletter)
Open Mon-Fri 8:30-5
Branches: 16
BIBLIOTHEQUE PUBLIQUE DE CAP-PELE, 2638, Chemin Acadie, Cap-Pele, E4N 1E3. Tel: 506-577-2090. FAX: 506-577-2094. E-mail: bibliocp@gnb.ca. *Libr Mgr,* Michele-Ann Goguen; E-mail: michele-ann.goguen@gnb.ca
Open Tues 1-5 & 6-8, Wed-Sat 10-12:30 & 1:30-5
BIBLIOTHEQUE PUBLIQUE DE ROGERSVILLE, 65, rue de l'Ecole, Unit 1, Rogersville, E4Y 1V4. Tel: 506-775-2102. FAX: 506-775-2087. E-mail: bibliorog@gnb.ca. *Libr Mgr,* Annick Goguen; E-mail: annick.goguen@gnb.ca
Open Tues 1-5 & 6-8, Wed-Sat 10-12 & 1-5
BIBLIOTHEQUE PUBLIQUE GERALD-LEBLANC DE BOUCTOUCHE, 84 boul Irving, Unite 100, Bouctouche, E4S 3L4, SAN 373-1847. Tel: 506-743-7263. FAX: 506-743-7263. E-mail: biblioPB@gnb.ca. *Libr Mgr,* Monique Langis; E-mail: monique.langis@gnb.ca
Open Tues, Wed, Fri & Sat 10-12 & 1-5, Thurs 1-5 & 6-8
DIEPPE PUBLIC, 333 Acadie Ave, Dieppe, E1A 1G9, SAN 366-6034. Tel: 506-877-7945. FAX: 506-877-7897. E-mail: bibliopd@gnb.ca. *Libr Dir,* Nathalie Brun; E-mail: nathalie.brun@gnb.ca
Open Tues, Fri & Sat 10-5, Wed & Thurs 10-8
DORCHESTER PUBLIC, 3516 Cape Rd, Dorchester, E4K 2X5, SAN 366-6069. Tel: 506-379-3032. FAX: 506-379-3033. E-mail: DorchPL@gnb.ca. *Libr Mgr,* Krista Johansen; E-mail: krista.johansen@gnb.ca
Open Thurs 1-5 & 6-8, Fri 10-12 & 1-4, Sat 10-12 & 1-3
HILLSBOROUGH PUBLIC, 2849 Main St, Unit 2, Hillsborough, E4H 2X7, SAN 366-6093. Tel: 506-734-3722. FAX: 506-734-3711. E-mail: hillsborough.publiclibrary@gnb.ca. *Libr Mgr,* Victoria Stroud; E-mail: victoria.stroud@gnb.ca
Open Tues, Wed, Fri & Sat 10-12 & 1-5, Thurs 1-5 & 6-8
MEMRAMCOOK PUBLIC, 540 Centrale St, Unit 1, Memramcook, E4K 3S6, SAN 366-6271. Tel: 506-758-4029. FAX: 506-758-4030. E-mail: bibliopm@gnb.ca. *Libr Mgr,* Lynn Bourgeois; E-mail: lynn.bourgeois@gnb.ca
Open Tues 1-5 & 6-8, Wed-Sat 10-12 & 1-5
MONCTON PUBLIC, 644 Main St, Ste 101, E1C 1E2, SAN 366-6158. Tel: 506-869-6000. FAX: 506-869-6040. E-mail: mplib@gnb.ca. *Libr Dir,* Chantale Bellemare; E-mail: chantale.bellemare@gnb.ca
Open Mon & Thurs-Sun 10-5, Tues & Wed 10-9
OMER-LEGER PUBLIC LIBRARY, 4556 Principale St, Ste 100, Saint-Antoine, E4V 1R3, SAN 366-6263. Tel: 506-525-4028. FAX: 506-525-4199. E-mail: BiblioSA@gnb.ca. *Libr Mgr,* Sylvie Hebert; E-mail: sylvie.hebert@gnb.ca
Open Tues, Wed, Fri & Sat 10-12 & 1-5, Thurs 1-5 & 6-8
PETITCODIAC PUBLIC, Six Kay St, Ste 101, Petitcodiac, E4Z 4K6, SAN 366-6166. Tel: 506-756-3144. FAX: 506-756-3142. E-mail: petitcodiac.publiclibrary@gnb.ca. *Libr Mgr,* Danny Jacobs; E-mail: danny.jacobs@gnb.ca
Open Tues, Wed, Fri & Sat 10-1 & 2-5, Thurs 1-5 & 6-8
PORT ELGIN PUBLIC, 33 Moore Rd, Port Elgin, E4M 2E6, SAN 366-6182. Tel: 506-538-9001. E-mail: portepl@gnb.ca. *Libr Mgr,* Kathleen Grigg; E-mail: kathleen.grigg@gnb.ca
Open Tues & Thurs-Sat 10-12 & 1-5, Wed 1-5 & 6-8
RICHIBUCTO PUBLIC, 9376 Main St, Richibucto, E4W 4C9, SAN 366-6190. Tel: 506-523-7851. FAX: 506-523-2019. E-mail: bibliori@gnb.ca. *Libr Mgr,* Sylvie Bourque; E-mail: sylvie.bourque@gnb.ca
Open Tues, Wed, Fri & Sat 10-1 & 2-5, Thurs 1-5 & 6-8
RIVERVIEW PUBLIC, 34 Honour House Ct, Riverview, E1B 3Y9, SAN 366-6212. Tel: 506-387-2108. FAX: 506-387-7120. E-mail: rplib@gnb.ca. *Libr Dir,* Elizabeth Boutilier; E-mail: elizabeth.boutilier@gnb.ca
Open Tues 10-8, Wed, Fri & Sat 10-5, Thurs 1-8
SACKVILLE PUBLIC, 66 Main St, Sackville, E4L 4A7, SAN 366-6247. Tel: 506-364-4915. E-mail: spublib@gnb.ca. *Libr Mgr,* Allan Alward; E-mail: allan.alward@gnb.ca
Open Tues 1-5 & 6-8, Wed-Sat 10-12 & 1-5
SALISBURY PUBLIC, 3215 Main St, Salisbury, E4J 2K7, SAN 366-628X. Tel: 506-372-3240. FAX: 506-372-3261. E-mail: salisbury.publiclibrary@gnb.ca. *Libr Mgr,* Cathy MacDonald; E-mail: cathy.macdonald@gnb.ca
Library Holdings: Bk Vols 10,000
Open Tues & Thurs-Sat 10-12 & 1-5, Wed 1-5 & 6-8
SHEDIAC PUBLIC, 290 Main St, Unit 100, Shediac, E4P 2E3, SAN 366-6301. Tel: 506-532-7014. FAX: 506-532-8400. E-mail: bibliosh@gnb.ca. *Libr Mgr,* Gabrielle Leblanc; E-mail: gabrielle.leblanc@gnb.ca
Open Tues, Fri & Sat 10-5, Wed 10-8, Thurs 1-8
Bookmobiles: 1

C CRANDALL UNIVERSITY*, George A Rawlyk Library, 333 Gorge Rd, E1C 3H9. (Mail add: Box 6004, E1C 9L7), SAN 324-1203. Tel: 506-858-8970, Ext 171. FAX: 506-863-6460. Web Site: www.crandallu.ca/student-life/george-a-rawlyk-library. *Head Librn,* David Purdy; E-mail: david.purdy@crandallu.ca
Founded 1949. Enrl 735; Fac 65; Highest Degree: Bachelor
Library Holdings: Bk Vols 57,000; Per Subs 155
Subject Interests: Art, Lit, Maritime Can hist, Music, Relig
Wireless access
Open Mon & Thurs 8:30am-10pm, Tues & Wed 8:30-11:15 & 1-10, Fri 8:30-5, Sat 9-5

M HORIZON HEALTH NETWORK*, Library Services, 135 MacBeath Ave, E1C 6Z8. SAN 318-9341. Tel: 506-857-5447. FAX: 506-857-5785. E-mail: Library@HorizonNB.ca. *Regional Mgr, Libr Serv,* Lori Leger; Tel: 506-870-2546, E-mail: Lori.Leger@HorizonNB.ca; *Libr Tech,* Karen Darrach; E-mail: Karen.Darrach@HorizonNB.ca; *Libr Tech,* Shannon MacTavish; E-mail: Shannon.MacTavish@HorizonNB.ca. Subject Specialists: *Health,* Karen Darrach; *Health,* Shannon MacTavish; Staff 3 (MLS 1, Non-MLS 2)
Apr 2019-Mar 2020. Mats Exp (CAN) $888,000, Books (CAN) $45,000, Per/Ser (Incl. Access Fees) (CAN) $350,000, Electronic Ref Mat (Incl. Access Fees) (CAN) $450,000
Library Holdings: e-books 219; e-journals 75; Bk Titles 5,000
Automation Activity & Vendor Info: (Acquisitions) EBSCO Online; (OPAC) Inmagic, Inc.; (Serials) EBSCO Online
Wireless access
Partic in Council of Atlantic Academic Libraries (CAAL)
Open Mon-Fri 8-4:30
Friends of the Library Group

C NEW BRUNSWICK COMMUNITY COLLEGE*, Moncton Campus Library Learning Commons, 1234 Mountain Rd, E1C 8H9. SAN 329-7322. Tel: 506-856-2226. Web Site: nbcc.libguides.com. *Coordr,* Caroline Baab; E-mail: caroline.baab@nbcc.ca
Founded 1965. Enrl 1,200; Fac 200
Library Holdings: Bk Titles 13,000; Per Subs 50
Special Collections: Disability Information Coll, bks, mag, pamphlets. Canadian and Provincial
Subject Interests: Civil engr, Electronics
Automation Activity & Vendor Info: (Cataloging) Follett Software; (Circulation) Follett Software; (OPAC) Follett Software
Wireless access
Special Services for the Deaf - Spec interest per
Open Mon-Fri 7-5:30

C UNIVERSITE DE MONCTON*, Bibliotheque Champlain, 18, ave Antonine-Maillet, E1A 3E9. SAN 366-6336. Tel: 506-858-4012. Interlibrary Loan Service Tel: 506-858-4185. Reference Tel: 506-858-4998. FAX: 506-858-4086. E-mail: bichamp@umoncton.ca. Web Site: www.umoncton.ca/umcm-bibliotheque-champlain. *Chief Librn,* Marthe Brideau; E-mail: marthe.brideau@umoncton.ca; *Asst Chief Librn,* Pauline Simard; E-mail: pauline.simard@umoncton.ca; *Head, ILL,* Denise M Savoie; E-mail: denise.m.savoie@umoncton.ca; *Head, Pub Serv, Librn,* Hector Alvarez; Tel: 506-858-4911, E-mail: hector.alvarez@umoncton.ca; *Ref Librn,* Pierre Goguen; E-mail: pierre.goguen@umoncton.ca; *Ref Librn,* Marc Harper; E-mail: marc.harper@umoncton.ca; *Ref Librn,* Adel Labidi; E-mail: adel.labidi@umoncton.ca; *Ref Librn,* Nathalie Richard; E-mail:

nathalie.richard@umoncton.ca; *Ref Librn,* Victoria Volkanova; E-mail: victoria.volkanova@umoncton.ca; Staff 10 (MLS 7, Non-MLS 3)
Founded 1965. Enrl 5,200; Fac 280; Highest Degree: Doctorate
Library Holdings: Bk Vols 434,000; Per Subs 1,595
Special Collections: Acadian Literature & History; Can; French Canadian Literature
Automation Activity & Vendor Info: (Acquisitions) SirsiDynix; (Cataloging) SirsiDynix; (Circulation) SirsiDynix; (ILL) Relais International; (OPAC) SirsiDynix; (Serials) SirsiDynix
Partic in Canadian Research Knowledge Network; Council of Atlantic Academic Libraries (CAAL)
Departmental Libraries:
CL BIBLIOTHEQUE DE DROIT MICHEL-BASTARCHE, Pavillon Adrein-J Cormier (MAC), 409 ave de l'Universite, E1A 3E9. (Mail add: Pavillon Leopold-Taillon, 18 ave Antonine-Maillet, E1A 3E9). Tel: 506-858-4547. FAX: 506-858-4518. E-mail: bibliodroit@umoncton.ca. Web Site: www.umoncton.ca/umcm-bibliotheque-droit. *Librn,* Michele LeBlanc; Tel: 506-858-4776, E-mail: michel.leblanc@umoncton.ca; Staff 6 (MLS 2, Non-MLS 4)
Founded 1978. Enrl 106; Highest Degree: Master
Library Holdings: Electronic Media & Resources 40; Bk Vols 150,000; Per Subs 350
Subject Interests: Common law
Automation Activity & Vendor Info: (Acquisitions) Infor Library & Information Solutions; (Cataloging) Infor Library & Information Solutions; (Circulation) Infor Library & Information Solutions; (Course Reserve) Infor Library & Information Solutions; (ILL) Infor Library & Information Solutions; (Media Booking) Infor Library & Information Solutions; (OPAC) Infor Library & Information Solutions; (Serials) Infor Library & Information Solutions
Open Mon-Thurs 8am-9pm, Fri 8-6, Sat & Sun Noon-6
C BIBLIOTHEQUE DU CAMPUS DE SHIPPAGAN, 218 Blvd J-D-Gauthier, Shippagan, E8S 1P6, SAN 370-6478. Tel: 506-336-3418, 506-336-3420. Toll Free Tel: 800-363-8336. FAX: 506-336-3434. E-mail: umcsbiblio@umoncton.ca. *Mgr,* Hélène McLaughlin
Library Holdings: Bk Titles 40,000; Per Subs 325
Open Mon-Thurs 8:30am-10:45pm, Fri 8:30-6
CENTRE DE RESSOURCES PEDAGOGIQUES, Pavillon Jeanne-de-Valois, local B-010, 68, rue Notre-Dame-du-Sacré-Coeur, E1A 3E9. (Mail add: Pavillon Leopold-Taillon, 18 ave Antonine-Maillet, E1A 3E9). Tel: 506-858-4356. FAX: 506-858-4317. E-mail: crp@umoncton.ca. Web Site: www.umoncton.ca/umcm-bibliotheque-crp. *Pub Serv,* Marie-Josée Robichaud; E-mail: marie-josee.robichaud@umoncton.ca
Founded 1973. Fac 35; Highest Degree: Doctorate
Library Holdings: Bk Vols 32,000
Subject Interests: Educ
Open Mon-Fri 8-5, Sun 12-5
CENTRE D'ETUDES ACADIENNES, Champlain Library (MCH), 415 ave de l'Universite, E1A 3E9. (Mail add: 18, Ave Antonine-Maillet, E1A 3E9). Tel: 506-858-4085. FAX: 506-858-4530. E-mail: cea-um@umoncton.ca. Web Site: www.umoncton.ca/umcm-ceaac. *Documentation Tech,* Francois J LeBlanc; E-mail: francois.j.leblanc@umoncton.ca
Library Holdings: Bk Vols 13,000; Per Subs 100
Special Collections: Acadian History. Oral History
Publications: Contact-Acadie
Open Mon-Wed & Fri 8:30-4:30, Thurs 8:30-4:30 & 7-10

PRINCE WILLIAM

S KINGS LANDING LIBRARY, 5804 Rte 102, E6K 0A5. SAN 377-077X. Tel: 506-363-4999. FAX: 506-363-4989. Web Site: kingslanding.nb.ca. *Res Mgr,* Evelyn Fidler; Tel: 506-476-1905, E-mail: evelyn.fidler@gnb.ca
Library Holdings: Bk Titles 5,000
Restriction: Not open to pub

SACKVILLE

C MOUNT ALLISON UNIVERSITY LIBRARIES & ARCHIVES, Ralph Pickard Bell Library, 49 York St, E4L 1C6. SAN 366-645X. Tel: 506-364-2568. FAX: 506-364-2617. E-mail: archives@mta.ca, circ@mta.ca. Web Site: libraryguides.mta.ca. *Dean of Libraries & Archives,* Rachel Rubin; Tel: 506-364-2567, E-mail: university_librarian@mta.ca; *Data & Digital Services Librn,* Elizabeth Stregger; Tel: 506-364-2610, E-mail: estregger@mta.ca; *Research & Teaching Librn,* Laura Landon; Tel: 506-364-2572, E-mail: llandon@mta.ca; *Tech Serv & Syst Librn,* Anne LePage; Tel: 506-364-2691, E-mail: alepage@mta.ca; *Univ Archivist,* David Mawhinney; Tel: 506-364-2563, E-mail: dmawhinney@mta.ca; Staff 29 (MLS 9, Non-MLS 20)
Founded 1862. Enrl 2,200; Fac 140; Highest Degree: Master
Library Holdings: Bk Titles 450,000; Bk Vols 500,000; Per Subs 1,250
Special Collections: Folklore, Ballads & Poetry (Mary Mellish Archibald Coll), a-tapes, bks, per & rec; Local History Archives; Maritime Provinces (Winthrop Pickard Bell Coll), bks, maps, micro & per; Mount Allison University Archives
Automation Activity & Vendor Info: (Acquisitions) SirsiDynix; (Cataloging) SirsiDynix; (ILL) Relais International; (OPAC) SirsiDynix
Wireless access
Publications: Bell Catalogue of Acadiana; Bibliography of George Frances Gilman Stanley; Catalogue of Canadian Folk Music; Classified Catalogue of Canadian Music; Lawren Phillips Harris: A Bibliography; Maritime Literature Reprint Series; Scores & Recordings
Partic in Council of Atlantic Academic Libraries (CAAL); Novanet; Utlas
Open Mon-Thurs 8:10am-11pm, Fri 8:10am-9pm, Sat Noon-8, Sun 1pm-11pm
Departmental Libraries:
ALFRED WHITEHEAD MUSIC LIBRARY, 134 Main St, E4L 1A6. Tel: 506-364-2561. Administration Tel: 506-364-2214. E-mail: musiclibrary@mta.ca. Web Site: libraryguides.mta.ca/music_library. *Libr Asst,* Jakob Roberts; E-mail: jaroberts@mta.ca; Staff 2 (MLS 1, Non-MLS 1)
Enrl 2,000; Fac 16; Highest Degree: Master
Special Collections: Canadian Music Coll
Restriction: Limited access for the pub, Open by appt only, Open to fac, students & qualified researchers, Open to students, fac & staff

SAINT ANDREWS

S SUNBURY SHORES ARTS & NATURE CENTRE, INC LIBRARY*, 139 Water St, E5B 1A7. SAN 320-3190. Tel: 506-529-3386. E-mail: info@sunburyshores.org. Web Site: www.sunburyshores.org. *Library Contact,* Joe McEachern
Founded 1964
Library Holdings: Bk Titles 1,000; Per Subs 10
Special Collections: Kronenburg Memorial Art Coll
Subject Interests: Art educ, Conserv, Ecology, Natural hist
Wireless access
Open Tues-Sat 10-4

SAINT JOHN

L COX & PALMER*, Law Library, One Brunswick Sq, Ste 1500, One Germain St, E2L 4H8. SAN 326-4696. Tel: 506-632-8900. FAX: 506-632-8809. E-mail: saintjohn@coxandpalmer.com. Web Site: coxandpalmerlaw.com. *Librn,* Marilyn Brown; E-mail: sjlaw@nbnet.nb.ca
Library Holdings: Bk Titles 4,000
Restriction: Not open to pub, Private libr

P FUNDY LIBRARY REGION*, One Market Sq, E2L 4Z6. SAN 318-9414. Tel: 506-643-7222. FAX: 506-643-7225. E-mail: nbplsfundyadministrativestaff@gnb.ca. Web Site: www1.gnb.ca/0003/pages/en/biblio-e.asp?code=fr. *Regional Dir,* Amy Heans; E-mail: amy.heans@gnb.ca; *Regional Resource Librarian,* Keith MacKinnon; E-mail: keith.mackinnon@gnb.ca; *Acting Collections Mgmt Librn,* Robin Sexton-Mayes; E-mail: robin.sexton-mayes@gnb.ca; *Pub Serv Librn,* Nora Kennedy; E-mail: nora.kennedy@gnb.ca; Staff 10 (MLS 4, Non-MLS 6)
Pop 111,519
Automation Activity & Vendor Info: (Acquisitions) SirsiDynix; (Cataloging) SirsiDynix; (Circulation) SirsiDynix; (Media Booking) SirsiDynix; (OPAC) SirsiDynix; (Serials) SirsiDynix
Wireless access
Special Services for the Deaf - Bks on deafness & sign lang
Special Services for the Blind - Bks on cassette; Bks on CD; Braille alphabet card; Children's Braille; Extensive large print coll; Large print bks; Large print bks & talking machines; Talking bk & rec for the blind cat; Talking bks
Open Mon-Fri 8:30-5
Branches: 10
BIBLIOTHEQUE LE CORMORAN, Centre Samuel de Champlain, 67 Ragged Point Rd, E2K 5C3, SAN 373-7837. Tel: 506-658-4610. FAX: 506-658-3984. E-mail: bibliolc@gnb.ca. *Libr Dir,* Mireille Mercure; E-mail: mireille.mercure@gnb.ca
Founded 1985
Open Mon & Wed-Fri 9-5, Tues 9-8
CAMPOBELLO PUBLIC LIBRARY, Three Welshhpool St, Campobello Parish, E5E 1G3, SAN 326-5803. Tel: 506-752-7082. FAX: 506-752-7083. E-mail: campbopl@gnb.ca. *Actg Libr Mgr,* Stephanie Gough; E-mail: stephanie.gough@gnb.ca
Open Tues 2-5 & 6-8, Wed-Fri 10-12 & 1-4
GRAND MANAN LIBRARY, 1144, Rte 776, Grand Manan, E5G 4E8. Tel: 506-662-7099. FAX: 506-662-7094. E-mail: grandmananlibrary@gnb.ca. *Libr Mgr,* Kendra Neves; E-mail: kendra.neves@gnb.ca
Open Mon, Tues, Thurs & Fri 9-4:30, Wed 9-4 & 5-7:45

KENNEBECASIS PUBLIC LIBRARY, One Landing Ct, Quispamsis, E2E 4R2. Tel: 506-849-5314. E-mail: kennebpl@gnb.ca. Web Site: www1.gnb.ca/0003/pages/en/biblio-e.asp?code=fk. *Libr Dir,* Norah Emerson; E-mail: norah.emerson@gnb.ca; Staff 5 (MLS 1, Non-MLS 4)
Founded 1984
Function: 24/7 Electronic res, 24/7 Online cat, Activity rm, Adult bk club, Art exhibits, Audio & video playback equip for onsite use, Audiobks on Playaways & MP3, AV serv, Bk club(s), Bks on CD, CD-ROM, Children's prog, Computers for patron use, Digital talking bks, Doc delivery serv, Electronic databases & coll, Extended outdoor wifi, Family literacy, Free DVD rentals, Games, Holiday prog, Homebound delivery serv, ILL available, Internet access, Large print keyboards, Magazines, Magnifiers for reading, Meeting rooms, Music CDs, Online cat, Outreach serv, OverDrive digital audio bks, Photocopying/Printing, Prog for adults, Prog for children & young adult, Ref & res, Scanner, STEM programs, Story hour, Study rm, Summer reading prog, Tax forms, Wheelchair accessible
Special Services for the Deaf - Bks on deafness & sign lang
Special Services for the Blind - Audio mat; Bks on cassette; Blind Club (monthly newsletter); Children's Braille; Large print bks; Talking bks; VIEW (Visually Impaired Educational Workstation)
Open Tues, Wed, Fri & Sat 10-4, Thurs 1-7

ROSS MEMORIAL LIBRARY, 110 King St, Saint Andrews, E5B 1Y6. Tel: 506-529-5125. FAX: 506-529-5129. E-mail: standrpl@gnb.ca. *Libr Mgr,* Lesley Wells; E-mail: lesley.wells@gnb.ca
Open Tues 12-7, Wed-Fri 10-4, Sat 10-12:30 & 1:30-4
Friends of the Library Group

ST CROIX PUBLIC LIBRARY, 11 King St, Saint Stephen, E3L 2C1. Tel: 506-466-7529. FAX: 506-466-7574. E-mail: ststeppl@gnb.ca. *Libr Dir,* Rebekah Wheaton; E-mail: rebekah.wheaton@gnb.ca
Open Tues 2-4 & 5-8, Wed-Sat 10-12 & 1-5

SAINT JOHN FREE PUBLIC LIBRARY, CENTRAL BRANCH, One Market Sq, E2L 4Z6. Tel: 506-643-7236. E-mail: sjfpl@gnb.ca. *Libr Dir,* Laura Corscadden; E-mail: laura.corscadden@gnb.ca
Special Collections: Local Family History Coll; Microforms; New Brunswickana, Canadian, Atlantic Seabord & Local History (Victorian Era Coll); Newspapers, dating back to 1785. Canadian and Provincial
Subject Interests: Genealogy, Local hist
Open Tues, Wed, Fri & Sat 10-5, Thurs 1-8

SAINT JOHN FREE PUBLIC LIBRARY, EAST BRANCH, 55 McDonald St, E2J 0C7. Tel: 506-643-7250. E-mail: eastbranch.publiclibrary@gnb.ca. *Libr Mgr,* Emily King; E-mail: emily.king@gnb.ca
Open Tues 1-7, Wed-Sat 10-4

SAINT JOHN FREE PUBLIC LIBRARY, WEST BRANCH, Lancaster Mall, 621 Fairville Blvd, E2M 4X5, SAN 326-257X. Tel: 506-643-7260. E-mail: westbranch.publiclibrary@gnb.ca. *Libr Dir,* Laura Corscadden
Open Tues & Thurs-Sat 10-4, Wed 1-7

SUSSEX REGIONAL LIBRARY, 46 Magnolia Ave, Sussex, E4E 2H2. Tel: 506-432-4585. FAX: 506-432-4583. E-mail: sussexpl@gnb.ca. *Libr Dir,* Vanessa Black; E-mail: vanessa.black@gnb.ca
Special Collections: Microforms
Open Tues & Thurs-Sat 11-4:30, Wed 1-7:30

J NEW BRUNSWICK COMMUNITY COLLEGE*, L R Fulton Library & Audiovisual Center, 950 Grandview Ave, E2L 3V1. Tel: 506-658-6727. FAX: 506-643-2853. Web Site: nbcc.libguides.com?b=5. *Librn,* Elizabeth Weaver; E-mail: elizabeth.weaver@nbcc.ca; Staff 3 (MLS 1, Non-MLS 2)
Library Holdings: Bk Vols 15,000; Per Subs 300
Automation Activity & Vendor Info: (Cataloging) Follett Software; (Circulation) Follett Software; (OPAC) Follett Software; (Serials) Surpass
Wireless access
Open Mon, Wed & Thurs 8:15am-10pm, Tues 7:45am-10pm, Fri 8:15-4:30, Sat & Sun 12-5

S NEW BRUNSWICK MUSEUM ARCHIVES & RESEARCH LIBRARY*, 277 Douglas Ave, E2K 1E5. SAN 318-9406. Tel: 506-643-2322. Toll Free Tel: 888-268-9595. FAX: 506-643-2360. E-mail: archives@nbm-mnb.ca. Web Site: www.nbm-mnb.ca. *Head Librn,* Felicity Osepchook; Tel: 506-643-2324; *Libr Asst,* Jennifer Longon; Staff 3 (Non-MLS 3)
Founded 1931
Library Holdings: Bk Titles 45,000; Per Subs 500
Special Collections: Art & Canadiana (Webster Coll); New Brunswickana (Ganong Coll)
Subject Interests: Botany, Decorative art, Fine arts, Geol, Shipping, Zoology
Library has been temporarily relocated as of Oct 2023 to the Collections & Research Centre at 228 Lancaster Ave

L SAINT JOHN LAW SOCIETY LIBRARY*, Ten Peel Plaza, E2L 4Y9. (Mail add: PO Box 5001, E2L 4Y9), SAN 373-8302. Tel: 506-658-2542. E-mail: sjlaw@nbnet.nb.ca. Web Site: lawsociety-barreau.nb.ca/en/public/law-libraries. *Librn,* Marilyn Brown; Staff 1 (Non-MLS 1)
Library Holdings: Bk Vols 10,000
Open Mon-Fri 8:30-4:30

M SAINT JOHN REGIONAL HOSPITAL*, Library Services, 400 University Ave, E2L 4L2. SAN 326-002X. Tel: 506-648-6763. FAX: 506-648-6859. E-mail: library@horizonnb.ca.
Wireless access
Open Mon-Fri 8-4:30

C UNIVERSITY OF NEW BRUNSWICK, SAINT JOHN CAMPUS*, Hans W Klohn Commons, 100 Tucker Park Rd, E2L 4L5. (Mail add: PO Box 5050, E2L 4L5), SAN 318-9422. Tel: 506-648-5710. Interlibrary Loan Service Tel: 506-648-5705. Reference Tel: 506-648-5888. Administration Tel: 506-648-5700. E-mail: hwkcommons@unb.ca. Web Site: www.lib.unb.ca. *Head Librn, Head, Res Serv,* David Ross; Tel: 506-648-5832, E-mail: drross@unb.edu; *Librn,* Alex Goudreau; *Librn,* Philip Taber; Staff 12 (MLS 3, Non-MLS 9)
Founded 1965. Enrl 2,000; Fac 125
Library Holdings: e-books 1,000,000; e-journals 80,000; Bk Titles 140,000
Special Collections: Science Fiction & Fantasy
Subject Interests: Bahav sci, Hist, Marine biol, Nursing, Soc sci
Wireless access
Function: Archival coll, Distance learning, Doc delivery serv, Equip loans & repairs, ILL available, Mail & tel request accepted, Online info literacy tutorials on the web & in blackboard, Outside serv via phone, mail, e-mail & web, Photocopying/Printing, Ref serv available, VHS videos

SUSSEX

CR KINGSWOOD UNIVERSITY*, Earle & Marion Trouten Library, 248 Main St, E4E 1R3. (Mail add: PO Box 5125, E4E 5L2), SAN 370-5625. Tel: 506-432-4417. Circulation Tel: 506-432-4437. FAX: 506-432-4425. E-mail: library@kingswood.edu. Web Site: www.kingswood.edu/library. *Dir, Libr Serv,* Virnna Sabine; E-mail: sabinev@kingswood.edu; *Libr Asst,* Amanda McFadzen; Staff 2 (MLS 1, Non-MLS 1)
Founded 1945. Enrl 140; Fac 11; Highest Degree: Master
Library Holdings: Bk Titles 33,596; Bk Vols 36,000
Subject Interests: Biblical studies, Theol
Automation Activity & Vendor Info: (Cataloging) TLC (The Library Corporation); (Circulation) TLC (The Library Corporation); (Course Reserve) TLC (The Library Corporation); (ILL) OCLC WorldShare Interlibrary Loan; (OPAC) TLC (The Library Corporation)
Wireless access
Partic in Association of Christian Librarians
Open Mon-Thurs 8am-10pm, Sat 12-5

WATERVILLE

M UPPER RIVER VALLEY HOSPITAL LIBRARY*, 11300 Rte 130, E7P 0A4. SAN 328-2309. Tel: 506-375-2740. FAX: 506-375-2680. E-mail: library@horizonnb.ca. Web Site: en.horizonnb.ca.
Library Holdings: Bk Titles 500; Per Subs 40
Partic in Maritimes Health Libraries Association
Open Mon-Fri 10-2:30

NEWFOUNDLAND & LABRADOR

Date of Statistics: Not provided.

ARNOLD'S COVE

P ARNOLD'S COVE PUBLIC LIBRARY*, Five Highliner Dr, A0B 1A0. (Mail add: PO Box 239, A0B 1A0). Tel: 709-463-8707. E-mail: arnoldscove@nlpl.ca. *Librn,* Beverly Best
Library Holdings: Bk Vols 11,000; Per Subs 22
Automation Activity & Vendor Info: (Cataloging) SirsiDynix; (Circulation) SirsiDynix; (OPAC) SirsiDynix
Wireless access
Function: ILL available, Magazines, Photocopying/Printing, Story hour
Open Tues 12-5, Wed 5-9, Thurs & Fri 10-3:30

BAY ROBERTS

P BAY ROBERTS PUBLIC LIBRARY, PO Box 610, A0A 1G0. Tel: 709-786-9629. FAX: 709-786-9674. Web Site: nlpl.ca. *Librn,* Marilyn Clarke; E-mail: mclarke@nlpl.ca
Wireless access
Open Tues & Thurs 10:30-5 & 7-9, Wed 10:30-5, Fri & Sat 10:30-3

BELL ISLAND

P BELL ISLAND PUBLIC LIBRARY*, Provincial Bldg, 20 Bennett St, A0A 4H0. (Mail add: PO Box 760, A0A 4H0). Tel: 709-488-2413. FAX: 709-488-2413. *Div Mgr,* Andrew Lockhart; E-mail: alockhart@nlpl.ca; *Librn,* Melanie Butler
Library Holdings: Per Subs 24
Wireless access
Open Tues & Fri 9-5, Sat 10-2

BONAVISTA

P BONAVISTA MEMORIAL PUBLIC LIBRARY, 32 Church St, A0C 1B0. (Mail add: PO Box 400, A0C 1B0). Tel: 709-468-2185. Web Site: nlpl.ca. *Librn,* Brenda Wilton
Founded 1945. Pop 3,800; Circ 10,000
Library Holdings: Bk Vols 14,000; Per Subs 25
Wireless access
Open Mon-Wed 1:30-5 & 7-9, Sat 1:30-5 (Fall); Mon-Wed 1:30-5 & 7-9, Fri 1:30-5 (Summer)

BRIGUS

P BRIGUS PUBLIC LIBRARY*, Seven S St, A0A 1K0. Tel: 709-528-3156. *Div Mgr,* Andrew Lockhart; *Library Contact,* Raelene Wall; E-mail: rwall@nlpl.ca
Library Holdings: Bk Titles 25,000; Per Subs 8
Wireless access
Open Mon 7pm-9pm, Tues & Thurs 12-5, Wed 10-5

BURIN BAY ARM

P BURIN MEMORIAL PUBLIC LIBRARY, 48 B Main St, A0E 1G0. (Mail add: PO Box 219, A0E 1G0). Tel: 709-891-1924. E-mail: burin@nlpl.ca. Web Site: nlpl.ca/locations-hours/bbn.
Library Holdings: Bk Vols 10,000; Per Subs 40
Automation Activity & Vendor Info: (Cataloging) SirsiDynix-Enterprise; (OPAC) SirsiDynix-Enterprise
Wireless access
Open Tues & Thurs 2-5:30 & 7-9, Wed 10-12 & 2-5:30, Sat 11-4

CARBONEAR

P CARBONEAR PUBLIC LIBRARY*, 256 Water St, A1Y 1C4. (Mail add: PO Box 928, A1Y 1C4). Tel: 709-596-3382. E-mail: carbonear@nlpl.ca. *Librn,* Tracey Vaughan-Evans
Library Holdings: Bk Vols 15,000; Per Subs 35
Wireless access
Function: Computer training, ILL available, Photocopying/Printing, Scanner, Story hour
Special Services for the Blind - Talking bks
Open Tues 11-4:30, Wed 2-8, Thurs 2-6:45, Fri 10:30-4:30, Sat 12-4

CATALINA

P TRINITY BAY NORTH PUBLIC LIBRARY, PO Box 69, A0C 1J0. Tel: 709-469-3045. FAX: 709-469-3045. E-mail: trinitybaynorth@nlpl.ca. Web Site: nlpl.ca/component/jumi/library.html?site_id=bca. *Div Mgr,* Andrew Lockhart; *Librn,* Kim Johnson
Founded 1937
Library Holdings: Bk Vols 9,157
Wireless access
Open Tues & Thurs 2-5 & 7-9, Wed 1-4, Sat 2-4

CLARENVILLE

P CLARENVILLE PUBLIC LIBRARY*, 98 Manitoba Dr, A5A 1K7. Tel: 709-466-7634. E-mail: clarenville@nlpl.ca. *Librn,* Kaitlyn Penney
Library Holdings: Bk Vols 21,560
Wireless access
Function: ILL available, Magazines, Photocopying/Printing, Story hour
Open Tues 12-5, Wed 12-7:30, Thurs 10-5, Fri 10-4

CONCEPTION BAY SOUTH

P CONCEPTION BAY SOUTH PUBLIC LIBRARY, Ten Remembrance Sq, A1X 0M2. Tel: 709-834-3620. E-mail: conceptionbaysouth@nlpl.ca. Web Site: nlpl.ca/locations-hours/acs.
Library Holdings: Bk Titles 45,000; Per Subs 16
Automation Activity & Vendor Info: (Cataloging) SirsiDynix-Enterprise; (OPAC) SirsiDynix-Enterprise
Wireless access
Open Tues 12-6, Wed & Thurs 10-8, Fri & Sat 10-6

CORNER BROOK

M WESTERN MEMORIAL REGIONAL HOSPITAL*, Health Sciences Library, One Brookfield Ave, A2H 6J7. (Mail add: PO Box 2005, A2H 6J7), SAN 329-9759. Tel: 709-784-5395. E-mail: library@westernhealth.nl.ca. Web Site: westernhealth.nl.ca/careers/learning-western-health/library-services. *Librn III, Team Leader,* Kim Hancock; Tel: 709-784-5218, E-mail: kimhancock@westernhealth.nl.ca; Staff 2 (MLS 2)
Library Holdings: Bk Titles 11,000; Per Subs 250
Subject Interests: Allied health, Med, Nursing
Open Mon-Fri 8am-10pm
Restriction: Restricted borrowing privileges

FORTUNE

P FORTUNE PUBLIC LIBRARY, One Temple St, A0E 1P0. (Mail add: PO Box 400, A0E 1P0). Tel: 709-832-0232. E-mail: fortune@nlpl.ca. Web Site: nlpl.ca/locations-hours/bfe.
Library Holdings: Bk Vols 7,350; Per Subs 20
Automation Activity & Vendor Info: (Cataloging) SirsiDynix-Enterprise; (OPAC) SirsiDynix-Enterprise
Wireless access
Open Tues & Wed 11-4, Thurs 5-7, Fri 9-2

FOX HARBOUR

P FOX HARBOUR PUBLIC LIBRARY, Two Southside Rd, A0B 1V0. Tel: 709-227-2135. E-mail: foxharbour@nlpl.ca. Web Site: nlpl.ca/locations-hours/afh.
Library Holdings: Bk Vols 5,280; Per Subs 14
Automation Activity & Vendor Info: (Cataloging) SirsiDynix-Enterprise; (OPAC) SirsiDynix-Enterprise
Wireless access
Open Tues 2:30-5:30 & 6-7, Wed 10-2, Sat 10:30-12:30 & 1-5

GARNISH

P GARNISH PUBLIC LIBRARY, Garnish Town Hall, 614 Sunset Dr, A0E 1T0. (Mail add: PO Box 40, A0E 1T0). Tel: 709-826-2371. E-mail: garnish@nlpl.ca. Web Site: nlpl.ca/locations-hours/bgh.
Library Holdings: Bk Vols 6,600; Per Subs 21
Automation Activity & Vendor Info: (Cataloging) SirsiDynix; (OPAC) SirsiDynix
Wireless access
Open Tues & Thurs 1-4, Wed 1-3 & 6-8, Sat 2-5

GRAND BANK

P GRAND BANK PUBLIC LIBRARY*, Church St, A0E 1W0. (Mail add: PO Box 1000, A0E 1W0). Tel: 709-832-0310. FAX: 709-832-0310. Web Site: www.nlpl.ca. *Librn,* Karen Anderson; E-mail: kanderson@nlpl.ca
Library Holdings: Bk Vols 12,000; Per Subs 27
Wireless access
Open Mon & Fri 2-5, Tues 9-12 & 2-5, Wed 2-5 & 6-9, Thurs 1-5

HARBOUR GRACE

P HARBOUR GRACE PUBLIC LIBRARY, 106 Harvey St, A0A 2M0. (Mail add: PO Box 40, A0A 2M0). Tel: 709-596-3894. E-mail: harbourgrace@nlpl.ca. Web Site: nlpl.ca/component/jumi/library.html?site_id=ahg. *Div Mgr,* Andrew Lockhart; *Librn,* Doreen Quinn
Library Holdings: Bk Vols 11,000; Per Subs 25
Wireless access
Open Tues & Wed 10:30-12:30 & 1-4, Thurs 2-5 & 5:30-8, Sat 12-4

HARE BAY

P HARE BAY-DOVER PUBLIC LIBRARY, Jane Collins Academy, 22 Anstey's Rd, A0G 2P0. (Mail add: PO Box 117, A0G 2P0). Tel: 709-537-2391. FAX: 709-537-2374. Web Site: nlpl.ca/component/jumi/library.html?site_id=ghb&view=article&id=145&Itemid=413. *Librn,* Stephanie Skelloway; E-mail: skelloway@nlpl.ca
Founded 1972. Pop 1,580
Library Holdings: Bk Vols 6,200; Per Subs 17
Automation Activity & Vendor Info: (Cataloging) Horizon; (Circulation) Horizon; (ILL) Horizon
Wireless access
Open Mon-Thurs 3-8:30

HOLYROOD

P HOLYROOD PUBLIC LIBRARY*, Holyrood Access Rd, Exit 36, A0A 2R0. (Mail add: PO Box 263, A0A 2R0). Tel: 709-229-7852. Administration Tel: 709-737-3508. FAX: 709-229-7852. Administration FAX: 709-737-3571. Web Site: www.nlpl.ca/component/jumi/library.html?site_id=ahd. *Librn,* Michelle Potter; E-mail: mpotter@nlpl.ca
Library Holdings: Large Print Bks 300; Bk Titles 15,200; Per Subs 27
Special Collections: Local Geneaology (Harbour Main/Holyrood Coll)
Wireless access
Open Tues & Thurs 2-5 & 6-8, Wed & Fri 10-12:30 & 1:45-5, Sat 1-4

MARYSTOWN

P MARYSTOWN PUBLIC LIBRARY, Sacred Heart Academy, Columbia Dr, A0E 2M0. (Mail add: PO Box 1270, A0E 2M0). Tel: 709-279-1507. FAX: 709-279-1507. E-mail: marystown@nlpl.ca. Web Site: nlpl.ca/locations-hours/bmn.
Library Holdings: Bk Vols 6,000; Per Subs 20
Automation Activity & Vendor Info: (Cataloging) SirsiDynix-Enterprise; (OPAC) SirsiDynix-Enterprise
Wireless access
Open Mon, Thurs & Sat 2:30-5, Tues 2:30-7, Fri 2:30-6

MOUNT PEARL

P MOUNT PEARL PUBLIC LIBRARY*, 65 Olympic Dr, A1N 5H6. Tel: 709-368-3603. E-mail: mountpearl@nlpl.ca. *Librn,* Cindy Hall
Pop 26,000
Library Holdings: Bk Vols 28,500
Automation Activity & Vendor Info: (Cataloging) SirsiDynix; (Circulation) SirsiDynix; (OPAC) SirsiDynix
Wireless access
Function: Bk club(s), ILL available, Magazines, Photocopying/Printing, Scanner
Special Services for the Blind - Talking bks
Open Tues 1-4, Wed & Thurs 9:30-8, Fri & Sat 9:30-4

OLD PERLICAN

P OLD PERLICAN PUBLIC LIBRARY, Town Hall, 299 Blow Me Down Dr, A0A 3G0. (Mail add: PO Box 265, A0A 3G0). Tel: 709-587-2028. E-mail: oldperlican@nlpl.ca. Web Site: www.nlpl.ca/component/jumi/library.html?site_id=aop, www.townofoldperlican.ca/library.php. *Librn,* Cathy Hatch
Library Holdings: Bk Vols 8,757; Per Subs 23
Wireless access
Open Tues 12:30-6:30, Wed 5:30-8:30, Thurs 10:30-4:30

PLACENTIA

P PLACENTIA PUBLIC LIBRARY, 14 Atlantic Ave, A0B 2Y0. (Mail add: PO Box 119, A0B 2Y0). Tel: 709-227-3621. E-mail: placentia@nlpl.ca. Web Site: www.nlpl.ca/component/jumi/library.html?site_id=apa. *Libr Tech,* Shyla Powes
Library Holdings: Bk Titles 2,000; Per Subs 65
Automation Activity & Vendor Info: (Cataloging) Horizon; (Circulation) Horizon
Wireless access
Open Tues & Thurs 10-12:30 & 1:30-5, Wed 2-8, Fri & Sat 10-2

POUCH COVE

P POUCH COVE PUBLIC LIBRARY, PO Box 40, A0A 3L0. Tel: 709-335-2652. FAX: 709-335-2652. E-mail: pouchcove@nlpl.ca. Web Site: nlpl.ca/component/jumi/library.html?site_id=apc. *Div Mgr,* Andrew Lockhart; *Librn,* Laura Bragg
Library Holdings: Per Subs 29
Wireless access
Open Mon 12-5, Tues & Wed 10-12, Thurs 6:30-8:30

ST. BRIDE'S

P ST BRIDES PUBLIC LIBRARY, Council Bldg, Main Rd, General Delivery, A0B 1E0. Tel: 709-337-2360. Web Site: www.nlpl.ca/component/jumi/library.html?site_id=ast. *Librn,* Sharon McGrath
Library Holdings: Bk Vols 5,000
Wireless access
Open Mon 9-5, Tues 9-4, Wed & Thurs 9-2

ST. JOHN'S

G CANADA-NEWFOUNDLAND OFFSHORE PETROLEUM BOARD LIBRARY*, West Campus Hall, Ste 7100, 240 Waterford Bridge Rd, A1E 1E2. SAN 323-9268. Tel: 709-778-1474. FAX: 709-778-4249. Web Site: www.cnlopb.ca. *Information & Privacy Coord,* Trevor Bennett
Library Holdings: Bk Titles 2,000

C COLLEGE OF THE NORTH ATLANTIC LIBRARY SERVICES*, Prince Philip Drive Campus, One Prince Philip Dr, A1C 5P7. (Mail add: PO Box 1693 Stn C, A1C 5P7), SAN 366-6573. Tel: 709-758-7274, Interlibrary

Loan Service Tel: 709-758-7447. FAX: 709-758-7231. E-mail: LibPP@cna.nl.ca. Web Site: www.cna.nl.ca/MyCNA/Academic-Support/Libraries.aspx. *Librn III,* Andrew Wood; Tel: 709-758-7448, E-mail: andrew.wood@cna.nl.ca; Staff 1 (MLS 1)
Founded 1963. Enrl 1,800; Fac 100
Library Holdings: Bk Titles 14,000; Bk Vols 16,000; Per Subs 200
Special Collections: Can & Prov
Wireless access

Departmental Libraries:

BAY ST GEORGE, Library Learning Commons, DSB Fowlow Bldg, 432 Massachusetts Dr, Stephenville, A2N 2Z6. (Mail add: PO Box 5400 Stn Main, Stephenville, A2N 2Z6), SAN 377-8487. Tel: 709-643-7752. Administration Tel: 709-643-7762. FAX: 709-643-7786. E-mail: LibBG@cna.nl.ca. *Librn III,* Lisa Marshall; E-mail: lisa.marshall@cna.nl.ca; Staff 4 (MLS 1, Non-MLS 3)
Enrl 900; Fac 90
Library Holdings: Bk Vols 14,000; Per Subs 150
Subject Interests: Archives, Folklore, Nfld & Labrador, Rare bks

BONAVISTA CAMPUS, 301 Confederation Dr, Bonavista, A0C 1B0. (Mail add: PO Box 670, Bonavista, A0C 1B0). Tel: 709-468-1716. FAX: 709-468-2004. E-mail: LibBO@cna.nl.ca. *Libr Tech II,* Tracy Mouland; E-mail: tracy.mouland@cna.nl.ca; Staff 1 (Non-MLS 1)
Library Holdings: Bk Titles 3,500
Function: Res libr

L A BOWN BUILDING LIBRARY, Bay St George Campus - L A Bown Bldg, Rm 29, 15 Washington Dr, Stephenville, A2N 2V5. (Mail add: Bay St George Campus - L A Bown Bldg, Rm 29, PO Box 5400 Stn Main, Stephenville, A2N 2Z6). Tel: 709-643-7787. FAX: 709-643-7784. E-mail: libbb@cna.nl.ca. *Libr Tech II,* Patricia Woodrow; E-mail: Patricia.Woodrow@cna.nl.ca

BURIN CAMPUS, 105 Main St, Burin Bay Arm, A0E 1G0. (Mail add: PO Box 370, Burin Bay Arm, A0E 1G0). Tel: 709-891-5621. FAX: 709-891-2256. E-mail: LibBU@cna.nl.ca. *Librn II,* Chelsea Heighton; E-mail: chelsea.heighton@cna.nl.ca
Library Holdings: Bk Titles 8,000; Per Subs 25

FRED CAMPBELL & RON BENNETT LIBRARY, Bay St George Campus - Martin Gallant Bldg, Rm 116, PO Box 5400 Stn Main, Stephenville, A2N 2Z6. Tel: 709-646-5704. FAX: 709-646-5717. E-mail: LibBX@cna.nl.ca. *Libr Tech II,* Theresa Hynes; E-mail: Theresa.Hynes@cna.nl.ca

CARBONEAR CAMPUS, Four Pikes Lane, Carbonear, A1Y 1A7, SAN 377-8541. Tel: 709-596-8925, 709-596-8940. FAX: 709-596-2688. E-mail: LibCA@cna.nl.ca. *Librn II,* Stephen Nolan; E-mail: stephen.nolan@cna.nl.ca; *Libr Tech II,* Brenda Peach; E-mail: brenda.peach@cna.nl.ca
Library Holdings: Bk Titles 4,000; Per Subs 20
Automation Activity & Vendor Info: (Serials) EBSCO Online

CLARENVILLE CAMPUS, 69 Pleasant St, Clarenville, A5A 1V9, SAN 377-8568. Tel: 709-466-6900. FAX: 709-466-2771. E-mail: LibCL@cna.nl.ca. *Library Contact,* Maisie Caines; E-mail: maisie.caines@cna.nl.ca
Enrl 700; Fac 27
Library Holdings: Bk Vols 7,000; Per Subs 40

CORNER BROOK CAMPUS, 141 O'Connell Dr, Corner Brook, A2H 6H6. (Mail add: PO Box 822 Stn Main, Corner Brook, A2H 6H6), SAN 377-8584. Tel: 709-637-8528. FAX: 709-634-2126. E-mail: LibCB@cna.nl.ca. *Librn II,* Brent Slade; E-mail: brent.slade@cna.nl.ca; *Libr Tech,* Amanda Thompson; E-mail: amanda.thomson@cna.nl.ca; Staff 1 (Non-MLS 1)
Library Holdings: Bk Vols 10,122; Per Subs 14,476; Videos 1,099
Special Collections: NFLD Coll
Subject Interests: Early childhood educ, Engr, Indust trade, Natural res
Automation Activity & Vendor Info: (Cataloging) SirsiDynix-WorkFlows; (Circulation) SirsiDynix-WorkFlows; (Course Reserve) SirsiDynix-WorkFlows; (ILL) SirsiDynix-WorkFlows; (Media Booking) SirsiDynix-WorkFlows; (OPAC) SirsiDynix-iLink; (Serials) SirsiDynix-WorkFlows
Function: Computers for patron use, Doc delivery serv, Electronic databases & coll, Free DVD rentals, ILL available, Internet access, Magazines, Mail & tel request accepted, Meeting rooms, Movies, Photocopying/Printing, Ref & res, Ref serv available, Study rm, Wheelchair accessible
Special Services for the Deaf - Assisted listening device; Assistive tech
Special Services for the Blind - Aids for in-house use; Assistive/Adapted tech devices, equip & products; Computer access aids; Computer with voice synthesizer for visually impaired persons; Copier with enlargement capabilities; Low vision equip; Magnifiers; PC for people with disabilities; Screen enlargement software for people with visual disabilities; Screen reader software
Restriction: Open to fac, students & qualified researchers, Open to pub for ref & circ; with some limitations, Open to students, fac, staff & alumni, Photo ID required for access, Registered patrons only

GANDER CAMPUS, One Magee Rd, Gander, A1V 1W8. (Mail add: PO Box 395 Stn Main, Gander, A1V 1W8), SAN 377-8606. Tel: 709-651-4815. FAX: 709-651-4854. E-mail: LibGR@cna.nl.ca. *Librn II,* Karen Patzold; E-mail: karen.patzold@cna.nl.ca; Staff 1 (MLS 1)
Founded 1963. Fac 40; Highest Degree: Associate
Library Holdings: DVDs 300; Bk Vols 5,200; Per Subs 40; Spec Interest Per Sub 10
Subject Interests: Adult basic educ, Aircraft maintenance & engr, Auto repair, Electronics, Local interest
Automation Activity & Vendor Info: (Cataloging) SirsiDynix; (Circulation) SirsiDynix; (Course Reserve) SirsiDynix; (ILL) SirsiDynix; (OPAC) SirsiDynix-iLink; (Serials) SirsiDynix
Function: Audio & video playback equip for onsite use, CD-ROM, Computers for patron use, Electronic databases & coll, Free DVD rentals, ILL available, Instruction & testing, Internet access, Learning ctr, Online cat, Orientations, Outside serv via phone, mail, e-mail & web, Photocopying/Printing, Ref & res, Ref serv available, Telephone ref, VHS videos, Wheelchair accessible
Restriction: Open to pub for ref & circ; with some limitations, Open to students, fac & staff

GRAND FALLS-WINDSOR CAMPUS, Five Cromer Ave, Grand Falls-Windsor, A2A 1X3, SAN 377-8622. Tel: 709-292-5637. FAX: 709-489-5765. E-mail: LibGF@cna.nl.ca. *Librn III,* John L Whelan; E-mail: John.Whelan@cna.nl.ca; Staff 2 (MLS 1, Non-MLS 1)
Library Holdings: Bk Vols 5,000
Special Collections: Grand Falls-Windsor Campus Archive
Automation Activity & Vendor Info: (Cataloging) SirsiDynix; (Circulation) SirsiDynix; (Course Reserve) SirsiDynix; (ILL) SirsiDynix; (OPAC) SirsiDynix-iLink; (Serials) SirsiDynix
Function: Archival coll, Art exhibits, Audio & video playback equip for onsite use, AV serv, Bks on cassette, CD-ROM, Computers for patron use, Distance learning, Doc delivery serv, Electronic databases & coll, For res purposes, Free DVD rentals, Health sci info serv, ILL available, Internet access, Learning ctr, Mail & tel request accepted, Mail loans to mem, Microfiche/film & reading machines, Online cat, Online info literacy tutorials on the web & in blackboard, Online ref, Orientations, Outreach serv, Outside serv via phone, mail, e-mail & web, Photocopying/Printing, Prof lending libr, Ref & res, Ref serv available, Res libr, Scanner, Spoken cassettes & CDs, Telephone ref, VHS videos, Wheelchair accessible
Restriction: Open to pub for ref & circ; with some limitations, Open to students, fac, staff & alumni

HAPPY VALLEY-GOOSE BAY CAMPUS, 219 Hamilton River Rd, Happy Valley-Goose Bay, A0P 1E0. (Mail add: PO Box 1720, Happy Valley-Goose Bay, A0P 1E0), SAN 377-8649. Tel: 709-896-6300. FAX: 709-896-3733. E-mail: LibHV@cna.nl.ca. *Librn II,* Ashley McKnight; Tel: 709-896-6772, E-mail: ashley.mcknight@cna.nl.ca; *Libr Tech I,* Marjorie Barnes; E-mail: marjorie.barnes@cna.nl.ca
Special Collections: Labrador Coll, texts; Labrador Institute Archives, photog, original mat. Canadian and Provincial; Oral History

LABRADOR WEST CAMPUS, Raymond J Condon Memorial Library, 1600 Nichols-Adams Hwy, Labrador City, A2V 0B8, SAN 377-8665. Tel: 709-944-6862. FAX: 709-944-6581. *Librn II,* Brent Slade; E-mail: Brent.Slade@cna.nl.ca; Staff 2 (MLS 1, Non-MLS 1)
Founded 1989
Library Holdings: DVDs 12; Bk Vols 5,000; Per Subs 60; Videos 700
Special Collections: Newfoundland Coll
Subject Interests: Mining tech

PLACENTIA CAMPUS, One Roosevelt Ave, Placentia, A0B 2Y0. (Mail add: PO Box 190, Placentia, A0B 2Y0). Tel: 709-227-6264. FAX: 709-227-7185. E-mail: libpl@cna.nl.ca. *Libr Assoc,* Rose Power; E-mail: rose.power@cna.nl.ca

PORT AUX BASQUES CAMPUS, 59 Grand Bay Rd, Port aux Basques, A0M 1C0. (Mail add: William Thornhill Library, PO Box 760, Port aux Basques, A0M 1C0), SAN 377-8703. Tel: 709-695-3343. FAX: 709-695-2963. E-mail: LibPB@cna.nl.ca. *Libr Tech II,* Pamela Hardy; E-mail: pamela.hardy@cna.nl.ca

RIDGE ROAD CAMPUS LIBRARY, 153 Ridge Rd, Rm 111, A1C 6L8. (Mail add: Ridge Road Campus Learning Commons, PO Box 1150 Stn C, A1C 6L8). Tel: 709-793-3305. FAX: 709-758-7059. E-mail: LibRR@cna.nl.ca. *Libr Tech II,* Jason MacKenzie; E-mail: jason.mackenzie@cna.nl.ca

ST ANTHONY CAMPUS, 83-93 East St, Rm 120, St. Anthony, A0K 4S0. (Mail add: PO Box 550, St. Anthony, A0K 4S0). Tel: 709-454-3559. FAX: 709-454-8808. E-mail: LibSA@cna.nl.ca. *Library Contact,* Elizabeth-Ann Critchley; E-mail: elizabeth-ann.critchley@cna.nl.ca

SEAL COVE CAMPUS, 1670 Conception Bay Hwy, Conception Bay South, A1X 5C7. (Mail add: PO Box 19003 Stn Main, Conception Bay South, A1X 5C7), SAN 373-5354. Tel: 709-744-2047. FAX: 709-744-3929. E-mail: LibSC@cna.nl.ca. *Libr Tech II,* Crystal Mercer; E-mail: crystal.mercer@cna.nl.ca; Staff 1 (MLS 1)
Founded 1992. Enrl 200; Fac 23; Highest Degree: Certificate
Library Holdings: CDs 50; High Interest/Low Vocabulary Bk Vols 30; Bk Titles 2,700; Bk Vols 3,000; Per Subs 50; Videos 300
Special Collections: Newfoundland

Subject Interests: Adult educ, Culinary arts, Electrical trades, Heating syst, Petroleum
Automation Activity & Vendor Info: (Acquisitions) SirsiDynix; (Cataloging) SirsiDynix; (Circulation) SirsiDynix; (Course Reserve) SirsiDynix; (ILL) SirsiDynix; (Media Booking) SirsiDynix; (OPAC) SirsiDynix
Special Services for the Deaf - Assistive tech
Special Services for the Blind - Assistive/Adapted tech devices, equip & products

L DEPARTMENT OF JUSTICE & PUBLIC SAFETY, Law Library, East Block, Confederation Bldg, 5th Flr, 100 Prince Philip Dr, A1B 4J6. (Mail add: PO Box 8700, A1B 4J6), SAN 372-3577. Tel: 709-729-0285. FAX: 709-729-2129. Web Site: www.gov.nl.ca/jps. *Law Librn,* Brenda Blundon; E-mail: brendab@gov.nl.ca; Staff 1 (Non-MLS 1)
Library Holdings: Bk Vols 5,000; Per Subs 5
Subject Interests: Govt
Function: Govt ref serv

G DEPARTMENT OF NATURAL RESOURCES, GOVERNMENT OF NEWFOUNDLAND & LABRADOR*, Geological Survey Library, Natural Resources Bldg, 50 Elizabeth Ave, A1B 4J6. (Mail add: PO Box 8700, A1B 4J6), SAN 318-9503. Tel: 709-729-3419. FAX: 709-729-4270. Web Site: www.nr.gov.nl.ca/nr/mines/geoscience. *Dir,* Dorothea Hanchar; E-mail: dorotheahanchar@gov.nl.ca; *Library Contact,* Cindy Saunders; Tel: 709-729-6280
Library Holdings: Bk Vols 1,000; Per Subs 20
Special Collections: Mineral Resources & Geology Technical Library, publs, rpts; Mineral Resources, Geology & Mineral Exploration - Newfoundland & Labrador, co & govt rpts
Subject Interests: Geol, Mineral exploration
Open Mon-Fri 8:30-4:30; Mon-Fri 8:30-4 (Summer)
Restriction: Restricted pub use

P MICHAEL DONOVAN LIBRARY, 655 Topsail Rd, A1E 2E3. Tel: 709-737-2621. E-mail: michaeldonovan@nlpl.ca. Web Site: www.nlpl.ca/component/jumi/library.html?site_id=sjb. *Librn,* Marianne King
Library Holdings: Bk Vols 23,400
Open Tues & Thurs-Sat 9:30-5, Wed 9:30-8

EASTERN HEALTH

S ADDICTIONS SERVICES LIBRARY*, Mount Pearl Sq, 760 Topsail Rd, A1B 4A4. (Mail add: PO Box 13122, A1B 4A4), SAN 373-3157. Tel: 709-752-4120, 709-752-4121. FAX: 709-752-4412. E-mail: ads.library@easternhealth.ca. *Librn,* Kate Shore; E-mail: kate.shore@easternhealth.ca; *Tech Support,* Leslie Stafford; E-mail: leslie.noftallstafford@easternhealth.ca
Library Holdings: CDs 170; DVDs 50; Bk Vols 5,200; Per Subs 10; Videos 1,000
Function: AV serv, For res purposes, Photocopying/Printing, Wheelchair accessible
Open Mon-Fri 8:30-4:30
Restriction: Access at librarian's discretion, Clients only, Lending to staff only, Open to pub for ref & circ; with some limitations

CM CENTRE FOR NURSING STUDIES LEARNING RESOURCE CENTRE*, 100 Forest Rd, A1A 1E5, SAN 318-9465. Tel: 709-777-8192. Interlibrary Loan Service Tel: 709-777-8194. Reference Tel: 709-777-8189. FAX: 709-777-8193. Web Site: www.cns.nf.ca. *Librn,* Karen Hutchens; Tel: 709-777-8189; Staff 3 (MLS 1, Non-MLS 2)
Founded 1996. Enrl 550; Fac 50; Highest Degree: Bachelor
Library Holdings: AV Mats 420; Bk Vols 9,400; Per Subs 65
Automation Activity & Vendor Info: (Cataloging) LibraryWorld, Inc; (Circulation) LibraryWorld, Inc
Open Mon-Thurs 8:30am-10pm, Fri 8:30-4:30, Sat 12-5, Sun 12-10
Restriction: Open to students, fac & staff

M ST CLAIRE'S MERCY HOSPITAL LIBRARY*, 154 Le Marchant Rd, A1C 5B8, SAN 327-5434. Tel: 709-777-5414. FAX: 709-777-5812. *Librn,* Jordan Pike; Staff 1 (MLS 1)
Founded 1954
Library Holdings: Bk Titles 1,500; Per Subs 90
Automation Activity & Vendor Info: (Cataloging) BiblioMondo; (Circulation) BiblioMondo
Function: ILL available
Open Mon-Fri 8-4

M WATERFORD HOSPITAL LIBRARY & INFORMATION SERVICES*, Waterford Bridge Rd, A1E 4J8, SAN 318-952X. Tel: 709-777-3368. FAX: 709-777-3319. Web Site: www.hccsj.nf.ca. *Librn,* Kate Shore; E-mail: kate.shore@easternhealth.ca
Founded 1969
Library Holdings: Bk Titles 300; Per Subs 80
Subject Interests: Geriatrics, Mental health, Psychiat
Open Mon-Fri 8:30-4:30

L LAW SOCIETY OF NEWFOUNDLAND LAW LIBRARY*, 196-198 Water St, A1C 5M3. (Mail add: PO Box 1028, A1C 5M3), SAN 318-9481. Tel: 709-753-7770. FAX: 709-753-0054. E-mail: lawlibrary@lsnl.ca. Web Site: www.lsnl.ca/law-library. *Law Librn,* Jenny Thornhill; E-mail: jthornhill@lsnl.ca; *Libr Tech,* Leah Griffiths; Staff 2 (MLS 1, Non-MLS 1)
Library Holdings: Bk Vols 10,000
Subject Interests: British law, Can
Automation Activity & Vendor Info: (Cataloging) ResourceMATE; (Circulation) ResourceMATE; (OPAC) ResourceMATE
Wireless access
Open Mon-Fri 9-5
Restriction: Not a lending libr, Open to pub for ref only

MEMORIAL UNIVERSITY OF NEWFOUNDLAND

C DR C R BARRETT LIBRARY (MARINE INSTITUTE)*, 155 Ridge Rd, A1C 5R3. (Mail add: PO Box 4920, A1C 5R3), SAN 318-9449. Tel: 709-778-0662. Reference Tel: 709-778-0615. FAX: 709-778-0316. E-mail: barrett@mi.mun.ca. Web Site: www.mi.mun.ca/library. *Head, Pub Serv,* Catherine Lawton; E-mail: catherine.lawton@mi.mun.ca; Staff 7 (MLS 1, Non-MLS 6)
Founded 1985. Enrl 1,500; Highest Degree: Master
Library Holdings: AV Mats 1,600; Bk Vols 44,000; Per Subs 495
Subject Interests: Architectural engr tech, Electrical, Environ engr, Fisheries tech, Food tech, Geomatics, Marine engr, Nautical sci, Naval archit, Ocean environ, Petroleum engr, Shipbuilding
Automation Activity & Vendor Info: (Acquisitions) SirsiDynix; (Cataloging) SirsiDynix; (Circulation) SirsiDynix; (Course Reserve) SirsiDynix; (ILL) SirsiDynix; (Media Booking) SirsiDynix; (OPAC) SirsiDynix; (Serials) SirsiDynix
Function: Res libr
Partic in Canadian Research Knowledge Network
Open Mon-Fri 8:30-5

CM HEALTH SCIENCES LIBRARY*, Memorial University, 300 Prince Philip Dr, A1B 3V6, SAN 366-6727. Circulation Tel: 709-777-6671. Reference Tel: 709-777-6672. Administration Tel: 709-777-7036. FAX: 709-777-6866. E-mail: hslinfo@mun.ca. Web Site: www.library.mun.ca/hsl. *Actg Assoc Univ Librn,* Pamela Morgan; Tel: 709-777-6025, E-mail: pmorgan@mun.ca; *Head, Pub Serv,* Linda Barnett; Tel: 709-777-6676, E-mail: lbarnett@mun.ca; Staff 22 (MLS 7, Non-MLS 15)
Founded 1967
Special Collections: History of Medicine
Subject Interests: Allied health, Med, Nursing, Pharm
Automation Activity & Vendor Info: (Acquisitions) SirsiDynix-Unicorn; (Cataloging) SirsiDynix-Unicorn; (Circulation) SirsiDynix-Unicorn; (Course Reserve) SirsiDynix-Unicorn; (ILL) Relais International; (OPAC) SirsiDynix-Unicorn; (Serials) SirsiDynix-Unicorn
Partic in Association of Faculties of Medicine of Canada; Council of Atlantic Academic Libraries (CAAL)
Publications: Library Guides; Library Links (Newsletter)

C FERRISS HODGETT LIBRARY*, University Dr, Corner Brook, A2H 6P9, SAN 366-6662. Tel: 709-637-6267. Interlibrary Loan Service Tel: 709-637-6271. FAX: 709-637-6273, 709-639-8125. Web Site: www.library.mun.ca, www.swgc.mun.ca. *Assoc Univ Librn,* Elizabeth Behrens; E-mail: ebehrens@swgc.mun.ca; *Circ,* Beverly Greene; *Ref Serv,* Louise McGillis; Tel: 709-637-6200, Ext 6122
Founded 1975. Enrl 1,124; Fac 60
Library Holdings: Bk Vols 125,000; Per Subs 550
Automation Activity & Vendor Info: (Acquisitions) SirsiDynix; (Cataloging) SirsiDynix; (Circulation) SirsiDynix; (Course Reserve) SirsiDynix; (ILL) SirsiDynix; (Media Booking) SirsiDynix; (OPAC) SirsiDynix; (Serials) SirsiDynix
Open Mon-Thurs 8am-11pm, Fri 8-5, Sat 1-5, Sun 2-10

C LABRADOR INSTITUTE OF NORTHERN STUDIES INFORMATION CENTRE LIBRARY*, Sta B, PO Box 490, Labrador, A0P 1E0, SAN 326-8144. Tel: 709-896-6210. FAX: 709-896-2970. *Library Contact,* Beatrice Dickers; E-mail: beatrice.dickers@mun.ca
Founded 1983
Library Holdings: Bk Titles 3,000; Per Subs 10
Special Collections: Labrador-Arctic Reference Materials - 1919-present
Subject Interests: Environ issues, Labrador mats, Northern studies
Automation Activity & Vendor Info: (Acquisitions) SirsiDynix; (Cataloging) SirsiDynix; (Circulation) SirsiDynix; (Course Reserve) SirsiDynix; (ILL) SirsiDynix; (Media Booking) SirsiDynix; (OPAC) SirsiDynix; (Serials) SirsiDynix
Open Mon-Fri 8:30-4:30

C QUEEN ELIZABETH II LIBRARY*, 234 Elizabeth Ave, A1B 3Y1, SAN 366-6638. Tel: 709-737-7428. Circulation Tel: 709-737-7423. Interlibrary Loan Service Tel: 709-737-7424. Administration Tel: 709-737-3862. Information Services Tel: 709-737-7427. FAX: 709-737-2153. Web Site: www.library.mun.ca. *Univ Librn,* Dianne Keeping; *Div Head, Syst Coordr,* Lisa Goddard; Tel: 709-737-2124, E-mail: lgoddard@mun.ca; *Head, Coll Develop,* Christopher Dennis; Tel: 709-737-3214, E-mail: cdennis@mun.ca; *Head, Info Serv, Ref (Info Servs),* Karen Lippold; Staff 139.5 (MLS 29.5, Non-MLS 110)

Founded 1925. Fac 925; Highest Degree: Doctorate
Library Holdings: Bk Vols 1,542,859; Per Subs 37,532
Special Collections: Newfoundlandia Coll, AV & maps. Canadian and Provincial
Automation Activity & Vendor Info: (Acquisitions) SirsiDynix; (Cataloging) SirsiDynix; (Circulation) SirsiDynix; (Course Reserve) SirsiDynix; (ILL) SirsiDynix; (OPAC) SirsiDynix; (Serials) SirsiDynix
Partic in Canadian Association of Research Libraries; Council of Atlantic Academic Libraries (CAAL)
Open Mon-Fri 8:30-5

P MARJORIE MEWS PUBLIC LIBRARY*, 12 Highland Dr, A1A 3C4. Tel: 709-737-3020. Web Site: www.nlpl.ca. *Librn,* Julia Mayo; E-mail: juliamayo@nlpl.ca; Staff 2.5 (Non-MLS 2.5)
Library Holdings: Bk Titles 28,000
Automation Activity & Vendor Info: (Acquisitions) SirsiDynix
Wireless access
Function: 24/7 Electronic res, 24/7 Online cat, After school storytime, Bks on CD, Children's prog, Computers for patron use, E-Readers, E-Reserves, Electronic databases & coll, Family literacy, Free DVD rentals, Holiday prog, ILL available, Internet access, Magazines, Mail & tel request accepted, Makerspace, Online cat, Online ref, Orientations, Outreach serv, OverDrive digital audio bks, Photocopying/Printing, Preschool outreach, Preschool reading prog, Prog for adults, Ref serv available, Scanner, Serves people with intellectual disabilities, STEM programs, Story hour, Summer reading prog, Wheelchair accessible, Writing prog
Open Tues, Wed & Fri 9:30-5, Thurs 9:30-8:30, Sat (Sept-June) 9:30-5
Restriction: Free to mem
Friends of the Library Group

S NEWFOUNDLAND & LABRADOR HISTORICAL SOCIETY LIBRARY, (Formerly Newfoundland Historical Society Library), 95 Bonaventure Ave, Ste 500, A1B 2X5. (Mail add: Churchill Sq, PO Box 23154, A1B 4J9), SAN 377-2411. Tel: 709-722-3191. FAX: 709-722-9035. E-mail: nlhistsociety@gmail.com. Web Site: www.nlhistory.ca. *Pres,* Patrick Kennedy; *Libr Office Mgr,* Uli Brown; Staff 1 (Non-MLS 1)
Founded 1905
Library Holdings: Bk Titles 600; Bk Vols 650; Per Subs 11
Special Collections: Archival Coll
Subject Interests: Hist, Labrador, Nfld & Labrador
Function: ILL available
Restriction: Not a lending libr

S NEWFOUNDLAND & LABRADOR TEACHERS' ASSOCIATION LIBRARY*, Three Kenmount Rd, A1B 1W1. SAN 377-3302. Tel: 709-726-3223. FAX: 709-726-4302. Web Site: www.nlta.nl.ca. *Library Contact,* Samantha Lee; E-mail: slee@nlta.nl.ca
Library Holdings: Bk Titles 5,000
Open Mon-Fri 8:30-4:30; Mon-Thurs 8:30-4:30, Fri 8:30-1 (Summer)

P PROVINCIAL INFORMATION & LIBRARY RESOURCES BOARD*, Provincial Resource Library Division, Arts & Culture Ctr, 125 Allandale Rd, A1B 3A3. Tel: 709-737-3418. Circulation Tel: 709-737-2133. Reference Tel: 709-737-3950. FAX: 709-737-2660. *Div Mgr,* Susan Prior; E-mail: sprior@nlpl.ca; *Librn,* Kim Kelly; Staff 32 (MLS 4, Non-MLS 28)
Founded 1935. Pop 102,172; Circ 454,171
Library Holdings: CDs 9,800; DVDs 22,602; Bk Vols 183,226; Per Subs 232; Talking Bks 1,812
Special Collections: Newfoundland, bks, mss, maps, newsp, per & photogs
Automation Activity & Vendor Info: (Acquisitions) SirsiDynix; (Cataloging) SirsiDynix; (Circulation) SirsiDynix; (OPAC) SirsiDynix
Wireless access
Partic in Canadian Urban Libr Coun
Special Services for the Blind - Bks available with recordings; Bks on cassette; Bks on CD; Copier with enlargement capabilities; Digital talking bk; Home delivery serv; Large print & cassettes; Large print bks; Recorded bks; Talking bks
Open Mon 1-5, Tues-Thurs 9:30-8:30, Fri & Sat 9:30-5
Friends of the Library Group

CR QUEEN'S COLLEGE LIBRARY*, 210 Prince Philip Dr, Ste 3000, A1B 3R6. SAN 371-7550. Tel: 709-753-0116. Toll Free Tel: 877-753-0116. FAX: 709-753-1214. E-mail: queens@mun.ca. Web Site: queenscollegenl.ca?page_id=433.
Founded 1841. Enrl 35; Fac 4; Highest Degree: Master
Library Holdings: Bk Titles 17,000; Bk Vols 17,800; Per Subs 60
Subject Interests: Theol
Wireless access
Restriction: Not a lending libr

ST. LAWRENCE

P ST LAWRENCE PUBLIC LIBRARY, PO Box 366, A0E 2V0. Tel: 709-873-2650. *Div Mgr,* Andrew Lockhart; *Librn,* Vicki Lockyer
Library Holdings: Bk Vols 8,500
Wireless access
Open Mon 2-7, Tues-Thurs 10-3

STEPHENVILLE

G PROVINCIAL INFORMATION & LIBRARY RESOURCES BOARD*, 48 St. George's Ave, A2N 1K9. SAN 366-6751. Tel: 709-643-0900, 709-643-0902. FAX: 709-643-0925. Web Site: www.nlpl.ca. *Exec Dir,* Andrew Hunt; E-mail: ahunt@nlpl.ca; Staff 19 (MLS 19)
Founded 1935. Pop 568,349; Circ 1,989,335
Library Holdings: Bk Vols 1,700,000
Special Collections: Oral History
Subject Interests: Hist
Automation Activity & Vendor Info: (Acquisitions) SirsiDynix; (Cataloging) SirsiDynix; (Circulation) SirsiDynix
Wireless access
Open Mon-Fri 8:30-4:30

TORBAY

P TORBAY PUBLIC LIBRARY, 1339C Torbay Rd, A1K 1B2. Tel: 709-437-6571. Web Site: www.nlpl.ca/component/jumi/library.html?site_id=ato. *Librn,* Mercia Harris
Library Holdings: Bk Vols 12,000; Per Subs 30
Wireless access
Open Tues-Thurs 1-6, Sat 10-12

TREPASSEY

P TREPASSEY PUBLIC LIBRARY*, Molloy's Rd, A0A 4B0. (Mail add: PO Box 183, A0A 4B0). Tel: 709-438-2224. FAX: 709-438-2224. Web Site: nlpl.ca/component/jumi/library.html?site_id=aty. *Div Mgr,* Andrew Lockhart; Tel: 709-737-3909, E-mail: alockhart@nlpl.ca; *Librn,* Patricia McCormack
Library Holdings: Bk Vols 6,000; Per Subs 18
Wireless access
Open Mon-Thurs 11-3

VICTORIA

P VICTORIA PUBLIC LIBRARY, Municipal Ctr, 2nd Flr, Main Rd, Rte 74, A0A 4G0. (Mail add: PO Box 190, A0A 4G0). Tel: 709-596-3682. Web Site: nlpl.ca/locations-hours/ava. *Librn,* Shona Colbourne
Library Holdings: Bk Vols 3,500; Per Subs 16
Automation Activity & Vendor Info: (Cataloging) SirsiDynix; (OPAC) SirsiDynix
Wireless access
Open Tues-Thurs 10-2

WHITBOURNE

P WHITBOURNE PUBLIC LIBRARY*, 494 Main St, A0B 3K0. (Mail add: PO Box 400, A0B 3K0). Tel: 709-759-2461. E-mail: whitbourne@nlpl.ca. *Librn,* Gloria Somerton; E-mail: gsomerton@nlpl.ca
Library Holdings: Bk Vols 6,291
Wireless access
Function: ILL available, Photocopying/Printing, Scanner
Open Tues 1-8, Fri 1-5, Sat 11-4

WINTERTON

P WINTERTON PUBLIC LIBRARY, Perlwin Elementary School, 102 Main Rd, A0B 3M0. (Mail add: PO Box 119, A0B 3M0). Tel: 709-583-2119. E-mail: winterton@npl.ca. Web Site: nlpl.ca/component/jumi/library.html?site_id=awn, winterton.ca/residents/library. *Librn,* Sarah Morgan
Library Holdings: Bk Vols 4,388; Per Subs 21
Wireless access
Function: Computers for patron use, Internet access, Photocopying/Printing, Scanner
Open Tues & Thurs 12-6

NORTHWEST TERRITORIES

Date of Statistics: Not provided.

INUVIK

J AURORA COLLEGE*, Aurora Research Institute Library, No 87 Gwich'in Rd, X0E 0T0. (Mail add: PO Box 1008, X0E 0T0), SAN 324-1629. Tel: 867-777-3298, Ext 234. Administration Tel: 867-777-7814. FAX: 867-777-4264. E-mail: inlibrary@auroracollege.nt.ca. Web Site: auroracollege.libguides.com. *Librn,* Melanie Adams; E-mail: melanie.adams@auroracollege.nt.ca; Staff 1 (Non-MLS 1)
Founded 1965
Library Holdings: Bk Titles 20,000; Per Subs 72; Spec Interest Per Sub 35; Videos 210
Special Collections: Arctic Research (Thesis Coll); Northern Material & Arctic Research (Rare Books Coll)
Subject Interests: Agr res, Alaskana, Arctic geol, Arctic res, Botany, Fisheries res, Native studies, Natural sci, Oral hist, Permafrost, Wildlife res
Wireless access
Function: For res purposes, ILL available, Internet access, Prof lending libr, Res libr, VHS videos
Open Mon-Thurs 8:30-12 & 1-9, Fri 8:30-12 & 1-5, Sun 4pm-9pm; Mon-Fri 8:30-12 & 1-5 (Summer)

P INUVIK CENTENNIAL LIBRARY*, 100 Mackenzie Rd, X0E 0T0. (Mail add: PO Box 1640, X0E 0T0), SAN 318-9694. Tel: 867-777-8620. FAX: 867-777-8621. E-mail: lfrontdesk@inuvik.ca. Web Site: www.inuvik.ca/en/getting-active/library.asp. *Libr Serv Mgr,* Tom Samoil; E-mail: lsm@inuvik.ca; Staff 10 (Non-MLS 10)
Founded 1967. Pop 3,600
Library Holdings: Bk Vols 30,000; Per Subs 72
Special Collections: Dick Hill/Northern Coll
Automation Activity & Vendor Info: (Acquisitions) SirsiDynix; (Cataloging) SirsiDynix; (Circulation) SirsiDynix; (Course Reserve) SirsiDynix; (ILL) SirsiDynix; (OPAC) SirsiDynix; (Serials) SirsiDynix
Wireless access
Special Services for the Blind - Bks on CD; Large print bks; Low vision equip
Open Mon & Wed 9:30-12 & 1-8, Tues, Thurs & Fri 9:30-12 & 1-5, Sat 1-5

NORMAN WELLS

P NORMAN WELLS COMMUNITY LIBRARY*, PO Box 97, X0E 0V0. SAN 318-9716. Tel: 867-587-3714. FAX: 867-587-3714. E-mail: nw_library@gov.nt.ca. *Librn,* Debra Ann Walker
Library Holdings: Bk Titles 10,000; Per Subs 15
Open Tues & Thurs 4-8, Wed & Fri 4-7, Sat 1-4
Friends of the Library Group

YELLOWKNIFE

G GOVERNMENT OF THE NORTHWEST TERRITORIES*, Departments of Environment & Natural Resources, Industry, Tourism & Investment & Lands-Resource Centre, Scotia Centre, Basement, 5102 50th Ave, Ste 600, X1A 3S8. SAN 370-1255. Tel: 867-767-9170, Ext 15505. E-mail: enriti_library@gov.nt.ca. Web Site: www.enr.gov.nt.ca/en/enr-iti-lands-resource-centre. *Mgr, Info Serv,* Julie Rodger; E-mail: julie_rodger@gov.nt.ca; Staff 2 (Non-MLS 2)
Founded 1980
Library Holdings: Bk Titles 22,000; Per Subs 100
Special Collections: Traditional Knowledge. Canadian and Provincial
Subject Interests: Bio-diversity, Climate change, Conserv, Environ, Forestry, Mining, Wildlife
Automation Activity & Vendor Info: (Cataloging) EOS International; (Circulation) EOS International; (OPAC) EOS International
Function: Doc delivery serv, Govt ref serv, ILL available, Mail & tel request accepted, Mail loans to mem, Online cat, Ref serv available, VHS videos
Publications: Recent Acquisitions (Acquisition list)
Open Mon-Fri 8:30-12 & 1-5
Restriction: Circ limited, Closed stack

G LEGISLATIVE LIBRARY OF THE NORTHWEST TERRITORIES*, Legislative Assembly Bldg, 4570 - 48th St, X1A 2L9. (Mail add: PO Box 1320, X1A 2L9), SAN 318-9783. Tel: 867-767-9132, Ext 12054. FAX: 867-873-0207. Web Site: www.ntassembly.ca/library. *Legislative Librn,* Lisc Daley; E-mail: lisc_daley@ntassembly.ca; Staff 4 (MLS 2, Non-MLS 2)
Founded 1973
Library Holdings: Bk Vols 35,000; Per Subs 8
Special Collections: Canadian and Provincial
Subject Interests: Aboriginal issues, Northern issues
Automation Activity & Vendor Info: (Acquisitions) Koha; (Cataloging) Koha; (Circulation) Koha; (OPAC) Koha
Open Mon-Fri 8:30-5

P YELLOWKNIFE PUBLIC LIBRARY*, Centre Square Mall, 5022 49th St, 2nd Flr, X1A 2N5. (Mail add: PO Box 694, X1A 2N5), SAN 318-9791. Tel: 867-920-5642. Information Services Tel: 867-669-3403. FAX: 867-920-5671. E-mail: library@yellowknife.ca. Web Site: www.yellowknife.ca/en/living-here/public-library.asp. *Pub Serv Librn,* John Mutford; E-mail: jmutford@yellowknife.ca; Staff 7 (MLS 2, Non-MLS 5)
Founded 1949. Pop 18,500; Circ 87,000
Library Holdings: High Interest/Low Vocabulary Bk Vols 400; Bk Titles 70,000; Per Subs 127
Special Collections: Northern Coll
Subject Interests: Can arctic
Automation Activity & Vendor Info: (Cataloging) SirsiDynix; (Circulation) SirsiDynix; (OPAC) SirsiDynix
Function: ILL available
Open Mon & Thurs 9:30-8:30, Tues & Wed 9:30-6, Fri 10-6, Sat 10-5, Sun (Oct-April) 1-5
Restriction: Circ limited
Friends of the Library Group

NOVA SCOTIA

Date of Statistics: FY 2023-2024
Population: 1,058,694
Population Served by Public Libraries 1,058,694
Total Volumes in Public Libraries: 1,748,490
Digital Resources:
Total e-books: 180,493
Audio/Video (physical items): 155,235
E-magazines: 12,417
Total computers for use by the public: 1,187
Municipalities: 49
Library Systems: 9
Service Points: 78
Information provided courtesy of: Dale MacMillan, Data Management Technician, Client Services; Nova Scotia Provincial Library

AMHERST

P CUMBERLAND PUBLIC LIBRARIES*, 21 Acadia St, 2nd Flr, B4H 4W3. (Mail add: PO Box 220, B4H 3Z2), SAN 366-7057. Tel: 902-667-2135. FAX: 902-667-1360. E-mail: information@cumberlandpubliclibraries.ca. Web Site: www.cumberlandpubliclibraries.ca. *Chief Librn,* Denise Corey; E-mail: denise.corey@cumberlandpubliclibraries.ca; *Dep Chief Librn,* Chantelle Taylor; E-mail: chantelle.taylor@cumberlandpubliclibraries.ca; Staff 3 (MLS 3)
Founded 1967. Pop 31,355; Circ 129,618
Library Holdings: Bk Vols 80,830; Per Subs 96
Wireless access
Function: 24/7 Electronic res, Adult bk club, Bk club(s), Bks on CD, Children's prog, Computer training, Computers for patron use, Doc delivery serv, E-Readers, Free DVD rentals, ILL available, Magazines, Mail & tel request accepted, Mail loans to mem, Movies, Online cat, Online ref, OverDrive digital audio bks, Photocopying/Printing, Prog for adults, Prog for children & young adult, Story hour, Summer reading prog, Telephone ref, Workshops
Friends of the Library Group
Branches: 7
ADVOCATE LIBRARY, Fundy Tides Recreation Ctr, 93 Mills Rd, Advocate Harbour, B0M 1A0. (Mail add: PO Box 1, Advocate Harbour, B0M 1A0), SAN 325-4259. Tel: 902-392-2214. *Br Asst,* Terry Gulliver
Function: ILL available, Photocopying/Printing
Open Wed & Fri 10-12 & 1-4, Thurs 2-8, Sat 9-1
FOUR FATHERS MEMORIAL, 21 Acadia St, B4H 3L5. (Mail add: PO Box 220, B4H 3Z2), SAN 366-7081. Tel: 902-667-2549. FAX: 902-667-1360. *Br Asst,* Position Currently Open
Function: 24/7 Electronic res, Adult bk club, Audiobks via web, Bks on CD, Children's prog, Computer training, Computers for patron use, E-Readers, Free DVD rentals, ILL available, Magazines, Movies, Online cat, Photocopying/Printing, Prog for adults, Prog for children & young adult, Scanner, Summer reading prog, Teen prog, Wheelchair accessible
Open Mon, Fri & Sat 10-5, Tues-Thurs 10-8 (Winter); Mon-Thurs & Fri 10-5, Tues & Wed 10-8, Sat 10-1 (Summer)
Friends of the Library Group
OXFORD LIBRARY, 22 Water St, Oxford, B0M 1P0, SAN 366-7111. Tel: 902-447-2440. *Br Asst,* Helen Cole; *Br Asst,* Megan McNutt
Function: Bks on CD, Children's prog, Computers for patron use, E-Readers, Free DVD rentals, ILL available, Magazines, Online cat, Photocopying/Printing
Open Wed & Fri 11-1 & 2-5, Thurs 2-5 & 6-8, Sat 10-3 (Summer); Tues & Fri 11-1 & 2-5, Wed & Thurs 2-5 & 6-8, Sat 10-3 (Winter)
PARRSBORO LIBRARY, 91 Queen St, Parrsboro, B0M 1S0, SAN 366-7146. Tel: 902-254-2046. *Br Asst,* Amber Allard; *Br Asst,* Cindy Walker
Function: Adult bk club, Bks on CD, Children's prog, Computers for patron use, E-Readers, Free DVD rentals, ILL available, Magazines, Online cat, OverDrive digital audio bks, Photocopying/Printing, Summer reading prog, Teen prog
Open Tues & Wed 1-4 & 6-8, Thurs & Fri 10-1 & 2-5, Sat 10-3
PUGWASH LIBRARY, 10222 Durham St, Pugwash, B0K 1L0, SAN 329-5591. Tel: 902-243-3331. *Br Asst,* Mary Hartling; *Br Asst,* Archan Knotz
Function: Adult bk club, Bks on CD, Children's prog, Computers for patron use, E-Readers, Free DVD rentals, ILL available, Magazines, Online cat, Photocopying/Printing, Summer reading prog
Open Tues & Fri Noon-5, Wed & Thurs 2-7, Sat 9-2 (Summer); Mon & Tues 11-4, Wed & Thurs 2-7, Fri Noon-5, Sat 10-1 (Winter)
Friends of the Library Group
RIVER HEBERT LIBRARY, 2730 Barronsfield Rd, River Hebert, B0L 1G0, SAN 329-563X. Tel: 902-251-2324. *Br Asst,* Rosemary Ulch
Function: Adult bk club, Bks on CD, Children's prog, Computers for patron use, E-Readers, Free DVD rentals, ILL available, Magazines, Online cat, OverDrive digital audio bks, Photocopying/Printing, Summer reading prog
Open Wed & Fri 10-1 & 2-4, Thurs 2-7, Sat 10-3
SPRINGHILL MINERS MEMORIAL LIBRARY, 85 Main St, Springhill, B0M 1X0, SAN 366-7170. Tel: 902-597-2211. *Br Asst,* Cathy Canning; *Br Asst,* Allison Watson
Function: Adult bk club, Audiobks via web, Children's prog, Computer training, Computers for patron use, Free DVD rentals, Home delivery & serv to seniorr ctr & nursing homes, ILL available, Magazines, Movies, Online cat, OverDrive digital audio bks, Photocopying/Printing, Summer reading prog
Open Tues 11-1 & 2-8, Wed & Thurs 10-1 & 2-6, Fri 11-1 & 2-8, Sat 10-1 (Summer); Tues 11-1 & 2-8, Wed & Thurs 10-1 & 2-6, Fri 11-1 & 2-5, Sat 10-1 (Winter)

ANTIGONISH

C SAINT FRANCIS XAVIER UNIVERSITY*, Angus L MacDonald Library, 3080 Martha Dr, B2G 2W5. SAN 366-7596. Tel: 902-867-2228. FAX: 902-867-5153. Circulation E-mail: library@stfx.ca. Web Site: www.mystfx.ca/library. *Univ Librn,* Sandy Iverson; Tel: 902-867-3931, E-mail: siverson@stfx.ca; *Spec Coll Librn,* Susan Cameron; Tel: 902-867-5328, E-mail: scameron@stfx.ca; *Archivist,* Kathleen MacKenzie; Tel: 902-867-2201, E-mail: kmackenz@stfx.ca; *ILL,* Angela Hagar; Tel: 902-867-2421, E-mail: ahagar@stfx.ca; Staff 21 (MLS 6, Non-MLS 15)
Founded 1852. Enrl 5,453; Fac 237; Highest Degree: Master
Library Holdings: Bk Vols 215,562; Per Subs 160
Special Collections: Celtic Coll
Wireless access
Partic in Council of Atlantic Academic Libraries (CAAL); Novanet
Open Mon-Thurs 7:30am-11:30pm, Fri 7:30am-9:30pm, Sat 11-8, Sun 8:30am-11:30pm
Departmental Libraries:
MARIE MICHAEL LIBRARY, Coady International Institute, B2G 2W5. (Mail add: PO Box 5000, B2G 2W5), SAN 366-7626. Tel: 902-867-3964. FAX: 902-867-3907. Web Site: www.coady.stfx.ca/library.

Libr Spec, Catherine Irving; E-mail: cirving@stfx.ca; Staff 2 (Non-MLS 2)
Founded 1959
Library Holdings: CDs 100; DVDs 600; e-journals 20; Bk Vols 12,500; Per Subs 95; Videos 200
Special Collections: Antigonish Movement Coll
Subject Interests: Adult educ, Credit unions, Develop studies
Automation Activity & Vendor Info: (Cataloging) Ex Libris Group; (OPAC) Ex Libris Group
Publications: Gender & Sustainable Rural Development: A Resource Directory (1996); Toward Total Wellness: Women in the Caribbean (1994)
Open Mon-Fri 9-5

BADDECK

S ALEXANDER GRAHAM BELL NATIONAL HISTORIC SITE OF CANADA*, Reference Library & Archives, 559 Chebucto St, B0E 1B0. (Mail add: PO Box 159, B0E 1B0), SAN 370-775X. Tel: 902-295-2069. FAX: 902-295-3496. E-mail: information@pc.gc.ca. Web Site: pc.gc.ca/en/lhn-nhs/ns/grahambell, www.parkscanada.gc.ca. *Mgr,* Madeline Harvey; E-mail: madeline.harvey@canada.ca
Founded 1977
Library Holdings: Bk Titles 450; Bk Vols 620
Special Collections: Alexander Graham Bell Coll, incl AEA bulletins, Beinn Bhreagh recorder, dictated, home & lab notes, letter bks, secondary res mat
Wireless access
Restriction: Open by appt only

BARRINGTON

S CAPE SABLE HISTORICAL SOCIETY ARCHIVES & LIBRARY*, 2401 Hwy 3, B0W 1E0. (Mail add: PO Box 67, B0W 1E0), SAN 370-7253. Tel: 902-637-2185. E-mail: barmuseumcomplex@eastlink.ca. Web Site: capesablehistoricalsociety.com. *Dir,* Samantha Brannen; E-mail: barrmuseum.director@gmail.com
Founded 1933
Library Holdings: Bk Vols 800
Subject Interests: Genealogy, Local hist
Wireless access
Restriction: Open by appt only

BARRINGTON PASSAGE

S SHELBURNE COUNTY ARCHIVES & GENEALOGICAL SOCIETY LIBRARY*, 3541 Hwy 3, B0W 1G0. (Mail add: PO Box 24, B0W 1G0), SAN 377-1245. Tel: 902-637-3824. E-mail: society@shelburnecountyarchives.ca. Web Site: www.shelburnecountyarchives.ca. *Archives Mgr,* Position Currently Open
Founded 1987
Library Holdings: CDs 10; Bk Titles 3,600; Per Subs 10
Wireless access
Open Mon-Sat 9-4:30 (Summer); Sat 9-5 (Winter)
Restriction: Not a lending libr

BERWICK

P ANNAPOLIS VALLEY REGIONAL LIBRARY*, Administrative Office, 236 Commercial St, B0P 1E0. (Mail add: PO Box 510, B0P 1E0), SAN 366-7235. Tel: 902-538-2665. Toll Free Tel: 866-922-0229. E-mail: administration@valleylibrary.ca. Web Site: www.valleylibrary.ca. *Chief Exec Officer,* Julia Merritt; *Commun Serv Coordr,* Wendy Trimper; E-mail: wtrimper@valleylibrary.ca; Staff 27 (MLS 3, Non-MLS 24)
Founded 1949. Pop 103,836; Circ 573,720
Library Holdings: Bk Vols 283,899; Per Subs 260
Wireless access
Restriction: Not open to pub
Friends of the Library Group
Branches: 11
ANNAPOLIS ROYAL BRANCH, 143 Ritchie St, Annapolis Royal, B0S 1A0. (Mail add: PO Box 579, Annapolis Royal, B0S 1A0), SAN 366-726X. Tel: 902-532-2226. *Br Mgr,* Christie Surprise-Tolj
Library Holdings: Bk Vols 10,869
Open Mon & Fri 10-5, Wed & Thurs 10-8, Sat 10-2
Friends of the Library Group
BERWICK & DISTRICT LIBRARY, 236 Commercial St, B0P 1E0. (Mail add: PO Box 510, B0P 1E0), SAN 366-7294. Tel: 902-538-4030. *Br Mgr,* Barbara Lipp
Library Holdings: Bk Vols 8,597
Open Tues & Wed 10-5, Thurs & Fri 12-6, Sat 10-2
Friends of the Library Group
BRIDGETOWN & AREA LIBRARY, 38 Queen St, Bridgetown, B0S 1C0. (Mail add: PO Box 39, Bridgetown, B0S 1C0), SAN 366-7324. Tel: 902-665-2758. *Br Mgr,* Pam Ellis
Library Holdings: Bk Vols 6,956
Open Tues 2-5 & 6:30-8:30, Thurs & Fri 10-5, Sat 10-1
Friends of the Library Group
ISABEL & ROY JODREY MEMORIAL LIBRARY - HANTSPORT, 10 Main St, Hantsport, B0P 1P0. (Mail add: PO Box 467, Hantsport, B0P 1P0), SAN 366-7359. Tel: 902-684-0103. *Br Mgr,* Leah Winter
Library Holdings: Bk Vols 11,552
Open Mon & Thurs 10-8, Wed & Sat 10-2
Friends of the Library Group
KENTVILLE BRANCH, 440 Main St, Kentville, B4N 1K8, SAN 366-7383. Tel: 902-679-2544. *Br Mgr,* Julie Johnson
Library Holdings: Bk Vols 12,740
Open Mon, Wed, Fri & Sat 10-5, Tues & Thurs 10-8
Friends of the Library Group
KINGSTON BRANCH, 671 Main St, Kingston, B0P 1R0. (Mail add: PO Box 430, Kingston, B0P 1R0), SAN 366-7413. Tel: 902-765-3631. *Br Mgr,* Shelly Cox
Library Holdings: Bk Vols 10,222
Open Tues & Thurs 2-5 & 6:30-8:30, Fri 6:30pm-8:30pm, Sat 10-2
Friends of the Library Group
ROSA M HARVEY MIDDLETON & AREA LIBRARY - MIDDLETON, 45 Gates Ave, Middleton, B0S 1P0. (Mail add: PO Box 667, Middleton, B0S 1P0), SAN 366-7472. Tel: 902-825-4835. *Br Mgr,* Sue Aldred
Library Holdings: Bk Vols 12,004
Open Tues & Thurs 10-5 & 6:30-8:30, Wed, Fri & Sat 10-5
Friends of the Library Group
DR FRANK W MORSE MEMORIAL LIBRARY - LAWRENCETOWN, 489 Main St, Lawrencetown, B0S 1M0. (Mail add: PO Box 88, Lawrencetown, B0S 1M0). Tel: 902-584-3044. *Br Mgr,* Jaki Fraser
Open Tues & Fri 2-5 & 6:30-8:30, Wed & Sat 10-1, Thurs 2-5
Friends of the Library Group
MURDOCH C SMITH MEMORIAL LIBRARY - PORT WILLIAMS, 1045 Main St, Port Williams, B0P 1T0. (Mail add: PO Box 70, Port Williams, B0P 1T0), SAN 366-7502. Tel: 902-542-3005. FAX: 902-542-3005. *Br Mgr,* Sue Mullen
Library Holdings: Bk Vols 10,271
Open Mon & Fri 2-5 & 6:30-8:30, Wed 10-5, Sat 10-2
Friends of the Library Group
WINDSOR REGIONAL LIBRARY, 195 Albert St, Windsor, B0N 2T0. (Mail add: PO Box 106, Windsor, B0N 2T0), SAN 366-7537. Tel: 902-798-5424. *Br Mgr,* Cathy Lothian
Library Holdings: Bk Vols 13,426
Open Tues-Thurs 10-8, Fri & Sat 10-5, Sun 2-5
Friends of the Library Group
WOLFVILLE BRANCH, 21 Elm Ave, Wolfville, B4P 2A1, SAN 366-7561. Tel: 902-542-5760. FAX: 902-542-5780. *Br Mgr,* Lisa Rice
Library Holdings: Bk Vols 16,604
Open Tues-Thurs 10-8, Fri & Sat 10-5, Sun 1-5
Friends of the Library Group
Bookmobiles: 2

BRIDGEWATER

P SOUTH SHORE PUBLIC LIBRARIES*, 135 North Park St, Unit B, B4V 9B3. Tel: 902-543-2548. Administration Tel: 877-455-2548. E-mail: info@southshorepubliclibraries.ca. Web Site: www.southshorepubliclibraries.ca. *Chief Librn,* Ashley Nunn-Smith; *Dep Chief Librn,* Jeff Mercer; E-mail: jmercer@southshorepubliclibraries.ca; Staff 3 (MLS 3)
Founded 1972
Automation Activity & Vendor Info: (Cataloging) SirsiDynix; (Circulation) SirsiDynix
Branches: 4
ALEAN FREEMAN LIBRARY, 5060 Hwy 210, Greenfield, B0T 1E0. Tel: 902-685-5400.
Open Wed 5pm-8pm, Sat 10-1
MARGARET HENNIGAR PUBLIC LIBRARY, 135 North Park St, Unit B, B4V 9B3, SAN 366-7685. Tel: 902-543-9222. *Br Coordr,* Katherine Sharp
Open Mon, Fri & Sat 10-5, Tues & Thurs 10-9, Sun 12-4
LUNENBURG BRANCH, 19 Pelham St, Lunenburg, B0J 2C0, SAN 366-7715. Tel: 902-634-8008. E-mail: lunenburg@southshorepubliclibraries.ca.
Open Mon-Wed, Fri & Sat 10-5, Thurs 10-8, Sun Noon-4
THOMAS H RADDALL LIBRARY, 145 Old Bridge St, Liverpool, B0T 1K0, SAN 366-7707. Tel: 902-354-5270.
Open Tues, Wed & Fri 10-5, Thurs 10-8, Sat 10-2, Sun 12-4
Bookmobiles: 1

CHERRY BROOK

S BLACK CULTURAL CENTRE FOR NOVA SCOTIA LIBRARY*, Ten Cherry Brook Rd, B2Z 1A8. SAN 374-6178. Tel: 902-434-6223. Toll Free Tel: 800-465-0767. FAX: 902-434-2306. E-mail: contact@bccns.com. Web Site: web1.bccnsweb.com/. *Exec Dir,* Russell Grosse
Founded 1983

Library Holdings: Bk Titles 3,000
Special Collections: Black Culture. Oral History
Publications: Out of the Past Into the Future; Out of the Past Into the Future, Vol 1; Publications List; Traditional Lifetime Stories, Vol 1; Traditional Lifetime Stories, Vol 2
Open Mon-Fri 10-4, Sat (June-Sept) Noon-3

CHURCH POINT

C UNIVERSITE SAINTE-ANNE*, Bibliotheque Louis-R-Comeau, 1695 Hwy 1, B0W 1M0. SAN 318-9813. Tel: 902-769-2114, Ext 7158. Web Site: www.usainteanne.ca/bibliotheque. *Dir,* Pamela Maher; Tel: 902-769-2114, Ext 7161, E-mail: pamela.maher@usainteanne.ca; *Dir, Res Serv,* Valerie Lalande; Tel: 902-769-2114, Ext 7196, E-mail: valerie.lalande@usainteanne.ca; *Libr Asst II,* Rosalie Robicheau; Tel: 902-769-2114, Ext 7170; *Libr Asst I,* Jason Saulnier; Tel: 902-769-2114, Ext 7158; Staff 2 (MLS 2)
Founded 1890. Enrl 407; Fac 45; Highest Degree: Master
Library Holdings: Bk Titles 78,000; Bk Vols 80,000; Per Subs 204
Special Collections: History & Folklore (Acadiana), bks, micro, newsp
Subject Interests: Children's lit
Automation Activity & Vendor Info: (Acquisitions) BiblioMondo; (Cataloging) BiblioMondo; (Circulation) BiblioMondo; (Course Reserve) BiblioMondo; (ILL) BiblioMondo; (Media Booking) BiblioMondo; (OPAC) BiblioMondo; (Serials) BiblioMondo
Wireless access
Function: Doc delivery serv, ILL available, Photocopying/Printing, Wheelchair accessible
Partic in Canadian Research Knowledge Network; Council of Atlantic Academic Libraries (CAAL)
Open Mon-Thurs 1-6, Fri 1-4:30
Restriction: Clients only, Fee for pub use

DARTMOUTH

G CANADA DEPARTMENT OF FISHERIES & OCEANS*, Bedford Institute of Oceanography Library, Holland Bldg, 4th Flr, One Challenger Dr, B2Y 4A2. (Mail add: PO Box 1006, B2Y 4A2), SAN 318-983X. Tel: 902-426-3683. FAX: 902-496-1544. E-mail: dartmouth.library-bibliotheque@dfo-mpo.gc.ca. Web Site: science-libraries.canada.ca/eng/fisheries-oceans, www.bio.gc.ca.
Founded 1962
Library Holdings: Bk Titles 18,000; Bk Vols 125,000; Per Subs 1,100
Special Collections: Arctic & Eastern Canadian Projects (Environmental Assessment Document Coll); Marine Sciences Coll
Subject Interests: Marine sci, Oceanography
Function: ILL available
Open Mon-Fri 8-5
Restriction: Lending to staff only, Open to pub for ref only

M CAPITAL HEALTH/NOVA SCOTIA HOSPITAL*, W James Meredith Health Sciences Library, Hugh Bell Bldg, Rm 200, 300 Pleasant St, B2Y 3Z9. (Mail add: PO Box 1004, B2Y 3Z9), SAN 324-5861. Tel: 902-464-3254. FAX: 902-464-4804. Web Site: library.nshealth.ca. *Librn/Educator,* Lara Killian; Tel: 902-464-3144; *Libr Tech,* Jackie Zoppa; Tel: 902-464-3146, E-mail: jackie.zoppa@nshealth.ca; *Libr Tech,* MacKenzie Rob; Tel: 902-464-3255, E-mail: robertb.mackenzie@nshealth.ca; Staff 4 (MLS 1, Non-MLS 3)
Founded 1860
Library Holdings: Bk Titles 3,330; Per Subs 114
Subject Interests: Mental illness, Psychiat, Psychol
Automation Activity & Vendor Info: (Cataloging) Inmagic, Inc.; (OPAC) Inmagic, Inc.
Wireless access
Partic in Atlantic Health Knowledge Partnership
Open Tues-Fri 8:30-4:30
Restriction: Hospital staff & commun

S DARTMOUTH HERITAGE MUSEUM LIBRARY, Evergreen House, 26 Newcastle St, B2Y 3M5. SAN 377-3353. Tel: 902-464-2300. E-mail: info@dartmouthmuseum.ca. Web Site: dartmouthheritagemuseum.ns.ca. *Exec Dir,* Amanda Furniss; Tel: 902-464-2916, E-mail: manager@dartmouthmuseum.ca; *Colls Mgr,* Shannon Baxter; Tel: 902-464-2004, E-mail: collections@dartmouthmuseum.ca; Staff 2 (Non-MLS 2)
Library Holdings: Bk Titles 400; Bk Vols 500; Per Subs 20
Mem of Halifax Public Libraries
Open Tues-Fri 10-5
Friends of the Library Group

G ENVIRONMENT & CLIMATE CHANGE CANADA*, Atlantic Region Library, Queen Sq, 5th Flr, 45 Alderney Dr, B2Y 2N6. SAN 327-5450. Tel: 902-426-7232. E-mail: ec.bibliotheque-library.ec@canada.ca. Web Site: science-libraries.canada.ca/eng/environment, www.canada.ca/en/environment-climate-change/corporate/contact/find-office. *Chief, Library Services,* Angela Ward Smith; E-mail: angela.wardsmith@ec.gc.ca; Staff 1 (MLS 1)
Library Holdings: Bk Vols 3,000
Wireless access
Partic in Council of Federal Libraries Consortium
Restriction: Open by appt only

P HALIFAX PUBLIC LIBRARIES*, 60 Alderney Dr, B2Y 4P8. SAN 366-7928. Tel: 902-490-5744. Interlibrary Loan Service Tel: 902-490-5821. Information Services Tel: 902-490-5753. FAX: 902-490-5762. E-mail: agadmin@halifax.ca. Web Site: www.halifaxpubliclibraries.ca. *Chief Librn/CEO,* Asa Kachan; Tel: 902-490-5868, E-mail: libraryceo@halifax.ca; *Serv Area Mgr,* Maureen Collier; E-mail: colliem@halifax.ca; *Serv Area Mgr,* Janice Fiander; E-mail: fiandej@halifax.ca; *Serv Area Mgr,* Kathleen Peverill; E-mail: peverik@halifax.ca; *Serv Area Mgr,* Helen Thexton; E-mail: thextoh@halifax.ca; Staff 316 (MLS 50, Non-MLS 266)
Pop 372,858; Circ 4,709,496
Library Holdings: CDs 36,037; DVDs 79,662; Bk Titles 340,491
Special Collections: Reference Halifax Coll
Subject Interests: Archit, Art, Hist
Wireless access
Function: Homebound delivery serv, ILL available, Prog for adults, Prog for children & young adult, Ref serv available, Summer reading prog, Wheelchair accessible
Publications: Bibliographies; Branch Profiles (Library statistics & report); Community Directories, Library Guide, Resource Lists; Halifax Public Libraries Library Guide (Library handbook)
Member Libraries: Dartmouth Heritage Museum Library
Open Mon-Fri 8:30-4:30
Restriction: Non-circulating coll
Branches: 14
ALDERNEY GATE BRANCH, 60 Alderney Dr, B2Y 4P8. Tel: 902-490-5745, 902-490-5748. Web Site: www.halifaxpubliclibraries.ca/locations/AG. *Librn,* Lynn Lavoie; Staff 22 (MLS 5, Non-MLS 17)
Founded 1989. Pop 28,572; Circ 474,455
Special Services for the Deaf - TDD equip
Open Mon-Thurs 9-9, Fri 9-6, Sat 10-5, Sun (Sept-May) 2-5
BEDFORD BRANCH, Wardour Ctr, 15 Dartmouth Rd, Bedford, B4A 3X6, SAN 376-8597. Tel: 902-490-5740. FAX: 902-490-5752. Web Site: www.halifaxpubliclibraries.ca/locations/BED. *Librn,* Jocelyn Covert; Staff 7 (MLS 2, Non-MLS 5)
Founded 1990. Pop 18,271; Circ 316,602
Library Holdings: CDs 2,420; DVDs 2,998; Videos 868
Open Tues-Thurs 9-9, Fri 9-6, Sat 10-5, Sun (Sept-May) 2-5
CAPTAIN WILLIAM SPRY BRANCH, 16 Sussex St, Halifax, B3R 1N9, SAN 366-7960. Tel: 902-490-5818. Circulation Tel: 902-490-5734. FAX: 902-490-5741. Web Site: www.halifaxpubliclibraries.ca/locations/CWS. *Librn,* Ella Leving; Staff 10 (MLS 2, Non-MLS 8)
Founded 1986. Pop 27,746; Circ 202,919
Open Tues-Thurs 9-9, Fri 9-5, Sat 10-5, Sun (Sept-May) 2-5
CENTRAL LIBRARY, 5440 Spring Garden Rd, Halifax, B3J 1E9, SAN 376-8686. Tel: 902-490-5700. Web Site: www.halifaxpubliclibraries.ca/locations/sga. *Asst Br Mgr,* Danielle Dungey; E-mail: dungeyd@halifax.ca; Staff 35 (MLS 8, Non-MLS 27)
Founded 1951. Pop 51,730; Circ 717,856
Function: Prog for adults, Prog for children & young adult, Ref serv available, Summer reading prog
Open Mon-Thurs 9-9, Fri & Sat 9-6, Sun (Sept-May) Noon-6
Restriction: Non-circulating coll
COLE HARBOUR BRANCH, 51 Forest Hills Pkwy, Cole Harbour, B2W 6C6, SAN 376-8619. Tel: 902-490-3820. FAX: 902-490-3829. Web Site: www.halifaxpubliclibraries.ca/locations/CH. *Librn,* Darcy Johns; Staff 11 (MLS 2, Non-MLS 9)
Founded 1989. Pop 50,785; Circ 397,838
Open Tues-Thurs 9-9, Fri 9-6, Sat 10-5, Sun (Sept-May) 2-5
DARTMOUTH NORTH BRANCH, 105 Highfield Park, B3A 0C2, SAN 376-8627. Tel: 902-490-5840. FAX: 902-490-5842. Web Site: www.halifaxpubliclibraries.ca/locations/DN. *Librn,* Carla Foxe; Staff 4 (MLS 1, Non-MLS 3)
Founded 1996. Pop 7,025; Circ 69,204
Open Mon 12-5, Tues-Thurs 9-9, Fri 9-5, Sat 10-5
KESHEN GOODMAN BRANCH, 330 Lacewood Dr, Halifax, B3S 0A3, SAN 370-0208. Tel: 902-490-5738. FAX: 902-490-6407. Web Site: www.halifaxpubliclibraries.ca/locations/KG. *Mgr,* Position Currently Open; *Serv Mgr,* Hannah Colville; E-mail: colvilh@halifax.ca; Staff 29 (MLS 5, Non-MLS 24)
Founded 1989. Pop 54,492; Circ 948,496
Open Mon-Thurs 9-9, Fri & Sat 10-5, Sun 12-5
HALIFAX NORTH MEMORIAL, 2285 Gottingen St, Halifax, B3K 3B6, SAN 366-7952. Tel: 902-490-5723. Information Services Tel: 902-490-5811. Web Site: www.halifaxpubliclibraries.ca/locations/N. *Librn,* Sarah Ziolkowska; Staff 10 (MLS 2, Non-MLS 8)

Founded 1966. Pop 8,316; Circ 126,688
Open Tues-Thurs 9-9, Fri 9-5, Sat 10-5
MUSQUODOBOIT HARBOUR BRANCH, Village Plaza, 7900 Hwy 7, Musquodoboit Harbour, B0J 2L0, SAN 376-8651. Tel: 902-889-2227. Web Site: www.halifaxpubliclibraries.ca/locations/MH. *Librn,* Ashley Norton; Staff 3 (MLS 1, Non-MLS 2)
Founded 1997. Pop 5,985; Circ 82,829
Open Tues-Thurs 9-8, Fri 9-5, Sat 10-5
SACKVILLE BRANCH, 636 Sackville Dr, Lower Sackville, B4C 2S3, SAN 376-866X. Tel: 902-865-8653. Reference Tel: 902-865-3744. FAX: 902-865-2370. Web Site: www.halifaxpubliclibraries.ca/locations/SA. *Librn,* Tara Eldershaw; Staff 14 (MLS 3, Non-MLS 11)
Founded 1996. Pop 42,473; Circ 447,037
Open Tues-Thurs 9-9, Fri 9-6, Sat 10-5, Sun (Sept-May) 2-5
J D SHATFORD MEMORIAL, 10353 St Margaret Bay Rd, Hubbards, B0J 1T0, SAN 376-8635. Tel: 902-857-9176. FAX: 902-857-1397. Web Site: www.halifaxpubliclibraries.ca/locations/HU. *User Serv Librn,* Eric Drew; Staff 2 (Non-MLS 2)
Founded 1969. Pop 1,059; Circ 57,196
Open Tues 12-7, Wed & Thurs 1-8, Fri & Sat 10-3
SHEET HARBOUR BRANCH, Blue Water Business Ctr, 22756 Hwy 7, Sheet Harbour, B0J 3B0, SAN 376-8678. Tel: 902-885-2391. FAX: 902-885-2749. Web Site: www.halifaxpubliclibraries.ca/locations/sh. *Librn,* Ashlee Norton; Staff 3 (MLS 1, Non-MLS 2)
Founded 1992. Pop 3,141; Circ 37,913
Open Tues & Fri 10-4, Wed 12-6, Thurs 3-8, Sat 10-1
TANTALLON PUBLIC, 3646 Hammonds Plains Rd, Upper Tantallon, B3Z 1H3. Tel: 902-826-3330. FAX: 902-826-3328. Web Site: www.halifaxpubliclibraries.ca/locations/TA. *Br Serv Librn,* Shannon Higgins; Staff 12 (MLS 2, Non-MLS 10)
Founded 2001. Pop 19,825; Circ 304,654
Function: Prog for children & young adult
Open Tues-Thurs 9-9, Fri 9-6, Sat 10-5, Sun (Sept-May) 2-5
WOODLAWN PUBLIC, 31 Eisener Blvd, B2W 0J1, SAN 376-8708. Tel: 902-490-2636. Web Site: www.halifaxpubliclibraries.ca/locations/W. *Ad,* Lara McAllister; Staff 21 (MLS 4, Non-MLS 17)
Founded 1975. Pop 26,795; Circ 425,350
Function: Prog for adults, Prog for children & young adult, Summer reading prog
Open Mon-Thurs 9-9, Fri 9-6, Sat 10-5, Sun (Sept-May) 2-5
Bookmobiles: 1

S NORTHWEST ATLANTIC FISHERIES ORGANIZATION LIBRARY*, 2 Morris Dr, Ste 100, B3B 1K8. SAN 373-3165. Tel: 902-468-5590. FAX: 902-468-5538. E-mail: info@nafo.int. Web Site: www.nafo.int/publications. *Library Contact,* Sarah Guile; E-mail: sguile@nafo.int
Library Holdings: Bk Titles 50; Bk Vols 100
Function: Ref & res
Restriction: Access at librarian's discretion

GLACE BAY

S CAPE BRENTON MINERS' MUSEUM LIBRARY*, 17 Museum St, B1A 5T8. (Mail add: PO Box 310, B1A 5T8), SAN 324-0029. Tel: 902-849-4522. E-mail: info@minersmuseum.com. Web Site: www.minersmuseum.com. *Exec Dir,* Mary Pat Mombourquette
Founded 1967
Library Holdings: Bk Titles 500
Special Collections: Technical Information on Coal Mining Pre-1965
Wireless access

HALIFAX

S ATLANTIC PROVINCES SPECIAL EDUCATION AUTHORITY LIBRARY, 102-7071 Bayers Rd, B3L 2C2. Tel: 902-423-8094. FAX: 902-423-8694. E-mail: library@apsea.ca. Web Site: www.apsea.ca. *Libr Tech,* Ann Terese MacDonald; E-mail: annterese_macdonald@apsea.ca; *Libr Tech,* Gail Simms; E-mail: gail_simms@apsea.ca
Wireless access
Special Services for the Deaf - Am sign lang & deaf culture; Bks on deafness & sign lang; Closed caption videos
Special Services for the Blind - Bks on CD; Braille bks; Braille equip; Braille music coll; Braille paper; Children's Braille; Large print bks; Lending of low vision aids; Transcribing serv
Restriction: Mem organizations only, Students only

R ATLANTIC SCHOOL OF THEOLOGY LIBRARY*, 624 Francklyn St, B3H 3B4. SAN 318-9899. Tel: 902-423-7986. Circulation E-mail: astcirc@astheology.ns.ca. Reference E-mail: astref@astheology.ns.ca. Web Site: www.astheology.ns.ca/library. *Chair, Coll Assessment, Coll Develop Librn,* Emily Cooke; Tel: 902-496-7948, E-mail: ewoodcock@astheology.ns.ca; *Instruction Librn,* Robert Martel; Tel: 902-420-1669, E-mail: rmartel@astheology.ns.ca; Staff 5 (MLS 3, Non-MLS 2)
Founded 1971. Highest Degree: Master
Library Holdings: AV Mats 1,667; Bk Vols 85,000; Per Subs 350; Videos 384
Special Collections: Church History; Ecumenical; J B Hardie Arabic & Islamic Library; Presbyterian Canadian Missionary
Subject Interests: Relig, Theol
Automation Activity & Vendor Info: (Acquisitions) OCLC WorldShare Interlibrary Loan; (Cataloging) OCLC WorldShare Interlibrary Loan; (Circulation) OCLC WorldShare Interlibrary Loan; (Course Reserve) OCLC WorldShare Interlibrary Loan
Wireless access
Publications: John B Hardie Arabic & Islamic Collection (Collection catalog)
Partic in Council of Atlantic Academic Libraries (CAAL); Novanet
Open Mon-Fri 8:30-4:30

S CANADA DEPARTMENT OF NATIONAL DEFENCE*, Cambridge Military Library, Royal Artillery Park, Bldg No 3, 5460 Royal Artillery Court, B3J 0A8. SAN 325-2604. Tel: 902-427-4494. FAX: 902-427-4495. Web Site: www.cafconnection.ca/Halifax/CML.aspx. *Pres,* Peter Dawson; Tel: 902-427-0774, E-mail: peter.dawson@forces.gc.ca; *Librn,* Coral Peterson; E-mail: coral.peterson@forces.gc.ca; Staff 1 (MLS 1)
Founded 1817
Library Holdings: Bk Vols 12,500
Special Collections: Corfu Coll
Subject Interests: Local hist, Mil
Automation Activity & Vendor Info: (Cataloging) Inmagic, Inc.
Restriction: Open by appt only

C DALHOUSIE UNIVERSITY*, Killam Memorial Library, 6225 University Ave, B3H 4H8. (Mail add: PO Box 15000, B3H 4R2), SAN 366-7804. Administration Tel: 902-494-3621. FAX: 902-494-2062. E-mail: killiam.library@dal.ca, killmref@dal.ca. Web Site: libraries.dal.ca/hours-locations/killam.html. *Head of Libr,* Sarah Stevenson; Tel: 902-494-1325, E-mail: sarah.stevenson@dal.ca
Founded 1867. Highest Degree: Doctorate
Special Collections: Australian Literature; Early Imprints & Fine Bindings (Douglas Cockerell Coll); Francis Bacon Coll; J J Stewart Maritime Coll; K G T Webster Castle Coll; Oscar Wilde Coll; Rudyard Kipling (James MacGregor Stewart Coll); Thomas Chandler Haliburton Coll; Thomas Raddall Manuscripts & Papers; William Gilpin Coll
Subject Interests: Arts, Bus & mgt, Computer sci, Humanities, Sci, Soc sci
Automation Activity & Vendor Info: (Acquisitions) Ex Libris Group; (Cataloging) Ex Libris Group; (Circulation) Ex Libris Group; (ILL) Relais International; (OPAC) Ex Libris Group
Wireless access
Partic in Canadian Association of Research Libraries; Canadian Research Knowledge Network; Council of Atlantic Academic Libraries (CAAL); Novanet

Departmental Libraries:

CL SIR JAMES DUNN LAW LIBRARY, 6061 University Ave, B3H 4R2. (Mail add: PO Box 15000, B3H 4R2), SAN 366-7863. Tel: 902-494-2124. Administration Tel: 902-494-2640. FAX: 902-494-6669. E-mail: lawref@dal.ca. Web Site: libraries.dal.ca/hours-locations/dunn.html. *Head Librn,* Anne Matthewman; E-mail: anne.matthewman@dal.ca
Founded 1883
Library Holdings: Bk Vols 275,408; Per Subs 600
Subject Interests: Intl law, Law of the sea
Publications: Marine Affairs Bibliography
Open Mon-Thurs 8am-10pm, Fri 8-4, Sat Noon-6, Sun Noon-8

CM W K KELLOGG HEALTH SCIENCES LIBRARY, Sir Charles Tupper Medical Bldg, 5850 College St, B3H 4R2. (Mail add: PO Box 15000, B3H 4R2). Circulation Tel: 902-494-2479. Interlibrary Loan Service Tel: 902-494-2469. Reference Tel: 902-717-5244. Administration Tel: 902-494-2458. Interlibrary Loan Service FAX: 902-494-3750. E-mail: kellogg.library@dal.ca. Web Site: libraries.dal.ca/hours-locations/kellogg.html. *Head of Libr,* Melissa Helwig; E-mail: melissa.helwig@dal.ca
Founded 1890
Library Holdings: Bk Vols 208,000
Subject Interests: Dentistry, Health serv admin, Human communication disorders, Med, Nursing, Occupational therapy, Pharm, Physiotherapy
Automation Activity & Vendor Info: (Cataloging) Ex Libris Group; (Circulation) Ex Libris Group; (OPAC) Ex Libris Group; (Serials) EBSCO Online
Open Mon-Thurs 8am-9pm, Fri 8-5, Sat Noon-4

SEXTON DESIGN & TECHNOLOGY LIBRARY, Bldg B, 3rd Flr, 5260 DaCosta Row, B3H 4R2. (Mail add: PO Box 15000, B3H 4R2), SAN 319-0102. Tel: 902-494-3240. FAX: 902-494-6089. E-mail: sexton.library@dal.ca. Web Site: libraries.dal.ca/hours-locations/sexton.html. *Head Librn,* Michelle Paon; Tel: 902-476-8437, E-mail: michelle.paon@dal.ca; Staff 4 (MLS 4)
Founded 1949. Enrl 3,000; Fac 110; Highest Degree: Doctorate

Library Holdings: Bk Titles 45,000; Bk Vols 141,000; Per Subs 740
Subject Interests: Agr engr, Applied math, Archit, Chem engr, Civil engr, Computer sci, Electrical engr, Engr, Environ, Food sci, Metallurgical, Mining engr, Rural planning, Urban

M IWK HEALTH*, Health Sciences Library, 5850/5980 University Ave, B3K 6R8. SAN 325-5913. Tel: 902-470-8646. E-mail: hslibrary@iwk.nshealth.ca. Web Site: www.iwk.nshealth.ca/page/health-sciences-library. *Librn,* Darlene Chapman; E-mail: darlene.chapman@iwk.nshealth.ca; *ILL,* Pamela Parker; Staff 2 (MLS 1, Non-MLS 1)
Library Holdings: Bk Titles 1,000; Bk Vols 32,170; Per Subs 800
Subject Interests: Neonatology, Obstetrics, Pediatrics, Women's health
Wireless access
Open Mon-Fri 9-5

L LEGAL INFORMATION SOCIETY OF NOVA SCOTIA LIBRARY*, 1741 Brunswick St, Ste 150B, B3J 3X8. SAN 373-644X. Tel: 902-454-2198. FAX: 902-455-3105. E-mail: lisns@legalinfo.org. Web Site: www.legalinfo.org. *Legal Info Mgr,* Wendy Turner
Library Holdings: Bk Titles 2,500; Bk Vols 3,000; Per Subs 20
Partic in Novanet
Restriction: Not open to pub

S MARITIME MUSEUM OF THE ATLANTIC*, Niels Jannasch Library, 1675 Lower Water St, B3J 1S3. SAN 325-6294. Tel: 902-424-6442. FAX: 902-424-0612. E-mail: mmalibry@gov.ns.ca. Web Site: maritimemuseum.novascotia.ca/research/niels-jannasch-library. *Curator,* Dr Roger Marsters; E-mail: roger.marsters@novascotia.ca
Library Holdings: Bk Titles 6,000; Per Subs 39
Special Collections: Nautical Charts; Photographs Coll; Vessel Plans
Restriction: Open by appt only

L MCINNES COOPER LIBRARY*, 1300-1969 Upper Water St, B3J 2V1. (Mail add: PO Box 730, B3J 2V1), SAN 328-0861. Tel: 902-444-8468. FAX: 902-425-6350. Web Site: www.mcinnescooper.com. *Regional Mgr, Libr Serv,* Kate Greene Stanhope; E-mail: kate.stanhope@mcinnescooper.com; Staff 4 (MLS 2, Non-MLS 2)
Automation Activity & Vendor Info: (Acquisitions) Inmagic, Inc.; (Cataloging) Inmagic, Inc.; (Serials) Inmagic, Inc.
Partic in Can Asn of Law Librs

C MOUNT SAINT VINCENT UNIVERSITY LIBRARY & ARCHIVES*, 15 Lumpkin Rd, B3M 2J6. SAN 318-9988. Tel: 902-457-6250. FAX: 902-457-6445. E-mail: library@msvu.ca. Web Site: www.msvu.ca/academics/library. *Univ Librn,* Tanja Harrison; Tel: 902-457-6108, E-mail: tanja.harrison@msvu.ca; *Colls Librn,* Meg Raven; Tel: 902-457-6403, E-mail: meg.raven@msvu.ca; *Research & E-Learning Librn,* Denyse Rodrigues; Tel: 902-457-6200, E-mail: denyse.rodrigues@msvu.ca; *Syst Librn,* Stanislav Orlov; E-mail: stan.orlov@msvu.ca; *Access Serv, Libr Operations,* Corinne Gilroy; Tel: 902-457-6204, E-mail: corinne.gilroy@msvu.ca; Staff 21 (MLS 5, Non-MLS 16)
Founded 1873. Enrl 3,959; Fac 330; Highest Degree: Doctorate
Library Holdings: AV Mats 2,035; e-books 405,400; e-journals 32,957; Bk Titles 224,149; Bk Vols 241,208; Per Subs 8,242
Special Collections: Canadian Drama Coll; English Literature (MacDonald Coll); Lesbian Pulp Fiction Coll; Women & Peace Coll; Women's Studies (Centennial, Gerritsen & Women's History), bks, micro. Canadian and Provincial
Subject Interests: Child & youth study, Cultural studies, Educ, Family studies, Gerontology, Human nutrition, Info tech, Pub relations, Tourism, Women's studies
Automation Activity & Vendor Info: (Acquisitions) Ex Libris Group; (Cataloging) Ex Libris Group; (Circulation) Ex Libris Group; (Course Reserve) Ex Libris Group; (ILL) Relais International; (OPAC) Ex Libris Group; (Serials) Ex Libris Group
Wireless access
Function: Archival coll, CD-ROM, Distance learning, Doc delivery serv, E-Reserves, ILL available, Magnifiers for reading, Online info literacy tutorials on the web & in blackboard, Online ref, Orientations, Ref serv available, Spoken cassettes & CDs, Telephone ref, VHS videos, Workshops
Publications: Guide to Resources in Women's Studies (Research guide)
Partic in Council of Atlantic Academic Libraries (CAAL); Novanet
Open Mon-Thurs 8am-10pm, Fri 8-6, Sat 9-6, Sun 9-9

L NOVA SCOTIA BARRISTERS' SOCIETY*, Library & Information Services, The Law Courts, 7th Flr, 1815 Upper Water St, B3J 1S7. SAN 319-0005. Tel: 902-425-2665. FAX: 902-422-1697. E-mail: nsbslib@nsbs.org. Web Site: www.nsbs.org/library_services. *Libr Tech,* Jennifer Haimes; E-mail: jhaimes@nsbs.org; *Libr Tech,* Lisa Woo Shue; E-mail: lisaw@nsbs.org; Staff 3 (MLS 3)
Founded 1797
Library Holdings: Bk Vols 15,000
Special Collections: Unreported Nova Scotia Decisions
Subject Interests: Can law
Automation Activity & Vendor Info: (Serials) Inmagic, Inc.
Wireless access
Publications: Nova Scotia Current Law (Monthly); Nova Scotia Law News (Quarterly)
Restriction: Mem only

C NOVA SCOTIA COLLEGE OF ART & DESIGN UNIVERSITY LIBRARY, 5163 Duke St, B3J 3J6. SAN 319-0013. Tel: 902-494-8196. Interlibrary Loan Service Tel: 902-494-8255. FAX: 902-425-2420. E-mail: librarycirc@nscad.ca. Web Site: library.nscad.ca/libraryhome. *Dir, Libr Serv,* Rebecca Young; Tel: 902-444-7212, E-mail: ryoung@nscad.ca; Staff 6 (MLS 2, Non-MLS 4)
Founded 1887. Enrl 730; Fac 45; Highest Degree: Master
Library Holdings: Bk Titles 50,000; Per Subs 225
Subject Interests: 20th Century art hist, Contemporary art, Environ planning, Graphic design, Photog
Automation Activity & Vendor Info: (Acquisitions) Infor Library & Information Solutions; (Cataloging) Infor Library & Information Solutions; (Circulation) Infor Library & Information Solutions; (OPAC) Infor Library & Information Solutions; (Serials) Infor Library & Information Solutions
Wireless access
Partic in Council of Atlantic Academic Libraries (CAAL); Novanet

NOVA SCOTIA COMMUNITY COLLEGE

J AKERLEY CAMPUS LIBRARY*, 21 Woodlawn Rd, Dartmouth, B2W 2R7. Tel: 902-491-4968. FAX: 902-491-2012. E-mail: library.akerley@nscc.ca. Web Site: www.library.nscc.ca. *Campus Librn,* Pam Eakin; Tel: 902-491-3580, E-mail: pam.eakin@nscc.ca; *Libr Asst,* Karen Marshall; E-mail: karen.marshall@nscc.ca; *Libr Tech,* Terry Matthews; E-mail: terry.matthews@nscc.ca
Library Holdings: Bk Vols 8,122
Automation Activity & Vendor Info: (Acquisitions) Ex Libris Group; (Cataloging) Ex Libris Group; (Circulation) Ex Libris Group; (Course Reserve) Ex Libris Group; (ILL) Ex Libris Group; (Media Booking) Ex Libris Group; (OPAC) Ex Libris Group; (Serials) Ex Libris Group
Open Mon-Thurs 8-4:30, Fri 8-4

J ANNAPOLIS VALLEY - LAWRENCETOWN CAMPUS LIBRARY*, 50 Elliot Rd, RR 1, Lawrencetown, B0S 1M0, SAN 366-7448. Tel: 902-584-2102. FAX: 902-584-2085. E-mail: library.avlawrencetown@nscc.ca. Web Site: www.library.nscc.ca. *Campus Librn,* Trish LeBlanc; E-mail: trish.leblanc@nscc.ca
Library Holdings: Bk Vols 5,000
Partic in Novanet
Open Mon-Fri 8:30-4:30

J ANNAPOLIS VALLEY - MIDDLETON CAMPUS LIBRARY*, 295 Commercial St, Middleton, B0S 1P0. (Mail add: 50 Elliott Rd, RR 1, Lawrencetown, B0S 1M0). Tel: 902-825-2930, 902-825-5481. E-mail: library.avlawrencetown@nscc.ca. *Libr Asst,* Natalie Catto; E-mail: natalie.catto@nscc.ca
Open Tues-Thurs 8:30-4:30 (Sept-May)

J BURRIDGE CAMPUS LIBRARY*, 372 Pleasant St, Yarmouth, B5A 2L2. Tel: 902-742-3416. FAX: 902-742-0519. E-mail: library.burridge@nscc.ca. Web Site: www.library.nscc.ca. *Dir, Libr & Educ,* Andrea Stewart; E-mail: andrea.stewart@nscc.ca; *Libr Tech,* Terri Noble; E-mail: terri.noble@nscc.ca
Library Holdings: Bk Vols 3,128
Automation Activity & Vendor Info: (Cataloging) Infor Library & Information Solutions; (Circulation) Infor Library & Information Solutions; (Course Reserve) Infor Library & Information Solutions; (ILL) Infor Library & Information Solutions; (Media Booking) Infor Library & Information Solutions; (OPAC) Infor Library & Information Solutions
Open Mon-Fri 8-4:30

J CUMBERLAND CAMPUS LIBRARY*, One Main St, Springhill, B0M 1X0. (Mail add: PO Box 550, Springhill, B0M 1X0). Tel: 902-597-4109. E-mail: library.cumberland@nscc.ca. Web Site: www.nscc.ca/library/about-nscc-libraries/locations/cumberland.asp. *Libr Tech,* Jo-Ann Potter; E-mail: jo-ann.potter@nscc.ca
Library Holdings: Bk Titles 2,000; Bk Vols 2,106
Open Mon-Fri 8-4

J INSTITUTE OF TECHNOLOGY LIBRARY*, 5685 Leeds St, B3J 3C4. (Mail add: PO Box 2210, B3J 3C4), SAN 319-0072. Tel: 902-491-4694. FAX: 902-491-2015. E-mail: library.institute@nscc.ca. Web Site: www.library.nscc.ca. *Campus Librn,* Carly Brake; E-mail: carly.brake@nscc.ca; Staff 1 (MLS 1)
Founded 1972. Enrl 1,100
Library Holdings: Bk Vols 7,809
Special Collections: Student Technical Reports
Subject Interests: Trades
Partic in Council of Atlantic Academic Libraries (CAAL)
Open Mon & Wed 8-5, Tues & Thurs 8-7, Fri 8-4

J IVANY CAMPUS LIBRARY*, 80 Mawiomi Pl, Dartmouth, B2Y 0A5. Tel: 902-491-1035. FAX: 902-491-1037. E-mail: library.ivany@nscc.ca. Web Site: www.library.nscc.ca/contact_us/campuses/waterfront. *Campus*

Librn, Ann Roman; E-mail: ann.roman@nscc.ca; *Libr Tech,* Robin Allen; E-mail: robin.allen@nscc.ca; Staff 4 (MLS 2, Non-MLS 2)
Founded 2007. Enrl 1,900
Open Mon-Thurs 8-4:30, Fri 8-4

J KINGSTEC CAMPUS LIBRARY*, 236 Belcher St, Kentville, B4N 0A6, SAN 371-7151. Tel: 902-679-7380. Reference Tel: 902-679-7379. FAX: 902-679-5187. E-mail: library.kingstec@nscc.ca. Web Site: www.library.nscc.ca. *Campus Librn,* Terri Milton; E-mail: terri.milton@nscc.ca; *Libr Tech,* Carolyn Armstrong; *Libr Tech,* Paula J Coldwell; E-mail: paula.coldwell@nscc.ca; Staff 3 (MLS 1, Non-MLS 2)
Founded 1964. Enrl 1,000; Fac 75
Library Holdings: Bk Titles 14,000; Bk Vols 19,000; Per Subs 30
Special Collections: Local Radio Station Record Coll, 45 & 33 1/3; Self-Esteem Coll
Subject Interests: Bus, Entrepreneurship, Health serv, Trades
Automation Activity & Vendor Info: (Cataloging) Ex Libris Group; (Circulation) Ex Libris Group
Function: Computers for patron use, Doc delivery serv, Electronic databases & coll, Health sci info serv, ILL available, Internet access, Learning ctr, Mail & tel request accepted, Online cat, Online ref, Orientations, Outside serv via phone, mail, e-mail & web, Photocopying/Printing, Ref serv available, Scanner, Telephone ref, VHS videos, Wheelchair accessible, Workshops
Special Services for the Deaf - Bks on deafness & sign lang
Open Mon-Thurs 8-8, Fri 8-5, Sat Noon-3 (Sept-May); Mon-Fri 8-5 (June-Sept)

J LUNENBURG CAMPUS LIBRARY*, 75 High St, Bridgewater, B4V 1V8. Tel: 902-543-0684. FAX: 902-543-0190. E-mail: library.lunenburg@nscc.ca. Web Site: www.library.nscc.ca. *Campus Librn,* Mary Jane Pittman; Tel: 902-543-0690, E-mail: mary.pittman@nscc.ca; *Libr Tech,* Marc Vollebekk; E-mail: marc.vollebekk@nscc.ca
Library Holdings: Bk Titles 2,801

J MARCONI CAMPUS LIBRARY*, 1240 Grand Lake Rd, Sydney, B1P 6J7. (Mail add: PO Box 1042, Sydney, B1P 6J7). Tel: 902-563-2102. FAX: 902-563-0511. E-mail: library.marconi@nscc.ca. Web Site: www.library.nscc.ca. *Campus Librn,* Kara Thompson; E-mail: kara.thompson@nscc.ca; *Libr Tech,* Nicole MacDonald; E-mail: nicole.macdonald@nscc.ca; Staff 3 (MLS 1, Non-MLS 2)
Library Holdings: Bk Titles 3,000
Automation Activity & Vendor Info: (Cataloging) Ex Libris Group; (Circulation) Ex Libris Group; (Course Reserve) Ex Libris Group; (ILL) Ex Libris Group; (OPAC) Ex Libris Group
Function: 24/7 Electronic res, 24/7 Online cat, Doc delivery serv, Electronic databases & coll, ILL available, Online cat, Online ref, Prof lending libr, Ref & res, Ref serv available
Partic in Council of Atlantic Academic Libraries (CAAL)
Open Mon-Fri 8-4

J PICTOU CAMPUS LIBRARY*, 39 Acadia Ave, Stellarton, B0K 1S0. (Mail add: PO Box 820, Stellarton, B0K 1S0). Tel: 902-755-7201. FAX: 902-755-7909. E-mail: library.pictou@nscc.ca. Web Site: www.library.nscc.ca/contact_us/campuses/pictou. *Dir of Libr,* Andrea Stewart; E-mail: andrea.stewart@nscc.ca; *Campus Librn,* Debbie Kaleva; E-mail: debbie.kaleva@nscc.ca; *Campus Librn,* Wendy McInnis; E-mail: wendy.mcinnis@nscc.edu
Library Holdings: Bk Vols 4,665; Per Subs 50
Subject Interests: Local Celtic hist
Function: Computer training, Computers for patron use, Distance learning, Doc delivery serv, E-Reserves, Electronic databases & coll, Equip loans & repairs, Free DVD rentals, ILL available, Instruction & testing, Internet access, Online cat, Online ref, Orientations, Photocopying/Printing, Ref & res, Ref serv available, Scanner, Story hour, Wheelchair accessible, Workshops

J SHELBURNE CAMPUS LIBRARY*, 1575 Lake Rd, Shelburne, B0T 1W0. (Mail add: PO Box 760, Shelburne, B0T 1W0). Tel: 902-875-8669. FAX: 902-875-3797. E-mail: library.shelburne@nscc.ca. Web Site: www.library.nscc.ca. *Libr Tech,* Susan Balkam; E-mail: susan.balkam@nscc.ca
Library Holdings: Bk Vols 1,045
Automation Activity & Vendor Info: (Cataloging) Ex Libris Group; (Circulation) Ex Libris Group; (OPAC) Ex Libris Group; (Serials) Ex Libris Group
Open Mon 9:30am-12:30pm, Tues & Fri 8am-11:30am, Wed & Thurs 10-2

J STRAIT AREA CAMPUS LIBRARY*, 226 Reeves St, Port Hawkesbury, B9A 2W2, SAN 372-7327. Tel: 902-625-4364. FAX: 902-625-0193. E-mail: library.straitarea@nscc.ca. Web Site: www.nscc.ns.ca/About_NSCC/Locations/Strait.asp. *Campus Librn,* April Sampson; Tel: 902-625-4075, E-mail: april.sampson@nscc.ca; *Libr Tech,* Margaret Eager; E-mail: margie.eager@nscc.ca; Staff 1 (MLS 1)
Library Holdings: Bk Titles 6,000; Bk Vols 10,091; Per Subs 80
Special Collections: Marine Engineering & Navigation
Open Mon-Fri 8-4

J TRURO CAMPUS LIBRARY*, McCarthy Hall, 36 Arthur St, Truro, B2N 1X5, SAN 319-020X. Tel: 902-893-5326. FAX: 902-893-6693. E-mail: library.truro@nscc.ca. Web Site: www.library.nscc.ca. *Regional Librn,* Charmaine Borden; E-mail: charmaine.borden@nscc.ca; Staff 3 (MLS 1, Non-MLS 2)
Founded 1995. Enrl 1,000
Library Holdings: Bk Vols 30,000; Per Subs 150
Special Collections: Community Economic Development
Subject Interests: Acad upgrading, Commun develop, Corrections
Publications: Handbook; Periodical Holdings list
Open Mon-Thurs 8-5, Fri 8-4:30

G NOVA SCOTIA DEPARTMENT OF EDUCATION & EARLY CHILDHOOD DEV*, Departmental Library, 2021 Brunswick St, B3J 2S9. SAN 329-2371. Tel: 902-424-5168. Reference Tel: 902-424-5264. Web Site: educationlibrary.ednet.ns.ca. *Librn,* Lynda Silver; E-mail: lynda.silver@novascotia.ca; *Libr Tech,* Visnja Parker; E-mail: visnja.parker@novascotia.ca; Staff 2 (MLS 1, Non-MLS 1)
Founded 1986
Library Holdings: Bk Vols 12,000; Per Subs 75
Special Collections: Nova Scotia Educational System (Departmental Archives)
Open Mon-Fri 8:30-4:30

G NOVA SCOTIA DEPARTMENT OF NATURAL RESOURCES & RENEWABLES, Natural Sciences Library, Founders Sq, 1701 Hollis St, 3rd Flr, B3J 3M8. (Mail add: PO Box 698, B3J 2T9), SAN 324-7465. Tel: 902-424-8633. FAX: 902-424-7735. E-mail: natural.sciences@novascotia.ca. Web Site: novascotia.ca/natr/library. Staff 2 (MLS 1, Non-MLS 1)
Founded 1960
Library Holdings: Microforms 20,000; Bk Titles 35,000; Per Subs 30
Special Collections: Annual Reports (Geological Survey of Canada, Nova Scotia Department of Mines, Nova Scotia Department of Lands & Forests); Company Exploration Reports; GSC Publications & Maps on Nova Scotia; NSDNR Publications & Maps
Subject Interests: Forestry, Geoscience, Land use, Mining, Resource mgt, Wildlife
Automation Activity & Vendor Info: (Cataloging) SirsiDynix; (OPAC) SirsiDynix
Wireless access
Function: Archival coll, ILL available, Online cat, Ref serv available, Wheelchair accessible
Open Mon-Fri 8:30-4
Restriction: Open to pub for ref & circ; with some limitations

G NOVA SCOTIA GOVERNMENT, Department of Justice Library, 1690 Hollis St, B3J 3J9. (Mail add: PO Box 7, B3J 2L6), SAN 366-810X. Tel: 902-717-3603. FAX: 902-424-1730. *Knowledge & Resource Mgmt Specialist,* Susan Cochrane; E-mail: susan.cochrane@novascotia.ca
Founded 1972
Library Holdings: Bk Titles 4,500; Bk Vols 9,000; Per Subs 30
Special Collections: Law
Subject Interests: Can, Criminology, English law, Police sci
Restriction: Staff use only

L NOVA SCOTIA LEGAL AID LIBRARY*, 5475 Spring Garden Rd, Ste 401, B3J 3T2. SAN 375-345X. Tel: 902-420-6590. Web Site: www.nslegalaid.ca. *Research Coordr,* Andrew Waugh; E-mail: Andrew.Waugh@nslegalaid.ca; Staff 1 (MLS 1)
Library Holdings: Bk Titles 680; Per Subs 12
Restriction: Staff use only

G NOVA SCOTIA LEGISLATIVE LIBRARY*, Province House, 2nd Flr, B3J 2P8. (Mail add: PO Box 396, B3J 2P8), SAN 318-9961. Tel: 902-424-5932. E-mail: leglib@novascotia.ca. Web Site: nslegislature.ca/about/supporting-offices/legislative-library. *Legislative Librn,* David McDonald; E-mail: David.McDonald@novascotia.ca; *Info Serv Librn,* Heather Ludlow; E-mail: Heather.Ludlow@novascotia.ca; *Mgr, Info Serv,* Anne Van Iderstine; E-mail: anne.vaniderstine@novascotia.ca; *Syst Mgr, Tech Mgr,* Yi Yu; E-mail: Yi.Yu@novascotia.ca; Staff 7 (MLS 4, Non-MLS 3)
Founded 1862
Library Holdings: Bk Vols 200,000
Special Collections: Novascotiana Coll
Subject Interests: Can hist, Fed, Nova Scotiana, Polit sci, Prov govt doc
Publications: A History of Province House; Nova Scotia Book of Days; Publications of the Province of Nova Scotia (Annual & Monthly)
Open Mon-Fri 8:30-4:30

S NOVA SCOTIA MUSEUM LIBRARY*, 1747 Summer St, 3rd Flr, B3H 3A6. SAN 319-0080. Tel: 902-424-6548. FAX: 902-424-0560. E-mail: museum@novascotia.ca. Web Site: museum.novascotia.ca. *Archives, Exec*

Dir, Stephanie Smith; Tel: 902-424-7344; *Colls Mgr,* Sean McKeane; Tel: 902-424-6453
Founded 1884
Library Holdings: Bk Vols 13,000; Per Subs 100
Subject Interests: Decorative art, Early tech, Museology, Natural hist, NS soc hist
Wireless access
Restriction: Open by appt only, Open to pub for ref only

G NOVA SCOTIA PROVINCIAL LIBRARY*, 6016 University Ave, 5th Flr, B3H 1W4. SAN 366-8223. Tel: 902-424-2457. FAX: 902-424-0633. E-mail: nspl@novascotia.ca. Web Site: library.novascotia.ca. *Dir,* Lynn Somers; E-mail: lynn.somers@novascotia.ca; *Mgr, Syst & Coll Access,* Dyan Bader; E-mail: dyan.bader@novascotia.ca; *Client Serv Mgr,* Kelli Woo Shue; E-mail: kelli.wooshue@novascotia.ca; *Coord, Finance & Admin,* Krista Wadman; E-mail: krista.wadman@novascotia.ca; Staff 15 (MLS 9, Non-MLS 6)
Founded 1952
Subject Interests: Libr sci
Automation Activity & Vendor Info: (Acquisitions) SirsiDynix; (Cataloging) SirsiDynix; (Circulation) SirsiDynix; (OPAC) SirsiDynix
Publications: Nova Scotia Provincial-Regional Libraries Annual Report
Restriction: Not open to pub, Staff use only

S PUBLIC ARCHIVES OF NOVA SCOTIA*, Nova Scotia Archives, 6016 University Ave, B3H 1W4. SAN 319-0110. Tel: 902-424-6060. Reference Tel: 902-424-6055. FAX: 902-424-0628. E-mail: archives@novascotia.ca. Web Site: www.novascotia.ca/archives. *Actg Archivist,* Patti Bannister; Tel: 902-424-6076, E-mail: bannispl@gov.ns.ca
Founded 1931
Library Holdings: Bk Vols 50,000
Special Collections: Akins Library Coll (static); Genealogical Research Resources; NS Historical Newspaper Coll (static). Canadian and Provincial
Subject Interests: Govt doc, Nova Scotiana
Wireless access
Open Mon, Tues, Thurs & Fri 8:30-4:30, Wed 8:30am-9pm, Sat 9-5
Restriction: Non-circulating to the pub

C SAINT MARY'S UNIVERSITY*, Patrick Power Library, 923 Robie St, B3H 3C3. SAN 366-8401. Tel: 902-420-5547. Interlibrary Loan Service Tel: 902-420-5542. Reference Tel: 902-420-5544. FAX: 902-420-5561. E-mail: research@smu.ca. Web Site: smu.ca/academics/the-patrick-power-library.html. *Univ Librn,* Suzanne van den Hoogen; Tel: 902-420-5532, E-mail: suzanne.vandenhoogen@smu.ca; *Assoc Univ Librn, Info Syst,* Peter Webster; Tel: 902-420-5507, E-mail: peter.webster@smu.ca; *Archives Librn,* Hansel Cook; Tel: 902-420-5508, E-mail: hansel.cook@smu.ca; *Res & Ref Librn,* Nicole Carter; Tel: 902-420-5540, E-mail: nicole.carter@smu.ca; *Mgr, Access Serv,* Susan Cannon; Tel: 902-420-5656, E-mail: susan.cannon@smu.ca; *Mgr, Acq Serv,* Terri Winchcombe; Tel: 902-420-5535, E-mail: terri.winchcombe@smu.ca; Staff 43 (MLS 9, Non-MLS 34)
Founded 1802. Enrl 8,541; Fac 237; Highest Degree: Doctorate
Special Collections: Atlantic Canada; Eric; Irish Studies; Latin America
Subject Interests: Educ, Relig studies
Automation Activity & Vendor Info: (Acquisitions) Ex Libris Group; (Cataloging) Ex Libris Group; (Circulation) Ex Libris Group; (Course Reserve) Ex Libris Group; (ILL) Relais International; (OPAC) Ex Libris Group; (Serials) Ex Libris Group
Wireless access
Publications: A Guide to the Patrick Power Library; Annual Report; Patrick Power Library Workbook; Psychology Workbook; Research Works; Sociology Workbook; The Perfect Term Paper
Partic in Can On-Line Enquiry; Council of Atlantic Academic Libraries (CAAL); Proquest Dialog; Univ of Toronto Libr Automation Syst

S SCHIZOPHRENIA SOCIETY OF NOVA SCOTIA RESOURCES*, 5571 Cunard St, Unit 101, B3K 1C5. SAN 373-6105. Tel: 902-465-2601. Toll Free Tel: 800-465-2601. FAX: 902-465-5479. E-mail: contact@ssns.ca. Web Site: www.ssns.ca/resources.html. *Exec Dir,* Diane MacDougall; E-mail: director@ssns.ca
Library Holdings: Bk Vols 70
Restriction: Open by appt only

L STEWART MCKELVEY, Law Library, 600-1741 Upper Water St, B3J 0J2. SAN 322-7014. Tel: 902-420-3200. FAX: 902-420-1417. E-mail: dlfwlibrary@stewartmckelvey.com. Web Site: stewartmckelvey.com. Staff 3.5 (MLS 1, Non-MLS 2.5)
Founded 1867
Library Holdings: Bk Vols 15,000; Per Subs 250
Restriction: Access for corporate affiliates, Co libr, Employee & client use only, Not a lending libr

C UNIVERSITY OF KING'S COLLEGE LIBRARY*, 6350 Coburg Rd, B3H 2A1. SAN 319-0129. Tel: 902-422-1271. FAX: 902-423-3357. E-mail: library@ukings.ca. Web Site: www.ukings.ca/campus-community/library. *Interim Univ Librn,* Janet Hathaway; Tel: 902-422-1271, Ext 175, E-mail: janet.hathaway@ukings.ca; *Head, Acq & Ser,* Alaina MacKenzie; E-mail: alaina.mackenzie@ukings.ca; *Asst Librn, Access Serv,* Patricia L Chalmers; E-mail: patricia.chalmers@ukings.ca
Founded 1789. Fac 24; Highest Degree: Bachelor
Library Holdings: Bk Vols 80,000
Special Collections: Dr Bray Associates Libraries; Tractarian Theology (Bishop Kingdon Coll); University Archives; Weldon Loyalist China Coll
Subject Interests: Classics, Hist, Journalism, Lit, Philos, Theol
Wireless access
Partic in Council of Atlantic Academic Libraries (CAAL); Novanet
Open Mon-Thurs 9am-11pm, Fri 9-5, Sat Noon-5, Sun Noon-11; Mon-Fri 9-5 (Summer)

MULGRAVE

P EASTERN COUNTIES REGIONAL LIBRARY*, 390 Murray St, B0E 2G0. (Mail add: PO Box 2500, B0E 2G0), SAN 366-8460. Tel: 902-747-2597. FAX: 902-747-2500. Web Site: ecrl.library.ns.ca. *Chief Librn,* Laura Emery; E-mail: lemery@ecrl.ca; *Dep Chief Librn,* Patricia McCormick; E-mail: pmccormi@ecrl.ca; *Mgr, Br,* Amanda Campbell; E-mail: acampbell@ecrl.ca
Founded 1969. Pop 41,830; Circ 145,513
Library Holdings: Bk Vols 104,800; Per Subs 200
Special Collections: Acadian Culture Coll
Subject Interests: Genealogy, Local hist
Wireless access
Open Mon-Fri 8-5
Branches: 8
CANSO BRANCH, 169 Main St, Canso, B0H 1H0. Tel: 902-366-2955. FAX: 902-366-2955. E-mail: canso@ecrl.ca. *Library Contact,* Sandra Dixon
Founded 1969
Library Holdings: Bk Vols 6,500
Open Mon & Thurs 1-4 & 6-8, Tues & Fri 10-12 & 1-4, Sat 11-2
COADY & TOMPKINS MEMORIAL, 7972 Cabot Trail Rd, Margaree Forks, B0E 2A0. Tel: 902-248-2821. FAX: 902-248-2821. E-mail: margaree@ecrl.ca. *Library Contact,* Anne LeBlanc
Founded 1978
Library Holdings: Bk Vols 8,000
Open Mon 1:30-4:30 & 6:30-8:30, Tues & Wed 6:30pm-8:30pm, Thurs 10-12, 1:30-4:30 & 6:30-8:30, Fri & Sat 1:30-4:30
ALEXANDER DOYLE PUBLIC LIBRARY, Dalbrae Academy, 11156 Rte 19, Mabou, B0E 1X0. Tel: 902-945-2257. E-mail: mabou@ecrl.ca. *Library Contact,* Madonna Macinnis
PETIT DE GRAT BRANCH, 3435 Hwy, No 206, Petit de Grat, B0E 2L0. Tel: 902-226-3534. FAX: 902-226-3534. E-mail: petitdeg@ecrl.ca. *Library Contact,* Kenneth David
Founded 1982
Library Holdings: Bk Vols 12,000
Open Mon, Tues & Thurs 2-8, Wed & Sat 10-4
PORT HAWKESBURY BRANCH, 304 Pitt St (SAERC), Unit 3, Port Hawkesbury, B9A 2T9. Tel: 902-625-2729. FAX: 902-625-2729. E-mail: porthawk@ecrl.ca. *Library Contact,* Joyce Olivar-Snair
Founded 1969
Library Holdings: Bk Vols 10,000
Special Services for the Blind - Closed circuit TV
Open Mon-Fri 3pm-8pm, Sat 11-2
SHERBROOKE BRANCH, 11 Main St, Sherbrooke, B0J 3C0. Tel: 902-522-2180. FAX: 902-522-2180. E-mail: sherbroo@ecrl.ca. *Library Contact,* Marcia Anderson
Founded 1969
Library Holdings: Bk Vols 6,500
Open Mon-Wed 2-5 & 6-8, Thurs 2-5, Fri 10:30-4, Sat 11-2
ST PETER'S BRANCH, 10036 Grenville St, Unit C, St. Peter's, B0E 3B0. Tel: 902-535-2465. E-mail: stpeters@ecrl.ca. *Library Contact,* Sharon McGrath
CYRIL WARD MEMORIAL, 27 Pleasant St, Guysborough, B0H 1N0. Tel: 902-533-3586. E-mail: guysborough@ecrl.ca. *Library Contact,* Terri Simpson
Founded 1986
Library Holdings: Bk Vols 8,300
Open Mon, Tues & Thurs 2-7, Fri & Sat 10-2

NEW GLASGOW

M ABERDEEN HOSPITAL*, Dr G R Douglas Memorial Library, 835 E River Rd, B2H 3S6. SAN 371-9960. Tel: 902-759-1786. FAX: 902-755-6764. *Libr Tech,* Lana MacEachern; Staff 1 (Non-MLS 1)
Library Holdings: DVDs 38; e-books 50; e-journals 86; Bk Titles 500; Per Subs 20; Videos 2

Subject Interests: Allied health, Med, Nursing
Function: Ref & res, Res libr
Open Mon-Fri 8-4
Restriction: Badge access after hrs, Circulates for staff only, Hospital employees & physicians only, Open to others by appt

P PICTOU - ANTIGONISH REGIONAL LIBRARY*, 182 Dalhousie St, B2H 5E3. (Mail add: PO Box 276, B2H 5E3), SAN 366-8649. Tel: 902-755-6031. Toll Free Tel: 866-779-7761. FAX: 902-755-6775. E-mail: info@parl.ns.ca. Web Site: www.parl.ns.ca. *Chief Librn,* Eric Stackhouse; E-mail: estackhouse@parl.ns.ca; Staff 48 (MLS 3, Non-MLS 45)
Founded 1951. Pop 68,272; Circ 380,294
Library Holdings: Bk Vols 142,071; Per Subs 359
Automation Activity & Vendor Info: (Acquisitions) MultiLIS; (Circulation) MultiLIS
Wireless access
Open Mon-Fri 8-4
Friends of the Library Group
Branches: 7
ANTIGONISH TOWN & COUNTY LIBRARY, 283 Main St, Antigonish, B2G 2C3, SAN 366-8673. Tel: 902-863-4276. E-mail: antigonish@parl.ns.ca. *Ch Serv Librn, Supvr,* Kristel Fleuren-Hunter
Library Holdings: Bk Vols 30,123
Open Wed, Fri & Sat 10-5, Tues & Thurs 10-9
Friends of the Library Group
NEW GLASGOW LIBRARY, 182 Dalhousie St, B2H 5E3. (Mail add: PO Box 276, B2H 5E3), SAN 366-8703. Tel: 902-752-8233. FAX: 902-752-6737. E-mail: newglasgow@parl.ns.ca. *Supvr, Tech Serv Librn,* Greg Hayward
Library Holdings: Bk Vols 146,220
Open Tues-Fri 10-9, Sat 10-5, Sun (Winter) 2-5
PICTOU LIBRARY, 40 Water St, Pictou, B0K 1H0. (Mail add: PO Box 622, Pictou, B0K 1H0), SAN 366-8738. Tel: 902-485-5021. E-mail: pictou@parl.ns.ca. *Br Asst,* Bonnie Allan
Library Holdings: Bk Vols 20,288
Open Tues-Thurs 12-9, Wed, Fri & Sat 10-5
RIVER JOHN LIBRARY, 2725 W Branch Rd, River John, B0K 1N0. (Mail add: PO Box 104, River John, B0K 1N0), SAN 374-3519. Tel: 902-351-2599. E-mail: riverjohn@parl.ns.ca. *Br Asst,* Samantha Allan
Library Holdings: Bk Vols 14,201
Open Tues & Thurs 2-5 & 7-9, Wed & Fri 10-1 & 2-5, Sat 10-12 & 1-4
STELLARTON LIBRARY, 248 Foord St, Stellarton, B0K 1S0. (Mail add: PO Box 1372, Stellarton, B0K 1S0), SAN 366-8762. Tel: 902-755-1638. E-mail: stellarton@parl.ns.ca. *Br Asst,* Ellie Smith
Library Holdings: Bk Vols 14,542
Open Tues & Thurs 2-5 & 7-9, Wed & Fri 9-12 & 2-5, Sat 10-12 & 1-4
TRENTON LIBRARY, 122 Main St, Trenton, B0K 1X0. (Mail add: PO Box 612, Trenton, B0K 1X0), SAN 366-8797. Tel: 902-752-5181. E-mail: trenton@parl.ns.ca. *Br Asst,* Barbara Ervin
Library Holdings: Bk Vols 6,827
Open Tues & Thurs 2-5 & 7-9, Wed & Fri 9-12 & 2-5, Sat 10-12 & 1-4
WESTVILLE LIBRARY, 2042 Queen St, Unit 3, Westville, B0K 2A0. (Mail add: PO Box 627, Westville, B0K 2A0), SAN 366-8827. Tel: 902-396-5022. E-mail: westville@parl.ns.ca. *Br Asst,* Gina Snell
Library Holdings: Bk Vols 11,514
Open Tues & Thurs 2-5 & 7-9, Wed & Fri 9-12 & 2-5, Sat 10-12 & 1-4

STELLARTON

S NOVA SCOTIA MUSEUM OF INDUSTRY LIBRARY*, 147 N Foord St, B0K 1S0. SAN 375-0361. Tel: 902-755-5425. FAX: 902-755-7045. E-mail: industry@novascotia.ca. Web Site: museumofindustry.novascotia.ca/collections-research/library. *Curator of Coll,* Erika Wilson
Founded 1986
Library Holdings: Bk Vols 2,600; Per Subs 35
Special Collections: Oral History
Subject Interests: Econ, Mining, Railway hist, Steelmaking
Restriction: Non-circulating to the pub, Open by appt only, Ref only

SYDNEY

G CANADA DEPARTMENT OF FISHERIES & OCEANS*, Canadian Coast Guard College John Adams Library, 1190 Westmount Rd, B1R 2J6. SAN 319-017X. Tel: 902-564-3660, Ext 1128. E-mail: cgclibrary@dfo-mpo.gc.ca. Web Site: www.ccg-gcc.gc.ca/college. *Librn,* Rachelle Brown; E-mail: rachelle.brown@dfo-mpo.gc.ca; Staff 3 (MLS 1, Non-MLS 2)
Founded 1965
Library Holdings: AV Mats 500; Bk Titles 65,000; Bk Vols 70,000; Per Subs 75
Special Collections: Ships Magnetism
Subject Interests: Marine engr, Mechanical engr, Navigation
Partic in OCLC Online Computer Library Center, Inc

P CAPE BRETON REGIONAL LIBRARY*, James McConnell Memorial Library, 50 Falmouth St, B1P 6X9. SAN 319-0188. Tel: 902-562-3279. FAX: 902-564-0765. E-mail: inssc@nssc.library.ns.ca. Web Site: www.cbrl.ca. *Regional Librn,* Lisa Mulak; E-mail: lmulak@cbrl.ca; *Asst Regional Dir, Coll Librn,* Theresa MacDonald; E-mail: tmacdona@cbrl.ca; *Br Mgr,* Emily Chasse; Tel: 902-562-3161, E-mail: echasse@cbrl.ca; *ILL,* Barbara MacLean; Staff 51 (MLS 8, Non-MLS 43)
Founded 1950
Apr 2018-Mar 2019 Income (Main & Associated Libraries) (CAN) $2,967,367, Provincial (CAN) $1,993,581, County (CAN) $706,900, Locally Generated Income (CAN) $226,927, Other (CAN) $39,959. Sal (CAN) $1,905,177
Library Holdings: Audiobooks 1,999; DVDs 8,279; e-books 25,719; Microforms 1,171; Bk Vols 215,072; Per Subs 190
Special Collections: Local History (Nova Scotia), bks, micro, playscripts. Canadian and Provincial
Subject Interests: Local hist
Automation Activity & Vendor Info: (Acquisitions) SirsiDynix; (Cataloging) SirsiDynix; (Circulation) SirsiDynix; (ILL) SirsiDynix; (OPAC) SirsiDynix
Wireless access
Function: 24/7 Online cat, 3D Printer, Activity rm, Adult bk club, Archival coll, Audiobks via web, Bk club(s), Bks on CD, Chess club, Children's prog, Computer training, Computers for patron use, Digital talking bks, Electronic databases & coll, Family literacy, Free DVD rentals, ILL available, Internet access, Large print keyboards, Life-long learning prog for all ages, Magazines, Magnifiers for reading, Mail & tel request accepted, Microfiche/film & reading machines, Movies, Online cat, Orientations, OverDrive digital audio bks, Photocopying/Printing, Preschool reading prog, Prog for adults, Prog for children & young adult, Ref & res, Scanner, Senior computer classes, Story hour, Summer reading prog, Teen prog, Wheelchair accessible, Workshops
Publications: Annual Report
Special Services for the Deaf - Assistive tech
Special Services for the Blind - Accessible computers
Open Mon 9-5, Tues-Thurs 10-8, Fri & Sat 10-5
Friends of the Library Group
Branches: 11
BADDECK PUBLIC, 520 Chebucto St, Baddeck, B0E 1B0. (Mail add: PO Box 88, Baddeck, B0E 1B0). Tel: 902-295-2055. E-mail: baddeck@cbrl.ca. *Librn,* Erin Phillips; Tel: 902-562-3279
Open Tues-Thurs 12-5 & 6-8, Fri & Sat 10-12 & 1-5
DOMINION PUBLIC, 78 Commercial St, Unit A, Dominion, B1G 1B4. Tel: 902-849-3590. E-mail: dominion@cbrl.ca. *Br Supvr,* Clare MacKillop; Tel: 902-562-3279, E-mail: cmackill@cbrl.ca
Open Tues & Wed 1-5:30 & 6-8, Thurs & Fri 10-12 & 1-5:30, Sat 10-12 & 1-5
FLORENCE PUBLIC, 676 Bras d'or Florence Rd, Florence, B1Y 1E4. Tel: 902-736-7583. E-mail: florence@cbrl.ca. *Br Supvr,* Clare MacKillop
Open Tues & Thurs 1-5 & 6-8, Wed & Fri 1-5, Sat 10-1
GLACE BAY PUBLIC, 143 Commercial St, Glace Bay, B1A 3B9. Tel: 902-849-8657. E-mail: glacebay@cbrl.ca. *Librn,* Cynthia Tiller
Open Mon 12:30-8, Tues-Thurs 9:30-8, Fri 9:30- 6, Sat 9:30-5
MARTHA HOLLETT MEMORIAL, One Fraser Ave, Sydney Mines, B1V 2B8. Tel: 902-736-3219. E-mail: sydneymines@cbrl.ca. *Br Supvr,* Clare MacKillop
Open Mon 1:30-5:30 & 7-9, Tues-Thurs 10-5:30 & 7-9, Fri 10-5:30, Sat 10-12 & 1-5
W W LEWIS MEMORIAL, Ten Upper Warren St, Louisbourg, B1C 1M6. Tel: 902-733-3608. E-mail: louisbou@cbrl.ca. *Br Supvr,* Clare MacKillop
Special Collections: Huntington Diaries
Open Tues & Thurs 2-5 & 6-8, Wed & Sat 2-5, Fri 10-11:30 & 2-5:30
MAIN-A-DIEU PUBLIC, 2886 Louisbourg-Main-a-Dieu Rd, Main-a-Dieu, B1C 1X5. Tel: 902-733-5708. E-mail: mainadie@cbrl.ca. *Br Supvr,* Clare MacKillop; Tel: 902-562-3279, E-mail: cmackill@cbrl.ca
Open Tues 1-5 & 6-8, Fri 10-1 & 2-5, Sat 2-5
NEW WATERFORD BRANCH, 3390 Plummer Ave, New Waterford, B1H 4K4. (Mail add: PO Box 12, New Waterford, B1H 4K4). Tel: 902-862-2892. E-mail: newwaterford@cbrl.ca. *Br Supvr,* Clare MacKillop
Open Mon 1:30-5:30 & 7-9, Tues-Thurs 10-9, Fri 10-7, Sat 10-5
WILFRED ORAM CENTENNIAL, 309 Commercial St, North Sydney, B2A 1B9. Tel: 902-794-3272. E-mail: northsydney@cbrl.ca. *Br Supvr,* Clare MacKillop
Open Mon 1:30-5:30 & 7-9, Tues-Thurs 10-9, Fri 10-6, Sat 10-5
TOMPKINS MEMORIAL, Tompkins Pl, 2249 Sydney Rd, Unit 3, Reserve Mines, B1E 1J9. Tel: 902-849-6685. E-mail: reservem@cbrl.ca. *Br Supvr,* Clare MacKillop; Tel: 902-562-3279, E-mail: cmackill@cbrl.ca
Open Mon, Tues & Fri 2-5:30, Wed & Thurs 2-5:30 & 6-8
VICTORIA NORTH REGIONAL, 36243 Cabot Trail, Ingonish, B0C 1K0. Tel: 902-285-2544. E-mail: ingonish@cbrl.ca. *Librn,* Erin Phillips
Open Tues-Thurs 12-5 & 6-8, Fri 9-12 & 1-5, Sat 10-12 & 1-5

C CAPE BRETON UNIVERSITY LIBRARY*, 1250 Grand Lake Rd, B1P 6L2. (Mail add: PO Box 5300, B1P 6L2), SAN 366-8851. Tel: 902-563-1320. Interlibrary Loan Service Tel: 902-563-1995. Reference Tel: 902-563-1387. FAX: 902-563-1177. E-mail: library_infoservices@cbu.ca. Web Site: www.cbu.ca/library. *Dean, Libr & Multicultural Learning,* Catherine Arseneau; E-mail: catherine_arseneau@cbu.ca; *Librn,* Cathy Chisholm; Tel: 902-563-1993, E-mail: cathy_chisholm@cbu.ca; *Librn,* Laura Syms; E-mail: laura_syms@cbu.ca. Subject Specialists: *Nursing, Sci,* Cathy Chisholm; *Bus,* Laura Syms; Staff 17 (MLS 6, Non-MLS 11)
Founded 1951. Enrl 3,600; Fac 160; Highest Degree: Master
Library Holdings: Bk Titles 250,000; Bk Vols 296,000; Per Subs 700
Special Collections: Bras d'Or Studies; Economic & Social History of Cape Breton Island, pamphlets, rpts, etc; Folklore; Scottish Coll (Gaelic & English)
Subject Interests: Local hist
Automation Activity & Vendor Info: (Acquisitions) Ex Libris Group; (Cataloging) Ex Libris Group; (Circulation) Ex Libris Group; (Course Reserve) Ex Libris Group; (OPAC) Ex Libris Group; (Serials) Ex Libris Group
Wireless access
Partic in Council of Atlantic Academic Libraries (CAAL); Novanet
Special Services for the Blind - Assistive/Adapted tech devices, equip & products
Open Mon-Thurs 8:30am-10pm, Fri 8:30-5, Sat 11-4, Sun 12-9
Friends of the Library Group
Departmental Libraries:
BEATON INSTITUTE ARCHIVES, 1250 Grand Lake Rd, B1P 6L2. (Mail add: PO Box 5300, B1P 6L2), SAN 366-8886. Tel: 902-563-1329. Automation Services FAX: 902 562-8899. E-mail: beaton@cbu.ca. Web Site: www.cbu.ca/campus/beaton-institute. *Dir, Cultural Resources,* Catherine Arseneau; Tel: 902-563-1326, E-mail: catherine_arseneau@cbu.ca; *Archivist,* Jane Arnold; Tel: 902-563-1690, E-mail: jane_arnold@cbu.ca
Founded 1957
Library Holdings: AV Mats 3,500; Bk Titles 1,700; Bk Vols 1,800; Per Subs 15
Special Collections: Cape Breton, bks, ms, micro, newsp, pamphlets; Gaelic & Scottish Coll, rare bks & ms. Oral History
Subject Interests: Local hist
Function: Archival coll, Res libr
Publications: Guide to the Genealogical Holdings; Guide to the Manuscript Holdings
Open Tues & Wed 1-4, Thurs & Fri 9-12 & 1-4
Restriction: Non-circulating

M NOVA SCOTIA HEALTH AUTHORITY*, Cape Breton Regional Hospital Library, 1482 George St, 3rd Flr, Rm 3613-1, B1P 1P3. SAN 373-3181. Web Site: library.nshealth.ca. *Librn,* Amanda Andrews; Tel: 902-574-1327, E-mail: amanda.andrews@nshealth.ca; Staff 1 (MLS 1)
Library Holdings: Bk Vols 2,000
Subject Interests: Allied health, Family med, Geriatrics, Med, Nursing, Obstetrics, Oncology, Pediatrics, Psychiat
Function: Res libr
Open Mon-Wed 8:30-4:30

TRURO

P COLCHESTER-EAST HANTS PUBLIC LIBRARY*, Truro Branch, 754 Prince St, B2N 1G9. SAN 366-8916. Tel: 902-895-4183. FAX: 902-895-7149. E-mail: anstc@cehpubliclibrary.ca. Web Site: www.lovemylibrary.ca. *Chief Exec Officer,* Tiffany Bartlett; E-mail: tbartlett@cehpubliclibrary.ca; *Head, Adult Serv, Head, Circ,* Lesley Brann; *Head, Syst, Head, Tech Serv,* Bill Morgan; *Head, Youth Serv,* Jenn Atkinson
Founded 1950. Pop 69,975; Circ 326,487
Library Holdings: Bk Vols 142,896; Per Subs 271
Wireless access
Open Mon 1-4, Tues-Thurs 10-8, Fri 10-6, Sat 10-5
Friends of the Library Group
Branches: 4
ELMSDALE BRANCH, Lloyd E Matheson Ctr, Ste 100, 15 Commerce Court, Elmsdale, B2S 3K5. Tel: 902-883-9838. FAX: 902-883-4935. E-mail: elmsdale@cehpubliclibrary.ca. *Br Mgr,* Patti Miller
Founded 1989. Pop 10,500; Circ 537,500
Library Holdings: Bk Vols 21,330
Open Tues & Thurs 10-8:30, Wed 1-5, Fri & Sat 10-5
MOUNT UNIACKE BRANCH, 555 Hwy One, Mount Uniacke, B0N 1Z0. Tel: 902-866-0124. FAX: 902-866-0519. E-mail: mtuniack@cehpubliclibrary.ca. *Br Mgr,* Kim Legge
Founded 2004. Pop 3,500
Library Holdings: Bk Vols 4,400
Automation Activity & Vendor Info: (Circulation) SirsiDynix; (OPAC) SirsiDynix
Open Tues 1-8, Thurs 3-8, Fri 2-5, Sat 10-1
STEWIACKE BRANCH, 295 George St, Stewiacke, B0N 2J0. Tel: 902-639-2481. E-mail: stewiack@cehpubliclibrary.ca. *Br Mgr,* Denise Sheppard
Founded 1951. Pop 4,305; Circ 42,958
Library Holdings: Bk Vols 17,200
Open Tues 1-5, Thurs 10-12, 1-5 & 6:30-8:30, Fri 1-5 & 7-9, Sat 12-4
TATAMAGOUCHE BRANCH, 170 Main St, Tatamagouche, B0N 2J0. Tel: 902-657-3064. E-mail: tatamago@cehpubliclibrary.ca. *Br Mgr,* Desirée Jans
Founded 1951. Pop 3,150; Circ 16,178
Library Holdings: Bk Vols 11,000
Open Tues & Thurs 11-5 & 6-8, Wed 10-2, Fri 1-5, Sat 10-1
Bookmobiles: 1

S COLCHESTER HISTORICAL SOCIETY ARCHIVES*, 29 Young St, B2N 3W3. SAN 375-7501. Tel: 902-895-6284. FAX: 902-895-9530. E-mail: research@colchesterhistoreum.ca. Web Site: colchesterhistoreum.ca. *Archive Researcher,* Joanne Hunt; Staff 2 (MLS 2)
Library Holdings: Microforms 2,000; Bk Titles 3,000
Subject Interests: Colchester County History, Genealogies, Planter History
Function: Archival coll
Restriction: Authorized personnel only, External users must contact libr, Free to mem, Internal use only, Non-circulating, Open to pub for ref only

C JANE NORMAN COLLEGE*, Russell Resource Library, 60 Lorne St, Ste 1, B2N 3K3. Tel: 902-893-3342. E-mail: info@janenorman.ca. Web Site: janenorman.ca/current-students/russell-resource-library. *Libr Coord,* Emily Scott; E-mail: emily.scott@janenorman.ca
Highest Degree: Certificate
Library Holdings: Bk Titles 8,000; Per Subs 17; Videos 700
Subject Interests: Early childhood, Spec educ
Automation Activity & Vendor Info: (Cataloging) LibraryWorld, Inc; (Circulation) LibraryWorld, Inc; (OPAC) LibraryWorld, Inc
Wireless access
Open Mon-Fri 8:30-4:30

L PATTERSON PALMER LIBRARY*, PO Box 1068, B2N 5B9. SAN 321-7000. Tel: 902-897-2000. FAX: 902-893-3071. *Librn,* Patti Sharpe; E-mail: psharpe@pattersonlaw.ca
Founded 1932
Library Holdings: Bk Titles 2,500; Bk Vols 6,500; Per Subs 15
Subject Interests: Commercial, Family, Income tax, Ins, Probate law, Real estate
Restriction: Not open to pub

WOLFVILLE

C ACADIA UNIVERSITY, Vaughan Memorial Library, 50 Acadia St, B4P 2R6. (Mail add: PO Box 4, B4P 2R6), SAN 366-8975. Tel: 902-585-1249. FAX: 902-585-1748. E-mail: ref-desk@acadiau.ca. Web Site: library.acadiau.ca. *Acting Dean, Library & Archives,* Jennifer Richard; Tel: 902-670-0294, E-mail: jennifer.richard@acadiau.ca; *Acad Librn,* Ann Smith; Tel: 902-585-1198, E-mail: ann.smith@acadiau.ca; *Mgr, Libr Serv,* Jason Levy; Tel: 902-670-9139, E-mail: jason.levy@acadiau.ca; *Archivist,* Wendy Robicheau; E-mail: wendy.robicheau@acadiau.ca; Staff 36 (MLS 10, Non-MLS 26)
Founded 1841. Highest Degree: Doctorate
Library Holdings: Bk Vols 520,000
Special Collections: Atlantic Baptist Archives; Esther Clark Wright Archives
Subject Interests: Med
Wireless access
Function: For res purposes
Partic in Canadian Research Knowledge Network; Council of Atlantic Academic Libraries (CAAL); Novanet
Restriction: Pub use on premises

YARMOUTH

S FIREFIGHTERS' MUSEUM OF NOVA SCOTIA LIBRARY*, 451 Main St, B5A 1G9. SAN 326-1867. Tel: 902-742-5525. FAX: 902-742-5525. Web Site: firefightersmuseum.novascotia.ca. *Curator,* David Darby; E-mail: darbydl@gov.ns.ca
Founded 1974
Library Holdings: Bk Vols 500; Per Subs 15
Open Mon-Fri 9-4

P WESTERN COUNTIES REGIONAL LIBRARY*, 405 Main St, B5A 1G3. SAN 366-9092. Tel: 902-742-2486. FAX: 902-742-6920. E-mail: ansy@nsy.library.ns.ca. Web Site: www.westerncounties.ca. *Exec Dir, Regional Librn,* Erin Comeau; E-mail: director@westerncounties.ca; *Br Coordr, Dep Dir,* Joanne Head; E-mail: jhead@nsy.library.ns.ca; Staff 5 (MLS 4, Non-MLS 1)
Founded 1969. Pop 65,135; Circ 258,228
Library Holdings: Bk Vols 149,044

Special Collections: H R Banks Nova Scotiana Coll, bks, per, pamphlets; Nova Scotia History, bks, micro
Automation Activity & Vendor Info: (Acquisitions) SirsiDynix; (Cataloging) SirsiDynix; (Circulation) SirsiDynix; (OPAC) SirsiDynix
Wireless access
Open Mon-Fri 8:30-4:30
Friends of the Library Group
Branches: 10
BARRINGTON MUNICIPAL, 3533 Hwy 3, Barrington Passage, B0W 1G0. (Mail add: PO Box 310, Barrington Passage, B0W 1G0), SAN 366-9106. Tel: 902-637-3348. E-mail: barrington@westerncounties.ca.
Founded 1981
Open Tues 10-5, Wed-Fri 12:30-5 & 6-8, Sat 10-2
Friends of the Library Group
CLARE, 29 Chemin Hache, Meteghan, B0W 2J0. (Mail add: PO Box 265, Meteghan, B0W 2J0), SAN 366-9114. Tel: 902-645-3350. E-mail: clare@westerncounties.ca.
Founded 1981
Open Mon 5-8, Tues & Thurs 10-4 & 6-8, Wed & Fri 10-4, Sat 10-12
CLARK'S HARBOUR BRANCH, 2648 Main St, Clark's Harbour, B0W 1P0. (Mail add: PO Box 189, Clark's Harbour, B0W 1P0), SAN 366-9122. Tel: 902-745-2885. E-mail: clarksharbour@westerncounties.ca.
Founded 1974
Open Tues & Thurs 5:30-8, Wed 12:30-5, Fri 10-12:30 & 1:30-5, Sat 10-12:30
LILLIAN B BENHAM LIBRARY, 35 North St, Lockeport, B0T 1L0. (Mail add: PO Box 265, Lockeport, B0T 1L0), SAN 366-9181. Tel: 902-656-2817. E-mail: lockeport@westerncounties.ca.
Founded 1973
Open Tues & Thurs 2:30-5 & 6-7:30, Wed 10:30-1 & 2:30-5, Fri 2:30-5, Sat 10-12
Friends of the Library Group
MCKAY MEMORIAL LIBRARY, 17 Glasgow St, Shelburne, B0T 1W0. (Mail add: PO Box 158, Shelburne, B0T 1W0), SAN 366-9246. Tel: 902-875-3615. FAX: 902-875-1015. E-mail: shelburne@westerncounties.ca.
Founded 1970
Open Tues-Thurs 12:30-5 & 6-8, Fri 10-5, Sat 10-2
Restriction: Restricted pub use
Friends of the Library Group
PUBNICO BRANCH, 35 Hwy 335, Pubnico Head, B0W 2W0. (Mail add: PO Box 22, Pubnico, B0W 2W0), SAN 366-9211. Tel: 902-762-2204. FAX: 902-762-3208. E-mail: pubnico@westerncounties.ca.
Founded 1978
Open Tues-Thurs 3-7, Wed 10-1 & 3-5:30, Fri 3-5:30, Sat 10-12
WESTPORT BRANCH, 17 Second St, Westport, B0V 1H0, (Mail add: PO Box 1194, Westport, B0V 1H0), SAN 322-6328. Tel: 902-839-2955. E-mail: westport@westerncounties.ca.
Founded 1983
Open Mon, Tues, Thurs & Sun 2-5, Wed 5-8
Friends of the Library Group
WEYMOUTH BRANCH, 4577 Hwy One, Weymouth, B0W 3T0. (Mail add: PO Box 340, Weymouth, B0W 3T0), SAN 366-9254. Tel: 902-837-4596. E-mail: weymouth@westerncounties.ca.
Open Tues & Fri 12-4:30 & 6-8, Wed & Thurs 12-4:30, Sat 10-1
ISAIAH W WILSON MEMORIAL, 84 Warwick St, Digby, B0V 1A0. (Mail add: PO Box 730, Digby, B0V 1A0), SAN 366-9157. Tel: 902-245-2163. E-mail: digby@westerncounties.ca.
Founded 1970
Open Tues-Thurs 12:30-5 & 6-8, Fri 10-5, Sat 10-2
YARMOUTH BRANCH, 405 Main St, B5A 1G3, SAN 366-9262. Tel: 902-742-5040. FAX: 902-742-6920. E-mail: yarmouth@westerncounties.ca. ; Staff 8 (MLS 1, Non-MLS 7)
Open Mon-Thurs 10-8, Fri 10-5, Sat 10-4

S YARMOUTH COUNTY MUSEUM & ARCHIVES*, 22 Collins St, B5A 3C8. SAN 319-0218. Tel: 902-742-5539. FAX: 902-749-1120. E-mail: ycarchives@eastlink.ca. Web Site: yarmouthcountymuseum.ca. *Archivist,* Lisette Gaudet; Staff 1 (MLS 1)
Founded 1935
Library Holdings: Bk Titles 3,000
Special Collections: Bob Brooks Photo Coll; Dominion Textiles Coll; RCAF Station Yarmouth, 1940-1945
Subject Interests: Local photog, Marine hist, Mus artifacts, NS hist, Yarmouth County genealogies, Yarmouth County hist, Yarmouth newsps
Wireless access
Publications: Butter the Size of an Egg 2001; Historic Yarmouth 1997; Historigram (Monthly newsletter); Index to Yarmouth Shipping; Surname Index of Births, Marriages, Deaths to the Yarmouth County Newspapers Vol 1 (1830-1839), Vol 2 (1840-1849), Vol 3 (1850-1859), Vol 4 (1860-1869); Vital Records of Township of Yarmouth 1792-1811; Yarmouth 1821; Yarmouth 1918; Yarmouth Past & Present 1902
Restriction: Non-circulating

NUNAVUT

Date of Statistics: Not provided.

BAKER LAKE

P NUNAVUT PUBLIC LIBRARY SERVICES, PO Box 270, X0C 0A0. Tel: 867-793-3353. FAX: 867-793-3360. Web Site: www.publiclibraries.nu.ca. *Mgr,* Ron Knowling; E-mail: rknowling@gov.nu.ca; *Tech Serv,* Kevin Iksiktaaryuk; Tel: 867-793-3351, E-mail: kiksiktaaryuk@gov.nu.ca
Automation Activity & Vendor Info: (Cataloging) Koha; (OPAC) Koha
Branches: 9
AMITTURMIUT LIBRARY, PO Box 30, Igloolik, X0A 0L0, SAN 321-6047. Tel: 867-934-8153. *Librn,* Nayru Gates
Library Holdings: Bk Vols 10,000; Per Subs 18
Special Collections: Arctica/Inuit Literature in Inuktitut
Open Mon-Thurs 6pm-9pm, Sat 12-4 & 6-9
CLYDE RIVER COMMUNITY LIBRARY, PO Box 150, Clyde River, X0A 0E0. Tel: 867-924-6565. FAX: 867-924-6570. E-mail: clyderiver@nupl.ca. Web Site: www.publiclibraries.nu.ca/index.php/en/crcl. *Librn,* Leveena Ashevak
Open Mon-Fri 9-12 & 1-5
MAY HAKONGAK COMMUNITY LIBRARY, PO Box 2106, Cambridge Bay, X0B 0C0. Tel: 867-983-2163. FAX: 867-983-3397. E-mail: cambridgebay@nupl.ca. Web Site: www.publiclibraries.nu.ca/en/cbl. *Librn,* Leggie Cristobal; *Librn,* Pam Langan; E-mail: plangan@kitikmeotherritage.ca
Open Mon-Fri 10-12 & 1-3:30
REBECCA P IDLOUT LIBRARY, PO Box 580, Pond Inlet, X0A 0S0. Tel: 867-899-8972. FAX: 867-899-8175. E-mail: pondinlet@nupl.ca. Web Site: www.publiclibraries.nu.ca/en/pil. *Librn,* Aileen Hope
Open Mon, Tues, Fri & Sat 1-6, Wed 1-5 & 7-9
ILITAQSINIQ LIBRARY, PO Box 519, Rankin Inlet, X0C 0G0. Tel: 867-645-2121. E-mail: info@nunavutliteracy.ca, rankininlet@nupl.ca. Web Site: www.publiclibraries.nu.ca/en/ril.
Open Mon-Fri 9-12
IQALUIT CENTENNIAL LIBRARY, PO Box 189A, Iqaluit, X0A 0H0, SAN 318-9651. Tel: 867-975-5595. FAX: 867-979-1373. Web Site: www.publiclibraries.nu.ca/en/iql. *Librn,* Keith Johnston; E-mail: kjohnston1@gov.nu.ca
Library Holdings: Bk Vols 32,000; Per Subs 80
Special Collections: T H Manning Coll (Arctica & Antarctica)
Open Mon, Wed & Fri 1-6, Tues & Thurs 3-8, Sat 1-4
KUGLUKTUK COMMUNITY LIBRARY, PO Box 190, Kugluktuk, X0E 0E0. Tel: 867-982-4406. FAX: 867-982-3404. E-mail: kugluktuk@nupl.ca. *Librn,* Carole Etokana
Open Mon-Fri 3:30-7:30
QIMIRUVIK LIBRARY, PO Box 403, Pangnirtung, X0A 0R0, SAN 318-9724. Tel: 867-473-8678. FAX: 819-473-8685. E-mail: pangnirtung@nupl.ca. Web Site: www.publiclibraries.nu.ca/en/qml. *Librn,* Lorna Nauyuq
Library Holdings: Bk Vols 33,000; Per Subs 25
Open Mon, Wed & Fri 1-5, Tues, Thurs & Sat 2-5
DONALD SULUK LIBRARY, PO Box 4000, Arviat, X0C 0E0. Tel: 867-857-2579. FAX: 867-857-4048. E-mail: arviat@nupl.ca. Web Site: www.publiclibraries.nu.ca/en/dsl. *Librn,* Sarah Voisey
Open Mon, Wed & Fri 3-8, Tues & Thurs 10-12 & 3-8, Sat 1-4

CAMBRIDGE BAY

J NUNAVUT ARCTIC COLLEGE, Kitikmeot Campus Library, PO Box 54, X0B 0C0. Tel: 867-983-4111. E-mail: ktikmeot@arcticcollege.ca. Web Site: www.arcticcollege.com.
Restriction: Open to students, fac & staff

IQALUIT

J NUNAVUT ARCTIC COLLEGE*, Nunatta Campus Library, 502 Niaqungusiariaq Dr, X0A 0H0. (Mail add: PO Box 600, X0A 0H0), SAN 372-7203. Tel: 867-979-7220. FAX: 867-979-7102. Web Site: arcticcollege.ca/library-services. *Circ, Ref,* Maureen Elizabeth Gunn; E-mail: elizabeth.gunn@arcticcollege.ca; Staff 2 (MLS 1, Non-MLS 1)
Founded 1986. Enrl 1,000; Fac 23
Library Holdings: DVDs 2,600; Bk Titles 12,000; Bk Vols 16,000; Per Subs 140
Special Collections: Arctic Discovery - Exploration (Pilot Coll); Northern - Arctic Studies (Cooke Coll)
Automation Activity & Vendor Info: (Cataloging) Innovative Interfaces, Inc; (Circulation) Innovative Interfaces, Inc; (OPAC) Innovative Interfaces, Inc; (Serials) Innovative Interfaces, Inc
Wireless access
Open Mon, Wed & Fri 8:45-12 & 1-4:45, Tues & Thurs 8:45-12, 1-4:45 & 6-8, Sat 1-4

GL NUNAVUT COURT OF JUSTICE LAW LIBRARY*, Nunavut Court of Justice Centre, Bldg 510, X0A 0H0. (Mail add: PO Box 1551, X0A 0H0). Tel: 867-975-6134. FAX: 867-975-6380. E-mail: courtlibrary@gov.nu.ca. Web Site: www.nunavutcourts.ca/index.php/library. *Librn,* Greg Hughes
Open Mon-Fri 8:30-12 & 1-5

RANKIN INLET

J NUNAVUT ARCTIC COLLEGE*, Kivalliq Campus Library, Bag 002, X0C 0G0. Tel: 867-645-4170. Toll Free Tel: 866-979-7222. FAX: 867-645-2387. Web Site: arcticcollege.com/library-services. *Mgr, Libr Serv,* Katharine Tagak; Tel: 867-979-7219, E-mail: ktagak@arcticcollege.ca
Highest Degree: Bachelor
Library Holdings: Bk Vols 18,000
Wireless access
Open Mon-Thurs 6pm-8pm, Sat 3-5 (Sept-April)

ONTARIO

Date of Statistics: FY 2023
Population, 2021 Canadian Census: 16,171,802
Population, 2021 per Statistics Canada: 16,171,802
Population Served by Public Libraries: 14,988,965
Total Active Cardholders: 4,367,107
Total Circulating Volumes Held: 28,159,513
Total Public Library Circulation: 74,940,588
Digital Resources: 33,120,653
Total e-book & e-audio book titles: 23,460,439
Total CD & DVD Titles Held: 2,678,574
Total Public Computers with Internet Access: 8,332
Income and Expenditures:
Total Operating Expenditures: $861,424,837
Total Expenditures Per Capita: $54.14
Total Public Library Income: $870,129,986
Provincial Operating Funding: $22,513,187
Municipal Funding: $800,793,852
Information provided courtesy of: Adam Haviaras, Culture Services Advisor ; Culture Services Advisor; Ministry of Tourism, Culture and Gaming, Programs and Services Branch

ADDISON

P ELIZABETHTOWN-KITLEY TOWNSHIP PUBLIC LIBRARY*, New Dublin, 4103 County Rd 29, K6V 5T4. SAN 319-0226. Tel: 613-498-3338. E-mail: elizndub@ektwp.ca. Web Site: www.elizabethtown-kitley.on.ca/content/public-library. *Chairperson,* Jill Yeatman; *Chief Exec Officer, Head Librn,* Ruth Blanchard
Pop 9,724; Circ 17,689
Library Holdings: Bk Vols 25,000; Per Subs 10
Wireless access
Mem of Ontario Library Service
Open Mon 9-12 & 1-6, Wed 4-8, Thurs 9-12 & 1-8, Sat 9-1
Branches: 2
KITLEY BRANCH, 424 Hwy 29, Toledo, K0E 1Y0. FAX: 613-275-2093. *Librn,* Charlotte Hoy
Open Mon 1-6, Thurs 2-7
LYN BRANCH, 14 Main St, Lyn, K0E 1M0. (Mail add: Box 158, Lyn, K0E 1M0). Tel: 613-345-0033. *Br Mgr,* Kristi Donovan
Open Tues 1-7, Fri 1-5

AJAX

P AJAX PUBLIC LIBRARY*, 55 Harwood Ave S, L1S 2H8. SAN 366-9270. Tel: 905-683-4000. FAX: 905-683-6944. E-mail: libraryinfo@ajaxlibrary.ca. Web Site: www.ajaxlibrary.ca. *Chief Librn, Exec Officer,* Donna Bright; Tel: 905-683-4000, Ext 8825, E-mail: donna.bright@ajaxlibrary.ca; *Colls Mgr, Commun Engagement Mgr,* Cindy Poon; Tel: 905-683-4000, Ext 8801, E-mail: cindy.poon@ajaxlibrary.ca; *Mgr, Coop Serv,* Susan Burrill; Tel: 905-683-4000, Ext 8822, E-mail: susan.burrill@ajaxlibrary.ca; *Customer Serv Mgr,* Dan Gioiosa; Tel: 905-683-4000, Ext 8824, E-mail: dan.gioiosa@ajaxlibrary.ca; *Manager, Customer Engagement,* Sarah Dodge; Tel: 905-683-4000, Ext 8802, E-mail: sarah.dodge@ajaxlibrary.ca; *Customer Serv Coordr,* Anna Galanis; Tel: 905-683-4000, Ext 8814, E-mail: anna.galanis@ajaxlibrary.ca; *Coord, Corp Services,* Cathy Fitzsimmons; Tel: 905-683-4000, Ext 8821, E-mail: cathy.fitzsimmons@ajaxlibrary.ca; *Marketing & Communications Coord,* Michael Barry; Tel: 905-683-4000, Ext 8819, E-mail: michael.barry@ajaxlibrary.ca; *Tech Serv Coordr,* Christofer Zorn; Tel: 905-683-4000, Ext 8838, E-mail: christofer.zorn@ajaxlibrary.ca; Staff 10 (MLS 5, Non-MLS 5)
Founded 1952
Library Holdings: Bk Titles 156,506; Per Subs 252
Special Collections: Local History Coll; Multilingual Coll. Canadian and Provincial
Automation Activity & Vendor Info: (Acquisitions) Koha; (Cataloging) Koha; (Circulation) Koha; (OPAC) Koha
Wireless access
Function: 24/7 Electronic res, 24/7 Online cat, 3D Printer, Activity rm, Adult bk club, Adult literacy prog, Archival coll, Art exhibits, Audiobks via web, Bk club(s), Bks on CD, CD-ROM, Children's prog, Citizenship assistance, Computer training, Computers for patron use, Digital talking bks, Electronic databases & coll, Free DVD rentals, Games & aids for people with disabilities, Genealogy discussion group, Govt ref serv, Holiday prog, Home delivery & serv to seniorr ctr & nursing homes, Homebound delivery serv, Homework prog, ILL available, Instruction & testing, Internet access, Large print keyboards, Life-long learning prog for all ages, Literacy & newcomer serv, Magazines, Magnifiers for reading, Mail & tel request accepted, Meeting rooms, Microfiche/film & reading machines, Movies, Music CDs, Online cat, Online ref, Outreach serv, Outside serv via phone, mail, e-mail & web, OverDrive digital audio bks, Photocopying/Printing, Preschool outreach, Preschool reading prog, Printer for laptops & handheld devices, Prog for adults, Prog for children & young adult, Ref serv available, Scanner, Senior computer classes, Senior outreach, Serves people with intellectual disabilities, Spanish lang bks, STEM programs, Story hour, Study rm, Summer & winter reading prog, Summer reading prog, Tax forms, Teen prog, Telephone ref, Wheelchair accessible
Publications: What's On (Bimonthly)
Special Services for the Deaf - Assisted listening device; Closed caption videos
Special Services for the Blind - Accessible computers; Aids for in-house use; Assistive/Adapted tech devices, equip & products; Bks on CD; Closed circuit TV magnifier; Computer with voice synthesizer for visually impaired persons; Daisy reader; Dragon Naturally Speaking software; Extensive large print coll; Home delivery serv; Large print bks; Large screen computer & software; Web-Braille
Open Mon-Fri 9:30-9, Sat 10-5, Sun 1-5
Restriction: Circ to mem only
Branches: 2
AUDLEY BRANCH LIBRARY, 1955 Audley Rd, L1Z 0L2. Tel: 905-683-4000, Ext 8871. Circulation Tel: 905-683-4000, Ext 8870.
MCLEAN BRANCH, 95 Magill Dr, L1T 4M5, SAN 374-8154. Tel: 905-683-4000, Ext 8903. Circulation Tel: 905-683-4000, Ext 8901. FAX: 905-428-3743.
Library Holdings: Bk Titles 38,000
Open Mon & Fri 1-9, Tues-Thurs 10-9, Sat 10-5, Sun (Oct-April) 1-5
Friends of the Library Group

ALLISTON

P NEW TECUMSETH PUBLIC LIBRARY*, 17 Victoria St E, L9R 1V6. (Mail add: PO Box 399, L9R 1V6), SAN 372-4034. Tel: 705-435-0250. FAX: 705-435-0750. Web Site: www.ntpl.ca. *Chief Exec Officer,* Jessica Mole; E-mail: jmole@ntpl.ca; *Admin Coordr,* Linda Jazwinski; E-mail: ljazwinski@ntpl.ca
Founded 1924. Pop 28,000; Circ 326,643
Library Holdings: AV Mats 6,757; Large Print Bks 1,277; Bk Titles 90,668; Bk Vols 118,667; Per Subs 115
Special Collections: New Tecumseth Digital History; Sir Frederick Banting Digital Library
Subject Interests: Govt doc, Local hist
Automation Activity & Vendor Info: (Cataloging) SirsiDynix; (Circulation) SirsiDynix; (OPAC) SirsiDynix

Wireless access
Friends of the Library Group
Branches: 3
D A JONES BRANCH, 42 Main St W, Beeton, L0G 1A0. (Mail add: PO Box 399, L9R 1V6), SAN 319-0455. Tel: 905-729-3726. *Br Mgr,* Lory Whittenmore; Staff 3 (Non-MLS 3)
Library Holdings: Bk Vols 20,000
Open Mon-Sat 10-5
PAM KIRKPATRICK BRANCH, 139 Queen St N, Tottenham, L0G 1W0. (Mail add: PO Box 399, L9R 1V6), SAN 319-5791. Tel: 905-936-2291. *Br Mgr,* Lory Whittemore
Library Holdings: Bk Vols 20,000
Open Tues-Thurs 10-6, Fri & Sat 10-5
MEMORIAL BRANCH, 17 Victoria St E, L9R 1V6. (Mail add: PO Box 399, L9R 1V6), SAN 319-0250. Tel: 705-435-5651. FAX: 705-435-0750. *Br Mgr,* Graeme Peters; Staff 6 (Non-MLS 6)
Library Holdings: Bk Vols 33,000
Open Tues-Thurs 10-6, Fri & Sat 10-5

ALMONTE

P MISSISSIPPI MILLS LIBRARIES*, Almonte Library, 155 High St, K0A 1A0. (Mail add: PO Box 820, K0A 1A0), SAN 319-0269. Tel: 613-256-1037. Web Site: missmillslibrary.com. *Chief Exec Officer,* Christine Row; E-mail: crow@mississippimills.ca; Staff 1 (MLS 1)
Pop 12,000
Library Holdings: Bk Vols 70,000; Per Subs 32
Subject Interests: Local hist
Wireless access
Mem of Ontario Library Service
Partic in Ont Pub Libr Info Network
Open Mon, Tues & Thurs 1-8, Wed 10-8, Fri 10-6, Sat 10-4
Branches: 1
PAKENHAM LIBRARY, 128 MacFarlane St, Pakenham, K0A 2X0. (Mail add: PO Box 250, Pakenham, K0A 2X0), SAN 319-3594. Tel: 613-624-5306. *Chief Exec Officer,* Christine Row; E-mail: crow@mississippimills.ca
Founded 1971. Pop 1,800; Circ 14,000
Library Holdings: Large Print Bks 30; Bk Titles 11,560; Bk Vols 11,578; Per Subs 15; Talking Bks 389; Videos 1,281
Automation Activity & Vendor Info: (Cataloging) L4U Library Software; (Circulation) L4U Library Software; (OPAC) L4U Library Software
Open Tues-Thurs 1-8, Fri 10-6, Sat 10-2

AMHERSTBURG

S FORT MALDEN NATIONAL HISTORIC SITE OF CANADA RESOURCE CENTRE*, 100 Laird Ave, N9V 2Z2. (Mail add: PO Box 38, N9V 2Z2), SAN 319-0277. Tel: 519-736-5416. FAX: 519-736-6603. E-mail: pc.fortmalden.pc@canada.ca. Web Site: www.parkscanada.gc.ca/malden.
Founded 1939
Library Holdings: Bk Titles 3,950; Per Subs 12
Special Collections: Archival Documents Relating to Fort's History
Subject Interests: British mil to 1860, Hist of Fort Malden, Local hist to 1860, Local Indian groups, Pioneer life, Rebellion of 1837, War of 1812
Function: Res libr
Restriction: Open by appt only, Open to pub for ref only

ANCASTER

C REDEEMER UNIVERSITY*, Peter Turkstra Library, 777 Garner Rd E, L9K 1J4. SAN 324-010X. Tel: 905-648-2131. Circulation Tel: 905-648-2139, Ext 4266. Toll Free Tel: 877-779-0913. FAX: 905-648-2134. E-mail: library@redeemer.ca. Web Site: libguides.redeemer.ca, www.redeemer.ca/academics/Library. *Libr Dir,* Marlene Power; E-mail: mpower@redeemer.ca; *Asst Librn,* Position Currently Open; *Circ Serv Supvr,* David Rowlandson; *Libr Tech,* Jennifer deBlieck; E-mail: jdeblieck@redeemer.ca; Staff 3.9 (MLS 2, Non-MLS 1.9)
Enrl 900; Fac 46
Library Holdings: Bk Titles 75,000; Bk Vols 90,000; Per Subs 330
Special Collections: Dutch Reformed Theology Coll; Science & Christian Faith Coll
Subject Interests: Educ, English, Faith, Hist, Lit, Philos, Psychol, Sci, Theol
Wireless access
Publications: Annual Report
Partic in OCLC Online Computer Library Center, Inc
Open Mon-Fri 8am-11pm, Sat 9-5 (Fall & Winter); Mon-Fri 8:30-4:30 (Summer)

ANGUS

P ESSA PUBLIC LIBRARY*, 8505 County Rd 10, Unit 1, L0M 1B1. SAN 319-0285. Tel: 705-424-6531. Administration Tel: 705-424-2679. FAX: 705-424-5512. E-mail: essalib@essa.library.on.ca. Web Site: www.essa.library.on.ca. *Chief Exec Officer,* Laura Wark; E-mail: ceo@essa.library.on.ca; *Mgr, Libr Serv,* Glenda Newbatt; E-mail: gnewbatt@essa.library.on.ca; *Coordr, Support Serv,* Angie Wishart; E-mail: awishart@essa.library.on.ca; Staff 2 (MLS 2)
Founded 1967. Pop 18,500; Circ 140,000
Library Holdings: Audiobooks 10,000; Large Print Bks 300; Bk Vols 65,000; Per Subs 350
Automation Activity & Vendor Info: (Acquisitions) SirsiDynix; (Cataloging) SirsiDynix; (Circulation) SirsiDynix; (OPAC) SirsiDynix; (Serials) SirsiDynix
Wireless access
Function: Art exhibits, Children's prog, Computers for patron use, Digital talking bks, Free DVD rentals, Homebound delivery serv, Homework prog, ILL available, Magnifiers for reading, Mail & tel request accepted, Music CDs, Online cat, OverDrive digital audio bks, Photocopying/Printing, Preschool outreach, Preschool reading prog, Prog for adults, Prog for children & young adult, Scanner, Spoken cassettes & CDs, Story hour, Summer reading prog, Wheelchair accessible
Mem of Ontario Library Service
Partic in County of Simcoe Libr Coop
Special Services for the Deaf - High interest/low vocabulary bks
Special Services for the Blind - Aids for in-house use; Bks on CD; Home delivery serv; Large print bks; Magnifiers; PC for people with disabilities
Open Mon-Thurs 10-8, Fri & Sat 10-4
Restriction: Circ to mem only
Branches: 1
THORNTON BRANCH, 34 Robert St, Thornton, L0L 2N0. Tel: 705-458-2549. FAX: 705-458-2549. *Chief Exec Officer,* Laura Wark
Automation Activity & Vendor Info: (Acquisitions) Horizon; (Cataloging) Horizon; (Circulation) Horizon; (OPAC) Horizon
Open Mon-Thurs 2-7, Fri & Sat 10-3

APSLEY

P NORTH KAWARTHA LIBRARY*, 175 Burleigh St, K0L 1A0. (Mail add: PO Box 335, K0L 1A0), SAN 319-0293. Tel: 705-656-4333. FAX: 705-656-2538. E-mail: info@northkawarthalibrary.com. Web Site: www.northkawarthalibrary.com. *Chief Exec Officer, Librn,* Debbie Hall; E-mail: d.hall@northkawarthalibrary.com; *Tech Serv Coordr,* Shawn Tucker
Founded 1971. Pop 2,200; Circ 22,000
Library Holdings: Large Print Bks 150; Bk Titles 15,500; Bk Vols 16,600; Per Subs 18; Talking Bks 150
Wireless access
Mem of Ontario Library Service
Open Tues-Fri 9:30-5, Sat 9-2
Branches: 1
WOODVIEW BRANCH, 66 Northeys Bay Rd, Woodview, K0L 3E0. Tel: 705-654-1071. *Librn,* Janet Grice
Open Tues, Thurs & Sat 10-2

ARNPRIOR

P ARNPRIOR PUBLIC LIBRARY*, 21 Madawaska St, K7S 1R6. SAN 319-0307. Tel: 613-623-2279. FAX: 613-623-0281. E-mail: library@arnpriorlibrary.ca. Web Site: www.arnpriorlibrary.ca. *Chief Librn,* Karen DeLuca; Staff 2 (Non-MLS 2)
Founded 1895. Pop 10,295
Library Holdings: Bk Vols 54,775; Per Subs 48
Automation Activity & Vendor Info: (Acquisitions) Insignia Software; (Cataloging) Insignia Software; (Circulation) Insignia Software
Wireless access
Function: AV serv, ILL available
Mem of Ontario Library Service
Special Services for the Blind - Accessible computers; Aids for in-house use; Assistive/Adapted tech devices, equip & products
Open Mon Noon-7, Tues-Thurs Noon-6, Fri 10-5, Sat 10-2

ATHENS

P TOWNSHIP OF ATHENS PUBLIC LIBRARY, Five Central St, K0E 1B0. (Mail add: PO Box 309, K0E 1B0), SAN 319-0315. Tel: 613-924-2048. E-mail: athenspubliclibrary@gmail.com. Web Site: athenslibrary.ca. *Chief Librn/CEO,* Diane Benschop; *Ch Serv Librn,* Karen DeJong
Pop 3,100; Circ 9,435
Library Holdings: Audiobooks 81; Braille Volumes 4; DVDs 393; Electronic Media & Resources 3,043; Large Print Bks 469; Bk Titles 9,153; Bk Vols 9,163
Special Collections: Children's Themed Backpacks
Automation Activity & Vendor Info: (Acquisitions) SirsiDynix-WorkFlows; (Cataloging) SirsiDynix-WorkFlows; (Circulation) SirsiDynix-WorkFlows

Wireless access
Function: 24/7 Electronic res, 24/7 Online cat, Adult bk club, Art exhibits, Bks on CD, Children's prog, Computers for patron use, E-Readers, Free DVD rentals, Games, Holiday prog, Home delivery & serv to seniorr ctr & nursing homes, ILL available, Internet access, Large print keyboards, Magazines, Makerspace, Movies, Museum passes, Online cat, OverDrive digital audio bks, Photocopying/Printing, Prog for children & young adult, Senior outreach, Summer reading prog, Wheelchair accessible
Mem of Ontario Library Service
Special Services for the Blind - Accessible computers; Bks on CD; Braille bks; Daisy reader; Digital talking bk machines; Extensive large print coll; Large print bks; Talking bks & player equip
Open Tues & Wed 3-7:30, Thurs & Sat 9:30-1:30
Restriction: Non-resident fee

ATIKOKAN

P ATIKOKAN PUBLIC LIBRARY*, Civic Centre, P0T 1C0. SAN 319-0323. Tel: 807-597-4406. FAX: 807-597-1514. Web Site: aplibrary.org. *Chief Exec Officer, Librn,* Tracey Sinclair; E-mail: tracey@aplibrary.org
Founded 1952. Pop 3,100; Circ 66,000
Library Holdings: Bk Vols 35,000; Per Subs 67
Special Collections: Municipal Document Depository
Subject Interests: Local hist
Automation Activity & Vendor Info: (Cataloging) Winnebago Software Co; (Circulation) Winnebago Software Co; (ILL) Fretwell-Downing; (OPAC) Winnebago Software Co
Wireless access
Publications: Annual Report
Open Tues & Wed Noon-7, Thurs 10-7, Fri & Sat Noon-5
Friends of the Library Group

S QUETICO PROVINCIAL PARK*, John B Ridley Research Library, Quetico Provincial Park, P0T 1C0. (Mail add: PO Box 2430, P0T 1C0), SAN 373-7926. Tel: 807-929-2571, Ext 224. FAX: 807-929-2123. *Superintendent,* Jason Blier; E-mail: jason.blier@ontario.ca; Staff 1 (MLS 1)
Founded 1986
Library Holdings: Bk Titles 5,000; Per Subs 15
Special Collections: Quetico Park Coll, bks, photog, slides. Oral History
Automation Activity & Vendor Info: (Cataloging) Inmagic, Inc.
Restriction: Open to pub for ref only

AURORA

P AURORA PUBLIC LIBRARY*, 15145 Young St, L4G 1M1. SAN 319-0331. Tel: 905-727-9494. Circulation Tel: 905-727-9494, Ext 211. FAX: 905-727-9374. Circulation E-mail: circulation@aurorapl.ca. Web Site: www.aurorapl.ca. *Chief Exec Officer,* Bruce Gorman; E-mail: bgorman@aurorapl.ca; Staff 14 (MLS 4, Non-MLS 10)
Founded 1855. Pop 49,000; Circ 550,000
Wireless access
Open Mon-Thurs 9:30-9, Fri 9:30-6, Sat 9:30-5

BADEN

P REGION OF WATERLOO LIBRARY*, 2017 Nafziger Rd, N3A 3H4. (Mail add: 150 Frederick St, 2nd Flr, Kitchener, N2G 4J3), SAN 368-8119. Tel: 519-575-4590. FAX: 519-634-5371. TDD: 519-575-4608. E-mail: libhq@regionofwaterloo.ca. Web Site: www.rwlibrary.ca. *Mgr, Libr Serv,* Sheryl Tilley; E-mail: stilley@regionofwaterloo.ca; Staff 6 (MLS 4, Non-MLS 2)
Founded 1968. Pop 55,491; Circ 368,787
Library Holdings: AV Mats 3,830; Bks on Deafness & Sign Lang 68; High Interest/Low Vocabulary Bk Vols 189; Large Print Bks 1,495; Bk Titles 109,126; Bk Vols 168,316; Per Subs 258; Talking Bks 1,944
Automation Activity & Vendor Info: (Cataloging) SirsiDynix; (Circulation) SirsiDynix; (OPAC) SirsiDynix
Function: ILL available, Photocopying/Printing, Telephone ref
Mem of Ontario Library Service
Partic in Ontario Library Consortium
Friends of the Library Group
Branches: 10
AYR BRANCH, 137 Stanley St, Ayr, N0B 1E0. (Mail add: PO Box 1179, Ayr, N0B 1E0), SAN 368-8143. Tel: 519-632-7298. E-mail: ayrlib@regionofwaterloo.ca. *Libr Asst Supvr,* Lee Puddephatt; Staff 1 (MLS 1)
Friends of the Library Group
BADEN BRANCH, 115 Snyder's Rd E, N3A 2V4, SAN 368-8178. Tel: 519-634-8933. E-mail: badenlib@regionofwaterloo.ca. *Asst Br Supvr,* Christine Baechler; Staff 1 (Non-MLS 1)
BLOOMINGDALE BRANCH, 860A Sawmill Rd, Bloomingdale, N0B 1K0, SAN 368-8208. Tel: 519-745-3151. E-mail: bloomlib@regionofwaterloo.ca. *Asst Br Supvr,* Susan O'Toole
ELMIRA BRANCH, 65 Arthur St S, Elmira, N3B 2M6, SAN 368-8216. Tel: 519-669-5477. E-mail: elmlib@regionofwaterloo.ca. *Libr Supvr,* Position Currently Open; Staff 1 (MLS 1)
Founded 1888
Function: Home delivery & serv to seniorr ctr & nursing homes, Homebound delivery serv, ILL available, Photocopying/Printing, Prog for children & young adult, Summer reading prog, Telephone ref, Wheelchair accessible
LINWOOD BRANCH, 5279 Ament Line, Linwood, N0B 2A0, SAN 368-8224. Tel: 519-698-2700. E-mail: linwdlib@regionofwaterloo.ca. *Asst Br Supvr,* Gayna McGarrity
NEW DUNDEE BRANCH, 1176 Queen St., New Dundee, N0B 2E0. (Mail add: PO Box 269, New Dundee, N0B 2E0), SAN 368-8232. Tel: 519-696-3041. E-mail: ndlib@regionofwaterloo.ca. *Asst Br Supvr,* Lynn Weiss
NEW HAMBURG BRANCH, 145 Huron St, New Hamburg, N3A 1K1, SAN 368-8240. Tel: 519-662-1112. E-mail: nhlib@regionofwaterloo.ca. *Libr Supvr,* Twyla Knight
ST CLEMENTS BRANCH, 3605 Lobsinger Line, St. Clements, N0B 2M0, SAN 368-8259. Tel: 519-699-4341. E-mail: stclemlib@regionofwaterloo.ca. *Asst Br Supvr,* Lois Johnson
ST JACOBS BRANCH, 29 Queensway Dr, St. Jacobs, N0B 2N0. (Mail add: PO Box 507, St. Jacobs, N0B 2N0), SAN 368-8267. Tel: 519-664-3443. E-mail: stjaclib@regionofwaterloo.ca. *Asst Br Supvr,* Anna Van Rootselaar
WELLESLEY BRANCH, 1137 Henry St, Wellesley, N0B 2T0. (Mail add: PO Box 190, Wellesley, N0B 2T0), SAN 368-8291. Tel: 519-656-2001. E-mail: wellslib@regionofwaterloo.ca. *Libr Asst Supvr,* Robin Holmes

BALA

S WAHTA MOHAWKS*, First Nation Library, 2664 Meskoa Rd 38, P0C 1A0. (Mail add: PO Box 260, P0C 1A0), SAN 377-4716. Tel: 705-756-2354, Ext 233. FAX: 705-756-2376. Web Site: www.wahtamohawks.com. *Library Contact,* Carol Holmes
Library Holdings: Bk Vols 8,000; Per Subs 10
Open Mon-Thurs 8-4:30, Fri 8-2

BALMERTOWN

P BALMERTOWN PUBLIC LIBRARY*, 12 Fifth St, P0V 1C0. (Mail add: PO Box 280, P0V 1C0), SAN 319-034X. Tel: 807-735-2110. FAX: 807-735-2110. E-mail: rllib212@yahoo.com. *Librn,* Lisa Johnson; Staff 1 (Non-MLS 1)
Founded 1970. Pop 2,113
Library Holdings: DVDs 500; Large Print Bks 97; Bk Titles 13,101; Bk Vols 13,500; Per Subs 10; Talking Bks 200
Wireless access
Open Mon-Fri 11-7

BANCROFT

P BANCROFT PUBLIC LIBRARY*, North Hastings Public Library, 14 Flint Ave, K0L 1C0. (Mail add: PO Box 127, K0L 1C0), SAN 319-0358. Tel: 613-332-3380. E-mail: info@northhastingslibrary.ca. Web Site: www.northhastingslibrary.ca. *Chief Exec Officer, Head Librn,* Debbie Dailey; Staff 4 (MLS 1, Non-MLS 3)
Founded 1901. Pop 5,200
Library Holdings: CDs 300; DVDs 1,000; e-books 67,000; Large Print Bks 150; Bk Titles 23,000; Per Subs 35; Talking Bks 120
Wireless access
Function: 24/7 Electronic res, 24/7 Online cat, Activity rm, Adult literacy prog, After school storytime, Archival coll, Audiobks via web, AV serv, Bks on CD, Children's prog, Computer training, Computers for patron use, Digital talking bks, Doc delivery serv, E-Readers, Electronic databases & coll, Family literacy, For res purposes, Free DVD rentals, Games & aids for people with disabilities, Govt ref serv, Holiday prog, Home delivery & serv to seniorr ctr & nursing homes, ILL available, Instruction & testing, Internet access, Large print keyboards, Life-long learning prog for all ages, Literacy & newcomer serv, Magazines, Magnifiers for reading, Mail & tel request accepted, Meeting rooms, Music CDs, Online cat, Online ref, Outreach serv, OverDrive digital audio bks, Photocopying/Printing, Preschool reading prog, Printer for laptops & handheld devices, Prog for adults, Prog for children & young adult, Ref & res, Ref serv available, Senior outreach, Story hour, Summer & winter reading prog, Workshops
Mem of Ontario Library Service
Open Tues & Fri 10-3, Wed Noon-6, Thurs 10-6, Sat 10-2
Friends of the Library Group

P CARLOW-MAYO PUBLIC LIBRARY*, c/o Hermon Public School, 124 Fort Stewart Rd, K0L 1C0. SAN 319-0366. Tel: 613-332-2544. E-mail: carlowmayopl@gmail.com. Web Site: carlowmayo.ca/services/library, carlowmayopubliclibrary.ca. *Chief Exec Officer, Head Librn,* Carrie McKenzie
Founded 1970. Circ 5,700

Library Holdings: Bk Titles 9,410; Bk Vols 10,410; Per Subs 20; Videos 500
Wireless access
Open Tues & Thurs 5-8, Fri & Sat 10-4
Friends of the Library Group

BARRIE

P BARRIE PUBLIC LIBRARY, 60 Worsley St, L4M 1L6. SAN 319-0374. Tel: 705-728-1010. E-mail: askus@barrielibrary.ca. Web Site: www.barrielibrary.ca. *Chief Exec Officer,* Lauren Jessop; Tel: 705-728-1010, Ext 2100, E-mail: lauren.jessop@barrie.ca; *Dir, Corporate Serv,* Christopher Vanderkruys; Tel: 705-728-1010, Ext 2200, E-mail: christopher.vanderkruys@barrie.ca; *Dir, Community, Connections & Content,* Laura LaFleshe; Tel: 705-728-1010, Ext 2400, E-mail: laura.lafleshe@barrie.ca; *Colls Mgr,* Vivien Keiling; Tel: 705-728-1010, Ext 2420, E-mail: vivien.keiling@barrie.ca; *Mgr, Human Res,* Jane Little; Tel: 705-728-1010, Ext 2120, E-mail: jane.little@barrie.ca
Founded 1862. Pop 143,000
Special Collections: Local History (Fred Grant Coll & Montagu Leeds Coll), microfilm; Ontario Genealogical Society, Simcoe County Branch Research Coll. Canadian and Provincial
Automation Activity & Vendor Info: (Acquisitions) Innovative Interfaces, Inc; (Cataloging) Innovative Interfaces, Inc; (Circulation) Innovative Interfaces, Inc; (ILL) OCLC; (OPAC) BiblioCommons; (Serials) Innovative Interfaces, Inc
Wireless access
Function: 24/7 Electronic res, Computers for patron use, Photocopying/Printing, Scanner
Publications: @ Your Library (Newsletter); Information Barrie Community Directory (Business & organization papers & directories)
Mem of Ontario Library Service
Special Services for the Deaf - Bks on deafness & sign lang; High interest/low vocabulary bks
Open Mon-Thurs 9:30-9, Fri-Sun 9:30-5
Branches: 2
HOLLY BRANCH, 555 Essa Rd, L4N 6A9. Web Site: www.barrielibrary.ca/about-bpl/branches/holly. *Commun Libr Mgr,* Darcy Glidden; Tel: 705-728-1010, Ext 4310
Founded 2022
Function: Meeting rooms, Photocopying/Printing, Scanner
Open Mon-Thurs 9:30-9, Fri-Sun 9:30-5
PAINSWICK BRANCH, 48 Dean Ave, L4N 0C2. (Mail add: 60 Worsley St, L4M 1L6). Web Site: www.barrielibrary.ca/about-bpl/branches/painswick. *Commun Libr Mgr,* Darcy Glidden; Tel: 705-728-1010, Ext 4310; Staff 7.3 (MLS 3, Non-MLS 4.3)
Founded 2012
Automation Activity & Vendor Info: (Circulation) Horizon; (OPAC) BiblioCommons
Function: Adult bk club, Audiobks via web, Bk club(s), Bks on CD, Children's prog, Computer training, Computers for patron use, Digital talking bks, Electronic databases & coll, Free DVD rentals, ILL available, Museum passes, Music CDs, Online cat, Online ref, OverDrive digital audio bks, Photocopying/Printing, Prog for adults, Prog for children & young adult, Ref serv available, Scanner, Senior computer classes, Senior outreach, Spanish lang bks, Summer reading prog, Teen prog, Wheelchair accessible, Workshops
Special Services for the Blind - Audio mat; Bks on CD; Digital talking bk; Extensive large print coll; Home delivery serv; Large print bks; Talking bks from Braille Inst
Open Mon, Sat & Sun 9:30-5, Tues-Fri 9:30-9
Restriction: ID required to use computers (Ltd hrs), In-house use for visitors, Non-resident fee

C GEORGIAN COLLEGE*, Barrie Library, One Georgian Dr, L4M 3X9. SAN 319-0390. Tel: 705-728-1968. Circulation Tel: 705-722-5139. Interlibrary Loan Service Tel: 705-728-1968, Ext 1682. Toll Free Tel: 877-890-8477. FAX: 705-722-5122. Reference FAX: 705-722-1508. E-mail: library@georgiancollege.ca. Web Site: library.georgiancollege.ca. *Librn,* Karen Halliday; E-mail: Karen.Halliday@GeorgianCollege.ca; *Librn,* Jennifer Varcoe; E-mail: Jennifer.Varcoe@GeorgianCollege.ca
Founded 1967. Enrl 10,500
Library Holdings: DVDs 6,000; e-books 48,000; Bk Vols 62,500; Per Subs 420
Automation Activity & Vendor Info: (Acquisitions) SirsiDynix; (Cataloging) SirsiDynix; (Circulation) SirsiDynix; (Media Booking) SirsiDynix; (OPAC) SirsiDynix; (Serials) SirsiDynix
Wireless access
Partic in Ontario Colleges Library Service (OCLS)
Open Mon-Thurs 7:30am-11pm, Fri 7:30-7, Sat 10-5, Sun 1-8

M ROYAL VICTORIA REGIONAL HEALTH CENTRE, Health Library, 201 Georgian Dr, L4M 6M2. SAN 373-6725. Tel: 705-728-9090, Ext 42631. FAX: 705-739-5693. E-mail: healthlibrary@rvh.on.ca. Web Site: www.rvh.on.ca/patient-visitors/health-library. *Libr Tech,* Donna Smith-Roselle; Tel: 705-728-9090, Ext 42630, E-mail: roselled@rvh.on.ca; Staff 1 (Non-MLS 1)
Library Holdings: Bk Vols 1,412
Special Collections: Biomedical Coll; Nursing & Allied Health Coll
Subject Interests: Consumer health, Med, Nursing
Automation Activity & Vendor Info: (Cataloging) OPALS (Open-source Automated Library System); (Circulation) OPALS (Open-source Automated Library System); (Course Reserve) OPALS (Open-source Automated Library System); (OPAC) OPALS (Open-source Automated Library System)
Wireless access
Partic in Health Science Information Consortium of Toronto; Ontario Health Library & Information Association
Open Tues-Thurs 9:30-4, Fri 1-4

BARRY'S BAY

P MADAWASKA VALLEY PUBLIC LIBRARY, 19474 Opeongo Line, K0J 1B0. (Mail add: PO Box 970, K0J 1B0), SAN 319-0404. Tel: 613-756-2000. E-mail: admin@madawaskavalleylibrary.ca. Web Site: madawaskavalleylibrary.ca. *Chief Exec Officer,* Natalie Barrington
Founded 1960. Pop 4,385; Circ 17,772
Library Holdings: Bk Vols 22,436; Per Subs 14
Wireless access
Function: 24/7 Electronic res, 24/7 Online cat, Adult bk club, Archival coll, Art exhibits, Audiobks on Playaways & MP3, Audiobks via web, Bks on CD, Children's prog, Computer training, Computers for patron use, Electronic databases & coll, Free DVD rentals, Holiday prog, ILL available, Internet access, Laminating, Magazines, Mango lang, Microfiche/film & reading machines, Museum passes, Music CDs, OverDrive digital audio bks, Photocopying/Printing, Prog for adults, Prog for children & young adult, Ref & res, Scanner, STEM programs, Story hour, Summer reading prog, Teen prog, Wheelchair accessible, Workshops
Mem of Ontario Library Service
Open Tues, Wed & Fri 10-12 & 1-5, Thurs 1-4 & 5-8, Sat 10-3
Restriction: Non-resident fee

BATH

G CORRECTIONAL SERVICE OF CANADA, Millhaven Institution Inmate Library, Hwy 33, K0H 1G0. (Mail add: PO Box 280, K0H 1G0), SAN 329-0840. Tel: 613-351-8000. Administration Tel: 613-351-8219. FAX: 613-351-8136. *Librn,* Holly Hiscoe; E-mail: holly.hiscoe@csc-scc.gc.ca
Library Holdings: Bk Titles 10,000
Special Collections: Arabic Coll; Multilingual (Asian) Coll; Native Coll
Restriction: Staff & inmates only

BEACHBURG

P WHITEWATER REGION PUBLIC LIBRARY*, Beachburg Branch, Beachburg Public School, 20 Cameron St, K0J 1C0. (Mail add: PO Box 159, K0J 1C0), SAN 319-0439. Tel: 613-582-7090. Web Site: libraries.whitewaterregion.ca. *Chief Librn/CEO,* Marilyn Labow; E-mail: mlabow@nrtco.net; Staff 1 (Non-MLS 1)
Pop 693; Circ 1,687
Library Holdings: Large Print Bks 200; Bk Titles 4,600; Bk Vols 5,000; Per Subs 20; Talking Bks 300
Wireless access
Mem of Ontario Library Service
Open Mon & Thurs 6pm-8pm, Tues 10-5, Sat 9-Noon

BEAMSVILLE

P LINCOLN PUBLIC LIBRARY*, 5020 Serena Dr, L0R 1B0. (Mail add: Box 460, L0R 1B0), SAN 367-0058. Tel: 905-563-7014. FAX: 905-563-1810. E-mail: admin@lppl.ca. Web Site: lppl.ca. *Chief Exec Officer,* Julie Andrews; E-mail: jandrews@lppl.ca; Staff 13 (MLS 2, Non-MLS 11)
Founded 1851. Pop 22,000; Circ 240,000
Library Holdings: Bk Vols 74,000; Per Subs 46
Special Collections: Local History Coll. Canadian and Provincial
Automation Activity & Vendor Info: (Cataloging) Evergreen; (Circulation) Evergreen; (OPAC) Evergreen
Wireless access
Function: 24/7 Electronic res, 24/7 Online cat, 3D Printer, Activity rm, Adult bk club, After school storytime, Archival coll, Art exhibits, Art programs, Audiobks on Playaways & MP3, Audiobks via web, AV serv, Bk club(s), Bks on CD, Children's prog, Computer training, Computers for patron use, Digital talking bks, Electronic databases & coll, Free DVD rentals, Holiday prog, Home delivery & serv to seniorr ctr & nursing homes, Homebound delivery serv, ILL available, Internet access, Large print keyboards, Life-long learning prog for all ages, Magazines, Mail & tel request accepted, Makerspace, Mango lang, Meeting rooms, Microfiche/film & reading machines, Movies, Music CDs, Online cat, Online info literacy tutorials on the web & in blackboard, Outreach serv,

OverDrive digital audio bks, Photocopying/Printing, Preschool outreach, Preschool reading prog, Prog for adults, Prog for children & young adult, Scanner, Senior computer classes, Senior outreach, STEM programs, Story hour, Study rm, Summer reading prog, Teen prog, Wheelchair accessible, Workshops
Mem of Ontario Library Service
Special Services for the Deaf - Assistive tech
Special Services for the Blind - Accessible computers
Open Mon-Thurs 10-8, Fri 1-5, Sat 10-5, Sun (Sept-June) 1-5
Branches: 1
MOSES F RITTENHOUSE BRANCH, 4080 John Charles Blvd, Vineland, L0R 2C0. (Mail add: PO Box 460, L0R 1B0). Tel: 905-562-5711. FAX: 905-562-3454. *Chief Exec Officer,* Julie Andrews; E-mail: jandrews@lppl.ca; Staff 13 (MLS 2, Non-MLS 11)
Library Holdings: Bk Titles 74,000; Per Subs 46
Subject Interests: Local hist
Automation Activity & Vendor Info: (Cataloging) Evergreen; (Circulation) Evergreen; (OPAC) Evergreen
Function: Adult bk club, After school storytime, Art exhibits, Bk club(s), Bks on CD, Chess club, Children's prog, Computer training, Computers for patron use, Electronic databases & coll, Free DVD rentals, Holiday prog, Home delivery & serv to seniorr ctr & nursing homes, Homebound delivery serv, ILL available, Internet access, Large print keyboards, Life-long learning prog for all ages, Magazines, Mango lang, Meeting rooms, Microfiche/film & reading machines, Movies, Music CDs, Online cat, Outreach serv, OverDrive digital audio bks, Photocopying/Printing, Preschool reading prog, Prog for adults, Prog for children & young adult, Scanner, Senior computer classes, Senior outreach, Story hour, Study rm, Summer reading prog, Teen prog, Telephone ref, Wheelchair accessible
Open Mon-Thurs 10-8, Fri 1-5, Sat 10-5
Restriction: Non-resident fee

BEAVERTON

P BROCK TOWNSHIP PUBLIC LIBRARY*, 401 Simcoe St, L0K 1A0. (Mail add: PO Box 310, L0K 1A0). Tel: 249-702-2255. Administration Tel: 705-426-9283. FAX: 705-426-9353. E-mail: info@brocklibraries.ca. Web Site: brocklibraries.ca. *Chief Exec Officer,* Katie-Scarlett MacGillivray; Staff 2 (MLS 2)
Founded 1853. Pop 11,797; Circ 68,684
Special Collections: Local history items
Automation Activity & Vendor Info: (Acquisitions) SirsiDynix; (Cataloging) SirsiDynix; (Circulation) SirsiDynix; (OPAC) SirsiDynix
Wireless access
Function: Computers for patron use
Open Tues & Thurs 10-7:30, Wed 2-5, Fri 10-4, Sat 10-3
Friends of the Library Group
Branches: 2
TIMOTHY FINDLEY MEMORIAL LIBRARY - CANNINGTON, 38 Laidlaw St, Cannington, L0E 1E0. (Mail add: PO Box 89, Cannington, L0E 1E0). Tel: 705-432-2867. FAX: 705-432-3282. E-mail: canningtonbranch@brocklibraries.ca.
Founded 1889
Library Holdings: DVDs 300; Large Print Bks 300; Bk Titles 8,000; Per Subs 120
Open Tues & Fri 2-7:30, Wed & Thurs 10-3, Sat 10-2
Friends of the Library Group
SUNDERLAND PUBLIC LIBRARY, 41 Albert St S, Sunderland, L0C 1H0. Tel: 705-357-3109. E-mail: sunderlandbranch@brocklibraries.ca.
Founded 1900
Open Tues 10-3, Wed & Thurs 3-8, Sat 10-2 (Summer); Tues-Thurs 3-8, Sat 10-2 (Winter)
Friends of the Library Group

BELLEVILLE

P BELLEVILLE PUBLIC LIBRARY*, 254 Pinnacle St, K8N 3B1. SAN 367-0147. Tel: 613-968-6731. FAX: 613-968-6841. E-mail: infoserv@bellevillelibrary.com. Web Site: www.bellevillelibrary.ca. *Chief Exec Officer,* Trevor Pross; Tel: 613-968-6731, Ext 2022, E-mail: tpross@bellevillelibrary.ca; Staff 36 (MLS 5, Non-MLS 31)
Founded 1876. Pop 48,000; Circ 345,000
Library Holdings: High Interest/Low Vocabulary Bk Vols 600; Large Print Bks 5,300; Bk Titles 100,000; Bk Vols 140,000; Per Subs 125; Talking Bks 3,000; Videos 5,000
Special Collections: Canadiana; Local Authors (Canadiana Room). Canadian and Provincial
Subject Interests: Genealogy
Automation Activity & Vendor Info: (Acquisitions) SirsiDynix; (Cataloging) SirsiDynix; (Circulation) SirsiDynix; (OPAC) SirsiDynix
Mem of Ontario Library Service
Open Mon-Thurs 9:30-8, Fri 9:30-5, Sat 9:30-5:30, Sun 1-5
Friends of the Library Group

J THE PARROTT CENTRE*, Loyalist College Library, 376 Wallbridge-Loyalist Rd, K8N 5B9. (Mail add: PO Box 4200, K8N 5B9), SAN 319-0463. Tel: 613-969-1913, Ext 2249. Circulation Tel: 613-969-1913, Ext 2141, 613-969-1913, Ext 2696. Interlibrary Loan Service Tel: 613-969-1913, Ext 2175. Administration Tel: 613-969-1913, Ext 2339. Automation Services Tel: 613-969-1913, Ext 2183, 613-969-1913, Ext 2216. Information Services Tel: 613-969-1913, Ext 2317. Toll Free Tel: 888-569-2547. FAX: 613-969-5183. E-mail: library@loyalistc.on.ca. Web Site: www.loyalistlibrary.com. *Dir, Libr & Res Serv,* Ross W Danaher; E-mail: rdanaher@loyalistcollege.com; *Info Serv, ILL,* Jennifer Dupuis; E-mail: jdupuis@loyalistic.on.ca; *Electronic Res, Libr Tech,* Mrs Dayle Gorsline; E-mail: dgorsline@loyalistic.on.ca; *Cat, Libr Tech, Tech Serv,* Danielle Emon; Tel: 613-969-1913, Ext 2183, E-mail: emon@loyalistic.on.ca; *Circ,* Cheryl Steele; E-mail: csteele@loyalistc.on.ca; *Circ,* Carla Williamson; E-mail: cwilliam@loyalistc.on.ca; *Libr Tech,* Cindy Fort; Tel: 613-969-1913, Ext 2595, E-mail: cfort@loyalistc.on.ca; *Libr Tech, Copyright,* Vanessa Lee; E-mail: vlee@loyalistc.on.ca; Staff 10 (MLS 1, Non-MLS 9)
Founded 1967. Enrl 3,000; Fac 145
Library Holdings: AV Mats 10,025; e-books 28,348; e-journals 14,000; Bk Titles 30,674; Bk Vols 55,000; Per Subs 292
Special Collections: John Peterson Photography Coll; Lorraine Monk Coll; Loyalist College Archives
Automation Activity & Vendor Info: (Acquisitions) Mandarin Library Automation; (Cataloging) Mandarin Library Automation; (Circulation) Mandarin Library Automation; (Course Reserve) Mandarin Library Automation; (Media Booking) Mandarin Library Automation; (OPAC) Mandarin Library Automation
Wireless access
Function: Audiobks via web, Computers for patron use, Digital talking bks, Distance learning, Electronic databases & coll, Microfiche/film & reading machines, Online cat, Orientations, Photocopying/Printing, Wheelchair accessible
Open Mon-Thurs 8am-9pm, Fri 8-4:30, Sat 9-4, Sun 12-4
Restriction: Borrowing privileges limited to fac & registered students, ID required to use computers (Ltd hrs), In-house use for visitors, Open to fac, students & qualified researchers, Open to students, fac & staff, Pub use on premises

BLIND RIVER

P BLIND RIVER PUBLIC LIBRARY, Eight Woodward Ave, P0R 1B0. (Mail add: PO Box 880, P0R 1B0), SAN 319-0471. Tel: 705-356-7616. FAX: 705-356-7343. E-mail: blindriverlibrary@gmail.com. Administration E-mail: brpl.ceo@gmail.com. Web Site: blindriver.olsn.ca. *Chief Exec Officer, Head Librn,* Jennifer Fortin
Founded 1926. Pop 3,549
Library Holdings: Bk Vols 18,000; Per Subs 3
Automation Activity & Vendor Info: (Cataloging) SirsiDynix; (Circulation) SirsiDynix
Wireless access
Function: 24/7 Electronic res, 24/7 Online cat, 24/7 wireless access, Adult bk club, Archival coll, Bk club(s), Bks on CD, Children's prog, Computer training, Computers for patron use, Digital talking bks, Distance learning, Extended outdoor wifi, Free DVD rentals, Games, Games & aids for people with disabilities, Genealogy discussion group, Holiday prog, Home delivery & serv to seniorr ctr & nursing homes, Homebound delivery serv, ILL available, Instruction & testing, Internet access, Laminating, Magazines, Mail & tel request accepted, Makerspace, Movies, Online cat, OverDrive digital audio bks, Photocopying/Printing, Preschool outreach, Preschool reading prog, Printer for laptops & handheld devices, Prog for adults, Prog for children & young adult, Ref & res, Ref serv available, Scanner, Senior computer classes, Senior outreach, Serves people with intellectual disabilities, STEM programs, Story hour, Summer & winter reading prog, Summer reading prog, Teen prog, Wheelchair accessible
Special Services for the Blind - Bks on CD; Copier with enlargement capabilities; Daisy reader; Home delivery serv; Large print bks
Open Mon-Thurs 10-7, Fri & Sat 10-2

BOLTON

P CALEDON PUBLIC LIBRARY*, Albion Bolton Branch, 150 Queen St S, L7E 1E3. SAN 319-0498. Tel: 905-857-1400. FAX: 905-857-8280. E-mail: bolton@caledon.library.on.ca. Web Site: www.caledon.library.on.ca. *Chief Librn/CEO,* Colleen Lipp; Tel: 905-857-1400, Ext 215, E-mail: clipp@caledon.library.on.ca; *Br Mgr,* Gillian Booth-Moyle; Tel: 905-857-1400, Ext 217, E-mail: gboothmoyle@caledon.library.on.ca; *Br Mgr,* Samantha Dillane; Tel: 905-857-1400, Ext 225, E-mail: sdillane@caledon.library.on.ca; *Mgr, Communications, Mgr, Community Dev,* Mary Maw; Tel: 905-857-1400, Ext 228, E-mail: mmaw@caledon.library.on.ca; *Mgr, Info Serv,* Megan Renkema; Tel: 905-857-1400, Ext 232, E-mail: mrenkema@caledon.library.on.ca; *Mgr, Info Tech,* Mojgan Schmalenberg; Tel: 905-857-1400, Ext 237, E-mail: mschmale@caledon.library.on.ca; *Mgr, Pub Serv,* Kelley Potter; Tel: 905-857-1400, Ext 238, E-mail: kpotter@caledon.library.on.ca; *Mgr, Youth*

Serv, Laurie Groe; Tel: 905-857-1400, Ext 231, E-mail: lgroe@caledon.library.on.ca
Founded 1974. Pop 69,000; Circ 425,000
Automation Activity & Vendor Info: (Cataloging) SirsiDynix; (Circulation) SirsiDynix; (OPAC) SirsiDynix
Wireless access
Mem of Ontario Library Service
Partic in Ontario Library Consortium
Open Tues & Fri 12-4, Wed & Sat 10-2, Thurs 4-8
Friends of the Library Group
Branches: 7
ALTON BRANCH, 35 Station Rd, Alton, L7K 0E2, SAN 320-0655. Tel: 519-941-5480. E-mail: alton@caledon.library.on.ca.
Open Tues 12-4, Wed & Sat 10-2, Thurs 4-8
Friends of the Library Group
CALEDON EAST BRANCH, 6500 Old Church Rd, Caledon East, L0N 1E0, SAN 320-068X. Tel: 905-584-1456. E-mail: ceast@caledon.library.on.ca.
Open Tues & Fri 12-4, Wed & Sat 10-2, Thurs 4-8
Friends of the Library Group
CALEDON VILLAGE, 18313 Hurontario St, Caledon Village, L7K 0X7, SAN 320-0671. Tel: 519-927-5800. E-mail: village@caledon.library.on.ca.
Open Tues & Fri 12-4, Wed & Sat 10-2, Thurs 4-8
Friends of the Library Group
INGLEWOOD BRANCH, 15825 McLaughlin Rd, Inglewood, L7C 1H4, SAN 320-0698. Tel: 905-838-3324. E-mail: inglewood@caledon.library.on.ca.
Open Wed 10-2, Fri 2-6
Friends of the Library Group
SOUTHFIELDS VILLAGE BRANCH, 225 Dougall Ave, Caledon, L7C 3M7. Tel: 905-843-1158. E-mail: southfields@caledon.library.on.ca.
Open Tues & Fri 12-4, Wed & Sat 10-2, Thurs 4-8
Friends of the Library Group
MARGARET DUNN VALLEYWOOD BRANCH, 20 Snellcrest Dr, Mayfield, L7C 1B5, SAN 378-1682. Tel: 905-843-0457. E-mail: dunn@caledon.library.on.ca.
Open Tues & Fri 12-4, Thurs 4-8, Sat 10-2
Friends of the Library Group

BONFIELD

P BONFIELD PUBLIC LIBRARY*, 365 Hwy 531, P0H 1E0. SAN 319-0501. Tel: 705-776-2396. FAX: 705-776-1154. E-mail: bonfieldlibrary@gmail.com. Web Site: www.bonfieldpubliclibrary.ca. *Chief Exec Officer, Chief Librn,* Jeannette Shields; Staff 2 (Non-MLS 2)
Founded 1974. Pop 2,000; Circ 8,097
Library Holdings: Bk Vols 19,652; Per Subs 9
Automation Activity & Vendor Info: (Circulation) Follett Software
Wireless access
Function: ILL available
Open Mon 10-3:30, Tues & Thurs 4:30-7:30, Wed 10-7:30, Sat 10-1
Friends of the Library Group

BORDEN

CANADA DEPARTMENT OF NATIONAL DEFENCE
G BASE BORDEN PUBLIC & MILITARY LIBRARY*, CFB BORDEN, 41 Kapyong Rd, L0M 1C0, SAN 367-0201. Tel: 705-424-1200, Ext 2273. *Chief Librn,* Don Allen; E-mail: don.allen@forces.gc.ca
Library Holdings: Bk Vols 45,000; Per Subs 20
Subject Interests: Mil
Partic in County of Simcoe Libr Coop
Open Tues-Fri 12-8, Sat 12-4
Friends of the Library Group
GM CANADIAN FORCES HEALTH SERVICES TRAINING CENTRE*, CFB Borden, 0-166, 30 Ortona Rd, Rm 1113, L0M 1C0. (Mail add: PO Box 1000, Sta Main, L0M 1C0), SAN 367-0236. Tel: 705-424-1200, Ext 3627. FAX: 705-423-2613.
Library Holdings: AV Mats 660; Bk Vols 15,000; Per Subs 40
Subject Interests: Emergency med, Mil med, Nursing, Preventive med

BOWMANVILLE

P CLARINGTON PUBLIC LIBRARY*, Bowmanville Branch, 163 Church St, L1C 1T7. SAN 367-0295. Tel: 905-623-7322, Ext 2712. FAX: 905-623-8608. E-mail: info@clarington-library.on.ca. Web Site: www.clarington-library.on.ca. *Chief Exec Officer,* Monika Machacek; Tel: 905-623-7322 x2727, E-mail: mmachacek@clarington-library.on.ca
Founded 1974. Pop 80,000; Circ 346,616
Library Holdings: Bk Vols 78,448; Per Subs 3,000
Automation Activity & Vendor Info: (Cataloging) SirsiDynix; (Circulation) SirsiDynix
Wireless access
Mem of Ontario Library Service
Open Mon-Fri 9-9, Sat 9-5, Sun 12-5
Branches: 3
COURTICE BRANCH, 2950 Courtice Rd, Courtice, L1E 2H8. Tel: 905-404-0707. Administration Tel: 905-404-0707, Ext 223. *Coordr, Commun Engagement,* Kiley Percy
Open Mon-Thurs 10-8, Fri 10-6, Sat 10-5, Sun 12-5
NEWCASTLE VILLAGE BRANCH, 150 King Ave E, Newcastle, L1B 1L5, SAN 367-035X. Tel: 905-987-4844. Administration Tel: 905-987-9844, Ext 223. *Coordr,* Alison Dee
Open Mon-Wed 1-8, Tues & Thurs 10-6, Fri 1-6, Sat 10-5, Sun 12-5
ORONO BRANCH, 127 Church St, Orono, L0B 1M0. (Mail add: PO Box 299, Orono, L0B 1M0), SAN 367-0325. Tel: 905-983-5507. *Coordr, Br Serv,* Position Currently Open
Open Mon, Tues, Thurs & Fri 1-6, Wed 1-8, Sat 10-2

BRACEBRIDGE

P BRACEBRIDGE PUBLIC LIBRARY*, 94 Manitoba St, P1L 2B5. SAN 319-051X. Tel: 705-645-4171. FAX: 705-645-6551. E-mail: info@bracebridgelibrary.ca. Web Site: bracebridgelibrary.ca. *Chief Librn/CEO,* Crystal Bergstrome; E-mail: crystal.bergstrome@bracebridgelibrary.ca; *Digital Serv Librn, Info Serv Librn,* Cindy Buhn; E-mail: illo@bracebridgelibrary.ca; *Digital Serv Librn, Info Serv Librn,* Sarah MacNeal; *Digital Serv Librn, Info Serv Librn,* Justine Splane; *Ch Serv, Youth Serv,* Ashleigh Whipp; E-mail: ashleigh.whipp@bracebridgelibrary.ca; *ILL,* Nancy Beasley; Staff 4 (MLS 4)
Founded 1908. Pop 15,652; Circ 137,526
Library Holdings: e-books 14,865; Bk Titles 42,226; Bk Vols 52,986; Per Subs 128
Special Collections: Muskoka Coll; Prov; Rene Caisse Coll
Automation Activity & Vendor Info: (Cataloging) SirsiDynix; (Circulation) SirsiDynix; (OPAC) SirsiDynix
Wireless access
Open Mon & Fri 9-6, Tues-Thurs 9-8, Sat 9-4
Friends of the Library Group

BRADFORD

P BRADFORD-WEST GWILLIMBURY PUBLIC LIBRARY*, 425 Holland St W, L3Z 0J2. SAN 319-0528. Tel: 905-775-3328. Circulation Tel: 905-775-3328, Ext 6100. Information Services Tel: 905-775-3328, Ext 6109. E-mail: bwgmailbox@bradford.library.on.ca. Web Site: www.bradford.library.on.ca. *Chief Exec Officer,* Matthew Corbett; Tel: 905-775-3328, Ext 6101, E-mail: mcorbett@bradford.library.on.ca; *Dep Chief Exec Officer,* Nina Cunniff; Tel: 905-775-3328, Ext 6105, E-mail: ncunniff@bradford.library.on.ca; *Borrower & Tech Services Mgr,* Andrea Ciurria; Tel: 905-775-3328, Ext 6106, E-mail: aciurria@bradford.library.on.ca
Founded 1879
Library Holdings: Bk Vols 100,000; Per Subs 150
Subject Interests: Local hist
Wireless access
Mem of Ontario Library Service
Open Mon, Fri & Sat 10-4, Tues & Thurs 10-7
Friends of the Library Group

BRAMPTON

P BRAMPTON LIBRARY*, 65 Queen St E, L6W 3L6. SAN 367-0384. Tel: 905-793-4636. FAX: 905-453-0810. TDD: 866-959-9994. E-mail: info@bramlib.on.ca. Web Site: www.bramptonlibrary.ca.
Founded 1974. Pop 750,000; Circ 4,500,000
Special Collections: Can & Prov; Community Information (Multilingual Literary French, large print, talking books)
Subject Interests: Archit, Art, Behav sci, Law, Local hist, Soc sci
Automation Activity & Vendor Info: (Acquisitions) SirsiDynix; (Cataloging) SirsiDynix; (Circulation) SirsiDynix; (OPAC) SirsiDynix
Wireless access
Function: 24/7 Electronic res, 24/7 Online cat, 3D Printer, Accelerated reader prog, Adult bk club, Adult literacy prog, Art programs, Audiobks via web, Bi-weekly Writer's Group, Bilingual assistance for Spanish patrons, Bk club(s), Bks on CD, CD-ROM, Children's prog, Citizenship assistance, Computer training, Computers for patron use, Digital talking bks, Distance learning, E-Reserves, Electronic databases & coll, Equip loans & repairs, Family literacy, For res purposes, Free DVD rentals, Games & aids for people with disabilities, Genealogy discussion group, Health sci info serv, Holiday prog, Home delivery & serv to seniorr ctr & nursing homes, Homebound delivery serv, Homework prog, ILL available, Internet access, Large print keyboards, Life-long learning prog for all ages, Literacy & newcomer serv, Magazines, Magnifiers for reading, Mail & tel request accepted, Makerspace, Mango lang, Meeting rooms, Microfiche/film & reading machines, Movies, Museum passes, Music CDs, Notary serv, Online cat, Online Chat, Online info literacy tutorials on the web & in blackboard, Online ref, Outreach serv, OverDrive digital audio bks, Photocopying/Printing, Preschool outreach, Preschool reading prog, Printer for laptops & handheld devices, Prog for adults, Prog for children

& young adult, Ref serv available, Res assist avail, Scanner, Senior computer classes, Senior outreach, Serves people with intellectual disabilities, Spanish lang bks, Spoken cassettes & CDs, Spoken cassettes & DVDs, STEM programs, Story hour, Study rm, Summer & winter reading prog, Summer reading prog, Teen prog, Telephone ref, Visual arts prog, Wheelchair accessible, Winter reading prog, Workshops, Writing prog
Open Mon-Thurs 10-9, Fri 10-6, Sat 10-5, Sun 1-5
Branches: 8
CHINGUACOUSY BRANCH, Brampton Civic Ctr, 150 Central Park Dr, L6T 1B4, SAN 367-0449. Tel: 905-793-4636, Ext 74120. FAX: 905-793-0506. *Br Mgr,* Julie Mandal; E-mail: jmandal@bramlib.on.ca
Special Collections: Community Information Centre
Subject Interests: Genealogy, Law, Literacy, Multilingual
Open Mon-Thurs 10-9, Fri 10-6, Sat 10-5, Sun 1-5
CYRIL CLARK BRANCH, 20 Loafers Lake Lane, L6Z 1X9, SAN 322-6034. Tel: 905-793-4636, Ext 74403. FAX: 905-846-4278. *Br Mgr,* Dominique China; E-mail: dchina@bramlib.on.ca
Subject Interests: Literacy, Multilingual
Friends of the Library Group
FOUR CORNERS BRANCH, 65 Queen St E, L6W 3L6, SAN 367-0414. Tel: 905-793-4636, Ext 74321. FAX: 905-453-4602. *Br Mgr,* Neil Arsenault; E-mail: narsenault@bramlib.on.ca
Subject Interests: Literacy, Multilingual
Open Mon-Thurs 10-9, Fri 10-6, Sat 10-5, Sun 1-5
GORE MEADOWS BRANCH, 10150 The Gore Rd, L6P 0A6. Tel: 905-793-4636, Ext 74707. *Br Mgr,* Zarena Cassar; E-mail: zcassar@bramlib.on.ca
Special Services for the Deaf - TTY equip
Special Services for the Blind - Daisy reader
Open Mon-Thurs 10-9, Fri & Sat 10-6, Sun 1-5
MOUNT PLEASANT VILLAGE BRANCH, 100 Commuter Dr, L7A 0G2. Tel: 905-793-4636, Ext 74231. *Br Mgr,* Jenny Omstead; E-mail: jomstead@bramlib.on.ca
Open Mon-Thurs 2-9, Fri 2-6, Sat 10-5, Sun 1-5
SOUTH FLETCHER'S BRANCH, 500 Ray Lawson Blvd, L6Y 5B3, SAN 376-9658. Tel: 905-793-4636, Ext 74267. FAX: 905-453-8425. *Br Mgr,* Katrina Doktor; E-mail: kdoktor@bramlib.on.ca
Open Mon-Thurs 10-9, Fri 10-6, Sat 10-5, Sun 1-5
SOUTH WEST BRANCH, 8405 Financial Dr, L6Y 1M1. *Br Mgr,* Jenny Omstead; E-mail: jomstead@bramlib.on.ca

BRANTFORD

S BRANT HISTORICAL SOCIETY LIBRARY*, Brant Museum & Archives, 57 Charlotte St, N3T 2W6. SAN 320-8788. Tel: 519-752-2483. E-mail: information@brantmuseums.ca, research@brantmuseums.ca. Web Site: www.brantmuseums.ca. *Exec Dir,* Mrs Marion McGeein; E-mail: mmcgeein@brantmuseums.ca; *Commun Coordr, Curator, Programming,* Nathan Etherington; E-mail: nathan.etherington@brantmuseums.ca
Founded 1908
Library Holdings: Bk Titles 800
Special Collections: Brant County History Coll
Open Mon-Fri 12-5, Sat 10-5

P BRANTFORD PUBLIC LIBRARY*, 173 Colborne St, N3T 2G8. SAN 319-0544. Tel: 519-756-2220. FAX: 519-756-4979. E-mail: info@brantford.library.on.ca. Web Site: brantford.library.on.ca. *Chief Librn/CEO,* Rae-Lynne Aramburo; Tel: 519-756-2220, Ext 3319, E-mail: raramburo@brantford.library.on.ca; *Services Administrator,* Ken Symons; Tel: 519-756-2220, Ext 3320, E-mail: ksymons@brantford.library.on.ca; *Mgr, Libr Res,* Laura Warner; Staff 64 (MLS 8, Non-MLS 56)
Founded 1884. Pop 92,000; Circ 1,000,000
Library Holdings: Bk Titles 153,923; Bk Vols 189,727; Per Subs 255
Special Collections: Can & Prov
Subject Interests: Adult literacy, Local hist
Automation Activity & Vendor Info: (Acquisitions) SirsiDynix; (Cataloging) SirsiDynix; (Circulation) SirsiDynix; (Serials) SirsiDynix
Wireless access
Mem of Ontario Library Service
Open Mon-Sat 9:30-5
Branches: 1
ST PAUL AVENUE BRANCH, 441 St Paul Ave, N3R 4N8, SAN 324-0258. Tel: 519-756-2220. FAX: 519-753-3557. *Chief Librn/CEO,* Rae-Lynne Aramburo
Library Holdings: Bk Titles 42,398; Bk Vols 46,379; Per Subs 65
Open Tues-Sat 9:30-5

BRIDGENORTH

P SELWYN PUBLIC LIBRARY*, Bridgenorth Library, 836 Charles St, K0L 1H0. (Mail add: PO Box 500, K0L 1H0), SAN 373-7373. Tel: 705-292-5065. FAX: 705-292-6695. Web Site: www.selwyntownship.ca/en/library/library.aspx. *Chief Exec Officer,* Sara Hennessey; E-mail: shennessey@mypubliclibrary.ca; *Librn,* Heather Jamieson; Staff 4 (Non-MLS 4)
Founded 1972. Pop 16,900; Circ 170,000
Library Holdings: Bk Titles 45,000; Bk Vols 65,000; Per Subs 75
Automation Activity & Vendor Info: (Acquisitions) Mandarin Library Automation; (Cataloging) Mandarin Library Automation; (Circulation) Mandarin Library Automation; (OPAC) Mandarin Library Automation
Wireless access
Open Mon, Tues, Thurs & Fri 10-5, Wed 10-7, Sat 10-2
Branches: 2
ENNISMORE BRANCH, c/o Ennismore Post Office, 551 Ennis Rd, Ennismore, K0L 1T0, SAN 319-1257. Tel: 705-292-8022. FAX: 705-292-8687. *Librn,* Sarah Jones
Founded 1971
Library Holdings: Bk Vols 22,000; Per Subs 20
Open Mon, Tues & Sat 10-2, Wed & Fri 1-5, Thurs 10-6
Friends of the Library Group
LAKEFIELD BRANCH, Eight Queen St, K0L 2H0. (Mail add: PO Box 2200, Lakefield, K0L 2H0), SAN 367-6021. Tel: 705-652-8623. FAX: 705-652-8878. *Librn,* Kacie Gardiner
Founded 1897. Pop 17,000; Circ 135,000
Library Holdings: Bk Vols 70,000
Special Collections: Local History Coll
Open Tues & Fri 10-5, Wed 10-3, Thurs 10-8, Sat 10-2

BRIGHTON

P BRIGHTON PUBLIC LIBRARY*, 35 Alice St, K0K 1H0. (Mail add: PO Box 129, K0K 1H0), SAN 319-0579. Tel: 613-475-2511. Web Site: www.brightonlibrary.ca. *Chief Exec Officer,* Heather Ratz; E-mail: brightonceo@brightonlibrary.ca; *Asst Librn,* Kim Reaman; Staff 3 (MLS 3)
Pop 10,500; Circ 140,000
Library Holdings: Bk Titles 30,000; Per Subs 72
Wireless access
Mem of Ontario Library Service
Open Mon, Wed & Fri 10-6, Tues & Thurs 10-8, Sat 10-4
Friends of the Library Group
Branches: 1
CODRINGTON BRANCH, 2992 County Rd 30, Codrington, K0K 1R0. Tel: 613-475-5628. *Librn,* Penny Kingyens; E-mail: pkingyens@brightonlibrary.ca
Function: Computers for patron use, ILL available, Meeting rooms, Photocopying/Printing
Open Tues 9:30-12:30, Fri 1-4, Sun 10-1

BRITT

P BRITT AREA LIBRARY*, Britt Public School, 841 Riverside Dr, P0G 1A0. (Mail add: PO Box 2, P0G 1A0), SAN 324-1211. Tel: 705-383-2292. FAX: 705-383-0077. E-mail: brittlibrary3@gmail.com. *Chief Librn,* Barbara Wohleber; E-mail: sbwohleber@gmail.com; Staff 5 (Non-MLS 5)
Founded 1979. Pop 600
Library Holdings: Bk Vols 10,000; Per Subs 25
Special Collections: Canadian Aviation History
Subject Interests: Can aviation, Folk tales
Wireless access
Publications: Brochure
Open Mon-Wed & Fri 9-3, Thurs 9-3 & 7-8:30
Friends of the Library Group

P MAGNETAWAN FIRST NATION PUBLIC LIBRARY*, Ten Regional Rd & Hwy 529, P0G 1A0. SAN 372-6630. Tel: 705-383-2477. FAX: 705-383-2566. E-mail: bandoffice@magfn.com. Web Site: www.magfn.com/library-repository. *Librn,* Wanda Noganosh
Founded 1985. Pop 90; Circ 12,500
Library Holdings: DVDs 30; High Interest/Low Vocabulary Bk Vols 200; Large Print Bks 100; Bk Titles 5,000; Bk Vols 7,000
Special Collections: First Nations Coll. Canadian and Provincial; Municipal Document Depository
Subject Interests: Local hist
Automation Activity & Vendor Info: (Cataloging) Follett Software; (Circulation) Follett Software
Wireless access
Publications: Magnetawan First Nation (Newsletter)
Special Services for the Deaf - Bks on deafness & sign lang; Closed caption videos; Staff with knowledge of sign lang
Special Services for the Blind - Large print bks
Open Mon-Thurs 8-4:30, Fri 9-12

BROCKVILLE

P AUGUSTA TOWNSHIP PUBLIC LIBRARY*, 4500 County Rd 15, RR 2, K6V 5T2. Tel: 613-926-2449. E-mail: staff@augustalibrary.com. Web Site: augustalibrary.com. *Librn,* Angie Knights; Staff 1 (Non-MLS 1)
Pop 7,600; Circ 20,170
Library Holdings: Bk Vols 24,000
Wireless access

Mem of Ontario Library Service
Open Mon, Tues & Thurs 1-7, Wed & Sat 9-1

P BROCKVILLE PUBLIC LIBRARY*, 23 Buell St, K6V 5T7. (Mail add: Box 100, K6V 5T7), SAN 319-0587. Tel: 613-342-3936. FAX: 613-342-9598. E-mail: info@brockvillelibrary.ca. Web Site: www.brockvillelibrary.ca. *Chief Exec Officer,* Emily Farrell; *Mgr,* Laura Julien; *Customer Serv Coordr,* Margie Bentley; *Youth Serv Coordr,* Lisa Cirka; Staff 11 (MLS 3, Non-MLS 8)
Founded 1903. Pop 22,000
Library Holdings: Bk Vols 70,000; Per Subs 50
Automation Activity & Vendor Info: (Acquisitions) SirsiDynix
Wireless access
Publications: Newsletter
Open Mon 9-1, Tues-Thurs 9-8, Fri & Sat 9-5, Sun (Sept-June) 1-5
Friends of the Library Group

C ST LAWRENCE COLLEGE LIBRARY, Brockville Campus, 2288 Parkedale Ave, K6V 5X3. SAN 367-0473. Tel: 613-345-0660, Ext 3104. E-mail: libraries@sl.on.ca. Web Site: stlawrencecollege.libguides.com. *Libr Tech,* Carrie Cousineau; E-mail: ccousineau@sl.on.ca; Staff 1 (Non-MLS 1)
Founded 1970. Enrl 500; Fac 50; Highest Degree: Bachelor
Library Holdings: Bk Vols 2,000
Subject Interests: Health sci, Law, Musical theatre
Automation Activity & Vendor Info: (Acquisitions) Ex Libris Group; (Cataloging) Ex Libris Group; (Circulation) Ex Libris Group; (Media Booking) Ex Libris Group; (OPAC) Ex Libris Group
Wireless access

BRUCE MINES

P BRUCE MINES & PLUMMER ADDITIONAL UNION PUBLIC LIBRARY*, 33 Desbarats St, P0R 1C0. (Mail add: PO Box 249, P0R 1C0), SAN 319-0609. Tel: 705-785-3370. FAX: 705-785-3370. E-mail: bmpalibrary@bellnet.ca. Web Site: brucemines.olsn.ca.
Pop 1,130; Circ 12,197
Library Holdings: AV Mats 350; Bk Titles 9,327; Talking Bks 225
Automation Activity & Vendor Info: (Cataloging) SirsiDynix-WorkFlows; (Circulation) SirsiDynix-WorkFlows; (OPAC) SirsiDynix-iBistro; (Serials) SirsiDynix-WorkFlows
Wireless access
Function: Homebound delivery serv, ILL available, Internet access, Photocopying/Printing, Prog for children & young adult, Summer reading prog, Telephone ref, Wheelchair accessible, Workshops
Open Tues & Thurs 10-7:30, Wed & Fri 11-6, Sat 10-Noon
Friends of the Library Group

BURK'S FALLS

P BURK'S FALLS, ARMOUR & RYERSON UNION PUBLIC LIBRARY, 39 Copeland St, P0A 1C0. (Mail add: PO Box 620, P0A 1C0), SAN 319-0617. Tel: 705-382-3327. FAX: 705-382-3327. E-mail: burksfallslibrary@gmail.com. Web Site: www.burksfallslibrary.com. *Chief Exec Officer,* Nieves Guijarro; Staff 3 (Non-MLS 3)
Founded 1896. Pop 3,752
Library Holdings: Bk Vols 11,000; Per Subs 23
Special Collections: History of Burk's Falls Ontario & District
Wireless access
Open Tues-Fri 10-6, Sat 10-3
Friends of the Library Group

BURLINGTON

P BURLINGTON PUBLIC LIBRARY*, 2331 New St, L7R 1J4. SAN 367-0538. Tel: 905-639-3611. FAX: 905-681-7277. Web Site: www.bpl.on.ca. *Chief Exec Officer,* Lita Barrie; Tel: 905-639-3611, Ext 1100, E-mail: barriel@bpl.on.ca; Staff 23 (MLS 21, Non-MLS 2)
Founded 1872. Pop 170,000; Circ 1,700,000
Special Collections: Canadian and Provincial
Automation Activity & Vendor Info: (Acquisitions) Innovative Interfaces, Inc - Sierra; (Cataloging) Innovative Interfaces, Inc - Sierra; (Circulation) Innovative Interfaces, Inc; (Serials) Innovative Interfaces, Inc - Sierra
Wireless access
Function: 24/7 Electronic res, 24/7 Online cat, 3D Printer, Activity rm, Adult bk club, Archival coll, Audio & video playback equip for onsite use, Audiobks via web, AV serv, Bk club(s), Bk reviews (Group), Children's prog, Citizenship assistance, Computer training, Computers for patron use, Digital talking bks, Distance learning, Doc delivery serv, E-Readers, E-Reserves, Electronic databases & coll, Equip loans & repairs, Family literacy, For res purposes, Free DVD rentals, Genealogy discussion group, Govt ref serv, Health sci info serv, Holiday prog, Home delivery & serv to seniorr ctr & nursing homes, Homebound delivery serv, Homework prog, ILL available, Internet access, Large print keyboards, Life-long learning prog for all ages, Magazines, Magnifiers for reading, Mail & tel request accepted, Mango lang, Meeting rooms, Microfiche/film & reading machines, Movies, Music CDs, Online cat, Online info literacy tutorials on the web & in blackboard, Online ref, Outreach serv, Outside serv via phone, mail, e-mail & web, OverDrive digital audio bks, Photocopying/Printing, Preschool outreach, Preschool reading prog, Printer for laptops & handheld devices, Prog for adults, Prog for children & young adult, Ref & res, Ref serv available, Res assist avail, Res libr, Res performed for a fee, Satellite serv, Scanner, Senior computer classes, Senior outreach, Serves people with intellectual disabilities, Story hour, Summer & winter reading prog, Summer reading prog, Teen prog, Telephone ref, Visual arts prog, Wheelchair accessible, Winter reading prog, Writing prog
Mem of Ontario Library Service
Special Services for the Deaf - Bks on deafness & sign lang
Special Services for the Blind - Assistive/Adapted tech devices, equip & products; Audio mat; Bks on CD; Daisy reader; Extensive large print coll; Home delivery serv; Info on spec aids & appliances; Internet workstation with adaptive software; Large print & cassettes; Large print bks; Large screen computer & software; Low vision equip; Magnifiers; Networked computers with assistive software; Screen enlargement software for people with visual disabilities; Screen reader software; Sound rec; Talking bks; Talking bks & player equip; Text reader; Vera Arkenstone; VisualTek equip; ZoomText magnification & reading software
Open Mon-Thurs 9-9, Fri 9-6, Sat 9-5, Sun (Nov-April) 1-5
Branches: 6
ALDERSHOT, 550 Plains Rd E, L7T 2E3, SAN 367-0562. Tel: 905-333-9995. *Br Mgr,* James Dekens; E-mail: dekensj@bpl.on.ca
Open Tues, Wed & Fri 10-6, Thurs 10-9, Sat 10-5
ALTON, 3040 Tim Dobbie Dr, L7M 0M3. Tel: 905-634-3686. *Br Mgr,* Frances Hanemaayer; Tel: 905-639-3611 ext;1405, E-mail: hanemaayerf@bpl.on.ca
Open Mon-Thurs 9-9, Fri 9-6, Sat 9-5
BRANT HILLS, 2255 Brant St, L7P 5C8, SAN 367-0651. Tel: 905-335-2209. *Br Supvr,* James Dekens; E-mail: dekens@bpl.on.ca
Open Mon-Thurs 9-9, Fri 9-6, Sat 9-5
KILBRIDE, Kilbride School, 6611 Panton St, L7P 0L8, SAN 367-0597. Tel: 905-335-4011. *Br Supvr,* James Dekens; E-mail: dekens@bpl.on.ca
Open Mon & Wed 6pm-9pm, Sat 9-Noon
NEW APPLEBY, 676 Appleby Line, L7L 5Y1, SAN 367-0627. Tel: 905-639-6373. *Team Leader,* Denise Fung; E-mail: fungd@bpl.on.ca
Open Tues, Thurs & Fri 10-6, Wed 10-9, Sat 9-5
TANSLEY WOODS, 1996 Itabashi Way, L7M 4J8, SAN 377-6948. Tel: 905-336-5583. *Br Mgr,* Frances Hanemaayer; E-mail: hanemaayerf@bpl.on.ca
Open Mon-Thurs 9-9, Fri 9-6, Sat 9-5, Sun 1-5

S ENVIRONMENT CANADA LIBRARY*, Canada Centre for Inland Waters Library, 867 Lakeshore Rd, L7S 1A1. (Mail add: PO Box 5050, L7R 4A6), SAN 319-0625. Tel: 905-336-4982. FAX: 905-336-4428. E-mail: ec.bibliotech-library.ec@canada.ca. *Head of Libr,* Francesco Lai; *Client Serv Librn,* Mary Orlik; Staff 3 (MLS 2, Non-MLS 1)
Founded 1968
Library Holdings: Bk Vols 3,000
Subject Interests: Fisheries, Great Lakes, Hydraulics, Hydrographic surveying, Limnology, Wastewater tech, Water pollution
Automation Activity & Vendor Info: (Acquisitions) Horizon; (Cataloging) Horizon; (Circulation) Horizon; (ILL) OCLC; (OPAC) Horizon; (Serials) Horizon
Wireless access
Partic in Council of Federal Libraries Consortium; Proquest Dialog
Open Mon-Fri 8-4
Restriction: Non-circulating to the pub, Open to fac, students & qualified researchers

S ROYAL BOTANICAL GARDENS LIBRARY*, 680 Plains Rd W, L7T 4H4. (Mail add: PO Box 399, Hamilton, L8N 3H8), SAN 319-0633. Tel: 905-527-1158, Ext 259. FAX: 905-577-0375. Web Site: www.rbg.ca. *Knowledge Res Spec,* Erin Aults; E-mail: eaults@rbg.ca
Founded 1946
Library Holdings: Bk Titles 14,000; Per Subs 90
Special Collections: Checklists & Registration Lists; Nursery & Seed Trade Catalogs
Subject Interests: Botany, Conserv, Natural hist, Ornamental hort
Restriction: Not open to pub

CALABOGIE

P GREATER MADAWASKA PUBLIC LIBRARY*, 12629 Lanark Rd, K0J 1H0. (Mail add: PO Box 160, K0J 1H0), SAN 325-0326. Tel: 613-752-2317. FAX: 613-752-1720. E-mail: gmpl@bellnet.ca. Web Site: www.greatermadawaska.com/en/play-and-discover/library.aspx. *Chief Exec Officer, Chief Librn,* Tracy Strudwick
Founded 1978
Library Holdings: Bk Titles 11,686
Wireless access

Function: 24/7 Online cat, Adult bk club, Art programs, Audiobks via web, Bk club(s), Bks on CD, Children's prog, Computers for patron use, Electronic databases & coll, Family literacy, Free DVD rentals, ILL available, Internet access, Laminating, Magazines, Mango lang, Movies, Museum passes, Music CDs, Online cat, Outreach serv, OverDrive digital audio bks, Photocopying/Printing, Preschool outreach, Preschool reading prog, Printer for laptops & handheld devices, Prog for adults, Prog for children & young adult, Scanner, Serves people with intellectual disabilities, STEM programs, Story hour, Summer & winter reading prog, Summer reading prog
Mem of Ontario Library Service
Open Tues & Wed 9-6, Thurs & Fri 9-1, Sat 9-2

CAMBRIDGE

CR HERITAGE COLLEGE & SEMINARY LIBRARY, 175 Holiday Inn Dr, N3C 3T2. SAN 322-6468. Tel: 519-651-2869. FAX: 519-651-2870. E-mail: library@heritagecs.edu. Web Site: discoverheritage.ca/library. *Interim Libr Dir,* Heather Okrafka; Staff 1 (Non-MLS 1)
Founded 1976. Enrl 350; Fac 32; Highest Degree: Master
Library Holdings: Bk Titles 43,000; Per Subs 175
Special Collections: Old Elementary Coll; Pre-1900 Baptist Periodicals; Works by & about John Bunyan
Subject Interests: Anabaptists, Baptist hist, Puritans
Automation Activity & Vendor Info: (Cataloging) Koha; (Circulation) Koha; (OPAC) Koha
Wireless access
Open Mon 8am-9:30pm, Tues-Thurs 8am-10pm, Fri 8-4:30, Sat 11-4

P IDEA EXCHANGE*, One North Sq, N1S 2K6. SAN 367-0686. Tel: 519-621-0460. FAX: 519-621-2080. Web Site: www.ideaexchange.org. *Chief Exec Officer,* Helen Kelly; *Dir, Finance & Fac,* Ellen Lehman; E-mail: elehman@ideaexchange.org; *Dir, Programming, Dir, Promotion,* Jaime Griffis; E-mail: jgriffis@ideaexchange.org; *Dir, Pub Libr Serv,* Cathy Kiedrowski; E-mail: ckiedrowski@ideaexchange.org; *Digital Serv Dir,* Betty Wilson; E-mail: bwilson@ideaexchange.org; *Gallery Dir,* Aidan Ware; E-mail: aware@ideaexchange.org; *Br Mgr,* Jamie Kamula; E-mail: jkamula@ideaexchange.org
Founded 1973. Pop 136,810; Circ 966,417
Library Holdings: Bk Vols 135,548; Per Subs 235
Subject Interests: Local hist
Automation Activity & Vendor Info: (Acquisitions) Innovative Interfaces, Inc
Wireless access
Function: 24/7 Electronic res, 24/7 Online cat, 3D Printer, Activity rm, Art exhibits, Audiobks via web, AV serv, Bk reviews (Group), Bks on CD, Children's prog, Citizenship assistance, Computer training, Computers for patron use, Electronic databases & coll, Family literacy, Free DVD rentals, Holiday prog, Home delivery & serv to seniorr ctr & nursing homes, Homebound delivery serv, ILL available, Large print keyboards, Literacy & newcomer serv, Magnifiers for reading, Mail & tel request accepted, Makerspace, Mango lang, Meeting rooms, Microfiche/film & reading machines, Movies, Museum passes, Music CDs, Online cat, Online ref, Outreach serv, OverDrive digital audio bks, Photocopying/Printing, Printer for laptops & handheld devices, Prog for adults, Prog for children & young adult, Ref serv available, Scanner, Senior outreach, Spoken cassettes & CDs, Spoken cassettes & DVDs, STEM programs, Story hour, Study rm, Summer reading prog, Teen prog, Telephone ref, Wheelchair accessible
Special Services for the Blind - Reader equip
Open Mon-Thurs 9:30-8:30, Fri & Sat 9:30-5:30, Sun 1-5
Branches: 4
CLEMENS MILL, 50 Saginaw Pkwy, N1T 1W2. (Mail add: PO Box 546, N1R 5W1), SAN 377-6778. Tel: 519-740-6294. FAX: 519-621-2080. *Mgr,* Carroll Chapman; E-mail: cchapman@ideaexchange.org
Library Holdings: Bk Vols 59,000
Open Mon-Thurs 10-8:30, Fri Noon-5:30, Sat 9:30-5:30, Sun (Sept-June) 1-5
HESPELER, Five Tannery St E, N3C 2C1, SAN 367-0716. Tel: 519-658-4412. FAX: 519-621-2080. *Mgr,* Susan Hastings; E-mail: shastings@ideaexchange.org
Library Holdings: Bk Vols 50,000
Open Mon-Thurs Noon-8:30, Fri 10-5:30, Sat 9:30-5:30, Sun (Sept-May) 1-5
PRESTON, 435 King St E, N3H 3N1, SAN 367-0740. Tel: 519-653-3632. FAX: 519-621-2080. *Mgr,* Greg Bester; E-mail: gbester@ideaexchange.org
Library Holdings: Bk Vols 60,000
Open Mon-Thurs 10-8:30, Fri Noon-5:30, Sat 9:30-5:30, Sun (Sept-May) 1-5

CARDINAL

P EDWARDSBURGH CARDINAL PUBLIC LIBRARY, Cardinal Branch, 618 County Rd 2, K0E 1E0. Tel: 613-657-3822. E-mail: cardinal@edcarlibrary.ca. Web Site: www.edcarlibrary.ca. *Chief Exec Officer,* Donna Gladstone; E-mail: donna.gladstone@edcarlibrary.ca; *Br Supvr,* Margaret Ann Gaylord
Library Holdings: CDs 300; DVDs 50; Large Print Bks 200; Bk Titles 20,000; Per Subs 15
Wireless access
Function: Wheelchair accessible
Open Mon & Wed 5pm-8pm, Tues & Thurs 1-5, Sat 9-12
Friends of the Library Group
Branches: 1
SPENCERVILLE BRANCH, Five Henderson St, Spencerville, K0E 1X0, SAN 319-4264. Tel: 613-658-5575. FAX: 613-658-5575. E-mail: spencerville@edcarlibrary.ca. *Chief Exec Officer,* Donna Gladstone; *Libr Asst,* Sarah De Visser
Pop 4,397; Circ 9,706
Library Holdings: Bk Vols 10,000; Per Subs 24
Mem of Ontario Library Service
Open Tues & Thurs 1-5, Wed 5pm-8pm, Sat 10-1:30
Friends of the Library Group

CARLETON PLACE

P CARLETON PLACE PUBLIC LIBRARY*, 101 Beckwith St, K7C 2T3. SAN 319-0706. Tel: 613-257-2702. E-mail: library@carletonplace.ca. Web Site: www.carletonplacelibrary.ca. *Chief Exec Officer,* Meriah Caswell; E-mail: mcaswell@carletonplace.ca; *Asst Librn, Ch Serv,* Heidi Sinnett; E-mail: hsinnett@carletonplace.ca; Staff 4 (Non-MLS 4)
Founded 1846. Pop 10,565
Library Holdings: Bk Vols 50,746; Per Subs 134
Wireless access
Mem of Ontario Library Service
Open Mon-Thurs 10:30-8, Fri & Sat 10-5:30

CHAPLEAU

P CHAPLEAU PUBLIC LIBRARY*, 20 Pine St W, P0M 1K0. (Mail add: PO Box 910, P0M 1K0), SAN 319-0757. Tel: 705-864-0852. FAX: 705-864-0295. E-mail: library@chapleau.ca. Web Site: chapleau.ca/visitors/facilities/library. *Chief Admin Officer,* Denis Duguay; E-mail: cao@chapleau.ca
Pop 2,800; Circ 35,104
Library Holdings: DVDs 400; Bk Titles 16,944; Per Subs 35; Talking Bks 85; Videos 200
Special Collections: Local History Coll
Wireless access
Function: Bks on cassette, Bks on CD, Computer training, Computers for patron use, ILL available, Photocopying/Printing, VHS videos, Wheelchair accessible
Open Mon, Thurs & Fri 1-5, Tues & Wed 1-7
Friends of the Library Group

CHATHAM

P CHATHAM-KENT PUBLIC LIBRARY*, 120 Queen St, N7M 2G6. SAN 319-0765. Tel: 519-354-2940. Administration Tel: 519-354-7352. FAX: 519-354-7366. Administration FAX: 519-354-2602. E-mail: cklibrary@chatham-kent.ca. Web Site: www.ckpl.ca. *Chief Librn/CEO,* Tania Sharpe; E-mail: tanias@chatham-kent.ca; *Mkt Mgr, Outreach Mgr,* Sarah Hart Coatsworth; *Mgr, Pub Serv,* Cassey Beauvais; E-mail: casseyb@chatham-kent.ca; *Mgr, Support Serv,* Heidi Wyma; Staff 9 (MLS 9)
Founded 1890. Pop 104,000; Circ 803,767
Library Holdings: Bk Vols 304,638
Special Collections: Local Hist (Hist of City of Chatham & Kent County & the Underground Railway) bks, microflm
Automation Activity & Vendor Info: (Acquisitions) Innovative Interfaces, Inc - Sierra; (Cataloging) Innovative Interfaces, Inc - Sierra; (Circulation) Innovative Interfaces, Inc - Sierra; (OPAC) Innovative Interfaces, Inc - Sierra
Wireless access
Open Mon-Thurs 9:30-8:30, Fri 9:30-6, Sat 9:30-5
Friends of the Library Group
Branches: 10
BLENHEIM BRANCH, 16 George St, Blenheim, N0P 1A0, SAN 367-0805. Tel: 519-676-3174. *Br Head,* Lucy Lavigne
Open Tues & Thurs 12-8, Wed & Fri 10-3, Sat 12-4
BOTHWELL BRANCH, 320 Main St, Bothwell, N0P 1C0, SAN 367-083X. Tel: 519-695-2844. *Br Head,* Vera Todd-Roberts; Staff 1 (Non-MLS 1)
Open Tues & Thurs 3-8, Fri & Sat 10-1
DRESDEN BRANCH, 187 Brown St, Dresden, N0P 1M0, SAN 367-0864. Tel: 519-683-4922. *Br Head,* Tamar Malic; Staff 2 (Non-MLS 2)
Open Tues & Thurs 12-8, Wed 12-5, Fri 10-3, Sat 10-2
Friends of the Library Group
HIGHGATE BRANCH, 291 King St, Highgate, N0P 1T0, SAN 367-0899. Tel: 519-678-3313. *Br Head,* Vera Todd-Roberts; Staff 1 (Non-MLS 1)
Open Mon & Wed 3-8, Fri 10-3

MERLIN BRANCH, 13 Aberdeen St, Merlin, N0P 1W0, SAN 367-0929. Tel: 519-689-4944. *Br Head,* Lucy Lavigne; Staff 1 (Non-MLS 1)
Open Mon 1-5, Tues & Thurs 4-8, Sat 10-2
RIDGETOWN BRANCH, 54 Main St, Ridgetown, N0P 2C0, SAN 367-0953. Tel: 519-674-3121. *Br Head,* Vera Todd-Roberts; Staff 3 (Non-MLS 3)
Open Mon & Fri Noon-5, Tues & Thurs Noon-8, Sat 10-2
Friends of the Library Group
THAMESVILLE BRANCH, Three London Rd, Thamesville, N0P 2K0, SAN 367-0988. Tel: 519-692-4251. *Br Head,* Tamar Malic; Staff 1 (Non-MLS 1)
Open Tues & Thurs 1-5, Wed 4-8, Sat 10-2
TILBURY BRANCH, Two Queen St, Tilbury, N0P 2L0. (Mail add: PO Box 999, Tilbury, N0P 2L0), SAN 367-1011. Tel: 519-682-0100. *Br Head,* Amy Osborne; E-mail: amyo@chatham-kent.ca; Staff 3 (Non-MLS 3)
Open Mon & Fri Noon-5, Tues & Thurs Noon-8, Sat 10-2
WALLACEBURG BRANCH, 209 James St, Wallaceburg, N8A 2N4, SAN 367-1046. Tel: 519-627-5292. *Br Head,* Stacey VanDeale; E-mail: staceyva@chatham-kent.ca; Staff 4 (Non-MLS 4)
Subject Interests: Genealogy, Local hist
Open Mon & Wed 10-6, Tues & Thurs Noon-8, Fri & Sat 10-5
WHEATLEY BRANCH, 35 Talbot St W, Wheatley, N0P 2P0, SAN 367-1070. Tel: 519-825-7131. *Br Head,* Amy Osborne; E-mail: amyo@chatham-kent.ca; Staff 1 (Non-MLS 1)
Open Tues & Thurs 4-8, Wed & Sat 10-2

J ST CLAIR COLLEGE*, Chatham Campus Library, 1001 Grand Ave W, N7M 5W4. SAN 324-167X. Tel: 519-354-9100, Ext 3232, 519-354-9100, Ext 3273. Circulation Tel: 519-354-9100, Ext 3287. Web Site: www.stclaircollege.ca. *Libr Tech,* Jeanette Giroux; E-mail: jgiroux@stclaircollege.ca; *Libr Tech,* Cheryl Smith; E-mail: csmith@stclaircollege.ca; Staff 2 (Non-MLS 2)
Library Holdings: CDs 88; DVDs 197; Bk Titles 4,980; Bk Vols 6,361; Per Subs 10
Automation Activity & Vendor Info: (Cataloging) Surpass; (Circulation) Surpass; (Course Reserve) Surpass; (ILL) Surpass; (OPAC) Surpass
Wireless access
Function: 24/7 Electronic res, 24/7 Online cat
Open Mon-Fri 8-4

CLINTON

P HURON COUNTY LIBRARY*, Administration Office, 77722B London Rd, RR 5 Hwy 4, N0M 1L0. SAN 367-2638. Tel: 519-482-5457. FAX: 519-482-7820. E-mail: libraryadmin@huroncounty.ca. Web Site: www.huroncounty.ca/library. *County Librn,* Beth Rumble; Staff 2 (MLS 2)
Founded 1967. Pop 59,068; Circ 358,327
Library Holdings: Bk Titles 148,225; Bk Vols 250,462; Per Subs 2,694
Special Collections: Canadiana. Canadian and Provincial
Automation Activity & Vendor Info: (Acquisitions) SirsiDynix; (Cataloging) SirsiDynix; (Circulation) SirsiDynix; (OPAC) SirsiDynix
Wireless access
Mem of Ontario Library Service
Open Mon-Fri 8:30-4:30
Friends of the Library Group
Branches: 12
BAYFIELD BRANCH, 18 Main St, Bayfield, N0M 1G0. (Mail add: PO Box 2090, Bayfield, N0M 1G0), SAN 367-2697. Tel: 519-565-2886. E-mail: bayfieldlibrary@huroncounty.ca. *Br Mgr,* Helen Gianoulis
Special Collections: Local History
Open Mon & Fri 1-5, Tues 10-12 & 1-5, Wed & Thurs 1-5 & 6-8, Sat 10-2
Friends of the Library Group
BLYTH BRANCH, 392 Queen St, Blyth, N0M 1H0. (Mail add: PO Box 388, Blyth, N0M 1H0), SAN 367-2816. Tel: 519-523-4400. E-mail: blythlibrary@huroncounty.ca. *Br Mgr,* Paula Mackie
Library Holdings: Bk Vols 3,000
Open Tues & Thurs 1-5 & 6-8, Fri & Sat 10-2
Friends of the Library Group
BRUSSELS BRANCH, 402 Turnberry St, Brussels, N0G 1H0. (Mail add: PO Box 80, Brussels, N0G 1H0), SAN 367-2875. Tel: 519-887-6448. E-mail: brusselslibrary@huroncounty.ca. *Br Mgr,* Anne Dodington
Open Tues & Thurs 1-5 & 6-8, Wed, Fri & Sat 10-2
CLINTON BRANCH, 27 Albert St, N0M 1L0. (Mail add: PO Box 370, N0M 1L0), SAN 367-2905. Tel: 519-482-3673. E-mail: clintonlibrary@huroncounty.ca. *Br Mgr,* Michelle Carter
Open Mon, Tues & Thurs 1-8, Wed & Sat 10-2, Fri 10-5, Sun (Winter) 1-5
EXETER BRANCH, 330 Main St, Exeter, N0M 1S6. (Mail add: PO Box 609, Exeter, N0M 1S6), SAN 367-3081. Tel: 519-235-1890. E-mail: exeterlibrary@huroncounty.ca. *Br Mgr,* Jenni Boles
Open Mon, Tues & Thurs 1-8, Wed, Fri & Sat 10-5, Sun (Winter) 1-5
Friends of the Library Group
GODERICH BRANCH, 52 Montreal St, Goderich, N7A 2G4, SAN 367-3146. Tel: 519-524-9261. E-mail: goderichlibrary@huroncounty.ca. *Br Mgr,* Helen Gianoulis
Open Mon-Fri 10-8, Sat 10-5, Sun (Winter) 1-5
Friends of the Library Group
HENSALL BRANCH, 108 King St, Hensall, N0M 1X0. (Mail add: PO Box 249, Hensall, N0M 1X0), SAN 367-3200. Tel: 519-262-2445. E-mail: hensalllibrary@huroncounty.ca. *Br Mgr,* Jenni Boles
Open Tues & Thurs 1-5 & 6-8, Wed & Sat 10-2
Friends of the Library Group
HOWICK BRANCH, 45088 Harriston Rd, RR 1, Gorrie, N0G 1X0. (Mail add: c/o Alice Munro Branch/Huran County Library, PO Box 280, Wingham, N0G 2W0). Tel: 519-335-6899. E-mail: howicklibrary@huroncounty.ca. *Br Mgr,* Paula Mackie
Open Tues-Thurs 4-8, Fri 1-5, Sat 10-2
KIRKTON BRANCH, c/o Kirkton-Woodham Community Ctr, 70497 Perth Rd 164, RR 1, Kirkton, N0K 1K0, SAN 367-326X. Tel: 519-229-8854. E-mail: kirktonlibrary@huroncounty.ca. *Br Mgr,* Jenni Boles
Open Tues 10-12 & 1-5, Thurs 1-5 & 6-8, Sat 9-Noon
Friends of the Library Group
ALICE MUNRO PUBLIC LIBRARY, 281 Edward St, Wingham, N0G 2W0. (Mail add: PO Box 280, Wingham, N0G 2W0), SAN 367-3448. Tel: 519-357-3312. E-mail: winghamlibrary@huroncounty.ca. *Br Mgr,* Paula Mackie
Open Tues-Thurs 10-8, Fri 10-5, Sat 10-3, Sun (Winter) 1-5
Friends of the Library Group
SEAFORTH BRANCH, 108 Main St S, Seaforth, N0K 1W0. (Mail add: PO Box 490, Seaforth, N0K 1W0), SAN 367-3383. Tel: 519-527-1430. E-mail: seaforthlibrary@huroncounty.ca. *Br Mgr,* Anne Dodington
Open Mon, Tues & Thurs 1-8, Wed & Sat 10-2, Fri 10-5, Sun (Winter) 1-5
ZURICH BRANCH, Ten Goshen St N, Zurich, N0M 2T0. (Mail add: PO Box 190, Zurich, N0M 2T0), SAN 367-3472. Tel: 519-236-4965. E-mail: zurichlibrary@huroncounty.ca. *Br Mgr,* Michelle Carter
Open Mon 1-5, Tues & Thurs 1-5 & 6-8, Wed, Fri & Sat 10-2
Friends of the Library Group

COBALT

P COBALT PUBLIC LIBRARY*, 30 Lang St, P0J 1C0. (Mail add: PO Box 170, P0J 1C0), SAN 319-0803. Tel: 705-679-8120. FAX: 705-679-8120. E-mail: cobaltpubliclibrary@gmail.com. Web Site: www.cobaltlibrary.com. *Chief Exec Officer,* Kendra Lacarte
Founded 1961. Pop 1,200; Circ 13,000
Library Holdings: DVDs 500; Large Print Bks 1,500; Bk Vols 12,000; Per Subs 32; Talking Bks 80; Videos 500
Automation Activity & Vendor Info: (Acquisitions) LiBRARYSOFT; (Cataloging) LiBRARYSOFT; (Circulation) LiBRARYSOFT; (OPAC) LiBRARYSOFT
Wireless access
Function: Audio & video playback equip for onsite use, Bks on cassette, Bks on CD, Computers for patron use, Free DVD rentals, Govt ref serv, Homebound delivery serv, ILL available, Internet access, Mail & tel request accepted, Online ref, Photocopying/Printing, Ref serv available, Scanner, VHS videos
Open Mon, Wed & Fri Noon-5, Tues & Thurs 1-7, Sat 2-5 (Winter); Mon-Fri Noon-5 (Summer)

COBOURG

P COBOURG PUBLIC LIBRARY*, 200 Ontario St, K9A 5P4. SAN 319-0811. Tel: 905-372-9271. FAX: 905-372-4538. E-mail: info@cobourg.library.on.ca. Web Site: www.cobourg.ca/en/library.aspx. *Chief Exec Officer,* Tammy Robinson; Tel: 905-372-9271, Ext 6200, E-mail: trobinson@cobourg.library.on.ca; *Pub Serv Mgr,* Kate Davis; Tel: 905-372-9271, Ext 6260, E-mail: kdavis@cobourg.library.on.ca
Founded 1886. Pop 28,000; Circ 261,969
Subject Interests: Local hist
Automation Activity & Vendor Info: (Acquisitions) Horizon
Wireless access
Mem of Ontario Library Service
Open Mon-Wed 10-8, Thurs-Sat 10-5, Sun 1-5

COCHRANE

P COCHRANE PUBLIC LIBRARY*, 178 Fourth Ave, P0L 1C0. (Mail add: PO Box 700, P0L 1C0), SAN 319-082X. Tel: 705-272-4178. FAX: 705-272-4165. E-mail: library@cochraneontario.com. Web Site: cochrane.olsn.ca. *Chief Exec Officer,* Christina Blazecka; E-mail: christina.blazecka@cochraneontario.com; *Asst Chief Exec Officer,* Jessica Horne; E-mail: jessica.horne@cochraneontario.com; Staff 3 (Non-MLS 3)
Founded 1921. Pop 5,330; Circ 17,244
Library Holdings: CDs 1,289; DVDs 2,400; Large Print Bks 500; Bk Vols 27,875; Per Subs 75; Talking Bks 300; Videos 640
Special Collections: Local History & Genealogy Coll

Automation Activity & Vendor Info: (Acquisitions) Follett Software; (Cataloging) Follett Software; (OPAC) Follett Software
Wireless access
Function: Archival coll, Art exhibits, Bks on cassette, Bks on CD, CD-ROM, Children's prog, Computer training, Computers for patron use, E-Reserves, Electronic databases & coll, Family literacy, Free DVD rentals, Holiday prog, Home delivery & serv to seniorr ctr & nursing homes, Homebound delivery serv, Homework prog, ILL available, Large print keyboards, Magnifiers for reading, Music CDs, Online cat, Photocopying/Printing, Ref & res, Ref serv available, Senior computer classes, Serves people with intellectual disabilities, Story hour, Summer reading prog, Teen prog, VHS videos, Wheelchair accessible, Winter reading prog
Partic in Ont Libr Serv-North
Open Mon, Tues, Thurs & Fri 10-5, Wed 10-7, Sat 10-2
Friends of the Library Group

COE HILL

P WOLLASTON PUBLIC LIBRARY*, 5629-A Hwy 620, K0L 1P0. (Mail add: PO Box 280, K0L 1P0), SAN 319-0838. Tel: 613-337-5183. FAX: 613-337-5183. E-mail: wollastonpubliclibrary@gmail.com. Web Site: wollastonpubliclibrary.ca. *Chief Exec Officer, Librn,* Temple Cameron
Pop 1,487; Circ 10,599
Library Holdings: Bk Vols 6,000
Wireless access
Mem of Ontario Library Service
Open Mon-Fri 12-5, Sat 10-1

COLBORNE

P TOWNSHIP OF CRAMAHE PUBLIC LIBRARY*, Colborne Branch, Six King St, K0K 1S0. (Mail add: PO Box 190, K0K 1S0), SAN 319-0846. Tel: 905-355-3722. FAX: 905-355-3430. E-mail: info@cramahelibrary.ca. Web Site: www.cramahelibrary.ca. *Chief Exec Officer,* Mary Norton; E-mail: libraryceo@cramahetownship.ca
Founded 1914. Pop 6,079; Circ 49,000
Library Holdings: Bk Vols 28,627
Subject Interests: Local hist of Colborne
Wireless access
Function: Homebound delivery serv
Publications: History of Colborne
Open Mon 3-8, Tues & Thurs 11-8, Fri & Sat 11-4

COLDWATER

P SEVERN TOWNSHIP PUBLIC LIBRARY*, Coldwater Memorial Branch, 31 Coldwater Rd, L0K 1E0. (Mail add: PO Box 278, L0K 1E0), SAN 319-0854. Tel: 705-686-3601. FAX: 705-686-3741. E-mail: library@severn.ca. Web Site: www.coldwater.library.on.ca. *Chief Librn,* Dee Byers
Founded 1937. Pop 11,600
Library Holdings: Audiobooks 22,373; CDs 4,413; DVDs 233; e-books 86,975; Bk Vols 15,403; Per Subs 41
Wireless access
Mem of Ontario Library Service
Open Mon, Tues, Thurs & Fri 9-3, Sat 11-2

COLLINGWOOD

P COLLINGWOOD PUBLIC LIBRARY*, 55 Ste. Marie St, L9Y 0W6. SAN 319-0862. Tel: 705-445-1571. FAX: 705-445-3704. E-mail: info@collingwoodpuliclibrary.ca. Web Site: www.collingwoodpubliclibrary.ca. *Chief Exec Officer,* Audrey Kulchychi; E-mail: akulchychi@collingwood.ca; *Mgr, Coll & Fac Serv,* Lynda Reid; Tel: 705-445-1571, Ext 6223, E-mail: lreid@collingwood.ca; Staff 14 (MLS 2, Non-MLS 12)
Pop 18,000; Circ 162,066
Library Holdings: CDs 2,471; DVDs 673; Large Print Bks 1,977; Bk Titles 65,352; Bk Vols 74,999; Per Subs 128; Talking Bks 324; Videos 3,199
Special Collections: Municipal Document Depository
Subject Interests: Genealogy, Local hist
Automation Activity & Vendor Info: (Acquisitions) SirsiDynix; (Cataloging) SirsiDynix; (Circulation) SirsiDynix; (OPAC) SirsiDynix
Wireless access
Mem of Ontario Library Service
Open Mon-Thurs 10-9, Fri 10-8, Sat 10-5, Sun (Sept-June) 1-4
Friends of the Library Group

COOKSTOWN

P INNISFIL PUBLIC LIBRARY*, Cookstown Branch, 20 Church St, L0L 1L0. SAN 319-0870. Tel: 705-431-7410. Interlibrary Loan Service Tel: 705-436-1681. FAX: 705-458-1294. E-mail: info@innisfilidealab.ca. Web Site: www.innisfil.library.on.ca. *Chief Librn/CEO,* Erin Scuccimarri; E-mail: escuccimarri@innisfilidealab.ca; *Dep Chief Librn,* Jayne Asselstine; E-mail: jasselstine@innisfill.library.on.ca; *Coll Mgr,* Susan Baues; E-mail: sbaues@innisfill.library.on.ca
Pop 1,500; Circ 45,000
Library Holdings: Bk Vols 15,000; Per Subs 25
Open Tues-Thurs 10-8, Fri & Sat 10-5
Friends of the Library Group

CORNWALL

P CORNWALL PUBLIC LIBRARY*, Bibliothèque Publique de Cornwall, 45 Second St E, K6H 1Y2. (Mail add: PO Box 939, K6H 5V1), SAN 319-0889. Tel: 613-932-4796. FAX: 613-932-2715. E-mail: generalmail@library.cornwall.on.ca. Web Site: library.cornwall.on.ca. *Chief Librn/CEO,* Dawn Kiddell; Staff 6 (MLS 3, Non-MLS 3)
Founded 1895. Pop 46,589; Circ 323,517
Library Holdings: AV Mats 16,029; e-books 13,272; Bk Titles 111,808; Bk Vols 124,466; Per Subs 146
Automation Activity & Vendor Info: (Acquisitions) Innovative Interfaces, Inc; (Circulation) Innovative Interfaces, Inc; (ILL) Fretwell-Downing; (OPAC) Innovative Interfaces, Inc; (Serials) Innovative Interfaces, Inc
Wireless access
Function: 24/7 Electronic res, 24/7 Online cat, 3D Printer, Activity rm, Adult bk club, Adult literacy prog, After school storytime, Archival coll, Art exhibits, Audio & video playback equip for onsite use, Audiobks via web, AV serv, BA reader (adult literacy), Bk club(s), Bks on CD, Chess club, Children's prog, Computers for patron use, Digital talking bks, Distance learning, Electronic databases & coll, Family literacy, Free DVD rentals, Genealogy discussion group, Holiday prog, Homebound delivery serv, ILL available, Instruction & testing, Internet access, Large print keyboards, Life-long learning prog for all ages, Literacy & newcomer serv, Magazines, Magnifiers for reading, Mail & tel request accepted, Mango lang, Meeting rooms, Microfiche/film & reading machines, Movies, Museum passes, Music CDs, Online cat, Orientations, OverDrive digital audio bks, Photocopying/Printing, Preschool outreach, Preschool reading prog, Prog for adults, Prog for children & young adult, Ref serv available, Scanner, Spoken cassettes & CDs, Spoken cassettes & DVDs, STEM programs, Story hour, Study rm, Summer & winter reading prog, Summer reading prog, Teen prog, Telephone ref, Wheelchair accessible, Writing prog
Mem of Ontario Library Service
Special Services for the Deaf - Bks on deafness & sign lang; High interest/low vocabulary bks
Special Services for the Blind - Accessible computers; Bks on CD; Daisy reader; Large print & cassettes; Large print bks; Magnifiers; Talking bk serv referral; Talking bks & player equip; ZoomText magnification & reading software
Open Mon-Thurs 9-8:30, Fri & Sat 9:30-5, Sun (Sept-May) 1-5

C ST LAWRENCE COLLEGE LIBRARY*, Cornwall Campus, Two Saint Lawrence Dr, K6H 4Z1. SAN 319-0897. Tel: 613-933-6080, Ext 2701. E-mail: clibrary@sl.on.ca. Web Site: stlawrencecollege.libguides.com, www.stlawrencecollege.ca/services/campus-services/libraries. *Assoc Dir, Libraries & Student Success,* Leigh Cunningham; Tel: 613-544-5400, Ext 1156, E-mail: ldcunningham@sl.on.ca; *Libr Coord,* Ann Small; Tel: 613-544-5400, Ext 2171, E-mail: asmall@sl.on.ca; Staff 1 (MLS 1)
Founded 1967
Library Holdings: Bk Vols 10,000; Per Subs 51; Videos 600
Subject Interests: Behav sci, Soc sci
Automation Activity & Vendor Info: (Circulation) SirsiDynix; (OPAC) SirsiDynix
Wireless access
Open Mon-Thurs 8am-9pm, Fri 8-4, Sat 11-3

P STORMONT, DUNDAS & GLENGARRY COUNTY LIBRARY*, 26 Pitt St, Ste 106, K6J 3P2. Tel: 613-936-8777. FAX: 613-936-2532. E-mail: generalinfo@sdglibrary.ca. Web Site: www.sdglibrary.ca. *Dir, Libr Serv,* Rebecca Luck; Tel: 613-936-8777, Ext 211, E-mail: rluck@sdglibrary.ca; *Communications Librn, Mkt Librn,* Susan Wallwork; Tel: 613-936-8777, Ext 226, E-mail: swallwork@sdglibrary.ca; *Info Serv Coordr,* Cheryl Servais; E-mail: cservais@sdglibrary.ca; *Cat/Acq Tech,* Erica Sutton; Tel: 613-936-8777, Ext 213, E-mail: esutton@sdglibrary.ca; *Cat/Acq Tech,* Lindsey Schulz; Tel: 613-936-8777, Ext 225, E-mail: lschulz@sdglibrary.ca; Staff 48 (MLS 2, Non-MLS 46)
Founded 1971. Pop 65,000; Circ 213,186
Library Holdings: Audiobooks 2,456; AV Mats 8,872; DVDs 4,242; e-books 3,261; e-journals 47,330; Electronic Media & Resources 16; Large Print Bks 3,603; Bk Titles 74,416; Bk Vols 116,991; Per Subs 187
Special Collections: Local History Coll. Canadian and Provincial
Automation Activity & Vendor Info: (Acquisitions) Innovative Interfaces, Inc; (Cataloging) Innovative Interfaces, Inc; (Circulation) Innovative Interfaces, Inc; (OPAC) Innovative Interfaces, Inc; (Serials) EBSCO Online
Wireless access
Function: Adult bk club, After school storytime, Art exhibits, Audio & video playback equip for onsite use, Audiobks via web, Bk club(s), Bks on

CD, CD-ROM, Children's prog, Computer training, Computers for patron use, Digital talking bks, Electronic databases & coll, Equip loans & repairs, Family literacy, Games & aids for people with disabilities, Holiday prog, Home delivery & serv to seniorr ctr & nursing homes, Homebound delivery serv, Homework prog, ILL available, Internet access, Large print keyboards, Mail & tel request accepted, Mail loans to mem, Museum passes, Online cat, Online ref, Orientations, Outreach serv, Outside serv via phone, mail, e-mail & web, OverDrive digital audio bks, Photocopying/Printing, Prog for adults, Prog for children & young adult, Ref serv available, Scanner, Senior computer classes, Senior outreach, Serves people with intellectual disabilities, Spoken cassettes & CDs, Spoken cassettes & DVDs, Story hour, Summer reading prog, Teen prog, Telephone ref

Publications: Assorted Subject/Services (Consumer guide); SDG Navigator (Quarterly)

Partic in Knowledge Ontario

Special Services for the Deaf - Accessible learning ctr; Bks on deafness & sign lang; Closed caption videos

Special Services for the Blind - Accessible computers; Assistive/Adapted tech devices, equip & products; Audio mat; Bks on CD; Computer access aids; Computer with voice synthesizer for visually impaired persons; Copier with enlargement capabilities; Daisy reader; Digital talking bk; Extensive large print coll; Home delivery serv; Internet workstation with adaptive software; Playaways (bks on MP3); Recorded bks; Screen enlargement software for people with visual disabilities; Screen reader software; Sub-lending agent for Braille Inst Libr; Talking bks; Talking bks & player equip; Text reader

Restriction: Circ to mem only, Lending limited to county residents, Non-resident fee

Friends of the Library Group

Branches: 15

ALEXANDRIA BRANCH, 170A MacDonald Blvd, Alexandria, K0C 1A0, SAN 377-6913. Tel: 613-525-3241. E-mail: alexandrialib@sdglibrary.ca. *District Supervisor,* Darlene Atkins; E-mail: datkins@sdglibrary.ca; Staff 3 (Non-MLS 3)

Open Mon 3-8, Tues-Thurs 10-8, Fri 12-5, Sat 10-2

AVONMORE BRANCH, 16299 Fairview Dr, Avonmore, K0C 1C0, SAN 377-693X. Tel: 613-346-2137. E-mail: avonmorelib@sdglibrary.ca. *Libr Serv Tech,* Lorna Platts

Open Tues 3-8, Wed 10-3, Thurs 4-8, Fri 1-4, Sat 10-1

CHESTERVILLE BRANCH, One Mill St, Chesterville, K0C 1H0, SAN 377-6972. Tel: 613-448-2616. E-mail: chestervillelib@sdglibrary.ca. *Libr Support Serv Asst,* Jennifer Harper

Open Tues 3-8, Wed 10-1, Thurs 3-8, Sat 10-2

CRYSLER BRANCH, 16 Third St, Crysler, K0C 1G0, SAN 377-6999. Tel: 613-987-2090. E-mail: cryslerlib@sdglibrary.ca. *Libr Support Serv Asst,* Josee Beauchamp

Open Mon & Sat 10-1, Tues & Thurs 3-8, Wed 9-1

FINCH BRANCH, 17 George St, Finch, K0C 1K0, SAN 377-7022. Tel: 613-984-2807. E-mail: finchlib@sdglibrary.ca. *District Supervisor,* Kate Jones Miner; E-mail: kminer@sdglibrary.ca

Open Tues 4-8, Wed 3-8, Thurs 10-3, Sat 10-1

INGLESIDE BRANCH, Ten Memorial Sq, Ingleside, K0C 1M0, SAN 377-7065. Tel: 613-537-2592. E-mail: inglesidelib@sdglibrary.ca. *District Supervisor,* Cheryl Servais; E-mail: cservais@sdglibrary.ca; *Br Support,* Linda Prieur; E-mail: lprier@sdglibrary.ca

Open Mon 4-9, Tues-Thurs 10-8, Fri 12-5, Sat 10-2

Friends of the Library Group

IROQUOIS BRANCH, One Dundas St & Elizabeth St, Iroquois, K0E 1K0. Tel: 613-652-4377. E-mail: Iroquoislib@sdglibrary.ca. *Libr Support Serv Asst,* Jeannette Devries; *Libr Support Serv Asst,* Eleanor Piertsma

Open Tues & Thurs 3-8, Wed 10-2, Fri 1-4, Sat 10-1

LANCASTER BRANCH, 195 S Rd Military, Lancaster, K0C 1N0. (Mail add: 26 Pitt St, K6J 3P2), SAN 377-7081. Tel: 613-347-2311. E-mail: lancasterlib@sdglibrary.ca. *District Supervisor,* Lorna Platts; E-mail: lplatts@sdglibrary.ca

Function: 24/7 Electronic res, 24/7 Online cat, 24/7 wireless access, Audiobks via web, Bk club(s), Bks on CD, Children's prog, Computers for patron use, Electronic databases & coll, Free DVD rentals, Games, ILL available, Internet access, Magazines, Mango lang, Movies, Museum passes, Online cat, Photocopying/Printing, Prog for adults, Prog for children & young adult, Summer reading prog

Open Mon 9-2, Tues-Thurs 10-8, Fri Noon-5, Sat 10-2

LONG SAULT BRANCH, 50 Milles Roches Rd (Fire Hall), Long Sault, K0C 1P0, SAN 377-712X. Tel: 613-534-2605. E-mail: longsaultlib@sdglibrary.ca. *Br Support,* Mrs Chris Denis; E-mail: cdenis@sdglibrary.ca

Open Tues & Thurs 10-8, Wed 4-8, Fri 1-4, Sat 10-1

Friends of the Library Group

MAXVILLE BRANCH, Two Spring St, Maxville, K0C 1T0, SAN 377-7146. Tel: 613-527-2235. E-mail: maxvillelib@sdglibrary.ca. *Libr Support Serv Asst,* Emily Andrews

Open Tues 4-8, Wed & Sat 10-2, Thurs 4-8

Friends of the Library Group

MORRISBURG BRANCH, 34 Ottawa St, Morrisburg, K0C 1X0, SAN 377-7200. Tel: 613-543-3384. E-mail: morrisburglib@sdglibrary.ca. *Libr Support Serv Asst,* Kate Jones Miner; *Libr Support Serv Asst,* Stacey Piticco

Open Mon & Fri Noon-5, Tues-Thurs 10-8, Sat 10-2

SOUTH MOUNTAIN BRANCH, 10543 Main St, South Mountain, K0E 1W0, SAN 377-7057. Tel: 613-989-2199. E-mail: southmountainlib@sdglibrary.ca. *Libr Support Serv Asst,* Ginette Tibben

Open Tues 4-8, Wed 10-2, Thurs 3-8, Sat 10-1

Friends of the Library Group

WILLIAMSBURG BRANCH, 12333 County Rd 18, Williamsburg, K0C 2H0, SAN 377-7073. Tel: 613-535-2185. E-mail: williamsburglib@sdglibrary.ca. *Libr Support Serv Asst,* Christina Thompson

Open Tues-Thurs 4-8, Sat 10-2

WILLIAMSTOWN BRANCH, 19641 County Rd 19, Williamstown, K0C 2J0, SAN 377-709X. Tel: 613-347-3397. E-mail: williamstownlib@sdglibrary.ca. *Libr Support Serv Asst,* Position Currently Open

Open Mon 2-6, Wed 10-2, Thurs 3-7, Sat 9-2

Friends of the Library Group

WINCHESTER BRANCH, 547 St Lawrence St, Winchester, K0C 2K0, SAN 377-7111. Tel: 613-774-2612. E-mail: winchesterlib@sdglibrary.ca. *District Supervisor,* Jenna Larmarche

Open Mon 9-2, Tues-Thurs 10-8, Fri 12-5, Sat 10-2

S UNITED EMPIRE LOYALISTS' ASSOCIATION OF CANADA LIBRARY*, Cornwall Community Museum, 160 Water St W, K6H 5T5. SAN 321-7248. Tel: 416-591-1783. E-mail: communications@uelac.org. Web Site: www.uelac.org. *Archivist,* Carl W Stymiest; Tel: 778-822-4290, E-mail: archivist@uelac.org

Founded 1968

Library Holdings: Bk Titles 1,540

Special Collections: American Revolution; American Revolutionary War Coll; Genealogy Coll (Family Histories of Descendants of Loyalists); Loyalist Landings; Provinces of Nova Scotia, New Brunswick, Prince Edward Island, Newfoundland, Upper Canada (Ontario), Lower Canada (Quebec)

Wireless access

Function: Ref serv available, Res libr, Res performed for a fee

Publications: American Revolutionary War; Early History & Genealogical Publication; Index to the Loyalist Gazette; Loyalist Gazette

Restriction: Access at librarian's discretion, Authorized patrons, Authorized personnel only, Authorized scholars by appt, By permission only, Circ to mem only, Not open to pub

DEEP RIVER

P DEEP RIVER PUBLIC LIBRARY*, W B Lewis Public Library Bldg, 55 Ridge Rd, K0J 1P0. (Mail add: PO Box 278, K0J 1P0), SAN 319-0943. Tel: 613-584-4244. FAX: 613-584-1405. Web Site: www.deepriverlibrary.ca. *Chief Exec Officer,* Naomi Balla-Boudreau; E-mail: nballa-boudreau@deepriverlibrary.ca; Staff 3.7 (MLS 1, Non-MLS 2.7)

Founded 1947. Pop 4,200

Library Holdings: Bk Vols 33,500; Per Subs 90

Automation Activity & Vendor Info: (Cataloging) Insignia Software; (Circulation) Insignia Software; (OPAC) Insignia Software

Wireless access

Open Mon-Fri 10-5 & 7-9, Sat 10-3

Friends of the Library Group

P LAURENTIAN HILLS PUBLIC LIBRARY, Point Alexander Branch, RR1 - 34465 Hwy 17, K0J 1P0. SAN 319-0951. Tel: 613-584-2714. FAX: 613-584-9145. E-mail: library@laurentianhills.ca. Web Site: library.laurentianhills.ca. *Chief Exec Officer,* Scott Jones

Founded 1974. Pop 2,800

Library Holdings: Large Print Bks 386; Bk Vols 21,900; Per Subs 45; Talking Bks 496; Videos 415

Automation Activity & Vendor Info: (Acquisitions) Insignia Software; (Cataloging) Insignia Software; (Circulation) Insignia Software; (OPAC) Insignia Software

Wireless access

Mem of Ontario Library Service

Open Mon 1-6, Tues & Thurs 10-3, Wed 10-12 & 6-8, Sat 12-3

Friends of the Library Group

Branches: 1

CHALK RIVER BRANCH, 15 Main St, Chalk River, K0J 1J0. Tel: 613-589-2966. FAX: 613-589-9759. E-mail: crlibrary@laurentianhills.ca. *Br Librn,* Jenny Dickson

Library Holdings: Bk Vols 7,800

Open Mon & Wed 3-5, Tues & Thurs 6-9, Sat 12-2

Friends of the Library Group

DESERONTO

P DESERONTO PUBLIC LIBRARY*, 358 Main St, K0K 1X0. (Mail add: PO Box 302, K0K 1X0), SAN 319-0978. Tel: 613-396-2744. FAX: 613-396-3466. Web Site: www.deserontopubliclibrary.ca. *Chief Exec Officer, Librn,* Julie Lane; E-mail: ceo@deserontopubliclibrary.ca; Staff 1 (Non-MLS 1)
Founded 1896. Pop 2,853; Circ 2,000
Library Holdings: Bk Titles 25,000; Per Subs 20
Special Collections: North American Indian Coll
Subject Interests: Local hist
Wireless access
Publications: In Review-Canadian Books for Children; Ontario Library Review
Open Mon & Wed 10-7, Fri & Sat 10-2

DORION

P DORION PUBLIC LIBRARY*, 170 Dorion Loop Rd, P0T 1K0. SAN 319-1036. Tel: 807-857-2289. FAX: 807-857-2203. E-mail: dorlib@tbaytel.net. Web Site: doriontownship.ca/living/library. *Librn,* Simone Marchand
Founded 1961. Pop 700; Circ 6,000
Library Holdings: Bk Vols 10,000
Wireless access
Open Mon & Fri 7pm-9pm, Wed 12:30-3 & 7-9

DRYDEN

P DRYDEN PUBLIC LIBRARY*, 36 Van Horne Ave, P8N 2A7. SAN 319-1095. Tel: 807-223-1475. FAX: 807-223-4312. E-mail: library@dryden.ca. Web Site: www.dryden.ca/en/explore/library.aspx.
Founded 1925. Pop 7,800; Circ 95,000
Library Holdings: Bk Vols 40,000; Per Subs 32
Subject Interests: Local hist
Open Mon-Thurs 10-8, Fri & Sun 10-5, Sat 1-5; Mon-Thurs 10-7, Fri & Sat 9-4 (Summer)

DUNDALK

P SOUTHGATE RUTH HARGRAVE MEMORIAL LIBRARY*, 80 Proton St N, N0C 1B0. (Mail add: PO Box 190, N0C 1B0), SAN 319-1117. Tel: 519-923-3248. E-mail: library@southgate.ca. Web Site: www.southgate-library.com. *Chief Exec Officer, Librn,* Lacy Russell
Pop 4,000; Circ 19,615
Library Holdings: Bk Vols 12,500; Per Subs 23
Special Collections: Dundalk Herald Weekly Newspaper, microfilm; Local Area Genealogy Records, digitized
Wireless access
Open Tues-Thurs 11-8, Fri 11-5, Sat 10-2
Friends of the Library Group

DUNNVILLE

P HALDIMAND COUNTY PUBLIC LIBRARY*, 317 Chestnut St, N1A 2H4. SAN 319-0668. Tel: 289-674-0400, 905-318-5932, Ext 6111. E-mail: library@haldimandcounty.on.ca. Web Site: www.haldimandcounty.ca/haldimand-county-public-library. *Chief Exec Officer,* Paul Diette; Staff 4 (MLS 1, Non-MLS 3)
Founded 2001. Pop 41,000; Circ 369,000
Library Holdings: Bk Vols 190,000; Per Subs 278
Automation Activity & Vendor Info: (Acquisitions) SirsiDynix; (Cataloging) SirsiDynix; (Circulation) SirsiDynix; (OPAC) SirsiDynix
Wireless access
Friends of the Library Group
Branches: 6
CALEDONIA BRANCH, 100 Haddington St, Unit 2, Caledonia, N3W 2N4, SAN 377-6573. E-mail: lcaledonia@haldimandcounty.ca. *Mgr,* Teresa Thompson; *Br Coordr,* Roberta Chapman
Library Holdings: Bk Vols 53,000; Per Subs 55
Open Mon-Thurs 10-8, Fri & Sat 10-5
CAYUGA BRANCH, 19 Talbot St W, Cayuga, N0A 1E0. (Mail add: PO Box 550, Cayuga, N0A 1E0), SAN 329-3386. E-mail: lcayuga@haldimandcounty.ca. *Chief Exec Officer,* Paul Diette; E-mail: pdiette@haldimandcounty.on.ca
Library Holdings: Bk Vols 16,000; Per Subs 31
Open Mon-Thurs 10-8, Fri & Sat 10-5
DUNNVILLE BRANCH, 317 Chestnut St, N1A 2H4, SAN 319-1133. E-mail: ldunnville@haldimandcounty.ca. *Sr Asst Librn,* Lynn Harrison; *Br Coordr,* Paul Diette
Founded 1854. Pop 11,460; Circ 170,000
Library Holdings: Bk Vols 55,000; Per Subs 58
Open Mon-Thurs 10-8, Fri & Sat 10-5
Friends of the Library Group
HAGERSVILLE BRANCH, 13 Alma St N, Hagersville, N0A 1H0. (Mail add: PO Box 219, Hagersville, N0A 1H0), SAN 329-336X. E-mail: lhagersville@haldimandcounty.ca. *Sr Librn, Pub,* Teresa Thompson; *Br Coordr,* Roberta Chapman
Library Holdings: Bk Vols 22,000; Per Subs 30
Open Tues-Thurs 10-8, Sat 10-5
JARVIS BRANCH, Two Monson St, Jarvis, N0A 1J0. E-mail: ljarvis@haldimandcounty.ca. *Br Coordr,* Roberta Chapman
Library Holdings: Bk Vols 21,000; Per Subs 20
Open Mon 12-8, Thurs 10-8, Fri & Sat 10-5
Friends of the Library Group
SELKIRK BRANCH, 34 Main St W, Selkirk, N0A 1P0. (Mail add: PO Box 130, Selkirk, N0A 1P0), SAN 319-4140. E-mail: lselkirk@haldimandcounty.ca. *Chief Exec Officer,* Paul Diette; E-mail: pdiette@haldimandcounty.on.ca; Staff 2 (MLS 1, Non-MLS 1)
Founded 1890. Pop 19,000; Circ 26,800
Library Holdings: Bk Titles 21,000; Bk Vols 22,000; Per Subs 40
Subject Interests: Local hist
Open Mon 12-5, Tues 10-8, Wed 12-8, Sat 10-5
Friends of the Library Group

DURHAM

P WEST GREY PUBLIC LIBRARY*, 453 Garafraxa St S, N0G 1R0. (Mail add: PO Box 706, N0G 1R0), SAN 319-1141. Tel: 519-369-2107. FAX: 519-369-9966. E-mail: info@westgreylibrary.com. Web Site: www.westgreylibrary.com. *Chief Librn/CEO,* Kim Storz; E-mail: kim@westgreylibrary.com; Staff 8 (Non-MLS 8)
Founded 1859. Pop 13,500; Circ 44,000
Library Holdings: Bk Vols 44,000; Per Subs 20
Special Collections: Durham Newspapers, dating back to 1859, 1985-present on microfiche; Genealogy Coll
Subject Interests: Local hist
Wireless access
Function: ILL available, Photocopying/Printing
Mem of Ontario Library Service
Open Tues & Thurs 10-8, Wed & Fri 10-5, Sat 11-3
Friends of the Library Group
Branches: 3
AYTON BRANCH, 610 Alfred St, Ayton, N0G 1C0. Tel: 519-665-2342.
Open Tues & Fri 1-7
ELMWOOD RESOURCE CENTRE, 12 Dirstein St S, Elmwood, N0G 1S0. Tel: 519-369-2107.
Founded 1905
Open Thurs 3-7
NEUSTADT BRANCH, 511 Mill St, Neustadt, N0G 2M0, SAN 328-1043. Tel: 519-799-5830. FAX: 519-799-5830.
Founded 1985
Open Thurs 11-7, Sat 11-3
Friends of the Library Group

EAR FALLS

P EAR FALLS PUBLIC LIBRARY*, Two Willow Crescent, P0V 1T0. (Mail add: Box 369, P0V 1T0), SAN 319-115X. Tel: 807-222-3209. FAX: 807-222-3432. E-mail: efpl@hotmail.ca. Web Site: ear-falls.com/residents/community-services/library-services. *Libr Dir,* Susan Carey
Pop 1,150; Circ 20,000
Library Holdings: Bk Titles 15,591; Per Subs 9
Wireless access
Open Tues, Thurs & Fri 10-4, Wed 10-4 & 6-8, Sat 10-2 (Winter); Mon, Tues & Thurs 10-4, Wed 6-8, Sat 10-2 (Summer)

EARLTON

P ARMSTRONG TOWNSHIP PUBLIC LIBRARY*, 35 Tenth St, P0J 1E0. (Mail add: PO Box 39, P0J 1E0), SAN 319-1168. Tel: 705-563-2717. FAX: 705-563-2093. E-mail: earltonlibrary@ntl.sympatico.ca. Web Site: www.olsn.ca/armstrong. *Chief Exec Officer, Head Librn,* Samara Cull; *Asst Librn,* Bernice Lockhart
Founded 1977. Pop 1,334; Circ 15,036
Library Holdings: Bk Vols 10,300; Per Subs 12
Open Mon 9-12 & 1-5, Tues 9-4, Thurs 9-12, 1-4 & 6-8, Fri 9-12 & 1-4

EGANVILLE

P BONNECHERE UNION PUBLIC LIBRARY*, 74 Maple St, K0J 1T0. (Mail add: PO Box 40, K0J 1T0), SAN 319-1176. Tel: 613-628-2400, 613-628-3101, Ext 2400. FAX: 613-628-5377. E-mail: info@bonnechereupl.com. Web Site: www.bonnechereupl.com. *Chief Exec Officer, Head Librn,* Susan Artymko; E-mail: ceo@bonnechereupl.com; Staff 5 (MLS 1, Non-MLS 4)
Pop 4,000; Circ 17,407
Library Holdings: Bk Titles 12,732; Per Subs 30
Wireless access

Mem of Ontario Library Service
Open Mon & Sat 10-3, Tues-Thurs 10-8, Fri 10-6
Friends of the Library Group

ELGIN

P RIDEAU LAKES PUBLIC LIBRARY*, 26 Halladay St, K0G 1E0. (Mail add: PO Box 189, K0G 1E0), SAN 367-1283. Tel: 613-359-5334. FAX: 613-359-5418. Administration E-mail: elgin@rlpl.ca. Web Site: www.rideaulakeslibrary.ca. *Chief Exec Officer,* Vicki Stevenson; E-mail: vicki@rlpl.ca
Library Holdings: Bk Titles 37,000; Per Subs 60
Special Collections: Large Print Coll; Local History Coll, bks, doc; Talking Books Coll
Wireless access
Publications: Walking & Driving Tours of North Leeds
Open Mon 5-8, Tues & Thurs 1-8, Wed 10-4, Fri & Sun 1-4, Sat 9:30-12:30
Branches: 5
DELTA BRANCH, 18 King St, Unit 2, Delta, K0E 1G0, SAN 367-1348. Tel: 613-928-2991. FAX: 613-928-2991. E-mail: delta@rlpl.ca. *Librn,* Liz Pribe
Open Tues 4-7, Thurs 1-4, Sat 9:30-12:30
ELGIN/ADMINISTRATION BRANCH, 24 Halladay St, K0G 1E0. (Mail add: PO Box 189, K0G1E0), SAN 367-1313. Tel: 613-359-5315. E-mail: admin@rlpl.ca. *Adminr,* Jamie Gipson
Open Mon 4-7, Tues & Thurs 1-7, Wed 10-4, Fri & Sun 1-4, Sat 9:30-12:30
Friends of the Library Group
NEWBORO BRANCH, Ten Brock St, Newboro, K0G 1P0, SAN 378-1895. Tel: 613-272-0241. FAX: 613-272-0241. E-mail: newboro@rlpl.ca. *Librn,* Elva McCann
Open Tues 4-7, Thurs 1-5, Fri 9-Noon, Sat 1-4
PORTLAND BRANCH, 2792 Hwy 15, Portland, K0G 1V0, SAN 367-1437. Tel: 613-272-2832. FAX: 613-272-2832. E-mail: portland@rlpl.ca. *Librn,* Sharon Riviere
Open Mon 4-7, Wed 2-5, Fri 9:30-12:30, Sat 1-4
SOUTH ELMSLEY BRANCH, 441 Hwy 15, Lombardy, K0G 1L0. Tel: 613-284-9827. E-mail: southelmsley@rlpl.ca.
Special Services for the Blind - BiFolkal kits
Open Tues 9-12, Wed 2-5, Thurs 4-7, Sat 9:30-12:30, Sun 1-4

ELK LAKE

P JAMES TOWNSHIP PUBLIC LIBRARY, 19 First St, P0J 1G0. (Mail add: PO Box 218, P0J 1G0), SAN 322-8037. Tel: 705-678-2340. FAX: 705-678-1166. E-mail: jamestwppl@gmail.com. Web Site: www.elklake.ca/library. *Chief Exec Officer,* Cyndi Stockman; *Libr Asst,* Amanda Miller-Marion
Founded 1971. Pop 450; Circ 603
Library Holdings: Bks on Deafness & Sign Lang 2; Braille Volumes 5; DVDs 800; Bk Titles 10,000; Per Subs 12
Wireless access
Function: 24/7 Electronic res, 24/7 Online cat, 3D Printer, Adult bk club, Art exhibits, Bks on CD, Children's prog, Computers for patron use, Electronic databases & coll, Free DVD rentals, Holiday prog, ILL available, Internet access, Laminating, Magazines, Mail & tel request accepted, Mango lang, Online cat, OverDrive digital audio bks, Photocopying/Printing, Printer for laptops & handheld devices, Prog for adults, Prog for children & young adult, Scanner, Spoken cassettes & DVDs, Summer reading prog
Special Services for the Blind - Assistive/Adapted tech devices, equip & products
Open Tues & Thurs 7pm-9pm, Wed & Sat 12:30-4:30

ELLIOT LAKE

P ELLIOT LAKE PUBLIC LIBRARY*, Pearson Plaza, 40 Hillside Dr S, P5A 1M7. SAN 319-1192. Tel: 705-848-2287, Ext 2800. FAX: 705-848-2120. Web Site: www.elliotlake.ca/en/library. *Chief Librn,* Pat McGurk; E-mail: pat.mcgurk@city.elliotlake.on.ca
Founded 1959. Pop 11,300; Circ 101,332
Library Holdings: Bk Vols 64,320; Per Subs 39
Subject Interests: Local hist, Mine decommissioning, Nuclear develop
Automation Activity & Vendor Info: (Acquisitions) Follett Software; (Cataloging) Follett Software; (Circulation) Follett Software; (OPAC) Follett Software
Wireless access
Function: Art exhibits, AV serv, Bks on cassette, Bks on CD, CD-ROM, Children's prog, Computers for patron use, Electronic databases & coll, Equip loans & repairs, ILL available, Internet access, Orientations, Photocopying/Printing, Prog for children & young adult, Serves people with intellectual disabilities, Summer reading prog, Telephone ref, Wheelchair accessible
Open Mon-Wed & Fri 9:30-6, Thurs 9:30-8, Sat 10-5
Restriction: Access for corporate affiliates

EMO

P EMO PUBLIC LIBRARY*, 36 Front St, P0W 1E0. (Mail add: PO Box 490, P0W 1E0), SAN 319-1230. Tel: 807-482-2575. FAX: 807-482-2575. E-mail: emolib@bellnet.ca. Web Site: emo.ca/emo-public-library. *Librn,* Nick Donaldson
Founded 1940. Pop 1,440; Circ 17,407
Library Holdings: Bk Vols 10,513
Automation Activity & Vendor Info: (Acquisitions) SirsiDynix; (Cataloging) SirsiDynix; (Circulation) SirsiDynix; (Course Reserve) SirsiDynix; (ILL) SirsiDynix; (Media Booking) SirsiDynix; (OPAC) SirsiDynix; (Serials) SirsiDynix
Wireless access
Open Mon, Wed & Fri 1-5, Tues 10-7, Thurs 1-7, Sat 10-2 (Winter); Mon & Wed 1-5, Tues 10-7, Thurs 1-7, Fri 9-5 (Summer)

ENGLEHART

P ENGLEHART PUBLIC LIBRARY, 71 Fourth Ave, P0J 1H0. (Mail add: PO Box 809, P0J 1H0), SAN 319-1249. Tel: 705-544-2100. FAX: 705-544-2238. Web Site: www.englehart.ca/p/englehart-public-library. *Librn,* Stephanie Carrier; E-mail: scarrier@englehartpubliclibrary.ca
Founded 1961. Pop 3,700; Circ 21,800
Library Holdings: Audiobooks 1,100; AV Mats 1,200; Bks on Deafness & Sign Lang 4; Braille Volumes 3; CDs 20; DVDs 1,100; Large Print Bks 908; Bk Titles 17,409; Bk Vols 24,927; Per Subs 23; Talking Bks 1,300
Special Collections: Canadian and Provincial; Municipal Document Depository
Subject Interests: Local hist
Automation Activity & Vendor Info: (Cataloging) Follett Software; (Circulation) Follett Software
Wireless access
Function: 24/7 Electronic res, 24/7 Online cat, 24/7 wireless access, Accelerated reader prog, Activity rm, Adult bk club, After school storytime, Art exhibits, Art programs, Bks on CD, Children's prog, Computer training, Computers for patron use, Free DVD rentals, Games, Holiday prog, ILL available, Internet access, Laminating, Literacy & newcomer serv, Magazines, Movies, Online cat, OverDrive digital audio bks, Photocopying/Printing, Wheelchair accessible
Special Services for the Blind - Braille bks
Open Tues & Thurs 12-5, Wed 12-9, Fri 10-1, Sat 10-3
Restriction: Access at librarian's discretion
Friends of the Library Group

ESPANOLA

P ESPANOLA PUBLIC LIBRARY*, 245 Avery Dr, P5E 1S4. SAN 319-1265. Tel: 705-869-2940. FAX: 705-869-6463. E-mail: library@espanola.ca. Web Site: www.espanola.library.on.ca. *Chief Librn/CEO,* Rosemary Rae; Staff 3 (MLS 1, Non-MLS 2)
Founded 1958. Pop 6,200
Library Holdings: Bk Titles 45,000; Bk Vols 46,000; Per Subs 100
Subject Interests: Local hist
Automation Activity & Vendor Info: (Cataloging) SirsiDynix-WorkFlows; (Circulation) SirsiDynix-WorkFlows; (OPAC) SirsiDynix-Enterprise
Wireless access
Function: 24/7 Electronic res, 24/7 Online cat, Activity rm, Adult bk club, Archival coll, Audiobks on Playaways & MP3, Audiobks via web, AV serv, Bks on CD, CD-ROM, Children's prog, Computer training, Computers for patron use, Digital talking bks, E-Readers, Electronic databases & coll, Equip loans & repairs, Free DVD rentals, Home delivery & serv to seniorr ctr & nursing homes, Homebound delivery serv, ILL available, Internet access, Laminating, Large print keyboards, Magazines, Mango lang, Meeting rooms, Microfiche/film & reading machines, Movies, Music CDs, Online cat, OverDrive digital audio bks, Photocopying/Printing, Prog for adults, Prog for children & young adult, Ref serv available, Scanner, Senior computer classes, Story hour, Summer reading prog, Wheelchair accessible
Special Services for the Blind - Bks on CD
Open Mon-Thurs 9-8, Fri 9-5, Sat 10-2 (Winter); Mon-Thurs 9-8, Fri 9-5 (Summer)
Friends of the Library Group

ESSEX

P ESSEX COUNTY LIBRARY*, Administrative Offices, 360 Fairview Ave W, Ste 101, N8M 1Y3. SAN 367-1496. Tel: 519-776-5241. FAX: 519-776-6851. Web Site: www.essexcountylibrary.ca. *Chief Librn/CEO,* Adam Craig; E-mail: acraig@essexcountylibrary.ca; *Commun Serv Mgr,* Manuela Denes; E-mail: mdenes@essexcountylibrary.ca; *IT Mgr,* Dan Henricks; *Pub Serv Mgr,* Chelsie Abraham; Staff 109 (MLS 6, Non-MLS 103)
Founded 1966. Pop 177,891; Circ 978,496
Library Holdings: CDs 21,561; DVDs 9,863; e-books 8,007; e-journals 7,355; Bk Titles 157,696; Bk Vols 321,969; Per Subs 159

Automation Activity & Vendor Info: (Acquisitions) SirsiDynix; (Cataloging) SirsiDynix; (Circulation) SirsiDynix; (OPAC) SirsiDynix
Wireless access
Special Services for the Deaf - Bks on deafness & sign lang
Branches: 14
AMHERSTBURG BRANCH, 232 Sandwich St S, Amherstburg, N9V 2A4, SAN 367-1526. Tel: 226-946-1549, Ext 240. *Supvr,* Dot Marchand
Open Mon & Tues 1-8, Wed & Thurs 10-8, Fri 10-6, Sat 10-5
COMBER BRANCH, 6400 Main St, Comber, N0P 1J0, SAN 367-1550. Tel: 226-946-1529, Ext 222. *Supvr,* Katie Nagy
Open Mon & Thurs 5-8, Tues 2:30-5:30, Sat 10-1
COTTAM BRANCH, 122 Fox St, Cottam, N0R 1B0, SAN 367-1585. Tel: 226-946-1529, Ext 212. *Supvr,* Elaine Buschman
Open Mon & Thurs 5-8, Tues 2:30-5:30, Sat 10-1
ESSEX BRANCH, 35 Gosfield Townline W, N8M 0A1, SAN 367-164X. Tel: 226-946-1529, Ext 250. *Supvr,* Cathy Humphrey
Open Mon & Tues 1-8, Wed & Thurs 10-8, Fri 10-6, Sat 10-5
HARROW BRANCH, 140 King St W, Harrow, N0R 1G0, SAN 367-1674. Tel: 226-946-1529, Ext 260. *Supvr,* Cathy Humphrey
Open Mon-Thurs 1:30-8, Sat 10-4
KINGSVILLE - HIGHLINE BRANCH, 40 Main St W, Kingsville, N9Y 1H3, SAN 367-1704. Tel: 226-946-1529, Ext 270. *Supvr,* Elaine Buschman
Open Mon & Tues 1-8, Wed & Thurs 10-8, Fri 10-6, Sat 10-5
LAKESHORE - TOLDO BRANCH, 447 Renaud Line Rd, Belle River, N0R 1A0, SAN 367-1615. Tel: 226-946-1529, Ext 280. *Supvr,* Katie Nagy
Open Mon-Thurs 1-8, Fri 10-6, Sat 10-4, Sun (Oct-May) Noon-4
LASALLE - BILL VARGA BRANCH, 5950 Malden Rd, LaSalle, N9H 1S4, SAN 367-1739. Tel: 226-946-1529, Ext 210. *Supvr,* Donna Spickett
Open Mon-Thurs 10-8, Fri 10-6, Sat 10-5, Sun (Oct-May) Noon-4
LEAMINGTON BRANCH, One John St, Leamington, N8H 1H1, SAN 378-0600. Tel: 226-946-1529, Ext 220. *Supvr,* Sue Tuck
Open Mon-Thurs 10-8, Fri 10-6, Sat 10-5, Sun (Oct-May) Noon-4
LIBRO CENTRE - WOODSLEE BRANCH, 1925 S Middle Rd, Woodslee, N0R 1V0, SAN 367-1925. Tel: 226-946-1529, Ext 231. *Supvr,* Katie Nagy
Open Mon, Wed & Thurs 5-8, Tues 2:30-5:30, Sat 10-3
MCGREGOR BRANCH, 9571 Walker Rd, McGregor, N0R 1J0, SAN 367-1798. Tel: 226-946-1529, Ext 211. *Supvr,* Cathy Humphrey
Open Mon, Wed & Thurs 5-8, Tues 2:30-5:30, Sat 10-3
RUTHVEN BRANCH, 1695 Elgin St, Ruthven, N0P 2G0, SAN 367-1828. Tel: 226-946-1529, Ext 221. *Supvr,* Elaine Buschman
Open Tues 2:30-5:30, Wed & Sat 10-1, Thurs 5-8
STONEY POINT BRANCH, 6690 Tecumseh Rd, Stoney Point, N0R 1N0, SAN 367-1887. Tel: 226-946-1529, Ext 232. *Supvr,* Gisele Levesque
TECUMSEH - CADA BRANCH, 13675 St Gregory's Rd, Tecumseh, N8N 3E4, SAN 367-1852. Tel: 226-946-1529, Ext 230. *Supvr,* Shannon McGuire
Open Mon-Thurs 10-8, Fri 10-6, Sat 10-5, Sun (Oct-May) Noon-4

S PROVERBS HERITAGE ORGANIZATION*, John Freeman Walls Historic Site & Underground Railroad Museum Library, 932 Lakeshore Rd 107, RR 3, N8M 2X7. SAN 376-0782. Tel: 519-727-6555. FAX: 519-727-5793. Web Site: www.undergroundrailroadmuseum.org. *Curator,* Dr Bryan Walls; Tel: 519-727-4866, E-mail: bryanugrr@aol.com
Library Holdings: Bk Vols 100
Restriction: Open by appt only

FERGUS

P WELLINGTON COUNTY LIBRARY*, Headquarters, 190 Saint Andrews St W, N1M 1N5. SAN 367-2271. Tel: 519-787-7805. FAX: 519-787-4608. Web Site: www.wellington.ca/en/library.aspx. *Chief Librn,* Rebecca Hine; E-mail: rebeccah@wellington.ca; *Asst Chief Librn,* Chanda Gilpin; *Libr Tech-ILLO,* Deanna Jensen; Tel: 519-846-0918, E-mail: deannaj@wellington.ca; *Cat,* Elaine Salter; Tel: 519-846-0918, Ext 6229, E-mail: elaines@wellington.ca; *Info Serv,* Jessica Zeldman; E-mail: jessicaz@wellington.ca; *Info Serv,* Laura Shtern; E-mail: lauras@wellington.ca; Staff 15 (MLS 1, Non-MLS 14)
Founded 1974
Library Holdings: Bk Vols 100,000; Per Subs 250
Wireless access
Open Mon-Fri 8:30-4:30
Branches: 14
ABOYNE, 552 Wellington Rd 18, N1M 2W3, SAN 367-2336. Tel: 519-846-0918. E-mail: aboynelib@wellington.ca. *Br Supvr,* Joyce Tenhage
Open Mon-Fri 10-8, Sat 10-5, Sun 1-5
ARTHUR BRANCH, 110 Charles St E, Arthur, N0G 1A0. (Mail add: PO Box 550, Arthur, N0G 1A0), SAN 367-2301. Tel: 519-848-3999. FAX: 519-848-6423. E-mail: arthurlib@wellington.ca. *Chief Librn,* Rebecca Hine; E-mail: rebeccah@wellington.ca
Open Tues-Thurs 10-8, Fri 10-5, Sat 10-3
CLIFFORD BRANCH, Seven Brown St N, Clifford, N0G 1M0. (Mail add: PO Box 14, Clifford, N0G 1M0), SAN 367-2360. Tel: 519-327-8328. FAX: 519-327-8345. E-mail: cliffordlib@wellington.ca. *Chief Librn,* Rebecca Hine; E-mail: rebeccah@wellington.ca
Open Tues 10-8, Wed & Thurs 2-8, Fri 10-6, Sat 10-3
DRAYTON BRANCH, 106 Wellington St S, Drayton, N0G 1P0. (Mail add: PO Box 130, Drayton, N0G 1P0), SAN 319-1087. Tel: 519-638-3788. FAX: 519-638-3881. E-mail: draytonlib@wellington.ca. *Br Supvr,* Valerie Denton; E-mail: valeried@wellington.ca
Open Mon & Fri 10-5, Tues-Thurs 10-8, Sat 10-3
ELORA BRANCH, 144 Geddes St, Elora, N0B 1S0, SAN 319-1214. Tel: 519-846-0190. FAX: 519-846-0344. E-mail: eloralib@wellington.ca. *Br Supvr,* Danielle Arial; E-mail: daniellea@wellington.ca
Open Mon, Wed & Fri 10-5, Tues & Thurs 10-8, Sat 10-3
ERIN BRANCH, 14 Boland Dr, Erin, N0B 1T0. (Mail add: PO Box 250, Erin, N0B 1TO), SAN 367-2395. Tel: 519-833-9762. E-mail: erinlib@wellington.ca. *Br Supvr,* Jeanine Morine
Open Mon-Thurs 10-8, Fri 10-5, Sat 10-3
FERGUS BRANCH, 190 St Andrew St W, N1M 1N5. Tel: 519-843-1180. FAX: 519-843-5743. E-mail: ferguslib@wellington.ca. *Br Supvr,* Rebecca Hine; E-mail: rebeccah@wellington.ca
Open Mon-Thurs 10-8, Fri 10-5, Sat 10-3
HARRISTON BRANCH, 88 Mill St, Harriston, N0G 1Z0. (Mail add: PO Box 130, Harriston, N0G 1Z0), SAN 319-163X. Tel: 519-338-2396. FAX: 519-338-5139. E-mail: harristonlib@wellington.ca. *Chief Librn,* Rebecca Hine; E-mail: rebeccah@wellington.ca
Open Mon-Thurs 10-8, Fri 10-6, Sat 10-3
HILLSBURGH BRANCH, Nine Station St, Hillsburgh, N0G 1Z0. (Mail add: PO Box 490, Hillsburgh, N0G 1Z0), SAN 319-1702. Tel: 519-855-4010. FAX: 519-855-4873. E-mail: hillsburglib@wellington.ca. *Br Supvr,* Andrew Whitefield; E-mail: andrewwh@wellington.ca
Pop 7,651; Circ 65,056
Library Holdings: Bk Vols 23,000; Per Subs 48
Mem of Ontario Library Service
Open Mon 2-5, Tues-Thurs 10-8, Fri 10-5, Sat 10-3, Sun (June-Aug) 1-5
MARDEN BRANCH, 7368 Wellington Rd 30, RR 5, Guelph, N1H 6J2. Tel: 519-763-7445. FAX: 519-763-0706. E-mail: mardenlib@wellington.ca. *Br Supvr,* Spencer Melch; E-mail: spencerm@wellington.ca
Open Mon & Wed 10-8, Tues & Thurs 2-8, Sat 10-5, Sun 1-5
MOUNT FOREST BRANCH, 118 Main St N, Mount Forest, N0G 2L0. (Mail add: PO Box 309, Mount Forest, N0G 2L0), SAN 319-2695. Tel: 519-323-4541. FAX: 519-323-0119. E-mail: mtforestlib@wellington.ca. *Chief Librn,* Rebecca Hine; E-mail: rebeccah@wellington.ca
Open Mon, Tues & Thurs 10-8, Wed & Fri 10-5, Sat 10-3
PALMERSTON BRANCH, 265 Bell St, Palmerston, N0G 2P0. (Mail add: PO Box 340, Palmerston, N0G 2P0), SAN 367-2425. Tel: 519-343-2142. FAX: 519-343-4236. E-mail: palmerstolib@wellington.ca. *Br Supvr,* Valerie Denton; E-mail: valeried.wellington.ca
Open Tues-Thurs 10-8, Fri 10-5, Sat 10-3
PUSLINCH BRANCH, 29 Brock Rd S, Puslinch, N0B 2J0, SAN 328-9850. Tel: 519-763-8026. FAX: 519-763-4122. E-mail: puslinchlib@wellington.ca. *Br Supvr,* Brittany Schauntz
Open Tues & Thurs 10-8, Fri 10-6, Sat 10-5
ROCKWOOD BRANCH, 121 Rockmosa Dr, Rockwood, N0B 2K0, SAN 319-3853. Tel: 519-856-4851. FAX: 519-856-2990. E-mail: rockwoodlib@wellington.ca. *Chief Librn,* Rebecca Hine; E-mail: rebeccah@wellington.ca
Pop 5,800; Circ 21,543
Library Holdings: Bk Vols 22,000; Per Subs 35
Open Mon-Thurs 10-8, Fri 10-5, Sat 10-4

S WELLINGTON COUNTY MUSEUM & ARCHIVES*, 0536 Wellington Rd 18, RR 1, N1M 2W3. SAN 370-5579. Tel: 519-846-0916, Ext 5225. FAX: 519-846-9630. Web Site: www.wellington.ca/museum. *Archivist,* Karen Wagner; Tel: 519-837-2600, Ext 5235, E-mail: karenw@wellington.ca; *Curator,* Hailey Johnston; E-mail: haileyj@wellington.ca; Staff 4 (MLS 4)
Founded 1976
Library Holdings: Bk Vols 2,300
Special Collections: Architecture (Couling Coll) slides; Genealogy Coll; Municipal Records, County of Wellington, bks, ledgers, film
Wireless access
Function: Archival coll, Photocopying/Printing
Publications: CIRCA (Newsletter)
Restriction: Pub use on premises

FLESHERTON

P GREY HIGHLANDS PUBLIC LIBRARY*, Flesherton Public Library, 101 Highland Dr, N0C 1E0. (Mail add: Box 280, N0C 1E0), SAN 319-1303. Tel: 519-924-2241. FAX: 519-924-2562. E-mail: fleshertonlibrary@greyhighlands.ca. Web Site: www.greyhighlandspubliclibrary.com. *Chief Exec Officer,* Wilda Allen
Founded 1908. Pop 11,000; Circ 21,000

Library Holdings: AV Mats 500; Large Print Bks 300; Bk Vols 14,000; Per Subs 50; Talking Bks 200
Subject Interests: Local hist
Automation Activity & Vendor Info: (Circulation) Koha
Wireless access
Open Tues 10-8:30, Wed & Fri 1-5, Thurs 1-5 & 6:30-8:30, Sat 9-2 (Sept-June); Tues 10-8:30, Wed & Fri 10-5, Thurs 1-5 & 6:30-8:30, Sat 9-2 (July-Aug)
Friends of the Library Group
Branches: 2
WALTER HARRIS MEMORIAL LIBRARY, 75 Walker St, Markdale, N0C 1H0. (Mail add: PO Box 499, Markdale, N0C 1H0), SAN 319-2385. Tel: 519-986-3436. FAX: 519-986-4799. E-mail: whml@greyhighlands.ca.
Founded 1915
Library Holdings: Bk Titles 22,000; Per Subs 47
Subject Interests: Local hist
Open Tues, Wed & Fri 10-5:30, Thurs 1-8:30, Sat 10-3:30
Friends of the Library Group
KIMBERLEY PUBLIC LIBRARY, Kimberley Memorial Hall, 235309 Grey Rd 13, Kimberley, N0C 1G0, SAN 319-1877. Tel: 519-599-6990. FAX: 519-599-6146. E-mail: kimberleylibrary@greyhighlands.ca.
Founded 1896
Library Holdings: Bk Titles 8,000
Open Tues 1-5, Thurs & Sat 10-2
Friends of the Library Group

FONTHILL

P PELHAM PUBLIC LIBRARY*, 43 Pelham Town Sq, L0S 1E0. (Mail add: PO Box 830, L0S 1E0), SAN 319-132X. Tel: 905-892-6443. FAX: 905-892-3392. Administration E-mail: admin@pelhamlibrary.on.ca. Web Site: www.pelhamlibrary.on.ca. *Dep Chief Exec Officer,* Amy Guilmette; E-mail: aguilmette@pelhamlibrary.on.ca
Founded 1852. Pop 17,110; Circ 171,372
Library Holdings: Bk Vols 58,000
Automation Activity & Vendor Info: (Cataloging) Evergreen; (Circulation) Evergreen; (OPAC) Evergreen
Wireless access
Function: 24/7 Electronic res, 24/7 Online cat, Activity rm, Adult literacy prog, Art exhibits, Audiobks via web, Bk club(s), Children's prog, Computers for patron use, E-Readers, Electronic databases & coll, Govt ref serv, Homebound delivery serv, Homework prog, ILL available, Life-long learning prog for all ages, Magazines, Meeting rooms, Movies, Online cat, Outreach serv, OverDrive digital audio bks, Photocopying/Printing, Preschool outreach, Preschool reading prog, Printer for laptops & handheld devices, Prog for adults, Prog for children & young adult, Ref & res, Ref serv available, Scanner, Senior computer classes, Senior outreach, Serves people with intellectual disabilities, Story hour, Study rm, Summer reading prog, Teen prog
Open Mon, Tues & Thurs 10-8, Wed & Fri 10-5, Sat 1-5
Friends of the Library Group
Branches: 1
MAPLE ACRE, 781 Canboro Rd, Fenwick, L0S 1C0. (Mail add: PO Box 294, Fenwick, L0S 1C0), SAN 376-8171. Tel: 905-892-5226.
Open Tues & Fri 11-5, Wed 11-8, Thurs 11-7, Sat 9-12
Friends of the Library Group

FORESTERS FALLS

P WHITEWATER REGION PUBLIC LIBRARY*, Foresters Falls Branch, 2022 Foresters Fall Rd, K0J 1V0. (Mail add: PO Box 69, K0J 1V0), SAN 319-1338. Tel: 613-646-2543. E-mail: fflib@nrtco.net. Web Site: libraries.whitewaterregion.ca. *Br Librn,* Debbie Byce; E-mail: debbiebyce@yahoo.ca
Pop 1,700; Circ 2,450
Library Holdings: Bk Vols 6,000; Per Subs 13
Wireless access
Open Tues 2-8, Thurs 3-8, Sat 9-12

FORT ERIE

P FORT ERIE PUBLIC LIBRARY*, Centennial Library, 136 Gilmore Rd, L2A 2M1. SAN 367-245X. Tel: 905-871-2546. Web Site: www.fepl.ca. *Chief Exec Officer,* Craig Shufelt; Tel: 905-871-2546, Ext 303, E-mail: cshufelt@fepl.ca; *Ad,* Sean Fleming; Tel: 905-871-2546, Ext 304, E-mail: sfleming@fepl.ca; *Children & Teen Librn,* Karissa Fast; Tel: 905-871-2546, Ext 306, E-mail: kfast@fepl.ca; *Syst Adminr,* Michael Schell; Tel: 905-871-2546, Ext 301, E-mail: mschell@fepl.ca; *Bus Mgr,* Maria Brigantino; Tel: 905-871-2546, Ext 307, E-mail: mbrigantino@fepl.ca; Staff 22 (MLS 3, Non-MLS 19)
Founded 1891. Pop 28,300; Circ 20,000
Library Holdings: Bk Vols 56,000; Per Subs 71
Subject Interests: Local hist
Wireless access
Open Mon-Wed 9:30-9, Thurs 1-9, Fri 9:30-5, Sat 10-5
Branches: 2
CRYSTAL RIDGE, 89 Ridge Rd S, Ridgeway, L0S 1N0, SAN 367-2484. Tel: 905-894-1281. *Br Serv Coordr,* Dawn Gangarossa; Tel: 905-871-2546 x310, E-mail: dgangarossa@fepl.ca
Library Holdings: Bk Vols 28,000; Per Subs 36
Open Mon-Wed 9:30-9, Thurs 1-9, Fri 1-5, Sat 10-5
Friends of the Library Group
STEVENSVILLE BRANCH, 2508 Stevensville Rd, Stevensville, L0S 1S0, SAN 367-2549. Tel: 905-382-2051. *Br Head,* Deborah Ashworth; E-mail: dashworth@fepl.ca
Library Holdings: Bk Vols 11,000; Per Subs 23
Open Mon 10:30-3, Tues & Thurs 1:30-6, Wed 3:30-8, Sat 12:30-5
Friends of the Library Group

FORT FRANCES

P FORT FRANCES PUBLIC LIBRARY TECHNOLOGY CENTRE*, 601 Reid Ave, P9A 0A2. SAN 319-1354. Tel: 807-274-9879. FAX: 807-274-4496. E-mail: ffpltc@gmail.com. Web Site: ffpltc.ca.
Founded 1914. Pop 8,200; Circ 157,000
Library Holdings: Bk Vols 54,000; Per Subs 143
Automation Activity & Vendor Info: (Acquisitions) SirsiDynix
Friends of the Library Group

S UNITED NATIVE FRIENDSHIP CENTRE*, Literacy Department Library, 516 Portage Ave, P9A 3N1. (Mail add: PO Box 752, P9A 3N1), SAN 373-7578. Tel: 807-274-8541. FAX: 807-274-4110. E-mail: inquiry@unfc.org. Web Site: www.unfc.org. *Exec Dir,* Sheila McMahon; E-mail: smcmahon@unfc.org; Staff 2 (MLS 2)
Library Holdings: Bk Titles 400; Per Subs 50
Special Services for the Deaf - High interest/low vocabulary bks
Open Mon-Fri 8:30-4:30

GANANOQUE

P GANANOQUE PUBLIC LIBRARY*, 100 Park St, K7G 2Y5. SAN 319-1370. Tel: 613-382-2436. E-mail: gplp@bellnet.ca. Web Site: www.gananoquelibrary.ca. *Chief Exec Officer, Librn,* Deirdre Crichton
Pop 5,000; Circ 39,400
Library Holdings: Bk Titles 19,000; Bk Vols 19,500; Per Subs 40
Special Collections: Gananoque History Coll
Wireless access
Open Tues, Thurs & Fri 10-4, Wed 10-7, Sat 10-2

GEORGETOWN

P HALTON HILLS PUBLIC LIBRARY*, Nine Church St, L7G 2A3. SAN 367-2573. Tel: 905-873-2681. FAX: 905-873-6118. E-mail: askus@haltonhills.ca. Web Site: www.hhpl.on.ca. *Chief Librn,* Melanie Southern; Tel: 905-873-2681, Ext 2513; *Supvr,* Sherry Farago; Staff 6 (MLS 6)
Founded 1880. Pop 60,000; Circ 490,000
Special Collections: Local Hist
Automation Activity & Vendor Info: (Acquisitions) SirsiDynix; (Cataloging) SirsiDynix; (Circulation) SirsiDynix; (OPAC) SirsiDynix
Wireless access
Publications: Index to Births, Marriage, Deaths for Georgetown Herald, Acton Free Press, Canadian Champion Newspapers
Partic in Halinet
Open Mon 1-8:30, Tues & Thurs 9:30-8:30, Fri & Sat 9:30-5, Sun (Oct-May) 1-5
Friends of the Library Group
Branches: 1
ACTON BRANCH, 17 River St, Acton, L7J 1C2, SAN 367-2603. Tel: 519-853-0301. FAX: 519-853-3110. *Supvr,* Alison Crawley; Tel: 905-873-2681, Ext 2551
Open Tues-Thurs 9:30-8:30, Fri & Sat 9:30-5, Sun 1-5
Friends of the Library Group

GERALDTON

P GREENSTONE PUBLIC LIBRARY*, Geraldton (Main Library), 405 Second St W, P0T 1M0. (Mail add: PO Box 40, P0T 1M0), SAN 319-1397. Tel: 807-854-1490. Administration Tel: 807-854-2421. FAX: 807-854-2351. Administration FAX: 807-854-2421. E-mail: greenlibger@gmail.com. Web Site: www.greenstone.ca/content/greenstone-public-library. *Chief Exec Officer,* Mari Mannisto; *Br Librn,* Maria Smith
Founded 1947. Pop 5,600; Circ 33,662
Library Holdings: Bk Titles 25,000; Bk Vols 30,000; Per Subs 25
Wireless access
Partic in Can Libr Asn; Ont Libr Asn
Open Mon & Wed 1-5 & 7-9, Tues, Thurs & Sat 1-5

Branches: 3
BEARDMORE BRANCH, 285 Main St, Beardmore, P0T 1G0. (Mail add: PO Box 240, Beardmore, P0T 1G0), SAN 319-0447. Tel: 807-875-2212. FAX: 807-875-2618. *Br Mgr,* Kim Brunet
Pop 360; Circ 3,091
Library Holdings: Bk Titles 10,700
Subject Interests: Canadiana
Open Mon & Wed 6pm-9pm, Tues 12:30-4, Thurs 6:30-9
LONGLAC BRANCH, 110 Kenogami Rd, Longlac, P0T 2A0, SAN 319-2296. Tel: 807-876-4515. FAX: 807-876-4886. *Br Mgr,* Nicole Belisle
Founded 1955
Library Holdings: Bk Vols 24,965; Per Subs 15
Open Mon 12:30-4:30 & 6:30-8:30, Tues 1-5, Wed 9-12, Thurs 1-5 & 7-9, Sat 9-12
NAKINA BRANCH, 216 North St, Nakina, P0T 2H0. (Mail add: PO Box 300, Nakina, P0T 2H0), SAN 319-2709. Tel: 807-329-5906. FAX: 807-329-5984. *Br Librn,* Jade Antonson
Pop 650; Circ 9,000
Library Holdings: Bk Vols 16,500; Per Subs 20
Open Mon & Wed 1-4, Tues & Thurs 6:30pm-8:30pm

GODERICH

L HURON LAW ASSOCIATION*, Huron County Courthouse Library, One Courthouse, 3rd Flr, N7A 1M2. SAN 325-1373. Tel: 519-524-7962. FAX: 519-524-1065. E-mail: huronlaw@hurontel.on.ca. *Librn,* Barb Alcook
Library Holdings: Bk Vols 7,800
Special Collections: Canadian Statutes back to 1852
Restriction: Staff & mem only

GORE BAY

P GORE BAY UNION PUBLIC LIBRARY*, 15 Water St, P0P 1H0. (Mail add: PO Box 225, P0P 1H0), SAN 319-1419. Tel: 705-282-2221. FAX: 705-282-2221. E-mail: gorebaylibrary@gorebaycable.com. Web Site: gorebayunionpubliclibrary.ca, www.gorebay.ca/discover/library. *Chief Librn,* Johanna Allison
Pop 900; Circ 12,721
Library Holdings: Bk Titles 35,020; Per Subs 4
Wireless access
Open Mon & Tues 2-5, Thurs 2-8, Fri 10-1 & 2-5, Sat 10-1

GRAND VALLEY

P GRAND VALLEY PUBLIC LIBRARY*, Four Amaranth St E, L9W 5L2. SAN 319-1435. Tel: 519-928-5622. FAX: 519-928-2586. E-mail: gvpl_info@townofgrandvalley.ca. Web Site: www.townofgrandvalley.ca/en/library-landing.aspx. *Chief Exec Officer,* Joanne Stevenson
Founded 1913. Pop 2,100; Circ 40,000
Automation Activity & Vendor Info: (Cataloging) Koha; (Circulation) Koha; (OPAC) Koha
Wireless access
Mem of Ontario Library Service
Open Mon, Tues, Thurs & Fri 10-6, Wed 10-8, Sat 10-4

GRAVENHURST

P GRAVENHURST PUBLIC LIBRARY*, 180 Sharpe St W, P1P 1J1. SAN 319-1443. Tel: 705-687-3382. FAX: 705-687-7016. E-mail: library@gravenhurst.ca. Web Site: www.gravenhurst.ca/en/library/library.asp. *Chief Librn/CEO,* Julia Reinhart; Staff 6.6 (MLS 1, Non-MLS 5.6)
Pop 12,125; Circ 47,906
Library Holdings: Bk Vols 45,791; Per Subs 41
Automation Activity & Vendor Info: (Cataloging) SirsiDynix; (Circulation) SirsiDynix; (OPAC) SirsiDynix
Wireless access
Mem of Ontario Library Service
Open Mon & Fri 10-5, Tues-Thurs 10-8, Sat 10-4

GRIMSBY

P GRIMSBY PUBLIC LIBRARY*, 18 Carnegie Lane, L3M 1Y1. SAN 319-1451. Tel: 905-945-5142. Web Site: www.grimsby.ca/en/parks-recreation-culture/library.aspx. *Chief Librn,* Ashleigh Whipp; E-mail: awhipp@grimsbylibrary.ca; Staff 15 (MLS 2, Non-MLS 13)
Founded 1871. Pop 27,314; Circ 104,347
Library Holdings: AV Mats 10; Bk Vols 50,000; Per Subs 100
Wireless access
Function: 24/7 Electronic res, 24/7 Online cat, 3D Printer, Activity rm, Adult bk club, Art exhibits, Audio & video playback equip for onsite use, Audiobks via web, AV serv, Bk club(s), Bks on CD, Chess club, Children's prog, Computer training, Computers for patron use, Digital talking bks, Family literacy, For res purposes, Free DVD rentals, Holiday prog, Home delivery & serv to seniorr ctr & nursing homes, Homebound delivery serv, ILL available, Internet access, Life-long learning prog for all ages, Literacy & newcomer serv, Magazines, Makerspace, Mango lang, Microfiche/film & reading machines, Movies, Online cat, Online ref, Outreach serv, Photocopying/Printing, Preschool reading prog, Printer for laptops & handheld devices, Prog for adults, Prog for children & young adult, Ref & res, Ref serv available, Scanner, Senior outreach, Story hour, Summer reading prog, Teen prog, Wheelchair accessible, Workshops
Open Mon-Thurs 9-9, Fri & Sat 9-5, Sun 1-5 (Sept-June); Mon-Thurs 9-8, Fri & Sat 9-5 (July-Aug)

GUELPH

S FARM & FOOD CARE ONTARIO LIBRARY*, 660 Speedvale Ave W, Unit 302, N1K 1E5. SAN 373-6792. Tel: 519-837-1326. FAX: 519-837-3209. E-mail: info@farmfoodcare.org. Web Site: www.farmfoodcare.org. *Exec Dir,* Kelly Daynard
Founded 1988
Library Holdings: Bk Titles 50; Per Subs 20
Wireless access
Publications: Food for Thought (Booklet & video)

P GUELPH PUBLIC LIBRARY*, 100 Norfolk St, N1H 4J6. SAN 319-146X. Tel: 519-824-6220. FAX: 519-824-8342. E-mail: askus@guelphpl.ca. Web Site: www.guelphpl.ca. *Chief Exec Officer,* Steven Kraft; Tel: 519-824-6220, Ext 224, E-mail: skraft@guelphpl.ca; *Dir, Operations,* Dan Atkins; Tel: 519-824-6220, Ext 313, E-mail: datkins@guelphpl.ca; *Prog Coordr,* Andrea Curtis; Tel: 519-824-6220, Ext 263, E-mail: acurtis@guelphpl.ca; *Children & Teen Librn,* Ben Robinson; Tel: 519-824-6220, Ext 277, E-mail: brobinson@guelphpl.ca; *ILL,* Deb Quaile; Tel: 519-824-6220, Ext 261, E-mail: dquaile@guelphpl.ca; *E-Librn,* Meg Forestell-Page; Tel: 519-824-6220, Ext 306, E-mail: mforestell@guelphpl.ca; Staff 42 (MLS 13, Non-MLS 29)
Founded 1883. Pop 100,000; Circ 1,200,000
Library Holdings: AV Mats 16,400; e-books 3,400; High Interest/Low Vocabulary Bk Vols 120; Large Print Bks 7,000; Bk Titles 195,700; Bk Vols 300,650; Per Subs 185; Talking Bks 1,500
Special Collections: Can & Prov
Subject Interests: Local hist
Automation Activity & Vendor Info: (Acquisitions) Innovative Interfaces, Inc; (Cataloging) Innovative Interfaces, Inc; (Circulation) Innovative Interfaces, Inc
Wireless access
Special Services for the Blind - Assistive/Adapted tech devices, equip & products; Bks on CD; Daisy reader; Home delivery serv; Large print bks; Magnifiers; Playaways (bks on MP3); Talking bks; ZoomText magnification & reading software
Open Mon-Thurs 9-9, Fri & Sat 9-5, Sun 1-5 (Sept-May); Mon-Thurs 9-8, Fri & Sat 9-5 (June-Aug)
Friends of the Library Group
Branches: 5
BULLFROG MALL BRANCH, 380 Eramosa Rd, N1E 6R2. Tel: 519-829-4401. *Br Supvr,* Eleni Hughes; E-mail: ehughes@guelphpl.ca
Open Mon-Thurs 9-8, Fri & Sat 9-5, Sun (Winter) 1-5
Friends of the Library Group
EAST SIDE BRANCH, One Starwood Dr, N1E 0H5. Tel: 519-829-4405. *Br Supvr,* April Norcross-Love; E-mail: anorcross@guelphpl.ca
Open Mon-Fri 10-8, Sat 9-5, Sun (Winter) 1-5
SCOTTSDALE CENTRE BRANCH, 650 Scottsdale Dr, N1G 3M2. Tel: 519-829-4402. *Br Supvr,* Christy Giesler; E-mail: cgiesler@guelphpl.ca
Open Mon-Fri 10-8, Sun (Winter) 1-5
WEST END BRANCH, 21 Imperial Rd S, N1K 1X3. Tel: 519-829-4403. *Br Supvr,* Christopher Raso; E-mail: craso@guelphpl.ca
Open Mon-Fri 10-9, Sat 9-5, Sun 1-5
WESTMINSTER SQUARE BRANCH, 100-31 Farley Dr, N1L 0B7. Tel: 519-829-4404. *Br Supvr,* Michelle Campbell; E-mail: mcampbell@guelphpl.ca
Open Mon-Fri 10-8, Sat 9-5, Sun (Winter) 1-5
Bookmobiles: 1

S OPIRG GUELPH RADICAL RESOURCE LIBRARY*, University of Guelph, 24 Trent Lane, N1G 2W1. SAN 325-6014. Tel: 519-824-2091. FAX: 519-824-8990. E-mail: opirg@uoguelph.ca. Web Site: www.opirgguelph.org. *Library Contact,* Bradley Evoy; E-mail: organizational@opirgguelph.org; Staff 1 (Non-MLS 1)
Founded 1976
Library Holdings: AV Mats 50; Bk Titles 1,500; Per Subs 20; Spec Interest Per Sub 10
Special Collections: Radical Zine Archive
Wireless access
Function: 24/7 Online cat, Adult bk club, AV serv, Bus archives, Computers for patron use, Electronic databases & coll, For res purposes, Free DVD rentals, ILL available, Magazines, Meeting rooms, Orientations, Photocopying/Printing, Res libr, Spoken cassettes & CDs, Workshops

Special Services for the Blind - Bks on CD
Open Mon-Thurs 11-5
Restriction: Circ to mem only, Limited access for the pub, Mem only, Open to pub for ref & circ; with some limitations

C UNIVERSITY OF GUELPH*, McLaughlin Library, 50 Stone Rd E, N1G 2W1. SAN 319-1508. Tel: 519-824-4120, Ext 53617. Reference Tel: 519-824-4120, Ext 53618. FAX: 519-824-6931. E-mail: library@uoguelph.ca. Web Site: www.lib.uoguelph.ca. *Interim Univ Librn,* Amanda Etches; *Dir, Admin Serv,* Kelly Bertrand; Tel: 519-824-4120, Ext 53359, E-mail: kbertran@uoguelph.ca; *Librn, Colls & Content,* Helen Salmon; Tel: 519-824-4120, Ext 52121, E-mail: hsalmon@uoguelph.ca; Staff 36 (MLS 28, Non-MLS 8)
Founded 1968. Enrl 14,300; Fac 939; Highest Degree: Doctorate
Library Holdings: e-journals 65,000; Bk Vols 1,000,250; Per Subs 7,609
Special Collections: Agricultural Government Publications from many countries; Agricultural History; Apiculture; Early Canadian Travel Coll; Family Studies; FAO, Can & Prov, ERIC; Guelph Spring Festival; Landscape Architecture; Literary & Theatre Archives (Blyth Festival, Black Theatre Canada, Factory Theatre, NDWT, LM Montgomery, Pheonix Theatre, Shaw Festival Theatre, Theatre Columbus, Theatre Francais de Toronto, Le Theatre du P'tit Bonheur, Theatre Passe Maraille, Tarragon Theatre, Theatre of Toronto, Toronto Free Theatre, Toronto Workshop Production, Young People's & Open Circle Theatre of Toronto); National Board Archives; Scottish Studies; Upper Canada History
Subject Interests: Agr, Biol sci, Consumer studies, Environ sci, Family studies, Food admin, Hotel, Veterinary med
Automation Activity & Vendor Info: (Acquisitions) Ex Libris Group; (Cataloging) Ex Libris Group; (Circulation) Ex Libris Group; (Course Reserve) Ex Libris Group; (ILL) Ex Libris Group; (Media Booking) Ex Libris Group; (OPAC) Ex Libris Group; (Serials) Ex Libris Group
Wireless access
Publications: Bernard Shaw on Stage; Bibliography Series; Collection Update; Shaw Festival Production Record; Technical Report Series; Theater Archives
Partic in Association of Research Libraries; Canadian Association of Research Libraries; Ontario Council of University Libraries
Departmental Libraries:
STUDENT ACCESSIBILITY SERVICES, University Centre, Level 2, 50 Stone Rd E, N1G 2W1. Tel: 519-824-4120, Ext 56208. FAX: 519-824-9689. E-mail: lasd@uoguelph.ca. *Mgr,* Athol Gow; Tel: 519-824-1420, Ext 52312, E-mail: agow@uogueph.ca
Open Mon-Fri 8:30-4:30

S UPPER GRAND DISTRICT SCHOOL BOARD*, Terry James Resource Library, 500 Victoria Rd N, N1E 6K2. SAN 329-9732. Tel: 519-822-4420, Ext 554. E-mail: terryjames.library@ugdsb.on.ca. Web Site: sites.google.com/ugcloud.ca/terryjamesresourcecentre. *Media Serv, Supvr,* Lauren Bull; E-mail: lauren.bull@ugdsb.on.ca. Subject Specialists: *Educ, Info studies, Libr,* Lauren Bull; Staff 10 (MLS 1, Non-MLS 9)
Founded 1972
Subject Interests: Spec educ
Automation Activity & Vendor Info: (Cataloging) Insignia Software; (Circulation) Insignia Software; (Media Booking) Insignia Software; (OPAC) Insignia Software
Wireless access
Publications: Bibliographies
Restriction: Open to staff only

L WELLINGTON LAW ASSOCIATION LIBRARY*, Court House, 74 Woolwich St, N1H 3T9. SAN 328-0160. Tel: 519-763-6365. E-mail: lawlibwell@gmail.com. Web Site: wellingtonlaw.org. *Librn,* John Eddie Kerr
Library Holdings: Bk Vols 6,000
Open Mon-Thurs 9:30-2:30

HALIBURTON

P HALIBURTON COUNTY PUBLIC LIBRARY*, Administrative Ctr, 78 Maple Ave, K0M 1S0. (Mail add: PO Box 119, K0M 1S0), SAN 319-1524. Tel: 705-457-2241. FAX: 705-457-9586. E-mail: info@haliburtonlibrary.ca. Web Site: olco.ent.sirsidynix.net/client/en_US/haliburton. *Br Serv Librn, Dep Chief Exec Officer,* Erin Kernohan-Berning; E-mail: ekernohan@haliburtonlibrary.ca; *Coll Develop Coordr,* Sherrill Sherwood; E-mail: ssherwood@haliburtonlibary.ca; Staff 5 (MLS 2, Non-MLS 3)
Founded 1965. Pop 16,000; Circ 100,746
Library Holdings: Audiobooks 1,149; DVDs 2,814; Large Print Bks 2,214; Bk Vols 474,811; Per Subs 42
Automation Activity & Vendor Info: (Acquisitions) SirsiDynix-WorkFlows; (Cataloging) SirsiDynix-WorkFlows; (Circulation) SirsiDynix-WorkFlows; (ILL) SirsiDynix-WorkFlows; (OPAC) SirsiDynix-WorkFlows
Wireless access
Mem of Ontario Library Service
Partic in Ontario Library Consortium
Open Mon-Fri 8:30-4:30
Friends of the Library Group
Branches: 7
CARDIFF BRANCH, 2778 Monck Rd, Cardiff, K0L 1M0. Tel: 613-339-2712. *Supvr,* Cathy Passaretti; E-mail: cpassaretti@haliburtonlibrary.ca
Open Tues 2-6, Wed 6:30-8:30, Fri & Sat 10-Noon
DYSART BRANCH, 78 Maple Ave, K0M 1S0. Tel: 705-457-1791. *Supvr,* Victoria Fraser; E-mail: vfraser@haliburtonlibrary.ca
Open Tues-Thurs 1:30-6, Fri & Sat 10-2:30
GOODERHAM BRANCH, 1032 Gooderham St, Gooderham, K0M 1R0. Tel: 705-447-3163. *Supvr,* Marilyn Billings; E-mail: mbillings@haliburtonlibrary.ca
Open Tues 6pm-8pm, Wed & Thurs 1-4, Sat 10-Noon
HIGHLAND GROVE BRANCH, 5373 Loop Rd, Highland Grove, K0L 2A0. Tel: 705-448-2652. *Supvr,* Tessa Iles; E-mail: tiles@haliburtonlibrary.ca
Open Tues & Sat 12-3:30, Thurs 6:30pm-8:30pm
MINDEN HILLS BRANCH, 176 Bobcaygeon Rd, Minden, K0M 2K0. Tel: 705-286-2491. *Supvr,* Margaret Graham; E-mail: mgraham@haliburtonlibrary.ca
Open Tues-Thurs 10:30-6, Fri & Sat 10-2:30
STANHOPE BRANCH, 1109 N Shore Rd, Algonquin Highlands, K0M 1J0. Tel: 705-489-2402. *Supvr,* Gayle Wetmore; E-mail: gwetmore@haliburtonlibrary.ca
Open Tues 12-2 & 6-9, Wed 10-2, Thurs & Sat 10-Noon
WILBERFORCE BRANCH, 1101 Holmes Rd, Wilberforce, K0L 3C0. Tel: 705-448-2510. *Supvr,* Tessa Iles
Open Tues, Thurs & Sat 10-2:30

HAMILTON

S ART GALLERY OF HAMILTON*, Muriel Bostwick Library, 123 King St W, L8P 4S8. SAN 325-6359. Tel: 905-527-6610. FAX: 905-577-6940. E-mail: info@artgalleryofhamilton.com. Web Site: www.artgalleryofhamilton.com/collections/library. *Pres & Chief Exec Officer,* Shelly Falconer; E-mail: shelley@artgalleryofhamilton.com; *Chief Curator, Dir, Exhibitions & Coll,* Tobi Bruce; E-mail: tobi@artgalleryofhamilton.com; *Colls Mgr,* Christine Braun; E-mail: christine@artgalleryofhamilton.com; *Sr Curator,* Melissa Bennett; E-mail: melissa@artgalleryofhamilton.com
Library Holdings: Bk Vols 1,200
Wireless access

R CANADIAN BAPTIST ARCHIVES*, McMaster Divinity College, 1280 Main St W, L8S 4K1. SAN 319-1532. Tel: 905-525-9140, Ext 23511. FAX: 905-577-4782. E-mail: cbarch@mcmaster.ca. Web Site: mcmasterdivinity.ca/canadian-baptist-archives. *Archives Dir,* Dr Gordon Heath; Tel: 905-525-9140, Ext 26409, E-mail: gheath@mcmaster.ca; *Archivist,* Adam McCulloch; E-mail: amccull@mcmaster.ca
Founded 1865
Special Collections: Brethren Coll; C H Spurgeon Coll; French Canadian Protestant Coll; John Milton Society for the Blind in Canada Coll; McMaster University Coll (to 1957)
Subject Interests: Biographies of ministers, Bks about Baptists, Bks by Baptists, Can Baptist Church life, Doctrine, Educ work, Hist, Lay leaders
Restriction: Open by appt only

G CANADIAN CENTRE FOR OCCUPATIONAL HEALTH & SAFETY*, P K Abeytunga Resource Centre, 135 Hunter St E, L8N 1M5. SAN 321-9054. Tel: 905-572-2981, Ext 4454. FAX: 905-572-4500. E-mail: docdel@ccohs.ca. Web Site: www.ccohs.ca. *Supvr,* Janice Carey; Staff 1 (Non-MLS 1)
Founded 1981
Library Holdings: AV Mats 250; CDs 186; DVDs 135; e-journals 17; Electronic Media & Resources 150; Microforms 301,700; Bk Titles 35,000; Bk Vols 67,000; Per Subs 45; Spec Interest Per Sub 42; Videos 190
Special Collections: CIS Occupational Health & Safety (Switzerland), microfiche 1969-1998, CDs 1999-2014; NIOSHtic (United States), microfiche 1971-1998; Occupational Health & Safety (Canadiana), 1990-present; OSHline® Journals 1999-2007. Canadian and Provincial
Subject Interests: Occupational health, Occupational safety
Automation Activity & Vendor Info: (Acquisitions) EBSCO Online; (Cataloging) FileMaker; (Circulation) FileMaker; (ILL) Amicus; (Serials) Inmagic, Inc.
Publications: Canadiana; CIS; OSHline
Open Mon-Fri 8:30-5
Restriction: Restricted loan policy

CR CANADIAN REFORMED THEOLOGICAL SEMINARY LIBRARY, 110 W 27th St, L9C 5A1. Tel: 905-575-3688. FAX: 905-575-0799. Web Site: www.canadianreformedseminary.ca. *Librn,* Margaret Alkema; Tel: 905-575-3688, Ext 28, E-mail: malkema@crts.ca; Staff 1 (MLS 1)

Founded 1969. Enrl 30; Fac 5; Highest Degree: Master
Library Holdings: Bk Vols 35,592
Special Collections: 16th Century Books
Subject Interests: Calvinism, Church hist
Automation Activity & Vendor Info: (Acquisitions) Innovative Interfaces, Inc; (Cataloging) Innovative Interfaces, Inc; (Circulation) Innovative Interfaces, Inc; (Course Reserve) Innovative Interfaces, Inc; (OPAC) Innovative Interfaces, Inc; (Serials) Innovative Interfaces, Inc
Wireless access
Function: 24/7 Electronic res, 24/7 Online cat, 24/7 wireless access
Partic in Christian Library Consortium
Open Mon-Fri 8:30-4:30
Restriction: Use of others with permission of librn

M HAMILTON HEALTH SCIENCES LIBRARY SERVICES*, 293 Wellington St N, Ste 125, L8L 8E7. SAN 319-1559. Tel: 905-527-4322. FAX: 905-527-8458. E-mail: libraryg@hhsc.ca. Web Site: www.hamiltonhealthsciences.ca.
Founded 1931
Library Holdings: Bk Vols 3,500; Per Subs 135
Subject Interests: Cardiology, Neurology, Nursing, Nutrition, Rehabilitation, Trauma
Open Mon-Fri 9-4
Restriction: Staff use only

L HAMILTON LAW ASSOCIATION, Anthony Pepe Memorial Law Library, John Sopinka Courthouse, 45 Main St E, Ste 500, L8N 2B7. SAN 319-1567. Tel: 905-522-1563. FAX: 905-572-1188. E-mail: reference@hamiltonlaw.on.ca. Web Site: www.hamiltonlaw.on.ca. Staff 3 (MLS 1, Non-MLS 2)
Founded 1879
Library Holdings: Bk Vols 28,000
Automation Activity & Vendor Info: (OPAC) Ex Libris Group
Wireless access
Publications: Members' Handbook; News Magazine: The HLA Journal (Bimonthly)
Open Mon-Fri 8-4
Restriction: Pub by appt only

P HAMILTON PUBLIC LIBRARY*, 55 York Blvd, L8R 3K1. (Mail add: PO Box 2700, L8N 4E4), SAN 367-3537. Tel: 905-546-3200. FAX: 905-546-3202. Web Site: www.hpl.ca. *Chief Librn/CEO,* Paul Takala; Tel: 905-546-3200, Ext 3215, E-mail: ptakala@hpl.ca; *Dir, Pub Serv,* Dawna Wark; Tel: 905-546-3200, Ext 3285, E-mail: dwark@hpl.ca; *Dir, Finance & Fac,* Tony Del Monaco; Tel: 905-546-3200, Ext 3226, E-mail: tdelmona@hpl.ca; *Dir, Human Res,* Lisa Dupelle; Tel: 905-546-3200, Ext 3290, E-mail: ldupelle@hpl.ca; Staff 255 (MLS 38, Non-MLS 217)
Founded 1889. Pop 535,234; Circ 6,980,582
Special Collections: Canadiana, bks, micro; Local History (Hamilton), bks, micro; Rare Books (incl Cummer, Lyle, Mullin & Witton Colls); Resource Center for Disabled Persons; War of 1812, bks & maps
Subject Interests: Fiction, Fine arts, Soc sci
Automation Activity & Vendor Info: (Acquisitions) Innovative Interfaces, Inc; (Cataloging) Innovative Interfaces, Inc; (Circulation) Innovative Interfaces, Inc; (Discovery) EBSCO Discovery Service
Wireless access
Function: Adult bk club, Adult literacy prog, Archival coll, Art exhibits, Audio & video playback equip for onsite use, Audiobks via web, Bk club(s), Bk reviews (Group), Bks on CD, Children's prog, Citizenship assistance, Computer training, Computers for patron use, Digital talking bks, E-Reserves, Electronic databases & coll, Equip loans & repairs, Free DVD rentals, Health sci info serv, Home delivery & serv to seniorr ctr & nursing homes, Homebound delivery serv, Homework prog, ILL available, Internet access, Learning ctr, Literacy & newcomer serv, Magnifiers for reading, Microfiche/film & reading machines, Music CDs, Online cat, Online ref, Orientations, Outreach serv, OverDrive digital audio bks, Photocopying/Printing, Prog for adults, Prog for children & young adult, Ref serv available, Senior computer classes, Senior outreach, Story hour, Summer reading prog, Teen prog, Telephone ref, Wheelchair accessible
Publications: What's Happening (Newsletter)
Mem of Ontario Library Service
Open Mon-Thurs 9-9, Fri 9-6, Sat 9-5, Sun 1-5
Friends of the Library Group
Branches: 21
ANCASTER, 300 Wilson St E, Ancaster, L9G 2B9, SAN 367-4258. Tel: 905-648-6911. *Br Mgr,* Leslie Muirhead; Tel: 905-546-3200, Ext 3463, E-mail: lmuirhead@hpl.ca
Circ 370,291
Function: Adult bk club, Audiobks via web, Bks on CD, Children's prog, Computer training, Computers for patron use, E-Reserves, Electronic databases & coll, Free DVD rentals, ILL available, Music CDs, Online cat, OverDrive digital audio bks, Photocopying/Printing, Preschool outreach, Prog for adults, Prog for children & young adult, Ref serv available, Story hour, Summer reading prog, Teen prog, Wheelchair accessible
Open Mon-Thurs 10-9, Sat 10-5
Friends of the Library Group
BARTON, 571 Barton St E, L8L 2Z4, SAN 367-3561. Tel: 905-546-3450. *Br Mgr,* Carol Wilkinson; Tel: 905-546-3200, Ext 3452, E-mail: cwilkins@hpl.ca
Circ 151,732
Function: Adult bk club, Children's prog, Computers for patron use, E-Reserves, Electronic databases & coll, Free DVD rentals, ILL available, OverDrive digital audio bks, Photocopying/Printing, Prog for adults, Prog for children & young adult, Ref serv available, Story hour, Summer reading prog, Teen prog, Wheelchair accessible
Open Mon & Wed 1-8, Tues, Thurs & Sat 10-5, Fri 10-6
Friends of the Library Group
BINBROOK BRANCH, 2641 Hwy 56, Binbrook, L0R 1C0. (Mail add: PO Box 89, Binbrook, L0R 1C0), SAN 367-4282. Tel: 905-692-3323. *Br Mgr,* Caitlin Fralick; Tel: 905-546-3200, Ext 1022, E-mail: cfralick@hpl.ca
Circ 83,299
Function: Audiobks via web, Bks on CD, Children's prog, Computers for patron use, Electronic databases & coll, Free DVD rentals, ILL available, Music CDs, Online cat, OverDrive digital audio bks, Photocopying/Printing, Prog for adults, Prog for children & young adult, Ref serv available, Story hour, Summer reading prog, Teen prog, Wheelchair accessible
Open Mon & Wed 10-8, Tues, Thurs & Fri 10-6, Sat 10-5
Friends of the Library Group
CARLISLE BRANCH, 1496 Centre Rd, Carlisle, L0R 1H0. (Mail add: PO Box 320, Carlisle, L0R 1H0), SAN 367-4312. Tel: 905-689-8769. *Br Mgr,* Melissa McSweeney; Tel: 905-546-3200, Ext 6603, E-mail: mmcsween@hpl.ca
Circ 45,240
Function: Audiobks via web, Bks on CD, Children's prog, Computers for patron use, Electronic databases & coll, Free DVD rentals, ILL available, Music CDs, Online cat, OverDrive digital audio bks, Photocopying/Printing, Prog for adults, Prog for children & young adult, Ref serv available, Story hour, Summer reading prog, Teen prog, Wheelchair accessible
Open Mon-Wed 2-8, Thurs & Sat 10-5
Friends of the Library Group
CONCESSION, 565 Concession St, L8V 1A8, SAN 367-3650. Tel: 905-546-3415. *Br Mgr,* Caitlin Fralick
Circ 214,496
Function: Adult bk club, Audiobks via web, Children's prog, Computers for patron use, Digital talking bks, E-Reserves, Electronic databases & coll, Free DVD rentals, ILL available, Music CDs, Online cat, OverDrive digital audio bks, Photocopying/Printing, Prog for adults, Prog for children & young adult, Ref serv available, Story hour, Teen prog, Wheelchair accessible
Open Tues & Thurs 10-8, Wed & Fri 10-6, Sat 10-5
Friends of the Library Group
DUNDAS BRANCH, 18 Ogilvie St, Dundas, L9H 2S2, SAN 319-1125. Tel: 905-627-3507. *Br Mgr,* Meg Uttangi-Matsos; Tel: 905-627-3507, Ext 1404, E-mail: muttangi@hpl.ca
Founded 1883. Circ 412,119
Special Collections: Arts & Crafts Coll; Children's French Coll; Dundas History Coll
Subject Interests: Can poetry
Function: Adult bk club, Bks on CD, Children's prog, Computer training, Computers for patron use, Digital talking bks, E-Reserves, Electronic databases & coll, Free DVD rentals, Homework prog, ILL available, Internet access, Music CDs, Online cat, OverDrive digital audio bks, Photocopying/Printing, Prog for adults, Prog for children & young adult, Ref serv available, Story hour, Summer reading prog, Teen prog, Wheelchair accessible
Open Mon & Fri 10-6, Tues-Thurs 10-9, Sat 10-5, Sun 1-5
Friends of the Library Group
FREELTON BRANCH, 1803 Brock Rd, Freelton, L0R 1K0. (Mail add: PO Box 15, Freelton, L0R 1K0), SAN 367-4347. Tel: 905-659-7639. *Br Mgr,* Melissa McSweeney
Circ 28,755
Function: Audiobks via web, Bks on CD, Children's prog, Computers for patron use, E-Reserves, Electronic databases & coll, Free DVD rentals, ILL available, Music CDs, Online cat, OverDrive digital audio bks, Photocopying/Printing, Prog for adults, Prog for children & young adult, Story hour, Summer reading prog, Teen prog, Wheelchair accessible
Open Mon & Wed 3:30-8, Tues & Thurs 1:30-5, Fri 10-2, Sat 1-5
Friends of the Library Group
GREENSVILLE, 59 Kirby Ave, Unit 5, Greensville, L9H 4H6, SAN 367-4401. Tel: 905-627-4951. *Br Mgr,* Meg Uttangi-Matsos
Circ 28,755
Function: Adult bk club, Audiobks via web, Bks on CD, Children's prog, Computers for patron use, E-Reserves, Electronic databases & coll, Free DVD rentals, ILL available, Music CDs, Online cat, OverDrive

digital audio bks, Photocopying/Printing, Ref serv available, Story hour, Summer reading prog, Wheelchair accessible
Open Mon & Wed 4-8, Tues, Thurs & Sat 2-5
Friends of the Library Group
KENILWORTH, 103 Kenilworth Ave N, L8H 4R6, SAN 367-3596. Tel: 905-546-3960. *Br Mgr,* Carol Wilkinson
Circ 237,816
Function: Adult bk club, Audiobks via web, Bks on CD, Children's prog, Computers for patron use, Electronic databases & coll, Free DVD rentals, ILL available, Internet access, Music CDs, Online cat, OverDrive digital audio bks, Photocopying/Printing, Prog for adults, Prog for children & young adult, Ref serv available, Story hour, Summer reading prog, Teen prog, Wheelchair accessible
Open Mon & Wed 10-6, Tues & Thurs 10-8, Sat 10-5
Friends of the Library Group
LOCKE, 285 Locke St S, L8P 4C2, SAN 367-3626. Tel: 905-546-3492. *Br Mgr,* Amy Hunter; Tel: 905-546-3200, Ext 3400, E-mail: ahunter@hpl.ca
Circ 178,482
Function: Adult bk club, Audiobks via web, Bks on CD, Children's prog, Computers for patron use, E-Reserves, Electronic databases & coll, Free DVD rentals, ILL available, Music CDs, Online cat, OverDrive digital audio bks, Photocopying/Printing, Prog for adults, Prog for children & young adult, Ref serv available, Story hour, Summer reading prog, Teen prog, Wheelchair accessible
Open Mon, Wed & Sat 10-5, Tues & Thurs 1-8
Friends of the Library Group
LYNDEN BRANCH, 79 Lynden Rd, Lynden, L0R 1T0. (Mail add: PO Box 9, Lynden, L0R 1T0), SAN 367-4436. Tel: 519-647-2571. *Br Mgr,* Leslie Muirhead
Circ 48,693
Function: Audiobks via web, Bks on CD, Children's prog, Computers for patron use, E-Reserves, Electronic databases & coll, Free DVD rentals, ILL available, Music CDs, Online cat, OverDrive digital audio bks, Photocopying/Printing, Prog for adults, Prog for children & young adult, Ref serv available, Story hour, Summer reading prog
Open Mon & Wed 3-8, Tues, Thurs & Fri 10-3, Sat 12-5
Friends of the Library Group
MOUNT HOPE, 3027 Homestead Dr, RR 1, Mount Hope, L0R 1W0, SAN 367-4371. Tel: 905-679-6445. *Br Mgr,* Caitlin Fralick
Circ 30,120
Function: Audiobks via web, Bks on CD, Children's prog, Computers for patron use, E-Reserves, Electronic databases & coll, Free DVD rentals, ILL available, Music CDs, Online cat, OverDrive digital audio bks, Photocopying/Printing, Story hour, Summer reading prog, Wheelchair accessible
Open Mon & Wed 2-5, Tues & Thurs 2-8
Friends of the Library Group
RED HILL, 695 Queenston Rd, L8G 1A1, SAN 367-3715. Tel: 905-546-2069. *Br Mgr,* Kat Drennan-Scace; Tel: 905-546-3200, Ext 2976, E-mail: kdrennan@hpl.ca
Circ 360,816
Function: Adult bk club, Audiobks via web, Bks on CD, Children's prog, Citizenship assistance, Computer training, Computers for patron use, E-Reserves, Free DVD rentals, ILL available, Music CDs, Online cat, OverDrive digital audio bks, Photocopying/Printing, Preschool outreach, Prog for adults, Prog for children & young adult, Story hour, Summer reading prog, Teen prog, Wheelchair accessible
Open Mon 1-9, Tues-Thurs 10-9, Fri 10-6, Sat 10-5, Sun 1-5
Friends of the Library Group
SALTFLEET, 131 Gray Rd, Stoney Creek, L8G 3V3, SAN 367-455X. Tel: 905-662-8611. *Br Mgr,* Jen Gal; Tel: 905-546-3200, Ext 3417, E-mail: jgal@hpl.ca
Circ 251,648
Function: Adult bk club, Audiobks via web, Bks on CD, Children's prog, Computers for patron use, E-Reserves, Electronic databases & coll, Free DVD rentals, ILL available, Music CDs, Online cat, OverDrive digital audio bks, Photocopying/Printing, Prog for adults, Prog for children & young adult, Ref serv available, Story hour, Summer reading prog, Teen prog, Wheelchair accessible
Open Mon-Wed 10-9, Thurs 10-6, Sat 10-5
Friends of the Library Group
SHERWOOD, 467 Upper Ottawa St, L8T 3T3, SAN 367-374X. Tel: 905-546-3249. *Br Mgr,* Ania Van Minnen; Tel: 905-546-3200, Ext 3436, E-mail: avanminn@hpl.ca
Circ 295,224
Function: Adult bk club, Audiobks via web, Bks on CD, Children's prog, Computer training, Computers for patron use, E-Reserves, Electronic databases & coll, Free DVD rentals, Homework prog, Music CDs, Online cat, OverDrive digital audio bks, Photocopying/Printing, Prog for adults, Prog for children & young adult, Ref serv available, Story hour, Summer reading prog, Teen prog, Wheelchair accessible
Open Mon, Wed & Thurs 10-9, Tues 10-6, Sat 10-5
Friends of the Library Group
STONEY CREEK BRANCH, 777 Hwy 8, Stoney Creek, L8E 5J4, SAN 367-4614. Tel: 905-643-2912. *Br Mgr,* Jen Gal
Circ 107,273
Function: Adult bk club, Audiobks via web, Bks on CD, Children's prog, Computer training, Computers for patron use, E-Reserves, Free DVD rentals, ILL available, Music CDs, Online cat, OverDrive digital audio bks, Photocopying/Printing, Preschool outreach, Prog for adults, Prog for children & young adult, Ref serv available, Senior computer classes, Story hour, Summer reading prog, Teen prog, Wheelchair accessible
Open Mon & Wed 1-8, Tues, Thurs & Sat 10-5
Friends of the Library Group
TERRYBERRY, 100 Mohawk Rd W, L9C 1W1, SAN 367-3774. Tel: 905-546-3921. *Br Mgr,* Dijia Qin; Tel: 905-546-3200, Ext 7065, E-mail: dqin@hpl.ca
Circ 277,746
Function: Adult bk club, Audiobks via web, Bks on CD, Children's prog, Computer training, Computers for patron use, E-Reserves, Electronic databases & coll, Free DVD rentals, Homework prog, ILL available, Music CDs, Online cat, OverDrive digital audio bks, Photocopying/Printing, Prog for adults, Prog for children & young adult, Ref serv available, Story hour, Summer reading prog, Teen prog, Wheelchair accessible
Open Mon-Thurs 10-9, Sat 10-5, Sun 1-5
Friends of the Library Group
TURNER PARK, 352 Rymal Rd E, L9B 1C2, SAN 367-3685. Tel: 905-546-4790. *Br Mgr,* Lorie Travi; Tel: 905-546-3200, Ext 4224, E-mail: ltravi@hpl.ca
Circ 635,311
Function: Adult bk club, Audiobks via web, Bks on CD, Children's prog, Computers for patron use, E-Reserves, Electronic databases & coll, Free DVD rentals, ILL available, Music CDs, Online cat, OverDrive digital audio bks, Photocopying/Printing, Prog for adults, Prog for children & young adult, Ref serv available, Story hour, Summer reading prog, Wheelchair accessible
Open Mon-Thurs 10-9, Fri 10-6, Sat 10-5, Sun 1-5
Friends of the Library Group
VALLEY PARK, 970 Paramount Dr, L8J 1Y2, SAN 367-4495. Tel: 905-573-3141. *Br Mgr,* Ania Van Minnen
Circ 163,496
Function: Adult bk club, Audiobks via web, Bks on CD, Citizenship assistance, Computers for patron use, E-Reserves, Electronic databases & coll, Free DVD rentals, Homework prog, ILL available, Music CDs, Online cat, OverDrive digital audio bks, Photocopying/Printing, Prog for adults, Prog for children & young adult, Ref serv available, Story hour, Summer reading prog, Teen prog, Wheelchair accessible
Open Mon-Thurs 10-8, Sat 10-5
Friends of the Library Group
WATERDOWN BRANCH, 163 Dundas St E, Waterdown, L9H 7H7, SAN 367-4649. Tel: 905-689-6269. *Br Mgr,* Melissa McSweeney
Circ 185,577
Function: Adult bk club, Audiobks via web, Bks on CD, Children's prog, Computers for patron use, E-Reserves, Free DVD rentals, Homework prog, ILL available, Music CDs, Online cat, OverDrive digital audio bks, Photocopying/Printing, Prog for adults, Prog for children & young adult, Ref serv available, Story hour, Summer reading prog, Teen prog, Wheelchair accessible
Open Mon-Thurs 10-9, Sat 10-5, Sun 1-5
Friends of the Library Group
WESTDALE, 955 King St W, L8S 1K9, SAN 367-3804. Tel: 905-546-3456. *Br Mgr,* Amy Hunter
Circ 291,387
Function: Adult bk club, Audiobks via web, Bks on CD, Children's prog, Computers for patron use, E-Reserves, Electronic databases & coll, Free DVD rentals, Homework prog, ILL available, Music CDs, Online cat, OverDrive digital audio bks, Photocopying/Printing, Prog for adults, Prog for children & young adult, Ref serv available, Story hour, Summer reading prog, Teen prog, Wheelchair accessible
Open Mon & Fri 10-6, Tues-Thurs 10-9, Sat 10-5
Friends of the Library Group
Bookmobiles: 2. Mgr, Susan Beattie

R HAMILTON WENTWORTH CATHOLIC DISTRICT SCHOOL BOARD*, Nicholas Mancini Library Information Center, 44 Hunt St, L8R 3R1. SAN 322-8649. Tel: 905-525-2930. FAX: 905-523-0247. Web Site: www.hwcdsb.ca. *Libr Mgr,* Paola Kontic; E-mail: konticp@hwcdsb.ca; Staff 10 (MLS 1, Non-MLS 9)
Library Holdings: Bk Titles 7,000; Per Subs 150
Special Collections: Language Arts (Primary & Literature Loan Service Coll)
Publications: Learning Materials Catalogue; New at the Professional Library; Professional Bks List
Special Services for the Deaf - Spec interest per
Open Mon-Fri 8-4:30

M JURAVINSKI CANCER CENTRE*, Patient & Family Resource Centre, 699 Concession St, L8V 5C2. SAN 324-6663. Tel: 905-387-9495, Ext 65109. E-mail: jccpfrcentre@hhsc.ca. Web Site: www.jcc.hhsc.ca. *Libr Tech,* Victoria Chambers; Staff 1 (Non-MLS 1)
Library Holdings: Bk Titles 750; Per Subs 2
Subject Interests: Illness, Oncology, Patient educ, Wellness
Automation Activity & Vendor Info: (Cataloging) Eloquent Systems Inc
Open Mon-Fri 8:30-4:30
Restriction: Open to staff, patients & family mem

C MCMASTER UNIVERSITY LIBRARY*, Mills Memorial Library, 1280 Main St W, L8S 4L6. SAN 367-3863. Tel: 905-525-9140, Ext 22077. Reference Tel: 905-525-9140, Ext 22533. FAX: 905-524-9850. E-mail: library@mcmaster.ca. Web Site: library.mcmaster.ca. *Univ Librn,* Vivian Lewis; Tel: 905-525-9140, Ext 23883, E-mail: lewisvm@mcmaster.ca; *Assoc Univ Librn,* Wade Wyckoff; Tel: 905-525-9140, Ext 26557, E-mail: wyckoff@mcmaster.ca; Staff 43 (MLS 43)
Founded 1887. Enrl 36,450; Fac 1,050; Highest Degree: Doctorate
Library Holdings: Bk Vols 1,973,349; Per Subs 124,174
Special Collections: Bertrand Russell Archives, bks, ms, flms, tapes; British Literature (18th Century Coll); Canadian Literary Papers (eg Pierre Berton, Farley Mowat); Canadian Publishing Papers (Macmillan of Canada, McClelland & Stewart, Clarke Irwin, etc); Fed & Prov; Holocaust & Underground Resistance Movements; War & Peace (Vera Brittain Archives, Canadian Participation in the World Wars)
Subject Interests: British hist, English lit, Geol, Nuclear physics, Relig studies
Automation Activity & Vendor Info: (Acquisitions) SirsiDynix; (Circulation) SirsiDynix
Wireless access
Function: Telephone ref
Publications: McMaster University Library Research News
Partic in Canadian Association of Research Libraries; Canadian Research Knowledge Network; Hamilton & District Health Library Network; Ontario Council of University Libraries
Open Mon-Thurs 8am-11pm, Fri 8-6, Sat 10:30-6, Sun 10:30am-11pm

Departmental Libraries:

CM HEALTH SCIENCES LIBRARY, 1280 Main St W, L8S 4K1, SAN 367-3898. Tel: 905-525-9140, Ext 22327. FAX: 905-528-3733. E-mail: hslib@mcmaster.ca. *Dir,* Jennifer McKinnell; Tel: 905-525-9140, Ext 24381, E-mail: mckinn@mcmaster.ca; *Operations Mgr,* Sheryl Derry; Tel: 905-525-9140, Ext 22320, E-mail: derrys@mcmaster.ca; *Coll Serv, Tech Serv,* Andrea McLellan; Tel: 905-525-9140, Ext 24169, E-mail: mclell@mcmaster.ca; *Pub Serv, Syst Serv,* Neera Bhatnagar; Tel: 905-525-9140, Ext 23775, E-mail: bhatnag@mcmaster.ca; Staff 23 (MLS 8, Non-MLS 15)
Founded 1971. Enrl 34,870
Library Holdings: Bk Titles 57,350; Per Subs 4,430
Special Collections: History of Health & Medicine Coll
Partic in Ontario Council of University Libraries; Ontario Learning Resources for NursingConsortium

H G THODE LIBRARY OF SCIENCE & ENGINEERING, 1280 Main St W, L8S 4P5. Tel: 905-525-9140, Ext 22000. FAX: 905-546-0625. *Mgr,* Ann Pearce; Tel: 905-525-9140, Ext 28691, E-mail: apearce@mcmaster.ca

J MOHAWK COLLEGE LIBRARY*, Cummings Library, 135 Fennell Ave W, L9C 0E5. SAN 367-4010. Information Services Tel: 905-575-2077. E-mail: library@mohawkcollege.ca. Web Site: library.mohawkcollege.ca/home. *Academic Services, Dir of Libr,* Lynn Coleman; E-mail: lynn.coleman@mohawkcollege.ca; *Colls Librn, Liaison Librn,* Meg Tyrell; Tel: 905-575-1212, Ext 3129, E-mail: meaghan.tyrell@mohawkcollege.ca; *Digital Syst Librn,* Robert Soulliere; Tel: 905-575-1212, Ext 3936, E-mail: robert.soulliere@mohawkcollege.ca; *Health Sci Librn, Liaison Librn,* Laura Riggs; Tel: 905-575-1212, Ext 6720, E-mail: laura.riggs@mohawkcollege.ca; Staff 18 (MLS 3, Non-MLS 15)
Founded 1967. Enrl 12,500; Fac 425; Highest Degree: Bachelor
Library Holdings: Bk Vols 50,400; Per Subs 800
Subject Interests: Chem, Computers
Automation Activity & Vendor Info: (Acquisitions) Evergreen; (Cataloging) Evergreen; (Circulation) Evergreen; (OPAC) Evergreen; (Serials) Evergreen
Wireless access
Partic in Ontario Colleges Library Service (OCLS)
Open Mon-Thurs 8-8, Fri 8-6

Departmental Libraries:

IAHS (INSTITUTE FOR APPLIED HEALTH SCIENCES) LIBRARY, 1400 Main St W, L8S 1C7. (Mail add: PO Box 2034, L8N 3T2). Tel: 905-540-4247, Ext 26835. Information Services Tel: 905-540-4247, Ext 26834. FAX: 905-528-5307. *Liaison Librn,* Laura Riggs; Tel: 905-575-1212 x6720, E-mail: laura.riggs@mohawkcollege.ca; Staff 5 (MLS 1, Non-MLS 4)
Founded 1978. Enrl 1,500; Fac 120; Highest Degree: Bachelor
Library Holdings: Bk Vols 10,978; Per Subs 140
Subject Interests: Allied health, Nursing
Function: ILL available, Ref serv available
Open Mon-Thurs 8:30-7, Fri 8:30-4:30, Sat 11-3

STARRT (SKILLED TRADES & APPRENTICESHIP RESEARCH, RESOURCES & TRAINING) LIBRARY, 481 Barton St E, Stoney Creek, L8E 2L7, SAN 320-5452. Tel: 905-575-2504. Information Services Tel: 905-575-1212, Ext 5038. FAX: 905-575-2549. *Libr Serv Tech,* April Speare; Tel: 905-575-2504, Ext 5028, E-mail: april.speare@mohawkcollege.ca; Staff 1 (Non-MLS 1)
Library Holdings: Bk Vols 7,600; Per Subs 45
Open Mon-Thurs 8-7, Fri 8-4

M ST JOSEPH HEALTHCARE CENTRE FOR MOUNTAIN HEALTH SERVICES*, Library Resource Centre, 100 W Fifth St, L8N 3K7. (Mail add: PO Box 585, L8N 3K7), SAN 324-6604. Tel: 905-522-1155, Ext 36322. FAX: 905-575-6035. E-mail: library@stjoes.ca. Web Site: www.stjoes.ca/patients-visitors/support-services/library-services. *Dir, Libr Serv,* Karin Dearness
Library Holdings: Bk Titles 1,500; Per Subs 75
Subject Interests: Psychiat disciplines, Related disciplines
Restriction: Open to students, fac & staff

M SAINT JOSEPH'S HOSPITAL*, Sherman Library, 50 Charlton Ave E, L8N 4A6. SAN 319-1583. Tel: 905-522-4941, Ext 33410. FAX: 905-540-6504. E-mail: library@stjoes.ca. Web Site: www.stjoes.ca/patients-visitors/support-services/library-services. *Dir, Libr Serv,* Karin Dearness
Founded 1964
Library Holdings: AV Mats 40; Bk Vols 2,500; Per Subs 120
Special Collections: History of Medicine; Osler Coll
Automation Activity & Vendor Info: (Cataloging) Eloquent Systems Inc
Wireless access
Open Mon, Wed & Fri 8-6, Tues & Thurs 8-8

HANOVER

P HANOVER PUBLIC LIBRARY*, 451 Tenth Ave, N4N 2P1. SAN 319-1621. Tel: 519-364-1420. FAX: 519-364-1747. E-mail: hanpub@hanover.ca. Web Site: hanoverlibrary.ca. *Chief Exec Officer, Chief Librn,* Agnes Rivers-Moore; Staff 5 (MLS 1, Non-MLS 4)
Founded 1906. Pop 7,500; Circ 75,000
Library Holdings: Audiobooks 1,300; AV Mats 4,900; CDs 1,700; DVDs 3,500; e-books 35,000; e-journals 21,000; High Interest/Low Vocabulary Bk Vols 70; Large Print Bks 2,350; Microforms 6; Bk Titles 26,900; Bk Vols 27,000; Per Subs 80; Talking Bks 1,580
Special Collections: Canadian and Provincial
Subject Interests: Local hist
Automation Activity & Vendor Info: (Cataloging) Koha; (Circulation) Koha; (OPAC) Koha; (Serials) Koha
Wireless access
Function: 24/7 Electronic res, 24/7 Online cat, Bks on CD, Children's prog, Computer training, Computers for patron use, Digital talking bks, E-Reserves, Electronic databases & coll, Free DVD rentals, Home delivery & serv to seniorr ctr & nursing homes, Homebound delivery serv, ILL available, Internet access, Large print keyboards, Literacy & newcomer serv, Magazines, Magnifiers for reading, Mail & tel request accepted, Microfiche/film & reading machines, Music CDs, Online cat, Outside serv via phone, mail, e-mail & web, OverDrive digital audio bks, Photocopying/Printing, Preschool reading prog, Prog for adults, Prog for children & young adult, Scanner, Senior computer classes, Story hour, Summer reading prog, Wheelchair accessible
Mem of Ontario Library Service
Partic in OLA
Special Services for the Deaf - Bks on deafness & sign lang; High interest/low vocabulary bks
Special Services for the Blind - Accessible computers; Assistive/Adapted tech devices, equip & products; Bks on CD; Daisy reader; Extensive large print coll; Home delivery serv; Magnifiers; Talking bks
Open Mon-Thurs 10-8, Fri & Sat 10-5, Sun 1-5

HAWKESBURY

P HAWKESBURY PUBLIC LIBRARY*, 550 Higginson St, K6A 1H1. SAN 319-1680. Tel: 613-632-0106, Ext 2250. FAX: 613-636-2097. E-mail: info@bibliotheque.hawkesbury.on.ca. Web Site: www.bibliotheque.hawkesbury.on.ca. *Chief Exec Officer,* Lynn Belle-Isle; Tel: 613-632-0106, Ext 2251; Staff 10 (MLS 1, Non-MLS 9)
Founded 1963. Pop 10,300
Library Holdings: Bk Vols 75,500; Per Subs 80
Special Collections: Genealogy (French)
Automation Activity & Vendor Info: (Cataloging) Mandarin Library Automation; (Circulation) Mandarin Library Automation; (OPAC) Mandarin Library Automation
Wireless access
Mem of Ontario Library Service

Partic in Mandarin
Open Mon, Tues, Thurs & Fri 10-5, Wed 10-7
Friends of the Library Group
Bookmobiles: 1

HEARST

P HEARST PUBLIC LIBRARY, 801 George St, P0L 1N0. (Mail add: PO Box 15000, P0L 1N0), SAN 319-1699. Tel: 705-372-2843. FAX: 705-372-2833. E-mail: tech@bibliohearst.on.ca. Web Site: bibliohearst.on.ca. *Dir, Libr Serv,* Julie Portelance; E-mail: director@bibliohearst.on.ca; *Libr Serv Tech,* Ariane Comeau
Founded 1975. Pop 6,000
Library Holdings: Bk Vols 26,000; Per Subs 60
Automation Activity & Vendor Info: (Cataloging) SirsiDynix; (Circulation) SirsiDynix-WorkFlows
Wireless access
Open Mon-Thurs 9:30-5, Fri 9:30-7, Sat 9:30-4
Friends of the Library Group

HILTON BEACH

P HILTON UNION PUBLIC LIBRARY*, 3085 Marks St, P0R 1G0. (Mail add: RR 1, P0R 1G0), SAN 319-1710. Tel: 705-255-3520. E-mail: hiltonlibrary@hotmail.ca. Web Site: hiltonunion.library.on.ca. *Chief Exec Officer,* Melanie Dorscht
Founded 1920. Pop 370; Circ 5,500
Library Holdings: Bk Vols 8,550
Special Collections: St Joseph's Island (Pioneer to Present)
Open Mon 3-5 & 7-9, Wed & Sat 1-5
Friends of the Library Group

HONEY HARBOUR

P TOWNSHIP OF GEORGIAN BAY PUBLIC LIBRARY*, Honey Harbour Public Library, 2586 Honey Harbour Rd, P0E 1E0. (Mail add: PO Box 220, P0E 1E0), SAN 319-2318. Tel: 705-756-8851. FAX: 705-756-9084. E-mail: honeyharbourpl@gmail.com. Web Site: gbpl.ca/locations. *Chief Librn/CEO,* Sarah Papple
Pop 2,000; Circ 5,372
Library Holdings: Bk Vols 9,183
Automation Activity & Vendor Info: (Cataloging) SirsiDynix-WorkFlows; (Circulation) SirsiDynix
Wireless access
Open Tues-Sat 9:30-5
Branches: 2
MACTIER PUBLIC, 12 Muskota Rd, MacTier, P0C 1H0. Tel: 705-375-5430. FAX: 705-375-5430. E-mail: mactierpl@gmail.com. *Libr Asst,* Carol McCron
Open Tues-Sat 9:30-5
PORT SEVERN PUBLIC, 71 Lone Pine Rd, Port Severn, L0K 1S0. Tel: 705-818-7749. E-mail: portsevernpl@gmail.com. *Libr Asst,* Jeanette Moreno
Open Tues & Thurs-Sat 9:30-5

HORNEPAYNE

P HORNEPAYNE PUBLIC LIBRARY*, 68 Front St, P0M 1Z0. (Mail add: PO Box 539, P0M 1Z0), SAN 319-1729. Tel: 807-868-2332. FAX: 807-868-3111. E-mail: hplstaff@hotmail.com. Web Site: hornepayne.olsn.ca, www.townshipofhornepayne.ca/our_community/hornepayne_public_library. *Chairperson,* David Turgeon; *Chief Exec Officer,* Darnelle Hill; E-mail: dhill@ontera.net; *Circ,* Margarita LeFort
Founded 1967. Pop 1,041; Circ 12,000
Library Holdings: Bk Vols 15,000; Per Subs 15
Wireless access
Open Tues 10:30-5, Wed & Sat 1:30-5, Thurs & Fri 1:30-5 & 7-9

HUNTSVILLE

P HUNTSVILLE PUBLIC LIBRARY*, Seven Minerva St E, P1H 1W4. SAN 319-1737. Tel: 705-789-5232. Toll Free Tel: 888-696-4255, Ext 3403. Web Site: www.huntsvillelibrary.ca. *Chief Exec Officer, Chief Librn,* David Tremblay
Founded 1885. Pop 20,000; Circ 199,027
Library Holdings: Bk Vols 52,000; Per Subs 143
Special Collections: Muskoka Coll. Canadian and Provincial
Wireless access
Function: 24/7 Electronic res, 24/7 Online cat, 3D Printer, Activity rm, Adult bk club, Archival coll, Art exhibits, Audio & video playback equip for onsite use, Audiobks on Playaways & MP3, Audiobks via web, Bk club(s), Bks on CD, Chess club, Children's prog, Citizenship assistance, Computer training, Computers for patron use, Digital talking bks, Distance learning, E-Readers, Electronic databases & coll, Family literacy, Home delivery & serv to seniorr ctr & nursing homes, ILL available, Internet access, Large print keyboards, Life-long learning prog for all ages, Meeting rooms, Microfiche/film & reading machines, Movies, Music CDs, Online cat, OverDrive digital audio bks, Photocopying/Printing, Prog for adults, Prog for children & young adult, Ref & res, Ref serv available, Scanner, Senior computer classes, Senior outreach, Summer & winter reading prog, Summer reading prog, Wheelchair accessible
Mem of Ontario Library Service
Open Mon-Fri 10-6, Sat 10-4
Friends of the Library Group

IGNACE

P IGNACE PUBLIC LIBRARY*, 36 Main St, P0T 1T0. SAN 319-1745. Tel: 807-934-2280. Web Site: ignace.olsn.ca. *Chief Exec Officer, Librn,* Susan Gagne; E-mail: ceoignacelibrary@gmail.com
Pop 1,202; Circ 14,174
Automation Activity & Vendor Info: (OPAC) SirsiDynix-Unicorn
Wireless access
Function: Children's prog, Computers for patron use, Digital talking bks, Free DVD rentals, Holiday prog, ILL available, Music CDs, Online cat, OverDrive digital audio bks, Photocopying/Printing, Scanner, Wheelchair accessible
Open Wed 3-8, Thurs 10-3, Fri & Sat Noon-5
Friends of the Library Group

IRON BRIDGE

P HURON SHORES PUBLIC LIBRARY*, Ten Main St, P0R 1H0. (Mail add: PO Box 460, P0R 1H0), SAN 319-1753. Tel: 705-843-2192. FAX: 705-843-2035. E-mail: hslibrary@hotmail.ca. Web Site: huronshores@olsn.ca. *Chief Exec Officer, Librn,* Terri Beharriell
Founded 1974. Pop 1,794; Circ 2,275
Library Holdings: Bk Titles 4,424; Bk Vols 4,956
Function: 24/7 Electronic res, 24/7 Online cat, Activity rm, Adult bk club, Bk club(s), Bks on CD, CD-ROM, Computers for patron use, Free DVD rentals, Govt ref serv, ILL available, Internet access, Magazines, Makerspace, Movies, Photocopying/Printing
Open Tues & Fri 1-7
Restriction: Access at librarian's discretion

KAGAWONG

P BILLINGS TOWNSHIP PUBLIC LIBRARY*, 18 Upper St, P0P 1J0. (Mail add: PO Box 37, P0P 1J0), SAN 319-1788. Tel: 705-282-2944. E-mail: billingslibrary@vianet.ca. Web Site: olsn.ca/billingslibrary. *Chief Exec Officer, Librn,* Jill Ferguson
Founded 1968. Pop 500; Circ 5,548
Library Holdings: CDs 400; DVDs 400; Bk Titles 7,137; Per Subs 10; Videos 200
Wireless access
Open Tues & Thurs 4-7, Sat 10-1 (Fall-Spring); Tues-Sat 9-12 & 1-5 (Summer)
Friends of the Library Group

KANATA

S CANADIAN WILDLIFE FEDERATION*, 350 Michael Cowpland Dr, K2M 2W1. SAN 326-8632. Tel: 613-599-9594. Toll Free Tel: 800-563-9453. FAX: 613-599-4428. E-mail: info@cwf-fcf.org. Web Site: www.cwf-fcf.org. *Library Contact,* Chad Gardner; E-mail: chadg@cwf-fcf.org
Library Holdings: e-books 7,000
Special Collections: Canadian Wildlife Federation Archives
Publications: Annual Report of the Canadian Wildlife Federation; Biosphere; Canadian Wildlife; Endangered Species Fact Sheet; Habitat 2000 Wildlife Habitat Improvement Series for Youth; Poaching Report; Project Wild; Your Big Backyard

KAPUSKASING

P KAPUSKASING PUBLIC LIBRARY*, 24 Mundy Ave, P5N 1P9. SAN 319-180X. Tel: 705-335-3363. FAX: 705-335-2464. E-mail: library@kapuskasing.ca. *Chief Exec Officer,* Julie Latimer; *Treas,* Aliela Simard; E-mail: library.admin@kapuskasing.ca
Founded 1964. Pop 9,501; Circ 42,391
Library Holdings: Audiobooks 998; DVDs 1,910; Large Print Bks 849; Bk Titles 29,447; Bk Vols 36,397; Per Subs 39; Talking Bks 1,133
Subject Interests: Bilingual, Bks, English lang, Fr lang
Wireless access
Special Services for the Deaf - Bks on deafness & sign lang
Special Services for the Blind - Assistive/Adapted tech devices, equip & products; Bks on CD; Daisy reader; Extensive large print coll; Large print bks; Lending of low vision aids; Magnifiers; Playaways (bks on MP3)
Open Mon, Tues & Thurs 10-8, Wed 4-8, Fri 10-5, Sat 12-4
Friends of the Library Group

KEARNEY

P KEARNEY & AREA PUBLIC LIBRARY*, Eight Main St, P0A 1M0. (Mail add: PO Box 220, P0A 1M0), SAN 319-1818. Tel: 705-636-5849. E-mail: kearneylibrary@hotmail.ca. Web Site: kearney.olsn.ca. *Librn,* Brandi Nolan
Pop 800; Circ 7,000
Library Holdings: Bk Vols 9,290; Per Subs 13
Wireless access
Function: Homebound delivery serv, ILL available, Prog for children & young adult, Ref serv available, Summer reading prog, Wheelchair accessible

KEENE

P OTONABEE-SOUTH MONAGHAN TOWNSHIP PUBLIC LIBRARY*, Gayle Nelson Keene Public Library, 3252 CR 2, K0L 2G0. (Mail add: PO Box 9, K0L 2G0), SAN 319-1826. Tel: 705-295-6814. E-mail: keene_library@nexicom.net. Web Site: www.otosoumon.library.on.ca. *Chief Exec Officer,* Carolanne Nadeau; Staff 7 (Non-MLS 7)
Pop 6,200; Circ 46,000
Library Holdings: Bk Vols 32,000; Per Subs 100
Open Tues & Thurs 12-8, Sat 11-4
Friends of the Library Group
Branches: 2
BAILIEBORO BRANCH, Hwy 28, Bailieboro, K0L 1B0. (Mail add: PO Box 9, K0L 2G0). Tel: 705-939-6510. FAX: 705-939-6510.
Open Tues & Thurs 1-7:30, Sat 10-3
Friends of the Library Group
STEWART HALL, 1490 Matchett Line, Peterborough, K9J 6Y3. (Mail add: Box 9, K0L 2G0). Tel: 705-749-5642.
Open Wed 3-8, Sat 11-2:30
Friends of the Library Group

KEMPTVILLE

P NORTH GRENVILLE PUBLIC LIBRARY*, Norenberg Bldg, One Water St, K0G 1J0. (Mail add: PO Box 538, K0G 1J0), SAN 319-1850. Tel: 613-258-4711. FAX: 613-258-4134. E-mail: info@ngpl.ca. Web Site: www.ngpl.ca. *Chief Exec Officer,* Rachel Brown; Tel: 613-258-4711, Ext 6; *Mgr, Info Serv,* Patricia Evans; E-mail: pevans@ngpl.ca; *Mgr, Serv Delivery,* Sierra Jones-Martel; E-mail: sjones@ngpl.ca; *Children's & Teen Serv Coordr,* Sue Bergeron; Tel: 613-258-4711, Ext 5, E-mail: kids@ngpl.ca; *Coordr, Commun Engagement,* Liz Dwyer; E-mail: ldwyer@ngpl.ca; Staff 4 (MLS 1, Non-MLS 3)
Founded 1998. Pop 15,085; Circ 95,232
Automation Activity & Vendor Info: (Cataloging) SirsiDynix; (Circulation) SirsiDynix; (ILL) Fretwell-Downing; (OPAC) SirsiDynix
Wireless access
Partic in Ontario Library Consortium
Special Services for the Blind - Talking bks
Open Mon, Tues & Thurs 10-7, Fri 1-5, Sat 10-2
Friends of the Library Group
Branches: 1
BURRITTS RAPIDS BRANCH, One Grenville St, Burritts Rapids, K0G 1B0. Tel: 613-269-3636. *Mgr, Info Serv,* Patricia Evans
Open Sat 10-2
Friends of the Library Group

KENORA

P KENORA PUBLIC LIBRARY*, 24 Main St S, P9N 1S7. SAN 319-1869. Tel: 807-467-2081. FAX: 807-467-2085. E-mail: kpl@kenora.ca. Web Site: www.kenorapubliclibrary.org. *Chief Exec Officer, Librn,* Crystal Alcock; E-mail: cralcock@kenora.ca; *Head, Children's Servx,* Kathleen Todd; E-mail: ktodd@kenora.ca; *Head, Ref,* Lori Jackson; E-mail: ljackson@kenora.ca; Staff 3 (Non-MLS 3)
Founded 1885. Pop 15,000; Circ 214,582
Library Holdings: Bk Vols 64,000; Per Subs 140
Subject Interests: Local hist
Wireless access
Open Mon & Fri 9-5, Tues & Thurs 9-7, Wed 9-8, Sat 9-2
Branches: 1
KEEWATIN BRANCH, 221 Main St, Keewatin, P0X 1C0. Tel: 807-547-2145. FAX: 807-547-3145. *Br Mgr,* Lyn Mackay; E-mail: lmackay@kenora.ca; Staff 3 (Non-MLS 3)
Founded 1973
Open Tues & Fri 11-4, Thurs 2-7, Sat 10-2

KESWICK

P GEORGINA PUBLIC LIBRARY*, Keswick Branch, 90 Wexford Dr, L4P 3P7. SAN 370-0151. Tel: 905-476-7233. FAX: 905-476-8724. Web Site: www.georginalibrary.ca. *Libr Dir & Chief Exec Officer,* Valerie Stevens; E-mail: vstevens@georgina.ca; Staff 14 (MLS 5, Non-MLS 9)
Founded 1971. Pop 30,000; Circ 305,242
Library Holdings: Bk Vols 75,000
Wireless access
Function: 24/7 Electronic res, 24/7 Online cat, 3D Printer, Activity rm, Adult bk club, After school storytime, Art exhibits, Audiobks via web, Bks on CD, Children's prog, Computer training, Electronic databases & coll, Govt ref serv, Holiday prog, ILL available, Internet access, Magazines, Meeting rooms, Movies, Music CDs, Online cat, OverDrive digital audio bks, Photocopying/Printing, Prog for adults, Prog for children & young adult, Ref & res, Story hour, Summer reading prog, Teen prog, Wheelchair accessible
Mem of Ontario Library Service
Open Tues-Thurs 10-9, Fri 10-6, Sat 9-5, Sun 1-5
Friends of the Library Group
Branches: 2
PETER GZOWSKI BRANCH, 5279 Black River Rd, Sutton, L0E 1R0. (Mail add: PO Box 338, Sutton, L0E 1R0), SAN 367-4797. Tel: 905-722-5702. FAX: 905-722-6309. *Mgr, E-Serv,* Becky George; Staff 1 (MLS 1)
Function: 3D Printer, Activity rm, Audiobks via web, Bk club(s), Bks on CD, Children's prog, Computers for patron use, Electronic databases & coll, Free DVD rentals, Homebound delivery serv, ILL available, Internet access, Online cat, Photocopying/Printing, Prog for adults, Prog for children & young adult, Ref & res, Scanner
Special Services for the Blind - Bks on CD; Large print bks; Talking bks; ZoomText magnification & reading software
Open Tues-Thurs 10-9, Fri 10-6, Sat 9-2, Sun 1-5
Friends of the Library Group
PEFFERLAW BRANCH, 76 Petes Lane, Pefferlaw, L0E 1N0. (Mail add: PO Box 220, Pefferlaw, L0E 1N0), SAN 367-4762. Tel: 705-437-1514. FAX: 705-437-4143. *Customer Serv Mgr,* Sarah James
Library Holdings: Bk Vols 100,000; Per Subs 66
Open Tues-Thurs 10-9, Fri 10-6, Sat 9-2, Sun 1-5
Friends of the Library Group

KING CITY

P KING TOWNSHIP PUBLIC LIBRARY*, 1970 King Rd, L7B 1A6. (Mail add: PO Box 392, L7B 1A6), SAN 319-1885. Tel: 905-833-5101. FAX: 905-833-0824. Web Site: kinglibrary.ca. *Actg Chief Exec Officer,* Adele Reid; E-mail: a.reid@kinglibrary.ca; Staff 8 (MLS 5, Non-MLS 3)
Founded 1893. Pop 24,512; Circ 150,000
Library Holdings: CDs 1,800; DVDs 4,000; e-books 1,000; e-journals 2,000; Bk Titles 67,252; Per Subs 80; Talking Bks 3,000
Special Collections: Archives (Local History); Can & Prov
Automation Activity & Vendor Info: (Acquisitions) SirsiDynix; (Cataloging) SirsiDynix; (Circulation) SirsiDynix; (Course Reserve) SirsiDynix; (OPAC) SirsiDynix
Wireless access
Partic in Ontario Library Consortium
Special Services for the Blind - Assistive/Adapted tech devices, equip & products; Bks on cassette; Bks on CD; Computer with voice synthesizer for visually impaired persons; Copier with enlargement capabilities; Home delivery serv; PC for people with disabilities; Ref serv; Spec prog; Talking bks; Volunteer serv
Open Mon-Fri 10-8, Sat 10-5, Sun (Oct-May) 1-4

J SENECA COLLEGE OF APPLIED ARTS & TECHNOLOGY*, King Campus, Suddick Resource Centre, 13990 Dufferin St N, L7B 1B3. SAN 368-9212. Tel: 416-491-5050. FAX: 905-833-1106. Web Site: seneca.libguides.com/aboutus. *Dir of Libr,* Joy Muller; E-mail: joy.muller@senecapolytechnic.ca; *Assoc Dir, Libr Serv,* Joy Muller; E-mail: joy.muller@senecacollege.ca
Subject Interests: Diving, Early childhood educ, Golf course landscaping, Golf course maintenance, Law enforcement, Nursing, Recreation, Tourism, Veterinary sci
Wireless access
Partic in Dobis
Open Mon-Thurs 7:30-7:30, Fri 7:30-5
Departmental Libraries:
NEWNHAM CAMPUS (MAIN), 1750 Finch Ave E, North York, M2J 2X5, SAN 368-9204. Tel: 416-491-5050, Ext 22099. FAX: 416-491-3349. *Dir,* Joy Muller; E-mail: joy.muller@senecapolytechnic.ca; *Librn,* Kelly Donaldson; Tel: 416-491-5050, Ext 26139, E-mail: kelly.donaldson@senecacollege.ca; *Digital Serv Librn, E-Learning Librn,* Jennifer Peters; Tel: 416-491-5050, Ext 22070, E-mail: jennifer.peters@senecacollege.ca; *Data Librn, Syst Librn,* Jane Foo; Tel: 416-491-5050, Ext 22011, E-mail: jane.foo@senecacollege.ca
Library Holdings: Bk Vols 50,000; Per Subs 472
Special Collections: Women in Canada
Partic in Dobis
Open Mon-Thurs 7:30am-11pm, Fri 7:30am-10pm, Sat 8:30-5, Sun 9-5

SENECA @ YORK, 70 The Pond Rd, North York, M3J 3M6. Tel: 416-491-5050, Ext 33055. *Coll, Quality Assurance Coord,* Pamela Bolan; E-mail: pamela.bolan@senecacollege.edu; Staff 10 (MLS 4, Non-MLS 6)
Enrl 4,000; Highest Degree: Bachelor
Library Holdings: Bk Titles 15,000
Open Mon-Fri 8am-10:30pm, Sat & Sun 9-5

KINGSTON

S CANADIAN ARMY COMMAND & STAFF COLLEGE, Fort Frontenac Army Library, 317 Ontario St, K7K 7B4. (Mail add: PO Box 17000, Sta Forces, K7K 7B4), SAN 319-1907. Tel: 613-541-5010, Ext 5815. FAX: 613-541-4468. E-mail: fortfrontenac@forces.gc.ca. Web Site: www.canada.ca/en/army/services/line-sight/library. *Chief Librn,* Kristen Coulas; Staff 3 (MLS 2, Non-MLS 1)
Founded 1947. Circ 12,000
Library Holdings: Bk Titles 100,000; Per Subs 100
Special Collections: The Study of Conflict & Land Warfare in the Canadian Context, artifacts, doc, monographs, vols
Subject Interests: Army, Behav sci, Defense, Intl relations, Leadership, Mil art, Mil hist, Operations
Open Mon-Fri 8-4

L THE FRONTENAC LAW ASSOCIATION LIBRARY*, Frontenac County Court House, Five Court St, K7L 2N4. SAN 370-7776. Tel: 613-542-0034. FAX: 613-887-2080. E-mail: library@cfla.on.ca. Web Site: www.cfla.on.ca. *Libr Tech,* Jackie Hassefras
Library Holdings: Bk Vols 9,000

P KINGSTON FRONTENAC PUBLIC LIBRARY*, 130 Johnson St, K7L 1X8. SAN 367-4827. Tel: 613-549-8888. FAX: 613-549-8476. E-mail: contact@kfpl.ca. Web Site: www.kfpl.ca. *Chief Librn/CEO,* Laura Carter; E-mail: lcarter@kfpl.ca; *Dir, Human Res,* Shelagh Quigley; E-mail: squigley@kfpl.ca; *Dir, Outreach & Tech,* Lester Webb; E-mail: lwebb@kfpl.ca; *Br Operations Mgr,* Elizabeth Coates; E-mail: lcoates@kfpl.ca; *Mgr, Prog & Outreach,* Kimberly Sutherland Mills; E-mail: kmills@kfpl.ca; Staff 60 (MLS 15, Non-MLS 45)
Founded 1834. Pop 150,000
Library Holdings: Bk Titles 270,000; Bk Vols 425,000; Per Subs 400
Special Collections: Local History (Grant Allen Coll); Local Newspaper Coll, 1810-present, micro
Subject Interests: Genealogy, Local hist
Automation Activity & Vendor Info: (Acquisitions) Infor Library & Information Solutions; (Cataloging) Infor Library & Information Solutions; (Circulation) Infor Library & Information Solutions; (Course Reserve) Infor Library & Information Solutions; (ILL) Infor Library & Information Solutions; (Media Booking) Infor Library & Information Solutions; (OPAC) Infor Library & Information Solutions; (Serials) Infor Library & Information Solutions
Wireless access
Open Mon-Thurs 9-8, Fri & Sat 9-5, Sun 1-5
Friends of the Library Group

Branches: 15

ARDEN BRANCH, 5998 Arden Rd, Arden, K0H 1B0, SAN 367-4851. Tel: 613-335-2570.
Library Holdings: Bk Vols 3,000
Open Tues 2-6, Thurs 5-8, Sat 10-1
Friends of the Library Group

CALVIN PARK BRANCH, 88 Wright Crescent, K7L 4T9, SAN 370-355X. Tel: 613-546-2582.
Library Holdings: Bk Vols 48,000
Open Mon-Thurs 9-9, Fri & Sat 9-5
Friends of the Library Group

CLOYNE BRANCH, 1011 Little Pond Rd, Cloyne, K0H 1K0, SAN 367-4916. Tel: 613-336-8744.
Library Holdings: Bk Vols 11,000
Open Tues 10-3, Wed 5-8, Fri 12-4, Sat 9-12
Friends of the Library Group

HARTINGTON BRANCH, 5597 Hwy 38, Hartington, K0H 1W0, SAN 367-4940. Tel: 613-372-2524.
Library Holdings: Bk Vols 6,000
Open Mon & Wed 1-5 & 6-8, Sat 1-4
Friends of the Library Group

HOWE ISLAND BRANCH, 50 Baseline Rd, Howe Island, K7G 2V6, SAN 325-4003. Tel: 613-549-7972.
Library Holdings: Bk Vols 2,800
Open Tues 3-5, Thurs 6-8, Sat 10-Noon
Friends of the Library Group

MOUNTAIN GROVE BRANCH, 1045 Mill Rd, Mountain Grove, K0H 2E0, SAN 367-5033. Tel: 613-335-5360.
Library Holdings: Bk Vols 2,600
Open Tues & Fri 2-5, Wed 5:30-7:30, Sat 12:30-2:30
Friends of the Library Group

PARHAM BRANCH, 1282 Wagarville Rd, Parham, K0H 2K0, SAN 367-5076. Tel: 613-375-6400.
Library Holdings: Bk Vols 2,000
Open Tues 4-6, Thurs 6-8, Sat 10-Noon
Friends of the Library Group

PITTSBURGH BRANCH, 80 Gore Rd, K7K 6X6, SAN 367-4886. Tel: 613-542-8222.
Library Holdings: Bk Vols 27,000
Open Tues-Thurs 10-8, Sat 9-5
Friends of the Library Group

PLEVNA BRANCH, 6638 Buckshot Lake Rd, Plevna, K0H 2M0, SAN 377-7510. Tel: 613-479-2542.
Library Holdings: Bk Vols 1,800
Open Tues & Thurs 2-4 & 5-7, Fri & Sat 10-1
Friends of the Library Group

RIDEAU HEIGHTS BRANCH, 85 MacCauley St, K7K 2V8.
Open Mon & Wed 10-8, Fri & Sat 9-5
Friends of the Library Group

SHARBOT LAKE BRANCH, 1037 Robert St, Sharbot Lake, K0H 2P0, SAN 367-5092. Tel: 613-279-2583.
Library Holdings: Bk Vols 6,000
Open Tues & Thurs 1-5 & 6-8, Fri 2-5, Sat 10-2
Friends of the Library Group

STORRINGTON BRANCH, 3910 Battersea Rd, Battersea, K0H 1H0, SAN 367-4975. Tel: 613-353-6333.
Library Holdings: Bk Vols 3,700
Open Tues & Thurs 1-5 & 6-8, Sat 1-4
Friends of the Library Group

SYDENHAM BRANCH, 4412 Wheatley St, Sydenham, K0H 2T0, SAN 367-5122. Tel: 613-376-3437.
Library Holdings: Bk Vols 11,000
Open Mon 10-6, Tues & Thurs 1-8, Fri 10-5, Sat 10-2
Friends of the Library Group

ISABEL TURNER BRANCH, 935 Gardiners Rd, K7M 9A9, SAN 367-5009. Tel: 613-389-2611.
Library Holdings: Bk Vols 102,000
Open Mon-Thurs 9-9, Fri & Sat 9-5
Friends of the Library Group

WOLFE ISLAND BRANCH, Ten Hwy 95, Wolfe Island, K0H 2Y0, SAN 322-5925. Tel: 613-385-2112.
Library Holdings: Bk Vols 5,700
Open Tues & Thurs 1-5 & 6-8, Fri 2-5, Sat 10-1
Friends of the Library Group

S MARINE MUSEUM OF THE GREAT LAKES AT KINGSTON*, Audrey Rushbrook Memorial Library, 53 Yonge St, K7M 6G4. SAN 370-6427. Tel: 613-542-2261. FAX: 613-542-0043. Web Site: www.marmuseum.ca. *Mgr,* Doug Cowie; E-mail: manager@marmuseum.ca; Staff 1 (MLS 1)
Library Holdings: Bk Titles 12,000; Per Subs 250
Publications: Jib Gems
Restriction: Open by appt only

M PROVIDENCE CARE MENTAL HEALTH SERVICES*, Staff Library, 752 King St W, K7L 4X3. (Mail add: PO Box 603, K7L 4X3), SAN 324-0487. Tel: 613-546-1101, Ext 5745. E-mail: library@providencecare.ca. Web Site: providencecare.ca. *Librn,* Sarah Kittmer; E-mail: kittmers@providencecare.ca; Staff 1.4 (MLS 1, Non-MLS 0.4)
Founded 1965
Library Holdings: Bk Titles 4,600; Per Subs 50
Subject Interests: Mental health, Nursing, Occupational therapy, Psychiat, Psychol
Open Mon-Fri 8:30-4:30

C QUEEN'S UNIVERSITY*, Joseph S Stauffer Library, 101 Union St, K7L 2N9. SAN 367-536X. Tel: 613-533-2524. Interlibrary Loan Service Tel: 613-533-2526. Reference Tel: 613-533-2527. Toll Free Tel: 866-267-7404. Reference E-mail: inforef@queensu.ca. Web Site: library.queensu.ca. *Univ Librn, Vice Provost,* Mark Asberg; Tel: 613-533-6000, Ext 74536, E-mail: mark.asberg@queensu.ca; *Assoc Univ Librn, Univ Archivist,* Ken Hernden; Tel: 613-533-6000, Ext 79267, E-mail: ken.hernden@queensu.ca; *Assoc Univ Librn,* Heather McMullen; Tel: 613-533-6000, Ext 79293, E-mail: heather.mcmullen@queensu.ca; *Assoc Univ Librn,* Michael Vandenburg; Tel: 613-533-6000, Ext 78844, E-mail: michael.vandenburg@queensu.ca
Founded 1841. Highest Degree: Doctorate
Library Holdings: Bk Vols 2,410,869
Special Collections: Map & Air Photo Coll
Wireless access
Partic in Association of Research Libraries; Canadian Association of Research Libraries; Ontario Council of University Libraries
Open Mon-Sun 8am-11pm

Departmental Libraries:

BRACKEN HEALTH SCIENCES LIBRARY, Botterell Hall, Ground Flr, 18 Stuart St, K7L 3N6. Tel: 613-533-2510. Reference Toll Free Tel: 877-209-5641. E-mail: bracken.library@queensu.ca. Web Site:

library.queensu.ca/locations/bracken-health-sciences-library. *Head of Libr,* Sarah Wickett; Tel: 613-533-6000, Ext 77078, E-mail: wicketts@queensu.ca
Subject Interests: Health, Life sci
Open Mon-Thurs 8:30am-11pm, Fri 8:30am-8pm, Sat 10-5, Sun 10-8 (Winter); Mon-Fri 8-4:30 (Summer)

EDUCATION LIBRARY, Duncan McArthur Hall, 511 Union St at Sir John A Macdonald Blvd, K7M 5R7, SAN 367-5572. Tel: 613-533-2191. Toll Free Tel: 866-267-7406. FAX: 613-533-2010. E-mail: education.library@queensu.ca. Web Site: guides.library.queensu.ca/education. *Head, Educ Libr,* Brenda Reed; Tel: 613-533-6000, Ext 77644, E-mail: brenda.reed@queensu.ca; Staff 6.5 (MLS 2, Non-MLS 4.5)
Founded 1968
Open Mon-Thurs 8am-9pm, Fri 8-4:30, Sat & Sun 10-5

ENGINEERING & SCIENCE LIBRARY, Douglas Library, 93 University Ave, K7L 5C4. Tel: 613-533-2610. Reference Tel: 613-533-2524. Toll Free Tel: 866-267-7407. E-mail: engsci@queensu.ca. Web Site: library.queensu.ca/locations/douglas-library. *Actg Head Librn,* Michael White; Tel: 613-533-6000, Ext 36785, E-mail: michael.white@queensu.ca
Open Mon-Thurs 8:30am-11pm, Fri 8:30am-9pm, Sat 10-9, Sun 10am-11pm

W D JORDAN RARE BOOKS & SPECIAL COLLECTIONS, Douglas Library, 6th Level, 2nd Flr, 93 University Ave, K7L 5C4. Tel: 613-533-2839. E-mail: jordan.library@queensu.ca. Web Site: library.queensu.ca/locations/wd-jordan-rare-books-special-collections. *Assoc Univ Librn, Univ Archivist,* Ken Hernden; E-mail: ken.hernden@queensu.ca; *Curator, Rare Books & Special Colls,* Brendan Edwards; Tel: 613-533-6320, E-mail: brendan.edwards@queensu.ca
Open Mon-Fri 8:30-4:30

CL LEDERMAN LAW LIBRARY, Law Bldg, 128 Union St, K7L 3N6, SAN 367-5696. Tel: 613-533-2842. Circulation Tel: 613-533-6346. Reference Tel: 613-533-2465. Administration Tel: 613-533-3179. FAX: 613-533-2594. Web Site: library.queensu.ca/law. *Head Law Librn,* Amy Kaufman; Tel: 613-533-2843, E-mail: kaufman@queensu.ca; Staff 5 (MLS 2.5, Non-MLS 2.5)
Founded 1957. Enrl 600; Fac 36; Highest Degree: Doctorate
Special Collections: Canadian and Provincial
Subject Interests: Can legal mat
Function: Computers for patron use, Electronic databases & coll, ILL available, Photocopying/Printing, Ref serv available, Scanner, Telephone ref, Wheelchair accessible
Open Mon-Thurs 8:30am-11pm, Fri 8:30-4:30, Sat & Sun 10-4:30
Restriction: Open to pub for ref & circ; with some limitations

J ST LAWRENCE COLLEGE LIBRARY*, Kingston Campus, 100 Portsmouth Ave, K7L 5A6. SAN 319-1966. Tel: 613-544-5400, Ext 1705. Reference Tel: 613-544-5400, Ext 1248. FAX: 613-545-3914. E-mail: klibrary@sl.on.ca. Web Site: stlawrencecollege.libguides.com. *Assoc Dir of Libr,* Leigh Cunningham; Tel: 613-544-5400, Ext 1156, E-mail: ldcunningham@sl.on.ca; Staff 1 (MLS 1)
Founded 1967. Enrl 5,000; Fac 195
Library Holdings: Bk Vols 45,000; Per Subs 250
Automation Activity & Vendor Info: (Cataloging) SirsiDynix; (Circulation) SirsiDynix; (Course Reserve) SirsiDynix; (OPAC) SirsiDynix
Wireless access
Open Mon-Thurs 8am-9pm, Fri 8-5, Sat 12-4

KIRKLAND LAKE

P TECK CENTENNIAL LIBRARY*, Ten Kirkland St E, P2N 1P1. SAN 319-1990. Tel: 705-567-7966. FAX: 705-568-6303. Web Site: teckcentennialpl.ca. *Chief Exec Officer,* Cheryl Lafreniere; Staff 6 (MLS 1, Non-MLS 5)
Founded 1928. Pop 7,980; Circ 17,220
Library Holdings: Audiobooks 1,000; DVDs 250; Large Print Bks 2,000; Bk Titles 23,973; Bk Vols 34,803; Per Subs 76; Talking Bks 350; Videos 1,500
Special Collections: Northern Daily News, 1923-present, microfilm
Wireless access
Partic in Ont Libr Serv-North
Special Services for the Deaf - Bks on deafness & sign lang
Special Services for the Blind - Audio mat
Open Tues-Fri 10-7, Sat 9-3

KITCHENER

C CONESTOGA COLLEGE*, Library Services-Doon Campus, 299 Doon Valley Dr, N2G 4M4. SAN 319-2008. Tel: 519-748-5220, Ext 3361. E-mail: lrcinfo@conestogac.on.ca. Web Site: library.conestogac.on.ca. *Customer Experience Mgr, Operations Mgr,* Rachel Caldwell; E-mail: rcaldwell@conestogac.on.ca; *Educ Mgr, Mgr, Access Serv,* Chris Woodley; E-mail: cwoodley@conestogac.on.ca; Staff 31 (MLS 6, Non-MLS 25)
Founded 1968
Library Holdings: Bk Vols 40,000; Per Subs 225
Automation Activity & Vendor Info: (OPAC) SirsiDynix
Wireless access
Departmental Libraries:
LIBRARY SERVICES-BRANTFORD CAMPUS, 274 Colborne St, Rm 138, Brantford, N3T 2L6. Tel: 519-748-5220, Ext 7343. E-mail: brantsupportdesk@conestogac.on.ca. *Libr Tech,* Brown Stacy-Ann; E-mail: sybrown@conestogac.on.ca

LIBRARY SERVICES-CAMBRIDGE CAMPUS, 850 Fountain St S, Cambridge, N3H 0A8. Tel: 519-748-5220, Ext 4526. E-mail: lrccamb@conestogac.on.ca.

S DOON HERITAGE CROSSROADS LIBRARY*, Ten Huron Rd, N2P 2R7. SAN 373-7810. Tel: 519-748-1914. FAX: 519-748-0009. Web Site: www.waterlooregionmuseum.ca. *Coll Curator,* Stacy McLennan; Tel: 519-748-1914, Ext 3268, E-mail: smclennan@regionofwaterloo.ca; Staff 1 (MLS 1)
Founded 1983
Library Holdings: Bk Titles 2,000; Per Subs 10
Special Collections: Oral History
Subject Interests: Local hist, Mat culture
Open Mon-Fri 8:30-4:30

R EMMANUEL BIBLE COLLEGE*, Edna Pridham Memorial Library, 100 Fergus Ave, N2A 2H2. SAN 324-6094. Tel: 519-894-8900, Ext 234, 519-894-8900, Ext 269. FAX: 519-894-5331. E-mail: rathornton@emmanuelbiblecollege.ca. Web Site: www.emmanuelbiblecollege.ca. *Libr Mgr,* Ruth Anne Thornton; E-mail: rathornton@emmanuelbiblecollege.ca; Staff 1 (Non-MLS 1)
Enrl 100; Fac 9; Highest Degree: Bachelor
Library Holdings: Audiobooks 19; CDs 100; DVDs 353; e-books 1,074; Bk Titles 19,000; Bk Vols 24,000; Per Subs 36; Videos 37
Special Collections: Canada East; Christian Womens' Temperance League; Evangelical Missionary Church
Subject Interests: Biblical theol, Counseling, Hist, Psychol, Theol
Wireless access
Function: Electronic databases & coll
Open Tues-Thurs 10-4

M GRAND RIVER HOSPITAL*, Library Services, 835 King St W, N2G 1G3. (Mail add: PO Box 9056, N2G 1G3), SAN 319-2016. Tel: 519-749-4300, Ext 2235. E-mail: libraryservices@grhosp.on.ca. *Med Librn,* Caroline Yeomans
Founded 1954
Library Holdings: Bk Titles 4,000; Per Subs 150
Subject Interests: Allied health, Med, Nursing
Wireless access
Partic in Wellington-Waterloo-Dufferin Health Library Network
Open Mon, Tues & Thurs 8:30-3:15

P KITCHENER PUBLIC LIBRARY*, 85 Queen St N, N2H 2H1. SAN 367-5939. Tel: 519-743-0271. FAX: 519-743-1261. Web Site: www.kpl.org. *Chief Exec Officer,* Mary Chevreau; E-mail: mary.chevreau@kpl.org; *Dep Chief Exec Officer,* Penny-Lynn Fielding; E-mail: Penny-Lynn.Fielding@kpl.org; *Dir, Bus Services & Infrastructure,* Angela Riddell; E-mail: angela.riddell@kpl.org; *Dir, Innovation & Integration,* Lesa Balch; E-mail: lesa.balch@kpl.org; *Sr Mgr, Human Res,* Sarah Jewitt; E-mail: sarah.jewitt@kpl.org
Founded 1884. Pop 233,700; Circ 2,437,926
Special Collections: Waterloo County Historical Society Coll
Subject Interests: Local hist
Automation Activity & Vendor Info: (Acquisitions) Innovative Interfaces, Inc; (Cataloging) Innovative Interfaces, Inc; (Circulation) Innovative Interfaces, Inc; (OPAC) Innovative Interfaces, Inc; (Serials) Innovative Interfaces, Inc
Wireless access
Mem of Ontario Library Service
Open Mon-Thurs 9:30-9, Fri 9:30-5:30, Sat 9-5:30, Sun 1-5
Branches: 5
COUNTRY HILLS COMMUNITY, 1500 Block Line Rd, N2C 2S2. Tel: 519-743-3558. FAX: 519-743-3558, Ext 297. *Br Mgr,* Alison Schroeder

FOREST HEIGHTS, 251 Fischer-Hallman Rd, N2H 2H1, SAN 367-5963. Tel: 519-743-0644. FAX: 519-743-0644. *Librn,* Chris Schnarr
Open Mon-Thurs 9:30-9, Fri 9:30-5:30, Sat 9-5:30

GRAND RIVER STANLEY PARK, 175 Indian Rd, N2B 2S7, SAN 367-5998. Tel: 519-896-1736. FAX: 519-896-1736. *Librn,* Robyn Zondervan
Open Mon-Thurs 9:30-9, Fri 9:30-5:30, Sat 9-5:30
Friends of the Library Group

PIONEER PARK, 150 Pioneer Dr, N2H 2H1, SAN 367-598X. Tel: 519-748-2740. FAX: 519-748-2740. *Librn,* Maureen Plomske
Open Mon-Thurs 9:30-9, Fri 9:30-5:30, Sat 9-5:30

GRACE SCHMIDT ROOM OF LOCAL HISTORY, 85 Queen St N, N2H 2H1, SAN 329-2215. Tel: 519-743-0271, Ext 252. FAX: 519-743-1261. Web Site: www.kpl.org/services/local-history-and-genealogy. *Librn,*

Karen Ball-Pyatt; E-mail: karen.ball-pyatt@kpl.org; Staff 2 (MLS 1, Non-MLS 1)
Library Holdings: Bk Vols 500
Special Collections: Oral History
Subject Interests: Genealogy, Local hist
Publications: Waterloo Historical Society Annual Reports
Restriction: Open to pub for ref only

M ST MARY'S GENERAL HOSPITAL, Medical Library, 911 Queen's Blvd, N2M 1B2. SAN 319-2032. Tel: 519-749-6549. E-mail: library@smgh.ca. Web Site: www.smgh.ca. *Librn,* Laura Paprocki; Staff 1 (MLS 1)
Founded 1962
Library Holdings: Bk Titles 350
Subject Interests: Cardiology, Med, Nursing, Ophthalmology, Rheumatology
Wireless access
Restriction: Staff use only

L WATERLOO REGION LAW ASSOCIATION, 85 Frederick St, N2H 0A7. SAN 370-6001. Tel: 519-742-0872. Toll Free Tel: 866-201-0168. FAX: 519-742-4102. Web Site: waterloolaw.org. *Exec Dir, Libr Mgr,* Pia Williams; E-mail: pwilliams@waterloolaw.org; *Libr Tech,* Najla Nureddin; E-mail: nnureddin@waterloolaw.org; *Libr Asst,* Merve Turhan; E-mail: mturhan@waterloolaw.org; Staff 3 (MLS 1, Non-MLS 2)
Founded 1894
Library Holdings: Bk Vols 15,500; Per Subs 16
Wireless access
Publications: WRLA Newsletter (Monthly)
Restriction: Mem only, Not open to pub

KLEINBURG

S MCMICHAEL CANADIAN ART COLLECTION, Library/Archives, 10365 Islington Ave, L0J 1C0. SAN 323-7192. Tel: 905-893-1121, Ext 2255. FAX: 905-893-2588. E-mail: library@mcmichael.com. Web Site: mcmichael.com/about/library-archives. *Archivist/Librn,* Linda Morita; Staff 1 (MLS 1)
Special Collections: Artist Archives (Canadian artists especially Group of Seven); Canadian Art Coll (focus on Group of Seven); Canadian Indigenous Art & Culture Coll; Norman E Hallendy Archives
Subject Interests: Canadian historical art, Group of Seven, Indigenous art & culture, Inuit art
Automation Activity & Vendor Info: (Cataloging) Lucidea - GeniePlus; (OPAC) Lucidea - GeniePlus
Wireless access
Restriction: Non-circulating, Open by appt only

LANSDOWNE

P LEEDS & THE THOUSAND ISLANDS PUBLIC LIBRARY*, 1B Jessie St, K0E 1L0. (Mail add: PO Box 219, K0E 1L0), SAN 319-2059. Tel: 613-659-3885. FAX: 613-659-4192. E-mail: staff@ltipl.net. Web Site: www.ltipl.net. *Chief Exec Officer,* Dayna DeBenedet; Staff 1 (MLS 1)
Founded 1974. Pop 4,387
Library Holdings: Bk Vols 26,000; Per Subs 38
Wireless access
Open Mon, Tues & Thurs 1:30-7:30, Wed 9:30-7:30, Fri 12:30-4:30, Sat 10:30-1:30
Friends of the Library Group
Branches: 3
ARCHIVES, 1365 County Rd 2, Mallorytown, K0E 1R0. (Mail add: PO Box 332, K0E 1L0), SAN 319-2342. Tel: 613-659-3800. FAX: 613-659-3800. *Interim Archivist,* Pierre Mercier; E-mail: archivist@ltiarchives.ca
Founded 1975
Restriction: Open by appt only
Friends of the Library Group
LYNDHURST BRANCH, 426 Lyndhurst Rd, Lyndhurst, K0E 1N0. SAN 367-1372. Tel: 613-928-2277. FAX: 613-928-2277. E-mail: lyndhurst@ltipl.net. *Br Coordr,* Lisa Marston
Open Mon 1:30-5:30, Wed 1:30-7:30, Fri 2:30-5:30, Sat 9:30-12:30
SEELEY'S BAY BRANCH, 150 Main St, Seeley's Bay, K0H 2N0, SAN 367-1461. Tel: 613-387-3909. E-mail: seeleysbay@ltipl.net. *Br Coordr,* Position Currently Open
Open Tues 1:30-5:30, Thurs 1:30-7:30, Fri 9:30-12:30, Sat 2:30-5:30

LARDER LAKE

P LARDER LAKE PUBLIC LIBRARY, 69 Fourth Ave, P0K 1L0. (Mail add: PO Box 189, P0K 1L0), SAN 319-2067. Tel: 705-643-2222. E-mail: llpublib@larderlake.ca. Web Site: www.larderlakepubliclibrary.ca. *Chief Exec Officer, Librn,* Patricia Bodick
Founded 1940. Pop 800; Circ 12,000
Library Holdings: DVDs 525; Bk Titles 13,000; Per Subs 45
Automation Activity & Vendor Info: (Acquisitions) SirsiDynix
Wireless access
Function: 24/7 Electronic res, 24/7 Online cat, 24/7 wireless access, Children's prog, Computer training, Computers for patron use, E-Readers, Electronic databases & coll, Free DVD rentals, Holiday prog, ILL available, Internet access, Laminating, Large print keyboards, Magazines, Movies, Online cat, Photocopying/Printing, Prog for adults, Prog for children & young adult, Scanner, Serves people with intellectual disabilities, Summer reading prog, Wheelchair accessible
Special Services for the Blind - Accessible computers; Assistive/Adapted tech devices, equip & products
Open Tues & Thurs 1-8, Wed & Sat 1-4

LEAMINGTON

G POINT PELEE NATIONAL PARK LIBRARY*, 1118 Point Pelee Dr, N8H 3V4. Tel: 519-322-5700, Ext 21. Toll Free Tel: 888-773-8888. FAX: 519-322-1277. TDD: 866-787-8888. E-mail: pc.pelee.info.pc@canada.ca. Web Site: www.pc.gc.ca/en/pn-np/on/pelee. *Mgr,* Monique Oltrop
Library Holdings: Bk Titles 5,000; Per Subs 24
Special Collections: Botany (Herbarium Coll), specimens; Entomology (Insects Coll), specimens
Restriction: Staff use only

LEFAIVRE

P ALFRED & PLANTAGENET PUBLIC LIBRARY SYSTEM*, 1963 Hotel de ville St, K0B 1J0. (Mail add: PO Box 280, Plantagenet, K0B 1L0), SAN 319-3691. Tel: 613-679-4928. FAX: 613-679-4928. E-mail: bibliolefaivre@yahoo.ca. Web Site: www.alfred-plantagenet.com/en/living-here/bibliotheques.aspx. *Library Contact,* Lyne Brazeau
Pop 2,650; Circ 7,483
Library Holdings: Bk Vols 10,430
Wireless access
Open Tues & Thurs 1-4:30 & 6-8
Branches: 5
ALFRED BRANCH, 555 Saint-Philippe St, Alfred, K0B 1A0, SAN 321-1681. Tel: 613-679-2663. FAX: 613-679-2663. *Br Head,* Ginette Peladeau; E-mail: peladeaug@yahoo.ca
Circ 16,713
Library Holdings: Bk Vols 11,172
Open Mon 4-7, Tues & Thurs 1-8, Wed 10-12 & 2-5, Sat 10-3
Friends of the Library Group
CURRAN BRANCH, 791 Mill St Box 29, Curran, K0B 1C0, SAN 324-7074. Tel: 613-673-2072. FAX: 613-673-2072. E-mail: bibliothequecurran@yahoo.ca. *Br Head,* Carol Mainville
Circ 10,907
Library Holdings: Bk Vols 11,324
Open Tues & Thurs 1:30-4:30 & 6:30-8:30, Sat 10-1
LEFAIVRE BRANCH, 1963 Hotel de Ville St, K0B 1J0, SAN 377-6867. E-mail: bibliolefaivre@yahoo.ca. *Br Head,* Lyne Brazeau
Circ 6,905
Library Holdings: Bk Vols 10,672
Open Tues 1-4:30 & 6-8, Thurs 11-12, 1-4:30 & 6-8
Friends of the Library Group
PLANTAGENET BRANCH, 550 Albert St, Plantagenet, K0B 1L0. Tel: 613-673-2051. FAX: 613-673-2051. E-mail: biblioplant@yahoo.com. *Br Head,* Lyne Brazeau
Open Mon 5pm-8pm, Wed & Fri 1:30-5:30 & 6:30-8:30
WENDOVER BRANCH, 5000 rue du Centre, Wendover, K0A 3K0, SAN 324-7082. Tel: 613-673-2923. FAX: 613-673-2923. E-mail: bibliowend@yahoo.ca. *Br Head,* Anne St-Pierre
Circ 4,412
Library Holdings: Bk Vols 7,988
Open Tues 6pm-8pm, Thurs 11:30-4:30 & 6-8, Sat 10-1

LINDSAY

P KAWARTHA LAKES PUBLIC LIBRARY*, Headquarters, 190 Kent St W, Lower Level, K9V 2Y6. SAN 367-6080. Tel: 705-324-9411, Ext 1291. Reference Tel: 705-324-9411, Ext 1268. FAX: 705-878-1859. E-mail: libraryadministration@kawarthalakes.ca. Web Site: www.kawarthalakeslibrary.ca. *Libr Dir & Chief Exec Officer,* Jamie Anderson; E-mail: janderson@kawarthalakeslibrary.ca; *South Area Libr Coord,* Marieke Junkin; Tel: 705-324-9411, Ext 1265, E-mail: mjunkin@kawarthalakeslibrary.ca; *North Area Libr Coord,* Debbie Spivey; Tel: 705-887-6300, E-mail: dspivey@kawarthalakeslibrary.ca; Staff 6 (MLS 1, Non-MLS 5)
Founded 2001. Pop 75,000
Library Holdings: Bk Vols 170,267
Wireless access
Mem of Ontario Library Service
Open Mon-Thurs 10-8, Fri & Sat 10-5, Sun (Oct-June) 1-4
Friends of the Library Group

Branches: 14
BETHANY BRANCH, 1474 Hwy 7A, Bethany, L0A 1K0. Tel: 705-324-9411, Ext 3544.
Open Tues 3-7, Wed & Sat 10-2, Thurs 11-7
BOBCAYGEON BRANCH, 21 Canal St, Bobcaygeon, K0M 1A0, SAN 367-6110. Tel: 705-738-2088.
Open Mon & Thurs 12:30-7, Tues, Wed & Fri 10-5, Sat 10-3
COBOCONK BRANCH, Nine Grandy Rd, Coboconk, K0M 1K0, SAN 367-620X. Tel: 705-324-9411, Ext 3504.
Open Mon & Thurs 8:30-7, Tues, Wed & Fri 8:30-4:30, Sat 10-2
DALTON BRANCH, 13 Rumohr Dr, Sebright, L0K 1W0, SAN 367-6269. Tel: 705-833-2858.
Open Mon & Sat 10-2, Wed 3-7
DUNSFORD BRANCH, 26 Community Centre Rd, Dunsford, K0M 1L0, SAN 367-6323. Tel: 705-793-3037.
Open Tues 2-7, Wed 10-1, Sat 10-2
FENELON FALLS BRANCH, 19 Market St, Fenelon Falls, K0M 1N0, SAN 367-6382. Tel: 705-887-6300.
Open Mon, Wed & Fri 10-5, Tues & Thurs 10-8, Sat 10-3
KINMOUNT BRANCH, 3980 County Rd 121, Kinmount, K0M 2A0, SAN 367-6412. Tel: 705-488-3199.
Open Tues & Sat 10-2, Wed 3-7, Thurs 11-7
KIRKFIELD LIBRARY, Seven Monroe St, Kirkfield, K0M 2B0, SAN 367-6358. Tel: 705-324-9411, Ext 3564.
Open Tues 11-7, Wed 3-7, Thurs & Sat 10-2
LINDSAY BRANCH, 190 Kent St W, K9V 2Y6. Tel: 705-324-9411, Ext 1263.
Open Mon-Thurs 10-8, Fri & Sat 10-5, Sun (Dec-June) 1-4
LITTLE BRITAIN BRANCH, Nine Arena Rd, Little Britain, K0M 2C0, SAN 367-6447. Tel: 705-786-2088.
Open Mon & Sat 10-2, Thurs 3-7
NORLAND BRANCH, 3448 County Rd 45, Norland, K0M 2L0, SAN 367-6501. Tel: 705-454-8552.
Open Tues & Sat 10-2, Thurs 3-7
OAKWOOD BRANCH, 932 Hwy 7, Oakwood, K0M 2M0, SAN 367-6536. Tel: 705-953-9060.
Open Tues 11-7, Wed & Sat 10-2
OMEMEE BRANCH, 24 King St E, Omemee, K0L 2W0, SAN 367-6560. Tel: 705-799-5711.
Open Tues & Sat 10-2, Wed 3-7, Thurs 11-7
WOODVILLE BRANCH, 78 King St, Woodville, K0M 2T0, SAN 367-6595. Tel: 705-439-2160.
Open Mon & Thurs 1-7, Fri & Sat 10-2

C SIR SANDFORD FLEMING COLLEGE OF APPLIED ARTS & TECHNOLOGIES, Frost Campus Library, School of Environmental & Natural Resources, 200 Albert St S, K9V 5E6. (Mail add: PO Box 8000, K9V 5E6), SAN 319-2113. Tel: 705-878-9319. FAX: 705-878-9313. E-mail: library@flemingcollege.ca. Web Site: library.flemingcollege.ca.
Founded 1968
Subject Interests: Arboriculture, Ecosystem mgt, Environ tech, Fish, Forestry, Geol, Heavy equip, Natural res law, Outdoor recreation, Park operations, Res drilling & blasting, Wildlife
Automation Activity & Vendor Info: (Circulation) Ex Libris Group; (Course Reserve) Ex Libris Group; (ILL) Ex Libris Group; (OPAC) Ex Libris Group
Wireless access
Open Mon-Fri 8:30-4:30

LISTOWEL

P NORTH PERTH PUBLIC LIBRARY*, 260 Main St W, N4W 1A1. SAN 319-2121. Tel: 519-291-4621. Toll Free Tel: 888-714-1993. FAX: 519-291-2235. E-mail: npl@northperth.ca. Web Site: www.northperth.ca/en/explore-and-discover/north-perth-public-library.aspx. *Interim Chief Exec Officer,* Ellen Whelan; Tel: 519-291-4621
Founded 1907. Pop 12,000; Circ 103,177
Library Holdings: Bk Titles 52,699; Bk Vols 59,414; Per Subs 89
Subject Interests: Biog, Can hist
Wireless access
Mem of Ontario Library Service
Partic in Perth County Information Network
Open Mon-Thurs 10-8, Fri 10-5, Sat 10-3
Friends of the Library Group
Branches: 2
ATWOOD BRANCH, 218A Main St, Atwood, N4W 3W1. Tel: 519-356-2455.
Open Tues 3-7, Thurs 11-2, Sat 1-3
MONKTON BRANCH, 200 Nelson St, Monkton, N0K 1P0. Tel: 519-347-2703.
Open Tues 11-2, Thurs 3-7, Sat 10-12

LITTLE CURRENT

P AUNDECK OMNI KANING FIRST NATION PUBLIC LIBRARY, 1300 Hwy 540, P0P 1K0. (Mail add: Box 21, P0P 1K0), SAN 319-2148. Tel: 705-368-0739. Administration Tel: 705-368-2228. FAX: 705-368-3563. E-mail: aoktent@aoksn.com.
Founded 1975. Pop 500; Circ 2,000
Library Holdings: Bk Vols 2,100
Special Collections: Native Coll, bks, videos
Automation Activity & Vendor Info: (Cataloging) SirsiDynix; (OPAC) SirsiDynix
Open Mon-Fri 8:30-4

P NEMI PUBLIC LIBRARY*, 50 Meredith St W, P0P 1K0. (Mail add: PO Box 459, P0P 1K0), SAN 319-213X. Tel: 705-368-2444. FAX: 705-368-0708. E-mail: nemilib@vianet.ca. Web Site: nemi.olsn.ca/location. *Chief Exec Officer, Head Librn,* Kathy Berry
Pop 2,300; Circ 24,000
Library Holdings: Bk Titles 13,540; Per Subs 16
Wireless access
Open Tues, Wed, Fri & Sat 10-5, Thurs 10-7

LONDON

CR BRESCIA UNIVERSITY COLLEGE*, Beryl Ivey Library, 1285 Western Rd, N6G 1H2. SAN 319-2164. Tel: 519-432-8353, Ext 28250. FAX: 519-858-5137. E-mail: beryliveylibrary@uwo.ca. Web Site: www.brescia.uwo.ca/library. *Dir, Libr Serv,* Caroline Whippey; E-mail: caroline.whippey@uwo.ca; Staff 6 (MLS 3, Non-MLS 3)
Founded 1919. Enrl 1,500; Highest Degree: Master
Library Holdings: Bk Titles 52,000
Automation Activity & Vendor Info: (Acquisitions) Ex Libris Group; (Cataloging) Ex Libris Group; (Circulation) Ex Libris Group; (OPAC) Ex Libris Group
Wireless access

J FANSHAWE COLLEGE*, Library & Media Services, 1001 Fanshawe College Blvd, N5Y 5R6. (Mail add: PO Box 7005, N5Y 5R6), SAN 319-2199. Tel: 519-452-4240. FAX: 519-452-4473. E-mail: library@fanshawec.ca. Web Site: www.fanshawelibrary.com. *Dir,* Jessica Bugorski; E-mail: jbugorski@fanshawec.ca; *Curric Librn, Research Librn,* Megan Anderson; E-mail: manderson@fanshawec.ca; *Curric Librn, Research Librn,* Linda Crosby; E-mail: lcrosby@fanshawec.ca; Staff 16 (MLS 4, Non-MLS 12)
Founded 1967. Enrl 10,000; Highest Degree: Bachelor
Library Holdings: e-books 20,000; Bk Titles 60,000; Per Subs 450; Videos 5,000
Special Collections: Can & Prov
Subject Interests: Applied arts, Health sci
Automation Activity & Vendor Info: (Cataloging) SirsiDynix; (Circulation) SirsiDynix; (OPAC) SirsiDynix
Wireless access
Open Mon-Thurs 8:30am-10pm, Fri 8:30-4:30, Sun 1-5

C HURON UNIVERSITY COLLEGE*, Library & Learning Services, 1349 Western Rd, N6G 1H3. SAN 319-2202. Tel: 519-438-7224, Ext 213. E-mail: huclibrary@uwo.ca. Web Site: huronuc.ca/library. *Learning Librn,* Rachel Melis; Tel: 519-438-7224, Ext 235, E-mail: rmelis@uwo.edu; *Content & Collection Librn,* Melissa Rapp; Tel: 519-438-7224, Ext 283, E-mail: mrapp2@uwo.edu; *Digital Scholarship Librn,* Ryan Rabie; Tel: 519-438-7224, Ext 195, E-mail: rrabie@uwo.edu; Staff 5 (MLS 2, Non-MLS 3)
Founded 1863. Enrl 1,200; Fac 75; Highest Degree: Master
Library Holdings: Bk Vols 170,000; Per Subs 172
Subject Interests: Chinese, Econ, English, Hist, Philos, Psychol, Theol
Wireless access
Open Mon-Fri 8:30-4

CR KING'S UNIVERSITY COLLEGE AT THE UNIVERSITY OF WESTERN ONTARIO*, G Emmett Cardinal Carter Library, 266 Epworth Ave, N6A 2M3. SAN 319-2210. Tel: 519-433-3491, Ext 4390. Circulation Tel: 519-433-3491, Ext 4505. Reference Tel: 519-433-3491, Ext 4327. Toll Free Tel: 800-265-4406, Ext 4390. FAX: 519-963-0307. Web Site: www.kings.uwo.ca/library. *Dir of Libr,* Adrienne Co-Dyre; *Head, Res & Info Serv,* Emma Swiatek; E-mail: emma.swiatek@kings.uwo.ca; *Assoc Librn, Head, Tech & Info Res,* Linda M Whidden; Tel: 519-433-3491, Ext 4506, E-mail: lwhidden@uwo.ca. Subject Specialists: *Philos, Psychol, Relig,* Adrienne Co-Dyre; *English, Soc work, Sociol,* Emma Swiatek; *Econ, Hist, Polit sci,* Linda M Whidden; Staff 6 (MLS 3, Non-MLS 3)
Founded 1954. Enrl 3,800; Fac 185; Highest Degree: Master
Library Holdings: CDs 106; DVDs 881; e-books 102,905; Microforms 1,888; Bk Titles 125,712; Per Subs 325
Special Collections: Cardinal Carter Archives; Georges Bernanos (William Bush Coll); Henry Edward Dormer Archives; Malcolm Muggeridge (Ian A. Hunter Coll); S & M Clouston 15th-18th Century Coll

Subject Interests: Peace studies, Relig, Soc justice, Soc work, Thanatology
Automation Activity & Vendor Info: (Acquisitions) Innovative Interfaces, Inc; (Cataloging) Innovative Interfaces, Inc; (Circulation) Innovative Interfaces, Inc; (Course Reserve) Innovative Interfaces, Inc; (ILL) Innovative Interfaces, Inc; (OPAC) Innovative Interfaces, Inc; (Serials) Innovative Interfaces, Inc
Wireless access
Function: Photocopying/Printing, Ref serv available
Special Services for the Deaf - Assistive tech
Special Services for the Blind - Assistive/Adapted tech devices, equip & products
Restriction: Open to students, fac & staff

L LERNERS LLP LIBRARY*, 85 Dufferin Ave, N6A 4G4. (Mail add: PO Box 2335, Sta A, N6A 4G4), SAN 326-1972. Tel: 519-640-6355. FAX: 519-932-3355. E-mail: lerner.london@lerners.ca. Web Site: www.lerners.ca. *Dir, Libr & Res Serv,* Michelle LaPorte; E-mail: mlaporte@lerners.ca. Subject Specialists: *Law,* Michelle LaPorte; Staff 4 (MLS 1, Non-MLS 3)
Library Holdings: e-books 3,000; Bk Titles 4,000; Bk Vols 10,000
Automation Activity & Vendor Info: (Acquisitions) EOS International; (Cataloging) EOS International; (Circulation) EOS International; (OPAC) EOS International; (Serials) EOS International
Wireless access
Restriction: Staff use only

M LONDON HEALTH SCIENCES CENTRE, Library Services, 800 Commissioners Rd E, N6A 4G5. SAN 373-6415. Tel: 519-685-8500, Ext 75934. FAX: 519-667-6641. Web Site: www.lhsc.on.ca. *Clinical Librarian Specialist,* Darren Hamilton; E-mail: darren.hamilton@lhsc.on.ca; *Clinical Librn,* Gabriel Boldt; E-mail: gabriel.boldt@lhsc.on.ca; *Clinical Librn,* Allison Fairbairn; E-mail: allison.fairbairn@lhsc.on.ca; *Clinical Librn,* Alla Iansavitchene; E-mail: alla.iansavitchene@lhsc.on.ca; Staff 4 (MLS 4)
Founded 1995
Library Holdings: AV Mats 250; e-books 150; Bk Titles 6,000; Per Subs 1,750
Subject Interests: Med, Nursing
Automation Activity & Vendor Info: (Acquisitions) Inmagic, Inc.; (Cataloging) Inmagic, Inc.; (Circulation) Inmagic, Inc.; (Serials) Inmagic, Inc.
Wireless access
Function: Doc delivery serv, For res purposes, ILL available, Outside serv via phone, mail, e-mail & web, Photocopying/Printing, Prof lending libr, Ref serv available, Telephone ref
Partic in Canadian Health Libraries Association; Ontario Health Libraries Association
Open Mon-Fri 8-4
Restriction: Open to students, fac & staff

P LONDON PUBLIC LIBRARY*, Central, 251 Dundas St, N6A 6H9. SAN 367-6625. Tel: 519-661-4600. FAX: 519-663-9013. TDD: 519-432-8835. E-mail: info@lpl.ca. Web Site: www.londonpubliclibrary.ca. *Chief Librn/CEO,* Michael Ciccone; E-mail: michael.ciccone@lpl.ca; *Dir, Br Operations, Dir, Customer Serv,* Nancy Collister; Tel: 519-661-5100, Ext 5136, E-mail: nancy.collister@lpl.ca; Staff 222 (MLS 54, Non-MLS 168)
Founded 1894. Pop 40,000; Circ 3,412,777
Library Holdings: AV Mats 6,396; CDs 1,014; DVDs 48,954; e-books 5,773; Large Print Bks 23,427; Bk Vols 554,170; Per Subs 1,632; Talking Bks 1,664
Special Collections: Can & Prov; Local History (London Room Coll) a-tapes, bks, microfilm, pictures. Oral History
Subject Interests: Archit, Art, Hist, Humanities, Music
Wireless access
Publications: Access (Monthly bulletin); Annual Report; Subject-Specific Booklists
Partic in Ont Pub Libr Info Network
Special Services for the Deaf - Bks on deafness & sign lang; High interest/low vocabulary bks; Staff with knowledge of sign lang; TTY equip
Open Mon-Thurs 9-9, Fri 9-6, Sat 9-5
Friends of the Library Group
Branches: 16
BEACOCK, 1280 Huron St, N5Y 4M2, SAN 367-6862. Tel: 519-451-8140. *Br Librn,* Maria Forte
Library Holdings: Bk Vols 58,483
Open Tues-Thurs 9-9, Fri 9-6, Sat 9-5
Friends of the Library Group
BOSTWICK, Bostwick Community Ctr, 501 Southdale Rd W, N6K 3X4. Tel: 519-473-4708. *Br Librn,* Sarah Andrews
Open Tues-Thurs 9-9, Fri 9-6, Sat 9-5
Friends of the Library Group
BYRON MEMORIAL, 1295 Commissioners Rd W, N6K 1C9, SAN 367-6714. Tel: 519-471-4000. *Br Librn,* Debra Franke
Library Holdings: Bk Vols 58,542
Open Tues-Thurs 9-9, Fri 9-6, Sat 9-5
Friends of the Library Group
W O CARSON, 465 Quebec St, N5W 3Y4, SAN 376-9720. Tel: 519-438-4287. *Br Librn,* Maria Forte
Library Holdings: Bk Vols 22,670
Open Tues & Thurs 1-5 & 6-9, Wed, Fri & Sat 9-12 & 1-5
Friends of the Library Group
CHERRYHILL, 301 Oxford St W, N6H 1S6, SAN 367-6927. Tel: 519-439-6456. *Br Librn,* Cathy McLandress
Library Holdings: Bk Vols 53,334
Open Tues-Thurs 9-9, Fri 9-6, Sat 9-5
Friends of the Library Group
CHILDREN'S, 251 Dundas St, N6A 6H9, SAN 367-6773. *Children's Coordr,* Lisa Manax
Library Holdings: Bk Vols 50,701
Open Mon-Thurs 9-9, Fri 9-6, Sat 9-5
Friends of the Library Group
R E CROUCH, 550 Hamilton Rd, N5Z 1S4, SAN 367-6803. Tel: 519-673-0111. *Br Librn,* Kevin Davidson
Library Holdings: Bk Vols 43,699
Open Tues-Thurs 9-9, Fri 9-6, Sat 9-5
Friends of the Library Group
EAST LONDON, 2016 Dundas St, N5V 1R1, SAN 367-665X. Tel: 519-451-7600. *Br Librn,* Barbara Adams
Library Holdings: Bk Vols 41,681
Open Tues-Thurs 9-9, Fri 9-6, Sat 9-5
Friends of the Library Group
GLANWORTH, 2950 Glanworth Dr, N6N 1N6, SAN 376-9739. Tel: 519-681-6797. *Br Librn,* Sarah Andrews
Library Holdings: Bk Vols 2,686
Open Tues 7pm-9pm, Sat 10-Noon
Friends of the Library Group
JALNA, 1119 Jalna Blvd, N6E 3B3, SAN 323-9365. Tel: 519-685-6465. *Br Librn,* Jodi Lewis
Library Holdings: Bk Vols 63,698
Open Tues-Thurs 9-9, Fri 9-6, Sat 9-5
Friends of the Library Group
LAMBETH, 7112 Beattie St, Lambeth, N6P 1A2, SAN 376-9747. Tel: 519-652-2951. *Br Librn,* Sarah Andrews
Library Holdings: Bk Vols 20,180
Open Tues & Thurs 1-5 & 6-9, Wed, Fri & Sat 9-12 & 1-5
Friends of the Library Group
LANDON, 167 Wortley Rd, N6C 3P6, SAN 367-6838. Tel: 519-439-6240. *Br Librn,* Jennifer Quinton
Library Holdings: Bk Vols 40,496
Open Tues-Thurs 9-9, Fri 9-6, Sat 9-5
Friends of the Library Group
MASONVILLE, 30 North Centre Rd, N5X 3W1, SAN 376-2165. Tel: 519-660-4646. *Br Librn,* Jessica Kipp
Library Holdings: Bk Vols 54,309
Open Tues-Thurs 9-9, Fri 9-6, Sat 9-5
Friends of the Library Group
POND MILLS, 1166 Commissioners Rd E, N5Z 4W8, SAN 323-8407. Tel: 519-685-1333. *Br Librn,* Kevin Moore
Library Holdings: Bk Vols 48,607
Open Tues-Thurs 9-9, Fri 9-6, Sat 9-5
Friends of the Library Group
SHERWOOD FOREST, Sherwood Forest Mall, 1225 Wonderland Rd N, #32, N6G 2V9, SAN 328-9699. Tel: 519-473-9965. *Br Librn,* Heather Lavalle
Library Holdings: Bk Vols 53,406
Open Tues-Thurs 9-9, Fri 9-6, Sat 9-5
Friends of the Library Group
STONEY CREEK, 920 Sunningdale Rd E, N5X 0H5. Tel: 519-930-2065. *Br Librn,* Brian Rhoden
Open Tues-Thurs 9-9, Fri 9-6, Sat 9-5
Friends of the Library Group

L MIDDLESEX LAW ASSOCIATION*, Law Library, Ground Flr, Unit N, 80 Dundas St, N6A 6A1. SAN 319-2253. Tel: 519-679-7046. E-mail: library@middlaw.on.ca. Web Site: middlaw.on.ca/library-resources. *Exec Dir,* Tracy Fawdry; E-mail: tracy@middlaw.on.ca; *Librn,* Cynthia Simpson; *Libr Tech,* Shabira Tamachi; Staff 3 (MLS 1, Non-MLS 2)
Founded 1879
Library Holdings: Bk Vols 21,000
Special Collections: Historical Coll of City (London) Directories
Wireless access
Restriction: Not open to pub, Private libr

M PARKWOOD INSTITUTE MENTAL HEALTH CARE LIBRARY*, 550-Wellington Rd, N6C 5J1. SAN 324-4962. Tel: 519-455-5110. E-mail: rmhcl_library@sjhc.london.on.ca. Web Site: sjhc.london.on.ca. *Med Librn,* Elizabeth Russell; Tel: 519-455-5110, Ext 49685, E-mail: elizabeth.russell@sjhc.london.on.ca; *Libr Asst,* Allison Fairnbairn; E-mail: allison.fairnbairn@sjhc.london.on.ca; Staff 2 (MLS 1, Non-MLS 1)
Founded 1964

Library Holdings: Bk Titles 2,694; Per Subs 116
Subject Interests: Mental health, Psychiat, Psychol
Automation Activity & Vendor Info: (Cataloging) Inmagic, Inc.; (Circulation) Inmagic, Inc.; (OPAC) Inmagic, Inc.; (Serials) Inmagic, Inc.
Wireless access
Open Mon-Fri 8:30-4:15

S PARMALAT CANADA, LTD*, Research & Development Library, 65 Bathurst St, N6B 1N8. SAN 329-9430. Tel: 519-667-7709. FAX: 519-667-7725. Web Site: www.parmalat.ca. *Library Contact,* Brigitte Bowen; Tel: 519-667-7769, E-mail: brigitte_bowen@parmalat.ca
Library Holdings: Bk Vols 450
Subject Interests: Dairy, Engr, Food sci, Nutrition
Open Mon-Fri 8:30-4:30
Restriction: Restricted access

R SAINT PETER'S SEMINARY*, A P Mahoney Library, 1040 Waterloo St N, N6A 3Y1. SAN 319-227X. Tel: 519-646-7125. FAX: 519-432-0964. E-mail: library@uwo.ca. Web Site: www.stpetersseminary.ca/Library/50. *Dir of Libr,* Adrienne Co-Dyre; Tel: 519-433-3491, Ext 4390, E-mail: adrienne.co-dyre@kings.uwo.ca; *Assoc Librn,* Jordan Patterson; E-mail: jpatte64@uwo.ca; Staff 2 (MLS 2)
Founded 1926
Library Holdings: AV Mats 2,041; Per Subs 110
Subject Interests: Philos, Theol
Automation Activity & Vendor Info: (Acquisitions) Innovative Interfaces, Inc - Sierra; (Cataloging) Innovative Interfaces, Inc - Sierra; (Circulation) Innovative Interfaces, Inc - Sierra; (Course Reserve) Innovative Interfaces, Inc - Sierra; (OPAC) Innovative Interfaces, Inc - Sierra
Wireless access
Function: 24/7 Online cat
Open Mon-Fri 8:30-4:30, Sat 1-5 (Sept-Apr); Mon-Fri 8:30-12:30 & 1-4:30 (May-Aug)

L SISKIND, CROMARTY, IVEY & DOWLER*, Law Library, 680 Waterloo St, N6A 3V8. (Mail add: PO Box 2520, N6A 3V8), SAN 328-0446. Tel: 519-672-2121. FAX: 519-672-6065. E-mail: library@siskinds.com. Web Site: www.siskinds.com. *Librn, Res Officer,* Michael McAlpine; E-mail: michael.mcalpine@siskinds.com; Staff 1 (MLS 1)
Library Holdings: Bk Titles 200
Function: CD-ROM, Doc delivery serv, For res purposes, Govt ref serv, Internet access, Ref serv available, VHS videos
Restriction: Co libr, Open to staff only

C UNIVERSITY OF WESTERN ONTARIO*, Faculty of Information & Media Studies Graduate Library, FNB 3020, N6A 5B9. SAN 324-4938. Tel: 519-661-2111, Ext 88488. E-mail: fimslib@uwo.ca. Web Site: lib.fims.uwo.ca. *Libr Dir,* Marni Harrington; E-mail: mharring@uwo.ca; *Libr Asst,* Kendall Sturgeon; E-mail: ksturge3@uwo.ca; Staff 4 (MLS 1, Non-MLS 3)
Founded 1966. Enrl 300; Highest Degree: Doctorate
Library Holdings: Bk Titles 1,500; Per Subs 150
Subject Interests: Health sci, Journalism, Libr sci, Media studies, Popular culture, Popular music
Wireless access
Function: Ref serv available
Restriction: Authorized patrons, Badge access after hrs, Borrowing privileges limited to fac & registered students, Borrowing requests are handled by ILL, ID required to use computers (Ltd hrs), Non-circulating coll

C WESTERN UNIVERSITY LIBRARIES*, 1151 Richmond St, Ste 200, N6A 3K7. SAN 367-6951. Tel: 519-661-3166. Administration Tel: 519-661-2111, Ext 84796. FAX: 519-661-3493. E-mail: libadmin@uwo.edu. Web Site: www.lib.uwo.ca. *Vice Provost & Chief Librn,* Catherine Steeves; Tel: 519-661-2111, Ext 83165, E-mail: csteeves@uwo.ca; *Chief Librn,* Bobby Glushko; Tel: 519-661-2111, Ext 82740, E-mail: rglushko@uwo.ca; *Dep Chief Librn,* Jennifer Robinson; Tel: 519-661-2111, Ext 86897, E-mail: jrobins@uwo.ca; Staff 62 (MLS 45, Non-MLS 17)
Founded 1908. Enrl 35,000; Fac 1,400; Highest Degree: Doctorate
Library Holdings: e-books 800,000; e-journals 79,327; Bk Vols 3,162,463; Per Subs 6,852; Videos 6,000
Special Collections: Canadian and Provincial
Subject Interests: Applied health sci, Dentistry, Educ, Engr, Humanities, Journalism, Kinesiology, Law, Med, Music, Nursing, Sci, Soc sci
Automation Activity & Vendor Info: (Acquisitions) Innovative Interfaces, Inc; (Cataloging) Innovative Interfaces, Inc; (Circulation) Innovative Interfaces, Inc; (OPAC) Innovative Interfaces, Inc; (Serials) Innovative Interfaces, Inc
Wireless access
Publications: A Guide to Selected Microform Collections & Sets in The D B Weldon Library; Bibliography of Hitchins Coll; Catalogue of the R M Bucke Coll; Guide to Canadian Newspapers on Microfilm in The D B Weldon Library
Partic in Ontario Council of University Libraries
Friends of the Library Group

Departmental Libraries:

ARCHIVES & RESEARCH COLLECTIONS CENTRE, The D B Weldon Library, 1151 Richmond St, Ste 2, N6A 3K7. Tel: 519-661-4046. FAX: 519-850-2979. E-mail: archive.services@uwo.ca. Web Site: www.lib.uwo.ca/archives. *Head Archivist,* Tom Belton; E-mail: tbelton@uwo.ca; Staff 12 (MLS 5, Non-MLS 7)
Founded 1900
Library Holdings: Electronic Media & Resources 1,652,000; Microforms 13,839; Bk Vols 80,000; Spec Interest Per Sub 15,381
Special Collections: Aviation History (Beatrice Hitchins Memorial Coll); Canadian Newspapers, microfilm; Canadian Quaker Archives, 1789-1950, microfilm; Canadian, American & British Government Publs; Edwardian Writers (John Galt Coll); French Enlightenment & the Revolution; History of Science & Medicine (Hannah Coll); John Milton & Miltonia (G William Stuart Jr Coll); Richard Maurice Buckle Coll; Southwestern Ontario Regional Coll; University Archives
Subject Interests: Local hist
Restriction: Non-circulating

CL JOHN & DOTSA BITOVE FAMILY LAW LIBRARY, Josephine Spencer Niblett Law Bldg, 2nd Flr, 1151 Richmond St, N6A 3K7, SAN 367-7109. Tel: 519-661-3171. FAX: 519-661-2012. E-mail: lawcirc@uwo.ca. Web Site: www.lib.uwo.ca/law. *Dir,* Stephen Spong; E-mail: sspong@uwo.ca; Staff 7 (MLS 2, Non-MLS 5)
Founded 1959. Enrl 850; Fac 40; Highest Degree: Doctorate
Library Holdings: Bk Vols 194,377; Per Subs 1,207
Subject Interests: Can law, Taxation
Function: Computers for patron use, Electronic databases & coll, ILL available, Photocopying/Printing, Ref & res, Ref serv available, Res libr, Wheelchair accessible
Open Mon-Fri 9-4:30
Friends of the Library Group

EDUCATION RESOURCE CENTRE, John George Althouse Bldg, Rm 1135, 1137 Western Rd, N6G 1G7, SAN 367-701X. Tel: 519-661-2111, Ext 89031. FAX: 519-661-3822. Web Site: www.lib.uwo.ca/education. *Head, User Serv,* Bruce Fyfe; E-mail: bfyfe@uwo.ca; Staff 2 (MLS 2)
Founded 1965. Enrl 873; Fac 42; Highest Degree: Doctorate
Library Holdings: Microforms 620,000; Bk Vols 650,000; Per Subs 342
Special Collections: Complete ERIC Coll, microfiche
Subject Interests: Elem educ
Function: Wheelchair accessible
Open Mon-Fri 12-4
Friends of the Library Group

C B JOHNSTON LIBRARY, Richard Ivey Bldg, Rm 1250, 1255 Western Rd, N6G 0N1, SAN 367-6986. Tel: 519-661-3941. FAX: 519-661-2158. E-mail: buslib@ivey.uwo.ca. Web Site: www.lib.uwo.ca/business. *Dir,* Elizabeth Marshall; Tel: 519-661-2111, Ext 84842, E-mail: emarsha3@uwo.ca; Staff 7 (MLS 2, Non-MLS 5)
Founded 1961. Enrl 1,169; Fac 93; Highest Degree: Doctorate
Library Holdings: Bk Vols 80,581; Per Subs 293
Special Collections: Canadian & US Company Data, microfiche. Canadian and Provincial
Subject Interests: Acctg, Finance, Labor relations, Mkt, Operation res
Special Services for the Deaf - ADA equip; Videos & decoder
Special Services for the Blind - Accessible computers
Open Mon-Fri 9-5
Friends of the Library Group

MUSIC LIBRARY, Talbot College, Rm 234, 1151 Richmond St, N6A 3K7, SAN 367-7133. Tel: 519-661-3913. E-mail: musref@uwo.ca. Web Site: www.lib.uwo.ca/music. *Dir,* Brian McMillan; Tel: 519-661-2111, Ext 85334, E-mail: bmcmill2@uwo.ca. Subject Specialists: *Dance, Music,* Brian McMillan; Staff 8 (MLS 2, Non-MLS 6)
Founded 1963. Enrl 661; Fac 42; Highest Degree: Doctorate
Library Holdings: AV Mats 53,912; Microforms 11,782; Music Scores 69,587; Bk Vols 35,806; Per Subs 557; Videos 453
Special Collections: Gustav Mahler, Alfred Rose & Bruno Walter (Mahler-Rose Coll), scores; Opera Coll, 1600-Early 20th Century
Subject Interests: Applied music, Hist, Music educ, Popular music, Theory of music
Function: Wheelchair accessible
Open Mon-Fri 9-5
Friends of the Library Group

ALLYN & BETTY TAYLOR LIBRARY, Natural Sciences Centre, 1151 Richmond St, N6A 5B7, SAN 367-7079. Tel: 519-661-3168. FAX: 519-661-3435. E-mail: taylib@uwo.ca. Web Site: www.lib.uwo.ca/taylor. *Mgr, User Serv,* Bruce Fyfe; E-mail: bfyfe@uwo.ca; Staff 26 (MLS 9, Non-MLS 17)
Founded 1882. Enrl 11,573; Fac 738; Highest Degree: Doctorate
Library Holdings: Bk Vols 360,712; Per Subs 900
Subject Interests: Chem, Chem engr, Communications, Communicative disorders, Conserv, Dentistry, Earth sci, Electrical engr, Life sci, Mat

engr, Math sci, Mechanical engr, Med, Natural hist, Nursing, Occupational therapy, Phys therapy
Function: Wheelchair accessible
Open Mon-Fri 9-8, Sat & Sun 10:30-5
Friends of the Library Group

THE D B WELDON LIBRARY, 1151 Richmond St, N6A 3K7. Tel: 519-661-3166. E-mail: dbwlib@uwo.ca. Web Site: www.lib.uwo.ca/weldon. *Head, User Serv,* Bruce Fyfe; E-mail: bfyfe@uwo.edu; Staff 100 (MLS 28, Non-MLS 72)
Founded 1934. Enrl 15,000; Fac 430; Highest Degree: Doctorate
Library Holdings: Microforms 2,929,162; Bk Titles 1,500,687; Per Subs 3,346
Subject Interests: Arts, Humanities, Journalism, Libr, Media studies, Soc sci
Function: Wheelchair accessible
Partic in Canadian Association of Research Libraries
Open Mon-Fri 8am-11:30pm, Sat & Sun 10:30-5
Friends of the Library Group

L'ORIGNAL

L PRESCOTT & RUSSELL LAW ASSOCIATION*, Henri Proulx Law Library, 1027 Queen St, K0B 1K0. (Mail add: PO Box 540, K0B 1K0), SAN 377-3310. Tel: 613-675-2424. FAX: 613-675-1003. E-mail: prescott.law@bellnet.ca. Web Site: www.prla-bdpr.ca/law-library. *Libr Asst,* Michelle Landriault
Library Holdings: Bk Titles 1,000; Bk Vols 1,100
Wireless access
Restriction: Not open to pub

MADOC

P MADOC PUBLIC LIBRARY*, 20 Davidson St, K0K 2K0. (Mail add: PO Box 6, K0K 2K0), SAN 319-2326. Tel: 613-473-4456. E-mail: frontdesk@madocpubliclibrary.ca. Web Site: madocpubliclibrary.ca. *Chief Exec Officer, Librn,* Tammie Adams-Wagner; E-mail: ceo@madocpubliclibrary.ca
Pop 1,266; Circ 20,000
Library Holdings: Bk Titles 23,867; Per Subs 18
Wireless access
Open Tues & Thurs 2:30-7:30, Wed & Fri 10-5, Sat 10-1
Friends of the Library Group

MANITOUWADGE

P MANITOUWADGE PUBLIC LIBRARY*, Community Ctr, Two Manitou Rd, P0T 2C0. SAN 319-2350. Tel: 807-826-3913. FAX: 807-826-4640. E-mail: library@manitouwadge.ca. Web Site: manitouwadge.olsn.ca. *Chief Exec Officer, Librn,* Tammy Langevin
Founded 1961. Pop 2,300; Circ 33,032
Library Holdings: Bk Titles 25,815
Special Collections: Geco Mining Coll. Canadian and Provincial
Subject Interests: Geol sci
Automation Activity & Vendor Info: (Cataloging) SirsiDynix; (Circulation) SirsiDynix; (OPAC) SirsiDynix; (Serials) SirsiDynix
Wireless access
Function: Bks on cassette, Computer training, Free DVD rentals, Holiday prog, Homebound delivery serv, ILL available, Magnifiers for reading, Music CDs, Photocopying/Printing, Prog for children & young adult, Scanner, Summer reading prog
Open Mon-Wed 10-7, Thurs & Fri Noon-4:30
Friends of the Library Group

MARATHON

P MARATHON PUBLIC LIBRARY*, 22 Peninsula Rd, P0T 2E0. (Mail add: PO Box 400, P0T 2E0), SAN 319-2377. Tel: 807-229-0740. FAX: 807-229-3336. E-mail: marpublib@shaw.ca. Web Site: marathon.olsn.ca. *Chief Exec Officer, Head Librn,* Tamara Needham; Tel: 807-229-1340, Ext 2266, E-mail: marpublib.ceo@outlook.com; Staff 5 (Non-MLS 5)
Founded 1948. Pop 4,400; Circ 35,000
Library Holdings: Bk Vols 21,000; Per Subs 12
Automation Activity & Vendor Info: (Acquisitions) Follett Software; (Cataloging) Follett Software; (Circulation) Follett Software; (OPAC) Follett Software
Wireless access
Open Mon-Fri 12-5

MARKHAM

P MARKHAM PUBLIC LIBRARY*, Administration Centre & Support Services, 6031 Hwy 7, L3P 3A7. SAN 319-4442. Tel: 905-513-7977. Automation Services Tel: 905-474-5966. FAX: 905-471-6015. E-mail: mplchats@markham.library.on.ca. Web Site: www.markhampubliclibrary.ca. *Chief Exec Officer,* Catherine Biss; Tel: 905-513-7977, Ext 5999, E-mail: cbiss@markham.library.on.ca; *Dir, Admin Serv,* Michelle Sawh; Tel: 905-513-7977, Ext 4233, E-mail: msawh@markham.library.on.ca; Staff 128 (MLS 9, Non-MLS 119)
Pop 317,453
Special Collections: Black Heritage Coll
Automation Activity & Vendor Info: (Circulation) SirsiDynix
Wireless access
Mem of Ontario Library Service
Special Services for the Blind - Bks available with recordings; Bks on cassette; Bks on CD; Home delivery serv; Large print bks
Open Mon-Fri 9-5
Branches: 8

AANIIN BRANCH, 5665 14th Ave, L3S 3K5. Tel: 905-513-7977, Ext 4470. *Br Mgr,* Angela Tse; Tel: 905-513-7977, Ext 4477, E-mail: atse@markham.public.on.ca
Function: 3D Printer, Computers for patron use, Makerspace, Meeting rooms, Study rm

ANGUS GLEN BRANCH, 3990 Major Mackenzie Dr E, L6C 1P8. Tel: 905-513-7977, Ext 7100.
Function: 24/7 Electronic res, Activity rm, Adult bk club, Adult literacy prog, Bk club(s), Bks on cassette, Bks on CD, CD-ROM, Children's prog, Citizenship assistance, Computer training, Computers for patron use, Digital talking bks, E-Reserves, Family literacy, Games & aids for people with disabilities, Holiday prog, ILL available, Internet access, Life-long learning prog for all ages, Literacy & newcomer serv, Magazines, Magnifiers for reading, Meeting rooms, Microfiche/film & reading machines, Movies, Museum passes, Online cat, Online ref, Outside serv via phone, mail, e-mail & web, OverDrive digital audio bks, Photocopying/Printing, Preschool outreach, Preschool reading prog, Prog for adults, Prog for children & young adult, Scanner, Senior computer classes, Serves people with intellectual disabilities, Story hour, Study rm, Summer & winter reading prog, Summer reading prog, Teen prog, Telephone ref, Wheelchair accessible, Workshops
Special Services for the Deaf - Coll on deaf educ
Open Mon-Thurs 9:30-9, Fri 9:30-5, Sat 9-5, Sun 1-5

CORNELL BRANCH, 3201 Burr Oak Ave, L6B 0T2. Tel: 905-513-7977, Ext 3460.
Subject Interests: Med
Automation Activity & Vendor Info: (Serials) BiblioCommons
Special Services for the Blind - Bks on cassette

MARKHAM VILLAGE BRANCH, 6031 Hwy 7, L3P 3A7, SAN 321-947X. Tel: 905-513-7977, Ext 4271. *Br Mgr,* Leah Rucchetto; Tel: 905-513-7977, Ext 4277, E-mail: lrucchetto@markham.library.on.ca
Open Mon-Thurs 9:30-9, Fri 9:30-5, Sat 9-5, Sun 1-5

MILLIKEN MILLS BRANCH, 7600 Kennedy Rd, Unit 1, Unionville, L3R 9S5, SAN 374-6356. Tel: 905-513-7977, Ext 5337.
Automation Activity & Vendor Info: (Serials) BiblioCommons

THORNHILL COMMUNITY CENTRE BRANCH, 7755 Bayview Ave, Thornhill, L3T 4P1, SAN 321-9488. Tel: 905-513-7977, Ext 3521. *Br Mgr,* Harman Malhi; Tel: 905-513-7977, Ext 3524, E-mail: hmalhi@markham.library.on.ca
Automation Activity & Vendor Info: (Serials) BiblioCommons
Open Mon-Thurs 9:30-9, Fri 9:30-5, Sat 9-5, Sun 1-5

THORNHILL VILLAGE BRANCH, Ten Colborne St, Thornhill, L3T 1Z6, SAN 321-9496. Tel: 905-513-7977, Ext 3481. *Br Mgr,* Kenneth Cheung; Tel: 905-513-7977, Ext 3524, E-mail: kcheung@markham.library.on.ca
Automation Activity & Vendor Info: (Serials) BiblioCommons
Open Tues & Thurs 12-8, Wed, Fri & Sat 9-5, Sun 1-5

UNIONVILLE BRANCH, 15 Library Lane, Unionville, L3R 5C4, SAN 321-950X. Tel: 905-513-7977, Ext 5517. *Br Mgr,* Fred Whitmarsh; Tel: 905-513-7977, Ext 5551, E-mail: fwhitmarsh@markham.library.on.ca
Automation Activity & Vendor Info: (Serials) BiblioCommons
Open Mon-Thurs 9:30-9, Fri 9:30-5, Sat 9-5, Sun 1-5

M MARKHAM STOUFFVILLE HOSPITAL LIBRARY*, 381 Church St, L3P 7P3. SAN 373-6334. Tel: 905-472-7061. Web Site: www.oakvalleyhealth.ca/our-hospitals/markham-stouffville-hospital. *Librn,* Abiola Ajayi; E-mail: aajayi@oakvalleyhealth.ca; Staff 1 (MLS 1)
Founded 1990
Library Holdings: CDs 34; DVDs 35; e-books 220; e-journals 20; Electronic Media & Resources 28; Large Print Bks 40; Bk Titles 4,000; Per Subs 40; Videos 381
Partic in Health Science Information Consortium of Toronto
Open Mon-Thurs 8-4, Fri 9-1

MARMORA

P MARMORA & LAKE PUBLIC LIBRARY*, 37 Forsyth St, K0K 2M0. (Mail add: PO Box 340, K0K 2M0), SAN 319-2393. Tel: 613-472-3122. E-mail: info@marmoralibrary.ca. Web Site: marmoralibrary.ca. *Chief Exec Officer, Librn,* Kathy Farrell; E-mail: ceo@mamoralibrary.ca; *Asst Librn,* Kim Hornak
Founded 1920. Pop 4,200
Library Holdings: Bk Vols 13,369; Per Subs 6
Wireless access

Open Tues & Fri 10-5, Wed & Thurs 3-7, Sat 10-2
Friends of the Library Group

MASSEY

P SABLES-SPANISH RIVERS PUBLIC LIBRARY*, Massey Main Branch, 185 Grove St, P0P 1P0. SAN 319-2407. Tel: 705-865-2641. FAX: 705-865-1781. E-mail: infomasseylibrary@gmail.com. Web Site: masseylibrary.com. *Chief Librn/CEO,* Rashad Ahmad
Founded 1960. Pop 3,500; Circ 15,000
Library Holdings: Audiobooks 313; CDs 26; DVDs 223; High Interest/Low Vocabulary Bk Vols 2,636; Large Print Bks 520; Bk Vols 19,358; Per Subs 35; Talking Bks 184; Videos 8
Special Collections: French Coll; German Coll
Wireless access
Special Services for the Deaf - Bks on deafness & sign lang
Special Services for the Blind - Accessible computers; Assistive/Adapted tech devices, equip & products; Audio mat; Bks on cassette; Bks on CD; Daisy reader; Extensive large print coll; Large print bks; Large screen computer & software; Low vision equip; Magnifiers
Open Mon, Wed & Fri 10-7, Tues & Thurs 10-5, Sat 11-1
Branches: 1
WEBBWOOD BRANCH, 16 Main St, Webbwood, P0P 1P0. Tel: 705-869-4147. FAX: 705-869-4147. E-mail: webbwoodlibrary@hotmail.com. *Br Librn,* Linda Lendrum
Library Holdings: Audiobooks 14; DVDs 228; High Interest/Low Vocabulary Bk Vols 11; Large Print Bks 64; Bk Titles 6,311; Bk Vols 91; Per Subs 3; Spec Interest Per Sub 1; Talking Bks 14
Open Mon, Wed & Thurs 6-8, Tues 12-2 & 6-8, Fri 10-12 & 6-8, Sat 2-4

MATTAWA

P MATTAWA PUBLIC LIBRARY*, John Dixon Public Library, 370 Pine St, P0H 1V0. (Mail add: PO Box 920, P0H 1V0), SAN 319-2423. Tel: 249-996-0080. FAX: 705-744-1714. E-mail: johndixonpubliclibrary@gmail.com. Web Site: olsn.ent.sirsidynix.net/client/en_us/mattawa. *Chief Exec Officer,* Gabrielle Lahaie
Pop 2,644; Circ 5,000
Library Holdings: Bk Vols 50,000; Per Subs 22
Wireless access
Open Mon-Fri 1-5
Friends of the Library Group

MATTICE

P MATTICE-VAL COTE PUBLIC LIBRARY*, 189 Balmoral Ave, P0L 1T0. SAN 320-071X. Tel: 705-364-5301. E-mail: biblimat@matticevalcote.ca. Web Site: www.matticevalcote.ca/en/bibliothèque (url needs accent mark). *Exec Dir,* Vicki Dion
Library Holdings: Bk Vols 11,000; Per Subs 45
Wireless access
Open Tues & Wed 12-4:30 & 6-8, Thurs 12-4:30, Fri 9-1

MAYNOOTH

P HASTINGS HIGHLANDS PUBLIC LIBRARY*, 33011 Hwy 62 N, K0L 2S0. SAN 319-2431. Tel: 613-338-2262. FAX: 613-338-5534. E-mail: info@hastingshighlandslibrary.ca. Web Site: hastingshighlandslibrary.ca. *Chief Exec Officer,* Wendy Keating; E-mail: ceo@hastingshighlandslibrary.ca
Pop 4,000; Circ 16,000
Wireless access
Mem of Ontario Library Service
Open Tues-Thurs 10-6, Fri & Sat 10-3

MCKELLAR

P MCKELLAR TOWNSHIP PUBLIC LIBRARY*, 701 Hwy 124, P0G 1C0. (Mail add: PO Box 10, P0G 1C0), SAN 321-8015. Tel: 705-389-2611. FAX: 705-389-2611. E-mail: mckellarlib@vianet.ca. Web Site: www.mckellarpubliclibrary.ca. *Librn,* Joan Ward; Staff 1 (MLS 1)
Founded 1982. Pop 1,400; Circ 4,672
Library Holdings: Bk Titles 7,732; Per Subs 18; Talking Bks 106
Automation Activity & Vendor Info: (Acquisitions) SirsiDynix-WorkFlows; (Cataloging) SirsiDynix-WorkFlows; (Circulation) SirsiDynix-WorkFlows; (Course Reserve) SirsiDynix-WorkFlows; (ILL) SirsiDynix-WorkFlows; (Media Booking) SirsiDynix-WorkFlows; (OPAC) SirsiDynix-WorkFlows; (Serials) SirsiDynix-WorkFlows
Wireless access
Open Wed & Thurs 12-5, Tues 12-5 & 7-9, Sat 10-1

MEAFORD

P MEAFORD PUBLIC LIBRARY*, 11 Sykes St N, N4L 1V6. SAN 319-244X. Tel: 519-538-3500. FAX: 519-538-1808. E-mail: libraryinfo@meaford.ca. Web Site: www.meaford.ca/en/explore-play/library.aspx. *Chief Exec Officer,* Rob Armstrong; *Mgr, Libr Serv,* Lynne Fascinato; E-mail: lfascinato@meaford.ca; *Children's Serv Coordr, Youth Serv Coordr,* Lori Pierce; *Commun Outreach Coordr,* Amy Solecki; *Pub Serv Coordr,* Lori Ledingham
Pop 11,000; Circ 70,000
Library Holdings: Bk Vols 40,000; Per Subs 35
Wireless access
Open Mon, Wed & Fri 10-5, Tues & Thurs 10-8
Friends of the Library Group

MERRICKVILLE

P MERRICKVILLE PUBLIC LIBRARY*, 446 Main St W, K0G 1N0. (Mail add: PO Box 460, K0G 1N0), SAN 319-2458. Tel: 613-269-3326. FAX: 613-269-3326. E-mail: merrickville_library@bellnet.ca. Web Site: www.merrickvillelibrary.ca. *Chief Exec Officer, Librn,* Mary Kate Laphen; Staff 1 (MLS 1)
Founded 1856. Pop 3,378; Circ 31,400
Library Holdings: Bk Titles 21,418; Per Subs 26
Special Collections: Merrickville Historical Society Digital Archives; Merrickville-Wolford Genealogy Records
Automation Activity & Vendor Info: (Cataloging) Mandarin Library Automation; (Circulation) Mandarin Library Automation; (OPAC) Mandarin Library Automation
Wireless access
Function: Adult bk club, Bks on cassette, Bks on CD, Children's prog, Computers for patron use, ILL available, Online cat, Photocopying/Printing, Ref serv available, Scanner, Story hour, Summer reading prog, Wheelchair accessible
Mem of Ontario Library Service
Open Mon, Wed & Thurs 1-5 & 6-8, Tues 10-12 & 1-5, Fri 1-5, Sat 10-4
Friends of the Library Group

MIDHURST

G ONTARIO OFFICE OF THE FIRE MARSHAL & EMERGENCY MANAGEMENT*, Fire Sciences Library & OFC Resource Centre, 2284 Nursery Rd, L9X 1N8. SAN 320-3395. Tel: 705-571-1560. E-mail: library.ofmem@ontario.ca. Web Site: www.ontario.ca/page/firefighter-training-and-certification#section-3. *Librn,* Ginette McCoy; E-mail: ginette.mccoy@ontario.ca; Staff 1 (MLS 1)
Founded 1961
Apr 2017-Mar 2018. Mats Exp (CAN) $41,700, Books (CAN) $18,000, Per/Ser (Incl. Access Fees) (CAN) $9,000, Other Print Mats (CAN) $4,700, AV Equip (CAN) $9,000, Electronic Ref Mat (Incl. Access Fees) (CAN) $1,000
Library Holdings: AV Mats 1,600; Bk Titles 9,500; Per Subs 150
Special Collections: Annual Reports of Dominion Fire Commissioner & Ontario Fire Marshall; Fire Journal from 1903; Ontario Fires, newsp clippings, audio-visual mat
Automation Activity & Vendor Info: (Cataloging) Inmagic, Inc.; (Circulation) Inmagic, Inc.; (OPAC) Inmagic, Inc.
Function: ILL available, Photocopying/Printing
Publications: Bibliographies; List of Monthly Acquisitions
Open Mon-Fri 8:30-4:30

P TOWNSHIP OF SPRINGWATER PUBLIC LIBRARY*, Midhurst Branch, 12 Finlay Mill Rd, L9X 0N7. (Mail add: PO Box 129, L0L 1X0), SAN 319-2547. Tel: 705-737-5650. FAX: 705-737-3594. E-mail: midhurst.library@springwater.ca. Web Site: www.springwater.library.on.ca. *Chief Exec Officer,* Jodie Delgado-Player; E-mail: Jodie.Delgado@springwater.ca; *Mgr,* Kathy Cook; E-mail: kathy.cook@springwater.ca
Pop 18,000; Circ 123,800
Library Holdings: Bk Titles 32,000; Per Subs 60
Wireless access
Function: Bks on CD, Children's prog, Computers for patron use, Free DVD rentals, Holiday prog, ILL available, Online cat, Photocopying/Printing, Preschool reading prog, Wheelchair accessible
Mem of Ontario Library Service
Open Tues 12-7, Wed 12-5, Thurs 10-7, Fri 10-5, Sat 10-3
Friends of the Library Group
Branches: 2
ELMVALE BRANCH, 50 Queen St W, Elmvale, L0L 1P0, SAN 319-1206. Tel: 705-322-1482. FAX: 705-322-0173. E-mail: elmvale.library@springwater.ca. *Mgr,* Jessica Brown
Library Holdings: Bk Vols 24,000; Per Subs 27
Open Tues & Thurs 10-7, Wed & Fri 10-5, Sat 10-3
Friends of the Library Group

MINESING BRANCH, Minesing Community Ctr, 2347 Ronald Rd, Minesing, L0L 1Y0. (Mail add: PO Box 131, Minesing, L0L 1Y0), SAN 375-3034. Tel: 705-722-6440. FAX: 705-722-6511. E-mail: minesing.library@springwater.ca. *Mgr,* Katie Moore; *Mgr,* Linda Potje
Library Holdings: Bk Vols 1,000
Open Tues 1-7, Thurs 1-5, Fri 9-5
Friends of the Library Group

MIDLAND

S HURONIA MUSEUM*, Library & Archives, 549 Little Lake Park Rd, L4R 4P4. (Mail add: PO Box 638, L4R 4P4), SAN 373-6849. Tel: 705-526-2844. FAX: 705-527-6622. E-mail: huroniamuseum@gmail.com. Web Site: huroniamuseum.com. *Curator,* Genevieve Carter
Library Holdings: Bk Titles 3,300
Special Collections: 16th Century Huronia. Oral History
Function: Archival coll, For res purposes, Photocopying/Printing
Open Mon-Fri 9-5, Sat & Sun (Summer) 9-5
Restriction: Non-circulating

P MIDLAND PUBLIC LIBRARY*, 320 King St, L4R 3M6. SAN 319-2482. Tel: 705-526-4216. Circulation Tel: 705-526-4216, Ext 3300. Information Services Tel: 705-526-4216, Ext 3304. FAX: 705-526-1474. E-mail: midlandlibrary@gmail.com. Web Site: midlandlibrary.com. *Interim Chief Exec Officer,* Amy Clennett; *Children's Serv Coordr,* Kelsi Maracle; *Adult & Teen Serv,* Jennifer Paquette
Founded 1880. Pop 16,400; Circ 160,000
Library Holdings: AV Mats 3,000; CDs 2,500; DVDs 200; e-books 6,800; Electronic Media & Resources 75; Large Print Bks 1,000; Bk Vols 50,000; Per Subs 125; Talking Bks 2,000; Videos 500
Special Collections: Sainte Marie Historical Coll (Local History). Canadian and Provincial
Automation Activity & Vendor Info: (Circulation) Auto-Graphics, Inc; (OPAC) Auto-Graphics, Inc
Wireless access
Mem of Ontario Library Service
Open Mon, Tues, Thurs & Fri 9:30-6, Wed 9:30-8, Sat 9:30-4
Friends of the Library Group

MILLBROOK

P THE CAVAN MONAGHAN LIBRARIES*, Millbrook Branch, One Dufferin St, L0A 1G0. SAN 319-2504. Tel: 705-932-2919. E-mail: questions@cavanmonaghanlibraries.ca. Web Site: cavanmonaghanlibraries.ca. *Chief Exec Officer, Chief Librn,* Karla Buckborough; *Br Librn,* Erin Stewart
Founded 1894. Pop 10,017; Circ 28,000
Library Holdings: Bk Titles 30,000; Per Subs 50
Wireless access
Mem of Ontario Library Service
Special Services for the Blind - Bks on CD
Open Tues 10-7, Wed-Fri 10-5, Sat 10-3
Branches: 1
BRUCE JOHNSTON BRANCH, 2199 Davis Rd, Cavan Monaghan, K9J 0G5. Tel: 705-741-1253. *Asst Librn,* Kimberly Lackie
Open Tues 10-7, Thurs 10-5, Sat 10-3

MILTON

L HALTON COUNTY LAW ASSOCIATION*, Court House Library, 491 Steeles Ave E, L9T 1Y7. SAN 328-0322. Tel: 905-878-1272. FAX: 905-878-8298. E-mail: info@haltoncountylaw.ca. *Librn,* Karen Cooper; *Librn,* Arielle Vaca; Staff 1 (Non-MLS 1)
Library Holdings: Bk Vols 8,000; Per Subs 40
Wireless access
Open Mon-Fri 9-4:30

P MILTON PUBLIC LIBRARY*, 1010 Main St E, L9T 6H7. SAN 810-1345. Tel: 905-875-2665. FAX: 905-875-4324. TDD: 905-875-1550. E-mail: information@beinspired.ca. Web Site: www.beinspired.ca. *Interim Chief Librn, Mgr, Support Serv,* Kanta Kapoor; Tel: 905-875-2665, Ext 3259, E-mail: kanta.kapoor@beinspired.ca; *Dep Chief Librn,* Dave Hook; Tel: 905-875-2665, Ext 3233, E-mail: david.hook@beinspired.ca; *Financial Admin Officer,* Cyndi Duncan; Tel: 905-875-2665, Ext 3255, E-mail: cyndi.duncan@beinspired.ca; *Sr Mgr, Human Res,* Vito Montesano; Tel: 905-875-2665, Ext 3232, E-mail: vito.montesano@beinspired.ca; *Mgr, Br,* Maria Petricko; Tel: 905-875-2665, Ext 3290, E-mail: maria.petricko@beinspired.ca; *Mkt & Communications Mgr,* Ashley Directo; Tel: 905-875-2665, Ext 3295, E-mail: ashley.directo@beinspired.ca; *Mgr, Pub Serv,* Lee Puddephatt; Tel: 905-875-2665, Ext 3260, E-mail: lee.puddephatt@beinspired.ca
Wireless access
Open Mon-Thurs 9:30-9, Fri & Sat 9:30-5, Sun 1-5
Friends of the Library Group

MILVERTON

P PERTH EAST PUBLIC LIBRARY*, 19 Mill St E, N0K 1M0. SAN 319-2512. Tel: 519-595-8395. E-mail: pel@pertheastpl.ca. Web Site: pertheastpl.ca. *Interim Chief Exec Officer,* Laura Bere; E-mail: lbere@pertheastpl.ca; Staff 7 (Non-MLS 7)
Pop 12,300; Circ 74,588
Library Holdings: Bk Vols 20,816; Per Subs 17
Subject Interests: Christian
Automation Activity & Vendor Info: (Acquisitions) Horizon; (Cataloging) Horizon; (Circulation) Horizon; (Course Reserve) Horizon; (ILL) Horizon; (OPAC) Horizon; (Serials) Horizon
Wireless access
Function: 24/7 Electronic res, 24/7 Online cat, Activity rm, Adult bk club, Adult literacy prog, Art exhibits, Bk club(s), Bks on CD, Chess club, Children's prog, Computer training, Computers for patron use, Digital talking bks, Electronic databases & coll, Family literacy, Free DVD rentals, Govt ref serv, Holiday prog, Home delivery & serv to seniorr ctr & nursing homes, Homebound delivery serv, Homework prog, ILL available, Instruction & testing, Internet access, Large print keyboards, Life-long learning prog for all ages, Meeting rooms, Movies, Music CDs, Online cat, Online ref, Outside serv via phone, mail, e-mail & web, OverDrive digital audio bks, Photocopying/Printing, Preschool outreach, Preschool reading prog, Prog for children & young adult, Ref serv available, Scanner, Story hour, Summer reading prog, Wheelchair accessible
Partic in Perth County Information Network
Open Mon & Sat 9-1, Tues-Thurs 9-8
Restriction: Access at librarian's discretion
Friends of the Library Group

MINDEMOYA

P CENTRAL MANITOULIN PUBLIC LIBRARIES*, 6020 Hwy 542, P0P 1S0. (Mail add: PO Box 210, P0P 1S0), SAN 319-2520. Tel: 705-377-5334. FAX: 705-377-5334. E-mail: bookworm@amtelecom.net. Web Site: www.centralmanitoulin.ca/central-manitoulin/library. *Chief Librn/CEO,* Claire Cline
Founded 1957. Pop 1,910; Circ 14,000
Library Holdings: Bk Vols 15,000
Open Tues, Wed, Fri & Sat 10-5, Thurs 1-8; Tues, Wed, Fri & Sat 10-4, Thurs 1-7 (Summer)
Friends of the Library Group
Branches: 1
PROVIDENCE BAY BRANCH, 11 Mutchmor St, Providence Bay, P0P 1T0, SAN 376-8856. Tel: 705-377-4503. *Asst Librn,* Sally Miller
Library Holdings: Bk Vols 8,000
Open Tues 6:30pm-8:30pm, Wed 1-3:30, Fri 1-4:30
Friends of the Library Group

MINESING

G SIMCOE COUNTY ARCHIVES, 1149 Hwy 26, L9X 0Z7. SAN 319-2539. Tel: 705-726-9331. Administration Tel: 705-726-9300, Ext 1287. Toll Free Tel: 866-893-9300, Ext 1287. FAX: 705-725-5341. E-mail: archives@simcoe.ca. Web Site: simcoe.ca/explore/simcoe-county-archives. *Archivist,* Matthew Fells; Tel: 705-726-9300, Ext 1285, E-mail: matthew.fells@simcoe.ca; *Corporate & Municipal Records Archivist,* Ellen Millar; Tel: 705-726-9300, Ext 1288, E-mail: ellen.millar@simcoe.ca; *Private Colls Archivist,* Jenn Huddleston; Tel: 705-726-9300, Ext 1295, E-mail: jennifer.huddleston@simcoe.ca; *Ref Serv Coordr,* Christina MacBain; Tel: 705-726-9300, Ext 1292, E-mail: chris.macbain@simcoe.ca; *Microfilm Tech,* Jamie Levy; Tel: 705-726-9300, Ext 1289, E-mail: Jamie.Levy@simcoe.ca; Staff 6 (MLS 4, Non-MLS 2)
Founded 1966
Special Collections: Ardagh & Gowan Papers; Barrie Gas Company Fonds; Barrie Sports Hall of Fame Coll; Beck Lumber Company Records; Cavana Survey Records Coll; County & Municipal Records; County of Simcoe & Lower Tier Government Records; Fred Grant Coll; History of Simcoe County Coll; Norman D Clarke Coll; Sir Frederick Banting Papers
Automation Activity & Vendor Info: (Acquisitions) Inmagic, Inc.; (Cataloging) Inmagic, Inc.; (OPAC) Inmagic, Inc.
Wireless access
Function: Archival coll, AV serv, Bus archives, Computers for patron use, For res purposes, Govt ref serv, Magnifiers for reading, Microfiche/film & reading machines, Online cat, Photocopying/Printing, Ref serv available
Special Services for the Deaf - TTY equip
Closed for renovation Dec 2024-June 2025
Restriction: Access at librarian's discretion, Access for corporate affiliates, Closed stack, Non-circulating, Non-circulating coll, Non-circulating of rare bks, Non-circulating to the pub, Not a lending libr

MISSISSAUGA

S GOLDER ASSOCIATES LTD LIBRARY*, 6925 Century Avenue, Ste 100, L5N 7K2. SAN 325-6642. Tel: 905-567-4444. FAX: 905-567-6561. E-mail: misinfocentre@golder.com. Web Site: www.golder.ca. *Librn,* Noelle Dube
Library Holdings: Bk Vols 3,500; Per Subs 400

P MISSISSAUGA LIBRARY SYSTEM*, Central Library, 301 Burnhamthorpe Rd W, L5B 3Y3. SAN 367-7435. Tel: 905-615-3500. FAX: 905-615-3625. E-mail: info.library@mississauga.ca. Web Site: web.mississauga.ca/library. *Dir, Libr Serv,* Lori Kelly; E-mail: lori.kelly@mississauga.ca; *Mgr,* Laura Reed; E-mail: laura.reed@mississauga.a
Automation Activity & Vendor Info: (Acquisitions) SirsiDynix; (Cataloging) SirsiDynix; (Circulation) SirsiDynix; (OPAC) SirsiDynix
Wireless access
Open Mon-Thurs 9-9, Fri 9-6, Sat 9-5, Sun 1-5
Friends of the Library Group
Branches: 17
BURNHAMTHORPE, 3650 Dixie Rd, L4Y 3V9, SAN 367-7400. Tel: 905-615-4635. *Libr Mgr,* Melanie Southern; E-mail: melanie.southern@mississauga.ca
Open Mon-Thurs 10-9, Fri 10-6, Sat 9-5
Friends of the Library Group
CHURCHILL MEADOWS, 3801 Thomas St, L5M 7G2. Tel: 905-615-4735. *Libr Mgr,* Amy Colson; E-mail: amy.colson@missisauga.ca
Open Mon-Thurs 10-9, Fri 10-6, Sat 9-5
Friends of the Library Group
CLARKSON, 2475 Truscott Dr, L5J 2B3, SAN 367-7559. Tel: 905-615-4840. FAX: 905-615-4841. *Libr Mgr,* Katie-Scarlett MacGillivray; E-mail: katie-scarlett.macgillivray@mississauga.ca
Open Tues & Wed 12-9, Thurs 10-9, Fri 10-6, Sat 9-5
Friends of the Library Group
COOKSVILLE, 3024 Hurontario St, Ste 212, L5B 4M4. Tel: 905-615-4855. *Libr Mgr,* Lina Vanvelzen; E-mail: lina.vanvelzen@mississauga.ca
Open Tues & Wed 12-9, Thurs 10-9, Fri 10-6, Sat 9-5
Friends of the Library Group
COURTNEYPARK, 730 Courtneypark Dr W, L5W 1L9, SAN 367-7370. Tel: 905-615-4745. *Libr Mgr,* Shannan Sword; E-mail: shannan.sword@mississauga.ca
Open Mon-Thurs 10-9, Fri 10-6, Sat 9-5
Friends of the Library Group
ERIN MEADOWS, 2800 Erin Centre Blvd, L5M 6R5. Tel: 905-615-4750. *Libr Mgr,* David Penteliuk; E-mail: david.penteliuk@mississauga.ca
Open Mon-Thurs 10-9, Fri 10-6, Sat 9-5
Friends of the Library Group
LAKEVIEW, 1110 Atwater Ave, L5E 1M9. (Mail add: 301 Burnhamthorpe Rd W, L5B 3Y3), SAN 367-7494. Tel: 905-615-4805. FAX: 905-615-3625. *Libr Mgr,* Melanie Southern
Open Tues & Wed 12-9, Thurs 10-9, Fri 10-6, Sat 9-5
Friends of the Library Group
LORNE PARK, 1474 Truscott Dr, L5J 1Z2, SAN 367-746X. Tel: 905-615-4845. FAX: 905-615-4846. *Libr Mgr,* Katie-Scarlett MacGillivray
Open Mon-Thurs 10-9, Fri 10-6, Sat 9-5
Friends of the Library Group
MALTON BRANCH, 3540 Morningstar Dr, Malton, L4T 1Y2, SAN 367-7524. Tel: 905-615-4640. *Libr Mgr,* Shannan Sword
Open Mon-Thurs 10-9, Fri 10-6, Sat 9-5
Friends of the Library Group
FRANK MCKECHNIE BRANCH, 310 Bristol Rd E, L4Z 3V5. Tel: 905-615-4660. FAX: 905-615-3625. *Libr Mgr,* Laura Higginson; E-mail: laura.higginson@mississauga.ca
Open Mon-Thurs 10-9, Fri 10-6, Sat 9-5
Friends of the Library Group
MEADOWVALE, 6655 Glen Erin Dr, L5N 3L4, SAN 367-7540. Tel: 905-615-4710. *Libr Mgr,* Amy Colson
Open Mon-Thurs 10-9, Fri 10-6, Sat 9-5
Friends of the Library Group
MISSISSAUGA VALLEY, 1275 Mississauga Valley Blvd, L5A 3R8, SAN 367-7532. Tel: 905-615-4670. FAX: 905-615-4671. *Libr Mgr,* Laura Higginson
Open Tues-Thurs 10-9, Fri 10-6, Sat 9-5
Friends of the Library Group
PORT CREDIT, 20 Lakeshore Rd E, L5G 1C8, SAN 367-7583. Tel: 905-615-4835. FAX: 905-615-4751. *Libr Mgr,* Lina Vanzelzen
Open Tues-Thurs 10-9, Fri 10-6, Sat 9-5
Friends of the Library Group
SHERIDAN, 2225 Erin Mills Pkwy, L5K 1T9, SAN 367-7613. Tel: 905-615-4815. FAX: 905-615-4816. *Libr Mgr,* Katie-Scarlett MacGillivray
Open Mon, Wed & Sat 11-5, Tues & Thurs 11-5, Fri 1-5
Friends of the Library Group
SOUTH COMMON, 2233 S Millway Dr, L5L 3H7, SAN 367-7478. Tel: 905-615-4770. FAX: 905-615-4771. *Libr Mgr,* James Cooper; E-mail: james.cooper@mississauga.ca
Open Mon-Thurs 10-9, Fri 10-6, Sat 9-5
Friends of the Library Group
STREETSVILLE, 112 Queen St S, L5M 1K8, SAN 367-7648. Tel: 905-615-4785. *Libr Mgr,* David Penteliuk
Open Tues-Thurs 10-9, Fri 10-6, Sat 9-5
Friends of the Library Group
WOODLANDS, 3255 Erindale Station Rd, L5C 1Y5, SAN 367-7672. Tel: 905-615-4825. FAX: 905-615-4826. *Libr Mgr,* James Cooper
Open Tues-Thurs 10-9, Fri 10-6, Sat 9-5
Friends of the Library Group

S PEEL DISTRICT SCHOOL BOARD*, J A Turner Professional Library, 5650 Hurontario St, L5R 1C6. SAN 319-2644. Tel: 905-890-1099, Ext 2601. FAX: 905-890-4780. E-mail: proflib@peelsb.com. Web Site: peelschools.org. *Librn,* Melanie Mulcaster; Staff 1.5 (Non-MLS 1.5)
Founded 1970
Library Holdings: Bk Titles 10,000; Bk Vols 11,000
Special Collections: Curriculum Coll; Education Coll; Leadership Coll
Subject Interests: Educ
Automation Activity & Vendor Info: (Acquisitions) SirsiDynix; (Cataloging) SirsiDynix; (Circulation) SirsiDynix; (Course Reserve) SirsiDynix; (ILL) SirsiDynix; (Media Booking) SirsiDynix; (OPAC) SirsiDynix
Wireless access
Open Mon-Fri 8:30-4:30

S STANDARDBRED CANADA LIBRARY*, 2150 Meadowvale Blvd, L5N 6R6. SAN 326-1751. Tel: 905-858-3060. FAX: 905-858-3111. Web Site: www.standardbredcanada.ca. *Library Contact,* Linda Bedard; E-mail: lbedard@standardbredcanada.ca
Library Holdings: Bk Titles 800; Bk Vols 1,500; Per Subs 50
Wireless access
Open Mon-Fri 8:30-4:30

M TRILLIUM HEALTH PARTNERS - CREDIT VALLEY HOSPITAL*, Dr Keith G MacDonald Health Sciences Library, 2200 Eglinton Ave W, L5M 2N1. SAN 377-4767. Tel: 905-813-2411. FAX: 905-813-3969. E-mail: library-thp@trilliumhealthpartners.ca. Web Site: trilliumhealthpartners.ca/education/aboutus. *Sr Librn,* Penka Stoyanova; Tel: 905-813-2111, Ext 6479, E-mail: penka.stoyanova@thp.ca; Staff 3 (MLS 2, Non-MLS 1)
Founded 1985
Apr 2015-Mar 2016. Mats Exp (CAN) $295,000, Books (CAN) $5,000, Per/Ser (Incl. Access Fees) (CAN) $120,000, Electronic Ref Mat (Incl. Access Fees) (CAN) $170,000
Library Holdings: e-journals 10,000; Bk Titles 3,000; Bk Vols 3,300; Per Subs 500
Automation Activity & Vendor Info: (Cataloging) SirsiDynix-WorkFlows; (Circulation) SirsiDynix-WorkFlows; (OPAC) SirsiDynix-WorkFlows
Function: Doc delivery serv, Electronic databases & coll, Health sci info serv, ILL available, Internet access, Mail & tel request accepted, Online cat, Online ref, Orientations, Photocopying/Printing, Ref & res, Scanner, VHS videos, Workshops
Partic in Health Science Information Consortium of Toronto
Open Mon-Fri 9-5
Restriction: Borrowing requests are handled by ILL, Circulates for staff only, Hospital staff & commun, In-house use for visitors

MITCHELL

P WEST PERTH PUBLIC LIBRARY*, 105 Saint Andrew St, N0K 1N0. (Mail add: PO Box 100, N0K 1N0), SAN 319-2679. Tel: 519-348-9234. E-mail: askwppl@pcin.on.ca. Web Site: www.westperthpl.ca. *Chief Exec Officer,* Rosemary Minnella; E-mail: rminnella@pcin.on.ca; *ILL, Libr Asst,* Sherri Bennewies; E-mail: sbennewies@pcin.on.ca; *Libr Asst,* Visnja Cuturic; E-mail: vcuturic@pcin.on.ca; *Libr Asst,* Alana La Grave; *Programmer,* Jennifer Barr; E-mail: jbarr@pcin.on.ca; *Programmer,* Pamela Morgan; E-mail: pmorgan@pcin.on.ca; *Programmer,* DeAnna Schouwstra
Founded 1910. Pop 9,000
Library Holdings: Bk Vols 20,000; Per Subs 35
Wireless access
Function: 24/7 Electronic res, 24/7 Online cat, Activity rm, Art exhibits, Audiobks via web, Bks on CD, Children's prog, Computer training, Computers for patron use, Electronic databases & coll, Free DVD rentals, Home delivery & serv to seniorr ctr & nursing homes, ILL available, Internet access, Large print keyboards, Life-long learning prog for all ages, Magazines, Mail & tel request accepted, Meeting rooms, Online cat, Online ref, Outside serv via phone, mail, e-mail & web, OverDrive digital audio bks, Photocopying/Printing, Preschool outreach, Prog for adults, Prog for children & young adult, Ref & res, Scanner, Story hour, Summer reading prog, Telephone ref, Wheelchair accessible
Partic in Perth County Information Network

Special Services for the Blind - Bks on CD; Braille bks; Daisy reader
Open Mon-Thurs 10-8, Fri & Sat 10-5
Friends of the Library Group

MOONBEAM

P BIBLIOTHEQUE PUBLIQUE DE MOONBEAM*, 53 St-Aubin Ave, P0L 1V0. (Mail add: Box 370, P0L 1V0), SAN 320-0728. Tel: 705-367-2462. FAX: 705-367-2120. E-mail: biblio@moonbeam.ca. Web Site: biblio.moonbeam.ca. *Chief Librn,* Gisele Belisle; *Librn,* Angèle Lauzon-Albert; Staff 2 (Non-MLS 2)
Founded 1977. Pop 1,170
Library Holdings: Bk Vols 20,000; Per Subs 40
Automation Activity & Vendor Info: (Acquisitions) Mandarin Library Automation; (Cataloging) Mandarin Library Automation
Wireless access
Function: Bks on CD, Children's prog, Computer training, E-Readers, Free DVD rentals, ILL available, Internet access, Laminating, Large print keyboards, Magazines, Mail & tel request accepted, Movies, Online cat, Photocopying/Printing, Printer for laptops & handheld devices, Ref serv available, Scanner, Spoken cassettes & CDs, Story hour, VHS videos
Special Services for the Blind - Large print bks
Open Mon 12-4:30 & 6:30-8:30, Tues, Wed & Fri 10-11:30 & 12:30-4:30, Thurs Noon-4:30
Friends of the Library Group

NAPANEE

P LENNOX & ADDINGTON COUNTY PUBLIC LIBRARY*, Information Services Administration Office, 97 Thomas St E, K7R 4B9. SAN 367-7702. Tel: 613-354-4883. FAX: 613-354-3112. Web Site: www.lennox-addington.on.ca/library-services. *Mgr, Libr Serv,* Catherine Coles; Tel: 613-354-4883, Ext 3237, E-mail: ccoles@lennox-addington.on.ca; Staff 2 (Non-MLS 2)
Founded 1972. Pop 42,000; Circ 152,000
Library Holdings: DVDs 500; Large Print Bks 10,000; Bk Vols 100,000; Per Subs 65
Special Collections: Fed & Prov
Wireless access
Mem of Ontario Library Service
Open Mon-Fri 8:30-4:30
Branches: 5
AMHERSTVIEW BRANCH, 322 Amherst Dr, Amherstview, K7N 1S9, SAN 367-7737. Tel: 613-389-6006. FAX: 613-389-0077. E-mail: amhbrch@lennox-addington.on.ca. Web Site: www.lennox-addington.on.ca/library-services/library-locations. *Br Mgr,* Amy Kay
Library Holdings: Bk Vols 23,070
Open Mon-Thurs 10-8, Fri & Sat 10-5
BATH BRANCH, 197 Davey St, Bath, K0H 1G0. (Mail add: PO Box 400, Bath, K0H 1G0), SAN 367-7761. Tel: 613-352-5600. E-mail: bathbrch@lennox-addington.on.ca. *Br Coordr,* Karen Scott
Library Holdings: Bk Vols 3,500
Open Mon & Wed 4-8, Tues, Thurs & Sat 10-2
NAPANEE BRANCH, 25 River Rd, K7R 3S6, SAN 367-7826. Tel: 613-354-2525. FAX: 613-354-7527. E-mail: napbrch@lennox-addington.on.ca. *Br Coordr,* Marg Wood
Library Holdings: Bk Vols 26,265
Open Mon-Thurs 10-8, Fri & Sat 10-5
TAMWORTH BRANCH, One Ottawa St, Tamworth, K0K 3G0. (Mail add: PO Box 10, Tamworth, K0K 3G0), SAN 367-7974. Tel: 613-379-3082. E-mail: tambrch@lennox-addington.on.ca. *Br Coordr,* Karen Nurbrum
Library Holdings: Bk Vols 3,500
Open Mon & Wed 4-8, Tues, Thurs & Sat 10-2
YARKER BRANCH, 4315 County Rd 1, Yarker, K0K 3N0, SAN 367-8008. Tel: 613-377-1673. E-mail: yarbrch@lennox-addington.on.ca. *Librn,* Kelly O'Neil
Library Holdings: Bk Titles 3,000
Open Mon & Wed 4-8, Tues, Thurs & Sat 10-2

NAUGHTON

P ATIKAMEKSHENG ANISHINAWBEK LIBRARY*, c/o Atikameksheng Kendaasii-Gamik, PO Box 39, P0M 2M0. SAN 319-2717. Tel: 705-692-9901. FAX: 705-692-5010. E-mail: library@wlfn.com. Web Site: atikamekshenganishnawbek.ca/service/library. *Librn,* Mary Fraser; E-mail: mfraser@wlfn.com
Pop 668; Circ 1,000
Library Holdings: Bk Titles 3,000; Bk Vols 3,100
Wireless access
Open Mon & Thurs 9-12 & 4:30-7, Tues, Wed & Fri 9-12 & 4-8

NEWMARKET

P NEWMARKET PUBLIC LIBRARY*, 438 Park Ave, L3Y 1W1. SAN 319-2741. Tel: 905-953-5110. FAX: 905-953-5104. E-mail: npl@newmarketpl.ca. Web Site: www.newmarketpl.ca. *Chief Exec Officer,* Todd Kyle; *Head, Children's Servx,* Susan Hoffman; E-mail: shoffman@newmarketpl.ca; *Librn,* Robert Caldwell; E-mail: rcaldwell@newmarketpl.ca; *Librn,* Alex Karlovski; E-mail: akarlovski@newmarketpl.ca; *Mgr, Libr Operations,* Benjamin Shaw; E-mail: bshaw@newmarketpl.ca; *Mgr, Libr Serv,* Jennifer Leveridge; E-mail: jleveridge@newmarketpl.ca; *Syst Mgr,* Simon Chong; E-mail: schong@newmarketpl.ca; Staff 7 (MLS 6, Non-MLS 1)
Founded 1956. Pop 84,000; Circ 500,000
Jan 2020-Dec 2020 Income (CAN) $3,668,895, Provincial (CAN) $64,401, City (CAN) $3,465,422, Locally Generated Income (CAN) $139,072. Mats Exp (CAN) $391,337, Books (CAN) $164,764, Per/Ser (Incl. Access Fees) (CAN) $11,100, AV Mat (CAN) $27,200, Electronic Ref Mat (Incl. Access Fees) (CAN) $157,530. Sal (CAN) $2,131,578
Library Holdings: Bk Titles 146,000; Bk Vols 175,000; Per Subs 258
Automation Activity & Vendor Info: (Acquisitions) Innovative Interfaces, Inc; (Cataloging) Innovative Interfaces, Inc; (Circulation) Innovative Interfaces, Inc; (OPAC) Innovative Interfaces, Inc; (Serials) Innovative Interfaces, Inc
Wireless access
Function: 24/7 Electronic res, 24/7 Online cat, 3D Printer, Activity rm, Adult bk club, Archival coll, Art exhibits, Art programs, Audiobks on Playaways & MP3, Audiobks via web, Bk club(s), Bks on CD, Chess club, Children's prog, Computer training, Computers for patron use, Digital talking bks, Distance learning, Electronic databases & coll, Equip loans & repairs, Free DVD rentals, Homebound delivery serv, ILL available, Internet access, Large print keyboards, Life-long learning prog for all ages, Magazines, Makerspace, Mango lang, Meeting rooms, Microfiche/film & reading machines, Movies, Music CDs, Online cat, Online info literacy tutorials on the web & in blackboard, Online ref, Outreach serv, Outside serv via phone, mail, e-mail & web, OverDrive digital audio bks, Preschool outreach, Preschool reading prog, Prog for adults, Prog for children & young adult, Ref & res, Ref serv available, Scanner, STEM programs, Story hour, Study rm, Summer reading prog, Teen prog, Telephone ref, Visual arts prog, Wheelchair accessible
Mem of Ontario Library Service
Open Tues-Thurs 9:30-9, Fri & Sat 9:30-5, Sun 1-5

NIAGARA FALLS

P NIAGARA FALLS PUBLIC LIBRARY*, 4848 Victoria Ave, L2E 4C5. SAN 367-8032. Tel: 905-356-8080. FAX: 905-356-9498. Web Site: my.nflibrary.ca. *Chief Exec Officer,* Alicia Kilgour; E-mail: askilgour@nflibrary.ca; *Libr Serv Mgr,* Christopher Dunn; E-mail: cdunn@nflibrary.ca; *Info Res Mgr,* Ashleigh Dronyk; E-mail: adronyk@nflibrary.ca; *Mgr Community Develop & Prog,* Laura Martin; E-mail: lmartin@nflibrary.ca; *Mgr, Customer Serv,* Susan DiBattista; E-mail: sdibattista@nflibrary.ca; Staff 45 (MLS 9, Non-MLS 36)
Founded 1878. Pop 88,000
Library Holdings: DVDs 25,000; e-books 55,500; e-journals 45,800; Bk Titles 150,000; Bk Vols 250,000; Talking Bks 2,000
Special Collections: Can
Subject Interests: Local hist
Automation Activity & Vendor Info: (OPAC) Infor Library & Information Solutions
Wireless access
Function: 24/7 Electronic res, 3D Printer, Art exhibits, Audio & video playback equip for onsite use, Audiobks on Playaways & MP3, Audiobks via web, Bks on CD, ILL available, Internet access, Magazines, Meeting rooms, Microfiche/film & reading machines, Movies, Music CDs, Online cat, Summer reading prog
Open Mon-Thurs 9-9, Fri & Sat 9-5:30, Sun (Winter) 1-5
Branches: 3
CHIPPAWA, 3763 Main St, L2G 6B3, SAN 367-8067. Tel: 905-295-4391.
Open Mon & Tues 1-8, Wed 9-5:30, Sat 10-4
COMMUNITY CENTER, 7150 Montrose Rd, L2H 3N3. Tel: 905-371-1200.
Open Mon-Thurs 10-8, Fri & Sat 10-5:30
STAMFORD CENTRE, Town & Country Plaza, 3643 Portage Rd N, L2J 2K8, SAN 367-8121. Tel: 905-357-0410.
Open Mon & Thurs 10-8, Tues, Wed, Fri & Sat 10-5:30

S NIAGARA PARKS BOTANICAL GARDENS & SCHOOL OF HORTICULTURE*, C H Henning Library, 2565 Niagara Pkwy N, L2E 6S4. (Mail add: PO Box 150, L2E 6T2), SAN 322-7413. Tel: 905-356-8554, Ext 6207. FAX: 905-356-5488. E-mail: info@niagaraparks.com. Web Site: niagaraparks.com. *Librn,* Ruth Stoner; Staff 1 (Non-MLS 1)
Library Holdings: CDs 45; DVDs 40; Bk Titles 4,700; Per Subs 120; Videos 130
Subject Interests: Arboriculture, Hort, Landscape archit

NIAGARA-ON-THE-LAKE

S GENAIRE LTD LIBRARY*, 468 Niagara Stone Rd, Unit D, L0S 1J0. SAN 377-4694. Tel: 905-684-1165. FAX: 905-684-2412. Web Site: www.genaireltd.com. *Tech Librn,* Amy Whittingham; Staff 1 (Non-MLS 1)
Library Holdings: Bk Vols 10,000
Restriction: Circulates for staff only, Not open to pub

P NIAGARA-ON-THE-LAKE PUBLIC LIBRARY*, Ten Anderson Lane, L0S 1J0. (Mail add: PO Box 430, L0S 1J0), SAN 367-8156. Tel: 905-468-2023. FAX: 905-468-3334. Web Site: notlpubliclibrary.org. *Chief Librn,* Cathy Simpson; *Libr Mgr,* Laura Tait; E-mail: ltait@notlpl.org; Staff 8 (MLS 1, Non-MLS 7)
Founded 1800. Pop 15,000; Circ 103,000
Library Holdings: Bk Titles 45,000; Per Subs 135
Special Collections: History of Niagara & the War of 1812 (Janet Carnochan Coll)
Automation Activity & Vendor Info: (Acquisitions) Evergreen; (Cataloging) Evergreen; (Circulation) Evergreen; (OPAC) Evergreen
Wireless access
Function: Art exhibits, CD-ROM, Home delivery & serv to seniorr ctr & nursing homes, ILL available, Photocopying/Printing, Prog for children & young adult, Ref serv available, Summer reading prog
Publications: Landmarks & People of Niagara; Records of Niagara - Inventory
Mem of Ontario Library Service
Special Services for the Blind - Talking bks
Open Mon-Thurs 9-8, Fri & Sat 9-5, Sun 1-5
Friends of the Library Group

NIPIGON

P CORPORATION OF THE TOWNSHIP OF NIPIGON PUBLIC LIBRARY BOARD, Nipigon Public Library, 52 Front St, P0T 2J0. (Mail add: PO Box 728, P0T 2J0), SAN 319-2784. Tel: 807-887-3142. FAX: 807-887-3142. E-mail: nipigonpl@gmail.com. Web Site: www.nipigon.net/living-here/culture-recreation/library. *Librn,* Sumiye Sugawara; Staff 1 (Non-MLS 1)
Founded 1958. Pop 1,473; Circ 6,444
Library Holdings: Audiobooks 195; DVDs 2,000; Large Print Bks 422; Bk Titles 9,773; Bk Vols 10,000; Per Subs 5
Subject Interests: Local hist, Local newsp
Automation Activity & Vendor Info: (Acquisitions) SirsiDynix-WorkFlows; (Cataloging) SirsiDynix-WorkFlows; (Circulation) SirsiDynix-WorkFlows; (Course Reserve) SirsiDynix-WorkFlows; (ILL) Fretwell-Downing; (Media Booking) SirsiDynix-WorkFlows; (OPAC) SirsiDynix-WorkFlows; (Serials) SirsiDynix-WorkFlows
Wireless access
Function: 24/7 Electronic res, 24/7 Online cat, 24/7 wireless access, Adult bk club, Audio & video playback equip for onsite use, Audiobks via web, Bk club(s), Bks on CD, Children's prog, Computers for patron use, Digital talking bks, E-Reserves, Electronic databases & coll, Equip loans & repairs, Extended outdoor wifi, Free DVD rentals, Games, Holiday prog, Homebound delivery serv, ILL available, Internet access, Laminating, Large print keyboards, Magazines, Mail & tel request accepted, Movies, Online cat, OverDrive digital audio bks, Photocopying/Printing, Prog for adults, Prog for children & young adult, Scanner, Senior outreach, Summer reading prog, Wheelchair accessible, Workshops
Publications: NPL (Annual report)
Special Services for the Blind - Bks on CD; Daisy reader; Large print bks; Talking bks & player equip
Open Tues & Wed 1:30-5:30 & 6-8, Thurs 10-1 & 1:30-5:30, Fri 1:30-5:30, Sat 10-2

NOELVILLE

P FRENCH RIVER PUBLIC LIBRARY*, 15 Dollard St, P0M 2N0. (Mail add: PO Box 130, P0M 2N0), SAN 319-2792. Tel: 705-898-2965. E-mail: staff@frenchriverlibrary.ca. Web Site: www.frenchriver.ca/p/french-river-public-library. *Librn,* Ms Chris Charron
Pop 1,564; Circ 7,742
Library Holdings: Large Print Bks 30; Bk Titles 11,478; Bk Vols 11,584; Per Subs 30; Talking Bks 40
Function: ILL available, Photocopying/Printing
Special Services for the Blind - Large print bks
Open Tues & Thurs 10-3, Wed 1-6
Branches: 1
ALBAN BRANCH, 796 Hwy 64, Unit A, Alban, P0M 1A0. (Mail add: PO Box 158, Alban, P0M 1A0). Tel: 705-857-1771. FAX: 705-857-1771. *Librn,* Ms Chris Charron
Open Tues & Thurs 10-3

NORTH BAY

L NIPISSING DISTRICT LAW ASSOCIATION LIBRARY*, 360 Plouffe St, P1B 9L5. SAN 375-3654. Tel: 705-495-3271. Toll Free Tel: 866-899-6439. FAX: 705-495-3487. E-mail: nipilaws@onlink.net. *Law Librn,* Amanda Adams
Library Holdings: Bk Vols 8,500; Per Subs 106
Wireless access
Open Mon-Thurs 8:30-3, Fri 8:30-12:30

P NORTH BAY PUBLIC LIBRARY*, 271 Worthington St E, P1B 1H1. SAN 319-2814. Tel: 705-474-4830. Reference Tel: 705-474-3332. FAX: 705-495-4010. E-mail: library@cityofnorthbay.ca. Web Site: www.cityofnorthbay.ca/library. *Chief Exec Officer,* Ravil Veli; E-mail: ravil.veli@cityofnorthbay.ca; *Head, Adult Serv,* Judith Bouman; E-mail: judith.bouman@cityofnorthbay.ca; *Head, Children's Servx,* Nora Elliott-Coutts; E-mail: nora.elliott-coutts@cityofnorthbay.ca; *Head, Info Serv,* Rebecca Larocque; E-mail: rebecca.larocque@cityofnorthbay.ca; Staff 27 (MLS 4, Non-MLS 23)
Founded 1895. Pop 54,982; Circ 450,000
Library Holdings: Bk Vols 146,090; Per Subs 191
Special Collections: Canadiana; French Coll, bks, pamphlets, rec; Picture File. Canadian and Provincial
Automation Activity & Vendor Info: (Acquisitions) Evergreen
Wireless access
Function: Adult bk club, Archival coll, Audiobks via web, Bks on CD, CD-ROM, Children's prog, Computer training, Computers for patron use, Digital talking bks, Electronic databases & coll, Family literacy, Free DVD rentals, Genealogy discussion group, Govt ref serv, Holiday prog, Homebound delivery serv, Homework prog, ILL available, Internet access, Magnifiers for reading, Music CDs, Online cat, OverDrive digital audio bks, Photocopying/Printing, Preschool outreach, Prog for children & young adult, Ref serv available, Res performed for a fee, Scanner, Senior computer classes, Senior outreach, Spoken cassettes & CDs, Story hour, Summer & winter reading prog, Summer reading prog, Wheelchair accessible
Open Mon-Thurs 9:30-9, Fri 9:30-6, Sat 9:30-4

NORTH YORK

G TORONTO DISTRICT SCHOOL BOARD, Professional Library Services, Three Tippett Rd, M3H 2V1. SAN 320-3484. Tel: 416-395-8289. FAX: 416-395-8292. E-mail: professionallibrary@tdsb.on.ca. Web Site: sigles-symbols.bac-lac.gc.ca/eng/Search/Details?Id=6063. *Libr Tech,* Tara Ferrier-Clarke; Tel: 416-395-8293, E-mail: tara.ferrier-clarke@tdsb.on.ca
Founded 1956
Library Holdings: Bk Titles 20,000; Per Subs 450
Subject Interests: Educ
Open Mon-Fri 8-4

C YORK UNIVERSITY LIBRARIES*, Scott Library, 4700 Keele St, M3J 1P3. SAN 367-1135. Tel: 416-736-5150, Ext 55150, 416-736-5601. FAX: 416-736-5451. E-mail: scottref@yorku.ca. Web Site: www.library.yorku.ca. *Dean of Libr,* Joy Kirchner; E-mail: joyk@yorku.ca; *Dir of Libr Advan,* Michelle Ariga; E-mail: ariga@yorku.ca; *Univ Archivist,* Michael Moir; Tel: 416-736-2100, Ext 22457, E-mail: mmoir@yorku.ca; Staff 54 (MLS 39, Non-MLS 15)
Founded 1959. Enrl 37,546; Fac 1,170; Highest Degree: Doctorate
Library Holdings: Bk Vols 2,487,083; Per Subs 17,356
Special Collections: American & English Literature of the 19th & 20th Centuries, bks & ms; Canadiana, bks & ms; Music, Theatre & Visual Arts Coll. Canadian and Provincial
Automation Activity & Vendor Info: (Acquisitions) SirsiDynix; (Cataloging) SirsiDynix; (Circulation) SirsiDynix
Wireless access
Partic in Association of Research Libraries; Canadian Association of Research Libraries; NELLCO Law Library Consortium, Inc.; OCLC Online Computer Library Center, Inc
Departmental Libraries:
PETER F BRONFMAN BUSINESS LIBRARY, Schulich School of Business, Seymour Schulich Bldg, Rm S237, 111 Ian McDonald Blvd, M3J 1P3, SAN 367-116X. Tel: 416-736-5139. FAX: 416-736-5687. E-mail: bronfref@yorku.ca. Web Site: www.library.yorku.ca/web/bbl. *Bus Librn,* Angie An; E-mail: angiean@yorku.ca; Staff 3 (MLS 3)
Founded 2003
Library Holdings: e-journals 10,000; Electronic Media & Resources 30; Bk Vols 25,000; Per Subs 360
Automation Activity & Vendor Info: (OPAC) SirsiDynix
Open Mon-Thurs 9am-10pm, Fri 9-5
Restriction: Open to researchers by request, Open to students, fac & staff
LESLIE FROST LIBRARY, GLENDON CAMPUS, 2275 Bayview Ave, M4N 3M6, SAN 319-5783. Tel: 416-487-6726. Reference Tel: 416-487-6729. FAX: 416-487-6705. Web Site:

www.library.yorku.ca/web/frost. *Access Serv Mgr,* Tanya Prince; E-mail: tprince@yorku.ca; Staff 9 (MLS 4, Non-MLS 5)
Founded 1960. Enrl 2,000; Fac 100; Highest Degree: Master
Library Holdings: Bk Vols 275,000
Special Collections: Bilingual (French/English) Translation Materials
Subject Interests: Humanities, Intl studies, Liberal arts, Linguistics, Soc sci
Open Mon-Thurs 8:30-6:30, Fri 8:30-4:30, Sat 10-6 (Summer); Mon-Thurs 8am-11pm, Fri 8-8, Sat 10-6, Sun Noon-5 (Winter)

MAP LIBRARY, Scott Library, Main Flr, 4700 Keele St, M3J 1P3. Tel: 416-736-2100, Ext 33353. FAX: 416-736-5838. E-mail: gislib@yorku.ca. Web Site: www.library.yorku.ca/web/map. *Maps Librn,* Rosa Orlandini; E-mail: rorlan@yorku.ca; *Coordr,* Janet Neate; E-mail: jneate@yorku.ca
Library Holdings: Bk Vols 6,600

NELLIE LANGFORD ROWELL WOMEN'S STUDY LIBRARY, 204 Founders College, 4700 Keele St, M4J 1P3, SAN 322-7391. Tel: 416-736-5735. E-mail: nlrowell@yorku.ca. Web Site: www.yorku.ca/laps/nellie-library. *Coordr,* Position Currently Open
Founded 1969
Library Holdings: Bk Vols 21,500; Per Subs 90
Special Collections: Caribbean Women; Women in the Visual & Performing Arts (Janet E Hutchison Memorial Coll); Women's Movement Ephemera
Subject Interests: Feminism, Women, Women's studies
Publications: Margins of the Blackboard; Nellie Langford Rowell; Pamphlets on Pay Equity, Equality in Sports
Open Mon-Fri 9:30-4:30

CL OSGOODE HALL LAW SCHOOL LIBRARY, 92 Scholar's Walk, Keele Campus, Toronto, M3J 1P3. (Mail add: Ignat Kafeff Bldg, 4700 Keele St, Toronto, M3J 1P3), SAN 367-1224. Tel: 416-736-5206. Reference Tel: 416-736-5207. FAX: 416-736-5298. E-mail: library@osgoode.yorku.ca. Web Site: www.osgoode.yorku.ca/library. *Chief Law Librn,* Yemisi Dina; Tel: 416-650-8404, E-mail: ydina@osgoode.yorku.ca; *Head, Tech Serv,* Tim F Knight; Tel: 416-650-8403, E-mail: tknight@osgoode.yorku.ca; *Ref Librn,* Daniel Perlin; Tel: 416-736-5380, E-mail: dperlin@osgoode.yorku.ca; *Ref Librn,* Sharon Wang; Tel: 416-736-5893, E-mail: swang@osgoode.yorku.ca; Staff 14 (MLS 6, Non-MLS 8)
Founded 1892. Enrl 1,042; Fac 60; Highest Degree: Doctorate
Special Collections: Early Anglo-American Legal Materials; Early Legal Canadiana
Subject Interests: Can & commonwealth, Can legal lit & hist, Gen law, Legal hist
Automation Activity & Vendor Info: (Cataloging) SirsiDynix; (Circulation) SirsiDynix; (OPAC) SirsiDynix
Partic in Ontario Council of University Libraries

STEACIE SCIENCE & ENGINEERING LIBRARY, 136 Campus Walk, Keele Campus, M3J 1P3, SAN 367-1259. Tel: 416-736-5084. FAX: 416-736-5452. Reference E-mail: steacref@yorku.ca. Web Site: www.library.yorku.ca/web/steacie. *Sci Librn,* John Dupuis; E-mail: jdupuis@yorku.ca; Staff 5 (MLS 3, Non-MLS 2)
Founded 1970
Library Holdings: Bk Titles 74,000; Bk Vols 178,000

NORWICH

S NORWICH & DISTRICT HISTORICAL SOCIETY ARCHIVES*, 91 Stover St N, RR3, N0J 1P0. SAN 373-6253. Tel: 519-863-3638. Administration Tel: 519-863-3101. FAX: 519-863-2343. E-mail: archives@norwichdhs.ca. Web Site: www.norwichdhs.ca/archives. *Adminr, Curator,* Matthew Lloyd; E-mail: norwichdhs@execulink.com; *Archivist,* Janet Hilliker
Founded 1979
Special Collections: Genealogy, bks, fiche, files, flm, pictures & maps; Municipal. Oral History
Function: Archival coll, Ref serv available
Restriction: Open by appt only

NORWOOD

P ASPHODEL-NORWOOD PUBLIC LIBRARY*, Norwood Branch, 2363 County Rd 45, K0L 2V0. (Mail add: PO Box 100, K0L 2V0), SAN 319-2822. Tel: 705-639-2228. E-mail: norwood@anpl.org. Web Site: www.anpl.org. *Chief Exec Officer, Head Librn,* Trish Reed; *Asst Librn,* Cheryl Sanford; *Libr Asst,* Laurie Strawbridge; Staff 3 (Non-MLS 3)
Founded 1872. Pop 4,500
Library Holdings: Bk Vols 22,000; Per Subs 50
Automation Activity & Vendor Info: (Cataloging) SirsiDynix-WorkFlows; (Circulation) SirsiDynix-WorkFlows
Wireless access
Function: 24/7 Electronic res, 24/7 Online cat, 3D Printer, Adult bk club, After school storytime, Audiobks via web, Bk club(s), Bks on CD, Children's prog, Citizenship assistance, Computer training, Computers for patron use, Electronic databases & coll, Family literacy, Free DVD rentals, Holiday prog, Home delivery & serv to seniorr ctr & nursing homes, ILL available, Internet access, Laminating, Life-long learning prog for all ages, Literacy & newcomer serv, Magazines, Magnifiers for reading, Online cat, OverDrive digital audio bks, Photocopying/Printing, Preschool outreach, Preschool reading prog, Prog for adults, Prog for children & young adult, Ref & res, Res assist avail, Senior computer classes, Serves people with intellectual disabilities, STEM programs, Story hour, Summer & winter reading prog, Wheelchair accessible, Workshops, Writing prog
Mem of Ontario Library Service
Open Tues & Thurs 2-7, Wed & Fri 9-1, Sat 1-3
Branches: 1
WESTWOOD BRANCH, 312 Centre Line, Westwood, K0L 3B0. Tel: 705-768-2548. E-mail: westwood@anpl.org. *Chief Exec Officer, Head Librn,* Trish Reed; *Libr Asst,* Laurie Strawbridge
Library Holdings: Bk Vols 22,000
Open Mon & Wed 4-7, Thurs 9-Noon, Sat 10-Noon

OAKVILLE

S GOLF CANADA LIBRARY & ARCHIVES*, 1333 Dorval Dr, Ste 1, L6M 4X7. SAN 370-6117. Tel: 905-849-9700. FAX: 905-845-7040. E-mail: cghf@golfcanada.ca, info@golfcanada.ca. Web Site: heritage.golfcanada.ca/library, www.cghf.org. *Dir,* Meggan Gardner; Tel: 905-849-9700, Ext 412, E-mail: mgardner@golfcanada.ca
Founded 1975
Library Holdings: Bk Vols 7,300; Per Subs 20
Wireless access
Open Mon-Sun 10-5

P OAKVILLE PUBLIC LIBRARY*, 120 Navy St, L6J 2Z4. SAN 367-8210. Tel: 905-815-2042. FAX: 905-815-2024. Web Site: www.opl.on.ca. *Chief Exec Officer,* Tara Wong; Tel: 905-815-2042, Ext 2027, E-mail: tara.wong@oakville.ca; *Customer Experience Dir,* Caitlyn Hicks; E-mail: Caitlyn.Hicks@oakville.ca; *Dir, Innovation & Integration,* Joseph Moncada; E-mail: Joseph.Moncada@oakville.ca; Staff 130 (MLS 20, Non-MLS 110)
Founded 1895. Pop 230,000
Special Collections: Canadian and Provincial
Subject Interests: Local hist
Automation Activity & Vendor Info: (Acquisitions) SirsiDynix; (Cataloging) SirsiDynix; (Circulation) SirsiDynix; (OPAC) SirsiDynix; (Serials) SirsiDynix
Wireless access
Restriction: Access at librarian's discretion
Friends of the Library Group
Branches: 7
CENTRAL, 120 Navy St, L6J 2Z4. Tel: 905-815-2042. FAX: 905-815-2024. Reference E-mail: oplreference@oakville.ca. *Br Mgr,* Andra Steele; Tel: 905-815-2042, Ext 5063, E-mail: andra.steele@oakville.ca
Open Tues-Thurs 11:30-7, Fri & Sat 9:30-5
Friends of the Library Group
CLEARVIEW NEIGHBOURHOOD, 2860 Kingsway Dr, L6J 6R3. Tel: 905-815-2033. FAX: 905-815-2034. *Br Mgr,* Cathy Burke; Tel: 905-338-4247, Ext 5906, E-mail: cathy.burke@oakville.ca
Founded 2007
Open Tues-Thurs 4-7, Sat 9:30-5
Friends of the Library Group
GLEN ABBEY, 1415 Third Line, L6M 3G2, SAN 371-3512. Tel: 905-815-2039. FAX: 905-815-5978. *Br Mgr,* Lila Saab; Tel: 905-815-2039, Ext 3596, E-mail: lsaab@oakville.ca
Open Tues-Thurs 11:30-7, Fri & Sat 9:30-5
Friends of the Library Group
IROQUOIS RIDGE, 1051 Glenashton Dr, L6H 6Z4. Tel: 905-338-4247. FAX: 905-338-4248. *Br Mgr,* Cathy Burke
Open Tues-Thurs 11:30-7, Fri & Sat 9:30-5
Friends of the Library Group
SIXTEEN MILE BRANCH, 3070 Neyagawa Blvd, L6M 4L6. Tel: 905-815-6112. *Br Mgr,* Cathy Burke; Tel: 905-338-4247, Ext 5906, E-mail: cathy.burke@oakville.ca
Open Tues & Thurs 11:30-7, Fri & Sat 9:30-5
Friends of the Library Group
WHITE OAKS, 1070 McCraney St E, L6H 2R6, SAN 367-8245. Tel: 905-815-2038. FAX: 905-815-5972. *Br Mgr,* Emma Primeau; E-mail: emma.primeau@oakville.ca
Open Tues-Thurs 3-7, Sat 10-5
Friends of the Library Group
WOODSIDE, 1274 Rebecca St, L6L 1Z2, SAN 367-827X. Tel: 905-815-2036. FAX: 905-815-2036. *Br Mgr,* Emma Primeau; Tel: 905-815-2036, Ext 5141
Subject Interests: Literacy, Parenting, Pre-sch children
Open Tues-Thurs 11:30-7, Fri & Sat 9:30-5
Friends of the Library Group

C SHERIDAN COLLEGE LIBRARY*, Trafalgar Learning Commons, 1430 Trafalgar Rd, L6H 2L1. SAN 367-830X. Tel: 905-845-9430, Ext 2483. E-mail: library@sheridancollege.ca. Web Site:

www.sheridancollege.ca/life-at-sheridan/student-services/library-services. *Assoc Vice Provost, Academic & Career Learning Resources,* Joan Sweeney Marsh; Tel: 905-845-9430, Ext 2480, E-mail: joan.sweeneymarsh@sheridancollege.ca; *Coll Develop Librn,* Ahtasham Rizvi; Tel: 905-845-9430, Ext 2495, E-mail: ahtasham.rizvi@sheridancollege.ca; *Acq Assoc,* Kirti Mistry; Tel: 905-459-7533, Ext 2487, E-mail: kirti.mistry@sheridancollege.ca; *Circulation & Ref Support Tech,* Kimberly Haney; Tel: 905-845-9438, Ext 2482, E-mail: kimberly.haney@sheridancollege.ca; *Ref & Instruction,* Madeleine Crew; Tel: 905-459-7533, Ext 2574, E-mail: madeleine.crew@sheridancollege.ca; Staff 6.5 (MLS 3.5, Non-MLS 3)
Founded 1967. Enrl 11,500; Fac 409; Highest Degree: Bachelor
Library Holdings: Bk Vols 40,000; Per Subs 130
Subject Interests: Art
Automation Activity & Vendor Info: (Acquisitions) SirsiDynix; (Cataloging) SirsiDynix; (Circulation) SirsiDynix; (Course Reserve) SirsiDynix; (OPAC) SirsiDynix; (Serials) SirsiDynix
Wireless access
Function: Audio & video playback equip for onsite use, ILL available, Photocopying/Printing, Ref serv available, VHS videos, Wheelchair accessible
Open Mon-Thurs 8:30am-10pm, Fri 8:30-4, Sat & Sun 11-4 (Sept-June); Mon-Fri 8:30-4:30 (July & Aug)
Departmental Libraries:
DAVIS CAMPUS, 7899 McLaughlin Rd, Brampton, L6V 1G6, SAN 367-8369. Tel: 905-459-7533, Ext 4338. Reference Tel: 905-459-7533, Ext 5280, 905-459-7533, Ext 5281. *Dir, Learning Serv,* Danielle Palombi; Tel: 905-459-7533, Ext 5476, E-mail: danielle.palombi@sheridanc.on.ca; *Mgr, User Serv,* Johnathan Pring; E-mail: johnathan.pring@sheridanc.on.ca; *Cat, Syst Tech,* Irene Sillius; E-mail: irene.sillius@sheridanc.on.ca; Staff 5 (MLS 1, Non-MLS 4)
Founded 1967. Enrl 4,000
Library Holdings: Bk Titles 18,000; Per Subs 80
Open Mon-Thurs 8:30am-9pm, Fri 8:30-4:30
HAZEL MCCALLION CAMPUS, 4180 Duke of York Blvd, Mississauga, L5B 0G5. Tel: 905-485-9430, Ext 5912. *Institutional Repository Coord,* Adam Duguay; Tel: 905-845-9430, Ext 5583, E-mail: adam.duguay@sheridancollege.ca; *Ref & Instruction,* Elizabeth Schembri; Tel: 905-845-9430, Ext 2467, E-mail: elizabeth.schembri@sheridancollege.ca; *User Services Tech,* Ravi Balasubramanian; Tel: 905-845-9430, Ext 2473, E-mail: ravichandran.balasubramanian@sheridancollege.ca
Open Mon-Fri 8:30-4:30

ORANGEVILLE

P ORANGEVILLE PUBLIC LIBRARY*, One Mill St, L9W 2M2. SAN 319-2849. Tel: 519-941-0610. FAX: 519-941-4698. E-mail: infolibrary@orangeville.ca. Web Site: www.orangevillelibrary.ca. *Chief Exec Officer,* Darla Fraser; Tel: 519-941-0610, Ext 5222; *Coll & Syst Coordr,* Kim Carson; Tel: 519-941-0610, Ext 5226, E-mail: kcarson@orangeville.ca; *Prog & Res Coordr,* Lauren Tilly; Tel: 519-941-0610, Ext 5230, E-mail: ltilly@orangeville.ca; *Pub Serv Coordr,* Kathryn Creelman; Tel: 519-941-0610, Ext 5232, E-mail: kcreelman@orangeville.ca; Staff 7 (MLS 2, Non-MLS 5)
Pop 32,000; Circ 231,000
Library Holdings: Bk Titles 78,000
Subject Interests: Genealogy, Local hist
Wireless access
Mem of Ontario Library Service
Open Mon-Thurs 10-9, Fri 10-6, Sat 10-5, Sun 1-4
Friends of the Library Group

ORILLIA

C GEORGIAN COLLEGE*, Orillia Library, 825 Memorial Ave, L3V 6S2. (Mail add: PO Box 2316, L3V 6S2). Tel: 705-329-3101. Circulation Tel: 705-325-2740, Ext 3050. Interlibrary Loan Service Tel: 705-329-2740, Ext 3052. Reference Tel: 705-325-2740, Ext 3054. FAX: 705-329-3107. Web Site: library.georgiancollege.ca. *Dir of Libr,* Joanna Coulthard; E-mail: joanna.coulthard@georgiancollege.ca; Staff 6 (MLS 3, Non-MLS 3)
Founded 1968. Enrl 1,300; Fac 43
Library Holdings: AV Mats 1,258; Bk Vols 20,000; Per Subs 119
Automation Activity & Vendor Info: (Acquisitions) SirsiDynix; (Cataloging) SirsiDynix; (Circulation) SirsiDynix; (OPAC) SirsiDynix; (Serials) SirsiDynix
Wireless access
Open Mon-Thurs 8:30-7, Fri 8:30-4:30, Sat 10-2
Restriction: Open to students, fac & staff

P STEPHEN LEACOCK MEMORIAL MUSEUM LIBRARY*, 50 Museum Dr, L3V 6K5. (Mail add: Box 625, L3V 6K5), SAN 371-117X. Tel: 705-329-1908. FAX: 705-326-5578. Web Site: www.orillia.ca/en/visiting/leacock-museum.aspx. *Admin Coordr,* Jenny Martynyshyn; E-mail: jmartynyshyn@orillia.ca
Founded 1936
Library Holdings: Bk Vols 6,000
Wireless access
Open Mon-Sun 10-4

G ONTARIO PROVINCIAL POLICE*, Eric Silk Library, 777 Memorial Ave, L3V 7V3. SAN 326-5579. Tel: 705-329-6886. FAX: 705-329-6887. E-mail: opp.ghq.library@opp.ca. Web Site: www.opp.ca. *Librn/Mgr,* Catherine Dowd; E-mail: catherine.dowd@opp.ca. Subject Specialists: *Can & Ont legislation & case law, Police sci,* Catherine Dowd; Staff 1 (MLS 1)
Library Holdings: Audiobooks 75; CDs 77; DVDs 263; Bk Vols 6,554; Per Subs 95; Spec Interest Per Sub 13; Videos 193
Subject Interests: Law, Law enforcement
Automation Activity & Vendor Info: (OPAC) Inmagic, Inc.; (Serials) EBSCO Online
Wireless access
Publications: Acquisitions List (Bimonthly)
Open Mon-Fri 8:30-4:30

P ORILLIA PUBLIC LIBRARY*, 36 Mississaga St W, L3V 3A6. SAN 319-2865. Tel: 705-325-2338. FAX: 705-327-1744. E-mail: info@orilliapubliclibrary.ca. Web Site: www.orilliapubliclibrary.ca. *Chief Exec Officer,* Bessie Sullivan; *Director, Children & Youth Services,* Meagan Wilkinson; *Dir, Info Serv,* Kelli Absalom; Staff 8.1 (MLS 5.2, Non-MLS 2.9)
Founded 1911. Pop 31,128; Circ 237,119
Library Holdings: Bk Titles 65,541; Bk Vols 69,578; Per Subs 129
Special Collections: Stephen Leacock Coll. Oral History
Subject Interests: Local hist, Orilliana
Automation Activity & Vendor Info: (Acquisitions) TLC (The Library Corporation); (Cataloging) Infor Library & Information Solutions; (Circulation) Infor Library & Information Solutions; (Course Reserve) Infor Library & Information Solutions; (ILL) Infor Library & Information Solutions; (Media Booking) Infor Library & Information Solutions; (OPAC) Infor Library & Information Solutions; (Serials) Infor Library & Information Solutions
Wireless access
Function: Teen prog
Mem of Ontario Library Service
Open Tues-Fri 10-6, Sat 9-5
Friends of the Library Group

OSHAWA

L DURHAM REGION LAW ASSOCIATION*, Terrence V Kelly Law Library, 150 Bond St E, L1G 0A2. SAN 372-7319. Tel: 905-579-9554. Toll Free Tel: 866-742-4316. FAX: 905-579-1801. E-mail: drlalaw@bellnet.ca. Web Site: durhamregionlawassociation.com. *Pres,* Mark Jacula; *Librn,* Jennie Clarke
Library Holdings: Bk Titles 7,000
Wireless access
Restriction: Mem only

M LAKERIDGE HEALTH, Oshawa Hospital Health Sciences Library, One Hospital Ct, L1G 2B9. SAN 321-6810. Tel: 905-576-8711, Ext 33754. FAX: 905-721-4759. Web Site: www.lakeridgehealth.on.ca. *Managing Librn,* Justin Johnston; Staff 2 (MLS 1, Non-MLS 1)
Founded 1973
Library Holdings: Bk Titles 1,000; Per Subs 75
Subject Interests: Med, Nursing
Partic in Health Science Information Consortium of Toronto

S ROBERT MCLAUGHLIN GALLERY LIBRARY*, Civic Centre, 72 Queen St, L1H 3Z3. SAN 328-3216. Tel: 905-576-3000. Web Site: www.rmg.on.ca. *Sr Curator,* Leila Timmins; E-mail: ltimmins@rmg.on.ca; *Curator,* Sonya Jones; Tel: 905-576-3000, Ext 110
Founded 1967
Library Holdings: Bk Titles 4,500; Per Subs 6
Special Collections: "Painters Eleven" Archives; Thomas Bouckley Photography Archives
Subject Interests: Can art
Automation Activity & Vendor Info: (OPAC) MINISIS Inc
Wireless access
Function: Archival coll, Art exhibits, Internet access, Magazines, Online cat, Res libr, Wheelchair accessible
Publications: Art Exhibition Catalogues (Annual report)
Restriction: Authorized scholars by appt, Circ to mem only, Closed stack, In-house use for visitors, Non-circulating of rare bks, Open by appt only, Restricted access, Visitors must make appt to use bks in the libr

P OSHAWA PUBLIC LIBRARY*, McLaughlin Library, 65 Bagot St, L1H 1N2. SAN 367-8482. Tel: 905-579-6111, Ext 5200. Interlibrary Loan Service Tel: 905-579-6111, Ext 5235. Administration Tel: 905-579-6111, Ext 5213. FAX: 905-433-8107. Web Site: www.oshawalibrary.on.ca. *Chief Exec Officer,* Frances Newman; E-mail: opladmin@oshawalibrary.on.ca;

Dir, Serv Delivery, Ellen Stroud; E-mail: estroud@oshawalibrary.on.ca; *Mgr, Access Serv, Mgr, Coll Serv,* Jennifer Green; E-mail: jgreen@oshawalibrary.on.ca; Staff 16 (MLS 16)
Founded 1864. Pop 160,000
Library Holdings: Bk Vols 336,018; Per Subs 791
Special Collections: Automotive & Transportation, bks; Can & Prov; Canadiana & Oshawa History, bks, maps, vf. State Document Depository
Automation Activity & Vendor Info: (Acquisitions) Infor Library & Information Solutions; (Cataloging) Infor Library & Information Solutions; (Circulation) Infor Library & Information Solutions; (Course Reserve) Infor Library & Information Solutions; (OPAC) Infor Library & Information Solutions; (Serials) Infor Library & Information Solutions
Wireless access
Publications: Annual Report
Mem of Ontario Library Service
Special Services for the Deaf - Bks on deafness & sign lang; Staff with knowledge of sign lang
Open Mon-Thurs 10-6, Fri & Sat 10-5
Friends of the Library Group
Branches: 3
DELPARK, 1661 Harmony Rd N, L1H 7K5. Tel: 905-436-5461. *Mgr,* Beckie McDonald; Staff 14 (MLS 2, Non-MLS 12)
Function: Adult bk club
Open Mon-Thurs 10-6, Fri & Sat 10-5
JESS HANN BRANCH, Lake Vista Sq, 199 Wentworth St W, L1J 6P4, SAN 367-8512. Tel: 905-579-6111, Ext 5860. *Mgr,* Gail Canonaco
Library Holdings: Bk Vols 44,000
Open Tues-Thurs 10-6, Fri & Sat 10-5
Friends of the Library Group
NORTHVIEW, 250 Beatrice St E, L1G 7T6, SAN 367-8547. Tel: 905-576-6040. *Mgr,* Gail Canonaco
Library Holdings: Bk Vols 54,300
Open Mon-Thurs 10-6, Fri & Sat 10-5
Friends of the Library Group

C UNIVERSITY OF ONTARIO INSTITUTE OF TECHNOLOGY LIBRARY*, Durham College Library, 2000 Simcoe St N, L1H 7K4. (Mail add: PO Box 385, L1H 7L7), SAN 760-3614. Tel: 905-721-3082. Interlibrary Loan Service Tel: 905-721-2412. FAX: 905-721-3029. E-mail: library@uoit.ca. Web Site: durhamcollege.ca/student-life/campus-services/library, uoit.ca/sites/library. *Chief Librn,* Catherine Davidson; E-mail: catherine.davidson@uoit.ca; Staff 5 (MLS 5)
Founded 2000. Enrl 10,000; Fac 250; Highest Degree: Doctorate
Library Holdings: DVDs 500; e-books 40,000; e-journals 45,000; Electronic Media & Resources 22,000; Bk Titles 80,000; Bk Vols 100,000; Per Subs 500; Videos 2,500
Special Collections: Canadian and Provincial
Subject Interests: Computer sci, Energy, Health sci, Nuclear, Sci, Tech
Automation Activity & Vendor Info: (Acquisitions) SirsiDynix; (Cataloging) SirsiDynix; (Circulation) SirsiDynix; (Course Reserve) SirsiDynix; (ILL) OCLC; (Media Booking) SirsiDynix; (OPAC) SirsiDynix; (Serials) SirsiDynix
Wireless access
Partic in Canadian Research Knowledge Network; Ontario Council of University Libraries
Open Mon-Thurs 8am-Midnight, Fri 8-7, Sat & Sun 10-6

OTTAWA

GL ADMINISTRATIVE TRIBUNALS SUPPORT SERVICES OF CANADA, ISST Library, CD Howe Bldg West Tower, 6th Flr, 240 rue Sparks St 645F, K1A 0E1. (Mail add: Internal Services ISST Library, K1A 0E1), SAN 319-308X. Tel: 613-990-1809. E-mail: library-bibliotheque@tribunal.gc.ca. *Info Mgr, Libr Serv Mgr,* Angela Foran; Tel: 343-598-8514, E-mail: angela.foran@tribunal.gc.ca; *Libr Coord, Libr Tech,* Pierre Robichaud; E-mail: pierre.robichaud@tribunal.gc.ca; Staff 1 (Non-MLS 1)
Founded 1967
Apr 2025-Mar 2026. Mats Exp (CAN) $15,430, Books (CAN) $15,000, Per/Ser (Incl. Access Fees) (CAN) $30, Electronic Ref Mat (Incl. Access Fees) (CAN) $400
Library Holdings: DVDs 30; e-books 3; e-journals 8; Bk Titles 7,099; Bk Vols 10,000; Per Subs 52
Special Collections: Canadian and Provincial
Subject Interests: Arbitration, Dispute resolution, Labor relations in the public sector, Mediation
Automation Activity & Vendor Info: (Cataloging) EOS International; (Circulation) EOS International; (OPAC) EOS International; (Serials) EOS International
Function: 24/7 Online cat, 24/7 wireless access, 3D Printer
Publications: Acquisitions List; Periodicals List
Partic in Can Asn of Law Librs; Council of Federal Libraries Consortium
Open Mon-Fri 8-4
Restriction: Authorized patrons, Authorized personnel only, Restricted access

G AGRICULTURE & AGRI-FOOD CANADA*, Canadian Agriculture Library, Tower 6, Flr 1, 1341 Baseline Rd, K1A 0C5. SAN 367-8571. Tel: 613-773-1433. FAX: 613-773-1499. E-mail: aafc.cal-bca.aac@canada.ca. Reference E-mail: CAL-BCA-ref@agr.gc.ca. Web Site: agriculture.canada.ca. *Dir,* Tania Costanzo; E-mail: tania.constanzo@canada.ca; *Actg Mgr,* Pierre Di Campo; E-mail: pierre.dicampo@agr.gc.ca; Staff 31 (MLS 14, Non-MLS 17)
Founded 1910
Library Holdings: e-journals 11,000; Bk Vols 1,000,000; Per Subs 250
Special Collections: Historical Agriculture (Chapais Coll)
Automation Activity & Vendor Info: (Acquisitions) Innovative Interfaces, Inc - Sierra; (Cataloging) Innovative Interfaces, Inc - Sierra; (Circulation) Innovative Interfaces, Inc - Sierra; (Discovery) SerialsSolutions; (ILL) OCLC; (OPAC) Innovative Interfaces, Inc - Sierra; (Serials) Innovative Interfaces, Inc - Sierra
Partic in Council of Federal Libraries Consortium
Open Mon-Fri 8:30-4:30

J ALGONQUIN COLLEGE LIBRARY*, Ottawa Campus, 1385 Woodroffe Ave, Rm C350, K2G 1V8. SAN 367-8784. Tel: 613-727-4723, Ext 5834. FAX: 613-727-7642. E-mail: library@algonquincollege.com. Web Site: www.algonquincollege.com/library. *Mgr,* Tammy Thornton; E-mail: thorntt@algonquincollege.edu; *Coordr, Librn,* Brenda Mahoney; Tel: 613-727-4723, Ext 5284, E-mail: mahoneb@algonquincollege.com; *Coordr, Librn,* Maureen Sheppard; Tel: 613-727-4723, Ext 5944, E-mail: sheppam@algonquincollege.com; *Admin Officer,* Sandra Brown; Tel: 613-727-4723, Ext 5288, E-mail: browns@algonquincollege.edu
Founded 1967
Library Holdings: AV Mats 6,269; e-books 16,695; Bk Vols 67,823; Per Subs 309
Subject Interests: Applied arts, Bus, Computer sci, Health sci, Tech, Trades
Automation Activity & Vendor Info: (Circulation) SirsiDynix; (Course Reserve) SirsiDynix; (Media Booking) SirsiDynix; (OPAC) SirsiDynix; (Serials) SirsiDynix
Wireless access
Open Mon-Thurs 7:30am-9pm, Fri 7:30-5, Sat 10-4
Departmental Libraries:
PEMBROKE CAMPUS, One College Way, Rm 145, Pembroke, K8A 0C8, SAN 367-9055. Tel: 613-735-4700, Ext 2707. FAX: 613-735-8801. E-mail: illpemb@algonquincollege.com. *Coordr, Librn,* Patricia Kim; Tel: 613-735-4700, Ext 2779, E-mail: kimp@algonquincollege.com
Open Mon-Thurs 8-7, Fri 8-5
PERTH CAMPUS, Seven Craig St, Rm 117, Perth, K7H 1X7, SAN 367-8938. Tel: 613-267-2859, Ext 5644. FAX: 613-267-3950. E-mail: illpert@algonquincollege.com. *Libr Tech,* Kendra Swallow; Tel: 613-267-2859, Ext 6225, E-mail: swallok@algonquincollege.com
Library Holdings: e-books 16,695; Bk Vols 10,000; Per Subs 30

SR ASSOCIATION FOR BAHA'I STUDIES*, Reference Library, 34 Copernicus St, K1N 7K4. SAN 374-4019. Tel: 613-233-1903, Press 2. FAX: 613-233-3644. E-mail: abs-na@bahai-studies.ca. Web Site: www.bahai-studies.ca. *Librn,* Mrs Nilufar Gordon
Founded 1971
Library Holdings: Bk Titles 1,700; Bk Vols 3,000; Per Subs 32
Special Collections: Early Baha'i Periodicals
Open Mon-Fri 9-5
Restriction: Open to pub for ref only

G BANK OF CANADA*, Knowledge & Information Services Archives, 234 Wellington St, K1A 0G9. SAN 319-2911. Tel: 613-782-8881. FAX: 613-782-7387. E-mail: knowlinfoserv@bankofcanada.ca. Web Site: www.bankofcanada.ca/about/archives. *Asst Dir, Knowledge Serv,* Beverly Graham; Staff 18.5 (MLS 9, Non-MLS 9.5)
Founded 1935
Library Holdings: Bk Titles 35,000; Per Subs 6,000
Subject Interests: Cent banking, Econ, Finance, Macro econ policy
Automation Activity & Vendor Info: (Cataloging) SirsiDynix; (ILL) A-G Canada Ltd
Function: Res libr
Restriction: Open to pub by appt only

M BIBLIOTHEQUE DE L'HOPITAL MONTFORT*, 713 Chemin Montreal, 2D-113, K1K 0T2. SAN 324-4016. Tel: 613-746-4621, Ext 6045. FAX: 613-748-4922. E-mail: biblio@montfort.on.ca. *Librn,* Veronique Synnett; Staff 1 (MLS 1)
Library Holdings: e-books 250; Bk Titles 1,054; Per Subs 4
Special Collections: Health professionals
Subject Interests: Med, Nursing
Automation Activity & Vendor Info: (Cataloging) Inmagic, Inc.; (Circulation) Inmagic, Inc.; (ILL) Amicus

Wireless access
Partic in Canadian Health Libraries Association; Ontario Health Libraries Association

CR BIBLIOTHEQUE DU COLLEGE UNIVERSITAIRE DOMINICAIN*, Dominican University College Library, 96 Empress Ave, K1R 7G3. SAN 319-325X. Tel: 613-233-5696, Ext 216. FAX: 613-233-6064. E-mail: library.info@dominicanu.ca. Web Site: udominicaine.ca/bibliotheque. *Head Student Librn,* Caleb Mondoux; E-mail: librarian@dominicanu.ca; *Assistant Student Librn,* Brandon Tran; Staff 6 (Non-MLS 6)
Founded 1884. Highest Degree: Doctorate
Library Holdings: Bk Vols 140,000; Per Subs 400
Subject Interests: Behav studies, Hist, Philos, Relig studies, Soc
Automation Activity & Vendor Info: (Cataloging) Koha; (OPAC) Koha
Wireless access
Open Mon-Fri 9-4

L BORDEN LADNER GERVAIS LLP LIBRARY, World Exchange Plaza, 100 Queen St, Ste 1300, K1P 1J9. SAN 374-5880. Tel: 613-237-5160. Toll Free Tel: 855-660-6003. FAX: 613-230-8842. Web Site: www.blg.com/en/about-us/offices/ottawa. *Library Colls & Procurement Tech,* Kathy Heney; E-mail: kheney@blg.com; Staff 2 (MLS 1, Non-MLS 1)
Library Holdings: Bk Vols 6,000; Per Subs 400
Automation Activity & Vendor Info: (Acquisitions) Horizon; (Cataloging) Horizon; (Circulation) Horizon; (Serials) Horizon
Restriction: Private libr

S CANADA AVIATION & SPACE MUSEUM*, Library & Archives, 11 Aviation Pkwy, K1K 4R3. (Mail add: PO Box 9724, Sta T, K1G 5A3), SAN 371-7445. Tel: 343-548-4368. Toll Free Tel: 800-463-2038 (Canada only). FAX: 613-990-3655. E-mail: library@ingeniumcanada.org. Web Site: ingeniumcanada.org/aviation. *Head, Info Serv,* F Smith Hale; *Asst Librn,* Sylvie Bertrand. Subject Specialists: *Can aviation,* Sylvie Bertrand; Staff 2 (MLS 1, Non-MLS 1)
Library Holdings: Bk Titles 12,000; Per Subs 120
Subject Interests: Aeronaut
Automation Activity & Vendor Info: (Acquisitions) SirsiDynix; (Cataloging) SirsiDynix; (Circulation) SirsiDynix; (Serials) SirsiDynix
Wireless access
Restriction: Open by appt only

S CANADA COUNCIL FOR THE ARTS*, Reference & Documentation Centre, 150 Elgin St, 2nd Flr, K2P 1L4. (Mail add: PO Box 1047, K1P 5V8), SAN 371-7739. Tel: 613-566-4414, Ext 4051. Toll Free Tel: 800-263-5588, Ext 4051. FAX: 613-566-4390. Web Site: www.canadacouncil.ca. *Asst Admin,* Melissa-Renee Boulrice; Tel: 613-566-4414, E-mail: melissa-renee.boulrice@canadacouncil.ca; Staff 4 (Non-MLS 4)
Founded 1980
Library Holdings: Bk Titles 5,000; Spec Interest Per Sub 300
Special Collections: Canada Council History Coll
Subject Interests: Arts, Culture
Function: Ref serv available
Partic in Canadian Fed Librs
Restriction: Non-circulating to the pub, Open by appt only

GL CANADA DEPARTMENT OF JUSTICE LIBRARY*, Headquarters, EMB, Rm A-370, 284 Wellington St, K1A 0H8. SAN 319-3004. Tel: 613-957-4606. Interlibrary Loan Service Tel: 613-957-4598. Administration Tel: 613-957-4609. Reference FAX: 613-952-5792. Administration FAX: 613-952-3491. E-mail: information.services@justice.gc.ca. Web Site: www.justice.gc.ca/eng/cv/admin/isb-dsi.html#s7. *Dir,* Nora Ballantyne; Tel: 613-957-4611, E-mail: nora.ballantyne@justice.gc.ca; Staff 16 (MLS 9, Non-MLS 7)
Founded 1868
Library Holdings: AV Mats 35,350; CDs 100; e-books 1,788; e-journals 20; Electronic Media & Resources 20; Bk Titles 28,855; Bk Vols 160,000; Per Subs 1,570; Talking Bks 130; Videos 235
Subject Interests: Law
Automation Activity & Vendor Info: (Acquisitions) Innovative Interfaces, Inc; (Cataloging) Innovative Interfaces, Inc; (Circulation) Innovative Interfaces, Inc; (ILL) Amicus; (OPAC) Innovative Interfaces, Inc; (Serials) Innovative Interfaces, Inc
Wireless access
Function: Audio & video playback equip for onsite use, CD-ROM, Doc delivery serv, Electronic databases & coll, ILL available, Internet access, Online cat, Orientations, Photocopying/Printing, Ref serv available, Res libr, Scanner, VHS videos, Wheelchair accessible, Workshops
Publications: AWACOU; Guide to Services (Library handbook); New Acquisitions - Nouvelles Acquisitions (Current awareness service); Service Pamphlets (Research guide)
Partic in Council of Federal Libraries Consortium
Open Mon-Fri 8:30-5
Restriction: Employees only

S CANADA SCIENCE & TECHNOLOGY MUSEUM*, Library & Information Services, 1865 St Laurent, K1G 5A3. (Mail add: PO Box 9724, Stn T, K1G 5A3), SAN 368-0282. Tel: 343-548-4368. E-mail: library@ingeniumcanada.org. Web Site: ingeniumcanada.org/scitech/collection-research/library-and-archives.php. *Dir, Libr & Archive Serv,* Fiona Smith Hale; Tel: 613-993-2303; *Library Services,* Sylvie Bertrand; Tel: 613-990-5015, E-mail: library@ingeniumcanada.org; Staff 4 (MLS 1, Non-MLS 3)
Founded 1967
Library Holdings: Bk Titles 26,000; Per Subs 300
Special Collections: Canadian National Railway Photographs Coll; Cycling (Shields Coll); Railway Engineering Drawings; Trade Literature
Subject Interests: Agr, Astronomy, Communications, Energy, Forestry, Graphic arts, Hist of sci & tech, Indust tech, Land transportation, Marine transportation, Mining, Phys sci, Radar, Space
Automation Activity & Vendor Info: (Acquisitions) SirsiDynix; (Cataloging) SirsiDynix; (Circulation) SirsiDynix; (OPAC) SirsiDynix; (Serials) SirsiDynix
Wireless access
Function: Archival coll, Ref serv available
Restriction: In-house use for visitors

S CANADIAN ARTISTS' REPRESENTATION*, Publication Archives, Two Daly Ave, Ste 250, K1N 6E2. SAN 375-2577. Tel: 613-233-6161. FAX: 613-233-6162. E-mail: communications@carfac.ca. Web Site: www.carfac.ca. *Exec Dir,* April Britski
Library Holdings: Bk Vols 3,000; Per Subs 34
Open Mon-Fri 10-5

M CANADIAN ASSOCIATION OF OCCUPATIONAL THERAPISTS*, Resource Centre, 103-2685 Queensview Dr, K2B 8K2. SAN 375-8052. Tel: 613-523-2268. Toll Free Tel: 800-434-2268. FAX: 613-523-2552. Web Site: caot.ca/client/product2. *Chief Exec Officer,* Helene Sabourin; E-mail: hsabourin@caot.ca
Library Holdings: e-books 30; Bk Titles 50

S CANADIAN CHILD CARE FEDERATION*, Resource Centre, 700 Industrial Ave, Ste 600, K1G 0Y9. SAN 373-6687. Tel: 613-729-5289. Toll Free Tel: 800-858-1412. FAX: 613-729-3159. E-mail: info@cccf-fcsge.ca. Web Site: www.cccf-fcsge.ca. *Chief Exec Officer,* Don Giesbrecht; Tel: 613-729-5289, Ext 220, E-mail: dgiesbrecht@cccf.fcsge.ca; Staff 2 (MLS 1, Non-MLS 1)
Founded 1988
Library Holdings: Bk Titles 5,000
Special Collections: Provincial Child Care Legislation (Special Coll), bk, files
Subject Interests: Child care, Families
Automation Activity & Vendor Info: (Acquisitions) Inmagic, Inc.; (Cataloging) Inmagic, Inc.; (Serials) Inmagic, Inc.
Restriction: Mem only, Open by appt only

G CANADIAN FORCES HEALTH SERVICES CENTRE LIBRARY*, c/o 101 Colonel By Rd, K1A 0K2. SAN 370-7849. Tel: 613-901-1608. FAX: 613-901-1756. E-mail: librarycfhs-bibliothequessfc@forces.gc.ca. Web Site: www.canada.ca/en/department-national-defence/services/bases-support-units.
Library Holdings: Bk Vols 4,095
Partic in Hosp Librs Group; Ontario Health Library & Information Association
Restriction: Not open to pub, Staff use only

G CANADIAN INTERNATIONAL TRADE TRIBUNAL LIBRARY*, 333 Laurier Ave W, 15th Flr, K1A 0G7. SAN 374-4035. Tel: 613-990-2452. FAX: 613-990-2431. *Library Contact,* Tierney Markey; E-mail: tierney.markey@tribunal.gc.ca
Founded 1989
Library Holdings: Bk Titles 7,832; Per Subs 666
Special Collections: Canadian International Trade Tribunal Reports; Tariff Board Reports; USITC Decisions Since 1954; World Trade Organization Documents
Subject Interests: Intl trade
Automation Activity & Vendor Info: (Cataloging) SydneyPlus; (Circulation) SydneyPlus; (OPAC) SydneyPlus; (Serials) SydneyPlus
Restriction: Open by appt only

M CANADIAN MEDICAL ASSOCIATION*, T Clarence Routley Library, 1410 Blair Towers Place, Ste 500, K1J 9B9. SAN 319-3209. Tel: 613-731-9331, Ext 8432. Toll Free Tel: 800-663-7336, Ext 8432. FAX: 613-731-2076. Web Site: www.cma.ca. *Ref Librn,* Elizabeth Czanyo; E-mail: elizabeth.czanyo@cma.ca; Staff 5 (MLS 3, Non-MLS 2)
Founded 1911
Library Holdings: Bk Titles 4,000; Per Subs 250

Subject Interests: Health econ, Health policy, Health promotion, Med ethics
Automation Activity & Vendor Info: (Acquisitions) Inmagic, Inc.; (Cataloging) Inmagic, Inc.; (Circulation) Inmagic, Inc.; (ILL) Inmagic, Inc.; (OPAC) Inmagic, Inc.; (Serials) Inmagic, Inc.
Open Mon-Fri 8:30-4:30

G CANADIAN NUCLEAR SAFETY COMMISSION LIBRARY*, 280 Slater St, K1P 1C2. (Mail add: PO Box 1046, Sta B, K1P 5S9), SAN 322-8061. Tel: 613-995-5894. Interlibrary Loan Service Tel: 613-995-1359. FAX: 613-995-5086. E-mail: cnsc.library.bibliotheque.ccsn@canada.ca. Web Site: www.nuclearsafety.gc.ca. *Librn,* Sarah Ghazi; E-mail: sarah.ghazi@canada.ca; *ILL/Doc Delivery Serv, Ref Serv,* Carole Blais; E-mail: carole.blais@canada.ca; Staff 2 (MLS 1, Non-MLS 1)
Library Holdings: CDs 240; DVDs 25; e-books 2,300; e-journals 70; Electronic Media & Resources 45; Bk Titles 52,000; Per Subs 220; Videos 160
Subject Interests: Engr, Nuclear nonproliferation, Nuclear sci, Phys sci, Radiation protection, Radioactive waste
Automation Activity & Vendor Info: (Acquisitions) Horizon; (Cataloging) Horizon; (Circulation) Horizon; (OPAC) Horizon; (Serials) Horizon
Function: ILL available, Wheelchair accessible
Publications: Monthly Acquisitions List (Online only); Periodical list (Online only)
Partic in Council of Federal Libraries Consortium; Horizon Users Group
Open Mon-Fri 8-5

G CANADIAN RADIO-TELEVISION & TELECOMMUNICATIONS COMMISSION INFORMATION RESOURCE CENTRE*, One Promenade du Portage, K1A 0N2. SAN 319-3217. Tel: 819-997-4484. FAX: 819-994-6337. Web Site: www.crtc.gc.ca. *Librn,* Michel Richard; E-mail: oort@crtc.gc.ca; Staff 6 (MLS 2, Non-MLS 4)
Founded 1971
Library Holdings: Bk Titles 6,700; Per Subs 151
Special Collections: Canadian Radio
Subject Interests: Broadcasting, Internet, Media, Policy, Regulation, Telecommunication
Automation Activity & Vendor Info: (OPAC) Inmagic, Inc.
Wireless access

G CANADIAN WAR MUSEUM*, Hartland Molson Library, One Vimy Pl, K1A 0M8. SAN 368-0258. Tel: 819-776-8652. FAX: 819-776-8623. E-mail: vimy.biblio@warmuseum.ca. Web Site: www.warmuseum.ca/learn/research-collections/military-history-research-centre/. *Supvr,* Paul Durand; *Librn,* Vincent Lafond
Founded 1969
Library Holdings: Bk Vols 65,000; Per Subs 70
Special Collections: Military Technical Manuals; Newspaper Clippings; Rare Book Coll; Regimental Histories
Subject Interests: Art, Can mil hist, Heraldry
Automation Activity & Vendor Info: (Acquisitions) OCLC; (Cataloging) OCLC; (Circulation) OCLC
Wireless access
Function: ILL available
Partic in Council of Federal Libraries Consortium; OCLC Online Computer Library Center, Inc

C CARLETON UNIVERSITY LIBRARY*, MacOdrum Library, 1125 Colonel By Dr, K1S 5B6. SAN 319-3241. Tel: 613-520-2735. Circulation Tel: 613-520-2733. FAX: 613-520-2786. E-mail: university_librarian@carleton.ca. Web Site: www.library.carleton.ca. *Univ Librn,* Amber Lannon; Tel: 613-520-2600, Ext 8189, E-mail: amber.lannon@carleton.ca; *Head, Access Serv,* Joanne Rumig; Tel: 613-520-2600, Ext 1018, E-mail: joanne.rumig@carleton.ca; *Head, Acq,* David Sharp; Tel: 613-520-2600, Ext 8372, E-mail: david.sharp@carleton.ca; *Head, Archives & Spec Coll,* Chris Trainor; Tel: 613-520-2600, Ext 6030, E-mail: chris.trainor@carleton.ca; *Head, Cat & Metadata Serv,* Erika Banski; Tel: 613-520-2600, Ext 4563, E-mail: erika.banski@carleton.ca; *Head, Res Support Serv,* Patti Harper; Tel: 613-520-2600, Ext 8066, E-mail: patti.harper@carleton.ca; *Head, Tech & Syst Serv,* Edward Bilodeau; Tel: 613-520-2600, Ext 6040, E-mail: ed.bilodeau@carleton.ca. Subject Specialists: *Digitization,* Erika Banski; Staff 102.6 (MLS 31.8, Non-MLS 70.8)
Founded 1942. Highest Degree: Doctorate
Library Holdings: CDs 27,407; e-books 811,272; e-journals 72,709; Music Scores 33,519; Bk Titles 1,066,991; Bk Vols 1,069,744; Per Subs 915
Special Collections: Broadside Poetry Coll; Canadian, British & American Small-Press Poetry; Douglas Cardinal Archives; French Revolution; George Bemi Archives; Herb Stovel Archives; Heritage Canada; Heritage Conservation Coll International & National; Maps, Atlases & Cartographic References; Maureen McTeer & Joe Clark fonds; Novosti Press Agency Photograph Files; Ottawa Regional Resource Coll; Siskind Coll; Ugandan Immigration Coll; Ukrainian Politics, 19th-20th Century (Batchinsky Coll). Canadian and Provincial
Automation Activity & Vendor Info: (Acquisitions) Innovative Interfaces, Inc - Sierra; (Cataloging) Innovative Interfaces, Inc - Sierra; (Circulation) Innovative Interfaces, Inc - Sierra; (Course Reserve) Atlas Systems; (ILL) Fretwell-Downing; (OPAC) Innovative Interfaces, Inc - Sierra; (Serials) Innovative Interfaces, Inc - Sierra
Wireless access
Partic in Canadian Association of Research Libraries; Canadian Research Knowledge Network; Ontario Council of University Libraries
Special Services for the Deaf - Assistive tech; Closed caption videos; TTY equip
Special Services for the Blind - Accessible computers; Blind students ctr; Braille equip; Braille paper; Braille servs; Closed circuit TV magnifier; Computer access aids; Dragon Naturally Speaking software; Inspiration software; Internet workstation with adaptive software; Large screen computer & software; Magnifiers; Networked computers with assistive software; Ref serv; Screen enlargement software for people with visual disabilities; Screen reader software; Transcribing serv; ZoomText magnification & reading software

M CHILDREN'S HOSPITAL OF EASTERN ONTARIO*, Conway Library, 401 Smyth Rd, K1H 8L1. SAN 324-4105. Tel: 613-737-7600, Ext 2206. FAX: 613-738-4806. E-mail: library@cheo.on.ca. Web Site: www.cheo.on.ca. *Mgr, Libr Serv,* Margaret Sampson; Staff 2 (MLS 1, Non-MLS 1)
Founded 1974
Library Holdings: Bk Titles 3,500; Per Subs 120
Subject Interests: Pediatrics
Wireless access
Open Mon-Fri 8-4
Restriction: Circulates for staff only

GL COUNTY OF CARLETON LAW LIBRARY*, Gordon F Henderson Library, Ottawa Court House, 2004-161 Elgin St, K2P 2K1. SAN 319-3292. Tel: 613-233-7386, Ext 221. FAX: 613-238-3788. E-mail: library@ccla-abcc.ca. Web Site: www.ccla-abcc.ca/page/Library. *Head Librn,* Jennifer Walker; Tel: 613-233-7386, Ext 225, E-mail: jwalker@ccla-abcc.ca; *Ref Librn,* Brenda Lauritzen; Tel: 613-233-7386, Ext 222, E-mail: blauritzen@ccla-abcc.ca; *Libr Tech,* Amanda Elliott; Tel: 613-233-7386, Ext 230, E-mail: aelliott@ccla-abcc.ca; Staff 4 (MLS 3, Non-MLS 1)
Founded 1888
Library Holdings: Bk Vols 35,000; Per Subs 80
Special Collections: Abridgements; Digests; Law Reports; Periodicals & Texts
Subject Interests: Legal
Wireless access
Publications: CCLA Bulletin
Restriction: Not open to pub

G DEPARTMENT OF CANADIAN HERITAGE*, Canadian Conservation Institute Library, 1030 Innes Rd, K1B 4S7. SAN 374-5341. Tel: 613-998-3721, Ext 157. FAX: 613-998-4721. E-mail: pch.iccbibliotheque-ccilibrary.pch@canada.ca. Web Site: www.canada.ca/en/conservation-institute/services/canadian-conservation-institute-library.html. *Dir Gen,* Jerome Moisan; E-mail: jerome.moisan@canada.ca; Staff 2 (MLS 1, Non-MLS 1)
Founded 1972
Library Holdings: Bk Titles 13,000; Per Subs 370; Videos 191
Subject Interests: Conserv, Museology, Restoration
Automation Activity & Vendor Info: (Acquisitions) Inmagic, Inc.; (Cataloging) Inmagic, Inc.; (OPAC) Inmagic, Inc.; (Serials) Inmagic, Inc.
Open Mon-Fri 9-12 & 1-4

G DEPARTMENT OF FINANCE CANADA LIBRARY*, 9022-90 Elgin St, 9th Flr, K1A 0G5. SAN 319-2970. Tel: 613-369-3386. FAX: 613-369-3436. E-mail: fin.library-bibliotheque.fin@canada.ca. Web Site: fin-ca.libguides.com/home-accueil.
Founded 1947
Library Holdings: Bk Vols 15,000; Per Subs 40
Subject Interests: Acctg, Auditing, Econ, Finance, Govt prog, Indust relations, Personnel admin, Pub admin, Pub policy
Automation Activity & Vendor Info: (Acquisitions) Insignia Software; (Cataloging) Insignia Software; (Circulation) Insignia Software; (OPAC) Insignia Software; (Serials) Insignia Software
Restriction: Open by appt only

G GLOBAL AFFAIRS CANADA*, Jules Leger Library, Lester B Pearson Bldg, 125 Sussex Dr, K1A 0G2. SAN 319-2962. Reference Tel: 343-203-6150. FAX: 613-944-0222. E-mail: library-biblio.sicl@international.gc.ca. Web Site: www.international.gc.ca/gac-amc/programs-programmes/jll-bjl/index.aspx.

Dir, Libr Serv, Fiona Scannell; Tel: 343-203-2644; Staff 16 (MLS 12, Non-MLS 4)
Founded 1909
Library Holdings: Bk Titles 35,000; Bk Vols 150,000; Per Subs 200
Subject Interests: Can foreign relations, Commerce, Develop, Econ, Intl law, Intl relations, Polit sci
Automation Activity & Vendor Info: (Acquisitions) Innovative Interfaces, Inc - Millennium; (Cataloging) Innovative Interfaces, Inc - Millennium; (Circulation) Innovative Interfaces, Inc - Millennium; (OPAC) Innovative Interfaces, Inc - Millennium

GOVERNMENT OF CANADA

L COURTS ADMINISTRATION SERVICE, TAX LIBRARY*, 200 Kent St, K1A 0M1, SAN 322-7251. Tel: 613-992-1704. FAX: 613-943-8449. Web Site: www.cas-satj.gc.ca. *Librn,* Denis Roussel; Staff 2 (MLS 1, Non-MLS 1)
Founded 1982
Library Holdings: Bk Titles 2,250; Bk Vols 12,485; Per Subs 180
Subject Interests: Acctg, Goods, Income tax, Law, Serv tax, Taxation
Automation Activity & Vendor Info: (OPAC) SydneyPlus

GL FEDERAL COURTS & TAX COURT OF CANADA, COURTS ADMINISTRATION SERVICE-LIBRARY SERVICES*, 90 Sparks St, K1A 0H9, SAN 326-1344. Tel: 613-995-1382. Reference Tel: 613-995-1267. FAX: 613-943-5303. Reference E-mail: reference@cas-satj.gc.ca. *Dir, Libr & Info Serv,* Jean Weerasinghe; *Br Mgr,* Denis Roussel; Tel: 613-992-1704, Fax: 613-943-8449; *Head, Coll Develop,* Christina-Anne Boyle; Tel: 613-947-3906, E-mail: christina-anne.boyle@cas-satj.gc.ca; *Head, Libr Syst & Cat,* Lawrence Wardroper; Tel: 613-996-8735, E-mail: lawrence.wardroper@cas-satj.gc.ca; *Client Serv Librn,* Karon J Crummey; Tel: 613-943-0839, E-mail: karon.crummey@cas-satj.gc.ca. Subject Specialists: *Tax,* Denis Roussel; Staff 11 (MLS 4, Non-MLS 7)
Library Holdings: AV Mats 200; e-books 2,100; Bk Vols 40,000
Subject Interests: Admin law, Citizenship, Competition law, Employment insurance, Immigration, Intellectual property, Maritime, Native law, Tax
Automation Activity & Vendor Info: (Acquisitions) SydneyPlus; (Cataloging) SydneyPlus; (Circulation) SydneyPlus; (ILL) SydneyPlus; (OPAC) SydneyPlus; (Serials) SydneyPlus
Partic in Federal Librs Consortium
Publications: Acquisitions List; Library Guide; Table of Contents Service
Restriction: Not open to pub

R GREENBERG FAMILIES LIBRARY*, 21 Nadolny Sachs PR, K2A 1R9. SAN 321-3382. Tel: 613-798-9818, Ext 245. E-mail: library@jccottawa.com. Web Site: jccottawa.com/our-facility/greenberg-families-library. *Sr Librn,* Carlie MacPherson; Staff 2 (MLS 1, Non-MLS 1)
Founded 1955
Library Holdings: Bk Titles 15,000; Per Subs 6
Subject Interests: Judaica
Wireless access
Open Mon-Thurs 9-5, Fri 9-2, Sun 10-4

G INNOVATION, SCIENCE & ECONOMIC DEVELOPMENT*, Library & Knowledge Centre, 235 Queen St, 2nd Flr, W Tower, K1A 0H5. SAN 319-3136. Tel: 343-291-3035. Administration Tel: 343-291-3035. FAX: 343-291-3027. E-mail: library-bibliotheque@ised-isde.gc.ca. *Dir,* Alain-Phillipe Bruneau; Tel: 343-291-1569; *Mgr, Info Serv,* Marguerite Lewis; Tel: 343-291-3033, E-mail: marguerite.lewis@ised-isde.gc.ca; Staff 9 (MLS 5, Non-MLS 4)
Founded 1918
Library Holdings: Bk Titles 63,000; Per Subs 1,000
Subject Interests: Bus info, Corp, Develop, Economy, Indust policy, Sci, Sci policy, Small bus, Tech innovation
Automation Activity & Vendor Info: (Acquisitions) Innovative Interfaces, Inc - Sierra; (Cataloging) Innovative Interfaces, Inc - Sierra; (Circulation) Innovative Interfaces, Inc - Sierra; (Discovery) EBSCO Discovery Service; (OPAC) Innovative Interfaces, Inc - Sierra; (Serials) Innovative Interfaces, Inc - Sierra
Wireless access
Open Mon-Fri 9-5

S INSTITUT CANADIEN FRANCAIS D'OTTAWA BIBLIOTHECAIRE*, 316 Dalhousie St, K1N 7E7. SAN 326-9442. Tel: 613-241-3522. FAX: 613-241-3611. E-mail: secretaire@icfo.ca. Web Site: icfo.blog.
Founded 1852
Library Holdings: Bk Vols 3,500
Restriction: Mem only

S INTERNATIONAL DEVELOPMENT RESEARCH CENTRE, 45 O'Connor St, K1G 3H9. (Mail add: PO Box 8500, K1G 3H9), SAN 321-2343. E-mail: informationservices@idrc.ca. Web Site: idrc-crdi.ca/en/contact-us. Staff 3 (MLS 2, Non-MLS 1)
Founded 1971
Special Collections: Brundtland Commission Archives; IDRC Digital Library; Rio Summit Archives
Subject Interests: Develop res, Info & communication technologies, Poverty alleviation, Sustainable develop
Open Mon-Fri 8-5

R KEHILLAT BETH ISRAEL, Malca Pass Library, 1400 Coldrey Ave, K1Z 7P9. SAN 319-289X. Tel: 613-728-3501, Ext 232. E-mail: library@kehillatbethisrael.com. Web Site: www.kehillatbethisrael.com/welcome/malca-pass-library. *Vols Coordr,* Norma Goldsmith; E-mail: nrgoldsmith@gmail.com; Staff 1 (MLS 1)
Founded 1960
Library Holdings: CDs 300; DVDs 50; Bk Titles 3,500; Videos 150
Subject Interests: Judaica
Open Thurs 10:30-2:30

G LIBRARY & ARCHIVES CANADA, Bibliothèque et Archives Canada, 395 Wellington St, K1A 0N4. (Mail add: 550 de la Cité Blvd, Gatineau, J8T 0A7), SAN 319-3403. Tel: 613-996-5115. Reference Toll Free Tel: 1-866-578-7777. FAX: 613-995-6274. Web Site: https://library-archives.canada.ca/eng/services/public/ask-us-question/pages/ask-us-question.aspx, library-archives.canada.ca/eng. *Librn & Archivist,* Leslie Weir
Founded 2004
Special Collections: Archival Documents; Genealogy Coll; Jacob M Lowy Coll; Reference Coll
Subject Interests: Can documentary heritage
Wireless access
Partic in OCLC Online Computer Library Center, Inc
Open Mon-Fri 9-4
Restriction: Open to pub for ref & circ; with some limitations
Friends of the Library Group

G LIBRARY OF PARLIAMENT*, Library of Parliament, K1A 0A9. SAN 368-0649. Information Services Tel: 613-992-4793. Toll Free Tel: 866-599-4999. E-mail: info@parl.gc.ca. Web Site: lop.parl.ca.
Founded 1867
Special Collections: Audubon Double Elephant Folio Birds of America; Canadian Political Pamphlets; Parliamentary Papers of France, Australia, United Kingdom, United Nations; Sessional Papers (1810-present); United Kingdom CTTEES (1715-present); United States (Congressional Papers). Canadian and Provincial
Subject Interests: Can studies, Canadiana, Govt, Intl relations, Law, Law Can, Legislation, Parliamentary affairs, Parliamentary hist, Parliamentary procedure, Polit sci, Soc sci with emphasis on Canada
Automation Activity & Vendor Info: (Acquisitions) SirsiDynix; (Cataloging) SirsiDynix; (Circulation) SirsiDynix; (OPAC) SirsiDynix; (Serials) SirsiDynix
Publications: Educational Resources; Electronic Services Offered to Parliamentarians by the Library of Parliament; History of the Federal Electoral Ridings since 1867; Legislative Summaries; Library of Parliament - Annual Report; Library of Parliament - Strategic Outlook; Research Publications

Branches:

BRANCHES & INFORMATION SERVICE, 125 Sparks St, K1A 0A6. Tel: 613-992-4793. Toll Free Tel: 866-599-4999. FAX: 613-992-1273. E-mail: info@parl.gc.ca. *Parliamentary Librarian,* Heather Lank

S NATIONAL GALLERY OF CANADA LIBRARY & ARCHIVES, 380 Sussex Dr, K1N 9N4. SAN 319-339X. Tel: 613-714-6000, Ext 6323. Interlibrary Loan Service Tel: 613-714-6000, Ext 6162. E-mail: erefel@gallery.ca. Web Site: www.gallery.ca/research/library-archives. *Sr Mgr, Library, Archives & Research Fellowship Program,* Amy Rose; Tel: 613-714-6000, Ext 6146, E-mail: arose@gallery.ca; *Archivist,* Philip Dombowsky; E-mail: pdombowsky@gallery.ca; *Archivist,* Carly Roberts; E-mail: croberts@gallery.ca; *Acq,* Catherine Laplante; E-mail: claplante@gallery.ca; *Cat,* Kathleen O'Reilly; E-mail: koreilly@gallery.ca; *ILL,* Annie Arseneault; E-mail: aarseneault@gallery.ca; *Presv,* Yves Neron; E-mail: yneron@gallery.ca; *Ref Serv,* Dominique Taylor; E-mail: dtaylor@gallery.ca; *Ser,* Mike Saunders; E-mail: msaunders@gallery.ca; Staff 9 (MLS 4, Non-MLS 5)
Founded 1918
Library Holdings: Bk Vols 431,000; Per Subs 550
Special Collections: Art Metropole; Artist's Books & Multiples; Auction Catalogues; Canadian Art Documentation Files; Canadiana; National Gallery of Canada Archives; National Gallery of Canada Personal & Corporate Archives
Subject Interests: Archit, Can art, Graphic arts, Post-mediaeval western painting, Sculpture
Automation Activity & Vendor Info: (Acquisitions) Innovative Interfaces, Inc; (Cataloging) Innovative Interfaces, Inc; (Circulation) Innovative

Interfaces, Inc; (OPAC) Innovative Interfaces, Inc; (Serials) Innovative Interfaces, Inc
Wireless access
Publications: Art at Auction: A Bibliographical Listing of Nineteenth-Century Canadian Catalogues (2000); Artists in Canada: A Union List of Artists' Files (1999); Index to National Gallery of Canada Exhibition Catalogues & Checklists, 1880-1930 (2007); Index to Nineteenth-Century Canadian Catalogues of Art (2004); Index to the National Gallery of Canada Bulletin & Annual Bulletin (1998); Library & Archives Collection Development Policy (1997)
Partic in AG Canada; Canadian Heritage Information Network; OCLC Online Computer Library Center, Inc
Open Tues-Fri 10-5

NATURAL RESOURCES CANADA

G BIBLIOTHEQUE DE RESSOURCES NATURELLES CANADA*, 580 Booth St, K1A 0E4, SAN 367-9144. Tel: 613-996-3919. Interlibrary Loan Service Tel: 613-996-0839. FAX: 613-943-8742. E-mail: bibliothequerncan.nrcanlibrary@nrcan.gc.ca, nrcanlibrary@nrcan.gc.ca. Web Site: www.nrcan.gc.ca/library/home. *Head of Libr,* Margaret Ahearn
Founded 1854
Special Collections: Contract Reports, Research Reports. Can & prov; Early Exploration Coll; Ehnography, Fauna, Flora & Geography; Forestry, Energy, Earth Sciences, Mineral & Metals Specialized Colls; Map Archival Coll; Minproc; Mintec; Photo Coll (1842-present); Rare Books on Geology & Mineral Exploration; Science of Geology Coll; Sir William Logan Coll
Subject Interests: Botany, Chem, Climate change, Earth sci, Entomology, Forestry, Geol, Geomatics, Hydrology (environment), Physics, Renewable energy
Partic in Council of Federal Libraries Consortium
Open Mon-Fri 8:30-4:30

G NATIONAL AIR PHOTO LIBRARY*, 615 Booth St, Rm 180, K1A 0E9, SAN 324-0657. Tel: 613-995-4560. FAX: 613-995-4568. E-mail: napl@nrcan.gc.ca. Web Site: nrcan.gc.ca/earth-sciences/home. *Mgr,* Florin Savopol; Tel: 613-943-0234
Founded 1925

G OFFICE OF THE AUDITOR GENERAL OF CANADA*, Knowledge Centre Library, West Tower, 240 Sparks St, 11th Flr, K1A 0G6. SAN 370-6923. Tel: 613-952-0213. Reference Tel: 613-952-0213, Ext 6204. E-mail: AEA_KCL-AMA_CCB@oag-bvg.gc.ca. *Libr Mgr,* Susan Ross; *Research Librn,* Colleen Martin; Staff 2 (MLS 2)
Founded 1979
Special Collections: Canadian and Provincial
Subject Interests: Acctg, Auditing
Automation Activity & Vendor Info: (Acquisitions) SirsiDynix; (Cataloging) SirsiDynix; (Circulation) SirsiDynix; (OPAC) SirsiDynix; (Serials) SirsiDynix
Wireless access

S OTTAWA CITIZEN LIBRARY COLLECTION*, 1101 Baxter Rd, K2C 3M4. SAN 319-3438. Tel: 613-596-3744. Toll Free Tel: 800-267-6100, Ext 3744. FAX: 613-726-1198. Web Site: www.ottawacitizen.com. *Researcher,* Liisa Tuominen; E-mail: ltuominen@postmedia.com
Founded 1940
Library Holdings: Bk Vols 300

M OTTAWA HOSPITAL, Medical Library (General Campus), 501 Smyth Rd, Rm M1404, K1H 8L6. SAN 319-3446. Tel: 613-737-8899, Ext 78530. FAX: 613-737-8521. E-mail: learningservices@toh.ca. Web Site: www.ottawahospital.on.ca. *Dir,* Position Currently Open; *Librn,* Risa Shorr; Staff 3 (MLS 2, Non-MLS 1)
Founded 1935
Library Holdings: e-journals 3,725; Bk Vols 7,735; Per Subs 3,000
Subject Interests: Allied health, Med, Nursing, Sexual abuse
Automation Activity & Vendor Info: (Cataloging) Inmagic, Inc.; (OPAC) Inmagic, Inc.; (Serials) Inmagic, Inc.
Function: ILL available
Open Mon-Fri 8:30-4:30
Restriction: Circulates for staff only, Med staff only
Branches:
CIVIC CAMPUS LIBRARY, 1053 Carling Ave, D-1, K1Y 4E9, SAN 321-6837. Tel: 613-798-5555, Ext 14450.
Founded 1960
Library Holdings: Bk Titles 3,000; Bk Vols 4,500; Per Subs 20
Restriction: Med staff only

P OTTAWA PUBLIC LIBRARY/BIBLIOTHEQUE PUBLIQUE D'OTTAWA*, Main Library, 120 Metcalfe St, K1P 5M2. SAN 368-0401. Tel: 613-580-2945. Circulation Tel: 613-580-2945, Ext 32106. Interlibrary Loan Service Tel: 613-580-2045, Ext 32162. Reference Tel: 613-580-2945, Ext 32164. Administration Tel: 613-580-2943. Automation Services Tel: 613-580-2424, Ext 41588. Information Services Tel: 613-580-2940, FAX: 613-567-8815. Automation Services FAX: 613-580-2711. Reference E-mail: ref@biblioottawalibrary.ca. Web Site: www.biblioottawalibrary.ca. *Chief Exec Officer,* Danielle McDonald; *Mgr,* Donna Clark; E-mail: donna.clark@BiblioOttawaLibrary.ca; Staff 452.4 (MLS 99.2, Non-MLS 353.2)
Founded 1906. Pop 790,000; Circ 9,711,880
Library Holdings: Electronic Media & Resources 77; Bk Titles 287,935; Bk Vols 2,404,076; Per Subs 4,777
Special Collections: Bilingual Coll (English & French); Local History (Ottawa Room), bks, pamphlets; Multilingual Coll. Canadian and Provincial
Automation Activity & Vendor Info: (Acquisitions) Horizon; (Cataloging) Horizon; (Circulation) Horizon; (OPAC) Horizon; (Serials) Horizon
Wireless access
Function: Adult literacy prog, Art exhibits, AV serv, BA reader (adult literacy), Bk club(s), Bk reviews (Group), Bks on cassette, Bks on CD, CD-ROM, Children's prog, Citizenship assistance, Computer training, Computers for patron use, Digital talking bks, E-Reserves, Electronic databases & coll, Family literacy, Free DVD rentals, Govt ref serv, Holiday prog, Home delivery & serv to seniorr ctr & nursing homes, Homebound delivery serv, Homework prog, ILL available, Internet access, Large print keyboards, Literacy & newcomer serv, Magnifiers for reading, Mail & tel request accepted, Museum passes, Music CDs, Online cat, Online ref, Orientations, Outside serv via phone, mail, e-mail & web, OverDrive digital audio bks, Photocopying/Printing, Preschool outreach, Prog for adults, Prog for children & young adult, Ref & res, Ref serv available, Senior computer classes, Senior outreach, Spoken cassettes & CDs, Spoken cassettes & DVDs, Summer reading prog, Teen prog, Telephone ref, VHS videos, Wheelchair accessible, Workshops
Publications: Preview/En primeur (Quarterly)
Mem of Ontario Library Service
Special Services for the Deaf - Assistive tech; Bks on deafness & sign lang; Closed caption videos; High interest/low vocabulary bks; Spec interest per
Special Services for the Blind - Assistive/Adapted tech devices, equip & products; Audio mat; Bks & mags in Braille, on rec, tape & cassette; Bks on cassette; Bks on CD; Cassettes; Computer access aids; Computer with voice synthesizer for visually impaired persons; Daisy reader; Descriptive video serv (DVS); Home delivery serv; Large print & cassettes; Large print bks; Large screen computer & software; Micro-computer access & training; PC for people with disabilities; Scanner for conversion & translation of mats; Screen enlargement software for people with visual disabilities; Sound rec; Text reader; Visunet prog (Canada); Volunteer serv; ZoomText magnification & reading software
Open Mon-Thurs 10-9, Fri 10-6, Sat 10-5
Friends of the Library Group
Branches: 32
ALTA VISTA, 2516 Alta Vista Dr, K1V 7T1, SAN 368-0436. *Br Mgr,* Jennifer Calhoun
Library Holdings: Bk Vols 130,038
Open Mon-Thurs 10-8:30, Fri 1-6, Sat 10-5
Friends of the Library Group
BEAVERBROOK BRANCH, 2500 Campeau Dr, K2K 2W3, SAN 319-1796. *Actg Br Mgr,* Catherine Flegg
Pop 14,000; Circ 450,000
Library Holdings: Bk Vols 80,000; Per Subs 250
Open Mon-Thurs 10-9, Fri 10-6, Sat 10-5
BLACKBURN HAMLET, 199 Glen Park Dr, K1B 5B8, SAN 367-9748. *Br Mgr,* Sarah Macintyre
Library Holdings: Bk Vols 52,892
Open Mon-Thurs 10-8:30, Fri 1-6, Sat 10-5
Friends of the Library Group
CARLINGWOOD, 281 Woodroffe Ave, K2A 3W4, SAN 368-0460. *Br Mgr,* Yvonne van Lith
Library Holdings: Bk Vols 112,091
Open Mon-Thurs 10-8:30, Fri 1-6, Sat 10-5
Friends of the Library Group
CARP BRANCH, 3911 Carp Rd, K0A 1L0. *Actg Br Mgr,* Catherine Flegg
Founded 1997. Pop 5,000
Library Holdings: Bk Vols 33,848
Open Mon 10-6, Tues-Thurs 10-8:30, Fri 1-6, Sat 10-5
CENTENNIAL, 3870 Old Richmond Rd, K2H 5C4, SAN 368-0371. *Br Mgr,* Yvonne van Lith
Open Mon-Thurs 10-8:30, Fri 1-6, Sat 10-5
Friends of the Library Group
CONSTANCE BAY BRANCH, 262 Len Purcell, K0A 1L0. *Actg Br Mgr,* Catherine Flegg
Founded 1982. Pop 4,950
Library Holdings: Bk Vols 3,000
Open Mon & Thurs 4:30-8:30, Tues 10-1 & 4:30-8:30
CUMBERLAND BRANCH, 1599 Tenth Line Rd, K1E 3E8, SAN 325-2639. *Br Mgr,* Sarah Macintyre; Staff 4 (MLS 2, Non-MLS 2)
Founded 1978. Pop 32,300; Circ 184,956
Library Holdings: Bk Titles 36,064; Bk Vols 41,191; Per Subs 99

Open Mon-Thurs 10-9, Fri 10-6, Sat 10-5
Friends of the Library Group
RUTH E DICKINSON BRANCH, Walter Baker Sports Centre, 100 Malvern Dr, K2J 2G5, SAN 368-0363. *Br Mgr,* Karen Beiles
Open Mon-Thurs 10-8:30, Fri 1-6, Sat 10-5
Friends of the Library Group
ELMVALE ACRES, Elmvale Acres Shopping Ctr, 1910 St Laurent Blvd, K1G 1A4, SAN 368-0495. *Br Mgr,* Jennifer Calhoun
Library Holdings: Bk Vols 61,121
Open Mon-Thurs 10-8:30, Fri 1-6, Sat 10-5
Friends of the Library Group
EMERALD PLAZA, 1547 Merivale Rd, K2G 4V3, SAN 368-0347. *Br Mgr,* Yvonne van Lith
Open Mon-Thurs 10-8:30, Fri 1-6, Sat 10-5
Friends of the Library Group
FITZROY HARBOUR BRANCH, Fitzroy Harbour Community Ctr, 100 Clifford Campbell, K0A 1X0. *Actg Br Mgr,* Catherine Flegg
Pop 2,835
Library Holdings: Bk Vols 4,500
Open Mon 5:30-8:30, Thurs 10-1 & 5:30-8:30, Sat 10-1
GREELY BRANCH, 1448 Meadow Dr, K4P 1B1, SAN 324-7031. *Br Mgr,* Jennifer Calhoun
Open Mon & Wed 10-1 & 4:30-8:30, Tues 10-1, Thurs 4:30-8:30, Fri 3-6, Sat 10-2
GREENBORO DISTRICT LIBRARY, 363 Lorry Greenberg Dr, K1T 3P8, SAN 367-9772. *Br Mgr,* Jennifer Calhoun
Library Holdings: Bk Vols 45,421
Open Mon-Thurs 10-9, Fri 10-6, Sat 10-5
Friends of the Library Group
HAZELDEAN BRANCH, 50 Castlefrank Rd, K2L 2N5. *Actg Br Mgr,* Catherine Flegg
Library Holdings: Bk Vols 60,000
Open Mon-Thurs 10-8:30, Fri 1-6, Sat 10-5
MANOTICK BRANCH, 5499 S River Dr, K4M 1A4. *Br Mgr,* Karen Beiles
Founded 1982. Pop 10,000
Library Holdings: Bk Vols 30,000
Open Tues-Thurs 10-8:30, Fri 1-6, Sat 10-5
METCALFE BRANCH, 2782 Eighth Line Rd, K0A 2P0, SAN 324-704X. *Br Mgr,* Jennifer Calhoun
Open Mon 5:30pm-8:30pm, Tues & Thurs 10-1 & 5:30-8:30, Wed 4:30-8:30, Sat 10-2
MUNSTER BRANCH, 7749 Bleeks Rd, K0A 3P0. *Br Mgr,* Karen Beiles
Founded 1982. Pop 3,315
Library Holdings: Bk Vols 11,056
Open Mon-Thurs 2:30-5:30 & 6:30-8:30, Sat 10-2
NEPEAN CENTREPOINTE BRANCH, 101 Centrepointe Dr, K2G 5K7. *Br Mgr,* Yvonne van Lith
Library Holdings: Bk Vols 148,072
Open Mon-Thurs 10-9, Fri 10-6, Sat 10-5
NORTH GLOUCESTER, 2036 Ogilvie Rd, K1J 7N8, SAN 367-9802. *Br Mgr,* Sarah Mcintyre
Pop 22,095
Library Holdings: Bk Vols 88,000; Per Subs 100
Open Mon-Thurs 10-8:30, Fri 1-6, Sat 10-5
Friends of the Library Group
NORTH GOWER BRANCH, 6579 Fourth Line Rd, K0A 2T0. *Br Mgr,* Karen Beiles
Library Holdings: Bk Vols 16,000; Per Subs 35
Open Mon 5-8:30, Tues 10-8:30, Wed 10-12:30 & 1-5, Thurs 1-8:30, Sat 10-2
ORLEANS BRANCH, 1705 Orleans Blvd, K1C 4W2, SAN 367-9713. *Br Mgr,* Sarah Mcintyre
Library Holdings: Bk Vols 87,604
Open Mon-Thurs 10-8:30, Fri 1-6, Sat 10-5
Friends of the Library Group
OSGOODE BRANCH, 5630 Osgoode Main St, K0A 2W0. (Mail add: PO Box 459, K0A 2W0), SAN 319-2466. *Br Mgr,* Jennifer Calhoun
Pop 9,850; Circ 35,680
Library Holdings: Bk Titles 27,746; Bk Vols 31,487; Per Subs 64
Open Mon 10-1 & 2-5, Tues 10-1 & 5:30-8:30, Wed & Thurs 2-5 & 5:30-8:30, Sat 10-2
RICHMOND BRANCH, 6240 Perth St, K0A 2Z0. *Br Mgr,* Karen Beiles
Library Holdings: Bk Vols 21,937
Open Mon, Wed & Thurs 1:30-5 & 6-8:30, Tues 10-12:30, 1:30-5 & 6-8:30, Fri 1:30-5, Sat 10-2
RIDEAU, 377 Rideau St, K1N 5Y6, SAN 368-0525. *Br Mgr,* Philip Robert
Library Holdings: Bk Vols 51,374
Open Mon-Thurs 10-8:30, Fri 1-6, Sat 10-5
Friends of the Library Group
ROCKCLIFFE PARK, 380 Springfield Rd, K1M 0K7, SAN 319-3837. *Br Mgr,* Philip Robert
Founded 1993. Pop 10,000
Library Holdings: Bk Vols 15,000
Open Mon & Wed 10-5, Tues & Thurs 1-8:30, Fri 2-6, Sat 10-2
Friends of the Library Group
ROSEMOUNT BRANCH, 1207 Wellington West/Ouest, K1Y 2Z8, SAN 368-0614. *Br Mgr,* Tony Westenbroek
Pop 33,995
Library Holdings: Bk Vols 41,076
Open Mon-Thurs 10-8:30, Fri 1-6, Sat 10-5
Friends of the Library Group
ST-LAURENT, 515 Cote St, K1K 0Z0, SAN 368-055X. *Br Mgr,* Philip Robert
Library Holdings: Bk Vols 82,776
Open Mon-Thurs 10-8:30, Fri 1-6, Sat 10-5
Friends of the Library Group
STITTSVILLE BRANCH, 1637 Stittsville Main St, K2S 1A9, SAN 319-4299. *Br Mgr,* Karen Beiles
Founded 1974. Pop 45,125; Circ 120,000
Library Holdings: Bk Titles 47,000; Bk Vols 72,000; Per Subs 85
Special Collections: Local Historical Society Information
Open Mon-Thurs 10-8:30, Fri 1-6, Sat 10-5
Friends of the Library Group
SUNNYSIDE, 1049 Bank St, K1S 3W9, SAN 368-0584. *Br Mgr,* Tony Westenbroek
Pop 32,545
Library Holdings: Bk Vols 129,463
Open Mon-Thurs 10-8:30, Fri 1-6, Sat 10-5
Friends of the Library Group
VANIER BRANCH, 310 Pères Blancs Ave, K1L 7L5, SAN 319-5848. *Br Mgr,* Philip Robert
Founded 1944. Pop 43,490
Library Holdings: Bk Titles 50,000; Bk Vols 54,000; Per Subs 40
Open Mon-Wed 10-8:30, Thurs & Fri 1-6, Sat 10-5
VERNON BRANCH, 8682 Bank St, K0A 3J0, SAN 324-7066, *Br Mgr,* Jennifer Calhoun
Open Tues 10-1 & 5:30-8:30, Wed 3-8:30, Thurs 5:30pm-8:30pm, Sat 10-2
Bookmobiles: 2. Libr Operations, Richard Stark

S PLANETARY ASSOCIATION FOR CLEAN ENERGY INC, 100 Bronson Ave, Ste 1001, K1R 6G8. SAN 328-4158. Tel: 613-236-6265. FAX: 613-235-5876. E-mail: paceincnet@gmail.com. Web Site: pacenet.homestead.com, pacenetwork.org. *Pres,* Dr Andrew Michrowski; *Library Contact,* Monique Michaud
Founded 1979
Jan 2024-Dec 2024 Income (CAN) $29,000, Federal (CAN) $4,000, Locally Generated Income (CAN) $25,000. Mats Exp (CAN) $22,000, Books (CAN) $2,000, Per/Ser (Incl. Access Fees) (CAN) $1,000, Other Print Mats (CAN) $2,000, Electronic Ref Mat (Incl. Access Fees) (CAN) $15,000, Presv (CAN) $2,000. Sal (CAN) $2,000
Library Holdings: CDs 250; DVDs 100; e-books 30; Electronic Media & Resources 50; Bk Titles 6,250; Videos 300
Special Collections: Andrija Puharich Coll, res notes; Biological Communication Technologies Coll, replications, res notes; Brown's Gas Coll, R&D, replications; Electromagnetic Field Bioeffect Research Notes; Energy From the Vacuum Coll, R&D, replications; Environmental Hypersensitivity Coll, case studies, res notes; Free Energy Systems Coll, R&D, replications; Nikola Tesla Coll, replications, res notes; Nuclear Transmutation- Nuclear Waste Decontamination Coll, R&D, replications
Subject Interests: United Nations
Wireless access
Function: Res libr
Open Mon-Fri 9-5
Restriction: Non-circulating of rare bks

G PRIVY COUNCIL OFFICE*, Library Information Centre, 85 Sparks St, Rm 1000, K1A 0A3. SAN 322-7197. Tel: 613-957-5125. FAX: 613-957-5043. E-mail: info@pco-bcp.gc.ca. Web Site: www.canada.ca/en/privy-council.
Founded 1920
Library Holdings: Bk Titles 35,000; Per Subs 350
Subject Interests: Current events, Hist, Polit sci, Pub admin, Pub policy
Automation Activity & Vendor Info: (Acquisitions) Sydney; (Cataloging) Sydney; (Circulation) Sydney; (OPAC) Sydney; (Serials) Sydney
Publications: Acquisitions List; Bibliography
Partic in Consortium of Fed Librs
Open Mon-Fri 9-5

M ROYAL OTTAWA HEALTH CARE GROUP*, Royal Ottawa Mental Health Centre Library, 1145 Carling Ave, K1Z 7K4. SAN 324-0495. Tel: 613-722-6521, Ext 6268. E-mail: library@theroyal.ca. *Mgr, Libr Serv,* Sascha Davis; E-mail: sascha.davis@theroyal.ca
Founded 1968
Library Holdings: Bk Titles 3,700; Per Subs 180
Subject Interests: Psychiat, Psychol

Automation Activity & Vendor Info: (Acquisitions) Inmagic, Inc.; (Cataloging) Inmagic, Inc.; (OPAC) Inmagic, Inc.; (Serials) Inmagic, Inc.
Restriction: Staff use only

S THE ROYAL SOCIETY OF CANADA LIBRARY*, Walter House, 282 Somerset St W, K2P 0J6. SAN 371-8875. Tel: 613-991-6990. FAX: 613-991-6996. Web Site: www.rsc-src.ca. *Mgr, Publications & Communications,* Erika Kujawski; E-mail: ekujawski@rsc-src.ca
Library Holdings: Bk Titles 600
Publications: Calendar (1954 to date); Index (1882-1982); Presentations (1943 to 2001); Proceedings (1882 to 1999); Transactions (1882 to 2000)
Restriction: Mem only

CR SAINT PAUL UNIVERSITY LIBRARY*, Jean-Leon Allie Library, Guides Hall, 1st Flr, 223 Main St, K1S 1C4. SAN 319-3497. Tel: 613-236-1393, Ext 2357. Toll Free Tel: 800-637-6859, Ext 2357. FAX: 613-751-4031. E-mail: biblio@ustpaul.ca. Web Site: ustpaul.ca/jean-leon-allie-omi-library.php. *Chief Librn,* Jeremie LeBlanc; Tel: 613-236-1393, Ext 2220, E-mail: jleblanc@ustpaul.ca; *Coll Develop Librn,* Marta Samokishyn; Tel: 613-236-1393, Ext 2313, E-mail: msamokishyn@ustpaul.ca; Staff 12 (MLS 3, Non-MLS 9)
Founded 1937. Enrl 835; Fac 66; Highest Degree: Doctorate
Library Holdings: Bk Titles 426,716; Bk Vols 452,813; Per Subs 793
Special Collections: Rare Books; Roman Catholic liturgy
Subject Interests: Canon law, Medieval studies, Theol
Automation Activity & Vendor Info: (Acquisitions) SirsiDynix-WorkFlows; (Cataloging) SirsiDynix-WorkFlows; (Circulation) SirsiDynix-WorkFlows; (OPAC) SirsiDynix; (Serials) SirsiDynix-WorkFlows
Wireless access
Function: Res libr
Restriction: Borrowing privileges limited to fac & registered students

S STATISTICS CANADA LIBRARY*, R H Coats Bldg, 2nd Flr, 100 Tunney's Pasture Driveway, K1A 0T6. SAN 319-3535. Tel: 613-951-8219. FAX: 613-951-0939. E-mail: statcan.library-bibliotheque.statcan@canada.ca, statcan.library-reference-bibliotheque-reference.statcan@statcan.gc.ca. Web Site: www.statcan.gc.ca/library-bibliotheque/index-eng.html, www.statcan.gc.ca/library-bibliotheque/index-fra.html.
Founded 1918
Special Collections: Statistics (Statistics Canada Coll, Foreign Statistics Coll)
Subject Interests: Demography, Econ, Labor, Math, Methodology, Sociol, Statistical theory
Automation Activity & Vendor Info: (Cataloging) SirsiDynix-WorkFlows; (Circulation) SirsiDynix-WorkFlows; (OPAC) SirsiDynix; (Serials) SirsiDynix-WorkFlows
Special Services for the Blind - Computer with voice synthesizer for visually impaired persons; ZoomText magnification & reading software
Restriction: Not open to pub

GL SUPREME COURT OF CANADA LIBRARY*, 301 Wellington St, K1A 0J1. SAN 319-3543. Tel: 613-996-8120. FAX: 613-952-2832. E-mail: library-bibliotheque@scc-csc.ca. Web Site: www.scc-csc.ca/lib-bib. *Dir,* Alicia Loo; Tel: 613-996-7996, E-mail: alicia.loo@scc-csc.ca; *Actg Mgr, Coll Develop,* Cheryl Murphy; E-mail: collection@scc-csc.ca; *Cat Mgr, Mgr, Libr Syst,* Carole Brisson; Tel: 613-947-0628, E-mail: carole.brisson@scc-csc.ca; *Mgr, Res, Ref Mgr,* Michel-Adrien Sheppard; Tel: 613-944-7723, E-mail: michel-adrien.sheppard@scc-csc.ca; Staff 13 (MLS 7, Non-MLS 6)
Founded 1875
Library Holdings: Bk Titles 106,015; Bk Vols 363,991; Per Subs 2,418
Subject Interests: Civil law, Common law
Automation Activity & Vendor Info: (Acquisitions) SirsiDynix; (Cataloging) SirsiDynix; (Circulation) SirsiDynix; (Discovery) EBSCO Online; (ILL) Relais International; (OPAC) SirsiDynix; (Serials) EBSCO Discovery Service
Function: 24/7 Online cat
Publications: New Journal Articles; New Library Titles (Acquisition list)
Partic in Canadian Fed Librs; NELLCO Law Library Consortium, Inc.
Restriction: Authorized patrons, Authorized scholars by appt, Badge access after hrs, By permission only

S TRANSPORTATION ASSOCIATION OF CANADA*, Transportation Information Service, 401-1111 Prince of Wales Dr, K2C 3T2. SAN 319-3470. Tel: 613-736-1350, Ext 244. FAX: 613-736-1395. E-mail: tis@tac-atc.ca. Web Site: www.tac-atc.ca/en/bookstore-and-resources/library. *Library Contact,* Glenn Cole; E-mail: gcole@tac-atc.ca; Staff 1 (Non-MLS 1)
Founded 1956
Library Holdings: Bk Titles 19,500; Per Subs 200
Special Collections: Great Britain Transportation & Road Research Laboratory Reports; National Association of Australia State Road Authority Publications; Transportation Association of Canada Annual Proceeds; Transportation Research Board Reports
Subject Interests: Bridges, Roads, Traffic engr, Transportation, Urban transportation
Automation Activity & Vendor Info: (Acquisitions) Inmagic, Inc.; (Cataloging) Inmagic, Inc.; (Circulation) Inmagic, Inc.; (ILL) Inmagic, Inc.; (OPAC) Inmagic, Inc.; (Serials) Inmagic, Inc.

C UNIVERSITY OF OTTAWA LIBRARIES*, University of Ottawa Library, 65 University Private, K1N 6N5. SAN 368-136X. Tel: 613-562-5213. FAX: 613-562-5195. E-mail: bibliolibrary@uOttawa.ca. Web Site: biblio.uottawa.ca. *Univ Librn, Vice Provost,* Talia Chung; Tel: 613-562-5880, E-mail: talia.chung@uottawa.ca; *Assoc Univ Librn, Learning & User Services,* Joan Cavanagh; Tel: 613-562-5690, E-mail: joan.cavanagh@uottawa.ca; *Chief Admin Officer,* Daniel Legault; Tel: 613-562-5800, Ext 3646, E-mail: daniel.legault@uottawa.ca; *Head, Res Support Serv, Head, Spec Coll,* Sarah Simpkin; E-mail: sarah.simpkin@uottawa.ca; Staff 53 (MLS 46, Non-MLS 7)
Founded 1848. Enrl 42,670; Fac 1,630; Highest Degree: Doctorate
Library Holdings: e-books 1,030,312; e-journals 115,849; Bk Vols 2,335,854
Special Collections: Canadian Women's Movement Archives; Literary Archives (Related to 19th century French literature); Slovak Archives. Canadian and Provincial; UN Document Depository
Subject Interests: Fr, Law, Med
Automation Activity & Vendor Info: (Acquisitions) Innovative Interfaces, Inc; (Cataloging) Innovative Interfaces, Inc; (Circulation) Innovative Interfaces, Inc; (Course Reserve) Innovative Interfaces, Inc; (ILL) OCLC; (Media Booking) Innovative Interfaces, Inc; (OPAC) Innovative Interfaces, Inc; (Serials) Innovative Interfaces, Inc
Wireless access
Function: Computers for patron use, Online cat, Photocopying/Printing, Wheelchair accessible
Partic in Canadian Association of Research Libraries; Canadian Research Knowledge Network; Ontario Council of University Libraries
Special Services for the Deaf - ADA equip; Closed caption videos
Special Services for the Blind - Accessible computers; Computer with voice synthesizer for visually impaired persons; Dragon Naturally Speaking software; Screen reader software; ZoomText magnification & reading software
Restriction: External users must contact libr
Friends of the Library Group

Departmental Libraries:

CL BRIAN DICKSON LAW LIBRARY, Pavillion Fauteux, 4e et 5e etages, 57 rue Louis Pasteur Private, K1N 6N5, SAN 368-1424. Circulation Tel: 613-562-5812. FAX: 613-562-5279. E-mail: droitlaw@uottawa.ca. Web Site: biblio.uottawa.ca/en/brian-dickson-law-library. *Law Librn,* Richard Harkin; Tel: 613-562-5800, Ext 3359, E-mail: rjharkin@uottawa.ca; Staff 3 (MLS 3)
Library Holdings: Bk Vols 220,000; Per Subs 1,000
Subject Interests: Civil law, Common law

ISOBEL FIRESTONE MUSIC LIBRARY, Perez Hall, 50 University Private, K1N 6N5, SAN 373-5613. Tel: 613-562-5209. Web Site: biblio.uottawa.ca/en/music-library. *Coordr,* Ann Hemingway; E-mail: ann.hemingway@uottawa.ca; Staff 1 (MLS 1)
Special Collections: Scandinavian Music
Automation Activity & Vendor Info: (Circulation) Innovative Interfaces, Inc; (Course Reserve) Innovative Interfaces, Inc; (OPAC) Innovative Interfaces, Inc; (Serials) Innovative Interfaces, Inc

GEOGRAPHIC, STATISTICAL & GOVERNMENT INFORMATION CENTRE, Morisset Hall, 3rd Flr, 65 University, K1N 9A5, SAN 373-5591. Tel: 613-562-5211. FAX: 613-562-5195. E-mail: gsg@uottawa.ca. Web Site: biblio.uottawa.ca/en/gsg-centre. *Geography Librn,* Rene Duplain; E-mail: rene.duplain@uottawa.ca; *Research Librn,* Chantal Ripp; E-mail: chantal.ripp@ottawa.c; Staff 3 (MLS 3)
Library Holdings: Bk Vols 866,059; Per Subs 16
Special Collections: Maps Coll-Canada, Western Europe, US, Amazonia & French-Speaking Africa
Publications: Acquisitions List

CM HEALTH SCIENCES LIBRARY, Roger-Guindon Hall, Rm 1020, 451 Smyth Rd, K1H 8M5, SAN 368-1459. Tel: 613-562-5407. E-mail: bibliorgnlibrary@uottawa.ca. Web Site: biblio.uottawa.ca/en/health-sciences-library. *Lead Librn,* Isabelle Castonguay; E-mail: icastong@uottawa.ca; *Health Sci Librn,* Marie-Cecile Domecq; E-mail: mdomecq@uottawa.ca; Staff 9 (MLS 3, Non-MLS 6)
Founded 1982
Subject Interests: Audiology, Med, Nursing, Nutrition, Occupational therapy, Physiotherapy, Speech pathology
Automation Activity & Vendor Info: (ILL) Fretwell-Downing
Partic in Ontario Council of University Libraries
Open Mon-Thurs 8am-10:30pm, Fri 8-8, Sat & Sun 9-7

MORISSET LIBRARY (ARTS & SCIENCES), 65 University Private, K1N 9A5, SAN 368-1394. Tel: 613-562-5213. Web Site: biblio.uottawa.ca/en/morisset-library. *Art Librn,* Tea Rokolj; E-mail: tea.rokolj@uottawa.ca; Staff 15 (MLS 14, Non-MLS 1)
Automation Activity & Vendor Info: (Circulation) Innovative Interfaces, Inc; (Course Reserve) Innovative Interfaces, Inc; (Media Booking) Innovative Interfaces, Inc; (OPAC) Innovative Interfaces, Inc; (Serials) Innovative Interfaces, Inc

OWEN SOUND

C GEORGIAN COLLEGE, Owen Sound Library, Main Bldg, 1st Flr, Rm 206, 1450 Eighth St E, N4K 5R4. Tel: 519-372-3211. Toll Free Tel: 877-890-8477. E-mail: library@georgiancollege.ca. Web Site: library.georgiancollege.ca. *Libr Tech,* Shannon Rankin; E-mail: shannon.rankin@georgiancollege.ca
Library Holdings: Bk Vols 6,254; Per Subs 40
Wireless access
Open Mon-Thurs 8-8, Fri 8-5, Sat 10-4

M GREY BRUCE HEALTH SERVICES*, Health Sciences Library, 1800 Eighth St E, N4K 6M9. SAN 323-9047. Tel: 519-376-2121, Ext 2043. FAX: 519-372-3947. *Libr Tech,* Christine Fenton-Stone; E-mail: cfentonstone@gbhs.on.ca; Staff 1 (MLS 1)
Library Holdings: e-books 85; e-journals 2,700; Bk Titles 500; Per Subs 15
Wireless access
Partic in Western Ontario Health Knowledge Network

P OWEN SOUND & NORTH GREY UNION PUBLIC LIBRARY*, 824 First Ave W, N4K 4K4. SAN 319-3586. Tel: 519-376-6623. FAX: 519-376-7170. E-mail: info@owensound.library.on.ca. Web Site: olco.ent.sirsidynix.net/client/en_US/owensound. *Chief Librn/CEO,* Tim Nicholls Harrison; E-mail: tnicholls-harrison@owensound.library.on.ca; *Chief Librn,* Nadia Danyluk; E-mail: ndanyluk@owensound.library.on.ca; *Fac Mgr,* Lindsey Harris; Staff 14.5 (MLS 3, Non-MLS 11.5)
Founded 1855. Pop 41,069; Circ 301,110
Library Holdings: Audiobooks 2,016; CDs 1,099; DVDs 2,643; e-books 32,535; Large Print Bks 1,848; Bk Titles 75,564; Bk Vols 81,734; Per Subs 214
Special Collections: Local History & Genealogy of Grey & Bruce Counties Coll. Oral History
Subject Interests: Genealogy, Local hist
Automation Activity & Vendor Info: (Acquisitions) SirsiDynix; (Cataloging) SirsiDynix; (Circulation) SirsiDynix; (OPAC) SirsiDynix
Wireless access
Function: Adult literacy prog, Bks on CD, Children's prog, Computer training, Computers for patron use, Family literacy, Free DVD rentals, Homebound delivery serv, ILL available, Large print keyboards, Magnifiers for reading, Music CDs, Online cat, Photocopying/Printing, Prog for children & young adult, Ref serv available, Senior computer classes, Story hour, Teen prog, Telephone ref, Wheelchair accessible
Mem of Ontario Library Service
Partic in Ontario Library Consortium
Open Mon-Thurs 9:30-9, Fri & Sat 9:30-5, Sun 2-5
Friends of the Library Group

PARIS

P COUNTY OF BRANT PUBLIC LIBRARY*, Paris Branch, 12 William St, N3L 1K7. SAN 324-1637. Tel: 519-442-2433. FAX: 519-442-7582. Web Site: olco.ent.sirsidynix.net/client/en_US/brant. *Chief Exec Officer,* Kelly Bernstein; E-mail: kelly.bernstein@brant.ca; Staff 33 (MLS 7, Non-MLS 26)
Pop 40,000; Circ 430,000
Library Holdings: Bk Titles 34,000; Per Subs 70
Wireless access
Mem of Ontario Library Service
Open Mon-Thurs 10-8, Fri & Sat 10-5
Friends of the Library Group
Branches: 4
BURFORD BRANCH, 24 Park Ave, Burford, N0E 1A0. (Mail add: Box 267, Burford, N0E 1A0). Tel: 519-449-5371. FAX: 519-449-5371. *Chief Librn,* Gay Kozak Selby; *Br Coordr,* Chris Scrivener; *Ch,* Zeta Phillipo
Library Holdings: Bk Vols 5,000
Open Tues & Thurs 10-8, Wed 3-8, Fri & Sat 10-2
GLEN MORRIS BRANCH, 474 E River Rd, Glen Morris, N0B 1W0. (Mail add: PO Box 40, Glen Morris, N0B 1W0). Tel: 519-740-2122. FAX: 519-740-2122.
Library Holdings: Bk Vols 8,000
Open Tues & Sat 10-2, Wed & Thurs 5-8
ST GEORGE BRANCH, 78 Main St N, St. George, N0E 1N0. (Mail add: PO Box 310, St. George, N0E 1N0). Tel: 519-448-1300. FAX: 519-448-4608.
Library Holdings: Bk Vols 4,000
Open Tues-Thurs 10-8, Fri 10-5, Sat 10-4, Sun Noon-4
SCOTLAND-OAKLAND BRANCH, 281 Oakland Rd, Scotland, N0E 1R0. (Mail add: PO Box 40, Scotland, N0E 1R0). Tel: 519-446-0181. FAX: 519-446-0077.
Library Holdings: Bk Vols 5,000
Open Tues & Thurs 3-8, Wed 10-5, Fri 12-5, Sat 10-2

PARRY SOUND

P PARRY SOUND PUBLIC LIBRARY*, 29 Mary St, P2A 1E3. SAN 319-3616. Tel: 705-746-9601. FAX: 705-746-9601. E-mail: askus@pspl.ca. Web Site: www.parrysoundlibrary.com. *Chief Exec Officer,* Selena Martens; E-mail: semartens@pspl.ca; Staff 4 (MLS 1, Non-MLS 3)
Founded 1898. Pop 6,900; Circ 53,245
Library Holdings: Bk Titles 35,000; Bk Vols 44,010; Per Subs 45
Automation Activity & Vendor Info: (Acquisitions) SirsiDynix; (Cataloging) SirsiDynix; (Circulation) SirsiDynix; (OPAC) SirsiDynix
Wireless access
Publications: District of Parry Sound Bibliography; Notes & Sketches on the History of Parry Sound
Open Tues-Thurs 10-7, Fri 10-5, Sat 10-2
Friends of the Library Group

PEMBROKE

P PEMBROKE PUBLIC LIBRARY*, 237 Victoria St, K8A 4K5. SAN 319-3624. Tel: 613-732-8844. FAX: 613-732-1116. E-mail: info@pembrokelibrary.ca. Web Site: pembrokelibrary.ca. *Chief Exec Officer,* Karthi Rajamani; E-mail: krajamani@pembrokelibrary.ca; Staff 11 (MLS 1, Non-MLS 10)
Founded 1901. Pop 23,500; Circ 172,036
Library Holdings: AV Mats 5,954; e-books 8,237; Large Print Bks 2,205; Bk Vols 72,000; Per Subs 103; Talking Bks 1,004
Subject Interests: Genealogy, Local hist
Automation Activity & Vendor Info: (Cataloging) Follett Software; (Circulation) Follett Software; (OPAC) Follett Software
Wireless access
Function: AV serv, Homebound delivery serv, ILL available, Outside serv via phone, mail, e-mail & web, Photocopying/Printing, Prog for children & young adult, Ref serv available, Serves people with intellectual disabilities, Summer reading prog, Wheelchair accessible
Mem of Ontario Library Service
Special Services for the Blind - Audio mat; Home delivery serv; Large print bks; Micro-computer access & training; PC for people with disabilities
Open Mon-Thurs 10-8, Fri & Sat 10-5:30
Friends of the Library Group

L RENFREW COUNTY LAW ASSOCIATION*, James W Fraser Law Library, 297 Pembroke St E, Ste 1211, K8A 3K2. SAN 328-0780. Tel: 613-732-4880. FAX: 613-732-1314. E-mail: library@rcla.on.ca. Web Site: www.rcla.on.ca/?page_id=9. *Librn,* Laurie Stoddard
Library Holdings: Bk Titles 5,600
Open Mon-Fri 9-4

PENETANGUISHENE

P PENETANGUISHENE PUBLIC LIBRARY*, 24 Simcoe St, L9M 1R6. SAN 319-3640. Tel: 705-549-7164. FAX: 705-549-3932. E-mail: penlibbk@gmail.com. Web Site: www.penetanguishene.library.on.ca. *Chief Exec Officer,* Linda Keenan; E-mail: lkeenan@penetanguishene.ca; Staff 6 (Non-MLS 6)
Pop 8,962; Circ 30,968
Library Holdings: e-books 4,400; Bk Vols 30,632; Per Subs 42
Automation Activity & Vendor Info: (Acquisitions) SirsiDynix; (Cataloging) SirsiDynix; (Circulation) SirsiDynix; (Course Reserve) SirsiDynix; (ILL) SirsiDynix; (Media Booking) SirsiDynix; (OPAC) SirsiDynix; (Serials) SirsiDynix
Wireless access
Mem of Ontario Library Service
Partic in County of Simcoe Libr Coop
Open Mon, Tues & Fri 9-6, Wed & Thurs 9-7, Sat 9-2
Friends of the Library Group

PERTH

P PERTH & DISTRICT UNION PUBLIC LIBRARY*, Perth & District Library, 30 Herriott St, K7H 1T2. SAN 319-3659. Tel: 613-267-1224. E-mail: info@perthunionlibrary.ca. Web Site: www.perthunionlibrary.ca. *Chief Exec Officer, Chief Librn,* Erika Heesen; E-mail: eheesen@perthunionlibrary.ca; Staff 3 (MLS 1, Non-MLS 2)
Founded 1832. Pop 19,300; Circ 140,000

Library Holdings: Bk Vols 50,000; Per Subs 70
Automation Activity & Vendor Info: (Circulation) Insignia Software
Wireless access
Function: 24/7 Electronic res, 24/7 Online cat, 3D Printer, Activity rm, Adult bk club, Audiobks via web, Bk club(s), Bks on CD, Children's prog, Computer training, Computers for patron use, Digital talking bks, E-Readers, Electronic databases & coll, Free DVD rentals, Home delivery & serv to seniorr ctr & nursing homes, Homebound delivery serv, Homework prog, ILL available, Instruction & testing, Internet access, Laminating, Large print keyboards, Life-long learning prog for all ages, Meeting rooms, Movies, Museum passes, Outreach serv, OverDrive digital audio bks, Photocopying/Printing, Preschool reading prog, Printer for laptops & handheld devices, Prog for adults, Prog for children & young adult, Ref serv available, Senior computer classes, Story hour, Study rm, Summer reading prog, Tax forms, Teen prog
Partic in Ontario Library Consortium
Special Services for the Blind - Accessible computers; Bks on CD; Computer access aids; Daisy reader; Digital talking bk; Internet workstation with adaptive software; Large print bks; Magnifiers
Open Mon & Fri 10-5, Tues-Thurs 10-7, Sat 10-4
Friends of the Library Group

PETAWAWA

P PETAWAWA PUBLIC LIBRARY*, 16 Civic Centre Rd, K8H 3H5. SAN 319-3667. Tel: 613-687-2227. FAX: 613-687-2527. Web Site: www.petawawapubliclibrary.ca. *Interim Chief Exec Officer,* Lynn Tweedie; Tel: 613-687-2227, Ext 2202, E-mail: l.tweedie@petawawapubliclibrary.ca; Staff 5.5 (MLS 1, Non-MLS 4.5)
Founded 1975. Pop 17,900; Circ 82,846
Library Holdings: Bk Titles 45,657; Bk Vols 45,826
Special Collections: French Coll; Heritage Coll, large print; Military & Family Resource Coll; Snowshoes & Walking Poles Coll
Wireless access
Function: 24/7 Electronic res, 24/7 Online cat, Activity rm, Adult bk club, Audiobks via web, AV serv, Bk club(s), Bks on CD, Children's prog, Computer training, Computers for patron use, Digital talking bks, Doc delivery serv, Electronic databases & coll, Equip loans & repairs, Family literacy, For res purposes, Free DVD rentals, Holiday prog, Home delivery & serv to seniorr ctr & nursing homes, Homebound delivery serv, ILL available, Internet access, Life-long learning prog for all ages, Magazines, Mango lang, Meeting rooms, Microfiche/film & reading machines, Museum passes, Music CDs, Online cat, Outreach serv, OverDrive digital audio bks, Photocopying/Printing, Preschool reading prog, Prog for adults, Prog for children & young adult, Ref & res, Ref serv available, Scanner, Senior computer classes, Senior outreach, Serves people with intellectual disabilities, Story hour, Summer & winter reading prog, Teen prog, Telephone ref, VHS videos, Wheelchair accessible
Mem of Ontario Library Service
Open Mon-Thurs 10-8, Fri 10-6, Sat 10-5

PETERBOROUGH

G ONTARIO MINISTRY OF NATURAL RESOURCES & FORESTRY*, Library Services, North Tower, 1st Flr, 300 Water St, K9J 3C7. SAN 323-4886. Tel: 705-755-1888. Administration Tel: 705-755-1879. FAX: 705-755-1882. E-mail: mnr.library@ontario.ca. *Sr Librn,* Allison Killins; Staff 3 (MLS 2, Non-MLS 1)
Founded 1942
Apr 2019-Mar 2020. Mats Exp (CAN) $86,000, Books (CAN) $1,000, Per/Ser (Incl. Access Fees) (CAN) $65,000, Electronic Ref Mat (Incl. Access Fees) (CAN) $20,000
Library Holdings: AV Mats 500; CDs 247; e-books 50; e-journals 50; Bk Vols 100,000; Per Subs 90; Talking Bks 25; Videos 500
Special Collections: Canadian and Provincial
Automation Activity & Vendor Info: (Cataloging) Inmagic, Inc.; (Circulation) Inmagic, Inc.; (OPAC) Inmagic, Inc.; (Serials) Inmagic, Inc.
Partic in Ont Govt Libr Coun
Open Mon-Fri 9-4

P PETERBOROUGH PUBLIC LIBRARY*, 345 Aylmer St N, K9H 3V7. SAN 368-1548. Tel: 705-745-5382. FAX: 705-745-8958. Web Site: www.ptbolibrary.ca/en. *Chief Exec Officer,* Jennifer Jones; Tel: 705-745-5382, Ext 2370, E-mail: jjones@peterborough.ca; *Libr Serv Mgr,* Mark Stewart; Tel: 705-745-5382, Ext 2380; *Access Serv Librn,* Marisa Giuliani; Tel: 705-745-5382, Ext 2351, E-mail: mgiuliani@peterborough.ca; *Ch Serv Librn,* Laura Murray; Tel: 705-745-5382, Ext 2362, E-mail: lmurray@peterborough.ca; *Coll Develop Librn,* Laura Gardner; Tel: 705-745-5382, Ext 2361, E-mail: lgardner@peterborough.ca; *Adult Programming, Outreach Librn,* Karen Bisschop; Tel: 705-745-5382, Ext 2352, E-mail: kbisschop@peterborough.ca; *Marketing & Communications Coord,* Becky Waldman; Tel: 705-745-5382, Ext 2324, E-mail: bwaldman@peterborough.ca
Founded 1910. Pop 78,698; Circ 620,655

Special Collections: Local History (Peterborough Coll)
Wireless access
Function: 24/7 Electronic res, Adult bk club, Audiobks on Playaways & MP3, Bk club(s), Bks on CD, Children's prog, Computer training, Computers for patron use, Electronic databases & coll, Free DVD rentals, Govt ref serv, Homebound delivery serv, ILL available, Internet access, Large print keyboards, Magazines, Magnifiers for reading, Mail & tel request accepted, Meeting rooms, Microfiche/film & reading machines, Music CDs, Online cat, Online ref, Outside serv via phone, mail, e-mail & web, OverDrive digital audio bks, Photocopying/Printing, Prog for adults, Prog for children & young adult, Ref serv available, Res performed for a fee, Scanner, Summer reading prog, Teen prog, Wheelchair accessible
Mem of Ontario Library Service
Open Tues & Thurs 10-8, Wed-Sat 10-5
Friends of the Library Group
Branches: 1
DELAFOSSE, 729 Park St S, K9J 3T3, SAN 368-1572. Tel: 705-745-8653.
Open Tues & Thurs 2:30-7:30, Sat 10-3
Friends of the Library Group

J SIR SANDFORD FLEMING COLLEGE OF APPLIED ARTS & TECHNOLOGY*, Sutherland Campus Library, 599 Brealey Dr, K9J 7B1. SAN 368-1602. Tel: 705-749-5530, Ext 1516. E-mail: library@flemingcollege.ca. Web Site: fleming.libguides.com/library. *Director, Student Learning,* David Luinstra; E-mail: david.luinstra@flemingcollege.ca; Staff 1 (MLS 1)
Founded 1968. Enrl 5,850; Fac 329
Library Holdings: Electronic Media & Resources 1,254; Bk Titles 29,283; Per Subs 87
Subject Interests: Art, Bus, Commun health, Commun serv, Computer sci, Computer tech, Heritage, Hospitality, Justice, Law, Nursing, Recreation, Tourism
Wireless access
Open Mon-Fri 8:30-4:30

C TRENT UNIVERSITY*, Thomas J Bata Library, 1600 West Bank Dr, K9J 7B8. SAN 368-1661. Tel: 705-748-1011. FAX: 705-748-1126. E-mail: library@trentu.ca. Web Site: www.trentu.ca/library. *Actg Univ Librn,* Suzanne Bailey; E-mail: sjbailey@trentu.ca; *Head, Maps, Data & Govt Info Ctr,* Barbara Znamirowski; Tel: 705-748-1011, Ext 7470, E-mail: bznamirowski@trentu.ca; *Learning Librn, Liaison Librn,* Ellen Olsen-Lynch; E-mail: ellenolsenlynch@trentu.ca; *Scholarly Resources Librn, Scholarly Services Librn,* Coralee Leroux; Tel: 705-748-1011, Ext 7196, E-mail: coraleeleroux@trent.ca; *Mgr, Libr Serv,* Kristy McKeown; Tel: 705-748-1011, Ext 7195, E-mail: kristymckeown@trentu.ca; *Archivist,* Karen Suurtramm; Tel: 705-748-1011, Ext 7410, E-mail: karensuurtramm@trentu.ca; Staff 31 (MLS 9, Non-MLS 22)
Founded 1963. Fac 350; Highest Degree: Doctorate
Library Holdings: Electronic Media & Resources 6,000; Bk Vols 600,000; Per Subs 2,000
Special Collections: Canadian Literature (Shell Coll); Canadiana; Native Studies; Trent Coll (Trent Valley Region)
Wireless access
Partic in Ontario Council of University Libraries; Ontario Univs Libr Coop Syst
Departmental Libraries:
ARCHIVES, Thomas J Bata Library, 1st Flr, 1600 W Bank Dr, K9J 7B8. Tel: 705-748-1011, Ext 7410. Web Site: www.trentu.ca/library/archives. *Archivist,* Jodi Aoki; E-mail: jaoki@trentu.ca
Open Mon-Fri 9-4
DURHAM GREATER TORONTO AREA CAMPUS LIBRARY & LEARNING CENTRE, 55 Thornton Rd S, Ste 102, Oshawa, L1J 5Y1. Tel: 905-435-5102, Ext 5061. Web Site: www.trentu.ca/library/oshawa/index.htm. *Libr Mgr,* Rob McLeod; Tel: 905-435-5102, Ext 5064, E-mail: rmcleod@trentu.ca; *Libr Assoc,* Rachel Podlowski; Tel: 905-435-5102, Ext 5062, E-mail: rachelpodlowski@trentu.ca; Staff 4 (MLS 1, Non-MLS 3)
Founded 2010. Enrl 1,000; Fac 30; Highest Degree: Master
Open Mon-Thurs 8:30am-9:30pm, Fri 8:30-5, Sat & Sun 11-5

PICKERING

P PICKERING PUBLIC LIBRARY*, Administrative Office, One The Esplanade, L1V 2R6. (Mail add: PO Box 368, L1V 2R6), SAN 368-1726. Tel: 905-831-6265. Toll Free Tel: 888-831-6266. FAX: 905-831-6927. Web Site: pickeringlibrary.ca. *Chief Exec Officer, Dir of Libr,* Jackie Flowers; Tel: 905-831-6265, Ext 6222, E-mail: jackieflowers@pickeringlibrary.ca; *Dir, Support Serv,* Elaine Bird; Tel: 905-831-6265, Ext 6231, E-mail: elainebird@pickeringlibrary.ca; *Mgr, Br Serv,* Doug Mirams; Tel: 905-831-6265, Ext 6003, E-mail: douglasmirams@pickeringlibrary.ca; Staff 53 (MLS 12, Non-MLS 41)
Founded 1967. Pop 94,000; Circ 1,193,956
Library Holdings: Bk Vols 150,000
Subject Interests: Local hist

Automation Activity & Vendor Info: (Acquisitions) SirsiDynix; (Cataloging) SirsiDynix; (Circulation) SirsiDynix; (Course Reserve) SirsiDynix; (ILL) SirsiDynix; (Media Booking) SirsiDynix; (OPAC) SirsiDynix; (Serials) SirsiDynix
Wireless access
Mem of Ontario Library Service
Open Tues-Fri 11-7, Sat 9:30-4:30
Branches: 2
GEORGE ASHE LIBRARY, 470 Kingston Rd, L1V 1A4, SAN 368-184X. Tel: 905-420-2254. FAX: 905-420-2860. *Mgr, Br Serv,* Doug Mirams
Library Holdings: Bk Vols 53,000
Open Mon, Thurs & Fri 3-7, Tues & Wed 9:30-1 & 3-7, Sat 11-3
CLAREMONT BRANCH, 4941 Old Brock Rd, Claremont, L1Y 1A9, SAN 368-1815. Tel: 905-649-3341. FAX: 905-649-2065. *Mgr, Br Serv,* Doug Mirams
Library Holdings: Bk Vols 9,400
Open Tues 3-7, Sat 2-5
Friends of the Library Group

PICTON

P PRINCE EDWARD COUNTY PUBLIC LIBRARY*, Picton Branch Library (Headquarters), 208 Main St, K0K 2T0. (Mail add: PO Box 260, K0K 2T0), SAN 319-3683. Tel: 613-476-5962. FAX: 613-476-3325. E-mail: ceo@peclibrary.org. Web Site: www.peclibrary.org. *Dir/Chief Exec Officer,* Barbara Sweet; E-mail: bsweet@peclibrary.org; *Children's Serv Coordr,* Position Currently Open
Pop 23,000
Library Holdings: Bk Vols 90,000; Per Subs 80
Subject Interests: Local hist
Wireless access
Mem of Ontario Library Service
Open Tues-Fri 10-5, Sat 10-4
Friends of the Library Group
Branches: 5
AMELIASBURGH BRANCH - AL PURDY LIBRARY, 809 Whitney Rd, Ameliasburgh, K0K 1A0. Tel: 613-968-9327. FAX: 613-961-7992. E-mail: ameliasburgh@peclibrary.org.
Founded 2001
Library Holdings: Bk Vols 15,000; Per Subs 10
Open Tues & Thurs 2-5, Wed & Fri 10-1, Sat 10-3
Friends of the Library Group
BLOOMFIELD BRANCH, 300 Main St, Bloomfield, K0K 1G0. (Mail add: PO Box 9, Bloomfield, K0K 1G0), SAN 319-048X. Tel: 613-393-3400. FAX: 613-393-1887. E-mail: bloomfield@peclibrary.org. Web Site: peclibrary.org/bloomfield.
Library Holdings: Bk Vols 9,000
Open Tues & Thurs 2-5, Wed 10-1, Sat 10-3
Friends of the Library Group
CONSECON BRANCH, 211 County Rd 29, Consecon, K0K 1T0. Tel: 613-392-1106. FAX: 613-392-4461. E-mail: consecon@peclibrary.org. Web Site: peclibrary.org/consecon.
Founded 1926
Library Holdings: Bk Vols 10,000
Open Tues & Thurs 10-1, Wed & Fri 2-5, Sat 10-3
Friends of the Library Group
ANN FARWELL BRANCH LIBRARY, 3053 County Rd 10, Milford, K0K 2P0, SAN 373-7918. Tel: 613-476-4130. FAX: 613-476-6527. E-mail: milford@peclibrary.org. Web Site: peclibrary.org/milford.
Founded 1951. Pop 2,210; Circ 13,966
Library Holdings: DVDs 200; Bk Vols 9,000
Subject Interests: Genealogy, Local hist
Open Tues & Thurs 10-1, Wed 2-5, Sat 10-3
Friends of the Library Group
WELLINGTON BRANCH, 261 Main St, Wellington, K0K 3L0. (Mail add; PO Box 370, Wellington, K0K 3L0), SAN 319-6038. Tel: 613-399-2023. FAX: 613-399-2391. E-mail: wellington@peclibrary.org. Web Site: peclibrary.org/wellington.
Founded 1926. Circ 24,873
Library Holdings: Bk Titles 12,000; Bk Vols 13,000; Per Subs 32
Mem of Ontario Library Service
Open Tues & Thurs 10-5, Wed, Fri & Sat 10-4
Friends of the Library Group

PORT CARLING

P MUSKOKA LAKES PUBLIC LIBRARY*, The Norma & Miller Alloway Muskoka Lakes Library, 69 Joseph St, P0B 1J0. (Mail add: Box 189, P0B 1J0), SAN 377-8118. Tel: 705-765-5650, 705-765-6477. FAX: 705-765-0422. E-mail: muskokalakes@pclib.ca. Web Site: www.muskokalakes.ca/library. *Chief Librn/CEO,* Cathy Duck; E-mail: cduck@pclib.ca
Library Holdings: CDs 229; DVDs 307; e-books 1,321; Large Print Bks 362; Music Scores 54; Bk Vols 50,000; Per Subs 33; Talking Bks 443; Videos 573
Automation Activity & Vendor Info: (Cataloging) SirsiDynix; (Circulation) SirsiDynix; (OPAC) SirsiDynix; (Serials) SirsiDynix
Wireless access
Function: 24/7 Electronic res, Activity rm, Computers for patron use, Laminating, Magazines, Movies, Online cat, Study rm
Open Tues, Wed & Fri 10:30-4:30, Thurs 10:30-6, Sat 10:30-2:30
Friends of the Library Group
Branches: 1
BALA LIBRARY, 1008 Maple St, Bala, P0C 1A0. (Mail add: Box 189, P0C 1J0), SAN 326-7318. Tel: 705-762-1086.
Founded 1979
Special Collections: Bala & Muskoka Coll
Open Tues & Thurs 9-3

PORT COLBORNE

P PORT COLBORNE PUBLIC LIBRARY*, 310 King St, L3K 4H1. SAN 368-1904. Tel: 905-834-6512. FAX: 905-835-5775. E-mail: library@portcolborne.ca. Web Site: portcolbornelibrary.org. *Chief Exec Officer,* Scott Luey; E-mail: CAO@portcolborne.ca; *Dir, Libr Serv,* Susan Therrien; E-mail: susantherrien@portcolborne.ca
Founded 1886. Pop 18,000; Circ 130,000
Library Holdings: Bk Vols 65,000; Per Subs 100
Automation Activity & Vendor Info: (Acquisitions) SirsiDynix; (Cataloging) SirsiDynix; (Circulation) SirsiDynix; (Course Reserve) SirsiDynix; (OPAC) SirsiDynix; (Serials) SirsiDynix
Wireless access
Open Mon, Tues & Thurs 10-8, Wed 10-5, Fri & Sat 9-5
Friends of the Library Group

PORT DOVER

S NORFOLK HISTORICAL SOCIETY*, 420 Main St, N0A 1N0. (Mail add: PO Box 1466, N0A 1N0). Toll Free Tel: 1-833-968-7647. Toll Free FAX: 1-844-557-7733. E-mail: info@norfolkhistoricalsociety.ca. Web Site: www.norfolkhistoricalsociety.ca. *Pres,* Michele Grant
Restriction: Open by appt only

PORT ELGIN

P BRUCE COUNTY PUBLIC LIBRARY*, 1243 MacKenzie Rd, N0H 2C6. SAN 368-1963. Tel: 519-832-6935. FAX: 519-832-9000. E-mail: libraryinfo@brucecounty.on.ca. Web Site: library.brucecounty.on.ca. *Dir,* Nicole Charles; E-mail: ncharles@brucecounty.on.ca; *Asst Dir,* Kathy Samson; E-mail: ksamson@brucecounty.on.ca; Staff 2 (MLS 2)
Founded 1967. Pop 63,000; Circ 460,410
Library Holdings: Bk Titles 110,000; Bk Vols 150,000; Per Subs 140
Special Collections: Local History
Wireless access
Open Mon-Fri 8:30-4:30
Branches: 17
CARGILL BRANCH, 1012 Greenock Brant, Cargill, N0G 1J0. (Mail add: PO Box 98, Cargill, N0G 1J0), SAN 368-2021. Tel: 519-366-9990. FAX: 519-366-9990. E-mail: calib@brucecounty.on.ca. Web Site: library.brucecounty.on.ca/branch/cargill. *Br Supvr,* Tracey Knapp
Open Tues 3-7, Thurs & Fri 10-2, Sat 10-1
CHESLEY BRANCH, 72 Second Ave SE, Chesley, N0G 1L0. (Mail add: PO Box 220, Chesley, N0G 1L0), SAN 368-2056. Tel: 519-363-2239. FAX: 519-363-0726. E-mail: chlib@brucecounty.on.ca. Web Site: library.brucecounty.on.ca/branch/chesley. *Br Supvr,* Grant Robertson
Open Open Mon & Wed 10-5, Tues 10-6, Thurs 10-7, Fri 10-3, Sat 10-2
Friends of the Library Group
KINCARDINE BRANCH, 727 Queen St, Kincardine, N2Z 1Z9, SAN 368-217X. Tel: 519-396-3289. FAX: 519-396-3289. E-mail: kilib@brucecounty.on.ca. Web Site: library.brucecounty.on.ca/branch/kincardine. *Br Supvr,* Michaela Posthumus
Open Mon 10-4, Tues & Wed 10-8, Thurs & Fri 10-5, Sat 10-3, Sun 1-4
LION'S HEAD BRANCH, 90 Main St, Lion's Head, N0H 1W0. (Mail add: PO Box 965, Lion's Head, N0H 1W0), SAN 368-220X. Tel: 519-793-3844. FAX: 519-793-3844. E-mail: lhlib@brucecounty.on.ca. Web Site: library.brucecounty.on.ca/branch/lions-head. *Br Supvr,* Kathryn Hauck
Open Mon & Fri 9:30-5, Wed 2-6, Thurs 10-2, Sat 9:30-2
Friends of the Library Group
LUCKNOW BRANCH, 526 Campbell St, Lucknow, N0G 2H0. (Mail add: PO Box 130, Lucknow, N0G 2H0), SAN 368-2234. Tel: 519-528-3011. E-mail: lulib@brucecounty.on.ca. Web Site: library.brucecounty.on.ca/branch/lucknow. *Br Supvr,* Cassie Wood
Open Tues 3-8, Wed-Fri 10-5, Sat 10-1
MILDMAY-CARRICK BRANCH, 51 Elora St, Mildmay, N0G 2J0. (Mail add: PO Box 87, Mildmay, N0G 2J0), SAN 368-2269. Tel: 519-367-2814. FAX: 519-367-2814. E-mail: mclib@brucecounty.on.ca. Web Site: library.brucecounty.on.ca/branch/mildmay. *Br Supvr,* Carolyn McKeeman
Founded 1929. Pop 1,200

Function: Activity rm, Adult bk club, Audiobks via web, Bks on cassette, Bks on CD, Children's prog, Computers for patron use, Digital talking bks, Free DVD rentals, ILL available, Magazines, Mail & tel request accepted, Music CDs, Online cat, OverDrive digital audio bks, Photocopying/Printing, Scanner, Story hour, Summer reading prog, Wheelchair accessible
Open Tues 11:30-7:30, Thurs 12-5, Fri 10-3, Sat 10-1
PAISLEY BRANCH, 274 Queen St, Paisley, N0G 2N0. (Mail add: PO Box 219, Paisley, N0G 2N0), SAN 368-2293. Tel: 519-353-7225. FAX: 519-353-7225. E-mail: palib@brucecounty.on.ca. Web Site: library.brucecounty.on.ca/branch/paisley. *Br Supvr,* Grant Robertson
Open Tues & Thurs 1-6, Fri 10-4, Sat 10-3
Friends of the Library Group
PORT ELGIN BRANCH, 708 Goderich St, N0H 2C0. (Mail add: PO Box 609, N0H 2C0), SAN 368-2323. Tel: 519-832-2201. E-mail: pelib@brucecounty.on.ca. Web Site: library.brucecounty.on.ca/branch/port-elgin. *Br Supvr,* Kathy Samson
Open Mon, Tues, Fri & Sat 10-5, Wed & Thurs 10-7, Sun 1-4
Friends of the Library Group
RIPLEY BRANCH, 23 Jessie St, Ripley, N0G 2R0. (Mail add: PO Box 207, Ripley, N0G 2R0), SAN 368-2358. Tel: 519-395-5919. E-mail: rilib@brucecounty.on.ca. Web Site: library.brucecounty.on.ca/branch/ripley. *Br Supvr,* Cassie Wood
Open Tues 2-7, Wed & Fri 1-5, Thurs 10-3, Sat 10-1
SAUBLE BEACH, 27 Community Centre Dr, Sauble Beach, N0H 2G0, SAN 368-2382. Tel: 519-422-1283. FAX: 519-422-1283. E-mail: salib@brucecounty.on.ca. Web Site: library.brucecounty.on.ca/branch/sauble-beach. *Actg Br Supvr,* Heather McCarron
Open Mon & Wed-Fri 10-6, Sat 11-4, Sun 12-4
Friends of the Library Group
SOUTHAMPTON BRANCH, 215 High St, Southampton, N0H 2L0. (Mail add: PO Box 130, Southampton, N0H 2L0), SAN 368-2412. Tel: 519-797-3586. FAX: 519-797-3586. E-mail: solib@brucecounty.on.ca. Web Site: library.brucecounty.on.ca/branch/southampton. *Br Supvr,* Kathy Samson
Open Tues, Thurs & Fri 10-5, Wed 10-7, Sat 10-4, Sun 1-4
Friends of the Library Group
TARA BRANCH, 67 Yonge St, Tara, N0H 2N0. (Mail add: PO Box 59, Tara, N0H 2N0), SAN 368-2447. Tel: 519-934-2626. E-mail: talib@brucecounty.on.ca. Web Site: library.brucecounty.on.ca/branch/tara. *Br Supvr,* Grant Robertson
Open Tues 12-6, Wed 10-4, Thurs & Sat 10-3, Fri 1-4
Friends of the Library Group
TEESWATER BRANCH, Two Clinton St, Teeswater, N0G 2S0. (Mail add: PO Box 430, Teeswater, N0G 2S0), SAN 368-2471. Tel: 519-392-6801. FAX: 519-392-6801. E-mail: telib@brucecounty.on.ca. Web Site: library.brucecounty.on.ca/branch/teeswater. *Br Supvr,* Carolyn McKeeman
Open Tues & Thurs 10-12:30 & 1-5:30, Wed 1-6, Fri 10-3, Sat 10-1
TIVERTON BRANCH, 56 King St, Tiverton, N0G 2T0. (Mail add: PO Box 174, Tiverton, N0G 2T0), SAN 368-2501. Tel: 519-368-5655. E-mail: tilib@brucecounty.on.ca. Web Site: library.brucecounty.on.ca/branch/tiverton. *Br Supvr,* Michaela Posthumus
Open Mon, Tues & Thurs 2-7, Fri & Sat 10-3
TOBERMORY BRANCH, 22 Bay St, Tobermory, N0H 2R0. (Mail add: PO Box 159, Tobermory, N0H 2R0), SAN 368-2536. Tel: 519-596-2446. E-mail: tolib@brucecounty.on.ca. Web Site: library.brucecounty.on.ca/branch/tobermory. *Br Supvr,* Kathryn Hauck
Open Tues & Sun 12:30-4:30, Wed & Thurs 10-6, Fri 10-5, Sat 10-3
Friends of the Library Group
WALKERTON BRANCH, 253 Durham St E, Walkerton, N0G 2V0. (Mail add: PO Box 250, Walkerton, N0G 2V0), SAN 368-2560. Tel: 519-881-3240. FAX: 519-881-3240. E-mail: walib@brucecounty.on.ca. Web Site: library.brucecounty.on.ca/branch/walkerton. *Br Supvr,* Tracey Knapp
Open Mon, Wed, Fri & Sat 10-5, Tues & Thurs 12-8
WIARTON BRANCH, 578 Brown St, Wiarton, N0H 2T0. (Mail add: PO Box 250, Wiarton, N0H 2T0), SAN 368-2595. Tel: 519-534-2602. FAX: 519-534-2602. E-mail: wilib@brucecounty.on.ca. Web Site: library.brucecounty.on.ca/branch/wiarton. *Br Supvr,* Heather McCarron
Open Tues & Thurs 10-7, Wed & Fri 10-6, Sat 10-4, Sun 1-5
Friends of the Library Group
Bookmobiles: 1

PORT HOPE

P PORT HOPE PUBLIC LIBRARY*, Mary J Benson Branch, 31 Queen St, L1A 2Y8. SAN 319-3713. Tel: 905-885-4712. E-mail: library@phpl.ca. Web Site: porthopepubliclibrary.ca. *Chief Exec Officer, Chief Librn,* Margaret Scott; E-mail: mscott@phpl.ca
Founded 1912. Pop 17,000; Circ 120,000
Library Holdings: Bk Titles 49,000; Per Subs 35
Special Collections: Historical Newspaper Name Index, 1980, microfilm; Port Hope Evening Guide 1832-2013
Subject Interests: Local hist
Automation Activity & Vendor Info: (Acquisitions) BiblioCommons; (Cataloging) BiblioCommons; (Circulation) BiblioCommons; (Course Reserve) BiblioCommons; (ILL) OCLC; (OPAC) BiblioCommons; (Serials) BiblioCommons
Wireless access
Open Mon-Thurs 10-8, Fri & Sat 10-5; Mon-Thurs 10-8, Fri 10-5 Sat 10-2 (Summer)
Friends of the Library Group
Branches: 1
HUB AT CANTON, 5325 County Rd 10, Canton, L1A 3V5. Tel: 905-753-0031. *Chief Librn,* Margaret Scott; E-mail: mscott@phpl.ca
Open Mon & Sat 10-1, Tues 4-7, Wed 1-4
Friends of the Library Group

PORT MCNICOLL

P TAY TOWNSHIP PUBLIC LIBRARY*, J & M Young Branch, 715 Fourth Ave, L0K 1R0. (Mail add: PO Box 490, L0K 1R0). Tel: 705-534-3511. FAX: 705-534-3511. E-mail: library@tay.ca. Web Site: www.tay.library.on.ca. *Actg Chief Exec Officer,* Jody Bressette; E-mail: jbressette@tay.ca; *Br Librn,* Heather Delong; E-mail: hdelong@tay.ca
Library Holdings: Bk Vols 48,311
Automation Activity & Vendor Info: (Acquisitions) SirsiDynix; (Cataloging) SirsiDynix; (Circulation) SirsiDynix; (Discovery) EBSCO Discovery Service; (ILL) SirsiDynix; (OPAC) SirsiDynix; (Serials) SirsiDynix
Wireless access
Function: Bks on CD, CD-ROM, Computers for patron use, Homebound delivery serv, ILL available, Online cat, Photocopying/Printing
Open Tues & Wed 11-8, Thurs 11-5, Fri 1-5, Sat 10-2
Branches: 2
THEO & ELAINE BERNARD BRANCH, 145 Albert St, Victoria Harbour, L0K 2A0. (Mail add: PO Box 158, Victoria Harbour, L0K 2A0), SAN 810-0985. Tel: 705-534-3581. FAX: 705-534-3581. E-mail: library@tay.ca. *Libr Serv Coordr,* Heather Fitzgerald; E-mail: hfitzgerald@tay.ca
Function: Computers for patron use
Open Tues 11-6, Wed & Thurs 11-8, Fri 11-5, Sat 10-2
WAUBAUSHENE BRANCH, 17 Thiffault St, Waubaushene, L0K 2C0. (Mail add: PO Box 280, Waubaushene, L0K 2C0). Tel: 705-538-1122. FAX: 705-538-1122. *Br Librn,* Jennylynn Brown
Function: Computers for patron use
Open Tues 1-6, Thurs 1-8, Fri 1-5, Sat 10-2

PORT PERRY

P SCUGOG MEMORIAL PUBLIC LIBRARY*, 231 Water St, L9L 1A8. (Mail add: PO Box 1049, L9L 1A8), SAN 319-3721. Tel: 905-985-7686. Web Site: www.scugoglibrary.ca. *Chief Exec Officer,* Amy Caughlin; E-mail: acaughlin@scugoglibrary.ca; Staff 6 (MLS 2, Non-MLS 4)
Founded 1856. Pop 22,500; Circ 138,064
Jan 2019-Dec 2019 Income (CAN) $826,401. Mats Exp (CAN) $232,217. Sal (CAN) $592,136
Library Holdings: Bk Titles 46,700; Bk Vols 49,000; Per Subs 79
Subject Interests: Local hist
Automation Activity & Vendor Info: (Acquisitions) Koha; (Cataloging) Koha; (Circulation) Koha; (OPAC) Koha; (Serials) Koha
Wireless access
Function: Art exhibits, ILL available, Music CDs, Photocopying/Printing, Prog for adults, Prog for children & young adult, Ref serv available, Spoken cassettes & CDs, Spoken cassettes & DVDs, Summer reading prog, Telephone ref, VHS videos, Wheelchair accessible
Mem of Ontario Library Service
Open Tues-Fri 11-6, Sat 11-3

POWASSAN

P POWASSAN & DISTRICT UNION PUBLIC LIBRARY*, 324 Clark St, P0H 1Z0. (Mail add: PO Box 160, P0H 1Z0), SAN 319-373X. Tel: 705-724-3618. FAX: 705-724-5525. E-mail: powlib@gmail.com. Information Services E-mail: info@powassanlibrary.ca. Web Site: www.powassanlibrary.com. *Chief Exec Officer,* Marie Rosset; E-mail: mrosset@powassanlibrary.ca; Staff 1 (Non-MLS 1)
Founded 2012. Pop 6,453; Circ 46,000
Library Holdings: Large Print Bks 549; Bk Titles 20,000; Bk Vols 30,505; Per Subs 40; Talking Bks 347
Automation Activity & Vendor Info: (Cataloging) SirsiDynix; (Circulation) SirsiDynix
Wireless access
Function: 24/7 Electronic res, 24/7 Online cat, Activity rm, Adult bk club, Art exhibits, Audio & video playback equip for onsite use, Audiobks on Playaways & MP3, Audiobks via web, Bi-weekly Writer's Group, Bk club(s), Bks on CD, Children's prog, Computer training, Computers for patron use, Digital talking bks, E-Readers, Electronic databases & coll, Equip loans & repairs, Family literacy, Free DVD rentals, Genealogy discussion group, Govt ref serv, Holiday prog, Home delivery & serv to

seniorr ctr & nursing homes, ILL available, Internet access, Laminating, Large print keyboards, Life-long learning prog for all ages, Magazines, Magnifiers for reading, Mail & tel request accepted, Meeting rooms, Movies, Online cat, Online ref, Outside serv via phone, mail, e-mail & web, OverDrive digital audio bks, Photocopying/Printing, Preschool outreach, Preschool reading prog, Printer for laptops & handheld devices, Prog for adults, Prog for children & young adult, Ref & res, Ref serv available, Res assist avail, Scanner, Senior computer classes, Senior outreach, STEM programs, Story hour, Summer reading prog, Teen prog, Visual arts prog, Wheelchair accessible, Workshops, Writing prog
Special Services for the Blind - Bks on cassette; Large print bks
Open Mon, Wed & Fri 10-5, Tues & Thurs 10-7, Sat 10-2
Friends of the Library Group

PRESCOTT

P PRESCOTT PUBLIC LIBRARY*, 360 Dibble St W, K0E 1T0. (Mail add: PO Box 430, K0E 1T0), SAN 319-3748. Tel: 613-925-4340. FAX: 613-925-0100. E-mail: library@prescott.ca. Web Site: www.prescott.ca/our-websites/library. *Chief Exec Officer, Chief Librn,* Anne Gillard; E-mail: agillard@prescott.ca; *Asst Librn,* Susen Kaylo; Staff 4 (Non-MLS 4)
Founded 1895. Pop 4,189; Circ 23,744
Library Holdings: Braille Volumes 5; DVDs 1,000; Large Print Bks 750; Bk Titles 31,417; Bk Vols 31,520; Per Subs 15; Talking Bks 525
Automation Activity & Vendor Info: (Cataloging) SirsiDynix; (Circulation) SirsiDynix; (ILL) Fretwell-Downing; (OPAC) SirsiDynix
Wireless access
Function: Adult literacy prog, AV serv, Computers for patron use, Distance learning, Games & aids for people with disabilities, Govt ref serv, Home delivery & serv to seniorr ctr & nursing homes, Homebound delivery serv, ILL available, Large print keyboards, Magnifiers for reading, OverDrive digital audio bks, Photocopying/Printing, Prog for children & young adult, Ref serv available, Scanner, Summer reading prog
Mem of Ontario Library Service
Special Services for the Deaf - Adult & family literacy prog; Bks on deafness & sign lang; High interest/low vocabulary bks
Special Services for the Blind - Assistive/Adapted tech devices, equip & products; Computer with voice synthesizer for visually impaired persons; Dragon Naturally Speaking software; HP Scan Jet with photo-finish software; Inspiration software; Large print & cassettes; Large screen computer & software; Reader equip; Screen reader software; ZoomText magnification & reading software
Open Mon-Thurs 11-7, Fri 11-5, Sat 10-2
Friends of the Library Group

RAINY RIVER

P RAINY RIVER PUBLIC LIBRARY*, 334 Fourth St, P0W 1L0. (Mail add: PO Box 308, P0W 1L0), SAN 319-3756. Tel: 807-852-3375. FAX: 807-852-3375. E-mail: rrpl.board@gmail.com. Web Site: www.facebook.com/profile.php?id=100064897833693. *Chief Exec Officer, Librn,* Michael Dawber
Founded 1971. Pop 2,100; Circ 12,900
Library Holdings: Bk Vols 12,000; Per Subs 15
Special Collections: Local History Coll, photos, scrapbks, tapes & written mat
Wireless access
Publications: Annual Report; Librarian's Annual Report, Local Library History
Open Tues & Thurs 1-6, Fri & Sat 10-2
Friends of the Library Group

RAMARA

P RAMARA TOWNSHIP PUBLIC LIBRARY, Ramara Centre Branch, 5482 Hwy 12 S, L3V 0S2. (Mail add: PO Box 158, Brechin, L0K 1B0). Tel: 705-325-5776. FAX: 705-325-8176. E-mail: info@ramarapubliclibrary.org. Web Site: www.ramarapubliclibrary.org. *Chief Exec Officer,* Elise Schofield; E-mail: ceo@ramarapubliclibrary.org; Staff 5 (MLS 1, Non-MLS 4)
Founded 1982. Pop 9,000
Library Holdings: Bk Vols 22,000
Automation Activity & Vendor Info: (Acquisitions) SirsiDynix; (Cataloging) SirsiDynix; (Circulation) SirsiDynix; (ILL) SirsiDynix; (OPAC) SirsiDynix; (Serials) SirsiDynix
Wireless access
Function: Bks on CD, CD-ROM, Computers for patron use, Photocopying/Printing
Special Services for the Deaf - Assistive tech
Special Services for the Blind - Audio mat
Open Tues-Thurs 10-8, Fri 10-6, Sat 9-3
Friends of the Library Group

Branches: 1
BRECHIN BRANCH, 2297 Hwy 12, Brechin, L0K 1B0. (Mail add: PO Box 158, Brechin, L0K 1B0). Tel: 705-484-0476. FAX: 705-484-0476.
Library Holdings: Bk Vols 10,000
Open Tues, Wed & Fri 10-6, Thurs 12-8, Sat 10-2

RED ROCK

P RED ROCK PUBLIC LIBRARY BOARD*, 42 Salls St, P0T 2P0. (Mail add: PO Box 285, P0T 2P0), SAN 319-3772. Tel: 807-886-2558. FAX: 807-886-2558. E-mail: rrocklib@gmail.com. Web Site: redrock.olsn.ca. *Chief Exec Officer, Head Librn,* Nancy Carrier; *Sr Asst Librn,* Stephanie Kivilahti; *Asst Librn,* Jean Brooke
Founded 1965. Pop 890; Circ 10,000
Library Holdings: Bk Vols 18,000; Per Subs 15
Subject Interests: Local hist
Wireless access
Mem of Ontario Library Service
Open Mon-Thurs 2-5 & 6:30-8:30, Fri 6:30-8:30
Friends of the Library Group

RENFREW

P RENFREW PUBLIC LIBRARY*, 13 Railway Ave, K7V 3A9. SAN 319-3780. Tel: 613-432-8151. FAX: 613-432-7680. E-mail: renfrewlib@cogeco.net. Web Site: www.renfrew.ca/library-welcome.cfm. *Chief Librn,* Kelly Thompson; E-mail: kthompson@renfrew.library.on.ca; Staff 5.5 (MLS 1, Non-MLS 4.5)
Founded 1898. Pop 8,500; Circ 100,900
Library Holdings: AV Mats 2,057; e-books 1,508; e-journals 1,650; Large Print Bks 4,300; Bk Titles 37,350; Per Subs 36; Talking Bks 670
Special Collections: DVDs; Large Print & Talking Book Coll; Video Games. Municipal Document Depository; State Document Depository
Subject Interests: Early Can, Ottawa valley hist
Automation Activity & Vendor Info: (Acquisitions) Insignia Software; (Cataloging) Insignia Software; (Circulation) Insignia Software; (OPAC) Insignia Software
Wireless access
Mem of Ontario Library Service
Open Mon-Thurs 10:30-8, Fri 10:30-5, Sat 10-4
Friends of the Library Group

RICHARDS LANDING

P ST JOSEPH TOWNSHIP PUBLIC LIBRARY*, 1240 Richard St, P0R 1J0. (Mail add: PO Box 9, P0R 1J0), SAN 319-3802. Tel: 705-246-2353. FAX: 705-246-2353. E-mail: sjtlibrary@gmail.com. Web Site: stjosephtownship.com/community/libraries. *Librn,* Kristina Leith
Founded 1942. Pop 2,000; Circ 11,551
Library Holdings: Large Print Bks 87; Bk Vols 8,400; Per Subs 20
Wireless access
Open Mon 5-8, Wed & Sat 10-3, Thurs 3-8 (Winter); Mon, Wed & Thurs 10-8, Tues & Fri 1-6, Sat 10-6 (Summer)

RICHMOND HILL

M MACKENZIE RICHMOND HILL HOSPITAL LIBRARY*, Ten Trench St, L4C 4Z3. SAN 375-1759. Tel: 905-883-1212, Ext 7224. E-mail: libraryservices@mackenziehealth.ca. Web Site: www.mackenziehealth.ca. *Librn,* Kimberly Aslett
Library Holdings: Bk Titles 800; Per Subs 100

P RICHMOND HILL PUBLIC LIBRARY*, One Atkinson St, L4C 0H5. SAN 368-2714. Tel: 905-884-9288. Administration Tel: 905-770-0310. FAX: 905-770-0312, 905-884-6544. Web Site: www.rhpl.richmondhill.on.ca. *Chief Exec Officer,* Darren Solomon; E-mail: dsolomon@rhpl.ca; *Dir, Commun Relations,* Catherine Charles; E-mail: ccharles@rhpl.ca; *Dir, Content Prog,* Mary Jane Celsie; E-mail: mjcelsie@rhpl.ca; *Dir Customer Experience, Main,* Barbara Ransom; E-mail: bransom@rhpl.ca; *Dir, Technology,* Yunmi Hwang; E-mail: yhwang@rhpl.ca
Founded 1852. Pop 200,000; Circ 2,213,713
Special Collections: Local History. Canadian and Provincial
Automation Activity & Vendor Info: (Acquisitions) SirsiDynix; (Cataloging) SirsiDynix; (Circulation) SirsiDynix; (Course Reserve) SirsiDynix; (OPAC) SirsiDynix; (Serials) SirsiDynix
Wireless access
Open Mon-Thurs 9:30-9, Fri 9:30-6, Sat 10-5, Sun 12-5
Branches: 3
OAK RIDGES MORAINE LIBRARY, 13085 Yonge St, Unit 12, L4E 3L2, SAN 368-2749. Tel: 905-773-5533. FAX: 905-773-8107. *Br Mgr,* Greg Patterson; E-mail: gpatterson@rhpl.ca
Open Mon-Thurs 10-9, Fri 10-6, Sat 10-5

RICHMOND GREEN LIBRARY, One William F Bell Pkwy, L4S 2T9. Tel: 905-780-0711. FAX: 905-780-1155. *Br Mgr,* Len Wong; E-mail: lwong@rhpl.ca; Staff 3 (MLS 3)
Function: 24/7 Electronic res, 24/7 Online cat, 3D Printer
Open Mon-Thurs 10-8, Fri 10-6, Sat 10-5

RICHVALE LIBRARY, 40 Pearson Ave, L4C 6T7, SAN 368-2773. Tel: 905-889-2847. FAX: 905-889-2435. *Br Mgr,* Brian Bell
Open Tues & Wed 10-8, Thurs & Fri 10-6, Sat 10-5

RIDGETOWN

C UNIVERSITY OF GUELPH*, Ridgetown Campus Library, 120 Main St E, N0P 2C0. SAN 319-3829. Tel: 519-674-1500, Ext 63540. FAX: 519-674-1539. E-mail: rclibrary@uoguelph.ca. Web Site: www.ridgetownc.com/library. *Libr Assoc,* Becky Clark
Founded 1954
Library Holdings: Bk Vols 16,000; Per Subs 500
Subject Interests: Agr, Biores mgt, Environ, Hort, Veterinary tech
Automation Activity & Vendor Info: (Acquisitions) Ex Libris Group; (Cataloging) Ex Libris Group; (Circulation) Ex Libris Group; (Course Reserve) Ex Libris Group; (ILL) Ex Libris Group; (Media Booking) Ex Libris Group; (OPAC) Ex Libris Group; (Serials) Ex Libris Group
Wireless access
Publications: Current Awareness Bulletin
Open Mon-Thurs 8:30am-9pm, Fri 8:30-4:30, Sat 1-4 (Winter); Mon 8:30am-9pm, Tues-Fri 8:30-4:30 (Summer)

ROCKLAND

P CLARENCE-ROCKLAND PUBLIC LIBRARY*, 1525 du Parc Ave, Unit 2, K4K 1C3. SAN 319-3845. Tel: 613-446-5680. E-mail: biblioinfo@bpcrpl.ca. Web Site: bpcrpl.ca. *Chief Exec Officer,* Catherina Rouse; E-mail: crouse@bpcrpl.ca
Founded 1972. Pop 24,512; Circ 79,150
Library Holdings: Bk Vols 46,000; Per Subs 30
Wireless access
Function: 24/7 Electronic res, 24/7 Online cat, Activity rm, Adult bk club, Art exhibits, Art programs, Audiobks via web, AV serv, Bk club(s), Bks on CD, Children's prog, Computer training, Computers for patron use, E-Readers, Electronic databases & coll, Equip loans & repairs, For res purposes, Free DVD rentals, Games & aids for people with disabilities, Home delivery & serv to seniorr ctr & nursing homes, ILL available, Internet access, Magazines, Mail & tel request accepted, Mango lang, Meeting rooms, Movies, Museum passes, Music CDs, Online cat, Online ref, OverDrive digital audio bks, Photocopying/Printing, Preschool outreach, Preschool reading prog, Prog for adults, Prog for children & young adult, Ref & res, Ref serv available, Scanner, Senior outreach, Serves people with intellectual disabilities, STEM programs, Story hour, Study rm, Summer & winter reading prog, Summer reading prog, Teen prog, Telephone ref, Visual arts prog, Wheelchair accessible, Winter reading prog
Mem of Ontario Library Service
Open Mon-Thurs 9-8, Fri 9-5, Sat 9-1
Branches: 2

BOURGET BRANCH, 2240 Dollard St, Box 208, Bourget, K0A 1E0, SAN 321-7167. Tel: 613-487-9488.
Founded 1950. Pop 26,505; Circ 112,000
Library Holdings: Bk Vols 47,000; Per Subs 10
Function: 24/7 Electronic res, 24/7 Online cat, 24/7 wireless access, Audiobks on Playaways & MP3, Audiobks via web, Bks on CD, Children's prog, Computers for patron use, Electronic databases & coll, Equip loans & repairs, Free DVD rentals, Games, Games & aids for people with disabilities, Holiday prog, Home delivery & serv to seniorr ctr & nursing homes, Homework prog, ILL available, Internet access, Laptop/tablet checkout, Magazines, Magnifiers for reading, Mango lang, Movies, Museum passes, Online cat, Outreach serv, OverDrive digital audio bks, Photocopying/Printing, Preschool reading prog, Printer for laptops & handheld devices, Prog for adults, Prog for children & young adult, Ref serv available, Scanner, Senior computer classes, Senior outreach, Serves people with intellectual disabilities, Spoken cassettes & CDs, STEM programs, Story hour, Study rm, Summer & winter reading prog, Summer reading prog, Tax forms, Teen prog, Wheelchair accessible
Open Mon & Wed 2-7, Tues 2-5, Thurs 9-Noon
Restriction: Circ to mem only, In-house use for visitors

RUSSELL

P TOWNSHIP OF RUSSELL PUBLIC LIBRARY*, 1053 Concession St, Box 280, K4R 1E1. Tel: 613-445-5331. FAX: 613-445-8014. E-mail: mylibrary@russellbiblio.com. Web Site: www.russellbiblio.com. *Chief Exec Officer,* France Séguin-Couture; E-mail: france.seguin@russellbiblio.com; *Br Head,* Helene Quesnel; E-mail: helene.quesnel@russellbiblio.com; Staff 2 (MLS 1, Non-MLS 1)
Pop 15,000
Library Holdings: DVDs 1,000; e-books 50,000; Electronic Media & Resources 200; Large Print Bks 350; Bk Titles 21,500; Bk Vols 22,000; Per Subs 30; Talking Bks 600
Special Collections: French Talking Books; St-Jacques Parish Records, genealogical database, microfilm. Municipal Document Depository
Wireless access
Open Mon, Wed, Fri & Sat 10-5, Tues & Thurs 10-8
Friends of the Library Group
Branches: 1

EMBRUN BRANCH, 1215 St Augustin St, Embrun, K0A 1W1, SAN 319-1222. Tel: 613-443-3636. FAX: 613-443-0668. *Br Head,* Melina Matte; E-mail: melina.matte@russellbiblio.com; Staff 1 (MLS 1)
Founded 1972. Pop 19,598
Library Holdings: DVDs 1,000; e-books 50,000; Bk Titles 21,500; Bk Vols 22,000; Per Subs 30; Talking Bks 150
Open Mon, Fri & Sat 10-5, Tues-Thurs 10-8
Friends of the Library Group

SAINT CHARLES

P ST CHARLES PUBLIC LIBRARY*, 22 St Anne, Rm 216-217, P0M 2W0. SAN 319-3934. Tel: 705-867-5332. FAX: 705-867-2511. E-mail: stcharles_library@yahoo.ca. Web Site: stcharlesontario.ca/resident-services/public-library. *Chief Librn,* Nicole Lafontaine
Founded 1970. Pop 1,208; Circ 10,625
Library Holdings: Bk Titles 8,500; Bk Vols 8,750; Per Subs 15
Subject Interests: Fiction (Fr & English), Genealogy, Geog, Hist
Function: Art exhibits, AV serv, Bk club(s), CD-ROM, Games & aids for people with disabilities, Govt ref serv, Home delivery & serv to seniorr ctr & nursing homes, Homebound delivery serv, Homework prog, ILL available, Internet access, Photocopying/Printing, Prog for children & young adult, Ref serv available, Spoken cassettes & DVDs, Summer reading prog, Telephone ref, VHS videos, Wheelchair accessible
Open Mon & Sat 11-2, Tues 9-Noon, Wed & Thurs 11-7, Fri 9-3; Tues & Fri 9-1, Wed & Thurs Noon-7, Sat 11-2 (Summer)
Restriction: Non-resident fee
Friends of the Library Group

SARNIA

J LAMBTON COLLEGE*, Library Resource Centre, 1457 London Rd, N7S 6K4. SAN 319-4000. Tel: 519-541-2441. Interlibrary Loan Service Tel: 519-542-7751, Ext 3288. FAX: 519-541-2426. E-mail: asklibrary@lambtoncollege.ca. Web Site: www.lambtoncollege.ca/Library/Library-Overview. *Dir, Campus Serv & Libr Res Ctr,* Kurtis Gray; Tel: 519-542-7751, Ext 3428, E-mail: Kurtis.Gray@lambtoncollege.ca; *Coll Develop, Electronic Res,* Angela Ashton; Tel: 519-542-7751, Ext 3453, E-mail: angela.ashton@lambtoncollege.ca; Staff 6 (Non-MLS 6)
Founded 1967. Enrl 2,495; Fac 110
Library Holdings: Bk Vols 24,000; Per Subs 236
Open Mon-Thurs 7:30-8, Fri 7:30-4:30, Sun 9-4:30

SAULT STE. MARIE

C ALGOMA UNIVERSITY*, Arthur A Wishart Library, 1520 Queen St E, P6A 2G4. SAN 319-4035. Tel: 705-949-2101. FAX: 705-949-6583. Web Site: library.algomau.ca. *Univ Librn,* Tracy Spurway; Tel: 705-949-2101, Ext 4612, E-mail: tracy.spurway@algomau.ca; *Acad Librn,* Lisl Schoner-Saunders; Tel: 705-949-2101, Ext 4614, E-mail: lisl.schoner-saunders@algomau.ca; Staff 6 (MLS 1, Non-MLS 5)
Founded 1967. Fac 35; Highest Degree: Master
Library Holdings: e-books 500,000; e-journals 20,000; Bk Vols 106,000; Per Subs 250
Subject Interests: Gen sci, Humanities, Liberal arts, Soc sci
Automation Activity & Vendor Info: (Acquisitions) SirsiDynix; (Cataloging) SirsiDynix; (Circulation) SirsiDynix; (Course Reserve) SirsiDynix; (ILL) SirsiDynix; (Media Booking) SirsiDynix; (OPAC) SirsiDynix; (Serials) SirsiDynix
Wireless access
Partic in Ontario Council of University Libraries
Open Mon-Thurs 8:30am-10pm, Fri 8:30-8, Sat 11-4 (Fall & Winter); Tues-Thurs 8:30-4:30 (Summer); Mon-Fri 8:30-8 (Spring)
Friends of the Library Group

G NATURAL RESOURCES CANADA LIBRARY*, 1219 Queen St E, P6A 2E5. SAN 319-4051. Tel: 705-541-5501. FAX: 705-541-5712. E-mail: bibliothequeRNCan.NRCanlibrary@nrcan.gc.ca. Web Site: science-libraries.canada.ca/eng/natural-resources. Staff 2 (MLS 2)
Founded 1947
Library Holdings: Bk Titles 8,000; Per Subs 180
Subject Interests: Bacteriology, Botany, Chem, Econ, Entomology, Forestry
Wireless access
Open Mon-Fri 8:30-4:30

M SAULT AREA HOSPITAL*, Health Sciences Library, 750 Great Northern Rd, P6B 2A8. SAN 324-489X. Tel: 705-759-3434, Ext 4368. FAX: 705-759-3847. *Health Sci Librn,* Amanda Caputo; E-mail: caputoa@sah.on.ca; Staff 1 (MLS 1)
Founded 1979
Library Holdings: e-books 4,000; e-journals 1,000; Bk Titles 1,000; Per Subs 1
Subject Interests: Critical care, Med, Nursing, Psychiat, Res
Automation Activity & Vendor Info: (Acquisitions) TDNet; (Cataloging) TDNet; (Circulation) TDNet; (OPAC) TDNet
Wireless access
Function: ILL available
Partic in Canadian Health Libraries Association; Health Science Information Consortium of Toronto; Ont Libr Asn
Restriction: Access at librarian's discretion, In-house use for visitors, Restricted borrowing privileges, Restricted pub use, Staff & mem only

J SAULT COLLEGE LIBRARY*, 443 Northern Ave, Rm H1112, P6B 4J3. SAN 319-406X. Tel: 705-759-2554, Ext 2711. Administration Tel: 705-759-2554, Ext 2402. E-mail: library@saultcollege.ca. Web Site: saultcollegelibrary.ca. *Mgr, Libr Serv,* Jason Bird; E-mail: jason.bird@saultcollege.ca; Staff 1 (MLS 1)
Founded 1965. Enrl 2,219
Library Holdings: Bk Vols 25,000; Per Subs 140
Automation Activity & Vendor Info: (Circulation) SirsiDynix; (Course Reserve) SirsiDynix; (Media Booking) SirsiDynix; (OPAC) SirsiDynix; (Serials) SirsiDynix
Wireless access
Function: AV serv, ILL available, Internet access
Open Mon-Thurs 8-8, Fri 8-4:30, Sat 12-4, Sun 12-8

P SAULT STE MARIE PUBLIC LIBRARY, James L McIntyre Centennial Library, 50 East St, P6A 3C3. SAN 368-3281. Tel: 705-759-5242. Circulation Tel: 705-759-5231. Reference Tel: 705-759-5236. FAX: 705-759-8752. Administration E-mail: admin.library@cityssm.on.ca. Web Site: ssmpl.ca. *Chief Exec Officer,* Matthew MacDonald; Tel: 705-759-5246, E-mail: m.macdonald@cityssm.on.ca; *Business Admin,* Kaltrin Aaltonen; Tel: 705-759-5275, E-mail: k.aaltonen@cityssm.on.ca; *Colls Librn,* Julie Ringrose; Tel: 705-759-5234, E-mail: j.ringrose@cityssm.on.ca; *Commun Engagement Mgr,* Elise Schofield; Tel: 705-759-5243, E-mail: e.schofield@cityssm.on.ca; *Mgr, Technology & Collections,* Michael Lysyj; Tel: 705-759-5245, E-mail: m.lysyj@cityssm.on.ca; Staff 63 (MLS 5, Non-MLS 58)
Founded 1896. Pop 80,000; Circ 564,128
Special Collections: Archives. Canadian and Provincial
Wireless access
Special Services for the Blind - Braille bks; Descriptive video serv (DVS); Reader equip; Talking bks
Open Mon-Thurs 9-9, Fri 9-6, Sat 9-5, Sun 2-5; Mon 9-8, Tues-Fri 9-6, Sat 9-5 (Summer)
Friends of the Library Group
Branches: 1
NORTH BRANCH, 232 C Northern Ave, P6B 4H6. Tel: 705-759-5248.
Open Mon 10-6, Tues-Thurs 10-8, Fri & Sat 10-5; Mon, Tues, Thurs & Fri 10-5, Wed 10-8, Sat 10-1 (Summer)

SCARBOROUGH

C CENTENNIAL COLLEGE OF APPLIED ARTS & TECHNOLOGY*, Centennial College Libraries, 941 Progress Ave, M1G 3T8. (Mail add: PO Box 631, Sta A, M1K 5E9), SAN 368-3400. Tel: 416-289-5000. FAX: 416-289-5228. E-mail: library@centennialcollege.ca. Web Site: library.centennialcollege.ca. *Dir,* Jane Burpee; Tel: 416-289-5000, Ext 5402, E-mail: jburpee@centennialcollege.ca; Staff 26 (MLS 6, Non-MLS 20)
Founded 1966. Enrl 14,000; Fac 500; Highest Degree: Bachelor
Library Holdings: Bk Titles 70,000; Per Subs 350
Special Collections: Centennial Writes Coll; Daher Folk Tales Coll; John & Molly Pollock Holocaust Coll
Automation Activity & Vendor Info: (Acquisitions) SirsiDynix; (Cataloging) SirsiDynix; (Circulation) SirsiDynix; (OPAC) SirsiDynix; (Serials) SirsiDynix
Partic in BiblioNet
Special Services for the Deaf - Closed caption videos
Special Services for the Blind - Accessible computers; Aids for in-house use; Assistive/Adapted tech devices, equip & products; Audio mat; Cassette playback machines; Closed caption display syst; Computer with voice synthesizer for visually impaired persons; Dragon Naturally Speaking software; Inspiration software; Integrated libr/media serv; Internet workstation with adaptive software; Large screen computer & software; Lending of low vision aids; Magnifiers; PC for people with disabilities; Ref serv; Scanner for conversion & translation of mats; Screen enlargement software for people with visual disabilities; Screen reader software; Text reader; VisualTek equip; ZoomText magnification & reading software
Open Mon-Fri 8am-10pm, Sat & Sun 9-4:30

Departmental Libraries:
ASHTONBEE CAMPUS, 75 Ashtonbee Rd, Rm L-202, M1L 4N4. (Mail add: PO Box 631, Sta A, M1K 5E9), SAN 368-3435. Tel: 416-289-5000, Ext 7000. FAX: 416-289-5017. *Librn,* Jennifer Easter; E-mail: jeaster@centennialcollege.ca; Staff 5 (MLS 1, Non-MLS 4)
Subject Interests: Aircraft, Automotive, Avionics, Heavy-duty equip, Transportation
Partic in BiblioNet
Open Mon-Thurs 8am-10pm, Fri 8-4, Sat & Sun 9-4:30
Restriction: Open to students, fac, staff & alumni
MORNINGSIDE CAMPUS, 755 Morningside Ave, Rm 160, M1C 5J9. (Mail add: PO Box 631, Sta A, Toronto, M1K 5E9). Tel: 416-289-5000, Ext 8000. FAX: 416-289-5156. E-mail: library@centennialcollege.ca. *Librn,* Joanna Blair; E-mail: jblair@centennialcollege.ca; *Librn,* Jennifer Easter; E-mail: jeaster@centennialcollege.ca; Staff 8 (MLS 2, Non-MLS 6)
Open Mon-Thurs 8am-10pm, Fri 8-4, Sat & Sun 11-3
PROGRESS CAMPUS, 941 Progress Ave, L3-06, M1G 3T8. (Mail add: PO Box 631, Sta A, Toronto, M1K 5E9), SAN 368-346X. Tel: 416-289-5000, Ext 5400. FAX: 416-289-5242. *Librn,* Eva McDonald; *Librn,* Richard Sims; E-mail: rsims@centennialcollege.ca; Staff 14 (MLS 3, Non-MLS 11)
Subject Interests: Bus, Engr tech
Open Mon-Thurs 8am-10pm, Fri 8-8, Sat & Sun 9-4:30
STORY ARTS CENTRE, 951 Carlaw Ave, Rm 109, Toronto, M4K 3M2. (Mail add: PO Box 631, Sta A, M1K 5E9), SAN 376-9674. Tel: 416-289-5000, Ext 8600. FAX: 416-289-5118. *Librn,* Gail Alexander; Staff 3 (MLS 1, Non-MLS 2)
Subject Interests: Communication arts, Newsmedia
Open Mon-Thurs 8am-10pm, Fri 8-4, Sat & Sun 9-4:30

S MASARYK MEMORIAL INSTITUTE INC*, Czech & Slovak Library, Bldg B, 2nd Flr, 450 Scarborough Golf Club Rd, M1G 3V7. SAN 376-1827. Administration Tel: 416-439-4354. E-mail: office@masaryktown.ca. Web Site: www.masaryktown.ca/library-1.
Library Holdings: Bk Vols 9,500
Special Collections: 68 Publishers; Exile Literature; T.G. Masaryk Coll
Automation Activity & Vendor Info: (Cataloging) FileMaker
Restriction: Private libr

R SAINT AUGUSTINE'S SEMINARY LIBRARY*, 2661 Kingston Rd, M1M 1M3. SAN 320-7986. Tel: 416-261-7207, Ext 271. Circulation Tel: 416-261-7207, Ext 279. FAX: 416-261-2529. E-mail: library@staugustines.on.ca. Web Site: www.staugustines.on.ca/library. *Chief Admin,* Maryam Rezai-Atrie; Staff 2 (MLS 1, Non-MLS 1)
Founded 1913. Enrl 129; Fac 47; Highest Degree: Master
Library Holdings: AV Mats 1,195; CDs 233; DVDs 199; Bk Vols 49,347; Per Subs 112
Subject Interests: Theol
Automation Activity & Vendor Info: (Cataloging) Ex Libris Group; (OPAC) Ex Libris Group
Wireless access
Restriction: Authorized patrons

S THE SALVATION ARMY ARCHIVES*, Canada & Bermuda Territory, 26 Howden Rd, M1R 3E4. Tel: 416-285-4344. FAX: 416-285-7763. E-mail: heritage_centre@can.salvationarmy.org. Web Site: salvationist.ca/archives-and-museum/about-us. *Dir,* Major Ron Millar; E-mail: ron_millar@can.salvationarmy.org; Staff 3 (Non-MLS 3)
Founded 1982
Library Holdings: Bk Titles 1,000
Special Collections: Salvation Army Immigration Coll, Ship Logs 1911-1929; The Salvation Army Canada & Bermuda Territory, artifacts, bks, flm, music, photos, prints. Oral History
Automation Activity & Vendor Info: (Acquisitions) Inmagic, Inc.; (Cataloging) Inmagic, Inc.; (Circulation) Inmagic, Inc.; (Serials) Inmagic, Inc.
Function: Archival coll, For res purposes, Photocopying/Printing, Ref serv available, Res libr, Wheelchair accessible
Restriction: Open by appt only

SCARBOROUGH HOSPITAL
M HEALTH INFORMATION RESOURCE CENTRE*, 3050 Lawrence Ave E, M1P 2V5, SAN 319-4108. Tel: 416-431-8200, Ext 6593. FAX: 416-431-8232. E-mail: librarygen@tsh.to. *Libr Tech,* Judy Ng; Staff 1 (Non-MLS 1)
Library Holdings: e-books 40; e-journals 1,700; Bk Titles 5,000; Per Subs 300; Videos 30
Partic in Health Science Information Consortium of Toronto
Restriction: Staff use only
M HEALTH INFORMATION RESOURCE CENTRE, BIRCHMOUNT CAMPUS*, 3030 Birchmount Rd, M1W 3W3. Tel: 416-495-2437. FAX: 416-495-2562. E-mail: library@shn.ca. *Librn,* Solaiman Talut; Staff 2 (MLS 1, Non-MLS 1)
Open Mon-Fri 8:30-4:30

SCHREIBER

P SCHREIBER PUBLIC LIBRARY*, 314 Scotia St, P0T 2S0. (Mail add: Box 39, P0T 2S0), SAN 319-4124. Tel: 807-824-2477. FAX: 807-824-2996. E-mail: libinfo@schreiber.ca, library@schreiber.ca. Web Site: www.schreiberlibrary.ca. *Chief Exec Officer,* Linda Williamson
Founded 1891. Pop 1,000; Circ 14,800
Library Holdings: AV Mats 237; CDs 106; DVDs 87; Large Print Bks 241; Bk Titles 17,544; Bk Vols 17,758; Per Subs 25; Videos 575
Special Collections: Local History Coll, photogs. Oral History
Wireless access
Open Tues 11-5 & 6-8, Wed-Sat 1-5
Friends of the Library Group

SHANNONVILLE

P TYENDINAGA TOWNSHIP PUBLIC LIBRARY*, 852 Melrose Rd, K0K 3A0. SAN 319-4159. Tel: 613-967-0606. FAX: 613-396-2080. E-mail: tyendinagatwplibrary@xplornet.ca. Web Site: www.ttpl.ca. *Chief Exec Officer,* Kristin Farrel
Pop 3,769; Circ 12,000
Library Holdings: Bk Titles 9,500; Bk Vols 12,000
Automation Activity & Vendor Info: (Acquisitions) Follett Software; (Cataloging) Follett Software; (Circulation) Follett Software; (OPAC) Follett Software; (Serials) Follett Software
Wireless access
Mem of Ontario Library Service
Open Tues-Thurs 10-8, Sat 10-4
Friends of the Library Group

SHELBURNE

P SHELBURNE PUBLIC LIBRARY*, 201 Owen Sound St, L9V 3L2. (Mail add: PO Box 127, L9V 3L2), SAN 319-4175. Tel: 519-925-2168. FAX: 519-925-6555. E-mail: info@shelburnelibrary.ca. Web Site: www.shelburnelibrary.ca. *Chief Exec Officer, Head Librn,* Rose Dotten; E-mail: rdotten@shelburnelibrary.ca
Founded 1912. Pop 7,090; Circ 8,492
Library Holdings: Bk Vols 35,000; Per Subs 45
Automation Activity & Vendor Info: (Cataloging) Koha; (Circulation) Koha
Wireless access
Mem of Ontario Library Service
Open Mon, Tues & Fri 12-6, Thurs 2-8, Sat 1-4

SIMCOE

S NORFOLK COUNTY ARCHIVES*, 109 Norfolk St S, N3Y 2W3. SAN 320-3328. Tel: 519-426-1583. FAX: 519-426-1584. E-mail: archives@norfolkcounty.ca. Web Site: www.nca-ebdm.ca. *Archivist,* Josh Klar; Staff 2 (MLS 1, Non-MLS 1)
Founded 1900
Library Holdings: CDs 25; Bk Titles 3,500; Per Subs 10
Special Collections: Canadian/American Genealogy
Subject Interests: Antiques, Genealogy, Hist, Local hist
Wireless access
Publications: Local History Pamphlets
Open Tues-Sat 10-4:30
Restriction: Open to pub for ref only
Friends of the Library Group

P NORFOLK COUNTY PUBLIC LIBRARY*, Simcoe Branch, 46 Colborne St S, N3Y 4H3. Tel: 519-426-3506, Ext 5. FAX: 519-582-8376. Web Site: olc.ncpl.ca. *Chief Exec Officer,* Heather King; Tel: 519-426-3506 x1253, E-mail: julie.kent@norfolkcounty.ca; *Mgr, Coll Develop, Tech Mgr,* Heidi Goodale; Tel: 519-426-3506, Ext 1250, E-mail: heidi.goodale@norfolkcounty.ca; *Admin Coordr,* Kasey Whitwell; Tel: 519-426-3506, Ext 1258, E-mail: kasey.whitwell@norfolkcounty.ca; Staff 46 (MLS 3, Non-MLS 43)
Pop 61,000
Library Holdings: Bk Vols 169,827; Per Subs 232; Talking Bks 2,866; Videos 6,797
Special Collections: Bibliography of History in Norfolk Libraries; Bibliography of Holdings of Norfolk County; Canadiana-Local History, bks, per, tapes; History of Simcoe Public Library; Selected Bibliography of Haldimand-Norfolk History, bks, newsp, per
Automation Activity & Vendor Info: (Cataloging) MINISIS Inc; (Circulation) MINISIS Inc; (OPAC) MINISIS Inc
Wireless access
Mem of Ontario Library Service
Open Mon-Thurs 10-8, Fri 10-6, Sat 10-4
Friends of the Library Group
Branches: 4
DELHI BRANCH, 192 Main St of Delhi, Delhi, N4B 2M1, SAN 319-096X. Tel: 519-426-3506, Ext 2.
Founded 1894
Special Collections: Preserving Our Tobacco History; The Tobacco Leaf Yesterday & Today; Tobacco History of Norfolk Area, photos. Oral History
Open Tues 10-5, Wed & Thurs 12-7, Fri 10-6, Sat 10-4
Friends of the Library Group
PORT DOVER BRANCH, 713 Saint George St, Port Dover, N0A 1N0, SAN 319-3705. Tel: 519-426-3506, Ext 3. FAX: 519-583-3496.
Founded 1888
Subject Interests: Local hist
Open Tues 10-5, Wed & Thurs 12-7, Fri 10-6, Sat 10-4
Friends of the Library Group
PORT ROWAN BRANCH, 1034 Bay St, Port Rowan, N0E 1M0. Tel: 519-426-3506, Ext 4. FAX: 519-586-3297.
Open Tues 10-5, Wed & Thurs 12-7, Fri 10-6, Sat 10-4
Friends of the Library Group
WATERFORD BRANCH, 15 Main St S, Waterford, N0E 1Y0, SAN 319-5929. Tel: 519-426-3506, Ext 6. FAX: 519-443-6540.
Founded 1898
Open Tues 10-5, Wed & Thurs 12-7, Fri 10-6, Sat 10-4
Friends of the Library Group

SIOUX LOOKOUT

P SIOUX LOOKOUT PUBLIC LIBRARY*, 21 Fifth Ave, P8T 1B3. (Mail add: PO Box 1028, P8T 1B3), SAN 319-4191. Tel: 807-737-3660. FAX: 807-737-4046. E-mail: slpl@live.ca. Web Site: www.slpl.on.ca. *Chief Librn/CEO,* Shawn Bethke; E-mail: ceo@slpl.on.ca; Staff 2 (MLS 1, Non-MLS 1)
Founded 1958. Pop 5,200; Circ 40,000
Library Holdings: Bk Titles 32,000; Per Subs 85
Special Collections: Oral History
Wireless access
Function: 24/7 Electronic res, 24/7 Online cat, Activity rm, Adult bk club, Archival coll, Audio & video playback equip for onsite use, Audiobks on Playaways & MP3, Audiobks via web
Mem of Ontario Library Service
Open Tues & Wed 10-7, Thurs & Fri 10-5

SIOUX NARROWS

P TOWNSHIP OF SIOUX NARROWS-NESTOR FALLS*, Nestor Falls Public Library, Municipal Office Bldg, 5NF Airport Rd, P0X 1N0. (Mail add: PO Box 417, P0X 1N0), SAN 319-4205. Tel: 807-484-2777. FAX: 807-226-5712. E-mail: library@kmts.ca. Web Site: www.snnf.ca/stay/library. *Librn,* Judy Holden
Founded 1975. Pop 300; Circ 5,683
Library Holdings: Bk Titles 13,830; Per Subs 26
Special Collections: National Geographic Coll
Open Mon & Thurs 9-4
Branches: 1
SIOUX NARROWS PUBLIC LIBRARY, 5689 Hwy 71, P0X 1N0. (Mail add: PO Box 417, P0X 1N0). Tel: 807-226-5204. *Librn,* Alice Motlong
Open Mon & Tues 4-8, Wed & Sun Noon-4 (Summer); Mon-Wed 4-7, Sun Noon-3 (Winter)

SMITHS FALLS

P SMITHS FALLS PUBLIC LIBRARY*, 81 Beckwith St N, K7A 2B9. SAN 319-4213. Tel: 613-283-2911. FAX: 613-283-9834. E-mail: smithsfallslibrary@vianet.ca. Web Site: www.smithsfallslibrary.ca. *Chief Librn,* Karen Schecter; *Ch Serv,* Debra Kuehl; *Circ,* Deborah Andre; *Ref Serv, Ad,* Beth Lavender; Staff 6 (MLS 1, Non-MLS 5)
Founded 1903. Pop 12,000
Library Holdings: Large Print Bks 616; Bk Titles 41,655; Bk Vols 43,500; Per Subs 50
Subject Interests: Local hist
Automation Activity & Vendor Info: (Cataloging) Mandarin Library Automation; (Circulation) Mandarin Library Automation; (OPAC) Mandarin Library Automation
Wireless access
Publications: Periodical Indexing
Mem of Ontario Library Service
Open Mon-Thurs 1-8, Fri 10-5, Sat 10-4:30
Friends of the Library Group

SMITHVILLE

P WEST LINCOLN PUBLIC LIBRARY*, Smithville Public Library, 177 West St, L0R 2A0. Tel: 905-957-3756. FAX: 905-957-3219. E-mail: smithville@westlincolnlibrary.ca. Web Site: www.westlincolnlibrary.ca.
Library Holdings: Bk Vols 25,000; Per Subs 37
Automation Activity & Vendor Info: (Acquisitions) Evergreen
Wireless access
Open Mon & Fri 3-8, Tues-Thurs & Sat 10-5
Friends of the Library Group

Branches: 2
CAISTORVILLE BRANCH, 9549 York St, Caistorville, N0A 1C0. Tel: 905-692-4290. FAX: 905-692-4290.
Library Holdings: Bk Vols 11,000
Open Wed & Thurs 6-9, Tues 2-5, Fri & Sat 10-4
Friends of the Library Group
WELLANDPORT BRANCH, 5042 Canborough Rd, Wellandport, L0R 2J0. (Mail add: Box 68, Wellandport, L0R 2J0). Tel: 905-386-6792.
Library Holdings: Bk Vols 10,000
Open Mon, Tues & Thurs 6:30-8:30, Wed & Sat 9-4
Friends of the Library Group

SMOOTH ROCK FALLS

P SMOOTH ROCK FALLS PUBLIC LIBRARY*, 120 Ross Rd, P0L 2B0. (Mail add: PO Box 670, P0L 2B0), SAN 319-4221. Tel: 705-338-2318. FAX: 705-338-2330. E-mail: smooth03@live.ca. Web Site: smoothrockfalls.ca/living-here/recreation-activities/library. *Chief Exec Officer,* Lise Gagnon; E-mail: lgagnon@townsrf.ca
Pop 1,800; Circ 25,448
Library Holdings: Bk Titles 24,918; Per Subs 67
Wireless access
Open Mon-Fri 1-5

SOUTH PORCUPINE

C NORTHERN COLLEGE*, Timmins Campus - Learning Resource Centre, 4715 Hwy 101 E, P0N 1H0. (Mail add: PO Box 3211, Timmins, P4R 8R6), SAN 319-423X. Tel: 705-235-7150. FAX: 705-235-7279. E-mail: libraryt@northern.on.ca. Web Site: www.northernc.on.ca/lrc. *Sr Libr Tech,* Shannon Arsenault; Tel: 705-235-3211, Ext 6816, E-mail: arsenaults@northern.on.ca; Staff 5 (Non-MLS 5)
Founded 1967. Enrl 1,500; Fac 300
Library Holdings: AV Mats 1,400; CDs 200; DVDs 400; Electronic Media & Resources 1,000; Bk Titles 30,000; Bk Vols 35,000; Per Subs 300; Videos 1,000
Special Collections: ECE Coll; Map Coll. Canadian and Provincial
Subject Interests: Behav sci, Econ, Mining, Soc sci, Welding
Automation Activity & Vendor Info: (Acquisitions) SirsiDynix; (Cataloging) SirsiDynix; (Circulation) SirsiDynix; (OPAC) SirsiDynix
Wireless access
Publications: Library Handbook; Student Success Handbook
Partic in Ontario Colleges Library Service (OCLS)
Open Mon-Thurs 8-8, Fri 8-6, Sat & Sun 10-3
Restriction: Access at librarian's discretion, Authorized patrons, Open to pub for ref only
Departmental Libraries:
HAILEYBURY CAMPUS LIBRARY, 640 Latchford St, Haileybury, P0J 1K0. (Mail add: PO Box 2060, Haileybury, P0J 1K0), SAN 367-3502. Tel: 705-672-3376, Ext 8806. FAX: 705-672-5404. E-mail: libraryh@northern.on.ca. *Libr Tech,* Brenda Morissette; E-mail: morissetteb@northern.on.ca
Enrl 450; Fac 25
Library Holdings: e-books 45,000; Bk Titles 4,000; Per Subs 30
Partic in Ontario Colleges Library Service (OCLS)
Open Mon-Thurs 8-8, Fri 8-4, Sat & Sun 10-3 (Fall-Winter); Mon-Fri 8-1 & 2-4 (Summer)
KIRKLAND LAKE CAMPUS LIBRARY, 140 Government Rd E, Kirkland Lake, P2N 3H7. (Mail add: Postal Bag 250, Kirkland Lake, P2N 3H7), SAN 319-1982. Tel: 705-567-9291, Ext 3700. E-mail: libraryk@northern.on.ca. *Libr Tech,* Wenlian Wang; Staff 2 (MLS 1, Non-MLS 1)
Founded 1962. Enrl 200; Fac 35; Highest Degree: Bachelor
Library Holdings: DVDs 450; Bk Vols 10,446; Per Subs 46
Partic in Ontario Colleges Library Service (OCLS)
Open Mon-Thurs 8-8, Fri 8-4, Sat 10-3 (Sept-April)

SOUTH RIVER

P SOUTH RIVER-MACHAR UNION PUBLIC LIBRARY*, 63 Marie St, P0A 1X0. (Mail add: PO Box 190, P0A 1X0), SAN 319-4248. Tel: 705-386-0222. FAX: 705-386-0222. E-mail: osrmlibrary@hotmail.com. Web Site: southriver.olsn.ca.
Founded 1973. Pop 2,000; Circ 20,179
Library Holdings: Bks on Deafness & Sign Lang 2; CDs 27; DVDs 258; e-books 2,000; Electronic Media & Resources 1,000; High Interest/Low Vocabulary Bk Vols 1,137; Large Print Bks 106; Bk Titles 7,500; Bk Vols 7,522; Per Subs 13; Talking Bks 99
Subject Interests: Local hist
Automation Activity & Vendor Info: (Cataloging) SirsiDynix-WorkFlows; (Circulation) SirsiDynix-WorkFlows; (ILL) OCLC; (Media Booking) SirsiDynix-WorkFlows; (OPAC) SirsiDynix-iBistro; (Serials) SirsiDynix-WorkFlows
Wireless access
Function: 24/7 Electronic res, 24/7 Online cat, Archival coll, Art exhibits, Bks on CD, Children's prog, Computer training, Computers for patron use, Digital talking bks, Electronic databases & coll, Free DVD rentals, Holiday prog, Homebound delivery serv, ILL available, Internet access, Life-long learning prog for all ages, Magazines, Online cat, OverDrive digital audio bks, Photocopying/Printing, Ref & res, Scanner, Senior computer classes, Summer reading prog, Wheelchair accessible
Partic in Ont Libr Serv-North
Special Services for the Deaf - Bks on deafness & sign lang; Closed caption videos
Special Services for the Blind - Audio mat; Bks on CD; Daisy reader; Digital talking bk; Extensive large print coll; Large print bks; Large screen computer & software; Playaways (bks on MP3); Talking bks
Open Mon & Wed 3-5 & 6-8, Tues & Thurs 10:30-12:30 & 1-5, Fri 1-5, Sat 10-Noon
Restriction: Non-resident fee

SPANISH

P SPANISH PUBLIC LIBRARY*, Eight Trunk Rd, P0P 2A0. (Mail add: PO Box 329, P0P 2A0), SAN 319-4256. Tel: 705-844-2555. FAX: 705-844-2555. E-mail: library@townofspanish.com. Web Site: spanish.olsn.ca. *Chief Exec Officer, Librn,* Gwendlyn Goulet
Pop 749; Circ 3,000
Library Holdings: Bk Vols 8,045
Wireless access
Open Mon 6-8, Tues & Thurs 10-5, Wed 10-5 & 6-8, Fri 10-2

ST. CATHARINES

S BABY'S BREATH LIBRARY, 5 Race St, L2R 3M1. (Mail add: PO Box 5005, L2R 7T4), SAN 375-2542. Tel: 905-688-8884. Toll Free Tel: 800-363-7437 (Canada only). FAX: 905-688-3300. E-mail: info@babysbreathcanada.ca. Web Site: www.babysbreathcanada.ca. *Exec Dir,* Mary Margaret Murphy; Staff 2 (MLS 2)
Founded 1973
Restriction: Open to pub for ref only

C BROCK UNIVERSITY*, James A Gibson Library, 1812 Sir Isaac Brock Way, L2S 3A1. SAN 319-3896. Tel: 905-688-5550, Ext 4583. FAX: 905-988-5490. E-mail: libhelp@brocku.ca. Web Site: www.brocku.ca/library. *Univ Librn,* Mark Robertson; Tel: 905-688-5550, Ext 5980, E-mail: mrobertson3@brocku.ca; *Assoc Univ Librn,* Nicole Nolan; Tel: 905-688-5550, Ext 5868, E-mail: nnolan@brocku.ca; *Coll Librn, Head of Liaison Services,* Laurie Morrison; Tel: 905-688-5550, Ext 5281, E-mail: lmorrison@brocku.ca; *Head, Spec Coll, Univ Archivist,* David Sharron; Tel: 905-688-5550, Ext 3264, E-mail: dsharron@brocku.ca; *Librn III,* Ian Gordon; Tel: 905-688-5550, Ext 3727, E-mail: igordon@brocku.ca; Staff 62 (MLS 19, Non-MLS 43)
Founded 1964. Enrl 18,053; Fac 550; Highest Degree: Doctorate
Library Holdings: AV Mats 21,988; e-books 386,429; e-journals 25,500; Music Scores 2,999; Bk Titles 400,000; Bk Vols 1,254,826; Per Subs 13,650; Videos 1,814
Special Collections: Niagara Regional Coll
Subject Interests: Applied health sci, Bus, Educ, Humanities
Automation Activity & Vendor Info: (Acquisitions) Innovative Interfaces, Inc; (Cataloging) Innovative Interfaces, Inc; (Circulation) Innovative Interfaces, Inc; (ILL) Fretwell-Downing; (OPAC) Innovative Interfaces, Inc; (Serials) Innovative Interfaces, Inc
Wireless access
Partic in Canadian Association of Research Libraries; Canadian Research Knowledge Network; Ontario Council of University Libraries
Open Mon, Thurs & Fri 7:30am-2:30am, Tues 7:30am-9pm, Wed 8-5, Sat 9am-11pm, Sun 9-2:30

L LINCOLN COUNTY LAW ASSOCIATION LIBRARY*, Robert S K Welch Courthouse, 59 Church St, L2R 3C3. SAN 377-3655. Tel: 905-685-9094. FAX: 905-685-0981. E-mail: library@thelcla.ca. Web Site: thelcla.ca. *Librn,* Kelly Elliott
Library Holdings: Bk Vols 9,000
Wireless access
Open Mon-Fri 9-5

M NIAGARA HEALTH SYSTEM, Library Services, 1200 Fourth Ave, L2S 0A9. SAN 329-4196. Tel: 905-378-4647, Ext 44354. Web Site: www.niagarahealth.on.ca/site/st-catharines-site. *Libr Tech,* Nina Kelly; *Libr Tech,* Janice Russell
Founded 1978
Library Holdings: Bk Titles 1,000; Per Subs 125
Special Collections: Hospital Archives
Subject Interests: Allied health, Med, Nursing
Restriction: Hospital employees & physicians only

G ONTARIO MINISTRY OF TRANSPORTATION LIBRARY, 301 St Paul St, 4th Flr, L2R 7R4. SAN 319-1079. Tel: 905-704-2171. E-mail: mto.library@ontario.ca. Web Site: www.library.mto.gov.on.ca. *Librn,* Patricia Bartel; E-mail: patricia.bartel@ontario.ca; Staff 1 (MLS 1)

Founded 1960
Library Holdings: Bk Titles 15,000
Special Collections: MTO Reports. Canadian and Provincial
Subject Interests: Econ, Transportation
Automation Activity & Vendor Info: (Cataloging) SydneyPlus
Function: ILL available
Restriction: Open by appt only

S ST CATHARINES MUSEUM*, Research Centre, 1932 Welland Canals Pkwy, L2R 7K6. (Mail add: PO Box 3012, L2R 7C2), SAN 319-3926. Tel: 905-984-8880. Toll Free Tel: 800-305-5134. FAX: 905-984-6910. E-mail: museum@stcatharines.ca. Web Site: www.stcatharinesmuseum.ca. *Curator,* Kathleen Powell
Founded 1965
Library Holdings: Bk Vols 1,600; Per Subs 20
Special Collections: Alan Howard Marine Coll, photog; Algoma Marine Coll; Benson Family Papers; Calder Family Papers; Craig Swayze Coll; DeCew Falls Waterworks Coll (1875-1970); Figure Skating (Winter Club of St Catharines Coll); Frank Scott & Sons Account; Fred Pattison Aviation Coll incl Records of No 9 EFTS (1920-1950); Girl Guides Coll; Grantham High School Coll; Grape & Wine Industry, Bright's Wines (George Hostetter Coll); Graves Shipping Papers, 19th Century; Heritage St Catharines Coll; Ingersoll Papers (Family & Business Accounts 1835-1909); Lalor Estate Coll; Maps & Plans (St Catharines Planning Dept & St Catharines Engineering Dept); Marine & Business Papers (Sylvester Neelon Coll); Marine (James Kidd Coll), photog; Marine, English Electric & W S Tyler (Jim Gilmore Coll); Mayor Joe Reid Coll; Mayor Roy Adams Coll; McCordick Family (Anne McPherson Coll); McCordick Family Papers; Merritt Family Papers (Wendy Young Coll); Merritton High School Coll; Mid-19th Century Shipping Business Papers (Norris & Neelon Coll); Niagara Grape & Wine Festival Archives (1955-present); Niagara North Land Registry Property Records; Old Courthouse Coll (1800-1920); Ontario Winter Games Coll, 1983; Papermaking (Lincoln Sulphite Mill Coll); Press Theatre Coll; Property Records (Robert Nunnenmacher Coll); Rob Sharik Marine Coll, ship photog; Robertson Farm (Janice Partlow Coll); Royal Canadian Legion Br 24 Coll; Skip Gillham Marine Coll; Sports Columns "Through the Sports Gate" (Jack Gatecliff Coll); St Catharines & Lincoln Historical Society Coll; St Catharines' Centennial (1976) Coll; St Catharines Equestrian Club Coll; St Catharines Standard Coll; St Catharines Wine Co Coll; Standard Fine Printing Coll; Third Welland Canal Construction (St Lawrence Seaway Coll); Welch's, Cadbury-Schweppes-Powell (Jack Collard Coll); Welland Canals Preservation Association Coll; Welland Vale Mfg Co Ltd (Ray Sheehan & Norman Shopland Coll); William Hamilton Merritt Papers, micro; World Rowing Championships (1999) Coll
Subject Interests: Artifact res, Great Lakes marine hist, Local hist, Welland Canals
Wireless access
Open Mon, Wed & Fri 12:30-4:30
Restriction: Non-circulating, Open to pub for ref only

P ST CATHARINES PUBLIC LIBRARY*, Central Library, 54 Church St, L2R 7K2. SAN 368-2803. Tel: 905-688-6103. FAX: 905-688-6292. E-mail: info@myscpl.ca. Web Site: www.myscpl.ca. *Chief Exec Officer,* Ken Su; E-mail: qksu@myscpl.ca; *Libr Bus Adminr,* Karen Smith Curtis; E-mail: ksmithcurtis@myscpl.ca; *Mgr, Ad Serv,* Diane Andrusko; E-mail: dandrusko@myscpl.ca; *Mgr, Br Serv,* Rita Di Marcantonio; E-mail: rdimarcantonio@myscpl.ca; *Commun Serv Mgr, Mgr, Ch Serv,* Ann McKenzie; E-mail: amckenzie@myscpl.ca; *Circ Mgr,* Joanna Spera; E-mail: jspera@myscpl.ca; *Mgr, Info Tech, Network Serv,* David Bott; E-mail: dbott@myscpl.ca; *Mgr, Tech Serv,* John Dunn; E-mail: jdunn@myscpl.ca; Staff 70 (MLS 15, Non-MLS 55)
Founded 1888. Pop 130,926
Library Holdings: AV Mats 38,291; CDs 16,000; DVDs 16,000; e-journals 46,500; Large Print Bks 7,000; Bk Titles 211,685; Bk Vols 327,139; Per Subs 681
Subject Interests: Genealogy, Local hist
Automation Activity & Vendor Info: (Acquisitions) SirsiDynix; (Cataloging) SirsiDynix; (Circulation) SirsiDynix; (ILL) SirsiDynix; (OPAC) SirsiDynix; (Serials) SirsiDynix
Wireless access
Mem of Ontario Library Service
Special Services for the Deaf - TDD equip
Open Tues-Thurs 10-9, Fri 10-6, Sat 9-5, Sun (Winter) 1:30-5
Branches: 3
DR HUQ FAMILY LIBRARY, 425 Carlton St, L2M 4W8, SAN 368-2838. Tel: 905-688-6103, Ext 300.
Founded 1888. Pop 50,000
Library Holdings: Bk Vols 58,917; Per Subs 50
Open Tues-Fri 10-8, Sat 9-5
WILLIAM HAMILTON MERRITT BRANCH, 149 Hartzel Rd, L2P 1N6, SAN 370-2251. Tel: 905-688-6103, Ext 400.
Library Holdings: Bk Vols 34,331; Per Subs 50
Open Tues-Fri 10-8, Sat 9-5
PORT DALHOUSIE BRANCH, 23 Brock St, L2N 5E1, SAN 368-2897. Tel: 905-688-6103, Ext 500.
Library Holdings: Bk Vols 9,455; Per Subs 25
Subject Interests: Local hist
Open Tues 1-8, Thurs 10-8, Sat 11-4

ST. ISIDORE

P NATION MUNICIPALITY PUBLIC LIBRARY*, St Isidore Public Library, 4531 Ste-Catherine St, K0C 2B0. SAN 319-3950. Tel: 613-524-2252. FAX: 613-524-2545. E-mail: biblioinfo@nationmun.ca. Web Site: www.nationmunbiblio.ca. *Chief Exec Officer,* Jeanne Leroux; E-mail: jeanneleroux@nationmun.ca; *ILL, Libr Asst,* Lynn Paquette; E-mail: lpaquette@nationmun.ca
Founded 1974. Pop 10,499; Circ 36,000
Library Holdings: DVDs 400; Bk Vols 41,000; Per Subs 407
Automation Activity & Vendor Info: (Cataloging) Mandarin Library Automation; (Circulation) Mandarin Library Automation; (OPAC) Mandarin Library Automation
Wireless access
Mem of Ontario Library Service
Open Mon, Wed & Thurs 1:30-5:30, Tues & Fri 2-8, Sat 9-12
Branches: 2
LIMOGES BRANCH, 205 Limoges Rd, Limoges, K0A 2M0. Tel: 613-443-1630. FAX: 613-443-9643. *Chief Exec Officer,* Jeanne Leroux
Open Mon 2:30-6:30, Tues & Wed 5-8, Thurs 4-8, Fri 3-8, Sat 10-1
ST ALBERT BRANCH, St Albert Community Centre, 201 Principale St, Saint Albert, K0A 3C0. (Mail add: St Albert Branch, c/o 25 rue de l'arena, Saint Isidore, K0C 2B0). Tel: 613-987-2143. FAX: 613-987-2909. *Chief Exec Officer,* Jeanne Leroux
Open Mon & Thurs 5-8, Tues & Wed 2:30-6:30, Fri 3-8, Sat 10-1

ST. MARYS

P ST MARY'S PUBLIC LIBRARY*, 15 Church St N, N4X 1B4. (Mail add: PO Box 700, N4X 1B4), SAN 319-3969. Tel: 519-284-3346. FAX: 519-284-2630. E-mail: libraryinfo@stmaryspubliclibrary.ca. Web Site: www.stmaryspubliclibrary.ca. *Chief Exec Officer,* Sarah Andrews; Staff 9 (MLS 1, Non-MLS 8)
Founded 1904. Circ 111,000
Library Holdings: Bk Vols 30,000; Per Subs 60
Subject Interests: Local hist
Automation Activity & Vendor Info: (Acquisitions) SirsiDynix; (Cataloging) SirsiDynix; (Circulation) SirsiDynix
Wireless access
Function: 24/7 Electronic res, 24/7 Online cat, 3D Printer, Audiobks via web, Children's prog, Computers for patron use, Digital talking bks, E-Reserves, Electronic databases & coll, Free DVD rentals, Home delivery & serv to seniorr ctr & nursing homes, Homebound delivery serv, ILL available, Internet access, Laminating, Magazines, Makerspace, Mango lang, Meeting rooms, Music CDs, Online cat, OverDrive digital audio bks, Photocopying/Printing, Printer for laptops & handheld devices, Prog for adults, Prog for children & young adult, Ref & res, Scanner, Wheelchair accessible, Winter reading prog
Mem of Ontario Library Service
Partic in Perth County Information Network
Open Mon-Thurs 10:30-8, Fri 10:30-5, Sat 10-4
Friends of the Library Group

ST. THOMAS

P ELGIN COUNTY LIBRARY*, County Administration Bldg, 450 Sunset Dr, N5R 5V1. SAN 368-2927. Tel: 519-631-1460, Ext 148. FAX: 519-631-9209. Web Site: elgincounty.ca/library. *Dir, Cultural Serv, Dir, Commun Serv,* Brian Masschaele; E-mail: bmasschaele@elgin-county.on.ca; Staff 12 (MLS 2, Non-MLS 10)
Founded 1936. Pop 50,000; Circ 271,347
Library Holdings: Audiobooks 3,869; AV Mats 529; CDs 3,185; DVDs 4,113; e-books 37,458; e-journals 32,469; Large Print Bks 4,539; Bk Titles 107,202; Bk Vols 162,717; Per Subs 126; Videos 2,607
Subject Interests: Local hist
Automation Activity & Vendor Info: (Cataloging) SirsiDynix; (Circulation) SirsiDynix
Wireless access
Function: CD-ROM
Partic in Ontario Library Consortium
Open Mon-Fri 8:30-4:30
Friends of the Library Group
Branches: 10
AYLMER OLD TOWN HALL LIBRARY, 38 John St S, Aylmer, N5H 2C2, SAN 368-2951. Tel: 519-773-2439. FAX: 519-773-2420. E-mail: aylmerlib@elgin.ca. *Br Supvr,* Dalene Van Zyl; Staff 8 (MLS 1, Non-MLS 7)
Founded 1936
Open Mon, Tues & Thurs 9:30-8:30, Fri & Sat 9:30-5

BELMONT LIBRARY, 14134 Belmont Rd, Belmont, N0L 1B0, SAN 368-2986. Tel: 519-644-1560. FAX: 519-644-1560. E-mail: belmontlib@elgin.ca. *Br Supvr,* Leah Ede-Pisano; Staff 4 (Non-MLS 4)
Founded 1936
Open Mon & Thurs 1-8, Tues 10-8, Fri 2-5, Sat 10-1:30

FRED BODSWORTH PUBLIC LIBRARY OF PORT BURWELL, 21 Pitt St, Port Burwell, N0J 1T0, SAN 368-3044. Tel: 519-874-4754. FAX: 519-874-4436. E-mail: ptburwelllib@elgin.ca. *Br Supvr,* Susan Morrell; Staff 4 (Non-MLS 4)
Founded 1936
Open Mon 2-5, Tues 2-7, Thurs 11-5, Sat 10-Noon

JOHN KENNETH GALBRAITH REFERENCE LIBRARY-DUTTON BRANCH, 236 Shackleton St, Dutton, N0L 1J0, SAN 368-301X. Tel: 519-762-2780. FAX: 519-762-0707. E-mail: duttonlib@elgin.ca. *Br Supvr,* Shelley Fleming; Staff 6 (MLS 1, Non-MLS 5)
Founded 1936
Open Mon & Tues 10-8, Thurs Noon-8, Fri & Sat 10-5
Friends of the Library Group

PORT STANLEY LIBRARY, 302 Bridge St, Port Stanley, N5L 1C3, SAN 368-3079. Tel: 519-782-4241. FAX: 519-782-4861. E-mail: ptstanleylib@elgin.ca. *Br Supvr,* Emily Finch; Staff 5 (Non-MLS 5)
Founded 1936
Open Mon, Tues & Thurs 10-8:30, Fri 1-5, Sat 9-1

RODNEY LIBRARY, 207 Furnival Rd, Rodney, N0L 2C0, SAN 368-3109. Tel: 519-785-2100. FAX: 519-785-1734. E-mail: rodneylib@elgin.ca. *Br Supvr,* Shelley Fleming; Staff 5 (Non-MLS 5)
Founded 1936
Open Tues & Thurs 2-8, Fri 10-5, Sat 10-12

SHEDDEN LIBRARY-SOUTHWOLD TOWNSHIP LIBRARY, 35921 Talbot Line, Shedden, N0L 2E0, SAN 368-3133. Tel: 519-764-2081. FAX: 519-764-2789. E-mail: sheddenlib@elgin.ca. *Br Supvr,* Emily Finch; Staff 3 (Non-MLS 3)
Founded 1936
Open Tues 2-8, Thurs 2-7, Fri 10-5, Sat 2-5

SPRINGFIELD LIBRARY, Malahida Community Pl, 12105 Whittaker Rd, Springfield, N0L 2J0, SAN 368-3168. Tel: 519-765-4515. FAX: 519-765-4453. E-mail: springfieldlib@elgin.ca. *Br Supvr,* Leah Ede-Pisano; Staff 2 (Non-MLS 2)
Founded 1936
Open Mon 1-5, Tues 2-8, Thurs 10-8, Sat 2-5

STRAFFORDVILLE LIBRARY, 9366 Plank Rd, Straffordville, N0J 1Y0. (Mail add: PO Box 209, Straffordville, N0J 1Y0), SAN 368-3192. Tel: 519-866-3584. FAX: 519-866-3219. E-mail: straffordvillelib@elgin.ca. *Br Supvr,* Susan Morrell; Staff 4 (Non-MLS 4)
Founded 1936
Open Mon, Tues & Thurs 10-8, Fri 10-5, Sat 1-4

WEST LORNE LIBRARY, 160A Main St, West Lorne, N0L 2P0, SAN 368-3257. Tel: 519-768-1150. FAX: 519-768-0773. E-mail: westlornelib@elgin.ca. *Br Supvr,* Shelley Fleming; Staff 4 (Non-MLS 4)
Founded 1936
Open Tues 10-8, Thurs 2-8, Fri 2-5, Sat 10-12

P ST THOMAS PUBLIC LIBRARY*, 153 Curtis St, N5P 3Z7. SAN 319-3977. Tel: 519-631-6050. Circulation Tel: 519-631-6050, Ext 8011. FAX: 519-631-1987. E-mail: info@stthomaspubliclibrary.ca. Web Site: www.stthomaspubliclibrary.ca. *Chief Exec Officer,* Heather Robinson; Tel: 519-631-6050, Ext 8027, E-mail: hrobinson@stthomaspubliclibrary.ca; Staff 10 (MLS 4, Non-MLS 6)
Founded 1884. Pop 38,100; Circ 436,299
Library Holdings: Bk Titles 131,961; Bk Vols 151,069; Per Subs 204
Subject Interests: Local hist
Wireless access
Function: Activity rm, Adult bk club, Art exhibits, Bks on CD, Children's prog, Computer training, Computers for patron use, E-Readers, Electronic databases & coll, Free DVD rentals, Homebound delivery serv, ILL available, Internet access, Life-long learning prog for all ages, Magazines, Movies, Online cat, Outreach serv, OverDrive digital audio bks, Photocopying/Printing, Prog for adults, Prog for children & young adult, Summer reading prog, Teen prog, Wheelchair accessible
Open Mon-Fri 9-8:30, Sat 9-5
Friends of the Library Group

STAYNER

P CLEARVIEW PUBLIC LIBRARY*, Stayner Branch, 269 Regina St, L0M 1S0. SAN 319-4272. Tel: 705-428-3595. FAX: 705-428-3595. Web Site: www.clearview.library.on.ca. *Chief Exec Officer,* Jennifer La Chapelle; E-mail: jlachapelle@clearview.ca; Staff 11 (MLS 1, Non-MLS 10)
Founded 1994. Pop 15,000; Circ 154,000
Library Holdings: Bk Titles 67,410; Per Subs 116
Subject Interests: Fed-prov govt doc, Local hist
Automation Activity & Vendor Info: (Acquisitions) SirsiDynix; (Cataloging) SirsiDynix; (Circulation) SirsiDynix; (ILL) SirsiDynix; (OPAC) SirsiDynix
Wireless access
Mem of Ontario Library Service
Open Tues-Fri 10-9, Sat 10-4
Branches: 2

CREEMORE BRANCH, 165 Library St, Creemore, L0M 1G0, SAN 319-0927. Tel: 705-466-3011. FAX: 705-466-3011. *Chief Exec Officer,* Jennifer LaChapelle
Open Tues-Fri 10-5 & 7-9, Sat 10-4
Friends of the Library Group

NEW LOWELL BRANCH, 5237 Simcoe County Rd 9, New Lowell, L0M 1N0, SAN 319-2733. Tel: 705-424-6288. FAX: 705-424-6288. *Chief Exec Officer,* Jennifer La Chapelle
Open Tues & Fri 1-6, Wed & Thurs 10-8, Sat 10-2

STIRLING

P STIRLING-RAWDON PUBLIC LIBRARY*, 43 W Front St, K0K 3E0. SAN 319-4280. Tel: 613-395-2837. E-mail: info@stirlinglibrary.com. Web Site: stirlinglibrary.com. *Chief Exec Officer,* Jaye Bannon; E-mail: jaye@stirlinglibrary.com; *Asst Librn,* Theresa Brennan; E-mail: theresa@stirlinglibrary.com; *Ch,* Haley Letch; E-mail: haley@stirlinglibrary.com; Staff 3 (Non-MLS 3)
Founded 1903. Pop 4,613; Circ 34,000
Library Holdings: Bk Titles 22,006; Per Subs 15
Wireless access
Mem of Ontario Library Service
Open Tues-Thurs 10-7, Fri & Sat 10-3
Friends of the Library Group

STITTSVILLE

S BREWERS ASSOCIATION OF CANADA LIBRARY*, Beer Canada Library, PO Box 654, K2S 1A7. SAN 325-5875. Tel: 613-232-9601. E-mail: cheers@beercanada.com. Web Site: www.beercanada.com. *Dir, Res,* Ed Gregory; E-mail: egregory@beercanada.com. Subject Specialists: *Brewing, Statistics,* Ed Gregory
Founded 1943
Library Holdings: Bk Titles 580; Per Subs 20
Restriction: Staff use only

STONECLIFFE

P HEAD, CLARA & MARIA TOWNSHIP PUBLIC LIBRARY*, 15 Township Hall Rd, K0J 2K0. SAN 319-4302. Tel: 613-586-1950. FAX: 613-586-2596. E-mail: hcmlibra13@gmail.com. Web Site: www.hcmpubliclibrary.ca.
Pop 300; Circ 1,800
Library Holdings: Bk Vols 2,400
Wireless access
Mem of Ontario Library Service
Open Mon, Wed & Fri 8:30-4, Tues 8:30-4 & 6-8:30, Sat 12:30-3

STOUFFVILLE

P WHITCHURCH-STOUFFVILLE PUBLIC LIBRARY, Two Park Dr, L4A 4K1. SAN 319-4329. Tel: 905-642-7323. Toll Free Tel: 888-603-4292. FAX: 905-640-1384. Web Site: wsplibrary.ca. *Chief Exec Officer,* Margaret Wallace; E-mail: margaret.wallace@wsplibrary.ca; *Mgr, Libr Serv,* Marcia Frignette; E-mail: marcia.frignette@wsplibrary.ca; *Coordr, Ch Serv,* Anne Houle; Tel: 905-642-7323, Ext 5228, E-mail: anne.houle@wsplibrary.ca; Staff 12 (MLS 5, Non-MLS 7)
Founded 1899. Pop 50,000; Circ 267,850
Library Holdings: Bk Titles 85,969; Bk Vols 86,985; Per Subs 126
Wireless access
Function: 24/7 Electronic res, 24/7 Online cat, 3D Printer, Adult bk club, Adult literacy prog, Archival coll, Art programs, Audio & video playback equip for onsite use, Audiobks on Playaways & MP3, Audiobks via web, Bk club(s), Bks on CD, Chess club, Children's prog, Citizenship assistance, Computer training, Computers for patron use, Digital talking bks, E-Reserves, Electronic databases & coll, Equip loans & repairs, Family literacy, Free DVD rentals, Games, Games & aids for people with disabilities, Genealogy discussion group, Govt ref serv, Holiday prog, Homebound delivery serv, Homework prog, ILL available, Internet access, Laptop/tablet checkout, Large print keyboards, Life-long learning prog for all ages, Literacy & newcomer serv, Magazines, Magnifiers for reading, Mail & tel request accepted, Makerspace, Mango lang, Meeting rooms, Microfiche/film & reading machines, Movies, Museum passes, Online cat, Online ref, Outreach serv, Photocopying/Printing, Preschool outreach, Preschool reading prog, Printer for laptops & handheld devices, Prog for adults, Prog for children & young adult, Ref serv available, Scanner, Senior computer classes, Senior outreach, Spanish lang bks, STEM programs, Story hour, Study rm, Summer & winter reading prog, Summer reading prog, Teen prog, Telephone ref, Wheelchair accessible, Wifi hotspot checkout, Winter reading prog, Workshops, Writing prog
Open Mon-Thurs 10-8:30, Fri 10-6, Sat 10-5, Sun 12-5 (Winter); Mon-Thurs 10-8:30, Fri & Sat 10-4 (Summer)

STRATFORD

P STRATFORD PUBLIC LIBRARY*, 19 Saint Andrew St, N5A 1A2. SAN 319-4337. Tel: 519-271-0220. FAX: 519-271-3843. Web Site: www.stratford.library.on.ca. *Actg Chief Exec Officer, Syst Librn,* Krista Robinson; Tel: 519-271-0220, Ext 112, E-mail: krobinson@stratfordcanada.ca; *Dir, Pub Serv,* Wendy Hicks; Tel: 519-271-0220, Ext 111, E-mail: whicks@stratfordcanada.ca; Staff 7 (MLS 7)
Founded 1846. Pop 33,000; Circ 368,755
Library Holdings: AV Mats 7,013; Bk Vols 102,132; Per Subs 173; Talking Bks 1,138
Special Collections: Chalmers Public Theatre Resource Coll; Fed & Prov
Subject Interests: Performing arts, Theatre
Automation Activity & Vendor Info: (Cataloging) BiblioCommons; (Circulation) BiblioCommons; (OPAC) BiblioCommons
Wireless access
Mem of Ontario Library Service
Open Mon-Thurs 10-9, Fri 10-6, Sat 10-5, Sun 2-5
Friends of the Library Group

STRATHROY

P MIDDLESEX COUNTY LIBRARY*, 34-B Frank St, N7G 2R4. SAN 366-9335. Tel: 519-245-8237. Interlibrary Loan Service Tel: 519-245-8237, Ext 4026. FAX: 519-245-8238. E-mail: librarian@middlesex.ca. Web Site: library.middlesex.ca. *Dir, Libr Serv,* Lindsay Brock; Tel: 519-245-8237, Ext 4022; *Ch & Youth Librn,* Shauna Dereniowski; Tel: 519-245-8237, Ext 4027, E-mail: sdereniowski@middlesex.ca; *Ref Librn,* Chris Harrington; Tel: 519-245-1290, E-mail: charrington@middlesex.ca; *Coordr, Pub Serv,* Liz Adema; Tel: 519-245-8237, Ext 4021, E-mail: eadema@middlesex.ca; Staff 14 (MLS 7, Non-MLS 7)
Founded 1963. Pop 71,000; Circ 389,048
Library Holdings: AV Mats 3,906; Large Print Bks 3,201; Bk Titles 185,000; Per Subs 434; Talking Bks 1,072
Subject Interests: Local hist
Automation Activity & Vendor Info: (Cataloging) SirsiDynix; (Circulation) SirsiDynix; (OPAC) SirsiDynix
Wireless access
Mem of Ontario Library Service
Partic in Ontario Library Consortium
Special Services for the Blind - Talking bks
Open Mon-Fri 8:30-4:30
Friends of the Library Group
Branches: 14
AILSA CRAIG BRANCH, 147 Main St, Ailsa Craig, N0M 1A0, SAN 366-936X. Tel: 519-293-3441. E-mail: acraig_staff@middlesex.ca. *Supvr,* Doug Warnock; E-mail: dwarnock@middlesex.ca; Staff 3 (Non-MLS 3)
Open Tues-Thurs 2-8, Fri 10-4, Sat 10-1
DELAWARE BRANCH, 29 Young St, Delaware, N0L 1E0, SAN 366-9815. Tel: 519-652-9978. E-mail: delaware_circ@middlesex.ca. *Supvr,* Tiffany Bolton; Staff 1 (Non-MLS 1)
Open Tues 4-8, Thurs 6-8, Sat 10-12
DORCHESTER BRANCH, 2123 Dorchester Rd, Dorchester, N0L 1G0. (Mail add: PO Box 463, Dorchester, N0L 1G0), SAN 366-9513. Tel: 519-268-3451. E-mail: dorchester_staff@middlesex.ca. *Supvr,* Kathryn Suffoletta; E-mail: ksuffoletta@middlesex.ca; *Br Asst,* Kathy Campeau; Staff 4 (Non-MLS 4)
Open Mon & Wed 2:30-8:30, Tues & Thurs 10-8:30, Fri 10-8, Sat 10-4
GLENCOE BRANCH, 123 McKellar St, Glencoe, N0L 1M0, SAN 366-9572. Tel: 519-287-2735. *Supvr,* Courtney Joris; E-mail: cjoris@middlesex.ca; Staff 3 (Non-MLS 3)
Open Tues-Thurs 2-8, Fri 10-4, Sat 10-1
ILDERTON BRANCH, 40 Heritage Dr, Ilderton, N0M 2A0, SAN 366-9661. Tel: 519-666-1599. *Supvr,* Karen Donaldson; E-mail: kdonaldson@middlesex.ca; Staff 3 (Non-MLS 3)
Open Tues-Thurs 2-8, Fri 10-4, Sat 10-1
KOMOKA BRANCH, One Tunks Lane, Komoka, N0L 1R0, SAN 366-984X. Tel: 519-657-1461. ; Staff 4 (Non-MLS 4)
Open Mon & Sat 10-4, Tues 10-8, Wed-Fri 2-8
LUCAN BRANCH, 270 Main St, Lucan, N0M 2J0, SAN 366-9726. Tel: 519-227-4682. *Supvr,* Leigh Robinson; E-mail: lrobinson@middlesex.ca; Staff 2 (Non-MLS 2)
Open Mon, Fri & Sat 10-4, Tues & Thurs 2-8, Wed 10-8
Friends of the Library Group
MELBOURNE BRANCH, 6570 Longwoods Rd, Melbourne, N0L 1T0, SAN 366-9750. Tel: 519-289-2405. E-mail: melbourne_circ@middlesex.ca. *Supvr,* Carolee Higgith; Staff 1 (Non-MLS 1)
Open Tues 3:30-5:30, Thurs 3:30-7:30, Fri 10-12
MOUNT BRYDGES BRANCH, 22501 Adelaide Rd, Mount Brydges, N0L 1W0, SAN 366-9785. Tel: 519-264-1061. *Supvr,* Vanessa Gay; E-mail: vgay@middlesex.ca; Staff 2 (Non-MLS 2)
Open Tues-Thurs 2-8, Fri 10-4, Sat 10-1
NEWBURY BRANCH, 22894 Hagerty St, Newbury, N0L 1Z0, SAN 366-9874. Tel: 519-693-4275. E-mail: newbury_circ@middlesex.ca. *Supvr,* Diana Watson
Open Mon & Thurs 2-5, Wed 6:30pm-8:30pm
PARKHILL BRANCH, 229 B Main St, Parkhill, N0M 2K0, SAN 366-9939. Tel: 519-294-6583. *Supvr,* Doug Warnock; E-mail: dwarnock@middlesex.ca; Staff 2 (Non-MLS 2)
Open Mon, Fri & Sat 10-4, Tues & Thurs 2-8, Wed 10-8
STRATHROY BRANCH, 34 Frank St, N7G 2R4, SAN 378-2409. Tel: 519-245-1290. *Supvr,* Jean Moir; E-mail: jmoir@middlesex.ca; Staff 6 (MLS 2, Non-MLS 4)
Special Collections: Middlesex County Local History
Open Mon-Fri 10-8:30, Sat 10-4
Friends of the Library Group
THORNDALE BRANCH, 21790 Fairview Rd, Thorndale, N0M 2P0. (Mail add: PO Box 88, Thorndale, N0M 2P0), SAN 367-0023. Tel: 519-461-1150. *Supvr,* Debbie Guy; E-mail: dguy@middlesex.ca; Staff 2 (Non-MLS 2)
Open Tues-Thurs 2-8:30, Fri 10-4:30, Sat 10-2
Friends of the Library Group
WARDSVILLE BRANCH, 21935 Hagerty Rd, Wardsville, N0L 2N0, SAN 366-9998. Tel: 519-693-4208. E-mail: wardsville_circ@middlesex.ca. *Supvr,* Marie Williams; Staff 1 (Non-MLS 1)
Open Tues 2-5, Thurs 5-8, Fri 10-2

STURGEON FALLS

P WEST NIPISSING PUBLIC LIBRARY*, 225 Holditch St, Ste 107, P2B 1T1. SAN 319-4353. Tel: 705-753-2620. FAX: 705-753-2131. E-mail: info@wnpl.ca, mail@wnpl.ca. Web Site: www.wnpl.ca. *Chief Exec Officer,* Emelie Bisaillon; E-mail: ebisaillon@wnpl.ca
Founded 1963
Automation Activity & Vendor Info: (Cataloging) Evergreen; (Circulation) Evergreen; (OPAC) Evergreen
Wireless access
Function: 24/7 Electronic res, 24/7 Online cat, Adult bk club, After school storytime, Archival coll, Audiobks on Playaways & MP3, BA reader (adult literacy), Bks on CD, CD-ROM, Children's prog, Computer training, Computers for patron use, E-Readers, Electronic databases & coll, Free DVD rentals, Games & aids for people with disabilities, Home delivery & serv to seniorr ctr & nursing homes, ILL available, Internet access, Laminating, Large print keyboards, Magazines, Magnifiers for reading, Mail & tel request accepted, Makerspace, Mango lang, Meeting rooms, Movies, Music CDs, Online cat, OverDrive digital audio bks, Photocopying/Printing, Preschool reading prog, Printer for laptops & handheld devices, Prog for adults, Prog for children & young adult, Ref serv available, Scanner, Senior computer classes, Serves people with intellectual disabilities, STEM programs, Story hour, Summer & winter reading prog, Summer reading prog, Wheelchair accessible, Workshops
Special Services for the Blind - Bks on CD; Daisy reader; Digital talking bk; Large print bks; Playaways (bks on MP3); Talking bks
Open Mon, Wed & Fri 9-5, Tues & Thurs 9-7, Sat 10-4
Branches: 4
CACHE BAY BRANCH, 55 Cache St, Cache Bay, P0H 1G0. (Mail add: PO Box 10, Cache Bay, P0H 1G0), SAN 319-065X. Tel: 705-753-9393. FAX: 705-753-9393. E-mail: cachebay@wnpl.ca. *Br Head,* Deborah Bidal
Open Mon 9-4, Wed 12-6
FIELD BRANCH, 110 Morin St, Field, P0H 1M0. (Mail add: PO Box 10, Field, P0H 1M0), SAN 319-129X. Tel: 705-758-6610. FAX: 705-758-6610. E-mail: field@wnpl.ca. *Br Head,* Gisele Labelle
Founded 1972
Open Mon 10-3, Wed 1-6
RIVER VALLY BRANCH, Seven Forget Ave, River Valley, P0H 1C0. Tel: 705-758-1186. FAX: 705-758-1186. E-mail: rivervalley@wnpl.ca. *Br Head,* Lise Bigras
Open Tues & Thurs 2-6
VERNER BRANCH, 11790 Hwy 64, Verner, P0H 2M0. Tel: 705-594-2800. FAX: 705-594-2800. E-mail: verner@wnpl.ca. *Br Head,* Carole Bidal
Open Tues 10-4, Thurs 12-6

SUDBURY

J CAMBRIAN COLLEGE LIBRARY*, 1400 Barrydowne Rd, 3rd Flr, Rm 3021, P3A 3V8. SAN 368-394X. Tel: 705-524-7333. Information Services Tel: 705-566-8101, Ext 7650. FAX: 705-566-6163. E-mail: library@cambriancollege.ca. Web Site: cambriancollege.ca/academic-services/library, cambriancollege.libguides.com/libraryhomepage. *Libr Mgr,* Marnie Seal; Tel: 705-524-7651, E-mail: marnie.seal@cambriancollege.ca; *Libr Tech,* Hilary Kelly; E-mail: hilary.kelly@cambriancollege.ca; *Libr Tech,* Ellen Mooney; E-mail: ellen.mooney@cambriancollege.ca; Staff 7 (MLS 1, Non-MLS 6)
Founded 1967. Enrl 4,000; Fac 185

Library Holdings: CDs 1,550; DVDs 750; Music Scores 950; Bk Titles 30,000; Per Subs 250; Videos 1,300
Special Collections: College Art Coll
Automation Activity & Vendor Info: (Cataloging) OCLC; (Circulation) Mandarin Library Automation; (OPAC) Mandarin Library Automation
Wireless access
Open Mon-Thurs 8am-2am, Fri 8-8, Sat & Sun 11-10; Mon-Fri 8:30-4:30 (Summer)

P GREATER SUDBURY PUBLIC LIBRARY*, Bibliotheque Publique de Grand Sudbury, 74 MacKenzie St, P3C 4X8. SAN 368-4121. Tel: 705-673-1155. FAX: 705-673-0554. Web Site: www.sudburylibraries.ca/en. *Chief Exec Officer, Chief Librn,* Brian Harding; E-mail: brian.harding@greatersudbury.ca; *Mgr, Libr Heritage Res,* Chelsie Abraham; Staff 49 (MLS 8, Non-MLS 41)
Founded 1912. Pop 155,000
Library Holdings: Bk Vols 600,000
Special Collections: Oral History
Subject Interests: Local hist
Automation Activity & Vendor Info: (Acquisitions) Innovative Interfaces, Inc; (Cataloging) Innovative Interfaces, Inc; (Circulation) Innovative Interfaces, Inc; (Course Reserve) Innovative Interfaces, Inc; (ILL) Innovative Interfaces, Inc; (Media Booking) Innovative Interfaces, Inc; (OPAC) Innovative Interfaces, Inc; (Serials) Innovative Interfaces, Inc
Wireless access
Open Mon & Thurs 8:30am-9pm, Tues, Wed & Fri 8:30-5, Sat 10-2
Friends of the Library Group
Branches: 12
CAPREOL PUBLIC LIBRARY-FRANK R MAZZUCA BRANCH, Citizen Service Ctr, Nine Morin St, Capreol, P0M 1H0, SAN 319-0684. Tel: 705-688-3958. FAX: 705-858-1085. *Lead Librn,* Ginette Mallette
Library Holdings: Bk Vols 13,000; Per Subs 14
Open Mon, Wed & Fri 9-5, Tues & Thurs 12-8
CHELMSFORD PUBLIC LIBRARY-NORMAN HUNEAULT BRANCH, Citizen Service Centre, 3502 Errington St, Chelmsford, P0M 1L0, SAN 319-0781. Tel: 705-688-3963. FAX: 705-855-4629. *Lead Librn,* Lise Paquette-Lalonde
Founded 1971. Pop 14,745; Circ 77,516
Library Holdings: Bk Vols 37,000; Per Subs 143
Open Mon & Wed 8:30-8, Tues, Thurs & Fri 8-5, Sat 10-2
CONISTON PUBLIC LIBRARY-MIKE SOLSKI BRANCH, 30 Second Ave, Coniston, P0M 1M0. Tel: 705-688-3953. FAX: 705-694-0992. *Lead Librn,* Jessica Watts
Open Mon & Thurs 3-8, Tues Noon-5, Wed 10-2
COPPER CLIFF PUBLIC LIBRARY, 11 Balsam St, Copper Cliff, P0M 1N0. (Mail add: PO Box 790, Copper Cliff, P0M 1N0), SAN 368-4156. Tel: 705-688-3954. FAX: 705-682-0484. *Lead Librn,* Jessica Watts
Library Holdings: Bk Vols 20,000
Open Mon & Thurs 3-8, Tues Noon-5, Wed 10-2
DOWLING PUBLIC LIBRARY-LIONEL RHEAUME BRANCH, Citizen Service Centre, 79 Main St W, Dowling, P0M 1R0, SAN 321-7302. Tel: 705-688-3956. FAX: 705-855-2591. *Lead Librn,* Lise Paquette-Lalonde
Library Holdings: Bk Vols 35,000
Open Mon, Wed & Fri 9-5, Tues & Thurs 12-8
Friends of the Library Group
GARSON PUBLIC LIBRARY, Citizen Service Centre, 214 Orell St, Garson, P3L 1V2, SAN 319-1389. Tel: 705-688-3957. FAX: 705-693-5540. *Lead Librn,* Jessica Watts
Founded 1972
Library Holdings: Bk Vols 66,141; Per Subs 36
Open Mon, Wed & Fri 9-5, Tues & Thurs 12-8
LEVACK/ONAPING PUBLIC LIBRARY-EARLE JARVIS BRANCH, One Hillside Ave, Onaping, P0M 2R0, SAN 373-0158. Tel: 705-688-3951. FAX: 705-966-1769. *Lead Librn,* Lise Paquette-Lalonde
Pop 5,954; Circ 54,632
Library Holdings: Bk Vols 15,400; Per Subs 17
Open Mon 10-2, Tues-Thurs 3-8
Friends of the Library Group
LIVELY PUBLIC LIBRARY-EARL MUMFORD BRANCH, Citizen Service Centre, 15 Kin Dr, Unit A, Lively, P3Y 1M3. Tel: 705-688-3959. FAX: 705-692-4261. *Lead Librn,* Jessica Watts
Open Mon & Wed 8:30-8, Tues, Thurs & Fri 8:30-5, Sat 10-2
NEW SUDBURY PUBLIC LIBRARY, 1346 Lasalle Blvd, P3A 1Z6, SAN 368-4245. Tel: 705-688-3952. FAX: 705-524-2868. *Lead Librn,* Rebecca McArthur; Staff 9 (MLS 1, Non-MLS 8)
Founded 1960
Library Holdings: Bk Vols 47,000; Per Subs 100
Special Collections: Children's Story Hour Coll
Open Mon & Thurs 9-9, Tues, Wed & Fri 9-5, Sat 10-2
Friends of the Library Group
AZILDA GILLES PELLAND LIBRARY, 120 Ste-Agnus St, Azilda, P0M 1B0. (Mail add: PO Box 818, Azilda, P0M 1B0), SAN 329-7659. Tel: 705-983-3955. FAX: 705-983-4119. *Lead Librn,* Lise Paquette-Lalonde
Open Mon 10-2, Tues-Thurs 3-8
SOUTH END PUBLIC LIBRARY, 1991 Regent St, P3E 5V3, SAN 368-4210. Tel: 705-688-3950. FAX: 705-522-7788. *Lead Librn,* Rebecca McArthur
Library Holdings: Bk Vols 42,114
Open Mon & Thurs 9-9, Tues, Wed & Fri 9-5, Sat 10-2
VALLEY EAST PUBLIC LIBRARY, Citizen Service Ctr, 4100 Elmview Dr, Hanmer, P3P 1J7, SAN 319-5821. Tel: 705-688-3961. FAX: 705-969-7787. *Lead Librn,* Ginette Mallette; Staff 8 (MLS 1, Non-MLS 7)
Founded 1971
Library Holdings: Bk Vols 70,000; Per Subs 110
Subject Interests: Local hist
Open Mon & Wed 8:30-8, Tues, Thurs & Fri 8:30-5, Sat 10-2

C HUNTINGTON UNIVERSITY*, J W Tate Library, Laurentian Campus, 935 Ramsey Lake Rd, P3E 2C6. SAN 326-5560. Tel: 705-673-4126, Ext 220. FAX: 705-673-6917. E-mail: jwtatelibrary@huntingtonu.ca. Web Site: www.huntingtonu.ca/students/library. *Head Librn,* Dr Natasha Gerolami; Tel: 705-673-4126, Ext 248, E-mail: ngerolami@huntingtonu.ca; Staff 1 (MLS 1)
Founded 1961. Fac 20; Highest Degree: Master
Library Holdings: DVDs 1,000; e-journals 43; Bk Vols 12,115; Per Subs 30; Videos 1,150
Subject Interests: Communication studies, Ethics, Gerontology, Relig studies, Theol
Automation Activity & Vendor Info: (Acquisitions) Evergreen; (Cataloging) Evergreen; (Circulation) Evergreen; (Course Reserve) Evergreen; (OPAC) Evergreen
Wireless access
Function: Prof lending libr
Open Mon-Thurs 9-9, Fri 9-4 (Winter); Mon-Fri 9-4:30 (Summer)

C LAURENTIAN UNIVERSITY LIBRARY & ARCHIVES*, 935 Ramsey Lake Rd, P3E 2C6. SAN 368-4032. Tel: 705-675-4800, Administration Tel: 705-675-1151, Ext 3302. Toll Free Tel: 800-661-1058. FAX: 705-675-4877. E-mail: bibdesmaraislib@laurentian.ca. Web Site: biblio.laurentian.ca. *Univ Librn,* Brent Roe; Tel: 705-675-1151, Ext 4841, E-mail: broe@laurentian.ca; *Librn,* Natasha Gerolami; Tel: 705-675-1151, E-mail: ngerolami@laurentian.ca; *Librn,* Alain Lamothe; Tel: 705-675-1151, Ext 3304, E-mail: alamothe@laurentian.ca; *Librn,* Leila Saadaoui; Tel: 705-675-1151, Ext 3319, E-mail: laadaoui@laurentian.ca; *Librn,* Daniel Scott; Tel: 705-675-1151, Ext 3315, E-mail: dscott@laurentian.ca. Subject Specialists: *Fr lang,* Leila Saadaoui; Staff 13.7 (MLS 5, Non-MLS 8.7)
Founded 1960. Enrl 6,600; Fac 250; Highest Degree: Doctorate
May 2022-Apr 2023. Mats Exp (CAN) $1,700,000. Sal (CAN) $2,000,000
Special Collections: Franco-Ontarienne Coll; Mining Environment
Subject Interests: Admin, Commerce, Educ, Engr, Humanities, Justice, Law, Nursing, Soc work
Automation Activity & Vendor Info: (Acquisitions) Ex Libris Group; (Cataloging) Ex Libris Group; (Circulation) Ex Libris Group; (Course Reserve) Ex Libris Group; (Discovery) Ex Libris Group; (ILL) OCLC WorldShare Interlibrary Loan; (Media Booking) Ex Libris Group; (OPAC) Ex Libris Group; (Serials) Ex Libris Group
Wireless access
Publications: Regional & Local Bibliographies
Partic in Canadian Research Knowledge Network; Ontario Council of University Libraries
Open Mon-Thurs 9am-10pm, Fri 9-8, Sat & Sun Noon-8pm

G MINISTRY OF NORTHERN DEVELOPMENT & MINES*, John B Gammon Geoscience Library, 933 Ramsey Lake Rd, Level A-3, P3E 6B5. SAN 319-5376. Tel: 705-670-5614. Toll Free Tel: 888-415-9845, Ext 5614. FAX: 705-670-5770. E-mail: mines.library.ndm@ontario.ca. Web Site: www.infogo.gov.on.ca/infogo/home.html#orgProfile/7101/en. *Archives, Tech, Libr Tech,* Johanne Roux; Staff 1 (Non-MLS 1)
Library Holdings: Bk Vols 100,000; Per Subs 40
Subject Interests: Engr geol, Geol of Ont, Maps, Mining, Theses
Automation Activity & Vendor Info: (Cataloging) Inmagic, Inc.
Open Mon-Fri 8:30-5

C UNIVERSITY OF SUDBURY LIBRARY*, 935 Ramsey Lake Rd, P3E 2C6. SAN 319-4388. Tel: 705-673-5661. FAX: 705-673-4912. Web Site: www.usudbury.ca. *Dir, Libr & Archives,* Paul Laverdure; Tel: 705-673-5661, Ext 208, E-mail: plaverdure@usudbury.ca; *IT Tech,* Patrick Picard; E-mail: ppicard@usudbury.ca; Staff 1 (Non-MLS 1)
Founded 1958. Highest Degree: Bachelor
Library Holdings: Bk Vols 30,000; Per Subs 80
Special Collections: College Sacre-Coeur de Sudbury; French Canadian Folklore (Luc Lacourciere Coll); Jesuit Archives
Subject Interests: Ethnology, Folklore, Indigenous studies, Journalism, Philos, Relig studies
Automation Activity & Vendor Info: (Acquisitions) OMNI; (Cataloging) OMNI; (Circulation) OMNI; (OPAC) OMNI; (Serials) EBSCO Discovery Service

Wireless access
Function: Archival coll, Art exhibits, AV serv, Bk club(s), Computers for patron use, Distance learning, Doc delivery serv, Electronic databases & coll, Equip loans & repairs, ILL available, Internet access, Magazines, Movies, Music CDs, Online cat, Orientations, Outside serv via phone, mail, e-mail & web, Photocopying/Printing, Ref serv available, Study rm, Wheelchair accessible, Workshops
Restriction: Authorized patrons, Authorized personnel only, Authorized scholars by appt, Borrowing requests are handled by ILL, Open by appt only

SUNDRIDGE

P SUNDRIDGE-STRONG UNION PUBLIC LIBRARY*, 110 Main St, P0A 1Z0. (Mail add: PO Box 429, P0A 1Z0), SAN 319-440X. Tel: 705-384-7311. FAX: 705-384-7311. E-mail: sundridgelibrary@gmail.com. Web Site: sundridge.olsn.ca. *Librn,* Melinda Kent; *Asst Librn,* Penny Erven
Founded 1978. Pop 2,800; Circ 12,000
Library Holdings: Braille Volumes 4; CDs 200; DVDs 900; e-books 147,141; Large Print Bks 5,000; Bk Titles 10,069; Bk Vols 10,116; Per Subs 17; Talking Bks 75
Special Collections: Legos & Puzzles; Local History Coll
Automation Activity & Vendor Info: (Acquisitions) SirsiDynix-WorkFlows; (Cataloging) SirsiDynix-WorkFlows; (Circulation) SirsiDynix-WorkFlows; (Serials) SirsiDynix-WorkFlows
Wireless access
Function: 24/7 Electronic res, 24/7 Online cat, Archival coll, Audiobks on Playaways & MP3, Audiobks via web, Bk club(s), Bks on CD, Children's prog, Computers for patron use, Digital talking bks, Electronic databases & coll, ILL available, Internet access, Laminating, Large print keyboards, Life-long learning prog for all ages, Magazines, Makerspace, Online cat, OverDrive digital audio bks, Photocopying/Printing, Preschool reading prog, Printer for laptops & handheld devices, Scanner, Summer reading prog
Partic in Ont Libr Serv-North
Special Services for the Blind - Bks on CD; Daisy reader; Digital talking bk; Large print bks; Playaways (bks on MP3)
Open Mon, Fri & Sat 10-3, Tues 10-5, Wed 10-3 & 6:30-8:30, Thurs 1:30-6:30

TERRACE BAY

P TERRACE BAY PUBLIC LIBRARY*, 13 Selkirk Ave, P0T 2W0. (Mail add: PO Box 369, P0T 2W0), SAN 319-4418. Tel: 807-825-3315, Ext 222. FAX: 807-825-1249. E-mail: library@terracebay.ca. Web Site: terracebay.library.on.ca. *Chief Exec Officer,* Mary Deschatelets; Tel: 807-825-3315, Ext 234, E-mail: m.deschatelets@terracebay.ca
Founded 1947. Pop 1,650; Circ 20,700
Library Holdings: Bk Titles 18,000; Bk Vols 20,000; Per Subs 50
Subject Interests: Foreign lang, Local hist
Automation Activity & Vendor Info: (Acquisitions) SirsiDynix-WorkFlows; (Cataloging) SirsiDynix-WorkFlows; (Circulation) SirsiDynix-WorkFlows; (ILL) SirsiDynix-WorkFlows; (OPAC) SirsiDynix-iBistro; (Serials) SirsiDynix-WorkFlows
Wireless access
Function: Archival coll, Audio & video playback equip for onsite use, CD-ROM, Computer training, Electronic databases & coll, Homebound delivery serv, ILL available, Internet access, Magnifiers for reading, Mail & tel request accepted, Orientations, Photocopying/Printing, Preschool outreach, Prog for children & young adult, Senior computer classes, Spoken cassettes & CDs, Spoken cassettes & DVDs, Summer reading prog, Telephone ref, VHS videos, Wheelchair accessible
Publications: Birchwood Terrace (Local historical information); History of Jackfish (Local historical information); Terrace Bay - First 50 Years (Local historical information)
Special Services for the Deaf - Bks on deafness & sign lang
Special Services for the Blind - Audio mat; Bks & mags in Braille, on rec, tape & cassette; Bks on cassette; Bks on CD; Braille bks; Cassette playback machines; Daisy reader; Large print bks; Large screen computer & software; Talking bks
Open Mon-Wed 10-5 & 6-8, Thurs & Fri 10-5, Sat (Winter) 12:30-4:30

THESSALON

P THESSALON PUBLIC LIBRARY*, 187 Main St, P0R 1L0. (Mail add: PO Box 549, P0R 1L0). Tel: 705-842-2306. FAX: 705-842-5690. E-mail: thessalonlib@hotmail.com. Web Site: www.thesslibcap.com. *Chief Exec Officer, Librn,* Norma LeBlanc
Library Holdings: Bk Vols 10,000
Wireless access
Open Mon 1-5, Tues, Thurs & Fri 1-5 & 7-9, Wed 9-1, Sat 10-1

THORNBURY

P THE BLUE MOUNTAINS PUBLIC LIBRARY*, Leonard E Shore Memorial Library, 173 Bruce St S, N0H 2P0. (Mail add: PO Box 580, N0H 2P0), SAN 319-4426. Tel: 519-599-3681. FAX: 519-599-7951. E-mail: libraryinfo@thebluemountains.ca. Web Site: www.thebluemountainslibrary.ca. *Pub Serv,* Emma Barker; *Tech Serv,* Elisa Chandler
Founded 1995. Pop 6,500; Circ 80,000
Library Holdings: Bk Vols 40,000; Per Subs 48
Wireless access
Function: Audiobks on Playaways & MP3, Audiobks via web, Bk club(s), Bks on CD, Children's prog, Computer training, Computers for patron use, Electronic databases & coll, Equip loans & repairs, Family literacy, For res purposes, Free DVD rentals, Holiday prog, Home delivery & serv to seniorr ctr & nursing homes, Homebound delivery serv, ILL available, Internet access, Large print keyboards, Life-long learning prog for all ages, Magazines, Mail & tel request accepted, Mango lang, Meeting rooms, Microfiche/film & reading machines, Movies, Online cat, Online ref, Outreach serv, OverDrive digital audio bks, Photocopying/Printing, Preschool outreach, Preschool reading prog, Printer for laptops & handheld devices, Prof lending libr, Prog for adults, Prog for children & young adult, Ref & res, Ref serv available, Scanner, Senior computer classes, Senior outreach, Serves people with intellectual disabilities, Story hour, Summer & winter reading prog, Summer reading prog, Teen prog, Visual arts prog, Wheelchair accessible, Winter reading prog, Workshops, Writing prog
Mem of Ontario Library Service
Open Mon, Wed, Fri & Sat 10-5, Tues & Thurs 10-7

THORNHILL

S ANTHROPOSOPHICAL SOCIETY IN CANADA LIBRARY*, 130A-1 Hesperus Rd, L4J 0G9. Tel: 416-892-3656. Toll Free Tel: 877-892-3656. FAX: 905-886-4989. E-mail: info@anthroposophy.ca. Web Site: www.anthroposophy.ca/en/membership/resources. *Adminr,* Jeffrey Saunders
Founded 1953
Library Holdings: Bk Titles 3,100; Bk Vols 4,000; Per Subs 12
Subject Interests: Anthroposophy, esp the works of Rudolf Steiner

THOROLD

P THOROLD PUBLIC LIBRARY*, 14 Ormond St N, L2V 1Y8. SAN 368-427X. Tel: 905-227-2581. E-mail: info@thoroldpubliclibrary.ca. Web Site: www.thoroldpubliclibrary.ca. *Chief Librn,* Joanne DeQuadros; *Pub Serv Librn,* Rebecca Lazarenko; E-mail: rlazarenko@thoroldpubliclibrary.ca; *Libr Tech,* Cheryl Bowman; E-mail: cheryl@thoroldpubliclibrary.ca; Staff 3 (MLS 2, Non-MLS 1)
Founded 1858. Pop 18,500; Circ 175,000
Library Holdings: Bk Vols 83,000; Per Subs 27
Special Collections: Fred Campbell Coll, photog, scrapbks; Thorold History; Thorold Sports Reunion Photographs
Subject Interests: Genealogy, Local hist
Automation Activity & Vendor Info: (Cataloging) Evergreen; (Circulation) Evergreen; (OPAC) Evergreen
Wireless access
Friends of the Library Group

THUNDER BAY

L BUSET LLP*, Law Library, 1121 Barton St, P7B 5N3. SAN 372-3534. Tel: 807-623-2500. FAX: 807-622-7808. Web Site: busetlaw.com. *Librn,* Carolyn Enns; E-mail: cenns@busetlaw.com; Staff 1 (Non-MLS 1)
Library Holdings: Bk Vols 2,800
Subject Interests: Aboriginal law, Civil litigation, Commercial law, Corporate law, Employment law, Estates, Family law, Ins, Labor law, Municipal law, Personal injury, Real estate, Taxation, Wills
Wireless access

J CONFEDERATION COLLEGE LIBRARY*, Paterson Library Commons, 1450 Nakina Dr, P7C 4W1. (Mail add: PO Box 398, P7C 4W1), SAN 319-4469. Circulation Tel: 807-475-6219. E-mail: infodesk@confederationcollege.ca. Web Site: www.confederationcollege.ca/department/library. *Libr Mgr,* Dayna DeBenedet; Tel: 807-475-6639, E-mail: ddebenedet@confederationcollege.ca; Staff 8 (MLS 1, Non-MLS 7)
Founded 1967. Enrl 3,186; Fac 144
Library Holdings: AV Mats 4,559; e-books 5,000; High Interest/Low Vocabulary Bk Vols 100; Bk Vols 27,000; Per Subs 318
Subject Interests: Aboriginal studies, Applied arts, Learning disabilities, Literacy, Women's studies
Automation Activity & Vendor Info: (Acquisitions) SirsiDynix; (Cataloging) SirsiDynix; (Circulation) SirsiDynix; (Course Reserve) SirsiDynix; (OPAC) SirsiDynix; (Serials) SirsiDynix
Wireless access
Function: Archival coll, Audio & video playback equip for onsite use, AV serv, Computers for patron use, Electronic databases & coll, Equip loans &

repairs, ILL available, Internet access, Music CDs, Online cat, Online ref, Photocopying/Printing, Ref serv available, Scanner, Telephone ref, VHS videos, Wheelchair accessible
Publications: Faculty Focus (Newsletter); Faculty Information Guide (Library handbook); General Guide to the Paterson Library Commons (Reference guide); LibGuides (Online only); Program Resource Guide (Reference guide); What's New (Newsletter)
Special Services for the Deaf - Assistive tech; Bks on deafness & sign lang; Closed caption videos; High interest/low vocabulary bks; TDD equip
Special Services for the Blind - Assistive/Adapted tech devices, equip & products; Bks on cassette; GEAC Advance
Open Mon-Thurs 8-8, Fri 8-4:30, Sat & Sun 12-5

G FORT WILLIAM HISTORICAL PARK*, Jean Morrison Canadian Fur Trade Library, 1350 King Rd, P7K 1L7. SAN 324-203X. Tel: 807-473-2337, 807-473-2344. E-mail: info@fwhp.ca, library@fwhp.ca. Web Site: fwhp.ca/our-collection/library.
Library Holdings: Bk Titles 5,000; Per Subs 60
Special Collections: Contains materials related to Fort William and the early 19th century British North American fur trade including the Selkirk Papers, copies of North West Company and Hudson's Bay Company papers from the Archives of Canada, engagé contracts from the Archives Nationales du Quebec, archival material from the Fort William Archaeological Project, and National Heritage League papers following the reconstruction of Fort William Historical Park.
Subject Interests: Fur trade, Trade
Wireless access
Restriction: Open by appt only

C LAKEHEAD UNIVERSITY*, Chancellor Paterson Library, 955 Oliver Rd, P7B 5E1. SAN 368-4369. Tel: 807-343-8205. Circulation Tel: 807-343-8225. Interlibrary Loan Service Tel: 807-343-8135. Information Services Tel: 807-343-8165. FAX: 807-343-8007. Reference E-mail: circdesk@lakeheadu.ca. Web Site: library.lakeheadu.ca. *Univ Librn,* Robin Canuel; Tel: 807-343-8010, Ext 8125, E-mail: rcanuel@lakeheadu.ca; *Univ Archivist,* Sara Janes; Tel: 807-252-8010, Ext 8272, E-mail: sjanes1@lakeheadu.ca; *Head, Coll Serv,* Evelyn Feldman; Tel: 807-343-8856, E-mail: efeldman@lakeheadu.ca; *Head, Digital Initiatives,* Qing (Jason) Zou; Tel: 807-343-8251, E-mail: qzou@lakeheadu.ca; *Copyright Librn, Health Sci Librn,* Debra Gold; Tel: 807-343-8129, E-mail: debra.gold@lakeheadu.ca; *Educ Librn,* Gisella Scalese; Tel: 807-343-8719, E-mail: gscalese@lakeheadu.ca; *Scholarly Communications Librn,* Nicole Stradiotto; Tel: 807-343-8315, E-mail: nicole.stradiotto@lakeheadu.ca; *Makerspace Librn,* Valerie Gibbons; E-mail: valerie.gibbons@lakeheadu.ca; *Spec Coll Librn,* Trudy Russo; Tel: 807-343-8302, E-mail: trusso@lakeheadu.ca; *User Experience Librn,* Janice Mutz; Tel: 807-343-8147, E-mail: jmutz@lakeheadu.ca; Staff 11 (MLS 11)
Founded 1948. Enrl 7,671; Fac 317; Highest Degree: Doctorate
Library Holdings: Microforms 491,222; Bk Titles 333,777; Bk Vols 352,126
Special Collections: Local Finnish History; Northern Studies
Automation Activity & Vendor Info: (Acquisitions) Ex Libris Group; (Cataloging) Ex Libris Group; (Circulation) Ex Libris Group; (Course Reserve) Ex Libris Group; (OPAC) Ex Libris Group; (Serials) Ex Libris Group
Wireless access
Partic in Ontario Council of University Libraries
Open Mon-Thurs 8am-11:30pm, Fri 8am-9pm, Sat 10-7, Sun (Sept-March) 11-9

Departmental Libraries:

EDUCATION LIBRARY, Bora Laskin Bldg, 1st Flr, 955 Oliver Rd, P7B 5E1, SAN 368-4393. Tel: 807-343-8718. FAX: 807-346-8007. E-mail: edlib@lakeheadu.ca. Web Site: library.lakeheadu.ca/libraries-and-collections/education. *Educ Librn,* Gisella Scalese; Tel: 807-343-8719, E-mail: gscalese@lakeheadu.ca; *Libr Tech,* Elisabeth Boileau; Tel: 807-343-8718, E-mail: eboileau@lakeheadu.ca
Library Holdings: Microforms 453,243; Bk Titles 40,000
Subject Interests: Educ

ORILLIA, 500 University Ave, Orillia, L3Z 0B9. Tel: 705-330-4010, Ext 2250. E-mail: orlib@lakeheadu.ca. Web Site: library.lakeheadu.ca/libraries-and-collections/harvie-legacy-library. *Librn,* Chris Tomasini; Tel: 705-330-2260, E-mail: ctomasin@lakeheadu.ca
Library Holdings: Bk Titles 10,000
Open Mon-Thurs 8am-7:30pm, Fri 8-5, Sat 11-4

S NORTHWESTERN ONTARIO SPORTS HALL OF FAME LIBRARY*, 219 May St S, P7E 1B5. SAN 373-8248. Tel: 807-622-2852. FAX: 807-622-2736. E-mail: nwosport@tbaytel.net. Web Site: www.nwosportshalloffame.com. *Exec Dir,* Diane Imrie; *Curator,* Kathryn Dwyer; Staff 2 (Non-MLS 2)
Founded 1978
Library Holdings: Bk Vols 1,000
Subject Interests: Sports hist
Function: Archival coll
Open Tues-Sat 12-5

S THUNDER BAY HISTORICAL MUSEUM SOCIETY*, Dr Thorold Tronrud Research Library, 425 Donald St E, P7E 5V1. SAN 329-1642. Tel: 807-623-0801. FAX: 807-622-6880. E-mail: info@thunderbaymuseum.com. Web Site: www.thunderbaymuseum.com. *Exec Dir,* Scott Bradley; E-mail: director@thunderbaymuseum.com; *Archivist, Curator,* Michael deJong; E-mail: curatorial@thunderbaymuseum.com; Staff 1 (MLS 1)
Founded 1908
Library Holdings: Bk Titles 3,500; Per Subs 4
Special Collections: Archival Coll. Oral History
Wireless access
Publications: The Thunder Bay Historical Museum Society Papers & Records (Annual)
Restriction: Non-circulating to the pub, Open by appt only

L THUNDER BAY LAW ASSOCIATION LIBRARY*, Thunder Bay Courthouse, 2nd Flr, 125 Brodie St N, P7C 0A3. SAN 328-235X. Tel: 807-344-3481. FAX: 807-345-9091. E-mail: library@tbla.ca. Web Site: www.tbla.ca. *Librn,* Helen Heerema; Staff 1 (Non-MLS 1)
Founded 1905
Library Holdings: Bk Vols 4,850; Per Subs 5
Wireless access
Open Mon-Fri 9-4:30

P THUNDER BAY PUBLIC LIBRARY*, Waverley Community Hub, 285 Red River Rd, P7B 1A9. SAN 368-4423. Tel: 807-345-8275. Reference Tel: 807-624-4200. Administration Tel: 807-684-6803. FAX: 807-345-8727. Administration FAX: 807-344-5119. E-mail: comments@tbpl.ca. Reference E-mail: reference@tbpl.ca. Web Site: www.tbpl.ca. *Chief Librn/CEO,* John Pateman; Tel: 807-684-6802, E-mail: jpateman@tbpl.ca; *Dir of Communities,* Tina Tucker; Tel: 807-684-6813, E-mail: ttucker@tbpl.ca; *Dir of Coll,* Angela Meady; Tel: 807-684-6810, E-mail: ameady@tbpl.ca; *Dir, Libr Res,* Cherri Braye; Tel: 807-684-6804, E-mail: cbraye@tbpl.ca; *Dir, Libr Syst,* Stephen Hurrell; Tel: 807-684-6807, E-mail: shurrell@tbpl.ca
Founded 1970. Pop 109,000; Circ 921,369
Automation Activity & Vendor Info: (Acquisitions) Innovative Interfaces, Inc - Millennium; (Cataloging) Innovative Interfaces, Inc - Millennium; (Circulation) Innovative Interfaces, Inc - Millennium
Wireless access
Publications: Annual Report; Newsletter (Quarterly)
Special Services for the Blind - Audio mat; Bks on cassette; Bks on CD; Children's Braille; Daisy reader; Home delivery serv; Internet workstation with adaptive software; Large print & cassettes; Large print bks; Magnifiers
Open Mon-Thurs 10-9, Fri & Sat 10-5, Sun 1-5
Friends of the Library Group

Branches: 3

MARY J L BLACK COMMUNITY HUB, 901 S Edward St, P7E 6R2, SAN 368-4482. Tel: 807-345-8275. FAX: 807-475-7855.
Library Holdings: Bk Vols 42,692
Open Mon, Wed, Fri & Sat 10-5, Tues & Thurs 1-9
Friends of the Library Group

BRODIE COMMUNITY HUB, 216 S Brodie St, P7E 1C2, SAN 368-4512. Tel: 807-345-8275. Reference Tel: 807-624-4200. FAX: 807-623-0875.
Founded 1911
Library Holdings: Bk Vols 108,788
Open Mon-Wed 10-9, Thurs-Sat 10-5, Sun 12-4

COUNTY PARK COMMUNITY HUB, 1020 Dawson Rd, P7B 1K6, SAN 368-4520. Tel: 807-345-8275. FAX: 807-768-0233.
Library Holdings: Bk Vols 30,949
Open Mon & Tues 1-6, Wed Noon-8, Thurs-Sat 10-5, Sun Noon-4

TIMMINS

S OJIBWAY & CREE CULTURAL CENTRE*, 150 Brousseau Ave, Unit B, P4N 5Y4. SAN 329-1723. Tel: 705-267-7911. FAX: 705-267-4988. E-mail: info@occc.ca. Web Site: www.occc.ca. *Exec Dir,* Dianne Riopel; Staff 1 (MLS 1)
Library Holdings: Bk Titles 6,500
Special Collections: Native Oriented Resource Centre. Oral History
Open Mon-Fri 8:30-4:30

P TIMMINS PUBLIC LIBRARY*, 320 Second Ave, P4N 4A8. SAN 368-4547. Tel: 705-360-2623, Ext 8519. FAX: 705-360-2688. E-mail: library@timmins.ca. Web Site: tpl.timmins.ca. *Chief Exec Officer,* Carole-Ann Demers; E-mail: caroleann.demers@timmins.ca; Staff 2 (MLS 2)
Founded 1924. Pop 41,788
Library Holdings: Bk Titles 96,155; Bk Vols 110,839
Special Collections: Northern Ontario Heritage Coll
Subject Interests: Mining

Automation Activity & Vendor Info: (Acquisitions) SirsiDynix; (Cataloging) SirsiDynix; (Circulation) SirsiDynix-WorkFlows; (OPAC) SirsiDynix-Enterprise; (Serials) SirsiDynix
Wireless access
Function: 24/7 Electronic res, 24/7 Online cat, Activity rm, Adult bk club, Bks on CD, Children's prog, Computer training, Computers for patron use, Electronic databases & coll, Free DVD rentals, ILL available, Internet access, Laminating, Magazines, Prog for adults, Prog for children & young adult, Ref serv available, Scanner, Senior computer classes, Study rm, Summer reading prog, Teen prog
Open Mon-Thurs 10-8, Fri & Sat 10-5, Sun (Sept-June) 1-5
Branches: 1
C M SHIELDS CENTENNIAL BRANCH, 99 Bloor Ave, South Porcupine, P0N 1H0, SAN 368-4601. Tel: 705-360-2623, Ext 8590. FAX: 705-360-2688. *Br Head,* Louise Gaudette; E-mail: louise.gaudette@timmins.ca
Circ 18,455
Library Holdings: Bk Vols 18,747; Per Subs 30
Function: 24/7 Electronic res, 24/7 Online cat, Children's prog, Electronic databases & coll, Free DVD rentals, Photocopying/Printing, Prog for adults, STEM programs, Summer reading prog
Open Mon 10-5, Tues & Wed Noon-8, Thurs-Sat 9-5; Mon 10-5, Tues & Wed Noon-8, Thurs & Fri 9-5 (Summer)

TORONTO

L AIRD & BERLIS LLP, Law Library, Brookfield Pl, Ste 1800, 181 Bay St, M5J 2T9. (Mail add: PO Box 754, M5J 2T9), SAN 326-8551. Tel: 416-863-1500. FAX: 416-863-1515. Web Site: www.airdberlis.com. *Supvr, Libr Serv,* Ken Cummings; Staff 1.5 (MLS 1, Non-MLS 0.5)
Library Holdings: Bk Vols 3,000; Per Subs 200
Automation Activity & Vendor Info: (OPAC) Inmagic, Inc.
Restriction: Not open to pub

S R V ANDERSON ASSOCIATES LTD LIBRARY*, 2001 Sheppard Ave E, Ste 400, M2J 4Z8. SAN 370-5471. Tel: 416-497-8600, Ext 1230. FAX: 416-497-0342. Web Site: www.rvanderson.com. *Library Contact,* Leah Swift; E-mail: lswift@rvanderson.com; Staff 2 (MLS 1, Non-MLS 1)
Library Holdings: Bk Titles 5,764; Per Subs 234
Automation Activity & Vendor Info: (Acquisitions) Inmagic, Inc.; (Cataloging) Inmagic, Inc.; (Circulation) Inmagic, Inc.; (ILL) Inmagic, Inc.; (OPAC) Inmagic, Inc.
Function: Ref & res
Open Mon-Fri 9-5
Restriction: Circulates for staff only

S ARCADIS CORPORATE LIBRARY, (Formerly IBI Group Library), 55 St Clair Ave W, 7th Flr, M4V 2Y7. SAN 323-7362. Tel: 416-596-1930, Ext 61332. *Coop Librn,* Jennifer Osther; E-mail: jennifer.osther@arcadis.com; *Libr Tech,* Karin Valdmanis; *Libr Tech,* Cindy Wong; Staff 3 (MLS 2, Non-MLS 1)
Founded 1974
Library Holdings: Bk Titles 800; Bk Vols 4,000; Per Subs 70
Special Collections: Reports by IBI Group
Subject Interests: Archit, Transportation, Urban design, Urban planning
Automation Activity & Vendor Info: (Cataloging) Lucidea - GeniePlus; (Circulation) Lucidea - GeniePlus; (OPAC) Lucidea - GeniePlus; (Serials) Lucidea - GeniePlus
Wireless access
Function: Electronic databases & coll, ILL available, Internet access, Orientations, Ref & res, Res libr
Restriction: Borrowing requests are handled by ILL, Employees only

G ARCHIVES OF ONTARIO LIBRARY, 134 Ian Macdonald Blvd, M7A 2C5. SAN 319-4574. Tel: 416-327-1600. Toll Free Tel: 800-668-9933. FAX: 416-327-1999. Reference E-mail: reference@ontario.ca. Web Site: www.archives.gov.on.ca. *Librn,* Frank van Kalmthout; E-mail: frank.vankalmthout@ontario.ca; Staff 1 (MLS 1)
Founded 1903
Library Holdings: Per Subs 25
Special Collections: Historical Pamphlets; Imperial Blue Books; Ontario Government Publications; Ontario Municipal Publications; Ontario School Textbooks; Ontario Voters Lists
Subject Interests: Archival sci, Conserv, Info mgt, Local hist, Ont govt publications, Ont hist, Presv
Automation Activity & Vendor Info: (Acquisitions) MINISIS Inc; (Cataloging) MINISIS Inc; (OPAC) MINISIS Inc
Wireless access
Function: Online cat
Partic in Ont Govt Libr Coun
Open Mon-Fri 8:30-5

S THE ARQUIVES: CANADA'S LGBTQ2S+ ARCHIVES*, James Fraser Library, 34 Isabella St, M4Y 1N1. (Mail add: PO Box 699, STN F, 663 Yonge St, M4Y 2N6), SAN 321-6691. Tel: 416-777-2755. E-mail: queeries@arquives.ca. Web Site: www.arquives.ca. Staff 4 (MLS 2, Non-MLS 2)
Founded 1973
Library Holdings: Bk Vols 10,000; Per Subs 6,100; Spec Interest Per Sub 2,300
Special Collections: Audio-visual Coll; Poster Coll; Realia Coll; Vertical Files Coll. Canadian and Provincial; Oral History
Subject Interests: Bisexual, Gay, Homosexuality, Lesbian
Function: Art exhibits
Publications: Gay Archivies (Newsletter); Lesbian & Gay Archivist (Newsletter); Photographs Catalogue & Finding Aid
Open Tues-Thurs 6:30-9, Fri 1-5
Restriction: Closed stack, Non-circulating, Not a lending libr, Off-site coll in storage - retrieval as requested

S ART GALLERY OF ONTARIO*, Edward P Taylor Library & Archives, 317 Dundas St W, M5T 1G4. SAN 319-4582. Tel: 416-979-6642. FAX: 416-979-6602. E-mail: library.archives@ago.ca. Web Site: ago.ca/research/library-and-archives. *Head of Libr & Archives,* Amy Furness; *Outreach Librn, Programming Librn,* Adrienne Connelly; *Ref Librn,* Donald Rance; *Archivist,* Marilyn Nazar; *Cataloger,* Deborah Mills. Subject Specialists: *Can art, Spec coll,* Amy Furness; *Artists bks,* Donald Rance; *Can art,* Marilyn Nazar; Staff 5 (MLS 5)
Founded 1933
Library Holdings: Bk Vols 300,000; Per Subs 450
Special Collections: Art Sales Catalogues, 1800-current; Artist Documentation Files; Canadian Art & Artists' Archives; Exhibition Catalogues; Fine Illustrated Books; Museum Archives & Records
Subject Interests: Can art, European decorative arts (15th-19th century), European miniature painting, Hist of Western art, Photog, Tribal art (Oceania, North Am)
Automation Activity & Vendor Info: (Acquisitions) SirsiDynix; (Cataloging) SirsiDynix; (Circulation) SirsiDynix; (OPAC) SirsiDynix; (Serials) SirsiDynix
Wireless access
Function: Archival coll, Art exhibits, Computers for patron use, E-Reserves, ILL available, Internet access, Microfiche/film & reading machines, Online cat, Online ref, Outreach serv, Outside serv via phone, mail, e-mail & web, Photocopying/Printing, Prog for adults, Ref serv available, Res libr, Study rm, Wheelchair accessible
Restriction: Non-circulating, Open by appt only, Open to pub for ref only, Open to students

S ARTS & LETTERS CLUB LIBRARY*, 14 Elm St, M5G 1G7. SAN 325-2035. Tel: 416-597-0223. FAX: 416-597-9544. E-mail: archives@artsandlettersclub.ca. Information Services E-mail: info@artsandlettersclub.ca. Web Site: www.artsandlettersclub.ca. *Librn,* William Denton; *Archivist,* Scott James
Founded 1908
Library Holdings: Bk Titles 4,700; Bk Vols 5,950; Per Subs 24
Special Collections: Canadian Art Coll, ms
Subject Interests: Archit, Art, Can, Lit, Painting, Theatre
Publications: Lampsletters (Newsletter)
Restriction: Not open to pub

R BETH TZEDEC CONGREGATION*, Max & Beatrice Wolfe Library, 1700 Bathurst St, M5P 3K3. SAN 319-4639. Tel: 416-781-3514, Ext 225. Administration Tel: 416-781-3511. FAX: 416-781-0150. E-mail: info@beth-tzedec.org. Web Site: www.beth-tzedec.org. *Dir of Educ, Dir, Programming,* Daniel Silverman; E-mail: dsilverman@beth-tzedec.org; Staff 2 (MLS 2)
Founded 1956
Library Holdings: Bk Vols 13,000; Per Subs 15
Subject Interests: Hebraica, Judaica
Automation Activity & Vendor Info: (Acquisitions) Follett Software; (Cataloging) Follett Software; (Circulation) Follett Software
Publications: Beth Tzedec Congregation Bulletin
Partic in Asn of Jewish Librs
Open Mon 10-6, Tues 9-6, Wed 12:30-6, Sun 10-2

L BLAKE, CASSELS & GRAYDON LLP*, Law Library, Commerce Ct W, 199 Bay St, Ste 4000, M5L 1A9. SAN 319-4647. Tel: 416-863-2650. Reference Tel: 416-863-3885. FAX: 416-863-2653. E-mail: research@blakes.com. Web Site: blakes.com. *Supvr, Libr Res,* Brenda Desjardins; *Mgr, Res Serv,* Leanne Notenboom; *Coordr, Electronic Res,* Harsev Gill; E-mail: harsev.gill@blakes.com; Staff 7 (MLS 2, Non-MLS 5)
Founded 1858
Library Holdings: Electronic Media & Resources 400; Bk Titles 5,000; Per Subs 350
Special Collections: Blakes Historical Coll; Lex Mundi Files; Statutes - Provincial, Canada, International
Subject Interests: Commercial law, Computer, Constitutional, Corporate law, Entertainment, Environ law, Estates, Insolvency, Intellectual property, Litigation, Real estate, Securities law, Tax

Wireless access
Function: ILL available
Publications: Blakes Current Law (Newsletter)
Restriction: Staff use only

L BLANEY MCMURTRY LLP*, Law Library, Two Queen St E, Ste 1500, M5C 3G5. SAN 324-0517. Tel: 416-593-1221, Ext 3550. FAX: 416-593-5437. E-mail: info@blaney.com. Web Site: www.blaney.com. Staff 1 (Non-MLS 1)

M BRIDGEPOINT ACTIVE HEALTHCARE*, Health Science Library, One Bridgepoint Dr, M4M 2B5. SAN 372-5871. Tel: 416-461-8252, Ext 2436. E-mail: clinicallibrary@sinaihealth.ca. *Clinical Libr Tech,* Patricia Petruga; Staff 1 (Non-MLS 1)
Library Holdings: Bk Titles 200; Per Subs 4
Wireless access
Partic in Health Science Information Consortium of Toronto
Restriction: Staff use only

SR CANADIAN BIBLE SOCIETY LIBRARY*, Ten Carnforth Rd, M4A 2S4. SAN 326-5366. Tel: 416-757-4171. FAX: 416-757-3376. Web Site: biblesociety.ca. *Library Contact,* Joanna Costopoulos; E-mail: jcostopoulos@biblesociety.ca
Library Holdings: Bk Vols 400; Per Subs 15
Special Collections: Old Bibles, 1477-1900s (CBS Library Museum), bks; Scripture in languages other than English (World Scriptures Coll), bks, pamphlets

CANADIAN BROADCASTING CORP
G RADIO ARCHIVES*, 205 Wellington St W, M5G 3G7. (Mail add: Box 500 Sta A, M5W 1E6), SAN 372-5863. Tel: 416-205-5880. FAX: 416-205-8602. *Mgr,* Allison Lennox; *Sr Librn,* Elizabeth Headlam; *Sr Librn,* Linda Partington; *Sr Librn,* Ken Puley; *Coordr,* Heather Palmer
Founded 1959
Library Holdings: Bk Vols 1,900
Subject Interests: Current events, Drama, Music
Restriction: Open by appt only

G REFERENCE & IMAGE RESEARCH LIBRARIES*, 250 Front St W, M5V 3G5. (Mail add: PO Box 500, Sta A, M5W 1E6), SAN 368-4849. Tel: 416-205-3244. FAX: 416-205-3733. E-mail: reference_library@cbc.ca. *Mgr,* Stew Moore; Tel: 416-205-7153, E-mail: stew.moore@cbc.ca; Staff 10 (MLS 3, Non-MLS 7)
Founded 1946
Library Holdings: Bk Titles 20,000; Per Subs 150
Special Collections: CBC Still Photo Coll
Subject Interests: Broadcasting media, Canadiana, Gen news
Automation Activity & Vendor Info: (Acquisitions) Inmagic, Inc.; (Cataloging) Inmagic, Inc.; (Circulation) Inmagic, Inc.; (Serials) Inmagic, Inc.
Restriction: Internal use only, Limited access for the pub

S CANADIAN COPPER & BRASS DEVELOPMENT ASSOCIATION LIBRARY*, 65 Overlea Blvd, Ste 210, M4H 1P1. SAN 373-7012. Tel: 416-391-5599. FAX: 416-391-3823. E-mail: library@copperalliance.ca. Web Site: en.coppercanada.ca. *Exec Dir,* Stephen J Knapp
Founded 1965
Library Holdings: Bk Titles 400; Per Subs 65

L CANADIAN ENVIRONMENTAL LAW FOUNDATION, Resource Library for the Environment & the Law, (Formerly Canadian Environmental Law Association), 55 University Ave, Ste 1500, M5J 2H7. SAN 325-0261. Tel: 416-960-2284. FAX: 416-960-9392. Web Site: celafoundation.ca. *Info Coordr,* Kesi Disha; Tel: 416-960-2284, Ext 7211, E-mail: kesi@cela.ca
Library Holdings: Bk Titles 2,100; Per Subs 90
Special Collections: Technical & Scientific Reports
Subject Interests: Environ, Environ law, Law reform
Wireless access
Function: Electronic databases & coll
Restriction: Open by appt only

S CANADIAN FEDERATION OF INDEPENDENT BUSINESS*, Information Research Centre, 401-4141 Yonge St, M2P 2A6. SAN 328-4956. Tel: 416-222-8022. FAX: 416-222-4337. E-mail: msont@cfib.ca. Web Site: www.cfib-fcei.ca/en. *Public Affairs Mgr,* Milena Stanoeva; Staff 2 (MLS 2)
Founded 1980
Library Holdings: Bk Titles 2,000
Special Collections: Conference Papers of Small Business Conferences
Automation Activity & Vendor Info: (Acquisitions) Inmagic, Inc.; (Cataloging) Inmagic, Inc.; (OPAC) Inmagic, Inc.; (Serials) Inmagic, Inc.
Function: ILL available

L CANADIAN FOUNDATION FOR CHILDREN, YOUTH & THE LAW*, Justice for Children & Youth Library, 55 University Ave, 15th Flr, M5J 2H7. SAN 329-8647. Tel: 416-920-1633. Toll Free Tel: 866-999-5329. FAX: 416-920-5855. E-mail: info@jfcy.org. Web Site: www.jfcy.org. *Exec Dir,* Mary Birdsell
Subject Interests: Child abuse, Educ law, Mental health, Young offenders
Open Mon-Fri 9-5

S CANADIAN LIFE & HEALTH INSURANCE ASSOCIATION, INC*, Resource & Information Library, 79 Wellington St W, Ste 2300, M5K 1G8. SAN 372-6770. Tel: 416-777-2221, Ext 3070. FAX: 416-777-1895. E-mail: info@clhia.ca. Web Site: www.clhia.ca. *Sr Mgr,* Kolette Taber; Staff 1.5 (MLS 1, Non-MLS 0.5)
Founded 1938
Library Holdings: Bk Titles 850; Per Subs 96
Subject Interests: Employee benefits, Law, Life ins, Pensions, Tax
Automation Activity & Vendor Info: (Acquisitions) Inmagic, Inc.; (Cataloging) Inmagic, Inc.; (Circulation) Inmagic, Inc.; (ILL) Inmagic, Inc.; (OPAC) Inmagic, Inc.; (Serials) Inmagic, Inc.
Restriction: Access at librarian's discretion

CM CANADIAN MEMORIAL CHIROPRACTIC COLLEGE*, Health Sciences Library, 6100 Leslie St, M2H 3J1. SAN 319-4809. Tel: 416-482-2340, Ext 158. Interlibrary Loan Service Tel: 416-482-2340, Ext 160. FAX: 416-482-4816. Web Site: www.cmcc.ca/library. *Dir,* Natalia Tukhareli; Tel: 416-482-2340, Ext 159, E-mail: ntukhareli@cmcc.ca; *Archivist, Coll Develop Librn,* Steve Zoltai; Tel: 416-482-2340, Ext 206, E-mail: szoltai@cmcc.ca; *Ref Serv,* Kent Murnaghan; Tel: 416-482-2340, Ext 205; Staff 3 (MLS 3)
Founded 1945. Enrl 739; Fac 138; Highest Degree: Doctorate
Library Holdings: AV Mats 850; e-journals 113; Bk Titles 13,735; Bk Vols 16,822; Per Subs 204
Special Collections: History of Chiropractic, Canada
Subject Interests: Anatomy, Athletic injuries, Chiropractic, Neurology, Nutrition, Orthopedics, Radiology
Automation Activity & Vendor Info: (Acquisitions) EOS International; (Cataloging) EOS International; (Circulation) EOS International; (Course Reserve) EOS International; (OPAC) EOS International; (Serials) EBSCO Online
Wireless access
Publications: Chiropractic Research Abstracts Coll (1984, 85, 87, 90); Index to Chiropractic Literature
Partic in Canadian Health Libraries Association; Chiropractic Libr Consortium; Medical Library Association; Ont Libr Asn; Toronto Health Libraries Association
Open Mon-Thurs 7:30am-10pm, Fri 7:30am-8pm, Sat 9-4, Sun 12-5
Restriction: Non-circulating to the pub

S CANADIAN MUSIC CENTRE LIBRARIES*, 20 St Joseph St, M4Y 1J9. SAN 321-7043. Tel: 416-961-6601. E-mail: info@cmccanada.org. Web Site: cmccanada.org. *Dir, Libr Serv,* Position Currently Open; *Circ Mgr, Mgr, Info & Libr Serv,* Andrea Ayotte; E-mail: andrea.ayotte@cmccanada.org; Staff 2 (MLS 1, Non-MLS 1)
Founded 1959
Library Holdings: AV Mats 14,000; CDs 1,000; Music Scores 26,000
Subject Interests: Can composers, Music
Wireless access
Function: 24/7 Electronic res, 24/7 Online cat, Archival coll, Audio & video playback equip for onsite use, Computers for patron use, Electronic databases & coll, Internet access, Magazines, Mail & tel request accepted, Mail loans to mem, Music CDs, Online cat, Online ref, Telephone ref
Open Mon-Fri 9-5
Branches:
ONTARIO REGION LIBRARY, 20 St Joseph St, M4Y 1J9, SAN 324-4865. Tel: 416-961-6601, Ext 007. Circulation Tel: 416-961-6601, Ext 201. *Regional Dir,* Joseph Glaser; E-mail: joseph.glaser@cmccanada.org; *Nat Librn,* Peter Gorman; E-mail: peter.gorman@cmccanada.org
Founded 1983
Library Holdings: AV Mats 17,000; CDs 2,000; Music Scores 31,000; Bk Titles 300; Per Subs 35
Special Collections: Ann Southam Audio Archive; Canadian Composer Vertical Files, bios, concert notes, photos, press
Subject Interests: Can composers, Concert mus
Function: Archival coll, Audio & video playback equip for onsite use, Computers for patron use, Doc delivery serv, Homebound delivery serv, Internet access, Music CDs, Online cat, Online ref, Orientations, Photocopying/Printing, Ref serv available, Satellite serv, Workshops
Publications: Notations (Newsletter)
Open Mon-Fri 10-3
Restriction: Circ limited
QUEBEC REGIONAL LIBRARY, 1085 Cote du Beaver Hall, Montreal, H2Z 1S5, SAN 321-706X. Tel: 514-866-3477. FAX: 514-866-0456. E-mail: quebec@cmccanada.org. *Regional Dir,* Claire Marchand; E-mail: claire.marchand@cmccanada.org

Founded 1986
Library Holdings: AV Mats 6,000; Bk Titles 15,271; Per Subs 2,100
Subject Interests: Can composers, Music
Publications: Alternance (Newsletter)
Open Mon-Fri 9-12 & 1-5

S CANADIAN NATIONAL INSTITUTE FOR THE BLIND*, Library for the Blind, 1929 Bayview Ave, M4G 3E8. SAN 319-4817. Toll Free Tel: 800-486-2500. FAX: 416-486-2500. E-mail: info@cnib.ca. Web Site: www.cnib.ca. *Pres & Chief Exec Officer,* John Rafferty
Founded 1906. Pop 100,000; Circ 1,500,000
Library Holdings: Bk Titles 60,000; Bk Vols 500,000; Per Subs 60
Special Collections: Music Braille Coll; Rehabilitative Aspects of Blindness, ref
Publications: Acquisitions Lists; Children's Audio Magazine, Music Magazine (Audio); CNIB Library Newsletter
Special Services for the Blind - Braille bks; Braille music coll; Spec cats; Talking bks

S CANADIAN OPERA CO*, The Margo Sandor Music Library, 227 Front St E, M5A 1E8. SAN 329-868X. Tel: 416-363-6671. Web Site: www.coc.ca. *Librn,* Ondrej Golias; E-mail: ondrejg@coc.ca
Library Holdings: Bk Vols 6,000
Special Collections: Vocal & Orchestral Music Materials
Subject Interests: Hist of opera in Toronto, Opera performance mat
Restriction: Not open to pub

S CANADIAN TAX FOUNDATION*, Douglas J Sherbaniuk Research Centre, 145 Wellington St W, Ste 1400, M5J 1H8. SAN 319-4868. Tel: 416-599-0283. Toll Free Tel: 877-733-0283. FAX: 416-599-9283. Web Site: www.ctf.ca. *Librn,* Judy Singh; E-mail: jsingh@ctf.ca; Staff 2 (MLS 1, Non-MLS 1)
Founded 1946
Library Holdings: Bk Titles 10,000; Per Subs 235
Special Collections: Canadian Federal & Provincial Budgets; Dictionaries & encyclopedias; Rare books; Tax Reform
Subject Interests: Econ, Fed govt finance, Intl taxation, Local govt admin, Pub finance, Taxation
Automation Activity & Vendor Info: (Acquisitions) SydneyPlus; (Cataloging) SydneyPlus; (Circulation) SydneyPlus; (OPAC) SydneyPlus; (Serials) SydneyPlus
Wireless access
Function: Archival coll, Computers for patron use, Doc delivery serv, Electronic databases & coll, ILL available, Internet access, Mail loans to mem, Online cat, Photocopying/Printing, Ref & res
Open Mon-Fri 9-5
Friends of the Library Group

S CENTRE FOR ADDICTION & MENTAL HEALTH LIBRARY*, 1025 Queen St W, M5S 2S1. SAN 319-4523. Tel: 416-535-8501, Ext 36991. FAX: 416-595-6601. E-mail: library@camh.ca. Web Site: www.camh.ca/en/health-info/camh-library. *Libr Mgr,* Daphne Horn; Staff 7.5 (MLS 4, Non-MLS 3.5)
Founded 1958
Library Holdings: AV Mats 1,500; e-books 125; e-journals 4,000; Bk Titles 40,000; Bk Vols 60,000; Per Subs 223
Special Collections: CAMH Staff Publications; Drug Education Materials; Temperance
Automation Activity & Vendor Info: (Acquisitions) SydneyPlus; (Cataloging) SydneyPlus; (Circulation) SydneyPlus; (OPAC) SydneyPlus; (Serials) SydneyPlus
Wireless access
Function: Res assist avail
Open Mon-Fri 9-5

S CHARTERED PROFESSIONAL ACCOUNTANTS OF CANADA*, Information Services Library, 277 Wellington St W, M5V 3H2. SAN 326-9000. Tel: 416-204-3307. FAX: 416-977-8585. E-mail: customerservice@cpacanada.ca. *Info Spec,* Katharine Matte; Tel: 416-204-3227
Founded 1980
Library Holdings: Bk Titles 10,000; Per Subs 200
Restriction: Not open to pub

S CSA GROUP*, Information Centre, 178 Rexdale Blvd, M9W 1R3. SAN 319-3799. Tel: 416-747-4059. E-mail: informationcentre@csagroup.org. *Archivist, Info Mgr,* Alice Desrocher; E-mail: alice.desrocher@csagroup.org; Staff 1 (MLS 1)
Founded 1970
Special Collections: Engineering Standards, doc
Subject Interests: Engr standards, Hist of Can Standards Asn, Production liability, Quality assurance, Standardization

L DALE & LESSMANN LIBRARY, 181 University Ave, Ste 2100, M5H 3M7. SAN 377-3175. Tel: 416-863-1010. FAX: 416-863-1009. Web Site: www.dalelessmann.com. *Librn,* Anna Tiemersma; E-mail: atiemersma@dalelessmann.com; Staff 1 (MLS 1)
Library Holdings: Bk Vols 2,000
Restriction: Staff use only

L DAVIES, WARD, PHILLIPS & VINEBERG*, Law Library, 155 Wellington St W, M5V 3J7. SAN 373-3254. Tel: 416-863-0900. FAX: 416-863-0871. Web Site: www.dwpv.com. *Dir, Libr Serv,* Gaye Lefebvre; Tel: 416-863-5533, E-mail: glefebvre@dwpv.com; Staff 5 (MLS 3, Non-MLS 2)
Restriction: Private libr

G DEFENCE RESEARCH & DEVELOPMENT CANADA, Toronto Research Centre Library, 1133 Sheppard Ave W, M3K 2C9. SAN 319-1052. Tel: 416-635-2070. FAX: 416-635-2104. E-mail: sic@drdc-rddc.gc.ca. *Head of Libr,* Stewart Harrison; Staff 1 (Non-MLS 1)
Founded 1951
Library Holdings: Bk Vols 16,000; Per Subs 8
Subject Interests: Aviation med, Environ physiology, Human factors, Hyperbaric med, Life support systs
Automation Activity & Vendor Info: (Cataloging) BiblioMondo; (OPAC) BiblioMondo
Partic in Council of Federal Libraries Consortium
Restriction: Not open to pub

L DENTONS CANADA LLP, 77 King St W, Ste 400, M5K 0A1. SAN 371-7755. Tel: 416-863-4511. FAX: 416-863-4592. Web Site: www.dentons.com/en/global-presence/canada/toronto. *Dir, Info Serv,* Yasmin Chandra; E-mail: yasmin.chandra@dentons.com; Staff 2 (MLS 1, Non-MLS 1)
Founded 1956
Restriction: Not open to pub

L DENTONS CANADA LLP*, Law Library, 77 King St W, Ste 400, M5K 0A1. SAN 326-8942. Tel: 416-863-4511. FAX: 416-863-4592. Web Site: www.dentons.com/en/global-presence/canada/toronto. *Dir,* Yvonne MacDonald; *Librn,* Ian Colvin; *Library Contact,* Ronny Tse; E-mail: ronny.tse@dentons.com; Staff 4 (MLS 2, Non-MLS 2)
Library Holdings: Bk Titles 10,500; Bk Vols 11,000; Per Subs 65
Automation Activity & Vendor Info: (Cataloging) EOS International; (OPAC) EOS International; (Serials) EOS International
Partic in Can Asn of Law Librs; Toronto Asn of Law Librs

L DICKINSON WRIGHT LLP LIBRARY, 199 Bay St, Ste 2200, M5L 1G4. (Mail add: PO Box 447, Commerce Ct W, M5L 1G4), SAN 375-3441. Tel: 416-777-0101. FAX: 416-865-1398. *Librn,* Mrs Micky Wylie; E-mail: mwylie@dickinsonwright.com; Staff 1 (MLS 1)
Library Holdings: Electronic Media & Resources 5; Bk Titles 2,000; Bk Vols 5,000; Per Subs 20
Wireless access
Restriction: Staff use only

S DYING WITH DIGNITY CANADA LIBRARY*, 802-55 Eglinton Ave E, M4P 1G8. SAN 374-6712. Tel: 416-486-3998. Toll Free Tel: 800-495-6156. FAX: 416-486-5562. E-mail: info@dyingwithdignity.ca. Web Site: www.dyingwithdignity.ca. *Chief Exec Officer,* Helen Long; *Coordr, Libr Adminr,* Debora Aguillon; Staff 9 (Non-MLS 9)
Founded 1980
Library Holdings: Bk Vols 500
Subject Interests: Law, Philos
Function: Prof lending libr
Publications: Newsletter
Restriction: Mem only

L FASKEN*, Toronto Library, Bay Adelaide Ctr, 333 Bay St, Ste 2400, M5H 2T6. (Mail add: PO Box 20, M5H 2T6), SAN 320-880X. Tel: 416-865-5143. Interlibrary Loan Service Tel: 416-865-4500. FAX: 416-364-7813. Web Site: www.fasken.com. *Sr Dir, Knowledge Services & Infrastructure,* Jennifer McNenly; E-mail: jmcnenly@fasken.com; *Mgr, Knowledge Services,* Nathifa Grier-Coward; E-mail: ngrier-coward@fasken.com; Staff 7 (MLS 5, Non-MLS 2)
Library Holdings: Bk Vols 10,000; Per Subs 300
Subject Interests: Law
Automation Activity & Vendor Info: (Acquisitions) Lucidea - GeniePlus; (Cataloging) Lucidea - GeniePlus; (Circulation) Lucidea - GeniePlus; (ILL) Lucidea - GeniePlus; (OPAC) Lucidea; (Serials) Lucidea - GeniePlus
Wireless access
Publications: Legislative Snapshots (Newsletter)
Restriction: Open to others by appt

L FILION WAKELY THORUP ANGELETTI LLP*, Law Library, 333 Bay St, M5H 2R2. SAN 372-3666. Tel: 416-408-3221. FAX: 416-408-4814. Web Site: www.filion.on.ca. *Library Contact,* Amanda Holmes; E-mail: aholmes@filion.on.ca; Staff 2 (MLS 1, Non-MLS 1)
Library Holdings: Bk Vols 11,000; Per Subs 29
Subject Interests: Employment, Human rights, Occupational health, Occupational safety, Workers compensation
Open Mon-Fri 9-5

L GARDINER ROBERTS LLP LIBRARY, Bay Adelaide Centre-East Tower, 22 Adelaide St W, Ste 3600, M5H 4E3. SAN 377-4678. Tel: 416-865-6600. FAX: 416-865-6636. Web Site: www.grllp.com. *Librn,* Anjali Dandekar; E-mail: adandekar@grllp.com; Staff 2 (MLS 1, Non-MLS 1)
Library Holdings: Bk Vols 2,000
Automation Activity & Vendor Info: (Cataloging) Inmagic, Inc.
Restriction: Staff use only

C GEORGE BROWN COLLEGE LIBRARY LEARNING COMMONS, (Formerly George Brown College of Applied Arts & Technology), PO Box 1015, Sta B, M5T 2T9. SAN 760-3606. Tel: 416-415-5000, Ext 8255. Interlibrary Loan Service E-mail: illo@georgebrown.ca. Web Site: www.georgebrown.ca/library-learning-commons. *Sr Manager, Library Services,* Pearl Raju; E-mail: praju2@georgebrown.ca; *Mgr, Digital & Technical Servs,* Sarah Gillard; E-mail: sgillard@georgebrown.ca; *Syst Librn,* Sarah Wiebe; E-mail: swiebe@georgebrown.ca; Staff 27 (MLS 14, Non-MLS 13)
Enrl 28,584; Fac 557; Highest Degree: Bachelor
Library Holdings: Bk Titles 35,000; Per Subs 150
Subject Interests: Commerce, Commun serv, Graphic design, Hospitality, Nursing
Automation Activity & Vendor Info: (Acquisitions) Ex Libris Group; (Cataloging) Ex Libris Group; (Circulation) Ex Libris Group; (Course Reserve) Ex Libris Group; (ILL) Ex Libris Group
Wireless access
Partic in Ontario Colleges Library Service (OCLS)
Open Mon-Fri 8am-10pm, Sat 9-5, Sun 10-2

C GEORGE BROWN COLLEGE OF APPLIED ARTS & TECHNOLOGY*, Casa Loma Campus Library Learning Commons, Bldg C, 3rd Flr, Rm C330, 160 Kendal Ave, M5R 1M3. (Mail add: PO Box 1015, Sta B, M5T 2T9), SAN 368-511X. Tel: 416-415-5000, Ext 8255. Reference Tel: 416-415-5000, Ext 4625. Toll Free Tel: 800-265-2002. FAX: 416-415-4765. Web Site: www.georgebrown.ca/library-learning-commons/visit/casa-loma. *Librn,* Andrea Hall; Tel: 416-415-5000, Ext 4635, E-mail: andrea.hall@georgebrown.ca; *Librn,* Bill McAskill; Tel: 416-415-5000, Ext 3702, E-mail: bmcaskil@georgebrown.ca; Staff 2 (MLS 2)
Founded 1968. Enrl 9,016; Fac 735
Library Holdings: Bk Titles 27,000; Per Subs 160
Subject Interests: Archit tech, Arts, Bus, Child care, Commerce, Dental hygiene, Dental tech, Engr, Fashion, Food tech, Info tech, Jewelry, Manufacturing, Microelectronics, Nursing
Wireless access
Special Services for the Deaf - Bks on deafness & sign lang; High interest/low vocabulary bks; Spec interest per; Staff with knowledge of sign lang
Open Mon-Fri 7:30am-11pm, Sat 9-6, Sun 10-5

S GOETHE-INSTITUT TORONTO LIBRARY*, North Tower, 100 University Ave, Ste 201, M5J 1V6. SAN 373-6377. Tel: 416-593-5257, Ext 208. FAX: 416-593-5145. E-mail: bib-toronto@goethe.ca. Web Site: www.goethe.de/toronto. *Head Librn,* Michelle Kay; Staff 1 (MLS 1)
Library Holdings: Bk Titles 5,500; Per Subs 15
Special Collections: Contemporary German Literature & Plays, AV & bks; German Language Textbooks
Function: Adult bk club, Audio & video playback equip for onsite use, Bks on CD, ILL available, Music CDs
Publications: Acquisitions List
Open Tues 1-8, Wed & Thurs 3-8, Sat 9:30-2:30

L GOODMANS LLP LIBRARY*, Bay Adelaide Ctr, 333 Bay St, Ste 3400, M5H 2S7. SAN 321-5547. Tel: 416-979-2211, Ext 6070. FAX: 416-979-1234. E-mail: library@goodmans.ca. Web Site: www.goodmans.ca. *Dir, Libr Serv,* Yasmin Chandra; Staff 6 (MLS 4, Non-MLS 2)
Library Holdings: Bk Vols 8,000; Per Subs 225
Subject Interests: Law
Automation Activity & Vendor Info: (Acquisitions) EOS International; (Cataloging) EOS International; (Serials) EOS International
Wireless access
Restriction: Staff use only

L GOWLING WLG (CANADA) LIBRARY, One First Canadian Pl, 100 King St W, Ste 1600, M5X 1G5. SAN 370-7148. Tel: 416-862-5735. Interlibrary Loan Service Tel: 416-862-3505. Reference Tel: 416-862-6261. FAX: 416-862-7661. Web Site: gowlingwlg.com. *Dir,* Roslyn Theodore-McIntosh; E-mail: roslyn.theodoremcintosh@ca.gowlingwlg.com; *Sr Ref Librn,* Suzanna LaRose; E-mail: suzanna.larose@ca.gowlingwlg.com; *Librn,* Mikaela Cookson; E-mail: mikaela.cookson@ca.gowlingwlg.com; *Librn,* Tracey Cote; E-mail: tracey.cote@ca.gowlingwlg.com; *Librn,* Lily Mac; E-mail: lily.mac@ca.gowlingwlg.com; *Ref Librn/Trainer,* Joanne Berent; E-mail: joanne.berent@ca.gowlingwlg.com; *Ref Librn/Trainer,* Elizabeth Dingman; E-mail: elizabeth.dingman@ca.gowlingwlg.com; *Senior Reference Tech,* Glenda O'Brien; E-mail: glenda.obrien@ca.gowlingwlg.com; *Libr Tech,* Roxanne Thomas; E-mail: roxanne.thomas@ca.gowlingwlg.com; *Libr Tech,* Peyton Biswas; E-mail: peyton.biswas@ca.gowling.com; *Ref Tech,* Helen Jarvis; E-mail: helen.jarvis@ca.gowlingwlg.com; Staff 11 (MLS 4, Non-MLS 7)
Automation Activity & Vendor Info: (Acquisitions) Inmagic, Inc.; (Cataloging) Inmagic, Inc.; (Circulation) Inmagic, Inc.; (Course Reserve) Inmagic, Inc.; (ILL) Inmagic, Inc.; (OPAC) Inmagic, Inc.; (Serials) Inmagic, Inc.
Wireless access
Publications: Acquisitions List; Information Packages; Library Brochure

L HICKS MORLEY HAMILTON STEWART & STORIE LLP, Law Library, Box 371, TD Ctr, 77 King St W, 39th Flr, M5H 1K8. SAN 375-4960. Tel: 416-362-1011. FAX: 416-362-9680. Web Site: hicksmorley.com. *Libr Tech,* Amy Barton; Tel: 416-362-1011, Ext 7012, E-mail: amy-barton@hicksmorley.com; Staff 1 (Non-MLS 1)
Founded 1972
Library Holdings: Bk Vols 7,500; Per Subs 90
Special Collections: Labour & Employment Law Coll. Canadian and Provincial
Subject Interests: Educ, Environ law, Pensions, Workers compensation
Wireless access
Function: Res libr
Publications: Client Update (Newsletter); FTR Now (Monthly bulletin)
Partic in Toronto Asn of Law Librs
Restriction: Not open to pub

M HOLLAND BLOORVIEW KIDS REHABILITAION HOSPITAL*, Health Sciences Library, 150 Kilgour Rd, M4G 1R8. SAN 370-8942. Tel: 416-425-6220, Ext 3517. Toll Free Tel: 800-363-2440, Ext 3517. FAX: 416-425-6376. E-mail: library@hollandbloorview.ca. Web Site: www.hollandbloorview.ca. *Mgr, Health Sci Libr & Archives,* Iveta Lewis; Staff 2 (MLS 1, Non-MLS 1)
Library Holdings: Bk Titles 4,000; Per Subs 50
Automation Activity & Vendor Info: (Acquisitions) SirsiDynix-WorkFlows; (Cataloging) SirsiDynix-WorkFlows; (Circulation) SirsiDynix-WorkFlows; (OPAC) SirsiDynix-WorkFlows; (Serials) SirsiDynix-WorkFlows
Wireless access
Partic in Health Science Information Consortium of Toronto
Open Mon-Fri 8:30-4:30

M HOSPITAL FOR SICK CHILDREN*, Hospital Library, 555 University Ave, M5G 1X8. SAN 319-5074. Tel: 416-813-6693. Interlibrary Loan Service Tel: 416-813-6591. FAX: 416-813-7523. E-mail: hospital.library@sickkids.ca. Web Site: www.sickkids.ca/en/learning/support-services/library.
Founded 1919
Library Holdings: DVDs 56; e-books 3,627; e-journals 1,091; Bk Titles 9,269; Bk Vols 9,749; Per Subs 61; Videos 164
Special Collections: Pediatrics Coll
Subject Interests: Pediatrics
Automation Activity & Vendor Info: (Cataloging) Ex Libris Group; (Circulation) Ex Libris Group; (OPAC) Ex Libris Group; (Serials) Ex Libris Group
Wireless access
Partic in Health Science Information Consortium of Toronto
Open Mon-Fri 9-5

S C D HOWE INSTITUTE LIBRARY*, 67 Yonge St, Ste 300, M5E 1J8. SAN 325-1632. Tel: 416-865-1904, Ext 2606. FAX: 416-865-1866. E-mail: library@cdhowe.org. Web Site: www.cdhowe.org. *Research Coordr,* Christa Perez; E-mail: cperez@cdhowe.org; Staff 1 (Non-MLS 1)
Founded 1973
Library Holdings: Bk Titles 3,500; Per Subs 100
Subject Interests: Econ, Pub policy
Automation Activity & Vendor Info: (Acquisitions) Inmagic, Inc.; (Cataloging) Inmagic, Inc.; (Circulation) Inmagic, Inc.; (Course Reserve) Inmagic, Inc.; (ILL) Inmagic, Inc.
Wireless access
Function: Res libr
Restriction: Staff & mem only

J HUMBER COLLEGE*, North Campus Libraries, 205 Humber College Blvd, M9W 5L7. SAN 374-4280. Tel: 416-675-5079. Reference Tel: 416-675-6622, Ext 4421. FAX: 416-675-7439. Web Site: library.humber.ca. *Libr Dir,* Cynthia Mckeich; E-mail: cynthia.mckeich@humber.ca; *Syst Librn,* Lisa Dibarbora; Tel: 416-675-6622, Ext 4692, E-mail: lisa.dibarbora@humber.ca
Library Holdings: Bk Titles 80,937; Bk Vols 90,421; Per Subs 969
Wireless access
Open Mon-Thurs 7:30am-10pm, Fri 7:30am-8pm, Sat 9-6
Departmental Libraries:
LAKESHORE CAMPUS LIBRARY, 3199 Lakeshore Blvd W, M8V 1K8, SAN 368-5292. Tel: 416-675-6622, Ext 3250. Reference Tel: 416-675-6622, Ext 3351. FAX: 416-252-0918. *Assoc Dir,* Alexandra Ross; E-mail: alexandra.ross@humber.ca; *Coordr,* Janet Hollingsworth
Founded 1968
Library Holdings: Bk Vols 20,000; Per Subs 216
Open Mon-Thurs 7:30am-10pm, Fri 7:30-6, Sat & Sun 9-6

M HUMBER RIVER HOSPITAL, Health Sciences Library, 1235 Wilson Ave, M3M 0B2. SAN 329-1901. Tel: 416-242-1000, Ext 81201. E-mail: hsl@hrh.ca. Web Site: onesearch.library.utoronto.ca/library-info/hrrh_hosp. Staff 1 (MLS 1)
Library Holdings: e-journals 15,000; Bk Vols 1,400; Per Subs 350
Subject Interests: Allied health sci, Med, Nursing
Partic in Health Science Information Consortium of Toronto

S HYDROCEPHALUS CANADA, Resource Centre, 16 Four Seasons Pl, Ste 111, M9B 6E5. SAN 373-7357. Tel: 416-214-1056. Toll Free Tel: 800-387-1575. FAX: 416-214-1446. E-mail: info@hydrocephalus.ca. Web Site: www.hydrocephalus.ca. *Dir, Info Serv, Dir, Programs,* Shauna Beaudoin
Founded 1973
Library Holdings: CDs 30; DVDs 25; Bk Titles 3,062; Per Subs 15; Videos 50
Subject Interests: Disabilities, Educ, Employment, Hydrocephalus, Lifestyle, Sexuality, Spina bifida
Publications: Library Listing; Video Listing
Open Mon-Fri 9-4:30

S INSURANCE INSTITUTE OF ONTARIO LIBRARY*, 18 King St E, 6th Flr, M5C 1C4. SAN 373-6830. Tel: 416-362-8586. FAX: 416-362-4239. Web Site: www.insuranceinstitute.ca. *Library Contact,* Kamila Edwards; E-mail: kedwards@insuranceinstitute.ca
Library Holdings: Bk Titles 100; Per Subs 20
Restriction: Mem only

S ITALIAN CULTURAL INSTITUTE LIBRARY*, 496 Huron St, M5R 2R3. SAN 374-7859. Tel: 416-921-3802. FAX: 416-962-2503. Web Site: www.iictoronto.esteri.it/IIC_Toronto/Menu/La_Biblioteca. *Dir,* Veronica Manson; E-mail: veronica.manson@esteri.it
Library Holdings: Bk Vols 5,587
Open Mon-Fri 9-1 & 2-5
Restriction: Open to pub for ref only

S JAPAN FOUNDATION, Toronto Library, Two Bloor St E, Ste 300, M4W 1A8. (Mail add: PO Box 130, M4W 1A8), SAN 377-0915. Tel: 416-966-1600, Ext 239, 416-966-2935. FAX: 416-966-0957. E-mail: library_jftoronto@jpf.go.jp. Web Site: tr.jpf.go.jp/library. *Librn,* Risa Hatanaka; E-mail: risa_hatanaka@jpf.go.jp
Library Holdings: Per Subs 65
Wireless access
Partic in Can Libr Asn; Coun on East Asian Librs; Nat Coord Comt on Japanese Libr Resources; OCLC Online Computer Library Center, Inc
Open Mon, Tues, Fri & Sat 11:30-4:30, Thurs 11:30-6:30

L LAW SOCIETY OF UPPER CANADA*, Great Library, Osgoode Hall, 130 Queen St W, M5H 2N6. SAN 319-5155. Tel: 416-947-3315, Ext 2510. Toll Free Tel: 800-668-7380, Ext 2510. E-mail: refstaff@lso.ca. Web Site: lso.ca/great-library. *Dir,* Olcay Atacan; E-mail: oatacan@lso.ca; *Head, Libr Syst,* Olcay Atacan; E-mail: oatacan@lso.ca; Staff 19 (MLS 8, Non-MLS 11)
Founded 1829
Library Holdings: Bk Titles 40,000; Bk Vols 120,000; Per Subs 1,700
Subject Interests: Canadiana, Govt doc, Law
Automation Activity & Vendor Info: (Acquisitions) Ex Libris Group; (Cataloging) Ex Libris Group; (OPAC) Ex Libris Group; (Serials) Ex Libris Group
Wireless access
Function: Ref serv available, Res libr
Open Mon-Fri 9am-10pm, Sat 9-5, Sun Noon-5 (Winter); Mon-Thurs 9am-10pm, Fri 9-5 (Summer)
Restriction: Mem only, Open to pub by appt only

C MICHENER INSTITUTE OF EDUCATION AT UHN*, Learning Resource Centre, 222 Saint Patrick St, 2nd Flr, M5T 1V4. SAN 320-3417. Tel: 416-596-3123. E-mail: lrc@michener.ca. Web Site: michener.ca/students/library. *Sr Dir,* Ann Russell; *Librn,* Juanita Richardson; E-mail: jrichardson@michener.ca; *Assoc Librn,* Graham Lavender; E-mail: glavender@michener.ca; Staff 2 (MLS 2)
Founded 1972. Enrl 850; Fac 80
Special Collections: Board Examination Questions
Subject Interests: Anesthesia tech, Cardiovascular perfusion, Chiropody, Cytology, Echocardiography, Genetics, Health, Nuclear med, Radiography, Respiratory tech
Wireless access

M MOUNT SINAI HOSPITAL*, Sidney Liswood Library, 600 University Ave, Rm 18-234, M5G 1X5. SAN 319-5260. Tel: 416-586-4800, Ext 4614. FAX: 416-586-4998. E-mail: library.msh@sinaihealthsystem.ca. Web Site: www.mountsinai.on.ca/education/educational-and-resource-centre/library. *Dir,* Chris Walsh; Staff 5 (MLS 2, Non-MLS 3)
Founded 1967
Library Holdings: e-books 1,190; e-journals 2,000; Bk Titles 2,000; Per Subs 100
Automation Activity & Vendor Info: (Acquisitions) SirsiDynix; (Cataloging) SirsiDynix; (Circulation) SirsiDynix; (Course Reserve) SirsiDynix; (ILL) SirsiDynix; (Media Booking) SirsiDynix; (OPAC) SirsiDynix; (Serials) SirsiDynix
Wireless access
Function: Res libr
Partic in Health Science Information Consortium of Toronto
Open Mon-Fri 8:30-6
Restriction: Circ limited

SR NEUBERGER HOLOCAUST EDUCATION CENTRE, Frank & Anita Ekstein Holocaust Resource Library, 4600 Bathurst St, 4th Flr, M2R 3V2. SAN 319-5686. Tel: 416-635-2996. FAX: 416-635-0925. Web Site: hec.emersonmedia.com/anitaekstein. Staff 1 (MLS 1)
Founded 2005
Library Holdings: CDs 73; DVDs 863; Bk Titles 7,715; Bk Vols 9,000; Per Subs 11; Spec Interest Per Sub 8
Special Collections: Anti-Semitism, Genocide & Racism; Camps & Ghettos During WWII; Children's Books on the Holocaust; History of German & Austrian Jews; Holocaust History in Different Countries; Holocaust Survivors' Oral Video Testimonies; Jewish Communities in Canada; Rare Books Coll; Righteous During WWII. Canadian and Provincial; Oral History
Subject Interests: Anti-Semitism, Art, Genealogy, Genocide, Holocaust, Human rights, Jewish hist, Philos, Politics, Racism, Relig, World hist
Automation Activity & Vendor Info: (Cataloging) Mandarin Library Automation; (Circulation) Mandarin Library Automation; (OPAC) Mandarin Library Automation
Wireless access
Function: 24/7 Online cat, Adult literacy prog, Archival coll, Online cat
Open Mon-Thurs 8:30-4:30, Fri 9-2
Friends of the Library Group

M NORTH YORK GENERAL HOSPITAL*, W Keith Welsh Library, 4001 Leslie St, M2K 1E1. SAN 368-8445. Tel: 416-756-6142. E-mail: library@nygh.on.ca. Web Site: www.nygh.on.ca/Default.aspx?cid=1261&lang=1. *Librn,* Julie Waddick; Staff 1 (MLS 1)
Founded 1968
Library Holdings: Bk Vols 3,700; Per Subs 10
Wireless access
Open Mon-Fri 9-5

C OCAD UNIVERSITY*, Dorothy H Hoover Library, Bldg MCC, 2nd Flr, 113 McCaul St, M5T 1W1. (Mail add: 100 McCaul St, M5T 1W1), SAN 319-5309. Tel: 416-977-6000, Ext 358. Reference Tel: 416-977-6000, Ext 334. FAX: 416-977-6006. E-mail: circulation@ocadu.edu. Web Site: www.ocadu.ca/services/library.htm. *Univ Librn,* Tony White; Tel: 416-977-6000, Ext 348, E-mail: twhite@ocadu.ca; *Syst Librn,* Ling He; Tel: 416-977-6000, Ext 3703, E-mail: lhe@ocadu.ca; Staff 5 (MLS 5)
Founded 1876. Enrl 3,500; Fac 255; Highest Degree: Master
Library Holdings: e-books 675,000; Electronic Media & Resources 56,000; Bk Vols 74,000; Per Subs 215; Videos 3,800
Subject Interests: Art, Design
Automation Activity & Vendor Info: (Acquisitions) SirsiDynix; (Cataloging) SirsiDynix; (Circulation) SirsiDynix; (Course Reserve) SirsiDynix; (OPAC) SirsiDynix; (Serials) SirsiDynix
Wireless access
Partic in OCLC Research Library Partnership; Ontario Council of University Libraries
Friends of the Library Group

J ONTARIO ARCHAEOLOGICAL SOCIETY LIBRARY*, 1444 Queen St E, Ste 102, M4L 1E1. SAN 329-2398. Tel: 416-406-5959. FAX: 416-406-5959. E-mail: info@ontarioarchaeology.org. Web Site: www.ontarioarchaeology.org. *Exec Dir,* Chiara Williamson; E-mail: execdirector@ontarioarchaeology.org
Founded 1950
Library Holdings: Bk Titles 550
Subject Interests: Local hist
Wireless access
Restriction: Open by appt only

S ONTARIO CAMPS ASSOCIATION LIBRARY*, 70 Martin Ross Ave., M3J 2L4. SAN 377-4201. Tel: 416-485-0425. Toll Free Tel: 844-485-0425. FAX: 416-485-0422. E-mail: info@ontariocamps.ca. Web Site: www.ontariocampsassociation.ca/. *Exec Dir,* Joy Levy
Library Holdings: Bk Vols 500; Per Subs 10
Open Mon-Fri 9-5
Restriction: Open to pub for ref only

S ONTARIO GENEALOGICAL SOCIETY LIBRARY, Toronto Reference Library, Humanities & Social Services Dept, 789 Yonge St, M4W 2G8. (Mail add: 2100 Steeles Ave, Unit 202, Concord, L4K 2V1). SAN 326-6362. Tel: 416-393-7175. Administration Tel: 416-489-0734. E-mail: trlhss@torontopubliclibrary.ca. Information Services E-mail: info@ogs.on.ca. Web Site: www.ogs.on.ca. *Admin Coordr,* Coral Harkies; Tel: 416-489-0734, Ext 201, E-mail: info@ogs.on.ca; Staff 1 (MLS 1)
Library Holdings: Bk Titles 10,000; Per Subs 200
Special Collections: Ontario Genealogical Society Coll, bks, fiche, maps, microfilm
Subject Interests: Genealogy
Wireless access
Open Mon-Fri 9-8:30, Sat 9-5, Sun (Sept-June) 1:30-5

P ONTARIO LIBRARY SERVICE*, 1504 One Yonge St, Ste107, M5E 1E5. (Mail add: Head Office, 334, rue Regent St, Sudbury, P3C 4E2). Tel: 416-961-1669. E-mail: info@olservice.ca. Web Site: www.olservice.ca. *Chief Exec Officer,* Mellissa D'Onofrio-Jones; E-mail: mdonofrio.jones@olservice.ca
Member Libraries: Arnprior Public Library; Asphodel-Norwood Public Library; Augusta Township Public Library; Bancroft Public Library; Barrie Public Library; Belleville Public Library; Bonnechere Union Public Library; Bradford-West Gwillimbury Public Library; Brantford Public Library; Brighton Public Library; Burlington Public Library; Caledon Public Library; Carleton Place Public Library; Clarence-Rockland Public Library; Clarington Public Library; Clearview Public Library; Cobourg Public Library; Collingwood Public Library; Cornwall Public Library; County of Brant Public Library; Edwardsburgh Cardinal Public Library; Elizabethtown-Kitley Township Public Library; Essa Public Library; Georgina Public Library; Grand Valley Public Library; Gravenhurst Public Library; Greater Madawaska Public Library; Haliburton County Public Library; Hamilton Public Library; Hanover Public Library; Hastings Highlands Public Library; Havelock Public Library; Hawkesbury Public Library; Head, Clara & Maria Township Public Library; Huntsville Public Library; Huron County Library; Kawartha Lakes Public Library; Kitchener Public Library; Laurentian Hills Public Library; Lennox & Addington County Public Library; Lincoln Public Library; Madawaska Valley Public Library; Markham Public Library; Merrickville Public Library; Middlesex County Library; Midland Public Library; Mississippi Mills Libraries; Nanticoke Public Library; Nation Municipality Public Library; Newmarket Public Library; Niagara-on-the-Lake Public Library; Norfolk County Public Library; North Kawartha Library; North Perth Public Library; Orangeville Public Library; Orillia Public Library; Oshawa Public Library; Ottawa Public Library/Bibliothèque publique d'Ottawa; Owen Sound & North Grey Union Public Library; Oxford County Library; Pembroke Public Library; Penetanguishene Public Library; Petawawa Public Library; Peterborough Public Library; Pickering Public Library; Prescott Public Library; Prince Edward County Public Library; Quinte West Public Library; Red Rock Public Library Board; Region of Waterloo Library; Renfrew Public Library; Scugog Memorial Public Library; Severn Township Public Library; Shelburne Public Library; Sioux Lookout Public Library; Smiths Falls Public Library; St Catharines Public Library; St Mary's Public Library; Stirling-Rawdon Public Library; Stratford Public Library; The Blue Mountains Public Library; The Cavan Monaghan Libraries; Township of Athens Public Library; Township of Springwater Public Library; Tyendinaga Township Public Library; Wellington County Library; West Grey Public Library; Westport Public Library; Whitby Public Library; Whitewater Region Public Library; Windsor Public Library; Wollaston Public Library; Woodstock Public Library

G ONTARIO MINISTRY OF EDUCATION, Brian Fleming Research Library, College Park, 777 Bay St, Ste 3201, M7A 1L2. SAN 319-4906. Tel: 416-215-0855. E-mail: brianfleming.library@ontario.ca. Web Site: www.ontario.ca/page/ministry-education. *Libr Mgr,* Andrea Sequeira; *Research Librn,* Corrina Taccone; Staff 2 (MLS 2)
Founded 1973
Library Holdings: Bk Vols 18,000; Per Subs 6
Special Collections: Ministry Documents Coll
Subject Interests: Educ, Mgt training
Function: ILL available, Ref serv available
Restriction: Not open to pub, Open by appt only

G ONTARIO MINISTRY OF FINANCE*, Finance Library, 95 Grosvenor St, 1st Flr, M7A 1Y8. SAN 319-5392. Tel: 416-325-1200. FAX: 416-325-1212. E-mail: financelibrary.fin@ontario.ca. *Sr Research Coord,* Daniel Gouthro; Tel: 416-325-1204, E-mail: danielgouthro@ontario.ca; Staff 3 (MLS 3)
Founded 1944
Library Holdings: Bk Vols 33,000; Per Subs 125
Special Collections: Ontario Budget, 1870-present; Ontario Public Accounts, 1867-present; Ontario Statutes, 1792-present
Subject Interests: Econ, Pub finance, Pub mgt
Automation Activity & Vendor Info: (Acquisitions) SydneyPlus; (Cataloging) SydneyPlus; (Circulation) SydneyPlus; (OPAC) SydneyPlus; (Serials) SydneyPlus
Function: ILL available
Publications: Library Update
Restriction: Open by appt only

GL ONTARIO MINISTRY OF THE ATTORNEY GENERAL, Law Library, McMurtry-Scott Bldg, 720 Bay St, Main Flr, M7A 2S9. SAN 319-5252. Tel: 416-326-4561. FAX: 416-326-4562. E-mail: library.mag@ontario.ca. Web Site: sigles-symbols.bac-lac.gc.ca/eng/Search/Details?Id=6026, www.ontario.ca/page/ministry-attorney-general. Staff 4 (MLS 3, Non-MLS 1)
Founded 1967
Library Holdings: Bk Vols 30,000
Special Collections: English Reports
Subject Interests: Civil, Constitutional law, Criminal
Automation Activity & Vendor Info: (Cataloging) Inmagic, Inc.; (Circulation) Inmagic, Inc.
Partic in Ont Govt Libr Coun
Restriction: Not open to pub

G ONTARIO MINISTRY OF THE ENVIRONMENT, CONSERVATION & PARKS, Information Research Centre, 40 Saint Clair Ave W, 12th Flr, M4V 1M2. SAN 374-5023. E-mail: irc.irc.moe@ontario.ca. *Libr & Info Spec,* Denise Angeloni; E-mail: denise.angeloni@ontario.ca; Staff 1 (MLS 1)
Founded 1984
Subject Interests: Pesticides, Risk assessment, Toxicology
Automation Activity & Vendor Info: (Cataloging) Inmagic, Inc.; (OPAC) Inmagic, Inc.
Restriction: Circulates for staff only, Employees & their associates, External users must contact libr, In-house use for visitors, Limited access for the pub, Open to pub by appt only, Staff use, pub by appt

G ONTARIO SECURITIES COMMISSION LIBRARY*, 20 W Queen St, 20th Flr, M5H 3S8. SAN 326-2944. Tel: 416-593-2303. Interlibrary Loan Service Tel: 416-593-8336. FAX: 416-593-3661. Web Site: www.osc.gov.on.ca. *Mgr, Knowledge Mgt Serv,* Laura Knapp; E-mail: lknapp@osc.gov.on.ca. Subject Specialists: *Bus, Legal res,* Laura Knapp; Staff 3 (MLS 2, Non-MLS 1)
Founded 1984
Library Holdings: Bk Titles 3,000; Per Subs 200
Special Collections: Ontario Securities Commission Bulletins (1949 to present)
Subject Interests: Admin law, Securities law
Automation Activity & Vendor Info: (Acquisitions) Sydney; (Cataloging) Sydney; (Circulation) Sydney; (OPAC) Sydney; (Serials) Sydney
Function: Doc delivery serv, For res purposes, Govt ref serv, ILL available, Internet access, Ref serv available, Workshops
Restriction: By permission only, Circulates for staff only, Not open to pub

G ONTARIO WORKPLACE TRIBUNALS LIBRARY, 505 University Ave, 7th Flr, M5G 2P2. SAN 368-5470. Tel: 416-314-3700. E-mail: owtl@wsiat.ca. Web Site: www.owtlibrary.on.ca. *Ref Librn,* Emily Sinclair; E-mail: emily.sinclair@wsiat.ca; Staff 2 (MLS 2)
Founded 1998
Library Holdings: Bk Titles 4,000; Bk Vols 13,400; Per Subs 150
Special Collections: Ontario Employment Standards Decisions; Ontario Labour Relations Board Reports; Workplace Safety & Insurance Appeals
Subject Interests: Human rights, Labor law, Pay equity, Workplace safety law
Partic in Can Asn of Law Librs; Ont Govt Libr Coun; Toronto Asn of Law Librs
Open Mon-Fri 8:30-4:30

L OSLER, HOSKIN & HARCOURT LIBRARY*, One First Canadian Pl, Ste 6200, 100 King St W, M5X 1B8. (Mail add: PO Box 50, 100 King St W, M5X 1B8), SAN 329-9406. Tel: 416-862-4239. FAX: 416-862-6666. Web Site: www.osler.com. *Sr Mgr,* Martin Tomlinson; E-mail: mtomlinson@osler.com; Staff 9 (MLS 5, Non-MLS 4)
Library Holdings: Bk Titles 3,000; Bk Vols 20,000; Per Subs 500
Special Collections: Can Gov
Subject Interests: Law
Restriction: Not open to pub

SR PRESBYTERIAN CHURCH IN CANADA ARCHIVES*, 50 Wynford Dr, M3C 1J7. SAN 375-0191. Tel: 416-441-1111, Ext 310. Toll Free Tel: 800-619-7301, Ext 310. FAX: 416-441-2825. E-mail: archives@presbyterian.com. Web Site: www.presbyterianarchives.ca. *Library Contact,* Nicole D'Angela; E-mail: ndangela@presbyterian.ca
Library Holdings: Bk Vols 600
Subject Interests: Church hist, Genealogy, Soc hist
Wireless access
Open Mon-Fri 9-4:45; Mon-Fri 9-4 (July & Aug)

S PRICEWATERHOUSECOOPERS*, National Tax Research Services, PwC Tower, 18 York St, Ste 2600, M5J 0B2. SAN 325-1128. Tel: 416-814-5890. FAX: 416-814-3200. *Mgr, Info Serv,* Kathryn Kingston; E-mail: kathryn.e.kingston@pwc.com; *Info Technician,* Bettina Krebs; E-mail: bettina.u.krebs@pwc.com; Staff 3 (MLS 3)
Library Holdings: Bk Titles 4,000; Per Subs 100
Subject Interests: Law, Taxation
Function: For res purposes
Restriction: Co libr, Staff use only

G PUBLIC HEALTH ONTARIO*, Public Health Laboratories Resource Centre, 661 University Ave, 17th Flr, M5G 1H1. SAN 319-6054. Tel: 647-792-3179. FAX: 416-235-6196. E-mail: phol-library@oahpp.ca. Web Site: www.publichealthontario.ca. *Tech Serv,* Gabrielle Gaedecke; Staff 1 (Non-MLS 1)
Founded 1963
Library Holdings: Bk Titles 3,800; Bk Vols 4,000; Per Subs 150; Spec Interest Per Sub 150
Special Collections: CLSI Guidelines
Subject Interests: Infectious diseases, Microbiology, Pub health
Partic in Health Science Information Consortium of Toronto; Ont Govt Libr Coun; Ontario Public Health Libraries Association
Restriction: Staff use only

CR REGIS COLLEGE LIBRARY*, 100 Wellesley St W, M5S 2Z5. SAN 319-5511. Tel: 416-922-5474, Ext 234. Reference Tel: 416-922-5474, Ext 235. FAX: 416-922-2898. E-mail: regis.library@utoronto.ca. Web Site: www.regiscollege.ca/library. *Chief Librn,* Teresa Helik; E-mail: teresa.helik@utoronto.ca; *Libr Tech,* Candice Park; Tel: 416-922-5474, Ext 236, E-mail: candice.park@utoronto.ca; Staff 1 (MLS 1)
Founded 1930. Highest Degree: Doctorate
Library Holdings: AV Mats 140; Bk Vols 78,000; Per Subs 175; Videos 22
Special Collections: Lonergan Research Center
Subject Interests: Jesuits, Theol
Automation Activity & Vendor Info: (Acquisitions) Ex Libris Group; (Cataloging) Ex Libris Group; (Circulation) Ex Libris Group; (OPAC) Ex Libris Group
Wireless access
Function: Res libr, Wheelchair accessible
Partic in LYRASIS; Univ of Toronto Libr Automation Syst
Open Mon-Fri 8:30-4:30
Restriction: In-house use for visitors, Open to fac, students & qualified researchers

S ROYAL CANADIAN MILITARY INSTITUTE LIBRARY, 426 University Ave, M5G 1S9. SAN 319-5570. Tel: 416-597-0286, Ext 128. Toll Free Tel: 800-585-1072. FAX: 416-597-6919. *Librn,* Penny Lipman; E-mail: penny.lipman@rcmi.org; *Honorary Librn,* Arthur Manvell; Staff 2 (MLS 1, Non-MLS 1)
Founded 1890
Library Holdings: Bk Titles 15,000
Special Collections: British Army Lists; Canadian Militia Lists
Subject Interests: Art, Mil hist, Sci
Automation Activity & Vendor Info: (Cataloging) SoutronGLOBAL; (Circulation) SoutronGLOBAL; (OPAC) SoutronGLOBAL
Wireless access
Function: Res libr
Restriction: Access at librarian's discretion, Circ to mem only, Mem only, Open to pub by appt only, Open to pub for ref only

S ROYAL ONTARIO MUSEUM*, Library & Archives, 100 Queen's Park, M5S 2C6. SAN 368-5500. Tel: 416-586-5595. FAX: 416-586-5519. E-mail: library@rom.on.ca. Web Site: www.rom.on.ca/en/collections-research/library-archives. *Actg Head,* Dr Max Dionisio; Tel: 416-586-5740; *Archivist,* Charlotte Chaffey; Tel: 416-586-8000, Ext 4033, E-mail: cchaffey@rom.on.ca. Subject Specialists: *Bibliog, East Asian studies, Japanese,* Dr Max Dionisio; Staff 6 (MLS 3, Non-MLS 3)
Apr 2021-Mar 2022. Mats Exp (CAN) $70,300, Books (CAN) $26,000, Per/Ser (Incl. Access Fees) (CAN) $43,000, Presv (CAN) $1,300
Library Holdings: Bk Vols 407,000
Special Collections: Asian Decorative Arts & Archaeology (Bishop White Committee Library of East Asia); Early North American Discovery & Exploration (Sigmund Samuel Canadiana Coll); Ornithology & Natural History (Fleming Coll)
Subject Interests: Anthrop, Archaeology, Astronomy, Botany, Canadiana, Decorative art, Entomology, Ethnology, Geol, Herpetology, Ichthyology, Mammalogy, Mineralogy, Museology, Ornithology, Paleontology, Textiles
Automation Activity & Vendor Info: (Cataloging) Ex Libris Group; (Circulation) Ex Libris Group; (Course Reserve) Ex Libris Group; (ILL) OCLC FirstSearch; (OPAC) Ex Libris Group; (Serials) Ex Libris Group
Wireless access
Function: Archival coll, Art exhibits, Bus archives, Computers for patron use, Electronic databases & coll, ILL available, Internet access, Magazines, Microfiche/film & reading machines, Online cat, Online ref, Photocopying/Printing, Ref serv available, Res libr, Scanner
Partic in Univ of Toronto Libr Automation Syst
Restriction: Authorized patrons, Authorized personnel only, Authorized scholars by appt, Circ limited, Circulates for staff only, Closed stack, External users must contact libr, In-house use for visitors, Lending to staff only, Non-circulating of rare bks, Non-circulating to the pub, Off-site coll in storage - retrieval as requested, Open to pub for ref only, Ref only to non-staff, Researchers by appt only, Restricted borrowing privileges, Visitors must make appt to use bks in the libr

C RYERSON UNIVERSITY LIBRARY*, 350 Victoria St, 2nd Flr, M5B 2K3. SAN 368-556X. Tel: 416-979-5055. FAX: 416-979-5215. E-mail: refdesk@ryerson.ca. Web Site: library.ryerson.ca. *Chief Librn,* Carol Shepstone; Tel: 416-979-5000, Ext 5142, E-mail: cshepstone@ryerson.ca; *Head, AV,* Susan Banerjee; Tel: 416-979-5000, Ext 4834, E-mail: sbanerjee@ryerson.ca; *Head, Borrowing & Lending Services,* Kelly Kimberley; Tel: 416-979-5000, Ext 4833, E-mail: kkimberley@ryerson.ca; *Acting Head Archivist, Head, Acq, Head, Coll Serv,* Brian Cameron; Tel: 416-979-5000, Ext 5146, E-mail: bcameron@ryerson.ca; *Head, Libr Info Tech,* Fangmin Wang; Tel: 416-979-5000, Ext 557034, E-mail: fwang@ryerson.ca; Staff 71 (MLS 23, Non-MLS 48)
Founded 1948. Enrl 18,300; Fac 550
Library Holdings: Electronic Media & Resources 21,434; Bk Vols 514,204; Per Subs 2,212
Special Collections: Canadian and Provincial
Subject Interests: Applied arts, Bus, Commun serv, Engr
Automation Activity & Vendor Info: (Acquisitions) Innovative Interfaces, Inc; (Cataloging) Innovative Interfaces, Inc; (Circulation) Innovative Interfaces, Inc; (OPAC) Innovative Interfaces, Inc
Wireless access
Partic in Canadian Association of Research Libraries; Ontario Council of University Libraries
Open Mon-Fri 7am-1am, Sat & Sun 10am-1am

M ST JOSEPH'S HEALTH CENTRE (UNITY HEALTH TORONTO)*, George Pennal Library, 30 The Queensway, M6R 1B5. SAN 319-5589. Tel: 416-530-6726. FAX: 416-530-6244. Web Site: library.stjoestoronto.ca. *Mgr, Health Inf & Knowledge Mobilization,* Zachary Osborne; E-mail: zachary.osborne@unityhealth.to; Staff 9 (MLS 7, Non-MLS 2)
Founded 1963
Library Holdings: e-books 85; e-journals 1,500; Bk Vols 1,000; Per Subs 38
Automation Activity & Vendor Info: (Cataloging) SirsiDynix-WorkFlows
Partic in Health Science Information Consortium of Toronto
Open Mon-Fri 8-6

M ST MICHAEL'S HOSPITAL*, Health Sciences Library, 209 Victoria St, M5B 1W8. (Mail add: 30 Bond St, M5B 1W8), SAN 320-3409. Tel: 416-864-5059. Interlibrary Loan Service Tel: 416-864-5419. FAX: 416-864-5296. E-mail: hslibrary@smh.ca. Web Site: www.stmichaelshospital.com/education/library.php. *Mgr,* Zachary Osborne; Tel: 416-864-6060, Ext 77694; Staff 7 (MLS 5, Non-MLS 2)
Founded 1961
Library Holdings: Bk Titles 3,000; Per Subs 500
Subject Interests: Med
Open Mon-Fri 8-6

S SAINT VLADIMIR INSTITUTE LIBRARY*, 620 Spadina Ave, M5S 2H4. SAN 321-091X. Tel: 416-923-3318. FAX: 416-923-8266. E-mail: library@stvladimir.ca, svi@stvladimir.ca. Web Site: www.stvladimir.ca. *Librn,* Halyna Ostapchuk; Staff 1 (Non-MLS 1)
Founded 1970

Library Holdings: Bk Vols 19,000; Per Subs 15
Special Collections: Canadian Ukrainians in Canadian Press, 1921 to present; Rare Book Coll; Ukrainians in Toronto, posters
Subject Interests: Archaeology, Hist, Lit, Music, Relig
Open Tues 2-8, Wed & Fri 10-3, Thurs 3-8, Sat 11-2
Restriction: Access at librarian's discretion

L SHIBLEY RIGHTON LLP*, Law Library, 250 University Ave, Ste 700, M5H 3E5. SAN 326-3932. Tel: 416-214-5294. Interlibrary Loan Service Tel: 416-214-5427. FAX: 416-214-5400. Interlibrary Loan Service FAX: 416-214-5426. Web Site: www.shibleyrighton.com. *Librn,* Joan Hudson; E-mail: joan.hudson@shibleyrighton.com; Staff 2 (MLS 1, Non-MLS 1)
Library Holdings: Bk Titles 2,500; Per Subs 400
Automation Activity & Vendor Info: (Serials) Inmagic, Inc.
Publications: Weekly Bulletin
Restriction: Staff use only

L STIKEMAN ELLIOTT*, Information Services Department, 5300 Commerce Ct W, 199 Bay St, M5L 1B9. (Mail add: PO Box 85, M5L 1B9), SAN 328-2090. Tel: 416-869-5500. FAX: 416-947-0866. Web Site: www.stikeman.com. *Dir, Knowledge Mgt,* Adrianna DeMarco; E-mail: ademarco@stikeman.com
Founded 1975
Library Holdings: Bk Vols 20,000; Per Subs 200
Subject Interests: Banking, Corporate-commercial, Environ, Labor, Real estate, Securities, Tax
Wireless access
Restriction: Not open to pub

SUNNYBROOK HEALTH SCIENCES CENTRE - LIBRARY SERVICES

M HOLLAND ORTHOPAEDIC & ARTHRITIC CENTRE*, 43 Wellesley St E, M4Y 1H1, SAN 373-1464. Tel: 416-967-8545. FAX: 416-967-8605. E-mail: library.requests@sunnybrook.ca. *Librn,* Carmen Genuardi; Staff 1.3 (MLS 1.3)
Library Holdings: Bk Titles 1,105; Per Subs 16
Subject Interests: Arthritis, Arthroscopy, Orthopedic surgery, Orthopedics, Rehabilitation, Rheumatology
Partic in Health Sci Libr Info Consortium
Open Mon-Fri 9-5
Restriction: Hospital employees & physicians only, In-house use for visitors

M DR R IAN MACDONALD LIBRARY*, 2075 Bayview Ave, M4N 3M5, SAN 319-5627. Tel: 416-480-6100, Ext 4562. Administration Tel: 416-480-6100, Ext 2560. FAX: 416-480-6848. *Mgr, Libr Serv,* Dr Farid Miah; Staff 6 (MLS 2, Non-MLS 4)
Founded 1968
Library Holdings: AV Mats 1,227; e-books 10; e-journals 185; Bk Titles 3,294; Per Subs 120; Videos 250
Subject Interests: Hospital admin, Med, Mentally challenged adults, Nursing, Women's health
Automation Activity & Vendor Info: (Acquisitions) EOS International; (Cataloging) EOS International; (Circulation) EOS International; (OPAC) EOS International; (Serials) EOS International
Open Mon-Fri 9-5, Sat & Sun 1-6

M SUNNYBROOK LIBRARY SERVICES*, 2075 Bayview Ave, Rm EG-29, M4N 3M5, SAN 319-5767. Tel: 416-480-4562. FAX: 416-480-6848. E-mail: library.requests@sunnybrook.ca. *Mgr, Libr Serv,* Md Farid Miah; Tel: 416-480-6100, Ext 2560; *Info Spec,* Henry Lam; Tel: 416-480-6100, Ext 2562, E-mail: henry.lam@sunnybrook.ca
Founded 1965
Library Holdings: e-books 100; e-journals 2,000; Electronic Media & Resources 100; Bk Vols 6,000; Per Subs 131
Subject Interests: Aging, Cancer, Cardiology, Critical care, Dermatology, Gynecology, Internal med, Neuroscience, Orthopedics, Perinatology, Pop health, Trauma, Women's health
Automation Activity & Vendor Info: (Acquisitions) SirsiDynix-WorkFlows; (Cataloging) SirsiDynix-WorkFlows; (Circulation) SirsiDynix-WorkFlows; (OPAC) SirsiDynix-WorkFlows; (Serials) SirsiDynix-WorkFlows
Partic in Health Science Information Consortium of Toronto
Open Mon-Fri 9-5

C TARTU INSTITUTE*, Dr Endel Aruja Archives & Library, 310 Bloor St W, M5S 1W4. SAN 370-7024. Tel: 416-925-9405. FAX: 416-925-2295. E-mail: vemu@tartucollege.ca. *Head Archivist,* Piret Noorhani; E-mail: piret@tartucollege.ca; *Archivist,* Roland Weiler; Tel: 905-627-3856, E-mail: rweiler7@cogeco.ca
Founded 1971
Special Collections: Archival Materials Related to Estonians in Canada; Estonian Literature. Oral History
Wireless access
Publications: Annual Reports
Restriction: Open by appt only

S TORONTO BOTANICAL GARDEN*, Weston Family Library, 777 Lawrence Ave E, M3C 1P2. SAN 319-0986. Tel: 416-397-1343. E-mail: librarian@torontobotanicalgarden.ca. Web Site: library.torontobotanicalgarden.ca. *Librn,* Mark Stewart; Staff 1 (MLS 1)
Founded 1959
Library Holdings: Bk Vols 9,500; Per Subs 30
Special Collections: Horticulture (Canadiana & Historical Coll)
Subject Interests: Botany, Ecology, Floral design, Garden design, Hort
Automation Activity & Vendor Info: (Cataloging) Koha; (Circulation) Koha; (OPAC) Koha
Wireless access
Function: 24/7 Online cat, Adult bk club, Archival coll, Art exhibits, Bk club(s), Butterfly Garden, Children's prog, Computers for patron use, For res purposes, Free DVD rentals, Internet access, Large print keyboards, Movies, Online cat, Outside serv via phone, mail, e-mail & web, Prof lending libr, Ref & res, Ref serv available, Res assist avail, Story hour, Visual arts prog, Wheelchair accessible
Open Mon-Fri 10-4, Sat & Sun 12-4
Restriction: Circ to mem only, Free to mem, In-house use for visitors, Non-circulating of rare bks

S TORONTO INTERNATIONAL FILM FESTIVAL INC*, TIFF Film Reference Library, TIFF Bell Lightbox, 350 King St W, M5V 3X5. SAN 321-5091. Tel: 416-599-8433. E-mail: libraryservices@tiff.net. Web Site: tiff.net/library. *Librn,* Fatima Mercado; *Sr Mgr,* Michelle Lovegrove Thomson; *Mgr, Coll Serv,* Natania Sherman; *Senior Coord,* Kate Watson; *Coordr, Cat, Database Coordr,* Krista Keller; Staff 5 (MLS 2, Non-MLS 3)
Founded 1968
Library Holdings: AV Mats 20,000; CDs 4,000; DVDs 9,515; Bk Titles 24,000; Per Subs 80; Videos 15,000
Special Collections: Cronenberg Archive Coll; Egoyan Archive Coll
Subject Interests: Film
Wireless access
Open Mon-Wed & Fri 12-5, Thurs 12-7
Restriction: Closed stack, Open to pub for ref only

GL TORONTO LAWYERS ASSOCIATION LIBRARY*, Courthouse, 3rd Flr, 361 University Ave, M5G 1T3. SAN 319-4922. Tel: 416-327-5700. FAX: 416-947-9148. E-mail: library@tlaonline.ca. Web Site: www.tlaonline.ca. *Exec Dir, Libr Dir,* Joan Rataic-Lang; Tel: 416-327-6012, E-mail: jrataiclang@tlaonline.ca; Staff 4 (MLS 3, Non-MLS 1)
Founded 1885
Library Holdings: Bk Vols 30,000
Automation Activity & Vendor Info: (Cataloging) Ex Libris Group
Wireless access
Open Mon-Fri 9-5

G TORONTO PUBLIC HEALTH LIBRARY*, 277 Victoria St, 6th Flr, M5B 1W2. SAN 326-1522. Tel: 416-338-7865. FAX: 416-338-0489. E-mail: hlibrary@toronto.ca. *Coll Develop, Sr Librn, Supvr,* Bruce Gardham; Tel: 416-338-8284, E-mail: Bruce.Gardham@toronto.ca; *Librn,* Minakshi Sharma; Tel: 416-338-0049, E-mail: Minakshi.Sharma@toronto.ca; *Info Officer, ILL,* Graciela Latan; Tel: 416-338-7862, E-mail: glatan@toronto.ca. Subject Specialists: *Health,* Minakshi Sharma; Staff 3 (MLS 2, Non-MLS 1)
Founded 1985
Jan 2019-Dec 2019 Income (CAN) $450,000. Mats Exp (CAN) $160,000, Books (CAN) $10,000, Per/Ser (Incl. Access Fees) (CAN) $95,000, Electronic Ref Mat (Incl. Access Fees) (CAN) $50,000
Library Holdings: e-books 35; e-journals 15,000; Electronic Media & Resources 65; Bk Vols 14,000; Per Subs 125
Subject Interests: Health, Health admin, Health policy, Health promotion, Pub health
Automation Activity & Vendor Info: (Acquisitions) SoutronGLOBAL; (Cataloging) SoutronGLOBAL; (Circulation) SoutronGLOBAL; (OPAC) SoutronGLOBAL; (Serials) SoutronGLOBAL
Partic in Health Science Information Consortium of Toronto; Knowledge Ontario; Ontario Public Health Libraries Association
Open Mon-Fri 8:30-4:30
Restriction: Clients only, External users must contact libr, In-house use for visitors

P TORONTO PUBLIC LIBRARY*, 789 Yonge St, M4W 2G8. SAN 368-5683. Tel: 416-393-7131. FAX: 416-393-7229. TDD: 416-393-7030. Web Site: www.torontopubliclibrary.ca. *Pres, Toronto Pub Libr Found,* Jennifer Jones; E-mail: jjones@tpl.ca; *City Librn,* Ms Vickery Bowles; E-mail: citylibrarian@tpl.ca; *Dir, Br Operations,* Mr Moe Hosseini-Ara; E-mail: branchoperations@tpl.ca; *Dir of Coll,* Susan Caron; E-mail: scaron@@tpl.ca; *Dir, Communications, Dir, Programming,* Linda Hazzan; E-mail: lhazzan@@tpl.ca; *Dir of Finance,* Larry Hughsam; E-mail: lhughsam@@tpl.ca; *Dir, Human Res,* Dan Keon; E-mail: dkeon@@tpl.ca; *Dir, Planning, Policy & E-Serv Delivery,* Elizabeth Glass; E-mail: eglass@tpl.ca; *Dir, Serv Develop,* Pam Ryan; E-mail: pryan@tpl.ca
Founded 1883. Pop 2,771,770; Circ 32,016,790

Library Holdings: Bk Vols 11,129,221
Special Collections: Art Room; Arthur Conan Doyle Coll; Black & Caribbean Heritage Coll; Business Information Centre; Canadian Theatre Record; Canadiana; Children's Literature Resource Coll; Consumer Health Information Service; Digital Coll; Electronic Books; Historicity:Toronto Then & Now; History of Canada (Baldwin Room); Jewish Mosaic; John Ross Robertson Coll; Languages Centre; Languages, Literature & Fine Arts; Local History Resources; Map Coll; Marguerite G Bagshaw Coll, puppetry, creative drama & theatre for children; Merril Coll of Science Fiction, Speculation & Fantasy; Native Peoples Coll; Osborne Coll of Early Children's Books; Performing Arts Centre; TD Audubon Coll; Theatre Coll Room; Toronto Star Newspaper Centre; Urban Affairs Library
Wireless access
Special Services for the Deaf - Sign lang interpreter upon request for prog
Special Services for the Blind - Braille bks; Talking bks
Open Mon-Fri 9-8:30, Sat 9-5
Friends of the Library Group

Branches: 100

AGINCOURT LIBRARY, 155 Bonis Ave, M1T 3W6, SAN 368-3524. Tel: 416-396-8943. FAX: 416-396-8956.
Circ 1,140,779
Library Holdings: Bk Vols 230,071
Special Services for the Blind - Screen enlargement software for people with visual disabilities
Open Mon-Fri 9-8:30, Sat 9-5, Sun (Sept-June) 1:30-5

ALBION BRANCH, 1515 Albion Rd, M9V 1B2, SAN 367-1976. Tel: 416-394-5170. FAX: 416-394-5185.
Circ 398,064
Library Holdings: Bk Vols 116,372
Special Services for the Blind - Screen enlargement software for people with visual disabilities
Open Mon-Fri 9-8:30, Sat 9-5, Sun (Sept-June) 1:30-5

ALDERWOOD BRANCH, Two Orianna Dr, M8W 4Y1, SAN 367-200X. Tel: 416-394-5310. FAX: 416-394-5313.
Circ 176,482
Library Holdings: Bk Vols 42,220
Special Services for the Blind - Screen enlargement software for people with visual disabilities
Open Mon 10-8:30, Tues, Wed & Fri 10-6, Thurs 12:30-8:30, Sat 9-5

AMESBURY PARK BRANCH, 1565 Lawrence Ave W, M6L 1A8, SAN 368-8593. Tel: 416-395-5420. FAX: 416-395-5432.
Circ 140,935
Library Holdings: Bk Vols 32,992
Special Services for the Blind - Screen enlargement software for people with visual disabilities
Open Tues & Thurs 12:30-8:30, Wed & Fri 10-6, Sat 9-5

ANNETTE STREET BRANCH, 145 Annette St, M6P 1P3, SAN 368-5713. Tel: 416-393-7692. FAX: 416-393-7412.
Circ 192,045
Library Holdings: Bk Vols 31,063
Special Services for the Blind - Screen enlargement software for people with visual disabilities
Open Mon 10-8:30, Tues & Thurs 12:30-8:30, Wed & Fri 10-6, Sat 9-5

ARMOUR HEIGHTS BRANCH, 2140 Avenue Rd, M5M 4M7, SAN 368-8607. Tel: 416-395-5430. FAX: 416-395-5433.
Circ 191,894
Library Holdings: Bk Vols 27,106
Special Services for the Blind - Screen enlargement software for people with visual disabilities
Open Tues, Thurs & Fri 10-6, Wed 12:30-8:30, Sat 9-5

BAYVIEW BRANCH, 123A Bayview Village Shopping Ctr, 2901 Bayview Ave, M2K 1E6, SAN 368-8658. Tel: 416-395-5460. FAX: 416-395-5434.
Circ 452,713
Library Holdings: Bk Vols 50,556
Special Services for the Blind - Screen enlargement software for people with visual disabilities
Open Mon 10-8:30, Tues & Thurs 12:30-8:30, Wed & Fri 10-6, Sat 9-5

BEACHES BRANCH, 2161 Queen St E, M4L 1J1, SAN 368-5748. Tel: 416-393-7703. FAX: 416-393-7422.
Circ 347,125
Library Holdings: Bk Vols 45,955
Special Services for the Blind - Screen enlargement software for people with visual disabilities
Open Mon-Thurs 9-8:30, Fri & Sat 9-5

BENDALE BRANCH, 1515 Danforth Rd, M1J 1H5, SAN 368-3559. Tel: 416-396-8910. FAX: 416-396-3608.
Circ 200,129
Library Holdings: Bk Vols 36,567
Special Services for the Blind - Screen enlargement software for people with visual disabilities
Open Tues & Thurs 12:30-8:30, Wed & Fri 10-6, Sat 9-5

BLACK CREEK BRANCH, North York Sheridan Mall, 1700 Wilson Ave, M3L 1B2, SAN 368-8682. Tel: 416-395-5470. FAX: 416-395-5435.
Circ 114,375
Library Holdings: Bk Vols 33,860
Special Services for the Blind - Screen enlargement software for people with visual disabilities
Open Tues & Thurs 12:30-8:30, Wed & Fri 10-6, Sat 9-5

BLOOR/GLADSTONE BRANCH, 1101 Bloor St W, M6H 1M7, SAN 368-5772. Tel: 416-393-7674. FAX: 416-393-7502.
Circ 441,779
Library Holdings: Bk Vols 78,297
Special Services for the Blind - Screen enlargement software for people with visual disabilities
Open Mon-Fri 9-8:30, Sat 9-5, Sun (Sept-June) 1:30-5

BRENTWOOD BRANCH, 36 Brentwood Rd N, M8X 2B5, SAN 367-2034. Tel: 416-394-5240. FAX: 416-394-5257.
Circ 405,716
Library Holdings: Bk Vols 80,307
Special Services for the Blind - Screen enlargement software for people with visual disabilities
Open Mon-Fri 9-8:30, Sat 9-5, Sun (Sept-June) 1:30-5

BRIDLEWOOD BRANCH, Bridlewood Mall, Lower Level, 2900 Warden Ave, M1W 2S8, SAN 368-3583. Tel: 416-396-8960. FAX: 416-396-3604.
Circ 493,667
Library Holdings: Bk Vols 62,310
Special Services for the Blind - Screen enlargement software for people with visual disabilities
Open Mon-Fri 9-8:30, Sat 9-5

BROOKBANKS BRANCH, 210 Brookbanks Dr, M3A 2T8, SAN 368-8712. Tel: 416-395-5480. FAX: 416-395-5436.
Circ 191,741
Library Holdings: Bk Vols 44,408
Special Services for the Blind - Screen enlargement software for people with visual disabilities
Open Tues & Thurs 12:30-8:30, Wed & Fri 10-6, Sat 9-5

BURROWS HALL BRANCH, 1081 Progress Ave, M1B 5Z6, SAN 378-2263. Tel: 416-396-8740. FAX: 416-396-3559.
Circ 193,458
Library Holdings: Bk Vols 46,094
Special Services for the Blind - Screen enlargement software for people with visual disabilities
Open Tues & Thurs 12:30-8:30, Wed & Fri 10-6, Sat 9-5

ALBERT CAMPBELL BRANCH, 496 Birchmount Rd, M1K 1N8, SAN 368-3613. Tel: 416-396-8890. FAX: 416-396-8901.
Circ 397,563
Library Holdings: Bk Vols 103,106
Special Services for the Blind - Screen enlargement software for people with visual disabilities
Open Mon-Fri 9-8:30, Sat 9-5, Sun (Sept-June) 1:30-5

CEDARBRAE BRANCH, 545 Markham Rd, M1H 2A1, SAN 368-3648. Tel: 416-396-8850. FAX: 416-396-8864.
Circ 583,940
Library Holdings: Bk Vols 123,731
Special Services for the Blind - Screen enlargement software for people with visual disabilities
Open Mon-Fri 9-8:30, Sat 9-5, Sun (Sept-June) 1:30-5

CENTENNIAL BRANCH, 578 Finch Ave W, M2R 1N7, SAN 368-8747. Tel: 416-395-5490. FAX: 416-395-5437.
Circ 311,490
Library Holdings: Bk Vols 43,266
Special Services for the Blind - Screen enlargement software for people with visual disabilities
Open Mon 10-8:30, Tues & Thurs 12:30-8:30, Wed & Fri 10-6, Sat 9-5

CITY HALL BRANCH, Nathan Phillips Sq, 100 Queen St W, M5H 2N3, SAN 368-5861. Tel: 416-393-7650. FAX: 416-393-7421.
Circ 360,042
Library Holdings: Bk Vols 32,425
Special Services for the Blind - Screen enlargement software for people with visual disabilities
Open Mon-Fri 10-6

CLIFFCREST BRANCH, Cliffcrest Plaza, 3017 Kingston Rd, M1M 1P1, SAN 368-3672. Tel: 416-396-8916. FAX: 416-396-3605.
Circ 174,837
Library Holdings: Bk Titles 29,030
Special Services for the Blind - Screen enlargement software for people with visual disabilities
Open Tues & Thurs 12:30-8:30, Wed & Fri 10-6, Sat 9-5

COLLEGE-SHAW BRANCH, 766 College St, M6G 1C4, SAN 322-6255. Tel: 416-393-7668. FAX: 416-393-7418.
Circ 194,176
Library Holdings: Bk Vols 30,051
Special Services for the Blind - Screen enlargement software for people with visual disabilities
Open Mon 10-8:30, Tues & Thurs 12:30-8:30, Wed & Fri 10-6, Sat 9-5

DANFORTH/COXWELL BRANCH, 1675 Danforth Ave, M4C 5P2, SAN 329-6555. Tel: 416-393-7783. FAX: 416-393-7578.
Circ 306,292

Library Holdings: Bk Vols 46,286
Special Services for the Blind - Screen enlargement software for people with visual disabilities
Open Mon-Thurs 9-8:30, Fri & Sat 9-5
DAVENPORT BRANCH, 1246 Shaw St, M6G 3P1, SAN 329-6571. Tel: 416-393-7732. FAX: 416-393-7588.
Circ 120,530
Library Holdings: Bk Vols 11,718
Special Services for the Blind - Screen enlargement software for people with visual disabilities
Open Mon, Wed & Fri 10-6, Tues & Thurs 12:30-8:30, Sat 9-5
DAWES ROAD BRANCH, 416 Dawes Rd, M4B 2E8, SAN 368-508X. Tel: 416-396-3820. FAX: 416-396-3825.
Circ 207,552
Library Holdings: Bk Vols 54,646
Special Services for the Blind - Screen enlargement software for people with visual disabilities
Open Mon 10-8:30, Tues & Thurs 12:30-8:30, Wed & Fri 10-6, Sat 9-5
DEER PARK BRANCH, 40 St Clair Ave E, M4T 1M9, SAN 368-5926. Tel: 416-393-7657. FAX: 416-393-7417.
Circ 409,300
Library Holdings: Bk Vols 72,613
Special Services for the Blind - Screen enlargement software for people with visual disabilities
Open Mon-Thurs 9-8:30, Fri & Sat 9-5
DON MILLS BRANCH, 888 Lawrence Ave E, M3C 1P6, SAN 368-8801. Tel: 416-395-5710. FAX: 416-395-5715.
Circ 600,127
Library Holdings: Bk Vols 115,216
Special Services for the Blind - Screen enlargement software for people with visual disabilities
Open Mon-Fri 9-8:30, Sat 9-5, Sun (Sept-June) 1:30-5
DOWNSVIEW BRANCH, 2793 Keele St, M3M 2G3, SAN 368-8836. Tel: 416-395-5720. FAX: 416-395-5727.
Circ 240,865
Library Holdings: Bk Vols 82,227
Special Services for the Blind - Screen enlargement software for people with visual disabilities
Open Mon-Thurs 9-8:30, Fri & Sat 9-5
DUFFERIN/ST CLAIR BRANCH, 1625 Dufferin St, M6H 3L9, SAN 368-5950. Tel: 416-393-7712. FAX: 416-393-7410.
Circ 145,949
Library Holdings: Bk Vols 38,638
Special Services for the Blind - Screen enlargement software for people with visual disabilities
Open Mon 10-8:30, Tues & Thurs 12:30-8:30, Wed & Fri 10-6, Sat 9-5
EATONVILLE BRANCH, 430 Burnhamthorpe Rd, M9B 2B1, SAN 367-2069. Tel: 416-394-5270. FAX: 416-394-5276.
Circ 511,266
Library Holdings: Bk Vols 68,977
Special Services for the Blind - Screen enlargement software for people with visual disabilities
Open Mon-Thurs 9-8:30, Fri & Sat 9-5
EGLINTON SQUARE BRANCH, Eglinton Square Shopping Ctr, One Eglinton Sq, Unit 126, M1L 2K1, SAN 368-3702. Tel: 416-396-8920. FAX: 416-396-3557.
Circ 259,982
Library Holdings: Bk Vols 38,780
Special Services for the Blind - Screen enlargement software for people with visual disabilities
Open Mon-Thurs 9-8:30, Fri & Sat 9-5
ELMBROOK PARK BRANCH, Two Elmbrook Crescent, M9C 5B4, SAN 370-2030. Tel: 416-394-5290. FAX: 416-394-5295.
Circ 167,200
Library Holdings: Bk Vols 29,311
Special Services for the Blind - Screen enlargement software for people with visual disabilities
Open Tues & Fri 10-6, Wed & Thurs 12:30-8:30, Sat 9-5
FAIRVIEW BRANCH, 35 Fairview Mall Dr, M2J 4S4, SAN 368-8860. Tel: 416-395-5750. FAX: 416-395-5756.
Circ 697,503
Library Holdings: Bk Vols 219,826
Open Mon-Fri 9-8:30, Sat 9-5, Sun (Sept-June) 1:30-5
FLEMINGDON PARK BRANCH, 29 St Dennis Dr, M3C 3J3, SAN 368-8895. Tel: 416-395-5820. FAX: 416-395-5438.
Circ 153,543
Library Holdings: Bk Vols 37,208
Special Services for the Blind - Screen enlargement software for people with visual disabilities
Open Tues & Thurs 12:30-8:30, Wed & Fri 10-6, Sat 9-5
FOREST HILL BRANCH, 700 Eglinton Ave W, M5N 1B9, SAN 368-5985. Tel: 416-393-7706. FAX: 416-393-7611.
Circ 205,210
Library Holdings: Bk Vols 45,130
Special Services for the Blind - Screen enlargement software for people with visual disabilities
Open Mon-Thurs 9-8:30, Fri & Sat 9-5
FORT YORK BRANCH, 190 Fort York Blvd, M5V 0E7. Tel: 416-393-6240.
Circ 132,032
Library Holdings: Bk Vols 35,376
Open Mon-Thurs 9-8:30, Fri & Sat 9-5
BARBARA FRUM LIBRARY, 20 Covington Rd, M6A 3C1, SAN 368-8623. Tel: 416-395-5440. FAX: 416-395-5447.
Circ 584,874
Library Holdings: Bk Vols 128,094
Open Mon-Fri 9-8:30, Sat 9-5, Sun (Sept-June) 1:30-5
GERRARD/ASHDALE BRANCH, 1432 Gerrard St E, M4L 1Z6, SAN 368-6043. Tel: 416-393-7717. FAX: 416-393-7779.
Circ 182,005
Library Holdings: Bk Vols 40,826
Special Services for the Blind - Screen enlargement software for people with visual disabilities
Open Mon 10-8:30, Tues & Thurs 12:30-8:30, Wed & Fri 10-6, Sat 9-5
GOLDHAWK PARK BRANCH, 295 Alton Towers Circle, M1V 4P1, SAN 373-854X. Tel: 416-396-8964. FAX: 416-396-3561.
Circ 286,203
Library Holdings: Bk Vols 43,326
Special Services for the Blind - Screen enlargement software for people with visual disabilities
Open Mon-Thurs 9-8:30, Fri & Sat 9-5
EVELYN GREGORY BRANCH, 120 Trowell Ave, M6M 1L7. Tel: 416-394-1006. FAX: 416-394-1035.
Circ 83,231
Library Holdings: Bk Vols 37,672
Special Services for the Blind - Screen enlargement software for people with visual disabilities
Open Mon 10–8:30, Tues & Thurs 12:30–8:30, Wed & Fri 10–6, Sat 9–5
GUILDWOOD BRANCH, Guildwood Plaza, 123 Guildwood Pkwy, M1E 4V2, SAN 368-3737. Tel: 416-396-8872. FAX: 416-396-3610.
Circ 124,635
Library Holdings: Bk Vols 29,881
Special Services for the Blind - Screen enlargement software for people with visual disabilities
Open Tues & Thurs 12:30-8:30, Wed & Fri 10-6, Sat 9-5
HIGH PARK BRANCH, 228 Roncesvalles Ave, M6R 2L7, SAN 368-6078. Tel: 416-393-7671. FAX: 416-393-7411.
Circ 334,288
Library Holdings: Bk Vols 46,745
Special Services for the Blind - Screen enlargement software for people with visual disabilities
Open Mon-Thurs 9-8:30, Fri & Sat 9-5
HIGHLAND CREEK BRANCH, 3550 Ellesmere Rd, M1C 3Z2, SAN 368-3761. Tel: 416-396-8876. FAX: 416-396-3562.
Circ 191,982
Library Holdings: Bk Vols 40,546
Special Services for the Blind - Screen enlargement software for people with visual disabilities
Open Tues & Thurs 12:30-8:30, Wed & Fri 10-6, Sat 9-5
HILLCREST BRANCH, 5801 Leslie St, M2H 1J8, SAN 368-8925. Tel: 416-395-5830. FAX: 416-395-5439.
Circ 363,435
Library Holdings: Bk Vols 46,881
Open Tues & Thurs 12:30-8:30, Wed & Fri 10-6, Sat 9-5
HUMBER BAY BRANCH, 200 Park Lawn Rd, M8Y 3J1, SAN 367-2093. Tel: 416-394-5300. FAX: 416-394-5072.
Circ 181,114
Library Holdings: Bk Vols 23,857
Open Tues & Fri 10-6, Wed & Thurs 12:30-8:30, Sat 9-5
HUMBER SUMMIT BRANCH, 2990 Islington Ave, M9L 2K6, SAN 368-895X. Tel: 416-395-5840. FAX: 416-395-5426.
Circ 78,361
Library Holdings: Bk Vols 22,724
Open Tues & Thurs 12:30-8:30, Wed & Fri 10-6, Sat 9-5
HUMBERWOOD BRANCH, 850 Humberwood Blvd, M9W 7A6, SAN 376-9682. Tel: 416-394-5210. FAX: 416-394-5215.
Circ 90,586
Library Holdings: Bk Vols 39,945
Open Tues & Thurs 12:30–8:30, Wed & Fri 10-6, Sat 9–5
JANE/DUNDAS BRANCH, 620 Jane St, M6S 4A6, SAN 368-475X. Tel: 416-394-1014. FAX: 416-394-1025.
Circ 284,989
Library Holdings: Bk Vols 55,348
Open Mon-Thurs 9–8:30, Fri & Sat 9–5
JANE/SHEPPARD BRANCH, 1906 Sheppard Ave W, M3L 1Y7, SAN 370-0933. Tel: 416-395-5966. FAX: 416-395-5427.
Circ 128,712
Library Holdings: Bk Vols 33,896
Open Mon 10-8:30, Tues & Thurs 12:30-8:30, Wed & Fri 10-6, Sat 9-5

JONES BRANCH, 118 Jones Ave, M4M 2Z9, SAN 368-6108. Tel: 416-393-7715. FAX: 416-393-7416.
Circ 178,651
Library Holdings: Bk Vols 29,724
Open Mon & Fri 10-6, Tues 10-8:30, Wed & Thurs 12:30-8:30, Sat 9-5
KENNEDY-EGLINTON BRANCH, Liberty Square Shopping Plaza, 2380 Eglinton Ave E, M1K 2P3, SAN 329-6547. Tel: 416-396-8924. FAX: 416-396-8928.
Circ 194,228
Library Holdings: Bk Vols 35,752
Open Tues & Thurs 12:30-8:30, Wed & Fri 10-6, Sat 9-5
LEASIDE BRANCH, 165 McRae Dr, M4G 1S8, SAN 368-5020. Tel: 416-396-3835. FAX: 416-396-3840.
Circ 362,645
Library Holdings: Bk Vols 55,091
Open Mon-Thurs 9-8:30, Fri & Sat 9-5
LOCKE BRANCH, 3083 Yonge St, M4N 2K7, SAN 368-6019. Tel: 416-393-7730. FAX: 416-393-7581.
Circ 347,352
Library Holdings: Bk Vols 68,102
Open Mon-Thurs 9-8:30, Fri & Sat 9-5
LONG BRANCH, 3500 Lakeshore Blvd W, M8W 1N6, SAN 367-2123. Tel: 416-394-5320. FAX: 416-394-5326.
Circ 138,524
Library Holdings: Bk Vols 34,309
Open Tues & Thurs 12:30-8:30, Wed & Fri 10-6, Sat 9-5
MAIN STREET BRANCH, 137 Main St, M4E 2V9, SAN 368-6132. Tel: 416-393-7700. FAX: 416-393-7505.
Circ 252,777
Library Holdings: Bk Vols 41,400
Open Mon-Thurs 9-8:30, Fri & Sat 9-5
MALVERN BRANCH, 30 Sewells Rd, M1B 3G5, SAN 368-377X. Tel: 416-396-8969. FAX: 416-396-3560.
Circ 442,480
Library Holdings: Bk Vols 132,514
Open Mon-Fri 9-8:30, Sat 9-5, Sun (Sept-June) 1:30-5
MARYVALE BRANCH, Parkway Mall, Unit 16, 85 Ellesmere Rd, M1R 4B9, SAN 368-3788. Tel: 416-396-8931. FAX: 416-396-3603.
Circ 239,773
Library Holdings: Bk Vols 49,899
Open Mon 10-8:30, Tues & Thurs 12:30-8:30, Wed & Fri 10-6, Sat 9-5
MCGREGOR PARK BRANCH, 2219 Lawrence Ave E, M1P 2P5, SAN 368-3796. Tel: 416-396-8935. FAX: 416-396-3609.
Circ 234,412
Library Holdings: Bk Vols 39,951
Open Tues & Thurs 12:30-8:30, Wed & Fri 10-6, Sat 9-5
MIMICO CENTENNIAL LIBRARY, 47 Station Rd, M8V 2R1, SAN 367-2158. Tel: 416-394-5330. FAX: 416-394-5338.
Circ 169,205
Library Holdings: Bk Vols 49,909
Open Tues & Wed 12:30-8:30, Thurs & Fri 10-6, Sat 9-5
MORNINGSIDE BRANCH, Morningside Mall, 255 Morningside Ave, M1E 2S8, SAN 368-3826. Tel: 416-396-8881. FAX: 416-396-3606.
Circ 189,536
Library Holdings: Bk Vols 42,946
Open Mon-Thurs 9-8:30, Fri & Sat 9-5
MOUNT DENNIS BRANCH, 1123 Weston Rd, M6N 3S3, SAN 368-4784. Tel: 416-394-1008. FAX: 416-394-1036.
Circ 114,699
Library Holdings: Bk Vols 40,307
Open Mon 10-8:30, Tues & Thurs 12:30-8:30, Wed & Fri 10-6, Sat 9-5
MOUNT PLEASANT BRANCH, 599 Mount Pleasant Rd, M4S 2M5, SAN 372-0047. Tel: 416-393-7737. FAX: 416-393-7414.
Circ 152,204
Library Holdings: Bk Vols 21,790
Open Tues & Thurs 12:30-8:30, Wed & Fri 10-6, Sat 9-5
NEW TORONTO BRANCH, 110 Eleventh St, M8V 3G5, SAN 367-2182. Tel: 416-394-5350. FAX: 416-394-5358.
Circ 127,437
Library Holdings: Bk Vols 40,747
Open Tues & Fri 10–6, Wed & Thurs 12:30–8:30, Sat 9–5
NORTH YORK CENTRAL LIBRARY, 5120 Yonge St, M2N 5N9, SAN 368-8771. Tel: 416-395-5535. FAX: 416-395-5668.
Circ 1,611,707
Library Holdings: Bk Vols 651,615
Special Services for the Deaf - TTY equip
Special Services for the Blind - Screen enlargement software for people with visual disabilities; Screen reader software
Open Mon-Fri 9-8:30, Sat 9-5, Sun (Sept-June) 1:30-5
Friends of the Library Group
NORTHERN DISTRICT BRANCH, 40 Orchard View Blvd, M4R 1B9, SAN 368-6167. Tel: 416-393-7610. FAX: 416-393-7742.
Circ 464,258
Library Holdings: Bk Vols 125,597
Open Mon-Fri 9-8:30, Sat 9-5, Sun (Sept-June) 1:30-5
NORTHERN ELMS BRANCH, 123B Rexdale Blvd, Unit 5, M9W 1P1, SAN 372-5227. Tel: 416-394-5230. FAX: 416-394-5235.
Circ 89,744
Library Holdings: Bk Vols 25,978
Open Tues & Wed 12:30-8:30, Thurs & Fri 10-6, Sat 9-5
OAKWOOD VILLAGE LIBRARY & ARTS CENTRE, 341 Oakwood Ave, M6E 2W1, SAN 377-7855. Tel: 416-394-1040. FAX: 416-394-1039.
Circ 132,013
Library Holdings: Bk Vols 36,083
Open Mon 10-8:30, Tues & Thurs 12:30-8:30, Wed & Fri 10-6, Sat 9-5
PALMERSTON BRANCH, 560 Palmerston Ave, M6G 2P7, SAN 368-6191. Tel: 416-393-7680. FAX: 416-393-7420.
Circ 218,313
Library Holdings: Bk Vols 33,551
Open Mon 10-8:30, Tues & Thurs 12:30-8:30, Wed & Fri 10-6, Sat 9-5
PAPE/DANFORTH BRANCH, 701 Pape Ave, M4K 3S6, SAN 368-5896. Tel: 416-393-7727. FAX: 416-393-7503.
Circ 424,013
Library Holdings: Bk Vols 57,394
Open Mon-Fri 9-8:30, Sat 9-5, Sun (Sept-June) 1:30-5
PARKDALE BRANCH, 1303 Queen St W, M6K 1L6, SAN 368-6221. Tel: 416-393-7686. FAX: 416-393-7705.
Circ 372,164
Library Holdings: Bk Vols 73,616
PARLIAMENT STREET BRANCH, 269 Gerrard St E, M5A 2G3, SAN 368-6256. Tel: 416-393-7663. FAX: 416-393-7413.
Circ 238,812
Library Holdings: Bk Vols 58,895
PERTH/DUPONT BRANCH, 1589 Dupont St, M6P 3S5, SAN 368-6280. Tel: 416-393-7677. FAX: 416-393-7724.
Circ 90,891
Library Holdings: Bk Vols 18,976
Open Tues & Thurs 12:30-8:30, Wed & Fri 10-6, Sat 9-5
PLEASANT VIEW BRANCH, 575 Van Horne Ave, M2J 4S8, SAN 368-8984. Tel: 416-395-5940. FAX: 416-395-5419.
Circ 238,569
Library Holdings: Bk Vols 31,030
Open Tues & Thurs 12:30-8:30, Wed & Fri 10-6, Sat 9-5
PORT UNION BRANCH, 5450 Lawrence Ave E, M1C 3B2, SAN 368-3850. Tel: 416-396-8885. FAX: 416-396-3558.
Circ 230,936
Library Holdings: Bk Vols 35,979
Open Mon 10-8:30, Tues & Thurs 12:30-8:30, Wed & Fri 10-6, Sat 9-5
QUEEN/SAULTER BRANCH, 765 Queen St E, M4M 1H3, SAN 368-6299. Tel: 416-393-7723. FAX: 416-393-7423.
Circ 115,755
Library Holdings: Bk Vols 21,619
Open Tues & Thurs 12:30-8:30, Wed & Fri 10-6, Sat 9-5
REXDALE BRANCH, 2243 Kipling Ave, M9W 4L5, SAN 367-2212. Tel: 416-394-5200. FAX: 416-394-5205.
Circ 80,634
Library Holdings: Bk Vols 30,180
Open Tues & Fri 10-6, Wed & Thurs 12:30-8:30, Sat 9-5
RICHVIEW BRANCH, 1806 Islington Ave, M9P 3N3, SAN 367-2247. Tel: 416-394-5120. FAX: 416-394-5158.
Circ 599,026
Library Holdings: Bk Vols 156,662
Open Mon-Fri 9-8:30, Sat 9-5, Sun (Sept-June) 1:30-5
RIVERDALE BRANCH, 370 Broadview Ave, M4K 2M8, SAN 368-6310. Tel: 416-393-7720. FAX: 416-393-7424.
Circ 306,035
Library Holdings: Bk Vols 58,419
Open Mon-Thurs 9-8:30, Fri & Sat 9-5
RUNNYMEDE BRANCH, 2178 Bloor St W, M6S 1M8, SAN 368-6345. Tel: 416-393-7697. FAX: 416-393-7574.
Circ 448,415
Library Holdings: Bk Vols 58,286
Open Mon-Thurs 9-8:30, Fri & Sat 9-5
SAINT JAMES TOWN BRANCH, 495 Sherbourne St, M4X 1K7. Tel: 416-393-7744. FAX: 416-393-7562.
Circ 281,414
Library Holdings: Bk Vols 52,878
Open Mon & Sat 9-5, Tues-Fri 9-8:30
SAINT LAWRENCE BRANCH, 171 Front St E, M5A 4H3, SAN 368-6361. Tel: 416-393-7655. FAX: 416-393-7419.
Circ 219,009
Library Holdings: Bk Vols 28,597
Open Mon-Thurs 9-8:30, Wed 10-6, Sat 9-5
SANDERSON BRANCH, 327 Bathurst St, M5T 1J1, SAN 368-5837. Tel: 416-393-7653. FAX: 416-393-7702.
Circ 264,444
Library Holdings: Bk Vols 49,387
Open Mon-Thurs 9-8:30, Fri & Sat 9-5

SCARBOROUGH CIVIC CENTRE, 156 Borough Dr, M1P 4N7. Tel: 416-396-3599.
Library Holdings: Bk Vols 28,527
Open Mon-Thurs 9-8:30, Fri & Sat 9-5
MARIA A SHCHUKA BRANCH, 1745 Eglinton Ave W, M6E 2H4, SAN 368-4768. Tel: 416-394-1000. FAX: 416-394-1034.
Circ 232,498
Library Holdings: Bk Titles 96,601
Open Mon-Fri 9-8:30, Sat 9-5, Sun (Sept-June) 1:30-5
LILLIAN H SMITH BRANCH, 239 College St, M5T 1R5, SAN 368-5802. Tel: 416-393-7746. FAX: 416-393-7609.
Circ 431,048
Library Holdings: Bk Vols 107,182
Open Mon-Fri 9-8:30, Sat 9-5, Sun (Sept-June) 1:30-5
SPADINA ROAD BRANCH, Ten Spadina Rd, M5R 2S7, SAN 368-637X. Tel: 416-393-7666. FAX: 416-393-7415.
Circ 160,837
Library Holdings: Bk Vols 32,751
Special Collections: Native Peoples' Coll
Open Tues & Thurs 12:30-8:30, Wed & Fri 10-6, Sat 9-5
ST CLAIR/SILVERTHORN BRANCH, 1748 St Clair Ave W, M6N 1J3, SAN 368-6353. Tel: 416-393-7709. FAX: 416-393-7409.
Circ 58,693
Library Holdings: Bk Vols 15,452
Open Tues & Thurs 12:30-8:30, Wed & Fri 10-6, Sat 9-5, Sun 1:30-5
STEELES BRANCH, Bamburgh Gardens Shopping Plaza, C107-375 Bamburgh Circle, M1W 3Y1, SAN 328-915X. Tel: 416-396-8975. FAX: 416-396-3602.
Circ 224,923
Library Holdings: Bk Vols 44,344
Open Mon-Fri 9-8:30, Sat 9-5
S WALTER STEWART BRANCH, 170 Memorial Park Ave, M4J 2K5, SAN 368-4997. Tel: 416-396-3975. FAX: 416-396-3842.
Circ 425,201
Library Holdings: Bk Vols 96,127
Open Mon-Fri 9-8:30, Sat 9-5, Sun (Sept-June) 1:30-5
SWANSEA MEMORIAL BRANCH, 95 Lavinia Ave, M6S 3H9, SAN 368-640X. Tel: 416-393-7695. FAX: 416-393-7552.
Circ 44,895
Library Holdings: Bk Vols 9,019
Open Tues & Thurs 10-6, Wed 1-8, Sat 10-5
TAYLOR MEMORIAL BRANCH, 1440 Kingston Rd, M1N 1R3, SAN 368-3885. Tel: 416-396-8939. FAX: 416-396-3601.
Circ 133,225
Library Holdings: Bk Vols 27,998
Open Tues & Thurs 12:30-8:30, Wed & Fri 10-6, Sat 9-5
THORNCLIFFE BRANCH, 48 Thorncliffe Park Dr, M4H 1J7, SAN 368-5055. Tel: 416-396-3865. FAX: 416-396-3866.
Circ 201,781
Library Holdings: Bk Vols 46,444
Open Mon-Fri 9-8:30, Sat 9-5
TODMORDEN ROOM, 1081 1/2 Pape Ave (at Torrens), M4K 3W6, SAN 378-228X. Tel: 416-396-3875. FAX: 416-396-3864.
Circ 56,153
Library Holdings: Bk Vols 7,844
Open Tues & Thurs 12:30-8:30, Wed & Sat 9-5
TORONTO REFERENCE LIBRARY, 789 Yonge St, M4W 2G8. Tel: 416-395-5577. FAX: 416-393-7147.
Circ 507,688
Library Holdings: Bk Vols 1,776,834
Special Services for the Deaf - TTY equip
Special Services for the Blind - Daisy reader; Magnifiers; Screen enlargement software for people with visual disabilities; Screen reader software; Talking bks
Open Mon-Fri 9-8:30, Sat 9-5, Sun (Sept-June) 1:30-5
Friends of the Library Group
VICTORIA VILLAGE BRANCH, 184 Sloane Ave, M4A 2C4, SAN 368-9077. Tel: 416-395-5950. FAX: 416-395-5418.
Circ 104,930
Library Holdings: Bk Vols 27,180
Open Tues & Thurs 12:30-8:30, Wed & Fri 10-6, Sat 9-5
WESTON BRANCH, Two King St, M9N 1K9, SAN 368-4814. Tel: 416-394-1016. FAX: 416-394-1037.
Circ 137,092
Library Holdings: Bk Vols 43,909
Open Mon 10-8:30, Tues & Thurs 12:30-8:30, Wed & Fri 10-6, Sat 9-5
WOODSIDE SQUARE BRANCH, Woodside Square Mall, 1571 Sandhurst Circle, M1V 1V2, SAN 368-3915. Tel: 416-396-8979. FAX: 416-395-3563.
Circ 457,735
Library Holdings: Bk Vols 56,896
Open Mon-Thurs 9-8:30, Fri & Sat 9-5
WOODVIEW PARK BRANCH, 16 Bradstock Rd, M9M 1M8, SAN 368-9107. Tel: 416-395-5960. FAX: 416-395-5417.
Circ 79,695
Library Holdings: Bk Vols 20,889
Open Tues, Wed & Fri 10-6, Thurs 12:30-8:30, Sat 9-5
WYCHWOOD BRANCH, 1431 Bathurst St, M5R 3J2, SAN 368-6434. Tel: 416-393-7683. FAX: 416-393-7665.
Circ 208,249
Library Holdings: Bk Vols 39,892
YORK WOODS BRANCH, 1785 Finch Ave W, M3N 1M6, SAN 368-9131. Tel: 416-395-5980. FAX: 416-395-5991.
Circ 289,475
Library Holdings: Bk Vols 105,126
Open Mon-Fri 9-8:30, Sat 9-5, Sun 1:30-5
YORKVILLE BRANCH, 22 Yorkville Ave, M4W 1L4, SAN 368-6469. Tel: 416-393-7660. FAX: 416-393-7725.
Circ 324,279
Library Holdings: Bk Vols 63,434
Open Mon-Thurs 9-8:30, Fri & Sat 9-5
Bookmobiles: 2

M TORONTO REHAB*, Library Services, 550 University Ave, Rm 2-055, M5G 2A2. SAN 323-9004. Tel: 416-597-3422, Ext 3050. FAX: 416-591-6515. Web Site: www.uhn.ca. *Libr Tech,* Raluca Serban; E-mail: raluca.serban@uhn.ca; Staff 6 (MLS 3, Non-MLS 3)
Founded 1998
Library Holdings: Bk Titles 5,000; Bk Vols 6,000; Per Subs 125
Function: ILL available
Partic in Health Science Information Consortium of Toronto
Open Mon-Fri 8:30-5

S TORONTO STAR NEWSPAPERS LTD LIBRARY, Eight Spadina Ave, M5V 0S8. SAN 319-5708. Tel: 416-869-4491. E-mail: tsnllibr@thestar.ca. Web Site: www.thestar.ca. *Supvr,* Astrid Lange; Staff 2 (MLS 2)
Library Holdings: Bk Vols 150; Per Subs 22
Special Collections: Electronic Clip Files; Events, Places, Subjects & People, photog; Personalities, micro
Subject Interests: Biog, Current events, Regional happenings
Wireless access
Restriction: Not open to pub, Staff use only

L TORYS LLP LIBRARY*, 79 Wellington St W, Ste 3000, M5K 1N2. (Mail add: Toronto-Dominion Ctr, PO Box 270, M5K 1N2), SAN 325-6529. Tel: 416-865-8158. FAX: 416-865-7380. E-mail: libserv@torys.com. *Dir,* Louis Mirando; E-mail: lmirando@torys.com; *Ref Librn,* Clare Mauro; Tel: 416-945-7737, E-mail: cmauro@torys.com. Subject Specialists: *Civil procedure, Law, Litigation,* Clare Mauro; Staff 10.5 (MLS 4, Non-MLS 6.5)
Library Holdings: Bk Titles 20,000
Special Collections: Legal Memoranda
Subject Interests: Corporate law, Finance, Financial institutions, Securities
Automation Activity & Vendor Info: (Acquisitions) SoutronGLOBAL; (Cataloging) SoutronGLOBAL; (Circulation) SoutronGLOBAL; (OPAC) SoutronGLOBAL; (Serials) SoutronGLOBAL
Wireless access
Function: ILL available
Publications: Legal Research Handbook; Library Handbook; Library Report
Restriction: Employee & client use only

CR TYNDALE UNIVERSITY COLLEGE & SEMINARY*, J William Horsey Library, 3377 Bayview Ave, M2M 3S4. SAN 319-6119. Tel: 416-226-6380. Circulation Tel: 416-226-6620, Ext 2131. Reference Tel: 416-226-6620, Ext 2126. FAX: 416-218-6765. E-mail: library@tyndale.ca. Web Site: www.tyndale.ca/library. *Dir,* Hugh Rendle; Tel: 416-226-6620, Ext 6716, E-mail: hrendle@tyndale.ca; *Acq,* Becky Wismer; Tel: 416-226-6620, Ext 2128, E-mail: bwismer@tyndale.ca; *Pub Serv,* Isabella Guthrie-McNaughton; *Tech Serv,* Maria Ho; Staff 9 (MLS 3, Non-MLS 6)
Founded 1894. Enrl 1,300; Fac 40; Highest Degree: Master
Library Holdings: CDs 300; DVDs 200; e-books 200,000; Bk Vols 132,000; Per Subs 500
Special Collections: Percival J Baldwin Puritan Coll
Subject Interests: Biblical studies, Christian ministry, Theol
Automation Activity & Vendor Info: (Acquisitions) OCLC WorldShare Interlibrary Loan; (Cataloging) OCLC Connexion; (Circulation) OCLC; (Course Reserve) OCLC; (ILL) OCLC WorldShare Interlibrary Loan; (OPAC) OCLC; (Serials) OCLC
Wireless access
Open Mon-Thurs 8am-10:30pm, Fri 8-7, Sat 10-5

S UNIFOR LIBRARY*, 115 Gordon Baker Rd, M2H 0A8. SAN 373-8361. Tel: 416-497-4110. FAX: 416-495-6552. E-mail: library@unifor.org. Web Site: www.unifor.org. *Info Serv,* Lisa Diaz; Tel: 416-718-8481; Staff 1 (Non-MLS 1)
Founded 1986
Library Holdings: Bk Titles 1,500; Per Subs 175

Automation Activity & Vendor Info: (Cataloging) Inmagic, Inc.; (Circulation) Inmagic, Inc.; (Serials) Inmagic, Inc.
Restriction: Authorized scholars by appt

S UNITED STEELWORKERS LIBRARY*, 234 Eglinton Ave E, 8th Flr, M4P 1K7. SAN 323-7311. Tel: 416-487-1571. FAX: 416-482-5548. Web Site: www.usw.ca, www.usw.org. *Educ Coordr,* Jackie Edwards; Tel: 416-544-5976, E-mail: jedwards@usw.ca
Library Holdings: Bk Titles 800
Special Collections: Stelabor Coll dating back to the 1940s, per
Partic in Toronto Indust Relations Librns
Restriction: Open by appt only

C UNIVERSITY COLLEGE LIBRARY, UNIVERSITY OF TORONTO*, East Hall, Rm 266, 15 King's College Circle, M5S 3H7. SAN 328-705X. Tel: 416-978-8107. Web Site: www.uc.utoronto.ca/students-current-students-university-college-library. *Librn,* Gabrielle Fournier; Tel: 416-978-4634, E-mail: gabrielle.fourneir@utoronto.ca; *Librn,* Margaret Fulford; Tel: 416-978-4634, E-mail: margaret.fulford@utoronto.ca
Library Holdings: Bk Vols 32,590
Special Collections: Canadian Literature (Al Purdy Coll)
Subject Interests: Can studies, Drama, Health studies, Sexual diversity studies
Wireless access

UNIVERSITY HEALTH NETWORK

M HEALTH SCIENCES LIBRARY*, 610 University Ave, 5th Flr, M5G 2M9, SAN 319-5295. Tel: 416-946-4482. Interlibrary Loan Service Tel: 416-340-4121. FAX: 416-946-2084. Web Site: www.uhn.ca/Education/library_services.asp. *Dir,* Bogusia Trojan
Founded 1957
Library Holdings: Bk Vols 15,000
Subject Interests: Hematology, Med biophysics, Molecular biol, Oncology, Radiotherapy
Automation Activity & Vendor Info: (Acquisitions) SydneyPlus; (Cataloging) SydneyPlus; (Circulation) SydneyPlus; (OPAC) SydneyPlus; (Serials) SydneyPlus
Partic in Health Science Information Consortium of Toronto
Open Mon-Fri 8:30-7

M TORONTO GENERAL HOSPITAL HEALTH SCIENCES LIBRARY*, 200 Elizabeth St, ENI 418, M5G 2C4, SAN 319-5678. Tel: 416-340-3429. FAX: 416-340-4384. Web Site: www.uhn.ca/Education/Libraries/Pages/default.aspx. *Interim Mgr,* Jessica Babineau; E-mail: jessica.babineau@uhn.ca
Founded 1964
Library Holdings: Bk Vols 22,000
Special Collections: History of Medicine
Subject Interests: Cardiology, Neuroscience, Oncology, Transplantation
Automation Activity & Vendor Info: (Cataloging) EOS International; (Circulation) EOS International; (OPAC) EOS International; (Serials) EOS International
Partic in Health Science Information Consortium of Toronto
Open Mon-Fri 8:30-5, Sat 10-5

C UNIVERSITY OF TORONTO LIBRARIES*, 130 St George St, M5S 1A5. SAN 368-6493. Tel: 416-978-8450. Reference Tel: 416-978-6215. FAX: 416-978-1608. E-mail: library.info@utoronto.ca. Web Site: onesearch.library.utoronto.ca. *Chief Univ Librn,* Larry Alford; Tel: 416-978-2292, E-mail: larry.alford@utoronto.ca; *Dep Chief Librn,* Julie Hannaford; Tel: 416-978-1702, E-mail: j.hannaford@utoronto.ca
Founded 1827. Enrl 91,286; Fac 14,434; Highest Degree: Doctorate
Jan 2019-Dec 2019. Mats Exp (CAN) $34,000,000
Library Holdings: Bk Vols 15,000,000
Wireless access
Publications: Annual Report; Noteworthy: News from the University of Toronto Libraries
Partic in Canadian Association of Research Libraries; OCLC Research Library Partnership; Ontario Council of University Libraries
Friends of the Library Group

Departmental Libraries:

A D ALLEN CHEMISTRY LIBRARY, Lash Miller Laboratories, Rm 480, 80 St George St, M5S 3H6, SAN 368-6825. Tel: 416-978-3587. FAX: 416-978-8775. Web Site: guides.library.utoronto.ca/chemistry. *Chem Librn,* Patricia Meindl; E-mail: pmeindl@chem.utoronto.ca; Staff 1 (MLS 1)
Highest Degree: Doctorate
Library Holdings: Bk Vols 21,151
Open Mon-Thurs 9-9, Fri 9-5 (Sept-April); Mon-Fri 9-5 (May-Jun); Mon-Fri 9-4:30 (July-Aug)

ARCHITECTURE, LANDSCAPE & DESIGN, EBERHARD ZEIDLER LIBRARY, One Spadina Crescent, M5S 2J5, SAN 368-6647. Tel: 416-978-2649. FAX: 416-971-2094. Web Site: www.daniels.utoronto.ca/resources/library/eberhard-zeidler-library. *Librn,* Irene Puchalski; Tel: 416-978-6787, E-mail: irene.puchalski@daniels.utoronto.ca; *Libr Tech,* Lisa Doherty; E-mail: lisa.doherty@daniels.utoronto.ca
Library Holdings: Bk Vols 32,000
Open Mon-Thurs 9-9, Fri 9-7, Sat 12-5

ASTRONOMY & ASTROPHYSICS LIBRARY, 60 St George St, Rm 1306, M5S 3H8. (Mail add: 50 St George St, M5S 3H4), SAN 368-6671. Tel: 416-978-4268. FAX: 416-946-7287. E-mail: library@astro.utoronto.ca. Web Site: www.astro.utoronto.ca/AALibrary. *Head Librn,* Lee Robbins; E-mail: robbins@astro.utoronto.ca
Founded 1935
Library Holdings: Bk Vols 25,000
Special Collections: David Dunlap Observatory Coll
Function: Archival coll
Open Mon-Fri 9-5

CENTRE OF CRIMINOLOGY & SOCIOLEGAL STUDIES, 14 Queens Park Crescent W, M5S 3K9, SAN 368-6949. Tel: 416-946-5824, 416-978-7124. FAX: 416-978-4195. E-mail: criminology.library@utoronto.ca. Web Site: criminology.utoronto.ca/library. *Librn,* Andrea Shier; Tel: 416-946-5745, E-mail: andrea.shier@utoronto.ca
Library Holdings: Bk Vols 30,000
Open Mon-Fri 9-5

CHENG YU TUNG EAST ASIAN LIBRARY, John P Robarts Research Library, 130 St George St, 8th Flr, M5S 1A5, SAN 368-7007. Tel: 416-864-8211, 416-978-3300. FAX: 416-978-0863. E-mail: ref.eal@utoronto.ca. Web Site: east.library.utoronto.ca. *Dir,* Hana Kim; Tel: 416-987-7690, E-mail: hn.kim@utoronto.ca; *Info Serv Librn,* Lucy Gan; Tel: 416-978-1025, E-mail: lucy.gan@utoronto.ca
Library Holdings: Bk Vols 400,000
Open Mon-Thurs 9-7, Fri 9-6

MASSEY COLLEGE, ROBERTSON DAVIES LIBRARY, Massey College, Four Devonshire Pl, M5S 2E1, SAN 368-7392. Tel: 416-978-2893. FAX: 416-978-1759. E-mail: library@masseycollege.ca. Web Site: www.masseycollege.ca/library. *Librn,* PJ MacDougall; E-mail: pjmacdougall@masseycollege.ca; Staff 2 (MLS 1, Non-MLS 1)
Founded 1963
Library Holdings: Bk Vols 46,000; Per Subs 16
Special Collections: 19th Century Colour Printing, Bookbinding & Illustration Processes (Ruari McLean Coll); Carl Dair Archives; Working 19th Century Printing Presses
Restriction: Closed stack, External users must contact libr, Non-circulating, Open to pub by appt only

CM DENTISTRY LIBRARY, 124 Edward St, Rm 267, M5G 1G6, SAN 368-6973. Tel: 416-864-8211. E-mail: library.dentistry@utoronto.ca. Web Site: dentistry.library.utoronto.ca. *Head of Libr,* Helen Yueping He; Tel: 416-864-8213, E-mail: helen.he@dentistry.utoronto.ca; Staff 3 (MLS 2, Non-MLS 1)
Library Holdings: Bk Vols 30,000

DEPARTMENT OF ART, Sidney Smith Hall, Rm 6032B, 100 St George St, M5S 3G3, SAN 368-7155. Tel: 416-978-5006. FAX: 416-978-1491. Web Site: arthistory.utoronto.ca/research/reference-service. *Librn,* Margaret English; E-mail: margaret.english@utoronto.ca
Founded 1930. Highest Degree: Doctorate
Library Holdings: Bk Vols 30,000
Subject Interests: Exhibition catalogs
Function: Ref serv available
Restriction: Non-circulating

EMMANUEL COLLEGE LIBRARY, 75 Queen's Park Crescent E, M5S 1K7. Tel: 416-585-4550.

ENGINEERING & COMPUTER SCIENCE LIBRARY, Sandford Fleming Bldg, Rm 2402, Ten King's College Rd, M5S 1A5. (Mail add: Engineering and Computer Science Library, University of Toronto, M5S 1A5), SAN 368-7066. Tel: 416-978-6494. Reference Tel: 416-978-6578. FAX: 416-971-2091. E-mail: engineering.library@utoronto.ca. Web Site: engineering.library.utoronto.ca. *Eng Librn,* Tracy Zahradnik; Tel: 416-946-5966, E-mail: tracy.zahradnik@utoronto.ca
Library Holdings: Bk Vols 200,000
Open Mon-Thurs 8:30am-10:30pm, Fri 8:30-6, Sat 9-5, Sun 1-6

FACULTY OF MUSIC LIBRARY, Edward Johnson Bldg, 80 Queens Park Crescent, M5S 2C5, SAN 368-7422. Tel: 416-978-3734. FAX: 416-946-3353. Web Site: music.library.utoronto.ca. *Head Librn,* Janneka Guise; Tel: 416-978-6920, E-mail: jan.guise@utoronto.ca; *Actg Head,* Tim Neufeldt; E-mail: tim.neufeldt@utoronto.ca
Library Holdings: Bk Vols 203,817

FIRST NATIONS HOUSE LIBRARY, Bordon Bldg N, 563 Spadina Ave, 3rd Flr, M5S 1A5. Tel: 416-978-0413. FAX: 416-978-1893. Web Site: studentlife.utoronto.ca/fnh/academic-support. *Coordr,* Jeff Kiyoshk Ross; E-mail: jeffrey.ross@utoronto.ca
Founded 1992
Library Holdings: Bk Vols 1,000; Per Subs 25
Function: Photocopying/Printing
Open Mon-Fri 9-5

THOMAS FISHER RARE BOOKS LIBRARY, 120 St George St, 2nd flr, M5S 1A5. Tel: 416-978-5285. FAX: 416-978-1667. E-mail: fisher.library@utoronto.ca. Web Site: fisher.library.utoronto.ca. *Assoc Chief Librn,* Loryl MacDonald; Tel: 416-978-7656, E-mail: loryl.macdonald@utoronto.ca
Founded 1973
Library Holdings: Bk Vols 700,000
Open Mon-Fri 9-5
Restriction: Non-circulating

GERSTEIN SCIENCE INFORMATION CENTRE, Sigmund Samuel Library Bldg, Nine Kings College Circle, M5S 1A5. Tel: 416-978-2280. FAX: 416-971-2848. E-mail: ask.gerstein@utoronto.ca. Web Site: gerstein.library.utoronto.ca. *Asst Dir/Res Librn,* Helen Cunningham; E-mail: h.cunningham@utoronto.ca; *Admin Assoc,* Vidya Mahadeo; Tel: 416-978-6434, E-mail: vidya.mahadeo@utoronto.ca
Library Holdings: Bk Vols 945,000
Subject Interests: Med
Function: Doc delivery serv, ILL available, Photocopying/Printing, Ref serv available
Open Mon-Thurs 8:30am-11pm, Fri 8:30am-10pm, Sat 9am-10pm, Sun 10-10

INNIS COLLEGE LIBRARY, Two Sussex Ave, 2nd Flr, M5S 1J5, SAN 328-7017. Tel: 416-978-4497. FAX: 416-946-0168. Web Site: innis.utoronto.ca/library. *Librn,* Kate Johnson; E-mail: katej.johnson@utoronto.ca
Library Holdings: Bk Vols 5,000
Special Collections: Cinema Studies
Subject Interests: Cinema

PETRO JACYK CENTRAL & EAST EUROPEAN RESOURCE CENTRE, Robarts Library, 130 St George St,3rd Flr, Rm 3008, M5S 1A5. Tel: 416-978-0588. Administration Tel: 416-978-1288. FAX: 416-971-2636. E-mail: jacyk.centre@utoronto.ca. Web Site: pjrc.library.utoronto.ca. *Head of Libr,* Dr Ksenya Kiebuzinski; Tel: 416-978-4826, E-mail: ksenya.kiebuzinski@utoronto.ca; *Ref Spec,* Wasyl Sydorenko; Tel: 416-978-0588, E-mail: wasyl.sydorenko@utoronto.ca; Staff 4 (MLS 2, Non-MLS 2)
Library Holdings: Bk Vols 5,000
Subject Interests: Cent Europe, Eastern Europe, Russia, Slavic studies
Function: Ref & res
Open Mon-Fri 10-6
Restriction: Ref only

CR JOHN M KELLY LIBRARY, University of St Michael's College, 81 St Mary St, M5S 1J4, SAN 368-7813. Tel: 416-926-7263. Web Site: stmikes.utoronto.ca. *Chief Librn,* Sheril Hook; Tel: 416-926-7263, E-mail: sheril.hook@utoronto.ca; *Assoc Chief Librn,* David Hagelaar; Tel: 416-926-7250, E-mail: d.hagelaar@utoronto.ca; Staff 11.8 (MLS 6, Non-MLS 5.8)
Founded 1852. Highest Degree: Doctorate
Library Holdings: Bk Vols 372,000
Special Collections: Centre d'Eludes sur le Naturalisme (Zola); Centre d'Etudes Romantiques; Chesterton Coll; New Man Coll; Recusant & Counter-Reformation Materials; Soulerin Coll
Automation Activity & Vendor Info: (Cataloging) SirsiDynix-WorkFlows
Function: Archival coll, Art exhibits, Audio & video playback equip for onsite use, Bks on CD, CD-ROM, Computers for patron use, Doc delivery serv, E-Reserves, Electronic databases & coll, Free DVD rentals, ILL available, Internet access, Mail & tel request accepted, Music CDs, Online cat, Online info literacy tutorials on the web & in blackboard, Online ref, Orientations, Photocopying/Printing, Res libr, Scanner, Spoken cassettes & CDs, Spoken cassettes & DVDs, Telephone ref, VHS videos, Wheelchair accessible, Workshops, Writing prog
Open Mon-Fri 8:30am-11:30pm, Sat 10am-11:30pm, Sun 1-11:30 (Winter); Mon-Thurs 8:30-7:30, Fri 8:30-4:30 (Summer)
Restriction: Authorized patrons
Friends of the Library Group

CR KNOX COLLEGE CAVEN LIBRARY, Knox College, 59 St George St, M5S 2E6, SAN 368-7783. Tel: 416-978-4504, 416-978-6719. E-mail: knox.college@utoronto.ca, knox.readerservices@utoronto.ca. Web Site: knox.utoronto.ca/caven-library. *Dir, Libr Serv,* Joan Pries; Tel: 416-978-6090, E-mail: joan.pries@utoronto.ca; *Cataloger, Tech Serv,* Anne McGillivray; Tel: 416-978-6719, E-mail: anne.mcgillivray@utoronto.ca; *Coordr, Spec Coll, Libr Asst,* Laura Alary; E-mail: knox.readerservices@utoronto.ca. Subject Specialists: *Interdisciplinary studies, Theol,* Joan Pries; *Theol,* Anne McGillivray; *Biblical studies, New Testament, Theol,* Laura Alary; Staff 3 (MLS 2, Non-MLS 1)
Founded 1844. Highest Degree: Doctorate
Library Holdings: Bk Vols 80,000; Per Subs 60
Subject Interests: Presbyterianism, Reform Church hist, Theol
Automation Activity & Vendor Info: (Acquisitions) Ex Libris Group; (Cataloging) Ex Libris Group; (Circulation) Ex Libris Group; (Course Reserve) Ex Libris Group; (OPAC) Ex Libris Group; (Serials) Ex Libris Group
Open Mon-Fri 8:30-4:30

LAIDLAW LIBRARY, UNIVERSITY COLLEGE, 15 King's College Circle, Rm 215, M5S 3H7.

CL BORA LASKIN LAW LIBRARY, Flavelle House, 78 Queen's Park Crescent, M5S 2C5, SAN 368-7279. Tel: 416-978-1073. Interlibrary Loan Service Tel: 416-946-7833. Reference Tel: 416-978-1072. FAX: 416-978-8396. E-mail: law.ref@utoronto.ca. Web Site: library.law.utoronto.ca. *Chief Law Librn,* Gian Medves; Tel: 416-978-5537, E-mail: gian.medves@utoronto.ca
Library Holdings: AV Mats 56,002; Bk Vols 265,000; Per Subs 2,413
Open Mon-Fri 9-5

RICHARD CHARLES LEE CANADA-HONG KONG LIBRARY (CHKL), Roberts Library, 130 Saint George St, 8th Flr, M5S 1A5. Tel: 416-946-8978.

MAP & DATA LIBRARY, John P Robarts Library, 130 St George St, 5th Flr, M5S 1A5, SAN 368-7368. Tel: 416-978-3931 (Govt & map info), 416-978-5589 (Data Library & GIS Service). FAX: 416-946-0522. E-mail: mdl@library.utoronto.ca. Web Site: mdl.library.utoronto.ca. *Actg Head, Data Librn,* Leanne Trimble; Tel: 416-978-5365, E-mail: leanne.trimble@utoronto.ca
Library Holdings: Bk Vols 410,000
Open Mon-Fri 11-5

MATHEMATICAL SCIENCES, Bahen Centre for Information Technology, 40 St George St, Rm 6141, M5S 1A1, SAN 368-7406. Tel: 416-978-8624. FAX: 416-978-4107. E-mail: math.library@utoronto.ca. Web Site: math.library.utoronto.ca. *Head Librn,* Bruce Garrod; E-mail: bruce.garrod@utoronto.ca. Subject Specialists: *Math,* Bruce Garrod
Library Holdings: Bk Vols 33,411
Open Mon-Fri 9-5

MEDIA COMMONS, Robarts Library, 130 St George St, 3rd flr, M5S 1A5, SAN 368-6701. Tel: 416-978-6015, 416-978-6520. FAX: 416-978-8707. E-mail: media.commons@utoronto.ca. Web Site: mediacommons.library.utoronto.ca. *Dept Head,* Brock Silversides; Tel: 416-978-7119, E-mail: brock.silversides@utoronto.ca
Library Holdings: Bk Vols 472
Open Mon-Thurs 8:30am-9:30pm, Fri 8:30-6, Sat & Sun 12-5

THE MILT HARRIS LIBRARY, Joseph L Rotman School of Management, 105 St George St, South Bldg , Rm 5005, M5S 3E6, SAN 368-7333. Tel: 416-978-3421. FAX: 416-978-1920. E-mail: bicstaff@rotman.utoronto.ca. Web Site: www.rotman.utoronto.ca/FacultyAndResearch/BIC.aspx. *Dir,* Sean Forbes; E-mail: forbes@rotman.utoronto.ca
Library Holdings: Bk Vols 19,500
Open Mon-Thurs 8:45-9:30, Fri 8:45-5, Sat 12-5

MISSISSAUGA LIBRARY, HAZEL MCCALLION ACADEMIC LEARNING CENTRE, Hazel McCallion Academic Learning Centre, 3359 Mississauga Rd N, Mississauga, L5L 1C6, SAN 368-7120. Tel: 905-828-5236. FAX: 905-569-4320. Reference E-mail: askutml.utm@utoronto.ca. Web Site: library.utm.utoronto.ca. *Interim Chief Librn,* Paula Hannaford; E-mail: paula.hannaford@utoronto.ca
Library Holdings: Bk Vols 340,000

NEW COLLEGE - D G IVEY LIBRARY, 20 Willcocks St, M5S 1C6, SAN 328-7033. Tel: 416-978-2493. FAX: 416-978-0554. Web Site: www.newcollege.utoronto.ca/academics/new-college-academic-programs/d-g-ivey-library. *Col Librn,* Jeff Newman; E-mail: jeff.newman@utoronto.ca; *Pub Serv Librn,* Aneta Kwak; E-mail: aneta.kwak@utoronto.ca
Library Holdings: Bk Vols 25,000
Subject Interests: Women's studies
Open Mon-Fri 10-6

JEAN & DOROTHY NEWMAN INDUSTRIAL RELATIONS LIBRARY, 121 St George St, M5S 2E8, SAN 368-7244. Tel: 416-946-7003. Automation Services Tel: 416-978-0191. FAX: 416-978-5696. E-mail: cirhr.library@utoronto.ca. Web Site: cirhr.library.utoronto.ca. *Head Librn,* Victoria Skelton; E-mail: victoria.skelton@utoronto.ca; *Tech Librn,* Monica Hypher; E-mail: monica.hypher@utoronto.ca
Library Holdings: Bk Vols 11,500

NORANDA EARTH SCIENCES LIBRARY, Five Bancroft Ave, 2nd Flr, Room 2091, M5S 1A5, SAN 368-6760. Tel: 416-978-3024. FAX: 416-971-2101. E-mail: earth.sciences@utoronto.ca. Web Site: earth.library.utoronto.ca. *Librn,* Jennifer Robertson; Tel: 416-978-6673, E-mail: jen.robertson@utoronto.ca
Library Holdings: Bk Vols 107,000
Open Mon-Thurs 9-9, Fri 9-6

OISE LIBRARY, 252 Bloor St W, Ground Flr, M5S 1V6. Tel: 416-978-1850.

PHYSICS LIBRARY, McLennan Physical Laboratories, 60 St George St, Rm 211C, M5S 1A7, SAN 368-7546. Tel: 416-978-5188. FAX: 416-978-5919. E-mail: library@physics.utoronto.ca. Web Site: www.physics.utoronto.ca/physics-at-uoft/library. *Librn,* Dylanne Dearborn; E-mail: dearborn@physics.utoronto.ca. Subject Specialists: *Physics,* Dylanne Dearborn
Library Holdings: Bk Vols 35,570
Open Mon-Fri 9-5

PONTIFICAL INSTITUTE FOR MEDIAEVAL STUDIES, St Michael's College, 113 St Joseph St, 4th Flr, M5S 1J4, SAN 368-7600. Tel: 416-926-7146. FAX: 416-926-7292. E-mail: pims.library@utoronto.ca. Web Site: www.pims.ca/library/general-information-hours-access-staff. *Librn,* Greti Dinkova-Bruun; E-mail: greti.dinkova.bruun@utoronto.ca; *Ref Librn,* William Edwards; Tel: 416-926-1300, Ext 3423; *Curator, Rare Bks,* James Farge; Tel: 416-926-7283, E-mail: james.farge@utoronto.ca
Library Holdings: Bk Vols 150,000
Special Collections: Mediaeval Manuscripts; Microfilms of Manuscripts; Monastic Foundations Image Coll
Open Mon-Thurs 9:30-5, Fri 9:30-4:30 (Summer); Mon-Thurs 9:30-7, Fri 9:30-5, Sat Noon-5 (Winter)

REGIS COLLEGE LIBRARY, 100 Wellesley St W, M5S 2Z5. Tel: 416-922-5474, Ext 234.

ROBARTS LIBRARY, 130 St George St, M5S 1A5, SAN 118-9948. FAX: 416-978-8450. E-mail: libraryhelp@utoronto.ca. *Dir, Info Serv, Head, User Serv,* Lari Langford; Tel: 416-978-2898, E-mail: lari.langford@utoronto.ca
Library Holdings: Bk Titles 100,424; Bk Vols 9,346,479; Per Subs 26,382
Subject Interests: Humanities
Open Mon-Fri 8:30am-11pm, Sat & Sun 10-10

CR SAINT AUGUSTINE'S SEMINARY LIBRARY, 2661 Kingston Rd, Scarborough, M1M 1M3.

SCARBOROUGH UTSC LIBRARY, Academic Resource Ctr, 1265 Military Trail, Scarborough, M1C 1A4, SAN 368-766X. Tel: 416-287-7500. FAX: 416-287-7486. Web Site: utsc.library.utoronto.ca. *Chief Librn,* Angela Hamilton; Tel: 416-208-5174, E-mail: angela.hamilton@utoronto.ca
Library Holdings: Bk Vols 357,000; Per Subs 700
Partic in Utlas

TRINITY COLLEGE, JOHN W GRAHAM LIBRARY, Munk School of Global Affairs Bldg, 3 Devonshire Pl, East House, M5S 3K7. (Mail add: Trinity College, Six Hoskin Ave, M5S 1H8). Administration Tel: 416-978-4398. Information Services Tel: 416-978-5851. FAX: 416-978-2797. E-mail: ask.grahamlibrary@utoronto.ca. Web Site: www.trinity.utoronto.ca/library_archives. *Nicholls Librn & Dir Graham Libr,* John Papadopoulos; E-mail: john.papadopoulos@utoronto.ca; Staff 7.5 (MLS 3.5, Non-MLS 4)
Founded 1852. Highest Degree: Doctorate
Library Holdings: Bk Vols 200,000
Special Collections: Churchill Coll; SPCK Coll; Strachan Coll; Works of Richard Hooker (W Speed Hill Coll)
Subject Interests: Anglican Church hist, English (Lang), English lit, Intl relations, Theol
Automation Activity & Vendor Info: (Acquisitions) SirsiDynix-WorkFlows; (Cataloging) SirsiDynix-WorkFlows; (Circulation) SirsiDynix-WorkFlows; (OPAC) SirsiDynix; (Serials) SirsiDynix-WorkFlows
Function: Archival coll, Audio & video playback equip for onsite use, Computers for patron use, Electronic databases & coll, ILL available, Online cat, Online info literacy tutorials on the web & in blackboard, Orientations, Photocopying/Printing, Ref serv available, Wheelchair accessible
Publications: Ex Libris (Friends of the Library) (Periodical)
Open Mon-Thurs 8:30am-11:45pm, Fri 8:30am-8:45pm, Sat 10-8:45, Sun 10am-11:45pm
Restriction: Open to fac, students & qualified researchers
Friends of the Library Group

UNIVERSITY OF TORONTO ARCHIVES & RECORDS MANAGEMENT (UTARMS), Thomas Fisher Rare Book Library, 120 Saint George St, M5S 1A5. Tel: 416-978-5344.

VICTORIA UNIVERSITY, CENTRE FOR REFORMATION & RENAISSANCE STUDIES, Victoria University, E J Pratt Library, Rm 301, 71 Queen's Park Crescent E, M5S 1K7, SAN 368-6795. Tel: 416-585-4468. FAX: 416-585-4430. E-mail: crrs.info@vicu.utoronto.ca. Web Site: crrs.ca/library-2. *Dir,* Ethan Matt Kavaler; Tel: 416-585-4461, E-mail: matt.kavaler@utoronto.ca
Library Holdings: Bk Vols 25,000
Special Collections: Erasmus Coll; Rare Book Coll
Subject Interests: Confraternities, Erasmus, Humanism, Northern renaissance, Reformation
Publications: A Reformation Debate: Karlstadt, Emser & Eck on Sacred Images; An Annotated Catalogue of Early Editions of Erasmas at the Centre for Reformation & Renaissance Studies, Toronto; Bibles, Theological Treatise & other Religious Literature, 1491-1700, at the CRRS; Galateo: A Renaissance Treatise on Manners; Humanist Editions of Statues & Histories at the CRRS; Humanist Editions of the Classics at the CRRS; International Directory of Renaissance & Reformation Associations & Institutes (1993); Language & literature: Early Printed Books at the CRRS; Published Books (1499-1700) on science, medicine & natural history at the CRRS; Register of Sermons Preached at Paul's Cross 1534-1642; Seven Dialogues; The Layman on Wisdom & the Mind; The Profession of the Religious & the Falsely-Believed & Forged Donation of Constantine
Open Mon-Fri 9-5; Mon-Fri 9:15-4:30 (Summer)
Restriction: Non-circulating

VICTORIA UNIVERSITY, E J PRATT LIBRARY, 71 Queens Park Crescent E, M5S 1K7, SAN 368-7872. Tel: 416-585-4471. Interlibrary Loan Service Tel: 416-585-4470. FAX: 416-585-4591. E-mail: victoria.library@utoronto.ca. Web Site: library.vicu.utoronto.ca. *Chief Librn,* Lisa J Sherlock; Tel: 416-585-4472, E-mail: l.sherlock@utoronto.ca; *Head, Reader Serv,* Roma Kail; E-mail: r.kail@utoronto.ca; *Syst Librn,* Doug Fox; E-mail: douglasfox@utoronto.ca; *Head, Bibliog Serv,* Beth Shoemaker; E-mail: beth.shoemaker@vicu.utoronto.ca. Subject Specialists: *Theol,* Doug Fox; Staff 20 (MLS 8, Non-MLS 12)
Fac 8; Highest Degree: Doctorate
Library Holdings: Bk Vols 261,171
Special Collections: A P Coleman, Geologist, 1852-1939; Baxter Coll, prints; Bloomsbury: Books, Art & Design; Canadian Literary Manuscripts; Claire Pratt Coll; Coburn Coll; E J Pratt Coll, bks, ms; Erasmus Coll; Guide to Canadian Manuscript Coll; Guide to the Northrop Frye Papers; Norman Jewison Archive; Northrop Frye, books, ms; Reformation & Renaissance Coll; S T Coleridge Coll, bks, ms; Tennyson Coll; V Woolf-Bloomsbury-Hogarth Press Coll; Wesleyana Coll; William Blake & His Contemporaries: An exhibition selected from the Bentley Coll at Victoria University; William Blake Coll
Subject Interests: Church hist, Humanities, Soc sci, Theol
Special Services for the Blind - Computer access aids; Computer with voice synthesizer for visually impaired persons; Internet workstation with adaptive software; Scanner for conversion & translation of mats; Screen enlargement software for people with visual disabilities; Screen reader software; ZoomText magnification & reading software
Friends of the Library Group

M WEST PARK HEALTHCARE CENTRE*, Health Disciplines Library, 82 Buttonwood Ave, M6M 2J5. SAN 323-6110. Tel: 416-243-3600, Ext 2048. FAX: 416-243-8947. *Librn,* Wynne DeJong; E-mail: Wynne.DeJong@westpark.org; Staff 1 (MLS 1)
Founded 1979
Library Holdings: Bk Titles 1,000; Per Subs 60
Special Collections: TB History (DR Gale Coll), bks, journals, med instruments, med recs, pathological specimens, photog, plaques. Oral History
Subject Interests: Respiratory med, Tuberculosis
Partic in Health Science Information Consortium of Toronto
Restriction: Staff use only

G WORKPLACE SAFETY & INSURANCE BOARD*, Reference Library, 200 Front St W, 17th Flr, M5V 3J1. SAN 319-5406. Tel: 416-344-4962. FAX: 416-344-4050. E-mail: reference_library@wsib.on.ca. *Digital Content Spec, Info Res Spec,* Melanie Browne; E-mail: melanie_browne@wsib.on.ca; *Info Res Spec,* David A Roy; Tel: 416-344-4585, E-mail: david_a_roy@wsib.on.ca; Staff 3 (MLS 2, Non-MLS 1)
Founded 1988
Library Holdings: Bk Vols 7,500; Per Subs 40
Special Collections: Canadian Workers' Compensation Systems
Subject Interests: Legal, Med, Occupational health, Safety, Vocational rehabilitation, Workers compensation
Automation Activity & Vendor Info: (Cataloging) Sydney Enterprise; (Circulation) Sydney Enterprise; (OPAC) Sydney Enterprise; (Serials) Sydney Enterprise
Function: 24/7 Electronic res, Doc delivery serv, Electronic databases & coll, ILL available, Internet access, Online cat, Ref & res
Open Mon-Fri 9-4
Restriction: Circulates for staff only, Pub use on premises, Ref only to non-staff, Restricted borrowing privileges, Restricted loan policy, Restricted pub use, Staff use only

TRENTON

P QUINTE WEST PUBLIC LIBRARY*, Seven Creswell Dr, K8V 6X5. SAN 368-7996. Tel: 613-394-3381. FAX: 613-394-2079. Web Site: www.library.quintewest.ca. *Chief Exec Officer,* Suzanne Humphreys; Tel: 613-394-3381, Ext 3315, E-mail: suzanneh@quintewest.ca; *Pub Serv Librn,* Vanessa Pritchard; Tel: 613-394-3381, Ext 3311, E-mail: vanessa.pritchard@quintewest.ca; *Pub Serv Librn,* Krista Richardson; Tel: 613-394-3381, Ext 3325, E-mail: kristar@quintewest.ca. Subject Specialists: *Ch,* Vanessa Pritchard; *Adult,* Krista Richardson; Staff 3 (MLS 3)
Founded 1920. Pop 43,577; Circ 219,433
Subject Interests: Local hist
Automation Activity & Vendor Info: (Acquisitions) SirsiDynix; (Cataloging) SirsiDynix; (Circulation) SirsiDynix; (ILL) Fretwell-Downing; (OPAC) SirsiDynix; (Serials) SirsiDynix
Wireless access
Function: 24/7 Electronic res, 24/7 Online cat, Adult bk club, Archival coll, Audiobks via web, Bk club(s), Bk reviews (Group), Bks on CD,

Chess club, Children's prog, Computer training, Computers for patron use, Digital talking bks, Electronic databases & coll, For res purposes, Free DVD rentals, Genealogy discussion group, Holiday prog, Home delivery & serv to seniorr ctr & nursing homes, Homebound delivery serv, ILL available, Internet access, Magazines, Mail & tel request accepted, Meeting rooms, Microfiche/film & reading machines, Music CDs, Online cat, OverDrive digital audio bks, Photocopying/Printing, Preschool reading prog, Printer for laptops & handheld devices, Prog for adults, Prog for children & young adult, Ref & res, Ref serv available, Scanner, Senior computer classes, Senior outreach, Serves people with intellectual disabilities, Story hour, Study rm, Summer reading prog, Teen prog, Wheelchair accessible
Mem of Ontario Library Service
Special Services for the Blind - Assistive/Adapted tech devices, equip & products
Open Mon-Wed 9:30-8, Thurs & Fri 9:30-6, Sat 9:30-4
Friends of the Library Group

UXBRIDGE

P UXBRIDGE PUBLIC LIBRARY*, Nine Toronto St S, L9P 1P7. (Mail add: PO Box 279, L9P 1P7), SAN 319-5813. Tel: 905-852-9747. E-mail: uxbridgelibrary@uxlib.com. Web Site: uxlib.com. *Chief Exec Officer,* Amanda Ferraro; E-mail: aferraro@uxbridge.ca; *Libr Mgr,* Corrinne Morrison; E-mail: corrinne.morrison@uxlib.com; Staff 4 (MLS 1, Non-MLS 3)
Founded 1870. Pop 23,005; Circ 130,633
Library Holdings: Bk Titles 49,512; Bk Vols 51,043; Per Subs 62
Subject Interests: Gen databases
Wireless access
Open Mon, Wed, Fri & Sat 10-5, Tues & Thurs 10-8, Sun 10-4
Friends of the Library Group
Branches: 1
ZEPHYR BRANCH, 13000 Concession 39, Zephyr, L0E 1T0. (Mail add: PO Box 51, Zephyr, L0E 1T0), SAN 377-6751. Tel: 905-473-2375. E-mail: zephrylibrary@uxlib.com. *Librn,* Peggy Kennedy; E-mail: peggy.kennedy@uxlib.com
Library Holdings: Bk Vols 14,300
Open Tues & Thurs 3-7, Sat 10-3
Friends of the Library Group

VANKLEEK HILL

P CHAMPLAIN LIBRARY, 94 Main St E, K0B 1R0. (Mail add: PO Box 520, K0B 1R0), SAN 319-5856. Tel: 613-678-2216. FAX: 613-678-2216. E-mail: library@bc-cl.ca. Web Site: bc-cl.ca. *Chief Exec Officer, Head Librn,* Cynthia Martin; E-mail: cmartin@bc-cl.ca; *Ad,* Karin Dierckx; E-mail: kdierckx@bc-cl.ca; *Ch Serv Librn,* Alicia Heinzle; E-mail: aheinzle@bc-cl.ca; *Commun Outreach Coordr,* Micheal Igaz; E-mail: migaz@bc-cl.ca
Pop 8,665; Circ 22,380
Library Holdings: Bk Vols 24,000; Per Subs 22
Automation Activity & Vendor Info: (Cataloging) Mandarin Library Automation; (Circulation) Mandarin Library Automation; (ILL) OCLC WorldShare Interlibrary Loan; (OPAC) Mandarin Library Automation
Wireless access
Function: 24/7 Electronic res, 24/7 Online cat, Adult bk club, Art exhibits, Art programs, Audiobks on Playaways & MP3, Audiobks via web, Bk club(s), Bks on CD, CD-ROM, Children's prog, Computer training, Computers for patron use, Digital talking bks, Electronic databases & coll, Free DVD rentals, Games, Games & aids for people with disabilities, Holiday prog, Home delivery & serv to seniorr ctr & nursing homes, Homebound delivery serv, Homework prog, ILL available, Internet access, Life-long learning prog for all ages, Magazines, Magnifiers for reading, Mail & tel request accepted, Meeting rooms, Movies, Museum passes, Music CDs, Online cat, Outreach serv, OverDrive digital audio bks, Photocopying/Printing, Preschool reading prog, Prog for adults, Prog for children & young adult, Scanner, Senior computer classes, Senior outreach, STEM programs, Story hour, Summer reading prog, Teen prog, Visual arts prog, Wheelchair accessible, Winter reading prog, Workshops
Open Mon & Wed 1-8, Tues & Thurs 10-6, Fri 1-6, Sat 10-1
Friends of the Library Group

VAUGHAN

P VAUGHAN PUBLIC LIBRARIES*, Civic Centre Resource Library, 2191 Major MacKenzie Dr, L6A 4W2. SAN 810-0454. Tel: 905-653-7323. FAX: 905-709-1530. Web Site: www.vaughanpl.info. *Chief Exec Officer,* Margie Singleton; E-mail: margie.singleton@vaughan.ca
Founded 1957
Library Holdings: Bk Titles 195,085; Bk Vols 399,775; Per Subs 434
Automation Activity & Vendor Info: (Acquisitions) Innovative Interfaces, Inc; (Cataloging) Innovative Interfaces, Inc; (Circulation) Innovative Interfaces, Inc
Wireless access
Function: 24/7 Electronic res, 24/7 Online cat, 3D Printer, Accelerated reader prog, Activity rm, Adult bk club, Adult literacy prog, After school storytime, Homebound delivery serv, ILL available, Photocopying/Printing, Ref serv available, Telephone ref
Open Mon-Thurs 9-9, Fri 9-6, Sat & Sun 9-5
Branches: 10
ANSLEY GROVE LIBRARY, 350 Ansley Grove Rd, Woodbridge, L4L 5C9. Tel: 905-653-7323. FAX: 905-856-6151. *Libr Mgr,* Tim Pate
Founded 1957
Function: 24/7 Electronic res, 24/7 Online cat, 3D Printer, Accelerated reader prog, Activity rm, Adult bk club, Adult literacy prog, After school storytime
Open Tues-Thurs 10-9, Fri & Sat 10-5, Sun 1-5
BATHURST CLARK RESOURCE LIBRARY, 900 Clark Ave W, Thornhill, L4J 8C1. Tel: 905-653-7323. FAX: 905-709-1099. *Area Mgr,* Melanie Raymond; *Libr Mgr,* Colleen Williamson
Founded 1957
Function: 24/7 Electronic res, 24/7 Online cat, 3D Printer, Accelerated reader prog, Activity rm, Adult bk club, Adult literacy prog, After school storytime
Open Mon 1-9, Tues-Thurs 10-9, Fri & Sat 10-5, Sun 1-5
PIERRE BERTON RESOURCE LIBRARY, 4921 Rutherford Rd, Woodbridge, L4L 1A6. Tel: 905-653-7323. FAX: 905-856-5706. *Area Mgr,* Jessica Chapman; *Libr Mgr,* Richard Anderson
Founded 1957
Function: 24/7 Electronic res, 24/7 Online cat, 3D Printer, Accelerated reader prog, Activity rm, Adult bk club, Adult literacy prog, After school storytime
Open Mon 1-9, Tues-Thurs 10-9, Fri & Sat 10-5, Sun 1-5
DUFFERIN CLARK LIBRARY, 1441 Clark Ave W, Thornhill, L4J 7R4. Tel: 905-653-7323. FAX: 905-660-7202. *Libr Mgr,* Ruthanne Price
Founded 1957
Function: 24/7 Electronic res, 24/7 Online cat, 3D Printer, Accelerated reader prog, Activity rm, Adult bk club, Adult literacy prog, After school storytime
Open Mon-Thurs 10-9, Sat 10-5, Sun 1-5
KLEINBURG LIBRARY, 10341 Islington Ave N, Kleinburg, L0J 1C0. Tel: 905-653-7323. FAX: 905-893-2736. *Libr Mgr,* Urszula Jambor
Founded 1957
Function: 24/7 Electronic res, 24/7 Online cat, Activity rm, Adult bk club, Adult literacy prog, After school storytime
Open Mon, Wed & Thurs 1-8, Tues 10-8, Sat (Sept-June) 1-5
MACKENZIE HEALTH VAUGHAN LIBRARY, 3200 Major Mackenzie Dr W, L6A 4Z3. Tel: 905-653-7323, Ext 4616. Web Site: www.vaughanpl.info/libraries/view/14. *Libr Mgr,* Urszula Jambor; E-mail: urszula.jambor@vaughan.ca
Library Holdings: Audiobooks 44; Bk Vols 10,000; Per Subs 63
Function: Photocopying/Printing, Scanner, Study rm
Open Mon-Thurs 9-9, Fri 9-6, Sat & Sun 9-5
MAPLE LIBRARY, 10190 Keele St, Maple, L6A 1G3. Tel: 905-653-7323. FAX: 905-832-4971. *Libr Mgr,* Miranda Yu
Open Mon-Thurs 10-9, Fri 10-6, Sat 10-5, Sun 1-5
WOODBRIDGE LIBRARY, 150 Woodbridge Ave, Woodbridge, L4L 2S7. Tel: 905-653-7323. FAX: 905-851-2322. *Libr Mgr,* Andrea Arsenault
Founded 1957
Function: 24/7 Electronic res, 24/7 Online cat, 3D Printer, Accelerated reader prog, Activity rm, Adult bk club, Adult literacy prog, After school storytime
Open Mon-Thurs 10-9, Sat 10-5, Sun 1-5

VIRGINIATOWN

P MCGARRY PUBLIC LIBRARY, One 27th St, P0K 1X0. SAN 319-5880. Tel: 705-634-2312. FAX: 705-634-2312. E-mail: mcgarrypubliclibrary@outlook.com. Web Site: www.facebook.com/mcgarrylibrary. *Chief Exec Officer, Librn,* Samantha Goulet; Staff 1 (MLS 1)
Founded 1946. Pop 800; Circ 12,098
Library Holdings: Bk Vols 14,000; Per Subs 31
Special Collections: French & English Videos (Entertainment & Educational, Adult & Juvenile)
Wireless access
Function: ILL available
Open Tues 9-12, Wed 12-4, Thurs 5-8, Sat 1-3
Friends of the Library Group

WAINFLEET

P WAINFLEET TOWNSHIP PUBLIC LIBRARY*, 31909 Park St, L0S 1V0. (Mail add: PO Box 118, L0S 1V0), SAN 319-5899. Tel: 905-899-1277. FAX: 905-899-2495. E-mail: dariusz@wainfleetlibrary.ca. Web Site: www.wainfleetlibrary.ca. *Chief Librn,* Lorrie Atkinson; E-mail: latkinson@wainfleetlibrary.ca; Staff 9 (MLS 1, Non-MLS 8)
Founded 1966. Pop 6,373; Circ 34,282
Library Holdings: Bk Vols 29,500

Subject Interests: Genealogy, Wainfleet hist
Wireless access
Function: Archival coll, AV serv, ILL available, Photocopying/Printing, Prog for children & young adult, Ref serv available, Summer reading prog, Wheelchair accessible
Restriction: In-house use for visitors

WASAGA BEACH

P WASAGA BEACH PUBLIC LIBRARY*, 120 Glenwood Dr, L9Z 2K5. SAN 319-5910. Tel: 705-429-5481, Ext 2401. E-mail: info.wbpl@wasagabeach.com. Web Site: www.wasagabeach.library.on.ca. *Chief Exec Officer, Chief Librn,* Pam Pal; Tel: 705-429-5481, Ext 2404, E-mail: ceo.wbpl@wasagabeach.com; Staff 15 (MLS 1, Non-MLS 14)
Founded 1972
Automation Activity & Vendor Info: (ILL) SirsiDynix-WorkFlows
Wireless access
Function: 24/7 Online cat, Accelerated reader prog, Adult bk club, Art programs, Audiobks on Playaways & MP3, Audiobks via web, Bi-weekly Writer's Group, Bk club(s), Bk reviews (Group), Bks on CD, Children's prog, Computer training, Computers for patron use, Digital talking bks, E-Readers, Electronic databases & coll, Family literacy, Free DVD rentals, Homebound delivery serv, ILL available, Internet access, Large print keyboards, Life-long learning prog for all ages, Magazines, Magnifiers for reading, Meeting rooms, Outreach serv, OverDrive digital audio bks, Photocopying/Printing, Preschool outreach, Prog for adults, Prog for children & young adult, Satellite serv, Senior computer classes, STEM programs, Story hour, Summer reading prog, Teen prog, Visual arts prog, Writing prog
Open Tues-Fri 10-8, Sat 10-4, Sun 12-4
Friends of the Library Group
Bookmobiles: Pub Serv Coord, Val Dickson. Bk vols 2,000

WATERLOO

C CONRAD GREBEL UNIVERSITY COLLEGE*, Milton Good Library, 140 Westmount Rd N, N2L 3G6. SAN 321-3439. Tel: 519-885-0220, Ext 34400. Administration Tel: 519-885-0220, Ext 24238. FAX: 519-885-0014. E-mail: Libcgc@library.uwaterloo.ca. Web Site: uwaterloo.ca/grebel/milton-good-library. *Librn & Archivist,* Laureen Harder-Gissing; E-mail: lharderg@uwaterloo.ca; *Asst Librn,* Mandy Macfie; E-mail: mmacfie@uwaterloo.ca. Subject Specialists: *Mennonites, Peace & conflict studies, Theol studies,* Laureen Harder-Gissing; *Music,* Mandy Macfie; Staff 3 (MLS 1, Non-MLS 2)
Founded 1964. Fac 14; Highest Degree: Master
Library Holdings: CDs 2,625; DVDs 212; Bk Vols 44,932; Per Subs 11,867; Videos 145
Special Collections: Mennonite Archives of Ontario Coll, doc & unbound paper. Oral History
Subject Interests: Biblical studies, Hist, Mennonite-Anabaptist theol, Music, Peace studies
Automation Activity & Vendor Info: (Acquisitions) Ex Libris Group; (Cataloging) Ex Libris Group; (Circulation) Ex Libris Group
Wireless access
Partic in OCLC Online Computer Library Center, Inc; OMNI
Open Mon-Thurs 8:30am-10pm, Fri 8:30-6, Sat 1-5 (Fall & Winter); Mon-Fri 8:30-4:30 (Spring)

JR GREAT LAKES BIBLE COLLEGE LIBRARY*, Waterloo Campus, 470 Glenelm Crescent, N2L 5C8. Tel: 519-342-3040. Toll Free FAX: 888-316-7678. Web Site: www.glbc.ca. *Pres,* Paul Rasmussen; E-mail: paulprasmussen@gmail.com
Library Holdings: Bk Titles 4,000

C RENISON UNIVERSITY COLLEGE LIBRARY*, Lusi Wong Library, 240 Westmount Rd N, N2L 3G4. Tel: 519-884-4404, Ext 28646. E-mail: renison.library@uwaterloo.ca. Web Site: uwaterloo.ca/renison/lusi-wong-library. *Libr Asst,* Tammy Kavanaugh; E-mail: tammy.kavanaugh@uwaterloo.ca; Staff 1 (MLS 1)
Highest Degree: Master
Library Holdings: Bk Titles 6,000; Per Subs 25
Subject Interests: Applied lang studies, Cultural studies, English as a second lang, Soc develop, Soc work
Automation Activity & Vendor Info: (Acquisitions) Ex Libris Group; (Cataloging) Ex Libris Group; (Circulation) Ex Libris Group; (Course Reserve) ARIS-Atlantic Rim Information Systems; (OPAC) Ex Libris Group
Wireless access
Open Mon-Wed 9:15-8, Thurs & Fri 9:15-4:30

CR SAINT JEROME'S UNIVERSITY LIBRARY*, 290 Westmount Rd N, N2L 3G3. SAN 319-597X. Tel: 519-884-8111, Ext 28271. Circulation Tel: 519-884-8110, Ext 28285. FAX: 519-884-5759. Web Site: www.sju.ca/library. *Univ Librn,* Lorna Rourke; E-mail: lerourke@uwaterloo.ca; *Libr Assoc,* Deborah Addesso; E-mail: daddesso@uwaterloo.ca; Staff 3 (MLS 1, Non-MLS 2)
Founded 1962. Enrl 1,050; Fac 60; Highest Degree: Master
Library Holdings: Bk Vols 40,000; Per Subs 320
Special Collections: Archives of Saint Jerome's College & the Congregation of the Resurrection
Subject Interests: English, Family, Hist, Liberal arts, Marriage, Psychol, Relig studies, Sociol
Automation Activity & Vendor Info: (Acquisitions) Ex Libris Group; (Cataloging) Ex Libris Group; (Circulation) Ex Libris Group; (Course Reserve) Ex Libris Group; (OPAC) Ex Libris Group; (Serials) Ex Libris Group
Wireless access

C UNIVERSITY OF WATERLOO LIBRARY*, Dana Porter Library, 200 University Ave W, N2L 3G1. SAN 368-8054. Tel: 519-888-4567, Ext 84883. Circulation Tel: 519-888-4567, Ext 84600. Interlibrary Loan Service Tel: 519-888-4567, Ext 32598. Reference Tel: 519-888-4567, Ext 35763. FAX: 519-888-4320. Web Site: www.lib.uwaterloo.ca. *Univ Librn,* Beth Sandore Namachchivaya; Tel: 519-888-4567, Ext 33568, E-mail: bsnamachchivaya@uwaterloo.ca; *Assoc Univ Librn, Res & Digital Discovery Serv,* Alison Hitchens; Tel: 519-888-4567, Ext 35980, E-mail: ahitchen@uwaterloo.ca; *Dir, Organizational Serv,* Sharon Lamont; Tel: 519-888-4567, Ext 33519, E-mail: sharon.lamont@uwaterloo.ca; *Head, Cat,* Betty Graf; Tel: 519-888-4567, Ext 46584, E-mail: bgraf@uwaterloo.ca; *Head, Circ Serv,* Alex McCulloch; Tel: 519-888-4567, Ext 45326, E-mail: iamccull@uwaterloo.ca; *Head, Coll Develop,* Ian Robson; Tel: 519-888-4567, Ext 41586, E-mail: ian.robson@uwaterloo.ca; *Head, Digital Initiatives,* Andrew McAlorum; Tel: 519-888-4567, Ext 39127, E-mail: amcalorum@uwaterloo.ca; *Head, Info Serv & Res,* Kathy MacDonald; Tel: 519-888-4567, Ext 33312, E-mail: kamacdonald@uwaterloo.ca; *Head, Libr Tech & Fac Serv,* Adam Savage; Tel: 519-888-4567, Ext 44141, E-mail: asavage@uwaterloo.ca; *Head, Spec Coll & Archives,* Nick Richbell; Tel: 519-888-4567, Ext 32445, E-mail: nick.richbell@uwaterloo.ca; Staff 40 (MLS 35, Non-MLS 5)
Founded 1957. Enrl 35,100; Fac 1,115; Highest Degree: Doctorate
Library Holdings: e-books 409,653; e-journals 35,553; Bk Vols 2,070,392
Special Collections: Breithaupt Hewetson Clark Coll; British Women's periodicals, 1893-1977; Canadiana (Sol Eisen Coll); Eric Gill Coll, bks, engravings; Euclid's Elements & History of Mathematics; Golden Cockerel & Nonesuch (Private Press Coll), bks, ephemera; Henry H Crapo Dance Coll; Kitchener-Waterloo YWCA Papers, 1905-1985; KW Oktoberfest Inc Archives; K-W Record Photographic Negative Coll; Library of George Santayana; Robert Southey (B R Davis Coll); Rosa Breithaupt Clark Architecture Coll; Seagram Museum Library & Archives; William Blake Coll; Women's Studies (Lady Aberdeen Coll), bks, ephemera
Automation Activity & Vendor Info: (Acquisitions) Ex Libris Group; (Cataloging) Ex Libris Group; (Circulation) Ex Libris Group; (OPAC) Ex Libris Group
Wireless access
Publications: News @ Your Library
Partic in Association of Research Libraries; Canadian Association of Research Libraries; Canadian Research Knowledge Network; OCLC Research Library Partnership; Ontario Council of University Libraries; TriUniversity Group of Libraries; Wellington-Waterloo-Dufferin Health Library Network
Friends of the Library Group

Departmental Libraries:

DAVIS CENTRE LIBRARY, 200 University Ave W, N2L 3G1. Tel: 519-888-4567, Ext 36913. FAX: 519-888-4311. *Head, Info Serv & Res,* Jennifer Haas; Tel: 519-888-4567, Ext 37469, E-mail: j2haas@uwaterloo.ca. Subject Specialists: *Engr, Math, Sci,* Jennifer Haas
Friends of the Library Group

MUSAGETES ARCHITECTURE LIBRARY, Seven Melville St S, Cambridge, N1S 2H4. Circulation Tel: 519-888-4567, Ext 27607. E-mail: libarch@library.uwaterloo.ca. Web Site: uwaterloo.ca/library/musagetes. *Archit Librn,* Evan Schilling; Tel: 519-888-4567, Ext 27620, E-mail: evan.schilling@uwaterloo.ca

WITER LEARNING RESOURCE CENTRE, Optometry Bldg, Rm 2101, N2L 3G1. Tel: 519-888-4567, Ext 84005. Web Site: uwaterloo.ca/witer-learning-resource-centre. *Circ Supvr,* Mirka Freemantle; Tel: 519-888-4567, Ext 38875, E-mail: mirka.freemantle@uwaterloo.ca
Special Collections: Optometry & Physiological Optics Materials Coll

P WATERLOO PUBLIC LIBRARY*, 35 Albert St, N2L 5E2. SAN 319-5988. Tel: 519-886-1310, Ext 110. Web Site: www.wpl.ca. *Chief Exec Officer,* Kelly Kipfer; Tel: 519-886-1310, Ext 123; *Dep Chief Exec Officer,* Laura Dick; E-mail: ldick@wpl.ca; *Info Serv Mgr,* Janet Seally; Tel: 519-886-1310, Ext 126, E-mail: jseally@wpl.ca; Staff 70 (MLS 9, Non-MLS 61)
Founded 1897. Pop 103,813; Circ 900,000
Library Holdings: CDs 12,985; DVDs 21,190; Bk Vols 335,700; Per Subs 325
Special Collections: Prov

Wireless access
Function: AV serv, For res purposes, Govt ref serv, Homebound delivery serv, ILL available, Magnifiers for reading, Outside serv via phone, mail, e-mail & web, Prog for children & young adult, Summer reading prog, Telephone ref, Wheelchair accessible
Open Mon-Thurs 9:30-9, Fri & Sat 9:30-5:30, Sun 1-4
Branches: 3
EASTSIDE, 2001 University Ave E, N2K4K4. Tel: 519-886-1310, Ext 410.
Open Mon-Thurs 9:30-9, Fri & Sat 9:30-5:30
JOHN M HARPER BRANCH, 500 Fischer Hallman Rd N, N2L 0B1. Tel: 519-886-1310, Ext 310.
Open Mon-Thurs 9:30-9, Fri & Sat 9:30-5:30
MCCORMICK BRANCH, 500 Parkside Dr, N2L 5J4, SAN 377-8452. Tel: 519-886-1310, Ext 213. *Mgr, Br,* Laura Dick
Open Tues-Thurs 9:30-9, Fri & Sat 9:30-5:30

C WILFRID LAURIER UNIVERSITY LIBRARY*, 75 University Ave W, N2L 3C5. SAN 319-5945. Tel: 519-884-0710, Ext 3222. Interlibrary Loan Service Tel: 519-884-0710, Ext 4970, 519-884-0710, Ext 4979. Administration Tel: 519-884-0710, Ext 3381. Automation Services Tel: 519-884-0710, Ext 3999. E-mail: libweb@wlu.ca. Web Site: library.wlu.ca. *Univ Librn,* Gohar Ashoughian; Tel: 519-884-0710, Ext 3380, E-mail: gashoughian@wlu.ca; *Admin Mgr,* Jennifer Knechtel; Tel: 519-884-0710, Ext 3642, E-mail: jknechtel@wlu.ca; *Assoc Univ Librn,* Gordon Bertrand; Tel: 519-884-0710, Ext 4923, E-mail: gbertrand@wlu.ca; *Assoc Univ Librn,* Scott Gillies; Tel: 519- 884-0710, Ext 3117, E-mail: sgillies@wlu.ca; *Head, Cat & Metadata Serv,* Matt Tales; Tel: 519-884-0710, Ext 3839, E-mail: mtales@wlu.ca; *Head, Coll & Acq,* Charlotte Innerd; Tel: 519-884-0710, Ext 2073, E-mail: cinnerd@wlu.edu; *Head, Digital Initiatives,* Dillon Moore; Tel: 519-884-0701, Ext 4126, E-mail: dimoore@wlu.ca; *Head, Spec Coll & Archives,* Amanda Oliver; Tel: 519-884-0710, Ext 3825, E-mail: aoliver@wlu.ca; *Govt Info Librn, Political Science Librarian,* Helene LeBlanc; Tel: 519-884-0710, Ext 3743, E-mail: hleblanc@wlu.ca; *Copyright & Reserves Supervisor,* Lauren Bourdages; Tel: 519-884-0710, Ext 4916, E-mail: lbourdages@wlu.ca; Staff 81 (MLS 26, Non-MLS 55)
Founded 1911. Enrl 19,000; Fac 719; Highest Degree: Doctorate
Library Holdings: CDs 5,985; DVDs 3,366; e-books 311,516; e-journals 63,642; Microforms 153,546; Music Scores 121,553; Bk Titles 603,465; Per Subs 777; Videos 1,519
Special Collections: Lutheran Church; University Archives
Subject Interests: Environ, Environ law, Environ studies, Liberal arts, Music, Relig
Automation Activity & Vendor Info: (Acquisitions) Ex Libris Group; (Cataloging) Ex Libris Group; (Circulation) Ex Libris Group; (Course Reserve) Ex Libris Group; (ILL) Ex Libris Group; (OPAC) Ex Libris Group; (Serials) Ex Libris Group
Wireless access
Publications: Annual Report of Librarian; Bibliographical & Reference Aids
Partic in Ontario Council of University Libraries

WAWA

P WAWA PUBLIC LIBRARY, 40 Broadway Ave, P0S 1K0. (Mail add: PO Box 1730, P0S 1K0), SAN 319-5996. Tel: 705-856-2244. Circulation Tel: 705-856-2244, Ext 290. Administration Tel: 705-856-2244, Ext 291. E-mail: circulation@wawa.cc. Web Site: wawa.olsn.ca. *Chief Exec Officer, Head Librn,* Suzanne Jarrell; E-mail: sjarrell@wawa.cc; Staff 1 (Non-MLS 1)
Founded 1954. Pop 2,700; Circ 23,400
Automation Activity & Vendor Info: (Cataloging) SirsiDynix-WorkFlows; (Circulation) SirsiDynix-WorkFlows
Wireless access
Function: 24/7 Electronic res, 24/7 Online cat, 24/7 wireless access, 3D Printer, Adult bk club, Homebound delivery serv, ILL available, Photocopying/Printing, Prog for children & young adult, Summer reading prog, Wheelchair accessible
Special Services for the Deaf - Bks on deafness & sign lang; Closed caption videos
Special Services for the Blind - Audio mat; Bks on CD; Large print bks; Ref serv; Talking bks
Open Tues-Thurs 11-7, Fri 11-5, Sat 11-2

WELLAND

J NIAGARA COLLEGE OF APPLIED ARTS & TECHNOLOGY*, Welland Campus Library, 100 Niagara College Blvd, L3C 7L3. SAN 319-602X. Tel: 905-735-2211, Ext 7767. E-mail: library@niagaracollage.ca. Web Site: nclibraries.niagaracollege.ca. *Tech Coordr,* Bianca Parisi; E-mail: bparisi@niagaracollege.ca; Staff 11 (MLS 3, Non-MLS 8)
Founded 1967. Enrl 6,200; Fac 240; Highest Degree: Bachelor
Library Holdings: Bk Vols 26,000; Per Subs 84
Subject Interests: Broadcasting, Commun studies, Communications, Health
Automation Activity & Vendor Info: (Acquisitions) Evergreen
Wireless access
Partic in Ontario Colleges Library Service (OCLS)
Open Mon-Thurs 8-10, Fri 8-5, Sat & Sun 1-5
Departmental Libraries:
DANIEL J PATTERSON CAMPUS LIBRARY, 135 Taylor Rd, SS 4, Niagara-on-the-Lake, L0S 1J0, SAN 378-1569. Tel: 905-641-2252, Ext 4413. *Libr Mgr,* Gordana Vitez; Tel: 905-641-2252, Ext 4223, E-mail: gvitez@niagaracollege.ca; Staff 4 (MLS 1, Non-MLS 3)
Founded 1967. Enrl 6,200; Fac 240; Highest Degree: Bachelor
Library Holdings: Bk Vols 14,000; Per Subs 86
Automation Activity & Vendor Info: (Circulation) Evergreen
Partic in College Bibliocentre
Open Mon-Thurs 8-10, Fri 8-5, Sat & Sun 1-5

P WELLAND PUBLIC LIBRARY*, 50 The Boardwalk, L3B 6J1. SAN 368-8321. Tel: 905-734-6210. FAX: 905-734-8955. E-mail: info@wellandlibrary.ca. Web Site: wellandlibrary.ca. *Chief Exec Officer,* Julianne Brunet; E-mail: jbrunet@wellandlibrary.ca; Staff 8 (MLS 5, Non-MLS 3)
Founded 1922. Circ 267,837
Library Holdings: CDs 2,285; Large Print Bks 2,916; Bk Titles 83,364; Per Subs 196; Talking Bks 932; Videos 4,287
Special Collections: French Language Coll; Welland County Local History Coll. Canadian and Provincial
Subject Interests: Multilingual
Automation Activity & Vendor Info: (Cataloging) SirsiDynix; (Circulation) SirsiDynix; (OPAC) SirsiDynix
Wireless access
Function: 24/7 Electronic res, 3D Printer, Adult bk club, Art programs, Audiobks via web, Bk club(s), Chess club, Children's prog, Electronic databases & coll, Free DVD rentals, Homebound delivery serv, Large print keyboards, Life-long learning prog for all ages, Magazines, Makerspace, Meeting rooms, Outreach serv, Photocopying/Printing, Prog for adults, Prog for children & young adult, Ref & res, Scanner, Story hour, Study rm, Summer reading prog, Workshops
Partic in Ontario Library Consortium

WESTPORT

P WESTPORT PUBLIC LIBRARY*, Three Spring St, K0G 1X0. (Mail add: PO Box 28, K0G 1X0), SAN 319-6062. Tel: 613-273-3223. FAX: 613-273-3460. E-mail: library@rideau.net. Web Site: westportontariolibrary.wordpress.com. *Librn,* Pamela Stuffles; Staff 1 (Non-MLS 1)
Founded 1947. Pop 680; Circ 8,756
Library Holdings: Bk Titles 13,500; Bk Vols 13,700
Wireless access
Function: 24/7 Electronic res, 24/7 Online cat, Adult bk club, Archival coll, Children's prog, Computers for patron use, Free DVD rentals, ILL available, Internet access, Online cat, OverDrive digital audio bks, Photocopying/Printing, Scanner, Story hour, Summer reading prog
Mem of Ontario Library Service
Open Mon & Fri 1-5, Tues & Sat 10-2, Thurs 2-5
Restriction: Circ to mem only, In-house use for visitors, Non-circulating coll, Non-circulating of rare bks
Friends of the Library Group

WHITBY

P WHITBY PUBLIC LIBRARY*, 405 Dundas St W, L1N 6A1. SAN 368-8380. Tel: 905-668-6531. FAX: 905-668-7445. Administration E-mail: admin@whitbylibrary.ca. Web Site: www.whitbylibrary.ca. *Chief Librn/CEO,* Rhonda Jessup; E-mail: rjessup@whitbylibrary.ca; Staff 49 (MLS 6, Non-MLS 43)
Founded 1852. Pop 110,000; Circ 1,081,120
Library Holdings: Bk Titles 140,433; Bk Vols 214,596; Per Subs 274
Special Collections: Canadian and Provincial
Automation Activity & Vendor Info: (Acquisitions) SirsiDynix; (Cataloging) SirsiDynix; (Circulation) SirsiDynix; (OPAC) SirsiDynix
Wireless access
Function: Art exhibits, CD-ROM, Computer training, Electronic databases & coll, Homebound delivery serv, ILL available, Mail & tel request accepted, Music CDs, Online ref, Photocopying/Printing, Prog for adults, Prog for children & young adult, Spoken cassettes & CDs, Summer reading prog, Telephone ref, VHS videos, Wheelchair accessible
Publications: Booklists; Monthly Bulletin of Events
Mem of Ontario Library Service
Open Mon-Fri 10-6, Sat 10-5
Branches: 3
BROOKLIN BRANCH, Eight Vipond Rd, Brooklin, L1M 1B3, SAN 368-8410. Tel: 905-655-3191. E-mail: askbrooklin@whitbylibrary.ca. *Br Supvr,* Sandra Mammone; Staff 4 (Non-MLS 4)
Open Mon-Fri 10-1 & 2-6, Sat 10-1 & 2-5

ROSSLAND BRANCH, 701 Rossland Rd E, L1N 8Y9, SAN 370-1352. Tel: 905-668-1886. E-mail: askrossland@whitbylibrary.ca. *Br Supvr,* Cheryl Schwass; Staff 3 (Non-MLS 3)
Open Tues, Wed & Fri 10-1 & 2-5

WHITBY ARCHIVES, 405 Dundas St W, L1N 6A1, SAN 373-7470. Tel: 905-668-6531, Ext 6. E-mail: archives@whitbylibrary.on.ca. *Archivist,* Sarah Ferencz; Staff 2 (MLS 1, Non-MLS 1)
Founded 1968
Special Collections: Genealogy; Land Records; Newspapers; Photographs; Private Coll
Function: Archival coll, Electronic databases & coll, Outreach serv
Open Mon-Fri 9:30-5
Restriction: Non-circulating, Open evenings by appt, Open to pub for ref only

WHITE RIVER

P WHITE RIVER PUBLIC LIBRARY*, 123 Superior St, P0M 3G0. (Mail add: PO Box 458, P0M 3G0), SAN 319-6070. Tel: 807-822-1113. FAX: 807-822-1488. E-mail: whiteriverlibrary@bellnet.ca. Web Site: www.whiteriverlibrary.com. *Chief Exec Officer,* Janet Ramage; *Asst Librn,* Diane Volf
Library Holdings: Bk Vols 5,000
Wireless access
Open Mon 2:30-5, Wed & Fri 6-8:30, Sat 10-12:30 (Sept-June); Mon, Tues, Thurs & Fri 10-5, Wed Noon-8 (July-Aug)

WINDSOR

L ESSEX LAW ASSOCIATION LAW LIBRARY*, Superior Courthouse, 245 Windsor Ave, N9A 1J2. SAN 320-3492. Tel: 519-252-8418. Toll Free Tel: 800-815-1112. FAX: 519 252-9686. E-mail: essexlaw@mnsi.net. *Libr Dir,* Douglas Hewitt
Founded 1884
Library Holdings: Bk Vols 15,000
Subject Interests: Can law
Open Mon-Fri 9-5

S MULTICULTURAL COUNCIL OF WINDSOR & ESSEX COUNTY LIBRARY*, 245 Janette Ave, N9A 4Z2. SAN 377-3396. Tel: 519-255-1127. FAX: 519-255-1435. E-mail: contact@themcc.com. Web Site: www.themcc.com.
Library Holdings: Bk Vols 500

J ST CLAIR COLLEGE OF APPLIED ARTS & TECHNOLOGY LIBRARY*, 2000 Talbot Rd W, N9A 6S4. SAN 319-6151. Tel: 519-972-2739. FAX: 519-972-2757. E-mail: library@stclaircollege.ca. Web Site: www.stclaircollege.ca/library. *Mgr, Libr Serv,* Cynthia Crump
Founded 1967
Library Holdings: Bk Vols 40,000; Per Subs 200
Special Collections: Government Documents
Subject Interests: Applied arts, Trades
Wireless access
Open Mon-Thurs 7:30am-10pm, Fri 7:30-6, Sat 9-5

C UNIVERSITY OF WINDSOR*, J Francis Leddy Library, 401 Sunset Ave, N9B 3P4. SAN 368-9220. Tel: 519-253-3000, Ext 3402. Interlibrary Loan Service Tel: 519-253-3000, Ext 3195. Reference Tel: 519-253-3000, Ext 3190. FAX: 519-971-3638. E-mail: leddylibrary@uwindsor.ca. Web Site: leddy.uwindsor.ca. *Univ Librn,* Selinda Berg; Tel: 519-253-3000, Ext 3196, E-mail: sberg@uwindsor.ca; *Assoc Univ Librn,* Tamsin Bolton-Bacon; Tel: 519-253-3000, Ext 3197, E-mail: tamsin.bacon@uwindsor.ca; *Assoc Univ Librn,* Karen Pillon; Tel: 519-253-3000, Ext 3201, E-mail: karen@uwindsor.ca; *Head, Access Serv,* Dave Johnston; Tel: 519-253-3000, Ext 3208, E-mail: djohnst@uwindsor.ca; *Bibliog Serv, Head, Acq,* Shuzhen Zhao; Tel: 519-253-3000, Ext 3162, E-mail: zhaoszf@uwindsor.ca; *Head, Syst,* Jennifer Soutter; E-mail: jsoutter@uwindsor.ca; *Scholarly Communications Librn,* Pascal Calarco; E-mail: pcalarco@uwindsor.ca; Staff 25 (MLS 23, Non-MLS 2)
Founded 1857. Enrl 15,525; Fac 524; Highest Degree: Doctorate
Library Holdings: Bk Vols 2,039,958
Special Collections: Classics & Misc (Leddy Coll); Katherine Mansfield Coll, bks & letters
Automation Activity & Vendor Info: (Acquisitions) Ex Libris Group; (Cataloging) Ex Libris Group; (Circulation) Ex Libris Group; (Course Reserve) Ex Libris Group; (Discovery) Ex Libris Group; (ILL) OCLC; (OPAC) Ex Libris Group; (Serials) Ex Libris Group
Wireless access
Function: 24/7 Online cat, Archival coll, Computers for patron use, Doc delivery serv, E-Reserves, Electronic databases & coll, For res purposes, Internet access, Microfiche/film & reading machines, Online cat, Online Chat, Online ref, Orientations, Outreach serv, Outside serv via phone, mail, e-mail & web, Photocopying/Printing, Printer for laptops & handheld devices, Ref & res, Ref serv available, Res assist avail, Res libr, Scanner, Study rm, Wheelchair accessible
Partic in Canadian Association of Research Libraries; Ontario Council of University Libraries
Restriction: Authorized patrons, Non-circulating of rare bks, Open to students, fac, staff & alumni, Pub use on premises

Departmental Libraries:

CL PAUL MARTIN LAW LIBRARY, Ron W Ianni Law Bldg, 401 Sunset Ave, N9B 3P4. Tel: 519-253-3000, Ext 2977. FAX: 519-973-7064. E-mail: lawcirc@uwindsor.ca. Web Site: www.uwindsor.ca/law/library. *Law Librn,* Annette Demers; Tel: 519-253-3000, Ext 2976, E-mail: lawlibrarian@uwindsor.ca; Staff 10 (MLS 2, Non-MLS 8)
Founded 1967. Enrl 600; Highest Degree: Bachelor
Library Holdings: Bk Vols 232,501; Per Subs 1,436
Subject Interests: Commonwealth, Law Can, US
Automation Activity & Vendor Info: (Acquisitions) Ex Libris Group; (Cataloging) Ex Libris Group; (Circulation) Ex Libris Group; (Course Reserve) Ex Libris Group; (Discovery) Ex Libris Group; (ILL) OCLC; (OPAC) Ex Libris Group; (Serials) Ex Libris Group
Open Mon-Thurs 8:30am-11:50pm, Fri 8:30-4:50, Sat 11-4:50, Sun 1-11:50

P WINDSOR PUBLIC LIBRARY*, 850 Ouellette Ave, N9A 4M9. SAN 368-931X. Tel: 519-255-6770. FAX: 519-255-7207. Web Site: www.windsorpubliclibrary.com. *Chief Exec Officer,* Kitty Pope; E-mail: KPope@windsorpubliclibrary.com; *Dir, Corporate Serv,* Chris Woodrow; E-mail: CWoodrow@windsorpubliclibrary.com; *Mgr, Pub Serv,* Christine Rideout-Arkell; E-mail: CArkell@windsorpubliclibrary.com
Founded 1894. Pop 212,000; Circ 1,500,000
Library Holdings: Bk Vols 640,818; Per Subs 250
Special Collections: Canadian and Provincial
Automation Activity & Vendor Info: (Acquisitions) BiblioCommons; (Cataloging) BiblioCommons; (Circulation) BiblioCommons; (OPAC) BiblioCommons
Wireless access
Mem of Ontario Library Service
Partic in Info-globe; Infomart; Proquest Dialog
Friends of the Library Group

Branches: 9

BRIDGEVIEW LIBRARY, 1295 Campbell Ave, N9B 3M7, SAN 368-9379. Tel: 519-255-6770, Ext 2200. FAX: 519-253-3472.
Library Holdings: Bk Vols 42,000
Open Mon & Wed 12-8, Tues & Thurs 10-6, Fri & Sat 9-5
Friends of the Library Group

NIKOLA BUDIMIR MEMORIAL LIBRARY, 1310 Grand Marais Rd W, N9E 1E4, SAN 368-9409. Tel: 519-255-6770, Ext 3300. FAX: 519-969-7947.
Library Holdings: Bk Vols 64,326
Open Mon-Wed 10-9, Thurs 10-6, Fri & Sat 9-5, Sun 1-5 (Winter); Mon & Wed Noon-8, Tues & Thurs 10-6, Fri & Sat 9-5 (Summer)
Friends of the Library Group

CENTRAL LIBRARY, 850 Ouellette Ave, N9A 4M9. Tel: 519-255-6770.
Library Holdings: Bk Vols 491,186
Special Collections: Automotive History Coll; Municipal Archives
Subject Interests: Local hist
Special Services for the Deaf - TDD equip
Open Mon-Thurs 9-9, Fri & Sat 9-5, Sun 1-5 (Winter); Mon-Thurs 9-8, Fri & Sat 9-5 (Summer)
Friends of the Library Group

W F CHISHOLM LIBRARY, 1075 Ypres Ave, N8W 4W4, SAN 368-9417. Tel: 519-255-6770, Ext 5500. FAX: 519-966-3854.
Library Holdings: Bk Vols 20,000
Open Mon & Wed Noon-8, Tues & Thurs 10-6, Sat 9-5 (Winter); Mon & Wed Noon-8, Tues & Thurs 10-6, Fri & Sat 9-5 (Summer)
Friends of the Library Group

FONTAINEBLEAU LIBRARY, 3030 Rivard Ave, N8T 2J2. Tel: 519-255-6770, Ext 5000.
Founded 2005
Library Holdings: Bk Vols 52,000
Open Mon & Wed Noon-8, Tues & Thurs 10-6, Sat 9-5 (Winter); Mon & Wed Noon-8, Tues & Thurs 10-6, Fri & Sat 9-5 (Summer)

FOREST GLADE-OPTIMIST LIBRARY, 3211 Forest Glade Dr, N8R 1W7, SAN 368-9522. Tel: 519-255-6635, Ext 5400.
Library Holdings: Bk Vols 53,627
Open Mon & Wed 12-8, Tues & Thurs 10-6, Fri & Sat 9-5
Friends of the Library Group

RIVERSIDE LIBRARY, 6305 Wyandotte St E, N8S 4N5, SAN 368-9433. Tel: 519-255-6770, Ext 6600. FAX: 519-945-2871.
Library Holdings: Bk Vols 56,000
Open Mon-Wed 10-9, Thurs 10-6, Fri & Sat 9-5, Sun 1-5 (Winter); Mon & Wed Noon-8, Tues & Thurs 10-6, Fri & Sat 9-5 (Summer)
Friends of the Library Group

SANDWICH LIBRARY, 3312 Sandwich St, N9C 1B1. Tel: 519-255-6770, Ext 7700.
Library Holdings: Bk Vols 35,000
Open Mon & Wed Noon-8, Tues & Thurs 10-6, Sat 9-5 (Winter); Mon & Wed Noon-8, Tues & Thurs 10-6, Fri & Sat 9-5 (Summer)

SEMINOLE LIBRARY, 4285 Seminole St, N8Y 1Z5, SAN 368-9468. Tel: 519-255-6770, Ext 8800. FAX: 519-945-3404.
Library Holdings: Bk Vols 42,584
Open Mon & Wed Noon-8, Tues & Thurs 10-6, Sat 9-5 (Winter); Mon & Wed Noon-8, Tues & Thurs 10-6, Fri & Sat 9-5 (Summer)
Friends of the Library Group

M WINDSOR REGIONAL HOSPITAL*, Health Sciences Library, WRH Health Sciences Library, 1030 Ouellette Ave, N9A 1E1. SAN 374-4914. Tel: 519-254-5577, Ext 33178. Administration E-mail: orien.duda@wrh.on.ca. Web Site: h91000.eos-intl.net/H91000/OPAC/Miscellaneous/LibraryInformation.aspx. *Coordr, Libr Serv; Librn,* Orien Duda; Tel: 519-254-5577, Ext 33178, E-mail: orien.duda@wrh.on.ca; Staff 1 (MLS 1)
Founded 1911
Automation Activity & Vendor Info: (Acquisitions) EOS International; (Cataloging) EOS International; (Circulation) EOS International; (Course Reserve) EOS International; (Media Booking) EOS International; (OPAC) EOS International
Wireless access
Partic in Midwest Collaborative for Library Services; Ontario Health Libraries Association
Open Mon-Fri 8-4

WOODSTOCK

P OXFORD COUNTY LIBRARY*, Headquarters, 21 Reeve St, N4S 7Y3. (Mail add: PO Box 1614, N4S 7Y3), SAN 368-9557. Tel: 519-539-9800, Ext 3260. FAX: 519-421-4712. Web Site: www.ocl.net. *Chief Librn/CEO,* Lisa Marie Williams; E-mail: lmwilliams@ocl.net; Staff 2 (MLS 2)
Founded 1965. Pop 51,140; Circ 329,496
Library Holdings: Bk Titles 152,974; Bk Vols 202,182; Per Subs 58
Special Collections: Canadian and Provincial
Automation Activity & Vendor Info: (Acquisitions) SirsiDynix; (Cataloging) SirsiDynix; (Circulation) SirsiDynix; (Serials) SirsiDynix
Wireless access
Mem of Ontario Library Service
Partic in Ontario Library Consortium
Open Mon-Fri 8:30-4:30
Friends of the Library Group
Branches: 14
BROWNSVILLE BRANCH, 292240 Culloden Rd, Brownsville, N0L 1C0. (Mail add: PO Box 29, Brownsville, N0L 1C0), SAN 368-9611. Tel: 519-877-2938. FAX: 519-877-2261. E-mail: brownsvillelibrary@ocl.net.
Open Tues & Sat 10-2, Wed 4-8
BURGESSVILLE BRANCH, 604 Main St S, Burgessville, N0J 1C0. (Mail add: PO Box 70, Burgessville, N0J 1C0), SAN 368-9646. Tel: 519-424-2404. FAX: 519-424-9422. E-mail: burgessvillelibrary@ocl.net.
Open Tues & Thurs 4-8, Fri 2-5, Sat 9-1
EMBRO BRANCH, Embro Town Hall, 135 Huron St, Embro, N0J 1J0. (Mail add: PO Box 193, Embro, N0J 1J0), SAN 368-9735. Tel: 519-475-4172. FAX: 519-475-6301. E-mail: embrolibrary@ocl.net.
Open Tues & Thurs 5:30pm-8:30pm, Wed 2-5, Sat 10-1
HARRINGTON BRANCH, 539 Victoria St, Harrington, N0J 1J0. (Mail add: PO Box 18, Harrington, N0J 1J0). Tel: 519-475-6909. FAX: 519-475-4115. E-mail: harringtonlibrary@ocl.net.
Open Tues 10-1, Thurs & Fri 5-8
INGERSOLL BRANCH, The Town Ctr, 130 Oxford St, Ingersoll, N5C 2V5, SAN 368-9824. Tel: 519-485-2505. FAX: 519-485-3857. E-mail: ingersolllibrary@ocl.net.
Open Mon-Thurs 9:30-8:30, Fri 9:30-5:30, Sat 10-5:30
Friends of the Library Group
INNERKIP BRANCH, Innerkip Community Ctr, 695566 17th Line, Innerkip, N0J 1M0. (Mail add: PO Box 104, Innerkip, N0J 1M0), SAN 368-9859. Tel: 519-469-3824. FAX: 519-469-3185. E-mail: innerkiplibrary@ocl.net.
Open Tues & Thurs 5-8, Wed 2-5, Sat 10-1
MOUNT ELGIN BRANCH, Mount Elgin Community Ctr, 333204 Plank Line, Mount Elgin, N0J 1N0, SAN 368-9913. Tel: 519-485-0134. FAX: 519-485-1812. E-mail: mountelginlibrary@ocl.net.
Open Tues & Sat 11-2, Wed & Thurs 5pm-8pm
NORWICH BRANCH, Ten Tidey St, Norwich, N0J 1P0. (Mail add: PO Box 249, Norwich, N0J 1P0), SAN 368-9948. Tel: 519-863-3307. FAX: 519-863-5356. E-mail: norwichlibrary@ocl.net.
Open Tues & Fri 9-5, Wed & Thurs 12:30-8, Sat 9-1
OTTERVILLE BRANCH, 207 Main St W, Otterville, N0J 1R0. (Mail add: PO Box 212, Otterville, N0J 1R0), SAN 368-9972. Tel: 519-879-6984. FAX: 519-879-6586. E-mail: ottervillelibrary@ocl.net.
Open Tues 10-1, Wed & Thurs 5-8, Sat 1:30-4:30
PLATTSVILLE BRANCH, Plattsville & District Public School, 112 Mill St E, Plattsville, N0J 1S0. (Mail add: PO Box 40, Plattsville, N0J 1S0), SAN 369-0008. Tel: 519-684-7390. FAX: 519-684-7512. E-mail: plattsvillelibrary@ocl.net.
Open Tues & Thurs 9-12 & 3-8:30, Wed 2-6, Sat 10-2
PRINCETON BRANCH, 25 Main St S, Princeton, N0J 1V0. (Mail add: PO Box 99, Princeton, N0J 1V0), SAN 369-0032. Tel: 519-458-4416. FAX: 519-458-8623. E-mail: princetonlibrary@ocl.net.
Open Tues & Thurs 3pm-7pm, Wed 12-4, Sat 9-1
Friends of the Library Group
TAVISTOCK BRANCH, 40 Woodstock St S, Tavistock, N0B 2R0. (Mail add: PO Box 190, Tavistock, N0B 2R0), SAN 369-0067. Tel: 519-655-3013. FAX: 519-655-3276. E-mail: tavistocklibrary@ocl.net.
Open Tues & Thurs 10-8, Wed 10-5, Fri & Sat 10-2
THAMESFORD BRANCH, 165 Dundas St, Thamesford, N0M 2M0. (Mail add: PO Box 220, Thamesford, N0M 2M0), SAN 369-0091. Tel: 519-285-3219. FAX: 519-285-3575. E-mail: thamesfordlibrary@ocl.net.
Open Tues & Thurs 10-8, Wed 12-8, Fri 2-6, Sat 11-2
Friends of the Library Group
TILLSONBURG PUBLIC LIBRARY, Two Library Lane, Tillsonburg, N4G 2S7, SAN 319-4493. Tel: 519-842-5571. FAX: 519-842-2941. E-mail: tillsonburglibrary@ocl.net.
Founded 1915. Pop 14,000; Circ 124,727
Library Holdings: Bk Vols 33,000; Per Subs 50
Subject Interests: Small libr admin
Open Mon-Thurs 9:30-8:30, Fri 9:30-6, Sat 9:30-4

L OXFORD LAW ASSOCIATION LIBRARY*, Courthouse, 415 Hunter St, 3rd Flr, N4S 4G6. (Mail add: PO Box 1678, N4S 0A9), SAN 372-6231. Tel: 519-539-7711. Toll Free Tel: 866-750-5169. FAX: 519-539-7962. Web Site: www.libraryco.ca/library/oxford-county-law-association. *Librn,* Carolyne Alsop; E-mail: oxfordlaw@ocl.net; Staff 1 (MLS 1)
Library Holdings: Bk Titles 750; Bk Vols 2,000
Automation Activity & Vendor Info: (OPAC) Ex Libris Group
Function: For res purposes
Restriction: Not open to pub

P WOODSTOCK PUBLIC LIBRARY*, 445 Hunter St, N4S 4G7. SAN 319-6186. Tel: 519-539-4801. FAX: 519-539-5246. Web Site: www.mywpl.ca. *Chief Exec Officer, Chief Librn,* Lindsay Harris; E-mail: lharris@mywpl.ca; *Mgr, Pub Serv,* Megan Cook; E-mail: mcook@mywpl.ca; *Operations Mgr,* Michael Cruickshank; E-mail: mcruickshank@mywpl.ca; Staff 24 (MLS 8, Non-MLS 16)
Founded 1835. Pop 40,900; Circ 273,280
Jan 2020-Dec 2020 Income (CAN) $2,700,242, Provincial (CAN) $60,168, Locally Generated Income (CAN) $32,116, Parent Institution (CAN) $2,531,340, Other (CAN) $76,618. Mats Exp (CAN) $285,926, Books (CAN) $169,056, Electronic Ref Mat (Incl. Access Fees) (CAN) $116,870
Library Holdings: Audiobooks 19,268; DVDs 21,899; e-books 76,876; e-journals 4,001; Electronic Media & Resources 8; Bk Titles 70,582; Bk Vols 77,899; Per Subs 190
Special Collections: Local History Pertaining to Woodstock & to Oxford County
Automation Activity & Vendor Info: (Cataloging) SirsiDynix-WorkFlows; (Circulation) SirsiDynix-WorkFlows; (Discovery) BiblioCommons; (ILL) SirsiDynix-WorkFlows; (OPAC) BiblioCommons
Wireless access
Function: 24/7 Electronic res, 24/7 Online cat, Activity rm, Adult bk club, Audiobks via web, Bk club(s), Bks on CD, CD-ROM, Children's prog, Computer training, Computers for patron use, Digital talking bks, Electronic databases & coll, Holiday prog, ILL available, Internet access, Magazines, Meeting rooms, Microfiche/film & reading machines, Music CDs, Online cat, Photocopying/Printing, Printer for laptops & handheld devices, Prog for adults, Prog for children & young adult, Ref & res, Story hour, Summer reading prog, Teen prog, Wheelchair accessible
Mem of Ontario Library Service
Partic in Ontario Library Consortium
Open Mon-Thurs 10-8:30, Fri & Sat 10-5, Sun (Sept-June) 1-5
Friends of the Library Group

WYOMING

P LAMBTON COUNTY LIBRARY*, Headquarters, 787 Broadway St, N0N 1T0. (Mail add: PO Box 3100, N0N 1T0), SAN 369-027X. Tel: 519-845-3324. Toll Free Tel: 866-324-6912. FAX: 519-845-0700. E-mail: Library.Contact@county-lambton.on.ca. Web Site: www.lclibrary.ca. *Gen Mgr,* John Innes; Tel: 519-845-0801; Staff 205 (MLS 10, Non-MLS 195)
Founded 1967. Pop 126,000; Circ 996,322
Library Holdings: Audiobooks 5,335; CDs 9,100; DVDs 16,100; Bk Titles 275,821; Bk Vols 500,591; Per Subs 497; Videos 4,000
Special Collections: Local History (Lambton Coll). Canadian and Provincial
Automation Activity & Vendor Info: (Acquisitions) Infor Library & Information Solutions; (Cataloging) Infor Library & Information Solutions; (Circulation) Infor Library & Information Solutions; (OPAC) Infor Library & Information Solutions
Wireless access
Function: Archival coll, AV serv, Homebound delivery serv, ILL available, Prog for children & young adult, Ref serv available, Summer reading prog

Publications: Leaflet (Newsletter)
Open Mon-Fri 9-5
Branches: 25
ALVINSTON BRANCH, 3251 River St, Alvinston, N0N 1A0. (Mail add: PO Box 44, Alvinston, N0N 1A0), SAN 369-030X. Tel: 519-898-2921.
Open Tues, Thurs & Fri 2-8:30, Sat 10-1:30
ARKONA BRANCH, 16 Smith St, Arkona, N0M 1B0. (Mail add: PO Box 12, Arkona, N0M 1B0), SAN 369-0334. Tel: 519-828-3406.
Open Tues 4-8, Thurs 3-8, Sat 10-1
BRIGDEN BRANCH, 1540 Duncan St, Brigden, N0N 1B0. (Mail add: PO Box 339, Brigden, N0N 1B0), SAN 369-0369. Tel: 519-864-1142.
Open Mon, Tues & Thurs 4-9, Wed 9:30-12:30 & 4-7, Sat 9-1
BRIGHTS GROVE BRANCH, 2618 Hamilton Rd, Brights Grove, N0N 1C0. (Mail add: PO Box 339, Brights Grove, N0N 1C0), SAN 369-0393. Tel: 519-869-2351.
Open Mon-Thurs 9:30-8, Sat & Sun 11-3
CAMLACHIE BRANCH, 6745 Camlachie Rd, Camlachie, N0N 1E0, SAN 369-0423. Tel: 519-899-2202.
Open Mon, Wed & Thurs 4-8, Sat 9-1
CORUNNA BRANCH, 417 Lyndock St, Corunna, N0N 1G0, SAN 369-0458. Tel: 519-862-1132.
Open Mon-Thurs 10-8, Fri & Sat 10-2
COURTRIGHT BRANCH, 1533 Fourth St, Courtright, N0N 1H0. (Mail add: PO Box 182, Courtright, N0N 1H0), SAN 369-0482. Tel: 519-867-2712.
Open Tues & Thurs 3-7, Sat 9-1
FLORENCE BRANCH, 6213 Mill St, Florence, N0P 1R0. (Mail add: PO Box 102, Florence, N0P 1R0), SAN 369-0504. Tel: 519-692-3213.
Open Tues & Thurs 4-8, Sat 10-2
FOREST BRANCH, 61 King St W, Forest, N0N 1J0, SAN 369-0512. Tel: 519-786-5152.
Open Mon-Fri 9:30-9, Sat 9:30-5
GRAND BEND BRANCH, 15 Gill Rd, Grand Bend, N0M 1T0. (Mail add: PO Box 117, Grand Bend, N0M 1T0), SAN 369-0547. Tel: 519-238-2067.
Open Mon-Thurs 9-4 & 5-8, Fri 9-3, Sat 10-1
INWOOD BRANCH, 6504 James St, Inwood, N0N 1K0. (Mail add: PO Box 41, Inwood, N0N 1K0), SAN 369-0571. Tel: 519-844-2491.
Open Tues & Thurs 4-8, Sat 9-1
MALLROAD BRANCH, 1362 Lambton Mall Rd, Sarnia, N7S 5A1, SAN 369-0601. Tel: 519-542-2580.
Open Mon-Fri 9:30-8, Sat 9:30-5, Sun 12-5
MOORETOWN BRANCH, Mooretown Sports Complex, 1166 Emily St, Mooretown, N0N 1M0, SAN 369-0644. Tel: 519-867-2823.
Open Mon & Wed 4-8, Sat 9-1
OIL SPRINGS BRANCH, 4596 Oil Springs Line, Oil Springs, N0N 1P0. (Mail add: PO Box 126, Oil Springs, N0N 1P0), SAN 369-0660. Tel: 519-834-2670.
Open Tues & Thurs 4-8, Sat 9-1
PETROLIA BRANCH, 4200 Petrolia Line, Petrolia, N0N 1R0, SAN 369-0695. Tel: 519-882-0771.
Open Mon-Fri 9:30-8:30, Sat 9-4:30, Sun 11-4
POINT EDWARD BRANCH, 220 Michigan Ave, Point Edward, N7V 1E8, SAN 372-5200. Tel: 519-336-3291.
Open Mon & Wed Noon-5, Tues & Fri 2-7, Sat 10-3
PORT FRANKS BRANCH, 9997 Port Franks Rd, Unit 2, Port Franks, N0M 2L0, SAN 369-0725. Tel: 519-243-2820.
Open Mon 4-8, Wed 3-8, Sat 9-12
PORT LAMBTON BRANCH, 507 Stoddard St, Port Lambton, N0P 2B0. (Mail add: PO Box 250, Port Lambton, N0P 2B0), SAN 369-075X. Tel: 519-677-5217.
Open Mon, Wed, & Thurs 6pm-9pm, Sat 9-12
SARNIA BRANCH, 124 Christina St S, Sarnia, N7T 8E1, SAN 319-4027. Tel: 519-337-3291. FAX: 519-344-3041.
Founded 1900. Pop 128,975
Special Collections: Canadian and Provincial
Open Mon-Thurs 9:30-9, Fri & Sat 9:30-5:30, Sun 2-5
SHETLAND BRANCH, 1279 Shetland Rd, RR 2, Florence, N0P 1R0, SAN 369-0784. Tel: 519-695-3330.
Open Mon & Wed 4-8, Sat 1-5
SOMBRA BRANCH, 3536 St Clair Pkwy, Sombra, N0P 2H0. (Mail add: PO Box 211, Sombra, N0P 2H0), SAN 369-0814. Tel: 519-892-3711.
Web Site: www.lclibrary.ca/en/visit/sombra-library.aspx.
Open Tues 3-7, Thurs & Fri 10-2
THEDFORD BRANCH, Legacy Ctr, 16 Allen St, Thedford, N0M 2N0. (Mail add: PO Box 70, Thedford, N0M 2N0), SAN 369-0849. Tel: 519-296-4459.
Open Tues 4-8, Thurs 3-8, Sat 10-1
WATFORD BRANCH, 5317 Nauvoo Rd, Watford, N0M 2S0. (Mail add: PO Box 9, Watford, N0M 2S0), SAN 369-0938. Tel: 519-876-2204.
Open Mon, Tues & Thurs 10-7, Fri 10-3, Sat 11-2
WILKESPORT BRANCH, 1349 Wilkesport Line, Wilkesport, N0P 2R0, SAN 369-0946. Tel: 519-864-4000.
Open Mon, Wed & Thurs 5-8, Sat 9-12
WYOMING BRANCH, 536 Niagara St, N0N 1T0. (Mail add: PO Box 357, N0N 1T0), SAN 369-0962. Tel: 519-845-0181.
Open Mon-Thurs 12-8, Fri & Sat 9-5
Bookmobiles: 1

PRINCE EDWARD ISLAND

Date of Statistics: FY April 1 2023 - March 31, 2024
Population, 2021 Canadian Census: 154,331
Total Volumes in Public Libraries: 201,204 (not including digital titles)
Volumes Per Capita: 1.30
Total Public Library Circulation: 681,680
Circulation Per Capita: 4.41
Digital Resources:
Total e-books & downloadable audiobooks: 18,130
Income and Expenditures:
Total Public Library Income: $3,429,400
Source of Income: Appropriations
Expenditures Per Capita: $22.22
Number of County or Multi-County Libraries: 1
Information provided courtesy of: Grace Dawson, Director of Libraries and Archives; Prince Edward Island Public Library Service

CHARLOTTETOWN

P CHARLOTTETOWN LIBRARY LEARNING CENTRE, Charlottetown Public Library, 97 Queen St, C1A 4A9. (Mail add: 100-97 Queen St, C1A 4A9), SAN 319-6208. Tel: 902-368-4642. E-mail: charlottetown@gov.pe.ca. Web Site: www.princeedwardisland.ca/en/point-interest/charlottetown-library-learning-centre. *Regional Librn,* Beth Clinton; Tel: 902-368-4654, E-mail: elclinton@gov.pe.ca; *Supvr, Pub Serv,* Lisa Newcombe; E-mail: lenewcombe@gov.pe.ca; Staff 21 (MLS 3, Non-MLS 18)
Founded 1965. Pop 37,400; Circ 108,405
Library Holdings: Bk Titles 100,920
Special Collections: Prince Edward Island Coll
Automation Activity & Vendor Info: (Acquisitions) SirsiDynix; (Cataloging) SirsiDynix; (Circulation) SirsiDynix; (Media Booking) SirsiDynix
Wireless access
Special Services for the Blind - Talking bks
Open Mon-Thurs 9:30-8:30, Fri & Sat 9:30-5, Sun 12:30-5
Friends of the Library Group

C HOLLAND COLLEGE LIBRARY SERVICES*, 140 Weymouth St, C1A 4Z1. SAN 372-6541. Tel: 902-566-9558. E-mail: library@hollandcollege.com. Web Site: hollandcollege.libguides.com. *Mgr, Libr Serv,* Patricia Doucette; Tel: 902-566-9350, E-mail: pmdoucette@hollandcollege.com; *Electronic Serv Librn,* Larry Tweed; Tel: 902-566-9578, E-mail: ldtweed@hollandcollege.com; *Instrul Librn,* Emily MacIsaac; Tel: 902-566-9308, E-mail: ermacisaac@hollandcollege.com; *Res Ctr Mgr,* Andrea Cameron; Tel: 902-853-0020, E-mail: ancameron@hollandcollege.com; *Res Ctr Mgr,* Leslie Holt; Tel: 902-566-9636, E-mail: ljholt@hollandcollege.com; *Res Ctr Mgr,* Jean Lykow; Tel: 902-888-6738, E-mail: jlykow@hollandcollege.com; *Libr Tech,* Rose MacDonald; Tel: 902-894-6837, E-mail: romacdonald@hollandcollege.com; Staff 7 (MLS 3, Non-MLS 4)
Founded 1969. Fac 175
Library Holdings: Per Subs 50
Automation Activity & Vendor Info: (Acquisitions) Horizon; (Cataloging) Horizon; (Circulation) Horizon; (OPAC) Horizon; (Serials) Horizon
Wireless access
Function: ILL available
Partic in Council of Atlantic Academic Libraries (CAAL)
Open Mon-Fri 8:30am-10pm, Sat 9-5, Sun 12-6

L LAW SOCIETY OF PRINCE EDWARD ISLAND LIBRARY*, 42 Water St, C1A 1A4. SAN 377-2837. Tel: 902-368-6099. FAX: 902-368-7557. Web Site: lawsocietypei.ca/law-library. *Law Librn,* Pam Borden; E-mail: pborden@lspei.pe.ca; Staff 1 (Non-MLS 1)
Library Holdings: Bk Titles 1,055; Bk Vols 14,000; Per Subs 20
Restriction: Non-circulating, Open by appt only

M PRINCE EDWARD ISLAND ASSOCIATION FOR COMMUNITY LIVING*, Resource Library, 40 Enman Crescent, Rm 273, C1E 1E6. SAN 375-6815. Tel: 902-439-4607. E-mail: familysupport@peiacl.org. Web Site: peiacl.org. *Exec Dir,* Julie Smith; E-mail: executivedirector@peiacl.org; Staff 2 (MLS 1, Non-MLS 1)
Founded 1956
Library Holdings: AV Mats 100; Bks on Deafness & Sign Lang 20; Bk Titles 1,500; Per Subs 20; Talking Bks 10
Subject Interests: Attention deficit disorder, Autism, Communication, Employment, Housing, Parenting, Self help, Sexuality
Open Mon-Fri 9-4

M QUEEN ELIZABETH HOSPITAL*, Frank J MacDonald Library, 60 Riverside Dr, C1A 8T5. (Mail add: PO Box 6600, C1A 8T5), SAN 324-461X. Tel: 902-894-2371. FAX: 902-894-2424. E-mail: qehlibrary@ihis.org. Web Site: www.qehlibrarypei.ca. *Librn,* Julie A Cole; E-mail: jacole@ihis.org; *Library Contact,* Melissa Stanley; E-mail: mmstanley@ihis.org
Founded 1982
Library Holdings: Bk Titles 500; Per Subs 85
Subject Interests: Health sci
Automation Activity & Vendor Info: (Cataloging) Inmagic, Inc.
Open Mon-Fri 8-4

C UNIVERSITY OF PRINCE EDWARD ISLAND*, Robertson Library, 550 University Ave, C1A 4P3. SAN 319-6224. Tel: 902-566-0343. Circulation Tel: 902-566-0583. Interlibrary Loan Service Tel: 902-566-0445. FAX: 902-628-4305. E-mail: reference@upei.ca. Web Site: library.upei.ca. *Univ Librn,* Donald Moses; E-mail: dmoses@upei.ca; *Archives & Spec Coll Librn,* Simon Lloyd; E-mail: slloyd@upei.ca; *Colls Librn, User Experience Librn,* Melissa Belvadi; E-mail: mbelvadi@upei.ca; *Digital Infrastructure, Discovery Librn,* Rosemary Le Faive; E-mail: rlefaive@upei.ca; *Digital Initiatives & Syst Librn,* Robert Drew; E-mail: rdrew@upei.ca; *Health Sci Librn, Scholarly Communications Librn,* Kim Mears; E-mail: kmears@upei.ca; Staff 21 (MLS 5, Non-MLS 16)
Founded 1969. Enrl 3,000; Fac 180; Highest Degree: Doctorate
Library Holdings: Bk Titles 307,552
Special Collections: Prince Edward Island Coll
Automation Activity & Vendor Info: (Acquisitions) SirsiDynix; (Cataloging) SirsiDynix; (Circulation) SirsiDynix; (Course Reserve) SirsiDynix; (ILL) Relais International; (OPAC) SirsiDynix; (Serials) SirsiDynix
Wireless access
Function: Photocopying/Printing, Scanner, Study rm
Partic in Council of Atlantic Academic Libraries (CAAL); Proquest Dialog
Open Mon-Thurs 8am-10pm, Fri 8-6, Sat 11-5, Sun 12-9
Friends of the Library Group

G VETERAN AFFAIRS CANADA LIBRARY*, 125 Maple Hills Ave, C1C 0B6. SAN 329-210X. Tel: 782-377-1025. E-mail: library-bibliotheque@veterans.gc.ca. Web Site: www.veterans.gc.ca. *Librn,* Heidi Lund; E-mail: heidi.lund@veterans.gc.ca; Staff 1 (MLS 1)

Library Holdings: Bk Titles 5,000; Per Subs 50
Subject Interests: Govt doc, Healthcare, Mil hist, Veterans
Function: Govt ref serv, ILL available
Publications: Veterans' Health Research Alert
Restriction: Access for corporate affiliates, Authorized personnel only, Borrowing requests are handled by ILL, Circulates for staff only, Employees only

MORELL

P PRINCE EDWARD ISLAND PUBLIC LIBRARY SERVICE*, 89 Red Head Rd, C0A 1S0. (Mail add: PO Box 7500, C0A 1S0), SAN 369-0997. Tel: 902-961-7320. Interlibrary Loan Service Tel: 902-961-7324. FAX: 902-961-7322. E-mail: plshq@gov.pe.ca. Web Site: www.library.pe.ca. *Prov Librn,* Kathleen Eaton; Tel: 902-961-7316; *Syst Librn,* Liam O'Hare; Tel: 902-961-7323, E-mail: lfohare@gov.pe.ca
Founded 1933. Pop 152,000; Circ 813,000
Library Holdings: Bk Vols 325,400; Per Subs 100
Special Collections: Can; Prince Edward Island History, bks, micro
Automation Activity & Vendor Info: (Acquisitions) SirsiDynix; (Cataloging) SirsiDynix; (Circulation) SirsiDynix; (OPAC) SirsiDynix
Wireless access
Open Mon-Fri 8-4
Branches: 26
ALBERTON PUBLIC LIBRARY, 11 Railway St, Alberton, C0B 1B0, SAN 369-111X. Tel: 902-231-2090. E-mail: alberton@gov.pe.ca.
Open Tues 3-8, Wed & Fri 10-4, Sat 10-2
Friends of the Library Group
BIBLIOTHEQUE PUBLIQUE D'ABRAM-VILLAGE, 1596 Rte 124, Wellington, C0B 2E0, SAN 369-108X. Tel: 902-854-2491. FAX: 902-854-2981. E-mail: abram@gov.pe.ca.
Open Tues 4-8, Thus 9-5, Sat 9-1
BORDEN-CARLETON PUBLIC LIBRARY, 244 Borden Ave, Borden, C0B 1X0, SAN 369-1144. Tel: 902-437-6492. E-mail: borden-carleton@gov.pe.ca.
Open Mon 10-2, Wed 4-8, Sat 9-1
BREADALBANE PUBLIC LIBRARY, 4023 Dixon Rd, Breadalbane, C0A 1E0, SAN 369-1179. Tel: 902-964-2520. E-mail: breadalbane@gov.pe.ca.
Open Tues 10-1:30, Thurs 3-8, Sat 2-5:30
CHARLOTTETOWN LIBRARY LEARNING CENTRE
See Separate Entry under Charlottetown Library Learning Centre in Charlottetown
CHARLOTTETOWN LIBRARY LEARNING CENTRE, 100-97 Queen St, Charlottetown, C1A 4A9. (Mail add: PO Box 7000, Charlottetown, C1A 8G8). Tel: 902-368-4642. FAX: 902-368-4652. E-mail: charlottetown@gov.pe.ca. *Regional Librn,* Beth Clinton
Open Mon, Fri & Sat 9:30-5, Tues-Thurs 9:30-8:30, Sun 12:30-5
Friends of the Library Group
CORNWALL PUBLIC LIBRARY, 15 Mercedes Dr, Cornwall, C0A 1H0, SAN 322-6069. Tel: 902-629-8415. E-mail: cornwall@gov.pe.ca.
Open Tues & Wed 1-8:30, Thurs-Sat 9:30-5:30
CRAPAUD PUBLIC LIBRARY, 20424 Trans Canada Hwy, Crapaud, C0A 1J0, SAN 369-1209. Tel: 902-658-2297. E-mail: crapaud@gov.pe.ca.
Open Wed 9-2, Thurs 3-8, Sat 9:30-12:30
BIBLIOTHEQUE PUBLIQUE DR J EDMOND-ARSENAULT, Five Acadian Dr, Charlottetown, C1C 1M2, SAN 374-4302. Tel: 902-368-6092. E-mail: carrefour@gov.pe.ca.
Open Tues 8:30-3:30, Thurs 12-8, Sat 9-1
GEORGETOWN GENEVIEVE SOLOMAN MEMORIAL LIBRARY, 36 Kent St, Georgetown, C0A 1L0, SAN 369-1233. Tel: 902-652-2832. E-mail: georgetown@gov.pe.ca.
Open Tues 4-7, Thurs 10-2, Fri 10-3
MURRAY RIVER LEONA GIDDINGS MEMORIAL LIBRARY, 1066 McInnis Rd, Murray River, C0A 1W0, SAN 369-1446. Tel: 902-962-2667. E-mail: murray_river@gov.pe.ca.
Open Tues 4-7, Wed & Thurs 10-1, Sat 1-4
BIBLIOTHEQUE PUBLIQUE J HENRI-BLANCHARD, Five Maris Stella Ave, Summerside, C1N 6M9. Tel: 902-432-2748. FAX: 902-888-1686. E-mail: blanchard@gov.pe.ca.
Founded 2003
Open Tues 9-2:30, Wed 4-8, Sat 9-1
Friends of the Library Group
HUNTER RIVER MEMORIAL LIBRARY, 19816 Rte 2, Hunter River, C0A 1N0, SAN 369-1268. Tel: 902-964-2800. E-mail: hunter_river@gov.pe.ca.
Open Tues 4-8, Wed 2-6, Fri 9:30-2:30, Sat 9:30-1:30
KENSINGTON HERITAGE LIBRARY, Six Commercial St, Kensington, C0B 1M0, SAN 369-1292. Tel: 902-836-3721. E-mail: kensington@gov.pe.ca.
Open Tues, Fri & Sat 10-4, Wed 12-6, Thurs 2-8
KINKORA PUBLIC LIBRARY, 45 Anderson Rd, Kinkora, C0B 1N0, SAN 369-1306. Tel: 902-887-2172. E-mail: kinkora@gov.pe.ca.
Open Mon 11-3, Tues 3-7, Thurs 9-1
MONTAGUE ROTARY LIBRARY, 53 Wood Islands Rd, Montague, C0A 1R0, SAN 369-1322. Tel: 902-838-2928. E-mail: montague@gov.pe.ca. *Regional Librn,* Grace Dawson
Open Mon, Fri & Sat 10-4, Tues 10-5, Wed & Thurs 10-8
Friends of the Library Group
MORELL PUBLIC LIBRARY, 89 Red Head Rd, C0A 1S0, SAN 369-1357. Tel: 902-961-3389. E-mail: morell@gov.pe.ca.
Open Tues & Thurs 3-6, Wed 10-2, Sat 10-3
MOUNT STEWART PUBLIC LIBRARY, 104 Main St, Mount Stewart, C0A 1T0, SAN 369-1381. Tel: 902-676-2050. E-mail: mtstewart@gov.pe.ca.
Open Tues & Thurs 10-2:30, Wed 3-6
MURRAY HARBOUR PUBLIC LIBRARY, 27 Faye Fraser Dr, Murray Harbour, C0A 1V0, SAN 369-1411. Tel: 902-962-3875. E-mail: murray_harbour@gov.pe.ca.
Open Tues 11-3, Wed 3-7, Fri 10-3, Sat 9:30-12:30
O'LEARY PUBLIC LIBRARY, 18 Community St, O'Leary, C0B 1V0, SAN 369-1470. Tel: 902-859-8788. E-mail: o'leary@gov.pe.ca.
Open Tues 10-4, Thurs 4-8, Fri 12-4, Sat 10-2
ST PETERS PUBLIC LIBRARY, 1968 Cardigan Rd, St. Peters, C0A 2A0, SAN 369-1500. Tel: 902-961-3415. E-mail: st_peters@gov.pe.ca.
Open Tues & Thurs 10-1:30, Wed 2-7
SOURIS PUBLIC LIBRARY, 75 Main St, Souris, C0A 2B0, SAN 369-1535. Tel: 902-687-2157. E-mail: souris@gov.pe.ca.
Open Tues & Thurs 2-6, Fri & Sat 10-3:30
STRATFORD PUBLIC LIBRARY, 25 Hopeton Rd, Stratford, C1B 1T6. Tel: 902-569-7441. E-mail: stratford@edu.pe.ca.
Founded 2001
Open Tues & Wed 9:30-8:30, Thurs-Sat 9:30-5:30
SUMMERSIDE ROTARY LIBRARY, 57 Central St, Summerside, C1N 3K9, SAN 369-156X. Tel: 902-436-7323, 902-888-8370. FAX: 902-888-8055. E-mail: summerside@gov.pe.ca. *Regional Librn,* Rebecca Boulter
Subject Interests: Local hist
Open Mon 12-8, Tues 10-9, Wed & Thurs 10-6, Fri & Sat 10-5, Sun 12-5
Friends of the Library Group
TIGNISH PUBLIC LIBRARY, 103 School St, Tignish, C0B 2B0, SAN 369-1594. Tel: 902-882-7363. E-mail: tignish@gov.pe.ca.
Open Tues 11-5, Thurs 2-8, Sat 10-1
TYNE VALLEY PUBLIC LIBRARY, 19 Allen Rd, Tyne Valley, C0B 2C0, SAN 369-1624. Tel: 902-831-2928. E-mail: tyne_valley@gov.pe.ca.
Open Wed 1-5, Thurs 4-8, Sat 10-2

SUMMERSIDE

S PRINCE COUNTY HOSPITAL*, Medical Library, 65 Roy Boates Ave, C1N 2A9. (Mail add: PO Box 3000, C1N 2A9), SAN 325-7932. Tel: 902-438-4520. FAX: 902-438-4102. Web Site: www.princeedwardisland.ca. *Health Res Ctr Coordr,* Lori Sharpe; E-mail: lrsharpe@ihis.org
Library Holdings: Bk Vols 3,000; Per Subs 30
Open Mon-Fri 8-4
Friends of the Library Group

QUEBEC

Date of Statistics: Not provided.

AKWESASNE

L THE MOHAWK COUNCIL OF AKWESASNE*, Research Library & Archival Services, PO Box 90, H0M 1A0. SAN 321-8406. Tel: 613-575-2250. FAX: 613-575-2181. E-mail: info@akwesasne.ca. Web Site: www.akwesasne.ca. *Supvr,* Sharon Peters; E-mail: sharon.peters@akwesasne.ca
Founded 1977
Library Holdings: Bk Titles 400
Special Collections: St Regis Band Council Archives
Subject Interests: Environ contaminants, Indian rights, Law
Open Mon-Fri 8-4

ALMA

P BIBLIOTHEQUE MUNICIPALE D'ALMA*, 500 rue Collard, G8B 1N2. SAN 325-0229. Tel: 418-669-5140. FAX: 418-669-5089. E-mail: bibliotheque@ville.alma.qc.ca. Web Site: www.ville.alma.qc.ca/biblio. *Libr Coord,* Emilie Guertin; Tel: 418-669-5140, Ext 5139, E-mail: emilie.guertin@ville.alma.qc.ca; Staff 5 (MLS 1, Non-MLS 4)
Founded 1968. Pop 31,000; Circ 191,000
Library Holdings: AV Mats 2,800; Bk Vols 78,000; Per Subs 128; Talking Bks 180
Special Collections: Municipal Document Depository
Subject Interests: Regional lit
Automation Activity & Vendor Info: (Acquisitions) SirsiDynix; (Cataloging) SirsiDynix; (Circulation) SirsiDynix; (ILL) OCLC; (OPAC) SirsiDynix
Wireless access
Open Mon-Thurs 10:30-8, Fri 10:30-5 (Summer); Mon-Fri 10:30-6, Sat & Sun 10-4:30 (Winter)

AMOS

P BIBLIOTHEQUE MUNICIPALE DE AMOS*, 222 Front St E, J9T 1H3. SAN 319-6259. Tel: 819-732-6070. FAX: 819-732-3242. E-mail: bibliotheque@ville.amos.qc.ca. Web Site: amos.quebec/loisirs-et-culture/culture-et-patrimoine/bibliotheque. *Mgr,* Michelle Bourque
Circ 9,200
Library Holdings: Bk Vols 39,600
Wireless access
Open Mon-Fri 9-12 & 1:30-9, Sat 10-5, Sun 1-5
Friends of the Library Group

ASBESTOS

P BIBLIOTHEQUE MUNICIPALE D'ASBESTOS*, 351 Saint Luc Blvd, J1T 2W4. SAN 319-6283. Tel: 819-879-7171, Ext 3400. FAX: 819-879-2343. E-mail: bibliotheque@ville.asbestos.qc.ca. Web Site: ville.asbestos.qc.ca/bibliotheque-municipale. *Dir,* Julie Fontaine; Tel: 819-879-7171, Ext 3401; Staff 2 (MLS 1, Non-MLS 1)
Founded 1958. Pop 7,000; Circ 50,067
Library Holdings: Bk Vols 18,980
Open Mon & Wed 5-8, Tues 10-1 & 2-5, Thurs 2-5, Fri 2-6, Sat 9-12, Sun 1-4

BAIE COMEAU

P BIBLIOTHEQUE MUNICIPALE ALICE-LANE*, Six Ave Radisson, G4Z 1W4. SAN 319-6291. Tel: 418-296-8304. Information Services Tel: 418-589-1519. FAX: 418-296-8328. E-mail: biblio@ville.baie-comeau.qc.ca. Web Site: ville.baie-comeau.qc.ca/culture/bibliotheque-municipale-alice-lane. *Dir,* Marie Amiot; E-mail: mamiot@ville.baie-comeau.qc.ca
Founded 1961. Pop 25,951
Library Holdings: Bk Vols 90,000; Per Subs 159
Wireless access
Open Mon-Wed 10-8, Thurs & Sat 10-5, Fri & Sun Noon-5 (Winter); Mon-Wed 10-6, Thurs & Sat 10-5, Fri Noon-5 (Summer)
Friends of the Library Group

C CEGEP DE BAIE-COMEAU*, Bibliotheque, 537 boul Blanche, G5C 2B2. SAN 322-8029. Tel: 418-589-5707, Ext 325. Reference Tel: 418-589-5707, Ext 322. Toll Free Tel: 800-463-2030, Ext 325. E-mail: biblio@cegepbc.ca. Web Site: cegep-baie-comeau.qc.ca/etudiants/bibliotheque. *Admin Support Coordr,* Nadyne Ducharme; E-mail: nducharme@cegepbc.ca; *Libr Tech,* Position Currently Open; Staff 3 (MLS 1, Non-MLS 2)
Founded 1959. Enrl 660; Fac 70
Library Holdings: Bk Vols 53,000; Per Subs 155
Special Collections: Canadian and Provincial
Subject Interests: Humanities, Natural sci
Open Mon-Thurs 8-5, Fri 8-4

BAIE-D'URFE

P BIBLIOTHEQUE BAIE-D'URFE*, 20551 chemin du Bord du Lac, H9X 1R3. SAN 319-6305. Tel: 514-457-3274. E-mail: biblio@baie-durfe.qc.ca. Web Site: www.bibliobaiedurfe.com. *Pres,* Nadia Bissada; *Librn,* Christopher Marsh
Founded 1966. Pop 3,900; Circ 19,618
Library Holdings: AV Mats 2,516; Bk Titles 30,360; Bk Vols 32,923; Per Subs 47
Special Collections: Early Childhood Education Coll. Municipal Document Depository
Wireless access
Partic in Mandarin
Open Mon, Thurs & Fri 2:30-5, Tues 2:30-5 & 7-9, Wed 2:30-9, Sat & Sun 1:30-4

BEACONSFIELD

P BIBLIOTHEQUE DE BEACONSFIELD*, 303 Beaconsfield Blvd, H9W 4A7. SAN 319-6313. Tel: 514-428-4460. Reference Tel: 514-428-4400, Ext 4470. E-mail: bibliotheque@beaconsfield.ca. Web Site:

www.beaconsfieldbiblio.ca. *Head Librn,* Elizabeth Lemyre; Tel: 514-428-4400, Ext 4474, E-mail: elizabeth.lemyre@beaconsfield.ca; Staff 20 (MLS 4, Non-MLS 16)
Founded 1951. Pop 19,300; Circ 153,000
Library Holdings: Bk Titles 80,000; Per Subs 300
Special Collections: Foreign Language Books (German & Spanish)
Subject Interests: Children's lit, Local hist
Automation Activity & Vendor Info: (Acquisitions) SirsiDynix; (Cataloging) SirsiDynix; (Circulation) SirsiDynix; (OPAC) SirsiDynix; (Serials) SirsiDynix
Wireless access
Open Mon 1-9, Tues-Fri 10-9, Sat 10-5, Sun 1-5
Friends of the Library Group

BELOEIL

P BIBLIOTHEQUE DE BELOEIL*, 620 rue Richelieu, J3G 5E8. SAN 319-6321. Tel: 450-467-7872. FAX: 450-467-3257. E-mail: biblio@beloeil.ca. Web Site: beloeil.ca/divertir/bibliotheque. *Dir,* Johanne Guevremont
Founded 1960. Pop 19,306; Circ 100,000
Library Holdings: Bk Vols 60,000; Per Subs 125
Wireless access
Open Mon-Thurs 9-12 & 1-4, Fri 9-12:30

BOUCHERVILLE

P BIBLIOTHEQUE MONTARVILLE-BOUCHER DE LA BRUERE*, 501 Chemin Du Lac, J4B 6V6. SAN 319-633X. Tel: 450-449-8650. FAX: 450-449-6865. E-mail: bibliotheque@boucherville.ca. Web Site: bibliotheque.ville.boucherville.qc.ca. *Libr Mgr,* Genevieve Cadieux
Founded 1962. Circ 451,141
Library Holdings: Bk Vols 140,420
Subject Interests: Canadiana, Genealogy
Wireless access
Open Tues-Sat 1-6

BROSSARD

P BIBLIOTHEQUE DE BROSSARD*, Georgette Lepage, 7855 ave San Francisco, J4X 2A4. SAN 328-3151. Tel: 450-923-6304. FAX: 450-923-7042. E-mail: bibliotheque@brossard.ca. Web Site: biblio.brossard.ca. *Dir,* Suzanne Payette; E-mail: suzanne.payette@brossard.ca; Staff 28 (MLS 9, Non-MLS 19)
Founded 1972. Pop 66,110; Circ 572,532
Library Holdings: Bk Vols 220,000; Per Subs 350
Subject Interests: Local hist
Automation Activity & Vendor Info: (Acquisitions) BiblioMondo; (Cataloging) BiblioMondo; (Circulation) BiblioMondo; (ILL) BiblioMondo; (OPAC) BiblioMondo; (Serials) BiblioMondo
Wireless access
Function: 24/7 Electronic res, 24/7 Online cat, 3D Printer, Activity rm, Adult bk club, Adult literacy prog, Audiobks via web, Bk club(s), Children's prog, Computer training, Family literacy, Large print keyboards, Literacy & newcomer serv, Magazines, Magnifiers for reading, Mail & tel request accepted, Makerspace, Meeting rooms, Movies, Online ref, Photocopying/Printing, Preschool reading prog, Printer for laptops & handheld devices, Ref & res, Ref serv available, Scanner, Summer reading prog
Publications: History of Brossard (Local historical information)
Open Mon-Fri 10-9, Sat 10-5
Friends of the Library Group

CAP-CHAT

P CENTRE REGIONAL DE SERVICE AUX BIBLIOTHEQUE PUBLIQUE DE PRET GASPESIE ISLE DE LA MADELENE*, 31 Rue des Ecoliers, CP 430, G0J 1E0. SAN 321-2637. Tel: 418-786-5597. Toll Free Tel: 800-737-3281. FAX: 418-786-2024. Web Site: www.reseaubibliogim.qc.ca/fr. *Dir,* Julie Blais; E-mail: julie.blais@reseaubibliogim.qc.ca
Pop 84,500
Library Holdings: Bk Vols 140,000
Open Mon-Thurs 8-4, Fri 8-12:30

CHARLESBOURG

C COLLEGE DE LIMOILOU-CAMPUS DE CHARLESBOURG*, Centre des Medias, 7600 Third Ave E, G1H 7L4. SAN 375-3840. Tel: 418-647-6600, Ext 3611. Reference Tel: 418-647-6600, Ext 3653. E-mail: bibliotheques@cegeplimoilou.ca. Web Site: www.cegeplimoilou.ca/etudiants/carrefour-de-l-information/bibliotheques. *Libr Mgr,* Marc Julien; Tel: 418-647-6600, Ext 3713; Staff 5 (MLS 1, Non-MLS 4)
Founded 1991. Enrl 1,650; Fac 100
Library Holdings: Bk Titles 28,000; Bk Vols 30,000; Per Subs 120
Automation Activity & Vendor Info: (Acquisitions) SirsiDynix; (Cataloging) SirsiDynix; (Circulation) SirsiDynix
Wireless access
Function: Res libr
Partic in RESDOC
Open Mon-Thurs 7:30am-8:30pm, Fri 7:30-5

CHARNY

P CENTRE REGIONAL DE SERVICES AUX BIBLIOTHEQUES PUBLIQUES DE LA CAPITALE-NATIONALE ET DE LA CHAUDIERE-APPALACHES INC*, Réseau BIBLIO CNCA, 3189 rue Albert-Demers, G6X 3A1. SAN 321-1738. Tel: 418-832-6166. Toll Free Tel: 866 446-6166. FAX: 418-832-6168. E-mail: info@reseaubibliocnca.qc.ca. Web Site: www.reseaubibliocnca.qc.ca. *Exec Dir,* Isabelle Poirier; E-mail: ipoirier@reseaubibliocnca.qc.ca; Staff 16 (MLS 3, Non-MLS 13)
Founded 1977. Pop 218,713
Library Holdings: Bk Titles 171,437; Bk Vols 617,678
Automation Activity & Vendor Info: (Acquisitions) SirsiDynix; (Cataloging) SirsiDynix; (Circulation) SirsiDynix; (OPAC) SirsiDynix; (Serials) SirsiDynix
Wireless access
Publications: Annual Report; Guides; Le Passeur (Bulletin)
Open Mon-Fri 8:30-12 & 1-4:30

CHATEAUGUAY

P BIBLIOTHEQUE RAYMOND-LABERGE*, 25 Maple Blvd, J6J 3P7. SAN 319-6372. Tel: 450-698-3080. E-mail: biblio@ville.chateauguay.qc.ca. *Dir,* Patricia Robitaille; E-mail: patricia.robitaille@ville.chateauguay.qc.ca; *Librn,* Marcotte Veronique; E-mail: veronique.marcotte@ville.chateauguay.qc.ca; *Acq & Cat, Adult Coll,* Johanne Beausejour; E-mail: johanne.beausejour@ville.chateauguay.qc.ca; *Acq, Cat, Ch Serv,* Nancy Bilodeau; E-mail: nancy.bilodeau@ville.chateauguay.qc.ca; *Tech Serv,* Annie Bonneau; E-mail: annie.bonneau@ville.chateauguay.qc.ca; *Tech Serv,* Marie-Eve Boyer; E-mail: marie-eve.boyer@ville.chateauguay.qc.ca; Staff 1 (MLS 1)
Founded 1968. Pop 51,614
Library Holdings: Bks on Deafness & Sign Lang 86,000; Bk Vols 106,000; Per Subs 215
Wireless access
Function: 24/7 Electronic res, 24/7 Online cat, 24/7 wireless access, Activity rm, Adult bk club, Audiobks on Playaways & MP3, Bk club(s), Bks on CD, Children's prog, Computer training, Computers for patron use, Digital talking bks, Electronic databases & coll, Free DVD rentals, Games, Genealogy discussion group, Home delivery & serv to seniorr ctr & nursing homes, ILL available, Internet access, Magazines, Meeting rooms, Museum passes, Music CDs, Online cat, Photocopying/Printing, Preschool reading prog, Prog for adults, Prog for children & young adult, Ref & res, Scanner, Senior computer classes, Story hour, Study rm, Summer reading prog, Wheelchair accessible
Open Mon Noon-9, Tues & Wed 9-9, Thurs 9-8, Fri 9-5, Sat & Sun 12-5
Bookmobiles: 1. Librn, Veronique Marcotte. Bk vols 5,000

CHICOUTIMI

P BANQ SAGUENAY*, 930 rue Jacques Cartier E Bureau C-103, Saguenay, G7H 7K9. SAN 319-6240. Tel: 418-698-3516. FAX: 418-698-3758. E-mail: archives.saguenay@banq.qc.ca. Web Site: www.banq.qc.ca. *Archivist,* Sonia Lachance; E-mail: sonia.lachance@banq.qc.ca
Pop 26,322; Circ 311,354
Library Holdings: Bk Vols 2,000,000
Open Mon-Fri 8:30-12 & 1-4:30

M BIBLIOTHEQUE DU CIUSSS DU SAGUENAY-LAC-SAINT-JEAN*, 305 rue Saint Vallier, CP 5006, G7H 5H6. SAN 325-7916. Tel: 418-541-1234, Ext 2496. FAX: 418-541-1145. *Library Contact,* Helene Marcoux; E-mail: helene.marcoux.chs@ssss.gouv.qc.ca
Library Holdings: Bk Vols 5,000
Wireless access
Open Mon-Thurs 8-4

P BIBLIOTHEQUE PUBLIQUE DE CHICOUTIMI*, 155, rue Racine Est, G7H 1R5. SAN 319-6399. Tel: 418-698-5350. Reference Tel: 418-698-5350, Ext 4184. FAX: 418-698-5359. E-mail: webbiblio@ville.saguenay.qc.ca. Web Site: ville.saguenay.ca/activites-et-loisirs/bibliotheque. *Chef de Div,* Luc-Michel Belley; E-mail: luc-michel.belley@ville.saguenay.qc.ca; Staff 29 (MLS 2, Non-MLS 27)
Founded 1950. Pop 65,000
Library Holdings: AV Mats 11,128; CDs 4,512; DVDs 947; Bk Vols 153,627; Per Subs 275; Talking Bks 450; Videos 5,669
Special Collections: Youth Coll. Canadian and Provincial
Automation Activity & Vendor Info: (Cataloging) SirsiDynix-Unicorn; (Circulation) SirsiDynix-WorkFlows; (Serials) EBSCO Online

Function: Art exhibits, Children's prog, Computer training, Computers for patron use, Electronic databases & coll, Free DVD rentals, Internet access, Mail & tel request accepted, Music CDs, Online cat, Photocopying/Printing, Spoken cassettes & CDs, Story hour, Summer reading prog, Telephone ref, Wheelchair accessible
Open Tues-Fri 10-8, Sat & Sun 10-5; Tues-Thurs 10-8, Fri & Sat 10-5 (Summer)

J CEGEP DE CHICOUTIMI BIBLIOTHEQUE*, 534, rue Jacques-Cartier, Est, G7H 1Z6. SAN 319-6402. Tel: 418-549-9520, Ext 2229. FAX: 418-549-1315. E-mail: cdmpret@cegep-chicoutimi.qc.ca. Web Site: cchic.ca/bibliotheque. *Libr Coord,* Michele Deshaies; E-mail: mdeshaies@cegep-chicoutimi.qc.ca; Staff 2 (MLS 2)
Founded 1967. Enrl 2,600; Fac 275
Library Holdings: Bk Titles 62,000; Bk Vols 70,000; Per Subs 225
Subject Interests: Archit, Art, Computers, Flight training, Hist, Med
Wireless access
Partic in Regard
Open Mon-Wed 8-5, Thurs & Fri 8:15-3:45

C UNIVERSITE DU QUEBEC A CHICOUTIMI*, Paul-Emile-Boulet Library, 555 Blvd de l'Universite E, G7H 2B1. SAN 319-6437. Tel: 418-545-5011, Ext 5630. Toll Free Tel: 800-463-9880, Ext 5630. FAX: 418-693-5896. E-mail: biblio@uqac.ca. Web Site: bibliotheque.uqac.ca. *Dir,* Nathalie Villeneuve; E-mail: nathalie2_villeneuve@uqac.ca; Staff 43 (MLS 13, Non-MLS 30)
Founded 1969. Enrl 4,132; Fac 199; Highest Degree: Doctorate
Library Holdings: Bk Vols 250,000; Per Subs 4,200
Special Collections: Canadiana
Wireless access
Partic in Proquest Dialog; SDC Info Servs

COATICOOK

P BIBLIOTHEQUE DE COATICOOK, INC*, 34 rue Main Est, J1A 1N2. SAN 319-6445. Tel: 819-849-4013. FAX: 819-849-0479. E-mail: biblcoat@bibliotheque.coaticook.qc.ca. Web Site: www.bibliotheque.coaticook.qc.ca. *Dir,* Bonoit Bouthillette
Founded 1958. Pop 9,800; Circ 44,384
Library Holdings: AV Mats 3,380; Bk Vols 28,892; Per Subs 88
Wireless access
Open Tues & Wed Noon-5, Thurs & Fri Noon-8, Sat 9-1, Sun Noon-3

COTE SAINT-LUC

P ELEANOR LONDON COTE SAINT LUC PUBLIC LIBRARY*, Cote Saint-Luc Public Library, 5851 Blvd Cavendish, H4W 2X8. SAN 319-6453. Tel: 514-485-6900. Reference Tel: 514-485-6900, Ext 4107. FAX: 514-485-6966. E-mail: reference@cotesaintluc.org. Web Site: csllibrary.org. *Dir, Libr Serv,* Janine West; Tel: 514-485-6900, Ext 4202, E-mail: jwest@cotesaintluc.org
Founded 1966. Pop 32,500; Circ 475,650
Library Holdings: Bk Vols 198,750
Wireless access
Open Mon-Thurs 10-8, Fri-Sun 10-6

DE SOREL TRACY

P BIBLIOTHEQUE DE SOREL TRACY*, Marie-Didace Library, 3015 Place des Loisirs, J3R 5S5. (Mail add: PO Box 368, Sorel-Tracy, J3R 1C2), SAN 370-6788. Tel: 450-780-5600, Ext 4442. FAX: 450-764-8894. E-mail: bibliotheque@ville.sorel-tracy.qc.ca. Web Site: bibliotheque.ville.sorel-tracy.qc.ca. *Head Librn,* Renaud Vernet; Staff 1 (MLS 1)
Founded 1987. Pop 12,900
Library Holdings: Bk Titles 106,000; Per Subs 86
Special Collections: State Document Depository
Wireless access
Open Mon & Tues 10-12 & 1:30-5, Wed-Fri 10-12 & 1:30-8, Sat 9-12 & 1-5, Sun 1-5

DEUX-MONTAGNES

P BIBLIOTHEQUE DE DEUX-MONTAGNES*, 200 rue Henri-Dunant, J7R 4W6. SAN 326-503X. Tel: 450-473-2796. Circulation Tel: 450-473-2796 (Option 5). FAX: 450-473-2816. Web Site: bibliotheque.ville.deux-montagnes.qc.ca. *Dir, Libr & Cultural Serv,* Ms Pascale Dupuis; E-mail: pdupuis@ville.deux-montagnes.qc.ca; Staff 4 (MLS 2, Non-MLS 2)
Pop 17,998
Library Holdings: Audiobooks 176; AV Mats 1,726; CDs 1,895; DVDs 67; e-books 640; Electronic Media & Resources 6; Bk Vols 83,041; Per Subs 128
Automation Activity & Vendor Info: (Cataloging) Koha; (Circulation) Koha; (OPAC) Koha
Wireless access
Function: 24/7 Electronic res, 24/7 Online cat, Activity rm, Adult bk club, Art exhibits, Bk club(s), Bks on CD, Children's prog, Computer training, Computers for patron use, Digital talking bks, Electronic databases & coll, Magazines, Music CDs, Online cat, Prog for adults, Ref serv available, Story hour, Summer & winter reading prog, Writing prog
Open Mon, Tues, Thurs & Fri 1-8, Wed 10-8, Sat 10-4:30, Sun (Winter) 1-4:30

DOLLARD-DES-ORMEAUX

P BIBLIOTHEQUE DE DOLLARD-DES-ORMEAUX*, 12001 Blvd de Salaberry, H9B 2A7. Tel: 514-684-1496. FAX: 514-684-9569. E-mail: bibliotheque@ddo.qc.ca. Web Site: ville.ddo.qc.ca. *Div Mgr, Libr & Culture,* Helen Diamond; Tel: 514-684-1496, Ext 422, E-mail: hdiamond@ddo.qc.ca; Staff 6 (MLS 5, Non-MLS 1)
Founded 1992. Pop 50,114; Circ 294,704
Jan 2018-Dec 2018 Income (CAN) $2,997,831, Provincial (CAN) $103,650, City (CAN) $2,854,422, Locally Generated Income (CAN) $39,759. Mats Exp (CAN) $264,958, Books (CAN) $192,124, Per/Ser (Incl. Access Fees) (CAN) $24,325, AV Mat (CAN) $15,865, Electronic Ref Mat (Incl. Access Fees) (CAN) $32,644. Sal (CAN) $2,236,702
Library Holdings: Audiobooks 1,665; DVDs 5,274; e-books 20,129; e-journals 8,648; Electronic Media & Resources 24; Bk Titles 113,735; Bk Vols 116,123; Per Subs 239; Talking Bks 4,057
Automation Activity & Vendor Info: (Acquisitions) Infor Library & Information Solutions; (Cataloging) Infor Library & Information Solutions; (Circulation) Infor Library & Information Solutions; (Discovery) Infor Library & Information Solutions; (ILL) OCLC; (Media Booking) Koha; (OPAC) Infor Library & Information Solutions; (Serials) Infor Library & Information Solutions
Wireless access
Function: 24/7 Electronic res, 24/7 Online cat, Activity rm, Adult bk club, Adult literacy prog, Audiobks via web, AV serv, Bk club(s), Bk reviews (Group), Bks on CD, CD-ROM, Chess club, Children's prog, Citizenship assistance, Computer training, Computers for patron use, Digital talking bks, E-Reserves, Electronic databases & coll, Free DVD rentals, Home delivery & serv to seniorr ctr & nursing homes, Homebound delivery serv, Homework prog, ILL available, Internet access, Large print keyboards, Life-long learning prog for all ages, Literacy & newcomer serv, Magnifiers for reading, Mail & tel request accepted, Music CDs, Online cat, Online info literacy tutorials on the web & in blackboard, Online ref, Orientations, Outreach serv, Outside serv via phone, mail, e-mail & web, OverDrive digital audio bks, Photocopying/Printing, Preschool outreach, Preschool reading prog, Prog for adults, Prog for children & young adult, Ref & res, Ref serv available, Scanner, Spoken cassettes & DVDs, Story hour, Study rm, Summer & winter reading prog, Summer reading prog, Teen prog, Telephone ref, Wheelchair accessible, Winter reading prog, Workshops, Writing prog
Special Services for the Blind - Aids for in-house use; Bks on CD; Large print bks; Low vision equip; Magnifiers; Screen enlargement software for people with visual disabilities; Telesensory screen enlarger
Open Mon-Fri 10-9, Sat & Sun 9-5
Restriction: Circ to mem only, ID required to use computers (Ltd hrs), Non-resident fee

DORVAL

P BIBLIOTHEQUE DE DORVAL, Dorval Library, 1401 Chemin du Bord du Lac, H9S 2E5. SAN 369-1683. Tel: 514-633-4170. FAX: 514-633-4177. E-mail: biblio@ville.dorval.qc.ca. *Actg Chief,* Marjorie Le Cavalier-Parant
Founded 1967. Pop 17,715; Circ 243,389
Library Holdings: Bk Vols 68,320
Subject Interests: Aviation, Local hist
Wireless access
Open Mon-Thurs 10-9, Fri-Sun (Winter) 10-5

G TRANSPORT CANADA, Centre de Reference Technique, Civil Aviation, NAS-CRT, Rm 0135, 700 Leigh Capreol St, H4Y 1G7. SAN 374-499X. Tel: 514-633-3589. FAX: 514-420-5801. *Head, Info Serv,* Jacques Bisson; *Librn,* Igor Abramenko; E-mail: igor.abramenko@tc.gc.ca. Subject Specialists: *Aircraft,* Jacques Bisson; Staff 1 (Non-MLS 1)
Founded 1956
Library Holdings: Bk Titles 4,000; Per Subs 6
Subject Interests: Aircraft maintenance, Aviation
Function: Govt ref serv
Restriction: Authorized personnel only

DRUMMONDVILLE

P BIBLIOTHEQUE MUNICIPALE COME-SAINT-GERMAIN*, 425 rue des Forges, J2B 0G4. SAN 319-647X. Tel: 819-474-8841, 819-478-6573. Circulation Tel: 819-478-6590. FAX: 819-478-0399. E-mail: bibliotheque@drummondville.ca. Web Site: drummondville.ca/culture-loisirs-et-sports/bibliotheque.
Founded 1949. Circ 238,818

Library Holdings: Bk Vols 105,000; Per Subs 430
Special Collections: Can & Prov Doc Dep
Subject Interests: Agr, Area, Drummondville, Genealogy, Quebec lit
Publications: Archives on Video; Feuillet d'information; listes bibliographiques; Recquil de gestion (non public); seasonal leaflets
Open Mon 12-8, Tues-Fri 9:30-8, Sat & Sun 9:30-5

FARNHAM

P BIBLIOTHEQUE DE FARNHAM, INC*, Bibliotheque Municipale Louise-Hall, 479 rue Hotel de Ville, J2N 2H3. SAN 319-6488. Tel: 450-293-3326, Ext 268. FAX: 450-293-2989. E-mail: bibliotheque@ville.farnham.qc.ca. Web Site: www.ville.farnham.qc.ca/bibliotheque-municipale-louise-hall. *Libr Mgr,* Dino Coude; E-mail: dcoude@ville.farnham.qc.ca
Founded 1957. Pop 7,000; Circ 36,000
Library Holdings: Bk Vols 32,000
Subject Interests: Applied sci, Computers, Countries, Political problems, Pure
Wireless access
Publications: Special Thematic
Open Tues 9-6, Wed-Fri 1-8, Sat 9-Noon

FERMONT

P BIBLIOTHEQUE PUBLIQUE DE FERMONT*, 100 Place Daviault, G0G 1J0. (Mail add: CP 2010, G0G 1J0), SAN 372-7300. Tel: 418-287-3227. FAX: 418-287-3274. E-mail: biblio@villedefermont.qc.ca. *Chief Librn,* Diane Mainville; Staff 1 (MLS 1)
Founded 1979. Pop 3,400
Library Holdings: Bk Titles 20,000; Bk Vols 22,000; Per Subs 27
Open Tues-Thurs 1:30-4:30 & 6:30-8:30, Fri-Sun 1:30-4:30

GASPE

G GOVERNMENT OF QUEBEC - AGRICULTURE FISHERIES & FOODS*, Centre de Documentation des Peches et de l'Aquaculture, 96 Montee de Sandy-Beach, Rez-de-chaussee, G4X 2V6. SAN 373-7977. Tel: 418-368-6371. FAX: 418-360-8400. Web Site: www.merinov.ca/en. *Br Adminr,* Léa Richard; E-mail: lea.richard@merinov.ca
Founded 1946
Library Holdings: Bk Titles 12,000; Per Subs 100
Special Collections: Agriculture, bks, serials; Fisheries, bks, serials

GATINEAU

M BIBLIOTHEQUE DU CISSS DE L'OUTAOUAIS*, CISSS de l'Outaouais - Hôpital Pierre-Janet, 20 rue Pharand, J9A 1K7. SAN 325-2094. Tel: 819-771-7761, Ext 8380. FAX: 819-771-1506. E-mail: 07_cissso_biblio@ssss.gouv.qc.ca. Web Site: catalogue.santecom.qc.ca. *Team Leader,* Annie Carreau; Tel: 819-966-6050, E-mail: annie_carreau@ssss.gouv.qc.ca; *Libr Tech,* Brigitte Ouellette; Tel: 819-966-6187; Staff 3 (MLS 1, Non-MLS 2)
Subject Interests: Med, Psychiat, Psychol
Wireless access
Restriction: Staff use only

P BIBLIOTHEQUE MUNICIPALE DE GATINEAU*, Ville de Gatineau, CP 1970 Succ. Hull, J8X 3Y9. SAN 325-2434. Tel: 819-243-2345. Web Site: www.gatineau.ca/portail/default.aspx?p=accueil. *Head Librn,* Raphael Lavoie; E-mail: lavoie.raphael@gatineau.ca; *Ad,* Marie-Hélène Rock; *Ch Serv Librn,* Nancy Bilodeau; *Outreach Librn,* Kayleigh Felice; *Pub Serv Librn,* Claudine Patry; *Syst Librn,* Marie-Chantal Paraskevas; *Ref Serv Mgr,* Martine Plouffe; *Res Mgr,* Jasmine Bouchard; *Res Mgr,* Noëlle Gratton-Tétreault
Founded 1938. Pop 254,549; Circ 1,624,003
Library Holdings: Audiobooks 1,220; AV Mats 32,566; CDs 15,606; DVDs 10,838; Electronic Media & Resources 7; Large Print Bks 3,728; Microforms 2,828; Bk Titles 234,190; Bk Vols 569,405; Per Subs 367; Videos 6,122
Special Collections: Canadiana (on Gatineau) genealogy
Subject Interests: Local hist
Automation Activity & Vendor Info: (Acquisitions) SirsiDynix; (Cataloging) SirsiDynix; (Circulation) SirsiDynix; (OPAC) SirsiDynix; (Serials) SirsiDynix
Wireless access
Publications: Annual Report
Open Mon & Thurs 10-9, Fri 10-6, Sat & Sun 11-5
Friends of the Library Group
Branches: 2
BIBLIOTHEQUE AURELIEN-DOUCET, 207 Mont-Bleu Blvd, J8Z 3G3, SAN 370-1107. Tel: 819-595-7460. FAX: 819-595-7376.
Library Holdings: Bk Titles 15,000; Bk Vols 27,000
Open Mon-Thurs 12-9, Fri 12-6, Sat 11-5
Friends of the Library Group
BIBLIOTHEQUE LUCIEN-LALONDE, 225 rue Berri, J8Y 4K1, SAN 369-1772. FAX: 819-595-7479.
Library Holdings: Bk Titles 28,500; Bk Vols 47,000
Open Mon-Thurs 10-9, Fri 10-6, Sat & Sun 10-5

G CANADA DEPARTMENT OF ABORIGINAL AFFAIRS & NORTHERN DEVELOPMENT*, Departmental Library, Ten Wellington St, Rm 1400, 14th Flr, K1A 0H4. SAN 319-2989. Tel: 819-997-0811. Interlibrary Loan Service Tel: 819-994-1347. FAX: 819-953-5491. Reference E-mail: aadnc.hqlibraryreference.aandc@canada.ca. Web Site: www.sac-isc.gc.ca/eng/1100100010124/1590587072006.
Founded 1966
Library Holdings: e-books 5,000; e-journals 10,000; Bk Vols 60,000; Per Subs 900
Subject Interests: Aboriginal people, Arctic Can
Automation Activity & Vendor Info: (Cataloging) Innovative Interfaces, Inc; (Circulation) Innovative Interfaces, Inc; (OPAC) Innovative Interfaces, Inc; (Serials) Innovative Interfaces, Inc
Function: ILL available
Publications: Acquisitions List; Various Subject Bibliographies
Open Mon-Fri 8:30-4:30

G CANADA SCHOOL OF PUBLIC SERVICE LIBRARY*, Asticou Centre, 241 de la Cite-des-Jeunes Blvd, Rm 1323, K1N 6Z2. SAN 328-1671. Tel: 819-934-7702. FAX: 819-953-1702. E-mail: csps.librarybibliotheque@canada.ca. Web Site: www.csps-efpc.gc.ca. *Libr Tech,* France Viau; Tel: 613-462-7631, E-mail: france.viau2@canada.ca; *Libr Asst,* Melanie Fortier; Staff 6 (MLS 4, Non-MLS 2)
Founded 1991
Library Holdings: DVDs 1,300; Bk Titles 10,000; Per Subs 120; Videos 50
Special Collections: Coll on Diversity
Subject Interests: Leadership, Mgt, Pub admin, Training lang
Partic in Council of Federal Libraries Consortium
Open Mon-Fri 8-4

S CANADIAN MUSEUM OF HISTORY LIBRARY*, 100 Laurier St, K1A 0M8. SAN 328-784X. Tel: 819-776-7173. Interlibrary Loan Service Tel: 819-776-7174. FAX: 819-776-7152. E-mail: library@historymuseum.ca. Web Site: historymuseum.ca/learn/resource-centre. *Coll Spec, Ref Serv,* Anneh Fletcher; Staff 3 (MLS 1, Non-MLS 2)
Founded 1854
Library Holdings: AV Mats 1,000; CDs 100; e-books 1,000; Bk Titles 61,000; Bk Vols 76,000; Per Subs 2,400
Special Collections: Indians of North America Coll. Canadian and Provincial
Subject Interests: Archaeology, Ethnology, Folklore, Hist, Mus studies
Automation Activity & Vendor Info: (Acquisitions) OCLC Worldshare Management Services; (Cataloging) OCLC Worldshare Management Services; (Circulation) OCLC Worldshare Management Services; (OPAC) OCLC Worldshare Management Services; (Serials) OCLC Worldshare Management Services
Function: Archival coll, Audio & video playback equip for onsite use, Doc delivery serv, Electronic databases & coll, For res purposes, ILL available, Internet access, Online cat, Outside serv via phone, mail, e-mail & web, Photocopying/Printing, Ref serv available, Res libr, Telephone ref
Publications: Bibliography Series
Partic in Canadian Fed Librs
Special Services for the Deaf - TDD equip
Open Mon-Fri 9-4:30
Restriction: Non-circulating of rare bks, Open to pub for ref only, Pub use on premises, Restricted borrowing privileges

G CANADIAN MUSEUM OF NATURE LIBRARY & ARCHIVES*, 1740 Pink Rd, J9J 3N7. (Mail add: PO Box 3443, Stn D, Ottawa, K1P 6P4), SAN 368-0193. Tel: 613-364-4047. FAX: 613-364-4026. E-mail: cmnlib@mus-nature.ca. Web Site: www.nature.ca. *Cataloger & Acq, Officer,* Mylène Philippe-Gagnon; Tel: 613-566-4734, E-mail: mpgagnon@nature.ca; *Coll Serv,* Laura Smyk; Tel: 613-364-4046, E-mail: lsmyk@nature.ca; Staff 3 (MLS 1, Non-MLS 2)
Founded 1842
Library Holdings: Bk Titles 35,000; Per Subs 110
Special Collections: Archives; Mammology Anderson Coll, bks, per; Nature Art Coll; Paleontology (C M Sternberg Coll), reprints; Photographs Coll; Rare Books Coll
Subject Interests: Botany, Geol, Natural sci, Ornithology, Paleobiology, Taxonomy, Zoology
Automation Activity & Vendor Info: (Acquisitions) Infor Library & Information Solutions; (Cataloging) Infor Library & Information Solutions; (Circulation) Infor Library & Information Solutions; (OPAC) Infor Library & Information Solutions; (Serials) Infor Library & Information Solutions
Wireless access
Function: Res libr
Restriction: Open by appt only

M CENTRE HOSPITALIER DES VALLEES DE L'OUTAOUAIS BIBLIOTHEQUE*, Hospital de Hull, 116, Blvd Lionel-Emond, local C-001, J8Y 1W7. SAN 319-6542. Tel: 819-966-6050. FAX: 819-966-6098. E-mail: 07_cissso_biblio@ssss.gouv.qc.ca. *Documentation Tech,* Brigitte Ouellette; *ILL,* Annie Carreau
Founded 1961
Library Holdings: Bk Vols 800; Per Subs 30
Function: Prof lending libr
Restriction: Mem only
Friends of the Library Group

G DEPARTMENT OF CANADIAN HERITAGE*, Knowledge Centre, 15 Eddy St, J8X 4B3. SAN 319-6550. Tel: 819-953-0527. FAX: 819-953-7988. E-mail: pch.bibliotheque-library.pch@canada.ca. Web Site: www.canada.ca/en/canadian-heritage/contact-us. *Client Serv Librn,* Sarah Coffin; E-mail: sarah.coffin@canada.ca; Staff 11 (MLS 2, Non-MLS 9)
Founded 1993
Library Holdings: CDs 125; DVDs 215; e-books 750; e-journals 40; Electronic Media & Resources 40; Bk Vols 59,000; Per Subs 300; Videos 460
Special Collections: Canadian and Provincial
Subject Interests: Amateur sport, Art & archit, Can cultural content, Can hist, Cultural industries, Historic sites, Human rights, Multiculturalism, Nat parks, Official langs, Shared citizenship, Soc cohesion
Automation Activity & Vendor Info: (Cataloging) Infor Library & Information Solutions; (Circulation) Infor Library & Information Solutions; (ILL) Relais International; (OPAC) Infor Library & Information Solutions; (Serials) Infor Library & Information Solutions
Function: Doc delivery serv, For res purposes, Govt ref serv, ILL available, Photocopying/Printing, Ref serv available, Res libr, Wheelchair accessible
Partic in Council of Federal Libraries Consortium
Special Services for the Deaf - Assistive tech; Bks on deafness & sign lang; Staff with knowledge of sign lang; TDD equip
Special Services for the Blind - Assistive/Adapted tech devices, equip & products; Braille equip; Dragon Naturally Speaking software
Restriction: Co libr, In-house use for visitors, Open to pub for ref only, Open to students, Pub use on premises

G ENVIRONMENT & CLIMATE CHANGE CANADA*, Departmental Library, 351 St Joseph Blvd, Place Vincent Massey Annex, 1st Flr, K1A 0H3. SAN 324-3397. Tel: 819-420-7570. E-mail: ec.bibliotheque-library.ec@canada.ca. Web Site: science-libraries.canada.ca/eng/environment. *Head, Libr Serv,* Angela Ward-Smith; Tel: 902-426-7232, E-mail: angela.wardsmith@canada.ca; Staff 9 (MLS 4, Non-MLS 5)
Founded 1971
Library Holdings: e-journals 95; Bk Titles 65,000
Subject Interests: Bio-diversity, Climatology, Environ, Environ chem, Environ impact analysis, Global warming, Meteorology, Pollution, Pollution prevention, Sustainable develop, Water res
Automation Activity & Vendor Info: (Acquisitions) SirsiDynix; (Cataloging) SirsiDynix; (Circulation) SirsiDynix; (OPAC) SirsiDynix; (Serials) SirsiDynix
Partic in Council of Federal Libraries Consortium
Open Mon-Fri 8-4
Restriction: Open to pub for ref only

G INNOVATION, SCIENCE & ECONOMIC DEVELOPMENT CANADA, Canadian Intellectual Property Office Resource Centre, 50 Victoria St, Rm 309, Place du Portage Phase I, K1A 0C9. SAN 325-5891. Tel: 873-455-5798. E-mail: cipocrc-croopic@ised-isde.gc.ca. *Sr Librn,* Cheryl Cohen; Tel: 873-455-5104; Staff 4 (MLS 1, Non-MLS 3)
Subject Interests: Intellectual property, Sci, Tech
Automation Activity & Vendor Info: (Acquisitions) Innovative Interfaces, Inc - Sierra; (Cataloging) Innovative Interfaces, Inc - Sierra; (Circulation) Innovative Interfaces, Inc - Sierra; (Discovery) EBSCO Discovery Service; (ILL) OCLC Tipasa; (OPAC) Innovative Interfaces, Inc; (Serials) Innovative Interfaces, Inc - Sierra
Wireless access
Function: ILL available, Ref serv available
Partic in Council of Federal Libraries Consortium

S SOCIETE DE GENEALOGIE DE L'OUTAOUAIS BIBLIOTHEQUE*, 855, blvd de la Gappe, J8T 8H9. SAN 373-8051. Tel: 819-243-0888. E-mail: sgo@genealogieoutaouais.com. Web Site: genealogieoutaouais.com. *Adminr,* Hélène Valentine
Founded 1978
Library Holdings: e-journals 10; Bk Titles 1,600; Bk Vols 1,800
Special Collections: Parish Registers on microfilm
Subject Interests: Genealogy
Publications: L'Outaouais Genealogique (Quarterly newsletter)
Restriction: Open to researchers by request

S TRANSLATION BUREAU DOCUMENTATION CENTRE*, 70 Cremazie St, 8th Flr, K1A 0S5. E-mail: btdocumentation.tbdocumentation@tpsgc-pwgsc.gc.ca. *Mgr,* Melanie Lefebvre; Tel: 613-294-7569, E-mail: melanie.lefebvre@tpsgc-pwgsc.gc.ca; Staff 12 (MLS 6, Non-MLS 6)
Library Holdings: Bk Titles 26,000
Special Collections: Annual Statutes of Canada. Canadian and Provincial
Wireless access
Open Mon-Fri 8-5

C UNIVERSITE DU QUEBEC EN OUTAOUAIS, Service de la Bibliotheque, 283, Blvd Alexandre-Tache, CP 1250, succursale Hull, J8X 3X7. SAN 319-6569. Tel: 819-595-3900. Circulation Tel: 819-595-3900, Ext 1624, 819-595-3900, Ext 2370. Interlibrary Loan Service Tel: 819-595-3900, Ext 1798. Reference Tel: 819-595-3900, Ext 1628, 819-595-3900, Ext 2375. Toll Free Tel: 800-567-1283. E-mail: bibliotheque@uqo.ca. Web Site: uqo.ca/biblio. *Dir, Libr Serv,* David Fournier-Viger; Tel: 819-595-3900, Ext 2690, E-mail: david.fournier-viger@uqo.ca; *Librn,* Simon Bouisset; Tel: 819-595-3900, Ext 2373, E-mail: simon.bouisset@uqo.ca; Staff 7 (MLS 7)
Founded 1972. Enrl 3,499; Fac 183; Highest Degree: Doctorate
Library Holdings: AV Mats 13,684; CDs 656; DVDs 1,310; e-books 8,000; e-journals 13,000; Bk Titles 189,680; Per Subs 1,370; Videos 2,332
Subject Interests: Acctg, Admin, Arts, Computer sci, Educ, Health, Indust relations, Soc sci, Soc work
Automation Activity & Vendor Info: (ILL) Fretwell-Downing
Wireless access
Publications: Annual Report; Bibliographies; Guides
Partic in Bureau de cooperation Interuniversitaire; Canadian Research Knowledge Network
Open Mon-Thurs 8am-9:30pm, Fri 8-6, Sat & Sun 10-5 (Fall-Spring); Mon-Fri 8:30-4:30 (Summer)

GRANBY

P BIBLIOTHEQUE PAUL-O-TREPANIER*, 11 rue Dufferin, J2G 4W5. SAN 319-6518. Tel: 450-776-8320. FAX: 450-776-8313. E-mail: bibliotheque@ville.granby.qc.ca. Web Site: biblio.ville.granby.qc.ca. *Dir,* Linda Laberge
Pop 45,223; Circ 167,228
Library Holdings: Bk Vols 80,353; Per Subs 219
Wireless access
Open Mon-Wed 12:30-8, Thurs & Fri 10-8, Sat & Sun 10-4; Mon-Wed Noon-8, Thurs & Fri 10-8, Sat 10-4 (Summer)

C CEGEP DE GRANBY*, Bibliotheque et technologies educatives, 235 Saint Jacques St, J2G 3N1. (Mail add: PO Box 7000, J2G 3N1), SAN 322-7006. Tel: 450-372-6614, Ext 1204. FAX: 450-372-6565. E-mail: biblio@cegepgranby.qc.ca. Web Site: www.cegepgranby.ca/services-offerts/bibliotheque. *Librn,* Position Currently Open; *Documentation Tech,* Élise Laplante; *Documentation Tech,* Ginette St-Martin; Staff 2 (MLS 1, Non-MLS 1)
Founded 1970. Enrl 3,700; Fac 190
Library Holdings: CDs 7,698; DVDs 8,987; Bk Titles 75,674; Per Subs 67; Videos 3,785
Special Collections: Federal Govt; Tourisme -Voyages. Canadian and Provincial
Wireless access
Publications: User Guide

P HISTORICAL SOCIETY OF HAUTE-YAMASKA LIBRARY*, 135 rue Principale, J2G 2V1. SAN 370-6354. Tel: 450-372-4500. FAX: 450-372-9904. E-mail: info@shhy.org. Web Site: www.shhy.info. *Managing Dir,* Cecilia Capocchi; E-mail: cecilia.capocchi@shhy.info; Staff 3 (MLS 2, Non-MLS 1)
Founded 1976. Pop 70,000
Library Holdings: Bk Titles 10,000
Special Collections: Agriculture (French Canadian Breeders Association); Industry (Miner Rubber Coll), doc; Quebec-Eastern Townships
Wireless access

JOLIETTE

C CEGEP REGIONAL DE LANAUDIERE A JOLIETTE*, 20, rue Saint-Charles-Borromee Sud, J6E 4T1. SAN 319-6585. Tel: 450-759-1661. FAX: 450-759-7120. Web Site: lanaudiere.portail-biblio.collecto.ca. *Admin Officer,* Lorraine Depelteau; E-mail: lorraine.depelteau@cegep-lanaudiere.qc.ca; *Libr Tech,* Amélie Gauthier; E-mail: amelie.gauthier@cegep-lanaudiere.qc.ca; *Libr Tech,* Amelie Lepage; E-mail: amelie.lepage@cegep-lanaudiere.qc.ca
Library Holdings: Bk Vols 100,000; Per Subs 450
Wireless access
Partic in RESDOC
Open Mon-Thurs 7:30-5, Fri 7:30-4

JONQUIERE

P BIBLIOTHEQUE MUNICIPALE DE JONQUIERE*, 2850 Davis Pl, G7X 7W7. SAN 319-6607. Tel: 418-699-6068, 418-699-6069. FAX: 418-699-6046. E-mail: webbiblio@ville.saguenay.qc.ca. Web Site: www.ville.saguenay.qc.ca. *Library Contact,* Isabel Nepton
Founded 1944. Pop 56,503; Circ 267,614
Library Holdings: Bk Titles 78,659; Bk Vols 155,443; Per Subs 98
Special Collections: Canadian and Provincial
Subject Interests: Genealogy, Local hist
Automation Activity & Vendor Info: (Cataloging) SirsiDynix; (Circulation) SirsiDynix; (OPAC) SirsiDynix; (Serials) SirsiDynix
Open Tues-Fri 10-8, Sat & Sun 10-5

J CEGEP DE JONQUIERE*, Centre de Resources Educatives, 2505 rue St Hubert, G7X 7W2. SAN 319-6615. Tel: 418-547-2191, Ext 6268. E-mail: pretcre@cegepjonquiere.ca. Web Site: bibliotheque.cegepjonquiere.ca. *Libr Coord,* Marie Briand; Tel: 418-547-2191, Ext 6303, E-mail: mariebriand@cegepjonquiere.ca; *AV,* Mathieu Arseneault; E-mail: mathieuarseneault@cegepjonquiere.ca; *Ref (Info Servs),* Fabienne Simard; E-mail: fabiennesimard@cegepjonquiere.ca; Staff 10 (MLS 1, Non-MLS 9)
Founded 1958. Enrl 3,200
Library Holdings: AV Mats 200; Bk Titles 95,000; Bk Vols 98,000; Per Subs 282
Special Collections: State Document Depository
Subject Interests: Art, Communications, Media, Nautical sci, Rare bks
Automation Activity & Vendor Info: (Serials) EBSCO Online
Wireless access
Function: Photocopying/Printing, Ref serv available
Open Mon-Thurs 8-5, Fri 8-4

KIRKLAND

P KIRKLAND PUBLIC LIBRARY*, 17100 Hymus Blvd, H9J 2W2. SAN 326-646X. Tel: 514-630-2726. FAX: 514-630-2716. Web Site: biblioweb.ville.kirkland.qc.ca. *Div Head,* Omar Soto-Rodriguez; E-mail: osotorodriguez@ville.kirkland.qc.ca; *Head, Ref Serv, Pub Serv,* Annie Tetreault; E-mail: atetreault@ville.kirkland.qc.ca; *Head, Youth Serv, Tech Serv,* Arianne Parent-Touchette; E-mail: Aparent@ville.kirkland.qc.ca; Staff 21 (MLS 3, Non-MLS 18)
Founded 1988. Pop 20,150; Circ 256,000
Library Holdings: Bk Vols 57,965
Wireless access
Function: 24/7 Electronic res, 24/7 Online cat, Activity rm, Adult bk club, After school storytime, Art exhibits, Audiobks via web, AV serv, Bk club(s), Bks on CD, Children's prog, Computer training, Computers for patron use, Digital talking bks, Distance learning, E-Readers, Electronic databases & coll, Free DVD rentals, Holiday prog, Home delivery & serv to seniorr ctr & nursing homes, Homebound delivery serv, ILL available, Internet access, Large print keyboards, Magazines, Magnifiers for reading, Mail & tel request accepted, Mango lang, Meeting rooms, Music CDs, Online cat, OverDrive digital audio bks, Photocopying/Printing, Prog for adults, Prog for children & young adult, Ref & res, Ref serv available, Scanner, Senior computer classes, Story hour, Study rm, Summer & winter reading prog, Summer reading prog, Teen prog, Wheelchair accessible, Workshops, Writing prog
Open Mon-Fri 10-9, Sat & Sun (Winter) Noon-4

LA BAIE

P BIBLIOTHEQUE DE LA BAIE*, 1911 Sixth Ave, G7B 1S1. SAN 319-8405. Tel: 418-698-5350. Interlibrary Loan Service Tel: 418-698-5350, Ext 6. Administration Tel: 418-698-5350, Ext 4. FAX: 418-697-5087. E-mail: webbiblio@ville.saguenay.qc.ca. Web Site: ville.saguenay.ca/fr/activites-et-loisirs/bibliotheque/horaire-et-coordonnees.
Founded 1961. Pop 21,647
Library Holdings: Bk Vols 70,000; Per Subs 70
Special Collections: Can
Wireless access
Open Tues-Fri 10-8, Sat & Sun 10-5

LA MALBAIE

P BIBLIOTHEQUE PUBLIQUE DE LA MALBAIE*, Bibliotheque Laure-Conan, 395 rue Saint-Etienne, G5A 1S8. SAN 319-6658. Tel: 418-665-3747, Ext 5283. FAX: 418-665-6481. E-mail: biblio@ville.lamalbaie.qc.ca. Web Site: www.ville.lamalbaie.qc.ca/ville-animee/bibliotheques/bibliotheque-laure-conan. *Dir,* Dominic Marier
Founded 1962. Pop 9,150
Library Holdings: CDs 500; Bk Vols 16,000; Per Subs 50
Wireless access
Open Tues-Thurs 12-7, Fri 10-6, Sat & Sun 10-4

LA POCATIERE

J CEGEP DE LA POCATIERE*, Bibliotheque Francois-Hertel, 140 Fourth Ave, G0R 1Z0. SAN 322-6891. Tel: 418-856-1525, Ext 2230. FAX: 418-856-4589. E-mail: fhertel@cageplapocatiere.qc.ca. Web Site: bibliofh-mgagnon.profweb.ca. *Libr Dir,* Martin Berube; Tel: 418-856-1525, Ext 2203, E-mail: maberube@cegeplapocatiere.qc.ca; *Libr Serv Mgr,* Mathieu Coulombe; Tel: 418-856-1525, Ext 2229, E-mail: matcoulombe@cepeglapocatiere.qc.ca; *Tech Serv Mgr,* Marc Gagnon; Tel: 418-856-1525, Ext 2232, E-mail: marcgagnon@cegeplapocatiere.qc.ca; Staff 6 (MLS 1, Non-MLS 5)
Library Holdings: Bk Titles 49,000; Per Subs 100
Special Collections: Canada & Quebec Gov; Oeuvres de Francois Hertel; Robotic Coll
Wireless access
Publications: Guide de l'usager, Catalogue des Productions Audiovisuelles et des Publications du cegep de La Pocatiere; La Recherche Documentaire
Open Mon-Thurs 7:50-6, Fri 7:50-4:30

J INSTITUT DE TECHNOLOGIE AGROALIMENTAIRE, CAMPUS LA POCATIERE, Centre multimédia, 401 rue Poire, local 202, G0R 1Z0. SAN 319-6623. Tel: 418-856-1110, Ext 1279. FAX: 418-856-1719. E-mail: lpmultimedias@itaq.ca. Web Site: bibliolp.itaq.ca/centre-multimedia. *Libr Tech,* Marie-Josée Lettre; E-mail: marie-josee.lettre@itaq.ca; *Libr Tech,* Hélène Talbot; Tel: 418-856-1110, Ext 1257, E-mail: helene.talbot@itaq.ca
Enrl 350
Library Holdings: Bk Vols 32,000; Per Subs 102
Subject Interests: Agr
Wireless access
Open Mon-Fri 8:30-4:30 (Sept-May)

S SOCIETE HISTORIQUE DE LA COTE-DU-SUD*, Archives de la Cote - du Sud et du College de Sainte-Anne, 100 4e Ave Painchaud, G0R 1Z0. SAN 375-0752. Tel: 418-856-2104. FAX: 418-856-2104. E-mail: archsud@bellnet.ca. Web Site: www.shcds.org/archives.html. *Pres,* Gaetan Godbout; *Dir,* Francois Taillon
Library Holdings: Bk Vols 2,500; Per Subs 25
Subject Interests: Genealogy, Hist
Wireless access
Friends of the Library Group

LA PRAIRIE

P CENTRE REGIONAL DE SERVICES AUX BIBLIOTHEQUES PUBLIQUES DE LA MONTEREGIE*, 275 rue Conrad-Pelletier, J5R 4V1. SAN 321-0987. Tel: 450-444-5433. FAX: 450-659-3364. Web Site: www.reseaubibliomonteregie.qc.ca. *Dir, Admin Serv,* Luce Brunell; E-mail: luce.brunell@reseaubibliomonteregie.qc.ca; Staff 12 (MLS 3, Non-MLS 9)
Founded 1978
Library Holdings: Bk Titles 314,487; Bk Vols 625,553
Special Collections: Canadian and Provincial
Automation Activity & Vendor Info: (Acquisitions) SirsiDynix; (Cataloging) SirsiDynix; (Circulation) SirsiDynix; (ILL) OCLC; (OPAC) SirsiDynix
Wireless access
Function: 24/7 Electronic res, 24/7 Online cat, Audiobks via web, Bk club(s), Children's prog, Digital talking bks, Distance learning, Doc delivery serv, Electronic databases & coll, ILL available, Magazines, OverDrive digital audio bks, Summer reading prog, Visual arts prog
Publications: Annual Report; Osez lire! (Periodical)
Restriction: Not open to pub

LA TUQUE

P BIBLIOTHEQUE MUNICIPALE DE LA TUQUE*, Bibliotheque Annie-St-Arnealt, 575 rue St-Eugene, G9X 2T5. (Mail add: 375 rue St-Joseph, G9X 1L5), SAN 319-6704. Tel: 819-523-3100. FAX: 819-523-4487. E-mail: bibliotheque@ville.latuque.qc.ca. Web Site: www.ville.latuque.qc.ca/fr/citoyens/loisir-et-culture. *Head Librn,* Position Currently Open
Founded 1961. Pop 11,000; Circ 50,000
Library Holdings: CDs 5,000; DVDs 400; Large Print Bks 250; Bk Vols 35,000; Per Subs 106
Function: Adult bk club, Art exhibits, CD-ROM, Homebound delivery serv, ILL available, Photocopying/Printing, Prog for children & young adult, Ref serv available, Spoken cassettes & CDs, Spoken cassettes & DVDs, Summer reading prog, Wheelchair accessible, Workshops
Open Tues & Wed 9:30-12 & 1:30-5, Thurs & Fri 9:30-12 & 1:30-8, Sat 9-12 & 1-4:30 (Sept-May); Tues & Wed 9-12 & 1:30-4:30, Thurs & Fri 9-12 & 1:30-8 (June-Aug)

LAC SAINT-CHARLES

P BIBLIOTHEQUE LE TOURNESOL*, Centre Communitaire Paul-Emile-Beaulieu, 530 rue Delage, Ste 2, G3G 1J2. SAN 321-3196. Tel: 418-641-6121. FAX: 419-849-2849. E-mail:

courrier@bibliothequedequebec.qc.ca. Web Site: www.bibliothequedequebec.qc.ca/bibliotheques/hautesaintcharles/le_tournesol.aspx. *Librn,* Julie Michaud
Founded 1981. Pop 9,064
Library Holdings: Bk Titles 8,000
Wireless access
Open Mon, Wed, Fri & Sat 10-5, Tues & Thurs 1-8, Sun 12-5

LAC-BROME

P BIBLIOTHEQUE COMMEMORATIVE PETTES*, Pettes Memorial Library, 276 chemin Knowlton, J0E 1V0. SAN 319-6712. Tel: 450-243-6128. FAX: 450-243-5272. E-mail: pettes.bpl@gmail.com. Web Site: pettes.ca. *Exec Dir,* Jana Marie Valasek; Staff 4 (MLS 1, Non-MLS 3)
Founded 1894. Pop 5,500; Circ 41,404
Library Holdings: Bk Vols 20,967; Per Subs 50; Talking Bks 627
Subject Interests: Local hist
Automation Activity & Vendor Info: (Cataloging) Mandarin Library Automation; (Circulation) Mandarin Library Automation; (OPAC) Mandarin Library Automation
Open Tues-Sat 10-4

LACHUTE

P BIBLIOTHEQUE JEAN-MARC-BELZILE*, 378, rue Principale, J8H 1Y2. SAN 319-6771. Tel: 450-562-4578. Interlibrary Loan Service Tel: 450-562-3781, Ext 214. FAX: 450-562-1431. E-mail: biblio@ville.lachute.qc.ca. Web Site: www.ville.lachute.qc.ca/biblio/votre-bibliotheque. *Head Librn,* Claudia Tremblay; Tel: 450-562-3781, Ext 255, E-mail: ctremblay@ville.lachute.qc.ca; Staff 9 (MLS 1, Non-MLS 8)
Founded 1959. Pop 16,000; Circ 100,000
Library Holdings: Bk Titles 50,000; Per Subs 96
Subject Interests: Genealogy, Hort
Automation Activity & Vendor Info: (Cataloging) SirsiDynix; (Circulation) SirsiDynix; (OPAC) SirsiDynix
Wireless access
Open Tues & Fri 10:30-6, Wed & Thurs 10:30-8, Sat & Sun 10:30-4
Restriction: Access for corporate affiliates

LASALLE

C CENTRE DE DOCUMENTATION COLLEGIALE*, 1111 rue Lapierre, H8N 2J4. SAN 374-6259. Tel: 514-364-3327. FAX: 514-364-2627. E-mail: info@cdc.qc.ca. Web Site: cdc.qc.ca. *Head Librn,* Isabelle Laplante; Tel: 514-364-3327, Ext 1, E-mail: isabelle.laplante@cdc.qc.ca; *Indexer, Librn,* Andree Dagenais; Tel: 514-364-3327, Ext 2, E-mail: andree.dagenais@cdc.qc.ca; *Cat, Circ,* Gaelle Tchepelev; Staff 4 (MLS 3, Non-MLS 1)
Founded 1969
Library Holdings: e-books 300; Electronic Media & Resources 5,000; Bk Titles 29,000; Spec Interest Per Sub 25
Special Collections: College Education
Subject Interests: Educ
Wireless access
Function: 24/7 Electronic res, 24/7 Online cat, Archival coll, Doc delivery serv, Electronic databases & coll, For res purposes, ILL available, Mail & tel request accepted, Mail loans to mem, Online cat, Online info literacy tutorials on the web & in blackboard, Outside serv via phone, mail, e-mail & web, Ref & res, Ref serv available, Res libr, Wheelchair accessible, Workshops
Restriction: Access at librarian's discretion, Authorized scholars by appt, Borrowing privileges limited to fac & registered students, External users must contact libr, In-house use for visitors, Open by appt only, Open to researchers by request, Open to students, fac & staff, Teacher & adminr only

L'ASSOMPTION

C COLLEGE DE L'ASSOMPTION*, Bibliotheque Secondaire, 270 boul l'Ange-Gardien, J5W 1R7. SAN 319-664X. Tel: 450-589-5621, Ext 258. FAX: 450-589-2910. E-mail: direction.generale@classomption.qc.ca. Web Site: www.classomption.qc.ca. *Librn,* Kevin Beaucage-Roy; E-mail: beaucke@classomption.qc.ca; *Tech Serv,* Pascal Belanger; E-mail: pascal.belanger@classomption.qc.ca
Founded 1833. Highest Degree: Doctorate
Library Holdings: Bk Titles 18,000; Per Subs 200
Special Collections: Prov; Theatre (Fonds Charbonneau)
Wireless access
Open Mon-Fri 8am-8:30pm

LAVAL

C COLLEGE MONTMORENCY BIBLIOTHEQUE*, 475 Boul de L Avenir, H7N 5H9. SAN 322-9033. Tel: 450-975-6274. FAX: 450-381-2263. E-mail: biblio@cmontmorency.qc.ca. Web Site: www.cmontmorency.qc.ca. *Asst Dir,* Emy Daniel; Tel: 450-975-6100, Ext 6364, E-mail: Emy.Daniel@cmontmorency.qc.ca; Staff 11 (MLS 1, Non-MLS 10)
Library Holdings: Bk Titles 60,000; Bk Vols 70,000
Automation Activity & Vendor Info: (Acquisitions) BiblioMondo; (Cataloging) BiblioMondo; (Circulation) BiblioMondo; (OPAC) BiblioMondo; (Serials) BiblioMondo
Wireless access
Publications: Nouveaute's
Open Mon-Thurs 7:45-7, Fri 7:45-6

C INRS - INSTITUT ARMAND-FRAPPIER - BIBLIOTHEQUE*, 531 blvd des Prairies, H7V 1B7. SAN 328-3801. Tel: 450-687-5010, Ext 4265. FAX: 450-686-5501. E-mail: sdis@adm.inrs.ca. Web Site: sdis.inrs.ca. *Librn,* Michel Courcelles; E-mail: michel.courcelles@iaf.inrs.ca; Staff 1 (MLS 1)
Founded 1938. Highest Degree: Doctorate
Library Holdings: e-journals 4,260; Bk Vols 7,000; Per Subs 4,600
Subject Interests: Animal health, Bacteriology, Epidemiology, Human health, Immunology, Microbiology, Toxicology, Virology
Wireless access
Function: Computers for patron use, Electronic databases & coll, For res purposes, Health sci info serv, ILL available, Internet access, Online cat, Photocopying/Printing, Ref & res
Partic in Bureau de cooperation Interuniversitaire; Canadian Research Knowledge Network
Open Mon-Fri 9-5
Restriction: External users must contact libr

LEVIS

P BIBLIOTHEQUE ALBERT ROUSSEAU*, 711 ave Albert Rousseau, G6J 1Z7. SAN 321-2785. Tel: 418-831-6492. FAX: 418-831-6107. E-mail: bibliolevis@ville.levis.qc.ca, levis@ville.levis.qc.ca. *Dir,* Rene Tremblay; Tel: 418-839-2002
Library Holdings: Bk Vols 30,000; Per Subs 25
Open Tues-Thurs 12-8, Fri 9-5, Sat & Sun 1-5

P BIBLIOTHEQUE ANNE-MARIE-FILTEAU*, 601 Route des Rivieres, G7A 1T7. SAN 321-2742. Tel: 418-835-8588. FAX: 418-835-5297. E-mail: bibliolevis@ville.levis.qc.ca. Web Site: www.ville.levis.qc.ca/culture/bibliotheques/carte-horaires. *Library Contact,* Position Currently Open
Library Holdings: Bk Vols 45,000
Special Collections: French Coll, bks, novels, mag
Open Tues-Thurs 9-8, Fri 12-8, Sat 9-5, Sun 1-5

P BIBLIOTHEQUE FRANCINE-MCKENZIE*, 100 Place Centre-Ville, G6Z 3B9. SAN 319-8944. Tel: 418-839-0012. FAX: 418-839-8818. E-mail: bibliolevis@ville.levis.qc.ca. Web Site: ville.levis.qc.ca. *Mgr,* Position Currently Open
Founded 1964. Pop 10,604; Circ 52,905
Library Holdings: Bk Vols 34,472; Per Subs 79
Subject Interests: Govt
Open Tues-Thurs 9-8, Fri Noon-8, Sat 9-5, Sun 1-5

P BIBLIOTHEQUE MUNICIPALE DE LEVIS*, Bibliotheque Pierre-Georges Roy, Seven rue Monsigneur-Gosselin, G6V 5J9. SAN 373-7780. Tel: 418-835-8570, 418-838-4122. FAX: 418-838-4124. E-mail: bibliolevis@ville.levis.qc.ca, levis@ville.levis.qc.ca. Web Site: www.ville.levis.qc.ca/culture/bibliotheques. *Dir,* Position Currently Open
Founded 1974. Pop 39,000
Library Holdings: Bk Vols 63,324
Wireless access
Open Tues-Thurs 9-8, Fri Noon-8, Sat 9-5, Sun 1-5

LONGUEUIL

P BIBLIOTHEQUES PUBLIQUES DE LONGUEUIL*, 100 rue Saint-Laurent Ouest, J4H 1M1. SAN 369-1802. Tel: 450-463-7180. E-mail: bibliotheques@longueuil.quebec. Web Site: www.longueuil.quebec/services/bibliotheques. *Dir,* Olivier Barrette; Staff 5 (MLS 5)
Founded 1967. Pop 135,634; Circ 1,006,446
Library Holdings: AV Mats 30,000; Bk Vols 500,000; Per Subs 364
Special Collections: History (J-Z-Leon Patenaude Coll)
Subject Interests: Genealogy, Handicraft, Lore, Quebec hist
Automation Activity & Vendor Info: (Acquisitions) MultiLIS; (Cataloging) MultiLIS
Wireless access

Publications: Bulletin (Quarterly)
Open Tues-Thurs 10-9, Fri 10-6, Sat 10-5
Branches: 10
BIBLIOTHEQUE HUBERT-PERRON, 1100, rue Beauregard, J4K 2L1. Web Site: longueuil.quebec/fr/bibliotheque-hubert-perron-0.
BIBLIOTHEQUE J-W-GENDRON, Ecole Mgr-A-M-Parent, 3875 Grand Allee, J4T 2V8. Web Site: longueuil.quebec/fr/bibliotheque-j-w-gendron-0.
Open Mon-Thurs 3-8, Sat 10-4, Sun 1-4
BIBLIOTHEQUE JACQUES-FERRON, ADULT LIBRARY, 100 Saint-Laurent St W, J4H 1M1. Web Site: www.longueuil.quebec/fr/bibliotheque-jacques-ferron.
Open Tues-Thurs 10-9, Fri 10-6, Sat & Sun 10-5; Tues-Thurs 10-9, Fri 10-6, Sat 10-5 (Summer)
BIBLIOTHEQUE JACQUES-FERRON, CHILDREN'S LIBRARY, 100 Saint-Laurent St W, J4H 1M1.
Open Tues 10-8, Wed & Thurs 1-8, Fri 1-6, Sat & Sun 10-5; Tues 10-8, Wed & Thurs 1-8, Fri 1-6, Sat 10-5 (Summer)
BIBLIOTHEQUE MUNICIPALE DE GREENFIELD PARK, 225 rue Empire, Greenfield Park, J4V 1T9, SAN 325-2396. Web Site: longueuil.quebec/fr/bibliotheque-de-greenfield-park. ; Staff 2 (MLS 2)
Circ 90,000
Library Holdings: Bk Vols 43,547; Per Subs 63
Special Collections: Large Print Coll- Pocket Books Coll
Open Mon, Tues, Thurs & Fri 1-9, Sat & Sun 1-4:30; Mon, Tues & Thurs 1-9, Fri 10-6, Sat 1-4:30 (Summer)
CLAUDE-HENRI GRIGNON BRANCH, 1660 rue Bourassa, J4J 3A4, SAN 369-1837. Web Site: www.longueuil.quebec/fr/bibliotheque-claude-henri-grignon.
Library Holdings: Bk Vols 42,000
Subject Interests: Genealogy, Quebec hist
Open Tues 10-9, Wed & Thurs 1-9, Fri 1-6, Sat & Sun 10-5; Tues 10-9, Wed & Thurs 1-9, Fri 1-6, Sat 10-5 (Summer)
BIBLIOTHEQUE RAYMOND LEVESQUE, 7025 boul Cousineu, J3Y 0H1. Web Site: longueuil.quebec/fr/bibliotheque-raymond-levesque.
Open Mon 1-9, Tues-Thurs 10-9, Fri 10-6, Sat 10-5, Sun Noon-5
ST-JEAN-BAPTISTE BRANCH, 700, rue Duvernay, J4K 4L1.
SUCCURSALE FATIMA, 2130 rue Jean-Louis, J4H 1M1. (Mail add: c/o Succursale Jaques Ferron, Five rue St Laurent Quest, J4H 1M1), SAN 369-1845. Web Site: longueuil.quebec/fr/bibliotheque-fatima-0.
Library Holdings: Bk Vols 5,487
Open Tues & Wed 1-8, Thurs & Fri 1-5, Sat Noon-3
SUCCURSALE GEORGES-DOR, 2760 Chemin de Chambly, J4L 1M7, SAN 369-1861. Web Site: longueuil.quebec/fr/bibliotheque-georges-dor.
Library Holdings: Bk Vols 43,799
Open Tues-Thurs 10-9, Fri 10-6, Sat & Sun 10-5; Tues-Thurs 10-9, Fri 10-6, Sat 10-5 (Summer)

J COLLEGE EDOUARD-MONTPETIT BIBLIOTHEQUE*, 945 Chemin de Chambly, J4H 3M6. SAN 369-1896. Tel: 450-679-2631, Ext 6047. Interlibrary Loan Service Tel: 450-679-2631, Ext 2486. E-mail: bibliolong@cegepmontpetit.ca. Web Site: bibli.cegepmontpetit.ca. *Coordr of Libr,* Nancie Lamontagne; E-mail: nancie.lamontagne@cegepmontpetit.ca; *Educ Spec,* Marilyne Cote; E-mail: marilyne.cote@cegepmontpetit.ca; Staff 2 (MLS 2)
Founded 1967. Enrl 6,700; Highest Degree: Associate
Library Holdings: CDs 400; DVDs 1,000; Bk Titles 75,000; Bk Vols 100,000; Per Subs 314; Videos 6,000
Special Collections: State Document Depository
Subject Interests: Archit, Art, Behav sci, Econ, Natural sci, Soc sci
Automation Activity & Vendor Info: (Acquisitions) SirsiDynix; (Cataloging) SirsiDynix; (Circulation) SirsiDynix; (OPAC) SirsiDynix; (Serials) SirsiDynix
Wireless access
Open Mon-Thurs 7:45am-8pm, Fri 7:45-6, Sat 9-1
Departmental Libraries:
ECOLE NATIONALE D'AEROTECHNIQUE BIBLIOTHEQUE, 5555, rue de l'ENA, J3Y 0Y3, SAN 374-728X. Tel: 450-678-3561, Ext 4599. FAX: 450-678-3240. E-mail: biblioena@cegepmontpetit.ca. *Librn,* Nathalie Ouellet; Staff 1 (MLS 1)
Founded 1964. Enrl 700
Library Holdings: Bk Titles 17,000; Bk Vols 25,000; Per Subs 50
Subject Interests: Aeronaut
Open Mon-Thurs 8-6, Fri 8-4:30

MANIWAKI

G BIBLIOTHEQUE MUNICIPALE JR L'HEUREUX*, 14 Comeau St, J9E 2R8. SAN 328-8145. Tel: 819-449-2738. FAX: 819-449-7626. E-mail: admmaniwaki@crsbpo.qc.ca. Web Site: www.ville.maniwaki.qc.ca/index.php/services/loisirs-et-culture/bibliotheque-j-r-l-heureux. *Coordr,* Archambault Colette
Founded 1967
Library Holdings: Bk Vols 8,000; Per Subs 15
Open Mon-Fri 2-7, Sat (Sept-May) 1-4

MARIEVILLE

P BIBLIOTHEQUE COMMEMORATIVE DESAUTELS*, 603 rue Claude-De Ramezay, J3M 1J7. SAN 319-6887. Tel: 450-460-4444, Ext 272. FAX: 450-460-3526. E-mail: biblio-marieville@ville.marieville.qc.ca. Web Site: www.ville.marieville.qc.ca/fr/loisirs-et-culture/bibliotheque. *Dir,* Daniel Lalonde; E-mail: d.lalonde@ville.marieville.qc.ca; Staff 3 (MLS 1, Non-MLS 2)
Founded 1967. Pop 7,000; Circ 50,900
Library Holdings: Bk Vols 42,000
Special Collections: Can
Automation Activity & Vendor Info: (Cataloging) SirsiDynix; (Circulation) SirsiDynix
Wireless access
Open Tues & Fri 8:30-12 & 1-4:30, Wed & Thurs 8:30-12 & 1-8, Sat 9-Noon

MONT-LAURIER

P BIBLIOTHEQUE MUNICIPALE DE MONT-LAURIER*, 385 rue du Pont, J9L 2R5. SAN 319-6895. Tel: 819-623-1221, Ext 750. FAX: 819-623-7079. E-mail: bibliotheque@villemont.qc.ca. Web Site: biblio.villemontlaurier.qc.ca/in/faces/homeInBook.xhtml. *Librn,* Sophie Monette; E-mail: smonette@villemontlaurier.qc.ca; Staff 2 (MLS 1, Non-MLS 1)
Pop 13,891
Library Holdings: DVDs 301; Large Print Bks 259; Bk Titles 36,472; Bk Vols 44,297; Per Subs 71
Automation Activity & Vendor Info: (Acquisitions) BiblioMondo; (Cataloging) BiblioMondo; (Circulation) BiblioMondo; (OPAC) BiblioMondo; (Serials) BiblioMondo
Wireless access
Open Mon-Fri 10-8, Sat 10-4:30

MONTREAL

M ALLAN MEMORIAL INSTITUTE OF PSYCHIATRY*, Eric D Wittkower Library, Royal Victoria Hospital, 1025 Pine Ave W, H3A 1A1. SAN 319-695X. Tel: 514-934-1934, Ext 34528. FAX: 514-843-1731. E-mail: ami.library@muhc.mcgill.ca. Web Site: www.muhclibraries.ca/libraries/ami. *Mgr, Libr Serv,* Julia Kleinberg; E-mail: julia.kleinberg@muhc.mcgill.ca
Subject Interests: Psychiat, Psychoanalysis, Psychopharmacology
Open Tues & Fri 9-1, Wed & Thurs 9-12:30
Friends of the Library Group

R ARCHIVES PROVINCIALES DES CAPUCINS, 3650 Blvd de la Rousseliere, H1A 2X9. SAN 370-6605. Tel: 514-642-5391. FAX: 514-642-5033. E-mail: archprovmtl@outlook.com. *Archivist/Librn,* Andre Chicone; Tel: 514-642-5391, Ext 345; *Documentation Tech,* France Guilbert; Tel: 514-642-5391, Ext 347
Founded 1977
Jan 2024-Dec 2024. Mats Exp (CAN) $1,400, Books (CAN) $550, AV Mat (CAN) $550, Presv (CAN) $300. Sal (CAN) $36,000
Library Holdings: DVDs 100; Bk Vols 7,000; Per Subs 6; Videos 85
Wireless access
Function: Electronic databases & coll, Res libr
Publications: Les Capucins de l'Est du Canada 1632 a nos jours, 1982; Les Capucins francophones du Canada
Restriction: Authorized scholars by appt, External users must contact libr, In-house use for visitors, Internal circ only, Internal use only, Open to researchers by appointment, Restricted borrowing privileges, Restricted pub use, Visitors must make appt to use bks in the libr

S ARTEXTE INFORMATION CENTRE, Two Saint-Catherine St Est, Rm 301, H2X 1K4. SAN 323-6676. Tel: 514-874-0049. E-mail: collections@artexte.ca. Web Site: www.artexte.ca. *Dir,* Manon Tourigny; *Librn,* Kate Lewis; *Documentation Tech,* Jonathan Lachance; Staff 2 (MLS 1, Non-MLS 1)
Founded 1981
Library Holdings: CDs 200; DVDs 200; Electronic Media & Resources 2,000; Bk Titles 32,000; Per Subs 50
Special Collections: Artists Files; Exhibition Catalogs
Subject Interests: Contemporary art
Wireless access
Function: Photocopying/Printing, Ref serv available
Publications: The Directory of Publications on Canadian Contemporary Art
Open Wed-Sat 12-5
Restriction: Non-circulating

S ASSOCIATION PARITAIRE POUR LA SANTE ET LA SECURITE DU TRAVAIL - SECTEUR AFFAIRES MUNICIPALES*, Centre de Documentation, 715 Square Victoria, Ste 710, H2Y 2H7. SAN 328-5359. Tel: 514-849-8373, Ext 235. Toll Free Tel: 800-465-1754. FAX:

514-849-8873. Toll Free FAX: 800-465-6578. E-mail: apsamdoc@apsam.com, apssap@apssap.qc.ca, info@apsam.com. Web Site: apssap.qc.ca, www.apsam.com/a-propos/centre-de-documentation. *Librn,* Gladys Aragon; E-mail: garagon@apsam.com; Staff 1 (Non-MLS 1)
Founded 1983
Library Holdings: CDs 21; DVDs 29; Bk Vols 3,865; Per Subs 35; Videos 121
Special Collections: NFPA Codes (Updated)
Subject Interests: Fire fighters, Law enforcement, Occupational health, Occupational safety, Pub transportation, Sewage treatment
Automation Activity & Vendor Info: (Cataloging) Isacsoft Inc (ISF); (Circulation) Isacsoft Inc (ISF); (Serials) Isacsoft Inc (ISF)
Open Mon-Fri 8-12 & 1-4

S BCA RESEARCH GROUP LIBRARY*, 1002 Sherbrooke St W, Ste 1600, H3A 3L6. SAN 375-5592. Toll Free Tel: 800-724-2942. FAX: 514-843-1763. Web Site: www.bcaresearch.com. *Res Serv, VPres, Info Res,* Meital Klod; E-mail: meital@bcaresearch.com
Founded 1992
Library Holdings: Bk Titles 2,000; Per Subs 400
Subject Interests: Finance
Automation Activity & Vendor Info: (Cataloging) Inmagic, Inc.
Restriction: Not open to pub

M DONALD BERMAN MAIMONIDES*, Health Information Centre, 5795 Caldwell Ave, H4W 1W3. SAN 321-673X. Tel: 514-483-2121, Ext 2217. FAX: 514-483-1086. E-mail: mhgclibrary@ssss.gouv.qc.ca. Web Site: www.donaldbermanmaimonides.net. *Head, Archives & Patient Info,* Nidaa Karnib; Tel: 514-483-2121, Ext 2299
Founded 1966
Library Holdings: Bk Titles 2,000; Per Subs 100
Automation Activity & Vendor Info: (Cataloging) Inmagic, Inc.; (Circulation) Inmagic, Inc.; (OPAC) Inmagic, Inc.
Publications: Resource Subject Guide
Open Mon-Fri 9-5

SR BIBLIOTHEQUE ALBERT-LE-GRAND*, Institut de pastorale des Dominicains, 2715, chemin de la Côte Ste-Catherine, H3T 1B6. SAN 325-8335. Tel: 514-731-3603, Ext 307. FAX: 514-731-0676. E-mail: albertlegrand1221@yahoo.ca. Web Site: www.ipastorale.ca/fr/bibliotheque. *Dir,* Patrick Dionne
Library Holdings: Bk Vols 80,000
Open Mon-Thurs 10:30-1:30 & 2:30-6
Friends of the Library Group

R BIBLIOTHEQUE DE LA COMPAGNIE DE JESUS*, Bibliothèque des Jésuites/Jesuit Library, Collège Jean-de-Brebeuf, Local B4-25, 3200 Chemin Côte-Sainte-Catherine, H3T 1C1. SAN 372-6908. Tel: 514-342-9342, Ext 5466. E-mail: bcj@brebeuf.qc.ca. Web Site: www.brebeuf.qc.ca/bibliotheques/bibliotheque-de-compagnie-de-jesus. *Librn,* Marc Mambuku Umba. Subject Specialists: *Classical studies, Law,* Marc Mambuku Umba; Staff 1 (MLS 1)
Founded 1882
Library Holdings: Per Subs 128
Special Collections: 15th to 19th Manuscripts; Ancient & Rare Books (16th Century & On); Corpus christianorum, series graeca (CGT), 1977; Corpus christianorum, series latina (CCL),1954; Corpus scriptorum christianorum orientalium (CSCO), 1903; Corpus scriptorum ecclesiasticorum latinorum (CSEL),1866; Die griechischen chrislichen Schriftsteller der ersten drei Jahrhunderte,(GCS), 1897; Patrologia orientalis (PO), 1903; Patrologia syriaca (PS), 1894; Philosophy & Theology (Jesuit Education); Rare Books from the Former Jesuit College of Quebec, Founded in 1635, (New France Books); Sources chretiennes (SC), 1941; Texte und Untersuchungen...(TU), 1882. Canadian and Provincial
Subject Interests: Canadiana, Classical studies, Philos, Relig, Sci, Theol
Wireless access
Function: 24/7 Online cat, For res purposes, Internet access, Magazines, Mail loans to mem, Microfiche/film & reading machines, Online cat, Photocopying/Printing, Res libr, Scanner
Open Mon-Fri 8:30-12 & 1-4:30
Restriction: Access at librarian's discretion, By permission only, External users must contact libr, Open to fac, students & qualified researchers, Open to pub for ref & circ; with some limitations, Open to pub upon request, Open to qualified scholars, Open to researchers by request, Open to students, fac & staff, Open to students, fac, staff & alumni, Private libr, Use of others with permission of librn, Visitors must make appt to use bks in the libr
Friends of the Library Group

G BIBLIOTHEQUE ET ARCHIVES NATIONALES DU QUEBEC*, 475 de Maisonneuve E, H2L 5C4. SAN 319-7069. Tel: 514-873-1100, Option 3. Toll Free Tel: 800-363-9028. FAX: 514-873-9312. E-mail: info@banq.ca, pdg@banq.qc.ca. Web Site: www.banq.qc.ca. *Pres & Chief Exec Officer,* Marie Gregoire; *Libr Dir,* Danielle Chagnon; Tel: 514-873-1101, Ext 3245; *Dir of Educ,* Jean-Luc Murray; Tel: 514-873-1101, Ext 6714, E-mail: jl.murray@banq.qc.ca; *Curator, Dir, Archives,* Helene Laverdure; Tel: 514-873-1101, Ext 6408, E-mail: helene.laverdure@banq.qc.ca; *Dir, Human Res,* Lise Morin; Tel: 514-873-1101, Ext 3241, E-mail: lise.morin@banq.qc.ca. Subject Specialists: *Cultural prog,* Jean-Luc Murray; *Admin,* Lise Morin
Founded 1967
Wireless access
Publications: A Rayons Ouverts
Open Tues-Fri 9-9, Sat & Sun 9-5
Friends of the Library Group

R BIBLIOTHEQUE FRANCISCAINE PROVINCIALE DES CAPUCINS*, 3650 boul de la Rousseliere, H1A 2X9. SAN 370-7385. Tel: 514-354-1161, 514-642-5391. FAX: 514-642-5033. E-mail: capucins.info@gmail.com. *Librn,* Position Currently Open
Jan 2016-Dec 2016. Mats Exp (CAN) $2,000, Books (CAN) $700, Electronic Ref Mat (Incl. Access Fees) (CAN) $600, Presv (CAN) $700. Sal (CAN) $2,000
Library Holdings: Bk Vols 21,000; Per Subs 200
Special Collections: Franciscan Coll
Subject Interests: Missions, Theol
Wireless access
Function: Archival coll, Electronic databases & coll, Photocopying/Printing
Publications: Repertoire des Livres Franciscains des Capucins de l'Est du Canada, 1993
Restriction: Internal circ only, Open to pub by appt only

G BIBLIOTHEQUE, INSTITUT DE TOURISME ET D'HOTELLERIE DU QUEBEC*, 3535, rue Saint-Denis, Local 1.97, H2X 3P1. SAN 329-2967. Tel: 514-282-5111, Ext 5114. Toll Free Tel: 800-361-5111, Ext 5114. E-mail: bibliotheque@ithq.qc.ca. Web Site: www.ithq.qc.ca. *Libr Serv Mgr,* Guylaine Simard; Tel: 514-282-5111, Ext 4525, E-mail: guylaine.simard@ithq.qc.ca; Staff 4 (MLS 1, Non-MLS 3)
Founded 1975
Library Holdings: AV Mats 3,073; e-books 120,000; Electronic Media & Resources 20; Bk Titles 21,522; Bk Vols 22,860; Per Subs 178
Special Collections: Professional Recipes; Restaurant menus
Subject Interests: Cookery, Food, Food serv mgt, Hotel mgt, Recipes, Restaurant mgt, Tourism, Wine
Automation Activity & Vendor Info: (Acquisitions) BiblioMondo; (Cataloging) BiblioMondo; (Circulation) BiblioMondo; (Media Booking) BiblioMondo; (OPAC) BiblioMondo; (Serials) BiblioMondo
Wireless access
Function: ILL available
Open Mon-Fri 8:30-4:30

C BIBLIOTHEQUE LAURENT-MICHEL-VACHER*, College Ahuntsic Bibliotheque, 9155 rue St-Hubert, H2M 1Y8. SAN 319-728X. Tel: 514-389-5921, Ext 2240. FAX: 514-389-1422. E-mail: bibliotheque@collegeahuntsic.qc.ca. Web Site: www.collegeahuntsic.qc.ca/bibliotheque. *Coordr,* Anne Le Blanc; E-mail: anne.le-blanc@collegeahuntsic.qc.ca
Founded 1973
Library Holdings: AV Mats 21,000; Bk Vols 68,000; Per Subs 225
Automation Activity & Vendor Info: (Cataloging) Koha
Wireless access
Open Mon-Thurs 7:45am-8pm, Fri 7:45-5

P BIBLIOTHEQUE PUBLIQUE JUIVE*, Jewish Public Library, 5151 Cote Ste Catherine, H3W 1M6. SAN 319-7085. Tel: 514-345-2627. Circulation Tel: 514-345-2627, Ext 3003. Reference Tel: 514-345-2627, Ext 3001. Administration Tel: 514-345-2627, Ext 3332. FAX: 514-342-6477. E-mail: info@jplmontreal.org. Web Site: www.jewishpubliclibrary.org. *Exec Dir,* Michael Crelinsten; *Director, Children's Library,* Nicole Beaudry; E-mail: nicole.beaudry@jplmontreal.org; *Head Biblio & Info Serv,* Eddie Paul; E-mail: eddie.paul@jplmontreal.org; *Head, Libr Serv,* Karen Biskin; E-mail: karen.biskin@jplmontreal.org; Staff 16 (MLS 5, Non-MLS 11)
Founded 1914. Pop 70,000; Circ 160,000
Library Holdings: Bk Titles 180,000
Special Collections: 15th-19th Century Judaica (Rare Book Coll); Archives, ms, photog, etc; German Judaica, 19th-20th Centuries; Irving Layton Library; Jewish Canadiana Coll, ephemera; Yiddish Periodicals; Yizkor Coll
Subject Interests: Gen fiction, Judaica
Automation Activity & Vendor Info: (Cataloging) SirsiDynix-WorkFlows; (Circulation) SirsiDynix-WorkFlows; (Discovery) SirsiDynix; (ILL) SirsiDynix; (OPAC) SirsiDynix; (Serials) SirsiDynix
Wireless access
Function: Bks on CD, CD-ROM, Chess club, Children's prog, Computer training, Computers for patron use, Doc delivery serv, Electronic databases & coll, Homebound delivery serv, ILL available, Internet access, Magazines, Microfiche/film & reading machines, Museum passes, Music

CDs, Online cat, Online ref, Orientations, Outreach serv, Outside serv via phone, mail, e-mail & web, Photocopying/Printing, Prog for adults, Prog for children & young adult, Ref & res, Ref serv available, Res libr, Scanner, Senior computer classes, Spoken cassettes & CDs, Study rm, Summer & winter reading prog, Telephone ref, Workshops, Writing prog
Special Services for the Deaf - Assistive tech
Special Services for the Blind - Audio mat; Bks available with recordings; Bks on cassette; Bks on CD; Large print bks
Open Mon-Thurs 10-8, Fri 10-1, Sun (Sept-June) 10-5
Restriction: Access at librarian's discretion, Borrowing requests are handled by ILL, By permission only, Circ limited, Circ to mem only, Closed stack, In-house use for visitors, Non-circulating coll, Non-circulating of rare bks
Friends of the Library Group

P BIBLIOTHEQUES DE MONTREAL*, Pavillon Prince, 801 rue Brennan, 5e etage, H3C 0G4. SAN 369-3279. Tel: 514-872-1608. FAX: 514-872-5588. Web Site: bibliomontreal.com. *Dir of Libr,* Ivan Filion; E-mail: ifilion@ville.montreal.qc.ca; *Div Chief, Programming Serv,* Chloé Baril; Tel: 514-872-1609, E-mail: chloe.baril@ville.montreal.qc.ca; *Libr Serv Section Chief,* Nathalie Bellemare; Tel: 514-872-1542, E-mail: nathalie.bellemare@ville.montreal.qc.ca; *Central Servs Mgr, Div Chief,* Alexandra Court; Tel: 514-872-6563; *Libr Serv Section Chief,* David Koné; Tel: 514-872-6308, E-mail: david.kone@ville.montreal.qc.ca; *Div Chief,* Amélie Harbec; Tel: 514-872-3160, E-mail: amelie.harbec@ville.montreal.qc.ca; *District Prog Mgr, Libr Serv Section Chief,* Nathalie Martin; Tel: 514-872-2449, E-mail: nathaliemartin@ville.montreal.qc.ca. Subject Specialists: *Construction, Renovation,* Amélie Harbec; Staff 708 (MLS 166.8, Non-MLS 541.2)
Founded 1902. Pop 1,765,616; Circ 12,031,263
Jan 2018-Dec 2018. Mats Exp (CAN) $7,715,308, Books (CAN) $5,452,544, Per/Ser (Incl. Access Fees) (CAN) $553,526, AV Mat (CAN) $598,031, Electronic Ref Mat (Incl. Access Fees) (CAN) $1,108,615. Sal (CAN) $63,097,943
Library Holdings: Audiobooks 21,914; AV Mats 354,616; Braille Volumes 33; CDs 123,317; DVDs 209,912; e-books 104,130; e-journals 133,927; Electronic Media & Resources 249,446; Large Print Bks 27,554; Microforms 18; Music Scores 5,712; Bk Titles 803,939; Bk Vols 3,439,323; Per Subs 12,111; Talking Bks 21,914; Videos 210,060
Special Collections: Dr Armand Frappier's Personal Coll; Genealogy Coll; History Coll; Music Scores; Nautical Maps; Stamps; Yves Ryan's Archives
Automation Activity & Vendor Info: (Acquisitions) Innovative Interfaces, Inc; (Cataloging) Innovative Interfaces, Inc; (Circulation) Innovative Interfaces, Inc; (Media Booking) Innovative Interfaces, Inc; (OPAC) Innovative Interfaces, Inc; (Serials) Innovative Interfaces, Inc
Wireless access
Partic in Consortium d'acquisition de ressources electroniques du Quebec
Friends of the Library Group
Branches: 45

AHUNTSIC, 10300 rue Lajeunesse, H3L 2E5, SAN 369-3368. Tel: 514-872-0568. *Chef de Div,* Isabelle Pilon; Tel: 514 872-0850, E-mail: isabelle.pilon@montreal.ca; Staff 22 (MLS 4, Non-MLS 18)
Founded 1953. Circ 533,345
Library Holdings: Audiobooks 825; AV Mats 11,401; CDs 2,859; DVDs 7,279; Electronic Media & Resources 78; Large Print Bks 1,012; Microforms 1; Music Scores 800; Bk Vols 122,418; Per Subs 486; Talking Bks 825; Videos 7,466
Open Mon 12-6, Tues & Wed 1-9, Thurs 10-9, Fri 10-6, Sat 10-5, Sun 12-5

BELLEVILLE, 10400 Ave de Belleville, Montreal-Nord, H1H 4Z7, SAN 369-4925. Tel: 514-328-4000, Ext 4140. *Chef de Div,* Marie Desilets; E-mail: marie.desilets@montreal.ca; *Chef de Section,* Dominique Riberdy; Tel: 514-328-4000, Ext 4220, E-mail: dominique.riberdy@ville.montreal.qc.ca; Staff 4 (Non-MLS 4)
Founded 1973. Circ 54,777
Library Holdings: Audiobooks 36; AV Mats 3,624; CDs 1,162; DVDs 2,279; Electronic Media & Resources 1; Bk Vols 36,853; Per Subs 98; Talking Bks 36; Videos 2,358
Open Mon 10-8, Tues-Thurs 9-8, Fri 9-1, Sat & Sun 12-5

BENNY, 6400 Ave de Monkland, H4B 1H3, SAN 369-3422. Tel: 514-872-4147 (Adult), 514-872-4636 (Youth). *Chef de Div,* Raymond Carrier; Tel: 514-868-4021, E-mail: raymond.carrier@montreal.ca; *Bibliothecaire Responsable,* Irinel-Maria Stingaciu; Tel: 514-280-3637, E-mail: irinel-maria.stingaciu@ville.montreal.qc.ca; Staff 26.6 (MLS 5.8, Non-MLS 20.8)
Founded 1956. Circ 458,128
Library Holdings: Audiobooks 1,261; AV Mats 12,673; CDs 4,691; DVDs 6,110; Electronic Media & Resources 146; Large Print Bks 1,271; Microforms 1; Music Scores 199; Bk Vols 121,121; Per Subs 202; Talking Bks 1,261; Videos 6,201
Open Mon, Thurs & Fri 10-6, Tues & Wed 12-7:30, Sat & Sun 10-5

CARTIERVILLE, 5900 rue De Salaberry, H4J 1J8, SAN 369-3333. Tel: 514-872-6989. *Chef de Div,* Isabelle Pilon; Tel: 514-872-0850, E-mail: isabelle.pilon@montreal.ca; *Chef de Section,* Sylvie Cantin; Tel: 514-868-5916, E-mail: sylvie.cantin@ville.montreal.qc.ca; Staff 10 (MLS 3, Non-MLS 7)
Founded 1966. Circ 152,171
Library Holdings: Audiobooks 383; AV Mats 5,752; CDs 1,038; DVDs 4,086; Electronic Media & Resources 9; Large Print Bks 169; Music Scores 8; Bk Vols 61,941; Per Subs 357; Talking Bks 383; Videos 4,161
Open Mon 1-8, Tues & Wed 10-8, Thurs 10-6, Fri 12-6, Sat 10-5, Sun 12-5

COTE-DES-NEIGES, 5290 chemin de la Cote-des-Neiges, H3T 1Y2, SAN 322-6077. Tel: 514-872-5118 (Children's Serv), 514-872-6603 (Adult). *Chef de Div,* Raymond Carrier; Tel: 514-868-4021, E-mail: raymond.carrier@montreal.ca; *Chef de Section,* Robert Chamberot; Tel: 514-872-2935, E-mail: rchamberot@ville.montreal.qc.ca; Staff 20 (MLS 2, Non-MLS 18)
Founded 1983. Circ 270,795
Library Holdings: Audiobooks 799; AV Mats 7,171; CDs 803; DVDs 5,160; Electronic Media & Resources 11; Large Print Bks 957; Microforms 1; Music Scores 60; Bk Vols 105,558; Per Subs 498; Talking Bks 799; Videos 5,308
Open Mon, Thurs & Fri 10-6, Tues & Wed 12-7:30, Sat & Sun 10-5

DE SALABERRY, 4170 rue De Salaberry, H4J 1H1, SAN 369-3872. Tel: 514-872-1521. *Chef de Div,* Isabelle Pilon; Tel: 514-872-0850, E-mail: isabelle.pilon@montreal.ca; *Chef de Section,* Sylvie Cantin; Tel: 514-868-5916, E-mail: sylvie.cantin@ville.montreal.qc.ca; Staff 6 (MLS 1, Non-MLS 5)
Founded 1964. Circ 107,393
Library Holdings: Audiobooks 12; AV Mats 1,563; Braille Volumes 1; CDs 12; DVDs 1,317; Electronic Media & Resources 2; Music Scores 2; Bk Vols 28,862; Per Subs 67; Talking Bks 12; Videos 1,342
Open Mon, Thurs & Fri 9-5, Tues & Wed 9-6, Sat 10-5, Sun 12-5

DU BOISE, 2727 Blvd Thimens, Saint-Laurent, H4R 1T4. Tel: 514-855-6130. *Chef de Div,* Andree Tremblay; Tel: 514-855-6130, Ext 4722, E-mail: andree.tremblay@ville.montreal.qc.ca; *Chef de Section,* Abir Ossman; Tel: 514-855-6130, Ext 4728, E-mail: abir.ossman@ville.montreal.qc.ca; Staff 38 (MLS 6, Non-MLS 32)
Founded 2013. Circ 479,673
Library Holdings: Audiobooks 977; AV Mats 16,032; CDs 4,026; DVDs 9,272; Electronic Media & Resources 13; Large Print Bks 1,335; Bk Vols 142,328; Per Subs 460; Talking Bks 977; Videos 9,659
Open Mon-Wed 11-9, Thurs & Fri 11-8, Sat & Sun 10-5

FRONTENAC, 2550 rue Ontario Est, H2K 1W7, SAN 370-4572. Tel: 514-872-7888. *Chef de Div,* Gina Tremblay; Tel: 514-872-0831; *Chef de Section,* Marie-Ève Lima; Tel: 514-872-7889, E-mail: marie-eve.lima@ville.montreal.qc.ca; Staff 11.6 (MLS 3.2, Non-MLS 8.4)
Founded 1989. Circ 177,803
Library Holdings: Audiobooks 389; AV Mats 6,210; CDs 2,028; DVDs 3,349; Electronic Media & Resources 7; Large Print Bks 554; Music Scores 11; Bk Vols 67,449; Per Subs 161; Talking Bks 389; Videos 3,374
Open Mon & Fri Noon-6, Tues-Thurs 10-8, Sat 10-5, Sun Noon-5

GEORGES-VANIER, 2450 rue Workman, H3J 1L8, SAN 369-3937. Tel: 514-872-2001 (Adult Serv), 514-872-2002 (Children's Serv). *Chef de Div,* Chantal Beaulieu; Tel: 514-872-3067, E-mail: chantalbeaulieu@montreal.ca; *Chef de Section,* Éliane Béliveau-Cantin; Tel: 514-872-3763, E-mail: eliane.beliveau-cantin@ville.montreal.qc.ca; Staff 8.5 (MLS 1.5, Non-MLS 7)
Founded 1985. Circ 112,230
Library Holdings: Audiobooks 2; AV Mats 5,634; Braille Volumes 1; CDs 1,367; DVDs 3,701; Electronic Media & Resources 14; Large Print Bks 5; Microforms 1; Music Scores 11; Bk Vols 38,409; Per Subs 109; Talking Bks 2; Videos 3,848
Open Mon 12-6, Tues 10-8, Wed 1-8, Thurs & Fri 10-6, Sat & Sun 10-5

HAUT-ANJOU, 7070 rue Jarry Est, Anjou, H1J 1G4. Tel: 514-493-8271. *Chef de Div,* Magdalena Michalowska; Tel: 514-493-8262, E-mail: mmichalowska@ville.montreal.qc.ca; *Chef de Section,* Véronic Papineau-Archambault; Tel: 514-493-8270, E-mail: veronic.papineau-archambault@ville.montreal.qc.ca; Staff 3.6 (MLS 0.4, Non-MLS 3.2)
Founded 1990. Circ 44,529
Library Holdings: Audiobooks 1; AV Mats 798; CDs 3; DVDs 751; Large Print Bks 15; Music Scores 2; Bk Vols 15,468; Per Subs 56; Talking Bks 1; Videos 754
Open Mon-Fri 12-8, Sat 9:30-5, Sun 11-5

HENRI-BOURASSA, 5400 Blvd Henri-Bourassa Est, Montreal-Nord, H1G 2S9, SAN 369-4895. Tel: 514-328-4000, Ext 4125 (Adult Serv), 514-328-4000, Ext 4134 (Children's Serv). *Chef de Div,* Marie Desilets; E-mail: marie.desilets@montreal.ca; *Chef de Section,* Isabelle Moreau; Tel: 514-328-4000, Ext 5620, E-mail: isabelle.moreau@ville.montreal.qc.ca; Staff 25.7 (MLS 4, Non-MLS 21.7)
Founded 1970. Circ 185,461

Library Holdings: Audiobooks 396; AV Mats 8,116; CDs 3,079; DVDs 4,260; Electronic Media & Resources 33; Large Print Bks 630; Music Scores 2; Bk Vols 70,660; Per Subs 301; Talking Bks 396; Videos 4,437
Open Mon 10-8, Tues-Thurs 9-8, Fri 9-5, Sat & Sun 10-5

HOCHELAGA, 1870 rue Davidson, H1W 2Y6, SAN 369-3570. Tel: 514-872-3666. *Chef de Div,* Frederic Steben; *Chef de Section,* Marie-Eve Leprohon; Tel: 514-872-6733, E-mail: marie-eve.leprohon@ville.montreal.qc.ca; Staff 1.9 (MLS 1.1, Non-MLS 0.8)
Founded 1964. Circ 70,874
Library Holdings: Audiobooks 16; AV Mats 1,430; Braille Volumes 3; CDs 335; DVDs 1,007; Electronic Media & Resources 2; Bk Vols 26,354; Per Subs 47; Talking Bks 16; Videos 1,027
Open Mon, Thurs & Fri 10-6, Tues & Wed 1-6, Sat & Sun 10-4

ILE-DES-SOEURS, 260 rue Elgar, Verdun, H3E 1C9, SAN 373-6202. Tel: 514-765-7266. *Chef de Div,* Nancy Raymond; Tel: 514-765-7154, E-mail: nancy.raymond@montreal.ca; *Bibliothecaire Responsable,* Marie Badogombwa; Tel: 514-765-7169, E-mail: marie.badogombwa@ville.montreal.qc.ca; Staff 8.3 (MLS 2.4, Non-MLS 5.9)
Founded 1990. Circ 132,691
Library Holdings: Audiobooks 217; AV Mats 5,733; CDs 1,581; DVDs 3,418; Electronic Media & Resources 1; Large Print Bks 186; Bk Vols 44,838; Per Subs 141; Talking Bks 217; Videos 3,557
Open Mon, Wed & Thurs 1-9, Tues 10-9, Fri 10-6, Sat & Sun 12-5

INTERCULTURELLE, 6767 chemin de la Cote-des-Neiges, H3S 2T6. Tel: 514-868-4715 (Adult), 514-868-4716. *Chef de Div,* Raymond Carrier; Tel: 514-868-4021, E-mail: raymond.carrier@montreal.ca; *Bibliothecaire Responsable,* Stéphane G Gauthier; Tel: 514-872-7367, E-mail: sg.gauthier@ville.montreal.qc.ca; Staff 12.2 (MLS 4.6, Non-MLS 7.6)
Founded 2005. Circ 232,426
Library Holdings: Audiobooks 1,000; AV Mats 13,359; CDs 4,082; DVDs 6,370; Electronic Media & Resources 333; Large Print Bks 351; Microforms 1; Music Scores 56; Bk Vols 108,375; Per Subs 393; Talking Bks 1,000; Videos 6,753
Open Mon, Thurs & Fri 10-6, Tues & Wed 12-7:30, Sat & Sun 10-5

JACQUELINE-DE REPENTIGNY, 5955 rue Bannantyne, Verdun, H4H 1H6, SAN 369-5646. Tel: 514-765-7172 (Adult serv), 514-765-7173 (Children's serv). *Chef de Div,* Nancy Raymond; Tel: 514-765-7154, E-mail: nancy.raymond@montreal.ca; *Bibliothecaire Responsable,* Susana Martins Fernandes; Tel: 514 765-7125, E-mail: susana.martinsfernandes@ville.montreal.qc.ca; Staff 16 (MLS 2.7, Non-MLS 13.3)
Founded 1975. Circ 132,691
Library Holdings: Audiobooks 518; AV Mats 11,687; Braille Volumes 1; CDs 5,921; DVDs 4,619; Electronic Media & Resources 46; Large Print Bks 315; Music Scores 172; Bk Vols 120,114; Per Subs 291; Talking Bks 518; Videos 4,886
Open Mon, Wed & Thurs 1-9, Tues 10-9, Fri 10-6, Sat & Sun 12-5

JEAN-CORBEIL, 7500 Ave Goncourt, Anjou, H1K 3X9. Tel: 514-493-8260. E-mail: bibliotheque.jean.corbeil@ville.montreal.qc.ca. *Chef de Div,* Magdalena Michalowska; Tel: 514-493-8262, E-mail: mmichalowska@ville.montreal.qc.ca; *Chef de Section,* Véronic Papineau-Archambault; Tel: 514-493-8270, E-mail: veronic.papineau-archambault@ville.montreal.qc.ca; Staff 14.5 (MLS 4, Non-MLS 10.5)
Founded 1984. Circ 204,399
Library Holdings: Audiobooks 456; AV Mats 9,429; Braille Volumes 2; CDs 4,512; DVDs 4,302; Large Print Bks 1,119; Music Scores 369; Bk Vols 96,738; Per Subs 188; Talking Bks 456; Videos 4,322
Open Mon-Fri 12-8, Sat 9:30-5, Sun 11-5

LA PETITE-PATRIE, 6707 Ave de Lorimier, H2G 2P8, SAN 328-8811. Tel: 514-872-1732 (Children's serv), 514-872-1733 (Adult serv). *Chef de Div,* Brigitte Lefebvre; Tel: 514-868-3880; *Chef de Section,* Émilie Paquin; Tel: 514-872-3910, E-mail: emilie.paquin@ville.montreal.qc.ca; Staff 10.4 (MLS 2.8, Non-MLS 7.6)
Founded 1987. Circ 189,392
Library Holdings: Audiobooks 527; AV Mats 9,282; Braille Volumes 1; CDs 3,660; DVDs 4,526; Electronic Media & Resources 19; Large Print Bks 535; Music Scores 66; Bk Vols 69,339; Per Subs 278; Talking Bks 527; Videos 4,653
Open Mon 1-6, Tues 1-8, Wed 10-8, Thurs 10-7, Fri 10-6, Sat & Sun 10-5

LANGELIER, 6473 rue Sherbrooke Est, H1N 1C5, SAN 369-3597. Tel: 514-872-2640 (Adult Serv), 514-872-4227 (Children's Serv). *Chef de Div,* Frederic Steben; *Chef de Section,* Jessica Lecavalier; Tel: 514-872-1529, E-mail: jessica.lecavalier@ville.montreal.qc.ca; Staff 15.1 (MLS 3.2, Non-MLS 11.9)
Founded 1980. Circ 271,992
Library Holdings: Audiobooks 462; AV Mats 9,853; Braille Volumes 2; CDs 2,603; DVDs 6,046; Electronic Media & Resources 53; Large Print Bks 286; Microforms 1; Music Scores 6; Bk Vols 52,358; Per Subs 249; Talking Bks 462; Videos 6,146
Open Mon, Sat & Sun 10-5, Tues & Wed 12-8, Thur & Fri 10-6

LE PREVOST, 7355 Ave Christophe-Colomb, H2R 2S5, SAN 322-6387. Tel: 514-872-1523 (Adult Serv), 514-872-1526 (Children's Serv). *Chef de Div,* Andréanne Leclerc; Tel: 514-868-3444, E-mail: andreanne.leclerc-marceau@ville.montreal.qc.ca; *Chef de Section,* Marc-André Huot; Tel: 514-872-1525, E-mail: marc-andre.huot@ville.montreal.qc.ca; Staff 16.2 (MLS 2.9, Non-MLS 13.3)
Founded 1983. Circ 324,316
Library Holdings: Audiobooks 455; AV Mats 5,172; Braille Volumes 1; CDs 1,056; DVDs 3,376; Electronic Media & Resources 77; Large Print Bks 237; Microforms 1; Music Scores 16; Bk Vols 83,779; Per Subs 365; Talking Bks 455; Videos 3,435
Open Mon 1-6, Tues 12-8, Wed 10-8, Thurs & Fri 10-6, Sat & Sun 10-5

L'ILE-BIZARD, 500 montee de l'Eglise, L'Ile-Bizard, H9C 1G9. Tel: 514-620-6257. *Bibliothecaire de Liaison,* Sophie David; Tel: 514-620-6257, E-mail: sophie.david@montreal.ca; Staff 6 (MLS 1, Non-MLS 5)
Founded 1971. Circ 101,325
Function: 24/7 Electronic res, 24/7 Online cat, Activity rm, Art exhibits, Bks on CD, Children's prog, Computers for patron use, Digital talking bks, Equip loans & repairs, Free DVD rentals, Games, ILL available, Internet access, Music CDs, Online cat, OverDrive digital audio bks, Photocopying/Printing, Preschool reading prog, Prog for adults, Prog for children & young adult, Story hour, Study rm, Summer reading prog, Wheelchair accessible, Workshops
Open Tues-Thurs 10-7, Fri 10-6, Sat & Sun 11-4

L'OCTOGONE, 1080 Ave Dollard, LaSalle, H8N 2T9, SAN 319-6674. Tel: 514-367-6376. *Chef de Div,* Melanie Poitras; *Chef de Section,* Christiane Côté; Tel: 514-367-6000, Ext 6385, E-mail: christiane.cote@ville.montreal.qc.ca; Staff 31.5 (MLS 7, Non-MLS 24.5)
Founded 1984. Circ 468,269
Library Holdings: Audiobooks 957; AV Mats 19,756; CDs 5,954; DVDs 12,536; Electronic Media & Resources 79; Large Print Bks 10; Music Scores 49; Bk Vols 183,252; Per Subs 1,025; Talking Bks 957; Videos 12,586
Open Mon-Thurs 10-9, Fri-Sun 10-5
Friends of the Library Group

MAISON CULTURELLE ET COMMUNAUTAIRE, 12002 Blvd Rolland, Montreal-Nord, H1G 3W1. Tel: 514-328-4000, Ext 5626. *Chef de Div,* Marie Desilets; E-mail: marie.desilets@montreal.ca; *Chef de Section,* Dominique Riberdy; Tel: 514-328-4000, Ext 4220, E-mail: dominique.riberdy@montreal.ca; Staff 14.1 (MLS 3, Non-MLS 11.1)
Founded 2006. Circ 138,266
Library Holdings: Audiobooks 198; AV Mats 5,799; CDs 1,489; DVDs 3,272; Electronic Media & Resources 7; Large Print Bks 466; Music Scores 401; Bk Vols 52,274; Per Subs 195; Talking Bks 198; Videos 3,385
Open Mon 10-9, Tues-Thurs 9-9, Fri 9-5, Sat & Sun 10-5

MAISONNEUVE, 4120 rue Ontario Est, H1V 1J9, SAN 369-3643. Tel: 514-872-4213 (Adult Serv), 514-872-4214 (Children's Serv). *Chef de Div,* Frederic Steben; *Chef de Section,* Marie-Ève Leprohon; Tel: 514-872-6733, E-mail: marie-eve.leprohon@ville.montreal.qc.ca; Staff 4.5 (MLS 1.5, Non-MLS 3)
Founded 1981. Circ 214,089
Library Holdings: Audiobooks 164; AV Mats 12,294; Braille Volumes 1; CDs 4,174; DVDs 7,961; Electronic Media & Resources 7; Large Print Bks 150; Bk Vols 53,227; Per Subs 105; Talking Bks 164; Videos 7,992
Open Mon, Thurs & Fri 12-7, Tues & Wed 10-9, Sat & Sun 10-5

MARC-FAVREAU, 500 Blvd Rosemont, H2S 1Z3. Tel: 514-872-7272. *Chef de Div,* Brigitte Lefebvre; Tel: 514-868-3880; *Chef de Section,* France Genest; Tel: 514-872-8231, E-mail: france.genest@ville.montreal.qc.ca; Staff 24.6 (MLS 5.3, Non-MLS 19.3)
Founded 2013. Circ 459,860
Library Holdings: Audiobooks 1,210; AV Mats 13,426; Braille Volumes 1; CDs 5,544; DVDs 6,585; Electronic Media & Resources 3; Large Print Bks 1,261; Music Scores 1,188; Bk Vols 126,625; Per Subs 468; Talking Bks 1,210; Videos 6,644
Open Mon 10-7, Tues 10-8, Wed & Thurs 1-8, Fri 1-7, Sat & Sun 10-5

MARIE-UGUAY, 6052 rue Monk, H4E 3H6, SAN 369-3929. Tel: 514-872-4097 (Adult serv), 514-872-4414 (Children's serv). *Chef de Div,* Chantal Beaulieu; Tel: 514-872-3067, E-mail: chantalbeaulieu@montreal.ca; *Chef de Section,* François Bureau-Seixo; Tel: 514-872-2313, E-mail: francois.bureau-seixo@ville.montreal.qc.ca; Staff 10.2 (MLS 2, Non-MLS 8.2)
Founded 1982. Circ 149,216
Library Holdings: Audiobooks 432; AV Mats 9,276; CDs 3,809; DVDs 4,655; Electronic Media & Resources 40; Large Print Bks 31; Microforms 1; Music Scores 46; Bk Vols 55,653; Per Subs 170; Talking Bks 432; Videos 4,828
Open Mon, Thurs & Fri 10-6, Tues 1-8, Wed 10-8, Sat 10-5, Sun 12-5

MERCIER, 8105 rue Hochelaga, H1L 2K9, SAN 370-4580. Tel: 514-872-8738 (Adult serv). *Chef de Div,* Frederic Steben; *Chef de Section,* Sylvie Alix; Tel: 514-872-8737, E-mail: sylvie.alix@ville.montreal.qc.ca; Staff 13.2 (MLS 3, Non-MLS 10.2)

Founded 1989. Circ 218,003
Library Holdings: Audiobooks 295; AV Mats 8,544; CDs 3,055; DVDs 4,674; Electronic Media & Resources 14; Large Print Bks 136; Microforms 1; Music Scores 55; Bk Vols 68,066; Per Subs 245; Talking Bks 295; Videos 4,738
Open Mon, Sat & Sun 10-5, Tues-Thurs 11-7, Fri 10-6

MORDECAI-RICHLER, 5434 Ave du Parc, H2V 4G7, SAN 369-3678. Tel: 514-872-2141 (Adult serv), 514-872-2142 (Children's serv). *Chef de Div,* Marie-Christine Lavallee; Tel: 514-248-0488, E-mail: mariechristine.lavallee@ville.montreal.qc.ca; *Chef de Section,* Abigail Cabrera; Tel: 514-872-9202, E-mail: abigail.cabrera@ville.montreal.qc.ca; Staff 13.4 (MLS 2, Non-MLS 11.4)
Founded 1982. Circ 165,539
Library Holdings: Audiobooks 474; AV Mats 8,088; CDs 2,737; DVDs 4,474; Electronic Media & Resources 34; Large Print Bks 318; Music Scores 21; Bk Vols 70,159; Per Subs 288; Talking Bks 474; Videos 4,506
Open Mon & Thurs 10-6, Tues & Wed 10-8, Fri Noon-6, Sat 10-5, Sun Noon-5

NOTRE-DAME-DE-GRACE, 3755 rue Botrel, H4A 3G8, SAN 328-879X. Tel: 514-872-2377 (Children's serv), 514-872-2398 (Adult serv). *Chef de Div,* Raymond Carrier; Tel: 514-868-4021, E-mail: raymond.carrier@montreal.ca; *Chef de Section,* Robert Chamberot; Tel: 514-872-2935, E-mail: rchamberot@ville.montreal.qc.ca; Staff 10.5 (MLS 2, Non-MLS 8.5)
Founded 1984. Circ 112,760
Library Holdings: Audiobooks 591; AV Mats 4,121; CDs 589; DVDs 3,102; Electronic Media & Resources 26; Large Print Bks 306; Microforms 1; Music Scores 1; Bk Vols 46,660; Per Subs 183; Talking Bks 591; Videos 3,221
Open Mon, Thurs & Fri 10-6, Tues & Wed 12-7:30, Sat & Sun 10-5

PARC-EXTENSION, 421 rue Saint-Roch, H3N 1K2, SAN 378-1828. Tel: 514-872-6071. *Chef de Div,* Marc-Andre Huot; Tel: 514-294-7810, E-mail: marc-andre.huot@montreal.ca; *Chef de Section,* Alex Bourdon-Charest; Tel: 514-872-7416, E-mail: alex.bourdon-charest@ville.montreal.qc.ca; Staff 17.1 (MLS 4.6, Non-MLS 12.5)
Founded 2004. Circ 239,722
Library Holdings: Audiobooks 369; AV Mats 7,897; CDs 2,630; DVDs 3,616; Electronic Media & Resources 40; Music Scores 27; Bk Vols 92,482; Per Subs 221; Talking Bks 369; Videos 3,723
Open Mon & Fri Noon-6, Tues & Wed 10-8:30, Thurs 10-6, Sat 10-5, Sun 11-5

PERE-AMBROISE, 2093 rue de la Visitation, H2L 3C9, SAN 373-5877. Tel: 514-872-1633. *Chef de Div,* Gina Tremblay; Tel: 514-872-0831; *Chef de Section,* Cecile Lointier; Tel: 514-872-9541, E-mail: cecile.lointier@ville.montreal.qc.ca; Staff 11.6 (MLS 2.8, Non-MLS 8.8)
Founded 1941. Circ 132,542
Library Holdings: Audiobooks 304; AV Mats 7,132; Braille Volumes 3; CDs 2,223; DVDs 4,025; Electronic Media & Resources 69; Large Print Bks 187; Music Scores 7; Bk Vols 59,369; Per Subs 132; Talking Bks 304; Videos 4,097
Open Mon 1-6, Tues & Wed 10-8, Thurs & Fri 10-6, Sat 10-5, Sun 12-5

PIERREFONDS, 13555 Blvd Pierrefonds, Pierrefonds, H9A 1A6. Tel: 514-626-1800. *Chef de Div,* Louise Zampini; Tel: 514-258-5593, E-mail: louise.zampini@montreal.ca; *Chef de Section,* Amélie Coutu; Tel: 514-242-0224, E-mail: amelie.coutu@montreal.ca; *Chef de Section,* Sophie Lecoq; Tel: 514-295-2540, E-mail: sophie.lecoq@montreal.ca; Staff 23.6 (MLS 4.5, Non-MLS 19.1)
Founded 1960. Circ 71,156
Library Holdings: Audiobooks 1,194; Braille Volumes 1; CDs 1,767; DVDs 5,963; Large Print Bks 1,804; Music Scores 47; Bk Vols 136,168; Per Subs 5,269
Open Mon 1-9, Tues-Fri 10-9, Sat & Sun 10-5

PLATEAU-MONT-ROYAL, 465 Ave du Mont-Royal E, H2J 1W3, SAN 328-8838. Tel: 514-872-2270 (Adult serv), 514-872-2271 (Children's serv). *Chef de Div,* Marie-Christine Lavallée; Tel: 514-248-0488, E-mail: mariechristine.lavallee@ville.montreal.qc.ca; *Chef de Section,* Abigail Cabrera; Tel: 514-872-9202, E-mail: abigail.cabrera@ville.montreal.qc.ca; Staff 13 (MLS 2, Non-MLS 11)
Founded 1984. Circ 233,564
Library Holdings: Audiobooks 385; AV Mats 5,068; CDs 393; DVDs 3,938; Electronic Media & Resources 19; Large Print Bks 373; Music Scores 661; Bk Vols 58,750; Per Subs 346; Talking Bks 385; Videos 3,993
Open Mon & Fri Noon-6, Tues & Wed 10-8, Thurs Noon-8, Sat 10-5, Sun Noon-5

POINTE-AUX-TREMBLES, 14001 rue Notre-Dame Est, H1A 1T9, SAN 371-344X. Tel: 514-872-6987 (Adult serv), 514-872-9170 (Children's serv). *Chef de Div,* Claude Toupin; Tel: 514-872-2102; *Chef de Section,* Valérie Doucet; Tel: 514-872-0644, E-mail: valerie.doucet@ville.montreal.qc.ca; Staff 13.6 (MLS 4, Non-MLS 9.6)
Founded 1983. Circ 192,025
Library Holdings: Audiobooks 373; AV Mats 3,015; Braille Volumes 1; CDs 376; DVDs 1,999; Electronic Media & Resources 19; Large Print Bks 617; Music Scores 33; Bk Vols 66,951; Per Subs 184; Talking Bks 373; Videos 2,069
Open Mon & Sun Noon-5, Tues & Wed 10-8, Thurs & Fri 10-6, Sat 10-5

RIVIERE-DES-PRAIRIES, 9001 Blvd Perras, H1E 3J7, SAN 376-026X. Tel: 514-872-9425 (Adult serv), 514-872-9494 (Children's serv). *Chef de Div,* Claude Toupin; Tel: 514-872-2102; *Chef de Section,* Valérie Doucet; Tel: 514-872-9386, E-mail: valerie.doucet@ville.montreal.qc.ca; Staff 15 (MLS 4, Non-MLS 11)
Founded 1995. Circ 172,280
Library Holdings: Audiobooks 265; AV Mats 3,736; CDs 286; DVDs 2,490; Electronic Media & Resources 13; Large Print Bks 492; Microforms 1; Music Scores 161; Bk Vols 89,094; Per Subs 255; Talking Bks 265; Videos 2,641
Open Mon & Sun Noon-5, Tues & Wed 10-8, Thurs & Fri 10-6, Sat 10-5

ROBERT-BOURASSA, 41 Ave Saint-Just, Outremont, H2V 4T7, SAN 319-8324. Tel: 514-495-6208. *Chef de Div,* Anne-Marie Poitras; Tel: 514-495-6270, E-mail: apoitras@ville.montreal.qc.ca; *Chef de Section,* Christiane St-Onge; Tel: 514-495-6209, E-mail: christianestonge@ville.montreal.qc.ca; Staff 12.8 (MLS 2.8, Non-MLS 10)
Founded 1965. Circ 180,814
Library Holdings: Audiobooks 716; AV Mats 6,256; CDs 3,595; DVDs 2,152; Electronic Media & Resources 2; Large Print Bks 534; Music Scores 93; Bk Vols 70,956; Per Subs 303; Talking Bks 716; Videos 2,330
Open Mon-Fri 12-8, Sat & Sun 10-5

ROSEMONT, 3131 Blvd Rosemont, H1Y 1M4, SAN 369-3724. Tel: 514-872-4701 (Adult serv), 514-872-6139 (Children's serv). *Chef de Div,* Brigitte Lefebvre; Tel: 514-868-3880; *Chef de Section,* Émilie Paquin; Tel: 514-872-1734, E-mail: emilie.paquin@ville.montreal.qc.ca; *Bibliothecaire Responsable,* Véronique L'Helgouach; Tel: 514-872-4735, E-mail: veroniquelhelgouach@ville.montreal.qc.ca; Staff 11.6 (MLS 2.7, Non-MLS 8.9)
Founded 1951. Circ 340,838
Library Holdings: Audiobooks 418; AV Mats 12,713; CDs 4,769; DVDs 6,528; Electronic Media & Resources 192; Large Print Bks 749; Microforms 1; Music Scores 68; Bk Vols 80,485; Per Subs 339; Talking Bks 418; Videos 6,596
Open Mon & Tues 1-8, Wed & Fri 10-6, Thurs 10-7, Sat & Sun 10-5

SAINT-CHARLES, 2333 rue Mullins, H3K 3E3, SAN 369-3759. Tel: 514-872-3035 (Children's serv), 514-872-3092 (Adult serv). *Chef de Div,* Chantal Beaulieu; Tel: 514-872-3067, E-mail: chantalbeaulieu@montreal.ca; *Chef de Section,* Éliane Béliveau-Cantin; Tel: 514 872-3763, E-mail: eliane.beliveau-cantin@ville.montreal.qc.ca; Staff 9.1 (MLS 2, Non-MLS 7.1)
Founded 1976. Circ 118,421
Library Holdings: Audiobooks 8; AV Mats 6,447; Braille Volumes 2; CDs 2,206; DVDs 3,939; Electronic Media & Resources 6; Large Print Bks 50; Microforms 1; Music Scores 1; Bk Vols 41,717; Per Subs 90; Talking Bks 8; Videos 4,005
Open Mon, Thurs & Fri 9-6, Tues & Wed 1-8, Sat 10-5, Sun 12-5

SAINT-HENRI, 4707 rue Notre-Dame Ouest, H4C 1S9, SAN 369-3694. Tel: 514-872-2879. *Chef de Div,* Chantal Beaulieu; Tel: 514-872-3067, E-mail: chantalbeaulieu@montreal.ca; *Chef de Section,* François Bureau-Seixo; Tel: 514-872-2313, E-mail: francois.bureau-seixo@ville.montreal.qc.ca; Staff 7.3 (MLS 1.5, Non-MLS 5.8)
Founded 1965. Circ 82,098
Library Holdings: Audiobooks 29; AV Mats 4,860; Braille Volumes 1; CDs 1,251; DVDs 3,175; Electronic Media & Resources 2; Large Print Bks 308; Microforms 1; Music Scores 9; Bk Vols 40,257; Per Subs 113; Talking Bks 29; Videos 3,217
Open Mon, Thurs & Fri 10-6, Tues 1-8, Wed 10-8, Sat 10-5, Sun 12-5

SAINT-LEONARD, 8420 Blvd Lacordaire, Saint-Leonard, H1R 3G5, SAN 319-8936. Tel: 514-328-8500, Ext 2. *Chef de Div,* Karyne St-Pierre; Tel: 514-328-8500, Ext 8517, E-mail: karynestpierre@ville.montreal.qc.ca; *Chef de Section,* Valérie Medzalabanleth; Tel: 514-328-8500, Ext 8594, E-mail: valerie.medzalabanleth@ville.montreal.qc.ca; Staff 22.6 (MLS 6, Non-MLS 16.6)
Founded 1966. Circ 311,598
Library Holdings: Audiobooks 334; AV Mats 11,010; Braille Volumes 1; CDs 4,563; DVDs 4,900; Electronic Media & Resources 49; Large Print Bks 1,251; Music Scores 35; Bk Vols 142,804; Per Subs 438; Talking Bks 334; Videos 5,018
Open Mon 1-9, Tues & Wed 10-9, Thurs & Fri 10-6, Sat 10-5, Sun 1-5

SAINT-MICHEL, 7601 rue Francois-Perrault, H2A 3L6, SAN 369-3813. Tel: 514-872-3899 (Adult serv), 514-872-4250 (Children's serv). *Chef de Div,* Marc-Andre Huot; Tel: 5142947810, E-mail: marc-andre.huot@montreal.ca; *Chef de Section,* Hélène Gervais; Tel: 514-872-3910, E-mail: helene.gervais@ville.montreal.qc.ca; Staff 14.5 (MLS 4.1, Non-MLS 10.4)
Founded 1970. Circ 198,179

Library Holdings: Audiobooks 314; AV Mats 5,812; Braille Volumes 4; CDs 2,462; DVDs 2,616; Electronic Media & Resources 12; Large Print Bks 375; Microforms 1; Music Scores 37; Bk Vols 84,886; Per Subs 331; Talking Bks 314; Videos 2,711
Open Mon 12-6, Tues 12-8, Wed 10-8, Thurs & Fri 10-6, Sat 10-5, Sun 11-5

SAINT-PIERRE, 183 rue des Erables, Lachine, H8R 1B1. Tel: 514-634-3471, Ext 826. *Chef de Div,* Dominique Gazo; Tel: 514-634-3471, Ext 304, E-mail: dominique.gazo@ville.montreal.qc.ca; *Chef de Section,* Melanie Bosse; Tel: 514-872-5077, E-mail: melanie.bosse@ville.montreal.qc.ca; Staff 2 (Non-MLS 2)
Founded 1966. Circ 26,035
Library Holdings: Audiobooks 25; AV Mats 2,283; Braille Volumes 1; CDs 656; DVDs 1,346; Large Print Bks 129; Bk Vols 19,615; Per Subs 30; Talking Bks 25; Videos 1,397
Open Mon-Wed 1-9, Thurs-Sat 9-5, Sun 12-5

SAUL-BELLOW, 3100 rue Saint-Antoine, Lachine, H8S 4B8, SAN 319-6755. Tel: 514-872-5080 (Young adult). *Chef de Div,* Dominique Gazo; Tel: 514-634-3471, Ext 304, E-mail: dominique.gazo@ville.montreal.qc.ca; *Chef de Section,* Melanie Bosse; Tel: 514 872-5077, E-mail: melanie.bosse@ville.montreal.qc.ca; Staff 9.3 (MLS 4, Non-MLS 5.3)
Founded 1973. Circ 265,684
Library Holdings: Audiobooks 908; AV Mats 9,801; CDs 4,619; DVDs 4,177; Large Print Bks 1,515; Music Scores 803; Bk Vols 89,792; Per Subs 340; Talking Bks 908; Videos 4,438
Open Mon-Thurs 10-9, Fri-Sun 10-5

VIEUX-SAINT-LAURENT, 1380 rue de l'Eglise, Saint-Laurent, H4L 2H2, SAN 319-8928. Tel: 514-855-6130. *Chef de Div,* Andree Tremblay; Tel: 514-855-6130, Ext 4722, E-mail: andree.tremblay@ville.montreal.qc.ca; *Chef de Section,* Christine Fillion; Tel: 514-855-6130, Ext 4726, E-mail: christine.fillion@ville.montreal.qc.ca; Staff 26.1 (MLS 6.5, Non-MLS 19.6)
Founded 1950. Circ 280,966
Library Holdings: Audiobooks 1,113; AV Mats 19,576; Braille Volumes 2; CDs 7,175; DVDs 10,361; Electronic Media & Resources 3; Large Print Bks 2,431; Bk Vols 91,185; Per Subs 319; Talking Bks 1,113; Videos 10,777
Open Mon, Tues & Wed 10-8, Thurs & Fri 10-6, Sat & Sun 10-5

WILLIAM G BOLL LIBRARY, 110 rue Cartier, Roxboro, H8Y 1G8, SAN 319-8766. Tel: 514-684-8247. *Chef de Div,* Louise Zampini; Tel: 514-626-0397, E-mail: louise.zampini@montreal.ca; *Chef de Section,* Amélie Coutu; Tel: 514-242-0224, E-mail: amelie.coutu@montreal.ca; *Chef de Section,* Sophie Lecoq; Tel: 514-295-2540, E-mail: sophie.lecoq@montreal.ca; Staff 5.6 (MLS 1.3, Non-MLS 4.3)
Founded 1961. Circ 111,521
Library Holdings: Audiobooks 428; Braille Volumes 2; CDs 910; DVDs 2,933; Large Print Bks 423; Bk Vols 35,037; Per Subs 1,869
Open Mon 10-8, Tues-Thurs 1-8, Fri-Sun 10-5

YVES-RYAN, 4740 rue de Charleroi, Montreal-Nord, H1H 1V2, SAN 369-4917. Tel: 514-328-4000, Ext 4135 (Youth), 514-328-4000, Ext 4238 (Adult). E-mail: biblio.mtlnord@montreal.ca. *Chef de Div,* Marie Desilets; E-mail: marie.desilets@montreal.ca; *Chef de Section,* Isabelle Moreau; Tel: 514-328-4000, Ext 5620, E-mail: isabelle.moreau@ville.montreal.qc.ca; Staff 7.3 (Non-MLS 7.3)
Founded 1970. Circ 75,086
Library Holdings: Audiobooks 158; AV Mats 4,617; Braille Volumes 1; CDs 1,622; DVDs 2,271; Electronic Media & Resources 40; Large Print Bks 170; Music Scores 73; Bk Vols 42,008; Per Subs 169; Talking Bks 158; Videos 2,551
Open Mon 10-8, Tues-Thurs 9-8, Fri 9-1, Sat & Sun 12-5
Bookmobiles: 4

L BORDEN LADNER GERVAIS LLP LIBRARY*, 1000 de la Gauchetiere W, Ste 900, H3B 5H4. SAN 325-8408. Tel: 514-954-3159. FAX: 514-954-1905. Web Site: www.blg.com. *Dir, Libr & Info Serv,* Jacquelyn DeGreeve; E-mail: jdegreeve@blg.com; *Res Serv Spec,* Nawal Zaarab; *Acq,* Catherine Dufresne; *Tech Serv,* Danielle Babin; Staff 4 (MLS 2, Non-MLS 2)
Founded 1980
Library Holdings: Bk Titles 8,000; Bk Vols 20,000; Per Subs 350
Automation Activity & Vendor Info: (Acquisitions) Horizon; (Cataloging) Horizon; (Circulation) GRCI; (OPAC) Horizon; (Serials) Horizon
Wireless access
Function: Res libr

G CANADA DEPARTMENT OF JUSTICE MONTREAL HEADQUARTERS LIBRARY*, East Tower, 9th flr, No 200 Quest boul Rene-Levesque W, H2Z 1X4. SAN 326-0046. Tel: 514-283-6674, 514-283-8739. FAX: 514-283-6425. E-mail: information.services@justice.gc.ca. *Libr Tech,* Lynda Cryans; *Libr Tech,* Michael Hamdinero; Staff 2 (MLS 2)
Founded 1982
Library Holdings: Bk Titles 24,000; Per Subs 250
Subject Interests: Law, Law enforcement
Publications: Acquisitions List

SR CANADIAN CENTRE FOR ECUMENISM LIBRARY*, 2715, Chemin de la Cote Sainte-Catherine, H3T 1B6. SAN 319-7131. Tel: 514-937-9176. E-mail: info@oikoumene.ca. Web Site: www.oikoumene.ca/library. *Exec Dir,* Adriana Bara, PhD; E-mail: abara@oikoumene.ca; *Chief Editor,* Mrs Denitsa Tsvetkova; E-mail: denitsa@oikoumene.ca; Staff 3 (MLS 3)
Founded 1963
Library Holdings: CDs 50; DVDs 50; Bk Titles 7,000; Bk Vols 7,250; Per Subs 150
Special Collections: Histoire de l'Eglise (2000 Ans de Christianisme); World Council of Churches, Geneva, Switzerland, Publications
Subject Interests: Bible, Can churches, Christian churches, Ecology, Ecumenism, Ethics, Hist of relig, Inter-church, Interfaith dialogue, Ministry, Native people, Relig freedom, Spirituality, Theol, World relig
Publications: Ecumenism (Quarterly); Oecumenisme (Quarterly)

S CEGEP DU VIEUX MONTREAL LIBRARY*, 255 Ontario St E, H2X 1X6. SAN 328-3119. Tel: 514-982-3437. FAX: 514-982-3448. E-mail: reference@cvm.qc.ca. Web Site: www.cvm.qc.ca/bibliotheque. *Head of Libr,* Ariane Legault-Venne; Tel: 514-982-3437, Ext 2210, E-mail: alegaultvenne@cvm.qc.ca
Library Holdings: Bk Vols 100,000; Per Subs 500
Subject Interests: Art
Open Mon-Thurs 7:45am-9pm, Fri 7:45-5

J CEGEP MARIE-VICTORIN BIBLIOTHEQUE*, 7000 rue Marie-Victorin, Rm G-130, H1G 2J6. SAN 319-7360. Tel: 514-325-0150. Circulation Tel: 514-325-0150, Ext 2311. FAX: 514-328-3830. E-mail: biblio@collegemv.qc.ca. Web Site: www.collegemv.qc.ca. *Coordr,* Pierre Bélanger; E-mail: pierre.belanger@collegemv.qc.ca
Founded 1965
Library Holdings: Bk Vols 80,000
Subject Interests: Behav sci, Humanities, Natural sci, Relig studies, Soc sci
Wireless access
Open Mon-Thurs 7:45am-8:15pm, Fri 7:45-4:30

S CENTRE CANADIEN D'ARCHITECTURE/CANADIAN CENTRE FOR ARCHITECTURE, 1920 rue Baile, H3H 2S6. SAN 322-8878. Tel: 514-939-7000. Circulation Tel: 514-939-7011. FAX: 514-939-7020. E-mail: ref@cca.qc.ca. Web Site: cca.on.worldcat.org/discovery, www.cca.qc.ca. *Head, Coll Access,* Gwen Mayhew; E-mail: gmayhew@cca.qc.ca; Staff 8 (MLS 6, Non-MLS 2)
Founded 1979
Library Holdings: Bk Titles 222,625; Bk Vols 225,258; Per Subs 440
Special Collections: Architectural Toys & Games; Architectural Trade Catalogues; Early Architectual Treatises; English Country House Guides; Fortifications; Frank Lloyd Wright; Italian Regional Histories & City Guides; Portraits of Architects; Russian Architecture; World Fairs
Subject Interests: Archit, Archit hist, Landscape design, Urban planning
Automation Activity & Vendor Info: (Acquisitions) OCLC Worldshare Management Services; (Cataloging) OCLC Worldshare Management Services; (Circulation) OCLC Worldshare Management Services; (OPAC) OCLC Worldshare Management Services; (Serials) OCLC Worldshare Management Services
Wireless access
Partic in OCLC Online Computer Library Center, Inc
Restriction: Open by appt only

L CENTRE D'ACCES A L'INFORMATION JURIDIQUE/LEGAL INFORMATIN ACCESS CENTER*, 480 Saint-Laurent, Bur 503, H2Y 3Y7. SAN 319-7018. Tel: 514-844-2245. Interlibrary Loan Service Tel: 418-525-0057. Administration Tel: 514-866-2049. Toll Free Tel: 866-878-2049, 877-666-2057. FAX: 514-879-8592, 844-596-2245. Interlibrary Loan Service FAX: 418-525-4208. Administration FAX: 514-866-8852. Toll Free FAX: 866-301-8852, 866-879-9470. Web Site: www.caij.qc.ca. *Exec Dir,* Nancy J Trudel; *Dir, Acq,* Chantal Lamarre; *Dir, Info Tech,* Dave Hinse; E-mail: dhinse@caij.qc.ca; *Dir, Libr Network,* Isabelle Pilon; E-mail: ipilon@caij.qc.ca; *Dir, Mkt & Communications,* Vicki Ng-Wan; E-mail: vngwan@caij.qc.ca; *Chief Libr Officer,* Julie Brousseau; E-mail: jbrousseau@caij.qc.ca; Staff 19 (MLS 7, Non-MLS 12)
Founded 1828
Library Holdings: Electronic Media & Resources 26; Microforms 8; Bk Titles 36,709; Bk Vols 287,263; Per Subs 2,036
Subject Interests: Law
Wireless access
Function: 24/7 Electronic res, Activity rm, Bks on CD, Computers for patron use, Distance learning, Doc delivery serv, Electronic databases & coll, ILL available, Internet access, Mail loans to mem, Microfiche/film & reading machines, Online cat, Online ref, Outside serv via phone, mail,

e-mail & web, Photocopying/Printing, Ref serv available, Res performed for a fee, Study rm, Wheelchair accessible
Restriction: Authorized patrons, Circ to mem only, Non-circulating of rare bks, Not open to pub

S CENTRE D'ANIMATION, DE DEVELOPPEMENT ET DE RECHERCHE*, 1940 Est Blvd Henri Bourassa, H2B 1S2. SAN 319-7247. Tel: 514-381-8891, Ext 246. Toll Free Tel: 888-381-8891, Ext 241. FAX: 514-381-4086. Web Site: www.cadre21.org. *Dir,* Jacques Cool; Tel: 514-381-8891, Ext 241, E-mail: jacques.cool@cadre21.org; *Librn,* Manon Dufresne; E-mail: dufresnem@feep.qc.ca; Staff 1 (MLS 1)
Founded 1968
Library Holdings: Bk Titles 7,100; Per Subs 40
Subject Interests: Primary educ, Pvt educ, Secondary educ
Automation Activity & Vendor Info: (Cataloging) CDS-ISIS (Unesco)

S CENTRE DE DOCUMENTATION SUR L'EDUCATION DES ADULTES ET LA CONDITION FEMININE*, 469 rue Jean Talon Ouest, bureau 229, H3N 1R4. SAN 323-7052. Tel: 514-876-1180. Toll Free Tel: 866-972-1180 (Canada only). FAX: 514-876-1325. E-mail: info@cdeacf.ca. Web Site: www.cdeacf.ca. *Dir Gen,* Judith Rouan; *Head Librn,* Allison Harvey; Staff 11 (MLS 2, Non-MLS 9)
Founded 1983
Library Holdings: CDs 226; DVDs 199; e-books 1,825; e-journals 82; Electronic Media & Resources 7,623; High Interest/Low Vocabulary Bk Vols 545; Bk Titles 22,562; Spec Interest Per Sub 106; Videos 678
Special Collections: Directory of Researchers & Research in Adult Education & Literacy in Canada; Feminist Archives; Literacy & Adult Basic Education Coll; Organizations Working in Adult Education & Women's Issues
Subject Interests: Adult learning, Adult literacy, Women's studies
Wireless access
Function: 24/7 Online cat, Archival coll, Audio & video playback equip for onsite use, CD-ROM, Distance learning, Doc delivery serv, For res purposes, ILL available, Online cat, Outside serv via phone, mail, e-mail & web, Photocopying/Printing, Ref serv available, Res performed for a fee, Scanner
Publications: Bibliographie sElective; EFA (Bibliographies); Horizon Alpha (Annual report); NetFemmes (Monthly bulletin); Pour voir plus loin (Acquisition list)
Partic in ASTED
Open Mon, Tues & Thurs 10-12 & 1-5, Wed 1-5

M CENTRE HOSPITALIER DE L'UNIVERSITE DE MONTREAL*, Hôpital St Luc Library, Documentation Centre, 3840, rue Saint-Urbain, H2W 1T8. SAN 325-5166. Tel: 514-890-8000, Ext 14355. FAX: 514-412-7194. E-mail: biblio.chum@ssss.gouv.qc.ca. Web Site: bibliothequeduchum.ca/index.php. *Mgr,* Diane St-Aubin; Staff 4 (MLS 1, Non-MLS 3)
Library Holdings: Bk Titles 12,200; Per Subs 400
Subject Interests: Alcohol abuse, Drug abuse, Hospital admin
Automation Activity & Vendor Info: (Acquisitions) Koha; (Cataloging) Koha; (Circulation) Koha; (OPAC) Koha; (Serials) Koha
Wireless access
Partic in Association des Bibliothequès de la Sante Affiliees a L'Universite de Montreal

M CENTRE INTEGRE UNIVERSITAIRE DE SANTE ET DE SERVICES SOCIAUX DU CENTRE-SUD-DE-L'ILE-DE-MONTREAL - INSTITUT UNIVERSITAIRE DE GERIATRIE DE MONTREAL*, Medical Library, 4565 Chemin Queen Mary, H3W 1W5. SAN 319-809X. Tel: 514-340-2800, Ext 3262. FAX: 514-340-2815. E-mail: biblio.iugm@ssss.gouv.qc.ca. Web Site: ccsmtl-biblio.ca/fr. *Chief Librn,* Audrey Attia; E-mail: audrey.attia.ccsmtl@ssss.gouv.qc.ca; Staff 2 (MLS 1, Non-MLS 1)
Founded 1947
Library Holdings: Bk Titles 23,000; Per Subs 20
Subject Interests: Aging, Chronic care, Geriatrics, Gerontology, Long term care, Neuroscience, Tech
Wireless access

G CENTRE JEUNESSE DE MONTREAL - INSTITUT UNIVERSITAIRE*, Bibliotheque, 1001 boul de Maisonneuve est, 5ieme etage, H2L 4P9. SAN 325-8270. Tel: 514-896-3396. FAX: 514-896-3483. E-mail: bibliotheque.cjm.ccsmtl@ssss.gouv.qc.ca. *Librn,* Paule Asselin; *Libr Tech,* Jade St-Vincent; *Libr Tech,* David Talbot; Staff 3 (MLS 1, Non-MLS 2)
Library Holdings: AV Mats 1,446; Bk Titles 30,000; Per Subs 80
Subject Interests: Child welfare, Juv delinquency, Youth
Function: For res purposes

GL CHAMBRE DES NOTAIRES DU QUEBEC*, Bibliothèque notariale, 1801 Ave McGill College, Bur 600, H3A 0A7. SAN 328-4832. Tel: 514-879-1793, Ext 5043. FAX: 514-879-1697. E-mail: bibliotheque.notariale@cnq.org. Web Site: www.cnq.org. *Asst Dir,* Sophie Lecoq
Library Holdings: e-journals 13,622; Bk Titles 7,612; Per Subs 190
Subject Interests: Law
Wireless access
Publications: Cours de perfectionnement du notariat (Journal); Entracte (Quarterly); Minute L'Infolettre de la profession (Newsletter); Répertoire de droit/Nouvelle série - Doctrine (Documents); Répertoire de droit/Nouvelle série - Modèles d'actes (Online only); Revue du notariat (Journal)
Open Mon-Fri 8:30-5

M CHU SAINTE-JUSTINE BIBLIOTHEQUE*, 3175 Chemin de la Sainte-Catherine, Bur 5971, H3T 1C5. SAN 319-7565. Tel: 514-345-4931, Ext 4681. FAX: 514-345-4806. E-mail: biblio.hsj@ssss.gouv.qc.ca. Web Site: enseignement.chusj.org/fr/bibliotheques. *Head Librn,* Philippe Dodin; Staff 6 (MLS 2, Non-MLS 4)
Founded 1936
Library Holdings: AV Mats 2,700; e-journals 230; Bk Vols 9,500; Per Subs 420
Special Collections: Mediatheque, AV mat; Parent Information Resources
Subject Interests: Child, Gynecology, Neonatology, Pediatric nursing, Pediatrics
Automation Activity & Vendor Info: (Acquisitions) Koha; (Cataloging) Koha; (Circulation) Koha; (OPAC) Koha; (Serials) Koha
Wireless access
Publications: Guide Info-Famille (2008) (Reference guide)
Open Mon-Thurs 8-5, Fri 8-4

M CHUM, HOPITAL NOTRE-DAME*, Bibliothèque du CHUM, 1000 Saint-Denis, Pavillon B, porte B1.8021, H2X 0C1. SAN 319-7964. Tel: 514-890-8000, Ext 32835. E-mail: biblio.chum@ssss.gouv.qc.ca. Web Site: www.bibliothequeduchum.ca. *Chief Librn,* Position Currently Open
Founded 1930
Library Holdings: Bk Vols 30,000; Per Subs 286
Subject Interests: Allied sci, Med
Automation Activity & Vendor Info: (Acquisitions) Infor Library & Information Solutions; (Cataloging) Infor Library & Information Solutions; (Circulation) Infor Library & Information Solutions; (Course Reserve) Infor Library & Information Solutions; (OPAC) Infor Library & Information Solutions; (Serials) Infor Library & Information Solutions
Partic in Association des Bibliotheques de la Sante Affiliees a L'Universite de Montreal

S CINEMATHEQUE QUEBECOISE*, Mediatheque Guy-L-Cote, 335 boul de Maisonneuve est, H2X 1K1. SAN 324-5209. Tel: 514-842-9768, Ext 262. FAX: 514-842-1816. E-mail: mediatheque@cinematheque.qc.ca. Web Site: www.cinematheque.qc.ca/en/mediatheque. *Head of Libr,* Élisabeth Meunier; E-mail: emeunier@cinematheque.qc.ca; *Head, Coll Serv,* Marina Gallet; E-mail: mgallet@cinematheque.qc.ca; Staff 6 (MLS 1, Non-MLS 5)
Founded 1970
Library Holdings: Bk Titles 45,000; Per Subs 450
Subject Interests: Cinema, Television, Video
Publications: Reperes Bibliographiques (irregular)
Open Tues-Fri 9-12:30 & 1:30-5

G CNESST*, Centre d'information scientifique et technique, 1199 rue de Bleury, 4th Flr, H3B 3J1. SAN 324-7430. Tel: 844-838-0808. E-mail: centreist@cnesst.gouv.qc.ca. Web Site: centredoc.cnesst.gouv.qc.ca.
Founded 1979
Library Holdings: AV Mats 1,500; Bk Titles 60,000; Bk Vols 120,000; Per Subs 200
Subject Interests: Occupational health, Occupational safety
Automation Activity & Vendor Info: (Acquisitions) BiblioMondo; (Cataloging) BiblioMondo; (Circulation) BiblioMondo; (OPAC) BiblioMondo; (Serials) BiblioMondo
Publications: Bibliographies sélectives; Bulletin de veille; Liste des Nouvelles Acquisitions; Thesaurus

C COLLEGE DE BOIS-DE-BOULOGNE BIBLIOTHEQUE*, 10555, ave de Bois-de-Boulogne, H4N 1L4. SAN 372-8404. Tel: 514-332-3000, Ext 6460. FAX: 514-332-0083. E-mail: bibliotheque@bdeb.qc.ca, info@bdeb.qc.ca. Web Site: www.bdeb.qc.ca/services-aux-etudiants/bibliotheque. *Dir,* Guillaume D'Amours; Tel: 514-332-3000, Ext 7540, E-mail: guillaume.damours@bdeb.qc.ca; Staff 1 (MLS 1)
Founded 1968. Enrl 2,800
Library Holdings: DVDs 522; Electronic Media & Resources 16; Bk Titles 47,811; Bk Vols 56,328; Per Subs 125
Automation Activity & Vendor Info: (Acquisitions) BiblioMondo; (Cataloging) BiblioMondo; (Circulation) BiblioMondo; (Course Reserve) BiblioMondo; (OPAC) BiblioMondo; (Serials) BiblioMondo
Wireless access
Open Mon-Thurs 7:30-6, Fri 7:30-5

C COLLEGE DE MAISONNEUVE CENTRE DES MEDIAS, Gabriel-Allard Bibliotheque, 3800 Est rue Sherbrooke E, 4th Flr, Rm D-4690, H1X 2A2. SAN 319-731X. Tel: 514-254-7131. Circulation Tel: 514-254-7131, Ext 4221. Reference Tel: 514-254-7131, Ext 4733. E-mail: biblio@cmaisonneuve.qc.ca. Web Site: www.cmaisonneuve.qc.ca/bibliotheque. *Librn,* Guillaume Cloutier; Tel: 514-254-7131, Ext 4279, E-mail: gcloutier@cmaisonneuve.qc.ca; *Librn,* Mario Paille; Tel: 514-254-7131, Ext 4770, E-mail: mpaille@cmaisonneuve.qc.ca; Staff 3 (MLS 3)
Founded 1952. Enrl 7,082
Library Holdings: e-books 107,200; Electronic Media & Resources 20; Bk Vols 95,000; Per Subs 75
Special Collections: Canadian and Provincial
Automation Activity & Vendor Info: (Acquisitions) SirsiDynix; (Cataloging) SirsiDynix; (Circulation) SirsiDynix; (OPAC) SirsiDynix; (Serials) SirsiDynix
Wireless access
Function: AV serv, Res libr
Publications: Fiche Technique d Utilisation De Canadian Reference Center; Guide cle Recherche du Catalogue; Guide de Recherche E-STAT; Guide de Recherche Internet; Guide de Recherche sur Biblio Branchee; Guide de Recherche sur Repere; Guide des Cederoms; Guide pour citer un Document electronique; Guide pour citer un document paper ou audiovisuel; List of Periodicals; Methodologie de Recherche; Rapport Annuel

C COLLEGE DE MONTREAL BIBLIOTHEQUE*, 1931 rue Sherbrooke Ouest, H3H 1E3. SAN 319-7328. Tel: 514-933-7397, Ext 291. FAX: 514-933-3225. E-mail: cdm@college-montreal.qc.ca. Web Site: www.college-montreal.qc.ca. *Documentation Tech,* Vanina Delmonaco; E-mail: delmonacov@college-montreal.qc.ca
Founded 1961
Library Holdings: Bk Vols 10,000
Special Collections: Canadian & French History (secondary school)
Subject Interests: Secondary sch educ
Wireless access
Open Mon-Fri 8-4:30

J COLLEGE DE ROSEMONT (CEGEP) BIBLIOTHEQUE*, 6400 16th Ave, H1X 2S9. SAN 319-7336. Tel: 514-376-1620, Ext 7265. E-mail: biblio@crosemont.qc.ca. Web Site: biblio.crosemont.qc.ca. *Librn,* Josee Corriveau; E-mail: jcorriveau@crosemont.qc.ca; *Acq,* Anne Beaudoin; E-mail: abeaudoin@crosemont.qc.ca; *Cat,* Christian Alaire; E-mail: calaire@crosemont.qc.ca; *User Serv,* Alexis Havard-Trepanier; E-mail: ahtrepanier@crosemont.qc.ca
Founded 1969
Library Holdings: AV Mats 4,413; Bk Titles 60,000; Per Subs 60
Wireless access
Open Mon-Thurs 8-6:30, Fri 8-4:30

M COLLEGE DES MEDECINS DU QUEBEC, Centre de Documentation, 3500-1250 Rene-Levesque Blvd W, H3B 0G2. SAN 319-8049. Tel: 514-933-4441. FAX: 514-933-3276. E-mail: gda@cmq.org. Web Site: www.cmq.org. *Archivist,* Marie-Eve Barsalou; Tel: 514-933-4441, Ext 5308, E-mail: mbarsalou@cmq.org
Founded 1961
Subject Interests: Health serv, Med educ, Med ethics
Restriction: Not open to pub

S COLLEGE JEAN-DE-BREBEUF*, Bibliotheque de Niveau Collegial, 5625 rue Decelles, H3T 1W4. SAN 319-7344. Tel: 514-342-9342, Ext 5346. FAX: 514-342-1558. E-mail: bibliocol@brebeuf.qc.ca. Web Site: www.brebeuf.qc.ca/bibliotheques. *Head of Libr, Librn,* Violaine Fortier; Tel: 514-342-9342, Ext 5374, E-mail: violaine.fortier@Brebeuf.qc.ca; *Circ,* Marie-Josee Emard; Tel: 514-342-9342, Ext 5361; Staff 7 (MLS 3, Non-MLS 4)
Founded 1958. Enrl 1,550; Fac 116
Library Holdings: Bk Titles 63,796; Bk Vols 70,338; Per Subs 325
Subject Interests: Can hist, Cinema, Fine arts, Philos, Polit sci
Open Mon-Thurs 8-7, Sat 8-5

C COLLEGE LASALLE*, Centre de Documentation, 2000 Saint Catherine St W, 4th Flr, H3H 2T2. SAN 323-9101. Tel: 514-939-2006, Ext 4503. Toll Free Tel: 800-363-3541. E-mail: centredoc@collegelasalle.com. Web Site: centredoc.clasalle.com. *Coordr,* Position Currently Open; *AV Tech,* Position Currently Open; Tel: 514-939-2006, Ext 4251; *Libr Tech,* Sylvie Auger; Tel: 514-939-2006, Ext 4389, E-mail: sylvie.auger@collegelasalle.com; *Libr Tech,* Miriam Bouchdoug; Tel: 514-939-2006, Ext 4439, E-mail: miriam.bouchdoug@collegelasalle.com; Staff 4 (MLS 1, Non-MLS 3)
Enrl 2,000; Highest Degree: Master
Library Holdings: AV Mats 1,500; Bk Titles 10,000; Bk Vols 12,000; Per Subs 125
Subject Interests: Computer sci, Fashion, Hotel, Mgt, Tourism
Wireless access
Publications: New Acquisitions List
Open Tues-Thurs 7:30-6:30 (Fall-Winter); Mon-Fri 9-5 (Summer)

C COLLEGE NOTRE DAME LIBRARY*, 3791 Queen Marie Rd, H3V 1A8. SAN 319-7379. Tel: 514-739-3371. FAX: 514-739-4833. E-mail: info@collegenotredame.com. Web Site: collegenotredame.com/services-a-leleve/bibliotheque.
Library Holdings: Bk Titles 50,000; Per Subs 110
Open Mon-Fri 8-7

C COLLEGE O'SULLIVAN LIBRARY*, 1191 de la Montagne, H3G 1Z2. SAN 323-6501. Tel: 514-866-4622, Ext 117. Toll Free Tel: 800-621-8055. FAX: 514-866-0668. Web Site: www.osullivan.edu. *Libr Coord,* Soukaina Kadouri; E-mail: skadouri@osullivan.edu
Founded 1976. Enrl 500; Fac 10
Library Holdings: Bk Titles 3,200; Bk Vols 5,000; Per Subs 23
Open Mon-Fri 8:30-6

C CONCORDIA UNIVERSITY LIBRARIES*, Webster Library, 1400 de Maisonneuve Blvd W, LB 2, H3G 1M8. (Mail add: 1455 de Maisonneuve Blvd W, LB 2, H3G 1M8), SAN 369-2221. Tel: 514-848-2424, Ext 7777. Interlibrary Loan Service Tel: 514-848-2424, Ext 7716. Administration Tel: 514-848-2424, Ext 7695. Information Services Tel: 514-848-2424, Ext 7706. FAX: 514-848-2882. Interlibrary Loan Service FAX: 514-848-2801. Web Site: library.concordia.ca. *Univ Librn,* Dr Guylaine Beaudry; E-mail: guylaine.beaudry@concordia.ca; *Assoc Univ Librn, Coll & Serv,* Pat Riva; Tel: 514-848-2424, Ext 5255, E-mail: pat.riva@concordia.ca; *Assoc Univ Librn, Info Tech & Syst,* Jean-Marc Edwards; Tel: 514-848-2424, Ext 7732, E-mail: jean-marc.edwards@concordia.ca; *Assoc Univ Librn, Learning & Teaching,* Dianne Cmor; Tel: 514-848-2424, Ext 7693, E-mail: dianne.cmor@concordia.ca; *Mgr, Budget & Fac,* Alexander Konyari; Tel: 514-848-2424, Ext 7761, E-mail: alex.konyari@concordia.ca; Staff 40 (MLS 35, Non-MLS 5)
Founded 1974. Highest Degree: Doctorate
Library Holdings: CDs 41,992; DVDs 5,599; e-books 331,762; Microforms 1,305,078; Music Scores 3,609; Bk Titles 1,668,267; Bk Vols 1,840,355; Per Subs 63,686
Special Collections: Adrien Arcand Coll; Christopher Fry's Works; Concordia Theses & MBA Papers; Gay & Lesbian Coll; Irving Layton Coll; James Card Coll; Peter Desbarats Coll; Quinn Coll; René Balcer Archives. Canadian and Provincial
Subject Interests: Admin, Arts, Commerce, Computer sci, Engr, Fine arts, Sci
Automation Activity & Vendor Info: (Cataloging) Innovative Interfaces, Inc; (Circulation) Innovative Interfaces, Inc; (ILL) Innovative Interfaces, Inc; (OPAC) Innovative Interfaces, Inc
Wireless access
Partic in Bureau de cooperation Interuniversitaire; Canadian Association of Research Libraries; Canadian Research Knowledge Network

Departmental Libraries:

COUNSELLING & DEVELOPMENT, CAREER RESOURCE CENTRE, Henry F Hall Bldg, 1455 de Maisonneuve Blvd W, H-440, H3G 1M8. Tel: 514-848-2424, Ext 3556. FAX: 514-848-4534. Web Site: concordia.ca/students/success/resource-centre. *Coordr,* Ann McLaughlin; Staff 2 (MLS 2)
Founded 1950. Enrl 32,530; Fac 2,000; Highest Degree: Doctorate
Library Holdings: CDs 50; DVDs 80; Bk Titles 2,749; Per Subs 30; Spec Interest Per Sub 22; Videos 30
Special Collections: Disabled, Women & Labour
Subject Interests: Career planning, Educ planning, Financial aid, Job hunting techniques, Travel
Automation Activity & Vendor Info: (Acquisitions) FileMaker; (Cataloging) FileMaker; (Circulation) FileMaker; (OPAC) FileMaker
Function: CD-ROM, Computers for patron use, Internet access, Ref serv available, Telephone ref
Publications: Acquisitions List
Restriction: Access at librarian's discretion, Open to pub for ref & circ; with some limitations, Open to students, fac & staff

FACULTY OF FINE ARTS SLIDE LIBRARY, 1395 Rene Levesque Blvd W, H3G 2M5. (Mail add: VA Bldg, Rm VA433, 1455 de Maisonneuve Blvd W, H3G 1M8), SAN 370-9183. *Art Librn,* John Latour; Tel: 514-848-2424, Ext 7811, E-mail: john.latour@concordia.ca; Staff 1 (Non-MLS 1)
Founded 1969. Highest Degree: Doctorate
Library Holdings: AV Mats 300,000
Special Collections: Canadian Sculpture, Mid-19th & 20th Century; Quebec Stained Glass
Subject Interests: 20th Century Can art, Archit, Art hist, Ceramics, Contemporary art hist, Fibres
Open Mon-Thurs 8:15-6, Fri 8:15-4
Restriction: Open to fac, students & qualified researchers

VANIER LIBRARY, 7141 Sherbrooke St W, H4B 1R6. Tel: 514-848-2424, Ext 7766. Circulation Tel: 514-848-2424, Ext 7770. Web Site: library.concordia.ca/locations/vanier.php. *Head of Libr,* Danielle Dennie; Tel: 514-848-2424, Ext 7725, E-mail: danielle.dennie@concordia.ca
Open Mon-Thurs 9-9, Fri 9-5, Sat & Sun 10-5

S CONSERVATOIRE DE MUSIQUE DE MONTREAL BIBLIOTHEQUE*, 4750 Ave Henri-Julien, 3rd Flr, H2T 2C8. SAN 369-2167. Tel: 514-873-4031. Interlibrary Loan Service Tel: 514-873-4031, Ext 248. FAX: 514-873-4601. E-mail: cmm.bib@conservatoire.gouv.qc.ca. Web Site: biblio.cmadq.gouv.qc.ca. *Librn,* Catherine Jolicoeur; Tel: 514 873-4031, Ext 261, E-mail: catherine.jolicoeur@conservatoire.gouv.qc.ca; *Libr Tech,* Anjela Rousiouk; Tel: 514-873-4031, Ext 250, E-mail: anjela.rousiouk@conservatoire.gouv.qc.ca; Staff 6 (MLS 1, Non-MLS 5)
Founded 1942. Highest Degree: Master
Library Holdings: Per Subs 81
Special Collections: Music (Cooper Coll, Arthur Garami Coll, Jean Deslauriers Coll); Scores & Manuscripts of the 16th, 17th & 18th Centuries; Wilfrid Pelletier Coll
Subject Interests: Analysis, Chamber music, Composition, Hist, Opera, Orchestra, Theory
Automation Activity & Vendor Info: (Acquisitions) BiblioMondo; (Cataloging) BiblioMondo; (Circulation) BiblioMondo; (OPAC) BiblioMondo; (Serials) BiblioMondo
Publications: Foldings on Research Strategy; Foldings on Service; List of New Acquisitions
Open Mon-Thurs 8:50-7, Fri 8:50-5:30, Sat Noon-4:30

L DE GRANDPRE CHAIT LIBRARY, 800 Blvd Rene-Levesque, 26th Flr, H3B 1X9. SAN 375-3670. Tel: 514-878-4311. FAX: 514-878-4333. Web Site: www.dgchait.com/en/contact. *Libr Coord,* Audreanne Noel; E-mail: anoel@dgchait.com; Staff 2 (MLS 1, Non-MLS 1)
Founded 1928
Library Holdings: Bk Titles 5,000
Wireless access
Partic in Muse; Soquiz
Restriction: Not open to pub, Private libr

C ECOLE DE TECHNOLOGIE SUPERIEURE (SERVICE DE LA BIBLIOTHEQUE), 1100 rue Notre-Dame Ouest, H3C 1K3. SAN 375-488X. Tel: 514-396-8960. Interlibrary Loan Service Tel: 514-396-8585. Reference Tel: 514-396-8591. FAX: 514-396-8633. Reference E-mail: bibref@etsmtl.ca. Web Site: bibliotheque.etsmtl.ca/en/accueil. *Dir,* Vicky Gagnon; E-mail: vicky.gagnon@etsmtl.ca; *Librn,* Diane Girard; E-mail: diane.girard@etsmtl.ca; *Acq/Cat Tech,* Anne Goyette; E-mail: anne.goyette@etsmtl.ca; Staff 16 (MLS 9, Non-MLS 7)
Founded 1974. Enrl 7,708; Fac 282; Highest Degree: Doctorate
Library Holdings: AV Mats 410; e-books 74,000; Electronic Media & Resources 1,905; Bk Vols 74,000; Per Subs 25,000
Special Collections: Rapports techniques de l'ETS
Subject Interests: Engr
Wireless access
Publications: Biblio-listes (Reference guide)
Open Mon-Sun 8:30am-10pm

L FASKEN MARTINEAU DUMOULIN LLP, Knowledge Services, 800 Victoria Sq, Ste 3500, H4Z 1E9. SAN 372-7424. Tel: 514-397-7400. Toll Free Tel: 800-361-6266 (Ontario & Quebec only). FAX: 514-397-7600. Web Site: www.fasken.com. *Mgr,* Esther Belanger; E-mail: ebelanger@fasken.com; Staff 6 (MLS 4, Non-MLS 2)
Founded 1907
Library Holdings: e-journals 28; Electronic Media & Resources 139; Bk Titles 8,493; Per Subs 428; Videos 10
Special Collections: Canadian and Provincial
Function: Res libr
Open Mon-Fri 8-6
Restriction: Mem only

M FEDERATION DES MEDECINS SPECIALISTES DU QUEBEC BIBLIOTHEQUE*, Two Complexe Desjardins, Ste 3000, H5B 1G8. (Mail add: CP 216 Succ Desjardins, H5B 1G8), SAN 372-9028. Tel: 514-350-5000. FAX: 514-350-5100. E-mail: documentation@fmsq.org. Web Site: www.fmsq.org. *Librn,* Angele L'Heureux
Library Holdings: e-books 4,000; Bk Vols 5,000; Per Subs 150
Subject Interests: Med
Restriction: Staff use only

S FEDERATION DES TRAVAILLEURS ET TRAVAILLEUSES DU QUEBEC, Centre de Documentation, 565 Cremazie Blvd E, 12th Flr, H2M 2W3. SAN 373-7322. Tel: 514-383-8000. Toll Free Tel: 877-897-0057. FAX: 514-383-8000. E-mail: info@ftq.qc.ca. Web Site: ftq.qc.ca/centre-documentation-3. Staff 1 (MLS 1)
Founded 1957
Library Holdings: AV Mats 480; CDs 81; DVDs 24; Bk Titles 11,000; Per Subs 74; Videos 375
Subject Interests: Economy, Labor, Soc sci, Unions
Restriction: Non-circulating, Open by appt only

C HEC MONTREAL LIBRARY*, 3000, chemin de la Cote-Sainte-Catherine, H3T 2A7. SAN 319-745X. Tel: 514-340-6220. Interlibrary Loan Service Tel: 514-340-6230. Reference Tel: 514-340-3851. FAX: 514-340-5639. E-mail: biblio.info@hec.ca. Web Site: www.hec.ca/biblio. *Dir,* Bernard Bizimana; Tel: 514-340-6689, E-mail: bernard.bizimana@hec.ca; *Librn,* Caroline Archambault; Tel: 514-340-6221, E-mail: caroline.archambault@hec.ca; *Librn,* Daphnee Belizaire; E-mail: daphnee.belizaire@hec.ca; *Digital Initiatives Librn,* Jean-Yves Cote; Tel: 514-340-3657, E-mail: jean-yves.cote@hec.ca; *Systems/Technical Processing Mgmt,* Cinzia Di Labio; Tel: 514-340-6215, E-mail: cinzia.di-labio@hec.ca; Staff 8 (MLS 8)
Founded 1910. Enrl 11,000; Fac 240; Highest Degree: Doctorate
Library Holdings: AV Mats 14,737; e-books 219,302; Electronic Media & Resources 52,230; Microforms 17,101; Bk Titles 123,221; Bk Vols 366,280; Per Subs 1,050
Subject Interests: Acctg for bus mgt, Bus admin, Distribution mgt, Econ, Electronic commerce, Financial mgt, Info syst, Mgt, Mkt, Operations mgt, Production mgt, Retail mgt
Automation Activity & Vendor Info: (Acquisitions) SirsiDynix; (Cataloging) SirsiDynix; (Circulation) SirsiDynix; (ILL) Fretwell-Downing; (OPAC) SirsiDynix; (Serials) SirsiDynix
Function: Doc delivery serv, ILL available, Internet access, Ref serv available
Open Mon-Thurs 8am-11:30pm, Fri 8am-10pm, Sat & Sun 10-10

M HOPITAL HOTEL-DIEU DU CHUM*, Centre de Documentation, 3840 rue St-Urbain, H2W 1T8. SAN 319-7530. Tel: 514-890-8000, Ext 35867. Reference Tel: 514-890-8000, Ext 14355. Administration Tel: 514-890-8000, Ext 14269. E-mail: biblio.chum@ssss.gouv.qc.ca. Web Site: bibliothequeduchum.ca. *Dir,* Diane St-Aubin; E-mail: diane.st-aubin.chum@ssss.gouv.qc.ca; *Acq,* Thuy Le; E-mail: biblio.admin.chum@ssss.gouv.qc.ca; *Doc Delivery,* Bin Chen; E-mail: biblio.chum@ssss.gouv.qc.ca; Staff 3 (MLS 1, Non-MLS 2)
Founded 1947
Library Holdings: e-journals 200; Bk Titles 1,000; Per Subs 200
Subject Interests: Med
Automation Activity & Vendor Info: (ILL) Relais International; (OPAC) Infor Library & Information Solutions
Partic in Association des Bibliotheques de la Sante Affiliees a L'Universite de Montreal
Open Mon-Fri 8:30-4:30

M HOPITAL MAISONNEUVE-ROSEMONT*, Bibliotheque Medicale, 5415 boul de l'Assomption, H1T 2M4. SAN 319-7549. Tel: 514-252-3463. FAX: 514-252-3574. E-mail: biblio.hmr@ssss.gouv.qc.ca. Web Site: biblio-hmr.ca. *Librn,* Guillaume Trottier; E-mail: guillaume.trottier.cemtl@ssss.gouv.qc.ca; *ILL,* Olivier Lafortune; E-mail: olafortune.hmr@ssss.gouv.qc.ca; Staff 2 (MLS 1, Non-MLS 1)
Founded 1955
Library Holdings: CDs 9; DVDs 20; e-books 119; e-journals 206; Electronic Media & Resources 15; Bk Titles 1,982; Bk Vols 2,260; Per Subs 67; Videos 15
Subject Interests: Bone marrow transplant, Family med, Hematology, Immunology, Kidney transplant, Med, Nursing, Oncology, Ophthalmology, Para-nursing, Pediatrics, Psychiat
Automation Activity & Vendor Info: (Acquisitions) BiblioMondo; (Cataloging) BiblioMondo; (Circulation) BiblioMondo; (OPAC) BiblioMondo; (Serials) BiblioMondo
Wireless access
Function: Computers for patron use, Doc delivery serv, Electronic databases & coll, Health sci info serv, ILL available, Photocopying/Printing
Publications: Patients & Family Booklets (Documents)
Partic in Association des Bibliotheques de la Sante Affiliees a L'Universite de Montreal; Consortium des Bibliotheques du RUIS Universite Laval
Restriction: Access at librarian's discretion, Authorized patrons, Clients only, Hospital employees & physicians only, Hospital staff & commun, Lending to staff only, Med & nursing staff, patients & families, Not open to pub

M HOSPITAL SANTA CABRINI*, Centre de Documentation, 5655 est Saint Zotique, H1T 1P7. SAN 324-4032. Tel: 514-252-4897. *Tech Serv,* Josee Berthelette; E-mail: josee.berthelette.santc@ssss.gouv.qc.ca
Library Holdings: AV Mats 50; e-journals 13; Bk Titles 2,170; Per Subs 128
Subject Interests: Emergency med, Family practice, Gynecology, Internal med, Nursing, Obstetrics, Surgery
Restriction: Staff use only

CR INSTITUT DE FORMATION THEOLOGIQUE DE MONTREAL BIBLIOTHEQUE*, 2065, rue Sherbrooke Ouest, H3H 1G6. SAN 326-3991. Tel: 514-935-1169, Ext 220. E-mail: biblio@iftm.ca. Web Site: ifti.ca/bibliotheque. *Librn,* Patrick Dionne; E-mail: pdionne@iftm.ca; Staff 1 (Non-MLS 1)
Founded 1841. Enrl 108; Highest Degree: Master
Library Holdings: CDs 73; DVDs 149; Bk Vols 190,000; Per Subs 700; Videos 357
Special Collections: Patrology Coll
Subject Interests: Philos, Theol
Wireless access
Open Tues & Thurs 12-7, Sat 10-5

M INSTITUT DE READAPTION GINGRAS-LINDSAY-DE-MONTREAL BIBLIOTHEQUE*, Lindsay Pavillon, 2nd Flr, 6363 Hudson Rd, H3S 1M9. SAN 325-8386. Tel: 514-340-2085, Ext 142270. E-mail: biblio.irglm.ccsmtl@ssss.gouv.qc.ca. Web Site: ccsmtl-biblio.ca/fr. *Libr Tech,* Noemie Delarosbil; Staff 1 (Non-MLS 1)
Apr 2016-Mar 2017 Income (CAN) $90,000. Mats Exp (CAN) $30,422, Books (CAN) $2,600, Presv (CAN) $350. Sal (CAN) $52,918 (Prof (CAN) $52,918)
Library Holdings: CDs 16; DVDs 21; e-books 455; e-journals 14; Bk Vols 3,264; Per Subs 4
Subject Interests: Neuropsychology, Nursing, Occupational therapy, Phys therapy, Physiatry, Rehabilitation
Wireless access
Partic in Association des Bibliotheques de la Sante Affiliees a L'Universite de Montreal
Open Mon-Fri 8:30-12 & 1-4:30

M INSTITUT UNIVERSITAIRE DE SANTE MENTALE DE MONTREAL*, Centre de Documentation, Pavilion Bedard, 3rd Flr, Rm BE-316-34, 7401 Hochelaga St, H1N 3M5. SAN 319-7697. Tel: 514-251-4000, Ext 2964. FAX: 514-251-0270. E-mail: centrededocumentation.iusmm@ssss.gouv.qc.ca. Web Site: www.iusmm.ca/centre-de-documentation.html. *Librn Spec,* Marie Desilets; Tel: 514-251-4000, Ext 2332, E-mail: mdesilets.iusmm@ssss.gouv.qc.ca. Subject Specialists: *Psychiat,* Marie Desilets; Staff 4 (MLS 1, Non-MLS 3)
Founded 1948
Library Holdings: Bk Vols 6,000; Per Subs 100
Subject Interests: Psychiat
Open Mon-Fri 8:30-4

S INSTITUTE PHILIPPE PINEL DE MONTREAL BIBLIOTHEQUE*, Centre de Documentation Jacques-Talbot, 10905 Henri Bourassa Blvd E, H1C 1H1. SAN 319-7662. Tel: 514-648-8461, Ext 557. FAX: 514-881-3706. Web Site: www.pinel.qc.ca/centre-de-documentation-jacques-talbot. *Librn,* Pan Hongyue; E-mail: hongyue.pan.ippm@ssss.gouv.qc.ca
Founded 1970
Library Holdings: Bk Titles 8,000; Per Subs 130
Subject Interests: Criminology, Legal psychiat, Psychiat
Restriction: Open by appt only

SR INTERNATIONAL INSTITUTE OF INTEGRAL HUMAN SCIENCES LIBRARY*, 1974 de Maisonneuve W, H3H 1K5. (Mail add: PO Box 1387, Sta H, H3G 2N3), SAN 329-224X. Tel: 514-937-8359. FAX: 514-937-5380. E-mail: info@iiihs.org. Web Site: www.iiihs.org/IIIHS_2.html. *Library Contact,* Dr Marilyn Rossner
Founded 1976. Enrl 200; Fac 10
Library Holdings: Bk Vols 10,000
Subject Interests: Comparative relig, Consciousness studies, Healing
Wireless access
Function: Ref serv available, Res libr
Open Mon-Fri 9-9

S ITALIAN CULTURAL INSTITUTE OF MONTREAL LA BIBLIOTHEQUE*, 1200 Dr Penfield Ave, H3A 1A9. SAN 328-3941. Tel: 514-849-3473. FAX: 514-849-2569. E-mail: iicmontreal@esteri.it. Web Site: iicmontreal.esteri.it/iic_montreal/en/la_biblioteca. *Dir,* Francesco D'Arelli; *Coordr,* Barbara Celli; E-mail: cours.iicmontreal@esteri.it
Library Holdings: Bk Titles 6,000; Per Subs 119
Open Mon-Thurs 2-5

S JARDIN BOTANIQUE DE MONTREAL BIBLIOTHEQUE*, 4101, rue Sherbrooke est, H1X 2B2. SAN 329-7748. Tel: 514-872-1824. E-mail: jbm_bibliotheque@montreal.ca. Web Site: bibliojardin.espacepourlavie.ca, espacepourlavie.ca/en/jardin-botanique-library. *Librn,* Ariane L Mathieu; Staff 1 (MLS 1)
Founded 1940
Library Holdings: Bk Vols 30,000; Per Subs 250
Special Collections: Curtis Botanical Illustration Mag, bd per, watercolors; Documentation Center on Japanese Horticulture & Japan
Subject Interests: Botany, Hort, Landscape archit, Urban forestry
Wireless access
Publications: Publications au Jardin Botanique de Montreal
Open Tues & Thurs 9-4:30

M JEWISH GENERAL HOSPITAL*, Health Sciences Library, 3755 Cote Ste Catherine Rd, Rm 200, H3T 1E2. SAN 369-237X. Tel: 514-340-8222, Ext 25927. FAX: 514-340-7552. Web Site: archive.jgh.ca. *Team Leader,* Julia Kleinberg; Tel: 514-340-8222, Ext 22391, E-mail: jkleinberg@jgh.mcgill.ca; *Circ, Libr Tech,* Heather Vesely; Tel: 514-340-8222, Ext 25931, E-mail: heather.vesely.ccomti@ssss.gouv.qc.ca; *Ref & Instruction,* Kendra Johnston; Tel: 514-340-8222, Ext 22453, E-mail: kendr.johnston.ccmti@ssss.gouv.qc.ca; Staff 5 (MLS 2, Non-MLS 3)
Founded 1950
Library Holdings: Bk Titles 47,000; Per Subs 300
Special Collections: Drazin Memorial Library on Judaica & Medical Ethics; Patient & Family Resource Centre Consumer Health Coll
Subject Interests: Clinical med, Hospital admin, Med, Nursing, Nutrition, Phys therapy, Related sci, Speech pathology
Publications: Medical Library Newsletter (Biannually)
Partic in Can-Ole; Canadian Health Libraries Association; Montreal Health Libr Asn
Open Mon-Fri 8:30-4:30
Friends of the Library Group

Branches:

HOPE & COPE LIBRARY, 3755 Cote Ste Catherine Rd, H3T 1E2. Tel: 514-340-8255. FAX: 514-340-8605. *Dir,* Suzanne O'Brien
Library Holdings: Bk Vols 1,000
Special Collections: Palliative; Radiotherapy
Subject Interests: Cancer patients, Families
Open Mon-Fri 8:30-4:30

DR HENRY KRAVITZ LIBRARY-INSTITUTE OF COMMUNITY & FAMILY PSYCHIATRY, 4333 Cote Ste Catherine Rd, H3T 1E4, SAN 322-6360. Tel: 514-340-8210, Ext 5243. FAX: 514-340-8104. E-mail: icfplib.jgh@mail.mcgill.ca. Web Site: www.jgh.ca. *Librn,* Teodora Constantinescu; Staff 1 (MLS 1)
Library Holdings: Bk Vols 2,300
Subject Interests: Psychiat

G LABORATOIRE DE SCIENCES JUDICIAIRES ET DE MEDECINE LEGALE*, Centre de Documentation, Ministere de la Securite Publique Edifice Wilfrid Derome, 1701 rue Parthenais, 12th Flr, H2K 3S7. SAN 326-3762. Tel: 514-873-3301, Ext 61435. FAX: 514-873-4847. E-mail: lsjml-bib@msp.gouv.qc.ca. *Coordr,* Judith Desharnais; E-mail: judith.desharnais@msp.gouv.qc.ca; Staff 2 (MLS 1, Non-MLS 1)
Founded 1968
Library Holdings: e-journals 30; Bk Titles 5,000; Per Subs 70
Special Collections: Dr Wilfrid Derome Coll
Subject Interests: Forensic medicine, Forensic sci
Automation Activity & Vendor Info: (Acquisitions) Inmagic, Inc.; (Cataloging) Inmagic, Inc.; (Media Booking) Inmagic, Inc.; (OPAC) Inmagic, Inc.; (Serials) Inmagic, Inc.
Function: Govt ref serv
Publications: Liste des nouvelles acquisitions (Acquisition list)
Open Mon-Fri 9-12 & 1-3
Restriction: External users must contact libr
Friends of the Library Group

G LOTO-QUEBEC*, Documentation Centre, 500 Sherbrooke W, H3A 3G6. SAN 326-2979. Tel: 514-282-8000. E-mail: centred@loto-quebec.com. Web Site: societe.lotoquebec.com/en/media-and-partners/documentation-centre. *Librn,* Stephanie Cadieux; *Librn,* Mirjana Martic; E-mail: mirjana.martic@loto-quebec.com; *Library Contact,* Alexis Beauchamp; E-mail: alexis.beauchamp@loto-quebec.com; Staff 2 (MLS 2)
Founded 1978
Subject Interests: Gambling
Open Mon-Fri 8:30-4

S LOWER CANADA COLLEGE LIBRARY*, 4090 Royal Ave, H4A 2M5. SAN 372-7742. Tel: 514-482-9797, Ext 473. FAX: 514-482-0195. Web Site: www.lcc.ca/academics/library. *Head Librn,* Laura Sanders; E-mail: lsanders@lcc.ca; Staff 5 (MLS 1, Non-MLS 4)
Library Holdings: Bk Titles 27,000
Wireless access
Restriction: Students only

M MCGILL UNIVERSITY HEALTH CENTRE - GLEN SITE*, McConnell Resource Centre - Medical Library, 1001 Boul DeCarie, Rm B RC 0078, H4A 3J1. SAN 369-4232. Tel: 514-934-1934, Ext 35290. FAX: 514-843-1483. E-mail: library.glen@muhc.mcgill.ca. Web Site: muhclibraries.ca/libraries/glen. *Librn,* Amy Bergeron; E-mail: amy.bergeron@muhc.mcgill.ca; *Librn,* Taline Ekmekjian; Tel: 514-934-1934, Ext 22554, E-mail: taline.ekmekjian@muhc.mcgill.ca; *Librn,* Paule Kelly-Rheaume; Tel: 514-934-1934, Ext 32593, E-mail:

paule.kelly-rheaume@muhc.mcgill.ca; *Patient Educ Librn,* Dahlal Mohr-Elzeki; Tel: 514-934-1934, Ext 22054, E-mail: dahlal.mohr-elzeki@muhc.mcgill.ca; *Documentation Tech,* Stephanie Bouchard-Lord; E-mail: stephanie.bouchard-lord@muhc.mcgill.ca; *Documentation Tech,* Vincent Caétano; Tel: 514-934-1934, Ext 22374, E-mail: vincent.caetano@muhc.mcgill.ca; Staff 6 (MLS 4, Non-MLS 2)
Founded 1945
Library Holdings: Bk Titles 3,000; Per Subs 175
Open Mon-Fri 8-5

C MCGILL UNIVERSITY LIBRARIES*, McLennan Library Bldg, 3459 McTavish St, H3A 0C9. SAN 369-2612. Tel: 514-398-4677. FAX: 514-398-7356. E-mail: assistant_dean.libraries@mcgill.ca. Web Site: www.mcgill.ca/library. *Dean of Libr,* C Colleen Cook, PhD; *Assoc Dean, Coll Serv,* Joseph Hafner; Tel: 514-398-4788, Fax: 514-398-8919, E-mail: joseph.hafner@mcgill.ca; *Assoc Dean, Digital Initiatives,* Jenn Riley; Tel: 514-398-3642, E-mail: jenn.riley@mcgill.ca; *Assoc Dean, User Serv,* Jeffry Archer; Tel: 514-398-4735, E-mail: jeffry.archer@mcgill.ca; *Coll Serv, Sr Dir,* Louis Houle; Tel: 514-398-4763, Fax: 514-398-3903, E-mail: louis.houle@mcgill.ca; *Dir, Academic Affairs,* Carole Urbain; Tel: 514-398-5725, Fax: 514-398-7184, E-mail: carole.urbain@mcgill.ca; *Assoc Dir, Planning & Res,* Diane Koen; Tel: 514-398-2149, E-mail: diane.koen@mcgill.ca; Staff 65 (MLS 64, Non-MLS 1)
Founded 1821. Enrl 33,258; Fac 2,575; Highest Degree: Doctorate
Special Collections: 16th & 17th Century Tracts (Redpath Coll); Architecture (Blackader Coll); Blake Coll; Canadiana (Arkin Coll & Lande Coll); Early Geology (Adams Coll); Entomology (Lyman Coll); History of Science & Medicine (Osler Coll); Hume Coll; Kierkegaard Coll; Leacock Coll; Marionettes (Stearn Coll); Napoleon Coll; Natural History & Ornithology (Blacker-Wood Coll); Printing (Colgate Coll); Shakespeare Coll; UN, Can, Prov & Food/Agr Orgn
Automation Activity & Vendor Info: (Acquisitions) Ex Libris Group; (Cataloging) Ex Libris Group; (Circulation) Ex Libris Group; (Course Reserve) Ex Libris Group; (ILL) Fretwell-Downing; (Media Booking) Ex Libris Group; (OPAC) Ex Libris Group; (Serials) Ex Libris Group
Wireless access
Publications: Fontanus
Partic in Association of Research Libraries; Bureau de cooperation Interuniversitaire; Canadian Association of Research Libraries; Canadian Research Knowledge Network
Special Services for the Deaf - ADA equip
Special Services for the Blind - Accessible computers
Friends of the Library Group

Departmental Libraries:

MARVIN DUCHOW MUSIC LIBRARY, Elizabeth Wirth Music Bldg, 3rd Flr, 527 Sherbrooke St W, H3A 1E3, SAN 369-3120. Tel: 514-398-4692. FAX: 514-398-8276. Web Site: mcgill.ca/library/branches/music. *Head Librn,* Houman Behzadi; Tel: 514-398-4694, E-mail: houman.behzadi@mcgill.ca
Library Holdings: AV Mats 89,993; CDs 27,632; DVDs 1,934; Microforms 194; Music Scores 52,359; Bk Titles 24,243; Bk Vols 28,034; Per Subs 237; Videos 307
Special Collections: Bassoon (Bruce Bower Coll), music, parts, scores; David Edelberg/Handel Coll, bks, scores, sound rec; Fonds Discographique Noël-Vallerand; Marvin Duchow Coll, correspondence, ms compositions, teaching mat; Sheet Music Coll (incl Roger Doucet Coll), 19th & Early 20th Centuries
Open Mon-Thurs 9am-11pm, Fri 9-6, Sat 10-6, Sun Noon-11

EDUCATION CURRICULUM RESOURCES CENTRE, 3700 McTavish St, 1st Flr, H3A 1Y2, SAN 369-2973. Tel: 514-398-5726. FAX: 514-398-2165. E-mail: education.library@mcgill.ca. Web Site: www.mcgill.ca/library/branches/education. *Liaison Librn,* Marcela Y Isuster; E-mail: marcela.isuster@mcgill.ca
Library Holdings: e-books 504; Bk Titles 105,570; Bk Vols 120,533; Per Subs 503
Open Mon-Fri 9-5

CL NAHUM GELBER LAW LIBRARY, 3660 Peel St, H3A 1W9, SAN 369-2701. Tel: 514-398-4715, Ext 00171. FAX: 514-398-3585. E-mail: law.library@mcgill.ca. Web Site: www.mcgill.ca/library/branches/law. *Head Librn,* Daniel Boyer; E-mail: daniel.boyer@mcgill.ca; Staff 12 (MLS 4, Non-MLS 8)
Founded 1998. Enrl 818; Fac 39; Highest Degree: Doctorate
Library Holdings: Bk Titles 79,413; Bk Vols 96,485; Per Subs 2,574
Special Collections: J P Humphrey Human Rights Coll; Wainwright Pre-Napoleanic French Law
Subject Interests: Civil law, Common law, Comparative law, Human rights, Intl law

GEOGRAPHIC INFORMATION CENTRE, Burnside Hall Bldg, 5th Flr, 805 Sherbrooke St W, H3A 2K6, SAN 369-2876. Tel: 514-398-7438. FAX: 514-398-7437. E-mail: gicsupport@mcgill.ca. Web Site: gic.geog.mcgill.ca. *Dir,* Dr Tim Elrick; *Chief Librn,* Ruilan Shi; E-mail: ruilan.shi@mcgill.ca; Staff 1 (MLS 1)
Library Holdings: AV Mats 231,969; Electronic Media & Resources 200; Bk Titles 3,808; Bk Vols 3,934; Per Subs 25
Special Collections: Airphotos; Geospatial Data; Maps, Atlases & Globes
Open Mon-Thurs 10-9, Fri 10-5, Sat & Sun 12-5

HUMANITIES & SOCIAL SCIENCES LIBRARY, McLennan-Redpath Library Complex, 3459 McTavish St, H3A 0C9, SAN 369-2760. Tel: 514-398-4734. FAX: 514-398-7184. E-mail: hssl.library@mcgill.ca. Web Site: www.mcgill.ca/library/branches/hssl. *Head Librn,* Eamon Duffy; E-mail: eamon.duffy@mcgill.ca
Founded 1893
Library Holdings: e-books 148; Bk Titles 1,001,781; Bk Vols 1,219,939; Per Subs 3,561
Friends of the Library Group

ISLAMIC STUDIES, Morrice Hall, 3485 McTavish St, H3A 1Y1, SAN 369-3031. Tel: 514-398-3662. FAX: 514-398-8189. Web Site: www.mcgill.ca/library/branches/islamic. *Head Librn,* Anaïs Salamon; Tel: 514-398-4688, E-mail: anais.salamon@mcgill.ca; Staff 4 (MLS 1, Non-MLS 3)
Founded 1952. Enrl 500; Fac 23; Highest Degree: Doctorate
Library Holdings: Bk Vols 130,927; Per Subs 363
Subject Interests: Islamic world
Function: Art exhibits, Computers for patron use, E-Reserves, Electronic databases & coll, ILL available, Internet access, Online ref, Orientations, Photocopying/Printing, Ref & res, Ref serv available, Res assist avail, Res libr, Wheelchair accessible
Restriction: Non-circulating of rare bks

MACDONALD CAMPUS LIBRARY, Barton Bldg, 21111 Lakeshore Rd, Sainte-Anne-de-Bellevue, H9X 3V9, SAN 369-2736. Tel: 514-398-7881. FAX: 514-398-7960. E-mail: macdonald.library@mcgill.ca. Web Site: www.mcgill.ca/library/branches/macdonald. *Head Librn,* Emily MacKenzie; Tel: 514-398-7876, E-mail: emily.mackenzie@mcgill.ca; Staff 7 (MLS 3, Non-MLS 4)
Founded 1907. Highest Degree: Doctorate
Library Holdings: Bk Titles 48,416; Bk Vols 53,384; Per Subs 694
Special Collections: Canadian, Quebec & FAO Documents. UN Document Depository
Subject Interests: Agr, Environ sci, Food, Nutrition, Parasitology

OSLER LIBRARY OF THE HISTORY OF MEDICINE, McIntyre Medical Sciences Bldg, 3655 Promenade Sir William Osler, H3G 1Y6, SAN 369-2825. Tel: 514-398-4475, Ext 09873. FAX: 514-398-5747. E-mail: osler.library@mcgill.ca. Web Site: www.mcgill.ca/library/branches/osler. *Head Librn,* Mary Yearl; E-mail: mary.yearl@mcgill.ca
Library Holdings: Bk Titles 90,773
Friends of the Library Group

SCHULICH LIBRARY OF PHYSICAL SCIENCE, LIFE SCIENCES, & ENGINEERING, Macdonald Stewart Library Bldg, 809 Sherbrooke St W, H3A 2K6, SAN 369-318X. Tel: 514-398-4769. FAX: 514-398-3903. E-mail: schulich.library@mcgill.ca. Web Site: www.mcgill.ca/library/branches/schulich. *Head Librn,* Natalie Waters; Tel: 514-398-1204, E-mail: natalie.waters@mcgill.ca; Staff 13 (MLS 5, Non-MLS 8)
Library Holdings: Bk Titles 121,973; Bk Vols 151,830; Per Subs 1,465

L MCMILLAN LIBRARY, 1000 Sherbrooke St W, 27th Flr, H3A 3G4. SAN 374-5619. Tel: 514-987-5000. FAX: 514-987-1213. Web Site: mcmillan.ca. *Libr Tech,* Brynne England
Library Holdings: Bk Titles 2,700; Bk Vols 5,000
Restriction: Mem only

G MONTREAL CITY PLANNING DEPARTMENT*, Centre de Documentation SUM, 303 Notre-Dame est Bureau 5A-37, H2Y 3Y8. SAN 329-7667. Tel: 514-872-4119. Web Site: www.stm.info/en. *Info Res, Librn,* Ginette Dugas; E-mail: ginette.dugas@montreal.ca; Staff 1 (MLS 1)
Library Holdings: Per Subs 70
Special Collections: Municipal Document Depository
Subject Interests: Archaeology, Archit, Sustainable develop, Urban planning
Function: Res libr
Restriction: Access for corporate affiliates, External users must contact libr, Internal circ only, Limited access for the pub, Open to dept staff only, Open to others by appt

M MONTREAL GENERAL HOSPITAL*, Medical Library, 1650 Cedar Ave, Rm E6-157, H3G 1A4. SAN 319-7867. Tel: 514-934-1934, Ext 43058. FAX: 514-934-8250. E-mail: library.mgh@muhc.mcgill.ca. Web Site: www.muhclibraries.ca/library/mgh. *Libr Dir,* Ibtisam Mahmoud; Tel: 514-934-1934, Ext 43057, E-mail: ibtisam.mahmoud@muhc.mcgill.ca; *Librn,* Linsay Hales; E-mail: lindsay.hales@muhc.mcgill.ca; Staff 3 (MLS 2, Non-MLS 1)
Founded 1955
Library Holdings: Bk Titles 2,200; Per Subs 100
Subject Interests: Consumer health info, Dentistry, Med, Surgery
Open Mon-Fri 8-5

S MONTREAL MUSEUM OF FINE ARTS*, Archives & Library, 2189 Bishop St, H3G 2E8. SAN 319-7883. Tel: 514-285-1600, Ext 160, 514-285-1600, Ext 202. E-mail: biblio@mbamtl.org. Web Site: www.mbam.qc.ca, www.mbam.qc.ca/en/explore-the-museum/archives-and-library-department. *Head of Libr & Archives,* Jean-Bruno Giard; Staff 3 (MLS 1, Non-MLS 2)
Founded 1882
Library Holdings: Bk Vols 82,200; Per Subs 631
Special Collections: Canadian Artists, clippings, auction catalogues
Subject Interests: Applied arts, Canadiana, Decorative art, Fine arts
Automation Activity & Vendor Info: (Acquisitions) SirsiDynix-Symphony; (Cataloging) SirsiDynix-Symphony; (Circulation) SirsiDynix-Symphony; (OPAC) SirsiDynix-Enterprise; (Serials) SirsiDynix-Symphony
Wireless access
Restriction: Open by appt only

M MONTREAL NEUROLOGICAL INSTITUTE HOSPITAL LIBRARY, 3801 University St, Rm 285, H3A 2B4. SAN 319-7891. Tel: 514-398-1980. E-mail: library.neuro@mcgill.ca. Web Site: www.muhclibraries.ca/libraries/mnih. *Librn,* Selin Altuntur; E-mail: selin.altuntur@muhc.mcgill.ca; *Librn,* Paule Kelly-Rheaume; E-mail: paule.kelly-rheaume@muhc.mcgill.ca; Staff 2 (MLS 2)
Founded 1934
Library Holdings: Bk Titles 14,000; Per Subs 109
Automation Activity & Vendor Info: (Acquisitions) Inmagic, Inc.; (Cataloging) Inmagic, Inc.; (Circulation) Inmagic, Inc.; (OPAC) Inmagic, Inc.; (Serials) Inmagic, Inc.
Wireless access
Open Mon-Fri 8-4

S MORNEAU SHEPELL*, 1060 Boul Robert-Bourassa, Ste 900, H3B 4V3. SAN 370-6036. Tel: 514-878-9090. FAX: 514-395-8773. Web Site: www.morneaushepell.com. *Librn,* Anne Marie Quiring; E-mail: aquiring@morneaushepell.com
Library Holdings: Bk Titles 5,000; Per Subs 150
Open Mon-Fri 8-5

S NATIONAL FILM BOARD OF CANADA, NFB Montreal, 1501 Bleury St, H3A 0H3. (Mail add: PO Box 6100, Station Centre-Ville, H3C 3H5), SAN 376-2181. Tel: 514-283-9045. E-mail: research@nfb.ca. Web Site: www.nfb.ca. *Cataloguing & Indexing Librn,* Helene-Marie Hegyes; E-mail: hm.hegyes@nfb.ca; Staff 1 (MLS 1)
Founded 1939
Library Holdings: AV Mats 10,000; Bk Titles 15,000; Per Subs 40
Special Collections: Films-Notebooks
Subject Interests: Cinema
Automation Activity & Vendor Info: (Acquisitions) Mandarin Library Automation; (Cataloging) Mandarin Library Automation; (OPAC) Marcive, Inc
Wireless access
Function: Electronic databases & coll, Online ref
Restriction: Employee & client use only

S NATIONAL THEATRE SCHOOL OF CANADA LIBRARY*, 5030 rue Saint-Denis, H2J 2L8. SAN 319-793X. Tel: 514-842-7954, Ext 125. FAX: 514-842-5661. Web Site: thalia.ent-nts.ca. *Dir,* Simon Barry; E-mail: simonbarry@ent-nts.ca; *Libr Asst,* Manon Garneau; Tel: 514-842-7954, Ext 147, E-mail: manongarneau@ent-nts.ca; *Libr Asst,* Marie-Claude Verdier; Tel: 514-842-7954, Ext 136, E-mail: mcverdier@ent-nts.ca; *Libr Tech,* Marianne Boudreau; Tel: 514-842-7954, Ext 112, E-mail: mboudreau@ent-nts.ca; Staff 5 (MLS 1, Non-MLS 4)
Founded 1941
Library Holdings: AV Mats 1,250; CDs 750; DVDs 1,000; Electronic Media & Resources 4; Bk Titles 80,000; Per Subs 50; Videos 900
Special Collections: Architecture Coll; Costume History Coll; Fine Arts Coll; Performing Arts Coll; Theatre Coll
Subject Interests: Archives
Automation Activity & Vendor Info: (Acquisitions) BiblioMondo; (Cataloging) BiblioMondo; (Circulation) BiblioMondo; (ILL) Amicus; (OPAC) BiblioMondo; (Serials) BiblioMondo
Wireless access
Open Mon & Thurs 10-8, Tues & Wed 10-6, Fri Noon-3

L NORTON ROSE FULBRIGHT CANADA LLP LIBRARY*, One Place Ville Marie, Ste 2500, H3B 1R1. SAN 319-7980. Tel: 514-847-4701. FAX: 514-286-5474. E-mail: MTLbiblio@nortonrosefulbright.com. Web Site: www.nortonrosefulbright.com/ca/en/offices/montreal. *Libr Serv Mgr,* Carole Mehu; E-mail: carole.mehu@nortonrosefulbright.com; *Ref Serv,* Julie Lavallee; *Ref Serv,* Carol Slutsky; *Tech Serv,* Caroline Brisson
Founded 1879
Library Holdings: Bk Vols 20,000
Special Collections: Canadian Law
Automation Activity & Vendor Info: (Acquisitions) SirsiDynix-WorkFlows
Wireless access

S POLISH INSTITUTE OF ARTS & SCIENCES LIBRARY*, 4220 rue Drolet, H2W 2L6. SAN 325-8424. Tel: 514-379-4220. Web Site: www.polishinstitute.org/library. *Librn,* Stefan Wladysiuk; E-mail: stefan.wladysiuk@mail.mcgill.ca; Staff 2 (MLS 2)
Founded 1943
Library Holdings: Bk Vols 48,000
Publications: Biuletyn Informacyjny (Annual)
Open Mon 10-7:30, Thurs 4-7:30, Sat 1-5

C POLYTECHNIQUE MONTREAL LIBRARY*, Campus de l'Universite de Montreal, 2500, chemin de Polytechnique, 2900, boul Edouard-Montpetit, H3T 1J4. (Mail add: CP 6079, succ Centre-ville, H3C 3A7), SAN 319-7468. Tel: 514-340-4666. Circulation Tel: 514-340-4849. Interlibrary Loan Service Tel: 514-340-4846. Reference Tel: 514-340-4665. FAX: 514-340-4026. E-mail: biblio@polymtl.ca. Web Site: www.polymtl.ca/biblio/en. *Dir,* Melissa Beaudry; Tel: 514-340-4711, Ext 4652, E-mail: melissa.beaudry@polymtl.ca; *Head, Client Serv,* Maryse Breton; Tel: 514-340-4711, Ext 4659, E-mail: maryse.breton@polymtl.ca; *Head, Tech Serv,* Marie-Hélène Vézina; Tel: 514-340-4711, Ext 4641, E-mail: marie-helene.vezina@polymtl.ca; *Section Head, Info Consult Serv,* Manon Du Ruisseau; Tel: 514-340-4711, Ext 7205, E-mail: manon.du-ruisseau@polymtl.ca; *Principal Advisor, Coll Dev,* Christine Chahal; Tel: 514-340-4711, Ext 7207, E-mail: christine.chahal@polymtl.ca; Staff 13 (MLS 13)
Founded 1873. Enrl 9,500; Fac 7; Highest Degree: Doctorate
Special Collections: Technical Standards
Subject Interests: Applied sci, Engr
Wireless access
Partic in Bureau de cooperation Interuniversitaire; Canadian Research Knowledge Network
Open Mon-Thurs 9-5, Fri 9-12

CR PRESBYTERIAN COLLEGE LIBRARY*, The Joseph C McLelland Library, 3495 University St, H3A 2A8. SAN 319-8022. Tel: 514-288-5256. FAX: 514-288-8072. *Librn,* Dr Daniel J Shute; E-mail: dshute@presbyteriancollege.ca; Staff 2 (MLS 1, Non-MLS 1)
Founded 1867. Enrl 30; Fac 6; Highest Degree: Master
Library Holdings: Bk Titles 35,000; Per Subs 30
Subject Interests: Hist, Reformed theol, Theol
Wireless access
Open Tues-Thurs 9-12 & 1-5

G QUEBEC COMMISSION DES SERVICES JURIDIQUES LIBRARY*, Two Complexe Desjardins, Ste 1404, H5B 1B3. (Mail add: CP 123, Succ Desjardins, H5B 1B3), SAN 371-764X. Tel: 514-873-3562. E-mail: info@csj.qc.ca. *Documentalist,* Position Currently Open
Founded 1973
Library Holdings: Bk Titles 3,800; Per Subs 100
Subject Interests: Law
Function: Res libr
Restriction: Not open to pub

L ROBINSON, SHEPPARD & SHAPIRO*, Law Library, 800 Place Victoria, Ste 4700, H4Z 1H6. SAN 328-4506. Tel: 514-393-4004. FAX: 514-878-1865. Web Site: www.rsslex.com. *Library Contact,* Chantel Noel; E-mail: cnoel@rsslex.com
Library Holdings: Bk Vols 12,500
Partic in EUREKA; SOQUIJ
Restriction: Staff use only

M SAINT MARY'S HOSPITAL*, Health Sciences Library, 3830 Lacombe Ave, H3T 1M5. SAN 319-812X. Tel: 514-345-3511, Ext 3317. Web Site: ciusss-odim.inlibro.net/. *Libr Mgr,* Maggy Wassef; E-mail: maggy.wassef@douglas.mcgill.ca; Staff 1 (MLS 1)
Founded 1952
Library Holdings: Bk Vols 2,000; Per Subs 125
Subject Interests: Family med, Gynecology, Med, Nursing, Obstetrics, Psychiat, Surgery

S SIMONE DE BEAUVOIR LIBRARY*, Concordia Univ, Simone de Beauvoir Inst, ER-630, 2155 Guy St, 6th Flr, H3G 1M8. (Mail add: Concordia Univ, Simone de Beauvoir Inst; MU-401, 1455 de Maisonneuve Blvd W, H3G 1M8). Tel: 514-848-2424, Ext 2377. Administration Tel: 514-848-2424, Ext 2370. Web Site: www.concordia.ca. *Librn,* Isabelle Lamoureux; E-mail: isabelle.lamoureux@concordia.ca; Staff 1 (MLS 1)
Founded 1978
Library Holdings: AV Mats 55; Bk Titles 2,500
Subject Interests: Aboriginal studies, Environ issues, Feminism, Gay & lesbian, Peace studies, Sexuality, Women's health, Women's studies
Wireless access

Open Mon-Thurs 10-4
Friends of the Library Group

S SNC-LAVALIN, INC LIBRARY*, 455 boul Rene-Levesque ouest, H2Z 1Z3. SAN 319-8235. Tel: 514-393-1000. FAX: 514-866-0795. Web Site: www.snclavalin.com/en/projects/the-box. *Librn,* Dorothy Gartner; E-mail: dorothy.gartner@snclavalin.com
Founded 1911
Library Holdings: Bk Vols 4,000; Per Subs 150
Subject Interests: Engr
Publications: Biblio-Bulletin (library bulletin); New Acquisitions

G SOCIETE DE TRANSPORT DE MONTREAL*, Centre de Documentation, 800 rue de la Gauchetiere St Ouest, Bur 6600, H5A 1J6. SAN 319-7913. Tel: 514-786-4636. FAX: 514-280-6126. E-mail: archives@stm.info. Web Site: www.stm.info. *Archivist,* Position Currently Open
Founded 1968
Library Holdings: Bk Titles 2,500; Bk Vols 4,500; Per Subs 350
Subject Interests: Engr, Finance, Law, Policy, Pub transit
Wireless access
Function: Archival coll, Doc delivery serv, Res libr, Telephone ref
Restriction: Open by appt only

S SOCIETE GENEALOGIQUE CANADIENNE-FRANCAISE BIBLIOTHEQUE, 3440 rue Davidson, H1W 2Z5. SAN 373-7985. Tel: 514-527-1010. E-mail: info@sgcf.com. Web Site: sgcf.com/bibliotheque. *Coordr,* Dominique Ritchot
Founded 1943
Library Holdings: Bk Titles 15,000; Bk Vols 18,000; Per Subs 307
Subject Interests: Genealogy, Hist
Wireless access
Function: 24/7 Electronic res, 24/7 Online cat, Activity rm, Archival coll, CD-ROM, Computers for patron use, Doc delivery serv, For res purposes, Genealogy discussion group, Internet access, Ref & res, Res performed for a fee, Workshops
Publications: Memoires
Open Mon & Tues 4:30-9, Thurs-Sat 9:30-4
Restriction: Authorized patrons, Employee & client use only, Free to mem

S UNIVERSITE DU QUEBEC*, Bibliotheque des Arts, CP 8889, Succ Centre-Ville, 1255 Rue St Denis, Locale-A-1200, H3C 3P3. SAN 319-8243. Tel: 514-987-6134. FAX: 514-987-0262. Web Site: www.uqam.ca. *Librn,* Marie-Christine Beaudry; E-mail: beaudry.mc@uqam.ca; *Librn,* Adèle Flannery; E-mail: flannery.adele@uqam.ca; *Librn,* Jean-Michel Lapointe; E-mail: lapointe.jean-michel@uqam.ca. Subject Specialists: *Art hist, Dance, Museology,* Marie-Christine Beaudry; *Design, Media arts, Visual arts,* Adèle Flannery; *Lit, Theatre,* Jean-Michel Lapointe
Founded 1925
Library Holdings: Bk Vols 80,000
Special Collections: Fine Arts Coll

C UNIVERSITE DU QUEBEC A MONTREAL BIBLIOTHEQUE*, 400 rue Ste-Catherine Est, Local A-M100, H2L 2C5. (Mail add: CP 8889, Succursale Centreville, H3C 3P3), SAN 319-8251. Tel: 514-987-6114. FAX: 514-987-3542. E-mail: bibliotheques@uqam.ca. Web Site: www.bibliotheques.uqam.ca. *Gen Mgr,* Frederic Giuliano; E-mail: giuliano.frederic@uqam.ca; *Mgr, Coll Develop,* Carole Brouillette; Staff 44 (MLS 42, Non-MLS 2)
Founded 1969. Highest Degree: Doctorate
Library Holdings: AV Mats 19,183; Bk Titles 1,598,814; Per Subs 8,972
Special Collections: Digital Image; Maps & Aerial Photographs; Rare Books
Subject Interests: Archit, Art, Educ, Humanities, Music
Wireless access
Publications: InfoSphere
Open Mon-Fri 8:30am-10pm, Sat & Sun 11-5

C VANIER COLLEGE LIBRARY*, 821 Ave Sainte-Croix, H4L 3X9. SAN 321-7086. Tel: 514-744-7500, Ext 7540. Interlibrary Loan Service Tel: 514-744-7500, Ext 7544. FAX: 514-744-7545. E-mail: library@vaniercollege.qc.ca. Web Site: www.vaniercollege.qc.ca/library.
Founded 1969. Enrl 5,800; Fac 450
Library Holdings: Bk Vols 75,000; Per Subs 100
Automation Activity & Vendor Info: (Acquisitions) Koha; (Cataloging) Koha; (Circulation) Koha; (OPAC) Koha; (Serials) Koha
Wireless access

MONTREAL-EST

P BIBLIOTHEQUE DE MONTREAL-EST*, Micheline Gagnon Library, 11370 rue Notre-Dame, 3rd Flr, H1B 2W6. SAN 319-8294. Tel: 514-905-2145. E-mail: bibliotheque.montreal-est@montreal-est.ca. Web Site: ville.montreal-est.qc.ca/culture-est-loisirs/bibliotheque-micheline-gagnon. *Libr Tech,* Anne-Marie Dufort; Tel: 514-905-2144, E-mail: anne-marie.dufort@montreal-est.ca; Staff 1 (MLS 1)
Founded 1967. Pop 3,796; Circ 42,000
Library Holdings: Bk Vols 28,371
Wireless access
Open Mon-Fri 10-7, Sat 9-5; Mon-Wed 9-7, Thurs & Fri 9-5 (Summer)

NICOLET

R CENTRE D'ARCHIVES REGIONALES SEMINAIRE DE NICOLET LIBRARY*, 645, boul Louis-Frechette, J3T 1L6. SAN 319-8316. Tel: 819-293-4838. FAX: 819-293-4543. E-mail: seminairedenicolet@sogetel.net. Web Site: www.archivesseminairenicolet.wordpress.com. *Archivist,* Marie Pelletier
Founded 1825
Library Holdings: Bk Vols 100,000
Subject Interests: Art, Hist, Relig studies
Open Mon-Fri 9-12 & 1-4:30

S ECOLE NATIONALE DE POLICE DU QUEBEC*, Carrefour de l'Information et du Savoir (CIS) Bibliotheque, 350 rue Marguerite d'Youville, J3T 1X4. SAN 329-4145. Tel: 819-293-8631, Ext 22. E-mail: cis@enpq.qc.ca. Web Site: cis.enpq.qc.ca/services/bibliotheque.
Founded 1970
Library Holdings: AV Mats 591; Bk Vols 7,200; Per Subs 102
Wireless access
Restriction: Employees only

PINCOURT

P BIBLIOTHEQUE MUNICIPALE DE PINCOURT*, 225 boul Pincourt, J7W 9T2. SAN 319-8340. Tel: 514-425-1104. E-mail: bibliotheque@villepincourt.qc.ca. Web Site: www.villepincourt.qc.ca. *Libr Mgr,* Sylvie de Repentigny
Founded 1965. Pop 15,074; Circ 91,750
Library Holdings: Audiobooks 51; CDs 1,256; DVDs 6,492; e-books 1,094; Bk Vols 35,815; Per Subs 55
Wireless access
Open Mon-Thurs 10-8:30, Fri 10-5, Sat 10-4

POINTE-CLAIRE

P BIBLIOTHEQUE PUBLIQUE DE POINTE-CLAIRE, Centrale, 100 ave Douglas-Shand, H9R 4V1. SAN 369-495X. Tel: 514-630-1218. Circulation Tel: 514-630-1218, Ext 1623. Interlibrary Loan Service Tel: 514-630-1218, Ext 1692. Reference Tel: 514-630-1218, Ext 1630. FAX: 514-630-1261. E-mail: bibliotheque@ville.pointe-claire.qc.ca. Interlibrary Loan Service E-mail: ill@ville.pointe-claire.qc.ca. Web Site: biblio.pointe-claire.ca. *Sr Mgr,* Katya Borras; Tel: 514-630-1217, E-mail: katya.borras@pointe-claire.ca; *Mgr,* Marie-Andree Dubreuil-Moisan; E-mail: marie-andree.dubreuil-moisan@pointe-claire.ca; Staff 21 (MLS 8, Non-MLS 13)
Founded 1965. Pop 35,429; Circ 414,489
Library Holdings: Audiobooks 3,875; AV Mats 3,105; Braille Volumes 11; CDs 3,448; DVDs 9,823; e-books 10,780; e-journals 46,148; Electronic Media & Resources 38; Large Print Bks 2,940; Bk Vols 141,981; Per Subs 210
Automation Activity & Vendor Info: (Acquisitions) BiblioMondo; (Cataloging) BiblioMondo; (Circulation) BiblioMondo; (OPAC) BiblioMondo; (Serials) BiblioMondo
Wireless access
Function: 24/7 Electronic res, 24/7 Online cat, 24/7 wireless access, Adult bk club, Bk club(s), Chess club, Computer training, Computers for patron use, Digital talking bks, Doc delivery serv, E-Readers, Electronic databases & coll, Equip loans & repairs, Family literacy, Free DVD rentals, Games, Games & aids for people with disabilities, Genealogy discussion group, Home delivery & serv to seniorr ctr & nursing homes, ILL available, Internet access, Large print keyboards, Magazines, Mail & tel request accepted, Movies, Music CDs, Online cat, Outreach serv, Outside serv via phone, mail, e-mail & web, Photocopying/Printing, Preschool outreach, Preschool reading prog, Prog for adults, Prog for children & young adult, Ref & res, Ref serv available, Res assist avail, Res libr, Scanner, Senior outreach, Serves people with intellectual disabilities, Spoken cassettes & CDs, STEM programs, Story hour, Summer & winter reading prog, Summer reading prog, Teen prog, Wheelchair accessible, Winter reading prog, Workshops, Writing prog
Open Mon-Fri 10-9, Sat 9-5, Sun 1-5
Restriction: Circ to mem only
Friends of the Library Group
Branches: 1
VALOIS BRANCH, 68 Prince-Edward Ave, H9R 4C7, SAN 369-5018. Tel: 514-630-1219. FAX: 514-695-9924. *Sr Libr Tech,* Kathy Wilson; Tel: 514-630-1218, Ext 1661, E-mail: kathy.wilson@pointe-claire.ca
Founded 1991

Open Mon, Wed & Fri 1-9, Sat 1-5
Friends of the Library Group

S FPINNOVATIONS*, 570 Blvd St-Jean, H9R 3J9. SAN 318-8264. Tel: 514-630-4100, Option 9. E-mail: library@fpinnovations.ca. Web Site: web.fpinnovations.ca. *Head Librn,* Roberta Roberts; E-mail: roberta.roberts@fpinnovations.ca; *Libr Tech,* Arielle Gatbonton; Staff 2 (MLS 1, Non-MLS 1)
Founded 1927
Library Holdings: Bk Titles 10,000; Per Subs 150
Subject Interests: Composite products, Forest mgt, Forestry, Papermaking, Plywood, Pulping, Saw milling, Trucking, Wood, Wood anatomy, Wood chem
Automation Activity & Vendor Info: (Cataloging) Inmagic, Inc.
Publications: Bibliographies
Restriction: Not open to pub

QUEBEC

G ARCHIVES NATIONALES A QUEBEC, Pavillon Louis Jacques Casault, Campus de l'Universite Laval, 1055 ave du Seminaire, G1V 5C8. SAN 372-7246. Tel: 418-643-8904. FAX: 418-646-4254. E-mail: anq-biblio@banq.qc.ca. Web Site: www.banq.qc.ca. *Archivist,* Renald Lessard; *Documentation Tech,* Annie Labrecque; Staff 1 (Non-MLS 1)
Founded 1920
Library Holdings: Microforms 14,000; Bk Vols 27,000; Per Subs 24
Special Collections: Archives & Records Management; Genealogy Coll; Government Institutions Coll; History of French America Coll
Automation Activity & Vendor Info: (Acquisitions) BiblioMondo; (Cataloging) BiblioMondo; (OPAC) BiblioMondo; (Serials) BiblioMondo
Wireless access
Open Mon, Tues, Thurs & Fri 9-12 & 1-5, Wed 9-12 & 1-8

G ASSEMBLEE NATIONALE DU QUEBEC BIBLIOTHEQUE*, Edifice Pamphile-Lemay, 1035 rue des Parlementaires, G1A 1A3. SAN 319-8421. Tel: 418-643-4408. FAX: 418-646-3207. E-mail: bibliotheque@assnat.qc.ca. Web Site: www.assnat.qc.ca. *Dir,* Jacques Gagnon; Staff 43 (MLS 12, Non-MLS 31)
Founded 1802
Library Holdings: Bk Titles 451,000; Bk Vols 955,000; Per Subs 942
Special Collections: Canadiana (Fonds Pierre-Joseph-Olivier Chauveau); Droit (Fonds Pollette); Government Documents (British Parliamentary Papers)
Subject Interests: Behav sci, Econ, Hist, Law, Parliamentary procedure, Polit sci, Soc
Automation Activity & Vendor Info: (Acquisitions) BiblioMondo; (Cataloging) BiblioMondo; (Circulation) BiblioMondo; (ILL) BiblioMondo; (OPAC) BiblioMondo; (Serials) BiblioMondo
Wireless access
Publications: Annual report; Bibliographie et Documentation; Bibliographies, Dictionaire des Parlementaires Quebecois, 1792-1992; Bulletin; Catalogue des Publications; Debats de l'Assemblee Legislative, 1867-1962; Journal des D-ebats: Index
Partic in Riseau Informatisi des Bibliothhques Gouvernementales du Quibec
Open Mon-Fri 8:30-4:30

P BIBLIOTHEQUE CHARLES-H BLAIS*, 1445 Ave Maguire, G1T 2W9. SAN 373-7314. Tel: 418-641-6276. FAX: 418-684-2169. E-mail: courrier@bibliothequedequebec.qc.ca. Web Site: www.bibliothequesdequebec.qc.ca/bibliotheques/saintefoysillerycaprouge/charles_h_blais.aspx. *Library Contact,* Position Currently Open; Staff 2 (MLS 1, Non-MLS 1)
Founded 1982. Pop 12,519; Circ 97,092
Library Holdings: Bk Titles 39,000; Bk Vols 43,015; Per Subs 102
Wireless access
Special Services for the Deaf - Bks on deafness & sign lang
Open Mon & Sat 10-5, Tues-Thurs 10-8, Fri Noon-6, Sun Noon-5

P BIBLIOTHEQUE CHRYSTINE-BROUILLET*, 264, rue Racine, G2B 1E6. SAN 319-6860. Tel: 418-641-6120. E-mail: courrier@bibliothequedequebec.qc.ca. Web Site: www.bibliothequedequebec.qc.ca/bibliotheques/hautesaintcharles/chrystine_brouillet.aspx. *Coordr,* Nancy Duchesneau; E-mail: nancy.duchesneau@bibliothequedequebec.qc.ca
Founded 2002. Pop 15,000
Library Holdings: Bk Vols 40,000; Per Subs 100
Automation Activity & Vendor Info: (Cataloging) SirsiDynix-Unicorn; (Circulation) SirsiDynix-Unicorn; (OPAC) SirsiDynix-Unicorn
Wireless access
Open Mon 1-8, Tues-Thurs 10-8, Fri-Sun 10-5

J BIBLIOTHEQUE DU CEGEP LIMOILOU, 1300 Eighth Ave, G1J 5L5. SAN 369-5220. Tel: 418-647-6600, Ext 6767. E-mail: bibliotheques@cegeplimoilou.ca. Web Site: www.cegeplimoilou.ca/etudiants/carrefour-de-l-information/bibliotheques. *Head of Libr,* Alexandra Lavallee; Tel: 418-647-6600, Ext 6884; Staff 12 (MLS 1, Non-MLS 11)
Founded 1967. Enrl 7,000; Fac 500
Library Holdings: AV Mats 2,299; Bk Vols 80,950; Per Subs 370
Special Collections: Gabriel-Garcia-Marquez Coll
Automation Activity & Vendor Info: (Acquisitions) LibLime Koha; (Cataloging) LibLime Koha; (Circulation) LibLime Koha; (OPAC) LibLime Koha; (Serials) LibLime Koha
Wireless access
Function: Photocopying/Printing
Partic in RESDOC
Open Mon-Thurs 7:30am-8:30pm, Fri 7:30-5

P BIBLIOTHEQUE GABRIELLE ROY*, 350 rue Saint-Joseph Est, G1K 3B2. SAN 369-5042. Tel: 418-641-6789. FAX: 418-641-6787. E-mail: courrier@bibliothequedequebec.qc.ca. Web Site: bibliothequedequebec.qc.ca. *Dir,* Eric Therrien; Staff 8 (MLS 8)
Founded 1848. Pop 166,000
Library Holdings: Bk Vols 447,000
Subject Interests: Art
Wireless access
Publications: Annual report
Open Mon-Fri 8am-9pm, Sat & Sun 9-5
Branches: 15
BIBLIOTHEQUE ALIETTE-MARCHAND, Complexe Jean-Paul-Nolin, 243 blvd Pierre-Bertrand, G1M 2C7. Tel: 418-641-6223.
Open Mon & Thurs-Sun 10-5, Tues & Wed 1-8
BIBLIOTHEQUE CANARDIERE, 1601 chemin de la Canardiere, G1J 2E1, SAN 369-5077. Tel: 418-641-6793.
Open Mon 1-5, Tues & Fri-Sun 10-5, Wed & Thurs 1-8
BIBLIOTHEQUE CHRYSTINE-BROUILLET, Centre Saint-Louis, 264 rue Racine, G2B 1E6. Tel: 418-641-6120.
Open Mon 1-8, Tues-Thurs 10-8, Fri-Sun 10-5
BIBLIOTHEQUE CLAIRE-MARTIN, 755 rue Saint-Jean, G1R 1R1, SAN 369-5212. Tel: 418-641-6798.
Open Mon, Tues & Fri-Sun 10-5, Wed & Thurs 1-8
BIBLIOTHEQUE COLLEGE DES JESUITES, 1120 blvd Rene-Levesques Ouest, G1S 4W4, SAN 369-5190. Tel: 418-641-6792.
Open Mon, Wed & Fri 9:30-5:30, Tues & Thurs 9:30-8, Sat & Sun 9:30-5
BIBLIOTHEQUE ETIENNE-PARENT, 3515 rue Clemenceau, G1C 7R5, SAN 321-2955. Tel: 418-641-6110. Web Site: www.bibliothequedequebec.qc.ca/bibliotheques/beauport/etienne_parent.aspx. *Libr Mgr,* Sophie Loiselle; *Tech Coordr,* Sylvie A Rheaume
Founded 1982. Pop 77,000; Circ 555,000
Library Holdings: Bk Titles 63,500; Bk Vols 80,400; Per Subs 126
Subject Interests: Local hist
Automation Activity & Vendor Info: (Acquisitions) SirsiDynix; (Cataloging) SirsiDynix; (Circulation) SirsiDynix; (Course Reserve) SirsiDynix; (ILL) SirsiDynix; (Media Booking) SirsiDynix; (OPAC) SirsiDynix; (Serials) SirsiDynix
Open Mon-Fri 8-9, Sat & Sun 8-5
Friends of the Library Group
BIBLIOTHEQUE JEAN-BAPTISTE-DUBERGER, 2475 blvd Central, G1P 4S1, SAN 378-1690. Tel: 418-641-6799.
Open Mon & Wed 1-8, Tues & Thurs-Sun 10-5
BIBLIOTHEQUE LE TOURNESOL, Centre communautaire Paul-Emile-Beaulieu, 530 rue Delage, Ste 2, G3G 1J2. Tel: 418-641-6121.
Open Mon, Wed, Fri & Sat 10-5, Tues & Thurs 1-8, Sun 12-5
BIBLIOTHEQUE LEBOURGNEUF, Centre communautaire Lebourgneuf, 1650 blvd La Morille, bur 230, G2K 2L2, SAN 376-9666. Tel: 418-641-6264.
Open Mon, Wed & Fri 1-5, Tues & Thurs 1-8, Sat & Sun 10-5
BIBLIOTHEQUE NEUFCHATEL, 4060 rue Blain, G2B 5C3, SAN 369-5182. Tel: 418-641-6794.
Open Mon, Fri & Sat 10-5, Tues-Thurs 10-8
BIBLIOTHEQUE ROMAIN-LANGLOIS, 2035 blvd Masson, G1P 1J3, SAN 369-5131. Tel: 418-641-6796.
Open Mon, Wed & Fri-Sun 10-5, Tues & Thurs 10-8
BIBLIOTHEQUE SAINT-ANDRE, Centre communautaire Charles-Auguste-Savard, 2155 blvd Bastien, G2B 1B8, SAN 325-4070. Tel: 418-641-6790.
Open Mon, Tues, Thurs, Sat & Sun 10-5, Wed & Fri 1-8
BIBLIOTHEQUE SAINT-CHARLES, 400 Fourth Ave, G1J 2Z9, SAN 325-4038. Tel: 418-641-6795.
Open Mon 1-5, Tues & Thurs 1-8, Wed & Fri-Sun 10-5
BILBIOTHEQUE SAINT-ALBERT, Five rue des Ormes, G1L 1M5, SAN 325-4054. Tel: 418-641-6791.
Open Mon, Tues & Fri 1-8, Wed, Thurs, Sat & Sun 10-5

MAISON DE LA LITTERATURE, 40 rue Sainte-Stanislas, G1R 4H1, SAN 369-5239. Tel: 418-641-6797. E-mail: info@maisondelalitterature.qc.ca. Web Site: www.maisondelalitterature.qc.ca. *Dir,* Dominique Lemieux; Tel: 418-641-6788, Ext 7780, E-mail: dominique.lemieux@institutcanadien.qc.ca; *Librn,* Jean-Philippe Marcoux-Fortier; Tel: 418-641-6788, Ext 7814, E-mail: jean-philippe.marcoux-fortier@institutcanadien.qc.ca
Open Tues-Fri 10-8, Sat 10-7, Sun 10-5
Friends of the Library Group

P BIBLIOTHEQUE MONIQUE-CORRIVEAU*, 1100 route de l'Eglise, G1V 3V9. SAN 319-8995. Tel: 418-641-6277. E-mail: courrier@bibliothequedequebec.qc.ca. Web Site: www.bibliothequedequebec.qc.ca. *Adminr,* Position Currently Open
Founded 1968. Pop 103,345; Circ 567,637
Library Holdings: Bk Titles 119,203
Subject Interests: Archit, Art, Genealogy, Musical scores
Wireless access
Open Mon 9-6, Tues-Fri 9-9, Sat & Sun 9-5

P BIBLIOTHEQUE PAUL-AIME-PAIEMENT*, 7950 First Ave, G1H 2Y4. SAN 321-2769. Tel: 418-641-6287. FAX: 418-624-7886. E-mail: courrier@bibliothequedequebec.qc.ca. Web Site: bibliothequedequebec.qc.ca/bibliotheques/charlesbourg/paul_aime_paiement.aspx.
Pop 73,000
Library Holdings: Bk Titles 106,000
Wireless access
Open Mon-Fri 9-8, Sat 9-5, Sun 12-5

C CEGEP GARNEAU BIBLIOTHEQUE*, 1660 Blvd de l'Entente, G1S 4S3. SAN 319-8502. Tel: 418-688-8310, Ext 2220, 418-688-8310, Ext 2225. FAX: 418-688-0087. E-mail: biblio@cegepgarneau.ca. Web Site: www.cegepgarneau.ca/services/bibliotheque.
Founded 1970. Enrl 6,000
Library Holdings: Bk Titles 90,000; Per Subs 290
Function: Ref serv available
Open Mon-Thurs 7:30am-9pm, Fri 7:30-6, Sun 12-5

L CENTRE D'ACCES A L'INFORMATION JURIDIQUE-BIBLIOTHEQUE DE QUEBEC*, 300 boul Jean-Lesage, 3.5 Local, G1K 8K6. SAN 319-8448. Tel: 418-525-0057. Toll Free Tel: 866-473-3035. FAX: 418-525-4208. Toll Free FAX: 866-473-3034. Web Site: www.caij.qc.ca. *Head of Libr,* Johanne Paquin; E-mail: jpaquin@caij.qc.ca
Founded 1849
Library Holdings: Bk Vols 40,000
Special Collections: Jurisprudence (Law Reviews)
Open Mon-Fri 8:30-5

S CENTRE DE DOCUMENTATION ET D'ARCHIVES YVON-CHARBONNEAU, Centre de Documentation Centrale des syndicats du Quebec, (Formerly Centrale des Syndicats du Quebec), 320, rue St-Joseph Est, bur 100, G1K 9E7. SAN 319-8464. Tel: 418-649-8888. FAX: 418-649-8800. E-mail: documentation@lacsq.org. Web Site: documentation.lacsq.org, www.lacsq.org. *Dir,* Francois Gagnon; E-mail: gagnon.francois@lacsq.org; Staff 3 (MLS 1, Non-MLS 2)
Founded 1965
Library Holdings: Bk Titles 26,000; Per Subs 144
Special Collections: Archives de la CSQ
Subject Interests: Econ, Educ, Labor unions, Trade unions
Wireless access
Function: 24/7 Online cat
Publications: Publications de la Centrale (Documents)
Restriction: Open by appt only

M CENTRE DE PEDOPSYCHIATRIE DU CHUQ*, Bibliotheque Medicale, One Ave Du-Sacre Coeur, G1N 2W1. SAN 328-5405. Tel: 418-529-6851, Ext 20278. FAX: 418-691-0751. E-mail: biblio.ciusssc n@ssss.gouv.qc.ca. *Head of Libr,* Marie-Marthe Gagnon; Staff 1 (MLS 1)
Library Holdings: Bk Titles 4,000; Per Subs 35
Subject Interests: Psychiat

C COLLEGE BART BIBLIOTHEQUE*, 751 cote d'Abraham, Rm D-13, G1R 1A2. SAN 375-3905. Tel: 418-522-3906. FAX: 418-522-5456. E-mail: info@bart.ca. Web Site: bart.ca. *Librn,* Romain Hulo; E-mail: romain.hulo@bart.ca
Founded 1974. Enrl 300
Library Holdings: Bk Vols 5,064; Per Subs 30
Subject Interests: Law

C COLLEGE MERICI - BIBLIOTHEQUE*, 755 Grande Allée Ouest, G1S 1C1. SAN 325-2507. Tel: 418-683-1591, Toll Free Tel: 800-208-1463. FAX: 418-682-8938. Web Site: www.merici.ca/outils/carrefour_de_linformation.html. *Librn,* Maryse Messely; Tel: 418-683-2104, Ext 2213; *Cat, Tech Serv,* Tina Latulippe; Tel: 418-683-2104, Ext 2249, E-mail: tlatulippe@merici.ca; Staff 4 (MLS 1, Non-MLS 3)
Enrl 900
Library Holdings: CDs 175; DVDs 2,300; e-books 535; e-journals 1; Electronic Media & Resources 15; Bk Vols 37,000; Per Subs 75; Videos 300
Subject Interests: Arts, Food serv mgt, Hotel bus, Liberal arts, Orthotic, Prosthetics, Restaurant, Sci, Tourism
Wireless access
Partic in Regard
Open Mon-Thurs 8-8, Fri 8-5

G COMMISSION D'ACCES A L'INFORMATION*, Centre de Documentation, 525 boul Rene-Levesque Est, Bur 236, G1R 5S9. SAN 373-8310. Tel: 418-528-7741. FAX: 418-528-2969. E-mail: cai.communications@cai.gouv.qc.ca. Web Site: www.cai.gouv.qc.ca/english. *Doc/Ref Serv,* Remi Bedard; E-mail: responsable.acces@cai.gouv.qc.ca
Founded 1983
Library Holdings: Bk Vols 2,000; Per Subs 50

G COMMISSION DE TOPONYMIE DU QUEBEC BIBLIOTHEQUE, 750, boul Charest Est, RC, G1K 9K4. SAN 373-9023. Tel: 418-643-4575. FAX: 418-528-1373. E-mail: qqolf@oqlf.gouv.qc.ca. Web Site: www.toponymie.gouv.qc.ca. *Libr Tech,* Elodie Bluteau; *Libr Tech,* Carolane Lacombe; Staff 2 (MLS 2)
Founded 1977
Library Holdings: Bk Titles 8,200; Per Subs 11
Special Collections: Geographical Names Coll; Municipality History Coll; Toponymy Coll
Partic in Reseau Informatise des Bibliotheques du Gouvernement du Quebec
Open Mon-Fri 8:30-4:30

S CONSERVATOIRE DE MUSIQUE DE QUEBEC BIBLIOTHEQUE*, 270 rue Jacques-Parizeau, G1R 5G1. SAN 372-6746. Tel: 418-643-2190, Ext 234. FAX: 418-644-9658. Web Site: www.conservatoire.gouv.qc.ca/quebec. *Head of Libr,* Marie-Eve Simard; Tel: 418-643-2190, Ext 224, E-mail: marie-eve.simard@conservatoire.gouv.qc.ca; *Cat,* Claire Tremblay; Tel: 418-643-2190, Ext 232; *Circ,* Robert Deblois; Staff 2 (Non-MLS 2)
Founded 1944
Library Holdings: Bk Titles 33,000; Bk Vols 60,000; Per Subs 32
Special Collections: Music History & Local (Fonds Vezina Coll), Archives
Subject Interests: Music
Automation Activity & Vendor Info: (Cataloging) BiblioMondo; (OPAC) BiblioMondo
Function: ILL available
Partic in Reseau Informatise des Bibliotheques du Gouvernement du Quebec
Open Mon-Thurs 9:30-Noon & 1-4, Fri 10-Noon & 1-4

C ECOLE NATIONALE D'ADMINISTRATION PUBLIQUE BIBLIOTHEQUE, 555 Blvd Charest Est, 2e etage, G1K 9E5. SAN 322-7308. Tel: 418-641-3000. FAX: 418-641-3060. Web Site: bibliotheque.enap.ca/fr/accueil.aspx. *Librn,* Karine Lamontagne; E-mail: karine.lamontagne@enap.ca
Founded 1969
Library Holdings: Bk Titles 60,157; Per Subs 407
Subject Interests: Econ, Psychol, Pub admin, Pub mgt, Sociol
Publications: Bulletin signaletique des acquisitions; Guide bibliographique en administration publique; Liste des publications et rapports de recherche du personnel de l'Enap; Vient de paraitre
Open Mon-Thurs 8:30am-10pm, Fri 8:30-5, Sat 10-5

Departmental Libraries:

MONTREAL CAMPUS, 4750 Ave Henri-Julien, 3e etage, Montreal, H2T 3E5, SAN 325-4445. Tel: 514-849-3989. FAX: 514-849-3369. *Head of Libr,* Karine Lamontagne; E-mail: karine.lamontagne@enap.ca; Staff 4 (MLS 1, Non-MLS 3)
Library Holdings: Bk Vols 54,077; Per Subs 1,662
Subject Interests: Intl admin, Local admin, Pub admin
Open Mon & Thurs 9-6, Tues & Wed 9-8, Fri 9-5, Sat 12-4

M HOPITAL DE L'ENFANT JESUS*, Bibliotheque Charles-Auguste-Gauthier, 1401 18e Rue, G1J 1Z4, SAN 321-6853. Tel: 418-525-4444, Ext 65686. FAX: 418-649-5627. E-mail: bibliotheque@chudequebec.ca. *Librn,* Zorica Djordjevic; Tel: 418-525-4444, Ext 82132; *Libr Tech,* Lucie Cote
Founded 1964
Library Holdings: Bk Titles 3,500; Per Subs 175
Subject Interests: Neurology
Wireless access
Open Mon-Fri 8:30-4:30

M HOSPITAL DU SAINT-SACREMENT, Bibliotheque Delage-Couture, 1050, Chemin Sainte-Foy, G1S 4L8. Tel: 418-525-4444, Ext 82128. FAX: 418-682-7730. E-mail: biblio.hss.ens@chudequebec.ca. Web Site: sigles-symbols.bac-lac.gc.ca/eng/search/details?id=6950. *Librn,* Zorica Djordjevic
Library Holdings: Bk Titles 2,422; Bk Vols 99
Restriction: Non-circulating

G INSTITUT DE LA STATISTIQUE DU QUEBEC*, Centre d'Information et de Documentation, 200 Chemin Ste Foy, 3e etage, G1R 5T4. SAN 374-6062. Tel: 418-691-2401. Toll Free Tel: 800-463-4090. FAX: 418-643-4129. E-mail: cid@stat.gouv.qc.ca. Web Site: www.stat.gouv.qc.ca. *Coordr,* Manon Leclerc; E-mail: manon.leclerc@stat.gouv.qc.ca; Staff 6 (MLS 1, Non-MLS 5)
Founded 1978
Library Holdings: Bk Titles 7,000; Bk Vols 18,000; Per Subs 45
Special Collections: Statistics Canada Coll, bks, CD-ROM
Open Mon-Fri 8:30-4:30

C INSTITUT NATIONAL DE LA RECHERCHE SCIENTIFIQUE*, 490 de la Couronne, G1K 9A9. SAN 373-7713. Tel: 418-654-2577. Reference Tel: 418-654-2663. E-mail: sdis@inrs.ca. Web Site: sdis.inrs.ca. *Libr Mgr,* Jean-Daniel Bourgault; E-mail: jean-daniel.bourgault@ete.inrs.ca; *Circ,* Pascale Dion; E-mail: pascale.dion@ete.inrs.ca; *Tech Serv,* Anne Robitaille; Tel: 418-654-2588, E-mail: anne.robitaille@ete.inrs.ca; Staff 4 (MLS 1, Non-MLS 3)
Founded 1970. Enrl 200; Fac 40; Highest Degree: Doctorate
Library Holdings: e-books 3,200; e-journals 4,500; Bk Titles 28,000; Per Subs 15
Special Collections: INRS-Eau Terre Environnement / Rapports de recherche
Subject Interests: Earth sci, Environ sci, Water sci
Automation Activity & Vendor Info: (Cataloging) OCLC Worldshare Management Services; (Circulation) OCLC Worldshare Management Services; (Discovery) OCLC Worldshare Management Services; (ILL) Fretwell-Downing; (OPAC) OCLC
Wireless access
Partic in Bureau de cooperation Interuniversitaire; Canadian Research Knowledge Network

GM INSTITUT UNIVERSITAIRE DE CARDIOLOGIE ET DE PNEUMOLOGIE DE QUEBEC BIBLIOTHEQUE*, 2725 Chemin Ste-Foy, Bibliotheque Y2244, G1V 4G5. SAN 322-8835. Tel: 418-656-4563. FAX: 418-656-4720. E-mail: iucpq.bibliotheque@ssss.gouv.qc.ca. Web Site: bibliotheque.iucpq.qc.ca/nous-joindre. *Librn,* Francine Aumont; E-mail: francine.aumont@ssss.gouv.qc.ca; Staff 2 (MLS 1, Non-MLS 1)
Founded 1960
Library Holdings: Per Subs 166
Subject Interests: Cardiology, Internal med, Respiratory med
Function: Health sci info serv

M INSTITUT UNIVERSITAIRE EN SANTE MENTALE*, Centre de Documentation, 2601 rue de la Canardiere, G1J 2G3. SAN 319-8472. Tel: 418-663-5300. FAX: 418-666-9416. E-mail: biblio@crulrg.ulaval.ca. *Adminr,* Murielle Lavoie; E-mail: murielle_lavoie@ssss.gouv.qc.ca; Staff 2 (Non-MLS 2)
Founded 1927
Library Holdings: Bk Vols 3,000; Per Subs 50
Subject Interests: Psychiat
Restriction: Mem organizations only

S LES ARCHIVES DE LA VILLE DE QUEBEC*, 350 rue Saint Joseph E, 4th Flr, G1K 3B2. SAN 370-713X. Tel: 418-641-6214. FAX: 418-641-6702. E-mail: archives@ville.quebec.qc.ca. Web Site: www.ville.quebec.qc.ca/citoyens/patrimoine/archives. *Dir, Div Archives,* Jerome Begin
Library Holdings: Bk Titles 5,000
Open Tues-Fri 8:30-12 & 1-4

S LITERARY & HISTORICAL SOCIETY OF QUEBEC LIBRARY*, 44 Chaussee des Ecossais, G1R 4H3. SAN 319-857X. Tel: 418-694-9147, Ext 227. FAX: 418-694-0754. E-mail: info@morrin.org. Web Site: www.morrin.org/en/explore-the-library. *Libr Mgr,* Kathleen Hulley; Tel: 418-694-9147, Ext 229, E-mail: kathleenhulley@morrin.org
Founded 1824
Library Holdings: Large Print Bks 200; Bk Vols 30,000; Per Subs 20; Talking Bks 25
Special Collections: Canadiana
Subject Interests: Local hist
Wireless access
Function: Prof lending libr
Open Tues 12-8, Wed-Fri & Sun 12-4, Sat 10-4

G MINISTERE DE L'EMPLOI ET DE LA SOLIDARITE SOCIALE*, Bibliothèque Cecile-Rouleau, Marie-Guyart Bldg, RC, 700 rue Jacques-Parizeau, G1R 5E5. SAN 319-8626. Tel: 418-643-1515. Toll Free Tel: 855-643-1515. E-mail: bcr@mtess.gouv.qc.ca. Web Site: www.bibliotheques.gouv.qc.ca. *Libr Mgr,* Dominic Jargaille; E-mail: dominic.jargaille@mtess.gouv.qc.ca; Staff 7 (MLS 7)
Founded 1972
Special Collections: Canadian and Provincial
Subject Interests: Computer sci, Economy, Educ, Environ, Intergovernmental affairs, Mgt, Native people, Pub admin, Quebec law, Road safety, Tourism
Automation Activity & Vendor Info: (Acquisitions) BiblioMondo; (Cataloging) BiblioMondo; (Circulation) BiblioMondo; (OPAC) BiblioMondo; (Serials) BiblioMondo
Wireless access
Open Mon-Fri 8:30-4:30

G MINISTERE DE L ENERGIE ET DES RESSOURCES NATURELLES DU QUEBEC*, 5700 4e Ave Ouest, B-205, G1H 6R1. SAN 319-8456. Tel: 418-627-8686. FAX: 418-644-1124. E-mail: bibliotheque@mern-mffp.gouv.qc.ca. Web Site: www.mern.gouv.qc.ca. *Librn,* Francis Bedard; E-mail: francis.bedard@mern.gouv.qc.ca; *ILL,* Louis-Philippe Lapointe; Staff 4 (MLS 1, Non-MLS 3)
Founded 1969
Library Holdings: Bk Titles 55,000; Bk Vols 57,000; Per Subs 500
Special Collections: Forestry & Geology (Ministere des Ressources Naturelles, USDA Forest Service, Forest Canada); Geological Survey of Canada; Mines (US Bureau of Mines)
Subject Interests: Chem, Conserv, Energy, Entomology, Forest econ, Forestry, Geol, Hydraulics, Hydrol, Land surveying geodesy, Law, Metallurgy, Meteorology, Mines, Mining, Pollution, Wildlife
Automation Activity & Vendor Info: (Acquisitions) BiblioMondo; (Cataloging) BiblioMondo; (Circulation) BiblioMondo; (OPAC) BiblioMondo; (Serials) BiblioMondo
Function: Computers for patron use, Electronic databases & coll, Online cat, Outside serv via phone, mail, e-mail & web, Photocopying/Printing, Prof lending libr, Ref serv available, Wheelchair accessible
Partic in Reseau Informatise des Bibliotheques du Gouvernement du Quebec
Restriction: Circulates for staff only

S MUSEE DE LA CIVILISATION - BIBLIOTHEQUE DU SEMINAIRE DE QUEBEC*, Direction des Collections, 9 rue de l'Universite, G1R 5K1. (Mail add: 16 rue de la Barricade, G1K 8W9), SAN 377-4945. Tel: 418-643-2158, Ext 796. Toll Free Tel: 866-710-8031, Ext 796. FAX: 418-692-5206. E-mail: collections@mcq.org. Web Site: www.mcq.org. *Dir,* Dany Brown; *Archivist, Coordr,* Anne Laplante; *Archivist,* Peter Gagné; *Tech Serv,* Adam Proulx
Library Holdings: Bk Vols 184,000
Subject Interests: Econ, Hist, Rare bks, Sci
Function: Ref serv available
Restriction: Non-circulating coll, Open by appt only

S MUSEE NATIONAL DES BEAUX-ARTS DU QUEBEC BIBLIOTHEQUE*, Parc des Champs-de-Bataille, G1R 5H3. SAN 320-3549. Tel: 418-644-6460. Reference Tel: 418-644-6460, Ext 3344. E-mail: biblio@mnbaq.org. Web Site: www.mnbaq.org. *Documentation Tech,* Nicole Gastonguay
Founded 1933
Library Holdings: AV Mats 56; CDs 35; DVDs 102; Electronic Media & Resources 64; Microforms 190; Bk Titles 40,000; Spec Interest Per Sub 86; Videos 138
Special Collections: Artists Archives; Artists Files; Research Archives
Subject Interests: Fine arts, Mus studies
Automation Activity & Vendor Info: (Acquisitions) BiblioMondo; (Cataloging) BiblioMondo; (Circulation) BiblioMondo; (OPAC) BiblioMondo
Partic in Reseau Informatise des Bibliotheques Gouvernementales du Quebec

G QUEBEC MINISTERE DE LA JUSTICE BIBLIOTHEQUE, 1200 Rte de l'Eglise, Local 415, G1V 4M1. SAN 322-7553. Tel: 418-643-8409. FAX: 418-643-9749. E-mail: biblio.justice@justice.gouv.qc.ca. *Librn,* Marc Lacerte; E-mail: marc.lacerte@justice.gouv.qc.ca; Staff 1 (Non-MLS 1)
Founded 1965
Subject Interests: Admin of justice, Criminology, Law
Restriction: Staff use only

G REVENU QUEBEC CENTRE DE DOCUMENTATION, 3800 rue de Marly, Secteur 5-1-10, G1X 4A5. SAN 320-3522. Tel: 418-652-5765. E-mail: centredoc-legal@revenuquebec.ca. *Librn,* Veronique Cayouette; E-mail: veronique.cayouette@revenuquebec.ca; Staff 2 (MLS 1, Non-MLS 1)
Founded 1961
Library Holdings: Bk Titles 10,000; Bk Vols 13,000; Per Subs 75

Subject Interests: Income, Law, Taxation
Automation Activity & Vendor Info: (Cataloging) BiblioMondo; (Circulation) BiblioMondo; (OPAC) BiblioMondo
Wireless access
Restriction: Open to govt employees only

S SOCIETE DE GENEALOGIE DE QUEBEC*, Pavillon Louis-Jacques-Casault/Cite Universitaire Laval, 1055 av du Seminaire, Local 4240, G1V 4A8. (Mail add: CP 9066 Succ Sainte-Foy, G1V 4A8), SAN 373-8337. Tel: 418-651-9127. FAX: 418-651-2643. E-mail: sgq@uniserve.com. Web Site: www.sgq.qc.ca/centre-de-documentation/bibliotheque. *Pres,* Guy Auclair
Founded 1961
Library Holdings: Bk Titles 3,000; Bk Vols 4,000; Per Subs 35
Subject Interests: Genealogy
Wireless access
Publications: L'Ancetre

C TELUQ UNIVERSITY*, Bibliotech at distance, 455 rue du Parvis, F015-B, G1K 9H6. SAN 375-0868. Tel: 418-657-2747, Ext 5397. Toll Free Tel: 888-843-4333 (Canada only). FAX: 418-657-2094. E-mail: biblio@teluq.ca. Web Site: bibliotheque.teluq.ca. *Dir,* Francois Ouellette; Tel: 418-657-2262, Ext 5044, E-mail: fracois.ouellette@teluq.ca; *Librn,* Marie-Josee Drolet; Tel: 418-657-2262, Ext 5333, E-mail: marie-josee.drolet@teluq.ca; *Doc Librn,* Mylene Lalonde; Tel: 418-657-2262, Ext 2057, E-mail: mylene.lalonde@teluq.ca
Library Holdings: Bk Vols 37,925; Per Subs 21,062
Subject Interests: Distance educ
Wireless access
Open Mon-Fri 8:30-12 & 1-4:30

C UNIVERSITE LAVAL BIBLIOTHEQUE, Bibliotheque des Sciences Humaines et Sociales, Pavillon Jean-Charles-Bonenfant, 2345, allée des Bibliothèques, G1V 0A6. Tel: 418-656-3344. Circulation Tel: 418-656-2131, Ext 5351. E-mail: bibl@bibl.ulaval.ca. Web Site: www.bibl.ulaval.ca. *Dir,* Loubna Ghaouti; E-mail: loubna.ghaouti@bibl.ulaval.ca; *Dir, Admin Serv,* Charles Berube; *Dir, Info Res,* Maryse Legault; *Director, Research Support,* Marie-Eve Paridis; *Asst Dir,* Marie-Claude Mailhot; Staff 50 (MLS 50)
Founded 1852. Highest Degree: Doctorate
Automation Activity & Vendor Info: (Acquisitions) SirsiDynix; (Cataloging) SirsiDynix; (Circulation) SirsiDynix; (Serials) SirsiDynix
Wireless access
Function: Homebound delivery serv, ILL available, Photocopying/Printing, Ref serv available, Res libr
Partic in Canadian Association of Research Libraries; Canadian Research Knowledge Network
Open Mon-Fri 8am-11pm, Sat & Sun 10-5:30
Restriction: Open to students, fac & staff

QUEBEC CITY

G NATURAL RESOURCES CANADA-FORESTRY*, Laurentian Forestry Centre Library, 1055 rue du PEPS, G1V 4C7. (Mail add: PO Box 10380, Stn Sainte-Foy, G1V 4C7), SAN 319-9037. Tel: 418-648-4850. Web Site: www.nrcan.gc.ca/forests/research-centres/lfc/13473. *Mgr, Libr Serv,* Deirdre Moore; E-mail: deirdre.moore@canada.ca; *Libr Tech,* Eve Montminy; Tel: 418-648-4428, E-mail: eve.montminy@canada.ca; Staff 2 (MLS 1, Non-MLS 1)
Founded 1952
Library Holdings: AV Mats 100; e-books 450; Bk Titles 12,000; Per Subs 150
Subject Interests: Botany, Entomology, Forest res, Forestry econs, Mycology, Silviculture, Vegetal genetics

REPENTIGNY

P BIBLIOTHEQUE EDMOND-ARCHAMBAULT*, 231, blvd J A Pare, J5Z 4M6. Reference Tel: 450-470-3001, Ext 3428. E-mail: bibliotheque@ville.repentigny.qc.ca. Web Site: bibliotheques.repentigny.ca. *Head, Libraries Div,* Chantal Brodeur
Open Tues-Thurs 1-9, Fri 9-5, Sat & Sun 1-5

P BIBLIOTHEQUE ROBERT-LUSSIER*, One Place d'Evry, J6A 8H7. SAN 319-8677. Tel: 450-470-3420. Reference Tel: 450-470-3001, Ext 3428. E-mail: bibliotheque@ville.repentigny.qc.ca. Web Site: bibliotheques.repentigny.ca, repentigny.ca/culture-loisirs/culture/bibliotheques/robert-lussier. *Head, Libraries Div,* Chantal Brodeur; Staff 7 (MLS 3, Non-MLS 4)
Founded 1964. Pop 74,485; Circ 407,763
Library Holdings: AV Mats 7,831; Large Print Bks 916; Bk Titles 137,741; Bk Vols 183,466; Per Subs 183
Subject Interests: Child, Fiction, Govt publ, Non-fiction bks for adults
Wireless access
Open Mon-Thurs 10-9, Fri & Sat 9-5, Sun 1-5

RIMOUSKI

P BIBLIOTHEQUE LISETTE-MORIN (MUNICIPALE DE RIMOUSKI)*, 110 de l'Eveche est, CP 710, G5L 7C7. SAN 321-2602. Tel: 418-724-3164. E-mail: bibliotheque.lisette-morin@ville.rimouski.qc.ca. Web Site: www.ville.rimouski.qc.ca. *Librn,* Nicole Gagnon
Pop 45,000
Library Holdings: Bk Vols 100,000
Open Mon-Fri 9:30-8, Sat 9:30-4:30, Sun 1-4:30

C UNIVERSITE DU QUEBEC A RIMOUSKI - SERVICE DE LA BIBLIOTHEQUE*, 300 Allee des Ursulines, G5L 3A1. SAN 321-3692. Tel: 418-723-1986, Ext 1470. Circulation Tel: 418-723-1986, Ext 1476. Interlibrary Loan Service Tel: 418-723-1986, Ext 1437. FAX: 418-724-1621. E-mail: bibliotheque@uqar.ca. Web Site: biblio.uqar.ca. *Dir,* Isabelle-Annie Lévesque; E-mail: Isabelle-annie_Levesque@uqar.ca; *Librn,* Marie-Eve Emond-Beaulieu; Tel: 418-833-8800, Ext 3287, E-mail: marie-eve_emond-beaulieu@uqar.ca; *Librn,* Louis Michaud; Tel: 418-723-1986, Ext 1213, E-mail: louis_michaud@uqar.ca; *Librn,* Jean-Francois Rioux; Tel: 418-723-1986, Ext 1669, E-mail: jean-francois_rioux@uqar.ca; *Librn,* Sandrine Vachon; Tel: 418-723-1986, Ext 1481, E-mail: sandrine_vachon@uqar.ca; *Coordr, Tech Serv & Syst,* Suzie Pelletier; Tel: 418-723-1986, Ext 1502, E-mail: suzie_pelletier@uqar.ca; *Info Access Coordr,* Josee Pelletier; Tel: 418-723-1986, Ext 1479, E-mail: josee_pelletier@uqar.ca; *Advisory Ref, Tech Serv,* Thomas Aubert; Tel: 418-723-1986, Ext 1463, E-mail: thomas_aubert@uqar.ca. Subject Specialists: *Educ, Nursing, Soc work,* Marie-Eve Emond-Beaulieu; *Engr, Sci,* Louis Michaud; *Archives, Hist,* Jean-Francois Rioux; *Lit, Nursing, Soc work,* Sandrine Vachon; Staff 23 (MLS 8, Non-MLS 15)
Founded 1969. Enrl 3,915; Fac 198; Highest Degree: Doctorate
Library Holdings: AV Mats 3,169; Electronic Media & Resources 304,084; Microforms 1,860; Bk Titles 167,512; Per Subs 148
Special Collections: Documentation Regionale de l'Est du Quebec; Patrimoniale de l'Institut Maurice-Lamontagne Coll
Automation Activity & Vendor Info: (Acquisitions) OCLC Worldshare Management Services; (Cataloging) OCLC Worldshare Management Services; (Circulation) OCLC Worldshare Management Services; (Course Reserve) OCLC Worldshare Management Services; (Discovery) OCLC Worldshare Management Services; (ILL) OCLC Worldshare Management Services; (OPAC) OCLC Worldshare Management Services; (Serials) OCLC Worldshare Management Services
Wireless access
Function: 24/7 Electronic res, 24/7 Online cat, Archival coll, AV serv, Computers for patron use, Electronic databases & coll, ILL available, Internet access, Magazines, Microfiche/film & reading machines, Online cat, Photocopying/Printing, Ref serv available, Study rm, Wheelchair accessible
Open Mon-Thurs 8:30am-10pm, Fri 8:30-8, Sat & Sun Noon-5

RIVIERE-DU-LOUP

P BIBLIOTHEQUE MUNICIPALE FRANCOISE-BEDARD*, 67 rue du Rocher, G5R 1J8. SAN 319-8715. Tel: 418-862-4252. FAX: 418-862-3478. E-mail: bibliotheque@ville.riviere-du-loup.qc.ca. Web Site: villerdl.ca/en/leasure/bibliotheque/votre-bibliotheque. *Chief Librn,* Sylvie Michaud; Tel: 418-867-6669, E-mail: sylvie.michaud@ville.riviere-du-loup.qc.ca; Staff 2.5 (MLS 1, Non-MLS 1.5)
Founded 1980. Pop 19,974; Circ 100,057
Library Holdings: Audiobooks 543; CDs 5,122; DVDs 479; Large Print Bks 2,011; Bk Titles 62,458; Bk Vols 68,136; Per Subs 106
Subject Interests: Caregiving, Genealogy, Local hist
Automation Activity & Vendor Info: (Cataloging) SirsiDynix-WorkFlows; (Circulation) SirsiDynix-WorkFlows; (OPAC) SirsiDynix-iBistro
Wireless access
Function: 24/7 Electronic res, Online cat, Wheelchair accessible
Special Services for the Blind - Accessible computers; Assistive/Adapted tech devices, equip & products; Bks on CD; Large print bks; Magnifiers; PC for people with disabilities; Playaways (bks on MP3); Talking bks; ZoomText magnification & reading software
Open Mon-Fri 12-8, Sat 10-5, Sun 1-5

C CEGEP RIVIERE DU-LOUP-BIBLIOTHEQUE, 80 rue Frontenac, G5R 1R1. SAN 323-5807. Tel: 418-862-6903, Ext 2579. FAX: 418-862-4959. E-mail: biblio@cegeprdl.ca. Web Site: www.cegeprdl.ca/grand-public/bibliotheque. *Head of Libr,* Jeremie Pouliot; *Librn,* Elise Martin; E-mail: elise.martin@cegeprdl.ca; Staff 5 (MLS 1, Non-MLS 4)
Enrl 970; Fac 15
Library Holdings: Per Subs 81
Wireless access

P RESEAU BIBLIOTHEQUES DU BAS-SAINT-LAURENT*, 465 St Pierre, G5R 4T6. SAN 321-0979. Tel: 418-867-1682. FAX: 418-867-3434. E-mail: crsbp@crsbp.net. Web Site: www.reseaubibliobsl.qc.ca. *Dir Gen,* Jacques Cote; Tel: 418-867-1682, Ext 112, E-mail: jacques.cote@crsbp.net; *Librn,* Sarah-Kim Poirier; Tel: 418-714-6007
Founded 1979. Pop 101,443; Circ 489,077
Library Holdings: Bk Titles 139,245; Bk Vols 489,077
Special Collections: Bas-St-Laurent Area
Automation Activity & Vendor Info: (Acquisitions) SirsiDynix; (Cataloging) SirsiDynix; (Circulation) SirsiDynix; (OPAC) SirsiDynix
Wireless access

ROSEMERE

P BIBLIOTHEQUE H J HEMENS*, Bibliothèque de Rosemère, 339 Chemin Grande-Cote, J7A 1K2. SAN 319-8731. Tel: 450-621-3500, Ext 7221. FAX: 450-621-6131. E-mail: biblio@ville.rosemere.qc.ca. Web Site: biblio.ville.rosemere.qc.ca. *Dir,* Marc Bineault; *Tech Serv Team Leader,* Tania Lobo; E-mail: tlobo@ville.rosemere.qc.ca
Founded 1946. Pop 14,193; Circ 138,728
Library Holdings: Audiobooks 626; CDs 1,650; DVDs 300; Bk Titles 72,400; Bk Vols 77,000; Per Subs 174
Automation Activity & Vendor Info: (Cataloging) BiblioMondo; (Circulation) BiblioMondo; (Course Reserve) BiblioMondo; (OPAC) BiblioMondo
Wireless access
Open Mon-Thurs 1-9, Fri & Sat 10-5, Sun Noon-4:30; Mon-Thurs 10-9, Fri & Sat 10-5 (Summer)

ROUYN-NORANDA

P BIBLIOTHEQUE MUNICIPALE DE ROUYN-NORANDA*, 201 Ave Dallaire, J9X 4T5. SAN 319-874X. Tel: 819-762-0944. FAX: 819-797-7564. E-mail: info@biblrn.qc.ca. Web Site: www.biblrn.qc.ca. *Dir, Libr Serv,* Miriam Lefebvre; E-mail: direction.generale@biblrn.qc.ca; Staff 5 (MLS 1, Non-MLS 4)
Founded 1947. Pop 29,600; Circ 350,000
Library Holdings: Bk Vols 100,000; Per Subs 100
Subject Interests: English, Multilingual
Publications: Annual report
Open Mon-Fri 12-8

C CEGEP DE L'ABITIBI - TEMISCAMINGUE BIBLIOTHEQUE*, 425 Boul du College, J9X 5M5. SAN 369-5344. Tel: 819-762-0931, Ext 1234. FAX: 819-762-2071. E-mail: aide.bibliotheque@uqat.ca. Web Site: bib.uqat.ca. *Dir,* David Fournier-Viger; E-mail: david.fournier-viger@uqat.ca; *Librn,* Marie-Marcelle Dubuc; E-mail: marie-marcelle-dubuc@uqat.ca; *Documentation Tech,* Camee Toupin-Lefebvre; E-mail: camee.toupin-lefebvre@uqat.ca; Staff 2 (MLS 2)
Founded 1953. Enrl 2,300
Library Holdings: DVDs 6,200; Bk Vols 225,036; Per Subs 700
Special Collections: Northwestern Quebec, bk, microform. Canadian and Provincial
Wireless access
Open Mon-Thurs 8am-9:45pm, Fri 8am-8:45pm, Sat & Sun Noon-4:15

P RESEAU BIBLIO ABITIBI-TEMISCAMINQUE-NORD-DU-QUEBEC*, Centre Regional Biblio, 20 Quebec Ave, J9X 2E6. SAN 321-2629. Tel: 819-762-4305. FAX: 819-762-5309. E-mail: info@reseaubiblioatnq.qc.ca. Web Site: mabiblio.quebec. *Exec Dir,* Louis Dallaire; Tel: 819-762-4305, Ext 23, E-mail: louis.dallaire@reseaubiblioatnq.qc.ca; Staff 9 (MLS 4, Non-MLS 5)
Founded 1976. Pop 58,299; Circ 269,439
Library Holdings: Bk Titles 75,507; Bk Vols 142,645; Per Subs 660
Special Collections: Provincial
Publications: L'Echange (Bimonthly)
Open Mon-Fri 9-12 & 1-4

SAINT BRUNO-DE-MONTARVILLE

P BIBLIOTHEQUE MUNICIPALE DE SAINT-BRUNO-DE-MONTARVILLE*, Georges-Brossard Library, 82 Seigneurial W, J3V 5N7. SAN 319-8782. Tel: 450-645-2950. FAX: 450-441-8485. E-mail: bibliotheque@stbruno.ca. Web Site: biblio.stbruno.ca, stbruno.ca/loisirs-et-culture/bibliotheque-municipale. *Dir,* Oleria Bedoieva; Staff 9 (MLS 1, Non-MLS 8)
Founded 1961. Pop 25,000; Circ 175,000
Library Holdings: Bk Titles 75,000; Bk Vols 85,000; Per Subs 137
Special Collections: Canadian and Provincial
Automation Activity & Vendor Info: (Acquisitions) BiblioMondo; (Cataloging) BiblioMondo; (Circulation) BiblioMondo; (OPAC) BiblioMondo; (Serials) BiblioMondo
Wireless access
Open Mon-Fri 9-8, Sat & Sun 10-5 (Winter); Mon-Fri 9-8, Sat 10-5, Sun 1-5 (Summer)

SAINT CHARLES BORROMEE

M CENTRE DE SANTE ET DE SERVICES SOCIAUX DU NORD DE LANAUDIERE BIBLIOTHEQUE*, Medical Staff Library, 1000 Blvd Ste-Anne, J6E 6J2. SAN 319-6577. Tel: 450-759-8222, Ext 2325. FAX: 450-759-7343. E-mail: bibliotheque.cissslan@ssss.gouv.qc.ca. Web Site: bibliocissslanaudiere.visard.ca. *Librn,* Nancy Gadoury; Tel: 450-759-8222, Ext 2326, E-mail: nancy.gadoury@ssss.gouv.qc.ca; *Documentation Tech,* Christiane Rondeau; E-mail: christiane.rondeau@ssss.gouv.qc.ca
Founded 1964
Library Holdings: Bk Titles 2,000; Per Subs 150
Subject Interests: Med, Nursing, Psychiat, Psychol
Open Mon-Fri 8:30-12 & 1-4:30
Branches:
BIBLIOTHEQUE DE L'HOPITAL PIERRE-LE GARDEUR, 911, montée des Pionniers, Terrebonne, J6V 2H2. Tel: 450-654-7525, Ext 22207. E-mail: documentation@cssssl.ca. *Documentation Tech,* Manon Therrien; E-mail: manon.therrien@ssss.gouv.qc.ca
Open Mon & Wed 8:30-Noon & 1-4:30, Tues, Thurs & Sat 8-4:30

SAINT CONSTANT

S EXPORAIL ARCHIVES LIBRARY*, The Canadian Railway Museum, 110 rue, St-Pierre, J5A 1G7. SAN 325-9846. Tel: 450-638-1522, Ext 237. FAX: 450-638-1522. E-mail: info@exporail.org. Web Site: www.exporail.org. *Archivist,* Mylene Belanger; E-mail: mylene.belanger@exporail.org
Library Holdings: Bk Titles 6,000; Per Subs 800
Subject Interests: Railway hist
Wireless access

SAINT EUSTACHE

P BIBLIOTHEQUE MUNICIPALE GUY-BELISLE SAINT EUSTACHE*, 12 chemin de la Grande-Cote, J7P 1AZ. SAN 322-676X. Tel: 450-974-5035. FAX: 450-974-5054. Web Site: www.saint-eustache.ca/bibliotheque. *Chief Librn,* Nicole Grimard; E-mail: ngrimard@saint-eustache.qc.ca; Staff 2 (MLS 2)
Pop 45,000
Library Holdings: Bk Vols 132,840; Per Subs 240
Special Collections: Canada & Quebec Govt
Subject Interests: Genealogy, Hist, Patrimony
Automation Activity & Vendor Info: (Acquisitions) Koha; (Cataloging) Koha; (Circulation) Koha; (Media Booking) Koha; (OPAC) Koha; (Serials) Koha
Function: 24/7 Electronic res, 24/7 Online cat, Activity rm, Adult bk club, Audiobks on Playaways & MP3, Audiobks via web, Bks on CD, CD-ROM, Children's prog, Computer training, E-Readers, E-Reserves, Electronic databases & coll, Free DVD rentals, Genealogy discussion group, ILL available, Internet access, Magazines, Online cat, Online info literacy tutorials on the web & in blackboard, Online ref, Orientations, Outreach serv, Prog for children & young adult, Ref & res, Ref serv available, Res assist avail, Scanner, Teen prog, Wheelchair accessible
Open Mon-Fri 9-9, Sat & Sun 9-5

SAINT FELICIEN

P BIBLIOTHEQUE MUNICIPALE DE SAINT FELICIEN*, 1209 Blvd Sacre-Coeur, G8K 2R5. SAN 319-8790. Tel: 418-679-2100, Ext 2245. FAX: 418-679-1449. E-mail: info@ville.stfelicien.qc.ca. Web Site: www.ville.stfelicien.qc.ca/fr/citoyens/bibliotheque-de-saint-felicien. *Libr Tech,* Bruno Forget; E-mail: bruno.forget@ville.stfelicien.qc.ca
Founded 1962. Pop 9,058; Circ 19,281
Library Holdings: DVDs 2,816; e-books 1,224; Bk Vols 36,520; Per Subs 56
Open Tues-Thurs 12-9, Fri 12-6, Sat 9-Noon, Sun 12-3

C CEGEP DE SAINT FELICIEN*, Centre de Documentation, 1105 boul Hamel, G8K 2R8. (Mail add: PO Box 7300, G8K 2R8), SAN 322-8371. Tel: 418-679-5412, Ext 284. FAX: 418-679-1040. E-mail: biblio@cegepstfe.ca. Web Site: www.cegepstfe.ca/centre_documentation. *ILL, Ref,* Diane Bernier; E-mail: dbernier@cegepstfe.ca; Staff 3 (MLS 1, Non-MLS 2)
Founded 1971. Enrl 998
Library Holdings: Bk Titles 65,000; Per Subs 125
Subject Interests: Natural sci
Wireless access
Open Mon-Thurs 8-6, Fri 8-5

SAINT GEORGES-DE-BEAUCE

C CEGEP BEAUCE APPALACHES*, Jean-Marie Darouin Bibliotheque, 1055 116e rue, G5Y 3G1. SAN 372-7475. Tel: 418-228-8896, Ext 2310. FAX: 418-228-0562. E-mail: bibli@cegepba.qc.ca. Web Site: biblio.cegepba.qc.ca. *Head Librn,* Aurelia Giusti; Tel: 418-228-8896, Ext 2314, E-mail: agiusti@cegepba.qc.ca

Library Holdings: Bk Vols 46,420; Per Subs 105
Automation Activity & Vendor Info: (Cataloging) Koha; (OPAC) Koha
Wireless access

SAINT JACQUES

P BIBLIOTHEQUE MUNICIPALE MARCEL-DUGAS*, 16 rue Marechal, J0K 2R0. SAN 319-8855. Tel: 450-831-2296. FAX: 450-839-2387. E-mail: biblio@st-jacques.org. Web Site: www.st-jacques.org/index.jsp?p=19. *Head, Tech Serv, Libr Tech,* JoAnie Buisson; Tel: 450-839-3671, Ext 7682
Pop 4,100; Circ 13,847
Library Holdings: Bk Vols 20,000
Open Mon & Tues 1-6, Thurs 1-8, Sat 9-Noon

SAINT JEROME

P BIBLIOTHEQUE MARIE-ANTOINETTE-FOUCHER*, 101 Place du Cure-Labelle, J7Z 1X6. SAN 319-8898. Tel: 450-432-0569. FAX: 450-436-1211. Web Site: www.vsj.ca. *Dir,* Claudine Richer; Tel: 450-436-1512, Ext 3330, E-mail: cricher@vsj.ca; *Libr Asst,* Sophie Boivin; E-mail: sboivin@vsj.ca; Staff 19 (MLS 1, Non-MLS 18)
Founded 1949. Pop 60,000
Library Holdings: Bk Vols 50,000; Per Subs 100
Automation Activity & Vendor Info: (Acquisitions) MultiLIS; (Cataloging) MultiLIS; (Circulation) MultiLIS; (OPAC) MultiLIS
Wireless access
Open Mon-Fri 12-8, Sat 9-5, Sun 12-4

SAINT LAMBERT

J CHAMPLAIN REGIONAL COLLEGE AT SAINT-LAMBERT*, George Wallace Library, 900 Riverside Dr, J4P 3P2. SAN 319-8901. Tel: 450-672-7360. Circulation Tel: 450-672-7360, Ext 3221. Reference Tel: 450-672-7360, Ext 3345. FAX: 450-672-2152. Reference E-mail: reference-stlambert@crcmail.net. Web Site: libraryguides.champlainonline.com/library. *Coordr,* Nicole Hache; E-mail: nhache@crcmail.net; Staff 6 (MLS 2, Non-MLS 4)
Founded 1972. Enrl 2,400; Fac 165
Library Holdings: Bk Vols 60,000; Per Subs 10
Automation Activity & Vendor Info: (OPAC) SirsiDynix
Wireless access
Open Mon-Thurs 7:30-5:30, Fri 7:30-4:30

P SAINT LAMBERT MUNICIPAL LIBRARY*, 490 Mercille Ave, J4P 2L5. SAN 369-5433. Tel: 450-466-3910. FAX: 450-923-6512. E-mail: bibliotheque@saint-lambert.ca. Web Site: www.saint-lambert.ca/en/recreation-services/library. *Dir,* Marie-Josee Benoit; E-mail: marie-josee.benoit@saint-lambert.ca; Staff 1 (MLS 1)
Founded 1954. Pop 21,700; Circ 203,500
Library Holdings: Bk Titles 101,786; Per Subs 151
Automation Activity & Vendor Info: (Acquisitions) BiblioMondo; (Cataloging) BiblioMondo; (Circulation) BiblioMondo; (Course Reserve) BiblioMondo; (ILL) BiblioMondo; (Media Booking) BiblioMondo; (OPAC) BiblioMondo; (Serials) BiblioMondo
Open Mon & Fri Noon-6, Tues-Thurs 10-9, Sat & Sun 10-5
Friends of the Library Group

SAINT-CASIMIR

P BIBLIOTHEQUE JEAN-CHARLES MAGNAN*, 510 boul de la Montagne, G0A 3L0. SAN 321-3099. Tel: 418-339-2909. FAX: 418-339-3105. E-mail: jcmagnan@hotmail.ca. Web Site: reseaubibliocnca.qc.ca/fr/ma-bibliotheque/b407/bibliotheque-jean-charles-magnan-saint-casimir. *Mgr,* Ange-Aimee Asselin
Founded 1980. Pop 1,437
Library Holdings: Bk Vols 2,000; Per Subs 10
Open Tues 1:30-3:30, Thurs 6:30pm-8:30pm, Sat 10-Noon

SAINT-CLEMENT

P BIBLIOTHEQUE MUNICIPALE, 25A rue Saint Pierre, G0L 2N0. SAN 321-2505. Tel: 418-963-2258. Web Site: www.st-clement.ca/loisirs?menuindex=0. *Library Contact,* Therese St-Pierre
Library Holdings: Bk Vols 1,500
Automation Activity & Vendor Info: (OPAC) MultiLIS
Open Wed 7pm-8:30pm

SAINTE-ANNE-DE-BELLEVUE

P BIBLIOTHEQUE MUNICIPALE DE SAINTE-ANNE-DE-BELLEVUE*, 40, rue Saint-Pierre, H9X 1Y6. Tel: 514-457-1940. FAX: 514-457-7146. E-mail: biblio@sadb.qc.ca. Web Site: www.ville.sainte-anne-de-bellevue.qc.ca. *Libr Tech,* Annie Gauthier
Founded 1980. Pop 5,035; Circ 28,815
Library Holdings: AV Mats 819; CDs 450; DVDs 175; Bk Vols 18,000
Automation Activity & Vendor Info: (Cataloging) OPALS (Open-source Automated Library System); (Circulation) OPALS (Open-source Automated Library System); (Course Reserve) OPALS (Open-source Automated Library System); (OPAC) OPALS (Open-source Automated Library System)
Wireless access
Open Mon & Tues Noon-8, Wed 10-1:30, Thurs 10-8, Fri 3-8, Sat & Sun 11-4 (Winter); Mon, Tues & Thurs 10-8, Wed 10-5, Fri 3-8 (Summer)

C JOHN ABBOTT COLLEGE*, Library Media Services, 21275 Lakeshore Dr, H9X 3L9. SAN 326-4335. Tel: 514-457-6610, Ext 5337. Circulation Tel: 514-457-6610, Ext 5330. Reference Tel: 514-457-6610, Ext 5331. Reference E-mail: library.ref@johnabbott.qc.ca. Web Site: jac.cegep.opalsinfo.net. *Chairperson, Librn,* Marek Pukteris; E-mail: marek.pukteris@johnabbott.qc.ca; Staff 10 (MLS 3, Non-MLS 7)
Founded 1972. Enrl 6,000; Fac 400
Library Holdings: AV Mats 4,000; Bk Titles 61,000; Bk Vols 85,000; Per Subs 65
Special Collections: Canadian and Provincial
Wireless access
Open Mon-Fri 8-4

MCGILL UNIVERSITY
See Montreal

SAINTE-ANNE-DES-MONTS

S SOCIETE D'HISTOIRE DE LA HAUTE-GASPESIE*, 5B First Ave W, G4V 1B4. SAN 370-6338. Tel: 418-763-7871. E-mail: genealogie@globetrotter.net. *Gen Mgr,* Marc-Antoine DeRoy; *Archivist,* Allison Servant; Staff 1 (MLS 1)
Founded 1970
Library Holdings: Bk Vols 5,000
Special Collections: Oral History
Subject Interests: Genealogy, Local hist
Wireless access

SAINTE-FOY

C CEGEP DE SAINTE-FOY BIBLIOTHEQUE*, 2410 Chemin Sainte-Foy, G1V 1T3. SAN 319-9029. Tel: 418-659-6600, Ext 3714. FAX: 418-659-4563. E-mail: biblio@csfoy.ca. Web Site: csfoy.ca/services-aux-etudiants/aide-aux-etudes/bibliotheque. *Coordr,* Claire Giroux; E-mail: claire.giroux@csfoy.ca; Staff 6 (MLS 6)
Founded 1918. Enrl 6,100
Library Holdings: Bk Vols 90,000; Per Subs 400
Wireless access
Open Mon-Thurs 7:15am-8:45pm, Fri 7:15-6

G CONSEIL SUPERIEUR DE L'EDUCATION*, Centre de Documentation, 1175 ave Lavigerie, Bur 180, G1V 5B2. SAN 323-908X. Tel: 418-643-2845. FAX: 418-644-2530. E-mail: panorama@cse.gouv.qc.ca. Web Site: www.cse.gouv.qc.ca. *Libr Tech,* Johane Beaudoin; Tel: 418-528-0608; *Libr Tech,* Daves Couture; E-mail: daves.couture@CSE.gouv.qc.ca; Staff 2 (Non-MLS 2)
Founded 1965
Library Holdings: e-books 153; Bk Titles 7,500; Per Subs 45
Subject Interests: Educ
Restriction: Staff use only

SAINTE-THERESE

P BIBLIOTHEQUE MUNICIPALE DE SAINTE-THERESE, 150 Boul du Seminaire, J7E 1Z2. SAN 322-8258. Tel: 450-434-1440, Ext 2400. FAX: 450-434-6070. E-mail: biblio@sainte-therese.ca. Web Site: biblio.sainte-therese.ca. *Dir,* Christine Dufour; Staff 9 (MLS 2, Non-MLS 7)
Founded 1975. Pop 27,000
Library Holdings: AV Mats 1,646; Bk Vols 89,000; Per Subs 250; Talking Bks 500
Special Collections: Canadian and Provincial
Subject Interests: Travel
Automation Activity & Vendor Info: (Acquisitions) BiblioMondo; (Cataloging) BiblioMondo; (Circulation) BiblioMondo
Function: 24/7 Electronic res, 24/7 Online cat, Adult bk club, Audiobks via web, Bks on CD, Electronic databases & coll, ILL available, Internet access, Large print keyboards, Magazines, Music CDs, Online cat, Online ref, Photocopying/Printing, Prog for adults, Prog for children & young adult, Ref & res, Spanish lang bks, Story hour, Wheelchair accessible
Open Mon-Fri 10-9, Sat & Sun 10-5

SAINT-FABIAN DE PANET

P BIBLIOTHEQUE MUNICIPALE DE SAINT-FABIEN DE PANET*, 199B, rue Bilodeau, G0R 2J0. SAN 321-3048. Tel: 418-249-4471, Ext 2. FAX: 418-249-4470. E-mail: munpanet@saintfabiendepanet.com. Web Site:

www.saintfabiendepanet.com/loisirs-et-vie-communautaire/bibliotheque-coordonnes-et-horaire. *Head Librn,* Alice Lenoir
Founded 1980. Pop 946
Open Mon, Tues, Thurs & Fri 9-12 & 1-4

SAINT-HYACINTHE

CR BIBLIOTHEQUE DU SEMINAIRE DE SAINT-HYACINTHE*, 650 rue Girouard Est, J2S 2Y2. SAN 374-518X. Tel: 450-774-5560, Ext 109. FAX: 450-774-7101. E-mail: biblio@seminairesth.org. Web Site: www.bibssh.qc.ca. *Librn,* Bernard Auger. Subject Specialists: *Indexing,* Bernard Auger; Staff 1 (MLS 1)
Founded 1811
Jul 2023-Jun 2024 Income (CAN) $50,000. Mats Exp (CAN) $5,000, Books (CAN) $2,500, Per/Ser (Incl. Access Fees) (CAN) $2,500. Sal (CAN) $48,000
Library Holdings: Bk Vols 265,000
Special Collections: Rare Religious Books, 1511-1900
Subject Interests: Can hist, Fr lit, Roman Catholic relig
Automation Activity & Vendor Info: (Acquisitions) Concepts Logiques 4DI Inc; (Cataloging) Concepts Logiques 4DI Inc; (Circulation) Concepts Logiques 4DI Inc; (ILL) Concepts Logiques 4DI Inc; (OPAC) Concepts Logiques 4DI Inc; (Serials) Concepts Logiques 4DI Inc
Function: Ref serv available
Open Mon-Thurs 8-12 & 12:30-4:30

G CANADA AGRICULTURE & AGRI-FOOD CANADA*, CAL Information Center-St-Hyacinthe, 3600 Blvd Casavant W, J2S 8E3. SAN 372-6401. Tel: 450-768-9618, 450-768-9619. FAX: 450-768-7851. E-mail: aafc.libraryst-hyacinthebibliotheque.aac@agr.gc.ca. Web Site: www.agr.gc.ca. *Head, Libr & Info Serv,* Pierre Di Campo; E-mail: Pierre.DiCampo@AGR.GC.CA; *Libr Tech,* Veronique Laroche; E-mail: Veronique.Laroche@AGR.GC.CA; Staff 2 (MLS 1, Non-MLS 1)
Library Holdings: Bk Titles 10,000; Per Subs 45
Open Mon-Fri 8:30-5

R CEGEP DE SAINT-HYACINTHE BIBLIOTHEQUE*, 3000 rue Boulle, J2S 1H9. SAN 319-8839. Tel: 450-773-6800, Ext 2213. Administration Tel: 450-773-6800, Ext 2211. FAX: 450-773-9971. E-mail: biblio@cegepsth.qc.ca. Web Site: www.cegepsth.qc.ca/eludiants/services-generaux/bibliotheque-et-centre-des-medias. *Librn,* Sylviane Houle; E-mail: shoule@cegepsth.qc.ca
Founded 1929
Library Holdings: Bk Vols 80,000; Per Subs 250
Special Collections: Canadiana
Subject Interests: Educ, Humanities, Sci, Textiles
Wireless access
Open Mon-Thurs 8am-8:30pm, Fri 8-5

M CENTRE DE SANTE ET DE SERVICES SOCIAUX RICHELIEU-YAMASKA*, Bibliotheque Romeo-Germain, 2750 boul Laframboise, J2S 4Y8. SAN 375-3646. Tel: 450-771-3333, Ext 793242. FAX: 450-771-3304. Web Site: www.lesommetavotreportee.qc.ca/info/Bibliotheque. *Mgr,* Mr Alain Dery; E-mail: alain.dery.csssry16@ssss.gouv.qc.ca
Library Holdings: Bk Vols 5,000; Per Subs 80
Subject Interests: Med

P MEDIATHEQUE MASKOUTAINE*, 2750 rue Dessaulles, J2S 2V7. SAN 325-2116. Tel: 450-773-1830. FAX: 450-773-3398. E-mail: info@mediatheque.qc.ca. Web Site: www.mediatheque.qc.ca. *Admin Dir,* Yves Tanguay; E-mail: tanguayy@mediatheque.qc.ca; Staff 77 (MLS 3, Non-MLS 74)
Founded 1954. Pop 63,624; Circ 380,522
Jan 2017-Dec 2017 Income (CAN) $1,798,074, Provincial (CAN) $180,900, City (CAN) $1,473,312, Federal (CAN) $13,244, County (CAN) $1,850, Locally Generated Income (CAN) $112,268, Other (CAN) $16,500. Mats Exp (CAN) $722,983, Books (CAN) $192,873, Per/Ser (Incl. Access Fees) (CAN) $17,657, AV Equip (CAN) $51,688, AV Mat (CAN) $390,639, Electronic Ref Mat (Incl. Access Fees) (CAN) $70,126. Sal (CAN) $1,000,884
Library Holdings: CDs 14,211; DVDs 21,949; e-books 14,528; Electronic Media & Resources 14; Large Print Bks 2,559; Bk Titles 169,873; Bk Vols 244,509; Per Subs 325; Talking Bks 1,681; Videos 26,688
Special Collections: Maskoutana
Automation Activity & Vendor Info: (Acquisitions) SirsiDynix-Unicorn; (Cataloging) SirsiDynix-Unicorn; (Circulation) SirsiDynix-Unicorn; (Course Reserve) SirsiDynix-Unicorn; (OPAC) SirsiDynix-iBistro; (Serials) SirsiDynix-Unicorn
Wireless access
Publications: Liste Collective des Periodiques des Bibliotheques de la Monteregie
Open Mon-Thurs 12-9, Fri 10-9, Sat & Sun 10-5
Friends of the Library Group

SAINT-JACQUES DE LEEDS

P BIBLIOTHEQUE LA RESSOURCE DE LA MUNIPALITE DE SAINT-JACQUES-DE-LEEDS, 415 rue Principale, G0N 1J0. SAN 321-2874. Tel: 418-424-3321, Ext 228. E-mail: biblio@saintjacquesdeleeds.ca. Web Site: biblio.saintjacquesdeleeds.ca.
Founded 1984. Pop 769
Function: Story hour
Open Tues 12:30-3 & 7-8, Wed 1-1:30, Thurs 12:30-3

SAINT-JEAN-SUR-RICHELIEU

P BIBLIOTHEQUE MUNICIPALE DE SAINT-JEAN-SUR-RICHELIEU*, 180, rue Laurier, J3B 7B2. SAN 319-8863. Tel: 450-357-2111. E-mail: biblio@sjsr.ca. Web Site: www.ville.saint-jean-sur-richelieu.qc.ca/bibliotheques. *Head Librn,* Johanne Jacob; Tel: 450-357-2111, Ext 2112, E-mail: j.jacob@sjsr.ca; Staff 41 (MLS 4, Non-MLS 37)
Founded 1959. Pop 97,087; Circ 558,308
Jan 2018-Dec 2018 Income (CAN) $3,644,213, Provincial (CAN) $241,000, City (CAN) $3,330,213, Locally Generated Income (CAN) $73,000. Mats Exp (CAN) $455,000, Books (CAN) $390,000, Per/Ser (Incl. Access Fees) (CAN) $18,000, AV Mat (CAN) $22,000, Electronic Ref Mat (Incl. Access Fees) (CAN) $25,000. Sal (CAN) $1,904,000 (Prof (CAN) $392,000)
Library Holdings: CDs 10,178; DVDs 14,716; e-books 7,567; Electronic Media & Resources 7,024; Large Print Bks 5,000; Bk Titles 157,328; Bk Vols 239,637; Per Subs 270; Talking Bks 4,812
Special Collections: Local History, bk, flm & micro
Automation Activity & Vendor Info: (Acquisitions) BiblioMondo; (Cataloging) BiblioMondo; (Circulation) BiblioMondo; (OPAC) BiblioMondo; (Serials) BiblioMondo
Wireless access
Function: 24/7 Electronic res, 24/7 Online cat, Adult bk club, Art exhibits, AV serv, Bks on CD, Children's prog, Computer training, Computers for patron use, Distance learning, Electronic databases & coll, Free DVD rentals, Holiday prog, ILL available, Internet access, Magazines, Magnifiers for reading, Mail & tel request accepted, Microfiche/film & reading machines, Music CDs, Online cat, Orientations, Outreach serv, Photocopying/Printing, Preschool outreach, Preschool reading prog, Prog for adults, Prog for children & young adult, Ref & res, Ref serv available, Scanner, Senior computer classes, Spanish lang bks, Spoken cassettes & CDs, Spoken cassettes & DVDs, Story hour, Summer reading prog, Wheelchair accessible, Workshops
Special Services for the Deaf - Assisted listening device
Special Services for the Blind - Accessible computers; Bks on CD; Large print bks; Low vision equip; ZoomText magnification & reading software
Open Mon-Fri 1-8:30, Sat & Sun 10-5
Restriction: Non-resident fee

C CEGEP ST JEAN SUR RICHELIEU BIBLIOTHEQUE*, 30 boul du Seminaire Nord, J3B 5J4. SAN 322-7499. Tel: 450-347-5301, Ext 2283, 450-347-5301, Ext 2333. FAX: 450-347-3329. E-mail: bibliotheque@cstjean.qc.ca. Web Site: bibliotheque.cstjean.qc.ca. *Coordr,* Suzie Roy; E-mail: suzie.roy@cstjean.qc.ca; Staff 7 (MLS 1, Non-MLS 6)
Founded 1961. Enrl 2,300; Fac 300
Library Holdings: AV Mats 25,000; CDs 500; DVDs 15; Bk Titles 63,000; Bk Vols 75,000; Per Subs 175; Videos 1,500
Subject Interests: Hist
Wireless access
Partic in RESDOC
Open Mon-Thurs 7:45-6, Fri 7:45-5

C COLLEGE MILITAIRE ROYAL DE SAINT-JEAN LIBRARY*, Lahie Bldg, Rm 210, 15 rue Jaques-Cartier Nord, J3B 8R8. SAN 319-8871. Tel: 450-358-6777, Ext 5866. E-mail: bibliotheque@cmrsj-rmcsj.ca, library@cmrsj-rmcsj.ca. Web Site: www.cmrsj-rmcsj.forces.gc.ca/bib-lib/bib-lib-eng.asp. *Actg Head Librn,* Joanie Tremblay; E-mail; joanie.tremblay@cmrsj-rmcsj.ca; Staff 4 (MLS 4)
Founded 1952. Enrl 700; Highest Degree: Master
Library Holdings: Bk Vols 185,000; Per Subs 750
Subject Interests: Computer sci, Mil, Strategic studies
Wireless access
Partic in Dobis; Utlas
Open Mon-Thurs 8am-9pm, Fri 8-4, Sat 1-8 (Fall & Winter); Mon-Fri 8-4 (Summer)

SAINT-LAURENT

J CEGEP DE SAINT-LAURENT BIBLIOTHEQUE*, 625 Ave Sainte-Croix, H4L 3X7. SAN 319-7212. Tel: 514-747-6521. E-mail: bibliotheque@cegepsl.qc.ca. Web Site: biblio.cegepsl.qc.ca. *Librn,* Jean-Philippe Bourdon; Tel: 514-747-6521, Ext 7211, E-mail: jpbourdon@cegepsl.qc.ca; *Libr Tech,* Rosalie Methot; Tel: 514-747-6521, Ext 7213, E-mail: rmethot@cegepsl.qc.ca; Staff 7 (MLS 1, Non-MLS 6)

Founded 1968. Enrl 3,800; Fac 19; Highest Degree: Associate
Library Holdings: CDs 590; DVDs 164; e-books 10,980; e-journals 6,000; Electronic Media & Resources 25,000; Music Scores 3,228; Bk Titles 39,800; Bk Vols 40,780; Per Subs 114; Videos 17,910
Subject Interests: Arts, Humanities, Music, Sciences
Automation Activity & Vendor Info: (Acquisitions) BiblioMondo; (Cataloging) BiblioMondo; (Circulation) BiblioMondo; (OPAC) BiblioMondo; (Serials) BiblioMondo
Wireless access
Function: 24/7 Electronic res, 24/7 Online cat, Computers for patron use, Electronic databases & coll, Internet access, Magazines, Mail & tel request accepted, Music CDs, Online cat, Online ref, Photocopying/Printing, Res assist avail, Scanner, Wheelchair accessible
Publications: Guide & bibliographies
Open Mon-Thurs 7:45-6:30, Fri 7:45-4
Restriction: Circ to mem only, ID required to use computers (Ltd hrs), Limited access for the pub, Open to students, fac & staff

S NATIONAL FILM BOARD OF CANADA*, Information Management, 3155 Cote-de-Liesse Rd, H4N 2N4. (Mail add: PO Box 6100, Montreal, H3C 3H5), SAN 369-3961. Tel: 514-496-1044. FAX: 514-283-9811. Web Site: www.nfb.ca. *Develop Dir,* Nathalie Bourdon; E-mail: n.bourdon@nfb.ca; Staff 3 (MLS 3)
Founded 1940
Library Holdings: Bk Vols 15,000; Per Subs 1,100
Special Collections: Challenge For Change, Norman McLaren
Subject Interests: Canadiana, Moving pictures, Television, Video

SAINT-LEONARD DE PORTNEUF

P BIBLIOTHEQUE FLEUR DE LIN*, 260 Pettigrew St, G0A 4A0. SAN 321-320X. Tel: 418-337-3961. FAX: 418-337-6742. E-mail: bibliofleurdelin@hotmail.com. Web Site: st-leonard.com/loisirs-et-activites/bibliotheque-fleur-de-lin. *Librn,* Ginette Poquet
Pop 1,059
Library Holdings: Bk Vols 1,200; Per Subs 12
Wireless access

SAINT-SIMEON

P BIBLIOTHEQUE HENRI-BRASSARD*, 505A rue Saint-Laurent, G0T 1X0. SAN 321-3021. Tel: 418-471-0550. Web Site: www.reseaubibliocnca.qc.ca/fr/ma-bibliotheque/b401/bibliotheque-henri-brassard-saint-simeon. *Dir,* Isabelle Poirier; E-mail: ipoirier@reseaubiblioonca.qc.ca
Library Holdings: Bk Vols 1,500
Wireless access
Open Tues & Thurs 6:30-8, Sat 10-Noon

SALABERRY-DE-VALLEYFIELD

J COLLEGE DE VALLEYFIELD*, Bibliotheque Armand-Frappier, 80 rue Saint Thomas, J6T 4J7. SAN 319-938X. Tel: 450-370-4860, 450-370-9441, Ext 470. FAX: 450-377-6011. E-mail: biblio.a.frappier@colval.qc.ca. Web Site: www.colval.qc.ca/bibliotheque. *Librn,* Virna Duplessis; Tel: 450-373-9441, Ext 350; *Town Librn,* Roxanne Poissant; Tel: 450-373-9441, Ext 200, E-mail: roxanne.poissant@ville.valleyfield.qc.ca; Staff 2 (MLS 2)
Founded 1997
Library Holdings: Bk Vols 100,000; Per Subs 139
Special Collections: UN Document Depository
Wireless access
Open Mon-Fri 8-8, Sat 10-4, Sun 12-4

SEPT ILES

P BIBLIOTHEQUE LOUIS-ANGE-SANTERRE*, 500, ave Jolliet, G4R 2B4. SAN 319-907X. Tel: 418-964-3355. FAX: 418-964-3353. Web Site: www.septiles.ca. *Supvr,* Pascale Malenfant; E-mail: pascale.malenfant@septiles.ca; *Libr Asst Supvr,* Lyne Remillard; E-mail: lyne.remillard@septiles.ca; Staff 1 (MLS 1)
Founded 1953. Pop 25,000; Circ 121,000
Library Holdings: Audiobooks 950; CDs 8,500; DVDs 6,450; Large Print Bks 1,500; Bk Vols 78,000; Per Subs 130
Subject Interests: Local hist
Automation Activity & Vendor Info: (OPAC) Koha
Wireless access
Function: 24/7 Online cat, Art exhibits, Internet access, Magazines, Movies, Music CDs, Photocopying/Printing, Scanner

P RESEAU BIBLIO DE LA COTE-NORD*, 59 ave Napoleon, G4R 5C5. SAN 321-0960. Tel: 418-962-1020. FAX: 418-962-5124. E-mail: biblio@reseaubibliocn.qc.ca. Web Site: www.reseaubibliocn.qc.ca. *Dir,* Marie-Soleil Vigneault; Tel: 418-962-1020, Ext 222, E-mail: msvigneault@reseaubibliocn.qc.ca; Staff 4 (MLS 2, Non-MLS 2)
Founded 1979. Pop 25,714
Library Holdings: Bk Titles 64,498; Bk Vols 79,959; Per Subs 10
Special Collections: Cote Nord; Hunting & Fishing (French & English); Plants & Shrubs (French)
Wireless access
Partic in ASTED
Special Services for the Blind - Bks & mags in Braille, on rec, tape & cassette; Bks available with recordings; Bks on CD
Open Mon-Thurs 8:30-Noon & 1-4:30, Fri 8:30-Noon

SHAWINIGAN

P BIBLIOTHEQUE DE LA VILLE DE SHAWINIGAN*, Bibliotheque Fabien-LaRochelle, 205 6e rue de la Pointe, G9N 6V3. SAN 319-9088. Tel: 819-536-7218. Web Site: biblio.shawinigan.ca. *Dir,* Catherine Patry; Tel: 819-537-4989, Ext 227, E-mail: cpatry@shawinigan.ca; Staff 1 (MLS 1)
Founded 1923. Pop 21,000; Circ 92,812
Library Holdings: Bk Titles 65,000; Per Subs 155; Videos 1,450
Open Tues-Fri 1-5:30, Sat 10-4:30

SHERBROOKE

P BIBLIOTHEQUE MUNICIPALE EVA-SENECAL*, Sherbrooke Municipal Library, 450 Marquette St, J1H 1M4, SAN 319-910X. Tel: 819-821-5596. FAX: 819-822-6110. E-mail: bibliotheque@sherbrooke.ca. Web Site: bibliotheques.sherbrooke.ca/bibliotheque-eva-senecal, ville.sherbrooke.qc.ca. *Chef de Section,* Linda Travis; *Head, Children's Servx,* Marie Eve Cloutier; Staff 38 (MLS 4, Non-MLS 34)
Founded 1954. Pop 146,000; Circ 639,000
Library Holdings: AV Mats 29,000; Bk Titles 166,000; Bk Vols 185,000; Per Subs 372; Talking Bks 1,800
Automation Activity & Vendor Info: (Acquisitions) Isacsoft Inc (ISF); (Cataloging) Isacsoft Inc (ISF); (Circulation) Isacsoft Inc (ISF); (OPAC) Isacsoft Inc (ISF); (Serials) Isacsoft Inc (ISF)
Wireless access
Open Mon, Wed, Fri-Sun 10-5, Tues & Thurs 10-8

C BISHOP'S UNIVERSITY, Library Learning Commons, 2600 College St, J1M 1Z7. SAN 319-6801. Tel: 819-822-9600, Ext 2605. Interlibrary Loan Service Tel: 819-822-9600, Ext 2710. Web Site: www.ubishops.ca/library. *Univ Librn,* Catherine Lavallee-Welch; Tel: 819-822-9600, Ext 2483, E-mail: catherine.lavallee-welch@ubishops.ca; *Learning Commons Librn,* Gary McCormick; Tel: 819-822-9600, Ext 2800, E-mail: gary.mccormick@ubishops.ca; Staff 17 (MLS 6, Non-MLS 11)
Founded 1843. Enrl 2,650; Fac 117; Highest Degree: Master
Special Collections: Canadiana (McKinnon Coll), bks & micro; Local History (Eastern Townships Historical Coll). Canadian and Provincial
Subject Interests: Bus, Educ, Humanities
Automation Activity & Vendor Info: (Acquisitions) OCLC Worldshare Management Services
Wireless access
Function: 24/7 Electronic res, 24/7 Online cat, Archival coll, Audio & video playback equip for onsite use, Computers for patron use, Distance learning, Electronic databases & coll, For res purposes, ILL available, Internet access, Magazines, Magnifiers for reading, Movies, Music CDs, Online cat, Online Chat, Orientations, Photocopying/Printing, Ref & res, Ref serv available, Res assist avail, Scanner, Study rm, Wheelchair accessible
Publications: Student Guides to Reference Sources; Subject Lists
Partic in Canadian Research Knowledge Network

C CEGEP DE SHERBROOKE*, Centre des Medias, 475 rue du Cegep, J1E 4K1. SAN 373-7551. Tel: 819-564-6350, Ext 5231, 819-564-6350, Ext 5233. Administration Tel: 819-564-6350, Ext 5195. FAX: 819-564-4025. E-mail: c-medias@cegepsherbrooke.qc.ca. Web Site: www.cegepsherbrooke.qc.ca. *Dir,* Petra Funk; E-mail: petra.funk@cegepsherbrooke.qc.ca; *Librn,* Rene-Pierre Custeau; E-mail: rene-pierre.custeau@cegepsherbrooke.qc.ca; Staff 4 (MLS 1, Non-MLS 3)
Founded 1968. Enrl 6,500; Fac 500
Library Holdings: e-books 2,000; Bk Titles 94,000; Bk Vols 100,000; Per Subs 167
Subject Interests: Computer, Ecology, Mechanics, Music, Nursing
Automation Activity & Vendor Info: (Cataloging) Koha; (OPAC) Koha
Wireless access
Function: ILL available
Open Mon-Thurs 8am-7:45pm, Fri 8-4:45

M CENTRE HOSPITALIER UNIVERSITAIRE DU SHERBROOKE*, Hotel-Dieu Bibliotheque Medicale, 580 rue Bowen Sud, Piece 1110, J1G 2E8. SAN 319-9118. Tel: 819-346-1110, Ext 21126. FAX: 819-822-6745. Web Site: www.chus.qc.ca/en/academique-ruis/bibliotheque-medicale. *Mgr,* Mykola Krupko; E-mail: mkrupko.chus@ssss.gouv.qc.ca; Staff 1 (MLS 1)
Founded 1954
Library Holdings: Bk Vols 5,600; Per Subs 161

Subject Interests: Cardiology, Hospital admin, Internal med, Nursing, Surgery
Restriction: Staff use only

R GRAND SEMINAIRE DES SAINTS APOTRES LIBRARY*, Archeveche de Sherbrooke Cathedrale, 130 rue de la Cathedrale, J1H 4M1. SAN 319-9126. Tel: 819-563-9934, Ext 209. FAX: 819-562-0125. E-mail: cure.st.michel@diocesedesherbrooke.org. Web Site: diocesedesherbrooke.org/fr/basilique-cathedrale-saint-michel. *Coordr,* Elisabeth Gouin
Founded 1940
Library Holdings: Bk Vols 28,000; Per Subs 130
Special Collections: Migne Coll
Subject Interests: Theol
Open Mon-Thurs 1:30-4

S LA SOCIETE D'HISTOIRE DE SHERBROOKE*, Sherbrooke Historical Society, 275, rue Dufferin, J1H 4M5. SAN 319-9134. Tel: 819-821-5406. FAX: 819-821-5417. E-mail: info@histoiresherbrooke.org. Web Site: www.histoiresherbrooke.org. *Exec Dir,* Michel Harnois; E-mail: michel.harnois@histoiresherbrooke.org; *Archivist,* Karine Savary; E-mail: karine.savary@histoiresherbrooke.org
Founded 1927
Library Holdings: Bk Titles 8,000; Per Subs 30
Special Collections: Local History Archives, newsp
Subject Interests: Eastern Townships in the Province of Quebec, Especially Sherbrooke region
Wireless access
Restriction: Authorized personnel only

C UNIVERSITE DE SHERBROOKE SERVICE DES BIBLIOTHEQUES ET ARCHIVES*, Pavillion George-Cabana B2, 2500 boul de l'Universite, J1K 2R1. SAN 369-5492. Tel: 819-821-7550. Toll Free Tel: 866-506-2433. FAX: 819-821-7096. E-mail: info.biblio@usherbrooke.ca. Web Site: usherbrooke.ca/biblio. *Exec Dir,* Sylvie Fournier; E-mail: sylvie.fournier2@usherbrooke.ca; Staff 26 (MLS 23, Non-MLS 3)
Founded 1954. Enrl 18,000; Fac 850; Highest Degree: Doctorate
Library Holdings: CDs 12,440; e-books 109,000; e-journals 60,970; Bk Titles 552,167; Bk Vols 840,000; Per Subs 14,386; Videos 4,440
Special Collections: Canadian and Provincial
Automation Activity & Vendor Info: (Acquisitions) SirsiDynix; (Cataloging) SirsiDynix; (Circulation) SirsiDynix; (ILL) Fretwell-Downing; (OPAC) SerialsSolutions; (Serials) SirsiDynix
Wireless access
Partic in Canadian Association of Research Libraries

SOREL-TRACY

P BIBLIOTHEQUE MUNICIPALE DE SOREL-TRACY*, Le Survenant Library, 145 rue George, J3P 7K1. (Mail add: CP 368, J3P 7K1), SAN 319-9193. Tel: 450-780-5600. FAX: 450-780-5758. E-mail: bibliotheque@ville.sorel-tracy.qc.ca. Web Site: bibliotheque.ville.sorel-tracy.qc.ca. *Librn,* Pierre Plante; E-mail: pierre.plante@ville.sorel-tracy.qc.ca
Founded 1947. Pop 25,000
Library Holdings: Bk Titles 49,000; Per Subs 100
Special Collections: Can & Prov
Subject Interests: Genealogy, Rare bks
Open Mon-Thurs 9-8, Fri 9-5

S RIO TINTO IRON & TITANIUM INC*, 1625 Rte Marie-Victorin, J3R 1M6. SAN 319-9207. Tel: 450-746-3000, 450-746-3077. FAX: 450-746-3391. Web Site: riotinto.com/en. *Librn,* Marc Duval; Tel: 450-746-3160, Fax: 450-746-9412, E-mail: marc.duval@riotinto.com. Subject Specialists: *Metallurgy,* Marc Duval; Staff 1 (MLS 1)
Founded 1950
Library Holdings: Bk Titles 8,000; Per Subs 50
Special Collections: Patents
Subject Interests: Chem, Physics
Open Mon-Fri 9-4

STANBRIDGE EAST

S MISSISQUOI HISTORICAL SOCIETY, Doris Jones McIntosh Annex, Two River St, J0J 2H0. SAN 319-9215. Tel: 450-248-3153. FAX: 450-248-0420. Web Site: www.missisquoimuseum.ca. *Archivist,* Mrs Rolande Lagacé Laduke; E-mail: rladuke@museemissisquoi.ca; *Curator,* Tyson Rosberg. Subject Specialists: *Res,* Mrs Rolande Lagacé Laduke
Founded 1964
Special Collections: Genealogical Reference (Archives Annex Coll)
Subject Interests: Antiques, Can hist, Canadiana, Genealogy, Old books, Rare
Wireless access
Publications: Biennial History Reports

SUTTON

P BIBLIOTHEQUE MUNICIPALE ET SCOLAIRE DE SUTTON*, 19 Highland St, J0E 2K0. SAN 319-9231. Tel: 450-538-5843. FAX: 450-538-4286. E-mail: bibliotheque@sutton.ca. Web Site: www.reseaubibliomonteregie.qc.ca/fr/bibliotheques-horaire-et-localisation/b7/bibliotheque. *Coordr,* Lisa Charbonneau
Pop 3,981; Circ 23,500
Library Holdings: Bk Titles 20,000
Automation Activity & Vendor Info: (Acquisitions) SirsiDynix; (Cataloging) SirsiDynix; (Circulation) SirsiDynix; (Course Reserve) SirsiDynix; (ILL) SirsiDynix; (Media Booking) SirsiDynix; (OPAC) SirsiDynix; (Serials) SirsiDynix
Wireless access
Open Mon, Wed, Fri & Sat 10-12, Tues & Thurs 10-12 & 6:30-8:30

TEMISCAMING

P BIBLIOTHEQUE MUNICIPALE*, 40 rue Boucher, J0Z 3R0. SAN 319-924X. Tel: 819-627-6623. E-mail: biblio@temiscaming.net. Web Site: www.temiscaming.net/city-services/leisure-sports-and-cultural/library. *Libr Tech,* Nathalie Labrosse; E-mail: bibliotemis@gmail.com
Pop 2,097
Library Holdings: Bk Vols 12,000
Open Mon-Wed 6pm-8pm, Thurs 4-6 (Winter); Mon 6pm-8pm, Tues-Thurs 1-3 (Summer)

TEMISCOUATA-SUR-LE-LAC

P BIBLIOTHEQUE MUNICIPALE DE NOTRE-DAME-DU-LAC*, 2448 rue Commerciale Sud, G0L 1X0. SAN 321-2483. Tel: 418-899-2528. E-mail: biblio.ndlac@crsbp.net. Web Site: www.blct.ca. *Dir,* Francis Touzin; Tel: 418-899-2528, Ext 301, E-mail: direction@blct.ca
Library Holdings: Bk Vols 1,000
Automation Activity & Vendor Info: (Circulation) MultiLIS
Wireless access
Open Tues & Wed 7pm-8pm, Thurs 2:30-4 & 7-8

TERREBONNE

P BIBLIOTHEQUE MUNICIPALE*, 855 Place de l'Île-des-Moulins, J6W 4N7. SAN 319-9258. Tel: 450-961-2001, Ext 1252. *Dir,* Jacques Francois Levesque; Staff 58 (MLS 6, Non-MLS 52)
Pop 269,413; Circ 714,028
Library Holdings: Bk Vols 234,253
Subject Interests: Genealogy, Local hist
Wireless access
Function: 24/7 Electronic res, 24/7 Online cat, Activity rm, Adult bk club, Adult literacy prog, After school storytime

TROIS-PISTOLES

P BIBLIOTHEQUE MUNICIPALE ANNE-MARIE-D'AMOURS*, Centre Culturel de Trois-Pistoles, 145, rue de l'Arena, G0L 4K0. SAN 319-9274. Tel: 418-851-2374. FAX: 418-851-3567. Web Site: www.ville-trois-pistoles.ca. *Libr Mgr,* Karen Dionne; E-mail: k.dionne@ville-trois-pistoles.ca
Founded 1967. Pop 4,551; Circ 19,783
Library Holdings: Bk Vols 12,000
Wireless access
Open Mon & Thurs 6:30pm-8:30pm, Tues & Wed 1:30-5, Fri 1:30-5 & 6:30-8:30, Sat 9:30-11:30; Tues & Fri 1-5 & 6:30-8:30, Wed & Thurs 1-5, Sat 9-Noon (Summer)

TROIS-RIVIERES

P BIBLIOTHEQUES DE TROIS-RIVIERES*, Bibliotheque Gatien-Lapointe, 1425 Place de l'Hotel de Ville, G9A 5L9. (Mail add: CP 1723, G9A 5L9), SAN 319-9290. Tel: 819-372-4615. FAX: 819-693-1892. E-mail: bgl@v3r.net. Reference E-mail: bglreference@v3r.net. Web Site: www.v3r.net/activites-et-loisirs/bibliotheques. *Dir,* Jessie Daigle; Tel: 819-372-4641, Ext 4622, E-mail: jdaigle@v3r.net; *Team Leader,* Julie Moreau; E-mail: jmoreau@v3r.net; *Ref Serv,* Marie-Claude Taillon; Tel: 819-372-4641, Ext 4317, E-mail: mtaillon@v3r.net; *Tech Serv,* Odette Pelletier; Tel: 819-372-4641, Ext 4251, E-mail: opelletier@v3r.net; Staff 6 (MLS 5, Non-MLS 1)
Founded 1946. Pop 128,000; Circ 980,000
Library Holdings: Per Subs 200
Special Collections: Trifluviana
Automation Activity & Vendor Info: (Acquisitions) BiblioMondo; (Cataloging) BiblioMondo; (Circulation) BiblioMondo; (Course Reserve) BiblioMondo; (ILL) BiblioMondo; (Media Booking) BiblioMondo; (OPAC) BiblioMondo; (Serials) BiblioMondo
Publications: Annual Report; Library Handbook
Partic in ASTED
Open Mon-Fri 10-9, Sat & Sun 10-5

Branches: 4
BIBLIOTHEQUE ALINE-PICHE, 5575 boul Jean-XXIII, G8Z 4A8. Tel: 819-374-6525. FAX: 819-374-5126. E-mail: bap@v3r.net. *Team Leader,* Denise Lemay; *Team Leader,* Sandra Mercier
Open Tues-Fri 10-8, Sat 10-5
BIBLIOTHEQUE DE POINTE-DU-LAC (SIMONE-L-ROY), 500 rue de la Grande-Allee, G0X 1Z0. Tel: 819-377-4289. FAX: 819-377-7116. E-mail: BSR@v3r.net. *Team Leader,* Simone Paquet
Open Tues & Wed 1-8, Thurs-Sat 10-5
BIBLIOTHEQUE MAURICE-LORANGER, 70 rue Pare, G8T 6V8, SAN 319-6348. Tel: 819-378-8206. FAX: 819-378-5539. E-mail: BML@v3r.net. *Team Leader,* Yves Lesage
Circ 26,093
Library Holdings: Bk Vols 30,000; Per Subs 75
Open Tues-Fri 10-8, Sat 10-5
BIBLIOTHEQUE DE LA FRANCIADE, 100 rue de la Mairie, G8W 1S1. Tel: 819-374-6419. E-mail: BLF@v3r.net. *Team Leader,* Sandra Thissault
Open Tues & Wed 1-8, Thurs & Fri 1-5, Sat 10-5

C CEGEP DU TROIS-RIVIERES BIBLIOTHEQUE*, 3175 Laviolette, G9A 5E6. (Mail add: 3500 de Courval CP97, G9A 5E6), SAN 319-9339. Tel: 819-376-1721, Ext 2633. FAX: 819-693-3844. E-mail: bibliotheque@cegeptr.qc.ca, comptoir.biblio@cegeptr.qc.ca. Web Site: bibliotheque.cegeptr.qc.ca. *Admin Support Coordr,* Manon Champagne; Staff 12 (MLS 3, Non-MLS 9)
Founded 1968. Enrl 4,300
Library Holdings: AV Mats 69,823; CDs 392; DVDs 176; Bk Vols 96,000; Per Subs 300; Videos 4,194
Special Collections: Materiautheque Coll; Mediatheque Coll; Pulp & Paper Coll
Publications: Guide de la Bibliothique; Liste des Periodiques Courants; Liste Regionale des Periodiques
Partic in RESDOC
Open Mon-Thurs 8-7:50, Fri 8-4:50

M CENTRE HOSPITALIER REGIONAL TROIS-RIVIERES PAVILLON STE-MARIE*, 1991 boul du Carmel, G8Z 3R9. SAN 319-9312. Tel: 819-697-3333, Ext 69878. FAX: 819-378-9850. E-mail: 04BiblioCHAUR@ssss.gouv.qc.ca. *Libr Dir,* Josee Aylwin
Founded 1961
Library Holdings: Bk Titles 3,200; Per Subs 65
Partic in OCLC Online Computer Library Center, Inc

P CENTRE REGIONAL DE SERVICES AUX BIBLIOTHEQUES PUBLIQUES*, Centre-du-Quebec-Lanaudiere-Mauricie, 3125 rue Girard, G8Z 2M4. SAN 319-9282. Tel: 819-375-9623. FAX: 819-375-0132. E-mail: crsbp@reseaubibliocqlm.qc.ca. Web Site: www.reseaubibliocqlm.qc.ca. *Exec Dir,* France Rene; E-mail: france.rene@reseaubibliocqlm.qc.ca
Founded 1962. Pop 222,837; Circ 850,030
Library Holdings: Bk Vols 498,185
Open Mon-Fri 8:30-12 & 1:30-4:30; Mon-Thurs 8:30-12 & 1-4, Fri 8:30-Noon (Summer)

S LE SEMINAIRE SAINT-JOSEPH DE TROIS-RIVIERES*, Archives du Seminaire de Trois-Rivieres, 858 rue Laviolette, local 221, G9A 5S3. SAN 328-1485. Tel: 819-376-4459, Ext 135. FAX: 819-378-0607. E-mail: astr@ssj.qc.ca. Web Site: ssj.qc.ca/ssjarchives. *Archivist,* Christian Lalancette
Founded 1918
Library Holdings: Bk Vols 10,000
Special Collections: Manuscripts, Maps, Photographs
Subject Interests: Educ, Families, Hist, Politics, Relig
Function: Archival coll, Photocopying/Printing, Ref serv available, Telephone ref
Open Wed & Thurs 9-12 & 1:30-4
Restriction: In-house use for visitors, Not a lending libr

G MINISTERE DE LA CULTURE, Conservatory of Music, 587 rue Radisson, G9A 2C8. SAN 325-2027. Tel: 819-371-6748, Ext 228. E-mail: cmtr@conservatoire.gouv.qc.ca. Web Site: biblio.cmadq.gouv.qc.ca, www.conservatoire.gouv.qc.ca/fr/conservatoires/trois-rivieres. *Librn,* Pascal Pepin; E-mail: pascal.pepin@conservatoire.gouv.qc.ca
Founded 1979
Library Holdings: Bk Titles 400
Special Collections: Anais Allard Rousseau Coll, bks, musical scores, parts
Restriction: Open to students

C UNIVERSITE DU QUEBEC A TROIS-RIVIERES*, Service de la bibliotheque, Pavillon Albert-Tessier, 3351 Blvd des Forges, G9A 5H7. (Mail add: Pavillon Albert-Tessier, CP 500, G9A 5H7), SAN 319-9347. Tel: 819-376-5005. FAX: 819-376-5032. E-mail: biblio.infodoc@uqtr.ca. Web Site: www.uqtr.ca/biblio. *Dir,* Etienne Audet; Tel: 819-376-5011, Ext 2254, E-mail: Etienne.Audet@uqtr.ca; *Asst Dir,* Eve Marie Houyoux; Tel: 819-376-5011, Ext 2266, E-mail: Eve-Marie.Houyoux@uqtr.ca; Staff 11 (MLS 11)
Founded 1969. Enrl 6,896; Fac 340; Highest Degree: Doctorate
Special Collections: Etudes Quebecoises. Canadian and Provincial
Subject Interests: Acctg, Arts, Biochem, Biology, Biophysics, Bus, Chem, Chiropractic, Communication, Computer sci, Educ, Engr, Fr Can studies, Geog, Hist, Math, Nursing, Philos, Physics, Psychol, Sports leisure

VAL-D'OR

P BIBLIOTHEQUE MUNICIPALE DE VAL-D'OR*, 600, 7e Rue, J9P 3P3. SAN 319-9355. Tel: 819-824-2666, Ext 4225. FAX: 819-825-3062. E-mail: bibliotheques@ville.valdor.qc.ca. Web Site: www.ville.valdor.qc.ca/bibliotheques. *Head of Libraries,* Michelle Bourque; Tel: 819-874-7469, Ext 4233
Founded 1952. Pop 30,000; Circ 225,000
Library Holdings: Bk Vols 70,000; Per Subs 110
Wireless access
Open Mon-Fri 1-9, Sat 10-5, Sun 1-5

VAUDREUIL-DORION

P BIBLIOTHEQUE MUNICIPALE*, 51, rue Jeannotte, J7V 6E6. SAN 377-0672. Tel: 450-455-3371, Ext 6. FAX: 450-455-5653. E-mail: biblio@ville.vaudreuil-dorion.qc.ca. Web Site: www.ville.vaudreuil-dorion.qc.ca/en/recreation-and-culture/library. *Chef de Div,* Annick Lemay
Library Holdings: Bk Titles 50,000; Bk Vols 60,000; Per Subs 200
Wireless access
Open Mon-Fri 10-9, Sat & Sun 10-4:30

VICTORIAVILLE

P BIBLIOTHEQUE CHARLES-EDOUARD-MAILHOT*, Two, rue de L'Ermitage, G6P 6T2. (Mail add: CP 370, G6P 6T2), SAN 319-941X. Tel: 819-758-8441. FAX: 819-758-9432. E-mail: bibliotheque@victoriaville.ca. Web Site: www.victoriaville.ca/page/865/bibliotheques.aspx. *Library Contact,* Position Currently Open
Founded 1948. Pop 40,853
Library Holdings: CDs 6,225; DVDs 263; Large Print Bks 515; Bk Vols 119,552; Per Subs 215; Talking Bks 623
Special Collections: Local History (Fonds Alcide-Fleury Coll)
Automation Activity & Vendor Info: (Acquisitions) BiblioMondo; (Cataloging) BiblioMondo; (Circulation) BiblioMondo; (OPAC) BiblioMondo; (Serials) BiblioMondo
Wireless access
Function: Home delivery & serv to seniorr ctr & nursing homes, Magnifiers for reading, Photocopying/Printing, Prog for children & young adult, Ref serv available, Summer reading prog, Telephone ref, Wheelchair accessible
Publications: Livraison Spéciale (Serials catalog)
Partic in Consortium d'acquisition de ressources electroniques du Quebec
Special Services for the Deaf - Assistive tech
Special Services for the Blind - Assistive/Adapted tech devices, equip & products
Open Mon 5-8, Tues 1-8, Wed & Thurs 10-8, Fri 10-5, Sat & Sun 10-4
Restriction: Badge access after hrs
Branches: 1
BIBLIOTHEQUE ALCIDE-FLEURY, 841, blvd des Bois-Francs Sud, G6P 5W3. (Mail add: Two, rue de l'Ermitage, Case postale 370, G6P 6T2), SAN 374-4450. Tel: 819-357-8240. Administration Tel: 819-758-8441. FAX: 819-357-2099. Administration FAX: 819-758-9432. *Pub Serv, Ref Serv,* Helene St-Martin; Staff 5 (Non-MLS 5)
Founded 1958
Library Holdings: AV Mats 909; Bk Titles 36,883; Bk Vols 38,940; Per Subs 45

J CEGEP DE VICTORIAVILLE*, Centre de Documentation, 475 rue Notre Dame E, G6P 4B3. SAN 369-5700. Tel: 819-758-6401, Ext 2485. E-mail: bibliotheque@cegepvicto.ca. Web Site: cegepvictobiblio.weebly.com. *Adminr,* Sylvain Cote; Tel: 819-758-6401, Ext 2485, E-mail: cote.sylvain@cegepvicto.ca
Founded 1963
Library Holdings: Bk Vols 52,000; Per Subs 300
Special Collections: Woodworking Coll
Subject Interests: Regional hist
Wireless access
Open Mon-Wed 8am-9pm, Thurs 8-5, Fri 8-4
Departmental Libraries:
E'COLE QUEBECOISE DU MEUBLE ET DU BOIS OUVRE, 765 Est Notre Dame, G6P 4B3, SAN 369-5735. Tel: 819-758-6401, Ext 2621. FAX: 819-758-2729. *Librn,* Marjo Bechard

M CIUSSS DE LA MAURICIE ET DU CENTRE DU QUEBEC*, Bibliotheque Dr Claude Richard, 5 rue des Hospitalieres, G6P 6N2. SAN 319-6267. Tel: 819-357-2030, Ext 2185. FAX: 819-357-6060. *Documentation Tech,* Annie Lemay; E-mail: annie_lemay_csssae@ssss.gouv.qc.ca
Founded 1960
Library Holdings: Bk Titles 1,000; Per Subs 40
Friends of the Library Group

WARWICK

P BIBLIOTHEQUE MUNICIPALE DE WARWICK*, Bibliotheque P -Rodolphe Baril, 181, rue Saint-Louis, J0A 1M0. SAN 319-9428. Tel: 819-358-4325. FAX: 819-358-4326. E-mail: bibliotheque@ville.warwick.qc.ca. Web Site: villedewarwick.quebec/bibliotheque-p-rodolphe-baril. *Dir,* Katia Houle
Founded 1969. Pop 4,764
Library Holdings: Bk Titles 26,013; Bk Vols 29,135; Per Subs 60
Function: Doc delivery serv
Open Mon & Fri 1-5 & 6-8, Wed 10-11:30 & 1-5, Sat 9:30-Noon; Mon & Fri 1-5 & 6-9, Wed 9-11:30 & 1-5 (Summer)

WATERLOO

P WATERLOO PUBLIC LIBRARY*, 650 Rue de la Cour, J0E 2N0. SAN 319-9436. Tel: 450-539-2268. E-mail: biblio@cacwaterloo.qc.ca. *Library Contact,* Nathalie Masse
Founded 1900. Circ 25,000
Library Holdings: Large Print Bks 200; Bk Vols 25,000; Per Subs 75
Special Collections: Journal de Waterloo 1921-53; Waterloo Advertiser 1856-1924
Wireless access
Open Mon-Fri 9:30-11:30 & 1-5, Sat 9-12 & 1-4

WESTMOUNT

S ATWATER LIBRARY & COMPUTER CENTRE*, 1200 Atwater Ave, H3Z 1X4. SAN 319-6984. Tel: 514-935-7344. FAX: 514-935-1960. E-mail: info@atwaterlibrary.ca. Web Site: www.atwaterlibrary.ca. *Exec Dir,* Lynn Verge; *Head Librn,* Kimberly Ryan; Staff 2 (Non-MLS 2)
Founded 1828
Library Holdings: Bk Vols 38,000; Per Subs 70
Special Collections: Archives of the Mechanics' Institute of Montreal, 1828-present; Quebec Writers' Federation Coll; The Scottish Coll
Subject Interests: Art, Biog, Can hist, Computer sci, Fiction, Geog, Local hist
Automation Activity & Vendor Info: (Acquisitions) Mandarin Library Automation; (Cataloging) Mandarin Library Automation; (Circulation) Mandarin Library Automation; (OPAC) Mandarin Library Automation
Wireless access
Function: Adult bk club, Adult literacy prog, Bks on cassette, Citizenship assistance, Computer training, Computers for patron use, Electronic databases & coll, Govt ref serv, Literacy & newcomer serv, Photocopying/Printing, Prog for adults, Ref serv available, Scanner, Senior computer classes, Senior outreach, Workshops
Publications: Annual report; Newsletter
Open Mon & Wed 10-8, Tues, Thurs & Fri 10-6, Sat 10-5

J DAWSON COLLEGE LIBRARY*, 3040 Sherbrooke St W, H3Z 1A4. SAN 319-7425. Tel: 514-931-8731. Circulation Tel: 514-931-8731, Ext 1620. Reference Tel: 514-931-8731, Ext 1731. FAX: 514-931-3567. Reference E-mail: libreference@dawsoncollege.qc.ca. Web Site: library.dawsoncollege.qc.ca. *Dir,* Monique Magnan; Tel: 514-931-8731, Ext 1204, E-mail: mmagnan@dawsoncollege.qc.ca; *Pub Serv Librn,* Claire Elliot; Tel: 514-931-8731, Ext 1736, E-mail: celliot@dawsoncollege.qc.ca; *Pub Serv Librn,* Stavroula Vitoratos; Tel: 514-931-8731, Ext 1798, E-mail: svitoratos@dawsoncollege.qc.ca; *Cat, ILL,* Margaret Black; Tel: 514-931-8731, Ext 1795, E-mail: mblack@dawsoncollege.qc.ca; Staff 12 (MLS 12)
Founded 1969. Enrl 7,000; Fac 450
Library Holdings: Bk Titles 92,000; Bk Vols 107,200; Per Subs 320
Automation Activity & Vendor Info: (Acquisitions) MultiLIS; (Cataloging) MultiLIS; (Circulation) MultiLIS; (Course Reserve) MultiLIS; (OPAC) MultiLIS; (Serials) MultiLIS
Wireless access
Open Mon-Thurs 8-6:30, Fri 8-5

SASKATCHEWAN

Date of Statistics: FY 2023
Population, 2021: 1,133,594
Population Served by Public Libraries: 1,133,594
Total Volumes in Public Libraries: 3,545,183
Volumes Per Capita: 3.13
Total Public Library Circulation: 8,833,303
Circulation Per Capita: 7.79
Number of Public Libraries: 11
Public Library Systems, including seven Regional Library Systems, three Municipal library Systems and One Federation of Northern Libraries.
Information provided courtesy of: Jack Ma, Accountability & Assessment Officer; Provincial Library & Literacy Office, Ministry of Education.

AIR RONGE

P PAHKISIMON NUYE?AH LIBRARY SYSTEM*, 118 Avro Pl, S0J 3G0. (Mail add: Bag Service 6600, La Ronge, S0J 1L0), SAN 374-6003. Tel: 306-425-4525. Toll Free Tel: 866-396-8818. FAX: 306-425-4572. E-mail: PNLSOffice@pnls.lib.sk.ca. Web Site: pahkisimon.ca. *Dir,* James Hope Howard; E-mail: director@pnls.lib.sk.ca; *Asst Dir,* Harriet Roy; E-mail: hroy@pnls.lib.sk.ca; *Archives, Historian,* Graham Guest; E-mail: archives@pnls.lib.sk.ca; Staff 8 (MLS 2, Non-MLS 6)
Founded 1990. Pop 36,557
Library Holdings: Bk Vols 64,781; Per Subs 30
Special Collections: Aboriginal, multimedia; Fur trade; Northern Saskatchewan, multimedia
Automation Activity & Vendor Info: (Cataloging) Innovative Interfaces, Inc - Millennium; (Circulation) Innovative Interfaces, Inc - Millennium; (ILL) Innovative Interfaces, Inc - Millennium; (OPAC) Innovative Interfaces, Inc - Millennium
Publications: Word's Worth
Member Libraries: Alex Robertson Public Library; Ayamicikiwikamik Public Library; Beauval Public Library; Dave O'Hara Community Library; Ile a la Crosse Public Library; Keethanow Public Library; Peayamechikee Public Library; Tawowikamik Public Library; Wisewood Library
Partic in Saskatchewan Electronic Resources Partnership; Saskatchewan Information & Library Services
Special Services for the Deaf - Bks on deafness & sign lang; High interest/low vocabulary bks
Special Services for the Blind - Braille bks; Talking bks
Open Mon-Fri 8-5

BEAUVAL

P BEAUVAL PUBLIC LIBRARY*, Valley View School Library, Laliberte St, S0M 0G0. (Mail add: Bag Service 9000, S0M 0G0). Tel: 306-288-2022, Ext 3316. FAX: 306-288-2222. E-mail: sb@pnls.lib.sk.ca. *Librn,* Ida Gauthier
Library Holdings: Bk Vols 15,000; Per Subs 15
Wireless access
Mem of Pahkisimon Nuye?ah Library System
Open Tues-Fri 9-12

BUFFALO NARROWS

P WISEWOOD LIBRARY*, PO Box 309, S0M 0J0. Tel: 306-235-4520. FAX: 306-235-4511. E-mail: sbn@pnls.lib.sk.ca. Web Site: pahkisimon.ca/branch/211. *Librn,* Nick Anderson
Library Holdings: Bk Vols 25,000
Wireless access
Mem of Pahkisimon Nuye?ah Library System
Open Mon-Fri 1-5

CARONPORT

CR BRIERCREST COLLEGE & SEMINARY*, Archibald Library, 510 College Dr, S0H 0S0. SAN 319-9487. Tel: 306-756-3252. Circulation Tel: 306-756-3248. Administration Tel: 306-756-3262. FAX: 306-756-5521. E-mail: library@briercrest.ca. Web Site: briercrest.ca/library. *Libr Dir,* Abigail Durkee; Tel: 306-756-3435; *Libr Supvr,* Carla Hoffmann; Staff 6 (MLS 1, Non-MLS 5)
Founded 1935. Enrl 800; Fac 40; Highest Degree: Master
Library Holdings: e-books 192,000; e-journals 14,000; Music Scores 2,153; Bk Vols 80,000; Per Subs 180
Special Collections: Eric Coll, microfiche
Subject Interests: Bible, Christian ministry, Theol
Automation Activity & Vendor Info: (Acquisitions) Horizon; (Cataloging) Horizon; (Circulation) Horizon; (ILL) Amicus; (OPAC) Horizon; (Serials) Horizon
Wireless access
Partic in Saskatchewan Electronic Resources Partnership
Open Mon-Thurs 8:15am-10pm, Fri 8:30-7:30, Sat 11-7:30

ESTON

C ESTON COLLEGE*, A D Marshall Library, 730 First St SE, S0L 1A0. (Mail add: PO Box 579, S0L 1A0), SAN 327-1234. Tel: 306-962-3621. Toll Free Tel: 888-440-3424. FAX: 306-962-3810. Web Site: www.estoncollege.ca. *Head Librn,* Ron Baker; E-mail: rbaker@estoncollege.ca; Staff 1 (MLS 1)
Founded 1979. Enrl 50; Fac 7; Highest Degree: Bachelor
Library Holdings: e-books 725; e-journals 100; Bk Titles 16,430; Per Subs 15
Subject Interests: Relig
Function: Audio & video playback equip for onsite use, CD-ROM, Electronic databases & coll, ILL available, Internet access, Mail & tel request accepted, Mail loans to mem, Orientations, Photocopying/Printing, Ref & res, Ref serv available, Telephone ref, VHS videos, Wheelchair accessible

ILE A LA CROSSE

P ILE A LA CROSSE PUBLIC LIBRARY, Bag Service 540, S0M 1C0. Tel: 306-833-3027. FAX: 306-833-2189. E-mail: sil@pnls.lib.sk.ca. Web Site: pahkisimon.ca/index.php/branch/203. *Librn,* Nicole Dalton
Library Holdings: Bk Vols 19,000
Mem of Pahkisimon Nuye?ah Library System
Open Mon-Thurs 4pm-9pm

LA LOCHE

P DAVE O'HARA COMMUNITY LIBRARY, Bag Service, No 4, S0M 1G0. Tel: 306-822-2151. FAX: 306-822-2151. E-mail: sll@pnls.lib.sk.ca. Web Site: pahkisimon.ca/branch/201. *Librn,* Priscilla Wolverine
Library Holdings: Bk Vols 18,000
Wireless access

Mem of Pahkisimon Nuye?ah Library System
Open Mon-Fri 9-5
Friends of the Library Group

LA RONGE

P ALEX ROBERTSON PUBLIC LIBRARY*, 1212 Hildebrand Dr, S0J 1L0. (Mail add: PO Box 5680, S0J 1L0). Tel: 306-425-2160. FAX: 306-425-3883. E-mail: arpl@pnls.lib.sk.ca. Web Site: pahkisimon.ca/branch/206. *Libr Adminr,* Sean Stares; E-mail: sa.stares@pnls.lib.sk.ca; Staff 2 (Non-MLS 2)
Founded 1962
Library Holdings: AV Mats 2,500; Bk Vols 24,000; Per Subs 24
Automation Activity & Vendor Info: (Acquisitions) Innovative Interfaces, Inc. - Polaris; (Cataloging) Innovative Interfaces, Inc. - Polaris; (Circulation) Innovative Interfaces, Inc. - Polaris; (Course Reserve) Innovative Interfaces, Inc. - Polaris; (ILL) Innovative Interfaces, Inc. - Polaris; (OPAC) Innovative Interfaces, Inc. - Polaris
Wireless access
Function: Adult bk club, Adult literacy prog, Children's prog
Mem of Pahkisimon Nuye?ah Library System
Open Mon-Fri 10-5:30, Sat 1-5
Friends of the Library Group

LLOYDMINSTER

J LAKELAND COLLEGE*, Lloydminster Campus Library, 2602 59 Ave, Bag 6600, T9V 3N7. Tel: 780-871-5709. Web Site: web.lakelandcollege.ca/commons/library. *Chair,* Jackie Bender; Tel: 780-871-5528, E-mail: jackie.bender@lakelandcollege.ca; *Pub Serv Librn,* Ben Harrison; Tel: 780-871-5797, E-mail: ben.harrison@lakelandcollege.ca
Library Holdings: Bk Vols 26,000
Wireless access
Open Mon-Thurs 7:30am-10pm, Fri 7:30am-8pm, Sat 1-8, Sun 1-8

MOOSE JAW

P PALLISER REGIONAL LIBRARY*, 366 Coteau St W, S6H 5C9. SAN 319-955X. Tel: 306-693-3669. E-mail: palliser@palliserlibrary.ca. Web Site: palliserlibrary.ca. *Dir,* Janet Smith; E-mail: director@palliserlibrary.ca; *Asst Dir, Rural Br Supvr,* Arwen Rudolph; Staff 6 (MLS 5, Non-MLS 1)
Founded 1973. Pop 54,200; Circ 553,300
Library Holdings: Audiobooks 5,590; AV Mats 388; CDs 4,957; DVDs 21,525; e-books 37,000; Large Print Bks 9,814; Bk Vols 271,750; Per Subs 615
Subject Interests: Local hist
Automation Activity & Vendor Info: (Acquisitions) Innovative Interfaces, Inc; (Cataloging) Innovative Interfaces, Inc; (Circulation) Innovative Interfaces, Inc; (ILL) OCLC WorldShare Interlibrary Loan; (Media Booking) IME; (OPAC) Innovative Interfaces, Inc; (Serials) Innovative Interfaces, Inc
Wireless access
Function: 24/7 Electronic res, Accelerated reader prog, Adult bk club, Adult literacy prog, After school storytime, Archival coll, Art exhibits, Audiobks via web, Bk club(s), Bks on cassette, Bks on CD, CD-ROM, Children's prog, Computer training, Computers for patron use, Digital talking bks, Distance learning, E-Readers, Electronic databases & coll, Equip loans & repairs, Family literacy, Free DVD rentals, Genealogy discussion group, Govt ref serv, Holiday prog, Home delivery & serv to seniorr ctr & nursing homes, Homebound delivery serv, ILL available, Instruction & testing, Internet access, Literacy & newcomer serv, Magazines, Mail & tel request accepted, Mail loans to mem, Mango lang, Masonic res mat, Meeting rooms, Microfiche/film & reading machines, Movies, Music CDs, Online cat, Orientations, Outreach serv, Outside serv via phone, mail, e-mail & web, OverDrive digital audio bks, Photocopying/Printing, Preschool outreach, Preschool reading prog, Printer for laptops & handheld devices, Prog for adults, Prog for children & young adult, Ref serv available, Scanner, Senior computer classes, Senior outreach, Spoken cassettes & CDs, Spoken cassettes & DVDs, Story hour, Summer & winter reading prog, Summer reading prog, Teen prog, Telephone ref, VHS videos, Wheelchair accessible, Winter reading prog, Words travel prog, Workshops, Writing prog
Publications: For the Record (Newsletter); Update
Partic in Saskatchewan Electronic Resources Partnership; Saskatchewan Information & Library Services
Friends of the Library Group
Branches: 20

ASSINIBOIA & DISTRICT PUBLIC LIBRARY, 201 Third Ave W, Assiniboia, S0H 0B0. (Mail add: Box 940, Assiniboia, S0H 0B0), SAN 321-1428. Tel: 306-642-3631. E-mail: assiniboia@palliserlibrary.ca. Web Site: palliserlibrary.ca/branch/216. *Librn,* Lori Crighton; *Asst Librn,* Gus Gere; *Asst Librn,* Lois Seeley; Staff 1 (Non-MLS 1)
Pop 3,665; Circ 42,611
Library Holdings: Bk Vols 21,547
Open Mon, Tues, Thurs & Fri 10-6, Wed 10-8, Sat 1-6

AVONLEA BRANCH, 201 Main St W, Avonlea, S0H 0C0. (Mail add: Box 351, Avonlea, S0H 0C0), SAN 321-1436. Tel: 306-868-2076. FAX: 306-868-2075. E-mail: avonlea@palliserlibrary.ca. Web Site: palliserlibrary.ca/branch/217. *Librn,* Randi Edmonds; Staff 1 (Non-MLS 1)
Pop 608; Circ 7,186
Library Holdings: Bk Vols 8,296
Open Tues 5-8, Wed 1-5, Thurs 12-5, Fri 10-2

BETHUNE BRANCH, Community Hall, 524 East St, Bethune, S0G 0H0. (Mail add: Box 116, Bethune, S0G 0H0), SAN 321-1444. Tel: 306-638-3046. E-mail: bethune@palliserlibrary.ca. Web Site: palliserlibrary.ca/branch/219. *Librn,* Robbie Curtis
Pop 962; Circ 7,022
Library Holdings: Bk Vols 7,598
Open Tues 2-8, Wed 9:30-4:30, Fri 10-3

BRIERCREST BRANCH, Community Ctr, Main St, Briercrest, S0H 0K0. (Mail add: Box 97, Briercrest, S0H 0K0), SAN 321-1452. Tel: 306-799-2137. E-mail: briercrest@palliserlibrary.ca. Web Site: palliserlibrary.ca/branch/218. *Librn,* Sharon Duncan
Pop 474; Circ 2,953
Library Holdings: Bk Vols 6,074
Open Tues 1-4:15, Wed 9:30-2, Thurs 6pm-9pm

CORONACH BRANCH, 111A Centre St, Coronach, S0H 0Z0. (Mail add: Box 30, Coronach, S0H 0Z0), SAN 321-1487. Tel: 306-267-3260. E-mail: coronach@palliserlibrary.ca. Web Site: palliserlibrary.ca/branch/220. *Librn,* Marlene McBurney
Pop 975; Circ 9,786
Library Holdings: Bk Vols 12,562
Open Tues & Wed 9:30-12:30 & 1-6, Thurs 9-12 & 1-6, Sat 9:30-12:30 & 1-4:30

CRAIK BRANCH, 611 First Ave, Craik, S0G 0V0. (Mail add: Box 339, Craik, S0G 0V0), SAN 321-1495. Tel: 306-734-2388. E-mail: craik@palliserlibrary.ca. Web Site: palliserlibrary.ca/branch/221. *Librn,* Jo McAlpine; Staff 1 (Non-MLS 1)
Pop 762; Circ 8,397
Library Holdings: Bk Vols 8,500
Open Tues 10-12, 1:30-5 & 6:30-8:30, Wed & Thurs 1:30-5, Fri 10-1:30

DAVIDSON BRANCH, 314 Washington Ave, Davidson, S0G 1A0. (Mail add: Box 754, Davidson, S0G 1A0), SAN 321-1509. Tel: 306-567-2022. FAX: 306-567-2081. E-mail: davidson@palliserlibrary.ca. Web Site: palliserlibrary.ca/branch/222. *Librn,* Victoria Martin; *Asst Librn,* Debbie Shearwood
Pop 1,519; Circ 15,752
Library Holdings: Bk Vols 10,103
Open Tues, Thurs & Fri 9:30-5, Wed 1-8, Sat 1-5

ELBOW BRANCH, 402 Minto St, Elbow, S0H 1J0. (Mail add: Box 10, Elbow, S0H 1J0), SAN 321-1517. Tel: 306-854-2220. E-mail: elbow@palliserlibrary.ca. Web Site: palliserlibrary.ca/branch/223. *Librn,* Sandra Dean
Pop 495; Circ 7,873
Library Holdings: Bk Vols 9,143
Open Wed-Fri 12:30-5:30

HOLDFAST BRANCH, 125 Robert St, Holdfast, S0G 2H0. (Mail add: Box 205, Holdfast, S0G 2H0), SAN 321-1525. Tel: 306-488-2101. E-mail: holdfast@palliserlibrary.ca. Web Site: palliserlibrary.ca/branch/224. *Librn,* Katherine Middleton
Pop 581; Circ 5,403
Library Holdings: Bk Vols 5,743
Open Tues 11:45-5:30, Thurs 12-7

IMPERIAL BRANCH, 310 Royal St, Imperial, S0G 2J0. (Mail add: Box 238, Imperial, S0G 2J0), SAN 321-1533. Tel: 306-963-2272. FAX: 306-963-2445. E-mail: imperial@palliserlibrary.ca. Web Site: palliserlibrary.ca/branch/225. *Librn,* Bruni King
Pop 593; Circ 10,110
Library Holdings: Bk Vols 9,235
Function: Bks on cassette, Bks on CD, Wheelchair accessible
Open Tues 11-4, Wed 9:30-4:30, Thurs 12-7:30

LOREBURN BRANCH, 528 Main St, Loreburn, S0H 2S0. (Mail add: Box 172, Loreburn, S0H 2S0), SAN 321-1541. Tel: 306-644-2026. E-mail: loreburn@palliserlibrary.ca. Web Site: palliserlibrary.ca/branch/226. *Librn,* Sue Ann Abbott
Pop 378; Circ 2,744
Library Holdings: Bk Vols 4,653
Open Wed 1-5:30, Thurs 10-1 & 2-5

MOOSE JAW BRANCH, 461 Langdon Crescent, S6H 0X6, SAN 321-155X. Tel: 306-692-2787. FAX: 306-692-3368. E-mail: ask@moosejawlibrary.ca. Web Site: palliserlibrary.ca/branch/228. *Librn,* Gwen Fisher; Staff 16.9 (MLS 3, Non-MLS 13.9)
Founded 1913. Pop 33,000; Circ 307,012
Library Holdings: Audiobooks 6,836; CDs 4,692; DVDs 5,767; e-books 18,477; Microforms 1,055; Bk Vols 130,263; Per Subs 500; Talking Bks 2,072; Videos 954
Special Collections: Archives Coll
Subject Interests: Local hist

Automation Activity & Vendor Info: (ILL) Innovative Interfaces, Inc - Millennium
Function: Adult bk club, After school storytime, Archival coll, Audio & video playback equip for onsite use, Audiobks via web, BA reader (adult literacy), Bk club(s), Bks on cassette, Bks on CD, CD-ROM, Children's prog, Computer training, Computers for patron use, Digital talking bks, Doc delivery serv, Electronic databases & coll, Family literacy, Free DVD rentals, Holiday prog, Home delivery & serv to seniorr ctr & nursing homes, Homebound delivery serv, ILL available, Magnifiers for reading, Mail & tel request accepted, Music CDs, Online cat, Orientations, Outreach serv, Outside serv via phone, mail, e-mail & web, OverDrive digital audio bks, Photocopying/Printing, Printer for laptops & handheld devices, Prog for adults, Prog for children & young adult, Ref & res, Ref serv available, Scanner, Senior computer classes, Spoken cassettes & CDs, Spoken cassettes & DVDs, Story hour, Summer reading prog, Teen prog, Telephone ref, VHS videos, Wheelchair accessible
Publications: Lines & Links (Newsletter)
Special Services for the Blind - Closed circuit TV; Reader equip
Open Mon-Thurs 9:30-9, Fri & Sat 9:30-6, Sun (Sept-July) 1-5
Friends of the Library Group

MORTLACH BRANCH, 118 Rose St, Mortlach, S0H 3E0. (Mail add: Box 36, Mortlach, S0H 3E0), SAN 321-1568. Tel: 306-355-2202. E-mail: mortlach@palliserlibrary.ca. Web Site: palliserlibrary.ca/branch/229. *Librn,* Angela Molde
Pop 438; Circ 4,466
Library Holdings: Bk Vols 4,760
Open Tues 9:30-4, Thurs 12-5

MOSSBANK BRANCH, 310 Main St, Mossbank, S0H 3G0. (Mail add: Box 422, Mossbank, S0H 3G0), SAN 321-1576. Tel: 306-354-2474. E-mail: mossbank@palliserlibrary.ca. Web Site: palliserlibrary.ca/branch/227. *Librn,* Kimberly Miller
Pop 727; Circ 10,835
Library Holdings: Bk Vols 10,099
Open Tues & Thurs 9:30-11:30 & 12:30-5, Wed 12:30-5

RIVERHURST BRANCH, 324 Teck St, Riverhurst, S0H 3P0. (Mail add: Box 37, Riverhurst, S0H 3P0), SAN 321-1584. Tel: 306-353-2130. E-mail: riverhurst@palliserlibrary.ca. Web Site: palliserlibrary.ca/branch/232. *Librn,* Brittany Bennett
Pop 281; Circ 5,348
Library Holdings: Bk Vols 5,544
Open Tues 11-5, Thurs 9:30-3

ROCKGLEN BRANCH, 1018 Centre St, Rockglen, S0H 3R0. (Mail add: Box 148, Rockglen, S0H 3R0), SAN 321-1592. Tel: 306-476-2350. E-mail: rockglen@palliserlibrary.ca. Web Site: palliserlibrary.ca/branch/231. *Librn,* Angela Stewart
Pop 837; Circ 9,167
Library Holdings: Bk Vols 6,389
Open Tues 10:30-5, Wed 11:45-5, Thurs 12-5

ROULEAU BRANCH, 113 Main St, Rouleau, S0G 4H0. (Mail add: Box 238, Rouleau, S0G 4H0), SAN 321-1606. Tel: 306-776-2322. E-mail: rouleau@palliserlibrary.ca. Web Site: palliserlibrary.ca/branch/233. *Librn,* Marla Gellvear
Pop 578; Circ 5,276
Library Holdings: Bk Vols 7,031
Open Mon & Wed 5-9, Tues & Fri 1-5

TUGASKE BRANCH, 106 Ogema St, Tugaske, S0H 4B0. (Mail add: Box 10, Tugaske, S0H 4B0), SAN 321-1614. Tel: 306-759-2215. E-mail: tugaske@palliserlibrary.ca. Web Site: palliserlibrary.ca/branch/234. *Librn,* Violet Beaudry
Pop 657; Circ 4,594
Library Holdings: Bk Vols 4,952
Open Wed 3:30-7:30, Thurs 9-2, Fri 3:30-6:30

WILLOW BUNCH BRANCH, Two Ave F S, Willow Bunch, S0H 4K0. (Mail add: Box 280, Willow Bunch, S0H 4K0), SAN 321-1622. Tel: 306-473-2393. E-mail: willowbunch@palliserlibrary.ca. Web Site: palliserlibrary.ca/branch/235. *Librn,* Barb Gibbons
Pop 430; Circ 5,018
Library Holdings: Bk Vols 6,746
Open Tues 1-5, Wed 2-8:30, Thurs 11:30-3:30

WOOD MOUNTAIN BRANCH, Two Second Ave, Wood Mountain, S0H 4L0. (Mail add: Box 62, Wood Mountain, S0H 4L0), SAN 321-1630. Tel: 306-266-2110. E-mail: woodmountain@palliserlibrary.ca. Web Site: palliserlibrary.ca/branch/236. *Librn,* Jocelyn Todd
Pop 183; Circ 3,001
Library Holdings: Bk Vols 3,608
Open Tues 9-12 & 12:30-3

C SIAST-SASKATCHEWAN INSTITUTE OF APPLIED SCIENCE & TECHNOLOGY*, Moose Jaw Campus Library, 600 Saskatchewan St W, S6H 4R4. SAN 319-9576. Tel: 306-691-8233. FAX: 306-691-8586. E-mail: help.library@saskpolytech.ca, moosejaw.library@saskpolytech.ca. Web Site: library.saskpolytech.ca. *Dir, Libr Serv,* Rian Misfeldt; Tel: 306-775-7710, E-mail: rian.misfeldt@saskpolytech.ca; *Dept Adminr,* Rhonda Starchuck; Tel: 306-775-7709, E-mail: rhonda.starchuck@saskpolytech.ca; *Libr Mgr,* Juliet Nielsen; Tel: 306-775-7412, E-mail: nielsenju@saskpolytech.ca; Staff 2 (MLS 2)
Founded 1961. Enrl 1,700
Library Holdings: Bk Vols 19,000; Per Subs 200
Subject Interests: Indust
Automation Activity & Vendor Info: (Acquisitions) SirsiDynix; (Cataloging) SirsiDynix; (Circulation) SirsiDynix; (Course Reserve) SirsiDynix; (ILL) Fretwell-Downing; (Media Booking) SirsiDynix; (OPAC) SirsiDynix; (Serials) SirsiDynix
Wireless access
Open Mon-Thurs 7:30am-9pm, Fri 7:30-4:30, Sat & Sun 1-5

MUENSTER

C SAINT PETER'S COLLEGE LIBRARY*, 100 College Dr, S0K 2Y0. (Mail add: PO Box 40, S0K 2Y0), SAN 319-9592. Tel: 306-682-7860, 306-682-7861. FAX: 306-682-4402. E-mail: library@stpeters.sk.ca. Web Site: www.stpeterscollege.ca/students1/library.php. *Libr Serv Mgr,* Position Currently Open
Founded 1903
Library Holdings: Bk Vols 50,000; Per Subs 100
Subject Interests: German Americana, German Canadiana, Monastic hist, Theol
Wireless access
Partic in Saskatchewan Electronic Resources Partnership
Open Mon-Thurs 8:30-8, Fri 8:30-5, Sat 11-4 (Sept-April); Mon-Fri 8:30-5 (May-Aug)

NIPAWIN

SR NIPAWIN BIBLE COLLEGE LIBRARY*, Hwy 35 S, S0E 1E0. (Mail add: PO Box 1986, S0E 1E0), SAN 370-565X. Tel: 306-862-5095. Toll Free Tel: 888-862-5095. FAX: 306-862-3651. E-mail: info@nipawin.org. Web Site: nipawin.org/academics/resources/. *Librn,* Myra Schmidt
Founded 1934
Library Holdings: Bk Titles 10,500; Per Subs 160
Special Collections: Religious Volumes
Wireless access

NORTH BATTLEFORD

P LAKELAND LIBRARY REGION*, Headquarters, 1302 100 St, S9A 0V8. SAN 319-9614. Tel: 306-445-6108. FAX: 306-445-5717. Web Site: lakelandlibrary.ca. *Dir,* Darrell Yates; E-mail: director@lakeland.lib.sk.ca; *Mgr, Libr Admin,* Irene Nones; E-mail: admin.manager@lakeland.lib.sk.ca; *Commun Serv Librn,* Colin Evans; E-mail: csl@lakeland.lib.sk.ca; Staff 11 (MLS 2, Non-MLS 9)
Founded 1972. Pop 77,400
Automation Activity & Vendor Info: (Acquisitions) Innovative Interfaces, Inc; (Cataloging) Innovative Interfaces, Inc; (Circulation) Innovative Interfaces, Inc; (OPAC) Innovative Interfaces, Inc
Wireless access
Special Services for the Blind - Bks on CD; Talking bks
Open Mon-Fri 8:30-5
Branches: 31

BATTLEFORD BRANCH, 201 22nd St W, Battleford, S0M 0E0. (Mail add: PO Box 220, Battleford, S0M 0E0). Tel: 306-937-2646. FAX: 306-937-6631. E-mail: battleford.lib@lakeland.lib.sk.ca.
Open Mon & Fri 12:30-6, Wed 10:30-6, Thurs 1-8:30

BORDEN BRANCH, 303 First Ave, Borden, S0K 0N0. (Mail add: PO Box 58, Borden, S0K 0N0). Tel: 306-997-2220. E-mail: bordon.lib@lakeland.lib.sk.ca.
Open Tues 3-6, Wed 10-3, Fri 1-4

CUT KNIFE BRANCH, 115 Broad St, Cut Knife, S0M 0N0. (Mail add: PO Box 595, Cut Knife, S0M 0N0). Tel: 306-398-2342. E-mail: cutknife.lib@lakeland.lib.sk.ca.
Library Holdings: Bk Vols 4,243
Open Tues & Thurs 1-4, Wed 1-5

DENZIL BRANCH, 405 Brooks Ave, Denzil, S0L 0S0. (Mail add: PO Box 188, Denzil, S0L 0S0). Tel: 306-358-2118. FAX: 306-358-4828. E-mail: denzil.lib@lakeland.lib.sk.ca.
Library Holdings: Bk Vols 2,763
Open Fri 9:30-4:30

EDAM BRANCH, 1000 Main St, Edam, S0M 0V0. (Mail add: PO Box 203, Edam, S0M 0V0). Tel: 306-397-2223. FAX: 306-397-2626. E-mail: edam.lib@lakeland.lib.sk.ca.
Open Mon 11-6, Thurs 3-6

GLASLYN BRANCH, 182 Main St, Glaslyn, S0M 0Y0. Tel: 306-342-4748. E-mail: glaslyn.lib@lakeland.lib.sk.ca.
Open Tues & Thurs 1-5

GOODSOIL BRANCH, First Ave, Goodsoil, S0M 1A0. (Mail add: PO Box 129, Goodsoil, S0M 1A0). Tel: 306-238-2155. E-mail: goodsoil.lib@lakeland.lib.sk.ca.
Open Wed & Thurs 9:30-4

HAFFORD BRANCH, 17 Main St, Hafford, S0J 1A0. (Mail add: PO Box 520, Hafford, S0J 1A0). Tel: 306-549-2373. FAX: 306-549-2333. E-mail: hafford.lib@lakeland.lib.sk.ca.
Partic in MnPALS
Open Tues & Thurs 12-4, Wed 12-3

LASHBURN BRANCH, 95 Main St E, Lashburn, S0M 1H0. (Mail add: PO Box 160, Lashburn, S0M 1H0). Tel: 306-285-4144. E-mail: lashburn.lib@lakeland.lib.sk.ca.
Library Holdings: Bk Vols 7,329
Open Tues 9-Noon, Wed 6:30-9:30, Thurs 1:30-4:30, Fri 10-3

LOON LAKE BRANCH, 414 Main St, Loon Lake, S0M 1L0. (Mail add: PO Box 216, Loon Lake, S0M 1L0). Tel: 306-837-2186. E-mail: loonlake.lib@lakeland.lib.sk.ca.
Open Tues 10-4, Thurs 11-5

MACKLIN BRANCH, 5001 Press Ave, Macklin, S0L 2C0. (Mail add: PO Box 652, Macklin, S0L 2C0). Tel: 306-753-2933. FAX: 306-753-3234. E-mail: macklin.lib@lakeland.lib.sk.ca.
Open Tues & Wed 1-6, Thurs 10-2

MAIDSTONE BRANCH, 102B 108 - First Ave W, Maidstone, S0M 1M0. (Mail add: PO Box 429, Maidstone, S0M 1M0). Tel: 306-893-4153. E-mail: maidstone.lib@lakeland.lib.sk.ca.
Open Tues 9:30-1 & 1:30-5, Wed 1-5 & 5:30-8, Fri 9:30-1

MAKWA BRANCH, Hwy 304, Makwa, S0M 1N0. (Mail add: General Delivery, Makwa, S0M 1N0). Tel: 306-236-3995. E-mail: makwa.lib@lakeland.lib.sk.ca.
Open Wed 10-4

MARSDEN BRANCH, 104 Centre St, Marsden, S0M 1P0. (Mail add: PO Box 328, Marsden, S0M 1P0). Tel: 306-826-5666. E-mail: marsden.lib@lakeland.lib.sk.ca.
Open Tues & Thurs 10-5

MARSHALL BRANCH, 13 Main St, Marshall, S0M 1R0. (Mail add: PO Box 273, Marshall, S0M 1R0). Tel: 306-387-6155. E-mail: marshall.lib@lakeland.lib.sk.ca.
Library Holdings: Bk Vols 4,000
Open Tues 1:30-6, Thurs 10-3

MAYFAIR BRANCH, Railway Ave, Mayfair, S0M 1S0. (Mail add: PO Box 70, Mayfair, S0M 1S0). Tel: 306-246-4465. E-mail: mayfair.lib@lakeland.lib.sk.ca.
Library Holdings: Bk Titles 20,000; Per Subs 12
Open Tues 10-2, Wed 5pm-8pm, Thurs 10-1

MAYMONT BRANCH, PO Box 102, Maymont, S0M 1T0. Tel: 306-389-2006. E-mail: maymont.lib@lakeland.lib.sk.ca.
Founded 1972
Open Tues 1-6, Fri 9-2

MEADOW LAKE BRANCH, 320 Centre St, Meadow Lake, S9X 1V8. (Mail add: PO Box 1351, Meadow Lake, S9X 1Z1). Tel: 306-236-5396. FAX: 306-236-6282. E-mail: meadowlake.lib@lakeland.lib.sk.ca. *Br Mgr,* Audrey Marsh
Open Mon & Fri 10-6, Tues-Thurs 10-9

MEDSTEAD BRANCH, 209 Second Ave, Medstead, S0M 1W0. (Mail add: PO Box 13, Medstead, S0M 1W0). Tel: 306-342-4988. E-mail: medstead.lib@lakeland.lib.sk.ca.
Open Wed 10:30-4:30, Thurs 2-6

MEOTA BRANCH, PO Box 214, Meota, S0M 1X0. Tel: 306-892-2004. E-mail: meota.lib@lakeland.lib.sk.ca.
Open Tues & Sat 9:30am-12:30pm, Wed & Thurs 2-6

NEILBURG BRANCH, 108 Centre St, Neilburg, S0M 2C0. (Mail add: PO Box 174, Neilburg, S0M 2C0). Tel: 306-823-4234. E-mail: neilburg.lib@lakeland.lib.sk.ca. Web Site: lakelandlibrary.ca/branch/186.
Open Tues 11-6, Thurs 1-6, Fri 11-5

NORTH BATTLEFORD PUBLIC LIBRARY, 1392-101 St, S9A 1A2, SAN 376-2173. Tel: 306-445-3206. FAX: 306-445-6454. E-mail: librarian.northbattleford@lakeland.lib.sk.ca. Web Site: www.northbattlefordlibrary.com. *Head Librn,* Caroline Popadick; Staff 2 (MLS 2)
Founded 1916. Pop 14,500
Library Holdings: Bk Vols 83,000; Per Subs 121
Function: 24/7 Electronic res, 24/7 Online cat, Adult bk club, After school storytime, Bks on CD, Children's prog, Computer training, Computers for patron use, Digital talking bks, Electronic databases & coll, Free DVD rentals, Govt ref serv, Holiday prog, Home delivery & serv to seniorr ctr & nursing homes, ILL available, Internet access, Magazines, Meeting rooms, Microfiche/film & reading machines, Movies, Online cat, Orientations, Outreach serv, OverDrive digital audio bks, Photocopying/Printing, Preschool reading prog, Printer for laptops & handheld devices, Prog for adults, Prog for children & young adult, Ref & res, Ref serv available, Summer & winter reading prog, Summer reading prog, Teen prog, Winter reading prog
Open Mon 12:30-9, Tues 10:30-8, Wed 10:30-9, Thurs-Sat 10:30-6, Sun 2-5:30

PARADISE HILL BRANCH, 104 - Second Ave, Paradise Hill, S0M 2G0. (Mail add: PO Box 187, Paradise Hill, S0M 2G0). Tel: 306-344-4741. E-mail: paradisehill.lib@lakeland.lib.sk.ca.
Open Tues 4:30-8:30, Wed 10-1, Fri 10-5

PAYNTON BRANCH, 205 First St E, Paynton, S0M 2J0. (Mail add: General Delivery, Paynton, S0M 2J0). Tel: 306-895-2175. E-mail: paynton.lib@lakeland.lib.sk.ca.
Open Tues 12:30-5:30, Thurs 3-8

PIERCELAND BRANCH, PO Box 250, Pierceland, S0M 2K0. Tel: 306-839-2166. E-mail: pierceland.lib@lakeland.lib.sk.ca.
Library Holdings: Bk Vols 2,000
Open Wed 10-3, Thurs 1-6

RABBIT LAKE BRANCH, 104 Main St, Rabbit Lake, S0M 2L0. (Mail add: PO Box 146, Rabbit Lake, S0M 2L0). Tel: 306-841-7079. E-mail: rabbitlake.lib@lakeland.lib.sk.ca.
Open Wed 12:30-5:30, Fri 9:30am-2:30pm

RADISSON BRANCH, 329 Main St, Radisson, S0K 3L0. (Mail add: PO Box 161, Radisson, S0K 3L0). Tel: 306-827-4521. E-mail: radisson.lib@lakeland.lib.sk.ca.
Open Tues 1-5, Wed 3-7, Fri 2-5

ST WALBURG BRANCH, 124 Main St, St. Walburg, S0M 2T0. (Mail add: PO Box 154, St. Walburg, S0M 2T0). Tel: 306-248-3250. E-mail: stwalburg.lib@lakeland.lib.sk.ca.
Open Tues 10-3, Wed 2-5:30, Thurs 10-5:30

SASKATCHEWAN HOSPITAL, One Jersey St, S9A 2X8. (Mail add: PO Box 39, S9A 2X8). Tel: 306-440-3940. FAX: 306-446-6810. E-mail: saskhospital.lib@lakeland.lib.sk.ca.
Library Holdings: Bk Vols 1,600; Per Subs 44
Open Tues 10-4

SPEERS BRANCH, Main St, Speers, S0M 2V0. (Mail add: General Delivery, Speers, S0M 2V0). Tel: 306-246-4866. E-mail: speers.lib@lakeland.lib.sk.ca.
Open Mon & Thurs 1:30-5, Wed 9:30-12:30

TURTLEFORD BRANCH, 212 Main St, Turtleford, S0M 2Y0. (Mail add: PO Box 146, Turtleford, S0M 2Y0). Tel: 306-845-2074. E-mail: turtleford.lib@lakeland.lib.sk.ca.
Open Mon-Fri 10-2

PELICAN NARROWS

P TAWOWIKAMIK PUBLIC LIBRARY, PO Box 100, S0P 0E0. Tel: 306-632-2161. E-mail: spn@pnls.lib.sk.ca. Web Site: pahkisimon.ca/branch/210. *Libr Adminr,* Margaret Brass; E-mail: mbrass@pbcn.ca
Library Holdings: Bk Vols 15,000; Per Subs 50
Automation Activity & Vendor Info: (Cataloging) Chancery SMS; (Circulation) Chancery SMS; (OPAC) Chancery SMS
Mem of Pahkisimon Nuye?ah Library System
Open Mon-Fri 9-12 & 1-4:30

PINEHOUSE LAKE

P PEAYAMECHIKEE PUBLIC LIBRARY*, Pinehouse Ave, S0J 2B0. (Mail add: PO Box 160, S0J-2B0). Tel: 306-884-4888. FAX: 306-884-2164. E-mail: splm@pnls.lib.sk.ca. Web Site: pahkisimon.ca/branch/208. *Librn,* Chad Ratt
Founded 1999
Library Holdings: AV Mats 150; Bk Vols 5,000; Per Subs 17
Wireless access
Mem of Pahkisimon Nuye?ah Library System
Open Mon-Fri 10-4

PRINCE ALBERT

C GABRIEL DUMONT INSTITUTE LIBRARY*, 48 12th St E, S6V 1B2. SAN 371-8441. Tel: 306-922-6466. FAX: 306-763-4834. E-mail: pa.library@gdins.org. *Librn,* Nicolle DeGagne; E-mail: nicolle.degagne@gdi.gdins.org; Staff 1 (Non-MLS 1)
Founded 1989. Enrl 200; Fac 17; Highest Degree: Master
Library Holdings: CDs 500; DVDs 200; Music Scores 200; Bk Vols 20,000; Per Subs 30
Subject Interests: Multicultural studies, Teacher educ
Partic in Saskatchewan Electronic Resources Partnership
Open Mon-Fri 8-4:30

M PRINCE ALBERT PARKLAND HEALTH REGION LIBRARY*, 1200 24th St W, S6V 4N5. SAN 319-9657. Tel: 306-765-6026. FAX: 306-765-6062. E-mail: library@saskhealthauthority.ca. Web Site: saskhealthauthority.libguides.com/about/victoria. *Lead Librn,* Susan Baer; E-mail: susan.baer@saskhealthauthority.ca
Subject Interests: Med, Pub health, Surgical
Wireless access
Function: Health sci info serv
Open Mon-Fri 8:30-4:30
Restriction: Non-circulating to the pub

P PRINCE ALBERT PUBLIC LIBRARY*, John M Cuelenaere Public Library, 125 12th St E, S6V 1B7. SAN 810-1035. Tel: 306-763-8496. FAX: 306-763-3816. E-mail: contactus@princealbertlibrary.ca. Web Site:

www.princealbertlibrary.ca. *Dir,* Greg Elliott; E-mail: gelliott@princealbertlibrary.ca; Staff 10 (MLS 4, Non-MLS 6)
Founded 1973. Pop 40,000; Circ 358,395
Library Holdings: AV Mats 4,623; CDs 3,617; DVDs 701; High Interest/Low Vocabulary Bk Vols 656; Large Print Bks 4,513; Bk Titles 109,509; Bk Vols 127,477; Per Subs 498; Talking Bks 150
Automation Activity & Vendor Info: (Acquisitions) Innovative Interfaces, Inc. - Polaris; (Cataloging) Innovative Interfaces, Inc. - Polaris; (Circulation) Innovative Interfaces, Inc. - Polaris; (Course Reserve) Innovative Interfaces, Inc. - Polaris; (ILL) Innovative Interfaces, Inc. - Polaris; (Media Booking) Innovative Interfaces, Inc. - Polaris; (OPAC) Innovative Interfaces, Inc. - Polaris; (Serials) Innovative Interfaces, Inc. - Polaris
Wireless access
Function: Govt ref serv, Health sci info serv, Home delivery & serv to seniorr ctr & nursing homes, ILL available, Wheelchair accessible
Partic in Saskatchewan Electronic Resources Partnership; Saskatchewan Information & Library Services
Open Mon-Thurs 8:30am-9pm, Fri & Sat 8:30-5

C SIAST LIBRARIES*, Woodland Campus, 1100 15th St E, S6V 6G1. SAN 370-6818. Tel: 306-765-1550. Toll Free Tel: 866-460-4430. FAX: 306-765-1829. E-mail: princealbert.library@saskpolytech.ca. Web Site: library.saskpolytech.ca. *Dir,* Aidan Meegan; E-mail: meegana@saskpolytech.ca; *Digital Res Librn,* Martine Morency; Tel: 306-765-1547, E-mail: morency@saskpolytech.ca; *Libr Mgr,* Regan Balfour; Tel: 306-765-1533, E-mail: regan.balfour@saskpolytech.ca; *Libr Supvr,* Jacquie Goertzen; Tel: 306-765-1546, E-mail: goertzenja@saskpolytech.ca; Staff 6 (MLS 2, Non-MLS 4)
Founded 1988. Enrl 2,500; Highest Degree: Doctorate
Library Holdings: DVDs 7,500; e-books 322,000; e-journals 107,000; Bk Vols 35,000; Per Subs 400
Automation Activity & Vendor Info: (Acquisitions) SirsiDynix; (Cataloging) SirsiDynix; (Circulation) SirsiDynix; (OPAC) SirsiDynix; (Serials) SirsiDynix
Wireless access
Function: ILL available
Special Services for the Deaf - Bks on deafness & sign lang; Staff with knowledge of sign lang
Open Mon-Fri 8-6
Restriction: Restricted borrowing privileges

P WAPITI REGIONAL LIBRARY*, 145 12th St E, S6V 1B7. SAN 319-9665. Tel: 306-764-0712. FAX: 306-922-1516. E-mail: wapiti@wapitilibrary.ca. Web Site: wapitilibrary.ca. *Chief Exec Officer, Regional Dir,* Tony Murphy; *IT Mgr,* Lorne Moffat; E-mail: lmoffat@wapitilibrary.ca; Staff 114 (MLS 6, Non-MLS 108)
Founded 1950. Pop 119,392; Circ 744,381
Library Holdings: Bk Vols 509,665
Automation Activity & Vendor Info: (Acquisitions) Innovative Interfaces, Inc; (Cataloging) Innovative Interfaces, Inc; (Circulation) Innovative Interfaces, Inc; (Course Reserve) Innovative Interfaces, Inc; (ILL) Innovative Interfaces, Inc; (Media Booking) Innovative Interfaces, Inc; (OPAC) Innovative Interfaces, Inc; (Serials) Innovative Interfaces, Inc
Wireless access
Publications: Wapiti
Partic in Saskatchewan Electronic Resources Partnership
Open Mon-Fri 8-5
Branches: 44
ALVENA PUBLIC LIBRARY, Business/Commerce Complex, 101 Main St, Alvena, S0K 0E0. (Mail add: Box 94, Alvena, S0K 0E0). Tel: 306-943-2003. Circulation E-mail: alvcirc@wapitilibrary.ca. *Br Librn,* Beverly Hilkewich
Open Tues 9-5, Thurs 10-1
ARBORFIELD PUBLIC LIBRARY, 201 Main St, Arborfield, S0E 0A0. (Mail add: PO Box 223, Arborfield, S0E 0A0). Circulation E-mail: arbcirc@wapitilibrary.ca. *Br Librn,* Julie Gray
Open Tues 11:30-6, Thurs 9:30-4
ARCHERWILL PUBLIC LIBRARY, First Ave, Archerwill, S0E 0B0. (Mail add: Box 174, Archerwill, S0E 0B0). Tel: 306-323-2128. Circulation E-mail: arccirc@wapitilibrary.ca. *Br Librn,* Robin Toews
Library Holdings: Bk Vols 3,000
Open Tues 11-4, Thurs 1-6
BIG RIVER PUBLIC LIBRARY, 606 First St N, Big River, S0J 0E0. (Mail add: Box 154, Big River, S0J 0E0). Tel: 306-469-2152. Circulation E-mail: bigcirc@wapitilibrary.ca. *Br Librn,* Melissa Clapper; *Br Librn,* Pat Warren
Open Mon, Wed & Fri 10:30-4:30
BIRCH HILLS PUBLIC LIBRARY, 126 McCallum Ave, Birch Hills, S0J 0G0. (Mail add: Box 396, Birch Hills, S0J 0G0). Tel: 306-749-3281. Circulation E-mail: bircirc@wapitilibrary.ca. *Br Librn,* Joanne Bzdel
Open Tues 11-4 & 5-8, Thurs 9-12 & 1-6
BJORKDALE PUBLIC LIBRARY, 105 Hara Ave, Bjorkdale, S0E 0E0. (Mail add: Box 210, Bjorkdale, S0E 0E0). Tel: 308-886-2119. Circulation E-mail: bjocirc@wapitilibrary.ca. *Br Librn,* Ashley Babcock
Open Tues & Thurs 9-4, Wed 9-12
BLAINE LAKE PUBLIC LIBRARY, CNR Sta, Blaine Lake, S0J 0J0. (Mail add: Box 491, Blaine Lake, S0J 0J0). Tel: 306-497-3130. Circulation E-mail: blacirc@wapitilibrary.ca. *Br Librn,* Louise Diehl
Open Wed 12-6, Fri 1-5, Sat 12-4
CANWOOD PUBLIC LIBRARY, 660 Main St, Canwood, S0J 0K0. (Mail add: Box 23, Canwood, S0J 0K0). Tel: 306-468-2501. E-mail: cancirc@wapitilibrary.ca. *Br Librn,* Judy Stempien
Open Tues & Fri 1-5, Thurs 10-4
CARROT RIVER PUBLIC LIBRARY, Town Office/Library Complex, Main St, Carrot River, S0E 0L0. (Mail add: Box 1001, Carrot River, S0E 0L0). Tel: 306-768-2501. Circulation E-mail: carcirc@wapitilibrary.ca. *Br Librn,* Coreen Holmen
Open Tues & Thurs 11-4, Wed 11-5
CHOICELAND PUBLIC LIBRARY, 116 First St E, Choiceland, S0J 0M0. (Mail add: Box 250, Choiceland, S0J 0M0). Tel: 306-428-2216. Circulation E-mail: chocirc@wapitilibrary.ca. *Br Librn,* Rita Holmen
Open Tues & Thurs 10-5, Wed 1-6
CHRISTOPHER LAKE PUBLIC LIBRARY, District of Lakeland Bldg, Hwy 263, Christopher Lake, S0J 0N0. (Mail add: Box 27, Christopher Lake, S0J 0N0). Tel: 306-982-4763. Circulation E-mail: chrcirc@wapitilibrary.ca. *Br Librn,* Kristin Burton
Open Wed & Thurs 1-7, Sat 10-2
CUDWORTH PUBLIC LIBRARY, 426 Second Ave, Cudworth, S0K 1B0. (Mail add: Box 321, Cudworth, S0K 1B0). Tel: 306-256-3530. Circulation E-mail: cudcirc@wapitilibrary.ca. *Librn,* Kathy Shawaga
Open Tues & Thurs 12-4, Fri 4:30-7:30
DEBDEN PUBLIC LIBRARY, 3 204 Second Ave E, Debden, S0J 0S0. (Mail add: Box 143, Debden, S0J 0S0). Tel: 306-724-2240. Circulation E-mail: debcirc@wapitilibrary.ca. *Br Librn,* Aline Hannon
Open Mon 2-7, Tues 10-4
DUCK LAKE PUBLIC LIBRARY, 410 Victoria Ave, Duck Lake, S0K 1J0. (Mail add: Box 490, Duck Lake, S0K 1J0), SAN 327-8417. Tel: 306-467-2016. Circulation E-mail: duccirc@wapitilibrary.ca. *Br Librn,* Diane Perrin
Open Mon-Wed 1-5
GRONLID PUBLIC LIBRARY, One Railway Ave, Gronlid, S0E 0W0. (Mail add: Box 192, Gronlid, S0E 0W0). Tel: 306-277-4633. FAX: 306-277-2170. Circulation E-mail: grocirc@wapitilibrary.ca. *Br Librn,* Cheryl Ens
Founded 1973
Open Wed 9-4, Thurs 9-3
HUDSON BAY PUBLIC LIBRARY, 130 Main St, Hudson Bay, S0E 0Y0. (Mail add: Box 1109, Hudson Bay, S0E 0Y0). Tel: 306-865-3110. Circulation E-mail: hudcirc@wapitilibrary.ca. Web Site: wapitilibrary.ca/index.php/branch/279. *Br Librn,* Linda Erickson; *Br Librn,* Tracey Knihnitski
Open Mon 9:30-3:30, Tues & Thurs 12:30-5:30, Wed 2:30-7:30, Fri 11:30-5:30
Friends of the Library Group
HUMBOLDT REID-THOMPSON PUBLIC LIBRARY, 705 Main St, Humboldt, S0K 2A0. (Mail add: Box 1330, Humboldt, S0K 2A0). Tel: 306-682-2034. FAX: 306-682-3035. Circulation E-mail: humcirc@wapitilibrary.ca. *Br Librn,* Michael Langhorst
Open Mon-Thurs 10-8, Fri 10-6, Sat 10-4
KINISTINO PUBLIC LIBRARY, 210 Kinistino Ave, Kinistino, S0J 1H0. (Mail add: Box 774, Kinistino, S0J 1H0). Tel: 306-864-2537. Circulation E-mail: kincirc@wapitilibrary.ca. *Br Librn,* Susan Turner
Function: Audiobks via web, AV serv, Bks on cassette, Bks on CD, Bus archives, Children's prog, Computers for patron use, Free DVD rentals, Games, Internet access, Laminating, Magazines, Music CDs, Online cat, Online ref, Photocopying/Printing, Spoken cassettes & CDs, Spoken cassettes & DVDs, Summer reading prog
Open Mon Noon-4, Tues 9:30-1:30, Wed & Thurs 12:30-5:30
LEASK PUBLIC LIBRARY, 231 First Ave, Leask, S0J 1M0. (Mail add: Box 117, Leask, S0J 1M0). Tel: 306-466-4577. E-mail: leacirc@wapitilibrary.ca. *Br Librn,* Beryle Peake; *Br Librn,* Connie Peake
Open Tues 1-5:30, Fri 10:30-5, Sat 1-5
LEOVILLE PUBLIC LIBRARY, Village Office, Main St, Leoville, S0J 1N0. (Mail add: Box 129, Leoville, S0J 1N0). Tel: 306-984-2057. Circulation E-mail: leocirc@wapitilibrary.ca. *Br Librn,* Debby Alberts
Open Wed 10-4, Thurs 10-3
MARCELIN PUBLIC LIBRARY, 100 First Ave, Marcelin, S0J 1R0. Tel: 306-226-2110. Circulation E-mail: marcirc@wapitilibrary.ca. *Br Librn,* Marilyn Crawford
Open Tues 2-6, Wed 2-8, Sat 10-2
MELFORT PUBLIC LIBRARY, 106 Crawford Ave W, Melfort, S0E 1A0. (Mail add: Box 429, Melfort, S0E 1A0). Tel: 306-752-2022. Circulation E-mail: melcirc@wapitilibrary.ca. *Br Librn,* Penny Markland
Open Mon & Fri 8:30-6, Tues-Thurs 8:30-9, Sat 10-5

MISTATIM PUBLIC LIBRARY, Old School Bldg, Railway Ave, Mistatim, S0E 1B0. (Mail add: Box 10, Mistatim, S0E 1B0). Tel: 306-889-2008. Circulation E-mail: miscirc@wapitilibrary.ca. *Br Librn,* Colleen Kapeller
Open Wed & Thurs 9-4:30

NAICAM PUBLIC LIBRARY, 109 Centre St, Naicam, S0K 2Z0. (Mail add: Box 587, Naicam, S0K 2Z0). Tel: 306-874-2156. Circulation E-mail: naicirc@wapitilibrary.ca. *Br Librn,* Darla Christianson
Open Tues-Thurs 1-5, Fri 12-5

NIPAWIN PUBLIC LIBRARY, 501 Second St E, Nipawin, S0E 1E0. (Mail add: Box 1720, Nipawin, S0E 1E0). Tel: 306-862-4867. Circulation E-mail: nipcirc@wapitilibrary.ca. *Br Librn,* Nancy Budd
Open Mon & Fri 9-6, Tues-Thurs 9-8, Sat 1-6

PADDOCKWOOD PUBLIC LIBRARY, Old School Bldg, First St N, Paddockwood, S0J 1Z0. (Mail add: Box 178, Paddockwood, S0J 1Z0). Circulation E-mail: padcirc@wapitilibrary.ca. *Br Librn,* Kyla Fremont
Open Tues 1-5, Wed 10-3, Thurs 12-5

PILGER PUBLIC LIBRARY, 622 Main St, Pilger, S0K 3G0. (Mail add: Box 116, Pilger, S0K 3G0). Tel: 306-367-4809. Circulation E-mail: pilcirc@wapitilibrary.ca. *Br Librn,* Crystal Gudmundson
Open Tues & Fri 3-7, Thurs 2-6

PORCUPINE PLAIN PUBLIC LIBRARY, 302 Pine St W, Porcupine Plain, S0E 1H0. (Mail add: Box 162, Porcupine Plain, S0E 1H0). Tel: 306-278-2488. Circulation E-mail: porcirc@wapitilibrary.ca. *Br Librn,* Joanne Yacyshyn
Open Tues & Wed 9:30-12 & 12:30-5, Thurs 9:30-12 & 12:30-4

PRAIRIE RIVER PUBLIC LIBRARY, Two Arras St, Prairie River, S0E 1J0. (Mail add: General Delivery, Prairie River, S0E 1J0). Tel: 306-889-4521. Circulation E-mail: pracirc@wapitilibrary.ca. *Br Librn,* Patricia Danku; *Br Librn,* Liudmyla Tokar
Open Tues-Fri 9-1

ST BENEDICT PUBLIC LIBRARY, Center St, Saint Benedict, S0K 3T0. (Mail add: Box 10, Saint Benedict, S0K 3T0). Tel: 306-289-2072. Circulation E-mail: sbencirc@wapitilibrary.ca. *Br Librn,* Lee Ann Hannotte
Open Tues 11-5, Fri 4-8

ST BRIEUX PUBLIC LIBRARY, 50 Third Ave, St. Brieux, S0K 3V0. (Mail add: Box 70, St. Brieux, S0K 3V0). Tel: 306-275-2133. Circulation E-mail: sbricirc@wapitilibrary.ca. *Br Librn,* Audrey Piatt
Open Tues & Wed 8-9 & 3:30-6:30, Thurs 8-9 & 3:30-5:30

ST LOUIS PUBLIC LIBRARY, 205 Second St, St. Louis, S0J 2C0. (Mail add: Box 70, St. Louis, S0J 2C0). Tel: 306-422-8511. Circulation E-mail: sloucirc@wapitilibrary.ca. *Br Librn,* Janice Bernier
Open Tues & Thur 4-8, Wed 4-7

SHELL LAKE PUBLIC LIBRARY, Main St, Village Office, Shell Lake, S0J 2G0. Tel: 306-427-2272. Circulation E-mail: shllcirc@wapitilibrary.ca. *Br Librn,* Pat Pelchat
Open Tues & Wed 12-4

SHELLBROOK PUBLIC LIBRARY, 105 Railway Ave W, Shellbrook, S0J 2E0. (Mail add: Box 490, Shellbrook, S0J 2E0). Tel: 306-747-3419. Circulation E-mail: shbrcirc@wapitilibrary.ca. *Br Librn,* Diana Campbell
Open Mon & Thurs 2-6:30, Tues & Wed 2-8, Fri 9-4

SMEATON PUBLIC LIBRARY, Village Office, Main St, Smeaton, S0J 2J0. (Mail add: Box 149, Smeaton, S0J 2J0). Tel: 306-426-2049. Circulation E-mail: smecirc@wapitilibrary.ca. *Br Librn,* Gail Olson
Open Tues & Wed 11-5

JAMES SMITH PUBLIC LIBRARY, Box 3848, Melfort, S0E 1A0. Tel: 306-864-2955. Circulation E-mail: jsfncirc@wapitilibrary.ca. *Br Librn,* Marcelynn Constant
Open Mon-Fri 8:30-3:30 (Sept-June)

SPIRITWOOD PUBLIC LIBRARY, 200 Main St, Spiritwood, S0J 2M0. (Mail add: Box 177, Spiritwood, S0J 2M0). Tel: 306-883-2337. Circulation E-mail: spicirc@wapitilibrary.ca. *Br Librn,* Joyce Carriere
Open Tues, Wed & Fri 9-4:30

STAR CITY PUBLIC LIBRARY, 400 Fourth St, Star City, S0E 1P0. (Mail add: Box 371, Star City, S0E 1P0). Tel: 306-863-4364. Circulation E-mail: stacirc@wapitilibrary.ca. *Librn,* Dena MacKenzie
Open Mon 5:30-8:30, Tues & Thurs 1-4:30, Wed 9-12

STURGEON LAKE PUBLIC LIBRARY, 721 White Buffalo Lane, Shellbrook, S0J 2E1. Tel: 306-764-5506. E-mail: sturgeonlakelibrary@gmail.com. *Br Librn,* Sharon Daniels
Open Wed 9-3

TISDALE COMMUNITY LIBRARY, 800 - 101st St, Tisdale, S0E 1T0. (Mail add: Box 2499, Tisdale, S0E 1T0). Tel: 306-873-4767. Circulation E-mail: tiscirc@wapitilibrary.ca. *Librn,* Isabel Hankins-Wilk
Open Mon-Thurs 8-8, Fri 8-5, Sat 1-5

VONDA PUBLIC LIBRARY, 204 Main St, Vonda, S0K 4N0. (Mail add: Box 160, Vonda, S0K 4N0). Tel: 306-258-2035. Circulation E-mail: voncirc@wapitilibrary.ca. *Br Librn,* Rebecca Fehr
Open Mon 10-2:30, Wed 5-9, Fri 2:30-7

WAKAW PUBLIC LIBRARY, 121 Main St, Wakaw, S0K 4P0. (Mail add: Box 464, Wakaw, S0K 4P0). Tel: 306-233-5552. Circulation E-mail: wakcirc@wapitilibrary.ca. Web Site: wapitilibrary.ca/index.php/branch/313. *Br Librn,* Vera Trembach; Tel: 306-233-5552
Open Tues, Wed & Fri 10-5, Sat 10-1

WELDON PUBLIC LIBRARY, Ten First Ave, Weldon, S0J 3A0. (Mail add: Box 55, Weldon, S0J 3A0). Tel: 306-887-4466. Circulation E-mail: welcirc@wapitilibrary.ca. *Br Librn,* Karen Fletcher
Open Mon & Wed 12:30-5

WHITE FOX PUBLIC LIBRARY, 301 Elinor St, White Fox, S0J 3B0. Tel: 306-276-5800. Circulation E-mail: whicirc@wapitilibrary.ca. *Br Librn,* Eileen Lane
Open Wed 10-6, Thurs 9-5

REGINA

C FIRST NATIONS UNIVERSITY OF CANADA*, Regina Campus Library, One First Nations Way, S4S 7K2. SAN 327-1137. Tel: 306-790-5950, Ext 3425. FAX: 306-790-5990. Web Site: fnuniv.ca. *Librn III,* Paula Daigle; Tel: 306-790-5950, Ext 3425, E-mail: pdaigle@fnuniv.ca; *Libr Tech II,* Joseph Cliff; Tel: 306-790-5950, Ext 3427, E-mail: jcliff@fnuniv.ca; Staff 2 (MLS 1, Non-MLS 1)
Founded 1977. Highest Degree: Master
Library Holdings: Bk Titles 60,000; Per Subs 35
Special Collections: First Nations University Special Coll; Native North American Rare Book Coll, hist, linguistics. Canadian and Provincial
Automation Activity & Vendor Info: (Acquisitions) Ex Libris Group; (Cataloging) Ex Libris Group; (Circulation) Ex Libris Group; (Course Reserve) Ex Libris Group; (ILL) Ex Libris Group; (Media Booking) Ex Libris Group; (OPAC) Ex Libris Group; (Serials) Ex Libris Group
Wireless access
Open Mon-Thurs 8am-9pm, Fri 8-4, Sat Noon-4 (Winter); Mon-Fri 8:30-4:30 (Summer)

Departmental Libraries:

NORTHERN CAMPUS LIBRARY, 1301 Central Ave, Prince Albert, S6V 4W1, SAN 377-7472. Tel: 306-765-3333. Toll Free Tel: 866-526-6578, Ext 7425. FAX: 306-765-3330. Web Site: www.fnuniv.ca/library-locations/northern-campus-library. *Libr Tech II,* Otto Ripoll-Leal; E-mail: oripoll-leal@fnuniv.ca; Staff 1 (MLS 1)
Founded 1991
Library Holdings: Bk Vols 15,000; Per Subs 60
Special Collections: Canadian and Provincial
Open Mon-Thurs 8:30-9, Fri 8:30-4:30 (Winter); Mon-Fri 8:30-4:30 (Summer)

SASKATOON CAMPUS LIBRARY, 229 Fourth Ave S, Rm 302, Saskatoon, S7K 4K3, SAN 377-7456. Tel: 306-931-1800, Ext 5430. FAX: 306-931-1847. *Libr Tech II,* Hongru Liu; E-mail: hliu@fnuniv.ca; Staff 1 (MLS 1)
Founded 1985. Highest Degree: Master
Library Holdings: Bk Vols 4,000
Special Collections: Canadian and Provincial
Open Mon-Fri 8:30-4:30

C GABRIEL DUMONT INSTITUTE LIBRARY - REGINA, 102-1235 Second Ave N, S4R 0X5. SAN 329-7705. Tel: 306-347-4124. Circulation Tel: 306-347-4117. Web Site: gdins.org/students-services/library.
Founded 1980. Highest Degree: Bachelor
Special Collections: Metis Historical Archive. Canadian and Provincial
Automation Activity & Vendor Info: (ILL) Ex Libris Group; (OPAC) Ex Libris Group
Wireless access

L LAW SOCIETY OF SASKATCHEWAN LIBRARIES*, Court House, 2425 Victoria Ave, 2nd Flr, S4P 3M3. (Mail add: PO Box 5032, S4P 3M3), SAN 369-5883. Tel: 306-569-8020. FAX: 306-569-0155. Reference E-mail: reference@lawsociety.sk.ca. Web Site: www.lawsociety.sk.ca/legal-resources-library. *Co-Dir, Librn,* Alan Kilpatrick; E-mail: alan.kilpatrick@lawsociety.sk.ca; *Librn,* Sara Stanley; E-mail: sara.stanley@lawsociety.sk.ca
Founded 1905
Library Holdings: Bk Vols 50,000
Special Collections: Law Reports; Law Text Books; Unreported Saskatchewan judgements
Automation Activity & Vendor Info: (Acquisitions) Inmagic, Inc.; (Cataloging) Inmagic, Inc.; (Circulation) Inmagic, Inc.; (Course Reserve) Inmagic, Inc.; (ILL) Inmagic, Inc.; (Media Booking) Inmagic, Inc.; (OPAC) Inmagic, Inc.; (Serials) Inmagic, Inc.
Publications: Builders' Lien Act-A Practitioners' Manual; Queen's Bench Rules of Saskatchewan Annotated
Open Mon-Fri 9-12 & 1-4

Branches:

SASKATOON COURT HOUSE, 520 Spadina Crescent E, Saskatoon, S7K 3G7, SAN 369-5913. Tel: 306-933-5141. FAX: 306-933-5166. *Librn,* Ken Fox; E-mail: ken.fox@lawsociety.sk.ca
Library Holdings: Bk Vols 15,000
Open Mon-Fri 9-12 & 1-4

S MUSEUMS ASSOCIATION OF SASKATCHEWAN*, Resource Library, 424 McDonald St, S4N 6E1. SAN 375-9261. Tel: 306-780-9279. FAX: 306-780-9463. E-mail: mas@saskmuseums.org. Web Site:

www.saskmuseums.org. *Exec Dir,* Wendy Fitch; Tel: 306-780-9280, E-mail: ex.director@saskmuseum.org
Library Holdings: Bk Titles 1,400; Per Subs 19
Subject Interests: Mus mgt
Function: Mail loans to mem
Open Mon-Fri 8-4

P PROVINCIAL LIBRARY & LITERACY OFFICE*, 409A Park St, S4N 5B2. SAN 319-9959. Tel: 306-787-2976. Circulation Tel: 306-787-2987. Administration FAX: 306-787-2029. Web Site: www.saskatchewan.ca/residents/education-and-learning/library-system-in-saskatchewan. *Exec Dir, Prov Librn,* Alison Hopkins; Tel: 306-787-2972, E-mail: alison.hopkins@gov.sk.ca; Staff 22 (MLS 10, Non-MLS 12)
Founded 1953. Pop 1,099,995; Circ 21,770
Apr 2020-Mar 2020. Mats Exp (CAN) $54,500, Books (CAN) $35,500, Per/Ser (Incl. Access Fees) (CAN) $10,000, Electronic Ref Mat (Incl. Access Fees) (CAN) $9,000
Library Holdings: Bk Titles 73,270
Special Collections: Last Copy Fiction; Library Science Coll; Multilingual Coll. Canadian and Provincial
Automation Activity & Vendor Info: (Acquisitions) Innovative Interfaces, Inc. - Polaris; (Cataloging) Innovative Interfaces, Inc. - Polaris; (Circulation) Innovative Interfaces, Inc. - Polaris; (ILL) OCLC; (OPAC) Innovative Interfaces, Inc. - Polaris; (Serials) Innovative Interfaces, Inc. - Polaris
Partic in Saskatchewan Electronic Resources Partnership; Saskatchewan Information & Library Services

P REGINA PUBLIC LIBRARY*, Library Directors Office, 2311 12th Ave, S4P 0N3. (Mail add: PO Box 2311, S4P 3Z5), SAN 369-5948. Tel: 306-777-6099. Circulation Tel: 306-777-6022. Web Site: www.reginalibrary.ca. *Chief Exec Officer, Libr Dir,* Jeff Barber; E-mail: jbarber@reginalibrary.ca; *Dep Dir,* Julie McKenna; E-mail: jmckenna@reginalibrary.ca; Staff 94 (MLS 41, Non-MLS 53)
Founded 1909. Pop 189,400; Circ 2,734,411
Library Holdings: Bk Vols 388,754
Special Collections: Dunlop Art Gallery; Prairie History Coll
Subject Interests: Archit, Art, Econ, Literacy, Local hist
Publications: Community Information Directory 1988-89; On the Street Where You Live; RPL Film Catalogue
Partic in Saskatchewan Electronic Resources Partnership
Special Services for the Blind - Reader equip
Open Mon-Fri 10-6, Sun 1-5
Branches: 8
ALBERT, Mamaweyatitan Ctr, 3355 Sixth Ave, S4T 4L8, SAN 369-5972. Tel: 306-777-6076. FAX: 306-949-7265. E-mail: al@reginalibrary.ca.
Library Holdings: Bk Vols 24,084
Special Collections: Native Indian Coll
Open Mon-Sat 10-6, Sun 1-5
GEORGE BOTHWELL BRANCH, 2965 Gordon Rd, S4S 6H7, SAN 326-7849. Tel: 306-777-6091. FAX: 306-949-7267. E-mail: gb@reginalibrary.ca.
Open Mon-Fri 10-6, Sun 1-5
CONNAUGHT, 3435 13th Ave, S4T 1P8, SAN 369-6006. Tel: 306-777-6078. E-mail: co@reginalibrary.ca.
Library Holdings: Bk Vols 30,370
Open Mon-Sat 10-6, Sun 1-5
GLEN ELM, 1601 Dewdney Ave E, S4N 4N6, SAN 369-6030. Tel: 306-777-6080. FAX: 306-949-7268. E-mail: ge@reginalibrary.ca.
Library Holdings: Bk Vols 58,745
Open Mon-Sat 10-6, Sun 1-5
PRINCE OF WALES, 445-14th Ave, S4N 6T5, SAN 369-6057. Tel: 306-777-6085. FAX: 306-949-7272. E-mail: pw@reginalibrary.ca.
Library Holdings: Bk Vols 18,590
Open Mon-Sat 10-6, Sun 1-5
REGENT PLACE, 331 Albert St, S4R 2N6, SAN 369-6065. Tel: 306-777-6086. FAX: 306-949-7269. E-mail: rp@reginalibrary.ca.
Library Holdings: Bk Vols 41,087
Open Mon-Sat 10-6, Sun 1-5
SHERWOOD VILLAGE, 6121 Rochdale Blvd, S4X 2R1, SAN 369-6073. Tel: 306-777-6088. FAX: 306-949-7270. E-mail: sv@reginalinrary.ca.
Library Holdings: Bk Vols 60,733
Open Mon-Sat 10-6, Sun 1-5
SUNRISE, 3130 E Woodhams Dr, S4V 2P9, SAN 373-0913. Tel: 306-777-6095. FAX: 306-949-7271. E-mail: su@reginalibrary.ca.
Open Mon-Sat 10-6, Sun 1-5

M REGINA QU'APPELLE HEALTH REGION*, Health Sciences Library, 1440 14th Ave, S4P 0W5. SAN 319-9819. Tel: 306-766-4142. FAX: 306-766-3839. E-mail: library@rqhealth.ca. Web Site: www.rqhealth.ca/departments/health-sciences-library-and-archives. *Dir,* Susan Baer; Tel: 306-766-3830, E-mail: susan.baer@rqhealth.ca; Staff 10 (MLS 5, Non-MLS 5)
Subject Interests: Health sci
Wireless access
Open Mon-Fri 8-4:30
Restriction: Badge access after hrs

REGINA-QU'APPELLE HEALTH REGION
M HEALTH SCIENCES LIBRARY-WASCANA*, 2180 23rd Ave, S4S 0A5, SAN 321-561X. Tel: 306-766-5441. FAX: 306-766-5460. *Librn,* Joan Harmsworth Dow; Staff 1 (Non-MLS 1)
Founded 1958
Library Holdings: Bk Titles 2,500; Per Subs 100
Subject Interests: Geriatrics, Phys med, Physically handicapped, Rehabilitation
Automation Activity & Vendor Info: (Acquisitions) Ex Libris Group; (Cataloging) Ex Libris Group; (Circulation) Ex Libris Group
Function: Doc delivery serv
Partic in Murlin
Open Mon-Thurs 8:30-4:30
M PASQUA HOSPITAL LIBRARY*, 4101 Dewdney Ave, S4T 1A5, SAN 320-8087. Tel: 306-766-2370. FAX: 306-766-2565. *Libr Tech,* Lily Walter-Smith; E-mail: lily.waltersmith@rqhealth.ca; Staff 1 (Non-MLS 1)
Founded 1953
Library Holdings: Bk Vols 800; Per Subs 75
Automation Activity & Vendor Info: (Acquisitions) Ex Libris Group; (Cataloging) Ex Libris Group; (Circulation) Ex Libris Group; (Serials) EBSCO Online
Restriction: Not open to pub

S ROYAL CANADIAN MOUNTED POLICE RESOURCE CENTRE, DEPOT DIVISION LIBRARY*, 5600 11th Ave W, S4P 3J7. (Mail add: PO Box 6500, S4P 3J7), SAN 327-103X. Tel: 639-625-3537, 639-625-3552. E-mail: RCMP.DepotLibrary-DepotBibliotheque.GRC@rcmp-grc.gc.ca. Web Site: depotlibrary.com. *Mgr,* Amy Rankin; Staff 4 (MLS 2, Non-MLS 2)
Library Holdings: Bk Vols 10,000; Per Subs 273; Videos 1,500
Subject Interests: Can law, Law enforcement
Automation Activity & Vendor Info: (Acquisitions) Ex Libris Group; (Cataloging) Ex Libris Group; (Circulation) Ex Libris Group; (Course Reserve) Ex Libris Group; (ILL) Ex Libris Group; (Media Booking) Ex Libris Group; (OPAC) Ex Libris Group; (Serials) Ex Libris Group
Partic in Multitype Libr Coun; RegLIN Consortium; Saskatchewan Electronic Resources Partnership
Open Mon-Fri 8-5
Restriction: Open to pub by appt only, Restricted access

S SASKATCHEWAN CHORAL FEDERATION LIBRARY*, 1415-B Albert St, S4K 2R8. SAN 376-186X. Tel: 306-780-9230. E-mail: information@saskchoral.ca. Web Site: www.saskchoral.ca/music-library. *Exec Dir,* Sheryl Neher; E-mail: director@saskchoral.ca
Open Mon-Fri 8:30-5

S SASKATCHEWAN GENEALOGICAL SOCIETY LIBRARY*, 110 - 1514 11th Ave, S4P 0H2. (Mail add: PO Box 1894, S4P 3E1), SAN 327-1110. Tel: 306-780-9207. FAX: 306-780-3615. E-mail: saskgenealogy@sasktel.net. Web Site: www.saskgenealogy.com/index.php/library-catalogues. *Exec Dir,* Deanne Cairns; Staff 2 (MLS 1, Non-MLS 1)
Founded 1969
Library Holdings: Bk Titles 22,166; Per Subs 153
Special Collections: Family Histories; Germans to America Series, Volumes 1-67; Index to 1881 Census for England & Wales; Index to Births, Marriages, & Deaths - England & Wales; Index to Ontario Vital Statistics, 1867 to most recent release; Metis Scrip Records; National Burial Index for England & Wales, 2nd Edition; Ontario Cemetery Records, microfilm & paper; Ontario Land Records; Saskatchewan Cemetery Records; Saskatchewan Henderson's Directories; Saskatchewan Local History Books; Saskatchewan Obituary File; Saskatchewan Residents Index (SRI); Zichydorf Village Association Coll
Subject Interests: Genealogy, Hist, Maps
Publications: The Bulletin (Quarterly)
Open Mon-Fri 10-4:30

SASKATCHEWAN JUSTICE
GL CIVIL LAW LIBRARY*, 900 - 1874 Scarth St, S4P 4B3, SAN 369-6456. Tel: 306-787-8955. FAX: 306-787-0581. *Library Contact,* Vicki Strickland; Tel: 306-787-8382, E-mail: vicki.strickland@gov.sk.ca
Restriction: Not open to pub
GL COURT OF APPEAL LIBRARY*, Court House, 2425 Victoria Ave, S4P 4W6, SAN 369-6391. Tel: 306-787-7399. FAX: 306-787-0505. *Librn,* Ann Marie Melvie; E-mail: amelvie@sasklawcourts.ca; Staff 1 (MLS 1)
Library Holdings: Bk Vols 5,000; Per Subs 30
GL COURT OF THE QUEEN'S BENCH*, Court House, 2425 Victoria Ave, S4P 3V7, SAN 369-6421. Tel: 306-787-7809. FAX: 306-787-7160. *Mgr,* Sharon West
Subject Interests: Law
Restriction: Not open to pub

G SASKATCHEWAN LEGISLATIVE LIBRARY*, 234-2405 Legislative Dr, S4S 0B3. SAN 319-9762. Tel: 306-787-2276. Circulation Tel: 306-787-1823. Administration Tel: 306-787-2277. FAX: 306-787-5856. Administration FAX: 306-787-1772. Reference E-mail: reference@legassembly.sk.ca. Web Site: www.legassembly.sk.ca/library. *Dir, Ref,* Leslie Polsom; Tel: 306-787-1825, E-mail: lpolsom@legassembly.sk.ca; *Dir, Support Serv,* Greg Salmers; Tel: 306-787-2278, Fax: 306-787-7400, E-mail: gsalmers@legassembly.sk.ca; *Legislative Librn,* Melissa Bennett; E-mail: mbennett@legassembly.sk.ca; Staff 19 (MLS 8, Non-MLS 11)
Founded 1887
Special Collections: Saskatchewan Government Publications (official repository); Saskatchewan Local Histories. Canadian and Provincial
Subject Interests: Govt doc, Hist, Law, Political, Soc sci with emphasis on Canada
Automation Activity & Vendor Info: (Acquisitions) Ex Libris Group; (Cataloging) Ex Libris Group; (Circulation) Ex Libris Group; (Discovery) Ex Libris Group; (OPAC) Ex Libris Group; (Serials) Ex Libris Group
Wireless access
Publications: Annual Report; Checklist of Saskatchewan Government Publications (Accession list); Publications of the Governments of the Northwest Territories, 1876-1905 & the Province of Saskatchewan, 1905-1952 (Bibliographies); Saskatchewan Local Histories at the Legislative Library (Bibliographies)
Partic in Saskatchewan Electronic Resources Partnership
Open Mon-Fri 9-5

S SASKATCHEWAN PARKS & RECREATION ASSOCIATION, SPRA Resource Centre, 100-1445 Park St, S4N 4C5. SAN 370-5498. Tel: 306-780-9439. Circulation Tel: 306-780-9206. Toll Free Tel: 800-563-2555. FAX: 306-780-9257. E-mail: resourcecentre@spra.sk.ca. Web Site: www.spra.sk.ca/resources-and-advocacy. Staff 3 (MLS 2, Non-MLS 1)
Founded 1984
Library Holdings: CDs 1,041; DVDs 1,926; Electronic Media & Resources 104; Bk Titles 2,120; Per Subs 14
Special Collections: Parks & Open Spaces; Physical Activity & Fitness; Recreation & Facility Management; Volunteer & Nonprofit Management
Automation Activity & Vendor Info: (Acquisitions) Sydney Enterprise; (Cataloging) Sydney Enterprise; (Circulation) Sydney Enterprise; (OPAC) Sydney Enterprise; (Serials) EBSCO Online
Partic in Saskatchewan Electronic Resources Partnership
Open Mon-Fri 8:30-4:30

C SASKATCHEWAN POLYTECHNIC*, Regina Campus Library, 4500 Wascana Pkwy, S4P 3A3. SAN 369-6480. Tel: 306-775-7408. Toll Free Tel: 866-460-4430. FAX: 306-775-7408. E-mail: regina.library@saskpolytech.ca. Web Site: library.saskpolytech.ca. *Libr Dir,* Aidan Meegan; Tel: 306-775-7936, E-mail: meegana@saskpolytech.ca; *Syst Adminr,* Holly Adamson; Tel: 306-665-7403, E-mail: holly.adamson@saskpolytech.ca; *Libr Mgr,* Juliet Nielsen; Tel: 306-775-7412, E-mail: nielsenju@saskpolytech.ca; *Digital Res Librn,* Robin Canham; Tel: 306-775-7409, E-mail: canhamr@saskpolytech.ca; *Ref & Info Serv Librn,* Erin Langman; Tel: 306-775-7411, E-mail: erin.langman@saskpolytech.ca; *Teaching & Learning Librn,* Diane Zerr; Tel: 306-775-7413, E-mail: zerrdi@saskpolytech.ca; Staff 43 (MLS 13, Non-MLS 30)
Founded 1961. Enrl 15,000; Fac 13; Highest Degree: Bachelor
Library Holdings: Bk Titles 40,000; Per Subs 500
Subject Interests: Agr, Allied health, Basic educ, Dental assisting, Dental hygiene, Early childhood educ, Literacy, Nursing, Off educ
Automation Activity & Vendor Info: (Acquisitions) SirsiDynix; (Cataloging) SirsiDynix; (Circulation) SirsiDynix; (Course Reserve) SirsiDynix; (Media Booking) SirsiDynix; (OPAC) SirsiDynix; (Serials) SirsiDynix
Wireless access
Function: Archival coll, Art exhibits, Audio & video playback equip for onsite use, CD-ROM, Computers for patron use, Doc delivery serv, E-Readers, E-Reserves, Electronic databases & coll, Equip loans & repairs, ILL available, Instruction & testing, Internet access, Laminating, Learning ctr, Mail & tel request accepted, Movies, Online cat, Online info literacy tutorials on the web & in blackboard, Online ref, Orientations, Photocopying/Printing, Ref serv available, Res libr, Scanner, Telephone ref, Wheelchair accessible
Partic in Province-wide Libr Electronic Info Syst; Saskatchewan Electronic Resources Partnership
Special Services for the Deaf - Assistive tech
Special Services for the Blind - Assistive/Adapted tech devices, equip & products
Open Mon-Fri 8-6
Restriction: Borrowing requests are handled by ILL, Non-circulating to the pub, Pub use on premises

S SASKTEL CORPORATE LIBRARY*, 2121 Saskatchewan Dr, 12th Flr, S4P 3Y2. SAN 319-9967. Tel: 306-777-2899. FAX: 306-359-9022. E-mail: sasktel.corporatelibrary@sasktel.com. *Librn,* Charlene Kramer; Staff 1 (Non-MLS 1)
Founded 1980
Library Holdings: Bk Vols 5,500; Per Subs 350
Subject Interests: Bus, Info tech, Telecommunication
Automation Activity & Vendor Info: (Cataloging) SydneyPlus
Wireless access
Function: 24/7 Online cat, Bks on CD, Computers for patron use, Electronic databases & coll, For res purposes, Free DVD rentals, Internet access, Magazines, Mail & tel request accepted, Mail loans to mem, Online cat, Online ref, Orientations, Ref & res, Ref serv available, Res assist avail, Res libr
Publications: Daily Headline News
Restriction: Not open to pub, Restricted loan policy

UNIVERSITY OF REGINA

C DR JOHN ARCHER LIBRARY*, 3737 Wascana Pkwy, S4S 0A2, SAN 319-9983. Tel: 306-585-4295. Circulation Tel: 306-585-4133. Reference Tel: 306-585-4134. FAX: 306-585-4878. Web Site: www.uregina.ca/library. *Head of Libr,* Barbara Nelke; Tel: 306-585-5099, E-mail: barbara.nelke@uregina.ca; Staff 22 (MLS 19, Non-MLS 3)
Founded 1967. Enrl 10,014; Fac 406; Highest Degree: Doctorate
Library Holdings: AV Mats 13,612; CDs 14,118; e-books 192,262; e-journals 95,396; Microforms 1,216,291; Music Scores 10,531; Bk Titles 677,951; Bk Vols 1,083,037; Per Subs 805; Videos 2,690
Automation Activity & Vendor Info: (Acquisitions) Ex Libris Group; (Cataloging) Ex Libris Group; (Circulation) Ex Libris Group; (Course Reserve) Ex Libris Group; (OPAC) Ex Libris Group; (Serials) Ex Libris Group
Function: Audio & video playback equip for onsite use, ILL available, Ref serv available, Res libr
Partic in Canadian Association of Research Libraries; Canadian Research Knowledge Network; Council of Prairie & Pacific University Libraries; OCLC Online Computer Library Center, Inc; Saskatchewan Electronic Resources Partnership
Special Services for the Blind - Computer with voice synthesizer for visually impaired persons
Open Mon-Thurs & Sun 8am-11pm, Fri & Sat 8-7:30

C LUTHER COLLEGE LIBRARY*, 3737 Wascana Pkwy, S4S 0A2, SAN 326-453X. Tel: 306-585-5030. FAX: 306-585-5267. E-mail: luther.library@uregina.ca. Web Site: https://www.luthercollege.edu/university/academics/luther-library. *Coordr,* Carla L Flengeris; E-mail: carla.flengeris@uregina.ca; Staff 1 (Non-MLS 1)
Founded 1971. Enrl 800; Fac 20; Highest Degree: Bachelor
Library Holdings: AV Mats 170; Bk Vols 20,000; Per Subs 46
Subject Interests: Art hist, Geog, Lit, Lutheran Church, Musicology, Psychol, Relig, Renaissance hist, Sociol, Tourism
Automation Activity & Vendor Info: (Acquisitions) Ex Libris Group; (Cataloging) Ex Libris Group; (Circulation) Ex Libris Group; (Course Reserve) Ex Libris Group; (ILL) Ex Libris Group; (OPAC) Ex Libris Group
Open Mon-Thurs 8:15am-10pm, Fri 8:15-5, Sat 1-5, Sun 1-10
Restriction: Borrowing privileges limited to fac & registered students

SANDY BAY

P AYAMICIKIWIKAMIK PUBLIC LIBRARY*, PO Box 240, S0P 0G0. Tel: 306-754-2139. FAX: 306-754-2130. E-mail: ssbp@pnls.lib.sk.ca. Web Site: pahkisimon.ca/branch/199. *Librn,* Geraldine Merasty; E-mail: geraldinemerasty@nlsb113.ca
Library Holdings: Bk Vols 16,000; Per Subs 35; Videos 100
Wireless access
Mem of Pahkisimon Nuye?ah Library System
Open Mon-Fri 8:30-4

SASKATOON

R HORIZON COLLEGE & SEMINARY*, Alvin C Schindel Library, 604 Webster St, S7N 3P9. Tel: 306-374-6655, Ext 234. FAX: 306-373-6968. E-mail: library@horizon.edu. Web Site: www.horizon.edu/students/library. *Libr Dir,* Karina Dunn; *Libr Tech,* Richelle Bekkattla
Wireless access
Open Mon-Thurs 8:30am-9pm, Fri 8:30-3:30, Sat 1-5 (Fall & Winter); Mon-Fri 8:30-3:30 (Summer)

L MCKERCHER LLP, Law Library, 500-211 19th St E, S7K 5R6. SAN 329-1138. Tel: 306-653-2000. FAX: 306-653-2699. *Library Contact,* Sandy Welsh; Tel: 306-664-1324, E-mail: s.welsh@mckercher.ca; Staff 1 (Non-MLS 1)
Founded 1986
Library Holdings: e-books 2; e-journals 8; Bk Titles 841; Bk Vols 1,206; Per Subs 9; Spec Interest Per Sub 21

Automation Activity & Vendor Info: (Cataloging) Insignia Software; (Circulation) Insignia Software; (ILL) Insignia Software; (OPAC) Insignia Software
Wireless access
Function: Res libr
Restriction: Staff use only

S NUTANA COLLEGIATE INSTITUTE*, Memorial Library & Art Gallery, 411 11th St E, S7N 0E9. SAN 320-0094. Tel: 306-683-7580. FAX: 306-683-7587. E-mail: nutanaschool@spsd.sk.ca.
Founded 1909
Library Holdings: Bk Vols 10,000; Per Subs 20
Special Collections: Canadian Artists (Memorial Art Gallery), paintings & wood cuts
Automation Activity & Vendor Info: (Acquisitions) Follett Software; (Cataloging) Follett Software; (Circulation) Follett Software; (Course Reserve) Follett Software; (ILL) Follett Software; (Media Booking) Follett Software; (OPAC) Follett Software; (Serials) Follett Software
Open Mon-Fri 8:30-4

S S E D SYSTEMS, INC LIBRARY*, 18 Innovation Blvd, S7K 3P7. (Mail add: PO Box 1464, S7K 3P7), SAN 320-0108. Tel: 306-931-3425. FAX: 306-933-1486. *Librn,* Amanda Luther; E-mail: a.luther@sedsystems.ca
Founded 1968
Library Holdings: Bk Titles 1,500; Per Subs 50
Subject Interests: Satellite communications, Space systs
Open Mon-Fri 8-4
Restriction: Open to pub for ref only

M ST PAUL'S HOSPITAL OF SASKATOON, Medical Library, 1702 20th St W, S7M 0Z9. SAN 321-6780. Tel: 306-655-5224. E-mail: library@saskhealthauthority.ca. *Libr Tech,* Jessica Kelly
Founded 1960
Library Holdings: Bk Titles 300; Per Subs 100
Restriction: Staff use only

C SAINT THOMAS MORE COLLEGE-UNIVERSITY OF SASKATCHEWAN*, Shannon Library, 1437 College Dr, S7N 0W6. SAN 320-0124. Tel: 306-966-8916. FAX: 306-966-8909. Web Site: www.stmcollege.ca. *Libr Dir,* Dr Donna Brockmeyer; Tel: 306-966-8962, E-mail: donna.brockmeyer@usask.ca; Staff 2 (MLS 1, Non-MLS 1)
Founded 1936. Fac 35; Highest Degree: Bachelor
Library Holdings: Bk Titles 45,000; Bk Vols 57,000; Per Subs 150
Special Collections: Canadian Catholic Church Coll; Catholic Authors; Elizabethan & Jacobean Studies; St Thomas More
Automation Activity & Vendor Info: (Acquisitions) Innovative Interfaces, Inc; (Cataloging) Innovative Interfaces, Inc; (Circulation) Innovative Interfaces, Inc; (Course Reserve) Innovative Interfaces, Inc; (ILL) Innovative Interfaces, Inc; (Media Booking) Innovative Interfaces, Inc; (OPAC) Innovative Interfaces, Inc; (Serials) Innovative Interfaces, Inc
Wireless access
Publications: Women & The Church
Open Mon-Thurs 8:30am-10pm, Fri 8:30-5, Sat 10-5, Sun Noon-9 (Winter); Mon-Fri 10-2 (Summer)

S SASKATCHEWAN INDIAN CULTURAL CENTRE*, Library & Information Services, 305-2555 Grasswood Rd E, S7T 0K1. SAN 320-0035. Tel: 306-244-1146. FAX: 306-665-6520. E-mail: info@sicc.sk.ca. Web Site: www.sicc.sk.ca/library-information-services. *Libr Tech,* Jessica Generoux
Founded 1973. Highest Degree: Master
Library Holdings: Bk Titles 8,200; Bk Vols 11,237; Per Subs 28
Subject Interests: Mat on Indian people of North Am
Wireless access
Open Mon-Thurs 8:30-5, Fri 8:30-4

S SASKATCHEWAN TEACHERS' FEDERATION*, Emma Stewart Resource Centre, 2311 Arlington Ave, S7J 2H8. SAN 320-0140. Tel: 306-373-1660. Toll Free Tel: 800-667-7762. FAX: 306-374-1122. E-mail: src@stf.sk.ca. Web Site: www.stf.sk.ca. *Librn,* Joan Elliott; E-mail: joan.elliott@stf.sk.ca; Staff 5 (MLS 2, Non-MLS 3)
Founded 1970
Library Holdings: Bk Titles 28,000; Per Subs 250
Subject Interests: Econ, Educ, Psychol
Wireless access
Partic in Saskatchewan Electronic Resources Partnership
Open Mon-Fri 8:30-5

P SASKATOON PUBLIC LIBRARY*, Frances Morrison Library, 311-23rd St E, S7K 0J6. SAN 369-660X. Tel: 306-975-7558. Web Site: saskatoonlibrary.ca. *Chief Exec Officer, Dir of Libr,* Carol Cooley; E-mail: c.cooley@saskatoonlibrary.ca; Staff 132 (MLS 37, Non-MLS 95)
Founded 1913. Pop 206,800; Circ 4,028,803
Library Holdings: Bk Vols 845,927; Per Subs 1,200
Special Collections: Canada Coll; Historical Children's Coll; Local History, bks, micro, pamphlets
Subject Interests: Performing arts
Automation Activity & Vendor Info: (Acquisitions) Innovative Interfaces, Inc - Millennium; (Cataloging) Innovative Interfaces, Inc - Millennium; (Circulation) Innovative Interfaces, Inc - Millennium; (OPAC) Innovative Interfaces, Inc - Millennium; (Serials) Innovative Interfaces, Inc - Millennium
Wireless access
Function: Wheelchair accessible
Publications: Annual Report; Programme brochures
Partic in Saskatchewan Information & Library Services
Special Services for the Blind - Assistive/Adapted tech devices, equip & products; Daisy reader; Newsp reading serv; Talking bks
Open Mon-Thurs 10-9, Fri & Sat 10-6, Sun (Sept-May) 1-5:30
Friends of the Library Group
Branches: 8
DR FREDA AHENAKEW BRANCH, 100-219 Ave K S, S7M 2C7. Tel: 306-975-7508.
Open Mon-Thurs 10-9, Fri & Sat 10-6, Sun 1-5:30
Friends of the Library Group
CARLYLE KING BRANCH, Cosmo Civic Ctr, 3130 Laurier Dr, S7L 5J7, SAN 369-6634. Tel: 306-975-7592. FAX: 306-975-7588.
Open Mon 1-9, Tues-Fri 10-9, Sat 10-6, Sun (Sept-May) 1-5:30
Friends of the Library Group
RUSTY MACDONALD BRANCH, 225 Primrose Dr, S7K 5E4, SAN 378-1933. Tel: 306-975-7600. FAX: 306-975-7603.
Open Mon-Fri 10-9, Sat 10-6, Sun (Sept-May) 1-5:30
Friends of the Library Group
MAYFAIR BRANCH, 602 33rd St W, S7L 0W1, SAN 369-6642. Tel: 306-975-7591.
Open Mon-Thurs 10-9, Fri & Sat 10-6, Sun (Sept-May) 1-5:30
Friends of the Library Group
ROUND PRAIRIE BRANCH, 170-250 Hunter Rd, S7T 0Y4. Tel: 306-986-9700.
Open Mon-Thurs 10-9, Fri & Sat 10-6, Sun 1-5:30
Friends of the Library Group
ALICE TURNER BRANCH, 110 Nelson Rd, S7S 1K7, SAN 378-195X. Tel: 306-975-8127. FAX: 306-975-8130.
Open Mon-Wed 10-9, Thurs-Sat 10-6, Sun (Sept-May) 1-5:30
Friends of the Library Group
J S WOOD BRANCH, 1801 Lansdowne Ave, S7H 2C4, SAN 369-6669. Tel: 306-975-7590. FAX: 306-975-7636.
Open Mon-Fri 1-9, Sat 10-6, Sun (Sept-May) 1-5:30
Friends of the Library Group
CLIFF WRIGHT BRANCH, Lakewood Civic Ctr, 1635 McKercher Dr, S7H 5J9, SAN 328-7157. Tel: 306-975-7550. FAX: 306-975-7632.
Open Mon-Fri 10-9, Sat 10-6, Sun (Sept-May) 1-5:30
Friends of the Library Group

R SASKATOON THEOLOGICAL UNION LIBRARY*, 1121 College Dr, S7N 0W3. Tel: 639-398-5561. E-mail: library@saskatoontheologicalunion.ca. Web Site: standrews.ca/college-library. *Sr Libr Tech,* Rachel Kotei; E-mail: rachel.kotei@saskatoontheologicalunion.ca; Staff 1.7 (MLS 0.2, Non-MLS 1.5)
Enrl 93; Fac 9; Highest Degree: Doctorate
Library Holdings: Bk Titles 85,000; Per Subs 41
Subject Interests: Biblical studies, Can Church, Eastern Christianity, Feminist, Liberation theol, Liturgical design, Reformation, Reformed theol, Soc justice, Systematic theol
Wireless access
Function: 24/7 Electronic res, 24/7 Online cat, AV serv, Computers for patron use, Distance learning, Electronic databases & coll, Internet access, Mail & tel request accepted, Mail loans to mem, Online cat, Online info literacy tutorials on the web & in blackboard, Orientations, Outside serv via phone, mail, e-mail & web, Photocopying/Printing, Ref & res, Ref serv available, Res assist avail, Res libr, Scanner
Open Mon-Thurs 8-4:30, Fri 8-3

C SIAST-SASKATCHEWAN INSTITUTE OF APPLIED SCIENCE & TECHNOLOGY*, Saskatoon Campus Library, 1130 Idylwyld Dr, S7K 3R5. (Mail add: PO Box 1520, S7K 3R5). Tel: 306-659-4040. Toll Free Tel: 866-460-4430. FAX: 306-659-4200. E-mail: saskatoon.library@saskpolytech.ca. Web Site: library.saskpolytech.ca. *Libr Mgr,* Regan Balfour; Tel: 306-765-1533, E-mail: regan.balfour@saskpolytech.ca; *Borrower Serv Librn, Colls Librn,* Fabian Harrison; Tel: 306-659-4240, E-mail: harrisonf@saskpolytech.ca; Staff 12 (MLS 2, Non-MLS 10)
Founded 1963. Enrl 10,444; Fac 320; Highest Degree: Associate
Library Holdings: Bk Titles 20,000; Bk Vols 35,000; Per Subs 400; Videos 5,000
Subject Interests: Adult basic educ, Natural sci, Nursing, Technologies, Trades

Automation Activity & Vendor Info: (Acquisitions) SirsiDynix; (Cataloging) SirsiDynix; (Circulation) SirsiDynix; (Media Booking) SirsiDynix; (OPAC) SirsiDynix; (Serials) SirsiDynix
Wireless access
Open Mon-Thurs 7:30am-9pm, Fri 7:30-5, Sat & Sun 10-5 (Sept-June); Mon-Fri 8-4:30 (July-Aug)

S UKRAINIAN CANADIAN CONGRESS - SASKATCHEWAN PROVINCIAL COUNCIL INC*, Library Resource Centre, 4-2345 Avenue C North, S7L 5Z5. SAN 374-7611. Tel: 306-652-5850. Toll Free Tel: 888-652-5850. FAX: 306-665-2127. E-mail: uccspc@ucc.sk.ca. Web Site: www.ucc.sk.ca. *Exec Dir,* Danylo Puderak; E-mail: d.puderak@ucc.sk.ca
Founded 1971
Library Holdings: Bk Vols 1,800
Function: Photocopying/Printing, Scanner
Open Mon-Fri 10-5
Restriction: Not a lending libr

S UKRAINIAN MUSEUM OF CANADA LIBRARY*, 910 Spadina Crescent E, S7K 3H5. SAN 326-7423. Tel: 306-244-3800. FAX: 306-652-7620. E-mail: ukrmuse@sasktel.net. Web Site: umcnational.ca/library-archives-and-collection. *Dir,* Janet Danyliuk
Founded 1936
Library Holdings: Bk Titles 11,000; Bk Vols 12,000
Special Collections: History & Ethnography (Save The Ukrainian Canadian Heritage Coll), three dimensional, print, photogs, oral hist, archival mats
Subject Interests: Lit
Wireless access
Publications: Embroidery Designs & Stitches; Heritage Patterns; Museum News; Pysanka Kit; Pysanka: Icon of the Universe; Saskatchewan's Ukrainian historic sites along the Yellowhead route; Ukrainian Historic Sites of Central Saskatchewan: Travel Guide
Restriction: Open by appt only
Friends of the Library Group

C UNIVERSITY OF SASKATCHEWAN LIBRARIES*, Murray Library, Three Campus Dr, S7N 5A4. SAN 369-6693. Tel: 306-966-5958. Interlibrary Loan Service Tel: 306-966-5963. Reference E-mail: library.services@usask.ca. Web Site: library.usask.ca. *Dean, Univ Libr,* Melissa Just; Tel: 306-966-6094, E-mail: melissa.just@usask.ca; *Assoc Dean,* Rachel Sarjeant-Jenkins; E-mail: rachel.sarjeant-jenkins@usask.ca; *Assoc Dean of Libr,* Charlene Sorensen; E-mail: charlene.sorensen@usask.ca; Staff 55 (MLS 30, Non-MLS 25)
Founded 1912. Enrl 24,000; Fac 1,000; Highest Degree: Doctorate
Library Holdings: e-books 1,149,857; Bk Titles 2,856,222; Bk Vols 3,394,247
Special Collections: Canadiana (Shortt Coll); Conrad Aiken Coll; John G Diefenbaker Archives; Pitrim A Sorokin Coll; Sexual & Gender Diversity Coll
Subject Interests: Agr, Dentistry, Engr, Humanities, Law, Med, Nursing, Pharm, Soc sci, Veterinary
Automation Activity & Vendor Info: (OPAC) Innovative Interfaces, Inc - Sierra; (Serials) Ex Libris Group
Wireless access
Partic in Association of Research Libraries; Canadian Association of Research Libraries; Canadian Research Knowledge Network; Saskatchewan Electronic Resources Partnership
Open Mon-Fri 9-9, Sat & Sun 10-6

Departmental Libraries:

LESLIE & IRENE DUBE HEALTH SCIENCES LIBRARY, Academic Health Sciences Bldg, Rm E1400, 104 Clinic Pl, S7N 2Z4, SAN 369-6847. Tel: 306-966-5991. E-mail: library.services@usask.ca. Web Site: library.usask.ca/hsl. ; Staff 9 (MLS 5, Non-MLS 4)
Enrl 3,509; Fac 1,193; Highest Degree: Doctorate
Subject Interests: Commun health, Dentistry, Epidemiology, Kinesiology, Med, Nursing, Nutrition, Pharm, Pub health, Rehabilitation
Open Mon-Fri 9-9, Sat & Sun 10-6

EDUCATION & MUSIC LIBRARY, Education Bldg, Rm 2003, 28 Campus Dr, S7N 0X1. Tel: 306-966-5973. Web Site: library.usask.ca/education. *Liaison Librn,* Carolyn Doi; Tel: 306-966-2433, E-mail: carolyn.doi@usask.ca
Library Holdings: Bk Vols 22,000
Special Collections: Professional & Curriculum Materials, multi-media

CL LAW, Law Bldg, Rm 8, 15 Campus Dr, S7N 5A6, SAN 369-6812. Tel: 306-966-6053. Circulation Tel: 306-966-1445. E-mail: library.services@usask.ca. Web Site: library.usask.ca/law. *Librn,* Greg Wurzer; Tel: 306-966-6020, E-mail: greg.wurzer@usask.ca
Library Holdings: AV Mats 793; e-journals 1,549; Bk Titles 42,766; Bk Vols 167,488; Per Subs 2,134
Automation Activity & Vendor Info: (OPAC) Innovative Interfaces, Inc
Open Mon-Fri 9-5

SCIENCE LIBRARY, 180 Geology Bldg, 114 Science Pl, S7N 5E2, SAN 369-6782. Tel: 306-966-6047. E-mail: library.services@usask.ca. Web Site: library.usask.ca/science.
Library Holdings: AV Mats 240; Bk Vols 168,878
Subject Interests: Chem, Chem engr, Geol, Nutrition, Physics
Open Tues-Fri 9-5

S WESTERN DEVELOPMENT MUSEUM*, George Shepherd Library, 2935 Melville St, S7J 5A6. SAN 324-6175. Tel: 306-934-1400. FAX: 306-934-4467. E-mail: info@wdm.ca. Web Site: www.wdm.ca/special_feature/george-shepherd. *Curator,* Julie Jackson; Tel: 306-934-1400, Ext 230, E-mail: jjackson@wdm.ca; Staff 1 (Non-MLS 1)
Founded 1972
Library Holdings: AV Mats 10,000; Bk Titles 3,500; Bk Vols 10,000; Per Subs 25
Special Collections: Agricultural Machinery Catalogue Coll
Subject Interests: Agr, Transportation, Western Can hist
Automation Activity & Vendor Info: (Cataloging) LibraryWorld, Inc; (OPAC) LibraryWorld, Inc
Function: Res libr
Restriction: Non-circulating, Open by appt only

P WHEATLAND REGIONAL LIBRARY*, Headquarters, 806 Duchess St, S7K 0R3. SAN 320-0183. Tel: 306-652-5077. Administration Tel: 306-652-5077, Ext 0. FAX: 306-931-7611. E-mail: admin@wheatland.sk.ca, branchmanager@wheatland.sk.ca. Web Site: www.wheatland.sk.ca. *Exec Dir,* Kim Hebig; Staff 12 (MLS 1, Non-MLS 11)
Founded 1967. Pop 86,105; Circ 521,969
Library Holdings: Bk Titles 346,519; Per Subs 14,600; Talking Bks 11,200
Automation Activity & Vendor Info: (Acquisitions) Mandarin Library Automation; (Cataloging) Mandarin Library Automation; (Circulation) Mandarin Library Automation; (Course Reserve) Mandarin Library Automation; (ILL) Mandarin Library Automation; (Media Booking) Mandarin Library Automation; (OPAC) Mandarin Library Automation; (Serials) Mandarin Library Automation
Wireless access
Publications: Annual Report; Don't Cry Baby, We'll Be Back (Brochure)
Partic in Saskatchewan Electronic Resources Partnership; Saskatchewan Information & Library Services
Special Services for the Blind - Talking bks
Open Mon-Thurs 8:30-4:30, Fri 8:30-4

Branches: 45

ABERDEEN BRANCH, 207 Main St, Aberdeen, S0K 0A0. (Mail add: Box 130, Aberdeen, S0K 0A0). Tel: 306-253-4349. E-mail: aberdeen.library@wheatland.sk.ca. Web Site: www.wheatland.sk.ca/index.php/branch/55.
Open Mon 10-1 & 5-8, Tues 12-3 & 5:30-8:30, Thurs 5:30-8:30, Sat 10-1

ALLAN BRANCH, 224 Main St, Allan, S0K 0C0. Tel: 306-257-4222. E-mail: allan.library@wheatland.sk.ca. Web Site: www.wheatland.sk.ca/index.php/branch/56.
Open Tues 4:30-8, Thurs 3:30-8:30, Fri 9-2

BEECHY BRANCH, 212 Main St, Beechy, S0L 0C0. Tel: 306-859-2032. E-mail: beechy.library@wheatland.sk.ca. Web Site: www.wheatland.sk.ca/index.php/branch/57.
Library Holdings: Bk Titles 4,500
Open Tues, Thurs & Fri 12-5

BIGGAR BRANCH, 202 Third Ave W, Biggar, S0K 0M0. (Mail add: PO Box 157, Biggar, S0K 0M0), SAN 374-7042. Tel: 306-948-3911. E-mail: biggar.library@wheatland.sk.ca. Web Site: www.wheatland.sk.ca/index.php/branch/58.
Pop 3,000
Special Services for the Deaf - Bks on deafness & sign lang; High interest/low vocabulary bks; Spec interest per; Staff with knowledge of sign lang
Open Tues & Thurs 10-9, Wed & Sat 1-6

BRUNO BRANCH, 522 Main St, Bruno, S0K 0C0. (Mail add: Box 2, Bruno, S0K 0S0). Tel: 306-369-2353. E-mail: bruno.library@wheatland.sk.ca. Web Site: www.wheatland.sk.ca/index.php/branch/59.
Open Mon-Wed & Fri 3:30-6:30, Thurs 7pm-9:30pm

COLEVILLE BRANCH, 200 Main St, Coleville, S0L 0K0. Tel: 306-965-2551. E-mail: coleville.library@wheatland.sk.ca. Web Site: www.wheatland.sk.ca/index.php/branch/60.
Open Mon & Wed 5-8:30, Sun 12-2

COLONSAY BRANCH, 100 Jura St, Colonsay, S0K 0Z0. (Mail add: Box 172, Colonsay, S0K 0Z0). Tel: 306-255-2232. E-mail: colonsay.library@wheatland.sk.ca. Web Site: www.wheatland.sk.ca/index.php/branch/62.
Library Holdings: Bk Titles 4,000; Per Subs 10
Open Mon 5:30-8:30, Tues & Fri 1-5

CONQUEST BRANCH, 401 Pacific Ave, Conquest, S0L 0L0. Tel: 306-856-4555. E-mail: conquest.library@wheatland.sk.ca. Web Site: www.wheatland.sk.ca/index.php/branch/61.
Library Holdings: Bk Titles 10,000
Open Tues 10-1 & 3-6

DALMENY BRANCH, 301 Railway Ave, Dalmeny, S0K 1E0. Tel: 306-254-2119. E-mail: dalmeny.library@wheatland.sk.ca. Web Site: www.wheatland.sk.ca/index.php/branch/63.
Open Tues & Wed 12-7, Thurs 9-3

DELISLE BRANCH, 201 First St W, Delisle, S0L 0P0. Tel: 306-493-8288. E-mail: delisle.library@wheatland.sk.ca. Web Site: www.wheatland.sk.ca/index.php/branch/64.
Open Mon Noon-4, Wed 12-4 & 7-9, Fri 9:30-4:30

DINSMORE BRANCH, 100 Main St, Dinsmore, S0L 0T0. (Mail add: Box 369, Dinsmore, S0L 0T0). Tel: 306-846-2011. E-mail: dinsmore.library@wheatland.sk.ca. Web Site: www.wheatland.sk.ca/index.php/branch/65.
Library Holdings: Bk Titles 5,000; Per Subs 15
Open Tues & Wed 3:30-6:30, Thurs 12:30-4:30pm, Sat 10-1

DODSLAND BRANCH, 125 Second Ave, Dodsland, S0L 2R0. (Mail add: Box 100, Dodsland, S0L 0V0). Tel: 306-356-2180. E-mail: dodsland.library@wheatland.sk.ca. Web Site: www.wheatland.sk.ca/index.php/branch/67.
Open Mon 1:30-7, Tues 2-8, Thurs 10-4

DRAKE BRANCH, 117 Francis St, Drake, S0K 1H0. Tel: 306-363-2101. E-mail: drake.library@wheatland.sk.ca. Web Site: www.wheatland.sk.ca/index.php/branch/68.
Open Tues 5-8, Wed 9-Noon, Thurs 10:30-2:30

DUNDURN BRANCH, 300 Third Ave, Dundurn, S0K 1K0. Tel: 306-492-2366. E-mail: dundurn.library@wheatland.sk.ca. Web Site: www.wheatland.sk.ca/index.php/branch/66.
Open Tues & Thurs 4-7, Wed & Fri 1-4

EATONIA BRANCH, 100 Railway Ave, Eatonia, S0L 0Y0. Tel: 306-967-2224. E-mail: eatonia.library@wheatland.sk.ca. Web Site: www.wheatland.sk.ca/index.php/branch/69.
Open Tues 11-4, Wed 2-7, Thurs 11-2

ELROSE BRANCH, 401 Main St, Elrose, S0L 0Z0. Tel: 306-378-2808. E-mail: elrose.library@wheatland.sk.ca. Web Site: www.wheatland.sk.ca/index.php/branch/70.
Library Holdings: Bk Titles 15,000
Open Tues & Thurs 9-2, Wed 10:30-1 & 1:30-7

ESTON BRANCH, 218 Main St, Eston, S0L 1A0. (Mail add: Box 487, Eston, S0L 1A0). Tel: 306-962-3513. E-mail: eston.library@wheatland.sk.ca. Web Site: www.wheatland.sk.ca/index.php/branch/71.
Open Mon, Tues, Thurs 2-5:30, Wed 2-8, Fri 10-12 & 3-5

HAGUE BRANCH, 210 Main St, Hague, S0K 1X0. Tel: 306-225-4326. E-mail: hague.library@wheatland.sk.ca. Web Site: www.wheatland.sk.ca/index.php/branch/73.
Open Tues & Thurs 6pm-9pm, Wed 9-12 & 2-5

HANLEY BRANCH, 110 B Lincoln St, Hanley, S0G 2E0. Tel: 306-544-7567. E-mail: hanley.library@wheatland.sk.ca. Web Site: www.wheatland.sk.ca/index.php/branch/72.
Open Tues 1-6, Wed 9:30-12:30, Thurs 2-6

KENASTON BRANCH, 501 Third St, Kenaston, S0G 2N0. Tel: 306-252-2130. E-mail: kenaston.library@wheatland.sk.ca. Web Site: www.wheatland.sk.ca/index.php/branch/76.
Open Mon 4-7, Wed 11-5, Thurs 9-4

KERROBERT BRANCH, 433 Manitoba Ave, Kerrobert, S0L 1R0. Tel: 306-834-5211. E-mail: kerrobert.library@wheatland.sk.ca. Web Site: www.wheatland.sk.ca/index.php/branch/74.
Open Tues & Thurs 10-12 & 1-5, Wed 2-8, Fri 10-1

KINDERSLEY BRANCH, 104 Princess St, Kindersley, S0L 1S2. Tel: 306-463-4141. E-mail: kindersley.library@wheatland.sk.ca. Web Site: www.wheatland.sk.ca/index.php/branch/75.
Open Tues & Fri 10-5, Wed & Thurs 1-9, Sat 1-5

KYLE BRANCH, 116 Centre St, Kyle, S0L 1T0. Tel: 306-375-2566. E-mail: kyle.library@wheatland.sk.ca. Web Site: www.wheatland.sk.ca/index.php/branch/77.
Library Holdings: Bk Titles 15,000; Per Subs 39
Open Mon, Tues & Thurs 10:30-5, Wed 10:30-6:30

LANDIS BRANCH, 100 Princess St, Landis, S0K 2K0. Tel: 306-658-2177. E-mail: landis.library@wheatland.sk.ca. Web Site: www.wheatland.sk.ca/index.php/branch/78.
Open Tues 1-5:30, Thurs 10-2:30

LANGHAM BRANCH, 302 Railway St, Langham, S0K 2L0. Tel: 306-283-4362. E-mail: langham.library@wheatland.sk.ca. Web Site: www.wheatland.sk.ca/index.php/branch/80.
Open Mon 10-12 & 4-8, Tues-Thurs 4-8

LANIGAN BRANCH, 40 Downing Dr, Lanigan, S0K 2M0. (Mail add: Box 70, Lanigan, S0K 2M0). Tel: 306-365-2472. E-mail: lanigan.library@wheatland.sk.ca. Web Site: www.wheatland.sk.ca/index.php/branch/81.
Open Mon & Wed 3-7, Tues & Thurs 11-4

LUCKY LAKE BRANCH, 101 First Ave S, Lucky Lake, S0L 1Z0. Tel: 306-858-2246. E-mail: luckylake.library@wheatland.sk.ca. Web Site: www.wheatland.sk.ca/index.php/branch/79.
Open Tues & Fri 12-5, Thurs 12-6

LUSELAND BRANCH, 510 Grand Ave, Luseland, S0L 2A0. Tel: 306-372-4808. E-mail: luseland.library@wheatland.sk.ca. Web Site: www.wheatland.sk.ca/branch/82. *Head Librn,* Kate Hughes
Open Tues & Thurs 10-2 & 4-7, Sat 10-12 & 1-4

MARTENSVILLE BRANCH, 66 Main St, Martensville, S0K 2T0. (Mail add: Box 1180, Martensville, S0K 2T0). Tel: 306-956-7311. E-mail: martensville.library@wheatland.sk.ca. Web Site: www.wheatland.sk.ca/index.php/branch/83.
Open Mon, Wed & Fri 9:30-6, Tues & Thurs 9:30-8, Sat 9:30-2

MILDEN BRANCH, 109 Centre St, Milden, S0L 2L0. Tel: 306-935-4600. E-mail: milden.library@wheatland.sk.ca. Web Site: www.wheatland.sk.ca/index.php/branch/84.
Open Wed 10:30-2 & 5-7:30

NOKOMIS BRANCH, 101 Third Ave W, Nokomis, S0G 3R0. Tel: 306-528-2251. E-mail: nokomis.library@wheatland.sk.ca. Web Site: www.wheatland.sk.ca/index.php/branch/85.
Open Mon 6pm-9pm, Wed & Thurs 1-5

OSLER BRANCH, 228 Willow Dr, Osler, S0K 3A0. (Mail add: Box 9, Osler, S0K 3A0). Tel: 306-239-4774. E-mail: osler.library@wheatland.sk.ca. Web Site: www.wheatland.sk.ca/index.php/branch/86.
Open Mon & Fri 10-12 & 12:30-5, Tues & Thurs 2-7

OUTLOOK BRANCH, 505 Franklin St S, Outlook, S0L 2N0. Tel: 306-867-8823. E-mail: outlook.library@wheatland.sk.ca. Web Site: www.wheatland.sk.ca/index.php/branch/87.
Open Tues & Thurs 9-9, Fri 8:30-12 & 1-5, Sat 9-Noon

PERDUE BRANCH, 1124 Tenth St, Perdue, S0K 3C0. Tel: 306-237-4227. E-mail: perdue.library@wheatland.sk.ca. Web Site: www.wheatland.sk.ca/index.php/branch/88.
Open Tues 11-3, Thurs 3-8

PLENTY BRANCH, 420 Grand Ave, Plenty, S0L 2R0. Tel: 306-932-4455. E-mail: plenty.library@wheatland.sk.ca. Web Site: www.wheatland.sk.ca/index.php/branch/89.
Open Tues 2-8, Wed 10-6

ROSETOWN BRANCH, 201 Fifth Ave E, Rosetown, S0L 2V0. Tel: 306-882-3566. E-mail: rosetown.library@wheatland.sk.ca. Web Site: www.wheatland.sk.ca/index.php/branch/91.
Open Mon-Wed & Fri 11-5, Thurs 11-6

ROSTHERN BRANCH, 1029 Sixth St, Rosthern, S0K 3R0. Tel: 306-232-5377. E-mail: rosetown.library@wheatland.sk.ca. Web Site: www.wheatland.sk.ca/index.php/branch/90.
Open Tues Noon-5, Wed 4-7, Thurs 2-7, Fri 2-5

STRANRAER BRANCH, One Prospect Ave, Stranraer, S0L 3B0. Tel: 306-377-2144. E-mail: stranraer.library@wheatland.sk.ca. Web Site: www.wheatland.sk.ca/index.php/branch/92.
Open Mon-Thurs 9-4:30, Fri 9-12

UNITY BRANCH, 100 First Ave W, Unity, S0K 4L0. Tel: 306-228-2802. E-mail: unity.library@wheatland.sk.ca. Web Site: www.wheatland.sk.ca/index.php/branch/93.
Open Mon 9-1, Tues & Thurs 1-9

VISCOUNT BRANCH, 319 Bangor Ave, Viscount, S0K 4M0. Tel: 306-944-2155. E-mail: viscount.library@wheatland.sk.ca. Web Site: www.wheatland.sk.ca/index.php/branch/94.
Open Mon 9-1, Wed 4-8, Fri 2-5

WALDHEIM BRANCH, 409 Main St, Waldheim, S0K 4R0. Tel: 306-945-2221. E-mail: waldheim.library@wheatland.sk.ca. Web Site: www.wheatland.sk.ca/index.php/branch/98.
Open Mon & Wed 10-4, Tues & Thurs 3-8, Fri 9-Noon

WARMAN BRANCH, 700 Gowan Rd, Warman, S0K 4S0. Tel: 306-933-4387. E-mail: warman.library@wheatland.sk.ca. Web Site: www.wheatland.sk.ca/index.php/branch/99.
Open Mon & Tues 10-7, Wed & Thurs 10-9, Fri 10-6, Sat 10-4

WATROUS BRANCH, 306 Main St, Watrous, S0K 4T0. Tel: 306-946-2244. E-mail: watrous.library@wheatland.sk.ca. Web Site: www.wheatland.sk.ca/index.php/branch/95.
Open Tues & Wed 11-6, Thurs 11-7, Fri & Sat 11-3

WILKIE BRANCH, 202 Second Ave E, Wilkie, S0K 4W0. Tel: 306-843-2616. E-mail: wilkie.library@wheatland.sk.ca. Web Site: www.wheatland.sk.ca/index.php/branch/97.
Open Tues & Thurs 11-4, Wed 4-8

YOUNG BRANCH, 114 Main St, Young, S0K 4Y0. Tel: 306-259-2227. E-mail: young.library@wheatland.sk.ca. Web Site: www.wheatland.sk.ca/branch/100. *Commun Librn,* Maria Vanderbie
Open Tues & Fri 10-2, Wed 3-7

STANLEY MISSION

P KEETHANOW PUBLIC LIBRARY, PO Box 70, S0J 1G0. Tel: 306-635-2104. FAX: 306-635-2050. E-mail: ssk@pnls.lib.sk.ca. Web Site: pahkisimon.ca/branch/205. *Librn,* Kristen Kehler
Library Holdings: DVDs 55; Bk Vols 8,000; Per Subs 9; Videos 100

Mem of Pahkisimon Nuye?ah Library System
Open Mon-Fri 1-4

SWIFT CURRENT

P CHINOOK REGIONAL LIBRARY*, Headquarters, 1240 Chaplin St W, S9H 0G8. SAN 320-0205. Tel: 306-773-3186. FAX: 306-773-0434. E-mail: chinook@chinook.lib.sk.ca. Web Site: chinooklibrary.ca. *Dir,* Kathryn Foley; E-mail: kfoley@chinook.lib.sk.ca
Founded 1971. Pop 53,000; Circ 313,589
Library Holdings: Audiobooks 675; Bk Vols 158,707; Videos 662
Automation Activity & Vendor Info: (Acquisitions) Innovative Interfaces, Inc - Millennium; (Cataloging) Innovative Interfaces, Inc - Millennium; (Circulation) Innovative Interfaces, Inc - Millennium; (OPAC) Innovative Interfaces, Inc - Millennium
Partic in Saskatchewan Electronic Resources Partnership
Open Mon-Fri 8-12 & 1-5
Branches: 31
ABBEY BRANCH, 336 Cathedral Ave, Abbey, S0N 0A0. (Mail add: PO Box 185, Abbey, S0N 0A0). Tel: 306-689-2202. E-mail: abbey@chinook.lib.sk.ca. *Librn,* Brandi Sorenson
Founded 1971
Open Mon & Fri 12-5, Wed 9-12
BURSTALL BRANCH, 428 Martin St, Burstall, S0N 0H0. (Mail add: PO Box 309, Burstall, S0N 0H0). Tel: 306-679-2177. E-mail: burstall@chinook.lib.sk.ca. *Librn,* Karen Dieterle
Founded 1979
Open Mon 12-5, Wed 1-5 & 7-9, Thurs 1-5
CABRI BRANCH, Town Hall, 202 Centre St, Cabri, S0N 0J0. Tel: 306-587-2911. E-mail: cabri@chinook.lib.sk.ca. *Librn,* Alanna Pawluk
Founded 1971
Open Mon 12:30-5, Wed 9-12, & 12:30-5
CENTRAL BUTTE BRANCH, 271 Butte St, Central Butte, S0H 0T0. Tel: 306-796-4660. E-mail: centralbutte@chinook.lib.sk.ca. *Librn,* Karina Layton
Founded 1972
Open Tues 9:30-2, Wed 5pm-9pm, Fri 2-6
CHAPLIN BRANCH, Second Ave Hall Complex, Chaplin, S0H 0V0. (Mail add: PO Box 225, Chaplin, S0H 0V0). Tel: 306-395-2524. E-mail: chaplin@chinook.lib.sk.ca. *Librn,* Gayla Gane
Founded 1973
Open Mon & Wed 12-5, Fri 9-12
CLIMAX BRANCH, 102 Main St, Climax, S0N 0N0. Tel: 306-293-2229. E-mail: climax@chinook.lib.sk.ca. *Librn,* Nancy Glenn
Founded 1974
Open Tues & Fri 1-6, Wed 1-4
CONSUL BRANCH, 102 Pescod St, Consul, S0N 0P0. Tel: 306-299-2118. E-mail: consul@chinook.lib.sk.ca. *Librn,* Linda Brown
Founded 1972
Open Mon & Wed 1-4, Fri 9-12
EASTEND BRANCH, Eastend Memorial Hall, Oak Ave N, Eastend, S0N 0T0. (Mail add: PO Box 91, Eastend, S0N 0T0). Tel: 306-295-3788. E-mail: eastend@chinook.lib.sk.ca. *Librn,* Kristel Grant; *Librn,* Catherine Myhr
Founded 1971
Open Tues & Sat 1:30-4:30, Wed 12:30-4:30, Thurs 9:30-12:30
FOX VALLEY BRANCH, 85 Centre St E, Fox Valley, S0N 0V0. (Mail add: Box 145, Fox Valley, S0N 0V0). Tel: 306-666-2045. E-mail: foxvalley@chinook.lib.sk.ca. *Librn,* Valerie Reinboldt
Founded 1974
Open Tues 11:30-4, Wed 6pm-9:30pm
FRONTIER BRANCH, 211 First St W, Frontier, S0N 0W0. (Mail add: Box 269, Frontier, S0N 0W0). Tel: 306-296-4667. E-mail: frontier@chinook.lib.sk.ca. *Librn,* Carmen Andrejcin
Founded 1971
Open Wed 12:30-5:30, Thurs 3-8
GLENTWORTH BRANCH, Glentworth School, First Ave, Glentworth, S0H 1V0. (Mail add: PO Box 209, Glentworth, S0H 1V0). Tel: 306-266-4804, 306-266-4940. E-mail: glentworth@chinook.lib.sk.ca. *Librn,* Yvonne Dubois
Founded 1974
Open Thurs 9-12 & 12:30-2:30
GRAVELBOURG BRANCH, Maillard Cultural Ctr, 133 Fifth Ave E, Gravelbourg, S0H 1X0. Tel: 306-648-3177. E-mail: gravelbourg@chinook.lib.sk.ca. *Librn,* Karen Frank
Founded 1974
Open Tues 9:30-11:30 & 12-5, Wed 1:30-6, Thurs 12-4
GULL LAKE BRANCH, 1377 Conrad Ave, Gull Lake, S0N 1A0. (Mail add: PO Box 653, Gull Lake, S0N 1A0). Tel: 306-672-3277. E-mail: gulllake@chinook.lib.sk.ca. *Librn,* Carla Orton
Founded 1971
Open Tues & Thurs 10-5, Wed 12-5, Fri 1-5
HAZLET BRANCH, 105 Main St, Hazlet, S0N 1E0. (Mail add: PO Box 73, Hazlet, S0N 1E0). Tel: 306-678-2155. E-mail: hazlet@chinook.lib.sk.ca. *Librn,* Elaine Little
Founded 1974
Open Tues 12:30-5, Thurs 11-4
HERBERT BRANCH, 517 Herbert Ave, Herbert, S0H 2A0. (Mail add: Box 176, Herbert, S0H 2A0). Tel: 306-784-2484. E-mail: herbert@chinook.lib.sk.ca. *Librn,* Evelyn Nickel
Founded 1972. Circ 6,077
Open Mon & Wed 6pm-9pm, Tues 8-11 & 1:30-5, Fri 1:30-5, Sat 9-Noon
HODGEVILLE BRANCH, Main St, Hodgeville, S0H 2B0. (Mail add: PO Box 68, Hodgeville, S0H 2B0). Tel: 306-677-2223. E-mail: hodgeville@chinook.lib.sk.ca. *Librn,* Missy Priebe
Founded 1971
Open Tues 10-2, Wed 1-6, Fri 1-5
KINCAID BRANCH, Village Office, Dominion Ave, Kincaid, S0H 2J0. (Mail add: Box 146, Kincaid, S0H 2J0). Tel: 306-264-3910. E-mail: kincaid@chinook.lib.sk.ca. *Librn,* Debbie Robertson
Founded 1971
Open Tues & Thurs 12-4
LAFLECHE BRANCH, 157 Main St, Lafleche, S0H 2K0. (Mail add: Box 132, Lafleche, S0H 2K0). Tel: 306-472-5466. E-mail: lafleche@chinook.lib.sk.ca. Web Site: chinooklibrary.ca/branch/38. *Librn,* Julia Byrnes
Founded 1975
Function: 24/7 Electronic res, 24/7 Online cat, Audiobks via web, Bks on CD, Computers for patron use, Digital talking bks, Free DVD rentals, Games, ILL available, Internet access, Magazines, Mail & tel request accepted, Movies, Music CDs, Online cat, Photocopying/Printing, Wifi hotspot checkout
Open Tues 10-1, Wed 4-7, Thurs 9:30-2, Fri 2-5
LEADER BRANCH, 151 First St W, Leader, S0N 1H0. (Mail add: Box 40, Leader, S0N 1H0). Tel: 306-628-3830. E-mail: leader@chinook.lib.sk.ca. *Librn,* Doreen Miller
Founded 1971
Open Mon 1-5, Tues-Thurs 9-12 & 1-5, Fri 9-12 & 1-3
MANKOTA BRANCH, Village Office Complex, First Ave, Mankota, S0H 2W0. (Mail add: PO Box 373, Mankota, S0H 2W0). Tel: 306-478-2401. E-mail: mankota@chinook.lib.sk.ca. Web Site: chinooklibrary.ca/branch/40. *Br Librn,* Sophie Geerts
Founded 1972
Open Mon-Thurs 1-5
MAPLE CREEK BRANCH, Town Office Complex, 205 Jasper St, Maple Creek, S0N 1N0. (Mail add: PO Box 760, Maple Creek, S0N 1N0). Tel: 306-662-3522. E-mail: maplecreek@chinook.lib.sk.ca. *Librn,* Violet Wong
Founded 1971. Pop 3,000; Circ 20,000
Open Mon & Wed-Fri 10-1 & 2-5, Tues 12-4 & 5-8, Sat 12-5
MORSE BRANCH, Saskatchewan 644, Morse, S0H 3C0. (Mail add: Box 64, Morse, S0H 3C0). Tel: 306-629-3335. E-mail: morse@chinook.lib.sk.ca. *Librn,* Velma Deobald
Founded 1971
Open Tues & Wed 1-5, Thurs 1-4
PENNANT BRANCH, 229 Standard St, Pennant, S0N 1X0. Tel: 306-626-3316. E-mail: pennant@chinook.lib.sk.ca. *Librn,* Doreen Fliegel
Founded 1975
Open Tues & Fri 12:30-5
PONTEIX BRANCH, 130 First Ave E, Ponteix, S0N 1Z0. (Mail add: Box 700, Ponteix, S0N 1Z0). Tel: 306-625-3353. E-mail: ponteix@chinook.lib.sk.ca. *Librn,* Roxanne Bedard
Founded 1971
Open Tues 1-5:30, Wed 9:30-11:30, 1-5:30 & 7-8:30, Thurs 1-5
SCEPTRE BRANCH, R M Office, 128 Kingsway St, Sceptre, S0N 2H0. (Mail add: Box 128, Sceptre, S0N 2H0). Tel: 306-623-4244. E-mail: sceptre@chinook.lib.sk.ca. *Librn,* Sherry Egeland
Founded 1975
Open Tues 1:30-4:30
SHAUNAVON BRANCH, Grand Coteau Heritage & Cultural Ctr, 440 Centre St, Shaunavon, S0N 2M0, (Mail add: Box 1116, Shaunavon, S0N 2M0). Tel: 306-297-3844. E-mail: shaunavon@chinook.lib.sk.ca. *Librn,* Joanne Hofmann
Founded 1971
Open Mon, Wed, Fri & Sat 12-5, Tues & Thurs 12-7:30
STEWART VALLEY BRANCH, Senior Ctr, 20 Charles St, Stewart Valley, S0N 2P0. E-mail: stewartvalley@chinook.lib.sk.ca. *Librn,* Kathy King
Founded 1971
Open Mon 2-5 & 7-9, Fri 2-5
SWIFT CURRENT BRANCH, R C Dahl Ctr, 411 Herbert St E, S9H 1M5. Tel: 306-778-2752. E-mail: sc@chinook.lib.sk.ca. Web Site: www.swiftcurrentlibrary.ca. *Mgr,* Andrea McCrimmon
Founded 1971
Function: Photocopying/Printing, Ref serv available
Open Mon-Thurs 9-9, Fri 9-6, Sat 10-5, Sun 1-5

TOMPKINS BRANCH, Main St, Tompkins, S0N 2S0. (Mail add: Box 203, Tompkins, S0N 2S0). Tel: 306-622-2255. E-mail: tompkins@chinook.lib.sk.ca. *Librn,* Lynne Baumann
Founded 1973
Open Tues & Thurs 9:30-4:30

VAL MARIE BRANCH, Val Marie Village Complex, 101 Centre St, Val Marie, S0N 2T0. (Mail add: PO Box 93, Val Marie, S0N 2T0). Tel: 306-298-2133. E-mail: valmarie@chinook.lib.sk.ca. *Librn,* Judy Gunter
Founded 1972
Open Tues & Wed 9:30-4

VANGUARD BRANCH, Library/Musem Bldg, Dominion St, Vanguard, S0N 2V0. (Mail add: Box 85, Vanguard, S0N 2V0). Tel: 306-582-7722. E-mail: vanguard@chinook.lib.sk.ca. *Librn,* Jen Hiebert
Founded 1971
Open Tues & Thurs 10-1, Wed 5-8

WEYBURN

P SOUTHEAST REGIONAL LIBRARY*, 49 Bison Ave, S4H 0H9. SAN 320-0221. Tel: 306-848-3100. FAX: 306-842-2665. E-mail: library.srl@southeastlibrary.ca. Web Site: southeastlibrary.ca. *Libr Dir,* Kate-Lee Nolin; E-mail: knolin@southeastlibrary.ca; Staff 91 (MLS 4, Non-MLS 87)
Founded 1966. Pop 97,000; Circ 363,114
Library Holdings: AV Mats 31,378; e-books 66,818; e-journals 84; Bk Vols 393,343
Automation Activity & Vendor Info: (Acquisitions) SirsiDynix; (Cataloging) SirsiDynix; (Circulation) SirsiDynix; (Course Reserve) SirsiDynix; (ILL) SirsiDynix; (Media Booking) SirsiDynix; (OPAC) SirsiDynix; (Serials) SirsiDynix
Wireless access
Function: Computers for patron use, Distance learning, Homebound delivery serv, ILL available, Ref serv available
Partic in Saskatchewan Electronic Resources Partnership
Special Services for the Blind - Talking bks
Open Mon-Fri 8-4:30
Branches: 47

ALAMEDA BRANCH, 200-Fifth St, Alameda, S0C 0A0. (Mail add: Box 144, Alameda, S0C 0A0). Tel: 306-489-2066. E-mail: alameda@southeastlibrary.ca. *Br Librn,* Dianne Miller
Library Holdings: Bk Vols 7,128
Open Mon & Fri 12:30-4:30, Wed 9:30-2, Sat 1-4:30

ARCOLA BRANCH, 127 Main St, Arcola, S0C 0G0. (Mail add: Box 389, Arcola, S0C 0G0). Tel: 306-455-2321. E-mail: arcola@southeastlibrary.ca. Web Site: southeastlibrary.ca/branch/319. *Br Librn,* Kyla Vanderhulst
Library Holdings: Bk Vols 6,000
Function: AV serv, Homebound delivery serv
Special Services for the Blind - Home delivery serv; Large print & cassettes; Talking bks
Open Tues 9-1 & 2-5, Wed 11-2 & 3-7, Thurs 10:30-1:30 & 2-5

BALGONIE BRANCH, 137 Lewis St, Balgonie, S0G 0E0. (Mail add: Box 389, Balgonie, S0G 0E0). Tel: 306-771-0044. E-mail: balgonie@southeastlibrary.ca. *Br Librn,* Celine Farley
Library Holdings: Bk Vols 15,000
Function: AV serv, Homebound delivery serv
Special Services for the Blind - Home delivery serv; Large print & cassettes; Talking bks
Open Mon 3:30-7, Tues & Thurs 3:30-8, Wed 9-1:30, Fri 1-5:30, Sat 10-1:30

BENGOUGH BRANCH, 301 Main St, Bengough, S0C 0K0. (Mail add: Box 71, Bengough, S0C 0K0). Tel: 306-268-2022. E-mail: bengough@southeastlibrary.ca. *Br Librn,* Fay Adam
Library Holdings: Bk Vols 10,000
Function: AV serv, Homebound delivery serv
Special Services for the Blind - Home delivery serv; Large print & cassettes; Talking bks
Open Tues 9-12 & 12:30-2:30, Wed 2:30-6 & 6:30-8, Thurs 11:30-1:30 & 2-5

BIENFAIT BRANCH, 414 Main St, Bienfait, S0C 0M0. (Mail add: Box 520, Bienfait, S0C 0M0). Tel: 306-388-2995. E-mail: bienfait@southeastlibrary.ca. *Br Librn,* Sheila Farstad
Library Holdings: Bk Vols 8,500
Function: AV serv, Homebound delivery serv
Special Services for the Blind - Home delivery serv; Large print & cassettes; Talking bks
Open Tues 9:30-2 & 3-6, Wed 9-1:30, Thurs 5-8

BROADVIEW BRANCH, 515 Main St, Broadview, S0G 0K0. (Mail add: Box 590, Broadview, S0G 0K0). Tel: 306-696-2414. E-mail: broadview@southeastlibrary.ca. *Br Librn,* Christine Judy
Library Holdings: Bk Vols 7,000
Function: AV serv, Homebound delivery serv
Special Services for the Blind - Home delivery serv; Large print & cassettes; Talking bks
Open Wed & Fri 10-1 & 2-5, Sat 12-3

CARLYLE BRANCH, 119 Souris Ave W, Carlyle, S0C 0R0. (Mail add: Box 417, Carlyle, S0C 0R0). Tel: 306-453-6120. E-mail: carlyle@southeastlibrary.ca. *Br Librn,* Jonathan Nicoll
Library Holdings: Bk Vols 6,200
Function: AV serv, Homebound delivery serv
Special Services for the Blind - Home delivery serv; Large print & cassettes; Talking bks
Open Tues & Thurs 10-12 & 1-5, Wed 10-1 & 2-6, Sat 10-12 & 12:30-4:30

CARNDUFF BRANCH, Carnduff Education Complex, 506 Anderson Ave, Carnduff, S0C 0S0. (Mail add: Box 6, Carnduff, S0C 0S0). Tel: 306-482-3255. E-mail: carnduff@southeastlibrary.ca. *Br Librn,* Linda Kimball
Library Holdings: Bk Vols 9,000
Function: AV serv, Homebound delivery serv
Special Services for the Blind - Home delivery serv; Large print & cassettes; Talking bks
Open Mon 1-6, Tues & Thurs 1-5, Wed 3-7, Fri 9-1, Sat 1-4

ESTEVAN BRANCH, Leisure Ctr, 701 Souris Ave N, Estevan, S4A 2T1. Tel: 306-636-1620. FAX: 306-634-5830. E-mail: estevan@southeastlibrary.ca. *Actg Br Mgr,* Roxy Blackmore; Staff 8 (MLS 1, Non-MLS 7)
Founded 1908. Pop 10,000; Circ 46,000
Library Holdings: Audiobooks 450; Bk Vols 33,000
Special Collections: Canadian and Provincial
Function: AV serv, Homebound delivery serv
Special Services for the Blind - Home delivery serv; Large print & cassettes; Talking bks
Open Mon-Thurs 9-8, Fri & Sat 9:30-6, Sun 1-5

FILLMORE BRANCH, 51 Main St, Fillmore, S0G 1N0. (Mail add: Box 68, Fillmore, S0G 1N0). Tel: 306-722-3369. E-mail: fillmore@southeastlibrary.ca. *Br Librn,* Koreana Bjarnason-stomp
Library Holdings: Bk Vols 9,400
Function: AV serv, Homebound delivery serv
Special Services for the Blind - Home delivery serv; Large print & cassettes; Talking bks
Open Wed 4:30-7:30, Thurs 9:30-12:30 & 1:30-5:30

FORT QU'APPELLE BRANCH, 140 Company Ave S, Fort Qu'Appelle, S0G 1S0. (Mail add: Box 218, Fort Qu'Appelle, S0G 1S0). Tel: 306-332-6411. E-mail: fortquappelle@southeastlibrary.ca. *Br Librn,* Malinda Heard
Library Holdings: Bk Vols 4,700
Function: AV serv, Homebound delivery serv
Special Services for the Blind - Home delivery serv; Large print & cassettes; Talking bks
Open Tues-Thurs 10-1 & 1:30-6, Fri 10-2:30, Sat 10-1

GAINSBOROUGH BRANCH, 401 Railway Ave, Gainsborough, S0C 0Z0. (Mail add: Box 57, Gainsborough, S0C 0Z0). Tel: 306-685-2229. E-mail: gainsborough@southeastlibrary.ca. *Br Librn,* Felicia Seymour
Library Holdings: Bk Vols 9,000
Function: AV serv, Homebound delivery serv
Special Services for the Blind - Home delivery serv; Large print & cassettes; Talking bks
Open Tues 1-4, Wed 9-12, Thurs 1:30-5:30

GLENAVON BRANCH, 311 Railway Ave, Glenavon, S0G 1Y0. (Mail add: Box 162, Glenavon, S0G 1Y0). Tel: 306-429-2180. E-mail: glenavon@southeastlibrary.ca. *Br Librn,* Angela Englot
Library Holdings: Bk Vols 11,000
Function: AV serv, Homebound delivery serv
Special Services for the Blind - Home delivery serv; Large print & cassettes; Talking bks
Open Tues 10-1 & 1:30-4:30, Fri 10-2

GRENFELL BRANCH, 710 Desmond St, Grenfell, S0G 2B0. (Mail add: Box 876, Grenfell, S0G 2B0). Tel: 306-697-2455. E-mail: grenfell@southeastlibrary.ca. *Br Librn,* Sheila Warne-Peter
Library Holdings: Bk Vols 9,700
Function: AV serv, Homebound delivery serv
Special Services for the Blind - Home delivery serv; Large print & cassettes; Talking bks
Open Tues 9:30-12:30 & 1-6, Thurs 9:30-12:30 & 1-5, Fri 12:30-5

INDIAN HEAD BRANCH, 419 Grand Ave, Indian Head, S0G 2K0. (Mail add: Box 986, Indian Head, S0G 2K0). Tel: 306-695-3922. E-mail: indianhead@southeastlibrary.ca. *Br Librn,* Colleen Reynard
Library Holdings: Bk Vols 9,405
Open Tues 12-4, Wed 10-12, 1-5 & 5:30-7:30, Fri 9:30-12 & 12:30-5, Sat 10-12 & 1-5

KENNEDY BRANCH, 235 Scott St, Kennedy, S0G 2R0. (Mail add: Box 217, Kennedy, S0G 2R0). Tel: 306-538-2020. E-mail: kennedy@southeastlibrary.ca. *Br Librn,* Carolyn McMillan
Library Holdings: Bk Vols 6,700
Function: AV serv, Homebound delivery serv
Special Services for the Blind - Home delivery serv; Large print & cassettes; Talking bks
Open Tues 12-1:30 & 2-6, Fri 9:30-2

KIPLING BRANCH, 207 Sixth Ave, Kipling, S0G 2S0. (Mail add: Box 608, Kipling, S0G 2S0). Tel: 306-736-2911. E-mail: kipling@southeastlibrary.ca. *Br Librn,* Charla Smyth
Library Holdings: Bk Vols 14,000
Function: AV serv, Homebound delivery serv
Special Services for the Blind - Home delivery serv; Large print & cassettes; Talking bks
Open Mon 3-7, Tues 12:30-5, Wed 4-8, Thurs 9:30-12:30 & 1-4:30, Fri 10-12:30 & 1-4:30

LAKE ALMA BRANCH, Hwy 18, Lake Alma, S0C 1M0. (Mail add: Box 216, Lake Alma, S0C 1M0). Tel: 306-447-2061. E-mail: lakealma@southeastlibrary.ca. *Br Librn,* Elizabeth Ager
Library Holdings: Bk Vols 4,000
Function: AV serv, Homebound delivery serv
Special Services for the Blind - Home delivery serv; Large print & cassettes; Talking bks
Open Tues 1-5:30, Thurs 9:30-12:30 & 1-3:30

LAMPMAN BRANCH, 302 Main St, Lampman, S0C 1N0. (Mail add: Box 9, Lampman, S0C 1N0). Tel: 306-487-2202. E-mail: lampman@southeastlibrary.ca. *Br Librn,* Tawney Johnson
Library Holdings: Bk Vols 6,500
Function: AV serv, Homebound delivery serv
Special Services for the Blind - Home delivery serv; Large print & cassettes; Talking bks
Open Tues 11-2:30 & 3-6:30, Wed & Thurs 9:30-1 & 1:30-5:30

LUMSDEN BRANCH, 50 Third Ave, Lumsden, S0G 3C0. (Mail add: Box 496, Lumsden, S0G 3C0). Tel: 306-731-2665. E-mail: lumsden@southeastlibrary.ca. *Br Librn,* Carol Fisher
Library Holdings: Bk Vols 7,000
Function: AV serv, Homebound delivery serv
Special Services for the Blind - Home delivery serv; Large print & cassettes; Talking bks
Open Mon & Wed 1-5 & 5:30-8:30, Thurs-Sat 9:30-12:30 & 1-5

MANOR BRANCH, 23 Main St, Manor, S0C 1R0. (Mail add: Box 188, Manor, S0C 1R0). Tel: 306-448-2266. E-mail: manor@southeastlibrary.ca. *Br Librn,* Diane Nehrebecky
Library Holdings: Bk Vols 5,000
Function: AV serv, Homebound delivery serv
Special Services for the Blind - Home delivery serv; Large print & cassettes; Talking bks
Open Mon 10-12 & 1-5, Wed 5:30-8:30, Fri 3-7:30 Sat 9-12:30

MARYFIELD BRANCH, 201 Barrows St, Maryfield, S0G 3K0. (Mail add: Box 160, Maryfield, S0G 3K0). Tel: 306-646-2148. E-mail: maryfield@southeastlibrary.ca. *Br Librn,* Janet Percy
Library Holdings: Bk Vols 6,000
Function: AV serv, Homebound delivery serv
Special Services for the Blind - Home delivery serv; Large print & cassettes; Talking bks
Open Tues 9-12 & 12:30-3:30, Wed 2:30-6:30

MIDALE BRANCH, Civic Ctr, 128 Haslem St, Midale, S0C 1S0. (Mail add: Box 478, Midale, S0C 1S0). Tel: 306-458-2263. E-mail: midale@southeastlibrary.ca. *Br Librn,* Vanessa Lund
Library Holdings: Bk Vols 7,500
Function: AV serv, Homebound delivery serv
Special Services for the Blind - Home delivery serv; Large print & cassettes; Talking bks
Open Mon & Tues 2:30-5:30 & 6-8, Fri 9:30-12 & 12:30-3

MILESTONE BRANCH, 112 Main St, Milestone, S0G 3L0. (Mail add: Box 549, Milestone, S0G 3L0). Tel: 306-436-2112. E-mail: milestone@southeastlibrary.ca. *Br Librn,* Shelley Sentes
Library Holdings: Bk Vols 1,000
Function: AV serv, Homebound delivery serv
Special Services for the Blind - Home delivery serv; Large print & cassettes; Talking bks
Open Mon & Thurs 10-1, Wed 2-5 & 6-8, Fri 2-6

MONTMARTRE BRANCH, 136 Central Ave, Montmartre, S0G 3M0. (Mail add: Box 360, Montmartre, S0G 3M0). Tel: 306-424-2029. E-mail: montmartre@southeastlibrary.ca. *Br Librn,* Lillian Ripplinger
Library Holdings: Bk Vols 7,500
Function: AV serv, Homebound delivery serv
Special Services for the Blind - Home delivery serv; Large print & cassettes; Talking bks
Open Mon & Fri 12:30-5, Wed 10:30-12:30 & 1-5:30, Thurs 3-7:30

MOOSOMIN BRANCH, 701 Main St, Moosomin, S0G 3N0. (Mail add: Box 845, Moosomin, S0G 3N0). Tel: 306-435-2107. E-mail: moosomin@southeastlibrary.ca. *Br Librn,* Maegan Nielsen
Library Holdings: Bk Vols 11,000
Function: AV serv, Homebound delivery serv
Special Services for the Blind - Home delivery serv; Large print & cassettes; Talking bks
Open Mon-Wed & Fri 9-12 & 1-5, Thurs 12-4 & 5-8

OGEMA BRANCH, 117 Main St, Ogema, S0C 1Y0. (Mail add: Box 460, Ogema, S0C 1Y0). Tel: 306-459-2985. E-mail: ogema@southeastlibrary.ca. *Br Librn,* Sheri Jackson Mead
Library Holdings: Bk Vols 9,000
Function: AV serv, Homebound delivery serv
Special Services for the Blind - Home delivery serv; Large print & cassettes; Talking bks
Open Mon 9-1:30, Tues 1:30-4:30 & 5-8, Thurs 1:30-6

OUNGRE BRANCH, Lyndale School, Hwy 18, Oungre, S0C 1Z0. (Mail add: Box 88, Oungre, S0C 1Z0). Tel: 306-456-2662. E-mail: oungre@southeastlibrary.ca. *Br Librn,* Katie Bloor
Library Holdings: Bk Vols 8,100
Function: AV serv, Homebound delivery serv
Special Services for the Blind - Home delivery serv; Large print & cassettes; Talking bks
Open Tues-Thurs 9:30-12:30 & 1-3

OXBOW BRANCH, 516 Prospect Ave, Oxbow, S0C 2B0. (Mail add: Box 510, Oxbow, S0C 2B0). Tel: 306-483-5175. E-mail: oxbow@southeastlibrary.ca. *Br Librn,* Shealyn Wenzel
Library Holdings: Audiobooks 250; AV Mats 25; Bk Vols 8,100; Per Subs 14
Function: AV serv, Homebound delivery serv
Special Services for the Blind - Home delivery serv; Large print & cassettes; Talking bks
Open Tues & Fri 9-1 & 2:30-6, Wed 2-5 & 5:30-8:30, Thurs 2:30-6:30

PANGMAN BRANCH, 120 Mergen St, Pangman, S0C 2C0. (Mail add: Box 151, Pangman, S0C 2C0). Tel: 306-442-2119. E-mail: pangman@southeastlibrary.ca. *Br Librn,* Teresa Whiteman
Library Holdings: Bk Vols 6,200
Function: AV serv, Homebound delivery serv
Special Services for the Blind - Home delivery serv; Large print & cassettes; Talking bks
Open Tues 10-1 & 1:30-4:30, Thurs 2-6

PILOT BUTTE BRANCH, Recreation Complex, Third St & Second Ave, Pilot Butte, S0G 3Z0. (Mail add: Box 668, Pilot Butte, S0G 3Z0). Tel: 306-781-3403. E-mail: pilotbutte@southeastlibrary.ca. *Br Librn,* Connie LaRonge-Mohr
Library Holdings: Bk Vols 3,500
Function: AV serv, Homebound delivery serv
Special Services for the Blind - Home delivery serv; Large print & cassettes; Talking bks
Open Tues & Thurs 1:30-4:30 & 5-8, Wed & Fri 9-12 & 1-5, Sun 1-4

QU'APPELLE BRANCH, 16 Qu'Appelle St, Qu'Appelle, S0G 4A0. (Mail add: Box 450, Qu'Appelle, S0G 4A0). Tel: 306-699-2902. E-mail: quappelle@southeastlibrary.ca. *Br Librn,* Elizabeth Fries
Library Holdings: Audiobooks 200; Bk Vols 4,000
Function: AV serv, Homebound delivery serv
Special Services for the Blind - Home delivery serv; Large print & cassettes; Talking bks
Open Tues 5-8, Wed 2-5 & 6-8, Thurs & Fri 10-1 & 2-5

RADVILLE BRANCH, 420 Floren St, Radville, S0C 2G0. (Mail add: Box 791, Radville, S0C 2G0). Tel: 306-869-2742. E-mail: radville@southeastlibrary.ca. *Br Librn,* Janine Mazenc
Library Holdings: Bk Vols 10,500
Function: AV serv, Homebound delivery serv
Special Services for the Blind - Home delivery serv; Large print & cassettes; Talking bks
Open Tues Thurs 10-1 & 2-6

REDVERS BRANCH, 23B Railway Ave, Redvers, S0C 2H0. (Mail add: Box 392, Redvers, S0C 2H0). Tel: 306-452-3255. E-mail: redvers@southeastlibrary.ca. *Br Librn,* Michelle Jensen
Library Holdings: Bk Vols 2,000
Function: AV serv, Homebound delivery serv
Open Mon 1-5, Tues & Thurs 9:30-12:30 & 1-5:30, Wed 3:30-8, Fri 9:30-12:30 & 1-4

REGINA BEACH BRANCH, Cultural Ctr, 133 Donovel Crescent, Regina Beach, S0G 4C0. (Mail add: Box 10, Regina Beach, S0G 4C0). Tel: 306-729-2062. E-mail: reginabeach@southeastlibrary.ca. *Br Librn,* Krista Hannan
Library Holdings: Bk Vols 8,500
Function: AV serv, Homebound delivery serv
Special Services for the Blind - Home delivery serv; Large print & cassettes; Talking bks
Open Tues & Thurs 4-8, Wed, Fri & Sat 10-2

ROCANVILLE BRANCH, 218 Ellice St, Rocanville, S0A 3L0. (Mail add: Box 263, Rocanville, S0A 3L0). Tel: 306-645-2088. E-mail: rocanville@southeastlibrary.ca. *Br Librn,* Carol Greening
Library Holdings: Bk Vols 9,000
Function: AV serv, Homebound delivery serv
Special Services for the Blind - Home delivery serv; Large print & cassettes; Talking bks
Open Tues & Thurs 1:30-5, Wed 9-12:30 & 2-6:30

SEDLEY BRANCH, 224 Broadway St, Sedley, S0G 4K0. (Mail add: Box 231, Sedley, S0G 4K0). Tel: 306-885-4505. E-mail: sedley@southeastlibrary.ca. *Br Librn,* Connie Perras
Library Holdings: Bk Vols 7,300
Function: AV serv, Homebound delivery serv

Special Services for the Blind - Home delivery serv; Large print & cassettes; Talking bks
Open Tues & Thurs 4-7, Wed 10-2
STOUGHTON BRANCH, 232 Main St, Stoughton, S0G 4T0. (Mail add: Box 595, Stoughton, S0G 4T0). Tel: 306-457-2484. E-mail: stoughton@southeastlibrary.ca. *Br Librn,* Laura Sabados
Library Holdings: Bk Vols 7,000
Function: AV serv, Computers for patron use, Homebound delivery serv
Special Services for the Blind - Home delivery serv; Large print & cassettes; Talking bks
Open Tues 2-5 & 5:30-7, Wed & Thurs 10-1 & 2-5, Sat 10-1
VIBANK BRANCH, 101 Second Ave, Vibank, S0G 4Y0. (Mail add: Box 241, Vibank, S0G 4Y0). Tel: 306-762-2270. E-mail: vibank@southeastlibrary.ca. *Br Librn,* Betty Kuntz
Library Holdings: Bk Vols 11,000
Function: AV serv, Homebound delivery serv
Special Services for the Blind - Home delivery serv; Large print & cassettes; Talking bks
Open Mon 1-4:30, Wed 5-8, Fri 9-12:30
WAPELLA BRANCH, 519 S Railway St, Wapella, S0G 4Z0. (Mail add: Box 130, Wapella, S0G 4Z0). Tel: 306-532-4419. E-mail: wapella@southeastlibrary.ca. *Br Librn,* Sharon Matheson
Library Holdings: Bk Vols 3,500
Function: AV serv, Homebound delivery serv
Special Services for the Blind - Home delivery serv; Large print & cassettes; Talking bks
Open Tues & Thurs 3-6:30, Wed 9-12
WAWOTA BRANCH, 308 Railway Ave, Wawota, S0G 5A0. (Mail add: Box 65, Wawota, S0G 5A0). Tel: 306-739-2375. E-mail: wawota@southeastlibrary.ca. *Br Librn,* Kayla Porter
Library Holdings: Bk Vols 10,000
Function: AV serv, Homebound delivery serv
Special Services for the Blind - Home delivery serv; Large print & cassettes; Talking bks
Open Tues 10-12 & 1-5, Wed 1-5:30, Thurs 10-2:30
WEYBURN BRANCH, 45 Bison Ave NE, S4H 0H9. Tel: 306-842-4352. FAX: 306-842-1255. E-mail: weyburn@southeastlibrary.ca. *Br Librn,* Matthew Rankin; Staff 5 (MLS 1, Non-MLS 4)
Founded 1920. Pop 10,000
Library Holdings: CDs 200; DVDs 100; Bk Vols 40,000
Function: AV serv, Homebound delivery serv
Special Services for the Blind - Home delivery serv; Large print & cassettes; Talking bks
Open Mon-Thurs 9:30-8:30, Fri & Sat 9:30-6, Sun 1-5
WHITE CITY BRANCH, Community Ctr, 12 Ramm Ave, White City, S4L 5B1. (Mail add: Box 308, White City, S0G 5B0). Tel: 306-781-2118. E-mail: whitecity@southeastlibrary.ca. *Br Librn,* Lori-Lee Harris
Library Holdings: Bk Vols 9,300
Function: AV serv, Homebound delivery serv
Special Services for the Blind - Home delivery serv; Large print & cassettes; Talking bks
Open Mon-Wed 12:30-4:30 & 5-8, Thurs & Fri 9:30-12:30 & 1-5, Sat 9:30-12:30 & 1-3
WHITEWOOD BRANCH, 731 Lalonde St, Whitewood, S0G 5C0. (Mail add: Box 488, Whitewood, S0G 5C0). Tel: 306-735-4233. E-mail: whitewood@southeastlibrary.ca. *Br Librn,* Krista Williams
Library Holdings: Bk Vols 5,000
Function: AV serv, Homebound delivery serv
Special Services for the Blind - Home delivery serv; Large print & cassettes; Talking bks
Open Tues 10-1 & 2-5, Thurs 10:30-1:30 & 4:30-8, Fri 12:30-4
WINDTHORST BRANCH, 202 Angus St, Windthorst, S0G 5G0. (Mail add: Box 220, Windthorst, S0G 5G0). Tel: 306-224-2159. E-mail: windthorst@southeastlibrary.ca. *Br Librn,* Jill Taylor
Library Holdings: Bk Vols 6,000
Function: AV serv, Homebound delivery serv
Special Services for the Blind - Home delivery serv; Large print & cassettes; Talking bks
Open Tues & Wed 5-8, Thurs 10:30-12:30 & 1-5
WOLSELEY BRANCH, RM Office, 500 Front St, Wolseley, S0G 5H0. (Mail add: Box 398, Wolseley, S0G 5H0). Tel: 306-698-2221. E-mail: woseley@southeastlibrary.ca. *Br Librn,* April Dahnke
Library Holdings: Bk Vols 3,000
Function: AV serv, Homebound delivery serv
Special Services for the Blind - Home delivery serv; Large print & cassettes; Talking bks
Open Tues & Thurs 9-12 & 1-4:30, Wed 1-4
YELLOW GRASS BRANCH, 213 Souris St, Yellow Grass, S0G 5J0. (Mail add: Box 381, Yellow Grass, S0G 5J0). Tel: 306-465-2574. E-mail: yellowgrass@southeastlibrary.ca. *Br Librn,* Betty Guest
Library Holdings: Bk Vols 9,000
Function: AV serv, Homebound delivery serv
Special Services for the Blind - Home delivery serv; Large print & cassettes; Talking bks
Open Mon 3:30-6:30, Wed 3-7, Fri 9-Noon

YORKTON

P PARKLAND REGIONAL LIBRARY-SASKATCHEWAN*, Hwy 52 W, S3N 3Z4. (Mail add: PO Box 5049, S3N 3Z4), SAN 320-0256. Tel: 306-783-7022. FAX: 306-782-2844. E-mail: office@parklandlibrary.ca. Web Site: parklandlibrary.ca. *Dir,* Helen McCutcheon; E-mail: hmccutcheon@parklandlibrary.ca; *Bus Mgr,* Candy Gellert; *Database Mgr, Syst Coordr,* Mathis Patrick; E-mail: mpatrick@parklandlibrary.ca; *Info Serv,* Morgan Stiles; E-mail: mstiles@parklandlibrary.ca; Staff 3 (MLS 3)
Founded 1968. Pop 92,200
Library Holdings: DVDs 3,723; e-journals 7,000; Large Print Bks 4,833; Bk Titles 45,866; Bk Vols 56,194; Talking Bks 7,363
Automation Activity & Vendor Info: (Acquisitions) Innovative Interfaces, Inc; (Cataloging) Innovative Interfaces, Inc; (Circulation) Innovative Interfaces, Inc
Partic in Saskatchewan Electronic Resources Partnership; Saskatchewan Information & Library Services
Branches: 54
ANNAHEIM BRANCH, 523 Second Ave N, Annaheim, S0K 0G0. Tel: 306-598-2155. E-mail: annaheim@parklandlibrary.ca.
Open Tues 1-5, Wed 2-6, Thurs 10-2
BALCARRES BRANCH, 209 Main St, Balcarres, S0G 0C0. Tel: 306-334-2966. E-mail: balcarres@parklandlibrary.ca.
Open Mon-Wed & Fri 2-6
BREDENBURY BRANCH, 201 Third St, Bredenbury, S0A 0H0. Tel: 306-898-4683. E-mail: bredenbury@parklandlibrary.ca.
Open Tues 10-4, Wed & Thurs 2-6
BUCHANAN BRANCH, 315 Central Ave, Buchanan, S0A 0J0. Tel: 306-592-2137. E-mail: buchanan@parklandlibrary.ca.
Open Tues 1-5, Thurs & Fri 2-6
Friends of the Library Group
CALDER PUBLIC LIBRARY, 181 One Ave, Calder, S0A 0K0. Tel: 306-621-7941. E-mail: calder@parklandlibrary.ca.
Open Mon & Wed 12-4
CANORA BRANCH, 223 Eighth Ave E, Canora, S0A 0L0. Tel: 306-563-6877. E-mail: canora@parklandlibrary.ca.
Open Mon 3:30-8, Tues 1-5, Wed 2:30-8, Thurs 11-5, Fri 3:30-7:30, Sat 12-5
CHURCHBRIDGE BRANCH, 114 Rankin Rd, Churchbridge, S0A 0M0. Tel: 306-896-2322. E-mail: churchbridge@parklandlibrary.ca.
Open Tues 1-7, Wed-Fri 1-5
CUPAR BRANCH, 217 Stanley St, Cupar, S0A 0Y0. Tel: 306-723-4749. E-mail: cupar@parklandlibrary.ca.
Open Wed & Fri 10-6
DYSART PUBLIC LIBRARY, 108 Main St, Dysart, S0G 1H0. Tel: 306-432-4442. E-mail: dysart@parklandlibrary.ca.
Open Mon 1-5, Tues 10-12 & 1-7
EARL GREY BRANCH, 133 Main St, Earl Grey, S0A 1J0. Tel: 306-939-2212. E-mail: earlgrey@parklandlibrary.ca.
Open Tues 2-7, Thurs 6-9, Fri 2-6
ELFROS BRANCH, 100 Nacka St, Elfros, S0A 0V0. Tel: 306-328-2175. E-mail: elfros@parklandlibrary.ca.
Open Tues & Thurs 3-7
ENGLEFELD BRANCH, 201 First Ave W, Englefeld, S0K 1N0. Tel: 306-280-7770. E-mail: englefeld@parklandlibrary.ca.
Open Tues & Thurs 10-2, Wed 4-8
ESTERHAZY BRANCH, 624 Main St, Esterhazy, S0A 0X0. Tel: 306-745-6406. E-mail: esterhazy@parklandlibrary.ca.
Open Tues-Thurs 9-12 & 12:30-5:30, Fri 12-4, Sat 10-3
FOAM LAKE BRANCH, 402 Cameron St, Foam Lake, S0A 1A0. Tel: 306-272-3660. E-mail: foamlake@parklandlibrary.ca.
Open Tues, Wed & Fri 10:30-4:30
GOVAN BRANCH, 317 Monk Ave, Govan, S0G 1Z0, SAN 325-1012. Tel: 306-484-2122. E-mail: govan@parklandlibrary.ca.
Library Holdings: Bk Vols 3,000
Special Collections: Saskatchewan History Room Coll, bks, pictures
Open Tues & Thurs 9:30-12:30 & 1-5
INVERMAY BRANCH, 301 Fourth Ave N, Invermay, S0A 1M0. Tel: 306-593-4990. E-mail: invermay@parklandlibrary.ca.
Open Tues & Wed 11-5
ITUNA BRANCH, 24 First St NE, Ituna, S0A 1N0. Tel: 306-795-2672. E-mail: ituna@parklandlibrary.ca.
Open Tues & Wed 11:30-4:30, Thurs 10:30-4:30
JANSEN BRANCH, 121 Main St, Jansen, S0K 2B0. Tel: 306-364-2122. E-mail: jansen@parklandlibrary.ca.
Open Tues 3-7 & Thurs 10-2
KAMSACK BRANCH, 235 Second St, Kamsack, S0A 1S0. Tel: 306-542-3787. E-mail: kamsack@parklandlibrary.ca.
Open Mon & Fri 4-7:30, Tues & Thurs 11-5, Wed 2-7:30, Sat 1-4:30
KELLIHER BRANCH, 413 Second Ave, Kelliher, S0A 1V0. Tel: 306-675-2110. E-mail: kelliher@parklandlibrary.ca.
Open Tues 11:30-5:30, Wed & Thurs 10-2

KELVINGTON BRANCH, 201 Main St, Kelvington, S0A 1W0. Tel: 306-327-4322. E-mail: kelvington@parklandlibrary.ca.
Open Tues & Fri 10-2, Wed & Thurs 11-4
LAKE LENORE BRANCH, 217 Second Ave, Lake Lenore, S0K 2J0. Tel: 306-682-2500. E-mail: lakelenore@parklandlibrary.ca.
Open Tues-Thurs 4-8
LANGENBURG BRANCH, 202 Wells E, Langenburg, S0A 2A0. Tel: 306-743-5394. E-mail: langenburg@parklandlibrary.ca.
Special Services for the Blind - Large print bks
Open Mon & Thurs 12:30-6, Tues 9-1, Wed 3:30-7:30
LEMBERG BRANCH, 302 Main St, Lemberg, S0A 2B0. Tel: 306-335-2267. E-mail: lemberg@parklandlibrary.ca.
Open Tues 1-6, Wed 10-3, Thurs 10-2
LEROY BRANCH, 101 First Ave NE, LeRoy, S0K 2P0. Tel: 306-286-3356. E-mail: leroy@parklandlibrary.ca.
Open Mon 10-3, Wed 1-6, Fri 10-2
LESTOCK PUBLIC LIBRARY, 215 Millersdale St, Lestock, S0A 2G0. E-mail: lestock@parklandlibrary.ca.
Open Tues & Thurs 4-7
LINTLAW BRANCH, 109 Main St, Lintlaw, S0A 2H0. Tel: 306-325-2166. E-mail: lintlaw@parklandlibrary.ca.
Open Tues & Thurs 10-3
LIPTON BRANCH, 1103 Shamrock Ave, Lipton, S0G 3B0. Tel: 306-336-2288. E-mail: lipton@parklandlibrary.ca.
Open Wed & Thurs 11-6
MACNUTT BRANCH, 18 Railway Ave N, MacNutt, S0A 2K0. Tel: 306-742-4774. E-mail: macnutt@parklandlibrary.ca.
Open Tues 1-5, Fri 10-2
MELVILLE BRANCH, 444 Main St, Melville, S0A 2P0. Tel: 306-728-2171. E-mail: melville@parklandlibrary.ca.
Open Mon & Sat 1-5, Tues 11-5 & 6-9, Wed 11-8, Thurs & Fri 11-5, Sat 1-5
MUENSTER BRANCH, 307 Railway St, Muenster, S0K 2Y0. Tel: 306-682-5252. E-mail: muenster@parklandlibrary.ca.
Open Tues 10:30-4:30, Wed 2:30-7:30, Thurs 12-4
NEUDORF BRANCH, 103 Main St, Neudorf, S0A 2T0. Tel: 306-748-2553. E-mail: neudorf@parklandlibrary.ca.
Open Tues & Wed 4-8, Sat 1-5
NORQUAY BRANCH, 25 Main St, Norquay, S0A 2V0. Tel: 306-594-2766. E-mail: norquay@parklandlibrary.ca.
Open Tues & Thurs 12-4:30
Friends of the Library Group
PELLY BRANCH, 1300 Second St W, Pelly, S0A 2Z0. Tel: 306-595-2243. E-mail: pelly@parklandlibrary.ca.
Open Tues 11-5, Thurs 1-7
PREECEVILLE BRANCH, 27 Main St, Preeceville, S0A 3B0. Tel: 306-547-3444. E-mail: preeceville@parklandlibrary.ca.
Open Tues 2-6, Wed 11-6, Thurs & Fri 2-5:30
PUNNICHY BRANCH, 100 Main St, Punnichy, S0A 3C0. (Mail add: PO Box 550, Punnichy, S0A 3C0). Tel: 306-835-2265. E-mail: punnichy@parklandlibrary.ca.
Open Tues & Thurs 2-5
QUILL LAKE BRANCH, 54 Main St, Quill Lake, S0A 3E0. Tel: 306-383-2242. E-mail: quillLake@parklandlibrary.ca.
Open Tues & Thurs 9:30-12:30 & 1-4
RAYMORE BRANCH, 205 Main St, Raymore, S0A 3J0. Tel: 306-746-2166. E-mail: raymore@parklandlibrary.ca.
Open Tues 1-7, Wed 1-5, Thurs 9:30-12 & 12:30-4
ROSE VALLEY BRANCH, 316 First Ave N, Rose Valley, S0E 1M0. Tel: 306-322-2001. E-mail: rosevalley@parklandlibrary.ca.
Open Tues & Wed 12:30-4:30, Fri 10-2
SALTCOATS BRANCH, 117 Allan St, Saltcoats, S0A 3R0. Tel: 306-744-2911. E-mail: saltcoats@parklandlibrary.ca.
Open Tues & Thurs 3:30-7:30, Wed 9-12 & 12:30-3:30
SEMANS BRANCH, 103 King St, Semans, S0A 3S0. Tel: 306-524-2224. E-mail: semans@parklandlibrary.ca.
Open Tues & Thurs 1-5, Wed 9-12 & 1-4
SOUTHEY BRANCH, 260 Keats St, Southey, S0G 4P0. Tel: 306-726-2907. E-mail: southey@parklandlibrary.ca.
Open Tues & Wed 9:30-2:30, Thurs 9:30-4:30
SPALDING BRANCH, 103 Centre St, Spalding, S0K 4C0. Tel: 306-872-2184. E-mail: spalding@parklandlibrary.ca.
Open Tues 1-5, Thurs 9-4
SPRINGSIDE BRANCH, 18 Main St, Springside, S0A 3V0. Tel: 306-792-4743. E-mail: springside@parklandlibrary.ca.
Open Tues 1-7, Thurs 1-6, Fri 9:30-12:30
SPY HILL BRANCH, 316 Main St, Spy Hill, S0A 3W0. Tel: 306-534-2122. E-mail: spyhill@parklandlibrary.ca.
Open Tues & Thurs 12:30-5:30
STOCKHOLM BRANCH, 202 Ohlen St, Stockholm, S0A 3Y0. Tel: 306-793-2102. E-mail: stockholm@parklandlibrary.ca.
Open Wed & Thurs 10-12 & 12:30-5:30
STRASBOURG BRANCH, 113 Pearson St, Strasbourg, S0G 4V0. Tel: 306-725-3239. E-mail: strasbourg@parklandlibrary.ca.
Open Tues 10:30-2:30 & 3-6, Thurs & Fri 10:30-4:30
STURGIS BRANCH, 222 Main St, Sturgis, S0A 4A0. Tel: 306-548-2824. E-mail: sturgis@parklandlibrary.ca.
Open Tues 2-6, Wed 12-6, Thurs 11-5
THEODORE BRANCH, 102 Main St, Theodore, S0A 4C0. Tel: 306-621-4097. E-mail: theodore@parklandlibrary.ca.
Open Mon 10-12 & 1-5, Tues & Thurs 1-5
WADENA BRANCH, 86 First St NE, Wadena, S0A 4J0. Tel: 306-338-2293. E-mail: wadena@parklandlibrary.ca.
Open Wed & Thurs 12-6, Fri 10-4
WATSON BRANCH, 300 Main St, Watson, S0K 4V0. Tel: 306-287-3642. E-mail: watson@parklandlibrary.ca.
Open Tues-Thurs 11-5
WISHART BRANCH, 111 Main St, Wishart, S0A 4T0. Tel: 306-576-2150. E-mail: wishart@parklandlibrary.ca.
Open Tues & Fri 10-2
WYNYARD BRANCH, 434 Boxworth St, Wynyard, S0A 4T0. Tel: 306-554-3321. E-mail: wynyard@parklandlibrary.ca.
Open Tues 11-6, Wed & Thurs 12-6, Fri & Sat 10-2
YORKTON PUBLIC LIBRARY & REFERENCE CENTRE, 93 Broadway St W, S3N 0L9, SAN 376-2076. Tel: 306-783-3523. FAX: 306-782-5524. E-mail: yorkton@parklandlibrary.ca.
Founded 1912. Pop 20,000; Circ 100,000
Open Mon, Thurs & Fri 9-6, Tues & Wed 9-9, Sat & Sun 1-5

YUKON

Date of Statistics: Not provided.

DAWSON CITY

S DAWSON CITY MUSEUM*, Klondike History Library, 595 Fifth Ave, Y0B 1G0. (Mail add: PO Box 303, Y0B 1G0). Tel: 867-993-5291, Ext 23. FAX: 867-993-5839. E-mail: info@dawsonmuseum.ca. Web Site: www.dawsonmuseum.ca/archives. *Exec Dir,* Alex Somerville; Tel: 867-993-5291, Ext 21, E-mail: asomerville@dawsonmuseum.ca; *Archivist,* Angela Fornelli
Library Holdings: Bk Titles 1,000
Special Collections: Dawson Photog Coll. Oral History
Subject Interests: Local hist
Open Tues-Sat 1-4 (May-Sept)
Restriction: Non-circulating

WHITEHORSE

G DEPARTMENT OF COMMUNITY SERVICES, GOVERNMENT OF YUKON*, Yukon Public Libraries, 1171 First Ave, Y1A 0G9. (Mail add: PO Box 2703, Y1A 2C6), SAN 369-6960. Tel: 867-667-5239. FAX: 867-393-6333. E-mail: whitehorse.library@gov.yk.ca. Web Site: yukon.ca/en/libraries. *Dir, Pub Libr Serv,* Melissa Yu Schott; E-mail: melissa.yuschott@yukon.ca; *Librn,* Joyce Kashman; Tel: 867-332-0970, E-mail: Joyce.Kashman@gov.yk.ca; *Pub Prog Librn,* Mairi Macrae; E-mail: Mairi.Macrae@gov.yk.ca; *Tech Serv Librn,* Debbie Hawco; E-mail: Debbie.Hawco@gov.yk.ca; *Commun Serv,* Don Allen; E-mail: Don.Allen@gov.yk.ca; Staff 13 (MLS 3, Non-MLS 10)
Founded 1962. Pop 36,701; Circ 180,000
Library Holdings: Bk Titles 145,423; Per Subs 340
Special Collections: Northern Books Coll; Yukon History Coll
Subject Interests: Alaskana
Automation Activity & Vendor Info: (Cataloging) TLC (The Library Corporation); (Circulation) TLC (The Library Corporation)
Wireless access
Function: Audio & video playback equip for onsite use, AV serv, Games & aids for people with disabilities, Govt ref serv, ILL available, Large print keyboards, Magnifiers for reading, Photocopying/Printing, Prog for adults, Prog for children & young adult, Ref serv available, Summer reading prog, Telephone ref, Wheelchair accessible
Open Mon-Fri 10-9, Sat 10-6, Sun 1-9
Friends of the Library Group

Branches:

BEAVER CREEK COMMUNITY, Beaver Creek Fire Hall, Beaver Creek, Y0B 1A0. (Mail add: General Delivery, Beaver Creek, Y0B 1A0), SAN 378-1356. Tel: 867-862-7622. FAX: 867-862-7904. E-mail: bclib@klondiker.com.
Open Sat & Sun 9-1

BURWASH LANDING COMMUNITY, 17 Sedata St, Burwash Landing, Y0B 1V0. (Mail add: PO Box 18, Burwash Landing, Y0B 1V0), SAN 378-1372. Tel: 867-841-4707. FAX: 867-841-5904. E-mail: bllib@klondiker.com.
Open Mon 10-1, Tues 3-5, Wed 10:30-1

CARMACKS COMMUNITY, 121 Tantalus Crescent, Carmacks, Y0B 1C0. (Mail add: PO Box 131, Carmacks, Y0B 1C0), SAN 325-4232. Tel: 867-863-5901. FAX: 867-863-5814. E-mail: cmlib@klondiker.com.
Open Mon-Thurs 3:15-8

DAWSON CITY COMMUNITY, Robert Service School, 967 Fifth Ave, Dawson City, Y0B 1G0. (Mail add: PO Box 1410, Dawson City, Y0B 1G0), SAN 369-6995. Tel: 867-993-5571. E-mail: dclib@klondiker.com. Web Site: yukon.ca/en/places/dawson-city-community-library. ; Staff 5 (Non-MLS 5)
Founded 1897. Pop 2,000
Special Collections: Klondike Goldrush Coll
Function: 24/7 Online cat, Bks on CD, Computers for patron use, Free DVD rentals, ILL available, Internet access, Magazines, Online cat, Online ref, Photocopying/Printing, Ref serv available, Res assist avail, Scanner, Summer reading prog, Wheelchair accessible, Writing prog
Open Mon-Fri 12-6:30, Sat 1-4

FARO COMMUNITY, Del Van Gorder School, 447 Campbell St, Faro, Y0B 1K0. (Mail add: PO Box 279, Faro, Y0B 1K0), SAN 369-7053. Tel: 867-994-2684. FAX: 867-994-2236, 867-994-3342. E-mail: flib@klondiker.com.
Open Tues 5pm-7pm, Wed-Fri 4:30-8:30, Sat 11-2

HAINES JUNCTION COMMUNITY, James Smith Bldg, Ste 201A, 112 Haines Rd, Haines Junction, Y0B 1L0. (Mail add: PO Box 5350, Haines Junction, Y0B 1L0), SAN 369-7088. Tel: 867-634-2215. FAX: 867-634-2400. E-mail: hjlib@klondiker.com.
Special Collections: Mountaineering (Kluane National Park Coll)
Open Tues-Thurs 1-5, Fri 10-11 & 1-5, Sat 1-4

ISABELLE PRINGLE COMMUNITY LIBRARY, 1152 Tagish Ave, Carcross, Y0B 1B0, SAN 325-4216. Tel: 867-821-3801. FAX: 867-821-3801. E-mail: iplib@klondiker.com.
Open Wed 2:30-9, Thurs-Sat 2:30-8

MAYO COMMUNITY, Mayo Administration Bldg, 18 Centre St, Mayo, Y0B 1M0. (Mail add: PO Box 158, Mayo, Y0B 1M0), SAN 369-7118. Tel: 867-996-2541. FAX: 867-996-2203. E-mail: mlib@klondiker.com.
Open Mon-Wed 12-5, Thurs 12-4

OLD CROW COMMUNITY, Chief Zzeh Gittlit School, Old Crow, Y0B 1N0. (Mail add: PO Box 101, Old Crow, Y0B 1N0). Tel: 867-966-3031. E-mail: oclib@klondiker.com.
Open Mon & Thurs 7pm-9pm, Sat 4-6

PELLY CROSSING COMMUNITY, Eliza Van Bibber School, Pelly Crossing, Y0B 1P0. (Mail add: PO Box 108, Pelly Crossing, Y0B 1P0). Tel: 867-537-3041. FAX: 867-537-3103. E-mail: pclib@klondiker.com.
Open Tues-Fri 4:30-7:30

ROSS RIVER COMMUNITY, Ross River School, Ross River, Y0B 1S0. (Mail add: General Delivery, Ross River, Y0B 1S0), SAN 329-6199. Tel: 867-969-2909. E-mail: rrlib@klondiker.com.
Open Mon 4-6:30, Wed 4-6, Thurs 6-8:30, Sat 10-1

TAGISH COMMUNITY, Tagish Community Association Bldg, Tagish, Y0B 1T0. (Mail add: PO Box 69, Tagish, Y0B 1T0). Tel: 867-399-3418. E-mail: tglib@klondiker.com.
Special Services for the Blind - Talking bks
Open Wed & Sat 12-5

TESLIN COMMUNITY, Teslin Community Bldg, Teslin, Y0A 1B0. (Mail add: PO Box 58, Teslin, Y0A 1B0), SAN 369-7134. Tel: 867-390-2802. E-mail: tslib@klondiker.com.
Open Mon-Wed 12-5:30, Thurs 9:30-3

WATSON LAKE COMMUNITY, Watson Lake Administration Bldg, 710 Adela Trail, Watson Lake, Y0A 1C0. (Mail add: PO Box 843, Watson Lake, Y0A 1C0), SAN 369-7142. Tel: 867-536-7517. FAX: 867-536-7515. E-mail: wllib@klondiker.com.
Subject Interests: Alaska hwy
Open Tues-Thurs 10-6, Fri & Sat 12:30-4:30
Friends of the Library Group

WHITEHORSE PUBLIC, 1171 Front St, Y1A 0G9. (Mail add: Box 2703 C-23, Y1A 2C6).
Founded 1961. Pop 31,587
Library Holdings: Bk Vols 75,000
Special Collections: Klondike Goldrush Coll. Canadian and Provincial
Automation Activity & Vendor Info: (OPAC) TLC (The Library Corporation)
Function: 24/7 Electronic res, 24/7 Online cat, Adult bk club, Audio & video playback equip for onsite use, Audiobks via web, AV serv, Bks on CD, Children's prog, Computers for patron use, Doc delivery serv, Electronic databases & coll, Free DVD rentals, Holiday prog, ILL available, Internet access, Magazines, Meeting rooms, OverDrive digital audio bks, Photocopying/Printing, Prog for adults, Ref & res, Summer reading prog, Teen prog
Open Mon-Thurs 10-9, Fri-Sun 10-6
Friends of the Library Group

S LEARNING DISABILITES ASSOCIATION OF YUKON, LDAY Resource Library, 128A Copper Rd, Y1A 2Z6. Tel: 867-668-5167. FAX: 867-668-6504. E-mail: office@ldayukon.com. Web Site: www.ldayukon.com/library. *Exec Dir,* Stephanie Hammond; E-mail: ed@ldayukon.com
Founded 1973
Library Holdings: Bk Titles 1,400; Bk Vols 2,200
Wireless access
Restriction: Open by appt only

J YUKON COLLEGE LIBRARY*, 500 College Dr, Y1A 5K4. (Mail add: PO Box 2799, Y1A 5K4), SAN 324-3842. Tel: 867-668-8870. Web Site: www.yukoncollege.yk.ca/student-life/learning-matters/library-services. *Managing Librn,* Duke Burke; Tel: 867-456-8549, E-mail: dburke@yukoncollege.yk.ca; *Circ Tech, Librn,* Genevieve O'Neil; E-mail: goneil@yukoncollege.yk.ca; *Cat/Syst Librn,* Derek Yap; E-mail: dyap@yukoncollege.yk.ca; *Info Literacy, Ref Librn,* Aline Goncalves; E-mail: agoncalves@yukoncollege.yk.ca; *Acq, Ser Tech,* Patricia Boleen; E-mail: pboleen@yukoncollege.yk.ca; Staff 6 (MLS 3, Non-MLS 3)
Founded 1983
Library Holdings: Bk Titles 40,000; Per Subs 500
Special Collections: Northern Economic Development, Northern Studies, Northern Building Construction
Wireless access
Publications: Acquisitions List; Newsletter (Irregular)
Partic in British Columbia Electronic Library Network; Electronic Health Library of British Columbia

G YUKON ENERGY MINES & RESOURCES LIBRARY*, 335-300 Main St, Y1A 2B5. SAN 373-8884. Tel: 867-667-3111. Toll Free Tel: 800-661-0408, Ext 3111. FAX: 867-456-3888. E-mail: emrlibrary@gov.yk.ca. Web Site: yukon.ca/en/department-energy-mines-resources. *Libr Mgr,* Anna Pearson; E-mail: anna.pearson@gov.yk.ca; Staff 3 (MLS 2, Non-MLS 1)
Founded 1991
Library Holdings: Bk Titles 51,000; Per Subs 102
Special Collections: Aerial Photos Coll; Earth Sciences Coll; Map Coll
Automation Activity & Vendor Info: (Acquisitions) Innovative Interfaces, Inc; (Cataloging) Innovative Interfaces, Inc; (Circulation) Innovative Interfaces, Inc; (Serials) Innovative Interfaces, Inc
Wireless access
Open Mon-Fri 8:30-4:30

GL YUKON PUBLIC LAW LIBRARY*, Yukon Law Courts, 2134 Second Ave, Y1A 2C6. (Mail add: Box 2703, J-3C, Y1A 2C6). Tel: 867-667-3086. E-mail: yukon.law.library@yukon.ca. Web Site: yukon.ca/en/public-law-library. *Librn,* Aimee Ellis; *Librn,* Natalie Wing
Library Holdings: Bk Titles 15,000; Per Subs 50
Open Mon-Fri 9-1 & 2-4

LIBRARY INFORMATION

Networks and Consortia

Library Schools and Training Courses

Library Systems

Libraries for the Blind
and Physically Handicapped

Libraries Serving the
Deaf and Hearing Impaired

State and Provincial
Public Library Agencies

State School Library Agencies

National Interlibrary Loan Codes
for the United States

NETWORKS, CONSORTIA & OTHER COOPERATIVE LIBRARY ORGANIZATIONS

These organizations are listed alphabetically by state or province.

ALABAMA

ALABAMA HEALTH LIBRARIES ASSOCIATION, INC*, (ALHeLa), University of Alabama, Lister Hill Library, 1530 Third Ave S, Birmingham, 35294-0013. SAN 372-8218. Tel: 205-975-8313. FAX: 205-934-2230. Web Site: alhela.org/. *Pres,* Andrea Wright; Tel: 205-348-1335, E-mail: alwright1@ua.edu
Founded 1980
Member Libraries: 43
Primary Functions: Increase & maintain the total health science information resources & services available; strengthen & promote existing health libraries & the professional skills of health information personnel by providing opportunities for continuing education; encourage the formation of new libraries & provide consulting services to developing Alabama health science libraries; through joint effort, utilize more effectively the resources of individual libraries

JEFFERSON COUNTY LIBRARY COOPERATIVE INC, (JCLC), 2100 Park Place, Birmingham, 35203-2794. Tel: 205-226-3615. FAX: 205-226-3617. Web Site: www.jclc.org. *Dir,* Tobin Cataldo; *Syst Librn, Web Serv Mgr,* Elizabeth Swift
Founded 1985
Member Libraries: 37
Primary Functions: Foster a culture of collaboration & community; support cooperative collection development & resource sharing; provide professional development, training & networking opportunities; adopt those technologies & services which enhance the user experience; practice fiscally responsible stewardship of member library resources

LIBRARY MANAGEMENT NETWORK, INC, (LMN), 1405 Plaza St SE, Decatur, 35603. SAN 322-3906. Tel: 256-822-2371. Administration E-mail: charlotte@lmnconnect.org. Web Site: lmnconnect.org. *Syst Coordr,* Charlotte Moncrief; E-mail: charlotte@lmnconnect.org
Founded 1983
Member Libraries: 3
Primary Functions: To operate an automated integrated library system; to offer access to the collective resources of the region to members & to the public via maintaining a web site; to establish a common database among members using MARC standards; to provide on a cooperative basis, automated management services for member libraries, i.e. circulation, MARC bibliographic processing, online public access catalog, federated searching & web-mail services.

NETWORK OF ALABAMA ACADEMIC LIBRARIES*, c/o Alabama Commission on Higher Education, 100 N Union St, Montgomery, 36104. (Mail add: PO Box 302000, Montgomery, 36130-2000), SAN 322-4570. Tel: 334-242-2211. FAX: 334-242-0270. Web Site: libguides.jsu.edu/NAAL. *Dir,* Sheila Snow-Croft; E-mail: sheila.snow-croft@ache.edu
Founded 1984
Member Libraries: 21 acad, 8 affiliates, 1 pub & 6 spec
Primary Functions: Collection development; digital collection development; interlibrary loan; continuing education; preservation; electronic access to information

ALASKA

ALASKA LIBRARY NETWORK*, (ALN), PO Box 230051, Anchorage, 99523-0051. SAN 371-0688. Tel: 907-786-0618. FAX: 907-786-1834. E-mail: info@aklib.net. Web Site: aklib.net. *Exec Dir,* Steve Rollins
Founded 2007
Member Libraries: 65
Primary Functions: Coordinate statewide digital resources including EBSCO & other commercial databases; manage the Alaska Digital Library & OCLC group contract; fiscal & administrative agent for Alaskan library group services & cooperative projects

CALIFORNIA

CALIFA*, 330 Townsend St, Ste 133, San Francisco, 94107. Tel: 888-239-2289. Toll Free Tel: 888-239-2289 (CA only). E-mail: califa@califa.org. Web Site: www.califa.org. *Exec Dir,* Paula MacKinnon; E-mail: pmackinnon@califa.org; *Asst Dir,* Veronda Pitchford; E-mail: veronda@califa.org; *Broadband Project Mgr,* Christian DeLay; E-mail: christian@califa.org
Founded 2003
Member Libraries: 250
Primary Functions: Delivery of cost effective services for members

CONSUMER HEALTH INFORMATION PROGRAM & SERVICES*, (CHIPS), 12350 Imperial Hwy, Norwalk, 90650. SAN 372-8110. Tel: 562-868-4003. Reference E-mail: referenceservices@library.lacounty.gov. Web Site: lacountylibrary.org/collections.
Founded 1976
Member Libraries: 88 county
Primary Functions: Provide information & extended reference service on health, diseases, disorders, types of therapy, prescription drugs & physician credentials

49-99 COOPERATIVE LIBRARY SYSTEM*, c/o Southern California Library Cooperative, 254 N Lake Ave, Pasadena, 91101. SAN 301-6218. Tel: 626-359-6111. FAX: 626-283-5949. *Exec Dir,* Diane Z Bednarski; E-mail: dbednarski@socallibraries.org
Founded 1977
Member Libraries: 6
Primary Functions: Provide communication and delivery services to member libraries; administer grant projects

GOLD COAST LIBRARY NETWORK*, 3437 Empresa Dr, Ste C, San Luis Obispo, 93401-7355. Tel: 805-543-6082. FAX: 805-543-9487. Web Site: www.goldcoastlibraries.org. *Admin Dir,* Maureen Theobald; E-mail: mtheobald@blackgold.org
Member Libraries: 11 acad, 8 pub & 19 spec
Primary Functions: Serves academic, public & special libraries in San Luis Obispo, Santa Barbara & Ventura counties & provides services that facilitate resource sharing & connectivity among its members

NORTHERN & CENTRAL CALIFORNIA PSYCHOLOGY LIBRARIES*, (NCCPL), c/o Wright Institute Library, 2728 Durant Ave, Berkeley, 94704. SAN 371-9006. Web Site: www.nccpl.org. *Pres,* Jason Strauss; Tel: 510-841-9230, E-mail: jstrauss@wi.edu
Founded 1985
Member Libraries: 18 acad & med
Primary Functions: Facilitate exchange of information & resources among Northern California libraries specializing in psychology studies; develop policies for resource sharing

NORTHERN CALIFORNIA ASSOCIATION OF LAW LIBRARIES*, (NOCALL), 268 Bush St, No 4006, San Francisco, 94104. SAN 323-5777. Administration E-mail: admin@nocall.org. Web Site: nocall.org. *Pres,* Delia Montesinos; E-mail: president@nocall.org; *VPres,* Jeremy Sullivan
Founded 1979
Member Libraries: 400
Primary Functions: Union list for participating libraries; consultant committees for law firms; educational seminars relating to law librarianship; government relations committee; Internet committee

PENINSULA LIBRARY SYSTEM, 32 W 25th Ave, Ste 201, Suite 201, San Mateo, 94403-4000. SAN 371-5035. Tel: 650-349-5538. FAX: 650-349-5089. Web Site: plsinfo.org. *Exec Dir,* Carol Frost; E-mail: frost@plpinfo.org; *Dir, Info Tech,* Farrukh Farid; E-mail: farid@plsinfo.org; *Database Mgr,* Vanessa Walden; E-mail: walden@plsinfo.org
Founded 1982
Member Libraries: 9 incl col, commun & pub
Primary Functions: Shared automated circulation, cataloging & online catalog system

SANTA CLARITA INTERLIBRARY NETWORK*, (SCILNET), College of the Canyons, Valencia Campus, 26455 Rockwell Canyon Rd, Santa Clarita, 91355-1899. SAN 371-8964. Tel: 661-362-3758. FAX: 661-362-2719. *Head Librn,* Peter Hepburn; E-mail: peter.hepburn@canyons.edu
Founded 1985
Member Libraries: 16 acad, pub, sch & spec
Primary Functions: Improve quality of service to citizens of Santa Clarita through interlibrary cooperation, including mutual borrowing privileges, union listings, shared technology & continuing education workshops

SERRA COOPERATIVE LIBRARY SYSTEM*, c/o SCLC, 254 N Lake Ave, No 874, Pasadena, 91101. SAN 301-3510. Tel: 626-283-5949. Web Site: www.serralib.org. *Exec Dir,* Diane Z Bednarski; E-mail: dbednarski@socallibraries.org
Member Libraries: 13
Primary Functions: Provide communication & delivery services to member libraries; administer grant projects

SOUTHERN CALIFORNIA LIBRARY COOPERATIVE*, (SCLC), 254 N Lake Ave, No 874, Pasadena, 91101. SAN 371-3865. Tel: 626-283-5949. FAX: 626-283-5949. E-mail: sclcadmin@socallibraries.org. Web Site: www.socallibraries.org. *Interim Exec Dir,* Wayne Walker; E-mail: wwalker@socallibraries.org
Founded 1965
Member Libraries: 40
Primary Functions: Provide communication & delivery services to member libraries; administer grant projects

STATEWIDE CALIFORNIA ELECTRONIC LIBRARY CONSORTIUM*, (SCELC), 617 S Olive St, Ste 1210, Los Angeles, 90014. Tel: 310-775-9807. Toll Free FAX: 888-715-7167. E-mail: officemanager@scelc.org. Web Site: scelc.org. *Exec Dir,* Teri Oaks Gallaway; E-mail: teri@scelc.org; *Libr Relations Mgr,* Eric Chao; E-mail: eric@scelc.org
Member Libraries: 300
Primary Functions: To collaborate on access to & the effective use of library resources & services

COLORADO

COLORADO ALLIANCE OF RESEARCH LIBRARIES*, 3801 E Florida Ave, Ste 515, Denver, 80210. SAN 322-3760. Tel: 303-759-3399. FAX: 303-759-3363. E-mail: help@coalliance.org. Web Site: www.coalliance.org. *Exec Dir,* George Machovec; Tel: 303-759-3399, Ext 101, E-mail: george@coalliance.org; *Asst Dir,* Rose Nelson; Tel: 303-759-3399, Ext 103, E-mail: rose@coalliance.org
Founded 1974
Member Libraries: 16
Primary Functions: Vehicle for members to cooperate for the benefit of their users & the public; Prospector Union Catalog, Cooperative purchasing of e-resources; Alliance Shared Print Trust, Software Development such as a library content comparison system & work in Bibframe & linked data. Includes 15 academic libraries & one public library in Colorado & Wyoming

COLORADO ASSOCIATION OF LAW LIBRARIES*, c/o William A Wise Law Library, 2450 Kittredge Loop Dr, 402 UCB, Boulder, 80309. SAN 322-4325. FAX: 303-492-2707. E-mail: coall@coallnet.org. Web Site: www.coallnet.org. *Pres,* Rachel Nelson; E-mail: nelson@narf.org
Founded 1977
Member Libraries: 100
Primary Functions: General networking & resource sharing; continuing education; information programs

COLORADO COUNCIL OF MEDICAL LIBRARIANS*, (CCML), PO Box 101058, Denver, 80210-1058. SAN 370-0755. Tel: 303-724-2124. FAX: 303-724-2154. E-mail: ccml.internet@gmail.com. Web Site: www.ccmlnet.org. *Pres,* Ben Harnke; E-mail: ben.harnke@ucdenver.edu
Founded 1957
Member Libraries: 108 med
Primary Functions: Provides opportunities for professional growth through networking, educational & organizational participation; collaborates with other organizations to increase public understanding & support of our profession; monitors developments in health care & information science & assesses their impact on the profession & its future.

COLORADO LIBRARY CONSORTIUM*, (CLiC), 7400 E Arapahoe Rd, Ste 75, Centennial, 80112. SAN 371-3970. Tel: 303-422-1150. Toll Free Tel: 888-206-2695. FAX: 303-431-9752. Web Site: www.clicweb.org. *Exec Dir,* Jim Duncan; E-mail: jduncan@clicweb.org; *Dep Dir,* Sara Wright; E-mail: swright@clicweb.org
Founded 2004
Member Libraries: 453
Primary Functions: Colleague on Call Consulting; Talent Development, Training & Continuing Education; Cooperative Purchasing; Fiscal Agency & related Support Services; Management of statewide courier system including links to other states and a discarded book-recycle program; Management of a Koha-based ILS for more than 150 member libraries

CONNECTICUT

BIBLIOMATION INC*, 24 Wooster Ave, Waterbury, 06708. Tel: 203-577-4070. Toll Free Tel: 800-327-4765 (CT only). FAX: 203-577-4077. Web Site: biblio.org. *Exec Dir,* Carl DeMilia; Tel: 203-577-4070, Ext 106, E-mail: cdemilia@biblio.org; *Dir, User Serv,* Amy Terlaga; Tel: 203-577-4070, Ext 101, E-mail: terlaga@biblio.org; *Bus Mgr,* Debbie Daiss; Tel: 203-577-4070, Ext 104, E-mail: ddaiss@biblio.org
Founded 1980
Member Libraries: 68 pub, 8 sch & 3 spec
Primary Functions: Evergreen open source integrated library system; database services; integration of community resources; network support & maintenance; technology management support

CONNECTICUT LIBRARY CONSORTIUM*, 234 Court St, Middletown, 06457-3304. SAN 322-0389. Tel: 860-344-8777. FAX: 860-344-9199. E-mail: clc@ctlibrarians.org. Web Site: www.ctlibrarians.org. *Exec Dir,* Ellen Paul; E-mail: epaul@ctlibrarians.org
Founded 2003
Member Libraries: Over 800 Connecticut public, academic, school, & special libraries
Primary Functions: Statewide membership collaborative serving all types of Connecticut libraries by helping them strengthen their ability to serve their users.

CONNECTICUT STATE COLLEGE & UNIVERSITY LIBRARY CONSORTIUM*, 61 Woodland St, Hartford, 06105. Tel: 860-723-0168. Web Site: www.ct.edu/libraries. *Prog Mgr,* Patrick Carr; E-mail: carrp@ct.edu; *Syst Librn,* Travis Feder; Tel: 860-723-0273, E-mail: federt@ct.edu
Member Libraries: 18
Primary Functions: Empowering library collaboration in support of success, equity, diversity, social justice, and access to resources that spark creativity and intellectual enrichment

CTW LIBRARY CONSORTIUM*, Wesleyan University, Olin Memorial Library, 252 Church St, Middletown, 06459. SAN 329-4587. Tel: 860-685-3887. FAX: 860-685-2661. *Access & Delivery Librn,* Nathan Mealey; E-mail: nmealey@wesleyan.edu
Founded 1987
Member Libraries: 3
Primary Functions: CTW Library Consortium, consisting of Connecticut College in New London, Trinity College in Hartford, and Wesleyan University in Middletown, CT. Shared computer system; resource sharing through a delivery service; FAX network

LIBRARIES ONLINE, INC*, (LION), 100 Riverview Ctr, Ste 252, Middletown, 06457. SAN 322-3922. Tel: 860-347-1704. FAX: 860-346-3707. Web Site: www.lioninc.org. *Exec Dir,* Joseph Farara; E-mail: jfarara@lioninc.org; *Assoc Dir,* Andrew Gardner; E-mail: agardner@lioninc.org
Founded 1982
Member Libraries: 22
Primary Functions: Provides members with an integrated library system, shared bibliographic database & cataloging utility, telecommunications, wide & local area network services, internet, email, web services & electronic databases

LIBRARY CONNECTION, INC*, 599 Matianuck Ave, Windsor, 06095-3567. Tel: 860-937-8263. FAX: 860-298-5328. Web Site: www.libraryconnection.info. *Bibliog Serv, Syst Librn,* Judy Njoroge; *Pub Serv, Syst Librn,* Sam Cook; E-mail: scook@libraryconnection.info; *Pub Serv Spec,* Max Rowe; *Cataloger,* Yi Liu
Founded 1981
Member Libraries: 30
Primary Functions: Shared online public access catalog & information system (SIERRA/ENCORE)

DISTRICT OF COLUMBIA

ASSOCIATION OF RESEARCH LIBRARIES*, (ARL), 21 Dupont Circle NW, Ste 800, Washington, 20036. Tel: 202-296-2296. FAX: 202-872-0884. E-mail: webmgr@arl.org. Web Site: www.arl.org. *Exec Dir,* Andrew Pace; E-mail: andrew@arl.org; *Dep Exec Dir,* Sue Baughman; E-mail: sue@arl.org; *Sr Dir, Diversity, Equity & Inclusion,* DeLa Dos

COUNCIL FOR CHRISTIAN COLLEGES & UNIVERSITIES*, 321 Eighth St NE, Washington, 20002. SAN 322-0524. Tel: 202-546-8713. FAX: 202-546-8913. E-mail: council@cccu.org. Web Site: www.cccu.org. *Pres,* Shirley V Hoogstra
Founded 1976
Member Libraries: 105 col
Primary Functions: Sharing resources that deal with the integration of Christian faith, learning & living; publication of Choose a Christian College

FEDERAL LIBRARY & INFORMATION NETWORK, (FEDLINK), Library of Congress FEDLINK, Adams Bldg, Rm 217, 101 Independence Ave SE, Washington, 20540-4935. SAN 322-0761. Tel: 202-707-4800. FAX: 202-707-4818. Web Site: loc.gov/flicc. *Exec Dir,* Melissa Blaschke; Tel: 202-707-2457, E-mail: mebl@loc.gov; *Admin Officer,* Tarsha Moon; Tel: 202-707-9452, E-mail: tamo@loc.gov; *Mgr,* Jocelyn Shapiro; Tel: 202-707-4168, E-mail: jshapiro@loc.gov
Founded 1965
Member Libraries: 1355 fed libr & info centers
Primary Functions: To achieve better utilization of federal library & information resources; to provide the most cost-effective & efficient administrative mechanism for providing necessary services & materials to federal libraries & information centers; to serve as a forum for discussion of federal library & information policies, programs & procedures; to help inform Congress, federal agencies & others concerned with libraries & information centers

WASHINGTON THEOLOGICAL CONSORTIUM*, 487 Michigan Ave NE, Washington, 20017-1585. SAN 322-0842. Tel: 202-832-2675. FAX: 202-526-0818. E-mail: wtc@washtheocon.org. Web Site: www.washtheocon.org. *Exec Dir,* Larry Golemon; E-mail: lgolemon@washtheocon.org
Founded 1967
Member Libraries: 16
Primary Functions: Interlibrary loan; acquisitions; Union List of Serials

FLORIDA

CONSORTIUM OF SOUTHERN BIOMEDICAL LIBRARIES*, (CONBLS), c/o Harriet F Ginsburg Health Sciences Library, 6850 Lake Nona Blvd, Orlando, 32867. SAN 370-7717. Web Site: musc.libguides.com/conbls. *Chair,* Nadine Dexter; Tel: 407-266-1421, E-mail: nadine.dexter@ucf.edu
Founded 1982
Member Libraries: 21 med
Primary Functions: To exchange information & share resources; to participate in cooperative programs

FLORIDA LIBRARY INFORMATION NETWORK, (FLIN), State Library & Archives of Florida, R A Gray Bldg, 500 S Bronough St, Tallahassee, 32399-0250. SAN 322-0869. Tel: 850-245-6600. E-mail: state.library@dos.myflorida.com. Web Site: dos.myflorida.com/library-archives/library-development/digital/resource-sharing/flin. *Bur Chief,* Cathy Moloney; Tel: 850-245-6687, E-mail: cathy.moloney@dos.myflorida.com
Founded 1968
Member Libraries: 84 acad, 1 inst, 1 K-12, 2 media ctr, 123 pub, 32 spec & 3 state agencies
Primary Functions: Statewide cooperative for interlibrary loan & resource sharing. The State Library serves as network headquarters; receives title, photocopy & subject requests by e-mail, OCLC & FAX from over 525 libraries in Florida & fills & refers them to member libraries; using FLIN protocols based on geographic proximity

FLORIDA VIRTUAL CAMPUS, LIBRARY SERVICES*, (FLVC), 1753 W Paul Dirac Dr, Tallahassee, 32310. Tel: 850-922-6044. FAX: 850-922-4869. Web Site: libraries.flvc.org/. *Exec Dir,* Elijah Scott; E-mail: EScott@flvc.org
Member Libraries: 40 acad inst, 150 col campus libr
Primary Functions: Provide catalogue, databases, digital services to colleges, as well as an integrated library system

LIBRARY & INFORMATION RESOURCES NETWORK*, (LIRN), 25400 US 19 N, Ste 220, Clearwater, 33763. Tel: 727-536-0214. FAX: 727-530-3126. E-mail: sales@lirn.net, support@lirn.net. Web Site: www.lirn.net. *Pres & Chief Exec Officer,* Andrew Anderson; E-mail: andrew@lirn.net
Founded 1997
Member Libraries: 296 acad

MIDWEST ARCHIVES CONFERENCE, (MAC), 2598 E Sunrise Blvd, Ste 2104, Fort Lauderdale, 33304. E-mail: membership@midwestarchives.org. Web Site: www.midwestarchives.org.
Founded 1972
Member Libraries: 800
Primary Functions: To support individuals & institutions in the archives field through advocacy, education, publication & networking

NORTHEAST FLORIDA LIBRARY INFORMATION NETWORK*, (NEFLIN), 2233 Park Ave, Ste 402, Orange Park, 32073. Tel: 904-278-5620. FAX: 904-278-5625. E-mail: office@neflin.org. Web Site: www.neflin.org. *Exec Dir,* Brad Ward; E-mail: brad@neflin.org; *Continuing Educ Coordr,* Raymond Neal; E-mail: raymond@neflin.org
Founded 1992
Member Libraries: 54 (24 acad, 19 pub, 8 sch & 3 spec)
Primary Functions: Establish a member expert database; facilitate multitype networking opportunities; develop networks for school & special libraries; expand training opportunities; assist libraries with staff training; enhance technology training; create a toolkit for advocacy specific to Florida; support member collaboration with Friends Groups & Library Advisory Boards; assist members with promotion & demonstrating value; offer activities that highlight emerging technologies; support innovation in member libraries; assist members with developing innovative funding streams

PANHANDLE LIBRARY ACCESS NETWORK*, (PLAN), Five Miracle Strip Loop, Ste 8, Panama City Beach, 32407-8410. SAN 370-047X. Tel: 850-233-9051. FAX: 850-235-2286. Web Site: www.plan.lib.fl.us. *Exec Dir,* Charles Mayberry; E-mail: cmayberry@plan.lib.fl.us
Founded 1991
Member Libraries: 46 acad, pub, sch & spec
Primary Functions: To provide services & programs which promote & enhance resource sharing amoung libraries in a 16-county region of the Florida Panhandle; Current projects include cooperative purchasing, library staff training, conferences, scholarships, digitization support, consulting for libraries on technical and organizational issues.

SOUTHEAST FLORIDA LIBRARY INFORMATION NETWORK, INC*, (SEFLIN), Florida Atlantic University, Wimberly Library, Office 452, 777 Glades Rd, Boca Raton, 33431. SAN 370-0666. Tel: 561-208-0984. Toll Free Tel: 877-733-5460. FAX: 561-208-0995. Web Site: www.seflin.org. *Exec Dir,* Brock Peoples; E-mail: peoples@seflin.org; *Dir, Staff Develop,* Sara Gassaway; E-mail: gassaway@seflin.org; *Dir, Res Sharing,* Melanie Lorraine Zaskey; E-mail: zaskey@seflin.org; *Mrg, Admin Serv,* Irina Galilova; E-mail: galilova@seflin.org; *Mgr, Communications, Tech Mgr,* Anna Arenas; E-mail: arenas@seflin.org
Founded 1984
Member Libraries: 39 acad, pub & sch
Primary Functions: To cultivate cooperation & coordination among libraries of all types, nurture efficient & effective information resource sharing; advance technological innovation; provide staff development opportunities; advocate for our libraries & their patrons

SOUTHWEST FLORIDA LIBRARY NETWORK*, (SWFLN), 13120 Westlinks Tr, Unit 3, Fort Myers, 33913. Tel: 239-313-6338. Toll Free FAX: 888-662-3233. Web Site: www.swfln.org. *Exec Dir,* Brian Chase; *Board Pres,* Anthony Valenti; E-mail: anthony.valenti@fsw.edu
Founded 1993
Member Libraries: 31
Primary Functions: Provide member libraries with cost-effective sharing of library materials, staff training & evaluation; help libraries make the best technology decisions

TAMPA BAY LIBRARY CONSORTIUM, INC, 1600 E 8th Ave, No A200, Tampa, 33605. (Mail add: PO Box 75498, Tampa, 33675), SAN 322-371X. Tel: 813-622-8252, Ext 102. Web Site: www.tblc.org. *Exec Dir,* Dr James H Walther; E-mail: jim@tblc.org
Founded 1979
Member Libraries: 102 acad, pub, sch & spec
Primary Functions: Providing essential services, connecting staff through active engagement; creating an environment of continuous learning & innovation

GEORGIA

ASSOCIATION OF SOUTHEASTERN RESEARCH LIBRARIES, (ASERL), c/o Robert W Woodruff Library, 540 Asbury Circle, Ste 316, Atlanta, 30322-1006. SAN 322-1555. Tel: 404-727-0137. Web Site: www.aserl.org. *Pres,* Jeff Steely; *Exec Dir,* John Burger; E-mail: jburger@aserl.org
Founded 1956
Member Libraries: 38 res libr in 12 states
Primary Functions: To promote cooperative enterprises among member research libraries

ATLANTA REGIONAL COUNCIL FOR HIGHER EDUCATION*, (ARCHE), 133 Peachtree St, Ste 4925, Atlanta, 30303. SAN 322-0990. Tel: 404-651-2668. FAX: 404-880-9816. E-mail: arche@atlantahighered.org. Web Site: www.atlantahighered.org. *Exec Dir,* Tracy Brantley
Founded 1938
Member Libraries: 19 pub & pvt col & univ, plus six affiliated libr
Primary Functions: Interlibrary loan & interlibrary use; other cooperative activities in areas of civil rights holdings & professional development

GOLD RESOURCE SHARING NETWORK FOR GEORGIA'S LIBRARIES*, (GOLD), c/o Georgia Public Library Service, 2872 Woodcock Blvd, Ste 250, Atlanta, 30341. SAN 322-094X. Tel: 404-235-7128. FAX: 404-235-7201. Web Site: georgialibraries.org/gold/. *Project Mgr,* Elaine Hardy; Tel: 404-235-7128, E-mail: ehardy@georgialibraries.org
Member Libraries: 211 acad, county, hosp, pub, regional, sch & spec libraries
Primary Functions: Statewide interlibrary lending network; group access capability through OCLC

LYRASIS*, 1438 W Peachtree St NW, Ste 150, Atlanta, 30309. SAN 322-0974. Toll Free Tel: 800-999-8558. FAX: 404-892-7879. Web Site: lyrasisnow.org, www.lyrasis.org. *Chief Exec Officer,* Robert Miller; Tel: 800-999-8558, Ext 4898, E-mail: robert.miller@lyrasis.org; *Chief Financial Officer,* Vern Ritter; Tel: 800-999-8558, Ext 4828, E-mail: vern.ritter@lyrasis.org
Founded 1973
Member Libraries: 2700 col, commun col, pub, sch, spec & state
Primary Functions: A non-profit, mission-driven leader in open technologies, hosting, data migration, content licensing, and community supported software programs for libraries, archives, museums and research organizations worldwide.

PUBLIC INFORMATION NETWORK FOR ELECTRONIC SERVICES*, (PINES), Georgia Public Library Service, 2872 Woodcock Blvd, Ste 250, Atlanta, 30341. Tel: 404-235-7200. Web Site: pines.georgialibraries.org. *Prog Dir,* Elizabeth McKinney; Tel: 404-235-7141, E-mail: emckinney@georgialibraries.org; *Prog Mgr,* Terran McCanna; Tel: 404-235-7138, E-mail: tmccanna@georgialibraries.org; *Syst Adminr,* Chris Sharp; Tel: 404-235-7147, E-mail: csharp@georgialibraries.org
Founded 1999
Member Libraries: 300 (incl 60 libr syst
Primary Functions: PINES (Public Information Network for Electronic Services) is Georgia's "borderless library" system that allows PINES card holders free access to books & other materials in all member libraries & affiliated service locations throughout the state.

HAWAII

HAWAII-PACIFIC CHAPTER OF THE MEDICAL LIBRARY ASSOCIATION, (HPC-MLA), Health Sciences Library, 651 Ilalo St MEB, Honolulu, 96813. SAN 371-3946. Tel: 808-692-0810. FAX: 808-692-1244. E-mail: hpchmla@gmail.com. Web Site: hpcmla.mlanet.org. *Chair,* Melissa Kahili-Heede; E-mail: mkahili@hawaii.edu; *Continuing Educ Chair,* Lauree H Ohigashi Oasay; E-mail: luree@hawaii.edu
Founded 1969
Member Libraries: 27
Primary Functions: Promote professional excellence among health care information providers; offer opportunities for educational & professional growth; provide leadership in the health care information field in Hawaii & the Pacific; provide a forum for the exchange of ideas & information; promote cooperation among health science libraries; represent the chapter & its members before the Medical Library Association & other organizations

IDAHO

COOPERATIVE INFORMATION NETWORK, (CIN), Community Library Network, Post Falls Branch, 821 N Spokane St, Post Falls, 83854. SAN 323-7656. Web Site: cinlibraries.org. *Pres,* Michael Priest; Tel: 208-769-2315, Ext 436, E-mail: mpriest@cdalibrary.org
Founded 1984
Member Libraries: 15
Primary Functions: Shared automated database for cataloging, circulation, OPAC

LIBRARY CONSORTIUM OF EASTERN IDAHO*, (LCEI), 110 N State, Rigby, 83442-1313. SAN 323-7699. Tel: 208-745-8231. Web Site: lcei.lili.org. *Pres,* Marilyn Kamoe; E-mail: rcity1@ida.net; *Treas,* Trina Bonman; E-mail: tbonman@marchallpl.org
Founded 1999
Member Libraries: 20 pub
Primary Functions: Shared automated circulation system

LYNX! CONSORTIUM*, c/o Boise Public Library, 715 S Capitol Blvd, Boise, 83702-7195. SAN 375-0086. Tel: 208-384-4238, 208-384-4485. FAX: 208-384-4025. Web Site: lynx.lili.org, www.boisepubliclibrary.org. *Dir,* Jessica Dorr; E-mail: jdorr@cityofboise.org
Founded 1979
Member Libraries: 11
Primary Functions: Shared automated circulation & online public access catalog

ILLINOIS

AMERICAN THEOLOGICAL LIBRARY ASSOCIATION*, (Atla), 200 S Wacker Dr, Ste 3100, Chicago, 60606-5829. SAN 371-9022. Tel: 872-310-4200. Toll Free Tel: 888-665-2852. E-mail: connect@atla.com. Web Site: www.atla.com. *Exec Dir,* Brenda Bailey-Hainer; Tel: 872-310-4229, E-mail: bbailey-hainer@atla.com; *Dir, Member Programs,* Gillian Harrison Cain; Tel: 872-310-4215, E-mail: gcain@atla.com
Founded 1946
Member Libraries: 321 libr & 460 individuals
Primary Functions: Foster professional growth of members; facilitate closer working relationship among members; provide continuing education programs; interpret role of libraries in theological and religious studies education; improve theological and religious studies libraries; develop & implement standards for theological & religious studies libraries & librarians; support scholarly communication in religious studies including creation, dissemination, transformation & preservation of information; create scholarly tools & aids; promote research & experimental projects including digital humanities; work with other scholarly or learned societies in bibliographic control & dissemination of religious studies information; support & aid education for theological and religious studies librarianship worldwide

ASSOCIATION OF CHICAGO THEOLOGICAL SCHOOLS*, (ACTS), Univ of St Mary of the Lake, 1000 E Maple Ave, Mundelein, 60060. Web Site: www.actschicago.org/libraries/library-locations-and-hours. *Coordr,* Jennifer Ould; E-mail: jould@mccormick.edu
Founded 1968
Member Libraries: 12
Primary Functions: Provides student cross registration; library cooperation; faculty interest groups; joint programs

BIG TEN ACADEMIC ALLIANCE, (BTAA), 1819 S Neil St, Ste D, Champaign, 61820-7271. Tel: 217-333-8475. FAX: 217-244-7127. E-mail: info@btaa.org. Web Site: www.btaa.org. *Exec Dir,* Keith A Marshall, PhD; Tel: 217-244-5756, E-mail: keith.marshall@btaa.org; *Dir, Libr Initiatives,* Maurice York; Tel: 217-300-0945, E-mail: maurice.york@btaa.org
Founded 1958
Member Libraries: 15 univ
Primary Functions: Interlibrary lending network; collaboration on content licensing; increasing cataloging capacity through shared expertise in over 40 languages; shared purchasing & investment for building library collections; seeking sustainable business models for strengthening open scholarship; pilot in purchasing e-book content universally available across institutions

CENTER FOR RESEARCH LIBRARIES*, 6050 S Kenwood, Chicago, 60637-2804. SAN 322-1032. Tel: 773-955-4545. Toll Free Tel: 800-621-6044. FAX: 773-955-4339. Web Site: www.crl.edu. *Pres,* Jacob Nadal; E-mail: jnadal@crl.edu
Founded 1949
Member Libraries: 220 col, independent res librs & univ
Primary Functions: Houses, preserves & circulates research materials for use by member libraries; purchases materials for cooperative use

CONSORTIUM OF ACADEMIC & RESEARCH LIBRARIES IN ILLINOIS, (CARLI), 1704 Interstate Dr, Champaign, 61822. SAN 322-3736. Tel: 217-244-7593. Toll Free Tel: 866-904-5843. FAX: 217-244-4664. E-mail: support@carli.illinois.edu. Web Site: www.carli.illinois.edu. *Sr Dir,* Anne Craig; Tel: 217-300-0375, E-mail: abcraig@uillinois.edu; *Dir, Coll Serv,* Elizabeth Clarage; Tel: 217-300-2624, E-mail: clarage@uillinois.edu; *Dir, Membership & Communications,* Margaret Chambers; Tel: 217-333-2618, E-mail: mchamber@uillinois.edu; *Asst Dir, Electronic Resources,* Jenny Taylor; Tel: 217-265-8437, E-mail: emanuelj@uillinois.edu
Founded 2005
Member Libraries: 128
Primary Functions: Electronic resource purchases; collection assessment; union catalog/resource sharing services; management of ILDS

EAST CENTRAL ILLINOIS CONSORTIUM, (ECIC), c/o CARLE Foundation Hospital, 611 W Park St, Urbana, 61801. SAN 322-1040. Tel: 217-383-4513. *Coordr,* Frances Drone-Silvers; E-mail: frances.drone-silvers@carle.com
Founded 1975
Member Libraries: 10 acad, med & spec
Primary Functions: Interlibrary loan; reference

ILLINOIS LIBRARY & INFORMATION NETWORK*, (ILLINET), c/o Illinois State Library, Gwendolyn Brooks Bldg, 300 S Second St, Springfield, 62701-1796. SAN 322-1148. Tel: 217-785-5600. Web Site: www.cyberdriveillinois.com/departments/library/libraries/illinet.html. *Dir,* Greg McCormick; Tel: 217-782-3504, E-mail: gmccormick@ilsos.gov; *Communications Mgr,* Kyle Peebles; Tel: 217-558-4029, E-mail: kpeebles@ilsos.gov
Founded 1975
Member Libraries: 5150 acad, pub, sch & spec librs, 3 libr systs
Primary Functions: Interlibrary loan; cooperative reference; access to research & reference centers; delivery; cooperative collection development; continuing education; services to the blind & physically handicapped; access to OCLC & staff support for training & administration of its use; access to electronic resources

LIBRAS, INC, c/o North Central College, 30 N Brainard St, Naperville, 60540. SAN 322-1172. E-mail: communications@libras.org. Web Site: libras.org. *Pres,* Michelle Boule-Smith; E-mail: mlboulesmith@noctrl.edu; *Dir, Communications,* Shoshana Frank; E-mail: shoshanafrank@aurora.edu
Founded 1965
Member Libraries: 20
Primary Functions: Resource sharing; staff development & continuing education

MEDICAL LIBRARY ASSOCIATION*, (MLA), 225 W Wacker Dr, Ste 650, Chicago, 60606-1210. Tel: 312-419-9094. FAX: 312-419-8950. E-mail: websupport@mail.mlahq.org. Web Site: www.mlanet.org. *Exec Dir,* Kevin Baliozian; E-mail: baliozian@mail.mlahq.org
Founded 1898
Member Libraries: 400
Primary Functions: Educates health information professionals, supports health information research, & promotes access to the world's health sciences information

NETWORK OF ILLINOIS LEARNING RESOURCES IN COMMUNITY COLLEGES*, (NILRC), c/o Kishwaukee College, 21193 Malta Rd, Malta, 60150. (Mail add: PO Box 5365, Buffalo Grove, 60089). Tel: 262-287-8017. Web Site: nilrc.org. *Dir, Member Relations,* Lois Bruno; E-mail: director@nilrc.org
Founded 1975
Member Libraries: 42 acad
Primary Functions: Enhance the service provided by post-secondary resource center libraries & alternative delivery programs to their institutions & respective communities

ROCK RIVER LIBRARY CONSORTIUM*, c/o Sterling Public Library, 102 W Third St, Sterling, 61081. Tel: 815-625-1370. Web Site: librarylearning.org/rock-river-library-consortium. *Dir,* Jennifer Slaney; E-mail: jennifer.slaney@sterlingpubliclibrary.org
Primary Functions: To effectively & efficiently share taxpayer library resources among residents in the towns represented by member libraries

SYSTEM WIDE AUTOMATED NETWORK*, (SWAN), c/o Metropolitan Library System, 800 Quail Ridge Dr, Westmont, 60559. Tel: 630-734-5153. Toll Free Tel: 844-792-6542. FAX: 630-734-5050. E-mail: media@swanlibraries.net. Web Site: swanlibraries.net. *Exec Dir,* Aaron Skog; E-mail: aaron@swanlibraries.net
Founded 1974
Member Libraries: 100 (2 col, 95 pub, 1 sch, 2 spec)
Primary Functions: Shared online public access catalog; centralized cataloging & software services; library staff support; networking opportunities & knowledge/resource sharing; library accessibility through modern technology

INDIANA

CONSORTIUM OF COLLEGE & UNIVERSITY MEDIA CENTERS*, (CCUMC), Indiana University, Franklin Hall 0009, 601 E Kirkwood Ave, Bloomington, 47405-1223. SAN 322-1091. Tel: 812-855-6049. FAX: 812-855-2103. E-mail: ccumc@ccumc.org. Web Site: www.ccumc.org. *Exec Dir,* Kristy Howard; *Admin Serv,* Kat Cross
Founded 1971
Member Libraries: 750 univ
Primary Functions: Advocate the accessibility & effective use of educational media; provide leadership in the development of standards for the effective implementation & management of instructional technology in higher education; foster cooperative efforts among colleges & universities & other institutions, agencies, foundations & organizations in the solution of mutual problems; gather & disseminate information about educational, professional & operational issues, including statistics important to the profession; develop & provide programs & services that will enable members to most effectively support the missions of their institutions; provide profesional development opportunities for members; inspire, generate & coordinate research & scholarship that advances the mission of the Consortium

EVERGREEN INDIANA LIBRARY CONSORTIUM, Indiana State Library, 315 W Ohio St, Indianapolis, 46202. (Mail add: Indiana State Library, 140 N Senate Ave, Indianapolis, 46204). Tel: 317-232-3691. FAX: 317-232-3713. E-mail: coordinator@evergreenindiana.org. Web Site: blog.evergreen.lib.in.us, www.in.gov/library/evergreen.htm. *Dir,* Courtney Brown
Founded 2008
Member Libraries: 132
Primary Functions: Cooperative, open-source, integrated library automation services; facilitating resource sharing among multi-type member libraries; cataloging; statistics

INDIANA LIBRARY FEDERATION*, (ILF), 941 E 86th St, Ste 260, Indianapolis, 46240. Tel: 317-257-2040. E-mail: askus@ilfonline.org. Web Site: www.ilfonline.org. *Exec Dir,* Lucinda Nord; Tel: 317-257-2040, Ext 101; *Communications Mgr,* Tisa Davis; Tel: 317-257-2040, Ext 104
Open Mon-Fri 8-5
Member Libraries: 2000 acad, pub, sch & spec librs
Primary Functions: Advocacy, education & library services

IOWA

NATIONAL NETWORK OF LIBRARIES OF MEDICINE REGION 6*, Univ of Iowa Hardin Libr for Health Sci, 600 Newton Rd, Iowa City, 52242-1098. E-mail: region6-rml@uiowa.edu. Web Site: nnlm.gov/about/regions/region6. *Dir,* Linda Walton; Tel: 319-335-6431, E-mail: linda-walton@uiowa.edu; *Assoc Dir,* Derek Johnson; Tel: 319-335-4997, E-mail: derek-d-johnson@uiowa.edu
Founded 1965
Member Libraries: 1350
Primary Functions: Serves Illinois, Indiana, Iowa, Michigan, Minnesota, Ohio & Wisconsin. By collaborating, training & funding over 1,100 health centers, health departments, community organizations, as well as medical, public & school libraries in a seven state region, the office supports the mission of NNLM: to provide US researchers, health professionals, public health workforce, educators & the public with equal access to biomedical & health information resources & data

POLK COUNTY BIOMEDICAL CONSORTIUM*, c/o Unity Point Health Sciences Library, 1200 Pleasant St, Des Moines, 50309. Tel: 515-241-6490. *Treas,* Paula Whannell; E-mail: paula.whannell@unitypoint.org; *Medical Educ Librn,* Rachel Sindelar; E-mail: rsindelar@broadlawns.org
Member Libraries: 12
Primary Functions: Interlibrary loan; in-service education activities; resource sharing

STATE OF IOWA LIBRARIES ONLINE*, (SILO), State Library of Iowa, 1112 E Grand, Des Moines, 50319. SAN 322-1415. Tel: 515-281-4105. Toll Free Tel: 800-248-4483. FAX: 515-281-6191. Web Site: www.statelibraryofiowa.org/ld/q-s/silo. *State Librn,* Michael Scott; E-mail: michael.scott@lib.state.ia.us
Founded 1995
Member Libraries: 500
Primary Functions: Provide libraries with interlibrary loans; email service; web hosting

KANSAS

GREATER WESTERN LIBRARY ALLIANCE*, (GWLA), 5200 W 94th Terrace, Ste 200, Prairie Village, 66027. Tel: 913-370-4422. Web Site: www.gwla.org. *Exec Dir,* Joni Blake, PhD; E-mail: joni@gwla.org; *Program Officer for Scholarly Communication,* Nora Dethloff; E-mail: nora@gwla.org
Founded 1998
Member Libraries: 39 acad
Primary Functions: Interlibrary loan; shared electronic resources, cooperative collection development

STATE LIBRARY OF KANSAS*, Statewide Services Division, 300 SW Tenth Ave, Rm 312-N, Topeka, 66612-1593. SAN 329-5621. Tel: 785-296-3296. FAX: 785-368-7291. E-mail: audiobooks@ks.gov. Web Site: kslib.info. *Dir,* Ray C Walling; Tel: 785-296-5466, E-mail: ray.walling@ks.gov; *Digital Coll Librn,* Andrew Schafer; Tel: 785-296-8152, E-mail: andy.schafer@ks.gov; *Res Sharing Librn,* Nicole Hansen; Tel: 785-296-5110, E-mail: nicole.hansen@ks.gov; *Statewide Servs Asst,* Erika Taylor; Tel: 785-296-2146, E-mail: erika.l.taylor@ks.gov
Founded 2005
Primary Functions: Administers & manages statewide research, reading & resource sharing programs; Coordinates the federal E-rate program for public libraries within Kansas

KENTUCKY

ASSOCIATION OF INDEPENDENT KENTUCKY COLLEGES & UNIVERSITIES*, (AIKCU), 484 Chenault Rd, Frankfort, 40601. SAN 322-1490. Tel: 502-695-5007. FAX: 502-695-5057. E-mail: info@aikcu.org. Web Site: www.aikcu.org. *Pres,* Dr OJ Oleka
Founded 1970
Member Libraries: 20 acad
Primary Functions: Interlibrary cooperation

KENTUCKIANA METROVERSITY, INC*, 200 W Broadway, Ste 800, Louisville, 40202. SAN 322-1504. Web Site: www.metroversity.org. *Dir, Libr Serv,* C Martin Rosen; Tel: 812-941-2262, E-mail: crosen@ius.edu
Founded 1969
Member Libraries: 7 col, univ & sem
Primary Functions: Interlibrary loan; Union List of Serials; Union Film Catalog

KENTUCKY MEDICAL LIBRARY ASSOCIATION*, University of Louisville Bldg D, Rm 110A, 500 S Preston St,, Louisville, 40292. SAN 370-0623. Tel: 859-323-8008. E-mail: KentuckyMLA@gmail.com. Web Site: www.kentuckymla.com/. *Pres,* Stephanie Henderson; E-mail: stephanie.henderson@uky.edu
Founded 1972
Member Libraries: 25
Primary Functions: Cooperative services; continuing education

LOUISIANA

HEALTH SCIENCES LIBRARY ASSOCIATION OF LOUISIANA*, (HSLAL), c/o National World War II Museum Library, 945 New Orleans, Shreveport, 70130. SAN 375-0035. Tel: 318-675-5679. Web Site: www.hslal.org. *Pres,* Wesley Lucas; Tel: 501-528-1944, Ext 469, E-mail: wesley.lucas@nationalww2museum.org; *Chair,* Diana Schaubhut; E-mail: dschaubhut@uhcno.edu
Founded 1976
Member Libraries: 48
Primary Functions: To encourage & promote cooperation & communication among the librarians & library managers of health sciences institutions in the state of Louisiana

LOAN SYSTEM HELPING AUTOMATE RETRIEVAL OF KNOWLEDGE*, (LoanSHARK), State Library of Louisiana, 701 North Fourth St, Baton Rouge, 70802. SAN 371-6880. Tel: 225-342-4918. FAX: 225-219-4725. Interlibrary Loan Service E-mail: ill@state.lib.la.us. Web Site: www.state.lib.la.us/state-employees/interlibrary-loan/libraries. *Adminr,* Kytara Christophe; E-mail: kgaudin@state.lib.la.us
Founded 1987
Member Libraries: 68 pub
Primary Functions: Provides an automated interlibrary loan referral system & use of statewide online catalog

LOUISIANA LIBRARY NETWORK*, (LOUIS), 1201 N Third St, Ste 6-200, Baton Rouge, 70802. (Mail add: PO Box 3677, Baton Rouge, 70821-3677). Tel: 225-342-4253. E-mail: louislibraries@laregents.edu. Web Site: louislibraries.org. *Exec Dir,* Laurie Blandino; E-mail: laurie.blandino@laregents.edu
Founded 1992
Member Libraries: 44 acad & 2 spec
Primary Functions: Provide library automation, digital library, & interlibrary loan support & services for member libraries; license access to electronic resources for all Louisiana public & private academic libraries.

MARYLAND

MARYLAND INTERLIBRARY LOAN ORGANIZATION*, (MILO), c/o Enoch Pratt Free Library, 400 Cathedral St, Baltimore, 21201-4484. SAN 343-8600. Tel: 410-396-5498. FAX: 410-396-5837. E-mail: milo@prattlibrary.org. Web Site: www.prattlibrary.org. *Pres & Chief Exec Officer,* Heidi Daniel
Member Libraries: 536
Primary Functions: Interlibrary loan; document delivery; information-reference service; consultation; service to Maryland government agencies

NATIONAL NETWORK OF LIBRARIES OF MEDICINE*, (NNLM), Office of Engagement & Training, National Library of Medicine, Two Democracy Plaza, Ste 510, 6707 Democracy Blvd, Bethesda, 20894. SAN 373-0905. Tel: 301-496-4777. FAX: 301-480-1467. Web Site: www.nnlm.gov. *Head, National Network Coordinating Office,* Amanda J Wilson; E-mail: amanda.wilson@nih.gov
Founded 1967
Member Libraries: 7800 health sci
Primary Functions: Administers program to ensure equal access to information to all US health professionals and the general public; programs funded by the National Library of Medicine & carried out in eight geographic regions through contracts with eight major medical libraries

NATIONAL NETWORK OF LIBRARIES OF MEDICINE REGION 1*, Univ Md Health Scis & Human Servs Libr, 601 W Lombard St, Baltimore, 21201-1512. SAN 322-1644. Tel: 410-706-2855. Toll Free Tel: 800-338-7657. FAX: 410-706-0099. E-mail: region1@nnlm.gov. Web Site: nnlm.gov/about/regions/region1. *Exec Dir,* Faith Steele; E-mail: fsteele@hshsl.umaryland.edu; *Outreach Librn,* Nancy Patterson; Tel: 410-706-2858, E-mail: npatters@hshsl.umaryland.edu
Founded 1983
Member Libraries: Over 940 health sci librs
Primary Functions: Serves Delaware, Kentucky, Maryland, New Jersey, North Carolina, Pennsylvania, Virginia, West Virginia & the District of Columbia. Program emphasizes provision of basic level of information services to health care providers through network by: promoting training & library development at the community level; encouraging state & local cooperative library efforts; coordinating regional interlibrary loan network; training of health professionals in the use of the US National Library of Medicine's products & services; provides referral information for health professionals needing information; exhibits at health professional meetings; funds projects related to provision of information to health care provider especially in rural areas or those who serve minority populations

SOUTHEASTERN CHAPTER OF THE AMERICAN ASSOCIATION OF LAW LIBRARIES*, (SEAALL), c/o University of Baltimore School of Law, 1420 N Charles St, Baltimore, 21201. Web Site: seaall.wildapricot.org. *Pres,* Charles Pipins; Tel: 410-837-4373, E-mail: cpipins@ubalt.edu
Founded 1954
Member Libraries: 500
Primary Functions: Promote law librarianship; develop & increase the usefulness of law libraries, particularly those in the southeastern US

US NATIONAL LIBRARY OF MEDICINE*, (NLM), 8600 Rockville Pike, Bethesda, 20894. SAN 322-1652. Tel: 301-594-5983. Toll Free Tel: 888-346-3656. FAX: 301-402-1384. E-mail: custserv@nlm.nih.gov. Web Site: www.nlm.nih.gov. *Dir,* Patti Brennan; E-mail: NLMDirector@nih.gov
Founded 1836
Member Libraries: Domestic & international health sci librs, health professionals, researchers & gen public
Primary Functions: Delivers authoritative health information to Americans & to people around the world through services including: MEDLINE/PubMed, MedlinePlus, the NLM Gateway, ClinicalTrials.gov, LocatorPlus, TOXNET, Images from the History of Medicine & Profiles in Science. NLM's mission, in conjunction with its National Network of Libraries of Medicine (NN/LM), is to assist the advancement of medical & related sciences & to aid the dissemination & exchange of scientific & other information important to the progress of medicine & to the public health

WASHINGTON RESEARCH LIBRARY CONSORTIUM*, (WRLC), 901 Commerce Dr, Upper Marlboro, 20774. SAN 373-0883. Tel: 301-390-2000. FAX: 301-390-2020. Web Site: www.wrlc.org. *Exec Dir,* Mark Jacobs; E-mail: jacobs@wrlc.org; *Libr Dir, User Serv,* Aaron Krebeck; E-mail: krebeck@wrlc.org; *Dir, Admin & Finance,* Timothy Connolly; E-mail: connolly@wrlc.org; *Dir, Info Tech,* Donald Gourley; E-mail: gourley@wrlc.org
Founded 1987
Member Libraries: 9 univ
Primary Functions: Shared integrated library system, online catalog & discovery tool; cooperative collection development; shared offsite storage facility; resource sharing, reciprocal borrowing & document delivery; professional development

MASSACHUSETTS

BOSTON LIBRARY CONSORTIUM, INC*, Teb Milk St, Ste 354, Boston, 02108. SAN 322-1733. Tel: 617-262-0380. FAX: 617-262-0163. Administration E-mail: admin@blc.org. Web Site: www.blc.org. *Exec Dir,* Charlie Barlow; Tel: 617-262-6244, E-mail: cbarlow@blc.org
Founded 1970
Member Libraries: 19 acad, pub, res & state
Primary Functions: Support resource sharing & enhancement of services to users through programs in cooperative collecting, access to electronic resources & physical collections & enhanced resource sharing; facilitate access to research materials at member institutions by member online catalogs & other information resources, interlibrary loan enhanced by the virtual catalog, on-site use of most member libraries & borrowing privileges for qualified researchers

BOSTON THEOLOGICAL INTERRELIGIOUS CONSORTIUM*, PO Box 391069, Cambridge, 02139. Tel: 207-370-5275. E-mail: btioffice@bostontheological.org. Web Site: bostontheological.org. *Exec Dir,* Stephanie Edwards; E-mail: edwards@bostontheological.org
Founded 1968
Member Libraries: 10 acad

CAPE LIBRARIES AUTOMATED MATERIALS SHARING NETWORK*, (CLAMS), 270 Communication Way, Unit 4E, Hyannis, 02601. SAN 370-579X. Tel: 508-790-4399. FAX: 508-771-4533. Web Site: www.clamsnet.org. *Exec Dir,* Eileen Chandler; E-mail: echandler@clamsnet.org
Founded 1988
Member Libraries: 36
Primary Functions: Resource sharing network via automated integrated library system

FENWAY LIBRARY ORGANIZATION*, (FLO), c/o Wentworth Institute Technology, Schumann Library & Learning Commons, 550 Huntington Ave, 2nd Flr, Boston, 02115. SAN 373-9112. Tel: 617-989-5032. FAX: 617-442-1519. Web Site: www.flo.org. *Exec Dir,* Walter Stine; E-mail: walter@flo.org
Founded 1987
Member Libraries: 10 acad & mus
Primary Functions: Provides online library & information services, including a shared bibliographic database, cataloging, acquisitions & serials control

MASSACHUSETTS HEALTH SCIENCES LIBRARY NETWORK*, (MAHSLIN), Lamar soutter Library, UMass Medical School, 55 Lake Ave, n, Worcester, 01655. SAN 372-8293. Tel: 508-856-1966. Web Site: www.mahslin.org. *Pres,* Jessie Casella; E-mail: jessie.casella@va.gov
Founded 1970
Member Libraries: 129 med
Primary Functions: Enhancement of health services & health information access for the people of Massachusetts

MERRIMACK VALLEY LIBRARY CONSORTIUM*, (MVLC), Four High St, Ste 175, North Andover, 01845. SAN 322-4384. Tel: 978-557-1050. Web Site: mvlc.ent.sirsi.net/client/en_US/mvlc. *Exec Dir,* Patty DiTullio; Tel: 978-557-5409, E-mail: pditullio@mvlcstaff.org
Founded 1982
Member Libraries: 36 pub

Primary Functions: Cataloging; circulation control; interlibrary loan; resource sharing; public access catalog; acquisitions; serials control; online periodical databases; shared eContent collections; e-mail; group purchases; support; training; consulting; centralized copy cataloging; library staff access to the Internet

MINUTEMAN LIBRARY NETWORK, Ten Strathmore Rd, Natick, 01760-2419. SAN 322-4252. Tel: 508-655-8008. FAX: 508-655-1507. Web Site: www.minlib.net. *Exec Dir,* Philip McNulty; E-mail: phil@minlib.net
Founded 1983
Member Libraries: 36 pub & 5 acad
Primary Functions: Resource sharing network; integrated library system; cataloging; Automated system: Innovative Interfaces Sierra; Catalog: Aspen Discovery

NATIONAL NETWORK OF LIBRARIES OF MEDICINE REGION 7*, Univ of Massachusetts Chan Med Sch, Lamar Soutter Libr, 55 Lake Ave N, Rm S4-241, Worcester, 01655. SAN 372-5448. Tel: 508-856-6099. Toll Free Tel: 800-338-7657. FAX: 508-856-5977. E-mail: nnlm-region7@umassmed.edu. Web Site: nnlm.gov/about/regions/region7. *Dir,* Mary Piorun; Tel: 508-856-2206, E-mail: mary.piorun@umassmed.edu; *Assoc Dir,* Jessica Kilham; E-mail: jessica.kilham@umassmed.edu
Founded 1991
Member Libraries: 1564
Primary Functions: Serves Connecticut, Massachusetts, Maine, New Hampshire, New York, Rhode Island & Vermont. Provides free access to information to all health care providers in New England

NORTH OF BOSTON LIBRARY EXCHANGE, INC*, (NOBLE), 42A Cherry Hill Dr, Danvers, 01923. SAN 322-4023. Tel: 978-777-8844. E-mail: staff@noblenet.org. Web Site: www.noblenet.org. *Exec Dir,* Ronald A Gagnon; E-mail: gagnon@noblenet.org; *Mgr, Libr Serv,* Elizabeth B Thomsen; *Syst Coordr,* Martha J Driscoll
Founded 1980
Member Libraries: 6 acad, 17 pub, 1 sch & 1 spec
Primary Functions: Resource sharing; automated circulation control; online union catalog; cooperative cataloging; acquisitions; serials; gateway services; collection management; PC support; Internet services; electronic resources; digital library & repository

SAILS LIBRARY NETWORK*, Ten Riverside Dr, Ste 102, Lakeville, 02347. SAN 378-0058. Tel: 508-946-8600. FAX: 508-946-8605. E-mail: support@sailsinc.org. Web Site: www.sailsinc.org. *Exec Dir,* Katherine Lussier; E-mail: klussier@sailsinc.org
Founded 1995
Member Libraries: 71 libr & branches
Primary Functions: Administration of a multi-type resource sharing network

MICHIGAN

DETROIT AREA LIBRARY NETWORK*, (DALNET), 5150 Anthony Wayne Dr, Detroit, 48202. Tel: 313-577-6789. FAX: 313-577-1231. E-mail: info@dalnet.org. Web Site: www.dalnet.org. *Exec Dir,* John E Sterbenz, Jr; E-mail: jsterben@wayne.edu
Founded 1985
Member Libraries: 15 institutions (9 academic, 3 special, 2 medical, 1 K-12/special)
Primary Functions: To advance research & learning; run library systems for members; provide training & technical support; supports participation in group digital projects; encourage reciprocal borrowing & interlibrary loan; provides funding for state-wide delivery

LAKELAND LIBRARY COOPERATIVE, 4138 Three Mile Rd NW, Grand Rapids, 49534-1134. SAN 308-132X. Tel: 616-559-5253. FAX: 616-559-4329. E-mail: mail@llcoop.org. Web Site: www.llcoop.org. *Dir,* Carol Dawe; E-mail: carol@llcoop.org; *Fac Mgr,* Terry Cross; E-mail: terry@llcoop.org; *ILS Manager,* Ann Langlois; E-mail: ann@llcoop.org; *Mgr, Cat Serv,* Jeff Lezman; E-mail: jeff@llcoop.org; *Mgr, Mem Serv,* Amber McLain; E-mail: amber@llcoop.org
Founded 1978
Member Libraries: 42
Primary Functions: An array of support services, such as professional consultation & referrals including board & staff development, director recruiting & hiring, strategic planning, coaching & problem solving; cost savings & access to dozens of products & services local & state-wide group purchasing; assistance in implementing statewide advocacy initiatives by working with our partners; maintain shared catalog for digital & physical materials, online patron registration, mobile app access, text & phone notification & training & documentation for member library staff & patrons; catalogs physical & digital materials & coordinates interlibrary loan of books, audiovisual materials & other materials through a centralized delivery service to move materials among libraries

THE LIBRARY NETWORK, (TLN), 41365 Vincenti Ct, Novi, 48375. SAN 370-596X. Tel: 248-536-3100. Web Site: tln.lib.mi.us. *Controller,* Rick Rosekrans; E-mail: rosekrans@tln.lib.mi.us; *Exec Dir,* Steven Bowers; Tel: 248-536-3100, Ext 107, E-mail: sbowers@tln.lib.mi.us; *Mgr, Tech Serv,* James Flury; E-mail: jflury@tln.lib.mi.us; *Human Res Mgr,* Judith Kozakowski; E-mail: jkozakowski&tln.lib.mi.us; *Tech Mgr,* Damon Dye; E-mail: ddye@tln.lib.mi.us; *Shared Automation Syst Coordr,* Anne Neville; E-mail: aneville@tln.lib.mi.us
Founded 1978
Member Libraries: 74 pub
Primary Functions: Resource sharing & delivery; networking & technology; shared integrated library system & cataloging; acquisitions & group purchasing (electronic & print); consulting; continuing education

MICHIGAN HEALTH SCIENCES LIBRARIES ASSOCIATION, (MHSLA), 1407 Rensen St, Ste 4, Lansing, 48910. SAN 323-987X. Tel: 517-394-2774. FAX: 517-394-2675. Web Site: mhsla.wildapricot.org. *Pres,* Abraham Wheeler; Tel: 517-884-0893, E-mail: awheeler@msu.edu
Founded 1963
Member Libraries: 160 acad & med
Primary Functions: To promote excellence in health sciences librarianship by providing its membership with opportunities for professional growth, fostering communication between members & their regions, facilitating resource sharing, increasing awareness of new technologies, providing high-quality continuing education & conducting research in health sciences information services

MID-MICHIGAN LIBRARY LEAGUE*, (MMLL), 201 N Mitchell, Ste 302, Cadillac, 49601. SAN 307-9325. Tel: 231-775-3037. FAX: 231-775-1749. Web Site: www.mmll.org. *Dir,* Jennifer Balcom; E-mail: jbalcom@mmll.org
Member Libraries: 38 acad, pub & sch
Primary Functions: Professional support, services, guidance & consulting

MIDEASTERN MICHIGAN LIBRARY COOPERATIVE*, 503 S Saginaw St, Ste 839, Flint, 48502. SAN 346-5187. Tel: 810-232-7119. FAX: 810-232-6639. Web Site: www.mmlc.info. *Dir,* Eric Palmer; E-mail: epalmer@mmlc.info

MIDWEST COLLABORATIVE FOR LIBRARY SERVICES*, (MCLS), 1407 Rensen St, Ste 1, Lansing, 48910. Toll Free Tel: 800-530-9019. FAX: 517-492-3878. E-mail: services@mcls.org. Web Site: www.mcls.org. *Exec Dir,* Scott Garrison; E-mail: garrisons@mcls.org; *Chief Info Officer,* Mark Szidik; E-mail: szidikm@mcls.org
Primary Functions: To facilitate sharing resources & collaborate with other organizations for member libraries.

PALNET, 1040 W Bristol Rd, Flint, 48507. Tel: 810-766-4070.
Founded 1991
Member Libraries: 3 acad
Primary Functions: Library automation project that serves the libraries of Baker College (10 sites), Mott Community College (2 sites) & Kettering University

SOUTHEASTERN MICHIGAN LEAGUE OF LIBRARIES, (SEMLOL), UM-Dearborn Mardigian Library, 4901 Evergreen Rd, Dearborn, 48128. SAN 322-4481. Tel: 313-593-5617. Web Site: www.semlol.org. *Chair,* Amy Seipke; E-mail: aseipke@umich.edu; *Treas,* Suzanne Schimanski-Gross
Founded 1980
Member Libraries: 15
Primary Functions: Establish channels of communication among member libraries; create programs to encourage cooperative use of resources; undertake projects to address common issues; work to enhance the quality of service in member libraries

SOUTHWEST MICHIGAN LIBRARY COOPERATIVE*, 401 Dix St, Otsego, 49078. SAN 308-2156. Tel: 269-694-9690. Web Site: smlccooperative.com. *Dir,* Andrea Estelle; E-mail: aestelle@otsegolibrary.org
Founded 1977

SUBURBAN LIBRARY COOPERATIVE*, (SLC), 44750 Delco Blvd, Sterling Heights, 48313. SAN 373-9082. Tel: 586-685-5750. FAX: 586-685-5750. Web Site: www.libcoop.net. *Dir,* Tammy Turgeon; Tel: 586-685-5764, E-mail: turgeont@libcoop.net; *Head, Syst,* Chris Frezza; E-mail: chris@libcoop.net; *Syst Librn,* Amy Shaughnessy; E-mail: shaughna@libcoop.net; *Cataloger,* Lauren Boggs; E-mail: boggsl@libcoop.net
Founded 1978
Member Libraries: 21 pub
Primary Functions: Services to libraries: shared automated system (SIRSIDynix); negotiating contracts & quantity discounts; continuing education; publicity & public relations

UPPER PENINSULA REGION OF LIBRARY COOPERATION, INC*, 1615 Presque Isle Ave, Marquette, 49855. SAN 329-5540. Tel: 906-228-7697. Toll Free Tel: 800-562-8985 (Michigan only). FAX: 906-228-5627. Web Site: joomla.uproc.lib.mi.us/uproc. *Treas,* Pamela Malmsten; E-mail: pmalmsten@superiorlandlibrary.org
Founded 1984
Member Libraries: 100
Primary Functions: Facilitate the sharing of information resources among the libraries of Michigan's Upper Peninsula & Northern Lower Peninsula; encourage libraries to institute such cost-effective practices & procedures which may be made possible through interlibrary cooperation; enable libraries to link up & interact with other regional & national electronic bibliographic communication systems; shared ILS

VALLEY LIBRARY CONSORTIUM*, 3210 Davenport Ave, Saginaw, 48602-3495. Tel: 989-497-0925. FAX: 989-497-0918. E-mail: info@vlc.lib.mi.us. Web Site: www.vlc.lib.mi.us. *Exec Dir,* Randall Lee; Tel: 898-497-0925, Ext 5, E-mail: l.martin@valleylibrary.org
Founded 1980
Member Libraries: 25
Primary Functions: To provide the greater Saginaw Valley community with access to shared library & information resources through quality, cost-effective automated services for member libraries

WHITE PINE LIBRARY COOPERATIVE*, 429 N State St, Ste 207, Caro, 48723. Tel: 989-793-7126. Web Site: wplc.org. *Dir,* Kate Van Auken; E-mail: kvanauken@wplc.org
Open Mon-Fri 8-5

MINNESOTA

CAPITAL AREA LIBRARY CONSORTIUM*, (CALCO), c/o Attorney General Library, Bremer Tower, Ste 1050, 445 Minnesota St, Saint Paul, 55101-2109. SAN 374-6127. Tel: 651-757-1055. FAX: 651-296-7000. Web Site: mn.gov/library. *Consortium Contact,* Jason Smock; E-mail: jason.smock@ag.state.mn.us
Founded 1973
Member Libraries: 18 state & govt
Primary Functions: Cooperation among member libraries to enhance information services in state government

CENTRAL MINNESOTA LIBRARIES EXCHANGE*, (CMLE), 570 First St SE, Saint Cloud, 56304. SAN 322-3779. Tel: 320-257-1933. E-mail: admin@cmle.org. Web Site: cmle.org. *Exec Dir,* Dr Mary Wilkins-Jordan; E-mail: mary@cmle.org; *Information Technologist,* Angie Gentile-Jordan; E-mail: ajordan@cmle.org
Founded 1979
Member Libraries: 320
Primary Functions: We provide information & support to libraries; produce two podcasts: Linking Our Libraries (library training) and Books & Beverages Podcast (podcast book group); provide online & in-person training; organize networking opportunities; provide research & information to our members

METRONET*, 1619 Dayton Ave, Ste 314, Saint Paul, 55104. SAN 322-1989. Tel: 651-646-0475. FAX: 651-649-3169. E-mail: info@metrolibraries.net. Web Site: www.metrolibraries.net. *Exec Dir,* Ann Walker Smalley; E-mail: ann@metronet.lib.mn.us
Founded 1979
Member Libraries: 725
Primary Functions: Resource sharing; long-range planning; communications systems; continuing education

METROPOLITAN LIBRARY SERVICE AGENCY*, (MELSA), 1619 Dayton Ave, Ste 314, Saint Paul, 55104. SAN 371-5124. Tel: 651-645-5731. FAX: 651-649-3169. E-mail: melsa@melsa.org. Web Site: www.melsa.org. *Exec Dir,* Scott Vrieze; E-mail: scott@melsa.org; *Bus Mgr,* Mona Scott; E-mail: mona@melsa.org
Founded 1969
Member Libraries: 8 libr syst
Primary Functions: Manage state & federal grant aid for reciprocal services; internet services; collection development; database purchasing; homework help; smARTpass; automation reimbursement & assistance

MINITEX*, University of Minnesota, Wilson Library, Rm 60, 309 19th Ave S, Minneapolis, 55455. SAN 322-1997. Tel: 612-624-4002. Toll Free Tel: 800-462-5348. FAX: 612-624-4508. Web Site: www.minitex.umn.edu. *Dir,* Maggie Snow; E-mail: msnow@umn.edu
Founded 1969
Partic in MnPALS
Member Libraries: Over 2,000 acad, govt, pub, sch & spec
Primary Functions: Shared licensing of reference databases online, courier delivery systems (North Dakota, South Dakota, & Wisconsin); resource sharing; reference on instruction; Minnesota Digital Library, statewide Ebooks Minnesota collection, statewide pressbooks publishing service, virtual reference, workshops/webinars training; & cooperative purchasing.

MINNESOTA LIBRARY INFORMATION NETWORK*, (MnLINK), University of Minnesota-Minitex, Wilson Library, Rm 60, 309 19th Ave S, Minneapolis, 55455. Tel: 612-624-8096, 612-625-0886. Toll Free Tel: 800-462-5348. FAX: 612-624-4508. Web Site: www.mnlink.org. *Res Sharing Mgr,* Nick Banitt; E-mail: banit006@umn.edu; *Spec,* Kyle Triska; E-mail: tris0020@umn.edu
Founded 1997
Member Libraries: 600
Primary Functions: Coordinate with libraries to facilitate resource sharing & make Minnesota resources available to Minnesotans

MINNESOTA THEOLOGICAL LIBRARY ASSOCIATION*, (MTLA), Luther Seminary Library, 2375 Como Ave, Saint Paul, 55108. SAN 322-1962. Tel: 651-641-3447. Web Site: www.atla.com/learning-engagement/rg/mtla. *Dir,* Dale Dobias; E-mail: ddobias001@luthersem.edu
Member Libraries: 7
Primary Functions: Coordinates interlibrary loans, certain acquisitions, resource sharing, professional development & collection development

MNPALS*, Minnesota State University, Mankato, 3022 Memorial Library, Mankato, 56001. Tel: 507-389-2000. Toll Free Tel: 877-466-5465. Web Site: www.mnpals.org. *Exec Dir,* Johnna Horton; E-mail: johnna.horton@mnsu.edu
Founded 1979
Open Mon-Fri 8-4:30
Member Libraries: 60
Primary Functions: To provide effective communication, coordination & collaboration among diverse types of member libraries; support standards-based systems that allow flexibility & integration with the larger information universe; facilitate resource sharing & networking among member libraries; provide support, training, expertise & additional related services through a central office; ensure that sufficient financial resources are available to meet current & long range system development & maintenance needs & that these resources are spent wisely

NORTHERN LIGHTS LIBRARY NETWORK*, (NLLN), 1104 Seventh Ave S, Box 136, Moorhead, 56563. SAN 322-2004. Tel: 218-477-2934. Web Site: www.nlln.org. *Exec Dir,* Kathy Brock Enger; E-mail: kathy.enger@nlln.org
Founded 1979
Primary Functions: NLLN is a cooperative network of 280 library members in academic, public, school, and special libraries in 23 counties of North-central, North-west and West-central Minnesota. We work at the grassroots level to bring together all types of libraries and collections in the region to discover, enhance, and share resources through administrative, technological, and educational support.

PRAIRIELANDS LIBRARY EXCHANGE*, (Prairielands), 109 S Fifth St, Marshall, 56258. SAN 322-2039. Tel: 507-532-9013. FAX: 507-532-2039. E-mail: info@prairielands.org. Web Site: www.prairielands.org. *Exec Dir,* Shelly Grace; E-mail: shelly@prairielands.org
Founded 1979
Member Libraries: 210
Primary Functions: Continuing Education; one of seven multicounty multitype library systems in state

SOUTHEASTERN LIBRARIES COOPERATING*, (SELCO), 2600 19th St NW, Rochester, 55901-0767. SAN 308-7417. Tel: 507-288-5513. Toll Free Tel: 800-992-5061. FAX: 507-288-8697. Web Site: www.selco.info. *Exec Dir,* Krista Ross; *Automation Librn,* Donovan Lambright; E-mail: dlambright@selco.info; *Regional Librn,* Reagen Thalacker; E-mail: rthalacker@selco.info; *Tech Serv Librn,* Cheryl Hill; E-mail: chill@selco.info; *Coordr, Tech Support, Librn,* Tyler Irvin; E-mail: tirvin@selco.info
Founded 1971
Member Libraries: 124
Primary Functions: Management of an integrated library system connecting 90 independent locations and an 11-county wide area network; cataloging; web catalog; electronic resources; downloadable eBooks; PC support; public internet management; delivery; interlibrary loan coordination; hosting local library websites; cooperative programming; public relations & publicity; continuing education & training; management of indiviudal scholarships; consultation on library matters; and library advocacy.

TWIN CITIES BIOMEDICAL CONSORTIUM*, (TCBC), c/o Fairview Health Services, 2450 Riverside Ave, Minneapolis, 55455. SAN 322-2055. Tel: 612-273-3000. *Libr Mgr,* Kolleen Olsen; E-mail: kolsen6@fairview.org
Primary Functions: Develop a strong network of biomedical libraries in Twin Cities area & improve efficiency of access to biomedical information; provide educational opportunities to members

MISSISSIPPI

CENTRAL MISSISSIPPI LIBRARY COUNCIL*, (CMLC), c/o Millsaps College Library, 1701 N State St, Jackson, 39210. SAN 372-8250. Tel: 601-974-1070. FAX: 601-974-1082. Web Site: centralmiss.wordpress.com/. *Chairperson,* Stephen Parks; E-mail: sparks@courts.ms.gov
Founded 1976
Member Libraries: 20 acad, pub & spec
Primary Functions: Promote access to books & other informational materials among libraries in central Mississippi; provide reference services to patrons of member libraries; develop interlibrary loan cooperation & staff development opportunities

LONGLEAF LIBRARY CONSORTIUM*, 100 S Jackson St, Brookhaven, 39601. Tel: 601-833-5038. Web Site: www.llf.lib.ms.us/longleaf-consortium. *Dir,* Ryda Worthy; E-mail: rworthy@llf.lib.ms.us
Founded 2006
Member Libraries: 4 pub libr syst
Primary Functions: Circulation software; shared financial resources; expand the range of library resources to participating libraries' patrons

MISSOURI

HEALTH SCIENCES LIBRARY NETWORK OF KANSAS CITY, INC*, (HSLNKC), c/o Shook, Hardy & Bacon Medical Library & Scientific Resource Ctr - Joyce Sickel, 2555 Grand Blvd, Kansas City, 64108. SAN 322-2098. Tel:

816-235-1880. FAX: 816-235-6570. Web Site: hslnkc.org. *Pres,* Lee Williams; E-mail: leeawilliams@swbell.net
Founded 1974
Member Libraries: 27 hospital, med ctr, col & med soc
Primary Functions: Courier service; interlibrary loan; Union Lists of Serials; professional opportunities

KANSAS CITY LIBRARY SERVICE PROGRAM*, (KC-LSP), Kansas City Public Library, 14 W Tenth St, Kansas City, 64105-1702. Tel: 816-701-3520. Toll Free Tel: 866-755-5252. FAX: 816-701-3401. E-mail: kc-lspsupport@kclibrary.org. *ILS Adminr,* Ruben Noguera; *Dir, Info Syst,* Melissa Carle; *Automation Coordr,* Laura Welter
Founded 1991
Member Libraries: 23
Primary Functions: A service program of the Kansas City Public Library, providing a full-featured library automation system (SirsiDynix), complete with web-based public access & reporting; direct patron borrowing & access to 2.1 million circulating items

MID-AMERICA LIBRARY ALLIANCE*, (MALA), 15624 E US Hwy 24, Independence, 64050. SAN 322-2101. Tel: 816-521-7257. Toll Free Tel: 888-514-9271. Web Site: malalibraries.org. *Exec Dir,* Jane Mulvihill-Jones; E-mail: jane.mulvihill-jones@malalibraries.org
Founded 1978
Open Mon-Fri 8-4
Member Libraries: 900
Primary Functions: Centralized interlibrary loan communication & delivery service; staff development & continuing education

MISSOURI EVERGREEN, 1190 Meramec Station Rd, Ste 207, Ballwin, 63021-6902. Web Site: moevergreenlibraries.org. *Exec Dir,* Steven Potter; E-mail: director@moevergreenlibraries.org; *Cataloger,* Liz Rudloff; E-mail: cataloger@moevergreenlibraries.org
Member Libraries: 78
Primary Functions: Resource sharing for libraries in Missouri

MOBIUS*, 111 E Broadway, Ste 220, Columbia, 65203. Tel: 877-366-2487. FAX: 541-264-7006. Web Site: mobiusconsortium.org. *Exec Dir,* Donna Bacon; E-mail: donna@mobiusconsortium.org
Founded 1998
Partic in Association for Rural & Small Libraries
Member Libraries: 76 Member Libraries in Missouri, Oklahoma, Texas, Iowa and Kansas
Primary Functions: Shared ILS and Resource Sharing

SAINT LOUIS REGIONAL LIBRARY NETWORK, (SLRLN), c/o Amigos Library Services, 1190 Meramec Station Rd, Ste 207, Ballwin, 63021-6902. SAN 322-2209. Toll Free Tel: 800-843-8482, Ext 2899. FAX: 636-529-1396. E-mail: slrln@amigos.org. Web Site: www.slrln.org. *Pres,* Dr Katy Smith
Founded 1977
Member Libraries: 96 acad, health related, pub, sch & spec
Primary Functions: Reciprocal library services, including directory of area libraries, an INFO-PASS system, staff-development programs, cooperative purchasing, collection development & preservation, newsletter & information publications

WESTERN COUNCIL OF STATE LIBRARIES, INC, Amigos Library Services - Fiscal Officer, 1190 Meramec Station Rd, Ste 207, Ballwin, 63021-6902. Tel: 972-851-8000. Toll Free Tel: 800-843-8482. FAX: 636-529-1396. E-mail: westco@amigos.org. Web Site: www.westernco.org.
Founded 1977
Member Libraries: 22
Primary Functions: Improve library services through the Western State Libraries; provide means for communicating a position of western state librarians on national & regional matters of common concern; develop resource sharing; foster staff development between libraries.

MONTANA

TREASURE STATE ACADEMIC INFORMATION & LIBRARY SERVICES, (TRAILS), Montana State University Library, Centennial Mall, PO Box 173320, Bozeman, 59717-3320. Tel: 406-994-4432. Web Site: trailsmt.org. *Exec Dir,* Pamela Benjamin; E-mail: pamela.benjamin1@montana.edu
Founded 2016
Member Libraries: 24 acad & the Montana State Libr
Primary Functions: Supports student success & faculty research by providing seamless access to high-quality information resources

NEBRASKA

ICON LIBRARY CONSORTIUM, c/o Clarkson College Library, 101 S 42nd St, Omaha, 68131. Tel: 402-552-3387. E-mail: iconlibne@gmail.com. Web Site: iconlibrary.org. *Exec Secy,* Amy Masek; E-mail: masekamy@clarksoncollege.edu; *Consortium Contact,* Judith Bergjord; E-mail: bergjord@creighton.edu
Founded 1990
Member Libraries: 19, incl 7 inst
Primary Functions: Provide resources to health science libraries, libraries with either a health science program or public libraries with a consumer health science information focus & to individuals in health care occupations, either professional or in-training

NEVADA

INFORMATION NEVADA, Nevada State Library, Archives & Public Records, 100 N Stewart St, Carson City, 89701. SAN 322-2276. Tel: 775-431-0097. E-mail: libraryservices@admin.nv.gov. Web Site: nsla.nv.gov/information-nevada, nvlibrarycoop.org. *Dir,* Kari Ward; E-mail: kward@admin.nv.gov
Founded 1977
Member Libraries: 35
Primary Functions: Provide more effective access to library & information resources on a local, statewide & interstate basis using interlibrary loan

NEW HAMPSHIRE

COUNCIL OF STATE LIBRARY AGENCIES IN THE NORTHEAST, (COSLINE), New Hampshire State Library, 20 Park St, Concord, 03301. SAN 322-0451. Tel: 603-271-2397. *Pres,* Michael York; E-mail: michael.c.york@dncr.nh.gov
Founded 1972
Member Libraries: State libr agencies of CT, DE, MA, MD, ME, NH, NJ, NY, PA, RI, VT & WV
Primary Functions: Provides coordination of planning for regional multitype library cooperation

GMILCS, INC, 31 Mount Saint Mary's Way, Hooksett, 03106. E-mail: postmaster@gmilcs.org. Web Site: www.gmilcs.org. *Syst Adminr,* Kevin French; *Syst Librn,* Sarah St Martin
Founded 1992
Member Libraries: 1 academic, 12 public
Primary Functions: Shared automation system, discovery layer, and delivery service.

LIBRARIANS OF THE UPPER VALLEY COOP*, (LUV Coop), c/o Hanover Town Library, 130 Etna Rd, Etna, 03750. (Mail add: PO Box 207, Etna, 03750), SAN 371-6856. Tel: 603-643-3116. *Coordr,* Judith Russell; Tel: 603-795-4622, E-mail: jrussell@lymenhlibrary.org
Founded 1977
Member Libraries: 26 pub & 2 acad
Primary Functions: Improve library service through cooperative purchase of materials; interlibrary loan of materials; exchange of information; presentation of workshops & demonstrations of interest to school & public librarians

MERRI-HILL-ROCK LIBRARY COOPERATIVE*, c/o Kimball Library, Three Academy Ave, Atkinson, 03811-2299. SAN 329-5338. Tel: 603-362-5234. FAX: 603-362-4791. *Dir,* Deborah Hoadley; Tel: 603-887-3428, E-mail: director@sandownlibrary.us
Member Libraries: 20 pub & 2 acad
Primary Functions: Meet monthly to share ideas, speakers come to discuss topics of interest to librarians

NEW HAMPSHIRE COLLEGE & UNIVERSITY COUNCIL*, Three Barrell Ct, Ste 100, Concord, 03301-8543. SAN 322-2322. Tel: 603-225-4199. FAX: 603-225-8108. Web Site: www.nhcuc.org. *Pres,* Dr Debby Scire; E-mail: scire@compactnh.org
Founded 1966
Member Libraries: 18
Primary Functions: Interlibrary loan; joint acquisition; reciprocal borrowing privileges; Union List of Serials; NELINET participation; resource sharing

NUBANUSIT LIBRARY COOPERATIVE, c/o Keene Public Library, 60 Winter St, Keene, 03431. SAN 322-4600. *Chair,* Susan Bloom; Tel: 603-757-0613, E-mail: sbloom@keenenh.gov
Founded 1971
Member Libraries: 30
Primary Functions: Staff development; discussion of regional & statewide library issues

NEW JERSEY

BASIC HEALTH SCIENCES LIBRARY NETWORK*, (BHSL), Overlook Medical Center, 99 Beauvoir Ave, Summit, 07902. SAN 371-4888. Tel: 908-522-2886. FAX: 908-522-2274. *Libr Mgr,* Pat Regenberg; E-mail: pat.regenberg@atlantichealth.org
Founded 1986
Member Libraries: 460 acad & med
Primary Functions: Resource sharing; interlibrary loan

BERGEN COUNTY COOPERATIVE LIBRARY SYSTEM, INC*, BCCLS, 21-00 Route 208 S, Ste 130, Fair Lawn, 07410. Tel: 201-498-7300. FAX: 201-489-4215. E-mail: bccls@bccls.org. Web Site: www.bccls.org. *Exec Dir,* David Hanson; Tel: 201-498-7302, E-mail: dave@bccls.org; *Dir, Info Tech,* Eric Lozauskas; Tel: 201-498-7309, E-mail: eric@bccls.org; *Sr Cat Librn,* Yumi Choi; Tel:

201-498-7313, E-mail: yumi@bccls.org; *Cat Librn,* Kirsten Fagerlund; Tel: 201-498-7306, E-mail: kirsten@bccls.org; *Cat, ILS LIbrn,* Margaret Rose O'Keefe; Tel: 201-498-7316, E-mail: margaret@bccls.org; *Bus Mgr,* Christina Park; Tel: 201-498-7311, E-mail: christina@bccls.org; *Libr Develop Coordr, Web Serv,* Joseph Palmer; Tel: 201-498-7312, E-mail: joseph@bccls.org; *Mem Serv Coordr,* Darlene Swistock; Tel: 201-498-7301, E-mail: darlene@bccls.org; *IT Serv, Sr Libr Tech,* Joe Guida; Tel: 201-498-7317, E-mail: joe@bccls.org; *IT Tech,* Brian Simoes; Tel: 201-498-7315, E-mail: brian@bccls.org; *Syst Adminr,* Michael Grguev; Tel: 201-498-7314, E-mail: mike@bccls.org
Founded 1979
Member Libraries: 77
Primary Functions: Resource sharing, shared library automation software, delivery services, IT services and other library-related services.

LIBRARYLINKNJ, THE NEW JERSEY LIBRARY COOPERATIVE*, 44 Stelton Rd, Ste 330, Piscataway, 08854. SAN 371-5116. Tel: 732-752-7720. FAX: 732-752-7785. Web Site: librarylinknj.org. *Exec Dir,* Ralph S Bingham, III; E-mail: ralph@librarylinknj.org
Founded 1985
Member Libraries: 2000 acad, corp, inst, med, pub & sch
Primary Functions: LibraryLinkNJ empowers libraries to serve their clientele more effectively & enhances the value of member libraries to their communities

MAIN LIBRARY ALLIANCE, (Formerly Morris Automated Information Network), 16 Wing Dr, Ste 212, Cedar Knolls, 07927. SAN 322-4058. Tel: 973-862-4606. E-mail: main@mainlib.org. Web Site: www.mainlib.org. *Exec Dir,* Phillip Berg; Tel: 973-862-4606, E-mail: phillip.berg@mainlib.org
Founded 1979
Member Libraries: 50
Primary Functions: Shared services & technology; shared materials; technical support; digital resources; group purchasing; technical training; continuing education & professional development; networking

MORRIS-UNION FEDERATION*, 214 Main St, Chatham, 07928. SAN 310-2629. Tel: 973-635-0603. FAX: 973-635-7827. *Dir,* Karen Brodsky; E-mail: kbrodsky@chathamlibrary.org
Founded 1974
Member Libraries: 9
Primary Functions: Provides interlibrary services; member libraries contribute to budget to purchase specialty books & increase access to information for residents in membership area

NEW JERSEY HEALTH SCIENCES LIBRARY NETWORK, (NJHSN), Overlook Hospital Library, 99 Beauvoir Ave, Summit, 07902. SAN 371-4829. Tel: 908-522-2886. FAX: 908-522-2274. *Libr Mgr,* Patricia Regenberg; E-mail: pat.regenberg@atlantichealth.org
Founded 1980
Member Libraries: 36 med
Primary Functions: Interlibrary loan; resource sharing

NEW JERSEY LIBRARY NETWORK*, 185 W State St, Trenton, 08608. (Mail add: PO Box 520, Trenton, 08625-0520), SAN 372-8161. Tel: 609-278-2640, Ext 151. FAX: 609-278-2650. Web Site: www.njstatelib.org. *State Librn,* Jennifer Nelson; E-mail: jnelson@njstatelib.org; *Adminr,* Ruth Pallante; E-mail: rpallante@njstatelib.org
Founded 1984
Member Libraries: 2467 acad, inst, pub, sch & spec
Primary Functions: Provides residents with full & equal access to library programs & materials not available within their communities; promotes cooperation among libraries; provides a number of statewide services & additional services through the New Jersey State Library & Regional Library Cooperatives; reference services to supplement those provided by the member libraries; interlibrary loan services; delivery services for library materials; access to online databases; consultant services; in-service training; preservation; conservation & disaster-preparedness programs; public relations; provides supplemental reference in specific subjects to all Network member libraries through contracts with Newark Public Library, New Jersey State Library, Rutgers University & the University of Medicine & Dentistry of New Jersey

SHARING & TECHNOLOGY ENHANCING LOCAL LIBRARY ACCESS, (STELLA), (Formerly Libraries of Middlesex Automation Consortium), 27 Mayfield Ave, Edison, 08837. SAN 329-448X. Tel: 732-750-2525. E-mail: support@stellanj.org. Web Site: www.stellanj.org. *Exec Dir,* Eric Lozauskas
Founded 1986
Member Libraries: 52
Primary Functions: To operate a shared automation system for its members; to promote all aspects of cooperative automated projects & resource sharing

VIRTUAL ACADEMIC LIBRARY ENVIRONMENT*, (VALE), VALE/NJEdge, 625 Broad St, Ste 260, Newark, 07102-4418. Tel: 855-832-3343. Web Site: vale.njedge.net. *Prog Mgr,* Melissa Lena; E-mail: melissa.lena@njedge.net
Founded 1998
Member Libraries: 50 academic & the NJ State Library
Primary Functions: To facilitate access to scholarly resources by leveraging the group's purchasing power for cost-effective access to electronic databases; to promote resource sharing among member libraries

NEW MEXICO

ESTACADO LIBRARY INFORMATION NETWORK*, (ELIN), 509 N Shipp St, Hobbs, 88240. Tel: 575-397-9328. FAX: 575-397-1508. Web Site: www.elinlib.org. *Dir,* Sandy Farrell; E-mail: sfarrell@elinlib.org
Founded 1996
Member Libraries: 2 acad & 4 pub
Primary Functions: To share common items & patron databases & provide more online databases to all patrons, free of charge

NEW MEXICO CONSORTIUM OF ACADEMIC LIBRARIES*, (NMCAL), c/o UNM-Taos Library, 1157 County Rd 110, Ranchos de Taos, 87557. SAN 371-6872. Web Site: nmcal.net. *Pres,* Valerie Nye; Tel: 505-428-1506, E-mail: valerie.nye@sfcc.edu
Founded 1988
Member Libraries: 34
Primary Functions: Provides the means to present the unified position of New Mexico's public & private academic libraries on key issues affecting them to governmental committees, the public & other appropriate bodies provides the means to devise & carry out projects of common usefulness such as: enhanced library cooperation for resource sharing, collection development & improved funding for library acquisitions in all academic libraries

NEW YORK

ACADEMIC LIBRARIES OF BROOKLYN*, Long Island University Brooklyn Library-LLC 524A, One University Plaza, Brooklyn, 11201. SAN 322-2411. Tel: 718-488-1081. FAX: 718-780-4057. Web Site: www.liu.edu/brooklyn-library. *Dean, Univ Libr,* Ingrid Wang; Tel: 718-488-1680, E-mail: ingrid.wang@liu.edu
Founded 1963
Member Libraries: 8 col
Primary Functions: Interlibrary loan; open access; Union periodicals list; Brooklyn bibliography

ASSOCIATED COLLEGES OF THE SAINT LAWRENCE VALLEY, SUNY Potsdam, 288 Van Housen Extension, Potsdam, 13676. SAN 322-242X. Tel: 315-267-3331. E-mail: acslv@potsdam.edu. Web Site: associatedcolleges.org. *Exec Dir,* Karen Kus; E-mail: kkus@stlawu.edu
Founded 1970
Member Libraries: 4
Primary Functions: Interlibrary loan; professional development for staff

BROOKLYN-QUEENS-STATEN ISLAND-MANHATTAN-BRONX HEALTH SCIENCES LIBRARIANS*, (BQSIMB), 150 55th St, Brooklyn, 11220. Tel: 718-630-7200. FAX: 718-630-8918. Web Site: www.bqsimb.org. *Pres,* Paul Tremblay; E-mail: ptremblay@nycpm.edu
Founded 1968
Primary Functions: To bring together persons of this constituted geographic area engaged in providing professional health sciences library services for the following objectives: furthering their specialized knowledge; exchange of information; improvements & developments of resources; identifying special needs & coordinating all library services & activities with existing area groups, libraries & programs

CAPITAL DISTRICT LIBRARY COUNCIL*, (CDLC), 28 Essex St, Albany, 12206. SAN 322-2446. Tel: 518-438-2500. Web Site: www.cdlc.org. *Exec Dir,* Kathleen Gundrum; E-mail: kgundrum@cdlc.org; *Communications Librn, Tech,* Kariann Kakeh; E-mail: kkakeh@cdlc.org; *Mem Serv Librn,* Amy Hren; E-mail: ahren@cdlc.org; *Res Sharing Librn,* Meghan Wakeman; E-mail: mwakeman@cdlc.org; *Continuing Educ Coordr, Digital Serv,* Susan D'Entremont; E-mail: susan@cdlc.org; *Hospital Libr Serv Coordr,* Christopher Tosh; E-mail: ctosh@cdlc.org
Founded 1967
Member Libraries: 23 acad, 11 hospitals, 3 pub libr systs, 4 sch libr systs & 24 spec
Primary Functions: Partner with members to strengthen library service through education, shared collections, and local connections. Enhance access to information, encourage resource sharing and promote library interests for all members through a variety of regional and statewide programs & services; ILL; cataloging and metadata services; Hospital Library Service Program; digital collections; coordinated collection development; continuing education; consortial purchases; advocacy

CENTRAL NEW YORK LIBRARY RESOURCES COUNCIL*, (CLRC), 5710 Commons Park Dr, East Syracuse, 13057. SAN 322-2454. Tel: 315-446-5446. FAX: 315-446-5590. E-mail: info@clrc.org. Web Site: www.clrc.org. *Exec Dir,* Marc Wildman; E-mail: mwildman@clrc.org
Founded 1967
Open Mon-Fri 8:30-4:30
Member Libraries: 55 acad, med, pub, sch & spec
Primary Functions: Interlibrary loan processing; materials delivery; bibliographic access through union lists & catalogs & collection development; continuing education; conservation & preservation; local administration of specialized state & federal library programs for regional automation & hospital library services; promotion of interlibrary communication & cooperation for enhanced service to

library users in the region; Internet training & connectivity; documentary heritage & archives program; regional electronic list serv CNYLIB-L & web site http://clrc.org

CONNECTNY, INC*, CNY, 6721 US Hwy 11, Potsdam, 13676. Web Site: www.connectny.org. *Exec Dir,* Julia Proctor; E-mail: julia@connectny.org; *Mem Serv Coordr,* Janelle Toner; E-mail: janelle@connectny.org
Founded 2002
Member Libraries: 12 academic
Primary Functions: The mission of ConnectNY is to share collections, leverage resources, and enhance services through cooperative initiatives and coordinated activities.

LIBRARY ASSOCIATION OF ROCKLAND COUNTY*, (LARC), PO Box 917, New City, 10956-0917. E-mail: president@rocklandlibraries.org. Web Site: www.rocklandlibraries.org.
Member Libraries: 17 pub
Primary Functions: To support & promote public libraries, public library development & public library services in Rockland County

LIBRARY CONSORTIUM OF HEALTH INSTITUTIONS IN BUFFALO*, (LCHIB), Abbott Hall, SUNY at Buffalo, 3435 Main St, Buffalo, 14214. SAN 329-367X. Tel: 716-829-3900, Ext 143. FAX: 716-829-2211. E-mail: hubnet@buffalo.edu, Ulb-lchib@buffalo.edu. Web Site: hubnet.buffalo.edu. *Exec Dir,* Martin E Mutka; E-mail: Mmutka@buffalo.edu
Founded 1988
Member Libraries: 10
Primary Functions: Cooperative collection development, library services & interlibrary loan; manage & provide access to share electronics resources over wide area network HUB NET

LONG ISLAND LIBRARY RESOURCES COUNCIL, (LILRC), 627 N Sunrise Service Rd, Bellport, 11713. SAN 322-2489. Tel: 631-675-1570. Web Site: lilrc.org. *Exec Dir,* Tim Spindler; E-mail: tspindler@lilrc.org
Founded 1966
Member Libraries: 198 acad, med, pub, sch & spec
Primary Functions: Interlibrary loan location (last resort); direct access (Research Loan Program); cooperative acquisitions, Hospital Library Services Program; Coordinated Collection Development Program; continuing education programs & workshops; Internet Gateway & OCLC FirstSearch access; regional digitization program

MEDICAL & SCIENTIFIC LIBRARIES OF LONG ISLAND*, (MEDLI), Molloy College, 1000 Hempstead Ave, Rockville Centre, 11571. SAN 322-4309. Web Site: medli.org. *Pres,* Joan Wagner; E-mail: medlipresident@gmail.com; *Treas,* Theresa Rienzo; E-mail: trienzo@molloy.edu
Founded 1962
Member Libraries: 50
Primary Functions: Initiate, sponsor & contribute to any educational programs pertaining to medicine & related subjects

METROPOLITAN NEW YORK LIBRARY COUNCIL*, (METRO), 599 11th Ave, 8th Flr, New York, 10036. SAN 322-2500. Tel: 212-228-2320. FAX: 212-228-2598. E-mail: info@metro.org. Web Site: metro.org. *Exec Dir,* Nate Hill; E-mail: nhill@metro.org; *Chief Admin Officer,* Kyle Brown; E-mail: kbrown@metro.org
Founded 1964
Member Libraries: 270
Primary Functions: Training professional development in resource sharing; coordinate digitization projects

NELLCO LAW LIBRARY CONSORTIUM, INC.*, 756 Madison Ave, Ste 102, Albany, 12208. SAN 322-4244. Tel: 518-694-3025. FAX: 518-694-3027. Administration E-mail: admin@nellco.org. Web Site: www.nellco.org. *Exec Dir,* Corie Dugas; Tel: 518-694-3026, E-mail: corie.dugas@nellco.org; *Admin & Mem Support Mgr,* Theresa M McCue; E-mail: theresa.mccue@nellco.org
Founded 1983
Member Libraries: 120+ law libraries in the U.S., Canada, the U.K. & Australia
Primary Functions: Interlibrary loan; virtual reference; legal scholarship repository; collaborative web page development; internships & exchanges; newsletter; union catalog for members; cooperative acquisitions

NORTHERN NEW YORK LIBRARY NETWORK*, 6721 US Hwy 11, Potsdam, 13676. SAN 322-2527. Tel: 315-265-1119. FAX: 315-265-1881. Web Site: nnyln.org. *Exec Dir,* Meg Backus; Tel: 315-265-1119, Ext 1, E-mail: meg@nnyln.org; *Assoc Dir, Bus Serv,* Phil Jones; Tel: 315-265-1119, Ext 17, E-mail: philj@nnyln.org; *Regional Serv Librn,* Eric Alan; E-mail: eric@nnyln.oeg; *IT Coordr,* Charles Henry; E-mail: chuck@nnyln.org
Founded 1965
Member Libraries: 67 acad, hospital, pub, res, sch & spec
Primary Functions: Reciprocal borrowing; interlibrary loan; paper & electronic union lists & directories; electronic mail; cooperative acquisition of library materials; continuing education for librarians & archivists; publication program; catalog support; bibliographic center; joint grants & research projects; computerized literature searches; conservation & preservation of historical materials; hospital library program; library regional automation program; public relations; automated services; shared access to commercial online database; technical assistance to special collections, archives & historical documents repositories; regional web catalog (ICEPAC) - www.icepac.net & regional interlibrary loan system (ICICILL); newspaper digitization

PROCONSORT, (Formerly Westchester Academic Library Directors Organization), 118 N Bedford Rd, Ste 100, Mount Kisco, 10549. E-mail: support@proconsort.atlassian.net. Web Site: proconsort.com. *Chief Exec Officer,* John Stromquist; *Director, Admin,* Daniel Karen; *Develop Dir,* Danila Kuklov
Founded 2000
Member Libraries: Acad, hospital & pub libr
Primary Functions: Procurement & administration of electronic information services

ROCHESTER REGIONAL LIBRARY COUNCIL*, 3445 Winton Pl, Ste 204, Rochester, 14623. SAN 322-2535. Tel: 585-223-7570. FAX: 585-223-7712. E-mail: rrlc@rrlc.org. Web Site: rrlc.org. *Exec Dir,* Laura Osterhout; E-mail: losterhout@rrlc.org; *Outreach Librn,* Barbara Ciambar; E-mail: bciambor@rrlc.org; *Digital Initiatives Librn,* Ryan Hughes; E-mail: rhughes@rrlc.org; *Educ Serv Mgr,* Tina Broomfield; E-mail: cbroomfield@rrlc.org
Founded 1966
Member Libraries: 57 acad, hospital, pub, res, sch, seminary & spec
Primary Functions: Interlibrary loan; photocopies; consortial purchases of electronic resources; OCLC processing center courier service; hospital library services; regional borrower's card; coordinated collection development program; regional automation program; continuing education programs for staff development; gifts & exchange program; directory of area libraries & resources; Union List of Serials; Union List of Historical Maps; Union catalog on the web; preservation of library materials, grant applications; share databases, automation & technology

SOUTH CENTRAL REGIONAL LIBRARY COUNCIL*, Clinton Hall, 108 N Cayuga St, Ithaca, 14850. SAN 322-2543. Tel: 607-273-9106. FAX: 607-272-0740. E-mail: scrlc@scrlc.org. Web Site: www.scrlc.org. *Exec Dir,* Mary-Carol Lindbloom; E-mail: mclindbloom@scrlc.org
Founded 1967
Member Libraries: 75
Primary Functions: Resource sharing; continuing education; grantsmanship; consulting & focus groups; legislative advocacy; hospital library services program: consortial purchase of e-resources, regional digitizing program

SOUTHEASTERN NEW YORK LIBRARY RESOURCES COUNCIL*, (SENYLRC), 21 S Elting Corners Rd, Highland, 12528-2805. SAN 322-2551. Tel: 845-883-9065. FAX: 845-883-9483. Web Site: www.senylrc.org. *Exec Dir,* Tessa Killian; E-mail: killian@senylrc.org
Founded 1965
Member Libraries: Over 80 acad, med, pub, sch libr systs & spec; 24 assoc
Primary Functions: Coordinates cooperative automation, interlibrary loan, delivery, electronic resource group discounts & admin reference services & retrospective conversion; publishes Union Catalog; maintains Union List of Serials; offers staff-development workshops, continuing education & consultations; publishes directories brochures; database searching; hospital library program; database maintenance; archival assistance; Conservation & Preservation assistance

SUNYCONNECT*, Office of Library & Information Services, SUNY Plaza, Albany, 12246. Tel: 518-320-1477. FAX: 518-320-1554. E-mail: olis@suny.edu. Web Site: www.sunyconnect.suny.edu. *Assoc Provost for Academic Technologies & Info Services,* Carey Hatch; E-mail: carey.hatch@suny.edu; *Prog Mgr,* Maureen Zajkowski; E-mail: maureen.zajkowski@suny.edu
Founded 2000
Member Libraries: 64
Primary Functions: Share collection & services across State University of New York

UNITED NATIONS SYSTEM ELECTRONIC INFORMATION ACQUISITIONS CONSORTIUM*, (UNSEIAC), c/o United Nations Library, 450 E 42nd St, Rm L-0204, New York, 10017. SAN 377-855X. Tel: 212-963-3000. E-mail: unseiac@un.org. Web Site: research.un.org. *Coordr,* Joelle Sciboz; Tel: 212-963-1344, E-mail: sciboz@un.org
Founded 1998
Member Libraries: 55
Primary Functions: Share cost of & access to electronic information resources within the United Nations System

WESTERN NEW YORK LIBRARY RESOURCES COUNCIL*, Airport Commerce Park E, 495 Genesee St, Ste 170, Cheektowaga, 14225. SAN 322-2578. Tel: 716-633-0705. FAX: 716-288-9400. Web Site: www.wnylrc.org/. *Exec Dir,* Sheryl Knab; E-mail: sknab@wnylrc.org
Founded 1966
Member Libraries: 64 academic, corporate, hospital, special, public and school library systems
Primary Functions: To foster & develop multi-type interlibrary cooperation, sharing & interlibrary loan among junior college, college, university, public, research, industrial, school, technical, hospital & medical libraries; to extend & improve library services to the profession, business, industry & the general public

NORTH CAROLINA

COMMUNITY COLLEGE LIBRARIES IN NORTH CAROLINA, (CCLINC), North Carolina Community Colleges System, 200 W Jones St, Raleigh, 27603. SAN 322-2594. Tel: 919-807-7100. Web Site: www.nccommunitycolleges.edu/college-faculty-staff/student-services/library-services. *Dir, Libr Serv,* Birch Barnes; Tel: 919-807-7066, E-mail: barnesb@nccommunitycolleges.edu
Founded 1963
Member Libraries: 58 community col
Primary Functions: To manage a statewide system of community colleges; to assist the colleges in providing essential services including support to provide technical services support; to provide collection development/management services; to provide leadership in library information technology initiatives

NORTHWEST AHEC LIBRARY INFORMATION NETWORK, One Medical Center Blvd, Winston-Salem, 27157. SAN 322-4708. Tel: 336-618-0310. FAX: 336-713-7701. Web Site: go.northwestahec.wakehealth.edu. *Professional Outreach Librn,* Janice D Moore; E-mail: jdmoore@wakehealth.edu
Founded 1976
Member Libraries: 4
Primary Functions: Resource sharing; outreach; circuit librarian & consultation; computer searching

TRIANGLE RESEARCH LIBRARIES NETWORK*, Wilson Library, CB No 3940, Chapel Hill, 27514-8890. SAN 329-5362. Tel: 919-962-8022. FAX: 919-962-4452. Web Site: www.trln.org. *Exec Dir,* Lisa Croucher; E-mail: lisa@trln.org; *Prog Officer,* Kelly Farrell; E-mail: kelly@trln.org
Founded 1977
Member Libraries: 10
Primary Functions: Collaborative organization of Duke University, North Carolina Central University, North Carolina State University & The University of North Carolina at Chapel Hill, the purpose of which is to marshal the financial, human & information resources of their research libraries through cooperative efforts in order to create a rich & unparalleled knowledge environment that furthers the universities' teaching, research & service missions

WESTERN NORTH CAROLINA LIBRARY NETWORK*, (WNCLN), c/o Appalachian State University, 218 College St, Boone, 28608. SAN 376-7205. Tel: 828-668-2368. Web Site: wncln.wncln.org. *Network Librarian,* Ben Shirley; E-mail: shirleybd@appstate.edu
Founded 1985
Member Libraries: 3
Primary Functions: Maintenance & enhancement of an integrated library system (Innopac: wncln.wncln.org); sharing of library materials through a network delivery service; development of cooperative collection management policies

NORTH DAKOTA

CENTRAL DAKOTA LIBRARY NETWORK*, 515 N Fifth St, Bismarck, 58501. SAN 373-1391. Tel: 701-55-1480. E-mail: mortonmandanlibrary@cdln.info. Web Site: www.cdln.info.
Founded 1990
Member Libraries: 20
Primary Functions: Facilitate & enhance the sharing of resources & services; improve access to & dissemination of knowledge & information; provide online public access catalog

OHIO

ASSOCIATION OF CHRISTIAN LIBRARIANS, (ACL), PO Box 4, Cedarville, 45314. Tel: 937-766-2255. E-mail: info@acl.org. Web Site: www.acl.org. *Pres,* Jeremy Labosier; *VPres,* Nate Farley; *Exec Dir,* Janelle Mazelin; E-mail: mazelinj@acl.org
Founded 1956
Member Libraries: 630
Primary Functions: The mission of the Association of Christian Librarians is to strengthen libraries by equipping Christian librarians through professional development, scholarship, and spiritual encouragement for service primarily in higher education.

CHRISTIAN LIBRARY CONSORTIUM, (CLC), c/o ACL, PO Box 4, Cedarville, 45314. Tel: 937-766-2255. FAX: 937-766-5499. E-mail: info@acl.org. Web Site: acl.org. *Coll Serv Librn,* Beth Purtee; E-mail: clc@acl.org
Founded 1991
Member Libraries: 190
Primary Functions: Resource sharing; vendor discounts; purchasing agreement for religious and other e-books

CONSORTIUM OF OHIO LIBRARIES*, (COOL), 1500 W Lane Ave, Columbus, 43221. Tel: 614-484-1061. Toll Free Tel: 800-686-8975. E-mail: info@info.cool-cat.org. Web Site: info.cool-cat.org. *Chair,* Curtis Schafer; E-mail: cshafer.apl@gmail.com; *Vice Chair,* Joe Knueven; E-mail: joe@wilmington.lib.oh.us
Founded 2012
Member Libraries: 13 pub
Primary Functions: Members share an Evergreen open-source library management system to facilitate borrowing & lending between libraries

CONSORTIUM OF POPULAR CULTURE COLLECTIONS IN THE MIDWEST*, (CPCCM), c/o Browne Popular Culture Library, Bowling Green State University, Bowling Green, 43403-0600. SAN 370-5811. Tel: 419-372-2450. FAX: 419-372-7996. *Interim Head Librn,* Stefanie Dennis Hunker; Tel: 419-372-7893, E-mail: sdennis@bgsu.edu
Founded 1990
Member Libraries: 8 acad
Primary Functions: Seeks to promote popular culture materials through cooperative collection development, access, preservation & promotion of research

FIVE COLLEGES OF OHIO*, Oberlin College, 173 W Lorain St, Rm 208, Oberlin, 44074. Tel: 440-775-5500. E-mail: libraries@ohio5.org. Web Site: www.ohio5.org. *Exec Dir,* Lindsey Interlante; E-mail: interlantel@ohio5.org; *Dir, Consortia Library Systems,* Spenser Lamm
Founded 1995
Member Libraries: 5
Primary Functions: Collaborates to provide cost savings & cost avoidance, promote scholarship & innovation, & improve competitive advantage in admissions & faculty recruitment

NASA LIBRARY NETWORK*, c/o Glenn Research Center, 21000 Brookpark Rd, Cleveland, 44135.
Member Libraries: 11 NASA libr in US
Primary Functions: To procure agency-wide e-journal & e-book subscriptions, improve access to library resources & modernize & consolidate the services of NASA libraries

NORTHEAST OHIO REGIONAL LIBRARY SYSTEM*, (NEO-RLS), 1737 Georgetown Rd, Ste B, Hudson, 44236. SAN 322-2713. Tel: 330-655-0531. FAX: 330-655-0568. Web Site: www.neo-rls.org. *Exec Dir,* Betsy Lantz; Tel: 330-655-0531, Ext 101, E-mail: betsy.lantz@neo-rls.org; *Fiscal Officer,* Debbie Blair; Tel: 330-655-0531, Ext 102, E-mail: deb.blair@neo-rls.org; *Continuing Educ Coordr,* Melissa Lattanzi; Tel: 330-655-0531, Ext 103, E-mail: lattanzm@neo-rls.org; *Continuing Educ Coordr,* Ragan Snead; Tel: 330-655-0531, Ext 105, E-mail: ragan.snead@neo-rls.org
Founded 1972
Member Libraries: 99 acad, pub, sch & spec
Primary Functions: Continuing Education; Professional Development; Strategic Planning service; Staff Day planning service; emerging technology services and circulating tech kits; e-Rate filing; One-on-one Management Coaching

NORWELD*, 181 1/2 S Main St, Bowling Green, 43402. SAN 322-273X. Tel: 419-352-2903. FAX: 419-353-8310. Web Site: www.norweld.org/. *Exec Dir,* Janelle Thomas; E-mail: jthomas@norweld.org
Member Libraries: 50 pub
Primary Functions: Interlibrary loan; reference service; large print book circuit; public relations; regional & local library planning; consultant services; delivery service

OCLC ONLINE COMPUTER LIBRARY CENTER, INC*, 6565 Kilgour Pl, Dublin, 43017-3395. SAN 322-2748. Tel: 614-764-6000. Toll Free Tel: 800-848-5878. FAX: 614-764-6096. E-mail: oclc@oclc.org. Web Site: www.oclc.org. *Pres & Chief Exec Officer,* Skip Pritchard; E-mail: skip@oclc.org; *VPres, Libr Serv,* Bruce Crocco; E-mail: croccob@oclc.org; *Chief Financial Officer,* William J Rozek; E-mail: rozekb@oclc.org; *Chief Info Officer, Chief Tech Officer,* Bart Murphy; E-mail: murphyba@oclc.org
Founded 1967
Member Libraries: 17,983
Primary Functions: Engages in computer library services & research; OCLC systems help libraries locate, acquire, catalog & lend books & other library materials; OCLC reference services provide electronic journals & online information used by researchers, students, faculty & scholars, as well as professional librarians; NetLibrary, a division of OCLC, offers an easy-to-use information retrieval system for accessing the full text of reference, scholarly & professional books & other e-content; more than 52,000 libraries contribute to &/or use info in WorldCat (Online Union Catalog), the world's largest database of library bibliographic information; through affiliated US regional networks, service centers & distributors, provides cataloging, database services, resource sharing, conversion & contract cataloging in 95 countries & territories; publishes the Dewey Decimal Classification, the world's most widely used classification system; OCLC Digital Collection & Preservation Services provides high quality microfilming, access & dissemination options for libraries, archives & museums

OCLC RESEARCH LIBRARY PARTNERSHIP*, 6565 Kilgour Pl, Dublin, 43017. Tel: 614-764-6000. E-mail: oclcresearch@oclc.org. Web Site: oclc.org/research/partnership. *Exec Dir,* Rachel L Frick; E-mail: frickr@oclc.org
Member Libraries: 123
Primary Functions: Creates opportunities for collaboration & peer learning through working groups, interest groups, webinars & special events; leverages the deep expertise of OCLC Research & is informed by an international, system-wide perspective; shared OCLC research efforts & access to the Research team's expertise for local consultation

OHIO HEALTH SCIENCES LIBRARY ASSOCIATION, (OHSLA), c/o Ohio Health Riverside Methodist Hospital, 3535 Olentangy River Rd, Columbus, 43214. Tel: 614-566-5740. E-mail: ohsla.info@gmail.com. Web Site: www.ohsla.info. *Pres,* Stacy Gall; E-mail: stacy.gall@ohiohealth.com
Founded 1994
Member Libraries: 60
Primary Functions: Statewide networking with other health information professionals & opportunities for cooperative ventures with other Ohio health science libraries

OHIO LIBRARY & INFORMATION NETWORK, (OhioLINK), 1224 Kinnear Rd, Columbus, 43215. SAN 374-8014. Tel: 614-485-6722. E-mail: info@ohiolink.edu. Web Site: www.ohiolink.edu. *Exec Dir,* Amy Pawlowski; E-mail: apawlowski@ohiolink.edu
Founded 1989
Member Libraries: 118 acad & State Library of Ohio
Primary Functions: Provide Ohio students, faculty & researchers with the information they need for teaching & research; provide access to & delivery of millions of books & other library materials, millions of electronic articles, electronic research databases, e-books, images, videos, sounds, theses & dissertations from Ohio students

OHIO NETWORK OF AMERICAN HISTORY RESEARCH CENTERS*, Ohio Historical Society Archives-Library, 1982 Velma Ave, Columbus, 43211-2497. SAN 323-9624. Tel: 614-297-2510. FAX: 614-297-2546. Reference E-mail: reference@ohiohistory.org. Web Site: www.ohiohistory.org. *Dir, Mus & Libr Serv,* Jen Aultman; E-mail: jaultman@ohiohistory.org
Founded 1970
Open Mon & Tues 9-12, Wed-Fri 10-5
Primary Functions: The Ohio Network of American History Research Centers was established in 1970 to aid in the collection, preservation & use of research materials documenting the history of the state; member respositories include the University of Akron, Bowling Green State University, the University of Cincinnati, the Ohio Historical Society, Ohio University, the Western Reserve Historical Society, Wright State University & the Youngstown Historical Center of Industry & Labor

OHIO PUBLIC LIBRARY INFORMATION NETWORK*, (OPLIN), 2323 W Fifth Ave, Ste 130, Columbus, 43204. Tel: 614-728-5252. Toll Free Tel: 888-966-7546. FAX: 614-728-5256. E-mail: support@oplin.ohio.gov. Web Site: oplin.ohio.gov. *Exec Dir,* Don Yarman; E-mail: don@oplin.ohio.gov; *Libr Serv Mgr,* Laura Solomon
Founded 1996
Member Libraries: 251 pub lib sys
Primary Functions: To provide broadband internet connections & related information services to Ohio public library systems

OHIONET*, 1500 W Lane Ave, Columbus, 43221-3975. SAN 322-2764. Tel: 614-486-2966. Toll Free Tel: 800-686-8975. FAX: 614-486-1527. E-mail: ohionet@ohionet.org. Web Site: ohionet.org. *Chief Exec Officer, Exec Dir,* Katy Mathuews; E-mail: katym@ohionet.org; *Dep Dir,* Christine Morris; E-mail: christinem@ohionet.org
Founded 1977
Member Libraries: 300
Primary Functions: We are a membership-driven organization serving libraries and information centers of all types and sizes throughout Ohio, West Virginia and western Pennsylvania. By providing innovative technology solutions, products, and training, we support our members' efforts to meet the needs of the diverse communities they serve.

SERVING EVERY OHIOAN SERVICE CENTER, (SEO), 40780 Marietta Rd, Caldwell, 43724. SAN 356-4606. Tel: 740-783-5705. Toll Free Tel: 877-552-4262. Toll Free FAX: 800-446-4804. Web Site: servingeveryohioan.org. *Director, Operations & Tech,* John Stewart; E-mail: jstewart@library.ohio.gov; *Customer Serv Mgr,* Jay Miley; E-mail: jmiley@library.ohio.gov
Founded 1961
Member Libraries: 104
Primary Functions: Resource sharing among members libraries

SOUTHEAST REGIONAL LIBRARY SYSTEM*, (SERLS), 252 W 13th St, Wellston, 45692. SAN 322-2756. Tel: 740-384-2103. FAX: 740-384-2106. Web Site: www.serls.org. *Dir,* Jay Burton; E-mail: director@serls.org; *Fiscal Officer,* Brenda Hutchison; E-mail: ctserls@serls.org
Founded 1973
Member Libraries: 24
Primary Functions: Consulting services; interlibrary loan; references services; continuing education

SOUTHWEST OHIO & NEIGHBORING LIBRARIES*, (SWON), 10250 Alliance Rd, Ste 112, Cincinnati, 45242. SAN 322-2675. Tel: 513-751-4423. E-mail: info@swonlibraries.org. Web Site: www.swonlibraries.org. *Exec Dir,* Gayle Ecabert; *Continuing Educ Coordr,* Cassondra Vick; *Educ Tech Spec,* Chas Smith
Founded 1973
Member Libraries: 47
Primary Functions: Library consulting - all types; direct lending; continuing education; custom staff training; information exchange; group discounts; web site & discussion forums; jobs listings; applied technology training; technology to lend including makerspace components

STRATEGIC OHIO COUNCIL FOR HIGHER EDUCATION*, (SOCHE), (Formerly Southwestern Ohio Council for Higher Education), Miami Valley Research Park, 3155 Research Blvd, Ste 204, Dayton, 45420-4015. SAN 322-2659. Tel: 937-258-8890. FAX: 937-258-8899. E-mail: soche@soche.org. Web Site: www.soche.org. *Exec Dir,* Cassie Barlow; E-mail: cassie.barlow@soche.org
Founded 1967
Member Libraries: 21 acad, corp, law, med, mil, tech & theol
Primary Functions: Resource sharing; delivery system; 16mm film catalog; joint & cooperative acquisitions; staff development

OKLAHOMA

MID-AMERICA LAW LIBRARY CONSORTIUM*, (MALLCO), 800 N Harvey Ave, Oklahoma City, 73102. SAN 371-6813. Tel: 405-208-5393. Web Site: mallco.org. *Exec Dir,* Susan Urban; E-mail: mallcoexecutivedirector@gmail.com
Founded 1980
Member Libraries: 27 acad
Primary Functions: Promotion of resource sharing; cooperation among member schools

OKLAHOMA HEALTH SCIENCES LIBRARY ASSOCIATION, (OHSLA), University of Oklahoma - HSC Bird Health Science Library, 1101 N Stonewall, Oklahoma City, 73190. (Mail add: PO Box 26901, Oklahoma City, 73126-0901), SAN 375-0051. Tel: 405-271-2285, Ext 48755. FAX: 405-271-3297. Web Site: ohsla.pbworks.com/w/page/61886926/homepage. *Dir,* Joy Summers-Ables; E-mail: joy-summers@ouhsc.edu
Member Libraries: 6 col/univ, 7 misc librs & 20 hosp
Primary Functions: Continuing education; sharing of resources

OREGON

CHEMEKETA COOPERATIVE REGIONAL LIBRARY SERVICE, (CCRLS), 4000 Lancaster Dr NE, Salem, 97305. SAN 322-2837. Tel: 503-399-5165. E-mail: contact.us@ccrls.info. Web Site: www.ccrls.org. *Exec Dir,* Doug Yancey
Founded 1973
Member Libraries: 18
Primary Functions: To promote library services & facilitate resource sharing among member libraries in Marion, Polk & Yamhill counties

LIBRARIES IN CLACKAMAS COUNTY, (LINCC), (Formerly Library Information Network of Clackamas County), 1810 Red Soils Ct, Ste 110, Oregon City, 97045. SAN 322-2845. Tel: 503-723-4888. Web Site: lincc.ent.sirsi.net. *Operations Mgr,* Darrel Mally; Tel: 503-723-4853, E-mail: dmally@lincc.org
Founded 1977
Member Libraries: 13
Primary Functions: Courier service; materials handling; administration of automated library system; centralized MARC cataloging via OCLC; centralized ILL via OCLC; continuing education; committee & project support, administrative functions; SirsiDynix Symphony ILS

ORBIS CASCADE ALLIANCE*, PO Box 6007, Portland, 97228. SAN 377-8096. Tel: 541-246-2470. E-mail: info@orbiscascade.org. Web Site: www.orbiscascade.org. *Exec Dir,* Kim Armstrong; E-mail: karmstrong@orbiscascade.org; *Asst Dir, Prog Mgr,* Maija Anderson; E-mail: manderson@orbiscascade.org; *Finance Mgr,* Amy Wheeler; *Program Mgr, Resource Sharing & Fulfillment,* Lori Hilterbrand; *Program Mgr, Share Content,* Jesse Holden; *Program Support & Events Mgr,* Elizabeth Duell; *Program Mgr, Systems,* Tamara Marnell; *Program Mgr, Tech Services,* Lesley Lowery; *E-Resources Specialist,* Jaime Bogdash
Founded 1993
Member Libraries: 38 acad
Primary Functions: Shared integrated library system; patron-initiated borrowing direct; reciprocal borrowing agreement for onsite borrowing; electronic resource licensing projects; contract administrator for library courier services; northwest digital archives program

WASHINGTON COUNTY COOPERATIVE LIBRARY SERVICES*, 2350 NE Griffin Oaks St, Hillsboro, 97124. SAN 322-287X. Tel: 503-846-3222. FAX: 503-846-3220. Web Site: www.wccls.org. *Mgr,* Lisa Tattersall; E-mail: lisat@wccls.org
Founded 1976
Member Libraries: 16 pub
Primary Functions: Interlibrary communication; courier service; online searching & interlibrary loan service; extensive e-book collection and databases for patrons with a library card; library development for community libraries; universal access to all public libraries; outreach to homebound; youth services coordination; branch coordination; automation centralized cataloging, on-line public access catalog & circulation including Internet access; public relations, staff training & development; provide 65% of operating funding to member libraries; jail library support; Spanish language support; outreach to Daycare and schools; summer reading program coordination; management of the West Slope Library

PENNSYLVANIA

CENTRAL PENNSYLVANIA CONSORTIUM*, (CPC), c/o Franklin & Marshall College, Goethean Hall 101, Lancaster, 17604. (Mail add: PO Box 3003, Lancaster, 17604-3003), SAN 322-2896. Tel: 717-358-4282. Web Site: centralpennsylvaniaconsortium.org. *Provost,* Neil B Weissman; *Provost,* Cameron Wesson; *Provost,* Christopher Zappe
Founded 1968
Member Libraries: 3 acad
Primary Functions: Interlibrary loan; interconsortium cooperation; journals analysis & redistribution; audio tapes sharing; online network administration

EASTERN MENNONITE ASSOCIATED LIBRARIES & ARCHIVES, (EMALA), 431 Gridley Rd, Lancaster, 17602. SAN 372-8226. Tel: 717-393-9745.
Founded 1961
Member Libraries: 8 spec (Mennonite & Anabaptist coll)
Primary Functions: Promote cooperation & foster discussion concerning operations, collection management & resources of Mennonite libraries, archives & museums; provide financial support for publication of Mennonite & Anabaptist research

GREATER PHILADELPHIA LAW LIBRARY ASSOCIATION*, (GPLLA), PO Box 335, Philadelphia, 19105. SAN 373-1375. Web Site: gplla.org. *Pres,* Andrew Lang; E-mail: andlang@law.upenn.edu
Founded 1970
Member Libraries: 230
Primary Functions: Promote librarianship; develop & increase the usefulness of law libraries; cultivate the science of law librarianship; foster a spirit of cooperation among the members of the profession

HEALTH SCIENCES LIBRARIES CONSORTIUM*, (HSLC), 3600 Market St, Ste 550, Philadelphia, 19104-2646. SAN 323-9780. Tel: 215-222-1532. FAX: 215-222-0416. E-mail: support@hslc.org. Web Site: www.hslc.org. *Exec Dir,* Maryam Phillips; E-mail: phillips@hslc.org; *Dep Dir,* Vincent Mariner; E-mail: mariner@hslc.org; *Dir, Libr Serv,* Cindy A Pitchon; *Dir, Network Serv,* Alan C Simon
Founded 1988
Member Libraries: 2600
Primary Functions: Cooperative programs in automated systems; statewide electronic interlibrary loan system; statewide online union catalog; subscription database services; POWER Library program; Ask Here PA virtual reference service; Access PA Digital Repository

INTERLIBRARY DELIVERY SERVICE OF PENNSYLVANIA*, (IDS), c/o Bucks County IU, No 22, 705 N Shady Retreat Rd, Doylestown, 18901. SAN 322-2942. Tel: 215-348-2940, Ext 1625. FAX: 215-348-8315. E-mail: ids@bucksiu.org. Web Site: idspa.org. *Admin Dir,* Pamela Dinan; E-mail: pdinan@bucksiu.org
Member Libraries: 224 acad, pub, sch & spec
Primary Functions: Interlibrary loan; delivery service

KEYSTONE LIBRARY NETWORK*, (KLN), 2300 Vartan Way, Ste 207, Harrisburg, 17110. Tel: 717-720-4208. Web Site: www.klnpa.org. *Network Adminr,* Mike Dorshimer; E-mail: mrdorshimer@ship.edu; *Interim Coordr,* Richard Riccardi; E-mail: rriccardi@passhe.edu
Founded 1998
Member Libraries: 16 col, state & univ
Primary Functions: Collections sharing; common library system; electronic content licensing; training including information literacy videos; electronic content presentation; ILL; document delivery; bookbinding contract; Archives Space; CONTENTdm, Islandora

LEHIGH VALLEY ASSOCIATION OF INDEPENDENT COLLEGES*, 1309 Main St, Bethlehem, 18018. SAN 322-2969. Tel: 610-625-7888. FAX: 610-625-7891. Web Site: www.lvaic.org. *Exec Dir,* Diane Dimitroff; E-mail: dimitroffd@lvaic.org
Founded 1969
Member Libraries: 6 acad
Primary Functions: Mutual notification of purchase or intent to purchase; delivery services; photocopying services; production or maintenance of Union catalogs, lists & directories; reciprocal borrowing privileges; interlibrary loan system involving association member colleges & area public libraries

MONTGOMERY COUNTY LIBRARY & INFORMATION NETWORK CONSORTIUM*, (MCLINC), 520 Virginia Dr, Fort Washington, 19034. Tel: 610-238-0580. Web Site: www.mclinc.org. *Pres,* Lisa Clancy; E-mail: lclancy@mclinc.org; *Exec Dir,* Michelle Kehoe; E-mail: mkehoe@mclinc.org
Founded 1995
Member Libraries: 31 pub
Primary Functions: Connect all free libraries & provide for their computer needs throughout Montgomery county

PARTNERSHIP FOR ACADEMIC LIBRARY COLLABORATIVE & INNOVATION*, (PALCI), 1005 Pontiac Rd, Ste 330, Drexel Hill, 19026. Tel: 215-567-1755. E-mail: support@palci.org. Web Site: www.palci.org. *Exec Dir,* Jill Morris; E-mail: jill@palci.org; *Mem Serv Coordr,* Carl Piraneo; E-mail: carl@palci.org
Founded 1996
Member Libraries: 74 coll, univ & res librs in PA, WV, NJ, and NY
Primary Functions: To enable cost-effective & sustainable access to information resources & services for academic libraries in Pennsylvania & surrounding states

PENNSYLVANIA LIBRARY ASSOCIATION, 220 Cumberland Pkwy, Ste 10, Mechanicsburg, 17055. Tel: 717-766-7663. Web Site: www.palibraries.org. *Exec Dir,* Christi Buker; E-mail: christi@palibraries.org
Founded 1901
Member Libraries: 1,500 individuals, 300 institutions
Primary Functions: Provide leadership development, continuing education & advocacy on behalf of libraries

PHILADELPHIA AREA CONSORTIUM OF SPECIAL COLLECTIONS LIBRARIES, (PACSCL), c/o The Library Company, 1300 Locust St, Philadelphia, 19107. (Mail add: PO Box 1321, Doylestown, 18901), SAN 370-7504. Tel: 501-295-4215. Web Site: www.pacscl.org. *Managing Dir,* Beth Lander; E-mail: director@pacscl.org
Founded 1985
Member Libraries: 38
Primary Functions: Encourages diverse audiences to explore & engage with member libraries' uniquely rich holdings & through collaboration, strengthens these collections & the institutions that preserve them

SOUTHEASTERN PENNSYLVANIA THEOLOGICAL LIBRARY ASSOCIATION*, (SEPTLA), c/o Biblical Seminary, 200 N Main St, Hatfield, 19440. SAN 371-0793. Tel: 2215-368-5000, Ext 234. Web Site: www.septla.org. *Pres,* Greg Murray; *Exec Secy,* Jenifer Gundry; Tel: 609-497-7758, E-mail: jenifer.gundry@ptsem.edu
Founded 1965
Member Libraries: 19 acad
Primary Functions: Promote cooperation among member libraries for ILL, Union List of Serials, resource sharing & exchange of ideas particularly among the different denominations of member libraries

TRI-STATE COLLEGE LIBRARY COOPERATIVE*, (TCLC), c/o Rosemont College Library, 1400 Montgomery Ave, Rosemont, 19010. SAN 322-3078. Tel: 610-525-0796. E-mail: tclc@rosemont.edu. Web Site: tclclibs.org. *Pres,* Mary Anne Farrell; E-mail: farrell@dtcc.edu; *Coordr,* Position Currently Open
Founded 1967
Member Libraries: 30
Primary Functions: Educational programs; interlibrary loan; direct borrowing; continuing education awards; professional development opportunities

RHODE ISLAND

LIBRARY OF RHODE ISLAND NETWORK, (LORI), One Capitol Hill, Providence, 02908. SAN 371-6821. Tel: 401-574-9300. FAX: 401-574-9320. Web Site: www.olis.ri.gov. *Chief, Libr Serv,* Karen Mellor; E-mail: karen.mellor@olis.ri.gov; *Resource Sharing Coord,* Lori DeCesare; Tel: 401-574-9307, E-mail: lori.decesare@olis.ri.gov
Founded 1964
Member Libraries: 176 libr sys
Primary Functions: The Library of Rhode Island (LORI) is a multi-type statewide library network, administered by the Office of Library & Information Services (OLIS) to foster & facilitate resource sharing & cooperation among the state's libraries & library personnel. Network members agree to comply with LORI Standards & Regulations & annually certify to this effect. In addition to the LORI network, OLIS provides interlibrary delivery; statewide programming in libraries; state agency consulting services; electronic communications; library directories; talking books plus; library construction; continuing education

OCEAN STATE LIBRARIES*, (OSL), 300 Centerville Rd, Ste 103S, Warwick, 02886. SAN 329-4560. Tel: 401-738-2200. E-mail: support@oslri.net. Web Site: www.oslri.org. *Exec Dir,* Stephen Spohn; Tel: 401-593-2160, E-mail: sspohn@oslri.net; *Asst Dir,* Lisa Sallee; Tel: 401-593-2167, E-mail: lsallee@oslri.net; *Syst Dir,* Renée Palermo; Tel: 401-593-2162, E-mail: rpalermo@oslri.net
Founded 1982
Member Libraries: 50
Primary Functions: Provides statewide catalog access, digital downloads, & technical support to its member libraries so they all can better serve their patrons & communities.

SOUTH CAROLINA

NATIONAL NETWORK OF LIBRARIES OF MEDICINE REGION 2, MUSC James W Colbert Educ Ctr & Libr, 171 Ashley Ave, Ste 300, MSC 403, Charleston, 29425. Tel: 843-792-2381. Web Site: nnlm.gov/about/regions/region2. *Exec Dir,* Lorin Jackson; Tel: 267-648-6170, E-mail: jacklori@musc.edu; *Dir,* Shannon Jones; Tel: 843-792-8839, E-mail: joneshan@musc.edu; *Assoc Dir of Libr,* Heather Holmes; Tel: 843-792-0065, E-mail: holmesh@musc.edu
Member Libraries: 1337
Primary Functions: Serves Alabama, Florida, Georgia, Mississippi, South Carolina, Tennessee, Puerto Rico & US Virgin Islands

PARTNERSHIP AMONG SOUTH CAROLINA ACADEMIC LIBRARIES*, (PASCAL), 1122 Lady St, Ste 400, Columbia, 29201. Tel: 803-734-0900. FAX: 803-734-0901. E-mail: office@pascalsc.org. Web Site: pascalsc.libguides.com. *Exec Dir,* Rick Moul; E-mail: rick.moul@pascalsc.org
Founded 2001
Member Libraries: 55 acad
Primary Functions: Shared library services platform; statewide rapid print delivery service; core electronic resources

SOUTH CAROLINA AHEC, One S Park Circle, Ste 203, Charleston, 29407. SAN 329-3998. Tel: 843-792-4431. FAX: 843-792-4430. Web Site: www.scahec.net. *Exec Dir,* Ann Lefebvre; E-mail: lefebvre@musc.edu
Founded 1972
Member Libraries: 12
Primary Functions: Retains physicians & other health care providers in the state; provides educational programs to health care professionals

TENNESSEE

APPALACHIAN COLLEGE ASSOCIATION*, 7216 Jewel Bell Lane, Bristol, 37620. (Mail add: ACA OFC, 3816 Camelot Dr, Lexington, 40517). Tel: 859-986-4584. FAX: 859-986-9549. Web Site: www.acaweb.org. *Pres,* Beth Rushing; E-mail: beth.rushing@acaweb.org; *Dir of Libr Prog,* Heather Tompkins; E-mail: heather.tompkins@acaweb.org; *VP, Academic Programs,* Larry Hall; E-mail: larry.hall@acaweb.org
Founded 1991
Member Libraries: 33 acad
Primary Functions: To promote cooperation & collaboration among member institutions & to support scholarly & creative activities of faculty & students

KNOXVILLE AREA HEALTH SCIENCES LIBRARY CONSORTIUM*, (KAHSLC), UT Preston Med Libr, 1924 Alcoa Hwy, Knoxville, 37920. SAN 371-0556. Tel: 865-305-9525. FAX: 865-305-9527. Web Site: kahslc.wordpress.com/. *Pres,* Martha Earl; E-mail: mearl@utmck.edu
Founded 1976
Member Libraries: 15 acad, commun col, hosp, med, pub & spec
Primary Functions: For better communication between health science libraries; cooperate in exchange of information & share existing resources; continuing education

TENN-SHARE, PO Box 691, Alcoa, 37701. Tel: 615-669-8670. E-mail: execdir@tenn-share.org. Web Site: www.tenn-share.org. *Exec Dir,* Ari Baker; *Bus Mgr,* Teresa Kline
Founded 1992
Member Libraries: 771
Primary Functions: Tenn-Share is a member-driven organization serving Tennessee libraries by providing cost effective resources & services that help them better serve their communities

TENNESSEE HEALTH SCIENCE LIBRARY ASSOCIATION*, (THeSLA), Holston Valley Med Ctr Health Sciences Library, 130 W Ravine Rd, Kingsport, 37660. SAN 371-0726. Tel: 423-224-6870. FAX: 423-224-6014. Web Site: www.theslatn.org/. *Pres,* Rick Wallace; Tel: 423-439-3883, E-mail: wallacer@etsu.edu
Founded 1977
Member Libraries: 55 acad, hosp & med
Primary Functions: To promote the profession & to provide education by exchange of information & materials

TEXAS

ABILENE LIBRARY CONSORTIUM*, 3305 N Third St, Abilene, 79603. SAN 322-4694. Tel: 325-672-7081. Toll Free Tel: 888-395-9723. FAX: 325-672-7081. Web Site: www.alc.org. *Exec Dir,* Edward J Smith; E-mail: edwards@alc.org
Founded 1989
Member Libraries: 5
Primary Functions: To deliver higher quality library services to our communities through resource sharing & collaboration

AMIGOS LIBRARY SERVICES, INC, 4901 LBJ Freeway, Ste 150, Dallas, 75244-6179. SAN 322-3191. Tel: 972-851-8000. Toll Free Tel: 800-843-8482. FAX: 972-991-6061. E-mail: amigos@amigos.org, info@amigos.org. Web Site: www.amigos.org. *Pres & Chief Exec Officer,* Miguel Figueroa; Tel: 972-340-2820, E-mail: figueroa@amigos.org; *Chief Financial Officer,* Keith Gaertner; Tel: 972-340-2894, E-mail: gaertner@amigos.org; *Chief Programs Officer,* Tracy Byerly; Tel: 972-340-2893, E-mail: byerly@amigos.org
Founded 1974
Member Libraries: Over 533 acad, cultural heritage, pub, sch, spec & state inst
Primary Functions: Member discounts on databases & supplies; resource sharing; consulting & training on cataloging, digital imaging, preservation & library technologies

BORDER REGIONAL LIBRARY ASSOCIATION*, (BRLA), PO Box 5342, El Paso, 79954-5342. E-mail: brla@nmsu.edu. Web Site: www.brla.info. *Pres,* Debi Lopez; Tel: 915-491-6173, E-mail: debilpz@gmail.com
Founded 1966
Member Libraries: 100 librarians, libr friends, media specialists, paraprofessionals & trustees
Primary Functions: To promote library service & librarianship in the El Paso/Las Cruces/Juarez metroplex; to provide a forum for local issues which impact the future of all types of libraries in the region; to serve as a support group to promote libraries as important educational & cultural institutions which have a direct impact on communities & democratic action

COUNCIL OF RESEARCH & ACADEMIC LIBRARIES, (CORAL), c/o Southwest Research Institute, 6220 Culebra Rd, San Antonio, 78212. SAN 322-3213. E-mail: coralsatx@gmail.com. Web Site: coralsa.org. *Pres,* Vicky Hart; Tel: 210-486-5461, E-mail: vhart4@alamo.edu
Member Libraries: 18 acad, mil inst, pvt & pub
Primary Functions: The Council of Research & Academic Libraries is a consortium of libraries in the greater San Antonio area. CORAL develops & strengthens library information resources & services through the development of cooperative programs, by providing a forum for librarians from member institutions to discuss important issues & by promoting information literacy in the greater San Antonio area, as well as in member institutions Goals of CORAL: Support cooperative resource development, preservation, sharing & outreach; enhance communication & cooperation between member libraries; promote professional development through workshops, seminars & scholarships; provide service & liaison to other consortia; pursue grants to benefit all members of the organization

HARRINGTON LIBRARY CONSORTIUM*, 413 E Fourth Ave, Amarillo, 79101. (Mail add: PO Box 2171, Amarillo, 79189), SAN 329-546X. Tel: 806-378-6037. Toll Free Tel: 800-687-9771. FAX: 806-378-6038. Toll Free FAX: 800-765-7045. Web Site: harringtonlc.org. *Dir,* Amanda Barrera; Tel: 806-378-3050, E-mail: amanda.barrera@amarillolibrary.org
Founded 1979
Member Libraries: 132 (incl 5 acad, 33 pub & 94 sch)
Primary Functions: To promote resource sharing; to provide access to information through a common automated integrated system

HEALTH LIBRARIES INFORMATION NETWORK*, (Health LINE), 3500 Camp Bowie Blvd, LIB-222, Fort Worth, 76107-2699. SAN 322-3299. Tel: 817-735-2590. E-mail: dfwhealthline@gmail.com. Web Site: dfwhealthline.org/. *Chair,* Jamie Quinn
Founded 1989
Member Libraries: 20 hospital & health sci institutions
Primary Functions: Provide support network for health sciences librarians who provide service to physicians, nurses, hospital administrators, faculty, professional med students & technical personnel interlibrary loan

NATIONAL NETWORK OF LIBRARIES OF MEDICINE REGION 3*, UNT Health Sci Ctr, Gibson D Lewis Health Sci Libr, 3500 Camp Bowie Blvd, Rm 110, Fort Worth, 76107. Tel: 817-735-2223. E-mail: nnlmregion3@unthsc.edu. Web Site: nnlm.gov/about/regions/region3. *Exec Dir,* Brian Leaf; Tel: 817-735-2169, E-mail: brian.leaf@unthsc.edu; *Dep Dir,* Debbie Montenegro; Tel: 817-735-2469, E-mail: debbie.montenegro@unthsc.edu; *Tech Coordr,* Bailey Sterling; Tel: 817-735-2370, E-mail: bailey.sterling@unthsc.edu
Member Libraries: 891 health sci, pub & other libr inst
Primary Functions: Serves Arkansas, Kansas, Louisiana, Missouri, Nebraska, Oklahoma & Texas. Document delivery; consultation & outreach; training for academic, medical, hospital & public libraries, consumers, healthcare providers, & public health departments; resource sharing; consortia development; Internet training; bibliographic instruction; course development

PARTNERS LIBRARY ACTION NETWORK*, (PLAN), 5806 Mesa Dr, Ste 375, Austin, 78731. Tel: 512-583-0704. E-mail: info@libaction.net. Web Site: libaction.net. *Exec Dir,* Eric Lashley; E-mail: eric.lashley@libaction.net; *Asst Exec Dir,* Paul Waak; E-mail: paul.waak@libaction.net; *Prog Mgr,* Samanatha Simpson; E-mail: ssimpson@libaction.net
Founded 2021
Member Libraries: 176
Primary Functions: To assist member libraries with the daily challenges of running a public library in Texas.

SOUTH CENTRAL ACADEMIC MEDICAL LIBRARIES CONSORTIUM*, (SCAMeL), c/o Lewis Library-UNTHSC, 3500 Camp Bowie Blvd, Fort Worth, 76107. SAN 372-8269. Tel: 817-735-2380. FAX: 817-735-5158. Web Site: www.tulane.edu/~scamel/. *Dir,* Daniel Burgard; E-mail: daniel.burgard@unthsc.edu
Founded 1982
Member Libraries: 14 acad med ctr
Primary Functions: Provide interlibrary loan, cooperative acquisitions, continuing education & management training, research, statistical data comparison, networking

TEXAS COUNCIL OF ACADEMIC LIBRARIES*, (TCAL), VC/UHV Library, 2602 N Ben Jordan, Victoria, 77901. (Mail add: c/o Texas Library Association, 3355 Bee Cave Rd, Ste 401, Austin, 78746), SAN 322-337X. Tel: 361-570-4150. FAX: 361-570-4155. E-mail: tla@txla.org. Web Site: www.txla.org. *Exec Dir,* Shirley Robinson
Member Libraries: Pub & pvt col & univ
Primary Functions: State contract for binding & book acquisition; statistics compilation; legislative action; liaison with Coordinating Board for Institutions of Higher Learning in library matters; liaison with Texas Legislative Budget Board; development of networks to meet specific information needs

TEXSHARE - TEXAS STATE LIBRARY & ARCHIVES COMMISSION*, 1201 Brazos St, Austin, 78701. (Mail add: PO Box 12927, Austin, 78711-2927). Tel: 512-463-5455. Toll Free Tel: 800-252-9386. FAX: 512-936-2306. E-mail: texshare@tsl.texas.gov. Reference E-mail: info@tsl.texas.gov. Web Site: www.tsl.texas.gov/texshare. *Dir & Librn,* Mark Smith; Tel: 512-463-5460, E-mail: director.librarian@tsl.texas.gov
Founded 1988
Member Libraries: 700
Primary Functions: A consortium of Texas libraries joining together to share print & electronic materials, purchase online resources, & combine staff expertise.

UTAH

NATIONAL NETWORK OF LIBRARIES OF MEDICINE REGION 4*, Univ Utah, Spencer S Eccles Health Sci Libr, Bldg 589, 10 North 1900 East, Salt Lake City, 84112-5890. SAN 322-225X. Tel: 801-587-3412. Toll Free Tel: 800-338-7657. FAX: 801-581-3632. Web Site: nnlm.gov/about/regions/region4. *Exec Dir,* Catherine Soehner; E-mail: catherine.soehner@utah.edu; *Assoc Dir,* John Bramble; Tel: 801-585-9646, E-mail: john.bramble@utah.edu
Founded 2001
Member Libraries: 400
Primary Functions: Serves Arizona, Idaho, Colorado, Montana, New Mexico, North Dakota, South Dakota, Utah & Wyoming. Consultation; education; online training & services; improvement of medical library service for health professionals

UTAH ACADEMIC LIBRARY CONSORTIUM, (UALC), University of Utah, J Willard Marriott Library, 295 S 1500 E, Salt Lake City, 84112-0860. SAN 322-3418. Tel: 801-581-3852. FAX: 801-585-7185. E-mail: ualc-mail@lists.utah.edu. Web Site: ualc.net. *Chair,* Jennifer Duncan; Tel: 435-797-2687, E-mail: jennifer.duncan@usu.edu
Founded 1971
Member Libraries: 14
Primary Functions: Cooperate in continually improving the availability & delivery of library & information services to the higher education community in the state of Utah

VERMONT

CATAMOUNT LIBRARY NETWORK*, (CLN), 43 Main St, Springfield, 05156. Tel: 802-885-3108. E-mail: accounts@catamountlibraries.org. Web Site: www.catamountlibraries.org. *Pres,* Jennie Rozycki; E-mail: director@mcculloughlibrary.org; *Treas,* Sue Dowdell
Member Libraries: 23 pub
Primary Functions: Creating an open-source multi-library shared catalog & integrated library system, using the Koha platform, for a consortium of participating Vermont libraries.

COLLABORATIVE LIBRARIES OF VERMONT, (CLOVER), Vermont Dept of Libraries, 60 Washington St, Ste 2, Barre, 05641. SAN 322-3426. Tel: 802-636-0040. Web Site: libraries.vermont.gov. *Asst State Librn,* Thomas McMurdo; E-mail: thomas.mcmurdo@vermont.gov; *Ref Librn,* Position Currently Open
Member Libraries: 200 acad, pub, sch & spec
Primary Functions: Coordination of statewide interlibrary loan through online automated system; courier service to some members

VIRGINIA

AMERICAN INDIAN HIGHER EDUCATION CONSORTIUM, (AIHEC), 121 Oronoco St, Alexandria, 22314. SAN 329-4056. Tel: 703-838-0400. FAX: 703-838-0388. E-mail: info@aihec.org. Web Site: www.aihec.org. *Chief of Staff,* John Phillips; E-mail: jphillips@aihec.org; *Pres & Chief Exec Officer,* Ahniwake Rose; Tel: 703-838-0400, Ext 111; *Vice President, Finance & Admin,* Tina Cooper; Tel: 703-838-0400, Ext 101, E-mail: tcooper@aihec.org; *Dir, Institutional Research, Assessment & Accreditation,* Jana Hanson; E-mail: jhanson@aihec.org; *Head, Libr & Info Serv,* Gary McCone; Tel: 410-707-9307, E-mail: gmccone@aihec.org
Founded 1972
Member Libraries: 37 tribal col & univ
Primary Functions: Provides leadership & influences public policy on American Indian higher education issues through advocacy, research & program initiatives; promotes & strengthens indigenous languages, cultures, communities & tribal nations; serves member institutions & emerging TCUs

RICHMOND ACADEMIC LIBRARY CONSORTIUM, (RALC), Virginia Union University, Wilder Library, 1500 N Lombardy St, Richmond, 23220. SAN 322-3469. Tel: 804-257-5821. Web Site: ralc.edu. *Pres,* Pamela Foreman; E-mail: pforeman@vuu.edu
Founded 1972
Member Libraries: 10 acad
Primary Functions: Further the development of academic libraries; sponsor projects for the mutual benefit of its members; sponsor activities in professional development & continuing education; promote resource sharing through interlibrary lending, document delivery, direct borrowing by patrons, shared collection development & automated networking

SOUTHWESTERN VIRGINIA HEALTH INFORMATION LIBRARIANS*, (SWVAHILI), Sentara RMH Virginia Funkhouser Health Sciences Library, 2010 Health Campus Drive, Harrisonburg, 22801. SAN 323-9527. Tel: 540-689-1772. FAX: 540-689-1770. E-mail: RMH_RMHLibrary@sentara.com. *Librn,* Megan Khamphavong; E-mail: mdkhamph@sentara.com
Founded 1982
Member Libraries: 16 acad & med
Primary Functions: Exchange information & ideas; provide short programs on various health science library functions & activities; ILL

VIRGINIA INDEPENDENT COLLEGE & UNIVERSITY LIBRARY ASSOCIATION, (VICULA), c/o Alison Gregory, Marymount University, 2807 N Glebe Rd, Arlington, 22207. SAN 374-6089. Tel: 703-284-1673. Web Site: libguides.roanoke.edu/vicula. *Chair,* Alison S Gregory; E-mail: agregory@marymount.edu; *Info Officer,* Carol Creager; E-mail: ccreager@marybaldwin.edu
Member Libraries: 31 pvt acad
Primary Functions: ILL resource sharing; union listing; staff cooperation & communication; cooperative projects; library directories

VIRGINIA TIDEWATER CONSORTIUM FOR HIGHER EDUCATION*, (VTC), 4900 Powhatan Ave, Norfolk, 23529. SAN 329-5486. Tel: 757-683-3183. FAX: 757-683-4515. Web Site: vtc.odu.edu. *Pres,* Dr Lawrence G Dotolo; E-mail: lgdotolo@aol.com; *Prog Coordr,* Leslie Mason; E-mail: lmason@odu.edu
Founded 1973
Member Libraries: 13
Primary Functions: To determine the need for higher education programs; to provide increased educational opportunities; to encourage cooperative projects among the institutions of higher education; to establish linkages between the member institutions & business, industry, government & the military; to enrich existing academic opportunities, exchange & articulation programs; to work cooperatively with the local school divisions to serve the educational needs of teachers & administrators; to develop the use of technology to enhance the teaching & learning process; to enhance the economic development of the region by providing an opportunity for the development of a highly trained workforce

VIRGINIA'S ACADEMIC LIBRARY CONSORTIUM*, (VIVA), George Mason University, 4400 University Dr, Fenwick 5100, Fairfax, 22030. (Mail add: George Mason University, MSN 2FL, Fairfax, 22030). Tel: 703-993-4654. E-mail: viva@gmu.edu. Web Site: vivalib.org. *Actg Dir, Dep Dir,* Genya O'Gara; E-mail: gogara@gmu.edu; *Head, Operations & Budget,* Cutrice Harris; E-mail: charri29@gmu.edu; *Learning Librn,* Sophie Rondeau; E-mail: wrondeau@gmu.edu; *Learning Coordr,* Stephanie Westcott; E-mail: swestcot@gmu.edu; *Coordr, Digital Initiatives,* Jessica Kirschner; E-mail: jkirsch4@gmu.edu; *Outreach & Events Coord,* Katara Hofmann; E-mail: kwrightl@gmu.edu; *Tech Serv,* Bobby Reeves; E-mail: rreeves@gmu.edu
Founded 1994
Member Libraries: 71 acad
Primary Functions: Group acquisition of electronic resources & promotion of use of these products; promote & assist resource sharing & interlibrary loan among members; shared initiatives in open & affordable course content

WASHINGTON

ASSOCIATION FOR RURAL & SMALL LIBRARIES*, (ARSL), PO Box 33731, Seattle, 98133. Tel: 206-453-3579. E-mail: info@arsl.org. Web Site: www.arsl.org. *Pres,* Bailee Hutchinson; *Exec Dir,* Kate Laughlin
Member Libraries: 190
Primary Functions: To build strong communities through advocacy, professional development & elevating the impact of rural & small libraries

NATIONAL NETWORK OF LIBRARIES OF MEDICINE REGION 5, Univ of Washington, Health Sciences Bldg, Rm T230, 1959 NE Pacific St, Seattle, 98195. (Mail add: University of Washington, Box 357155, Seattle, 98195-7155), SAN 322-3485. Tel: 206-543-8262. E-mail: nnlm@uw.edu. Web Site: nnlm.gov/about/regions/region5. *Exec Dir,* Kathryn Vela; E-mail: kvela2@uw.edu; *Asst Dir,* Emily Hamstra; E-mail: ehamstra@uw.edu
Founded 1968
Member Libraries: 204 acad, 203 hospitals, 161 pub & 234 other
Primary Functions: Serves Alaska, California, Hawaii, Nevada, Oregon, Washington, US territories & Freely Associated States in the Pacific. Staff supports member organizations' health information services, resource sharing, community partnerships, outreach program development & evaluation. We offer or sponsor distance & on-site training about online health resources & provide funding to libraries & community-based partners to promote the use of quality health information. Network members & staff exhibit & present about health information topics & resources for diverse professionals & community groups

WASHINGTON COMMUNITY & TECHNICAL COLLEGES LIBRARY CONSORTIUM, (WACTCLC), c/o Big Ben Community College, 7662 Chanute St NE, Moses Lake, 98837. E-mail: wactclc@gmail.com. Web Site: wactclc.org. *Library Consortium Services Mgr,* Carleigh Hill; Tel: 509-795-0140, E-mail: carleighh@bigbend.edu
Founded 2016

Member Libraries: 33 acad
Primary Functions: Offers access to group licensing of selected electronic resources to qualified academic libraries

WISCONSIN

FOX RIVER VALLEY AREA LIBRARY CONSORTIUM*, (FRVALC), c/o Ascension Mercy Hospital Library, 500 S Oakwood Rd, Oshkosh, 54901. SAN 322-3531. Tel: 920-223-0340. Web Site: ascension-wi.libguides.com/frvalc. *Med Librn,* Michele Matucheski; E-mail: michele.matucheski@ascension.org
Founded 1975
Member Libraries: 16
Primary Functions: Shared resources; workshops; journal exchange; Union List of books, periodicals & catalogs

SOUTHEASTERN WISCONSIN INFORMATION TECHNOLOGY EXCHANGE, INC*, (SWITCH), 6801 N Yates Rd, Milwaukee, 53217-3985. SAN 371-3962. Tel: 414-351-2423. FAX: 414-228-4146. Web Site: www.switchinc.org. *Coordr,* Katie Utschig; E-mail: katie@switchinc.org
Founded 1988
Member Libraries: 8 acad
Primary Functions: Dedicated to the advancement of open information technologies & shared electronic resources among information-providing institutions; operates a union database & shared integrated library system utilizing Innovative Interfaces software

WILS*, 1360 Regent St, Ste 121, Madison, 53715-1255. SAN 322-3612. Tel: 608-216-8399. FAX: 608-237-2358. E-mail: information@wils.org. Web Site: www.wils.org. *Exec Dir,* Jennifer Chamberlain; Tel: 608-205-8591, E-mail: jennifer@wils.org
Founded 1972
Member Libraries: 59 acad, 155 pub, 260 sch districts, 22 spec, 10 state agency & 17 vo-tech
Primary Functions: Cooperative purchasing & licensing; consortial management; events & education; project management for Wisconsin libraries

WISCONSIN PUBLIC LIBRARY CONSORTIUM, (WPLC), c/o WiLS, 1360 Regent St, No 121, Madison, 53713. Tel: 608-218-4480. E-mail: wplc-info@wils.org. Web Site: www.wplc.info. *Project Mgr,* Jennifer Chamberlain
Founded 2000
Member Libraries: 15 pub libr syst
Primary Functions: Manages public library ebook consortium for the state; undertakes research & development &/or new technology projects for public library systems

WISCONSIN VALLEY LIBRARY SERVICE*, (WVLS), 300 N First St, Wausau, 54403. SAN 371-3911. Tel: 715-261-7250. FAX: 715-261-7259. Web Site: wvls.org. *Dir,* Marla Rae Sepnafski; E-mail: director@wvls.org; *IT Dir,* Joshua Klingbeil; Tel: 715-261-7252, E-mail: jklingbeil@wvls.org
Founded 1961
Member Libraries: 25 pub, 187 sch & 25 spec
Primary Functions: Provide backup reference, referral & courier services to member libraries; provide professional consultant services to member library personnel & trustees; administer the wide area network and ILS.

WISPALS LIBRARY CONSORTIUM, c/o WiLS, 1360 Regent St, No 121, Madison, 53715. Tel: 608-218-4480. FAX: 608-237-2358. E-mail: wispals-wils@wils.org. Web Site: www.wispals.org. *Communications & Consortia Mgr,* Andrea Coffin; Tel: 414-979-9457, E-mail: acoffin@wils.org
Founded 1989
Member Libraries: 11 tech col
Primary Functions: Provides member libraries shared access to an integrated library system, information resources, electronic databases & other services & technologies at reduced costs; promotes the exchange of knowledge, skills, & best practices for libraries; serves as a liaison between member libraries & local, state, & national library organizations & vendors

WYOMING

WYLD NETWORK, c/o Wyoming State Library, 2800 Central Ave, Cheyenne, 82002-0060. (Mail add: 2800 Central Ave, Cheyenne, 82002-0060), SAN 371-0661. Tel: 307-777-6333. Toll Free Tel: 800-264-1281. E-mail: support@wyldnetwork.org. Web Site: library.wyo.gov/wyld/network. *State Librn,* Abby Beaver; E-mail: abby.beaver@wyo.gov; *Prog Mgr,* Desiree Saunders; Tel: 307-777-6258, E-mail: desiree.saunders@wyo.gov
Founded 1984
Member Libraries: 40 voting members in our multi-type library system
Primary Functions: Support all aspects of the statewide SirsiDynix Symphony ILS as used by the multi-type library consortia

ALBERTA

THE ALBERTA LIBRARY*, (TAL), 623 Seven Sir Winston Churchill Sq NW, Edmonton, T5J 2V5. Tel: 780-414-0805. Administration E-mail: admin@thealbertalibrary.ab.ca. Web Site: www.thealbertalibrary.ca. *Chief Exec Officer,* ; E-mail: ceo@thealbertalibrary.ab.ca
Founded 1997
Member Libraries: 49
Primary Functions: Optimize resources & services among member libraries in a dynamic model of collaboration

COUNCIL OF PRAIRIE & PACIFIC UNIVERSITY LIBRARIES*, (COPPUL), 150B -1711 85th St NW, Calgary, T3R 1J3. Tel: 604-827-0578. Web Site: www.coppul.ca. *Exec Dir,* Vivian Stieda; Tel: 403-973-0149, E-mail: execdir@coppul.ca; *Licensing Coord,* Carol Stephenson; E-mail: carol@coppul.ca; *Shared Print Archive Network Coord,* Doug Brigham; E-mail: span@coppul.ca; *Digital Preserv,* Corey Davis; E-mail: cdsn@coppul.ca
Founded 1991
Member Libraries: 22
Primary Functions: The Council of Prairie and Pacific University Libraries (COPPUL) provides leadership in the development of collaborative solutions addressing the academic information resource needs, the staffing development needs, and the preservation needs of its member institutions.

NEOS LIBRARY CONSORTIUM, 5-07 Cameron Library, University of Alberta, Edmonton, T6G 2J8. Tel: 780-492-0075. Web Site: www.neoslibraries.ca. *Mgr,* Anne Carr-Wiggin; E-mail: anne.carr-wiggin@ualberta.ca
Founded 1994
Member Libraries: 18
Primary Functions: Resource & knowledge sharing; shared integrated library system & related services; centralized interlibrary loan; professional development & training

BRITISH COLUMBIA

BRITISH COLUMBIA ELECTRONIC LIBRARY NETWORK, (BCELN), WAC Bennett Library, 7th Flr, Simon Fraser University, 8888 University Dr, Burnaby, V5A 1S6. Tel: 778-782-7003. E-mail: office@bceln.ca. Web Site: www.bceln.ca. *Exec Dir,* Sunni Nishimura; E-mail: sunnin@bceln.ca
Founded 1989
Member Libraries: 34 acad
Primary Functions: Develop, promote & maintain system-wide mechanisms that allow post-secondary libraries to meet the expanding information needs of the province's learners, researchers & educators, at the lowest possible cost

CENTRE FOR ACCESSIBLE POST-SECONDARY EDUCATION RESOURCES*, (CAPER-BC), Langara College Library, 100 W 49th Ave, Vancouver, V5Y 2Z6. SAN 329-6970. Tel: 604-323-5639. Toll Free Tel: 855-729-2457. FAX: 604-323-5544. E-mail: caperbc@langara.ca. Web Site: caperbc.ca. *Dir,* Dr Debbie Schachter
Founded 1985
Member Libraries: 20 colleges served
Primary Functions: Locates, produces & provides library materials in forms accessible to students with print disabilities; interlibrary loan; electronic text, large print, digital audio & DAISY production & reference information service

ELECTRONIC HEALTH LIBRARY OF BRITISH COLUMBIA*, (e-HLbc), c/o Bennett Library, 8888 University Dr, Burnaby, V5A 1S6. Tel: 778-782-7003. FAX: 778-782-3023. E-mail: info@ehlbc.ca, office@ehlbc.ca. Web Site: ehlbc.ca. *Exec Dir,* Sunni Nishimura; E-mail: sunnin@bceln.ca; *Coordr,* Reba Ouimet; Tel: 236-333-2955, E-mail: rebao@bceln.ca
Founded 2006
Member Libraries: 51
Primary Functions: To provide BC's & Yukon's health care & post-secondary communities with equitable access to essential online health resources

NORTHWEST LIBRARY FEDERATION*, (NWLF), 1162 McGowan Dr, Prince George, V2M 6R1. (Mail add: Box 4722, Smithers, V0J 2N0). Tel: 250-981-3507. Web Site: nwlf.ca. *Dir,* Kaitlyn Vecchio; E-mail: director@nwlf.ca
Member Libraries: 7 pub, 1 col
Primary Functions: To create equitable & easy access to library services through resource sharing & collaboration

PUBLIC LIBRARY INTERLINK*, 5489 Byrne Rd, No 158, Burnaby, V5J 3J1. SAN 318-8272. Tel: 604-437-8441. FAX: 604-437-8410. E-mail: info@interlinklibraries.ca. Web Site: www.interlinklibraries.ca. *Exec Dir,* Michael Burris; E-mail: michael.burris@interlinklibraries.ca; *Operations Mgr,* Allie Douglas; E-mail: allie.douglas@interlinklibraries.ca
Founded 1994
Member Libraries: 18 pub
Primary Functions: Fosters & promotes the provision of quality library services to residents through open access to member libraries with free access & reciprocal borrowing

MANITOBA

MANITOBA LIBRARY CONSORTIUM, INC*, (MLCI), c/o Library Administration, University of Winnipeg, 515 Portage Ave, Winnipeg, R3B 2E9. SAN 372-820X. Tel: 204-786-9801. FAX: 204-783-8910. E-mail: manitobalibraryconsortium@gmail.com. Web Site: www.mlcinc.mb.ca. *Chair,* Heather Brydon
Founded 1991

Member Libraries: 54 acad, govt, health, pub, sch & spec
Primary Functions: Initiate & coordinate projects & activities related to resource sharing & library networking; maintain cooperative relationships with groups or agencies with similar goals

NOVA SCOTIA

COUNCIL OF ATLANTIC ACADEMIC LIBRARIES (CAAL), Conseil des bibliotheques postsecondaires de l'Atlantique (CBPA), 120 Western Pkwy, Ste 202, Bedford, B4B 0V2. Tel: 902-830-6467. E-mail: execdir@caul-cbua.ca. Web Site: caul-cbua.ca. *Committee Chair,* Suzanne van den Hoogen
Member Libraries: 20
Primary Functions: Provide a venue to influence public policy; advocate on matters relevant to members & the post-secondary community; foster cooperation & resource sharing; support consortial purchasing to achieve optimal savings; coordinate library services among member institutions; improve the delivery of information services; provide a network of colleagues

MARITIMES HEALTH LIBRARIES ASSOCIATION*, (MHLA-ABSM), WK Kellogg Health Sciences Library, 5850 College St, Halifax, B3H 1X5. SAN 370-0836. Tel: 902-494-2483. FAX: 902-494-3750. Web Site: library.nshealth.ca/MHLA. *Pres,* Sandra O'Driscoll; E-mail: sodriscoll.mlis@gmail.com
Member Libraries: 35 med
Primary Functions: Promote continuity among health science libraries; promote continuing education & development activities

NOVANET, A Consortium of Academic Libraries, 120 Western Pkwy, No 202, Bedford, B4B 0V2. SAN 372-4050. E-mail: office@novanet.ca. Web Site: www.novanet.ca. *Mgr,* Katie McCaskill; E-mail: katie.mccaskill@novanet.ca
Founded 1988
Member Libraries: 12 acad
Primary Functions: Enhance access to information & knowledge through cooperation among the member institutions for the benefit of their user communities

ONTARIO

CANADIAN ASSOCIATION OF RESEARCH LIBRARIES*, (CARL), 309 Cooper St, Ste 203, Ottawa, K2P 0G5. SAN 323-9721. Tel: 613-482-9344. E-mail: info@carl-abrc.ca. Web Site: www.carl-abrc.ca. *Exec Dir,* Susan Haigh; Tel: 613-482-9344, Ext 101, E-mail: susan.haigh@carl-abrc.ca; *Mrg, Admin & Prog,* Katherine McColgan; Tel: 613-482-9344, Ext 102, E-mail: katherine.mccolgan@carl-abrc.ca; *Admin Officer, Events Coord,* Katarzyna Kozyra-Kocikowska; Tel: 613-482-9344, Ext 103, E-mail: kasia.kozyra-kocikowska@carl-abrc.ca; *Sr Prog Officer,* Julie Morin; Tel: 613-482-9344, Ext 107, E-mail: julie.morin@carl-abrc.ca
Founded 1976
Member Libraries: 29 acad & 2 natl
Primary Functions: To provide leadership on behalf of Canada's research libraries & enhance capacity to advance research & higher education; to promote effective & sustainable knowledge creation, dissemination, & preservation, & public policy that enables broad access to scholarly information.

CANADIAN HEALTH LIBRARIES ASSOCIATION*, (CHLA-ABSC), 468 Queen St E, Ste LL-02, Toronto, M5A 1T7. SAN 370-0720. Tel: 416-646-1600. FAX: 416-646-9460. E-mail: info@chla-absc.ca. Web Site: www.chla-absc.ca. *Pres,* Tara Landry; E-mail: president@chla-absc.ca; *VPres,* Naz Torabi; E-mail: vicepresident@chla-absc.ca
Founded 1976
Member Libraries: 450 allied health sci & med
Primary Functions: To encourage the professional development of its members whose foremost concern is for the dissemination of health sciences information to those in research, education & patient care

CANADIAN HERITAGE INFORMATION NETWORK*, (CHIN), 1030 Innes Rd, Ottawa, K1B 4S7. SAN 329-3076. Tel: 613-998-3721. Toll Free Tel: 866-998-3721. FAX: 613-998-4721. E-mail: rcip-chin@pch.gc.ca. Web Site: www.canada.ca/chin. *Dir,* Bruno Lemay
Founded 1972
Primary Functions: The Canadian Heritage Information Network (CHIN), a Special Operating Agency within the Department of Canadian Heritage, assists Canadian museums in documenting, managing, and sharing information about their collections, to ensure that this information is accessible now and in the future. CHIN has three core areas of activity: - create and maintain an online point of entry to Canadian collections; - carry out research and development on collections documentation tools and standards; - provide guidance and training to cultural institutions on managing collections information.

CANADIAN RESEARCH KNOWLEDGE NETWORK*, (CRKN), 1309 Carling Ave, PO Box 35155 Westgate, Ottawa, K1Z 1A2. Tel: 613-907-7040. Web Site: crkn.ca. *Exec Dir,* Clare Appavoo; Tel: 613-907-7029, E-mail: cappavoo@crkn.ca
Founded 2004
Member Libraries: 78
Primary Functions: For our member organizations and the diverse communities they serve, CRKN empowers researchers, educators, and society with greater access to the world's research and Canada's preserved documentary heritage, now and for future generations. We deliver value to academic libraries, heritage organizations, and knowledge seekers within Canada in the following ways: Represent our membership in large-scale licensing and content acquisition activities; Collaborate to expand and enrich the digital knowledge ecosystem in Canada and the world; Advocate for fair and sustainable access to public research and content; Support the digital infrastructure required to preserve and access critical Canadian content; Mobilize our membership to transform scholarly communications in Canada.

HEALTH SCIENCE INFORMATION CONSORTIUM OF TORONTO*, c/o Gerstein Sci Info Ctr, Univ Toronto, Nine King's College Circle, Toronto, M5S 1A5. SAN 370-5080. Tel: 416-978-6359. FAX: 416-971-2637. Web Site: guides.hsict.library.utoronto.ca/welcome. *Exec Dir,* Lori Anne Oja; E-mail: lori.oja@utoronto.ca
Founded 1990
Member Libraries: 35 inst
Primary Functions: Collaborate to promote advances in health care through optimal use of information resources, technologies & collective expertise; ensure optimal access to electronic & print resources on a consortium-wide basis; coordinate new technology to streamline resources sharing; rationalize information services to allow for the most effective use of local institution library budgets; support the patient care, teaching, research & community outreach mandates of the Consortium members

ONTARIO COUNCIL OF UNIVERSITY LIBRARIES*, (OCUL), 130 Saint George St, 7th Flr, Toronto, M5S 1A5. Tel: 416-978-5338. E-mail: ocul@ocul.on.ca. Web Site: www.ocul.on.ca. *Interim Exec Dir,* Michael Vandenburg; Tel: 613-893-2665, E-mail: michael.vandenburg@ocul.on.ca
Founded 1967
Member Libraries: 21 acad
Primary Functions: Seeks to enhance information services through resource sharing, collective purchasing, document delivery & many similar activities

ONTARIO LIBRARY CONSORTIUM*, (OLC), c/o Georgina Public Library, 90 Wexford Dr, Keswick, L4P 3P7. Tel: 905-627-8662. Web Site: www.onlibcon.on.ca. *Pres,* Kelly Bernstein; E-mail: kelly.bernstein@brant.ca; *Coordr,* Katherine Slimman; E-mail: k.slimman@onlibcon.on.ca
Founded 1986
Member Libraries: 27 libr systs, 11 county & regional municipality, 16 medium-sized pub librs located in southern Ontario
Primary Functions: OLC continues to develop library processes together, through joint custom programming, negotiations of bulk rates with vendors, and co-operative training and support. Priorities, activities and membership costs of the OLC are determined by the members

PERTH COUNTY INFORMATION NETWORK, (PCIN), c/o Stratford Public Library, 19 St Andrew St, Stratford, N5A 1A2. Tel: 519-271-0220. Web Site: perthcountylibraries.ca. *Management Chair,* Sarah Andrews; E-mail: sandrews@stmaryspubliclibrary.ca; *Network Adminr,* Jordan Bulbrook; E-mail: jbulbrook@pcin.on.ca
Founded 2000
Member Libraries: 5 pub
Primary Functions: Public information access

TORONTO HEALTH LIBRARIES ASSOCIATION, (THLA), c/o University of Toronto Libraries, 130 Saint George St, Toronto, M5S 1A5. SAN 323-9853. Web Site: thla.chla-absc.ca. *Pres,* Kaitlyn Merriman; Tel: 416-978-2280, E-mail: kaitlyn.merriman@utoronto.ca
Founded 1965
Member Libraries: 80 acad, govt & med
Primary Functions: To promote the provision of quality library service to the health community in the Greater Toronto area by fostering & stimulating health sciences libraries; to encourage communication & cooperation among members & to actively promote their continuing education & professional development; to consult & collaborate with other professional, technical & scientific organizations in Toronto in matters of mutual interest

WOODSTOCK HOSPITAL REGIONAL LIBRARY SERVICES, Woodstock Hospital, 310 Juliana Dr, Woodstock, N4V 0A4. SAN 323-9500. Tel: 519-421-4233, Ext 2735. FAX: 519-421-4236. E-mail: library@woodstockhospital.ca. Web Site: wohkn.org/wh. *Librn,* Emma Carrataca
Member Libraries: 8 health organizations
Primary Functions: Provision of both reference & technical library services to contracted hospitals

QUEBEC

ASSOCIATION DES BIBLIOTHEQUES DE LA SANTE AFFILIEES A L'UNIVERSITE DE MONTREAL*, (ABSAUM), c/o Health Library Univ Montreal, Pavillon Roger-Gaudry, 2900 Boul Edouard-Montpetit, 6e Etage, Salle L-623, Montreal, H3C 3J7. SAN 370-5838. Tel: 514-343-6826. FAX: 514-343-2350. Web Site: www.bib.umontreal.ca/sa. *Librn,* Natalie Clairoux; Tel: 514-343-6111, Ext 3585, E-mail: natalie.clairoux@umontreal.ca
Founded 1979

Member Libraries: 15 acad
Primary Functions: Interlibrary loan services; sharing periodical development collection; mutual assistance

RESEAU BIBLIO DE L'OUTAOUAIS*, 2295 Saint-Louis St, Gatineau, J8T 5L8. SAN 319-6526. Tel: 819-561-6008. FAX: 819-561-6767. Web Site: www.crsbpo.qc.ca. *Dir Gen,* Sylvie Thibault; E-mail: sylvie.thibault@crsbpo.qc.ca
Founded 1964
Primary Functions: Maintain & develop document collections, document processing services & other technical or professional library science services; develop & maintain training & information sessions, activities & cultural development programs in the field of library science

LIBRARY SCHOOLS AND TRAINING COURSES

Library Schools are listed alphabetically by state or province.

This section provides the name of the school, its address, name of the director or dean, names of the staff members, number of yearly visiting faculty, date the program was established, type of school (private, public or denominational), entrance exams required, degrees offered, scholarships granted, and enrollment. The entries also list data on tuition for graduate and undergraduate students, the course offered, and the availability of evening and summer school classes.

The schools marked with an asterisk (*) are those which did not reply to the questionnaire sent to them.

The schools marked with a dagger (†) are those which have first professional degree programs that are accredited by the American Library Association Committee on Accreditation as of 1995 based on the Standards of Accreditations adopted by the ALA Council in 1972.

Once a program is accredited under these standards, periodic revisits for purposes of continuing accreditation are scheduled by the Committee.

A list of the programs accredited by the ALA is issued twice yearly and is available on request to: "Accredited List," American Library Association, 50 East Huron St., Chicago, Illinois 60611, or visit ALA website at www.ala.org.

ALABAMA

ALABAMA STATE UNIVERSITY, COLLEGE OF EDUCATION, Library Education Media Program, Ralph Abernathy Hall, 915 S Jackson St, Montgomery, 36104. (Mail add: PO Box 271, Montgomery, 36101-0271). Tel: 334-229-6829. Web Site: www.alasu.edu/_qa/college-education.php. *Instructional Support Programs,* Hannah O Jones; E-mail: hjones@alasu.edu
Prog estab 1949. Sch type: Pub. Scholarships offered
Tuition: Non-resident Graduate $824 Per credit hour; Resident Graduate $412 Per credit hour
Degrees & Hours Offered: M.Ed., 30-33 sem hrs; EdS
Special Courses: Administration of Media Programs, Advanced Educational Media Programs, Collection Development, Organization & Management of Information, Communications Technology & Instructional Design, Computer Based Instructional Technology, Current & Emerging Technology, Integration of Technology into the K-12 Curriculum, Legal Basis of Library Education, Literature for Children & Young Adults, Readings in Instructional Technology, Reference & Reference Service, Research in Library Media, Seminar in Library Media
Evening Session, Summer Session

AUBURN UNIVERSITY*, Department of Educational Foundations, Leadership & Technology, 4036 Haley Ctr, Auburn, 36849-5221. Tel: 334-844-4460. FAX: 334-844-3072. Web Site: www.auburn.edu. *Assoc Prof, Dir,* Susan H Bannon; E-mail: bannosh@auburn.edu
Prog estab 1969. Sch type: Pub; Enrl: Grad: 220
Tuition: Non-resident Graduate $6,345 Per semester; Resident Graduate $2,115 Per semester
Type of Training Offered: School
Degrees & Hours Offered: MS
Evening Session, Summer Session

JACKSONVILLE STATE UNIVERSITY*, Department of Counseling & Instructional Support, Library Media Program, 700 Pelham Rd N, Jacksonville, 36265. Tel: 256-782-5011, 256-782-5096. FAX: 256-782-5321, 256-782-8136. Web Site: jsu.edu. *Prog Chair,* Dr Wendy Stephens; E-mail: wstephens@jsu.edu
Prog estab 1965. Sch type: Pub; Enrl: Grad: 30
Type of Training Offered: School Library Media Certificate
Degrees & Hours Offered: MS, School Librarianship, 37 semester hours; EdS, School Librarianship; Information Technology, 30 semester hours
Special Courses: Library Automation, Library Management, Young Adult Literature
Continuing Education, Online Courses, Professional Development, Summer Session

† UNIVERSITY OF ALABAMA*, School of Library & Information Studies, 7035 Gorgas Library, Campus Box 870252, Tuscaloosa, 35487-0252. Tel: 205-348-4610. FAX: 205-348-3746. Web Site: slis.ua.edu. *Interim Dir,* Dr Jamie Campbell Naidoo; E-mail: jcnaidoo@ua.edu; *Asst Dir,* Dr Ann Bourne; E-mail: abourne@ua.edu; *Asst Dir, Assoc Prof,* Dr Steven Yates; E-mail: steven.d.yates@ua.edu; *Prof,* Dr Jim Elmborg; E-mail: jkelmborg@ua.edu; *Prof,* Anna Embree; E-mail: aembree@ua.edu; *Prof,* Dr Bharat Mehra; E-mail: bmehra@ua.edu; *Assoc Prof,* Dr Laurie Bonnici; E-mail: lbonnici@ua.edu; *Assoc Prof,* Dr Steven L MacCall; E-mail: smaccall@ua.edu; *Assoc Prof,* Dr Miriam Sweeney; E-mail: mesweeney@ua.edu; *Assoc Prof,* Dr Jeff Weddle; E-mail: jweddle@ua.edu; *Asst Prof,* Sarah Bryant; E-mail: shbryant@ua.edu; *Asst Prof,* Dr John Burgess; E-mail: jtfburgess@ua.edu; *Asst Prof,* Dr Hengyi Fu; E-mail: hfu4@ua.edu; *Asst Prof,* Dr Dimitrios Latsis; E-mail: dlatsis@ua.edu; *Asst Prof,* Dr Robert B Riter; E-mail: rbriter@ua.edu
Prog estab 1972. Sch type: Pub; Enrl: Grad: 263; Fac 15
Ent Req: GPA 3.0/4.0 scale
Tuition: Non-resident Graduate $15,125 Per semester; Resident Graduate $5,390 Per semester; Online Graduate $3,960 Per semester
Type of Training Offered: Public
Degrees & Hours Offered: MLIS, 36 sem hrs; Ph.D., 24-48 sem hrs; EdS, Sch Lib Media, 30-33 sem hrs; MFA, Bk Arts, 60 sem hrs
Special Courses: Archival Studies; Academic Libraries; Book Arts; Children's & Young Adult Literature; Digital Stewardship; Information Ethics; Information Literacy; information Policy; Information Science; Outreach to Diverse Populations; Printing & Book Design; Public Libraries; School Library Media; Social Justice; Special Libraries; Systems Analysis; Youth Librarianship
Evening Session, Online Courses, Summer Session, Weekend Session

UNIVERSITY OF SOUTH ALABAMA*, College of Education & Professional Studies, Educational Media Program, UCOM 3800, Mobile, 36688. Tel: 251-380-2861. FAX: 251-380-2713. E-mail: ceps@southalabama.edu. Web Site: www.southalabama.edu/coe. *Coordr,* Dr Pamela Moore; Tel: 251-380-2153, E-mail: prmoore@southalabama.edu
Sch type: Pub
Tuition: Online Graduate $525 Per credit hour
Degrees & Hours Offered: M.Ed., Educ Media, 30 sem hrs
Online Courses

ARIZONA

MESA COMMUNITY COLLEGE*, Library Information Technology Program, Paul A Elsner Library, 1833 W Southern Ave, Mesa, 85202. Tel: 480-461-7686. FAX: 480-461-7681. Web Site: www.mc.maricopa.edu/library/lbt. *Chair,* Marie Brown; *Libr Spec Supvr,* Michael Felix; E-mail: michael.felix@mesacc.edu
Prog estab 1967. Sch type: Pub; Enrl: Undergrad: 35; Fac 9
Ent Req: Open enrollment
Tuition: Non-resident Undergraduate $90 Per credit hour; Resident Undergraduate $65 Per credit hour
Type of Training Offered: Library & Information Science
Degrees & Hours Offered: AAS, Electronic Res, Libr Info Systs, Libr Tech Servs, Multimedia, Pub Servs, 24 sem hrs in LBT, 64 credit hr total; Certificate, Basic Certificate - Introduction to Libr Info Servs & Practical Skills, 20; Certificate, Advanced Certificate - Basic & Specialized courses

leading to thorough background as Libr Info Tech, 30; Certificate, Practitioners Certificate - Will qualify students working as Libr Mgr or Dir to apply for certification through the Regional Western Coun of State Librs Practitioner Certification Prog, 23; Certificate, Sch Libr Media Ctr Certificate - Prepares & upgrades the skills of staff working in sch libr media centers, 28
Continuing Education, Evening Session, Online Courses, Summer Session, Weekend Session

† UNIVERSITY OF ARIZONA*, School of Information, Harvill Bldg, 4th Flr, 1103 E Second St, Tucson, 85721. (Mail add: PO Box 210076, Tucson, 85721). Tel: 520-621-3565. E-mail: si-info@email.arizona.edu. Web Site: ischool.arizona.edu. *Assoc Prof, Dir,* Catherine Brooks; E-mail: cfbrooks@arizona.edu; *Asst Dir, Dir, Res,* Winslow Burleson; E-mail: win@arizona.edu; *Prof,* Hong Cui; E-mail: hongcui@arizona.edu; *Prof,* Dr Bryan Heidorn; E-mail: heidorn@arizona.edu; *Prof,* Cheryl Knott; E-mail: cherylknott@arizona.edu; *Prof,* Carla Stoffle; E-mail: stofflec@arizona.edu
Prog estab 1971. Sch type: Pub. Scholarships offered
Degrees & Hours Offered: BA, Info Sci & Arts; BA, Info Sci & eSociety; BS, Info Sci & Tech; Certificate; MA, Libr & Info Sci; MS, Info; Ph.D., Info
Continuing Education, Evening Session, Online & Blended Courses, Online Courses, Professional Development, Summer Session, Weekend Session

ARKANSAS

UNIVERSITY OF CENTRAL ARKANSAS*, Library & Information Technologies, College of Education, PO Box 4918, Conway, 72032-5001. Tel: 501-450-3177, 501-450-5497. FAX: 501-450-5680. Web Site: www.uca.edu. *Dean,* Dr Victoria Groves-Scott; *Asst Prof,* Erin Shaw; E-mail: erins@uca.edu
Prog estab 1980. Sch type: Pub; Fac 3
Tuition: Non-resident Graduate $300 Per credit hour; Resident Graduate $150 Per credit hour
Type of Training Offered: School
Degrees & Hours Offered: MS, Libr Media & Info Tech, 36
Evening Session, Summer Session

CALIFORNIA

CALIFORNIA STATE UNIVERSITY, LONG BEACH, Librarianship Program, Dept of Advanced Studies in Education & Counseling, 1250 Bellflower Blvd, Long Beach, 90840-2201. Tel: 562-985-4517. FAX: 562-985-4534. E-mail: ced-asec@csulb.edu. Web Site: www.csulb.edu/college-of-education/teacher-librarian-services-credential. *Librn, Prog Coordr,* Dr Jeanna Wersebe; E-mail: jeanna.wersebe@csulb.edu
Prog estab 1968. Sch type: Pub; Enrl: Grad: 45; Fac 4
Type of Training Offered: School Library Media Certificate
Degrees & Hours Offered: Certificate, Teacher Librn Servs Credential, 27 units; Certificate, Spec Class Authorization in Info & Digital Literacy for Teacher Librarians (who have current TL credential), 3 units; MA, Educ Tech & Media Leadership & Teacher Librn Servs Credential, 33 units; MS, Educ Tech & Media Leadership, 30 units
Special Courses: Digital Society & Culture; Education & the Internet; eLearning Design & Development; Information/Digital Literacies; Library Technologies; Management & Administration; Organization of Resources
Evening Session, Online Courses, Summer Session, Weekend Session

CITY COLLEGE OF SAN FRANCISCO*, Library Information Technology Program, 50 Frida Kahlo Way, Rm 517, San Francisco, 94112. Tel: 415-452-5519. FAX: 415-452-5478. Web Site: library.ccsf.edu. *Dept Chair,* Michele Alaniz; E-mail: malaniz@ccsf.edu
Sch type: Pub; Enrl: Undergrad: 100; Fac 6
Type of Training Offered: Professional Development for Public, Academic & Special Libraries
Degrees & Hours Offered: Certificate, Library Assisting, 17 units minimum; AS, Library Assisting, 19 units in the major & 42 units general education & electives
Special Courses: Continuing Education Workshops

HARTNELL COLLEGE*, Library-Media Technology Program, 411 Central Ave, Salinas, 93901. Tel: 831-755-6700, 831-755-6872. FAX: 831-759-6084. Reference E-mail: reference@hartnell.edu. Web Site: www.hartnell.edu/library. *Dean, Acad Affairs, Learning Support & Res,* Dr Sachiko Matsunaga; E-mail: smatsunaga@hartnell.edu; *VPres, Libr & Info Tech,* Matthew Coombs; *Head Librn,* Margaret Mayfield
Tuition: Non-resident Undergraduate $149 Per unit; Resident Undergraduate $26 Per unit
Degrees & Hours Offered: AA, Libr Med Tech; Certificate, Libr Med Tech
Special Courses: Children's Literature & Media (AV), Computers, Libraries & other Continuing Education
No Summer Sessions

PALOMAR COLLEGE*, Library & Information Technology Program, 1140 W Mission Rd, San Marcos, 92069-1487. Tel: 760-744-1150, Ext 2666. E-mail: library@palomar.edu. Web Site: www2.palomar.edu/pages/library/. *Dean,* Dr Pearl Ly; *Chairperson,* Marlene Forney; E-mail: mforney@palomar.edu
Prog estab 1965. Sch type: Pub; Enrl: Undergrad: 35; Fac 5
Tuition: Resident Undergraduate $46 Per unit
Type of Training Offered: Library Technician
Degrees & Hours Offered: AA, Libr Tech, 60 sem hrs; Certificate, 24 units
Special Courses: Children's Literature
Co-operative Education Prog, No Summer Sessions, Online Courses

† SAN JOSE STATE UNIVERSITY*, School of Information, Clark Hall 417, One Washington Sq, San Jose, 95192-0029. Tel: 408-924-2490. E-mail: ischool@sjsu.edu. Web Site: ischool.sjsu.edu. *Dir,* Dr Anthony Chow; E-mail: a.chow@sjsu.edu
Prog estab 1954. Sch type: Pub. Scholarships offered; Enrl: Grad: 2,000; Fac 137
Ent Req: B average
Tuition: Domestic Graduate $474 Per unit
Type of Training Offered: Information Systems
Degrees & Hours Offered: BS, Bachelor of Science in Information Science and Data Analytics Prepares students to work with data, technology and people., 60; Certificate, Post-Master's Certificate in Library and Information Science Focus Areas: Data science, digital curation, youth services, leadership and management, information architecture, emerging technologies, digital archives and records management, information intermediation and instruction, 16; Certificate, Advanced Certificate in Digital Assets and Services Focus Areas: Digital asset management, information governance, data analytics, 9; MLIS, Master of Library and Information Science Students can customize their studies with numerous electives from 14 career pathways (e.g., data science, digital curation, librarianship, emerging technologies, archival studies, & more) and build comprehensive skills for wide ranging careers in the information profession., 43; MS, Master of Archives and Records Administration Focus Areas: Archives, electronic records, information governance in non-library career environments, 42; MS, Informatics Focus Areas: Health, cybersecurity/privacy, 30
Special Courses: Cybersecurity, Information Visualization, Big Data Analytics & Management, Community Partnerships, Digital Curation, Digital Asset Management, User Experience, Web & Social Media Analytics, Data Mining.
Continuing Education

UNIVERSITY OF CALIFORNIA AT BERKELEY*, School of Information, 102 South Hall, No 4600, Berkeley, 94720-4600. Tel: 510-642-1464. FAX: 510-642-5814. Web Site: www.ischool.berkeley.edu. *Dean,* Jennifer Chayes; *Assoc Dean,* Hany Farid; E-mail: hfarid@ischool.berkeley.edu
Tuition: Non-resident Graduate $20,378 Per semester; Resident Graduate $14,256 Per semester
Type of Training Offered: Public
Degrees & Hours Offered: Ph.D., Info Mgt & Syst; MIMS; MIDS; MICS
Special Courses: Archives Management, Catalog Design, Children's Literature, Data Processing, Economics of Information, History of Printing & Publishing, Information Retrieval Theory, Information Systems Design, Information Systems Management, Law, Media (AV), Systems Analysis & Use of Database Management Systems

† UNIVERSITY OF CALIFORNIA, LOS ANGELES*, Department of Information Studies, Graduate School of Education & Information Studies, 2320 Moore Hall, Mail Box 951521, Los Angeles, 90095-1521. Tel: 310-825-8799. FAX: 310-206-3076. E-mail: info@gseis.ucla.edu. Web Site: is.gseis.ucla.edu. *VPres,* Noreen Webb; E-mail: webb@ucla.edu
Sch type: Pub; Enrl: Grad: 200
Tuition: Non-resident Graduate $25,810 Per year; Resident Graduate $10,768 Per year
Type of Training Offered: Special
Degrees & Hours Offered: Certificate, Archival Studies, Libr Studies, Informatics, 36 qtr hrs; MA, Moving Image Archive Studies, 72 qtr hrs; MLIS, Archival Studies, Libr Studies, Informatics, 72 qtr hrs; Ph.D., Info Studies: Evidence, Retrieval, Policy, Seeking, Structures, Inst & Professions, 72 qtr hrs; MLIS/MA, Latin Am Studies Articulated Prog, 84 qtr hrs; MLIS/MBA, 96 qtr hrs Concurrent Program
Special Courses: Advanced Issues in Archival Sciences, American Archives & Manuscripts, Analytical Bibliography, Automation of Library Processes, Development of Multimedia Resources, Health & Life Sciences Libraries, Human/Computer Communication, Information Seeking Behavior, Internship, Legal Bibliography, Preservation, Principles of Information Systems Analysis & Design, Public Libraries, Special Libraries, Thesaurus Construction, University & Research Libraries & User-Centered Design of Information Retrieval Systems

COLORADO

† UNIVERSITY OF DENVER*, Library & Information Science Program, Morgridge College of Education, Katherine A Ruffatto Hall, 1999 E Evans Ave, Denver, 80208. Toll Free Tel: 800-835-1607. E-mail: mce@du.edu. Web Site: morgridge.du.edu/academic-programs/library-information-science. *Assoc Prof, Dept Chair,* Mary C Stansbury, PhD; Tel: 303-871-3217, E-mail: mary.stansbury@du.edu; *Assoc Prof,* Shimelis Getu Assefa, PhD; Tel: 303-871-6072, E-mail: shimelis.assefa@du.edu; *Assoc Prof,* Krystyna Matusiak; Tel: 303-871-6163, E-mail: krystyna.matusiak@du.edu; *Asst Prof,* Spencer Acadia, PhD; Tel: 303-871-2838, E-mail: spencer.acadia@du.edu
Prog estab 1995. Sch type: Pvt; Enrl: Grad: 175
Ent Req: Undergrad degree & 2.5 GPA or higher. Does not require GRE
Tuition: Online Graduate $952 Per credit hour
Type of Training Offered: Special
Degrees & Hours Offered: Certificate, Res Data Mgt, 24 quarter credit hrs or 16 sem hrs; MLIS, 58 quarter credit hrs
Special Courses: Advocacy & Marketing; Career Development; Cataloging & Classification; Collection Management; Digital Libraries; Digitization; Info Access & Retrieval; Information Literacy Instruction; Introduction to Archives; Outreach, Privilege & Equity; Public Libraries; Reference; Web Content Management
Evening Session, Online Courses

CONNECTICUT

SOUTHERN CONNECTICUT STATE UNIVERSITY, Department of Information & Library Science, 501 Crescent St, New Haven, 06515. Tel: 203-392-5781. Toll Free Tel: 888-500-7278. FAX: 203-392-5780. Web Site: www.southernct.edu/ils. *Interim Dean,* Christopher Trombly; *Chairperson, Prof,* Dr Hak Joon Kim; Tel: 203-392-5703, E-mail: kimh1@southernct.edu; *Prof,* Dr Yan Quan Liu; Tel: 203-392-5763, E-mail: liuy1@southernct.edu; *Assoc Prof,* Dr Eino Sierpe; Tel: 203-392-6883, E-mail: sierpee1@southernct.edu; *Prof,* Cindy Schofield; Tel: 203-392-5778, E-mail: schofieldc2@southernct.edu; *Asst Prof,* Helene Murtha; Tel: 203-392-8387, E-mail: murthah1@southernct.edu; *Assoc Prof,* Saira Soroya; Tel: 203-392-6655, E-mail: soroyas1@southernct.edu; *Asst Prof,* Oghenere (Gabriel) Salubi; Tel: 203-392-5708, E-mail: salubio1@southernct.edu
Prog estab 1954. Sch type: Pub. Scholarships offered; Enrl: Grad: 160; Fac 7
Ent Req: Bachelor's degree from an accredited university; GPA 3.0 (on 4.0 scale), resume, essay & two letters of recommendation. Applicants for whom English is a second language, minimum score 600 on TOEFL (213 cBT or 80 iBT)
Tuition: Non-resident Graduate $8,313 Per semester; Non-resident Graduate $1,059 Per credit hour
Type of Training Offered: Special
Degrees & Hours Offered: MLS, 36 sem hrs
Special Courses: Digital Librarian, Information Seeking Behavior, Information Systems/Technology, Legal Bibliography, Media (AV), Medical Bibliography, Online Information Retrieval & Preservation of Library Materials, Special Topics - Current Relevant Issues Presented
Continuing Education, Evening Session, Online Courses, Professional Development, Summer Session

DISTRICT OF COLUMBIA

† CATHOLIC UNIVERSITY OF AMERICA*, Department of Library & Information Science, 620 Michigan Ave NE, Washington, 20064. (Mail add: Columbus School of Law, 3600 John McCormack Rd, NE, Ste 314, Washington, 20064). Tel: 202-319-5085. FAX: 202-319-5574. E-mail: cua-lis@cua.edu. Web Site: lis.catholic.edu. *Chair,* Dr Youngok Choi; Tel: 202-319-5085, E-mail: choiy@cua.edu; *Dean,* Thomas W Smith, PhD; *Prog Coordr, Syst Mgr,* Louise Gray; E-mail: grayl@cua.edu. Subject Specialists: *Acad,* Louise Gray
Prog estab 1938. Sch type: Den. Scholarships offered; Enrl: Grad: 100
Ent Req: Undergrad GPA of 3.0 OR GRE scores of 1000, plus 3 letters of reference, personal statement & transcripts
Type of Training Offered: School Library Media Certificate
Degrees & Hours Offered: Certificate, Sch Libr Media Studies, 24 credit hrs; Certificate, Cultural Heritage Info Mgt, 12 credit hrs; MSLIS, Libr Sci, Sch Libr Media Studies, 36 credit hrs; MSLIS, Libr Sci, Sch Libr Media Studies, 30 credit hrs with previous grad degree
Evening Session, Online Courses, Summer Session

FLORIDA

† FLORIDA STATE UNIVERSITY, COLLEGE OF COMMUNICATION & INFORMATION*, School of Library & Information Studies, 142 Collegiate Loop, Tallahassee, 32306-2100. (Mail add: Louis Shores Bldg, MC 2100, Tallahassee, 32306-2100). Tel: 850-644-5775. FAX: 850-644-9763. Web Site: cci.fsu.edu. *Dean, Col of Communication & Info,* Dr Lawrence W Dennis; Tel: 850-644-8741; *Asst Dean,* Ebrahim Randeree; Tel: 850-645-5674, E-mail: ebrahim.randeree@cci.fsu.edu; *Dir, Info Inst, Prof,* Dr Charles McClure; Tel: 850-644-8109, E-mail: charles.mcclure@cci.fsu.edu; *Assoc Prof, Dir, PALM Ctr,* Dr Nancy Everhart; Tel: 850-644-8122, E-mail: nancy.everhart@cci.fsu.edu; *Asst Prof, Assoc Dir, PALM Ctr,* Dr Marcia Mardis; Tel: 850-644-3392, E-mail: marcia.mardis@cci.fsu.edu
Prog estab 1947. Sch type: Pub. Scholarships offered; Enrl: Grad: 12, Grad: 51, Undergrad: 310, Grad: 569; Fac 30
Ent Req: GRE or other graduate admissions test, GPA of 3.0 on a 4.0 scale; letters of reference
Tuition: Non-resident Undergraduate $675 Per credit hour; Non-resident Graduate $1,059 Per credit hour; Resident Graduate $428 Per credit hour
Type of Training Offered: Special
Degrees & Hours Offered: BS, Information Technology, 120 semester hrs; Certificate, Information Architecture; Leadership & Management; Museum Studies; Reference Services; School Library Media Leadership; Youth Services, 12-15 credit hours; MA, Information Studies, 36 semester hrs; MS, Information Studies, 36 semester hrs; Ph.D., Information Studies, Varies, normally around 60. 24 credit hours in residence required by university; EdS, Specialist Degree; focused area of interest, 30 credit hours
Special Courses: Advanced Web Applications, Health Informatics, Information Architecture, Information Security, Information Storage & Retrieval, International & Comparative Information Services, International Literature for Youth, Introduction to Legal Resources, Leadership in Reading, Metadata, Multicultural Literature for Youth, Museum Studies, Storytelling, Usability Analysis
Evening Session, Online & Blended Courses, Online Courses, Summer Session, Weekend Session

† UNIVERSITY OF SOUTH FLORIDA*, School of Information, 4202 Fowler Ave, CIS 1040, Tampa, 33620-7800. Tel: 813-974-3520. FAX: 813-974-6840. E-mail: lisinfo@cas.usf.edu. Web Site: www.cas.usf.edu/lis. *Dir,* James E Andrews, PhD; Tel: 813-974-2108; *Asst Dir, Instr,* Diane Austin; E-mail: dianeaustin@usf.edu; *Distinguished Univ Prof,* Kathleen de la Pena McCook; E-mail: kmccook@tampabay.rr.com; *Prof,* Dr John Gathegi; Tel: 813-974-5322, E-mail: jgathegi@usf.edu; *Prof,* Vicki L Gregory; E-mail: gregory@usf.edu; *Assoc Prof,* Dr James Andrews; E-mail: jimandrews@usf.edu; *Assoc Prof,* Dr Cora Dunkley; E-mail: cdunkley@usf.edu; *Assoc Prof,* Dr Jung Won Yoon; E-mail: jyoon@usf.edu; *Asst Prof,* Dr Hong Huang; Tel: 813-974-6361, E-mail: honghuang@usf.edu; *Asst Prof,* Dr Jinfang Niu; Tel: 813-974-6837, E-mail: jinfang@usf.edu; *Asst Prof,* Dr Edward Schneider; Tel: 813-974-7540, E-mail: efschneider@usf.edu; *Instr,* Linda Alexander; E-mail: lalexander@usf.edu; *Instr,* Richard Austin; E-mail: raustin@usf.edu; *Instr,* Kiersten Cox; E-mail: kcox@usf.edu; *Instr,* Dr Heiko Haubitz; Tel: 813-974-7650, E-mail: heiko@usf.edu; *Instr,* Dr John Sullivan; Tel: 813-974-2370, E-mail: jjsullivan@usf.edu; *Instr,* Maria Treadwell; E-mail: mtreadwell@cas.usf.edu
Prog estab 1965. Sch type: Pub. Scholarships offered; Enrl: Grad: 600; Fac 28
Ent Req: GRE minimum 800, GPA of 3.0 on a 4.0 syst, or GRE minimum 1000
Tuition: Non-resident Graduate $855 Per credit hour; Resident Graduate $431 Per credit hour
Type of Training Offered: Special
Degrees & Hours Offered: MA, Libr & Info Sci, 39 sem hrs
Special Courses: Adult Services, Children's Literature, Genealogy, Health Sciences Librarianship, Information Science, Law Librarianship, Library Personnel Management, Media (AV), Organization of Knowledge, Web Page Design & Management, Young Adult Literature
Evening Session, Online Courses, Summer Session

GEORGIA

GEORGIA COLLEGE & STATE UNIVERSITY*, Education Library Media, Campus Box 079, Milledgeville, 31061. Tel: 478-445-5004, Ext 2515. FAX: 478-445-2513. Web Site: www.gcsu.edu/. *Prog Coordr,* Dr Diane Gregg; E-mail: diane.gregg@gcsu.edu
Prog estab 1933. Sch type: Pub; Enrl: Grad: 80
Ent Req: Bachelor's & graduation in upper half of class; writing test adminstered on campus
Tuition: Non-resident Graduate $450 Per credit hour; Resident Graduate $215 Per credit hour
Degrees & Hours Offered: M.Ed., Edu Tech- Major Libr, Media Servs, 36 sem hrs
Special Courses: Instructional technology, Web based Resources, Production of multi-media products
Evening Session, Summer Session

UNIVERSITY OF WEST GEORGIA, Department of Educational Technology & Foundations, 1601 Maple St, Carrollton, 30118. Tel: 678-839-6558. FAX: 678-839-6153. E-mail: media@westga.edu. Web Site: www.westga.edu. *Chair,* Dr Logan Arrington; Tel: 678-839-3937, E-mail: tlarring@westga.edu
Sch type: Pub; Enrl: Grad: 500; Fac 12

Tuition: Non-resident Graduate $935 Per credit hour; Resident Graduate $241 Per credit hour
Type of Training Offered: School
Degrees & Hours Offered: M.Ed., Media, 30 - 36 sem hrs (may be taken concurrently with Education Degree)
Special Courses: Children's Materials, Diffusion of Innovations, Distance Education Courses, Instructional Design, Issues in Instructional Technology, Media Production, Media Program & Microcomputer Technology, Planning Research in Education
Online Courses

† VALDOSTA STATE UNIVERSITY, Department of Library & Information Studies, Odum Library, 1500 N Patterson St, Valdosta, 31698. Tel: 229-333-5966. FAX: 229-259-5055. E-mail: mlis@valdosta.edu. Web Site: www.valdosta.edu/mlis. *Assoc Prof, Interim Dept Head,* Dr Lenese M Colson; E-mail: lcolson@valdosta.edu; *Assoc Prof,* Dr Nicole D Alemanne; Tel: 229-245-3742, E-mail: ndalemanne@valdosta.edu; *Assoc Prof,* Dr Yunseon Choi; Tel: 229-245-3725, E-mail: yunchoi@valdosta.edu; *Assoc Prof,* Dr Colette Drouillard; Tel: 229-245-3715, E-mail: cldrouillard@valdosta.edu; *Assoc Prof,* Dr Xiaoai Ren; Tel: 229-249-2726, E-mail: xren@valdosta.edu; *Assoc Prof,* Dr Changwoo Yang; Tel: 229-333-7185, E-mail: cyang@valdosta.edu; *Lecturer,* Dr Debra Carruth; Tel: 229-333-5657, E-mail: dlcarruth@valdosta.edu; *Lecturer,* Dr Ryan Rucker; E-mail: rdrucker@valdosta.edu
Prog estab 2001. Sch type: Pub; Enrl: Grad: 390; Fac 8
Tuition: Online Graduate $300 Per credit hour
Degrees & Hours Offered: MLIS, 39

HAWAII

† UNIVERSITY OF HAWAII*, Library & Information Science Program, 2550 McCarthy Mall, Hamilton Library, Rm 002, Honolulu, 96822. Tel: 808-956-7321. E-mail: LISinfo@hawaii.edu. Web Site: www.hawaii.edu/lis. *Assoc Prof, Prog Chair,* Dr Noriko Asato; E-mail: asaton@hawaii.edu; *Prof,* Dr Rich Gazan; E-mail: gazan@hawaii.edu; *Asst Prof,* Dr Vanessa Irvin; E-mail: irvinv@hawaii.edu; *Asst Prof,* Dr Tonia Sutherland; E-mail: tsuther@hawaii.edu; *Assoc Prof,* Dr Andrew Wertheimer; E-mail: wertheim@hawaii.edu; *Instr, Sch Libr Media Prog Coordr,* Meera Garud; E-mail: meera@hawaii.edu
Prog estab 1965. Sch type: Pub. Scholarships and fellowships offered; Enrl: Grad: 50; Fac 6
Ent Req: Applicants must have a four-year bachelor's degree (B.A. or B.S.) from an accredited college/university in any major. Minimum GPA 3.0. No GRE necessary.
Tuition: Non-resident Graduate $1,380 Per credit hour; Resident Graduate $650 Per credit hour
Type of Training Offered: Special
Degrees & Hours Offered: Certificate, 15 sem hrs & paper; MLIS, Advan Libr Info, 39 sem hrs
Special Courses: Asian Informatics, Asian Research Materials & Methods, Database Design & Creation, Digital Archives, Digital Instruction, Government Documents, Hawaiian & Pacific Librarianship, Indigenous Librarianship, Moving Image Archives, Preservation Management, Traditional Literature & Oral Narration
Evening Session, Online Courses, Summer Session

IDAHO

COLLEGE OF SOUTHERN IDAHO*, Library & Information Science Program, Gerald R Meyerhoeffer Bldg, Main Flr, 315 Falls Ave, Twin Falls, 83303. (Mail add: PO Box 1238, Twin Falls, 83303-1238). Tel: 208-732-6501. FAX: 208-736-3087. Web Site: csi.ent.sirsi.net/client/en_US/default. *Dept Chair, Dir,* Dr Teri Fattig; E-mail: tfattig@csi.edu
Sch type: Pub; Enrl: Undergrad: 15
Ent Req: HS Diploma or GED
Tuition: Non-resident Undergraduate $280 Per credit hour; Resident Undergraduate $130 Per credit hour
Degrees & Hours Offered: AA, Libr Sci, 61 sem hrs
Online Courses
Friends of the Library Group

ILLINOIS

CHICAGO STATE UNIVERSITY*, Library Science & Communications Media Program, Education Bldg, Rm 208, 9501 S King Dr, Chicago, 60628-1598. Tel: 773-995-2598. FAX: 773-821-2441. Web Site: csu.edu/collegeofeducation. *Chair,* Nancy Grim; E-mail: ngrim@csu.edu; *Prog Coordr,* Dr Rae-Anne Montague; E-mail: rmontagu@csu.edu
Sch type: Pub; Fac 3
Tuition: Non-resident Undergraduate $3,628 Per semester; Resident Undergraduate $1,479 Per semester
Degrees & Hours Offered: MS, Libr Sci, 38 sem hrs
Special Courses: Children's Literature, Government Documents, Information Science, Instructional Design, International Comparative Librarianship, Media (AV), TV & AV Production & Young Adult Literature & Storytelling
Evening Session, Summer Session

COLLEGE OF DUPAGE*, Library & Information Technology Program, 425 Fawell Blvd, Glen Ellyn, 60137. Tel: 630-942-3787. Web Site: www.cod.edu/lta. *Asst Prof,* Amanda Musacchio; Tel: 630-942-3787, E-mail: musacchioa@cod.edu
Enrl: Undergrad: 120
Tuition: Non-resident Undergraduate $325 Per semester hour; Resident Undergraduate $139 Per semester hour
Degrees & Hours Offered: AAS, Libr Tech, 64 sem hrs; Certificate, Libr Tech, 30 sem hrs
Evening Session, Online Courses, Summer Session, Video Courses, Weekend Session

† DOMINICAN UNIVERSITY*, Graduate School of Library & Information Science, Crown Library 300, 7900 W Division St, River Forest, 60305. Tel: 708-524-6845. FAX: 708-524-6657. E-mail: gradinfo@dom.edu. Web Site: www.dom.edu. *Dir,* Kate Marek; Tel: 708-524-6648, E-mail: kmarek@dom.edu; *Dir, PhD Prog,* Karen Snow; E-mail: ksnow@dom.edu; *Dir, Sch Libr Media Prog,* Don W Hamerly; E-mail: dhamerly@dom.edu
Prog estab 1930. Sch type: Pvt; Enrl: Grad: 250; Fac 13
Tuition: Resident Graduate $2,448 Per course
Type of Training Offered: Library & Information Science
Degrees & Hours Offered: Certificate, Archives & Cult Heritage; Data & Knowledge Mgmt; Digital Curation; Digital Libraries; Informatics; Web Design; Youth Services, 15-18 credit hrs beyond MLIS; MLIS, 36 credit hrs (12 courses); Ph.D., Libr & Info Sci, 36 credit hrs (beyond Master's degree) plus dissertation

ILLINOIS CENTRAL COLLEGE*, Library Technical Assistant Program, S113 Banwart Library, Student Ctr, One College Dr, East Peoria, 61635. Tel: 309-690-6958. Web Site: icc.edu/academics/catalog/academic-departments/business-legal-and-information-systems. *Prog Coordr,* Daniel Fuertges; E-mail: daniel.fuertges@icc.edu
Prog estab 1971. Sch type: Pub; Enrl: Undergrad: 15; Fac 7
Tuition: Resident Undergraduate $135 Per credit hour
Degrees & Hours Offered: Certificate, Lib Tech Asst, 24 credit hrs
Continuing Education, Evening Session, No Summer Sessions, Online Courses, Professional Development

† UNIVERSITY OF ILLINOIS AT URBANA-CHAMPAIGN, School of Information Sciences, Library & Information Science Bldg, 501 E Daniel St, Champaign, 61820-6211. Tel: 217-333-3280. Toll Free Tel: 800-982-0914. FAX: 217-244-3302. E-mail: ischool@illinois.edu. Web Site: www.ischool.illinois.edu. *Prof & Dean,* Eunice E Santos; *Interim Executive Assoc Dean, Vis Prof,* Jiangping Chen; *Assoc Dean, Acad Affairs, Prof,* Catherine Blake; *Assoc Dean, Res, Co-Director, HathiTrust Research Ctr, Prof,* J Stephen Downie; *Dir, Ctr for Children's Books, Prof,* Sara L Schwebel; *Dir, Ctr, Informatics Research in Science & Scholarship, Prof,* Bertram Ludascher; *MSIM Program Dir, Prof,* Jingrui He; *Prof,* Christopher Lueg; *Prof,* Allen Renear; *Prof,* Michael Twidale; *Prof,* Ted Underwood; *Prof,* Yang Wang; *Assoc Prof, Dir, Champaign-Urbana (CU) Community Fab Lab,* Kyungwon Koh; *Assoc Prof, MSLIS & CAS Program Director,* Maria Bonn; *Asst Teaching Prof, Undergraduate Programs Dir,* Brandon Batzloff; *Teaching Prof,* Judith Pintar; *Assoc Prof,* Rachel Adler; *Assoc Prof,* Masooda Bashir; *Assoc Prof,* Anita Say Chan; *Assoc Prof,* Ryan Cordell; *Assoc Prof,* Peter Darch; *Assoc Prof,* Elizabeth Hoiem; *Assoc Prof,* Yun Huang; *Assoc Prof,* Lori Kendall; *Assoc Prof,* Halil Kilicoglu; *Assoc Prof,* Emily Knox; *Assoc Prof,* Bonnie Mak; *Assoc Prof,* Kate McDowell; *Assoc Prof,* Sarah Park Dahlen; *Assoc Prof,* Jodi Schneider; *Assoc Prof,* Yoo-Seong Song; *Assoc Prof,* Carol Tilley; *Assoc Prof,* Vetle Torvik; *Assoc Prof,* Dong Wang; *Assoc Teaching Prof,* David Dubin; *Assoc Teaching Prof,* Martin Wolske; *Asst Prof,* Nigel Bosch; *Asst Prof,* Jessie Chin; *Asst Prof,* Kahyun Choi; *Asst Prof,* Yue Guo; *Asst Prof,* Zoe LeBlanc; *Asst Prof,* Yaoyao Liu; *Asst Prof,* Ismini Lourentzou; *Asst Prof,* Jiaqi Ma; *Asst Prof,* Emily Maemura; *Asst Prof,* Rachel M Magee; *Asst Prof,* Melissa Ocepek; *Asst Prof,* Madelyn Rose Sanfilippo; *Asst Prof,* JooYoung Seo; *Asst Prof,* Meicen Sun; *Asst Prof,* Matthew Turk; *Asst Prof,* Haohan Wang; *Asst Prof,* Travis L Wagner; *Asst Prof,* Karen Wickett; *Asst Teaching Prof,* David Charles; *Asst Teaching Prof,* Inkyung Choi; *Asst Teaching Prof,* Sharon Comstock; *Asst Teaching Prof,* Renee Hendricks; *Asst Teaching Prof,* David Hopping; *Asst Teaching Prof,* David Mussulman; *Asst Teaching Prof,* Jill Naiman; *Asst Teaching Prof,* Adam Rusch; *Asst Teaching Prof,* Craig Willis; *Asst Teaching Prof,* Yang Zhang; *Sr Lecturer,* Kevin Trainor; *Sr Lecturer,* John Weible; *Lecturer,* Craig Evans; *Lecturer,* Elizabeth Wickes
Prog estab 1893. Sch type: Pub. Scholarships offered; Enrl: Grad: 1,240, Undergrad: 818; Fac 68
Ent Req: For MS, CAS, PhD need GPA of 3.0 on a scale of 4.0; for MS need a Baccalaureate; for CAS need a MS in LIS; for PhD need a BA/BS or MS in LIS or closely related field
Type of Training Offered: Special
Degrees & Hours Offered: BS, 123 sem hrs; Certificate, Advan Studies, 40 sem hrs; MS, 40 sem hrs; Ph.D., 80 sem hrs

Special Courses: Archives, Business Information, Children's Literature, Community Information Systems, Designing Universally Accessible WWW Resources, Electronic Publishing & Information Processing Standards, Information Consulting, Information Retrieval, Inquiry Teaching & Learning, Interfaces to Information Systems, Legal Bibliography, Medical Reference, Music Bibliography, Preservation, Slavic Bibliography, Young Adult Literature
Online Courses, Summer Session

INDIANA

† INDIANA UNIVERSITY*, School of Library & Information Science, Wells Library 001, 1320 E Tenth St, Bloomington, 47405-3907. SAN 340-9805. Tel: 812-855-2018. Toll Free Tel: 888-335-7547. FAX: 812-855-6166. E-mail: ilsmain@indiana.edu. Web Site: www.slis.indiana.edu. *Chair, Prof, Libr Sci,* Ronald E Day, PhD; E-mail: roday@indiana.edu
Tuition: Non-resident Graduate $1,124 Per credit hour; Resident Graduate $386 Per credit hour
Type of Training Offered: Library & Information Science
Degrees & Hours Offered: MLS; Ph.D.; MIS; MIS/MLS; SpLIS
Special Courses: Archives & Manuscripts, Children's Sources & Services, Descriptive Bibliography, Electronic Commerce, Human Computer Interaction, Government Documents, Information Retrieval, Legal Bibliography, Online Information Retrieval, Preservation, Rare Books Librarianship, Web Management

IOWA

† UNIVERSITY OF IOWA*, School of Library & Information Science, 3087 Main Library, 125 W Washington St, Iowa City, 52242-1420. Tel: 319-335-5707. FAX: 319-335-5374. E-mail: slis@uiowa.edu. Web Site: slis.uiowa.edu. *Interim Dir,* Dr Jennifer Burek Pierce; E-mail: jennifer-burek-pierce@uiowa.edu; *Adminr, Prog Serv,* Katie McCullough; Tel: 319-384-1538, E-mail: katie-mccullough@uiowa.edu; *Asst Prof,* Micah Bateman; E-mail: micah-bateman@uiowa.edu; *Assoc Prof,* Jackie Biger; E-mail: jacqueline-biger@uiowa.edu; *Lecturer,* Kara Logsden; Tel: 319-335-5707, E-mail: kara-logsden@uiowa.edu; *Lecturer,* Colleen Theisen; E-mail: colleen-theisen@uiowa.edu; *Asst Prof,* Iulian Vamanu; Tel: 319-335-5714, E-mail: iulian-vamanu@uiowa.edu; *Assoc Prof,* Julie Leonard; E-mail: julia-leonard@uiowa.edu; *Assoc Prof,* Sara Langworthy; E-mail: sara-langworthy@uiowa.edu; *Prof Emeritus,* Dr David Eichmann; E-mail: david-eichmann@uiowa.edu; *Prof Emeritus,* Timothy Barrett; E-mail: timothy-barrett@uiowa.edu
Prog estab 1967. Sch type: Pub. Scholarships offered; Enrl: Grad: 110
Ent Req: BA, GPA of 3.0, statement of purpose, three letters of recommendation.
Tuition: Resident Graduate $5,608 Per semester; Resident Graduate $6,117 Per semester
Type of Training Offered: Special
Degrees & Hours Offered: MA, Libr & Info Sci, 36 sem hrs

UNIVERSITY OF NORTHERN IOWA*, School Library Studies, Schindler 107, University of Northern Iowa, Cedar Falls, 50614-0612. Tel: 319-273-2050. FAX: 319-273-5886. Web Site: www.uni.edu/sls. *Assoc Prof, Prog Coordr,* Karla Krueger; Tel: 319-273-7241, E-mail: karla.krueger@uni.edu
Prog estab 1969. Sch type: Pub. Scholarships offered; Enrl: Grad: 40; Fac 2
Ent Req: 3.0 GPA Teaching License or teacher education coursework
Tuition: Online Graduate $539 Per credit hour
Type of Training Offered: School Library Media
Degrees & Hours Offered: MA, School Library Studies, 33-36 sem hrs
Special Courses: Information Resources for Inquiry Learning, Library Resources for Children, Library Resources for Young Adults, Technologies for Libraries, School Library Curriculum Development, Leadership in the School Library Program, Organization of Information
Online Courses

KANSAS

† EMPORIA STATE UNIVERSITY*, School of Library & Information Management, One Kellogg Circle, Campus Box 4025, Emporia, 66801-4025. Tel: 620-341-5203. Toll Free Tel: 800-552-4770. FAX: 620-341-5233. E-mail: sliminfo@emporia.edu. Web Site: emporia.edu/slim. *Dean,* Wooseob Jeong; Tel: 800-552-4770, Ext 5203, E-mail: wjeong1@emporia.edu; *Academic Specialist,* Kathie Buckman; Tel: 620-757-9088, E-mail: kbuckman@emporia.edu
Prog estab 1902. Sch type: Pub; Enrl: Grad: 400; Fac 10
Tuition: Non-resident Graduate $9,263 Per year; Non-resident Graduate $515 Per credit hour; Resident Graduate $6,808 Per year; Resident Graduate $378 Per credit hour
Type of Training Offered: Librarianship
Degrees & Hours Offered: MLS, Sch Libr Media Certification, Legal Info Mgt Certificate, Info Mgt Certificate, Archives Studies Certificate, 36 hrs; Ph.D., Libr & Info Mgt, 52 hrs
Continuing Education

KENTUCKY

MURRAY STATE UNIVERSITY*, Library Media Program, College of Education & Human Services, 3201 Alexander Hall, Murray, 42071-3309. Tel: 270-809-2500. Toll Free Tel: 800-272-4678. FAX: 270-809-3799. Web Site: www.murraystate.edu. *Interim Assoc Dean,* Dr Susana Bloomdahl; Tel: 270-809-6471, E-mail: sbloomdahl@murraystate.edu; *Dept Chair,* Samir Patel; E-mail: spatel4@murraystate.edu; *Prog Coordr,* Terri Grief; E-mail: tgrief@murraystate.edu
Prog estab 1930. Sch type: Pub. Scholarships offered; Enrl: Grad: 10
Ent Req: 2.5 GPA
Tuition: Non-resident Graduate $800 Per semester hour; Resident Graduate $544 Per semester hour
Degrees & Hours Offered: MA, 30 credit hrs
Special Courses: Media, Preparation & Utilization of School Library Media & Print-Nonprint Curriculum
Evening Session, Online Courses

† UNIVERSITY OF KENTUCKY*, School of Information Science, 320 Little Library Bldg, Lexington, 40506-0224. Tel: 859-257-8876. FAX: 859-257-4205. E-mail: sis@uky.edu. Web Site: infosci.uky.edu. *Dir,* Dr Jeffrey T Huber; E-mail: jeffrey.huber@uky.edu; *Asst Prof,* Dr Shannon Barniskis; E-mail: barniskis@uky.edu; *Asst Prof,* Dr Sarah Barriage; E-mail: sarah.barriage@uky.edu; *Asst Prof,* Dr Beth Bloch; E-mail: beth.s.bloch@uky.edu; *Asst Dir,* Will Buntin; E-mail: will.buntin@uky.edu; *Asst Prof,* Dr Christopher Sean Burns; E-mail: sean.burns@uky.edu; *Assoc Prof,* Dr Maria Cahill; E-mail: maria.cahill@uky.edu; *Asst Prof,* Dr Yu Chi; E-mail: yu.chi@uky.edu; *Assoc Prof,* Dr Namjoo Choi; E-mail: namjoo.choi@uky.edu; *Asst Prof,* Dr Daniela DiGiacomo; E-mail: daniela.digiacomo@uky.edu; *Asst Prof,* Dr Soohyung Joo; E-mail: soohyung.joo@uky.edu; *Asst Prof,* Dr Shannon M Oltmann; E-mail: shannon.oltmann@uky.edu; *Asst Prof,* Dr Brian Real; E-mail: brian.real@uky.edu; *Coordr, Lecturer,* Ashley DeWitt; E-mail: ashdewitt@uky.edu
Prog estab 1933. Sch type: Pub. Scholarships offered; Enrl: Grad: 200; Fac 13
Ent Req: UGPA of 3.0
Tuition: Online Graduate $6,300 Per semester
Type of Training Offered: School Library Media Certificate
Degrees & Hours Offered: MS, Information Communication Technology, 36 sem hrs; MSLS, Library Science, 36 sem hrs
Special Courses: Information Retrieval, Information Policy, Medical Informatics
Online Courses, Summer Session

WESTERN KENTUCKY UNIVERSITY, SCHOOL OF TEACHER EDUCATION*, Library, Informatics & Technology in Education (LITE), Gary A Ransdell Hall, Office 1005, 1906 College Heights Blvd, No 61030, Bowling Green, 42101-1030. Tel: 270-745-2435, 270-745-5414. FAX: 270-745-6322. Web Site: www.wku.edu/lite. *Assoc Prof, Graduate Program Coord,* Dr Andrea Paganelli; Tel: 270-745-5414, E-mail: andrea.paganelli@wku.edu
Prog estab 1929. Sch type: Pub. Scholarships offered
Type of Training Offered: School Library Media Certificate
Degrees & Hours Offered: Certificate, Educ Tech for teacher certification, non-teacher prep, 12 credit hrs; MS, Libr Media Educ, P-12 Libr Media Spec, Educ Tech Spec, non-teacher certified Ky Pub Libr credential, non-teacher Educ Tech Spec, 30 credit hrs
Special Courses: Children's Literature; Collection Management; Informatics; Instructional Design; Integration of Technology; Issues in Educational Technology; Management of Educational Networks; Storytelling; Technology Production
Evening Session, Online Courses, Summer Session

LOUISIANA

† LOUISIANA STATE UNIVERSITY*, School of Library & Information Science, 267 Coates Hall, Baton Rouge, 70803. Tel: 225-578-3158, 225-578-3159. FAX: 225-578-4581. E-mail: slis@lsu.edu. Web Site: slis.lsu.edu. *Dir,* Dr Carol Barry; E-mail: carolbarry@lsu.edu; *Assoc Prof,* Dr Edward A Benoit, III; E-mail: ebenoit@lsu.edu; *Assoc Prof,* Tao Jin; E-mail: taojin@lsu.edu; *Assoc Prof,* Dr Yejun Wu; E-mail: wuyj@lsu.edu; *Prof,* Dr Boryung Ju; E-mail: bju1@lsu.edu; *Prof,* Dr Suzanne Stauffer; E-mail: stauffer@lsu.edu; *Bus Mgr,* Nicole Rozas; E-mail: nrozas@lsu.edu
Prog estab 1931. Sch type: Pub. Scholarships offered; Enrl: Grad: 180; Fac 11
Ent Req: BA, 3.0 GPA, GRE, TOEFL & letters of recommendation
Tuition: Non-resident Graduate $13,296 Per semester; Non-resident Graduate $1,988 Per 3 credit hour; Resident Graduate $4,256 Per semester; Resident Graduate $1,015 Per 3 credit hour

Type of Training Offered: Special
Degrees & Hours Offered: MLIS, 36 sem hrs
Special Courses: Archives, Health Sciences, Information Science, Joint Degree with Computer Science, Joint Degree with History
Evening Session, Online & Blended Courses, Online Courses, Summer Session

MCNEESE STATE UNIVERSITY*, Burton College of Education, 4205 Ryan St, Lake Charles, 70605. Tel: 337-475-5432, 337-475-5433. Toll Free Tel: 800-622-3352. FAX: 337-475-5467. Web Site: www.mcneese.edu. *Dean,* Dr Angelique Ogea; E-mail: aogea@mcneese.edu
Sch type: Pub; Fac 54
Tuition: Resident Undergraduate $1,165 Per semester hour; Resident Graduate $1,418 Per semester hour
Type of Training Offered: School
Degrees & Hours Offered: BA, Educ with Add - On Endorsement & Libr Sci, 18 sem hrs; BS, Educ with Add - On Endorsement & Libr Sci, 18 sem hrs
Special Courses: Cataloging & Classification, Children's Literature, Educational Technology, Library Administration, Reference & Young Adult Literature
Evening Session, Online Courses, Summer Session

SOUTHEASTERN LOUISIANA UNIVERSITY*, Department of Teaching & Learning, 1300 N General Pershing St, Hammond, 70402. (Mail add: PO Box 10549, Hammond, 70402). Tel: 985-549-2221. FAX: 985-549-5559. E-mail: Teaching.Learning@selu.edu. Web Site: www.southeastern.edu. *Dept Head,* Colleen Klein-Ezell; E-mail: colleen.klein-ezell@southeasternedu
Sch type: Pub
Type of Training Offered: School
Degrees & Hours Offered: Certificate, Libr Sci, 21 hrs
Special Courses: Bibliotherapy, Information Literacy, Technology for the Library
Evening Session, Summer Session

UNIVERSITY OF LOUISIANA AT LAFAYETTE*, Department of Education (Librarianship), Maxim Doucet Hall 101, 1405 Johnston St, Lafayette, 70503. (Mail add: PO Box 43722, Lafayette, 70504). Tel: 337-482-6405. FAX: 337-482-5904. Web Site: education.louisiana.edu. *Dept Head,* Dr Tony Daspit; Tel: 337-482-6409, E-mail: tdaspit@louisiana.edu
Prog estab 1939. Sch type: Pub; Enrl: Undergrad: 15
Type of Training Offered: School
Degrees & Hours Offered: BA, Libr Sci minor or Add-On Certification, 21 sem hrs; BS, Libr Sci minor or Add-On Certification, 21 sem hrs
Special Courses: Children's Literature, Young Adult Literature
Evening Session, Summer Session

UNIVERSITY OF NEW ORLEANS*, Department of Curriculum Instruction & Special Education Program in Library Science, College of Education, Rm 342, New Orleans, 70148. Tel: 504-280-7063. FAX: 504-280-1120. E-mail: coehd@uno.edu. Web Site: www.uno.edu/academics/colaehd/ehd/curriculum-instruction. *Asst Prof,* Dr Kenneth Farizo, PhD; E-mail: kpfarizo@uno.edu
Prog estab 1962. Sch type: Pub; Fac 2
Tuition: Non-resident Undergraduate $4,878 Per semester; Resident Undergraduate $1,356 Per semester
Type of Training Offered: School
Degrees & Hours Offered: Certificate, 21 sem hrs; M.Ed., Libr Sci, 33 sem hrs
Special Courses: Children's Literature, Teaching Information Literacy
Evening Session, Summer Session

MARYLAND

MCDANIEL COLLEGE, School Librarianship Program, Graduate Studies, Two College Hill, Westminster, 21157-4390. Tel: 410-857-2501. FAX: 410-857-2515. Web Site: www.mcdaniel.edu/graduate/your-plan/academic-programs/m.s.-in-school-librarianship. *Coordr, Prof,* Dr Ramona N Kerby; Tel: 410-857-2507, E-mail: rkerby@mcdaniel.edu
Sch type: Pvt; Enrl: Grad: 100; Fac 4
Ent Req: Baccalaureate Degree
Type of Training Offered: School
Degrees & Hours Offered: MS, Sch Librarianship, 36 sem hrs
Online & Blended Courses, Summer Session

† UNIVERSITY OF MARYLAND*, College of Information Studies, Hornbake Library, Ground Flr, Rm 0220, 4130 Campus Dr, College Park, 20742-4345. Tel: 301-405-2039. FAX: 301-314-9145. E-mail: mlisprogram@umd.edu. Web Site: ischool.umd.edu/mlis. *Dean,* Dr Keith Marzullo; E-mail: ischooldean@umd.edu; *Assoc Dean, Res,* Dr Susan Winter; E-mail: sjwinter@umd.edu; *Asst Dir, Fac Serv,* Ryan O'Grady; E-mail: rogrady1@umd.edu; *Prog Dir,* Ursula Gorham; E-mail: ugorham@umd.edu; *Prog Coordr,* Joseph Sherren; E-mail: jsherren@umd.edu
Prog estab 1965. Sch type: Pub. Scholarships offered; Enrl: Grad: 301
Ent Req: Bachelor's degree, letters of recommendation, supplemental questions, statement of purpose
Tuition: Non-resident Graduate $1,404 Per credit hour; Resident Graduate $651 Per credit hour
Type of Training Offered: Special
Degrees & Hours Offered: MLIS, Archives & Digital Curation; Diversity & Inclusion; Intelligence & Analytics; Legal Informatics; Sch Libr; Youth Experience (YX)., 36 credits; MA/MLIS, Archives & Digital Curation; Diversity & Inclusion; Intelligence & Analytics; Legal Informatics, 54 credits
Continuing Education, Evening Session, Online & Blended Courses, Online Courses, Professional Development, Summer Session

MASSACHUSETTS

BOSTON UNIVERSITY*, Educational Media & Technology Program, Wheelock College of Education & Human Development, No 2 Sherborn St, Boston, 02215. Tel: 617-353-3182. FAX: 617-353-3924. Web Site: www.bu.edu. *Asst Prof,* Lindsay Gibbons; Tel: 617-353-3182, E-mail: lgibbons@bu.edu
Prog estab 1960. Sch type: Pvt; Enrl: Grad: 45
On moratorium for 2016-2017
Ent Req: GRE or MAT & letters of recommendation; Statement of qualifications and objectives
Type of Training Offered: College
Degrees & Hours Offered: M.Ed., Educ Media & Tech, 36 sem hrs
Special Courses: Database & Web Integration for Educators, Designing Educational Multimedia, Distance Education, Instructional Video, Interactive Software Development, Internet & WWW for Educators
Evening Session, Summer Session

SALEM STATE UNIVERSITY*, Library Media Studies Program, Graduate School, 352 Lafayette St, Salem, 01970. Tel: 978-542-6000, 978-542-7044. FAX: 978-542-7215. Web Site: www.salemstate.edu. *Dean,* Stephanie Bellar; E-mail: stephanie.bellar@salemstate.edu; *Prog Coordr,* Valerie Diggs; E-mail: vdiggs@salemstate.edu
Prog estab 1973. Enrl: Grad: 30
Tuition: Non-resident Graduate $640 Per credit hour; Resident Graduate $550 Per credit hour
Type of Training Offered: School
Degrees & Hours Offered: M.Ed., Libr Media Servs, 36 credits
Evening Session, Summer Session

† SIMMONS UNIVERSITY, School of Library & Information Science, 300 The Fenway, Boston, 02115. Tel: 617-521-2800. FAX: 617-521-3192. E-mail: slis@simmons.edu. Web Site: www.simmons.edu/slis. *Dean, Prof,* Sanda Erdelez; E-mail: sanda.erdelez@simmons.edu; *Assoc Dean, Prof,* Laura Saunders; *Assoc Prof, MSLIS Program Dir,* Katherine Wisser; *Assoc Prof, PhD Prog Dir,* Kyong Eun Oh; *Prof,* Naresh Agarwal; *Prof,* Heather Hole; *Prof,* Lisa Hussey; *Prof,* Daniel Joudrey; *Prof,* Amy Pattee; *Asst Prof,* Rhiannon Bettivia; *Assoc Prof,* Peter Botticelli; *Assoc Prof,* Melanie Kimball; *Asst Prof,* Adam Kriesberg; *Asst Prof,* Don Simmons; *Asst Prof,* Rebecca Stallworth; *Asst Prof,* Mei Zhang; *Assoc Prof of Practice,* Donia Conn; *Asst Prof of Practice,* Arianna Lechan; *Asst Prof of Practice,* Molly Metevier; *Asst Prof of Practice,* Eric Poulin; *Asst Prof of Practice,* Stacie Williams
Prog estab 1902. Sch type: Pvt. Scholarships offered; Enrl: Grad: 821; Fac 20
Ent Req: BA or equivalent & 3.0 GPA
Type of Training Offered: Special
Degrees & Hours Offered: Certificate, Archives Management, 15; Certificate, School Library Teacher Licensure, 12; MA, Part of MA/MS dual-degree. MA in Children's Literature, 58-60 credit hrs; MA, Part of an MA/MS dual-degree. The MA is in History, the MS is with an Archives Management or Cultural Heritage Informatics concentration, 57 credit hrs; MS, 36 credit hrs; Ph.D., Library and Information Science (LIS), 36 credit hrs
Special Courses: Administration of Archives & Manuscript Collections, Applied Information Systems Design, Information/Organization Ethics, Intellectual Freedom & Censorship, Modern Publishing & Librarianship, Music Librarianship, Photographic Archives, Visual Information, Preservation Management, Digital Asset Management, Data Interoperability, Digital Preservation , Database Management, User Instruction

MICHIGAN

† UNIVERSITY OF MICHIGAN*, School of Information, 4322 North Quad, 105 S State St, Ann Arbor, 48109-1285. Tel: 734-763-2285. FAX: 734-764-2475. E-mail: umsi.admissions@umich.edu, umsi.human.resources@umich.edu, umsi.marcom@umich.edu. Web Site: www.si.umich.edu. *Dean,* Andrea Forte; E-mail: umsi.dean@umich.edu; *Assoc Dean, Acad Affairs,* Cliff Lampe; E-mail: cacl@umich.edu

Prog estab 1926. Sch type: Pub. Scholarships offered; Enrl: Grad: 1,216, Grad: 130; Fac 67
Ent Req: Doctoral
Tuition: Non-resident Undergraduate $28,317 Per semester; Non-resident Graduate $25,068 Per semester; Resident Undergraduate $8,940 Per semester; Resident Graduate $12,451 Per semester
Degrees & Hours Offered: Ph.D., 4-5 years; BSI, Info Analytics; User Experience Design & Res, 120 credit hrs; MADS, 34 credit hrs; MHI, 52 credit hrs; MSI, Archives & Rec Mgt; Digital Curation; Human-Computer Interaction; Info Analysis & Retrieval; Libr & Info Sci, 48 credit hrs

† WAYNE STATE UNIVERSITY*, School of Information Sciences, 106 Kresge Library, Detroit, 48202. Tel: 313-577-1825. Toll Free Tel: 877-263-2665. FAX: 313-577-7563. E-mail: asksis@wayne.edu. Web Site: sis.wayne.edu. *Dean,* Dr Jon E Cawthorne; Tel: 313-577-4020, E-mail: jon.cawthorne@wayne.edu; *Assoc Dean,* Dr Thomas D Walker; Tel: 313-577-0350, E-mail: tom.walker@wayne.edu; *Acad Serv Officer II,* Matthew D Fredericks; Tel: 313-577-2446, E-mail: aj8416@wayne.edu; *Acad Serv Officer III,* Megen R Drulia; Tel: 313-577-8543, E-mail: ay6086@wayne.edu; *Acad Serv Officer IV,* Jennifer L Bondy; Tel: 313-577-2523, E-mail: aa1676@wayne.edu; *Prof Emeritus,* Dr Robert P Holley; E-mail: aa3805@wayne.edu; *Prof,* Dr Dian E Walster; E-mail: ah1984@wayne.edu; *Assoc Prof,* Dr Hermina G B Anghelescu; E-mail: ag7662@wayne.edu; *Prof,* Dr Stephen Bajjaly; E-mail: bajjaly@wayne.edu; *Asst Prof,* Dr Joan Beaudoin; E-mail: ee4525@wayne.edu; *Asst Prof,* Dr Deborah Charbonneau; E-mail: ao8245@wayne.edu; *Asst Prof,* Dr Kafi Kumasi; E-mail: ak4901@wayne.edu; *Asst Prof,* Dr Xiangmin E Zhang; E-mail: ae9101@wayne.edu; *Sr Lecturer,* Dr Bin Li; E-mail: ax9064@wayne.edu; *Lecturer,* Kimberly A Schroeder; E-mail: ag1797@wayne.edu; *Mgr, Libr Student & Instrul Computing,* Mark Temnyk; Tel: 313-577-5328, E-mail: ai5487@wayne.edu; *Practicum Coordr,* Jennifer Gustafson; E-mail: ad9667@wayne.edu; *Prof in Residence,* Judith J Field; E-mail: aa4101@wayne.edu; *Asst Prof,* Dr Timothy Bowman; Tel: 888-497-8754, Ext 702, E-mail: timothy.d.bowman@wayne.edu; *Asst Prof,* Christine D'Arpa; E-mail: Christine.DArpa@wayne.edu; *Asst Prof,* Dr Laura Sheble; Tel: 313-577-3762, E-mail: aj0151@wayne.edu
Prog estab 1940. Sch type: Pub; Enrl: Grad: 435; Fac 13
Tuition: Non-resident Graduate $1,579 Per credit hour; Online Graduate $788 Per credit hour
Type of Training Offered: Special
Degrees & Hours Offered: Certificate, Archival Admin, 15 credit hrs; Certificate, Post Master-Specialist, 30 credit hrs; Certificate, Info Mgt, 15 plus 3 credit prerequisite; Certificate, Pub Libr Servs to Ch & YA, 15; MLIS, Library Services; Information Management; Archives and Digital Content Management, 36 credit hrs; MS, Information Management, 30; MLIS/MA, Hist, 57 credit hrs
Special Courses: Archives; Arts & Museum Librarianship; Cataloging & Classification; Children's Literature; Competitive Intelligence; Database Concepts & Applications; Digital Content Management; Digital Curation and Preservation; Digital Libraries; Educational Technology; Health & Scientific Data Management; Indexing & Abstracting; Information Analytics; Information Architecture; Information Behavior; Information Policy; Information Visualization; Integrated Library Systems; Metadata; Multicultural Information Services & Resources; Productivity Tools; Project Management; Records Management; User Experience; Urban Libraries; Web Development; Young Adult Literature

MINNESOTA

MINNESOTA STATE UNIVERSITY, MANKATO*, School Library & Information Studies Program, College of Education, Armstrong Hall AH 313, Mankato, 56001-8400. Tel: 507-389-1965. FAX: 507-389-5751. Web Site: ed.mnsu.edu/academic-programs/k12-secondary-programs/school-library-and-information-studies-ms. *Dept Chair,* Scott Page, PhD; Tel: 507-389-1788, E-mail: scott.page@mnsu.edu
Prog estab 1971. Sch type: Pub. Scholarships offered
Tuition: Resident Graduate $473 Per credit hour
Degrees & Hours Offered: Certificate, Sch Lib & Info Studies, 28 sem hrs; MA, Sch Lib & Info Studies, 34 credit hrs; MS, Sch Lib & Info Studies, 34 credit hrs
Special Courses: Children's Literature, Information Science, Media & Technology, Records Management
Online Courses, Summer Session

† SAINT CATHERINE UNIVERSITY*, Library & Information Science, 2004 Randolph Ave, Mailstop No 4125, Saint Paul, 55105. Tel: 651-690-6802. FAX: 651-690-8724. E-mail: imdept@stkate.edu. Web Site: www.stkate.edu. *Assoc Prof, Prog Dir,* Anthony Molaro, PhD; E-mail: agmolaro@stkate.edu; *Assoc Prof,* David Lesniaski, PhD; E-mail: DALesniaski@stkate.edu; *Assoc Prof,* Sook Lim, PhD; E-mail: SLim@stkate.edu; *Assoc Prof,* Sheri Ross, PhD; E-mail: svtross@stkate.edu; *Assoc Prof,* Kyunghye Yoon, PhD; E-mail: kyoon@stkate.edu; *Assoc Prof,* Joyce Yukawa, PhD; E-mail: JYukawa@stkate.edu
Prog estab 1918. Sch type: Pvt; Enrl: Grad: 144; Fac 9
Ent Req: 3.0 GPA
Tuition: Resident Graduate $960 Per credit hour
Degrees & Hours Offered: Certificate, School Library Media Specialist (SLMS) certification, 33 semester credits, hold Minnesota Teaching license; additional 19 semester credits w/o Minnesota Teaching license; MLIS, Library & Information Science, 36 semester credits; MLIS, School Library Media Specialist (SLMS)/MLIS, 36 semester credits, SLMS/MLIS with Minnesota Teaching License; additional 19 semester credits w/o Minnesota Teaching license
Evening Session

SAINT CLOUD STATE UNIVERSITY*, Library Media Graduate Program, Education Bldg A132, 720 Fourth Ave S, Saint Cloud, 56301-4498. Tel: 320-308-3007. FAX: 320-308-2933. E-mail: ed@stcloudstate.edu. Web Site: www.stcloudstate.edu/graduate/im-library. *Dir,* Jennifer Hill; Tel: 320-308-4057, E-mail: jchill@stcloudstate.edu
Sch type: Pub. Scholarships offered; Fac 5
Partic in MnPALS
Type of Training Offered: College
Degrees & Hours Offered: MS, Info Media: Libr Media, 39-42 sem hrs
Open Mon-Fri 8-4:30

MISSISSIPPI

† UNIVERSITY OF SOUTHERN MISSISSIPPI*, School of Library & Information Science, 129 Fritz-Gibbs Hall, 118 College Dr, No 5146, Hattiesburg, 39406-0001. Tel: 601-266-4228. FAX: 601-266-5774. E-mail: slis@usm.edu. Web Site: www.usm.edu/slis. *Dir,* Dr Teresa Welsh; E-mail: teresa.welsh@usm.edu
Prog estab 1926. Sch type: Pub; Fac 9
Tuition: Non-resident Undergraduate $6,180 Full-time; Non-resident Graduate $1,818 Per 3 credit hour; Non-resident Graduate $5,448 Full-time; Resident Undergraduatc $4,448 Full-time; Resident Graduate $2,571 Per credit hour; Resident Graduate $1,482 Per 3 credit hour; Resident Graduate $4,628 Full-time
Type of Training Offered: Special
Degrees & Hours Offered: BA, 39 sem hrs for major/124 hours total; Certificate, Archives and Special Collections, 18 hours post-master's (12 hours can be taken as part of master's); Certificate, Youth Services and Literature, 15 hours post-master's (12 hours can be taken as part of master's); Certificate, School library licensure endorsement, 21 hours, either graduate or undergraduate; MLIS, with or without Sch Libr Media specialization, 39 sem hrs
Special Courses: Archives, British Studies, Children's Literature
Evening Session, Online Courses, Summer Session, Video Courses

MISSOURI

UNIVERSITY OF CENTRAL MISSOURI*, Library Science & Information Services Program, Dept of Educational Technology & Library Science, Lovinger 4101, Warrensburg, 64093. Tel: 660-543-4910. Toll Free Tel: 877-729-8266. Web Site: www.ucmo.edu/lis. *Assoc Prof, Dept Chair,* Dr Rene Burress; Tel: 660-543-4910, E-mail: burress@ucmo.edu; *Assoc Prof, Prog Coordr,* Dr Jenna Kammer; E-mail: jkammer@ucmo.edu; *Asst Prof,* Dr Amanda Harrison; E-mail: aeharrison@ucmo.edu; *Instr,* Sandra Jenkins; Tel: 660-543-4150, E-mail: sjenkins@ucmo.edu
Prog estab 1964. Sch type: Pub. Scholarships offered; Enrl: Grad: 200
Ent Req: 2.75 GPA,personal interview
Tuition: Non-resident Undergraduate $294 Per credit hour; Non-resident Graduate $353 Per credit hour; Resident Undergraduate $294 Per credit hour; Resident Graduate $353 Per credit hour; International Graduate $353 Per credit hour
Type of Training Offered: School Library Media Certificate
Degrees & Hours Offered: MS, Sch Libr Media, 33 sem hrs; EdS, Professional Librarianship, 30 sem hrs
Special Courses: Action Research, Administration of the Library Media Center, Children's, Adolescent & Young Adult Literature, Curriculum & the Media Center, Foundations of Librarianship, Organizing Information, Using Online Resources
Online Courses

† UNIVERSITY OF MISSOURI-COLUMBIA*, School of Information Science & Learning Technology, 303 Townsend Hall, Columbia, 65211. Tel: 573-882-4546. Toll Free Tel: 877-747-5868. FAX: 573-884-0122. E-mail: sislt@missouri.edu. Web Site: lis.missouri.edu. *Dir,* Rose Marra; E-mail: rmarra@missouri.edu; *Prof,* Denice Adkins; E-mail: adkinsde@missouri.edu; *Assoc Prof,* Jenny Bossaller; E-mail: bossallerj@missouri.edu; *Assoc Prof,* Joi L Moore; E-mail: moorejoi@missouri.edu; *Assoc Prof,* Heather Moulaison Sandy; E-mail: moulaisonhe@missouri.edu; *Asst Prof,* Sarah Buchanan; E-mail: buchanans@missouri.edu; *Asst Prof,* Hyrim Cho; E-mail: hyrimcho@missouri.edu; *Asst Prof,* Danielle Oprean; E-mail: opreand@missouri.edu; *Asst Prof,* Xinhao XU; E-mail: xuxin@missouri.edu; *Learning Technologies Coordr, Teaching Prof,* Jane

Howland; E-mail: howlandj@missouri.edu; *Assoc Teaching Prof,* Beth Brendler; E-mail: brendlerb@missouri.edu; *Asst Teaching Prof,* Jason Alston; E-mail: alstonj@missouri.edu
Prog estab 1966. Sch type: Pub. Scholarships offered; Enrl: Grad: 250
Ent Req: Undergrad degree & 3.0 GPA (last 60 hrs) & GRE
Tuition: Non-resident Graduate $1,081 Per credit hour; Resident Graduate $395 Per credit hour
Type of Training Offered: Special
Degrees & Hours Offered: MA, Libr Sci, 42 hrs; M.Ed., Educ Tech, 32 hrs; Ph.D., Info Sci & Learning Tech, 66 hrs
Special Courses: Digital Humanities & Information, Digital Libraries, Emerging Technologies in Libraries, Ethics & Information, History of Books & Printing, Intellectual Freedom, International & Comparative Libraries, Materials for Children & Teens, Reader Advisory Services, Social Constructs of Information, Special Libraries & Information Centers, Web Usability
Co-operative Education Prog, Evening Session, Online & Blended Courses, Online Courses, Summer Session

MONTANA

MONTANA STATE UNIVERSITY*, Department of Education Library Media Certificate Program, Department of Education, 215 Reid Hall, Bozeman, 59717. (Mail add: PO Box 172880, Bozeman, 59717-2880). Tel: 406-994-6786. E-mail: edgrad@montana.edu, librarymedia@montana.edu. Web Site: www.montana.edu/education/grad/librarymedia. *Dir, Libr Media Prog,* Dr Deborah Rinio, PhD; Tel: 406-994-6898, E-mail: deborah.rinio@montana.edu; *Prof,* Mary Anne Hansen; E-mail: mhansen@montana.edu; *Assoc Prof,* Dr Ann Ewbank, PhD; E-mail: ann.ewbank@montana.edu; *Assoc Prof, Curriculum & Instruction Program Leader,* Dr Gilbert Kalonde
Prog estab 1967. Sch type: Pub; Enrl: Grad: 65; Fac 4
Ent Req: Grad sch libr media K-12 certification only for post BS teachers
Tuition: Non-resident Graduate $1,136 Per credit hour; Resident Graduate $283 Per credit hour
Type of Training Offered: School Library Media Certificate
Degrees & Hours Offered: Certificate, Sch Libr Media K-12, 21 credit hrs; M.Ed., Curric & Instruction, 9 credit hrs in addition to Libr Media Certificate
Special Courses: Library Media K-12
Online Courses

UNIVERSITY OF MONTANA*, Phyllis J Washington College of Education, 32 Campus Dr, Missoula, 59812-6346. Tel: 406-243-4841. FAX: 406-243-4908. Web Site: www.coehs.umt.edu/departments/currinst/libmedia/default.php. *Libr Media Endorsement Dir,* Tava Smathers; Tel: 406-243-6192, E-mail: tava.smathers@mso.umt.edu
Enrl: Grad: 30
Type of Training Offered: School Library Media Certificate
Degrees & Hours Offered: Certificate, 21 sem hrs; M.Ed., Library Media Endorsement, 37 sem hrs
Special Courses: Administration, Youth Lit for Librarians, Collection and Cataloging, Curriculum and Information Literacy, Practicum, Reference, Libraries and Technology
Online & Blended Courses, Online Courses, Summer Session

NEBRASKA

CHADRON STATE COLLEGE*, Library Media Specialist Program, 1000 Main St, Chadron, 69337. Tel: 308-432-6271. FAX: 308-432-6409. Web Site: www.csc.edu. *Dept Chair, Prof,* Donald King; E-mail: dking@csc.edu
Prog estab 1965. Enrl: Undergrad: 23
Degrees & Hours Offered: BA, Libr Media Specialist major, 21 sem hrs; BS, Libr Media Specials major & endorsement, 33 sem hrs
No Summer Sessions, Online Courses

UNIVERSITY OF NEBRASKA AT OMAHA*, Library Science Program, College of Education, Roskens Hall, Omaha, 68182. Tel: 402-554-2119. Toll Free Tel: 800-858-8648, Ext 2119. FAX: 402-554-2125. Web Site: www.unomaha.edu. *Prog Coordr,* Erica Rose; E-mail: ecrose@unomaha.edu; *Asst Prof,* Dr Sara Churchill; Tel: 402-554-3485, E-mail: schurchill@unomaha.edu
Sch type: Pub; Enrl: Undergrad: 100, Grad: 200
Type of Training Offered: School Library Media Certificate
Degrees & Hours Offered: BS, Libr Sci major, 30 sem hrs; MS, Elem Educ, Secondary Educ or Reading, 36 sem hrs
Co-operative Education Prog, Online & Blended Courses, Online Courses, Weekend Session

NEW JERSEY

† RUTGERS, THE STATE UNIVERSITY OF NEW JERSEY*, School of Communication & Information, Four Huntington St, New Brunswick, 08901-1071. Tel: 848-932-7500. E-mail: mcis@comminfo.rutgers.edu. Web Site: comminfo.rutgers.edu. *Assoc Prof,* Claire McInerney; E-mail: clairemc@rutgers.edu
Prog estab 1953. Sch type: Pub. Scholarships offered; Enrl: Grad: 304; Fac 18
Ent Req: GRE, 3.0 GPA, letters of recommendation & personal statement
Tuition: Non-resident Graduate $6,511 Per semester; Non-resident Graduate $500 Per credit hour; Resident Graduate $4,597 Per semester; Resident Graduate $338 Per credit hour
Type of Training Offered: Special
Degrees & Hours Offered: MLIS, Libr & Info Studies, 36 credit hrs; Ph.D., Communication, Info & Libr Studies
Special Courses: Academic Librarianship, Information Retrieval, Human Information Behavior, Information Science, Information Technology, Management Services, Scientific & Technical Information, Reference & Information Service, Services for Children & Young Adults, School Media Services, Special Librarianship, Technical Services
Evening Session, Summer Session

WILLIAM PATERSON UNIVERSITY*, School Library Media Concentration Program, College of Education, 1600 Valley Rd, Wayne, 07470. Tel: 973-720-3784. FAX: 973-720-2585. Web Site: www.wpunj.edu. *Prog Dir,* Dr Ellen Pozzi; E-mail: pozzie@wpunj.edu
Prog estab 1952. Sch type: Pub; Enrl: Grad: 51; Fac 2
Ent Req: GPA 3.0, NJ Teaching Certificate, GRE 450, MAT 388
Tuition: Non-resident Graduate $1,156 Per credit hour; Resident Graduate $746 Per credit hour
Type of Training Offered: School Library Media Certificate
Degrees & Hours Offered: M.Ed., Sch Libr Media Program, 36 credit hrs
Special Courses: Children's & Adolescent Literature, Field Experiences in School Library Media Centers, Foundations of School Librarianship, Information Sources & Services, Instructional Design, Management of the School Library Media Program, Technical Processes
Evening Session, Online Courses, Summer Session

NEW YORK

† LONG ISLAND UNIVERSITY*, Palmer School of Library & Information Science, C W Post Campus, 720 Northern Blvd, Brookville, 11548-1300. Tel: 516-299-2866, 516-299-2900. FAX: 516-299-4168. E-mail: palmer@liu.edu. Web Site: www.liu.edu/palmer. *Dir, PhD Prog, Prof,* Dr Gregory Hunter; Tel: 516-299-7171, E-mail: ghunter@liu.edu; *Dir, Sch Media Prog,* Dr Bea Baaden; Tel: 516-299-3818, E-mail: bea.baaden@liu.edu; *Prof,* Dr Heting Chu; E-mail: hchu@liu.edu; *Assoc Prof,* Dr Qiping Zhang; E-mail: qiping.zhang@liu.edu
Prog estab 1959. Sch type: Pvt. Scholarships offered; Enrl: Grad: 450; Fac 15
Ent Req: 3.0 GPA, letters of recommendation, transcripts, essay & resume
Type of Training Offered: Special
Degrees & Hours Offered: Certificate, Archives & Rec Mgt, 18 credits; Certificate, Pub Libr Mgt, 18 credits; MS, Libr & Info Sci, 36 credits; MS, Libr & Info Science: School Library Media; Ph.D., Info Studies, 60 credits; MLIS/MA, Dual-degree prog with New York Univ
Special Courses: Abstracting & Indexing, Archives, Artist's Books, Building Digital Libraries, Business & Economic Resources, Children's Literature, Descriptive Cataloging, Digital Preservation, Electronic Resources, Encoded Archival Description, Government Information, Health Sciences Sources & Services, History of the Book, Information Networks, Instructional Design & Leadership, Knowledge Management, Library Services for the Special Populations, Preservation, Rare Books, Records Management, School Media Centers, Special Collections of NYC, Storytelling, Subject Analysis
Evening Session, Online & Blended Courses, Summer Session, Weekend Session

† PRATT INSTITUTE*, School of Information, 144 W 14th St, 6th Flr, New York, 10011-7301. Tel: 212-647-7682. Toll Free Tel: 800-331-0834. FAX: 212-367-2492. E-mail: si@pratt.edu. Web Site: pratt.edu. *Dean,* Anthony Cocciolo; Tel: 212-647-7702, E-mail: acocciol@pratt.edu
Prog estab 1890. Sch type: Pvt; Enrl: Grad: 296; Fac 44
Ent Req: GPA 3.0, TOEFL minimum of 82
Tuition: Resident Graduate $1,553 Per credit hour
Type of Training Offered: Public
Degrees & Hours Offered: Certificate, Advan Certs in Archives are open only to MSLIS Students or individuals who already hold a master's degree, 18 credits each cert; Certificate, Advan Cert in Museum Studies is open only to Museums and Digital Culture students, dual degree program students, or individuals who already hold a master's degree, 12 credits; Certificate, Advan Cert in Conservation and Digital Curation is open only to MSLIS students, Museums and Digital Culture students, or individuals who already hold a master's degree, 12 credits; Certificate, Advan Certs in Digital Humanities or Spatial Analysis and Design are only open to MSLIS students, Data Analytics and Visutalization students, or individuals who already hold a master's degree, 12 credits each cert; Certificate, Advan Cert in User Experience may be taken as a stand-alone program by MSLIS students, MSLIS dual-degree students, Data Analytics and Visualization

students, or individuals who hold a master's degree, 12 credits; MS, Data Analytics and Visualization (see advanced certificates), 36 credits; MS, Information Experience Design (see advanced certificates), 36 credits; MS, Museums and Digital Culture (see advanced certificates), 36 credits; MLIS/MA, History of Art and Design, 60 credits; MSLIS, Archives, Special Collections, Rare Books and Digital Curation; Informtion Services, Organization, Management, and Use; Learning, Literacies, and Communities; Research and Data, Technology and Interfaces Design and Development, 36 credits
Special Courses: Information Policies and Politics, Research Design and Methods, Web Development, Art Documentation, Projects in Digital Archives, Archiving the Diaspora, Instructional Technologies, Usability Theory and Practice, Information Visualization, Information Architecture and Interaction Design
Summer Session

† QUEENS COLLEGE OF THE CITY UNIVERSITY OF NEW YORK*, Graduate School of Library & Information Studies, Benjamin Rosenthal Library, Rm 254, 65-30 Kissena Blvd, Flushing, 11367-1597. Tel: 718-997-3790. FAX: 718-997-3797. E-mail: qc_gslis@qc.cuny.edu. Web Site: sites.google.com/view/qcgslis, www.qc.cuny.edu/academics/degrees/dss/gslis/pages/homepage.aspx. *Dir, Prof,* Kwong Bor Ng; E-mail: kwongbor.ng@qc.cuny.edu; *Prof,* Roberta Brody; E-mail: roberta.brody@qc.cuny.edu; *Prof,* Harry Kibirige; E-mail: harry.kibirige@qc.cuny.edu; *Assoc Prof,* Ping Li; E-mail: ping.li@qc.cuny.edu; *Asst Prof,* James Lowry; E-mail: james.lowry@qc.cuny.edu; *Asst Prof,* Jose Sanchez; E-mail: jose.sanchez2@qc.cuny.edu; *Asst Prof,* Johnathan Thayer; E-mail: jthayer@qc.cuny.edu; *Asst Prof,* Shuheng Wu; E-mail: shuheng.wu@qc.cuny.edu
Prog estab 1955. Sch type: Pub. Scholarships offered; Fac 9
Tuition: Non-resident Graduate $855 Per credit hour; Resident Graduate $470 Per credit hour; Resident Graduate $5,545 Per semester
Degrees & Hours Offered: Certificate, Post-Master's Studies in Librarianship, 30 credits; Certificate, Ch & YA Servs in the Pub Libr, 12 credits; Certificate, Archives & Presv of Cultural Mats, 15 credits; MLS, 36 credits; MLS, Sch Libr Media Specialist, 45 credits; MLS, Sch Libr Media Specialist for Certified Teachers, 36 credits; MLS, Sch Libr Media Specialist Advan Certificate, 27 credits; MLS/MA, Libr Sci & Hist, 54 credits
Special Courses: Art Librarianship, Bibliographic Control of Non-print Materials, Business Reference, Children's Literature, Digital Libraries, Fundamentals of Library Conservation & Preservation, Geographic Information Science, Health Sciences, Issues & Applications, Law Librarianship, Library Conservation & Preservation, Media (AV), Mythology & Folklore for Children & Adolescents, Planning & Delivering Services to Youth in the Public Library, Public Library Services for Children & Young Adults, Reading Motivation Techniques for Children & Adolescents, Resources for the School Curriculum, Young Adult Literature
Evening Session, Summer Session

† ST JOHN'S UNIVERSITY*, Division of Library & Information Science, Saint Augustine Hall, Rm 408A, 8000 Utopia Pkwy, Jamaica, 11439. Tel: 718-990-6200. FAX: 718-990-2071. E-mail: dlis@stjohns.edu. *Assoc Prof, Dir, Library & Info Science,* James Vorbach, PhD; Tel: 718-990-1834, E-mail: vorbachj@stjohns.edu; *Assoc Prof,* Christine Angel, PhD; Tel: 718-990-1452, E-mail: angelc@stjohns.edu; *Assoc Prof,* Shari Lee, PhD; Tel: 718-990-1451, E-mail: lees2@stjohns.edu; *Assoc Prof,* Kevin Rioux, PhD; Tel: 718-990-1458, E-mail: riouxk@stjohns.edu; *Assoc Prof,* Rajesh Singh, PhD
Prog estab 1937. Sch type: Pvt; Enrl: Grad: 70; Fac 6
Ent Req: Bachelor's Degree, 3.0 min GPA, two letters of recommendation, statement of professional goals
Type of Training Offered: Special
Degrees & Hours Offered: Certificate, Academic Librarianship, Archival Studies, Law Librarianship, Public Librarianship, Special Librarianship, Youth Services, 24 sem hrs; MSLS, Academic Librarianship, Archival Studies, Law Librarianship, Public Librarianship, Special Librarianship, Youth Services, 36 sem hrs
Special Courses: Archives & Records, Children's Literature, Children & Young Adult Literature, Database Modeling and Design, Knowledge Management, Law Library Administration, Metadata, Materials and Services to Diverse Populations, Social Justice, Web Design
Evening Session, Online & Blended Courses, Online Courses, Summer Session

† SYRACUSE UNIVERSITY*, School of Information Studies, 114 Hinds Hall, Syracuse, 13244-1190. Tel: 315-443-4900. FAX: 315-443-5673. E-mail: ischool@syr.edu. Web Site: ischool.syr.edu. *Interim Dean,* David Seaman; Tel: 315-443-2736, E-mail: dseaman@syr.edu
Prog estab 1896. Sch type: Pvt. Scholarships offered; Enrl: Undergrad: 528, Grad: 1,466; Fac 44
Ent Req: GRE & letters of recommendation
Type of Training Offered: School Library Media Certificate
Degrees & Hours Offered: Certificate, Information Management & Technology; Certificate, Data Administration Concepts & Database Management; Certificate, Introduction to Data Science; Certificate, School Media CAS, 21; MLIS, Library & Information Science, 36; MLIS, Library & Information Science: School Media, 36; MS, Applied Data Science, 36 sem hrs; MS, Info Mgt, 42 sem hrs; MS, Enterprise Data Systems, 36 sem hrs; Ph.D., Information Science & Technology, 78 sem hrs
Special Courses: Reference and Information Literacy Services, Library Planning, Marketing, and Assessment, Information Resources: Organization and Access, Academic Libraries, Public Libraries, Preservation of Cultural Heritage, Organization/Management of Archival Collections, Digital Data and Services in Libraries, Collection Development and Access, Human Interaction with Computers, Copyright for Information Professionals, Accessible Library & Information Services, Instructional Strategies and Techniques for Information Professionals, Database Management, Information Resources Management, Information Policy, Information Science, Project Management, School Media Management, Youth Services
Evening Session, Online & Blended Courses, Online Courses, Summer Session

† UNIVERSITY AT ALBANY, STATE UNIVERSITY OF NEW YORK*, College of Emergency Preparedness, Homeland Security & Cybersecurity, Draper 015, 135 Western Ave, Albany, 12203. Tel: 518-442-5258. E-mail: infosci@albany.edu. Web Site: www.albany.edu/cehc. *Prof,* Dr Philip B Eppard; Tel: 518-442-5119; *Prof,* Dr Joette Stefl-Mabry; Tel: 518-442-5120, E-mail: jstefl@albany.edu; *Assoc Prof,* Dr Hemalata Iyer; Tel: 518-442-5116, E-mail: hiyer@albany.edu; *Assoc Prof,* Dr Abebe Rorissa; Tel: 518-442-5123, E-mail: arorissa@albany.edu; *Assoc Prof,* Dr Donghee Sinn; Tel: 518-442-5117, E-mail: dsinn@albany.edu; *Assoc Prof,* Dr Xiaojun Yuan; Tel: 518-591-8746, E-mail: xyuan@albany.edu; *Asst Prof,* Carol Anne Germain; E-mail: cgermain@albany.edu; *Lecturer,* Shannon Mersand; Tel: 518-888-6761, E-mail: smersand@albany.edu; *Graduate Studies Programs, Mgr,* Tiffany Williams-Hart; E-mail: tdwilliams@albany.edu
Prog estab 1926. Sch type: Pub. Scholarships offered; Enrl: Grad: 243
Ent Req: Bachelor's Degree, GRE or other grad degree, statement of goals, 3 letters of recommendation
Tuition: Non-resident Graduate $9,500 Per semester; Non-resident Graduate $1,075 Per credit hour; Resident Graduate $5,072 Per semester; Resident Graduate $583 Per credit hour
Type of Training Offered: Special
Degrees & Hours Offered: Certificate, Advanced Study, 30 credits; MS, Information Science, 36 credits; MS, School Library Media Specialist, 36 credits; Ph.D., Information Science, 60 credits; MIS/MA, Information Science with English or History, 53-59 credits
Special Courses: Archives, Children's Literature, Literature for Young Adults, Teaching Fundamentals for School Libraries, Fundamentals of XML, Preservation Management, Rare Books, Records Management,Public Libraries, Database Design & Development, Archival Representation, Information Literacy Instruction, Developing User Interface, Web Database Programming, Information Systems, Academic Libraries & Higher Education, Data Analytics, Intelligence Analysis, Predictive Modeling, Cybersecurity, Human Information Behavior, Emergency Preparedness College-at-Home Program, Continuing Education, Evening Session, Online & Blended Courses, Online Courses, Professional Development, Summer Session

† UNIVERSITY AT BUFFALO, THE STATE UNIVERSITY OF NEW YORK*, Department of Information Science, 534 Baldy Hall, Buffalo, 14260. Tel: 716-645-2412. FAX: 716-645-3775. E-mail: infosci-information@buffalo.edu. Web Site: ed.buffalo.edu/information.html. *Chair, Prof,* Dr Dan Albertson; *Prof,* Dr Heidi Julien; E-mail: heidijul@buffalo.edu; *Prof,* Dr Dagobert Soergel; *Assoc Prof,* Dr Ying Sun; *Assoc Prof,* Dr Amy VanScoy; *Assoc Prof,* Dr Jiangiang Wang; *Assoc Prof,* Dr Samuel Ambramovich; *Clinical Asst Prof,* Dr Brenda Battleson White; *Asst Prof,* Dr Samuel Dodson; *Asst Prof,* Dr Africa Hands
Prog estab 1966. Sch type: Pub. Scholarships offered; Enrl: Grad: 203; Fac 10
Ent Req: 3.0 GPA & letters of reference, BA or BS
Tuition: Resident Graduate $565 Per credit hour; Resident Graduate $5,655 Per semester; Online Graduate $565 Per credit hour; Online Graduate $5,655 Per semester
Type of Training Offered: Special
Degrees & Hours Offered: MS, Information and Library Science, 36 sem hrs; MS, School Librarianship, 39 sem hrs
Evening Session, Online Courses, Summer Session

NORTH CAROLINA

APPALACHIAN STATE UNIVERSITY*, Library Science Program, Reich College of Education, Ste 204, 151 College St, ASU Box 32086, Boone, 28608. Tel: 828-262-2243. Web Site: mls.appstate.edu. *Assoc Prof, Prog Dir,* Dr Kim Becnel; E-mail: becnelke@appstate.edu; *Assoc Prof,* Dr Robin Moeller; E-mail: moellerra@appstate.edu; *Asst Prof,* Dr Jennifer Luetkemeyer; E-mail: luetkemeyerjr@appstate.edu
Prog estab 1937. Sch type: Pub. Scholarships offered; Enrl: Grad: 60

Ent Req: GRE & 3.0 undergrad
Tuition: Non-resident Graduate $1,103 Per credit hour; Resident Graduate $269 Per credit hour
Type of Training Offered: School
Degrees & Hours Offered: MLS, Libr Sci; Sch (K-12) Pub Librarianship, 36 sem hrs
Evening Session, Online Courses, Summer Session, Weekend Session

EAST CAROLINA UNIVERSITY*, Department of Interdisciplinary Professions, 104B Ragsdale Hall, Greenville, 27858. (Mail add: 1000 E Fifth St, Mail Stop 172, Greenville, 27858). Tel: 252-328-6621. E-mail: mlsprogram@ecu.edu. Web Site: education.ecu.edu/idp. *Prof,* Dr Al Jones, Jr; Tel: 252-328-6803, E-mail: jonesp@ecu.edu; *Assoc Prof,* Dr Kaye Dotson; Tel: 252-328-2787, E-mail: dotsonl@ecu.edu; *Asst Prof,* Dr Kawanna Bright; Tel: 252-737-1150, E-mail: brightka19@ecu.edu; *Asst Prof,* Dr Africa Hands; Tel: 252-328-4389, E-mail: handsa19@ecu.edu; *Asst Prof, Prog Coordr,* Dr Barbara M Marson; Tel: 252-328-2345, E-mail: marsonb@ecu.edu; *Asst Prof,* Dr Rita Soulen; Tel: 252-737-4352, E-mail: soulenr19@ecu.edu; *Teaching Instructor,* Laura Mangum; Tel: 252-328-6391, E-mail: manguml19@ecu.edu
Prog estab 1939. Sch type: Pub. Scholarships offered; Enrl: Grad: 205
Ent Req: Minimum 2.7 GPA, undergrad degree & letters of recommendation
Tuition: Non-resident Graduate $864 Per credit hour; Resident Graduate $186 Per credit hour
Type of Training Offered: School
Degrees & Hours Offered: MLS, 39 sem hrs
Special Courses: Academic Libraries; Art of Storytelling; Collection Development; Digital Libraries; Electronic Resources in Library Collections; Financial Management of Public Library Organizations; Foundations of Library & Information Studies; Genealogy for Librarians; Government Publications; History of Books & Libraries; Information Literacy & Library Instruction; Instructional Foundations of the School Library Media Program; Instructional Strategies & Leadership for School Media Specialists; Intellectual Freedom; Introduction to Reference; Library Administration & Management; Library Advocacy; Library Services to Diverse & Special Populations; Materials for Children; Materials for Early Childhood; Materials for Young Adults; Organization of Information in Libraries; Public Libraries; Research Literacy in Library Science; Research Methods in Library & Information Studies; Technology for Library Services
Summer Session

† NORTH CAROLINA CENTRAL UNIVERSITY*, School of Library & Information Sciences, 1801 Fayetteville St, Durham, 27707. (Mail add: PO Box 19586, Durham, 27707-0021). Tel: 919-530-6485. FAX: 919-530-6402. Web Site: nccuslis.org. *Dean, Prof,* Jon Gant; E-mail: jpgant@nccu.edu; *Prof,* Eun-Young Yoo; E-mail: eunyoung@nccu.edu; *Adjunct Prof,* Barbara J Montgomery; E-mail: bjmontgomery@nccu.edu; *Assoc Prof,* Pauletta B Bracy; E-mail: pbracy@nccu.edu; *Assoc Prof,* Gabriel Peterson; E-mail: gpeterson@nccu.edu; *Asst Prof,* Alexandra Chassanoff; E-mail: chass@nccu.edu; *Asst Prof,* Siobahn Day; E-mail: sday@nccu.edu; *Asst Prof,* Patrick Roughen; E-mail: proughen@nccu.edu; *Asst Prof,* Deborah E Swain; E-mail: dswaine@nccu.edu; *Lecturer,* Gyesi Amaniampong; E-mail: gyesi@ieee.org; *Lecturer,* Kim Mayo; E-mail: kmayo@nccu.edu; *Lecturer,* Lori Payton-Johnson; E-mail: ljohn149@nccu.edu
Prog estab 1939. Sch type: Pub. Scholarships offered; Enrl: Grad: 237
Ent Req: GRE, SAT, GPA, Bachelor's, Letters of reference
Tuition: Non-resident Graduate $8,117 Per semester; Resident Graduate $2,520 Per semester
Type of Training Offered: Special
Degrees & Hours Offered: MLS, Archives, 36 sem hrs
Special Courses: African American Coll, Computer - Based Info Storage Retrieval Systems, Early Childhood Libr Specialist Program, Expert Systems, Ethnic Materials, Info Science Program & Meta-Data Analysis
Evening Session, Summer Session, Weekend Session

† UNIVERSITY OF NORTH CAROLINA AT CHAPEL HILL*, School of Information & Library Science, Manning Hall, 216 Lenoir Dr, Campus Box 3360, Chapel Hill, 27599-3360. Tel: 919-962-8366. FAX: 919-962-8071. E-mail: info@ils.unc.edu. Web Site: sils.unc.edu. *Dean,* Dr Gary Marchionini; E-mail: gary@ils.unc.edu; *Assoc Dean, Acad Affairs, Prof,* Brian Sturm; E-mail: sturm@ils.unc.edu
Prog estab 1931. Sch type: Pub. Scholarships offered; Enrl: Undergrad: 200, Grad: 325; Fac 30
Ent Req: 3.5 average GPA & letters of reference
Tuition: Non-resident Graduate $1,796 Per credit hour; Resident Graduate $780 Per credit hour
Type of Training Offered: Special
Degrees & Hours Offered: BS, Info Sci, 120 sem hrs; MS, Info Sci, 48 sem hrs; MS, Libr Sci, 48 sem hrs; Ph.D., Info & Libr Sci
Special Courses: Big Data & NoSQL for Data Science; Community Data Lab; Data Criticism; Data Mining: Methods & Applications; Developing with Fast Health Interoperability Resources; Digital Gazetteer of North Carolina; Foundations of Clinical Data Science; Health Care Systems in the US; Human-Centered Data Science Applications; Misinformation & Society; Natural Language Processing Applications in Health Care; Programming for Data Analysis; Real-Time Data Science in the Makerspace: Making Sense of the Everyday; Social Informatics; Systems Analysis in Healthcare
Online & Blended Courses, Professional Development

† UNIVERSITY OF NORTH CAROLINA AT GREENSBORO*, Department of Library & Information Science, School of Education Bldg, Rm 446, 1300 Spring Garden St, Greensboro, 27412. (Mail add: PO Box 26170, Greensboro, 27402-6170). Tel: 336-334-3477. FAX: 336-334-4120. E-mail: lis@uncg.edu. Web Site: lis.uncg.edu. *Assoc Prof, Dept Chair,* Dr Lisa O'Connor; E-mail: lgoconno@uncg.edu; *Assoc Prof, Dir, Grad Studies,* Nora J Bird, PhD; Tel: 336-256-1313, E-mail: njbird@uncg.edu; *Assoc Prof,* Anthony S Chow, PhD; E-mail: aschow@uncg.edu; *Assoc Prof,* Julie Hersberger, PhD; E-mail: jahersbe@uncg.edu; *Assoc Prof,* Dr Heather Moorefield-Lang; E-mail: hmmooref@uncg.edu; *Assoc Prof,* Fatih Oguz, PhD; E-mail: f_oguz@uncg.edu; *Asst Prof,* Dr April Dawkins; E-mail: amdawkin@uncg.edu; *Asst Prof,* Dr Noah Lenstra; E-mail: njlenstr@uncg.edu; *Asst Prof,* Dr Colin Post; E-mail: ccpost@uncg.edu; *Asst Prof,* Dr LaTesha Velez; E-mail: lmvelez@uncg.edu; *Clinical Asst Prof,* Sonia Archer-Capuzzo; E-mail: smarcher@uncg.edu; *Lecturer,* Dr Joanna DePolt; E-mail: jldepolt@uncg.edu
Sch type: Pub; Enrl: Grad: 250
Ent Req: Bachelor's degree & GRE or MAT : Exams may be waived for above 3.5 undergrad GPA
Tuition: Non-resident Graduate $672 Per credit hour; Non-resident Graduate $10,960 Per semester; Resident Graduate $255 Per credit hour; Resident Graduate $4,101 Per semester
Type of Training Offered: Special
Degrees & Hours Offered: MLIS, 36 sem hrs
Special Courses: Programs available face-to-face or online through distance education
Evening Session, Online & Blended Courses, Online Courses

NORTH DAKOTA

MAYVILLE STATE UNIVERSITY*, Library Science Program, 330 Third St NE, Mayville, 58257-1299. Tel: 701-788-4816. Toll Free Tel: 800-437-4104, Ext 34816. E-mail: library@mayvillestate.edu. Web Site: www.mayvillestate.edu. *Dir,* Kelly Kornkven; E-mail: Kelly.Kornkven@mayvillestate.edu
Sch type: Pub; Enrl: Undergrad: 10
Tuition: Resident Undergraduate $166 Per credit hour; Regional Undergraduate $249 Per credit hour
Type of Training Offered: School
Degrees & Hours Offered: BA, Educ with Libr Sci Minor, 25 sem hrs; BS, Educ with Libr Sci Minor, 25 sem hrs
Online Courses, Summer Session

VALLEY CITY STATE UNIVERSITY*, Library Media & Information Science Program, 327 E McFarland Hall, 101 College St SW, Valley City, 58072-4098. Tel: 701-845-7303. FAX: 701-845-7437. Web Site: catalog.vcsu.edu/graduate-catalog, catalog.vcsu.edu/undergraduate-catalog, www.vcsu.edu. *Dept Chair,* Dr James Boe; E-mail: jim.boe@vcsu.edu; *Dir,* Donna V James; E-mail: donna.james@vcsu.edu
Sch type: Pub; Enrl: Grad: 20, Undergrad: 20; Fac 3
Ent Req: GPA 3.0
Tuition: Resident Undergraduate $204 Per credit hour; Resident Graduate $339 Per credit hour
Type of Training Offered: School Library Media Certificate
Degrees & Hours Offered: BS, Libr Media & Info Sci minor, 24 sem hrs–minor; M.Ed., Library & Information Technologies Concentration, 37 sem hrs
Continuing Education, Online Courses, Summer Session

OHIO

† KENT STATE UNIVERSITY*, School of Information, College of Communication & Information, 314 University Library, 1125 Risman Dr, Kent, 44242-0001. (Mail add: 800 E Summit St, Kent, 44242). Tel: 330-672-2782. E-mail: iSchool@kent.edu. Web Site: www.kent.edu/iSchool. *Dir, Prof,* Kendra S Albright; E-mail: kalbrig7@kent.edu; *Prof,* Dr Karen Gracy; *Prof,* Dr Megan Harper; *Prof,* Dr Christine Hudak; *Prof,* Dr Athena Salaba; *Prof,* Dr Marcia Zeng; *Prof,* Dr Yin Zhang; *Assoc Prof,* Dr Belinda Boon; *Assoc Prof,* Dr Lala Hajibayova; *Assoc Prof,* Dr Marianne Martens; *Assoc Prof,* Dr Rebecca Meehan; *Assoc Prof,* Dr David Robins; *Assoc Prof,* Dr Paul Sherman; *Assoc Prof,* Dr Catherine Smith; *Asst Prof,* Elda Heggmann; *Asst Prof,* Campana Kathleen; *Asst Prof,* Heather Soyka; *Sr Lecturer,* Mary A Nichols
Prog estab 1946. Sch type: Pub. Scholarships offered; Enrl: Grad: 633; Fac 20
Ent Req: 3.0 GPA & BA or BS; or GRE

Tuition: Non-resident Graduate $999 Per credit hour; Resident Graduate $536 Per credit hour
Type of Training Offered: Special
Degrees & Hours Offered: MLIS, see below, 37 credit hrs; MS, Information Architecture and Knowledge Management – health informatics, knowledge management, user experience design, Varies by concentration
Special Courses: Academic Librarianship; Archives; Cataloging or Metadata; Children's Librarianship; Digital Librarianship; Digital Preservation; Information Technology & Information Science; K-12 School Librarianship; Library Management; Museum Studies; Public Librarianship; Reference Librarianship; Special Librarianship; Young Adult Librarianship; User Experience Design; Knowledge Management; Health Informatics
Continuing Education, Online & Blended Courses

OKLAHOMA

UNIVERSITY OF CENTRAL OKLAHOMA*, Instructional Media Education, 100 N University Dr, Edmond, 73034. (Mail add: Box 193 - LIB 124, Edmond, 73034-0193). Tel: 405-974-5437. FAX: 405-974-3857. Web Site: www.uco.edu. *Dept Chair,* Laressa Beliele, PhD; E-mail: lbeliele@uco.edu
Enrl: Grad: 60
Ent Req: Prior teaching certification; 3.0 undergrad GPA
Tuition: Non-resident Graduate $746 Per credit hour; Resident Graduate $329 Per credit hour
Type of Training Offered: School Library Media Certificate
Degrees & Hours Offered: M.Ed., Instrul Media - Libr Info, 36 sem hrs
Special Courses: Cataloging, Effective Writing, Elements of Web Design, Graphic & Video Production, Library Materials for Elementary Schools, Library Materials for Secondary Schools, Materials Selection, PR & Information Skills, Reference & Bibliography, School Library Administration
Evening Session, Online & Blended Courses, Online Courses, Summer Session, Weekend Session

† UNIVERSITY OF OKLAHOMA*, School of Library & Information Studies, Bizzell Memorial Library, 401 W Brooks, Rm 120, Norman, 73019-6032. Tel: 405-325-3921. Toll Free Tel: 800-522-0772,Ext 3921. E-mail: slisinfo@ou.edu. Web Site: slis.ou.edu. *Prof,* Dr June M Abbas, PhD; E-mail: jmabbas@ou.edu; *Assoc Prof, Dir,* Dr Susan Burke, PhD; E-mail: sburke@ou.edu; *Assoc Prof,* Dr Yong-Mi Kim, PhD; Tel: 918-660-3364, E-mail: yongmi@ou.edu; *Assoc Prof,* Dr Kun Lu, PhD; E-mail: kunlu@ou.edu; *Assoc Prof,* Dr Ellen Rubenstein, PhD; E-mail: erubenstein@ou.edu; *Assoc Prof,* Dr Kelvin White, PhD; E-mail: kwhite@ou.edu; *Asst Prof,* Jiqun Liu; E-mail: jiqunliu@ou.edu; *Asst Prof,* Yong Ju Jung; E-mail: yongju@ou.edu; *Lecturer,* Beverly Edwards, PhD; E-mail: buffy@ou.edu; *Lecturer,* Dr DH Monobe; E-mail: dh.monobe@ou.edu; *Lecturer,* Dr Yasser Youssef; E-mail: yyoussef@ou.edu
Prog estab 1929. Sch type: Pub. Scholarships offered; Enrl: Grad: 207; Fac 11
Ent Req: 3.0 GPA
Tuition: Non-resident Undergraduate $957 Per credit hour; Non-resident Graduate $806 Per credit hour; Resident Undergraduate $346 Per credit hour; Resident Graduate $293 Per credit hour
Type of Training Offered: Special
Degrees & Hours Offered: BA, Information Studies (BAIS), 120 sem hrs; MLIS, Library & Information Studies (MLIS), 36 sem hrs
Special Courses: Biomedical Information Program
Evening Session, Online & Blended Courses, Online Courses, Summer Session, Video Courses, Weekend Session

PENNSYLVANIA

† DREXEL UNIVERSITY*, College of Computing & Informatics, 3675 Market St, Ste 1000, Philadelphia, 19104. Tel: 215-895-2474. FAX: 215-895-2494. E-mail: cciinfo@drexel.edu. Web Site: drexel.edu/cci. *Dean,* Yi Deng, PhD; E-mail: yd362@drexel.edu
Prog estab 1892. Sch type: Pvt. Scholarships offered; Enrl: Undergrad: 1,181, Grad: 525; Fac 56
Ent Req: 4-year bachelor's degree; GRE (3.0 or higher; scores must be five years old or less) official transcripts; at least 1 letter of recommendation; essay/statement of purpose; resume
Type of Training Offered: Library & Information Science
Degrees & Hours Offered: BS, Info Syst, 187; BS, Data Sci, 187; BS, Software Eng, 188; BS, Computing & Security Tech, 188; Certificate, Healthcare Informatics, 9; Certificate, Computational Data Science, 15; Certificate, Applied Data Science, 15; MS, Libr & Info Sci, 45; MS, Info Syst, 45; MS, Software Eng, 45; MS, Data Science, 45; MS, Info Systems, 45; Ph.D., Info Science, 45; Ph.D., Computer Science, 45
Special Courses: Healthcare Informatics; Optional Concentrations in Archival Studies, Competitive Intelligence & Knowledge Management, Digital Libraries, Library & Information Services, School Library Media, & Youth Services
Evening Session, Online Courses, Professional Development, Summer Session

KUTZTOWN UNIVERSITY*, Department of Library & Learning Technologies, 12 Rohrbach Library, Kutztown, 19530. Tel: 610-683-4301. FAX: 610-683-1326. Web Site: www.kutztown.edu. *Prof,* Dr Andrea Harmer; Tel: 610-683-4301, E-mail: harmer@kutztown.edu; *Asst Prof,* Roseanne Perkins; Tel: 610-683-4902, E-mail: rperkins@kutztown.edu
Prog estab 1921. Sch type: Pub. Scholarships offered; Enrl: Undergrad: 60, Grad: 100; Fac 5
Ent Req: BA with 3.0 GPA or better & GRE
Tuition: Resident Undergraduate $3,858 Per semester; Resident Graduate $516 Per credit hour
Degrees & Hours Offered: BS, Educ with major in Libr Sci K-12, 120 sem hrs; MLS, Libr Sci, 30 sem hrs
Online Courses

NORTHAMPTON COMMUNITY COLLEGE, Library Technical Assistant Specialized Diploma, 3835 Green Pond Rd, Bethlehem, 18020. Tel: 610-861-4150. Web Site: www.northampton.edu/library-technical-assistant.htm. *Dir, Libr Serv,* Sandra L Sander; E-mail: ssander@northampton.edu
Prog estab 1968. Sch type: Pub; Enrl: Undergrad: 30
Tuition: Non-resident Undergraduate $216 Per credit hour
Degrees & Hours Offered: Diploma, 16 credit hrs
Online Courses

† PENNSYLVANIA WESTERN UNIVERSITY - CLARION*, Department of Information & Library Science, (Formerly Clarion University of Pennsylvania), 840 Wood St, Clarion, 16214. Tel: 814-393-2271. Toll Free Tel: 866-272-5612. FAX: 814-393-2150. Web Site: www.pennwest.edu/about/colleges-depts/ceah/lis/index.php. *Dept Chair,* Dr Linda Lillard; E-mail: llillard@pennwest.edu
Prog estab 1937. Sch type: Pub; Fac 8
Tuition: Non-resident Undergraduate $16,028 Per year; Non-resident Graduate $774 Per credit hour; Resident Undergraduate $11,149 Per year; Resident Graduate $516 Per credit hour; International Undergraduate $16,028 Per year
Type of Training Offered: Special
Degrees & Hours Offered: BS, Liberal Studies with Libr Sci concentration, 120 credits; Certificate, post-MS Certificate of Advan Study, 24 credits; MLIS/MA, MA in Applied Hist is offered in cooperation with Shippensburg Univ, 36 credits; MSLS, Library Science, 36 credits; MSLS, School Library Media, 36 credits; MSLS/JD, offered in cooperation with Widener Univ Sch of Law, 36 credits
Special Courses: Archival Management of Small Repositories, Business Reference Sources, Children's Literature, Digital Libraries, Instructional Strategies, Integrated Technologies, Multicultural Library Services, Online Information Retrieval, Preservation of Library Materials, Rural Library Services, Special Collection Representation & Records Management, Young Adult Literature

† UNIVERSITY OF PITTSBURGH*, School of Computing & Information, Information Science Bldg 5th Flr, 135 N Bellefield Ave, Pittsburgh, 15260. Tel: 412-624-5015. Web Site: www.sci.pitt.edu. *Interim Dean,* Bruce Childers; E-mail: childers@pitt.edu; *Chair,* Mary Kay Biagini; E-mail: biagini@pitt.edu
Prog estab 1962. Sch type: Pvt. Scholarships offered; Enrl: Grad: 606, Undergrad: 118; Fac 31
Ent Req: 2.0 GPA & 3rd yr standing
Tuition: Non-resident Undergraduate $17,976 Per semester; Non-resident Undergraduate $1,498 Per credit hour; Non-resident Graduate $20,976 Per semester; Non-resident Graduate $1,724 Per credit hour; Resident Undergraduate $10,228 Per semester; Resident Undergraduate $852 Per credit hour; Resident Graduate $12,371 Per semester; Resident Graduate $1,006 Per credit hour
Type of Training Offered: Public
Degrees & Hours Offered: BS, Info Sci, 30 credit hrs; MLIS, Libr & Info Sci, 36 credit hrs; MS, Info Sci, 36 credit hrs; MS, Telecom, 36 credit hrs; Ph.D., Info Sci & Tele, 72 credit hrs; Ph.D., Libr & Info Sci, 54 credit hrs
Special Courses: Archives & Records Management, Cognitive Science, Field Experience, Image Databases, Indexing & Abstracting, Information Storage & Retrieval, Information Systems Design, Law Librarianship, Management of Library Automation, Medical Informatics, Personnel Issues, Rare Books & Preservation, Research Methods & Statistics, Resources for Youth, School Librarianship, Systems Integration, Telecommunications & Networking
Evening Session, Summer Session

RHODE ISLAND

† UNIVERSITY OF RHODE ISLAND*, Graduate School of Library & Information Studies, Rodman Hall, 94 W Alumni Ave, Kingston, 02881-0815. Tel: 401-874-2878, 401-874-2947. FAX: 401-874-4964.

E-mail: gslis@etal.uri.edu. Web Site: www.uri.edu/artsci/lsc. *Assoc Prof, Prog Dir,* Valerie Karno; E-mail: vkarno@uri.edu; *Prof,* Yan Ma; E-mail: yanma@uri.edu; *Prof Emerita,* Dr Donna L Gilton; E-mail: dgilton@uri.edu
Prog estab 1963. Sch type: Pub. Scholarships offered; Enrl: Grad: 210; Fac 40
Ent Req: GRE, MAT or advanced degree; 3.0 GPA, Bachelor's; 2 letters of recommendation; resume
Tuition: Non-resident Graduate $29,082 Per year; Resident Graduate $15,964 Per year; Regional Graduate $23,012 Per year
Type of Training Offered: Special
Degrees & Hours Offered: Certificate, Library Media (TCP); Certificate, Information Literacy Instruction, 15 credit hrs; MLIS, 36 credit hrs
Special Courses: Digital Resources for Children & Youth, Health Sciences Librarianship, Information Ethics, Information Policy, Law Librarianship, Library Preservation, Multiculturalism in Libraries, Rare Book Librarianship, Special Collections & Archives, Visual Information Science
Evening Session, Online & Blended Courses, Online Courses, Summer Session

SOUTH CAROLINA

† UNIVERSITY OF SOUTH CAROLINA*, School of Information Science, 1501 Greene St, Columbia, 29208. Tel: 803-777-3858. E-mail: slisss@mailbox.sc.edu. Web Site: www.sc.edu/study/colleges_schools/cic/library_and_information_science/index.php. *Dean,* Tom Reichert, PhD; Tel: 803-777-4105, E-mail: reichert@sc.edu; *Interim Dir,* Karen W Gavigan, PhD; E-mail: kgavigan@mailbox.sc.edu; *Assoc Prof,* Jennifer Weil Arns, PhD; E-mail: jarns@mailbox.sc.edu; *Assoc Prof,* Darin Freeburg, PhD; E-mail: darinf@mailbox.sc.edu; *Assoc Prof,* Dick Kawooya, PhD; E-mail: kawooya@sc.edu; *Assoc Prof,* Susan R Rathbun-Grubb, PhD; E-mail: srathbun@mailbox.sc.edu; *Assoc Prof,* Feili Tu-Keefner, PhD; E-mail: feilitu@sc.edu; *Asst Prof,* Amir Karami, PhD; E-mail: karami@mailbox.sc.edu; *Instr,* Clayton A Copeland, PhD; E-mail: copelan2@mailbox.sc.edu; *Instr,* Elise C Lewis, PhD; E-mail: elewis@sc.edu
Enrl: Grad: 298
Tuition: Non-resident Graduate $1,240 Per credit hour; Resident Graduate $572 Per credit hour; Online Graduate $572 Per credit hour (out of state)
Type of Training Offered: Special
Degrees & Hours Offered: Certificate, Specialized Study in Info Sci, 12 sem hrs; MLIS, Libr & Info Sci, 36 sem hrs; Ph.D., Libr & Info Sci, 54 sem hrs; SLIS, Libr & Info Sci, 30 sem hrs
Special Courses: Automation, Business Information Services, Children's Literature, Information Retrieval, Information Science, Library Service to the Handicapped, Media (AV) & Young Adult Literature
Evening Session, Summer Session

SOUTH DAKOTA

BLACK HILLS STATE UNIVERSITY*, Library Media Program, E Y Berry Library Learning Ctr, 1200 University St, Unit 9676, Spearfish, 57799-9676. Tel: 605-642-6250, 605-642-6834. FAX: 605-642-6298. Web Site: iis.bhsu.edu/lis/librarymedia/index.cfm. *Instructor, Library Media,* Michael Tolan; Tel: 605-642-6356, E-mail: Michael.Tolan@bhsu.edu
Sch type: Pub; Fac 5
Tuition: Non-resident Undergraduate $391 Per credit hour; Resident Undergraduate $289 Per credit hour; Resident Graduate $367 Per credit hour
Type of Training Offered: School Library Media Certificate
Degrees & Hours Offered: BS, Library Media minor, 20; Certificate, Library Media online, 20
Special Courses: Library Technology
Online Courses, Summer Session

TENNESSEE

EAST TENNESSEE STATE UNIVERSITY*, Educational Media & Educational Technology, Dept Curriculum & Instruction, Warf-Pickel Hall, PO Box 70684, Johnson City, 37614-1709. Tel: 423-439-7595. FAX: 423-439-8362. E-mail: CUAI@etsu.edu. Web Site: www.etsu.edu/etsuhome. *Prog Coordr,* Renee Lyons; Tel: 423-439-7845, E-mail: lyonsrc@etsu.edu
Prog estab 1948. Sch type: Pub; Enrl: Grad: 45; Fac 5
Ent Req: 3.0 GPA
Tuition: Non-resident Graduate $841 Per credit hour; Resident Graduate $601 Per credit hour
Degrees & Hours Offered: M.Ed., Sch Libr Media, 36 sem hrs; M.Ed., Educ Tech, 36
Special Courses: Adult Literature, Children's Literature, Issues in Media, Media (AV), Storytelling
Evening Session, Online Courses, Summer Session, Weekend Session

MIDDLE TENNESSEE STATE UNIVERSITY*, Womack Educational Leadership Department, Master of Library Science Program, 1301 E Main St, Box 91, Murfreesboro, 37132. Tel: 615-898-5378. FAX: 615-898-2859. Web Site: mtsu.edu/programs/library-science-mls/. *Asst Prof, Prog Coordr,* Dr Frank Lambert; E-mail: Frank.Lambert@mtsu.edu
Prog estab 2016. Sch type: Pub; Enrl: 55; Grad: 70; Fac 3
Ent Req: For admission: 1) an earned bachelor's degree from an accredited university or college; 2) official transcripts from all previous college-and university-level work showing a minimum grade point average (GPA) of 2.75; 3) three letters of recommendations from professionals; 4) 500-word essay (Statement of Purpose) regarding applicant's reasons for seeking the MLS at MTSU.
Tuition: Non-resident Undergraduate $3,206 Per semester; Non-resident Undergraduate $515 Per credit hour; Non-resident Graduate $3,517 Per semester; Non-resident Graduate $606 Per credit hour; Resident Undergraduate $908 Per semester; Resident Undergraduate $147 Per credit hour; Resident Graduate $1,219 Per semester; Resident Graduate $238 Per credit hour
Type of Training Offered: School Library Media
Degrees & Hours Offered: MLS, School librarianship; Public librarianship; Academic librarianship, 36 sem hrs
Special Courses: Cataloging, Children's Literature, Integration of Curriculum, Learning Theory & Technology, Reference, Young Adult Literature
Online Courses, Summer Session

TENNESSEE TECHNOLOGICAL UNIVERSITY*, Library Science Program, Graduate Studies, Dewberry Hall 306, One William L Jones Dr, Cookeville, 38505. (Mail add: PO Box 5012, Cookeville, 38505-0001). Tel: 931-372-3233. FAX: 931-372-3497. E-mail: gradstudies@tntech.edu. Web Site: www.tntech.edu/graduatestudies. *Dean,* Dr Mark Stephens; Tel: 931-372-3224, E-mail: mstephens@tntech.edu; *Assoc Dean,* Dr Alice Camuti; Tel: 931-372-6006, E-mail: acamuti@tntech.edu; *Assoc Prof,* Dr Julie Stepp; Tel: 931-372-3103, E-mail: jstepp@tntech.edu; *Adminr,* Rebecca Blalock; E-mail: bblalock@tntech.edu
Sch type: Pub
Type of Training Offered: School
Degrees & Hours Offered: MA, Curric & Instruction, 33 sem hrs; MA, Libr Sci, 33 sem hrs; EdS, Libr Sci, 30 credit hrs; EdS, Curric & Instruction, 30 credit hrs
Special Courses: Applied Behavior Analysis; Curriculum; Early Childhood Education; Educational Technology; Elementary Education; Exercise Science; Family & Consumer Sciences; Library Science; Literacy; Secondary Education; Special Education; STEM Education
Evening Session, Online Courses, Summer Session

TREVECCA NAZARENE UNIVERSITY, Library & Information Science Program, School of Education, 333 Murfreesboro Rd, Nashville, 37210-2877. Tel: 615-248-1201, 615-248-1206. Toll Free Tel: 888-210-4868. FAX: 615-248-1597. Web Site: www.trevecca.edu/mlis. *Prog Dir,* Judy Bivens; E-mail: jbivens@trevecca.edu; *Assoc Prof,* Priscilla Speer
Sch type: Pvt; Enrl: Grad: 35
Ent Req: MAT or GRE, 2.7 GPA
Type of Training Offered: School
Degrees & Hours Offered: MLIS, Sch Libr or Ch/YA Servs, 30 credit hrs

UNIVERSITY OF MEMPHIS*, Instruction & Curriculum Leadership, 406 Ball Hall, Memphis, 38152. Tel: 901-678-2365. FAX: 901-678-3881. E-mail: coe@memphis.edu. Web Site: www.memphis.edu. *Chair,* Sandra Cooley Nichols; E-mail: smcooley@memphis.edu
Sch type: Pub. Scholarships offered; Enrl: Grad: 400; Fac 2
Ent Req: GRE 2.7 GPA
Tuition: Non-resident Graduate $704 Per credit hour; Resident Graduate $512 Per credit hour
Type of Training Offered: School
Degrees & Hours Offered: MS, 39 sem hrs; MAT
Evening Session, Summer Session

† UNIVERSITY OF TENNESSEE, KNOXVILLE*, School of Information Sciences, 451 Communications Bldg, 1345 Circle Park Dr, Knoxville, 37996-0332. Tel: 865-974-2148. E-mail: sis@utk.edu. Web Site: www.sis.utk.edu. *Assoc Dean, Res,* Suzie Allard; E-mail: sallard@utk.edu; *Interim Dir,* Carol Tenopir; E-mail: ctenopir@utk.edu; *Assoc Prof,* Vandana Singh; Tel: 865-974-2785, E-mail: vandana@utk.edu; *Prof,* Dania Bilal; E-mail: dania@utk.edu; *Prof,* Peiling Wang; *Clinical Assoc Prof,* Dr Cindy Welch; Tel: 865-974-7918, E-mail: cwelch11@utk.edu
Prog estab 1971. Sch type: Pub. Scholarships offered; Enrl: Grad: 225; Fac 12
Ent Req: GRE & 3.25 GPA
Tuition: Non-resident Graduate $1,650 Per credit hour; Resident Graduate $639 Per credit hour
Type of Training Offered: School Library Media Certificate
Degrees & Hours Offered: MS, 36 sem hrs
Special Courses: Youth Services in Public & School Libraries
Evening Session, Summer Session

TEXAS

SAM HOUSTON STATE UNIVERSITY*, Department of Library Science & Technology, 1905 Bobby K Marks Dr, Huntsville, 77340. (Mail add: PO Box 2236, Huntsville, 77341-2236). Tel: 936-294-1151. Toll Free Tel: 866-232-5287. FAX: 936-294-1153. E-mail: libraryscience@shsu.edu. Web Site: www.shsu.edu/libraryscience. *Chair, Prof,* Holly A Weimar; Tel: 936-294-1150, E-mail: hweimar@shsu.edu; *Asst Chair, Library Services, Assoc Prof, Prog Coordr,* Dr Karin Perry; Tel: 936-294-4641, E-mail: kperry@shsu.edu; *Prof,* Dr Teri Lesesne; Tel: 936-294-3673, E-mail: lis_tsl@shsu.edu; *Asst Prof,* Dr Rose Brock; Tel: 936-294-3158, E-mail: rmb043@shsu.edu; *Asst Prof,* Dr Elizabeth Gross; Tel: 936-294-4740, E-mail: eag041@shsu.edu
Prog estab 1937. Sch type: Pub. Scholarships offered; Enrl: Grad: 200
Ent Req: teacher certification, 2 years teaching, & 3.0 GPA or better
Tuition: Non-resident Graduate $503 Per credit hour; Resident Graduate $503 Per credit hour; Domestic Graduate $503 Per credit hour; Online Graduate $503 Per credit hour
Type of Training Offered: School Library Media Certificate
Degrees & Hours Offered: MLS, 36 sem hrs
Online Courses, Summer Session

TEXAS A&M UNIVERSITY - COMMERCE*, Department of Educational Leadership, Frank Young Education Bldg N, No 113, 2600 S Neal St, Commerce, 75428. (Mail add: PO BOX 3011, Commerce, 75429). Tel: 903-886-5520. FAX: 903-886-5507. Web Site: www.tamuc.edu/academics. *Assoc Prof, Interim Dept Head,* Peter Williams, PhD; E-mail: Peter.Williams@tamuc.edu
Enrl: Grad: 75
Ent Req: MS or school librarian certification only
Tuition: Non-resident Graduate $2,682 Per semester; Resident Graduate $1,455 Per semester
Type of Training Offered: Library & Information Science
Degrees & Hours Offered: M.Ed., 30 Sem hrs
Evening Session, Online & Blended Courses, Online Courses, Summer Session

† TEXAS WOMAN'S UNIVERSITY*, School of Library & Information Studies, Stoddard Hall, Rm 404, 304 Administration Dr, Denton, 76201. Tel: 940-898-2602. FAX: 940-898-2611. E-mail: slis@twu.edu. Web Site: twu.edu/slis. *Dir, Prof,* Dr Ling Jeng; E-mail: ljeng@twu.edu
Sch type: Pub. Scholarships offered; Enrl: Grad: 501; Fac 1
Partic in Amigos Library Services, Inc
Ent Req: BA, 3.0 GPA for last 60 hours
Tuition: Non-resident Graduate $692 Per credit hour; Resident Graduate $284 Per credit hour
Type of Training Offered: Public
Degrees & Hours Offered: MA, Libr Sci, 39 credits; MLS, Libr Sci, 36 credits
Special Courses: Academic Libraries, Public Libraries, Special Libraries, Texas School Librarian Certification, Evidence-Based Health Science Librarianship, Community Information
Online Courses, Summer Session

UNIVERSITY OF HOUSTON-CLEAR LAKE*, School Library & Information Science Program, 2700 Bay Area Blvd, Bayou Ste 1321, Houston, 77058. Tel: 281-283-3500. Web Site: www.uhcl.edu/academics/degrees/school-library-information-science-ms. *Assoc Prof, Prog Coordr,* Sheila Baker; Tel: 281-283-3515, E-mail: bakers@uhcl.edu; *Asst Prof,* Janice Newsum; Tel: 281-283-3537, E-mail: newsum@uhcl.edu
Prog estab 1974. Sch type: Pub; Enrl: Grad: 80; Fac 3
Ent Req: BA, Texas Teaching Certification & GRE
Tuition: Non-resident Graduate $9,539 Full-time; Resident Graduate $4,899 Full-time
Type of Training Offered: Library & Information Science
Degrees & Hours Offered: MS, Sch Librarianship, 30 sem hrs
Special Courses: Children's Literature; Librarians as Instructional Partners; Research in Library Science; School Library Collection Development Management; School Library Services Administration; School Library Systems & Services; Selection & Application of Media & Technology; Young Adult Literature
Online Courses, Professional Development, Summer Session

† UNIVERSITY OF NORTH TEXAS*, College of Information, Department of Information Science, 3940 N Elm St, Ste E292, Denton, 76207. (Mail add: 1155 Union Circle, No 311068, Denton, 76203-5017). Tel: 940-565-2445. Toll Free Tel: 877-275-7547. FAX: 940-565-3101. E-mail: CI-Advising@unt.edu. Web Site: informationscience.unt.edu. *Chair, Prof,* Dr Jiangping Chen; E-mail: Jiangping.Chen@unt.edu; *Assoc Dean, Prof,* Dr Yunfei Du; Tel: 940-565-3565, E-mail: Yunfei.Du@unt.edu; *Assoc Chair, Assoc Prof,* Barbara Schultz-Jones; E-mail: Barbara.Schultz-Jones@unt.edu; *Assoc Prof,* Dr Jeonghyun Annie Kim; E-mail: Jeonghyun.Kim@unt.edu; *Assoc Prof,* Dr Shawne Miksa; E-mail: Shawne.Miksa@unt.edu; *Assoc Prof,* Dr Daniella Smith; E-mail: Daniella.Smith@unt.edu; *Assoc Prof,* Dr Maurice Wheeler; E-mail: Maurice.Wheeler@unt.edu; *Assoc Prof,* Dr Oksana Zavalina; E-mail: Zavalina.Oksana@unt.edu; *Prof,* Dr Suliman Hawamdeh; E-mail: Suliman.Hawamdeh@unt.edu; *Prof,* Dr Brian C O'Connor; E-mail: Brian.O'Connor@unt.edu; *Prof Emeritus,* Dr Phillip Turner; E-mail: Philip.Turner@unt.edu; *Sr Lecturer,* Dr Larry Enoch; E-mail: Larry.Enoch@unt.edu
Prog estab 1939. Sch type: Pub. Scholarships offered; Enrl: Grad: 1,010, Undergrad: 47
Ent Req: ACT or SAT
Tuition: Non-resident Undergraduate $689 Per credit hour; Non-resident Graduate $686 Per credit hour; Resident Undergraduate $280 Per credit hour; Resident Graduate $277 Per credit hour
Type of Training Offered: Special
Degrees & Hours Offered: BS, Info Sci major, 120 sem hrs; MS, Libr Sci or Info Sci, 36 hrs; Ph.D., Info Sci, 60 sem hrs
Special Courses: Communications & the Use of Information, Economics of Information, Horizon Technologies for Library & Information Centers, Human Information & Communication Behavior, Information Networks, Information Resources & Services in Culturally Diverse Communities, Information Retrieval Design, Information Retrieval Theory, Internet Applications for Information Professionals, Legal Information & Access Services, Management of Information Resources in Organizations, Medical Informatics, Music Libraries, Preservation, Product Management for Information Systems, Rare Books, Records Management, Scholarly & Scientific Communication, Telecommunications for Information Professionals, Website Development, Youth Programs & Storytelling
Continuing Education, Evening Session, Online Courses, Professional Development, Summer Session, Weekend Session

† UNIVERSITY OF TEXAS AT AUSTIN*, School of Information, 1616 Guadalupe St, Ste 5.202, Austin, 78712-0390. (Mail add: MC-D 8600, Austin, 78701-1213). Tel: 512-471-3821. FAX: 512-471-3971. E-mail: info@ischool.utexas.edu. Web Site: www.ischool.utexas.edu. *Dean,* Eric T Meyer; E-mail: dean@ischool.utexas.edu; *Prof,* Andrew Dillon; *Prof,* R David Lankes; E-mail: rdlankes@utexas.edu
Prog estab 1948. Sch type: Pub. Scholarships offered; Enrl: Grad: 300
Ent Req: GRE & letters of reference
Tuition: Resident Undergraduate $11,400 Per semester; Resident Graduate $10,850 Per semester
Type of Training Offered: Special
Degrees & Hours Offered: MS, Info Studies, 36 sem hrs; Ph.D., Info Studies
Special Courses: Archives & Manuscripts, Architecture & Usability Studies, Audio Preservation & Reformatting, Children's Literature, Classification Theory, Cognitive Science, Competitive Intelligence, Database-Mgt Principles & Applications, Developing Media Collections, Electronic & Digital Records, Electronic Online Info Resources, Health Informatics, Image Processing, Indexing & Categorization of Informational Materials, Info Materials, Info Mgt, Info Policy, Info Resources in Business, Info Resources in Law, Info Services for Hispanic Americans, Issues in Contemporary Publishing, Library History, Mgt of Library Automation, Modern Info Retrieval, Network Security, Photograph & Cinema Archives, Preservation in Digital Environment, Preservation of Archival Material & Conservation of Library, Printing History, Rare Books & Special Collections, Records Mgt, Research in Library & Info Science, Subject Cataloging, Systems Analysis
Evening Session, Online Courses, Summer Session

UTAH

SOUTHERN UTAH UNIVERSITY GERALD R SHERRATT LIBRARY*, School Library Media Program, 351 W University Blvd, Cedar City, 84720. Tel: 435-586-7933. E-mail: library@suu.edu. Web Site: www.suu.edu/library/library-media-endorsement. *Dir, Libr Media Prog,* Caitlin Gerrity; Tel: 435-586-1908, E-mail: caitlingerrity@suu.edu
Prog estab 1980. Sch type: Pub; Enrl: Grad: 29, Undergrad: 29; Fac 9
Tuition: Non-resident Undergraduate $1,800 Per 6-credit semester; Non-resident Graduate $2,130 Per 6-credit semester; Resident Undergraduate $1,800 Per 6-credit semester; Resident Graduate $2,130 Per 6-credit semester
Type of Training Offered: College
Degrees & Hours Offered: BA, Libr Media Endorsement, 18 sem hrs; BA, Libr Media minor, 18 sem hrs; BS, Libr Media Endorsement, 18 sem hrs; BS, Libr Media minor, 18 sem hrs; M.Ed., Sch Libr Media Endorsement, 42 sem hrs; MIS, Sch Libr Media Endorsement, 30 sem hrs
Special Courses: Library Computer & Reference Skills, Library Media Practicum, Library Technical Services, Managing a Media Center, School Library Media Foundations, Technology for Library Media Teachers, Utilization of Literature in the Classroom
Online Courses

UTAH STATE UNIVERSITY, Department of Instructional Technology & Learning Sciences-School Library Media Administration, 2830 Old Main Hill, Education, Bldg 215, Logan, 84322. Tel: 435-797-2694. Toll Free Tel: 866-782-9301. FAX: 435-797-2693. Web Site: itls.usu.edu. *Professional*

Practice Asst Professor, Dr Kelli Munns; Tel: 435-797-1583, E-mail: kelli.munns@usu.edu; *Assoc Prof, Dept Head,* Andy Walker; Tel: 435-797-2614, E-mail: andy.walker@usu.edu
Prog estab 1966. Sch type: Pub; Enrl: Grad: 150; Fac 4
Ent Req: GPA 3.0
Tuition: Online Graduate $477 Per credit hour
Type of Training Offered: School Library Media Certificate
Degrees & Hours Offered: M.Ed., Sch Libr Media Admin, 37 sem hrs

VIRGINIA

OLD DOMINION UNIVERSITY, DARDEN COLLEGE OF EDUCATION*, Department of STEM & Professional Studies, Education Bldg-4101-A, 4301 Hampton Blvd, Norfolk, 23529. Tel: 757-683-4305. FAX: 757-683-5862. Web Site: www.education.odu.edu/eci/libsci. *Chair,* Petros Katsioloudis; E-mail: pkatsiol@odu.edu; *Assoc Prof, Prog Dir,* Sue Kimmel; E-mail: skimmel@odu.edu
Prog estab 1975. Sch type: Pub; Enrl: Grad: 100
Tuition: Non-resident Graduate $1,387 Per credit hour; Resident Graduate $551 Per credit hour
Type of Training Offered: Librarianship
Degrees & Hours Offered: M.Ed., Sch Librarianship, 30 credit hrs

WASHINGTON

HIGHLINE COLLEGE*, Library & Information Services Program, 2400 S 240th St, Bldg 25, Rm 416, Des Moines, 98198. (Mail add: PO Box 98000, Des Moines, 98198-9800). Tel: 206-592-3248. FAX: 206-870-3776. E-mail: lisinquiry@highline.edu. Web Site: lis.highline.edu. *Prog Coordr,* Hara Brook; E-mail: hbrook@highline.edu
Prog estab 1967. Sch type: Pub; Enrl: Undergrad: 100; Fac 8
Tuition: Non-resident Undergraduate $131 Per credit hour; Resident Undergraduate $116 Per credit hour; International Undergraduate $299 Per credit hour
Type of Training Offered: School Library Media Certificate
Degrees & Hours Offered: Certificate, K-12 Libr Media Endorsement, 32 credits
Special Courses: Collection Development; Computers in Libraries; Library Administration & Management; School Libraries; Technical Services & Cataloging for Small Libraries
Co-operative Education Prog, Evening Session, Online & Blended Courses, Online Courses, Professional Development, Weekend Session

† UNIVERSITY OF WASHINGTON*, Information School, Mary Gates Hall, Ste 370, Campus Box 352840, Seattle, 98195-2840. Tel: 206-543-1794. FAX: 206-616-3152. E-mail: iask@uw.edu. Web Site: ischool.uw.edu. *Prof & Dean,* Dr Anind K Dey; E-mail: anind@uw.edu; *Cleary Prof of Ch & Youth Serv, Prog Chair,* Dr Michelle H Martin; E-mail: mhmarti@uw.edu; *Assoc Dean, Assoc Prof, Faculty Servs,* Dr Joseph Tennis; E-mail: jtennis@uw.edu; *Prof in Residence, Prof of Practice,* Cindy Aden; E-mail: adenc@uw.edu; *Assoc Prof, Prog Chair,* Dr Hala Annabi; E-mail: hpannabi@uw.edu; *Assoc Prof, Prog Chair,* Dr Alexis Hiniker; E-mail: alexisr@uw.edu; *Assoc Prof,* Dr Jin Ha Lee; E-mail: jinhalee@uw.edu; *Asst Prof,* Dr Miranda Belarde-Lewis; E-mail: mhbl@uw.edu; *Asst Prof,* Dr Marika Cifor; E-mail: mcifor@uw.edu; *Asst Prof,* Dr Nicolas Weber; E-mail: nmweber@uw.edu; *Teaching Prof,* Helene Williams; E-mail: helenew@uw.edu; *Assoc Teaching Prof,* Mike Doane; E-mail: mtd@uw.edu; *Assoc Teaching Prof,* Chance Hunt; E-mail: cahunt@uw.edu; *Assoc Teaching Prof,* Dr Sandy Littletree; E-mail: sandy505@uw.edu
Prog estab 1911. Sch type: Pub. Scholarships offered; Enrl: Grad: 779, Undergrad: 693; Fac 63
Ent Req: BS-Admission to the University of Washington, application document & prerequisite courses
Tuition: Non-resident Undergraduate $13,580 Per quarter; Non-resident Graduate $872 Per credit hour; Resident Undergraduate $4,080 Per quarter; Resident Graduate $872 Per credit hour
Type of Training Offered: Special
Degrees & Hours Offered: BS, Informatics; MLIS; MS, Info Mgt; Ph.D., Info Sci
Special Courses: Digital humanities librarianship; design thinking for libraries; Indigenous systems of knowledge; information and ownership; metadata design; youth development and information behavior in a digital age; data science; social media data mining and analysis; information and social justice; participatory design; design methods for librarianship; policy and ethics in information management; digital preservation; information architecture; Capstone project planning and implementation; faculty-supported research; directed fieldwork
Online & Blended Courses

WISCONSIN

† UNIVERSITY OF WISCONSIN-MADISON*, School of Computer & Information Sciences, Helen C White Hall, Rm 4217, 600 N Park St, Madison, 53706. Tel: 608-263-2900. FAX: 608-263-4849. E-mail: info@ischool.wisc.edu. Web Site: ischool.wisc.edu. *Dir,* Tom Erickson; E-mail: tom.erickson@wisc.edu; *Dir, Prof,* Kyung-Sun Kim; E-mail: kskim@ischool.wisc.edu; *Assoc Dean, Prof,* Greg Downey; E-mail: greg.downey@wisc.edu; *Assoc Dir, Prof,* Kristin Eschenfelder; E-mail: eschenfelder@wisc.edu
Prog estab 1906. Sch type: Pub. Scholarships offered; Enrl: Grad: 257; Pop 235; Fac 1
Ent Req: Bachelor's, 3.0 GPA, 90 sem hrs of Liberal Arts & Scis, letters of ref (2 acad & 1 more either prof or acad)
Tuition: Non-resident Undergraduate $18,892 Per semester; Non-resident Graduate $12,753 Per semester; Resident Undergraduate $5,362 Per semester; Resident Graduate $6,089 Per semester
Type of Training Offered: School Library Media Certificate
Degrees & Hours Offered: Certificate, Specialist, 24 credits beyond MA with major paper & oral defense; MA, Libr & Info Studies, 39 Credits; Ph.D., 32 credit hrs
Special Courses: Archives, Children's & Young Adult Literature & Services, Corporate & Specialized Information Services, Database Design, Digital Divides & Differences, Geographies of Information, Government Information Sources, Health Information Systems, Information Architecture, Information Sources, Intellectual Freedom, Library History, Mass Media & Global Communication, Online Reference, Reading Interests of Adults, Reference Services & Materials, Research Methods, School Library Media Specialist, Storytelling & Oral Literature
Continuing Education, Professional Development

† UNIVERSITY OF WISCONSIN-MILWAUKEE*, School of Information Studies, NWQD, Rm 3860, 2025 E Newport, Milwaukee, 53211. (Mail add: PO Box 413, Milwaukee, 53201-0413). Tel: 414-229-4707. Toll Free Tel: 888-349-3432. FAX: 414-229-6699. E-mail: soisinfo@uwm.edu. Web Site: www.uwm.edu/dept/SOIS. *Prof,* Dr Dietmar Wolfram; E-mail: dwolfram@uwm.edu; *Asst Dean,* Chad Zahrt; Tel: 414-229-5421, E-mail: zahrt@uwm.edu; *Asst Prof,* Dr Abigail L Phillips; E-mail: abileigh@uwm.edu
Prog estab 1966. Sch type: Pub. Scholarships offered; Enrl: Grad: 350, Undergrad: 500; Fac 1
Ent Req: BA/BS and cumulative GPA of 2.75 or above.
Type of Training Offered: Special
Degrees & Hours Offered: BS, Info Resources, 120 sem hrs; Certificate, Advan Study in digital Libraries, 12 sem hrs; Certificate, Archives and Records Administration, 15 sem hrs; MLIS, 36 sem hrs; Ph.D., Info Sci, Educ & Media Tech
Special Courses: Archives, Archives Automation, Bibliometrics, Book Binding & Repair, Children's Literature, Computerized Information Systems, Electronic Networking & Information Services, Goverment Documents, Health Sciences & Information Services, Information Marketing, Information Systems Analysis & Designs, Information & Communications Technology, Microcomputers in Libraries, Law Librarianship, Law Library Administration, Legal Bibliography, Library Automation, Library Resources on the Internet, Map Librarianship, Media (AV), Multimedia, Music Librarianship, On-Line Information Retrieval, Records Management, Storytelling & Young Adult Literature
Evening Session, Online Courses, Summer Session

UNIVERSITY OF WISCONSIN OSHKOSH COLLEGE OF EDUCATION & HUMAN SERVICES*, Educational Leadership & Policy Graduate Program, 800 Algoma Blvd, Oshkosh, 54901. Tel: 920-424-0881. FAX: 920-424-0858. E-mail: edldrsp@uwosh.edu. Web Site: uwosh.edu/coehs/departments/edleadership. *Assoc Prof, Dept Chair,* Dr Joshua Garrison; E-mail: garrisoj@uwosh.edu; *Graduate Program Coord, Prof,* Marguerite W Penick, PhD; E-mail: penickm@uwosh.edu; *Assoc Prof, Graduate Program Coord,* Cathy Toll, PhD; E-mail: tollc@uwosh.edu
Prog estab 1951. Sch type: Pub
Tuition: Resident Graduate $700 Per credit hour
Type of Training Offered: School
Degrees & Hours Offered: MS, Educational Leadership & Policy, 30 sem hrs; EdD, Educational Leadership & Policy, 48 sem hrs
Special Courses: School Library Media Specialist
Evening Session, Online Courses, Summer Session, Weekend Session

UNIVERSITY OF WISCONSIN-WHITEWATER*, Educational Foundations Department, Library Media Program, Winther Hall 6035, 800 W Main St, Whitewater, 53190. Tel: 262-472-1463. FAX: 262-472-2841. Web Site: uww.edu/coeps/departments/edfound/library-media. *Prog Dir,* Sarah Beth Nelson; E-mail: nelsons@uww.edu
Enrl: Undergrad: 50, Grad: 20
Type of Training Offered: School Library Media Certificate
Degrees & Hours Offered: BA, Library Science minor, 24 sem hrs; BS, School Library Minor, 21 sem hrs plus 6 credit practicum; M.Ed., MSE-Professional Studies with Information, Technology, & Libraries Emphasis, 30
Evening Session, Online & Blended Courses, Summer Session

PUERTO RICO

† UNIVERSITY OF PUERTO RICO, RIO PIEDRAS CAMPUS*, Graduate School of Information Sciences & Technologies, PO Box 21906, San Juan, 00931-1906. Tel: 787-764-0000, Ext 8521, 787-764-6199. FAX: 787-764-2311. E-mail: portal.egcti@upr.edu. Web Site: egcti.uprrp.edu. *Assoc Prof, Interim Dir,* Noraida Dominguez Flores; Tel: 787-764-0000, Ext 85269, E-mail: noraida.dominguez@upr.edu; *Prof,* Eliut Flores-Caraballo; E-mail: eliut.flores@upr.edu; *Prof,* Jose Sanchez-Lugo; Tel: 787-764-0000, Ext 85272, E-mail: Jose.sanchez18@upr.edu; *Prof,* Carlos Suarez-Balseiro; Tel: 787-764-0000, Ext 85284, E-mail: carlos.suarez5@upr.edu; *Assoc Prof,* Betsaida Velez-Natal; E-mail: betsaida.velez@upr.edu
Prog estab 1969. Sch type: Pub; Enrl: Grad: 165; Fac 2
Ent Req: Bachelor's, 3.00 PAEG
Tuition: Non-resident Graduate $1,500 Per semester; Resident Graduate $75 Per credit hour
Type of Training Offered: Public
Degrees & Hours Offered: Certificate, Post Bachelor - School Librarian, 22 sem hrs; Certificate, Post Bachelor - Analyst in Electronic Resources, 21 sem hrs; Certificate, Post Bachelor - Archives & Records Mgt, 18 sem hrs; Certificate, Post Master - Legal Specialist, 18 sem hrs; Certificate, Post Master - Library Administrator, 16 sem hrs; Certificate, Post Master - Info Consultant, 20 sem hrs; MIS, 38 sem hrs
Special Courses: Abstracting & Indexing, Automation of Information Services, Bibliographic Instruction, Information Needs Analysis, Latin American Bibliography, Legal Bibliography, Music Bibliography, Systems Analysis
Evening Session

ALBERTA

MACEWAN UNIVERSITY*, Library & Information Technology Program, 10700-104 Ave NW 5-306W, Edmonton, T5J 4S2. Tel: 780-497-5162. E-mail: business@macewan.ca. Web Site: www.macewan.ca/academics/programs/library-and-information-technology. *Assoc Prof,* Dr Norene Erickson; Tel: 780-633-3541, E-mail: ericksonn7@macewan.ca; *Asst Prof,* Lisa Shamchuk; Tel: 780-633-3574, E-mail: shamchukl@macewan.ca
Prog estab 1971. Sch type: Pub. Scholarships offered; Enrl: Undergrad: 70
Tuition: Resident Undergraduate $210 Per credit hour
Type of Training Offered: Special
Degrees & Hours Offered: Diploma, 60 credit hrs

SAIT POLYTECHNIC*, Library Information Technology, School of Information Communication Technologies, 1301 - 16 Ave NW, Calgary, T2M 0L4. Tel: 403-284-7231, 403-284-8897. Toll Free Tel: 877-284-7248. FAX: 403-284-7238. E-mail: ict.info@sait.ca. Web Site: www.sait.ca. *Chair,* Sandra Lee; E-mail: sandra.lee@sait.ca
Prog estab 1968. Sch type: Pub
Type of Training Offered: Library Technician
Degrees & Hours Offered: Diploma, Libr Tech (2-year day prog), 1,460 hrs
Special Courses: Acquisitions & Serials, Cataloguing & Classification, Circulation, Collection Development (Children, Young Adult & Adult), Communication Skills, Designing Web Tools for Libraries, Information Services, Library Automation, Library Management, Library Marketing, Library Network Technology, Managing Digital Content, Records Management
Continuing Education, Online Courses

† UNIVERSITY OF ALBERTA*, School of Library & Information Studies, 7-104 Education N, University of Alberta, Edmonton, T6G 2G5. Tel: 780-492-7625. FAX: 780-492-2024. E-mail: slis@ualberta.ca. Web Site: www.ualberta.ca/school-of-library-and-information-studies. *Dir,* Kenneth Gariepy, PhD; *Prof,* Dinesh Rathi, PhD; *Prof,* Toni Samek, PhD; *Prof,* Ali Shiri, PhD; *Prof,* Dangzhi Zhao, PhD; *Assoc Prof,* Danielle Allard, PhD; *Assoc Prof,* Michael McNally, PhD; *Assoc Prof, Graduate Program Coord,* Tami Oliphant, PhD; *Asst Prof,* Brenda Reyes Ayala, PhD
Prog estab 1968. Sch type: Pub. Scholarships offered; Enrl: Grad: 300
Ent Req: 3.0 GPA, 4-Year Undergraduate Degree (except Bachelor in Library Science)
Type of Training Offered: Library & Information Science
Degrees & Hours Offered: MLIS, 39 credits; MLIS/MA, 45 credits + Thesis; MLIS/MBA, 81 credits
Special Courses: Advanced Research Methods, Archives, Children's Literature, Conservation & Preservation, Contemporary Theories & Practices of Reading, Globalization, Diversity & Information, Government Publications, History of the Book, Information Retrieval, Instructional Practices in Library & Information Services, Internet, Intellectual Freedom, Knowledge Management, Multi-media Texts for Young People, Practicum, Records Management, Young Adult Literature
Evening Session, Online & Blended Courses, Online Courses, Summer Session

BRITISH COLUMBIA

LANGARA COLLEGE, Library & Information Technology Program, 100 W 49th Ave, Vancouver, V5Y 2Z6. Tel: 604-323-5364. FAX: 604-323-5010. Reference E-mail: libtech@langara.ca. Web Site: langara.ca/programs-and-courses/programs/library-information-technology. *Dept Chair,* Fiona Hunt; E-mail: fhunt@langara.ca
Prog estab 1967. Sch type: Pub. Scholarships offered; Enrl: Undergrad: 200
Tuition: Resident Undergraduate $103 Per credit hour (CAN)
Type of Training Offered: Library Technician
Degrees & Hours Offered: Diploma, 61 credit hrs
Special Courses: Advanced Online Searching and Information Literacy, Cataloguing (AACR2, RDA, MARC, non-book materials), Reference Services, Technical Services and Circulation, Library Systems and Accessibility, Subject Analysis and Classification, Indigenous Knowledges and Libraries, Readers' Advisory, Children's Services, Young Adult Services, Managing Digital Collections, Special Libraries, Supervisory Skills, Introduction to Records Management, Introduction to Archives and Museums
Online & Blended Courses

† UNIVERSITY OF BRITISH COLUMBIA, School of Information, The Irving K Barber Learning Ctr, 1961 E Mall, Ste 470, Vancouver, V6T 1Z1. Tel: 604-822-2404. E-mail: ischool.info@ubc.ca. Web Site: www.ischool.ubc.ca. *Assoc Prof, Dir,* Dr Luanne Sinnamon; *Prof,* Erik Kwakkel; *Prof,* Victoria Lemieux; *Prof,* Heather O'Brien; *Assoc Prof,* Muhammad Abdul-Mageed; *Assoc Prof,* Richard Arias-Hernandez; *Assoc Prof,* Jennifer Douglas; *Assoc Prof,* Eric Meyers; *Assoc Prof,* Lisa Nathan; *Asst Prof,* Julia Bullard; *Asst Prof,* Alexander Ross; *Asst Prof,* Elizabeth Shaffer; *Asst Prof,* Hannah Turner; *Asst Professor of Teaching,* Fatemeh Salehian Kia; *Lecturer,* Tess Prendergast. Subject Specialists: *Teaching,* Richard Arias-Hernandez
Prog estab 1961. Sch type: Pub; Enrl: Grad: 320; Fac 16
Ent Req: Bachelor's & achieved a minimum overall average in the B+ grade range (76% at UBC) in third & fourth year level courses
Tuition: Resident Graduate $5,753 Per year (CAN); International Graduate $12,238 Per year (CAN)
Degrees & Hours Offered: MA, Children's Lit, 30 credits; MAS, 48 credits; MLIS, 48 credits; Ph.D., Archival, Libr & Info Studies, 24 credits; MAS/MLIS, 81 credits
Special Courses: Archival Administration, Archival Appraisal, Bibliographic Control, Community & Culture, Data Services, Electronic Records, First Nations Curriculum Concentration (FNCC), Human-Computer Interaction (HCI) Sub-Specialization, Information Interaction & Design, Information Retrieval, Librarianship, Management, Records Management, Serving Groups with Special Needs, Youth Literature & Services
Evening Session, Summer Session

MANITOBA

RED RIVER COLLEGE POLYTECHNIC*, Library & Information Technology Program, School of Continuing Education, E113-2055 Notre Dame Ave, Winnipeg, R3H 0J9. Tel: 204-694-1789. Toll Free Tel: 866-242-7073. FAX: 204-633-6489. E-mail: cde@rrc.ca. Web Site: catalogue.rrc.ca/Programs/WPG/PartTime/LIBIP-DP/Overview. *Prog Mgr,* Tammy Desmond; Tel: 204-632-2084, E-mail: tdesmond@rrc.ca
Prog estab 1963. Sch type: Pub; Enrl: Undergrad: 120; Fac 9
Degrees & Hours Offered: Diploma
Open Mon-Thurs 7:45-6:30, Fri 7:45-4:30; Mon-Fri (Summer) 8-4

NOVA SCOTIA

† DALHOUSIE UNIVERSITY*, School of Information Management, Kenneth C Rowe Management Bldg, Ste 4010, 6100 University Ave, Halifax, B3H 4R2. (Mail add: PO Box 15000, Halifax, B3H 4R2). Tel: 902-494-3656. FAX: 902-494-2451. E-mail: sim@dal.ca. Web Site: www.dal.ca/faculty/management/school-of-information-management.html. *Assoc Dean, Prof,* Dr Mike Smit; Tel: 902-494-1901, E-mail: mike.smit@dal.ca; *Asst Prof, Dir,* Dr Sandra Toze; Tel: 902-494-2488, E-mail: stoze@dal.ca; *Prof,* Dr Bertrum MacDonald; Tel: 902-494-2472, E-mail: bertrum.macdonald@dal.ca; *Prof,* Dr Louise Spiteri; Tel: 902-494-2473, E-mail: louise.spiteri@dal.ca; *Assoc Prof,* Dr Vivian Howard; Tel: 902-494-3031, E-mail: vivian.howard@dal.ca; *Asst Prof,* Dr Conrad Colin; Tel: 902-494-8378, E-mail: colin.conrad@dal.ca; *Asst Prof,* Dr Keith Lawson; Tel: 902-494-6123, E-mail: klawson@dal.ca; *Asst Prof,* Dr Joyline Makani; Tel: 902-494-3661, E-mail: joyline.makani@dal.ca; *Asst Prof,* Dr Philippe Mongeon; E-mail: pmongeon@dal.ca; *Asst Prof,* Dr Paulette Skerrett; Tel: 902-494-6119, E-mail: paulette.skerrett@dal.ca; *Lecturer,* Patti Bannister; E-mail: patti.bannister@dal.ca; *Lecturer,* Alison Brown; E-mail: alisonbrown@dal.ca; *Lecturer,* Jennifer Grek Martin; Tel: 902-494-2462, E-mail: jgrekmartin@dal.ca; *Lecturer,* Lindsay McNiff; E-mail: lindsay.mcniff@dal.ca; *Lecturer,* Sandi Stewart; E-mail: sandi.stewart@dal.ca
Prog estab 1969. Sch type: Pub. Scholarships offered

Type of Training Offered: Information Manager
Degrees & Hours Offered: MIM; MI, 48 credit hrs; MI/MPA, 91 credit hrs; MI/JD, 79-83 credit hrs; MI/MREM, 66 credit hrs

ONTARIO

ALGONQUIN COLLEGE OF APPLIED ARTS & TECHNOLOGY*, Library & Information Technician Program, School of Health & Community Studies, Rm C230, 1385 Woodroffe Ave, Ottawa, K2G 1V8. Tel: 613-727-4723. FAX: 613-727-7759. Web Site: www.algonquincollege.com. *Prof,* Helena Merriam; E-mail: merriah@algonquincollege.com
Prog estab 1967. Sch type: Pub; Enrl: Undergrad: 40
Type of Training Offered: Library Technician
Degrees & Hours Offered: Diploma
Continuing Education

SENECA COLLEGE OF APPLIED ARTS & TECHNOLOGY*, Library & Information Technician Diploma Program, 1750 Finch Ave E, Toronto, M2J 2X5. Tel: 416-491-5050. FAX: 416-491-4606. Web Site: www.senecac.on.ca. *Prof,* Delia Antonacci; Tel: 416-491-5050, Ext 33739, E-mail: delia.antonacci@senecacollege.ca; *Prof,* Katherine More; Tel: 416-491-5050, Ext 33701, E-mail: katherine.more@senecacollege.ca
Prog estab 1967. Sch type: Pub; Enrl: Undergrad: 120
Ent Req: High school diploma
Tuition: Resident Undergraduate $3,452 Per year (CAN)
Degrees & Hours Offered: Diploma
Evening Session, Summer Session

† UNIVERSITY OF TORONTO*, Faculty of Information, iSchool@Toronto, 140 St George St, Toronto, M5S 3G6. Tel: 416-978-3234. FAX: 416-978-5762. E-mail: inquire.ischool@utoronto.ca. Web Site: current.ischool.utoronto.ca, www.ischool.utoronto.ca. *Dean, Prof,* Wendy Duff; E-mail: wendy.duff@utoronto.ca; *Prof,* Dr Seamus Ross; Tel: 416-978-5763, E-mail: seamus.ross@utoronto.ca; *Prof,* Dr Leslie Shade; E-mail: leslie.shade@utoronto.ca; *Assoc Prof, Dir, Intl Prog,* Dr Nadia Caidi; E-mail: nadia.caidi@utoronto.ca; *Registrar & Dir, Student Serv,* Adriana Rossini; Tel: 416-978-8589, E-mail: adriana.rossini@utoronto.ca; *Assoc Prof,* Dr Costis Dallas; E-mail: costis.dallas@utoronto.ca
Prog estab 1928. Sch type: Pub. Scholarships offered; Enrl: Grad: 500, Undergrad: 25; Fac 39
Tuition: Domestic Graduate $10,280 Per year (CAN); International Graduate $38,590 Per year (CAN)
Type of Training Offered: Special
Degrees & Hours Offered: BA, Honours Bachelor of Arts in Interactive Digital Media This program is offered jointly by the Faculty of Information on the St. George CampusÂ, and the University of Toronto at Mississauga.; Ph.D., Doctor of Philosophy in Information Studies; MI, Master of Information Concentrations available: Library & Information Science; Archives & Records Management; Information Systems & Design; Knowledge Media & Design; Critical Information Studies; Knowledge Management & Information Management; MMSt, Master of Museum Studies; DAIS, Diploma of Advanced Study in Information Studies
Special Courses: Digital Preservation and Curation; Culture & Technology; Museum Studies; Knowledge Management; Project Management; Data Analytics; Health Informatics; Practicum (MI); Internship & Exhibitions courses (MMSt)
Continuing Education, Evening Session, Professional Development, Summer Session

† WESTERN UNIVERSITY, Faculty of Information & Media Studies, FIMS & Nursing Bldg, Rm 2020, London, N6A 5B9. Tel: 519-661-4017. FAX: 519-661-3506. E-mail: fims-gradservices@uwo.ca, lis-phd-info@uwo.ca, mlisinfo@uwo.ca. Web Site: www.fims.uwo.ca. *Dean, Prof,* Lisa Henderson; Tel: 519-661-2111, Ext 84235, E-mail: lhende44@uwo.ca; *Assoc Dean, Prof,* Anabel Quan-Haase; Tel: 519-661-2111, Ext 81405, E-mail: aquan@uwo.ca; *Asst Dean, Research, Assoc Prof,* Isola Ajiferuke; Tel: 519-661-2111, Ext 81364, E-mail: iajiferu@uwo.ca; *Assoc Prof, Chair, LIS PhD Program,* Melissa Adler; Tel: 519-661-2111, Ext 81034, E-mail: madler7@uwo.ca; *Assoc Prof, Chair, MLIS Prog,* Heather Hill; Tel: 519-661-2111, Ext 88013, E-mail: hhill6@uwo.ca; *Prof,* Jacquie Burkell; Tel: 519- 661-2111, Ext 88506, E-mail: jburkell@uwo.ca; *Prof,* Pam McKenzie; Tel: 519-661-2111, Ext 88514, E-mail: pmckenzi@uwo.ca; *Prof,* Victoria Rubin; Tel: 519-661-2111, Ext 88479, E-mail: vrubin@uwo.ca; *Prof,* Kamran Sedig; Tel: 519-661-2111, Ext 86612, E-mail: sedig@uwo.ca; *Assoc Prof,* Grant Campbell; Tel: 519-661-2111, Ext 88483, E-mail: gcampbel@uwo.ca; *Assoc Prof,* Ajit Pyati; Tel: 519-661-2111, Ext 85616, E-mail: apyati@uwo.ca; *Assoc Prof,* Paulette Rothbauer; Tel: 519-661-2111, Ext 88512, E-mail: prothba2@uwo.ca; *Asst Prof,* Alissa Centivany; Tel: 519-661-2111, Ext 88510, E-mail: acentiva@uwo.ca; *Asst Prof,* Shengnan Yang; Tel: 519-661-2111, Ext 84720, E-mail: syang859@uwo.ca
Prog estab 1966. Sch type: Pub; Enrl: Grad: 220, Grad: 26; Fac 45
Ent Req: For PhD: 4 yr undergrad degree & Master's degree preferably in Libr & Info Sci from ALA-accredited sch
Tuition: Domestic Graduate $2,120 Per term (Masters) (CAN); International Graduate $2,120 Per term (Doctorate) (CAN)
Type of Training Offered: Special
Degrees & Hours Offered: MLIS, 15 courses; Ph.D., Libr & Info Sci, 6 courses
Special Courses: Collective Memory Through Documents; Digital Humanitites & Library & Information Science; Information in the Age of Planet Google; Introduction to Data Librarianship; Introduction to Indigenizing & Decolonizing LIS; Public Library Services for Newcomers & Immigrants; Scholarly Communications & Open Access; Services & Materials for an Aging Population; Youth in Context: New Media & Digital Equity
Co-operative Education Prog, Evening Session, Summer Session

QUEBEC

CEGEP GARNEAU*, Techniques de la Documentation - Gestion de l'information, 1660 blvd de l'Entente, Quebec, G1S 4S3. Tel: 418-688-8310, Ext 2290. Web Site: www.cegepgarneau.ca/programmes-formations/techniques/techniques-documentation. *Prof,* Melanie De Buhan; E-mail: mdebuhan@cegepgarneau.ca; *Prof,* Nancy Drolet; E-mail: ndrolet@cegepgarneau.ca; *Prof,* Amelie Frenette; E-mail: afrenette@cegepgarneau.ca; *Prof,* Josee Gaudreau; E-mail: jgaudreau@cegepgarneau.ca; *Prof,* Mario Goupil; E-mail: mgoupil@cegepgarneau.ca; *Tech Serv,* Diane Bourget; E-mail: dbourget@cegepgarneau.ca
Prog estab 1971. Sch type: Pub. Scholarships offered; Enrl: Undergrad: 100; Fac 23
Type of Training Offered: Special
Special Courses: Archives & Documentation, Records Management

CEGEP TROIS-RIVIERES*, Dept Techniques Documentation, 3500 rue De Courval, Trois-Rivieres, G9A 5E6. (Mail add: CP 97, Trois-Rivieres, G9A 5E6). Tel: 819-376-1721, Ext 2824. E-mail: tech.documentation@cegeptr.qc.ca. Web Site: www.cegeptr.qc.ca/cours-cegep/programmes-techniques/documentation. *Coordr,* Sylvain Martel; E-mail: sylvain.martel@cegeptr.qc.ca
Prog estab 1968. Sch type: Pub
Type of Training Offered: Library Technician
Degrees & Hours Offered: Diploma, DEC Techniques de la Documentation - Libr Tech
Special Courses: Archives, Information & Library Technologies, Information Science, MARC21, RCAA2, RDDA, Records Management

COLLEGE DE MAISONNEUVE*, Techniques de la Documentation, 3800, rue Sherbrooke Est, Montreal, H1X 2A2. Tel: 514-254-7131. FAX: 514-251-9741. E-mail: communic@cmaisonneuve.qc.ca. Web Site: www.cmaisonneuve.qc.ca. *Prof,* Ginette Allard; *Prof,* Lise Brotherton; *Prof,* Guy Champagne
Prog estab 1975. Sch type: Pub; Enrl: Undergrad: 100
Tuition: Non-resident Undergraduate $754 Per year; Resident Undergraduate $754 Per year
Special Courses: Archives, Data Processing in Documentation, Information Retrieval, Media (AV) & Records Management

COLLEGE LIONEL-GROULX*, Department des Techniques de la Documentation, 100, rue Duquet, Sainte-Therese, J7E 3G6. Tel: 450-430-3120, Ext 2407. FAX: 450-971-7883. E-mail: formationcontinue@clg.qc.ca. Web Site: www.clg.qc.ca. *Prof,* Genevieve Fortin; E-mail: Genevieve.Fortin@clg.qc.ca
Prog estab 1972. Sch type: Pub; Enrl: Undergrad: 55
Special Courses: Media (AV) & Records Management

† MCGILL UNIVERSITY*, School of Information Studies, 3661 Peel St, Montreal, H3A 1X1. Tel: 514-398-4204. FAX: 514-398-7193. E-mail: sis@mcgill.ca. Web Site: www.mcgill.ca/sis. *Assoc Prof, Dir,* Joan Bartlett; E-mail: joan.bartlett@mcgill.ca; *Assoc Prof,* France Bouthillier; E-mail: france.bouthillier@mcgill.ca; *Assoc Prof,* Max Evans; E-mail: max.evans@mcgill.ca; *Assoc Prof,* Ilja Frissen; E-mail: ilja.frissen@mcgill.ca; *Prof,* Benjamin Fung; E-mail: ben.fung@mcgill.ca; *Prof,* Catherine Guastavino; E-mail: catherine.guastavino@mcgill.ca; *Assoc Prof,* Karyn Moffatt; E-mail: karyn.moffatt@mcgill.ca; *Asst Prof,* Rebekah Willson; E-mail: rebekah.willson@mcgill.ca; *Asst Prof,* Gracen Brilmyer; E-mail: gracen.brilmyer@mcgill.ca
Prog estab 1904. Sch type: Pub. Scholarships offered; Enrl: Grad: 205; Fac 10
Type of Training Offered: Library & Information Science
Degrees & Hours Offered: Certificate, Digital Archives Management, Information & Knowledge Management, Library and Information Studies, Cybersecurity (online), 15 credits; Ph.D., Information Studies; MISt, Archival Studies, Knowledge Mgt, Librarianship, HCI, 48 credits
Special Courses: Abstracting & Indexing, Archival Principles & Practice, Bibliographic & Factual Sources, Bioinformatics Resources, Business Information, Classification & Cataloging, Data Mining, Data Security, Descriptive Bibliography, Financial Management, Government Information, Health Sciences Information, History of Books & Printing, Humanities &

Social Sciences Information, Independent Study, Managing Information Systems, Information Policy, Web System Design and Management, Information System Design, Information Services and Users, Knowledge Management, Knowledge Taxonomies, Communities of Practice, Knowledge Networks, Law Information, Library Systems, Multimedia Systems, Organization of Information, Public Libraries, Practicum in Information Services, Research Principles & Analysis, Research Project, Scientific & Technical Information, Selected Topics in Library & Information Studies, Systems Thinking; Database Design and Management.

† UNIVERSITE DE MONTREAL*, Ecole de bibliotheconomie et des sciences de l'information, 3150, rue Jean-Brillant, bur C-2004, Montreal, H3T 1N8. (Mail add: CP 6128, succ Centre-ville, Montreal, H3C 3J7). Tel: 514-343-6044. FAX: 514-343-5753. E-mail: ebsiinfo@ebsi.umontreal.ca. Web Site: www.ebsi.umontreal.ca. *Dir, Prof,* Lyne Da Sylva; Tel: 514-343-7400, E-mail: lyne.da.sylva@umontreal.ca; *Prof,* Clément Arsenault; *Prof,* Dominic Forest; *Prof,* Vincent Larivière; *Asst Prof,* Guillaume Boutard; *Assoc Prof,* Nadine Desrochers; *Assoc Prof,* Christine Dufour; *Assoc Prof,* Audrey Laplante; *Assoc Prof,* Yvon Lemay; *Assoc Prof,* Eric Leroux; *Asst Prof,* Marie D Martel; *Assoc Prof,* Sabine Mas; *Assoc Prof,* Dominique Maurel; *Asst Prof,* Jean-Sébastien Sauvé; *Asst Prof,* Lubna Daraz; E-mail: lubna.daraz@umontreal.ca
Prog estab 1961. Sch type: Pub; Enrl: Grad: 250, Undergrad: 250; Fac 15
Ent Req: BA with B average for Master
Tuition: Domestic Undergraduate $1,300 Per semester (CAN); Domestic Graduate $1,300 Per semester (CAN)
Type of Training Offered: Library & Information Science
Degrees & Hours Offered: Certificate, Archival Studies, 30 credits; Certificate, Digital Info Mgt, 30 credits; Ph.D., Info Studies, 90 credits; MIS, Info Studies, 51 credits; MIS, Info Studies - Research track, 45 credits
Special Courses: Archives & Records Management, Digital Information Management, Information Science, Librarianship

SASKATCHEWAN

SASKATCHEWAN POLYTECHNIC LIBRARY & INFORMATION TECHNOLOGY*, 107 Fourth Ave S, Saskatoon, S7K 5X2. (Mail add: PO Box 1520, Saskatoon, S7K 3R5). Tel: 306-659-3846. Toll Free Tel: 866-467-4278. Web Site: saskpolytech.ca/. *Prog Head,* Chasity Berast; E-mail: berastc@saskpolytech.ca
Prog estab 1969. Sch type: Pub. Scholarships offered; Enrl: Undergrad: 30; Fac 2
Ent Req: Grade 12, English A & B
Tuition: Resident Undergraduate $5,600 Per year (CAN)
Degrees & Hours Offered: Diploma

LIBRARY SYSTEMS

This section describes the arrangement and or the function of state or province sponsored library systems in its jurisdiction, if applicable.

Complete data for each system can be found in the Library Section of this directory, unless the heading is followed by an (N), in which case the information can be found in the Network Section.

ALABAMA

The state of Alabama has the following Library Systems, which provide easily accessible services through branches and cooperating libraries.

Single County Systems (public libraries only):

Anniston-Calhoun County Library, Anniston
Baldwin County Library System, Robertsdale
DeKalb County Public Library, Fort Payne
Escambia County Cooperative Library System, Atmore
Harrison Regional Library, Columbiana
Jefferson County Library Cooperative, Birmingham
Lauderdale County Regional Library, Florence
Marengo Library System, Demopolis
Marshall County Cooperative Library, Guntersville
Pickens County Cooperative Library, Carrollton
Sumter County Library System, Livingston

Multi-County Systems (public libraries only):

Cheaha Regional Library, Heflin
Carl Elliott Regional Library, Jasper
Horseshoe Bend Regional Library, Dadeville
Northwest Regional Library, Winfield

ALASKA

Alaska has six public library systems, which operate multiple libraries either as a unit of borough government or as a consortium located within a single borough.

Anchorage Public Library, Anchorage
Bristol Bay Borough Libraries, Naknek
Fairbanks North Star Borough Public Library, Fairbanks
Juneau Public Library, Juneau
Mantanuska-Susitna Borough Libraries, Palmer
Tuzzy Consortium Library, Utqiagvik (formerly Barrow)

ARIZONA

The state of Arizona has fifteen county libraries of which eleven are Library Districts with secondary taxing authority.

Single-Type Library Districts:

Apache County Library District, Saint Johns
Cochise County Library District, Bisbee
Flagstaff City-Coconino County Public Library, Flagstaff
Gila County Library District, Globe
Maricopa County Library District, Phoenix
Mohave County Library District, Kingman
Navajo County Library District, Holbrook
Pinal County Library District, Florence
Pima County Public Library, Tucson
Yavapai County Free Library District, Prescott
Yuma County Library District, Yuma

Single-Type Library Co-ops:

Greenlee County Library System, Clifton
Nogales City-Santa Cruz County Library, Nogales
La Paz County Library Services, Parker
Safford City-Graham County Library, Safford

ARKANSAS

Public library service in Arkansas is provided through fifty-five library systems within five library development districts.

Library Development District I

Arkansas River Valley Regional Library, Dardanelle
Baxter County Library, Mountain Home
Bella Vista Public Library, Bella Vista
Bentonville Public Library, Bentonville
Boone County Library, Harrison
Carroll & Madison Library System, Berryville
Crawford County Library, Van Buren
Fayetteville Public Library, Fayetteville
Fort Smith Public Library, Fort Smith
Gentry Public Library, Gentry
Gravette Public Library, Gravette
Iva Jane Peek Public Library, Decatur
Marion County Library, Yellville
Newton County Library, Jasper
Pea Ridge Library, Pea Ridge
Pope County Library System, Russellville
Rogers Public Library, Rogers
Scott-Sebastian Regional Library, Greenwood
Searcy County Library, Marshall
Siloam Springs Public Library, Siloam Springs
Sulphur Springs Public Library, Sulphur Springs
Washington County Library, Fayetteville

Library Development District II

Ash Flat Library, Ash Flat
Crowley Ridge Regional Library, Jonesboro
East Central Arkansas Regional Library, Wynne
Forrest City Public Library, Forrest City
Independence County Library, Batesville
Jackson County Library, Newport
Lawrence County Library, Walnut Ridge
Mississippi-Crittenden County Library System, Blytheville
Northeast Arkansas Regional Library, Paragould
Trumann Public Library, Trumann
West Memphis Public Library, West Memphis
White River Regional Library, Mountain View
Woolfolk Library, Marion

Library Development District III

Central Arkansas Library System, Little Rock

Conway County Library, Morrilton
Fairfield Bay Library, Fairfield Bay
Faulkner-Van Buren Regional Library, Conway
Lonoke County Library, Lonoke
Mid-Arkansas Regional Library, Malvern
North Little Rock Public Library System, North Little Rock
Prairie County Library, Hazen
Saline County Public Library, Benton
White County Library System, Searcy

Library Development District IV

Calhoun County Library, Hampton
Clark County Library, Arkadelphia
Columbia County Library, Magnolia
Garland County Library, Hot Springs
Hempstead County Library, Hope
LaFayette County Library, Lewisville
Ouachita Mountains Regional Library System
Montgomery County Library, Mount Ida
Polk County Library, Mena
Public Library of Camden & Ouachita County, Camden
Southwest Arkansas Regional Library, Prescott
Texarkana Public Library, Texarkana
Tri-County Regional Library, Nashville
Union County Library, El Dorado

Library Development District V

Arkansas County Library, Stuttgart
Ashley County Library, Hamburg
Crossett Public Library, Crossett
Phillips-Lee-Monroe Regional Library, Helena
Public Library of Pine Bluff & Jefferson County, Pine Bluff
Southeast Arkansas Regional Library, Monticello

CALIFORNIA

The state of California has nine public library systems which provide resource sharing & interlibrary cooperation.

California Library Services Act (CLSA) Systems:

Black Gold Cooperative Library System; Arroyo Grande; six library jurisdictions
49-99 Cooperative Library System; Pasadena; six library jurisdictions
Inland Library System; Pasadena; 19 library jurisdictions
NorthNet Library System; San Mateo; 41 library jurisdictions
Pacific Library Partnership; San Mateo; 33 library jurisdictions
San Joaquin Valley Library System; Fresno; ten library jurisdictions
Santiago Library System; Pasadena; ten library jurisdictions
Serra Cooperative Library System, Pasadena; 13 library jurisdictions
Southern California Library Cooperative; Pasadena; 38 library jurisdictions

COLORADO

Colorado is a division of the state department of education and is charged with providing multi-type services for libraries throughout the state. Services to improve libraries and residents' access to materials are offered through technology-based programs, professional development, and direct consulting by staff. The Talking Book and State Publications Libraries meet walk-in needs.

CONNECTICUT (N)

Connecticut has the Connecticut Library Consortium, a statewide membership collaborative serving all types of Connecticut libraries.

DELAWARE

The state of Delaware has library governance at multiple levels, including: county, city, and independent libraries. Delaware Division of Libraries provides general direction to all Delaware public libraries including oversight of the networked integrated library system.

FLORIDA

Residents of the state of Florida have access to public library service through 40 countywide library systems, 8 multi-county regional library systems and 32 municipal libraries. There are also 5 multi-type library consortia that coordinate resource sharing and cooperative programming in 5 regions of the state.

Regional Public Libraries:

1) Heartland Library Cooperative, Sebring
2) New River Public Library Cooperative, Lake Butler
3) Northwest Regional Library System, Panama City
4) PAL Public Library Cooperative, Gainesville
5) Panhandle Public Library Cooperative System, Marianna
6) Suwannee River Regional Library, Live Oak
7) Three Rivers Regional Library System, Mayo
8) Wilderness Coast Public Libraries (WILD), Monticello

Countywide Public Libraries:

1) Brevard County Library System, Cocoa
2) Broward County Division of Libraries, Fort Lauderdale
3) Charlotte County Library System, Port Charlotte
4) Citrus County Library System, Beverly Hills
5) Clay County Public Library, Orange Park
6) Collier County Public Library, Naples
7) Columbia County Public Library, Lake City
8) Flagler County Public Library, Palm Coast
9) Gadsden County Public Library, Quincy
10) Hendry County Library System, Clewiston
11) Hernando County Library System, Brooksville
12) Hillsborough County Public Library Cooperative, Tampa
13) Indian River County Library, Vero Beach
14) Jacksonville Public Library System, Jacksonville
15) Lake County Public Library System, Tavares
16) Lee County Library System, Fort Myers
17) Leon County Public Library System, Tallahassee
18) Manatee County Public Library System, Bradenton
19) Marion County Public Library System, Ocala
20) Martin County Public Library, Stuart
21) Miami-Dade Public Library System, Miami
22) Monroe County Public Library, Key Largo
23) Nassau County Public Library, Fernandina Beach
24) Okaloosa County Public Library Cooperative, Niceville
25) Orange County Library District, Orlando
26) Osceola County Public Library System, Kissimmee
27) Palm Beach County Library System, West Palm Beach
28) Pasco County Library Cooperative, Hudson
29) Pinellas Public Library Cooperative Inc., Clearwater
30) Polk County Library Cooperative, Bartow
31) Saint Johns County Public Library, Saint Augustine
32) Saint Lucie County Library System, Fort Pierce
33) Santa Rosa County Library System, Milton
34) Sarasota County Library System, Sarasota
35) Seminole County Public Library System, Casselberry
36) Sumter County Library System, Wildwood
37) Volusia County Public Library System, Daytona Beach
38) Walton County Public Library System, DeFuniak Springs
39) Washington County Public Library, Chipley
40) West Florida Public Library System, Pensacola

Multi-type Library Cooperatives (MLCs):

Northeast Florida Library Information Network, Orange Park
Panhandle Library Access Network, Panama City Beach
Southeast Florida Library Information Network, Boca Raton
Southwest Florida Library Network, Fort Myers
Tampa Bay Library Consortium, Tampa

Municipal Libraries:

1) Altamonte Springs City Library, Altamonte Springs
2) Apalachicola Municipal Library, Apalachicola
3) Boca Raton Public Library, Boca Raton
4) Boynton Beach City Library, Boynton Beach
5) Brockway Memorial Library, Miami Shores
6) Citrus Springs Memorial Library, Citrus Springs
7) Delray Beach Public Library, Delray Beach
8) Eustis Memorial Library, Eustis
9) Flagler Beach Library, Flagler Beach
10) Fort Myers Beach Public Library, Fort Myers Beach
11) Doreen Gauthier Lighthouse Point Library, Lighthouse Point
12) Hialeah Public Libraries, Hialeah
13) Highland Beach Library, Highland Beach
14) Helen B Hoffman Plantation Library, Plantation
15) Indian Rocks Beach Library, Indian Rocks Beach
16) Lake Park Public Library, Lake Park
17) Lake Worth Public Library, Lake Worth
18) Lantana Public Library, Lantana
19) Lynn Haven Public Library, Lynn Haven
20) Maitland Public Library, Maitland
22) New Port Richey Public Library, New Port Richey
23) North Miami Beach Public Library, North Miami Beach
24) North Miami Public Library, North Miami
25) North Palm Beach Library, North Palm Beach
26) Oakland Park Library, Oakland Park
27) Palm Springs Public Library, Palm Springs
28) Parkland Library, Parkland
29) Riviera Beach Public Library, Rivera Beach

30) Sanibel Public Library District, Sanibel
32) West Palm Beach Public Library, West Palm Beach
33) Richard C Sullivan Public Library of Wilton Manors, Wilton Manors
34) Winter Park Public Library, Winter Park

GEORGIA

The state of Georgia has 34 Multi-county Regional Library Systems and 26 single County Library Systems. These systems provide comprehensive public library service to their service areas. All areas of the state are served by public libraries.

Multi-county Regional Systems:

Athens Regional Library System, Athens
Augusta-Richmond County Public Library System, Augusta
Azalea Regional Library System, Madison
Bartram Trail Regional Library System, Washington
Chattahoochee Valley Libraries, Columbus
Cherokee Regional Library System, LaFayette
Chestatee Regional Library System, Dawsonville
Coastal Plain Regional Library System, Tifton
De Soto Trail Regional Library System, Camilla
Flint River Regional Library, Griffin
Greater Clarks Hill Regional Library System, Evans
Sara Hightower Regional Library System, Rome
Kinchafoonee Regional Library System, Dawson
Lake Blackshear Regional Library System, Americus
Live Oak Public Libraries, Savannah
Middle Georgia Regional Library, Macon
Mountain Regional Library System, Young Harris
Northeast Georgia Regional Library System, Clarkesville
Northwest Georgia Regional Library System, Dalton
Ocmulgee Regional Libraries, Eastman
Oconee Regional Library System, Dublin
Ohoopee Regional Library System, Vidalia
Okefenokee Regional Library System, Waycross
Piedmont Regional Library System, Winder
Pine Mountain Regional Library System, Manchester
Satilla Regional Library System, Douglas
Screven-Jenkins Regional Library System, Sylvania
Sequoyah Regional Library System, Canton
South Georgia Regional Library, Valdosta
Southwest Georgia Regional Library, Bainbridge
Statesboro Regional Library System, Statesboro
Three Rivers Regional Library System, Brunswick
Troup-Harris Regional Library, La Grange
West Georgia Regional Library System, Carrollton

Single County Library Systems:

Bartow County Library System, Cartersville
Brooks County Public Library, Quitman
Catoosa County Library, Ringgold
Clayton County Library System, Jonesboro
Cobb County Public Library, Marietta
Conyers-Rockdale Library System, Conyers
Coweta Public Library System, Newnan
DeKalb County Public Library, Decatur
Dougherty County Public Library, Albany
Elbert County Public Library, Elberton
Forsyth County Public Library, Cumming
Fulton County Library System, Atlanta
Gwinnett County Public Library, Lawrenceville
Hall County Public Library, Gainesville
Hart County Library, Hartwell
Henry County Library System, McDonough
Houston County Public Library, Perry
Jefferson County Library System, Louisville
Lee County Library, Leesburg
Marshes of Glynn Libraries, Brunswick
Moultrie-Colquitt County Library System, Moultrie
Newton County Library System, Covington
Peach Public Libraries, Fort Valley
Roddenbery Memorial Library, Cairo
Thomas County Public Library System, Thomasville
Worth County Library, Sylvester

HAWAII

The state of Hawaii has one Public Library System, which administers free comprehensive statewide library resources and information services to the residents, government agencies, libraries and the library profession.

Library System:

Hawaii State Public Library System, Honolulu

IDAHO (N)

Definition: The Idaho Commission for Libraries defines a network as an electronic means of sharing resources among member libraries of a consortium. At a minimum, a network consists of a shared integrated library system that is web-accessible and allows multi-site searching both from within the network and remotely, and interlibrary loan service among all network members.

Library Networks:

Cooperative Information Network (CIN)
Inland Northwest Library Council (INCOL)
Library Consortium of Eastern Idaho (LCEI)
LIBRI Consortium (Libraries By A River)
LYNX! Consortium
Valley Library Network (VALNet)

Library Consortia:

Definition: The Idaho Commission for Libraries defines a consortium as a group of libraries that join together for one or more cooperative purposes. A consortium provides the infrastructure through which these services are delivered. A consortium has a mission, goals and objectives that are outlined in a long range or strategic planning document. It also has an organizational structure that includes governance, administration, staffing, and sustainable finding.
Idaho Digital Consortium (IDC)
Valley Mountain Library Consortium, VMLC

ILLINOIS

The state of Illinois has three regional library systems. Two multi-type library systems cover the state geographically with system membership held by public, academic, school and special libraries. The one public library system serves the city of Chicago. Each library system participates in SILC, the Statewide Illinois Library Catalog.

LIBRARY SYSTEMS

Chicago Public Library, Chicago
Illinois Heartland Library System, Edwardsville
Reaching Across Illinois Library System, Burr Ridge

INDIANA

The residents of the State of Indiana have access to 236 public library systems, through 34 city & town library systems, 31 partial county (half or more of the total townships) library systems, 24 countywide library systems, 143 township library systems and 4 endowed library systems.

Public Library Systems:

Adams Public Library System
Akron Carnegie Public Library
Alexandria-Monroe Public Library
Alexandrian Public Library
Allen County Public Library
Anderson Public Library
Andrews-Dallas Township Public Library
Argos Public Library
Attica Public Library
Aurora Public Library District
Avon-Washington Township Public Library
Bartholomew County Public Library
Barton Rees Pogue Memorial Public Library
Batesville Memorial Public Library
Bedford Public Library
Bell Memorial Public Library
Benton County Public Library
Berne Public Library
Bicknell-Vigo Township Public Library
Bloomfield-Eastern Greene County Public Library
Boonville-Warrick County Public Library
Boswell Grant Township Public Library
Bourbon Public Library
Brazil Public Library
Bremen Public Library
Bristol-Washington Township Public Library
Brook-Iroquois-Washington Township Public Library
Brookston-Prairie Township Public Library
Brown County Public Library
Brownsburg Public Library
Brownstown Public Library
Butler Carnegie Public Library
Cambridge City Public Library
Camden-Jackson Township Public Library

Carmel Clay Public Library
Carnegie Public Library of Steuben County
Centerville-Center Township Public Library
Charlestown Clark County Public Library
Churubusco Public Library
Clayton-Liberty Township Public Library
Clinton Public Library
Coatesville-Clay Township Public Library
Colfax-Perry Township Public Library
Converse-Jackson Township Public Library
Covington-Veedersburg Public Library
Crawford County Public Library
Crawfordsville District Public Library
Crown Point Community Public Library
Culver-Union Township Public Library
Danville-Center Township Public Library
Darlington Public Library
Delphi Public Library
Dublin Public Library
Dunkirk Public Library
Earl Park Public Library
East Chicago Public Library
Eckhart Public Library
Edinburgh Wright-Hageman Public Library
Elkhart Public Library
Evansville-Vanderburgh Public Library
Fairmount Public Library
Farmland Public Library
Fayette County Public Library
Flora-Monroe Public Library
Fort Branch-Johnson Township Public Library
Fortville-Vernon Township Public Library
Francesville-Salem Township Public Library
Frankfort-Clinton County Contractual Public Library
Franklin County Public Library District
Fremont Public Library
Fulton County Public Library
Garrett Public Library
Gary Public Library
Gas City-Mill Township Public Library
Goodland & Grant Township Public Library
Goshen Public Library
Greensburg Decatur County Contractual Public Library
Greentown & Eastern Howard School Public Library
Greenwood Public Library
Hagerstown-Jefferson Township Public Library
Hamilton East Public Library
Hamilton North Public Library
Hammond Public Library
Hancock County Public Library
Harrison County Public Library
Hartford City Public Library
Henry Henley Public Library
Huntingburg Public Library
Huntington City-Township Public Library
Hussey-Mayfield Memorial Public Library
Indianapolis-Marion County Public Library
Jackson County Public Library
Jasonville Public Library
Jasper County Public Library
Jasper-Dubois County Contractual Public Library
Jay County Public Library
Jefferson County Public Library
Jeffersonville Township Public Library
Jennings County Public Library
Johnson County Public Library
Jonesboro Public Library
Joyce Public Library
Kendallville Public Library
Kentland-Jefferson Township Public Library
Kewanna-Union Township Public Library
Kingman-Millcreek Public Library
Kirklin Public Library
Knightstown Public Library
Knox County Public Library
Kokomo-Howard County Public Library
La Crosse Public Library
La Grange Public Library
La Porte County Public Library
Ladoga-Clark Township Public Library
Lake County Public Library
Lawrenceburg Public Library
Lebanon Public Library
Ligonier Public Library
Lincoln Heritage Public Library
Linden Carnegie Public Library
Linton Public Library
Logansport-Cass County Public Library
Loogootee Public Library
Lowell Public Library
Marion Public Library
Matthews Public Library
Melton Public Library
Michigan City Public Library
Middlebury Community Public Library
Middletown Fall Creek Township Public Library
Milford Public Library
Mishawaka-Penn-Harris Public Library
Mitchell Community Public Library
Monon Town and Township Public Library
Monroe County Public Library
Monterey-Tippecanoe Township Public Library
Montezuma Public Library
Monticello-Union Township Public Library
Montpelier-Harrison Township Public Library
Mooresville Public Library
Morgan County Public Library
Morrisson Reeves Library
Muncie-Center Township Public Library
Nappanee Public Library
New Albany-Floyd County Public Library
New Carlisle & Olive Township Public Library
New Castle-Henry County Public Library
New Harmony Workingmen's Institute
Newburgh Chandler Public Library
Newton County Public Library
Noble County Public Library
North Judson-Wayne Township Public Library
North Madison County Public Library System
North Manchester Public Library
North Webster Community Public Library
Oakland City-Columbia Township Public Library
Odon Winkelpleck Public Library
Ohio County Public Library
Orleans Town & Township Public Library
Osgood Public Library
Otterbein Public Library
Owen County Public Library
Owensville Carnegie Public Library
Oxford Public Library
Paoli Public Library
Parke County Public Library
Peabody Public Library
Pendleton Community Public Library
Penn Township Public Library
Perry County Public Library
Peru Public Library
Pierceton & Washington Township Public Library
Pike County Public Library
Plainfield-Guilford Township Public Library
Plymouth Public Library
Porter County Public Library System
Poseyville Carnegie Public Library
Princeton Public Library
Pulaski County Public Library
Putnam County Public Library
Remington-Carpenter Township Public Library
Ridgeville Public Library
Roachdale-Franklin Township Public Library
Roann Paw-Paw Township Public Library
Roanoke Public Library
Royal Center-Boone Township Public Library
Rushville Public Library
Salem-Washington Township Public Library
Scott County Public Library
Shelby County Public Library
Sheridan Public Library
Shoals Public Library
South Whitley-Cleveland Township Public Library
Speedway Public Library
Spencer County Public Library
Spiceland Town Township Public Library
St Joseph County Public Library
Starke County Public Library System
Sullivan County Public Library
Swayzee Public Library
Switzerland County Public Library
Syracuse-Turkey Creek Township Public Library
Thorntown Public Library
Tippecanoe County Public Library

Tipton County Public Library
Tyson Library Association, Inc
Union City Public Library
Union County Public Library
Van Buren Public Library
Vermillion County Public Library
Vigo County Public Library
Wabash Carnegie Public Library
Wakarusa-Olive & Harrison Township Public Library
Walkerton-Lincoln Township Public Library
Walton & Tipton Township Public Library
Wanatah Public Library
Warren Public Library
Warsaw Community Public Library
Washington Carnegie Public Library
Washington Township Public Library
Waterloo Grant Township Public Library
Waveland-Brown Township Public Library
Wells County Public Library
West Lafayette Public Library
West Lebanon-Pike Township Public Library
Westchester Public Library
Westfield Washington Public Library
Westville-New Durham Township Public Library
Whiting Public Library
Willard Library of Evansville
Williamsport -Washington Township Public Library
Winchester Community Public Library
Wolcott Community Public Library
Worthington Jefferson Township Public Library
York Township Public Library
Yorktown-Mount Pleasant Township Public Library

IOWA

Iowa no longer has Regional Library Service Areas.

KANSAS

In 1965, Kansas Statutes K.S.A. 75-2547 and 75-2548 established seven regional systems to help local libraries provide library services to all citizens of the state. Through the use of joint planning and financing of library services, the systems improve existing library service and utilize what federal funding becomes available.

Originally the systems only served public libraries, but over time their roles have expanded to include school, academic and special libraries. Each system adapts its service to the needs of the libraries it serves, therefore there are services offered in one area that are not offered in another, however, they come together to work with the State Library to develop goals and determine plans for improving library service throughout the state.

Library Systems:

Central Kansas Library System, Great Bend
North Central Kansas Library System, Manhattan
Northeast Kansas Library System, Lawrence
Northwest Kansas Library System, Norton
South Central Kansas Library System, Hutchinson
Southeast Kansas Library System, Iola
Southwest Kansas Library System, Dodge City

KENTUCKY

Kentucky has Regional Library Consultants headquartered in five Regions who develop, extend and improve library service and provide information to the citizens of the Commonwealth.

LOUISIANA

In the 64 parishes, there are 68 public libraries. Sixty-one of these are parish-wide; one is a two-parish consolidated unit; three are municipal libraries in a parish without parish-wide service; one is a district library serving three towns and their outlying areas in a parish without parish-wide service; the other two are independent city libraries in parishes with parish-wide service.

MAINE

The state of Maine has one Regional Library System. The Maine Regional Library System was created to improve library service for the citizens of Maine. Membership consists of public, school, academic, & special libraries.

Library System:

The Maine Regional Library System is administered by the Maine State Library in Augusta.

Library Districts:

Recently, the Maine Library Commission created one statewide district with nine regions. The Library Development Division holds regional meetings throughout the course of the year instead of three annual meetings in three locations. This change was made to improve service delivery to all libraries given their geographic distribution. Consulting services will be delivered through statewide subject specialists. Each public library will have a designated MSL staff liaison to contact. This liaison will direct the library to the appropriate specialist for their question or need.

MARYLAND

The state of Maryland has one library System in each County and Baltimore City, for a total of 24 Library Systems. Additionally, Maryland's three Regional Libraries, by providing leadership in cooperative resource sharing, training, and technical assistance in non-metropolitan areas, plays a pivotal role in the delivery of information to Maryland residents, while the State Library Resource Center provides access to specialized materials and services in its reference and research collections. They are a vital part of the Maryland library network, a network recognized nationally for its excellence and innovation.

Library Systems:

Eastern Shore Regional Library, Salisbury
Pratt Free Library System-Baltimore
Southern Maryland Regional Library Association, Charlotte Hall
State Library Resource Center/Central Library of the Enoch Pratt Free Library, Baltimore
Western Maryland Public Libraries, Hagerstown

MASSACHUSETTS

The state of Massachusetts has one library system that provides services to 1,568 Massachusetts libraries throughout the Commonwealth.

Massachusetts Library System, Marlborough/Northampton

MICHIGAN (N)

With state funds authorized by Public Act 89 of 1977, Michigan has 11 Library Cooperatives. A Library Cooperative is the library or service center designated by the cooperative board to provide services as specified by the cooperative plan and provided to public libraries participating in the cooperative. Michigan in addition has one multi-type region of cooperation based on the cooperatives.

Cooperative Libraries:

Detroit Library Cooperative, Detroit
Lakeland Library Cooperative, Grand Rapids
Mideastern Michigan Library Cooperative, Flint
Mid-Michigan Library League, Cadillac
Northland Library Cooperative, Lapeer
Southwest Michigan Library Cooperative, Paw Paw
Superiorland Library Cooperative, Marquette
Suburban Library League, Sterling Heights
The Library Network, Novi
White Pine Library Cooperative, Saginaw
Woodlands Library Cooperative, Albion

Multi-Type Regions of Cooperation: (N)

Upper Peninsula Region of Library Cooperation, Marquette

MINNESOTA

The state of Minnesota has six federated regional public library systems and six consolidated regional public library systems. In a manner appropriate to their organizational structures, they support or provide minimum levels of library service to residents of the areas they serve. In addition, seven multi-county, multi-type library systems coordinate cooperative programs among academic, public, school, and special libraries - of which two are combined with a regional public library system.

Federated Public Library Systems:

Arrowhead Library System, Mountain Iron
Metropolitan Library Service Agency, Saint Paul
Plum Creek Library System, Worthington
Southeastern Libraries Cooperating, Rochester
Traverse des Sioux Library Cooperative, Mankato
Viking Library System, Fergus Falls

Consolidated Public Library Systems:

East Central Regional Library, Cambridge
Great River Regional Library, Saint Cloud
Kitchigami Regional Library, Pine River

Lake Agassiz Regional Library, Moorhead
Northwest Regional Library, Thief River Falls
Pioneerland Library System, Willmar

Multicounty, Multi-type Library Systems:

Arrowhead Library System, Mountain Iron
Central Minnesota Library Exchange, Saint Cloud
Metronet, Saint Paul
Northern Lights Library Network, Moorhead
Traverse des Sioux Library Cooperative, Mankato
Southeast Library System, Rochester
Prairielands Library Exchange, Marshall

MISSISSIPPI

The state of Mississippi has sixteen Regional Systems. In addition, there are thirty-five County or City-County Libraries in Mississippi. There are also two independent public libraries in the state.

Regional Libraries:

Central Mississippi Regional Library, Brandon
Copiah-Jefferson Regional Library, Hazlehurst
Dixie Regional Library, Pontotoc
East Mississippi Regional Library, Quitman
First Regional Library, Hernando
Jackson-George Regional Library, Pascagoula
Kemper-Newton Regional Library, Union
Lee-Itawamba Library System, Tupelo
Lincoln-Lawrence-Franklin Regional Library, Brookhaven
Mid-Mississippi Regional Library System, Kosciusko
Northeast Regional Library, Corinth
Pike-Amite-Walthall Library System, McComb
Pine Forest Regional Library, Richton
Sharkey-Issaquena County Library System, Rolling Fork
South Mississippi Regional Library, Columbia
Tombigbee Regional Library, West Point

MISSOURI

Interlibrary loan for public libraries in the state is done through an OCLC statewide license paid for by the Missouri State Library.

A statewide courier service supports materials delivery for public libraries.
A statewide, shared integrated library system to improve discovery and sharing of library resources is provided through a contract to serve as a low-cost alternative to systems owned and managed individually.
A statewide system for Internet access is partially supported for public libraries through an appropriation to the Missouri State Library.

MONTANA

The state of Montana has six Library Federations, which incorporate all city, county and district public libraries. Member libraries gain strength from a larger unit without losing individual control.

Library Federations:

Broad Valleys Federation, Bozeman Public Library, Bozeman
Golden Plains Federation, Sheridan County Library, Plentywood
Pathfinder Federation, Blaine County Library, Chinook
Sagebrush Federation, Miles City Public Library, Miles City
South Central Federation, Laurel Public Library, Laurel
Tamarack Federation, North Lake County Library, Polson

NEBRASKA

The state of Nebraska has four regional multi-type Library Systems that provide services to libraries within multi-county areas. The library systems provide continuing education and training, and other services for the benefit of library staff and library users.

Systems:

Central Plains Library System
Southeast Library System
Three Rivers Library System
Western Library System

NEVADA

The state of Nevada has eleven automated library networks, each of which provides interlibrary loan and resource sharing. Seven are based in public libraries, one is a regional network of central and northern Nevada public libraries, one is a community college, and two are housed at universities. The eleven networks communicate via a digital system for statewide resource sharing.

Automated Library Networks:

Amargosa Valley Library District
Douglas County Public Library
Henderson District Public Libraries
Nevada Library Cooperative (CoOp) Headquarters, Nevada State Library and Archives
Pahrump Community Library District
Smoky Valley Library District
Southern Network, Headquarters, Las Vegas/Clark County Library District
Truckee Meadows Community College
University of Nevada, Las Vegas
University of Nevada, Reno Library
Washoe County Library

NEW HAMPSHIRE

The New Hampshire State Library maintains an online statewide union catalog. 474 multi-type member libraries share access to the web-based system to contribute their holdings and to borrow Interlibrary Loan materials.

Multi-Type Library System:

New Hampshire Automated Information System

NEW JERSEY

The state of New Jersey has one Library Cooperative and two Statewide Services Contract Libraries which facilitate interlibrary reference and loan. The Library Cooperative, through contracts and partnerships with local libraries, provide direct access to expanded resources and services, such as material delivery, shares specialized service and staff skills and develops a coordinated plan of library services to serve patron needs. Membership is voluntary and multi-type (academic, institutional, public, school and special libraries). The cooperative is funded by The New Jersey State Library.

NEW MEXICO

The state of New Mexico has no library system.

NEW YORK

The state of New York supports twenty-three Public Library Systems, nine Reference and Research Library Resources Systems, and forty School Library Systems, which in partnership with the New York State Library support some 7,000 local public, academic, school, and special libraries in meeting the needs of their primary users through a wide range of collaborative services and resource sharing programs. BOCES are 'Boards of Cooperative Educational Services'.

Public Library Systems:

Brooklyn Public Library, Brooklyn
Buffalo & Erie County Public Library, Buffalo
Chautauqua-Cattaraugus Library System, Jamestown
Clinton-Essex-Franklin Library System, Plattsburgh
Finger Lakes Library System, Ithaca
Four County Library System, Vestal
Mid-Hudson Library System, Poughkeepsie
Mid York Library System, Utica
Mohawk Valley Library System, Schenectady
Monroe County Library System, Rochester
Nassau Library System, Uniondale
Nioga Library System, Lockport
North County Library System, Watertown
Onondaga County Public Library, Syracuse
OWWL Library System, Canandaigua
Queens Borough Public Library, Jamaica
Ramapo Catskill Library System, Middletown
Southern Adirondack Library System, Saratoga Springs
Southern Tier Library System, Painted Post
Suffolk Cooperative Library System, Bellport
The New York Public Library, New York
Upper Hudson Library System, Albany
Westchester Library System, Ardsley

Reference and Research Library Resources Systems:

Capital District Library Council, Albany
Central New York Library Resources Council, Syracuse
Long Island Library Resources Council Inc, Bellport
Metropolitan New York Library Council (METRO), New York
Northern New York Library Network, Potsdam
Rochester Regional Library Council, Fairport
South Central Regional Library Council, Ithaca
Southeastern New York Library Resources Council, Highland
Western New York Library Resources Council, Buffalo

School Library Systems:

Albany-Schoharie-Schenectady-Saratoga BOCES School Library System
Broome-Delaware-Tioga BOCES School Library System
Buffalo City School Library System
Cattaraugus-Allegany-Erie-Wyoming BOCES School Library System
Cayuga-Onondaga BOCES School Library System
Clinton-Essex-Warren-Washington BOCES School Library System
Delaware-Chenango-Madison-Otsego BOCES School Library System
Dutchess BOCES School Library System
Eastern Suffolk, (Suffolk 1) BOCES School Library System
Erie 1 BOCES School Library System
Erie 2-Chautauqua-Cattaraugus BOCES School Library System
Franklin-Essex-Hamilton BOCES School Library System
Genesee-Livingston-Steuben-Wyoming (Genesee Valley) BOCES School Library System
Hamilton-Fulton-Montgomery BOCES School Library System
Jefferson-Lewis BOCES School Library System
Madison-Oneida BOCES School Library System
Monroe 1-BOCES School Library System
Monroe 2-Orleans BOCES School Library System
Nassau School Library System
New York City School Library System
Oneida-Herkimer-Madison BOCES School Library System
Onondaga-Cortland-Madison BOCES School Library System
Ontario-Seneca-Yates-Cayuga-Wayne (Wayne-Finger Lakes) BOCES School Library System
Orange-Ulster BOCES School Library System
Orleans-Niagara BOCES School Library System
Otsego-Delaware-Schoharie-Greene (Otsego Northern Catskills) BOCES School Library System
Putnam Westchester BOCES School Library System
Rensselaer-Columbia-Greene (Questar III) BOCES School Library System
Rochester City School Library System
Rockland BOCES School Library System
St Lawrence-Lewis BOCES School Library System
Schuyler-Steuben-Chemung-Tioga-Allegany BOCES School Library System
Sullivan BOCES School Library System
Syracuse City School Library System
Tompkins-Seneca-Tioga BOCES School Library System
Ulster BOCES School Library System
Washington-Saratoga-Warren-Hamilton-Essex BOCES School Library System
Westchester (Southern Westchester or Westchester 2) BOCES School Library System
Western Suffolk, (Suffolk 2) BOCES School Library System
Yonkers City School Library System

NORTH CAROLINA

North Carolina public libraries are organized into twelve regional (multi-county) systems, 59 single-county systems and eleven independent municipal public libraries. These systems have a total of 393 service outlets.

NORTH DAKOTA

North Dakota has a statewide online library catalog.

OHIO

The state of Ohio has four chartered regional library systems which develop services and resources within a region to meet the needs of the users.

Chartered Regional Library Systems:

Northeast Ohio Regional Library System (NEO-RLS), Hudson
Northwest Regional Library System, (NORWELD), Bowling Green
Southeast Regional Library System (SERLS), Wellston
Southwest Ohio and Neighboring Libraries (SWON), Blue Ash

OKLAHOMA

The state of Oklahoma has eight Library Systems: six Multi-County; one County; and one City-County System. The Multi-County Systems provide public library service in two or more counties under a consolidated administration and governance, with a stable financial base.

Library Systems:

Eastern Oklahoma District Library System, Muskogee
Metropolitan Library System, Oklahoma City
Pioneer Library System, Norman
Southeastern Public Library System of Oklahoma, McAlester
Southern Oklahoma Library System, Ardmore
Southern Prairie Library System, Altus
Tulsa City-County Library, Tulsa
Western Plains Library System, Clinton

OREGON (N)

The state of Oregon has seven cooperative library systems, which derive their operating income exclusively from local tax sources. These systems provide a variety of services including, in some cases, cooperative automation, outreach services, interlibrary loan, courier service, books-by-mail, bookmobile, and reference back-up.

Cooperative Library Systems:

Chemeketa Cooperative Regional Library Service, Salem
Coos County Library Service District, Coos Bay
Libraries of Clackamas County, Oregon City
Lincoln County Library District, Newport
Umatilla County Special Library District, Pendleton
Wasco County Library Service District, The Dalles
Washington County Cooperative Library Services, Hillsboro

PENNSYLVANIA

The state of Pennsylvania has thirty-three Public Library Systems. The systems are federations of independent libraries which have joined together to serve a county or township. They provide interlibrary loan and, in some cases, centralized ordering and processing. The chief benefit is that residents of the county or township have free use of any library in the system.

Library Systems:

Adams County Library System, Gettysburg
Allegheny County Library Association, Pittsburgh
Beaver County Library System, Aliquippa
Bedford County Federated Library System, Bedford
Berks County Library System, Reading
Blair County Library System, Altoona
Bradford County Library System, Troy
Bucks County Free Library, Doylestown
Butler County Library System, Butler
Cambria County Library System, Johnstown
Centre County Federation of Public Libraries, State College
Chester County Library System, Exton
Clarion County Library System, Clarion
Crawford County Federated Library System, Meadville
Cumberland County Library System, Carlisle
Delaware County Library System, Media
Franklin County Library System, Chambersburg
Greene County Library System, Jefferson
Jefferson County Library System, Brockway
Lackawanna County Library System, Scranton
Lawrence County Federated Library System, New Castle
Lebanon County Library System, Lebanon
Library System of Lancaster County, Lancaster
Luzerne County Library System, Wilkes-Barre
Lycoming County Library System, Williamsport
Potter-Tioga County Library System, Coudersport
Schuylkill County Library System, Pottsville
Somerset County Federated Library System, Somerset
Union County Library System, Lewisburg
Washington County Library System, Washington
Wayne Library Authority, Honesdale
Westmoreland County Federated Library System, Greensburg
York County Library System, York

RHODE ISLAND (N)

The Library of Rhode Island (LORI) is the statewide library network consisting of the collected resources and services available from Rhode Island libraries. The network is coordinated and administered by the Office of Library and Information Services (OLIS) which annually certifies member libraries.

State of Rhode Island general law § 29-6-9, Rhode Island library network, established LORI in 1989, as a multi-type network to promote resource sharing and interlibrary cooperation. Approximately 177 library facilities belong to LORI, including public, academic, special and school libraries. Libraries annually certify that they comply with network regulations to receive: physical interlibrary delivery, interlibrary loan, FirstSearch and Clearinghouse services, and e-rate application support.

The LORI Standards and Regulations are online at: https://rules.SOS.ri.gov/regulations/part/220-60-15-3.

SOUTH CAROLINA

The state of South Carolina has 42 Public Library Systems. Each system provides services to an entire county or to a region composed of several counties, thus serving the entire state.

SOUTH DAKOTA (N)

The South Dakota Share-It system provides resource sharing, discovery & provision for in and out-of-state InterLibrary loan services. South Dakota Share-It is a federated overlay network of some 93 academic, special, public and school libraries administered by the South Dakota State Library.

TENNESSEE

The state of Tennessee has 9 multi-county regional library systems, which provide support services to public libraries in 91 counties.

Multi-County Library Systems:
Buffalo River Regional Library, Columbia
Clinch River Regional Library, Clinton
Falling Water River Regional Library, Cookeville
Hatchie River Regional Library, Jackson
Holston River Regional Library, Johnson City
Obion River Regional Library, Martin
Ocoee River Regional Library, Athens
Red River Regional Library, Clarksville
Stones River Regional Library, Murfreesboro

The state also has 4 single-county library systems that provide direct library services to residents of those counties.

Single-County Library Systems:
Chattanooga Public Library, Chattanooga
Knox County Public Library System, Knoxville
Memphis Public Libraries, Memphis
Nashville Public Library, Nashville

Other Library Systems with Multiple Branches:
Collegedale Public Library, Collegedale
East Ridge City Library, East Ridge
Germantown Community Library, Germantown
Grand Junction Public Library, Grand Junction
La Vergne Public Library, La Vergne
Lucius E & Elsie C Burch, Jr Library, Collierville
Millington Public Library, Millington
Oak Ridge Public Library, Oak Ridge
Sam T Wilson Public Library, Arlington
Signal Mountain Library, Town of Signal Mountain

TEXAS

Texas has no state-funded systems.

UTAH

In the State of Utah, public libraries are established by state statute under the jurisdiction of a city or a county government. There are 60 certified city public library systems and 12 from counties, as well as 7 Native American tribal libraries. In addition, the State Library provides mobile library services to 11 counties with seven bookmobiles equipped with computers and wireless Internet access serving rural and remote areas of the State. The State Library manages the state's digital library of government publications.

As a division of the Department of Cultural and Community Engagement, the State Library is also established under state statute to oversee the development of libraries across the state, and has adopted a vision to be the primary leadership resource for librarians, while providing equal access to information and enduring services for citizens. The State Library provides funding, training, professional advice, and technical assistance to library directors, staff, and trustees throughout Utah.

Through Utah's Online Public Library, the State Library offers all residents of the state access to a broad range of full-text premium databases featuring unique business resources, tools for research and homework, career information, genealogy research, and downloadable media. Additionally, the State Library assists residents of all ages who are blind, visually impaired, physically or print-disabled by providing digital books, books in large print and one of the largest collections of books in Braille in the world.

VERMONT

The state of Vermont has no library systems.

VIRGINIA

The state of Virginia has no library systems.

WASHINGTON

Washington State has twenty-seven public library districts serving an aggregate population of 5,921,635 across thirty-six of the state's thirty-nine counties. Another 1,830,375 people are served by thirty-three municipal libraries. At least one public library (either municipal, county or multi-county library) exists in every county in Washington State, serving at least a portion of the total population of that county.

WEST VIRGINIA

The state of West Virginia has thirteen service center libraries.

Service Center Libraries:
Cabell County Public Library, Huntington
Craft Memorial Library, Bluefield
Greenbrier County Public Library, Lewisburg
Kanawha County Public Library, Charleston
Keyser-Mineral County Public Library, Keyser
Martinsburg-Berkeley County Public Library, Martinsburg
Mary H Weir Public Library, Weirton
Morgantown Public Library, Morgantown
Moundsville-Marshall County Public Library, Moundsville
Parkersburg & Wood County Public Library, Parkersburg
Raleigh County Public Library, Beckley
South Charleston Public Library, South Charleston
Upshur County Public Library, Buckhannon

WISCONSIN

The state of Wisconsin has seventeen Public Library Systems which provide an organizational and service structure to make the most efficient use of library resources through cooperative arrangements among system members. The following are county and multi-county organizations.

Public Library Systems:
Arrowhead Library System, Milton
Bridges Library System, Waukesha
Indianhead Federated Library System (IFLS), Eau Claire
Kenosha County Library System, Kenosha
Lakeshores Library System, Waterford
Manitowoc-Calumet Library System, Manitowoc
Monarch Library System, Sheboygan
Milwaukee County Federated Library System, Milwaukee
Nicolet Federated Library System, Green Bay
Northern Waters Library Service, Ashland
Outagamie Waupaca Library System, Appleton
South Central Library System, Madison
Southwest Wisconsin Library System, Fennimore
Winding Rivers Library System, West Salem
Winnefox Library System, Oshkosh
Wisconsin Valley Library Service, Wausau

WYOMING

Each of the twenty-three counties in the state of Wyoming forms a Library System.

CANADA

ALBERTA

Alberta has seven Regional Library Systems serving 212 library boards, 307 municipalities, and 271 library service points. There are 322 total library service points across Alberta.

Library Systems:
Chinook Arch Regional Library System, Lethbridge
Marigold Library System, Strathmore
Northern Lights Library System, Elk Point
Parkland Regional Library, Lacombe
Peace Library System, Grande Prairie
Shortgrass Library System, Medicine Hat
Yellowhead Regional Library, Spruce Grove

Municipalities:

There are 351 municipalities in Alberta, including Metis Settlements, Improvement Districts and Special Areas. 317 municipalities provide access to municipal library service. The remaining 34 municipalities do not provide any level of public library service (many of these are Summer Villages).

BRITISH COLUMBIA

British Columbia has six Library Federations, two Integrated Public Library Systems, three Regional Library Districts, 30 Municipal Public Libraries & 36 Public Library Associations serving the province.

Library Federations:

InterLINK, Burnaby
IslandLink Library Federation, Victoria
Kootenay Library Federation, Castlegar
North Central Library Federation, Victoria
Northwest Library Federation, New Westminster
North East Library Federation, Victoria

Regional Library Districts:

Fraser Valley Regional Library, Abbotsford
Okanagan Regional Library District, Kelowna
Vancouver Island Regional Library, Nanaimo

Integrated Public Library Systems:

Cariboo Regional District Library System, Williams Lake
Thompson-Nicola Regional District Library System, Kamloops

MANITOBA

Manitoba has 110 public library service outlets organized under 60 municipal and regional public library systems. Additional "Community Collections" have been facilitated by the Public Library Services Branch to remote northern communities.

NEW BRUNSWICK

In New Brunswick, public library services are offered through a partnership between the provincial government and participating municipalities. New Brunswick Public Library Service (NBPLS) is the agency responsible for the management and development of public library services in the province. NBPLS has been part of the New Brunswick Department of Post-Secondary Education Training & Labour since February 14, 2006. NBPLS is made up of one provincial office, five regional offices, 52 public libraries, and eleven public-school libraries.

Provincial Office:

New Brunswick Public Library Service, Fredericton

Regional Offices:

Albert-Westmorland-Kent Library Region, Moncton
Chaleur Library Region, Campbellton
Fundy Library Region, Saint John
Haut-Saint-Jean Library Region, Edmundston
York Library Region, Fredericton

NEWFOUNDLAND & LABRADOR

The Provincial Information and Library Resources Board of Newfoundland and Labrador is responsible for public library services throughout the province. The Board operates 95 public libraries offering a range of services including: printed materials, DVDs, CDs, e-content, public access computers with free Internet access, Wi-Fi and a variety of library programs. Communities without public libraries are served through books-by-mail. The libraries are organized into four geographic divisions: Provincial Resource, Eastern, Central and West Newfoundland/Labrador. There are also three divisions located at the provincial headquarters, which have provincial responsibilities: Administration, Technical Services and Information Management. The Board's website is: www.nlpl.ca.

NORTHWEST TERRITORIES

There are 20 public libraries in the Northwest Territories, all community run and supported by Public Library Services, a government unit located in Hay River, NT, Canada.

NOVA SCOTIA

Public library service in Nova Scotia is provided by nine Regional Libraries serving 50 municipalities through 83 service points.

Regional Libraries:

Annapolis Valley Regional Library, Berwick
Cape Breton Regional Library, Sydney
Colchester - East Hants Public Library, Truro
Cumberland Public Libraries, Amherst
Eastern Counties Regional Library, Mulgrave
Halifax Public Libraries, Dartmouth
Pictou - Antigonish Regional Library, New Glasgow
South Shore Public Libraries, Bridgewater
Western Counties Regional Library, Yarmouth

NUNAVUT

The Nunavut Public Library Service has eleven community branches serving 70% of Nunavut's population. Programs and collections are offered in the Inuit languages, English, and French.

ONTARIO

Ontario's Public Libraries Act, administered by the Ministry of Tourism, Culture and Gaming, sets out a model of public library board governance for Ontario public libraries. Public library boards are appointed by municipal councils and have a four-year term concurrent with council.

Ontario's public library system includes public library boards, First Nation public libraries, Local Services Board public libraries, as well as municipalities, Local Services Boards and First Nation bands that contract for public library services with neighboring public libraries.

In 2023, Ontario had 261 public library boards and 34 First Nation Public Libraries. The public was served through 1327 public library service points with 8,332 public computer workstations with Internet access. 7,099 Full Time Equivalent staff included 1,590 librarians, 842 library technicians and 800 other professional staff.

The public visited Ontario public libraries 54,391,800 times in person, with 96,030,480 visits to library websites. Ontario public libraries offered 284,450 programs with 5,008,099 attendees. Library staff answered 4,395,600 reference inquiries (in person and electronic).

Programs included 239,526 early literacy and learning programs with 4,574,268 attendees, 10,608 class instruction at a library or school sessions with 305,348 attendees and 5,943 Newcomer focus programs with 75,177 attendees. Ontario public libraries reported 672 education sector partnerships, 818 cultural partnerships, 864 social media initiatives, 920 consortia initiatives, and 133 business partnerships.

PRINCE EDWARD ISLAND

The Prince Edward Island Public Library Service is responsible for the administration and operation of Prince Edward Island's province-wide public library system. Public library service on Prince Edward Island is a partnership between the provincial government - which supplies materials, staff, and administration - and participating communities, which provide and maintain library facilities.

QUEBEC

In 2019 Quebec had eleven Centres regionaux de services aux bibliotheques publiques (CRSBP), also called Reseaux BIBLIO, which promote library services in municipalities with populations under 5,000. 684 public libraries are served by CRSBP. 173 public libraries promote library service in municipalities with population over 5,000. Bibliothèque et Archives Nationales du Québec (BAnQ), a national institution, has as part of its mission to assemble, preserve permanently and disseminate Quebec's published documentary heritage together with any related document of cultural interest, and documents relating to Quebec that are published outside Quebec. It carries out its activities in 12 facilities which are open to the public across Quebec.

Bibliothèque et Archives Nationales du Québec (BAnQ), a national institution, has as part of its mission to assemble, preserve permanently and disseminate Quebec's published documentary heritage together with any related document of cultural interest, and documents relating to Quebec that are published outside Quebec. It carries out its activities in 12 facilities which are open to the public across Quebec.

SASKATCHEWAN

Saskatchewan has seven regional library systems, three municipal library systems, and a northern federation of educational and public libraries, which deliver public library services. All library systems in Saskatchewan cooperate with each other in extensive resource sharing to foster a one-province library system, which provides service to all residents. The Provincial Library and Literacy Office, in cooperation with all types of libraries, develops and coordinates library services throughout the province.

Regional Library Systems:

Chinook Regional Library, Swift Current
Lakeland Library Region, North Battleford
Palliser Regional Library, Moose Jaw
Parkland Regional Library, Yorkton
Southeast Regional Library, Weyburn
Wapiti Regional Library, Prince Albert
Wheatland Regional Library, Saskatoon

Municipal Library Systems:
The City of Prince Albert Public Library Board, Prince Albert
Regina Public Library, Regina
Saskatoon Public Library, Saskatoon

Federated System:
Pahkisimon Nuye Ah Library System, Air Ronge

Provincial Library and Literacy office

YUKON

Public Libraries Branch of the Community Development Division of the Department of Community Services provides public library service in Yukon through a distributed network with a central library in Whitehorse and fourteen community libraries. Public libraries provides centralized administrative and consultative services, an online catalogue of the holdings of public libraries plus the Yukon Archives Library, the cataloguing, processing and distribution of materials, programming and promotion, reference services and a Yukon-wide ILL network.

LIBRARIES FOR THE BLIND AND PHYSICALLY HANDICAPPED

Through designated regional and sub-regional libraries, the National Library Service for the Blind and Physically Handicapped (NLS), part of The Library of Congress, provides free library service to print-handicapped individuals. This index serves as a guide for locating those libraries, which provide recordings and Braille materials for their patrons.

Each regional library has an individual entry in the Library Section of this directory. Each sub-regional library has a sub-entry under the library of which it is a part. For statistics on NLS (Karen Keninger, Director), see the Library of Congress entry.

Also included are other libraries, U.S. and Canadian, with significant assets (equipment & services) dedicated to the blind and handicapped.

For Canada, this index lists the headquarters of the Canadian National Institute for the Blind (John M. Rafferty, President and CEO).

ALABAMA

Regional

Alabama Public Library Service, Regional Library for the Blind & Physically Disabled, Montgomery

Subregional

Alabama Institute for the Deaf & Blind, Library & Resource Center for the Blind & Print Disabled, Talladega
Huntsville-Madison County Public Library, Subregional Library for the Blind & Physically Handicapped, Huntsville

Other

Daphne Public Library, Daphne

ALASKA

Regional

Alaska State Library, Talking Book Center, Juneau

Other

Special Education Service Agency Library, Anchorage

ARIZONA

Regional

Arizona Talking Book Library, Phoenix

Other

Arizona State Schools for the Deaf & the Blind Library, Tucson Campus, Tucson
Foundation for Blind Children Library & Media Center, Arizona Instructional Resource Center, Phoenix

ARKANSAS

Regional

Arkansas State Library for the Blind & Print Disabled, Little Rock

Other

Boone County Library, Harrison

CALIFORNIA

Regional

Braille Institute Library, Los Angeles
California State Library, Braille & Talking Book Library, Sacramento

Subregional

Fresno County Public Library, Talking Book Library for the Blind, Fresno

Other

California School for the Blind Library, Fremont

San Francisco Public Library, San Francisco

Torrance Public Library, Katy Geissert Civic Center, Torrance

COLORADO

Regional

Colorado Talking Book Library, Denver

Other

Colorado State Library, Denver

CONNECTICUT

Regional

Connecticut State Library, Connecticut Library for Accessible Books, Middletown

Other

Greenwich Library, Greenwich

DELAWARE

Regional

State of Delaware, Delaware Library Access Services, Dover

DISTRICT OF COLUMBIA

Regional

District of Columbia Talking Book & Braille Library, Washington

Other
District of Columbia Public Library, Martin Luther King Jr Memorial, Washington
Library of Congress, National Library Service for the Blind & Print Disabled, Washington

FLORIDA

Regional
Florida Braille & Talking Book Library, Daytona Beach

Subregional
Broward County Libraries Division, Talking Book Library, Fort Lauderdale
Jacksonville Public Library, Talking Books for the Blind & Physically Handicapped, Jacksonville
Lee County Library System, Talking Books Library, Fort Myers
Miami-Dade Public Library System, Braille & Talking Books Library, Miami
Orange County Library System, Talking Books Section, Orlando
Pinellas Talking Book Library, Clearwater

Other
Alachua County Library District, Headquarters Library, Gainesville
Orange County Library System, Orlando Public Library, Orlando

GEORGIA

Regional
Georgia Library for Accessible Statewide Services, Atlanta

Subregional
Oconee Regional Library, Talking Book Center, Dublin

Other
Chattahoochee Valley Libraries, Columbus Public Library, Headquarters, Columbus
Hall County Library System, Gainesville Branch, Gainesville
Southwest Georgia Regional Library, Decatur County - Gilbert H Gragg Library, Bainbridge

HAWAII

Regional
Hawaii State Public Library System, Library for the Blind & Physically Handicapped, Honolulu

IDAHO

Regional
Idaho Commission for Libraries, Talking Book Service, Boise
Idaho School for the Deaf & Blind Library, Gooding

ILLINOIS

Regional
Illinois State Library, Talking Book & Braille Service, Springfield

Other
Glenview Public Library, Glenview
Illinois School for the Visually Impaired Library, Jacksonville
Illinois State Library, Springfield
Orland Park Public Library, Orland Park

INDIANA

Regional
Indiana State Library, Indiana Talking Book & Braille Library, Indianapolis

Subregional
Other
Bartholomew County Public Library, Columbus

IOWA

Regional
Iowa Regional Library for the Blind & Physically Handicapped, Des Moines

Other
University of Northern Iowa Library, Rod Library, Cedar Falls

KANSAS

Regional
Kansas State Library, Kansas Talking Books Service, Emporia
Southwest Kansas Library System, Talking Books, Dodge City

Subregional
Central Kansas Library System, Subregional Library for the Blind & Physically Handicapped, Great Bend

KENTUCKY

Regional
Kentucky Talking Book Library, Frankfort

Other
American Printing House for the Blind, Inc, M C Migel Library & Barr Research Library, Louisville
Kentucky Department for Libraries & Archives, Frankfort
Kentucky School for the Blind Library, Louisville

LOUISIANA

Regional
State Library of Louisiana, Talking Books & Braille Library, Baton Rouge

Other
East Baton Rouge Parish Library, Main Library, Baton Rouge
Rapides Parish Library, Alexandria
State Library of Louisiana, Baton Rouge

MAINE

Regional
Maine State Library, Talking Books Plus/Library for the Blind & Physically Handicapped, Augusta

MARYLAND

Regional
Maryland State Library for the Blind & Print Disabled, Baltimore

MASSACHUSETTS

Regional
Perkins School for the Blind, Perkins Library, Watertown

Subregional
Worcester Public Library, Worcester Talking Book Library, Worcester

Other
Perkins School for the Blind, Samuel P Hayes Research Library, Watertown

MICHIGAN

Regional
Michigan Bureau of Services for Blind Persons - Braille & Talking Book Library, Lansing

Subregional
Ann Arbor District Library, Washtenaw Library for the Blind & Physically Disabled, Ann Arbor
Detroit Public Library, Detroit

Detroit Public Library, Detroit Subregional Library for the Blind & Physically Handicapped, Detroit
Genesee District Library, Talking Book Center, Flint
Kent District Library, Library for the Blind & Physically Handicapped, Wyoming
Muskegon Area District Library, Blind & Physically Handicapped Library, Muskegon
Saint Clair County Library System, Blind & Physically Handicapped Library, Port Huron
Traverse Area District Library, Talking Book Library, Traverse City
Great Lakes Talking Books, Reader Advisory & Outreach Center, Marquette

Other
Albion College, Stockwell-Mudd Libraries, Albion
Clinton-Macomb Public Library, Clinton Township
Genesee District Library, Flint
Muskegon Area District Library, Muskegon
Rochester Hills Public Library, Rochester

MINNESOTA

Regional
Minnesota Braille & Talking Book Library, Faribault

Other
University of Minnesota Duluth, Kathryn A Martin Library, Duluth

MISSISSIPPI

Regional
Mississippi Library Commission, Talking Book Library Services, Jackson
Other
Mississippi Library Commission, Jackson

MISSOURI

Regional
Missouri State Library, Wolfner Talking Book & Braille Library, Jefferson City

Other
Missouri School for the Blind Library, Saint Louis
Saint Louis Community College, Meramec Campus Library, Saint Louis

MONTANA

Other
Montana School for the Deaf & Blind Library, Great Falls
Montana State Library, Helena

NEBRASKA

Regional
Nebraska Library Commission, Talking Book & Braille Service, Lincoln

Other
Christian Record Services for the Blind, Lending Library, Lincoln

NEVADA

Regional
Nevada State Library, Archives & Public Records, Regional Library for the Blind & Physically Handicapped, Carson City

NEW HAMPSHIRE

Regional
New Hampshire State Library, Talking Book Services, Concord

NEW JERSEY

Regional
New Jersey State Library, Talking Book & Braille Center, Trenton

Other
New Jersey State Library, Trenton

NEW MEXICO

Regional
New Mexico State Library, Library for the Blind and Print Disabled, Santa Fe

Other
New Mexico School for the Blind & Visually Impaired Library, Alamogordo

NEW YORK

Regional
The New York Public Library - Astor, Lenox & Tilden Foundations, Andrew Heiskell Braille & Talking Book Library, New York
New York State Library, Talking Book & Braille Library, Albany

Subregional

Other
JBI International, Jewish Braille Institute of America, New York
Plattekill Public Library, Modena
Suffolk Cooperative Library System, Long Island Talking Book Library, Bellport
Xavier Society for the Blind, National Catholic Press & Lending Library for the Visually Impaired, New York

NORTH CAROLINA

Regional
North Carolina Regional Library for the Blind & Physically Handicapped, Raleigh

Other
Gardner-Webb University, John R Dover Memorial Library, Boiling Springs

NORTH DAKOTA

Other
North Dakota Vision Services-School for the Blind, Vision Resource Center, Grand Forks

OHIO

Regional
Cleveland Public Library, Ohio Library for the Blind & Physically Disabled, Cleveland

Other
Preble County District Library, Eaton

OKLAHOMA

Regional
Oklahoma Library for the Blind & Physically Handicapped, Oklahoma City

Other
Stillwater Public Library, Stillwater

OREGON

Regional
Oregon State Library Talking Book & Braille Services, Salem

Other
Eugene Public Library, Downtown Library, Eugene

PENNSYLVANIA

Regional
Carnegie Library of Pittsburgh, Library for the Blind & Physically Handicapped, Pittsburgh

Free Library of Philadelphia, Library for the Blind & Physically Handicapped, Philadelphia

RHODE ISLAND

Regional

State of Rhode Island, Talking Books Library, Providence

SOUTH CAROLINA

Regional

South Carolina State Library, Talking Book Services, Columbia

Other

Greenville County Library System, Hughes Main Library, Greenville
South Carolina School for the Deaf & the Blind, Jesse Franklin Cleveland Learning Resource Center, Spartanburg

SOUTH DAKOTA

Regional

South Dakota State Library, Braille & Talking Book Program, Pierre

Other

South Dakota School for the Blind & Visually Impaired, Library Media Center, Aberdeen
South Dakota State Library, Pierre

TENNESSEE

Regional

Tennessee Regional Library for the Blind & Physically Handicapped, Tennessee Library for Accessible Books & Media, Nashville

Other

Tennessee State Library & Archives, Nashville

TEXAS

Regional

Texas State Library & Archives Commission, Talking Book Program, Austin

UTAH

Regional

Utah State Library Division, Program for the Blind & Disabled, Salt Lake City

VERMONT

Regional

Vermont Department of Libraries, ABLE Library, Barre

VIRGINIA

Regional

Virginia Department for the Blind & Vision Impaired, Library & Resource Center, Richmond

Subregional

Alexandria Library, Talking Books, Alexandria
Central Rappahannock Regional Library, Fredericksburg Subregional for the Blind-Physically Handicapped, Fredericksburg
Staunton Public Library, Talking Book Center, Staunton

Other

Braille Circulating Library For The Blind Inc, Richmond
Virginia Beach Public Library, Bayside Area & Special Services Library, Virginia Beach
Virginia Beach Public Library, Administration Office, Virginia Beach
Waynesboro Public Library, Waynesboro

WASHINGTON

Regional

Washington Talking Book & Braille Library, Seattle

Other

Washington State Library, Tumwater

WEST VIRGINIA

Subregional

Cabell County Public Library, Services for the Blind & Physically Handicapped, Huntington
Parkersburg & Wood County Public Library, Services for the Blind & Physically Handicapped, Parkersburg
West Virginia Schools for the Deaf & the Blind Library, Romney

WISCONSIN

Regional

Wisconsin Talking Book & Braille Library, Milwaukee

Other

Appleton Public Library, Appleton

PUERTO RICO

Regional

Puerto Rico Regional Library for the Blind & Physically Handicapped, Biblioteca Regional para Ciegos y Fisicamente Impedidos de Puerto Rico, San Juan

VIRGIN ISLANDS

Regional

Virgin Islands Division of Libraries, Archives & Museums, Regional Library for the Blind & Physically Handicapped, Christiansted

CANADA

ALBERTA

Calgary Public Library, Calgary
Edmonton Public Library, Stanley A Milner (Downtown) Library, Edmonton

NEW BRUNSWICK

New Brunswick Public Library Service (NBPLS), Service des bibliothèques publiques du Nouveau-Brunswick (SBPNB), Fredericton

NOVA SCOTIA

Atlantic Provinces Special Education Authority Library, Halifax

ONTARIO

Canadian National Institute for the Blind, Library for the Blind, Toronto
Carleton University Library, MacOdrum Library, Ottawa
Ottawa Public Library/Bibliothèque publique d'Ottawa, Main Library, Ottawa

LIBRARIES SERVING THE DEAF AND HEARING IMPAIRED

Many libraries in the U.S. and Canada offer extensive personal services and assistive technologies for the deaf or hearing impaired. These may include video relay equipment, captioned videos, or staff that provide interpreter or sign language services. What follows is an index to those libraries, which have certain technologies or a significant offering of technologies and personal services for the deaf and hearing impaired.

For specific information on specialized technologies and services available, please see the "Special Services for the Deaf" paragraph in each individual entry in the library section of this directory.

ALABAMA

Birmingham Public Library, West End, Birmingham
Bishop State Community College, Minnie Slade Bishop Library, Mobile
Columbiana Public Library, Columbiana
Leeds Jane Culbreth Public Library, Leeds
Mobile Public Library, Ben May Main Library, Mobile
Montgomery City-County Public Library System, Coliseum Boulevard Branch Library, Montgomery

ALASKA

Anchorage Public Library, Mountain View Branch, Anchorage
Anchorage Public Library, Z J Loussac Public Library, Anchorage
Special Education Service Agency Library, Anchorage

ARIZONA

Arizona State Prison Complex Florence Libraries, Florence
Arizona State Schools for the Deaf & the Blind Library, Tucson
Yuma County Free Library District, Main Library, Yuma

ARKANSAS

Arkansas School for the Deaf Library, Little Rock
Pope County Library System, Russellville Headquarters Branch, Russellville
Saline County Public Library, Bob Herzfeld Memorial Library, Benton

CALIFORNIA

Alameda County Library, Fremont Library, Fremont
Alameda Free Library, Alameda
California School for the Deaf Library, Riverside
California State University, Northridge, Delmar T Oviatt Library, Northridge
County of Los Angeles Public Library, Downey
Fresno County Public Library, Fresno
Lincoln Public Library, Lincoln
Los Angeles Public Library System, Central Library, Los Angeles
Los Angeles Valley College Library, Valley Glen
National University Library, San Diego
Oxnard Public Library, Oxnard
Riverside Public Library, Riverside
San Francisco Public Library, San Francisco
Santa Clara City Library, Santa Clara
Santa Maria Public Library, Santa Maria
South San Francisco Public Library, South San Francisco

COLORADO

Alamosa Public Library, Alamosa
Longmont Public Library, Longmont
Mamie Doud Eisenhower Public Library, Broomfield
Otero Junior College, Wheeler Library, La Junta
Pikes Peak Library District, Colorado Springs

CONNECTICUT

Greenwich Library, Greenwich
Hartford Public Library, Hartford
Northwestern Connecticut Community College Library, Winsted
West Hartford Public Library, Noah Webster Memorial Library, West Hartford

DISTRICT OF COLUMBIA

District of Columbia Public Library, Administration, Washington
District of Columbia Public Library, Martin Luther King Jr Memorial, Washington
District of Columbia Talking Book & Braille Library, Washington
Gallaudet University Library, Washington
Library of Congress, Washington
National Society of the Daughters of the American Revolution, DAR Library, Washington

FLORIDA

Alachua County Library District, Headquarters Library, Gainesville
Barbara S Ponce Public Library, Pinellas Park
Broward County Libraries Division, Broward County Library, Fort Lauderdale
Manatee County Public Library System, Downtown Library, Bradenton
Miami-Dade Public Library System, Main Library, Miami
Orange County Library System, Orlando Public Library, Orlando
Pasco County Library System, Administration & Support Services, Hudson
Saint Johns County Public Library System, Southeast Branch Library & Administrative Headquarters, Saint Augustine
Volusia County Public Library, Daytona Beach

GEORGIA

Hall County Library System, Gainesville Branch, Gainesville
Sara Hightower Regional Library, Cave Spring Branch, Cave Spring

HAWAII

Hawaii State Public Library System, Library for the Blind & Physically Handicapped, Honolulu

ILLINOIS

Chicago Public Library, Chicago
Gail Borden Public Library District, Main Library, Elgin
Glenview Public Library, Glenview
Illinois School for the Deaf, Library for the Deaf, Jacksonville
Illinois State Library, Springfield
Indian Prairie Public Library District, Darien
Lyons Public Library, Lyons
Messenger Public Library of North Aurora, North Aurora
Mount Prospect Public Library, Mount Prospect
Northbrook Public Library, Northbrook
Park Ridge Public Library, Park Ridge
Prairie State College Library, Chicago Heights
Schaumburg Township District Library, Schaumburg
Skokie Public Library, Skokie
Westmont Public Library, Westmont

INDIANA

Indianapolis Public Library, Library Service Center - Administrative Headquarters, Indianapolis
Scott County Public Library, Scottsburg Public, Scottsburg
West Lafayette Public Library, West Lafayette

IOWA

Ames Public Library, Ames
University of Northern Iowa Library, Rod Library, Cedar Falls

KANSAS

Johnson County Community College, Billington Library, Overland Park
Topeka & Shawnee County Public Library, Topeka

KENTUCKY

Boyle County Public Library, Danville
Scott County Public Library, Georgetown
Somerset Community College Learning Commons, Somerset

LOUISIANA

East Baton Rouge Parish Library, Main Library, Baton Rouge

MAINE

Wilton Free Public Library, Wilton

MARYLAND

DEVCOM Army Research Laboratory, Technical Library, Adelphi
Dorchester County Public Library, Cambridge
Enoch Pratt Free Library, Baltimore
Frederick County Public Libraries, Frederick
Howard County Library System, Administrative Offices, Ellicott City
Uniformed Services University of the Health Sciences, James A Zimble Learning Resource Center, Bethesda
Washington County Free Library, Hagerstown

MASSACHUSETTS

Adams Free Library, Adams
Goodnow Library, Sudbury
Millis Public Library, Millis

MICHIGAN

Albion College, Stockwell-Mudd Libraries, Albion
Baker College of Muskegon Library, Academic Resource Center, Muskegon
Holly Township Library, Holly
Novi Public Library, Novi
Presque Isle District Library, Rogers City

MINNESOTA

Duluth Public Library, Duluth
Hennepin County Library, Minnetonka
Saint Catherine University, Libraries, Media Services & Archives, Saint Paul
Saint Cloud Technical & Community College Library, Saint Cloud

MISSISSIPPI

University of Mississippi, John Davis Williams Library, University

MISSOURI

Saint Louis Community College, Meramec Campus Library, Saint Louis
Saint Louis County Library, Headquarters, Saint Louis
Sedalia Public Library, Sedalia

MONTANA

Montana School for the Deaf & Blind Library, Great Falls
Montana State Library, Helena

NEBRASKA

Hastings Public Library, Hastings
Scotia Public Library, Scotia

NEVADA

Washoe County Library System, Reno

NEW HAMPSHIRE

River Valley Community College, Charles P Puksta Library, Claremont

NEW JERSEY

Burlington County Library System, Westampton
Cumberland County Library, Bridgeton
Borough of Totowa Public Library, Dwight D Eisenhower Public Library, Totowa
East Orange Public Library, East Orange
Hamilton Township Public Library, Hamilton
Jersey City Free Public Library, Priscilla Gardner Main Library & Administrative Offices, Jersey City
Monmouth County Library, Headquarters, Manalapan
Monroe Township Public Library, Monroe Township
Morris County Library, Whippany
Mount Olive Public Library, Flanders
New Jersey Historical Society Library, Newark
Newark Public Library, Newark
Ocean County Library, Toms River
Penfield Public Library, Penfield
Sussex County Community College Library, Newton

NEW MEXICO

Belen Public Library, Belen

NEW YORK

Adelphi University, Swirbul Library, Garden City
College of Staten Island Library, Staten Island
Jervis Public Library Association, Inc, Rome
Long Beach Public Library, Long Beach
Northport-East Northport Public Library, Northport
Pawling Free Library, Pawling
Red Hook Public Library, Red Hook
RIT Libraries, Wallace Library, Rochester
Rochester Public Library, Rochester
Stony Brook University, Frank Melville Jr Memorial Library, Stony Brook
SUNY Broome Community College, Cecil C Tyrrell Learning Resource Center, Binghamton

NORTH CAROLINA

Cumberland County Public Library & Information Center, Headquarters, Fayetteville
Gardner-Webb University, John R Dover Memorial Library, Boiling Springs
Greensboro Public Library, Greensboro
New Bern-Craven County Public Library, New Bern

NORTH DAKOTA

University of North Dakota, Gordon Erickson Music Library, Grand Forks

OHIO

Columbus Metropolitan Library, Main Library, Columbus
Kent State University, Salem Campus Library, Salem
Mentor Public Library, Mentor
Ohio School for the Deaf Library, Columbus
Ohio University Libraries, Vernon R Alden Library, Athens
Preble County District Library, Eaton
Tuscarawas County Public Library, New Philadelphia

OKLAHOMA

Stillwater Public Library, Stillwater

OREGON

Deschutes Public Library District, Bend
Eugene Public Library, Downtown Library, Eugene
Lyons Public Library, Lyons

PENNSYLVANIA

Elizabethtown Public Library, Elizabethtown
Pennsylvania School for the Deaf Library, Philadelphia
Rosemont College Library, Gertrude Kistler Memorial Library, Rosemont

PUERTO RICO

Inter-American University of Puerto Rico, Information Access Center, San Juan
University of Puerto Rico Library System, San Juan

RHODE ISLAND

Rhode Island School for the Deaf Library, Providence

SOUTH CAROLINA

Charleston County Public Library, Charleston
Greenville County Library System, Hughes Main Library, Greenville
Harvin Clarendon County Library, Manning
Horry County Memorial Library, Administration, Conway
South Carolina School for the Deaf & the Blind, Jesse Franklin Cleveland Learning Resource Center, Spartanburg

SOUTH DAKOTA

Siouxland Libraries, Sioux Falls

TENNESSEE

Kingsport Public Library & Archives, J Fred Johnson Memorial Library, Kingsport
Nashville Public Library, Nashville
Nashville Public Library, Library Service for the Deaf & Hard of Hearing, Nashville
Perry County Public Library, Linden

TEXAS

Austin Public Library, Central Library, Austin
Dallas Public Library, Dallas
Groesbeck Maffett Public Library, Groesbeck
Howard County Junior College, Southwest Collegiate Institute for the Deaf - Library, Big Spring
Lamar State College, Gates Memorial Library, Port Arthur
Orange Public Library, Orange
Quitman Public Library, Quitman
Watauga Public Library, Watauga

UTAH

The Church of Jesus Christ of Latter-Day Saints, Family History Library, Salt Lake City

VERMONT

Goodrich Memorial Library, Newport

VIRGINIA

Alexandria Library, Alexandria
Arlington County Department of Libraries, Arlington Public Library, Arlington
Regent University, Law Library, Virginia Beach
Staunton Public Library, Staunton
Virginia State University, Johnston Memorial Library, Petersburg

WASHINGTON

Bellingham Public Library, Bellingham
Big Bend Community College Library, Bonaudi Library, Moses Lake
Eastern Washington University, John F Kennedy Memorial Library, Cheney
Puyallup Public Library, Puyallup
San Juan Island Library, Friday Harbor
The Seattle Public Library, Central Library & Administrative Offices, Seattle
Washington School for the Deaf, McGill Library, Vancouver

WEST VIRGINIA

West Virginia School for the Deaf & Blind Library, Romney

WISCONSIN

Bridges Library System, Waukesha
Brown County Library, Green Bay
Everett Roehl Marshfield Public Library, Marshfield
Menomonie Public Library, Menomonie
Milwaukee Public Library, Milwaukee
Northcentral Technical College Library, Wausau
Racine Public Library, Racine
T B Scott Library, Merrill Public Library, Merrill
Wisconsin School for the Deaf, WESP-DHH Educational Resource Library, Delavan

CANADA

ALBERTA

Alberta Bible College Library, Calgary
Alberta School for the Deaf Library, Edmonton Public School Division, Edmonton
Calgary Public Library, Calgary
Calgary Public Library, Bowness, Calgary
Calgary Public Library, Crowfoot, Calgary
Calgary Public Library, Fish Creek, Calgary
Calgary Public Library, Forest Lawn, Calgary
Calgary Public Library, Louise Riley Branch, Calgary
Calgary Public Library, Memorial Park, Calgary
Calgary Public Library, Nose Hill, Calgary
Calgary Public Library, Shawnessy, Calgary
Calgary Public Library, Southwood, Calgary
Calgary Public Library, W R Castell Central Library, Calgary
Edmonton Public Library, Stanley A Milner (Downtown) Library, Edmonton
Strathcona County Library, Sherwood Park

BRITISH COLUMBIA

Cariboo Regional District Library, Quesnel Branch, Quesnel
North Vancouver City Library, North Vancouver

ONTARIO

George Brown College of Applied Arts & Technology, Casa Loma Campus Library Learning Commons, Toronto
London Public Library, Central, London
Magnetawan First Nation Public Library, Britt
Oshawa Public Library, McLaughlin Library, Oshawa

QUEBEC

Department of Canadian Heritage, Knowledge Centre, Gatineau

SASKATCHEWAN

SIAST Libraries, Woodland Campus, Prince Albert
Wheatland Regional Library, Biggar Branch, Biggar

STATE AND PROVINCIAL PUBLIC LIBRARY AGENCIES

Listed here are the agencies (mostly state libraries) concerned with Public Library extension work in a given state or province. Entries include the names of the person in charge of this work, usually the state librarian. For detailed information see entries in the Library Section.

Also of interest is the National Library of Education (NLE) which conducts nationwide surveys of libraries, learning resources, and educational technology.

NATIONAL LIBRARY OF EDUCATION, 400 Maryland Ave SW, Rm 107, Washington, DC 20202-5523. Tel: 202-205-5015. E-mail: askalibrarian@ed.gov. *Dir,* Pamela Tripp-Melby (NLE conducts surveys of libraries, learning resources and educational technology.)

ALABAMA PUBLIC LIBRARY SERVICE, 6030 Monticello Dr, Montgomery 36130. Tel: 334-213-3900. FAX: 334-213-3993. *Dir,* Nancy Pack

ALASKA STATE LIBRARY, 395 Whittier Ave, Juneau 99801. (Mail add: PO Box 110571, 99811-0571). Tel: 907-465-2920. E-mail: asl@alaska.gov. *Dir, Libr, Archives & Mus,* Amy Phillips-Chan

ARIZONA STATE LIBRARY, ARCHIVES & PUBLIC RECORDS, 1700 W Washington, Ste 300, Phoenix 85007. Tel: 602-926-3870. FAX: 602-256-7984. E-mail: research@azlib.gov. *State Librn,* Holly Henley

ARKANSAS STATE LIBRARY, 900 W Capitol, Ste 100, Little Rock 72201-3108. Tel: 501-682-1527, 501-682-1526. FAX: 501-682-1899. *State Librn,* Jennifer Chilcoat

CALIFORNIA STATE LIBRARY, 900 N St, Sacramento 95814. (Mail add: PO Box 942837, 94237-0001). Tel: 916-654-0261. E-mail: cslsinfo@library.ca.gov. *State Librn,* Greg Lucas

COLORADO STATE LIBRARY, 201 E Colfax Ave, Rm 309, Denver 80203-1799. Tel: 303-866-6900. FAX: 303-866-6940. *Exec Dir,* Eugene Hainer

CONNECTICUT STATE LIBRARY, 231 Capitol Ave, Hartford 06106-1537. Tel: 860-757-6510. FAX: 860-757-6503. *State Librn,* Deborah Schander

STATE OF DELAWARE, DELAWARE DIVISION OF LIBRARIES, 121 Martin Luther King Jr, Blvd N Dover 19901. Tel: 302-739-4748. FAX: 302-739-6787. *Dir,* Dr Annie Norman

DISTRICT OF COLUMBIA PUBLIC LIBRARY, 901 G St NW, Washington, DC 20001-4599. Tel: 202-727-1101. FAX: 202-727-1129. *Exec Dir,* Richard Reyes-Gavilan

FLORIDA DEPARTMENT OF STATE, DIVISION OF LIBRARY & INFORMATION SERVICES, State Library & Archives of Florida, R A Gray Bldg, 500 S Bronough St, Tallahassee 32399-0250. Tel: 850-245-6600. E-mail:info@dos.myflorida.com. *State Librn,* Amy L Johnson

GEORGIA PUBLIC LIBRARY SERVICE, 1800 Century Place, Ste 150, Atlanta 30345-4304. Tel: 404-235-7200. FAX: 404-235-7201. *State Librn,* Dr Julie Walker

HAWAII STATE PUBLIC LIBRARY SYSTEM, Office of the State Librarian, 44 Merchant St, Honolulu 96813. Tel: 808-586-3704. FAX: 808-586-3715. *State Librn,* Stacey A Aldrich

IDAHO COMMISSION FOR LIBRARIES, Idaho State Library, 325 W State St, Boise 83702-6072. Tel: 208-334-2150. FAX: 208-334-4016. *State Librn,* Stephanie Bailey-White

ILLINOIS STATE LIBRARY, Gwendolyn Brooks Bldg, 300 S Second St, Springfield 62701-1713. Tel: 217-782-2994. E-mail: islinformationline@ilsos.net. *Dir,* Greg McCormick

INDIANA STATE LIBRARY, 315 W Ohio St, Indianapolis 46202. Tel: 317-232-3675. FAX: 317-232-3728. *State Librn,* Jacob Speer

STATE LIBRARY OF IOWA, 1112 E Grand Ave, Des Moines 50319. Tel: 515-281-4105. FAX: 515-281-6191. *State Librn,* Michael Scott

KANSAS STATE LIBRARY, State Capitol Bldg, 300 SW Tenth Ave, Rm 312N, Topeka 66612-1593. Tel: 785-296-3296. E-mail: kslc@.ks.gov. *State Librn,* Roy C. Walling

KENTUCKY DEPARTMENT FOR LIBRARIES & ARCHIVES, 300 Coffee Tree Rd, Frankfort 40601. (Mail Add: PO Box 537, 40602). Tel: 502-564-8300. FAX: 502-564-5773. *State Librn,* Denise Lyons

STATE LIBRARY OF LOUISIANA, 701 N Fourth St, Baton Rogue 70821-5232. (Mail add: PO Box 131, 70821-0131). Tel: 225-342-4923. E-mail: admin@state.lib.la.us. *State Librn,* Rebecca Hamilton. *Dep State Librn,* Meg Placke

MAINE STATE LIBRARY, LMA Bldg, 230 State St, Augusta 04333. (Mail Add: LMA Bldg, 64 State House Sta, 04333-0064). Tel: 207-287-5600. E-mail: reference.desk@maine.gov. *State Librn,* Lori Fisher

MARYLAND STATE DEPARTMENT OF EDUCATION, Division of Library Development & Services, 22 S Calhoun St, Baltimore 21223. Tel: 667-219-4800. FAX: 667-219-4798. *State Librn,* Irene Padilla

MASSACHUSETTS BOARD OF LIBRARY COMMISSIONERS, State House, 90 Canal St, Ste 500, Boston 02114. Tel: 617-727-2590. FAX: 617-727-9730. *Dir,* James Lonergan

LIBRARY OF MICHIGAN, 702 W Kalamazoo St, Lansing 48915. (Mail add: PO Box 30007, 48909-0007). Tel: 517-373-1580. E-mail: librarian@michigan.gov. *State Librn,* Randy Riley

MISSISSIPPI LIBRARY COMMISSION, 3881 Eastwood Dr, Jackson 39211. Tel: 601-432-4039. E-mail: mlcref@mlc.lib.ms.us; mslib@mlc.lib.ms.us. *Deputy Dir,* Tracy Carr

MISSOURI STATE LIBRARY, James C Kirkpatrick State Information Ctr, 600 W Main St, Jefferson City 65101-1532, (Mail add: PO Box 387, 65102-0387). Tel: 573-751-2751. E-mail: info@sos.mo.gov. *State Librn,* Robin Westphal

MONTANA STATE LIBRARY, 1515 E Sixth Ave, Helena 59620-1800. (Mail Add: PO Box 201800). Tel: 406-444-3115. E-mail: MSLReference@mt.gov. *State Librn,* Jennie Stapp

NEBRASKA LIBRARY COMMISSION, The Atrium, 1200 N St, Ste 120, Lincoln, 68508-2023. Tel: 402-471-2045. FAX: 402-471-2083. *Dir,* Rod Wagner

NEVADA STATE LIBRARY & ARCHIVES, 100 N Stewart St, Carson City 89701-4285. Tel: 775-684-3360. FAX: 775-684-3330. *Admin,* Mike Strom

NEW HAMPSHIRE STATE LIBRARY, 20 Park St, Concord 03301-6314. Tel: 603-271-2397. E-mail: michael.york@dncr.nh.gov. *State Librn,* Michael York

NEW JERSEY STATE LIBRARY, 185 W State St, Trenton 08618. (Mail add: PO Box 520, 08625-0520). Tel: 609-278-2640. E-mail: refdesk@njstatelib.org. *State Librn,* Jennifer Nelson

NEW MEXICO STATE LIBRARY, 1209 Camino Carlos Rey, Santa Fe 87507. Tel: 505-476-9700. FAX: 505-476-9701. *State Librn,* Eli Guinnee

NEW YORK STATE LIBRARY, State Education Department, Cultural Education Center, Empire State Plaza, Albany 12230. Tel: 518-474-5961. E-mail: nyslcirc@nysed.gov, nyslweb@nysed.gov. *State Librn,* Lauren Moore

STATE LIBRARY OF NORTH CAROLINA, 109 E Jones St, (Mail add: 4640 Mail Service Ctr, Raleigh 27699-4640). Tel: 919-814-6780. FAX: 919-733-8748. *State Librn,* Michelle Underhill

NORTH DAKOTA STATE LIBRARY, 604 East Blvd Ave, Dept 250, Bismarck 58505-0800. Tel: 701-328-2492. E-mail: statelib@nd.gov. *State Librn,* Mary Soucie

STATE LIBRARY OF OHIO, 274 E First Ave, Ste 100, Columbus 43201. Tel: 614-644-7061. E-mail: refhelp@library.ohio.gov. *State Librn,* Wendy Knapp

OKLAHOMA DEPARTMENT OF LIBRARIES, 200 NE 18th St, Oklahoma City 73105. Tel: 405-521-2502. FAX: 405-525-7804. *Dir,* Natalie Currie

OREGON STATE LIBRARY, 250 Winter St NE, Salem 97301-3950. Tel: 503-378-4243. E-mail: library.help@state.or.us. *State Librn,* Wendy Cornelisen

STATE LIBRARY OF PENNSYLVANIA, Forum Bldg , 607 South Dr, Harrisburg 17120-0600. Tel: 717-783-5950; 717-787-4307. FAX: 717-787-9127. *State Librn,* Susan Banks

STATE OF RHODE ISLAND OFFICE OF LIBRARY & INFORMATION SERVICES, One Capitol Hill, 4th Flr, Providence 02908. Tel: 401-574-9300. FAX: 401-574-9320. *Chief Librn,* Karen Mellor

SOUTH CAROLINA STATE LIBRARY, 1430-1500 Senate St, Columbia 29201. (Mail add: PO Box 11469, 29211). Tel: 803-734-8666. E-mail: reference@statelibrary.sc.gov. *Dir,* Leesa Aiken

SOUTH DAKOTA STATE LIBRARY, 800 Governors Dr, Pierre 57501-2294. Tel: 605-773-3131. FAX: 605-773-6962. E-mail: library@state.sd.us. *State Librn,* George Seamon

TENNESSEE STATE LIBRARY & ARCHIVES, 403 Seventh Ave N, Nashville 37243-0312. Tel: 615-741-2764. FAX: 615-741-6471, 615-532-2472. E-mail: reference.tsla@tn.gov. *State Librn,* James Ritter

TEXAS STATE LIBRARY & ARCHIVES COMMISSION, 1201 Brazos, Austin 78701. (Mail add: PO Box 12927, 78711-2927). Tel: 512-463-5460. FAX: 512-463-5436. E-mail: info@tsl.texas.gov. *Dir,* Gloria Meraz

UTAH STATE LIBRARY DIVISION, 250 N 1950 W, Ste A, Salt Lake City 84116-7901. Tel: 801-715-6777. FAX: 801-715-6767. *Dir,* Chaundra Johnson

STATE OF VERMONT DEPARTMENT OF LIBRARIES, 60 Washington St, Ste 2,Barre 05641. Tel: 802-636-0040. E-mail: lib.rls@state.vt.us. *State Librn,* Catherine Delneo

THE LIBRARY OF VIRGINIA, 800 E Broad St, Richmond 23219-8000. Tel: 804-692-3592. FAX: 804-692-3594. *State Librn,* Dennis T.Clark

WASHINGTON STATE LIBRARY, 6880 Capital Blvd S, Tumwater 98501-5513, (Mail add: PO Box 42460, Olympia 98504-2460). Tel: 360-704-5200. FAX: 360-586-7575. *State Librn,* Sarah Jones

WEST VIRGINIA LIBRARY COMMISSION, State Capital Complex, 1900 Kanawha Blvd, Charleston 25305-0620. Tel: 304-558-2041. E-mail: web_one@wvlc.lib.wv.us. *State Librn,* Donna Calvert

WISCONSIN DEPARTMENT OF PUBLIC INSTRUCTION, Division for Libraries, Technology & Community Learning, 125 S Webster St, Madison 53707. (Mail add: PO Box 7841, 53707-7841). Tel: 608-266-2205. FAX: 608-266-8770. *State Superintendent,* Jill Underly

WYOMING STATE LIBRARY, 2800 Central Ave, Cheyenne 82002. Tel: 307-777-6333. FAX: 307-777-7281. E-mail: refdesk@wyo.gov. *State Librn,* Abby Beaver

AMERICAN SAMOA OFFICE OF LIBRARY SERVICES, American Library Bldg, Pago Pago 96799. (Mail add: PO Box 1329, 96799-1329). Tel: 684-699-2170. FAX: 684-699-2193. *Asst Dir,* Talosia Uperesa

COMMONWEALTH OF PUERTO RICO, Library & Information Services Program, Cesar Gonzalez Ave, San Juan 00919. (Mail add: PO Box 190759, 00919-0759). Tel: 787-759-2000. FAX: 787-753-6945. *Dir,* Aixamar Gonzalez

VIRGIN ISLANDS DIVISION OF LIBRARIES, ARCHIVES & MUSEUMS, 4607 Tutu Park, Saint Thomas 00802. Tel: 340-774-0630. FAX: 340-693-9620. *Territorial Dir,* Ingrid Bough

ALBERTA DEPARTMENT OF CULTURE & COMMUNITY SPIRIT, Provincial Archives of Alberta, Reference Library, 8555 Roper Rd, Edmonton T6E 5W1. Tel: 780-427-1750. FAX: 780-427-4646. E-mail: paa@gov.ab.ca. *Exec Dir,* Leslie Latta

BRITISH COLUMBIA MINISTRY OF EDUCATION, Public Library Services Branch, 620 Superior St, Fifth Fl, Victoria V8V 1V2, (Mail add: PO Box 9831, Stn Prov Govt, V8W 9T1). Tel: 250-356-1791. FAX: 250-953-3225. E-mail: lib@gov.bc.ca. *Dir,* Mari Martin

NOVA SCOTIA PROVINCIAL LIBRARY, 6016 University Ave, 4th Flr, Halifax B3H 1W4. (Mail add: PO Box 456, B3J 2R5). Tel: 902-424-2457. E-mail: nspl@novascotia.ca. *Dir,* Lynn Somers

ARCHIVES OF ONTARIO LIBRARY, 134 Ian Macdonald Blvd, Toronto M7A 2C5. Tel: 416-327-1600. E-mail: reference@ontario.ca. *Librn,* Frank van Kalmthout

PRINCE EDWARD ISLAND PUBLIC LIBRARY SERVICE, 89 Red Head Rd, Morell C0A 1S0. (Mail add: PO Box 7500). Tel: 902-961-7320. E-mail: plshq@gov.pe.ca. *Prov Librn,* Kathleen Simmonds

SASKATCHEWAN PROVINCIAL LIBRARY, 409A Park St, Regina S4N 5B2. Tel: 306-787-2973. E-mail: alison.hopkins@gov.sk.ca. *Prov Librn,* Alison Hopkins

DEPARTMENT OF COMMUNITY SERVICES, Yukon Public Libraries, 2071 Second Ave, Whitehorse Y1A 2C6. (Mail add: PO Box 2703). Tel: 867-667-5239. E-mail: whitehorse.library@gov.yk.ca; reference.pls@gov.yk.ca. *Dir,* Ben YuSchott

STATE SCHOOL LIBRARY AGENCIES

Listed below are agencies (mostly state departments of education) concerned with management of public school libraries. Except where the agency is a state library, these entities tend not to be listed elsewhere in the directory. Included are core contact data points and the name and title of the person in charge.

ALABAMA DEPARTMENT OF EDUCATION, 5114 Gordon Persons Bldg, PO Box 302101, Montgomery 36104-2101. Tel: 334-242-9702. Fax: 334-242-9708. Web Site: www.alabamaachieves.org . *Superintendent of Educ,* Dr Eric G. Mackey. Tel: 334-242-9704. E-mail: superintendent@alsde.edu

ALASKA STATE LIBRARY, Alaska Department of Education & Early Development, 801 W Tenth St, Ste 200, Juneau 99801. Tel: 907-465-2802. Fax: 907-465-4156. *Commissioner of Educ,* Deena Bishop

ARIZONA DEPARTMENT OF EDUCATION, Bin 2, 1535 W Jefferson, Phoenix 85007-3280. Tel: 602-542-5460. Fax: 602-542-7378. Web Site: www.azed.gov. *Superintendent of Pub Instruction,* Tom Horne E-mail: adeinbox@azed.gov

ARKANSAS DEPARTMENT OF EDUCATION, Education Buildings, 304A, Four Capitol Mall, Little Rock 72201-1071. Tel: 501-682-4203. Fax: 501-682-1079. *Commissioner of Educ,* Jacob Oliva

CALIFORNIA STATE LIBRARY, Library & Courts Bldg1, Rm 220, 914 Capitol Mall, Sacramento 95814 (Mail add: PO Box 942837, 94237-0001). Tel: 916-323-9759. Fax: 916-654-0064. *State Libr Dir,* Greg Lucas. E-mail: csl_adm@library.ca.gov

COLORADO STATE LIBRARY, Colorado Department of Education, 201 E Colfax, Rm 500, Denver 80203. Tel: 303-866-6646. Fax: 303-866-6940. Web Site: www.cde.state.co.us. *Commissioner of Educ,* Susana Cordova. E-mail commissioner@cde.state.co.us

CONNECTICUT STATE DEPARTMENT OF EDUCATION, 450 Columbus Blvd, Hartford 06103.Tel: 860-713-6553. Fax: 860-713-7018. *Commissioner of Educ,* Charlene M. Russell-Tucker

DELAWARE STATE DEPARTMENT OF EDUCATION, John G Townsend Bldg, Ste 2, 401 Federal St, Dover 19901-1402, Tel: 302-739-4000. Fax: 302-739-4654. Web Site: www.doe.k12.de.us. *Secy of Educ,* Dr Mark A. Holodick E-mail: mark.holodick@doe.k12.de.us

FLORIDA DEPARTMENT OF EDUCATION, 325 W Gaines St, Turlington Bldg, Ste 1514, Tallahassee 32399. Tel: 850-245-0505. Fax: 850-245-0826. *Commissioner of Educ,* Manny Diaz, Jr . Tel: 850-245-9663. E-mail: commissioner@fldoe.org

GEORGIA DEPARTMENT OF EDUCATION, 1754 Twin Towers E, 205 Jesse Hill Jr Dr, Atlanta 30334. Tel: 404-222-1322. Fax: 404-656-5744. Web Site: www.doe.k12.ga.us. *Libr Media Res Spec,* Donita Hinckley. E-mail: dhinckley@doe.k12.ga.us

HAWAII STATE DEPARTMENT OF EDUCATION, School Library Services, 475 22nd Ave, Bldg 302, Rm 205, Honolulu 96816. Tel: 808-733-9150. Fax: 808-733-9154. Web Site:www.hawaiipublicschools.org . *Adminr,* Joanne Dunn. E-mail: joanna_dunn@hawaiidoe.org

IDAHO STATE DEPARTMENT OF EDUCATION, Commission for Libraries 650 W State St, PO Box 83720, Boise 83720-0027. Tel: 208-332-6800. Fax: 208-334-6908. *Academic Serv, Shannon Dunstan. Tel: 208-334-6908. E-mail: sdunstan@sde.idaho.gov*

ILLINOIS STATE BOARD OF EDUCATION, 100 N First St, Springfield 62777-0001. Tel: 217-782-0354. Fax: 217-782-7937. Web Site: www.isbe.net. *Principal Consult,* Jamey Baiter. E-mail: jbaiter@isbe.net

INDIANA DEPARTMENT OF EDUCATION, Center for School Improvement & Performance, 115 N Washington St, Indianapolis 46204. *Superintendent of Pub Instruction,* Dr Katie Jenner. Tel: 317-232-6610. E-mail:kjenner@doe.in.gov

KANSAS STATE DEPARTMENT OF EDUCATION, 900 SW Jackson St, Topeka 66612-1182. Tel 785-296-3202. Fax 785-296-3523. Web Site: www.ksde.org. *Commissioner of Educ,*Dr. Randy Watson. E-mail: rwatson@ksde.org

KENTUCKY STATE DEPARTMENT OF EDUCATION, 500 Mero St, Frankfort 40601. Tel: 502-564-2106, Ext 4500. Fax: 502-564-6470. Web Site: www.education.ky.gov

LOUISIANA STATE DEPARTMENT OF EDUCATION, Division Curriculum Standard, Claiborne Bldg 1201, N Third St, PO Box 94064, Baton Rouge 70804-9064. Tel: 225-342-9969. Fax: 225-342-0178. Web Site: www.doe.state.la.us. *Ancillary Res,* Dr Jackie Bobbett. E-mail: jackie.bobbett@la.gov

MAINE STATE LIBRARY, 64 State House Station, Augusta 04333. Tel: 207-624-6897.*Sch Libr & Tech Plan Coordr,*Position Vacant

MARYLAND STATE DEPARTMENT OF EDUCATION, Division of Instruction, 200 W Baltimore St, Baltimore 21201. Web Site: www.marylandpublicschools.org. *Asst State Superintendent for Instruction,* Henry Johnson. Tel: 410-767-0316. Fax: 410-333-2369. *Dir, Instrul Tech & Sch Libr Media,* Valerie Emrich. Tel: 410-767-0382. E-mail: vemrich@msde.state.md.us

MASSACHUSETTS DEPARTMENT OF EDUCATION, 135 Santilli Hwy, Everett, 02149. Tel: 781-338-3000. Fax: 781-338-3770. Web Site: www.doe.mass.edu. *Commissioner of Educ,* Jeffrey C.Riley

MISSISSIPPI STATE DEPARTMENT OF EDUCATION, 359 North West St, PO Box 771, Jackson 39205. Tel: 601-359-2586. Fax: 601-359-2040. Web Site: www.mde.k12.ms.us. *Visual & Performing Arts & Libr Media Spec,* Limeul Eubanks. E-mail: leubanks@mdek12.org

MISSOURI STATE DEPARTMENT OF EDUCATION, 205 Jefferson St, PO Box 480, Jefferson City 65102. Tel: 573-751-2721.*Asst Dir ,* Larry Thomas

MONTANA OFFICE OF PUBLIC INSTRUCTION, 1227 11th Ave, PO Box 202501, Helena 59620-2501. Tel: 406-444-3680. Fax: 406-444-2893. E-mail: opisupt@mt.gov. Web Site: www.opi.mt.gov. *Superintendent,* Elsie Arntzen. Tel: 406-444-5658, 406-444-9299

NEBRASKA DEPARTMENT Of EDUCATION, 301 S Centennial Mall South, PO Box 94987 Lincoln, NE 68509. Tel: 402-471-2295 Fax: 402-471-0117. Web Site: www.education.ne.gov. *E-Librarian,* Kristina Peters. Tel: 402-471-4366

NEVADA DEPARTMENT OF EDUCATION, Technology Team, 700 E Fifth St, Capitol Complex, Carson City 89701. Fax: 775-687-9202. Web Site: www.doe.nv.gov. *Superintendent,* Jhone Ebert Tel: 775-687-9217

NEW HAMPSHIRE STATE DEPARTMENT OF EDUCATION, 101 Pleasant St, Concord 03301-3860. Web Site: www.education.nh.gov. *Deputy Commissioner,* Christine Brennan. Tel: 603-271-3801. Fax: 603-271-1953. E-mail: christine.brennan@doe.nh.gov

NEW JERSEY STATE DEPARTMENT OF EDUCATION, Division of Education Standards & Programs, Office of Language Arts Literacy Education, 100 Riverview Plaza, (Mail add: PO Box 500, Trenton 08625-0500). Tel: 609-292-6245. Fax: 609-292-7276. *Spec,* Crystal Siniaki. Tel: 609-984-6163

NEW MEXICO STATE DEPARTMENT OF EDUCATION, Public Education Bldg, 300 Don Gaspar Ave, Santa Fe 87501-2786. Tel: 505-827-4278. Fax: 505-827-6694. *Coordr of Arts, Media & Libr,* Vicki Breen. E-mail: vicki.breen@state.nm.us

NEW YORK STATE EDUCATION DEPARTMENT, 89 Washington Ave, Education Bldg, Albany 12234. Web Site: www.nysed.gov. *Sch Libr Media Serv Assoc,* John Brock. Tel: 518-474-1672, Fax: 518-473-4884. E-mail: john.brock@nysed.gov

PUBLIC SCHOOLS OF NORTH CAROLINA, North Carolina Department of Public Instruction, K-12 Curriculum, Instruction & Technology Division, Instructional Technology Section, 6301 Mail Service Center, Raleigh 27699-6364. Tel: 984-236-2100. Fax: 984-236-2349. Web Site: www.dpi.state.nc.us *Instrul Tech Section Chief,* Kathy Parker. E-mail: Kathy.parker@dpi.nc.gov

NORTH DAKOTA STATE DEPARTMENT OF PUBLIC INSTRUCTION, State Capitol Bldg, Ninth Fl, 600 E Boulevard Ave, Bismarck 58505-0440. Tel: 701-328-2260. Web Site: www.dpi.state.nd.us. *Dir of Sch Approval & Opportunity,* Joe Kolosky. Tel: 701-328-2755. Fax: 701-328-4770. E-mail: jkolosky@nd.gov

OHIO DEPARTMENT OF EDUCATION, 25 S Front St, Columbus 43215-4183. Tel: 614-466-1317. Fax: 614-387-0421. Web Site: www.ode.state.oh.us. *Curric & Instruction, Sch Libr,* Shantelle Hill. Tel: 614-752-5070. E-mail: shantelle.hill@education.ohio.gov

OKLAHOMA STATE DEPARTMENT OF EDUCATION, 2500 N Lincoln Blvd, Oklahoma City 73105-4599. Tel: 405-521-3301. Fax: 405-521-6205. Web Site: www.sde.state.ok.us. Superintendent of Pub Instruction,Ryan Walters

Documents/Media Production Section. Tel: 405-521-3103. *Media Production Dir,* Marty Fulk.

PENNSYLVANIA DEPARTMENT OF EDUCATION, Resources for School Libraries, Commonwealth Libraries, 333 Market St, Harrisburg 17126-0333. Tel: 717-787-8007

RHODE ISLAND DEPARTMENT OF EDUCATION, Shepard Bldg, 255 Westminster St, Providence 02903-3414. Tel: 401-222-4600. Fax: 401-222-6178. Web Site: www.ride.ri.gov

SOUTH CAROLINA DEPARTMENT OF EDUCATION, District Technology Services, 1429 Senate St, Columbia 29201. Tel: 803-734-1434. Fax: 803-734-4064

SOUTH DAKOTA STATE LIBRARY, 800 Governors Dr, Pierre 57501-2294. Tel: 605-773-3131. Fax: 605-773-6962. Web Site: library.sd.gov. *State Librn,* George Seamon. E-mail: george.seamon@state.sd.us

TEXAS EDUCATION AGENCY, 1701 N Congress Ave, Austin 78701-1494. Tel: 512-463-9601. Fax: 512-463-3612

UTAH STATE OFFICE OF EDUCATION, Library Media, 250 E 500 S, PO Box 144200, Salt Lake City 84114-4200. Tel: 801-538-7616. Fax: 801-538-7769. Web Site: www.usoe.k12.ut.us/curr/library/. *Spec,* Davina Sauthoff. E-mail:davina.sauthoff@schools.utah.gov

VERMONT DEPARTMENT OF EDUCATION, One National Life Dr, Davis 5 Montipelier, 05620.Tel: 802-828-1130. Web Site: www.education.vermont.gov. *Secy of Educ,* Daniel French

VIRGINIA STATE DEPARTMENT OF EDUCATION, James Monroe Bldg, 101 N 14th St, PO Box 2120, Richmond 23218-2120. Tel: 804-225-2825. Fax: 804-371-2455. Web Site: www.doe.virginia.gov. *Off of Educ Tech & Libr Serv Dir,* Jean Weller. E-mail: Jean.Weller@doe.virginia.gov

WASHINGTON OFFICE OF THE STATE SUPERINTENDENT OF PUBLIC INSTRUCTION, Old Capitol Bldg, PO Box 47200, Olympia 98504-7200. TDD: 360-664-3631. Web Site: www.k12.wa.us. *Superintendent Pub Instruction,* Chris Reykdal. Tel: 360-725-6004. E-mail: chris.reykdal@k12.wa.us. *Dir, Title I, LAP, Title V,* Gayle Pauley. Tel: 360-725-6100. Fax: 360-586-3305. E-mail: Gayle.Pauley@k12.wa.us

WEST VIRGINIA STATE DEPARTMENT OF EDUCATION, 1900 Kanawha Blvd, Capitol Complex Bldg 6, Rm B-346, Charleston 25305. Tel: 304-558-7880. Fax: 304-558-2584. Web Site: www.wvde.state.wv.us. *Exec Dir, Off of Instrul Tech,* Brenda Morris. E-mail bmorris@k12.wv.us

WISCONSIN STATE DEPARTMENT OF PUBLIC INSTRUCTION, 125 S Webster St, PO Box 7841, Madison 53707. Tel: 608-266-2205. Fax: 608-266-8770. Web: www.dpi.wi.gov. *State Superintendent, Div for Libr Tech & Commun Learning,* Dr. Jill Underly

Instructional Media & Technology Team. *Dir,* Doug Benson. E-mail: doug.benson@dpi.wi.gov. , *Sch Libr Media Consult,* Monica Treptow

Public Library Development *Dir,* John Debacher

Interlibrary Loan & Resource Sharing. 2109 S Stoughton Rd, Madison 53716. Tel: 608-224-6161. Chief, Ref & ILL, Martha Berninger

Library & Statistical Information Center Team. *Librn,* Kay Ihlenfeldt

WYOMING DEPARTMENT OF EDUCATION, Hathaway Bldg, 2nd Flr, 2300 Capitol Ave, Cheyenne 82002-0050. Tel: 307-777-7675. Fax: 307-777-6234. *State Superintendent of Pub Instruction,* Megan Degenfelder. E-mail: superintendent@wyo.gov

GUAM PUBLIC SCHOOL SYSTEM, Curriculum & Instruction Improvement, PO Box DE, Hagatna 96932. Tel: 671-475-0457. Fax: 671-472-5003. Web Site: www.gdoe.net. *Dep Superintendent,* Jon J P Fernandez. Tel: 671-300-1247. E-mail: jfernandez@doe.edu.gu

NORTHERN MARIANA ISLANDS, Public School System Library Program. PO Box 501370, Saipan, 96950. Tel: 01-670-237-3061. *Contact,* Rita A Sablan. E-mail: sablanr@pss.cnmi.mp

COMMONWEALTH OF PUERTO RICO, DEPARTMENT OF EDUCATION, Public Library Services Division, PO Box 190759, San Juan 00919-0759. Tel: 787-754-1120. Fax: 787-754-0843. *Dir,* Aura Roderigues

VIRGIN ISLANDS DEPARTMENT OF EDUCATION, Media Library Services, 1834 Kongens Gade, Charlotte Amalie, Saint Thomas 00802-6742. Tel: 340-775-2250, Ext 8534. Fax: 340-777-3673. Web Site:/www.vide.vi. *Coordr Media Libr Serv,* Nancy Christie. E-mail: nchristie@sttj.k12.vi

Interlibrary Loan Code for the United States

The "Interlibrary Loan Code for the United States" is reprinted with permission of the Reference and User Services Association (RUSA), a division of the American Library Association (ALA), www.ala.org/rusa.

Prepared by the Interlibrary Loan Committee, Reference and User Services Association (RUSA), 1994, revised 2001. Revised 2008, by the Sharing and Transforming Access to Resources Section (STARS).

For more detailed information about the provisions of this code, please see the accompanying explanatory supplement.

Introduction

The Reference and User Services Association, acting for the American Library Association in its adoption of this code, recognizes that the sharing of material between libraries is an integral element in the provision of library service and believes it to be in the public interest to encourage such an exchange.

In the interest of providing quality service, libraries have an obligation to obtain material to meet the informational needs of users when local resources do not meet those needs. Interlibrary Loan (ILL), a mechanism for obtaining material, is essential to the vitality of all libraries.

The effectiveness of the national interlibrary loan system depends upon participation of libraries of all types and sizes.

This code establishes principles that facilitate the requesting of material by a library and the provision of loans or copies in response to those requests. In this code, "material" includes books, audiovisual materials, and other returnable items as well as copies of journal articles, book chapters, excerpts, and other non-returnable items.

1.0 Definition

1.1 Interlibrary loan is the process by which a library requests material from, or supplies material to, another library.

2.0 Purpose

2.1 The purpose of interlibrary loan as defined by this code is to obtain, upon request of a library user, material not available in the user's local library.

3.0 Scope

3.1 This code regulates the exchange of material between libraries in the United States.

3.2 Interlibrary loan transactions with libraries outside of the United States are governed by the International Federation of Library Associations and Institutions' International Lending: Principles and Guidelines for Procedure.

4.0 Responsibilities of the Requesting Library

4.1 Establish, promptly update, and make available an interlibrary borrowing policy.

4.2 Ensure the confidentiality of the user.

4.3 Describe completely and accurately the requested material following accepted bibliographic practice.

4.4 Identify libraries that own the requested material and check and adhere to the policies of potential supplying libraries.

4.5 When no libraries can be identified as owning the needed material, requests may be sent to libraries believed likely to own the material, accompanied by an indication that ownership is not confirmed.

4.6 Transmit interlibrary loan requests electronically whenever possible.

4.7 For copy requests, comply with the U.S. copyright law (Title 17, U.S. Code) and its accompanying guidelines.

4.8 Assume responsibility for borrowed material from the time it leaves the supplying library until it has been returned to and received by the supplying library. This includes all material shipped directly to and/or returned by the user. If damage or loss occurs, provide compensation or replacement, in accordance with the preference of the supplying library.

4.9 Assume full responsibility for user-initiated transactions.

4.10 Honor the due date and enforce any use restrictions specified by the supplying library. The due date is defined as the date the material is due to be checked-in at the supplying library.

4.11 Request a renewal before the item is due. If the supplying library does not respond, the requesting library may assume that a renewal has been granted extending the due date by the same length of time as the original loan.

4.12 All borrowed material is subject to recall. Respond immediately if the supplying library recalls an item.

4.13 Package material to prevent damage in shipping and comply with any special instructions stated by the supplying library.

4.14 Failure to comply with the provisions of this code may be reason for suspension of service by a supplying library.

5.0 Responsibilities of the Supplying Library

5.1 Establish, promptly update, and make available an interlibrary lending policy.

5.2 Consider filling all requests for material regardless of format.

5.3 Ensure the confidentiality of the user.

5.4 Process requests in a timely manner that recognizes the needs of the requesting library and/or the requirements of the electronic network or transmission system being used. If unable to fill a request, respond promptly and state the reason the request cannot be filled.

5.5 When filling requests, send sufficient information with each item to identify the request.

5.6 Indicate the due date and any restrictions on the use of the material and any special return packaging or shipping requirements. The due date is defined as the date the material is due to be checked-in at the supplying library.

5.7 Ship material in a timely and efficient manner to the location specified by the requesting library. Package loaned material to prevent loss or damage in shipping. Deliver copies electronically whenever possible.

5.8 Respond promptly to requests for renewals. If no response is sent, the requesting library may assume that a renewal has been granted extending the due date by the same length of time as the original loan.

5.9 Loaned material is subject to recall at any time.

5.10 Failure to comply with the provisions of this code may lead to suspension of service to the requesting library.

Supplemental Documentation

For more detailed information, please see the accompanying explanatory supplement.

Interlibrary Loan Code for the United States

For Use with the Interlibrary Loan Code for the United States (May 2008)

This Explanatory Supplement is intended to amplify specific sections of the Interlibrary Loan Code for the United States, providing fuller explanation and specific examples for text that is intentionally general and prescriptive. Topical headings refer to the equivalent sections in the Code. Libraries are expected to comply with the Code, using this Supplement as a source for general direction.[1]

Introduction

The U.S. Interlibrary Loan Code, first published in 1917 and adopted by The American Library Association in 1919, is designed to provide a code of behavior for requesting and supplying material within the United States. This code does not override individual or consortial agreements or regional or state codes which may be more liberal or more prescriptive. This national code is intended to provide guidelines for exchanges between libraries where no other agreement applies. The code is intended to be adopted voluntarily by U.S. libraries and is not enforced by an oversight body. However, as indicated below, supplying libraries may suspend service to borrowing libraries that fail to comply with the provisions of this code.

This interlibrary loan code describes the responsibilities of libraries to each other when requesting material for users. Increasingly, libraries are allowing users to request material directly from suppliers. This code makes provision for direct patron requesting and at the same time affirms the responsibility of the patron's library for the safety and return of the borrowed material, or for paying the cost of a non-returnable item sent directly to the patron.

Technology has expanded access options beyond traditional library-to-library transactions. Unmediated requests, direct-to-user delivery, purchase-on-demand options, and increasing full-text availability are exciting developments in resource sharing. At present, the Interlibrary Loan Code reflects established practices. However, libraries and other information centers are encouraged to explore and use nontraditional means where available to ensure maximum accessibility and convenience for users. More information for libraries interested in new ideas for resource sharing can be found at: http://www.ala.org/ala/rusa/rusaourassoc/rusasections/stars/starssection

1. Definition

The Interlibrary Code for the United States covers transactions between two libraries. Transactions between libraries and commercial document suppliers or library fee-based services are contractual arrangements beyond the scope of these guidelines.

The terms "requesting library" and "supplying library" are used in preference to "borrowing" and "lending" to cover the exchange of copies as well as loans.

2. Purpose

Interlibrary loan (ILL) is intended to complement local collections and is not a substitute for good library collections intended to meet the routine needs of users. ILL is based on a tradition of sharing resources between various types and sizes of libraries and rests on the belief that no library, no matter how large or well supported, is self-sufficient in today's world. It is also evident that some libraries are net borrowers (borrow more than they lend) and others are net lenders (lend more than they borrow), but the system of interlibrary loan still rests on the belief that all libraries should be willing to lend if they are willing to borrow.

3. Scope

The conduct of international interlibrary loan is regulated by the rules set forth in the *IFLA document International Lending: Principles and Guidelines for Procedure.*[2]

Although the U.S. shares a common border with Canada and Mexico, it is important to remember that these countries have their own library infrastructures and ILL codes. The *IFLA Principles and Guidelines* regulate the exchange of material between institutions across these borders. Further, U.S. librarians would be wise to inform themselves of customs requirements that take precedence over library agreements when material is shipped across these national borders, e.g., as described in the Association of Research Libraries' *Transborder Interlibrary Loan: Shipping Interlibrary Loan Materials from the U.S. to Canada.*[3]

4. Responsibilities of the Requesting Library

4.1 Written Policies

A library's interlibrary loan borrowing policy should be available in a written format that is readily accessible to all library users. Whenever possible the borrowing policy should be posted on the library's Web site as well as be available in paper copy at public service desks or wherever other library user handouts are provided.

4.2 Confidentiality

Interlibrary loan transactions, like circulation transactions, are confidential library records. Interlibrary loan personnel are encouraged to be aware of local/state confidentiality rules and laws as they relate to interlibrary loan transactions. Appropriate steps, such as using identification numbers or codes rather than users' names, should be taken to maintain confidentiality. However, it is not a violation of this code to include a user's name on a request submitted to a supplier. Policies and procedures should be developed regarding the retention of ILL records and access to this information. ILL personnel should also be aware of privacy issues when posting requests for assistance or using the text of ILL requests as procedural examples. ALA's Office for Intellectual Freedom has developed a number of policies regarding confidentiality of library records.[4]

ILL staff should adhere to the American Library Association's (ALA) Code of Ethics[5], specifically principle III, that states: "We protect each library user's right to privacy and confidentiality with respect to information sought or received and resources consulted, borrowed, acquired or transmitted."

4.3 Complete Bibliographic Citation

A good bibliographic description is the best assurance that the user will receive the item requested. Rather than detail these descriptive elements, the code requires the requesting library to include whatever data provides the best indication of the desired material, whether an alphanumeric string or an extensive bibliographic citation. The important point is that this description be exact enough to avoid unnecessary work on the part of the supplier and frustration on the part of the user. For example, journal title verification rather than article level verification would be sufficient.

4.4 Identifying Appropriate Suppliers

Requesting libraries should use all resources at their disposal to determine ownership of a particular title before sending a request to a potential supplier. Many libraries contribute their holdings to major bibliographic utilities such as DOCLINE and/or OCLC and make their individual catalogs freely available via the Internet. The interlibrary loan listserv (ill-l@webjunction.org) or other ILL-related lists are also excellent sources for the requesting library to verify and/or locate particularly difficult items.

The requesting library is encouraged to use resources such as the OCLC *Policies Directory* to determine lending policies including any applicable charges, before requesting material.

The requesting library should clearly state on the request an amount that meets or exceeds the charges of suppliers to which the request is sent. The requesting library is responsible for payment of any fees charged by the supplying library that are less than or equal to the amount stated on its request. Libraries are encouraged to use electronic invoicing capabilities such as OCLC's Interlibrary Loan Fee Management (IFM) system or the Electronic Fund Transfer System used by medical libraries.

4.5 Sending Unverified Requests

Despite the requirements in Sec. 4.4 and 4.5 that an item should be completely and accurately described and located, the code recognizes that it is not always possible to verify and/or locate a particular item. For example, a request may be sent to a potential supplier with strong holdings in a subject or to the institution at which the dissertation was written.

4.6 Transmitting the Request

The code recommends electronic communication. For many libraries, sending requests electronically means using the ILL messaging systems associated with DOCLINE, OCLC, other products that use the ISO ILL Protocol, or structured email requests.

Lacking the ability to transmit in this fashion, the requesting library should send a completed ALA interlibrary loan request form via fax, Internet transmission, or mail; use a potential supplier's web request form; or otherwise provide the necessary information via email message or conventional letter. Whatever communication method is used, the requesting library should identify and use the appropriate address or number for ILL requests.

The requesting library should include a street address, a postal box number, an IP address, a fax number, and an email address to give the supplying library delivery options. Any special needs, such as for a particular edition, language, or rush delivery, should be included on the request.

In addition, because the primary purpose of interlibrary loan is to provide material for relatively short term use by an individual, the requesting library should communicate with the supplying library in advance if the material is needed for other uses (such as course reserves, classroom or other group viewing of audio-visual material or for an extended loan period, especially of a textbook).

4.7 Copy Requests

The requesting library is responsible for complying with the provisions of Section 108(g)(2) Copyright Law[6] and the *Guidelines for the Proviso of Subsection* 108(g)(2) prepared by the National Commission on New Technological Uses of Copyrighted Works (the CONTU Guidelines).[7]

4.8 Responsibility of the Requester

The requesting library assumes an inherent risk when material is supplied through interlibrary loan. Although the number is small, some material is lost or damaged at some point along the route from the supplier and back again. The requesting library's responsibility for this loss is based on the concept that if the request had not been made, the material would not have left the supplier's shelf, and thus would not have been put at risk. This section clearly states that the requesting library is responsible for the material from the time it leaves the supplying library until its safe return to the supplying library.

If the requesting library asks for delivery at a location away from the library (such as to the user's home), the requesting library is likewise responsible for the material during this delivery and return process. In any case, a final decision regarding replacement, repair, or compensation rests with the supplying library.

Borrowed items should be returned in the condition in which they were received at the requesting library. In particular, adhesive labels or tape should not be affixed directly to any borrowed item.

It is the responsibility of the requesting library to pay invoices received or to notify the supplying library of any billing questions not later than six months from the billing date for the charges in question. The requesting library should also make every attempt to resolve billing questions within six months of notifying the supplying library of an apparent billing error.

Although the code stipulates that the requesting library is required to pay if billed for a lost or damaged item, the supplying library is not necessarily required to charge for a lost item. In the case of lost material, the requesting and supplying libraries may need to work together to resolve the matter. For instance, the library shipping the material may need to initiate a trace with the delivery firm.

4.9 Responsibility for Unmediated ILL Requests

Some requesting libraries permit users to initiate online ILL requests that are sent directly to potential supplying libraries. A requesting library that chooses to allow its users to order materials through interlibrary loan without mediation accepts responsibility for these requests as if they have been placed by library staff. The supplying library may assume that the user has been authenticated and authorized to place requests and that the requesting library assumes full responsibility for transaction charges, the safety and return of material, and the expense of replacement or repair.

4.10 Due Date and Use Restrictions

This code makes a departure from earlier codes that described due dates in terms of a "loan period" which was interpreted as the length of time a requesting library could retain the material before returning it. The primary object of this section is to provide a clear definition of due date as the date the material must be checked in at the supplying library. This definition brings ILL practice into alignment with automated circulation procedures and is intended to facilitate interoperability of ILL and circulation applications.

The requesting library should develop a method for monitoring due dates so that material can be returned to and checked in at the supplying library by the due date assigned by the supplying library.

The requesting library is responsible for ensuring compliance with any use restrictions specified by the supplying library such as "library use only" or "no photocopying."

4.11 Renewals

When the supplying library denies a renewal request the material should be returned by the original due date or as quickly as possible if the renewal is denied after the due date has passed.

4.12 Recalls

The response to a recall may be the immediate return of the material, or timely communication with the supplying library to negotiate a new due date.

When the material has been recalled, the requesting library is encouraged to return the material via an expedited delivery carrier such as UPS, FedEx, or USPS Priority Mail.

4.13 Shipping

It is the ultimate responsibility of the requesting library to return materials in the same condition in which they were received as noted in section 4.8 of the *Interlibrary Loan Code for the United States.*

It is the responsibility of the requesting library to follow the shipping and packaging requirements, including insurance and preferred shipping method, as stipulated by the supplying library. Packaging is defined as the outer material, which may be a box, padded envelope, etc. Wrapping is defined as an inner covering for the item such as paper or bubble wrap.

If no shipping or packaging methods are specified, the requesting library's regular form of shipment should be used.

If packaging material has been used previously, remove or mark out old addresses, postal marks, etc. to avoid misdirection. Do not reuse old, frayed, ripped, or decaying packaging and wrapping materials - discard it instead. Clearly address all packages with both the destination and return addresses properly attached to the packaging material.

In accordance with United States Postal Service guidelines, tape is the preferred sealing methods on all types of packages. Remember that wrapping and packaging materials will most likely be reused. So, please use tape judiciously. If staples must be used, do not use industrial (e.g. copper) staples if at all possible. Copper staples make it very difficult to reuse wrapping and packaging materials and are not ergonomically sound.

Use wrapping and packaging material that is appropriate to the size and format of the material being shipped. Too small or too large packaging will not adequately protect materials during transportation. Remember to use appropriate wrapping to avoid shifting and damage to the contents.

For special formats, consult the appropriate ALA Guidelines:

- American Library Association. Association for Library Collections and Technical Services. *Guidelines for Packaging and Shipping Magnetic Tape Recording and Optical Discs (CD-ROM and CD-R) Carrying Audio, Video, and/or Data,* n.d.
- American Library Association. Association for Library Collection and Technical Services. *Guidelines for Packaging and Shipping Microforms,* 1989.
- American Library Association. Association for Library Collections and Technical Services. *Guidelines for Preservation Photocopying of Replacement Pages,* 1990.
- American Library Association. Video Round Table. *Guidelines for the Interlibrary Loan of Audiovisual Formats,* 1998.
- American Library Association. Association of College and Research Libraries. Ad Hoc Committee on the Interlibrary Loan of Rate and Unique Materials. *Guidelines for the Interlibrary Loan of Rare and Unique Materials,* 2004.

4.14 Suspension of Service

Repeated or egregious breaches of this code may result in the requesting library's inability to obtain material. Examples of actions that may result in suspension include lost or damaged books, allowing "library use only" books to leave the library, or failing to pay the supplier's charges. A supplying library should not suspend service to a requesting library without first attempting to resolve the problem(s).

5. Responsibilities of the Supplying Library

5.1 Lending Policy

The lending policy should be clear, detailed, and readily available to requesting libraries. The policy should include among other things, schedule of fees and charges, overdue fines, non-circulating items/categories, current shipping instructions, calendar for service suspensions, penalties for late payments, etc. While a supplying library may charge additional fees for the rapid delivery of requested material, it is recommended that no additional fees be charged for the routine supply of documents via electronic means.

The supplying library is encouraged to make its lending policy available in print, on the library's Web site, and in resources such as the *OCLC Policies Directory.* The supplying library should be willing to fill requests for all types and classes of users, and all types of libraries, regardless of their size or geographic location.

5.2 Material Format

Supplying libraries are encouraged to lend as liberally as possible regardless of the format of the material requested, while retaining the right to determine what material will be supplied. It is the obligation of the supplying library to consider the loan of material on a case by case basis. Supplying libraries are encouraged to lend audiovisual material, newspapers, and other categories of material that have traditionally been non-circulating.

Supplying libraries are encouraged to follow *ACRL's Guidelines for the Interlibrary Loan of Rare and Unique Materials*[8] and the *Guidelines for Interlibrary Loan of Audiovisual Formats.*[9]

If permitted by copyright law, the supplying library should consider providing a copy in lieu of a loan rather than giving a negative response.

Supplying libraries should be aware of the provisions of license agreements for electronic resources that may either permit or prohibit use of an electronic resource to fill interlibrary copying requests.

5.3 Confidentiality

The supplying library has a responsibility to safeguard the confidentiality of the individual requesting the material. The sharing of the user's name between requesting and supplying library is not, of itself, a violation of confidentiality. However, the supplying library should not require the user's name if the requesting library chooses not to provide it. If the name is provided, the supplying library needs to take care not to divulge the identity of the person requesting the material.

5.4 Timely Processing

The supplying library has a responsibility to act promptly on all requests. If a supplying library cannot fill a request within a reasonable time then it should respond promptly. The response should be sent via the same method the requesting library used to send the request, or by otherwise contacting the requesting library directly. Some ILL messaging systems such as OCLC and DOCLINE have built-in time periods after which requests will either expire or be sent to another institution. The supplying library should respond before this time expires rather than allow requests to time-out.

Providing a reason for an unfilled request helps the requesting library determine what additional steps, if any, may be taken to access the requested item. For example, "non-circulating" indicates the item is likely available for on-site use while "in use" indicates that another request at a later date might be filled. Providing no reason or simply stating "policy problem" or "other" without providing additional information deprives the requesting library of important information and can lead to time-consuming follow-up for both libraries.

Timely processing of a loan or copy may involve other library departments, such as circulation, copy services, and the mailroom. The interlibrary loan department is responsible for ensuring that material is delivered expeditiously, irrespective of internal library organizational responsibilities.

The supplying library should, when charging for materials, make every effort to allow for a variety of payment options. Payment through electronic crediting and debiting services such as OCLC's ILL Fee Management (IFM) system or other non-invoicing payment forms such as IFLA vouchers should be encouraged. The supplying library that charges should make every effort to accept the use of vouchers, coupons, or credit cards.

It is the responsibility of the supplying library to send final bills for service not later than six months after the supply date, final overdue notices not later than six months after the final due date, and final bills for replacement of lost material not later than one year after the final due date. The supplying library should resolve billing questions within six months of receiving notice of an apparent billing error.

5.5 Identifying the Request

The supplying library should send sufficient identifying information with the material to allow the requesting library to identify the material and process the request quickly. Such information may include a copy of the request, the requestor's transaction number, or the user's ID or name. Failure to include identifying information with the material can unduly delay its processing and may risk the safety of the material.

Supplying libraries are encouraged to enclose an accurate and complete return mailing label.

5.6 Use Restrictions and Due Date

Although it is the responsibility of the requesting library to ensure the safe treatment and return of borrowed material, the supplying library should provide specific instructions when it is lending material that needs special handling. These instructions might include the requirement that material be used only in a monitored special collections area, no photocopying, library use only, specific return packaging/shipping instructions, etc. The supplying library should not send "library use only" material directly to a user.

The supplying library should clearly indicate the date on which it expects the loan to be discharged in its circulation system. As explained in section 4.10 above, this code has moved away from the concept of a loan period, to a definite date that accommodates the sending and return of material as well as sufficient time for the use of the material. For example, a supplying library might establish a due date of six (6) weeks for the purpose of providing one (1) week for shipping, four (4) weeks for use, and one (1) week for the return trip and check-in.

5.7 Delivery and Packaging

The location specified by the requesting library may include the requesting library, a branch or departmental library, or the individual user.

It is the responsibility of the supplying library:

- to judge whether an item is suitable for shipment and circulation. If a damaged item is sent, the supplying library should note all prior damage (such as loose pages or loose spine) and not hold the requesting library responsible for subsequent damage.
- to take care that the material it sends out is properly packaged to protect the item from damage even though the requesting library will be held responsible for material damaged in shipment to specify the shipping method, as well as insurance, for returning materials and if any special wrapping or packaging is required. See section 4.13 above for definitions and other important information regarding wrapping and packaging.
- to provide a complete street address if asking for return via UPS, FedEx, etc. (Many supplying libraries find it safer and more cost effective to ship all material via expedited carriers).
- to work with the requesting library when tracing a lost or damaged item if the commercial delivery firm is responsible for reimbursement for losses in transit.

5.8 Renewals

The supplying library should respond affirmatively or negatively to all renewal requests. The supplying library is encouraged to grant the renewal request if the material is not needed by a local user.

5.9 Recalls

The supplying library may recall material at its discretion at any time. Increasingly, some libraries are finding it more effective to request the material on ILL for a local user rather than to recall material in use by another library.

5.10 Service Suspension

A supplying library should not suspend service without first attempting to address the problem(s) with the requesting library.

References

[1] Boucher, Virginia. *Interlibrary Loan Practices Handbook.* Chicago, IL: American Library Association, 1997. Though written in light of an earlier code, the Practices Handbook contains many useful and practical details on interlibrary loan procedures.

[2] International Federation of Library Associations and Institutions. *International Lending: Principles and Guidelines for Procedure.* 2001.

[3] Transborder Interlibrary Loan: *Shipping Interlibrary Loan Materials from the U.S. to Canada.* 1999. (note: Pricing information is out of date)

[4] American Library Association. Office for Intellectual Freedom. *Policy on Confidentiality of Library Records.* 1986.

American Library Association. Office for Intellectual Freedom. *Policy Concerning Confidentiality of Personally Identifiable Information about Library Users.* 2004.

[5] American Library Association. Committee on Professional Ethics. *Code of Ethics.* Chicago, American Library Association, 1995.

[6] Copyright Law of the United States of America Chapter 1, Section 108: Limitations on the exclusive rights: *Reproduction by libraries and archives.*

[7] National Commission on New Technological Uses of Copyrighted Works. *Guidelines on Photocopying Under Interlibrary Loan Arrangements.*

[8] American Library Association. Association of College and Research Libraries. Ad Hoc Committee on the Interlibrary Loan of Rate and Unique Materials. *Guidelines for the Loan of Rare and Unique Materials.* 2004.

[9] American Library Association. Video Round Table. *Guidelines for Interlibrary Loan of Audiovisual Formats.* 1998.

[10] Hilyer, Lee. *Interlibrary loan and document delivery: best practices for operating and managing interlibrary loan services in all libraries.* New York: Haworth Information Press, 2006. (Co-published simultaneously as *Journal of interlibrary loan, document delivery & electronic reserve,* volume 16, numbers 1/2, 2006)

[11] Hilyer, Lee. *Interlibrary loan and document delivery in the larger academic library: a guide for university, research, and larger public libraries.* Binghamton, NY: Haworth Information Press, 2002. (Co-published simultaneously as *Journal of interlibrary loan, document delivery & information supply,* v. 13, nos. 1/2, 2002)

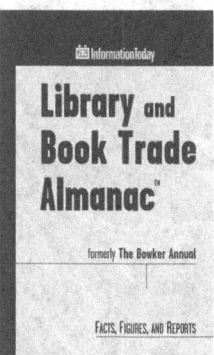

for the library, publishing, research, and business professional

[illegible]

American Library Directory

[illegible]

This comprehensive directory brings together nearly 5,000 retail and antiquarian book dealers [illegible]

[illegible]

INDEXES

Organization Index

Personnel Index

ORGANIZATION INDEX

Air Force, Army and Navy are listed under United States.

The letter (N) after an organization name indicates that the organization will be found in the Networks and Consortia section.

Letter-by-letter alphabetization is used. Universities, colleges or junior colleges named after a person are alphabetized by the person's first name, e.g., Sarah Lawrence College will be found under S. Any other library or institution named after a person will be alphabetized by the person's last name, e.g., Martin Luther King Libarary will be found under K.

A T Still University, Mesa AZ p. 66
A T Still University Library, Kirksville MO p. 1258
A&O Shearman Library, Washington DC p. 359
A&O Shearman Library, New York NY p. 1578
Aalfs Wilbur Library, *see* Sioux City Public Library, Sioux City IA p. 782
Aaniiih Nakoda College Library, Harlem MT p. 1295
Aaniin Branch, *see* Markham Public Library, Markham ON p. 2656
Aaron A H Health Sciences Library, *see* Kaleida Health - Buffalo General Medical Center, Buffalo NY p. 1509
Abbell Joseph J & Dora Library, *see* Congregation Rodfei Zedek, Chicago IL p. 559
Abbell Maxwell Library, *see* North Suburban Synagogue Beth El, Highland Park IL p. 599
Abbett Wheeler Taft Sr Library, *see* Pima County Public Library, Tucson AZ p. 82
Abbeville County Library System, Abbeville SC p. 2045
Abbeville Memorial Library, Abbeville AL p. 3
Abbey of Gethsemani Library, Trappist KY p. 876
Abbey of Regina Laudis Library, Bethlehem CT p. 302
Abbot Public Library, Marblehead MA p. 1031
Abbotsford Community Library, *see* Fraser Valley Regional Library, Abbotsford BC p. 2561
Abbotsford Public Library, Abbotsford WI p. 2419
Abbott Edith Memorial Library, *see* Grand Island Public Library, Grand Island NE p. 1316
Abbott Library, Sunapee NH p. 1382
Abbott Memorial Library, Dexter ME p. 923
Abbott Memorial Library, South Pomfret VT p. 2295
Abbottsfield-Penny McKee, *see* Edmonton Public Library, Edmonton AB p. 2536
Abell George T & Gladys H Library Center, *see* Austin College, Sherman TX p. 2243
Aberdeen District Library, Aberdeen ID p. 515
Aberdeen Hospital, New Glasgow NS p. 2621
Abernathy Public Library, Abernathy TX p. 2131
Abeytunga P K Resource Centre, *see* Canadian Centre for Occupational Health & Safety, Hamilton ON p. 2644
Abilene Christian University, Abilene TX p. 2131
Abilene Educational Center Library, *see* Cisco College, Abilene TX p. 2155
Abilene Library Consortium (N), Abilene TX p. 2775
Abilene Public Library, Abilene KS p. 795
Abilene Public Library, Abilene TX p. 2131
Abington College Library, *see* Pennsylvania State University, Abington PA p. 1903
Abington Community Library, Clarks Summit PA p. 1922
Abington Free Library, *see* Abington Township Public Library, Abington PA p. 1903
Abington Memorial Hospital, Abington PA p. 1903
Abington Memorial Library, *see* Arkansas State University, Beebe AR p. 90
Abington Presbyterian Church Library, Abington PA p. 1903
Abington Public Library, Abington MA p. 983
Abington Social Library, Abington CT p. 301
Abington Township Public Library, Abington PA p. 1903
ABLE Librry, *see* State of Vermont Department of Libraries VT p. 2278
ABLE Library, *see* Vermont Department of Libraries, Barre VT p. 2278
Abplanalp Josephine S Library, *see* University of New England Libraries, Portland ME p. 917
Abraham Baldwin Agricultural College, Tifton GA p. 500
Abraham Lincoln Presidential Library, Springfield IL p. 649
Abrahams Milton R & Pauline S Library, *see* Joslyn Art Museum, Omaha NE p. 1328
Abrahams Milton R, *see* Omaha Public Library, Omaha NE p. 1329
ABSAUM (N), *see* Association des Bibliotheques de la Sante Affiliees, Montreal QC p. 2778
Absecon Public Library, Absecon NJ p. 1387
ACA Library of Savannah College of Art & Design, Atlanta GA p. 460
Acacia Library, *see* Phoenix Public Library, Phoenix AZ p. 72
Academic Libraries of Brooklyn (N), Brooklyn NY p. 2770
Academic Resources Information Center, *see* United States Navy, Newport RI p. 2035
Academic Support Center Media Rental Library, *see* University of Missouri-Columbia, Columbia MO p. 1243
Academy Art Museum, Easton MD p. 964
Academy of Art University Library, San Francisco CA p. 223
Academy of Motion Picture Arts & Sciences, Beverly Hills CA p. 124
Academy of Natural Sciences of Drexel University, Philadelphia PA p. 1974
Acadia Municipal Library, Acadia Valley AB p. 2521
Acadia Parish Library, Crowley LA p. 888
Acadia University, Wolfville NS p. 2623
Accettola Charles N Medical Library, *see* Staten Island University Hospital Northwell Health, Staten Island NY p. 1645
Accokeek Foundation Library, Accokeek MD p. 949
Achilles Frances Mulhall Library, *see* Whitney Museum of American Art, New York NY p. 1604
Acker David D Library, Fort Belvoir VA p. 2318
Ackerman Irving P MD Health Sciences Library, *see* Kaiser-Permanente Medical Center, Los Angeles CA p. 162
Ackley Public Library, Ackley IA p. 729
ACL (N), *see* Association of Christian Librarians, Cedarville OH p. 2772
Acme Municipal Library, Acme AB p. 2521
Acopian Center for Conservation Learning, Orwigsburg PA p. 1973
Acorn Public Library District, Oak Forest IL p. 627
Acosta Moreno Esperanza Regional, *see* El Paso Public Library, El Paso TX p. 2174
ACT Information Resource Center, Iowa City IA p. 760
Acton Memorial Library, Acton MA p. 983
Acton Public Library, Old Saybrook CT p. 333
Acton Public Library, Acton ME p. 913
ACTS (N), *see* Association of Chicago Theological Schools, Mundelein IL p. 2764
Acuren Group, Inc Library, Edmonton AB p. 2534
Acushnet Public Library, Acushnet MA p. 983
Acworth Silsby Library, Acworth NH p. 1353
Ada Community Library, Boise ID p. 516
Ada Library, *see* College of Western Idaho, Boise ID p. 527
Ada Public Library, Ada OH p. 1743
Ada Public Library, Ada OK p. 1839
Ada Public Library, *see* Lake Agassiz Regional Library, Ada MN p. 1188
Adair County Public Library, Columbia KY p. 852
Adair County Public Library, Kirksville MO p. 1258
Adair Public Library, Adair IA p. 729
Adamany David Library, *see* Wayne State University Libraries, Detroit MI p. 1100
Adams & Reese LLP, New Orleans LA p. 900
Adams Center Free Library, Adams Center NY p. 1481
Adams County Historical Society, Gettysburg PA p. 1935
Adams County Historical Society Archives, Hastings NE p. 1317
Adams County Law Library, Gettysburg PA p. 1935
Adams County Library, Hettinger ND p. 1736
Adams County Library, Adams WI p. 2419
Adams County Library System, Gettysburg PA p. 1935
Adams County Public Library, Peebles OH p. 1814
Adams Dr & Mrs J F Memorial Library, *see* Cannon County Library System, Woodbury TN p. 2130
Adams Free Library, Adams MA p. 983

Adams Free Library, Adams NY p. 1481
Adams Henry C Memorial Library, Prophetstown IL p. 637
Adams James P Library, *see* Rhode Island College, Providence RI p. 2039
Adams Memorial Library, Latrobe PA p. 1953
Adams Memorial Library, Central Falls RI p. 2030
Adams Paul M Memorial Library, *see* Rocky Mountain College, Billings MT p. 1288
Adams Public Library, Adams OR p. 1871
Adams Public Library System, Decatur IN p. 678
Adams State University, Alamosa CO p. 263
Adams-Vines Library, *see* Arkansas Northeastern College, Blytheville AR p. 91
Adamstown Area Library, Adamstown PA p. 1903
Adamsville Public Library, Adamsville AL p. 3
Adath Israel Congregation, Cincinnati OH p. 1759
Adcock Ernest J Library, *see* Holmes Community College, Ridgeland MS p. 1232
Addictions Services Library, *see* Eastern Health, St. John's NL p. 2610
Addiego Peter Health Sciences Library, *see* Nassau University Medical Center, East Meadow NY p. 1528
Addison Public Library, Addison IL p. 535
Addison Public Library, Addison NY p. 1481
Addison Township Public Library, Leonard MI p. 1126
Addlestone Marlene & Nathan Library, *see* College of Charleston, Charleston SC p. 2050
Adel Public Library, Adel IA p. 729
Adelphi University, Brooklyn NY p. 1500
Adelphi University, Garden City NY p. 1536
Adelphi University, Hauppauge NY p. 1544
Adelson Library, Laboratory of Ornithology, *see* Cornell University Library, Ithaca NY p. 1551
Adirondack Community College Library, Queensbury NY p. 1625
Adirondack Correctional Facility Library, Ray Brook NY p. 1626
Adirondack Experience, the Museum on Blue Mountain Lake Library, Blue Mountain Lake NY p. 1495
Adkins Rocky J Public Library, Sandy Hook KY p. 874
Adler Pollock & Sheehan PC Library, Providence RI p. 2037
Adler University, Chicago IL p. 553
Administration Office, *see* Tangipahoa Parish Library, Amite LA p. 880
Administrative Office, *see* Lonesome Pine Regional Library, Wise VA p. 2354
Administrative Office of the United States Courts Library, Washington DC p. 359
ad, *see* Scenic Regional Library, Union MO p. 1283
Administrative Offices, *see* Sunflower County Library System, Indianola MS p. 1220
Administrative Offices & Archives, *see* Irving Public Library, Irving TX p. 2202
Administrative Service Center, *see* Timberland Regional Library, Tumwater WA p. 2388
Administrative Tribunals Support Services of Canada, Ottawa ON p. 2664
Admiral Nimitz National Museum of the Pacific War, Fredericksburg TX p. 2181
Adrian College, Adrian MI p. 1075
Adrian District Library, Adrian MI p. 1075
Adriance Memorial Library, *see* Poughkeepsie Public Library District, Poughkeepsie NY p. 1623
Adult Library, *see* First Presbyterian Church, Houston TX p. 2191
AdventHealth Hinsdale, Hinsdale IL p. 600
AdventHealth Orlando, Orlando FL p. 430
AdventHealth Shawnee Mission Medical Library, Shawnee Mission KS p. 836
AdventHealth Tampa, Tampa FL p. 448
AdventistHealth University, Orlando FL p. 430
Adventist Health Glendale, Glendale CA p. 148
Adventist HealthCare Shady Grove Medical Center, Rockville MD p. 973
Advocate Aurora Library, Milwaukee WI p. 2457
Advocate Illinois Masonic Medical Center, Chicago IL p. 553
Advocate Library, *see* Cumberland Public Libraries, Advocate Harbour NS p. 2615
Advocate Lutheran General Hospital, Park Ridge IL p. 633
Advocate/Times-Picayune Library, *see* Capital City Press, Baton Rouge LA p. 882
Advocates for Youth, Washington DC p. 359
Aerospace Corp, El Segundo CA p. 140
Aesthetic Realism Foundation Library, New York NY p. 1578
African American Library at the Gregory School, *see* Houston Public Library, Houston TX p. 2195
African-American Research Library & Cultural Center, *see* Broward County Libraries Division, Fort Lauderdale FL p. 396
Afro-American Historical Society Museum Library, Jersey City NJ p. 1409
Afro-American Studies Resource Center, *see* Howard University Libraries, Washington DC p. 369
Afton Free Library, Afton NY p. 1481
Agassiz Library, *see* Fraser Valley Regional Library, Agassiz BC p. 2561
Agat Public Library-Maria R Aguigui Memorial Library, *see* Guam Public Library System, Agat GU p. 2505
Agave Library, *see* Phoenix Public Library, Phoenix AZ p. 72
Agawam Public Library, Agawam MA p. 983
Agency Public Library, Agency IA p. 729
Agnes Scott College, Decatur GA p. 475
Agness Community Library, Agness OR p. 1871
Agriculture & Agri-Food Canada, Ottawa ON p. 2664
Aguilar Public Library, Aguilar CO p. 263
Ahmadiyya Movement In Islam Inc, Washington DC p. 359
Ahoskie Public Library, *see* Albemarle Regional Library, Ahoskie NC p. 1727
Ahrens Memorial Library, *see* United States Air Force, Holloman AFB NM p. 1469
AIDE Canada Library, Richmond BC p. 2575
Aiea Public Library, *see* Hawaii State Public Library System, Aiea HI p. 507
AIHEC (N), *see* American Indian Higher Education Consortium, Alexandria VA p. 2776
AIKCU (N), *see* Association of Independent Kentucky Colleges & Universities, Frankfort KY p. 2765
Aiken-Bamberg-Barnwell-Edgefield Regional Library, Aiken SC p. 2045
Aiken Technical College Library, Graniteville SC p. 2060
Aikins Law, Winnipeg MB p. 2592
Aims Community College, Greeley CO p. 284
Aina Haina Public Library, *see* Hawaii State Public Library System, Honolulu HI p. 507
Ainsworth Annie Porter Memorial Library, Sandy Creek NY p. 1636
Ainsworth Public Library, Ainsworth NE p. 1305
Ainsworth Public Library, Williamstown VT p. 2299
Air Force Flight Test Center, *see* United States Air Force, Edwards AFB CA p. 139
Air Force Research Lab, Tyndall Research Site, *see* United States Air Force, Tyndall AFB FL p. 451
Air Force Research Laboratory, Eglin AFB FL p. 394
Air Force Research Laboratory-Information Directorate Technical Library, *see* United States Air Force, Rome NY p. 1632
Air Force Research Laboratory, Wright Research Site, *see* United States Air Force, Wright-Patterson AFB OH p. 1834
Air Line Pilots Association International, McLean VA p. 2332
Aird & Berlis LLP, Toronto ON p. 2686
Airdrie Public Library, Airdrie AB p. 2521
Airway Heights Corrections Center, *see* Washington State Library, Airway Heights WA p. 2390
Aiso Library, Monterey CA p. 179
Aitkin Memorial District Library, Croswell MI p. 1095
Aitkin Public Library, *see* East Central Regional Library, Aitkin MN p. 1168
Ajax Public Library, Ajax ON p. 2627
Akin Free Library, Pawling NY p. 1616
Akin Gump Strauss Hauer & Feld LLP, Washington DC p. 359
Akin, Gump, Strauss, Hauer & Feld LLP, Dallas TX p. 2162
Akron Art Museum, Akron OH p. 1743
Akron Carnegie Public Library, Akron IN p. 667
Akron Law Library, Akron OH p. 1743
Akron Library, *see* Newstead Public Library, Akron NY p. 1481
Akron Public Library, Akron AL p. 3
Akron Public Library, Akron CO p. 263
Akron Public Library, Akron IA p. 729
Akron-Summit County Public Library, Akron OH p. 1743
Akwesasne Cultural Center Library, Hogansburg NY p. 1547
Alabama A&M University, Normal AL p. 31
Alabama College of Osteopathic Medicine, Dothan AL p. 14
Alabama Department of Archives & History Research Room, Montgomery AL p. 27
Alabama Department of Conservation & Natural Resources, Dauphin Island AL p. 14
Alabama Department of Corrections, Springville AL p. 36
Alabama Health Libraries Association, Inc (N), Birmingham AL p. 2761
Alabama Institute for the Deaf & Blind, Talladega AL p. 36
Alabama Power Co, Birmingham AL p. 6
Alabama Public Library Service, Montgomery AL p. 27, 28
Alabama Regional Library for the Blind & Physically Handicapped, *see* Alabama Public Library Service AL p. 27
Alabama State University, Montgomery AL p. 2781
Alabama Supreme Court & State Law Library, Montgomery AL p. 28
Alachua County Library District, Gainesville FL p. 406
Alamance Community College Library, Graham NC p. 1691
Alamance County Historic Properties Commission, Burlington NC p. 1676
Alamance County Public Libraries, Burlington NC p. 1676
Alamance Regional Medical Center; Div of Cone Health, Burlington NC p. 1676
Alameda County Library, Fremont CA p. 143
Alameda Free Library, Alameda CA p. 115
Alameda Health System Medical Library, Oakland CA p. 184
Alameda McCollough Research Library, *see* Tippecanoe County Historical Association, Lafayette IN p. 701
Alamo Colleges District, Universal City TX p. 2250
Alamogordo Public Library, Alamogordo NM p. 1459
Alamosa Library, *see* Albuquerque-Bernalillo County Library System, Albuquerque NM p. 1460
Alamosa Public Library, Alamosa CO p. 263
Alanson Area Public Library, Alanson MI p. 1076
Alaska Bible College Library, Palmer AK p. 49
Alaska Christian College, Soldotna AK p. 51
Alaska Department of Law, Juneau AK p. 47
Alaska Department of Natural Resources, Anchorage AK p. 41
Alaska Housing Finance Corp, Anchorage AK p. 41
Alaska Library Network (N), Anchorage AK p. 2761
Alaska Masonic Library & Museum, Anchorage AK p. 41
Alaska Native Medical Center, Anchorage AK p. 41
Alaska Oil & Gas Conservation Commission Library, Anchorage AK p. 41
Alaska Resources Library & Information Services ARLIS, Anchorage AK p. 41
Alaska State Court Law Library, Anchorage AK p. 41
Alaska State Department of Corrections, Eagle River AK p. 45
Alaska State Legislature, Juneau AK p. 47
Alaska State Library, Juneau AK p. 47
Alaska Vocational Technical Center, Seward AK p. 50
Albany College of Pharmacy & Health Sciences, Albany NY p. 1481
Albany County Public Library, Laramie WY p. 2496

Allendale County Library, *see* Allendale-Hampton-Jasper Regional Library, Allendale SC p. 2046
Allendale-Hampton-Jasper Regional Library, Allendale SC p. 2046
Allendale Township Library, Allendale MI p. 1077
Allens Hill Free Library, Bloomfield NY p. 1495
Allenstown Public Library, Allenstown NH p. 1353
Allentown Public Library, Allentown PA p. 1904
Allerton Public Library, Allerton IA p. 730
Allerton Public Library District, Monticello IL p. 619
Allerton Robert Art Library, *see* Honolulu Museum of Art, Honolulu HI p. 512
Alliance Public Library, Alliance NE p. 1305
Alliance Public Library, Alliance AB p. 2521
Alliance University, New York NY p. 1578
Alliant International University, Alhambra CA p. 115
Alliant International University, Fresno CA p. 144
Alliant International University, San Diego CA p. 214
Alliant International University, San Francisco CA p. 223
Allin Township Library, Stanford IL p. 651
Allina Health Library Services, Minneapolis MN p. 1182
Alling Dorothy Memorial Library, Williston VT p. 2299
Allison John Richard Library, *see* Regent College, Vancouver BC p. 2579
Allison Ora Byram Memorial Library, *see* Mid-America Baptist Theological Seminary, Cordova TN p. 2095
Allison Public Library, Allison IA p. 730
Alloway Norma & Miller, *see* Muskoka Lakes Public Library, Port Carling ON p. 2673
Alloway Norma Marion Library, *see* Trinity Western University, Langley BC p. 2569
Allyn Lyman Art Museum Library, New London CT p. 328
Alma-Bacon County Public, *see* Okefenokee Regional Library, Alma GA p. 503
Alma College Library, Alma MI p. 1077
Alma Learning Resource Center, *see* Coastal Pines Technical College, Alma GA p. 503
Alma Public Library, Alma AR p. 89
Alma Public Library, Alma MI p. 1077
Alma Public Library, Alma WI p. 2419
Almena City Library, Almena KS p. 795
Almont District Library, Almont MI p. 1077
Almonte Library, *see* Metropolitan Library System in Oklahoma County, Oklahoma City OK p. 1857
Almonte Library, *see* Mississippi Mills Libraries, Almonte ON p. 2628
ALN (N), *see* Alaska Library Network, Anchorage AK p. 2761
Alondra Library, *see* County of Los Angeles Public Library, Norwalk CA p. 135
Alpena Community College, Alpena MI p. 1078
Alpena County Library, Alpena MI p. 1078
Alpert-Solotken Library, *see* Congregation Beth-El Zedeck, Indianapolis IN p. 691
Alpha Park Public Library District, Bartonville IL p. 540
Alphin Albert Music Library, *see* Boston Conservatory, Boston MA p. 991
Alpine County Historical Society, Markleeville CA p. 173
Alpine County Library, Markleeville CA p. 173
Alpine County Museum Library, *see* Alpine County Historical Society, Markleeville CA p. 173
Alpine Public, *see* Apache County Library District, Alpine AZ p. 76
Alpine Public Library, Alpine TX p. 2133
Pottberg Alric CT Library, *see* Pasco-Hernando State College-West Campus, New Port Richey FL p. 428
Alsea Community Library, *see* Corvallis-Benton County Public Library, Alsea OR p. 1876
Alsip-Merrionette Park Public Library District, Alsip IL p. 536
Alston & Bird, LLP Library, New York NY p. 1578
Alta Community Library, Alta IA p. 730
Alta Vista Public Library, Alta Vista IA p. 730
Altadena Library District, Altadena CA p. 116
Altamont Free Library, Altamont NY p. 1485
Altamont Public Library, Altamont IL p. 536
Altamont Public Library, Altamont KS p. 795
Altamont Public Library, Altamont TN p. 2087
Altamonte Springs City Library, Altamonte Springs FL p. 383
Altamonte Springs Library, *see* City College, Altamonte Springs FL p. 383
Alternative Press Center Library, Baltimore MD p. 951
Altheimer Public Library, *see* Pine Bluff & Jefferson County Library System, Altheimer AR p. 107
Altman David Library, *see* Beth Hillel Congregation Bnai Emunah, Wilmette IL p. 663
Alton, *see* Burlington Public Library, Burlington ON p. 2634
Alton Library, Alton KS p. 795
Alton Public Library, Alton IA p. 730
Alton Public Library, *see* Oregon County Library District, Alton MO p. 1237
Altona Correctional Facility Library, *see* New York State Department of Corrections & Community Supervision, Altona NY p. 1486
Altona Reading Center, Altona NY p. 1485
Altoona Area Public Library, Altoona PA p. 1905
Altoona Public Library, Altoona IA p. 730
Altoona Public Library, Altoona KS p. 796
Altoona Public Library, Altoona WI p. 2419
Altschul Medical Library, *see* Monmouth Medical Center, Long Branch NJ p. 1414
Altus Public Library, Altus OK p. 1839
Alum Creek Public Library, *see* Lincoln County Libraries, Alum Creek WV p. 2403
Alumnae Library, *see* College of Our Lady of the Elms, Chicopee MA p. 1011
Alva Public Library, Alva OK p. 1840
Alvar Library, *see* New Orleans Public Library, New Orleans LA p. 903
Alvarado Public Library, Alvarado TX p. 2133
Alvena Public Library, *see* Wapiti Regional Library, Alvena SK p. 2745
Alvernia University, Reading PA p. 2000
Alverno College Library, Milwaukee WI p. 2457
Alvin Community College Library, Alvin TX p. 2133
Alvord Public Library, Alvord TX p. 2133
Alzheimer's Association, Chicago IL p. 554
Amador County Law Library, Jackson CA p. 153
Amador County Library, Jackson CA p. 153
Amagansett Free Library, Amagansett NY p. 1486
Amargosa Valley Library, Amargosa Valley NV p. 1343
Amarillo College, Amarillo TX p. 2134
Amarillo Museum of Art Library, Amarillo TX p. 2134
Amarillo Public Library, Amarillo TX p. 2134
Amasa Community Library, Amasa MI p. 1078
Amaury Veray Music Library, San Juan PR p. 2513
Amberg Health Sciences Library, *see* Spectrum Health, Grand Rapids MI p. 1111
Amberton University, Garland TX p. 2183
Amble Charles A Library, *see* Mid Michigan Community College, Harrison MI p. 1113
Ambrose Library, Calgary AB p. 2525
Ambrose Public Library, *see* Satilla Regional Library, Ambrose GA p. 476
Amelia County Historical Society Library, Amelia VA p. 2303
Ameliasburgh Branch Al Purdy Library, *see* Prince Edward County Public Library, Ameliasburgh ON p. 2673
Amenia Free Library, Amenia NY p. 1486
America's National Churchill Museum, *see* Westminster College, Fulton MO p. 1246
American Academy of Arts & Letters Library, New York NY p. 1578
American Academy of Dramatic Arts, Los Angeles CA p. 160
American Academy of Dramatic Arts, New York NY p. 1578
American Academy of Ophthalmology Library, San Francisco CA p. 223
American Academy of Pediatrics, Itasca IL p. 602
American Alpine Club Library, Golden CO p. 282
American Antiquarian Society Library, Worcester MA p. 1071
American Association of Advertising Agencies, New York NY p. 1578
American Association of Nurse Anesthetists, Rosemont IL p. 643
American Association of Orthodontists, Saint Louis MO p. 1269
American Association of State Highway & Transportation, Washington DC p. 359
American Association of Textile Chemists & Colorists Library, Research Triangle Park NC p. 1712
American Aviation Historical Society, Riverside CA p. 201
American Baptist College, Nashville TN p. 2118
American Bar Association Library, Washington DC p. 359
American Camellia Society Library, Fort Valley GA p. 479
American-Canadian Genealogical Society Library, Manchester NH p. 1371
American Chemical Society Information Resource Center, Washington DC p. 359
American Clock & Watch Museum, Inc, Bristol CT p. 304
American College of Obstetricians & Gynecologists, Washington DC p. 360
American Congregational Association, Boston MA p. 990
American Contract Bridge League, Horn Lake MS p. 1220
American Correctional Association, Alexandria VA p. 2303
American Council of Life Insurers Library, Washington DC p. 360
American Counseling Association, Alexandria VA p. 2303
American Dental Association Library & Archives, Chicago IL p. 554
American Donkey & Mule Society Library, Lewisville TX p. 2211
American Falls District Library, American Falls ID p. 515
American Federation of Astrologers, Inc Library, Tempe AZ p. 79
American Federation of State, County & Municipal Employees, Washington DC p. 360
American Folk Art Museum, Long Island City NY p. 1565
American Fork City Library, American Fork UT p. 2261
American-French Genealogical Society Library, Woonsocket RI p. 2044
American Geographical Society Library, *see* University of Wisconsin-Milwaukee Libraries, Milwaukee WI p. 2461
American Geological Institute Library, Alexandria VA p. 2303
American Graduate University Library, Covina CA p. 133
American Herb Association Library, Nevada City CA p. 182
American Heritage Center, Laramie WY p. 2496
American Heritage Library & Museum, Glendale CA p. 148
American Historical Society of Germans from Russia, Lincoln NE p. 1320
American Hospital Association, Chicago IL p. 554
American Hungarian Library & Historical Society, New York NY p. 1578
American Independence Museum Library, Exeter NH p. 1363
American Indian Higher Education Consortium (N), Alexandria VA p. 2776
American Institute for Biosocial & Medical Research Inc Library, Seattle WA p. 2376
American Institute for Economic Research, Great Barrington MA p. 1021
American Institute of Physics, College Park MD p. 962
American Institutes for Research Library, Silver Spring MD p. 977

Annawan-Alba Township Library, Annawan IL p. 537
Anne Arundel Community College, Arnold MD p. 951
Annenberg Library & Communications Center, *see* Pine Manor College, Chestnut Hill MA p. 1011
Annville Free Library, Annville PA p. 1906
Anoka County Historical Society, Anoka MN p. 1163
Anoka County Law Library, Anoka MN p. 1163
Anoka County Library, Blaine MN p. 1165
Anoka-Ramsey Community College, Cambridge MN p. 1167
Anoka-Ramsey Community College, Coon Rapids MN p. 1171
Anoka Technical College Library, Anoka MN p. 1163
Anschutz Library, *see* University of Kansas Libraries, Lawrence KS p. 819
Anselmo Learning Commons and Library, *see* Quincy College, Quincy MA p. 1048
Anshe Chesed Fairmount Temple, Beachwood OH p. 1749
Anshe Hesed Temple Library, Erie PA p. 1931
Ansley Grove Library, *see* Vaughan Public Libraries, Woodbridge ON p. 2701
Anson Public Library, Anson TX p. 2135
Ansonia Library, Ansonia CT p. 301
Ansted Public, *see* Fayette County Public Libraries, Ansted WV p. 2411
Antelope Valley College Library, Lancaster CA p. 156
Anthology Film Archives, New York NY p. 1579
Anthony Cardinal Bevilacqua Theological Research Center, Wynnewood PA p. 2025
Anthony Clarence E, *see* Palm Beach County Library System, South Bay FL p. 454
Anthony Public Library, Anthony KS p. 796
Anthroposophical Society In Canada Library, Thornhill ON p. 2684
Anti-Defamation League, New York NY p. 1579
Antietam National Battlefield Library, *see* National Park Service, Sharpsburg MD p. 977
Antigo Public Library, Antigo WI p. 2420
Antigonish Town & County Library, *see* Pictou - Antigonish Regional Library, Antigonish NS p. 2622
Antioch College, Yellow Springs OH p. 1835
Antioch Community Library, *see* Contra Costa County Library, Antioch CA p. 174
Antioch Public Library District, Antioch IL p. 537
Antioch University Library, Yellow Springs OH p. 1835
Antioch University Library, Seattle WA p. 2376
Antioch University New England Library, Keene NH p. 1369
Antique Boat Museum, Clayton NY p. 1518
Antique Stove Association Library, Faribault MN p. 1175
Antlers Public Library, Antlers OK p. 1840
Anythink Libraries, Thornton CO p. 296
Anza Library, *see* Riverside County Library System, Anza CA p. 201
AORN Center for Library Services & Archives, Denver CO p. 273
Apache County Library District, Saint Johns AZ p. 76
Apache Junction Public Library, Apache Junction AZ p. 55
Apalachicola Margaret Key Library, Apalachicola FL p. 383
Apalachin Library, Apalachin NY p. 1487
Aplington Legion Memorial Library, Aplington IA p. 732
Apollo Memorial Library, Apollo PA p. 1907
Apostle Islands National Lakeshore Library, *see* National Park Service, Bayfield WI p. 2423
Appalachian College Association (N), Bristol TN p. 2775
Appalachian Mountain Club Archives, Bretton Woods NH p. 1356
Appalachian Regional Library, West Jefferson NC p. 1721
Appalachian School of Law Library, Grundy VA p. 2322
Appalachian State University, Boone NC p. 1674, 2789
Appaloosa Museum & Heritage Center, Moscow ID p. 526
Appaloosa Museum Library, *see* Appaloosa Museum & Heritage Center, Moscow ID p. 526
Appleton City Public Library, Appleton City MO p. 1237
Appleton Public Library, Appleton MN p. 1164
Appleton Public Library, Appleton WI p. 2420
Appling County Public, *see* Okefenokee Regional Library, Baxley GA p. 503
Appomattox Court House Library, *see* National Park Service, Appomattox VA p. 2304
Appomattox Regional Library System, Hopewell VA p. 2326
Appoquinimink Community Library, Middletown DE p. 354
Appraisal Institute, Chicago IL p. 554
Aquinas College, Grand Rapids MI p. 1109
Aquinnah Public Library, Aquinnah MA p. 985
Arab Public Library, Arab AL p. 4
Arabian Library, *see* Scottsdale Public Library, Scottsdale AZ p. 77
Aram Public Library, Delavan WI p. 2431
Aransas County Public Library, Rockport TX p. 2233
Arapahoe Community College, Littleton CO p. 289
Arapahoe Library District, Englewood CO p. 279
Arapahoe Public Library, Arapahoe NE p. 1305
Arbor Road Church, Long Beach CA p. 158
Arboretum at Flagstaff Library, Flagstaff AZ p. 60
Arborfield Public Library, *see* Wapiti Regional Library, Arborfield SK p. 2745
Arcade Free Library, Arcade NY p. 1487
Arcade Library, *see* Sacramento Public Library, Sacramento CA p. 209
Arcadia Free Public Library, Arcadia WI p. 2421
Arcadia Public Library, Arcadia CA p. 117
Arcadia Township Library, Arcadia NE p. 1305
Arcadia University, Glenside PA p. 1937
Arcadis Corporate Library, Toronto ON p. 2686
Arcanum Public Library, Arcanum OH p. 1746
Archabbey Library, *see* Saint Meinrad Archabbey & School of Theology, Saint Meinrad IN p. 717
Archbishop Alemany Library, *see* Dominican University of California, San Rafael CA p. 236
Archbishop Alter Library, *see* Mount Saint Joseph University, Cincinnati OH p. 1761
Archbishop Iakovos Library, *see* Hellenic College, Brookline MA p. 1003
Archbishop Ireland Memorial Library, *see* University of Saint Thomas, Saint Paul MN p. 1202
Archbishop O'Brien Library, *see* Archdiocese of Hartford Pastoral Center, Bloomfield CT p. 302
Archbold Biological Station Library, Venus FL p. 452
Archbold Community Library, Archbold OH p. 1746
Archdiocese of Hartford Pastoral Center, Bloomfield CT p. 302
ARCHE (N), *see* Atlanta Regional Council for Higher Education, Atlanta GA p. 2764
Archer & Greiner Library, Voorhees NJ p. 1450
Archer Dr John Library, *see* University of Regina, Regina SK p. 2748
Archer Public Library, Archer IA p. 732
Archer Public Library, Archer City TX p. 2136
Archer Robert M & Janet L Library, *see* Ashland University Library, Ashland OH p. 1747
Archerwill Public Library, *see* Wapiti Regional Library, Archerwill SK p. 2745
Archibald Library, *see* Briercrest College & Seminary, Caronport SK p. 2741
Archibald Public Library, *see* Rancho Cucamonga Public Library, Rancho Cucamonga CA p. 197
Archives at Queens Library, *see* Queens Library, Jamaica NY p. 1553
Archives de la Cote - du Sud et du College de Sainte-Anne, *see* Societe Historique de la Cote-du-Sud, La Pocatiere QC p. 2714
Archives nationales a Quebec, Quebec QC p. 2729
Archives of Ontario Library, Toronto ON p. 2686
Archives of the Episcopal Church, Austin TX p. 2137
Archives of the Episcopal Church in Connecticut, Meriden CT p. 321
Archives Provinciales des Capucins, Montreal QC p. 2716
Arcola Public Library District, Arcola IL p. 537
Arden-Dimick Library, *see* Sacramento Public Library, Sacramento CA p. 209
Ardmore Free Library, Ardmore PA p. 1907
Ardmore Public Library, Ardmore OK p. 1840
Ardmore Public Library, Ardmore TN p. 2087
Ardsley Public Library, Ardsley NY p. 1487
Arecibo University College Library, *see* University of Puerto Rico, Arecibo PR p. 2509
Arent Fox PLLC Library, Washington DC p. 361
Argenta-Oreana Public Library District, Argenta IL p. 537
Argenta-Oreana Public Library District, Oreana IL p. 630
Argenta Public Library, *see* Argenta-Oreana Public Library District, Argenta IL p. 537
Argonne National Laboratory, Lemont IL p. 608
Argos Public Library, Argos IN p. 668
Argyle Free Library, Argyle NY p. 1488
Argyle Public Library, Argyle WI p. 2421
Aria Health, Philadelphia PA p. 1974
Arizona Christian University, Glendale AZ p. 61
Arizona City Community Library, Arizona City AZ p. 55
Arizona Department of Corrections, Douglas AZ p. 59
Arizona Department of Corrections, Buckeye AZ p. 57
Arizona Department of Corrections - Adult Institutions, Florence AZ p. 61
Arizona Department of Corrections, Globe AZ p. 62
Arizona Department of Corrections, Goodyear AZ p. 62
Arizona Department of Corrections, Phoenix AZ p. 68
Arizona Department of Corrections, Safford AZ p. 75
Arizona Department of Corrections, San Luis AZ p. 76
Arizona Department of Corrections, Tucson AZ p. 80
Arizona Department of Corrections, Winslow AZ p. 84
Arizona Department of Corrections, Safford AZ p. 75
Arizona Geological Survey at University of Arizona, Tucson AZ p. 81
Arizona Historical Society, Tucson AZ p. 81
Arizona Historical Society Museum Library & Archives, Tempe AZ p. 79
Arizona-Sonora Desert Museum Library, Tucson AZ p. 81
Arizona State Hospital Library, Phoenix AZ p. 68
Arizona State Library, Archives & Public Records, Phoenix AZ p. 69
Arizona State Museum Library, Tucson AZ p. 81
Arizona State Parks, Winslow AZ p. 84
Arizona State Prison Complex - Eyman Library, *see* Arizona Department of Corrections - Adult Institutions, Florence AZ p. 61
Arizona State Prison Complex Florence Libraries, Florence AZ p. 61
Arizona State Prison Complex - Globe Library, *see* Arizona Department of Corrections, Globe AZ p. 62
Lewis Library, *see* Arizona Department of Corrections, Buckeye AZ p. 57
Arizona State Schools for the Deaf & the Blind Library, Tucson AZ p. 81
Arizona State University, College of Law, Phoenix AZ p. 69
Arizona State University Libraries, Tempe AZ p. 79
Arizona Superior Court in Pima County, Tucson AZ p. 81
Arizona Talking Book Library, Phoenix AZ p. 69
Arizona Western College, Yuma AZ p. 85
Arkansas Arts Center, Little Rock AR p. 100
Arkansas Baptist College, Little Rock AR p. 100
Arkansas City Public Library, Arkansas City KS p. 796

ASHP Library, *see* American Society of Health-System Pharmacists (ASHP), Bethesda MD p. 959
Ashtabula County District Library, Ashtabula OH p. 1747
Ashtabula County Law Library, Jefferson OH p. 1792
Ashton Liz Campus Centre, *see* Camosun College, Victoria BC p. 2582
Ashton Public Library, Ashton IA p. 733
Ashurbanipal Library, *see* Assyrian Universal Alliance Foundation, Lincolnwood IL p. 609
Ashville Free Library, Ashville NY p. 1488
Ashville Public Library, *see* McCain Memorial Public Library, Ashville AL p. 5
Askwith Media Library, *see* University of Michigan, Ann Arbor MI p. 1080
Asnuntuck Community College Library, Enfield CT p. 311
Asotin County Library, Clarkston WA p. 2361
Aspen Hill Library, *see* Montgomery County Public Libraries, Rockville MD p. 974
Aspen Historical Society Archives, Aspen CO p. 264
Aspen Institute, Aspen CO p. 264
Asphodel-Norwood Public Library, Norwood ON p. 2662
Aspira Association Library, Washington DC p. 361
Aspirus Health, Wausau WI p. 2485
Assemblee Nationale du Quebec Bibliotheque, Quebec QC p. 2729
Assemblies of God Theological Seminary, Springfield MO p. 1280
Assiniboia & District Public Library, *see* Palliser Regional Library, Assiniboia SK p. 2742
Assiniboine Community College Library, Brandon MB p. 2585
Associated Colleges of the Saint Lawrence Valley (N), Potsdam NY p. 2770
Association des Bibliotheques de la Sante Affiliees (N), Montreal QC p. 2778
Association for Baha'i Studies, Ottawa ON p. 2664
Association for Research & Enlightenment, Virginia Beach VA p. 2349
Association for Rural & Small Libraries (N), Seattle WA p. 2776
Association of Chicago Theological Schools (N), Mundelein IL p. 2764
Association of Christian Librarians (N), Cedarville OH p. 2772
Association of Independent Kentucky Colleges & Universities (N), Frankfort KY p. 2765
Association of Research Libraries (N), Washington DC p. 2763
Association of Southeastern Research Libraries (N), Atlanta GA p. 2763
Association of the Bar of the City of New York Library, New York NY p. 1579
Association of the Free Library & Reading Room of Rowayton, Inc., *see* Rowayton Library, Rowayton CT p. 335
Association Paritaire Pour la Sante et la Securite du Travail, Montreal QC p. 2716
Assumption Abbey Library, Richardton ND p. 1739
Assumption College for Sisters Library, Denville NJ p. 1399
Assumption Parish Library, Napoleonville LA p. 899
Assumption Public Library District, Assumption IL p. 538
Assumption Seminary Library, San Antonio TX p. 2236
Assumption University, Worcester MA p. 1071
Assyrian Universal Alliance Foundation, Lincolnwood IL p. 609
Aston Public Library, Aston PA p. 1907
Astor County Library, *see* Lake County Library System, Astor FL p. 450
Astoria Community Library, *see* Queens Library, Long Island City NY p. 1554
Astoria Public Library, Astoria OR p. 1872
Astoria Public Library District, Astoria IL p. 538
Astronomical Society of the Pacific Library, San Francisco CA p. 223
AT&T Library & Technology Resource Center, *see* Harris-Stowe State University Library, Saint Louis MO p. 1271
Atalig Antonio C Memorial Public Library, *see* Joeten-Kiyu Public Library, Rota MP p. 2507
Atascadero Historical Society Museum Library, Atascadero CA p. 118
Atascadero State Hospital, Atascadero CA p. 118
Atchison County Library, Rock Port MO p. 1267
Atchison Public Library, Atchison KS p. 797
Atglen Public Library, Atglen PA p. 1907
Athabasca Municipal Library, Athabasca AB p. 2522
Athabasca University, Athabasca AB p. 2522
Athena Public Library, Athena OR p. 1872
Athenaeum Music & Arts Library, *see* Library Association of La Jolla, La Jolla CA p. 154
Athenaeum of Ohio, Cincinnati OH p. 1759
Athenaeum of Philadelphia, Philadelphia PA p. 1975
Athens Campus, *see* Trinity Valley Community College Library, Athens TX p. 2137
Athens-Clarke County Library, *see* Athens Regional Library System, Athens GA p. 458
Athens Community Library, Athens MI p. 1081
Athens County Public Libraries, Nelsonville OH p. 1805
Athens First United Methodist Church Library, Athens GA p. 458
Athens-Limestone Public Library, Athens AL p. 5
Athens Municipal Library, Athens IL p. 538
Athens Public Library, *see* Athens County Public Libraries, Athens OH p. 1805
Athens Regional Library System, Athens GA p. 458
Athens State University Library, Athens AL p. 5
Athens Technical College Library, Athens GA p. 459
Atherton Library, *see* Hawaii Pacific University Libraries, Kaneohe HI p. 506
Atherton Library, *see* San Mateo County Library, Atherton CA p. 235
Athol Public Library, Athol MA p. 986
Atikameksheng Anishinawbek Library, Naughton ON p. 2660
Atikokan Public Library, Atikokan ON p. 2629
Atkins J Murrey Library, *see* University of North Carolina at Charlotte, Charlotte NC p. 1681
Atkins Memorial Library, Corinth ME p. 922
Atkins Public Library, Atkins IA p. 733
Atkinson Library, *see* Jackson Community College, Jackson MI p. 1119
Atkinson Public Library, Atkinson NE p. 1306
Atkinson Public Library District, Atkinson IL p. 538
ATLA (N), *see* American Theological Library Association, Chicago IL p. 2764
Atlanta Botanical Garden, Atlanta GA p. 460
Atlanta Campus Library, *see* Richmont Graduate University, Atlanta GA p. 466
Atlanta-Fulton Public Library System, Atlanta GA p. 460
Atlanta History Center, Atlanta GA p. 462
Atlanta Metropolitan State College Library, Atlanta GA p. 462
Atlanta Public Library, Atlanta TX p. 2137
Atlanta Public Library & Museum, *see* Atlanta Public Library District, Atlanta IL p. 538
Atlanta Public Library District, Atlanta IL p. 538
Atlanta Regional Commission, Atlanta GA p. 462
Atlanta Regional Council for Higher Education (N), Atlanta GA p. 2764
Atlanta Technical College, Atlanta GA p. 462
Atlanta University Center, Atlanta GA p. 462
Atlantic Cape Community College, Atlantic City NJ p. 1387
Atlantic Cape Community College, Cape May Court House NJ p. 1394
Atlantic Cape Community College, Mays Landing NJ p. 1417
Atlantic City Campus - Worthington Information Commons, *see* Atlantic Cape Community College, Atlantic City NJ p. 1387
Atlantic City Free Public Library, Atlantic City NJ p. 1388
Atlantic County Historical Society Library, Somers Point NJ p. 1442
Atlantic County Library System, Mays Landing NJ p. 1417
Atlantic Provinces Special Education Authority Library, Halifax NS p. 2618
Atlantic Public Library, Atlantic IA p. 733
Atlantic Region Library, *see* Environment & Climate Change Canada, Dartmouth NS p. 2617
Atlantic School of Theology Library, Halifax NS p. 2618
AtlantiCare Regional Medical Center, Atlantic City NJ p. 1388
Atmore Public Library, Atmore AL p. 5
Atmospheric Turbulence & Diffusion Division Library, Oak Ridge TN p. 2123
Atoka County Library, *see* Southern Oklahoma Library System, Atoka OK p. 1841
Atrium Cabarrus Medical Library, *see* Cabarrus College Health Sciences Library, Concord NC p. 1682
Attalla-Etowah County Public Library, Attalla AL p. 5
Attica City Library, Attica KS p. 797
Attica Public Library, Attica IN p. 668
Attleboro Public Library, Attleboro MA p. 986
Attorney General's Law Library, *see* California Department of Justice, Sacramento CA p. 207
Attorney General's Office, Baltimore MD p. 951
Atwater Library & Computer Centre, Westmount QC p. 2739
Atwater Memorial, *see* North Branford Library Department, North Branford CT p. 330
Atwater Public Library, Atwater MN p. 1164
Atwood Alaska Resource Center, *see* Anchorage Museum, Anchorage AK p. 42
Atwood-Hammond Public Library, Atwood IL p. 538
Atwood Public Library, Atwood KS p. 797
Atwood Steven W Veterinary Medicine Library, *see* University of Pennsylvania Libraries, Philadelphia PA p. 1988
Au Sable Forks Free Library, Au Sable Forks NY p. 1488
Aubrey Area Library, Aubrey TX p. 2137
Auburn Avenue Research Library, *see* Atlanta-Fulton Public Library System, Atlanta GA p. 460
Auburn Correctional Facility Library, Auburn NY p. 1488
Auburn Hills Public Library, Auburn Hills MI p. 1081
Auburn Memorial Library, Auburn NE p. 1306
Auburn Public Library, Auburn AL p. 5
Auburn Public Library, Auburn IL p. 538
Auburn Public Library, Auburn IA p. 733
Auburn Public Library, Auburn ME p. 913
Auburn Public Library, Auburn MA p. 986
Auburn University, Auburn AL p. 5
Auburn University, Montgomery AL p. 28
Auburn University, Auburn AL p. 2781
Auburndale Community Library, *see* Queens Library, Flushing NY p. 1554
Auburndale Public Library, Auburndale FL p. 383
Audubon Public Library, Audubon IA p. 733
Audubon Regional Library, Clinton LA p. 887
Auer Library, *see* Fort Wayne Museum of Art, Fort Wayne IN p. 684
Auerbach Art Library, *see* Wadsworth Atheneum Museum of Art, Hartford CT p. 318
Auglaize County Law Library, Wapakoneta OH p. 1827
Auglaize County Libraries, Wapakoneta OH p. 1827
Augsburg University, Minneapolis MN p. 1182
Augusta County Library, Fishersville VA p. 2318
Augusta Memorial Public Library, Augusta WI p. 2421
Augusta Public Library, Augusta KS p. 797
Augusta Richmond County Historical Society, Augusta GA p. 466
Augusta-Richmond County Public Library, Augusta GA p. 466
Augusta State Medical Prison, *see* Georgia Department of Corrections, Grovetown GA p. 481
Augusta Technical College, Augusta GA p. 467
Augusta Township Public Library, Brockville ON p. 2633
Augusta University, Augusta GA p. 467
Augustana Campus Library, *see* University of Alberta, Camrose AB p. 2530
Augustana College Library, Rock Island IL p. 640

Baker May H Memorial Library, *see* Valley Forge Military Academy & College, Wayne PA p. 2019
Baker Memorial Timmonsville Public Library, *see* Florence County Library System, Timmonsville SC p. 2058
Baker Michael International Library, Moon Township PA p. 1965
Baker Solomon R Library, *see* Bentley University, Waltham MA p. 1061
Baker University, Baldwin City KS p. 797
Bakersfield College, Bakersfield CA p. 119
Bakerville Library, New Hartford CT p. 325
Bakken Lavola Research Library, *see* Douglas County Museum, Roseburg OR p. 1895
Bakken Library of Electricity in Life, *see* Bakken Museum, Minneapolis MN p. 1182
Bakken Museum, Minneapolis MN p. 1182
Bakwin Library, *see* American Academy of Pediatrics, Itasca IL p. 602
Bala Cynwyd Memorial Library, Bala Cynwyd PA p. 1908
Balaban Jack Memorial Library of Temple Sinai, Cinnaminson NJ p. 1396
Balch & Bingham LLP Library, Birmingham AL p. 7
Balch Alden Memorial Library, Lunenburg VT p. 2288
Balch Mr & Mrs Allan C Art Research Library, *see* Los Angeles County Museum of Art, Los Angeles CA p. 163
Balch Springs Library-Learning Center, Balch Springs TX p. 2144
Baldwin Borough Public Library, Pittsburgh PA p. 1990
Baldwin Cabin Public Library, Datil NM p. 1466
Baldwin City Library, Baldwin City KS p. 797
Baldwin County Library Cooperative, Inc, Robertsdale AL p. 34
Baldwin H Furlong Library, *see* Maryland Center for History & Culture Library, Baltimore MD p. 954
Baldwin-Kittler Memorial, *see* White County Regional Library System, Judsonia AR p. 109
Baldwin Library, *see* Abraham Baldwin Agricultural College, Tifton GA p. 500
Baldwin Mary University, Staunton VA p. 2347
Baldwin Memorial Library, Wells River VT p. 2297
Baldwin Public Library, Birmingham MI p. 1086
Baldwin Public Library, Baldwin NY p. 1490
Baldwin Public Library, Baldwin WI p. 2421
Baldwin State Prison, *see* Georgia Department of Corrections, Hardwick GA p. 482
Baldwin Wallace University, Berea OH p. 1750
Baldwinsville Public Library, Baldwinsville NY p. 1490
Balfour L G & Mildred Memorial, *see* Norton Public Library, Norton MA p. 1043
Ball Gerald J Library, *see* Ancilla College, Donaldson IN p. 679
Ball Ground Public, *see* Sequoyah Regional Library System, Ball Ground GA p. 469
Ball State University Libraries, Muncie IN p. 708
Ball Virgina Beall Library, *see* Indiana Youth Institute, Indianapolis IN p. 693
Ballad Health, Johnson City TN p. 2103
Ballad Health, Kingsport TN p. 2104
Ballard-Carlisle-Livingston County Public Library, Wickliffe KY p. 877
Ballard Nora Library, *see* Stanislaus County Library, Waterford CA p. 178
Ballard, Spahr LLP Library, Philadelphia PA p. 1975
Ballentine Branch, *see* Richland Library, Irmo SC p. 2054
Balloch Grace Memorial Library, Spearfish SD p. 2083
Ballston Spa Public Library, Ballston Spa NY p. 1490
Balmertown Public Library, Balmertown ON p. 2629
Balmorhea Public Library, Balmorhea TX p. 2144
Balsam Lake Public Library, Balsam Lake WI p. 2422
Baltimore Bar Library, *see* Library Company of the Baltimore Bar, Baltimore MD p. 954
Baltimore Branch / Griley Memorial, *see* Fairfield County District Library, Baltimore OH p. 1794
Baltimore City Community College, Baltimore MD p. 951
Baltimore City Department of Legislative Reference Library, Baltimore MD p. 951
Baltimore County Circuit Court Library, Towson MD p. 979
Baltimore County Historical Society Library, Hunt Valley MD p. 968
Baltimore County Public Library, Towson MD p. 979
Baltimore Museum of Art, Baltimore MD p. 952
Baltimore Museum of Industry, Baltimore MD p. 952
Baltimore Sun Library, *see* Tribune Publishing, Baltimore MD p. 957
Balzekas Museum of Lithuanian Culture, Chicago IL p. 554
Bamfield Marine Sciences Centre Library, *see* Western Canadian Universities, Bamfield BC p. 2562
Bancroft Library, *see* University of California, Berkeley, Berkeley CA p. 122
Bancroft Memorial Library, Hopedale MA p. 1025
Bancroft Public Library, Bancroft IA p. 734
Bancroft Public Library, Bancroft NE p. 1306
Bancroft Public Library, Salem NY p. 1635
Bancroft Public Library, Bancroft ON p. 2629
Bandini Library, *see* City of Commerce Public Library, Commerce CA p. 132
Bandon Public Library, Bandon OR p. 1873
Banff Centre, Banff AB p. 2522
Banff Public Library, Banff AB p. 2522
Bangor Historical Society Library, Bangor ME p. 915
Bangor Public Library, Bangor ME p. 915
Bangor Public Library, Bangor PA p. 1908
Bank of Canada, Ottawa ON p. 2664
Bank Street College of Education Library, New York NY p. 1579
Bankier Library, *see* Brookdale Community College, Lincroft NJ p. 1412
Banks Arthur C Jr Library, *see* Capital Community College Library, Hartford CT p. 316
Banks County Public Library, *see* Piedmont Regional Library System, Homer GA p. 482
Banks Public Library, Banks OR p. 1873
Banner & Witcoff, Ltd Library, Chicago IL p. 555
Banner Desert Medical Center Library, *see* Banner Health Library Services, Mesa AZ p. 66
Banner Health Library Services, Mesa AZ p. 66
Banner - University Medical Center - Phoenix, Phoenix AZ p. 69
Banning Library District, Banning CA p. 120
BAnQ Saguenay, Chicoutimi QC p. 2710
Bapst Library, *see* Boston College Libraries, Chestnut Hill MA p. 1011
Baptist Bible College & Theological Seminary, Springfield MO p. 1280
Baptist College of Florida, Graceville FL p. 408
Baptist General Convention of Texas, Waco TX p. 2252
Baptist Health - Fort Smith, Fort Smith AR p. 96
Baptist Health Lexington Library, Lexington KY p. 862
Baptist Health Louisville, Louisville KY p. 864
Baptist Health Madisonville, Madisonville KY p. 868
Baptist Health Sciences University, Memphis TN p. 2112
Baptist Health System, San Antonio TX p. 2236
Baptist Hospital of Miami, Miami FL p. 421
Baptist Memorial Health Care Library, *see* University Libraries, University of Memphis, Memphis TN p. 2115
Baptist Missionary Association, Jacksonville TX p. 2203
Baptist University of the Americas, San Antonio TX p. 2236
Savides T N Library, *see* University of Wisconsin Baraboo-Sauk County, Baraboo WI p. 2422
Barack, Ferrazzano, Kirshbaum & Nagelberg Library, Chicago IL p. 555
Baraga Correctional Facility Library, *see* Michigan Department of Corrections, Baraga MI p. 1082
Barbee G V Sr, *see* Brunswick County Library, Oak Island NC p. 1716
Barber Irving K Learning Centre, *see* University of British Columbia Library, Vancouver BC p. 2580
Barber Scotia College, Concord NC p. 1682
Barberton Public Library, Barberton OH p. 1748
Barbour Clifford E Library, *see* Pittsburgh Theological Seminary, Pittsburgh PA p. 1995
Barclay College, Haviland KS p. 812
Barclay Damon, LLP, Buffalo NY p. 1507
Barclay H Douglas Law Library, *see* Syracuse University College of Law, Syracuse NY p. 1650
Barclay Public Library District, Warrensburg IL p. 658
Barco Law Library, *see* University of Pittsburgh, Pittsburgh PA p. 1996
Bard College, Annandale-on-Hudson NY p. 1487
Bard College at Simon's Rock, Great Barrington MA p. 1022
Bard Graduate Center Library, New York NY p. 1579
Bard Library, *see* Baltimore City Community College, Baltimore MD p. 951
Bare Hill Correctional Facility Library, Malone NY p. 1567
Barger-Richardson LRC, *see* Oakland City University, Oakland City IN p. 712
Baright Hollis & Helen Public Library, Ralston NE p. 1333
Barker Darwin R Library Association, Fredonia NY p. 1535
Barker Public Library, Barker NY p. 1490
Barkerville Historic Town Library & Archives, Barkerville BC p. 2563
Barkman Frank & Marie, *see* Pueblo City-County Library District, Pueblo CO p. 293
Barksdale Medical Library, *see* Centra Virginia Baptist Hospital, Lynchburg VA p. 2329
Barlow Robert W Memorial Library, Iowa Falls IA p. 761
Barnard College, New York NY p. 1579
Barnard E T Library, *see* Otter Tail County Historical Society, Fergus Falls MN p. 1175
Barnard Library, La Crosse KS p. 818
Barnes Reading Room, Everest KS p. 807
Barnesville Hutton Memorial Library, Barnesville OH p. 1749
Barnesville-Lamar County Library, *see* Flint River Regional Library System, Barnesville GA p. 481
Barnesville Public Library, *see* Lake Agassiz Regional Library, Barnesville MN p. 1188
Barnet Public Library, Barnet VT p. 2278
Barnett Mary J Memorial Library, Guthrie Center IA p. 757
Barnett Trone Jean Memorial Library of East Berlin, *see* Adams County Library System, East Berlin PA p. 1935
Barneveld Free Library, Barneveld NY p. 1490
Barneveld Public Library, Barneveld WI p. 2422
Barnhart Joe Bee County Public Library, Beeville TX p. 2146
Barnsdall Public Library-Ethel Briggs Memorial Library, Barnsdall OK p. 1841
Barnstable Law Library, *see* Massachusetts Trial Court Law Libraries, Barnstable MA p. 987
Barnwell Public Library, Barnwell AB p. 2522
Baron-Forness Library, *see* Pennsylvania Western University - Edinboro, Edinboro PA p. 1929
Barr Burton Central Library, *see* Phoenix Public Library, Phoenix AZ p. 72
Barr Memorial Library, *see* Saint Thomas Aquinas Church, Ames IA p. 731
Barr Memorial Library, *see* United States Army, Fort Knox KY p. 855
Barret Paul Jr Library, *see* Rhodes College, Memphis TN p. 2114
Barrett Dr C R Library (Marine Institute), *see* Memorial University of Newfoundland, St. John's NL p. 2610
Barrett Kate Waller, *see* Alexandria Library, Alexandria VA p. 2302

Bethany Public Library, Bethany PA p. 1911
Bethea Katherine Shaw Hospital, Dixon IL p. 578
Bethel College, Mishawaka IN p. 706
Bethel College Library, North Newton KS p. 827
Bethel Library Association, Bethel ME p. 917
Bethel Park Public Library, Bethel Park PA p. 1911
Bethel Public Library, Bethel CT p. 302
Bethel Public Library, Bethel VT p. 2279
Bethel-Tulpehocken Public Library, Bethel PA p. 1911
Bethel University, McKenzie TN p. 2111
Bethel University Library, Saint Paul MN p. 1199
Bethesda Health - Bethesda Hospital East, Boynton Beach FL p. 386
Bethesda Mennonite Church Library, Henderson NE p. 1318
Bethesda United Methodist Church Library, Bethesda MD p. 959
Bethlehem Area Public Library, Bethlehem PA p. 1911
Bethlehem College & Seminary Library, Minneapolis MN p. 1183
Bethlehem Public Library, Bethlehem CT p. 302
Bethlehem Public Library, Bethlehem NH p. 1355
Bethlehem Public Library, Delmar NY p. 1524
Bethpage Public Library, Bethpage NY p. 1493
Bethune-Cookman University, Daytona Beach FL p. 392
Bethune Public, *see* Kershaw County Library, Bethune SC p. 2048
Betsie Valley District Library, Thompsonville MI p. 1153
Bettencourt Medical Library, *see* Shattuck Lemuel Hospital, Jamaica Plain MA p. 1026
Bettendorf Public Library, Bettendorf IA p. 734
Betts Merritt D American Indian Research Library, *see* Bacone College, Muskogee OK p. 1854
Bettsville Public Library, Bettsville OH p. 1751
Betze Stephen J Library, *see* Delaware Technical & Community College, Georgetown DE p. 353
Beulah Heights University, Atlanta GA p. 462
Beulah Public Library, Beulah ND p. 1729
Beveridge & Diamond, PC Library, Washington DC p. 361
Beverly Free Library, Beverly NJ p. 1390
Beverly Hills Public Library, Beverly Hills CA p. 124
Beverly Hospital, Montebello CA p. 179
Beverly Hospital Medical Library, Beverly MA p. 989
Beverly Public Library, Beverly MA p. 989
Bevevino Mary Kintz Library, *see* Misericordia University, Dallas PA p. 1925
Bevill State Community College, Fayette AL p. 16
Bevill Tom Public, *see* Cullman County Public Library System, Hanceville AL p. 13
Bexar County Law Library, San Antonio TX p. 2236
Bexar County Medical Society, San Antonio TX p. 2236
Bexley Public Library, Bexley OH p. 1751
Bezhigoogahbow Library, *see* Leech Lake Tribal College, Cass Lake MN p. 1169
BHSL (N), *see* Basic Health Sciences Library Network, Summit NJ p. 2769
Biane Paul A Library, *see* Rancho Cucamonga Public Library, Rancho Cucamonga CA p. 197
Bibby Basil G Library, *see* University of Rochester Medical Center, Rochester NY p. 1631
Bible Holiness Movement Library, Penticton BC p. 2573
Bibliomation Inc (N), Waterbury CT p. 2762
Biblioteca Carolina, *see* Universidad Ana G Mendez, Carolina PR p. 2510
Biblioteca Centro Educativo de la Communidad de Pinewoods Pinewoods Library, *see* Athens Regional Library System, Athens GA p. 458
Biblioteca CRAAI, *see* Universidad Central de Bayamon, Bayamon PR p. 2510
Biblioteca Dennis Soto, *see* Universidad Adventista de las Antillas, Mayaguez PR p. 2511
Biblioteca Regional para Ciegos y Fisicamente Impedidos de Puerto Rico, *see* Puerto Rico Regional Library for the Blind & Physically, San Juan PR p. 2513
Biblioteca Victor M Pons Gil, *see* University of Puerto Rico Library, Cayey Campus, Cayey PR p. 2510
Bibliotech at distance, *see* Teluq University, Quebec QC p. 2732
Bibliotheque Albert-le-Grand, Montreal QC p. 2717
Bibliotheque Albert Rousseau, Levis QC p. 2715
Bibliotheque Alcide-Fleury, *see* Bibliotheque Charles-Edouard-Mailhot, Victoriaville QC p. 2738
Bibliotheque Alfred-Monnin, *see* Universite de Saint-Boniface, Winnipeg MB p. 2594
Bibliothèque Allard Regional Library, Saint Georges MB p. 2590
Bibliotheque Anne-Marie-Filteau, Levis QC p. 2715
Bibliotheque Annie-St-Arnealt, *see* Bibliotheque Municipale de La Tuque, La Tuque QC p. 2714
Bibliotheque Armand-Frappier, *see* College de Valleyfield, Salaberry-de-Valleyfield QC p. 2736
Bibliotheque Baie-D'Urfe, Baie-D'Urfe QC p. 2709
Bibliotheque Cecile-Rouleau, *see* Ministère de l'Emploi et de la Solidarité sociale, Quebec QC p. 2731
Bibliotheque Charles-Auguste-Gauthier, *see* Hopital De L'Enfant Jesus, Quebec QC p. 2730
Bibliotheque Charles-Edouard-Mailhot, Victoriaville QC p. 2738
Bibliotheque Charles H Blais, Quebec QC p. 2729
Bibliotheque Chrystine-Brouillet, Quebec QC p. 2729
Bibliotheque Commemorative Desautels, Marieville QC p. 2716
Bibliotheque Commemorative Pettes, Lac-Brome QC p. 2715
Bibliotheque de Beaconsfield, Beaconsfield QC p. 2709
Bibliotheque de Beaumont Library, Beaumont AB p. 2523
Bibliotheque de Beloeil, Beloeil QC p. 2710
Bibliotheque de Brossard, Brossard QC p. 2710
Bibliotheque de Coaticook, Inc, Coaticook QC p. 2711
Bibliotheque de Deux-Montagnes, Deux-Montagnes QC p. 2711
Bibliotheque de Dollard-des-Ormeaux, Dollard-des-Ormeaux QC p. 2711
Bibliotheque de Dorval, Dorval QC p. 2711
Bibliotheque de Farnham, Inc, Farnham QC p. 2712
Bibliotheque de la Baie, La Baie QC p. 2714
Bibliotheque de la ville de Shawinigan, Shawinigan QC p. 2736
Bibliotheque de l'Hopital Montfort, Ottawa ON p. 2664
Bibliotheque de Montreal-Est, Montreal-Est QC p. 2728
Bibliotheque de Niveau Collegial, *see* College Jean-de-Brebeuf, Montreal QC p. 2723
Bibliotheque de Saint Isidore, St. Isidore AB p. 2555
Bibliotheque de Sorel Tracy, De Sorel Tracy QC p. 2711
Bibliotheque Delage-Couture, *see* Hospital du Saint-Sacrement, Quebec QC p. 2731
Bibliotheque Dentinger, Falher AB p. 2539
Bibliotheque Dr Claude Richard, *see* CIUSSS de la Mauricie-et-du-Centre-du-Quebec, Victoriaville QC p. 2739
Bibliotheque Dre-Marguerite-Michaud, *see* York Library Region, Fredericton NB p. 2602
Bibliotheque du Cegep Limoilou, Quebec QC p. 2729
Bibliothèque du CIUSSS du Saguenay-Lac-Saint-Jean, Chicoutimi QC p. 2710
Bibliotheque du College Universitaire Dominicain, Ottawa ON p. 2665
Bibliotheque du Seminaire de Saint-Hyacinthe, Saint-Hyacinthe QC p. 2735
Bibliotheque Edmond-Archambault, Repentigny QC p. 2732
Bibliotheque et Archives Nationales du Quebec, Montreal QC p. 2717
Bibliotheque e technologies educatives, *see* Cegep de Granby, Granby QC p. 2713
Bibliotheque Etienne-Parent, *see* Bibliotheque Gabrielle Roy, Quebec QC p. 2729
Bibliotheque Fabien-LaRochelle, *see* Bibliotheque de la ville de Shawinigan, Shawinigan QC p. 2736
Bibliotheque Fleur de Lin, Saint-Leonard de Portneuf QC p. 2736
Bibliotheque Francine-McKenzie, Levis QC p. 2715
Bibliotheque Franciscaine Provinciale des Capucins, Montreal QC p. 2717
Bibliotheque Francois-Hertel, *see* Cegep de La Pocatiere, La Pocatiere QC p. 2714
Bibliotheque Gabrielle Roy, Quebec QC p. 2729
Bibliotheque H J Hemens, Rosemere QC p. 2733
Bibliotheque Henri-Brassard, Saint-Simeon QC p. 2736
Bibliotheque Hubert-Perron, *see* Bibliotheques Publiques de Longueuil, Longueuil QC p. 2716
Bibliotheque, Institut de Tourisme et d'Hotellerie du Quebec, Montreal QC p. 2717
Bibliotheque J-W-Gendron, *see* Bibliotheques Publiques de Longueuil, Longueuil QC p. 2716
Bibliotheque Jacques-Ferron, Adult Library, *see* Bibliotheques Publiques de Longueuil, Longueuil QC p. 2716
Bibliotheque Jacques-Ferron, Children's Library, *see* Bibliotheques Publiques de Longueuil, Longueuil QC p. 2716
Bibliotheque Jean-Charles Magnan, Saint-Casimir QC p. 2734
Bibliotheque Jean-Marc-Belzile, Lachute QC p. 2715
Bibliotheque La Ressource de la Munipalite de Saint-Jacques-de-Leeds, Saint-Jacques de Leeds QC p. 2735
Bibliotheque Laure-Conan, *see* Bibliotheque Publique de La Malbaie, La Malbaie QC p. 2714
Bibliothèque Laurent-Michel-Vacher, Montreal QC p. 2717
Bibliothèque Le Cormoran, *see* Fundy Library Region, Saint John NB p. 2604
Bibliotheque Le Tournesol, Lac Saint-Charles QC p. 2714
Bibliothèque Lisette-Morin (Municipale de Rimouski), Rimouski QC p. 2732
Bibliotheque Louis-Ange-Santerre, Sept Iles QC p. 2736
Bibliotheque Louis-R-Comeau, *see* Universite Sainte-Anne, Church Point NS p. 2617
Bibliotheque Mallaig Library, Mallaig AB p. 2547
Bibliotheque Marie-Antoinette-Foucher, Saint Jerome QC p. 2734
Bibliotheque Monique-Corriveau, Quebec QC p. 2730
Bibliotheque Montarville-Boucher de la Bruere, Boucherville QC p. 2710
Bibliotheque Montcalm Library, Saint-Jean-Baptiste MB p. 2590
Bibliotheque Municipale, Saint-Clement QC p. 2734
Bibliotheque Municipale, Temiscaming QC p. 2737
Bibliotheque Municipale, Terrebonne QC p. 2737
Bibliotheque Municipale, Vaudreuil-Dorion QC p. 2738
Bibliotheque Municipale Alice-Lane, Baie Comeau QC p. 2709
Bibliotheque Municipale Anne-Marie-D'Amours, Trois-Pistoles QC p. 2737
Bibliotheque Municipale Come-Saint-Germain, Drummondville QC p. 2711
Bibliotheque Municipale d'Alma, Alma QC p. 2709
Bibliotheque Municipale d'Asbestos, Asbestos QC p. 2709
Bibliotheque Municipale de Amos, Amos QC p. 2709
Bibliotheque Municipale de Greenfield Park, *see* Bibliotheques Publiques de Longueuil, Longueuil QC p. 2716
Bibliotheque Municipale de Jonquiere, Jonquiere QC p. 2714
Bibliotheque Municipale de La Tuque, La Tuque QC p. 2714
Bibliotheque Municipale de levis, Levis QC p. 2715
Bibliotheque Municipale de Mont-Laurier, Mont-Laurier QC p. 2716
Bibliotheque Municipale de Notre-Dame-du-Lac, Temiscouata-sur-Le-Lac QC p. 2737
Bibliotheque Municipale de Pincourt, Pincourt QC p. 2728

Black Cultural Centre for Nova Scotia Library, Cherry Brook NS p. 2616
Black Earth Public Library, Black Earth WI p. 2424
Black Estelle M Library, *see* Rock Valley College, Rockford IL p. 641
Black Gold Cooperative Library System, Arroyo Grande CA p. 117
Black Hawk College, Galva IL p. 591
Black Hawk College, Moline IL p. 618
Black Heritage Library & Multicultural Center, Findlay OH p. 1785
Black Hills State University, Spearfish SD p. 2083, 2792
Black Marianna Library, Bryson City NC p. 1675
Black Mary J L Community Hub, *see* Thunder Bay Public Library, Thunder Bay ON p. 2685
Black River Falls Public Library, Black River Falls WI p. 2424
Black River Technical College Library, Pocahontas AR p. 108
Black Watch Memorial Library, Ticonderoga NY p. 1651
Blackburn College, Carlinville IL p. 549
Blackburn Correctional Complex Library, Lexington KY p. 862
Blackduck Community Library, Blackduck MN p. 1165
Blackfalds Public Library, Blackfalds AB p. 2523
Blackfeet Community College, Browning MT p. 1290
Blackfoot Public Library, Blackfoot ID p. 515
Blackhawk Technical College Library, Janesville WI p. 2443
Blackmore Library, *see* Capital University, Columbus OH p. 1772
Blackmur Memorial Library, Water Valley MS p. 1235
Blackstone James Memorial Library, Branford CT p. 303
Blackstone Library - Louis Spenser Epes Library, *see* Nottoway County Public Libraries, Blackstone VA p. 2314
Blackstone Public Library, Blackstone MA p. 990
Blackwater Regional Library, Courtland VA p. 2313
Blackwell Lucien E West Philadelphia Regional, *see* Free Library of Philadelphia, Philadelphia PA p. 1977
Blackwell Public Library, Blackwell OK p. 1842
Blackwell R E Memorial, *see* Covington County Library System, Collins MS p. 1214
Bladen Community College Library, Dublin NC p. 1683
Bladen County Public Library, Elizabethtown NC p. 1687
Blaine County Library, Chinook MT p. 1291
Blaine Lake Public Library, *see* Wapiti Regional Library, Blaine Lake SK p. 2745
Blaine Public Library, Blaine TN p. 2088
Blair-Caldwell African American Research Library, *see* Denver Public Library, Denver CO p. 275
Blair County Law Library, Hollidaysburg PA p. 1944
Blair County Library System, Altoona PA p. 1906
Blair Library, *see* Fayetteville Public Library, Fayetteville AR p. 95
Blair Memorial Library, Clawson MI p. 1091
Blair Memorial Library, *see* Kent State University, East Liverpool OH p. 1783
Blair-Preston Public Library, Blair WI p. 2424
Blair Public Library, Blair NE p. 1308
Blairstown Public Library, Blairstown IA p. 735
Blairsville Public Library, Blairsville PA p. 1913
Blaisdell F William Medical Library, *see* University of California, Davis, Sacramento CA p. 210
Blaisdell Memorial Library, Nottingham NH p. 1377
Blake, Cassels & Graydon LLP, Toronto ON p. 2686
Blake Library, *see* Martin County Library System, Stuart FL p. 444
Blake Library, *see* University of Maine at Fort Kent, Fort Kent ME p. 925
Blake Library (Main), *see* Martin County Library System, Stuart FL p. 445
Blake Memorial Library, East Corinth VT p. 2283
Blakesburg Public Library, Blakesburg IA p. 735
Blaksley Library, *see* Santa Barbara Botanic Garden, Santa Barbara CA p. 240
Blanchard Community Library, *see* Blanchard-Santa Paula Library District, Santa Paula CA p. 245
Blanchard Judith Rozier Library, *see* Tampa Museum of Art, Tampa FL p. 449
Blanchard Learning Resources Center, *see* Ohlone College, Fremont CA p. 143
Blanchard Public, *see* Pioneer Library System, Blanchard OK p. 1855
Blanchard-Santa Paula Library District, Santa Paula CA p. 245
Blanchardville Public Library, Blanchardville WI p. 2424
Blanchester Public Library, Blanchester OH p. 1751
Blanco County South Library District, Blanco TX p. 2148
Bland Correctional Center Library, *see* Virginia Department of Corrections, Bland VA p. 2307
Bland County Library, Bland VA p. 2307
Bland Schuyler Otis Memorial Library, *see* United States Merchant Marine Academy, Kings Point NY p. 1560
Bland W T Public Library, Mount Dora FL p. 427
Blanding Free Public Library, Rehoboth MA p. 1049
Blandinsville-Hire District Library, Blandinsville IL p. 542
Blaney McMurtry LLP, Toronto ON p. 2687
Blankenbuehler John H Memorial Library, *see* Hobart Institute of Welding Technology, Troy OH p. 1825
Blasco Raymond M MD Memorial Library, *see* Erie County Public Library, Erie PA p. 1931
Blauvelt Free Library, Blauvelt NY p. 1494
Blazer Paul G Library, *see* Kentucky State University, Frankfort KY p. 855
Bledsoe County Correctional Complex Library, *see* Tennessee Department of Corrections, Pikeville TN p. 2124
Bledsoe County Public Library, Pikeville TN p. 2124
Bleskacek G E Family Memorial, *see* Bloomer Public Library, Bloomer WI p. 2424
Blessing Health Professions Library, *see* Blessing-Rieman College of Nursing & Health Sciences, Quincy IL p. 637
Blessing-Rieman College of Nursing & Health Sciences, Quincy IL p. 637
Blind River Public Library, Blind River ON p. 2631
Blinn College Library, Brenham TX p. 2149
Bliss Memorial Library, *see* First United Methodist Church, Shreveport LA p. 907
Bliss Memorial Public Library, Bloomville OH p. 1751
Blissell Elisabeth S Library, *see* Pennsylvania State University, New Kensington, Upper Burrell PA p. 2016
Blitstein Institute, *see* Hebrew Theological College, Chicago IL p. 647
Bloch Isidore & Rose Memorial Library, *see* Congregation B'Nai Israel, Albuquerque NM p. 1461
Bloch Leon E Law Library, *see* University of Missouri-Kansas City Libraries, Kansas City MO p. 1258
Block Edward A Family Library, Indianapolis IN p. 690
Block Robert Library, *see* United States Sports University, Daphne AL p. 14
Block William D Memorial Law Library, Waukegan IL p. 660
Blodgett Mabel D Memorial Reading Center, Rushville NY p. 1634
Blodgett Memorial Library, Fishkill NY p. 1533
Blommer Science Library, *see* Georgetown University, Washington DC p. 368
Blommers Measurement Resources Library, *see* University of Iowa, Iowa City IA p. 760
Blood Mary L Memorial Library, West Windsor VT p. 2298
Bloom Library, *see* Mount Zion Temple, Saint Paul MN p. 1201
Bloomberg Industry Group Library, Arlington VA p. 2305
Bloomer Public Library, Bloomer WI p. 2424
Bloomfield College Library, Bloomfield NJ p. 1391
Bloomfield-Eastern Greene County Public Library, Bloomfield IN p. 670
Bloomfield Public Library, Bloomfield CT p. 303
Bloomfield Public Library, Bloomfield IA p. 735
Bloomfield Public Library, Bloomfield MO p. 1237
Bloomfield Public Library, Bloomfield NE p. 1308
Bloomfield Public Library, Bloomfield NJ p. 1391
Bloomfield Public Library, Bloomfield NM p. 1464
Bloomfield Public Library, Bloomfield NY p. 1495
Bloomfield Public Library, New Bloomfield PA p. 1968
Bloomfield Township Public Library, Bloomfield Township MI p. 1086
Bloomingdale Free Public Library, Bloomingdale NJ p. 1391
Bloomingdale Public Library, Bloomingdale IL p. 542
Bloomingdale Regional Public, *see* Tampa-Hillsborough County Public Library System, Valrico FL p. 448
Bloomington Public Library, Bloomington IL p. 542
Bloomington Public Library, Bloomington WI p. 2424
Bloomsburg Public Library, Bloomsburg PA p. 1913
Bloomsburg University of Pennsylvania, Bloomsburg PA p. 1913
Blossburg Memorial Library, Blossburg PA p. 1913
Blossom Memorial Library, *see* Desert Caballeros Western Museum, Wickenburg AZ p. 84
Blough-Weis Library, *see* Susquehanna University, Selinsgrove PA p. 2005
Blount County Public Library, Maryville TN p. 2111
Blount Library, Inc, Franklinville NY p. 1535
Blount Margaret Little Bethel Library, *see* Sheppard Memorial Library, Bethel NC p. 1694
Blount Mary B Library, *see* Averett University Library, Danville VA p. 2314
Blountsville Public Library, Blountsville AL p. 10
Blue Ash College Library, *see* University of Cincinnati, Cincinnati OH p. 1764
Blue Diamond Library, *see* Las Vegas-Clark County Library District, Blue Diamond NV p. 1346
Blue Earth Community Library, Blue Earth MN p. 1166
Blue Earth County Library System, Mankato MN p. 1181
Blue Hill Public Library, Blue Hill ME p. 918
Blue Hill Public Library, Blue Hill NE p. 1308
Blue Island Public Library, Blue Island IL p. 543
Blue Mound Library, *see* Linn County Library District No 3, Blue Mound KS p. 799
Blue Mound Memorial Library District, Blue Mound IL p. 543
Blue Mountain College, Blue Mountain MS p. 1212
Blue Mountain Community College Library, Pendleton OR p. 1890
Blue Mountain Public Library, *see* Northeast Regional Library, Blue Mountain MS p. 1215
Blue Mountains Public Library, Thornbury ON p. 2684
Blue Public Library, Blue AZ p. 56
Blue Rapids Public Library, Blue Rapids KS p. 799
Blue Ridge Community College, Weyers Cave VA p. 2352
Blue Ridge Community College Library, Flat Rock NC p. 1689
Blue Ridge Community Library, Blue Ridge AB p. 2524
Blue Ridge Regional Library, Martinsville VA p. 2331
Blue Ridge Summit Free Library, Blue Ridge Summit PA p. 1914
Blue Ridge Township Public Library, Mansfield IL p. 613
Blue River Library, *see* Metropolitan Community College, Independence MO p. 1256
Blue Springs Historical Society, Blue Springs MO p. 1237
Bluebonnet Regional, *see* East Baton Rouge Parish Library, Baton Rouge LA p. 883
Bluefield State University, Bluefield WV p. 2398
Bluefield University, Bluefield VA p. 2307
Bluegrass Community & Technical College, Lexington KY p. 862

Boston Free Library, Boston NY p. 1496
Boston Law Library, *see* New England Law, Boston MA p. 998
Boston Library Consortium, Inc (N), Boston MA p. 2766
Boston Psychoanalytic Society & Institute, Inc, Newton MA p. 1039
Boston Public Library, Boston MA p. 991
Boston Theological Interreligious Consortium (N), Cambridge MA p. 2766
Boston University, Boston MA p. 2786
Boston University Libraries, Boston MA p. 993
Bostwick Muriel Library, *see* Art Gallery of Hamilton, Hamilton ON p. 2644
Bostwick Public, *see* Putnam County Library System, Palatka FL p. 433
Boswell & Grant Township Public Library, Boswell IN p. 672
Boswell Mabel Memorial, *see* Saline County Public Library, Bryant AR p. 90
Boswell Thomas E Memorial Library, *see* First Presbyterian Church, Evanston IL p. 586
Bosworth Memorial Library, *see* Lexington Theological Seminary, Lexington KY p. 863
Botanical Research Institute of Texas Library, Fort Worth TX p. 2179
Botetourt County Libraries, Roanoke VA p. 2344
Bothell Campus/Cascadia College Library, *see* University of Washington Libraries, Bothell WA p. 2381
Bothell Library, *see* King County Library System, Bothell WA p. 2365
Bothwell George, *see* Regina Public Library, Regina SK p. 2747
Bottineau County Public Library, Bottineau ND p. 1730
Bottineau Pierre, *see* Hennepin County Library, Minneapolis MN p. 1186
Boulder City Library, Boulder City NV p. 1343
Boulder Community Hospital, Boulder CO p. 266
Boulder Community Library, *see* Jefferson County Library System, Boulder MT p. 1288
Boulder County Corrections Library, Boulder CO p. 266
Boulder Junction Public Library, Boulder Junction WI p. 2425
Boulder Laboratories Library, *see* United States Department of Commerce, Boulder CO p. 267
Boulder Public Library, Boulder CO p. 266
Boulet Paul Emile Library, *see* Universite du Quebec a Chicoutimi, Chicoutimi QC p. 2711
Boulevard Park Library, *see* King County Library System, Seattle WA p. 2365
Boundary County Library, Bonners Ferry ID p. 518
Bourbon Public Library, Bourbon IN p. 672
Bourbonnais Public Library District, Bourbonnais IL p. 544
Bourke Memorial Library, *see* Cayuga County Community College, Auburn NY p. 1488
Bourne Frances T Jacaranda Public Library, Venice FL p. 452
Bourne Jonathan Public Library, Bourne MA p. 1001
Bouse Public Library, Bouse AZ p. 56
Bouwhuis Andrew L Library, *see* Canisius College, Buffalo NY p. 1509
Bovard Sarah Stewart Memorial Library, Tionesta PA p. 2012
Bovey Public Library, Bovey MN p. 1166
Bovina Public Library, Bovina Center NY p. 1496
Bow Island Municipal Library, Bow Island AB p. 2524
Bowden Public Library, Bowden AB p. 2524
Bowditch & Dewey, Worcester MA p. 1071
Bowdle Public Library, Bowdle SD p. 2074
Bowdoin College Library, Brunswick ME p. 919
Bowdoinham Public Library, Bowdoinham ME p. 918
Bowen Island Public Library, Bowen Island BC p. 2563
Bowen Otis & Elizabeth Library, *see* Bethel College, Mishawaka IN p. 706
Bowerston Public Library, Bowerston OH p. 1752
Bowie Public Library, Bowie TX p. 2149
Bowie State University, Bowie MD p. 960
Bowlby Eva K Public Library, Waynesburg PA p. 2019
Bowld Kathryn Sullivan Music Library, *see* Southwestern Baptist Theological Seminary Libraries, Fort Worth TX p. 2180
Bowling Green Public Library, Bowling Green MO p. 1238
Bowling Green State University, Huron OH p. 1791
Bowling Green State University Libraries, Bowling Green OH p. 1752
Bowman & Brooke, Minneapolis MN p. 1183
Bowman Library, *see* Menlo College, Atherton CA p. 118
Bowman Mary Jane & James L, *see* Handley Regional Library System, Stephens City VA p. 2354
Bowman Regional Public Library, Bowman ND p. 1731
Bown L A Building Library, *see* College of the North Atlantic Library Services, Stephenville NL p. 2609
Boxer University Library, *see* Franklin Rosalind University of Medicine & Science, North Chicago IL p. 626
Boxford Town Library, Boxford MA p. 1001
Boyajian Mesrob G Library, *see* Armenian Museum of America, Inc, Watertown MA p. 1062
Boyce Ditto Public Library, Mineral Wells TX p. 2220
Boyce James P Centennial Library, *see* Southern Baptist Theological Seminary, Louisville KY p. 866
Boyce R Dudley Library, *see* Golden West College, Huntington Beach CA p. 151
Boyce Ronald N Library, *see* United States Courts Library - Tenth Circuit Court of Appeals, Salt Lake City UT p. 2272
Boyce William T Library, *see* Fullerton College, Fullerton CA p. 147
Boyceville Public Library, Boyceville WI p. 2425
Boyd County Public Library, Ashland KY p. 847
Boyd Dettre Betty Library & Research Center, *see* National Museum of Women in the Arts, Washington DC p. 372
Boyd J D Library, *see* Alcorn State University, Alcorn State MS p. 1211
Boyd Katharine L Library, *see* Sandhills Community College, Pinehurst NC p. 1707
Boyden Library, Foxborough MA p. 1019
Boyden Public Library, Boyden IA p. 735
Boydstun Q B Library, Fort Gibson OK p. 1847
Boydton Public Library (Headquarters), *see* Mecklenburg County Public Library, Boydton VA p. 2308
Boyer L R Memorial Library - Sumrall, *see* Lamar County Library System, Sumrall MS p. 1230
Boyer-Reinstein Julia Library, *see* Cheektowaga Public Library, Cheektowaga NY p. 1517
Boyertown Community Library, Boyertown PA p. 1914
Boyle County Public Library, Danville KY p. 853
Boyle Public Library, Boyle AB p. 2524
Boylston Public Library, Boylston MA p. 1001
Boyne District Library, Boyne City MI p. 1087
Boyne Regional Library, Carman MB p. 2586
Boynton Beach City Library, Boynton Beach FL p. 386
Boynton Public Library, Templeton MA p. 1059
Boy's Town National Research Hospital, Omaha NE p. 1327
Bozeman Public Library, Bozeman MT p. 1289
BQSIMB (N), *see* Brooklyn-Queens-Staten Island-Manhattan-Bronx Health Sciences, Brooklyn NY p. 2770
Bracebridge Public Library, Bracebridge ON p. 2632
Bracewell Neighborhood Library, *see* Houston Public Library, Houston TX p. 2195
Bracken Alexander M Library, *see* Ball State University Libraries, Muncie IN p. 708
Bracken County Public Library, Brooksville KY p. 849
Bracken Health Sciences Library, *see* Queen's University, Kingston ON p. 2650
Bracken Memorial Library, Woodstock CT p. 349
Brackett Library, *see* Harding University, Searcy AR p. 109
Brackett Library, *see* Indian River State College, Vero Beach FL p. 404
Brackin Harl V Library, *see* Museum of Flight, Seattle WA p. 2377
Braddock Carnegie Library, Braddock PA p. 1914
Bradenton Beach Public Library, *see* Tingley Memorial Library, Bradenton Beach FL p. 387
Bradenton Campus Library, *see* State College of Florida Manatee-Sarasota Library, Bradenton FL p. 387
Bradford Area Public Library, Bradford PA p. 1914
Bradford County Library System, Troy PA p. 2013
Bradford County Public Library, Starke FL p. 444
Bradford Memorial Library, El Dorado KS p. 805
Bradford Public Library, Bradford OH p. 1752
Bradford Public Library, Bradford VT p. 2280
Bradford Public Library District, Bradford IL p. 544
Bradford Regional Medical Center, Bradford PA p. 1914
Bradford-West Gwillimbury Public Library, Bradford ON p. 2632
Bradley Beach Public Library, Bradley Beach NJ p. 1391
Bradley Blanche Memorial Library, *see* Cathlamet Public Library, Cathlamet WA p. 2361
Bradley LLP, Birmingham AL p. 8
Bradley Public Library District, Bradley IL p. 544
Bradley University, Peoria IL p. 634
Bradner Eric J Library, *see* Schoolcraft College, Livonia MI p. 1127
Bradshaw H Grady Chambers County Library, Valley AL p. 39
Brady Library of the Health Sciences, *see* UPMC Mercy Hospital of Pittsburgh, Pittsburgh PA p. 1997
Braille Circulating Library For The Blind Inc, Richmond VA p. 2340
Braille Institute Library, Los Angeles CA p. 160
Brainerd Memorial Library, Haddam CT p. 315
Brainerd Memorial Library, Danville VT p. 2282
Brainerd Public Library, Brainerd MN p. 1166
Braintree Historical Society, Inc Library & Resource Center, Braintree MA p. 1001
Braken Vera Library, *see* Medicine Hat College Library, Medicine Hat AB p. 2548
Brakensiek Clifton M Library, *see* County of Los Angeles Public Library, Bellflower CA p. 135
Bramlage Dorothy Public Library, Junction City KS p. 816
Bramley Jordan Library, Jordan NY p. 1558
Brammer R Iris Public Library, Narrows VA p. 2333
Brampton Library, Brampton ON p. 2632
Branch District Library, Coldwater MI p. 1092
Branchville Correctional Facility, Branchville IN p. 672
Brandeis School of Law Library, *see* University of Louisville Libraries, Louisville KY p. 867
Brandeis University, Waltham MA p. 1061
Brandel Library, *see* North Park University, Chicago IL p. 566
Brandon Free Public Library, Brandon VT p. 2280
Brandon Public Library, Brandon MS p. 1212
Brandon Public Library, Brandon WI p. 2425
Brandon Regional Health Authority, Brandon MB p. 2585
Brandon Regional Library, *see* Tampa-Hillsborough County Public Library System, Brandon FL p. 448
Brandon Township Public Library, Ortonville MI p. 1139
Brandon University, Brandon MB p. 2585
Brandywine Community Library, Topton PA p. 2013
Brandywine Conservancy, Inc, Chadds Ford PA p. 1920
Brandywine Hundred Library, Wilmington DE p. 356
Brandywine River Museum Library, *see* Brandywine Conservancy, Inc, Chadds Ford PA p. 1920
Branford Public Library, *see* Suwannee River Regional Library, Branford FL p. 419
Branigan Thomas Memorial Library, *see* Las Cruces Public Libraries, Las Cruces NM p. 1470

British Columbia Courthouse Library Society, Prince George BC p. 2574
British Columbia Electronic Library Network (N), Burnaby BC p. 2777
British Columbia Genealogical Society, Surrey BC p. 2576
British Columbia Institute of Technology Library, Burnaby BC p. 2563
British Columbia Land Surveyors Foundation, Sidney BC p. 2576
British Columbia Legislative Library, Victoria BC p. 2582
British Columbia Ministry of Education, Victoria BC p. 2582
British Columbia Securities Commission, Vancouver BC p. 2578
Britt Area Library, Britt ON p. 2633
Britt Public Library, Britt IA p. 736
Brittingham Harold H Memorial Library, *see* Metrohealth Medical Center, Cleveland OH p. 1770
Britton Public Library, Britton SD p. 2074
BRLA (N), *see* Border Regional Library Association, El Paso TX p. 2775
Broad Brook Public Library, Broad Brook CT p. 304
Broad Channel Community Library, *see* Queens Library, Broad Channel NY p. 1554
Broad Robert Medical Library, *see* Cayuga Medical Center at Ithaca, Ithaca NY p. 1551
Broad Valleys Federation of Libraries, Helena MT p. 1295
Broadhurst Library, *see* First United Methodist Church, Tulsa OK p. 1864
Broadhurst William Library, *see* Nazarene Theological Seminary, Kansas City MO p. 1257
Broadlawns Medical Center, Des Moines IA p. 745
Broadneck Library, *see* Arundel Anne County Public Library, Annapolis MD p. 950
Broadview Public Library District, Broadview IL p. 545
Broadwater Public Library, Broadwater NE p. 1309
Broadwater School & Community Library, Townsend MT p. 1303
Broadway Community Library, *see* Queens Library, Long Island City NY p. 1554
Brock Benjamin L Medical Library, *see* Holley A G State Hospital, Lantana FL p. 417
Brock Township Public Library, Beaverton ON p. 2631
Brock University, St. Catharines ON p. 2679
Brockton Campus Library, *see* Massasoit Community College, Brockton MA p. 1003
Brockton Law Library, *see* Commonwealth of Massachusetts - Trial Court, Brockton MA p. 1002
Brockton Public Library, Brockton MA p. 1002
Brockville Public Library, Brockville ON p. 2634
Brockway Memorial Library, Miami Shores FL p. 426
Broder Aaron & Bertha Center for Jewish Education, *see* Temple Beth Zion, Buffalo NY p. 1510
Brodhead Memorial Public Library, Brodhead WI p. 2425
Brodsky Saul Jewish Community Library, Saint Louis MO p. 1269
Broken Bow Public Library, Broken Bow NE p. 1309
Broken Bow Public Library, Broken Bow OK p. 1843
Brokenhead River Regional Library, Beausejour MB p. 2585
Bromfield Louis Library, *see* Ohio State University LIBRARIES, Mansfield OH p. 1775
Bronfman Peter F Business Library, *see* York University Libraries, North York ON p. 2661
Bronson Methodist Hospital, Kalamazoo MI p. 1121
Bronson Public, *see* Levy County Public Library System, Bronson FL p. 387
Bronson Public Library, Bronson KS p. 799
Bronson Silas Library, Waterbury CT p. 343
Bronx Community College Library, Bronx NY p. 1497
Bronx County Historical Society, Bronx NY p. 1498
Bronxville Public Library, Bronxville NY p. 1500
Brook-Iroquois-Washington Public Library, Brook IN p. 672
Brookdale Community College, Lincroft NJ p. 1412
Brookdale University Hospital & Medical Center, Brooklyn NY p. 1501
Brooke County Public Library, Wellsburg WV p. 2417
Brooke-Gould Memorial, *see* Preble County District Library, Eaton OH p. 1784
Brookens Norris L Library, *see* University of Illinois at Springfield, Springfield IL p. 651
Brookes Bible College Library, Saint Ann MO p. 1268
Brookfield Free Public Library, Brookfield VT p. 2280
Brookfield Library, Brookfield CT p. 304
Brookfield Public Library, Brookfield MO p. 1239
Brookfield Public Library, Brookfield WI p. 2425
Brookfield Zoo Library, *see* Chicago Zoological Society, Brookfield IL p. 545
Brookgreen Gardens Library, Murrells Inlet SC p. 2066
Brookhaven Free Library, Brookhaven NY p. 1500
Brookhaven National Laboratory, Upton NY p. 1654
Brookings Institution Library, Washington DC p. 361
Brookings Public Library, Brookings SD p. 2074
Brookline Public Library, Brookline NH p. 1356
Brooklyn Bar Association Foundation Inc Library, Brooklyn NY p. 1501
Brooklyn Botanic Garden Library, Brooklyn NY p. 1501
Brooklyn College Library, Brooklyn NY p. 1501
Brooklyn Hospital Center, Brooklyn NY p. 1501
Brooklyn Law School Library, Brooklyn NY p. 1501
Brooklyn Museum, Brooklyn NY p. 1501
Brooklyn Park Library, *see* Arundel Anne County Public Library, Baltimore MD p. 950
Brooklyn Public Library, Brooklyn IA p. 736
Brooklyn Public Library, Brooklyn NY p. 1502
Brooklyn-Queens-Staten Island-Manhattan-Bronx Health Sciences (N), Brooklyn NY p. 2770
Brooklyn Town Library Association, Brooklyn CT p. 305
Brooks-Cork Library, *see* Shelton State Community College, Tuscaloosa AL p. 37
Brooks County Public Library, Quitman GA p. 493
Brooks Ellen West Memorial Library, Forney TX p. 2177
Brooks Ernest C Correctional Facility Library, *see* Michigan Department of Corrections, Muskegon MI p. 1089
Brooks Free Library, Harwich MA p. 1023
Brooks Gladys Memorial Library, *see* Mount Washington Observatory, North Conway NH p. 1376
Brooks Gwendolyn Library, *see* Chicago State University, Chicago IL p. 558
Brooks James E Library, *see* Central Washington University, Ellensburg WA p. 2363
Brooks Lyman Beecher Library, *see* Norfolk State University Library, Norfolk VA p. 2335
Brooks Marshall Library, *see* Principia College, Elsah IL p. 585
Brooks Memorial Library, Brattleboro VT p. 2280
Brooks Public Library, Brooks AB p. 2524
Brookside Congregational Church Library, Manchester NH p. 1372
Brookston - Prairie Township Public Library, Brookston IN p. 672
Brooksville Free Public Library, Inc, Brooksville ME p. 919
Brookswood Library, *see* Fraser Valley Regional Library, Langley BC p. 2561
Brookville Public Library, *see* Franklin County Public Library District, Brookville IN p. 673
Broome County Courts Law Library, *see* NYS Supreme Court Library - Binghamton, Binghamton NY p. 1494
Broome County Historical Society Library, Binghamton NY p. 1493
Broome County Public Library, Binghamton NY p. 1493
Brosville/Cascade, *see* Pittsylvania County Public Library, Danville VA p. 2311
Brother Edmond Drouin Library, *see* Walsh University, North Canton OH p. 1809
Broughton Hospital, Morganton NC p. 1704
Broward College, Davie FL p. 391
Broward County Libraries Division, Fort Lauderdale FL p. 396
Brown A H Public Library, Mobridge SD p. 2079
Brown Albert Church Memorial Library, China ME p. 922
Brown Arvin A Public Library, Richford VT p. 2293
Brown Barbara Moscato Memorial Library, *see* Cameron County Public Library, Emporium PA p. 1930
Brown Beverley J Library, *see* Jackson/Hinds Library System, Byram MS p. 1221
Brown Charles Ewing Library, *see* Mid-America Christian University, Oklahoma City OK p. 1858
Brown Charles L Science & Engineering Library, *see* University of Virginia, Charlottesville VA p. 2310
Brown City District Library, Brown City MI p. 1087
Brown County Historical Society, New Ulm MN p. 1190
Brown County Library, Green Bay WI p. 2438
Brown County Public Library, Nashville IN p. 709
Brown County Public Library, Mount Orab OH p. 1804
Brown County Public Library District, Mount Sterling IL p. 621
Brown D Memorial Library, Rosebud TX p. 2234
Brown-Daniel Library, *see* Tennessee State University, Nashville TN p. 2121
Brown Dee Library, *see* Central Arkansas Library System, Little Rock AR p. 101
Brown Deer Public Library, Brown Deer WI p. 2426
Brown George E Jr Library/Research Center, *see* National Academies of Sciences, Engineering & Medicine, Washington DC p. 371
Brown George H & Laura E Library, Washington NC p. 1721
Brown George Warren School of Social Work, *see* Washington University Libraries, Saint Louis MO p. 1277
Brown Hallie Q Memorial Library, *see* Central State University, Wilberforce OH p. 1831
Brown Herman Free Library, *see* Burnet County Library System, Burnet TX p. 2152
Brown James V Library, Williamsport PA p. 2023
Brown John A Library Media Center, *see* Wenatchee Valley College, Wenatchee WA p. 2395
Brown John Carter Library, *see* Brown University, Providence RI p. 2037
Brown LaVerne & Dorothy Library, *see* University of St Francis, Joliet IL p. 603
Brown Library, *see* Sterling College, Craftsbury Common VT p. 2282
Brown Library, *see* Tuscaloosa Public Library, Tuscaloosa AL p. 38
Brown Library, *see* Virginia Western Community College, Roanoke VA p. 2346
Brown Margaret & Herman Library, *see* Abilene Christian University, Abilene TX p. 2131
Brown Mary Berry Memorial Library, Midland City AL p. 25
Brown Memorial Library, Clinton ME p. 922
Brown Memorial Library, East Baldwin ME p. 923
Brown Memorial Library, Bradford NH p. 1355
Brown Memorial Library, Lewisburg OH p. 1795
Brown Nelle Memorial Library, *see* Ohoopee Regional Library System, Lyons GA p. 502
Brown P D Memorial, *see* Charles County Public Library, Waldorf MD p. 969
Brown Public Library, Northfield VT p. 2290
Brown Raiford A, *see* Jacksonville Public Library, Jacksonville FL p. 412
Brown Richard J Library, *see* Nicolet Area Technical College, Rhinelander WI p. 2472
Brown, Rudnick LLP, Boston MA p. 994
Brown Sammy Library, Carthage TX p. 2154
Brown University, Providence RI p. 2037
Brown W L Lyons Library, *see* Bellarmine University, Louisville KY p. 864
Brown William C, *see* DeKalb County Public Library, Decatur GA p. 475

Bureau of Land Management Library, Denver CO p. 273
Bureau of Prisons, El Reno OK p. 1846
Bureau of Reclamation Library, *see* United States Department of the Interior, Denver CO p. 277
Burger Warren E Library, *see* Mitchell Hamline School of Law, Saint Paul MN p. 1201
Burges Richard Regional, *see* El Paso Public Library, El Paso TX p. 2174
Burgess Marie Blair Library, *see* Spartanburg Methodist College, Spartanburg SC p. 2070
Burgettstown Community Library, Burgettstown PA p. 1916
Burin Memorial Public Library, Burin Bay Arm NL p. 2607
Burkburnett Library, Burkburnett TX p. 2151
Burke Carleton F Memorial Library, *see* California Thoroughbred Breeders Association, Arcadia CA p. 117
Burke Centre Library, *see* Fairfax County Public Library, Burke VA p. 2316
Burke County Library, *see* Greater Clarks Hill Regional Library System, Waynesboro GA p. 478
Burke County Public Library, Morganton NC p. 1704
Burke Ellen Coolidge, *see* Alexandria Library, Alexandria VA p. 2302
Burke Library, *see* Hamilton College, Clinton NY p. 1519
Burke Library, *see* Columbia University, New York NY p. 1583
Burke Marnie & John Memorial Library, *see* Spring Hill College, Mobile AL p. 26
Burkholder Dr Maurice M, *see* Saint Luke's Health System Libraries, Boise ID p. 518
Burkley Library & Resource Center, Dewitt NE p. 1312
Burk's Falls, Armour & Ryerson Union Public Library, Burk's Falls ON p. 2634
Burleson Public Library, Burleson TX p. 2152
Burlew Medical Library, *see* Saint Joseph Hospital & Childrens Hospital, Orange CA p. 189
Burley Public Library, Burley ID p. 518
Burling Library, *see* Grinnell College Libraries, Grinnell IA p. 756
Burlingame Community Library, Burlingame KS p. 799
Burlingame Public Library, Burlingame CA p. 125
Burlington County Historical Society, Burlington NJ p. 1393
Burlington County Library System, Westampton NJ p. 1453
Burlington Public, *see* Keyser-Mineral County Public Library, Burlington WV p. 2406
Burlington Public Library, Burlington CO p. 269
Burlington Public Library, Burlington CT p. 305
Burlington Public Library, Burlington IA p. 736
Burlington Public Library, Burlington MA p. 1003
Burlington Public Library, Burlington WA p. 2360
Burlington Public Library, Burlington WV p. 2399
Burlington Public Library, Burlington WI p. 2426
Burlington Public Library, Burlington ON p. 2634
Burlington Township Library, Burlington MI p. 1087
Burman Roberta L Medical Library, *see* Memorial Hospital at Gulfport, Gulfport MS p. 1218
Burman University Library, Lacombe AB p. 2545
Burnaby Hospital Library, *see* Fraser Health Authority, Burnaby BC p. 2563
Burnaby Public Library, Burnaby BC p. 2563
Burnap Harriet Call Memorial Library, *see* Clarkson University Libraries, Potsdam NY p. 1622
Burnet County Library System, Burnet TX p. 2152
Burnet, Duckworth & Palmer, LLP, Calgary AB p. 2526
Burnett Community Library, *see* Larsen Family Public Library, Webster WI p. 2486
Burnett Cordas C Library, *see* Assemblies of God Theological Seminary, Springfield MO p. 1280
Burnett Library & Learning Center, *see* Mecklenburg County Public Library, Clarksville VA p. 2308
Burnett Mary Couts Library, *see* Texas Christian University, Fort Worth TX p. 2181
Burnett Ron Library & Learning Commons, *see* Emily Carr University of Art & Design Library, Vancouver BC p. 2578
Burnett Tom Memorial Library, Iowa Park TX p. 2202
Burnette Maybelle, *see* Warren Public Library, Warren MI p. 1157
Burnham Guy H Map & Aerial Photography Library, *see* Clark University, Worcester MA p. 1071
Burnham Library, *see* Bridgewater Library Association, Bridgewater CT p. 304
Burnham Memorial Library, Colchester VT p. 2282
Burnley Memorial Library, Cottonwood Falls KS p. 803
Burns & Levinson, Boston MA p. 994
Burns Jacob Law Library, *see* George Washington University, Washington DC p. 367
Burns Lake Public Library, Burns Lake BC p. 2564
Burns Ollie, *see* Ouachita Parish Public Library, Richwood LA p. 898
Burns Public Library, Burns KS p. 800
Burnsville Public Library, Burnsville WV p. 2399
Burnsville Public Library, *see* Northeast Regional Library, Burnsville MS p. 1215
Burr & Forman Library, Birmingham AL p. 8
Burr Oak Community Library, Burr Oak KS p. 800
Burr Oak Township Library, Burr Oak MI p. 1088
Burrage Library, *see* University of Olivet, Olivet MI p. 1138
Burrell College of Osteopathic Medicine, Las Cruces NM p. 1470
Burrell Township Library, Black Lick PA p. 1912
Burritt Elihu Library, *see* Central Connecticut State University, New Britain CT p. 324
Burritt Memorial Library, Spencer TN p. 2127
Burroughs Learning Center, *see* Bethel University, McKenzie TN p. 2111
Burruss Correctional Training Center, *see* Georgia Department of Corrections, Forsyth GA p. 479
Burt County Museum, Inc Library, Tekamah NE p. 1338
Burt Klyte Memorial Public Library, Curtis NE p. 1312
Burt Public Library, Burt IA p. 736
Burtchville Township Branch Library, *see* Saint Clair County Library System, Lakeport MI p. 1142
Burton College of Education, *see* McNeese State University, Lake Charles LA p. 2786
Burton G B Memorial Library, Clarendon TX p. 2156
Burton Mamie Ethel Memorial Library, *see* East Central Community College, Decatur MS p. 1216
Burton Public Library, Burton OH p. 1753
Busch Dorothy M, *see* Warren Public Library, Warren MI p. 1157
Busch Michael E Annapolis Library, *see* Arundel Anne County Public Library, Annapolis MD p. 950
Buschow Edna Memorial Library, *see* Valley Center Public Library, Valley Center KS p. 840
Buset LLP, Thunder Bay ON p. 2684
Bush Barbara, *see* Harris County Public Library, Spring TX p. 2192
Bush David F Library, *see* Stanislaus County Library, Oakdale CA p. 178
Bush George H W Presidential Library & Museum, *see* National Archives & Records Administration, College Station TX p. 2157
Bush George W Presidential Library, *see* National Archives & Records Administration, Dallas TX p. 2167
Bush Laura Community Library, *see* Westbank Community Library District, Austin TX p. 2143
Bush Memorial Library, *see* Hamline University, Saint Paul MN p. 1199
Bush William H Memorial Library, Martinsburg NY p. 1569
Bushnell Public Library, Bushnell IL p. 547
Bushnell Public Library, *see* Sumter County Library System, Bushnell FL p. 455
Bushnell-Sage Library, Sheffield MA p. 1052
Bushnell University, Eugene OR p. 1878
Business Learning Center, *see* North Dakota State University Libraries, Fargo ND p. 1733
Business Resource & Innovaton Center, *see* Free Library of Philadelphia, Philadelphia PA p. 1977
Busse Library, *see* Mount Mercy University, Cedar Rapids IA p. 738
Bussey Community Library, Bussey IA p. 736
Buswell J Oliver Jr Library, *see* Covenant Theological Seminary, Saint Louis MO p. 1270
Buswell Memorial Library, *see* Wheaton College, Wheaton IL p. 662
Butler Area Public Library, Butler PA p. 1917
Butler Community College Library & Archives, El Dorado KS p. 805
Butler County Community College, Butler PA p. 1917
Butler County Federated Library System, Butler PA p. 1917
Butler County Historical-Genealogical Society Library, Greenville AL p. 19
Butler County Law Library, Butler PA p. 1917
Butler County Public Library, Morgantown KY p. 870
Butler E H Library, *see* Buffalo State University of New York, Buffalo NY p. 1508
Butler Hospital, Providence RI p. 2037
Butler Institute of American Art, Youngstown OH p. 1835
Butler Library, *see* Columbia University, New York NY p. 1584
Butler Memorial, *see* Mecklenburg County Public Library, Chase City VA p. 2308
Butler Memorial & Martin Luther King Center, *see* Lafayette Public Library, Lafayette LA p. 892
Butler Memorial Library, Cambridge NE p. 1309
Butler Public, *see* Pine Mountain Regional Library, Butler GA p. 488
Butler Public Library, Butler IN p. 673
Butler Public Library, Butler MO p. 1239
Butler Public Library, Butler NJ p. 1393
Butler Public Library, Butler WI p. 2426
Butler, Rubin, Saltarelli & Boyd LLP, Chicago IL p. 555
Butler University Libraries, Indianapolis IN p. 690
Butt-Holdsworth Memorial Library, Kerrville TX p. 2205
Butt Marshall W Library, *see* Portsmouth Naval Shipyard Museum, Portsmouth VA p. 2338
Butte College Library, Oroville CA p. 189
Butte County Library, Oroville CA p. 189
Butte County Public Law Library, Oroville CA p. 190
Butte-Silver Bow Public Library, Butte MT p. 1290
Butterfield Julia L Memorial Library, Cold Spring NY p. 1520
Butterfield Library, Westminster VT p. 2298
Butterfield Memorial Research Library, *see* Bay County Historical Society, Bay City MI p. 1083
Buxbaum Edith Library, *see* Seattle Psychoanalytic Society & Institute, Seattle WA p. 2379
Buxton Library, *see* Paradise Valley Community College, Phoenix AZ p. 71
Byers Jay C Memorial Library, Cleveland OK p. 1844
Byker Gary Memorial Library, Hudsonville MI p. 1117
Byrd John L Jr Technical Library, *see* United States Army, McAlester OK p. 1853
Byrd Polar Research Center, Columbus OH p. 1771
Byrd Richard Branch, *see* Fairfax County Public Library, Springfield VA p. 2316
Byrnes-Quanbeck Library, *see* Mayville State University, Mayville ND p. 1737
Byrom Fletcher L Earth & Mineral Sciences Library, *see* Pennsylvania State University Libraries, University Park PA p. 2015
Byron-Bergen Public Library, Bergen NY p. 1493
Byron Memorial, *see* London Public Library, London ON p. 2654
Byron Public, *see* Peach Public Libraries, Byron GA p. 480
Byron Public Library, Byron NE p. 1309
Byron Public Library District, Byron IL p. 547
Byzantine Catholic Seminary of Saints Cyril & Methodius Library, Pittsburgh PA p. 1990

Callaway Luther Public, *see* Levy County Public Library System, Chiefland FL p. 387
Callender Heritage Library, Callender IA p. 736
Callier Library, *see* University of Texas at Dallas, Dallas TX p. 2231
Calling Lake Public Library, Calling Lake AB p. 2529
Calloway County Public Library, Murray KY p. 870
Calmar Campus Library, *see* Northeast Iowa Community College, Calmar IA p. 776
Calmar Public Library, Calmar IA p. 736
Calmar Public Library, Calmar AB p. 2529
Calumet City Public Library, Calumet City IL p. 548
Calumet College of Saint Joseph, Whiting IN p. 726
Calumet Park Public Library, Calumet Park IL p. 548
Calumet Public Library, Calumet MN p. 1167
Calvary Hospital, Bronx NY p. 1498
Calvary Presbyterian Church USA Library, Riverside CA p. 201
Calvary University, Kansas City MO p. 1254
Calvert Janet Carlson Library, Franklin CT p. 313
Calvert Library, Prince Frederick MD p. 972
Calvert Marine Museum Library, Solomons MD p. 978
Calvin University & Calvin Theological Seminary, Grand Rapids MI p. 1110
Camanche Public Library, Camanche IA p. 736
Camano Island Library, *see* Sno-Isle Libraries, Camano Island WA p. 2370
Camarena Memorial Library, Calexico CA p. 126
Camargo Township District Library, Villa Grove IL p. 658
Camarillo Public Library, Camarillo CA p. 126
Camas County Public Library, Fairfield ID p. 520
Camas Public Library, Camas WA p. 2360
Cambie Branch, *see* Richmond Public Library, Richmond BC p. 2575
Cambria County Free Law Library, Ebensburg PA p. 1929
Cambria County Historical Society Library, Ebensburg PA p. 1929
Cambria County Library System & District Center, Johnstown PA p. 1947
Cambria Heights Community Library, *see* Queens Library, Cambria Heights NY p. 1554
Cambrian College Library, Sudbury ON p. 2682
Cambridge City Public Library, Cambridge City IN p. 673
Cambridge Community Library, Cambridge ID p. 519
Cambridge Community Library, Cambridge WI p. 2426
Cambridge Historical Commission Archive, Cambridge MA p. 1004
Cambridge Hospital-Cambridge Health Alliance, Cambridge MA p. 1004
Cambridge Memorial Library, Cambridge IA p. 736
Cambridge Military Library, *see* Canada Department of National Defence, Halifax NS p. 2618
Cambridge Public Library, Cambridge MA p. 1004
Cambridge Public Library, Cambridge NY p. 1512
Cambridge Public Library District, Cambridge IL p. 548
Cambridge Springs Public Library, Cambridge Springs PA p. 1917
Camden Archives & Museum Library, Camden SC p. 2048
Camden-Carroll Library, *see* Morehead State University, Morehead KY p. 869
Camden-Clark Memorial Center, Parkersburg WV p. 2411
Camden County College Library, Blackwood NJ p. 1390
Camden County Historical Society, Camden NJ p. 1394
Camden County Library, Camden NC p. 1677
Camden County Library District, Camdenton MO p. 1239
Camden County Library System, Voorhees NJ p. 1450
Camden County Public Library, Kingsland GA p. 484
Camden-Jackson Township Public Library, Camden IN p. 674
Camden Law Library, *see* Rutgers University Libraries, Camden NJ p. 1394
Camden Public Library, Camden ME p. 920
Camden Public Library, Camden NY p. 1512
Camden Township Library, Camden MI p. 1088
Camdenton Library, *see* Camden County Library District, Camdenton MO p. 1239
Cameron Angus L Medical Library, *see* Trinity Health, Minot ND p. 1738
Cameron Area Public Library, Cameron WI p. 2427
Cameron County Public Library, Emporium PA p. 1930
Cameron J Jarvis Troup Municipal Library, Troup TX p. 2249
Cameron Parish Library, Cameron LA p. 886
Cameron Public, *see* Moundsville-Marshall County Public Library, Cameron WV p. 2410
Cameron Public Library, Cameron MO p. 1239
Cameron Public Library, Cameron TX p. 2152
Cameron Science & Technology Library, Edmonton AB p. 2535
Cameron University Library, Lawton OK p. 1851
Camosun College, Victoria BC p. 2582
Camp Albert T Technical Library, *see* United States Navy, Indian Head MD p. 969
Camp Point Public Library, Camp Point IL p. 548
Camp Verde Community Library, Camp Verde AZ p. 57
Camp Wood Public Library, Camp Wood TX p. 2152
Campbell Albert Branch, *see* Toronto Public Library, Toronto ON p. 2694
Campbell Burchell Memorial Library, *see* Lexington Public Library, Lexington AL p. 24
Campbell Carlyle Library, *see* Meredith College, Raleigh NC p. 1708
Campbell County Health Library, Gillette WY p. 2494
Campbell County Public Library, Rustburg VA p. 2346
Campbell County Public Library District, Cold Spring KY p. 851
Campbell County Public Library System, Gillette WY p. 2494
Campbell Express Library, *see* Santa Clara County Library District, Campbell CA p. 127
Campbell Foundation Library, Memphis TN p. 2112
Campbell Frank D Memorial Library, Bessemer PA p. 1911
Campbell Fred & Ron Bennett Library, *see* College of the North Atlantic Library Services, Stephenville NL p. 2609
Campbell G Lynn Branch Library, *see* Saint Clair County Library System, Kimball MI p. 1142
Campbell James & Abigail Library, *see* University of Hawaii - West Oahu Library, Kapolei HI p. 513
Campbell John Bulow Library, *see* Columbia Theological Seminary, Decatur GA p. 475
Campbell Keith & Shirley Library, *see* Rowan University Library, Glassboro NJ p. 1405
Campbell Keith A Memorial Library, *see* Joint Base San Antonio Libraries, Fort Sam Houston TX p. 2178
Campbell Library, *see* Saint Joseph's University, Philadelphia PA p. 1985
Campbell Mary M Public Library, Marcus Hook PA p. 1958
Campbell Public Library, Campbell NE p. 1309
Campbell River Museum & Archives, Campbell River BC p. 2564
Campbell Ruth Camp Memorial, *see* Blackwater Regional Library, Franklin VA p. 2313
Campbell University, Buies Creek NC p. 1676
Campbell William J Library, *see* Library of the United States Courts of the Seventh Circuit, Chicago IL p. 563
Campbellsport Public Library, Campbellsport WI p. 2427
Campbellsville University, Campbellsville KY p. 850
Campbellton Centennial Library, *see* Chaleur Library Region, Campbellton NB p. 2599
Campobello Public Library, *see* Fundy Library Region, Campobello Parish NB p. 2604
Campton Public Library, Campton NH p. 1356
Campus Martius Museum Library, *see* Ohio Historical Society, Marietta OH p. 1799
Camrose Public Library, Camrose AB p. 2529
Canaan Public Library, Canaan ME p. 920
Canaan Town Library, Canaan NH p. 1356
Canada Agriculture & Agri-Food Canada, Saint-Hyacinthe QC p. 2735
Canada Aviation & Space Museum, Ottawa ON p. 2665
Canada Centre for Inland Waters Library, *see* Environment Canada Library, Burlington ON p. 2634
Canada Council for the Arts, Ottawa ON p. 2665
Canada Department of Aboriginal Affairs & Northern Development, Gatineau QC p. 2712
Canada Department of Fisheries & Oceans, Dartmouth NS p. 2617
Canada Department of Fisheries & Oceans, Sydney NS p. 2622
Canada Department of Justice, Edmonton AB p. 2535
Canada Department of Justice Library, Ottawa ON p. 2665
Canada Department of Justice Montreal Headquarters Library, Montreal QC p. 2721
Canada Department of National Defence, Halifax NS p. 2618
Canada Department of National Defence, Borden ON p. 2632
Canada Energy Regulator Library, Calgary AB p. 2527
Canada-Newfoundland Offshore Petroleum Board Library, St. John's NL p. 2608
Canada School of Public Service Library, Gatineau QC p. 2712
Canada Science & Technology Museum, Ottawa ON p. 2665
Canaday Mariam Coffin Library, *see* Bryn Mawr College, Bryn Mawr PA p. 1916
Canadian Agriculture Library-Fredericton, Fredericton NB p. 2600
Canadian Army Command & Staff College, Kingston ON p. 2650
Canadian Artists' Representation, Ottawa ON p. 2665
Canadian Association of Occupational Therapists, Ottawa ON p. 2665
Canadian Association of Research Libraries (N), Ottawa ON p. 2778
Canadian Baptist Archives, Hamilton ON p. 2644
Canadian Bible Society Library, Toronto ON p. 2687
Canadian Broadcasting Corp, Toronto ON p. 2687
Canadian Centre for Ecumenism Library, Montreal QC p. 2721
Canadian Centre for Occupational Health & Safety, Hamilton ON p. 2644
Canadian Child Care Federation, Ottawa ON p. 2665
Canadian Coast Guard College John Adams Library, *see* Canada Department of Fisheries & Oceans, Sydney NS p. 2622
Canadian Conference of Mennonite Brethren Churches, Winnipeg MB p. 2592
Canadian Conservation Institute Library, *see* Department of Canadian Heritage, Ottawa ON p. 2666
Canadian Copper & Brass Development Association Library, Toronto ON p. 2687
Canadian County Historical Museum Library, El Reno OK p. 1846
Canadian Environmental Law Foundation, Toronto ON p. 2687
Canadian Federation of Independent Business, Toronto ON p. 2687
Canadian Forces Health Services Centre Library, Ottawa ON p. 2665
Canadian Forces Health Services Training Centre, *see* Canada Department of National Defence, Borden ON p. 2632
Canadian Foundation for Children, Youth & the Law, Toronto ON p. 2687
Canadian Grain Commission Library, Winnipeg MB p. 2592
Canadian Health Libraries Association (N), Toronto ON p. 2778

Carlisle Public Library, Carlisle IA p. 736
Carlock Public Library District, Carlock IL p. 549
Carlos Albizu University Library, Miami FL p. 421
Carlow-Mayo Public Library, Bancroft ON p. 2629
Carlow University, Pittsburgh PA p. 1990
Carlsbad City Library, Carlsbad CA p. 127
Carlsbad Public Library, Carlsbad NM p. 1465
Carlsen Anne Learning Center, Jamestown ND p. 1736
Carlsen Memorial Library, *see* Saint Olaf Lutheran Church, Minneapolis MN p. 1185
Carlsmith Ball LLP Library, Honolulu HI p. 505
Carlson Dr James, *see* Fargo Public Library, Fargo ND p. 1733
Carlson Frank Library, Concordia KS p. 803
Carlson Rena M Library, *see* Pennsylvaia Western University - Clarion, Clarion PA p. 1922
Carlson Science & Engineering Library, *see* University of Rochester, Rochester NY p. 1631
Carlson William S Library, *see* University of Toledo, Toledo OH p. 1825
Carlton Albert-Cashiers Community Library, Cashiers NC p. 1677
Carlton Area Public Library, Carlton MN p. 1169
Carlton County Historical Society, Cloquet MN p. 1170
Carlton Fields, Tampa FL p. 448
Carmangay & District Municipal Library, Carmangay AB p. 2530
Carmel Clay Public Library, Carmel IN p. 674
Carmel Public Library, *see* Harrison Memorial Library, Carmel CA p. 128
Carmelitana Collection, Washington DC p. 362
Carmelitana Collection - Order of Carmelites (OCarm), *see* Society of Mount Carmel, Washington DC p. 376
Carmelite Monastery, Baltimore MD p. 952
Carmen Public Library, Carmen OK p. 1843
Carmi Public Library, Carmi IL p. 549
Carmichael Library, *see* Sacramento Public Library, Carmichael CA p. 209
Carmichael Oliver Cromwell Library, *see* University of Montevallo, Montevallo AL p. 27
Carmody, Torrance, Sandak, Hennessey LLP, Waterbury CT p. 343
Carnegie Andrew Free Library & Music Hall, Carnegie PA p. 1919
Carnegie Andrew Library, *see* Livingstone College, Salisbury NC p. 1714
Carnegie City-County Library, Vernon TX p. 2251
Carnegie Education Library, *see* Washburn University, Topeka KS p. 839
Carnegie Endowment for International Peace Library, Washington DC p. 362
Carnegie Evans Public Library Albia Public, Albia IA p. 729
Carnegie Free Library, Beaver Falls PA p. 1909
Carnegie Free Library, Connellsville PA p. 1924
Carnegie Free Library, Midland PA p. 1963
Carnegie Free Library of Swissvale, Pittsburgh PA p. 1991
Carnegie History Center, *see* Bryan College Station Public Library System, Bryan TX p. 2151
Carnegie Library, *see* Muncie Public Library, Muncie IN p. 708
Carnegie Library, *see* University of Georgia Libraries, Athens GA p. 459
Carnegie Library of Ballinger, Ballinger TX p. 2144
Carnegie Library of Homestead, Munhall PA p. 1967
Carnegie Library of McKeesport, McKeesport PA p. 1959
Carnegie Library of Pittsburgh, Pittsburgh PA p. 1991
Carnegie Mellon University, Pittsburgh PA p. 1992
Carnegie Memorial, *see* Calcasieu Parish Public Library System, Lake Charles LA p. 893
Carnegie Museum of Natural History Library, Pittsburgh PA p. 1992
Carnegie Observatories, Pasadena CA p. 193
Carnegie Perry Library, Perry OK p. 1860
Carnegie Public, *see* Saint Joseph Public Library, Saint Joseph MO p. 1269
Carnegie Public Library, Monte Vista CO p. 291
Carnegie Public Library, Clarksdale MS p. 1213
Carnegie Public Library, Albany MO p. 1237
Carnegie Public Library, Big Timber MT p. 1288
Carnegie Public Library, Las Vegas NM p. 1471
Carnegie Public Library, East Liverpool OH p. 1783
Carnegie Public Library, Washington Court House OH p. 1828
Carnegie Public Library, Carnegie OK p. 1843
Carnegie Public Library, Dell Rapids SD p. 2076
Carnegie Public Library, *see* Montague Public Libraries, Turners Falls MA p. 1060
Carnegie Public Library of Steuben County, Angola IN p. 668
Carnegie Regional Library, Grafton ND p. 1734
Carnegie-Schadde Memorial Public Library, Baraboo WI p. 2422
Carnegie-Schuyler Library, Pana IL p. 632
Carnegie-Stout Public Library, Dubuque IA p. 748
Carnegie Vincent Library, *see* Lincoln Memorial University, Harrogate TN p. 2100
Carnell Marion P Library, *see* Piedmont Technical College Library, Greenwood SC p. 2063
Carney, Badley & Spellman, Seattle WA p. 2376
Carney Claire T Library, *see* University of Massachusetts Dartmouth Library, North Dartmouth MA p. 1041
Caro Area District Library, Caro MI p. 1088
Carol Stream Public Library, Carol Stream IL p. 549
Carolina Population Center, Chapel Hill NC p. 1678
Carolina University, Winston-Salem NC p. 1724
Caroline County Public Library, Denton MD p. 964
Caroline Library, Inc, Milford VA p. 2333
Caroline Municipal Library, Caroline AB p. 2530
Carondelet Health Medical Libraries, Tucson AZ p. 81
Carothers Robert L Library & Learning Commons, *see* University of Rhode Island, Kingston RI p. 2033
Carp Lake Township Library, White Pine MI p. 1159
Carpenter Alma M Public Library, Sourlake TX p. 2244
Carpenter-Carse Library, Hinesburg VT p. 2286
Carpenter Coy C Medical Library, *see* Wake Forest University, Winston-Salem NC p. 1726
Carpenter Elizabeth Public Library, *see* Huntsville-Madison County Public Library, New Hope AL p. 22
Carpenter Josiah Library, Pittsfield NH p. 1378
Carpenter Juanita Library, *see* Oak Grove Lutheran Church, Richfield MN p. 1194
Carpenter Library, *see* South Piedmont Community College, Monroe NC p. 1708
Carpenter Memorial Library, Cle Elum WA p. 2362
Carpenter Rhys Library for Art, Archaeology & Cities, *see* Bryn Mawr College, Bryn Mawr PA p. 1916
Carpenter Technology Corp, Reading PA p. 2000
Carpenter Thomas G Library, *see* University of North Florida, Jacksonville FL p. 413
Carpinteria Community Library, Carpinteria CA p. 128
Carr Emily, *see* Greater Victoria Public Library, Victoria BC p. 2583
Carr James Dickson Library, *see* Rutgers University Libraries, Piscataway NJ p. 1424
Carrabassett Valley Public Library, Carrabassett ME p. 921
Carraway Gertrude Research Library, *see* Tryon Palace, New Bern NC p. 1706
Carrefour de l'Information et du Savoir (CIS) Bibliotheque, *see* Ecole Nationale de Police du Quebec, Nicolet QC p. 2728
Carrell Brandon MD Medical Library, *see* Texas Scottish Rite Hospital, Dallas TX p. 2168
Carriage Association of America Library, Lexington KY p. 862
Carrico Philip N, *see* Campbell County Public Library District, Fort Thomas KY p. 851
Carrier Judith J Library Southeast Campus, *see* Tarrant County College, Arlington TX p. 2136
Carrier Library, *see* James Madison University Libraries, Harrisonburg VA p. 2324
Carrier Mills-Stonefort Public Library District, Carrier Mills IL p. 550
Carrington City Library, Carrington ND p. 1731
Carroll & Madison Library System, Berryville AR p. 91
Carroll College, Helena MT p. 1295
Carroll Community College, Westminster MD p. 980
Carroll County District Library, Carrollton OH p. 1756
Carroll County Library, Huntingdon TN p. 2101
Carroll County Public, *see* Galax-Carroll Regional Library, Hillsville VA p. 2321
Carroll County Public Library, Carrollton KY p. 851
Carroll County Public Library, New Windsor MD p. 971
Carroll Lied Public Library, Carroll NE p. 1309
Carroll Medical Library, *see* University of Arkansas for Medical Sciences, Magnolia AR p. 103
Carroll Public Library, Carroll IA p. 737
Carroll University, Waukesha WI p. 2484
Carrollton North-Carrollton Public Library, Carrollton MS p. 1213
Carrollton Public, *see* Blackwater Regional Library, Carrollton VA p. 2313
Carrollton Public Library, Carrollton AL p. 11
Carrollton Public Library, Carrollton IL p. 550
Carrollton Public Library, Carrollton MO p. 1240
Carrollton Public Library, Carrollton TX p. 2153
Carrolltown Public Library, Carrolltown PA p. 1919
Carrot River Public Library, *see* Wapiti Regional Library, Carrot River SK p. 2745
Carruthers Center for Inner City Studies Library, *see* Northeastern Illinois University, Chicago IL p. 566
Carseland Community Library, Carseland AB p. 2530
Carson City Campus Library, *see* Western Nevada Community College, Carson City NV p. 1344
Carson City Correctional Facility Library, *see* Michigan Department of Corrections, Carson City MI p. 1089
Carson City Library, Carson City NV p. 1343
Carson City Public Library, Carson City MI p. 1089
Carson County Public Library, Panhandle TX p. 2225
Carson Lucy Memorial Library, *see* University of Montana Western, Dillon MT p. 1292
Carson Nancy Branch Library, *see* Aiken-Bamberg-Barnwell-Edgefield Regional Library, North Augusta SC p. 2045
Carson-Newman University, Jefferson City TN p. 2103
Carson Rachel Landmark Alliance, Silver Spring MD p. 977
Carstairs Public Library, Carstairs AB p. 2530
Carter Amon Museum of American Art, Fort Worth TX p. 2179
Carter County Library District, Van Buren MO p. 1284
Carter G Emmett Cardinal Library, *see* King's University College, London ON p. 2653
Carter James Earl Library, *see* Georgia Southwestern State University, Americus GA p. 457
Carter Jimmy Presidential Library & Museum, *see* National Archives & Records Administration, Atlanta GA p. 465
Carter, Ledyard & Milburn Library, New York NY p. 1580
Carter Memorial Library, Omro WI p. 2466
Carter Music Resources Center, *see* Louisiana State University Libraries, Baton Rouge LA p. 884
Carteret Community College Library, Morehead City NC p. 1704
Carteret County Public Library, Beaufort NC p. 1673
Carteret Public Library, Carteret NJ p. 1395
Carthage College, Kenosha WI p. 2444
Carthage Free Library, Carthage NY p. 1514
Carthage Library, *see* Henley Henry Public Library, Carthage IN p. 674
Carthage Public Library, Carthage MO p. 1241
Carthage Public Library District, Carthage IL p. 550
Cartographic Information Center, *see* Louisiana State University Libraries, Baton Rouge LA p. 884
Cartwright Arthur LRC Library, *see* Wayne County Community College District, Detroit MI p. 1099
Carus LLC, LaSalle IL p. 607

Centennial Correctional Facility Library, *see* Colorado Department of Corrections, Canon City CO p. 269
Centennial Hills Library, *see* Las Vegas-Clark County Library District, Las Vegas NV p. 1346
Centennial Memorial Library, Eastland TX p. 2172
Centennial Public Library, Salome AZ p. 76
Center for Advanced Study in the Behavioral Sciences Library, Stanford CA p. 248
Center for American Archeology, Kampsville IL p. 604
Center for Applications of Psychological Type, Gainesville FL p. 407
Center for Astrophysics Library / Harvard & Smithsonian Library, Cambridge MA p. 1004
Center for Behavioral Medicine Library, *see* Missouri Department of Mental Health, Kansas City MO p. 1256
Center for Brooklyn History, Brooklyn NY p. 1504
Center for Coastal Environmental Health & Biomolecular Research, Charleston SC p. 2048
Center for Communications Research Library, *see* Institute for Defense Analyses, Princeton NJ p. 1436
Center for Creative Leadership Library, Greensboro NC p. 1691
Center for Demography & Population Health, *see* Florida State University Libraries, Tallahassee FL p. 447
Center for Early Education Library, West Hollywood CA p. 258
Horn Point Library, *see* University of Maryland, Cambridge MD p. 960
Center for Fiction, Brooklyn NY p. 1504
Center for Health, Environment & Justice, Falls Church VA p. 2317
Center for Health Evidence, *see* Huntington Memorial Hospital, Pasadena CA p. 193
Center for Jewish History, New York NY p. 1580
Center for Modern Psychoanalytic Studies Library, New York NY p. 1581
Center for Molecular Nutrition & Sensory Disorders, Washington DC p. 362
Center for Naval Analyses Library, Arlington VA p. 2305
Center for Research Libraries (N), Chicago IL p. 2764
Center for Science & Social Science Information, *see* Yale University Library, New Haven CT p. 327
Center for the Study of Ethics, *see* Illinois Institute of Technology, Chicago IL p. 562
Center for Transportation Research Library, *see* University of Texas at Austin, Austin TX p. 2141
Center Line Public Library, Center Line MI p. 1089
Center Moriches Free Public Library, Center Moriches NY p. 1515
Center on Conscience & War Library, Washington DC p. 362
Center Point Outpost Public Library, *see* Doddridge County Public Library, Salem WV p. 2417
Center Point Public Library, Center Point IA p. 738
Center Raymond H Library, *see* Trinity College, Trinity FL p. 451
Center - Resources for Teaching & Learning Library, Arlington Heights IL p. 537
Centerburg Public Library, Centerburg OH p. 1757
Centers for Disease Control & Prevention, Atlanta GA p. 462
Centers for Disease Control & Prevention, Cincinnati OH p. 1759
Centers for Disease Control & Prevention, Morgantown WV p. 2409
Centerville Branch, *see* Queen Anne's County Free Library, Centreville MD p. 961
Centerville Branch, *see* Saint Mary Parish Library, Centerville LA p. 890
Centerville-Center Township Public Library, Centerville IN p. 674
Centerville Community Library, Centerville SD p. 2075
Centerville Public Library, Centerville MA p. 1009
Centinela State Prison, *see* California Department of Corrections Library System, Imperial CA p. 206
Centra Lynchburg General Hospital, Lynchburg VA p. 2329
Centra Virginia Baptist Hospital, Lynchburg VA p. 2329
CentraCare - Saint Cloud Hospital, Saint Cloud MN p. 1196
Central Alabama Community College, Alexander City AL p. 3
Central Arizona College, Apache Junction AZ p. 55
Central Arizona College, Coolidge AZ p. 58
Central Arkansas Library System, Little Rock AR p. 101
Central Arkansas Veterans Healthcare System, Little Rock AR p. 101
Central Baptist College, Conway AR p. 92
Central Baptist Theological Seminary Library, Shawnee KS p. 836
Central California Women's Facility, *see* California Department of Corrections Library System, Chowchilla CA p. 206
Central Carolina Community College, Sanford NC p. 1715
Central Carolina Technical College Library, Sumter SC p. 2071
Central Christian Church Library, Lexington KY p. 862
Central Christian College of Kansas, McPherson KS p. 824
Central Christian College of the Bible Library, Moberly MO p. 1262
Central Citizens' Library District, Clifton IL p. 572
Central City Library, *see* New Orleans Public Library, New Orleans LA p. 903
Central City Public Library, Central City IA p. 739
Central City Public Library, Central City NE p. 1309
Central College, Pella IA p. 776
Central Community College, Columbus NE p. 1310
Central Community College, Grand Island NE p. 1316
Central Community College, Hastings Campus Library, Hastings NE p. 1317
Central Connecticut State University, New Britain CT p. 324
Central Dakota Library Network (N), Bismarck ND p. 2772
Central Express Branch & Administrative Offices, *see* Maricopa County Library District, Phoenix AZ p. 70
Central Florida Reception Center, Orlando FL p. 431
Central Georgia Technical College Library, Macon GA p. 486
Central Georgia Technical College Library, Milledgeville GA p. 490
Central Georgia Technical College Library, Warner Robins GA p. 502
Central Great Plains Research Station Library, *see* USDA Agricultural Research Service, Akron CO p. 263
Central Islip Public Library, Central Islip NY p. 1516
Central Kansas Library System, Great Bend KS p. 810
Central Lake District Library, Central Lake MI p. 1089
Central Lakes College, Brainerd MN p. 1166
Central Library, *see* Halifax Public Libraries, Halifax NS p. 2617
Central Library, *see* Saint Louis Public Library, Saint Louis MO p. 1275
Central Library & Administrative Offices, *see* Seattle Public Library, Seattle WA p. 2379
Central Louisiana State Hospital, Pineville LA p. 905
Central Louisiana Technical Community College Library, Alexandria LA p. 879
Central Maine Community College Library, Auburn ME p. 914
Central Maine Medical Center, Lewiston ME p. 929
Central Manitoulin Public Libraries, Mindemoya ON p. 2658
Central Maryland Correctional Facility Library, Sykesville MD p. 978
Central Methodist University, Fayette MO p. 1245
Central Michigan University, Mount Pleasant MI p. 1134
Central Minnesota Libraries Exchange (N), Saint Cloud MN p. 2768
Central Mississippi Library Council (N), Jackson MS p. 2768
Central Mississippi Regional Library System, Brandon MS p. 1212
Central Nevada Museum & Historical Society, Tonopah NV p. 1351
Central New Mexico Community College Libraries, Albuquerque NM p. 1460
Central New York Library Resources Council (N), East Syracuse NY p. 2770
Central Oklahoma Juvenile Center Library, Tecumseh OK p. 1864
Central Oregon Community College Barber Library, Bend OR p. 1873
Central Penn College, Summerdale PA p. 2011
Central Pennsylvania Consortium (N), Lancaster PA p. 2774
Central Piedmont Community College Library, Charlotte NC p. 1679
Central Plains Library System, Hastings NE p. 1317
Central Presbyterian Church Library, Terre Haute IN p. 720
Central Rappahannock Regional Library, Fredericksburg VA p. 2319
Central Senior Services, *see* Free Library of Philadelphia, Philadelphia PA p. 1977
Central Skagit Library District, Sedro-Woolley WA p. 2383
Central Square Library, Central Square NY p. 1516
Central State University, Wilberforce OH p. 1831
Central Texas College, Killeen TX p. 2206
Central Texas Veterans Health Care System Library System, *see* Department of Veterans Affairs, Temple TX p. 2247
Central United Methodist Church Library, Albuquerque NM p. 1461
Central Utah Correctional Facility Library, *see* Utah Department of Corrections, Gunnison UT p. 2264
Central Virginia Community College Library, Lynchburg VA p. 2330
Central Virginia Regional Library, Farmville VA p. 2317
Central Washington University, Ellensburg WA p. 2363
Central Wyoming College Library, Riverton WY p. 2498
Centralhatchee Public Library, *see* West Georgia Regional Library, Franklin GA p. 469
Centralia College, Centralia WA p. 2361
Centralia Community Library, Centralia KS p. 801
Centralia Correctional Center Library, Centralia IL p. 551
Centralia Public Library, Centralia MO p. 1241
Centralia Regional Library District, Centralia IL p. 551
Centrastate Healthcare System Library, Freehold NJ p. 1404
Centre Canadien d'Architecture, Montreal QC p. 2721
Centre College of Kentucky, Danville KY p. 853
Centre County Law Library, Bellefonte PA p. 1910
Centre County Library & Historical Museum, Bellefonte PA p. 1910
Centre d'acces a l'information juridique/Legal Informatin Access, Montreal QC p. 2721
Centre d'Animation, de Developpement et de Recherche, Montreal QC p. 2722
Centre d'information scientifique et technique, *see* CNESST, Montreal QC p. 2722
Centre d'acces a l'Information Juridique, Quebec QC p. 2730
Centre d'Archives Regionales Seminaire de Nicolet Library, Nicolet QC p. 2728
Centre de Documentation Centrale des syndicats du Quebec, *see* Centre de documentation et d'archives Yvon-Charbonneau, Quebec QC p. 2730
Centre de documentation collegiale, LaSalle QC p. 2715

Chase Library, *see* Chase Township Public Library, Chase MI p. 1090
Chase Salmon P College of Law Library, *see* Northern Kentucky University, Highland Heights KY p. 859
Chase Township Public Library, Chase MI p. 1090
Chase Virginius H, *see* Bradley University, Peoria IL p. 634
Chastek Library, *see* Gonzaga University School of Law, Spokane WA p. 2383
Chateaugay Memorial Library, Chateaugay NY p. 1516
Chatelain Jane O'Brien West Bank Regional, *see* Jefferson Parish Library, Harvey LA p. 897
Chatfield College Library, Saint Martin OH p. 1819
Chatfield Music Lending Library, Chatfield MN p. 1169
Chatfield Public Library, Chatfield MN p. 1169
Chatham Area Public Library District, Chatham IL p. 553
Chatham Branch, *see* Jackson Parish Library, Chatham LA p. 892
Chatham College, Pittsburgh PA p. 1992
Chatham County Public Libraries, Pittsboro NC p. 1707
Chatham-Kent Public Library, Chatham ON p. 2635
Chatham Public Library, Chatham NY p. 1517
Chatham Public Library, *see* York Library Region, Miramichi NB p. 2602
Chatlos Library, *see* Florida College, Temple Terrace FL p. 451
Chatsworth Historical Society, Chatsworth CA p. 129
Chatsworth Township Library, Chatsworth IL p. 553
Chatsworth-Murray County, *see* Northwest Georgia Regional Library System, Chatsworth GA p. 474
Chattahoochee Technical College Library, Marietta GA p. 488
Chattahoochee Valley Community College, Phenix City AL p. 32
Chattahoochee Valley Libraries, Columbus GA p. 471
Chattanooga College Medical, Dental & Technical, Chattanooga TN p. 2091
Chattanooga Public Library, Chattanooga TN p. 2091
Chattanooga State Community College, Chattanooga TN p. 2091
Chatton Milton J Medical Library, *see* Santa Clara Valley Medical Center, San Jose CA p. 232
Chauncey Public, *see* Athens County Public Libraries, Chauncey OH p. 1805
Chautauqua-Cattaraugus Library System, Jamestown NY p. 1557
Chautauqua County Historical Society, Westfield NY p. 1664
Chautauqua Institution Library, *see* Smith Memorial Library, Chautauqua NY p. 1517
Chauvin Municipal Library, Chauvin AB p. 2531
Chavez Cesar Central Library Headquarters, *see* Stockton-San Joaquin County Public Library, Stockton CA p. 250
Chavez Cesar E, *see* Oakland Public Library, Oakland CA p. 186
Chavez Cesar E Library, *see* San Jose City College Library, San Jose CA p. 230
Chavez Cesar Library, *see* Phoenix Public Library, Laveen AZ p. 72
Chavez Cesar Library, *see* Salinas Public Library, Salinas CA p. 211
Chavez Fray Angelico History Library, *see* Museum of New Mexico, Santa Fe NM p. 1475
Chavis Vance H, *see* Greensboro Public Library, Greensboro NC p. 1692
Chazy Public Library, Chazy NY p. 1517
Cheaha Regional Library, Heflin AL p. 20
Cheatham County Public Library, Ashland City TN p. 2088
Chebeague Island Library, Chebeague Island ME p. 921
Cheboygan Area Public Library, Cheboygan MI p. 1090
Cheek James E Learning Resources Center, *see* Shaw University, Raleigh NC p. 1710
Cheektowaga Public Library, Cheektowaga NY p. 1517
Chelan Public Library, *see* North Central Washington Libraries, Chelan WA p. 2393
Chelmsford Public Library, Chelmsford MA p. 1010
Chelmsford Citizen Service Center Public Library, *see* Greater Sudbury Public Library, Chelmsford ON p. 2683
Chelsea District Library, Chelsea MI p. 1090
Chelsea Public Library, Chelsea AL p. 12
Chelsea Public Library, Chelsea IA p. 739
Chelsea Public Library, Chelsea MA p. 1010
Chelsea Public Library, Chelsea OK p. 1843
Chelsea Public Library, Chelsea VT p. 2281
Cheltenham Township Library System, Glenside PA p. 1937
Chemeketa Community College Library, Salem OR p. 1896
Chemeketa Cooperative Regional Library Service (N), Salem OR p. 2773
Chemung County Historical Society, Inc, Elmira NY p. 1530
Chemung County Library District, Elmira NY p. 1530
Chenango Memorial Hospital, Norwich NY p. 1609
Cheney Library, Hoosick Falls NY p. 1548
Cheney Mary Library, *see* Manchester Public Library, Manchester CT p. 320
Cheney Public Library, Cheney KS p. 801
Cheney's Grove Township Library, Saybrook IL p. 645
Cheng David & Lorraine Library, *see* William Paterson University, Wayne NJ p. 1451
Cheng Yu Tung East Asian Library, *see* University of Toronto Libraries, Toronto ON p. 2698
Chenoa Public Library, Chenoa IL p. 553
Cherokee Center Library, *see* Gadsden State Community College, Centre AL p. 18
Cherokee-City-County Public Library, Cherokee OK p. 1843
Cherokee County Public Library, Centre AL p. 11
Cherokee County Public Library, Gaffney SC p. 2059
Cherokee Garden Library, *see* Atlanta History Center, Atlanta GA p. 462
Cherokee Mental Health Institute, Cherokee IA p. 739
Cherokee Public Library, Cherokee AL p. 12
Cherokee Public Library, Cherokee IA p. 739
Cherokee Regional Library System, LaFayette GA p. 484
Cherry County Historical Society Archives, Valentine NE p. 1339
Cherry Hill Public Library, Cherry Hill NJ p. 1395
Cherry Hills Library, *see* Albuquerque-Bernalillo County Library System, Albuquerque NM p. 1460
Cherry Valley Memorial Library, Cherry Valley NY p. 1517
Cherry Valley Public Library District, Cherry Valley IL p. 553
Cherryfield Free Public Library, Cherryfield ME p. 922
Cherryvale Public Library, Cherryvale KS p. 801
Chesapeake & Ohio Canal National Historical Park Library, *see* National Park Service, Williamsport MD p. 981
Chesapeake & Ohio Historical Society Archives, Clifton Forge VA p. 2313
Chesapeake Bay Maritime Museum Library, Saint Michaels MD p. 976
Chesapeake Biological Laboratory Library, *see* University of Maryland Center for Environmental Science, Solomons MD p. 978
Chesapeake College, Wye Mills MD p. 981
Chesapeake Public Library, Chesapeake VA p. 2311
Cheshire Correctional Institution Library, Cheshire CT p. 305
Cheshire Public Library, Cheshire CT p. 305
Cheshire Public Library, Cheshire MA p. 1010
Chesley Memorial Library, Northwood NH p. 1377
Chesnutt Charles W Library, *see* Fayetteville State University, Fayetteville NC p. 1689
Chestatee Regional Library System, Dahlonega GA p. 474
Chester County Archives & Records Services Library, West Chester PA p. 2020
Chester County History Center Library, West Chester PA p. 2020
Chester County Law Library, West Chester PA p. 2020
Chester County Library, Chester SC p. 2052
Chester County Library & District Center, Exton PA p. 1932
Chester County Library System, Exton PA p. 1932
Chester County Public Library, Henderson TN p. 2101
Chester Library, Chester NJ p. 1396
Chester Mental Health Center, Chester IL p. 553
Chester Public Library, Chester CT p. 306
Chester Public Library, Chester IL p. 553
Chester Public Library, Chester NH p. 1357
Chester Public Library, Chester NY p. 1517
Chester Springs Library, Chester Springs PA p. 1921
Chesterfield County Library System, Chesterfield SC p. 2052
Chesterfield County Public Library, Chesterfield VA p. 2312
Chesterfield Public Library, Chesterfield MA p. 1010
Chesterfield Public Library, Chesterfield NH p. 1357
Chesterfield Township Library, Chesterfield MI p. 1091
Chestermere Public Library, Chestermere AB p. 2531
Chestnut Dr Walter Public Library, *see* Haut-Saint-Jean Regional Library, Hartland NB p. 2600
Chestnut Hill College, Philadelphia PA p. 1975
Chetco Community Public Library, Brookings OR p. 1875
Chetopa City Library, Chetopa KS p. 801
Chetwynd Public Library, Chetwynd BC p. 2564
Chevron Global Library, *see* Chevron Information Technology Company, Richmond CA p. 200
Chevron Information Technology Company, Richmond CA p. 200
Cheyenne Mountain Library, *see* Pikes Peak Library District, Colorado Springs CO p. 271
Cheyney University, Cheyney PA p. 1921
CHI Health Creighton University Medical Center-Bergan Mercy, Omaha NE p. 1327
CHI Health Medical Library, *see* Catholic Health Initiatives, Lincoln NE p. 1321
Chi John W Memorial Medical Library, *see* McLaren Greater Lansing, Lansing MI p. 1125
Chicago Academy of Sciences/Peggy Notebaert Nature Museum, Chicago IL p. 555
Chicago Heights Public Library, Chicago Heights IL p. 571
Chicago History Museum, Chicago IL p. 555
Chicago Institute for Psychoanalysis, Chicago IL p. 555
Chicago-Kent College of Law Library, *see* Illinois Institute of Technology, Chicago IL p. 562
Chicago Public Library, Chicago IL p. 555
Chicago Ridge Public Library, Chicago Ridge IL p. 571
Chicago School of Professional Psychology Library, Chicago IL p. 558
Chicago Sinai Congregation, Chicago IL p. 558
Chicago State University, Chicago IL p. 558, 2784
Chicago Theological Seminary, Chicago IL p. 558
Chicago Zoological Society, Brookfield IL p. 545
Chicano Studies Research Center Library & Archive, *see* University of California Los Angeles Library, Los Angeles CA p. 169
Chichester Town Library, Chichester NH p. 1358
Longstreet Thomas Library, *see* National Park Service, Fort Oglethorpe GA p. 479
Chickamauga Public, *see* Cherokee Regional Library System, Chickamauga GA p. 484
Chickasaw Public Library, Chickasaw AL p. 12
Chickasha Public Library, Chickasha OK p. 1844
Chico Center, *see* Butte College Library, Chico CA p. 189
Chico Public Library Inc, Chico TX p. 2155
Chicopee Public Library, Chicopee MA p. 1011
Chief Dull Knife College, Lame Deer MT p. 1298
Child Custody Evaluations Library, *see* Child Custody Research Library, Glenside PA p. 1937

City of Fairfax Regional Library, *see* Fairfax County Public Library, Fairfax VA p. 2316
City of Hope, Duarte CA p. 139
City of Langley Library, *see* Fraser Valley Regional Library, Langley BC p. 2561
City of Melissa Public Library, Melissa TX p. 2218
City of New York Department of Records & Information Services, New York NY p. 1582
City of Palo Alto Library, Palo Alto CA p. 191
City of Presidio Public Library, Presidio TX p. 2229
City of San Bernardino Library Services, San Bernardino CA p. 212
City of Sundown Library, Sundown TX p. 2246
City of Tavares Public Library, Tavares FL p. 450
City of Tonawanda Public Library, Tonawanda NY p. 1652
City of Wolfforth Library, Wolfforth TX p. 2258
City Terrace Library, *see* County of Los Angeles Public Library, Los Angeles CA p. 135
City University of New York, New York NY p. 1582
City University of Seattle Library, Seattle WA p. 2376
CIUSSS de la Mauricie-et-du-Centre-du-Quebec, Victoriaville QC p. 2739
Civic Center Library, *see* Oceanside Public Library, Oceanside CA p. 187
Civic Centre Resource Library, *see* Vaughan Public Libraries, Vaughan ON p. 2701
Civil Aerospace Medical Institute Library, *see* Federal Aviation Administration, Oklahoma City OK p. 1856
Clackamas Community College Library, Oregon City OR p. 1889
Clackamas County Library, Oak Grove OR p. 1889
Claflin University, Orangeburg SC p. 2066
Claiborne County Public Library, Tazewell TN p. 2127
Claiborne Parish Library, Homer LA p. 891
Clairton Public Library, Clairton PA p. 1922
Clallam Bay Correction Center, *see* Washington State Library, Clallam Bay WA p. 2390
Clallam County Law Library, Port Angeles WA p. 2373
CLAMS (N), *see* Cape Libraries Automated Materials Sharing Network, Hyannis MA p. 2766
Clapp Margaret Library, *see* Wellesley College, Wellesley MA p. 1063
Clapp Mary Norton Library, *see* Occidental College Library, Los Angeles CA p. 167
Clapp Memorial Library, Belchertown MA p. 988
Clara City Public Library, Clara City MN p. 1170
Clare Public Library, Clare IA p. 740
Claremont Colleges Library, Claremont CA p. 130
Claremont Public, *see* Blackwater Regional Library, Claremont VA p. 2313
Claremont School of Theology Library, Claremont CA p. 130
Clarence Public Library, Clarence IA p. 740
Clarence Public Library, Clarence NY p. 1518
Clarence-Rockland Public Library, Rockland ON p. 2676
Clarendon College, Clarendon TX p. 2156
Clarendon Hills Public Library, Clarendon Hills IL p. 572
Clarenville Public Library, Clarenville NL p. 2607
Claresholm Public Library, Claresholm AB p. 2531
Clarington Public Library, Bowmanville ON p. 2632
Clarion County Historical Society, Clarion PA p. 1922
Clarion Free Library, Clarion PA p. 1922
Clarion Public Library, Clarion IA p. 740
Clark A C Library, *see* Bemidji State University, Bemidji MN p. 1165
Clark C W Memorial Library, Oriskany Falls NY p. 1612
Clark College, Vancouver WA p. 2390
Clark County Historical Society, Springfield OH p. 1821
Clark County Law Library, Las Vegas NV p. 1346
Clark County Law Library, Vancouver WA p. 2390
Clark County Library, Arkadelphia AR p. 89
Clark County Library, Dubois ID p. 520
Clark County Library, *see* Las Vegas-Clark County Library District, Las Vegas NV p. 1346
Clark County Public Library, Winchester KY p. 878
Clark County Public Library, Springfield OH p. 1821
Clark Cyril, *see* Brampton Library, Brampton ON p. 2633
Clark David G Memorial Physics Library, *see* University of New Hampshire Library, Durham NH p. 1362
Clark Dr Eugene Library, Lockhart TX p. 2212
Clark Emma S Memorial Library, Setauket NY p. 1640
Clark Family Health Science Library, *see* Mercy Medical Center, Oshkosh WI p. 2467
Clark Family Library, *see* Washington & Jefferson College Library, Washington PA p. 2018
Clark Gladys H Memorial Library, *see* Thomas County Public Library System, Ochlocknee GA p. 499
Clark Harold T Library, *see* Cleveland Museum of Natural History, Cleveland OH p. 1767
Clark Hill PLC, Detroit MI p. 1097
Clark Hill PLC Library, Dallas TX p. 2163
Clark Library, *see* University of Portland, Portland OR p. 1894
Clark Memorial, *see* Puskarich Public Library, Freeport OH p. 1754
Clark Memorial Library, Bethany CT p. 302
Clark Memorial Library, Carolina RI p. 2030
Clark Memorial Library, *see* Shawnee State University, Portsmouth OH p. 1816
Clark Memorial Library, *see* Yavapai County Free Library District, Clarkdale AZ p. 74
Clark Pleasant Library, *see* Johnson County Public Library, New Whiteland IN p. 686
Clark Public Library, Clark NJ p. 1396
Clark Roger Memorial Library, Pittsfield VT p. 2291
Clark State Community College Library, Springfield OH p. 1821
Clark University, Worcester MA p. 1071
Clark W Dale Library, *see* Omaha Public Library, Omaha NE p. 1329
CLARK W Van Alan Library, *see* Tufts University, Boston MA p. 1034
Clark William Andrews Memorial Library, *see* University of California Los Angeles Library, Los Angeles CA p. 169
Clarke Bruce C Library Academic Services Division, *see* United States Army, Fort Leonard Wood MO p. 1246
Clarke Bruce C Library, *see* United States Army, Fort Leonard Wood MO p. 1246
Clarke County Library, *see* Handley Regional Library System, Berryville VA p. 2354
Clarke County-Quitman Public, *see* East Mississippi Regional Library System, Quitman MS p. 1231
Clark David A School of Law Library, *see* University of the District of Columbia, Washington DC p. 380
Clarke Historical Library, *see* Central Michigan University, Mount Pleasant MI p. 1135
Clarke J R Public Library, Covington OH p. 1778
Clarke John Henrik Africana Library, *see* Cornell University Library, Ithaca NY p. 1551
Clarkesville-Habersham County Library, Clarkesville GA p. 470
Clarkia District Library, Clarkia ID p. 519
Clarks Public Library, Clarks NE p. 1310
Clarksburg-Harrison Public Library, Clarksburg WV p. 2401
Clarksburg Town Library, Clarksburg MA p. 1012
Clarkson College Library, Omaha NE p. 1327
Clarkson Public Library, Clarkson NE p. 1310
Clarkson University Libraries, Potsdam NY p. 1622
Clarkston Independence District Library, Clarkston MI p. 1091
Clarksville-Montgomery County Public Library, Clarksville TN p. 2092
Clarksville Public Library, Clarksville IA p. 740
Clarkton Public, *see* Bladen County Public Library, Clarkton NC p. 1687
Clatskanie Library District, Clatskanie OR p. 1875
Clatsop Community College, Astoria OR p. 1872
Clausen Miller Research Services, Chicago IL p. 559
Claverack Free Library, Claverack NY p. 1518
Clay-Battelle Public Library, *see* Morgantown Public Library System, Blacksville WV p. 2409
Clay Center Carnegie Library, Clay Center KS p. 802
Clay Center for the Arts & Sciences of West Virginia, Charleston WV p. 2400
Clay Center Public Library, Clay Center NE p. 1310
Clay County Archives & Historical Library, Liberty MO p. 1259
Clay County Library, *see* Kinchafoonee Regional Library System, Fort Gaines GA p. 475
Clay County Public Library, Manchester KY p. 868
Clay County Public Library, Celina TN p. 2090
Clay County Public Library, Clay WV p. 2401
Clay County Public Library System, Fleming Island FL p. 396
Clay Public Library, Pinson AL p. 33
Clay Springs Public Library, Clay Springs AZ p. 58
Claymont Public Library, Claymont DE p. 351
Claymont Public Library, Uhrichsville OH p. 1826
Claysburg Area Public Library, Claysburg PA p. 1922
Clayton County Library System, Jonesboro GA p. 483
Clayton-Glass Library, *see* Motlow State Community College Libraries, Tullahoma TN p. 2128
Clayton-Liberty Township Public Library, Clayton IN p. 675
Clayton Library, *see* Contra Costa County Library, Clayton CA p. 174
Clayton Library, *see* Surrey Libraries, Surrey BC p. 2577
Clayton Library Center for Genealogical Research, *see* Houston Public Library, Houston TX p. 2195
Clayton Public Library District, Clayton IL p. 572
Clayton State University Library, Morrow GA p. 491
Clayville Library Association, Clayville NY p. 1519
CLC (N), *see* Christian Library Consortium, Cedarville OH p. 2772
Clear Creek Baptist Bible College, Pineville KY p. 873
Clear Lake City Library, Clear Lake SD p. 2075
Clear Lake Public Library, Clear Lake IA p. 740
Clear Lake Public Library, Clear Lake WI p. 2428
Clearbrook Library, *see* Fraser Valley Regional Library, Abbotsford BC p. 2561
Clearfield County Law Library, Clearfield PA p. 1922
Clearfield County Public Library, Curwensville PA p. 1925
Clearfield Public Library, Clearfield IA p. 740
Clearview Library District, Windsor CO p. 298
Clearview Neighbourhood, *see* Oakville Public Library, Oakville ON p. 2662
Clearview Public Library, Stayner ON p. 2681
Clearwater County Free Library District, Weippe ID p. 532
Clearwater Memorial Public Library, Orofino ID p. 528
Clearwater Public Library, Clearwater KS p. 802
Clearwater Public Library, Clearwater NE p. 1310
Clearwater Public Library System, Clearwater FL p. 388
Cleary, Gottlieb, Steen & Hamilton LLP Library, New York NY p. 1582
Cleary University Library, Howell MI p. 1117
Cleaves Nathan & Henry B Law Library, Portland ME p. 936
Cleburne County Library, Heber Springs AR p. 98
Cleburne Public Library, Cleburne TX p. 2156
Cleland Joseph Maxwell Atlanta VA Medical Center Library, Decatur GA p. 475
Clemens Library, *see* College of Saint Benedict, Saint Joseph MN p. 1199
Clement Whittington W Learning Resources Center, *see* Danville Community College, Danville VA p. 2314
Clementon Memorial Library, Clementon NJ p. 1396
Clements William L Library, *see* University of Michigan, Ann Arbor MI p. 1079
Clemons Library, *see* University of Virginia, Charlottesville VA p. 2310
Clemson University Libraries, Clemson SC p. 2052

Coffee Correctional Facility, *see* Georgia Department of Corrections, Nicholls GA p. 493
Coffee County Lannom Memorial Public Library, Tullahoma TN p. 2128
Coffee County-Manchester Library, Manchester TN p. 2110
Coffee Creek Correctional Facility, *see* Oregon State Penitentiary Library, Wilsonville OR p. 1896
Coffeeville Public Library, *see* Yalobusha County Public Library System, Coffeeville MS p. 1214
Coffey County Library, Burlington KS p. 799
Coffeyville Community College, Coffeyville KS p. 802
Coffeyville Public Library, Coffeyville KS p. 802
Coffman Cove Community Library, Coffman Cove AK p. 44
Cofrin David A Library, *see* University of Wisconsin-Green Bay, Green Bay WI p. 2439
Coggon Public Library, Coggon IA p. 741
Cogswell Free Public Library, Orwell NY p. 1612
Cohalan Supreme Court Library, *see* Tenth Judicial District Supreme Court Law Library, Central Islip NY p. 1516
Cohen Albert D Management Library, *see* University of Manitoba Libraries, Winnipeg MB p. 2595
Cohen Morris Raphael Library, *see* City College of the City University of New York, New York NY p. 1581
Cohen Ralph & Julia Library, *see* Wise Isaac M Temple Library, Cincinnati OH p. 1765
Cohen Rhoda & Aaron Library, *see* Temple Beth Sholom, Hamden CT p. 316
Cohocton Public Library, Cohocton NY p. 1520
Cohoes Public Library, Cohoes NY p. 1520
Coil Henry Wilson Library & Museum of Freemasonry, San Francisco CA p. 224
Coin Public Library, Coin IA p. 741
Cokato Library, *see* Great River Regional Library, Cokato MN p. 1196
Coke County Library, Robert Lee TX p. 2233
Coker Charles W & Joan S Library, *see* Coker University, Hartsville SC p. 2063
Coker University, Hartsville SC p. 2063
Colburn Phyllis Ann Memorial Family Library, *see* Children's Hospital of Michigan, Detroit MI p. 1097
Colby College Libraries, Waterville ME p. 945
Colby Community College, Colby KS p. 802
Colby Community Library, Colby WI p. 2428
Colby Memorial Library, Danville NH p. 1360
Colby-Sawyer College, New London NH p. 1375
Colby William E Memorial Library, *see* Sierra Club, Oakland CA p. 187
Colchester District Library, Colchester IL p. 573
Colchester-East Hants Public Library, Truro NS p. 2623
Colchester Historical Society Archives, Truro NS p. 2623
Cold Lake Public Library, Cold Lake AB p. 2532
Cold Spring Harbor Laboratory, Cold Spring Harbor NY p. 1520
Cold Spring Harbor Library, Cold Spring Harbor NY p. 1520
Cold Spring Harbor Whaling Museum Library, Cold Spring Harbor NY p. 1520
Cold Spring Library, *see* Great River Regional Library, Cold Spring MN p. 1196
Coldspring Area Public Library, Coldspring TX p. 2157
Coldwater Branch Library Main, *see* Branch District Library, Coldwater MI p. 1092
Coldwater Memorial Branch, *see* Severn Township Public Library, Coldwater ON p. 2637
Coldwater Public Library, Coldwater OH p. 1771
Coldwater-Wilmore Regional Library, Coldwater KS p. 803
Cole Donald M & Jameson Annex Library, *see* South Dakota State Penitentiary, Sioux Falls SD p. 2082
Cole Georgina Library, *see* Carlsbad City Library, Carlsbad CA p. 128
Cole Houston Library, *see* Jacksonville State University Library, Jacksonville AL p. 23
Cole Memorial Library, Enfield ME p. 924
Cole Norwood Library, *see* Skagit Valley College, Mount Vernon WA p. 2371
Cole Russell D Library, *see* Cornell College, Mount Vernon IA p. 771
Cole Thomas Winston Sr Library, *see* Wiley University, Marshall TX p. 2216
Colebrook Public Library, Colebrook NH p. 1358
Coleman Area Library, Coleman MI p. 1093
Coleman Bessie, *see* Chicago Public Library, Chicago IL p. 556
Coleman John B Library, *see* Prairie View A&M University, Prairie View TX p. 2229
Coleman Joseph E Northwest Regional, *see* Free Library of Philadelphia, Philadelphia PA p. 1978
Coleman L Zenobia Library, *see* Tougaloo College, Tougaloo MS p. 1233
Coleman-Pound Library, *see* Marinette County Library System, Coleman WI p. 2453
Coleman Public Library, Coleman TX p. 2157
Coleman Samuel H Memorial Library, *see* Florida Agricultural & Mechanical University Libraries, Tallahassee FL p. 446
Coleman William Tell Library, *see* Monterey Institute of International Studies, Monterey CA p. 179
Coleraine Public Library, Coleraine MN p. 1170
Coles County Historical Society, Mattoon IL p. 615
Coles Leroy R Jr Branch Library, *see* Buffalo & Erie County Public Library System, Buffalo NY p. 1508
Colesburg Public Library, Colesburg IA p. 741
Colfax-Perry Township Public Library, Colfax IN p. 675
Colfax Public Library, Colfax IA p. 741
Colfax Public Library, Colfax WI p. 2428
Colgate Rochester Crozer Divinity School, Rochester NY p. 1628
Colgate University, Hamilton NY p. 1543
Collaborative Libraries of Vermont (N), Barre VT p. 2776
Collector Car Appraisers Association Library, Buffalo NY p. 1509
Collectors Club Library, New York NY p. 1582
Collectors Club of Chicago Library, Chicago IL p. 559
College Ahuntsic Bibliotheque, *see* Bibliothèque Laurent-Michel-Vacher, Montreal QC p. 2717
College Bart Bibliotheque, Quebec QC p. 2730
College Church in Wheaton Library, Wheaton IL p. 661
College de Bois-de-Boulogne Bibliotheque, Montreal QC p. 2722
College de l'Assomption, L'Assomption QC p. 2715
College de Limoilou-Campus de Charlesbourg, Charlesbourg QC p. 2710
College de Maisonneuve, Montreal QC p. 2796
College de Maisonneuve Centre des Medias, Montreal QC p. 2723
College de Montreal Bibliotheque, Montreal QC p. 2723
College de Rosemont (Cegep) Bibliotheque, Montreal QC p. 2723
College de Valleyfield, Salaberry-de-Valleyfield QC p. 2736
College des Medecins Du Quebec, Montreal QC p. 2723
College Edouard-Montpetit Bibliotheque, Longueuil QC p. 2716
College Football Hall of Fame Library, *see* National Football Foundation's College, Atlanta GA p. 465
College for Creative Studies Library, Detroit MI p. 1097
College Hill Library, *see* Front Range Community College, Westminster CO p. 298
College Hill Library, *see* Westminster Public Library, Westminster CO p. 298
College Jean-de-Brebeuf, Montreal QC p. 2723
College LaSalle, Montreal QC p. 2723
College Lionel-Groulx, Sainte-Therese QC p. 2796
College Medical Center, Long Beach CA p. 158
College Merici - Bibliotheque, Quebec QC p. 2730
College Militaire Royal de Saint-Jean Library, Saint-Jean-Sur-Richelieu QC p. 2735
College Montmorency Bibliotheque, Laval QC p. 2715
College Notre Dame Library, Montreal QC p. 2723
College of Alameda, Alameda CA p. 115
College of Central Florida, Ocala FL p. 429
College of Central Florida Learning Resources, Lecanto FL p. 418
College of Charleston, Charleston SC p. 2050
College of Coastal Georgia, Brunswick GA p. 468
College of Computing & Informatics, *see* Drexel University, Philadelphia PA p. 2791
College of Dupage, Glen Ellyn IL p. 2784
College of DuPage Library, Glen Ellyn IL p. 593
College of Eastern Idaho, Idaho Falls ID p. 522
College of Environmental Design Library, *see* California State Polytechnic University Library, Pomona CA p. 196
College of Idaho, Caldwell ID p. 518
College of Information, Department of Information Science, *see* University of North Texas, Denton TX p. 2793
College of Lake County, Grayslake IL p. 595
College of Marin Library, Kentfield CA p. 154
College of Menominee Nation Library, Keshena WI p. 2445
College of Mount Saint Vincent, Bronx NY p. 1498
College of New Caledonia Library, Prince George BC p. 2574
College of New Jersey, Ewing NJ p. 1402
College of New Rochelle, New Rochelle NY p. 1577
College of Our Lady of the Elms, Chicopee MA p. 1011
College of Physicians & Surgeons, Vancouver BC p. 2578
College of Physicians of Philadelphia, Philadelphia PA p. 1975
College of Saint Benedict, Saint Joseph MN p. 1199
College of Saint Mary Library, Omaha NE p. 1327
College of Saint Scholastica Library, Duluth MN p. 1171
College of San Mateo Library, San Mateo CA p. 235
College of Southern Idaho, Twin Falls ID p. 2784
College of Southern Idaho Library, Twin Falls ID p. 531
College of Southern Maryland Library, La Plata MD p. 970
College of Southern Nevada, Las Vegas NV p. 1346
College of Staten Island Library, Staten Island NY p. 1644
College of the Albemarle Library, Elizabeth City NC p. 1687
College of the Atlantic, Bar Harbor ME p. 916
College of the Canyons Library, Santa Clarita CA p. 242
College of the Desert Library, Palm Desert CA p. 191
College of the Florida Keys, Key Largo FL p. 413
College of the Florida Keys, Key West FL p. 413
College of the Holy Cross, Worcester MA p. 1072
College of the Mainland Library, Texas City TX p. 2248
College of the Muscogee Nation Library, Okmulgee OK p. 1859
College of the North Atlantic Library Services, St. John's NL p. 2608
College of the Ouachitas, Malvern AR p. 103
College of the Ozarks, Point Lookout MO p. 1266
College of the Redwoods Library, Eureka CA p. 141
College of the Sequoias Library, Visalia CA p. 257
College of the Siskiyous Library, Weed CA p. 258
College of veterinary Medicine, William E Brook Memorial Library, *see* Oklahoma State University Libraries, Stillwater OK p. 1862
College of Virginia Beach Information Resource Center, *see* Hampton University, Virginia Beach VA p. 2349
College of Western Idaho, Nampa ID p. 527
College of William & Mary in Virginia, Williamsburg VA p. 2353
College of Wooster Libraries, Wooster OH p. 1832
College O'Sullivan Library, Montreal QC p. 2723
Collegedale Public Library, Collegedale TN p. 2094
Colleton County Memorial Library, Walterboro SC p. 2072

Convergence Zone Recreation Center Library, *see* United States Navy, Oak Harbor WA p. 2372
Converse College, Spartanburg SC p. 2069
Converse County Library, Douglas WY p. 2494
Converse Free Library, Lyme NH p. 1371
Converse Jackson Township Public Library, Converse IN p. 677
Converse Library, *see* Bryn Mawr Presbyterian Church, Bryn Mawr PA p. 1916
Converse Public Library, Converse TX p. 2159
Conway County Library Headquarters, Morrilton AR p. 105
Conway E A Medical Center Library, *see* Ochsner LSU Health Shreveport Monroe Medical Center, Monroe LA p. 898
Conway Library, *see* Children's Hospital of Eastern Ontario, Ottawa ON p. 2666
Conway Public Library, Conway NH p. 1360
Conway Springs City Library, Conway Springs KS p. 803
Conyers John Jr LRC Library, *see* Wayne County Community College District, Detroit MI p. 1099
Conyers-Rockdale Library System, Conyers GA p. 472
Cook Albert S Library, *see* Towson University, Towson MD p. 980
Cook County Law Library, Chicago IL p. 559
Cook County Workforce Development Resource Center, *see* Wiregrass Georgia Technical College Library, Sparks GA p. 497
Cook Inlet Pre-Trial Facility Library, Anchorage AK p. 42
Cook Jane Bancroft Library, *see* New College of Florida, Sarasota FL p. 443
Cook Library, *see* Western Theological Seminary, Holland MI p. 1116
Cook Mary L Public Library, Waynesville OH p. 1829
Cook Memorial Library, Tamworth NH p. 1382
Cook Memorial Library, La Grande OR p. 1883
Cook Memorial Public Library District, Libertyville IL p. 608
Cook Perry Memorial Public Library, Shauck OH p. 1820
Cook Public Library, Cook MN p. 1171
Cook William & Gayle Music Library, *see* Indiana University Bloomington, Bloomington IN p. 670
Cooke County Library, Gainesville TX p. 2182
Cooke Ethel Miner Historical & Genealogical Library, *see* Rocky Hill Historical Society Library, Rocky Hill CT p. 335
COOL (N), *see* Consortium of Ohio Libraries, Columbus OH p. 2772
COOL Cavile Outreach Opportunity Library, *see* Fort Worth Library, Fort Worth TX p. 2179
Cooley George R Science Library, *see* Colgate University, Hamilton NY p. 1543
Cooley Harold D Library, *see* Nashville Public Library, Nashville NC p. 1705
Cooley LLP, New York NY p. 1584
Coolidge Calvin Library, *see* Vermont State University - Castleton, Castleton VT p. 2281
Coolidge Library, Solon ME p. 940
Coolidge Public Library, Coolidge AZ p. 59
Coolidge Public Library, *see* Thomas County Public Library System, Coolidge GA p. 499
Coolville Public, *see* Athens County Public Libraries, Coolville OH p. 1805
Coon George Public Library, Princeton KY p. 873
Coon Rapids Public Library, Coon Rapids IA p. 742
Cooper E M Memorial Library, Wilmington NY p. 1666
Cooper-Hewitt, National Design Library, *see* Smithsonian Libraries, New York DC p. 375
Cooper John Hughes, *see* Richland Library, Columbia SC p. 2054
Cooper Landing Community Library, Cooper Landing AK p. 44
Cooper Library, *see* Bluegrass Community & Technical College, Lexington KY p. 862
Cooper Martha Library, *see* Pima County Public Library, Tucson AZ p. 82
Cooper Memorial Library, *see* Lake County Library System, Clermont FL p. 451
Cooper R M Library, *see* Clemson University Libraries, Clemson SC p. 2052
Cooper River Memorial, *see* Charleston County Public Library, Charleston SC p. 2049
Cooper-Siegel Community Library, Pittsburgh PA p. 1993
Cooper Thomas Library, *see* University of South Carolina, Columbia SC p. 2055
Cooper Union for Advancement of Science & Art Library, New York NY p. 1584
Cooperative Information Network (N), Post Falls ID p. 2764
Cooperman Leon & Toby Library, *see* Hunter College Libraries, New York NY p. 1588
Cooperstown Public Library, Cooperstown PA p. 1924
Coopersville Area District Library, Coopersville MI p. 1094
Coos Bay Public Library, Coos Bay OR p. 1876
Coos County Library Service District, Coos Bay OR p. 1876
Copeland Public Library, Copeland KS p. 803
Copiague Memorial Public Library, Copiague NY p. 1522
Copiah-Jefferson Regional Library System, Hazlehurst MS p. 1219
Copiah-Lincoln Community College, Mendenhall MS p. 1226
Copiah-Lincoln Community College, Natchez MS p. 1227
Copiah-Lincoln Community College, Wesson MS p. 1235
Copland Aaron School of Music Library, *see* Queens College, Flushing NY p. 1533
Coplay Public Library, Coplay PA p. 1924
Copley Helen K & James S Library, *see* University of San Diego, San Diego CA p. 222
Copper Mountain College, Joshua Tree CA p. 154
Copper Queen Library, Bisbee AZ p. 56
Copper Valley Community Library, Glennallen AK p. 46
Copperas Cove Public Library, Copperas Cove TX p. 2160
Coppin State College, Baltimore MD p. 952
COPPUL (N), *see* Council of Prairie & Pacific University Libraries, Calgary AB p. 2777
Coquille Public Library, Coquille OR p. 1876
Coquitlam Public Library, Coquitlam BC p. 2565
CORAL (N), *see* Council of Research & Academic Libraries, San Antonio TX p. 2775
Coralville Public Library, Coralville IA p. 742
Coraopolis Memorial Library, Coraopolis PA p. 1924
Corban University Library, Salem OR p. 1896
Corbett Lynn Library, *see* Southern Methodist College, Orangeburg SC p. 2067
Corbin Public Library, Corbin KY p. 852
Corbit-Calloway Memorial Library, Odessa DE p. 356
Cordell Public Library, *see* Western Plains Library System, Cordell OK p. 1845
Cordes Lakes Public Library, *see* Yavapai County Free Library District, Cordes Lakes AZ p. 75
Cordova District Library, Cordova IL p. 573
Cordova Public Library, Cordova AK p. 44
Corette Jack & Sallie Library, *see* Carroll College, Helena MT p. 1295
Corewell Health Niles Hospital, Niles MI p. 1137
Corfu Free Library, Corfu NY p. 1522
Corgan D Leonard Library, *see* King's College, Wilkes-Barre PA p. 2022
Corinth Free Library, Corinth NY p. 1522
Corinth Public Library, *see* Northeast Regional Library, Corinth MS p. 1216
Cornelia-Habersham County Library, Cornelia GA p. 473
Cornelius Public Library, Cornelius OR p. 1876
Cornell College, Mount Vernon IA p. 771
Cornell Ida, *see* Woodbury Public Library, Central Valley NY p. 1516
Cornell Julien & Virginia Library, *see* Vermont Law School, South Royalton VT p. 2295
Cornell Public Library, Cornell WI p. 2429
Cornell University Library, Ithaca NY p. 1551
Cornerstone University, Grand Rapids MI p. 1110
Cornette Library, *see* West Texas A&M University, Canyon TX p. 2153
Corning City Library, Corning KS p. 803
Corning Museum of Glass, Corning NY p. 1522
Corning Public Library, Corning AR p. 93
Corning Public Library, Corning IA p. 742
Corning Warren H Library, *see* Holden Arboretum, Kirtland OH p. 1793
Cornish College of the Arts Library, Seattle WA p. 2376
Cornwall Free Public Library, Cornwall VT p. 2282
Cornwall Library, Cornwall CT p. 306
Cornwall Public Library, Cornwall NY p. 1522
Cornwall Public Library, Cornwall ON p. 2637
Cornwall Public Library, *see* Prince Edward Island Public Library Service, Cornwall PE p. 2708
Corona Community Library, *see* Queens Library, Corona NY p. 1554
Corona Public Library, Corona CA p. 132
Coronado Public Library, Coronado CA p. 132
Coronation Memorial Library, Coronation AB p. 2532
Corporal Michael J Crescenz VA Medical Center, Philadelphia PA p. 1975
Corporation of the Township of Nipigon Public Library Board, Nipigon ON p. 2661
Corps of Engineers Buffalo Technical Library, *see* United States Army, Buffalo NY p. 1510
Corps of Engineers New England Library, *see* United States Army, Concord MA p. 1012
Corps of Engineers New Orleans Technical Library, *see* United States Army, New Orleans LA p. 904
Corps of Engineers Omaha Library, *see* United States Army, Omaha NE p. 1330
Corps of Engineers Saint Paul Technical Library, *see* United States Army, Saint Paul MN p. 1202
Corps of Engineers Technical Library, *see* United States Army, Jacksonville FL p. 413
Corpus Christi Museum of Science & History, Corpus Christi TX p. 2160
Corpus Christi Public Libraries, Corpus Christi TX p. 2160
Corrales Community Library, Corrales NM p. 1466
Correct Care Recovery Solutions Library, *see* Florida Department of Children & Families, Pembroke Pines FL p. 436
Correctional Institution for Women, Clinton NJ p. 1397
Correctional Reception Center Library, Orient OH p. 1810
Correctional Service of Canada, Bath ON p. 2630
Correctional Service of Canada-Pacific Region, Agassiz BC p. 2562
Correctional Services of Canada, Dorchester NB p. 2599
Correctionville Public Library, Correctionville IA p. 742
Corrigan Memorial Library, *see* Saint Joseph's Seminary, Yonkers NY p. 1667
Corriher-Linn-Black Library, *see* Catawba College, Salisbury NC p. 1714
Corry Public Library, Corry PA p. 1924
Corsicana Public Library, Corsicana TX p. 2161
Cortese Library, *see* California Christian College, Fresno CA p. 144
Corteva Agriscience, Johnston IA p. 762
Corteva Agriscience Library, Indianapolis IN p. 691
Cortez Public Library, Cortez CO p. 272
Cortland Community Library, Cortland IL p. 574
Cortland County Historical Society, Cortland NY p. 1522
Cortland Free Library, Cortland NY p. 1522
Corvallis-Benton County Public Library, Corvallis OR p. 1876
Corwith Public Library, Corwith IA p. 742
Cosbey Winifred Library, *see* Elkhart County Historical Society Museum, Inc, Bristol IN p. 672
Cosby Community Library, Cosby TN p. 2095
Coshocton Public Library, Coshocton OH p. 1778
COSLINE (N), *see* Council of State Library Agencies in the Northeast, Concord NH p. 2769
Cosmos Club Library, Washington DC p. 363
Cosmos Public Library, Cosmos MN p. 1171

Cossatot Community College of the University of Arkansas, De Queen AR p. 93
Costa Anthony Pio Memorial Library, *see* Fairfield Public Library, Fairfield NJ p. 1402
Costilla County Library, San Luis CO p. 295
Costin Gibson Corinne Memorial Public Library, *see* Northwest Regional Library System, Port Saint Joe FL p. 435
Cosumnes River College Library, Sacramento CA p. 208
Cote Saint-Luc Public Library, *see* London Eleanor Cote Saint Luc Public Library, Cote Saint-Luc QC p. 2711
Cottage Grove Public Library, Cottage Grove OR p. 1877
Cottage Health System, Santa Barbara CA p. 239
Cottet Gerard Library, *see* Pennsylvania College of Optometry at Salus University, Elkins Park PA p. 1930
Cottey College, Nevada MO p. 1264
Cotton G Robert Regional Correctional Facility Library, Jackson MI p. 1119
Cotton Mary Public Library, Sabetha KS p. 834
Cotton Plant Branch Library, *see* East Central Arkansas Regional Library, Cotton Plant AR p. 112
Cottonwood County Historical Society Library, Windom MN p. 1208
Cottonwood Public Library, Cottonwood AZ p. 59
Cottonwood Union Library, *see* Montana State Prison, Deer Lodge MT p. 1292
Cottrell E J Memorial Library, Atlanta NY p. 1488
Cotuit Library, Cotuit MA p. 1013
Coudersport Public Library, Coudersport PA p. 1924
Coulee Public Libraray, *see* North Central Washington Libraries, Coulee City WA p. 2393
Coulter Public Library, Coulter IA p. 742
Coulter Sidney B Library, *see* Onondaga Community College, Syracuse NY p. 1649
Coulterville Public Library, Coulterville IL p. 574
Council Bluffs Public Library, Council Bluffs IA p. 742
Council District Library, Council ID p. 520
Council for Advancement & Support of Education, Washington DC p. 363
Council for Christian Colleges & Universities (N), Washington DC p. 2763
Council Grove Public Library, Council Grove KS p. 803
Council of Atlantic Academic Libraries (N), Bedford NS p. 2778
Council of Prairie & Pacific University Libraries (N), Calgary AB p. 2777
Council of Research & Academic Libraries (N), San Antonio TX p. 2775
Council of State Library Agencies in the Northeast (N), Concord NH p. 2769
Council on Foreign Relations Library, New York NY p. 1584
Council on Foundations, Washington DC p. 363
Council Tree Library, *see* Poudre River Public Library District, Fort Collins CO p. 281
Council Valley Free Library, *see* Council District Library, Council ID p. 520
Country Hills Community, *see* Kitchener Public Library, Kitchener ON p. 2651
Country Music Hall of Fame & Museum, Nashville TN p. 2118
Countway Francis A Library of Medicine, *see* Harvard Library, Boston MA p. 1005
County College of Morris, Randolph NJ p. 1438
County of Brant Public Library, Paris ON p. 2671
County of Carleton Law Library, Ottawa ON p. 2666
County of Los Angeles Public Library, Downey CA p. 134
Coupeville Library, *see* Sno-Isle Libraries, Coupeville WA p. 2370
Courant Institute of Mathematical Sciences, *see* New York University, New York NY p. 1599
Court of Appeals Eleventh Circuit Library, Atlanta GA p. 463
Court of the Queen's Bench, *see* Saskatchewan Justice, Regina SK p. 2747
Courtland Community Library, Courtland KS p. 804
Courtland Public Library, Courtland AL p. 13
Courtright Memorial Library, *see* Otterbein University, Westerville OH p. 1830
Courts Administration Service, Tax Library, *see* Government of Canada, Ottawa ON p. 2667
Courville-Abbott Memorial Library, *see* White Memorial Medical Center, Los Angeles CA p. 170
Coutts Herbert T Education & Physical Education Library, *see* University of Alberta, Edmonton AB p. 2538
Coutts Municipal Library, Coutts AB p. 2532
Cove City-Craven County Public Library, Cove City NC p. 1683
Cove Library, Cove OR p. 1877
Covenant College, Lookout Mountain GA p. 485
Covenant Health Grey Nuns Community Hospital, Edmonton AB p. 2536
Covenant Health Misericordia Community Hospital, Edmonton AB p. 2536
Covenant Health System, Lubbock TX p. 2213
Covenant Medical Library, *see* Covenant Health System, Lubbock TX p. 2213
Covenant Theological Seminary, Saint Louis MO p. 1270
Coventry Public Library, Coventry RI p. 2030
Covina Public Library, Covina CA p. 133
Covington & Burling LLP, Washington DC p. 363
Covington Beach, *see* Kenton County Public Library, Covington KY p. 852
Covington County Library System, Collins MS p. 1214
Covington George W Memorial Library, *see* Copiah-Jefferson Regional Library System, Hazlehurst MS p. 1219
Covington-Veedersburg Public Library, Covington IN p. 677
COWAN-BLAKLEY MEMORIAL LIBRARY, *see* University of Dallas, Irving TX p. 2203
Cowen Public Library, Cowen WV p. 2401
Cowen Public Library, *see* Gadsden County Public Library, Chattahoochee FL p. 439
Coweta Public Library, Coweta OK p. 1845
Coweta Public Library System, Newnan GA p. 492
Cowles Harriet Cheney Memorial Library, *see* Whitworth University, Spokane WA p. 2385
Cowles Library, *see* Drake University, Des Moines IA p. 746
Cowley County Community College, Arkansas City KS p. 796
Cowley County Historical Society Museum Library, Winfield KS p. 844
Cox & Palmer, Saint John NB p. 2604
Cox Angie Williams Public Library, Pardeeville WI p. 2468
Cox Anne Spencer Library, *see* Northeast Regional Library, Baldwyn MS p. 1216
Cox, Castle & Nicholson LLP Library, Los Angeles CA p. 161
Cox Sidney Library of Music & Dance, *see* Cornell University Library, Ithaca NY p. 1551
Cox T Elmer Genealogical & Historical Library, *see* Greeneville Green County Public Library, Greeneville TN p. 2100
CoxHealth Libraries, Springfield MO p. 1280
Coxsackie Correctional Facility Library, Coxsackie NY p. 1523
Coyle Free Library, Chambersburg PA p. 1920
Cozby William T Public Library, Coppell TX p. 2159
Cozean C H Library, *see* Mineral Area College, Park Hills MO p. 1265
Cozen O'Connor, Philadelphia PA p. 1976
CPC (N), *see* Central Pennsylvania Consortium, Lancaster PA p. 2774
CPC Research Communications & Library Services, *see* Carolina Population Center, Chapel Hill NC p. 1678
CPCCM (N), *see* Consortium of Popular Culture Collections in the Midwest, Bowling Green OH p. 2772
Crab Orchard Public Library District, Marion IL p. 613
Crabtree James Correctional Center, Helena OK p. 1849
Cracchiolo Andrea Library, *see* Cochise College Library, Sierra Vista AZ p. 59
Cracchiolo Daniel F Law Library, *see* University of Arizona Libraries, Tucson AZ p. 83
Craemer Family Collection & Research Facility, *see* Marin History Museum Library, Novato CA p. 184
Craft Memorial Library, Bluefield WV p. 2398
Crafton Hills College Library, Yucaipa CA p. 262
Crafton Public Library, Pittsburgh PA p. 1993
Craftsbury Public Library, Craftsbury Common VT p. 2282
Cragin Memorial Library, Colchester CT p. 306
Craig Gladys J Memorial Library, Ashland ME p. 913
Craig Phyllis Legacy Library, Irma AB p. 2543
Craig Public Library, Craig AK p. 44
Craigsville Public Library, Craigsville WV p. 2401
Craik Donald W Engineering Library, *see* University of Manitoba Libraries, Winnipeg MB p. 2595
Cranberry Public Library, Cranberry Township PA p. 1924
Cranbrook Academy of Art Library, Bloomfield Hills MI p. 1086
Cranbrook Public Library, Cranbrook BC p. 2565
Cranbury Public Library, Cranbury NJ p. 1397
Crandall-Combine Community Library, Crandall TX p. 2161
Crandall Public Library, Glens Falls NY p. 1539
Crandall University, Moncton NB p. 2603
Crandon Public Library, Crandon WI p. 2429
Crane County Library, Crane TX p. 2161
Crane Julia E Memorial Library, *see* State University of New York College at Potsdam, Potsdam NY p. 1622
Crane Thomas Public Library, Quincy MA p. 1048
Cranford Free Public Library, Cranford NJ p. 1398
Cranston Public Library, Cranston RI p. 2031
Cravath Memorial Library, Hay Springs NE p. 1318
Craven Community College, New Bern NC p. 1705
Craven-Pamlico-Carteret Regional Library System, New Bern NC p. 1706
Crawford C C Memorial Library, *see* Dallas Christian College, Dallas TX p. 2163
Crawford County Historical Society, Meadville PA p. 1960
Crawford County Library, Grayling MI p. 1112
Crawford County Library District, Steelville MO p. 1282
Crawford County Library System, Van Buren AR p. 111
Crawford County Public Library, English IN p. 681
Crawford County Public, *see* Middle Georgia Regional Library System, Roberta GA p. 487
Crawford Ethelbert B Public Library, Monticello NY p. 1573
Crawford Library of the Health Sciences, Rockford, *see* University of Illinois at Chicago, Rockford IL p. 570
Crawford Pearle L Memorial Library, Dudley MA p. 1015
Crawford Public, *see* Columbus-Lowndes Public Library, Crawford MS p. 1215
Crawford Public, *see* Delta County Libraries, Crawford CO p. 286
Crawford Public Library, Crawford NE p. 1311
Crawfordsville District Public Library, Crawfordsville IN p. 677
Crawshaw Sonya Branch, *see* Poplar Creek Public Library District, Hanover Park IL p. 652
Crazy Horse Memorial Library, Crazy Horse SD p. 2075
Cream Riletta L, *see* Camden County Library System, Camden NJ p. 1450
Creech Dayle Library, *see* Northeastern Oklahoma A&M College, Miami OK p. 1853
Creech James Bryan Public Library, Four Oaks NC p. 1690
Creighton Public Library, Creighton NE p. 1311
Creighton University, Omaha NE p. 1328
Cremona Municipal Library, Cremona AB p. 2532
Crenshaw Cornelia Memorial Library, *see* Memphis Public Library, Memphis TN p. 2113
Crerar John Library, *see* University of Chicago Library, Chicago IL p. 569

Curry Charles F Library, *see* William Jewell College, Liberty MO p. 1260
Curry College, Milton MA p. 1036
Curry Memorial Library, *see* First Baptist Church, Salem OR p. 1896
Curry Public Library, Gold Beach OR p. 1880
Curtis Institute of Music, Philadelphia PA p. 1976
Curtis John B Free Public Library, Bradford ME p. 918
Curtis John Free Library, Hanover MA p. 1023
Curtis, Mallet-Prevost, Colt & Mosle Library, New York NY p. 1584
Curtis Martin Hendersonville Public Library, Hendersonville TN p. 2101
Curtis Mary Louise Library, *see* Settlement Music School, Philadelphia PA p. 1986
Curtis Memorial Library, Wheatland IA p. 791
Curtis Memorial Library, Brunswick ME p. 919
Curtis Township Library, Glennie MI p. 1109
Curtiss Glenn H Museum of Local History, Hammondsport NY p. 1544
Curtiss Lua e-Library, *see* Hialeah Public Libraries, Hialeah FL p. 409
Curwensville Public Branch Library, *see* Clearfield County Public Library, Curwensville PA p. 1925
Cushing Community Library, Cushing IA p. 743
Cushing Harvey, *see* Yale University Library, New Haven CT p. 327
Cushing Mary Beatrice Memorial Library, *see* Schoharie Free Association Library, Schoharie NY p. 1639
Cushing Memorial Library & Archives, *see* Texas A&M University Libraries, College Station TX p. 2157
Cushing Public Library, Cushing ME p. 922
Cushing Public Library, Cushing OK p. 1845
Cushman Library, Bernardston MA p. 989
Cushwa-Leighton Library, *see* Saint Mary's College, Notre Dame IN p. 711
Cusseta-Chattahoochee Public Library, *see* Chattahoochee Valley Libraries, Cusseta GA p. 472
Custer County Library, Custer SD p. 2075
Cutchogue-New Suffolk Free Library, Cutchogue NY p. 1524
Cutler Aaron Memorial Library, Litchfield NH p. 1371
Cutler Memorial Library, Plainfield VT p. 2291
Cutler Public Library, Cutler IL p. 575
Cutler T A Memorial Library, *see* Saint Louis Public Library, Saint Louis MI p. 1148
Cuyahoga Community College, Cleveland OH p. 1769
Cuyahoga County Archives Library, Cleveland OH p. 1769
Cuyahoga County Public Library, Parma OH p. 1813
Cuyahoga Falls Library, Cuyahoga Falls OH p. 1779
Cuyahoga Valley Historical Museum, *see* Peninsula Library & Historical Society, Peninsula OH p. 1814
Cuyamaca College Library, El Cajon CA p. 139
The Cybrarium, Homestead FL p. 409
CyFair Library, *see* Lone Star College System, Cypress TX p. 2196
Cylburn Arboretum Friends Library, Baltimore MD p. 952
Cynthiana-Harrison County Public Library, Cynthiana KY p. 853
Cypress College Library, Cypress CA p. 133
Cyrill Westside Library, *see* Spartanburg County Public Libraries, Spartanburg SC p. 2070
Czar Municipal Library, Czar AB p. 2532
Czech & Slovak Library, *see* Masaryk Memorial Institute Inc, Scarborough ON p. 2677
Czech Heritage Museum & Genealogy Center Library, Temple TX p. 2247
Czechoslovak Heritage Museum, Lombard IL p. 610
Dabney S Lancaster Community College Library-LRC, Clifton Forge VA p. 2313
Dacus Ida Jane Library, *see* Winthrop University, Rock Hill SC p. 2067
Dade County Public Library, *see* Cherokee Regional Library System, Trenton GA p. 484
Dadeville Public Library, Dadeville AL p. 13
Daemen University Library, Amherst NY p. 1486
Dafoe Elizabeth Library, *see* University of Manitoba Libraries, Winnipeg MB p. 2595
Daggett Eleanor Public Library, Chama NM p. 1465
Dahlgren Memorial Library, *see* Georgetown University, Washington DC p. 368
Dahlgren Public Library, Dahlgren IL p. 575
Dailey Memorial Library, Derby VT p. 2283
Daingerfield Public Library, Daingerfield TX p. 2162
Dakota City Public Library, Dakota City NE p. 1312
Dakota College at Bottineau Library, Bottineau ND p. 1730
Dakota County Historical Society, South Saint Paul MN p. 1204
Dakota County Library System, Eagan MN p. 1173
Dakota County Technical College Library, Rosemount MN p. 1195
Dakota State University, Madison SD p. 2078
Dakota Wesleyan University, Mitchell SD p. 2079
Daland Memorial Library, Mont Vernon NH p. 1374
Dale & Lessmann Library, Toronto ON p. 2688
Dale City Library, *see* Prince William Public Libraries, Dale City VA p. 2338
Dale Gertrude Angel Library, *see* Southeast Kentucky Community & Technical College, Cumberland KY p. 853
Daleville Public Library, Daleville AL p. 13
Daley Richard J Bridgeport, *see* Chicago Public Library, Chicago IL p. 556
Daley Richard J College Library, *see* City Colleges of Chicago, Chicago IL p. 558
Daley Richard J Library, *see* University of Illinois at Chicago, Chicago IL p. 570
Daley Richard M W Humboldt, *see* Chicago Public Library, Chicago IL p. 556
Dalhousie Centennial Library, *see* Chaleur Library Region, Dalhousie NB p. 2599
Dalhousie University, Halifax NS p. 2618, 2795
Dali Museum Library, *see* Dali Salvador Foundation Inc, Saint Petersburg FL p. 441
Dali Salvador Foundation Inc, Saint Petersburg FL p. 441
Dallam-Hartley County Library, Dalhart TX p. 2162
Dallas Baptist University, Dallas TX p. 2163
Dallas Christian College, Dallas TX p. 2163
Dallas College, Dallas TX p. 2164
Dallas College, Farmers Branch TX p. 2176
Dallas College, Irving TX p. 2202
Dallas College, Lancaster TX p. 2209
Dallas College, Mesquite TX p. 2219
Dallas County Historical Society, Buffalo MO p. 1239
Dallas County Law Library, Dallas TX p. 2164
Dallas County Library, Buffalo MO p. 1239
Dallas County Library, *see* Mid-Arkansas Regional Library, Fordyce AR p. 103
Dallas Historical Society, Dallas TX p. 2164
Dallas International University Library, Dallas TX p. 2164
Dallas Municipal Archives, Dallas TX p. 2164
Dallas Museum of Art, Dallas TX p. 2164
Dallas Public Library, Dallas OR p. 1877
Dallas Public Library, Dallas TX p. 2164
Dallas Theological Seminary, Dallas TX p. 2166
Dalles Public Library, *see* Wasco County Library District, The Dalles OR p. 1899
Dally Memorial Library, Sardis OH p. 1819
DALNET (N), *see* Detroit Area Library Network, Detroit MI p. 2767
Dalton Community Library, Dalton PA p. 1925
Dalton Free Public Library, Dalton MA p. 1013
Dalton Public Library, Dalton NE p. 1312
Dalton Public Library, Dalton NH p. 1360
Dalton State College, Dalton GA p. 474
Dalton-Whitfield Regional Library (Headquarters), *see* Northwest Georgia Regional Library System, Dalton GA p. 474
Daly City Public Library, Daly City CA p. 134
Daly Elizabeth Kerns Library, *see* Northern Wyoming Community College District - Gillette College, Gillette WY p. 2495
Daly John D, *see* Daly City Public Library, Daly City CA p. 134
D'Alzon Emmanuel Library, *see* Assumption University, Worcester MA p. 1071
Damascus Library, *see* Montgomery County Public Libraries, Damascus MD p. 974
D'Amour Library, *see* Western New England University, Springfield MA p. 1057
Dana Biomedical Library, *see* Dartmouth College Library, Hanover NH p. 1366
Dana John Cotton Library, *see* Rutgers University Libraries, Newark NJ p. 1428
Dana John Cotton Research Library & Archives, *see* Woodstock History Center, Woodstock VT p. 2300
Dana Medical Library, *see* University of Vermont Libraries, Burlington VT p. 2281
Danbury Hospital, Danbury CT p. 307
Danbury Law Library, *see* Connecticut Judicial Branch Law Libraries, Danbury CT p. 316
Danbury Museum & Historical Society, Danbury CT p. 307
Danbury Public Library, Danbury CT p. 307
Danbury Public Library, Danbury NC p. 1683
Dance Notation Bureau Library, New York NY p. 1584
Dandridge Memorial Library, Dandridge TN p. 2096
Dane County Law Library, *see* Wisconsin State Law Library, Madison WI p. 2453
Danforth Charles B Public Library, Barnard VT p. 2277
Danforth H Raymond Library, *see* New England College, Henniker NH p. 1367
Danforth Memorial Library, *see* Paterson Free Public Library, Paterson NJ p. 1433
Danforth Public Library, Danforth ME p. 922
D'Angelo Law Library, *see* University of Chicago Library, Chicago IL p. 570
D'Angelo Library, *see* Kansas City University, Kansas City MO p. 1256
Daniel John H, *see* Southside Virginia Community College, Keysville VA p. 2327
Daniel Library, *see* Citadel, Charleston SC p. 2050
Daniel Vista J Memorial, *see* Noxubee County Library System, Shuqualak MS p. 1225
Daniel Watha T/Shaw Neighborhood Library, *see* District of Columbia Public Library, Washington DC p. 364
Daniels County Free Library, Scobey MT p. 1302
Dannemora Free Library, Dannemora NY p. 1524
Dansville Library, *see* Capital Area District Libraries, Dansville MI p. 1124
Dansville Public Library, Dansville NY p. 1524
Danvers Township Library, Danvers IL p. 575
Danville Area Community College Library, Danville IL p. 575
Danville Community College, Danville VA p. 2314
Danville Library, *see* Contra Costa County Library, Danville CA p. 174
Danville Public, *see* Public Library of Mount Vernon & Knox County, Danville OH p. 1805
Danville Public Library, Danville IL p. 575
Danville Public Library, Danville IN p. 678
Danville Public Library, Danville VA p. 2315
Daphne Public Library, Daphne AL p. 13
DAR Library, *see* National Society of the Daughters of the American Revolution, Washington DC p. 373
Darby Community Public Library, Darby MT p. 1291
Darby Free Library, Darby PA p. 1926
Darby William O Ranger Memorial Foundation Inc, Fort Smith AR p. 96
Darcy Library of Beulah, Beulah MI p. 1085
Darden Graduate School of Business-Camp Library, *see* University of Virginia, Charlottesville VA p. 2310
Dare County Library, Manteo NC p. 1702
Dare Ruby E Library, *see* Greenville University, Greenville IL p. 596
Darien Library, Darien CT p. 308
Darien Public Library, Darien WI p. 2430
Darke County Law Library, *see* Greenville Law Library Association, Greenville OH p. 1788
Darling Hugh & Hazel Law Library, *see* University of California Los Angeles Library, Los Angeles CA p. 169
Darling Hugh & Hazel Library, *see* Hope International University, Fullerton CA p. 148

Deer Park Public Library, Deer Park WI p. 2430
Deere & Co Library, Moline IL p. 618
Deerfield Beach Percy White Branch, *see* Broward County Libraries Division, Deerfield Beach FL p. 397
Deerfield Correctional Center, Capron VA p. 2308
Deerfield Public Library, Deerfield IL p. 577
Deerfield Public Library, Deerfield WI p. 2430
Deering Public Library, Deering NH p. 1360
Dees Eula Memorial Library, *see* Northeast Mississippi Community College, Booneville MS p. 1212
Deets Harold & Mary Ellen Memorial Library, *see* Southwestern College, Winfield KS p. 845
Defence Research & Development Canada, Toronto ON p. 2688
Defense Security Corporation University, Wright-Patterson AFB OH p. 1834
Defense Technical Information Center, Fort Belvoir VA p. 2318
Defiance College, Defiance OH p. 1781
Defiance Public Library, Defiance OH p. 1781
deFord Library & Information Center, *see* American Society of International Law Library, Washington DC p. 360
DeForest Area Public Library, DeForest WI p. 2430
Degen John A Resource Room, *see* Florida State University Libraries, Tallahassee FL p. 447
Degenshein George A MD Memorial Library, *see* Maimonides Medical Center, Brooklyn NY p. 1505
Degenstein Community Library, Sunbury PA p. 2011
Degolyer & MacNaughton Library, Dallas TX p. 2166
DeGolyer Library of Special Collections, *see* Southern Methodist University, Dallas TX p. 2168
Degroodt Franklin T Library, Palm Bay FL p. 434
DeHart A Robert Learning Center, *see* De Anza College, Cupertino CA p. 133
Dehay Dell Law Library of Tarrant County, Fort Worth TX p. 2179
DeHoff Memorial Branch, *see* Stark County District Library, Canton OH p. 1755
DeKalb County Library System, Smithville TN p. 2126
DeKalb County Public Library, Fort Payne AL p. 18
DeKalb County Public Library, Decatur GA p. 475
DeKalb Public Library, DeKalb IL p. 577
DeKoven Center Library, *see* DeKoven Foundation, Racine WI p. 2471
DeKoven Foundation, Racine WI p. 2471
Del Mar College, Corpus Christi TX p. 2160
Del Norte County Historical Society Museum Library, Crescent City CA p. 133
Del Norte County Library District, Crescent City CA p. 133
Del Norte Public Library, Del Norte CO p. 273
Del Paso Heights Library, *see* Sacramento Public Library, Sacramento CA p. 209
Del Toro Fulladosa Josefina, Rare Books & Manuscripts, *see* University of Puerto Rico Library System, San Juan PR p. 2514
Webb Del Library at Indian Land, *see* Lancaster County Library, Indian Land SC p. 2064
Delafield Public Library, Delafield WI p. 2431
DeLaMare Library, *see* University of Nevada-Reno, Reno NV p. 1349
Delanco Public Library, Delanco NJ p. 1398
Deland Campus Library, *see* Daytona State College Library, Deland FL p. 392
DeLand Regional Library, *see* Volusia County Public Library, DeLand FL p. 393
Delaney Sadie Peterson African Roots Branch, *see* Poughkeepsie Public Library District, Poughkeepsie NY p. 1623
Delano Library, *see* Great River Regional Library, Delano MN p. 1196
DeLap Loyd Law Library, *see* Klamath County Library Services District, Klamath Falls OR p. 1883
Delavan Elizabeth Garnsey Library, Lodi NY p. 1565
Delaware Art Museum, Wilmington DE p. 356
Delaware City Public Library, Delaware City DE p. 351
Delaware County Community College Library, Media PA p. 1961
Delaware County District Library, Delaware OH p. 1781
Delaware County Historical Society, Media PA p. 1961
Delaware County Law Library, Delaware OH p. 1782
Delaware County Libraries, Media PA p. 1961
Delaware County Library, Jay OK p. 1851
Delaware County Supreme Court Law Library, Delhi NY p. 1524
Delaware Division of Substance Abuse & Mental Health, New Castle DE p. 354
Delaware Historical Society Research Library, Wilmington DE p. 357
Delaware Museum of Natural History Library, Wilmington DE p. 357
Delaware State University, Dover DE p. 352
Delaware Technical & Community College, Dover DE p. 352
Delaware Technical & Community College, Georgetown DE p. 353
Delaware Technical & Community College, Newark DE p. 355
Delaware Technical & Community College, Wilmington DE p. 357
Delaware Township Library, Valley Falls KS p. 841
Delaware Valley University, Doylestown PA p. 1927
Delburne Municipal Library, Delburne AB p. 2532
Delevan-Yorkshire Public Library, Delevan NY p. 1524
Delgado Community College, City Park Campus, New Orleans LA p. 900
Delhi Public Library, Delhi IA p. 745
Delia Municipal Library, Delia AB p. 2533
Dellinger Earl E & Dorothy J Learning Resources Center, *see* Southwest Virginia Community College Library, Cedar Bluff VA p. 2309
Delmar Public Library, Delmar DE p. 352
Delmont Public Library, Delmont PA p. 1926
DeLoria Vine, Jr Library, *see* Smithsonian Libraries, Suitland DC p. 375
Delphi Public Library, Delphi IN p. 679
Delphos Public Library, Delphos KS p. 804
Delphos Public Library, Delphos OH p. 1782
Delray Beach Public Library, Delray Beach FL p. 394
Delta City Library, Delta UT p. 2262
Delta College Library, University Center MI p. 1155
Delta Community Library, Delta Junction AK p. 44
Delta Correctional Center Library, *see* Colorado Department of Corrections, Delta CO p. 273
Delta County Libraries, Hotchkiss CO p. 286
Delta County Public Library, Cooper TX p. 2159
Delta Public Library, Delta OH p. 1782
Delta Public Library, *see* Delta County Libraries, Delta CO p. 286
Delta State University, Cleveland MS p. 1214
Delta Township District Library, Lansing MI p. 1124
Delton District Library, Delton MI p. 1097
Deltona Regional, *see* Volusia County Public Library, Deltona FL p. 393
DeMaio Paul Library Dania Beach, *see* Broward County Libraries Division, Dania Beach FL p. 397
Demarest Free Public Library, Demarest NJ p. 1398
DeMary Memorial Library, Rupert ID p. 530
Demmer Edward U Memorial Library, Three Lakes WI p. 2481
Demopolis Public Library, Demopolis AL p. 14
Denison Ella Strong Library, *see* Claremont Colleges Library, Claremont CA p. 130
Denison Public Library, Denison TX p. 2170
Denmark Public Library, Denmark ME p. 923
Denmark Technical College, Denmark SC p. 2057
Dennard Gladys S Library at South Fulton, *see* Atlanta-Fulton Public Library System, Union City GA p. 461
Dennis Memorial, *see* Sussex County Library System, Newton NJ p. 1429
Dennis Memorial Library Association, Dennis MA p. 1014
Dennis Public Library, Dennisport MA p. 1014
Denton Public Library, Denton MT p. 1292
Denton Public Library, Denton TX p. 2170
Bingham Greenebaum Doll LLP, Lexington KY p. 862
Dentons Canada LLP, Toronto ON p. 2688
Dentons Cohen & Grigsby PC, Pittsburgh PA p. 1993
Dentons United States LLP, Atlanta GA p. 463
Denton US, New York NY p. 1585
Dentons US LLP, Chicago IL p. 560
Denver Academy Library, Denver CO p. 275
Denver Art Museum, Denver CO p. 275
Denver Botanic Gardens, Denver CO p. 275
Denver Public Library, Denver CO p. 275
Denver Public Library, Denver IA p. 745
Denver Seminary, Littleton CO p. 290
Denver Women's Correctional Facility Library, *see* Colorado Department of Corrections, Denver CO p. 274
Denville Free Public Library, Denville NJ p. 1399
Department of Art, *see* University of Toronto Libraries, Toronto ON p. 2698
Department of Behavioral Health, St Elizabeths Hospital, Washington DC p. 363
Department of Canadian Heritage, Ottawa ON p. 2666
Department of Canadian Heritage, Gatineau QC p. 2713
Department of Community Services, Government of Yukon, Whitehorse YT p. 2757
Department of Environmental Protection Environmental Research Library, *see* New Jersey State Library, Trenton NJ p. 1448
Department of Finance Canada Library, Ottawa ON p. 2666
Department of Human Services-Youth Corrections, Colorado Springs CO p. 271
Department of Human Services, Englewood CO p. 279
Department of Human Services-Youth Corrections, Golden CO p. 283
Department of Human Services, Greeley CO p. 285
Department of Human Services-Youth Corrections, Pueblo CO p. 293
Department of Instructional Technology & Learning Sciences-School Library Media Administration, *see* Utah State University, Logan UT p. 2793
Department of Justice & Public Safety, St. John's NL p. 2610
Department of Library & Learning Technologies, *see* Kutztown University, Kutztown PA p. 2791
Department of Natural Resources, Government of Newfoundland, St. John's NL p. 2610
Department of Veteran Affairs, Tomah WI p. 2481
Department of Veterans Affairs, Tucson AZ p. 81
Department of Veterans Affairs, Loma Linda CA p. 157
Department of Veterans Affairs, San Francisco CA p. 224
Department of Veterans Affairs, Grand Junction CO p. 284
Department of Veterans Affairs, Washington DC p. 363
Department of Veterans Affairs, Boise ID p. 517
Department of Veterans Affairs, Hines IL p. 600
Department of Veterans Affairs, Indianapolis IN p. 691
Department of Veterans Affairs, Bedford MA p. 988
Department of Veterans Affairs, Ann Arbor MI p. 1078
Department of Veterans Affairs, Battle Creek MI p. 1083
Department of Veterans Affairs, Saginaw MI p. 1146
Department of Veterans Affairs, Minneapolis MN p. 1183
Department of Veterans Affairs, Kansas City MO p. 1255
Department of Veterans Affairs, Saint Louis MO p. 1270
Department of Veterans Affairs, Lyons NJ p. 1414
Department of Veterans Affairs, Bronx NY p. 1498
Department of Veterans Affairs, Northport NY p. 1608

Dillon County Library, Dillon SC p. 2058
Dillsboro Public, *see* Aurora Public Library District, Dillsboro IN p. 669
Dillsburg Area Public Library, Dillsburg PA p. 1926
Dillwyn Correctional Center Library, Dillwyn VA p. 2315
DiMenna-Nyselius Library, *see* Fairfield University, Fairfield CT p. 312
Dimeo Mary & James Library, *see* Sacred Heart Academy, Hamden CT p. 316
Dimmick Memorial Library, Jim Thorpe PA p. 1947
Dimmit County Public Library, Carrizo Springs TX p. 2153
Dinand Library, *see* College of the Holy Cross, Worcester MA p. 1072
Dine College, Tsaile AZ p. 80
Dine College, Crownpoint NM p. 1466
Dine College, Shiprock NM p. 1477
Dingell John D VA Medical Center, *see* Department of Veterans Affairs Library Service, Detroit MI p. 1097
Dingell John LRC Library, *see* Wayne County Community College, Taylor MI p. 1153
Dinsmore & Shohl Library, Cincinnati OH p. 1760
Diocesan of Providence Office of Faith Formation, Providence RI p. 2038
Diocesan Synod of Fredericton, Fredericton NB p. 2600
Diocese of Colorado Springs, Colorado Springs CO p. 271
DiPietro Frank S Library, *see* Franklin Pierce University Library, Rindge NH p. 1379
Dirac Paul A M Science Library, *see* Florida State University Libraries, Tallahassee FL p. 447
Direction des Collections, *see* Musee de la Civilisation, Quebec QC p. 2731
Disciples of Christ Historical Society, Bethany WV p. 2398
Distance Education Accrediting Commission, Washington DC p. 363
Distefano Memorial Library, *see* Central Louisiana State Hospital, Pineville LA p. 905
Distinctive Collections, *see* Massachusetts Institute of Technology Libraries, Cambridge MA p. 1008
District of Columbia Department of Corrections, Washington DC p. 363
District of Columbia Public Library, Washington DC p. 363
District of Columbia Superior Court Library, Washington DC p. 365
District of Columbia Talking Book & Braille Library, Washington DC p. 365
Dittrick Medical History Center, *see* Cleveland Health Sciences Library, Cleveland OH p. 1767
Diver Arvilla E Memorial Library, Schaghticoke NY p. 1637
Divernon Township Library, Divernon IL p. 578
Divide County Public Library, Crosby ND p. 1731
Divinity School Library, *see* Duke University Libraries, Durham NC p. 1684
Divinity School Library, *see* Yale University Library, New Haven CT p. 327
Division of Analytical Mechanics Associates, Inc Library, *see* Nielsen Engineering & Research, Inc, Santa Clara CA p. 241
Division of Asia Collections (Carl A Kroch Library), *see* Cornell University Library, Ithaca NY p. 1551
Division of Legislative Services Reference Center, Richmond VA p. 2340
Division of Mining, Land & Water Library, *see* Alaska Department of Natural Resources, Anchorage AK p. 41
Division of Rare & Manuscript Collections (Carl A Kroch Library), *see* Cornell University Library, Ithaca NY p. 1551
Dixie County Public Library, Cross City FL p. 391
Dixie Regional Library System, Pontotoc MS p. 1229
Dixie State University Library, Saint George UT p. 2270
Dixon Correctional Center Library, Dixon IL p. 579
Dixon Correctional Institute, Jackson LA p. 891
Dixon Gallery & Gardens Library, Memphis TN p. 2112
Dixon Homestead Library, Dumont NJ p. 1399
Dixon John Public Library, *see* Mattawa Public Library, Mattawa ON p. 2657
Dixon Julian Library, *see* County of Los Angeles Public Library, Culver City CA p. 135
Dixon Neighborhood Library, *see* Houston Public Library, Houston TX p. 2195
Dixon Public Library, Dixon IL p. 579
Dixon Public Library, *see* Solano County Library, Dixon CA p. 142
Dixon Township Library, Argonia KS p. 796
Dixonville Community Library, Dixonville AB p. 2533
DLA Piper (Canada) LLP, Vancouver BC p. 2578
DLA Piper US LLP, Chicago IL p. 560
DLA Piper US LLP, Baltimore MD p. 952
DLA Piper US LLP, New York NY p. 1585
Doane College, Crete NE p. 1311
Doane Dr Grace O Alden Public Library, Alden IA p. 730
Dobbs Ferry Public Library, Dobbs Ferry NY p. 1526
Doblitz Ray Memorial Library, *see* Ohev Shalom Synagogue, Wallingford PA p. 2017
Dobson Community Library, Dobson NC p. 1683
Dockery Dr Carl D Library, *see* Tri-County Community College, Murphy NC p. 1705
Doctor F Lee Library, Agra KS p. 795
Doctor's Hospital, Baptist Health, Coral Gables FL p. 390
Doctors Medical Center, Modesto CA p. 177
Doctors' Memorial Library, *see* Arkansas Methodist Hospital, Paragould AR p. 106
Doddridge County Public Library, West Union WV p. 2417
Dodge Center Public Library, Dodge Center MN p. 1171
Dodge City Community College, Dodge City KS p. 804
Dodge City Public Library, Dodge City KS p. 804
Dodge Correctional Institution Library, Waupun WI p. 2485
Dodge County Historical Society, Fremont NE p. 1314
Dodge County Historical Society Library, Mantorville MN p. 1182
Dodge County Library, *see* Ocmulgee Regional Library System, Eastman GA p. 477
Dodge Library, West Chazy NY p. 1661
Dodge Memorial Public Library, Olive Branch IL p. 629
Dodge State Prison, *see* Georgia Department of Corrections, Chester GA p. 470
Dodgeville Public Library, Dodgeville WI p. 2431
Doe Library, *see* University of California, Berkeley, Berkeley CA p. 122
Doerun Municipal Library, *see* Moultrie-Colquitt County Library, Doerun GA p. 492
Dog River Public Library, *see* West Georgia Regional Library, Douglasville GA p. 470
Doheny Eye Institute Library, Los Angeles CA p. 161
Doherty Grace Library, *see* Centre College of Kentucky, Danville KY p. 853
Doherty Robert Pace & Ada Mary Library, *see* University of Saint Thomas, Houston TX p. 2200
Dolan Springs Community Library, *see* Mohave County Library District, Dolan Springs AZ p. 64
Dolby Laboratories, Inc, San Francisco CA p. 224
Dole Ruth Memorial Library, Burrton KS p. 800
Dolgeville-Manheim Public Library, Dolgeville NY p. 1526
Dolores County Public Library, Dove Creek CO p. 278
Dolores Public Library, Dolores CO p. 278
Dolton Public Library District, Dolton IL p. 579
Dombrosky Margaret Swedesboro Public Library, *see* Gloucester County Library System, Swedesboro NJ p. 1423
Dominican College Library, Blauvelt NY p. 1494
Dominican House of Studies Library, *see* Dominican Theological Library, Washington DC p. 365
Dominican Sisters of San Rafael Library, San Rafael CA p. 236
Dominican Studies Institute Archives & Library, *see* City College of the City University of New York, New York NY p. 1581
Dominican Theological Library, Washington DC p. 365
Dominican University, River Forest IL p. 639, 2784
Dominican University College Library, *see* Bibliotheque du College Universitaire Dominicain, Ottawa ON p. 2665
Dominican University of California, San Rafael CA p. 236
Dominion Public, *see* Cape Breton Regional Library, Dominion NS p. 2622
Dominy Memorial Library, Fairbury IL p. 587
Don Bosco Technical Institute, Rosemead CA p. 205
Dona Ana Community College, Las Cruces NM p. 1470
Donahue Alice B Library & Archives, *see* Athabasca Municipal Library, Athabasca AB p. 2522
Donalda Public Library, Donalda AB p. 2533
Donaldson Frances Library, *see* Nashotah House, Nashotah WI p. 2463
Donaldsonville Branch (Headquarters), *see* Ascension Parish Library, Donaldsonville LA p. 889
Donatucci Thomas F Sr, *see* Free Library of Philadelphia, Philadelphia PA p. 1978
Dongola Public Library District, Dongola IL p. 579
Doniphan-Ripley County Library, Doniphan MO p. 1245
Donna Public Library, Donna TX p. 2171
Donnelley & Lee Library, *see* Lake Forest College, Lake Forest IL p. 606
Donnellson Public Library, Donnellson IA p. 748
Donnelly College, Kansas City KS p. 816
Donnelly Thomas C Library, *see* New Mexico Highlands University, Las Vegas NM p. 1471
Donora Public Library, Donora PA p. 1926
Donovan Michael Library, St. John's NL p. 2610
Donovan Richard J Correctional Facility, *see* California Department of Corrections Library System, San Diego CA p. 206
Dooly State Prison, *see* Georgia Department of Corrections, Unadilla GA p. 501
Doon Heritage Crossroads Library, Kitchener ON p. 2651
Doon Public Library, Doon IA p. 748
Door County Library, Sturgeon Bay WI p. 2479
Dora Public Library, Myrtle Point OR p. 1888
Dorcas Library, Prospect Harbor ME p. 938
Dorchester County Circuit Court, Cambridge MD p. 960
Dorchester County Library, Saint George SC p. 2069
Dorchester County Public Library, Cambridge MD p. 960
Dorchester Public Library, Dorchester NE p. 1313
Dorchester Public Library, Dorchester WI p. 2431
Dorchester Road Regional, *see* Charleston County Public Library, North Charleston SC p. 2049
Dordt University, Sioux Center IA p. 782
Doren Electra C, *see* Dayton Metro Library, Dayton OH p. 1779
Dorion Public Library, Dorion ON p. 2639
Dormann Library, Bath NY p. 1491
Dormont Public Library, Pittsburgh PA p. 1993
Dorn William Jennings Bryan VA Medical Center Medical Library, *see* Department of Veterans Affairs, Columbia SC p. 2053
Dorr Township Library, Dorr MI p. 1101
Dorsch Memorial, *see* Monroe County Library System, Monroe MI p. 1133
Dorset Village Library, Dorset VT p. 2283
Dorsey & Whitney, Minneapolis MN p. 1183
Dorsey Run Correctional Facility Library, Jessup MD p. 969
Dossin Great Lakes Museum, Detroit MI p. 1098
Dothan Houston County Library System, Dothan AL p. 14
Dothan Library, *see* Troy University, Dothan AL p. 15
Double Springs Public Library, Double Springs AL p. 15

Dunbar Paul Laurence, *see* Dallas Public Library, Dallas TX p. 2165
Dunbar Public, *see* Kanawha County Public Library, Dunbar WV p. 2400
Dunbarton Public Library, Dunbarton NH p. 1361
Duncan James M Jr, *see* Alexandria Library, Alexandria VA p. 2302
Duncan Mary Public Library, Benson NC p. 1674
Duncan Public Library, Duncan AZ p. 59
Duncan Public Library, Duncan OK p. 1845
Duncan-Traner Community Library, *see* Washoe County Library System, Reno NV p. 1350
Duncanville Public Library, Duncanville TX p. 2172
Duncombe Public Library, Duncombe IA p. 749
Dundalk Library, *see* Community College of Baltimore County, Baltimore MD p. 961
Dundee Library, Dundee NY p. 1527
Dundee Library, *see* Fox River Valley Public Library District, East Dundee IL p. 580
Dundee Public Library, Dundee FL p. 394
Dundy County Library, Benkelman NE p. 1308
Dunedin Public Library, Dunedin FL p. 394
Dunellen Public Library, Dunellen NJ p. 1399
Dunham Hall Library, *see* Windham Textile & History Museum, Willimantic CT p. 347
Dunham Public Library, Whitesboro NY p. 1665
Dunham Tavern Museum Library, Cleveland OH p. 1770
Dunkerton Public Library, Dunkerton IA p. 749
Dunkirk Public Library, Dunkirk IN p. 679
Dunkirk Public Library, Dunkirk NY p. 1527
Dunklin County Library, Kennett MO p. 1258
Dunlap Bailey H Memorial Public Library, La Feria TX p. 2207
Dunlap Public Library, Dunlap IA p. 749
Dunlap Public Library District, Dunlap IL p. 580
Dunlap S M Memorial Library, Italy TX p. 2203
Dunn Jess Leisure Library, *see* Oklahoma Department of Corrections, Taft OK p. 1863
Dunn Library, *see* Simpson College, Indianola IA p. 759
Dunn Public, *see* Harnett County Public Library, Dunn NC p. 1701
Dunn Sir James Law Library, *see* Dalhousie University, Halifax NS p. 2618
Dunn Willie Mae Library, *see* Copiah-Lincoln Community College, Natchez MS p. 1227
Dunnellon Public Library, *see* Marion County Public Library System, Dunnellon FL p. 430
Dunstable Free Public Library, Dunstable MA p. 1015
Dunwoody College of Technology, Minneapolis MN p. 1183
Duplin County Library, Kenansville NC p. 1698
duPont-Ball Library, *see* Stetson University, DeLand FL p. 393
duPont Jean Austin Veterinary Medicine Library, *see* University of Pennsylvania Libraries, Kennett Square PA p. 1988
DuPont Jessie Ball Library, *see* University of the South, Sewanee TN p. 2126
Dupont Jessie Ball Memorial Library, Stratford VA p. 2347
Dupré Edith Garland Library, *see* University of Louisiana at Lafayette, Lafayette LA p. 893
Duquesne University, Pittsburgh PA p. 1993
Duraleigh Road Community Library, *see* Wake County Public Library System, Raleigh NC p. 1711
Duran Linda Public Library, Decatur AL p. 14
Duran SPC Jesus D Eastside Library, *see* Riverside Public Library, Riverside CA p. 203
Durand Public Library, Durand WI p. 2431
Durango Public Library, Durango CO p. 278
Durant Public, *see* Mid-Mississippi Regional Library System, Durant MS p. 1224
Durbin Community Library, *see* Pocahontas County Free Libraries, Durbin WV p. 2408
Durfee Mike State Prison, Springfield SD p. 2083
Durham Charles L, *see* Free Library of Philadelphia, Philadelphia PA p. 1978
Durham College Library, *see* University of Ontario Institute of Technology Library, Oshawa ON p. 2664
Durham County Library, Durham NC p. 1685
Durham Greater Toronto Area Campus Library & Learning Centre, *see* Trent University, Oshawa ON p. 2672
Durham Public Library, Durham CT p. 309
Durham Public Library, Durham NH p. 1361
Durham Region Law Association, Oshawa ON p. 2663
Durham Technical Community College, Durham NC p. 1685
Durland Alternatives Library, Ithaca NY p. 1552
Durland Anne Carry Memorial Library, *see* Durland Alternatives Library, Ithaca NY p. 1552
Durr William E, *see* Kenton County Public Library, Independence KY p. 852
Durst Seymour B Library, *see* Real Estate Board of New York, New York NY p. 1600
Dutchess Community College Library, Poughkeepsie NY p. 1622
Dutchess County Genealogical Society Library, Poughkeepsie NY p. 1623
Dutchrss County Supreme Court Law Library, *see* New York State Supreme Court Ninth Judicial District, Poughkeepsie NY p. 1623
Dutton/Teton Public Library, Dutton MT p. 1292
Duval County Law Library, Jacksonville FL p. 411
Duval County-San Diego Public Library, San Diego TX p. 2240
Duxbury Free Library, Duxbury MA p. 1015
Dvoracek Memorial Library, Wilber NE p. 1340
Dwight Library, Dwight KS p. 805
Dyckman Free Library, Sleepy Eye MN p. 1204
Dye M R Public Library, *see* First Regional Library, Horn Lake MS p. 1220
Dyer Edythe L Community Library, Hampden ME p. 926
Dyer Library, Saco ME p. 939
Dyersburg State Community College, Dyersburg TN p. 2097
Dying With Dignity Canada Library, Toronto ON p. 2688
Dykes Archie R Library of Health Sciences, *see* University of Kansas Medical Center, Kansas City KS p. 817
Dykes Eva B Library, *see* Oakwood University, Huntsville AL p. 22
Dykes W I Library, *see* University of Houston-Downtown, Houston TX p. 2199
D'Youville College, Buffalo NY p. 1509
e-HLbc (N), *see* Electronic Health Library of British Columbia, Burnaby BC p. 2777
E&H Library, *see* Emory & Henry College, Emory VA p. 2315
EAA Library, Oshkosh WI p. 2467
Eager Free Public Library, Evansville WI p. 2434
Eagle Bend Library, *see* Great River Regional Library, Eagle Bend MN p. 1196
Eagle Free Library, Bliss NY p. 1495
Eagle Grove Memorial Library, Eagle Grove IA p. 750
Eagle Lake Public Library, Eagle Lake FL p. 394
Eagle Mountain Library, Eagle Mountain UT p. 2263
Eagle Nest Public Library, Eagle Nest NM p. 1467
Eagle Pass Public Library, Eagle Pass TX p. 2172
Eagle Public Library, Eagle AK p. 44
Eagle Public Library, Eagle ID p. 520
Eagle Public Library, *see* Eagle Valley Library District, Eagle CO p. 279
Eagle Rock Library, *see* Botetourt County Libraries, Eagle Rock VA p. 2344
Eagle Valley Library District, Eagle CO p. 279
Eaglesham Public Library, Eaglesham AB p. 2534
Eagleton Learning Resources Center, *see* Lincoln Trail College, Robinson IL p. 640
Ear Falls Public Library, Ear Falls ON p. 2639
Earl Park-Richland Township Public Library, Earl Park IN p. 680
Earlham College, Richmond IN p. 715
Earlham Public Library, Earlham IA p. 750
Earlville Free Library, Earlville NY p. 1527
Earlville Library District, Earlville IL p. 580
Early Public Library, Early IA p. 750
Earth Resources Observation & Science Center Library, *see* United States Geological Survey, Sioux Falls SD p. 2082
East Adams Library District, Ritzville WA p. 2375
East Albemarle Regional Library, Elizabeth City NC p. 1687
East Alton Public Library District, East Alton IL p. 580
East Arkansas Community College, Forrest City AR p. 95
East Athens Resource Center, *see* Athens Regional Library System, Athens GA p. 458
East Bank Regional Library, *see* Jefferson Parish Library, Metairie LA p. 897
East Baton Rouge Parish Library, Baton Rouge LA p. 882
East Bend Public Library, East Bend NC p. 1686
East Berlin Library Association, East Berlin CT p. 309
East Bonner County Library District, Sandpoint ID p. 530
East Bridgewater Public Library, East Bridgewater MA p. 1015
East Brookfield Public Library, East Brookfield MA p. 1015
East Brunswick Public Library, East Brunswick NJ p. 1399
East Burke Community Library, East Burke VT p. 2283
East Carolina University, Greenville NC p. 1693, 2790
East Carroll Parish Library, Lake Providence LA p. 894
East Central Arkansas Regional Library, Wynne AR p. 112
East Central College Library, Union MO p. 1283
East Central Community College, Decatur MS p. 1216
East Central Illinois Consortium (N), Urbana IL p. 2764
East Central Public Library, *see* Jackson-George Regional Library System, Moss Point MS p. 1228
East Central Regional Library, Cambridge MN p. 1167
East Central University, Ada OK p. 1839
East Cheltenham Free Library, *see* Cheltenham Township Library System, Cheltenham PA p. 1937
East Cheyenne County Library District, Cheyenne Wells CO p. 270
East Chicago Public Library, East Chicago IN p. 680
East Cleveland Public Library, East Cleveland OH p. 1783
East Columbus Library, *see* Columbus County Public Library, Riegelwood NC p. 1722
East County Regional, *see* Lee County Library System, Lehigh Acres FL p. 403
East Dubuque District Library, East Dubuque IL p. 580
East Elmhurst Community Library, *see* Queens Library, East Elmhurst NY p. 1554
East Fishkill Community Library, Hopewell Junction NY p. 1548
East Flagstaff Community Library, *see* Flagstaff City-Coconino County Public Library System, Flagstaff AZ p. 60
East Flushing Community Library, *see* Queens Library, Flushing NY p. 1554
East Georgia State College Library, Swainsboro GA p. 498
East Glastonbury Public Library, Glastonbury CT p. 313
East Granby Public Library, East Granby CT p. 309
East Grand Forks Campbell Library, East Grand Forks MN p. 1173
East Greenbush Community Library, East Greenbush NY p. 1527
East Greenwich Free Library, East Greenwich RI p. 2031
East Haddam Free Public Library, *see* East Haddam Library System, Moodus CT p. 323
East Haddam Library System, Moodus CT p. 323
East Hampton Library, East Hampton NY p. 1527
East Hampton Public Library, East Hampton CT p. 309
East Hancock Public Library, *see* Hancock County Library System, Diamondhead MS p. 1212

Eden Library, Eden NY p. 1529
Eden Public Library, Eden TX p. 2172
Edens J Drake Library, *see* Columbia College, Columbia SC p. 2053
Edgartown Free Public Library, Edgartown MA p. 1017
Edgecombe Community College, Tarboro NC p. 1718
Edgecombe County Memorial Library, Tarboro NC p. 1718
Edgeley Public, *see* South Central Area Library, Edgeley ND p. 1732
Edgemont Public Library, Edgemont SD p. 2076
Edgerton Public Library, Edgerton MN p. 1173
Edgerton Public Library, Edgerton WI p. 2433
Edgerton Public Library, Edgerton AB p. 2534
Edgewater Free Public Library, Edgewater NJ p. 1400
Edgewater Public Library, *see* Volusia County Public Library, Edgewater FL p. 393
Edgewood College Library, Madison WI p. 2449
Edgewood Community Library, Edgewood NM p. 1467
Edgewood Library, *see* Mellor C C Memorial Library, Edgewood PA p. 1929
Edgewood Public Library, Edgewood IA p. 750
Edinburgh Wright-Hageman Public Library, Edinburgh IN p. 680
Edison State Community College Library, Piqua OH p. 1815
Edison Township Free Public Library, Edison NJ p. 1400
Editorial Projects in Education Library, Bethesda MD p. 959
Edmeston Free Library, Edmeston NY p. 1529
Edmond-Arsenault Dr J, *see* Prince Edward Island Public Library Service, Charlottetown PE p. 2708
Edmonds College Library, Lynnwood WA p. 2370
Edmonds Library, *see* Sno-Isle Libraries, Edmonds WA p. 2370
Edmondson Memorial, *see* Dixie Regional Library System, Vardaman MS p. 1230
Edmonson County Public Library, Brownsville KY p. 850
Edmonton Garrison Community Library, Lancaster Park AB p. 2545
Edmonton Public Library, Edmonton AB p. 2536
Edmonton Public School Division, *see* Alberta School for the Deaf Library, Edmonton AB p. 2535
Edna Public Library, Edna KS p. 805
Edson & District Public Library, Edson AB p. 2539
Educational Communications Corp, Los Angeles CA p. 161
Educational Foundations Department, Library Media Program, *see* University of Wisconsin-Whitewater, Whitewater WI p. 2794
Educational Leadership & Policy Graduate Program, *see* University of Wisconsin Oshkosh College of Education & Human Services, Oshkosh WI p. 2794
Educational Resource Services Library, *see* Tulare County Office of Education, Visalia CA p. 257
Educational Testing Service, Princeton NJ p. 1436
Edward Waters College Library, Jacksonville FL p. 411
Edwards J Joel Public Library, *see* Flint River Regional Library System, Zebulon GA p. 481
Edwards Jacob Library, Southbridge MA p. 1055
Edwards Jessie J Public Library, *see* First Regional Library, Coldwater MS p. 1220
Edwards Joan C School of Medicine, *see* Marshall University Libraries, Huntington WV p. 2405
Edwards Jonathan Library, *see* Berkshire Community College, Pittsfield MA p. 1046
Edwards Kathleen Clay, *see* Greensboro Public Library, Greensboro NC p. 1692
Edwards Lois Morgan Memorial, *see* Union County Public Library, Marshville NC p. 1704
Edwards M Delmar MD Library, *see* Morehouse School of Medicine, Atlanta GA p. 465
Edwards Public Library, Southampton MA p. 1055
Edwards Public Library, Henrietta TX p. 2189
Edwards River Public Library District, Aledo IL p. 535
Edwardsburgh Cardinal Public Library, Cardinal ON p. 2635
Edwardsville Public Library, Edwardsville IL p. 581
Effigy Mounds National Monument Library, *see* United States National Park Service, Harpers Ferry IA p. 757
Effingham Community Library, Effingham KS p. 805
Effingham Public Library, Effingham IL p. 582
Effingham Public Library, Effingham NH p. 1362
EGAN JOSEPH F MEMORIAL SUPREME COURT LAW LIBRARY, *see* New York State Supreme Court Law Library, Schenectady NY p. 1638
Egan William A Library, *see* University of Alaska Southeast, Juneau AK p. 47
Egegik Village Library, Egegik AK p. 45
Egremont Free Library, South Egremont MA p. 1054
Egypt Lake Partnership Library, *see* Tampa-Hillsborough County Public Library System, Tampa FL p. 448
Eickhoff Emery & Almeda Genealogy Library, *see* Fillmore County History Center, Fountain MN p. 1175
Einstein Emanuel Memorial Library, *see* Free Public Library of the Borough of Pompton Lakes, Pompton Lakes NJ p. 1435
Eiseley Loren Corey, *see* Lincoln City Libraries, Lincoln NE p. 1321
Doris F Eisenberg Library of the Health Sciences, *see* Texas Tech University Health Sciences Center El Paso, El Paso TX p. 2174
Eisenhower Army Medical Center, *see* United States Army, Fort Gordon GA p. 479
Dwight D. Eisenhower Presidential Library, Museum & Boyhood Home, *see* National Archives & Records Administration, Abilene KS p. 795
Eisenhower Dwight D, *see* Borough of Totowa Public Library, Totowa NJ p. 1447
Eisenhower Mamie Doud Public Library, Broomfield CO p. 268
Eisenhower Medical Center, Rancho Mirage CA p. 197
Eisenhower Public Library District, Harwood Heights IL p. 597
Eisman Malcolm Memorial Library, *see* Temple Am Echad, Lynbrook NY p. 1566
Eisner Memorial Library, *see* Red Bank Public Library, Red Bank NJ p. 1439
Eiteljorg Museum of American Indians & Western Art, Indianapolis IN p. 691
Ekalaka Public Library, Ekalaka MT p. 1292
Ekstein Frank & Anita Holocaust Resource Library, *see* Neuberger Holocaust Education Centre, Toronto ON p. 2690
Ekstrom William F Library, *see* University of Louisville Libraries, Louisville KY p. 867
El Camino College, Torrance CA p. 252
El Camino Hospital Library & Information Center, Mountain View CA p. 181
El Camino Los Gatos Health Library, Los Gatos CA p. 170
El Camino Real Library, *see* County of Los Angeles Public Library, Los Angeles CA p. 136
El Centro Library & Learning Resource Center, *see* Northeastern Illinois University, Chicago IL p. 566
El Centro Public Library, El Centro CA p. 139
El Cerrito Library, *see* Contra Costa County Library, El Cerrito CA p. 174
El Cerrito Library, *see* Riverside County Library System, Corona CA p. 202
El Dorado Correctional Facility Library, *see* Kansas Department of Corrections, El Dorado KS p. 806
El Dorado County Law Library, Placerville CA p. 195
El Dorado County Library, Placerville CA p. 195
El Monte Museum of History Library, El Monte CA p. 140
El Paso Community College Library, El Paso TX p. 2173
El Paso Community Library, *see* White County Regional Library System, El Paso AR p. 110
El Paso County Law Library, El Paso TX p. 2173
El Paso Museum of Art, El Paso TX p. 2174
El Paso Public Library, El Paso IL p. 583
El Paso Public Library, El Paso TX p. 2174
El Progreso Memorial Library, Uvalde TX p. 2251
El Reno Carnegie Library, El Reno OK p. 1846
El Rito Public Library, El Rito NM p. 1467
El Segundo Public Library, El Segundo CA p. 140
El Sobrante Library, *see* Contra Costa County Library, El Sobrante CA p. 174
Ela Area Public Library District, Lake Zurich IL p. 607
Elaine Library, *see* Phillips-Lee-Monroe Regional Library, Elaine AR p. 98
Elba Public Library, Elba AL p. 15
Elberon Public Library, Elberon IA p. 750
Elbert County Public Library, Elberton GA p. 477
Elberta Public Library, Elberta AL p. 15
Elbin Paul N Library, *see* West Liberty University, West Liberty WV p. 2417
Elbridge Free Library, Elbridge NY p. 1529
Eldon Carnegie Public Library, Eldon IA p. 750
Eldon Public Library, *see* Heartland Regional Library System, Eldon MO p. 1249
Eldora Public Library, Eldora IA p. 750
Eldorado Memorial Public Library District, Eldorado IL p. 583
Eldredge Public Library, Chatham MA p. 1010
Electra Public Library, Electra TX p. 2175
Electronic Health Library of British Columbia (N), Burnaby BC p. 2777
Elfrida Library, *see* Cochise County Library District, Elfrida AZ p. 56
Elgin Community College, Elgin IL p. 583
Elgin Community Library, Elgin OK p. 1847
Elgin County Library, St. Thomas ON p. 2680
Elgin Mental Health Center Library, Elgin IL p. 584
Elgin Public Library, Elgin IA p. 751
Elgin Public Library, Elgin NE p. 1313
Elgin Public Library, Elgin ND p. 1732
Elgin Public Library, Elgin OR p. 1878
Elgin Public Library, Elgin TX p. 2175
ELIN (N), *see* Estacado Library Information Network, Hobbs NM p. 2770
Elizabeth City State University, Elizabeth City NC p. 1687
Elizabeth Public Library, Elizabeth NJ p. 1401
Elizabeth Township Public Library, Elizabeth IL p. 584
Elizabethton-Carter County Public Library, Elizabethton TN p. 2097
Elizabethtown College, Elizabethtown PA p. 1929
Elizabethtown Community & Technical College Library, Elizabethtown KY p. 854
Elizabethtown-Kitley Township Public Library, Addison ON p. 2627
Elizabethtown Library Association, Elizabethtown NY p. 1529
Elizabethtown Public Library, Elizabethtown PA p. 1929
Elk City Carnegie Library, Elk City OK p. 1847
Elk City Community Library, Elk City ID p. 520
Elk Grove Library, *see* Sacramento Public Library, Elk Grove CA p. 209
Elk Grove Village Public Library, Elk Grove Village IL p. 584
Elk Horn Public Library, Elk Horn IA p. 751
Elk Mountain Branch, *see* Carbon County Library System, Elk Mountain WY p. 2498
Elk Point Municipal Library, Elk Point AB p. 2539
Elk Rapids District Library, Elk Rapids MI p. 1103
Elk River Free Library District, Elk River ID p. 520
Elk River Library, *see* Great River Regional Library, Elk River MN p. 1196
Elk Township Library, Peck MI p. 1140
Elkader Public Library, Elkader IA p. 751
Elkford Public Library, Elkford BC p. 2566
Elkhart County Historical Society Museum, Inc, Bristol IN p. 672
Elkhart Lake Public Library, Elkhart Lake WI p. 2433
Elkhart Public Library, Elkhart IN p. 680
Elkhart Public Library District, Elkhart IL p. 584

Fayette County Historical Society Library, West Union IA p. 791
Fayette County Law Library, Lexington KY p. 862
Fayette County Law Library, Washington Court House OH p. 1828
Fayette County Law Library, Uniontown PA p. 2014
Fayette County Memorial Library, Fayette AL p. 17
Fayette County Public Libraries, Oak Hill WV p. 2410
Fayette County Public Library, Connersville IN p. 676
Fayette County Public Library, *see* Flint River Regional Library System, Fayetteville GA p. 481
Fayette Library, *see* Normal Memorial Library, Fayette OH p. 1785
Fayette Library, *see* Pennsylvania State University, Uniontown PA p. 2014
Fayette Public Library, La Grange TX p. 2207
Fayetteville Free Library, Fayetteville NY p. 1533
Fayetteville-Lincoln County Public Library, Fayetteville TN p. 2098
Fayetteville Public Library, Fayetteville AR p. 95
Fayetteville State University, Fayetteville NC p. 1689
Fayetteville Technical Community College, Fayetteville NC p. 1689
FCHM Library, *see* Freeborn County Historical Museum Library, Albert Lea MN p. 1163
Feather River College Library, Quincy CA p. 197
Federal Aviation Administration, Atlantic City NJ p. 1388
Federal Aviation Administration, Oklahoma City OK p. 1856
Federal Bureau of Investigation Library, *see* United States Department of Justice, Quantico VA p. 2339
Federal Bureau of Prisons Library, Washington DC p. 365
Federal Communications Commission Library, Washington DC p. 366
Federal Correctional Institution, Danbury CT p. 307
Federal Correctional Institution, Hopewell VA p. 2326
Federal Correctional Institution - Englewood Library, Littleton CO p. 290
Federal Correctional Institution Library, Tallahassee FL p. 445
Federal Correctional Institution Library, *see* Bureau of Prisons, El Reno OK p. 1846
Federal Courts & Tax Court of Canada, *see* Government of Canada, Ottawa ON p. 2667
Federal Deposit Insurance Corp Library, Washington DC p. 366
Federal Election Commission, Washington DC p. 366
Federal Highway Administration-Chief Counsel's Law Library, *see* United States Department of Transportation, Washington DC p. 379
Federal Judicial Center, Washington DC p. 366
Federal Law Enforcement Training Center Library, Glynco GA p. 481
Federal Library & Information Network (N), Washington DC p. 2763
Federal Maritime Commission Library, Washington DC p. 366
Federal Reserve Bank of Atlanta, Atlanta GA p. 463
Federal Reserve Bank of Boston, Boston MA p. 995
Federal Reserve Bank of Chicago, Chicago IL p. 561
Federal Reserve Bank of Cleveland, Cleveland OH p. 1770
Federal Reserve Bank of Dallas Library, Dallas TX p. 2166
Federal Reserve Bank of Minneapolis, Minneapolis MN p. 1183
Federal Reserve Bank of Philadelphia, Philadelphia PA p. 1977
Federal Reserve Bank of Richmond, Richmond VA p. 2340
Federal Reserve Bank of Saint Louis, Saint Louis MO p. 1270
Federal Trade Commission, Washington DC p. 366
Federal Trade Commission, Cleveland OH p. 1770
Federal Way Library, *see* King County Library System, Federal Way WA p. 2365
Federal Way 320th Library, *see* King County Library System, Federal Way WA p. 2365
Federation des Medecins Specialistes, Montreal QC p. 2724
Federation des Travailleurs et Travailleuses, Montreal QC p. 2724
Federation of American Scientists Library, Washington DC p. 366
Federman Hal, MD Health Sciences Library, *see* Northern Westchester Hospital, Mount Kisco NY p. 1574
FEDLINK (N), *see* Federal Library & Information Network, Washington DC p. 2763
Feehan Memorial Library, *see* University of Saint Mary of the Lake - Mundelein Seminary, Mundelein IL p. 622
Feffer Marian & Ralph Library, *see* Congregation Beth Israel, Scottsdale AZ p. 77
Feinberg Benjamin F Library, *see* State University of New York College at Plattsburgh, Plattsburgh NY p. 1619
Feinberg Harry & Anna Library, *see* Congregation Mishkan Tefila, Brookline MA p. 1003
Feinblatt Gordon LLC, Baltimore MD p. 953
Feldberg Business & Engineering Library, *see* Dartmouth College Library, Hanover NH p. 1366
Feldheym Norman F Central Library, *see* City of San Bernardino Library Services, San Bernardino CA p. 212
Feleti Barstow Public Library, Pago Pago AS p. 2503
Felhaber, Larson, Fenlon & Vogt, Minneapolis MN p. 1183
Felician University, Lodi NJ p. 1413
Fellin Octavia Public Library, Gallup NM p. 1468
Fendig Charles J Public Library, *see* Tampa-Hillsborough County Public Library System, Tampa FL p. 448
Fendrick Library, Mercersburg PA p. 1962
Fenimore Art Museum, Cooperstown NY p. 1521
Fennell Frederick & Elizabeth Ludwig Music Library, *see* Interlochen Center for the Arts, Interlochen MI p. 1118
Fennville District Library, Fennville MI p. 1104
Fenton Free Library, Binghamton NY p. 1494
Fenton History Center, Jamestown NY p. 1557
Fenton Public Library, Fenton IA p. 753
Fentress County Public Library, Jamestown TN p. 2103
Fenway Library Organization (N), Boston MA p. 2766
Fenwick & West LLP, Library, Mountain View CA p. 181
Fenwick Library, *see* George Mason University Libraries, Fairfax VA p. 2316
Fenwick Music Library, *see* College of the Holy Cross, Worcester MA p. 1072
Fergus Falls Public Library, Fergus Falls MN p. 1175
Ferguson Franklin Memorial Library, Cripple Creek CO p. 272
Ferguson Jim G Memorial, *see* Searcy County Library, Marshall AR p. 104
Ferguson Library, Stamford CT p. 338
Ferguson Municipal Public Library, Ferguson MO p. 1246
Fermi National Accelerator Laboratory Library, Batavia IL p. 540
Fern Ridge Public Library, Veneta OR p. 1901
Fernald Anna Field Library, Detroit ME p. 923
Fernbank Science Center Library, Atlanta GA p. 464
Ferndale Area District Library, Ferndale MI p. 1105
Fernie Heritage Library, Fernie BC p. 2566
Ferris Joel E Research Library & Archives, *see* Northwest Museum of Art & Culture, Spokane WA p. 2384
Ferris Library for Information, Technology & Education, *see* Ferris State University Library, Big Rapids MI p. 1085
Ferris Public Library, Ferris TX p. 2176
Ferris State University, Grand Rapids MI p. 1110
Ferris State University Library, Big Rapids MI p. 1085
Ferrum College, Ferrum VA p. 2318
Fertile Public Library, Fertile IA p. 753
Fertile Public Library, *see* Lake Agassiz Regional Library, Fertile MN p. 1188
Festus Public Library, Festus MO p. 1246
FHI 360, Washington DC p. 366
FHN Memorial Hospital, Freeport IL p. 590
Fiction & Popular Culture Library & Central Circulation Department, *see* Free Library of Philadelphia, Philadelphia PA p. 1978
Field-Carnegie Library, Odebolt IA p. 774
Field Evelyn S Library, *see* Raritan Valley Community College, Somerville NJ p. 1442
Field Library, Northfield MA p. 1043
Field Library, Peekskill NY p. 1616
Field Memorial Library, Conway MA p. 1013
Field Memorial Library, *see* Bolivar County Library System, Shaw MS p. 1214
Field Museum of Natural History, Chicago IL p. 561
Field Teen Center, *see* Free Library of Philadelphia, Philadelphia PA p. 1978
Fielding Graduate University, Santa Barbara CA p. 239
Fields Mildred G Memorial Library, Milan TN p. 2116
Fields Octavia Memorial, *see* Harris County Public Library, Humble TX p. 2192
Fife Branch, *see* Pierce County Library System, Fife WA p. 2386
Fife Lake Public Library, Fife Lake MI p. 1105
Fifth Appellate District Library, *see* California Court of Appeal, Fresno CA p. 144
Fig Garden Regional, *see* Fresno County Public Library, Fresno CA p. 146
Olga V Figueroa - Zapata County Public Library, Zapata TX p. 2259
Filer Public Library, Filer ID p. 520
Files Loyd Research Library, *see* Museum of Western Colorado, Grand Junction CO p. 284
Filger Public Library, Minonk IL p. 618
Filion Wakely Thorup Angeletti LLP, Toronto ON p. 2689
Fillmore County History Center, Fountain MN p. 1175
Fillmore Riley LLP, Winnipeg MB p. 2593
Filson Historical Society Library, Louisville KY p. 865
Financial Accounting Foundation Library Information Resource, Norwalk CT p. 331
Finch Lucy Cooper Library, *see* William Peace University, Raleigh NC p. 1712
Finch Memorial Public Library, Arnold NE p. 1306
Findlay-Hancock County District Public Library, Findlay OH p. 1785
Findley Alexander Community Library, Findley Lake NY p. 1533
Findley Timothy Memorial Library, *see* Brock Township Public Library, Cannington ON p. 2631
Fine Arts Museums of San Francisco Library & Archives, San Francisco CA p. 224
Finger Lakes Community College, Canandaigua NY p. 1512
Finger Lakes Library System, Ithaca NY p. 1552
Fingold George Library, *see* State Library of Massachusetts, Boston MA p. 1000
Fink Harold Memorial Library, *see* Coney Island Hospital, Brooklyn NY p. 1504
Finkelstein Memorial Library, Spring Valley NY p. 1644
Finlandia University, Hancock MI p. 1113
Finley Mary K Library & Administrative Offices, *see* Barton County Library, Lamar MO p. 1259
Finley Public Library, Finley ND p. 1733
Finnegan, Henderson, Farabow, Garrett & Dunner, Washington DC p. 366
Finney County Public Library, Garden City KS p. 809
Finney Memorial Library, *see* Columbia State Community College, Columbia TN p. 2094
Fintel Library, *see* Roanoke College, Salem VA p. 2346
Fiorello H LaGuardia Community College Library, Long Island City NY p. 1565

Flipper J S Library, *see* Allen University, Columbia SC p. 2053
FLO (N), *see* Fenway Library Organization, Boston MA p. 2766
Flomaton Public Library, Flomaton AL p. 17
Flora-Monroe Township Public Library, Flora IN p. 682
Flora Public Library, Flora IL p. 588
Flora Public Library, *see* Madison County Library System, Flora MS p. 1213
Floral Park Public Library, Floral Park NY p. 1533
Florala Public Library, Florala AL p. 17
Florence Community Library, Florence AZ p. 61
Florence County Library, Florence WI p. 2435
Florence County Library System, Florence SC p. 2058
Florence-Darlington Technical College Libraries, Florence SC p. 2059
Florence Griswold Museum, Old Lyme CT p. 332
Florence-Lauderdale Public Library, Florence AL p. 17
Florence Public, *see* Cape Breton Regional Library, Florence NS p. 2622
Florence Public Library, Florence KS p. 808
Florence Public Library, Florence MS p. 1216
Florence Public Library, Florence TX p. 2176
Florence Township Public Library, Roebling NJ p. 1440
Flores Neighborhood Library, *see* Houston Public Library, Houston TX p. 2195
Flores Nieves M Memorial Library, *see* Guam Public Library System, Hagatna GU p. 2505
Florham Park Public Library, Florham Park NJ p. 1403
Florida Agricultural & Mechanical University, Orlando FL p. 431
Florida Agricultural & Mechanical University Libraries, Tallahassee FL p. 446
Florida Atlantic University, Boca Raton FL p. 385
Florida Atlantic University, Fort Pierce FL p. 404
Florida Atlantic University, Jupiter FL p. 413
Florida Attorney General's Law Library, Tallahassee FL p. 446
Florida Auditor General Library, Tallahassee FL p. 446
Florida Braille & Talking Book Library, Daytona Beach FL p. 392
Florida College, Temple Terrace FL p. 451
Florida DEP-Geological Survey Research Library, Tallahassee FL p. 446
Florida Department of Agriculture & Consumer Services, Gainesville FL p. 407
Florida Department of Children & Families, Pembroke Pines FL p. 436
Florida Department of State, Tallahassee FL p. 446
Florida Department of Transportation, Tallahassee FL p. 446
Florida Free Library, Florida MA p. 1019
Florida Gateway College, Lake City FL p. 415
Florida Gulf Coast University Library, Fort Myers FL p. 402
Florida Historical Society, Cocoa FL p. 390
Florida Institute of Technology, Melbourne FL p. 420
Florida International University, Miami FL p. 421
Florida International University, North Miami FL p. 428
Florida Library Information Network (N), Tallahassee FL p. 2763
Florida Medical Entomology Laboratory Library, *see* University of Florida, Vero Beach FL p. 453
Florida Memorial University, Miami Gardens FL p. 425
Florida National University Library, Hialeah FL p. 408
Florida Polytechnic University Library, Lakeland FL p. 417
Florida Public, *see* Napoleon Public Library, Napoleon OH p. 1805
Florida Public Library, Florida NY p. 1533
Florida Southern College, Lakeland FL p. 417
Florida SouthWestern State College, Fort Myers FL p. 403
Florida SouthWestern State College, Naples FL p. 427
Florida SouthWestern State College, Punta Gorda FL p. 439
Florida State College at Jacksonville, Jacksonville FL p. 411
Florida State University, Tallahassee FL p. 2783
Florida State University College of Engineering Library, *see* Florida Agricultural & Mechanical University Libraries, Tallahassee FL p. 446
Florida State University Libraries, Tallahassee FL p. 446
Florida Supreme Court Library, Tallahassee FL p. 447
Florida Technical College Library, Orlando FL p. 431
Florida Today Newspaper Library, Melbourne FL p. 420
Florida Virtual Campus, Library Services (N), Tallahassee FL p. 2763
Florissant Public Library, *see* Rampart Library District, Florissant CO p. 299
Flossmoor Public Library, Flossmoor IL p. 588
Flower Judson H Jr Library, *see* Miles Community College, Miles City MT p. 1299
Flower Mound Public Library, Flower Mound TX p. 2177
Flower Roswell P Memorial Library, Watertown NY p. 1659
Flower-Sprecher Veterinary Library, *see* Cornell University Library, Ithaca NY p. 1551
Flowing Wells Branch, *see* Pima County Public Library, Tucson AZ p. 82
Floyd Carolyn Library, *see* Kodiak College, Kodiak AK p. 48
Floyd County Historical Society Museum Library, Charles City IA p. 739
Floyd County Library, Floydada TX p. 2177
Floyd County Public Library, Prestonsburg KY p. 873
Floyd Library, *see* Georgia Highlands College Libraries, Rome GA p. 494
Floyd Memorial Library, Greenport NY p. 1541
Flushing Hospital Medical Center, Flushing NY p. 1533
Flushing Library, *see* Queens Library, Flushing NY p. 1554
Fluvanna County Public Library, Palmyra VA p. 2336
Fluvanna Free Library, Jamestown NY p. 1557
FLVC (N), *see* Florida Virtual Campus, Library Services, Tallahassee FL p. 2763
Fly Fishers International, Livingston MT p. 1299
Fly Murry H Learning Resources Center, *see* Odessa College, Odessa TX p. 2223
FM, Norwood MA p. 1044
FMI-The Food Industry Association, Arlington VA p. 2305
Foard County Library, Crowell TX p. 2162
Fobes Memorial Library, Oakham MA p. 1044
Fogelman Raymond Library, *see* New School, New York NY p. 1592
Fogg James Lemont Memorial Library, *see* Art Center College of Design, Pasadena CA p. 192
Fogg Library, *see* Weymouth Public Libraries, South Weymouth MA p. 1068
Fogg William Library, Eliot ME p. 924
Fogler Raymond H Library, *see* University of Maine, Orono ME p. 934
Fohrell Public Library, *see* Mid-Arkansas Regional Library, Sparkman AR p. 103
FOI Services Inc Library, Clarksburg MD p. 962
Foley & Hoag LLP Library, Boston MA p. 995
Foley & Lardner, Milwaukee WI p. 2458
Foley & Lardner LLP, Los Angeles CA p. 161
Foley & Lardner LLP, Washington DC p. 366
Foley & Lardner LLP, Chicago IL p. 561
Foley Center Library, *see* Gonzaga University, Spokane WA p. 2383
Foley Doris Library for Historical Research, *see* Nevada County Community Library, Nevada City CA p. 182
Foley Library, *see* Great River Regional Library, Foley MN p. 1196
Foley Public Library, Foley AL p. 17
Folger Shakespeare Library, Washington DC p. 366
Folks Frances L Memorial Library, *see* Loogootee Public Library, Loogootee IN p. 704
Follett David L Memorial Library, *see* New York State Supreme Court Sixth District, Norwich NY p. 1609
Follett House Museum, *see* Sandusky Library, Sandusky OH p. 1819
Folsom Lake College Library, Folsom CA p. 142
Folsom Library, *see* Rensselaer Libraries, Troy NY p. 1652
Folsom Public Library, Folsom CA p. 142
Folsom State Prison, *see* California Department of Corrections Library System, Represa CA p. 206
Fond Du Lac Circuit Court, Fond du Lac WI p. 2435
Fond du Lac County Historical Society, Fond du Lac WI p. 2435
Fond Du Lac Public Library, Fond du Lac WI p. 2435
Fond du Lac Tribal & Community College, Cloquet MN p. 1170
Fonda Public Library, Fonda IA p. 753
Fondren Library, *see* Rice University, Houston TX p. 2197
Fondren Library, *see* Southern Methodist University, Dallas TX p. 2168
Fondulac Public Library District, East Peoria IL p. 581
Fontainebleau Library, *see* Windsor Public Library, Windsor ON p. 2704
Fontana Public Library, Fontana WI p. 2435
Fontana Regional Library, Bryson City NC p. 1675
Fontanelle Public Library, Fontanelle IA p. 753
Fontbonne University, Saint Louis MO p. 1270
Fontenot Memorial, *see* Calcasieu Parish Public Library System, Vinton LA p. 893
Food Development Centre Library, *see* Manitoba Agriculture, Food & Rural Initiatives, Portage la Prairie MB p. 2589
Foote Marvin W Youth Services Center, *see* Department of Human Services, Englewood CO p. 279
Foothill College, Los Altos Hills CA p. 159
Foothills Art Center, Golden CO p. 283
Foothills Correctional Institution Library, *see* North Carolina Department of Correction, Morganton NC p. 1704
FOR Sto-Rox Library, McKees Rocks PA p. 1959
Forbes Library, Northampton MA p. 1042
Forbes Regional Hospital, Monroeville PA p. 1964
Forbush Memorial Library, Westminster MA p. 1067
Ford Benson Research Center, *see* Ford Henry, Dearborn MI p. 1095
Ford Edith B Memorial Library, Ovid NY p. 1613
Ford Evon A Public Library, Taylorsville MS p. 1233
Ford Gerald R Presidential Library, *see* National Archives & Records Administration, Ann Arbor MI p. 1079
Ford Henry, Dearborn MI p. 1095
Ford Henry Centennial Library, *see* Dearborn Public Library, Dearborn MI p. 1095
Ford Henry Hospital, Detroit MI p. 1098
Ford Henry Wyandotte Hospital, Wyandotte MI p. 1160
Ford Library, *see* Duke University Libraries, Durham NC p. 1684
Ford Library-Learning Resources Center, *see* Southwest Mississippi Community College, Summit MS p. 1233
Ford-MacNichol Home, Wyandotte Museum, Archives, Wyandotte MI p. 1160
Ford Motor Company Library, *see* Tuskegee University, Tuskegee AL p. 38
Ford-Price Bernice Memorial Library, *see* Oklahoma Historical Society-Museum of the Western Prairie, Altus OK p. 1839
Ford Thomas Memorial Library, Western Springs IL p. 661
Ford William D LRC Library, *see* Wayne County Community College District, Belleville MI p. 1084
Fordham University Libraries, Bronx NY p. 1498
Fordham University School of Law, New York NY p. 1585

Gainesville Public Library, Silver Springs NY p. 1641
Gainesville VA Medical Center, *see* United States Department of Veterans Affairs, Gainesville FL p. 407
Gaithersburg Library, *see* Montgomery County Public Libraries, Gaithersburg MD p. 974
Galax-Carroll Regional Library, Galax VA p. 2321
Galax Public Library, *see* Galax-Carroll Regional Library, Galax VA p. 2321
Galbraith John Kenneth Reference Library, *see* Elgin County Library, Dutton ON p. 2681
Gale Family Library, *see* Minnesota Historical Society, Saint Paul MN p. 1201
Gale Free Library, Holden MA p. 1025
Gale Library, Newton NH p. 1376
Gale Medical Library, *see* Littleton Regional Healthcare, Littleton NH p. 1371
Galena Public Library, Galena KS p. 809
Galena Public Library District, Galena IL p. 590
Gales Ferry Library, *see* Ledyard Public Library, Gales Ferry CT p. 320
GALESBURG CHARLESTON MEMORIAL DISTRICT LIBRARY, Galesburg MI p. 1108
Galesburg Public Library, Galesburg IL p. 591
Galesville Public Library, Galesville WI p. 2436
Galeton Public Library, Galeton PA p. 1934
Galien Township Public Library, Galien MI p. 1108
Galion Public Library, Galion OH p. 1787
Gallagher Law Library, *see* University of Washington Libraries, Seattle WA p. 2382
Gallagher Library, *see* University of Calgary Library, Calgary AB p. 2529
Gallatin County Public Library, Warsaw KY p. 876
Gallatin Public Library, Gallatin TN p. 2099
Gallaudet University Library, Washington DC p. 367
Gallia County District Library, Gallipolis OH p. 1787
Gallier Florence, *see* Duplin County Library, Magnolia NC p. 1698
Gallison Memorial Library, Harrington ME p. 927
Gallitzin Public Library, Gallitzin PA p. 1934
Galt Ocean Mile Reading Center, *see* Broward County Libraries Division, Fort Lauderdale FL p. 397
Galter Health Sciences Library, *see* Northwestern University Libraries, Chicago IL p. 586
Galucci-Cirio Amelia V Library, *see* Fitchburg State University, Fitchburg MA p. 1019
Galva Public Library, Galva IA p. 754
Galva Public Library District, Galva IL p. 591
Galvan Robert J Law Library, *see* El Paso County Law Library, El Paso TX p. 2173
Galveston College, Galveston TX p. 2183
Galveston County Library System, Galveston TX p. 2183
Galvin Paul V Library, *see* Illinois Institute of Technology, Chicago IL p. 562
Galway Public Library, Galway NY p. 1536
Gambaiani Benny Public Library, Shell Rock IA p. 781
Gambier Public, *see* Public Library of Mount Vernon & Knox County, Gambier OH p. 1805
Gamble George Library, Danbury NH p. 1360
Gammon John B Geoscience Library, *see* Ministry of Northern Development & Mines, Sudbury ON p. 2683
Gananoque Public Library, Gananoque ON p. 2642
Gangwish Library, *see* Ottawa University, Ottawa KS p. 829
Gann Rae & Joseph Library, *see* Hebrew College, Newton MA p. 1039
Gannett Frank E Memorial Library, *see* Utica University, Utica NY p. 1656
Gannett-Tripp Library, *see* Elmira College, Elmira NY p. 1530
Gannon University, Erie PA p. 1931
Garbrecht Donald L Law Library, *see* University of Maine School of Law, Portland ME p. 937
Garcia Dr Clotilde P Public Library, *see* Corpus Christi Public Libraries, Corpus Christi TX p. 2160
Garcia Dr Hector P Memorial Library, Mercedes TX p. 2218
Garcia Sam Western Avenue Library, *see* Avondale Public Library, Avondale AZ p. 55
Garden City Community College, Garden City KS p. 809
Garden City Public, *see* Cullman County Public Library System, Garden City AL p. 13
Garden City Public Library, Garden City ID p. 521
Garden City Public Library, Garden City MI p. 1108
Garden City Public Library, Garden City NY p. 1536
Garden City Public Library, Garden City UT p. 2264
Garden Grove Main Library, *see* OC Public Libraries, Garden Grove CA p. 238
Garden Grove Public Library, Garden Grove IA p. 754
Garden Home Community Library, Portland OR p. 1891
Garden Plain Community Library, Garden Plain KS p. 809
Garden State Youth Correctional Facility Library, Crosswicks NJ p. 1398
Garden Valley District Library, Garden Valley ID p. 521
Gardena Mayme Dear Library, *see* County of Los Angeles Public Library, Gardena CA p. 136
Gardendale - Martha Moore Public Library, Gardendale AL p. 19
Gardenview Horticultural Park Library, Strongsville OH p. 1822
Gardiner Library, Gardiner NY p. 1537
Gardiner Public Library, Gardiner ME p. 926
Gardiner Roberts LLP Library, Toronto ON p. 2689
Gardner-Harvey Library, *see* Miami University Libraries, Middletown OH p. 1812
Gardner Isabella Stewart Museum Library, Boston MA p. 995
Gardner Joan P Library, *see* Atlanta-Fulton Public Library System, Atlanta GA p. 461
Gardner Leon P Health Science Library, *see* Ascension Saint Joseph-Juliet, Joliet IL p. 603
Gardner Priscilla Main Library & Administrative Offices, *see* Jersey City Free Public Library, Jersey City NJ p. 1409
Gardner Public Library, Wakefield NE p. 1339
Gardner-Webb University, Boiling Springs NC p. 1674
Garfield County Free Library, Jordan MT p. 1297
Garfield County Library, Burwell NE p. 1309
Garfield County-Panguitch City Library, Panguitch UT p. 2268
Garfield County Public Library District, Rifle CO p. 294
Garfield Library, *see* East Travis Gateway Library District, Del Valle TX p. 2169
Garfield Public Library, Garfield NJ p. 1404
Garfoot Rosemary Public Library, Cross Plains WI p. 2429
Garland County Library, Hot Springs AR p. 99
Garland Public Library, Garland UT p. 2264
Garland Thomas J Library, *see* Tusculum University, Greeneville TN p. 2100
Garnavillo Public Library, Garnavillo IA p. 754
Garner Correctional Institution Library, Newtown CT p. 330
Garner Public Library, Garner IA p. 754
Garnett Library, *see* Missouri State University-West Plains, West Plains MO p. 1286
Garnett Public Library, Garnett KS p. 809
Garnish Public Library, Garnish NL p. 2608
Garrard County Public Library, Lancaster KY p. 861
Garrett Bruce A Medical Library, *see* Baptist Health System, San Antonio TX p. 2236
Garrett Charlie Memorial Library, Gorman TX p. 2185
Garrett College, McHenry MD p. 971
Garrett County Circuit Court Library, Oakland MD p. 972
Garrett Eileen J Library, *see* Parapsychology Foundation Inc, Greenport NY p. 1542
Garrett-Evangelical Theological Seminary, Evanston IL p. 586
Garrett John Work Library, *see* Johns Hopkins University Libraries, Baltimore MD p. 954
Garrett Memorial Library, Moulton IA p. 771
Garrett Public Library, Garrett IN p. 686
Garrison Public Library, Garrison IA p. 754
Garrison Public Library, Garrison ND p. 1734
Garst Memorial Library, *see* Webster County Library, Marshfield MO p. 1261
Garwin Public Library, Garwin IA p. 755
Garwood Free Public Library, Garwood NJ p. 1405
Gary Library, *see* Vermont College of Fine Arts, Montpelier VT p. 2289
Gary Public Library, Gary IN p. 686
Gary Sam Branch Library, *see* Denver Public Library, Denver CO p. 275
Gas City-Mill Township Public Library, Gas City IN p. 687
Gas Technology Institute, Des Plaines IL p. 578
Gassaway Public Library, Gassaway WV p. 2403
Gast William C Business Library, *see* Michigan State University Libraries, East Lansing MI p. 1102
Gaston College, Dallas NC p. 1683
Gaston Community Library, Yamhill OR p. 1902
Gaston County Public Library, Gastonia NC p. 1690
Gasway Memorial Library, *see* Temple Judah, Cedar Rapids IA p. 738
Gates County Public Library, *see* Albemarle Regional Library, Gatesville NC p. 1727
Gates Memorial Library, *see* Lamar State College, Port Arthur TX p. 2228
Gates Public Library, Rochester NY p. 1628
Gatesville Public Library, Gatesville TX p. 2184
Gateway Community & Technical College, Edgewood KY p. 853
Gateway Community College Library, New Haven CT p. 325
Gateway Seminary, Centennial CO p. 270
Gateway Seminary, Vancouver WA p. 2391
Gateway Seminary Library, Ontario CA p. 188
Gateway Technical College, Elkhorn WI p. 2433
Gateway Technical College, Kenosha WI p. 2444
Gateway Technical College, Racine WI p. 2471
Gattis Boyd T & Mollie-Logan County, *see* Arkansas River Valley Regional Library System, Paris AR p. 93
Gauzza Maureen B Public Library, *see* Tampa-Hillsborough County Public Library System, Tampa FL p. 448
Gavilan College Library, Gilroy CA p. 148
Gay J Douglas Jr/Frances Carrick Thomas Library, *see* Transylvania University Library, Lexington KY p. 863
Gay John & Judy Library, *see* McKinney Memorial Public Library, McKinney TX p. 2218
Gay-Kimball Library, Troy NH p. 1382
Gaylord City Library, Gaylord KS p. 809
Gaylord Hospital, Wallingford CT p. 342
Gaylord Memorial Library, *see* South Hadley Public Library, South Hadley MA p. 1054
Gaylord Music Library, *see* Washington University Libraries, Saint Louis MO p. 1277
Gaylord Public Library, Gaylord MN p. 1176
Gaynor Family Regional Library, Selkirk MB p. 2590
Gays Mills Public Library, Gays Mills WI p. 2436
Gearn Helen Memorial Library, *see* Historical Society of Newburgh Bay & the Highlands, Newburgh NY p. 1605
Geary Library-Health Care Facility, *see* Roane County Public Library, Left Hand WV p. 2415
Geary Public Library, Geary OK p. 1848
Geauga County Historical Society, Burton OH p. 1753
Geauga County Law Library Resources Board, Chardon OH p. 1758
Geauga County Public Library, Chardon OH p. 1758
Geier Science Library, *see* Cincinnati Museum Center At Union Terminal, Cincinnati OH p. 1760
Geisel Library, *see* Saint Anselm College, Manchester NH p. 1372
Geisinger Health System, Danville PA p. 1926
Geisinger Wyoming Valley Medical Center, Wilkes-Barre PA p. 2022
Geisler Library, *see* Central College, Pella IA p. 776
Geissert Katy Civic Center, *see* Torrance Public Library, Torrance CA p. 253

Gerstenburg Carriage Reference Library, *see* Long Island Museum of American Art, History & Carriages, Stony Brook NY p. 1646
Gervasini Health Library, *see* SCLHS Saint Joseph Hospital, Denver CO p. 277
Getty Research Institute, Los Angeles CA p. 161
Gettysburg College, Gettysburg PA p. 1935
Gettysburg National Military Park Library, Gettysburg PA p. 1936
Getz Oscar Museum of Bourbon History Library, Bardstown KY p. 848
Getz Stan Media Center & Library, *see* Berklee College of Music Library, Boston MA p. 990
GHEC Library, *see* Mississippi Delta Community College, Greenville MS p. 1227
Ghost Ranch Library, Abiquiu NM p. 1459
GIA Library, *see* Liddicoat Richard T Gemological Library & Information Center, Carlsbad CA p. 128
Gibb Hamilton A R Islamic Seminar Library, *see* Harvard Library, Cambridge MA p. 1006
Gibbon Public Library, Gibbon MN p. 1176
Gibbon Public Library, Gibbon NE p. 1315
Gibbons Municipal Library, Gibbons AB p. 2541
Gibbons PC, Newark NJ p. 1426
Gibbs Library, Washington ME p. 944
Gibbs Memorial Library, Mexia TX p. 2219
Gibbsboro Public Library, Gibbsboro NJ p. 1405
Gibson Charles W Public Library, Buckhannon WV p. 2399
Gibson County Memorial Library, Trenton TN p. 2128
Gibson Dunn & Crutcher, Los Angeles CA p. 161
Gibson, Dunn & Crutcher, New York NY p. 1587
Gibson James A Library, *see* Brock University, St. Catharines ON p. 2679
Gibson James I Library, *see* Henderson District Public Libraries, Henderson NV p. 1345
Gibson Library, *see* Kentucky Mountain Bible College, Jackson KY p. 861
Gibson Memorial Library, Creston IA p. 743
Gibsons & District Public Library, Gibsons BC p. 2566
Giddings Leona Memorial Library, *see* Prince Edward Island Public Library Service, Murray River PE p. 2708
Giddings Public Library & Cultural Center, Giddings TX p. 2184
Giese Memorial Library, *see* East Central Regional Library, Wyoming MN p. 1168
Gila County Historical Museum Library, Globe AZ p. 62
Gila County Library District, Globe AZ p. 62
Gilbert Library, Inc, Northfield CT p. 331
Gilbert Public Library, Gilbert MN p. 1176
Gilbert Public Library, Friend NE p. 1315
Gilbertsville Free Library, Gilbertsville NY p. 1538
Gilbreath Memorial Library, Winnsboro TX p. 2258
Gilchrist County Public Library, Trenton FL p. 451
Gilcrease Thomas Institute of American History & Art, Tulsa OK p. 1864
Giles County Public Library, Pulaski TN p. 2124
Gilford Public Library, Gilford NH p. 1364
Gilkey Mary City Library, Dayton OR p. 1877
Gill Gail P Community Health Library, *see* Christiana Hospital Library, Newark DE p. 355
Gill Library, *see* College of New Rochelle, New Rochelle NY p. 1577
Gill Library, *see* Southwest Tennessee Community College, Memphis TN p. 2115
Gill Memorial Library, Paulsboro NJ p. 1433
Gillespie Public Library, Gillespie IL p. 592
Gillett Public Library, Gillett WI p. 2437
Gilliam County Public Library, Condon OR p. 1875
Gilliam Elvis Maxine Memorial Public Library, Wilmer TX p. 2258
Gillis Richard S Jr - Ashland Branch, *see* Pamunkey Regional Library, Ashland VA p. 2323
Gilliss James Melville Library, *see* United States Naval Observatory, Washington DC p. 379
Gilman-Danforth District Library, Gilman IL p. 592
Gilman Library, Alton NH p. 1353
Gilman Public Library, Gilman IA p. 755
Gilmanton Corner Public Library, Gilmanton NH p. 1364
Gilmanton Year-Round Library, Gilmanton Iron Works NH p. 1364
Gilmer Claud H Memorial Library, Rocksprings TX p. 2234
Gilmer County Public, *see* Sequoyah Regional Library System, Ellijay GA p. 469
Gilmer Public Library, Glenville WV p. 2403
Gilmore City Public Library, Gilmore City IA p. 755
Gilmore Irving S Music Library, *see* Yale University Library, New Haven CT p. 327
Gilpin County Public Library District, Black Hawk CO p. 266
Gilroy Library, *see* Santa Clara County Library District, Gilroy CA p. 127
Gilsum Public Library, Gilsum NH p. 1364
Giltner Public Library, Giltner NE p. 1315
Gimbel Adam & Sophie Design Library, *see* New School, New York NY p. 1593
Gingrich F Wilbur Library, *see* Albright College, Reading PA p. 2000
Ginn Edwin Library, *see* Tufts University, Medford MA p. 1034
Ginsberg Allen Library, *see* Naropa University Library, Boulder CO p. 267
Ginsburg Health Sciences Library, *see* Temple University Libraries, Philadelphia PA p. 1986
Giodone Tom L & Anna Marie Library, *see* Pueblo City-County Library District, Pueblo CO p. 293
Giovale Library, *see* Westminster College, Salt Lake City UT p. 2273
Girard Free Library, Girard OH p. 1788
Girard Public Library, Girard KS p. 809
Girard Township Library, Girard IL p. 592
Girl Scouts of the USA, Savannah GA p. 495
Gitenstein R Barbara Library, *see* College of New Jersey, Ewing NJ p. 1402
Giuffre Family Library, *see* Calgary Public Library, Calgary AB p. 2527
Given Memorial Library & Tufts Archives, Pinehurst NC p. 1707
Givin Amelia S Free Library, Mount Holly Springs PA p. 1966
Glace Bay Public, *see* Cape Breton Regional Library, Glace Bay NS p. 2622
Glacier Bay National Park & Preserve Library, *see* National Park Service, Gustavus AK p. 46
Glacier County Library, Cut Bank MT p. 1291
Gladbrook Public Library, Gladbrook IA p. 755
Glades County Public Library, Moore Haven FL p. 427
Gladewater Public Library, *see* Lee Public Library, Gladewater TX p. 2185
Gladhill Learning Commons, *see* Frederick Community College, Frederick MD p. 966
Gladstone Area School & Public Library, Gladstone MI p. 1109
Gladstone Public Library, Gladstone OR p. 1880
Gladwin County District Library, Gladwin MI p. 1109
Gladwyne Free Library, Gladwyne PA p. 1936
Glann John D Library, *see* Peninsula College Library, Port Angeles WA p. 2374
Glasco City Library, Glasco KS p. 809
Glascock County Library, *see* Oconee Regional Library, Gibson GA p. 477
Glasgow City-County Library, Glasgow MT p. 1293
Glasgow James A Library, *see* Northwest-Shoals Community College, Phil Campbell AL p. 33
Glasgow Public, *see* Rockbridge Regional Library System, Glasgow VA p. 2329
Glass D R Library, *see* Texas College, Tyler TX p. 2249
Glass Memorial Library, *see* Johnson University, Knoxville TN p. 2105
Glatfelter Dr Charles H Research Room, *see* Adams County Historical Society, Gettysburg PA p. 1935
Glatfelter Lee R Library, *see* Penn State University York, York PA p. 2026
Glatfelter Memorial Library, Spring Grove PA p. 2009
GlaxoSmithKline Pharmaceuticals, Philadelphia PA p. 1981
Gleason Ellen Library, *see* Santa Ynez Valley Historical Society, Santa Ynez CA p. 245
Gleason Memorial Library, Ringling OK p. 1861
Gleason Memorial Library, Gleason TN p. 2099
Gleason Public Library, Carlisle MA p. 1009
Glebe House Museum Library, *see* Seabury Society for the Preservation of the Glebe House, Inc, Woodbury CT p. 349
Gledhill Library, *see* Santa Barbara Historical Museum, Santa Barbara CA p. 240
Gleeson Richard A Library-Charles & Nancy Geschke Resource Center, *see* University of San Francisco, San Francisco CA p. 229
Gleichen & District Library, Gleichen AB p. 2541
Glen Avon Library, *see* Riverside County Library System, Jurupa Valley CA p. 202
Glen Burnie Library, *see* Arundel Anne County Public Library, Glen Burnie MD p. 950
Glen Carbon Centennial Library District, Glen Carbon IL p. 593
Glen Cove Public Library, Glen Cove NY p. 1538
Glen Elder Library, Glen Elder KS p. 810
Glen Ellyn Public Library, Glen Ellyn IL p. 593
Glen Lake Community Library, Empire MI p. 1103
Glen Oaks Community College Learning Commons, Centreville MI p. 1090
Glen Oaks Community Library, *see* Queens Library, Glen Oaks NY p. 1554
Glen Ridge Free Public Library, Glen Ridge NJ p. 1405
Glen Rock Public Library, Glen Rock NJ p. 1405
Glen Rose Public Library, Glen Rose TX p. 2185
Glen Ullin Public Library, Glen Ullin ND p. 1734
Glenbow Museum Library, Calgary AB p. 2528
Glencoe Public Library, Glencoe IL p. 593
Glencoe Public Library, Glencoe MN p. 1176
Glendale Area Public Library Inc, Coalport PA p. 1923
Glendale Community College Library, Glendale CA p. 148
Glendale Community College - Main, Glendale AZ p. 61
Glendale Community College - North, Glendale AZ p. 61
Glendale Community Library, *see* Queens Library, Glendale NY p. 1554
Glendale Library, Arts & Culture, Glendale CA p. 148
Glendale Public Library, Glendale AZ p. 62
Glendive Public Library, Glendive MT p. 1294
Glendora Public Library & Cultural Center, Glendora CA p. 149
Glenmary Novitiate Library, *see* Home Missioners of America, Fairfield OH p. 1785
Glenn Memorial United Methodist Church, Atlanta GA p. 465
Glennan Dr T Keith Memorial Library, *see* NASA Headquarters Library, Washington DC p. 371
Glenns Ferry Public Library, Glenns Ferry ID p. 521
Glennville Public, *see* Ohoopee Regional Library System, Glennville GA p. 502
Glenolden Library, Glenolden PA p. 1937
Glenrose Rehabilitation Hospital, Edmonton AB p. 2537
Glens Falls-Queensbury Historical Association, Glens Falls NY p. 1539
Glenshaw Public Library, Glenshaw PA p. 1937
Glenside Free Library, *see* Cheltenham Township Library System, Glenside PA p. 1937
Glenside Public Library District, Glendale Heights IL p. 593
Glenview Public Library, Glenview IL p. 594
Glenville State College, Glenville WV p. 2403
Glenwood & Souris Regional Library, Souris MB p. 2590
Glenwood City Public Library, Glenwood City WI p. 2437
Glenwood Community Library, *see* Greensboro Public Library, Greensboro NC p. 1692
Glenwood-Lynwood Public Library District, Lynwood IL p. 611
Glenwood Municipal Library, Glenwood AB p. 2541
Glenwood Public Library, Glenwood IA p. 755
Glenwood Public Library, Glenwood MN p. 1176
Glew William B MD Health Sciences Library, *see* Washington Hospital Center, Washington DC p. 381

Goss Sam & Carmena Memorial Branch, *see* Chambers County Library System, Mont Belvieu TX p. 2134
Gothenburg Public Library, Gothenburg NE p. 1316
Gottesman D Samuel Library, *see* Albert Einstein College of Medicine, Bronx NY p. 1497
Gottesman David S & Ruth L Research Library & Learning Center, *see* American Museum of Natural History Library, New York NY p. 1578
Gottesman Libraries, *see* Teachers College, Columbia University, New York NY p. 1602
Gottesman Mendel Library of Hebraica-Judaica, *see* Yeshiva University Libraries, New York NY p. 1604
Gottfredson Don M Library of Criminal Justice, *see* Rutgers University Libraries, Newark NJ p. 1428
Goucher College Library, Baltimore MD p. 953
Gould Clara Wood Memorial Library, *see* College of Coastal Georgia, Brunswick GA p. 468
Gould Laurence McKinley Library, *see* Carleton College, Northfield MN p. 1191
Goulston & Storrs PC, Boston MA p. 995
Gouverneur Correctional Facility, Gouverneur NY p. 1540
Gove City Library, Gove KS p. 810
Government of Canada, Ottawa ON p. 2667
Government of Quebec - Agriculture Fisheries & Foods, Gaspe QC p. 2712
Government of the Northwest Territories, Yellowknife NT p. 2613
Governors State University Library, University Park IL p. 655
Gowanda Free Library, Gowanda NY p. 1540
Gowling WLG (Canada) Library, Toronto ON p. 2689
Gowrie Public Library, Gowrie IA p. 755
GPLLA (N), *see* Greater Philadelphia Law Library Association, Philadelphia PA p. 2774
Grace Christian University, Grand Rapids MI p. 1110
Grace College & Grace Theological Seminary, Winona Lake IN p. 727
Grace District Library, Grace ID p. 521
Grace Library, *see* Carlow University, Pittsburgh PA p. 1990
Grace Lutheran Church Library, La Grange IL p. 605
Grace of Christ Presbyterian Church Library, Yakima WA p. 2395
Grace Presbyterian Church, Tuscaloosa AL p. 37
Graceland University, Lamoni IA p. 764
Graceville Public Library, Graceville MN p. 1176
Gradient, Cambridge MA p. 1005
Graduate Theological Union Library, Berkeley CA p. 122
Grady Oscar Public Library, Saukville WI p. 2475
Graese Clifford E Community Health Library, *see* Orlando Health, Orlando FL p. 432
Graettinger Public Library, Graettinger IA p. 755
Graff Lee Medical & Scientific Library, *see* City of Hope, Duarte CA p. 139
Grafton Community Library, Grafton NY p. 1540
Grafton Martha S Library, *see* Baldwin Mary University, Staunton VA p. 2347
Grafton Public Library, Grafton IA p. 755
Grafton Public Library, Grafton MA p. 1021
Grafton Public Library, Grafton NH p. 1365
Grafton Public Library, Grafton VT p. 2285
Grafton-Midview Public Library, Grafton OH p. 1788
Graham Community Library, Ralston AB p. 2551
Graham Correctional Center Library, Hillsboro IL p. 599
Graham County Public Library, Hill City KS p. 813
Graham County Public Library, Robbinsville NC p. 1713
Graham Dallas James, *see* Jacksonville Public Library, Jacksonville FL p. 412
Graham Hospital Association, Canton IL p. 548
Graham John Public Library, Newville PA p. 1970
Graham Library, *see* Coffeyville Community College, Coffeyville KS p. 802
Graham Library, *see* County of Los Angeles Public Library, Los Angeles CA p. 136
Graham Library, *see* Trinity Bible College, Ellendale ND p. 1732
Graham Public Library, Union Grove WI p. 2482
Graham Public Library, *see* Alamance County Public Libraries, Graham NC p. 1676
Grainfield City Library, Grainfield KS p. 810
Grainger Engineering Library, *see* University of Illinois Library at Urbana-Champaign, Urbana IL p. 656
Grambling State University, Grambling LA p. 890
Gramley Dale H Library, *see* Salem College, Winston-Salem NC p. 1725
Granby Free Public Library, Granby MA p. 1021
Granby Public Library, Granby CT p. 313
Grand Army of the Republic Civil War Museum & Archive, Philadelphia PA p. 1981
Grand Bank Public Library, Grand Bank NL p. 2608
Grand Canyon National Park Research Library, Grand Canyon AZ p. 62
Grand Canyon University Library, Phoenix AZ p. 70
Grand Canyon-Tusayan Community Library, *see* Flagstaff City-Coconino County Public Library System, Grand Canyon AZ p. 60
Grand Central Library, *see* New York Public Library - Astor, Lenox & Tilden Foundations, New York NY p. 1595
Grand County Historical Association Library, Hot Sulphur Springs CO p. 286
Grand County Library District, Granby CO p. 283
Grand County Public Library, Moab UT p. 2266
Grand Encampment Museum, Inc Library, Encampment WY p. 2494
Grand Falls Public Library, *see* Haut-Saint-Jean Regional Library, Grand Sault NB p. 2600
Grand Forks & District Public Library, Grand Forks BC p. 2566
Grand Forks Public Library, Grand Forks ND p. 1734
Grand Island Memorial Library, Grand Island NY p. 1540
Grand Island Public Library, Grand Island NE p. 1316
Grand Isle Free Library, Grand Isle VT p. 2285
Grand Junction Public Library, Grand Junction IA p. 755
Grand Junction Public Library, Grand Junction TN p. 2100
Grand Ledge Area District Library, Grand Ledge MI p. 1109
Grand Lodge AF&AM of Virginia, Richmond VA p. 2340
Grand Lodge of Ancient Free & Accepted Masons of Wyoming Library, Cheyenne WY p. 2492
Grand Lodge of Iowa, AF & AM, Cedar Rapids IA p. 738
Grand Lodge of Manitoba, Winnipeg MB p. 2593
Grand Lodge of Masons in Massachusetts, Boston MA p. 995
Grand Manan Library, *see* Fundy Library Region, Grand Manan NB p. 2604
Grand Marais Public Library, Grand Marais MN p. 1176
Grand Meadow Public Library, Grand Meadow MN p. 1177
Grand Portage National Monument Library, *see* United States National Park Service, Grand Portage MN p. 1177
Grand Prairie of the West Public Library District, Virden IL p. 658
Grand Prairie Public Library System, Grand Prairie TX p. 2185
Grand Rapids Area Library, Grand Rapids MN p. 1177
Grand Rapids Art Museum, Grand Rapids MI p. 1110
Grand Rapids Community College, Grand Rapids MI p. 1110
Grand Rapids Public Library, Grand Rapids MI p. 1111
Grand River Hospital, Kitchener ON p. 2651
Grand Saline Public Library, Grand Saline TX p. 2186
Grand Seminaire des Saints Apotres Library, Sherbrooke QC p. 2737
Grand Street, *see* Hoboken Public Library, Hoboken NJ p. 1408
Grand Valley Public Library, Orwell OH p. 1811
Grand Valley Public Library, Grand Valley ON p. 2643
Grand Valley State University Libraries, Allendale MI p. 1077
Grand View Library, *see* Eastern Owyhee County Library, Grand View ID p. 521
Grand View University Library, Des Moines IA p. 746
Grande Anne W Law Library, *see* Hennepin County Law Library, Minneapolis MN p. 1183
Grande Cache Municipal Library, Grande Cache AB p. 2541
Grande Prairie Public Library, Grande Prairie AB p. 2541
Grande Prairie Public Library District, Hazel Crest IL p. 598
Grande Prairie Regional College, Grande Prairie AB p. 2541
Grandfalls Public, *see* Ward County Library, Grandfalls TX p. 2220
Grandfield Public Library, Grandfield OK p. 1848
Grandview Heights Public Library, Columbus OH p. 1773
Grandview Library, Grandview WA p. 2365
Grandview Public Library, Grandview TX p. 2186
Granger Public Library, Granger IA p. 756
Grangeville Centennial Library, Grangeville ID p. 521
Granisle Public Library, Granisle BC p. 2567
Granite Falls Library, *see* Sno-Isle Libraries, Granite Falls WA p. 2370
Granite Falls Public, *see* Caldwell County Public Library, Granite Falls NC p. 1700
Granite Falls Public Library, Granite Falls MN p. 1177
Grant Area District Library, Grant MI p. 1112
Grant County Library, Ulysses KS p. 840
Grant County Library, Hyannis NE p. 1319
Grant County Library, John Day OR p. 1882
Grant County Library, *see* Mid-Arkansas Regional Library, Sheridan AR p. 103
Grant County Public Library, Milbank SD p. 2079
Grant County Public Library District, Williamstown KY p. 877
Grant David USAF Medical Center Learning Resource Center, *see* United States Air Force, Travis AFB CA p. 253
Grant Library, *see* United States Army, Fort Carson CO p. 280
Grant Nieman Journalism Reading Room, *see* University of Wisconsin-Madison, Madison WI p. 2451
Grant Parish Library, Colfax LA p. 887
Grant Park Public Library, Grant Park IL p. 595
Grant Public Library, Grant AL p. 19
Grant Public Library, *see* Hastings Memorial Library, Grant NE p. 1316
Granton Community Library, Granton WI p. 2437
Grants Public Library, Grants NM p. 1468
Grantsburg Public Library, Grantsburg WI p. 2438
Grantsville City Library, Grantsville UT p. 2264
Grantville Public Library, *see* Coweta Public Library System, Grantville GA p. 492
Granum Public Library, Granum AB p. 2541
Granville County Library System, Oxford NC p. 1707
Granville Public Library, Granville MA p. 1021
Granville Public Library, Granville OH p. 1788
Grapeland Public Library, Grapeland TX p. 2186
Grapevine Public Library, Grapevine TX p. 2186
Grasselli Library & Breen Learning Center, *see* John Carroll University, University Heights OH p. 1826
Grassland Public Library, Grassland AB p. 2541
Grassy Lake Community Library, Grassy Lake AB p. 2542
Gratz College, Melrose Park PA p. 1962
Graubner Library, *see* Romeo District Library, Washington MI p. 1157
Gravenhurst Public Library, Gravenhurst ON p. 2643
Graves County Public Library, Mayfield KY p. 868

Greenwell Springs Road Regional, *see* East Baton Rouge Parish Library, Baton Rouge LA p. 883
Greenwich Free Library, Greenwich NY p. 1542
Greenwich Historical Society, Cos Cob CT p. 306
Greenwich Hospital, Greenwich CT p. 314
Greenwich Library, Greenwich CT p. 314
Greenwich Public Library, *see* Huron County Community Library, Greenwich OH p. 1832
Greenwood County Historical Society Library, Eureka KS p. 807
Greenwood County Library, Greenwood SC p. 2062
Greenwood Genetic Center Library, Greenwood SC p. 2062
Greenwood Janet D Library, *see* Longwood University, Farmville VA p. 2318
Greenwood Lake Public Library, Greenwood Lake NY p. 1542
Greenwood-Leflore Public Library System, Greenwood MS p. 1217
Greenwood Library, *see* Mississippi Delta Community College, Greenwood MS p. 1227
Greenwood Public, *see* Sussex County Department of Libraries, Greenwood DE p. 353
Greenwood Public Library, Greenwood IN p. 688
Greenwood Public Library, Greenwood NE p. 1316
Greenwood Public Library, Greenwood WI p. 2440
Greenwood Public Library, Greenwood BC p. 2567
Greenwood Reading Center, Greenwood NY p. 1542
Greer Memorial, *see* Apache County Library District, Greer AZ p. 76
Greer Music Library, *see* Connecticut College, New London CT p. 329
Gregg-Graniteville Library, *see* University of South Carolina Aiken, Aiken SC p. 2046
Gregory Evelyn, *see* Toronto Public Library, Toronto ON p. 2695
Gregory Francis A Neighborhood, *see* District of Columbia Public Library, Washington DC p. 364
Gregory Public Library, Gregory SD p. 2076
Greig Memorial Library, Oneida IL p. 630
Grems-Doolittle Library, *see* Schenectady County Historical Society, Schenectady NY p. 1638
Grenola Public Library, Grenola KS p. 811
Gresham Newton Library, *see* Sam Houston State University, Huntsville TX p. 2201
Gretna Public Library, Gretna NE p. 1316
Grey Bruce Health Services, Owen Sound ON p. 2671
Grey Eagle Community Library, *see* Great River Regional Library, Grey Eagle MN p. 1197
Grey Highlands Public Library, Flesherton ON p. 2641
Greystone Park Psychiatric Hospital, Morris Plains NJ p. 1421
Gridley Public Library District, Gridley IL p. 596
Gries Library, *see* Suburban Temple Kol - Ami, Beachwood OH p. 1749
Griffin Campus Library, *see* Southern Crescent Technical College, Griffin GA p. 481
Griffin Free Public Library, Auburn NH p. 1354
Griffin Hospital, Derby CT p. 309
Griffin Memorial Hospital, Norman OK p. 1855
Griffin-Spalding County Library & Library System Headquarters, *see* Flint River Regional Library System, Griffin GA p. 481
Griffith-Calumet Township Branch, *see* Lake County Public Library, Griffith IN p. 705
Griffith Observatory Library, Los Angeles CA p. 162
Griffith Silas L Memorial Library, Danby VT p. 2282
Grifton Public Library, Grifton NC p. 1694
Grigg Medical Library, *see* HonorHealth John C Lincoln Medical Center, Phoenix AZ p. 70
Griggs County Public Library, Cooperstown ND p. 1731
Grignon Claude-Henri, *see* Bibliotheques Publiques de Longueuil, Longueuil QC p. 2716
Grimes Norma K Research Library, *see* Washington County Historical Society Library, Washington PA p. 2018
Grimes Public Library, Grimes IA p. 756
Grimsby Public Library, Grimsby ON p. 2643
Grimshaw Municipal Library, Grimshaw AB p. 2542
Grinnell College Libraries, Grinnell IA p. 756
Grinnell Library, Wappingers Falls NY p. 1658
Grisham Law Library, *see* University of Mississippi, University MS p. 1234
Grissom Virgil I, *see* Newport News Public Library System, Newport News VA p. 2334
Griswold Memorial Library, Colrain MA p. 1012
Griswold Public Library, Griswold IA p. 756
Groesbeck Maffett Public Library, Groesbeck TX p. 2186
Groffe Memorial Library, Grayville IL p. 595
Grolier Club of New York Library, New York NY p. 1587
Groninger Library, *see* United States Army, Fort Eustis VA p. 2319
Gronlid Public Library, *see* Wapiti Regional Library, Gronlid SK p. 2745
Grosse Pointe Public Library, Grosse Pointe Farms MI p. 1112
Grossmont College Library, El Cajon CA p. 139
Groton Free Public Library, Groton VT p. 2285
Groton Public Library, Groton CT p. 314
Groton Public Library, Groton MA p. 1022
Groton Public Library, Groton NY p. 1542
Grout Museum of History & Science, Waterloo IA p. 788
Grove City Community Library, Grove City PA p. 1939
Grove City Public Library, Grove City MN p. 1177
Grove Family Library, Chambersburg PA p. 1920
Grove Hill Public Library, Grove Hill AL p. 19
Grove Public Library, Grove OK p. 1848
Grove United Methodist Church Library, West Chester PA p. 2020
Groveland Correctional Facility Library, Sonyea NY p. 1642
Groves Public Library, Groves TX p. 2186
Groveton Public Library, Groveton TX p. 2187
Grovetown Library, *see* Greater Clarks Hill Regional Library System, Grovetown GA p. 478
Grundy County-Jewett Norris Library, Trenton MO p. 1282
Grundy Margaret R Memorial Library, Bristol PA p. 1915
Grunigen Medical Library, *see* University of California Irvine Libraries, Orange CA p. 153
Gruver City Library, Gruver TX p. 2187
Guam Community College, Mangilao GU p. 2505
Guam Law Library, Hagatna GU p. 2505
Guam Public Library System, Hagatna GU p. 2505
Guebert Arnold Library, *see* Concordia University of Edmonton, Edmonton AB p. 2536
Guelph Public Library, Guelph ON p. 2643
Guerneville Regional Library, *see* Sonoma County Library, Guerneville CA p. 204
Guernsey County District Public Library, Cambridge OH p. 1754
Guernsey County Law Library, Cambridge OH p. 1754
Guernsey Memorial Library, Norwich NY p. 1609
Guerra Joe A Laredo Public Library, Laredo TX p. 2209
Guerrieri Academic Commons, *see* Salisbury University, Salisbury MD p. 976
Guggenheim Memorial Library, *see* Monmouth University Library, West Long Branch NJ p. 1452
Guilderland Public Library, Guilderland NY p. 1542
Guildhall Public Library, Guildhall VT p. 2285
Guilford College, Greensboro NC p. 1692
Guilford Free Library, Guilford CT p. 315
Guilford Free Library, Guilford VT p. 2285
Guilford Hazel W Memorial, *see* Beaufort, Hyde & Martin County Regional Library, Aurora NC p. 1720
Guilford Memorial Library, Guilford ME p. 926
Guilford Technical Community College, Jamestown NC p. 1698
Guin Marilyn Potts Library, *see* Oregon State University, Newport OR p. 1889
Guinn Nancy Memorial Library, *see* Conyers-Rockdale Library System, Conyers GA p. 472
Guiteau Foundation Library, *see* Irvington Public Library, Irvington NY p. 1550
Gulf Beaches Public Library, Madeira Beach FL p. 419
Richard G Cox - Gulf Coast Library, *see* University of Southern Mississippi Library MS p. 1219
Gulf Coast State College Library, Panama City FL p. 435
Gulf Correctional Institution Library, Wewahitchka FL p. 454
Gulf Gate Public Library, Sarasota FL p. 442
Gulf Shores Learning Resources Center, *see* Coastal Alabama Community College, Gulf Shores AL p. 6
Gulfport Library, *see* Harrison County Library System, Gulfport MS p. 1217
Gulfport Public Library, Gulfport FL p. 408
Gum Spring Library, *see* Loudoun County Public Library, Aldie VA p. 2328
Gumberg Library, *see* Duquesne University, Pittsburgh PA p. 1993
Gund Jessica Memorial Library, *see* Cleveland Institute of Art, Cleveland OH p. 1767
Gundersen Adolf MD Health Sciences Library, *see* Gundersen Lutheran Health System, La Crosse WI p. 2446
Gundersen Lutheran Health System, La Crosse WI p. 2446
Gunlocke Memorial Library, *see* Wayland Free Library, Wayland NY p. 1661
Gunn Memorial Library, Inc, Washington CT p. 343
Gunn Memorial Public Library Caswell County Public Library, Yanceyville NC p. 1727
Gunnin Architecture Library, *see* Clemson University Libraries, Clemson SC p. 2052
Gunnison Civic Library, Gunnison UT p. 2264
Gunnison Public Library, Gunnison CO p. 285
Gunston Hall Plantation Library & Archives, Mason Neck VA p. 2332
Gunter Herman Library, *see* Florida DEP-Geological Survey Research Library, Tallahassee FL p. 446
Gunter Library, *see* University of Southern Mississippi-Gulf Coast, Ocean Springs MS p. 1228
Guntersville Public Library, Guntersville AL p. 20
Gurley Public Library, *see* Huntsville-Madison County Public Library, Gurley AL p. 22
Gustavus Public Library, Gustavus AK p. 46
Gutekunst Public Library, State Center IA p. 784
Gutenberg College Library, Eugene OR p. 1878
Guthrie Ben Lac Du Flambeau Public Library, Lac Du Flambeau WI p. 2447
Guthrie Memorial Library, Hanover PA p. 1939
Guthrie Public Library, Guthrie OK p. 1848
Guthrie Warren Learning Resource Center, *see* Pittsburgh Institute of Aeronautics, West Mifflin PA p. 2021
Gutman Monroe C Library, *see* Harvard Library, Cambridge MA p. 1006
Gutman Paul J Library, *see* Thomas Jefferson University-East Falls, Philadelphia PA p. 1987
Guttenberg Public Library, Guttenberg IA p. 757
Guyan River Public Library, *see* Lincoln County Libraries, Branchland WV p. 2403
Guymon Public Library & Arts Center, Guymon OK p. 1849
Guyton Library, *see* Blue Mountain College, Blue Mountain MS p. 1212
Gwinnett County Judicial Circuit, Lawrenceville GA p. 485
Gwinnett County Public Library, Lawrenceville GA p. 485
Gwinnett Technical College Library, Lawrenceville GA p. 485
GWLA (N), *see* Greater Western Library Alliance, Prairie Village KS p. 2765
Gwynedd Mercy University, Gwynedd Valley PA p. 1939
Gypsum Community Library, Gypsum KS p. 811
Gypsum Public Library, *see* Eagle Valley Library District, Gypsum CO p. 279
Gzowski Peter, *see* Georgina Public Library, Sutton ON p. 2649
H Councill Trenholm State Technical College Library, Montgomery AL p. 28
H J International Graduate School for Peace & Public Leadership, New York NY p. 1587
H O K, Inc, Houston TX p. 2191
Haakon County Public Library, Philip SD p. 2080

Hancock Community Library, Hancock MN p. 1177
Hancock County Law Library Association, Findlay OH p. 1785
Hancock County Library, *see* Azalea Regional Library System, Sparta GA p. 488
Hancock County Library System, Bay Saint Louis MS p. 1211
Hancock County Public Library, Greenfield IN p. 688
Hancock County Public Library, Hawesville KY p. 858
Hancock County Public Library, Sneedville TN p. 2126
Hancock Estabrook, LLP, Syracuse NY p. 1648
Hancock Free Public Library, Hancock VT p. 2285
Hancock Public Library, Hancock WI p. 2440
Hancock State Prison, *see* Georgia Department of Corrections, Sparta GA p. 497
Hancock Town Library, Hancock NH p. 1366
Hancock War Memorial, *see* Washington County Free Library, Hancock MD p. 968
Hand County Library, Miller SD p. 2079
Handelman Edith H Library, *see* Temple Israel of New Rochelle, New Rochelle NY p. 1577
Handley Regional Library System, Winchester VA p. 2354
Handley William R Health Sciences Library, *see* Hardin Memorial Hospital, Elizabethtown KY p. 854
Hands J J Library, Lohrville IA p. 766
Hanes Madlyn L Library, *see* Pennsylvania State University-Harrisburg Library, Middletown PA p. 1963
Hangar Flight Museum, Calgary AB p. 2528
Hankin Henrietta Branch, *see* Chester County Library & District Center, Chester Springs PA p. 1932
Hankinson Public Library, Hankinson ND p. 1735
Hanley T Edward & Tullah Library, *see* University of Pittsburgh at Bradford, Bradford PA p. 1914
Hann Jess, *see* Oshawa Public Library, Oshawa ON p. 2664
Hanna Alex A Law Library, *see* Saint Thomas University Library, Miami Gardens FL p. 425
Hanna Branch, *see* Carbon County Library System, Hanna WY p. 2498
Hanna Municipal Library, Hanna AB p. 2542
Hanna Walter J Memorial Library, Fairfield AL p. 16
Hannibal Free Library, Hannibal NY p. 1544
Hannibal Free Public Library, Hannibal MO p. 1247
Hannibal-LaGrange University, Hannibal MO p. 1247
Hannon Library, *see* Southern Oregon University, Ashland OR p. 1872
Hanover College, Hanover IN p. 689
Hanover Public, *see* Wyoming County Public Library, Hanover WV p. 2412
Hanover Public Library, Hanover KS p. 811
Hanover Public Library, Hanover ON p. 2647
Hanover Town Library, Etna NH p. 1363
Hanover Township Library, Hanover IL p. 597
Hansen Community Library, Hansen ID p. 522
Hansen Walter T A Memorial Library, Mars Hill ME p. 931
Hansford County Library, Spearman TX p. 2245
Hanska Community Library, Hanska MN p. 1177
Hanson Bridgett LLP, San Francisco CA p. 225
Hanson Clarence B Jr Library, *see* Birmingham Museum of Art, Birmingham AL p. 7
Hanson Luise V Library, *see* Waldorf University, Forest City IA p. 753
Hanson Public Library, Hanson MA p. 1023
Hanston City Library, Hanston KS p. 811
Happy Valley Library, Happy Valley OR p. 1881
Har Zion Temple, Penn Valley PA p. 1974
Harbaugh-Thomas Library, *see* Adams County Library System, Biglerville PA p. 1935
Harbin Memorial Library, *see* Muhlenberg County Libraries, Greenville KY p. 857
Harbor Beach Area District Library, Harbor Beach MI p. 1113
Harbor-Topky Memorial Library, Ashtabula OH p. 1748
Harborfields Public Library, Greenlawn NY p. 1541
Harbour Grace Public Library, Harbour Grace NL p. 2608
Harcourt Community Library, Harcourt IA p. 757
Harcum College, Bryn Mawr PA p. 1916
Hardee County Public Library, Wauchula FL p. 453
Hardeeville Community Library, *see* Allendale-Hampton-Jasper Regional Library, Hardeeville SC p. 2046
Hardesty Regional Library, *see* Tulsa City-County Library, Tulsa OK p. 1866
Hardin County Library, Savannah TN p. 2125
Hardin County Public Library, Elizabethtown KY p. 854
Hardin Library for the Health Sciences, *see* University of Iowa Libraries, Iowa City IA p. 761
Hardin Memorial Hospital, Elizabethtown KY p. 854
Hardin Northern Public Library, Dunkirk OH p. 1783
Hardin-Simmons University, Abilene TX p. 2132
Hardin Valley Library, *see* Pellissippi State Community College, Knoxville TN p. 2106
Harding School of Theology, Memphis TN p. 2112
Harding University, Searcy AR p. 109
Hardisty Public Library, Hardisty AB p. 2542
Hardtner Public Library, Hardtner KS p. 811
Hardy County Public Library, Moorefield WV p. 2409
Hardymon Philip B Medical Library, *see* Ohio State University LIBRARIES, Columbus OH p. 1775
Hare Bay-Dover Public Library, Hare Bay NL p. 2608
Harford Community College Library, Bel Air MD p. 958
Harford County Public Library, Belcamp MD p. 958
Hargis William J Jr Library, *see* Virginia Institute of Marine Science, Gloucester Point VA p. 2322
Hargraves Juanita Memorial, *see* Chambers County Library System, Winnie TX p. 2134
Hargrove Jean Gray Music Library, *see* University of California, Berkeley, Berkeley CA p. 123
Harker Heights Public Library, Harker Heights TX p. 2187
Harkins Bob, *see* Prince George Public Library, Prince George BC p. 2574
Harlan Community Library, Harlan IA p. 757
Harlan County Public Libraries, Harlan KY p. 858
Harlan William B Memorial Library, *see* Monroe County Public Library, Tompkinsville KY p. 876
Harlem Public Library, Harlem MT p. 1295
Harless Library, *see* Southern West Virginia Community & Technical College, Mount Gay WV p. 2410
Harlingen Public Library, Harlingen TX p. 2187
Harlowton Public Library, Harlowton MT p. 1295
Harmon Library, *see* Phoenix Public Library, Phoenix AZ p. 72
Harmony Library, *see* Front Range Community College, Fort Collins CO p. 281
Harmony Library, *see* Glocester Libraries, Harmony RI p. 2030
Harmony Library, *see* Poudre River Public Library District, Fort Collins CO p. 281
Harmony Public Library, Harmony MN p. 1177
Harness Racing Museum & Hall of Fame, Goshen NY p. 1540
Harnett County Public Library, Lillington NC p. 1700
Harney County Library, Burns OR p. 1875
Harnish Jerene Appleby Law Library, *see* Pepperdine University Libraries, Malibu CA p. 171
Harnsberger Ann I Biomedical Sciences Library, *see* American Red Cross Holland Laboratory, Rockville MD p. 973
Harper Grey LLP Library, Vancouver BC p. 2578
Harper John M Branch, *see* Waterloo Public Library, Waterloo ON p. 2703
Harper Margaret & James Library, *see* Brunswick County Library, Southport NC p. 1716
Harper Memorial, *see* Barton Public Library, Junction City AR p. 94
Harper Public Library, Harper KS p. 812
Harper Woods Public Library, Harper Woods MI p. 1113
Harrah Library, *see* Metropolitan Library System in Oklahoma County, Harrah OK p. 1857
Harrell George T Health Sciences Library, *see* Pennsylvania State University, College of Medicine, Hershey PA p. 1943
Harrell Memorial Library of Liberty County, *see* Northwest Regional Library System, Bristol FL p. 435
Harriman Public Library, Harriman TN p. 2100
Harrington Gladys Library, *see* Plano Public Library System, Plano TX p. 2227
Harrington Library, *see* Texas Tech University Health Sciences, Amarillo TX p. 2214
Harrington Library Consortium (N), Amarillo TX p. 2775
Harrington Park Public Library, Harrington Park NJ p. 1407
Harrington Public Library, Harrington DE p. 353
Harrington Public Library, Harrington WA p. 2365
Harris Al Library, *see* Southwestern Oklahoma State University, Weatherford OK p. 1868
Harris, Beach PLLC, Pittsford NY p. 1618
Harris Corporation, Palm Bay FL p. 434
Harris County Hainsworth Robert W Law Library, Houston TX p. 2191
Harris County Public Library, Houston TX p. 2192
Harris County Public Library, *see* Troup-Harris Regional Library System, Hamilton GA p. 484
Harris Elizabeth Library, *see* Lake Blackshear Regional Library System, Unadilla GA p. 458
Harris-Elmore Public Library, Elmore OH p. 1784
Harris Engineering LIbrary, *see* Harris Corporation, Palm Bay FL p. 434
Harris Frazee Memorial Library, *see* Saint John the Baptist Parish Library, Garyville LA p. 895
Harris Lillian & Milford Library, *see* Case Western Reserve University, Cleveland OH p. 1766
Harris Memorial Library, Otego NY p. 1613
Harris Memorial Library, *see* College Medical Center, Long Beach CA p. 158
Harris-Stowe State University Library, Saint Louis MO p. 1271
Harris Walter Memorial Library, *see* Grey Highlands Public Library, Markdale ON p. 2642
Harris Willard S Medical Library, *see* United States Department of Veterans Affairs, Tampa FL p. 449
Harrisburg Area Community College, Harrisburg PA p. 1940
Harrisburg Area Community College, Lancaster PA p. 1951
Harrisburg Area Community College, Lebanon PA p. 1953
Harrisburg Area Community College, York PA p. 2025
Harrisburg District Library, *see* Harrisburg Public Library District, Harrisburg IL p. 597
Harrisburg Public Library, Harrisburg OR p. 1881
Harrisburg Public Library District, Harrisburg IL p. 597
Harrisburg University of Science & Technology, Harrisburg PA p. 1940
Harrison A R Learning Resources Center, *see* Redlands Community College, El Reno OK p. 1847
Harrison B J Library, *see* Marshalltown Community College, Marshalltown IA p. 768
Harrison Community Library, Harrison MI p. 1113
Harrison County Historical Museum, Marshall TX p. 2216
Harrison County Law Library, Gulfport MS p. 1217
Harrison County Library System, Gulfport MS p. 1217
Harrison County Public Library, Corydon IN p. 677
Harrison Donald C Health Sciences Library, *see* University of Cincinnati Libraries, Cincinnati OH p. 1765
Harrison G Lamar Library, *see* Langston University, Langston OK p. 1851
Harrison Library, *see* Community Library of Allegheny Valley, Natrona Heights PA p. 1968
Harrison Mel Memorial Library, *see* Temple Judea, Coral Gables FL p. 390

Haworth Municipal Library, Haworth NJ p. 1407
Hawthorn Audrey & Harry Library & Archives at the UBC Museum, Vancouver BC p. 2579
Haxton Memorial Library, Oakfield NY p. 1609
Haxtun Public Library, Haxtun CO p. 285
Hay John Library, *see* Brown University, Providence RI p. 2037
Hay Lakes Municipal Library, Hay Lakes AB p. 2542
Hay Library, *see* Western Wyoming Community College, Rock Springs WY p. 2498
Hay Memorial Library, Sackets Harbor NY p. 1634
Hayden Branch, *see* Community Library Network, Hayden ID p. 522
Hayden Edward J Library, *see* Cumberland Public Library, Cumberland RI p. 2031
Hayden Library Humanities & Science, *see* Massachusetts Institute of Technology Libraries, Cambridge MA p. 1008
Hayden Memorial Library, *see* Citrus College, Glendora CA p. 149
Hayden Public Library, Hayden AZ p. 63
Hayden Public Library, *see* West Routt Library District, Hayden CO p. 285
Hayes Center Public Library, Hayes Center NE p. 1318
Hayes Helen Hospital, West Haverstraw NY p. 1662
Hayes Ira H Memorial Library, Sacaton AZ p. 75
Hayes Rutherford B Presidential Library & Museums, Fremont OH p. 1786
Hayes Samuel P Research Library, *see* Perkins School for the Blind, Watertown MA p. 1063
Hayner Public Library District, Alton IL p. 536
Haynes & Boone LLP, Dallas TX p. 2167
Haynes Library, Alexandria NH p. 1353
Haynesville Correctional Center, Haynesville VA p. 2325
Hayneville-Lowndes County Public Library, Hayneville AL p. 20
Hays Public Library, Hays KS p. 812
Hays Public Library, Hays AB p. 2542
Hays State Prison, *see* Georgia Department of Corrections, Trion GA p. 501
Haysi Public, *see* Lonesome Pine Regional Library, Haysi VA p. 2355
Haysville Community Library, Haysville KS p. 812
Haytaian & Maier Library, *see* Warren County Community College, Washington NJ p. 1451
Hayward Public Library, Hayward CA p. 150
Haywood Community College, Clyde NC p. 1682
Haywood County Public Library, Waynesville NC p. 1721
Hazard Community & Technical College, Jackson KY p. 860
Hazard Community & Technical College Library, Hazard KY p. 858
Hazard Library Association, Poplar Ridge NY p. 1620
Hazel Cross Library, *see* Western Plains Library System, Thomas OK p. 1845
Hazel Green Public Library, Hazel Green WI p. 2441
Hazel Park Memorial District Library, Hazel Park MI p. 1114
Hazelbaker Ralph E Library, *see* North Madison County Public Library System, Summitville IN p. 681
Hazelden Betty Ford Foundation Library, Center City MN p. 1169
Hazeltine Public Library, Jamestown NY p. 1557
Hazelton District Public Library, Hazelton BC p. 2567
Hazen Memorial Library, Shirley MA p. 1053
Hazen Public Library, Hazen ND p. 1735
Hazen Public Library Headquarters, *see* Prairie County Library System, Hazen AR p. 98
Hazlehurst Learning Resource Center, *see* Coastal Pines Technical College, Hazlehurst GA p. 503
Hazleton Area Public Library, Hazleton PA p. 1943
He Sapa College Center, *see* Oglala Lakota College, Rapid City SD p. 2077
Head, Clara & Maria Township Public Library, Stonecliffe ON p. 2681
Headingley Municipal Library, Headingley MB p. 2587
Headley-Whitney Museum Library, Lexington KY p. 862
Headquarters, *see* Kawartha Lakes Public Library, Lindsay ON p. 2652
Heafey Edwin A Law Library, *see* Santa Clara University Library, Santa Clara CA p. 242
Healdsburg Regional Library, *see* Sonoma County Library, Healdsburg CA p. 204
Healdton Community Library, *see* Southern Oklahoma Library System, Healdton OK p. 1841
Healey Joseph P Library, *see* University of Massachusetts at Boston, Boston MA p. 1000
Health & Human Services Library, Victoria BC p. 2583
Health Capital Consultants, LLC Library, Saint Louis MO p. 1271
Health Care Sciences Library, *see* VA Long Beach Health Care System, Long Beach CA p. 159
Health Law Institute Library, *see* University of Alberta, Edmonton AB p. 2538
Health Libraries Information Network (N), Fort Worth TX p. 2775
Health LINE (N), *see* Health Libraries Information Network, Fort Worth TX p. 2775
Health Science Information Consortium of Toronto (N), Toronto ON p. 2778
Health Science Library, *see* Our Lady of Fatima Hospital, North Providence RI p. 2036
Health Sciences Digital Library & Learning Center, *see* University of Texas Southwestern Medical Center, Dallas TX p. 2169
Health Sciences Libraries Consortium (N), Philadelphia PA p. 2774
Health Sciences Library, *see* Beebe Healthcare, Lewes DE p. 353
Health Sciences Library Association of Louisiana (N), Shreveport LA p. 2766
Health Sciences Library Network of Kansas City, Inc (N), Kansas City MO p. 2768
HealthAlliance Hospital - Broadway Campus, Kingston NY p. 1560
HealthPartners Libraries, Saint Louis Park MN p. 1199
Heard County Public Library, *see* West Georgia Regional Library, Franklin GA p. 470
Heard Jean & Alexander Libraries, *see* Vanderbilt University, Nashville TN p. 2121
Heard Museum, Phoenix AZ p. 70
Hearst Castle Staff Library, *see* Hearst San Simeon State Historical Monument, San Simeon CA p. 237
Hearst Free Library, Anaconda MT p. 1287
Hearst Public Library, Hearst ON p. 2648
Hearst San Simeon State Historical Monument, San Simeon CA p. 237
William Randolph Hearst Library, *see* International Center of Photography, New York NY p. 1589
Heart of America Library, Rugby ND p. 1740
Heart of the Valley Public Library, Terreton ID p. 531
Heartland Community College Library, Normal IL p. 625
Heartland Institute, Chicago IL p. 561
Heartland Library Cooperative, Sebring FL p. 444
Heartland Regional Library System, Iberia MO p. 1249
Heath Patrick Public Library, *see* Boerne Public Library, Boerne TX p. 2148
Heath Public Library, Heath MA p. 1024
Heavener Public Library, Heavener OK p. 1849
Hebert Effie & Wilton Public Library, Port Neches TX p. 2228
Hebert Paul M Law Center, *see* Louisiana State University Libraries, Baton Rouge LA p. 884
Hebrew College, Newton MA p. 1039
Hebrew Theological College, Skokie IL p. 647
Hebrew Union College-Jewish Institute of Religion, New York NY p. 1587
Hebrew Union College-Jewish Institute of Religion, Cincinnati OH p. 1760
Hebron & Josey Branch, *see* Carrollton Public Library, Carrollton TX p. 2154
Hebron Library, Hebron NH p. 1367
Hebron Public, *see* Porter County Public Library System, Hebron IN p. 722
Hebron Public Library, Hebron ND p. 1736
Hebron Secrest Library, Hebron NE p. 1318
HEC Montreal Library, Montreal QC p. 2724
Hector MacLean Public Library, *see* Robeson County Public Library, Fairmont NC p. 1702
Hector Public Library, Hector MN p. 1178
Hedberg Library, *see* Carthage College, Kenosha WI p. 2444
Hedberg Public Library, Janesville WI p. 2443
Hedgesville Public Library, *see* Martinsburg-Berkeley County Public Library, Hedgesville WV p. 2408
Hedrick Public Library, Hedrick IA p. 758
Heermance Memorial Library, Coxsackie NY p. 1523
Heffernan Margaret Avery Reference Library, *see* Sioux City Art Center, Sioux City IA p. 782
Hefner W G VA Medical Center Library, *see* Department of Veterans Affairs, Salisbury NC p. 1714
Hege Library & Learning Technologies, *see* Guilford College, Greensboro NC p. 1692
Heginbotham Library, Holyoke CO p. 286
Heidelberg University, Tiffin OH p. 1823
Height Dorothy I/Benning Neighborhood Library, *see* District of Columbia Public Library, Washington DC p. 364
Heights Neighborhood Library, *see* Houston Public Library, Houston TX p. 2195
Heilig Resource Center, *see* North Carolina Synod of the ELCA, Salisbury NC p. 1715
Heintzelman Donald S Wildlife Library, *see* Wildlife Information Center, Slatington PA p. 2007
Heisey Collectors of America, Inc, Newark OH p. 1807
Heiskell Andrew Braille & Talking Book Library, *see* New York Public Library - Astor, Lenox & Tilden Foundations, New York NY p. 1595
Heisler Municipal Library, Heisler AB p. 2542
Hekemian Samuel & Sandra Medical Library, *see* Hackensack University Medical Center, Hackensack NJ p. 1406
Hekman Library, *see* Calvin University & Calvin Theological Seminary, Grand Rapids MI p. 1110
Heldman Learning Resource Center, *see* West Los Angeles College Library, Culver City CA p. 133
Helix Public Library, Helix OR p. 1881
Hellenic College, Brookline MA p. 1003
Hellertown Area Library, Hellertown PA p. 1943
Helling Madelyn Library, *see* Nevada County Community Library, Nevada City CA p. 183
Hellmuth, Obata & Kassabaum, Inc Library, Dallas TX p. 2167
Helmerich Center for American Research, *see* Gilcrease Thomas Institute of American History & Art, Tulsa OK p. 1864
Helmerich Peggy V Library, *see* Tulsa City-County Library, Tulsa OK p. 1866
Helmke Walter E Library, *see* Indiana University-Purdue University, Fort Wayne IN p. 684
Helper City Library, Helper UT p. 2264
Helvetia Public Library, Helvetia WV p. 2404
Hemenway & Barnes, Boston MA p. 996
Hemet Public Library, Hemet CA p. 151
Hemingford Public Library, Hemingford NE p. 1318
Hemphill County Library, Canadian TX p. 2152
Hempstead County Library, Hope AR p. 98
Hempstead Public Library, Hempstead NY p. 1545
Henderson Community College, Henderson KY p. 859
Henderson County, Athens TX p. 2137
Henderson County Public Library, Henderson KY p. 859
Henderson County Public Library, Hendersonville NC p. 1695
Henderson County Public Library District, Biggsville IL p. 542
Henderson Curt B Law Library, McKinney TX p. 2217
Henderson District Public Libraries, Henderson NV p. 1345
Henderson Free Library, Henderson NY p. 1545

Highland County Public Library, Monterey VA p. 2333
Highland Falls Library, Highland Falls NY p. 1546
Highland Library, *see* Medina County District Library, Medina OH p. 1801
Highland Park Library, Highland Park TX p. 2190
Highland Park Presbyterian Church, Dallas TX p. 2167
Highland Park Public Library, Highland Park IL p. 599
Highland Park Public Library, Highland Park NJ p. 1408
Highland Park United Methodist Church Library, Dallas TX p. 2167
Highland Public Library, Highland NY p. 1546
Highland Township Public Library, Highland MI p. 1115
Highlands County Library, Sebring FL p. 444
Highline College, Des Moines WA p. 2794
Highline College Library, Des Moines WA p. 2363
Hightower Dorothy W Collaborative Learning Center & Library, *see* Gordon State College, Barnesville GA p. 468
Hightower Memorial, *see* Pine Mountain Regional Library, Thomaston GA p. 488
Hightower Memorial Library, York AL p. 40
Hightower Sara Regional Library, Rome GA p. 494
Highwood Public Library, Highwood IL p. 599
Hiland Mountain Correctional Center Library, *see* Alaska State Department of Corrections, Eagle River AK p. 45
Hilandar Research Library & Research Center for Medieval, *see* Ohio State University LIBRARIES, Columbus OH p. 1775
Hilbert College, Hamburg NY p. 1543
Hildebrand C B Public, *see* Burke County Public Library, Hildebran NC p. 1704
Hildebrand Memorial Library, Boscobel WI p. 2425
Hilding Medical & Health Sciences Library, *see* Saint Luke's Hospital, Duluth MN p. 1172
Hildreth Public Library, Hildreth NE p. 1318
Hill A P, *see* Petersburg Public Library, Petersburg VA p. 2337
Hill Arden G Memorial Library, *see* United States Air Force, Malmstrom AFB MT p. 1299
Hill B J Library, Holland TX p. 2190
Hill City Public Library, Hill City SD p. 2077
Hill College Library, Hillsboro TX p. 2190
Hill Correctional Center Library, Galesburg IL p. 591
Hill Emily S, *see* Duplin County Library, Faison NC p. 1698
Hill Jerome Reference Library, *see* Anthology Film Archives, New York NY p. 1579
Hill Jim Dan Library, *see* University of Wisconsin-Superior, Superior WI p. 2480
Hill Laurie Library, Heron MT p. 1297
Hill Leslie Pinckney Library, *see* Cheyney University, Cheyney PA p. 1921
Hill Lewis Dana Memorial Library, Center Lovell ME p. 921
Hill Library, Strafford NH p. 1381
Hill Lister Library of the Health Sciences, *see* University of Alabama at Birmingham, Birmingham AL p. 9
Hill Public Library, Hill NH p. 1367
Hill Ruth Library & Archives, *see* Peabody Historical Society & Museum, Peabody MA p. 1045
Hill Stella Memorial Library, Alto TX p. 2133
Hill Tillman D Public Library, *see* Huntsville-Madison County Public Library, Hazel Green AL p. 22
Hillcrest Community Library, *see* Queens Library, Flushing NY p. 1554
Hillcrest Hospital, Mayfield Heights OH p. 1800
Hillcrest Public Library, Cuba KS p. 804
Hillendahl Neighborhood Library, *see* Houston Public Library, Houston TX p. 2195
Hillman Library, *see* University of Pittsburgh Library System, Pittsburgh PA p. 1996
Hillsboro City Library, Hillsboro TX p. 2190
Hillsboro Community Library, Hillsboro NM p. 1469
Hillsboro Public Library, Hillsboro IL p. 599
Hillsboro Public Library, Hillsboro IA p. 758
Hillsboro Public Library, Hillsboro KS p. 813
Hillsboro Public Library, Hillsboro OR p. 1881
Hillsboro Public Library, Hillsboro WI p. 2441
Hillsboro Public Library, *see* Pocahontas County Free Libraries, Hillsboro WV p. 2408
Hillsborough Community College, Tampa FL p. 448
Hillsborough Public, *see* Somerset County Library System of New Jersey, Hillsborough NJ p. 1392
Hillsdale College, Hillsdale MI p. 1115
Hillsdale Community Library, Hillsdale MI p. 1115
Hillsdale Free Public Library, Hillsdale NJ p. 1408
Hillside Public Library, Hillside IL p. 599
Hillside Public Library, Hillside NJ p. 1408
Hillside Public Library, New Hyde Park NY p. 1576
Hillview Free Library, Diamond Point NY p. 1525
Hillwood Estate, Museum & Gardens Library, Washington DC p. 368
Hillyer Art Library, *see* Smith College Libraries, Northampton MA p. 1042
Hilo Public Library, *see* Hawaii State Public Library System, Hilo HI p. 507
Hilton Conrad N Library, *see* Culinary Institute of America, Hyde Park NY p. 1550
Hilton Union Public Library, Hilton Beach ON p. 2648
Hilton-Green Research Room, *see* University of West Florida Historic Trust, Pensacola FL p. 437
Hilty Mae Memorial Library, *see* Texas Chiropractic College, Pasadena TX p. 2225
Himmelfarb Paul Health Sciences Library, *see* George Washington University, Washington DC p. 367
Hinckley, Allen & Snyder LLP, Providence RI p. 2038
Hinckley Library, *see* Northwest College, Powell WY p. 2497
Hinckley Public Library, *see* East Central Regional Library, Hinckley MN p. 1168
Hinckley Public Library District, Hinckley IL p. 600
Hinds Community College, Raymond MS p. 1231
Hineline Richard H Research Library, *see* Camden County Historical Society, Camden NJ p. 1394
Hines Creek Municipal Library, Hines Creek AB p. 2543
Hingham Public Library, Hingham MA p. 1024
Louise & Lucille Hink Library, *see* Tama Public Library, Tama IA p. 786
Hinkle Walter C Memorial Library, *see* State University of New York, College of Technology, Alfred NY p. 1485
Hinkston Park Branch, *see* Waukegan Public Library, Waukegan IL p. 660
Hinsdale County Library District, Lake City CO p. 288
Hinsdale Public Library, Hinsdale IL p. 600
Hinsdale Public Library, Hinsdale MA p. 1024
Hinsdale Public Library, Hinsdale NH p. 1368
Hinton Elmer Memorial Library, *see* Portland Public Library of Sumner County, Portland TN p. 2124
Hinton Municipal Library, Hinton AB p. 2543
Hinton Public Library, Hinton OK p. 1849
Hiram College Library, Hiram OH p. 1790
Hirons Library, *see* Goldey-Beacom College, Wilmington DE p. 357
Hirsch Library, *see* Museum of Fine Arts, Houston, Houston TX p. 2197
Hirshhorn Museum & Sculpture Garden Library, *see* Smithsonian Libraries, Washington DC p. 375
Hispanic Society of America Library, New York NY p. 1587
Historic Arkansas Museum Library, Little Rock AR p. 101
Historic Bethlehem Partnership Library, Bethlehem PA p. 1911
Historic Beverly, Beverly MA p. 989
Historic Courthouse Museum Library, Lakeport CA p. 155
Historic Deerfield Inc & Pocumtuck Valley Memorial, Deerfield MA p. 1014
Historic House Museum Library, *see* Buck Pearl S Birthplace Foundation, Hillsboro WV p. 2404
Historic Hudson Valley Library, Tarrytown NY p. 1651
Historic Huguenot Street Library, New Paltz NY p. 1576
Historic Mobile Preservation Society, Mobile AL p. 26
Historic New England, Boston MA p. 996
Historic New Orleans Collection, New Orleans LA p. 901
Historic Northampton, Northampton MA p. 1042
Historic Restoration Resources Library, *see* Alamance County Historic Properties Commission, Burlington NC p. 1676
Historic Saint Mary's City, Saint Mary's City MD p. 976
Historic Westville Library, Columbus GA p. 472
Historic White Pine Village Research Library, *see* Mason County Historical Society, Ludington MI p. 1128
Historical & Genealogical Society of Indiana County, Indiana PA p. 1945
Historical Association of Catawba County, Newton NC p. 1706
Historical Society of Carroll County Library, Westminster MD p. 981
Historical Society of Cheshire County, Keene NH p. 1369
Historical Society of Dauphin County Library, Harrisburg PA p. 1940
Historical Society of Haddonfield Archives Center, Haddonfield NJ p. 1407
Historical Society of Haute-Yamaska Library, Granby QC p. 2713
Historical Society of Long Beach, Long Beach CA p. 158
The Historical Society of Mendocino County Archives, Ukiah CA p. 254
Historical Society of Michigan, Lansing MI p. 1124
Historical Society of Moorestown Library, Moorestown NJ p. 1420
Historical Society of Newburgh Bay & the Highlands, Newburgh NY p. 1605
Historical Society of Ocean Grove, Ocean Grove NJ p. 1431
Historical Society of Old Yarmouth Library, Yarmouth Port MA p. 1073
Historical Society of Palm Beach County, West Palm Beach FL p. 453
Historical Society of Pennsylvania, Philadelphia PA p. 1981
Historical Society of Princeton, Princeton NJ p. 1436
Historical Society of Quincy & Adams County Library, Quincy IL p. 637
Historical Society of Rockland County Library, New City NY p. 1575
Historical Society of the Cocalico Valley Library, Ephrata PA p. 1931
Historical Society of Western Pennsylvania, Pittsburgh PA p. 1994
Historical Society of York County, York PA p. 2026
Historical Society Serving Sleepy Hollow & Tarrytown, Tarrytown NY p. 1651
History Center in Tompkins County, Ithaca NY p. 1552
History Colorado, Denver CO p. 276
History Museum of Mobile, Mobile AL p. 26
History Museum of Western Virginia, Roanoke VA p. 2344
History Nebraska-Nebraska State Historical Society, *see* Nebraska History Library, Lincoln NE p. 1322
History of Science Library - Cabot Science Library, *see* Harvard Library, Cambridge MA p. 1007
History San Jose, San Jose CA p. 230
Hitchcock Memorial Museum & Library, Westfield VT p. 2298
Hitt John C Library, *see* University of Central Florida Libraries, Orlando FL p. 432
Hjorth Norman E Memorial Library, *see* Trinity Presbyterian Church Library, Cherry Hill NJ p. 1396
Ho-Ho-Kus Public Library, *see* Worth Pinkham Memorial Library, Ho-Ho-Kus NJ p. 1408
Ho Mui Fine Arts Library, *see* Cornell University Library, Ithaca NY p. 1551
Hoag Library, Albion NY p. 1484
Hoar Reuben Library, Littleton MA p. 1029

Honnold-Mudd Library, *see* Claremont Colleges Library, Claremont CA p. 130
Honokaa Public Library, *see* Hawaii State Public Library System, Honokaa HI p. 507
Honolulu Community College Library, Honolulu HI p. 512
Honolulu Museum of Art, Honolulu HI p. 512
Honorable Amdor Michael W Memorial Law Library, *see* Douglas County District Court, Omaha NE p. 1328
Honorable Sharon J Bell Library, *see* Knox County Governmental Law Library, Knoxville TN p. 2105
HonorHealth John C Lincoln Medical Center, Phoenix AZ p. 70
Hood College, Frederick MD p. 966
Hood County Public Library, Granbury TX p. 2185
Hood Theological Seminary Library, Salisbury NC p. 1714
Hood Warren A Library, *see* Belhaven University, Jackson MS p. 1221
Hoodland Library, Welches OR p. 1901
Hooker County Library, Mullen NE p. 1325
Hooker Ruth H Research Library, *see* Naval Research Laboratory, Washington DC p. 373
Hooks Benjamin L Central Library, *see* Memphis Public Library, Memphis TN p. 2112
Hooks Public Library, Hooks TX p. 2191
Hooksett Public Library, Hooksett NH p. 1368
Hooley-Bundschu Library/Learning Commons, *see* Avila University, Kansas City MO p. 1254
Hooper Dorothy Memorial Library, *see* First United Methodist Church, Alhambra CA p. 116
Hooper Public Library, Hooper NE p. 1318
Hoopeston Public Library, Hoopeston IL p. 601
Hoose Library of Philosophy, *see* University of Southern California Libraries, Los Angeles CA p. 170
Hoover Dorothy H Library, *see* OCAD University, Toronto ON p. 2690
Hoover Herbert Presidential Library-Museum, *see* National Archives & Records Administration, West Branch IA p. 790
Hoover Institution Library & Archives, *see* Stanford University Libraries, Stanford CA p. 248
Hoover Library, *see* McDaniel College, Westminster MD p. 981
Hoover Philip A MD Library, *see* WellSpan York Hospital, York PA p. 2026
Hoover Public Library, Hoover AL p. 21
Hope & Cope Library, *see* Jewish General Hospital, Montreal QC p. 2725
Hope College, Holland MI p. 1115
Hope Community Library, Hope KS p. 814
Hope International University, Fullerton CA p. 148
Hope John & Aurelia E Franklin Library, *see* Fisk University, Nashville TN p. 2118
Hope Library, Hope ND p. 1736
Hope Library, Hope RI p. 2032
Hope Library, *see* Fraser Valley Regional Library, Hope BC p. 2561
Hope Place Public Library, *see* Volusia County Public Library, Daytona Beach FL p. 393
Hopewell Culture National Historical Park Library, *see* United States National Park Service, Chillicothe OH p. 1759
Hopewell Furnace National Historic Site, *see* United States Department of Interior, National Park Service, Elverson PA p. 1930
Hopewell Public Library, Hopewell NJ p. 1409
Hopi Public Library, Kykotsmovi Village AZ p. 65
Hopital De L'Enfant Jesus, Quebec QC p. 2730
Hopital Hotel-Dieu du Chum, Montreal QC p. 2724
Hopital Maisonneuve-Rosemont, Montreal QC p. 2724
Hopkins & Carley Library, San Jose CA p. 230
Hopkins County-Madisonville Public Library, Madisonville KY p. 868
Hopkins Owen R Public Library, *see* Corpus Christi Public Libraries, Corpus Christi TX p. 2160
Hopkins Public Library, Hopkins MI p. 1116
Hopkinsville-Christian County Public Library, Hopkinsville KY p. 860
Hopkinsville Community College Library, Hopkinsville KY p. 860
Hopkinton Historical Society, Hopkinton NH p. 1368
Hopkinton Public Library, Hopkinton IA p. 758
Hopkinton Public Library, Hopkinton MA p. 1025
Hopkinton Town Library, Contoocook NH p. 1360
Hopkinton Town Library, Hopkinton NY p. 1548
Hopland Research & Extension Center Library, Hopland CA p. 151
Hopper George W Law Library, *see* University of Wyoming, Laramie WY p. 2496
Hopper Research Library, *see* Butler Institute of American Art, Youngstown OH p. 1835
Hopwood Library, *see* University of Pittsburgh Medical Center Shadyside, Pittsburgh PA p. 1997
Horgan Paul Library, *see* New Mexico Military Institute, Roswell NM p. 1474
Horicon Free Public Library, Brant Lake NY p. 1496
Horicon Public Library, Horicon WI p. 2441
Horizon College & Seminary, Saskatoon SK p. 2748
Horizon Health Network, Moncton NB p. 2603
Horn Everett Public Library, Lexington TN p. 2109
Horn Library, *see* Babson College, Babson Park MA p. 987
Hornbake R Lee Library, *see* University of Maryland Libraries, College Park MD p. 962
Hornell Public Library, Hornell NY p. 1548
Hornepayne Public Library, Hornepayne ON p. 2648
Horner Joseph Memorial Library, *see* German Society of Pennsylvania, Philadelphia PA p. 1980
Horrmann Library, *see* Wagner College, Staten Island NY p. 1645
Horry County Memorial Library, Conway SC p. 2056
Horry-Georgetown Technical College, Conway SC p. 2057
Horse Cave Free Public Library, Horse Cave KY p. 860
Horseheads Free Library, *see* Chemung County Library District, Horseheads NY p. 1530
Horseshoe Bend District Library, Horseshoe Bend ID p. 522
Horseshoe Bend Public Library, *see* Izard County Library, Horseshoe Bend AR p. 98
Horseshoe Bend Regional Library, Dadeville AL p. 13
Horsey J William Library, *see* Tyndale University College & Seminary, Toronto ON p. 2697
Horsham Township Library, Horsham PA p. 1944
Horst Janice, *see* San Bernardino County Library, Lucerne Valley CA p. 213
Horton Gail Library, *see* Montana Bible College, Bozeman MT p. 1289
Hortonville Public Library, Hortonville WI p. 2442
Hospers Public Library, Hospers IA p. 758
Hospital du Saint-Sacrement, Quebec QC p. 2731
Hospital for Sick Children, Toronto ON p. 2689
Hospital for Special Surgery, New York NY p. 1588
Hospital Santa Cabrini, Montreal QC p. 2724
Host Bruce J Center, *see* Collins LeRoy Leon County Public Library System, Tallahassee FL p. 445
Hostos Community College Library, Bronx NY p. 1498
Hot Springs County Library, Thermopolis WY p. 2499
Hot Springs Public Library, Hot Springs SD p. 2077
Hotchkiss Library of Sharon, Inc, Sharon CT p. 336
Hotchkiss Public, *see* Delta County Libraries, Hotchkiss CO p. 286
Hotel-Dieu Bibliotheque Medicale, *see* Centre Hospitalier Universitaire du Sherbrooke, Sherbrooke QC p. 2736
Houff Library, *see* Blue Ridge Community College, Weyers Cave VA p. 2352
Houghton Arthur A Jr Library, *see* SUNY Corning Community College, Corning NY p. 1522
Houghton Lake Public Library, Houghton Lake MI p. 1116
Houghton Library, *see* Harvard Library, Cambridge MA p. 1007
Houghton Memorial Library, *see* Huntingdon College, Montgomery AL p. 28
Houghton University, Houghton NY p. 1548
Houghton Willard J Library, *see* Houghton University, Houghton NY p. 1548
Houlka Public, *see* Dixie Regional Library System, Houlka MS p. 1230
Housatonic Community College Library, Bridgeport CT p. 304
House Memorial Public Library, Pender NE p. 1332
House Robert B Undergraduate, *see* University of North Carolina at Chapel Hill, Chapel Hill NC p. 1678
Houston Academy of Medicine, Houston TX p. 2193
Houston Baptist University, Houston TX p. 2194
Houston Chronicle Library, Houston TX p. 2194
Houston Community College-Central College, Houston TX p. 2194
Houston Community College - Northeast College, Houston TX p. 2194
Houston Community College - Northwest College, Houston TX p. 2194
Houston Community College - Southeast College, Houston TX p. 2194
Houston Community College - Southwest College, Houston TX p. 2195
Houston County Public Library, Erin TN p. 2098
Houston County Public Library System, Perry GA p. 493
Houston Metropolitan Research Center, *see* Houston Public Library, Houston TX p. 2196
Houston Museum of Natural Science, Houston TX p. 2195
Houston Public Library, Houston TX p. 2195
Houston Public Library, Houston BC p. 2567
Houston Sam Regional Library & Research Center, *see* Texas State Library & Archives Commission, Liberty TX p. 2141
Howard Beach Community Library, *see* Queens Library, Howard Beach NY p. 1554
Howard City Library, Howard KS p. 814
Howard College - San Angelo Library, San Angelo TX p. 2236
Howard Community College Library, Columbia MD p. 963
Howard County Junior College, Big Spring TX p. 2148
Howard County Library, Big Spring TX p. 2148
Howard County Library, *see* Tri-County Regional Library, Nashville AR p. 106
Howard County Library System, Ellicott City MD p. 965
Howard County Public Library, Fayette MO p. 1245
Howard Lake Library, *see* Great River Regional Library, Howard Lake MN p. 1197
Howard Payne University, Brownwood TX p. 2150
Howard Public Library, Hornell NY p. 1548
Howard Ray W Library, *see* Shoreline Community College, Shoreline WA p. 2383
Howard-Tilton Memorial Library, *see* Tulane University, New Orleans LA p. 903
Howard University Libraries, Washington DC p. 368
Howe C D Institute Library, Toronto ON p. 2689
Howe Community Library, Howe TX p. 2201
Howe David A Public Library, Wellsville NY p. 1661
Howe David W Memorial Library, *see* University of Vermont Libraries, Burlington VT p. 2281
Howe John Library, *see* Albany Public Library, Albany NY p. 1482
Howe Library, Hanover NH p. 1367
Howe Memorial Library, Breckenridge MI p. 1087
Howell Bruce I, *see* Wake Technical Community College, Raleigh NC p. 1711
Howell Carnegie District Library, Howell MI p. 1117
Howell Julian M Library, *see* Southside Virginia Community College Libraries, Alberta VA p. 2302
Howell William J Branch, *see* Central Rappahannock Regional Library, Fredericksburg VA p. 2320
Howells Public Library, Howells NE p. 1319
Hower Mary Medical Library, Akron OH p. 1745
Howey-in-the-Hills Library, *see* Beck Marianne Memorial Library, Howey in the Hills FL p. 410
Howison Philosophy Library, *see* University of California, Berkeley, Berkeley CA p. 123

Interlibrary Delivery Service of Pennsylvania (N), Doylestown PA p. 2774
Interlochen Center for the Arts, Interlochen MI p. 1118
Interlochen Public Library, Interlochen MI p. 1118
Intermountain Health, Butte MT p. 1290
International Business College Library, Indianapolis IN p. 696
International Center of Photography, New York NY p. 1589
International Crane Foundation, Baraboo WI p. 2422
International Development Research Centre, Ottawa ON p. 2667
International District/Chinatown Branch, *see* Seattle Public Library, Seattle WA p. 2379
International Falls Public Library, International Falls MN p. 1178
International Food Policy Research Institute, Washington DC p. 370
International Foundation of Employee Benefit Plans, Brookfield WI p. 2425
International Game Fish Association, Dania Beach FL p. 391
International Institute for Sport History Library, State College PA p. 2009
International Institute of Integral Human Sciences Library, Montreal QC p. 2725
International Longshore & Warehouse Union, San Francisco CA p. 225
International Mission Board, Southern Baptist Convention, Richmond VA p. 2340
International Museum of Surgical Science Library, Chicago IL p. 562
International Society Daughters of Utah Pioneers, Salt Lake City UT p. 2271
International Tennis Hall of Fame & Museum Library, Newport RI p. 2034
International Tsunami Information Center Library, *see* UNESCO-Intergovernmental Oceanographic Commission, Honolulu HI p. 512
International Wild Waterfowl Association, Spring Hope NC p. 1717
Interprofessional Health Sciences Library, *see* Seton Hall University Libraries, Nutley NJ p. 1430
Intertek Testing Services, Coquitlam BC p. 2565
Inuvik Centennial Library, Inuvik NT p. 2613
Inver Hills Community College Library, Inver Grove Heights MN p. 1179
Invermere Public Library, Invermere BC p. 2567
Inverness Public, *see* Sunflower County Library System, Inverness MS p. 1220
Inwood Public Library, Inwood IA p. 760
Inyo County Free Library, Independence CA p. 152
Inyo County Law Library, Independence CA p. 152
Iola Public Library, Iola KS p. 815
Iola Village Library, Iola WI p. 2442
Iona Branch, *see* Bonneville County Library District, Iona ID p. 515
Iona University, New Rochelle NY p. 1577
Ione Public Library, *see* Pend Oreille County Library District, Ione WA p. 2372
Ionia Community Library, Ionia IA p. 760
Ionia Community Library, Ionia MI p. 1118
Iosco-Arenac District Library, East Tawas MI p. 1102
Iowa Central Community College, Fort Dodge IA p. 754
Iowa City Public Library, Iowa City IA p. 760
Iowa Correctional Institution for Women Library, Mitchellville IA p. 770
Iowa Genealogical Society Library, Des Moines IA p. 746
Iowa History Research Center Des Moines, *see* State Historical Society of Iowa, Des Moines IA p. 747
Iowa History Research Center Iowa City, *see* State Historical Society of Iowa, Iowa City IA p. 760
Iowa Lakes Community College Libraries, Estherville IA p. 752
Iowa League of Cities Library, Des Moines IA p. 746
Iowa Masonic Library, *see* Grand Lodge of Iowa, AF & AM, Cedar Rapids IA p. 738
Iowa Methodist Medical Center, Des Moines IA p. 746
Iowa Regional Library for the Blind & Physically Handicapped, Des Moines IA p. 747
Iowa State Law Library, *see* State Library of Iowa, Des Moines IA p. 747
Iowa State University Library, Ames IA p. 731
Iowa Veteran's Home Library, Marshalltown IA p. 768
Iowa Wesleyan University, Mount Pleasant IA p. 771
Iowa Western Community College, Clarinda IA p. 740
Ipnatchiaq Public Library, Deering AK p. 44
Ipswich Public Library, Ipswich MA p. 1026
Iqaluit Centennial Library, *see* Nunavut Public Library Services, Iqaluit NU p. 2625
Ira Township Branch Library, *see* Saint Clair County Library System, Fair Haven MI p. 1142
Iraan Public Library, Iraan TX p. 2202
Iredell County Public Library, Statesville NC p. 1717
Ireland Billy Cartoon Library & Museum, *see* Ohio State University LIBRARIES, Columbus OH p. 1775
Iris Swedlund School & Public Library, Velva ND p. 1740
Iron Range Research Center Library, *see* Minnesota Discovery Center, Chisholm MN p. 1170
Iron Ridge Public Library, Iron Ridge WI p. 2442
Irondale Public Library, Irondale AL p. 23
Irondequoit Public Library, Rochester NY p. 1628
Ironwood Carnegie Public Library, Ironwood MI p. 1119
Ironwood Library, *see* Phoenix Public Library, Phoenix AZ p. 72
Ironwood State Prison Library, *see* California Department of Corrections Library System, Blythe CA p. 207
Iroquois County Genealogical Society, Watseka IL p. 659
Iroquois Indian Museum Library, Howes Cave NY p. 1548
Irricana & Rural Municipal Library, Irricana AB p. 2544
Irvine Commuity Library, *see* Irvine Community Library, Irvine AB p. 2544
Irvine Community Library, Irvine AB p. 2544
Irvine Valley College Library, Irvine CA p. 153
Irving Addison Beck Library, *see* Miriam Hospital, Providence RI p. 2039
Irving Harriet Library, *see* University of New Brunswick Libraries, Fredericton NB p. 2601
Meek Irving Jr Memorial Library, *see* McNairy County Libraries, Adamsville TN p. 2087
Irving Public Library, Irving TX p. 2202
Irvington Public Library, Irvington NJ p. 1409
Irvington Public Library, Irvington NY p. 1550
Irwin Army Community Hospital Medical Library, *see* United States Army, Fort Riley KS p. 808
Irwin Library, *see* Butler University Libraries, Indianapolis IN p. 690
Irwin Robert C Public Library, *see* First Regional Library, Tunica MS p. 1220
Irwindale Public Library, Irwindale CA p. 153
ISA - The International Society of Automation, Research Triangle Park NC p. 1712
Pringle Isabelle Community Library, *see* Department of Community Services, Government of Yukon, Carcross YT p. 2757
Isaly Samuel D Library, *see* Ohio Genealogical Society, Bellville OH p. 1750
Isanti County Historical Society, Cambridge MN p. 1168
ISB/PAB Library, *see* Salt River Project Library, Tempe AZ p. 79
Ische John P Library, *see* Louisiana State University Health Sciences Center, New Orleans LA p. 901
Ishpeming Carnegie Public Library, Ishpeming MI p. 1119
Islamic Da'wah Center Library, Houston TX p. 2196
Island Free Library, Block Island RI p. 2029
Island Library, *see* Eastern Shore Public Library, Chincoteague VA p. 2301
Island Park Public Library, *see* Fremont County District Library, Island Park ID p. 530
Island Park Public Library, Island Park NY p. 1550
Island Pond Public Library, Island Pond VT p. 2286
Island Trees Public Library, Levittown NY p. 1562
Isle La Motte Library, Isle La Motte VT p. 2286
Isleton Library, *see* Sacramento Public Library, Isleton CA p. 209
Islip Public Library, Islip NY p. 1551
Isothermal Community College Library, Spindale NC p. 1717
ISST Library, *see* Administrative Tribunals Support Services of Canada, Ottawa ON p. 2664
Istituto Italiano di Cultura, Biblioteca, New York NY p. 1589
Italian Cultural Institute Library, Toronto ON p. 2690
Italian Cultural Institute of Montreal La Bibliotheque, Montreal QC p. 2725
Itasca Community College Library, Grand Rapids MN p. 1177
Itasca Community Library, Itasca IL p. 602
Itasca County Historical Society, Grand Rapids MN p. 1177
Itawamba Community College, Fulton MS p. 1216
Itawamba Community College, Tupelo MS p. 1233
Ithaca College Library, Ithaca NY p. 1552
IU Ball Memorial Hospital, Muncie IN p. 708
IU Health Medical Library, Indianapolis IN p. 696
Iuka Public Library, *see* Northeast Regional Library, Iuka MS p. 1216
Ivanhoe Public Library, Ivanhoe MN p. 1179
Ivany Campus Library, *see* Nova Scotia Community College, Dartmouth NS p. 2619
Ivey Beryl Library, *see* Brescia University College, London ON p. 2653
Ivey Stinceon Memorial Library, *see* Fairmont First Baptist Church, Fairmont NC p. 1688
Ivins, Philips & Barker Library, Washington DC p. 370
Ivoryton Library Association, Ivoryton CT p. 319
Ivy Tech Community College, Anderson IN p. 668
Ivy Tech Community College, Evansville IN p. 682
Ivy Tech Community College, Indianapolis IN p. 697
Ivy Tech Community College, Lafayette IN p. 701
Ivy Tech Community College, Madison IN p. 704
Ivy Tech Community College, Sellersburg IN p. 717
Ivy Tech Community College, South Bend IN p. 718
Ivy Tech Community College, Terre Haute IN p. 721
Ivy Tech Community College, Fort Wayne IN p. 684
Ivy Tech Community College-Northwest, Gary IN p. 687
Ivy Tech Community College of Indiana, Bloomington IN p. 671
Ivy Tech Community College of Indiana, Logansport IN p. 703
Iwasaki Library, *see* Emerson College, Boston MA p. 995
IWK Health, Halifax NS p. 2619
Izard County Library, Calico Rock AR p. 92
Izard County Library, Horseshoe Bend AR p. 98
Izard County Library, Melbourne AR p. 104
J Sargeant Reynolds Community College Library, Richmond VA p. 2340
Jackman Public Library, Jackman ME p. 928
Jacksboro Public Library, Jacksboro TN p. 2102
Jackson-Butts County Public Library, *see* Flint River Regional Library System, Jackson GA p. 481
Jackson Center Memorial, *see* Shelby County Libraries, Jackson Center OH p. 1820
Jackson City Library, Jackson OH p. 1791
Jackson Community College, Jackson MI p. 1119
Jackson County Historical Society, Independence MO p. 1250
Jackson County Historical Society Library, Lakefield MN p. 1180
Jackson County Law Library, Jackson OH p. 1792
Jackson County Law Library, Medford OR p. 1886
Jackson County Law Library, Inc, Kansas City MO p. 1255
Jackson County Library, Newport AR p. 106
Jackson County Library, Jackson MN p. 1179
Jackson County Library, Kadoka SD p. 2077
Jackson County Library Services, Medford OR p. 1886
Jackson County Memorial Library, Edna TX p. 2173
Jackson County Public Library, Walden CO p. 297
Jackson County Public Library, McKee KY p. 869

Jefferson Township Public Library, Oak Ridge NJ p. 1430
Jeffersonville Headquarters Branch, *see* Western Sullivan Public Library, Jeffersonville NY p. 1558
Jeffersonville Township Public Library, Jeffersonville IN p. 698
Jellico Public Library, Jellico TN p. 2103
Jemez Pueblo Community Library & Archives, Jemez Pueblo NM p. 1470
Jemez Springs Public Library, Jemez Springs NM p. 1470
Jemison Public Library, *see* Chilton Clanton Public Library, Jemison AL p. 12
Jenkins Arthur D Library, *see* George Washington University Museum & The Textile Museum, Washington DC p. 367
Jenkins County Memorial Library, *see* Screven-Jenkins Regional Library, Millen GA p. 498
Jenkins Law Library, Philadelphia PA p. 1982
Jenkins Public, *see* Letcher County Public Library District, Jenkins KY p. 877
Jenkins Research Library, *see* International Mission Board, Southern Baptist Convention, Richmond VA p. 2340
Jenkins Sallie Harrell Memorial Library, *see* Albemarle Regional Library, Aulander NC p. 1727
Jenkins William R Architecture & Art Library, *see* University of Houston, Houston TX p. 2199
Jenkintown Library, Jenkintown PA p. 1947
Jenks Library, *see* Gordon College, Wenham MA p. 1064
Jenner & Block Library, Chicago IL p. 562
Jennings Carnegie Public Library, Jennings LA p. 892
Jennings City Library, Jennings KS p. 816
Jennings County Public Library, North Vernon IN p. 711
Jennings Library, *see* Caldwell University, Caldwell NJ p. 1393
Jennings Music Library, *see* Bennington College, Bennington VT p. 2279
Jennings Public Library, *see* Suwannee River Regional Library, Jennings FL p. 419
Jennings, Strouss & Salmon, Phoenix AZ p. 70
Jensen Lettie W Public Library, Amherst WI p. 2420
Jensen Lillian Anderson Memorial Library, *see* Mondak Heritage Center, Sidney MT p. 1302
Jensen Memorial Library, Minden NE p. 1325
Jericho Public Library, Jericho NY p. 1558
Jericho Town Library, Jericho VT p. 2287
Jermain John Memorial Library, Sag Harbor NY p. 1634
Jernigan James C Library, *see* Texas A&M University-Kingsville, Kingsville TX p. 2206
Jerome Public Library, Jerome AZ p. 63
Jerome Public Library, Jerome ID p. 523
Jersey City Free Public Library, Jersey City NJ p. 1409
Jersey Shore Public Library, Jersey Shore PA p. 1947
Jersey Shore University Medical Center, Neptune NJ p. 1423
Jerseyville Public Library, Jerseyville IL p. 603
Jervis Public Library Association, Inc, Rome NY p. 1632
Jessamine County Public Library, Nicholasville KY p. 870
Jessup Betty Sue Library, *see* Piedmont Virginia Community College, Charlottesville VA p. 2309
Jessup Correctional Institute, Jessup MD p. 969
Jesup Library, *see* Coastal Pines Technical College, Jesup GA p. 503
Jesup Memorial Library, Bar Harbor ME p. 916
Jesup Public Library, Jesup IA p. 762
Jet Propulsion Laboratory Library, *see* California Institute of Technology, Pasadena CA p. 193
Jetmore Public Library, Jetmore KS p. 816
Jeudevine Memorial Library, Hardwick VT p. 2285
Jewell Public Library, Jewell KS p. 816
Jewish Community Center, Louisville KY p. 865
Jewish Community Center of Greater Rochester, Rochester NY p. 1628
Jewish Community Center of Metropolitan Detroit, West Bloomfield MI p. 1158
Jewish Community Library, San Francisco CA p. 225
Jewish Community Relations Council, Minneapolis MN p. 1184
Jewish General Hospital, Montreal QC p. 2725
Jewish Historical Society of Central Jersey Library, New Brunswick NJ p. 1424
Jewish Historical Society of New Jersey, Whippany NJ p. 1455
Jewish Hospital, Cincinnati OH p. 1761
Jewish Museum of Maryland, Baltimore MD p. 953
Jewish Public Library, *see* Bibliotheque Publique Juive, Montreal QC p. 2717
Jewish Theological Seminary Library, New York NY p. 1589
JFCS Holocaust Center, San Francisco CA p. 225
JFK Medical Center, Edison NJ p. 1400
Jimenez Zenobia & Juan Ramon Room, *see* University of Puerto Rico Library System, San Juan PR p. 2515
Jimmy Swaggart Bible College & Seminary Library, Baton Rouge LA p. 883
JKM Library, *see* Lutheran School of Theology, Chicago IL p. 564
Joanne Cole-Mitte Memorial Library, *see* Burnet County Library System, Bertram TX p. 2152
Jocko Valley Library, Arlee MT p. 1287
Jodrey Isabel & Roy Memorial Library, *see* Annapolis Valley Regional Library, Hantsport NS p. 2616
Joeten-Kiyu Public Library, Saipan MP p. 2507
Johann Carl Memorial Library, *see* Culver-Stockton College, Canton MO p. 1240
John & Mable Ringling Museum of Art, Sarasota FL p. 443
John A Burns School of Medicine, Honolulu HI p. 512
John A Gupton College, Nashville TN p. 2118
John Abbott College, Sainte-Anne-de-Bellevue QC p. 2734
John Brown University Library, Siloam Springs AR p. 110
John Carroll University, University Heights OH p. 1826
John Clayton Fant Memorial Library, *see* Mississippi University For Women, Columbus MS p. 1215
Kennedy John F Memorial Library, *see* Hialeah Public Libraries, Hialeah FL p. 408
John F Kennedy University Libraries, Pleasant Hill CA p. 195
John Jay College of Criminal Justice, New York NY p. 1589
John Marshall Law School, Atlanta GA p. 465
John Van Puffelen Library, Mount Hope WV p. 2410
John Wood Community College Library, Quincy IL p. 637
Johns Hopkins University Libraries, Baltimore MD p. 954
Johns Hopkins University Libraries, Columbia MD p. 963
Johns Hopkins University-Peabody Conservatory of Music, Baltimore MD p. 954
Johns Hopkins University School of Advanced International, Washington DC p. 370
John's Island Regional, *see* Charleston County Public Library, Johns Island SC p. 2049
Johns Theodore R Sr Branch Library, *see* Beaumont Public Library System, Beaumont TX p. 2145
Johnsburg Public Library District, Johnsburg IL p. 603
Johnson & Wales University, Denver CO p. 276
Johnson & Wales University, Charlotte NC p. 1680
Johnson & Wales University Library, Providence RI p. 2038
Johnson A Holmes Memorial Library, *see* Kodiak Public Library, Kodiak AK p. 48
Johnson Andrew National Historic Site Library, *see* National Park Service, Greeneville TN p. 2100
Johnson Arthur Memorial Library, Raton NM p. 1473
Johnson C Smith University, Charlotte NC p. 1680
Johnson City Library District, Johnson City TX p. 2204
Johnson City Medical Center Learning Resources Center, *see* Ballad Health, Johnson City TN p. 2103
Johnson City Public Library, Johnson City TN p. 2104
Johnson Clarella Hackett Public Library, Sand Creek WI p. 2475
Johnson College, Scranton PA p. 2004
Johnson County Community College, Overland Park KS p. 829
Johnson County Historical Society, Warrensburg MO p. 1285
Johnson County Law Library, Olathe KS p. 828
Johnson County Library, Overland Park KS p. 830
Johnson County Library, Buffalo WY p. 2491
Johnson County Public Library, Franklin IN p. 686
Johnson County Public Library, Paintsville KY p. 872
Johnson County Public Library, Mountain City TN p. 2117
Johnson Creek Public Library, Johnson Creek WI p. 2443
Johnson Doris Library, *see* Southwestern Christian College, Terrell TX p. 2248
Johnson Ella Memorial Public Library District, Hampshire IL p. 596
Johnson Family Library, *see* Lorain County Historical Society, Elyria OH p. 1784
Johnson Free Public Library, Hackensack NJ p. 1406
Johnson George F Memorial Library, Endicott NY p. 1531
Johnson Georgie G, *see* Rapides Parish Library, Lecompte LA p. 880
Johnson Harold F Library Center, *see* Hampshire College Library, Amherst MA p. 984
Johnson J Fred Memorial Library, *see* Kingsport Public Library & Archives, Kingsport TN p. 2104
Johnson James Weldon, *see* Saint Petersburg Public Library, Saint Petersburg FL p. 441
Johnson Jay Public Library, Quinter KS p. 833
Johnson Jerry Crail Earth Sciences & Map Library, *see* University of Colorado Boulder, Boulder CO p. 268
Johnson Lawrence V Library, *see* Kennesaw State University Library System, Marietta GA p. 483
Johnson Library, *see* Olympic College, Shelton WA p. 2360
Johnson Lois Memorial Library, Oakdale NE p. 1327
Johnson Louis A VA Library Service, *see* Department of Veterans Affairs, Clarksburg WV p. 2401
Johnson Lyndon B National Historical Park, *see* National Park Service, Johnson City TX p. 2204
Lyndon Baines Johnson Presidential Library, *see* National Archives & Records Administration, Austin TX p. 2140
Johnson Martin & Osa Safari Museum, Chanute KS p. 801
Johnson Mary Lou Hardin County District Library, Kenton OH p. 1792
Johnson Memorial, *see* Defiance Public Library, Hicksville OH p. 1781
Johnson Memorial Library, *see* Dauphin County Library System, Millersburg PA p. 1940
Johnson Mildred Library, *see* North Dakota State College of Science, Wahpeton ND p. 1741
Johnson Milo P Library, *see* Mount San Jacinto College, San Jacinto CA p. 230
Johnson Neighborhood Library, *see* Houston Public Library, Houston TX p. 2196
Johnson Norman B Memorial Library, *see* First Reformed Church of Schenectady, Schenectady NY p. 1637
Johnson Orlen J Health Sciences Library, *see* McLaren Bay Region Health Sciences Library, Bay City MI p. 1083
Johnson Oscar Memorial Library, Silverhill AL p. 35
Johnson Pauline Library, Lundar MB p. 2588
Johnson Public Library, Johnson VT p. 2287
Johnson Public Library, Darlington WI p. 2430

Kahuku Public & School Library, *see* Hawaii State Public Library System, Kahuku HI p. 507
Kahului Public Library, *see* Hawaii State Public Library System, Kahului HI p. 508
Kaibab Paiute Public Library, Fredonia AZ p. 61
Kailua-Kona Public Library, *see* Hawaii State Public Library System, Kailua-Kona HI p. 508
Kailua Public Library, *see* Hawaii State Public Library System, Kailua HI p. 508
Kaimuki Public Library, *see* Hawaii State Public Library System, Honolulu HI p. 508
Kaiser Herman & Kate Library, *see* Tulsa City-County Library, Tulsa OK p. 1866
Kaiser Permanente, Portland OR p. 1891
Kaiser-Permanente Medical Center, Fontana CA p. 142
Kaiser-Permanente Medical Center, Los Angeles CA p. 162
Kaiser-Permanente Medical Center, Riverside CA p. 201
Kaiser-Permanente Medical Center, Sacramento CA p. 209
Kaiser-Permanente Medical Center, San Francisco CA p. 225
Kaiser-Permanente Medical Center, San Rafael CA p. 236
Kaiser Permanente Northwest Regional Libraries, Clackamas OR p. 1875
Kalama Public Library, Kalama WA p. 2367
Kalamazoo College Library, Kalamazoo MI p. 1121
Kalamazoo Institute of Arts, Kalamazoo MI p. 1121
Kalamazoo Public Library, Kalamazoo MI p. 1121
Kalamazoo Valley Community College Libraries, Kalamazoo MI p. 1121
Kaleida Health - Buffalo General Medical Center, Buffalo NY p. 1509
Kales Carl Memorial Library, *see* Beth El Temple Center, Belmont MA p. 988
Kalihi-Palama Public Library, *see* Hawaii State Public Library System, Honolulu HI p. 508
Kalkaska County Library, Kalkaska MI p. 1122
Kalmbach Media, Waukesha WI p. 2484
Kalona Public Library, Kalona IA p. 762
Kaltreider-Benfer Library, Red Lion PA p. 2001
Kanab City Library, Kanab UT p. 2265
Kanawha County Public Library, Charleston WV p. 2400
Kanawha Public Library, Kanawha IA p. 762
Kandiyohi County Historical Society, Willmar MN p. 1208
Kane County Law Library & Self Help Legal Center, Saint Charles IL p. 644
Kaneohe Public Library, *see* Hawaii State Public Library System, Kaneohe HI p. 508
Kaneville Public Library District, Kaneville IL p. 604
Kankakee Community College, Kankakee IL p. 604
Kankakee County Historical Society Museum Library, Kankakee IL p. 604
Kankakee Public Library, Kankakee IL p. 604
Kanopolis Public Library, Kanopolis KS p. 816
Kansas City Art Institute Library, Kansas City MO p. 1255
Kansas City Kansas Community College Library, Kansas City KS p. 816
Kansas City, Kansas Public Library, Kansas City KS p. 816
Kansas City Library Service Program (N), Kansas City MO p. 2769
Kansas City Public Library, Kansas City MO p. 1255
Kansas City University, Kansas City MO p. 1256
Kansas City VA Medical Center Library, *see* Department of Veterans Affairs, Kansas City MO p. 1255
Kansas Community Memorial Library, Kansas IL p. 604
Kansas Department of Corrections, El Dorado KS p. 806
Kansas Department of Corrections, Ellsworth KS p. 806
Kansas Department of Corrections, Hutchinson KS p. 814
Kansas Department of Corrections, Lansing KS p. 818
Kansas Department of Corrections, Larned KS p. 818
Kansas Department of Corrections, Topeka KS p. 838
Kansas Department of Transportation Library, Topeka KS p. 838
Kansas Heritage Center Library, Dodge City KS p. 804
Kansas Historical Society, Topeka KS p. 838
Kansas Juvenile Correctional Complex Library, *see* Kansas Department of Corrections, Topeka KS p. 838
Kansas Public Library, Kansas OK p. 1851
Kansas State Library, Emporia KS p. 807
Kansas State University at Salina, Salina KS p. 835
Kansas State University Libraries, Manhattan KS p. 822
Kansas Supreme Court, Topeka KS p. 838
Kansas University Medical Center, Kansas City KS p. 817
Kansas Wesleyan University, Salina KS p. 835
Kapaa Public Library, *see* Hawaii State Public Library System, Kapaa HI p. 508
Kapi'olani Community College Library, Honolulu HI p. 512
Kaplan Family Library & Learning Center, *see* Mount Saint Mary College, Newburgh NY p. 1605
Kaplan Mordecai M Library, *see* Reconstructionist Rabbinical College Library, Wyncote PA p. 2024
Kapolei Public Library, *see* Hawaii State Public Library System, Kapolei HI p. 508
Kapp Frederic T Memorial Library, *see* Cincinnati Psychoanalytic Institute, Cincinnati OH p. 1760
Kappe Library, *see* Southern California Institute of Architecture, Los Angeles CA p. 168
Kapuskasing Public Library, Kapuskasing ON p. 2648
Kardon-Northeast - Sol Schoenbach Library, *see* Settlement Music School, Philadelphia PA p. 1986
Kare Morley R Library, *see* Monell Chemical Senses Center, Philadelphia PA p. 1983
Kares Library, *see* Athens State University Library, Athens AL p. 5
Karjala Genealogy & History Research Center/Itasca Veterans, *see* Itasca County Historical Society, Grand Rapids MN p. 1177
Karlen Memorial Library, Beemer NE p. 1307
Karlstad Public Library, *see* Northwest Regional Library, Karlstad MN p. 1205
Karrmann Elton S Library, *see* University of Wisconsin - Platteville, Platteville WI p. 2470
Karnes City Public Library, Karnes City TX p. 2204
Karnes County Library System, Falls City TX p. 2176
Karre Fred Memorial Library, *see* Southeastern Community College Library, Keokuk IA p. 791
Kaskaskia College Library, Centralia IL p. 551
Kaslo & District Public Library, Kaslo BC p. 2568
Kasner Reference Library, *see* Catholic Archives of Texas, Austin TX p. 2139
Kass Judaic Library, *see* Bender Jewish Community Center of Greater Washington, Rockville MD p. 973
Kasson Public Library, Kasson MN p. 1179
Katahdin Public Library, Island Falls ME p. 927
Katonah Village Library, Katonah NY p. 1559
Katten Muchin Rosenman LLP, New York NY p. 1590
Katten, Muchin, Rosenman LLP Library, Chicago IL p. 562
Katz Bennett D Library, *see* University of Maine at Augusta Libraries, Augusta ME p. 915
Katz Herbert D Center for Advanced Judaic Studies Library, Philadelphia PA p. 1982
Katz Joel A Law Library, *see* University of Tennessee, Knoxville TN p. 2107
Katzen International Inc Library, Cincinnati OH p. 1761
Kauai Community College, Lihue HI p. 514
Kauai Community Correctional Center Library, Lihue HI p. 514
Kaubisch Memorial Public Library, Fostoria OH p. 1786
Kauffman Library, *see* Alliant International University, Fresno CA p. 144
Kaufman County Library, Kaufman TX p. 2204
Kaukauna Public Library, Kaukauna WI p. 2444
Kaw City Public Library, Kaw City OK p. 1851
Kawartha Lakes Public Library, Lindsay ON p. 2652
Kaweah Delta Health Care District Library, Visalia CA p. 257
KC-LSP (N), *see* Kansas City Library Service Program, Kansas City MO p. 2769
Keaau Public & School Library, *see* Hawaii State Public Library System, Keaau HI p. 508
Keach Family Library, *see* Nueces County Public Libraries, Robstown TX p. 2233
Kealakekua Public Library, *see* Hawaii State Public Library System, Kealakekua HI p. 508
Kean University, Union NJ p. 1448
Keansburg Waterfront Public Library, Keansburg NJ p. 1410
Kearl Jim & Mary Library of Cardston, Cardston AB p. 2530
Kearney & Area Public Library, Kearney ON p. 2649
Kearney Public Library, Kearney NE p. 1319
Kearny County Library, Lakin KS p. 818
Kearny Public Library, Kearny AZ p. 63
Kearny Public Library, Kearny NJ p. 1410
Keck Memorial Library, Wapello IA p. 788
Keefe Science Library, *see* Amherst College, Amherst MA p. 984
Keel Jimmie B Regional Library, *see* Tampa-Hillsborough County Public Library System, Tampa FL p. 449
Keeler Ruth Memorial Library, North Salem NY p. 1608
Keen Mountain Correctional Center, Oakwood VA p. 2336
Keen Sally Stretch Memorial Library, Vincentown NJ p. 1449
Keene Gayle Nelson Public Library, *see* Otonabee-South Monaghan Township Public Library, Keene ON p. 2649
Keene Memorial Library, Fremont NE p. 1314
Keene Public Library, Keene NH p. 1369
Keene Public Library, Keene NY p. 1559
Keene State College, Keene NH p. 1369
Keene Valley Library Association, Keene Valley NY p. 1559
Keeneland Association, Lexington KY p. 862
Keeneland Library, *see* Keeneland Association, Lexington KY p. 862
Keephills Public Library, Duffield AB p. 2534
Keeseville Free Library, Keeseville NY p. 1559
Keeter John Ed Public Library of Saginaw, *see* Saginaw Public Library, Saginaw TX p. 2235
Keethanow Public Library, Stanley Mission SK p. 2751
Keewatin Public Library, Keewatin MN p. 1179
Keffer Charles J Library, *see* University of Saint Thomas, Minneapolis MN p. 1203
Keg River Community Library, Keg River AB p. 2544
Kegler Brown Hill + Ritter, Columbus OH p. 1773
Kegoayah Kozga Public Library, Nome AK p. 49
Kehillat Beth Israel, Ottawa ON p. 2667
Kehillat Israel Reconstructionist Congregation Library, Pacific Palisades CA p. 191
Keiser Public, *see* Mississippi County Library System, Keiser AR p. 91
Keiser University Library System, Fort Lauderdale FL p. 401
Keiss Library & Learning Commons, *see* Gwynedd Mercy University, Gwynedd Valley PA p. 1939
Keleher Learning Commons - De Paul Library, *see* University of Saint Mary, Leavenworth KS p. 820
Kellar Library, *see* Baptist Missionary Association, Jacksonville TX p. 2203
Kellenberger Edward P Library, *see* Bushnell University, Eugene OR p. 1878
Keller Christoph Jr Library, *see* General Theological Seminary, New York NY p. 1586
Keller Helen Public Library, Tuscumbia AL p. 38
Keller J J & Associates, Inc, Neenah WI p. 2463

Krausz Charles E Library, *see* Temple University School of Podiatric Medicine, Philadelphia PA p. 1986
Krauth Memorial Library, *see* Lutheran Theological Seminary, Philadelphia PA p. 1982
Kravitz Dr Henry Library, *see* Jewish General Hospital, Montreal QC p. 2725
Kresge Anna Emma Memorial Library, *see* Covenant College, Lookout Mountain GA p. 485
Kresge Engineering Library, *see* University of California, Berkeley, Berkeley CA p. 123
Kresge Law Library, *see* University of Detroit Mercy School of Law, Detroit MI p. 1099
Kresge Law Library, *see* University of Notre Dame, Notre Dame IN p. 711
Kresge Learning Resource Center, *see* Meharry Medical College Library, Nashville TN p. 2119
Kresge Library, *see* Oakland University Library, Rochester MI p. 1144
Kresge Library, *see* Scripps Research Institute, La Jolla CA p. 154
Kretsch Brain Resource Library, *see* Chance to Grow, Minneapolis MN p. 1183
Krieble Library, *see* Lyme Academy College of Fine Arts, Old Lyme CT p. 332
Kripke-Veret Collection of the Jewish Federation, Omaha NE p. 1329
Krishnamurti Foundation of America, Ojai CA p. 188
Krishnamurti Library & Study Center, *see* Krishnamurti Foundation of America, Ojai CA p. 188
Kroeker Hilda Library, *see* Calvary University, Kansas City MO p. 1254
Kroemer Wayne & Barbara Library, *see* Concordia Theological Seminary, Fort Wayne IN p. 684
Krohn Memorial Library, Lebanon PA p. 1953
Kronkosky Bandera Public Library, *see* Kronkosky Albert & Bessie Mae Library, Bandera TX p. 2144
Krotona Institute of Theosophy Library, Ojai CA p. 188
Krotz Springs Municipal Public Library, Krotz Springs LA p. 892
Krueger Darrell W Library, *see* Winona State University, Winona MN p. 1209
Krum Public Library, Krum TX p. 2207
Krupp Douglas & Judith Library, *see* Bryant University, Smithfield RI p. 2042
Kubie Lawrence S Medical Library, *see* Sheppard Pratt Health Systems, Baltimore MD p. 956
Kuehner Fred C Memorial Library, *see* Reformed Episcopal Seminary, Blue Bell PA p. 1914
Kugluktuk Community Library, *see* Nunavut Public Library Services, Kugluktuk NU p. 2625
Kuhn Albin O Library & Gallery, *see* University of Maryland, Baltimore County, Baltimore MD p. 958
Kulish Psychoanalytic Library, *see* Michigan Psychoanalytic Institute & Society, Farmington Hills MI p. 1104
Kuna Library District, Kuna ID p. 523
Kurth Memorial Library, Lufkin TX p. 2214
Kusalaba Michael Branch Library, *see* Public Library of Youngstown & Mahoning County, Youngstown OH p. 1836
Kuskokwim Consortium Library, Bethel AK p. 43
Kutak Robert J Memorial Library, *see* United States Department of Justice, Aurora CO p. 265
Kutak Rock LLP, Omaha NE p. 1329
Kutztown Community Library, Kutztown PA p. 1949
Kutztown University, Kutztown PA p. 1949, 2791
Kuyper College, Grand Rapids MI p. 1111
Kwantlen Polytechnic University Library, Surrey BC p. 2576
Kyle Public Library, Kyle TX p. 2207
La Center Community Library, *see* Fort Vancouver Regional Library District, La Center WA p. 2391
La Conner Regional Library, La Conner WA p. 2368
La Crescent Public Library, La Crescent MN p. 1179
La Crete Community Library, La Crete AB p. 2544
La Crosse County Library, Holmen WI p. 2441
La Crosse Public Library, La Crosse IN p. 700
La Crosse Public Library, La Crosse WI p. 2446
La Farge Oliver Branch Library, *see* Santa Fe Public Library, Santa Fe NM p. 1476
La Fayette-Walker County Public Library, *see* Cherokee Regional Library System, LaFayette GA p. 484
La Follette Public Library, La Follette TN p. 2108
La Glace Community Library, La Glace AB p. 2544
La Grange Association Library, LaGrangeville NY p. 1561
La Grange College, LaGrange GA p. 484
La Grange Memorial Library, *see* Troup-Harris Regional Library System, LaGrange GA p. 484
La Grange Park Public Library District, La Grange Park IL p. 606
La Grange Public Library, La Grange IL p. 605
La Grange Public Library, *see* Neuse Regional Library, La Grange NC p. 1699
La Habra Library, *see* OC Public Libraries, La Habra CA p. 238
La Harpe Carnegie Public Library District, La Harpe IL p. 606
La Joya Municipal Library, La Joya TX p. 2207
La Marque Public Library, La Marque TX p. 2207
La Moisson Public, *see* Haut-Saint-Jean Regional Library, Saint Quentin NB p. 2600
La Moure School & Public Library, La Moure ND p. 1737
La Palma Library, *see* OC Public Libraries, La Palma CA p. 238
La Plata Public Library, La Plata MO p. 1259
La Porte County Public Library, La Porte IN p. 700
La Quinta Library, *see* Riverside County Library System, La Quinta CA p. 202
La Retama Central Library, *see* Corpus Christi Public Libraries, Corpus Christi TX p. 2160
La Roche University, Pittsburgh PA p. 1994
La Salle County Library - Encinal Branch, *see* Alexander Memorial Library, Cotulla TX p. 2161
La Salle University, Philadelphia PA p. 1982
La Societe d'Histoire de Sherbrooke, Sherbrooke QC p. 2737
La Societe Historique de Saint-Boniface Bibliotheque, Saint Boniface MB p. 2589
La Valle Public Library, La Valle WI p. 2447
La Vergne Public Library, La Vergne TN p. 2108
La Veta Public Library, *see* La Veta Regional Library District, La Veta CO p. 287
La Veta Regional Library District, La Veta CO p. 287
La Vista Public Library, La Vista NE p. 1320
Labette Community College Library, Parsons KS p. 831
Laboratoire de Sciences Judiciaires et de Medicine Legale, Montreal QC p. 2725
Laboure College, Milton MA p. 1036
Lac Courte Oreilles Ojibwa Community College, Hayward WI p. 2441
Lac Du Bonnet Regional Library, Lac du Bonnet MB p. 2588
Lac La Biche County Libraries, Lac La Biche AB p. 2544
Lac Qui Parle County Historical Society, Madison MN p. 1181
Laceyville Public Library, Laceyville PA p. 1950
LaChance Library, *see* Mount Wachusett Community College Library, Gardner MA p. 1020
Lackawanna College, Scranton PA p. 2004
Lackawanna County Law Library, Scranton PA p. 2004
Lackawanna County Library System, Scranton PA p. 2004
Lackawanna Historical Society Library, Scranton PA p. 2004
Lackawanna Public Library, Lackawanna NY p. 1561
Lacombe Public Library, Lacombe AB p. 2545
Lacon Public Library District, Lacon IL p. 606
Lacona Public Library, Lacona IA p. 763
Laconia Public Library, Laconia NH p. 1370
Ladd George & Helen Library, *see* Bates College, Lewiston ME p. 929
Ladd Public Library District, Ladd IL p. 606
Ladner Pioneer Library, *see* Fraser Valley Regional Library, Delta BC p. 2561
Ladoga-Clark Township Public Library, Ladoga IN p. 701
Ladson Genealogical Library, *see* Ohoopee Regional Library System, Vidalia GA p. 502
Ladson Research Library & Archives, *see* Sandy Spring Museum, Sandy Spring MD p. 977
Ladwig Jack R Memorial Library, *see* Hometown Public Library, Hometown IL p. 601
Lady Lake Public Library, Lady Lake FL p. 414
Ladysmith Public Library, *see* Rusk County Community Library, Ladysmith WI p. 2447
LA84 Foundation, Los Angeles CA p. 162
LAF Library, Chicago IL p. 563
Lafayette College, Easton PA p. 1928
Lafayette County-Oxford Public Library, *see* First Regional Library, Oxford MS p. 1220
Lafayette County Public Library, Lewisville AR p. 99
Lafayette County Public Library, Mayo FL p. 420
Lafayette Library, *see* Contra Costa County Library, Lafayette CA p. 174
Lafayette-Orinda Presbyterian Church Library, Lafayette CA p. 155
Lafayette Pilot Public Library, *see* Bradshaw H Grady Chambers County Library, Lafayette AL p. 39
Lafayette Public Library, Lafayette CO p. 288
Lafayette Public Library, Lafayette LA p. 892
LaFayette Public Library, LaFayette NY p. 1561
Lafayette Science Museum, Lafayette LA p. 893
Lafayette-Yalobusha Learning Resource Center Library, *see* Northwest Mississippi Community College, Oxford MS p. 1228
Lafourche Parish Public Library, Thibodaux LA p. 911
Lagace Raymond Public Library, *see* Chaleur Library Region, Atholville NB p. 2599
Lago Vista Public Library, Lago Vista TX p. 2208
LaGrange County Public Library, LaGrange IN p. 701
Laguna Beach Library, *see* OC Public Libraries, Laguna Beach CA p. 238
Laguna College of Art & Design (LCAD), Laguna Beach CA p. 155
Laguna Public Library, Laguna NM p. 1470
Laguna Vista Public Library, Laguna Vista TX p. 2208
Lahaina Public Library, *see* Hawaii State Public Library System, Lahaina HI p. 509
Lahey Hospital & Medical Center, Burlington MA p. 1004
Lahti Elisabeth Library, *see* Martin County Library System, Indiantown FL p. 445
Lai Him Mark Branch Library, *see* San Francisco Public Library, San Francisco CA p. 228
Laidlaw Library, University College, *see* University of Toronto Libraries, Toronto ON p. 2699
Laingsburg Public Library, Laingsburg MI p. 1123
Laird Flora M Memorial Library, *see* Myrtle Point Library, Myrtle Point OR p. 1888
Lake Agassiz Regional Library, Moorhead MN p. 1188
Lake Alfred Public Library, Lake Alfred FL p. 415
Lake Andes Carnegie Public Library, Lake Andes SD p. 2078
Lake Area Technical Institute Library, Watertown SD p. 2085
Lake Benton Public Library, Lake Benton MN p. 1179
Lake Blackshear Regional Library System, Americus GA p. 458
Lake Bluff Public Library, Lake Bluff IL p. 606
Lake Campus Library & Technology Center, *see* Wright State University, Celina OH p. 1757
Lake City Public Library, Lake City IA p. 763
Lake City Public Library, Lake City MN p. 1180
Lake City Public Library, *see* Florence County Library System, Lake City SC p. 2058
Lake City Public Library, *see* Hinsdale County Library District, Lake City CO p. 288
Lake County Historical Society, Painesville OH p. 1812

Lake County Historical Society Library, Tavares FL p. 450
Lake County Law Library, Lakeport CA p. 156
Lake County Library, Lakeport CA p. 156
Lake County Library District, Lakeview OR p. 1884
Lake County Library System, Tavares FL p. 450
Lake County Public Library, Leadville CO p. 289
Lake County Public Library, Merrillville IN p. 705
Lake Dallas Public Library, Lake Dallas TX p. 2208
Lake Elmo Branch, *see* Washington County Library, Lake Elmo MN p. 1210
Lake Elsinore Library, *see* Riverside County Library System, Lake Elsinore CA p. 202
Lake Erie College, Painesville OH p. 1812
Lake Erie College of Osteopathic Medicine, Erie PA p. 1931
Lake Forest College, Lake Forest IL p. 606
Lake Forest Library, Lake Forest IL p. 606
Lake Geneva Public Library, Lake Geneva WI p. 2447
Lake Helen Public, *see* Volusia County Public Library, Lake Helen FL p. 393
Lake Hills Library, *see* King County Library System, Bellevue WA p. 2366
Lake Land College Library, Mattoon IL p. 615
Lake Lillian Public Library, Lake Lillian MN p. 1180
Lake Los Angeles Library, *see* County of Los Angeles Public Library, Palmdale CA p. 136
Lake Mead National Recreation Area Library, Boulder City NV p. 1343
Lake Michigan College, Benton Harbor MI p. 1084
Lake Mills Public Library, Lake Mills IA p. 764
Lake Odessa Community Library, Lake Odessa MI p. 1123
Lake Oswego Public Library, Lake Oswego OR p. 1884
Lake Park Public Library, Lake Park FL p. 415
Lake Park Public Library, Lake Park IA p. 764
Lake Placid Memorial Library, *see* Highlands County Library, Lake Placid FL p. 444
Lake Placid Public Library, Lake Placid NY p. 1561
Lake Public Library, Lake MS p. 1224
Lake Region Community College, Laconia NH p. 1370
Lake Region Public Library, Devils Lake ND p. 1731
Lake Region State College, Devils Lake ND p. 1731
Lake Ridge Library, *see* Prince William Public Libraries, Woodbridge VA p. 2339
Lake Stevens Library, *see* Sno-Isle Libraries, Lake Stevens WA p. 2370
Lake-Sumter State College Library, Leesburg FL p. 418
Lake Superior College, Duluth MN p. 1172
Lake Superior State University, Sault Sainte Marie MI p. 1149
Lake Tahoe Community College, South Lake Tahoe CA p. 247
Lake Tahoe Prim Library, *see* University of Nevada-Reno, Incline Village NV p. 1349
Lake Tamarisk Library, *see* Riverside County Library System, Desert Center CA p. 202
Lake Travis Community Library, Austin TX p. 2139
Lake View Public Library, Lake View IA p. 764
Lake Villa District Library, Lindenhurst IL p. 609
Lake Village Memorial Township Library, *see* Newton County Public Library, Lake Village IN p. 702
Lake Wales Public Library, Lake Wales FL p. 416
Lake Washington Institute of Technology, Kirkland WA p. 2367
Lake Whitney Public Library, Whitney TX p. 2257
Lake Worth Beach City Library, Lake Worth Beach FL p. 416
Lake Wylie Public, *see* York County Library, Lake Wylie SC p. 2068
Lakehead University, Thunder Bay ON p. 2685
Lakehills Area Library, Lakehills TX p. 2208
Lakeland College, Lloydminster SK p. 2742
Lakeland College Library, Vermilion AB p. 2558
Lakeland Community College Library, Kirtland OH p. 1793
Lakeland Health Care, Saint Joseph MI p. 1148
Lakeland Library Cooperative (N), Grand Rapids MI p. 2767
Lakeland Library Region, North Battleford SK p. 2743
Lakeland Public Library, Lakeland FL p. 417
Lakeland Regional Library, Killarney MB p. 2587
Lakeland University, Plymouth WI p. 2470
Lakeport Library, *see* Lake County Library, Lakeport CA p. 156
Lakeridge Health, Oshawa ON p. 2663
Lakes Arthur Library, *see* Colorado School of Mines, Golden CO p. 282
Lakes Country Public Library, Lakewood WI p. 2447
Lakes Environmental Association, Bridgton ME p. 918
Lakes Regional, *see* Lee County Library System, Fort Myers FL p. 403
Lakeshore Museum Center Archives, Muskegon MI p. 1136
Lakeshore Technical College Library, Cleveland WI p. 2428
Lakeside Community Library, *see* Libraries of Stevens County, Nine Mile Falls WA p. 2369
Lakeside Library, *see* Riverside County Library System, Lake Elsinore CA p. 202
Lakeside Public Library, Lakeside OR p. 1884
Lakeview Area Public Library, Sandy Lake PA p. 2003
Lakeview College of Nursing, Danville IL p. 575
Lakeview Community Library, Random Lake WI p. 2472
Lakeview Public Library, Rockville Centre NY p. 1631
Lakeville Public Library, Lakeville MA p. 1026
Lakewood Historical Society Library, Lakewood OH p. 1793
Lakewood Memorial Library, Lakewood NY p. 1561
Lakewood Neighborhood Library, *see* Houston Public Library, Houston TX p. 2196
Lakewood Public Library, Lakewood OH p. 1793
Lakewood Ranch, *see* Manatee County Public Library System, Lakewood Ranch FL p. 387
Lakewood/Smokey Point Library, *see* Sno-Isle Libraries, Arlington WA p. 2370
Lakota City Library, Lakota ND p. 1737
Lakota Public Library, Lakota IA p. 764
Lallouise Florey McGraw Public Library, Vincent AL p. 39
Lam David Management Research Library, *see* University of British Columbia Library, Vancouver BC p. 2580
Lama Library, *see* Kapi'olani Community College Library, Honolulu HI p. 512
Laman William F Public Library, North Little Rock AR p. 106
Lamar Community College Library & Learning Resource Center, Lamar CO p. 289
Lamar County Library System, Purvis MS p. 1230
Lamar Memorial Library, *see* Maryville College, Maryville TN p. 2111
Lamar Public Library, Lamar CO p. 289
Lamar State College, Port Arthur TX p. 2228
Lamar State College Orange Library, Orange TX p. 2224
Lamar University, Beaumont TX p. 2146
Lamb County Library, Littlefield TX p. 2212
Lamb Frank I, *see* Pueblo City-County Library District, Pueblo CO p. 293
Lamb Miriam B Memorial, *see* Sampson-Clinton Public Library, Garland NC p. 1681
Lamberton Public Library, Lamberton MN p. 1180
Lambertville Free Public Library, Lambertville NJ p. 1411
Lambton College, Sarnia ON p. 2676
Lambton County Library, Wyoming ON p. 2705
Lameque Public Library, *see* Chaleur Library Region, Lameque NB p. 2599
LaMoille-Clarion Public Library District, LaMoille IL p. 607
Lamoni Public Library, Lamoni IA p. 764
Lamont Library, *see* Harvard Library, Cambridge MA p. 1007
Lamont Memorial Free Library, McGraw NY p. 1570
Lamont Public Library, Lamont IA p. 764
Lamont Public Library, Lamont AB p. 2545
Lampasas Public Library, Lampasas TX p. 2209
Lamson Herbert H Library, *see* Plymouth State University, Plymouth NH p. 1378
Lanai Public & School Library, *see* Hawaii State Public Library System, Lanai City HI p. 509
Lanark Public Library, Lanark IL p. 607
Lancaster Bible College, Lancaster PA p. 1951
Lancaster Campus Library, *see* Harrisburg Area Community College, Lancaster PA p. 1951
Lancaster Community Library, Kilmarnock VA p. 2327
Lancaster County Law Library, Lancaster PA p. 1951
Lancaster County Library, Lancaster SC p. 2064
Lancaster Public Library, Lancaster NY p. 1562
Lancaster Public Library, Lancaster PA p. 1951
Lancaster Public Library, *see* Schreiner Memorial Library, Lancaster WI p. 2447
Lancaster Theological Seminary Library, Lancaster PA p. 1951
Lancaster Veterans Memorial Library, Lancaster TX p. 2209
LancasterHistory, Lancaster PA p. 1951
LancasterHistory Research Center, Lancaster PA p. 1951
Land O'Lakes Public Library, Land O'Lakes WI p. 2448
Lander Branch Library & Headquarters, *see* Fremont County Library System, Lander WY p. 2496
Lander Clara Library, *see* Winnipeg Art Gallery, Winnipeg MB p. 2596
Lander Memorial Regional, *see* Anderson County Library, Williamston SC p. 2047
Lander University, Greenwood SC p. 2062
Landes John Community Center, *see* Oceanside Public Library, Oceanside CA p. 187
Landis Valley Village & Farm Museum, Lancaster PA p. 1951
Landman Bette E Library, *see* Arcadia University, Glenside PA p. 1937
Landmark College Library, Putney VT p. 2292
LandMark Communications, Greensboro NC p. 1692
Landmark Society of Western New York, Inc, Rochester NY p. 1628
Lane College Library, Jackson TN p. 2102
Lane Community College Library, Eugene OR p. 1878
Lane County Law Library, Eugene OR p. 1879
Lane County Library, Dighton KS p. 804
Lane Library, *see* Georgia Southern University, Savannah GA p. 495
Lane Library, *see* Ripon College, Ripon WI p. 2474
Lane Library District, Creswell OR p. 1877
Lane Medical Library, *see* Stanford University Libraries, Stanford CA p. 248
Lane Medical Library, *see* United States Army, Fort Carson CO p. 280
Lane Memorial Library, Hampton NH p. 1366
Lane Powell PC, Portland OR p. 1891
Lane Public Libraries, Hamilton OH p. 1789
Lanesboro Public Library, Lanesboro MN p. 1180
Lanesborough Public Library, Lanesborough MA p. 1027
Laney College, Oakland CA p. 185
Lanford Charles A MD Library, *see* Middle Georgia Regional Library System, Macon GA p. 487
Lang Memorial Library, Wilson KS p. 844
Lang Norman McKee Library, *see* Lester B Pearson College of the Pacific, Victoria BC p. 2583
Lang Stewart B Memorial Library, Cato NY p. 1514
Langara College, Vancouver BC p. 2795
Langara College Library, Vancouver BC p. 2579
Langdon Library, Newington NH p. 1376
Langenheim Memorial Library, *see* Thiel College, Greenville PA p. 1939
Langley-Adams Library, Groveland MA p. 1022
Langley Library, *see* Sno-Isle Libraries, Langley WA p. 2370
Langley Public Library, Langley OK p. 1851
Langlois Public Library, Langlois OR p. 1884
Langsam Walter C Library, *see* University of Cincinnati Libraries, Cincinnati OH p. 1764

Langson Library, *see* University of California Irvine Libraries, Irvine CA p. 153
Langston University, Langston OK p. 1851
Langworthy Public Library, Hope Valley RI p. 2033
Lanier Library Association, Tryon NC p. 1719
Lanier Technical College, Cumming GA p. 473
Lanier Technical College, Dawsonville GA p. 475
Lanier Technical College, Gainesville GA p. 480
Lankenau Institute for Medical Research, Wynnewood PA p. 2025
Lanpher Memorial Library, Hyde Park VT p. 2286
Lansdale Public Library, Lansdale PA p. 1952
Lansdowne Public Library, Lansdowne PA p. 1953
L'Anse Area School-Public Library, L'Anse MI p. 1123
Lansing Community College Library, Lansing MI p. 1124
Lansing Community Library, Lansing KS p. 818
Lansing Community Library, Lansing NY p. 1562
Lansing Correctional Facility Library, *see* Kansas Department of Corrections, Lansing KS p. 818
Lansing Public Library, Lansing IL p. 607
Lantana Public Library, Lantana FL p. 417
Lapeer District Library, Lapeer MI p. 1126
Lapidus Sam Memorial Public Library, *see* First Regional Library, Crenshaw MS p. 1220
Lara SSgt Salvador J Casa Blanca Library, *see* Riverside Public Library, Riverside CA p. 203
Larabee Nora E Memorial Library, Stafford KS p. 837
Laramie County Community College, Cheyenne WY p. 2492
Laramie County Library System, Cheyenne WY p. 2492
Laramie Plains Museum Association Inc Library, Laramie WY p. 2496
LARC (N), *see* Library Association of Rockland County, New City NY p. 2771
Larchmont Public Library, Larchmont NY p. 1562
Larchwood Public Library, Larchwood IA p. 764
Larder Lake Public Library, Larder Lake ON p. 2652
Laredo College, Laredo TX p. 2209
Largo Public Library, Largo FL p. 417
Larkin, Hoffman, Daly & Lindgren, Minneapolis MN p. 1184
Larkspur Public Library, Larkspur CA p. 156
Larned Correctional Mental Health Facility Library, *see* Kansas Department of Corrections, Larned KS p. 818
Larned State Hospital, Larned KS p. 818
Larsen Family Public Library, Webster WI p. 2486
Larsen-Sant Public Library, *see* Franklin County Library District, Preston ID p. 529
Lartz Memorial Library, *see* Penn State Shenango, Sharon PA p. 2006
Larue County Public Library, Hodgenville KY p. 859
Las Animas - Bent County Public Library, Las Animas CO p. 289
Las Cruces Public Libraries, Las Cruces NM p. 1470
Las Positas College Library, Livermore CA p. 156
Las Vegas-Clark County Library District, Las Vegas NV p. 1346
Las Vegas FamilySearch Genealogy Library, Las Vegas NV p. 1347
Lasalle Parish Library, Jena LA p. 891
LaSalle Public Library, LaSalle IL p. 607
Lasater Elliott Maysville Public Library, Maysville OK p. 1852
Lasell College, Newton MA p. 1039
Laskey Virginia Davis Research Library, Nashville TN p. 2118
Laskin Bora Law Library, *see* University of Toronto Libraries, Toronto ON p. 2699
Lassen Community College Library, Susanville CA p. 251
Lassen Library District, Susanville CA p. 251
Lassen Volcanic National Park Library, *see* National Park Service, Mineral CA p. 177
Latah County Historical Society Library, Moscow ID p. 526
Latah County Library District, Moscow ID p. 526
Latham & Watkins, San Diego CA p. 215
Latham & Watkins, Chicago IL p. 563
Latham & Watkins, New York NY p. 1590
Latham Memorial Library, Thetford VT p. 2296
Lathlin Oscar Research Library, *see* University College of the North Libraries, The Pas MB p. 2591
Latimer County Public Library, Wilburton OK p. 1869
Latimer Dale P Library, *see* Saint Vincent College & Seminary Library, Latrobe PA p. 1953
Latimer George Central, *see* Saint Paul Public Library, Saint Paul MN p. 1202
Latter Milton H Memorial Library, *see* New Orleans Public Library, New Orleans LA p. 903
Latzer Louis Memorial Public Library, Highland IL p. 599
Lauderdale County Library, Ripley TN p. 2125
Laughlin Library, *see* Las Vegas-Clark County Library District, Laughlin NV p. 1347
Laughlin Memorial Library, Ambridge PA p. 1906
Lauinger Joseph Mark Library, *see* Georgetown University, Washington DC p. 367
Laumeier Sculpture Park Library & Archive, Saint Louis MO p. 1271
Launders Science Library, *see* Saint Lawrence University, Canton NY p. 1514
Laupahoehoe Public & School Library, *see* Hawaii State Public Library System, Laupahoehoe HI p. 509
Laupus William E Health Sciences Library, *see* East Carolina University, Greenville NC p. 1693
Laurel Community Learning Center & Public Library, Laurel NE p. 1320
Laurel County Public Library District, London KY p. 864
Laurel Highlands Library, *see* State Correctional Institution, Somerset PA p. 2008
Laurel-Jones County Library, *see* Laurel-Jones County Library System, Inc, Laurel MS p. 1224
Laurel-Jones County Library System, Inc, Laurel MS p. 1224
Laurel Public Library, Laurel DE p. 353
Laurel Public Library, Laurel MT p. 1298
Laurel Public Library, *see* Franklin County Public Library District, Laurel IN p. 673
Laurelton Community Library, *see* Queens Library, Laurelton NY p. 1555
Laurens County Library, Laurens SC p. 2064
Laurens Public Library, Laurens IA p. 765
Laurentian Forestry Centre Library, *see* Natural Resources Canada-Forestry, Quebec City QC p. 2732
Laurentian Hills Public Library, Deep River ON p. 2638
Laurentian University Library & Archives, Sudbury ON p. 2683
Laurie Blanche & Irving Performing Arts Library, *see* Rutgers University Libraries, New Brunswick NJ p. 1425
Lauritsen Charles C Library, *see* Aerospace Corp, El Segundo CA p. 140
Lava Beds National Monument Research Library, *see* National Park Service, Tulelake CA p. 253
Lavaca Library, *see* Scott-Sebastian Regional Library, Lavaca AR p. 97
Laval-Goupil Public Library, *see* Chaleur Library Region, Shippagan NB p. 2599
LaValley Law Library, *see* University of Toledo, Toledo OH p. 1825
Lavery Library, *see* Saint John Fisher University, Rochester NY p. 1630
LaVista Correctional Facility Library, *see* Colorado Department of Corrections, Pueblo CO p. 293
Law Library, *see* Meserve, Mumper & Hughes, Los Angeles CA p. 166
Law Library, *see* Polsinelli, Kansas City MO p. 1257
Law Library, *see* Third Judicial Circuit Court, Wayne County, Detroit MI p. 1099
Law Library Association of Saint Louis, Saint Louis MO p. 1271
Law Library for San Bernardino County, San Bernardino CA p. 212
Law Library of Chiesa, Shahinian & Giantomasi, Roseland NJ p. 1440
Law Library of Kings County, Brooklyn, *see* New York State Supreme Court Library, Brooklyn NY p. 1505
Law Library of Louisiana, New Orleans LA p. 901
Law Library of Montgomery County, Norristown PA p. 1971
Law Library of the Massachusetts Attorney General, Boston MA p. 996
Law Society of New Brunswick Library, Fredericton NB p. 2600
Law Society of Newfoundland Law Library, St. John's NL p. 2610
Law Society of Prince Edward Island, Charlottetown PE p. 2707
Law Society of Saskatchewan Libraries, Regina SK p. 2746
Law Society of Upper Canada, Toronto ON p. 2690
Lawler Public Library, Lawler IA p. 765
Lawrence & Memorial Hospital, New London CT p. 329
Lawrence Carl G Library, *see* Durfee Mike State Prison, Springfield SD p. 2083
Lawrence Correctional Center Library, *see* Illinois Department of Corrections, Sumner IL p. 653
Lawrence County Federated Library System, New Castle PA p. 1968
Lawrence County Law Library, New Castle PA p. 1969
Lawrence County Bar Library Association, Ironton OH p. 1791
Lawrence County Library, Walnut Ridge AR p. 111
Lawrence County Public Library, Moulton AL p. 30
Lawrence County Public Library, Louisa KY p. 864
Lawrence County Public Library, Lawrenceburg TN p. 2108
Lawrence County Public Library, *see* Lincoln-Lawrence-Franklin Regional Library, Monticello MS p. 1213
Lawrence Jerry Memorial Library, *see* Harrison County Library System, D'Iberville MS p. 1217
Lawrence Law Library, Lawrence MA p. 1027
Lawrence Library, Pepperell MA p. 1046
Lawrence Livermore National Laboratory, Livermore CA p. 157
Lawrence Marian O Library, *see* Sacramento Public Library, Galt CA p. 209
Lawrence Marion Memorial Library, Gratis OH p. 1788
Lawrence Memorial District Library, Climax MI p. 1091
Lawrence Memorial Library, Bristol VT p. 2280
Lawrence Public Library, Lawrence KS p. 819
Lawrence Public Library, Fairfield ME p. 924
Lawrence Public Library, Lawrence MA p. 1027
Lawrence Public Library District, Lawrenceville IL p. 607
Lawrence Samuel Crocker Library, *see* Grand Lodge of Masons in Massachusetts, Boston MA p. 995
Lawrence Technological University Library, Southfield MI p. 1151
Lawrence University, Appleton WI p. 2420
Lawrenceburg Public Library District, Lawrenceburg IN p. 702
Laws Railroad Museum & Historical Site Library, Bishop CA p. 124
Lawson Edith S Library, *see* Jefferson Parish Library, Westwego LA p. 897
Lawson Research Library, *see* Kandiyohi County Historical Society, Willmar MN p. 1208
Lawson State Community College Library, Bessemer AL p. 6
Lawson State Community College Library, Birmingham AL p. 8
Lawton Memorial Library, La Farge WI p. 2447
Lawton Public Library, Lawton MI p. 1126
Lawton Public Library, Lawton OK p. 1852
Lay Park Resource Center, *see* Athens Regional Library System, Athens GA p. 458
Layland Museum, Cleburne TX p. 2156
LCEI (N), *see* Library Consortium of Eastern Idaho, Rigby ID p. 2764
LCHIB (N), *see* Library Consortium of Health Institutions in Buffalo, Buffalo NY p. 2771
LDAY Resource Library, *see* Learning Disabilites Association of Yukon, Whitehorse YT p. 2758

Lemieux A A Library, *see* Seattle University, Seattle WA p. 2380
Lemmon Public Library, Lemmon SD p. 2078
Lemon Gene & Cathie Art Research Library, *see* Phoenix Art Museum, Phoenix AZ p. 71
Lemont Public Library District, Lemont IL p. 608
LeMoyne-Owen College, Memphis TN p. 2112
Lena Community District Library, Lena IL p. 608
Lena Public Library, Lena WI p. 2448
Lena Sam, *see* Pima County Public Library, Tucson AZ p. 82
Lenawee District Library, Adrian MI p. 1075
Lenhardt Library of the Chicago Botanic Garden, Glencoe IL p. 593
Lenig-Focht Library, *see* Perry Historians, New Bloomfield PA p. 1968
Lennox & Addington County Public Library, Napanee ON p. 2660
Lenoir City Public Library, Lenoir City TN p. 2109
Lenoir Community College, Kinston NC p. 1699
Lenoir-Rhyne University, Columbia SC p. 2053
Lenoir-Rhyne University Libraries, Hickory NC p. 1696
Lenora Blackmore Branch, *see* Henry County Library, Windsor MO p. 1242
Lenora Public Library, Lenora KS p. 820
Lenox Gary J Library, *see* University of Wisconsin-Rock County Library, Janesville WI p. 2443
Lenox Library Association, Lenox MA p. 1027
Lenox Public Library, Lenox IA p. 765
Lenox Township Library, New Haven MI p. 1137
Dehon Leo Library, *see* Sacred Heart Seminary & School of Theology, Franklin WI p. 2436
Leola Public Library, Leola SD p. 2078
Leominster Public Library, Leominster MA p. 1028
Leon County Library, Centerville TX p. 2155
Leon Public Library, Leon IA p. 765
Leon Public Library, Leon KS p. 820
Leon-Saxeville Township Library, Pine River WI p. 2469
Leon Valley Public Library, Leon Valley TX p. 2211
Shore Leonard E Memorial Library, *see* Blue Mountains Public Library, Thornbury ON p. 2684
Leonard J Paul Library, *see* San Francisco State University, San Francisco CA p. 228
Leonard Public Library, Leonard TX p. 2211
Leonard William Public Library District, Robbins IL p. 640
Leonardtown Library (Headquarters), *see* Saint Mary's County Library, Leonardtown MD p. 971
Leonardville City Library, Leonardville KS p. 821
Leonia Public Library, Leonia NJ p. 1412
Leoville Public Library, *see* Wapiti Regional Library, Leoville SK p. 2745
LePage Georgette, *see* Bibliotheque de Brossard, Brossard QC p. 2710
Lepper Public Library, Lisbon OH p. 1796
Lerners LLP Library, London ON p. 2654
Leroy Community Library, LeRoy MI p. 1127
LeRoy Historical Society Library, LeRoy NY p. 1562
Les Archives de la Ville de Quebec, Quebec QC p. 2731
Les Cheneaux Community, *see* Superior District Library, Cedarville MI p. 1149
Lesack Bohdan Memorial Library, *see* Surrey Memorial Hospital, Surrey BC p. 2577
Lesbian, Bisexual, Gay & Transgender Community Center, New York NY p. 1590
Lesbian Herstory Archives, Brooklyn NY p. 1505
Lesbian Herstory Educational Foundation Inc, *see* Lesbian Herstory Archives, Brooklyn NY p. 1505
Lesley University, Cambridge MA p. 1008
Leslie County Public Library, Hyden KY p. 860
Leslie Library, *see* Capital Area District Libraries, Leslie MI p. 1124
Lester B Pearson College of the Pacific, Victoria BC p. 2583
Lester Charles & Joann Library, Nekoosa WI p. 2464
Lester Library, *see* Patrick Henry Community College, Martinsville VA p. 2332
Lester Louise R Library, *see* Beaufort County Community College, Washington NC p. 1720
Lester Public Library, Two Rivers WI p. 2482
Lester Public Library of Arpin, Arpin WI p. 2421
Lester Public Library of Rome, Nekoosa WI p. 2464
Lester Public Library of Vesper, Vesper WI p. 2482
Letcher County Public Library District, Whitesburg KY p. 877
Lethbridge College, Lethbridge AB p. 2546
Lethbridge Public Library, Lethbridge AB p. 2546
LeTourneau University, Longview TX p. 2213
Letts Public Library, Letts IA p. 765
Levack/Onaping Public Library-Earl Jarvis Branch, *see* Greater Sudbury Public Library, Onaping ON p. 2683
Leverett Library, Leverett MA p. 1028
Levesque Raymond Bibliotheque, *see* Bibliotheques Publiques de Longueuil, Longueuil QC p. 2716
Levi Heywood Memorial Library, Gardner MA p. 1020
Levin Louis R Memorial Library, *see* Curry College, Milton MA p. 1036
Levine Sklut Judaic Library, Charlotte NC p. 1680
Levitt Library, *see* Mercy Medical Center, Des Moines IA p. 747
Levittown Public Library, Levittown NY p. 1562
Levy County Public Library System, Bronson FL p. 387
Levy Economics Institute Library, *see* Bard College, Annandale-on-Hudson NY p. 1487
Levy Gustave L & Janet W Library, *see* Ican School of Medicine at Mount Sinai, New York NY p. 1588
Levy Leon Dental Medicine Library, *see* University of Pennsylvania Libraries, Philadelphia PA p. 1988
Lewellen Public Library, Lewellen NE p. 1320
Lewes Public Library, Lewes DE p. 354
Lewis & Clark College, Portland OR p. 1891
Lewis & Clark Community College, Godfrey IL p. 594
Lewis & Clark Library, Helena MT p. 1296
Lewis & Clark Trail Heritage Foundation, Inc, Great Falls MT p. 1294
Lewis A C Memorial Library, *see* Grambling State University, Grambling LA p. 890
Lewis Baach Kaufmann Middlemiss PLLC Library, Washington DC p. 370
Lewis, Brisbois, Bisgaard & Smith, Los Angeles CA p. 162
Lewis-Clark State College Library, Lewiston ID p. 524
Lewis County Law Library, Lowville NY p. 1566
Lewis County Law Library, Chehalis WA p. 2361
Lewis County Public Library, Vanceburg KY p. 876
Lewis County Public Library & Archives, Hohenwald TN p. 2101
Lewis Family Branch, *see* Ontario City Library, Ontario CA p. 188
Lewis Frank & Laura Library, *see* La Grange College, LaGrange GA p. 484
Lewis George & Leona Library, *see* Albany College of Pharmacy & Health Sciences, Albany NY p. 1481
Lewis Gibson D Health Science Library, *see* University of North Texas Health Science Center at Fort Worth, Fort Worth TX p. 2181
Lewis Hazel M Library, Powers OR p. 1895
Henrietta G Lewis Library, *see* Niagara County Community College, Sanborn NY p. 1635
Lewis Library, *see* Loyola University Chicago Libraries, Chicago IL p. 563
Lewis Library & Technology Center, *see* San Bernardino County Library, Fontana CA p. 213
Lewis Library of Glasgow, Glasgow MO p. 1247
Lewis Music Library, *see* Massachusetts Institute of Technology Libraries, Cambridge MA p. 1008
Lewis Paula A Branch Library, *see* Saint Lucie County Library System, Port Saint Lucie FL p. 405
Lewis Public Library & Heritage Center, Lewis IA p. 765
Lewis Roca Rothgerber Christie LLP, Denver CO p. 276
Lewis Ron E Library, *see* Lamar State College Orange Library, Orange TX p. 2224
Lewis Rufus A, *see* Montgomery City-County Public Library System, Montgomery AL p. 29
Lewis Science Library, *see* Princeton University, Princeton NJ p. 1437
Lewis University Library, Romeoville IL p. 642
Lewis W W Memorial, *see* Cape Breton Regional Library, Louisbourg NS p. 2622
Lewisboro Library, South Salem NY p. 1643
Lewisohn Irene Costume Reference Library, *see* Metropolitan Museum of Art, New York NY p. 1591
Lewison Memorial Library, *see* Mount Sinai Hospital Medical Center, Chicago IL p. 565
Lewiston-Auburn College Library, *see* University of Southern Maine Libraries, Lewiston ME p. 937
Lewiston City Library, Lewiston ID p. 524
Lewiston Public, *see* Montmorency County Public Libraries, Lewiston MI p. 1081
Lewiston Public Library, Lewiston ME p. 929
Lewiston Public Library, Lewiston NY p. 1563
Lewiston Public Library, Lewiston UT p. 2265
Lewistown Branch, *see* Northeast Missouri Library Service, Lewistown MO p. 1254
Lewistown Carnegie Public Library District, Lewistown IL p. 608
Lewistown Public Library, Lewistown MT p. 1298
Lewisville Community Library, *see* Chester County Library, Richburg SC p. 2052
Lewisville Legacy Library, Lewisville ID p. 524
Lewisville Public Library System, Lewisville TX p. 2211
Lexington County Public Library System, Lexington SC p. 2064
Lexington Historical Society, Lexington MA p. 1028
Lexington Public, *see* Mid-Mississippi Regional Library System, Lexington MS p. 1224
Lexington Public Library, Lexington AL p. 24
Lexington Public Library, Lexington KY p. 862
Lexington Public Library, Lexington NE p. 1320
Lexington Public Library District, Lexington IL p. 608
Lexington Theological Seminary, Lexington KY p. 863
Lexmark Library, *see* University of Kentucky Libraries, Lexington KY p. 863
Libby Memorial Library, Old Orchard Beach ME p. 934
Liberal Memorial Library, Liberal KS p. 821
Liberty Center Public Library, Liberty Center OH p. 1795
Liberty County Library, Chester MT p. 1290
Liberty Hill Public Library, Liberty Hill TX p. 2211
Liberty Lake Municipal Library, Liberty Lake WA p. 2368
Liberty Library, Liberty ME p. 929
Liberty Municipal Library, Liberty TX p. 2211
Liberty Mutual, Boston MA p. 996
Liberty Public Library, Liberty NY p. 1563
Liberty University Library, Lynchburg VA p. 2330
Libhart Jimmie Library, *see* Cochise County Library District, Bowie AZ p. 56
Librarians of the Upper Valley Coop (N), Etna NH p. 2769
Libraries at Rochester Regional Health, Rochester NY p. 1628
Libraries in Clackamas County (N), Oregon City OR p. 2773
Libraries of Foster, Foster RI p. 2032
Libraries of Stevens County, Loon Lake WA p. 2369
Libraries Online, Inc (N), Middletown CT p. 2762
Library & Academic Information Services, *see* Barnard College, New York NY p. 1579
Library & Academic Resource Center, *see* Central Wyoming College Library, Riverton WY p. 2498
Library & Archives, *see* Haggin Museum, Stockton CA p. 249
Library & Archives Canada, Ottawa ON p. 2667
Library & Information Resources Network (LIRN) (N), Clearwater FL p. 2763

Lincoln Land Community College Library, Springfield IL p. 650
Lincoln Law School of San Jose, San Jose CA p. 230
Lincoln-Lawrence-Franklin Regional Library, Brookhaven MS p. 1213
Lincoln Library, Springfield IL p. 650
Lincoln Library, Medicine Lodge KS p. 825
Lincoln Library, Lincoln VT p. 2287
Lincoln Library, *see* Veterans Home of California, Yountville CA p. 261
Lincoln Medical Center, Bronx NY p. 1499
Lincoln Memorial Library, Yountville CA p. 261
Lincoln Memorial Library, Dennysville ME p. 923
Lincoln Memorial Library, Lincoln ME p. 930
Lincoln Memorial Library, *see* Larue County Public Library, Hodgenville KY p. 859
Lincoln Memorial University, Harrogate TN p. 2100
Lincoln Park Public Library, Lincoln Park MI p. 1127
Lincoln Park Public Library, Lincoln Park NJ p. 1412
Lincoln Public Library, Lincoln AL p. 24
Lincoln Public Library, Lincoln AR p. 99
Lincoln Public Library, Lincoln CA p. 156
Lincoln Public Library, Lincoln MA p. 1028
Lincoln Public Library, Lincoln NH p. 1370
Lincoln Public Library, Lincoln RI p. 2033
Lincoln Public Library, Beamsville ON p. 2630
Lincoln Public Library District, Lincoln IL p. 609
Lincoln Sarah Bush Health Center, Mattoon IL p. 615
Lincoln Township Public Library, Stevensville MI p. 1152
Lincoln Trail College, Robinson IL p. 640
Lincoln University, Lincoln University PA p. 1956
Lincoln University Library, Oakland CA p. 185
Lincoln University of Missouri, Jefferson City MO p. 1252
Lincolnwood Public Library District, Lincolnwood IL p. 609
Lindell Library, *see* Augsburg University, Minneapolis MN p. 1182
Linden-Carnegie Public Library, Linden IN p. 703
Linden Free Public Library, Linden NJ p. 1412
Linden Municipal Library, Linden AB p. 2546
Linden Public Library, Linden IA p. 765
Lindenhurst Memorial Library, Lindenhurst NY p. 1563
Lindenwold Public Library, Lindenwold NJ p. 1412
Lindenwood University Library, Saint Charles MO p. 1268
Linderman Library, *see* Lehigh University, Bethlehem PA p. 1912
Lindgren Don O Library, *see* Nebraska Prairie Museum, Holdrege NE p. 1318
Lindoe Luke Library, *see* Alberta College of Arts, Calgary AB p. 2525
Lindsay Community Library, Lindsay OK p. 1852
Lindsay H Pat Library, *see* Coastal Alabama Community College, Gilbertown AL p. 6
Lindsay Kitty, *see* Richland Community College, Decatur IL p. 576
Lindsborg Community Library, Lindsborg KS p. 821
Lindsey Anne West District Library, Carterville IL p. 550
Lindsey J Stephen Medical Library, Richmond VA p. 2341
Lindsey Wilson College, Columbia KY p. 852
Lineberger Memorial Library, *see* Lenoir-Rhyne University, Columbia SC p. 2053
Linesville Community Public Library, Linesville PA p. 1956
Lineville City Library, Lineville AL p. 24
Linfield University, McMinnville OR p. 1885
Link Library, *see* Concordia University, Seward NE p. 1335
Linklaters, New York NY p. 1590
Linn-Benton Community College Library, Albany OR p. 1871
Linn County Law Library, Albany OR p. 1871
Linn County Library District No 5, Pleasanton KS p. 832
Linn County Library District Number 1, Parker KS p. 831
Linn County Library District No 3, Blue Mound KS p. 799
Linn County Library District No 2, La Cygne KS p. 818
Linn County Museum & Genealogy Library, Pleasanton KS p. 832
Linn Grove Public Library, Linn Grove IA p. 766
Linn Otto F Library, *see* Warner Pacific University, Portland OR p. 1894
Linnemann Kathryn, *see* Saint Charles City-County Library District, Saint Charles MO p. 1278
Linscheid Library, *see* East Central University, Ada OK p. 1839
Linton Public Library, Linton IN p. 703
Linton Public Library, Linton ND p. 1737
Linwood Community Library, Linwood KS p. 821
Linwood Community Library at Snowshoe, *see* Pocahontas County Free Libraries, Slatyfork WV p. 2408
Linwood Public Library, Linwood NJ p. 1412
LION (N), *see* Libraries Online, Inc, Middletown CT p. 2762
Lions Gate Hospital Library, *see* Vancouver Coastal Health, North Vancouver BC p. 2573
Lipscomb Library, *see* Randolph College, Lynchburg VA p. 2330
Lipscomb University, Nashville TN p. 2119
LIRN (N), *see* Library & Information Resources Network (LIRN), Clearwater FL p. 2763
Lisbon Library Department, Lisbon Falls ME p. 930
Lisbon Public Library, Lisbon IA p. 766
Lisbon Public Library, Lisbon NH p. 1370
Lisbon Public Library, Lisbon ND p. 1737
Lisle Free Library, Lisle NY p. 1563
Lisle Library District, Lisle IL p. 610
Liswood Sidney Library, *see* Mount Sinai Hospital, Toronto ON p. 2690
Litchfield Carnegie Public Library, Litchfield IL p. 610
Litchfield District Library, Litchfield MI p. 1127
Litchfield Historical Society, Litchfield CT p. 320
Litchfield Public Library, Litchfield MN p. 1180
Litchfield Public Library, Litchfield NE p. 1323
Litchfield Public Library, *see* Wolcott Oliver Library, Litchfield CT p. 320
Literary & Historical Society of Quebec Library, Quebec QC p. 2731
Lithgow Public Library, Augusta ME p. 914
Lithia Springs Public Library, *see* West Georgia Regional Library, Lithia Springs GA p. 470
Lithuanian Research & Studies Center, Inc, Chicago IL p. 563
Lititz Public Library, Lititz PA p. 1956
Little Big Horn College Library, Crow Agency MT p. 1291
Little Chute Public Library, Little Chute WI p. 2448
Little Compton Free Public Library, *see* Brownell Library, Little Compton RI p. 2034
Little Dixie Regional Libraries, Moberly MO p. 1262
Little E H Library, *see* Davidson College, Davidson NC p. 1683
Little Elm Public Library, Little Elm TX p. 2212
Little Falls Library, *see* Montgomery County Public Libraries, Bethesda MD p. 974
Little Falls Public Library, Little Falls NJ p. 1413
Little Falls Public Library, Little Falls NY p. 1563
Little Falls Public Library, *see* Great River Regional Library, Little Falls MN p. 1197
Little Ferry Free Public Library, Little Ferry NJ p. 1413
Little G R Library, *see* Elizabeth City State University, Elizabeth City NC p. 1687
Little Memorial Library, *see* Midway University, Midway KY p. 869
Little Priest Tribal College Library, Winnebago NE p. 1341
Little River Community Library, Little River KS p. 821
Little Rock Public Library, Little Rock IA p. 766
Little Saxton B Free Library, Inc, Columbia CT p. 306
Little Silver Public Library, Little Silver NJ p. 1413
Little Snake River Valley, *see* Carbon County Library System, Baggs WY p. 2498
Little Traverse History Museum Library, Petoskey MI p. 1140
Little Wood River District Library, Carey ID p. 519
Littlestown Library, *see* Adams County Library System, Littlestown PA p. 1935
Littleton Museum Research Center, Littleton CO p. 290
Littleton Public Library, Littleton NH p. 1371
Littleton Public Library, *see* Bemis Edwin A Public Library, Littleton CO p. 290
Littleton Regional Healthcare, Littleton NH p. 1371
Littman Barbara & Leonard, *see* New Jersey Institute of Technology, Newark NJ p. 1427
Live Oak County Library, George West TX p. 2184
Live Oak Library, *see* County of Los Angeles Public Library, Arcadia CA p. 137
Live Oak Public Libraries, Savannah GA p. 496
Lively Public Library-Earl Mumford Branch, *see* Greater Sudbury Public Library, Lively ON p. 2683
Livengood Charles H Jr Memorial Library, *see* North Carolina Department of Labor, Raleigh NC p. 1709
Livermore Mary Library, *see* University of North Carolina at Pembroke, Pembroke NC p. 1707
Livermore Public Library, Livermore CA p. 157
Livermore Public Library, Livermore IA p. 766
Livermore Public Library, Livermore ME p. 930
Liverpool Public Library, Liverpool NY p. 1564
Livingston A E Health Sciences Library, *see* Carle BroMenn Medical Center, Normal IL p. 625
Livingston County Library, Chillicothe MO p. 1242
Livingston Free Library, Livingston NY p. 1564
Livingston Library, *see* Shorter University, Rome GA p. 495
Livingston Library, *see* Webb Institute, Glen Cove NY p. 1539
Livingston Manor Free Library, Livingston Manor NY p. 1564
Livingston Municipal Library, Livingston TX p. 2212
Livingston Parish Library, Livingston LA p. 895
Livingston-Park County Public Library, Livingston MT p. 1299
Livingston Public Library, Livingston NJ p. 1413
Livingston Public Library, *see* Dietzman Allen Library, Livingston WI p. 2448
Livingstone College, Salisbury NC p. 1714
Livonia Public Library, Livonia MI p. 1127
Livonia Public Library, Livonia NY p. 1564
Lizard Butte Public Library, Marsing ID p. 525
Lizzadro Museum of Lapidary Art Library, Oak Brook IL p. 627
Llano County Library System, Llano TX p. 2212
Llano County Public Library, *see* Llano County Library System, Llano TX p. 2212
Lloyd Library & Museum, Cincinnati OH p. 1761
Lloydminster Public Library, Lloydminster AB p. 2547
LMI Library, Tysons Corner VA p. 2348
LMN (N), *see* Library Management Network, Inc, Decatur AL p. 2761
Loan System Helping Automate Retrieval of Knowledge (N), Baton Rouge LA p. 2766
LoanSHARK (N), *see* Loan System Helping Automate Retrieval of Knowledge, Baton Rouge LA p. 2766
Loar Barbara Branch, *see* DeKalb County Public Library, Tucker GA p. 476
Loch Raven Branch, *see* Baltimore County Public Library, Towson MD p. 979
Lock Haven University of Pennsylvania, Lock Haven PA p. 1956
Lock Museum of America, Inc Library, Terryville CT p. 341
Locke Don C Library, *see* Asheville-Buncombe Technical Community College, Asheville NC p. 1672
Locke E D Public Library, *see* McFarland Public Library, McFarland WI p. 2455
Locke Lord Bissell & Liddell LLP, Chicago IL p. 563
Lockesburg Public Library, *see* Tri-County Regional Library, Lockesburg AR p. 106

Madison Public Library, Madison MN p. 1181
Madison Public Library, Madison NE p. 1324
Madison Public Library, Madison NJ p. 1415
Madison Public Library, Madison OH p. 1798
Madison Public Library, Madison SD p. 2078
Madison Public Library, Madison WI p. 2449
Madison Public Library, *see* Huntsville-Madison County Public Library, Madison AL p. 22
Madison Public Library, *see* Suwannee River Regional Library, Madison FL p. 419
Madison Valley Public Library, Ennis MT p. 1292
Madisonville Community College, Madisonville KY p. 868
Madisonville Public Library, Madisonville TN p. 2110
Madoc Public Library, Madoc ON p. 2656
Madonna University Library, Livonia MI p. 1127
Madre Maria Teresa Guevara Library, *see* University of the Sacred Heart, Santurce PR p. 2515
Madrid Public Library, Madrid IA p. 766
Magale Library, *see* Southern Arkansas University, Magnolia AR p. 103
Magdalen College of the Liberal Arts, Warner NH p. 1383
Magdalena Public Library, Magdalena NM p. 1472
Magee Public Library, Magee MS p. 1225
Magee Rehabilitation Hospital, Philadelphia PA p. 1982
Magill James P Library, *see* Haverford College, Haverford PA p. 1942
Magness W H & Edgar Community House & Library, McMinnville TN p. 2111
Magnetawan First Nation Public Library, Britt ON p. 2633
Magnin George E Medical Library, *see* Marshfield Clinic, Marshfield WI p. 2454
Magnolia Library, *see* Baton Rouge Community College, Baton Rouge LA p. 882
Magnolia Library & Community Center, Gloucester MA p. 1021
Magoffin County Public Library, Salyersville KY p. 874
Magrath Library, *see* University of Minnesota Libraries-Twin Cities, Saint Paul MN p. 1185
Magrath Public Library, Magrath AB p. 2547
Maguire Charlotte Edwards Medical Library, *see* Florida State University Libraries, Tallahassee FL p. 447
Maguire Library, *see* New England Bible College & Seminary, Bangor ME p. 915
Maguire Raymer Jr Learning Resources Center, West Campus, *see* Valencia College, Orlando FL p. 433
Mahaffey Thomas Jr Business Library, *see* Hesburgh Libraries, Notre Dame IN p. 711
Mahan Edna Hall Library, *see* Correctional Institution for Women, Clinton NJ p. 1397
Mahan Oldham County Public, *see* Oldham County Public Library, Goshen KY p. 861
Mahanoy City Public Library, Mahanoy City PA p. 1957
Maharishi International University Library, Fairfield IA p. 752
Mahnomen Public Library, *see* Lake Agassiz Regional Library, Mahnomen MN p. 1188
Mahomet Public Library District, Mahomet IL p. 612
Mahoney A P Library, *see* Saint Peter's Seminary, London ON p. 2655
Mahoning County Law Library, Youngstown OH p. 1835
Mahopac Public Library, Mahopac NY p. 1567
MAHSLIN (N), *see* Massachusetts Health Sciences Library Network, Worcester MA p. 2766
Mahwah Public Library, Mahwah NJ p. 1415
Maimonides Medical Center, Brooklyn NY p. 1505
Main-a-Dieu Public, *see* Cape Breton Regional Library, Main-a-Dieu NS p. 2622
Main Branch, *see* Livingston Parish Library, Livingston LA p. 895
Main Library Alliance (N), Cedar Knolls NJ p. 2770
Main Line Health, Paoli Hospital, Paoli PA p. 1973
Main Line Reform Temple, Wynnewood PA p. 2025
Maine Charitable Mechanic Association Library, Portland ME p. 936
Maine College of Art, Portland ME p. 936
Maine Correctional Center Library, *see* Maine Department of Corrections, Windham ME p. 946
Maine Department of Corrections, Charleston ME p. 921
Maine Department of Corrections, South Portland ME p. 941
Maine Department of Corrections, Warren ME p. 944
Maine Department of Corrections, Windham ME p. 946
Maine Department of Transportation Library, Augusta ME p. 914
Maine Historical Society, Portland ME p. 936
Maine Irish Heritage Center Library, Portland ME p. 936
Maine Maritime Academy, Castine ME p. 921
Maine Maritime Museum, Bath ME p. 916
Maine State Law & Legislative Reference Library, Augusta ME p. 914
Maine State Library, Augusta ME p. 914
Maine State Library, Region 1, Portland ME p. 936
Maine State Prison Library, *see* Maine Department of Corrections, Warren ME p. 944
MaineGeneral Medical Center Library, Augusta ME p. 914
MaineHealth, Portland ME p. 936
Maitland Public Library, Maitland FL p. 419
Major Hillard Library, *see* Chesapeake Public Library, Chesapeake VA p. 2311
Majure Evelyn Taylor Library, *see* Jackson/Hinds Library System, Utica MS p. 1221
Makawao Public Library, *see* Hawaii State Public Library System, Makawao HI p. 509
Maki Library, *see* Finlandia University, Hancock MI p. 1113
Maki Sulo & Aileen Research Library, *see* Desert Research Institute, Las Vegas NV p. 1346
MALA (N), *see* Mid-America Library Alliance, Independence MO p. 2769
Malca Pass Library, *see* Kehillat Beth Israel, Ottawa ON p. 2667
Malcolm X College - Woodson Carter G Library, *see* City Colleges of Chicago, Chicago IL p. 558
Malden Public Library, Malden MA p. 1031
Mallaig Public Library, *see* Bibliotheque Mallaig Library, Mallaig AB p. 2547
Mallard Public Library, Mallard IA p. 766
MALLCO (N), *see* Mid-America Law Library Consortium, Oklahoma City OK p. 2773
Mallet Chemistry Library, *see* University of Texas Libraries, Austin TX p. 2142
Malley Henry A Memorial Library, Broadus MT p. 1290
Mallory Tracy Burr Memorial Library, *see* Massachusetts General Hospital, Boston MA p. 997
Malloy/Jordon East Winston Heritage Center, *see* Forsyth County Public Library, Winston-Salem NC p. 1725
Malone University, Canton OH p. 1755
Maloney Library, *see* Fordham University School of Law, New York NY p. 1585
Malpass Leslie F Library, *see* Western Illinois University, Macomb IL p. 612
Malta Community Center, *see* Round Lake Library, Malta NY p. 1633
Malta Township Public Library, Malta IL p. 612
Maltman Memorial Public Library, Wood River NE p. 1341
Malvern-Hot Spring County Library Headquarters, *see* Mid-Arkansas Regional Library, Malvern AR p. 103
Malvern Public Library, Malvern IA p. 766
Malvern Public Library, Malvern PA p. 1957
Malverne Public Library, Malverne NY p. 1567
Maly Eugene H Memorial Library, *see* Athenaeum of Ohio, Cincinnati OH p. 1759
Mamakating Library, Wurtsboro NY p. 1667
Mamaroneck Public Library, Mamaroneck NY p. 1567
Mamie's Place Children's Library, *see* Russell Adelia M Library, Alexander City AL p. 4
Mammoth Public Library, Mammoth AZ p. 66
Mammoth Spring Library, *see* Fulton County Library, Mammoth Spring AR p. 103
Manasquan Public Library, Manasquan NJ p. 1416
Manassas National Battlefield Park Library, Manassas VA p. 2331
Manatee County Law Library, Bradenton FL p. 386
Manatee County Public Library System, Bradenton FL p. 386
Manatt, Phelps & Phillips LLP, Washington DC p. 371
Mancelona Township Library, Mancelona MI p. 1128
Manchester-by-the-Sea Public Library, Manchester-by-the-Sea MA p. 1031
Manchester City Library, Manchester NH p. 1372
Manchester Community College Library, Manchester CT p. 320
Manchester Community College Library, Manchester NH p. 1372
Manchester Community Library, Manchester Center VT p. 2288
Manchester District Library, Manchester MI p. 1129
Manchester Historic Association Library, Manchester NH p. 1372
Manchester Historical Museum, Manchester-by-the-Sea MA p. 1031
Manchester Public Library, Manchester CT p. 320
Manchester Public Library, Manchester IA p. 767
Manchester Public Library, *see* Adams County Public Library, Manchester OH p. 1814
Manchester University, North Manchester IN p. 710
Manchester VA Medical Center Library, Manchester NH p. 1372
Mancini Nicholas Library Information Center, *see* Hamilton Wentworth Catholic District School Board, Hamilton ON p. 2646
Mancos Public Library, Mancos CO p. 291
Mancuso Neighborhood Library, *see* Houston Public Library, Houston TX p. 2196
Mandel Public Library of West Palm Beach, West Palm Beach FL p. 453
Manderino Louis L Library, *see* Pennsylvania Western University - California, California PA p. 1917
Maner Memorial Library, *see* Cisco College, Cisco TX p. 2155
Manhasset Public Library, Manhasset NY p. 1568
Manhattan Christian College Library, Manhattan KS p. 823
Manhattan College, Riverdale NY p. 1627
Manhattan Community Library, Manhattan MT p. 1299
Manhattan-Elwood Public Library District, Manhattan IL p. 613
Manhattan Public Library, Manhattan KS p. 823
Manhattan School of Music, New York NY p. 1590
Manhattanville University Library, Purchase NY p. 1624
Manheim Community Library, Manheim PA p. 1957
Manheim Township Public Library, Lancaster PA p. 1952
Manila Public, *see* Mississippi County Library System, Manila AR p. 91
Manilla Public Library, Manilla IA p. 767
Manistee County Historical Museum, Manistee MI p. 1129
Manistee County Library System, Manistee MI p. 1129
Manistique School & Public Library, Manistique MI p. 1129
Manitoba Agriculture, Food & Rural Initiatives, Portage la Prairie MB p. 2589
Manitoba Association of Playwrights, Winnipeg MB p. 2593
Manitoba Crafts Museum & Library, Winnipeg MB p. 2593
Manitoba Culture, Heritage & Tourism, Brandon MB p. 2586
Manitoba Department of Sport, Culture & Heritage, Winnipeg MB p. 2593
Manitoba Developmental Centre Memorial Library, Portage la Prairie MB p. 2589
Manitoba Genealogical Society Inc Library, Winnipeg MB p. 2593
Manitoba Hydro Library, Winnipeg MB p. 2593

Marist College, Poughkeepsie NY p. 1623
Marist College Library, Washington DC p. 371
Maritime Museum at Battleship Cove, Fall River MA p. 1018
Maritime Museum of British Columbia Library, Victoria BC p. 2583
Maritime Museum of San Diego, San Diego CA p. 215
Maritime Museum of the Atlantic, Halifax NS p. 2619
Maritimes Health Libraries Association (N), Halifax NS p. 2778
Markesan Public Library, Markesan WI p. 2454
Marketplace Library, *see* Saint Louis Public Library, Saint Louis MO p. 1275
Markham Public Library, Markham IL p. 614
Markham Public Library, Markham ON p. 2656
Markham Stouffville Hospital Library, Markham ON p. 2656
Markle Public Library, *see* Huntington City-Township Public Library, Markle IN p. 690
Markosian Library, *see* Salt Lake Community College Libraries, Taylorsville UT p. 2273
Markowitz Jewel K Library, *see* Beth David Reform Congregation, Gladwyne PA p. 1936
Marks Maud Smith, *see* Harris County Public Library, Katy TX p. 2193
Marks-Quitman County Library, Marks MS p. 1225
Markus Rita & Frits Library, *see* Rockefeller University, New York NY p. 1601
Marlboro County Library System, Bennettsville SC p. 2047
Marlboro Free Library, Marlboro NY p. 1569
Marlborough Public Library, Marlborough MA p. 1032
Marlette District Library, Marlette MI p. 1130
Marlin Public Library, *see* Chilton Pauline & Jane Memorial Marlin Public Library, Marlin TX p. 2215
Marlow Town Library, Marlow NH p. 1373
Marmion Academy Library, Aurora IL p. 539
Marmion Library, *see* Church of the Incarnation, Dallas TX p. 2163
Marmora & Lake Public Library, Marmora ON p. 2656
Maroa Public Library District, Maroa IL p. 614
Marple Public Library, Broomall PA p. 1915
Marquand Library of Art & Archaeology, *see* Princeton University, Princeton NJ p. 1437
Marquat Memorial Library, *see* United States Army, Fort Bragg NC p. 1689
Marques Rene Biblioteca, *see* Inter-American University of Puerto Rico, Arecibo PR p. 2509
Marquette Community Library, Marquette KS p. 824
Marquette Heights Public Library, Marquette Heights IL p. 614
Marquette Regional History Center, Marquette MI p. 1130
Marquette University, Milwaukee WI p. 2458
Marrero Lillian, *see* Free Library of Philadelphia, Philadelphia PA p. 1979
Marriott J Willard Library, *see* University of Utah, Salt Lake City UT p. 2272
Marrowbone Public Library District, Bethany IL p. 542
Mars Area Public Library, Mars PA p. 1958
Mars Hill University, Mars Hill NC p. 1703
Marseilles Public Library, Marseilles IL p. 614
Marsh J Frank Library, *see* Concord University, Athens WV p. 2397
Marshall & Melhorn, Toledo OH p. 1824
Marshall A D Library, *see* Eston College, Eston SK p. 2741
Marshall B Ketchum University, Fullerton CA p. 148
Marshall Community Health Library, Cameron Park CA p. 126
Marshall Community Library, Marshall WI p. 2454
Marshall County Cooperative Library, Albertville AL p. 3
Marshall County Historical Society Library, Lacon IL p. 606
Marshall County Historical Society Library, Plymouth IN p. 713
Marshall County Library System, Holly Springs MS p. 1220
Marshall County Memorial Library, Lewisburg TN p. 2109
Marshall County Public Library System, Benton KY p. 848
Marshall District Library, Marshall MI p. 1130
Marshall George C Foundation Library, Lexington VA p. 2328
Marshall John, *see* Fairfax County Public Library, Alexandria VA p. 2316
Marshall John, *see* Fauquier County Public Library, Marshall VA p. 2352
Marshall John Law School, Chicago IL p. 564
Marshall-Lyon County Library, Marshall MN p. 1182
Marshall Memorial Library, Deming NM p. 1467
Marshall Public Library, Pocatello ID p. 529
Marshall Public Library, Marshall IL p. 614
Marshall Public Library, Marshall MO p. 1260
Marshall Public Library, Marshall TX p. 2216
Marshall Thurgood, *see* Chicago Public Library, Chicago IL p. 557
Marshall Thurgood Law Library, *see* University of Maryland, Baltimore, Baltimore MD p. 957
Marshall Thurgood Library, *see* Bowie State University, Bowie MD p. 960
Marshall Thurgood School of Law Library, *see* Texas Southern University, Houston TX p. 2199
Marshall Thurgood State Law Library, Annapolis MD p. 950
Marshall University Libraries, Huntington WV p. 2405
Marshalltown Community College, Marshalltown IA p. 768
Marshalltown Public Library, Marshalltown IA p. 768
Marshallville Public, *see* Middle Georgia Regional Library System, Marshallville GA p. 487
Marshes of Glynn Libraries, Brunswick GA p. 468
Marshfield Campus Library, *see* Mid-State Technical College, Marshfield WI p. 2454
Marshfield Clinic, Marshfield WI p. 2454
Marston Memorial Historical Center & Archives, *see* Free Methodist Church USA, Indianapolis IN p. 692
Marstons Mills Public Library, Marstons Mills MA p. 1033
Martelle Public Library, Martelle IA p. 768
Marthas Vineyard Museum Lirary, Vineyard Haven MA p. 1060
Martin & Gail Press Health Professions Division Library, *see* Nova Southeastern University Libraries FL p. 402
Martin Army Community Hospital Medical Library, *see* United States Army, Fort Benning GA p. 479
Martin Bennett Public Library, *see* Lincoln City Libraries, Lincoln NE p. 1321
Martin Community College Library, Williamston NC p. 1722
Martin Correctional Institution Library, Indiantown FL p. 411
Martin County Historical Society, Inc, Fairmont MN p. 1174
Martin County Law Library, *see* Martin County Library System, Stuart FL p. 445
Martin County Library, Fairmont MN p. 1174
Martin County Library, Stanton TX p. 2245
Martin County Library System, Stuart FL p. 444
Martin County Public Library, Inez KY p. 860
Martin Elizabeth Rasmussen Memorial Library, New Hartford IA p. 772
Martin Francis, *see* New York Public Library - Astor, Lenox & Tilden Foundations, Bronx NY p. 1596
Martin Frank Lee Memorial Journalism Library, *see* University of Missouri-Columbia, Columbia MO p. 1244
Martin J W Library, *see* Northwestern Oklahoma State University, Alva OK p. 1840
Martin Kathryn A Library, *see* University of Minnesota Duluth, Duluth MN p. 1173
Martin Luther College Library, New Ulm MN p. 1190
Martin Marydean Library, *see* Nevada State University, Henderson NV p. 1346
Martin Memorial, *see* Beaufort, Hyde & Martin County Regional Library, Williamston NC p. 1720
Martin Memorial Library, York PA p. 2026
Martin Music Library, *see* New Orleans Baptist Theological Seminary, New Orleans LA p. 902
Martin Paul Law Library, *see* University of Windsor, Windsor ON p. 2704
Martin Public Library, Martin TN p. 2110
Martin Regional Library, *see* Tulsa City-County Library, Tulsa OK p. 1866
Martin Township Public Library, Colfax IL p. 573
Martindale Community Library, Martindale TX p. 2216
Martinez Library, *see* Contra Costa County Library, Martinez CA p. 174
Martins Ferry Public Library, *see* Belmont County District Library, Martins Ferry OH p. 1800
Martinsburg-Berkeley County Public Library, Martinsburg WV p. 2408
Martinsburg Community Library, Martinsburg PA p. 1958
Martinsburg Public Library, *see* Martinsburg-Berkeley County Public Library, Martinsburg WV p. 2408
Martinsville Public Library District, Martinsville IL p. 614
Marvell Library, *see* Phillips-Lee-Monroe Regional Library, Marvell AR p. 98
Marvin Dwight Library & Instructional Media Center, *see* Hudson Valley Community College, Troy NY p. 1652
Marvin Memorial Library, Shelby OH p. 1820
Marwayne Public Library, Marwayne AB p. 2547
Marx Robert S Law Library, *see* University of Cincinnati, Cincinnati OH p. 1764
Karl Mary Memorial, *see* Daytona State College Library, Daytona Beach FL p. 392
Maryland Center for History & Culture Library, Baltimore MD p. 954
Maryland Correctional Institution for Women Library, Jessup MD p. 969
Maryland Correctional Institution-Hagerstown Library, Hagerstown MD p. 967
Maryland Correctional Institution-Jessup Library, Jessup MD p. 969
Maryland Correctional Training Center Library, Hagerstown MD p. 968
Maryland Department of Legislative Services Library, Annapolis MD p. 951
Maryland Department of Planning Library, Baltimore MD p. 955
Maryland Institute College of Art, Baltimore MD p. 955
Maryland Interlibrary Loan Organization (N), Baltimore MD p. 2766
Maryland National Capital Park & Planning Commission, Clinton MD p. 962
Maryland Pharmacists Association Library, Columbia MD p. 963
Maryland State Library, Baltimore MD p. 955
Maryland State Library for the Blind & Print Disabled, Baltimore MD p. 955
Marymount California University Library, Rancho Palos Verdes CA p. 198
Marymount Manhattan College, New York NY p. 1591
Marymount University, Arlington VA p. 2305
Marystown Public Library, Marystown NL p. 2608
Marysville Library, *see* Sno-Isle Libraries, Marysville WA p. 2370
Marysville Public Library, Marysville KS p. 824
Marysville Public Library, Marysville OH p. 1800
Marysville-Rye Library, Marysville PA p. 1958
Maryville College, Maryville TN p. 2111
Maryville Community Library, Maryville IL p. 614
Maryville Public Library, Maryville MO p. 1261
Maryville University Library, Saint Louis MO p. 1271
Marywood University Library & Learning Commons, Scranton PA p. 2004
Masaryk Memorial Institute Inc, Scarborough ON p. 2677

Mayo Clinic Scottsdale Libraries, Scottsdale AZ p. 77
Mayor Joe V Sanchez Public Library, Weslaco TX p. 2256
Mayor Salvatore Mancini Union Free Public Library, *see* North Providence Union Free Library, North Providence RI p. 2036
Maysville Community & Technical College, Maysville KY p. 869
Maysville Public Library, *see* Neuse Regional Library, Maysville NC p. 1699
Maysville Public Library, *see* Piedmont Regional Library System, Maysville GA p. 482
Maytag Memorial Library, *see* Saint John Vianney College Seminary, Miami FL p. 424
Mayville District Public Library, Mayville MI p. 1131
Mayville Library, Mayville NY p. 1570
Mayville Public Library, Mayville ND p. 1737
Mayville Public Library, Mayville WI p. 2455
Mayville State University, Mayville ND p. 1737, 2790
Maywood Cesar Chavez Library, *see* County of Los Angeles Public Library, Maywood CA p. 137
Maywood Public Library, Maywood NJ p. 1417
Maywood Public Library District, Maywood IL p. 615
Mazamas Library & Archives, Portland OR p. 1892
Mazomanie Free Library, Mazomanie WI p. 2455
McAfee & Taft, Oklahoma City OK p. 1857
McAfee Memorial Library, *see* Park University Library, Parkville MO p. 1265
McAlester Public Library, McAlester OK p. 1853
McAllen Public Library, McAllen TX p. 2217
McArthur Public Library, Biddeford ME p. 917
MCAS New River Library, *see* United States Marine Corps, Jacksonville NC p. 1698
McAuliffe Christa Corrigan, *see* Framingham Public Library, Framingham MA p. 1019
McBain Community Library, McBain MI p. 1131
McBee Depot Library, *see* Chesterfield County Library System, McBee SC p. 2052
McBride & District Public Library, McBride BC p. 2569
McBride Library, *see* United States Air Force, Keesler AFB MS p. 1223
McBride Memorial Library, Berwick PA p. 1910
McBurney Memorial, *see* Davis Jefferson Parish Library, Welsh LA p. 892
McCabe Library, *see* Swarthmore College, Swarthmore PA p. 2011
McCain Andrew & Laura Public Library, *see* Haut-Saint-Jean Regional Library, Florenceville-Bristol NB p. 2600
McCain Library, *see* Agnes Scott College, Decatur GA p. 475
McCain Library, *see* Erskine College & Theological Seminary, Due West SC p. 2058
McCain Memorial Public Library, Ashville AL p. 5
McCain William David Library & Archives, *see* University of Southern Mississippi Library, Hattiesburg MS p. 1219
McCall Doy Leale Rare Book & Manuscript Library, *see* University of South Alabama Libraries, Mobile AL p. 27
McCall Public Library, McCall ID p. 525
McCallion Hazel Campus, *see* Sheridan College Library, Mississauga ON p. 2663
McCallum Jane Yelvington Public Library, *see* Wilson County Public Libraries, La Vernia TX p. 2177
McCammon Library, *see* South Bannock Library District, McCammon ID p. 520
McCardle Library, *see* Vicksburg & Warren County Historical Society, Vicksburg MS p. 1234
McCarter & English Library, Cherry Hill NJ p. 1396
McCarthy J Thomas Library, *see* Mount Saint Mary's University, Los Angeles CA p. 166
McCarthy Library, *see* Napa Valley College, Napa CA p. 182
McCarthy Tetrault LLP Library, Calgary AB p. 2528
McCarthy Tetrault LLP Library, Vancouver BC p. 2579
McCarthy Walter T Law Library, Arlington VA p. 2306
McCartney Library, *see* Geneva College, Beaver Falls PA p. 1909
McCauley Hannah V Library, *see* Ohio University-Lancaster Library, Lancaster OH p. 1794
McCaw Foundation Library of Asian Art, *see* Seattle Art Museum, Seattle WA p. 2378
McChord Library, *see* Joint Base Lewis-McChord Library System, Joint Base Lewis-McChord WA p. 2366
McClatchy Ella K Library, *see* Sacramento Public Library, Sacramento CA p. 209
McClellan Julia Crowder Memorial Library, Mounds OK p. 1854
McClintic Public Library, *see* Pocahontas County Free Libraries, Marlinton WV p. 2408
McCloskey Joseph F School of Nursing, *see* Lehigh Valley Health Network, Pottsville PA p. 1999
McCloskey Joseph F School of Nursing at Lehigh Valley Hospital, Pottsville PA p. 1999
McClung Mary Library, *see* West Georgia Technical College, Waco GA p. 502
McClung Nellie, *see* Greater Victoria Public Library, Victoria BC p. 2583
McClure Community Library, *see* Snyder County Libraries, McClure PA p. 2005
McClure Susie Library, *see* American Baptist College, Nashville TN p. 2118
McCollum Public, *see* Jefferson County Library System, Wrens GA p. 486
McComb Public Library, McComb OH p. 1801
McComb Public Library, *see* Pike-Amite-Walthall Library System, McComb MS p. 1225
McConathy Nancy L Public Library, Sauk Village IL p. 645
McCone George Memorial County Library, Circle MT p. 1291
McConnell Air Force Base Library, *see* United States Air Force, McConnell AFB KS p. 824
McConnell James Memorial Library, *see* Cape Breton Regional Library, Sydney NS p. 2622
McConnell John Preston Library, *see* Radford University, Radford VA p. 2339
McConnell Resource Centre - Medical Library, *see* McGill Univeristy Health Centre, Montreal QC p. 2725
McConnell Valdes, Hato Rey PR p. 2511
McConnico Jack Memorial Library, *see* McNairy County Libraries, Selmer TN p. 2087
McCook Learning Commons, *see* Mid-Plains Community College, McCook NE p. 1324
McCook Public Library, McCook NE p. 1324
McCook Public Library District, McCook IL p. 616
McCord Memorial Library, North East PA p. 1971
McCormick Barstow, LLP, Fresno CA p. 147
McCormick County Library, McCormick SC p. 2065
McCormick Library, *see* Harrisburg Area Community College, Harrisburg PA p. 1940
McCormick Riverfront Library, *see* Dauphin County Library System, Harrisburg PA p. 1940
McCormick Robert R Tribune Foundation Library, *see* Roosevelt University, Schaumburg IL p. 567
McCowan Memorial Library, Pitman NJ p. 1435
McCoy Larry W Learning Resource Center, *see* Northwest-Shoals Community College, Muscle Shoals AL p. 31
McCoy Memorial Library, McLeansboro IL p. 616
McCoy Public Library, Shullsburg WI p. 2477
McCracken County Public Library, Paducah KY p. 871
McCracken Public Library, McCracken KS p. 824
McCracken Research Library, *see* Buffalo Bill Historical Center, Cody WY p. 2493
McCrane Kashmere Gardens Neighborhood Library, *see* Houston Public Library, Houston TX p. 2196
McCrary Marjorie Walker Memorial Library (Headquarters), *see* Lonoke County Librraries, Lonoke AR p. 102
McCray Rube Memorial, *see* Columbus County Public Library, Lake Waccamaw NC p. 1722
McCreary County Public Library District, Whitley City KY p. 877
McCreedy James E MD Medical Library, *see* Logan Health Medical Library, Kalispell MT p. 1298
McCrory Branch Library, *see* East Central Arkansas Regional Library, McCrory AR p. 112
MCCS Library, *see* Marine Corps Logistics Bases, Albany GA p. 457
McCulloch County Library, Brady TX p. 2149
McCullough John G Free Library, North Bennington VT p. 2290
McCully-Moiliili Public Library, *see* Hawaii State Public Library System, Honolulu HI p. 509
McCune Osage Township Library, McCune KS p. 824
McDaniel College, Westminster MD p. 981, 2786
McDermott Eugene Library, *see* University of Texas at Dallas, Richardson TX p. 2231
McDermott Library, *see* United States Air Force Academy Libraries, USAF Academy CO p. 297
McDermott, Will & Emery Law Library, Chicago IL p. 564
McDonald Ben F, *see* Corpus Christi Public Libraries, Corpus Christi TX p. 2160
McDonald County Library, Pineville MO p. 1265
McDonald Elvin Horticultural Library, *see* Monmouth County Park System, Middletown NJ p. 1418
McDonald Hopkins, LLC, Cleveland OH p. 1770
McDonald W J, *see* Rapides Parish Library, Glenmora LA p. 880
McDonald Judy B Public Library, Nacogdoches TX p. 2221
McDonald Library, *see* Oregon National Primate Research Center, Beaverton OR p. 1873
McDonald Memorial Library, *see* Xavier University, Cincinnati OH p. 1765
McDonald Public Library, McDonald KS p. 824
McDowell County Public Library, Marion NC p. 1702
McDowell Public Library, Welch WV p. 2416
McDowell Technical Community College Library, Marion NC p. 1702
McDuffie Campus Library, *see* Augusta Technical College, Thomson GA p. 467
McEachern Annie Hubbard Public, *see* Robeson County Public Library, Saint Pauls NC p. 1702
McElroy, Deutsch, Mulvaney & Carpenter, LLP, Morristown NJ p. 1421
McElvain Catherine Library, *see* School for Advanced Research Library, Santa Fe NM p. 1477
McElveen Library, *see* United States Air Force, Shaw AFB SC p. 2069
McElwain Edward Memorial Library, Peach Springs AZ p. 68
McEntegart Hall Library, *see* Saint Joseph's College, Brooklyn NY p. 1506
McEwen Robert C Library, *see* United States Army, Fort Drum NY p. 1534
McFarland Library, *see* Southwest Minnesota State University Library, Marshall MN p. 1182
McFarland Public Library, McFarland WI p. 2455
McFarlin Library, *see* University of Tulsa Libraries, Tulsa OK p. 1867
McGarry Public Library, Virginiatown ON p. 2701
McGaw Library & Learning Center, *see* Alice Lloyd College, Pippa Passes KY p. 873
McGhee Lawson Library, *see* Knox County Public Library System, Knoxville TN p. 2105
McGill Library, *see* Washington School for the Deaf, Vancouver WA p. 2391
McGill Library, *see* Westminster College, New Wilmington PA p. 1970
McGill University, Sainte-Anne-de-Bellevue QC p. 2734
McGill University, Montreal QC p. 2796
McGill Univeristy Health Centre, Montreal QC p. 2725
McGill University Libraries, Montreal QC p. 2726
McGill William A Bill Pubic Library & Administrative Office, *see* Gadsden County Public Library, Quincy FL p. 439
McGinley Memorial Public Library, McGregor TX p. 2217
McGinnis, Lochridge, Austin TX p. 2140
McGlannan Health Sciences Library, Baltimore MD p. 955

Mecca Library, *see* Riverside County Library System, Mecca CA p. 202
Mechanic Falls Public Library, Mechanic Falls ME p. 931
Mechanics' Hall Library, *see* Maine Charitable Mechanic Association Library, Portland ME p. 936
Mechanics' Institute Library, San Francisco CA p. 226
Mechanicsburg Public Library, Mechanicsburg OH p. 1801
Mechanicsville Public Library, Mechanicsville IA p. 769
Mechanicville District Public Library, Mechanicville NY p. 1570
Mecklenburg County Public Library, Boydton VA p. 2308
Medaille College Library, Buffalo NY p. 1509
Medal of Honor Memorial Library, *see* United States Army, Fort George G Meade MD p. 965
Meder Charles J Library, *see* Finger Lakes Community College, Canandaigua NY p. 1512
Medfield Historical Society Library, Medfield MA p. 1033
Medfield Public Library, Medfield MA p. 1033
Medford Public Library, Medford MA p. 1033
Medford Public Library, Medford OK p. 1853
Medgar Evers College, Brooklyn NY p. 1505
Media-Upper Providence Free Library, Media PA p. 1961
Mediapolis Public Library, Mediapolis IA p. 769
Mediatheque Maskoutaine, Saint-Hyacinthe QC p. 2735
Medical & Scientific Libraries of Long Island (N), Rockville Centre NY p. 2771
Medical College of Wisconsin Libraries, Milwaukee WI p. 2458
Medical Library & Community Health Information Center, *see* Self Regional Healthcare, Greenwood SC p. 2063
Medical Library Association (N), Chicago IL p. 2765
Medical Library Services, *see* Hennepin County Medical Center, Minneapolis MN p. 1183
Medical-Nursing Library, *see* Ellis Medicine, Schenectady NY p. 1637
Medical Research Institute of Infectious Diseases Library, *see* United States Army, Frederick MD p. 967
Medical Research Library of Brooklyn, *see* State University of New York Downstate Health Sciences University, Brooklyn NY p. 1506
Medical University of South Carolina Libraries, Charleston SC p. 2051
Medicine Bow Branch, *see* Carbon County Library System, Medicine Bow WY p. 2498
Medicine Hat College Library, Medicine Hat AB p. 2548
Medicine Hat Public Library, Medicine Hat AB p. 2548
Medicine Spring Library, *see* Blackfeet Community College, Browning MT p. 1290
Medieval Institute Library, *see* Hesburgh Libraries, Notre Dame IN p. 711
Medina Community Library, Medina TX p. 2218
Medina County District Library, Medina OH p. 1801
Medina County Law Library Association, Medina OH p. 1802
MEDLI (N), *see* Medical & Scientific Libraries of Long Island, Rockville Centre NY p. 2771
MedStar Franklin Square Medical Center, Baltimore MD p. 955
MedStar Harbor Hospital, Baltimore MD p. 955
Medstar Union Memorial Hospital, Baltimore MD p. 956
Medway Public Library, Medway MA p. 1034
Medweganoonind Library, *see* Red Lake Nation College, Red Lake MN p. 1193
Meehan Memorial Lansing Public Library, Lansing IA p. 764
Meek Paul Library, *see* University of Tennessee at Martin, Martin TN p. 2111
Meeker Regional Library District, Meeker CO p. 291
Meekins Library, Williamsburg MA p. 1069
Meem Library, *see* Saint John's College, Santa Fe NM p. 1476
Meharry Medical College Library, Nashville TN p. 2119
Meherrin Regional Library, Lawrenceville VA p. 2327
Mehoopany Area Library, Mehoopany PA p. 1962
Meigs County - Decatur Public Library, Decatur TN p. 2096
Meigs County District Public Library, Pomeroy OH p. 1816
Meigs Public Library, *see* Thomas County Public Library System, Meigs GA p. 499
Meijer Hendrik Library, *see* Muskegon Community College, Muskegon MI p. 1136
Meinders Community Library, Pipestone MN p. 1193
Meir Golda Library, *see* University of Wisconsin-Milwaukee Libraries, Milwaukee WI p. 2461
Meisel Nancy Petricoff Library, *see* Adath Israel Congregation, Cincinnati OH p. 1759
Melbourne Beach Public Library, Melbourne Beach FL p. 421
Melbourne Public Library, Melbourne FL p. 421
Melbourne Public Library, Melbourne IA p. 769
Melbourne Public Library, *see* Izard County Library, Melbourne AR p. 104
Melcher-Dallas Public Library, Melcher-Dallas IA p. 769
Melcher Neighborhood Library, *see* Houston Public Library, Houston TX p. 2196
Melfort Public Library, *see* Wapiti Regional Library, Melfort SK p. 2745
Melick Library, *see* Eureka College, Eureka IL p. 585
Melissa Public Library, *see* City of Melissa Public Library, Melissa TX p. 2218
Melita Library, *see* Southwestern Manitoba Regional Library, Melita MB p. 2588
Mellinger Memorial Library, Morning Sun IA p. 771
Mellon Andrew W Foundation, New York NY p. 1591
Mellon Institute Library, *see* Carnegie Mellon University, Pittsburgh PA p. 1992
Mellon Jennie King Library, *see* Chatham College, Pittsburgh PA p. 1992
Mellor C C Memorial Library, Edgewood PA p. 1929
Melnyk Alice Public Library, Two Hills AB p. 2557
Melrose Library, *see* Great River Regional Library, Melrose MN p. 1197
Melrose Park Public Library, Melrose Park IL p. 616
Melrose Public Library, Melrose MA p. 1034
Melrose Public Library, *see* Putnam County Library System, Melrose FL p. 433
MELSA (N), *see* Metropolitan Library Service Agency, Saint Paul MN p. 2768
Melton Arthur W Library, *see* American Psychological Association, Washington DC p. 360
Melton Public Library, French Lick IN p. 686
Melville Frank Jr Memorial Library, *see* Stony Brook University, Stony Brook NY p. 1646
Melvin Public Library, Melvin IL p. 616
Melvin Public Library, Melvin IA p. 769
Melvindale Public Library, Melvindale MI p. 1131
Memorial & Library Association, Westerly RI p. 2043
Memorial Care Health Sciences Library, *see* Long Beach Memorial/Miller Children's Hospital, Long Beach CA p. 158
Memorial Hall Library, Andover MA p. 985
Memorial Health University Medical Center, Savannah GA p. 496
Memorial Healthcare System, Hollywood FL p. 409
Memorial Hospital at Gulfport, Gulfport MS p. 1218
Memorial Hospital Library, Belleville IL p. 541
Memorial Library of Little Valley, Little Valley NY p. 1563
Memorial Library of Nazareth & Vicinity, Nazareth PA p. 1968
Memorial Presbyterian Church, Midland MI p. 1132
Memorial Public Library of the Borough of Alexandria, Alexandria PA p. 1904
Memorial Regional Hospital Library, *see* Memorial Healthcare System, Hollywood FL p. 409
Memorial Sloan-Kettering Cancer Center Medical Library, New York NY p. 1591
Memorial University of Newfoundland, St. John's NL p. 2610
Memphis Brooks Museum of Art Library, Memphis TN p. 2112
Memphis Museum of Science & History, Memphis TN p. 2112
Memphis Public Library, Memphis TX p. 2218
Memphis Public Library, Memphis TN p. 2112
Memphis Theological Seminary Library, Memphis TN p. 2114
Menan Annis Grant Library, Menan ID p. 525
Menan-Annis, Grant Public Library, Menan ID p. 525
Menands Public Library, Menands NY p. 1570
Menard Public Library, Menard TX p. 2218
Menasha Public Library, Menasha WI p. 2455
Menaul Historical Library of the Southwest, Albuquerque NM p. 1461
Mendel Music Library, *see* Princeton University, Princeton NJ p. 1438
Mendenhall Public Library, Mendenhall MS p. 1226
Mendes & Mount, LLP, New York NY p. 1591
Mendham Borough Library, Mendham NJ p. 1418
Mendham Township Library, Brookside NJ p. 1393
Mendik Library, *see* New York Law School, New York NY p. 1594
Mendocino Art Center Library, Mendocino CA p. 175
Mendocino College Library, Ukiah CA p. 254
Mendocino County Law Library, Ukiah CA p. 254
Mendocino County Library District, Ukiah CA p. 254
Mendon Library, Mendon UT p. 2266
Mendon Public Library, Honeoye Falls NY p. 1548
Mendon Township Library, Mendon MI p. 1131
Mendota Mental Health Institute, Madison WI p. 2449
Mengle Memorial Library, Brockway PA p. 1915
Menifee County Public Library, Frenchburg KY p. 856
Menil Foundation, Houston TX p. 2197
Menlo College, Atherton CA p. 118
Menlo Park, *see* United States Geological Survey Library, Menlo Park CA p. 176
Menlo Park Public Library, Menlo Park CA p. 175
Menlo Public Library, Menlo IA p. 769
Menno-Simons Community Library, Cleardale AB p. 2531
Mennonite Historians of Eastern Pennsylvania, Harleysville PA p. 1939
Mennonite Historical Library, *see* Goshen College, Goshen IN p. 687
Mennonite Historical Library & Archives, *see* Mennonite Historians of Eastern Pennsylvania, Harleysville PA p. 1939
Mennonite Library & Archives, *see* Bethel College Library, North Newton KS p. 827
Mennonite Life, Lancaster PA p. 1952
Menominee County Library, Stephenson MI p. 1152
Menomonee Falls Public Library, Menomonee Falls WI p. 2455
Menomonie Public Library, Menomonie WI p. 2456
Mental Health America Library, Poughkeepsie NY p. 1623
Mentor Public Library, Mentor OH p. 1802
Mercantile Library Association, Cincinnati OH p. 1761
Merced College, Merced CA p. 176
Merced County Law Library, Merced CA p. 176
Merced County Library, Merced CA p. 176
Mercer Area Library, Mercer PA p. 1962
Mercer County Community College Library, West Windsor NJ p. 1453
Mercer County Correction Center Library, Trenton NJ p. 1447
Mercer County District Library, Celina OH p. 1757
Mercer County Law Library, Celina OH p. 1757
Mercer County Law Library, Mercer PA p. 1962
Mercer County Library, Princeton MO p. 1266
Mercer County Library System, Lawrenceville NJ p. 1411

Michigan Department of Corrections, Baraga MI p. 1082
Michigan Department of Corrections, Carson City MI p. 1089
Michigan Department of Corrections, Freeland MI p. 1108
Michigan Department of Corrections, Jackson MI p. 1120
Michigan Department of Corrections, Manistee MI p. 1129
Michigan Department of Corrections, Munising MI p. 1135
Michigan Department of Corrections, Muskegon MI p. 1136
Michigan Department of Health and Human Services, Saline MI p. 1148
Michigan Department of Natural Resources, Ann Arbor MI p. 1079
Michigan Department of Transportation Library, Lansing MI p. 1125
Michigan Health Sciences Libraries Association (N), Lansing MI p. 2767
Michigan Legislative Service Bureau Library, Lansing MI p. 1125
Michigan Maritime Museum, South Haven MI p. 1150
Michigan Masonic Museum & Library, Grand Rapids MI p. 1111
Michigan Psychoanalytic Institute & Society, Farmington Hills MI p. 1104
Michigan Public, *see* Carnegie Regional Library, Michigan ND p. 1734
Michigan Road, *see* Indianapolis Public Library, Indianapolis IN p. 696
Michigan Road Community Library, *see* Frankfort Community Public Library, Michigantown IN p. 685
Michigan State University College of Law Library, East Lansing MI p. 1101
Michigan State University Libraries, East Lansing MI p. 1102
Michigan Technological University, Houghton MI p. 1116
Mickel Library, *see* Converse College, Spartanburg SC p. 2069
Mickelsen Community Library, *see* United States Army, Fort Bliss TX p. 2177
Mid-America Baptist Theological Seminary, Cordova TN p. 2095
Mid-America Christian University, Oklahoma City OK p. 1858
Mid-America College of Funeral Service, Jeffersonville IN p. 698
Mid-America Law Library Consortium (N), Oklahoma City OK p. 2773
Mid-America Library Alliance (N), Independence MO p. 2769
Mid-America Reformed Seminary Library, Dyer IN p. 679
Mid-Arkansas Regional Library, Malvern AR p. 103
Mid-Atlantic Christian University, Elizabeth City NC p. 1687
Mid-City Library, *see* New Orleans Public Library, New Orleans LA p. 903
Mid-Columbia Libraries, Kennewick WA p. 2367
Mid-Continent Public Library, Independence MO p. 1250
Mid-County Regional Library, *see* Charlotte County Library System, Port Charlotte FL p. 438
Mid Florida Research & Education Center Library, *see* University of Florida, Apopka FL p. 383
Mid-Hudson Forensic Psychiatric Center Library, New Hampton NY p. 1576
Mid-Hudson Library System, Poughkeepsie NY p. 1623
Mid-Manhattan Library, *see* New York Public Library - Astor, Lenox & Tilden Foundations, New York NY p. 1596
Mid Michigan Community College, Harrison MI p. 1113
Mid-Michigan Library League (N), Cadillac MI p. 2767
Mid-Mississippi Regional Library System, Kosciusko MS p. 1224
Mid-Plains Community College, McCook NE p. 1324
Mid-State Technical College, Marshfield WI p. 2454
Mid-State Technical College, Stevens Point WI p. 2479
Mid-State Technical College, Wisconsin Rapids WI p. 2489
Mid-York Library System, Utica NY p. 1655
Mid-Plains Community College, North Platte NE p. 1327
MidAmerica Nazarene University, Olathe KS p. 828
Middle Country Public Library, Centereach NY p. 1515
Middle East Institute, Washington DC p. 371
Middle Georgia Regional Library System, Macon GA p. 486
Middle Georgia State University, Macon GA p. 487
Middle Georgia State University, Cochran Campus, Cochran GA p. 471
Middle Haddam Public Library, Middle Haddam CT p. 321
Middle Tennessee State University, Murfreesboro TN p. 2117, 2792
Middle Village Community Library, *see* Queens Library, Middle Village NY p. 1555
Middleborough Public Library, Middleborough MA p. 1035
Middleburg Community Library, *see* Snyder County Libraries, Middleburg PA p. 2005
Middleburgh Library, Middleburgh NY p. 1571
Middlebury College, Middlebury VT p. 2288
Middlebury Community Public Library, Middlebury IN p. 706
Middlebury Public Library, Middlebury CT p. 321
Middlefield Public Library, Middlefield MA p. 1035
Middlemas George & Sherry Arts & Humanities Library, *see* Pennsylvania State University Libraries, University Park PA p. 2015
Middlesborough-Bell County Public, Middlesboro KY p. 869
Middlesex College Library, Edison NJ p. 1401
Middlesex Community College, Middletown CT p. 322
Middlesex Community College, Bedford MA p. 988
Middlesex Community College, Lowell MA p. 1029
Middlesex County Adult Correction Center Library, North Brunswick NJ p. 1429
Middlesex County Courthouse, New Brunswick NJ p. 1424
Middlesex County Cultural & Heritage Commission, New Brunswick NJ p. 1424
Middlesex County Historical Society Library, Middletown CT p. 322
Middlesex County Library, Strathroy ON p. 2682
Middlesex County Public Library, Urbanna VA p. 2349
Middlesex Law Association, London ON p. 2654
Middlesex Law Library, Woburn MA p. 1070
Middlesex Public Library, Middlesex NJ p. 1418
Middlesex Reading Center, Middlesex NY p. 1571
Middleton Community Library, Middleton TN p. 2115
Middleton Public Library, Middleton ID p. 525
Middleton Public Library, Middleton WI p. 2457
Middleton Rosa M Harvey & Area Library, *see* Annapolis Valley Regional Library, Middleton NS p. 2616
Middletown Fall Creek Library, Middletown IN p. 706
Middletown Free Library, Media PA p. 1961
Middletown Law Library, *see* Connecticut Judicial Branch Law Libraries, Middletown CT p. 316
Middletown Public Library, Middletown PA p. 1962
Middletown Public Library, Middletown RI p. 2034
Middletown Springs Public Library, Middletown Springs VT p. 2289
Middletown Thrall Library, Middletown NY p. 1571
Middletown Township Public Library, Middletown NJ p. 1418
Middleville Free Library, Middleville NY p. 1572
Mideastern Michigan Library Cooperative (N), Flint MI p. 2767
Midkiff Public, *see* Rankin Public Library, Midkiff TX p. 2230
Midland City Library, *see* Brown Mary Berry Memorial Library, Midland City AL p. 25
Midland College, Midland TX p. 2219
Midland Community Library, *see* Haakon County Public Library, Midland SD p. 2080
Midland County Historical Society, Midland MI p. 1132
Midland County Public Library, Midland TX p. 2219
Midland Park Memorial Library, Midland Park NJ p. 1418
Midland Public Library, Midland ON p. 2658
Midland University, Fremont NE p. 1314
Midlands Technical College Library, West Columbia SC p. 2072
Midlothian Public Library, Midlothian IL p. 617
MidMichigan Medical Center, Midland MI p. 1132
MidPointe Library System, Middletown OH p. 1802
Midtown Hospital Medical Library, *see* Saint Thomas Health Services Library, Nashville TN p. 2120
Midvale Community Library, Midvale ID p. 525
Midway Public Library, Midway BC p. 2570
Midway University, Midway KY p. 869
Midwest Archeological Center Library, *see* National Park Service, Lincoln NE p. 1321
Midwest Archives Conference (N), Fort Lauderdale FL p. 2763
Midwest Collaborative for Library Services (N), Lansing MI p. 2767
Midwest Historical & Genealogical Society, Inc Library, Wichita KS p. 843
Midwestern Baptist Theological Seminary Library, Kansas City MO p. 1256
Midwestern State University, Wichita Falls TX p. 2257
Midwestern University, Downers Grove IL p. 579
Mifflin Community Library, Shillington PA p. 2006
Mifflin County Historical Society Library & Museum, Lewistown PA p. 1955
Mifflin County Library, Lewistown PA p. 1955
Migel M C Library & Barr Research Library, *see* American Printing House for the Blind, Inc, Louisville KY p. 864
Migrant Legal Action Program Library, Washington DC p. 371
Mikkelsen Library, *see* Augustana University, Sioux Falls SD p. 2081
Milaca Community Library, *see* East Central Regional Library, Milaca MN p. 1168
Milam Max, *see* Central Arkansas Library System, Perryville AR p. 101
Milan-Berlin Library District, Milan OH p. 1802
Milan Public Library, Milan MI p. 1132
Milan Public Library, Milan MN p. 1182
Milan Public Library, Milan NH p. 1373
Milanof-Schock Library, Mount Joy PA p. 1966
Milbridge Public Library, Milbridge ME p. 931
Miles City Public Library, Miles City MT p. 1299
Miles College, Fairfield AL p. 16
Miles Community College, Miles City MT p. 1299
Miles Davison Library, Calgary AB p. 2528
Miley Library, *see* Indian River State College, Fort Pierce FL p. 404
Milford District Library, Milford IL p. 617
Milford Free Library, Milford NY p. 1572
Milford Memorial Library, Milford IA p. 770
Milford Public Library, Milford CT p. 323
Milford Public Library, Milford DE p. 354
Milford Public Library, Milford IN p. 706
Milford Public Library, Milford MI p. 1132
Milford Public Library, Milford NJ p. 1419
Milford Public Library, Milford UT p. 2266
Milford Town Library, Milford MA p. 1035
Mililani Public Library, *see* Hawaii State Public Library System, Mililani HI p. 509
Military Occupational Specialty Library, *see* United States Army, Fort Wainwright AK p. 46
Milk Harvey Memorial, *see* San Francisco Public Library, San Francisco CA p. 228
Milk River Municipal Library, Milk River AB p. 2548
Mill City Library, Mill City OR p. 1886
Mill Creek Library, *see* Sno-Isle Libraries, Mill Creek WA p. 2370

Montes-Gallo Delia Library, *see* Texas Tech University Health Sciences Center El Paso, El Paso TX p. 2174
Montevideo Public Library, Montevideo MN p. 1187
Montezuma Public Library, Montezuma IN p. 707
Montezuma Public Library, Montezuma IA p. 770
Montezuma Public, *see* Middle Georgia Regional Library System, Montezuma GA p. 487
Montezuma Township Library, Montezuma KS p. 825
Montfort Public Library, Montfort WI p. 2462
Montgomery & Andrews, Santa Fe NM p. 1475
Montgomery Area Public Library, Montgomery PA p. 1965
Montgomery Botanical Center, Coral Gables FL p. 390
Montgomery City-County Public Library System, Montgomery AL p. 29
Montgomery City Public Library, Montgomery City MO p. 1263
Montgomery College Library, Rockville MD p. 973
Montgomery College Library, *see* Lone Star College System, Conroe TX p. 2197
Montgomery Community College Library, Troy NC p. 1719
Montgomery County Circuit Court, Rockville MD p. 974
Montgomery County Community College, Blue Bell PA p. 1913
Montgomery County Correctional Facility, *see* Montgomery County Public Libraries, Boyds MD p. 974
Montgomery County Department of History & Archives, Fonda NY p. 1534
Montgomery County Law Library, Montgomery AL p. 30
Montgomery County Law Library, Dayton OH p. 1780
Montgomery County Library, Mount Ida AR p. 105
Montgomery County Library, Troy NC p. 1719
Montgomery County Library & Information Network Consortium (N), Fort Washington PA p. 2774
Montgomery County Memorial Library System, Conroe TX p. 2159
Montgomery County-Norristown Public Library, Norristown PA p. 1971
Montgomery County Planning Commission Library, Norristown PA p. 1971
Montgomery County Public Libraries, Rockville MD p. 974
Montgomery County Public Library, Mount Sterling KY p. 870
Montgomery County Public Library, *see* Ohoopee Regional Library System, Mount Vernon GA p. 502
Montgomery-Floyd Regional Library System, Christiansburg VA p. 2312
Montgomery Frederick S Library, *see* Butte College Library, Oroville CA p. 189
Montgomery Free Library, Montgomery NY p. 1573
Montgomery G V VA Medical Center Library, Jackson MS p. 1223
Montgomery History, Rockville MD p. 975
Montgomery House Library, McEwensville PA p. 1959
Montgomery Library, *see* Campbellsville University, Campbellsville KY p. 850
Montgomery Library, *see* Montgomery Botanical Center, Coral Gables FL p. 390
Montgomery Library, *see* Westminster Theological Seminary, Glenside PA p. 1937
Montgomery, McCracken, Walker & Rhoads LLP Library, Philadelphia PA p. 1983
Montgomery Memorial Library, Jewell IA p. 762
Montgomery Presbyterian Church Library, Montgomery OH p. 1803
Montgomery Public, *see* Waseca-Le Sueur Regional Library, Montgomery MN p. 1207
Montgomery State Prison, *see* Georgia Department of Corrections, Mount Vernon GA p. 492
Montgomery Town Library, Montgomery Center VT p. 2289
Monticello Library, *see* Great River Regional Library, Monticello MN p. 1197
Monticello Public Library, Monticello WI p. 2462
Monticello-Union Township Public Library, Monticello IN p. 707
Montieth Library, *see* Alma College Library, Alma MI p. 1077
Montmorency County Public Libraries, Atlanta MI p. 1081
Montour Falls Memorial Library, Montour Falls NY p. 1573
Montpelier Harrison Township Public Library, Montpelier IN p. 707
Montpelier Public Library, Montpelier OH p. 1804
Montreal City Planning Department, Montreal QC p. 2726
Montreal General Hospital, Montreal QC p. 2726
Montreal Museum of Fine Arts, Montreal QC p. 2727
Montreal Neurological Institute Hospital Library, Montreal QC p. 2727
Montreat College, Montreat NC p. 1704
Montrose Public Library, Montrose IA p. 771
Montrose Regional Library District, Montrose CO p. 291
Montserrat College of Art, Beverly MA p. 989
Montvale Free Public Library, Montvale NJ p. 1420
Montvale Library, *see* Bedford Public Library System, Montvale VA p. 2306
Montverde Library, *see* Lehmann Helen Memorial Library, Montverde FL p. 426
Montville Township Public Library, Montville NJ p. 1420
Monument Library, *see* Pikes Peak Library District, Monument CO p. 271
Moody Bible Institute, Chicago IL p. 564
Moody Community Library, Moody TX p. 2220
Moody County Resource Center, Flandreau SD p. 2076
Moody Mary Northern Municipal Library, *see* Fairfield Library Association, Inc, Fairfield TX p. 2176
Moody Medical Library, *see* University of Texas Medical Branch, Galveston TX p. 2183
Moody Memorial Library, *see* Baylor University Libraries, Waco TX p. 2253
Moody Memorial Library, *see* Houston Baptist University, Houston TX p. 2194
Moody Neighborhood Library, *see* Houston Public Library, Houston TX p. 2196
Moody W L Jr Library, *see* Blinn College Library, Brenham TX p. 2149
Mooers Free Library, Mooers NY p. 1574
Mookini Edwin H Library, *see* University of Hawaii at Hilo Library, Hilo HI p. 505
Moomau Grant County Library, Petersburg WV p. 2412
Moon D R Memorial Library, Stanley WI p. 2478
Moon F Franklin Library, *see* State University of New York, Syracuse NY p. 1650
Moon Township Public Library, Moon Township PA p. 1965
Mooneyham Public Library, Forest City NC p. 1689
Moore & Van Allen PLLC, Charlotte NC p. 1680
Moore Ann Carroll Children's Library, *see* Utah State University, Logan UT p. 2265
Moore Arthur J Methodist Museum Library, *see* United Methodist Church - South Georgia Conference, Saint Simons Island GA p. 495
Moore Bessie Boehm Library, *see* Stone County Library, Mountain View AR p. 105
Moore Cecil B, *see* Free Library of Philadelphia, Philadelphia PA p. 1979
Moore Claude Health Sciences Library, *see* University of Virginia, Charlottesville VA p. 2310
Moore College of Art & Design, Philadelphia PA p. 1983
Moore County Library, Carthage NC p. 1677
Moore County Library System, Dumas TX p. 2172
Moore County Public Library, Lynchburg TN p. 2110
Moore Family Library, Grinnell KS p. 811
Moore Franklin F Library, *see* Rider University, Lawrenceville NJ p. 1411
Moore Free Library, Newfane VT p. 2290
Moore Haven Correctional Facility Library, Moore Haven FL p. 427
Moore Henry D Parrish House & Library, Steuben ME p. 942
Moore J Turner Memorial Library, Manalapan FL p. 419
Moore Mary C Public Library, *see* Lacombe Public Library, Lacombe AB p. 2545
Moore Memorial Library, Greene NY p. 1541
Moore Memorial Library District, Hillsdale IL p. 599
Moore Memorial Public Library, Texas City TX p. 2248
Moore Parlett Library, *see* Coppin State College, Baltimore MD p. 952
Moore Public, *see* Pioneer Library System, Moore OK p. 1855
Moore Public Library, Lexington MI p. 1127
Moore Public Library, Moore MT p. 1300
Moore William J, *see* University of Kansas, Department of Religious Studies, Lawrence KS p. 819
Moores Memorial Library, Christiana PA p. 1921
Moorestown Public Library, Moorestown NJ p. 1421
Mooresville Public Library, Mooresville IN p. 707
Mooresville Public Library, Mooresville NC p. 1704
Moorhead Public Library, *see* Lake Agassiz Regional Library, Moorhead MN p. 1188
Moorland-Spingarn Research Center, *see* Howard University Libraries, Washington DC p. 369
Moorpark City Library, Moorpark CA p. 180
Moorpark College Library, Moorpark CA p. 180
Moose Jaw Branch, *see* Palliser Regional Library, Moose Jaw SK p. 2742
Moose Jaw Campus Library, *see* SIAST-Saskatchewan Institute of Applied Science & Technology, Moose Jaw SK p. 2743
Moose Lake Public Library, Moose Lake MN p. 1189
Moose Pass Public Library, Moose Pass AK p. 49
Moosilauke Public Library, North Woodstock NH p. 1377
Mora Public Library, *see* East Central Regional Library, Mora MN p. 1168
Moraga Historical Society Archives, Moraga CA p. 180
Moraga Library, *see* Contra Costa County Library, Moraga CA p. 174
Moraine Park Technical College, West Bend WI p. 2487
Moraine Park Technical College Library, Beaver Dam WI p. 2423
Moraine Park Technical College Library, Fond du Lac WI p. 2435
Moraine Valley Community College Library, Palos Hills IL p. 632
Moran Jan Collier City Learning Library, *see* Broward County Libraries Division, Pompano Beach FL p. 398
Moran Pierre, *see* Elkhart Public Library, Elkhart IN p. 680
Moran Public Library, Moran KS p. 826
Moravia Public Library, Moravia IA p. 771
Moravian Archives, Bethlehem PA p. 1912
Moravian Church in America, Winston-Salem NC p. 1725
Moravian College & Moravian Theological Seminary, Bethlehem PA p. 1912
Moravian Historical Society, Nazareth PA p. 1968
Moravian Music Foundation, Winston-Salem NC p. 1725
Morbito Joseph F Architecture Library, *see* Kent State University Libraries, Kent OH p. 1792
Morehead Albert H Memorial Library, *see* American Contract Bridge League, Horn Lake MS p. 1220
Morehead State University, Morehead KY p. 869
Morehouse Parish Library, Bastrop LA p. 881
Morehouse School of Medicine, Atlanta GA p. 465
Morell Public Library, *see* Prince Edward Island Public Library Service, Morell PE p. 2708
Morella Connie Library, *see* Montgomery County Public Libraries, Bethesda MD p. 974
Morenci Community Library, Morenci AZ p. 67
Moreno Valley College Library, *see* Riverside Community College District, Moreno Valley CA p. 181

Mount Charleston Library, *see* Las Vegas-Clark County Library District, Las Vegas NV p. 1347
Mount Clemens Public Library, Mount Clemens MI p. 1134
Mt Cuba Astronomical Observatory Memorial Library, Wilmington DE p. 357
Mount Enterprise Public Library, *see* Rusk County Library System, Mount Enterprise TX p. 2189
Mount Gilead Public Library, Mount Gilead OH p. 1804
Mount Holly Town Library, Belmont VT p. 2279
Mount Holyoke College Library, South Hadley MA p. 1054
Mount Hood Community College Libraries, Gresham OR p. 1881
Mount Hope-Funks Grove Townships Library District, McLean IL p. 616
Mount Hope Public Library, Mount Hope KS p. 826
Mount Horeb Public Library, Mount Horeb WI p. 2463
Mount Jackson Community, *see* Shenandoah County Library, Mount Jackson VA p. 2315
Mount Jewett Memorial Library, Mount Jewett PA p. 1966
Mount Juliet-Wilson County Library, *see* Lebanon-Wilson County Library, Mount Juliet TN p. 2109
Mount Kisco Public Library, Mount Kisco NY p. 1574
Mount Laurel Library, Mount Laurel NJ p. 1422
Mount Laurel Library, *see* North Shelby County Library, Birmingham AL p. 8
Mt Lebanon Public Library, Pittsburgh PA p. 1994
Mount Lehman Library, *see* Fraser Valley Regional Library, Abbotsford BC p. 2562
Mount Logan Branch Library, *see* Chillicothe & Ross County Public Library, Chillicothe OH p. 1758
Mount Marty University, Yankton SD p. 2086
Mount Mary University, Milwaukee WI p. 2460
Mount Mercy University, Cedar Rapids IA p. 738
Mount Morris Library, Mount Morris NY p. 1574
Mount Morris Public Library, Mount Morris IL p. 620
Mount Olive Correctional Complex Library, Mount Olive WV p. 2410
Mount Olive Public Library, Mount Olive IL p. 621
Mount Olive Public Library, Flanders NJ p. 1403
Mount Pearl Public Library, Mount Pearl NL p. 2608
Mount Pleasant Free Public Library, Mount Pleasant PA p. 1966
Mt Pleasant Library, *see* Community Libraries of Providence, Providence RI p. 2038
Mount Pleasant Public Library, Mount Pleasant IA p. 771
Mount Pleasant Public Library, Pleasantville NY p. 1620
Mount Pleasant Public Library, Mount Pleasant TX p. 2220
Mount Pleasant Public Library, Mount Pleasant UT p. 2267
Mount Prospect Public Library, Mount Prospect IL p. 621
Mount Pulaski Public Library District, Mount Pulaski IL p. 621
Mount Royal University Library, Calgary AB p. 2528
Mount Saint Joseph University, Cincinnati OH p. 1761
Mount Saint Mary College, Newburgh NY p. 1605
Mount Saint Mary's University, Los Angeles CA p. 166
Mount Saint Mary's University, Emmitsburg MD p. 965
Mount Saint Vincent University Library & Archives, Halifax NS p. 2619
Mt San Antonio College Library, Walnut CA p. 258
Mount San Jacinto College, San Jacinto CA p. 230
Mount Sinai Hospital, Toronto ON p. 2690
Mount Sinai Hospital Medical Center, Chicago IL p. 565
Mount Sinai Medical Center, Miami Beach FL p. 425
Mount Sinai Phillips School of Nursing, Beth Israel, New York NY p. 1592
Mount Sinai Services-Queens Hospital Center Affiliation, Jamaica NY p. 1553
Mount Sinai South Nassau, Oceanside NY p. 1609
Mount Sinai West, New York NY p. 1592
Mount Sterling Public Library, Mount Sterling OH p. 1804
Mount Stewart Public Library, *see* Prince Edward Island Public Library Service, Mount Stewart PE p. 2708
Mount Vernon City Library, Mount Vernon WA p. 2371
Mount Vernon Nazarene University, Mount Vernon OH p. 1804
Mount Vernon Public Library, Mount Vernon AL p. 31
Mount Vernon Public Library, Mount Vernon NY p. 1575
Mount Wachusett Community College Library, Gardner MA p. 1020
Mount Washington Observatory, North Conway NH p. 1376
Mount Washington Public Library, Mount Washington MA p. 1037
Mount Zion District Library, Mount Zion IL p. 622
Mount Zion Public Library, *see* West Georgia Regional Library, Mount Zion GA p. 470
Mount Zion Temple, Saint Paul MN p. 1201
Mountain Area Health Education Center, Asheville NC p. 1672
Mountain Empire Community College, Big Stone Gap VA p. 2307
Mountain Home Public Library, Mountain Home ID p. 527
Mountain Iron Public Library, Mountain Iron MN p. 1190
Mountain Lake Public Library, Mountain Lake MN p. 1190
Mountain Lakes Public Library, Mountain Lakes NJ p. 1423
Mountain Regional Library, *see* Mountain Regional Library System, Young Harris GA p. 503
Mountain Regional Library System, Young Harris GA p. 503
Mountain Road Library, *see* Arundel Anne County Public Library, Pasadena MD p. 950
Mountain Top Library, Tannersville NY p. 1651
Mountain View Correctional Facility Library, Charleston ME p. 921
Mountain View Public & School Library, *see* Hawaii State Public Library System, Mountain View HI p. 510
Mountain View Public Library, Mountain View CA p. 181
Mountain View Public Library, Mountain View MO p. 1264
Mountainair Public Library, Mountainair NM p. 1473
Mountainburg Public Library, Mountainburg AR p. 105
Mountaineers Library, Seattle WA p. 2377
Mountainside Public Library, Mountainside NJ p. 1423
Mountaintop Public Library, Thomas WV p. 2415
Mountlake Terrace Library, *see* Sno-Isle Libraries, Mountlake Terrace WA p. 2371
Mount Hope Public Library, *see* Fayette County Public Libraries, Mount Hope WV p. 2411
Moweaqua Public Library, Moweaqua IL p. 622
Moye Library, *see* University of Mount Olive, Mount Olive NC p. 1705
Moyer District Library, Gibson City IL p. 592
Moyer Jane S Library, *see* Northampton County Historical & Genealogical Society, Easton PA p. 1929
Moyock Public Library, *see* Currituck County Public Library, Moyock NC p. 1673
MPR Associates, Inc, Alexandria VA p. 2303
MTLA (N), *see* Minnesota Theological Library Association, Saint Paul MN p. 2768
Muckleshoot Library, *see* King County Library System, Auburn WA p. 2366
Mudd Seeley G Library, *see* Lawrence University, Appleton WI p. 2420
Mudd Seeley G Library, *see* Northwestern University Libraries, Evanston IL p. 587
Mudd Seeley G Manuscript Library, *see* Princeton University, Princeton NJ p. 1438
Mudge E W Jr Ornithology Library, *see* Perot Museum of Nature & Science, Dallas TX p. 2167
Muehl Public Library, Seymour WI p. 2475
Mueller Dr Cheryl A Library, *see* University of Northwestern Ohio, Lima OH p. 1796
Mugar Memorial Library, *see* Boston University Libraries, Boston MA p. 993
Muhlenberg College, Allentown PA p. 1905
Muhlenberg Community Library, Laureldale PA p. 1953
Muhlenberg County Libraries, Greenville KY p. 857
Muhlenberg Medical Library, *see* Lehigh Valley Hospital, Bethlehem PA p. 1905
Muir John Health Medical Library, Walnut Creek CA p. 258
Muir Library, Winnebago MN p. 1209
Mukilteo Library, *see* Sno-Isle Libraries, Mukilteo WA p. 2371
Mukwonago Community Library, Mukwonago WI p. 2463
Mulberry Community Library, *see* Frankfort Community Public Library, Mulberry IN p. 685
Mulberry Public Library, Mulberry AR p. 106
Mulberry Public Library, Mulberry FL p. 427
Muldrow Public Library, Muldrow OK p. 1854
Mule Creek State Prison, *see* California Department of Corrections Library System, Ione CA p. 207
Muleshoe Area Public Library, Muleshoe TX p. 2221
Mulford Healh Science Library, *see* University of Toledo, Toledo OH p. 1825
Mullan Public Library, Mullan ID p. 527
Mullen John K of Denver Memorial Library, *see* Catholic University of America, Washington DC p. 362
Mullens Area Public, *see* Wyoming County Public Library, Mullens WV p. 2412
Mulliken District Library, Mulliken MI p. 1135
Mulreany Robert H Health Sciences Library, *see* Overlook Medical Center, Summit NJ p. 1445
Multicultural Council of Windsor & Essex County Library, Windsor ON p. 2704
Multnomah County Library, Portland OR p. 1892
Multnomah Law Library, Portland OR p. 1893
Mulva Miriam B & James J Library, *see* Saint Norbert College, De Pere WI p. 2430
Mulvane Public Library, Mulvane KS p. 826
Muncie Public Library, Muncie IN p. 708
Muncy Historical Society & Museum of History, Muncy PA p. 1967
Muncy Public Library, Muncy PA p. 1967
Mundare Municipal Public Library, Mundare AB p. 2548
Munday Pat & Bill Library, *see* Saint Edwards University, Austin TX p. 2140
Mundt Karl E Library, *see* Dakota State University, Madison SD p. 2078
Munford-Tipton Memorial Library, Munford TN p. 2117
Munger, Tolles & Olson LLP, Los Angeles CA p. 166
Municipal Research Library, Milwaukee WI p. 2460
Municipal Technical Advisory Service, Knoxville TN p. 2106
Munn Dozier M Pamplico Public Library, *see* Florence County Library System, Pamplico SC p. 2058
Munro Dr E H Library, *see* Saint Mary's Hospital, Grand Junction CO p. 284
Munsil Sarah A Free Library, Ellenburg Depot NY p. 1529
Munson Healthcare, Traverse City MI p. 1154
Munson Memorial, *see* Jones Library, Inc, South Amherst MA p. 984
Munson-Williams-Proctor Arts Institute Library, Utica NY p. 1655
Muntz Robert R Library, *see* University of Texas at Tyler Library, Tyler TX p. 2250
Murchison Clint W Memorial Library, *see* Henderson County, Athens TX p. 2137

Nashotah House, Nashotah WI p. 2463
Nashua Community College, Nashua NH p. 1374
Nashua Public Library, Nashua IA p. 772
Nashua Public Library, Nashua NH p. 1374
Nashville Public Library, Nashville IL p. 623
Nashville Public Library, Nashville NC p. 1705
Nashville Public Library, Nashville TN p. 2119
Nashville School of Law Library, Nashville TN p. 2120
Nashville State Technical Community College, Nashville TN p. 2120
Nassau Community College, Garden City NY p. 1537
Nassau County Public Library System, Fernandina Beach FL p. 395
Nassau County Supreme Court, Mineola NY p. 1572
Nassau Free Library, Nassau NY p. 1575
Nassau Library System, Uniondale NY p. 1654
Nassau University Medical Center, East Meadow NY p. 1528
Natchitoches Parish Library, Natchitoches LA p. 899
Natick Historical Society, Natick MA p. 1037
Nation Municipality Public Library, St. Isidore ON p. 2680
National Academies, Washington DC p. 371
National Academies of Sciences, Engineering & Medicine, Washington DC p. 371
National Academy of Social Insurance, Washington DC p. 371
National Agricultural Library, *see* United States Department of Agriculture, Beltsville MD p. 959
National Air & Space Intelligence Center, *see* United States Air Force, Wright-Patterson AFB OH p. 1834
National Air & Space Museum Library, *see* Smithsonian Libraries, Chantilly DC p. 375
National Air Photo Library, *see* Natural Resources Canada, Ottawa ON p. 2668
National Archives & Records Administration, Little Rock AR p. 101
National Archives & Records Administration, Simi Valley CA p. 246
National Archives & Records Administration, Yorba Linda CA p. 260
National Archives & Records Administration, Broomfield CO p. 268
National Archives & Records Administration, Atlanta GA p. 465
National Archives & Records Administration, Morrow GA p. 491
National Archives & Records Administration, Chicago IL p. 565
National Archives & Records Administration, West Branch IA p. 790
National Archives & Records Administration, Abilene KS p. 795
National Archives & Records Administration, College Park MD p. 962
National Archives & Records Administration, Boston MA p. 997
National Archives & Records Administration, Ann Arbor MI p. 1079
National Archives & Records Administration, Independence MO p. 1251
National Archives & Records Administration, Kansas City MO p. 1256
National Archives & Records Administration, Hyde Park NY p. 1550
National Archives & Records Administration, Philadelphia PA p. 1983
National Archives & Records Administration, Austin TX p. 2140
National Archives & Records Administration, College Station TX p. 2157
National Archives & Records Administration, Dallas TX p. 2167
National Archives & Records Administration, Seattle WA p. 2377
National Archives at Kansas City, *see* National Archives & Records Administration, Kansas City MO p. 1256
National Archives at San Francisco, San Bruno CA p. 214
National Archives of The Christian & Missionary Alliance, Colorado Springs CO p. 271
National Association of Insurance Commissioners, Kansas City MO p. 1256
National Association of Realtors, Chicago IL p. 565
National Baseball Hall of Fame & Museum, Inc, Cooperstown NY p. 1521
National Business & Disability Council at the Viscardi, Albertson NY p. 1484
National Center for Atmospheric Research Library, Boulder CO p. 267
National Center for Health Statistics Staff Research Library, *see* United States Department of Health & Human Services, Hyattsville MD p. 975
National Center for State Courts Library, Williamsburg VA p. 2353
National Centers for Environmental Information Library, *see* National Oceanic & Atmospheric Administration, Asheville NC p. 1673
National City Public Library, National City CA p. 182
National Concrete Masonry Association Library, Herndon VA p. 2326
National Conservation Library, *see* United States Fish & Wildlife Service, Shepherdstown WV p. 2414
National Cotton Council of America Library, Cordova TN p. 2095
National Cowboy & Western Heritage Museum, Oklahoma City OK p. 1858
National Defense University Library, *see* United States Department of Defense, Washington DC p. 378
National Economic Research Associates, Inc, White Plains NY p. 1664
National Emergency Training Center, *see* United States Fire Administration, Emmitsburg MD p. 965
National Endowment for Democracy Library, Washington DC p. 371
National Endowment for the Humanities Library, Washington DC p. 372
National Energy Technology Laboratory Library, *see* United States Department of Energy, Morgantown WV p. 2409
National Film Board of Canada, Montreal QC p. 2727
National Film Board of Canada, Saint-Laurent QC p. 2736
National Fire Protection Association, Quincy MA p. 1048
National Football Foundation's College, Atlanta GA p. 465
National Forest Service Library, Fort Collins CO p. 281
National Gallery of Art Library, Washington DC p. 372
National Gallery of Canada Library & Archives, Ottawa ON p. 2667
National Geodetic Survey Library, Silver Spring MD p. 977
National Geospatial-Intelligence Agency Research Library, *see* United States Department of Defense, Springfield VA p. 2347
National Ground Water Association, Westerville OH p. 1830
National Guard Memorial Library, Washington DC p. 372
National Highway Traffic Safety Administration-Technical, *see* United States Department of Transportation, Washington DC p. 379
National Hispanic Cultural Center Library, Albuquerque NM p. 1461
National Humanities Center Library, Research Triangle Park NC p. 1712
National Hurricane Center Library, *see* United States National Oceanic & Atmospheric, Miami FL p. 425
National Indian Law Library, *see* Native American Rights Fund, Boulder CO p. 267
National Institute of Arthritis & Musculoskeletal, Bethesda MD p. 959
National Institute of Environmental Health Sciences Library, Research Triangle Park NC p. 1712
National Institute of Justice, Washington DC p. 372
National Institute of Standards & Technology Library, Gaithersburg MD p. 967
National Institutes of Health Library, Bethesda MD p. 959
National Intelligence University Library, Washington DC p. 372
National Jewish Health, Denver CO p. 276
National Labor Relations Board Library, Washington DC p. 372
National Library of Education, Washington DC p. 372
National Library of International Trade, *see* United States International Trade Commission, Washington DC p. 379
National Library of Medicine, Bethesda MD p. 960
National Library Service for the Blind & Print Disabled, *see* Library of Congress, Washington DC p. 370
National Louis University Library, Chicago IL p. 565
National Marine Fisheries Service, Miami FL p. 424
National Marine Fisheries Service, Panama City FL p. 435
National Marine Fisheries Service, Pascagoula MS p. 1228
National Multiple Sclerosis Society, New York NY p. 1592
National Museum of American Jewish Military History Collections, Washington DC p. 372
National Museum of Asian Art Library Freer Gallery of Art, *see* Smithsonian Libraries, Washington DC p. 375
National Museum of Natural History Library, *see* Smithsonian Libraries, Washington DC p. 375
National Museum of Racing & Hall of Fame, Saratoga Springs NY p. 1636
National Museum of Transportation, Saint Louis MO p. 1272
National Museum of Women in the Arts, Washington DC p. 372
National Music Museum Library, *see* University of South Dakota, Vermillion SD p. 2084
National Network of Libraries of Medicine (N), Bethesda MD p. 2766
National Network of Libraries of Medicine Region 5 (N), Seattle WA p. 2776
National Network of Libraries of Medicine Region 4 (N), Salt Lake City UT p. 2776
National Network of Libraries of Medicine Region 1 (N), Baltimore MD p. 2766
National Network of Libraries of Medicine Region 7 (N), Worcester MA p. 2767
National Network of Libraries of Medicine Region 6 (N), Iowa City IA p. 2765
National Network of Libraries of Medicine Region 3 (N), Fort Worth TX p. 2775
National Network of Libraries of Medicine Region 2 (N), Charleston SC p. 2774
National Oceanic & Atmospheric Administration, Miami FL p. 424
National Oceanic & Atmospheric Administration, Silver Spring MD p. 977
National Oceanic & Atmospheric Administration, Asheville NC p. 1673
National Opinion Research Center Library, Chicago IL p. 565
National Park College Library, Hot Springs AR p. 99
National Park Service, Gustavus AK p. 46
National Park Service, Sitka AK p. 51
National Park Service, Tucson AZ p. 81
National Park Service, Mineral CA p. 177
National Park Service, San Francisco CA p. 226
National Park Service, Tulelake CA p. 253
National Park Service, Fort Oglethorpe GA p. 479
National Park Service, Kennesaw GA p. 484
National Park Service, Macon GA p. 487
National Park Service, Sharpsburg MD p. 977
National Park Service, Williamsport MD p. 981
National Park Service, Republic MO p. 1266
National Park Service, Van Buren MO p. 1284
National Park Service, Lincoln NE p. 1321
National Park Service, Omaha NE p. 1329
National Park Service, Morristown NJ p. 1422
National Park Service, Aztec NM p. 1463
National Park Service, Mountainair NM p. 1473
National Park Service, Stillwater NY p. 1646

Newark Public Library, Newark NY p. 1605
Newark Public Library, Newark TX p. 2222
Newark United Methodist Church, Newark DE p. 355
Newaygo Area District Library, Newaygo MI p. 1137
Newberg Public Library, Newberg OR p. 1888
Newbern City Library, Newbern TN p. 2122
Newberry College, Newberry SC p. 2066
Newberry Correctional Facility Library, Newberry MI p. 1137
Newberry County Library System, Newberry SC p. 2066
Newberry Library, Chicago IL p. 565
Newbrook Public Library, Newbrook AB p. 2549
Newburgh Chandler Public Library, Newburgh IN p. 709
Newburgh Free Library, Newburgh NY p. 1606
Newburgh Library, *see* Newburgh Chandler Public Library, Newburgh IN p. 710
Newbury Public Library, Newbury NH p. 1376
Newbury Town Library, Byfield MA p. 1004
Newburyport Public Library, Newburyport MA p. 1038
Newcastle Public, *see* Pioneer Library System, Newcastle OK p. 1855
Newcomerstown Public Library, Newcomerstown OH p. 1808
Newell Public Library, Newell IA p. 773
Newell Public Library, Newell SD p. 2080
Newfane Public Library, Newfane NY p. 1606
Newfield Public, *see* Gloucester County Library System, Newfield NJ p. 1423
Newfield Public Library, Newfield NY p. 1606
Newfield Village Library & Reading Room, West Newfield ME p. 946
Newfoundland & Labrador Historical Society Library, St. John's NL p. 2611
Newfoundland & Labrador Teachers' Association Library, St. John's NL p. 2611
Newfoundland Area Public Library, Newfoundland PA p. 1970
Newhall Public Library, Newhall IA p. 773
Newhope Library, *see* Santa Ana Public Library, Santa Ana CA p. 239
Newkirk Learning Commons, *see* Dunwoody College of Technology, Minneapolis MN p. 1183
Newkirk Public Library, Newkirk OK p. 1855
Newman Grove Public Library, Newman Grove NE p. 1326
Newman Jean & Dorothy Industrial Relations Library, *see* University of Toronto Libraries, Toronto ON p. 2699
Newman Judi Prokop Information Resource Center, *see* University of Miami Libraries, Coral Gables FL p. 391
Newman Library, *see* Virginia Polytechnic Institute & State University Libraries, Blacksburg VA p. 2307
Newman Regional Library District, Newman IL p. 624
Newman Riga Library, Churchville NY p. 1518
Newman Theological College Library, Edmonton AB p. 2537
Newman University, Wichita KS p. 843
Newman William & Anita Library, *see* Baruch College-CUNY, New York NY p. 1580
Newman William R Library, *see* University of Manitoba Libraries, Winnipeg MB p. 2595
Newmarket Public Library, Newmarket NH p. 1376
Newmarket Public Library, Newmarket ON p. 2660
Newnam Clara Drinkwater Library, *see* Mississippi County Library District, Charleston MO p. 1241
Newport Beach Public Library, Newport Beach CA p. 183
Newport Cultural Center, Newport ME p. 933
Newport Free Library, Newport NY p. 1606
Newport Historical Society Library, Newport RI p. 2034
Newport News Public Library System, Newport News VA p. 2334
Newport Public Library, Newport OR p. 1888
Newport Public Library, Newport PA p. 1970
Newport Public Library, Newport RI p. 2034
Newport Public Library, *see* Pend Oreille County Library District, Newport WA p. 2372
Newport Way Library, *see* King County Library System, Bellevue WA p. 2366
Newsday, Inc Library, Melville NY p. 1570
Newstead Public Library, Akron NY p. 1481
Newton Correctional Facility, Newton IA p. 773
Newton County Library System, Covington GA p. 473
Newton County Public Library, Jasper AR p. 99
Newton County Public Library, Lake Village IN p. 702
Newton County Public Library, Newton TX p. 2222
Newton Falls Public Library, Newton Falls OH p. 1808
Newton Free Library, Newton Centre MA p. 1039
Newton Learning Commons, *see* Bluegrass Community & Technical College, Lexington KY p. 862
Newton Phinehas S Library, Royalston MA p. 1050
Newton Public Library, Newton IA p. 773
Newton Public Library, Newton KS p. 826
Newton Public Library & Agricultural Museum, Newton AL p. 31
Newton Public Library & Museum, Newton IL p. 624
Newton Town Library, Newton UT p. 2267
Newtown Historic Association, Inc, Newtown PA p. 1970
Newtown Library Co, Newtown PA p. 1970
Newtown Public Library, Newtown Square PA p. 1970
Neyland Anita & W T Public Library, *see* Corpus Christi Public Libraries, Corpus Christi TX p. 2160
NHTI, Concord's Community College, Concord NH p. 1359
Niagara College of Applied Arts & Technology, Welland ON p. 2703
Niagara County Community College, Sanborn NY p. 1635
Niagara County Genealogical Society, Lockport NY p. 1564
Niagara Falls Public Library, Niagara Falls NY p. 1606
Niagara Falls Public Library, Niagara Falls ON p. 2660
Niagara Health System, St. Catharines ON p. 2679
Niagara-on-the-Lake Public Library, Niagara-on-the-Lake ON p. 2661
Niagara Parks Botanical Gardens & School of Horticulture, Niagara Falls ON p. 2660
Niagara Public Library, *see* Marinette County Library System, Niagara WI p. 2454
Niagara University Library, Niagara University NY p. 1606
Niceville Public Library, Niceville FL p. 428
Nicholas County Public Library, Carlisle KY p. 851
Nicholls Family Library, *see* Calgary Public Library, Calgary AB p. 2527
Nicholls Public Library, *see* Satilla Regional Library, Nicholls GA p. 476
Nicholls State University, Thibodaux LA p. 911
Nichols College, Dudley MA p. 1015
Nichols Fairchild Memorial, *see* Trumbull Library System, Trumbull CT p. 342
Nichols Gus Library, *see* Faulkner University, Montgomery AL p. 28
Nichols House Museum, Boston MA p. 998
Nichols James E Memorial Library, Center Harbor NH p. 1357
Nichols Library, *see* Naperville Public Library, Naperville IL p. 622
Nicholson Irma D Library, *see* Bevill State Community College, Jasper AL p. 17
Nicholson Jereld R Library, *see* Linfield University, McMinnville OR p. 1885
Nicholson Kathleen Wyatt Branch, *see* Lawton Public Library, Lawton OK p. 1852
Nicholson Memorial Library System, Garland TX p. 2183
Nicholson Robert A Library, *see* Anderson University, Anderson IN p. 668
Nickells J B Memorial Library, Luling TX p. 2214
Nickerson Public Library, Nickerson KS p. 827
Nicklaus Children's Hospital Medical Library, *see* Miami Children's Health System, Miami FL p. 422
Nicola Valley Institute of Technology, Merritt BC p. 2570
Nicolet Area Technical College, Rhinelander WI p. 2472
Nicolet Federated Library System, Green Bay WI p. 2438
Nicollet County Historical Society, Saint Peter MN p. 1203
Nicoma Park Library, *see* Metropolitan Library System in Oklahoma County, Nicoma Park OK p. 1857
Niederkorn W J Library, Port Washington WI p. 2470
Bohr Niels Library & Archives, *see* American Institute of Physics, College Park MD p. 962
Nielsen Engineering & Research, Inc, Santa Clara CA p. 241
Nielsen Library, *see* Adams State University, Alamosa CO p. 263
Nightingale Maggie Library, *see* Montgomery County Public Libraries, Poolesville MD p. 974
NIH, National Institute of Allergy & Infectious Diseases, Hamilton MT p. 1295
Nikolai Public Library, Nikolai AK p. 49
Niles District Library, Niles MI p. 1137
Niles-Maine District Library, Niles IL p. 624
Niles, Barton & Wilmer LLP, Baltimore MD p. 956
NILRC (N), *see* Network of Illinois Learning Resources in Community Colleges, Malta IL p. 2765
Nimitz Education & Research Center, *see* Admiral Nimitz National Museum of the Pacific War, Fredericksburg TX p. 2181
Nimitz Library, *see* United States Naval Academy, Annapolis MD p. 951
Ninety-Nines, Inc, Oklahoma City OK p. 1858
Nineveh Public Library of Colesville Township, Nineveh NY p. 1606
Ninilchik Community Library, Ninilchik AK p. 49
Niobrara County Library, Lusk WY p. 2497
Niobrara Public Library, Niobrara NE p. 1326
Nioga Library System, Lockport NY p. 1564
Niota Public Library, Niota TN p. 2122
Nipawin Bible College Library, Nipawin SK p. 2743
Nipawin Public Library, *see* Wapiti Regional Library, Nipawin SK p. 2746
Nipigon Public Library, *see* Corporation of the Township of Nipigon Public Library Board, Nipigon ON p. 2661
Nipissing District Law Association Library, North Bay ON p. 2661
Nippersink Public Library District, Richmond IL p. 638
Nissen Public Library, Saint Ansgar IA p. 780
Niton Library, Niton Junction AB p. 2549
Nitro Public, *see* Kanawha County Public Library, Nitro WV p. 2400
Nivison Michael Public Library, Cloudcroft NM p. 1465
Nix Clyde Public Library, *see* Northwest Regional Library, Hamilton AL p. 40
Nix Library, *see* New Orleans Public Library, New Orleans LA p. 903
Nixon Aphne Pattillo Public Library, Nixon TX p. 2222
Nixon Blanche A Library - Cobbs Creek Branch, *see* Free Library of Philadelphia, Philadelphia PA p. 1979
Nixon Ester Dewitt Branch, *see* Central Arkansas Library System, Jacksonville AR p. 101
Nixon L W Library, El Dorado Campus, *see* Butler Community College Library & Archives, El Dorado KS p. 805
Nixon Peabody, Chicago IL p. 566
Nixon Peabody LLP, Washington DC p. 373
Nixon Peabody LLP, Boston MA p. 998
Nixon Presidential Library & Museum, *see* National Archives & Records Administration, Yorba Linda CA p. 260
Nixon Research Library, *see* Chautauqua County Historical Society, Westfield NY p. 1664

North Fork Community Library, *see* Whatcom County Library System, Maple Falls WA p. 2359
North Fort Myers Public, *see* Lee County Library System, North Fort Myers FL p. 403
North Freedom Public Library, North Freedom WI p. 2465
North Garland Branch, *see* Nicholson Memorial Library System, Garland TX p. 2184
North Georgia Technical College Library, Blairsville GA p. 468
North Georgia Technical College Library, Clarkesville GA p. 470
North Gorham Public Library, Gorham ME p. 926
North Greenbush Public Library, Wynantskill NY p. 1667
North Greenville University, Tigerville SC p. 2071
North Grenville Public Library, Kemptville ON p. 2649
North Haledon Free Public Library, North Haledon NJ p. 1429
North Hampton Public Library, North Hampton NH p. 1376
North Harris College Library, *see* Lone Star College System, Houston TX p. 2197
North Hastings Public Library, *see* Bancroft Public Library, Bancroft ON p. 2629
North Haven Library, North Haven ME p. 933
North Haven Memorial Library, North Haven CT p. 331
North Hennepin Community College Library, Brooklyn Park MN p. 1167
North Hero Public Library, North Hero VT p. 2290
North Highlands/Antelope Library, *see* Sacramento Public Library, Antelope CA p. 210
North Hills Community Library, *see* Queens Library, Little Neck NY p. 1555
North Idaho College Library, Coeur d'Alene ID p. 519
North Idaho Correctional Institution Library, Cottonwood ID p. 520
North Indian River County Library, *see* Indian River County Library System, Sebastian FL p. 452
North Iowa Area Community College Library, Mason City IA p. 769
North Island College, Campbell River BC p. 2564
North Island College, Courtenay BC p. 2565
North Island College, Port Alberni BC p. 2573
North Island College, Port Hardy BC p. 2574
North Judson-Wayne Township Public Library, North Judson IN p. 710
North Kansas City Public Library, North Kansas City MO p. 1264
North Kawartha Library, Apsley ON p. 2628
North Kern State Prison, *see* California Department of Corrections Library System, Delano CA p. 207
North Kingstown Free Library, North Kingstown RI p. 2036
North Kohala Public Library, *see* Hawaii State Public Library System, Kapaau HI p. 510
North Las Vegas Library District, North Las Vegas NV p. 1348
North Liberty Library, North Liberty IA p. 773
North Logan City Library, North Logan UT p. 2267
North Loup Township Library, North Loup NE p. 1326
North Madison County Public Library System, Elwood IN p. 680
North Manchester Public Library, North Manchester IN p. 710
North Mankato Taylor Library, North Mankato MN p. 1190
North Merrick Public Library, North Merrick NY p. 1607
North Metro Campus Library, *see* Chattahoochee Technical College Library, Acworth GA p. 489
North Miami Beach Public Library, North Miami Beach FL p. 429
North Miami Public Library, North Miami FL p. 429
North Mississippi Health Services, Tupelo MS p. 1234
North Norfolk MacGregor Regional Library, MacGregor MB p. 2588
North of Boston Library Exchange, Inc (N), Danvers MA p. 2767
North Olympic Library System, Port Angeles WA p. 2373
North Palm Beach Public Library, North Palm Beach FL p. 429
North Park University, Chicago IL p. 566
North Perth Public Library, Listowel ON p. 2653
North Pike District Library, Griggsville IL p. 596
North Plainfield Library, *see* Somerset County Library System of New Jersey, North Plainfield NJ p. 1392
North Platte Learning Commons, *see* Mid-Plains Community College, North Platte NE p. 1327
North Platte Public Library, North Platte NE p. 1327
North Pocono Public Library, Moscow PA p. 1966
North Point Branch, *see* Baltimore County Public Library, Baltimore MD p. 980
North Port Public Library, North Port FL p. 429
North Powder Library, North Powder OR p. 1889
North Providence Union Free Library, North Providence RI p. 2036
North Richland Hills Public Library, North Richland Hills TX p. 2223
North Riverside Public Library District, North Riverside IL p. 626
North Sacramento-Hagginwood Library, *see* Sacramento Public Library, Sacramento CA p. 210
North Saint Paul Historical Society, North Saint Paul MN p. 1191
North Salem Free Library, *see* Keeler Ruth Memorial Library, North Salem NY p. 1608
North Scituate Public Library, North Scituate RI p. 2036
North Seattle Community College, Seattle WA p. 2377
North Shelby County Library, Birmingham AL p. 8
North Shore Community College Library, Danvers MA p. 1013
North Shore Community College Library, Lynn MA p. 1030
North Shore Library, Glendale WI p. 2437
North Shore Medical Center, Salem Hospital, Salem MA p. 1051
North Shore Public Library, Shoreham NY p. 1641
North Shore University Hospital, Manhasset NY p. 1568
North Smithfield Public Library, Slatersville RI p. 2041
North Suburban Library District, Loves Park IL p. 611
North Suburban Synagogue Beth El, Highland Park IL p. 599
North Suffolk Library, *see* Suffolk Public Library System, Suffolk VA p. 2348
North Texas State Hospital, Vernon TX p. 2251
North Tonawanda Public Library, North Tonawanda NY p. 1608
North Trails Public Library, West Sunbury PA p. 2021
North Valley Public Library, Stevensville MT p. 1302
North Valley Regional, *see* Maricopa County Library District, Anthem AZ p. 71
North Vancouver City Library, North Vancouver BC p. 2572
North Vancouver District Public Library, North Vancouver BC p. 2573
North Versailles Public Library, North Versailles PA p. 1971
North Wales Area Library, North Wales PA p. 1971
North Webster Community Public Library, North Webster IN p. 711
North-West Regional Library, Swan River MB p. 2591
North Woodstock Library, Woodstock CT p. 349
North York General Hospital, Toronto ON p. 2690
Northampton Area Public Library, Northampton PA p. 1972
Northampton Community College, Bethlehem PA p. 1912, 2791
Northampton County Historical & Genealogical Society, Easton PA p. 1929
Northampton County Law Library, Easton PA p. 1929
Northampton Free Library, *see* Eastern Shore Public Library, Nassawadox VA p. 2301
Northampton Memorial Library, *see* Albemarle Regional Library, Jackson NC p. 1727
Northborough Free Library, Northborough MA p. 1043
Northbrook Public Library, Northbrook IL p. 626
Northcentral Technical College Library, Wausau WI p. 2486
Northeast Alabama Community College, Rainsville AL p. 34
Northeast Alabama Regional Medical Center, Anniston AL p. 4
Northeast Arkansas Regional Library System, Paragould AR p. 107
Northeast Community College, Norfolk NE p. 1326
Northeast Correctional Center, *see* Missouri Department of Corrections, Bowling Green MO p. 1252
Northeast Fisheries Science Center, Woods Hole MA p. 1071
Northeast Florida Library Information Network (N), Orange Park FL p. 2763
Northeast Georgia Health System, Gainesville GA p. 480
Northeast Georgia Regional Library System, Clarkesville GA p. 471
Northeast Harbor Library, Northeast Harbor ME p. 933
Northeast Iowa Community College, Peosta IA p. 776
Northeast Kansas Library System, Lawrence KS p. 819
Northeast Lakeview College Library, *see* Alamo Colleges District, Universal City TX p. 2250
NorthEast-Millerton Library, Millerton NY p. 1572
Northeast Mississippi Community College, Booneville MS p. 1212
Northeast Missouri Library Service, Kahoka MO p. 1254
Northeast Neighborhood Library, *see* District of Columbia Public Library, Washington DC p. 364
Northeast Ohio Medical University, Rootstown OH p. 1818
Northeast Ohio Regional Library System (N), Hudson OH p. 2772
Northeast Regional Center Learning Commons, *see* Community College of Philadelphia Library, Philadelphia PA p. 1975
Northeast Regional Library, Corinth MS p. 1215
Northeast State Community College, Blountville TN p. 2088
Northeast Texas Community College, Mount Pleasant TX p. 2220
Northeast Wisconsin Masonic Library & Museum, Green Bay WI p. 2439
Northeast Wisconsin Technical College Library, Green Bay WI p. 2439
Northeastern Illinois University, Chicago IL p. 566
Northeastern Junior College, Sterling CO p. 296
Northeastern Nevada Museum Library, Elko NV p. 1345
Northeastern Oklahoma A&M College, Miami OK p. 1853
Northeastern State University, Tahlequah OK p. 1863
Northeastern Technical College Library, Cheraw SC p. 2051
Northeastern University Libraries, Oakland CA p. 185
Northeastern University Libraries, Boston MA p. 998
Northeastern University School of Law Library, Boston MA p. 999
Northeastern Vermont Regional Hospital, Saint Johnsbury VT p. 2294
Northern & Central California Psychology Libraries (N), Berkeley CA p. 2762
Northern Alberta Institute of Technology, Edmonton AB p. 2537
Northern Baptist Theological Seminary, Lisle IL p. 610
Northern California Association of Law Libraries (N), San Francisco CA p. 2762

Notre Dame de Namur University Library, Belmont CA p. 121
Notre Dame Seminary Graduate School of Theology, New Orleans LA p. 903
Nottage Library, *see* University of Maine at Augusta, Bangor ME p. 916
Nottawa Township Library, Centreville MI p. 1090
Nottoway County Public Libraries, Crewe VA p. 2314
Notus Public Library, Notus ID p. 528
Nova Scotia Barristers' Society, Halifax NS p. 2619
Nova Scotia College of Art & Design University Library, Halifax NS p. 2619
Nova Scotia Community College, Halifax NS p. 2619
Nova Scotia Department of Education & Early Childhood Dev, Halifax NS p. 2620
Nova Scotia Department of Natural Resources & Renewables, Halifax NS p. 2620
Nova Scotia Government, Halifax NS p. 2620
Nova Scotia Health Authority, Sydney NS p. 2623
Nova Scotia Legal Aid Library, Halifax NS p. 2620
Nova Scotia Legislative Library, Halifax NS p. 2620
Nova Scotia Museum Library, Halifax NS p. 2620
Nova Scotia Museum of Industry Library, Stellarton NS p. 2622
Nova Scotia Provincial Library, Halifax NS p. 2621
Nova Southeastern University, Fort Lauderdale FL p. 401
Nova Southeastern University Libraries, Fort Lauderdale FL p. 402
Novanet (N), Bedford NS p. 2778
Novant Health Library Services, Winston-Salem NC p. 1725
Novant Health Presbyterian Medical Center, Charlotte NC p. 1680
Novi Public Library, Novi MI p. 1138
Nowata City-County Library, Nowata OK p. 1856
Noxubee County Library System, Macon MS p. 1225
Noyes Library for Young Children, *see* Montgomery County Public Libraries, Kensington MD p. 975
Noyes Phoebe Griffin Library, *see* Old Lyme, Old Lyme CT p. 332
NPR RAD - Research Archive & Data Strategy, Washington DC p. 373
Nubanusit Library Cooperative (N), Keene NH p. 2769
Nucla Public Library, Nucla CO p. 292
Nuclear Energy Institute Library, Washington DC p. 373
Nueces County Public Libraries, Robstown TX p. 2233
Nueta Hidatsa Sahnish College, New Town ND p. 1739
Nugen H J Public Library, New London IA p. 772
Nunavut Arctic College, Cambridge Bay NU p. 2625
Nunavut Arctic College, Iqaluit NU p. 2625
Nunavut Arctic College, Rankin Inlet NU p. 2625
Nunavut Court of Justice Law Library, Iqaluit NU p. 2625
Nunavut Public Library Services, Baker Lake NU p. 2625
Nunez Community College Library, Chalmette LA p. 887
Nutana Collegiate Institute, Saskatoon SK p. 2749
Nute High School & Library, Milton NH p. 1374
Nutley Free Public Library, Nutley NJ p. 1430
Nutter Fort Library, Nutter Fort WV p. 2410
Nutter McClennen & Fish LLP, Boston MA p. 999
Nuview Library, *see* Riverside County Library System, Nuevo CA p. 202
NWLF (N), *see* Northwest Library Federation, Prince George BC p. 2777
Nyack Library, Nyack NY p. 1609
NYC Health & Hospital - Elmhurst, Elmhurst NY p. 1530
NYC Health & Hospitals - Coler, New York NY p. 1599
Nye George Jr Library, *see* County of Los Angeles Public Library, Lakewood CA p. 137
Nye Library, *see* United States Army, Fort Sill OK p. 1848
NYS Small Business Development Center Research Network, Albany NY p. 1483
NYS Supreme Court Library - Binghamton, Binghamton NY p. 1494
Nyssa Public Library, Nyssa OR p. 1889
NYU Grossman Long Island School of Medicine, Mineola NY p. 1572
NYU Langone Hospital, New York NY p. 1599
NYU Tandon School of Engineering, Brooklyn NY p. 1505
O'Brien Library, *see* United Theological Seminary, Dayton OH p. 1780
Oak Bluffs Public Library, Oak Bluffs MA p. 1044
Oak Brook Public Library, Oak Brook IL p. 627
Oak Creek Public Library, Oak Creek WI p. 2465
Oak Creek Public Library, *see* South Routt Library District, Oak Creek CO p. 292
Oak Forest Neighborhood Library, *see* Houston Public Library, Houston TX p. 2196
Oak Grove Baptist Church Library, Carrollton GA p. 469
Oak Grove Lutheran Church, Richfield MN p. 1194
Oak Grove Public, *see* Lamar County Library System, Hattiesburg MS p. 1230
Oak Harbor Library, *see* Sno-Isle Libraries, Oak Harbor WA p. 2371
Oak Harbor Public Library, Oak Harbor OH p. 1810
Oak Hill Public Library, Oak Hill OH p. 1810
Oak Hill Public Library, *see* Volusia County Public Library, Oak Hill FL p. 393
Oak Hills Christian College, Bemidji MN p. 1165
Oak Lawn Public Library, Oak Lawn IL p. 628
Oak Park Public Library, Oak Park IL p. 628
Oak Park Public Library, Oak Park MI p. 1138
Oak Point University Library, Chicago IL p. 567
Oak Ridge Public Library, Oak Ridge TN p. 2123
Oak Ridges Moraine Library, *see* Richmond Hill Public Library, Richmond Hill ON p. 2675
Oakalla Public Library, *see* Burnet County Library System, Oakalla TX p. 2152
Oakdale Public Library, Oakdale TN p. 2123
Oakes Public Library, Oakes ND p. 1739
Oakfield Public Library, Oakfield WI p. 2466
Oakland City-Columbia Township Public Library, Oakland City IN p. 712
Oakland City University, Oakland City IN p. 712
Oakland Community College, Auburn Hills MI p. 1082
Oakland Community College, Farmington Hills MI p. 1104
Oakland Community College, Royal Oak MI p. 1146
Oakland Community College, Southfield MI p. 1151
Oakland Community College, Waterford MI p. 1157
Oakland County Jail Library, Pontiac MI p. 1141
Oakland County Pioneer & Historical Society, Pontiac MI p. 1142
Oakland Public Library, Oakland CA p. 185
Oakland Public Library, Oakland ME p. 934
Oakland Public Library, Oakland NE p. 1327
Oakland Public Library, Oakland NJ p. 1430
Oakland Public Library, *see* Yalobusha County Public Library System, Oakland MS p. 1214
Oakland University Library, Rochester MI p. 1144
Oakley Free Library District, Oakley ID p. 528
Oakley Millard Library, Livingston TN p. 2109
Oakley Public Library, Oakley KS p. 828
Oakmont Carnegie Library, Oakmont PA p. 1972
Oakridge Public Library, Oakridge OR p. 1889
Oaks Correctional Facility Library, *see* Michigan Department of Corrections, Manistee MI p. 1129
Oakton College Library, Des Plaines IL p. 578
Oakton Community College Library, Skokie IL p. 647
Oakton Library, *see* Fairfax County Public Library, Oakton VA p. 2316
Oakville Public Library, Oakville ON p. 2662
Oakwood Public Library District, Oakwood IL p. 628
Oakwood University, Huntsville AL p. 22
Oakwood Village Library & Arts Centre, *see* Toronto Public Library, Toronto ON p. 2696
Obama Barack Learning Center, *see* Phoenix Public Library District, Phoenix IL p. 635
Obama Michelle Branch, *see* Long Beach Public Library, Long Beach CA p. 159
Oberlin City Library, Oberlin KS p. 828
Oberlin Public Library, Oberlin OH p. 1810
Oberndorf Meyera E Central Library, *see* Virginia Beach Public Library, Virginia Beach VA p. 2351
Obion County Public Library, Union City TN p. 2128
Obion River Regional Library, Martin TN p. 2110
Oblate School of Theology, San Antonio TX p. 2237
Oblon, Spivak, Alexandria VA p. 2303
Oboler Eli M Library, *see* Idaho State University, Pocatello ID p. 528
O'Brien Memorial Library, Blue River OR p. 1874
OC Public Libraries, Santa Ana CA p. 237
OCAD University, Toronto ON p. 2690
Ocala Public Library (Headquarters), *see* Marion County Public Library System, Ocala FL p. 430
OCallahan Science Library, *see* College of the Holy Cross, Worcester MA p. 1072
Occidental College Library, Los Angeles CA p. 167
Ocean City Free Public Library, Ocean City NJ p. 1430
Ocean City Historical Museum, Ocean City NJ p. 1431
Ocean County College Library, Toms River NJ p. 1446
Ocean County Historical Society, Toms River NJ p. 1446
Ocean County Library, Toms River NJ p. 1446
Ocean Park Memorial Library, Ocean Park ME p. 934
Ocean Shores Public Library, Ocean Shores WA p. 2372
Ocean Springs Municipal Library, *see* Jackson-George Regional Library System, Ocean Springs MS p. 1228
Ocean State Libraries (N), Warwick RI p. 2774
Ocean Township Historical Museum Library, Ocean NJ p. 1430
Ocean Vicinage Court User Resource Center, Toms River NJ p. 1447
Oceana Public, *see* Wyoming County Public Library, Oceana WV p. 2412
Oceanic Free Library, Rumson NJ p. 1441
Oceanographic Campus Library, *see* Nova Southeastern University Libraries, Dania Beach FL p. 402
Oceanside Library, Oceanside NY p. 1609
Oceanside Public Library, Oceanside CA p. 187
Ocheyedan Public Library, Ocheyedan IA p. 774
Ochsner LSU Health Shreveport Monroe Medical Center, Monroe LA p. 898
Ochsner Medical Library, New Orleans LA p. 903
OCLC Library, Archive & Museum, Dublin OH p. 1782
OCLC Online Computer Library Center, Inc (N), Dublin OH p. 2772
OCLC Research Library Partnership (N), Dublin OH p. 2772
Ocmulgee National Monument Library, *see* National Park Service, Macon GA p. 487
Ocmulgee Regional Library System, Eastman GA p. 477
Ocoee River Regional Library, Athens TN p. 2088
Oconee Campus Library, *see* University of North Georgia, Watkinsville GA p. 493
Oconee County Public Library, Walhalla SC p. 2072
Oconee Regional Library, Dublin GA p. 477
O'Connell Alfred C Library, *see* Genesee Community College, Batavia NY p. 1490
O'Connell Branch, *see* Cambridge Public Library, Cambridge MA p. 1004
O'Connor Catherine B Library, *see* Boston College Libraries, Weston MA p. 1011
O'Connor Dennis M Public Library, Refugio TX p. 2231
Oconomowoc Public Library, Oconomowoc WI p. 2466
Oconto Falls Community Library, Oconto Falls WI p. 2466
Oconto Public Library, Oconto NE p. 1327
Ocotillo Library & Workforce Literacy Center, *see* Phoenix Public Library, Phoenix AZ p. 72
Ocracoke School & Community Library, *see* Beaufort, Hyde & Martin County Regional Library, Ocracoke NC p. 1720

O'Leary Library, *see* University of Massachusetts Lowell Library, Lowell MA p. 1030
OLeary Public Library, *see* Prince Edward Island Public Library Service, O'Leary PE p. 2708
Olewine Madeline L Memorial Library, *see* Dauphin County Library System, Harrisburg PA p. 1940
OLI Systems, Inc Library, Parsippany NJ p. 1432
Olin & Uris Libraries, *see* Cornell University Library, Ithaca NY p. 1552
Olin Corp, Charleston TN p. 2091
Olin F W Library, *see* Drury University, Springfield MO p. 1280
Olin F W Library, *see* Northeastern University Libraries, Oakland CA p. 185
Olin John M Library, *see* Washington University Libraries, Saint Louis MO p. 1276
Olin Learning Resource Center, *see* Jarvis Christian College, Hawkins TX p. 2188
Olin Library, *see* Rollins College, Winter Park FL p. 455
Olin Library & Gordon Keith Chalmers Memorial Library, *see* Kenyon College Library & Information Services, Gambier OH p. 1787
Olin Memorial Library, *see* Wesleyan University, Middletown CT p. 322
Olin Public Library, Olin IA p. 774
Olive Free Library Association, West Shokan NY p. 1663
Olive-Harvey College Library, *see* City Colleges of Chicago, Chicago IL p. 559
Oliver J C Library, *see* Arkansas Baptist College, Little Rock AR p. 100
Oliver Springs Public Library, Oliver Springs TN p. 2123
Olivet Nazarene University, Bourbonnais IL p. 544
Olivia Public Library, Olivia MN p. 1191
Olmsted County Historical Society, Rochester MN p. 1194
Olmsted Public Library, Olmsted IL p. 629
Olney Central College, Olney IL p. 629
Olney Community Library & Arts Center, Olney TX p. 2223
Olney Library, *see* Montgomery County Public Libraries, Olney MD p. 975
Olney Public Library, Olney IL p. 630
Olneyville Library, *see* Community Libraries of Providence, Providence RI p. 2038
Olschner Quinerly Public Library, Ayden NC p. 1673
Olson Gordon B Library, *see* Minot State University, Minot ND p. 1738
Olson Lydia M Library, *see* Northern Michigan University, Marquette MI p. 1130
Olson Walter E Memorial Library, Eagle River WI p. 2432
Olton Area Library, Olton TX p. 2223
Olympic College, Bremerton WA p. 2360
Omaha Correctional Center Library, Omaha NE p. 1329
Omaha Public Library, Omaha NE p. 1329
Omaha World-Herald Library, Omaha NE p. 1330
O'Malley Mary Alice & Tom Library, *see* Manhattan College, Riverdale NY p. 1627
Oman Library, *see* Middle East Institute, Washington DC p. 371
Ombudsman Library, Fredericton NB p. 2601
O'Melveny & Myers LLP, Los Angeles CA p. 167
O'Melveny & Myers LLP, Newport Beach CA p. 183
O'Melveny & Myers LLP, Washington DC p. 373
O'Melveny & Myers LLP, New York NY p. 1599
Omer-Leger Public Library, *see* Albert-Westmorland-Kent Regional Library, Saint-Antoine NB p. 2603
Omohundro Institute of Early American History & Culture, Williamsburg VA p. 2353
Omro Public Library, *see* Carter Memorial Library, Omro WI p. 2466
Onalaska Public, *see* La Crosse County Library, Onalaska WI p. 2441
Onalaska Public Library, Onalaska TX p. 2223
Onarga Community Public Library District, Onarga IL p. 630
Onawa Public Library, Onawa IA p. 774
ONE National Gay & Lesbian Archives at the USC Libraries, Los Angeles CA p. 167
O'Neal Emmet Library, Mountain Brook AL p. 31
O'Neal S C Library & Technology Center, *see* Drake State Community & Technical College, Huntsville AL p. 21
Onebane Law Firm APC, Lafayette LA p. 893
Oneida Community Library, Oneida WI p. 2466
Oneida County Historical Center, Utica NY p. 1655
Oneida County Library, Malad City ID p. 525
Oneida Public, *see* Scott County Public Library, Oneida TN p. 2123
Oneida Public Library, Oneida NY p. 1611
O'Neill Eugene Theater Center, Waterford CT p. 344
O'Neill Public Library, O'Neill NE p. 1331
O'Neill Thomas P Jr Library, *see* Boston College Libraries, Chestnut Hill MA p. 1011
Oneonta Public Library, Oneonta AL p. 31
Onion Creek Library Station, *see* Libraries of Stevens County, Colville WA p. 2370
Onondaga Community College, Syracuse NY p. 1649
Onondaga County Public Libraries, Syracuse NY p. 1649
Onondaga Free Library, Syracuse NY p. 1649
Onoway Public Library, Onoway AB p. 2550
Onslow County Public Library, Jacksonville NC p. 1697
Ontario Archaeological Society Library, Toronto ON p. 2691
Ontario Camps Association Library, Toronto ON p. 2691
Ontario City Library, Ontario CA p. 188
Ontario Community Library, Ontario OR p. 1889
Ontario Council of University Libraries (N), Toronto ON p. 2778
Ontario County Historical Society Library, Canandaigua NY p. 1512
Ontario Genealogical Society Library, Toronto ON p. 2691
Ontario Library Consortium (N), Keswick ON p. 2778
Ontario Library Service, Toronto ON p. 2691
Ontario Ministry of Education, Toronto ON p. 2691
Ontario Ministry of Finance, Toronto ON p. 2691
Ontario Ministry of Natural Resources & Forestry, Peterborough ON p. 2672
Ontario Ministry of the Attorney General, Toronto ON p. 2691
Ontario Ministry of the Environment, Conservation & Parks, Toronto ON p. 2691
Ontario Ministry of Transportation Library, St. Catharines ON p. 2679
Ontario Office of the Fire Marshal & Emergency Management, Midhurst ON p. 2657
Ontario Provincial Police, Orillia ON p. 2663
Ontario Public Library, Ontario NY p. 1611
Ontario Public Library, Ontario WI p. 2466
Ontario Securities Commission Library, Toronto ON p. 2691
Ontario Workplace Tribunals Library, Toronto ON p. 2691
Ontonagon Township Library, Ontonagon MI p. 1139
Oostburg Public Library, Oostburg WI p. 2466
Opelika Campus Library, *see* Southern Union State Community College, Opelika AL p. 39
Opelika Public Library, Opelika AL p. 31
Opelousas Public Library, Opelousas LA p. 905
Opheim Community Library, Opheim MT p. 1300
OPIRG Guelph Radical Resource Library, Guelph ON p. 2643
OPLIN (N), *see* Ohio Public Library Information Network, Columbus OH p. 2773
Opp Public Library, Opp AL p. 32
Opperman Jacquelin E Memorial Library, Kingston MI p. 1122
Optometry & Health Sciences Library, *see* University of California, Berkeley, Berkeley CA p. 123
O'Quinn Law Library, *see* University of Houston, Houston TX p. 2199
Oracle Public Library, Oracle AZ p. 67
Oradell Free Public Library, Oradell NJ p. 1431
Oral Roberts University Library, Tulsa OK p. 1865
Oram Wilfred Centennial, *see* Cape Breton Regional Library, North Sydney NS p. 2622
Orange Beach Public Library, Orange Beach AL p. 32
Orange City Public Library, Orange City IA p. 775
Orange City Public Library, *see* Volusia County Public Library, Orange City FL p. 393
Orange Coast College Library, Costa Mesa CA p. 132
Orange County Community College Library, Middletown NY p. 1571
Orange County Global Medical Center, Santa Ana CA p. 239
Orange County Library System, Orlando FL p. 431
Orange County Museum of Art Library, Costa Mesa CA p. 132
Orange County Public Law Library, Santa Ana CA p. 239
Orange County Public Library, Hillsborough NC p. 1697
Orange County Public Library, Orange VA p. 2336
Orange County Regional History Center, Orlando FL p. 432
Orange County Supreme Court Law Library, *see* New York State Supreme Court Ninth Judicial District, Goshen NY p. 1540
Orange Grove Public, *see* Harrison County Library System, Gulfport MS p. 1218
Orange Grove School & Public Library, *see* Salinas Alicia City of Alice Public Library, Orange Grove TX p. 2133
Orange Park Public Library, *see* Clay County Public Library System, Orange Park FL p. 396
Orange Public Library, Orange NJ p. 1431
Orange Public Library, Orange TX p. 2224
Orange Public Library & History Center, Orange CA p. 188
Orangeburg-Calhoun Technical College Library, Orangeburg SC p. 2066
Orangeburg County Library, Orangeburg SC p. 2066
Orangeburg Library, Orangeburg NY p. 1612
Orangevale Library, *see* Sacramento Public Library, Orangevale CA p. 210
Orangeville Public Library, Orangeville PA p. 1973
Orangeville Public Library, Orangeville ON p. 2663
Orbach Raymond L Science Library, *see* University of California, Riverside, Riverside CA p. 203
Orbis Cascade Alliance (N), Portland OR p. 2773
Orcas Island Library District, Eastsound WA p. 2363
Orchard Park Public Library, Orchard Park NY p. 1612
Orchard Public Library, Orchard NE p. 1331
Ord Township Library, Ord NE p. 1331
Order of Servants of Mary (Servites), USA Province, Chicago IL p. 567
Oreana Public Library, *see* Argenta-Oreana Public Library District, Oreana IL p. 630
Oregon City Public Library, Oregon City OR p. 1890
Oregon Coast Community College Library, Newport OR p. 1888
Oregon Coast History Center, Newport OR p. 1888
Oregon College of Oriental Medicine Library, Portland OR p. 1893
Oregon County Library District, Alton MO p. 1237
Oregon Department of Transportation Library, Salem OR p. 1896
Oregon Health & Science University Library, Portland OR p. 1893
Oregon Historical Society, Portland OR p. 1893
Oregon Institute of Technology Library, Klamath Falls OR p. 1883
Oregon National Primate Research Center, Beaverton OR p. 1873
Oregon Public Library, Oregon MO p. 1264
Oregon Public Library, Oregon WI p. 2467
Oregon Public Library District, Oregon IL p. 630
Oregon Research Institute Library, Springfield OR p. 1899
Oregon School for the Deaf Library, Salem OR p. 1896
Oregon State Correctional Institution Library, Salem OR p. 1896

Patrick Jack B Information Tech Center, *see* Augusta Technical College, Augusta GA p. 467
Patrick Lynch Public Library, Poteau OK p. 1860
Pattee Library & Paterno Library, *see* Pennsylvania State University Libraries, University Park PA p. 2015
Patten Free Library, Bath ME p. 916
Patten John L Library, *see* Faith Baptist Bible College, Ankeny IA p. 732
Patten-North Haverhill Library, North Haverhill NH p. 1377
Patterson A Holly Library, *see* Nassau Community College, Garden City NY p. 1537
Patterson, Belknap, Webb & Tyler LLP Library, New York NY p. 1600
Patterson Daniel J Campus Library, *see* Niagara College of Applied Arts & Technology, Niagara-on-the-Lake ON p. 2703
Patterson Gilbert Memorial, *see* Robeson County Public Library, Maxton NC p. 1702
Patterson Library, Patterson NY p. 1615
Patterson Library, Westfield NY p. 1664
Patterson Lucy Hill Memorial Library, Rockdale TX p. 2233
Patterson Memorial Library, Wild Rose WI p. 2488
Patterson Palmer Library, Truro NS p. 2623
Pattillo Library, *see* Peachtree Presbyterian Church, Atlanta GA p. 466
Patton Melba Library, *see* Southeastern Illinois College, Harrisburg IL p. 597
Patton Museum of Cavalry & Armor Emert L Davis Memorial Library, *see* United States Army, Fort Knox KY p. 855
Patton Public Library, Patton PA p. 1973
Patton State Hospital, Patton CA p. 195
Patuxent Institution Library, Jessup MD p. 969
Elsner Paul A Library, *see* Mesa Community College Library, Mesa AZ p. 66
Paul D Camp Community College Library, Franklin VA p. 2319
Paul Hastings LLP, Los Angeles CA p. 167
Paul Memorial Library, Newfields NH p. 1376
Paul Quinn College, Dallas TX p. 2167
Paul Smiths College of Arts & Sciences, Paul Smiths NY p. 1615
Paul, Weiss, Rifkind, Wharton & Garrison LLP Library, New York NY p. 1600
Paulden Public Library, *see* Yavapai County Free Library District, Paulden AZ p. 75
Paulding County Carnegie Library, Paulding OH p. 1814
Paullina Public Library, Paullina IA p. 776
Pavo Public Library, *see* Thomas County Public Library System, Pavo GA p. 499
Paw Paw District Library, Paw Paw MI p. 1140
Paw Paw Public Library, Paw Paw WV p. 2412
Paw Paw Public Library District, Paw Paw IL p. 633
Pawhuska Public Library, Pawhuska OK p. 1860
Pawlet Public Library, Pawlet VT p. 2291
Pawling Free Library, Pawling NY p. 1616
Pawnee City Public Library, Pawnee City NE p. 1332
Pawnee Heights Library, Burdett KS p. 799
Pawnee Public Library, Pawnee IL p. 633
Pawnee Public Library, Pawnee OK p. 1860
Pawtucket Public Library, Pawtucket RI p. 2036
Paxton Carnegie Library, Paxton IL p. 633
Paxton Public Library, Paxton NE p. 1332
Payette Associates, Boston MA p. 999
Payette Public Library, Payette ID p. 528
Payne Bishop Library, *see* Virginia Theological Seminary, Alexandria VA p. 2303
Payne Theological Seminary, Wilberforce OH p. 1831
Paynesville Library, *see* Great River Regional Library, Paynesville MN p. 1197
Payson City Library, Payson UT p. 2269
Payson Daniel Carroll Medical Library, *see* North Shore University Hospital, Manhasset NY p. 1568
Payson Library, *see* Pepperdine University Libraries, Malibu CA p. 171
Payson Public Library, Payson AZ p. 68
Payton Benjamin F Learning Resources Center, *see* Benedict College Library, Columbia SC p. 2053
PCIN (N), *see* Perth County Information Network, Stratford ON p. 2778
Pea Ridge Community Library, Pea Ridge AR p. 107
Pea Ridge Military Park Library, *see* United States National Park Service, Garfield AR p. 96
Peabody Essex Museum, Rowley MA p. 1050
Peabody Frances W Research Library, *see* Greater Portland Landmarks, Inc, Portland ME p. 936
Peabody George Library, *see* Johns Hopkins University Libraries, Baltimore MD p. 954
Peabody Historical Society & Museum, Peabody MA p. 1045
Peabody Institute Library, Danvers MA p. 1013
Peabody Institute Library, Peabody MA p. 1045
Peabody Library, *see* Vanderbilt University, Nashville TN p. 2122
Peabody Memorial Library, Jonesport ME p. 928
Peabody Public Library, Columbia City IN p. 676
Peabody Robert S Museum of Archaeology, *see* Phillips Academy, Andover MA p. 985
Peabody Township Library, Peabody KS p. 831
Peace Library System, Grande Prairie AB p. 2541
Peace River Bible Institute Library, Sexsmith AB p. 2553
Peace River Municipal Library, Peace River AB p. 2550
Peace River Museum, Archives & Mackenzie Centre, Peace River AB p. 2550
Peach Public Libraries, Fort Valley GA p. 480
Peacham Library, Peacham VT p. 2291
Peachtree City Library, *see* Flint River Regional Library System, Peachtree City GA p. 481
Peachtree Presbyterian Church, Atlanta GA p. 466
Peapack & Gladstone Public, *see* Somerset County Library System of New Jersey, Peapack NJ p. 1392
Pearce B C Learning Resources Center, *see* Saint Johns River State College, Palatka FL p. 433
Pearisburg Public Library, Pearisburg VA p. 2337
Pearl City Public Library, *see* Hawaii State Public Library System, Pearl City HI p. 510
Pearl City Public Library District, Pearl City IL p. 633
Pearl Public Library, Pearl MS p. 1229
Pearl River Community College, Poplarville MS p. 1230
Pearl River County Library System, Picayune MS p. 1229
Pearl River Public Library, Pearl River NY p. 1616
Pearlington Public Library, *see* Hancock County Library System, Pearlington MS p. 1212
Pearsall Elizabeth Braswell Library, *see* North Carolina Wesleyan University, Rocky Mount NC p. 1713
Pearsall Public Library, Pearsall TX p. 2225
Pearse Memorial Library-Marine Lab, *see* Duke University Libraries, Beaufort NC p. 1684
Pearson Library, *see* California Lutheran University, Thousand Oaks CA p. 252
Pearson Public Library, *see* Satilla Regional Library, Pearson GA p. 476
Pease Public Library, Plymouth NH p. 1378
Peavey Memorial Library, Eastport ME p. 924
Peayamechikee Public Library, Pinehouse Lake SK p. 2744
Pecatonica Public Library District, Pecatonica IL p. 633
Peck Memorial Library, Marathon NY p. 1568
Peckar & Abramson, River Edge NJ p. 1439
McLeod Peden Library, *see* University of South Carolina, Walterboro SC p. 2046
Pederson Nellie Civic Library, Clifton TX p. 2156
Peebles Public Library, *see* Adams County Public Library, Peebles OH p. 1814
Peek Iva Jane Public Library, Decatur AR p. 93
Peel District School Board, Mississauga ON p. 2659
Pegues Godfrey Public Library, *see* Newark Public Library, Newark TX p. 2222
Peine H A District Library, Minier IL p. 618
Peirce College Library, Philadelphia PA p. 1983
Pejepscot History Center, Brunswick ME p. 919
Pekin Public Library, Pekin IL p. 634
Pelahatchie Public Library, Pelahatchie MS p. 1229
Pelham Library, Pelham MA p. 1045
Pelham Public Library, Pelham AL p. 32
Pelham Public Library, Pelham NH p. 1377
Pelham Public Library, Fonthill ON p. 2642
Pelican Bay State Prison, *see* California Department of Corrections Library System, Crescent City CA p. 207
Pelican Public Library, Pelican AK p. 50
Pelican Rapids Public Library, Pelican Rapids MN p. 1192
Pell City Library, Pell City AL p. 32
Pell Marine Science Library, *see* University of Rhode Island, Narragansett RI p. 2034
Pella Public Library, Pella IA p. 776
Pelland Azalea Gilles Library, *see* Greater Sudbury Public Library, Azilda ON p. 2683
Pellissippi State Community College, Friendsville TN p. 2099
Pellissippi State Community College, Knoxville TN p. 2106
Pember Library & Museum of Natural History, Granville NY p. 1540
Pemberton & District Public Library, Pemberton BC p. 2573
Pemberton Library, *see* Burlington County Library System, Browns Mills NJ p. 1454
Pemberville Public Library, Pemberville OH p. 1814
Pembina City Library, Pembina ND p. 1739
Pembroke Library, Pembroke ME p. 935
Pembroke Public, *see* Robeson County Public Library, Pembroke NC p. 1702
Pembroke Public Library, Pembroke GA p. 493
Pembroke Public Library, Pembroke MA p. 1046
Pembroke Public Library, Pembroke ON p. 2671
Pembroke Public Library District, Hopkins Park IL p. 601
Pembroke Town Library, Pembroke NH p. 1377
Pence Law Library, Washington College of Law, *see* American University, Washington DC p. 360
Pend Oreille County Library District, Newport WA p. 2372
Pender County Public Library, Burgaw NC p. 1676
Pender Island Public Library, *see* Southern Gulf Islands Community Libraries, Pender Island BC p. 2573
Pendergraft Ross Library, *see* Arkansas Tech University, Russellville AR p. 108
Pendergrass Webster C Agriculture & Veterinary Medicine, *see* University of Tennessee, Knoxville, Knoxville TN p. 2108
Pendergrast James Memorial Library, *see* Albany State University, Albany GA p. 457
Pendle Hill Library, Wallingford PA p. 2017
Pendleton Alice L Library, Islesboro ME p. 928
Pendleton Community Library, Pendleton IN p. 713
Pendleton Correctional Facility, Pendleton IN p. 713
Pendleton County Library, Franklin WV p. 2402
Pendleton County Public Library, Falmouth KY p. 854
Pendleton District Historical, Recreational, Pendleton SC p. 2067
Pendleton Public Library, Pendleton OR p. 1890
Penetanguishene Public Library, Penetanguishene ON p. 2671
Penfield Library, *see* Polk Museum of Art, Lakeland FL p. 417
Penfield Library, *see* State University of New York at Oswego, Oswego NY p. 1613
Penfield Public Library, Penfield NY p. 1616
Penhold & District Public Library, Penhold AB p. 2550
Peninsula Center Library, *see* Palos Verdes Library District, Rolling Hills Estates CA p. 204
Peninsula College Library, Port Angeles WA p. 2374
Peninsula Community Library, Traverse City MI p. 1154
Peninsula Library & Historical Society, Peninsula OH p. 1814
Peninsula Library System (N), San Mateo CA p. 2762
Peninsula Public Library, Lawrence NY p. 1562
Peninsula Temple Beth El Library, San Mateo CA p. 235
Penitas Public Library, Penitas TX p. 2226
Penn Area Library, Harrison City PA p. 1941
Penn Hills Library, Pittsburgh PA p. 1995

Peters Health Sciences Library, *see* Rhode Island Hospital, Providence RI p. 2040
Peters James J VA Medical Center Library, *see* Department of Veterans Affairs, Bronx NY p. 1498
Peters Township Public Library, McMurray PA p. 1959
Peters William Wesley Library, *see* Frank Lloyd Wright Foundation, Scottsdale AZ p. 77
Petersburg Public Library, Petersburg AK p. 50
Petersburg Public Library, Petersburg IL p. 635
Petersburg Public Library, Petersburg NE p. 1332
Petersburg Public Library, Petersburg TX p. 2226
Petersburg Public Library, Petersburg VA p. 2337
Petersburgh Public Library, Petersburgh NY p. 1617
Petersen Betty Memorial Library, *see* National Oceanic & Atmospheric Administration, College Park MD p. 977
Petersham Memorial Library, Petersham MA p. 1046
Peterson Dutton S Memorial Library, Odessa NY p. 1609
Peterson Marvin K Library, *see* University of New Haven, West Haven CT p. 346
Peterson Memorial Library, *see* Walla Walla University Libraries, College Place WA p. 2362
Peterson Walter R Library & Media Center, *see* Nashua Community College, Nashua NH p. 1374
Peterstown Public Library, Peterstown WV p. 2412
Petit-Rocher Public Library, *see* Chaleur Library Region, Petit-Rocher NB p. 2599
Petoskey District Library, Petoskey MI p. 1140
Petrie Harry L Public Library, *see* Linton Public Library, Linton ND p. 1737
Petroleum County Community Library, Winnett MT p. 1304
Petroleum Museum Library & Hall of Fame, Midland TX p. 2219
Petros Public Library, Petros TN p. 2124
Pettee Memorial Library, Wilmington VT p. 2299
Pettes Memorial Library, *see* Bibliotheque Commemorative Pettes, Lac-Brome QC p. 2715
Pettigrew Home & Museum Library, Sioux Falls SD p. 2082
Pettigrew Regional Library, Plymouth NC p. 1708
Pettis Olive G Memorial Library, Goshen NH p. 1365
Pew Charitable Trusts Library, Washington DC p. 374
Pew Joseph N Jr Medical Library, *see* Bryn Mawr Hospital Library, Bryn Mawr PA p. 1916
Pew Learning Center & Ellison Library, *see* Warren Wilson College, Swannanoa NC p. 1718
Pewaukee Public Library, Pewaukee WI p. 2469
Pfau John M Library, *see* California State University, San Bernardino, San Bernardino CA p. 212
Pfeiffer Annie Merner Library, *see* West Virginia Wesleyan College, Buckhannon WV p. 2399
Pfeiffer G A Library, *see* Pfeiffer University, Misenheimer NC p. 1703
Pfeiffer Library, *see* Tiffin University, Tiffin OH p. 1823
Pfeiffer Library at Charlotte, *see* Pfeiffer University, Charlotte NC p. 1703
Pfeiffer University, Misenheimer NC p. 1703
Pflugerville Public Library, Pflugerville TX p. 2226
Pfohl Anthony C Health Sciences Library, *see* Mercy Medical Center, Dubuque IA p. 749
Pharr Memorial Library, Pharr TX p. 2226
Phelan Memorial Library, *see* San Bernardino County Library, Phelan CA p. 213
Phelps Dunbar LLP, New Orleans LA p. 903
Phelps Dunbar, LLP, Jackson MS p. 1223
Phelps Library, Phelps NY p. 1617
Phelps Public, *see* Pike County Public Library District, Phelps KY p. 872
Phelps Public Library, Phelps WI p. 2469
Phelps Tavern Museum, *see* Simsbury Historical Society Archives, Simsbury CT p. 336
Phenix City-Russell County Library, Phenix City AL p. 33
Philadelphia Area Consortium of Special Collections Libraries (N), Philadelphia PA p. 2774
Philadelphia City Institute, *see* Free Library of Philadelphia, Philadelphia PA p. 1979
Philadelphia College of Osteopathic Medicine, Philadelphia PA p. 1984
Philadelphia Corporation for Aging Library, Philadelphia PA p. 1984
Philadelphia Historical Commission Library, Philadelphia PA p. 1984
Philadelphia Museum of Art Library, Philadelphia PA p. 1984
Philadelphia Public Library, Philadelphia TN p. 2124
Philadelphia Yearly Meeting of the Religious Society of Friends, Philadelphia PA p. 1984
Philander Smith College, Little Rock AR p. 101
Philbrick-James Library, Deerfield NH p. 1360
Philbrook Museum of Art, Tulsa OK p. 1865
Philip Read Memorial Library, *see* Plainfield Public Libraries, Plainfield NH p. 1373
Philippi Public Library, Philippi WV p. 2412
Philipsburg Public Library, Philipsburg MT p. 1301
Phillips Academy, Andover MA p. 985
Phillips Charles B Library, *see* Aurora University, Aurora IL p. 539
Phillips Charles B Public Library District, Newark IL p. 624
Phillips Collection Library, Washington DC p. 374
Phillips Community College of the University of Arkansas, DeWitt AR p. 94
Phillips Community College of the University of Arkansas, Helena AR p. 98
Phillips Community College of the University of Arkansas, Stuttgart AR p. 111
Phillips County Library, Malta MT p. 1299
Phillips County Library, *see* Phillips-Lee-Monroe Regional Library, Helena AR p. 98
Phillips Dr Walter Health Sciences Library, *see* Englewood Health, Englewood NJ p. 1401
Phillips Free Library, Homer NY p. 1547
Phillips Graduate University Library, Chatsworth CA p. 129
Phillips Hugh J Library, *see* Mount Saint Mary's University, Emmitsburg MD p. 965
Phillips L E Memorial Public Library, Eau Claire WI p. 2432
Phillips-Lee-Monroe Regional Library, Helena AR p. 98
Phillips Library, *see* Peabody Essex Museum, Rowley MA p. 1050
Phillips, Lytle LLP Library, Buffalo NY p. 1509
Phillips Memorial Library, *see* Providence College, Providence RI p. 2039
Phillips Murrah, Oklahoma City OK p. 1859
Phillips Public Library, Phillips ME p. 935
Phillips Public Library, Phillips WI p. 2469
Phillips Site Technical Library, *see* United States Air Force, Kirtland AFB NM p. 1470
Phillips 66 Research Library, Bartlesville OK p. 1842
Phillips State Prison, Buford GA p. 468
Phillips Stephen Memorial Library, *see* Penobscot Marine Museum, Searsport ME p. 940
Phillips T W Memorial Library, *see* Bethany College, Mary Cutlip Center, Bethany WV p. 2398
Phillips Theological Seminary Library, Tulsa OK p. 1865
Phillipsburg City Library, Phillipsburg KS p. 831
Phillipsburg Free Public Library, Phillipsburg NJ p. 1434
Phillipston Free Public Library, Phillipston MA p. 1046
Philmont Public Library, Philmont NY p. 1617
Philmont Scout Ranch Library, *see* National Scouting Museum, Cimarron NM p. 1465
Philo Public Library District, Philo IL p. 635
Philomath Community Library, *see* Corvallis-Benton County Public Library, Philomath OR p. 1876
Philosophical Research Society Library, Los Angeles CA p. 167
Hearst Phoebe Apperson Library - Lead Library, Lead SD p. 2078
Phoenicia Library, Phoenicia NY p. 1618
Phoenix Art Museum, Phoenix AZ p. 71
Phoenix Children's Hospital, Phoenix AZ p. 71
Phoenix College, Phoenix AZ p. 72
Phoenix Emerging Adult Career & Education (PEACE) Center, Saint Charles IL p. 644
Phoenix Indian Medical Center Library, *see* Indian Health Service, Phoenix AZ p. 70
Phoenix Public Library, Phoenix AZ p. 72
Phoenix Public Library, Phoenix NY p. 1618
Phoenix Public Library District, Phoenix IL p. 635
Phoenix Seminary Library, Scottsdale AZ p. 77
Phoenix VA Health Care System, Phoenix AZ p. 72
Phoenixville Public Library, Phoenixville PA p. 1989
Pi Beta Phi Patient/Family Library, *see* Texas Children's Hospital, Houston TX p. 2198
Piatt County Historical & Genealogical Society Library, Monticello IL p. 619
Picatinny Armaments Technical Library, Picatinny Arsenal NJ p. 1435
Pickaway Correctional Institution Library, Orient OH p. 1810
Pickaway County District Public Library, Circleville OH p. 1765
Pickaway County Law Library Association, Circleville OH p. 1766
Pickens County Cooperative Library, Carrollton AL p. 11
Pickens County Educational Center, *see* Bevill State Community College, Carrollton AL p. 17
Pickens County Library System, Easley SC p. 2058
Pickens County Public, *see* Sequoyah Regional Library System, Jasper GA p. 469
Pickens Grace M Public Library, Holdenville OK p. 1850
Pickens Public, *see* Mid-Mississippi Regional Library System, Pickens MS p. 1224
Pickering Educational Resources Library, *see* Boston University Libraries, Boston MA p. 993
Pickering Public Library, Pickering ON p. 2672
Pickerington Public Library, Pickerington OH p. 1815
Pickett County Public Library, Byrdstown TN p. 2090
Pickett Library, *see* Alderson-Broaddus University, Philippi WV p. 2412
Pickford Community Library, *see* Superior District Library, Pickford MI p. 1149
Pickler Memorial Library, *see* Truman State University, Kirksville MO p. 1258
Pickleweed Library, *see* San Rafael Public Library, San Rafael CA p. 237
Pictou - Antigonish Regional Library, New Glasgow NS p. 2622
Picture Butte Municipal Library, Picture Butte AB p. 2550
Piedmont Columbus Regional - Midtown, Columbus GA p. 472
Piedmont Community College, Roxboro NC p. 1714
Piedmont Public Library, Piedmont AL p. 33
Piedmont Public Library, Piedmont WV p. 2412
Piedmont Regional Library System, Jefferson GA p. 482
Piedmont Technical College Library, Greenwood SC p. 2063
Piedmont University Library, Demorest GA p. 476
Piedmont Valley Library, Piedmont SD p. 2080
Piedmont Virginia Community College, Charlottesville VA p. 2309
Pierce Allen F Free Library, Troy PA p. 2014
Pierce Art Library, *see* Bowdoin College Library, Brunswick ME p. 919
Pierce Atwood LLP, Portland ME p. 937
Pierce College Library, Woodland Hills CA p. 260
Pierce College Library, Lakewood WA p. 2368
Pierce County Law Library, Tacoma WA p. 2386
Pierce County Library System, Tacoma WA p. 2386
Pierce County Public, *see* Okefenokee Regional Library, Blackshear GA p. 503
Pierce Daniel Library, Grahamsville NY p. 1540
Pierce District Library, Pierce ID p. 528
Pierce Franklin School of Law Library, *see* University of New Hampshire School of Law, Concord NH p. 1360
Pierce, Goodwin, Alexander & Linville Library, Houston TX p. 2197
Pierce Lawrence J Library, *see* Rhododendron Species Foundation & Botanical Garden, Federal Way WA p. 2364
Pierce Library, *see* Eastern Oregon University, La Grande OR p. 1884

Platte Valley Youth Services Center Library, *see* Department of Human Services, Greeley CO p. 285
Plattekill Public Library, Modena NY p. 1573
Platteville Public Library, Platteville CO p. 292
Platteville Public Library, Platteville WI p. 2469
Plattsburgh Public Library, Plattsburgh NY p. 1619
Plattsmouth Public Library, Plattsmouth NE p. 1333
Pleak Mariam Library, *see* Hobart Historical Society, Inc, Hobart IN p. 689
Pleasant Grove Christian Church Library, Dallas TX p. 2167
Pleasant Grove City Library, Pleasant Grove UT p. 2269
Pleasant Grove Public Library, Pleasant Grove AL p. 33
Pleasant Hill Library, *see* Contra Costa County Library, Pleasant Hill CA p. 174
Pleasant Hill Public Library, Pleasant Hill IA p. 777
Pleasant Hills Public Library, Pleasant Hills PA p. 1997
Pleasant Mount Public Library, Pleasant Mount PA p. 1997
Pleasant Valley Free Library, Pleasant Valley NY p. 1619
Pleasant Valley State Prison, *see* California Department of Corrections Library System, Coalinga CA p. 207
Pleasanton Library & Information Center, Pleasanton TX p. 2227
Pleasanton Lincoln Library, *see* Linn County Library District No 5, Pleasanton KS p. 832
Pleasanton Public Library, Pleasanton CA p. 196
Pleasants County Public Library, Saint Marys WV p. 2414
Pleasantville Neighborhood Library, *see* Houston Public Library, Houston TX p. 2196
Plimoth Plantation, Plymouth MA p. 1047
Plough Library, *see* Christian Brothers University, Memphis TN p. 2112
Plover Public Library, Plover IA p. 777
Plum Borough Community Library, Plum Borough PA p. 1998
Plum City Public Library, Plum City WI p. 2470
Plum Creek Library System, Worthington MN p. 1210
Plum Helen M Memorial Public Library District, Lombard IL p. 611
Plum Lake Public Library, Sayner WI p. 2475
Plumas County Library, Quincy CA p. 197
Plumb Joseph H Memorial Library, Rochester MA p. 1049
Plumb Memorial Library, Shelton CT p. 336
Plummer Public Library, Plummer ID p. 528
Plunkett & Cooney, Bloomfield Hills MI p. 1086
Plymouth Church, Seattle WA p. 2378
Plymouth District Library, Plymouth MI p. 1141
Plymouth Historical Museum Archives, Plymouth MI p. 1141
Plymouth Law Library, Plymouth MA p. 1047
Plymouth Library Association, Plymouth CT p. 334
Plymouth Public Library, Plymouth IN p. 714
Plymouth Public Library, Plymouth MA p. 1047
Plymouth Public Library, Plymouth NE p. 1333
Plymouth Public Library, Plymouth PA p. 1998
Plymouth Public Library, Plymouth WI p. 2470
Plymouth State University, Plymouth NH p. 1378
Plympton Public Library, Plympton MA p. 1047
Poage W R Legislative Library, *see* Baylor University Libraries, Waco TX p. 2253
Pocahontas County Free Libraries, Marlinton WV p. 2408
Pocahontas Public Library, Pocahontas IA p. 777
Pocatello Women's Correctional Center Library, *see* Idaho State Correctional Institution Library, Pocatello ID p. 517
Pocono Mountain Public Library, Tobyhanna PA p. 2013
Poe Edgar Allen, *see* Charleston County Public Library, Sullivan's Island SC p. 2049
Poestenkill Public Library, Poestenkill NY p. 1620
Pogue Barton Rees Memorial Library, Upland IN p. 722
Pohick Regional, *see* Fairfax County Public Library, Burke VA p. 2316
Poindexter Library, *see* Richmont Graduate University, Chattanooga TN p. 2092
Point Loma Nazarene University, San Diego CA p. 216
Point Marion Public Library, Point Marion PA p. 1998
Point Park University Library, Pittsburgh PA p. 1995
Point Pelee National Park Library, Leamington ON p. 2652
Point Reyes National Seashore Research Library & Archives, *see* United States National Park Service, Point Reyes Station CA p. 196
Point University, West Point GA p. 503
Pointe Coupee Parish Library, New Roads LA p. 905
Pointer Emily Jones Public Library, *see* First Regional Library, Como MS p. 1220
Poland Public Library, Poland NY p. 1620
Polish Genealogical Society of Connecticut & The Northeast,Inc, New Britain CT p. 324
Polish Institute of Arts & Sciences in America, Inc, New York NY p. 1600
Polish Institute of Arts & Sciences Library, Montreal QC p. 2727
Polish Museum of America Library, Chicago IL p. 567
Politi Leo, *see* Fresno County Public Library, Fresno CA p. 146
Polk City Community Library, Polk City IA p. 777
Polk County Biomedical Consortium (N), Des Moines IA p. 2765
Polk County Historical & Genealogical Library, Bartow FL p. 384
Polk County Law Library, Bartow FL p. 384
Polk County Library, Mena AR p. 104
Polk County Library, Bolivar MO p. 1238
Polk County Public Library, Columbus NC p. 1682
Polk Library, *see* University of Wisconsin Oshkosh, Oshkosh WI p. 2467
Polk Museum of Art, Lakeland FL p. 417
Polk Public Library, Polk NE p. 1333
Polk State College, Winter Haven FL p. 455
Polkville Public Library, Morton MS p. 1227
Pollack Library Landowne Bloom Library, *see* Yeshiva University Libraries, New York NY p. 1605
Pollak Paulina June & George Library, *see* California State University, Fullerton, Fullerton CA p. 147
Leroy Pollard Memorial Library, New Braintree MA p. 1038
Pollard Memorial Library, Lowell MA p. 1029
Pollins Calvin E Memorial Library, *see* Westmoreland County Historical Society, Greensburg PA p. 1938
Pollocksville Public Library, *see* Neuse Regional Library, Pollocksville NC p. 1699
Polo Public Library District, Polo IL p. 636
Polsinelli, Kansas City MO p. 1257
Polsinelli PC, Saint Louis MO p. 1272
Polson City Library, Polson MT p. 1301
Polytechnique Montreal Library, Montreal QC p. 2727
Pomerantz Marvin A Business Library, *see* University of Iowa Libraries, Iowa City IA p. 761
Pomeroy Public Library, Pomeroy IA p. 777
Pomeroy Public, *see* Ashby Denny Memorial Library, Pomeroy WA p. 2373
Pomfret Public Library, Pomfret CT p. 334
Pomona Community Library, Pomona KS p. 832
Pomona Public Library, Pomona CA p. 196
Pomonok Community Library, *see* Queens Library, Flushing NY p. 1555
Ponca Carnegie Library, Ponca NE p. 1333
Ponca City Library, Ponca City OK p. 1860
Ponce Barbara S Public Library, Pinellas Park FL p. 437
Ponce Health Sciences University Library, Ponce PR p. 2512
Pond Creek City Library, Pond Creek OK p. 1860
Ponderosa Joint Use Library, *see* Anaheim Public Library, Anaheim CA p. 116
Ponoka Jubilee Library, Ponoka AB p. 2550
Pontiac Correctional Center Library, Pontiac IL p. 636
Pontiac Free Library, Warwick RI p. 2043
Pontiac Public Library, Pontiac IL p. 636
Pontiac Public Library, Pontiac MI p. 1142
Pontifical Catholic University, Mayaguez PR p. 2511
Pontifical Catholic University, Ponce PR p. 2512
Pontifical College Josephinum, Columbus OH p. 1777
Pontifical Institute for Mediaeval Studies, *see* University of Toronto Libraries, Toronto ON p. 2700
Pontificia Catholic University of Puerto Rico, Arecibo, Arecibo PR p. 2509
Pontious Learning Resource Center, *see* Warner University, Lake Wales FL p. 416
Pontotoc County Library, *see* Dixie Regional Library System, Pontotoc MS p. 1230
Poole James C Jr Memorial Library, Eutaw AL p. 16
Pope County Historical Society, Glenwood MN p. 1176
Pope County Library System, Russellville AR p. 109
Pope John XXIII National Seminary, Weston MA p. 1067
Pope Memorial Library, North Conway NH p. 1376
Pope Memorial Library, Danville VT p. 2283
Poplar Bluff Municipal Library, Poplar Bluff MO p. 1266
Poplar Creek Public Library District, Streamwood IL p. 652
Poplarville Public, *see* Pearl River County Library System, Poplarville MS p. 1229
Poppenhusen Community Library, *see* Queens Library, College Point NY p. 1555
Popular Library, *see* Chicago Public Library, Chicago IL p. 557
Population Council Library, New York NY p. 1600
Poquoson Public Library, Poquoson VA p. 2337
Porcupine Plain Public Library, *see* Wapiti Regional Library, Porcupine Plain SK p. 2746
Port Arthur Public Library, Port Arthur TX p. 2228
Port Austin Township Library, Port Austin MI p. 1142
Port Byron Library, Port Byron NY p. 1620
Port Carbon Public Library, Port Carbon PA p. 1998
Port Charlotte Public, *see* Charlotte County Library System, Port Charlotte FL p. 438
Port Chester-Rye Brook Public Library, Port Chester NY p. 1620
Port Clinton Public Library, *see* Rupp Ida Public Library, Port Clinton OH p. 1816
Port Colborne Public Library, Port Colborne ON p. 2673
Port Hope Public Library, Port Hope ON p. 2674
Port Isabel Public Library, Port Isabel TX p. 2228
Port Jefferson Free Library, Port Jefferson NY p. 1621
Port Jervis Free Library, Port Jervis NY p. 1621
Port Leyden Community Library, Port Leyden NY p. 1622
Port Library, Beloit KS p. 798
Port Moody Public Library, Port Moody BC p. 2574
Port Orange Public Library, *see* Volusia County Public Library, Port Orange FL p. 393
Port Orford Public Library District, Port Orford OR p. 1890
Port Saint John Public Library, Cocoa FL p. 390
Port Severn Public, *see* Township of Georgian Bay Public Library, Port Severn ON p. 2648
Port Tampa City Library, *see* Tampa-Hillsborough County Public Library System, Tampa FL p. 449
Port Townsend Public Library, Port Townsend WA p. 2374
Port Washington Public, *see* Niederkorn W J Library, Port Washington WI p. 2470
Port Washington Public Library, Port Washington NY p. 1622
Portage College Library, Lac La Biche AB p. 2545
Portage County District Library, Garrettsville OH p. 1787
Portage County Historical Society Museum & Library, Ravenna OH p. 1817
Portage County Law Library, Ravenna OH p. 1817

Preston J T L Library, *see* Virginia Military Institute, Lexington VA p. 2329
Preston Medical Library, *see* University of Tennessee Graduate School of Medicine, Knoxville TN p. 2107
Preston Public Library, Preston CT p. 334
Preston Public Library, Preston IA p. 778
Preston Public Library, Preston MN p. 1193
Preston Town-County Library of Hot Springs, Hot Springs MT p. 1297
Preston Tye Memorial Library, Canyon Lake TX p. 2153
Preti Flaherty Beliveau & Pachios, Portland ME p. 937
Pretlow Mary D Anchor Branch Library, *see* Norfolk Public Library, Norfolk VA p. 2335
Pretty Prairie Public Library, Pretty Prairie KS p. 833
Preus Library, *see* Luther College, Decorah IA p. 744
Prevention & Education Program & Monmouth County Prevention HUB, *see* Prevention First, a Division of Preferred Behavioral Health Group, West Long Branch NJ p. 1453
Prevention First, a Division of Preferred Behavioral Health Group, West Long Branch NJ p. 1453
Prewett Library, *see* Contra Costa County Library, Antioch CA p. 174
Price Allan Science Commons & Research Library, *see* University of Oregon Libraries, Eugene OR p. 1879
Price City Library, Price UT p. 2269
Price Hollis F Library, *see* LeMoyne-Owen College, Memphis TN p. 2112
Price Leontyne Library, *see* Rust College, Holly Springs MS p. 1220
Price-Pottenger Nutrition Foundation Library, Lemon Grove CA p. 156
PricewaterhouseCoopers, Toronto ON p. 2692
Prichard Public Library, Prichard AL p. 33
Pridham Edna Memorial Library, *see* Emmanuel Bible College, Kitchener ON p. 2651
Priest Lake Public Library, Priest Lake ID p. 529
Priestly Diana M Law Library, *see* University of Victoria Libraries, Victoria BC p. 2583
Primary Children's Hospital Medical Library, Salt Lake City UT p. 2271
Primghar Public Library, Primghar IA p. 778
Prince Albert Parkland Health Region Library, Prince Albert SK p. 2744
Prince Albert Public Library, Prince Albert SK p. 2744
Prince County Hospital, Summerside PE p. 2708
Prince Edward County Public Library, Picton ON p. 2673
Prince Edward Island Association for Community Living, Charlottetown PE p. 2707
Prince Edward Island Public Library Service, Morell PE p. 2708
Prince George Public Library, Prince George BC p. 2574
Prince George's Community College, Largo MD p. 970
Prince George's County, Upper Marlboro MD p. 980
Prince George's County Memorial, Largo MD p. 970
Prince John F Library, *see* Glendale Community College - Main, Glendale AZ p. 61
Prince Memorial Library, Cumberland ME p. 922
Prince R T Memorial, *see* Mize Public Library, Mize MS p. 1227
Prince Rupert Library, Prince Rupert BC p. 2574
Prince William County Law Library, Manassas VA p. 2331
Prince William Public Libraries, Prince William VA p. 2338
Princeton Area Library, *see* East Central Regional Library, Princeton MN p. 1168
Princeton Community Hospital Library, Princeton WV p. 2413
Princeton HealthCare System, Plainsboro NJ p. 1435
Princeton Library in New York, New York NY p. 1600
Princeton Public Library, Princeton IL p. 636
Princeton Public Library, Princeton IN p. 714
Princeton Public Library, Princeton ME p. 938
Princeton Public Library, Princeton MA p. 1048
Princeton Public Library, Princeton NJ p. 1436
Princeton Public Library, Princeton NC p. 1708
Princeton Public Library, Princeton WV p. 2413
Princeton Public Library, Princeton WI p. 2471
Princeton Theological Seminary Library, Princeton NJ p. 1436
Princeton University, Princeton NJ p. 1437
Princeville Public Library, *see* Hawaii State Public Library System, Princeville HI p. 510
Principal Financial Group, Des Moines IA p. 747
Principia College, Elsah IL p. 585
Prior John A Health Sciences Library, *see* Ohio State University LIBRARIES, Columbus OH p. 1776
Prior Lake Public Library, *see* Scott County Library System, Prior Lake MN p. 1203
Prior Walter F Medical Library, *see* Frederick Memorial Hospital, Frederick MD p. 966
Prisma Health System, Greenville SC p. 2062
Prittie Bob, *see* Burnaby Public Library, Burnaby BC p. 2563
Pritzker Legal Research Center, *see* Northwestern University Libraries, Chicago IL p. 587
Pritzker Military Museum & Library, Chicago IL p. 567
Privy Council Office, Ottawa ON p. 2669
Pro-Life Action League Library, Chicago IL p. 567
ProConsort (N), Mount Kisco NY p. 2771
Proctor Donald C Library, *see* State Fair Community College, Sedalia MO p. 1279
Proctor Free Library, Proctor VT p. 2292
Proctor Library, *see* Flagler College, Saint Augustine FL p. 439
Project for Public Spaces, Inc, New York NY p. 1600
ProMedica Toledo Hospital, Toledo OH p. 1824
Proskauer LLP Library, Washington DC p. 374
Proskauer Rose LLP, Los Angeles CA p. 167
Proskauer Rose LLP Library, New York NY p. 1600
Prospect Community Library, Prospect PA p. 1999
Prospect Free Library, Prospect NY p. 1624
Prospect Heights Public Library District, Prospect Heights IL p. 637
Prospect Park Free Library, Prospect Park PA p. 1999
Prospect Public Library, Prospect CT p. 334
Prosper Community Library, Prosper TX p. 2229
Prosser Public Library, *see* Bloomfield Public Library, Bloomfield CT p. 303
Protection Township Library, Protection KS p. 833
Proulx Henri Law Library, *see* Prescott & Russell Law Association, L'Orignal ON p. 2656
Proverbs Heritage Organization, Essex ON p. 2641
Providence Archives, Seattle WA p. 2378
Providence Athenaeum, Providence RI p. 2039
Providence Care Mental Health Services, Kingston ON p. 2650
Providence College, Providence RI p. 2039
Providence Historical Society, Clearwater FL p. 389
Providence Holy Cross Medical Center, Mission Hills CA p. 177
Providence Presbyterian Church Library, Virginia Beach VA p. 2349
Providence Public Library, Providence RI p. 2039
Providence Sacred Heart Medical Center, Spokane WA p. 2384
Providence Saint Joseph Medical Center, Burbank CA p. 125
Providence Saint Vincent Hospital & Medical Center, Portland OR p. 1894
Providence University College & Seminary, Otterburne MB p. 2588
Providence Willamette Falls Medical Center, Oregon City OR p. 1890
Provincetown Public Library, Provincetown MA p. 1048
Provincial Archives of Alberta, Reference Library, Edmonton AB p. 2537
Provincial Archives of New Brunswick, Fredericton NB p. 2601
Provincial Information & Library Resources Board, St. John's NL p. 2611
Provincial Information & Library Resources Board, Stephenville NL p. 2611
Provincial Library & Literacy Office, Regina SK p. 2747
Provo City Library, Provo UT p. 2269
Provost Municipal Library, Provost AB p. 2550
Prudential Financial, Newark NJ p. 1428
Prudential Insurance Law Library, *see* Prudential Financial, Newark NJ p. 1428
Prueter Ray D Library, *see* Ventura County Library, Port Hueneme CA p. 256
Pruitt Ken Campus Library, *see* Indian River State College, Port Saint Lucie FL p. 404
Pruitt Mary & Charles W Branch Library, *see* Nashville Public Library, Nashville TN p. 2120
Pruitt Molly Library, *see* San Antonio Public Library, San Antonio TX p. 2239
Pryor, Cashman LLP, New York NY p. 1600
Pryor Public Library, Pryor OK p. 1861
PSP Metrics Library, Pittsburgh PA p. 1996
Psychoanalytic Center of Philadelphia Library, Philadelphia PA p. 1985
PT Boats, Inc, Memphis TN p. 2114
Public Archives of Nova Scotia, Halifax NS p. 2621
Public Citizen Library, Washington DC p. 374
Public Health Ontario, Toronto ON p. 2692
Public Information Network for Electronic Services (N), Atlanta GA p. 2764
Public Law Library of King County, Seattle WA p. 2378
Public Libraries of Saginaw, Saginaw MI p. 1147
Public Library at Tellico Village, Loudon TN p. 2110
Public Library for Union County, Lewisburg PA p. 1955
Public Library InterLINK (N), Burnaby BC p. 2777
Public Library of Anniston-Calhoun County, Anniston AL p. 4
Public Library of Arlington, Arlington MA p. 985
Public Library of Brookline, Brookline MA p. 1003
Public Library of Camden & Ouachita County, *see* Ouachita County Libraries, Camden AR p. 92
Public Library of Catasauqua, Catasauqua PA p. 1919
Public Library of Cincinnati & Hamilton County, Cincinnati OH p. 1761
Public Library of Enid & Garfield County, Enid OK p. 1847
Public Library of Johnston County & Smithfield, Smithfield NC p. 1716
Public Library of Mount Vernon & Knox County, Mount Vernon OH p. 1804
Public Library of Selma & Dallas County, Selma AL p. 35
Public Library of Springfield, Illinois, *see* Lincoln Library, Springfield IL p. 650
Public Library of Steubenville & Jefferson County, Steubenville OH p. 1821
Public Library of Youngstown & Mahoning County, Youngstown OH p. 1835
Public Library Services Branch, *see* Manitoba Culture, Heritage & Tourism, Brandon MB p. 2586
Public Policy Forum, Milwaukee WI p. 2461
Public Utility Commission of Texas Library, Austin TX p. 2140
Puckett Public Library, Puckett MS p. 1230
Pueblo City-County Library District, Pueblo CO p. 293
Pueblo Community College Library, Pueblo CO p. 293
Pueblo de Abiquiu Library & Cultural Center, Abiquiu NM p. 1459
Pueblo Grande Museum & Archaeological Park, Phoenix AZ p. 72
Pueblo of Isleta Library, Albuquerque NM p. 1461
Pueblo of Pojoaque Public Library, Santa Fe NM p. 1476
Pueblo of San Felipe Community Library, San Felipe Pueblo NM p. 1474
Pueblo Youth Services Center Library, *see* Department of Human Services-Youth Corrections, Pueblo CO p. 293
Puente John G & Beverly A Library, *see* Capitol Technology University, Laurel MD p. 971
Puerto Rico Regional Library for the Blind & Physically, San Juan PR p. 2513

Ramirez Lorenzo A Library, *see* Santiago Canyon College, Orange CA p. 189
Mario E Ramirez, MD Library, *see* University of Texas Rio Grande Valley, Harlingen TX p. 2188
Rampart Library District, Woodland Park CO p. 298
Ramsay John W Research Center, *see* New England Air Museum, Windsor Locks CT p. 348
Ramsayer Research Library, *see* McKinley William Presidential Library & Museum, Canton OH p. 1755
Ramsdell Public Library, *see* Great Barrington Libraries, Housatonic MA p. 1022
Ramsey County Law Library, Saint Paul MN p. 1201
Ramsey County Library, Shoreview MN p. 1203
Ramsey D Hiden Library, *see* University of North Carolina at Asheville, Asheville NC p. 1673
Ramsey Free Public Library, Ramsey NJ p. 1438
Ramsey Public Library, Ramsey IL p. 638
Rancho Cordova Library, *see* Sacramento Public Library, Sacramento CA p. 210
Rancho Cucamonga Public Library, Rancho Cucamonga CA p. 197
Rancho Mirage Library & Observatory, Rancho Mirage CA p. 197
Rand Anne Research Library, *see* International Longshore & Warehouse Union, San Francisco CA p. 225
RAND Corporation Library, Santa Monica CA p. 244
Rand William H & Lucy F Memorial Library, North Troy VT p. 2290
Randall Library, Stow MA p. 1058
Randall Public Library, Randall KS p. 833
Randall University, Moore OK p. 1853
Randolph A Philip Memorial Library, *see* Borough of Manhattan Community College Library, New York NY p. 1580
Randolph College, Lynchburg VA p. 2330
Randolph Community College Library, Asheboro NC p. 1671
Randolph County Library, Pocahontas AR p. 108
Randolph County Library, *see* Kinchafoonee Regional Library System, Cuthbert GA p. 475
Randolph County Public Library, Asheboro NC p. 1672
Randolph-Decker Library, *see* Clyde Public Library, Clyde KS p. 802
Randolph Free Library, Randolph NY p. 1625
Randolph Library, *see* Hutchinson Memorial Library, Randolph WI p. 2472
Randolph Library, *see* Joint Base San Antonio Libraries, Randolph AFB TX p. 2230
Randolph-Macon College, Ashland VA p. 2306
Randolph Public Library, Randolph IA p. 778
Randolph Public Library, Randolph NH p. 1379
Randolph Township Free Public Library, Randolph NJ p. 1438
Raney Olivia Local History Library, *see* Wake County Public Library System, Raleigh NC p. 1711
Rangeley Public Library, Rangeley ME p. 938
Rangely Regional Library, Rangely CO p. 294
Ranger City Library, Ranger TX p. 2230
Ranger College, Ranger TX p. 2230
Rankin Library, *see* Hinds Community College, Pearl MS p. 1231
Rankin Public Library, Rankin TX p. 2230
Rankin Robert S Memorial Library, *see* United States Commission on Civil Rights, Washington DC p. 377
Rankin W A Memorial Library, Neodesha KS p. 826
Ransom Charles A District Library, Plainwell MI p. 1141
Ransom Harry Center, *see* University of Texas Libraries, Austin TX p. 2143
Ransom Memorial Public Library, Altona IL p. 536
Ransom Public Library, Ransom KS p. 833
Ransom Reverdy C Memorial Library, *see* Payne Theological Seminary, Wilberforce OH p. 1831
Ransomville Free Library, Ransomville NY p. 1625
Rantoul Public Library, Rantoul IL p. 638
Rapid City Public Library, Rapid City SD p. 2081
Rapid City Regional Library, Rapid City MB p. 2589
Rapides Parish Library, Alexandria LA p. 880
Rapides Regional Medical Center, Alexandria LA p. 880
Rappahannock Community College, Warsaw VA p. 2352
Rappahannock Community College Library, Glenns VA p. 2321
Rappahannock County Library, Washington VA p. 2352
Raquette Lake Free Library, Raquette Lake NY p. 1625
Raritan Public Library, Raritan NJ p. 1438
Raritan Valley Community College, Somerville NJ p. 1442
Rasey Memorial, *see* Monroe County Library System, Luna Pier MI p. 1134
Rasmuson Elmer E Library, *see* University of Alaska Fairbanks, Fairbanks AK p. 45
Rathbun Bryce C, *see* Kern County Library, Bakersfield CA p. 120
Rathbun Free Memorial Library, *see* East Haddam Library System, East Haddam CT p. 323
Rauchholz Memorial Library, Hemlock MI p. 1114
Raudenbush Hank Library, *see* HATCH LTK, Knowledge & Information Research Centre (KIRC), Ambler PA p. 1906
Raugust Library, *see* University of Jamestown, Jamestown ND p. 1736
Rauner Special Collections Library, *see* Dartmouth College Library, Hanover NH p. 1366
Raushenbush Esther Library, *see* Sarah Lawrence College, Bronxville NY p. 1500
Ravalli County Museum, Hamilton MT p. 1295
Raven Peter H Library, *see* Missouri Botanical Garden, Saint Louis MO p. 1272
Ravenna Public Library, Ravenna NE p. 1334
Rawlings Robert Hoag Public Library, *see* Pueblo City-County Library District, Pueblo CO p. 293
Rawlins Municipal Library, Pierre SD p. 2080
Rawls Walter Cecil Library, *see* Blackwater Regional Library, Courtland VA p. 2313
Rawlyk George A Library, *see* Crandall University, Moncton NB p. 2603
Rawson Deborah Memorial Library, Jericho VT p. 2287
Rawson Memorial District Library, Cass City MI p. 1089
Ray Brook Federal Correctional Institution Library, Ray Brook NY p. 1626
Ray County Historical Society & Museum Library, Richmond MO p. 1267
Ray County Library, Richmond MO p. 1267
Ray Isaac Medical Library, *see* Butler Hospital, Providence RI p. 2037
Ray Lewis A Library, *see* Cobb County Public Library System, Smyrna GA p. 489
Ray Township Public Library, Ray MI p. 1143
Rayburn Correctional Center Library, Angie LA p. 881
Rayburn Sam Library & Museum, Bonham TX p. 2148
Raymond Library, Oakdale CT p. 332
Raymond Library, *see* Yakima Valley College, Yakima WA p. 2395
Raymond Memorial Library, *see* East Hartford Public Library, East Hartford CT p. 310
Raymond Public Library, Raymond MN p. 1193
Raymond Public Library, Raymond AB p. 2551
Raymond Public Library, *see* Jackson/Hinds Library System, Raymond MS p. 1221
Raymond Village Library, Raymond ME p. 938
Rayner Thelma Memorial Library, *see* Bolivar County Library System, Merigold MS p. 1214
Raynham Public Library, Raynham MA p. 1049
Raynor Memorial Libraries, *see* Marquette University, Milwaukee WI p. 2458
Raytheon Co, Marlborough MA p. 1032
RCS Community Library, Ravena NY p. 1625
Reaching Across Illinois Library System (RAILS), Burr Ridge IL p. 546
Read Louise Adelia Memorial Library, Hancock NY p. 1544
Read Victoria, *see* Belmont County District Library, Flushing OH p. 1800
Reade International Corp, East Providence RI p. 2032
Readfield Community Library, Readfield ME p. 938
Reading Area Community College, Reading PA p. 2000
Reading Community Library, Reading MI p. 1143
Reading Public Library, Reading MA p. 1049
Reading Public Library, Reading PA p. 2000
Reading Public Library, Reading VT p. 2293
Reading Room Association of Gouverneur, Gouverneur NY p. 1540
Readington Township Library, Whitehouse Station NJ p. 1455
Readlyn Community Library, Readlyn IA p. 778
Readsboro Community Library, Readsboro VT p. 2293
Readstown Public Library, Readstown WI p. 2472
Ready Alma D Research Library, *see* Pimeria Alta Historical Society, Nogales AZ p. 67
Reagan County Library, Big Lake TX p. 2148
Ronald Reagan Presidential Library & Museum, *see* National Archives & Records Administration, Simi Valley CA p. 246
Real County Public Library Leakey, Leakey TX p. 2210
Real Estate Board of New York, New York NY p. 1600
Ream Louise Library, *see* Heisey Collectors of America, Inc, Newark OH p. 1807
Reaney Margaret Memorial Library, Saint Johnsville NY p. 1635
Reardan Memorial Library, Reardan WA p. 2375
Reber Memorial Library, Raymondville TX p. 2230
Rebok Memorial Library, *see* General Conference of Seventh-Day Adventists, Silver Spring MD p. 977
Reconstructionist Rabbinical College Library, Wyncote PA p. 2024
Record Library, Stockton CA p. 249
Rector Public Library, Rector AR p. 108
Red Bank Public Library, Red Bank NJ p. 1439
Red Bud Public Library, Red Bud IL p. 638
Red Clay State Historic Area Library, Cleveland TN p. 2093
Red Creek Free Library, Red Creek NY p. 1626
Red Deer & District Archives, Red Deer AB p. 2551
Red Deer College Library, Red Deer AB p. 2551
Red Deer Public Library, Red Deer AB p. 2551
Red Deer Regional Hospital Centre Knowledge Resource Services, *see* Alberta Health Services, Red Deer AB p. 2551
Red Earth Public Library, Red Earth Creek AB p. 2551
Red Feather Lakes Community Library, Red Feather Lakes CO p. 294
Red Hook Public Library, Red Hook NY p. 1626
Red Jacket Community Library, Manchester NY p. 1568
Red Lake Falls Public Library, *see* Northwest Regional Library, Red Lake Falls MN p. 1205
Red Lake Nation College, Red Lake MN p. 1193
Red Lodge Carnegie Library, Red Lodge MT p. 1301
Red Mill Museum Library, Clinton NJ p. 1397
Red Oak Public Library, Red Oak IA p. 778
Red Oak Public Library, Red Oak TX p. 2230
Red River College Polytechnic, Winnipeg MB p. 2795
Red River College Polytechnic Library, Winnipeg MB p. 2594
Red River County Public Library, Clarksville TX p. 2156
Red River Parish Library, Coushatta LA p. 887
Red River Public Library, Red River NM p. 1473
Red River Regional Library, Clarksville TN p. 2092
Red Rock Public Library Board, Red Rock ON p. 2675
Red Rocks Community College, Lakewood CO p. 288
Red Waller Community Library, Malakoff TX p. 2215
Red Wing Public Library, Red Wing MN p. 1194
Redbank Valley Public Library, New Bethlehem PA p. 1968
Redcliff Public Library, Redcliff AB p. 2552

Robinson Agnes Waterloo Public Library, Waterloo NE p. 1340
Robinson Arthur H Map Library, *see* University of Wisconsin-Madison, Madison WI p. 2451
Robinson Carl Correctional Institution Library, Enfield CT p. 311
Robinson-Carpenter Memorial Library, *see* Bolivar County Library System, Cleveland MS p. 1213
Robinson Floyd J Memorial Library, *see* Raleigh Public Library, Raleigh MS p. 1231
Robinson Health Sciences Library, *see* Hartford Hospital, Hartford CT p. 317
Robinson Layon F II Law Library, *see* Manatee County Law Library, Bradenton FL p. 386
Robinson Mary S Art Library, *see* Foothills Art Center, Golden CO p. 283
Robinson Music Library, *see* Cleveland Institute of Music, Cleveland OH p. 1767
Robinson Norma & Joseph Partnership Library at Sulphur Springs, *see* Tampa-Hillsborough County Public Library System, Tampa FL p. 449
Robinson Pauline, *see* Denver Public Library, Denver CO p. 275
Robinson Prezell R Library, *see* Saint Augustine's College, Raleigh NC p. 1710
Robinson Public Library District, Robinson IL p. 640
Robinson, Sheppard & Shapiro, Montreal QC p. 2727
Robinson Township Library, Pittsburgh PA p. 1996
Robinson Westchase Neighborhood Library, *see* Houston Public Library, Houston TX p. 2196
Robley Rex Department of Veterans Affairs Medical Center Library, Louisville KY p. 866
Robson Ed, *see* Maricopa County Library District, Sun Lakes AZ p. 71
Robson Library, *see* University of the Ozarks, Clarksville AR p. 92
Rochambeau Library, *see* Community Libraries of Providence, Providence RI p. 2038
Rochdale Village Community Library, *see* Queens Library, Jamaica NY p. 1555
Rochelle Park Library, Rochelle Park NJ p. 1440
Rochester Civic Garden Center, Inc Library, Rochester NY p. 1629
Rochester College, Rochester Hills MI p. 1145
Rochester Community & Technical College, Rochester MN p. 1194
Rochester Hills Public Library, Rochester MI p. 1144
Rochester Historical Society Library, Rochester NY p. 1630
Rochester Municipal Library, Rochester AB p. 2552
Rochester Museum & Science Center Library, Rochester NY p. 1630
Rochester Public Library, Rochester MN p. 1194
Rochester Public Library, Rochester NH p. 1380
Rochester Public Library, Rochester NY p. 1630
Rochester Public Library, Rochester PA p. 2002
Rochester Public Library, Rochester VT p. 2293
Rochester Public Library, Rochester WI p. 2474
Rochester Public Library District, Rochester IL p. 640
Rochester Regional Library Council (N), Rochester NY p. 2771
Rock County Community Library, Luverne MN p. 1180
Rock County Historical Society, Janesville WI p. 2443
Rock County Public Library, Bassett NE p. 1306
Rock Creek Public Library, Rock Creek OH p. 1817
Rock Falls Public Library District, Rock Falls IL p. 640
Rock Hill Public Library, Rock Hill MO p. 1267
Rock Hill Public Library, *see* York County Library, Rock Hill SC p. 2068
Rock Island County Illinois Genealogical Society Library, Moline IL p. 618
Rock Island County Law Library, Rock Island IL p. 641
Rock Island District Library, *see* United States Army Corps of Engineers, Rock Island IL p. 641
Rock Island Public Library, Rock Island IL p. 641
Rock Rapids Public Library, Rock Rapids IA p. 779
Rock River Library Consortium (N), Sterling IL p. 2765
Rock Springs Library, *see* Sweetwater County Library System, Rock Springs WY p. 2495
Rock Springs Public Library, Rock Springs WI p. 2474
Rock Valley College, Rockford IL p. 641
Rock Valley Public Library, Rock Valley IA p. 779
Rockaway Borough Public Library, Rockaway NJ p. 1440
Rockaway Township Free Public Library, Rockaway NJ p. 1440
Rockbridge Regional Library System, Lexington VA p. 2329
Rockcastle County Public Library, Mount Vernon KY p. 870
Rockdale Temple, Cincinnati OH p. 1763
Rockefeller John D Jr Library, *see* Brown University, Providence RI p. 2037
Rockefeller John D Jr Library, *see* Colonial Williamsburg Foundation, Williamsburg VA p. 2353
Rockefeller Laurance S Library, *see* California Institute of Integral Studies, San Francisco CA p. 223
Rockefeller University, New York NY p. 1601
Rockford Carnegie Library, Rockford OH p. 1818
Rockford Institute Library, Rockford IL p. 641
Rockford Public Library, Rockford AL p. 34
Rockford Public Library, Rockford IL p. 642
Rockford Public Library, Rockford IA p. 779
Rockford Public Library, *see* Great River Regional Library, Rockford MN p. 1197
Rockford University, Rockford IL p. 642
Rockhurst University, Kansas City MO p. 1257
Rockingham Community College, Wentworth NC p. 1721
Rockingham County Public Library, Eden NC p. 1686
Rockingham Free Public Library, Bellows Falls VT p. 2278
Rockland Community College Library, Suffern NY p. 1647
Rockland County Supreme Court Law Library, *see* New York State Supreme Court Ninth Judicial District, New City NY p. 1576
Rockland Memorial Library, Rockland MA p. 1049
Rockland Public Library, Rockland ME p. 939
Rockland School Community Library, Rockland ID p. 530
Rocklin Campus, *see* Sierra College Library, Rocklin CA p. 203
Rockport Public Library, Rockport ME p. 939
Rockport Public Library, Rockport MA p. 1050
Rockrimmon Library, *see* Pikes Peak Library District, Colorado Springs CO p. 271
Rocktown History Genealogy & Research Library, Dayton VA p. 2315
Rockville Centre Public Library, Rockville Centre NY p. 1632
Rockville Correctional Facility Library, Rockville IN p. 717
Rockville Law Library, *see* Connecticut Judicial Branch Law Libraries, Rockville CT p. 316
Rockville Memorial Library, *see* Montgomery County Public Libraries, Rockville MD p. 975
Rockville Public Library, Vernon CT p. 342
Rockwall County Library, Rockwall TX p. 2234
Rockwell City Public Library, Rockwell City IA p. 779
Rockwell Falls Public Library, Lake Luzerne NY p. 1561
Rockwell Public Library, Rockwell IA p. 779
Rockwood Public Library, Rockwood TN p. 2125
Rocky Boy Community Library, *see* Stone Child College, Box Elder MT p. 1289
Rocky Ford Public Library, Rocky Ford CO p. 294
Rocky Hill Historical Society Library, Rocky Hill CT p. 335
Rocky Mount Historical Association Library, Piney Flats TN p. 2124
Rocky Mountain Campus, *see* Gateway Seminary, Centennial CO p. 270
Rocky Mountain College, Billings MT p. 1288
Rocky Mountain College of Art & Design Library, Lakewood CO p. 289
Rocky Mountain House Public Library, Rocky Mountain House AB p. 2552
Rocky Mountain Laboratories Library, *see* NIH, National Institute of Allergy & Infectious Diseases, Hamilton MT p. 1295
Rocky Ridge, *see* Calgary Public Library, Calgary AB p. 2527
Rocky River Public Library, Rocky River OH p. 1818
Rocky Top Public Library, Rocky Top TN p. 2125
Rockyford Municipal Library, Rockyford AB p. 2552
Rockyview General Hospital Knowledge Centre, *see* Calgary Health Region, Calgary AB p. 2526
Rod Library, *see* University of Northern Iowa Library, Cedar Falls IA p. 737
Roddenbery Memorial Library, Cairo GA p. 468
Roddis Hamilton Memorial Library, *see* University of Wisconsin-Stevens Point, Marshfield WI p. 2454
Roddy Clyde W Library, Dayton TN p. 2096
Roden M E Memorial Library, *see* Ocmulgee Regional Library System, Hawkinsville GA p. 477
Rodenberg Billie Davis Memorial Library, *see* Temple Beth El, Hollywood FL p. 409
Rodeo Community Library, *see* Contra Costa County Library, Rodeo CA p. 175
Rodgers George H & Ella M Memorial Library, Hudson NH p. 1368
Rodham Olivia Memorial Library, Nelson NH p. 1375
Rodino Peter W Jr Law Library, *see* Seton Hall University School of Law, Newark NJ p. 1428
Rodman Public Library, Rodman NY p. 1632
Rodman Public Library, Alliance OH p. 1745
Rodolfo (Corky) Gonzales Branch Library, *see* Denver Public Library, Denver CO p. 276
Rodriguez Betty Regional Library, *see* Fresno County Public Library, Fresno CA p. 146
Rodriguez Rivera Nestor M Library, *see* University of Puerto Rico RP College, San Juan PR p. 2515
Roehl Everett Marshfield Public Library, Marshfield WI p. 2454
Roeliff Jansen Community Library, Hillsdale NY p. 1547
Roesch Library, *see* University of Dayton Libraries, Dayton OH p. 1780
Roger Williams University, Bristol RI p. 2029
Roger Williams University Library, Bristol RI p. 2029
Rogers Free Library, Bristol RI p. 2030
Rogers James A Library, *see* Francis Marion University, Florence SC p. 2059
Rogers John Memorial Public Library, Dodge NE p. 1312
Rogers Lauren Museum of Art Library, Laurel MS p. 1224
Rogers Library, *see* Pennsauken Free Public Library, Pennsauken NJ p. 1434
Rogers Memorial Library, Southampton NY p. 1643
Rogers Public Library, Rogers AR p. 108
Rogers State Prison, *see* Georgia Department of Corrections, Reidsville GA p. 493
Rogers State University Library, Claremore OK p. 1844
Rogers Will Library, Claremore OK p. 1844
Rogers Will Memorial Museum Library, Claremore OK p. 1844
Rogersville Public Library, Rogersville AL p. 35
Rohnert Park Cotati Regional Library, *see* Sonoma County Library, Rohnert Park CA p. 204
Rohrbach Library, *see* Kutztown University, Kutztown PA p. 1949
Rohrer William G Memorial Library, *see* Camden County Library System, Westmont NJ p. 1450
Rokeby Museum, Ferrisburg VT p. 2284
Roland Library, *see* Hannibal-LaGrange University, Hannibal MO p. 1247
Roland Public Library, Roland IA p. 779
Rolette City Library, Rolette ND p. 1739
Rolfe Public Library, Rolfe IA p. 779

Royal Victoria Regional Health Centre, Barrie ON p. 2630
Royalton Hartland Community Library, Middleport NY p. 1571
Royalton Library, *see* Great River Regional Library, Royalton MN p. 1197
Royalton Memorial Library, South Royalton VT p. 2295
Royalton Public Library District, Royalton IL p. 644
Royersford Public, *see* Montgomery County-Norristown Public Library, Royersford PA p. 1971
Royle Willis Library, *see* Connecticut Valley Hospital, Middletown CT p. 322
RTI International, Research Triangle Park NC p. 1712
Rubenstein David M Rare Book & Manuscript Library, *see* Duke University Libraries, Durham NC p. 1684
Rubin Hyman A Library, *see* Congregation Shaare Emeth, Saint Louis MO p. 1270
Rubin Tibor Library, *see* OC Public Libraries, Garden Grove CA p. 238
Rubinstein Jack H Library, *see* Cincinnati Children's Hospital, Cincinnati OH p. 1759
Rudd Public Library, Rudd IA p. 780
Rudisill Carl A Library, *see* Lenoir-Rhyne University Libraries, Hickory NC p. 1696
Rudisill Regional Library, *see* Tulsa City-County Library, Tulsa OK p. 1866
Rudofker Ida & Matthew Library, *see* Har Zion Temple, Penn Valley PA p. 1974
Rudolph Lorraine F Fine Arts Center Library, *see* Salem College, Winston-Salem NC p. 1726
Rudolph Richard C East Asian Library, *see* University of California Los Angeles Library, Los Angeles CA p. 169
Ruidoso Public Library, Ruidoso NM p. 1474
Ruiz Irene H Biblioteca de las Americas, *see* Kansas City Public Library, Kansas City MO p. 1255
Rumberger Kirk, Orlando FL p. 432
Rumford Public Library, Rumford ME p. 939
Rumsey Community Library, Rumsey AB p. 2552
Runge Public Library, Runge TX p. 2235
Runnells Community Library, Runnells IA p. 780
Runnemede Free Public Library, Runnemede NJ p. 1441
Rupert Public Library, Rupert WV p. 2414
Rupp Ida Public Library, Port Clinton OH p. 1816
Ruppel Harry Memorial Library, *see* Vandercook College of Music, Chicago IL p. 570
Rural Municipality of Argyle Public Library, Baldur MB p. 2585
Rural Retreat Public, *see* Wythe-Grayson Regional Library, Rural Retreat VA p. 2326
Rush Center Library, Rush Center KS p. 833
Rush Copley Medical Center, Aurora IL p. 539
Rush Public Library, Rush NY p. 1634
Rush Richard H Library, *see* Florida SouthWestern State College, Fort Myers FL p. 403
Rushbrook Audrey Memorial Library, *see* Marine Museum of the Great Lakes, Kingston ON p. 2650
Rushford Free Library, Rushford NY p. 1634
Rushford Public Library, Rushford MN p. 1195
Rushmore Memorial, *see* Woodbury Public Library, Highland Mills NY p. 1546
Rushville Public Library, Rushville IL p. 644
Rushville Public Library, Rushville IN p. 717
Rushville Public Library, Rushville NE p. 1334
Rusk County Community Library, Ladysmith WI p. 2447
Rusk County Library, *see* Rusk County Library System, Henderson TX p. 2189
Rusk County Library System, Henderson TX p. 2189
Ruskin Moscou Faltischek, PC, Uniondale NY p. 1654
Russell & District Regional Library, Russell MB p. 2589
Russell Adelia M Library, Alexander City AL p. 4
Russell Bessie K, *see* Huntsville-Madison County Public Library, Huntsville AL p. 22
Russell C M Museum Library, Great Falls MT p. 1294
Russell Cave National Monument Library, Bridgeport AL p. 10
Russell County Public Library, Jamestown KY p. 861
Russell County Public Library, Lebanon VA p. 2328
Russell Helen Crocker Library of Horticulture, *see* San Francisco Botanical Garden Society at Strybing Arboretum, San Francisco CA p. 226
Russell Jack Memorial Library, Hartford WI p. 2440
Russell Learning Resource Center, *see* Spoon River College Library, Canton IL p. 548
Russell Library, Middletown CT p. 322
Russell Lillie Memorial Library, Lindale TX p. 2212
Russell Memorial, *see* Chesapeake Public Library, Chesapeake VA p. 2311
Russell Memorial Library, Monkton VT p. 2289
Russell Memorial Public Library, Mill Creek WV p. 2408
Russell Public Library, Russell KS p. 834
Russell Public Library, Russell MA p. 1050
Russell Public Library, Russell NY p. 1634
Russell Resource Library, *see* Jane Norman College, Truro NS p. 2623
Russellville Public Library, Russellville AL p. 35
Rust College, Holly Springs MS p. 1220
Rutan & Tucker Library, Irvine CA p. 153
Rutgers, The State University of New Jersey, New Brunswick NJ p. 2788
Rutgers University Libraries, Camden NJ p. 1394
Rutgers University Libraries, New Brunswick NJ p. 1424
Rutgers University Libraries, Newark NJ p. 1428
Rutgers University Library for the Center for Law & Justice, Newark NJ p. 1428
Bach Ruth, *see* Long Beach Public Library, Long Beach CA p. 159
Culver Ruth Community Library, Prairie du Sac WI p. 2471
Rutherford County Library System, Murfreesboro TN p. 2117
Rutherford Humanities & Social Sciences Library, *see* University of Alberta, Edmonton AB p. 2538
Rutherford Library, South Bristol ME p. 941
Rutherford Public Library, Rutherford NJ p. 1441
Ruthmere Museum, Elkhart IN p. 680
Ruthven Public Library, Ruthven IA p. 780
Rutland Free Library, Rutland VT p. 2293
Rutland Free Public Library, Rutland MA p. 1050
Rutland Library, *see* Three Rivers College Library, Poplar Bluff MO p. 1266
Rutland Regional Medical Center, Rutland VT p. 2293
Rutledge Public Library, Rutledge TN p. 2125
Rutledge State Prison, *see* Georgia Department of Corrections, Columbus GA p. 472
Ryan T Calvin Library, *see* University of Nebraska at Kearney, Kearney NE p. 1319
Ryan Library, *see* Iona University, New Rochelle NY p. 1577
Ryan Library, *see* Point Loma Nazarene University, San Diego CA p. 216
Ryan Matura Library, *see* Sacred Heart University, Fairfield CT p. 312
Ryan Memorial Library, *see* Anthony Cardinal Bevilacqua Theological Research Center, Wynnewood PA p. 2025
Ryan W Gordon, *see* Portsmouth Public Library, Lucasville OH p. 1816
Rycroft Municipal Library, Rycroft AB p. 2552
Rye Free Reading Room, Rye NY p. 1634
Rye Historical Society, Rye NY p. 1634
Rye Public Library, Rye NH p. 1380
Ryerson & Burnham Libraries, *see* Art Institute of Chicago, Chicago IL p. 554
Ryerson Nature Library, Riverwoods IL p. 640
Ryerson University Library, Toronto ON p. 2692
Ryerss Museum & Library, Philadelphia PA p. 1985
Rylander Memorial Library, *see* San Saba County Library, San Saba TX p. 2241
S E D Systems, Inc Library, Saskatoon SK p. 2749
Sabina Public Library, Sabina OH p. 1818
Sabinal Public Library, Sabinal TX p. 2235
Sabine Parish Library, Many LA p. 896
Sable-Spanish Riversi Public Library, Massey ON p. 2657
Sabshin Melvin, MD Library & Archives, *see* American Psychiatric Association Foundation, Washington DC p. 360
Sac & Fox National Public Library & Archives, Stroud OK p. 1863
Sac City Public Library, Sac City IA p. 780
Sachem Public Library, Holbrook NY p. 1547
Sachs Hanns Medical Library, *see* Boston Psychoanalytic Society & Institute, Inc, Newton MA p. 1039
Sachs Samuel C, *see* Saint Louis County Library, Chesterfield MO p. 1274
Sachse Public Library, Sachse TX p. 2235
Sackler Medical Library, *see* Greenwich Hospital, Greenwich CT p. 314
Sacramento Area Council of Governments Data Resource Center, Sacramento CA p. 209
Sacramento City College, Sacramento CA p. 209
Sacramento County Public Law Library, Sacramento CA p. 209
Sacramento Public Library, Sacramento CA p. 209
Sacred Heart Academy, Hamden CT p. 316
Sacred Heart Library, *see* Providence Sacred Heart Medical Center, Spokane WA p. 2384
Sacred Heart Major Seminary, Detroit MI p. 1099
Sacred Heart Seminary & School of Theology, Franklin WI p. 2436
Sacred Heart University, Fairfield CT p. 312
Saddle Brook Free Public Library, Saddle Brook NJ p. 1441
Saddleback College, Mission Viejo CA p. 177
Saddletowne Library, *see* Calgary Public Library, Calgary AB p. 2527
Saegertown Area Library, Saegertown PA p. 2002
Safety Harbor Public Library, Safety Harbor FL p. 439
Saffell Thomas F Library, *see* Garden City Community College, Garden City KS p. 809
Safford City-Graham County Library, Safford AZ p. 76
Sagamore Hill National Historic Site Library, Oyster Bay NY p. 1614
Sage Colleges, Albany NY p. 1483
Sage Gardner A Library, *see* New Brunswick Theological Seminary, New Brunswick NJ p. 1424
SAGE Medical Library, *see* Cottage Health System, Santa Barbara CA p. 239
Sage Memorial Library, *see* Barber Scotia College, Concord NC p. 1682
Sage Russell College Libraries, Troy NY p. 1653
Sage Russell Foundation Library, New York NY p. 1601
Sagebrush Federation, Miles City MT p. 1299
Saginaw Art Museum, Saginaw MI p. 1147
Saginaw Chippewa Tribal Libraries, Mount Pleasant MI p. 1135
Saginaw Correctional Facility Library, *see* Michigan Department of Corrections, Freeland MI p. 1108
Saginaw Public Library, Saginaw TX p. 2235
Saginaw Valley State University, University Center MI p. 1155
Saguache Public Library, Saguache CO p. 295
Saguaro Library, *see* Phoenix Public Library, Phoenix AZ p. 72
Sahara West Library, *see* Las Vegas-Clark County Library District, Las Vegas NV p. 1347
Sahatdjian Library, *see* California State University, Fresno, Fresno CA p. 144
Sahuarita, *see* Pima County Public Library, Sahuarita AZ p. 82
Sahyun Library, *see* Santa Barbara County Genealogical Society, Santa Barbara CA p. 240
SAILS Library Network (N), Lakeville MA p. 2767
Saint Albans Community Library, *see* Queens Library, Saint Albans NY p. 1555
Saint Albans Free Library, Saint Albans VT p. 2293
Saint Albert Public Library, St. Albert AB p. 2555
Saint Alphonsus Regional Medical Center - Boise, Boise ID p. 518
Saint Ambrose University Library, Davenport IA p. 744
Saint Andrew's Abbey, Cleveland OH p. 1770
Saint Andrew's College Library, *see* University of Manitoba, Winnipeg MB p. 2594

Saint Louis Community College, Saint Louis MO p. 1272
Saint Louis County Law Library, Duluth MN p. 1172
Saint Louis County Law Library, Clayton MO p. 1242
Saint Louis County Library, Saint Louis MO p. 1273
Saint Louis District Library, *see* United States Army Corps of Engineers, Saint Louis MO p. 1276
Saint Louis Mercantile Library, Saint Louis MO p. 1274
Saint Louis Metropolitan Police Department, Saint Louis MO p. 1274
Saint Louis Police Library, *see* Saint Louis Metropolitan Police Department, Saint Louis MO p. 1274
Saint Louis Psychiatric Rehabilitation Center, Saint Louis MO p. 1274
Saint Louis Psychoanalytic Institute, Saint Louis MO p. 1274
Saint Louis Public Library, Saint Louis MI p. 1148
Saint Louis Public Library, Saint Louis MO p. 1274
Saint Louis Public Library, *see* Wapiti Regional Library, St. Louis SK p. 2746
Saint Louis Regional Library Network (N), Ballwin MO p. 2769
Saint Louis University, Saint Louis MO p. 1275
Saint Louis Zoo Library, Saint Louis MO p. 1276
Saint Lucie County Law Library, *see* Smith Rupert J Law Library of Saint Lucie County, Fort Pierce FL p. 405
Saint Lucie County Library System, Fort Pierce FL p. 404
Saint Lucie County Regional History Center, Fort Pierce FL p. 405
Saint Luke's College Library, Sioux City IA p. 782
Saint Luke's Episcopal Church Library, Kalamazoo MI p. 1122
Saint Luke's Health System Libraries, Boise ID p. 518
Saint Luke's Hospital, Duluth MN p. 1172
Saint Luke's Hospital, Kansas City MO p. 1257
Saint Luke's Hospital, Maumee OH p. 1800
Saint Maries Public Library, Saint Maries ID p. 530
Saint Mark's Episcopal Church, San Antonio TX p. 2237
Saint Mark's Hospital, Salt Lake City UT p. 2271
Saint Mark's Parish Library, Beaumont TX p. 2146
Saint Mark's Presbyterian Church Library, Tucson AZ p. 83
Saint Martin Parish Library, Saint Martinville LA p. 907
Saint Martin Public Library, *see* Jackson-George Regional Library System, Biloxi MS p. 1228
Saint Martin's University, Lacey WA p. 2368
Saint Mary Medical Center, Long Beach CA p. 159
Saint Mary-of-the-Woods College, Saint Mary-of-the-Woods IN p. 717
Saint Mary Parish Library, Franklin LA p. 889
Saint Mary Seminary, Wickliffe OH p. 1831
St Mary's Branch, *see* CMU Health, Saginaw MI p. 1146
Saint Mary's College, Notre Dame IN p. 711
Saint Mary's College Library, Moraga CA p. 180
Saint Mary's College of Maryland Library, Saint Mary's City MD p. 976
Saint Marys Community Public Library, Saint Marys OH p. 1819
Saint Marys Correctional Center Library, Saint Marys WV p. 2414
Saint Mary's County Historical Society, Leonardtown MD p. 971
Saint Mary's County Library, Leonardtown MD p. 971
Saint Mary's General Hospital, Kitchener ON p. 2652
Saint Marys Headquarters Library, *see* Pottawatomie Wabaunsee Regional Library, Saint Marys KS p. 834
Saint Mary's Hospital, Grand Junction CO p. 284
Saint Mary's Hospital, Waterbury CT p. 344
Saint Mary's Hospital, Montreal QC p. 2727
St Mary's Hospital Medical Library, Madison WI p. 2450
St Mary's Library, Saint Marys GA p. 495
Saint Marys Patients' Library, *see* Mayo Clinic Libraries, Rochester MN p. 1194
Saint Mary's Public Library, Saint Marys PA p. 2002
St Mary's Public Library, St. Marys ON p. 2680
Saint Mary's School for the Deaf Library, Buffalo NY p. 1510
Saint Mary's Seminary & University, Baltimore MD p. 956
Saint Mary's University, San Antonio TX p. 2237
Saint Mary's University, Halifax NS p. 2621
Saint Mary's University of Minnesota, Winona MN p. 1209
Saint Meinrad Archabbey & School of Theology, Saint Meinrad IN p. 717
Saint Michael Public Library, *see* Great River Regional Library, Saint Michael MN p. 1197
Saint Michael's Hospital, Toronto ON p. 2692
Saint Norbert Abbey, De Pere WI p. 2430
Saint Norbert College, De Pere WI p. 2430
Saint Olaf College, Northfield MN p. 1191
Saint Olaf Lutheran Church, Minneapolis MN p. 1185
Saint Paris Public Library, Saint Paris OH p. 1819
Saint Patrick's Seminary, Menlo Park CA p. 175
Saint Paul College Library, Saint Paul MN p. 1202
Saint Paul Library, Saint Paul NE p. 1334
Saint Paul Municipal Library, St. Paul AB p. 2555
Saint Paul of the Cross Province, Jamaica NY p. 1556
St Paul Public Library, Saint Paul AR p. 109
Saint Paul Public Library, Saint Paul MN p. 1202
Saint Paul School of Theology Library, Leawood KS p. 820
Saint Paul University Library, Ottawa ON p. 2670
Saint Paul's Episcopal Church Library, Maumee OH p. 1800
Saint Paul's Episcopal Church Library, Richmond VA p. 2342
Saint Paul's Hospital of Saskatoon, Saskatoon SK p. 2749
Saint Pete Beach Public Library, Saint Pete Beach FL p. 441
Saint Peter Public Library, Saint Peter MN p. 1203
Saint Peter Regional Treatment Center Libraries, Saint Peter MN p. 1203
Saint Peter's College Library, Muenster SK p. 2743
Saint Peter's Hospital, Albany NY p. 1483
Saint Peter's Hospital College of Nursing, Albany NY p. 1483
Saint Peters Public Library, *see* Prince Edward Island Public Library Service, St. Peters PE p. 2708
Saint Peter's Seminary, London ON p. 2655
Saint Peter's University, Englewood Cliffs NJ p. 1402
Saint Peter's University, Jersey City NJ p. 1410
Saint Peter's University Hospital Medical Library, New Brunswick NJ p. 1425
Saint Petersburg College, Pinellas Park FL p. 437
Saint Petersburg Museum of History, Saint Petersburg FL p. 441
Saint Petersburg Public Library, Saint Petersburg FL p. 441
Saint Philip's College, San Antonio TX p. 2238
Saint Rita's Medical Center, Lima OH p. 1796
Saint Simons Island Public Library, Saint Simons Island GA p. 495
Saint Tammany Parish Library, Covington LA p. 887
Saint Thomas Aquinas Church, Ames IA p. 731
Saint Thomas Aquinas College, Sparkill NY p. 1643
Saint Thomas Episcopal Church Library, Sunnyvale CA p. 251
Saint Thomas Health Services Library, Nashville TN p. 2120
Saint Thomas Library, Saint Thomas PA p. 2003
Saint Thomas More Catholic Newman Center, Tucson AZ p. 83
Saint Thomas More College-University of Saskatchewan, Saskatoon SK p. 2749
Saint Thomas Public Library, St. Thomas ON p. 2681
Saint Thomas University Library, Miami Gardens FL p. 425
Saint Tikhon's Orthodox Theological Seminary, South Canaan PA p. 2008
Saint Vincent College & Seminary Library, Latrobe PA p. 1953
Saint Vincent de Paul Regional Seminary Library, Boynton Beach FL p. 386
Saint Vincent Hospital, Worcester MA p. 1072
Saint Vladimir Institute Library, Toronto ON p. 2692
Saint Vladimir's Orthodox Theological Seminary Library, Yonkers NY p. 1667
Saint Volodymyr's Cultural Centre, Calgary AB p. 2529
Saint Walburg Monastery Archives, Covington KY p. 852
Saint Xavier University, Chicago IL p. 567
Sainte Genevieve County Library, Sainte Genevieve MO p. 1278
SAIT Polytechnic, Calgary AB p. 2795
Salado Public Library, Salado TX p. 2235
Salamanca Public Library, Salamanca NY p. 1635
Salem Athenaeum, Salem MA p. 1051
Salem Baptist Church Library, Salem VA p. 2347
Salem City Library, Salem UT p. 2270
Salem College, Winston-Salem NC p. 1725
Salem Community College Library, Carneys Point NJ p. 1395
Salem County Historical Society, Salem NJ p. 1441
Salem Free Public Library, Salem CT p. 335
Salem Free Public Library, Salem NJ p. 1441
Salem Health Community Health Education Center, Salem OR p. 1896
Salem Maritime National Historic Site Library, *see* United States National Park Service, Salem MA p. 1051
Salem Public Library, Salem IN p. 717
Salem Public Library, Salem MA p. 1051
Salem Public Library, Salem MO p. 1278
Salem Public Library, Salem OH p. 1819
Salem Public Library, Salem OR p. 1897
Salem Public Library, Salem VA p. 2347
Salem Public Library, *see* Fulton County Library, Salem AR p. 109
Salem-South Lyon District Library, South Lyon MI p. 1151
Salem State University, Salem MA p. 1051, 2786
Salem Township Library, Burnips MI p. 1088
Salem Township Public Library, Morrow OH p. 1804
Salem Township Public Library District, Yates City IL p. 665
Salem University, Salem WV p. 2414
Salem VA Health Care System Library, *see* Department of Veterans Affairs, Salem VA p. 2346
Salida Regional Library, Salida CO p. 295
Salina Library, Mattydale NY p. 1570
Salina Public Library, Salina KS p. 835
Salina Public Library, Salina UT p. 2270
Salinas Alicia City of Alice Public Library, Alice TX p. 2132
Salinas Public Library, Salinas CA p. 211
Salinas Pueblo Missions Research Library, *see* National Park Service, Mountainair NM p. 1473
Salinas Valley State Prison, *see* California Department of Corrections Library System, Soledad CA p. 207
Saline County Public Library, Benton AR p. 90
Saline District Library, Saline MI p. 1148
Salisbury Free Library, Salisbury NH p. 1380
Salisbury Public Library, Salisbury MA p. 1051
Salisbury Township Branch Library, *see* Pequea Valley Public Library, Gap PA p. 1946
Salisbury University, Salisbury MD p. 976
Salish Kootenai College, Pablo MT p. 1300
Salk Institute for Biological Studies, La Jolla CA p. 154
Salk Institute Library, *see* Salk Institute for Biological Studies, La Jolla CA p. 154
Salkehatchie Library, *see* University of South Carolina, Allendale SC p. 2046
Salmagundi Club Library, New York NY p. 1601
Salman Terry Branch, *see* Vancouver Public Library, Vancouver BC p. 2582
Salmen Joan Memorial, *see* Superior Public Library, Solon Springs WI p. 2480

Sanford Virtual Library, Fargo ND p. 1733
Sanford William K Town Library, Loudonville NY p. 1565
Sanger Public Library, Sanger TX p. 2241
Sangudo Public Library, Sangudo AB p. 2553
Sanibel Public Library District, Sanibel FL p. 442
Sanilac District Library, Port Sanilac MI p. 1143
Santa Ana College, Santa Ana CA p. 239
Santa Ana Public Library, Santa Ana CA p. 239
Santa Ana Pueblo Community Library, Bernalillo NM p. 1464
Santa Barbara Botanic Garden, Santa Barbara CA p. 240
Santa Barbara City College, Santa Barbara CA p. 240
Santa Barbara County Genealogical Society, Santa Barbara CA p. 240
Santa Barbara County Law Library, Santa Maria CA p. 243
Santa Barbara Historical Museum, Santa Barbara CA p. 240
Santa Barbara Mission, Santa Barbara CA p. 240
Santa Barbara Museum of Natural History Library, Santa Barbara CA p. 240
Santa Barbara News Press Library, Santa Barbara CA p. 240
Santa Barbara Public Library, Santa Barbara CA p. 240
Santa Clara City Library, Santa Clara CA p. 241
Santa Clara County Law Library, San Jose CA p. 232
Santa Clara County Library District, Campbell CA p. 126
Santa Clara Pueblo Community Library, Espanola NM p. 1467
Santa Clara University Library, Santa Clara CA p. 242
Santa Clara Valley Medical Center, San Jose CA p. 232
Santa Clara Valley Water District Library, San Jose CA p. 232
Santa Clarita Interlibrary Network (N), Santa Clarita CA p. 2762
Santa Clarita Public Library, Santa Clarita CA p. 242
Santa Cruz City-County Library System, Santa Cruz CA p. 242
Santa Cruz County Law Library, Santa Cruz CA p. 243
Santa Fe College, Gainesville FL p. 407
Santa Fe Community College Library, Santa Fe NM p. 1476
Santa Fe Institute Library, Santa Fe NM p. 1476
Santa Fe Public Library, Santa Fe NM p. 1476
Santa Fe Springs City Library, Santa Fe Springs CA p. 243
Santa Fe Trail Center Museum & Research Library, *see* Fort Larned Historical Society, Inc, Larned KS p. 818
Santa Maria Public Library, Santa Maria CA p. 243
Santa Monica College Library, Santa Monica CA p. 244
Santa Monica Public Library, Santa Monica CA p. 244
Santa Rita Express Branch Library, *see* Guerra Joe A Laredo Public Library, Laredo TX p. 2209
Santa Rosa County Library System, Milton FL p. 426
Santa Rosa Junior College, Santa Rosa CA p. 245
Santa Rosa Press Democrat, Santa Rosa CA p. 245
Santa Ynez Branch, *see* Goleta Valley Library, Santa Ynez CA p. 149
Santa Ynez Valley Historical Society, Santa Ynez CA p. 245
Santaquin City Library, Santaquin UT p. 2273
Santee Campus Library, *see* Nebraska Indian Community College Library, Niobrara NE p. 1326
Santiago Canyon College, Orange CA p. 189
Santiago Library System, Pasadena CA p. 194
Santiam Correctional Institution Library, Salem OR p. 1897
Santo Domingo Public Library, Santo Domingo Pueblo NM p. 1477
Santore Charles, *see* Free Library of Philadelphia, Philadelphia PA p. 1980
Sapp Raymond A Memorial Township Library, Wyanet IL p. 665
Sappi North America, Westbrook ME p. 946
SAR Genealogical Research Library, *see* National Society of the Sons of the American Revolution, Louisville KY p. 866
Sarah Lawrence College, Bronxville NY p. 1500
Saraland Public Library, *see* Mobile Public Library, Saraland AL p. 26
Saranac Lake Free Library, Saranac Lake NY p. 1636
Saranac Public Library, Saranac MI p. 1149
Sarasota County Library System, Sarasota FL p. 443
Saratoga Branch, *see* Carbon County Library System, Saratoga WY p. 2498
Saratoga Community Library, *see* Santa Clara County Library District, Saratoga CA p. 127
Saratoga Hospital, Saratoga Springs NY p. 1636
Saratoga Springs Public Library, Saratoga Springs NY p. 1636
Saratoga Springs Public Library, Saratoga Springs UT p. 2273
Sarcoxie Public Library, Sarcoxie MO p. 1279
Sardis City Public Library, Sardis City AL p. 35
Sardis Public Library, *see* First Regional Library, Sardis MS p. 1220
Sargeant Fernando de la Rosa Memorial Library, Alamo TX p. 2132
Sargent & Lundy, LLC, Chicago IL p. 567
Sargent Memorial Library, Boxborough MA p. 1001
Sargent Township Library, Sargent NE p. 1334
Sargentville Library Association, Sargentville ME p. 939
Sarris Frank Public Library, Canonsburg PA p. 1918
Sasaki Associates, Inc Library, Watertown MA p. 1063
Saskatchewan Choral Federation Library, Regina SK p. 2747
Saskatchewan Genealogical Society Library, Regina SK p. 2747
Saskatchewan Indian Cultural Centre, Saskatoon SK p. 2749
Saskatchewan Justice, Regina SK p. 2747
Saskatchewan Legislative Library, Regina SK p. 2748
Saskatchewan Parks & Recreation Association, Regina SK p. 2748
Saskatchewan Polytechnic, Regina SK p. 2748
Saskatchewan Polytechnic Library & Information Technology, Saskatoon SK p. 2797
Saskatchewan Teachers' Federation, Saskatoon SK p. 2749
Saskatoon Public Library, Saskatoon SK p. 2749
Saskatoon Theological Union Library, Saskatoon SK p. 2749
Sasktel Corporate Library, Regina SK p. 2748
Satellite Beach Public Library, Satellite Beach FL p. 443
Satilla Regional Library, Douglas GA p. 476
Satow Masao W Library, *see* County of Los Angeles Public Library, Gardena CA p. 138
Satre Memorial Library, Milnor ND p. 1738
Satsuma Public Library, Satsuma AL p. 35
Satterlee, Stephens LLP, New York NY p. 1601
Saucier Children's Library, *see* Harrison County Library System, Saucier MS p. 1218
Sauey Ron Memorial Library for Bird Conservation, *see* International Crane Foundation, Baraboo WI p. 2422
Saugatuck-Douglas District Library, Douglas MI p. 1101
Saugerties Public Library, Saugerties NY p. 1637
Sauk County Law Library, Baraboo WI p. 2422
Sauk Valley Community College, Dixon IL p. 579
Saul Ewing Arnstein & Lehr, Philadelphia PA p. 1985
Saul Ewing LLP, Baltimore MD p. 956
Saulnier Pere Zoel Public Library, *see* Chaleur Library Region, Tracadie-Sheila NB p. 2599
Sault Area Hospital, Sault Ste. Marie ON p. 2677
Sault College Library, Sault Ste. Marie ON p. 2677
Sault Sainte Marie Public Library, Sault Ste. Marie ON p. 2677
Saunders Robert W Sr Public Library, *see* Tampa-Hillsborough County Public Library System, Tampa FL p. 449
Sausalito Public Library, Sausalito CA p. 246
Savage John E Medical Library, *see* Greater Baltimore Medical Center, Baltimore MD p. 953
Savage Leslie J Library, *see* Western Colorado University, Gunnison CO p. 285
Savage Public Library, *see* Scott County Library System, Savage MN p. 1203
Savanna Municipal Library, Silver Valley AB p. 2553
Savanna Public Library District, Savanna IL p. 645
Savannah River National Applied Science Library, *see* Savannah River Site, Aiken SC p. 2045
Savannah River Site, Aiken SC p. 2045
Savannah State University, Savannah GA p. 496
Savannah Technical College, Hinesville GA p. 482
Savannah Technical College, Savannah GA p. 496
Savanuck SSG Paul D Memorial Library, Fort George G Meade MD p. 965
Savarino Rachel R Library, *see* Trocaire College Library, Buffalo NY p. 1510
Savery Library, *see* Talladega College, Talladega AL p. 36
Savitt Medical Library, *see* University of Nevada-Reno, Reno NV p. 1349
Savonburg Public Library, Savonburg KS p. 835
Savoy Hollow Library, Savoy MA p. 1052
Sawyer Library, *see* Williams College, Williamstown MA p. 1069
Sawyer Martha Community Library, Lebanon ME p. 929
Sawyer Mildred F Library, *see* Suffolk University, Boston MA p. 1000
Sawyer W Tom & Bonnie Library, *see* Husson University, Bangor ME p. 915
Sawyier Paul Public Library, Frankfort KY p. 856
Saxton Community Library, Saxton PA p. 2003
Sayers Carey B Memorial Library, *see* Chapelwood United Methodist Church, Houston TX p. 2191
Sayre Public Library, Sayre OK p. 1861
Sayre Public Library, Inc, Sayre PA p. 2003
Sayreville Public Library, Parlin NJ p. 1432
Sayville Library, Sayville NY p. 1637
SCAMeL (N), *see* South Central Academic Medical Libraries Consortium, Fort Worth TX p. 2775
Scandia City Library, Scandia KS p. 835
Scandinavia Public Library, Scandinavia WI p. 2475
Scappoose Public Library, Scappoose OR p. 1898
Scarborough Hospital, Scarborough ON p. 2677
Scarborough Library, *see* Shepherd University, Shepherdstown WV p. 2414
Scarborough Memorial Library, *see* University of the Southwest, Hobbs NM p. 1469
Scarborough Public Library, Scarborough ME p. 939
Scarborough UTSC Library, *see* University of Toronto Libraries, Scarborough ON p. 2700
Scarsdale Public Library, Scarsdale NY p. 1637
SCELC (N), *see* Statewide California Electronic Library Consortium, Los Angeles CA p. 2762
Scenic Regional Library, Union MO p. 1283
Scenic Woods Regional Libray, *see* Houston Public Library, Houston TX p. 2196
Schaber Gordon D Law Library, *see* University of the Pacific - McGeorge School of Law, Sacramento CA p. 210
Schaefer John F Law Library, *see* Michigan State University College of Law Library, East Lansing MI p. 1101
Schaffer Law Library, *see* Albany Law School, Albany NY p. 1482
Schaffer Library, *see* Union College, Schenectady NY p. 1638
Schaffer Library of Health Sciences, *see* Albany Medical College, Albany NY p. 1482
Schaffner Joseph Library, *see* Northwestern University Libraries, Chicago IL p. 587
Schaller Public Library, Schaller IA p. 780
Schalm Memorial Collection, *see* Vanguard College Library, Edmonton AB p. 2538
Schauerman Library, *see* El Camino College, Torrance CA p. 252
Schaumburg Township District Library, Schaumburg IL p. 645

Scottsdale Community College Library, Scottsdale AZ p. 77
Scottsdale Healthcare, Scottsdale AZ p. 77
Scottsdale Public Library, Scottsdale AZ p. 77
Scottsville Free Library, Scottsville NY p. 1639
Scotus Duns Library, *see* Lourdes University, Sylvania OH p. 1822
Scoville Memorial Library, Salisbury CT p. 335
Scranton E C Memorial Library, Madison CT p. 320
Scranton Public Library, Scranton PA p. 2004
Scranton Times-Tribune, Scranton PA p. 2005
Screven-Jenkins Regional Library, Sylvania GA p. 498
Scribner Lucy Library, *see* Skidmore College, Saratoga Springs NY p. 1636
Scribner Public Library, Scribner NE p. 1335
Scripps Mercy Hospital Medical Library, San Diego CA p. 221
Scripps Research Institute, La Jolla CA p. 154
Scripture William E & Elaine Memorial Library, *see* Rome Historical Society, Rome NY p. 1632
Scugog Memorial Public Library, Port Perry ON p. 2674
Scurry County Library, Snyder TX p. 2244
Sea Bright Library, Sea Bright NJ p. 1442
Sea Cliff Village Library, Sea Cliff NY p. 1639
Sea Girt Library, Sea Girt NJ p. 1442
SEAALL (N), *see* Southeastern Chapter of the American Association of Law Libraries, Baltimore MD p. 2766
Seabrook Library, Seabrook NH p. 1381
Seabury Learning Resource Center, *see* Southern California University of Health Sciences, Whittier CA p. 259
Seabury Society for the Preservation of the Glebe House, Inc, Woodbury CT p. 349
Seaford District Library, Seaford DE p. 356
Seaford Public Library, Seaford NY p. 1639
Seagoville Public Library, Seagoville TX p. 2242
Seal Beach-Mary Wilson Library, *see* OC Public Libraries, Seal Beach CA p. 238
Sealy Lloyd George Library, *see* John Jay College of Criminal Justice, New York NY p. 1589
Search Group, Inc Library, Sacramento CA p. 210
Searchlight Library, *see* Las Vegas-Clark County Library District, Searchlight NV p. 1347
Searcy County Library, Marshall AR p. 104
Searcy Cpl J R Memorial Library, *see* Ouachita Parish Public Library, West Monroe LA p. 898
SEARK Library & Learning Resource Center, *see* Southeast Arkansas College, Pine Bluff AR p. 107
Searls Historical Library, *see* Nevada County Historical Society, Nevada City CA p. 183
Sears Charles B Law Library, *see* University at Buffalo Libraries-State University of New York, Buffalo NY p. 1511
Sears Jacob Memorial Library, East Dennis MA p. 1015
Searsmont Town Library, Searsmont ME p. 940
Seashore Trolley Museum Library, *see* New England Electric Railway Historical Society, Kennebunkport ME p. 928
Seaside Community Library, *see* Queens Library, Rockaway Park NY p. 1555
Seaside Public Library, Seaside OR p. 1898
Seaside Square Library, *see* United States Marine Corps, Camp Pendleton CA p. 126
Seaton Memorial Library, *see* Riley County Historical Museum, Manhattan KS p. 823
Seattle Art Museum, Seattle WA p. 2378
Seattle Central College, Seattle WA p. 2378
Seattle Children's Hospital, Seattle WA p. 2378
Seattle Genealogical Society Library, Seattle WA p. 2378
Seattle Metaphysical Library, Seattle WA p. 2378
Seattle Pacific University Library, Seattle WA p. 2379
Seattle Psychoanalytic Society & Institute, Seattle WA p. 2379
Seattle Public Library, Seattle WA p. 2379
Seattle University, Seattle WA p. 2380
Seba Beach Public Library, Seba Beach AB p. 2553
Sebastian County Law Library, Fort Smith AR p. 96
Sebastian County Library, *see* Scott-Sebastian Regional Library, Greenwood AR p. 97
Sebastopol Public Library, Sebastopol MS p. 1232
Sebastopol Regional Library, *see* Sonoma County Library, Sebastopol CA p. 204
Sebewaing Township Library, Sebewaing MI p. 1150
Sebring Public Library, *see* Highlands County Library, Sebring FL p. 444
Secaucus Public Library, Secaucus NJ p. 1442
Sechelt Public Library, Sechelt BC p. 2575
Second Congregational United Church of Christ Library, Grand Rapids MI p. 1111
Second Presbyterian Church, Bloomington IL p. 543
Security Public Library, Security CO p. 295
Sedalia Public Library, Sedalia MO p. 1279
Sedan Public Library, Sedan KS p. 835
Seddiqui Omar Research Library, *see* Palo Alto University, Palo Alto CA p. 192
Sedgewick & District Municipal Library, Sedgewick AB p. 2553
Sedgwick County Law Library, Wichita KS p. 843
Sedgwick Library Association, Sedgwick ME p. 940
Seekonk Public Library, Seekonk MA p. 1052
Seeley Memorial Library, *see* Lackawanna College, Scranton PA p. 2004
SEFLIN (N), *see* Southeast Florida Library Information Network, Inc, Boca Raton FL p. 2763
Segars Library Health Sciences Campus, *see* Florence-Darlington Technical College Libraries, Florence SC p. 2059
Seguin Public Library, Seguin TX p. 2242
Seidman Morton & Norma Memorial & Dr Kaplan Harvey & Sharon Library & Media Center, *see* Kent State University College of Podiatric Medicine, Independence OH p. 1791
Seiling Public Library, *see* Western Plains Library System, Seiling OK p. 1845
Sekula Dustin Michael Memorial Library, Edinburg TX p. 2173
Selah Public Library, *see* Yakima Valley Libraries, Selah WA p. 2396
Selby Marie Botanical Gardens Research Library, Sarasota FL p. 443
Selby Public Library, Sarasota FL p. 443
Selby Township Library District, De Pue IL p. 576
Selbyville Public Library, Selbyville DE p. 356
SELCO (N), *see* Southeastern Libraries Cooperating, Rochester MN p. 2768
Selden Public Library, Selden KS p. 836
Seldovia Public Library, Seldovia AK p. 50
Self Regional Healthcare, Greenwood SC p. 2063
Seligman Public Library, *see* Yavapai County Free Library District, Seligman AZ p. 75
Selkirk College Library, Castlegar BC p. 2564
Sellers Health Sciences Library, *see* Hendrick Medical Center, Abilene TX p. 2132
Selma Public Library, Selma NC p. 1716
Selma University, Selma AL p. 35
Selover Public Library, Chesterville OH p. 1758
Seltzer, Caplan, McMahon, Vitek, San Diego CA p. 222
Selwyn Public Library, Bridgenorth ON p. 2633
Semans Hubert H Library, *see* Foothill College, Los Altos Hills CA p. 159
Semiahmoo Library, *see* Surrey Libraries, Surrey BC p. 2577
Seminole Community College, Oviedo FL p. 433
Seminole Community Library at Saint Petersburg College, Seminole FL p. 444
Seminole County Public Library, *see* Southwest Georgia Regional Library, Donalsonville GA p. 467
Seminole County Public Library System, Casselberry FL p. 388
Seminole Library, *see* Windsor Public Library, Windsor ON p. 2705
Seminole Nation Museum Library, Wewoka OK p. 1869
Seminole Public Library, Seminole OK p. 1861
Seminole State College, Seminole OK p. 1861
Seminole State College of Florida, Altamonte Springs FL p. 383
Seminole State College of Florida, Heathrow FL p. 408
Seminole State College of Florida, Sanford FL p. 442
Seminole Tribe of Florida, Okeechobee FL p. 430
SEMLOL (N), *see* Southeastern Michigan League of Libraries, Dearborn MI p. 2767
Semmes, Bowen & Semmes Library, Baltimore MD p. 956
Senate Library of Pennsylvania, Harrisburg PA p. 1941
Senatobia Public Library, *see* First Regional Library, Senatobia MS p. 1220
Senator John D Pinto Library, *see* Dine College, Shiprock NM p. 1477
Seneca @ York, *see* Seneca College of Applied Arts & Technology, North York ON p. 2650
Seneca College of Applied Arts & Technology, King City ON p. 2649
Seneca College of Applied Arts & Technology, Toronto ON p. 2796
Seneca County Law Library, Tiffin OH p. 1823
Seneca East Public Library, Attica OH p. 1748
Seneca Falls Historical Society Library, Seneca Falls NY p. 1639
Seneca Falls Library, Seneca Falls NY p. 1640
Seneca Free Library, Seneca KS p. 836
Seneca Nation Libraries, Salamanca NY p. 1635
Seneca Public Library District, Seneca IL p. 646
Senkfor Leonard Library, *see* Park Synagogue, Pepper Pike OH p. 1815
Senoia Area Public Library, *see* Coweta Public Library System, Senoia GA p. 492
Sentara College of Health Sciences, Chesapeake VA p. 2312
Sentara RMH Medical Center, Harrisonburg VA p. 2325
Sentinel Public Library, *see* Western Plains Library System, Sentinel OK p. 1845
SENYLRC (N), *see* Southeastern New York Library Resources Council, Highland NY p. 2771
SEO (N), *see* Serving Every Ohioan Service Cente, Caldwell OH p. 2773
SEPTLA (N), *see* Southeastern Pennsylvania Theological Library Association, Hatfield PA p. 2774
Sequatchie County Public Library, Dunlap TN p. 2097
Sequoyah Regional Library System, Canton GA p. 469
Sergeants Major Academy Learning Resources Center, *see* United States Army, Fort Bliss TX p. 2177
SERLS (N), *see* Southeast Regional Library System, Wellston OH p. 2773
Serra Cooperative Library System (N), Pasadena CA p. 2762
Serramonte Main Library, *see* Daly City Public Library, Daly City CA p. 134
Service des bibliothèques publiques du Nouveau-Brunswick (SBPNB), *see* New Brunswick Public Library Service, Fredericton NB p. 2601
Services for Older Adults, *see* Brooklyn Public Library, Brooklyn NY p. 1504
Serving Every Ohioan Service Cente (N), Caldwell OH p. 2773
Servite Provincial Library, *see* Order of Servants of Mary (Servites), USA Province, Chicago IL p. 567
Sesser Public Library, Sesser IL p. 646
Sessions Rube Memorial Library, Wells TX p. 2256
Seton Elizabeth Library, *see* College of Mount Saint Vincent, Bronx NY p. 1498
Seton Hall University, South Orange NJ p. 1443
Seton Hall University Libraries, Nutley NJ p. 1430
Seton Hall University Libraries, South Orange NJ p. 1443
Seton Hall University School of Law, Newark NJ p. 1428
Seton Hill University, Greensburg PA p. 1938
Settlement Music School, Philadelphia PA p. 1986
Seven Oaks General Hospital Library, *see* University of Manitoba, Winnipeg MB p. 2595
Seven Trees, *see* San Jose Public Library, San Jose CA p. 232

Shepard James E Memorial Library, *see* North Carolina Central University, Durham NC p. 1685
Shepard Memorial Library, *see* Dansville Public Library, Dansville NY p. 1524
Shepard-Pruden Memorial Library, Edenton NC p. 1686
Shepherd George Library, *see* Western Development Museum, Saskatoon SK p. 2750
Shepherd Public Library, Shepherd TX p. 2243
Shepherd University, Shepherdstown WV p. 2414
Shepherds Theological Seminary Library, Cary NC p. 1677
Shepherdstown Public Library, Shepherdstown WV p. 2414
Sheppard Bert Library & Archives, *see* Stockmen's Memorial Foundation Library, Cochrane AB p. 2531
Sheppard Memorial Library, Greenville NC p. 1694
Sheppard, Mullin, Richter & Hampton Library, Los Angeles CA p. 167
Sheppard Pratt Health Systems, Baltimore MD p. 956
Sheppard William H Library, *see* Stillman College, Tuscaloosa AL p. 37
Shepperd Leadership Institute, Odessa TX p. 2223
Sherbaniuk Douglas J Research Centre, *see* Canadian Tax Foundation, Toronto ON p. 2688
Sherborn Library, Sherborn MA p. 1053
Sherbrooke Historical Society, *see* La Societe d'Histoire de Sherbrooke, Sherbrooke QC p. 2737
Sherbrooke Municipal Library, *see* Bibliotheque Municipale Eva-Senecal, Sherbrooke QC p. 2736
Sherburne Memorial Library, Killington VT p. 2287
Sherburne Public Library, Sherburne NY p. 1640
Sheridan College Library, Oakville ON p. 2662
Sheridan Correctional Center Library, *see* Illinois Department of Corrections, Sheridan IL p. 646
Sheridan County Fulmer Public Library, *see* Sheridan County Public Library System, Sheridan WY p. 2498
Sheridan County Historical Society, Inc, Rushville NE p. 1334
Sheridan County Library, Hoxie KS p. 814
Sheridan County Library, Plentywood MT p. 1301
Sheridan County Public Library System, Sheridan WY p. 2498
Sheridan Libraries, *see* Johns Hopkins University Libraries, Baltimore MD p. 954
Sheridan Memorial Library, Sheridan TX p. 2243
Sheridan Public Library, Sheridan IN p. 718
Sheridan Public Library, Sheridan MT p. 1302
Sheridan Public Library, Sheridan OR p. 1898
Sheridan Public Library, *see* Arapahoe Library District, Sheridan CO p. 279
Sheriff Kathy June Library, *see* Sunflower County Library System, Moorhead MS p. 1221
Sherman Alvin Library, *see* Broward County Libraries Division, Fort Lauderdale FL p. 399
Sherman Alvin Library, Research & Information Technology Center, *see* Nova Southeastern University Libraries, Fort Lauderdale FL p. 402
Sherman Art Library, *see* Dartmouth College Library, Hanover NH p. 1367
Sherman College of Chiropractic, Boiling Springs SC p. 2048
Sherman County Library, Stratford TX p. 2246
Sherman Free Library, Port Henry NY p. 1621
Sherman Library, *see* Saint Joseph's Hospital, Hamilton ON p. 2647
Sherman Library & Gardens, Corona del Mar CA p. 132
Sherman Library Association, Sherman CT p. 336
Sherman Public, *see* Dixie Regional Library System, Sherman MS p. 1230
Sherman Public Library, Sherman ME p. 940
Sherman Public Library, Sherman TX p. 2243
Sherman Public Library District, Sherman IL p. 646
Sherman William P Library & Archives, *see* Lewis & Clark Trail Heritage Foundation, Inc, Great Falls MT p. 1294
Sherrard Public Library District, Sherrard IL p. 646
Sherratt Gerald R Library, *see* Southern Utah University, Cedar City UT p. 2262
Sherrill-Kenwood Free Library, Sherrill NY p. 1640
Sherrill Library, *see* Lesley University, Cambridge MA p. 1008
Sherrod Library, *see* East Tennessee State University, Johnson City TN p. 2103
Sherry Margaret, *see* Harrison County Library System, Biloxi MS p. 1218
Sherwin-Williams Automotive Finishes Corp Library, Cleveland OH p. 1770
Sherwood Public Library, Sherwood OR p. 1898
Sherwood Regional, *see* Fairfax County Public Library, Alexandria VA p. 2316
Shevchenko Scientific Society Inc, New York NY p. 1602
Shiawassee District Library, Owosso MI p. 1139
Shibley Righton LLP, Toronto ON p. 2693
Shields C M Centennial Branch, *see* Timmins Public Library, South Porcupine ON p. 2686
Shields Peter J Library, *see* University of California, Davis, Davis CA p. 134
Shiffman Vera P Medical Library, *see* Wayne State University Libraries, Detroit MI p. 1100
Shilo Community Library, Shilo MB p. 2590
Shiloh Museum of Ozark History Library, Springdale AR p. 110
Shiloh National Military Park Study Library, *see* National Park Service, Shiloh TN p. 2126
Shimberg Hinks & Elaine Health Sciences Library, *see* University of South Florida, Tampa FL p. 449
Shiner Public Library, Shiner TX p. 2243
Shinn-Lathrope Health Sciences Library, *see* Morristown Medical Center, Morristown NJ p. 1422
Shiocton Public Library, Shiocton WI p. 2477
Shipman Library, *see* Adrian College, Adrian MI p. 1075
Shippensburg Public Library, Shippensburg PA p. 2007
Shippensburg University, Shippensburg PA p. 2007
Shipper Mary F Library, *see* Potomac State College of West Virginia University, Keyser WV p. 2406
Shirley Ryan AbilityLab, Chicago IL p. 568
Shivers Allan Library & Museum, Woodville TX p. 2258
Shoals Public Library, Shoals IN p. 718
Shoalwater Bay Tribal Community Library, Tokeland WA p. 2388
Shodair Children's Hospital, Helena MT p. 1297
Shontz Margaret Memorial Library, Conneaut Lake PA p. 1924
Shook, Hardy & Bacon, Kansas City MO p. 1257
Shore Line Trolley Museum Library, East Haven CT p. 310
Shoreline Community College, Shoreline WA p. 2383
Shorewood Public Library, Shorewood WI p. 2477
Shorewood-Troy Public Library District, Shorewood IL p. 647
Shorter University, Rome GA p. 495
Shortgrass Library System, Medicine Hat AB p. 2548
Shoshone-Bannock Library, Fort Hall ID p. 521
Shoshone Public Library, Shoshone ID p. 531
Shoshoni Public Library, Shoshoni WY p. 2499
Shotwell Tony, *see* Grand Prairie Public Library System, Grand Prairie TX p. 2186
Shouldice Kenneth J Library, *see* Lake Superior State University, Sault Sainte Marie MI p. 1149
Show Low Public Library, Show Low AZ p. 78
Showers R Center, *see* Huntsville-Madison County Public Library, Huntsville AL p. 22
Shreve Memorial Library, Shreveport LA p. 908
Shreveport CON-SAH Library, *see* Northwestern State University College of Nursing & Allied Health, Shreveport LA p. 908
Shrewsbury Public Library, Shrewsbury MA p. 1053
Shrewsbury Public Library, Cuttingsville VT p. 2282
Shriners Hospital for Children, Honolulu HI p. 512
Shubert Byram, *see* Greenwich Library, Greenwich CT p. 314
Shubert Public Library & Museum, Shubert NE p. 1336
Shullsburg Public, *see* McCoy Public Library, Shullsburg WI p. 2477
Shumaker Library, *see* Central Baptist Theological Seminary Library, Shawnee KS p. 836
Shun Chan Centennial Library, *see* Southwestern Adventist University, Keene TX p. 2204
Shute Memorial, *see* Everett Public Libraries, Everett MA p. 1017
Shuter Library of Angel Fire, Angel Fire NM p. 1463
Shuts Environmental Library, Lancaster PA p. 1952
SIAST Libraries, Prince Albert SK p. 2745
SIAST-Saskatchewan Institute of Applied Science & Technology, Moose Jaw SK p. 2743
SIAST-Saskatchewan Institute of Applied Science & Technology, Saskatoon SK p. 2749
Sibley-Cone Memorial Library, *see* Georgia Military College, Milledgeville GA p. 491
Sibley Music Library, *see* University of Rochester, Rochester NY p. 1631
Sibley Public Library, Sibley IA p. 781
Sidell District Library, Sidell IL p. 647
Sidley Austin LLP, Washington DC p. 374
Sidley, Austin LLP, New York NY p. 1602
Sidley Austin LLP Library, Los Angeles CA p. 168
Sidley Austin LLP Library, Chicago IL p. 568
Sidney Center Branch, *see* Sidney Memorial Public Library, Unadilla NY p. 1641
Sidney Community Library, Sidney IL p. 647
Sidney Memorial Public Library, Sidney NY p. 1641
Sidney Public Library, Sidney IA p. 782
Sidney Public Library, Sidney NE p. 1336
Sidney-Richland County Library, Sidney MT p. 1302
Siebers James J Memorial Library, *see* Kimberly Public Library, Kimberly WI p. 2445
SIEC Library, *see* Centre for Suicide Prevention, Calgary AB p. 2528
Siegrist Edith B Vermillion Public Library, Vermillion SD p. 2084
Siena College, Loudonville NY p. 1566
Siena Heights University Library, Adrian MI p. 1076
Sierra Club, Oakland CA p. 187
Sierra College Library, Rocklin CA p. 203
Sierra Madre Public Library, Sierra Madre CA p. 246
Sierra Vista Public Library, Sierra Vista AZ p. 78
Sigma Alpha Epsilon Fraternity & Foundation, Evanston IL p. 587
Signal Hill Public Library, Signal Hill CA p. 246
Signal Mountain Public Library, Signal Mountain TN p. 2126
Signal Peak Library, *see* Central Arizona College, Coolidge AZ p. 58
Signature Healthcare - Brockton Hospital Library, Brockton MA p. 1003
Sigourney Public Library, Sigourney IA p. 782
Sikes Robert L F Public Library, Crestview FL p. 391
Sikeston Public Library, Sikeston MO p. 1279
Silber Saul Memorial Library, *see* Hebrew Theological College, Skokie IL p. 647
Siletz Public Library, Siletz OR p. 1898
Silk Eric Library, *see* Ontario Provincial Police, Orillia ON p. 2663
SILO (N), *see* State of Iowa Libraries Online, Des Moines IA p. 2765
Siloam Springs Public Library, Siloam Springs AR p. 110
Silsbee Public Library, Silsbee TX p. 2244
Silsby Free Public Library, Charlestown NH p. 1357
Silver Bay Public Library, Silver Bay MN p. 1204
Silver City Public Library, Silver City IA p. 782
Silver Cross Hospital Medical Library, New Lenox IL p. 624
Silver Falls Library District, Silverton OR p. 1899
Silver Hill Hospital, New Canaan CT p. 325
Silver Lake Library, Silver Lake KS p. 836
Silver Spring Library, *see* Montgomery County Public Libraries, Silver Spring MD p. 975
Silver Spring United Methodist Church, Silver Spring MD p. 978
Silverman Oscar A Library, *see* University at Buffalo Libraries-State University of New York, Buffalo NY p. 1511

Smith Alson H Jr Library, *see* Shenandoah University, Winchester VA p. 2354
Smith Bertha Library, *see* Luther Rice University & Seminary, Lithonia GA p. 485
Smith Betty Golde Library, *see* Saint Louis Psychoanalytic Institute, Saint Louis MO p. 1274
Smith Jean Burr Library, *see* Middlesex Community College, Middletown CT p. 322
Smith Calvin S, *see* Salt Lake County Library Services, Salt Lake City UT p. 2275
Smith Center Public Library, Smith Center KS p. 836
Smith College Libraries, Northampton MA p. 1042
Smith Community Library, Smith AB p. 2554
Smith County Public Library, Carthage TN p. 2090
Smith Dick Library, *see* Tarleton State University Library, Stephenville TX p. 2246
Smith Dillard Virginia, *see* Mobile Public Library, Mobile AL p. 26
Smith Dr Joseph F Medical Library, *see* Aspirus Health, Wausau WI p. 2485
Smith Dumas, *see* William Carey University Libraries, Hattiesburg MS p. 1219
Smith Edward, *see* North Branford Library Department, Northford CT p. 331
Smith Elisha D Public Library, *see* Menasha Public Library, Menasha WI p. 2455
Smith Ethel K Library, *see* Wingate University, Wingate NC p. 1724
Smith Frank A Jr Library Center, *see* Southwestern University, Georgetown TX p. 2184
Smith Frederick Madison Library, *see* Graceland University, Lamoni IA p. 764
Smith, Gambrell & Russell, Atlanta GA p. 466
Smith Garland Public Library, Marlow OK p. 1852
Smith George F Library, *see* Rutgers University Libraries, Newark NJ p. 1425
Smith Guilford Memorial Library, South Windham CT p. 337
Smith Harriotte B Library, *see* United States Marine Corps, Camp Lejeune NC p. 1677
Smith Harvey Library West End, *see* Winnipeg Public Library, Winnipeg MB p. 2596
Smith, Haughey, Rice & Roegge, Grand Rapids MI p. 1111
Smith Hill Library, *see* Community Libraries of Providence, Providence RI p. 2038
Smith J Eugene Library, *see* Eastern Connecticut State University, Willimantic CT p. 347
Smith James Public Library, *see* Wapiti Regional Library, Melfort SK p. 2746
Smith Jennie Stephens Library, *see* Union County Library, New Albany MS p. 1228
Smith Jesse M Memorial Library, Harrisville RI p. 2032
Smith John D/Eldorado Springs Branch, *see* Cedar County Library District, El Dorado Springs MO p. 1282
Smith John Peter Hospital, Fort Worth TX p. 2180
Smith Joseph F Library, *see* Brigham Young University-Hawaii, Laie HI p. 514
Smith Kathryn L Memorial, *see* Winter Haven Public Library, Winter Haven FL p. 455
Smith Kelvin Library, *see* Case Western Reserve University, Cleveland OH p. 1766
Smith-Kettlewell Eye Research Institute Library, San Francisco CA p. 229
Smith Library, *see* High Point University, High Point NC p. 1697
Smith Library of Regional History, Oxford OH p. 1812
Smith Lillian H, *see* Toronto Public Library, Toronto ON p. 2697
Smith Lou Library, *see* Antique Boat Museum, Clayton NY p. 1518
Smith Margaret Chase Library, Skowhegan ME p. 940
Smith Maxine A Library, *see* Southwest Tennessee Community College, Memphis TN p. 2115
Smith Melanee Memorial Library, Waller TX p. 2254
Smith Memorial Library, Chautauqua NY p. 1517
Smith Michelle Performing Arts Library, *see* University of Maryland Libraries, College Park MD p. 962
Smith Morgan Library, Jennings Campus, *see* SOWELA Technical Community College Library, Jennings LA p. 894
Smith Murdoch C Memorial Library, *see* Annapolis Valley Regional Library, Port Williams NS p. 2616
Smith Neighborhood Library, *see* Houston Public Library, Houston TX p. 2196
Smith P K Research Library, *see* Lake County Historical Society, Painesville OH p. 1812
Smith Paul Library of Southern York County, Shrewsbury PA p. 2007
Smith Preston Library, *see* Texas Tech University Health Sciences, Lubbock TX p. 2214
Smith Richard R Medical Library, Grand Rapids MI p. 1111
Smith Richard V Art Reference Library, *see* Everson Museum of Art Library, Syracuse NY p. 1648
Smith Rita & Truett Public Library, Wylie TX p. 2258
Smith Robert E Library, *see* New Orleans Public Library, New Orleans LA p. 903
Smith Roberta A University Library, *see* Muskingum University, New Concord OH p. 1806
Smith Rupert J Law Library of Saint Lucie County, Fort Pierce FL p. 405
Smith Samuel W Memorial Public Library, Port Allegany PA p. 1998
Smith State Prison, *see* Georgia Department of Corrections, Glennville GA p. 481
Smith Van K Consumer Health Information Service, *see* Mercy Health, Springfield MO p. 1280
Smith Warren Hunting Library, *see* Hobart & William Smith Colleges, Geneva NY p. 1538
Smith-Welch Memorial Library, Hearne TX p. 2188
Smith Wilbur Research Library & Archives, *see* Texarkana Museums System, Texarkana TX p. 2248
Smith William Henry Memorial Library, *see* Indiana Historical Society Library, Indianapolis IN p. 692
Smith William S Library, *see* South Georgia State College, Douglas GA p. 477
Smithers Public Library, Smithers BC p. 2576
Smithfield Branch, *see* Blackwater Regional Library, Smithfield VA p. 2313
Smithfield Library, *see* State Correctional Institution, Huntingdon PA p. 1945
Smithfield Public Library, Smithfield PA p. 2008
Smithfield Public Library, Smithfield UT p. 2273
Smiths Falls Public Library, Smiths Falls ON p. 2678
Smithsonian American Art Museum, *see* Smithsonian Libraries, Washington DC p. 376
Smithsonian Environmental Research Center Library, *see* Smithsonian Libraries, Edgewater DC p. 376
Smithsonian Libraries, Washington DC p. 375
Smithton Public Library, Smithton PA p. 2008
Smithton Public Library District, Smithton IL p. 648
Smithtown Library, Smithtown NY p. 1641
Smithville Public Library, Smithville TX p. 2244
Smithville Public Library, *see* West Lincoln Public Library, Smithville ON p. 2678
Smoky Hill Public Library, *see* Arapahoe Library District, Centennial CO p. 279
Smoky Lake Municipal Library, Smoky Lake AB p. 2554
Smoky Valley Library District, Round Mountain NV p. 1351
Smolt Lillian Memorial Library, *see* Ventura County Medical Center, Ventura CA p. 256
Smoot Lewis Egerton Memorial Library, King George VA p. 2327
Smooth Rock Falls Public Library, Smooth Rock Falls ON p. 2679
Smyrna Public Library, Smyrna DE p. 356
Smyrna Public Library, Smyrna GA p. 497
Smyrna Public Library, Smyrna NY p. 1642
Smyrna Public Library, *see* Rutherford County Library System, Smyrna TN p. 2118
Smyth County Public Library, Marion VA p. 2331
Smyth Herbert Weir Classical Library, *see* Harvard Library, Cambridge MA p. 1007
Smyth Public Library, Candia NH p. 1356
Snake River School Community Library, Blackfoot ID p. 516
SNC-Lavalin, Inc Library, Montreal QC p. 2728
Snead State Community College, Boaz AL p. 10
Sneden Margaret D Library, *see* Davenport University, Grand Rapids MI p. 1110
Snell Library, *see* Northeastern University Libraries, Boston MA p. 998
Sno-Isle Libraries, Marysville WA p. 2370
Snohomish Community Library, *see* Sno-Isle Libraries, Snohomish WA p. 2371
Snohomish County Law Library, Everett WA p. 2364
Snow College, Ephraim UT p. 2263
Snow John, Inc, Boston MA p. 999
Snow Lake Community Library, Snow Lake MB p. 2590
Snow Library, Orleans MA p. 1044
Snowden John G Memorial Library, *see* Lycoming College, Williamsport PA p. 2023
Snowflake-Taylor Public Library, Snowflake AZ p. 78
Snyder County Historical Society, Inc Library, Middleburg PA p. 1962
Snyder County Libraries, Selinsgrove PA p. 2005
Snyder Leonard P Memorial, *see* Washington County Free Library, Clear Spring MD p. 968
Snyder O J Memorial Library, *see* Philadelphia College of Osteopathic Medicine, Philadelphia PA p. 1984
Snyder Public Library, Snyder NE p. 1336
SOCHE (N), *see* Strategic Ohio Council for Higher Education, Dayton OH p. 2773
Societe d'histoire de la Haute-Gaspesie, Sainte-Anne-des-Monts QC p. 2734
Societe de Genealogie de l'Outaouais Bibliotheque, Gatineau QC p. 2713
Societe de Genealogie de Quebec, Quebec QC p. 2732
Societe de Transport de Montreal, Montreal QC p. 2728
Societe Genealogique Canadienne-Francaise Bibliotheque, Montreal QC p. 2728
Societe Historique de la Cote-du-Sud, La Pocatiere QC p. 2714
Society of Actuaries Library, Schaumburg IL p. 645
Society of Mount Carmel, Washington DC p. 376
Society of the Cincinnati Library, Washington DC p. 376
Society of the Four Arts, Palm Beach FL p. 434
Socorro Public Library, Socorro NM p. 1478
Soda Springs Public Library, Soda Springs ID p. 531
Sodus Community Library, Sodus NY p. 1642
Sodus Township Library, Sodus MI p. 1150
Sofia University Library, Palo Alto CA p. 192
Sola Gerardo Selles Library, *see* University of Puerto Rico Library System, San Juan PR p. 2515
Solano Community College Library, Fairfield CA p. 142
Solano County Library, Fairfield CA p. 142
Soldiers Grove Public Library, Soldiers Grove WI p. 2478
Soldiers Memorial Library, Hiram ME p. 927
Soldotna Public Library, Soldotna AK p. 51
Solheim Albert Library, *see* Pacific Northwest College of Art, Portland OR p. 1893
Soliz Albert H Library, *see* Ventura County Library, Oxnard CA p. 256
Solomon Blanche R Memorial Library, Headland AL p. 20
Solomon Public Library, Solomon KS p. 836
Solon Public Library, Solon IA p. 783
Solvang Branch, *see* Goleta Valley Library, Solvang CA p. 149
Solvay Public Library, Solvay NY p. 1642
Somers Library, Somers NY p. 1642
Somers Public Library, Somers CT p. 337
Somers Public Library, Somers IA p. 783
Somerset Community College Learning Commons, Somerset KY p. 875

South Plainfield Public Library, South Plainfield NJ p. 1443
South Plains College Library, Levelland TX p. 2211
South Pointe Hospital Library, Warrensville Heights OH p. 1828
South Portland Public Library, South Portland ME p. 941
South Providence Library, *see* Community Libraries of Providence, Providence RI p. 2038
South Puget Sound Community College Library, Olympia WA p. 2373
South Regional Library, *see* Lafayette Public Library, Lafayette LA p. 892
South River-Machar Union Public Library, South River ON p. 2679
South River Public Library, South River NJ p. 1444
South Routt Library District, Oak Creek CO p. 292
South Ryegate Public Library, Inc, South Ryegate VT p. 2295
South St Landry Community Library, Sunset LA p. 910
South Saint Paul Public Library, South Saint Paul MN p. 1204
South San Francisco Public Library, South San Francisco CA p. 247
South Seattle Community College, Seattle WA p. 2380
South Shore Campus Library, *see* Hillsborough Community College, Ruskin FL p. 448
South Shore Hospital, South Weymouth MA p. 1055
South Shore Public Libraries, Bridgewater NS p. 2616
South Sioux City Public Library, South Sioux City NE p. 1336
South Suburban College Library, South Holland IL p. 648
South Suburban Genealogical & Historical Society Library, Hazel Crest IL p. 598
South Texas College Library, McAllen TX p. 2217
South Texas College of Law Houston, Houston TX p. 2198
South Thomaston Public Library, South Thomaston ME p. 942
South Union Shaker Village, Auburn KY p. 848
South University, Royal Palm Beach FL p. 439
South University, Columbia SC p. 2055
South University Library, Montgomery AL p. 30
South University Library, Savannah GA p. 497
South Whitley Community Public Library, South Whitley IN p. 719
South Windsor Public Library, South Windsor CT p. 337
South Yarmouth Library, *see* Yarmouth Town Libraries, South Yarmouth MA p. 1055
Southampton Free Library, Southampton PA p. 2009
Southborough Library, Southborough MA p. 1055
Southbury Public Library, Southbury CT p. 337
Southcenter Library Connection, *see* King County Library System, Tukwila WA p. 2366
Southcoast Health Medical Library, New Bedford MA p. 1038
Southeast Arkansas College, Pine Bluff AR p. 107
Southeast Arkansas Regional Library, Monticello AR p. 104
Southeast Community College, Beatrice NE p. 1307
Southeast Correctional Center, *see* Missouri Department of Corrections, Charleston MO p. 1252
Southeast Florida Library Information Network, Inc (N), Boca Raton FL p. 2763
Southeast Kansas Library System, Iola KS p. 815
Southeast Kentucky Area Health Education Center, Hazard KY p. 859
Southeast Kentucky Community & Technical College, Cumberland KY p. 853
Southeast Kentucky Community & Technical College, Middlesboro KY p. 869
Southeast Kentucky Community & Technical College, Whitesburg KY p. 877
Southeast Library System (SELS), Rochester MN p. 1195
Southeast Library System (SLS), Lincoln NE p. 1323
Southeast Missouri State University, Cape Girardeau MO p. 1240
Southeast Missourian Newspaper Library, Cape Girardeau MO p. 1240
Southeast New Mexico College, Carlsbad NM p. 1465
Southeast Oklahoma Library System (SEOLS), McAlester OK p. 1853
Southeast Regional, *see* Maricopa County Library District, Gilbert AZ p. 71
Southeast Regional Library, Weyburn SK p. 2753
Southeast Regional Library System (N), Wellston OH p. 2773
Southeast Steuben County Library, Corning NY p. 1522
Southeastern Baptist College, Laurel MS p. 1225
Southeastern Baptist Theological Seminary Library, Wake Forest NC p. 1720
Southeastern Chapter of the American Association of Law Libraries (N), Baltimore MD p. 2766
Southeastern Community College, Whiteville NC p. 1722
Southeastern Community College Library, West Burlington IA p. 790
Southeastern Illinois College, Harrisburg IL p. 597
Southeastern Libraries Cooperating (N), Rochester MN p. 2768
Southeastern Louisiana University, Hammond LA p. 890, 2786
Southeastern Michigan League of Libraries (N), Dearborn MI p. 2767
Southeastern New York Library Resources Council (N), Highland NY p. 2771
Southeastern Oklahoma State University, Durant OK p. 1846
Southeastern Pennsylvania Theological Library Association (N), Hatfield PA p. 2774
Southeastern Railway Museum Library, *see* National Railway Historical Society, Atlanta Chapter, Duluth GA p. 477
Southeastern Technical College, Vidalia GA p. 502
Southeastern Technical College Library, Swainsboro GA p. 498
Southeastern University, Lakeland FL p. 417
Southeastern Wisconsin Information Technology Exchange, Inc (N), Milwaukee WI p. 2777
Southern Adirondack Library System, Saratoga Springs NY p. 1636
Southern Adventist University, Collegedale TN p. 2094
Southern Alberta Art Gallery Library, Lethbridge AB p. 2546
Southern Alberta Institute of Technology Library, Calgary AB p. 2529
Southern Area Library, Lost Creek WV p. 2407
Southern Arizona VA Healthcare System, *see* Department of Veterans Affairs, Tucson AZ p. 81
Southern Arkansas University, Magnolia AR p. 103
Southern Arkansas University Tech, Camden AR p. 92
Southern Baptist Historical Library & Archives, Nashville TN p. 2120
Southern Baptist Theological Seminary, Louisville KY p. 866
Southern Boone County Public Library, *see* Boone Daniel Regional Library, Ashland MO p. 1243
Southern Branch Library, *see* Orange County Public Library, Carrboro NC p. 1697
Southern California Genealogical Society, Burbank CA p. 125
Southern California Institute of Architecture, Los Angeles CA p. 168
Southern California Library Cooperative (N), Pasadena CA p. 2762
Southern California Library for Social Studies & Research, Los Angeles CA p. 168
Southern California University of Health Sciences, Whittier CA p. 259
Southern Campus Library, *see* Ohio University, Ironton OH p. 1791
Southern College of Optometry Library, Memphis TN p. 2114
Southern Connecticut State University, New Haven CT p. 326, 2783
Southern Crescent Technical College, Griffin GA p. 481
Southern Crescent Technical College Library, Thomaston GA p. 498
Southern Gulf Islands Community Libraries, Pender Island BC p. 2573
Southern Highland Craft Guild, Asheville NC p. 1673
Southern Illinois University Carbondale, Carbondale IL p. 549
Southern Illinois University Edwardsville, East Saint Louis IL p. 581
Southern Illinois University Edwardsville, Edwardsville IL p. 582
Southern Illinois University School of Medicine, Springfield IL p. 650
Southern Lehigh Public Library, Center Valley PA p. 1920
Southern Maine Community College Library, South Portland ME p. 941
Southern Maryland Regional Library Association, Inc, Charlotte Hall MD p. 961
Southern Methodist College, Orangeburg SC p. 2067
Southern Methodist University, Dallas TX p. 2167
Southern Nazarene University, Bethany OK p. 1842
Southern New Mexico Correctional Facility Library, *see* New Mexico Corrections Department, Las Cruces NM p. 1471
Southern Oaks Library, *see* Metropolitan Library System in Oklahoma County, Oklahoma City OK p. 1857
Southern Oklahoma Library System, Ardmore OK p. 1840
Southern Oregon University, Ashland OR p. 1872
Southern Pines Public Library, Southern Pines NC p. 1716
Southern Prairie Library System, Altus OK p. 1839
Southern Regional Area Health Education Center, Fayetteville NC p. 1689
Southern Regional Technical College Library Services, Thomasville GA p. 498
Southern State Community College Library, Hillsboro OH p. 1790
Southern Technical College, Fort Myers FL p. 404
Southern Tier Library System, Painted Post NY p. 1614
Southern Union State Community College, Wadley AL p. 39
Southern University, Baton Rouge LA p. 884
Southern University at Shreveport, Shreveport LA p. 910
Southern University in New Orleans, New Orleans LA p. 903
Southern Utah University, Cedar City UT p. 2262
Southern Utah University Gerald R Sherratt Library, Cedar City UT p. 2793
Southern Virginia University, Buena Vista VA p. 2308
Southern Wasco County Public Library, *see* Wasco County Library District, Maupin OR p. 1900
Southern Wesleyan University, Central SC p. 2048
Southern West Virginia Community & Technical College, Mount Gay WV p. 2410
Southern West Virginia Community & Technical College, Saulsville WV p. 2414
Southern West Virginia Community & Technical College, Williamson WV p. 2418
Southfield Public Library, Southfield MI p. 1151
Southgate Community Library, *see* Wake County Public Library System, Raleigh NC p. 1711
Southgate Library, *see* Sacramento Public Library, Sacramento CA p. 210
Southgate Ruth Hargrave Memorial Library, Dundalk ON p. 2639
Southgate Veterans Memorial Library, Southgate MI p. 1152
Southglenn Public Library, *see* Arapahoe Library District, Centennial CO p. 279
Southington Library, *see* Southington Public Library & Museum, Southington CT p. 337
Southington Public Library & Museum, Southington CT p. 337
Southlake Public Library, Southlake TX p. 2245
Southold Free Library, Southold NY p. 1643
Southold Historical Society Museum Library, Southold NY p. 1643
Southport Memorial Library, Southport ME p. 942

Spokane Public Library, Spokane WA p. 2385
Spokesman-Review, Spokane WA p. 2385
Spoon River College Library, Canton IL p. 548
Spoon River Public Library District, Cuba IL p. 575
Spooner Memorial Library, Spooner WI p. 2478
Spotswood Public Library, Spotswood NJ p. 1444
Sprague Harry A Library, *see* Montclair State University, Montclair NJ p. 1420
Sprague Public Library, Baltic CT p. 302
Sprague Public Library, Sprague WA p. 2385
Sprauve Elaine Ione Library, Saint John VI p. 2517
Elaine Ione Sprauve Library, *see* Virgin Islands Division of Libraries, Archives & Museums VI p. 2518
Spring Arbor University, Spring Arbor MI p. 1152
Spring Branch Memorial Branch, *see* Harris County Public Library, Houston TX p. 2193
Spring City Free Public Library, Spring City PA p. 2009
Spring Creek Correctional Center Library, Seward AK p. 51
Spring Green Community Library, Spring Green WI p. 2478
Spring Grove Hospital Center, Catonsville MD p. 961
Spring Hill College, Mobile AL p. 26
Spring Hill Public Library, Spring Hill TN p. 2127
Spring Lake District Library, Spring Lake MI p. 1152
Spring Lake Public Library, Spring Lake NJ p. 1444
Spring Township Library, Wyomissing PA p. 2025
Spring Valley Library, *see* Las Vegas-Clark County Library District, Las Vegas NV p. 1347
Spring Valley Library, *see* Yavapai County Free Library District, Mayer AZ p. 75
Spring Valley Public Library, Spring Valley MN p. 1204
Spring Valley Public Library, Spring Valley WI p. 2478
Springbank Township Library, Allen NE p. 1305
Springboro Public Library, Springboro PA p. 2009
Springdale Free Public Library, Springdale PA p. 2009
Springdale Public Library, Springdale AR p. 110
Springfield Art Association, Springfield IL p. 650
Springfield City Library, Springfield MA p. 1056
Springfield College, Springfield MA p. 1057
Springfield Free Public Library, Springfield NJ p. 1444
Springfield-Greene County Library District, Springfield MO p. 1281
Springfield Library, Springfield Center NY p. 1644
Springfield Memorial Library, Springfield NE p. 1337
Springfield Museum of Art Library, Springfield OH p. 1821
Springfield Public Library, Springfield MN p. 1204
Springfield Public Library, Springfield OR p. 1899
Springfield Technical Community College Library, Springfield MA p. 1057
Springfield Town Library, Springfield VT p. 2295
Springfield Township Library, Davisburg MI p. 1095
Springfield Township Library, Springfield PA p. 2009
Springhill Miners Memorial Library, *see* Cumberland Public Libraries, Springhill NS p. 2615
Springlake-Earth Community Library, Springlake TX p. 2245
Springmier Community Library, Tiffin IA p. 786
Springport Free Library, Union Springs NY p. 1654
Springstowne Library, *see* Solano County Library, Vallejo CA p. 142
Springtown Public Library, Springtown TX p. 2245
Springvale Public Library, Springvale ME p. 942
Springville Memorial Library, Springville IA p. 784
Springville Public Library, Springville AL p. 36
Springville Public Library, Springville UT p. 2273
Sprouse Nigel Memorial Library, Callaway NE p. 1309
Spruce Grove Public Library, Spruce Grove AB p. 2554
Spruce Pine Public Library, Spruce Pine NC p. 1717
Spruce View Community Library, Spruce View AB p. 2554
Squamish Public Library, Squamish BC p. 2576
Squire Eleanor Library, *see* Cleveland Botanical Garden, Cleveland OH p. 1766
Squire Patton & Boggs LLP, Washington DC p. 376
Squire Patton Boggs, Columbus OH p. 1777
Squires Patrick Library, *see* Desert Research Institute, Reno NV p. 1349
Squires William G Library, *see* Lee University, Cleveland TN p. 2093
SRI International, Menlo Park CA p. 176
SSM Health - Good Samaritan Hospital, Mount Vernon IL p. 622
Saint Peter's Branch, *see* Eastern Counties Regional Library, St. Peter's NS p. 2621
Staats Joan Library, *see* Jackson Laboratory, Bar Harbor ME p. 916
Staatsburg Library, Staatsburg NY p. 1644
Stacks Rare Coin Company of NY, New York NY p. 1602
Stacyville Public Library, Stacyville IA p. 784
Staff Library, *see* Spring Grove Hospital Center, Catonsville MD p. 961
Stafford Creek Correctional Center, *see* Washington State Library, Aberdeen WA p. 2390
Stafford J W & Lois Library, *see* Columbia College, Columbia MO p. 1243
Stafford Library, Stafford Springs CT p. 338
Stafford Peale Ruth Library, *see* Interchurch Center, New York NY p. 1589
Stafford R H, *see* Washington County Library, Woodbury MN p. 1210
Stahl John A Library, West Point NE p. 1340
Stair Public Library, Morenci MI p. 1134
Stake Family History Center, *see* Church of Jesus Christ of Latter-Day Saints, Broomall PA p. 1915
Staley Library, *see* Millikin University, Decatur IL p. 576
Stallo Francis J Memorial Library, *see* Auglaize County Libraries, Minster OH p. 1828
Stamford Carnegie Library, Stamford TX p. 2245
Stamford Community Library, Stamford VT p. 2295
Stamford History Center (Historical Society), Stamford CT p. 339
Stamford Hospital, Stamford CT p. 339
Stamford Law Library, *see* Connecticut Judicial Branch Law Libraries, Stamford CT p. 316
Stamford Village Library, Stamford NY p. 1644
Stamps H B Memorial Library, *see* Hawkins County Library System, Rogersville TN p. 2125
Stanaker Neighborhood Library, *see* Houston Public Library, Houston TX p. 2196
Standard Municipal Library, Standard AB p. 2555
Standardbred Canada Library, Mississauga ON p. 2659
Standish J Spencer & Patricia Library, *see* Siena College, Loudonville NY p. 1566
Standley Lake Library, *see* Jefferson County Public Library, Arvada CO p. 288
Stanfield Public Library, Stanfield OR p. 1899
Stanford Comprehensive Cancer Center, *see* Stanford Health Library, Stanford CA p. 192
Stanford Free Library, Stanfordville NY p. 1644
Stanford Health Library, Palo Alto CA p. 192
Stanford Hospital, *see* Stanford Health Library, Palo Alto CA p. 192
Stanford University Libraries, Stanford CA p. 248
Stanhope Public Library, Stanhope IA p. 784
Stanislaus County Law Library, Modesto CA p. 178
Stanislaus County Library, Modesto CA p. 178
Stanley Community Public Library, Stanley ID p. 531
Stanley Correctional Institution Library, Stanley WI p. 2478
Stanley Doris Memorial Library, Moody AL p. 30
Stanley Edmund Library, *see* Friends University, Wichita KS p. 842
Stanley Public Library, Stanley ND p. 1740
Stanley Thomas Library, *see* Ferrum College, Ferrum VA p. 2318
Stanley Tubbs Memorial Library, Sallisaw OK p. 1861
Stanly Community College Library, Albemarle NC p. 1671
Stanly County Public Library, Albemarle NC p. 1671
Stansbury Park Library, Stansbury Park UT p. 2273
Stansel Horace Memorial, *see* Sunflower County Library System, Ruleville MS p. 1221
Stanton County Public Library, Johnson KS p. 816
Stanton Public Library, Stanton IA p. 784
Stanton Public Library, Stanton NE p. 1337
Stanton Public Library, Stanton ND p. 1740
Stanton W H Memorial Library, *see* Azalea Regional Library System, Social Circle GA p. 488
Stanwood Library, *see* Sno-Isle Libraries, Stanwood WA p. 2371
Stanwood Public Library, Stanwood IA p. 784
Staples Public Library, *see* Great River Regional Library, Staples MN p. 1197
Stapleton Library, *see* Indiana University of Pennsylvania, Indiana PA p. 1946
Star City Public Library, *see* Wapiti Regional Library, Star City SK p. 2746
Star Learning Center, *see* Goddard Riverside Community Center, New York NY p. 1587
Star of the Republic Museum Library, Washington TX p. 2254
Star Tribune, Minneapolis MN p. 1185
Star Valley Branch, *see* Lincoln County Library System, Afton WY p. 2496
Starhill Forest Arboretum Library, Petersburg IL p. 635
Stark County District Library, Canton OH p. 1755
Stark County Law Library, Canton OH p. 1756
Homer M Stark Law Library, *see* Gwinnett County Judicial Circuit, Lawrenceville GA p. 485
Starke County Public Library System, Knox IN p. 699
Starkey Ranch Theatre Library & Cultural Center, *see* Pasco County Library System, Odessa FL p. 411
Starksboro Public Library, Starksboro VT p. 2295
Starkville-Oktibbeha County Public, Starkville MS p. 1233
Starr C V East Asian Library, *see* Columbia University, New York NY p. 1584
Starr C V East Asian Library, *see* University of California, Berkeley, Berkeley CA p. 123
Starr C V Library, *see* Japan Society, New York NY p. 1589
Starr County Public Library, Larosita TX p. 2210
Starr County Public Library, Roma TX p. 2234
Starr Dorothy C S Civil War Research Library, *see* Fort Ward Museum, Alexandria VA p. 2303
Starr Library, Rhinebeck NY p. 1626
STARRT, *see* Mohawk College Library, Stoney Creek ON p. 2647
Starsmore Center for Local History, *see* Colorado Springs Pioneers Museum, Colorado Springs CO p. 270
Start-Kilgour Memorial Library, *see* Simpson University, Redding CA p. 199
State College of Florida Manatee-Sarasota Library, Bradenton FL p. 387
State Correctional Institution, Albion PA p. 1904
State Correctional Institution, Bellefonte PA p. 1910
State Correctional Institution, Frackville PA p. 1934
State Correctional Institution, Houtzdale PA p. 1944
State Correctional Institution, Hunlock Creek PA p. 1944
State Correctional Institution, Huntingdon PA p. 1945
State Correctional Institution, Indiana PA p. 1946
State Correctional Institution, Somerset PA p. 2008
State Correctional Institution, Waymart PA p. 2018
State Correctional Institution Mercer Library, Mercer PA p. 1962
State Education Resource Center Library, Waterbury CT p. 344
State Fair Community College, Sedalia MO p. 1279
State Historical Society of Iowa, Des Moines IA p. 747
State Historical Society of Iowa, Iowa City IA p. 760
State Historical Society of Missouri, Kansas City MO p. 1257
State Historical Society of Missouri - Rolla, Rolla MO p. 1267

State Historical Society of Missouri Library, Columbia MO p. 1243
State Historical Society of North Dakota, Bismarck ND p. 1730
State Law Library of Mississippi, *see* State of Mississippi Judiciary, Jackson MS p. 1223
State Law Library of Montana, Helena MT p. 1297
State Library & Archives of Florida, *see* Florida Department of State, Tallahassee FL p. 446
State Library of Florida, Tallahassee FL p. 447
State Library of Iowa, Des Moines IA p. 747
State Library of Kansas, Topeka KS p. 839
State Library of Kansas (N), Topeka KS p. 2765
State Library of Louisiana, Baton Rouge LA p. 884, 885
State Library of Massachusetts, Boston MA p. 1000
State Library of North Carolina, Raleigh NC p. 1710
State Library of Ohio, Columbus OH p. 1777
State Library of Oregon, Salem OR p. 1897
State Library of Pennsylvania, Harrisburg PA p. 1941
State Line Public, *see* Pine Forest Regional Library System - Headquarters, State Line MS p. 1232
State of Delaware, Dover DE p. 352
State of Iowa Libraries Online (N), Des Moines IA p. 2765
State of Mississippi Judiciary, Jackson MS p. 1223
State of New Jersey - Department of Banking & Insurance, Trenton NJ p. 1448
State of Oregon Law Library, Salem OR p. 1897
State of Rhode Island, Providence RI p. 2041
State of Vermont Department of Libraries, Barre VT p. 2278
State University of New York, Brooklyn NY p. 1506
State University of New York, Morrisville NY p. 1574
State University of New York, Old Westbury NY p. 1610
State University of New York, Purchase NY p. 1625
State University of New York at Binghamton, Binghamton NY p. 1494
State University of New York at Fredonia, Fredonia NY p. 1535
State University of New York at Oswego, Oswego NY p. 1613
State University of New York College, Geneseo NY p. 1537
State University of New York College at Brockport, Brockport NY p. 1497
State University of New York College at Plattsburgh, Plattsburgh NY p. 1619
State University of New York College at Potsdam, Potsdam NY p. 1622
State University of New York, Syracuse NY p. 1650
State University of New York, College of Technology, Alfred NY p. 1485
State University of New York Downstate Health Sciences University, Brooklyn NY p. 1506
State University of New York - Jefferson Community College, Watertown NY p. 1660
State University of New York Maritime College, Bronx NY p. 1500
State University of New York Polytechnic Institute, Utica NY p. 1655
State University of New York, State College of Optometry, New York NY p. 1602
Staten Island Historical Society Library, Staten Island NY p. 1645
Staten Island Institute of Arts & Sciences, Staten Island NY p. 1645
Staten Island University Hospital Northwell Health, Staten Island NY p. 1645
Statesboro Regional Public Libraries, Statesboro GA p. 498
Statewide California Electronic Library Consortium (N), Los Angeles CA p. 2762
Statham Public Library, *see* Piedmont Regional Library System, Statham GA p. 482
Statistics Canada Library, Ottawa ON p. 2670
Statton Learning Commons, *see* Juniata College, Huntingdon PA p. 1945
Stauffer Joseph S Library, *see* Queen's University, Kingston ON p. 2650
Staunton Public Library, Staunton IL p. 651
Staunton Public Library, Staunton VA p. 2347
Staunton River Memorial, *see* Campbell County Public Library, Altavista VA p. 2346
Stautzenberger College Library, Maumee OH p. 1800
Stavely Municipal Library, Stavely AB p. 2555
Stayton Public Library, Stayton OR p. 1899
Steacie Science & Engineering Library, *see* York University Libraries, North York ON p. 2662
Steamboat Rock Public Library, Steamboat Rock IA p. 784
Stearns History Museum, Saint Cloud MN p. 1198
Stearns, Weaver, Miller, Weissler, Alhadeff & Sitterson, Miami FL p. 425
Steele Memorial, *see* Wayne County Public Library, Mount Olive NC p. 1691
Steele Memorial Library, *see* Chemung County Library District, Elmira NY p. 1530
Steele Public Library, Steele AL p. 36
Steele Public Library, Steele MO p. 1282
Steeleville Area Public Library District, Steeleville IL p. 651
Steelman Library, *see* Southeastern University, Lakeland FL p. 417
Steely W Frank Library, *see* Northern Kentucky University, Highland Heights KY p. 859
Steen Ralph W Library, *see* Stephen F Austin State University, Nacogdoches TX p. 2221
Steenbock Library, *see* University of Wisconsin-Madison, Madison WI p. 2452
Steep Falls Public Library, Steep Falls ME p. 942
Steffens Katherine Annex, *see* Secaucus Public Library, Secaucus NJ p. 1442
Steger-South Chicago Heights Public Library District, Steger IL p. 651
Steinbach Bible College Library, Steinbach MB p. 2590
Steinbeck John Library, *see* Salinas Public Library, Salinas CA p. 211
Steinberg Hedi Library, *see* Yeshiva University Libraries, New York NY p. 1605
Steiner Rudolf Library, Hudson NY p. 1549
Steinway Community Library, *see* Queens Library, Long Island City NY p. 1555
STELLA (N), *see* Sharing & Technology Enhancing Local Library Access, Edison NJ p. 2770
Stella Community Library, Stella NE p. 1337
Stephen F Austin State University, Nacogdoches TX p. 2221
Stephens-Burnett Memorial Library, *see* Carson-Newman University, Jefferson City TN p. 2103
Stephens Central Library, *see* Green Tom County Library System, San Angelo TX p. 2235
Stephens College, Columbia MO p. 1243
Stephens Henry Memorial Library, *see* Almont District Library, Almont MI p. 1077
Stephens Hugh Library, *see* Stephens College, Columbia MO p. 1243
Stephens Library, *see* Hazard Community & Technical College Library, Hazard KY p. 858
Stephens Mary L Davis Branch, *see* Yolo County Library, Davis CA p. 260
Stephenson Memorial Library, Greenfield NH p. 1365
Stephenson Public Library, *see* Marinette County Library System, Marinette WI p. 2453
Stephentown Memorial Library, Stephentown NY p. 1645
Stephenville Public Library, Stephenville TX p. 2245
Steptoe & Johnson Library, Washington DC p. 376
Sterling & Francine Clark Art Institute Library, Williamstown MA p. 1069
Sterling College, Sterling KS p. 837
Sterling College, Craftsbury Common VT p. 2282
Sterling Correctional Facility Library- West - East, *see* Colorado Department of Corrections, Sterling CO p. 296
Sterling County Public Library, Sterling City TX p. 2246
Sterling Free Public Library, Sterling KS p. 837
Sterling Heights Public Library, Sterling Heights MI p. 1152
Sterling Memorial Library, *see* Yale University Library, New Haven CT p. 328
Sterling Municipal Library, Baytown TX p. 2145
Sterling Public Library, Sterling CO p. 296
Sterling Public Library, Oneco CT p. 333
Sterling Public Library, Sterling IL p. 651
Sterling Public Library, Sterling NE p. 1337
Sterlington Memorial, *see* Ouachita Parish Public Library, Monroe LA p. 898
Sterne-Hoya House Museum & Library, Nacogdoches TX p. 2221
Sterne, Kessler, Goldstein & Fox Library, Washington DC p. 376
Sterne Mervyn H Library, *see* University of Alabama at Birmingham, Birmingham AL p. 9
Stetson Public Library, Stetson ME p. 942
Stetson University, DeLand FL p. 393
Stetson University College of Law Library, Gulfport FL p. 408
Stettenheim Ivan M Library, *see* Congregation Emanu-El of the City of New York, New York NY p. 1584
Stettler Public Library, Stettler AB p. 2555
Stevens Charles E American Atheist Library & Archives, Inc, Cranford NJ p. 1398
Stevens County Library, Hugoton KS p. 814
Stevens-German Library, *see* Hartwick College, Oneonta NY p. 1611
Stevens Henager College Library, Ogden UT p. 2267
Stevens Institute of Technology, Hoboken NJ p. 1408
Stevens Library, *see* Connecticut River Museum, Essex CT p. 311
Stevens Memorial Community Library, Attica NY p. 1488
Stevens Memorial Library, Ashburnham MA p. 986
Stevens Memorial Library, North Andover MA p. 1040
Stevens Museum - The John Hay Center, *see* Washington County Historical Society Library, Salem IN p. 717
Stevenson Charles P Jr Library, *see* Bard College, Annandale-on-Hudson NY p. 1487
Stevenson Community Library, *see* Fort Vancouver Regional Library District, Stevenson WA p. 2391
Stevenson George B Library, *see* Lock Haven University of Pennsylvania, Lock Haven PA p. 1956
Stevenson-Ives Library, *see* McLean County Museum of History, Bloomington IL p. 543
Stevenson Merck Library & Archives, *see* Greenwich Historical Society, Cos Cob CT p. 306
Stevenson Public Library, Stevenson AL p. 36
Stevenson University Library, Stevenson MD p. 978
Stevensville Library, *see* North Valley Public Library, Stevensville MT p. 1302
Steward Health Care, Warren OH p. 1828
Stewart Charles B - West Branch, *see* Montgomery County Memorial Library System, Montgomery TX p. 2159
Stewart County Public Library, Dover TN p. 2097
Stewart David Memorial Library, *see* Southfield Public Library, Southfield MI p. 1151
Stewart Emma Resource Centre, *see* Saskatchewan Teachers' Federation, Saskatoon SK p. 2749
Stewart Ewell Sale Library & Archives, *see* Academy of Natural Sciences of Drexel University, Philadelphia PA p. 1974
Stewart Free Library, Corinna ME p. 922
Stewart John Memorial Library, *see* Wilson College, Chambersburg PA p. 1921
Stewart Library, *see* Weber State University, Ogden UT p. 2268
Stewart McKelvey, Halifax NS p. 2621
Stewart Memorial Library, *see* Coe College, Cedar Rapids IA p. 738
Stewart Public Library, North Anson ME p. 933
Stewart Public Library, Stewart BC p. 2576
Stewart S Walter, *see* Toronto Public Library, Toronto ON p. 2697
Stewart-Swift Research Center, *see* Henry Sheldon Museum of Vermont History, Middlebury VT p. 2288
Stewartsville Library, *see* Bedford Public Library System, Vinton VA p. 2306
Stewartville Public Library, Stewartville MN p. 1205

Stey-Nevant Branch Library, *see* Community Library of the Shenango Valley, Farrell PA p. 2006
Stickney Crossing Library, *see* Great River Regional Library, Clearwater MN p. 1197
Stickney-Forest View Public Library District, Stickney IL p. 651
Stiern Walter W Library, *see* California State University, Bakersfield, Bakersfield CA p. 119
Stigler Public Library, Stigler OK p. 1862
Stikeman Elliott, Toronto ON p. 2693
Stillman College, Tuscaloosa AL p. 37
Stillwater County Library, Columbus MT p. 1291
Stillwater Public Library, Stillwater MN p. 1205
Stillwater Public Library, Stillwater NY p. 1646
Stillwater Public Library, Stillwater OK p. 1862
Stilwell Public library, New Sharon IA p. 773
Stilwell Public Library, Stilwell OK p. 1863
Stimley Blue Ridge Neighborhood Library, *see* Houston Public Library, Houston TX p. 2196
Stimson Library, *see* United States Army, Fort Sam Houston TX p. 2178
Stinson LLP, Minneapolis MN p. 1185
Stinson Memorial Public Library District, Anna IL p. 536
Stirling-Rawdon Public Library, Stirling ON p. 2681
Stirling Theodore Brandley Municipal Library, Stirling AB p. 2555
Stites & Harbison, Louisville KY p. 867
Stitt David L & Jane Library, *see* Austin Presbyterian Theological Seminary, Austin TX p. 2138
Stockbridge Library, *see* Capital Area District Libraries, Stockbridge MI p. 1124
Stockbridge Library Association, Stockbridge MA p. 1058
Stockmen's Memorial Foundation Library, Cochrane AB p. 2531
Stockport Public Library, Stockport IA p. 784
Stockton Public Library, Stockton KS p. 837
Stockton-San Joaquin County Public Library, Stockton CA p. 250
Stockton Springs Community Library, Stockton Springs ME p. 942
Stockton Township Public Library, Stockton IL p. 651
Stockton University, Galloway NJ p. 1404
Stockwell-Mudd Libraries, *see* Albion College, Albion MI p. 1076
Stoel Rives LLP, Portland OR p. 1894
Stoel Rives LLP, Seattle WA p. 2380
Stohlman Library, *see* Saint Elizabeth's Medical Center, Boston MA p. 999
Stokely Memorial Library, Newport TN p. 2122
Stokes Brown Public Library, Springfield TN p. 2127
Stokes Donald E Library, *see* Princeton University, Princeton NJ p. 1438
Stokes Louis Health Sciences Library, *see* Howard University Libraries, Washington DC p. 369
Stokes Rembert E Library & Information Commons, *see* Wilberforce University, Wilberforce OH p. 1831
Stone Charles H Memorial Library, Pilot Mountain NC p. 1707
Stone Child College, Box Elder MT p. 1289
Stone County Library, Mountain View AR p. 105
Stone County Library, Galena MO p. 1247
Stone Mattheis Xenopoulos & Brew PC Library, Washington DC p. 376
Stone Memorial Library, Conneautville PA p. 1924
Stone Olive Clifford Library, *see* Clymer Rolla A Research Library, El Dorado KS p. 806
Stone Ridge Public Library, Stone Ridge NY p. 1646
Stone-Robinson Library, *see* Selma University, Selma AL p. 35
Stone Science Library, *see* Boston University Libraries, Boston MA p. 994
Stoneham Public Library, Stoneham MA p. 1058
Stonehill College, Easton MA p. 1016
Stones River Regional Library, Murfreesboro TN p. 2118
Stonewall County Library, Aspermont TX p. 2137
Stonewall Library, *see* Stonewall National Museum, Archives & Library, Fort Lauderdale FL p. 402
Stonewall National Museum, Archives & Library, Fort Lauderdale FL p. 402
Stonewall Public, *see* East Mississippi Regional Library System, Stonewall MS p. 1231
Stonewall Public Library-Headquarters, *see* South Interlake Regional Library, Stonewall MB p. 2591
Stonington Free Library, Stonington CT p. 339
Stonington Historical Society, Stonington CT p. 339
Stonington Public Library, Stonington ME p. 943
Stonington Township Public Library, Stonington IL p. 652
Stony Brook University, Stony Brook NY p. 1646
Stony Creek Free Library, Stony Creek NY p. 1647
Stony Plain Public Library, Stony Plain AB p. 2555
James R Stookey Library, *see* West Virginia School of Osteopathic Medicine, Lewisburg WV p. 2407
Storm Lake Public Library, Storm Lake IA p. 785
Storm Memorial Library, *see* Scientific & Biomedical Information & Documentation Center, Fort Lauderdale FL p. 402
Stormont, Dundas & Glengarry County Library, Cornwall ON p. 2637
Storrowton Village Museum Library, West Springfield MA p. 1066
Storrs Congregational Church UCC, Storrs CT p. 339
Storrs Richard Salter Library, Longmeadow MA p. 1029
Story Library, *see* Central Baptist College, Conway AR p. 92
Story Margaret Library, *see* Snead State Community College, Boaz AL p. 10
Stott Explorers Library, *see* Johnson Martin & Osa Safari Museum, Chanute KS p. 801
Stoudenmire Vernice Public Library, Wilsonville AL p. 40
Stoughton Public Library, Stoughton MA p. 1058
Stoughton Public Library, Stoughton WI p. 2479
Stout Reference Library, *see* Indianapolis Museum of Art at Newfields, Indianapolis IN p. 693
Stow-Munroe Falls Public Library, Stow OH p. 1822
Stowe Free Library, Stowe VT p. 2295
Stowe Harriet Beecher Center Research Collections, Hartford CT p. 318
Stowell George H Free Library, Cornish Flat NH p. 1360
Stoxen Library, *see* Dickinson State University, Dickinson ND p. 1732
Stradling, Yocca, Carlson & Rauth, Newport Beach CA p. 183
Strahorn Library, *see* Illinois Railway Museum, Marengo IL p. 613
Strasburg Community, *see* Shenandoah County Library, Strasburg VA p. 2315
Strasburg-Heisler Library, Strasburg PA p. 2010
Strategic Ohio Council for Higher Education (N), Dayton OH p. 2773
Stratford Free Public Library, Stratford NJ p. 1444
Stratford Historical Society Library, Stratford CT p. 340
Stratford Library Association, Stratford CT p. 340
Stratford Public Library, Stratford IA p. 785
Stratford Public Library, North Stratford NH p. 1377
Stratford Public Library, Stratford ON p. 2682
Stratford Public Library, *see* Prince Edward Island Public Library Service, Stratford PE p. 2708
Stratford University, Baltimore MD p. 956
Strathcona County Library, Sherwood Park AB p. 2553
Strathearn Historical Park & Museum, Simi Valley CA p. 246
Strathmore Municipal Library, Strathmore AB p. 2556
Stratton Free Library, West Swanzey NH p. 1384
Stratton Public Library, Stratton CO p. 296
Stratton Public Library, Stratton ME p. 943
Stratton Public Library, Stratton NE p. 1337
Strauss Health Sciences Library, *see* University of Colorado Denver /Anschutz Medical Campus, Aurora CO p. 265
Strawberry Point Public Library, Strawberry Point IA p. 785
Strawbery Banke Museum, Portsmouth NH p. 1379
Strazzeri Medical Library, *see* Providence Holy Cross Medical Center, Mission Hills CA p. 177
Streator Public Library, Streator IL p. 652
Street John L Library, Cadiz KY p. 850
Streeter Centennial Library, Streeter ND p. 1740
Strickler Richard Lee Research Center, *see* Ocean County Historical Society, Toms River NJ p. 1446
Stroger John H Jr Hospital of Cook County, Chicago IL p. 569
Stromberg Medical Library, *see* Endeavor Health-Swedish Hospital, Chicago IL p. 560
Stromsburg Public Library, Stromsburg NE p. 1337
Strong B Elizabeth Memorial Library, Turin NY p. 1654
Strong Dr Joseph M Memorial Library, *see* University Hospital Elyria Medical Center, Elyria OH p. 1785
Strong Helman Frances Library, *see* Historical & Genealogical Society of Indiana County, Indiana PA p. 1945
Strong Kate Historical Library, *see* Long Island Museum of American Art, History & Carriages, Stony Brook NY p. 1646
Strong Museum, Rochester NY p. 1630
Strong Public, *see* Barton Public Library, Strong AR p. 94
Strong Public Library, Strong ME p. 943
Stroock & Stroock & Lavan Library, New York NY p. 1602
Strosacker Library, *see* Northwood University, Midland MI p. 1132
Stroud Public Library, Stroud OK p. 1863
Strozier Robert Manning Library, *see* Florida State University Libraries, Tallahassee FL p. 446
Struckman-Baatz Public Library, Western NE p. 1340
Strum Public Library, Strum WI p. 2479
Stuart Public Library, Stuart IA p. 785
Stuart Township Library, Stuart NE p. 1337
Stubblefield Helen Law Library, *see* Laboure College, Milton MA p. 1036
Stubbs Memorial Library, Holstein IA p. 758
Stuck Medical Library, *see* McLaren Macomb Medical Center, Mount Clemens MI p. 1134
Studebaker National Museum Archives, South Bend IN p. 719
Stuhr Museum, Grand Island NE p. 1316
Stump Robert & Rita Murphy, *see* Saint Xavier University, Chicago IL p. 567
Sturdivant Public Library, East Machias ME p. 923
Sturgeon Lake Public Library, *see* Wapiti Regional Library, Shellbrook SK p. 2746
Sturgis District Library, Sturgis MI p. 1153
Sturgis Horace W Library, *see* Kennesaw State University Library System, Kennesaw GA p. 483
Sturgis Library, Barnstable MA p. 987
Sturgis Public Library, Sturgis SD p. 2083
Sturgis Public Library, *see* Starkville-Oktibbeha County Public, Sturgis MS p. 1233
Roy & Christine Sturgis Library of Cleveland County, *see* Mid-Arkansas Regional Library, Rison AR p. 103
Sturm Elizabeth Library, *see* Truckee Meadows Community College, Reno NV p. 1349
Sturm Memorial Library, Manawa WI p. 2453
Stutsman County Library, *see* James River Valley Library System, Jamestown ND p. 1736
Stuttgart Public Library, Stuttgart AR p. 111
Styberg Library, *see* Garrett-Evangelical Theological Seminary, Evanston IL p. 586
Styles Mary Riley Public Library, Falls Church VA p. 2317
Sublett Sam Library, *see* Phoenix Emerging Adult Career & Education (PEACE) Center, Saint Charles IL p. 644
Sublette County Libraries, Pinedale WY p. 2497
Substance Abuse Treatment Faclity & State Prison, Corcoran, *see* California Department of Corrections Library System, Corcoran CA p. 207
Suburban Library Cooperative (N), Sterling Heights MI p. 2767

Swampscott Public Library, Swampscott MA p. 1059
SWAN (N), *see* System Wide Automated Network, Westmont IL p. 2765
Swan Hills Municipal Library, Swan Hills AB p. 2556
Swan Lake Public Library, Swan Lake MT p. 1303
Swan Paul Library, *see* Becker College, Leicester MA p. 1027
Swan Valley Branch, *see* Bonneville County Library District, Irwin ID p. 515
Swaney Memorial Library, New Cumberland WV p. 2410
Swans Island Educational Society, Swans Island ME p. 943
Swans Island Public Library, *see* Swans Island Educational Society, Swans Island ME p. 943
Swansea Free Public Library, Swansea MA p. 1059
Swanson Robert S Library & Learning Center, *see* University of Wisconsin-Stout, Menomonie WI p. 2456
Swanson W Clarke Branch, *see* Omaha Public Library, Omaha NE p. 1330
Swanton Local School District Public Library, Swanton OH p. 1822
Swanton Public Library, Swanton VT p. 2296
Swanville Library, *see* Great River Regional Library, Swanville MN p. 1197
Swarthmore College, Swarthmore PA p. 2011
Swarthmore Public Library, Swarthmore PA p. 2012
Swarthout Minor Memorial Library, *see* Curtiss Glenn H Museum of Local History, Hammondsport NY p. 1544
Swartwood Charles B Supreme Court Library, Elmira NY p. 1531
Swasey Ambrose Library, *see* Colgate Rochester Crozer Divinity School, Rochester NY p. 1628
Swayzee Public Library, Swayzee IN p. 720
Swea City Public Library, Swea City IA p. 786
Swedenborg Foundation Library, West Chester PA p. 2020
Swedenborg Library, *see* Bryn Athyn College, Bryn Athyn PA p. 1916
Swedenborgian Library & Archives, Berkeley CA p. 122
Swedish-American Archives of Greater Chicago, *see* North Park University, Chicago IL p. 566
Swedish Medical Center Library, Seattle WA p. 2380
Sween Jane C Research Library & Special Collections, *see* Montgomery History, Rockville MD p. 975
Sweet Briar College, Sweet Briar VA p. 2348
Sweet Corrine & Jack Library, *see* Salt Lake City Public Library, Salt Lake City UT p. 2272
Sweet Home Public Library, Sweet Home OR p. 1899
Sweet Springs Public Library, Sweet Springs MO p. 1282
Sweetkind Irene S Public Library, Cochiti Lake NM p. 1466
Sweetser Services for Children & Families, Saco ME p. 939
Sweetwater County-City Library, Sweetwater TX p. 2246
Sweetwater County Library, *see* Sweetwater County Library System, Green River WY p. 2495
Sweetwater County Library System, Green River WY p. 2495
Sweetwater Public Library, Sweetwater TN p. 2127
Swem Earl Gregg Library, *see* College of William & Mary in Virginia, Williamsburg VA p. 2353
Swenson Robert E Library, *see* Cabrillo College, Aptos CA p. 117
Swenson Swedish Immigration Research Center, Rock Island IL p. 641
Swett Morris J Technical Library, *see* United States Army, Fort Sill OK p. 1848
SWFLN (N), *see* Southwest Florida Library Network, Fort Myers FL p. 2763
Swilley Monroe F Jr Library, *see* Mercer University Atlanta, Atlanta GA p. 465
Swindle Harold S Public Library, *see* Piedmont Regional Library System, Nicholson GA p. 482
Swirbul Library, *see* Adelphi University, Garden City NY p. 1536
Swisher Carl S Library, *see* Jacksonville University, Jacksonville FL p. 413
Swisher Carl S Library, *see* Bethune-Cookman University, Daytona Beach FL p. 392
Swisher County Library, Tulia TX p. 2249
SWITCH (N), *see* Southeastern Wisconsin Information Technology Exchange, Inc, Milwaukee WI p. 2777
Switzerland County Public Library, Vevay IN p. 723
SWON (N), *see* SouthWest Ohio & Neighboring Libraries, Cincinnati OH p. 2773
SWVAHILI (N), *see* Southwestern Virginia Health Information Librarians, Harrisonburg VA p. 2776
Sycamore Public Library, Sycamore IL p. 653
Sykesville Public Library, Sykesville PA p. 2012
Sylvan Grove Public Library, Sylvan Grove KS p. 837
Sylvan Lake Municipal Library, Sylvan Lake AB p. 2556
Sylvan Oaks Library, *see* Sacramento Public Library, Citrus Heights CA p. 210
Sylvester Memorial Wellston Public Library, Wellston OH p. 1829
Sylvia Public Library, Sylvia KS p. 837
Syosset Public Library, Syosset NY p. 1648
Syracuse Public Library, Syracuse NE p. 1337
Syracuse Turkey Creek Township Public Library, Syracuse IN p. 720
Syracuse University, Syracuse NY p. 2789
Syracuse University College of Law, Syracuse NY p. 1650
Syracuse University Libraries, Syracuse NY p. 1650
System Wide Automated Network (N), Westmont IL p. 2765
T O H P Burnham Public Library, Essex MA p. 1017
Tabb Library, *see* York County Public Library, Yorktown VA p. 2355
Taber Elizabeth Library, Marion MA p. 1031
Taber Emily Public Library, Macclenny FL p. 419
Taber Lloyd Marina del Rey Library, *see* County of Los Angeles Public Library, Marina del Rey CA p. 138
Taber Public Library, Taber AB p. 2556
Table Rock Public Library, Table Rock NE p. 1338
Tabor City Public, *see* Columbus County Public Library, Tabor City NC p. 1722
Tabor College Library, Hillsboro KS p. 813
Tabor Public Library, Tabor IA p. 786
Tacoma Community College Library, Tacoma WA p. 2387
Tacoma Family History Center, Tacoma WA p. 2387
Tacoma Public Library, Tacoma WA p. 2387
Taft College Library, Taft CA p. 251
Taft Museum of Art Library, Cincinnati OH p. 1763
Taft Public Library, Mendon MA p. 1034
Taft Public Library, Taft TX p. 2246
Taft, Stettinius & Hollister LLP, Minneapolis MN p. 1185
Taft, Stettinius & Hollister Library, Cincinnati OH p. 1764
Taggart Law Library, *see* Ohio Northern University, Ada OH p. 1743
Tahlequah Public Library, Tahlequah OK p. 1863
Tahquamenon Area Library, Newberry MI p. 1137
Taitano Richard F Micronesian Area Research Center, *see* University of Guam, Mangilao GU p. 2505
Takoma Park Maryland Library, Takoma Park MD p. 979
TAL (N), *see* The Alberta Library, Edmonton AB p. 2777
Talbot Belmond Public Library, Belmond IA p. 734
Talbot County Free Library, Easton MD p. 964
Talbot Research Library & Media Services, Philadelphia PA p. 1986
Talbott Katharine Houk Library, *see* Rider University, Lawrenceville NJ p. 1411
Talcott Free Library, Rockton IL p. 642
Talihina Public Library, Talihina OK p. 1864
Talkeetna Public Library, Talkeetna AK p. 51
Talking Book Library, *see* Traverse Area District Library, Traverse City MI p. 1155
Talking Books Plus/Library for the Blind & Print Disabled, *see* Maine State Library ME p. 914
Talladega College, Talladega AL p. 36
Talladega County Law Library, Talladega AL p. 36
Tallahassee Community College Library, Tallahassee FL p. 447
Tallahatchie County Library, Charleston MS p. 1213
Tallapoosa Public Library, *see* West Georgia Regional Library, Tallapoosa GA p. 470
Tallassee Community Library, Tallassee AL p. 36
Tallmadge Historical Society Library, Tallmadge OH p. 1823
Talmage Public Library, Talmage KS p. 838
Talmage Public Library, Talmage NE p. 1338
Talmo Public Library, *see* Piedmont Regional Library System, Talmo GA p. 483
Tama County Historical Society & Genealogy Library, Toledo IA p. 786
Tama Public Library, Tama IA p. 786
Tamaqua Public Library, Tamaqua PA p. 2012
Tamarack District Library, Lakeview MI p. 1123
Tamarack Federation of Libraries, Missoula MT p. 1300
Tamiment Library/Robert F Wagner Labor Archives, *see* New York University, New York NY p. 1599
Tampa Bay Library Consortium, Inc (N), Tampa FL p. 2763
Tampa Bay Regional Planning Council, Pinellas Park FL p. 438
Tampa-Hillsborough County Public Library System, Tampa FL p. 448
Tampa Museum of Art, Tampa FL p. 449
Tanana Community-School Library, Tanana AK p. 51
Tangent Community Library, Tangent AB p. 2556
Tangipahoa Parish Library, Amite LA p. 880
Tanimura & Antle Family Memorial Library, *see* California State University - Monterey Bay, Seaside CA p. 246
Tankland Library, *see* American Society of Military History Museum, South El Monte CA p. 247
Taos Public Library, Taos NM p. 1478
Tappan Library, Tappan NY p. 1651
Tappan-Spaulding Memorial Library, Newark Valley NY p. 1605
Tarbell J A Library, Lyndeborough NH p. 1371
Tarkington Community Library, Cleveland TX p. 2156
Tarleton State University Library, Stephenville TX p. 2246
Tarpon Springs Public Library, Tarpon Springs FL p. 450
Tarrant County College, Arlington TX p. 2136
Tarrant County College, Fort Worth TX p. 2180
Tarrant County College, Hurst TX p. 2201
Tarrant Public Library, Tarrant AL p. 36
Tartt Ruby Pickens Public Library, Livingston AL p. 24
Tartu Institute, Toronto ON p. 2693
Tarver Jack Library, *see* Mercer University, Macon GA p. 486
Tate J W Library, *see* Huntington University, Sudbury ON p. 2683
Tateuchi East Asia Library, *see* University of Washington Libraries, Seattle WA p. 2382
Tatnuck Magnet Branch, *see* Worcester Public Library, Worcester MA p. 1073
Tatro Fred Research Library, *see* Boston Baptist College, Boston MA p. 991
Tattnall County Library, *see* Ohoopee Regional Library System, Reidsville GA p. 502
Tatum Community Library, Tatum NM p. 1478
Tatum Mary Lee Library, *see* Advocates for Youth, Washington DC p. 359
Tatum Public, *see* Rusk County Library System, Tatum TX p. 2189
Tauber Holocaust Library, *see* JFCS Holocaust Center, San Francisco CA p. 225
Taubman Health Sciences Library, *see* University of Michigan, Ann Arbor MI p. 1080
Taubman Museum of Art, Roanoke VA p. 2346
Taunton Public Library, Taunton MA p. 1059
Taussig Joseph Memorial Library, *see* Emanuel Congregation, Chicago IL p. 560

Texas Christian University, Fort Worth TX p. 2181
Texas College, Tyler TX p. 2249
Texas Commission on Environment Quality, Austin TX p. 2140
Texas Council of Academic Libraries (N), Victoria TX p. 2775
Texas County Library, Houston MO p. 1249
Texas Department of State Health Services, Austin TX p. 2140
Texas General Land Office, Austin TX p. 2140
Texas Grants Resource Center, Austin TX p. 2140
Texas Health Harris Methodist Fort Worth Hospital, Fort Worth TX p. 2181
Texas Health Presbyterian Hospital Library, Dallas TX p. 2168
Texas Historical Commission Library, Austin TX p. 2140
Texas Legislative Reference Library, Austin TX p. 2140
Texas Lutheran University, Seguin TX p. 2242
Texas Medical Association, Austin TX p. 2141
Texas Medical Center Library, *see* Houston Academy of Medicine, Houston TX p. 2193
Texas Ranger Hall of Fame & Museum, Waco TX p. 2254
Texas School for the Blind, Austin TX p. 2141
Texas Scottish Rite Hospital, Dallas TX p. 2168
Texas Southern University, Houston TX p. 2198
Texas State Court of Appeals, Eastland TX p. 2172
Texas State Law Library, Austin TX p. 2141
Texas State Library & Archives Commission, Austin TX p. 2141
Texas State Museum of Asian Cultures, Corpus Christi TX p. 2161
Texas State Technical College, Harlingen TX p. 2188
Texas State Technical College Library, Sweetwater TX p. 2246
Texas State Technical College, Waco TX p. 2254
Texas State University, San Marcos TX p. 2241
Texas Tech University, Lubbock TX p. 2213
Texas Tech University Health Sciences, Lubbock TX p. 2214
Texas Tech University Health Sciences Center El Paso, El Paso TX p. 2174
Texas Tech University Libraries, Lubbock TX p. 2214
Texas Wesleyan University, Fort Worth TX p. 2181
Texas Woman's University, Dallas TX p. 2168
Texas Woman's University, Denton TX p. 2793
Texhoma Public Library, Texhoma OK p. 1864
Texline Public Library, Texline TX p. 2249
TexSHARE - Texas State Library & Archives Commission (N), Austin TX p. 2776
Thacker Stephen B CDC Library, *see* Centers for Disease Control & Prevention, Atlanta GA p. 462
Thacker Stephen B CDC Library - Cincinnati Branch, *see* Centers for Disease Control & Prevention, Cincinnati OH p. 1759
Thacker Stephen B CDC Library-Morgantown Branch, *see* Centers for Disease Control & Prevention, Morgantown WV p. 2409
Thaddeus Stevens College of Technology, Lancaster PA p. 1952
Thalman James S, *see* San Bernardino County Library, Chino Hills CA p. 213
Thayer County Museum, Belvidere NE p. 1308
Thayer Friday Reading Club City Library, Thayer KS p. 838
Thayer Memorial Library, Lancaster MA p. 1026
Thayer Public, *see* Oregon County Library District, Thayer MO p. 1237
Thayer Public Library, Braintree MA p. 1001
Thayer Public Library, Ashuelot NH p. 1354
The Archives at Historic Newton, *see* The Jackson Homestead & Museum, Newton MA p. 1039
The Jackson Homestead & Museum, Newton MA p. 1039
The Mall Library Connection, *see* Fort Vancouver Regional Library District, Vancouver WA p. 2391
The Plains Public, *see* Athens County Public Libraries, The Plains OH p. 1805
ThedaCare Medical Library, Appleton WI p. 2420
Theological School of Protestant Reformed Churches Library, Wyoming MI p. 1160
Theosophical Library Center, Altadena CA p. 116
Theosophical Society in America, Wheaton IL p. 662
Theresa Free Library, Theresa NY p. 1651
Theresa Public Library, Theresa WI p. 2481
THeSLA (N), *see* Tennessee Health Science Library Association, Kingsport TN p. 2775
Thessalon Public Library, Thessalon ON p. 2684
Thief River Falls Public Library, *see* Northwest Regional Library, Thief River Falls MN p. 1205
Thiel College, Greenville PA p. 1939
Thiele Kaolin Co, Sandersville GA p. 495
Thigpin Library, *see* Volunteer State Community College Library, Gallatin TN p. 2099
Third District Appellate Court Library, Ottawa IL p. 631
Third District Court of Appeals, Miami FL p. 425
Third Judicial Circuit Court, Wayne County, Detroit MI p. 1099
Thistle Cottage History & Genealogy Annex, *see* Muhlenberg County Libraries, Greenville KY p. 857
THLA (N), *see* Toronto Health Libraries Association, Toronto ON p. 2778
Thode H G Library of Science & Engineering, *see* McMaster University Library, Hamilton ON p. 2647
Hall Thomas A Library, *see* Klein Ann Forensic Center, West Trenton NJ p. 1453
Thomas Aquinas College, Santa Paula CA p. 245
Thomas Carey S Library, *see* Denver Seminary, Littleton CO p. 290
Thomas College Library, Waterville ME p. 945
Thomas County Library, Thedford NE p. 1338
Thomas County Public Library System, Thomasville GA p. 499
Thomas Didymus Memorial Library, Remsen NY p. 1626
Thomas Florida B Library, *see* Hendry County Library System, Clewiston FL p. 389
Thomas Jefferson University, Philadelphia PA p. 1986
Thomas Jefferson University-East Falls, Philadelphia PA p. 1987
Thomas Julie Memorial Library, Morganville KS p. 826
Thomas Library, *see* Westchester Public Library, Chesterton IN p. 674
Thomas Library, *see* Wittenberg University, Springfield OH p. 1821
Thomas Memorial, *see* Sullivan County Public Library, Bluff City TN p. 2089
Thomas Memorial Library, Cape Elizabeth ME p. 920
Thomas More College of Liberal Arts, Merrimack NH p. 1373
Thomas More University Benedictine Library, Crestview Hills KY p. 852
Thomas Public Library, *see* Peach Public Libraries, Fort Valley GA p. 480
Thomas Saint Angelo Public Library, Cumberland WI p. 2429
Thomas Township Library, Saginaw MI p. 1147
Thomas University, Thomasville GA p. 500
Thomas-Wilhite Memorial Library, Perkins OK p. 1860
Thomason Dr John M Public Library, *see* Florence County Library System, Olanta SC p. 2059
Thomason James H Library, *see* Presbyterian College, Clinton SC p. 2052
Thomaston Public Library, Thomaston CT p. 341
Thomaston Public Library, Thomaston ME p. 943
Thomasville Public Library, Thomasville AL p. 37
Thomasville Public Library, *see* Oregon County Library District, Birch Tree MO p. 1237
Thompson & Knight, Dallas TX p. 2169
Thompson Alan Library, *see* Lower Columbia College, Longview WA p. 2369
Thompson Albert W Memorial Library, Clayton NM p. 1465
Thompson Branch, *see* Geauga County Public Library, Thompson OH p. 1758
Thompson Coburn LLP, Saint Louis MO p. 1276
Thompson Coburn LLP Library, Washington DC p. 377
Thompson Dr D A Memorial Library, *see* Chaleur Regional Hospital, Bathurst NB p. 2599
Thompson Falls Public Library, Thompson Falls MT p. 1303
Thompson Frances Willson Library, *see* University of Michigan-Flint, Flint MI p. 1107
Thompson Free Library, Dover-Foxcroft ME p. 923
Thompson-Hickman Free County Library, Virginia City MT p. 1303
Thompson Hine LLP, Cincinnati OH p. 1764
Thompson, Hine LLP, Cleveland OH p. 1770
Thompson Hine LLP, Dayton OH p. 1780
Thompson Home Public Library, Ithaca MI p. 1119
Thompson Ina Moss Point Library, *see* Jackson-George Regional Library System, Moss Point MS p. 1228
Thompson John Memorial Library, *see* Torrington Historical Society, Torrington CT p. 342
Thompson Nancy Learning Commons, *see* Kean University, Union NJ p. 1448
Thompson-Nicola Regional District Library System, Kamloops BC p. 2567
Thompson Paul H Library, *see* Fayetteville Technical Community College, Fayetteville NC p. 1689
Thompson-Pell Research Center, *see* Fort Ticonderoga Museum, Ticonderoga NY p. 1651
Thompson Public Library, North Grosvenordale CT p. 331
Thompson Public Library, Thompson IA p. 786
Thompson Public Library, Thompson MB p. 2591
Thompson Rivers University, Kamloops BC p. 2568
Thompson Rivers University, Williams Lake BC p. 2584
Thompson Roosevelt, *see* Central Arkansas Library System, Little Rock AR p. 101
Thompson-Sawyer Public Library, Quanah TX p. 2229
Thompson William Oxley Library, *see* Ohio State University LIBRARIES, Columbus OH p. 1776
Thomsen Jean M Memorial Library, Stetsonville WI p. 2479
Thomson Reuters Westlaw, Eagan MN p. 1173
Thomson Sandrea Reading Room, *see* Provincial Archives of Alberta, Reference Library, Edmonton AB p. 2537
Thorhild Library, Thorhild AB p. 2556
Thormodsgard Law Library, *see* University of North Dakota, Grand Forks ND p. 1734
Thornapple Kellogg School & Community Library, Middleville MI p. 1131
Thorndike Library, *see* College of the Atlantic, Bar Harbor ME p. 916
Thorne Bay Public Library, Thorne Bay AK p. 52
Thorne Library & Learning Resource Center, *see* Mount Vernon Nazarene University, Mount Vernon OH p. 1804
Thornton Harry Library, *see* Pensacola Museum of Art, Pensacola FL p. 436
Thornton Juanita E Shepherd Park Neighborhood Library, *see* District of Columbia Public Library, Washington DC p. 364
Thornton Public Library, Thornton IL p. 653
Thornton Public Library, Thornton IA p. 786
Thornton Public Library, Thornton NH p. 1382
Thornton Public Library, *see* Calhoun County Library, Thornton AR p. 97
Thornton Richard H Library, *see* Granville County Library System, Oxford NC p. 1707
Thorntown Public Library, Thorntown IN p. 721
Thorold Public Library, Thorold ON p. 2684
Thorp Public Library, Thorp WI p. 2481
Thorsby Municipal Library, Thorsby AB p. 2556
Thorsen Margaret Library, *see* Bailey-Matthews National Shell Museum & Aquarium, Sanibel FL p. 442
Thorson Memorial Public Library, Elbow Lake MN p. 1174
Thousand Island Park Library, Thousand Island Park NY p. 1651
Thousand Oaks Library, Thousand Oaks CA p. 252
Thousand Palms Library, *see* Riverside County Library System, Thousand Palms CA p. 202

United States Geological Survey, Fort Collins CO p. 281
United States Geological Survey, Sioux Falls SD p. 2082
United States Geological Survey, Ann Arbor MI p. 1079
United States Geological Survey Library, Flagstaff AZ p. 61
United States Geological Survey Library, Menlo Park CA p. 176
United States Geological Survey Library, Denver CO p. 277
United States Geological Survey Library, Reston VA p. 2340
United States Golf Association Museum & Archives, Liberty Corner NJ p. 1412
United States Government Accountability Office, Washington DC p. 379
United States Holocaust Memorial Museum Library, Washington DC p. 379
United States House of Representatives Library, Washington DC p. 379
United States International Trade Commission, Washington DC p. 379
United States Marine Band, Washington DC p. 379
United States Marine Corps, Yuma AZ p. 85
United States Marine Corps, Camp Pendleton CA p. 126
United States Marine Corps, Twentynine Palms CA p. 254
United States Marine Corps, Camp Lejeune NC p. 1677
United States Marine Corps, Cherry Point NC p. 1681
United States Marine Corps, Jacksonville NC p. 1698
United States Marine Corps, Beaufort SC p. 2047
United States Marine Corps, Parris Island SC p. 2067
United States Merchant Marine Academy, Kings Point NY p. 1560
United States Military Academy Library, West Point NY p. 1663
United States National Library of Medicine (N), Bethesda MD p. 2766
United States National Oceanic & Atmospheric, Miami FL p. 425
US National Park Service, Skagway AK p. 51
US National Park Service, Willcox AZ p. 84
United States National Park Service, Garfield AR p. 96
United States National Park Service, Point Reyes Station CA p. 196
United States National Park Service, San Diego CA p. 222
US National Park Service, Twentynine Palms CA p. 254
US National Park Service, La Junta CO p. 287
United States National Park Service, Washington DC p. 379
United States National Park Service, Savannah GA p. 497
United States National Park Service, Lincoln City IN p. 703
United States National Park Service, Harpers Ferry IA p. 757
United States National Park Service, Larned KS p. 818
United States National Park Service, Salem MA p. 1051
United States National Park Service, Wellfleet MA p. 1064
United States National Park Service, Grand Portage MN p. 1177
United States National Park Service, Diamond MO p. 1245
United States National Park Service, Beatrice NE p. 1307
United States National Park Service, Capulin NM p. 1465
United States National Park Service, Chillicothe OH p. 1759
US National Park Service, King of Prussia PA p. 1948
United States National Park Service, Townsend TN p. 2128
US National Park Service, Vancouver WA p. 2391
United States National Ski Hall of Fame, Ishpeming MI p. 1119
United States Naval Academy, Annapolis MD p. 951
United States Naval Observatory, Washington DC p. 379
United States Naval School of Music, Virginia Beach VA p. 2350
United States Naval War College Library, Newport RI p. 2035
United States Navy, Camp Pendleton CA p. 126
United States Navy, China Lake CA p. 129
United States Navy, San Diego CA p. 222
United States Navy, Groton CT p. 315
United States Navy, Pensacola FL p. 436
United States Navy, Great Lakes IL p. 595
United States Navy, Indian Head MD p. 969
United States Navy, Stennis Space Center MS p. 1233
United States Navy, Philadelphia PA p. 1987
United States Navy, Newport RI p. 2035
United States Navy, Charleston SC p. 2051
United States Navy, Corpus Christi TX p. 2161
United States Navy, Kingsville TX p. 2207
United States Navy, Dahlgren VA p. 2314
United States Navy, Norfolk VA p. 2336
United States Navy, Portsmouth VA p. 2338
United States Navy, Bremerton WA p. 2360
United States Navy, Oak Harbor WA p. 2372
United States Navy Library For Innovation & Technology (LIT), Patuxent River MD p. 972
United States Nuclear Regulatory Commission, Rockville MD p. 975
United States Patent & Trademark Office, Alexandria VA p. 2303
United States Postal Service Library, Washington DC p. 379
United States Railroad Retirement Board Library, Chicago IL p. 569
United States Securities & Exchange Commission Library, Washington DC p. 380
United States Senate Library, Washington DC p. 380
United States Sentencing Commission Library, Washington DC p. 380
United States Space & Rocket Center, Huntsville AL p. 22
United States Sports University, Daphne AL p. 14
United States Tax Court Library, Washington DC p. 380
United Steelworkers Library, Toronto ON p. 2698
United Theological Seminary, Dayton OH p. 1780
United Theological Seminary of the Twin Cities, New Brighton MN p. 1190
United Tribes Technical College Library, Bismarck ND p. 1730
Unity Archives, Unity Village MO p. 1284
Unity College, Unity ME p. 944
Unity Free Public Library, Unity NH p. 1382
Universal City Public Library, Universal City TX p. 2250
Universidad Adventista de las Antillas, Mayaguez PR p. 2511
Universidad Ana G Mendez, Carolina PR p. 2510
Universidad Central de Bayamon, Bayamon PR p. 2510
Universidad Central Del Caribe, Bayamon PR p. 2510
Universidad del Turabo, Gurabo PR p. 2511
Universite de Moncton, Moncton NB p. 2603
Universite de Montreal, Montreal QC p. 2797
Universite de Saint-Boniface, Winnipeg MB p. 2594
Universite de Sherbrooke Service des Bibliotheques et Archives, Sherbrooke QC p. 2737
Universite du Quebec, Montreal QC p. 2728
Universite du Quebec a Chicoutimi, Chicoutimi QC p. 2711
Université du Québec à Montréal Bibliotheque, Montreal QC p. 2728
Universite du Quebec a Rimouski - Service de la bibliotheque, Rimouski QC p. 2732
Universite du Quebec a Trois-Rivieres, Trois-Rivieres QC p. 2738
Universite du Quebec en Outaouais, Gatineau QC p. 2713
Universite Laval Bibliotheque, Quebec QC p. 2732
Universite Sainte-Anne, Church Point NS p. 2617
University at Albany, State University of New York, Albany NY p. 1483, 2789
University at Buffalo Libraries-State University of New York, Buffalo NY p. 1510
University at Buffalo,The State University of New York, Buffalo NY p. 2789
University Baptist Church Library, Baton Rouge LA p. 885
University Canada West, Vancouver BC p. 2580
University Center of Greenville Library, *see* University of South Carolina Upstate Library, Greenville SC p. 2070
University Center of Southern Oklahoma Library, Ardmore OK p. 1841
University City Public Library, University City MO p. 1284
University Club Library, New York NY p. 1603
University College Library, University of Toronto, Toronto ON p. 2698
University College of the North Libraries, The Pas MB p. 2591
University de Moncton, Edmundston NB p. 2600
University Health Network, Toronto ON p. 2698
University Hospital Elyria Medical Center, Elyria OH p. 1785
University Hospital of Northern British Columbia, Prince George BC p. 2574
University Hospitals Saint John Medical Center, Westlake OH p. 1830
University Libraries - Davis Library, *see* University of North Carolina at Chapel Hill, Chapel Hill NC p. 1678
University Libraries, University of Memphis, Jackson TN p. 2103
University Libraries, University of Memphis, Memphis TN p. 2115
University Library of Columbus, *see* Indiana University-Purdue University, Columbus IN p. 676
University of Akron Libraries, Orrville OH p. 1811
University of Akron, University Libraries, Akron OH p. 1745
University of Alabama, Tuscaloosa AL p. 38, 2781
University of Alabama at Birmingham, Birmingham AL p. 9
University of Alabama College of Community Health Sciences, Tuscaloosa AL p. 38
University of Alabama in Huntsville, Huntsville AL p. 22
University of Alaska Anchorage, Anchorage AK p. 43
University of Alaska Anchorage, Mat-Su College, Palmer AK p. 50
University of Alaska Fairbanks, Fairbanks AK p. 45
University of Alaska Fairbanks, Kotzebue AK p. 49
University of Alaska Southeast, Juneau AK p. 47
University of Alaska Southeast, Ketchikan AK p. 48
University of Alberta, Camrose AB p. 2530
University of Alberta, Edmonton AB p. 2537, 2795
University of Arizona, Tucson AZ p. 2782
University of Arizona Libraries, Tucson AZ p. 83
University of Arkansas at Hope-Texarkana, Hope AR p. 98
University of Arkansas at Little Rock, Little Rock AR p. 102
University of Arkansas at Monticello, Crossett AR p. 93
University of Arkansas Community College at Morrilton, Morrilton AR p. 105
University of Arkansas Community College Batesville, Batesville AR p. 90
University of Arkansas For Medical Sciences, Jonesboro AR p. 99
University of Arkansas for Medical Sciences, Texarkana AR p. 111
University of Arkansas for Medical Sciences Library, Little Rock AR p. 102
University of Arkansas for Medical Sciences, Magnolia AR p. 103
University of Arkansas Fort Smith, Fort Smith AR p. 96

University of Nebraska Medical Center, Omaha NE p. 1331
University of Nevada, Las Vegas Univ Libraries, Las Vegas NV p. 1347
University of Nevada-Reno, Reno NV p. 1349
University of New Brunswick Libraries, Fredericton NB p. 2601
University of New Brunswick, Saint John Campus, Saint John NB p. 2605
University of New England Libraries, Biddeford ME p. 917
University of New Hampshire at Manchester Library, Manchester NH p. 1372
University of New Hampshire Library, Durham NH p. 1361
University of New Hampshire School of Law, Concord NH p. 1360
University of New Haven, West Haven CT p. 346
University of New Mexico, Gallup NM p. 1468
University of New Mexico, Los Alamos NM p. 1472
University of New Mexico, Albuquerque NM p. 1462
University of New Orleans, New Orleans LA p. 904, 2786
University of North Alabama, Florence AL p. 17
University of North Carolina at Asheville, Asheville NC p. 1673
University of North Carolina at Chapel Hill, Chapel Hill NC p. 1678, 2790
University of North Carolina at Charlotte, Charlotte NC p. 1681
University of North Carolina at Greensboro, Greensboro NC p. 1693, 2790
University of North Carolina at Pembroke, Pembroke NC p. 1707
University of North Carolina School of the Arts Library, Winston-Salem NC p. 1726
University of North Carolina Wilmington Library, Wilmington NC p. 1723
University of North Dakota, Grand Forks ND p. 1734, 1735
University of North Florida, Jacksonville FL p. 413
University of North Georgia, Oakwood GA p. 493
University of North Texas, Denton TX p. 2793
University of North Texas Health Science Center at Fort Worth, Fort Worth TX p. 2181
University of North Texas Libraries, Denton TX p. 2170
University of Northern British Columbia Library, Prince George BC p. 2574
University of Northern Colorado Libraries, Greeley CO p. 285
University of Northern Iowa, Cedar Falls IA p. 2785
University of Northern Iowa Library, Cedar Falls IA p. 737
University of Northwestern Ohio, Lima OH p. 1796
University of Northwestern-St Paul, Saint Paul MN p. 1202
University of Notre Dame, Notre Dame IN p. 711
University of Oklahoma, Tulsa OK p. 1867
University of Oklahoma, Norman OK p. 2791
University of Oklahoma Health Sciences Center, Oklahoma City OK p. 1859
University of Oklahoma Libraries, Norman OK p. 1856
University of Olivet, Olivet MI p. 1138
University of Ontario Institute of Technology Library, Oshawa ON p. 2664
University of Oregon, Charleston OR p. 1875
University of Oregon Libraries, Eugene OR p. 1879
University of Ottawa Libraries, Ottawa ON p. 2670
University of Pennsylvania Libraries, Philadelphia PA p. 1987
University of Pikeville, Pikeville KY p. 872
University of Pittsburgh, Pittsburgh PA p. 2791
University of Pittsburgh at Bradford, Bradford PA p. 1914
University of Pittsburgh at Greensburg, Greensburg PA p. 1938
University of Pittsburgh at Titusville, Titusville PA p. 2013
University of Pittsburgh, Johnstown PA p. 1948
University of Pittsburgh Library System, Pittsburgh PA p. 1996
University of Pittsburgh, Pittsburgh PA p. 1996
University of Pittsburgh Medical Center Shadyside, Pittsburgh PA p. 1997
University of Portland, Portland OR p. 1894
University of Prince Edward Island, Charlottetown PE p. 2707
University of Providence Library, Great Falls MT p. 1294
University of Puerto Rico, Arecibo PR p. 2509
University of Puerto Rico, Mayaguez PR p. 2511
University of Puerto Rico, San Juan PR p. 2514
University of Puerto Rico Library, Cayey Campus, Cayey PR p. 2510
University of Puerto Rico Library System, San Juan PR p. 2514
University of Puerto Rico, Rio Piedras Campus, San Juan PR p. 2795
University of Puerto Rico RP College, San Juan PR p. 2515
University of Puget Sound, Tacoma WA p. 2387
University of Redlands, Redlands CA p. 199
University of Regina, Regina SK p. 2748
University of Rhode Island, Kingston RI p. 2033
University of Rhode Island, Narragansett RI p. 2034
University of Rhode Island, Providence RI p. 2041
University of Rhode Island, Kingston RI p. 2791
University of Richmond, Richmond VA p. 2342
University of Rio Grande, Rio Grande OH p. 1817
University of Rochester, Rochester NY p. 1631
University of Rochester Medical Center, Rochester NY p. 1631
University of St Augustine for Health Sciences, San Marcos CA p. 234
University of St Augustine for Health Sciences, Coral Gables FL p. 391
University of St Augustine for Health Sciences, Saint Augustine FL p. 440
University of St Augustine for Health Sciences, Austin TX p. 2141
University of St Augustine for Health Sciences, Irving TX p. 2203
University of St Francis, Joliet IL p. 603
University of Saint Francis, Fort Wayne IN p. 685
University of Saint Joseph, West Hartford CT p. 345
University of Saint Mary, Leavenworth KS p. 820
University of Saint Mary of the Lake - Mundelein Seminary, Mundelein IL p. 622
University of Saint Thomas, Saint Paul MN p. 1202
University of Saint Thomas, Houston TX p. 2200
University of San Diego, San Diego CA p. 222
University of San Francisco, San Francisco CA p. 229
University of Saskatchewan Libraries, Saskatoon SK p. 2750
University of Science & Arts of Oklahoma, Chickasha OK p. 1844
University of Scranton, Scranton PA p. 2005
University of Silicon Valley, San Jose CA p. 232
University of Sioux Falls, Sioux Falls SD p. 2083
University of South Alabama, Mobile AL p. 2781
University of South Alabama Libraries, Mobile AL p. 27
University of South Carolina, Allendale SC p. 2046
University of South Carolina, Columbia SC p. 2055, 2792
University of South Carolina Aiken, Aiken SC p. 2046
University of South Carolina at Beaufort Library, Bluffton SC p. 2047
University of South Carolina at Union Library, Union SC p. 2071
University of South Carolina Lancaster, Lancaster SC p. 2064
University of South Carolina Sumter, Sumter SC p. 2071
University of South Carolina Upstate Library, Spartanburg SC p. 2070
University of South Dakota, Sioux Falls SD p. 2083
University of South Dakota, Vermillion SD p. 2084
University of South Florida, Tampa FL p. 449, 2783
University of South Florida Saint Petersburg, Saint Petersburg FL p. 442
University of Southern California Libraries, Los Angeles CA p. 169
University of Southern Indiana, Evansville IN p. 682
University of Southern Maine Libraries, Portland ME p. 937
University of Southern Mississippi, Long Beach MS p. 1225
University of Southern Mississippi, Hattiesburg MS p. 2787
University of Southern Mississippi-Gulf Coast, Ocean Springs MS p. 1228
University of Southern Mississippi Library, Hattiesburg MS p. 1218
University of Sudbury Library, Sudbury ON p. 2683
University of Tampa, Tampa FL p. 450
University of Tennessee, Knoxville TN p. 2107
University of Tennessee, Memphis TN p. 2115
University of Tennessee at Chattanooga Library, Chattanooga TN p. 2092
University of Tennessee at Martin, Martin TN p. 2111
University of Tennessee Graduate School of Medicine, Knoxville TN p. 2107
University of Tennessee, Knoxville, Knoxville TN p. 2107, 2792
University of Tennessee Southern, Pulaski TN p. 2124
University of Texas, Houston TX p. 2200
University of Texas at Arlington Library, Arlington TX p. 2136
University of Texas at Austin, Austin TX p. 2141, 2793
University of Texas at Austin, Briscoe Center, Round Top TX p. 2234
University of Texas at Dallas, Richardson TX p. 2231
University of Texas at El Paso Library, El Paso TX p. 2175
University of Texas at San Antonio Libraries, San Antonio TX p. 2240
University of Texas at Tyler Library, Tyler TX p. 2250
University of Texas Health Science Center, San Antonio TX p. 2240
University of Texas Health Science Center at Tyler, Tyler TX p. 2250
University of Texas Libraries, Austin TX p. 2142
University of Texas Medical Branch, Galveston TX p. 2183
University of Texas of the Permian Basin, Odessa TX p. 2223
University of Texas Rio Grande Valley, Brownsville TX p. 2150
University of Texas Rio Grande Valley, Edinburg TX p. 2173
University of Texas Rio Grande Valley, Harlingen TX p. 2188
University of Texas Southwestern Medical Center, Dallas TX p. 2169
University of the Arts University Libraries, Philadelphia PA p. 1988
University of the Cumberlands, Williamsburg KY p. 877
University of the District of Columbia, Washington DC p. 380
University of the Fraser Valley, Abbotsford BC p. 2562
University of the Incarnate Word, San Antonio TX p. 2240
University of the Ozarks, Clarksville AR p. 92
University of the Pacific Libraries, Stockton CA p. 250
University of the Pacific - McGeorge School of Law, Sacramento CA p. 210
University of the Sacred Heart, Santurce PR p. 2515
University of the Sciences in Philadelphia, Philadelphia PA p. 1989
University of the South, Sewanee TN p. 2126
University of the Southwest, Hobbs NM p. 1469
University of the Virgin Islands, Kingshill VI p. 2517
University of the Virgin Islands, Saint Thomas VI p. 2517
University of Toledo, Toledo OH p. 1825
University of Toronto, Toronto ON p. 2796
University of Toronto Archives & Records Management (UTARMS), *see* University of Toronto Libraries, Toronto ON p. 2700

Validata Computer & Research Corp Library, Montgomery AL p. 30
Valier Public Library, Valier MT p. 1303
Valle Vista Community Library, *see* Mohave County Library District, Kingman AZ p. 65
Valle Vista Library, *see* Riverside County Library System, Hemet CA p. 203
Vallejo Naval & Historical Museum, Vallejo CA p. 255
Valley Campus Library, *see* Southern Union State Community College, Valley AL p. 39
Valley Center Public Library, Valley Center KS p. 840
Valley Children's Healthcare, Madera CA p. 171
Valley City Barnes County Public Library, Valley City ND p. 1740
Valley City State University, Valley City ND p. 2790
Valley City State University Library, Valley City ND p. 1740
Valley Community Library, Peckville PA p. 1974
Valley Cottage Free Library, Valley Cottage NY p. 1656
Valley District Public Library, Fairview IL p. 588
Valley Falls Free Library, Valley Falls NY p. 1657
Valley Forge Military Academy & College, Wayne PA p. 2019
Valley Head Public Library, Valley Head WV p. 2416
Valley Hi-North Laguna Library, *see* Sacramento Public Library, Sacramento CA p. 210
Valley Hospital, Ridgewood NJ p. 1439
Valley Library, *see* Oregon State University Libraries, Corvallis OR p. 1876
Valley Library Consortium (N), Saginaw MI p. 2768
Valley Mills Public Library, Valley Mills TX p. 2251
Valley of the Tetons Library, Victor ID p. 532
Valley Park Library, Valley Park MO p. 1284
Valley Public Library, Valley NE p. 1339
Valley Ranch Library, *see* Irving Public Library, Irving TX p. 2202
Valley Regional Library, Morris MB p. 2588
Valley State Prison, *see* California Department of Corrections Library System, Chowchilla CA p. 207
Valley Street Campus Library, *see* Gadsden State Community College, Gadsden AL p. 18
Valley View Library, *see* King County Library System, SeaTac WA p. 2366
Valleyview Municipal Library, Valleyview AB p. 2557
Valleywood Margaret Dunn Branch, *see* Caledon Public Library, Mayfield ON p. 2632
Valmeyer Public Library District, Valmeyer IL p. 657
Valparaiso Community Library, Valparaiso FL p. 452
Valparaiso Public, *see* Porter County Public Library System, Valparaiso IN p. 722
Valparaiso Public Library, Valparaiso NE p. 1339
Valparaiso University, Valparaiso IN p. 723
Van Alstyne Public Library, Van Alstyne TX p. 2251
Van Buren District Library, Decatur MI p. 1096
Van Buren Library, *see* Carter County Library District, Van Buren MO p. 1284
Van Buren Public Library, Van Buren AR p. 111
Van Buren Public Library, Van Buren IN p. 723
Van Buskirk Miro Branch, *see* Stockton-San Joaquin County Public Library, Stockton CA p. 250
Van Cleave Kevin Poole Memorial Library, *see* Wilkinson County Library System, Centreville MS p. 1236
Van Doren Dorris Branch, *see* El Paso Public Library, El Paso TX p. 2174
Van Etten Library, *see* Chemung County Library District, Van Etten NY p. 1530
Van Gorden-Williams Library & Archives, *see* Scottish Rite Masonic Museum & Library, Inc, Lexington MA p. 1028
Van Hoof Gerard H Library, *see* Little Chute Public Library, Little Chute WI p. 2448
Van Horn City County Library, Van Horn TX p. 2251
Van Horn Library, *see* Somerset County Historical Society, Bridgewater NJ p. 1392
Van Horn Public Library, Pine Island MN p. 1192
Van Horne Public Library, Van Horne IA p. 787
Van Houten Robert W Library, *see* New Jersey Institute of Technology, Newark NJ p. 1426
Van Meter Public Library, Van Meter IA p. 787
Van Ness Feldman Library, Washington DC p. 380
Van Noy Library, *see* United States Army, Fort Belvoir VA p. 2319
Van Oosten John Library, *see* United States Geological Survey, Ann Arbor MI p. 1079
Van Pelt J Robert & John & Ruanne Opie Library, *see* Michigan Technological University, Houghton MI p. 1116
Van Pelt Library, *see* University of Pennsylvania Libraries, Philadelphia PA p. 1987
Van Rensselear - Rankin Family Historic Cherry Hill Museum, Albany NY p. 1484
Van Trump James D Library, *see* Pittsburgh History & Landmarks Foundation, Pittsburgh PA p. 1995
Van Tyne Josselyn Memorial Library, *see* Wilson Ornithological Society, Ann Arbor MI p. 1081
Van Wagenen Library, *see* SUNY Cobleskill College of Agriculture & Technology, Cobleskill NY p. 1520
Van Wert County Law Library Association, Van Wert OH p. 1827
Van Wylen Library, *see* Hope College, Holland MI p. 1115
Van Zandt County Sarah Norman Library, Canton TX p. 2152
Van Zandt James E Medical Center Library, *see* Department of Veterans Affairs, Altoona PA p. 1906
Vance-Granville Community College, Henderson NC p. 1695
Vance Memorial Library, *see* Dallas Baptist University, Dallas TX p. 2163
Vance Township Library, Fairmount IL p. 587
Vanceboro Public Library, Vanceboro NC p. 1719
Vancleave Public Library, *see* Jackson-George Regional Library System, Vancleave MS p. 1228
VanCott Stuart Memorial Library, *see* Congregational Church of Patchogue, Patchogue NY p. 1615
Vancouver Art Gallery Library, Vancouver BC p. 2580
Vancouver Coastal Health, North Vancouver BC p. 2573
Vancouver Community College, Vancouver BC p. 2581
Vancouver Community Library, *see* Fort Vancouver Regional Library District, Vancouver WA p. 2391
Vancouver Holocaust Education Centre, Vancouver BC p. 2581
Vancouver Island Regional Library, Nanaimo BC p. 2570
Vancouver Island University Library, Nanaimo BC p. 2572
Vancouver Premier College, Richmond BC p. 2575
Vancouver Public Library, Vancouver BC p. 2581
Vancouver School of Theology, Vancouver BC p. 2582
Vandalia Correctional Center Library, Vandalia IL p. 657
Vanderbilt University, Nashville TN p. 2121
Vandercook College of Music, Chicago IL p. 570
Vandergrift Public Library Association, Vandergrift PA p. 2016
Vanderhoof Public Library, Vanderhoof BC p. 2582
VanDusen Gardens Library, *see* Wosk Yosef Library & Resource Centre, Vancouver BC p. 2582
Vanguard College Library, Edmonton AB p. 2538
Vanguard University of Southern California, Costa Mesa CA p. 132
Vanier College Library, Montreal QC p. 2728
Vanier Library, *see* Concordia University Libraries, Montreal QC p. 2724
Vann Lee & Jim Library, *see* University of Saint Francis, Fort Wayne IN p. 685
Varey Vida B Library, *see* Plymouth Church, Seattle WA p. 2378
Varnum Memorial Library, Jeffersonville VT p. 2287
Vassalboro Public Library, East Vassalboro ME p. 924
Vassar Brothers Medical Center, Poughkeepsie NY p. 1623
Vassar College Library, Poughkeepsie NY p. 1624
Vaughan John Library, *see* Northeastern State University, Tahlequah OK p. 1863
Vaughan Memorial Library, *see* Acadia University, Wolfville NS p. 2623
Vaughan Public Libraries, Vaughan ON p. 2701
Vaughn College Library, Flushing NY p. 1534
Vaughn James T Correctional Center Law Library, Smyrna DE p. 356
Vaughn Library, *see* Tyler Junior College, Tyler TX p. 2249
Vaughn Public Library, Vaughn NM p. 1479
Vaughn Public Library, Ashland WI p. 2421
Vaught Fred A Memorial Public Library, Hartsville TN p. 2101
Vauxhall Public Library, Vauxhall AB p. 2557
Vedder, Price, Chicago IL p. 570
Vedder Research Library, *see* Greene County Historical Society, Coxsackie NY p. 1523
Veedersburg Public, *see* Covington-Veedersburg Public Library, Veedersburg IN p. 677
Vegreville Centennial Library, Vegreville AB p. 2558
Venable LLP Library, Washington DC p. 381
Venable LLP Library, Baltimore MD p. 958
Venable LLP Library, Tysons Corner VA p. 2348
Venango County Law Library, Franklin PA p. 1934
Venice Campus Dr Bill Jervey Jr Library, *see* State College of Florida Manatee-Sarasota Library, Venice FL p. 387
Venice Public Library, Venice FL p. 452
Venice Public Library, Venice IL p. 657
Garcia Venito Public Library, Sells AZ p. 78
Ventress Memorial Library, Marshfield MA p. 1032
Ventura College, Ventura CA p. 255
Ventura County Law Library, Ventura CA p. 256
Ventura County Library, Ventura CA p. 256
Ventura County Medical Center, Ventura CA p. 256
Ventura Public Library, Ventura IA p. 787
Vera Dial Dickey Library, *see* Clarendon College, Clarendon TX p. 2156
Verde Valley Medical Center, Cottonwood AZ p. 59
Verdigre Public Library, Verdigre NE p. 1339
Vergara Lamar Bruni Inner City Branch Library, *see* Guerra Joe A Laredo Public Library, Laredo TX p. 2209
Vermilion Community College Library, Ely MN p. 1174
Vermilion Parish Library, Abbeville LA p. 879
Vermilion Public Library, Vermilion AB p. 2558
Vermillion County Public Library, Newport IN p. 710
Vermillion Public Library, Vermillion KS p. 841
Vermont College of Fine Arts, Montpelier VT p. 2289
Vermont Department of Libraries, Barre VT p. 2278
Vermont Grand Lodge Library, Barre VT p. 2278
Vermont Historical Society, Barre VT p. 2278
Vermont Law School, South Royalton VT p. 2295
Vermont Public Library, Vermont IL p. 657
Northern Vermont University - Johnson, Johnson VT p. 2287
Vermont State University - Castleton, Castleton VT p. 2281
Vermont State University - Lyndon, Lyndonville VT p. 2288
Vermont State University - Randolph, Randolph Center VT p. 2292
Vermont State University - Williston, Williston VT p. 2299
Vermont Veterans Home Library, Bennington VT p. 2279
Vermontville Township Library, Vermontville MI p. 1156
Vernon Area Public Library District, Lincolnshire IL p. 609
Vernon College, Vernon TX p. 2252
Vernon District Public Library, Vernon MI p. 1156
Vernon Free Library, Vernon VT p. 2296
Vernon Manfred C Library, *see* Whale Museum Library, Friday Harbor WA p. 2364
Vernon Parish Library, Leesville LA p. 895
Peeples Vernon Library-Charlotte Campus, *see* Florida SouthWestern State College, Punta Gorda FL p. 439

Vernon Public, *see* Apache County Library District, Vernon AZ p. 76
Vernon Public Library, Vernon NY p. 1657
Vernonia Public Library, Vernonia OR p. 1901
Verona Public Library, Verona NJ p. 1449
Verona Public Library, Verona WI p. 2482
Vershire Community Library, Vershire VT p. 2297
Vestal Public Library, Vestal NY p. 1657
Vestavia Hills Library in the Forest, Vestavia Hills AL p. 39
Vesterheim Norwegian-American Museum, Decorah IA p. 745
Veteran Affairs Canada Library, Charlottetown PE p. 2707
Veteran Municipal Library, Veteran AB p. 2558
Veterans Affairs Medical Library, Omaha NE p. 1331
Veterans Home of California, Yountville CA p. 261
Veterans Library, *see* City of Commerce Public Library, Commerce CA p. 132
Veterans Memorial Library, Patten ME p. 935
Veterans Memorial Library, *see* Chippewa River District Library, Mount Pleasant MI p. 1135
Veterans Memorial Library, *see* Osceola Library System, Saint Cloud FL p. 414
Viborg Public Library, Viborg SD p. 2085
Viburnum Branch, *see* Ozark Regional Library, Viburnum MO p. 1251
Vick G B Memorial Library, *see* Baptist Bible College & Theological Seminary, Springfield MO p. 1280
Vickery Park, *see* Dallas Public Library, Dallas TX p. 2166
Vicksburg & Warren County Historical Society, Vicksburg MS p. 1234
Vicksburg District Library, Vicksburg MI p. 1156
Victor Farmington Library, Victor NY p. 1657
Victor Michael II Art Library, *see* Springfield Art Association, Springfield IL p. 650
Victor Public Library, Victor CO p. 297
Victor Public Library, Victor IA p. 787
Victor Valley College Library, Victorville CA p. 256
Victoria College Library, *see* University of Houston, Victoria TX p. 2252
Victoria Conservatory of Music Library, Victoria BC p. 2583
Victoria Municipal Library, Holland MB p. 2587
Victoria North Regional, *see* Cape Breton Regional Library, Ingonish NS p. 2622
Victoria Public, *see* Lunenburg County Public Library System Inc, Victoria VA p. 2327
Victoria Public Library, Victoria TX p. 2252
Victoria Public Library, Victoria NL p. 2611
Victoria Public Library District, Victoria IL p. 657
Victoria University, E J Pratt Library, *see* University of Toronto Libraries, Toronto ON p. 2700
Victorville City Library, Victorville CA p. 256
VICULA (N), *see* Virginia Independent College & University Library Association, Arlington VA p. 2776
Vidalia-Toombs County Library, *see* Ohoopee Regional Library System, Vidalia GA p. 501
Vidor Public Library, Vidor TX p. 2252
Vienna Carnegie Public Library, Vienna IL p. 657
Vienna Correctional Center Library, Vienna IL p. 657
Vienna Public Library, Vienna WV p. 2416
View Park Bebe Moore Campbell Library, *see* County of Los Angeles Public Library, Los Angeles CA p. 138
View Royal Reading Centre, Victoria BC p. 2583
Vigil Samuel F Learning Resource Center, *see* Luna Community College, Las Vegas NM p. 1471
Vigo County Historical Museum Library, Terre Haute IN p. 721
Vigo County Public Library, Terre Haute IN p. 721
Viking Library System, Fergus Falls MN p. 1175
Viking Municipal Library, Viking AB p. 2558
Villa Maria College Library, Buffalo NY p. 1511
Villa Park Public Library, Villa Park IL p. 658
Villa Rica Public Library, *see* West Georgia Regional Library, Villa Rica GA p. 470
Village Church Library, Prairie Village KS p. 832
Village Library, *see* Massanutten Regional Library, Broadway VA p. 2325
Village Library of Cooperstown, Cooperstown NY p. 1522
Village Library of Morgantown, Morgantown PA p. 1966
Village Library of Morris, Morris NY p. 1574
Village Library of Wrightstown, Wrightstown PA p. 2024
Village of Avon Public Library, Avon IL p. 539
Village of Verdon Library, Verdon NE p. 1339
Village Regional Library, *see* Wake County Public Library System, Raleigh NC p. 1711
Villages Public Library at Belvedere, *see* Sumter County Library System, The Villages FL p. 455
Villages Public Library at Pinellas Plaza, *see* Sumter County Library System, Wildwood FL p. 455
Villanova University, Villanova PA p. 2017
Villasenor Paul, *see* City of San Bernardino Library Services, San Bernardino CA p. 212
Villisca Public Library, Villisca IA p. 787
Vilna Municipal Library, Vilna AB p. 2558
Vinalhaven Public Library, Vinalhaven ME p. 944
Vincennes University, Vincennes IN p. 724
Vincent D J Medical Library, *see* Ohio Health-Riverside Methodist Hospital, Columbus OH p. 1774
Vineland Historical & Antiquarian Society, Vineland NJ p. 1450
Vineland Public Library, Vineland NJ p. 1450
Vineyard Haven Public Library, Vineyard Haven MA p. 1060
Vineyard Library, *see* Northern Oklahoma College, Tonkawa OK p. 1864
Vining Library, *see* West Virginia University Institute of Technology, Montgomery WV p. 2408
Vinita Public Library, Vinita OK p. 1868
Vinson & Elkins, Houston TX p. 2200
Vinson Mary Memorial Library, *see* Twin Lakes Library System, Milledgeville GA p. 491
Vinson Neighborhood Library, *see* Houston Public Library, Houston TX p. 2196
Vinton Public Library, Vinton IA p. 788
Viola Public Library, Viola WI p. 2482
Viola Public Library, *see* Fulton County Library, Viola AR p. 111
Viola Public Library District, Viola IL p. 658
Viola Township Library, Viola KS p. 841
Violette Dr Lorne J Public Library, *see* Haut-Saint-Jean Regional Library, Saint Leonard NB p. 2600
Virden Public Library, Virden NM p. 1479
Virgin Islands Division of Libraries, Archives & Museums, Christiansted VI p. 2517
Virgin Islands Division of Libraries, Archives & Museums, Saint Thomas VI p. 2517
Virginia Aquarium & Marine Science Center, Virginia Beach VA p. 2350
Virginia Baptist Historical Society, Richmond VA p. 2343
Virginia Beach Higher Education Resource Center, *see* Norfolk State University Library, Virginia Beach VA p. 2335
Virginia Beach Public Library, Virginia Beach VA p. 2350
Virginia Commonwealth University Libraries, Richmond VA p. 2343
Virginia Department for the Blind & Vision Impaired, Richmond VA p. 2343
Virginia Department of Corrections, Bland VA p. 2307
Virginia Department of Corrections, Crozier VA p. 2314
Virginia Department of Historic Resources, Richmond VA p. 2343
Virginia Department of Transportation (VDOT) Research Library, Charlottesville VA p. 2310
Virginia Division of Geology & Mineral Resources Library, Charlottesville VA p. 2311
Virginia Highlands Community College Library, Abingdon VA p. 2301
Virginia Historical Society Library, Richmond VA p. 2344
Virginia Independent College & University Library Association (N), Arlington VA p. 2776
Virginia Institute of Marine Science, Gloucester Point VA p. 2322
Virginia Memorial Public Library, Virginia IL p. 658
Virginia Military Institute, Lexington VA p. 2329
Virginia Museum of Fine Arts Library, Richmond VA p. 2344
Virginia Office, *see* Venable LLP Library MD p. 958
Virginia Peninsula Community College Library, Hampton VA p. 2323
Virginia Polytechnic Institute & State University Libraries, Blacksburg VA p. 2307
Virginia Public Library, Virginia MN p. 1206
Virginia State Law Library, Richmond VA p. 2344
Virginia State University, Petersburg VA p. 2337
Virginia Theological Seminary, Alexandria VA p. 2303
Virginia Tidewater Consortium for Higher Education (N), Norfolk VA p. 2776
Virginia Union University, Richmond VA p. 2344
Virginia University of Lynchburg, Lynchburg VA p. 2331
Virginia War Museum, Newport News VA p. 2334
Virginia Wesleyan University, Virginia Beach VA p. 2351
Virginia Western Community College, Roanoke VA p. 2346
Virginia's Academic Library Consortium (N), Fairfax VA p. 2776
Virtua Health System, Voorhees Division, Voorhees NJ p. 1450
Virtual Academic Library Environment (N), Newark NJ p. 2770
Vise Doris & Harry Library, *see* Cumberland University, Lebanon TN p. 2108
Vista Grande Library, *see* Casa Grande Public Library, Casa Grande AZ p. 57
Vista Grande Public Library, Santa Fe NM p. 1477
Vista Hermosa Library, *see* Walla Walla County Rural Library District, Prescott WA p. 2392
Viterbo University, La Crosse WI p. 2446
VIVA (N), *see* Virginia's Academic Library Consortium, Fairfax VA p. 2776
Vivian Robert A, *see* Monroe County Library System, Monroe MI p. 1134
VMFH Franciscan Library, Tacoma WA p. 2388
Vogel Library, *see* Wartburg College Library, Waverly IA p. 789
Vogel Marylee, *see* Spencer County Public Library, Richland IN p. 716
Vogelson M Allan Regional Branch & Headquarters, *see* Camden County Library System, Voorhees NJ p. 1450
Voice Library, *see* Michigan State University Libraries, East Lansing MI p. 1102
Volga Public Library, Volga IA p. 788
Volpe Angelo & Jennette Library, *see* Tennessee Technological University, Cookeville TN p. 2095
Volpe John A National Transportation Systems Center, Cambridge MA p. 1009
Volunteer State Community College Library, Gallatin TN p. 2099
Voluntown Public Library, Voluntown CT p. 342
Volusia County Law Library, Daytona Beach FL p. 392
Volusia County Public Library, Daytona Beach FL p. 392
Von Braun Library & Archives, *see* United States Space & Rocket Center, Huntsville AL p. 22
Von Canon Library, *see* Southern Virginia University, Buena Vista VA p. 2308
Von KleinSmid Center Library, *see* University of Southern California Libraries, Los Angeles CA p. 170
Vonda Public Library, *see* Wapiti Regional Library, Vonda SK p. 2746
Vonore Public Library, Vonore TN p. 2129
Voorhees University, Denmark SC p. 2058
Voorheesville Public Library, Voorheesville NY p. 1657
Vose Library, Union ME p. 943
Voskuyl Roger John Library, *see* Westmont College, Santa Barbara CA p. 241
VTC (N), *see* Virginia Tidewater Consortium for Higher Education, Norfolk VA p. 2776
Vulcan Municipal Library, Vulcan AB p. 2558

Wabamun Public Library, Wabamun AB p. 2558
Wabasca Public Library, Wabasca AB p. 2558
Wabash Carnegie Public Library, Wabash IN p. 724
Wabash College, Crawfordsville IN p. 677
Wabash Valley College, Mount Carmel IL p. 620
Wabash Valley Correctional Facility, Carlisle IN p. 674
Wabasha Public Library, Wabasha MN p. 1206
Wabasso Public Library, Wabasso MN p. 1206
Wabeno Public Library, Wabeno WI p. 2483
Wachtell, Lipton, Rosen & Katz, New York NY p. 1603
Wachute Joseph W & Emma L Memorial, *see* Prairie du Chien Memorial Library, Prairie du Chien WI p. 2471
Waco-McLennan County Library System, Waco TX p. 2254
Wade David Correctional Center, Homer LA p. 891
Wade Marion E Center, *see* Wheaton College, Wheaton IL p. 662
Wade Richard & Glen Vyck McKinney Library, *see* Rio Grande Bible Institute & Language School, Edinburg TX p. 2173
Wadena City Library, Wadena MN p. 1206
Wadena Public Library, Wadena IA p. 788
Wadhams Free Library, Wadhams NY p. 1658
Wadleigh Memorial Library, Milford NH p. 1374
Wadley Campus Library, *see* Southern Union State Community College, Wadley AL p. 39
Wadley Public, *see* Jefferson County Library System, Wadley GA p. 486
Wadsworth Atheneum Museum of Art, Hartford CT p. 318
Wadsworth Library, Geneseo NY p. 1538
Wadsworth Public Library, *see* Everhard Ella M Public Library, Wadsworth OH p. 1827
Waelder Public Library, Waelder TX p. 2254
Waggoner Frances Banta Community Library, DeWitt IA p. 747
Waggoner Library, *see* Trevecca Nazarene University, Nashville TN p. 2121
Wagnalls Memorial Library, Lithopolis OH p. 1796
Wagner Albert C Youth Correctional Facility Library, Bordentown NJ p. 1391
Wagner Charles A, *see* Jefferson Parish Library, Metairie LA p. 897
Wagner College, Staten Island NY p. 1645
Wagner Free Institute of Science Library, Philadelphia PA p. 1989
Wagner Lois Memorial Library, Richmond MI p. 1144
Wagner Public Library, Wagner SD p. 2085
Wagoner City Public Library, Wagoner OK p. 1868
Wahab Public Law Library, *see* Virginia Beach Public Library, Virginia Beach VA p. 2351
Wahiawa Public Library, *see* Hawaii State Public Library System, Wahiawa HI p. 510
Wahlstrom Library, *see* University of Bridgeport, Bridgeport CT p. 304
Wahoo Public Library, Wahoo NE p. 1339
Wahta Mohawks, Bala ON p. 2629
Waialua Public Library, *see* Hawaii State Public Library System, Waialua HI p. 511
Waianae Public Library, *see* Hawaii State Public Library System, Waianae HI p. 511
Waidner-Spahr Library, *see* Dickinson College, Carlisle PA p. 1919
Waikiki-Kapahulu Public Library, *see* Hawaii State Public Library System, Honolulu HI p. 511
Wailuku Public Library, *see* Hawaii State Public Library System, Wailuku HI p. 511
Waimanalo Public & School Library, *see* Hawaii State Public Library System, Waimanalo HI p. 511
Waimea Public Library, *see* Hawaii State Public Library System, Waimea HI p. 511
Wainfleet Township Public Library, Wainfleet ON p. 2701
Wainwright Jonathan M Memorial VA Medical Center Library, Walla Walla WA p. 2392
Wainwright Public Library, Wainwright AB p. 2559
Waipahu Public Library, *see* Hawaii State Public Library System, Waipahu HI p. 511
Wakarusa-Olive & Harrison Township Public Library, *see* Wakarusa Public Library, Wakarusa IN p. 724
Wakarusa Public Library, Wakarusa IN p. 724
Wakaw Public Library, *see* Wapiti Regional Library, Wakaw SK p. 2746
Wake County Public Library System, Raleigh NC p. 1710
Wake Forest University, Winston-Salem NC p. 1726
Wake Technical Community College, Raleigh NC p. 1711
WaKeeney Public Library, WaKeeney KS p. 841
Wakefield Jessie Memorial Library, Port Lions AK p. 50
Wakefield Library Association, Wakefield NH p. 1383
Wakefield Public Library, Wakefield KS p. 841
Wakefield Public Library, Wakefield MI p. 1156
Wakulla County Public Library, Crawfordville FL p. 391
Walden Community Library, West Danville VT p. 2298
Walden University Library, Minneapolis MN p. 1186
Waldinger Henry Memorial Library, Valley Stream NY p. 1657
Waldo Community, *see* Kansas City Public Library, Kansas City MO p. 1255
Waldo Dwight B Library, *see* Western Michigan University, Kalamazoo MI p. 1122
Waldoboro Public Library, Waldoboro ME p. 944
Waldorf Branch, *see* Waseca-Le Sueur Regional Library, Waldorf MN p. 1207
Waldorf University, Forest City IA p. 753
Waldport Public Library, Waldport OR p. 1901
Waldron District Library, Waldron MI p. 1156
Waldrop Frances N Health Sciences Library, *see* Department of Behavioral Health, St Elizabeths Hospital, Washington DC p. 363
Waldwick Public Library, Waldwick NJ p. 1451
Wales Public Library, Wales MA p. 1061
Walhalla Public Library, Walhalla ND p. 1741
Walker e-Library, *see* Hialeah Public Libraries, Hialeah FL p. 409
Walker J B Memorial Library, *see* Hickman County Public Library, Centerville TN p. 2091
Walker James E Library, *see* Middle Tennessee State University, Murfreesboro TN p. 2117
Walker Management Library, *see* Vanderbilt University, Nashville TN p. 2122
Walker Memorial Library, Westbrook ME p. 946
Walker Memorial Library, *see* Howard Payne University, Brownwood TX p. 2150
Walker Public Library, Walker MN p. 1207
Walkerton-Lincoln Township Public Library, Walkerton IN p. 724
Wall Community Library, Wall SD p. 2085
Wall Lake Public Library, Wall Lake IA p. 788
Walla Walla Community College Library, Walla Walla WA p. 2392
Walla Walla County Law Library, Walla Walla WA p. 2392
Walla Walla County Rural Library District, Walla Walla WA p. 2392
Walla Walla Public Library, Walla Walla WA p. 2392
Walla Walla University Libraries, College Place WA p. 2362
Walla Walla VAMC Library, *see* Wainwright Jonathan M Memorial VA Medical Center Library, Walla Walla WA p. 2392
Wallace Community College, Dothan AL p. 15
Wallace Community College, Eufaula AL p. 16
Wallace Community College, Selma AL p. 35
Wallace DeWitt Library, *see* Macalester College, Saint Paul MN p. 1200
Wallace George Library, *see* Champlain Regional College at Saint-Lambert, Saint Lambert QC p. 2734
Wallace Library, *see* Criswell College, Dallas TX p. 2163
Wallace Lila Acheson Library, *see* Juilliard School, New York NY p. 1589
Wallace Madeleine Clark, *see* Wheaton College Library, Norton MA p. 1043
Wallace Public Library, Wallace ID p. 532
Wallace State College, Hanceville AL p. 20
Wallace Willoughby Memorial Library, Stony Creek CT p. 339
Walled Lake City Library, Walled Lake MI p. 1156
Wallenberg Library & Archives, *see* American Swedish Institute, Minneapolis MN p. 1182
Waller County Library, Hempstead TX p. 2189
Waller Sam Museum Library, The Pas MB p. 2591
Wallerstedt Learning Center, *see* Bethany College, Lindsborg KS p. 821
Wallingford Historical Society Inc, Library, Wallingford CT p. 342
Wallingford Public Library, Wallingford CT p. 342
Wallkill Public Library, Wallkill NY p. 1658
Wallowa County Library, Enterprise OR p. 1878
Wallowa Public Library, Wallowa OR p. 1901
Walls John Freeman, *see* Proverbs Heritage Organization, Essex ON p. 2641
Walls Public Library, *see* First Regional Library, Walls MS p. 1220
Walnut Cove Public Library, Walnut Cove NC p. 1720
Walnut Creek Historical Society, Walnut Creek CA p. 258
Walnut Grove Library, *see* Fraser Valley Regional Library, Langley BC p. 2562
Walnut Grove Library, *see* Sacramento Public Library, Walnut Grove CA p. 210
Walnut Grove Public, *see* Mid-Mississippi Regional Library System, Walnut Grove MS p. 1224
Walnut Public Library, Walnut IA p. 788
Walnut Public Library, Walnut KS p. 841
Walnut Public Library, *see* Northeast Regional Library, Walnut MS p. 1216
Walnut Public Library District, Walnut IL p. 658
Walpole Lewis Library, *see* Yale University Library, Farmington CT p. 328
Walpole Public Library, Walpole MA p. 1061
Walpole Town Library, Walpole NH p. 1383
Walsh College, Troy MI p. 1155
Walsh Library, *see* Seton Hall University Libraries, South Orange NJ p. 1443
Walsh Library at Rose Hill, *see* Fordham University Libraries, Bronx NY p. 1498
Walsh University, North Canton OH p. 1809
Walt Bess Dodson, *see* Lincoln City Libraries, Lincoln NE p. 1321
Walt Disney Imagineering, Glendale CA p. 149
Walt Joseph W Library, *see* Sigma Alpha Epsilon Fraternity & Foundation, Evanston IL p. 587
Walter & Haverfield LLP, Cleveland OH p. 1770
Walter Geology Library, *see* University of Texas Libraries, Austin TX p. 2143
Walter Library, *see* University of Minnesota Libraries-Twin Cities, Minneapolis MN p. 1186
Walter Library, *see* Alliant International University, San Diego CA p. 214
Walter Neighborhood Library, *see* Houston Public Library, Houston TX p. 2196
Walters Art Museum Library, Baltimore MD p. 958
Walters Elizabeth D Library, *see* Monroe County Historical Association, Stroudsburg PA p. 2011
Walters Public Library, Walters OK p. 1868
Walters State Community College, Morristown TN p. 2116
Walters W H Free Public Library, Alpha NJ p. 1387
Waltham Museum Inc Library, Waltham MA p. 1062
Waltham Public Library, Waltham MA p. 1062
Walthill Public Library, Walthill NE p. 1340
Walton & Tipton Township Public Library, Walton IN p. 724
Walton Community Library, Walton KS p. 841
Walton County Public Library System, De Funiak Springs FL p. 393
Walton-DeFuniak Library, *see* Walton County Public Library System, De Funiak Springs FL p. 393
Walton Public Library, *see* Roane County Public Library, Walton WV p. 2415
Waltz Howard B Music Library, *see* University of Colorado Boulder, Boulder CO p. 268
Walworth Memorial Library, Walworth WI p. 2483
Walworth-Seely Public Library, Walworth NY p. 1658
Wamego Public Library, Wamego KS p. 841

Washington Martha, *see* Fairfax County Public Library, Alexandria VA p. 2316
Washington Mary Ball Museum & Library, Inc, Lancaster VA p. 2327
Washington Mary Hospital, Fredericksburg VA p. 2320
Washington Memorial Library, *see* Middle Georgia Regional Library System, Macon GA p. 486
Washington Metropolitan Area Transit Authority, Washington DC p. 381
Washington Municipal Library, Washington LA p. 912
Washington National Cathedral, Washington DC p. 381
Washington Parish Library System, Franklinton LA p. 890
Washington Park Library, *see* Community Libraries of Providence, Providence RI p. 2038
Washington Phyllis J College of Education, *see* University of Montana, Missoula MT p. 2788
Washington Public Library, Washington IA p. 788
Washington Public Library, Washington KS p. 841
Washington Public Library, Washington MO p. 1285
Washington Public Library, Washington NJ p. 1451
Washington Research Library Consortium (N), Upper Marlboro MD p. 2766
Washington School for the Deaf, Vancouver WA p. 2391
Washington State Community College, Marietta OH p. 1799
Washington State Department of Natural Resources, Olympia WA p. 2373
Washington State History Research Center, Tacoma WA p. 2388
Washington State Law Library, Olympia WA p. 2373
Washington State Library, Tumwater WA p. 2390
Washington State Reformatory, *see* Washington State Library, Monroe WA p. 2390
Washington State University Libraries, Pullman WA p. 2374
Washington State University Libraries, Vancouver WA p. 2391
Washington State University Tri-Cities Library, Richland WA p. 2375
Washington Talking Book & Braille Library, Seattle WA p. 2382
Washington Talking Book & Braille Library, *see* Seattle Public Library WA p. 2380
Washington Theological Consortium (N), Washington DC p. 2763
Washington Township Free Public Library, Long Valley NJ p. 1414
Washington Township Historical Society Library, Long Valley NJ p. 1414
Washington University Libraries, Saint Louis MO p. 1276
Washington's Headquarters State Historic Site Library, *see* New York State Office of Parks, Recreation & Historic, Newburgh NY p. 1605
Washoe County Law Library, Reno NV p. 1350
Washoe County Library System, Reno NV p. 1350
Washougal Community Library, *see* Fort Vancouver Regional Library District, Washougal WA p. 2391
Washta Public Library, Washta IA p. 788
Washtenaw Community College, Ann Arbor MI p. 1081
Washtenaw Library for the Blind & Physically Disabled, *see* Ann Arbor District Library, Ann Arbor MI p. 1078
Wasilla Public Library, Wasilla AK p. 52
Waskom Public Library, Waskom TX p. 2254
Watanabe Family Library, *see* Eiteljorg Museum of American Indians & Western Art, Indianapolis IN p. 691
Watauga County Public Library, Boone NC p. 1675
Watauga Public Library, Watauga TX p. 2255
Water Valley Public Library, Water Valley AB p. 2559
Waterboro Public Library, East Waterboro ME p. 924
Waterbury Law Library, *see* Connecticut Judicial Branch Law Libraries, Waterbury CT p. 316
Waterbury Public Library, Waterbury VT p. 2297
Waterbury Republican & American Library, Waterbury CT p. 344
Waterfield Harry Lee Library, *see* Murray State University, Murray KY p. 870
Waterford Hospital Library & Information Services, *see* Eastern Health, St. John's NL p. 2610
Waterford Library Association, Waterford ME p. 944
Waterford Public Library, Waterford CT p. 344
Waterford Public Library, Waterford NY p. 1659
Waterford Public Library, Waterford PA p. 2018
Waterford Public Library, Waterford WI p. 2483
Waterford Township Public Library, Waterford MI p. 1158
Waterford Township Public Library, Atco NJ p. 1387
Waterloo-Grant Township Public Library, Waterloo IN p. 725
Waterloo Library & Historical Society, Waterloo NY p. 1659
Waterloo Public Library, Waterloo IA p. 789
Waterloo Public Library, Waterloo ON p. 2702
Waterloo Public Library, Waterloo QC p. 2739
Waterloo Region Law Association, Kitchener ON p. 2652
Waters Robbie, *see* Sacramento Public Library, Sacramento CA p. 210
Waters Velma K Library, *see* Texas A&M University-Commerce, Commerce TX p. 2158
Watertown Daily Times Library, Watertown NY p. 1660
Watertown Free Public Library, Watertown MA p. 1063
Watertown History Museum Library, Watertown CT p. 344
Watertown Library Association, Watertown CT p. 344
Watertown Public Library, Watertown WI p. 2484
Watertown Regional Library, Watertown SD p. 2085
Watertown Township Fostoria Library, Fostoria MI p. 1107
Waterville Historical Society Library, Waterville ME p. 945
Waterville Public, *see* Waseca-Le Sueur Regional Library, Waterville MN p. 1207
Waterville Public Library, Waterville IA p. 789
Waterville Public Library, Waterville KS p. 841
Waterville Public Library, Waterville ME p. 945
Waterville Public Library, Waterville NY p. 1660
Waterville Town Library, Waterville VT p. 2297
Watervliet District Library, Watervliet MI p. 1158
Watervliet Public Library, Watervliet NY p. 1660
Watkins College of Art & Design Library, Nashville TN p. 2122
Watkins Glen Public Library, Watkins Glen NY p. 1660
Watkins Woolen Mill State Historic Site Archives, *see* Missouri Department of Natural Resources, Lawson MO p. 1259
Watkinson Library, *see* Trinity College Library, Hartford CT p. 318
Watne Memorial Library, *see* Crown College, Saint Bonifacius MN p. 1195
Watonga Public Library, Watonga OK p. 1868
Watonwan County Library, Saint James MN p. 1198
Watseka Public Library, Watseka IL p. 659
Watson Chapel Public Library, *see* Pine Bluff & Jefferson County Library System, Pine Bluff AR p. 107
Watson Eugene P Memorial Library, *see* Northwestern State University Libraries, Natchitoches LA p. 900
Watson-Griffith Library, *see* Mid-Atlantic Christian University, Elizabeth City NC p. 1687
Watson Library, *see* University of Kansas Libraries, Lawrence KS p. 819
Watson Memorial Library, *see* University of Arkansas-Pine Bluff, Pine Bluff AR p. 108
Watson Randolph C Library, *see* Kilgore College, Kilgore TX p. 2205
Watson Sheppard Arthur Library, *see* Wilmington College, Wilmington OH p. 1832
Watson Thomas J Library, *see* Metropolitan Museum of Art, New York NY p. 1591
Watson Thomas J Library of Business & Economics, *see* Columbia University, New York NY p. 1584
Watson Thomas J Research Center Library, *see* IBM Corp, Yorktown Heights NY p. 1668
Watsonville Public Library, Watsonville CA p. 258
Watt Donald B Library & Information Commons, *see* SIT Graduate Institute/SIT Study Abroad, Brattleboro VT p. 2280
Watt, Tieder, Hoffar & Fitzgerald, McLean VA p. 2332
Watts Library Research Center, *see* History Museum of Western Virginia, Roanoke VA p. 2344
Watts Street Baptist Church Library, Durham NC p. 1686
Watzek Aubrey R Library, *see* Lewis & Clark College, Portland OR p. 1892
Waubay Public Library, Waubay SD p. 2085
Waubonsee Community College, Sugar Grove IL p. 652
Waucoma Public Library, Waucoma IA p. 789
Wauconda Area Public Library District, Wauconda IL p. 659
Waukee Public Library, Waukee IA p. 789
Waukegan Public Library, Waukegan IL p. 660
Waukesha County Historical Society & Museum, Waukesha WI p. 2484
Waukesha County Technical College Library, Pewaukee WI p. 2469
Waukesha Memorial Hospital, Waukesha WI p. 2484
Waukesha Public Library, Waukesha WI p. 2484
Waunakee Public Library, Waunakee WI p. 2485
Wauneta Public Library, Wauneta NE p. 1340
Waupaca Area Public Library, Waupaca WI p. 2485
Waupun Correctional Institution Library, Waupun WI p. 2485
Waupun Public Library, Waupun WI p. 2485
Waurika Public Library, Waurika OK p. 1868
Wausau Public Library, *see* Washington County Library, Wausau FL p. 388
Wausaukee Public Library, *see* Marinette County Library System, Wausaukee WI p. 2454
Wauseon Public Library, Wauseon OH p. 1829
Wautoma Public Library, Wautoma WI p. 2486
Wauwatosa Public Library, Wauwatosa WI p. 2486
Waveland-Brown Township Public Library, Waveland IN p. 725
Waveland Public Library, *see* Hancock County Library System, Waveland MS p. 1212
Waverley Community Hub, *see* Thunder Bay Public Library, Thunder Bay ON p. 2685
Waverly Free Library, Waverly NY p. 1661
Waverly Memorial Library, Waverly PA p. 2018
Waverly Public Library, Waverly IL p. 660
Waverly Public Library, Waverly IA p. 789
Waverly Reading Center, Saint Regis Falls NY p. 1635
Wawa Public Library, Wawa ON p. 2703
Waxman Joanne Library, *see* Maine College of Art, Portland ME p. 936
Way Public Library, Perrysburg OH p. 1815
Waycross Campus Library, *see* South Georgia State College, Waycross GA p. 503
Waycross-Ware County Public Library, *see* Okefenokee Regional Library, Waycross GA p. 503
Wayland Baptist University, Plainview TX p. 2227
Wayland Free Library, Wayland NY p. 1661
Wayland Free Public Library, Wayland MA p. 1063
Wayne City Public Library, Wayne City IL p. 660
Wayne College Library, *see* University of Akron Libraries, Orrville OH p. 1811
Wayne Community College Library, Goldsboro NC p. 1690
Wayne County Community College District, Belleville MI p. 1084
Wayne County Community College District, Detroit MI p. 1099
Wayne County Community College, Taylor MI p. 1153
Wayne County Historical Society, Corydon IA p. 742
Wayne County Historical Society Museum Library, Lyons NY p. 1566
Wayne County, Indiana, Historical Museum Library, Richmond IN p. 715
Wayne County Law Library, Wooster OH p. 1833
Wayne County Library, Jesup GA p. 483

Welter Donald R Library, *see* Three Rivers Community College, Norwich CT p. 332
Weltner Philip Library, *see* Oglethorpe University, Atlanta GA p. 465
Welty Eudora Library, *see* Jackson/Hinds Library System, Jackson MS p. 1221
Welty Hope Public Library District, Cerro Gordo IL p. 551
Wembley Public Library, Wembley AB p. 2559
Wenatchee Valley College, Wenatchee WA p. 2395
Wende Correctional Facility Library, Alden NY p. 1485
Wendell Free Library, Wendell MA p. 1064
Wendell Public Library, Wendell ID p. 532
Wenham Museum, Wenham MA p. 1064
Wenonah Free Public Library, Wenonah NJ p. 1452
Wenrich Memorial Library, *see* Landmark Society of Western New York, Inc, Rochester NY p. 1628
Wentworth Institute of Technology, Boston MA p. 1000
Wentworth Samuel H Library, Center Sandwich NH p. 1357
Wentz A R Library, *see* United Lutheran Seminary, Gettysburg PA p. 1936
Werner Blanche K Public Library, Trinity TX p. 2249
Werner Bud Memorial Library, Steamboat Springs CO p. 295
Werner Jack Memorial Library, *see* Alaska Vocational Technical Center, Seward AK p. 50
Wernersville Public Library, Wernersville PA p. 2019
Wertz Art & Architecture Library, *see* Miami University Libraries, Oxford OH p. 1812
Wescoat Herbert Memorial Library, McArthur OH p. 1801
Wesley Biblical Seminary Library, Ridgeland MS p. 1232
Wesley Public Library, Wesley IA p. 790
Wesley Susie Memorial, *see* Robinson Public Library District, Flat Rock IL p. 640
Wesley Theological Seminary Library, Washington DC p. 381
Wesleyan Church, Fishers IN p. 682
Wesleyan College, Macon GA p. 487
Wesleyan University, Middletown CT p. 322
WESP-DHH Educational Resource Library, *see* Wisconsin School for the Deaf, Delavan WI p. 2431
Wessels Library, *see* Newberry College, Newberry SC p. 2066
Wessington Public Library, Wessington SD p. 2085
Wessington Springs Carnegie Library, Wessington Springs SD p. 2085
West Acton Citizen's Library, West Acton MA p. 1065
West Allis Public Library, West Allis WI p. 2487
West Babylon Public Library, West Babylon NY p. 1661
West Baton Rouge Parish Library, Port Allen LA p. 906
West Bend Community Memorial Library, West Bend WI p. 2487
West Bend Public Library, West Bend IA p. 790
West Biloxi Library, *see* Harrison County Library System, Biloxi MS p. 1218
West Blocton Public Library, West Blocton AL p. 39
West Bloomfield Township Public Library, West Bloomfield MI p. 1158
West Bonner Library District, Priest River ID p. 529
West Branch District Library, West Branch MI p. 1159
West Branch Public Library, West Branch IA p. 790
West Bridgewater Public Library, West Bridgewater MA p. 1065
West Burke Public Library, West Burke VT p. 2298
West Buxton Public Library, Buxton ME p. 920
West Caldwell Public Library, West Caldwell NJ p. 1452
West Carroll Parish Library, Oak Grove LA p. 905
West Central Minnesota Historical Research Center, Morris MN p. 1189
West Charleston Library, *see* Las Vegas-Clark County Library District, Las Vegas NV p. 1347
West Chester Public Library, West Chester PA p. 2020
West Chester University, West Chester PA p. 2020
West Chicago Public Library District, West Chicago IL p. 660
West Concord Public Library, West Concord MN p. 1207
West Custer County Library District, Westcliffe CO p. 298
West Dade Regional, *see* Miami-Dade Public Library System, Miami FL p. 424
West Dennis Free Public Library, West Dennis MA p. 1065
West Deptford Free Public Library, West Deptford NJ p. 1452
West Des Moines Public Library, West Des Moines IA p. 791
West Elmira Library, *see* Chemung County Library District, Elmira NY p. 1530
West End Library, Laurelton PA p. 1953
West End Public Library, *see* Industry Public Library, Industry TX p. 2202
West End Synagogue, Nashville TN p. 2122
West Eunice & James L Library, *see* Texas Wesleyan University, Fort Worth TX p. 2181
West Fairlee Free Public Library, West Fairlee VT p. 2298
West Falmouth Library, West Falmouth MA p. 1065
West Fargo Public Library, West Fargo ND p. 1741
West Feliciana Parish Library, Saint Francisville LA p. 907
West Florida Public Library, Pensacola FL p. 437
West Fork Municipal Library, West Fork AR p. 112
West Frankfort Public Library, West Frankfort IL p. 660
West Georgia Regional Library, Carrollton GA p. 469
West Georgia Technical College, Waco GA p. 502
West Grey Public Library, Durham ON p. 2639
West Hartford Library, West Hartford VT p. 2298
West Hartford Public Library, West Hartford CT p. 345
West Haven Public Library, West Haven CT p. 346
West Helena Library, *see* Phillips-Lee-Monroe Regional Library, West Helena AR p. 98
West Hempstead Public Library, West Hempstead NY p. 1662
West Hennepin County Pioneers Association Library, Long Lake MN p. 1180
West Hills College Lemoore Library, Lemoore CA p. 156
West Hills Community College, Coalinga CA p. 131
West Hurley Public Library, West Hurley NY p. 1662
West Iron District Library, Iron River MI p. 1119
West Irving Library, *see* Irving Public Library, Irving TX p. 2203
West Islip Public Library, West Islip NY p. 1662
West Kendall Regional, *see* Miami-Dade Public Library System, Miami FL p. 424
West Kentucky Community & Technical College, Paducah KY p. 872
West Lafayette Public Library, West Lafayette IN p. 726
West Las Vegas Library, *see* Las Vegas-Clark County Library District, Las Vegas NV p. 1347
West Lawn-Wyomissing Hills Library, West Lawn PA p. 2021
West Lebanon-Pike Township Public Library, West Lebanon IN p. 726
West Liberty Free Public Library, West Liberty IA p. 791
West Liberty University, West Liberty WV p. 2417
West Lincoln Public Library, Smithville ON p. 2678
West Linn Public Library, West Linn OR p. 1902
West Los Angeles College Library, Culver City CA p. 133
West Melbourne Public Library, West Melbourne FL p. 453
West Memphis Public Library, West Memphis AR p. 112
West Milford Township Library, West Milford NJ p. 1453
West New York Public Library, West New York NJ p. 1453
West Newton Public Library, West Newton PA p. 2021
West Nipissing Public Library, Sturgeon Falls ON p. 2682
West Nyack Free Library, West Nyack NY p. 1662
West Orange Public Library, West Orange NJ p. 1453
West Paris Public Library, West Paris ME p. 946
West Park Healthcare Centre, Toronto ON p. 2700
West Perth Public Library, Mitchell ON p. 2659
West Pittston Library, West Pittston PA p. 2021
West Plains Public Library, West Plains MO p. 1286
West Point Public Library, West Point IA p. 791
West Polk Public Library, Benton TN p. 2088
West Public, *see* Mid-Mississippi Regional Library System, West MS p. 1224
West Public Library, West TX p. 2256
West Regional Center Learning Commons, *see* Community College of Philadelphia Library, Philadelphia PA p. 1975
West Routt Library District, Hayden CO p. 285
West Roxbury VA Medical Center, West Roxbury MA p. 1066
West Roy O Library, *see* DePauw University, Greencastle IN p. 687
West Rutland Free Library, West Rutland VT p. 2298
West Saint Petersburg Community Library, *see* Saint Petersburg Public Library, Saint Petersburg FL p. 442
West Salem Public Library, West Salem IL p. 660
West Sangamon Public Library, New Berlin IL p. 624
West Seneca Public Library, West Seneca NY p. 1663
West Shore Community College, Scottville MI p. 1150
West Slope Community Library, Portland OR p. 1895
West Springfield Public Library, West Springfield MA p. 1066
West Stockbridge Public Library, West Stockbridge MA p. 1066
West Texas A&M University, Canyon TX p. 2153
West Tisbury Free Public Library, Vineyard Haven MA p. 1061
West Union Community Library, West Union IA p. 791
West Union District Library, West Union IL p. 661
West Union Public Library, *see* Adams County Public Library, West Union OH p. 1814
West Valley Community College Library, Saratoga CA p. 245
West Vancouver Memorial Library, West Vancouver BC p. 2584
West Virginia & Regional History Center, *see* West Virginia University Libraries, Morgantown WV p. 2410
West Virginia Archives & History Library, Charleston WV p. 2400
West Virginia Junior College Library, Charleston WV p. 2400
West Virginia Legislative Reference Library, Charleston WV p. 2400
West Virginia Library Commission, Charleston WV p. 2401
West Virginia Northern Community College Library, Wheeling WV p. 2417
West Virginia School for the Deaf & Blind Library, Romney WV p. 2413
West Virginia School of Osteopathic Medicine, Lewisburg WV p. 2407
West Virginia Schools for the Deaf & the Blind Library, Romney WV p. 2413
West Virginia State Law Library, Charleston WV p. 2401
West Virginia State University, Institute WV p. 2406
West Virginia University, Charleston WV p. 2401
West Virginia University, Parkersburg WV p. 2411
West Virginia University Institute of Technology, Montgomery WV p. 2408
West Virginia University Libraries, Morgantown WV p. 2409
West Virginia Wesleyan College, Buckhannon WV p. 2399

Weyerhaeuser Charles A Memorial Museum, Little Falls MN p. 1180
Weymouth Public Libraries, Weymouth MA p. 1068
Whale Museum Library, Friday Harbor WA p. 2364
Whalley James E Museum & Library, Portsmouth NH p. 1379
Wharton County Junior College, Wharton TX p. 2256
Wharton County Library, Wharton TX p. 2256
Wharton Public Library, Wharton NJ p. 1454
What Cheer Public Library, What Cheer IA p. 791
Whatcom Community College Library, Bellingham WA p. 2359
Whatcom County Law Library, Bellingham WA p. 2359
Whatcom County Library System, Bellingham WA p. 2359
Wheat Law Library, *see* University of Kansas Libraries, Lawrence KS p. 820
Wheat Ridge Historical Society Library, Wheat Ridge CO p. 298
Wheatland Regional Library, Saskatoon SK p. 2750
Wheatland Township Library, Remus MI p. 1144
Wheatley Phillis, *see* Rochester Public Library, Rochester NY p. 1630
Wheaton College, Wheaton IL p. 662
Wheaton College Library, Norton MA p. 1043
Wheaton Community Library, Wheaton MN p. 1207
Wheaton Franciscan Healthcare - All Saints, Racine WI p. 2472
Wheaton Library, *see* Montgomery County Public Libraries, Silver Spring MD p. 975
Wheaton Public Library, Wheaton IL p. 662
Wheeler County Library, *see* Ocmulgee Regional Library System, Alamo GA p. 477
Wheeler Edith Memorial Library, Monroe CT p. 323
Wheeler J C Public Library, Martin MI p. 1131
Wheeler Katie Library, *see* OC Public Libraries, Irvine CA p. 239
Wheeler Library, North Stonington CT p. 331
Wheeler Library, *see* Otero Junior College, La Junta CO p. 287
Wheeler Memorial Library, Orange MA p. 1044
Wheeler Public Library, Wheeler TX p. 2257
Wheeling Jesuit University, Wheeling WV p. 2418
Wheelwright Mary Cabot Research Library, *see* Wheelwright Museum of the American Indian, Santa Fe NM p. 1477
Wheelwright Museum of the American Indian, Santa Fe NM p. 1477
Whelden Memorial Library, West Barnstable MA p. 1065
Whippanong Library, Whippany NJ p. 1455
Whipple Ethel L Memorial Library, Los Fresnos TX p. 2213
Whipple Free Library, New Boston NH p. 1375
Whistler Public Library, Whistler BC p. 2584
Whitaker Library, *see* Chowan University, Murfreesboro NC p. 1705
Whitaker Pauline Library, *see* Northwest Arkansas Community College, Bentonville AR p. 91
Whitbourne Public Library, Whitbourne NL p. 2611
Whitby Public Library, Whitby ON p. 2703
Whitchurch-Stouffville Public Library, Stouffville ON p. 2681
White & Case Law Library, New York NY p. 1604
White & Case LLP, Washington DC p. 381
White & Williams, LLP, Philadelphia PA p. 1989
White Center Library, *see* King County Library System, Seattle WA p. 2366
White City Public Library, White City KS p. 842
White Cloud Community Library, White Cloud MI p. 1159
White County Public Library, Cleveland GA p. 471
White County Public Library, Sparta TN p. 2127
White County Regional Library System, Searcy AR p. 109
White Earth Tribal & Community College Library, Mahnomen MN p. 1181
White Edward R & Minnie D Memorial Library, *see* Auglaize County Libraries, Waynesfield OH p. 1828
White Ernest Miller Library, *see* Louisville Presbyterian Theological Seminary, Louisville KY p. 866
White Fox Public Library, *see* Wapiti Regional Library, White Fox SK p. 2746
White Frances Hamilton Art Reference Library, *see* Mingei International Museum, San Diego CA p. 215
White Francis Beach Library, *see* New Hampshire Audubon, Concord NH p. 1359
White G W Blunt, *see* Mystic Seaport Museum, Mystic CT p. 324
White Hall Public Library, Whitehall AL p. 40
White Hall Public Library, *see* Pine Bluff & Jefferson County Library System, White Hall AR p. 107
White Hall Township Library, White Hall IL p. 662
White Haven Area Community Library, White Haven PA p. 2021
White House Public Library, White House TN p. 2129
White Hugh A & Edna C Library, *see* Spring Arbor University, Spring Arbor MI p. 1152
White James Herbert Library, *see* Mississippi Valley State University, Itta Bena MS p. 1221
White James Library, *see* Andrews University, Berrien Springs MI p. 1085
White James Memorial Library, East Freetown MA p. 1016
White Joe E Library, *see* Carl Albert State College, Poteau OK p. 1860
White Lake Community Library, Whitehall MI p. 1159
White Lake Township Library, White Lake MI p. 1159
White Maxine Public Library, *see* Sutherland Public Library, Sutherland NE p. 1337
White Memorial Chemistry Library, *see* University of Maryland Libraries, College Park MD p. 963
White Memorial Medical Center, Los Angeles CA p. 170
White Mountain Library, *see* Sweetwater County Library System, Rock Springs WY p. 2495
White Mountains Community College, Berlin NH p. 1355
White Oak Library, *see* Montgomery County Public Libraries, Silver Spring MD p. 975
White Oak Library District, Romeoville IL p. 643
White Peter Public Library, Marquette MI p. 1130
White Pigeon Township Library, White Pigeon MI p. 1159
White Pine County Library, Ely NV p. 1345
White Pine Library, Stanton MI p. 1152
White Pine Library Cooperative (N), Caro MI p. 2768
White Pine Public Library, White Pine TN p. 2129
White Plains Public Library, White Plains NY p. 1665
White River Library, *see* Johnson County Public Library, Greenwood IN p. 686
White River Public Library, White River ON p. 2704
White River Regional Library, Mountain View AR p. 105
White River Valley Museum Research Library, Auburn WA p. 2358
White Robert M Memorial Library, *see* Main Line Health, Paoli Hospital, Paoli PA p. 1973
White Rock Library, *see* Fraser Valley Regional Library, White Rock BC p. 2562
White Salmon Valley Community Library, *see* Fort Vancouver Regional Library District, White Salmon WA p. 2391
White Sam Library, *see* Lovelace Respiratory Research Institute, Albuquerque NM p. 1461
White Sands Test Facility Technical Library, *see* NASA, Las Cruces NM p. 1471
White Settlement Public Library, White Settlement TX p. 2257
White Smith Memorial Library, Jackson AL p. 23
White Springs Public Library, *see* Suwannee River Regional Library, White Springs FL p. 419
White Sulphur Springs Public Library, White Sulphur Springs WV p. 2418
White William Allen Library, *see* Emporia State University, Emporia KS p. 807
White William F Jr Library, *see* Del Mar College, Corpus Christi TX p. 2160
White William M Business Library, *see* University of Colorado Boulder, Boulder CO p. 268
Whitebird Community Library, Whitebird ID p. 533
Whitecourt & District Public Library, Whitecourt AB p. 2559
Whitefield Public Library, Whitefield NH p. 1384
Whitefish Bay Public Library, Whitefish Bay WI p. 2488
Whitefish Township Community Library, Paradise MI p. 1140
Whiteford, Taylor & Preston, LLP, Baltimore MD p. 958
Whitehall Community Library, *see* Jefferson County Library System, Whitehall MT p. 1289
Whitehall Free Library, Whitehall NY p. 1665
Whitehall Public Library, Pittsburgh PA p. 1997
Whitehall Public Library, Whitehall WI p. 2488
Whitehall Township Public Library, Whitehall PA p. 2021
Whitehaven Center Library, *see* Southwest Tennessee Community College, Memphis TN p. 2115
Whitehead Alfred Music Library, *see* Mount Allison University Libraries & Archives, Sackville NB p. 2604
Whitehead Charles Wewahitchka Public Library, *see* Northwest Regional Library System, Wewahitchka FL p. 436
Whitehead Elizabeth Augustus Library, *see* Whitehead Institute for Biomedical Research, Cambridge MA p. 1009
Whitehead Institute for Biomedical Research, Cambridge MA p. 1009
Whitehorse Public, *see* Department of Community Services, Government of Yukon, Whitehorse YT p. 2758
Whitehouse Community Library, Inc, Whitehouse TX p. 2257
Whiteriver Public Library, Whiteriver AZ p. 84
Whitesboro Public Library, Whitesboro TX p. 2257
Whitesburg Public Library, *see* West Georgia Regional Library, Whitesburg GA p. 470
Whitestone Community Library, *see* Queens Library, Whitestone NY p. 1556
Whitesville Public Library, Whitesville NY p. 1665
Whitetop Public, *see* Wythe-Grayson Regional Library, Whitetop VA p. 2326
Whitewater Memorial Library, Whitewater KS p. 842
Whitewater Region Public Library, Beachburg ON p. 2630
Whitewater Region Public Library, Foresters Falls ON p. 2642
Whitewood Public Library, Whitewood SD p. 2085
Whitewright Public Library, Whitewright TX p. 2257
Whitfield Bryan W Jr, *see* Harlan County Public Libraries, Harlan KY p. 858
Whitfield Henry State Museum, Guilford CT p. 315
Whitfield-Murray Historical Society, Dalton GA p. 474
Whiting Forensic Institute Library, Middletown CT p. 323
Whiting Library, Chester VT p. 2282
Whiting Public Library, Whiting IN p. 726
Whiting Public Library, Whiting IA p. 791
Whitingham Free Public Library, Jacksonville VT p. 2286
Whitinsville Social Library, Whitinsville MA p. 1068
Whitley County Library, Williamsburg KY p. 877
Whitman College, Walla Walla WA p. 2393
Whitman County Rural Library District, Colfax WA p. 2362
Whitman Memorial Library, Bryant Pond ME p. 919
Whitman Public Library, Whitman MA p. 1069
Whitman Stanley House Library, Farmington CT p. 313
Whitman Walt Birthplace Association, Huntington Station NY p. 1550
Whitman Walt, *see* Brooklyn Public Library, Brooklyn NY p. 1504
Whitmire Memorial, *see* Newberry County Library System, Whitmire SC p. 2066

Williams Sheridan & John Eddie, *see* Baylor University Libraries, Waco TX p. 2253
Williams Sue Cowan, *see* Central Arkansas Library System, Little Rock AR p. 101
Williamsburg Community Library, Williamsburg KS p. 844
Williamsburg County Library, Kingstree SC p. 2063
Williamsburg Public Library, Williamsburg IA p. 792
Williamsburg Public Library, Williamsburg PA p. 2023
Williamsburg Regional Library, Williamsburg VA p. 2353
Williamsburg Technical College Library, Kingstree SC p. 2063
Williamsfield Public Library, Williamsfield IL p. 663
Williamson County Center Library, *see* Columbia State Community College, Franklin TN p. 2094
Williamson County Public Library, Franklin TN p. 2098
Williamson Library, *see* Southeastern Community College, Whiteville NC p. 1722
Williamson Public Library, Williamson NY p. 1665
Williamson Public Library, Williamson WV p. 2418
Williamsport Memorial, *see* Washington County Free Library, Williamsport MD p. 968
Williamsport-Washington Township Public Library, Williamsport IN p. 726
Williamston Library, *see* Capital Area District Libraries, Williamston MI p. 1124
Williamstown Historical Museum Library, Williamstown MA p. 1069
Williamstown Library, Williamstown NY p. 1666
Williamsville Public Library & Museum, Williamsville IL p. 663
Williford Branch, *see* Sharp County Library, Williford AR p. 97
Willimantic Public Library, Willimantic CT p. 347
Willingboro Public Library, Willingboro NJ p. 1455
Willington Public Library, Willington CT p. 347
Willis Mary Library, *see* Bartram Trail Regional Library, Washington GA p. 502
Williston Community Library, Williston ND p. 1741
Williston Emily Memorial Library, Easthampton MA p. 1016
Williston Park Public Library, Williston Park NY p. 1666
Williston Public, *see* Levy County Public Library System, Williston FL p. 387
Williston State College, Williston ND p. 1741
Willkie Farr & Gallagher LLP, New York NY p. 1604
Willmar Public Library, Willmar MN p. 1208
Willoughby-Eastlake Public Library, Eastlake OH p. 1783
Willow Branch Township Library, Cisco IL p. 572
Willow Public Library, Willow AK p. 52
Willow Springs Public Library, Willow Springs MO p. 1286
Willowbrook Library, *see* County of Los Angeles Public Library, Los Angeles CA p. 138
Willows Public Library, Willows CA p. 259
Wills Eye Hospital, Philadelphia PA p. 1989
Willson Wicklund Research Center, *see* Olmsted County Historical Society, Rochester MN p. 1194
Wilmer Cutler Pickering Hale & Dorr LLP Library, Washington DC p. 381
Wilmer Memorial Medical Library, *see* Abington Memorial Hospital, Abington PA p. 1903
WilmerHale Library, Boston MA p. 1001
Wilmette Historical Museum, Wilmette IL p. 663
Wilmette Public Library District, Wilmette IL p. 663
Wilmington College, Wilmington OH p. 1832
Wilmington Memorial Library, Wilmington MA p. 1070
Wilmington Public Library, Wilmington DE p. 358
Wilmington Public Library District, Wilmington IL p. 663
Wilmington Public Library of Clinton County, Wilmington OH p. 1832
Wilmington University Library, New Castle DE p. 354
Wilmot Public Library, Wilmot NH p. 1384
WiLS (N), Madison WI p. 2777
Wilshire Boulevard Temple, Los Angeles CA p. 170
Wilson Anne Potter Music Library, *see* Vanderbilt University, Nashville TN p. 2122
Wilson Carolyn Munro Learning Resources Center, *see* Mayland Community College, Spruce Pine NC p. 1717
Wilson College, Chambersburg PA p. 1921
Wilson Community College Library, Wilson NC p. 1724
Wilson Community Library, Wilson NY p. 1666
Wilson County Historical Commission Archives, *see* Wilson County Public Libraries, Floresville TX p. 2177
Wilson County Historical Society Museum Library, Fredonia KS p. 809
Wilson County Public Libraries, Floresville TX p. 2177
Wilson County Public Library, Wilson NC p. 1724
Wilson Curtis Laws Library, Rolla MO p. 1268
Wilson Eleanor N, *see* Kern County Library, Bakersfield CA p. 120
Wilson Elvin & Betty Library, *see* University of La Verne, La Verne CA p. 155
Wilson Garnet A Public Library of Pike County, Waverly OH p. 1829
Wilson Isaiah W Memorial, *see* Western Counties Regional Library, Digby NS p. 2624
Wilson Jennifer Ann Dental Library, *see* University of Southern California Libraries, Los Angeles CA p. 170
Wilson Jodie, *see* Greenwood-Leflore Public Library System, Greenwood MS p. 1217
Wilson Memorial Library, Keota IA p. 763
Wilson Ornithological Society, Ann Arbor MI p. 1081
Wilson Public, *see* Mississippi County Library System, Wilson AR p. 91
Wilson Public Library, Cozad NE p. 1311
Wilson Public Library, *see* Southern Oklahoma Library System, Wilson OK p. 1841
Wilson Sam T Public Library, Arlington TN p. 2087
Wilson Seth Library, *see* Ozark Christian College, Joplin MO p. 1254
Wilson Seymour, *see* New Haven Free Public Library, New Haven CT p. 326
Wilson, Sonsini, Goodrich & Rosati, Palo Alto CA p. 192
Wilson Woodrow, *see* Fairfax County Public Library, Falls Church VA p. 2316
Wilson Woodrow International Center for Scholars Library, Washington DC p. 381
Wilson Woodrow Presidential Library & Museum, Staunton VA p. 2347
Wilsonville Public Library, Wilsonville NE p. 1341
Wilsonville Public Library, Wilsonville OR p. 1902
Wilton Free Public Library, Wilton ME p. 946
Wilton Library Association, Wilton CT p. 347
Wilton Public & Gregg Free Library, Wilton NH p. 1384
Wilton Public Library, Wilton IA p. 792
Wilton Public Library, Wilton WI p. 2489
Wimberley Village Library, Wimberley TX p. 2258
Wimberly S E Library, *see* Florida Atlantic University, Boca Raton FL p. 385
Wimodaughsian Free Library, Canisteo NY p. 1513
Winchester Community Library, Winchester IN p. 727
Winchester Engineering & Analytical Center Library, *see* United States Food & Drug Administration, Winchester MA p. 1070
Winchester Historical Society Library, Winsted CT p. 349
Winchester Public Library, Winchester IL p. 663
Winchester Public Library, Winchester KS p. 844
Winchester Public Library, Winchester MA p. 1070
Winchester Public Library, Winchester WI p. 2489
Windber Public Library, Windber PA p. 2024
Windels Marx Lane & Mittendorf, LLP Library, New York NY p. 1604
Winder Public Library, *see* Piedmont Regional Library System, Winder GA p. 483
Windham Free Library Association, Windham CT p. 348
Windham Kathryn Tucker Library & Museum, *see* Coastal Alabama Community College, Thomasville AL p. 6
Windham Public Library, Windham ME p. 946
Windham Public Library, Windham NY p. 1666
Windham Textile & History Museum, Willimantic CT p. 347
Windham Town Library, Windham VT p. 2299
Winding Rivers Library System, West Salem WI p. 2487
Windmill Library & District Headquarters, *see* Las Vegas-Clark County Library District, Las Vegas NV p. 1346
Windom Public Library, Windom MN p. 1208
Windsor Free Public Library, Windsor MA p. 1070
Windsor Historical Society Library, Windsor CT p. 348
Windsor Locks Public Library, Windsor Locks CT p. 348
Windsor Park Community Library, *see* Queens Library, Bayside NY p. 1556
Windsor Public, *see* Blackwater Regional Library, Windsor VA p. 2313
Windsor Public Library, Windsor CT p. 348
Windsor Public Library, Windsor VT p. 2299
Windsor Public Library, Windsor ON p. 2704
Windsor Regional Hospital, Windsor ON p. 2705
Windsor Regional Library, *see* Sonoma County Library, Windsor CA p. 204
Windsor Storm Memorial Public Library District, Windsor IL p. 663
Windward Campus, Barth Learning Resource Center, *see* Del Mar College, Corpus Christi TX p. 2160
Windward Community College Library, *see* University of Hawaii, Kaneohe HI p. 513
Windwood Presbyterian Church Library, Houston TX p. 2200
Wine Sherwin Library & Pivnick Library, *see* Congregation for Humanistic Judaism, Farmington Hills MI p. 1104
Winfield Community Library, Winfield AB p. 2560
Winfield Public Library, Winfield IL p. 663
Winfield Public Library, Winfield IA p. 792
Winfield Public Library, Winfield KS p. 845
Winfield Public Library, Winfield TN p. 2130
Winfield Public Library, *see* Northwest Regional Library, Winfield AL p. 40
Post Winfred L & Elizabeth C Foundation, Joplin MO p. 1254
Wingate University, Wingate NC p. 1724
Winhall Memorial Library, Bondville VT p. 2279
Winkelpleck Odon Public Library, Odon IN p. 712
Winkler County Library, Kermit TX p. 2205
Winkler Henry R, *see* University of Cincinnati Libraries, Cincinnati OH p. 1765
Winn Army Community Hospital Medical Library, *see* United States Army, Fort Stewart GA p. 479
Winn Correctional Center Library, Winnfield LA p. 912
Winn Parish Library, Winnfield LA p. 912
Winnebago County Court House, Oshkosh WI p. 2468
Winnebago County Law Library, Rockford IL p. 642
Winnebago Public Library District, Winnebago IL p. 664
Winneconne Public Library, Winneconne WI p. 2489
Winnefox Library System, Oshkosh WI p. 2468
Winner Bette Public Library, Gillam MB p. 2587
Winnetka-Northfield Public Library District, Winnetka IL p. 664
Winnett School Library, *see* Petroleum County Community Library, Winnett MT p. 1304
Winnipeg Art Gallery, Winnipeg MB p. 2596
Winnipeg Public Library, Winnipeg MB p. 2596
Winona County Historical Society, Winona MN p. 1209
Winona Public Library, Winona MN p. 1209
Winona State University, Winona MN p. 1209
Winooski Memorial Library, Winooski VT p. 2299
Winslow Medical Library, *see* Meadville Medical Center, Meadville PA p. 1960
Winslow Public Library, Winslow AZ p. 85
Winslow Public Library, Winslow ME p. 946
Winsted Public Library, Winsted MN p. 1209
Winston & Strawn Library, Houston TX p. 2200

Woodenlegs Dr John Memorial Library, *see* Chief Dull Knife College, Lame Deer MT p. 1298
Woodford County Historical Society, Versailles KY p. 876
Woodford County Library, Versailles KY p. 876
Woodgate Free Library, Woodgate NY p. 1667
Woodhaven Community Library, *see* Queens Library, Woodhaven NY p. 1556
Woodland Community Library, *see* Fort Vancouver Regional Library District, Woodland WA p. 2391
Woodland Park Public Library, *see* Rampart Library District, Woodland Park CO p. 298
Woodland Public Library, Woodland CA p. 260
Woodland Public Library, Baileyville ME p. 915
Woodlands Library Cooperative, Albion MI p. 1076
Woodlawn Library, Wilmington DE p. 358
Woodman Astronomical Library, *see* University of Wisconsin-Madison, Madison WI p. 2452
Woodmere Art Museum Library, Philadelphia PA p. 1989
Woodmont Library, *see* King County Library System, Des Moines WA p. 2366
Woodridge Public Library, Woodridge IL p. 664
Woodruff Community Library, Woodruff AZ p. 85
Woodruff Health Sciences Center Library, *see* Emory University Libraries, Atlanta GA p. 463
Woodruff Memorial Library, La Junta CO p. 287
Woodruff Robert W Library, *see* Atlanta University Center, Atlanta GA p. 462
Woodruff Robert W Library, *see* Emory University Libraries, Atlanta GA p. 463
Woodruff, Spradlin & Smart Library, Costa Mesa CA p. 133
Woods Alice Sunizona Library, *see* Cochise County Library District, Pearce AZ p. 56
Woods Hole Laboratory Library, *see* Northeast Fisheries Science Center, Woods Hole MA p. 1071
Woods Hole Oceanographic Institution Data Library & Archives, *see* Marine Biological Laboratory, Woods Hole MA p. 1071
Woods Hole Public Library, Woods Hole MA p. 1071
Woods Memorial, *see* Pima County Public Library, Tucson AZ p. 83
Woods Memorial Library, Barre MA p. 987
Woods Memorial Presbyterian Church Library, Severna Park MD p. 977
Woods Rogers, PLC, Roanoke VA p. 2346
Woodside Community Library, *see* Queens Library, Woodside NY p. 1556
Woodside Library, *see* San Mateo County Library, Woodside CA p. 236
Woodson Carter G, *see* Gary Public Library, Gary IN p. 686
Woodson Carter G Regional, *see* Chicago Public Library, Chicago IL p. 557
Woodson Harrie P Memorial Library, Caldwell TX p. 2152
Woodstock History Center, Woodstock VT p. 2300
Woodstock Hospital Regional Library Services (N), Woodstock ON p. 2778
Woodstock Public, *see* Sequoyah Regional Library System, Woodstock GA p. 469
Woodstock Public Library, Woodstock IL p. 665
Woodstock Public Library, Woodstock ON p. 2705
Woodstock Public Library District, Woodstock NY p. 1667
Woodstock Theological Center Library, Washington DC p. 381
Woodstown-Pilesgrove Public Library, Woodstown NJ p. 1456
Woodsville Free Public Library, Woodsville NH p. 1385
Woodville Community Library, Woodville WI p. 2490
Woodville Public Library, Woodville AL p. 40
Woodville Public Library, *see* Wilkinson County Library System, Woodville MS p. 1236
Woodward Felix G Library, *see* Austin Peay State University, Clarksville TN p. 2092
Woodward Library, *see* University of British Columbia Library, Vancouver BC p. 2580
Woodward Memorial Library, LeRoy NY p. 1562
Woodward Park Regional, *see* Fresno County Public Library, Fresno CA p. 146
Woodward Public Library, Woodward IA p. 793
Woodward Public Library, Woodward OK p. 1869
Woodworth Consolidated Library, *see* United States Army, Fort Gordon GA p. 479
Woodyard Dora Bee Memorial Library, Elizabeth WV p. 2402
Woolaroc Museum Library, Bartlesville OK p. 1842
Woolfolk Margaret Library, *see* Crittenden County Library, Marion AR p. 104
Woolmarket Library, *see* Harrison County Library System, Biloxi MS p. 1218
Woolworth Community Library, Jal NM p. 1470
Woolworth Richard W Library & Research Center, *see* Stonington Historical Society, Stonington CT p. 339
Woonsocket City Library, Woonsocket SD p. 2086
Woonsocket Harris Public Library, Woonsocket RI p. 2044
Wootters J H Crockett Public Library, Crockett TX p. 2161
Wor-Wic Community College, Salisbury MD p. 977
Worcester Art Museum Library, Worcester MA p. 1072
Worcester County Library, Snow Hill MD p. 978
Worcester Historical Museum, Worcester MA p. 1072
Worcester Law Library, *see* Massachusetts Court System, Worcester MA p. 1072
Worcester Polytechnic Institute, Worcester MA p. 1073
Worcester Public Library, Worcester MA p. 1073
Worcester Recovery Cneter & Hospital Library, Worcester MA p. 1073
Worcester-Schenevus Library, Worcester NY p. 1667
Worcester State University, Worcester MA p. 1073
Worcester Talking Book Library, *see* Worcester Public Library, Worcester MA p. 1073
Worch Memorial Public Library, Versailles OH p. 1827
Word Cecil B Learning Resources Center, *see* Northeast Alabama Community College, Rainsville AL p. 34
Worden Memorial Library, *see* Barclay College, Haviland KS p. 812
Worden Public Library District, Worden IL p. 665
Working Men's Institute Museum & Library, New Harmony IN p. 709
Workman & Temple Family Homestead Museum Library, City of Industry CA p. 130
Workplace Safety & Insurance Board, Toronto ON p. 2700
World Bank Group Library, Washington DC p. 382
World Book Publishing, Chicago IL p. 570
World Research Foundation Library, Sedona AZ p. 78
World Resources Institute, Washington DC p. 382
WW II PT Boats Museum Archives & Library, *see* PT Boats, Inc, Memphis TN p. 2114
Worley David Library, *see* Austin Graduate School of Theology, Austin TX p. 2138
Wornstaff Memorial Public Library, Ashley OH p. 1747
Woron Mykola Library & Archives, *see* Saint Volodymyr's Cultural Centre, Calgary AB p. 2529
Worsley & District Public Library, Worsley AB p. 2560
Worth County Library, Sylvester GA p. 498
Worth Pinkham Memorial Library, Ho-Ho-Kus NJ p. 1408
Worth Public Library District, Worth IL p. 665
Worthen Library, South Hero VT p. 2294
Worthington Biochemical Corp Library, Lakewood NJ p. 1411
Worthington Historical Society Library, Worthington OH p. 1833
Worthington-Jefferson Township Public Library, Worthington IN p. 727
Worthington Libraries, Worthington OH p. 1833
Worthington Library, Worthington MA p. 1073
Worthington West Franklin Community Library, Worthington PA p. 2024
Wosk Yosef Library & Resource Centre, Vancouver BC p. 2582
WPLC (N), *see* Wisconsin Public Library Consortium, Madison WI p. 2777
Wrangell Public Library, *see* Ingle Irene Public Library, Wrangell AK p. 53
Wray Public Library, Wray CO p. 299
Wregie Memorial Library, Oxford Junction IA p. 776
Wren Memorial Library, *see* Chatham County Public Libraries, Siler City NC p. 1708
Wren Public Library, *see* Tombigbee Regional Library System, Aberdeen MS p. 1236
Wrentham Public Library, Wrentham AB p. 2560
Wright & Greenhill PC, Austin TX p. 2144
Wright Cliff, *see* Saskatoon Public Library, Saskatoon SK p. 2749
Wright County Library, Hartville MO p. 1248
Wright Edelman Marian Public Library, *see* Marlboro County Library System, Bennettsville SC p. 2047
Wright Frank Lloyd Trust, Oak Park IL p. 628
Wright Hillman, *see* Montmorency County Public Libraries, Hillman MI p. 1081
Wright Institute Library, Berkeley CA p. 124
Wright John J Library, *see* La Roche University, Pittsburgh PA p. 1994
Wright John Shepard Memorial Library, *see* Indiana Academy of Science, Indianapolis IN p. 692
Wright Library, *see* Vernon College, Vernon TX p. 2252
Wright Memorial Public Library, Oakwood OH p. 1810
Wright-Potts Library, *see* Voorhees University, Denmark SC p. 2058
Wright Richard Library, *see* Jackson/Hinds Library System, Jackson MS p. 1222
Wright Shirley M Memorial Library, Trempealeau WI p. 2481
Wright Solomon Library, Pownal VT p. 2292
Wright State University, Celina OH p. 1757
Wright State University Libraries, Dayton OH p. 1780
Wright Wilbur College Library, *see* City Colleges of Chicago, Chicago IL p. 559
WRLC (N), *see* Washington Research Library Consortium, Upper Marlboro MD p. 2766
WSU Campus of Applied Sciences & Technology, Wichita KS p. 844
WVLS (N), *see* Wisconsin Valley Library Service, Wausau WI p. 2777
Wyalusing Public Library, Wyalusing PA p. 2024
Wyandanch Public Library, Wyandanch NY p. 1667
Wyandotte County Historical Museum, Bonner Springs KS p. 799
Wyandotte County Law Library, Kansas City KS p. 817
Wyckoff Heights Medical Center, Brooklyn NY p. 1506
Wyckoff Public Library, Wyckoff NJ p. 1456
WYLD Network (N), Cheyenne WY p. 2777
Wylie Zula Bryant Public Library, Cedar Hill TX p. 2154
Wyllie John Cook Library, *see* University of Virginia's College at Wise, Wise VA p. 2355
Wylliesburg Community, *see* Charlotte County Library, Wylliesburg VA p. 2309
Wymore Public Library, Wymore NE p. 1341
Wynnewood Public Library, Wynnewood OK p. 1869
Wyocena Public Library, Wyocena WI p. 2490
Wyoming Correctional Facility, Attica NY p. 1488
Wyoming County Public Library, Pineville WV p. 2412
Wyoming Department of Corrections, Riverton WY p. 2498
Wyoming Free Circulating Library, Wyoming NY p. 1667
Wyoming Free Library, Wyoming PA p. 2025
Wyoming Game & Fish Department Library, Casper WY p. 2492
Wyoming Honor Farm Library, *see* Wyoming Department of Corrections, Riverton WY p. 2498

PERSONNEL INDEX

Abeita, Jan A, Mgr, Access Serv, Oregon Institute of Technology Library, 3201 Campus Dr, Klamath Falls, OR, 97601-8801. Tel: 541-885-1772. p. 1883

Abel, Cynthia, ILL Spec, Creighton University, Health Sciences Library-Learning Resource Center, 2770 Webster St, Omaha, NE, 68178-0210. Tel: 402-280-5108. p. 1328

Abel, Jocelyn, Head, Tech Serv, Lancaster Bible College, Teague Learning Commons, 901 Eden Rd, Lancaster, PA, 17601-5036. Tel: 717-569-7071, Ext 5361. p. 1951

Abel, Patty, Librn, Champion Municipal Library, 132A Second St S, Champion, AB, T0L 0R0, CANADA. Tel: 403-897-3099. p. 2531

Abel-Smith, Smitty, Resource Librn, Villa Maria College Library, 240 Pine Ridge Rd, Buffalo, NY, 14225. Tel: 716-961-1864. p. 1511

Abele, Amy, Dir, Ogema Public Library, W 5005 State Rd 86, Ogema, WI, 54459. Tel: 715-767-5130. p. 2466

Abell, Donna, Dir, Libr Serv, Owensboro Community & Technical College Library, Learning Resource Ctr Bldg, 1st Flr, 4800 New Hartford Rd, Owensboro, KY, 42303. Tel: 270-686-4575. p. 871

Abell, Russell, Dir, Pratt Institute Libraries, 200 Willoughby Ave, Brooklyn, NY, 11205-3897. Tel: 718-399-4223. p. 1506

Abella, Elisa, Dir, Miami Dade College, Medical Center Campus Library & Information Resource Center, 950 NW 20th St, Miami, FL, 33127. Tel: 305-237-4498. p. 422

Abeln, Barb, Dir, South Dakota Developmental Center, 17267 W Third St, Redfield, SD, 57469-1001. Tel: 605-472-4210. p. 2081

Abend, Susan, Librn, Sierra Vista Public Library, 2600 E Tacoma, Sierra Vista, AZ, 85635. Tel: 520-458-4225. p. 78

Aber, Suzanne, Chief Info Officer, VPres for Info Serv, Trinity College Library, 300 Summit St, Hartford, CT, 06106. Tel: 860-297-2525. p. 318

Aberle, Jessica, Colls Librn, Research Librn, Harvard Library, Fine Arts Library, Littauer Ctr, 1805 Cambridge St, Cambridge, MA, 02138. Tel: 617-495-3374. p. 1006

Abernathy, Andrea, Dir, University of West Alabama, UWA Station 12, Livingston, AL, 35470. Tel: 205-652-3613. p. 24

Abernathy-Kuck, Gretchen, Dir, Archer Public Library, 105 N Center St, Archer City, TX, 76351. Tel: 940-574-4954. p. 2136

Abernathy-Morris, Jolyce, Circ Mgr, New Lenox Public Library District, 120 Veterans Pkwy, New Lenox, IL, 60451. Tel: 815-485-2605. p. 624

Abernethy, Braegan, Acq, Head, Res, Georgia State University, 100 Decatur St SE, Atlanta, GA, 30303-3202. Tel: 404-413-2796. p. 464

Abero, Gloria, Ch, Clifton Public Library, 292 Piaget Ave, Clifton, NJ, 07011. Tel: 973-772-5500. p. 1397

Abing, Kevin, Archivist, Milwaukee County Historical Society, 910 N Old World Third St, Milwaukee, WI, 53203. Tel: 414-273-7487, 414-273-8288. p. 2459

Abiola, Ufuoma, Head, Sci Libr, Princeton University, Lewis Science Library, Washington Rd, Princeton, NJ, 08544-0001. Tel: 609-258-6004. p. 1437

Able, Nell, Libr Tech 1, SCLHS Saint Joseph Hospital, 1375 E 19th Ave, 3rd Flr, Denver, CO, 80218-1191. Tel: 303-812-3625. p. 277

Abler, Mary, Libr Mgr, New Orleans Public Library, Dr Martin Luther King Jr Library, 1611 Caffin Ave, New Orleans, LA, 70117. Tel: 504-596-2695. p. 903

Ables, Rose, Mrs, Br Mgr, Barton Public Library, Norphlet Public, City Hall Bldg, 101 E Padgett St, Norphlet, AR, 71759. Tel: 870-546-2274. p. 94

Ables, Sharron, Coordr, Copper Valley Community Library, Mile 186 Glenn Hwy, Glennallen, AK, 99588. Tel: 907-822-5427. p. 46

Ables, Venita Ann, Librn, Calhoun County Library, Thornton Public Library, 220 Second St, Thornton, AR, 71766. Tel: 870-352-5990. p. 97

Ablove, Gayle, Librn, Roswell Park Comprehensive Cancer Center, Elm & Carlton Sts, Buffalo, NY, 14263. Tel: 716-845-5966. p. 1510

Abney, Eric, Dir, Fremont Public Library, Seven Jackie Bernier Dr, Fremont, NH, 03044. Tel: 603-895-9543. p. 1364

Abordonado, Valentina, PhD, Actg Dir, Hawaii Pacific University Libraries, 1060 Bishop St, Honolulu, HI, 96813-3192. Tel: 808-544-0210. p. 506

Abou-El-Kheir, Yasmine, Dir, Chicago Theological Seminary, 1407 E 60th St, Chicago, IL, 60637. Tel: 773-896-2450. p. 558

Abou-Farah, Cassandra, Asst Dir, Lawrence Public Library, 51 Lawrence St, Lawrence, MA, 01841. Tel: 978-620-3600. p. 1027

Abougoush, Riya, Library Services Asst, Portage College Library, 9531 94th Ave, Lac La Biche, AB, T0A 2C0, CANADA. Tel: 780-623-5650. p. 2545

Abounader, Angel, Libr Mgr, Piedmont Regional Library System, Commerce Public Library, 1344 S Broad St, Commerce, GA, 30529-2053. Tel: 706-335-5946. p. 482

Abraham, Chelsie, Pub Serv Mgr, Essex County Library, 360 Fairview Ave W, Ste 101, Essex, ON, N8M 1Y3, CANADA. Tel: 519-776-5241. p. 2640

Abraham, Chelsie, Mgr, Libr Heritage Res, Greater Sudbury Public Library, 74 MacKenzie St, Sudbury, ON, P3C 4X8, CANADA. Tel: 705-673-1155. p. 2683

Abraham, Dana, Head, Adult Serv, Coal City Public Library District, 85 N Garfield St, Coal City, IL, 60416. Tel: 815-634-4552. p. 572

Abraham, Latecia, Pub Info Coordr, Medical University of South Carolina Libraries, 171 Ashley Ave, Ste 419, Charleston, SC, 29425-0001. Tel: 843-792-5530. p. 2051

Abraham, Lila J, Sr Ref Librn, Nutter McClennen & Fish LLP, Seaport West, 155 Seaport Blvd, Boston, MA, 02210. Tel: 617-439-2000. p. 999

Abraham, Vanessa, Dir, Groton Public Library, 99 Main St, Groton, MA, 01450. Tel: 978-448-1167. p. 1022

Abrahamsen, Laura, Libr Dir, George Holmes Bixby Memorial Library, 52 Main St, Francestown, NH, 03043-3025. Tel: 603-547-2730. p. 1364

Abrahamson, Michelle, Libr Mgr, Des Moines Public Library, North Side, 3516 Fifth Ave, Des Moines, IA, 50313. Tel: 515-283-4152. p. 746

Abrahamson, Sue, Youth Serv Librn, Waupaca Area Public Library, 107 S Main St, Waupaca, WI, 54981-1521. Tel: 715-258-4414. p. 2485

Abram, Deborah, Libr Mgr, Vedder, Price, 222 N LaSalle, Chicago, IL, 60601. Tel: 312-609-7500. p. 570

Abram, Hannah, Dir, Mary E Seymour Memorial Free Library, 22 N Main St, Stockton, NY, 14784-0432. Tel: 716-595-3323. p. 1646

Abramenko, Igor, Librn, Transport Canada, Civil Aviation, NAS-CRT, Rm 0135, 700 Leigh Capreol St, Dorval, QC, H4Y 1G7, CANADA. Tel: 514-633-3589. p. 2711

Abrams, Ashley, Mgr, County of Los Angeles Public Library, Topanga Library, 122 N Topanga Canyon Blvd, Topanga, CA, 90290. Tel: 310-455-3480. p. 138

Abrams, Harvey, Pres, International Institute for Sport History Library, 237 S Fraser, Ste 732, State College, PA, 16804. Tel: 814-321-4018. p. 2009

Abrams, Israela, Head, Children's Servx, Swampscott Public Library, 61 Burrill St, Swampscott, MA, 01907. Tel: 781-596-8867. p. 1059

Abrams, Whitley, Circ, Libr Asst, Paradise Valley Community College, 18401 N 32nd St, Phoenix, AZ, 85032-1200. Tel: 602-787-7238. p. 71

Abramson, Anne, Foreign & Intl Law Librn, The John Marshall Law School, 300 S State St, 6th Flr, Chicago, IL, 60604. Tel: 312-427-2737. p. 564

Abramson, Dina, Disability Info & Referral Coord, Texas State Library & Archives Commission, 1201 Brazos St, Austin, TX, 78701. Tel: 512-463-5458. p. 2141

Abreu, Darcie, Human Res Mgr, Palatine Public Library District, 700 N North Ct, Palatine, IL, 60067. Tel: 847-907-3600. p. 631

Abreu, Sara, Dir, Inter-American University of Puerto Rico, Barrio San Daniel, Carretera 2, km 80.4, Arecibo, PR, 00614. Tel: 787-878-5475, Ext 2321. p. 2509

Abruzzo, Paul, Ref & Instrul Serv, Instr Coordr, New School, Raymond Fogelman Library, 55 W 13th St, New York, NY, 10011. Tel: 212-229-5307, Ext 3055. p. 1592

Absalom, Kelli, Dir, Info Serv, Orillia Public Library, 36 Mississaga St W, Orillia, ON, L3V 3A6, CANADA. Tel: 705-325-2338. p. 2663

Abt, Mary Jo, Circ Supvr, Putnam Public Library, 225 Kennedy Dr, Putnam, CT, 06260-1691. Tel: 860-963-6826. p. 334

Abu-Zeid, Barbara, Info Serv Coordr, Emory University Libraries, Woodruff Health Sciences Center Library, 1462 Clifton Rd NE, Atlanta, GA, 30322. Tel: 404-727-8727. p. 463

Abuhalimeh, Ameer, Exec Dir, Islamic Da'wah Center Library, 201 Travis St, Houston, TX, 77002. Tel: 713-223-3311. p. 2196

Acadia, Spencer, PhD, Asst Prof, University of Denver, Morgridge College of Education, Katherine A Ruffatto Hall, 1999 E Evans Ave, Denver, CO, 80208. Tel: 303-871-2838. p. 2783

Accardo, Chris, Dir, Weatherford Public Library, 1014 Charles St, Weatherford, TX, 76086. Tel: 817-598-4150. p. 2255

Accola, Dianne, Br Mgr, Scenic Regional Library, New Haven Branch, 200 Douglas St, New Haven, MO, 63068. Tel: 573-237-2189. p. 1283

Acerro, Heather, Head, Youth Serv, Rochester Public Library, 101 Second St SE, Rochester, MN, 55904-3776. Tel: 507-328-2339. p. 1194

Acevedo, Leslie, Dir of Libr Operations, Flint Public Library, 1026 E Kearsley St, Flint, MI, 48503. Tel: 810-249-2046. p. 1105

Acevedo, Marjorie, Assoc Dir, Res & Instruction, Mount Saint Mary's University, J Thomas McCarthy Library, Doheny Campus, Ten Chester Pl, Los Angeles, CA, 90007. Tel: 213-477-275. p. 166

Acevedo, Nicole, Librn, Libr Dir, Kendrick Memorial Library, 301 W Tate, Brownfield, TX, 79316-4387. Tel: 806-637-3848. p. 2150

Acevedo, Pat, Youth Serv Librn, Madison County Public Library, Berea Branch, 319 Chestnut St, Berea, KY, 40403. Tel: 859-986-7112. p. 874

Acevedo, Tamara S, Mgr, Knowledge Mgt, Mgr, Res, Moore & Van Allen PLLC, Bank of America Corporate Ctr, 100 N Tryon, Ste 4700, Charlotte, NC, 28202-4003. Tel: 704-331-1000, 704-331-3746. p. 1680

Acfalle, Marie, Libr Tech, United States Army, Grant Library, 1637 Flint St, Fort Carson, CO, 80913-4105. Tel: 719-526-2350. p. 280

Achee, Christopher, Asst Dir, Ascension Parish Library, 500 Mississippi St, Donaldsonville, LA, 70346. Tel: 225-473-8052. p. 889

Achee, Henri, Librn, Houston Community College - Southeast College, Eastside Campus Library, 6815 Rustic St, Houston, TX, 77087. Tel: 713-718-7050. p. 2194

Acheson, Phoebe, Adult Serv, Ref, Yarmouth Town Libraries, 312 Old Main St, South Yarmouth, MA, 02664. Tel: 508-760-4820, Ext 1314. p. 1055

Achille, Pamela, Asst Dir, Norwell Public Library, 64 South St, Norwell, MA, 02061-2433. Tel: 781-659-2015. p. 1043

Achilles, Elizabeth, Librn, South Ryegate Public Library, Inc, 140 Church St, South Ryegate, VT, 05069. Tel: 802-584-3675. p. 2295

Achipa, Joshua, Libr Dir, Southern Nazarene University, 4115 N College Ave, Bethany, OK, 73008. Tel: 405-491-6351, Ext 8148. p. 1842

Achterman, Douglas, Head Librn, Gavilan College Library, 5055 Santa Teresa Blvd, Gilroy, CA, 95020. Tel: 408-848-4809. p. 148

Acierno, Lou, Dir, Libr Serv, LIM College Library, 216 E 45th St, 2nd Flr, New York, NY, 10017. Tel: 646-218-4126. p. 1590

Acker, Connie, Br Mgr, Mineral County Public Library, Alberton Branch, 701 Railroad Ave, Alberton, MT, 59820. Tel: 406-722-3372. p. 1303

Acker, Jennifer, ILL, Hudson Valley Community College, 80 Vandenburgh Ave, Troy, NY, 12180. Tel: 518-629-7330. p. 1652

Acker Rothenberg, Lisa, Asst Dir, Lincoln Public Library, Three Bedford Rd, Lincoln, MA, 01773. Tel: 781-259-8465, Ext 202. p. 1028

Ackerly, Jean, Dir, Newbury Town Library, Zero Lunt St, Byfield, MA, 01922-1232. Tel: 978-465-0539. p. 1004

Ackerman, Cathy, Br Mgr, Pine Bluff & Jefferson County Library System, Redfield Public Library, 310 Brodie St, Redfield, AR, 72132. Tel: 501-397-5070. p. 107

Ackerman, Erin, Asst Dir, Pub Serv, The College of New Jersey, 2000 Pennington Rd, Ewing, NJ, 08628-1104. Tel: 609-771-2311. p. 1402

Ackerman, Linda, Youth Serv, Portland Public Library of Sumner County, 301 Portland Blvd, Portland, TN, 37148-1229. Tel: 615-325-2279. p. 2124

Ackerman, Rita, Br Mgr, Whitman County Rural Library District, Farmington Branch, E 203 Main St, Farmington, WA, 99128. Tel: 509-287-3302. p. 2362

Ackerman, Wendi, Dep Dir, SUNY Upstate Medical University, 766 Irving Ave, Syracuse, NY, 13210-1602. Tel: 315-464-8141. p. 1650

Ackermann, Jason, Digital Res Coordr, State of Rhode Island, Department of Administration, One Capitol Hill, 2nd Flr, Providence, RI, 02908. Tel: 401-574-9317. p. 2041

Acklin, Valerie, Adult Serv, Bellmore Memorial Library, 2288 Bedford Ave, Bellmore, NY, 11710. Tel: 516-785-2990. p. 1492

Acklin, Valerie, Libr Dir, Gloversville Public Library, 58 E Fulton St, Gloversville, NY, 12078. Tel: 518-725-2819. p. 1539

Acompanado, Gay P, Supvr, Old Dominion University Libraries, Elise N Hofheimer Art Library, Barry Arts Bldg, Rm 2008, 4600 Monarch Way, Norfolk, VA, 23529. Tel: 757-683-4059. p. 2336

Acosta, Migell, Dir, San Diego County Library, MS 070, 5560 Overland Ave, Ste 110, San Diego, CA, 92123. Tel: 858-694-2389. p. 216

Acosta, Ray, Libr Tech, Oxnard College Library, 4000 S Rose Ave, Oxnard, CA, 93033-6699. Tel: 805-986-5150. p. 190

Acosta, Stephenie, Br Mgr, Monmouth County Library, Marlboro Branch, One Library Ct, Marlboro, NJ, 07746-1102. Tel: 732-536-9406. p. 1416

Acree, Eric Kofi, Head of Libr, Cornell University Library, John Henrik Clarke Africana Library, 310 Triphammer Rd, Ithaca, NY, 14850. Tel: 607-255-5229. p. 1551

Actarian, Emanuel, Head, Coll Mgt, New Brunswick Public Library Service (NBPLS), 570 Two Nations Crossing, Ste 2, Fredericton, NB, E3A 0X9, CANADA. Tel: 506-453-2354. p. 2601

Adair, Jessica, Asst Dir, Morgan County Library, 600 N Hunter, Versailles, MO, 65084-1830. Tel: 573-378-5319. p. 1284

Adair, Vivian, Asst Librn, Villisca Public Library, 204 S Third Ave, Villisca, IA, 50864. Tel: 712-826-2452. p. 787

Adair Williams, Catherine, Asst Dir, Verona Public Library, 17 Gould St, Verona, NJ, 07044-1928. Tel: 973-857-4848. p. 1449

Adam, Doris, Br Mgr, San Diego County Library, Lakeside Branch, 9839 Vine St, Lakeside, CA, 92040-3199. Tel: 619-443-1811. p. 217

Adam, Fay, Br Librn, Southeast Regional Library, Bengough Branch, 301 Main St, Bengough, SK, S0C 0K0, CANADA. Tel: 306-268-2022. p. 2753

Adam, Joanne, Libr Dir, Huntington Public Library, 338 Main St, Huntington, NY, 11743. Tel: 631-427-5165, Ext 206. p. 1549

Adamcyk, William, Dir, Milton Public Library, 476 Canton Ave, Milton, MA, 02186-3299. Tel: 617-698-5757. p. 1036

Adami, Donna, Librn, Illinois Prairie District Public Library, Washburn Branch, 102 W Magnolia, Washburn, IL, 61570. Tel: 309-248-7429. p. 617

Adamkiewicz, Pat, Tech Serv, DeKalb Public Library, Haish Memorial Library Bldg, 309 Oak St, DeKalb, IL, 60115-3369. Tel: 815-756-9568. p. 577

Adamo, Marilyn, Adult Programs, Head Ref Librn, Island Trees Public Library, 38 Farmedge Rd, Levittown, NY, 11756. Tel: 516-731-2211. p. 1562

Adamowski, Betsy, Dir, Wheaton Public Library, 225 N Cross St, Wheaton, IL, 60187-5376. Tel: 630-668-1374. p. 662

Adamowski, Catherine, Dep Dir, Joliet Public Library, 150 N Ottawa St, Joliet, IL, 60432. Tel: 815-740-2660. p. 603

Adamowski, Catherine Yanikoski, Dep Dir, Joliet Public Library, Black Road Branch, 3395 Black Rd, Joliet, IL, 60431. Tel: 815-846-6519. p. 603

Adamowski, Mary, Asst Libr Dir, Orland Park Public Library, 14921 Ravinia Ave, Orland Park, IL, 60462. Tel: 708-428-5202. p. 630

Adams, Abigail, Librn, Platt Memorial Library, 279 Main St, Shoreham, VT, 05770. Tel: 802-897-2647. p. 2294

Adams, Aimee, Youth Serv Mgr, Ritter Public Library, 5680 Liberty Ave, Vermilion, OH, 44089. Tel: 440-967-3798. p. 1827

Adams, Aleah, Asst Librn, Madison Public Library, 827 N College Ave, Huntsville, AR, 72740. Tel: 479-738-2754. p. 99

Adams, Alyssa, Libr Support Spec, Allen Community College Library, 1801 N Cottonwood, Iola, KS, 66749-1648. Tel: 620-365-5116, Ext 6235. p. 815

Adams, Amanda, Law Librn, Nipissing District Law Association Library, 360 Plouffe St, North Bay, ON, P1B 9L5, CANADA. Tel: 705-495-3271. p. 2661

Adams, Amelia, Dir, Goose Creek District Library, 220 N Highway Ave, De Land, IL, 61839. Tel: 217-664-3572. p. 576

Adams, Andrea, Asst Dean for Learning Innovations & Design, James Madison University Libraries, 880 Madison Dr, MSC 1704, Harrisonburg, VA, 22807. Tel: 540-568-6568. p. 2324

Adams, Aranda, Head Librn, Bibliotheque Somerset Library, 289 Carlton Ave, Somerset, MB, R0G 2L0, CANADA. Tel: 204-744-2170. p. 2590

Adams, Bailey, Circ & Adult Serv Mgr, Council Bluffs Public Library, 400 Willow Ave, Council Bluffs, IA, 51503-9042. Tel: 712-323-7553, Ext 5418. p. 742

Adams, Barbara, Br Librn, London Public Library, East London, 2016 Dundas St, London, ON, N5V 1R1, CANADA. Tel: 519-451-7600. p. 2654

Adams, Becky, Mgr, Suwannee River Regional Library, Jasper Public Library, 311 Hatley St NE, Jasper, FL, 32052. Tel: 386-792-2285. p. 419

Adams, Betty, Dir, Leanna Hicks Public Library, 1086 Inkster Rd, Inkster, MI, 48141. Tel: 313-563-2822. p. 1118

Adams, Brinda Franceine, Dir, Coalmont Public Library, 7426 State Rte 56, Coalmont, TN, 37313-0334. Tel: 931-592-9373. p. 2094

Adams, Carrie D, Prog Dir, University of Florida Health Science Center-Jacksonville, 653-1 W Eighth St, Jacksonville, FL, 32209-6511. Tel: 904-244-3240. p. 413

Adams, Christine, Co-Dir, Head, Research & Academic Support, Youngstown State University, One University Plaza, Youngstown, OH, 44555-0001. Tel: 330-941-3681. p. 1836

Adams, Cindy, Circ Mgr, Campbell University, 113 Main St, Buies Creek, NC, 27506. Tel: 910-814-5563. p. 1676

Adams, Cori, City Librn, Parowan Public Library, 16 S Main St, Parowan, UT, 84761. Tel: 435-477-3491. p. 2269

Adams, Diane, Libr Dir, International Falls Public Library, 750 Fourth St, International Falls, MN, 56649. Tel: 218-283-8051. p. 1178

Adams, Emily, Instruction & Ref Librn, Walden University Library, 100 Washington Ave S, Ste 900, Minneapolis, MN, 55401. p. 1186

Adams, Eveann, Librn, Tingley Memorial Library, 111 Second St N, Bradenton Beach, FL, 34217. Tel: 941-779-1208. p. 387

Adams, Heidi Sue, Lead Med Librn, Logan Health Medical Library, 310 Sunnyview Lane, Kalispell, MT, 59901. Tel: 406-752-1739. p. 1298

Adams Hilliard, Linda, Dir, Andover Free Library, 40 Main St, Andover, NY, 14806. Tel: 607-478-8442. p. 1487

Adams, Jackie, Dir, Kent County Public Library, 408 High St, Chestertown, MD, 21620-1312. Tel: 410-778-3636. p. 961

Adams, Jalisha, Libr Mgr, Aiken-Bamberg-Barnwell-Edgefield Regional Library, Edgefield County, 105 Courthouse Sq, Edgefield, SC, 29824. Tel: 803-637-4025. p. 2045

Adams, January, Dir, Libr Serv, Franklin Township Free Public Library, 485 DeMott Lane, Somerset, NJ, 08873. Tel: 732-873-8700. p. 1442

Adams, Jennifer, Libr Serv Coordr, Holyoke Community College Library, Donahue Bldg, 2nd Flr, 303 Homestead Ave, Holyoke, MA, 01040-1099. Tel: 413-552-2733. p. 1025

Adams, Jennifer, Libr Dir, Jackson Community College, 2111 Emmons Rd, Jackson, MI, 49201-8399. Tel: 517-796-8622. p. 1119

Adams, Joel, Dir of Finance, Vancouver Island Regional Library, 6250 Hammond Bay Rd, Nanaimo, BC, V9T 6M9, CANADA. Tel: 250-729-2312. p. 2570

Adams, John L, Librn, Jones Day, 2727 N Harwood St, Dallas, TX, 75201-1515. Tel: 214-969-4823. p. 2167

Adams, Julie, Dir, New York Mills Public Library, 30 Main Ave N, New York Mills, MN, 56567-4318. Tel: 218-385-2436. p. 1190

Adams, Julie, Libr Dir, Tennessee Wesleyan College, 23 Coach Farmer Dr, Athens, TN, 37303. Tel: 423-746-5251. p. 2088

Adams, Kellie, Sr Law Librn, Queens County Supreme Court Library, General Court House, 88-11 Sutphin Blvd, Jamaica, NY, 11435. Tel: 718-298-1206. p. 1553

Adams, Keri, Head, Per, Johnson Free Public Library, 274 Main St, Hackensack, NJ, 07601-5797. Tel: 201-343-4169. p. 1406

Adams, Keri, Head, YA, Johnson Free Public Library, 274 Main St, Hackensack, NJ, 07601-5797. Tel: 201-343-4169. p. 1406

Adams, Louise, Info & Res Mgr, Kilpatrick Townsend & Stockton LLP, 1100 Peachtree St, Ste 2800, Atlanta, GA, 30309-4528. Tel: 404-815-6500. p. 465

Adams, Luisa, Circ/Reserves, Columbia College Library, 11600 Columbia College Dr, Sonora, CA, 95370-8581. Tel: 209-588-5119. p. 246

Adams, Lynnette, Asst Librn, Five Rivers Public Library, 301 Walnut St, Parsons, WV, 26287. Tel: 304-478-3880. p. 2411

Adams, Mararia, Asst Dir, Syst, Louisiana State University Health Sciences Center, 1501 Kings Hwy, Shreveport, LA, 71130. Tel: 318-675-5448. p. 908

Adams, Margaret S, Ref/Outreach Librn, Widener University, School of Law Library, 4601 Concord Pike, Wilmington, DE, 19803. Tel: 302-477-2039. p. 358

Adams, Mary, Law Librn, Louisiana Department of Justice Office of the Attorney General, 1885 N Third St, 4th Flr, Baton Rouge, LA, 70802. Tel: 225-326-6422. p. 883

Adams, Melanie, Librn, Aurora College, No 87 Gwich'in Rd, Inuvik, NT, X0E 0T0, CANADA. Tel: 867-777-3298, Ext 234. p. 2613

Adams, Melissa, Exec Dir, Reading Public Library, 100 S Fifth St, Reading, PA, 19602. Tel: 610-655-6355. p. 2000

Adams, Melissa, Librn, Tacoma Community College Library, Bldg 7, 6501 S 19th St, Tacoma, WA, 98466-6100. Tel: 253-566-5204. p. 2387

Adams, Melissa, Librn & Archivist, Union of British Columbia Indian Chiefs, 312 Main St, Vancouver, BC, V6A 2T2, CANADA. Tel: 604-684-0231. p. 2580

Adams, Michelanne, Acq, Circ, Reserves, Eastern Washington University, 600 N Riverpoint Blvd, Rm 230, Spokane, WA, 99202. Tel: 509-358-7930. p. 2383

Adams, Nacole, Librn, Holmes Community College, Ridgeland Campus, 412 W Ridgeland Ave, Ridgeland, MS, 39158-1410. Tel: 601-605-3303. p. 1232

Adams, Nancy, Librn, Court of Appeals Eleventh Circuit Library, Elbert P Tuttle US Court of Appeals Bldg, 56 Forsyth St NW, Atlanta, GA, 30303. Tel: 404-335-6500. p. 463

Adams, Nancy, Educ Librn, Instruction Librn, Pennsylvania State University, College of Medicine, Penn State Hershey, 500 University Dr, Hershey, PA, 17033. Tel: 717-531-8989. p. 1943

Adams, Rebecca, Librn, Atchison County Library, 200 S Main St, Rock Port, MO, 64482. Tel: 660-744-5404. p. 1267

Adams, Richard, Dr, Pub Serv, Reader Serv, Emory University Libraries, Pitts Theology Library, Candler School of Theology, 1531 Dickey Dr, Ste 560, Atlanta, GA, 30322-2810. Tel: 404-727-4166. p. 463

Adams, Robert, Libr Dir, Boston Architectural College, 320 Newbury St, Boston, MA, 02115. Tel: 617-585-0232. p. 990

Adams, Sabrena, Br Mgr, Phoenix Public Library, Palo Verde Library, 4402 N 51st Ave, Phoenix, AZ, 85031. p. 72

Adams, Sarah, Dir, Vaughn Public Library, 502 W Main St, Ashland, WI, 54806. Tel: 715-685-1668. p. 2421

Adams, Scott, Br Mgr, Jacksonville Public Library, Willowbranch Branch, 2875 Park St, Jacksonville, FL, 32205-8099. Tel: 904-381-8490. p. 412

Adams, Shanette, Br Librn, Middle Georgia Regional Library System, Shurling Branch, Shurlington Plaza, 1769 Shurling Dr, Macon, GA, 31211-2152. Tel: 478-744-0875. p. 487

Adams, Shannon, Mgr, Dallas Public Library, Martin Luther King Jr Branch, 2922 Martin Luther King Jr Blvd, Dallas, TX, 75215-2393. Tel: 214-670-0344. p. 2165

Adams, Sheila, Circ Mgr, Glenwood-Lynwood Public Library District, 19901 Stony Island Ave, Lynwood, IL, 60411. Tel: 708-758-0090. p. 611

Adams, Sheryll, Br Mgr, Chicago Public Library, McKinley Park, 1915 W 35th St, Chicago, IL, 60609. Tel: 312-747-6082. p. 557

Adams, Stephanie, Electronic Res, Tennessee Technological University, 1100 N Peachtree Ave, Cookeville, TN, 38505. Tel: 931-372-3326. p. 2095

Adams, Susan, Librn, Lincoln-Lawrence-Franklin Regional Library, Franklin County Public Library, 38 First St, Meadville, MS, 39653. Tel: 601-384-2997. p. 1213

Adams, Suzanne, Libr Dir, Bella Vista Public Library, 11 Dickens Pl, Bella Vista, AR, 72714-4603. Tel: 479-855-1753. p. 90

Adams, Tina, Dir, Southwestern Community College, 447 College Dr, Sylva, NC, 28779. Tel: 828-339-4288. p. 1718

Adams, Valarie, Coordr, Cat, University of Tennessee at Chattanooga Library, 400 Douglas Ave, Dept 6456, Chattanooga, TN, 37403-2598. Tel: 423-425-4501. p. 2092

Adams, Vanessa, Dir, Crowley Ridge Regional Library, 315 W Oak Ave, Jonesboro, AR, 72401. Tel: 870-935-5133. p. 99

Adams, Wanda, Coordr, Ser/Govt Doc, Benedictine College Library, 1020 N Second St, Atchison, KS, 66002-1499. Tel: 913-360-7610. p. 797

Adams, Warren, Dir, Cumberland County Historical Society, 981 Ye Greate St, Greenwich, NJ, 08323. Tel: 856-455-8580. p. 1406

Adams, Wendy, Dir, Normal Memorial Library, 301 N Eagle St, Fayette, OH, 43521. Tel: 419-237-2115. p. 1785

Adams, Wright R, Libr Dir, Cleveland County Library System, 104 Howie Dr, Shelby, NC, 28150. Tel: 704-487-9069. p. 1716

Adams-Cook, Vicki, Br Mgr, Cuyahoga County Public Library, Southeast Branch, 70 Columbus Rd, Bedford, OH, 44146-2836. Tel: 440-439-4997. p. 1813

Adams-Joanette, John J, Digital Serv Librn, Bureau of Land Management Library, Denver Federal Ctr, Bldg 85, W-5, Denver, CO, 80225. Tel: 303-236-6650. p. 273

Adams-O'Brien, Frances, Librn, Municipal Technical Advisory Service, 1610 University Ave, Knoxville, TN, 37921-6741. Tel: 865-974-9842. p. 2106

Adams-Wagner, Tammie, Chief Exec Officer, Librn, Madoc Public Library, 20 Davidson St, Madoc, ON, K0K 2K0, CANADA. Tel: 613-473-4456. p. 2656

Adamson, Holly, Syst Adminr, Saskatchewan Polytechnic, 4500 Wascana Pkwy, Regina, SK, S4P 3A3, CANADA. Tel: 306-665-7403. p. 2748

Adamson, Stephanie, Dir, Aberdeen District Library, 76 E Central, Aberdeen, ID, 83210. Tel: 208-397-4427. p. 515

Adar, Ilan, Educ Dir, Library Contact, Temple Sinai Library, 363 Penfield Rd, Rochester, NY, 14625. Tel: 585-381-6890. p. 1630

Adasiak, Paul, Pub Serv Coordr, University of Alaska Fairbanks, 1732 Tanana Dr, Fairbanks, AK, 99775. Tel: 907-474-5354. p. 45

Aday, Mike, Librn & Archivist, US National Park Service, National Park Services, 8440 State Hwy 73, Townsend, TN, 37882. Tel: 865-448-2247. p. 2128

Adcock, Michelle, Dir, Stokes Brown Public Library, 405 White St, Springfield, TN, 37172-2340. Tel: 615-384-5123. p. 2127

Adcox, Amy, Coordr, Alaska Christian College, 35109 Royal Pl, Soldotna, AK, 99669. Tel: 907-260-7422. p. 51

Adcox, James, Ch, Kenai Community Library, 163 Main St Loop, Kenai, AK, 99611. Tel: 907-283-4378. p. 48

Addesso, Deborah, Libr Assoc, Saint Jerome's University Library, 290 Westmount Rd N, Waterloo, ON, N2L 3G3, CANADA. Tel: 519-884-8111, Ext 28271. p. 2702

Addesso, Nanette, Access Serv Coordr, University of Connecticut, Music & Dramatic Arts Library, 1295 Storrs Rd, Unit 1153, Storrs, CT, 06269-1153. Tel: 860-486-2033. p. 340

Addington, Jennifer, District Dir, Palos Verdes Library District, 701 Silver Spur Rd, Rolling Hills Estates, CA, 90274. Tel: 310-377-9584. p. 204

Addison, Sarah, Librn, Pensacola State College, Bldg 20, 1000 College Blvd, Pensacola, FL, 32504-8998. Tel: 850-484-2084. p. 436

Addison, Watonka, Principal Librn, Pub Serv, Watsonville Public Library, 275 Main St, Ste 100, Watsonville, CA, 95076. Tel: 831-768-3400. p. 258

Addison-Amoyaw, Jane, Libr Mgr, New York Public Library - Astor, Lenox & Tilden Foundations, Mosholu Branch, 285 E 205th St, (Near Perry Ave), Bronx, NY, 10467. Tel: 718-882-8239. p. 1596

Addleman, Jayanti, Dir, Libr Serv, Hayward Public Library, 835 C St, Hayward, CA, 94541. Tel: 510-293-8685. p. 150

Addleman Ritter, Kristi, Ref & Instruction Librn, Pennsylvania State University, 320 Campus Dr, Mont Alto, PA, 17237. Tel: 717-749-6040. p. 1965

Addy, Cody, Dir, Newcomerstown Public Library, 123 E Main St, Newcomerstown, OH, 43832. Tel: 740-498-8228. p. 1808

Ade, Ryan, Network Adminr, Carthage College, 2001 Alford Park Dr, Kenosha, WI, 53140-1900. Tel: 262-551-5950. p. 2444

Adebola-Wilson, Francis, PhD, Dr, Sr Commun Libr Mgr, Contra Costa County Library, San Ramon Library, 100 Montgomery St, San Ramon, CA, 94583. Tel: 925-973-2850. p. 175

Adebonojo, Leslie, Student Serv/Outreach Librn, East Tennessee State University, Sherrod Library, Seehorn Dr & Lake St, Johnson City, TN, 37614-0204. Tel: 423-439-4308. p. 2104

Adelberg, Janet H, Librn, Cary Memorial Library, 17 Old Winthrop Rd, Wayne, ME, 04284. Tel: 207-685-3612. p. 945

Adelman, Elizabeth, Dir, Law Libr, Vice Dean, Legal Info Serv, University at Buffalo Libraries-State University of New York, Charles B Sears Law Library, John Lord O'Brian Hall, 211 Mary Talbert Way, Buffalo, NY, 14260-1110. Tel: 716-645-2089. p. 1511

Adema, Liz, Coordr, Pub Serv, Middlesex County Library, 34-B Frank St, Strathroy, ON, N7G 2R4, CANADA. Tel: 519-245-8237, Ext 4021. p. 2682

Aden, Christine, Head, Circ, Augustana College Library, 3435 9 1/2 Ave, Rock Island, IL, 61201-2296. Tel: 309-794-7819. p. 640

Aden, Cindy, Prof in Residence, Prof of Practice, University of Washington, Mary Gates Hall, Ste 370, Campus Box 352840, Seattle, WA, 98195-2840. Tel: 206-543-1794. p. 2794

Aden, Debbie, Libr Dir, Fairbury Public Library, 601 Seventh St, Fairbury, NE, 68352. Tel: 402-729-2843. p. 1313

Aden, Sara, Info Syst Mgr, North Platte Public Library, 120 W Fourth St, North Platte, NE, 69101-3993. Tel: 308-535-8036. p. 1327

Adenuga, Doyin, Electronic Res Librn, Ref & Instruction Librn, Houghton University, One Willard Ave, Houghton, NY, 14744. Tel: 585-567-9242. p. 1548

Adeogun, Margaret, Head, Patron Serv, Andrews University, 4190 Administration Dr, Berrien Springs, MI, 49104-1400. Tel: 269-471-3156. p. 1085

Ader, Meredith, Access Serv Librn, Roberts Wesleyan College & Northeastern Seminary, 2301 Westside Dr, Rochester, NY, 14624-1997. Tel: 585-594-6141. p. 1629

Ader, Meredith, Head, Res & Instruction, Regent University Library, 1000 Regent University Dr, Virginia Beach, VA, 23464-5037. Tel: 757-352-4184. p. 2349

Adermann, Anna, Dir, Assumption Public Library District, 205 N Oak St, Assumption, IL, 62510. Tel: 217-226-3915. p. 538

Adkins, Brian, Cat, Shook, Hardy & Bacon, 2555 Grand Blvd, 3rd Flr, Kansas City, MO, 64108-2613. Tel: 816-474-6550. p. 1257

Adkins, Delania, Dir, Pike County Public Library District, 119 College St, Pikeville, KY, 41502-1787. Tel: 606-432-9977. p. 872

Adkins, Denice, Prof, University of Missouri-Columbia, 303 Townsend Hall, Columbia, MO, 65211. Tel: 573-882-4546. p. 2787

Adkins, Elaine, Tech Serv, Carroll County Public Library, 1100 Green Valley Rd, New Windsor, MD, 21776. Tel: 410-386-4500. p. 971

Adkins, Guy, Br Mgr, Jacksonville Public Library, Murray Hill Branch, 918 Edgewood Ave S, Jacksonville, FL, 32205-5341. Tel: 904-384-2665. p. 412

Ahmadi, Shokria, Ref Librn, MGH Institute of Health Professions Library, Charlestown Navy Yard, 38 Third Ave, 4th Flr, Charlestown, MA, 02129. p. 1009
Ahmed, Khalil, Ref (Info Servs), J Sargeant Reynolds Community College Library, Downtown Campus-Library & Information Services, 700 E Jackson St, 2nd Flr, Rm 231, Richmond, VA, 23219-1543. Tel: 804-523-5211. p. 2341
Ahn, Hanna, Univ Archivist, Northeastern Illinois University, 5500 N Saint Louis Ave, Chicago, IL, 60625-4699. Tel: 773-442-4400. p. 566
Aho, Stacia, Virtual Libr Mgr, Arlington County Department of Libraries, 1015 N Quincy St, Arlington, VA, 22201. Tel: 703-228-5968. p. 2305
Ahola, Scott, Dir, Ref Librn, Black Hills State University, 1200 University St, Unit 9676, Spearfish, SD, 57799-9676. Tel: 605-642-6359. p. 2083
Ahrens, Debra, Br Mgr, Free Library of Philadelphia, Oak Lane Branch, 6614 N 12th St, Philadelphia, PA, 19126-3299. Tel: 215-685-2847. p. 1979
Ahrens, Tracy, Asst Dir, Comfort Public Library, 701 High St, Comfort, TX, 78013. Tel: 830-995-2398. p. 2158
Aiello, Pauline, Coordr, Libr Serv, Massasoit Community College, Canton Campus Library, 900 Randolph St, Canton, MA, 02021. Tel: 508-588-9100, Ext 2945. p. 1003
Aigner, Lorna, Dir, Muscoda Public Library, 400 N Wisconsin Ave, Muscoda, WI, 53573. Tel: 608-739-3510. p. 2463
Aikau, Fredericka P, Libr Tech, Hawaii State Archives, Iolani Palace Grounds, 364 S King St, Honolulu, HI, 96813. Tel: 808-586-0329. p. 506
Aiken, Jennie, Asst Librn, Sweet Springs Public Library, 217 Turner St, Sweet Springs, MO, 65351. Tel: 660-335-4314. p. 1282
Aiken, Julian, Access & Fac Serv Librn, Yale University Library, Lillian Goldman Library Yale Law School, 127 Wall St, New Haven, CT, 06511. Tel: 203-432-9616. p. 328
Aiken, Leesa M, Dir, South Carolina State Library, 1500 Senate St, Columbia, SC, 29201. Tel: 803-734-8666. p. 2054
Aikens, Dale, IT & Security Mgr, Warren Library Association, 205 Market St, Warren, PA, 16365. Tel: 814-723-4650. p. 2017
Aikens, Tonya, Pres & Chief Exec Officer, Howard County Library System, 9411 Frederick Rd, Ellicott City, MD, 21042. Tel: 410-313-7750. p. 965
Aikin, Louise, Lead Librn, Scottsdale Public Library, Palomino Library, 12575 E Via Linda, Ste 102, Scottsdale, AZ, 85259. Tel: 480-312-6011. p. 77
Ainsworth, Cynthia, Head Librn, Hartnell College Library, 411 Central Ave, Salinas, CA, 93901. p. 211
Ainsworth, Kyle, Spec Coll Librn, Stephen F Austin State University, 1936 North St, Nacogdoches, TX, 75962. Tel: 936-468-1590. p. 2221
Airoldi, Melissa, Libr Syst Adminr, Austin Community College, 5930 Middle Fiskville Rd, Austin, TX, 78752. Tel: 512-223-3464. p. 2137
Aitken, Eric, Br Mgr, Tuolumne County Public Library, Groveland Branch, 18990 Hwy 120, Groveland, CA, 95321. Tel: 209-962-6144. p. 247
Aitken, Eric, Libr Mgr, Tuolumne County Public Library, 480 Greenley Rd, Sonora, CA, 95370-5956. Tel: 209-533-5507. p. 247
Ajayi, Abiola, Librn, Markham Stouffville Hospital Library, 381 Church St, Markham, ON, L3P 7P3, CANADA. Tel: 905-472-7061. p. 2656
Ajiferuke, Isola, Asst Dean, Research, Assoc Prof, Western University, FIMS & Nursing Bldg, Rm 2020, London, ON, N6A 5B9, CANADA. Tel: 519-661-2111, Ext 81364. p. 2796
Ajmi, Ayyoub, Assoc Dir, University of Missouri-Kansas City Libraries, 500 E 52nd St, Kansas City, MO, 64110. Tel: 816-235-1650. p. 1258
Akao, Pamela, Br Mgr, Hawaii State Public Library System, Thelma Parker Memorial Public & School Library, 67-1209 Mamalahoa Hwy, Kamuela, HI, 96743. Tel: 808-887-6067. p. 510
Ake, Ryan, Asst Dir, Susquehanna University, 514 University Ave, Selinsgrove, PA, 17870-1050. Tel: 570-372-4324. p. 2005
Aked, Deborah, Librn, Toledo Zoological Society, 2700 Broadway St, Toledo, OH, 43609. Tel: 419-385-5721, Ext 2043. p. 1825
Aked, Michael, Acq Librn, Owens Community College Library, 30335 Oregon Rd, Perrysburg, OH, 43551. Tel: 567-661-7031. p. 1815
Akehurst-Moore, Scott, Coll Develop, Sr Law Librn, Northeastern University School of Law Library, 416 Huntington Ave, Boston, MA, 02115. Tel: 617-373-3331. p. 999
Aken'Ova, Andrea, Dir, Phoenix Children's Hospital, 1919 E Thomas Rd, Phoenix, AZ, 85016. Tel: 602-933-1400. p. 71
Akerman, James, Curator, Maps, Newberry Library, 60 W Walton St, Chicago, IL, 60610-3305. Tel: 312-255-3523. p. 565
Akerman, Patricia, Librn, Saint Cloud Technical & Community College Library, 1520 Whitney Ct, Saint Cloud, MN, 56303-1240. Tel: 320-308-5141. p. 1198
Akers, Carla, Mgr, Charlestown-Clark County Public Library, Borden Branch, 117 W Main St, Borden, IN, 47106. Tel: 812-258-9041. p. 674
Aki, Maxine, Br Mgr, Hawaii State Public Library System, Keaau Public & School Library, 16-571 Keaau-Pahoa Rd, Keaau, HI, 96749. Tel: 808-982-4281. p. 508
Akin, Jessi, Dir, Giddings Public Library & Cultural Center, 276 N Orange St, Giddings, TX, 78942-3317. Tel: 979-542-2716. p. 2184
Akin, Kelly, Dir, Med Libr, Indian Health Service, 4212 N 16th St, Phoenix, AZ, 85016. Tel: 602-263-1676. p. 70
Akin, Kelly, Libr Mgr, Valley Falls Free Library, 42 State St, Valley Falls, NY, 12185. Tel: 518-753-4230. p. 1657
Akin, Reimi, Outreach Library Asst, University of San Francisco, 2130 Fulton St, San Francisco, CA, 94117-1080. Tel: 415-422-5387. p. 229
Akins, Susan, Outreach & Children's Serv, Autauga Prattville Public Library, Marbury Community, 205 County Rd 20 E, Marbury, AL, 36051. Tel: 205-755-8575. p. 33
Aklus, Sue, Br Mgr, Moore County Library, Robbins Branch, 161 E Magnolia Dr, Robbins, NC, 27325. Tel: 910-948-4000. p. 1677
Akman, Jesse, Health Librarian, Life Sci Librn, Elon University, 308 N O'Kelly Ave, Elon, NC, 27244-0187. Tel: 336-278-6600. p. 1688
Akulich, Helen, Principal Law Librn, New York State Supreme Court, 45 Monroe Pl, Brooklyn, NY, 11201. Tel: 718-722-6356. p. 1505
Akus, Elizabeth, Cat Supvr, Delray Beach Public Library, 100 W Atlantic Ave, Delray Beach, FL, 33444. Tel: 561-266-0194. p. 394
Al-Shabibi, Amy, Tech Mgr, Champaign Public Library, 200 W Green St, Champaign, IL, 61820-5193. Tel: 217-403-2000. p. 551
Alagha, Emily, Clinical Serv Librn, Data Mgt, Georgetown University, Dahlgren Memorial Library, Preclinical Science Bldg GM-7, 3900 Reservoir Rd NW, Washington, DC, 20007. Tel: 202-687-2486. p. 368
Alaire, Christian, Cat, College de Rosemont (Cegep) Bibliotheque, 6400 16th Ave, Montreal, QC, H1X 2S9, CANADA. Tel: 514-376-1620, Ext 7265. p. 2723
Alamo, Ernest, Law Librn, Patterson, Belknap, Webb & Tyler LLP Library, 1133 Avenue of the Americas, New York, NY, 10036. Tel: 212-336-2000. p. 1600
Alan, Eric, Regional Serv Librn, Northern New York Library Network, 6721 US Hwy 11, Potsdam, NY, 13676. Tel: 315-265-1119. p. 2771
Alaniz, Lori, Access Serv Asst, University of California, Riverside, Raymond L Orbach Science Library, 900 University Ave, Riverside, CA, 92521. Tel: 951-827-3701. p. 203
Alaniz, Michele, Fac Librn, City College of San Francisco, 50 Frida Kahlo Way, 4th Flr, San Francisco, CA, 94112. Tel: 415-452-5433. p. 224
Alaniz, Michele, Dept Chair, City College of San Francisco, 50 Frida Kahlo Way, Rm 517, San Francisco, CA, 94112. Tel: 415-452-5519. p. 2782
Alardin, Victoria, Interim Br Mgr, Youth Serv, Harris County Public Library, Baldwin Boettcher Branch, 22306 Aldine Westfield Rd, Humble, TX, 77338. Tel: 832-927-5480. p. 2192
Alary, Laura, Coordr, Spec Coll, Libr Asst, University of Toronto Libraries, Knox College Caven Library, Knox College, 59 St George St, Toronto, ON, M5S 2E6, CANADA. Tel: 416-978-4504, 416-978-6719. p. 2699
Alaverdova, Liana, Managing Librn, Brooklyn Public Library, Kings Bay, 3650 Nostrand Ave, Brooklyn, NY, 11229. Tel: 718-368-1709. p. 1503
Alavi, Natasha, Libr Mgr, Avondale Public Library, 495 E Western Ave, Avondale, AZ, 85323. Tel: 623-333-2602. p. 55
Alba, Samantha, Libr Serv Mgr, Arcadia Public Library, 20 W Duarte Rd, Arcadia, CA, 91006. Tel: 626-821-5565. p. 117
Albanese, Holly, Dir, Flagler County Public Library, 2500 Palm Coast Pkwy NW, Palm Coast, FL, 32137. Tel: 386-446-6763. p. 434
Albano, Joanne, Asst Dir, Commack Public Library, 18 Hauppauge Rd, Commack, NY, 11725-4498. Tel: 631-499-0888. p. 1521
Albarelli, Devereux, Online Learning Info Services Librn, Northampton Community College, College Ctr, 3835 Green Pond Rd, Bethlehem, PA, 18020-7599. Tel: 610-861-3360. p. 1912
Albaugh, Sylvia, Dir, Shoals Public Library, 404 N High St, Shoals, IN, 47581. Tel: 812-247-3838. p. 718
Albear, Sandra, Regional Dir, Braille Institute Library, Anaheim Center, 527 N Dale Ave, Anaheim, CA, 92801. Tel: 714-821-5000. p. 160
Albee, Deborah, Circ Supvr, Fort Madison Public Library, 1920 Avenue E, Fort Madison, IA, 52627. Tel: 319-372-5721. p. 754
Alber, Merryl, Dir, University of Georgia, One Turkey Fountain Way, Sapelo Island, GA, 31327. Tel: 912-485-2221. p. 495
Albers, Erin, Ch, Caribou Public Library, 30 High St, Caribou, ME, 04736. Tel: 207-493-4214. p. 920
Albers, Kate, Br Mgr, Upper Arlington Public Library, Miller Park Branch, 1901 Arlington Ave, Upper Arlington, OH, 43212. Tel: 614-488-5710. p. 1778
Albers, Kimberly, Librn, Bunker Hill Public Library District, 220 E Warren St, Bunker Hill, IL, 62014. Tel: 618-585-4736. p. 545
Albers, Libby, Dir, Hesston Public Library, 300 N Main St, Hesston, KS, 67062. Tel: 620-327-4666. p. 813
Albers, Marian, Dir, Mascoutah Public Library, Three W Church St, Mascoutah, IL, 62258. Tel: 618-566-2562. p. 615
Albers, Natalie, Dir, Williamsville Public Library & Museum, 217 N Elm St, Williamsville, IL, 62693. Tel: 217-566-3520. p. 663
Albert, Allison, Asst Librn, Ch, Herrin City Library, 120 N 13th St, Herrin, IL, 62948-3233. Tel: 618-942-6109. p. 598
Albert, Christina, Asst Librn, Eldon Carnegie Public Library, 608 W Elm St, Eldon, IA, 52554. Tel: 641-652-7517. p. 750
Albert, Stuart Lee, Sr Libr Spec, University of Illinois Library at Urbana-Champaign, Classic Library Collection Reading Room, 225 Main Library, 1408 W Gregory Dr, Urbana, IL, 61801. Tel: 217-333-2220. p. 655
Alberth, Kimberly, Circ Mgr, Ella Johnson Memorial Public Library District, 109 S State St, Hampshire, IL, 60140. Tel: 847-683-4490. p. 596

Alberto, Rebecca, Libr Mgr, New York Public Library - Astor, Lenox & Tilden Foundations, Mulberry Street Branch, Ten Jersey St, New York, NY, 10012-3332. Tel: 212-966-3424. p. 1596

Alberts, Debby, Br Librn, Wapiti Regional Library, Leoville Public Library, Village Office, Main St, Leoville, SK, S0J 1N0, CANADA. Tel: 306-984-2057. p. 2745

Albertson, Dan, Dr, Chair, Prof, University at Buffalo, The State University of New York, 534 Baldy Hall, Buffalo, NY, 14260. Tel: 716-645-2412. p. 2789

Albertson, Lois, Libr Dir, Highland Beach Library, 3618 S Ocean Blvd, Highland Beach, FL, 33487. Tel: 561-278-5455. p. 409

Albertson-Denison, Kari, Circ Librn, Pub Serv Librn, Lewistown Public Library, 701 W Main St, Lewistown, MT, 59457. Tel: 406-538-5212. p. 1298

Albertus, Kris, Ms, Head, Res Serv, United States Court of Appeals, 110 E Court Ave, Ste 358, Des Moines, IA, 50309. Tel: 314-244-2665. p. 747

Albitz, Rebecca, Libr Dir, Marist College, 3399 North Rd, Poughkeepsie, NY, 12601-1387. Tel: 845-575-3196. p. 1623

Albrecht, Amy, Br Mgr, Beaumont Public Library System, Theodore R Johns Sr Branch Library, 4255 Fannett Rd, Beaumont, TX, 77705. Tel: 409-842-5233. p. 2145

Albrecht, Danette, Dir, Sodus Township Library, 3776 Naomi Rd, Sodus, MI, 49126-9783. Tel: 269-925-0903. p. 1150

Albrecht, Debbie, Dir, Lansing Public Library, 2750 Indiana Ave, Lansing, IL, 60438. Tel: 708-474-2447. p. 607

Albrecht, Jack, Dir, Thompson-Hickman Free County Library, 217 Idaho St, Virginia City, MT, 59755. Tel: 406-843-5346. p. 1303

Albrecht, Lynne, Tech Serv, Saint Helena Public Library, 1492 Library Lane, Saint Helena, CA, 94574-1143. Tel: 707-963-5244. p. 210

Albrecht, Marisa, Libr Dir, University of Indianapolis, 1400 E Hanna Ave, Indianapolis, IN, 46227-3697. Tel: 317-788-3268. p. 697

Albrecht, Rhonda K, Bus Mgr, Rushville Public Library, 130 W Third St, Rushville, IN, 46173-1899. Tel: 765-932-3496. p. 717

Albrecht, Susan, Fellowship Advisor & Library Visual Media Liaison, Wabash College, 301 W Wabash Ave, Crawfordsville, IN, 47933. Tel: 765-361-6216. p. 677

Albrecht, Tina, Ch, Nelson Public Library, Ten W Third St, Nelson, NE, 68961. Tel: 402-225-7111. p. 1326

Albright, Anita, Liaison & Instruction Librn, Salt Lake Community College Libraries, South City Campus, Main Bldg, Rm 1-022, 1575 S State St, Salt Lake City, UT, 84115. Tel: 801-957-3435. p. 2274

Albright, Eric, Dir, Tufts University, Hirsh Health Sciences Library, 145 Harrison Ave, Boston, MA, 02111. Tel: 617-636-6705. p. 1034

Albright, Gary, Dir of Mus, Tillamook County Pioneer Museum, 2106 Second St, Tillamook, OR, 97141. Tel: 503-842-4553. p. 1900

Albright, Hyesoo, Circ Supvr, Centralia College, 600 Centralia College Blvd, Centralia, WA, 98531. Tel: 360-623-8110. p. 2361

Albright, Jenifer, Asst City Librn, Pretty Prairie Public Library, 119 W Main St, Pretty Prairie, KS, 67570. Tel: 620-459-6392. p. 833

Albright, Julie, Youth Serv, Ventura County Library, Ojai Library, 111 E Ojai Ave, Ojai, CA, 93023. Tel: 805-646-1639. p. 256

Albright, Katie, Student Success Librn, Otterbein University, 138 W Main St, Westerville, OH, 43081. Tel: 614-823-1597. p. 1830

Albright, Kendra S, Dir, Prof, Kent State University, 314 University Library, 1125 Risman Dr, Kent, OH, 44242-0001. Tel: 330-672-2782. p. 2790

Albright, Phyllis, Dir, Nicholas County Public Library, 223 N Broadway St, Carlisle, KY, 40311. Tel: 859-289-5595. p. 851

Albright, Ruth, Librn, Bowerston Public Library, 200 Main St, Bowerston, OH, 44695. Tel: 740-269-8531. p. 1752

Albritton, Geri Lynn, Adminr, Escambia County Cooperative Library System, 700 E Church St, Atmore, AL, 36502. Tel: 251-368-4130. p. 5

Albrizio, Lori, Librn, Broward College, South Campus Library LRC, Bldg 81, 7300 Pines Blvd, Pembroke Pines, FL, 33024. Tel: 954-201-8825, 954-201-8896. p. 391

Albro, Maggie, Agr Librn, University of Tennessee, Knoxville, Webster C Pendergrass Agriculture & Veterinary Medicine Library, A-113 Veterinary Medical Ctr, 2407 River Dr, Knoxville, TN, 37996-4541. Tel: 865-974-7338. p. 2108

Alcantar, Jackie, Dir, Oglala Lakota College, He Sapa College Center, 127 Knollwood Dr, Rapid City, SD, 57709. Tel: 605-342-1513. p. 2077

Alcantara-Antoine, Sonia, Dir, Baltimore County Public Library, 320 York Rd, Towson, MD, 21204-5179. Tel: 410-887-6100. p. 979

Alcock, Crystal, Chief Exec Officer, Librn, Kenora Public Library, 24 Main St S, Kenora, ON, P9N 1S7, CANADA. Tel: 807-467-2081. p. 2649

Alcock, Tara, Libr Dir, Petersburg Public Library, 14 S Second St, Petersburg, AK, 99833. Tel: 907-772-3349. p. 50

Alcook, Barb, Librn, Huron Law Association, One Courthouse, 3rd Flr, Goderich, ON, N7A 1M2, CANADA. Tel: 519-524-7962. p. 2643

Alcorn, Dean, Outreach Librn, Pub Serv, Kellogg Community College, 450 North Ave, Battle Creek, MI, 49017-3397. Tel: 269-565-2876. p. 1083

Alcorn, Louise, Tech Coordr, West Des Moines Public Library, 4000 Mills Civic Pkwy, West Des Moines, IA, 50265-2049. Tel: 515-222-3573. p. 791

Alcorn, Patricia, Ref Librn, United States Army, Fort Stewart Main Post Library, 316 Lindquist Rd, Fort Stewart, GA, 31314-5126. Tel: 912-767-2260, 912-767-2828. p. 479

Alcorn, Shelby, Admin Assoc, Montana State University-Billings Library, 1500 University Dr, Billings, MT, 59101. Tel: 406-657-2262. p. 1288

Alcorta, Marissa, Br Mgr, Pima County Public Library, Quincie Douglas, 1585 E 36th St, Tucson, AZ, 85713. Tel: 520-594-5335. p. 82

Alcott, Martha, Asst Libr Dir, Head, Ref Serv, Chappaqua Public Library, 195 S Greeley Ave, Chappaqua, NY, 10514. Tel: 914-238-4779. p. 1516

Aldana, Lynda, Assoc Dir, Tech Serv, University of Maryland, Baltimore County, 1000 Hilltop Circle, Baltimore, MD, 21250. Tel: 410-455-2356. p. 958

Aldaz, Savannah, Librn, New Mexico Corrections Department, 2111 Lobo Canyon Rd, Grants, NM, 87020. Tel: 505-876-8300. p. 1469

Alden, Gail M, Dir, United States Army, Redstone Arsenal Family & MWR Library, 3323 Redeye Rd, Redstone Arsenal, AL, 35898. Tel: 256-876-4741. p. 34

Alder, Kate, Dir, Libr Serv, Metropolitan College of New York Library, 60 West St, 7th Flr, New York, NY, 10006. Tel: 212-343-1234, Ext 2001. p. 1591

Alderete, Kate, Dep State Librn, New Mexico State Library, 1209 Camino Carlos Rey, Santa Fe, NM, 87507-5166. Tel: 505-476-9712. p. 1475

Alderfer, Joel D, Colls Mgr, Mennonite Historians of Eastern Pennsylvania, 565 Yoder Rd, Harleysville, PA, 19438-1020. Tel: 215-256-3020. p. 1939

Alderman, Marlene, Libr Dir, Boston University Libraries, Pappas Law Library, 765 Commonwealth Ave, Boston, MA, 02215. Tel: 617-353-8870. p. 993

Alderman, Pamela, Libr Dir, Florida Atlantic University, 5600 US 1 N, Fort Pierce, FL, 34946. Tel: 772-242-2486. p. 404

Alderson, Craig, Circ/Reserves, University of California, Berkeley, Social Research Library, 227 Haviland Hall, Berkeley, CA, 94720-6000. Tel: 510-642-4432. p. 123

Aldmon, Bayley, Ch, Brazoria County Library System, Manvel Branch, 20514B Hwy 6, Manvel, TX, 77578. Tel: 281-489-7596. p. 2135

Aldred, Sue, Br Mgr, Annapolis Valley Regional Library, Rosa M Harvey Middleton & Area Library - Middleton, 45 Gates Ave, Middleton, NS, B0S 1P0, CANADA. Tel: 902-825-4835. p. 2616

Aldrich, Alan, Instrul Serv Librn, University of South Dakota, I D Weeks Library, 414 E Clark St, Vermillion, SD, 57069. Tel: 605-658-3384. p. 2084

Aldrich, Michael, Dir, Brigham Young University-Hawaii, BYU-Hawaii, No 1966, 55-220 Kulanui St, Bldg 5, Laie, HI, 96762-1294. Tel: 808-675-3851. p. 514

Aldrich, Nancy, Librn/Mgr, AdventHealth Orlando, 601 E Rollins, Orlando, FL, 32803. Tel: 407-303-1860. p. 430

Aldrich, Nina, Libr Tech II, Colorado Department of Corrections, Skyline Correctional Center Library, PO Box 300, Canon City, CO, 81215. Tel: 719-269-5420, Ext 3351. p. 269

Aldrich, Stacey, State Librn, Hawaii State Public Library System, Office of the State Librarian, 44 Merchant St, Honolulu, HI, 96813. Tel: 808-586-3704. p. 506

Aldrich, Stacey A, State Librn, Hawaii State Public Library System, Hana Public & School Library, 4111 Hana Hwy, Hana, HI, 96713. Tel: 808-586-3704. p. 507

Aldrich, Stacey A, State Librn, Hawaii State Public Library System, Kahuku Public & School Library, 56-490 Kamehameha, Kahuku, HI, 96731. Tel: 808-293-8935. p. 507

Aldrich, Stacey A, State Librn, Hawaii State Public Library System, Lanai Public & School Library, 555 Fraser Ave, Lanai City, HI, 96763. Tel: 808-565-7920. p. 509

Aldrich, Stacey A, State Librn, Hawaii State Public Library System, Makawao Public Library, 1159 Makawao Ave, Makawao, HI, 96768. Tel: 808-573-8785. p. 509

Aldrich, Stacey A, State Librn, Hawaii State Public Library System, Pahoa Public & School Library, 15-3070 Pahoa-Kalapana Rd, Pahoa, HI, 96778. Tel: 808-965-2171. p. 510

Aldrich, Stacey A, State Librn, Hawaii State Public Library System, Wahiawa Public Library, 820 California Ave, Wahiawa, HI, 96786. Tel: 808-622-6345. p. 510

Aldrich, Stacey A, State Librn, Hawaii State Public Library System, Waikiki-Kapahulu Public Library, 400 Kapahulu Ave, Honolulu, HI, 96815. Tel: 808-733-8488. p. 511

Aldrich, Tracy, Libr Dir, Hughes Ruth Memorial District Library, Attica Township Library, 4302 Peppermill Rd, Attica, MI, 48412-9624. Tel: 810-724-2007. p. 1118

Aldrich, Tracy, Libr Dir, Ruth Hughes Memorial District Library, 211 N Almont Ave, Imlay City, MI, 48444-1004. Tel: 810-724-8043. p. 1118

Aleccia, Jan, Dir, The Joint Commission, One Renaissance Blvd, Oakbrook Terrace, IL, 60181. Tel: 630-792-5474. p. 628

Aleem, Mahasin, Commun Libr Mgr, Contra Costa County Library, Antioch Community Library, 501 W 18th St, Antioch, CA, 94509. Tel: 925-757-9224. p. 174

Aleem, Mahasin, Commun Libr Mgr, Contra Costa County Library, Prewett Library, 4703 Lone Tree Way, Antioch, CA, 94531. Tel: 925-776-3060. p. 174

Alef, Julie, Branch Lead, Saint Clair County Library System, Saint Clair Branch Library, 310 S Second St, Saint Clair, MI, 48079. Tel: 810-329-3951. p. 1142

Alegria, Cindy, Br Librn, Chambers County Library System, Juanita Hargraves Memorial Branch, 924 Hwy 124, Winnie, TX, 77665. Tel: 409-296-8245. p. 2134

Alegria, Sara, Dr, Assoc Dir, Miami Dade College, North Campus Learning Resources, 11380 NW 27th Ave, Miami, FL, 33167. Tel: 305-237-1777. p. 422
Alejandro, Angela, Libr Mgr, Castroville Public Library, 802 London St, Castroville, TX, 78009. Tel: 830-931-4095. p. 2154
Aleksandravicius, Regina, Mgr, Ch Serv, Wethersfield Public Library, 515 Silas Deane Hwy, Wethersfield, CT, 06109. Tel: 860-529-2665. p. 347
Aleksic, Olha, Archivist, Bibliographer, Harvard Library, Ukrainian Research Institute Reference Library, 34 Kirkland St, Cambridge, MA, 02138. Tel: 617-496-5891. p. 1008
Aleman, Claudia, Interim Mgr, Durham County Library, Stanford L Warren Branch, 1201 Fayetteville St, Durham, NC, 27707. Tel: 919-560-0274. p. 1685
Aleman, Karla, Dean of Library & eLearning, Lorain County Community College, 1005 Abbe Rd N, North Elyria, OH, 44035-1691. Tel: 440-366-4026. p. 1809
Aleman, Selena, Archivist, Catholic Archives of Texas, 6225 Hwy 290 E, Austin, TX, 78723. Tel: 512-476-6296. p. 2139
Aleman, Stephanie, Dir, President Millard Fillmore Library, 25 S 100 West St, Fillmore, UT, 84631. Tel: 435-743-5314. p. 2263
Alemanne, Nicole D, Dr, Assoc Prof, Valdosta State University, Odum Library, 1500 N Patterson St, Valdosta, GA, 31698. Tel: 229-245-3742. p. 2784
Alendorf, Holly, Circ, Windsor Storm Memorial Public Library District, 102 S Maple, Windsor, IL, 61957. Tel: 217-459-2498. p. 663
Alessi, Lauren, Librn, Roswell Park Comprehensive Cancer Center, Elm & Carlton Sts, Buffalo, NY, 14263. Tel: 716-845-5966. p. 1510
Alessi, Mary, Resource Description Mgr, Maryland Institute College of Art, 1401 W Mount Royal Ave, Baltimore, MD, 21217. Tel: 410-225-2304, 410-225-2311. p. 955
Alessi, Robert, Dir, West Seneca Public Library, 1300 Union Rd, West Seneca, NY, 14224. Tel: 716-674-2928. p. 1663
Alexander, Adrian, Info Serv Mgr, Mount Laurel Library, 100 Walt Whitman Ave, Mount Laurel, NJ, 08054. Tel: 856-234-7319. p. 1422
Alexander, Amber L, Libr Dir, Presque Isle District Library, 181 E Erie St, Rogers City, MI, 49779-1709. Tel: 989-734-2477, Ext 222. p. 1145
Alexander, Cari, Music & Media Librn, Texas Christian University, 2913 Lowden St, TCU Box 298400, Fort Worth, TX, 76129. Tel: 817-257-7106. p. 2181
Alexander, Carita, Librn, Pulaski Technical College, 13000 Interstate 30, Little Rock, AR, 72210. Tel: 501-812-2811. p. 102
Alexander, Dan, Continuing Educ Coordr, Northeast Kansas Library System, 4317 W Sixth St, Lawrence, KS, 66049. Tel: 785-838-4090. p. 819
Alexander, David, Head, Res Mgt, University of South Dakota, I D Weeks Library, 414 E Clark St, Vermillion, SD, 57069. Tel: 605-658-3374. p. 2084
Alexander, David, Univ Librn, Vancouver Island University Library, 900 Fifth St, Nanaimo, BC, V9R 5S5, CANADA. Tel: 250-753-3245. p. 2572
Alexander, Debbie, Dir, Graysville Public Library, 315 S Main St, Graysville, AL, 35073. Tel: 205-674-3040. p. 19
Alexander, Elizabeth, Head, Circ, Bethel Public Library, 189 Greenwood Ave, Bethel, CT, 06801-2598. Tel: 203-794-8756. p. 302
Alexander, Ellen, Asst Dir, Coralville Public Library, 1401 Fifth St, Coralville, IA, 52241. Tel: 319-248-1850. p. 742
Alexander, Gail, Librn, Centennial College of Applied Arts & Technology, Story Arts Centre, 951 Carlaw Ave, Rm 109, Toronto, ON, M4K 3M2, CANADA. Tel: 416-289-5000, Ext 8600. p. 2677
Alexander, Heather, Access Serv, Asst Librn, Dominican College Library, 480 Western Hwy, Blauvelt, NY, 10913-2000. Tel: 845-848-7505. p. 1495
Alexander, Jean, Dir, McKenzie Memorial Library, 15 Broadway St, McKenzie, TN, 38201. Tel: 731-352-5741. p. 2111
Alexander, John, Br Mgr, Sevier County Public Library System, Kodak Branch, 319 W Dumplin Valley Rd, Kodak, TN, 37764. Tel: 865-933-0078. p. 2125
Alexander, Kristen, Acq Librn, Programming Librn, Virginia Museum of Fine Arts Library, 200 N Arthur Ashe Blvd, Richmond, VA, 23220-4007. Tel: 804-340-1495. p. 2344
Alexander, Laurie, Assoc Univ Librn, Learning & Teaching, University of Michigan, 818 Hatcher Graduate Library South, 913 S University Ave, Ann Arbor, MI, 48109-1190. Tel: 734-764-0400, p. 1080
Alexander, Laurie, Assoc Univ Librn, Learning & Teaching, University of Michigan, Harlan Hatcher Graduate Library, 913 S University Ave, Ann Arbor, MI, 48109-1190. Tel: 734-763-2381. p. 1080
Alexander, Laurie, Assoc Univ Librn, Learning & Teaching, University of Michigan, Shapiro Undergraduate Library, 919 S University Ave, Ann Arbor, MI, 48109-1185. Tel: 734-764-7490. p. 1080
Alexander, Linda, Pub Serv Mgr, Old Lyme, Two Library Lane, Old Lyme, CT, 06371. Tel: 860-434-1684. p. 333
Alexander, Linda, Librn, Ontario County Historical Society Library, 55 N Main St, Canandaigua, NY, 14424. Tel: 585-394-4975. p. 1512
Alexander, Linda, Instr, University of South Florida, 4202 Fowler Ave, CIS 1040, Tampa, FL, 33620-7800. Tel: 813-974-3520. p. 2783
Alexander, Lois, Head, Circ, Bergenfield Public Library, 50 W Clinton Ave, Bergenfield, NJ, 07621-2799. Tel: 201-387-4040. p. 1390
Alexander, Margaret, Veterinary Med Librn, Tuskegee University, 1200 W Old Mongtomery Rd, Ford Motor Company Library, Tuskegee, AL, 36088. Tel: 334-727-8780. p. 38
Alexander, Mike, Br Mgr, Harrison County Library System, Orange Grove Public, 12135 Old Hwy 49, Gulfport, MS, 39503. Tel: 228-832-6924. p. 1218
Alexander, O D, Dr, Libr Dir, Saint John Vianney College Seminary, 2900 SW 87th Ave, Miami, FL, 33165. Tel: 305-223-4561, Option 9. p. 424
Alexander, Patty, Libr Mgr, Joe Barnhart Bee County Public Library, 110 W Corpus Christi St, Beeville, TX, 78102-5604. Tel: 361-362-4901. p. 2146
Alexander, Rachel, Coll Serv Librn, Maynard Public Library, 77 Nason St, Maynard, MA, 01754-2316. Tel: 978-897-1010. p. 1033
Alexander, Rebecca, Access Serv, Visual Res Mgr, San Francisco Art Institute, 800 Chestnut St, San Francisco, CA, 94133. Tel: 415-749-4562. p. 226
Alexander, Rebecca, Librn, Washburn University, School of Law Library, 1700 SW College Ave, Topeka, KS, 66621. Tel: 785-670-1040. p. 840
Alexander, Rebecca, Mgr, Ref Serv, Tech Serv, University of Washington Botanic Gardens, 3501 NE 41st St, Seattle, WA, 98105. Tel: 206-543-0415. p. 2381
Alexander, Rose, Libr Mgr, Thorhild Library, 210 Seventh Ave, Thorhild, AB, T0A 3J0, CANADA. Tel: 780-398-3502. p. 2556
Alexander, Ruby, Libr Dir, First Baptist Church of Highland Park Library, James J McCord Education Bldg, Rm 200, 6801 Sheriff Rd, Landover, MD, 20785. Tel: 301-773-6655. p. 970
Alexander, Sarah, PhD, Dir, Colona District Public Library, 911 First St, Colona, IL, 61241. Tel: 309-792-0548. p. 573
Alexander, Shelly, Br Mgr, North Las Vegas Library District, Aliante Library, 2400 Deer Springs Way, North Las Vegas, NV, 89084. Tel: 702-839-2980. p. 1348
Alexander, Stephanie, Assoc Librn, California State University, East Bay Library, CSU East Bay Library, 25800 Carlos Bee Blvd, Hayward, CA, 94542-3052. Tel: 510-885-7674. p. 150
Alexander, Tamala, Br Mgr, Azalea Regional Library System, Jasper County Library, 319 E Green St, Monticello, GA, 31064. Tel: 706-468-6292. p. 488
Alexander, Tammy, Dir, Hill City Public Library, 341 Main St, Hill City, SD, 57745. Tel: 605-574-4529. p. 2077
Alexander, Tanya, Dir, Arab Public Library, 325 Second St NW, Arab, AL, 35016-1999. Tel: 256-586-3366. p. 4
Alexander, Teri, Director, Learning Spaces, Clemson University Libraries, 116 Sigma Dr, Clemson, SC, 29631. Tel: 864-656-5172. p. 2052
Alexander, Whitney, Dir, Law Libr, Santa Clara University Library, Edwin A Heafey Law Library, School of Law, 500 El Camino Real, Santa Clara, CA, 95053-0430. Tel: 408-554-4072. p. 242
Alexander-East, Jessie, Br Mgr, Springfield-Greene County Library District, The Library Center, 4653 S Campbell Ave, Springfield, MO, 65810-1723. Tel: 417-882-0714. p. 1281
Alexander-Friet, Debra, Asst Dir, Viterbo University, 900 Viterbo Dr, La Crosse, WI, 54601. Tel: 608-796-3265. p. 2446
Alexandre, Ritza, Libr Asst, Trinitas Regional Medical Center, 225 Williamson St, Elizabeth, NJ, 07207. Tel: 908-994-5371. p. 1401
Alfano, Kemma, Dir, Kiowa County Public Library District, 1305 Goff St, Eads, CO, 81036. Tel: 719-438-5581. p. 278
Alfano, Sharon, Bus Mgr, The Nyack Library, 59 S Broadway, Nyack, NY, 10960. Tel: 845-358-3370, Ext 233. p. 1609
Alfermann, Barbara, Dir, Saint Louis Psychiatric Rehabilitation Center, 5300 Arsenal St, Saint Louis, MO, 63139. Tel: 314-768-5051, 314-877-6500. p. 1274
Alfgren, Drew, Ref & Instruction Librn, University of Maryland, Baltimore County, 1000 Hilltop Circle, Baltimore, MD, 21250. Tel: 410-455-2356. p. 958
Alford, Angela, Adult Serv Supvr, DeSoto Public Library, 211 E Pleasant Run Rd, Ste C, DeSoto, TX, 75115. Tel: 972-230-9656. p. 2170
Alford, Becky, Librn, St John's Hospital, 800 E Carpenter, Springfield, IL, 62769. Tel: 217-757-6700. p. 650
Alford, Duncan, Assoc Dean, Dir, University of South Carolina, Law Library, 1525 Senate St, Columbia, SC, 29208. Tel: 803-777-5942. p. 2055
Alford, Frank, Asst Librn, University of North Carolina at Chapel Hill, School of Government Knapp Library, Knapp-Sanders Bldg, CB No 3330, Chapel Hill, NC, 27599-3330. Tel: 919-962-2760. p. 1679
Alford, Glynnis, Br Librn, Ascension Parish Library, Gonzales Branch, 708 S Irma Blvd, Gonzales, LA, 70737. Tel: 225-647-3955. p. 889
Alford, Heidi, Dir, Toole County Library, 229 Second Ave S, Shelby, MT, 59474. Tel: 406-424-8345. p. 1302
Alford, Larry, Chief Univ Librn, University of Toronto Libraries, 130 St George St, Toronto, ON, M5S 1A5, CANADA. Tel: 416-978-2292. p. 2698
Alford, Michelle, Info Syst, Library Technologist, Marshall University Libraries, One John Marshall Dr, Huntington, WV, 25755-2060. Tel: 304-696-2320. p. 2405
Alford, Tierney, Ch, Dillon County Library, 600 E Main St, Dillon, SC, 29536. Tel: 843-774-0330. p. 2058
Alfred, Sarah, Dir, Morrill Public Library, 119 E Webster, Morrill, NE, 69358. Tel: 308-247-2611. p. 1325

Alger, Annie, ILL/Ref Librn, Missoula Public Library, 301 E Main, Missoula, MT, 59802-4799. Tel: 406-721-2665. p. 1300
AlHusaini, Pamela, Libr Dir, Alvord Public Library, 109 N Wickham St, Alvord, TX, 76225-5325. Tel: 940-427-2842. p. 2133
Ali, Alyssa, Dir, Maxwell Memorial Library, 14 Genesee St, Camillus, NY, 13031. Tel: 315-672-3661. p. 1512
Ali, Diane, Head Librn, Valley Regional Library, 141 Main St S, Morris, MB, R0G 1K0, CANADA. Tel: 204-746-2136. p. 2588
Ali, Nazli R, Br Librn, Stockton-San Joaquin County Public Library, Linden Branch, 19059 E Main St, Hwy 26, Linden, CA, 95236. p. 250
Ali, Radwa, Dir, Roxbury Township Public Library, 103 Main St, Succasunna, NJ, 07876. Tel: 973-584-2400. p. 1445
Alicea, Maritza, Br Mgr, Orange County Library System, North Orange Branch, 1211 E Semoran Blvd, Apopka, FL, 32703. p. 431
Alifano, Alison, Libr Mgr, Mgr, Res, Downs Rachlin Martin PLLC, 199 Main St, Burlington, VT, 05401. Tel: 802-846-8345. p. 2281
Alimusa, Jacques, Br Assoc, Las Vegas-Clark County Library District, Goodsprings Library, 365 W San Pedro Ave, Goodsprings, NV, 89019. Tel: 702-874-1366. p. 1346
Alison, Gibson, Dir, Union Township Public Library, Russellville Branch Library, 280 W Main St, Russellville, OH, 45168-8730. Tel: 937-377-2700. p. 1817
Alita, John, Dir, Commun Serv, Stockton-San Joaquin County Public Library, 605 N El Dorado St, Stockton, CA, 95202. Tel: 209-937-8221. p. 250
Alix, Sylvie, Chef de Section, Bibliotheques de Montreal, Mercier, 8105 rue Hochelaga, Montreal, QC, H1L 2K9, CANADA. Tel: 514-872-8737. p. 2719
Alkema, Margaret, Librn, Canadian Reformed Theological Seminary Library, 110 W 27th St, Hamilton, ON, L9C 5A1, CANADA. Tel: 905-575-3688, Ext 28. p. 2644
Allan, Bonnie, Br Asst, Pictou - Antigonish Regional Library, Pictou Library, 40 Water St, Pictou, NS, B0K 1H0, CANADA. Tel: 902-485-5021. p. 2622
Allan, Katie, Adult Serv Mgr, Orland Park Public Library, 14921 Ravinia Ave, Orland Park, IL, 60462. Tel: 708-428-5155. p. 630
Allan, Mark, Asst Dir, Res & Instrul Serv, Angelo State University Library, 2025 S Johnson, San Angelo, TX, 76904-5079. Tel: 325-486-6535. p. 2235
Allan, Samantha, Br Asst, Pictou - Antigonish Regional Library, River John Library, 2725 W Branch Rd, River John, NS, B0K 1N0, CANADA. Tel: 902-351-2599. p. 2622
Allard, Amber, Cataloger, Syst Adminr, Spies Public Library, 940 First St, Menominee, MI, 49858-3296. Tel: 906-863-3911. p. 1131
Allard, Amber, Br Asst, Cumberland Public Libraries, Parrsboro Library, 91 Queen St, Parrsboro, NS, B0M 1S0, CANADA. Tel: 902-254-2046. p. 2615
Allard, Danielle, PhD, Assoc Prof, University of Alberta, 7-104 Education N, University of Alberta, Edmonton, AB, T6G 2G5, CANADA. Tel: 780-492-7625. p. 2795
Allard, Emily, Dir, Voluntown Public Library, 107 Main St, Voluntown, CT, 06384-1820. Tel: 860-376-0485. p. 342
Allard, Ginette, Prof, College de Maisonneuve, 3800, rue Sherbrooke Est, Montreal, QC, H1X 2A2, CANADA. Tel: 514-254-7131. p. 2796
Allard, Paula, Admin Supvr, The Record Library, 530 E Market St, Stockton, CA, 95202. Tel: 209-546-8271. p. 249
Allard, Suzie, Assoc Dean, Res, University of Tennessee, Knoxville, 451 Communications Bldg, 1345 Circle Park Dr, Knoxville, TN, 37996-0332. Tel: 865-974-2148. p. 2792
Allard, Victoria, Libr Dir, Centerville Public Library, 585 Main St, Centerville, MA, 02632. Tel: 508-790-6220. p. 1009
Allard, Wendy, Br Mgr, Harrison County Library System, Pass Christian Public, 111 Hiern Ave, Pass Christian, MS, 39571. Tel: 228-452-4596. p. 1218
Allbaugh, LaVern, Libr Coord, Summit Christian College Library, 2025 21st St, Gering, NE, 69341. Tel: 308-632-6933, Ext 208. p. 1315
Allbee, Robbyn, Admin Mgr, Round Lake Area Public Library District, 906 Hart Rd, Round Lake, IL, 60073. Tel: 847-546-7060, Ext 105. p. 643
Allbright, Shantay, Libr Mgr, New York Public Library - Astor, Lenox & Tilden Foundations, Jerome Park Branch, 118 Eames Pl, Bronx, NY, 10468. Tel: 718-549-5200. p. 1596
Allcorn, Linda, Dir, Ref (Info Servs), Boonslick Regional Library, 219 W Third St, Sedalia, MO, 65301. Tel: 660-827-7111. p. 1279
Alldridge, Corrine, Asst Dir, Coll Develop Mgr, Portage County District Library, 10482 South St, Garrettsville, OH, 44231. Tel: 330-527-5082, Ext 229. p. 1787
Allee, Nancy J, Libr Dir, University of Michigan Health-West, 5900 Byron Ctr Ave SW, Wyoming, MI, 49519. Tel: 616-252-7200 Ext 7021. p. 1160
Allegrina, Tony, Library Contact, Bodman PLC, Ford Field, 6th Flr, 1901 Saint Antoine St, Detroit, MI, 48226. Tel: 313-259-7777. p. 1097
Alleman, Angela, Public Services & Acquisitions Assoc, Louisiana State University Libraries, LSU School of Veterinary Medicine Library, Skip Bertman Dr, Baton Rouge, LA, 70803-8414. Tel: 225-578-7058. p. 884
Alleman, Michelle M, Dir, McKinley Memorial Library, 40 N Main St, Niles, OH, 44446-5082. Tel: 330-652-1704, Ext 5. p. 1808
Alleman, Sheryl, Tech Serv, Lincoln County Library System, 519 Emerald St, Kemmerer, WY, 83101. Tel: 307-877-6961. p. 2495
Alleman, Steve, Head, Coll Develop, University of Missouri-Kansas City Libraries, 800 E 51st St, Kansas City, MO, 64110. Tel: 816-235-1580. p. 1257
Allen, Allia, Youth Serv Spec, Central Skagit Library District, 110 W State St, Sedro-Woolley, WA, 98284-1551. Tel: 360-755-3985. p. 2383
Allen, Allison, Head, Youth Serv, Cheshire Public Library, 104 Main St, Cheshire, CT, 06410-2499. Tel: 203-272-2245. p. 305
Allen, Amy, Univ Archivist, University of Arkansas Libraries, 365 N McIlroy Ave, Fayetteville, AR, 72701-4002. Tel: 479-575-6370. p. 95
Allen, April, Info Serv & Instrul Librn, Indiana University-Purdue University Fort Wayne, 2101 E Coliseum Blvd, Fort Wayne, IN, 46805-1499. Tel: 260-481-6505. p. 684
Allen, Beverly, Dept Chair, Univ Archivist, Colorado State University - Pueblo, 2200 Bonforte Blvd, Pueblo, CO, 81001-4901. Tel: 719-549-2475. p. 293
Allen, Bonnie, Librn, Churchill Public Library, Town Centre Complex, 180 Laverendrye Ave, Churchill, MB, R0B 0E0, CANADA. Tel: 204-675-2731. p. 2586
Allen, Brad, Exec Dir, Lawrence Public Library, 707 Vermont St, Lawrence, KS, 66044-2371. Tel: 785-843-3833, Ext 102. p. 819
Allen, Brett, Libr Dir, Fairfield/Teton Public Library, 14 N Fourth St, Fairfield, MT, 59436. Tel: 406-467-2477. p. 1292
Allen, Chasidy, Asst Mgr, Saint Louis County Library, Lewis & Clark Branch, 9909 Lewis-Clark Blvd, Saint Louis, MO, 63136-5322. Tel: 314-994-3300, Ext 3450. p. 1274
Allen, Chris, Exec Dir, Kenosha County Historical Society, 220 51st Pl, Kenosha, WI, 53140. Tel: 262-654-5770. p. 2444
Allen, Christy, Dir, Putnam County Public Library, 115 S 16th St, Unionville, MO, 63565-1624. Tel: 660-947-3192. p. 1284
Allen, Christy, YA Serv, Youth Serv, Franklin County Library, 906 N Main St, Louisburg, NC, 27549-2199. Tel: 919-496-2111. p. 1701
Allen, Christy, Asst Dir, Discovery Serv, Furman University Libraries, 3300 Poinsett Hwy, Greenville, SC, 29613-4100. Tel: 864-294-2258. p. 2061
Allen, Colleen, Asst Dir, Luck Public Library, 301 S Main St, Luck, WI, 54853. Tel: 715-472-2770. p. 2448
Allen, Courtney, Sr Librn/Youth Serv, Norfolk Public Library, Two Liberty Lane, Norfolk, MA, 02056. Tel: 508-528-3380. p. 1040
Allen, Darla, Dir, Charles & Joann Lester Library, 100 Park St, Nekoosa, WI, 54457. Tel: 715-886-7879. p. 2464
Allen, Debra, Asst Dir, Orangeburg County Library, 510 Louis St, Orangeburg, SC, 29115-5030. Tel: 803-531-4636. p. 2066
Allen, Delene H, Dir, Libr Serv, Quitman Public Library, 202 E Goode St, Quitman, TX, 75783-2533. Tel: 903-763-4191. p. 2230
Allen, Denise, Asst Librn, Emery County Library System, Emery Branch, 100 North Ctr, Emery, UT, 84522. Tel: 435-286-2474. p. 2262
Allen, Don, Chief Librn, Canada Department of National Defence, Base Borden Public & Military Library, CFB BORDEN, 41 Kapyong Rd, Borden, ON, L0M 1C0, CANADA. Tel: 705-424-1200, Ext 2273. p. 2632
Allen, Don, Commun Serv, Department of Community Services, Government of Yukon, 1171 First Ave, Whitehorse, YT, Y1A 0G9, CANADA. Tel: 867-667-5239. p. 2757
Allen, Douglas, Operations Mgr, Rutgers University Libraries, Archibald Stevens Alexander Library, 169 College Ave, New Brunswick, NJ, 08901-1163. Tel: 848-932-6102. p. 1424
Allen, Ethan, Librn, Detroit Symphony Orchestra Library, 3711 Woodward Ave, Detroit, MI, 48201. Tel: 313-576-5111. p. 1098
Allen, Frank R, Admin Serv, Sr Assoc Dir, University of Central Florida Libraries, 12701 Pegasus Dr, Orlando, FL, 32816-8030. Tel: 407-823-2892. p. 432
Allen, George, Pub Serv Librn, Hillsdale College, 33 E College St, Hillsdale, MI, 49242. Tel: 517-607-4370. p. 1115
Allen, Ian, Reserves, Butte College Library, Chico Center, 2320 Forest Ave, Rm 219, Chico, CA, 95928. Tel: 530-879-4366. p. 189
Allen, Jacob, Libr Asst, McKendree University, 701 College Rd, Lebanon, IL, 62254-1299. Tel: 618-537-6558. p. 607
Allen, Janice, Tech Serv Spec, Northeast Texas Community College, 2886 Farm-to-Market Rd 1735, Mount Pleasant, TX, 75456. Tel: 903-434-8100. p. 2221
Allen, Janice E, Acq, Presv, John E Allen, Inc, 116 North Ave, Park Ridge, NJ, 07656. Tel: 570-676-4145, 570-676-4152. p. 1432
Allen, Jen, Asst Librn, Ossipee Public Library, 74 Main St, Center Ossipee, NH, 03814. Tel: 603-539-6390. p. 1357
Allen, Jennifer, Sr Librn, Lincoln Memorial Library, 240 California Dr, Yountville, CA, 94599-1445. Tel: 707-944-4792. p. 261
Allen, Jennifer, Sr Librn, Veterans Home of California, 250 California Dr, Yountville, CA, 94599-1446. Tel: 707-944-4916. p. 261
Allen, Jessica, Dir, Fultondale Public Library, 500 Byrd Lane, Fultondale, AL, 35068. Tel: 205-849-6335. p. 18
Allen, Joyce, Asst Librn, Robertsdale Public Library, 18301 Pennsylvania St, Robertsdale, AL, 36567. Tel: 251-947-8960. p. 34
Allen, Karen, Youth Serv Coordr, Lawrence Public Library, 707 Vermont St, Lawrence, KS, 66044-2371. Tel: 785-843-3833, Ext 121. p. 819
Allen, Karen, Youth Serv Mgr, Greenville County Library System, 25 Heritage Green Pl, Greenville, SC, 29601-2034. Tel: 864-242-5000, Ext 2249. p. 2061

Allen, Katherine, Librn, University of Minnesota Libraries-Twin Cities, Andersen Horticultural Library, 3675 Arboretum Dr, Chaska, MN, 55318. Tel: 612-301-1239. p. 1185
Allen, Kathy, Librn, Clare Public Library, 119 E Front St, Clare, IA, 50524. Tel: 515-546-6222. p. 740
Allen, Kaylee, Librn, Colony City Library, 339 Cherry St, Colony, KS, 66015. Tel: 620-852-3530. p. 803
Allen, Kelly, Br Mgr, Anythink Libraries, Anythink Brighton, 327 E Bridge St, Brighton, CO, 80601. Tel: 303-405-3230. p. 296
Allen, Kelly, Youth Serv Librn, Oregon Public Library, 256 Brook St, Oregon, WI, 53575. Tel: 608-835-3656. p. 2467
Allen, Kiersten, Libr Dir, Louisburg Public Library, 206 S Broadway, Louisburg, KS, 66053. Tel: 913-837-2217. p. 822
Allen, Kristin, Dir, Hugo Public Library, 522 Second Ave, Hugo, CO, 80821. Tel: 719-743-2325. p. 286
Allen, Leslie, Libr Mgr, Toccoa-Stephens County Public Library, 53 W Savannah St, Toccoa, GA, 30577. Tel: 706-886-6082. p. 500
Allen, Loni, Acq Tech, Messiah University, One University Ave, Ste 3002, Mechanicsburg, PA, 17055. Tel: 717-691-6006, Ext 7018. p. 1960
Allen, Marcia, Coll & Tech Serv Mgr, North Central Kansas Libraries System, 629 Poyntz Ave, Manhattan, KS, 66502. Tel: 785-776-4741. p. 823
Allen, Marguerite, Asst Librn, Inola Public Library, 15 North Broadway, Inola, OK, 74036. Tel: 918-543-8862. p. 1850
Allen, Martha, Chair, Res & Instrul Serv, Saint Louis University, 3650 Lindell Blvd, Saint Louis, MO, 63108-3302. Tel: 314-977-3596. p. 1275
Allen, Mary, Libr Mgr, Lawrence Livermore National Laboratory Library, 7000 East Ave, Livermore, CA, 94550. Tel: 925-423-8386. p. 157
Allen, Mary, Youth Serv Librn, Southwest Public Libraries, Westland Area Library, 4740 W Broad St, Columbus, OH, 43228. Tel: 614-878-1301. p. 1789
Allen, Megan, Dir, Thomas Crane Public Library, 40 Washington St, Quincy, MA, 02269-9164. Tel: 617-376-1331. p. 1048
Allen, Megan, Electronic Res, Case Western Reserve University, School of Law Library, 11075 East Blvd, Cleveland, OH, 44106-7148. Tel: 216-368-5223. p. 1766
Allen, Michael, Library Contact, Harvard Library, Child Memorial & English Tutorial Library, Widener Library, 3rd Flr, Harvard Yard, Cambridge, MA, 02138. Tel: 617-495-4681. p. 1005
Allen, Michelle, Youth Serv Librn, Memphis Public Library, Poplar-White Station Branch, 5094 Poplar, Memphis, TN, 38117-7629. Tel: 901-415-2777. p. 2113
Allen, Misty, Resource Sharing & Course Materials Mgr, Weber State University, 3921 Central Campus Dr, Dept 2901, Ogden, UT, 84408-2901. Tel: 801-626-7820. p. 2268
Allen, Mitchell, Bus Mgr, Avery-Mitchell-Yancey Regional Library System, 289 Burnsville School Rd, Burnsville, NC, 28714. Tel: 828-682-4476. p. 1677
Allen, Nancy, Librn, Lowell Community Library, 2170 Vermont Rte 100, Lowell, VT, 05847. Tel: 802-744-2317. p. 2287
Allen, Nichole, Technical Services Specialist II, Susquehanna University, 514 University Ave, Selinsgrove, PA, 17870-1050. p. 2006
Allen, Nora, Asst Librn, Carleton A Friday Memorial Library, 155 E First St, New Richmond, WI, 54017. Tel: 715-243-0431. p. 2465
Allen, Pat, Librn, Tipton Library, Main St, Tipton, KS, 67485. p. 838
Allen, Penny, Br Mgr, Iberville Parish Library, Rosedale Branch, 15695 Rosedale Rd, Rosedale, LA, 70772. Tel: 225-648-2213. p. 906
Allen, Ramona, Librn, Jackie Brannon Correctional Center Library, 900 N West St, McAlester, OK, 74501. Tel: 918-421-3349. p. 1853
Allen, Rich, Circ Supvr, Edwin A Bemis Public Library, 6014 S Datura St, Littleton, CO, 80120-2636. Tel: 303-795-3961. p. 290
Allen, Robbie, Librn, Palm Beach State College, 4200 Congress Ave, Mail Sta 17, Lake Worth, FL, 33461. Tel: 561-868-3800. p. 416
Allen, Robert, Asst Dir, Fordham University Libraries, Quinn Library at Lincoln Center, 140 W 62nd St, New York, NY, 10023. Tel: 212-636-6058. p. 1498
Allen, Robin, Libr Tech, Nova Scotia Community College, Ivany Campus Library, 80 Mawiomi Pl, Dartmouth, NS, B2Y 0A5, CANADA. Tel: 902-491-1035. p. 2620
Allen, Rochelle, Asst Librn, Eagle Mountain Library, 1650 E Stagecoach Run, Eagle Mountain, UT, 84005. Tel: 801-789-6623. p. 2263
Allen, Ruby, Ref Librn, Atlanta-Fulton Public Library System, Sandy Springs Branch, 395 Mount Vernon Hwy NE, Sandy Springs, GA, 30328. Tel: 404-612-7000. p. 461
Allen, Selicia, Archivist/Librn, Virginia Union University, 1500 N Lombardy St, Richmond, VA, 23220. Tel: 804-257-4117. p. 2344
Allen, Stacey, Chief of Operations, National Park Service, 1055 Pittsburg Landing Rd, Shiloh, TN, 38376. Tel: 731-689-5275. p. 2126
Allen, Teresa, Asst Librn, John Mosser Public Library District, 106 W Meek St, Abingdon, IL, 61410-1451. Tel: 309-462-3129. p. 535
Allen, Tonya, Access Serv Librn/YA, Digital & Electronic Serv, Hobbs Public Library, 509 N Shipp St, Hobbs, NM, 88240. Tel: 575-397-9328. p. 1469
Allen, Tracy, Assoc Dir, Rensselaer Libraries, Rensselaer Architecture Library, Greene Bldg 308, 3rd Flr, 110 Eighth St, Troy, NY, 12180-3590. Tel: 518-276-8310. p. 1652
Allen, Travis, Br Mgr, White County Regional Library System, Baldwin-Kittler Memorial, 612 Van Buren, Judsonia, AR, 72081. Tel: 501-729-3995. p. 109
Allen, Tricia, Br Mgr, Dare County Library, Kill Devil Hills Branch, 400 Mustian St, Kill Devil Hills, NC, 27948. Tel: 252-441-4331. p. 1702
Allen, Tricia, Youth Serv Librn, Ilsley Public Library, 75 Main St, Middlebury, VT, 05753. Tel: 802-388-4097. p. 2288
Allen, Virginia, Libr Spec Supvr, University of Louisiana at Monroe Library, 700 University Ave, Monroe, LA, 71209-0720. Tel: 318-342-1064. p. 899
Allen, Wilda, Chief Exec Officer, Grey Highlands Public Library, 101 Highland Dr, Flesherton, ON, N0C 1E0, CANADA. Tel: 519-924-2241. p. 2641
Allen, Yvonne, Libr Mgr, Wake County Public Library System, Olivia Raney Local History Library, 4016 Carya Dr, Raleigh, NC, 27610. Tel: 919-250-1196. p. 1711
Allen-Ward, Laura, Dir, Phillips 66 Research Library, 190 PLB PRC, Bartlesville, OK, 74003-6670. Tel: 918-977-5875. p. 1842
Allender, Rex, Librn, Central United Methodist Church Library, 201 University Blvd NE, Albuquerque, NM, 87106-4596. Tel: 505-243-7834. p. 1461
Allery, Laisee, Dir, Turtle Mountain Community College Library, PO Box 340, Belcourt, ND, 58316-0340. Tel: 701-477-7812, Ext 2081. p. 1729
Allessandria, Rebekah, Early Literacy Specialist, Outreach Specialist, Shaler North Hills Library, 1822 Mount Royal Blvd, Glenshaw, PA, 15116. Tel: 412-486-0211. p. 1937
Alley, Adam, Pub Serv Librn, Emory & Henry College, 30480 Armbrister Dr, Emory, VA, 24327. Tel: 276-944-6208. p. 2315
Alley, Pennie, Dir, South Thomaston Public Library, 54 Spruce Head Rd, South Thomaston, ME, 04858. Tel: 207-596-0022. p. 942
Allgeier, Donald, Dir, Operations, Multnomah County Library, 919 NE 19th Ave, Ste 250, Portland, OR, 97232. Tel: 503-988-5123. p. 1892
Alligood, Elaine, Chief, Libr Serv, West Roxbury VA Medical Center, 1400 Veterans of Foreign Wars Pkwy, West Roxbury, MA, 02132. Tel: 617-323-7700, Ext 35142. p. 1066
Allinder, Jon, Lead Librarian, Systems & Colls, Walden University Library, 100 Washington Ave S, Ste 900, Minneapolis, MN, 55401. p. 1186
Allington, Mary, Assoc Dir, Br Mgr, Ada Community Library, Star Branch, 10706 W State St, Star, ID, 83669. Tel: 208-286-9755. p. 516
Allison, Bethany, Br Mgr, Indianapolis Public Library, Eagle, 3905 Moller Rd, Indianapolis, IN, 46254. Tel: 317-275-4340. p. 694
Allison, Celia, Mgr, Coll Serv, Wethersfield Public Library, 515 Silas Deane Hwy, Wethersfield, CT, 06109. Tel: 860-529-2665. p. 347
Allison, Eden, Head Librn, Greene County Public Library, Cedarville Community Library, 20 S Miller St, Cedarville, OH, 45314-8556. Tel: 937-352-4006. p. 1834
Allison, Elise, Archivist, Greensboro Historical Museum Archives Library, 130 Summit Ave, Greensboro, NC, 27401-3004. Tel: 336-373-2976. p. 1692
Allison, James M, Head Librn, Bexar County Law Library, Bexar County Courthouse, 5th Flr, 100 Dolorosa, San Antonio, TX, 78205. Tel: 210-335-3189. p. 2236
Allison, Johanna, Chief Librn, Gore Bay Union Public Library, 15 Water St, Gore Bay, ON, P0P 1H0, CANADA. Tel: 705-282-2221. p. 2643
Allison, Joslyn, Instrul Librn, City Colleges of Chicago, Malcolm X College - Carter G Woodson Library, 1900 W Jackson St, 2nd Flr, Chicago, IL, 60612. Tel: 312-850-7244. p. 558
Allison, Kristy, Ch, Algona Public Library, 210 N Phillips St, Algona, IA, 50511. Tel: 515-295-5476. p. 730
Allison, Matthew, Commun Libr Mgr, Queens Library, Peninsula Community Library, 92-25 Rockaway Beach Blvd, Rockaway Beach, NY, 11693. Tel: 718-634-1110. p. 1555
Allison, Sarah, Head, Spec Coll & Univ Archives, California State University, Sacramento, 6000 J St, Sacramento, CA, 95819-6039. Tel: 916-278-6708. p. 208
Allison, Sarah, Head of Archives User Engagement, Ball State University Libraries, Archives & Special Collections, Bracken Library, Rm 210, Muncie, IN, 47306-0161. Tel: 765-285-3301. p. 708
Allison, Zane, Cat, Libr Asst, Virginia Museum of Fine Arts Library, 200 N Arthur Ashe Blvd, Richmond, VA, 23220-4007. Tel: 804-340-1495. p. 2344
Allison-Bunnell, Jodi, Head, Archives & Spec Coll, Univ Archivist, Montana State University Library, One Centennial Mall, Bozeman, MT, 59717. Tel: 406-994-5297. p. 1289
Allman, Deborah, Libr Mgr, New York Public Library - Astor, Lenox & Tilden Foundations, High Bridge Branch, 78 W 168th St, (@ Woodycrest Ave), Bronx, NY, 10452. Tel: 718-293-7800. p. 1595
Allman, Janice, Asst Dir, Tech Serv Librn, East Bridgewater Public Library, 32 Union St, East Bridgewater, MA, 02333. Tel: 508-378-1616. p. 1015
Allman, Kim, Cat Librn, Livingstone College, 701 W Monroe St, Salisbury, NC, 28144. Tel: 704-216-6325. p. 1714
Allmendinger, Carrie, Librn & Archivist, Historic Huguenot Street Library & Archives, 88 Huguenot St, New Paltz, NY, 12561. Tel: 845-255-1660. p. 1576
Allmon, Jessica, ILL, Programming, Duncan Public Library, 2211 N Hwy 81, Duncan, OK, 73533. Tel: 580-255-0636. p. 1846

Allmon, Treva, Br Mgr, Stanly County Public Library, Badin Branch, 62 Pine St, Badin, NC, 28009. Tel: 704-422-3218. p. 1671

Allmon, Warren, Dr, Dir, Paleontological Research Institution Library, 1259 Trumansburg Rd, Ithaca, NY, 14850. Tel: 607-273-6623, Ext 320. p. 1553

Allocco, Claudia, Dir, Libr Serv, Valley Hospital, 223 N Van Dien Ave, Ridgewood, NJ, 07450. Tel: 201-447-8285. p. 1439

Alloway, Catherine, Dir, Schlow Centre Region Library, 211 S Allen St, State College, PA, 16801-4806. Tel: 814-237-6236. p. 2010

Allred, Betty, Librn, Lilbourn Memorial Library, 210 E Lewis Ave, Lilbourn, MO, 63862. Tel: 573-688-2622. p. 1260

Allred, Kristin, Asst Libr Dir, Eagle Mountain Library, 1650 E Stagecoach Run, Eagle Mountain, UT, 84005. Tel: 801-789-6623. p. 2263

Allred, Nora, Asst Dir, Coll & Scholarly Communications, Michigan Technological University, 1400 Townsend Dr, Houghton, MI, 49931-1295. Tel: 906-487-3208. p. 1116

Allred, Tracy, Mgr, Stigler Public Library, 410 NE Sixth St, Stigler, OK, 74462. p. 1862

Allred, Zachary, Asst Dir, Salt Lake Community College Libraries, Taylorsville Redwood Campus, 4600 S Redwood Rd, Taylorsville, UT, 84123-3145. Tel: 801-957-4602. p. 2274

Allred, Zachary, Liaison & Instruction Librn, Salt Lake Community College Libraries, Miller Campus, Miller Free Enterprise Ctr, Rm 123, 9750 S 300 W, Sandy, UT, 84070. Tel: 801-957-5412. p. 2274

Allumbaugh, Jody, Ad, Atlantic Public Library, 507 Poplar St, Atlantic, IA, 50022. Tel: 712-243-5466. p. 733

Allums, Jeanna, Head Librn, South Georgia Regional Library System, 2906 Julia Dr, Valdosta, GA, 31602. Tel: 229-333-0086. p. 501

Allyn, Cathy, Libr Dir, New Durham Public Library, Two Old Bay Rd, New Durham, NH, 03855-2214. Tel: 603-859-2201. p. 1375

Almanzar, Karoline G, Libr Dir, Western University of Health Sciences, 287 E Third St, Pomona, CA, 91766. Tel: 909-469-5323. p. 196

Almberg, Jackie, Libr Mgr, Czar Municipal Library, 5005 49th Ave, Czar, AB, T0B 0Z0, CANADA. Tel: 780-857-3740. p. 2532

Almeida, Ann, Libr Tech, Berkley Public Library, Two N Main St, Berkley, MA, 02779. Tel: 508-822-3329. p. 989

Almeleh, Karen, Dir Bus Ops, Mount Prospect Public Library, Ten S Emerson St, Mount Prospect, IL, 60056. Tel: 847-253-5675. p. 621

Almeyda, Brenda, Med Librn, Charlotte AHEC Library, Medical Education Bldg, 1000 Blythe Blvd, Charlotte, NC, 28203-5812. Tel: 704-355-3129. p. 1679

Almgren, Shelley, Per, Syst Librn, Texas Wesleyan University, 1201 Wesleyan St, Fort Worth, TX, 76105. Tel: 817-531-4816. p. 2181

Almodovar, Milton, Circ Serv, Head Res Librn, Pace University, 861 Bedford Rd, Pleasantville, NY, 10570-2799. Tel: 914-773-3039. p. 1620

Almquist, Deborah, Dir, Libr Serv, North Shore Medical Center, Salem Hospital, 81 Highland Ave, Salem, MA, 01970. Tel: 978-354-4950. p. 1051

Aloenshon, Alexandria, Libr Mgr, New York Public Library - Astor, Lenox & Tilden Foundations, Webster Branch, 1465 York Ave, (Near E 78th St), New York, NY, 10021-8895. Tel: 212-288-5049. p. 1598

Aloisi, John, Dr, Acq Librn, Detroit Baptist Theological Seminary Library, 4801 Allen Rd, Allen Park, MI, 48101. Tel: 313-381-0111, Ext 412. p. 1077

Alomia, Sharyn, Br Mgr, Tuolumne County Public Library, Twain Harte Branch, 18701 Tiffeni Rd, Ste 1F, Twain Harte, CA, 95383. Tel: 209-586-4501. p. 247

Alongi, Nicholas, Head, Info Access Serv, Fordham University Libraries, Quinn Library at Lincoln Center, 140 W 62nd St, New York, NY, 10023. Tel: 212-636-6050. p. 1498

Alonso, Carmen, Cat, United States Air Force, 628 FSS/FSDL, 106 W McCaw St, Bldg 215, Charleston AFB, SC, 29404. Tel: 843-963-3320. p. 2051

Alos, Maryanne, YA Librn, West Springfield Public Library, 200 Park St, West Springfield, MA, 01089. Tel: 413-736-4561, Ext 5. p. 1066

Alpi, Kris, Assoc Dean of Libr, Mount Sinai Medical Center, 4300 Alton Rd, Miami Beach, FL, 33140. Tel: 305-674-2840. p. 425

Alpi, Kris, Univ Librn, Oregon Health & Science University Library, 3181 SW Sam Jackson Park Rd, MC LIB, Portland, OR, 97239-3098. Tel: 503-494-0455. p. 1893

Alpi, Kristine, Assoc Dean of Libraries & Info Sciences, Icahn School of Medicine at Mount Sinai, One Gustave L Levy Pl, New York, NY, 10029. Tel: 212-241-7791. p. 1588

Alquist, Lois, Libr Dir, M-C Community Library, 200 W Grace St, Cleghorn, IA, 51014. Tel: 712-436-2521. p. 740

Alsmeyer, Arlene, Librn, Scribner Public Library, 530 Main St, Scribner, NE, 68057. Tel: 402-664-3540. p. 1335

Alsop, Carolyne, Librn, Oxford Law Association Library, Courthouse, 415 Hunter St, 3rd Flr, Woodstock, ON, N4S 4G6, CANADA. Tel: 519-539-7711. p. 2705

Alston, Jason, Asst Teaching Prof, University of Missouri-Columbia, 303 Townsend Hall, Columbia, MO, 65211. Tel: 573-882-4546. p. 2788

Alston, Kay, Dean, Libr Serv, Campbellsville University, One University Dr, Campbellsville, KY, 42718-2799. Tel: 270-789-5360. p. 850

Alston, Nancy, Libr Adminr, Washington County Public Library, McIntosh Branch, Melva Jean Daughtery Bldg, 83 Olin Rd, McIntosh, AL, 36553. Tel: 251-944-2047. p. 11

Alston, Sarah, Ref & Instruction Librn, Bellevue University, 1028 Bruin Blvd, Bellevue, NE, 68005. Tel: 402-557-7302. p. 1308

Alsum-O'Donovan, Linda, Dir, Oakfield Public Library, 130 N Main St, Oakfield, WI, 53065-9563. Tel: 920-583-4552. p. 2466

Alsup, Kathleen, Asst Dir, Mercy Hospital, Tower B, Ste 1000, 621 S New Ballas Rd, Saint Louis, MO, 63141. Tel: 314-251-6340. p. 1271

Alt, Laura, Dir, Shelby Community Library, 648 N Walnut, Shelby, NE, 68662. Tel: 402-527-5256. p. 1336

Altamirano, Felipe, Asst Dir, Maywood Public Library District, 121 S Fifth Ave, Maywood, IL, 60153-1307. Tel: 708-343-1847, Ext 11. p. 615

Altamirano, Patricia, Web Coordr, Dallas County Law Library, George Allen Courts Bldg, 600 Commerce St, Rm 760, Dallas, TX, 75202-4606. Tel: 214-653-6947. p. 2164

Altan, Alex, Col Archivist, ILL Librn, Prairie State College Library, 202 S Halsted St, Chicago Heights, IL, 60411-8200. Tel: 708-709-3552. p. 571

Altenberg, Wayne, Ref Librn, Merced College, 3600 M St, Merced, CA, 95348. Tel: 209-381-6431. p. 176

Alter, Rachel, Dir, West Stockbridge Public Library, 21 State Line Rd, West Stockbridge, MA, 01266. Tel: 413-232-0300, Ext 308. p. 1066

Altieri, Marylene, Curator, Harvard Library, Arthur & Elizabeth Schlesinger Library on the History of Women in America, Three James St, Cambridge, MA, 02138-3766. Tel: 617-495-8647. p. 1007

Altilio, Barbara, Br Mgr, Clifton Public Library, Allwood Branch, 44 Lyall Rd, Clifton, NJ, 07012. Tel: 973-471-0555. p. 1397

Altman, Kelly, Children & Youth Serv Librn, Presque Isle District Library, 181 E Erie St, Rogers City, MI, 49779-1709. Tel: 989-734-2477. p. 1145

Altman, Leslie, Adult Collection Dev, Yarmouth Port Library, 297 Main St, Rte 6A, Yarmouth Port, MA, 02675. Tel: 508-362-3717. p. 1073

Altman, Lynn, Br Mgr, Presque Isle District Library, Posen Branch, 11919 M-65, Posen, MI, 49776. p. 1145

Altman, Mary, Librn, United States Air Force, Medical Center Library, 81st Medical Group/SGGMEL, 301 Fisher St, Rm 1A132, Keesler AFB, MS, 39534-2519. Tel: 228-376-4949. p. 1224

Altman, Micah, Dir, Res, Massachusetts Institute of Technology Libraries, Office of the Director, Bldg NE36-6101, 77 Massachusetts Ave, Cambridge, MA, 02139-4307. Tel: 617-324-8475. p. 1008

Altman, Rachael, Br Mgr, Bryan College Station Public Library System, Carnegie History Center, 111 S Main St, Bryan, TX, 77803. Tel: 979-209-5630. p. 2151

Altmeyer, Sue, Electronic Serv Librn, Cleveland State University, Cleveland-Marshall Law Library, Cleveland-Marshall College of Law, 1801 Euclid Ave, Cleveland, OH, 44115-2223. Tel: 216-687-4894. p. 1769

Altnau, Chris, Electronic Res, Tech Serv Librn, East Texas Baptist University, One Tiger Dr, Marshall, TX, 75670-1498. Tel: 903-923-2259. p. 2215

Altom, Clayton, Dir, Tennessee Regional Library for the Blind & Physically Handicapped, 403 Seventh Ave N, Nashville, TN, 37243. Tel: 615-741-3915. p. 2121

Alton, Beth, Libr Dir, Moody Community Library, 612 Ave D, Moody, TX, 76557. Tel: 254-853-2044. p. 2220

Altson, Traci, Librn, Yachats Public Library, 560 W Seventh St, Yachats, OR, 97498. Tel: 541-547-3741. p. 1902

Altuntur, Selin, Librn, Montreal Neurological Institute Hospital Library, 3801 University St, Rm 285, Montreal, QC, H3A 2B4, CANADA. Tel: 514-398-1980. p. 2727

Aluzzo, Adrienne, Digital Projects Librn, Lawrence Technological University Library, 21000 W Ten Mile Rd, Southfield, MI, 48075-1058. Tel: 248-204-2821. p. 1151

Alvarado Anderson, Martha, Dir Diversity, Head, Digital Serv, University of Arkansas Libraries, 365 N McIlroy Ave, Fayetteville, AR, 72701-4002. Tel: 479-575-4101. p. 95

Alvarado, Claudia, Coordr, Acq, Mount Saint Mary's University, J Thomas McCarthy Library, Doheny Campus, Ten Chester Pl, Los Angeles, CA, 90007. Tel: 213-477-2750. p. 166

Alvarado, Jessica, Br Mgr, Dallas Public Library, Vickery Park, 8333 Park Lane, Dallas, TX, 75231. Tel: 214-671-2101. p. 2166

Alvarado, Melissa, Librn II, Southwest Texas Junior College, 215 W Zavala St, Crystal City, TX, 78839. Tel: 830-374-2828, Ext 7611. p. 2162

Alvarado, Rasheima, Adult Programming, Mkt, Riverhead Free Library, 330 Court St, Riverhead, NY, 11901-2885. Tel: 631-727-3228. p. 1627

Alvarez, Alberto, Sr Librn, Los Angeles Public Library System, Exposition Park - Dr Mary McLeod Bethune Regional Library, 3900 S Western Ave, Los Angeles, CA, 90062. Tel: 323-290-3113. p. 164

Alvarez, Alma, Dir, Town of Chester Public Library, 6307 State Rte 9, Chestertown, NY, 12817. Tel: 518-494-5384. p. 1518

Alvarez, Alvaro, Innovative Media Librn, University of California, Riverside, 900 University Ave, Riverside, CA, 92521. Tel: 951-827-3220. p. 203

Alvarez Aponte, Pamela Marie, Coordr, Coll Mgt, Katten Muchin Rosenman LLP, 50 Rockefeller Plaza, New York, NY, 10020-1605. Tel: 312-577-8341. p. 1590

Alvarez, Barbara, Mgr, Dallas Public Library, Arcadia Park, 1302 N Justin Ave, Dallas, TX, 75211-1142. Tel: 214-670-6446. p. 2165

Alvarez, Daniel, Circ Mgr, Berklee College of Music Library, 150 Massachusetts Ave, Boston, MA, 02115. Tel: 617-747-2258. p. 990

Alvarez, Diane, Librn, Arizona Department of Corrections, Arizona State Prison Complex-Safford, 15500 S Fort Grant Rd, Safford, AZ, 85643. Tel: 928-828-3393, Ext 94508. p. 75

Alvarez, Hector, Head, Pub Serv, Librn, Universite de Moncton, 18, ave Antonine-Maillet, Moncton, NB, E1A 3E9, CANADA. Tel: 506-858-4911. p. 2603

Alvarez, Lily, Librn IV, Chicago Public Library, Rudy Lozano Library, 1805 S Loomis St, Chicago, IL, 60608. Tel: 312-746-4329. p. 557

Alvarez, Miguel, Circ, Ref (Info Servs), Pontifical Catholic University, Monsignor Fremiot Torres Oliver Law Library, 2250 Blvd Luis A Ferre Aguayo, Ste 544, Ponce, PR, 00717-9997. Tel: 787-841-2000, Ext 1850, 787-841-2000, Ext 1851. p. 2512

Alvarez, Minerva, Librn III, Ref & Circ Librn, South Texas College Library, 3201 W Pecan Blvd, McAllen, TX, 78501-6661. Tel: 956-872-3442. p. 2217

Alvarez, Samuel, Libr Dir, Reuben Hoar Library, 35 Shattuck St, Littleton, MA, 01460. Tel: 978-540-2600. p. 1029

Alvarez, Shaunta, Digital Coll Librn, Syst Librn, Elon University, 308 N O'Kelly Ave, Elon, NC, 27244-0187. Tel: 336-278-6600. p. 1688

Alvarez, Sophia, Libr Assoc, Grandview Library, 500 W Main St, Grandview, WA, 98930-1398. Tel: 509-882-7034, 509-882-7057. p. 2365

Alvarez-Lenda, Alina, Research & Information Services Mgr, Hunton Andrews Kurth, LLP, 200 Park Ave, New York, NY, 10166. Tel: 212-309-1078. p. 1588

Alvayay, Patty, Head, Tech Serv, University of Kentucky Libraries, Law Library, J David Rosenberg College of Law, 620 S Limestone St, Lexington, KY, 40506-0048. Tel: 859-257-2925. p. 863

Alvery-Henderson, Luke, Libr Dir, Durango Public Library, 1900 E Third Ave, Durango, CO, 81301. Tel: 970-375-3380. p. 278

Alves, Corrie, Coordr, Tech, Cranston Public Library, 140 Sockanosset Cross Rd, Cranston, RI, 02920-5539. Tel: 401-943-9080. p. 2031

Alves, Persephone, Circ, Swansea Free Public Library, 69 Main St, Swansea, MA, 02777. Tel: 508-674-9609. p. 1059

Alvey, Scott, Exec Dir, Kentucky Historical Society, 100 W Broadway St, Frankfort, KY, 40601. Tel: 502-782-8080. p. 855

Alvia, Manuel, Supvr, Pub Serv, Iona University, Helen T Arrigoni Library-Technology Center, 715 North Ave, New Rochelle, NY, 10801-1890. Tel: 914-633-2000, Ext 4165. p. 1577

Alvin, Glenda, Asst Dir, Coll Develop, Interim Exec Dir, Tennessee State University, 3500 John A Merritt Blvd, Nashville, TN, 37209. Tel: 615-963-5230. p. 2121

Alvino, Jennifer, Libr Dir, Windham Public Library, 217 Windham Center Rd, Windham, ME, 04062. Tel: 207-892-1908. p. 946

Alvis, Alexandra, Ref Librn, Smithsonian Libraries, Joseph F Cullman III, Library of Natural History, Nat Museum of Natural History, Tenth St & Constitution Ave NW, Washington, DC, 20560. Tel: 202-633-1177. p. 375

Alvord, Elizabeth, Libr Dir, Ivoryton Library Association, 106 Main St, Ivoryton, CT, 06442. Tel: 860-767-1252. p. 319

Alward, Allan, Libr Mgr, Albert-Westmorland-Kent Regional Library, Sackville Public, 66 Main St, Sackville, NB, E4L 4A7, CANADA. Tel: 506-364-4915. p. 2603

Alward, Judy, Info Spec, University of Alaska Anchorage, Environment & Natural Resources Institute Arctic Environment & Data Information Center Library, 707 A St, Anchorage, AK, 99501. Tel: 907-257-2732. p. 43

Alway, Joseph, Coordr, Tech Serv, Southwestern Adventist University, 101 W Magnolia St, Keene, TX, 76059. Tel: 817-202-6603. p. 2204

Alwine, Hope D, Digital Initiatives, Spec, Longwood University, Redford & Race St, Farmville, VA, 23909. Tel: 434-395-2873. p. 2318

Alyea, Beth, Br Head, Lake County Public Library, Dyer-Schererville Branch, 1001 W Lincoln Hwy, Schererville, IN, 46375-1552. Tel: 219-322-4731. p. 705

Amabile, Anthony, Asst Dir, Skadden, Arps, Slate, Meagher & Flom Library, One Manhattan W, New York, NY, 10036. Tel: 212-735-3000. p. 1602

Amack, April, Dir, Learning Res, Morgan Community College Library, 920 Barlow Rd, Fort Morgan, CO, 80701-4399. Tel: 970-542-3187. p. 282

Amadife, Nkechi, Coordr, Libr Instruction, Head, Pub Serv, Kentucky State University, 400 E Main St, Frankfort, KY, 40601-2355. Tel: 502-597-6817. p. 855

Amalong, Rebecca, Tech Serv Librn, Jasper County Public Library, 208 W Susan St, Rensselaer, IN, 47978. Tel: 219-866-5881. p. 714

Aman, Timothy, Librn, Spokane Community College/Community Colleges of Spokane Library, MS 2160, 1810 N Greene St, Spokane, WA, 99217-5399. Tel: 509-533-7054. p. 2384

Amanda, Brown, Librn, Roanoke Public Libraries, Melrose, 2502 Melrose Ave NW, Suite D, Roanoke, VA, 24017. Tel: 540-853-2648. p. 2345

Amaniampong, Gyesi, Lecturer, North Carolina Central University, 1801 Fayetteville St, Durham, NC, 27707. Tel: 919-530-6485. p. 2790

Amaral, Andria L, YA Mgr, Charleston County Public Library, 68 Calhoun St, Charleston, SC, 29401. Tel: 843-805-6801. p. 2048

Amaral, Ann, Asst Dir & Head, Adult Serv, Newport Public Library, 300 Spring St, Newport, RI, 02840. Tel: 401-847-8720. p. 2035

Amaral, Jean, Outreach Librn, Borough of Manhattan Community College Library, 199 Chambers St, S410, New York, NY, 10007. Tel: 212 220-8000, Ext 5114. p. 1580

Amaral, Kristin, Tech Coordr, Tiverton Public Library, 34 Roosevelt Ave, Tiverton, RI, 02878. Tel: 401-625-6796, Ext 8. p. 2042

Amatrudo, Christine, YA Serv, Marlborough Public Library, 35 W Main St, Marlborough, MA, 01752-5510. Tel: 508-624-6900. p. 1032

Amaya, Angela, Librn, Las Positas College Library, 3000 Campus Hill Dr, Livermore, CA, 94551. Tel: 925-424-1150. p. 156

Amaya, Guadalupe, Asst Librn, Virgil & Josephine Gordon Memorial Library, 917 N Circle Dr, Sealy, TX, 77474. Tel: 979-885-7469. p. 2242

Amaya, Rosie, Dir, Joe Barnhart Bee County Public Library, 110 W Corpus Christi St, Beeville, TX, 78102-5604. Tel: 361-362-4901. p. 2146

Amberths, Luis, Dir, Vineland Public Library, 1058 E Landis Ave, Vineland, NJ, 08360. Tel: 856-794-4244. p. 1450

Ambramovich, Samuel, Dr, Assoc Prof, University at Buffalo, The State University of New York, 534 Baldy Hall, Buffalo, NY, 14260. Tel: 716-645-2412. p. 2789

Ambriz, Lorely, Head Librn, El Paso Community College Library, Jenna Welch & Laura Bush Community Library, Northwest Campus, 6701 S Desert Rd, Rm L100, El Paso, TX, 79932. Tel: 915-831-8889. p. 2173

Ambrosait, Denise, Youth Serv, Titusville Public Library, 2121 S Hopkins Ave, Titusville, FL, 32780. Tel: 321-264-5026. p. 451

Ambrose, Amelia, Exec Dir, Franklin County Law Library Association, 100 Lincoln Way E, Ste E, Chambersburg, PA, 17201. Tel: 717-267-2071. p. 1920

Ambrose, Diane L, Dir, Citizens Library, 55 S College St, Washington, PA, 15301. Tel: 724-222-2400. p. 2018

Ambrose, Jan, Dir, Marseilles Public Library, 155 E Bluff St, Marseilles, IL, 61341-1499. Tel: 815-795-4437. p. 614

Ambrose-Dalton, Rebekah, Spec Coll Librn, Cape Cod Community College, 2240 Iyannough Rd, West Barnstable, MA, 02668-1599. Tel: 774-330-4445. p. 1065

Ambrosi, Tom, Head, Res Serv, University of Minnesota Duluth, 416 Library Dr, Duluth, MN, 55812. Tel: 218-726-7681. p. 1173

Ambrosino, Robin, Librn, Saratoga Hospital, 211 Church St, Saratoga Springs, NY, 12866. Tel: 518-583-8301. p. 1636

Ambrosius, Amy, Libr Dir, Rushville Public Library, 514 Maple Ave, Rushville, IL, 62681-1044. Tel: 217-322-3030. p. 644

Ambroziak, Marta, Head, Access Serv, New York Medical College, Basic Science Bldg, 15 Dana Rd, Valhalla, NY, 10595. Tel: 914-594-4204. p. 1656

Ambrus, Andre, Asst Prof, Res & Instruction Librn, University of La Verne, 2040 Third St, La Verne, CA, 91750. Tel: 909-593-3511, Ext 4305. p. 155

Ameen, Joe, Head, Access Serv, University of California, Merced Library, 5200 N Lake Rd, Merced, CA, 95343. Tel: 209-761-4512. p. 176

Amelsberg, Paula, Asst Law Librn, North Dakota Supreme Court, Judicial Wing, 2nd Flr, 600 E Boulevard Ave, Dept 182, Bismarck, ND, 58505-0540. Tel: 701-328-4496. p. 1730

Amemasor, James, Libr Spec, New Jersey Historical Society Library, 52 Park Pl, Newark, NJ, 07102-4302. Tel: 973-596-8500, Ext 249. p. 1426

Amen, Anna, Finance & Operations Mgr, Northbrook Public Library, 1201 Cedar Lane, Northbrook, IL, 60062-4581. Tel: 847-272-6224. p. 626

Amen, Kathy, Govt Doc, Saint Mary's University, Louis J Blume Library, One Camino Santa Maria, San Antonio, TX, 78228-8608. Tel: 210-436-3441. p. 2238

Amend, Lee Ann, Dir, Sharon Public Library, 11 N Main St, Sharon, MA, 02067-1299. Tel: 781-784-1578. p. 1052

Amenda, Matthew, Youth Serv, Bellaire City Library, 5111 Jessamine, Bellaire, TX, 77401-4498. Tel: 713-662-8160. p. 2147

Amerson, Amber, Libr Asst, East Georgia State College Library, 131 College Circle, Swainsboro, GA, 30401-2699. Tel: 478-289-2086. p. 498

Amerson, Robert, Instruction/Ref Serv, Syst Librn, University of South Carolina Aiken, 471 University Pkwy, Aiken, SC, 29801. Tel: 803-641-3320. p. 2046

Ames, Caleb, Syst Librn, Dixie State University Library, 225 S 700 E, Saint George, UT, 84770. Tel: 435-879-4321. p. 2270

Ames, Kathryn, Lead Librn, Muskegon Area District Library, Muskegon Township Branch, 1765 Ada Ave, Muskegon, MI, 49442. Tel: 231-760-4329. p. 1136

Ames, Katie, Lead Librn, Muskegon Area District Library, Ravenna Branch, 12278 Stafford, Ravenna, MI, 49451-9410. Tel: 231-853-6975. p. 1136

Ames, Wendy, Librn, Weld Free Public Library, 25 Church St, Weld, ME, 04285. Tel: 207-585-2439. p. 945

Amey, Jon, Libr Dir, Pennsylvania Institute of Technology Library, 800 Manchester Ave, Media, PA, 19063-4098. Tel: 610-892-1524. p. 1961

Amey, Tracey, Dir, Pennsylvania College of Technology, 999 Hagan Way, Williamsport, PA, 17701. Tel: 570-327-4523. p. 2023

Amici, Heidi, Asst Libr Dir, Monmouth County Library, 125 Symmes Dr, Manalapan, NJ, 07726. Tel: 732-431-7220. p. 1415

Aminy, Marina, Dean, Saddleback College, 28000 Marguerite Pkwy, Mission Viejo, CA, 92692. Tel: 949-582-4365. p. 177

Amiot, Marie, Dir, Bibliotheque Municipale Alice-Lane, Six Ave Radisson, Baie Comeau, QC, G4Z 1W4, CANADA. Tel: 418-296-8304. p. 2709
Amling, Jennifer, Head, Commun Serv, Mount Prospect Public Library, Ten S Emerson St, Mount Prospect, IL, 60056. Tel: 847-253-5675. p. 621
Amlong, Jennifer F, Dir, Elba Public Library, 406 Simmons St, Elba, AL, 36323. Tel: 334-897-6921. p. 15
Amlong, Terri, Interim Dean, Delaware County Community College Library, 901 S Media Line Rd, Media, PA, 19063-1094. Tel: 610-359-5133. p. 1961
Ammerman, Jackie, Assoc Univ Librn, Digital Initiatives & Open Access, Boston University Libraries, Mugar Memorial Library, 771 Commonwealth Ave, Boston, MA, 02215. Tel: 617-353-3710. p. 993
Ammerman, Nick, Librn, American Planning Association Library, 205 N Michigan Ave, Ste 1200, Chicago, IL, 60601. Tel: 312-431-9100, Ext 6353. p. 554
Ammon, Teresa, Cataloger, Libr Asst, Central Christian College of the Bible Library, 911 E Urbandale Dr, Moberly, MO, 65270. Tel: 660-263-2933. p. 1262
Ammons, Jessica, Educ Mat Ctr Librn, University of Wisconsin Oshkosh, 801 Elmwood Ave, Oshkosh, WI, 54901. Tel: 920-424-2320. p. 2467
Amoe, Veronica, Mgr, Sterne-Hoya House Museum & Library, 211 S Lanana St, Nacogdoches, TX, 75961. Tel: 936-560-5426. p. 2221
Amohror, Gaylene, Circ Asst, Arcadia Free Public Library, 730 Raider Dr, Ste 3140, Arcadia, WI, 54612. Tel: 608-323-7505. p. 2421
Amores, Michelle, Div Mgr, San Jose Public Library, 150 E San Fernando St, San Jose, CA, 95112-3580. Tel: 408-808-2186. p. 231
Amorosi, Chris, Head, Tech Serv, Peabody Institute Library, 15 Sylvan St, Danvers, MA, 01923. Tel: 978-774-0554. p. 1013
Amos, Beate, Circ, Kinnelon Public Library, 132 Kinnelon Rd, Kinnelon, NJ, 07405. Tel: 973-838-1321. p. 1410
Amos, Jeanne, Libr Dir, El Dorado County Library, 345 Fair Lane, Placerville, CA, 95667. Tel: 530-621-5546. p. 195
Amos, Laura, Library Contact, Armona Community Library, 11115 C St, Armona, CA, 93202. Tel: 559-583-5020, Ext 5005. p. 117
Amos, MK, Music Cataloging Tech, University of North Carolina at Greensboro, Harold Schiffman Music Library, School of Music Bldg, 100 McIver St, Greensboro, NC, 27412. Tel: 336-334-5868. p. 1693
Amoyaw, Sandy, Br Adminr, Yonkers Public Library, Riverfront Library, One Larkin Center, Yonkers, NY, 10701. Tel: 914-375-7941. p. 1668
Amsbary, Jen, Coordr, Youth Serv, Carpenter-Carse Library, 69 Ballards Corner Rd, Hinesburg, VT, 05461. Tel: 802-482-2878. p. 2286
Amsberry, Dawn, Ref & Instruction Librn, Pennsylvania State University Libraries, Library Learning Services, 216 Pattee Tower, University Park, PA, 16802-1803. Tel: 814-865-5093. p. 2015
Amsberryaugier, Lora, Assoc Dean of Libr, Info Serv, University of New Orleans, 2000 Lakeshore Dr, New Orleans, LA, 70148. Tel: 504-280-5563. p. 904
Amschl, Tiffany, Adult & Teen Serv Mgr, Asst Dir, Crete Public Library District, 1177 N Main St, Crete, IL, 60417. Tel: 708-672-8017. p. 574
Amstutz, Tim, Educ Res Librn, Bethel College, 1001 Bethel Circle, Mishawaka, IN, 46545. Tel: 574-807-7001. p. 706
Amulung, Johnene, Libr Mgr, Rolling Hills Public Library, 322 Fourth St, Rolling Hills, AB, T0J 2S0, CANADA. Tel: 403-964-2186. p. 2552
Amundsen, Michele Lee, Colls Mgr, Danbury Museum & Historical Society, 43 Main St, Danbury, CT, 06810. Tel: 203-743-5200. p. 307
Amundson, Anna, Dir, Mountain Iron Public Library, 5742 Mountain Ave, Mountain Iron, MN, 55768-9636. Tel: 218-735-8625. p. 1190
Amundson, Lauren, Librn & Archivist, Lowell Observatory Library, 1400 W Mars Hill Rd, Flagstaff, AZ, 86001. Tel: 928-714-7083. p. 60
An, Amy, Ref & Instruction Librn, Lynn University Library, 3601 N Military Trail, Boca Raton, FL, 33431-5598. Tel: 561-237-7072. p. 385
An, Angie, Bus Librn, York University Libraries, Peter F Bronfman Business Library, Schulich School of Business, Seymour Schulich Bldg, Rm S237, 111 Ian McDonald Blvd, North York, ON, M3J 1P3, CANADA. Tel: 416-736-5139. p. 2661
An-Dunning, Jin, Librn, College of the Desert Library, 43-500 Monterey Ave, Palm Desert, CA, 92260. Tel: 760-773-2563. p. 191
Anabel, Kate, Dir, Admin & Planning, Harvard Library, Social Sciences Program, Lamont Library, Level B, Harvard University, Cambridge, MA, 02138. Tel: 617-495-2106. p. 1007
Anastasio, Lauren, Circ, Palisades Free Library, 19 Closter Rd, Palisades, NY, 10964. Tel: 845-359-0136. p. 1614
Anastos, Ross, Libr Serv Mgr, University of California, Merced Library, 5200 N Lake Rd, Merced, CA, 95343. Tel: 209-201-6485. p. 176
Anaya, Amy, Head, Borrower Serv, Jones Library, Inc, 43 Amity St, Amherst, MA, 01002-2285. Tel: 413-259-3132. p. 984
Anaya, Andrea, Dir, Libr & Archives, The Salvation Army College for Officer Training at Crestmont, 30840 Hawthorne Blvd, Rancho Palos Verdes, CA, 90275. Tel: 310-265-6129, 310-377-0481. p. 198
Anaya, Joseph, Library Services Assoc III, University of Arizona Libraries, Health Sciences Library, 1501 N Campbell Ave, Tucson, AZ, 85724. Tel: 520-626-6125. p. 83
Anbler, Amy, Ch Serv, Free Library of Springfield Township, 8900 Hawthorne Lane, Wyndmoor, PA, 19038. Tel: 215-836-5300. p. 2025
Anchondo, Paul, Dir, Commun Serv, Eloy Santa Cruz Library, 1000 N Main St, Eloy, AZ, 85131. Tel: 520-466-3814. p. 60
Ancira, Leticia, Ch Serv, Outreach Specialist, Camp Verde Community Library, 130 N Black Bridge Rd, Camp Verde, AZ, 86322. Tel: 928-554-8387. p. 57
Andeen, Sarah, Dir, Knowledge Mgt, Dir, Res, Chapman & Cutler, 320 S Canal St, 27th Flr, Chicago, IL, 60606. Tel: 312-845-3000, 312-845-3749. p. 555
Andel, Ruth, Col Archivist, Allegheny College, 520 N Main St, Meadville, PA, 16335. Tel: 814-332-2398. p. 1959
Anderies, John, Dir, John J Wilcox Jr Archives & Library, William Way LGBT Community Ctr, 1315 Spruce St, Philadelphia, PA, 19107. Tel: 215-732-2220. p. 1989
Anders, Eleanor, ILL, Libr Assoc, Marshall University Libraries, One John Marshall Dr, Huntington, WV, 25755-2060. Tel: 304-696-2320. p. 2405
Anders, Erin, Dir, Fox Lake Public Library, 117 W State St, Fox Lake, WI, 53933-9505. Tel: 920-928-3223. p. 2436
Anders, Jessica, Libr Tech, Eastern Wyoming College Library, 3200 West C St, Torrington, WY, 82240. Tel: 307-532-8210. p. 2500
Anders, Justin, Dir, Libr Tech, Mount Royal University Library, 4825 Mount Royal Gate SW, Calgary, AB, T3E 6K6, CANADA. Tel: 403-440-6132. p. 2528
Anders, Kelly, Dep Dir, National Archives & Records Administration, 500 W US Hwy 24, Independence, MO, 64050-1798. Tel: 816-268-8200. p. 1251
Anders, Kelly Lynn, Dir, Jackson County Law Library, Inc, 1301 Oak St, Ste 310, Kansas City, MO, 64106. Tel: 816-221-2221. p. 1255
Anders, Tara, Assoc Librn, Spruce Pine Public Library, 142 Walnut Ave, Spruce Pine, NC, 28777. Tel: 828-765-4673. p. 1717
Andersen, Dana, Dir, Brown Deer Public Library, 5600 W Bradley Rd, Brown Deer, WI, 53223-3510. Tel: 414-357-0106. p. 2426
Andersen, Jill, Adult Ref Librn, Interim Dir, Carpenter-Carse Library, 69 Ballards Corner Rd, Hinesburg, VT, 05461. Tel: 802-482-2878. p. 2286
Andersen, Jon, Supvr, Riverside Public Library, SSgt Salvador J Lara Casa Blanca Library, 2985 Madison St, Riverside, CA, 92504-4480. Tel: 951-826-2120. p. 203
Andersen, Katie, Librn, Northwest Regional Library, Greenbush Public Library, 234 Main St N, Greenbush, MN, 56726. Tel: 218-782-2218. p. 1205
Andersen, Kevin, Prog Coordr, Wethersfield Historical Society, 150 Main St, Wethersfield, CT, 06109. Tel: 860-529-7656. p. 347
Andersen, Linda, Librn, Northwest Regional Library, Greenbush Public Library, 234 Main St N, Greenbush, MN, 56726. Tel: 218-782-2218. p. 1205
Andersen, Marcy, Libr Dir, Thomas County Library, 503 Main St, Thedford, NE, 69166. Tel: 308-645-2237. p. 1338
Andersen, Michael, Ref Librn, Morton College Library, 3801 S Central Ave, Cicero, IL, 60804. Tel: 708-656-8000, Ext 2321. p. 571
Andersen, Michelle, Dir, Atlantic Public Library, 507 Poplar St, Atlantic, IA, 50022. Tel: 712-243-5466. p. 733
Andersen, Patricia, Assessment Librn, User Experience Librn, Colorado School of Mines, 1400 Illinois St, Golden, CO, 80401-1887. Tel: 303-273-3652. p. 283
Andersen, Patricia M, Dir, South Dakota School of Mines & Technology, 501 E Saint Joseph St, Rapid City, SD, 57701-3995. p. 2081
Andersen, Ron, Dir, Eagle Nest Public Library, 74 N Tomboy Dr, Eagle Nest, NM, 87718. Tel: 575-377-0657. p. 1467
Anderson, A P, Res & Instruction Librn, Texas A&M University-Commerce, 2600 S Neal St, Commerce, TX, 75428. Tel: 903-886-5713. p. 2158
Anderson, Aaron, Bus Mgr, State Library of Louisiana, 701 N Fourth St, Baton Rouge, LA, 70802-5232. Tel: 225-342-4923. p. 885
Anderson, Amanda, YA Librn, Bristol Public Library, 701 Goode St, Bristol, VA, 24201. Tel: 276-821-6192. p. 2308
Anderson, Amy, Br Mgr, Wayne County Public Library, Creston Branch, 116 S Main St, Creston, OH, 44217. Tel: 330-804-4732. p. 1833
Anderson, Amy, Chief Exec Officer, Allegheny County Library Association (ACLA), 22 Wabash St, Ste 202, Pittsburgh, PA, 15220. Tel: 412-921-1123. p. 1990
Anderson, Amy, Dir, Libr Res, Southwestern University, 1100 E University Ave, Georgetown, TX, 78626. Tel: 512-863-1639. p. 2184
Anderson, Andrew, Pres & Chief Exec Officer, Library & Information Resources Network, 25400 US 19 N, Ste 220, Clearwater, FL, 33763. Tel: 727-536-0214. p. 2763
Anderson, Ann, Library Contact, Shuts Environmental Library, Three Nature's Way, Lancaster, PA, 17602. Tel: 717-295-2055. p. 1952
Anderson, AnneMarie, Instruction Librn, Northern Virginia Community College Libraries, Alexandria Campus, Bisdorf Bldg, Rm 232, 5000 Dawes Ave, Alexandria, VA, 22311. Tel: 703-845-6025. p. 2304
Anderson, Annette, Circ Librn, Galena Public Library District, 601 S Bench St, Galena, IL, 61036. Tel: 815-777-0200. p. 590
Anderson, Anthony, Ref Serv, University of Southern California Libraries, Von KleinSmid Center Library, Von KleinSmid Ctr, 3518 Trousdale Pkwy, Los Angeles, CA, 90089-0182. Tel: 213-740-1190. p. 170

Anderson, Bailey, Libr Dir, Black Earth Public Library, 1210 Mills St, Black Earth, WI, 53515. Tel: 608-767-4905. p. 2424

Anderson, Barbara, Head of Instruction & Learning, Roosevelt University, 430 S Michigan Ave, Chicago, IL, 60605. Tel: 312-341-3647. p. 567

Anderson, Beth, Libr Mgr, Bucks County Free Library, James A Michener Branch, 401 W Mill St, Quakertown, PA, 18951-1248. Tel: 215-536-3306. p. 1927

Anderson, Beth, Head, Acq, Virginia Polytechnic Institute & State University Libraries, 560 Drillfield Dr, Blacksburg, VA, 24061. Tel: 540-231-4884. p. 2307

Anderson, Brenda, Acq, Tech Serv, North Platte Public Library, 120 W Fourth St, North Platte, NE, 69101-3993. Tel: 308-535-8036. p. 1327

Anderson, Brianna, Br Librn, Stockton-San Joaquin County Public Library, Escalon Branch, 1540 Second St, Escalon, CA, 95320. p. 250

Anderson, Brooke, Librn, Muskingum County Genealogical Society Library, c/o John McIntire Public Library, 220 N Fifth St, Second Flr, Zanesville, OH, 43701-3508. Tel: 740-453-0391, Ext 139. p. 1836

Anderson, Carol, Dir, Bristol-Washington Township Public Library, 505 W Vistula St, Bristol, IN, 46507. Tel: 574-848-7458. p. 672

Anderson, Chandler, Head, Cat, Weber State University, 3921 Central Campus Dr, Dept 2901, Ogden, UT, 84408-2901. Tel: 801-626-6766. p. 2268

Anderson, Che, Mgr, Durham County Library, South Regional, 4505 S Alston Ave, Durham, NC, 27713. Tel: 919-560-7409. p. 1685

Anderson, Chela, Libr Serv Mgr, Daly City Public Library, 40 Wembley Dr, Daly City, CA, 94015-4399. Tel: 650-991-8023. p. 134

Anderson, Christopher, Collection Servs & Digital Initiatives Librarian, St John's University Library, Rittenberg Law Library, 8000 Utopia Pkwy, Jamaica, NY, 11439. Tel: 718-990-5074. p. 1556

Anderson, Christopher J, Spec Coll Librn/Curator, Day Missions Coll, Yale University Library, Divinity School Library, 409 Prospect St, New Haven, CT, 06511. Tel: 203-432-5289. p. 327

Anderson, Connie, Dir, Pierceton & Washington Township Library, 101 Catholic St, Pierceton, IN, 46562. Tel: 574-594-5474. p. 713

Anderson, Craig, Librn, Kean University, 1000 Morris Ave, Union, NJ, 07083. Tel: 908-737-4629. p. 1449

Anderson, Dave, Dir of Finance, Douglas County Libraries, 100 S Wilcox, Castle Rock, CO, 80104. Tel: 303-688-7623. p. 270

Anderson, Dave, Br Mgr, Campbell County Public Library District, 3920 Alexandria Pike, Cold Spring, KY, 41076. Tel: 859-781-6166. p. 851

Anderson, David, Dir, Crossett Public Library, 1700 Main St, Crossett, AR, 71635. Tel: 870-364-2230. p. 93

Anderson, Debbie, Asst Dir, South Bannock Library District, 18 N Main St, Downey, ID, 83234. Tel: 208-897-5270. p. 520

Anderson, Deborah, Asst Direc, Community Engagement & Education, County of Los Angeles Public Library, 7400 E Imperial Hwy, Downey, CA, 90242-3375. Tel: 562-940-4187. p. 134

Anderson, Deborah, Dir, Sabine Parish Library, 705 Main St, Many, LA, 71449-3199. Tel: 318-256-4150. p. 896

Anderson, Debra, Asst Dir, Head, Univ Archives & Area Res Ctr, University of Wisconsin-Green Bay, 2420 Nicolet Dr, Green Bay, WI, 54311-7001. Tel: 920-465-2539. p. 2439

Anderson, Dorothy, Ch, YA Librn, Franklin County Public Library, 355 Franklin St, Rocky Mount, VA, 24151. Tel: 540-483-3098. p. 2346

Anderson, Doug, Dr, Archivist, Ref Librn, Northwestern College, 101 Seventh St SW, Orange City, IA, 51041. Tel: 712-707-7402. p. 774

Anderson, Douglas, Dr, Dir, Marietta College, 215 Fifth St, Marietta, OH, 45750. Tel: 740-376-4757. p. 1798

Anderson, Elaine, Dir & Librn, Holly Public Library, 100 Tony Garcia Dr, Holly, CO, 81047-9149. Tel: 719-537-6520. p. 286

Anderson, Elizabeth, Libr Dir, Preston Public Library, 101 St Paul St NW, Preston, MN, 55965. Tel: 507-765-4511. p. 1193

Anderson, Elizabeth A, Dir, Burnsville Public Library, 235 Kanawha Ave, Burnsville, WV, 26335. Tel: 304-853-2338. p. 2399

Anderson, Elzena, Asst Dir, Waynesboro Public Library, 600 S Wayne Ave, Waynesboro, VA, 22980. Tel: 540-942-6746. p. 2352

Anderson, Emily, Libr Coord, New Mexico State University at Alamogordo, 2400 N Scenic Dr, Alamogordo, NM, 88310. Tel: 575-439-3650. p. 1459

Anderson, Emma J, Dir, Clairton Public Library, 616 Miller Ave, Clairton, PA, 15025-1497. Tel: 412-233-7966. p. 1922

Anderson, Freya, Head, Historical Coll, Head, Info Serv, Alaska State Library, Alaska Historical Collections, 395 Whittier St, Juneau, AK, 99801. Tel: 907-465-1315. p. 47

Anderson, Freya, Head, Info Serv, Alaska State Library, 395 Whittier St, Juneau, AK, 99801. Tel: 907-465-2920. p. 47

Anderson, Freya, Regional Librn, Alaska State Library, 395 Whittier St, Juneau, AK, 99801. Tel: 907-465-1315. p. 47

Anderson, Gaaren, Co-Dir, Tacoma Family History Center, 1102 S Pearl St, Tacoma, WA, 98465. Tel: 253-564-1103. p. 2387

Anderson, Gillian, Asst Dir, Milford Memorial Library, 1009 Ninth St, Ste 5, Milford, IA, 51351. Tel: 712-338-4643. p. 770

Anderson, Gina, Br Mgr, White County Regional Library System, Rose Bud Public, 548A Hwy 5, Rose Bud, AR, 71237. Tel: 501-556-4447. p. 110

Anderson, Glenn, Asst Dean, Coll Develop, Auburn University, Ralph Brown Draughon Library, 231 Mell St, Auburn, AL, 36849. Tel: 334-844-4500. p. 5

Anderson, Gordon, Sr Assoc, National Economic Research Associates, Inc, 360 Hamilton Ave, 10th Flr, White Plains, NY, 10601. Tel: 914-448-4000. p. 1664

Anderson, Harmony, Ad, Gilmanton Year-Round Library, 1385 NH Rte 140, Gilmanton Iron Works, NH, 03837. Tel: 603-364-2400. p. 1364

Anderson, Holly, Mgr, North Port Public Library, 13800 S Tamiami Trail, North Port, FL, 34287. Tel: 941-861-1300. p. 429

Anderson, J Theodore, Dir, Libr & Archives, The National Presbyterian Church, Administration Bldg, 2nd Flr, 4101 Nebraska Ave NW, Washington, DC, 20016. Tel: 202-537-7529. p. 373

Anderson, Jamie, Libr Dir & Chief Exec Officer, Kawartha Lakes Public Library, 190 Kent St W, Lower Level, Lindsay, ON, K9V 2Y6, CANADA. Tel: 705-324-9411, Ext 1291. p. 2652

Anderson, Janet, Dir, Minot Public Library, 516 Second Ave SW, Minot, ND, 58701-3792. Tel: 701-852-1045. p. 1738

Anderson, Jayme, Asst Dir, Milton Public Library, 430 E High St, Milton, WI, 53563. Tel: 608-868-7462. p. 2457

Anderson, Jeanne, Coll Develop Librn, Lake Agassiz Regional Library, 118 S Fifth St, Moorhead, MN, 56560-2756. Tel: 218-233-3757, Ext 122. p. 1188

Anderson, Jennifer, Ser & Electronic Res Librn, The Sage Colleges, 140 New Scotland Ave, Albany, NY, 12208. Tel: 518-292-1701. p. 1483

Anderson, Jennifer, Electronic Res Librn, Russell Sage College Libraries, 109 Second St, Troy, NY, 12180. Tel: 518-292-1701. p. 1653

Anderson, Jessica, Dir, Humboldt County Library, 85 E Fifth St, Winnemucca, NV, 89445. Tel: 775-623-6388. p. 1351

Anderson, Jessica, Mgr, Ser, University of Washington Botanic Gardens, 3501 NE 41st St, Seattle, WA, 98105. Tel: 206-543-0415. p. 2381

Anderson, Joanna, Health & Human Services Librn, Med Librn, Wright State University Libraries, 126 Dunbar Library, 3640 Colonel Glenn Hwy, Dayton, OH, 45435-0001. Tel: 937-775-3840. p. 1781

Anderson, Joanna, Distance Educ Librn, East Tennessee State University, Sherrod Library, Seehorn Dr & Lake St, Johnson City, TN, 37614-0204. Tel: 423-439-4714. p. 2103

Anderson, John M, Dir, Maps Librn, Louisiana State University Libraries, Cartographic Information Center, Dept of Geography & Anthropology, Howe-Russell-Kniffen Geoscience Complex, Rm 313, Baton Rouge, LA, 70803-4100. Tel: 225-578-6247. p. 884

Anderson, Jon R, Dir, Marian J Mohr Memorial Library, One Memorial Ave, Johnston, RI, 02919-3221. Tel: 401-231-4980. p. 2033

Anderson, Joseph, Digital Initiatives Librn, Fashion Institute of Technology-SUNY, Seventh Ave at 27th St, 227 W 27th St, New York, NY, 10001-5992. Tel: 212-217-4340. p. 1585

Anderson, Joseph, Asst Dir, Logan Library, 255 N Main, Logan, UT, 84321-3914. Tel: 435-716-9137. p. 2265

Anderson, Joye, Asst Librn, Albion Public Library, 437 S Third St, Albion, NE, 68620. Tel: 402-395-2021. p. 1305

Anderson, Jude, Libr Mgr, Sno-Isle Libraries, Snohomish Community Library, 311 Maple Ave, Snohomish, WA, 98290-2525. Tel: 360-568-2898. p. 2371

Anderson, Julie, Ch Serv, Thomas St Angelo Public Library, 1305 Second Ave, Cumberland, WI, 54829. Tel: 715-822-2767. p. 2429

Anderson, K-Dee, Electronic Res Librn, Lubbock Christian University Library, 5601 19th St, Lubbock, TX, 79407-2009. Tel: 806-720-7326. p. 2213

Anderson, Karen, Librn, Perkins Coie Library, 2901 N Central Ave, Ste 2000, Phoenix, AZ, 85012. Tel: 602-351-8213. p. 71

Anderson, Karen, Librn, Grand Bank Public Library, Church St, Grand Bank, NL, A0E 1W0, CANADA. Tel: 709-832-0310. p. 2608

Anderson, Karissa, Cataloger, Wabash Valley College, 2200 College Dr, Mount Carmel, IL, 62863. Tel: 618-263-5099. p. 620

Anderson, Kathy, Dir, Philander Smith College, 900 Daisy Bates Dr, Little Rock, AR, 72202. Tel: 501-370-5306. p. 101

Anderson, Katie, Ref, Rutgers University Libraries, Paul Robeson Library, 300 N Fourth St, Camden, NJ, 08102-1404. Tel: 856-225-2848, 856-225-6034. p. 1394

Anderson, Kaycee, Circ, North Platte Public Library, 120 W Fourth St, North Platte, NE, 69101-3993. Tel: 308-535-8036. p. 1327

Anderson, Keri, Dir, Hoesch Memorial Public Library, City Park W Second St, Alma, NE, 68920. Tel: 308-928-2600. p. 1305

Anderson, Kim, Dir, Callender Heritage Library, 505 Thomas St, Callender, IA, 50523. Tel: 515-548-3803. p. 736

Anderson, Kim, Library Contact, Multnomah County Library, Northwest, 2300 NW Thurman St, Portland, OR, 97210. p. 1892

Anderson, Kris, Libr Assoc, Modoc County Library, 212 W Third St, Alturas, CA, 96101. Tel: 530-233-6340. p. 116

Anderson, Kristen, Libr Dir, John A Burns School of Medicine, 651 Ilalo St, MEB 101, Honolulu, HI, 96813. Tel: 808-692-0823. p. 512

Anderson, Kristen, Dir, Winding Rivers Library System, 980 W Hwy 16, Ste 1, West Salem, WI, 54669. Tel: 608-789-7151. p. 2487

Anderson, Kristin, Br Mgr, Jackson County Library Services, Ashland Branch, 410 Siskiyou Blvd, Ashland, OR, 97520-2136. Tel: 541-774-6980. p. 1886

Anderson, Kristina, Assoc Dir, Digital Serv, Libr Tech, Seton Hall University School of Law, One Newark Ctr, Newark, NJ, 07102. Tel: 973-642-8764. p. 1428

Anderson, Lajmar, Archives, Ref (Info Servs), Sinclair Community College Library, 444 W Third St, Dayton, OH, 45402-1460. Tel: 937-512-3003. p. 1780

Anderson, Laurie, Programming, Princeton Public Library, 698 E Peru St, Princeton, IL, 61356. Tel: 815-875-1331. p. 636

Anderson, Lawrence, Librn, Houston Community College - Northeast College, Northline Library, 8001 Fulton St, Houston, TX, 77022. Tel: 713-718-8045. p. 2194

Anderson, Leah, Circ & ILL Mgr, Concordia College, 901 S Eighth St, Moorhead, MN, 56562. Tel: 218-299-4640. p. 1187

Anderson, Lisa, Archivist, Fac Librn, Muskegon Community College, 221 S Quarterline Rd, Muskegon, MI, 49442. Tel: 231-777-0274. p. 1136

Anderson, Liz, Asst Dir, Pub Serv Librn, Sherborn Library, Four Sanger St, Sherborn, MA, 01770-1499. Tel: 508-653-0770. p. 1053

Anderson, Lois, eCampus/Library Circulation Mgr, Garrett College, 687 Mosser Rd, McHenry, MD, 21541. Tel: 301-387-3009. p. 971

Anderson, Lynn, Br Mgr, Darlington County Library System, Society Hill Branch, 114 Carrigan St, Society Hill, SC, 29593. Tel: 843-378-0026. p. 2057

Anderson, Lynn, Tech Serv Librn, Snow College, 141 E Center St, Ephraim, UT, 84627. Tel: 435-283-7366. p. 2263

Anderson, Maija, Asst Dir, Prog Mgr, Orbis Cascade Alliance, PO Box 6007, Portland, OR, 97228. Tel: 541-246-2470. p. 2773

Anderson, Marcia, Library Contact, Eastern Counties Regional Library, Sherbrooke Branch, 11 Main St, Sherbrooke, NS, B0J 3C0, CANADA. Tel: 902-522-2180. p. 2621

Anderson, Marjorie, Admin Dir, Stevens Henager College Library, 1890 S 1350 West, Ogden, UT, 84401. Tel: 801-622-1567. p. 2267

Anderson, Mark, Br Mgr, Pasadena Public Library, 1201 Jeff Ginn Memorial Dr, Pasadena, TX, 77506. Tel: 713-477-0276. p. 2225

Anderson, Marlene, Dir, Libr Serv, Bismarck State College Library, 1500 Edwards Ave, Bismarck, ND, 58501. Tel: 701-224-5578. p. 1729

Anderson, Mary, Assoc Univ Librn, Palo Alto University, 1791 Arastradero Rd, Palo Alto, CA, 94304. Tel: 650-433-3816. p. 192

Anderson, Mary, Ch, Dir, Lincoln Carnegie Library, 203 S Third St, Lincoln, KS, 67455. Tel: 785-524-4034. p. 821

Anderson, Mary, Asst Librn, Caribou Public Library, 30 High St, Caribou, ME, 04736. Tel: 207-493-4214. p. 920

Anderson, Mary, Head, Circ Serv, University of Missouri-Kansas City Libraries, 800 E 51st St, Kansas City, MO, 64110. Tel: 816-235-1678. p. 1257

Anderson, Mary, Co-Dir, Tacoma Family History Center, 1102 S Pearl St, Tacoma, WA, 98465. Tel: 253-564-1103. p. 2387

Anderson, MaryAnn, Tech Serv, Norfolk Library, Nine Greenwoods Rd E, Norfolk, CT, 06058-1320. Tel: 860-542-5075. p. 330

Anderson, Matt, Libr Tech Spec, Mt Hood Community College Libraries, 26000 SE Stark St, Gresham, OR, 97030. Tel: 503-491-7671. p. 1881

Anderson, Maureen H, Asst Dir, Pub Serv, University of Dayton School of Law, 300 College Park, Dayton, OH, 45469-2772. Tel: 937-229-2314. p. 1780

Anderson, Megan, Coord, Ad Serv, Coordr, AV, Mansfield-Richland County Public Library, 43 W Third St, Mansfield, OH, 44902-1295. Tel: 419-521-3121. p. 1798

Anderson, Megan, Curric Librn, Research Librn, Fanshawe College, 1001 Fanshawe College Blvd, London, ON, N5Y 5R6, CANADA. Tel: 519-452-4240. p. 2653

Anderson, Melissa, Coord, Libr Coll, Field Museum of Natural History, 1400 S DuSable Lake Shore Dr, Chicago, IL, 60605-2496. Tel: 312-665-7892. p. 561

Anderson, Melissa, Dept Chair, Research Servs Librn, Southern Oregon University, 1250 Siskiyou Blvd, Ashland, OR, 97520. Tel: 541-552-6820. p. 1872

Anderson, Melissa, Libr Dir, Jefferson Public Library, 321 S Main St, Jefferson, WI, 53549-1772. Tel: 920-674-7733. p. 2443

Anderson, Michele K, Dir, Benton Public Library, 48 W Main St, Benton, WI, 53803. Tel: 608-759-2665. p. 2423

Anderson, Missy, Prog Coordr, Medical University of South Carolina Libraries, 171 Ashley Ave, Ste 419, Charleston, SC, 29425-0001. Tel: 843-792-2369. p. 2051

Anderson, Molly, Interim Circ Mgr, Northern Michigan University, 1401 Presque Isle Ave, Marquette, MI, 49855-5376. Tel: 906-227-2199. p. 1130

Anderson, Nadine, Asst Librn, University of Michigan-Dearborn, 4901 Evergreen Rd, Dearborn, MI, 48128-2406. Tel: 313-583-6324. p. 1096

Anderson, Nancy, Library Contact, The Manitoba Museum, 190 Rupert Ave, Winnipeg, MB, R3B 0N2, CANADA. Tel: 204-988-0692. p. 2594

Anderson, Nate, Ref Librn, Wisconsin State Law Library, Dane County Law Library, Courthouse Rm L1007, 215 S Hamilton St, Madison, WI, 53703. Tel: 608-266-6316. p. 2453

Anderson, Nick, Librn, Wisewood Library, PO Box 309, Buffalo Narrows, SK, S0M 0J0, CANADA. Tel: 306-235-4520. p. 2741

Anderson Painter, Tara, Dir, Glenwood Public Library, 109 N Vine St, Glenwood, IA, 51534. Tel: 712-527-5252. p. 755

Anderson, Pamalla, Archivist, Southern Methodist University, DeGolyer Library of Special Collections, 6404 Robert S Hyer Lane, Dallas, TX, 75275. Tel: 214-768-0829. p. 2168

Anderson, Pat, Libr Asst, Thorson Memorial Public Library, 117 Central Ave, Elbow Lake, MN, 56531. Tel: 218-685-6850. p. 1174

Anderson, Paul J, Curator, North Saint Paul Historical Society, 2666 E Seventh Ave, North Saint Paul, MN, 55109. Tel: 651-777-8965. p. 1191

Anderson, Rachel, Librn, Byron G Merrill Library, Ten Buffalo Rd, Rumney, NH, 03266. Tel: 603-786-9520. p. 1380

Anderson, Rebecca, Librn, Ouzinkie Tribal Council, 130 Third St, Ouzinkie, AK, 99644. Tel: 907-680-2323. p. 49

Anderson, Rebecca, Dir, Riter C Hulsey Public Library, 301 N Rockwall, Terrell, TX, 75160-2618. Tel: 972-551-6663. p. 2248

Anderson, Rebecca Lynn, Libr Dir, Rock Springs Public Library, 251 Railroad St, Rock Springs, WI, 53961. Tel: 608-737-1063. p. 2474

Anderson, Richard, Libr Mgr, Vaughan Public Libraries, Pierre Berton Resource Library, 4921 Rutherford Rd, Woodbridge, ON, L4L 1A6, CANADA. Tel: 905-653-7323. p. 2701

Anderson, Richita, Librn, Aesthetic Realism Foundation Library, 141 Greene St, New York, NY, 10012. Tel: 212-777-4490. p. 1578

Anderson, Richita, Librn, Aesthetic Realism Foundation Library, Eli Siegel Collection, 141 Greene St, New York, NY, 10012-3201. Tel: 212-777-4490. p. 1578

Anderson, Rick, Pres, New Providence Historical Society Library, c/o Memorial Library, 377 Elkwood Ave, New Providence, NJ, 07974. Tel: 908-665-1034. p. 1426

Anderson, Rick, Assoc Dean, Scholarly Res & Coll, University of Utah, J Willard Marriott Library, 295 S 1500 East, Salt Lake City, UT, 84112-0860. Tel: 801-587-9989. p. 2272

Anderson, Roni, Librn, Federal Aviation Administration, Civil Aerospace Medical Institute Library, 6500 S MacArthur, AAM-400a, Oklahoma City, OK, 73169. Tel: 405-954-4398. p. 1856

Anderson, S, Libr Asst, Tiskilwa Public Library, 119 E Main, Tiskilwa, IL, 61368. Tel: 815-646-4511. p. 654

Anderson, Sally, Res Mgr, Hallmark Cards, Inc, 2501 McGee Trafficway, MD 912, Kansas City, MO, 64108. Tel: 816-274-5525. p. 1255

Anderson, Samantha, Libr Dir, Kitimat Public Library Association, 940 Wakashan Ave, Kitimat, BC, V8C 2G3, CANADA. Tel: 250-632-8985. p. 2569

Anderson, Sandra, Ref Librn, Atlanta-Fulton Public Library System, Northside Branch, 3295 Northside Pkwy NW, Atlanta, GA, 30327. Tel: 404-613-6870. p. 461

Anderson, Sandra, Librn, Alberta Teachers' Association Library, 11010 142 St, Edmonton, AB, T5N 2R1, CANADA. Tel: 780-447-9400. p. 2535

Anderson, Sarah, Libr Tech, Richmond Community College Library, J Richard Conder Bldg, 1042 W Hamlet Ave, Hamlet, NC, 28345. Tel: 910-410-1752. p. 1694

Anderson, Sarah, Br Mgr, Whitman County Rural Library District, Garfield Branch, 109 N Third, Garfield, WA, 99130. Tel: 509-635-1490. p. 2362

Anderson, Shannon, Library Contact, Washburn County Law Library, Courthouse, 10 W Fourth Ave, 2nd Flr, Shell Lake, WI, 54871. Tel: 715-468-4677. p. 2477

Anderson, Sharon, Br Mgr, Polk County Library, Humansville Branch, 101 S Ohio St, Humansville, MO, 65674. Tel: 417-754-2455. p. 1238

Anderson, Sharon, Commun Libr Mgr, Queens Library, Far Rockaway Community Library, 1637 Central Ave, Far Rockaway, NY, 11691. Tel: 718-327-2549. p. 1554

Anderson, Shauna, Dir, Plymouth District Library, 223 S Main St, Plymouth, MI, 48170-1687. Tel: 734-453-0750. p. 1141

Anderson, Shelley, Dir, Stanton Public Library, 501 Elliott St, Ste A, Stanton, IA, 51573. Tel: 712-829-2290. p. 784

Anderson, Shelley, Librn, Library District Number One, Doniphan County, Elwood Branch, 410 N Ninth, Elwood, KS, 66024. Tel: 913-365-5625. p. 840

Anderson, Shelley, Librn, Library District Number One, Doniphan County, Wathena Branch, 206 St Joseph, Wathena, KS, 66090. Tel: 785-990-2665. p. 840

Anderson, Shelly, Librn Emeritus, Iowa Western Community College-Clarinda Campus, 923 E Washington, Clarinda, IA, 51632. Tel: 712-542-5117, Ext 2234. p. 740

Anderson, Stacey, Supvr, Tech Serv, University of Idaho Library, College of Law, 711 Rayburn St, Moscow, ID, 83844. Tel: 208-885-6521. p. 526

Anderson, Stacy, Assessment Librn, Ferris State University Library, 1010 Campus Dr, Big Rapids, MI, 49307-2279. Tel: 231-591-3500. p. 1085

Anderson, Stephen, Classroom Support Technician, Northwood Technical College, 1900 College Dr, Rice Lake, WI, 54868. Tel: 715-234-7082. p. 2473

Anderson, Steven P, Dir, Thurgood Marshall State Law Library, Courts of Appeals Bldg, 361 Rowe Blvd, Annapolis, MD, 21401. Tel: 410-260-1430. p. 950

Anderson, Sufa, Br Mgr, Las Vegas-Clark County Library District, Rainbow Library, 3150 N Buffalo Dr, Las Vegas, NV, 89128. Tel: 702-507-3710. p. 1347

Anderson, Susan, Dir, Redondo Beach Public Library, 303 N Pacific Coast Hwy, Redondo Beach, CA, 90277. Tel: 310-318-0675. p. 199

Anderson, Susan, Adminr, University of Rochester Medical Center, 601 Elmwood Ave, Rochester, NY, 14642. Tel: 716-275-3363. p. 1631

Anderson, Tami L, Libr Dir, Hartington Public Library, 106 S Broadway, Hartington, NE, 68739. Tel: 402-254-6245. p. 1317

Anderson, Terry, Ch, Wheaton Community Library, 901 First Ave N, Wheaton, MN, 56296. Tel: 320-563-8487. p. 1207

Anderson, Thomas, Coll Develop Librn, Montgomery City-County Public Library System, 245 High St, Montgomery, AL, 36104, Tel: 334-240-4975. p. 29

Anderson, Timothy, Tech Serv Mgr, Florence County Library System, 509 S Dargan St, Florence, SC, 29506. Tel: 843-662-8424. p. 2058

Anderson, Tosha, Libr Assoc, Saint Peter Public Library, 601 S Washington Ave, Saint Peter, MN, 56082. Tel: 507-934-7420. p. 1203

Anderson, Tracy, Dir, Mount Olive Public Library, 100 N Plum St, Mount Olive, IL, 62069-1755. Tel: 217-999-7311. p. 621

Anderson, Vanja K, Univ Librn, South Baylo University Library, 1126 N Brookhurst St, Anaheim, CA, 92801-1704. Tel: 714-533-1495. p. 116

Anderson, Vera, Mgr, Sharp County Library, Cave City Branch, 120 Spring St, Cave City, AR, 72521. Tel: 870-283-6947. p. 97

Anderson, Vicki, Librn, Northwest Regional Library, PO Box 26, Buffalo, SD, 57720-0026. Tel: 605-375-3835. p. 2075

Anderson, Vicky, Res Asst, Otter Tail County Historical Society, 1110 Lincoln Ave W, Fergus Falls, MN, 56537. Tel: 218-736-6038. p. 1175

Anderson-Ferdinand, Heidi, Br Librn, East Central Regional Library, Pine City Public Library, 300 Fifth St SE, Pine City, MN, 55063. Tel: 320-629-6403. p. 1168

Anderson-Hancock, Tracy, Tech Serv Mgr, Greenville County Library System, 25 Heritage Green Pl, Greenville, SC, 29601-2034. Tel: 864-242-5000, Ext 2265. p. 2061

Anderson-Strait, Malisa, Bus Librn, Emory University Libraries, Goizueta Business Library, 540 Asbury Circle, Atlanta, GA, 30322. Tel: 404-727-1641. p. 463

Anderton, Holly, Mgr, Carnegie Library of Pittsburgh, Downtown & Business, 612 Smithfield St, Pittsburgh, PA, 15222-2506. Tel: 412-281-7141. p. 1991

Anderzhon, Bevin, Circ, Shenandoah Public Library, 201 S Elm St, Shenandoah, IA, 51601. Tel: 712-246-2315. p. 781

Andes, Barbara, Br Mgr, Massanutten Regional Library, Village Library, 175 N Main St, Broadway, VA, 22815. Tel: 540-434-4475, Ext 7. p. 2325

Andolsen, Heather, Dir, Middletown Township Public Library, 55 New Monmouth Rd, Middletown, NJ, 07748. Tel: 732-671-3700. p. 1418

Andolsen, Heather, Exec Dir, Special Libraries Association, 1120 Rte 73, Ste 200, Mount Laurel, NJ, 08054. Tel: 703-647-4900. p. 1423

Andolsen, Heather, Asst Dir, Burlington County Library System, Five Pioneer Blvd, Westampton, NJ, 08060. Tel: 609-267-9660. p. 1453

Andra, Josh, Br Mgr, Mansfield-Richland County Public Library, Bellville Branch, 97 Bell St, Bellville, OH, 44813. Tel: 419-886-3811. p. 1798

Andrada-Tanega, Milagros, Br Mgr, Harris County Public Library, Evelyn Meador Branch Library, 2400 N Meyer Ave, Seabrook, TX, 77586. Tel: 281-474-9142. p. 2193

Andrade, Brooke, Libr Dir, National Humanities Center Library, Seven Alexander Dr, Research Triangle Park, NC, 27709. Tel: 919-549-0661. p. 1712

Andrade, Kate Pohjola, Dir, Woodlands Library Cooperative, PO Box 1048, Albion, MI, 49224. Tel: 517-629-9469. p. 1076

Andrade, Martha, Br Mgr, El Paso Public Library, Memorial Park, 3200 Copper Ave, El Paso, TX, 79930. Tel: 915-212-0448. p. 2174

Andrade, Sandra, Asst Libr Mgr, El Paso County Law Library, Court House, 12th Flr, 500 E San Antonio St, Rm 1202, El Paso, TX, 79901. Tel: 915-273-3699. p. 2174

Andrasik, Alex, Ad, Penn Yan Public Library, 214 Main St, Penn Yan, NY, 14527. Tel: 315-536-6114. p. 1617

Andre, Deborah, Circ, Smiths Falls Public Library, 81 Beckwith St N, Smiths Falls, ON, K7A 2B9, CANADA. Tel: 613-283-2911. p. 2678

Andrea, Ariel, Chem Librn, University of Wisconsin-Madison, Chemistry Library, Chemistry Bldg, 1101 University Ave, Rm 2132, Madison, WI, 53706. Tel: 608-262-4423. p. 2451

Andreae, Elizabeth, Dir, Scottsville Free Library, 28 Main St, Scottsville, NY, 14546. Tel: 585-889-2023. p. 1639

Andreasson, Amy, Dir, Eldredge Public Library, 564 Main St, Chatham, MA, 02633-2296. Tel: 508-945-5170. p. 1010

Andrejcin, Carmen, Librn, Chinook Regional Library, Frontier Branch, 211 First St W, Frontier, SK, S0N 0W0, CANADA. Tel: 306-296-4667. p. 2752

Andreou, Constantinos, Dir of Circ, Nova Southeastern University Libraries, 3100 Ray Ferrero Jr Blvd, Fort Lauderdale, FL, 33314. Tel: 954-262-4682. p. 402

Andres, Chloe, Librn, United States Navy, 1481 D St, Bldg 3016, Norfolk, VA, 23521. Tel: 757-462-7691. p. 2336

Andres, Cloe, Br Mgr, United States Army, 8640 Omaha Beach Rd, Virginia Beach, VA, 23459. Tel: 757-422-7600. p. 2350

Andres, Patricia, Dir, Neoga Public Library District, 550 Chestnut St, Neoga, IL, 62447. Tel: 217-895-3944. p. 623

Andresen, Christine, Res & Educ Informationist, Medical University of South Carolina Libraries, 171 Ashley Ave, Ste 419, Charleston, SC, 29425-0001. Tel: 843-792-7183. p. 2051

Andresen, Julie, Libr Dir, Hannibal-LaGrange University, 2800 Palmyra Rd, Hannibal, MO, 63401-1999. Tel: 573-629-3130. p. 1247

Andrew, Blake, Dir, Chazy Public Library, 1329 Fiske Rd, Chazy, NY, 12921. Tel: 518-846-7676. p. 1517

Andrew, Devonia, Asst to the Dir, Alachua County Library District, 401 E University Ave, Gainesville, FL, 32601-5453. Tel: 352-334-3900. p. 406

Andrew, Maud, Mgr, Brooklyn Public Library, Business & Career Center, Ten Grand Army Plaza, Brooklyn, NY, 11238. Tel: 718-623-7000. p. 1502

Andrews, Amanda, Librn, Nova Scotia Health Authority, 1482 George St, 3rd Flr, Rm 3613-1, Sydney, NS, B1P 1P3, CANADA. Tel: 902-574-1327. p. 2623

Andrews, Beth, Human Res Mgr, Whatcom County Library System, 5205 Northwest Dr, Bellingham, WA, 98226. Tel: 360-305-3600. p. 2359

Andrews, Brent, Librn, Lutheran Brethren Seminary, 1036 W Alcott Ave, Fergus Falls, MN, 56537. Tel: 218-739-1211. p. 1175

Andrews, Chase, Collection Dev & Engagement Librn, Linfield University, 900 SE Baker St, McMinnville, OR, 97128. Tel: 503-883-2261. p. 1885

Andrews, Danika, Libr Dir, Fort Nelson Public Library, Municipal Sq, 5315-50th Ave S, Fort Nelson, BC, V0C 1R0, CANADA. Tel: 250-774-6777. p. 2566

Andrews, Debra, Juv Coll Develop Librn, Kokomo-Howard County Public Library, 220 N Union St, Kokomo, IN, 46901-4614. Tel: 765-457-3242. p. 699

Andrews, Devon, Dir, Mansfield Public Library, 54 Warrenville Rd, Mansfield Center, CT, 06250. Tel: 860-423-2501. p. 321

Andrews, Donna, Ref Mgr, York County Library, 138 E Black St, Rock Hill, SC, 29730. Tel: 803-981-5844. p. 2068

Andrews, Ellery, Dep Dir, Fort Lauderdale Historical Society, 219 SW Second Ave, Fort Lauderdale, FL, 33301. Tel: 954-463-4431. p. 401

Andrews, Emily, Libr Support Serv Asst, Stormont, Dundas & Glengarry County Library, Maxville Branch, Two Spring St, Maxville, ON, K0C 1T0, CANADA. Tel: 613-527-2235. p. 2638

Andrews, Grace, Dir, Libr Serv, Wesley Biblical Seminary Library, 1880 E County Line rd, Ridgeland, MS, 39157. Tel: 601-366-8880. p. 1232

Andrews, James, Dr, Assoc Prof, University of South Florida, 4202 Fowler Ave, CIS 1040, Tampa, FL, 33620-7800. Tel: 813-974-3520. p. 2783

Andrews, James E, PhD, Dir, University of South Florida, 4202 Fowler Ave, CIS 1040, Tampa, FL, 33620-7800. Tel: 813-974-2108. p. 2783

Andrews, Jayne, Br Mgr, Augusta-Richmond County Public Library, Talking Book Center, 823 Telfair St, Augusta, GA, 30901. Tel: 706-821-2625. p. 467

Andrews, Jeanette, Spec Serv Librn, Urbandale Public Library, 3520 86th St, Urbandale, IA, 50322. Tel: 515-278-3945. p. 787

Andrews, Joy, Br Mgr, Robeson County Public Library, Annie Hubbard McEachern Public, 221 W Broad St, Saint Pauls, NC, 28384. Tel: 910-865-4002. p. 1702

Andrews, Judith, Br Mgr, Hawaii State Public Library System, Kealakekua Public Library, 81-6619 Mamalahoa Hwy, Kealakekua, HI, 96750. Tel: 808-323-7585. p. 508

Andrews, Julie, Chief Exec Officer, Lincoln Public Library, 5020 Serena Dr, Beamsville, ON, L0R 1B0, CANADA. Tel: 905-563-7014. p. 2630

Andrews, Julie, Chief Exec Officer, Lincoln Public Library, Moses F Rittenhouse Branch, 4080 John Charles Blvd, Vineland, ON, L0R 2C0, CANADA. Tel: 905-562-5711. p. 2631

Andrews, Kathy, Asst Librn, Ch, Lena Community District Library, 300 W Mason St, Lena, IL, 61048. Tel: 815-369-3180. p. 608

Andrews, Kristen, Pub Serv Dir, Surrey Libraries, 10350 University Dr, Surrey, BC, V3T 4B8, CANADA. Tel: 604-598-7300. p. 2577

Andrews, Mari, Law Librn, A Max Brewer Memorial Law Library, Harry T & Harriette V Moore Justice Ctr, 2825 Judge Fran Jamieson Way, Viera, FL, 32940. Tel: 321-617-7295. p. 453

Andrews, Michele, Libr Mgr, Parkland Library, 6620 University Dr, Parkland, FL, 33067. Tel: 954-757-4200. p. 436

Andrews, Nick, Dir, Elmwood Public Library, 111 N Main St, Elmwood, WI, 54740. Tel: 715-639-2615. p. 2434

Andrews, Nicole, Circ Asst, Edith B Siegrist Vermillion Public Library, 18 Church St, Vermillion, SD, 57069-3093. Tel: 605-677-7060. p. 2084

Andrews, Rayna, Archivist, College of Physicians of Philadelphia, 19 S 22nd St, Philadelphia, PA, 19103. Tel: 215-399-2301. p. 1975

Andrews, Robin, Circ, University of Alaska Fairbanks, 1732 Tanana Dr, Fairbanks, AK, 99775. Tel: 907-474-6699. p. 45

Andrews, Ruth, Librn, Palm Beach State College, 4200 Congress Ave, Mail Sta 17, Lake Worth, FL, 33461. Tel: 561-868-3800. p. 416

Andrews, Sarah, Br Librn, London Public Library, Bostwick, Bostwick Community Ctr, 501 Southdale Rd W, London, ON, N6K 3X4, CANADA. Tel: 519-473-4708. p. 2654

Andrews, Sarah, Br Librn, London Public Library, Glanworth, 2950 Glanworth Dr, London, ON, N6N 1N6, CANADA. Tel: 519-681-6797. p. 2654

Andrews, Sarah, Br Librn, London Public Library, Lambeth, 7112 Beattie St, Lambeth, ON, N6P 1A2, CANADA. Tel: 519-652-2951. p. 2654

Andrews, Sarah, Chief Exec Officer, St Mary's Public Library, 15 Church St N, St. Marys, ON, N4X 1B4, CANADA. Tel: 519-284-3346. p. 2680

Andrews, Sarah, Management Chair, Perth County Information Network, c/o Stratford Public Library, 19 St Andrew St, Stratford, ON, N5A 1A2, CANADA. Tel: 519-271-0220. p. 2778

Andrews, Star, Supvr, Tech Serv, Nova Southeastern University, 3200 S University Dr, Fort Lauderdale, FL, 33328. Tel: 954-262-3129. p. 401

Andrews, Terry, Br Mgr, Blackwater Regional Library, Smithfield Branch, 255 James St, Smithfield, VA, 23430. Tel: 757-357-2264. p. 2313

Andrews, Wanda, Info Spec, Pennsylvania State University, N Atherton St, State College, PA, 16801. Tel: 814-865-6531. p. 2010

Andrews, Wendi, Youth Serv, Scappoose Public Library, 52469 SE Second St, Scappoose, OR, 97056. Tel: 503-543-7123. p. 1898

Andriolo, Karen, Emerging Tech Librn, Bernards Township Library, 32 S Maple Ave, Basking Ridge, NJ, 07920-1216. Tel: 908-204-3031. p. 1388

Andrist, Suzan, Access & Technical Servs, Library Tech, Southwestern Oregon Community College Library, 1988 Newmark Ave, Coos Bay, OR, 97420. Tel: 541-888-7270. p. 1876

Andros, Anthony, Asst Admin, Tinley Park Public Library, 7851 Timber Dr, Tinley Park, IL, 60477-3398. Tel: 708-532-0160. p. 653

Andros, Anthony, Libr Mgr, Plano Public Library System, L E R Schimelpfenig Library, 5024 Custer Rd, Plano, TX, 75023. Tel: 972-769-4200. p. 2227

Androski, Kathryn, Dir, Kansas Department of Corrections, 500 Reformatory St, Hutchinson, KS, 67501. Tel: 620-625-7377. p. 814

Andrus, Miriam, Dir, Grace A Dow Memorial Library, 1710 W St Andrews Ave, Midland, MI, 48640-2698. Tel: 989-837-3430. p. 1132

Andrus, Sue, Br Librn, Oconee County Public Library, 501 W South Broad St, Walhalla, SC, 29691. Tel: 864-638-4133. p. 2072

Andrusko, Diane, Mgr, Ad Serv, St Catharines Public Library, 54 Church St, St. Catharines, ON, L2R 7K2, CANADA. Tel: 905-688-6103. p. 2680

Aneja, Kusum, Tech Serv, Valencia College, Raymer Maguire Jr Learning Resources Center, West Campus, 1800 S Kirkman Rd, Orlando, FL, 32811. Tel: 407-582-1210. p. 433

Ang, Vince, Operations Mgr, Hayward Public Library, 835 C St, Hayward, CA, 94541. Tel: 510-881-7987. p. 150

Angel, Christine, PhD, Assoc Prof, St John's University, Saint Augustine Hall, Rm 408A, 8000 Utopia Pkwy, Jamaica, NY, 11439. Tel: 718-990-1452. p. 2789

Angel, Eric, Info Res & Serv Support Spec, Pennsylvania State University Libraries, Mary M & Bertil E Lofstrom Library, 76 University Dr, Hazleton, PA, 18202. Tel: 570-450-3171. p. 2015

Angel, Jessie, Libr Asst III, Nashville State Technical Community College, 120 White Bridge Rd, Nashville, TN, 37209-4515. Tel: 615-353-3472. p. 2120

Angel, Michael, Sr Circ & Reserves Coordr, Champlain College Library, 95 Summit St, Burlington, VT, 05401. Tel: 802-383-6295. p. 2280

Angeli, Christine, Libr Dir, Milford Public Library, 57 New Haven Ave, Milford, CT, 06460. Tel: 203-783-3399. p. 323

Angell, Alli, Head, Children's & Tech Services, Benicia Public Library, 150 East L St, Benicia, CA, 94510-3281. Tel: 707-746-4343. p. 121

Angell, Katelyn, Coordr, Libr Instruction, Long Island University, One University Plaza, Brooklyn, NY, 11201. Tel: 718-780-4513. p. 1505

Angell, Kenneth, Assoc Librn, Henderson State University, 1100 Henderson St, Arkadelphia, AR, 71999-0001. Tel: 870-230-5506. p. 89

Angello, Stacey, Libr Dir, Nashville School of Law Library, 4013 Armory Oaks Dr, Nashville, TN, 37204. Tel: 615-256-3684, Ext 7. p. 2120

Angelloz, Anna, Br Mgr, Iberville Parish Library, Grosse Tete Branch, 18135 Willow Rd, Grosse Tete, LA, 70740. Tel: 225-648-2667. p. 906

Angelo, Catie, Cat Librn, ILL, North Kingstown Free Library, 100 Boone St, North Kingstown, RI, 02852-5150. Tel: 401-294-3306. p. 2036

Angelo, F Michael, Spec Coll Librn & Univ Archivist, Thomas Jefferson University, 1020 Walnut St, Philadelphia, PA, 19107. Tel: 215-503-8097. p. 1987

Angelo, Kate, Tech, Long Branch Free Public Library, 328 Broadway, Long Branch, NJ, 07740. Tel: 732-222-3900. p. 1413

Angeloni, Denise, Libr & Info Spec, Ontario Ministry of the Environment, Conservation & Parks, 40 Saint Clair Ave W, 12th Flr, Toronto, ON, M4V 1M2, CANADA. p. 2691

Angelow, Susan, Br Mgr, Brunswick County Library, G V Barbee Sr Branch, 8200 E Oak Island Dr, Oak Island, NC, 28465. Tel: 910-278-4283. p. 1716

Angelucci, Joyce, Libr Coord, Res & Instruction Librn, Bryn Mawr College, Lois & Reginald Collier Science Library, 101 N Merion Ave, Bryn Mawr, PA, 19104-2899. Tel: 610-526-7462. p. 1916

Anger, William, Librn, Miriam Hospital, Fain Bldg, Basement, 164 Summit Ave, Providence, RI, 02906. Tel: 401-793-2500. p. 2039

Anghelescu, Hermina G B, Dr, Assoc Prof, Wayne State University, 106 Kresge Library, Detroit, MI, 48202. Tel: 313-577-1825. p. 2787

Angione, Jeff, Circ Coordr, Vermont State University - Johnson, 337 College Hill, Johnson, VT, 05656. Tel: 802-635-1273. p. 2287

Angleone, Shannon, Digital Serv Librn, West Haven Public Library, 300 Elm St, West Haven, CT, 06516-4692. Tel: 203-937-4233. p. 346

Angleton, Matt, Librn II, Arizona Department of Corrections - Adult Institutions, 896 S Cook Rd, Safford, AZ, 85546. Tel: 928-428-4698, Ext 75508. p. 75

Anglim, Christopher, Ref/Archives Librn, University of the District of Columbia, Learning Resources Division, 4200 Connecticut Ave NW, Bldg 39, Level B, Washington, DC, 20008. p. 380

Anglin, Emily, Br Mgr, Williamson County Public Library, Leiper's Fork, 5333 Old Hwy 96, Franklin, TN, 37064-9357. Tel: 615-794-7019. p. 2098

Angregg, JJ, Youth Serv Librn, Logan Public Library, 121 E Sixth St, Logan, IA, 51546. Tel: 712-644-2551. p. 766

Angry-Smith, Evelyn, Ref Serv, Manchester Community College Library, Great Path, Manchester, CT, 06040. Tel: 860-512-2874. p. 320

Angstadt, Jeremy, Serv Mgr, Sandusky Library, Follett House Museum, 404 Wayne St, Sandusky, OH, 44870. Tel: 419-625-3834. p. 1819

Angstman, Jodi, Asst Librn, Dumont Community Library, 602 Second St, Dumont, IA, 50625. Tel: 641-857-3304. p. 749

Anguiano, Ian, Dir, Dickinson Area Public Library, 139 Third St W, Dickinson, ND, 58601-5147. Tel: 701-456-7703. p. 1732

Anguiano, Ian, Dir, Dickinson Area Public Library, Billings County Resource Center, PO Box 307, Medora, ND, 58645-0307. Tel: 701-623-4604. p. 1732

Anguiano, Veronica, Commun Outreach Librn, Nueces County Public Libraries, 100 Terry Shamsie Blvd, Robstown, TX, 78380. Tel: 361-387-3431. p. 2233

Angulas, Bonnie, Dir, Daland Memorial Library, Five N Main St, Mont Vernon, NH, 03057. Tel: 603-673-7888. p. 1374

Anhalt, Joy, Tech Serv, Tinley Park Public Library, 7851 Timber Dr, Tinley Park, IL, 60477-3398. Tel: 708-532-0160, Ext 7. p. 653

Anielski, Jennifer, Tech Serv Librn, Mariners' Museum & Park Library, 100 Museum Dr, Newport News, VA, 23606-3759. Tel: 757-591-7782. p. 2333

Ankarlo, Rob, Dir, Thomas St Angelo Public Library, 1305 Second Ave, Cumberland, WI, 54829. Tel: 715-822-2767. p. 2429

Anna, LeeAnn, Mgr, Carnegie Library of Pittsburgh, Lawrenceville, 279 Fisk St, Pittsburgh, PA, 15201-2847. Tel: 412-682-3668. p. 1991

Annabi, Hala, Dr, Assoc Prof, Prog Chair, University of Washington, Mary Gates Hall, Ste 370, Campus Box 352840, Seattle, WA, 98195-2840. Tel: 206-543-1794. p. 2794

Annable, Linda, Supv Librn, Youth Serv Librn, Newport Public Library, 35 NW Nye St, Newport, OR, 97365-3714. Tel: 541-265-2153. p. 1888

Anne, Barnard, ILS Coordr, Orion Township Public Library, 825 Joslyn Rd, Lake Orion, MI, 48362. Tel: 248-693-3000, Ext 339. p. 1123

Annen, Alexandra, Adult Serv Mgr, Homer Township Public Library District, 14320 W 151st St, Homer Glen, IL, 60491. Tel: 708-301-7908. p. 600

Annesi, Lori, Ref Librn/Spec Coll, Monroe Community College, LeRoy V Good Library, 1000 E Henrietta Rd, Rochester, NY, 14692. Tel: 585-292-2338. p. 1629

Annico, Alyssa, Curric Res Ctr Librn, Youngstown State University, One University Plaza, Youngstown, OH, 44555-0001. Tel: 330-941-2511. p. 1836

Anning, Chris, Librn, Minnesota Department of Revenue Library, 600 N Robert St, Saint Paul, MN, 55101. Tel: 651-556-6134. p. 1200

Annis, Ethan, Head, Access & Technical Services, Librn, Dominican University of California, 50 Acacia Ave, San Rafael, CA, 94901-2298. Tel: 415-482-1837. p. 236

Annis, Nicole, Libr Dir, Keosauqua Public Library, 608 First St, Keosauqua, IA, 52565. Tel: 319-293-3766. p. 763

Annis, Tyler, Libr Dir, Anderson-Lee Library, 43 Main St, Silver Creek, NY, 14136. Tel: 716-934-3468. p. 1641

Ansah, Samuel, Libr Mgr, New York Public Library - Astor, Lenox & Tilden Foundations, Sedgwick Branch, 1701 Martin Luther King Jr Blvd, Bronx, NY, 10453. Tel: 718-731-2074. p. 1597

Ansel, Carol, Libr Dir, Godfrey Memorial Library, 134 Newfield St, Middletown, CT, 06457-2534. Tel: 860-346-4375. p. 322

Ansell, Cindy, Libr Mgr, Lake Worth Beach City Library, 15 North M St, Lake Worth Beach, FL, 33460. Tel: 561-533-7354. p. 416

Ansell, Donna, Head, Circ, Sr Libr Tech, Blackstone Public Library, 86 Main St, Blackstone, MA, 01504. Tel: 508-883-1931. p. 990

Ansell, Melissa, Dir, Avella Area Public Library, 11 School Ct, Avella, PA, 15312. Tel: 724-587-5688. p. 1908

Ansley, John, Dir, Archives, Spec Coll, Marist College, 3399 North Rd, Poughkeepsie, NY, 12601-1387. Tel: 845-575-5217. p. 1623

Anspach, Judith Ford, Dir, Indiana University, Ruth Lilly Law Library, 530 W New York St, Indianapolis, IN, 46202-3225. Tel: 317-274-3884, 317-274-4028. p. 693

Anspach, Sarah, Head, Pub Serv, Security Public Library, 715 Aspen Dr, Security, CO, 80911-1807. Tel: 719-391-3190. p. 295

Anstine, Becky, Libr Tech, Harrisburg Area Community College, 2010 Pennsylvania Ave, York, PA, 17404. Tel: 717-801-3220. p. 2026

Anstiss, Terri, Libr Dir, Stevens Memorial Library, 20 Memorial Dr, Ashburnham, MA, 01430. Tel: 978-827-4115. p. 986

Ansty, Maggie, Librn for Blind & Physically Handicapped, Indiana State Library, 315 W Ohio St, Indianapolis, IN, 46202. Tel: 317-232-3675. p. 692

Antaya, Elizabeth, Libr Dir, Shelburne Free Public Library, 233 Shelburne Center Rd, Shelburne Falls, MA, 01370. Tel: 413-625-0307. p. 1052
Antaya, Jeff, Head Librn, Capital Area District Libraries, Leslie Library, 201 Pennsylvania St, Leslie, MI, 49251. Tel: 517-589-9400. p. 1124
Anteau, Joseph B, Asst Librn, Consumers Energy, Corporate Library, One Energy Plaza, EP1-244, Jackson, MI, 49201. Tel: 517-788-2520. p. 1119
Antelll, Suzy, Asst Dir, Admin Serv, Dep Dir, Oak Park Public Library, 834 Lake St, Oak Park, IL, 60301. Tel: 708-452-3410. p. 628
Antelman, Kristin, Univ Librn, University of California, Santa Barbara, UCEN Rd, Bldg 525, Santa Barbara, CA, 93106-9010. Tel: 805-893-3256. p. 241
Anteola, Marquel, Ref & Instruction Librn, Texas Wesleyan University, 1201 Wesleyan St, Fort Worth, TX, 76105. Tel: 817-531-4813. p. 2181
Anter, Stacey, Co-Dir, Pontiac Free Library, 101 Greenwich Ave, Warwick, RI, 02886. Tel: 401-737-3292. p. 2043
Anthony, Cathy, Librn, Norcatur Public Library, 301 E Ossipee St, Norcatur, KS, 67653. Tel: 785-693-3025. p. 827
Anthony, Mark, Mgr, Info Tech, Wood Buffalo Regional Library, One CA Knight Way, Fort McMurray, AB, T9H 5C5, CANADA. Tel: 780-743-7800. p. 2540
Anthony, Rachel, Educ Mgr, Tyler Museum of Art Library, 1300 S Mahon, Tyler, TX, 75701. Tel: 903-595-1001. p. 2250
Anthony, Sheri, Commun Serv Mgr, Wood Buffalo Regional Library, One CA Knight Way, Fort McMurray, AB, T9H 5C5, CANADA. Tel: 780-743-7800. p. 2540
Anthony, Vivienne, Access Serv, ILL Coordr, Assumption University, 500 Salisbury St, Worcester, MA, 01609. Tel: 508-767-7291. p. 1071
Antila, Kendra, Libr Dir, Lebanon Public Library, 55 Academy St, Lebanon, OR, 97355-3320. Tel: 541-258-4232. p. 1885
Antill, Robert, Exec Dir, Dorchester County Library, 506 N Parler Ave, Saint George, SC, 29477. Tel: 843-563-9189. p. 2069
Antley-Hearn, Lisa, Libr Spec, Lenoir-Rhyne University, 4201 N Main St, Columbia, SC, 29203. Tel: 803-461-3220, 803-461-3269. p. 2053
Antoine, Molly, Libr Supvr, Baptist Health Sciences University, 1003 Monroe Ave, Memphis, TN, 38104. Tel: 901-572-2680. p. 2112
Antolino, Lauren, Ch, Cranford Free Public Library, 224 Walnut Ave, Cranford, NJ, 07016-2931. Tel: 908-709-7272. p. 1398
Anton, Mary, Br Mgr, Handley Regional Library System, Mary Jane & James L Bowman Branch, 871 Tasker Rd, Stephens City, VA, 22655. Tel: 540-869-9000. p. 2354
Antonacci, Amanda, Br Mgr, York County Library, Clover Public, 107 Knox St, Clover, SC, 29710. Tel: 803-222-3474. p. 2068
Antonacci, Delia, Prof, Seneca College of Applied Arts & Technology, 1750 Finch Ave E, Toronto, ON, M2J 2X5, CANADA. Tel: 416-491-5050, Ext 33739. p. 2796
Antone, Alicia, Outreach Serv Mgr, Alachua County Library District, 401 E University Ave, Gainesville, FL, 32601-5453. Tel; 352-334-3991. p. 406
Antonellis, Mary Anne, Dir, MN Spear Memorial Library, Ten Cooleyville Rd, Shutesbury, MA, 01072-9766. Tel: 413-259-1213. p. 1053
Antonio, Roman, Sr Librn, Los Angeles Public Library System, Panorama City Branch Library, 14345 Roscoe Blvd, Panorama City, CA, 91402-4222. Tel: 818-894-4071. p. 165
Antonioni, Mike, Curator, US National Park Service, 1411 W St SE, Washington, DC, 20020. Tel: 202-426-5961. p. 379
Antoniuk, Donna, Librn, Rio Grande Bible Institute & Language School, 4300 S Business Hwy 281, Edinburg, TX, 78539-9650. Tel: 956-380-8100. p. 2173
Antonowicz, Sherrie, Librn, Westmininster Presbyterian Church Library, 3906 W Friendly Ave, Greensboro, NC, 27410. Tel: 336-299-3785. p. 1693
Antonson, Jade, Br Librn, Greenstone Public Library, Nakina Branch, 216 North St, Nakina, ON, P0T 2H0, CANADA. Tel: 807-329-5906. p. 2643
Antonucci, Carl, Dir, Libr Serv, Central Connecticut State University, 1615 Stanley St, New Britain, CT, 06050. Tel: 860-832-2099. p. 324
Antonucci, Kassie M, Libr Dir, Elko-Lander-Eureka County Library System, 720 Court St, Elko, NV, 89801. Tel: 775-738-3066. p. 1344
Antonucci, Robert, Librn, Finger Lakes Community College, 3325 Marvin Sands Dr, Canandaigua, NY, 14424-8405. Tel: 585-785-1371. p. 1512
Antonucci, Sean, Head, Adult Serv, Valley Cottage Free Library, 110 Rte 303, Valley Cottage, NY, 10989. Tel: 845-268-7700, Ext 134. p. 1656
Antonucci-Durgan, Dana, Head Librn, Suffolk County Community College, Montaukett Learning Center, 121 Speonk Riverhead Rd, Riverhead, NY, 11901-3499. Tel: 631-548-2540. p. 1627
Antosh, Marissa, Youth Serv Librn, Norwell Public Library, 64 South St, Norwell, MA, 02061-2433. Tel: 781-659-2015. p. 1043
Antrim, Brenda, Ref (Info Servs), Santa Monica College Library, 1900 Pico Blvd, Santa Monica, CA, 90405-1628. Tel: 310-434-4334. p. 244
Anwar, Moira, Archivist, Historian, Walnut Creek Historical Society, 2660 Ygnacio Valley Rd, Walnut Creek, CA, 94598. Tel: 925-935-7871. p. 258
Anzalone, Christina, Libr Dir, Rowayton Library, 33 Highland Ave, Rowayton, CT, 06853. Tel: 203-838-5038. p. 335
Anzalone, Filippa Marullo, Assoc Dean for Libr & Tech Serv, Boston College, 885 Centre St, Newton Centre, MA, 02459. Tel: 617-552-6809. p. 1039
Anzel, Andrew, Dir, League of American Orchestras, 520 8th Ave, Ste 2005, New York, NY, 10018. Tel: 212-262-5161. p. 1590
Aoki, Jodi, Archivist, Trent University, Archives, Thomas J Bata Library, 1st Flr, 1600 W Bank Dr, Peterborough, ON, K9J 7B8, CANADA. Tel: 705-748-1011, Ext 7410. p. 2672
Apelquest, Eva, Adult Prog Coordr, Tech Serv, Spooner Memorial Library, 421 High St, Spooner, WI, 54801. Tel: 715-635-2792. p. 2478
Apfelbaum, Danielle, Scholarly Communications, Farmingdale State College of New York, 2350 Broadhollow Rd, Farmingdale, NY, 11735-1021. Tel: 934-420-2040. p. 1532
Apolant, Kim, Librn I, Woodstock Public Library District, Five Library Lane, Woodstock, NY, 12498. Tel: 845-679-2213. p. 1667
Aponte, Sarah, Chief Librn, City College of the City University of New York, Dominican Studies Institute Archives & Library, NAC 2/202, 160 Convent Ave, New York, NY, 10031. Tel: 212-650-7170, 212-650-7496. p. 1581
Apostolos, Erin, Dir, Meredith Public Library, 91 Main St, Meredith, NH, 03253. Tel: 603-279-4303. p. 1373
Appavoo, Clare, Exec Dir, Canadian Research Knowledge Network, 1309 Carling Ave, PO Box 35155 Westgate, Ottawa, ON, K1Z 1A2, CANADA. Tel: 613-907-7029. p. 2778
Appel, Stephen, Geospatial Information Librarian, University of Wisconsin-Milwaukee Libraries, American Geographical Society Library, Golda Meir Library, 2311 E Hartford Ave, Milwaukee, WI, 53211. Tel: 414-229-3984, 414-229-6282. p. 2461
Appell, Nelson, Dir, Washington Public Library, 410 Lafayette St, Washington, MO, 63090. Tel: 636-390-1070. p. 1285
Appelt, Diane, Adjunct Librn, Harrisburg Area Community College, 2010 Pennsylvania Ave, York, PA, 17404. Tel: 717-801-3220. p. 2026
Appelt, Susan, Tech Serv, Oakland Community College, Library Systems, 2900 Featherstone Rd, MTEC A210, Auburn Hills, MI, 48326. Tel: 248-232-4480. p. 1082
Apperson, Carolee, Br Mgr, Camden County Library District, Climax Springs Branch, 14157 N State Hwy 7, Climax Springs, MO, 65324. Tel: 573-347-2722. p. 1239
Appleby, Cindy, Dir, Wells Public Library, 1434 Post Rd, Wells, ME, 04090-4508. Tel: 207-646-8181, Ext 206. p. 945
Appleby, Jade, Teen Librn, Marion County Public Library, 201 E Main St, Lebanon, KY, 40033-1133. Tel: 270-692-4698. p. 861
Appleby, Jean, Libr Mgr, Mannsville Free Library, 106 Lilac Park Dr, Mannsville, NY, 13661. Tel: 315-465-4049. p. 1568
Appleby, Melinda, Librn, Groveland Correctional Facility Library, 7000 Sonyea Rd, Sonyea, NY, 14556. Tel: 585-658-2871. p. 1642
Appleby, Rachel, Law Librn, Alberta Law Libraries, Judicial, Calgary Courts Ctr, 601-Five St SW, Ste 501N, Calgary, AB, T2P 5P7, CANADA. Tel: 403-592-4796. p. 2525
Appleby, Sarah, Univ Archivist, University of Mary Washington, 1801 College Ave, Fredericksburg, VA, 22401-5300. Tel: 540-654-1763. p. 2320
Applegarth, Crystal, Asst Librn, Central Christian College of the Bible Library, 911 E Urbandale Dr, Moberly, MO, 65270. Tel: 660-263-3933. p. 1262
Applegate, Jeff, Library Contact, Colusa County Free Library, Stonyford Branch, 5080 Stonyford-Lodoga Rd, Stonyford, CA, 95979. Tel: 530-963-3722. p. 131
Applegate, Laura, Assoc Librn, Ohio Agricultural Research & Development Center Library, 1680 Madison Ave, Wooster, OH, 44691-4096. Tel: 330-202-3580. p. 1833
Applegate, Sarah, Co-Dir, Coyle Free Library, 102 N Main St, Chambersburg, PA, 17201. Tel: 717-263-1054. p. 1920
Applegate, Tamara, Libr Mgr, Apache County Library District, Vernon Public, Ten County Rd 3142, Vernon, AZ, 85940. Tel: 928-532-5005. p. 76
Appleman, Laura, Commun Engagement Mgr, Licking County Library, 101 W Main St, Newark, OH, 43055-5054. Tel: 740-349-5523. p. 1807
Appleton, Scott, Library Contact, Alcona County Library System, Mikado Township, 2291 S F-41, Mikado, MI, 48745. Tel: 989-569-8175. p. 1113
Applin, Mary Beth, District Dean of Libraries, Hinds Community College, 505 E Main St, Raymond, MS, 39154. Tel: 601-857-3355. p. 1231
Applin, Mary Beth, Dr, Dean, Learning Res, Hinds Community College, McLendon Library, 505 E Main St, Raymond, MS, 39154. Tel: 601-857-3255. p. 1231
Appling, Sherryl, Cat, Tech, Logan County Public Library, 225 Armory Dr, Russellville, KY, 42276. Tel: 270-726-6129. p. 874
Apps, Michelle, Coll Develop, Ref, Broward College, Bldg 17, 3501 SW Davie Rd, Davie, FL, 33314. Tel: 954-201-6330. p. 391
Apsel, Charlaine, Exec Dir, Presbytery of Long Island, 42 Hauppauge Rd, Commack, NY, 11725. Tel: 631-499-7171. p. 1521
Apt, Robbie, Outreach Serv Mgr, Delaware County District Library, 84 E Winter St, Delaware, OH, 43015. Tel: 740-362-3861. p. 1781
Apterbach, Emily, Ref & Instruction Librn, Yeshiva University Libraries, Hedi Steinberg Library, 245 Lexington Ave, New York, NY, 10016. Tel: 646-592-4980. p. 1605
Aquila, Mary, Cat Librn, Athens State University, 407 E Pryor St, Athens, AL, 35611. Tel: 256-216-6650. p. 5
Aquila, Sam, Coordr, Cat, University of Victoria Libraries, McPherson Library, PO Box 1800, Victoria, BC, V8W 3H5, CANADA. Tel: 250-721-8211. p. 2583

Aquilanti, Rylee, Archives Specialist, Museum of York County, 210 E Jefferson St, York, SC, 29745. Tel: 803-329-2121. p. 2072
Aquino, Andy, Pub Serv Librn, Niagara County Community College, 3111 Saunders Settlement Rd, Sanborn, NY, 14132. Tel: 716-614-6705, 716-614-6780. p. 1635
Arabadjis, Chris, Dir, Visual & Multimedia Serv, Pratt Institute Libraries, 200 Willoughby Ave, Brooklyn, NY, 11205-3897. Tel: 718-399-4437. p. 1506
Aracena, Rebecca, Support Serv Coordr, Lincoln City Libraries, 136 S 14th St, Lincoln, NE, 68508-1899. Tel: 402-441-8576. p. 1321
Aragon, Gladys, Librn, Association Paritaire Pour la Sante et la Securite du Travail - Secteur Affaires Municipales, 715 Square Victoria, Ste 710, Montreal, QC, H2Y 2H7, CANADA. Tel: 514-849-8373, Ext 235. p. 2717
Aragon, Lynnelle, Library Contact, Laguna Public Library, 29 Rodeo Dr, Laguna, NM, 87026. Tel: 505-552-6280. p. 1470
Aragon, Ruben F, Libr Dir, New Mexico Highlands University, 802 National Ave, Las Vegas, NM, 87701. Tel: 505-454-3401. p. 1471
Aragon, Sherry, Libr Dir, Espanola Public Library, 313 N Paseo de Onate, Espanola, NM, 87532. Tel: 505-747-6087. p. 1467
Aragon, Tova, Coll, Poudre River Public Library District, 201 Peterson St, Fort Collins, CO, 80524-2990. Tel: 970-221-6740. p. 281
Araiza, William, Ref Librn, Chaffey College Library, 5885 Haven Ave, Rancho Cucamonga, CA, 91737-3002. Tel: 909-652-8119. p. 197
Aramburo, Rae-Lynne, Chief Librn/CEO, Brantford Public Library, 173 Colborne St, Brantford, ON, N3T 2G8, CANADA. Tel: 519-756-2220, Ext 3319. p. 2633
Aramburo, Rae-Lynne, Chief Librn/CEO, Brantford Public Library, St Paul Avenue Branch, 441 St Paul Ave, Brantford, ON, N3R 4N8, CANADA. Tel: 519-756-2220. p. 2633
Arana, Wilson, Dir, Info Tech, Westchester Library System, 570 Taxter Rd, Ste 400, Elmsford, NY, 10523-2337. Tel: 914-231-3248. p. 1531
Aranas, Pauline, Dir, Law Libr, Assoc Dean & Chief Info Officer, University of Southern California Libraries, Asa V Call Law Library, 699 Exposition Blvd, LAW 202, MC 0072, Los Angeles, CA, 90089-0072. Tel: 213-740-6482. p. 170
Arand, Betsy, Libr Mgr, Sno-Isle Libraries, Freeland Library, 5495 Harbor Ave, Freeland, WA, 98249. Tel: 360-331-7323. p. 2370
Aranda, Jose, Instrul Librn, Dona Ana Community College, East Mesa Library, 2800 N Sonoma Ranch Blvd, Las Cruces, NM, 88011. Tel: 575-528-7260. p. 1470
Aranda, Nicole, Pub Serv Librn, William Carey University Libraries, 710 William Carey Pkwy, Hattiesburg, MS, 39401. Tel: 601-318-6169. p. 1219
Arauz, Cynthia, Br Supvr, La Crosse Public Library, North Community, 1552 Kane St, La Crosse, WI, 54603. Tel: 608-789-7189. p. 2446
Arauz, Cynthia, Circ Mgr, La Crosse Public Library, 800 Main St, La Crosse, WI, 54601. Tel: 608-789-4909. p. 2446
Aravecz Shaw, Nancy, Libr Dir, Florham Park Public Library, 107 Ridgedale Ave, Florham Park, NJ, 07932. Tel: 973-377-2694. p. 1403
Arce Senati, Vanessa, Head, Ref, Lehman College, City University of New York, 250 Bedford Park Blvd W, Bronx, NY, 10468. Tel: 718-960-7765. p. 1499
Arceneaux, Keisa, Acq Librn, Terrebonne Parish Library, 151 Library Dr, Houma, LA, 70360. Tel: 985-876-5861. p. 891
Archambault, Caroline, Librn, HEC Montreal Library, 3000, chemin de la Cote-Sainte-Catherine, Montreal, QC, H3T 2A7, CANADA. Tel: 514-340-6221. p. 2724
Archambault, Kristin, Librn, Christ Church Library, 527 Pomfret St, Pomfret, CT, 06258. Tel: 860-315-7780, 860-576-7907. p. 334
Archer, Alyssa, Head, Res Serv, Radford University, 925 E Main St, Radford, VA, 24142. Tel: 540-831-5688. p. 2339
Archer, David, Libr Dir, Cook Memorial Public Library District, 413 N Milwaukee Ave, Libertyville, IL, 60048-2280. Tel: 847-362-2330. p. 608
Archer, Elizabeth, Library Contact, Thiele Kaolin Co, 520 Kaolin Rd, Sandersville, GA, 31082. Tel: 478-552-3951. p. 495
Archer, J, Libr Asst, Tiskilwa Public Library, 119 E Main, Tiskilwa, IL, 61368. Tel: 815-646-4511. p. 654
Archer, Jeffry, Dean, Univ Libr, Baylor University Libraries, 1312 S Third St, Waco, TX, 76798. Tel: 254-710-3590. p. 2252
Archer, Jeffry, Assoc Dean, User Serv, McGill University Libraries, McLennan Library Bldg, 3459 McTavish St, Montreal, QC, H3A 0C9, CANADA. Tel: 514-398-4735. p. 2726
Archer, Jenna, Dir, Hesseltine Public Library, 14 NW Division, Wilbur, WA, 99185. Tel: 509-647-5828. p. 2395
Archer, Laila, Br Mgr, Knox County Public Library System, Howard Pinkston Branch, 7732 Martin Mill Pike, Knoxville, TN, 37920. Tel: 865-573-0436. p. 2106
Archer, Mary, Youth Serv Librn, Princeton Public Library, 698 E Peru St, Princeton, IL, 61356. Tel: 815-875-1331. p. 636
Archer, Ruth, Circ Mgr, Holly Township Library, 1116 N Saginaw St, Holly, MI, 48442-1395. Tel: 248-634-1754. p. 1116
Archer, Sylvia, Outreach Librn, Avery-Mitchell-Yancey Regional Library System, 289 Burnsville School Rd, Burnsville, NC, 28714. Tel: 828-682-4476. p. 1677
Archer, Wendy, Adult Serv Mgr, YA Mgr, Scarsdale Public Library, 54 Olmsted Rd, Scarsdale, NY, 10583. Tel: 914-722-1300. p. 1637
Archer-Capuzzo, Sonia, Clinical Asst Prof, University of North Carolina at Greensboro, School of Education Bldg, Rm 446, 1300 Spring Garden St, Greensboro, NC, 27412. Tel: 336-334-3477. p. 2790
Archibald, Amanda, Libr Mgr, Caroline Municipal Library, 5023 50th Ave, Caroline, AB, T0M 0M0, CANADA. Tel: 403-722-4060. p. 2530
Archibald, Emily, Br Mgr, Tulsa City-County Library, Hardesty Regional Library, 8316 E 93rd St, Tulsa, OK, 74133. p. 1866
Archibald, Karen, Dir of Libr, Nicholson Memorial Library System, 625 Austin St, Garland, TX, 75040-6365. Tel: 972-205-2545. p. 2183
Archibald, Matthew, Br Mgr, Traverse Area District Library, East Bay Branch, 1989 Three Mile Rd N, Traverse City, MI, 49686. Tel: 231-922-2085. p. 1154
Archibald, Sylvia, Exec Dir, East Norwalk Improvement Association Library, 51 Van Zant St, Norwalk, CT, 06855. Tel: 203-838-0408, Ext 102. p. 331
Archibeque, Orlando, Researcher, Support Librn, Auraria Library, 1100 Lawrence St, Denver, CO, 80204-2095. Tel: 303-315-7741. p. 273
Archuletta, Susan, Asst Librn, Nesbitt Memorial Library, 529 Washington St, Columbus, TX, 78934-2326. Tel: 979-732-3392. p. 2158
Ard, Amber, Br Mgr, Nassau County Public Library System, Hilliard Branch, 15821 CR 108, Hilliard, FL, 32046. Tel: 904-530-6544. p. 395
Ard, Denise, Dir, North Valley Public Library, 208 Main St, Stevensville, MT, 59870. Tel: 406-777-5061. p. 1302
Ard, Pam, Librn, Rayburn Correctional Center Library, 27268 Hwy 21 N, Angie, LA, 70426. Tel: 985-661-6328. p. 881
Ardelle, Cindy, Head Cataloger, Manatee County Public Library System, 1301 Barcarrota Blvd W, Bradenton, FL, 34205-7522. Tel: 941-748-5555, Ext 6327. p. 386
Arden, Janet, Adult Programmer, Coordr, Hampstead Public Library, Nine Mary E Clark Dr, Hampstead, NH, 03841. Tel: 603-329-6411. p. 1366
Arden, Michael, AV Librn, United States Military Academy Library, Jefferson Hall Library & Learning Ctr, 758 Cullum Rd, West Point, NY, 10996. Tel: 845-938-8301. p. 1663
Ardoin, Charmetra, Asst Br Mgr, Bossier Parish Libraries, Benton Branch, 115 Courthouse Dr, Benton, LA, 71006. Tel: 318-965-2751. p. 886
Arecke, Konrad, Librn, Morgan Lewis & Bockius LLP, 1111 Pennsylvania Ave NW, Washington, DC, 20004-2541. Tel: 202-739-4636. p. 371
Aregbesola, Emmanuel, Libr Mgr, Natural Resources Canada Library, Hugh John Flemming Forestry Ctr, 1350 Regent St S, Rm 1-112, Fredericton, NB, E3B 5P7, CANADA. Tel: 506-452-3541. p. 2601
Arehart, Carrick, Asst Dir, Louisville Free Public Library, 301 York St, Louisville, KY, 40203-2205. Tel: 502-574-1712. p. 865
Arellano, Joyce, Ch Mgr, Fountaindale Public Library District, 300 W Briarcliff Rd, Bolingbrook, IL, 60440. Tel: 630-685-4180. p. 543
Arellano, Marcos, Head, Tech Serv, Stickney-Forest View Public Library District, 6800 W 43rd St, Stickney, IL, 60402. Tel: 708-749-1050. p. 651
Arellano, Oscar, Ref Serv, Tech Serv, Blue Island Public Library, 2433 York St, Blue Island, IL, 60406-2011. Tel: 708-388-1078, Ext 16. p. 543
Arena, Elizabeth, Ch Serv, North Babylon Public Library, 815 Deer Park Ave, North Babylon, NY, 11703-3812. Tel: 631-669-4020. p. 1607
Arena, Tom, Actg Dir, The Waltham Museum Inc Library, 25 Lexington St, Waltham, MA, 02452. Tel: 781-893-9020. p. 1062
Arenas, Anna, Mgr, Communications, Tech Mgr, Southeast Florida Library Information Network, Inc, Florida Atlantic University, Wimberly Library, Office 452, 777 Glades Rd, Boca Raton, FL, 33431. Tel: 561-208-0984. p. 2763
Arend, Mark, Asst Dir, Winnefox Library System, 106 Washington Ave, Oshkosh, WI, 54901-4985. Tel: 920-236-5220. p. 2468
Arends, Katherine, Br Mgr, Alamance County Public Libraries, Mebane Public Library, 101 S First St, Mebane, NC, 27302. Tel: 919-563-6431. p. 1676
Arends, Shannon, Br Mgr, Chicago Public Library, Mount Greenwood, 11010 S Kedzie Ave, Chicago, IL, 60655. Tel: 312-747-2805, 312-747-5693. p. 557
Arens, Addie, Dir, Drummond Public Library, 14990 Superior St, Drummond, WI, 54832. Tel: 715-739-6290. p. 2431
Arens, Layne, Br Mgr, Chicago Public Library, West Belmont, 3104 N Narragansett Ave, Chicago, IL, 60634. Tel: 312-746-5142. p. 557
Areson, Anna, Teen & Adult Librn, La Grange Association Library, 1110 Route 55, 2nd Flr, LaGrangeville, NY, 12540. Tel: 845-452-3141. p. 1561
Arevalo, Jonathan, Circ Mgr, Marymount Manhattan College, 221 E 71st St, New York, NY, 10021. Tel: 212-517-0815. p. 1591
Argandoña, José, Ad, Commerce Township Community Library, 180 E Commerce, Commerce Township, MI, 48382. Tel: 248-669-8101, Ext 110. p. 1093
Argentati, Carolyn, Dep Dir, North Carolina State University Libraries, D H Hill Jr Library, Two Broughton Dr, Raleigh, NC, 27695. Tel: 919-515-7188. p. 1709
Argentati, Carolyn, Dep Dir, North Carolina State University Libraries, James B Hunt Jr Library, 1070 Partners Way, Campus Box 7132, Raleigh, NC, 27606. p. 1709
Argo, Elizabeth, Youth Serv Coordr, Maryville Public Library, 509 N Main St, Maryville, MO, 64468. Tel: 660-582-5281. p. 1261
Argo, Melanie, ILL, Madison Public Library, 209 E Center St, Madison, SD, 57042. Tel: 605-256-7525. p. 2078
Argo, Suzanne, Head Librn, First Regional Library, B J Chain Public Library, 6619 Hwy 305 N, Olive Branch, MS, 38654. Tel: 662-895-5900. p. 1219

Argue, Gwen, Head Librn, Parkland Regional Library-Manitoba, Hamiota Branch, 43 Maple Ave E, Hamiota, MB, R0M 0T0, CANADA. Tel: 204-764-2680. p. 2586

Argueta, Jennifer, Asst Dir, Coll Mgt, University of La Verne, 320 E D St, Ontario, CA, 91764. Tel: 909-460-2064. p. 188

Arhipov, Sergei, Head Librn, Saint Tikhon's Orthodox Theological Seminary, St Tikhon's Rd, South Canaan, PA, 18459. Tel: 570-561-1818, Ext 5. p. 2008

Arial, Danielle, Br Supvr, Wellington County Library, Elora Branch, 144 Geddes St, Elora, ON, N0B 1S0, CANADA. Tel: 519-846-0190. p. 2641

Arias-Bautista, Omar, Pub Serv Coordr, Arlington Public Library System, East Arlington, 1817 New York Ave, Arlington, TX, 76010. p. 2136

Arias-Hernandez, Richard, Assoc Prof, University of British Columbia, The Irving K Barber Learning Ctr, 1961 E Mall, Ste 470, Vancouver, BC, V6T 1Z1, CANADA. Tel: 604-822-2404. p. 2795

Ariga, Michelle, Dir of Libr Advan, York University Libraries, 4700 Keele St, North York, ON, M3J 1P3, CANADA. Tel: 416-736-5150, Ext 55150, 416-736-5601. p. 2661

Arjona, Ed, Asst Dir, Support Serv, McAllen Public Library, 4001 N 23rd St, McAllen, TX, 78504. Tel: 956-681-3000. p. 2217

Arkelian, Nora, Libr Dir, Mercyhurst University, 501 E 38th St, Erie, PA, 16546. Tel: 814-824-2234. p. 1932

Arkoosh, Rachel, Coll Mgt Serv, Pacific University Libraries, 2043 College Way, Forest Grove, OR, 97116. Tel: 503-352-1411. p. 1880

Arkwright, Patti, Dir, Maury Loontjens Memorial Library, 35 Kingstown Rd, Narragansett, RI, 02882. Tel: 401-789-9507. p. 2034

Arlain, Mandi, Librn, University of Illinois Library at Urbana-Champaign, Social Sciences, Health & Education Library, 101 Main Library, MC-522, 1408 W Gregory Dr, Urbana, IL, 61801. Tel: 217-244-1864. p. 656

Arlitsch, Kenning, Dean of Libr, Montana State University Library, One Centennial Mall, Bozeman, MT, 59717. Tel: 406-994-6978. p. 1289

Armacost, J Andrew, Head, Coll Develop, Duke University Libraries, 411 Chapel Dr, Durham, NC, 27708. Tel: 919-660-5800. p. 1684

Armaza, Gustavo, Law Libr Asst, New York State Supreme Court Ninth Judicial District, 20 County Center, Ground Flr, Carmel, NY, 10512. Tel: 845-208-7804. p. 1514

Arment, Donna, Supvr, Coll Develop, Durango Public Library, 1900 E Third Ave, Durango, CO, 81301. Tel: 970-375-3386. p. 278

Arment, Shirley, Dir, K O Lee Aberdeen Public Library, 215 S E Fourth Ave, Aberdeen, SD, 57401. Tel: 605-626-7997. p. 2073

Armenti, Sarah, Librn, Keansburg Waterfront Public Library, 55 Shore Blvd, Keansburg, NJ, 07734. Tel: 732-787-0636. p. 1410

Armentrout, Philip, Librn, Bakerville Library, Six Maple Hollow Rd, New Hartford, CT, 06057. Tel: 860-482-8806. p. 325

Armington, Beth, Libr Asst, Vernon Free Library, 567 Governor Hunt Rd, Vernon, VT, 05354. Tel: 802-257-0150. p. 2296

Armington, Shawn, Dir, Flemington Free Public Library, 118 Main St, Flemington, NJ, 08822. Tel: 908-782-5733. p. 1403

Armond, David, Info Tech, Brigham Young University, Howard W Hunter Law Library, 256 JRCB, Provo, UT, 84602-8000. Tel: 801-422-3593. p. 2269

Armour, Keith, Mgr, Public Library of Cincinnati & Hamilton County, Homework Center, North Bldg, 1st Flr, 800 Vine St, Cincinnati, OH, 45202. Tel: 513-369-3121. p. 1762

Arms, Julianna, Ch Serv, Stone Ridge Public Library, 3700 Main St, Stone Ridge, NY, 12484. Tel: 845-687-7023, Ext 107. p. 1646

Arms, Kevin, Assoc Dean of Library & Learning Servs, Lake-Sumter State College Library, 9501 US Hwy 441, Leesburg, FL, 34788. Tel: 352-365-3563, 352-365-3590. p. 418

Arms, Michele, Asst Dir, Cherry Valley Public Library District, 755 E State St, Cherry Valley, IL, 61016-9699. Tel: 815-332-5161, Ext 35. p. 553

Arms, Wendi, Music Librn, Converse College, 580 E Main St, Spartanburg, SC, 29302. Tel: 864-596-9074. p. 2069

Armstrong, Alison, Assoc Dir, Res & Educ, Ohio State University LIBRARIES, William Oxley Thompson Library, 1858 Neil Ave Mall, Columbus, OH, 43210-1286. Tel: 614-292-6785. p. 1776

Armstrong, Andrew, Libr Dir, Christendom College, 263 St Johns Way, Front Royal, VA, 22630. Tel: 540-551-9157. p. 2320

Armstrong, Angela, Youth Serv Librn, Ardmore Public Library, 320 E St NW, Ardmore, OK, 73401. Tel: 580-223-8290. p. 1840

Armstrong, Anne, Dir, Archives, National Guard Memorial Library, One Massachusetts Ave NW, Washington, DC, 20001. Tel: 202-408-5890, 202-789-0031. p. 372

Armstrong, Betty Joe, Tech Serv, Oregon City Public Library, 606 John Adams St, Oregon City, OR, 97045. Tel: 503-657-8269. p. 1890

Armstrong, Bill, Library Contact, New Haven Free Public Library, Wilson Branch, 303 Washington St, New Haven, CT, 06511. Tel: 203-946-2228. p. 326

Armstrong, Brenda, Acq, Lee University, 260 11th St NE, Cleveland, TN, 37311. Tel: 423-614-8551. p. 2093

Armstrong, Callie, Dir, Marshall Community Library, 605 Waterloo Rd, Marshall, WI, 53559. Tel: 608-655-3123. p. 2454

Armstrong, Carolyn, Libr Tech, Nova Scotia Community College, Kingstec Campus Library, 236 Belcher St, Kentville, NS, B4N 0A6, CANADA. Tel: 902-679-7380. p. 2620

Armstrong, Cathy, Libr Mgr, Nampa Municipal Library, 10203 99th Ave, Nampa, AB, T0H 2R0, CANADA. Tel: 780-322-3805. p. 2549

Armstrong, Dana, Libr Mgr, Monterey County Free Libraries, Buena Vista, 18250 Tara Dr, Salinas, CA, 93908. Tel: 831-455-9699. p. 172

Armstrong, Darcy Davidson, Pub Serv Mgr, Eckhart Public Library, 603 S Jackson St, Auburn, IN, 46706-2298. Tel: 206-925-2414, Ext 504. p. 668

Armstrong, David, Librn, Bowditch & Dewey, 311 Main St, Worcester, MA, 01608. Tel: 508-926-3331. p. 1071

Armstrong, David, Librn, Wayne County Law Library, Wayne County Courthouse, 215 N Grant St, Wooster, OH, 44691. Tel: 330-287-7721. p. 1833

Armstrong, Gracie, Mrs, Dir, Stewart County Public Library, 102 Natcor Dr, Dover, TN, 37058. Tel: 931-232-3127. p. 2097

Armstrong, Janet, Librn, Missouri Department of Corrections, Women's Eastern Reception & Diagnostic Correctional Center, 1101 E Hwy 54, Vandalia, MO, 63382-2905. Tel: 573-594-6686. p. 1252

Armstrong, Jason, IT Dir, Allegany County Library System, 31 Washington St, Cumberland, MD, 21502. Tel: 301-777-1200. p. 963

Armstrong, Jenna, Ch, Sullivan County Public Libraries, 100 S Crowder St, Sullivan, IN, 47882. Tel: 812-268-4957. p. 719

Armstrong, Jody, Assoc Dir, Columbia University, Arthur W Diamond Law Library, 435 W 116th St, New York, NY, 10027. Tel: 212-854-1308. p. 1583

Armstrong, Kacie, Dir, Euclid Public Library, 631 E 222nd St, Euclid, OH, 44123-2091. Tel: 216-261-5300, Ext 101. p. 1785

Armstrong, Kathleen, Dir, Cahokia Public Library District, 140 Cahokia Park Dr, Cahokia, IL, 62206-2129. Tel: 618-332-1491. p. 547

Armstrong, Kim, Exec Dir, Orbis Cascade Alliance, PO Box 6007, Portland, OR, 97228. Tel: 541-246-2470. p. 2773

Armstrong, Leigh Galmiche, Br Librn, Plaquemines Parish Library, Buras Branch, 35572 Hwy 11, Buras, LA, 70041. Tel: 504-564-0921, 504-564-0944. p. 885

Armstrong, Leslie, Head, Youth Serv, Locust Valley Library, 170 Buckram Rd, Locust Valley, NY, 11560-1999. Tel: 516-671-1837. p. 1564

Armstrong, Matthew, Info & Tech Serv, Hancock County Library System, 312 Hwy 90, Bay Saint Louis, MS, 39520-3595. Tel: 228-467-5282. p. 1211

Armstrong, Melanie, Coordr, Sauk Valley Community College, 173 IL Rte 2, Dixon, IL, 61021-9112. Tel: 815-288-5511, Ext 210. p. 579

Armstrong, Melanie, Music Libr Assoc, University of Richmond, Mary Morton Parsons Music Library, Modlin Ctr for the Arts, 453 Westhampton Way, Richmond, VA, 23173. Tel: 804-287-6894. p. 2343

Armstrong, Melissa, Asst Dir, Caro Area District Library, 840 W Frank St, Caro, MI, 48723. Tel: 989-673-4329, Ext 107. p. 1088

Armstrong, Michelle, Assoc Dean, Boise State University, 1865 Cesar Chavez Lane, Boise, ID, 83725. Tel: 208-426-1204. p. 517

Armstrong, Oriana B, Librn, United States Army, 701 San Marco Blvd, Rm 430-W, Jacksonville, FL, 32207. Tel: 904-232-3643. p. 413

Armstrong, Pam, Libr Dir, Allegan District Library, 331 Hubbard St, Allegan, MI, 49010. Tel: 269-673-4625. p. 1076

Armstrong, Pamela, Asst Dir of Br, Jackson-George Regional Library System, 3214 Pascagoula St, Pascagoula, MS, 39567. Tel: 228-769-3227. p. 1228

Armstrong, Rhonda, Libr Dir, Lincoln Memorial University, 6965 Cumberland Gap Pkwy, Harrogate, TN, 37752. Tel: 423-869-6436. p. 2101

Armstrong, Rob, Chief Exec Officer, Meaford Public Library, 11 Sykes St N, Meaford, ON, N4L 1V6, CANADA. Tel: 519-538-3500. p. 2657

Armstrong, Sara, Assoc Dean, Tech Serv & Libr Syst, University of Detroit Mercy Libraries, 4001 W McNichols Rd, Detroit, MI, 48221-3038. Tel: 313-993-1074. p. 1099

Armstrong, Sheldon, Assoc Univ Librn, Coll, University of British Columbia Library, 1961 East Mall, Vancouver, BC, V6T 1Z1, CANADA. Tel: 604-822-5300. p. 2580

Armstrong, Tanya, Dr, Prog Dir, Nebraska Center for the Education of Children Who Are Blind or Visually Impaired, 824 Tenth Ave, Nebraska City, NE, 68410. Tel: 402-873-5513. p. 1325

Arn, Nancy L, Interim Dir, Barton Public Library, 200 E Fifth St, El Dorado, AR, 71730-3897. Tel: 870-863-5447. p. 94

Arnall, Darcy, Youth Serv Librn, Oconee County Public Library, 501 W South Broad St, Walhalla, SC, 29691. Tel: 864-638-4133. p. 2072

Arnason, Laurie, Librn, Pauline Johnson Library, 23 Main St, Lundar, MB, R0C 1Y0, CANADA. Tel: 204-762-5367. p. 2588

Arndell, Bettie, Genealogy & Per, Grayson County Public Library, 163 Carroll Gibson Blvd, Leitchfield, KY, 42754-1488. Tel: 270-259-5455. p. 861

Arndt, April, Dir, Ontario Public Library, 313 Main St, Ontario, WI, 54651. Tel: 608-337-4651. p. 2466

Arndt, Katherine, Bibliographer, Curator, Rare Bks & Maps, University of Alaska Fairbanks, 1732 Tanana Dr, Fairbanks, AK, 99775. Tel: 907-474-6671. p. 45

Arndt, Nathan Scott, Dir & Curator, University of Northern Iowa Library, 1227 W 27th St, Cedar Falls, IA, 50613-3675. Tel: 319-273-6922. p. 737

Arndt, Robert, Dir, Res Serv, University of North Carolina at Pembroke, One University Dr, Pembroke, NC, 28372. Tel: 910-521-6516. p. 1707
Arndt, Theresa, Assoc Dir, Libr Res & Admin, Dickinson College, 28 N College St, Carlisle, PA, 17013-2311. Tel: 717-245-1397. p. 1919
Arnhold, Laura, Libr Dir, Upper Merion Township Library, 175 W Valley Forge Rd, King of Prussia, PA, 19406-2399. Tel: 610-265-4805. p. 1948
Arnold, Alexandria, Exec Dir, Bernardsville Public Library, One Anderson Hill Rd, Bernardsville, NJ, 07924. Tel: 908-766-0118. p. 1390
Arnold, Allison, Libr Dir, Saint Clair County Library System, 210 McMorran Blvd, Port Huron, MI, 48060-4098. Tel: 810-987-7323. p. 1142
Arnold, Allison, Mgr, Ref & Adult Serv, Lake Oswego Public Library, 706 Fourth St, Lake Oswego, OR, 97034-2399. Tel: 503-534-5665. p. 1884
Arnold, Angela, Circ Supvr, University of California, Berkeley, Jean Gray Hargrove Music Library, Berkeley, CA, 94720-6000. Tel: 510-643-6196. p. 123
Arnold, Bonnie, Regional Librn, AdventHealth Hinsdale, 120 N Oak St, Hinsdale, IL, 60521. Tel: 630-856-7230. p. 600
Arnold, Bonnie, Regional Librn, Ascension Saint Joseph-Juliet, 333 N Madison St, Joliet, IL, 60435. Tel: 815-725-7133, Ext 3530. p. 603
Arnold, Bonnie, Dir, UChicago Medicine AdventHealth La Grange Hospital, 5101 Willow Springs Rd, La Grange, IL, 60525. Tel: 708-245-7230. p. 605
Arnold, Carrie, Librn Supvr, Hearst San Simeon State Historical Monument, 750 Hearst Castle Rd, San Simeon, CA, 93452. Tel: 805-927-2076. p. 237
Arnold, Christina, Librn, Frederick Memorial Hospital, 400 W Seventh St, Frederick, MD, 21701. Tel: 240-566-3459. p. 966
Arnold, Cindy, Librn, United States Army, Barr Memorial Library, 62 W Spearhead Division Ave, Bldg 400, Fort Knox, KY, 40121-5187. Tel: 502-624-1232, 502-624-4636. p. 855
Arnold, Diane, Digital Libr & Ref Coordr, Delaware County Libraries, Bldg 19, 340 N Middletown Rd, Media, PA, 19063-5597. Tel: 610-891-8622. p. 1961
Arnold, Eli, Dir & Univ Librn, Oglethorpe University, 4484 Peachtree Rd NE, Atlanta, GA, 30319. Tel: 404-364-8511. p. 465
Arnold, Emily, Youth Serv Librn, Scott County Library System, 200 N Sixth Ave, Eldridge, IA, 52748. Tel: 563-285-4794. p. 750
Arnold, Emily, Asst Ch, Circ, Teen Librn, Gallatin County Public Library, 209 W Market St, Warsaw, KY, 41095. Tel: 859-567-7323. p. 876
Arnold, Gretchen, Dir, University of Virginia, Claude Moore Health Sciences Library, Univ Va Health System, 1350 Jefferson Park Ave, Charlottesville, VA, 22908. Tel: 434-924-5444. p. 2310
Arnold, Jane, Archivist, Cape Breton University Library, Beaton Institute Archives, 1250 Grand Lake Rd, Sydney, NS, B1P 6L2, CANADA. Tel: 902-563-1690. p. 2623
Arnold, Jennifer, Dir, Libr Serv, Central Piedmont Community College Library, 1201 Elizabeth Ave, Charlotte, NC, 28235. Tel: 704-330-6635. p. 1679
Arnold, Laurin, Br Mgr, Garfield County Public Library District, Glenwood Springs Branch, 815 Cooper Ave, Glenwood Springs, CO, 81601. Tel: 970-945-5958. p. 294
Arnold, Lee, Dr, Librn Emeritus, Historical Society of Pennsylvania, 1300 Locust St, Philadelphia, PA, 19107-5699. Tel: 215-732-6200. p. 1981
Arnold, Marialisa, Head, Adult Serv, Baldwin Public Library, 2385 Grand Ave, Baldwin, NY, 11510-3289. Tel: 516-223-6228. p. 1490
Arnold, Michelle, Ref Supvr, Clearwater Public Library System, 100 N Osceola Ave, Clearwater, FL, 33755. Tel: 727-562-4970. p. 388
Arnold, Michelle, Reference Support Specialist, Bellevue University, 1028 Bruin Blvd, Bellevue, NE, 68005. Tel: 402-557-7081. p. 1308
Arnold, Michelle, Dir, Bainbridge Free Library, 13 N Main St, Bainbridge, NY, 13733. Tel: 607-967-5305. p. 1489
Arnold, Nicole, Ref & Instruction Librn, Muskingum University, Ten College Dr, New Concord, OH, 43762. Tel: 740-826-8154. p. 1806
Arnold, Pabby, Coordr, Spec Projects, Literacy Prog Coordr, East Baton Rouge Parish Library, 7711 Goodwood Blvd, Baton Rouge, LA, 70806-7625. Tel: 225-924-9389. p. 882
Arnold, Sarah, Head, Circ, Kewanee Public Library District, 102 S Tremont St, Kewanee, IL, 61443. Tel: 309-852-4505. p. 605
Arnold, Sharmain, Ch Serv, Riviera Beach Public Library, 600 W Blue Heron Blvd, Riviera Beach, FL, 33404-4398. Tel: 561-845-3428. p. 439
Arnold, Susan, Dir, Health Sci Libr, West Virginia University, 3110 MacCorkle Ave SE, Charleston, WV, 25304. Tel: 304-347-1285. p. 2401
Arnold, Susan, Dir, Health Sci Libr, West Virginia University Libraries, 1549 University Ave, Morgantown, WV, 26506. Tel: 304-293-4040. p. 2409
Arnold, Susan, Dir, West Virginia University Libraries, Health Sciences Library, Robert C Byrd Health Sciences Center N, One Medical Ctr Dr, Morgantown, WV, 26506. Tel: 304-293-2113. p. 2410
Arnold, Tiffany, Library Operations Assoc, Southern Illinois University Edwardsville, 601 James R Thompson Blvd, Bldg B, East Saint Louis, IL, 62201. Tel: 618-482-6357. p. 581
Arnott, Jennifer, Research Librn, Perkins School for the Blind, Samuel P Hayes Research Library, 175 N Beacon St, Watertown, MA, 02472. Tel: 617-972-7250. p. 1063
Arnott, Lesley, Dir, Libr Serv, Ochsner LSU Health Shreveport Monroe Medical Center, 4864 Jackson St, Monroe, LA, 71202. Tel: 318-330-7644. p. 898
Arns, Jennifer Weil, PhD, Assoc Prof, University of South Carolina, 1501 Greene St, Columbia, SC, 29208. Tel: 803-777-3858. p. 2792
Arntzen, Kim L, Libr Spec, Fox Valley Technical College, 1825 N Bluemound Dr, Rm G113, Appleton, WI, 54912. Tel: 920-735-4836. p. 2420
Arocho, Anibal, Mr, Libr Mgr, Hunter College Libraries, Centro - Center for Puerto Rican Studies Library, 2180 Third Ave, Rm 121, New York, NY, 10035. Tel: 212-396-7879. p. 1588
Aromire, Lami, Chief Info Officer, Dir, Info Tech, District of Columbia Public Library, 1990 K St NW, Washington, DC, 20006. Tel: 202-727-1101. p. 363
Aronoff, Nell, Sr Asst Librn, University at Buffalo Libraries-State University of New York, Health Sciences Library, Abbott Hall, 3435 Main St, Bldg 28, Buffalo, NY, 14214-3002. Tel: 716-829-5735. p. 1510
Aronoff, Shelley, Coll Develop Librn, Glendale Community College Library, 1500 N Verdugo Rd, Glendale, CA, 91208-2894. Tel: 818-240-1000, Ext 5581, 818-240-1000, Ext 5586. p. 148
Aronson, Heather, Youth Serv, Southbury Public Library, 100 Poverty Rd, Southbury, CT, 06488. Tel: 203-262-0626. p. 337
Aronson, Morgan, Librn, United States Naval Observatory, 3450 Massachusetts Ave NW, Washington, DC, 20392. Tel: 202-762-1463. p. 379
Arozena, Steven, Librn, California State Department of Transportation, 1120 N St, Rm 1315, Sacramento, CA, 95812. Tel: 916-654-2630. p. 208
Arpen, Audrey, Asst Librn, ILL, Chief Dull Knife College, One College Dr, Lame Deer, MT, 59043. Tel: 406-477-8293. p. 1298
Arpin, Danielle, Head, Circ & Tech Serv, Pelham Public Library, 24 Village Green, Pelham, NH, 03076. Tel: 603-635-7581. p. 1377
Arquitt, Myra, Librn, Crittenden County Library, Earle Branch, 703 Commerce St, Earle, AR, 72331. Tel: 870-792-8500. p. 104
Arras, Marlena, Dir, Finance & Gen Serv, Charlotte Community Library, 226 S Bostwick St, Charlotte, MI, 48813-1801. Tel: 517-543-8859. p. 1090
Arredondo, Charlotte, Head, Children's Servx, Stevens Memorial Library, 345 Main St, North Andover, MA, 01845. Tel: 978-688-9505. p. 1040
Arredondo, David, Coll Serv Librn, University of Nebraska at Kearney, 2508 11th Ave, Kearney, NE, 68849-2240. Tel: 308-865-8992. p. 1319
Arredondo, Laurie, Br Mgr, Grand Prairie Public Library System, Betty Warmack Branch Library, 760 Bardin Rd, Grand Prairie, TX, 75052. Tel: 972-237-5772. p. 2186
Arrenholtz, Jennifer, Asst Dir, Newton County Public Library, 9444 N 315 W, Lake Village, IN, 46349. Tel: 219-992-3490. p. 702
Arreola, Omelia, Info Literacy Librn, Laredo College, West End Washington St, Laredo, TX, 78040. Tel: 956-721-5813. p. 2209
Arrick, Laurie, Librn, Henry Ford Wyandotte Hospital, Rehabilitation Bldg, 4th Flr, 2333 Biddle Ave, Wyandotte, MI, 48192-4668. Tel: 734-246-7361. p. 1160
Arrighetti, Julie, Chief Librn, United States Department of State, A/GIS/IPS/LIBR, Rm 3239, 2201 C St NW, Washington, DC, 20520-2442. Tel: 202-647-3002. p. 378
Arrigo, Paul A, Libr Dir, Lee College Library, 150 Lee Dr, Baytown, TX, 77520. Tel: 281-425-6447. p. 2145
Arrington, Logan, Dr, Chair, University of West Georgia, 1601 Maple St, Carrollton, GA, 30118. Tel: 678-839-3937. p. 2783
Arrivee, Sally, Head Ref Librn, Madison Heights Public Library, 240 W 13 Mile Rd, Madison Heights, MI, 48071-1894. Tel: 248-588-7763. p. 1128
Arrowood, Chris, Asst Libr Dir, Bellaire City Library, 5111 Jessamine, Bellaire, TX, 77401-4498. Tel: 713-662-8166. p. 2147
Arroyo, Kerri, Br Mgr, Inglewood Public Library, Crenshaw-Imperial Branch Library, 11141 Crenshaw Blvd, Inglewood, CA, 90303-2338. p. 153
Arroyo, Luis A, Dir, Info Tech, Universidad del Turabo, Rd 189 Km 3.3, Gurabo, PR, 00778. Tel: 787-743-7979, Ext 4501. p. 2511
Arroyo, Lupita, Principal Librn, Youth Serv, Santa Ana Public Library, 26 Civic Ctr Plaza, Santa Ana, CA, 92701-4010. Tel: 714-647-5283. p. 239
Arsenault, Andrea, Libr Mgr, Vaughan Public Libraries, Woodbridge Library, 150 Woodbridge Ave, Woodbridge, ON, L4L 2S7, CANADA. Tel: 905-653-7323. p. 2701
Arsenault, Clément, Prof, Universite de Montreal, 3150, rue Jean-Brillant, bur C-2004, Montreal, QC, H3T 1N8, CANADA. Tel: 514-343-6044. p. 2797
Arsenault, Neil, Br Mgr, Brampton Library, Four Corners Branch, 65 Queen St E, Brampton, ON, L6W 3L6, CANADA. Tel: 905-793-4636, Ext 74321. p. 2633
Arsenault, Shannon, Sr Libr Tech, Northern College, 4715 Hwy 101 E, South Porcupine, ON, P0N 1H0, CANADA. Tel: 705-235-3211, Ext 6816. p. 2679
Arseneau, Catherine, Dean, Libr & Multicultural Learning, Cape Breton University Library, 1250 Grand Lake Rd, Sydney, NS, B1P 6L2, CANADA. Tel: 902-563-1320. p. 2623

Arseneau, Catherine, Dir, Cultural Resources, Cape Breton University Library, Beaton Institute Archives, 1250 Grand Lake Rd, Sydney, NS, B1P 6L2, CANADA. Tel: 902-563-1326. p. 2623

Arseneault, Annie, ILL, National Gallery of Canada Library & Archives, 380 Sussex Dr, Ottawa, ON, K1N 9N4, CANADA. Tel: 613-714-6000, Ext 6323. p. 2667

Arseneault, Mathieu, AV, Cegep de Jonquiere, 2505 rue St Hubert, Jonquiere, QC, G7X 7W2, CANADA. Tel: 418-547-2191, Ext 6268. p. 2714

Artabane, Lynn, Tech Info Spec, Pension Benefit Guaranty Corporation, 1200 K St NW, Ste 360, Washington, DC, 20005-4026. Tel: 202-326-4000, Ext 6061. p. 374

Arteaga, Adela, Mgr, Circ Serv, Frisco Public Library, 6101 Frisco Square Blvd, Frisco, TX, 75034-3000. Tel: 972-292-5669. p. 2182

Arteaga, Racheal, Ref & Instruction Librn, Butte College Library, Chico Center, 2320 Forest Ave, Rm 219, Chico, CA, 95928. Tel: 530-895-2956. p. 189

Arteaga, Roberto, Instruction & Ref Librn, Pacific Lutheran University, 12180 Park Ave S, Tacoma, WA, 98447-0001. Tel: 253-535-7500. p. 2386

Arthay, Aurora, Asst Dir, Palm Beach County Library System, 3650 Summit Blvd, West Palm Beach, FL, 33406-4198. Tel: 561-233-2600. p. 454

Arthen, Leona, Dir, Worthington Library, One Huntington Rd, Worthington, MA, 01098. Tel: 413-238-5565. p. 1073

Arthur, Angela, Youth Serv Mgr, Cabell County Public Library, 455 Ninth Street Plaza, Huntington, WV, 25701. Tel: 304-528-5700. p. 2404

Arthur, Anne, Br Mgr, Saint Louis County Library, Meramec Valley Branch, 1501 San Simeon Way, Fenton, MO, 63026-3479. Tel: 314-994-3300, Ext 3550. p. 1274

Arthur, Gwen, Univ Librn, Clark University, 950 Main St, Worcester, MA, 01610-1477. Tel: 508-793-7384. p. 1071

Arthur, John, Libr Dir, East Brunswick Public Library, Two Jean Walling Civic Ctr, East Brunswick, NJ, 08816-3599. Tel: 732-390-6950. p. 1399

Arthur, John, Dir, Englewood Public Library, 31 Engle St, Englewood, NJ, 07631. Tel: 201-568-2215, Ext 222. p. 1401

Arthur, Steve, Librn, Ellis Public Library, 907 Washington St, Ellis, KS, 67637. Tel: 785-726-3464. p. 806

Arthur, Susan, Br Mgr, Jacksonville Public Library, Dallas James Graham Branch, 2304 N Myrtle Ave, Jacksonville, FL, 32209-5099. Tel: 904-630-0922. p. 412

Arthur, Susan, Br Mgr, Jacksonville Public Library, Westbrook Branch, 2809 Commonwealth Ave, Jacksonville, FL, 32254-2599. Tel: 904-384-7424. p. 412

Artice-Moore, Melanie, Youth Serv Librn, Murrysville Community Library, 4130 Sardis Rd, Murrysville, PA, 15668. Tel: 724-327-1102. p. 1967

Artigas, Junn, Dir, Media Serv, Pacific Union College, One Angwin Ave, Angwin, CA, 94508-9705. Tel: 707-965-7221. p. 116

Artiglia, Susan Weart, Ref Librn, Joint Base San Antonio Libraries, 3011 Harney Path, Fort Sam Houston, TX, 78234. Tel: 210-221-4387, 210-221-4702. p. 2178

Artman, Julie, Assoc Dean, Chapman University, One University Dr, Orange, CA, 92866. Tel: 714-532-7756. p. 188

Artymko, Susan, Chief Exec Officer, Head Librn, Bonnechere Union Public Library, 74 Maple St, Eganville, ON, K0J 1T0, CANADA. Tel: 613-628-2400, 613-628-3101, Ext 2400. p. 2639

Aruin, Jane, Libr Asst, Northwestern Medicine Marianjoy Rehabilitation Hospital, 26 W 171 Roosevelt Rd, Wheaton, IL, 60187. p. 661

Arvidson, Susie, Dir, Libr Serv, Fort Scott Community College Library, 2108 S Horton, Fort Scott, KS, 66701. Tel: 620-223-2700, Ext 3441. p. 808

Arvin, Shelley, Ref & Instruction Librn, Indiana State University, 510 North 6 1/2 St, Terre Haute, IN, 47809. Tel: 812-237-3700. p. 720

Arwood, Katie, Libr Dir, Montcalm Community College Library, 2800 College Dr, Sidney, MI, 48885. Tel: 989-328-2111, Ext 261, 989-328-2111, Ext 291. p. 1150

Arzola, Rebecca, Govt Doc Librn, Lehman College, City University of New York, 250 Bedford Park Blvd W, Bronx, NY, 10468. Tel: 718-960-8831. p. 1499

Asaris, Eric, Access Serv Coordr, DeSales University, 2755 Station Ave, Center Valley, PA, 18034. Tel: 610-282-1100, Ext 1266. p. 1920

Asato, Noriko, Dr, Assoc Prof, Prog Chair, University of Hawaii, 2550 McCarthy Mall, Hamilton Library, Rm 002, Honolulu, HI, 96822. Tel: 808-956-7321. p. 2784

Asbell, Cameron, Regional Libr Dir, Ohoopee Regional Library System, 610 Jackson St, Vidalia, GA, 30474-2835. Tel: 912-537-9283, Ext 104. p. 501

Asbell, Jason, Library Contact, Selkirk College Library, Tenth Street Campus, 820 Tenth St, Nelson, BC, V1l 3C7, CANADA. Tel: 250-505-1359. p. 2564

Asberg, Mark, Univ Librn, Vice Provost, Queen's University, 101 Union St, Kingston, ON, K7L 2N9, CANADA. Tel: 613-533-6000, Ext 74536. p. 2650

Asbury, Edie, Librn, Penn State Health Holy Spirit Medical Center, 503 N 21st St, Camp Hill, PA, 17011. Tel: 717-763-2664. p. 1918

Asbury, Ivy, Libr Mgr, South Georgia Regional Library System, Allen Statenville Branch, US Hwy 129 & Jackson St, Statenville, GA, 31648. Tel: 229-559-8182. p. 501

Ascencio, Mario, Col Librn, Art Center College of Design, 1700 Lida St, Pasadena, CA, 91103. Tel: 626-396-2233. p. 192

Ascenzo, Sally Ellen, Co-Dir, Marrowbone Public Library District, 216 W Main St, Bethany, IL, 61914. Tel: 217-665-3014. p. 542

Asch, Emily, Dir, Libr & Archives, Saint Catherine University, 2004 Randolph Ave, Saint Paul, MN, 55105. Tel: 651-690-6650. p. 1201

Aschenbach, Jamie, Head, Access Serv, Southern Connecticut State University, 501 Crescent St, New Haven, CT, 06515. Tel: 203-392-5768. p. 326

Aschenbrenner, Erin, Dir, Lied Scottsbluff Public Library, 1809 Third Ave, Scottsbluff, NE, 69361-2493. Tel: 308-630-6251. p. 1335

Ascher, Marie, Dir, New York Medical College, Basic Science Bldg, 15 Dana Rd, Valhalla, NY, 10595. Tel: 914-594-4207. p. 1656

Aschim, Mary Jo, Librn, Toole County Library, Sunburst Branch, 105 First St N, Sunburst, MT, 59482. Tel: 406-937-6980. p. 1302

Aschliman, Jillian, Dir, Bettendorf Public Library Information Center, 2950 Learning Campus Dr, Bettendorf, IA, 52722. Tel: 563-344-4175. p. 734

Aschliman, Jillian, Dir, The Frances Banta Waggoner Community Library, 505 Tenth St, DeWitt, IA, 52742-1335. Tel: 563-659-5523. p. 747

Asdel, Bryan, Interim Dir, Barstow Community College, 2700 Barstow Rd, Barstow, CA, 92311. Tel: 760-252-2411, Ext 7270. p. 120

Asebedo, Samantha J, Dir, Elm Creek Township Library, 213 N Fifth St, Wilsey, KS, 66873-9768. Tel: 785-497-2289. p. 844

Asfeld, Carla, Br Mgr, Great River Regional Library, Annandale Public Library, 30 Cedar St E, Annandale, MN, 55302-1113. Tel: 320-274-8448. p. 1196

Asfeld, Carla, Libr Serv Coordr, Great River Regional Library, Kimball Library, Five Main St N, Kimball, MN, 55353. Tel: 320-398-3915. p. 1197

Ash, Melanie, Libr Mgr, Clive Public Library, 5107 50th St, Clive, AB, T0C 0Y0, CANADA. Tel: 403-784-3131. p. 2531

Ash, Suzanne, Librn, Midvale Community Library, 70 E Bridge St, Midvale, ID, 83645-2012. Tel: 208-355-2213. p. 525

Ashbrook, Leslie, Asst Dir, Head, Res Serv, University of Virginia, Arthur J Morris Law Library, 580 Massie Rd, Charlottesville, VA, 22903-1738. Tel: 434-243-2493. p. 2310

Ashbrook, Nancy A, Libr Dir, Ella Johnson Memorial Public Library District, 109 S State St, Hampshire, IL, 60140. Tel: 847-683-4490. p. 596

Ashby, Caroline, Dir, Nassau Library System, 900 Jerusalem Ave, Uniondale, NY, 11553-3039. Tel: 516-292-8920. p. 1654

Ashby, Hayley, Network Serv, Riverside Community College District, 4800 Magnolia Ave, Riverside, CA, 92506-1299. p. 201

Ashby, Jennifer, Dir, Asotin County Library, 417 Sycamore St, Clarkston, WA, 99403-2666. Tel: 509-758-5454, Ext 102. p. 2361

Ashby, Jennifer, Dir, Asotin County Library, Heights Branch, 2036 Fourth Ave, Clarkston, WA, 99403-1322. Tel: 509-758-4601. p. 2362

Ashby, Michael, Youth Reference Supervisor, Samuels Public Library, 330 E Criser Rd, Front Royal, VA, 22630. Tel: 540-635-3153. p. 2321

Ashby, Samantha, Acq & Ref, Peter White Public Library, 217 N Front St, Marquette, MI, 49855. Tel: 906-226-4309. p. 1130

Ashby, Susan DiRenzo, Libr Syst Coordr, University of Akron, University Libraries, 315 Buchtel Mall, Akron, OH, 44325-1701. Tel: 330-972-7240. p. 1745

Ashcraft, Misty, Br Librn, Webster County Public Library, Providence Branch, 230 Willow St, Providence, KY, 42450. Tel: 270-667-5658. p. 853

Ashcraft, Rachel, Dir, Flora-Monroe Township Public Library, 109 N Center St, Flora, IN, 46929-1004. Tel: 574-967-3912. p. 682

Ashdown, Maryn, Customer Experience Dir, Coquitlam Public Library, City Centre Branch, 1169 Pinetree Way, Coquitlam, BC, V3B 0Y1, CANADA. Tel: 604-554-7324. p. 2565

Ashdown, Maryn, Dir Customer Experience, Main, Coquitlam Public Library, 575 Poirier St, Coquitlam, BC, V3J 6A9, CANADA. Tel: 604-554-7324. p. 2565

Ashdown, Maryn, Dir, Neighborhood & Youth Services, Vancouver Public Library, 350 W Georgia St, Vancouver, BC, V6B 6B1, CANADA. Tel: 604-331-3603. p. 2581

Ashdown, Pamela, Asst Librn, Ch, Erie Public Library District, 802 Eighth Ave, Erie, IL, 61250. Tel: 309-659-2707. p. 585

Ashe, Casey, Supvr, Tulsa Community College Libraries, Metro Campus, 909 S Boston Ave, Tulsa, OK, 74119-2011. Tel: 918-595-7285. p. 1866

Ashe, Sue, Human Res Mgr, Naperville Public Library, Naper Boulevard, 2035 S Naper Blvd, Naperville, IL, 60565-3353. Tel: 630-961-4100, Ext 2229. p. 623

Asher, Alan, Dr, Assoc Dean, Learning Res, University of Mary Hardin-Baylor, 900 College St, UMHB Sta, Box 8016, Belton, TX, 76513-2599. Tel: 254-295-4637. p. 2147

Asher, Dorothy, Curator, Lizzadro Museum of Lapidary Art Library, 1220 Kensington Rd, Oak Brook, IL, 60523. Tel: 630-833-1616. p. 627

Asher, Norma J, Libr Asst, La Follette Public Library, 201 S Ninth St, La Follette, TN, 37766-3606. Tel: 423-562-5154. p. 2108

Asherbranner, Jennifer, Dir, Falkville Public Library, Seven N First Ave, Falkville, AL, 35622. Tel: 256-784-5822. p. 16

Ashevak, Leveena, Librn, Nunavut Public Library Services, Clyde River Community Library, PO Box 150, Clyde River, NU, X0A 0E0, CANADA. Tel: 867-924-6565. p. 2625

Ashford, Robin, E-Learning & Ref Librn, George Fox University, Portland Center Library, Hampton Plaza, 12753 SW 68th Ave, Portland, OR, 97223. Tel: 503-554-6130. p. 1888
Ashley, Amy, Youth Serv, Powell County Public Library, 725 Breckenridge St, Stanton, KY, 40380. Tel: 606-663-4511. p. 875
Ashley, Jeannie, Info Serv, Libr Mgr, Fulton County Courts, Justice Center Tower, J1-7001, 185 Central Ave SW, Atlanta, GA, 30303. Tel: 404-612-4544. p. 464
Ashley, Joanna, Br Mgr, Laurel-Jones County Library System, Inc, Ellisville Public, 201 Poplar St, Ellisville, MS, 39437. Tel: 601-477-9271. p. 1224
Ashley, Julie, Dir of Tutoring & Academic Support, Metropolitan Community College Library, 30th & Fort Sts, Bldg 23, Omaha, NE, 68111. Tel: 531-622-2306. p. 1329
Ashley, Peggy, Dir, Post Public Library, 105 E Main St, Post, TX, 79356. Tel: 806-990-2149. p. 2229
Ashley, Richard, Jr, Dir, Sharon Hill Public Library, 246 Sharon Ave, Sharon Hill, PA, 19079. Tel: 610-586-3993. p. 2006
Ashley, Teresa, Fac Librn, Austin Community College, Northridge Campus Library, 11928 Stone Hollow Dr, 2nd, Rm 1223, Austin, TX, 78758. Tel: 512-223-4742. p. 2138
Ashlin, Kerri, Adult & Teen Prog Coordr, Rice Lake Public Library, Two E Marshall St, Rice Lake, WI, 54868. Tel: 715-234-4861, Ext 1115. p. 2473
Ashlin, Scott, Tech Serv Asst, Thurgood Marshall State Law Library, Courts of Appeals Bldg, 361 Rowe Blvd, Annapolis, MD, 21401. Tel: 410-260-1430. p. 950
Ashman, Nic, Tech Serv Librn, Chippewa Valley Technical College Library, 620 W Clairemont Ave, Eau Claire, WI, 54701-6162. Tel: 715-831-7281. p. 2432
Ashmore, Ann, Ref (Info Servs), Delta State University, Laflore Circle at Fifth Ave, Cleveland, MS, 38733-2599. Tel: 662-846-4430. p. 1214
Ashmore, Chris, Libr Dir, Jacksonville Public Library, 201 W College Ave, Jacksonville, IL, 62650-2497. Tel: 217-243-5435. p. 602
Ashmun, Margery, Sci Librn, Drew University Library, 36 Madison Ave, Madison, NJ, 07940. Tel: 973-408-3483. p. 1414
Ashoughian, Gohar, Dean of Libr, Simon Fraser University - Burnaby Campus, 8888 University Dr, Burnaby, BC, V5A 1S6, CANADA. Tel: 778-782-4084. p. 2563
Ashoughian, Gohar, Univ Librn, Wilfrid Laurier University Library, 75 University Ave W, Waterloo, ON, N2L 3C5, CANADA. Tel: 519-884-0710, Ext 3380. p. 2703
Ashton, Andrew, Dir of Libr, Vassar College Library, 124 Raymond Ave, Box 20, Poughkeepsie, NY, 12604. Tel: 845-437-5787. p. 1624
Ashton, Angela, Coll Develop, Electronic Res, Lambton College, 1457 London Rd, Sarnia, ON, N7S 6K4, CANADA. Tel: 519-542-7751, Ext 3453. p. 2676
Ashton, Katrine, Syst & Tech Serv Librn, Huston-Tillotson University, 900 Chicon St, Austin, TX, 78702. Tel: 512-505-3088. p. 2139
Ashton, Terence, Libr Tech, Department of Veterans Affairs, 1901 Veterans Memorial Dr, 14LIB-T, Temple, TX, 76504. Tel: 254-743-0607. p. 2247
Ashurst, Jonathan, Librn, Blackburn Correctional Complex Library, 3111 Spurr Rd, Lexington, KY, 40511. Tel: 859-246-2366, Ext 6271. p. 862
Ashworth, Ann, Libr Asst, Emmanuel University, 2261 W Main St, Franklin Springs, GA, 30639. Tel: 706-245-7226, Ext 2848. p. 480
Ashworth, Deborah, Br Head, Fort Erie Public Library, Stevensville Branch, 2508 Stevensville Rd, Stevensville, ON, L0S 1S0, CANADA. Tel: 905-382-2051. p. 2642
Ashworth, Mickki, Librn, Congregation Beth-El Zedeck, 600 W 70th St, Indianapolis, IN, 46260. Tel: 317-253-3441. p. 691
Ashworth, Nicole, Br Mgr, Augusta-Richmond County Public Library, Appleby Branch, 2260 Walton Way, Augusta, GA, 30904. Tel: 706-736-6244. p. 466
Ashworth, Sandra, Libr Dir, Boundary County Library, 6370 Kootenai St, Bonners Ferry, ID, 83805. Tel: 208-267-3750. p. 518
Askew, Consuella, Dir, Rutgers University Libraries, John Cotton Dana Library, 185 University Ave, Newark, NJ, 07102. Tel: 973-353-5222. p. 1428
Askins, Joe, Mgr, Tech Serv, Fayetteville Public Library, 401 W Mountain St, Fayetteville, AR, 72701. Tel: 479-856-7000. p. 95
Aslett, Kimberly, Librn, Mackenzie Richmond Hill Hospital Library, Ten Trench St, Richmond Hill, ON, L4C 4Z3, CANADA. Tel: 905-883-1212, Ext 7224. p. 2675
Aspatore, Robert, Head, Access Serv, DeKalb Public Library, Haish Memorial Library Bldg, 309 Oak St, DeKalb, IL, 60115-3369. Tel: 815-756-9568. p. 577
Aspelin, Jackie, Librn, Sully Area Library, 500 S Eighth St, Onida, SD, 57564. Tel: 605-258-2133. p. 2080
Aspinwall, Marie, Manager, Family Services, New Canaan Library, 151 Main St, New Canaan, CT, 06840. Tel: 203-594-5011. p. 324
Asplund, Susan, Ser Librn, Eastern New Mexico University - Portales, 1500 S Ave K, Portales, NM, 88130-7402. Tel: 575-562-2629. p. 1473
Assefa, Shimelis Getu, PhD, Assoc Prof, University of Denver, Morgridge College of Education, Katherine A Ruffatto Hall, 1999 E Evans Ave, Denver, CO, 80208. Tel: 303-871-6072. p. 2783
Asselin, Ange-Aimee, Mgr, Bibliotheque Jean-Charles Magnan, 510 boul de la Montagne, Saint-Casimir, QC, G0A 3L0, CANADA. Tel: 418-339-2909. p. 2734
Asselin, Paule, Librn, Centre Jeunesse de Montreal - Institut universitaire, 1001 boul de Maisonneuve est, 5ieme etage, Montreal, QC, H2L 4P9, CANADA. Tel: 514-896-3396. p. 2722
Asselstine, Jayne, Dep Chief Librn, Innisfil Public Library, 20 Church St, Cookstown, ON, L0L 1L0, CANADA. Tel: 705-431-7410. p. 2637
Assenza, Amanda, Ad, East Fishkill Community Library, 348 Rte 376, Hopewell Junction, NY, 12533-6075. Tel: 845-221-9943, Ext 225. p. 1548
Assmus, Jenna, Dir, Rio Community Library, 324 W Lyons St, Rio, WI, 53960. Tel: 920-992-3206. p. 2473
Astiz, M Fernanda, Dr, Dir, Mount Morris Library, 121 Main St, Mount Morris, NY, 14510-1596. Tel: 585-658-4412. p. 1574
Astle, Becky, Ch, Lincoln County Library System, Star Valley Branch, 261 Washington, Afton, WY, 83110. Tel: 307-885-3158. p. 2496
Astleford, Sandra, Asst Dir, Head, Tech Serv, Bellevue Public Library, 1003 Lincoln Dr, Bellevue, NE, 68005. Tel: 402-293-3157. p. 1307
Aston, Christine, Mgr, Gulf Gate Public Library, 7112 Curtiss Ave, Sarasota, FL, 34231. Tel: 941-861-1230. p. 442
Aston, Rollah, Dir, Eastern New Mexico University - Roswell, 52 University Blvd, Roswell, NM, 88203. Tel: 575-624-7282. p. 1474
Astorga, Aracelli, Br Mgr, San Luis Obispo County Library, 995 Palm St, San Luis Obispo, CA, 93403. Tel: 805-781-5783. p. 233
Asu, Glynis, Instruction Coordr, Research Librn, Hamilton College, 198 College Hill Rd, Clinton, NY, 13323. Tel: 315-859-4482. p. 1519
Atacan, Olcay, Dir, Law Society of Upper Canada, Osgoode Hall, 130 Queen St W, Toronto, ON, M5H 2N6, CANADA. Tel: 416-947-3315, Ext 2510. p. 2690
Atacan, Olcay, Head, Libr Syst, Law Society of Upper Canada, Osgoode Hall, 130 Queen St W, Toronto, ON, M5H 2N6, CANADA. Tel: 416-947-3315, Ext 2510. p. 2690
Atchinson, Cadence, Research & Teaching Librn, University of New England Libraries, 11 Hills Beach Rd, Biddeford, ME, 04005. Tel: 207-602-2497. p. 917
Atchley, Kathy, Br Mgr, Western Plains Library System, Clinton Public Library, 721 Frisco Ave, Clinton, OK, 73601-3320. Tel: 580-323-2165. p. 1845
Aten, Rachel, Bus Mgr, Carroll University, 100 N East Ave, Waukesha, WI, 53186. Tel: 262-650-4893. p. 2484
Atene, Dathine, Librn, San Juan County Public Library, Navajo Mountain Branch, Navajo Mountain High School, Navajo Mountain Rd, Rte 16, Navajo Mountain, UT, 84510. Tel: 435-678-1287, Ext 2481. p. 2267
Athanas, Ryan, Dir, Harborfields Public Library, 31 Broadway, Greenlawn, NY, 11740. Tel: 631-757-4200. p. 1541
Atherton, Jessica, Asst Head Librn, Newburyport Public Library, 94 State St, Newburyport, MA, 01950-6619. Tel: 978-465-4428, Ext 224. p. 1038
Athey, Liz, Supv Librn, Pierce County Library System, Tillicum Branch, 14916 Washington Ave SW, Lakewood, WA, 98498. Tel: 253-548-3314. p. 2387
Atilano, Marcia, Libr Dir, Dripping Springs Community Library, 501 Sportsplex Dr, Dripping Springs, TX, 78620. Tel: 512-858-7825. p. 2171
Atkins, Allison, Asst Dir, Head, Adult Serv, Kennebunk Free Library, 112 Main St, Kennebunk, ME, 04043. Tel: 207-985-2173. p. 928
Atkins, Dan, Dir, Operations, Guelph Public Library, 100 Norfolk St, Guelph, ON, N1H 4J6, CANADA. Tel: 519-824-6220, Ext 313. p. 2643
Atkins, Darlene, District Supervisor, Stormont, Dundas & Glengarry County Library, Alexandria Branch, 170A MacDonald Blvd, Alexandria, ON, K0C 1A0, CANADA. Tel: 613-525-3241. p. 2638
Atkins, David, Librn, Montgomery County Library, 215 W Main, Troy, NC, 27371. Tel: 910-572-1311. p. 1719
Atkins, David, Dean, East Tennessee State University, Sherrod Library, Seehorn Dr & Lake St, Johnson City, TN, 37614-0204. Tel: 423-439-4337. p. 2103
Atkins, Janet, Librn, Storrs Congregational Church UCC, Two N Eagleville Rd, Storrs, CT, 06268. Tel: 860-423-5930. p. 339
Atkins, Kathy, Dir, Bloomington Public Library, 453 Canal St, Bloomington, WI, 53804. Tel: 608-994-2531. p. 2424
Atkins, Rodney, Dir, Jarvis Christian College, Hwy 80 E, Hawkins, TX, 75765. Tel: 903-730-4890, Ext 2171. p. 2188
Atkins, Sue, Libr Dir, Northwest Regional Library, Millport Public Library, 920 Black St, Millport, AL, 35576. Tel: 205-662-4286. p. 40
Atkinson, Beth, Librn, Ryerss Museum & Library, Burholme Park, 7370 Central Ave, Philadelphia, PA, 19111-3055. Tel: 215-685-0599. p. 1985
Atkinson, Jenn, Head, Youth Serv, Colchester-East Hants Public Library, 754 Prince St, Truro, NS, B2N 1G9, CANADA. Tel: 902-895-4183. p. 2623
Atkinson, John, Asst Librn, Signal Mountain Public Library, 1114 James Blvd, Signal Mountain, TN, 37377-2509. Tel: 423-886-7323. p. 2126
Atkinson, Lee, ILL Librn, Weeks Public Library, 36 Post Rd, Greenland, NH, 03840-2312. Tel: 603-436-8548. p. 1365
Atkinson, Lorrie, Chief Librn, Wainfleet Township Public Library, 31909 Park St, Wainfleet, ON, L0S 1V0, CANADA. Tel: 905-899-1277. p. 2701
Atkinson, Megan, Archivist, Tennessee Technological University, 1100 N Peachtree Ave, Cookeville, TN, 38505. Tel: 931-372-3326. p. 2095

Atkinson, Melissa, Dir, Distance & Online Library Services, Abilene Christian University, 221 Brown Library, ACU Box 29208, Abilene, TX, 79699-9208. Tel: 325-674-2316. p. 2131
Atkinson, Taylor, Libr Dir, University of South Carolina at Union Library, Union County Carnegie Library, 300 E South St, Union, SC, 29379. Tel: 864-427-7140. p. 2071
Atkinson, Taylor, Ms, Dir, Union County Carnegie Library, 300 E South St, Union, SC, 29379. Tel: 864-427-7140. p. 2071
Atkinson, Tiffany, Dir, La Crosse Public Library, 307 E Main St, La Crosse, IN, 46348. Tel: 219-754-2606. p. 700
Atteberry, Pam, Dir, Independent Township Library, 108 Main St, Claflin, KS, 67525. Tel: 620-587-3488. p. 801
Attebury, Rami, Assoc Dean, Ops & Access, University of Idaho Library, 850 S Rayburn St, Moscow, ID, 83844. Tel: 208-885-2503. p. 526
Attia, Audrey, Chief Librn, Centre intégré universitaire de santé et de services sociaux du Centre-Sud-de-l'Ile-de-Montréal - Institut Universitaire de Gériatrie de Montréal, 4565 Chemin Queen Mary, Montreal, QC, H3W 1W5, CANADA. Tel: 514-340-2800, Ext 3262. p. 2722
Attwell, Tami, Technical Spec, Saint Bonaventure University, 3261 W State Rd, Saint Bonaventure, NY, 14778. Tel: 716-375-2347. p. 1635
Atwater, Amanda, YA Librn, Indian River County Library System, North Indian River County Library, 1001 Sebastian Blvd, CR 512, Sebastian, FL, 32958. Tel: 772-400-6360. p. 452
Atwell, Mary, Archivist, Coll Develop Librn, Hood College, 401 Rosemont Ave, Frederick, MD, 21701. Tel: 301-696-3873. p. 966
Atwill, Jade, PhD, Librn, Pennsylvania State University Libraries, George & Sherry Middlemas Arts & Humanities Library, Pennsylvania State University, W 337 Pattee Library, University Park, PA, 16802-1801. Tel: 814-863-0738. p. 2016
Atwood, Beth, Br Mgr, Greenville County Library System, Taylors Branch, 316 W Main St, Taylors, SC, 29687. Tel: 864-527-9203. p. 2061
Atwood, Jonathan, Digital & Web Services Librarian, Otterbein University, 138 W Main St, Westerville, OH, 43081. Tel: 614-823-1027. p. 1830
Atwood, Melinda, Libr Dir, Abbott Library, 11 Soonipi Circle, Sunapee, NH, 03782. Tel: 603-763-5513. p. 1382
Atwood, Mindy, Adminr, Libr Operations, New Hampshire State Library, 20 Park St, Concord, NH, 03301. Tel: 603-271-2393. p. 1359
Atwood, Misty, Area Mgr, Albuquerque-Bernalillo County Library System, Erna Fergusson Library, 3700 San Mateo NE, Albuquerque, NM, 87110. Tel: 505-888-8100. p. 1460
Atwood, Pete, Sr Res Analyst, Sacramento Area Council of Governments Data Resource Center, 1415 L St, Ste 300, Sacramento, CA, 95814. Tel: 916-321-9000. p. 209
Atwood, Sheila, Libr Dir, New Portland Community Library, 899 River Rd, New Portland, ME, 04961. Tel: 207-628-6561. p. 933
Atwood, Susan, Dir, Winterport Memorial Library, 229 Main St, Winterport, ME, 04496. Tel: 207-223-5540. p. 947
Atwood, Thomas, Assoc Dean, University of Toledo, 2975 W Centennial Dr, Toledo, OH, 43606-3396. Tel: 419-530-2833. p. 1825
Au, Alison, Head Librn, Headingley Municipal Library, 49 Alboro St, Headingley, MB, R4J 1A3, CANADA. Tel: 204-888-5410. p. 2587
Au, Karen, Educ Spec, University of Hawaii West Hawaii Center, 81-964 Halekii St, Kealakekua, HI, 96750. Tel: 808-322-4858, 808-934-2530. p. 514
Aube, Megan, Librn, Belgrade Public Library, 124 Depot Rd, Belgrade, ME, 04917. Tel: 207-495-3508. p. 917
Aubert, Thomas, Advisory Ref, Tech Serv, Universite du Quebec a Rimouski - Service de la bibliotheque, 300 Allee des Ursulines, Rimouski, QC, G5L 3A1, CANADA. Tel: 418-723-1986, Ext 1463. p. 2732
Aubin, Mary Ann, Libr Dir, Kenrick-Glennon Seminary, 5200 Glennon Dr, Saint Louis, MO, 63119. Tel: 314-792-6302. p. 1271
Aubin, Nate, Tech Systems/E-Resources Librn, Texas Lutheran University, 1000 W Court St, Seguin, TX, 78155-5978. Tel: 830-372-8102, p. 2242
Aubin, Tina, Asst Dir, Ch, Putnam Public Library, 225 Kennedy Dr, Putnam, CT, 06260-1691. Tel: 860-963-6826. p. 334
Aubry, John, Dir, New School, Raymond Fogelman Library, 55 W 13th St, New York, NY, 10011. Tel: 212-229-5307. p. 1592
Aubry, John, Dir, New School, Adam & Sophie Gimbel Design Library, Two W 13th St, 2nd Flr, New York, NY, 10011. Tel: 212-229-5307. p. 1593
Auclair, Guy, Pres, Societe de Genealogie de Quebec, Pavillon Louis-Jacques-Casault/Cite Universitaire Laval, 1055 av du Seminaire, Local 4240, Quebec, QC, G1V 4A8, CANADA. Tel: 418-651-9127. p. 2732
Aucoin, Brendan, Head, Access Serv, SUNY Oneonta, 108 Ravine Pkwy, Oneonta, NY, 13820. Tel: 607-436-4141. p. 1611
Aucoin, Lisa, Asst Dir, Hudson Public Library, Three Washington St, Hudson, MA, 01749-2499. Tel: 978-568-9644. p. 1025
Audano, Brian, Info Serv Librn, Outreach Serv Librn, Rockport Public Library, 17 School St, Rockport, MA, 01966. Tel: 978-546-6934. p. 1050
Audet, Etienne, Dir, Universite du Quebec a Trois-Rivieres, Pavillon Albert-Tessier, 3351 Blvd des Forges, Trois-Rivieres, QC, G9A 5H7, CANADA. Tel: 819-376-5011, Ext 2254. p. 2738
Audiss, Sara, Ch Serv, New Carlisle & Olive Township Public Library, 408 S Bray St, New Carlisle, IN, 46552. Tel: 574-654-3046. p. 709
Audrain, Glenda, Dir, Washington County Library System, 1080 W Clydesdale Dr, Fayetteville, AR, 72701. Tel: 479-442-6253. p. 95
Auensen, Don, Cataloger, Librn, Chattahoochee Technical College Library, 980 S Cobb Dr, Marietta, GA, 30060. Tel: 770-528-6466. p. 488
Auerbach, Stevanne, Dr, Dir, Institute for Childhood Resources, 268 Bush St, San Francisco, CA, 94104. Tel: 510-540-0111. p. 225
Auerfeld, Maylynne, Youth Serv Dept Head, Moffat Library of Washingtonville, Six W Main St, Washingtonville, NY, 10992. Tel: 845-496-5483. p. 1659
Aufderhaar, Kathleen, Syst Librn, Bluffton University, One University Dr, Bluffton, OH, 45817-2104. Tel: 419-358-3414. p. 1751
Augelli, John F, Exec Dir, Galveston County Library System, 2310 Sealy Ave, Galveston, TX, 77550. Tel: 409-763-8854. p. 2183
Auger, Bernard, Librn, Bibliotheque du Seminaire de Saint-Hyacinthe, 650 rue Girouard Est, Saint-Hyacinthe, QC, J2S 2Y2, CANADA. Tel: 450-774-5560, Ext 109. p. 2735
Auger, Brian, Adminr, County Librn, Somerset County Library System of New Jersey, One Vogt Dr, Bridgewater, NJ, 08807-2136. Tel: 908-458-8401. p. 1392
Auger, Sylvie, Libr Tech, College LaSalle, 2000 Saint Catherine St W, 4th Flr, Montreal, QC, H3H 2T2, CANADA. Tel: 514-939-2006, Ext 4389. p. 2723
Augliera, John, Librn, National Psychological Association for Psychoanalysis, Inc, 40 W 13th St, New York, NY, 10011. Tel: 212-924-7440. p. 1592
August, Roberta, Librn, Saint Charles Parish Library, 160 W Campus Dr, Destrehan, LA, 70047. Tel: 985-764-2366. p. 888
Augusta, Caitlin, Head, Children's Servx, Stratford Library Association, 2203 Main St, Stratford, CT, 06615. Tel: 203-385-4165. p. 340
Augustin, Caitlin, Pub Serv, University of Tennessee Southern, 433 W Madison St, Pulaski, TN, 38478-2799. Tel: 931-363-9844, p. 2124
Augustine, Matthew, Tech Mgr, Euclid Public Library, 631 E 222nd St, Euclid, OH, 44123-2091. Tel: 216-261-5300, Ext 601. p. 1785
Augustine, Shelley, Dir, Yorkville Public Library, 902 Game Farm Rd, Yorkville, IL, 60560. Tel: 630-553-4354. p. 665
Augustniak, Ashley, Head, Ref, Reader Serv, Science History Institute Museum & Library, 315 Chestnut St, Philadelphia, PA, 19106. Tel: 215-873-8205. p. 1985
Augustson, Jessica, Outreach Serv Dir, Danville Public Library, 319 N Vermilion St, Danville, IL, 61832. Tel: 217-477-5227. p. 575
Augustus, Marva, Librn, California Department of Corrections Library System, California State Prison, Los Angeles County, 44750 60th St W, Lancaster, CA, 93536-7620. Tel: 661-729-2000, Ext 6148. p. 206
Auk, Phanary, Libr Asst, North Shore Community College Library, One Ferncroft Rd, Danvers Campus Library, Danvers, MA, 01923-4093. Tel: 978-739-5426. p. 1013
Aularkh, Jorja, Libr Serv Mgr, University of Texas Medical Branch, 914 Market St, Galveston, TX, 77555. Tel: 409-772-4164. p. 2183
Auld, Charles M, Chief Exec Officer, Anne Arundel County Public Library, Five Harry Truman Pkwy, Annapolis, MD, 21401. Tel: 410-222-7234. p. 950
Aulisio, George J, Dean of the Library, University of Scranton, 800 Linden St, Scranton, PA, 18510-4634. Tel: 570-941-4008. p. 2005
Aull, Kylah E, Mgr, North Dakota Legislative Council Library, 600 E Boulevard Ave, Bismarck, ND, 58505-0660. Tel: 701-328-4900. p. 1730
Aultman Becker, April, Dean, Libr & Info Tech, Sul Ross State University, PO Box C-109, Alpine, TX, 79832. Tel: 432-837-8123. p. 2133
Aultman, Jen, Dir, Mus & Libr Serv, Ohio Network of American History Research Centers, Ohio Historical Society Archives-Library, 1982 Velma Ave, Columbus, OH, 43211-2497. Tel: 614-297-2510. p. 2773
Aults, Erin, Knowledge Res Spec, Royal Botanical Gardens Library, 680 Plains Rd W, Burlington, ON, L7T 4H4, CANADA. Tel: 905-527-1158, Ext 259. p. 2634
Aultz, Kathy, Exec Dir, Douglas County Historical Society, 5730 N 30th St, No 11A, Omaha, NE, 68111. Tel: 402-455-9990. p. 1328
Auman, Heather, Head, Libr Serv, Western Allegheny Community Library, 181 Bateman Rd, Oakdale, PA, 15071-3906. Tel: 724-695-8150. p. 1972
Auman, Katie, Dir, Communications & Develop, Poudre River Public Library District, 201 Peterson St, Fort Collins, CO, 80524-2990. Tel: 970-221-6740. p. 281
Aumont, Francine, Librn, Institut universitaire de cardiologie et de pneumologie de Quebec Bibliotheque, 2725 Chemin Ste-Foy, Bibliotheque Y2244, Quebec, QC, G1V 4G5, CANADA. Tel: 418-656-4563. p. 2731
Aurand, Marilyn, Librn, Rae Hobson Memorial Library, 401 Pawnee Ave, Republic, KS, 66964. Tel: 785-361-2481. p. 833
Auriat, Nicole, Libr Serv Coordr, Edmonton Public Library, Castle Downs, 106 Lakeside Landing, 15379 Castle Downs Rd, Edmonton, AB, T5X 3Y7, CANADA. Tel: 780-496-2738. p. 2536
Ausel, Jill, Libr Dir, Chatham College, Woodland Rd, Pittsburgh, PA, 15232. Tel: 412-365-1244. p. 1992
Ausmus, Sarah, Tech Coordr, Lamar Public Library, 102 E Parmenter St, Lamar, CO, 81052-3239. Tel: 719-336-1296. p. 289

Ausmus, Shelly, Br Mgr, Whitman County Rural Library District, Tekoa Branch, S 139 Crosby, Tekoa, WA, 99033. Tel: 509-284-3121. p. 2362
Austad, Julie, Interim Dean of Libr, Clark College, Mail Stop LIB 112, 1933 Fort Vancouver Way, Vancouver, WA, 98663-3598. Tel: 360-992-2472. p. 2390
Austin, Amy, Dir, Beck Bookman Library, 420 W Fourth St, Holton, KS, 66436-1572. Tel: 785-364-3532. p. 813
Austin, Brodie, Asst Dir, Northbrook Public Library, 1201 Cedar Lane, Northbrook, IL, 60062-4581. Tel: 847-272-6224. p. 626
Austin, Cheryl, Dir, Weedsport Library, 2795 E Brutus St, Weedsport, NY, 13166. Tel: 315-834-6222. p. 1661
Austin, Diane, Asst Dir, Instr, University of South Florida, 4202 Fowler Ave, CIS 1040, Tampa, FL, 33620-7800. Tel: 813-974-3520. p. 2783
Austin, Donna, Br Mgr, Mississippi County Library System, Leachville Public, 105 S Main St, Leachville, AR, 72438. Tel: 870-539-6485. p. 91
Austin, Gary, Distance Learning/Bus Librn, Res & Instruction Librn, University of South Florida Saint Petersburg, 140 Seventh Ave S, POY118, Saint Petersburg, FL, 33701-5016. Tel: 727-873-4404. p. 442
Austin, Gayle, Asst Dir, Donnellson Public Library, 411 Main, Donnellson, IA, 52625. Tel: 319-835-5545. p. 748
Austin, Holy, Librn, Illinois Appellate Court, 14th & Main Sts, Mount Vernon, IL, 62864. Tel: 618-242-6414. p. 622
Austin, Jenna, Br Mgr, Halifax County-South Boston Regional Library, South Boston Public Library, 509 Broad St, South Boston, VA, 24592. Tel: 434-575-4228. p. 2322
Austin, Jennifer M, Dir, Coshocton Public Library, 655 Main St, Coshocton, OH, 43812-1697. Tel: 740-622-0956. p. 1778
Austin, Jill, Circ Supvr, Portage District Library, 300 Library Lane, Portage, MI, 49002. Tel: 269-329-4542, Ext 706. p. 1143
Austin, Joanne, Course Reserves Coord, University of California, Riverside, 900 University Ave, Riverside, CA, 92521. Tel: 951-827-3220. p. 203
Austin, Joanne, Supvr, Osterhout Free Library, North, 28 Oliver St, Wilkes-Barre, PA, 18705. Tel: 570-822-4660. p. 2022
Austin, Linda, Managing Librn, Bay County Library System, Auburn Area Branch Library, 235 W Midland Rd, Auburn, MI, 48611. Tel: 989-662-2381. p. 1083
Austin, Linda, Managing Librn, Bay County Library System, Pinconning Branch Library, 218 S Kaiser St, Pinconning, MI, 48650. Tel: 989-879-3283. p. 1083
Austin, Marcia, Br Dir, Plumb Memorial Library, Huntington Branch, 41 Church St, Shelton, CT, 06484-5804. Tel: 203-926-0111. p. 336
Austin, Michele, Libr Asst, Hillview Free Library, 3717 Lake Shore Dr, Diamond Point, NY, 12824. Tel: 518-668-3012. p. 1525
Austin, Nate, Dir, Allegany Public Library, 90 W Main St, Allegany, NY, 14706-1204. Tel: 716-373-1056. p. 1485
Austin, Peggy, Acq & Per Mgr, Cypress College Library, 9200 Valley View St, Cypress, CA, 90630-5897. Tel: 714-484-7066. p. 133
Austin, Reid, Dir, Newberry College, 2100 College St, Newberry, SC, 29108-2197. Tel: 803-321-5229. p. 2066
Austin, Richard, Instr, University of South Florida, 4202 Fowler Ave, CIS 1040, Tampa, FL, 33620-7800. Tel: 813-974-3520. p. 2783
Austin, Shellie, Instructor of Library Services, Interim Dir, Southwest Baptist University Libraries, 1600 University Ave, Bolivar, MO, 65613. Tel: 417-328-1626. p. 1238
Austin, Shellie, Interim Dir, Southwest Baptist University Libraries, Mountain View Campus Library, 209 W First St, Mountain View, MO, 65548. Tel: 417-934-5057. p. 1238
Austin, Trish, Dir, Divernon Township Library, 221 S Second St, Divernon, IL, 62530. Tel: 217-628-3813. p. 578
Austin, Whitney, Br Mgr, Springfield-Greene County Library District, Fair Grove Branch, 81 S Orchard Blvd, Fair Grove, MO, 65648-8421. Tel: 417-759-2637. p. 1281
Austin, Whitney, Br Mgr, Springfield-Greene County Library District, Strafford Branch, 101 S State Hwy 125, Strafford, MO, 65757-8998. Tel: 417-736-9233. p. 1282
Auston, Anthony, Libr Dir, Wilmette Public Library District, 1242 Wilmette Ave, Wilmette, IL, 60091-2558. Tel: 847-256-5025. p. 663
Auwen, Joan, Librn, United States Army, Nye Library, 1640 Randolph Rd, Fort Sill, OK, 73503-9022. Tel: 580-442-2048, 580-442-3806. p. 1848
Avagliano, Kim, Chief Librn, Monmouth County Library, Eastern Branch, 1001 Rte 35, Shrewsbury, NJ, 07702. Tel: 732-683-8980. p. 1416
Avaire, Carolyn, Br Librn, East Central Regional Library, Mille Lacs Lake Community Library, 285 Second Ave S, Isle, MN, 56342-0147. Tel: 320-676-3929. p. 1168
Avalos, Daniel, Asst Dir, San Rafael Public Library, 1100 E St, San Rafael, CA, 94901. Tel: 415-485-3323. p. 237
Avalos, Mary Helen, Dep Librn, Globe Public Library, 339 S Broad St, Globe, AZ, 85501. Tel: 928-425-6111. p. 62
Avans, Martha, Librn, Scottsboro Public Library, 1002 S Broad St, Scottsboro, AL, 35768. Tel: 256-574-4335. p. 35
Avara, Anne, Colls, Database & Digitization Asst, Houston Museum of Natural Science, 5555 Hermann Park Dr, Houston, TX, 77030-1799. Tel: 713-639-4670. p. 2195
Avasthi, Smita, Librn, Santa Rosa Junior College, 1501 Mendocino Ave, Santa Rosa, CA, 95401. Tel: 707-524-1839. p. 245
Averett, Catherine, Circ, Tidewater Community College Learning Resources Center, 300 Granby St, Norfolk, VA, 23510. Tel: 757-822-1124. p. 2336
Averett, Steve, Ref (Info Servs), Brigham Young University, Howard W Hunter Law Library, 256 JRCB, Provo, UT, 84602-8000. Tel: 801-422-3593. p. 2269
Averette, Kim, Librn I, Sheppard Memorial Library, 530 S Evans St, Greenville, NC, 27858. Tel: 252-329-4580. p. 1694
Averitt, Megan, Librn, Millstadt Library District, 115 W Laurel St, Millstadt, IL, 62260. Tel: 618-476-1887. p. 618
Avers, Robin, Asst Librn, Wellsville City Library, 115 W Sixth St, Wellsville, KS, 66092. Tel: 785-883-2870. p. 842
Aversano, Gloria, Librn, National Oceanic & Atmospheric Administration, Atlantic Oceanographic & Meteorological Lab, 4301 Rickenbacker Causeway, Miami, FL, 33149. Tel: 305-361-4428. p. 424
Aversano, Gloria, Librn, United States National Oceanic & Atmospheric Administration, 11691 SW 17 St, Miami, FL, 33165. Tel: 305-229-4406. p. 425
Avery, Amanda, Col Archivist, Info Serv Librn, Parkland College Library, 2400 W Bradley Ave, Champaign, IL, 61821-1899. p. 552
Avery, Amanda, Outreach Librn, Marywood University Library & Learning Commons, 2300 Adams Ave, Scranton, PA, 18509. Tel: 570-961-4707. p. 2004
Avery, Audrey, Head, Adult Serv, Dover Public Library, 35 Loockerman Plaza, Dover, DE, 19901. Tel: 302-736-7030. p. 352
Avery, Barbara, Ch Serv, Cove City-Craven County Public Library, 102 N Main St, Cove City, NC, 28523. Tel: 252-638-6363. p. 1683
Avery, Barbara, Librn, Marshall & Melhorn, Four SeaGate, 8th Flr, Toledo, OH, 43604. Tel: 419-249-7100. p. 1824
Avery, Brian, Libr Dir, Pawling Free Library, 11 Broad St, Pawling, NY, 12564. Tel: 845-855-3444. p. 1616
Avery, Connie, Asst Dir, Flagg-Rochelle Public Library District, 619 Fourth Ave, Rochelle, IL, 61068. Tel: 815-562-3431. p. 640
Avery, Connie, Dir, Solomon Public Library, 108 N Walnut St, Solomon, KS, 67480. Tel: 785-655-3521. p. 836
Avery, David, Interim Libr Dir, University of Connecticut, Avery Point Campus Library, 1084 Shenneeossett Rd, Groton, CT, 06340. Tel: 860-486-1582. p. 340
Avery, Louise, Exec Dir, Kitimat Museum & Archives, 293 City Ctr, Kitimat, BC, V8C 1T6, CANADA. Tel: 250-632-8950. p. 2569
Avery, Paula, Prog Spec, Harnett County Public Library, Dunn Public, 110 E Divine St, Dunn, NC, 28334. Tel: 910-892-2899. p. 1701
Aves, Sandy, Librn, Manly Public Library, 127 S Grant, Manly, IA, 50456. Tel: 641-454-2982. p. 767
Avila, Celia, Sr Librn, Los Angeles Public Library System, Junipero Serra Branch Library, 4607 S Main St, Los Angeles, CA, 90037-2735. Tel: 323-234-1685. p. 164
Avila, Salvador, Br Mgr, Las Vegas-Clark County Library District, Enterprise Library, 25 E Shelbourne Ave, Las Vegas, NV, 89123. Tel: 702-507-3760. p. 1346
Aviles, Jackie, Br Mgr, Osceola Library System, Poinciana Branch, 101 N Doverplum Ave, Kissimmee, FL, 34758. Tel: 407-742-8888. p. 414
Avis, Ellie, Br Mgr, Josephine Community Library District, Williams Branch, 20695 Williams Hwy, Williams, OR, 97544. Tel: 541-846-7020. p. 1880
Avise, Miriam, Activity Specialist I, Kansas Department of Corrections, 1607 State St, Ellsworth, KS, 67439. Tel: 785-472-5501, Ext 250, 785-472-6250. p. 806
Avitia, Anthony, Sr Res Librn, Reed Smith LLP, 355 S Grand Ave, Ste 2900, Los Angeles, CA, 90071. Tel: 213-457-8000. p. 167
Avolio, Robin, Libr Dir, South New Berlin Free Library, 3320 State Hwy 8, South New Berlin, NY, 13843. Tel: 607-859-2420. p. 1642
Avra, Lisa, Dir of Develop, University of Texas Libraries, Briscoe Center for American History, Sid Richard Hall, Unit 2, Rm 2106, 2300 Red River St, Austin, TX, 78712-1426. Tel: 512-495-4515. p. 2142
Avromov, Gig, Dir, McMillan Township Library, 200 Cedar St, Ewen, MI, 49925. Tel: 906-988-2515. p. 1104
Awalt, Jami, Dir, Presv Serv, Tennessee State Library & Archives, 403 Seventh Ave N, Nashville, TN, 37243-0312. Tel: 615-253-6446. p. 2121
Awgul, Brian, Librn, Good Samaritan Hospital, 1000 Montauk Hwy, West Islip, NY, 11795. Tel: 631-376-3380. p. 1662
Axel, Peggy, Coordr, Cat, Mohawk Valley Community College Libraries, 1101 Sherman Dr, Utica, NY, 13501-5394. Tel: 312-792-5339. p. 1655
Axel-Lute, Melanie, Co-Chair, First Unitarian Universalist Society of Albany, 405 Washington Ave, Albany, NY, 12206. p. 1482
Axel-Lute, Paul, Dep Dir, Rutgers University Library for the Center for Law & Justice, 123 Washington St, Newark, NJ, 07102-3094. Tel: 973-353-3121. p. 1428
Axel-Lute, Paul, Co-Chair, First Unitarian Universalist Society of Albany, 405 Washington Ave, Albany, NY, 12206. p. 1482
Axelsen, Shari, Libr Asst, La Crosse County Library, John Bosshard Memorial, 1720 Henry Johns Blvd, Bangor, WI, 54614. Tel: 608-486-4408. p. 2441
Ayala, Karla, Libr Spec III, Southern University in New Orleans, 6400 Press Dr, New Orleans, LA, 70126. Tel: 504-286-5225. p. 903

Ayala, Kevin, Asst Dir, Bay County Library System, 500 Center Ave, Bay City, MI, 48708. Tel: 989-894-2837. p. 1083
Ayala, Mari, Head, Tech Serv, Marple Public Library, 2599 Sproul Rd, Broomall, PA, 19008-2399. Tel: 610-356-1510. p. 1915
Ayala, Michael, Br Head, Lake County Public Library, Munster Branch, 8701 Calumet Ave, Munster, IN, 46321-2526. Tel: 219-836-8450. p. 706
Aybar Maki, Violeta, Ch, Union City Public Library, 324 43rd St, Union City, NJ, 07087-5008. Tel: 201-866-7500. p. 1449
Aycock, Anthony, Libr Dir, North Carolina Legislative Library, 500 Legislative Office Bldg, 300 N Salisbury St, Raleigh, NC, 27603-5925. Tel: 919-733-9390. p. 1709
Aycock, Laurie, Coll Develop, Interim Dir, Kennesaw State University Library System, 385 Cobb Ave NW, MD 1701, Kennesaw, GA, 30144. Tel: 470-578-4825. p. 483
Aydelott, Kathrine, Ref (Info Servs), University of New Hampshire Library, 18 Library Way, Durham, NH, 03824. Tel: 603-862-0657. p. 1362
Ayer, Sandy, Dir, Libr Serv, Ambrose Library, 150 Ambrose Circle SW, Calgary, AB, T3H 0L5, CANADA. Tel: 403-410-2947. p. 2525
Ayers, Dawn, Dir, Cameron Area Public Library, 506 Main St, Cameron, WI, 54822. Tel: 715-458-2267. p. 2427
Ayers, Janet, Dir, Burnley Memorial Library, 401 N Oak, Cottonwood Falls, KS, 66845. Tel: 620-273-9119. p. 803
Ayers, Lynn, Cataloger, Payne Theological Seminary, 1230 Wilberforce-Clifton Rd, Wilberforce, OH, 45384. Tel: 937-971-2853. p. 1831
Ayers, Meredith, Sci Librn, Northern Illinois University Libraries, 217 Normal Rd, DeKalb, IL, 60115-2828. Tel: 815-753-1872. p. 577
Aylett, Scott, Dir, Spanish Fork Public Library, 49 S Main St, Spanish Fork, UT, 84660-2030. Tel: 801-804-4480. p. 2273
Aylward, Emily, Mgr, Access Serv, Connecticut College, 270 Mohegan Ave, New London, CT, 06320-4196. Tel: 860-439-2655. p. 328
Aylward, James F, Dir, United States Navy, Academic Resources Information Center, 440 Meyerkord Rd, Newport, RI, 02841. Tel: 401-841-4352, 401-841-6631. p. 2035
Aylward, Susan, Interim Dir, North Kingstown Free Library, 100 Boone St, North Kingstown, RI, 02852-5150. Tel: 401-294-3306. p. 2036
Aylwin, Josee, Libr Dir, Centre Hospitalier Regional trois-Rivieres Pavillon Ste-Marie, 1991 boul du Carmel, Trois-Rivieres, QC, G8Z 3R9, CANADA. Tel: 819-697-3333, Ext 69878. p. 2738
Aymer, Ann-Marie, Head, Youth Serv, Summit Free Public Library, 75 Maple St, Summit, NJ, 07901-9984. Tel: 908-273-0350. p. 1445
Ayotte, Andrea, Circ Mgr, Mgr, Info & Libr Serv, Canadian Music Centre Libraries, 20 St Joseph St, Toronto, ON, M4Y 1J9, CANADA. Tel: 416-961-6601. p. 2687
Ayres, Laura-Ellen, Dir, Rapides Parish Library, 411 Washington St, Alexandria, LA, 71301-8338. Tel: 318-445-6436, Ext 1001. p. 880
Ayres, Melissa, Libr Asst, ILL, Windsor Public Library, 43 State St, Windsor, VT, 05089. Tel: 802-674-2556. p. 2299
Ayres, Tom, Head Librn, Canton Historical Society Library, 11 Front St, Collinsville, CT, 06019. Tel: 860-693-2793. p. 306
Aytac, Selenay, PhD, Cat Librn, Long Island University Post, 720 Northern Blvd, Brookville, NY, 11548. Tel: 516-299-3443. p. 1507
Ayton, Kieran, Electronic Resources & Tech Librn, Rhode Island College, 600 Mt Pleasant Ave, Providence, RI, 02908-1924. p. 2039
Azinheira, E, Info Res Mgr, Dolby Laboratories, Inc, 1275 Market St, San Francisco, CA, 94103. Tel: 415-558-0268. p. 224
Azodi, Susan, Evening Circ Supvr, Syst Coordr, Colby-Sawyer College, 541 Main St, New London, NH, 03257-4648. Tel: 603-526-3685. p. 1375
Azpiri, Dina, Mgr, Bus Serv, Nova Southeastern University Libraries, 3100 Ray Ferrero Jr Blvd, Fort Lauderdale, FL, 33314. Tel: 954-262-4546. p. 402
Azua, Sonia, Librn, New Mexico Corrections Department, 1983 Joe R Silva Blvd, Las Cruces, NM, 88004. Tel: 575-523-3398. p. 1471
Baab, Caroline, Coordr, New Brunswick Community College, 1234 Mountain Rd, Moncton, NB, E1C 8H9, CANADA. Tel: 506-856-2226. p. 2603
Baaden, Bea, Dr, Dir, Sch Media Prog, Long Island University, C W Post Campus, 720 Northern Blvd, Brookville, NY, 11548-1300. Tel: 516-299-3818. p. 2788
Baalman, Pat, Ms, Dir, Moore Family Library, 95 S Adams, Grinnell, KS, 67738. Tel: 785-824-3885. p. 811
Babal, Megan, Ad, Cranberry Public Library, Municipal Ctr, 2525 Rochester Rd, Ste 300, Cranberry Township, PA, 16066-6423. Tel: 724-776-9100, Ext 1126. p. 1924
Babay, J A, Dir, Montgomery House Library, 20 Church St, McEwensville, PA, 17749. Tel: 570-538-1381. p. 1959
Babbit, Jan R, Assoc Dir, Cleveland State University, Cleveland-Marshall Law Library, Cleveland-Marshall College of Law, 1801 Euclid Ave, Cleveland, OH, 44115-2223. Tel: 216-687-6913. p. 1769
Babcock, Ashley, Br Librn, Wapiti Regional Library, Bjorkdale Public Library, 105 Hara Ave, Bjorkdale, SK, S0E 0E0, CANADA. Tel: 308-886-2119. p. 2745
Babcock, Dalton, Libr Dir, Shenandoah Area Free Public Library, 15 W Washington St, Shenandoah, PA, 17976-1708. Tel: 570-462-9829. p. 2006
Babcock, Jamie, Br Supvr, Warren Public Library, Dorothy M Busch Branch, 23333 Ryan Rd, Warren, MI, 48091. Tel: 586-353-0580. p. 1157
Babcock, Jim, Tech Serv Supvr, Columbia University, Mathematics, 303 Mathematics, 2990 Broadway, MC 4702, New York, NY, 10027. Tel: 212-854-4181. p. 1583
Babcock, Melissa, Libr Dir, Josiah Carpenter Library, 41 Main St, Pittsfield, NH, 03263. Tel: 603-435-8406. p. 1378
Babcock, Susan, Youth Serv Librn, Rose Memorial Library, 79 E Main St, Stony Point, NY, 10980-1699. Tel: 845-786-2100. p. 1647
Babcock-Landry, Amy, Dir, Livingston Public Library, Ten Robert Harp Dr, Livingston, NJ, 07039. Tel: 973-992-4600. p. 1413
Baber, Holly, Dir, Dvoracek Memorial Library, 419 W Third St, Wilber, NE, 68465. Tel: 402-821-2832. p. 1340
Baber, Jessica, Mgr, Layland Museum, 201 N Caddo St, Cleburne, TX, 76031. Tel: 817-645-0940. p. 2156
Baber, Rebecca, Libr Asst, Crown College, 8700 College View Dr, Saint Bonifacius, MN, 55375-9002. Tel: 952-446-4241. p. 1195
Babin, Danielle, Tech Serv, Borden Ladner Gervais LLP Library, 1000 de la Gauchetiere W, Ste 900, Montreal, QC, H3B 5H4, CANADA. Tel: 514-954-3159. p. 2721
Babineau, Jessica, Interim Mgr, University Health Network, Toronto General Hospital Health Sciences Library, 200 Elizabeth St, ENI 418, Toronto, ON, M5G 2C4, CANADA. Tel: 416-340-3429. p. 2698
Babinsky, Jane, Exec Dir, Fenton History Center, 73 Forest Ave, Jamestown, NY, 14701. Tel: 716-664-6256. p. 1557
Babirye-Alibatya, Rebecca, Commun Libr Mgr, Queens Library, Richmond Hill Community Library, 118-14 Hillside Ave, Richmond Hill, NY, 11418. Tel: 718-849-7150. p. 1555
Babits, Ann, Supv Librn, Circ, Bernards Township Library, 32 S Maple Ave, Basking Ridge, NJ, 07920-1216. Tel: 908-204-3031. p. 1388
Babitske, Nel, Librn, Illinois Prairie District Public Library, Springbay Branch, 411 Illinois St, Springbay, IL, 61611. Tel: 309-822-0444. p. 617
Babka, Julie, Ref Librn, Pacific Lutheran University, 12180 Park Ave S, Tacoma, WA, 98447-0001. Tel: 253-535-7500. p. 2386
Babli, Linda, Info & Tech Librn, Winter Haven Public Library, 325 Ave A NW, Winter Haven, FL, 33881. Tel: 863-291-5880. p. 455
Babou, Robin, Librn, Rio Hondo College Library, 3600 Workman Mill Rd, 2nd Flr, Whittier, CA, 90601. Tel: 562-908-3375. p. 259
Baca, David, PhD, Dir, Libr Serv, Texas A&M University at Galveston, Bldg 3010, 200 Seawolf Pkwy, Galveston, TX, 77554. Tel: 409-740-4568. p. 2183
Baca, Margaret G, Dir, Tech Serv, Santa Fe Public Library, 145 Washington Ave, Santa Fe, NM, 87501. Tel: 505-955-6780. p. 1476
Baca, Maudie, Libr Asst, Imperial County Free Library, Salton City Branch, 1209 Van Buren Rd, Ste 2, Salton City, CA, 92275. Tel: 760-604-6956. p. 140
Baca, Sherri, Assoc Exec Dir, Pueblo City-County Library District, 100 E Abriendo Ave, Pueblo, CO, 81004-4290. Tel: 719-562-5652. p. 293
Baca, Sherri, Br Mgr, Shreve Memorial Library, Oil City Branch, 102 Allen St, Oil City, LA, 71061. Tel: 318-995-7975. p. 910
Baca, Terra, Asst Mgr, Saint Louis County Library, Meramec Valley Branch, 1501 San Simeon Way, Fenton, MO, 63026-3479. Tel: 314-994-3300, Ext 3550. p. 1274
Bacall, Jennifer, Br Mgr, Door County Library, Forestville Branch, 123 Hwy 42 S, Forestville, WI, 54213. Tel: 920-856-6886. p. 2480
Bacardi, Frances, Interim Libr Dir, Belleville Public Library & Information Center, 221 Washington Ave, Belleville, NJ, 07109-3189. Tel: 973-450-3434. p. 1389
Bacarella, Ellen, Bus Mgr, Eisenhower Public Library District, 4613 N Oketo Ave, Harwood Heights, IL, 60706. Tel: 708-867-7828. p. 597
Bacchiocchi, Donna, Mgr, Tech Serv, Bentley University, 175 Forest St, Waltham, MA, 02452-4705. Tel: 781-891-2168. p. 1061
Bach, Jessie, Mgr, Bibliog Serv, Marigold Library System, 710 Second St, Strathmore, AB, T1P 1K4, CANADA. Tel: 403-934-5334, Ext 258. p. 2555
Bach, Kathy, Regional Br Operations Mgr, Public Library of Cincinnati & Hamilton County, 800 Vine St, Cincinnati, OH, 45202-2009. Tel: 513-369-4418. p. 1761
Bach, Susan, Dir, Tecumseh District Library, 215 N Ottawa St, Tecumseh, MI, 49286-1564. Tel: 517-423-2238. p. 1153
Bache, Arlene, Br Mgr, Middle Georgia Regional Library System, East Wilkinson County Public Library, 154 E Main St, Irwinton, GA, 31042-2602. Tel: 478-946-2778. p. 487
Bachelder, Matt, Br Mgr, Mansfield-Richland County Public Library, Ontario Branch, 2221 Village Mall Dr, Mansfield, OH, 44906. Tel: 419-529-4912. p. 1798
Bachman, Amy, Ch, Conrad Public Library, 114 N Main St, Conrad, IA, 50621. Tel: 641-366-2583. p. 741
Bachman, Ann, Dir, House Memorial Public Library, 220 Thurston Ave, Pender, NE, 68047. Tel: 402-385-2521. p. 1332
Bachman, David, Librn, Saint Louis Psychoanalytic Institute, 7700 Clayton Rd, 2nd Flr, Saint Louis, MO, 63117. Tel: 314-361-7075, Ext 324. p. 1274
Bachman, Steven J, Exec Dir, Four County Library System, 304 Clubhouse Rd, Vestal, NY, 13850-3713. Tel: 607-723-8236. p. 1657
Bachmann, Julia, Outreach Serv Spec, Ohio County Public Library, 52 16th St, Wheeling, WV, 26003. Tel: 304-232-0244. p. 2417
Bachmann, Sandy, Circ Supvr, Indian River County Library System, North Indian River County Library, 1001 Sebastian Blvd, CR 512, Sebastian, FL, 32958. Tel: 772-400-6360. p. 452

Bachtold, Matthew, Dir, Upton Town Library, Two Main St, Upton, MA, 01568-1608. Tel: 508-529-6272. p. 1060

Bacik, Kimberly, Paralegal Adminr/Law Librn, MMSD Law Library, 260 W Seeboth St, Milwaukee, WI, 53204. Tel: 414-225-2098. p. 2460

Back, Andi, Librn, University of Kansas Libraries, Murphy Art & Architecture Library, 1301 Mississippi St, Lawrence, KS, 66045-7500. Tel: 785-864-3425. p. 820

Back, Mary Constance, Dir, Adult Serv, Rolling Meadows Library, 3110 Martin Lane, Rolling Meadows, IL, 60008. Tel: 847-259-6050. p. 642

Backenstose, Sharon, Tech Serv, United States Army, Fort Jackson Main Post Library, Thomas Lee Hall Main Post Library, Bldg 4679, Fort Jackson, SC, 29207. Tel: 803-751-4816, 803-751-5589. p. 2059

Backer, Lisa, Ref Librn, Fruitville Public Library, 100 Apex Rd, Sarasota, FL, 34240. Tel: 941-861-2500. p. 442

Backhus, Diane, Mgr, San Antonio Public Library, San Pedro, 1315 San Pedro Ave, San Antonio, TX, 78212. Tel: 210-207-9050. p. 2239

Backowski, Roxanne, Head, Acq, Head, Electronic Res, University of Wisconsin-Eau Claire, 103 Garfield Ave, Eau Claire, WI, 54701-4932. Tel: 715-836-3508. p. 2433

Backstrom, Priscilla, Dir, Maddock Community Library, 114 Central Ave, Maddock, ND, 58348. Tel: 701-438-2235. p. 1737

Backus, Meg, Exec Dir, Northern New York Library Network, 6721 US Hwy 11, Potsdam, NY, 13676. Tel: 315-265-1119, Ext 1. p. 2771

Bacon, Abigail, Head, Pub Serv, Hebrew Union College-Jewish Institute of Religion, 3101 Clifton Ave, Cincinnati, OH, 45220-2488. Tel: 513-487-3088. p. 1760

Bacon, Dave, Computer Network Mgr, Outagamie Waupaca Library System (OWLS), 225 N Oneida, Appleton, WI, 54911. Tel: 920-832-6193. p. 2420

Bacon, Donna, Exec Dir, MOBIUS, 111 E Broadway, Ste 220, Columbia, MO, 65203. Tel: 877-366-2487. p. 2769

Bacon, Gale, Dir, Belgrade Community Library, 106 N Broadway, Belgrade, MT, 59714. Tel: 406-388-4346. p. 1287

Bacon, Gina, Ad, Oregon City Public Library, 606 John Adams St, Oregon City, OR, 97045. Tel: 503-657-8269. p. 1890

Bacon, Maggie, Br Supvr, Belleville Public Library, West Branch, 3414 W Main St, Belleville, IL, 62226. Tel: 618-233-4366. p. 541

Bacon, Tammee, Tech Serv, Northwest Regional Library, 210 LaBree Ave N, Thief River Falls, MN, 56701. Tel: 218-681-1066. p. 1205

Badal, Lala, Head, Electronic Resources & Digital Content, California Lutheran University, 60 W Olsen Rd, No 5100, Thousand Oaks, CA, 91360. Tel: 805-493-3937. p. 252

Badarak, Mary, Libr Dir, Irene S Sweetkind Public Library, 6515A Hoochaneetsa Blvd, Cochiti Lake, NM, 87083. Tel: 505-465-2561. p. 1466

Baden, Martha, Pub Serv Mgr, Prescott Public Library, 215 E Goodwin St, Prescott, AZ, 86303. Tel: 928-777-1519. p. 73

Baden, Mary Kay, Librn, Scott County Library System, 1615 Weston Ct, Shakopee, MN, 55379. Tel: 952-496-8010. p. 1203

Bader, David, Ref Librn, Dallas County Law Library, George Allen Courts Bldg, 600 Commerce St, Rm 760, Dallas, TX, 75202-4606. Tel: 214-653-6027. p. 2164

Bader, David P, Sr Librn, Haynes & Boone LLP, 2323 Victory Ave, Ste 700, Dallas, TX, 75219. Tel: 214-651-5709. p. 2167

Bader, Dyan, Mgr, Syst & Coll Access, Nova Scotia Provincial Library, 6016 University Ave, 5th Flr, Halifax, NS, B3H 1W4, CANADA. Tel: 902-424-2457. p. 2621

Badertscher, Amy E, Assoc VPres, Libr Dir, Kenyon College Library & Information Services, Olin & Chalmers Libraries, 103 College Dr, Gambier, OH, 43022. Tel: 740-427-5605. p. 1787

Badger, Maureen, Dir, Dailey Memorial Library, 101 Junior High Dr, Derby, VT, 05829. Tel: 802-766-5063. p. 2283

Badger, Melissa, Cat, Streator Public Library, 130 S Park St, Streator, IL, 61364. Tel: 815-672-2729. p. 652

Badger, Nicole, Libr Dir, Sykesville Public Library, 21 E Main St, Sykesville, PA, 15865-0021. Tel: 814-894-5243. p. 2012

Badgett, Adrian, Br Mgr, Pittsylvania County Public Library, Gretna Branch Library, 207 Coffey St, Ste A, Gretna, VA, 24557. Tel: 434-656-2579. p. 2311

Badgett, Paula, User Serv Librn, Laramie County Community College, 1400 E College Dr, Cheyenne, WY, 82007-3204. Tel: 307-778-1378. p. 2492

Badgley, Nicholas, Br Librn, Genesee District Library, Goodrich Library, 10237 Hegel Rd, Goodrich, MI, 48438. Tel: 810-636-2489. p. 1106

Badics, Joe, Acq Librn, Eastern Michigan University, Administrative Office, Rm 200, 955 W Circle Dr, Ypsilanti, MI, 48197. Tel: 734-487-2402. p. 1160

Badilla, Sam, Dir, Bartley Public Library, 411 Commercial St, Bartley, NE, 69020. Tel: 308-692-3313. p. 1306

Badke, Angela, Librn, Ojibwa Community Library, 409 S Superior Ave, Baraga, MI, 49908. Tel: 906-353-8163. p. 1082

Badke, William, Assoc Librn, Trinity Western University, 22500 University Dr, Langley, BC, V2Y 1Y1, CANADA. Tel: 604-513-2023. p. 2569

Badogombwa, Marie, Bibliothecaire Responsable, Bibliotheques de Montreal, Ile-des-Soeurs, 260 rue Elgar, Verdun, QC, H3E 1C9, CANADA. Tel: 514-765-7169. p. 2719

Badore, Angela, Head, Children's Servx, Case Memorial Library, 176 Tyler City Rd, Orange, CT, 06477-2498. Tel: 203-891-2170. p. 333

Badowski, Caroline, Head, Adult Serv, Memorial & Library Association, 44 Broad St, Westerly, RI, 02891. Tel: 401-596-2877, Ext 307. p. 2044

Baechler, Christine, Asst Br Supvr, Region of Waterloo Library, Baden Branch, 115 Snyder's Rd E, Baden, ON, N3A 2V4, CANADA. Tel: 519-634-8933. p. 2629

Baehler, Mary, Circ Librn, Mineral Point Public Library, 137 High St, Ste 2, Mineral Point, WI, 53565. Tel: 608-987-2447. p. 2462

Baek, Daniel, Head, Tech Serv, Libr Coord, Vancouver School of Theology, 6015 Walter Gage Rd, Vancouver, BC, V6T 1Z1, CANADA. Tel: 604-822-9382. p. 2582

Baek, Tim, Ad, Closter Public Library, 280 High St, Closter, NJ, 07624-1898. Tel: 201-768-4197. p. 1397

Baele, Connie, Dir, Mineral-Gold Public Library District, 120 E Main St, Mineral, IL, 61344. Tel: 309-288-3971. p. 618

Baer, Amy, Dir, Ridgway Public Library, 300 Charles St, Ridgway, CO, 81432. Tel: 970-626-5252. p. 294

Baer, Catherine, Youth Serv Librn, Rosemary Garfoot Public Library, 2107 Julius St, Cross Plains, WI, 53528. Tel: 608-798-3881. p. 2429

Baer, Dan, Chief Financial Officer, Kitsap Regional Library, 1301 Sylvan Way, Bremerton, WA, 98310-3498. Tel: 360-405-9137. p. 2359

Baer, Eileen, Acq, Bedford Hills Free Library, 26 Main St, Bedford Hills, NY, 10507-1832. Tel: 914-666-6472. p. 1492

Baer, Katherine, Info & Res Mgr, Holland & Knight Law Library, 800 17th St NW, Washington, DC, 20006. Tel: 202-955-3000. p. 368

Baer, Nancy, Dir, Wales Public Library, 77 Main St, Wales, MA, 01081. Tel: 413-245-9072. p. 1061

Baer, Samantha, Dir, E M Cooper Memorial Library, 5751 Rte 86, Wilmington, NY, 12997. Tel: 518-946-7701. p. 1666

Baer, Susan, Lead Librn, Prince Albert Parkland Health Region Library, 1200 24th St W, Prince Albert, SK, S6V 4N5, CANADA. Tel: 306-765-6026. p. 2744

Baer, Susan, Dir, Regina Qu'Appelle Health Region, 1440 14th Ave, Regina, SK, S4P 0W5, CANADA. Tel: 306-766-3830. p. 2747

Baer, Thomas, Ref Librn, Jenkins Law Library, Ten Penn Ctr, 1801 Market St, Ste 900, Philadelphia, PA, 19103-6405. Tel: 215-574-7946. p. 1982

Baerkircher, Fred, Br Mgr, Akron-Summit County Public Library, Highland Square Branch, 807 W Market St, Akron, OH, 44303-1010. Tel: 330-376-2927. p. 1744

Baessler, Jane, Librn, Saint Paul's Episcopal Church Library, 310 Elizabeth St, Maumee, OH, 43537. Tel: 419-893-3381. p. 1800

Baeza, Emily, Libr Dir, Reeves County Library, 315 S Oak St, Pecos, TX, 79772-3735. Tel: 432-755-0914. p. 2226

Baeza, Oscar, Head Librn, El Paso Community College Library, 919 Hunter St, Rm C200, El Paso, TX, 79915. Tel: 915-831-2442. p. 2173

Baeza, Victor, Dir of Libr Grad & Res Serv, Oklahoma State University Libraries, Athletic Ave, 216, Stillwater, OK, 74078. Tel: 405-744-1241. p. 1862

Baffoni, Nicolette, Adult Serv Coordr, State of Rhode Island, Department of Administration, One Capitol Hill, 2nd Flr, Providence, RI, 02908. Tel: 401-574-9316. p. 2041

Baffour, Osei, Mgr, Fort Worth Library, East Berry, 4300 E Berry St, Fort Worth, TX, 76105. Tel: 817-392-5470. p. 2179

Baffour, Osei, Mgr, Fort Worth Library, East Regional, 6301 Bridge St, Fort Worth, TX, 76105. Tel: 817-892-5550. p. 2179

Baffour, Osei, Librn, Fort Worth Library, Summerglen, 4205 Basswood Blvd, Fort Worth, TX, 76137-1402. Tel: 817-392-5970. p. 2180

Bagby, Pamela, Asst Dir, Tech Serv, Henry County Public Library System, 1001 Florence McGarity Blvd, McDonough, GA, 30252. Tel: 678-432-5353. p. 490

Bagdasarian, Armine, ILL, Regis College Library, 235 Wellesley St, Weston, MA, 02493. Tel: 781-768-7306. p. 1068

Baggett, Patsy, Prog Spec, Harnett County Public Library, Dunn Public, 110 E Divine St, Dunn, NC, 28334. Tel: 910-892-2899. p. 1701

Baggett, Stacy, Electronic Res Librn, Shenandoah University, 1460 University Dr, Winchester, VA, 22601. Tel: 540-665-4819. p. 2354

Baggett, Tammy, Dir, Durham County Library, 300 N Roxboro St, Durham, NC, 27701. Tel: 919-560-0160. p. 1685

Baggili, Eva, Ad, Chicago Ridge Public Library, 10400 S Oxford Ave, Chicago Ridge, IL, 60415. Tel: 708-423-7753. p. 571

Baghetti, Amy, Librn, Northeast State Community College, 2425 Hwy 75, Blountville, TN, 37617. Tel: 423-354-2429. p. 2088

Bagley, Annette, Head, Commun Relations, Bellingham Public Library, 210 Central Ave, Bellingham, WA, 98225. Tel: 360-778-7206. p. 2358

Bagley, Carol Lynne, Sr Ref Librn, Chicopee Public Library, 449 Front St, Chicopee, MA, 01013. Tel: 413-594-1800. p. 1011

Bagley, Catlin, Instruction Librn, Gonzaga University, 502 E Boone Ave, Spokane, WA, 99258-0095. Tel: 509-313-6529. p. 2383

Bagley, Elizabeth Leslie, Dir, Libr Serv, Agnes Scott College, 141 E College Ave, Decatur, GA, 30030-3770. p. 475

Bagley, Lynette, Br Mgr, Dorchester County Public Library, Hurlock Branch, 222 S Main St, Hurlock, MD, 21643. Tel: 410-943-4331. p. 960

Bagley, Michelle, Dean, Portland Community College Library, 12000 SW 49th Ave, Portland, OR, 97219. p. 1893

Bagley, Nicole, Library Contact, Admiral Nimitz National Museum of the Pacific War, 311 E Austin St, Fredericksburg, TX, 78624. Tel: 830-997-4379, Ext 262. p. 2181
Bagley, Pamela, Research Coordr, Dartmouth College Library, Dana Biomedical Library, HB 6168, 37 Dewey Field Rd, 3rd Flr, Hanover, NH, 03755-1417. Tel: 603-650-1749. p. 1366
Baglin, Steve, Pub Serv Librn, Cedar Mill Community Library, Bethany Branch, 15325 NW Central Dr, Ste J-8, Portland, OR, 97229-0986. Tel: 503-617-7323. p. 1891
Bagnall, David, Curator, Dir, Coll & Interpretation, Frank Lloyd Wright Trust, 951 Chicago Ave, Oak Park, IL, 60302. Tel: 312-994-4035. p. 628
Bagwell, Ashley, Research Librn, Seminole State College, 2701 Boren Blvd, Seminole, OK, 74868. Tel: 405-382-9246. p. 1861
Bagwell, Cassie, Mrs, Circ, Stewart County Public Library, 102 Natcor Dr, Dover, TN, 37058. Tel: 931-232-3127. p. 2097
Bahde, Anne, Hist of Sci Librn/Curator, Oregon State University Libraries, Special Collections & Archives Research Center, 121 The Valley Library, 5th Flr, Corvallis, OR, 97331. Tel: 541-737-2075. p. 1877
Bahler, Kristen, Ref & Instruction Librn, Alliant International University, 5130 E Clinton Way, Fresno, CA, 93727. Tel: 916-561-3202. p. 144
Bahlinger, Tom, Ref Librn, San Antonio College, 1819 N Main Ave, San Antonio, TX, 78212. Tel: 210-486-0554. p. 2238
Bahnaman, Steve, Reference & Electronic Resources Librn, Campbell University, 113 Main St, Buies Creek, NC, 27506. Tel: 910-893-1760. p. 1676
Bahnsen, Tara, Head, Youth Serv, Kaubisch Memorial Public Library, 205 Perry St, Fostoria, OH, 44830-2265. Tel: 419-435-2813. p. 1786
Bahnson, Jane, Asst Director, Research & Instruction, Duke University Libraries, J Michael Goodson Law Library, 210 Science Dr, Durham, NC, 27708. Tel: 919-613-7113. p. 1684
Bahr, Ellen, Info Syst, Alfred University, Herrick Memorial Library, One Saxon Dr, Alfred, NY, 14802. Tel: 607-871-2976. p. 1485
Bahr, Philip, Head, Adult Serv, Fairfield Public Library, 1080 Old Post Rd, Fairfield, CT, 06824. Tel: 203-256-3155. p. 312
Bahr, William, Dir, Marks-Quitman County Library, 315 E Main St, Marks, MS, 38646. Tel: 662-326-7141. p. 1225
Bahret, Karla, Circ Librn, Silver Lake Library, 203 Railroad St, Silver Lake, KS, 66539. Tel: 785-582-5141. p. 836
Bahringer, Annie, Libr Dir, North Shore Library, 6800 N Port Washington Rd, Glendale, WI, 53217. Tel: 414-351-3461. p. 2437
Bai, Sheryl, Head, Libr Syst & Tech, UConn Health Sciences Library, 263 Farmington Ave, Farmington, CT, 06034-4003. Tel: 860-679-8371. p. 313
Baier, Susan, Exec Dir, Allen County Public Library, 900 Library Plaza, Fort Wayne, IN, 46802. Tel: 260-421-1200. p. 683
Baier, Susan, Libr Dir, McCracken County Public Library, 555 Washington St, Paducah, KY, 42003. Tel: 270-442-2510. p. 871
Baierl, Hans, Libr Serv Coordr, Moraine Park Technical College Library, 235 N National Ave, Fond du Lac, WI, 54936. Tel: 920-929-2470. p. 2435
Bailey, Alex, Br Librn, Stockton-San Joaquin County Public Library, Margaret K Troke Branch, 502 W Benjamin Holt Dr, Stockton, CA, 95207. p. 250
Bailey, Amy, Ref Librn, Loutit District Library, 407 Columbus Ave, Grand Haven, MI, 49417. Tel: 616-850-6924. p. 1109
Bailey, Amy, Librn, Missouri State Court of Appeals, University Plaza, 300 Hammons Pkwy, Ste 300, Springfield, MO, 65806. Tel: 417-895-1398. p. 1281
Bailey, Angela, Libr Dir, Huron Public Library, 521 Dakota Ave S, Huron, SD, 57350. Tel: 605-353-8530. p. 2077
Bailey, April, Dir, Heritage Public Library, 52 Fourth St, McDonald, PA, 15057. Tel: 724-926-8400. p. 1959
Bailey, Barb, Dir, Girard Public Library, 128 W Prairie Ave, Girard, KS, 66743-1498. Tel: 620-724-4317. p. 809
Bailey, Barb, Asst Librn, Beresford Public Library, 115 S Third St, Beresford, SD, 57004. Tel: 605-763-2782. p. 2074
Bailey, Barbara, Ch Mgr, Morley Library, 184 Phelps St, Painesville, OH, 44077-3926. Tel: 440-352-3383. p. 1812
Bailey, Barbara, Circ Supvr, Chester County Library & District Center, 450 Exton Square Pkwy, Exton, PA, 19341-2496. Tel: 610-344-5600. p. 1932
Bailey, Barbara J, Dir, Welles-Turner Memorial Library, 2407 Main St, Glastonbury, CT, 06033. Tel: 860-652-7719. p. 313
Bailey, Barry, Digital Librn, Johnson County Community College, 12345 College Blvd, Overland Park, KS, 66210. Tel: 913-469-8500, Ext 4841. p. 829
Bailey, Cheryl, Librn, Irvine Valley College Library, 5500 Irvine Center Dr, Irvine, CA, 92618-4399. Tel: 949-451-5761. p. 153
Bailey, Christopher, Librn, University of Illinois Library at Urbana-Champaign, Social Sciences, Health & Education Library, 101 Main Library, MC-522, 1408 W Gregory Dr, Urbana, IL, 61801. Tel: 217-300-8365. p. 656
Bailey, Cindy, Libr Asst III, University of Delaware Library, Chemistry, Brown Laboratory, Rm 202, 181 S College Ave, Newark, DE, 19717. Tel: 302-831-2455. p. 355
Bailey, Clare, Tech Serv, Bloomberg Industry Group Library, 1801 S Bell St, Arlington, VA, 22202. Tel: 703-341-3306. p. 2305
Bailey, Eric, Libr Dir, Lake Bluff Public Library, 123 E Scranton Ave, Lake Bluff, IL, 60044. Tel: 847-234-2540. p. 606
Bailey, Faith, Libr Asst, Becket Athenaeum, Inc, 3367 Main St, Becket, MA, 01223. Tel: 413-623-5483. p. 987
Bailey, Greg, University Archivist & Special Collections, Iowa State University Library, 302 Parks Library, 701 Morrill Rd, Ames, IA, 50011-2102. Tel: 515-294-4216. p. 731
Bailey, Janet, Operations Mgr, Manheim Township Public Library, 595 Granite Run Dr, Lancaster, PA, 17601. Tel: 717-560-6441. p. 1952
Bailey, Janet, Head, Tech Serv, ILL, Abilene Public Library, 202 Cedar St, Abilene, TX, 79601-5793. Tel: 352-676-6063. p. 2131
Bailey, Janice, Network Adminr, Wichita Falls Public Library, 600 11th St, Wichita Falls, TX, 76301-4604. Tel: 940-767-0868, Ext 4246. p. 2258
Bailey, Jeff, Dean of Libr, Arkansas State University, 322 University Loop Circle, State University, AR, 72401. Tel: 870-972-3077. p. 111
Bailey, Jo Ann, Cat, ILL, Florida Gateway College, 149 SE College Pl, Lake City, FL, 32025-2006. Tel: 386-754-4338. p. 415
Bailey, Joanna M, Libr Dir, Bay Minette Public Library, 205 W Second St, Bay Minette, AL, 36507. Tel: 251-580-1648. p. 6
Bailey, Jodi, Ms, Libr Dir, Poynette Area Public Library, 118 N Main St, Poynette, WI, 53955. Tel: 608-635-7577. p. 2470
Bailey, John, Admin Officer, Centers for Disease Control & Prevention, Robert A Taft Laboratories, 1090 Tusculum Ave, MS-P03, Cincinnati, OH, 45226. Tel: 513-533-8495. p. 1759
Bailey, Joy, Dir, South Fork Public Library, 320 Main St, South Fork, PA, 15956-9998. Tel: 814-495-4812. p. 2009
Bailey, Katie, Dir, Libr Serv, North Shelby County Library, 5521 Cahaba Valley Rd, Birmingham, AL, 35242. Tel: 205-439-5540. p. 8
Bailey, Katie, Libr Dir, North Shelby County Library, Mt Laurel Library, 111 Olmsted St, Birmingham, AL, 35242. Tel: 205-439-5540. p. 8
Bailey, Kellie, Libr Spec I, Okeechobee County Public Library, 206 SW 16th St, Okeechobee, FL, 34974. Tel: 863-763-3536. p. 430
Bailey, Kieren, Chair, Librn, Grande Prairie Regional College, 10726 106th Ave, Grande Prairie, AB, T8V 4C4, CANADA. Tel: 780-539-2202. p. 2541
Bailey, Kim, ILL, Ser, Vermont State University - Castleton, 178 Alumni Dr, Castleton, VT, 05735. Tel: 802-468-1256, p. 2281
Bailey, Kimberly, Ref & Instruction Librn, University of Pittsburgh at Bradford, 300 Campus Dr, Bradford, PA, 16701. Tel: 814-362-7621. p. 1914
Bailey, Lennadene, Bus Mgr, Montgomery County Public Libraries, 21 Maryland Ave, Ste 310, Rockville, MD, 20850. Tel: 240-777-0002. p. 974
Bailey, Marnie, Knowledge Services Librn, Fasken Martineau DuMoulin LLP Library, 2900-550 Burrard St, Vancouver, BC, V6C 0A3, CANADA. Tel: 604-631-3131. p. 2578
Bailey, Meghan, Youth Serv Coordr, Red Jacket Community Library, 89 S Main St, Manchester, NY, 14504. Tel: 585-289-3559. p. 1568
Bailey, Melissa, Youth Serv, Paso Robles City Library, 1000 Spring St, Paso Robles, CA, 93446-2207. Tel: 805-237-3870. p. 194
Bailey, Michelle M, Asst Dean of Libr, Scott Community College Library, 500 Belmont Rd, Bettendorf, IA, 52722. Tel: 563-441-4150. p. 735
Bailey, Nancy, Libr Mgr, Byron-Bergen Public Library, 13 S Lake Ave, Bergen, NY, 14416-9420. Tel: 585-494-1120. p. 1493
Bailey, Patty M, Dir, Yalobusha County Public Library System, 14432 Main St, Coffeeville, MS, 38922-2590. Tel: 662-675-8822. p. 1214
Bailey, Peter, Chief Exec Officer, St Albert Public Library, Five Saint Anne St, St. Albert, AB, T8N 3Z9, CANADA. Tel: 780-459-1530. p. 2555
Bailey, Robert, Educ Coordr, Cook Inlet Pre-Trial Facility Library, 1300 E Fourth Ave, Anchorage, AK, 99501. Tel: 907-269-0943. p. 42
Bailey, Robin, Br Mgr, Richland Parish Library, Delhi Branch, 520 Main St, Delhi, LA, 71232. Tel: 318-878-5121. p. 906
Bailey, Scott D, Dir, Research & Knowledge Servs, Eversheds Sutherland (US) LLP Library, 700 Sixth St NW, Ste 700, Washington, DC, 20001-3980. Tel: 202-383-0979. p. 365
Bailey, Stephanie, Br Mgr, Johnson County Library, Blue Valley, 9000 W 151st St, Overland Park, KS, 66221. p. 830
Bailey, Suzanne, Actg Univ Librn, Trent University, 1600 West Bank Dr, Peterborough, ON, K9J 7B8, CANADA. Tel: 705-748-1011. p. 2672
Bailey, Tim, Head, Libr Tech, Auburn University, 7440 East Dr, Montgomery, AL, 36117. Tel: 334-244-3200. p. 28
Bailey, Tristan, Shelving Supervisor, San Marcos Public Library, 625 E Hopkins, San Marcos, TX, 78666. Tel: 512-393-8200. p. 2241
Bailey-Hainer, Brenda, Exec Dir, American Theological Library Association, 200 S Wacker Dr, Ste 3100, Chicago, IL, 60606-5829. Tel: 872-310-4229. p. 2764
Bailey-McDaniel, Sara, Ch Mgr, Vermilion Parish Library, 405 E Saint Victor St, Abbeville, LA, 70510-5101. Tel: 337-893-2655. p. 879
Bailey-White, Stephanie, Dep State Librn, Idaho Commission for Libraries, 325 W State St, Boise, ID, 83702-6072. Tel: 208-334-2150. p. 517
Bailey-White, Stephanie, State Librn, Idaho Commission for Libraries, 325 W State St, Boise, ID, 83702-6072. Tel: 208-334-2150., State Librn, Idaho Commission for Libraries, 325 W State St, Boise, ID, 83702-6072. Tel: 208-334-2150. p. 517
Bailie, Colleen, Exec Dir, West Haven Public Library, 300 Elm St, West Haven, CT, 06516-4692. Tel: 203-937-4233. p. 346

Bailin, Kylie, Dir, Outreach & Access Services, Lafayette College, 710 Sullivan Rd, Easton, PA, 18042-1797. Tel: 610-330-5154. p. 1928
Baillargeon, Tara, Dean of Libr, Marquette University, 1355 W Wisconsin Ave, Milwaukee, WI, 53233. Tel: 414-288-5213. p. 2458
Baillie, Margaret, Asst Librn, Chester County History Center Library, 225 N High St, West Chester, PA, 19380. Tel: 610-692-4800, Ext 221. p. 2020
Bailon, Kathy, Dir, Fashion Institute of Design & Merchandising, 350 Tenth Ave, 3rd Flr, San Diego, CA, 92101. Tel: 619-235-2049. p. 215
Bailon, Kathy, Libr Dir, Fashion Institute of Design & Merchandising Library, 55 Stockton St, 5th Flr, San Francisco, CA, 94108. Tel: 415-675-5200. p. 224
Bain, Amanda, Dir, Smith County Public Library, 215 Main St N, Carthage, TN, 37030. Tel: 615-735-1326. p. 2090
Bain, M Rex, Exec Dir, Lawrence County Public Library, 401 College St, Moulton, AL, 35650. Tel: 256-974-0883. p. 30
Bain, Paul, PhD, Ref & Educ Librn, Harvard Library, Francis A Countway Library of Medicine, Ten Shattuck St, Boston, MA, 02115. Tel: 617-432-2136. p. 1005
Bain, Sandra, Dir, Appleton City Public Library, 105 W Fourth St, Appleton City, MO, 64724. Tel: 660-476-5513. p. 1237
Bainbridge, Erika, Acq & Ref, Librn, Ser Mgt, Harvard Library, Center for Hellenic Studies Library, 3100 Whitehaven St NW, Washington, MA, 20008. Tel: 202-745-4414. p. 1005
Bainter, Emily, Info Spec, State Library of Iowa, 1112 E Grand Ave, Des Moines, IA, 50319. Tel: 515-281-7574. p. 747
Bainum, Bobbie, Assoc Librn, Mount Ayr Public Library, 121 W Monroe St, Mount Ayr, IA, 50854. Tel: 641-464-2159. p. 771
Baiocchi, Matthew, Ref Librn, Driftwood Public Library, 801 SW Hwy 101, Ste 201, Lincoln City, OR, 97367-2720. Tel: 541-996-2277. p. 1885
Baione, Tom, Harold Boeschenstein Dir, American Museum of Natural History, 200 Central Park W, New York, NY, 10024-5192. Tel: 212-769-5417. p. 1578
Bair, David, Cat, Tech Serv Librn, Brookings Institution Library, 1775 Massachusetts Ave NW, Washington, DC, 20036. Tel: 202-797-6240. p. 361
Bair, Jeannette, Dir, Rochester Public Library, 22 S Main St, Rte 100, Rochester, VT, 05767. Tel: 802-767-3927. p. 2293
Baird, Candy, Dir, Delta Public Library, 402 Main St, Delta, OH, 43515. Tel: 419-822-3110. p. 1782
Baird, Catherine, Online & Outreach Serv Librn, Montclair State University, One Normal Ave, Montclair, NJ, 07043-1699. Tel: 973-655-7144. p. 1420
Baird, Pamela, Circ Coordr, The California Maritime Academy Library, 200 Maritime Academy Dr, Vallejo, CA, 94590. Tel: 707-654-1090. p. 255
Baird, Robin, Ref Serv, United States Department of the Army, CEHEC-ZL Casey Bldg, 7701 Telegraph Rd, Alexandria, VA, 22315-3860. Tel: 703-428-6388. p. 2303
Baird, Sandy, Cat Librn, User Serv, Georgetown College, 400 E College St, Georgetown, KY, 40324. Tel: 502-863-8410. p. 856
Baird, Tim, Adult Serv, White Plains Public Library, 100 Martine Ave, White Plains, NY, 10601. Tel: 914-422-1400. p. 1665
Baird, Zahra, Br Mgr, Yonkers Public Library, Crestwood, 16 Thompson St, Yonkers, NY, 10707. Tel: 914-779-3774. p. 1668
Baird-Adams, Jan, Br Mgr, Montgomery County Public Libraries, Germantown Library, 19840 Century Blvd, Germantown, MD, 20874. Tel: 240-773-0126. p. 974
Baitz, Alison, Librn, Butterfield Library, 3534 US Rte 5, Westminster, VT, 05158. Tel: 802-722-4891. p. 2298
Baiz, Elizabeth, Br Mgr, Riverside County Library System, Sun City Library, 26982 Cherry Hills Blvd, Menifee, CA, 92586. Tel: 951-679-3534. p. 202
Baiza, Rose, Commun Librn, Santa Clara County Library District, Los Altos Main Library, 13 S San Antonio Rd, Los Altos, CA, 94022. Tel: 650-948-7683. p. 127
Baiza, Rose, Commun Librn, Santa Clara County Library District, Woodland Branch, 1975 Grant Rd, Los Altos, CA, 94024. Tel: 650-969-6030. p. 127
Bajjaly, Stephen, Dr, Prof, Wayne State University, 106 Kresge Library, Detroit, MI, 48202. Tel: 313-577-1825. p. 2787
Bakaitis, Elvis, Head, Ref Serv, City University of New York, 365 Fifth Ave, New York, NY, 10016-4309. Tel: 212-817-7073. p. 1582
Baker, Adrianne, Syst Librn, Alberta Legislature Library, 216 Legislature Bldg, 10800-97 Ave NW, Edmonton, AB, T5K 2B6, CANADA. Tel: 780-415-2904. p. 2535
Baker, Amelia, Tech Serv Librn, Harding University, 915 E Market St, Searcy, AR, 72149-5615. Tel: 501-279-4235. p. 109
Baker, Amia, Dir, University of South Alabama Libraries, Joseph & Rebecca Mitchell Learning Resource Center, Mitchell College of Business, Rm 240, 5811 USA Dr S, Mobile, AL, 36688. Tel: 251-460-7998. p. 27
Baker, Anne, Librn, Department of Veterans Affairs Medical Center, 3001 Green Bay Rd, North Chicago, IL, 60064. Tel: 847-688-1900, Ext 83757. p. 626
Baker, Anwan, Dir, Libr Serv, Livermore Public Library, 1188 S Livermore Ave, Livermore, CA, 94550. Tel: 925-373-5500. p. 157
Baker, Anwan, Libr Dir, Lodi Public Library, 201 W Locust St, Lodi, CA, 95240. Tel: 209-333-5566. p. 157
Baker, Ari, Exec Dir, Tenn-Share, PO Box 691, Alcoa, TN, 37701. Tel: 615-669-8670. p. 2775
Baker, Barbara, Supvr, Deschutes Public Library District, East Bend Branch, 62080 Dean Swift Rd, Bend, OR, 97701. Tel: 541-330-3761. p. 1874
Baker, Barry B, Dir of Libr, University of Central Florida Libraries, 12701 Pegasus Dr, Orlando, FL, 32816-8030. Tel: 407-823-2564. p. 432
Baker, Becky, Libr Dir, Seward Memorial Library, 233 S Fifth St, Seward, NE, 68434. Tel: 402-643-3318. p. 1336
Baker, Betsy, Dir, Milton Free Public Library, 13 Main St, Milton Mills, NH, 03852. Tel: 603-473-8535. p. 1374
Baker, Bo, Dept Head, Pub Serv, Res, University of Tennessee at Chattanooga Library, 400 Douglas Ave, Dept 6456, Chattanooga, TN, 37403-2598. Tel: 423-425-4501. p. 2092
Baker, Bradley, Evening Librn, Ref Spec, Belmont Abbey College, 100 Belmont-Mt Holly Rd, Belmont, NC, 28012. Tel: 704-461-6748. p. 1674
Baker, Brandon, Ms, Ref Librn, Stacks Mgr, California Western School of Law Library, 290 Cedar St, San Diego, CA, 92101. Tel: 619-525-1425. p. 215
Baker, BreeAna, Online Learning Librn, D'Youville College, 320 Porter Ave, Buffalo, NY, 14201-1084. Tel: 716 597-6803. p. 1509
Baker, Brian, Library Services, Prog Mgr, Valley Children's Healthcare, 9300 Valley Children's Pl, Madera, CA, 93638-8762. Tel: 559-353-6178. p. 171
Baker, Brian, Acad Res Coordr, Juniata College, 1700 Moore St, Huntingdon, PA, 16652-2119. Tel: 814-641-3078. p. 1945
Baker, Carolyn, Library Contact, American Counseling Association, 2461 Eisenhower Ave, Alexandria, VA, 22331. Tel: 703-823-9800. p. 2303
Baker, Carri, Pub Serv Librn, Harding University, 915 E Market St, Searcy, AR, 72149-5615. Tel: 501-279-4349. p. 109
Baker, Cheryl, County Librn, Modoc County Library, 212 W Third St, Alturas, CA, 96101. Tel: 530-233-6340. p. 116
Baker, Cheryl, Librn, South China Public Library, 247 Village St, South China, ME, 04358. Tel: 207-445-3094. p. 941
Baker, Chris, Fac Mgr, Tech Serv Mgr, Saint Mary's University of Minnesota, 700 Terrace Heights, No 26, Winona, MN, 55987-1399. Tel: 507-457-8702. p. 1209
Baker, Chris, Metadata Librn, Shaw University, 118 E South St, Raleigh, NC, 27601. Tel: 919-546-8597. p. 1710
Baker, Christine, Asst Librn, Metadata Librn, Colorado School of Mines, 1400 Illinois St, Golden, CO, 80401-1887. Tel: 303-273-3446. p. 283
Baker, Colleen, Br Mgr, San Diego County Library, Ramona Branch, 1275 Main St, Ramona, CA, 92065. Tel: 760-788-5270. p. 217
Baker, Dara, Chief, Libr Serv, Federal Deposit Insurance Corp Library, 550 17th St NW, Washington, DC, 20429-0002. Tel: 202-898-3631. p. 366
Baker, Dawn, ILL & Periodicals Specialist, Hartwick College, One Hartwick Dr, Oneonta, NY, 13820. Tel: 607-431-4454. p. 1611
Baker, Deb, Libr Dir, Manchester Community College Library, 1066 Front St, Manchester, NH, 03102. Tel: 603-206-8150. p. 1372
Baker, Deborah, Adminr, University of Georgia, Alexander Campbell King Law Library, 225 Herty Dr, Athens, GA, 30602-6018. Tel: 706-542-1922. p. 459
Baker, Deborah, Libr Mgr, Timberland Regional Library, Oakville Branch, 204 Main St, Oakville, WA, 98568. Tel: 360-273-5305. p. 2389
Baker, Dennis, Fiscal Officer, Bradford Public Library, 138 E Main St, Bradford, OH, 45308-1108. Tel: 937-448-2612. p. 1752
Baker, Diane, Ref Librn, Lake Michigan College, 2755 E Napier Ave, Benton Harbor, MI, 49022. Tel: 269-927-8605. p. 1084
Baker, Diane, Bus Mgr, Project Mgr, Carson City Library, 900 N Roop St, Carson City, NV, 89701. Tel: 775-887-2244, Ext 7554. p. 1343
Baker, Dobie, Dir, Mabel D Blodgett Memorial Reading Center, 35 S Main St, Rushville, NY, 14544-9648. Tel: 585-554-3939. p. 1634
Baker, Doris, Asst Dir, Grundy County-Jewett Norris Library, 1331 Main St, Trenton, MO, 64683. Tel: 660-359-3577. p. 1282
Baker, Drew, Asst Libr Dir, Head, Tech Serv, Claremont School of Theology Library, 1325 N College Ave, Claremont, CA, 91711. Tel: 909-447-2513. p. 130
Baker, Drew, Theatre, Dance & Performance Studies Librn, University of Maryland Libraries, Michelle Smith Performing Arts Library, 8270 Alumni Dr, College Park, MD, 20742-1630. Tel: 301-314-0535. p. 963
Baker, Drew, Dr, Asst Libr Dir, Claremont School of Theology Library, Center for Process Studies, 1325 N College Ave, Claremont, CA, 91711-3154. Tel: 909-447-2533, 909-621-5330. p. 130
Baker, Eileen, Dir, Norwood Public Library, 513 Welcome Ave, Norwood, PA, 19074. Tel: 610-534-0693. p. 1972
Baker, Elizabeth, Dir, Carteret Community College Library, Michael J Smith Bldg, 201 College Circle, Morehead City, NC, 28557. Tel: 252-222-6216. p. 1704
Baker, Emily, Digital Serv Librn, Lucius E & Elsie C Burch Jr Library, 501 Poplar View Pkwy, Collierville, TN, 38017. Tel: 901-457-2600. p. 2094
Baker, Erin, Circ, Webster County Library, 219 W Jackson St, Marshfield, MO, 65706. Tel: 417-468-3335. p. 1261
Baker, Harrison, Asst Dir, Toledo Public Library, 173 NW Seventh St, Toledo, OR, 97391. Tel: 541-336-3132. p. 1900

Baker, Heather, Ch, Canton Public Library, 40 Dyer Ave, Canton, CT, 06019. Tel: 860-693-5800. p. 305

Baker, Heather, Children's & Youth Serv, Grove City Community Library, 125 W Main St, Grove City, PA, 16127-1569. Tel: 724-458-7320. p. 1939

Baker, Jamie J, Ms, Assoc Dean, Dir, Texas Tech University, 3311 18th St, Lubbock, TX, 79409. Tel: 806-742-3957. p. 2213

Baker, Jane, Communications & Develop Officer, Spokane County Library District, 4322 N Argonne Rd, Spokane, WA, 99212. Tel: 509-893-8200. p. 2384

Baker, Janet, Head, Circ, Township of Washington Public Library, 144 Woodfield Rd, Washington Township, NJ, 07676. Tel: 201-664-4586. p. 1451

Baker, Jaxon, Dir, Sam Waller Museum Library, 306 Fischer Ave, The Pas, MB, R9A 1K4, CANADA. Tel: 204-623-3802. p. 2591

Baker, Jean, Dean, Libr Serv, Dallas College, 12800 Abrams Rd, Dallas, TX, 75243. Tel: 972-238-6081. p. 2164

Baker, Jean, Lead Librn, Dallas College, 4849 W Illinois, Dallas, TX, 75211-6599. Tel: 214-860-8669. p. 2164

Baker, Jeff, Ref Librn, North Merrick Public Library, 1691 Meadowbrook Rd, North Merrick, NY, 11566. Tel: 516-378-7474. p. 1607

Baker, Jeff, Dir, Chili Public Library, 3333 Chili Ave, Rochester, NY, 14624. Tel: 585-889-2200. p. 1628

Baker, Jen R, Librn, Aurora Public Library, 14 W Second Ave N, Aurora, MN, 55705-1314. Tel: 218-229-2021. p. 1164

Baker, Jennifer, City Librn, Benicia Public Library, 150 East L St, Benicia, CA, 94510-3281. Tel: 707-746-4343. p. 121

Baker, Jenny, Dir, Libr Serv, Wisconsin Lutheran College Library, 8800 W Bluemound Rd, Milwaukee, WI, 53226. Tel: 414-443-8864. p. 2461

Baker, Joyce, Libr Mgr, Coolidge Public Library, 160 W Central Ave, Coolidge, AZ, 85128. Tel: 520-723-6030. p. 59

Baker, Julie, Bus Mgr, University of Central Oklahoma, Chambers Library, 100 N University Dr, Edmond, OK, 73034. Tel: 405-974-2884. p. 1846

Baker, Kate, Dir, NYS Small Business Development Center Research Network, Ten N Pearl St, Albany, NY, 12246. Tel: 518-944-2840. p. 1483

Baker, Kathy, Asst Dir, Head, Tech Serv, Everett Roehl Marshfield Public Library, 105 S Maple Ave, Marshfield, WI, 54449. Tel: 715-387-8494, Ext 2759. p. 2454

Baker, Kelly, Circ, Spring Arbor University, 106 E Main St, Spring Arbor, MI, 49283. Tel: 517-750-6442. p. 1152

Baker, Kelly Daniels, Head, Youth Serv, Sunderland Public Library, 20 School St, Sunderland, MA, 01375. Tel: 413-665-2642. p. 1058

Baker, Keri, Reference Librarian III, Nova Southeastern University Libraries, Oceanographic Campus Library, 8000 N Ocean Dr, Dania Beach, FL, 33004. Tel: 954-262-3643. p. 402

Baker, Larry L, Exec Dir, San Juan County Archaeological Research Center & Library at Salmon Ruins, 6131 US Hwy 64, Bloomfield, NM, 87413. Tel: 505-632-2013. p. 1464

Baker, Laura, Outreach Librn, Furman University Libraries, 3300 Poinsett Hwy, Greenville, SC, 29613-4100. Tel: 864-294-2277. p. 2061

Baker, Laura, Libr Dir, Pub Serv, Midlands Technical College Library, 1260 Lexington Dr, West Columbia, SC, 29170-2176. Tel: 803-822-3533. p. 2072

Baker, Laura, Assessment & User Experience Librn, Abilene Christian University, 221 Brown Library, ACU Box 29208, Abilene, TX, 79699-9208. Tel: 325-674-2316. p. 2131

Baker, Linda, Branch Experience Mgr, Evansville Vanderburgh Public Library, East Branch, 840 E Chandler Ave, Evansville, IN, 47713. Tel: 812-428-8231. p. 681

Baker, Lisa, Coordr, Learning Commons, Belmont College, 68094 Hammond Rd, Rm 1076, Saint Clairsville, OH, 43950-9735. Tel: 740-699-3835. p. 1818

Baker, Marie, Libr Asst, Charlotte E Hobbs Memorial Library, 227 Main St, Lovell, ME, 04051. Tel: 207-925-3177. p. 930

Baker, Mary, Pres, Longboat Library, 555 Bay Isles Rd, Longboat Key, FL, 34228. Tel: 941-383-2011. p. 419

Baker, Matthew, Head Librn, Columbia University, The Burke Library at Union Theological Seminary, 3041 Broadway, New York, NY, 10027. Tel: 212-851-5606. p. 1583

Baker, Megan W, Dir, Bolton Free Library, 4922 Lakeshore Dr, Bolton Landing, NY, 12814. Tel: 518-644-2233. p. 1495

Baker, Melissa, Mgr, Prog & Outreach, Lee County Library System, 2201 Second St, Ste 400, Fort Myers, FL, 33901. Tel: 239-533-4800. p. 403

Baker, Michelle, Asst Librn, Somersworth Public Library, 25 Main St, Somersworth, NH, 03878-3198. Tel: 603-692-4587. p. 1381

Baker, Pam, Librn, Oregon County Library District, Myrtle Public, 9040 V Hwy, Myrtle, MO, 65778. Tel: 417-938-4350. p. 1237

Baker, Patty, Librn, Sheridan Public Library, 103 W First St, Sheridan, IN, 46069. Tel: 317-758-5201. p. 718

Baker, Rachel, Youth Serv Librn, Elkins Public Library, Nine Center Rd, Canterbury, NH, 03224. Tel: 603-783-4386. p. 1356

Baker, Raymond, Dir, Miami-Dade Public Library System, 101 W Flagler St, Miami, FL, 33130-1523. Tel: 305-375-2665. p. 422

Baker, Ricky, Pub Serv Librn, Guilford Technical Community College, 601 E Main St, Jamestown, NC, 27282. Tel: 336-334-4822, Ext 50519. p. 1698

Baker, Ron, Head Librn, Eston College, 730 First St SE, Eston, SK, S0L 1A0, CANADA. Tel: 306-962-3621. p. 2741

Baker, Roxanne, Libr Dir, Wide Awake Club Library, 22 Genesee St, Fillmore, NY, 14735. Tel: 585-567-8301. p. 1533

Baker, Ryan, Libr Dir, Los Gatos Public Library, 100 Villa Ave, Los Gatos, CA, 95030-6981. Tel: 408-354-6891. p. 171

Baker, Sara, Circ Supvr, Valdez Consortium Library, 212 Fairbanks St, Valdez, AK, 99686. Tel: 907-835-4632. p. 52

Baker, Sarah, Tech Serv Mgr, Granville Public Library, 217 E Broadway, Granville, OH, 43023-1398. Tel: 740-587-0196. p. 1788

Baker, Scott, Librn, Washington County Library System, Greenland Branch Library, 8 E Ross St, Greenland, AR, 72737. Tel: 479-582-5992. p. 95

Baker, Sharon, Pub Serv Asst, Lutheran Theological Seminary, United Lutheran Seminary, 7301 Germantown Ave, Philadelphia, PA, 19119-1794. Tel: 215-248-6335. p. 1982

Baker, Shaunna, Mgr, Mission Support & Test Services, LLC, PO Box 98521, M/S 400, Las Vegas, NV, 89193-8521. p. 1347

Baker, Sheila, Assoc Prof, Prog Coordr, University of Houston-Clear Lake, 2700 Bay Area Blvd, Bayou Ste 1321, Houston, TX, 77058. Tel: 281-283-3515. p. 2793

Baker, Shelly, Br Mgr, Hightower Sara Regional Library, Chattooga Public Library, 360 Farrar Dr, Summerville, GA, 30747. Tel: 706-857-2553. p. 495

Baker, Sherry, Circ Librn, Silver Lake Library, 203 Railroad St, Silver Lake, KS, 66539. Tel: 785-582-5141. p. 836

Baker, Stacey, Supvr, Mid-Columbia Libraries, Benton City Branch, 810 Horne Dr, Benton City, WA, 99320. Tel: 509-588-6471. p. 2367

Baker, Steev, Head, Access Serv, Head, Circ, Sun Prairie Public Library, 1350 Linnerud Dr, Sun Prairie, WI, 53590. Tel: 608-825-7323. p. 2480

Baker, Stewart, Institutional Repository Librn, Western Oregon University, 345 N Monmouth Ave, Monmouth, OR, 97361-1396. Tel: 503-838-8890. p. 1887

Baker, Susan, Co-Dir, Chiniak Public Library, 43318 Spruce Way, Chiniak, AK, 99615. p. 44

Baker, Susan, Ref Librn, Durham Technical Community College, 1637 E Lawson St, Durham, NC, 27703. Tel: 919-536-7211, Ext 1631. p. 1685

Baker, Susannah, Youth Serv, Lancaster County Library, 313 S White St, Lancaster, SC, 29720. Tel: 803-285-1502. p. 2064

Baker, Tom, Chairperson, Telephone Museum of New Mexico Library, 110 Fourth St NW, Albuquerque, NM, 87102. Tel: 505-238-1952. p. 1462

Baker, Tricia, Libr Operations, Waldorf University, 106 S Sixth St, Forest City, IA, 50436. Tel: 641-585-8110. p. 753

Baker Wilkinson, Maureen, Dir, Warren County Library, Two Shotwell Dr, Belvidere, NJ, 07823. Tel: 908-818-1280. p. 1389

Baker-Jones, Daniel, Ref Librn, Capital University, Law School Library, 303 E Broad St, Columbus, OH, 43215. Tel: 614-236-6539. p. 1772

Bakkalbasi, Nisa, Coll, Columbia University, Butler Library, 535 W 114th St, New York, NY, 10027. Tel: 212-854-7309. p. 1582

Bakken, Melissa, Ad, Libr Dir, Leach Public Library, 417 Second Ave N, Wahpeton, ND, 58075. Tel: 701-642-5732. p. 1741

Bakos, Jenny, Exec Dir, Washington County Free Library, 100 S Potomac St, Hagerstown, MD, 21740. Tel: 301-739-3250. p. 968

Bakos, Judith, Dir, Monmouth Beach Library, 18 Willow Ave, Monmouth Beach, NJ, 07750. Tel: 732-229-1187. p. 1419

Bakos, Stephanie, Libr Dir, Berkeley Heights Public Library, 29 Park Ave, Berkeley Heights, NJ, 07922. Tel: 908-464-9333. p. 1390

Bakovka, Cierra, Dir, Henika District Library, 149 S Main St, Wayland, MI, 49348-1208. Tel: 269-792-2891. p. 1158

Baksh, Fazana, Ch, Altamonte Springs City Library, 281 N Maitland Ave, Altamonte Springs, FL, 32701. Tel: 407-571-8830. p. 383

Bakshi, Raja, Library Contact, Ropers Majeski, 1001 Marshall St, Ste 500, Redwood City, CA, 94063. Tel: 650-364-8200. p. 200

Balacco, Morris, Head, Coll Develop, Fort Lee Public Library, 320 Main St, Fort Lee, NJ, 07024. Tel: 201-592-3615. p. 1403

Balance, Rachel, Librn, Manly Public Library, 127 S Grant, Manly, IA, 50456. Tel: 641-454-2982. p. 767

Balasubramanian, Indra, Commun Libr Mgr, Queens Library, McGoldrick Community Library, 155-06 Roosevelt Ave, Flushing, NY, 11354. Tel: 718-461-1616. p. 1555

Balasubramanian, Ravi, User Services Tech, Sheridan College Library, Hazel McCallion Campus, 4180 Duke of York Blvd, Mississauga, ON, L5B 0G5, CANADA. Tel: 905-845-9430, Ext 2473. p. 2663

Balberchak, Debra, Asst Librn, Belgrade Public Library, 124 Depot Rd, Belgrade, ME, 04917. Tel: 207-495-3508. p. 917

Balcer, Tiffany, Operations Mgr, Pub Relations Mgr, William Jeanes Memorial Library, 4051 Joshua Rd, Lafayette Hill, PA, 19444-1400. Tel: 610-828-0441. p. 1950

Balch, Lesa, Dir, Innovation & Integration, Kitchener Public Library, 85 Queen St N, Kitchener, ON, N2H 2H1, CANADA. Tel: 519-743-0271. p. 2651

Balch, Peggy, Curator, University of Alabama at Birmingham, Reynolds-Finley Historical Library, Lister Hill Library of the Health Sciences, 1700 University Blvd, 3rd Flr, Birmingham, AL, 35233. Tel: 205-934-4475. p. 9

Balcom, Jennifer, Dir, Mid-Michigan Library League, 201 N Mitchell, Ste 302, Cadillac, MI, 49601. Tel: 231-775-3037. p. 2767

Ball-Pyatt, Karen, Librn, Kitchener Public Library, Grace Schmidt Room of Local History, 85 Queen St N, Kitchener, ON, N2H 2H1, CANADA. Tel: 519-743-0271, Ext 252. p. 2652

Balla, Amanda, Adult Serv Supvr, Hubbard Public Library, 436 W Liberty St, Hubbard, OH, 44425. Tel: 330-534-3512. p. 1790

Balla-Boudreau, Naomi, Libr Dir, McBride & District Public Library, 521 Main St, McBride, BC, V0J 2E0, CANADA. Tel: 250-569-2411. p. 2569

Balla-Boudreau, Naomi, Chief Exec Officer, Deep River Public Library, W B Lewis Public Library Bldg, 55 Ridge Rd, Deep River, ON, K0J 1P0, CANADA. Tel: 613-584-4244. p. 2638

Ballain, Craig, Dir, University of Alaska Anchorage, Mat-Su College, 8295 E College Dr, Palmer, AK, 99645. Tel: 907-745-9740. p. 50

Ballam, Anne Marie, Ch, Haverhill Library Association, 67 Court St, Haverhill, NH, 03765. Tel: 603-989-5578. p. 1367

Ballantyne, Nora, Dir, Canada Department of Justice Library, EMB, Rm A-370, 284 Wellington St, Ottawa, ON, K1A 0H8, CANADA. Tel: 613-957-4611. p. 2665

Ballard, Alyssa, Archivist, The Historical Society of Mendocino County Archives, Held-Poage Memorial Home, 603 W Perkins St, Ukiah, CA, 95482-4726. Tel: 707-462-6969. p. 254

Ballard, Angie, Br Librn, Preble County District Library, West Manchester Branch, 212 S High St, West Manchester, OH, 45382. Tel: 937-678-8503. p. 1784

Ballard, Angie, Librn, Preble County District Library, Eldorado Branch, 150 N Main St, Eaton, OH, 45321. Tel: 937-273-4933. p. 1784

Ballard, Arielle, Ch, Hyrum Library, 50 W Main, Hyrum, UT, 84319. Tel: 435-245-6411. p. 2265

Ballard, Darlita, Digital Archivist, Jackson State University, 1325 J R Lynch St, Jackson, MS, 39217. Tel: 601-979-2123, 601-979-4270. p. 1222

Ballard, Denise, Mgr, Brunswick County Library, 109 W Moore St, Southport, NC, 28461. Tel: 910-457-6237. p. 1716

Ballard, Donna, Reader Serv, East Meadow Public Library, 1886 Front St, East Meadow, NY, 11554-1705. Tel: 516-794-2570. p. 1528

Ballard, Jennifer, Dir & Librn, Jackson County Library, 213 Walnut St, Newport, AR, 72112. Tel: 870-523-2952. p. 106

Ballard, Linda, Asst Dir, Chelsea District Library, 221 S Main St, Chelsea, MI, 48118-1267. Tel: 734-475-8732, Ext 202. p. 1090

Ballard, Liz, Br Librn, Kiowa County Library, Haviland Branch, 112 N Main, Haviland, KS, 67059. Tel: 620-862-5350. p. 811

Ballard, Marilyn, Libr Dir, Camas County Public Library, 607 Soldier Rd, Fairfield, ID, 83327. Tel: 208-764-2553. p. 520

Ballard, Marsha, Tech Serv Librn, Scottsdale Community College Library, 9000 E Chaparral Rd, Scottsdale, AZ, 85256. Tel: 480-423-6638. p. 77

Ballard, Paula, Librn, McCain Memorial Public Library, 35717 US Hwy 231, Ashville, AL, 35953. Tel: 205-594-7954. p. 5

Ballard, Randall, Br Librn, Fayette County Public Libraries, Fayetteville Branch, 200 W Maple Ave, Fayetteville, WV, 25840. Tel: 304-574-0070. p. 2411

Ballard-Thrower, Rhea, Exec Dir, Howard University Libraries, 500 Howard Pl NW, Ste 203, Washington, DC, 20059. Tel: 202-806-7236. p. 368

Ballard-Thrower, Rhea, Dean of Libr, Univ Librn, University of Illinois at Chicago, MC 234, 801 S Morgan St, Chicago, IL, 60607. Tel: 312-996-2716. p. 570

Ballenge, Megan, Instrul Serv Librn, Heartland Community College Library, 1500 W Raab Rd, Normal, IL, 61761. Tel: 309-268-8284. p. 625

Ballenger, Norma, Head Librn, El Paso Community College Library, Mission del Paso Campus Library, 10700 Gateway E, Rm C-102, El Paso, TX, 79927. Tel: 915-831-7052. p. 2173

Ballentine, Glenda, Asst Dir, Homer Public Library, 141 W Main St, Homer, MI, 49245. Tel: 517-568-3450. p. 1116

Ballentyne, Robin, Libr Tech, City & County of Honolulu Municipal Reference Center, 558 S King St, Honolulu, HI, 96813-3006. Tel: 808-768-3765. p. 506

Balleste, Roy, Dir, Saint Thomas University Library, Alex A Hanna Law Library, 16401 NW 37th Ave, Miami Gardens, FL, 33054. Tel: 305-623-2330. p. 425

Ballett, Pamela, Dir, Schoolcraft Community Library, 330 N Centre St, Schoolcraft, MI, 49087. Tel: 269-679-5959. p. 1149

Ballhagen, Gayle, Libr Asst, Wheaton Community Library, 901 First Ave N, Wheaton, MN, 56296. Tel: 320-563-8487. p. 1207

Balli, Shayna, City Librn, Irwindale Public Library, 5050 N Irwindale Ave, Irwindale, CA, 91706. Tel: 626-430-2229. p. 153

Ballinger, Jennie, Tech Serv Librn, Fort Smith Public Library, 3201 Rogers Ave, Fort Smith, AR, 72903. Tel: 479-783-0229. p. 96

Ballock, Tracie, Asst Univ Librn, Coll, Metadata Serv, Duquesne University, 600 Forbes Ave, Pittsburgh, PA, 15282. Tel: 412-396-4560. p. 1993

Ballou, Barbara, Ch, Whipple Free Library, 67 Mont Vernon Rd, New Boston, NH, 03070. Tel: 603-487-3391. p. 1375

Ballou, Julie, Exec Dir, Metropolitan Library System in Oklahoma County, 300 Park Ave, Oklahoma City, OK, 73102. Tel: 405-606-3825. p. 1857

Ballou, Ken, Coordr, ILL, Libr Asst, Tech, Whipple Free Library, 67 Mont Vernon Rd, New Boston, NH, 03070. Tel: 603-487-3391. p. 1375

Ballou, Marlene, Coll Develop Librn, Norfolk State University Library, 700 Park Ave, Norfolk, VA, 23504-8010. Tel: 757-823-2428. p. 2335

Balmer, Abby, Asst Dir, Ephrata Public Library, 550 S Reading Rd, Ephrata, PA, 17522. Tel: 717-738-9291. p. 1930

Baloo, Lucinda, Libr Mgr, Apache County Library District, Sanders Public, I-40, Exit 339, 191 N Frontage Rd E, Sanders, AZ, 86512. Tel: 928-688-2677. p. 76

Balough, Sandra A, Dean, Libr Serv, Saint Francis University, 106 Franciscan Way, Loretto, PA, 15940. Tel: 814-472-3153. p. 1956

Baloyra, Bibi, Asst Dir, The Albuquerque Museum, 2000 Mountain Rd NW, Albuquerque, NM, 87104. Tel: 505-243-7255. p. 1460

Balsamello, Rick, Dir, Westville Public Library District, 233 S State St, Westville, IL, 61883. Tel: 217-267-3170. p. 661

Balsamo, Deborah, Project Mgr, Environmental Protection Agency Library, 109 Alexander Dr, Rm C261, Research Triangle Park, NC, 27711. Tel: 919-541-2777. p. 1712

Baltazar, Ashley, Head, Tech Serv, Richton Park Public Library District, 22310 Latonia Lane, Richton Park, IL, 60471. Tel: 708-481-5333. p. 638

Baltich Nelson, Becky, Clinical Librn, Cornell University Library, Samuel J Wood Library & C V Starr Biomedical Information Center, 1300 York Ave, C115, Box 67, New York, NY, 10065-4896. Tel: 646-962-2555. p. 1552

Baltiero, Anthony, Dir, Libr Serv, Blue Ridge Community College Library, 180 W Campus Dr, Flat Rock, NC, 28731. Tel: 828-694-1879. p. 1689

Baltierra, Yesenia, Asst Libr Dir, Placentia Library District, 411 E Chapman Ave, Placentia, CA, 92870. Tel: 714-528-1906, Ext 201. p. 195

Baltzer Kom, Stephanie, Head, Patron Serv, North Dakota State Library, Liberty Memorial Bldg, Dept 250, 604 East Blvd Ave, Bismarck, ND, 58505-0800. Tel: 701-328-4021. p. 1730

Baltzer, Randi, Ref/Tech Serv Librn, Arizona Christian University, One W Firestorm Way, Glendale, AZ, 85306. Tel: 602-489-5300, Ext 3033. p. 61

Bambenek, Jill, Access Serv Librn, Dominican University, 7900 W Division St, River Forest, IL, 60305-1066. Tel: 708-524-6875. p. 639

Bamberg, Christina, Interim Dir, Carthage Free Library, 412 Budd St, Carthage, NY, 13619. Tel: 315-493-2620. p. 1514

Bambrick, Kayla, Adult Programmer, Mkt Coordr, Allegan District Library, 331 Hubbard St, Allegan, MI, 49010. Tel: 269-673-4625. p. 1077

Bamburg, Mona, Libr Dir, Natchitoches Parish Library, 450 Second St, Natchitoches, LA, 71457-4649. Tel: 318-238-9226. p. 899

Bamburg, Mona, Libr Dir, Winn Parish Library, 200 N St John St, Winnfield, LA, 71483-2718. Tel: 318-628-4478. p. 912

Bamio, Monica, Supvr, Miami VA Healthcare System, 1201 NW 16th St, Miami, FL, 33125-1693. Tel: 305-575-3187. p. 424

Ban, Youngwoo, Research Librn, University of Nevada, Las Vegas Univ Libraries, Wiener-Rogers Law Library, William S Boyd School of Law, 4505 S Maryland Pkwy, Las Vegas, NV, 89154. Tel: 702-895-2400. p. 1348

Banas, Ray, Head Librn, Free Library of Philadelphia, Music, 1901 Vine St, Rm 126, Philadelphia, PA, 19103-1116. Tel: 215-686-5316. p. 1979

Banbor, Marianne, Br Mgr, Free Library of Philadelphia, Independence Branch, 18 S Seventh St, Philadelphia, PA, 19106. Tel: 215-685-1633. p. 1978

Banchs, Sarah, Dir, Luverne Public Library, 113 DeWitt St, Luverne, IA, 50560. Tel: 515-882-3436. p. 766

Bancroft, Carol, Dir, Clinton Community Library, 1215 Centre Rd, Rhinebeck, NY, 12572. Tel: 845-266-5530. p. 1626

Bancroft, Deborah, Librn, Grays Harbor College, 1620 Edward P Smith Dr, Aberdeen, WA, 98520. Tel: 360-538-4050. p. 2357

Bancroft, Donna, Librn, Beal University Library, 99 Farm Rd, Bangor, ME, 04401-6831. Tel: 207-307-3900. p. 915

Bancroft, Joan, Asst Dir, Newfoundland Area Public Library, 954 Main St, Newfoundland, PA, 18445. Tel: 570-676-4518. p. 1970

Bandel, Stephanie, Librn, Middle Tennessee State University, Center for Popular Music, John Bragg Media & Entertainment Bldg, Rm 140, 1301 E Main St, Murfreesboro, TN, 37132. Tel: 615-898-5512. p. 2117

Bandelier, Celia, Libr Dir, Roanoke Public Library, 314 N Main St, Ste 120, Roanoke, IN, 46783-1073. Tel: 260-672-2989. p. 716

Bandyopadhyay, Aditi, Res & Instruction Librn, Adelphi University, One South Ave, Garden City, NY, 11530. Tel: 516-877-4166. p. 1536

Banerjee, Susan, Head, AV, Ryerson University Library, 350 Victoria St, 2nd Flr, Toronto, ON, M5B 2K3, CANADA. Tel: 416-979-5000, Ext 4834. p. 2692

Bangilan, Joel, Br Mgr, Pasadena Public Library, Fairmont Branch Library, 4330 Fairmont Pkwy, Pasadena, TX, 77504. Tel: 713-848-5346. p. 2225

Banick, Cheryl R, Dir, Libr Serv, Department of Veterans Affairs, Library Service, 830 Chalkstone Ave, Providence, RI, 02908-4799. Tel: 401-457-3001. p. 2038

Banick, Michael, Dir, Millburn Free Public Library, 200 Glen Ave, Millburn, NJ, 07041. Tel: 973-376-1006, Ext 126. p. 1419

Banister, Jamie, Research Services Asst, Rockhurst University, 1100 Rockhurst Rd, Kansas City, MO, 64110-2561. Tel: 816-501-4142. p. 1257

Banister, Sarah, Head, Children's Servx, Grafton Public Library, 35 Grafton Common, Grafton, MA, 01519. Tel: 508-839-4649, Ext 1107, p. 1021

Banister, Stephen, Libr Dir, Germantown Community Library, 1925 Exeter Rd, Germantown, TN, 38138. Tel: 901-757-7323. p. 2099

Banitt, Nick, Res Sharing Mgr, Minnesota Library Information Network, University of Minnesota-Minitex, Wilson Library, Rm 60, 309 19th Ave S, Minneapolis, MN, 55455. Tel: 612-624-8096, 612-625-0886. p. 2768

Banker, Annette, Libr Dir, Milo Free Public Library, Four Pleasant St, Milo, ME, 04463. Tel: 207-943-2612. p. 932

Bankert, Ryan, Adult Serv Mgr, Interim Dir, Guthrie Memorial Library, Two Library Pl, Hanover, PA, 17331. Tel: 717-632-5183. p. 1939

Bankert, Trenton, Dir, Info Literacy, York College of Pennsylvania, 441 Country Club Rd, York, PA, 17403-3651. Tel: 717-815-1480. p. 2026

Banks, Ann, Librn, Fishers Island Library, 988 Oriental Ave, Fishers Island, NY, 06390. Tel: 631-788-7362. p. 1533

Banks, Brenda, Dir, Arma City Library, 508 E Washington, Arma, KS, 66712. Tel: 620-347-4811. p. 796

Banks, Heather, Head, Circ, Coal City Public Library District, 85 N Garfield St, Coal City, IL, 60416. Tel: 815-634-4552. p. 572

Banks, Justin, Supvry Archivist, National Archives & Records Administration, 2943 SMU Blvd, Dallas, TX, 75205. Tel: 214-346-1557. p. 2167

Banks, Justin, Archivist, Head, Spec Coll, Austin College, 900 N Grand Ave, Ste 6L, Sherman, TX, 75090-4402. Tel: 903-813-2557. p. 2243

Banks, Katie, Info Res Librn, Univ Archivist, Milligan College, 200 Blowers Blvd, Milligan College, TN, 37682. Tel: 423-461-8901. p. 2116

Banks, Lauren, Ch Serv, Nanuet Public Library, 149 Church St, Nanuet, NY, 10954. Tel: 845-623-4281, Ext 112. p. 1575

Banks, Leah, Acq & Cat, Libr Tech, Elizabeth City State University, 1704 Weeksville Rd, Elizabeth City, NC, 27909. Tel: 252-335-3429. p. 1687

Banks, Margaret Downie, PhD, Assoc Dir, University of South Dakota, National Music Museum Library, Corner of Clark & Yale St, 414 E Clark St, Vermillion, SD, 57069-2390. Tel: 605-658-3450. p. 2084

Banks, Melissa, Br Mgr, Ref Serv, Ad, Somerset County Library System of New Jersey, Peapack & Gladstone Public, School St, Peapack, NJ, 07977. Tel: 908-458-8440. p. 1392

Banks, Nalondria, Prog Coordr, Teen Librn, Glenwood-Lynwood Public Library District, 19901 Stony Island Ave, Lynwood, IL, 60411. Tel: 708-758-0090. p. 611

Banks, Susan, Commissioner of Libraries, Deputy Secretary, State Library of Pennsylvania, Forum Bldg, 607 South Dr, Harrisburg, PA, 17120. Tel: 717-787-5968. p. 1941

Bankson, John, Librn, United States Environmental Protection, 6201 Congdon Blvd, Duluth, MN, 55804-2595. Tel: 218-529-5000, 218-529-5085. p. 1173

Bannen, Sally, Ad, Cataloger, Windham Public Library, 217 Windham Center Rd, Windham, ME, 04062. Tel: 207-892-1908. p. 946

Banner, Shirly, Libr Spec, Kripke-Veret Collection of the Jewish Federation, 333 S 132nd St, Omaha, NE, 68154. Tel: 402-334-6462. p. 1329

Banner, Susan, Pub Serv Librn, Sherman Public Library, 421 N Travis St, Sherman, TX, 75090. Tel: 903-892-7240. p. 2243

Bannister, Lisa, Head, Tech Serv, Roanoke Public Libraries, 706 S Jefferson St, Roanoke, VA, 24016-5191. Tel: 540-853-2473. p. 2345

Bannister, Patti, Actg Archivist, Public Archives of Nova Scotia, 6016 University Ave, Halifax, NS, B3H 1W4, CANADA. Tel: 902-424-6076. p. 2621

Bannister, Patti, Lecturer, Dalhousie University, Kenneth C Rowe Management Bldg, Ste 4010, 6100 University Ave, Halifax, NS, B3H 4R2, CANADA. Tel: 902-494-3656. p. 2795

Bannon, Brian, Dir, The New York Public Library - Astor, Lenox & Tilden Foundations, 476 Fifth Ave, (@ 42nd St), New York, NY, 10018. Tel: 212-621-0587. p. 1594

Bannon, Jaye, Chief Exec Officer, Stirling-Rawdon Public Library, 43 W Front St, Stirling, ON, K0K 3E0, CANADA. Tel: 613-395-2837. p. 2681

Bannon, Paula, Head, Children's Servx, Schlow Centre Region Library, 211 S Allen St, State College, PA, 16801-4806. Tel: 814-237-6236. p. 2010

Bannon, Susan H, Assoc Prof, Dir, Auburn University, 4036 Haley Ctr, Auburn, AL, 36849-5221. Tel: 334-844-4460. p. 2781

Bannwart, Susan, Commun Engagement Mgr, La Porte County Public Library, 904 Indiana Ave, La Porte, IN, 46350. Tel: 219-362-6156. p. 700

Banski, Erika, Head, Cat & Metadata Serv, Carleton University Library, 1125 Colonel By Dr, Ottawa, ON, K1S 5B6, CANADA. Tel: 613-520-2600, Ext 4563. p. 2666

Bant, Suzanne, Children's & YA Librn, Henry County Public Library, 172 Eminence Terrace, Eminence, KY, 40019-1146. Tel: 502-845-5682. p. 854

Banta, Mykal, Exec Dir, Delray Beach Public Library, 100 W Atlantic Ave, Delray Beach, FL, 33444. Tel: 561-266-0198. p. 394

Banta, Rita, Asst Dir, W A Rankin Memorial Library, 502 Indiana St, Neodesha, KS, 66757. Tel: 620-325-3275. p. 826

Banta, Ryer, Librn, Centralia College, 600 Centralia College Blvd, Centralia, WA, 98531. Tel: 360-623-8121. p. 2361

Banz, Clint, Libr Dir, Lancaster Bible College, Teague Learning Commons, 901 Eden Rd, Lancaster, PA, 17601-5036. Tel: 717-560-8250. p. 1951

Banzhaf, Troy, Library Contact, US National Park Service, 15930 Hyw 62, Garfield, AR, 72732. Tel: 479-451-8122. p. 96

Bao, Bryant, Commun Librn, Santa Clara County Library District, Cupertino Library, 10800 Torre Ave, Cupertino, CA, 95014. Tel: 408-446-1677. p. 127

Bapiran, Loretto, Customer Serv Supvr, Parsippany-Troy Hills Free Public Library, 449 Halsey Rd, Parsippany, NJ, 07054. Tel: 973-887-5150. p. 1433

Baptiste, Melissa, Asst Librn, Chesterfield Public Library, 524 Rte 63, Chesterfield, NH, 03443-0158. Tel: 603-363-4621. p. 1357

Baptiste-Joseph, Judy, Access Serv Librn, Coll Mgr, Brooklyn Law School Library, 250 Joralemon St, Brooklyn, NY, 11201. Tel: 718-780-0670. p. 1501

Bara, Adriana, PhD, Exec Dir, Canadian Centre for Ecumenism Library, 2715, Chemin de la Cote Sainte-Catherine, Montreal, QC, H3T 1B6, CANADA. Tel: 514-937-9176. p. 2721

Bara, Sgefanie, Libr Dir, Ellis Memorial Library, 700 W Ave A, Port Aransas, TX, 78373. Tel: 361-749-4116. p. 2228

Barahona, Philip, Mgr, Res & Competitive Intelligence, Weil, Gotshal & Manges LLP, 767 Fifth Ave, New York, NY, 10153. Tel: 212-310-8444. p. 1603

Baran, Peter, Chief Tech Officer, Stradling, Yocca, Carlson & Rauth, 660 Newport Ctr, Ste 1600, Newport Beach, CA, 92660. Tel: 949-725-4000. p. 183

Baranowski, Richard, Hist Coll Librn, Way Public Library, 101 E Indiana Ave, Perrysburg, OH, 43551. Tel: 419-874-3135, Ext 110. p. 1815

Barash, Melanee, Library Contact, Santa Cruz City-County Library System, Capitola Branch, 2005 Wharf Rd, Capitola, CA, 95010-2002. Tel: 831-427-7706, Ext 7672. p. 242

Barash, Melanie, Interim Br Mgr, Santa Cruz City-County Library System, Felton Branch, 6299 Gushee St, Felton, CA, 95018-9140. Tel: 831-427-7700, Ext 5800. p. 243

Baratko, David, Asst Dir, Media Serv Tech, Connecticut College, 270 Mohegan Ave, New London, CT, 06320-4196. Tel: 860-439-2655. p. 328

Baratta, Paula, Br Mgr, Newark Public Library, North End, 722 Summer Ave, Newark, NJ, 07104. Tel: 973-733-7766. p. 1427

Barb, Trisha, Librn, Pocahontas County Free Libraries, Linwood Community Library at Snowshoe, 72 Snowshoe Dr, Slatyfork, WV, 26291. Tel: 304-572-2665. p. 2408

Barbanell, Robert, Br Serv Mgr, Elizabeth Public Library, Elizabeth Port, 102-110 Third St, Elizabeth, NJ, 07206-1717. Tel: 908-353-4820. p. 1401

Barbanell, Robert, Br Serv Mgr, Elizabeth Public Library, Elmora, 740 W Grand St, Elizabeth, NJ, 07202. Tel: 908-353-4820. p. 1401

Barbanell, Robert, Br Serv Mgr, Elizabeth Public Library, Lacorte, 418-424 Palmer St, Elizabeth, NJ, 07202. Tel: 908-353-4820. p. 1401

Barbara, Miles, Br Librn, Sweetwater County Library System, Bairoil Branch Library, 101 Blue Bell St, Bairoil, WY, 82322. Tel: 307-328-0239. p. 2495

Barbato, Kellie, Access Serv Librn, Palm Beach Atlantic University, 300 Pembroke Pl, West Palm Beach, FL, 33401-6503. Tel: 561-803-2210. p. 453

Barbeau, Dyan, Director of Library & Academic Support, Sacred Heart Seminary & School of Theology, 7335 Lovers Lane Rd, Franklin, WI, 53132. Tel: 414-858-4995. p. 2436

Barbeau, Dyan, Dir, Cardinal Stritch University Library, 6801 N Yates Rd, Milwaukee, WI, 53217. Tel: 414-410-4263. p. 2458

Barbel, Mara, Ch Serv, Outreach Librn, Shorewood-Troy Public Library District, 650 Deerwood Dr, Shorewood, IL, 60404. Tel: 815-725-1715. p. 647

Barber, Andrew, Asst Circ Librn, Prescott College Library, 220 Grove Ave, Prescott, AZ, 86301. Tel: 928-350-1300. p. 73

Barber, Anne, Dir, Morris Public Library, 102 E Sixth St, Morris, MN, 56267-1211. Tel: 320-589-1634. p. 1189

Barber, Chris, Libr Mgr, Tech Serv, Lee County Library System, 2201 Second St, Ste 400, Fort Myers, FL, 33901. Tel: 239-533-4800. p. 403

Barber, Chris, Libr Mgr, Tech Serv, Lee County Library System, Library Processing, 881 Gunnery Rd N, Ste 2, Lehigh Acres, FL, 33971-1246. Tel: 239-533-4170. p. 403

Barber, Jeff, Chief Exec Officer, Libr Dir, Regina Public Library, Library Directors Office, 2311 12th Ave, Regina, SK, S4P 0N3, CANADA. Tel: 306-777-6099. p. 2747

Barber, Judith, Head, Tech Serv, East Carolina University, Music Library, A J Fletcher Music Ctr, Rm A110, Greenville, NC, 27858. Tel: 252-328-1240. p. 1694

Barber, Katryna, Youth Serv Spec, La Conner Regional Library, 520 Morris St, La Conner, WA, 98257. Tel: 360-466-3352. p. 2368

Barber, Kyle, Mgr, Ad Serv, Nashville Public Library, 615 Church St, Nashville, TN, 37219-2314. Tel: 615-862-5839. p. 2119

Barber, Lesley, Coordr, Coll Mgt, DeKalb County Public Library, Darro C Willey Administrative Offices, 3560 Kensington Rd, Decatur, GA, 30032. Tel: 404-508-7190. p. 475

Barber, Maryke, Info Literacy & Outreach Librn, Hollins University, 7950 E Campus Dr, Roanoke, VA, 24020. Tel: 540-362-6592. p. 2345

Barber, Melissa, Br Mgr, Lubbock Public Library, Patterson Branch, 1836 Parkway Dr, Lubbock, TX, 79403. Tel: 806-767-3300. p. 2213

Barber, Porter, Librn, Orange County Community College Library, Newburgh Campus, One Washington Ctr, Newburgh, NY, 12550. Tel: 845-341-9049. p. 1571

Barber, Traci, Genealogy Serv, Okmulgee Public Library, 218 S Okmulgee Ave, Okmulgee, OK, 74447. Tel: 918-756-1448. p. 1860

Barbera, Chris, Ms, Libr Dir, Hubbardston Public Library, Seven Main St, Unit 8, Hubbardston, MA, 01452. Tel: 978-928-4775. p. 1025

Barberena, Corine, Sr Library Services Mgr; Community & Colls, Irving Public Library, 801 W Irving Blvd, Irving, TX, 75015. Tel: 972-721-2439. p. 2202

Barberi, Debra, Head, Emerging Technologies & Digital Content, Russell Library, 123 Broad St, Middletown, CT, 06457. Tel: 860-347-2528. p. 322

Barbieri, AnnMarie, Library Contact, Adelphi University, 55 Kennedy Dr, Hauppauge, NY, 11788-4001. Tel: 516-237-8610. p. 1544

Barbknecht, Kaley, ILL, Spoon River College Library, 23235 N County Hwy 22, Canton, IL, 61520. Tel: 309-649-6603. p. 548

Barbone, Patricia, Dir, Libr Serv, Hughes, Hubbard & Reed LLP Library, 1775 I St NW, Ste 600, Washington, DC, 20006-2401. Tel: 202-721-4600. p. 369

Barbone, Patricia E, Dir, Libr Serv, Hughes, Hubbard & Reed Library, One Battery Park Plaza, 16th Flr, New York, NY, 10004. Tel: 212-837-6594. p. 1588

Barbosa, Renaldo, Circ Supvr, The Master's Seminary Library, 13248 Roscoe Blvd, Sun Valley, CA, 91352. Tel: 818-909-5545. p. 251

Barbosa-Jerez, Mary, Head, Coll Develop, Saint Olaf College, Rolvaag Memorial Library, Hustad Science Library, Halvorson Music Library, 1510 Saint Olaf Ave, Northfield, MN, 55057-1097. Tel: 507-786-3634. p. 1191

Barbounis, Anna, Circ, Allentown Public Library, 1210 Hamilton St, Allentown, PA, 18102. Tel: 610-820-2400. p. 1904

Barbour, Brittney, Br Mgr, Forsyth County Public Library, Rural Hall Branch, 7125 Broad St, Rural Hall, NC, 27045. Tel: 336-703-2970. p. 1725

Barbour, Denise, Br Mgr, Atlanta-Fulton Public Library System, Martin Luther King Jr Branch, 409 John Wesley Dobbs Ave, Atlanta, GA, 30312-1342. Tel: 404-730-1185. p. 461

Barbour, Denise, Ch, Atlanta-Fulton Public Library System, Mechanicsville Branch, 400 Formwalt St SW, Atlanta, GA, 30312. Tel: 404-730-4779. p. 461

Barbour, Denise, Dir, Libr Serv, Southern Crescent Technical College, 501 Varsity Rd, Griffin, GA, 30223. Tel: 770-228-7348, 770-412-4755. p. 481

Barbour, Denise, Dir, Libr Serv, Southern Crescent Technical College, Bldg B, 1533 Hwy 19 S, Thomaston, GA, 30286. Tel: 706-646-6173. p. 498

Barbour, Katie, Bus Mgr, Public Library of Johnston County & Smithfield, 305 E Market St, Smithfield, NC, 27577-3919. Tel: 919-934-8146. p. 1716

Barbour, Maggie, Libr Mgr, New York Public Library - Astor, Lenox & Tilden Foundations, 67th Street Branch, 328 E 67th St, (Near First Ave), New York, NY, 10021-6296. Tel: 212-734-1717. p. 1597

Barbus, Colleen, Librn & Archivist, American Library Association Library & Information Resource Center, 225 N Michigan Ave, Ste 1300, Chicago, IL, 60601. Tel: 312-280-2153. p. 554

Barbush, Alexandra, Librn, Senate Library of Pennsylvania, Main Capitol Bldg, Rm 157, Harrisburg, PA, 17120-0030. Tel: 717-787-6120. p. 1941

Barcal, Rose, Libr Dir, La Vista Public Library, 9110 Giles Rd, La Vista, NE, 68128. Tel: 402-537-3900. p. 1320

Barcenas, Luis, Circ Serv, United States Air Force, 628 FSS/FSDL, 106 W McCaw St, Bldg 215, Charleston AFB, SC, 29404. Tel: 843-963-3320. p. 2051

Barckhaus, Wendy, Dir & Librn, Franklin Free Library, 334 Main St, Franklin, NY, 13775. Tel: 607-829-2941. p. 1534

Barclay, Amy, Br Mgr, Johnson County Library, Corinth, 8100 Mission Rd, Prairie Village, KS, 66208. p. 830

Barclay, Bella, Commun Libr Mgr, Queens Library, Baisley Park Community Library, 117-11 Sutphin Blvd, Jamaica, NY, 11436. Tel: 718-529-1590. p. 1554

Barclay, Donald, Dep Univ Librn, University of California, Merced Library, 5200 N Lake Rd, Merced, CA, 95343. Tel: 209-201-9724. p. 176

Bard, Brooks F, Vols Coordr, Everett C Benton Library, 75 Oakley Rd, Belmont, MA, 02478-0125. Tel: 617-484-0988. p. 988

Bard, Corey, Mr, Dir, Libr Serv, Bloomfield Public Library, 333 S First St, Bloomfield, NM, 87413-3559. Tel: 505-632-8315. p. 1464

Bard, Jan, Digital Serv Librn, Hutchinson Community College, 1300 N Plum St, Hutchinson, KS, 67501. Tel: 620-665-3547. p. 814

Bardascino, Katie, Head, Youth Serv, Stoneham Public Library, 431 Main St, Stoneham, MA, 02180. Tel: 781-438-1325. p. 1058

Barden, Daniel, Dir, Tech Serv, Cuyahoga County Public Library, 2111 Snow Rd, Parma, OH, 44134-2728. Tel: 216-398-1800. p. 1813

Barden, Kathryn, Head, Pub Serv, Westminster College, Reeves Memorial Library, 501 Westminster Ave, Fulton, MO, 65251-1299. Tel: 573-592-5245. p. 1246

Bardi, Gina, Ref Librn, San Francisco Maritime Library, Bldg E, 2nd Flr, Two Marina Blvd, San Francisco, CA, 94123. Tel: 415-561-7030. p. 227

Bardin, Connie, Asst Librn, Madill City County Library, 500 W Overton St, Madill, OK, 73446. Tel: 580-795-2749. p. 1852

Bardon, Jan, Mkt Mgr, Saint Charles City-County Library District, 77 Boone Hills Dr, Saint Peters, MO, 63376. Tel: 636-441-2300. p. 1277

Bardyn, Tania, Assoc Dean, Univ Libr, University of Washington Libraries, Box 352900, Seattle, WA, 98195-2900. Tel: 206-685-3299. p. 2381

Bardyn, Tania P, Dir, University of Washington Libraries, Health Sciences Library, T-334 Health Sciences Bldg, 1959 NE Pacific St, Box 357155, Seattle, WA, 98195-7155. Tel: 206-543-0427. p. 2382

Bare, Katherine, Ref Librn, Venable LLP Library, 750 E Pratt St, 9th Flr, Baltimore, MD, 21202. Tel: 410-244-7502. p. 958

Barefield, Lisa, Head, Teen Serv, Wheaton Public Library, 225 N Cross St, Wheaton, IL, 60187-5376. Tel: 630-868-7534. p. 662

Barefoot, Derrick, Dir, Mary Duncan Public Library, 100 W Main St, Benson, NC, 27504. Tel: 919-894-3724. p. 1674

Barefoot, Gary, Curator, University of Mount Olive, 646 James B Hunt Dr, Mount Olive, NC, 28365-1699. Tel: 919-658-7869, Ext 1416. p. 1705

Barefoot, Ruth, Libr Dir, Anacortes Public Library, 1220 Tenth St, Anacortes, WA, 98221-1988. Tel: 360-293-1910. p. 2357

Bareford, Lee, Head, Learning Commons, Georgia Southern University, 11935 Abercorn St, Savannah, GA, 31419. Tel: 912-344-3027. p. 495

Bares, Joan, Ref (Info Servs), United States Army, Stimson Library, Medical Department Ctr & School, Bldg 2840, Ste 106, 3630 Stanley Rd, Fort Sam Houston, TX, 78234-7697. Tel: 210-221-6900. p. 2178

Barfield, Holly, Asst Dir, Info Tech, Forsyth County Public Library, 585 Dahlonega St, Cumming, GA, 30040-2109. Tel: 770-781-9840. p. 473

Barfield, Laura, Syst, Trident Technical College, Main Campus Learning Resources Center, LR-M, PO Box 118067, Charleston, SC, 29423-8067. Tel: 843-574-6089. p. 2051

Barg, Jennifer, Chief Librn, Vanderhoof Public Library, 230 Stewart St E, Vanderhoof, BC, V0J 3A0, CANADA. Tel: 250-567-4060. p. 2582

Barger, Barb, Youth Serv Librn, Frankenmuth James E Wickson District Library, 359 S Franklin St, Frankenmuth, MI, 48734. Tel: 989-652-8323. p. 1107

Barger, Matthew, Circ Asst, Per Asst, Gardner-Webb University, 110 S Main St, Boiling Springs, NC, 28017. Tel: 704-406-4311. p. 1674

Bargmann, Lesa, Asst Librn, Bancroft Public Library, 103 E Poplar St, Bancroft, NE, 68004. Tel: 402-648-3350. p. 1306

Barham, Cecilia, Dir, Libr Serv, North Richland Hills Public Library, 9015 Grand Ave, North Richland Hills, TX, 76180. Tel: 817-427-6800. p. 2223

Barham, Winston K, Music Librn, University of Virginia, Music, Old Cabell Hall, Charlottesville, VA, 22904. Tel: 434-924-7041. p. 2310

Baril, Chloé, Div Chief, Programming Serv, Bibliotheques de Montreal, Pavillon Prince, 801 rue Brennan, 5e etage, Montreal, QC, H3C 0G4, CANADA. Tel: 514-872-1609. p. 2718

Baril, Kathleen, Dir, Ohio Northern University, 525 S Main St, Ada, OH, 45810. Tel: 419-772-2188. p. 1743

Baril, Rachel, Sr Libr Tech, College of Central Florida Learning Resources Center, 3800 S Lecanto Hwy, C2-202, Lecanto, FL, 34461. Tel: 352-249-1205. p. 418

Barillaro, Jake, Libr Dir, Mohave County Library District, 3269 N Burbank St, Kingman, AZ, 86402. p. 64

Bariola, Kristy, Librn, Mississippi Delta Community College, Greenwood Library, 207 W Park Ave, Greenwood, MS, 38930. Tel: 662-453-7377. p. 1227

Bariola, Kristy Aust, Dir, Libr Serv, Mississippi Delta Community College, 414 Hwy 3 S, Moorhead, MS, 38761. Tel: 662-246-6378. p. 1227

Barkdull, Cody, Asst Dir, Bandon Public Library, 1204 11th St SW, Bandon, OR, 97411. Tel: 541-347-3221. p. 1873

Barkema, Jodi, ILL, Libr Tech, Waldorf University, 106 S Sixth St, Forest City, IA, 50436. Tel: 641-585-8110. p. 753

Barker, Amanda, Br Mgr, Cooperstown Public Library, 182 N Main St, Cooperstown, PA, 16317. Tel: 814-374-4605. p. 1924

Barker, Amy, Interim Dir, Instrul Serv, Res, Kennesaw State University Library System, 385 Cobb Ave NW, MD 1701, Kennesaw, GA, 30144. Tel: 470-578-2861. p. 483

Barker, Anne, Humanities Librn, University of Missouri-Columbia, Elmer Ellis Library, 104 Ellis Library, Columbia, MO, 65201-5149. Tel: 573-882-6324. p. 1243

Barker, Apple, Br Mgr, Mesa County Public Library District, DeBeque Joint Branch, 730 Minter Ave, DeBeque, CO, 81630. Tel: 970-283-8625. p. 284

Barker, Bill, Archivist, Mariners' Museum & Park Library, 100 Museum Dr, Newport News, VA, 23606-3759. Tel: 757-591-7782. p. 2333

Barker, Emma, Pub Serv, The Blue Mountains Public Library, 173 Bruce St S, Thornbury, ON, N0H 2P0, CANADA. Tel: 519-599-3681. p. 2684

Barker, John, Archivist, Hawaiian Mission Children's Society Library, 553 S King St, Honolulu, HI, 96813. Tel: 808-531-0481. p. 512

Barker, Leo, Fr, Librn, Westminster Abbey Library, Seminary of Christ The King, 34224 Dewdney Trunk Rd, Mission, BC, V2V 6Y5, CANADA. Tel: 604-826-8975. p. 2570

Barker, Martha, Tech Serv Librn, Indiana University Kokomo Library, 2300 S Washington St, Kokomo, IN, 46902. Tel: 765-455-9265. p. 699

Barker, Mary, Dir, Coffey County Library, Lebo Branch, 327 S Ogden St, Lebo, KS, 66856-9306. Tel: 620-256-6452. p. 800

Barker, Mary, Dir, Pentwater Township Library, 402 E Park, Pentwater, MI, 49449. Tel: 231-869-8581. p. 1140

Barker, Melissa, Librn, Murphy Public Library, Nine Blumenthal St, Murphy, NC, 28906. Tel: 828-837-2417. p. 1705

Barnes, Sharon, Tech Consult, South Central Kansas Library System, 321 N Main St, South Hutchinson, KS, 67505. Tel: 620-663-3211. p. 837

Barnes, Sharon, Asst Dir, Watonga Public Library, 301 N Prouty, Watonga, OK, 73772. Tel: 580-623-7748. p. 1868

Barnes, Stephanie, Libr Dir, La Grange College, 601 Broad St, LaGrange, GA, 30240-2999. Tel: 706-880-8312. p. 484

Barnes, Tamika, Assoc Dean, Georgia State University, Alpharetta Campus, 3705 Brookside Pkwy, Alpharetta, GA, 30022. Tel: 770-274-5084. p. 464

Barnes, Tamika, Assoc Dean, Georgia State University, Clarkston Campus, 555 N Indian Creek Dr, Clarkston, GA, 30021. Tel: 770-274-5084. p. 464

Barnes, Tamika, Assoc Dean, Georgia State University, Decatur Campus, 3251 Panthersville Rd, Decatur, GA, 30034. Tel: 770-274-5084. p. 464

Barnes, Tamika, Assoc Dean, Georgia State University, Dunwoody Campus, 2101 Womack Rd, Dunwoody, GA, 30338. Tel: 770-274-5084. p. 464

Barnes, Tamika, Assoc Dean, Georgia State University, Newton Campus, 239 Cedar Lane, Newton, GA, 30014. Tel: 770-274-5084. p. 464

Barnes, Tamika, Assoc Dean, Library Services, Georgia State University, 100 Decatur St SE, Atlanta, GA, 30303-3202. Tel: 770-274-5084. p. 464

Barnes, Thelma, Ser, Cincinnati State Technical & Community College, 3520 Central Pkwy, Rm 170, Cincinnati, OH, 45223-2690. Tel: 513-569-1610. p. 1760

Barnes, Vivian, Librn, Elbert County Public Library, Bowman Branch, 21 Prince Ave, Bowman, GA, 30624. Tel: 706-245-0705. p. 478

Barnes, Wayne, Soc Sci Librn, University of Missouri-Columbia, Elmer Ellis Library, 104 Ellis Library, Columbia, MO, 65201-5149. Tel: 573-882-3310. p. 1243

Barnes, Windie, Tech Serv Supvr, Sandhills Community College, 3395 Airport Rd, Pinehurst, NC, 28374. Tel: 910-695-3818. p. 1707

Barnes-Long, Judith, Coordr, Access Serv, University of Massachusetts Lowell Library, Lydon Library, 84 University Ave, Lowell, MA, 01854-2896. Tel: 978-934-3552. p. 1030

Barnes-Sanchez, Kevyn, Ms, Mgr, Libr Serv, University of Texas at Austin, 3925 W Braker Lane, Ste 4.909, Austin, TX, 78759. Tel: 512-232-3130. p. 2141

Barnett, Andrew, Dir, McMillan Memorial Library, 490 E Grand Ave, Wisconsin Rapids, WI, 54494-4898. Tel: 715-422-5136. p. 2489

Barnett, Caroline, Head Librn, First Regional Library, M R Davis Public Library, 8554 Northwest Dr, Southaven, MS, 38671. Tel: 662-342-0102. p. 1219

Barnett, Catherine, Outreach & Programming Supvr, Chillicothe Public Library District, 430 N Bradley Ave, Chillicothe, IL, 61523-1920. Tel: 309-274-2719. p. 571

Barnett, Dawson, Asst Librn, Southeast Kentucky Area Health Education Center, 100 Medical Center Dr, Hazard, KY, 41701-9429. Tel: 606-439-6796. p. 859

Barnett, Debra, Tech Serv, Mayland Community College, 200 Mayland Dr, Spruce Pine, NC, 28777. Tel: 828-766-1211. p. 1717

Barnett, Kaya, Youth Serv Coordr, Cardington-Lincoln Public Library, 128 E Main St, Cardington, OH, 43315. Tel: 419-864-8181. p. 1756

Barnett, Kayci, Br Mgr, Pueblo City-County Library District, Tom L & Anna Marie Giodone Library, 24655 US Hwy 50 E, Pueblo, CO, 81006. p. 293

Barnett, Kristen, Librn, Mississippi Gulf Coast Community College, 2226 Switzer Rd, Gulfport, MS, 39507. Tel: 228-896-2536. p. 1218

Barnett, Linda, Head, Pub Serv, Memorial University of Newfoundland, Health Sciences Library, Memorial University, 300 Prince Philip Dr, St. John's, NL, A1B 3V6, CANADA. Tel: 709-777-6676. p. 2610

Barnett, Lindsay, Coll Develop Librn, Yale University Library, Harvey Cushing/John Hay Whitney Medical Library, Sterling Hall of Medicine, 333 Cedar St, New Haven, CT, 06510. Tel: 203-785-2883. p. 327

Barnett, Lynette, Circ Mgr, Kendallville Public Library, 221 S Park Ave, Kendallville, IN, 46755-2248. Tel: 260-343-2010. p. 698

Barnett, Marie M, Librn, Grand Lodge AF&AM of Virginia Library, Museum & Historical Foundation, 4115 Nine Mile Rd, Richmond, VA, 23223-4926. Tel: 804-222-3110, Ext 220. p. 2340

Barnett, Mertis, Br Mgr, Dillon County Library, Lake View Branch, 207 S Main St, Lake View, SC, 29563. Tel: 843-759-2692. p. 2058

Barnett, Pat, Asst Dir, Mary H Weir Public Library, 3442 Main St, Weirton, WV, 26062. Tel: 304-797-8510. p. 2416

Barnett, Philip, Div Chief, City College of the City University of New York, Science-Engineering, Marshak Bldg, Rm J29, 160 Convent Ave, New York, NY, 10031. Tel: 212-650-8243. p. 1582

Barnett, Roberta, Dir, Lane County Library, Healy Extension, 2009 W Hwy 4, Healy, KS, 67850-5088. Tel: 620-398-2267. p. 804

Barnett, Sharon, Libr Tech, Rutherford B Hayes Presidential Library & Museums, Spiegel Grove, Fremont, OH, 43420-2796. Tel: 419-332-2081. p. 1786

Barnett, Sheila, Librn, Fort Worth Library, Diamond Hill/Jarvis Branch, 1300 NE 35th St, Fort Worth, TX, 76106. Tel: 817-392-6010. p. 2179

Barnett, Sheila, Librn, Fort Worth Library, Northside, 601 Park St, Fort Worth, TX, 76106. Tel: 817-392-6641. p. 2179

Barnett, Sheila, Librn, Fort Worth Library, Northwest, 6228 Crystal Lake Dr, Fort Worth, TX, 76179. Tel: 817-392-5420. p. 2179

Barnett, Sheila, Librn, Fort Worth Library, Riverside, 2913 Yucca Ave, Fort Worth, TX, 76111. Tel: 817-392-5560. p. 2179

Barnett, Teri, Newspaper Librn, Abraham Lincoln Presidential Library, 112 N Sixth St, Springfield, IL, 62701. Tel: 217-558-0126. p. 649

Barnett-Ellis, Paula, Health Sci Librn, Jacksonville State University Library, 700 Pelham Rd N, Jacksonville, AL, 36265. Tel: 256-782-5758. p. 23

Barney, Emily, Digital Education & Internal Resource Librn, Illinois Institute of Technology, Chicago-Kent College of Law Library, 565 W Adams St, 9th Flr, Chicago, IL, 60661. Tel: 312-906-5630. p. 562

Barney, Jeremy, Spec Coll & Digital Projects Metadata Librn, Hope College, Van Wylen Library, 53 Graves Pl, Holland, MI, 49422. Tel: 616-395-7790. p. 1115

Barney, Maria, Asst Librn, Hispanic Society of America Library, 613 W 155th St, New York, NY, 10032. Tel: 212-926-2234, Ext 229. p. 1587

Barney, Maureen, Graduate Writing Specialist, Info Literacy Librn, Linfield University, 900 SE Baker St, McMinnville, OR, 97128. Tel: 503-883-2573. p. 1885

Barney, Ruth, Libr Assoc, Napa County Library, Yountville Branch, 6516 Washington St, Yountville, CA, 94599-1271. Tel: 707-944-1888. p. 182

Barnfield, Ann, Circ, Wheaton Public Library, 225 N Cross St, Wheaton, IL, 60187-5376. Tel: 630-868-7512. p. 662

Barnhardt, Jeff, Circ Mgr, Warner Pacific University, 2219 SE 68th Ave, Portland, OR, 97215. Tel: 503-517-1037. p. 1894

Barnhart, Amanda, Br Mgr, Kansas City Public Library, North-East, 6000 Wilson Rd, Kansas City, MO, 64123. Tel: 816-701-3589. p. 1255

Barnhart, Amber, Law Libr Dir/Law Librn, Akron Law Library, 209 S High St, 4th Flr, Akron, OH, 44308-1675. Tel: 330-643-2804. p. 1743

Barnhart, Andrew, Libr Supvr, San Francisco Conservatory of Music Library, 50 Oak St, San Francisco, CA, 94102. Tel: 415-503-6213, 415-503-6256. p. 227

Barnhart, Anne, Head, Assessment & Outreach, University of West Georgia, 1601 Maple St, Carrollton, GA, 30118. Tel: 678-839-6495. p. 469

Barnhart, Fred, Dean, Northern Illinois University Libraries, 217 Normal Rd, DeKalb, IL, 60115-2828. Tel: 815-753-9801. p. 577

Barnhart, Marcella, Dir, University of Pennsylvania Libraries, Lippincott-Wharton School, 3420 Walnut St, Philadelphia, PA, 19104-3436. Tel: 215-898-8755. p. 1988

Barnhart, Teresa, Dir, Wayne Public Library, 137 E Main St, Wayne, OH, 43466. Tel: 419-288-2708. p. 1829

Barnhill, Ashley, Br Mgr, Public Library of Cincinnati & Hamilton County, College Hill, 1400 W North Bend Rd, Cincinnati, OH, 45224. Tel: 513-369-6036. p. 1762

Barnhill, Ashley, Br Mgr, Public Library of Cincinnati & Hamilton County, Walnut Hills, 2533 Kemper Lane, Cincinnati, OH, 45206. Tel: 513-369-6053. p. 1763

Barnickel, Christopher, Dir, San Luis Obispo County Library, 995 Palm St, San Luis Obispo, CA, 93403. Tel: 805-781-5785. p. 233

Barnicle, Susan, AV, Morse Institute Library, 14 E Central St, Natick, MA, 01760. Tel: 508-647-6522. p. 1037

Barniskis, Shannon, Dr, Asst Prof, University of Kentucky, 320 Little Library Bldg, Lexington, KY, 40506-0224. Tel: 859-257-8876. p. 2785

Barnitz, LaTrobe Edward, Mr, Dir, Foxburg Free Library, 31 Main St, Foxburg, PA, 16036. Tel: 724-659-3431. p. 1934

Barnthouse, Erin, Coll Develop, Tech Serv, College of the Canyons Library, 26455 Rockwell Canyon Rd, Santa Clarita, CA, 91355-1899. Tel: 661-362-3854. p. 242

Barnum, Susan, Br Mgr, El Paso Public Library, Westside, 125 Belvidere St, El Paso, TX, 79912. Tel: 915-212-0445. p. 2174

Barnum, Terry, Br Mgr, Public Library of Cincinnati & Hamilton County, Madisonville, 4830 Whetsel Ave, Cincinnati, OH, 45227. Tel: 513-369-6029. p. 1762

Barnwell, Jane, Grants Mgr, University of Florida Libraries, 1545 W University Ave, Gainesville, FL, 32611-7000. Tel: 352-273-2782. p. 407

Baroff, Deborah, Curator, Museum of the Great Plains, 601 NW Ferris Ave, Lawton, OK, 73507. Tel: 580-581-3460. p. 1852

Baron, Courtney, Dir, University of Louisville Libraries, Margaret Bridwell Art Library, 2301 S Third St, Louisville, KY, 40208. Tel: 502-852-6741. p. 867

Baron, Sara, Dr, Univ Librn, Duquesne University, 600 Forbes Ave, Pittsburgh, PA, 15282. Tel: 412-396-6130. p. 1993

Baron, Shari, Head Bldg Serv, Sacred Heart University, 5151 Park Ave, Fairfield, CT, 06825-1000. Tel: 203-371-7702. p. 312

Barone, Deborah, Acq, United States Air Force, Air University - Muir S Fairchild Research Information Center, 600 Chennault Circle, Maxwell AFB, AL, 36112-6010. Tel: 334-953-2410. p. 25

Baros, Debbie, Libr Asst, Stanfield Public Library, 180 W Coe Ave, Stanfield, OR, 97875. Tel: 541-449-1254. p. 1899

Baroudi, Tonya, Dir, Libr Serv, Prince George's County, 14735 Main St, Rm M1400, Upper Marlboro, MD, 20772. Tel: 301-952-3438. p. 980

Barowich, Christy, Br Mgr, Carnegie Library of McKeesport, Duquesne Branch, 300 Kennedy Ave, Duquesne, PA, 15110. Tel: 412-469-9143. p. 1959

Baroza, Baron, Br Mgr, Hawaii State Public Library System, 402 Kapahulu Ave, Honolulu, HI, 96815. Tel: 808-733-8444. p. 511

Baroza, Hilda, Circ Mgr, John A Burns School of Medicine, 651 Ilalo St, MEB 101, Honolulu, HI, 96813. Tel: 808-692-0816. p. 512

Barr, Angela, Ref & Digital Librn, Georgetown University, Dahlgren Memorial Library, Preclinical Science Bldg GM-7, 3900 Reservoir Rd NW, Washington, DC, 20007. Tel: 202-687-1535. p. 368

Barr, Belinda, Asst Dean, Miami University Libraries, 151 S Campus Ave, Oxford, OH, 45056. Tel: 513-529-7096. p. 1811

Barr, Elissa, Cataloger, Researcher, Hopkinton Historical Society, 300 Main St, Hopkinton, NH, 03229. Tel: 603-746-3825. p. 1368

Barr, Jennifer, Programmer, West Perth Public Library, 105 Saint Andrew St, Mitchell, ON, N0K 1N0, CANADA. Tel: 519-348-9234. p. 2659

Barr, Katherine, Libr Mgr, Wake County Public Library System, Leesville Community Library, 5105 Country Trail, Raleigh, NC, 27613. Tel: 919-571-6661. p. 1711

Barr, Linda, Head Librn, Tech Serv & Automation, Austin Community College, 5930 Middle Fiskville Rd, Austin, TX, 78752. Tel: 512-223-3461. p. 2137

Barr, Robb, Br Mgr, Phoenix Public Library, South Mountain Community Library, 7050 S 24th St, Phoenix, AZ, 85042. Tel: 602-243-8187. p. 72

Barr, Tabitha, Tech Serv Librn, Ursuline College, 2550 Lander Rd, Pepper Pike, OH, 44124-4398. Tel: 440-449-4202. p. 1815

Barr-Walker, Jill, Clinical Librn, Zuckerberg San Francisco General Hospital, 1001 Potrero Ave, Bldg 30, San Francisco, CA, 94110. Tel: 628-206-6638. p. 230

Barrasso, Beata P, Head, Tech Serv, Syst Adminr, Summit Free Public Library, 75 Maple St, Summit, NJ, 07901-9984. Tel: 908-273-0350. p. 1445

Barratsingh, Felicia, Spec Asst, Budget & Payment Proc, New York State Supreme Court, First Judicial District Criminal Law Library, 100 Centre St, 17th Flr, New York, NY, 10013. Tel: 646-386-3889. p. 1598

Barratt, Donna, Head, Tech Serv, Thompson Coburn LLP, One US Bank Plaza, Saint Louis, MO, 63101-1693. Tel: 314-552-6347. p. 1276

Barravecchia, Mary N, Librn, United States Navy, Naval Undersea Warfare Center Division, Newport Technical Library, 1176 Howell St, Bldg 101, Newport, RI, 02841. Tel: 401-832-4338. p. 2036

Barraza, Vinny, Archivist, Digital Preservation Librn, Xavier University of Louisiana, One Drexel Dr, New Orleans, LA, 70125-1098. Tel: 504-520-7311. p. 904

Barre, Abby, Weekend Librn, Endicott College Library, 376 Hale St, Beverly, MA, 01915. Tel: 978-232-2279. p. 989

Barreca, Anne, Libr Mgr, New York Public Library - Astor, Lenox & Tilden Foundations, Battery Park City Library, 175 North End Ave, New York, NY, 10282. Tel: 212-790-3499. p. 1594

Barreiro, Christopher, Sr Librn, Los Angeles Public Library System, Sun Valley Branch Library, 7935 Vineland Ave, Sun Valley, CA, 91352-4477. Tel: 818-764-1338. p. 165

Barrera, Amanda, Dir, Amarillo Public Library, 413 E Fourth Ave, Amarillo, TX, 79101. Tel: 806-378-3050. p. 2134

Barrera, Amanda, Dir, Harrington Library Consortium, 413 E Fourth Ave, Amarillo, TX, 79101. Tel: 806-378-3050. p. 2775

Barrera, Gloria, Asst Dir, Tech Serv Librn, Wharton County Library, 1920 N Fulton St, Wharton, TX, 77488. Tel: 979-532-8080. p. 2256

Barrera, Steven, Libr Mgr, San Antonio Public Library, Pan American, 1122 W Pyron Ave, San Antonio, TX, 78221. Tel: 210-207-9150. p. 2239

Barrero, Camilo, Mgr, Miami-Dade Public Library System, Hispanic Branch, 1398 SW First St, Miami, FL, 33135. Tel: 305-643-8574. p. 423

Barreto, Ana, Mgr, Miami-Dade Public Library System, Edison Center Branch, 531 NW 62nd St, Miami, FL, 33150. Tel: 305-757-0668. p. 423

Barreto, Ana, Mgr, Miami-Dade Public Library System, Hialeah Gardens Branch, 11300 NW 87th Ct, Ste 112-114, Hialeah Gardens, FL, 33018. Tel: 305-820-8520. p. 423

Barrett, Ann Marie, Mgr, Salt Lake County Library Services, Holladay, 2150 E Murray-Holladay Rd, 4730 S, Salt Lake City, UT, 84117-5241. p. 2274

Barrett, Barbara, Head, Children's Servx, Jericho Public Library, One Merry Lane, Jericho, NY, 11753. Tel: 516-935-6790. p. 1558

Barrett, Chelsea, Bus Librn, Seton Hall University Libraries, Walsh Library Bldg, 400 S Orange Ave, South Orange, NJ, 07079. Tel: 973-275-2035. p. 1443

Barrett, Eileen, Local Hist Librn, Reading Public Library, 64 Middlesex Ave, Reading, MA, 01867-2550. Tel: 781-944-0840. p. 1049

Barrett, Elizabeth, Mgr, Richland Library, Wheatley, 931 Woodrow St, Columbia, SC, 29205. Tel: 803-799-5873. p. 2054

Barrett, Felicia A, Regional Head Librn, University of Illinois at Chicago, Crawford Library of the Health Sciences, Rockford, 1601 Parkview Ave, Rockford, IL, 61107. Tel: 815-395-5660. p. 570

Barrett, Justina, Dir of Education & Programs, Historical Society of Pennsylvania, 1300 Locust St, Philadelphia, PA, 19107-5699. Tel: 215-732-6200, Ext 246. p. 1981

Barrett, Kandis, Libr Dir, Davies Memorial Library, 532 Maple St, Lower Waterford, VT, 05848. Tel: 802-748-4609. p. 2287

Barrett, Kayla, Dir, Archives, Georgia Archives, 5800 Jonesboro Rd, Morrow, GA, 30260. Tel: 678-364-3781. p. 491

Barrett, Lisa, Libr Tech, Tech Serv, Lycoming College, One College Pl, Williamsport, PA, 17701. Tel: 570-321-4085. p. 2023

Barrett, Liza, Br Mgr, Onslow County Public Library, Sneads Ferry Branch, 1330 Hwy 210, Sneads Ferry, NC, 28460. Tel: 910-327-6471, Ext 1429. p. 1697

Barrett, Marcia, Head, Metadata Serv, University of California, 1156 High St, Santa Cruz, CA, 95064. Tel: 831-459-5166. p. 243

Barrett, Martin, Tech Serv, Cedar City Public Library in the Park, 303 N 100 East, Cedar City, UT, 84720. Tel: 435-586-6661. p. 2262

Barrett, Mary Ellin, Librn, Haines City Public Library, 111 N Sixth St, Haines City, FL, 33844. Tel: 863-421-3633. p. 408

Barrett, Matthew, Dir, Libr Serv, Dir, Rec Mgt, Los Angeles County Metropolitan Transportation Authority, One Gateway Plaza, 15th Flr, Mail Stop 99-15-1, Los Angeles, CA, 90012-2952. Tel: 213-922-4859. p. 163

Barrett, Michelle, Br Mgr, Chemung County Library District, West Elmira Library, 1231 W Water St, Elmira, NY, 14905. Tel: 607-733-0541. p. 1530

Barrett, Mindy, Br Supvr, Rutherford County Library System, Myrtle Glanton Lord Library, 521 Mercury Blvd, Murfreesboro, TN, 37130. Tel: 615-907-3429. p. 2118

Barrett, Sundi, Librn, Macon County Legal Law Library, Macon County Courthouse, 253 E Wood St, Rm 303, Decatur, IL, 62523. Tel: 217-424-1372. p. 576

Barrett, Timothy, Prof Emeritus, University of Iowa, 3087 Main Library, 125 W Washington St, Iowa City, IA, 52242-1420. Tel: 319-335-5707. p. 2785

Barrett, Walt, Asst Dir, Meridian-Lauderdale County Public Library, 2517 7th St, Meridian, MS, 39301. Tel: 601-693-6771, Ext 3001. p. 1226

Barrette, Katharine, Assoc Dean, Pub Serv, Mount Royal University Library, 4825 Mount Royal Gate SW, Calgary, AB, T3E 6K6, CANADA. Tel: 403-440-6126. p. 2528

Barrette, Olivier, Dir, Bibliotheques Publiques de Longueuil, 100 rue Saint-Laurent Ouest, Longueuil, QC, J4H 1M1, CANADA. Tel: 450-463-7180. p. 2715

Barriage, Sarah, Dr, Asst Prof, University of Kentucky, 320 Little Library Bldg, Lexington, KY, 40506-0224. Tel: 859-257-8876. p. 2785

Barrick, Noelle, Dir, WSU Campus of Applied Sciences & Technology, WSU South Campus, 3821 E Harry, Wichita, KS, 67218. Tel: 316-677-9492. p. 844

Barrie, Dale, Dir, Alberta Law Libraries, North Library, Law Courts North, 5th Flr, 1A Sir Winston Churchill Sq, Edmonton, AB, T5J 0R2, CANADA. Tel: 780-427-3327. p. 2535

Barrie, Dale, Libr Dir, Alberta Law Libraries, Edmonton, Law Courts Bldg, 2nd Flr S, 1A Sir Winston Churchill Sq, Edmonton, AB, T5J 0R2, CANADA. Tel: 780-422-2342. p. 2535

Barrie, Dale, Dir, Alberta Law Libraries - Lethbridge, Courthouse, 320-Four St S, Lethbridge, AB, T1J 1Z8, CANADA. Tel: 403-381-5639. p. 2546

Barrie, Dale, Dir, Alberta Law Libraries - Red Deer, Courthouse, 4909 - 48 Ave, Red Deer, AB, T4N 3T5, CANADA. Tel: 403-340-5499. p. 2551

Barrie, Laura, Co-Dir, Ocheyedan Public Library, 874 Main St, Ocheyedan, IA, 51354. Tel: 712-758-3352. p. 774

Barrie, Lita, Chief Exec Officer, Burlington Public Library, 2331 New St, Burlington, ON, L7R 1J4, CANADA. Tel: 905-639-3611, Ext 1100. p. 2634

Barrilleaux, Cynthia, Cat Librn, Tulane University, Law Library, Weinmann Hall, 3rd Flr, 6329 Freret St, New Orleans, LA, 70118-6231. Tel: 504-862-8867. p. 904

Barringer, Bob, Dir, Schultz-Holmes Memorial Library, 407 S Lane St, Blissfield, MI, 49228-1232. Tel: 517-486-2858. p. 1086

Barrington, Natalie, Chief Exec Officer, Madawaska Valley Public Library, 19474 Opeongo Line, Barry's Bay, ON, K0J 1B0, CANADA. Tel: 613-756-2000. p. 2630

Barrington, Susannah, Cat, Abilene Christian University, 221 Brown Library, ACU Box 29208, Abilene, TX, 79699-9208. Tel: 325-674-2316. p. 2131

Barrios, Tiffany, Supvr, Glendale Library, Arts & Culture, Chevy Chase, 3301 E Chevy Chase Dr, Glendale, CA, 91206. Tel: 818-548-2046. p. 149

Barrios, Tiffany, Supvr, Glendale Library, Arts & Culture, Montrose Library, 2465 Honolulu Ave, Montrose, CA, 91020. Tel: 818-548-2048. p. 149

Barritt, Amy, Br Mgr, Traverse Area District Library, Kingsley Branch, 213 S Brownson Ave, Kingsley, MI, 49649. Tel: 231-263-5484. p. 1154

Barron, Allison B, Dir, Washington Parish Library System, 825 Free St, Franklinton, LA, 70438. Tel: 985-839-7805. p. 890

Barron, Ari, Youth Serv Librn, Madison County Public Library, 507 W Main St, Richmond, KY, 40475. Tel: 859-623-6704. p. 874

Barron, Elizabeth, Ref Librn, University of Tampa, 401 W Kennedy Blvd, Tampa, FL, 33606-1490. Tel: 813-257-3741. p. 450

Barron, Joy, Asst Libr Dir, Towanda Public Library, 620 Highland, Towanda, KS, 67144-9042. Tel: 316-536-2464. p. 840

Barron, Lori, Dir, Brownsville Free Public Library, 100 Seneca St, Brownsville, PA, 15417-1974. Tel: 724-785-7272. p. 1915

Barron, Sandra, Dir, Guttenberg Public Library, 603 S Second St, Guttenberg, IA, 52052. Tel: 563-252-3108. p. 757

Barron, Shelley, Dir, Le Grand Pioneer Heritage Library, 204 N Vine St, Le Grand, IA, 50142. Tel: 641-479-2122. p. 765

Barron, Viviana, Libr Tech, United States Army, Grant Library, 1637 Flint St, Fort Carson, CO, 80913-4105. Tel: 719-526-2350. p. 280

Barroso, Violet, Research Librn, Santa Barbara News Press Library, 715 Anacapa St, Santa Barbara, CA, 93101. Tel: 805-564-5200, Ext 0. p. 240

Barroso-Ramirez, Essy, Br Mgr, Santa Cruz City-County Library System, Boulder Creek Branch, 13390 W Park Ave, Boulder Creek, CA, 95006-9301. Tel: 831-427-7703. p. 242

Barrow, Phyllis, Dir, Finance & Operations, Georgetown University, 37th & O St NW, Washington, DC, 20057-1174. Tel: 202-687-7454. p. 368

Barrow, William, Spec Coll Librn, Cleveland State University, Michael Schwartz Library, Rhodes Tower, Ste 501, 2121 Euclid Ave, Cleveland, OH, 44115-2214. Tel: 216-687-6998. p. 1769

Barrows, Gwen, Circ, Strasburg-Heisler Library, 143 Precision Ave, Strasburg, PA, 17579. Tel: 717-687-8969. p. 2010

Barrows, Kate, Asst Libr Dir, Griswold Memorial Library, 12 Main St, Colrain, MA, 01340. Tel: 413-624-3619. p. 1012

Barrows, Mary, Librn, First United Methodist Church Library, 501 Howe St, Green Bay, WI, 54301. Tel: 920-437-9252. p. 2438

Barry, Carol, Dr, Dir, Louisiana State University, 267 Coates Hall, Baton Rouge, LA, 70803. Tel: 225-578-3158, 225-578-3159. p. 2785

Barry, Jeff, Library Tech Developer, Washington & Lee University, University Library, 204 W Washington St, Lexington, VA, 24450-2116. Tel: 540-458-8643. p. 2329

Barry, Joe, Research Servs Librn, United States Air Force Academy Libraries, 2354 Fairchild Dr, Ste 3A15, USAF Academy, CO, 80840-6214. Tel: 719-333-4406. p. 297

Barry, Kevin, Libr Mgr, Plunkett & Cooney, 38505 Woodward Ave, Bloomfield Hills, MI, 48304. Tel: 248-901-4094. p. 1086

Barry, Lezlie, Dir, Maynard Community Library, 245 Main St W, Maynard, IA, 50655. Tel: 563-637-2330. p. 769

Barry, Lorraine, Head, Reader Serv, Head, Res Serv, Reading Public Library, 64 Middlesex Ave, Reading, MA, 01867-2550. Tel: 781-942-6703. p. 1049

Barry, Margaret, Br Mgr, Palm Beach County Library System, Wellington Branch, 1951 Royal Fern Dr, Wellington, FL, 33414. Tel: 561-790-6070. p. 454

Barry, Michael, Marketing & Communications Coord, Ajax Public Library, 55 Harwood Ave S, Ajax, ON, L1S 2H8, CANADA. Tel: 905-683-4000, Ext 8819. p. 2627

Barry, Simon, Dir, National Theatre School of Canada Library, 5030 rue Saint-Denis, Montreal, QC, H2J 2L8, CANADA. Tel: 514-842-7954, Ext 125. p. 2727

Barsalou, Marie-Eve, Archivist, College des Medecins du Quebec, 3500-1250 Rene-Levesque Blvd W, Montreal, QC, H3B 0G2, CANADA. Tel: 514-933-4441, Ext 5308. p. 2723

Barsanti, Michael J, Dr, Dir, Library Company of Philadelphia, 1314 Locust St, Philadelphia, PA, 19107. Tel: 215-546-3181, Ext 124. p. 1982

Barselle, Ellen, Librn, Brown Memorial Library, 78 W Main St, Bradford, NH, 03221-3308. Tel: 603-938-5562. p. 1355

Barsom, Michelle, Exec Dir, Libr Serv, West Georgia Technical College, 176 Murphy Campus Blvd, Waco, GA, 30182. Tel: 770-537-6066. p. 502

Barta, Carol R, Asst Dir, North Central Kansas Libraries System, 629 Poyntz Ave, Manhattan, KS, 66502. Tel: 785-776-4741, Ext 801. p. 823

Barta, Evan, Coordr, Tech, Warwick Public Library, 600 Sandy Lane, Warwick, RI, 02889-8298. Tel: 401-739-5440, Ext 9753. p. 2043

Barta, Stephanie, Asst Dir, Youth Serv Librn, Louttit Library, 274 Victory Hwy, West Greenwich, RI, 02817. Tel: 401-397-3434. p. 2043

Barta-Norton, Nancy, Acq, Cat Librn, Salve Regina University, 100 Ochre Point Ave, Newport, RI, 02840-4192. Tel: 401-341-2330. p. 2035

Bartek-Jensen, Autumn, Tech Serv Assoc, University of Nebraska at Kearney, 2508 11th Ave, Kearney, NE, 68849-2240. Tel: 308-865-8846. p. 1319

Bartel, Barbara, Dir, West Iron District Library, 116 W Genesee St, Iron River, MI, 49935-1437. Tel: 906-265-2831. p. 1119

Bartel, Cathy, Dir, Pub Serv, Toledo-Lucas County Public Library, 325 Michigan St, Toledo, OH, 43604. Tel: 419-259-5200. p. 1824

Bartel, Jeanie, Libr Dir, Hillsboro Public Library, 120 E Grand Ave, Hillsboro, KS, 67063. Tel: 620-947-3827. p. 813

Bartel, Patricia, Librn, Ontario Ministry of Transportation Library, 301 St Paul St, 4th Flr, St. Catharines, ON, L2R 7R4, CANADA. Tel: 905-704-2171. p. 2679

Bartell, Sandra, Br Mgr, Hamden Public Library, Brundage Community, 91 Circular Ave, Hamden, CT, 06514. Tel: 203-287-2675. p. 315

Bartelmann, Anya, Physics, Astronomy & Mat Librn, Princeton University, Lewis Science Library, Washington Rd, Princeton, NJ, 08544-0001. Tel: 609-258-3150. p. 1437

Bartelmo, Sara, Ch, West Hartford Public Library, 20 S Main St, West Hartford, CT, 06107-2432. Tel: 860-561-6950. p. 345

Bartels, Niels, Sr Librn, Los Angeles Public Library System, Edendale Branch Library, 2011 W Sunset Blvd, Los Angeles, CA, 90026. Tel: 213-207-3000. p. 164

Bartels, Suzanne M, Dir, Learning Tech, Libr Dir, Guilford College, 5800 W Friendly Ave, Greensboro, NC, 27410. Tel: 336-316-2046. p. 1692

Barten-McGrowen, Abigail, Dir, Collins Public Library, 2341 Main St, Collins, NY, 14034. Tel: 716-532-5129. p. 1521

Bartenfelder, Tom, Dir, Glenside Public Library District, 25 E Fullerton Ave, Glendale Heights, IL, 60139-2697. Tel: 630-260-1550. p. 593

Bartenhagen, Lynn, Coordr, Muscatine Art Center, 1314 Mulberry Ave, Muscatine, IA, 52761. Tel: 563-263-8282. p. 772

Barter, Scott, Mgr, Info Tech, Anne Arundel County Public Library, Five Harry Truman Pkwy, Annapolis, MD, 21401. Tel: 410-222-7371. p. 950

Barth, Christine, ILL Coordr, Wisconsin Department of Public Instruction, Resources for Libraries & Lifelong Learning, 2109 S Stoughton Rd, Madison, WI, 53716-2899. Tel: 608-224-6171. p. 2452

Barth, Christopher, Assoc Dean, Librn, United States Military Academy Library, Jefferson Hall Library & Learning Ctr, 758 Cullum Rd, West Point, NY, 10996. Tel: 845-938-8301. p. 1663

Barth, Derek, Cat Librn, Bath Township Public Library, 14033 Webster Rd, Bath, MI, 48808. Tel: 517-641-7111. p. 1082

Barth, Jen, Adult Serv, Henrietta Public Library, 625 Calkins Rd, Rochester, NY, 14623. Tel: 585-359-7092. p. 1628

Barth, JeNel, Dir, Drake Public Library, 115 Drake Ave, Centerville, IA, 52544. Tel: 641-856-6676. p. 739

Barth, Tami, Asst Librn, Stanton Public Library, 1009 Jackpine St, Stanton, NE, 68779. Tel: 402-439-2230. p. 1337

Barthelmess, Joann, Curator, Watertown History Museum Library, 401 Main St, Watertown, CT, 06795. Tel: 860-274-1050. p. 344

Barthol, Sue, Br Mgr, Morehouse Parish Library, Mer Rouge Branch, 107 S 16th St, Mer Rouge, LA, 71261. Tel: 318-647-5639. p. 882

Bartholomew, Audra, Br Mgr, Bossier Parish Libraries, Haughton Branch, 116 E McKinley Ave, Haughton, LA, 71037. Tel: 318-949-0196. p. 886

Bartholomew, Christina, Libr Dir, Shelbina Carnegie Public Library, 102 N Center St, Shelbina, MO, 63468. Tel: 573-588-2271. p. 1279

Bartholomew, Malik, Access Serv, Dillard University, 2601 Gentilly Blvd, New Orleans, LA, 70122. Tel: 504-816-4786. p. 901

Bartle, Lisa, Coord, Coll Develop, California State University, San Bernardino, 5500 University Pkwy, San Bernardino, CA, 92407-2318. Tel: 909-537-7552. p. 212

Bartles, John D, Cat & Syst Librn, Prince George's Community College Library, 301 Largo Rd, Largo, MD, 20774-2199. Tel: 301-546-0469. p. 970

Bartles, Maryanne, Libr Dir, Dearborn Public Library, 16301 Michigan Ave, Dearborn, MI, 48126. Tel: 313-943-2049. p. 1095

Bartleson, Tieana, Head Librn, Jessie Wakefield Memorial Library, 207 Spruce Dr, Port Lions, AK, 99550. Tel: 907-454-2012. p. 50

Bartlett, Bernadette, Librn, Mich Doc, Library of Michigan, 702 W Kalamazoo St, Lansing, MI, 48915. Tel: 517-373-2971. p. 1125

Bartlett, Diane, Br Mgr, Stanislaus County Library, Turlock Branch, 550 Minaret Ave, Turlock, CA, 95380-4198. Tel: 209-664-8100. p. 178

Bartlett, Elizabeth, Asst Libr Dir, Dir, Ch Serv, Ivoryton Library Association, 106 Main St, Ivoryton, CT, 06442. Tel: 860-767-1252. p. 319

Bartlett, Helen, Tech Serv Librn, Yale University Library, Irving S Gilmore Music Library, 120 High St, New Haven, CT, 06520. Tel: 203-432-0493. p. 327

Bartlett, Jennifer, Head, Ref, Manchester Public Library, 586 Main St, Manchester, CT, 06040. Tel: 860-643-2471. p. 320

Bartlett, Jennifer, Assoc Dean, Teaching, Learning & Res, University of Kentucky Libraries, 401 Hilltop Ave, Lexington, KY, 40506. Tel: 859-218-1881. p. 863

Bartlett, Joan, Assoc Prof, Dir, McGill University, 3661 Peel St, Montreal, QC, H3A 1X1, CANADA. Tel: 514-398-4204. p. 2796

Bartlett, Liz, Libr Mgr, Wake County Public Library System, Cary Community Library, 315 Kildaire Farm Rd, Cary, NC, 27511. Tel: 919-460-3350. p. 1710

Bartlett, Lynne, Dir, Tazewell County Public Library, 129 Main St, Tazewell, VA, 24651. Tel: 276-988-2541. p. 2348

Bartlett, Lynnette, Assoc Librn, Ref/Electronic Res Librn, Bluefield University, 3000 College Ave, Bluefield, VA, 24605. Tel: 276-326-4237. p. 2307

Bartlett, Mike, Libr Dir, Meeker Regional Library District, 490 Main St, Meeker, CO, 81641. Tel: 970-878-5911. p. 291

Bartlett, Nancy, Assoc Dir, University of Michigan, Bentley Historical Library, 1150 Beal Ave, Ann Arbor, MI, 48109-2113. Tel: 734-764-3482. p. 1079

Bartlett, Rebecca, Coll Serv Mgr, La Grange Public Library, Ten W Cossitt Ave, La Grange, IL, 60525. Tel: 708-215-3240. p. 605

Bartlett, Rhonda, Br Mgr, Lake Blackshear Regional Library System, Elizabeth Harris Library, 312 Harman St, Unadilla, GA, 31091. Tel: 478-627-9303. p. 458

Bartlett, Robin A, Dir, Richwood Public Library, Eight White Ave, Richwood, WV, 26261. Tel: 304-846-6222. p. 2413

Bartlett, Sandy, Dir, Morton Memorial Library & Community House, 82 Kelly St, Rhinecliff, NY, 12574. Tel: 845-876-2903. p. 1626

Bartlett, Sarah, Br Mgr, San Bernardino County Library, Twentynine Palms Branch, 6078 Adobe Rd, Twentynine Palms, CA, 92277. Tel: 760-367-9519. p. 213

Bartlett, Tiffany, Chief Exec Officer, Colchester-East Hants Public Library, 754 Prince St, Truro, NS, B2N 1G9, CANADA. Tel: 902-895-4183. p. 2623

Bartley, Ashley, Adult Serv, Speedway Public Library, 5633 W 25th St, Speedway, IN, 46224-3899. Tel: 317-243-8959. p. 719

Bartley, Barbara, Pub Serv Librn, Kennebec Valley Community College, 92 Western Ave, Fairfield, ME, 04937-1367. Tel: 207-453-5004. p. 924

Bartley, Julie, Ch, Old Lyme, Two Library Lane, Old Lyme, CT, 06371. Tel: 860-434-1684. p. 333

Bartley, Kelsa, Mgr, Ref & Educ Serv, University of Miami, Louis Calder Memorial Library, Miller School of Medicine, 1601 NW Tenth Ave, Miami, FL, 33136. Tel: 305-243-5530. p. 425
Bartley, Linda, Youth Serv Mgr, McCracken County Public Library, 555 Washington St, Paducah, KY, 42003. Tel: 270-442-2510. p. 872
Bartley, Margaret, Pres, The Seattle Metaphysical Library (As-You-Like-It Library), 3450 40th Ave W, Seattle, WA, 98199. Tel: 206-329-1794. p. 2379
Bartley, Peishan, Libr Dir, Sargent Memorial Library, 427 Massachusetts Ave, Boxborough, MA, 01719. Tel: 978-263-4680. p. 1001
Bartley, Robin, Dir, Wickliffe Public Library, 1713 Lincoln Rd, Wickliffe, OH, 44092. Tel: 440-944-6010. p. 1831
Bartley, Tara, Dir, Twin Falls Public Library, 201 Fourth Ave E, Twin Falls, ID, 83301-6397. Tel: 208-733-2964. p. 532
Bartling, Renee, Dir, Nora Springs Public Library, 45 N Hawkeye Ave, Nora Springs, IA, 50458. Tel: 641-749-5569. p. 773
Bartnik, Laura, Dir, Northlake Public Library District, 231 N Wolf Rd, Northlake, IL, 60164. Tel: 708-562-2301. p. 627
Bartok, Melissa, Dir, Mayville Library, 92 S Erie St, Mayville, NY, 14757. Tel: 716-753-7362. p. 1570
Bartoli, Tami, Dir, East Troy Lions Public Library, 3094 Graydon Ave, East Troy, WI, 53120. Tel: 262-642-6262. p. 2432
Bartolomeo, Kristen, Supvr, Circ, Northborough Free Library, 34 Main St, Northborough, MA, 01532-1942. Tel: 508-393-5025. p. 1043
Bartolotta, Fran, Head, Customer Serv, Grande Prairie Public Library, 101-9839 103 Ave, Grande Prairie, AB, T8V 6M7, CANADA. Tel: 780-357-7470. p. 2541
Bartolotto, Julie, Exec Dir, Historical Society of Long Beach, 4260 Atlantic Ave, Long Beach, CA, 90807. Tel: 562-424-2220. p. 158
Bartolucci, D, Libr Asst, Tiskilwa Public Library, 119 E Main, Tiskilwa, IL, 61368. Tel: 815-646-4511. p. 654
Barton, Alexander, Assoc Dir, Admin & Tech Serv, Boston College, 885 Centre St, Newton Centre, MA, 02459. Tel: 617-552-4475. p. 1039
Barton, Allie, Ch, Sherman Public Library, 421 N Travis St, Sherman, TX, 75090. Tel: 903-892-7240. p. 2243
Barton, Amanda, Librn, Livermore Public Library, 22 Church St, Livermore, ME, 04253-3699. Tel: 207-897-7173. p. 930
Barton, Amy, Libr Tech, Hicks Morley Hamilton Stewart & Storie LLP, Box 371, TD Ctr, 77 King St W, 39th Flr, Toronto, ON, M5H 1K8, CANADA. Tel: 416-362-1011, Ext 7012. p. 2689
Barton, Benjamin, Coll Develop Librn, Brenau University, 625 Academy St, Gainesville, GA, 30501-3343. Tel: 770-538-4723. p. 480
Barton, Christina, Sr Librn, Teen Serv, Haltom City Public Library, 4809 Haltom Rd, Haltom City, TX, 76117-3622. Tel: 817-222-7769. p. 2187
Barton, Jennifer, Libr Dir, Genoa Public Library District, 240 W Main St, Genoa, IL, 60135. Tel: 815-784-2627. p. 592
Barton, Jennifer, Asst Libr Dir, Munford-Tipton Memorial Library, 1476 Munford Ave, Munford, TN, 38058. Tel: 901-837-2665. p. 2117
Barton, Kevin, Libr Mgr, Geauga County Public Library, Thompson Branch, 6645 Madison Rd, Thompson, OH, 44086. Tel: 440-298-3831. p. 1758
Barton, Nancy, Readers' Advisory, Starke County Public Library System, 152 W Culver Rd, Knox, IN, 46534-2220. Tel: 574-772-7323. p. 699
Barton, Nancy, Circ Supvr, Davis County Library, Centerville Branch, 45 S 400 West, Centerville, UT, 84014. Tel: 801-451-1775. p. 2263
Barton, Sarah, Circ Supvr, Harvard Library, Eda Kuhn Loeb Music Library, Music Bldg, Three Oxford St, Cambridge, MA, 02138. Tel: 617-495-2794. p. 1007
Bartos, Dave, Coord, Ad Serv, Cranston Public Library, 140 Sockanosset Cross Rd, Cranston, RI, 02920-5539. Tel: 401-943-9080. p. 2031
Bartula, Angela, Br Mgr, Mesquite Public Library, North Branch, 2600 Oates Dr, Mesquite, TX, 75150. Tel: 972-681-0465. p. 2219
Bartusiewicz, Pam, Assoc Dir, Youth Services, East Chicago Public Library, 2401 E Columbus Dr, East Chicago, IN, 46312-2998. Tel: 219-397-2453. p. 680
Bartusik, LisaMarie, District Dept Head of Libr, Pensacola State College, Bldg 20, 1000 College Blvd, Pensacola, FL, 32504-8998. Tel: 850-484-2007. p. 436
Bartz, Jessica, Asst Dir, Westchester Public Library, 200 W Indiana Ave, Chesterton, IN, 46304. Tel: 219-926-7696. p. 674
Bartz, Vicki, Head Librn, Graceville Public Library, 415 Studdart Ave, Graceville, MN, 56240. Tel: 320-748-7332. p. 1176
Bartz, Vicki, Head Librn, Ortonville Public Library, 412 NW Second St, Ortonville, MN, 56278-1415. Tel: 320-839-2494. p. 1192
Baruzzi, Andrea, Sci Librn, Swarthmore College, 500 College Ave, Swarthmore, PA, 19081. Tel: 610-328-7685. p. 2011
Baruzzi, Andrea, Sci Librn, Swarthmore College, Cornell Science & Engineering, 500 College Ave, Swarthmore, PA, 19081. Tel: 610-328-7685. p. 2012
Barvoets, Peter, Interim Dir, SUNY Cobleskill College of Agriculture & Technology, 142 Schenectady Ave, Cobleskill, NY, 12043. Tel: 518-255-5841. p. 1520
Baryo, Kayleigh, Br Mgr, Scenic Regional Library, Wright City Branch, 60 Wildcat Dr, Wright City, MO, 63390. Tel: 636-384-1136. p. 1284
Barzel, Tamar, Head Music Libr, Stanford University Libraries, Music Library, Braun Music Ctr, 541 Lasuen Mall, Stanford, CA, 94305-3076. Tel: 650-723-1211. p. 249
Bascle, Brenda, Br Mgr, Lafourche Parish Public Library, Lockport Branch, 720 Crescent Ave, Lockport, LA, 70374. Tel: 985-532-3158. p. 911
Baseggio, Sara, Dir, Libr Serv, Sidley Austin LLP Library, One S Dearborn St, Chicago, IL, 60603. Tel: 312-853-7475. p. 568
Basel, William, Head, Ref, Cheshire Public Library, 104 Main St, Cheshire, CT, 06410-2499. Tel: 203-272-2245. p. 305
Bases, Grace, Tech Serv Mgr, Martin Luther College Library, 1995 Luther Ct, New Ulm, MN, 56073-3965. Tel: 507-354-8221, Ext 364. p. 1190
Bash, Cassaundra, Dir, Libr Serv, Ancilla College, 9601 S Union Rd, Donaldson, IN, 46513. Tel: 574-936-8898, Ext 323. p. 679
Basham, Debra, Asst Dir, Libr Mgr, West Virginia Archives & History Library, Culture Ctr, 1900 Kanawha Blvd E, Charleston, WV, 25305-0300. Tel: 304-558-0230, Ext 702. p. 2400
Bashaw, Debra, Dir, McMullen Memorial Library, 900 N Main St, Huntington, TX, 75949. Tel: 936-876-4516. p. 2201
Bashir, Masooda, Assoc Prof, University of Illinois at Urbana-Champaign, Library & Information Science Bldg, 501 E Daniel St, Champaign, IL, 61820-6211. Tel: 217-333-3280. p. 2784
Bashore, Matthew, Ref Serv Librn, Brighton Memorial Library, 2300 Elmwood Ave, Rochester, NY, 14618. Tel: 585-784-5300. p. 1628
Bashus, Laura, Adminr, University of Nebraska Medical Center, 600 S 42nd St, Omaha, NE, 68198. Tel: 462-559-7080. p. 1331
Basiliere, Teresa, Library Contact, Winnebago County Court House, Court House, 415 Jackson St, Oshkosh, WI, 54903-4794. Tel: 920-236-4808. p. 2468
Basinger, Andrea, Adult Serv, Garrett Public Library, 107 W Houston St, Garrett, IN, 46738. Tel: 260-357-5485. p. 686
Basinger, Jan, Dir, Gabbs Community Library, 530 E Ave, Gabbs, NV, 89409. p. 1345
Baskette, Shawna, Dean of Libr, Cerritos College Library, 11110 Alondra Blvd, Norwalk, CA, 90650. Tel: 562-860-2451, Ext 2430. p. 184
Baskin, Sandra, Dir, Sherman County Library, 719 N Main St, Stratford, TX, 79084. Tel: 806-366-2200. p. 2246
Bass, April, Libr Spec, Johnston Community College Library, Learning Resource Ctr, Bldg E, 245 College Rd, Smithfield, NC, 27577. Tel: 919-464-2259. p. 1716
Bass, Brittany, Dir, Olney Public Library, 400 W Main St, Olney, IL, 62450. Tel: 618-392-3711. p. 630
Bass, Catharine, Circ, Metropolis Public Library, 317 Metropolis St, Metropolis, IL, 62960. Tel: 618-524-4312. p. 617
Bass, Catherine, Dir, Jericho Town Library, Seven Jericho Ctr Circle, Jericho, VT, 05465. Tel: 802-899-4686. p. 2287
Bass, David, Sr Developer, Digital Initiatives, Western Washington University, 516 High St, MS 9103, Bellingham, WA, 98225. Tel: 360-650-3084. p. 2358
Bass, Erica, Chief, Libr Serv, Department of Veterans Affairs, 11201 Benton St, Loma Linda, CA, 92357. Tel: 909-422-3000, Ext 2970. p. 157
Bass, Jimmy, Dir of Libr, Coweta Public Library System, 85 Literary Lane, Newnan, GA, 30265. Tel: 770-683-2052. p. 492
Bass, Kim, Children's Spec, Libr Spec I, Okeechobee County Public Library, 206 SW 16th St, Okeechobee, FL, 34974. Tel: 863-763-3536. p. 430
Bass, Lisa, Dir, Bruneau District Library, 32073 Ruth St, Bruneau, ID, 83604. Tel: 208-845-2131. p. 518
Bass, Liz, Library Contact, George Mason University Libraries, Arlington Campus Library, 3351 Fairfax Dr, MSN IDI, Founders Hall, Rm 201, Arlington, VA, 22201. Tel: 703-993-8188. p. 2317
Bass, Marcia, Head, Ref, Ludington Public Library, Five S Bryn Mawr Ave, Bryn Mawr, PA, 19010-3471. Tel: 610-525-1776. p. 1916
Bass, Marlene, YA Librn, Wayne County Public Library, 157 Rolling Hills Blvd, Monticello, KY, 42633. Tel: 606-348-8565. p. 869
Bass, Mary, Youth Serv Supvr, Kankakee Public Library, 201 E Merchant St, Kankakee, IL, 60901. Tel: 815-939-4564. p. 604
Bass, Michelle, Clinical Information Librarian, Pennsylvania Hospital, 800 Spruce St, Philadelphia, PA, 19107. Tel: 215-829-3370. p. 1984
Bass, Michelle, Librn, Pennsylvania Hospital, Medical Library, Three Pine Ctr, 800 Spruce St, Philadelphia, PA, 19107-6192. Tel: 215-829-3370. p. 1984
Bass, Sheryl, Dir, Durham Public Library, 49 Madbury Rd, Durham, NH, 03824. Tel: 603-868-6699. p. 1361
Bass, Tammy, Teen Librn, East Morgan County Library District, 500 Clayton St, Brush, CO, 80723-2110. Tel: 970-842-4596. p. 269
Bass, Vanessa, Coordr, Libr Serv, Piedmont Community College, Caswell Learning Commons, 331 Piedmont Dr, Yanceyville, NC, 27379. Tel: 336-694-5707, Ext 8072. p. 1714
Bass, Vanessa L, Coordr, Libr Serv, Piedmont Community College, 1715 College Dr, Roxboro, NC, 27573. Tel: 336-322-2127. p. 1714
Bassett, Christa, Adult Serv & Outreach Coordr, Cumberland County Library System, 400 Bent Creek Blvd, Ste 150, Mechanicsburg, PA, 17050. Tel: 717-240-6175. p. 1960
Bassett, Dawn, Managing Librn, Summerland Research & Development Centre, 4200 Hwy 97, Summerland, BC, V0H 1Z0, CANADA. Tel: 250-494-2100. p. 2576
Bassett, Pegeen, Doc Librn, Northwestern University Libraries, Pritzker Legal Research Center, 375 E Chicago Ave, Chicago, IL, 60611. Tel: 312-503-7344. p. 587

Bassford, Karen, Librn, Idaho State Correctional Institution Library, 13500 S Pleasant Valley Rd, Boise, ID, 83707. Tel: 208-336-0740. p. 517
Bassford, Rebecca, Librn, Colorado Department of Corrections, 3600 Havana St, Denver, CO, 80239. Tel: 303-307-2500, Ext 2659, 303-307-2721. p. 274
Basso, Mary, Humanities Librn, Georgian Court University, 900 Lakewood Ave, Lakewood, NJ, 08701-2697. Tel: 732-987-2427. p. 1410
Basso, Toni, Dir, Worcester-Schenevus Library, 170 Main St, Worcester, NY, 12197. Tel: 607-397-7309. p. 1667
Bastian, Jessica, Electronic Res Librn, Illinois Central College, Kenneth L Edward Library Administration Bldgs, L312, One College Dr, East Peoria, IL, 61635-0001. Tel: 309-690-6961. p. 581
Bastin, Judy, Archives, Dir of Libr, Butler Community College Library & Archives, Library 600 Bldg, 901 S Haverhill Rd, El Dorado, KS, 67042-3280. Tel: 316-322-3235. p. 805
Bastin, Judy, Res & Instruction Librn, Butler Community College Library & Archives, Butler of Andover Library, Library Rm 5012, 715 E 13th St, Andover, KS, 67002. Tel: 316-218-6371. p. 806
Basye, Jonatha, Ch, Glenwood Public Library, 109 N Vine St, Glenwood, IA, 51534. Tel: 712-527-5252. p. 755
Batchelder, Ashley, Dir, Mount Zion District Library, 115 W Main St, Mount Zion, IL, 62549. Tel: 217-864-3622. p. 622
Batchelor, Chelle, Dean of Library & Academic Innovation, Western Oregon University, 345 N Monmouth Ave, Monmouth, OR, 97361-1396. Tel: 503-838-8886. p. 1887
Batchelor, Lori, Asst Libr Mgr, Boyce Ditto Public Library, 2300 Martin Luther King Jr St, Mineral Wells, TX, 76067. Tel: 940-328-7880. p. 2220
Batchen, Joan, Libr Dir, Kirkland & Ellis LLP Library, 300 N LaSalle St, 11th Flr, Chicago, IL, 60654. Tel: 312-862-2358. p. 562
Bateman, Amy, Br Mgr, Norfolk Public Library, Lafayette Branch, 1610 Cromwell Rd, Norfolk, VA, 23509. Tel: 757-441-2842. p. 2335
Bateman, Andre L, Librn, Georgia Department of Corrections, Rogers State Prison, 1978 Georgia Hwy 147, Reidsville, GA, 30453. Tel: 912-557-7019. p. 493
Bateman, Kristy, Operations Mgr, Spokane County Library District, Fairfield Library, 305 E Main, Fairfield, WA, 99012. Tel: 509-893-8320. p. 2384
Bateman, Micah, Asst Prof, University of Iowa, 3087 Main Library, 125 W Washington St, Iowa City, IA, 52242-1420. Tel: 319-335-5707. p. 2785
Bateman, Patti, Dir, Libr & Cultural Serv, Aurora Public Library, 14949 E Alameda Pkwy, Aurora, CO, 80012. Tel: 303-739-6594. p. 264
Bateman, Trenton, Libr Dir, North Logan City Library, 475 E 2500 N, North Logan, UT, 84341. Tel: 435-755-7169. p. 2267
Bates, Amy, Ch, Talbot Belmond Public Library, 440 E Main St, Belmond, IA, 50421-1224. Tel: 641-444-4160. p. 734
Bates, Angie, Libr Dir, Farmville Public Library, 4276 W Church St, Farmville, NC, 27828. Tel: 252-753-3355. p. 1688
Bates, Aryana, Dean, Libr & Learning Res, North Seattle Community College, 9600 College Way N, Seattle, WA, 98103. Tel: 206-527-3607. p. 2377
Bates, Cara, Librn, United States Army, Fort Irwin Post Library, National Training Ctr, Bldg 331, Second St & F Ave, Fort Irwin, CA, 92310. Tel: 760-380-3462. p. 143
Bates, Caroline, Librn, University of South Dakota, I D Weeks Library, 414 E Clark St, Vermillion, SD, 57069. Tel: 605-658-3390. p. 2084
Bates, Chris, Libr Dir, Union Presbyterian Seminary Library, 5141 Sharon Rd, Charlotte, NC, 28210. Tel: 980-636-1700, Ext 661. p. 1681
Bates, Christy, Circ Supvr, Rumford Public Library, 56 Rumford Ave, Rumford, ME, 04276-1919. Tel: 207-364-3661. p. 939
Bates, Kathy, Br Mgr, Lawrence County Library, Driftwood Public, 28 S Hwy 25, Lynn, AR, 72440. Tel: 870-528-3506. p. 112
Bates, Kim, Librn, University of Alberta, John Alexander Weir Memorial Law Library, Law Ctr, 111 St & 89 Ave, Edmonton, AB, T6G 2H5, CANADA. Tel: 780-492-3371. p. 2538
Bates, Mary, Br Mgr, Southeast Arkansas Regional Library, Eudora Branch, 161 N Cherry St, Eudora, AR, 71640. Tel: 870-355-2450. p. 104
Bates, Mikel, Program Coord, Sr, University of Arizona Libraries, Health Sciences Library, 1501 N Campbell Ave, Tucson, AZ, 85724. Tel: 520-626-2921. p. 83
Bates, Rachel, Acq, Supvr, Res Mgr, Northeastern University School of Law Library, 416 Huntington Ave, Boston, MA, 02115. Tel: 617-373-3553. p. 999
Bates, Robin W, Head Law Librn, Essex Law Library, J Michael Ruane Judicial Ctr, 56 Federal St, Salem, MA, 01970. Tel: 978-741-0674. p. 1051
Bates, Sara, Law Librn, Washoe County Law Library, 75 Courth St, Rm 101, Reno, NV, 89501. Tel: 775-328-3250. p. 1350
Bates, Scott, Circ Mgr, Capital University, One College & Main, Columbus, OH, 43209. Tel: 614-236-6614. p. 1772
Bates, Sheida, Asst Br Mgr, Johnson County Library, Antioch, 8700 Shawnee Mission Pkwy, Merriam, KS, 66202. p. 830
Bates-Tarrant, Donna, Head, Tech Serv, Grafton Public Library, 35 Grafton Common, Grafton, MA, 01519. Tel: 508-839-4649, Ext 1106. p. 1021
Bates-Ulibani, Mary, Libr Mgr, Central New Mexico Community College Libraries, 525 Buena Vista SE, Albuquerque, NM, 87106-4023. Tel: 505-224-4000, Ext 52552. p. 1460
Bath, Raman, County Librn, Fresno County Public Library, 2420 Mariposa St, Fresno, CA, 93721. Tel: 559-600-7323. p. 145
Bathe, Jessica, Tech Serv Librn, Elizabeth Titus Memorial Library, Two W Water St, Sullivan, IL, 61951. Tel: 217-728-7221. p. 652
Batista, David, Head, Ref & Res Serv, Rutgers University Libraries, Camden Law Library, 217 N Fifth St, Camden, NJ, 08102-1203. Tel: 856-225-6469. p. 1394
Batista, Elizabeth, Libr Supvr, University of Miami, 1311 Miller Dr, Coral Gables, FL, 33146. Tel: 305-284-2251. p. 390
Baton, Martha, Asst Dir, Langworthy Public Library, 24 Spring St, Hope Valley, RI, 02832-1620. Tel: 401-539-2851. p. 2033
Batschelet, Tammy, Ch, Dare County Library, 700 N Hwy 64-264, Manteo, NC, 27954. Tel: 252-473-2372. p. 1702
Batson, Jennifer, Cat Librn, University of Mary Hardin-Baylor, 900 College St, UMHB Sta, Box 8016, Belton, TX, 76513-2599. Tel: 254-295-5002. p. 2147
Batson, Lill, Dir, Viola Public Library District, 1701 17th St, Viola, IL, 61486. Tel: 309-596-2620. p. 658
Batson, Rebecca E, Dr, Dean, Univ Libr, Delaware State University, 1200 N Dupont Hwy, Dover, DE, 19901-2277. Tel: 302-857-7887. p. 352
Battad, Maria Teresa, Circ, Milford Public Library, 57 New Haven Ave, Milford, CT, 06460. Tel: 203-783-3304. p. 323
Battaglia, Alyssa, Ref/YA, Township of Washington Public Library, 144 Woodfield Rd, Washington Township, NJ, 07676. Tel: 201-664-4586. p. 1451
Battcher, Ray, Curator, Librn, Bristol Historical & Preservation Society Library, 48 Court St, Bristol, RI, 02809. Tel: 401-253-7223. p. 2029
Battelle, Rene, Br Mgr, Onondaga County Public Libraries, The Galleries of Syracuse, 447 S Salina St, Syracuse, NY, 13202-2494. Tel: 315-435-1900. p. 1649
Batterson, Mary, Access Serv Librn, Columbia College, 1001 Rogers St, Columbia, MO, 65216. Tel: 573-875-7373. p. 1243
Battis, Abby, Assoc Dir, Coll, Historic Beverly, 117 Cabot St, Beverly, MA, 01915. Tel: 978-922-1186, Ext 202. p. 989
Battistini, Nina, Librn, Alexandria Technical College Library, 1601 Jefferson St, Rm 302, Alexandria, MN, 56308. Tel: 320-762-4465. p. 1163
Battle, Shawna, Interlibrary Serv Coordr, Hollins University, 7950 E Campus Dr, Roanoke, VA, 24020. Tel: 540-362-7465. p. 2345
Battles, Barbara, Head, Outreach Serv, South Brunswick Public Library, 110 Kingston Lane, Monmouth Junction, NJ, 08852. Tel: 732-329-4000, Ext 7637. p. 1419
Battles De Ramos, Stacey, Access Serv Librn, Boston University Libraries, School of Theology Library, 745 Commonwealth Ave, 2nd Flr, Boston, MA, 02215. Tel: 617-353-3034. p. 993
Battles, Jason, Dean of Libr, University of Arkansas Libraries, 365 N McIlroy Ave, Fayetteville, AR, 72701-4002. Tel: 479-575-4101. p. 95
Battley, Joan, Dir, North Chicago Public Library, 2100 Argonne Dr, North Chicago, IL, 60064. Tel: 847-689-0125, Ext 110. p. 626
Battley, Tammy, Libr Operations Coordr, Chattahoochee Valley Libraries, 3000 Macon Rd, Columbus, GA, 31906-2201. Tel: 706-243-2702. p. 471
Batzel, Patricia, Human Res Mgr, Saint Charles City-County Library District, 77 Boone Hills Dr, Saint Peters, MO, 63376. Tel: 636-441-2300. p. 1277
Batzloff, Brandon, Asst Teaching Prof, Undergraduate Programs Dir, University of Illinois at Urbana-Champaign, Library & Information Science Bldg, 501 E Daniel St, Champaign, IL, 61820-6211. Tel: 217-333-3280. p. 2784
Baucicaut, Guerda, ILL & Reserves Coordr, Borough of Manhattan Community College Library, 199 Chambers St, S410, New York, NY, 10007. Tel: 212-220-8000, Ext 7211. p. 1580
Baucom, Erin, Digital Archivist, University of Montana Missoula, 32 Campus Dr, Missoula, MT, 59812. Tel: 406-243-6866. p. 1300
Bauder, Deborah, Res, Instruction & Outreach Librn, State University of New York at Oswego, SUNY Oswego, 7060 State Rte 104, Oswego, NY, 13126-3514. Tel: 315-312-3010. p. 1613
Bauder, Julia, Soc Studies & Data Serv Librn, Grinnell College Libraries, 1111 Sixth Ave, Grinnell, IA, 50112-1770. Tel: 641-269-4431. p. 756
Baudino, Frank, Research Librn, Northwest Missouri State University, 800 University Dr, Maryville, MO, 64468-6001. Tel: 660-562-1193. p. 1261
Baudouin, Eleanor, Ref Librn, Air Force Research Laboratory, Technical Library, 203 W Eglin Blvd, Ste 300, Eglin AFB, FL, 32542-6843. Tel: 850-882-3212, 850-882-5586. p. 395
Bauer, Avi, Digital Initiatives & Scholarly Communication Specialist, Boston College, 885 Centre St, Newton Centre, MA, 02459. Tel: 617-552-8602. p. 1039
Bauer, Deb, Asst to the Dir, Fontanelle Public Library, 303 Washington St, Fontanelle, IA, 50846. Tel: 641-745-4981. p. 753
Bauer, Ellen, Br Mgr, Pine Bluff & Jefferson County Library System, White Hall Public Library, 300 Anderson Ave, White Hall, AR, 71602. Tel: 870-247-5064. p. 107
Bauer, Hella, Head Librn, Raymond A Whitwer Tilden Public Library, 202 S Center St, Tilden, NE, 68781. Tel: 402-368-5306. p. 1338
Bauer, Jessica, Head, Youth Serv, Somerset County Library System of New Jersey, Hillsborough Public, Hillsborough Municipal Complex, 379 S Branch Rd, Hillsborough, NJ, 08844. Tel: 908-458-8420. p. 1392
Bauer, Kathleen, Coll, Dir, Discovery & Access, Trinity College Library, 300 Summit St, Hartford, CT, 06106. Tel: 860-297-2258. p. 318

Bauer, Lisa, Children's Prog, Iola Village Library, 180 S Main St, Iola, WI, 54945-9689. Tel: 715-445-4330. p. 2442
Bauer, Martha, Dir, Brewer Public Library, 325 N Central Ave, Richland Center, WI, 53581. Tel: 608-647-6444. p. 2473
Bauer, Melissa, Online Learning Librn, Kent State University, 6000 Frank Ave NW, North Canton, OH, 44720-7548. Tel: 330-244-3320. p. 1809
Bauer, Mike, Adult Programming, Coordr, East Bonner County Library District, 1407 Cedar St, Sandpoint, ID, 83864-2052. Tel: 208-263-6930. p. 531
Bauer, Miranda, Youth Serv, Benbrook Public Library, 1065 Mercedes St, Benbrook, TX, 76126. Tel: 817-249-6632. p. 2147
Bauer-Fisher, Becky, Asst Librn, Jesup Public Library, 721 Sixth St, Jesup, IA, 50648. Tel: 319-827-1533. p. 762
Bauersfeld, Diane, Circuit Librn, US Courts Library - Tenth Circuit Court of Appeals, Byron Rogers Courthouse, 1929 Stout St, Rm 430, Denver, CO, 80294. Tel: 303-335-2654. p. 277
Bauersfeld, Diane, Circuit Librn, US Courts Library - Tenth Circuit Court of Appeals, Federal Bldg, Rm 2314, 2120 Capital Ave, Cheyenne, WY, 82001. Tel: 307-433-2427. p. 2493
Baues, Susan, Coll Mgr, Innisfil Public Library, 20 Church St, Cookstown, ON, L0L 1L0, CANADA. Tel: 705-431-7410. p. 2637
Baugh, Tina, Br Mgr, San Luis Obispo County Library, Cambria Library, 1043 Main St, Cambria, CA, 93428. Tel: 805-927-4336. p. 234
Baughan, Betty, Library Contact, Charlotte County Library, Keysville Branch, 300 King St, Keysville, VA, 23947. Tel: 434-736-0083. p. 2309
Baughan, Betty, Librn, Charlotte County Library, Wylliesburg Community, Hwy 15, Wylliesburg, VA, 23976. Tel: 434-735-8812. p. 2309
Baughman, Colleen, Asst Dir, Nancy L McConathy Public Library, 21737 Jeffery Ave, Sauk Village, IL, 60411. Tel: 708-757-4771. p. 645
Baughman, Megan, Adult Serv Mgr, Coshocton Public Library, 655 Main St, Coshocton, OH, 43812-1697. Tel: 740-622-0956. p. 1778
Baughman, Monica, Dep Dir, Worthington Libraries, 820 High St, Worthington, OH, 43085. Tel: 614-807-2602. p. 1834
Baughman, Sue, Dep Exec Dir, Association of Research Libraries, 21 Dupont Circle NW, Ste 800, Washington, DC, 20036. Tel: 202-296-2296. p. 2763
Baule, John, Archivist, Dir, Emeritus, Yakima Valley Museum, 2105 Tieton Dr, Yakima, WA, 98902. Tel: 509-248-0747. p. 2396
Baulne, Connie, Librn, North Central Washington Libraries, Moses Lake Public Library, 418 E Fifth Ave, Moses Lake, WA, 98837-1797. Tel: 509-765-3489. p. 2394
Bauman, David, Library Contact, Osterhout Free Library, Plains Township, 126 N Main St, Plains, PA, 18705. Tel: 570-824-1862. p. 2022
Bauman, David J, Dir, West Pittston Library, 200 Exeter Ave, West Pittston, PA, 18643-2442. Tel: 570-654-9847. p. 2021
Bauman, Kara, Dir, Lyons Regional Library, 451 Fourth Ave, Lyons, CO, 80540. Tel: 303-823-5165. p. 291
Baumann, Corey, Delivery Serv Coordr, South Central Library System, 4610 S Biltmore Lane, Ste 101, Madison, WI, 53718-2153. Tel: 608-266-4695. p. 2450
Baumann, Kristin, Libr Dir, Aldrich Public Library, Six Washington St, Barre, VT, 05641. Tel: 802-476-7550, Ext 307. p. 2278
Baumann, Kristin J, Dir, Island Free Library, Nine Dodge St, Block Island, RI, 02807. Tel: 401-466-3233. p. 2029
Baumann, Laurie, Head, Circ, Cocoa Beach Public Library, 550 N Brevard Ave, Cocoa Beach, FL, 32931. Tel: 321-868-1104. p. 390
Baumann, Lynne, Librn, Chinook Regional Library, Tompkins Branch, Main St, Tompkins, SK, S0N 2S0, CANADA. Tel: 306-622-2255. p. 2753
Baumann, Mauri, Libr Dir, West Melbourne Public Library, 2755 Wingate Blvd, West Melbourne, FL, 32904. Tel: 321-952-4508. p. 453
Baumann, Michael, Dir, Toulon Public Library District, 617 E Jefferson St, Toulon, IL, 61483. Tel: 309-286-5791. p. 654
Baumann, Patrick N, Head, Coll & Instruction Div/Librn, New Mexico Highlands University, 802 National Ave, Las Vegas, NM, 87701. Tel: 505-454-3408. p. 1471
Baumeister, Cindy, Br Mgr, Crown Point Community Library, Winfield, 10771 Randolph St, Crown Point, IN, 46307. Tel: 219-662-4039. p. 678
Baumeister, Dean, Ref (Info Servs), Memorial Hall Library, 2 N Main St, Andover, MA, 01810. Tel: 978-623-8400. p. 985
Baumgarn, Chris, Pub Serv Librn, Winterset Public Library, 123 N Second St, Winterset, IA, 50273-1508. Tel: 515-462-1731. p. 792
Baumgart, Lori, Educ Spec, Mkt & Communications Spec, Nicolet Federated Library System, 1595 Allouez Ave, Ste 4, Green Bay, WI, 54311. Tel: 920-448-4410. p. 2439
Baumle, Robert, Librn, South Plains College Library, 1401 S College Ave - Box E, Levelland, TX, 79336. Tel: 806-716-4888. p. 2211
Baures, Lisa, Ref & Instruction Librn, Minnesota State University, Mankato, 601 Maywood Ave, Mankato, MN, 56001. Tel: 507-389-5952. p. 1181
Bause, George, Dr, Curator, Wood Library-Museum of Anesthesiology, 1061 American Lane, Schaumburg, IL, 60173. Tel: 847-825-5586. p. 645
Bausman, Margaret, Head of Libr, Hunter College Libraries, Schools of Social Work & Public Health Library, 2180 Third Ave, New York, NY, 10035. Tel: 212-396-7659. p. 1588
Bautista, Cynthia, Sr Librn, Long Beach Public Library, Ruth Bach Branch, 4055 N Bellflower Blvd, Long Beach, CA, 90808. Tel: 562-570-1038. p. 159
Bautz, Kim, Outreach Serv Mgr, Dayton Metro Library, 215 E Third St, Dayton, OH, 45402. Tel: 937-496-8956. p. 1779
Bautz, Travis, Dir, MidPointe Library System, 125 S Broad St, Middletown, OH, 45044. Tel: 513-424-1251. p. 1802
Baxley, Wanda, Br Mgr, Williamsburg County Library, Hemingway Branch, 306 N Main St, Hemingway, SC, 29554. Tel: 843-558-7679. p. 2063
Baxter, Brian, Mgr, Tech Serv, DLA Piper US LLP, 6225 Smith Ave, Baltimore, MD, 21209-3600. Tel: 410-580-4653. p. 952
Baxter, James, Asst Dir, Tarrant County College, Northwest Campus Walsh Library, 4801 Marine Creek Pkwy, Fort Worth, TX, 76179. Tel: 817-515-7725. p. 2180
Baxter, Julie, Asst Librn, Franklin County Library, 100 Main St, Mount Vernon, TX, 75457. Tel: 903-537-4916. p. 2221
Baxter, Karen, Visual Arts Librn, California Institute of the Arts, 24700 McBean Pkwy, Valencia, CA, 91355. Tel: 661-253-7880. p. 255
Baxter, Kate, Dir, Bethany Public Library, Eight Court St, Bethany, PA, 18431-9516. Tel: 570-253-4349. p. 1911
Baxter, Rosemary, Libr Dir, Metropolis Public Library, 317 Metropolis St, Metropolis, IL, 62960. Tel: 618-524-4312. p. 617
Baxter, Shannon, Colls Mgr, Dartmouth Heritage Museum Library, Evergreen House, 26 Newcastle St, Dartmouth, NS, B2Y 3M5, CANADA. Tel: 902-464-2004. p. 2617
Baxter, Sydney, Librn, Tofield Municipal Library, 5407 50 St, Tofield, AB, T0B 4J0, CANADA. Tel: 780-662-3838. p. 2557
Baxter, Tammy, Br Mgr, Heartland Regional Library System, Belle Branch, 206 B S Alvarado, Belle, MO, 65013. Tel: 573-859-6285. p. 1249
Bay, Kelly, Dir, Orrington Public Library, 15 School St, Orrington, ME, 04474. Tel: 207-825-4938. p. 934
Bay-Winslow, Karen, Dir, Cambridge City Public Library, 600 W Main St, Cambridge City, IN, 47327. Tel: 765-478-3335. p. 673
Bayahy, Zaineb, Head Librn, Tech Serv, Capital University, One College & Main, Columbus, OH, 43209. Tel: 614-236-6614. p. 1772
Bayan, Anne-Solene, Asst Curator, Telfair Museum of Art, 207 W York St, Savannah, GA, 31401. Tel: 912-790-8800. p. 497
Bayer, Marc Dewey, Asst Libr Dir, Buffalo State University of New York, 1300 Elmwood Ave, Buffalo, NY, 14222. Tel: 716-878-6305. p. 1508
Bayer, Vicki, Asst Librn, Yoakum County Library, 901 Ave E, Plains, TX, 79355. Tel: 806-456-8725. p. 2227
Bayes, Amy, Youth Serv, Newton Public Library, 720 N Oak, Newton, KS, 67114. Tel: 316-283-2890. p. 826
Baykoucheva, Svetla, Head Librn, University of Maryland Libraries, White Memorial Chemistry Library, 4176 Campus Dr, College Park, MD, 20742. Tel: 301-405-9078. p. 963
Bayles, Kelly, Br Mgr, Tulsa City-County Library, Brookside, 1207 E 45th Pl, Tulsa, OK, 74105. p. 1866
Bayless, Paul, Br Mgr, Saint Louis County Library, Grand Glaize Branch, 1010 Meramec Station Rd, Manchester, MO, 63021-6943. Tel: 314-994-3300, Ext 3300. p. 1273
Bayless, Stephanie, Dir, The National Archives at San Francisco, 1000 Commodore Dr, San Bruno, CA, 94066-2350. Tel: 650-238-3501. p. 214
Baylis, Lisa, Circ Serv, ILL, Groton Public Library, 99 Main St, Groton, MA, 01450. Tel: 978-448-1167, Ext 1318. p. 1022
Baylor, Ralph, Libr Dir, University Club Library, One W 54th St, New York, NY, 10019. Tel: 212-572-3418. p. 1603
Bayne, Angie, Mgr, Children's Dept, Missouri River Regional Library, 214 Adams St, Jefferson City, MO, 65101. Tel: 573-634-2464. p. 1252
Bayne, Cathy, Dir, Fairfax Public Library, 313 Vanderbilt St, Fairfax, IA, 52228. Tel: 319-846-2994. p. 752
Bayne, Virginia, Circ, Oak Ridge Public Library, 1401 Oak Ridge Tpk, Oak Ridge, TN, 37830-6224. Tel: 865-425-3455. p. 2123
Baynes, Patricia, Dir, Palmyra Community Library, 402 E Main St, Palmyra, NY, 14522. Tel: 315-597-5276. p. 1614
Bayness, Aisha, Libr Mgr, Timberland Regional Library, Winlock Branch, 322 NE First St, Winlock, WA, 98596. Tel: 360-785-3461. p. 2390
Bayonne, Phara, Dir, University of Connecticut, Jeremy Richard Library, Stamford Campus, One University Pl, Stamford, CT, 06901-2315. Tel: 203-251-8523. p. 340
Bays, Brian, Pub Serv Librn, University of Hawaii at Hilo Library, 200 W Kawili St, Hilo, HI, 96720. Tel: 808-932-7310. p. 505
Bays, Mary, Asst Dir, Marshall Public Library, 214 N Lafayette, Marshall, MO, 65340. Tel: 660-886-3391, Ext 4. p. 1260
Baysinger, Richard, Media Librn, Eastern New Mexico University - Portales, 1500 S Ave K, Portales, NM, 88130-7402. Tel: 575-562-2602. p. 1473
Bazemore, Trudy, Asst Dir, Georgetown County Library, 405 Cleland St, Georgetown, SC, 29440-3200. Tel: 843-545-3300. p. 2060
Bazile, Grace, Librn, Lincoln Medical Center, 234 E 149th St, Rm 2D4, Bronx, NY, 10451. Tel: 718-579-5000, 718-579-5745. p. 1499
Bazile, Paul, Dir, North Miami Public Library, 835 NE 132nd St, North Miami, FL, 33161. Tel: 305-891-5535. p. 429
Bazilus, Meridith, Ref Librn, Middlesex Public Library, 1300 Mountain Ave, Middlesex, NJ, 08846. Tel: 732-356-6602. p. 1418
Bazinet, Gail, Br Mgr, Allen Parish Libraries, 320 S Sixth St, Oberlin, LA, 70655. Tel: 318-491-4543. p. 905

Bazzano, Rody, Librn, Archdiocese of Hartford Pastoral Center, 467 Bloomfield Ave, Bloomfield, CT, 06002. Tel: 860-242-5573, Ext 2623. p. 302
Beaber, Tammie, Learning Commons Coord, Kent State University, 330 University Dr NE, New Philadelphia, OH, 44663-9452. Tel: 330-308-7471. p. 1807
Beach, Gail, Libr Asst, Gilchrist County Public Library, 105 NE 11th Ave, Trenton, FL, 32693-3803. Tel: 352-463-3176. p. 451
Beach, Gretchen, Cat, Digital Serv Librn, Marshall University Libraries, One John Marshall Dr, Huntington, WV, 25755-2060. Tel: 304-696-2312. p. 2405
Beach, Jennifer, Instrul & Res Librn, Longwood University, Redford & Race St, Farmville, VA, 23909. Tel: 434-395-2257. p. 2318
Beach, Marcia, Youth Serv Mgr, Highland Park Public Library, 494 Laurel Ave, Highland Park, IL, 60035-2690. Tel: 847-432-0216. p. 599
Beach, Sherry, Dir, Will Rogers Library, 1515 N Florence Ave, Claremore, OK, 74017. Tel: 918-341-1564. p. 1844
Beacom, Matthew, Cataloger, Spec Projects, Yale University Library, Beinecke Rare Book & Manuscript Library, 121 Wall St, New Haven, CT, 06511. Tel: 202-432-4947. p. 327
Beacom, Natalie, Dir, New Berlin Public Library, 15105 Library Lane, New Berlin, WI, 53151. Tel: 262-785-4980. p. 2464
Beagle, Donald, Dir, Libr Serv, Belmont Abbey College, 100 Belmont-Mt Holly Rd, Belmont, NC, 28012. Tel: 704-461-6748. p. 1674
Beaird, Kathy, Dir, Adult Serv, Norman Williams Public Library, Ten The Green, Woodstock, VT, 05091. Tel: 802-457-2295. p. 2300
Beal, Charlie, Archives Coordr, Florence Griswold Museum, 96 Lyme St, Old Lyme, CT, 06371. Tel: 860-434-5542. p. 332
Beal, Darry, Finance Mgr, Eugene Public Library, 100 W Tenth Ave, Eugene, OR, 97401. Tel: 541-682-5450. p. 1878
Beal, Mary Rogers, Dir, Talking Bks, Mississippi Library Commission, 3881 Eastwood Dr, Jackson, MS, 39211. Tel: 601-432-4116. p. 1222
Beal, Susan, Bus Off Mgr, Indian Trails Public Library District, 355 S Schoenbeck Rd, Wheeling, IL, 60090. Tel: 847-459-4100. p. 662
Bealer, Rebecca, Head, Ser, Louisiana State University Health Sciences Center, 433 Bolivar St, Box B3-1, New Orleans, LA, 70112-2223. Tel: 504-568-6108. p. 901
Beall, Cassie, Cataloger, Tech Asst, Conway County Library Headquarters, 101 W Church St, Morrilton, AR, 72110. Tel: 501-354-5204. p. 105
Beall, Connie, Co-Dir, Addison Public Library, Six South St, Addison, NY, 14801. Tel: 607-359-3888. p. 1481
Beall, Mary, City Librn, Southfield Public Library, 26300 Evergreen Rd, Southfield, MI, 48076. Tel: 248-796-4200. p. 1151
Beall, Mary, Dep Librn, Southfield Public Library, 26300 Evergreen Rd, Southfield, MI, 48076. Tel: 248-796-4302. p. 1151
Bealle, Penny J, Libr Instruction, Ref, Suffolk County Community College, Montaukett Learning Center, 121 Speonk Riverhead Rd, Riverhead, NY, 11901-3499. Tel: 631-548-2541. p. 1627
Beals, Blake, Asst Dir, Reference & Access Services, The University of Memphis, One N Front St, Memphis, TN, 38103. Tel: 901-678-5462. p. 2115
Beals, Brynn, Librn, VMFH Franciscan Library, St Joseph Medical Ctr, 1717 S J St, Tacoma, WA, 98405. Tel: 253-426-6778. p. 2388
Beals, Jessica, Circ Librn, Elizabeth Titus Memorial Library, Two W Water St, Sullivan, IL, 61951. Tel: 217-728-7221. p. 652
Beam, Jonathan, ILL, Libr Tech, Colorado Mountain College, 1275 Crawford Ave, Steamboat Springs, CO, 80487. Tel: 970-870-4449. p. 295
Beam, Pam, Circ Asst, Arcadia Free Public Library, 730 Raider Dr, Ste 3140, Arcadia, WI, 54612. Tel: 608-323-7505. p. 2421
Beamer, Michele B, Br Librn, Orange County Public Library, Wilderness, 6421 Flat Run Rd, Locust Grove, VA, 22508. Tel: 540-854-5310. p. 2336
Beamon, Lennie, Br Mgr, Madison County Library System, Paul E Griffin Library, 116 Parkside Ave, Camden, MS, 39045. Tel: 662-468-0309. p. 1213
Beams, Daniel J, Curator, The Old Stone Fort Museum, 145 Fort Rd, Schoharie, NY, 12157. Tel: 518-295-7192. p. 1638
Beams, Nicholas, Law Librn, Connecticut Judicial Branch Law Libraries, Putnam Law Library, Putnam Courthouse, 155 Church St, Putnam, CT, 06260. Tel: 860-928-3716. p. 316
Bean, Ashley, Distance Learning Librn, First Year Experience Librn, Rogers State University Library, 1701 W Will Rogers Blvd, Claremore, OK, 74017-3252. Tel: 918-343-7786. p. 1844
Bean, Barbara, Ref Librn, Michigan State University College of Law Library, Law College Bldg, Rm 115, 648 N Shaw Lane, East Lansing, MI, 48824-1300. Tel: 517-432-6878. p. 1102
Bean, Beth, Br Mgr, Greater Clarks Hill Regional Library System, Warren County Library, Ten Warren St, Warrenton, GA, 30828. Tel: 706-465-2656. p. 478
Bean, Christina, Dir, Atkins Memorial Library, 360 Main St, Corinth, ME, 04427. Tel: 207-285-7226. p. 922
Bean, Christopher A, Dir of Libr, Shenandoah University, 1460 University Dr, Winchester, VA, 22601. Tel: 540-665-4553. p. 2354
Bean, Elaine, Tech Serv Librn, Rivier University, 420 S Main St, Nashua, NH, 03060-5086. Tel: 603-897-8672. p. 1375
Bean, Jenny, Head, Res, Hammond Public Library, 564 State St, Hammond, IN, 46320-1532. Tel: 219-931-5100, Ext 329. p. 689
Bean, Kerry, Asst Librn, Otis Library & Museum, 48 N Main Rd, Otis, MA, 01253. Tel: 413-269-0100, Ext 117, 413-269-0109. p. 1045
Bean, Nancy, Libr Supvr, Warren General Hospital, Two Crescent Park W, Warren, PA, 16365. Tel: 814-723-4973, Ext 1825. p. 2017
Bean, Pam, Adult Serv, Head, Ref, Southern Oklahoma Library System, 601 Railway Express St, Ardmore, OK, 73401. Tel: 580-223-3164. p. 1840
Bean, Phoebe, Assoc Dir, Rhode Island Historical Society, 121 Hope St, Providence, RI, 02906. Tel: 401-273-8107, Ext 424. p. 2039
Bean, Steven, Fac Librn, Itasca Community College Library, 1851 E Hwy 169, Grand Rapids, MN, 55744. Tel: 218-322-2351. p. 1177
Beane, Susan, Libr Assoc, Maine State Law & Legislative Reference Library, 43 State House Sta, Augusta, ME, 04333-0043. Tel: 207-287-1600. p. 914
Bear Killer, Darlene, Circ & ILL, Oglala Lakota College, Three Mile Creek Rd, Kyle, SD, 57752. Tel: 605-455-6069. p. 2077
Bear, Kylee, Libr Dir, George Culver Community Library, 615 Phillips Blvd, Sauk City, WI, 53583-1159. Tel: 608-643-8346. p. 2475
Bearce, Lisa, Head, Youth Serv, Peterborough Town Library, Two Concord St, Peterborough, NH, 03458. Tel: 603-924-8040. p. 1378
Beard, Alison, Dir, Caldwell Community College & Technical Institute, 2855 Hickory Blvd, Hudson, NC, 28638. Tel: 828-726-2311. p. 1697
Beard, Anita, Br Librn, Pike-Amite-Walthall Library System, Walthall, 707 Union Rd, Tylertown, MS, 39667. Tel: 601-876-4348. p. 1226
Beard, Barbara S, Br Mgr, Beaumont Public Library System, Maureen Gray Literacy Center, 801 Pearl St, Beaumont, TX, 77701. Tel: 409-835-7924. p. 2145
Beard, Craig, Ref Librn, University of Alabama at Birmingham, Mervyn H Sterne Library, 917 13th St S, Birmingham, AL, 35205. Tel: 205-934-6364. p. 9
Beard, Louan, Asst Dir, Morton-James Public Library, 923 First Corso, Nebraska City, NE, 68410. Tel: 402-873-5609. p. 1325
Beard, Regina, Assoc Librn, Florida Gulf Coast University Library, 10501 FGCU Blvd S, Fort Myers, FL, 33965. Tel: 239-590-4372. p. 403
Beard, Renee, Br Mgr, Newburgh Chandler Public Library, 4111 Lakeshore Dr, Newburgh, IN, 47630-2274. Tel: 812-583-5468, Ext 305. p. 709
Beard, Renee, Br Mgr, Newburgh Chandler Public Library, Newburgh Library, 30 W Water St, Newburgh, IN, 47630. Tel: 812-858-1437. p. 710
Beard, Sherry, Librn, Gadsden State Community College, Allen Hall, Rms 204 & 220, 1001 George Wallace Dr, Gadsden, AL, 35903. Tel: 256-549-8333. p. 18
Bearden, Cole, Adult Serv Mgr, Poplar Bluff Municipal Library, 318 N Main St, Poplar Bluff, MO, 63901. Tel: 573-686-8639, Ext 22. p. 1266
Beardslee, Elizabeth, Nonfiction & IT/Webmaster Librn, Richmond Memorial Library, 19 Ross St, Batavia, NY, 14020. Tel: 585-343-9550. p. 1491
Beardsley, Renee, Libr Mgr, New Woodstock Free Library, 2106 Main St, New Woodstock, NY, 13122-8718. Tel: 315-662-3134. p. 1577
Bearman, Alan, Dr, Dean, Univ Libr, Washburn University, 1700 SW College Ave, Topeka, KS, 66621. Tel: 785-670-1179. p. 839
Bearre, Denise, Libr Dir, Curtis Township Library, 4884 Bamfield Rd, Glennie, MI, 48737. Tel: 989-735-2601. p. 1109
Bearre, Denise, Libr Dir, Alcona County Library System, 312 W Main, Harrisville, MI, 48740. Tel: 989-724-6796. p. 1113
Bearse, Carrie, Admin Dir, Ch, Yarmouth Port Library, 297 Main St, Rte 6A, Yarmouth Port, MA, 02675. Tel: 508-362-3717. p. 1073
Beary, Camille, Asst Dir, Lyon College, 2300 Highland Rd, Batesville, AR, 72501-3699. Tel: 870-307-7444. p. 90
Beasecker, Robert, Curator, Rare Bks, Grand Valley State University Libraries, One Campus Dr, Allendale, MI, 49401-9403. Tel: 616-331-8556. p. 1077
Beasley, Allison, Dir, Kankakee Public Library, 201 E Merchant St, Kankakee, IL, 60901. Tel: 815-939-4564. p. 604
Beasley, Deborah, Youth Serv, Blue Island Public Library, 2433 York St, Blue Island, IL, 60406-2011. Tel: 708-388-1078, Ext 22. p. 543
Beasley, Elizabeth, Coordr, Alabama Power Co, 600 N 18th St, Birmingham, AL, 35203-2206. Tel: 205-257-4466. p. 6
Beasley, Emily, Librn, Grifton Public Library, 568 Queen St, Grifton, NC, 28530. Tel: 252-524-0345. p. 1694
Beasley, Gerald, Vice Provost & Chief Librn, University of Alberta, University Library, 5-02 Cameron Libr, Edmonton, AB, T6G 2J8, CANADA. Tel: 780-492-3790. p. 2538
Beasley, Gerald R, Univ Librn, Cornell University Library, 201 Olin Library, Ithaca, NY, 14853. Tel: 607-255-4144. p. 1551
Beasley, Joanna, Archivist, Tech Serv Librn, North Greenville University, 100 Donnan Blvd, Tigerville, SC, 29688. Tel: 864-977-7091. p. 2071
Beasley, Kathleen, Libr Mgr, San Mateo County Library, Belmont Library, 1110 Alameda de las Pulgas, Belmont, CA, 94002. Tel: 650-591-8286, Ext 227. p. 235
Beasley, Meaghan, Ref Serv, Dare County Library, Kill Devil Hills Branch, 400 Mustian St, Kill Devil Hills, NC, 27948. Tel: 252-441-4331. p. 1702
Beasley, Nancy, ILL, Bracebridge Public Library, 94 Manitoba St, Bracebridge, ON, P1L 2B5, CANADA. Tel: 705-645-4171. p. 2632
Beasley, Paula, Co-Director, Library Services, Sr Asst Librn, Bluefield University, 3000 College Ave, Bluefield, VA, 24605. Tel: 276-326-4269. p. 2307

Beathard, Lana, Bus Mgr, Montgomery County Memorial Library System, 104 I-45 N, Conroe, TX, 77301-2720. Tel: 936-788-8377, Ext 6238. p. 2159

Beaton, Rebecca, Br Head, Thompson-Nicola Regional District Library System, Blue River Branch, 829 Cedar St, Blue River, BC, V0E 1J0, CANADA. Tel: 250-673-8235. p. 2567

Beatson, Leigh, Tech Serv, Fried, Frank, Harris, Shriver & Jacobson LLP, 801 17th St NW, Ste 600, Washington, DC, 20006. Tel: 202-639-7000. p. 367

Beattie, Lyn, Law Librn, Alberta Law Libraries, Judicial, Calgary Courts Ctr, 601-Five St SW, Ste 501N, Calgary, AB, T2P 5P7, CANADA. Tel: 403-297-8234. p. 2525

Beatty, Amy, Dean, Libr Serv, Southeastern University, 1000 Longfellow Blvd, Lakeland, FL, 33801. Tel: 863-667-5523. p. 417

Beatty, Janet, Bus Mgr, Jackson-George Regional Library System, 3214 Pascagoula St, Pascagoula, MS, 39567. Tel: 228-769-3092. p. 1228

Beatty, John R, Faculty Scholarship Librn, University at Buffalo Libraries-State University of New York, Charles B Sears Law Library, John Lord O'Brian Hall, 211 Mary Talbert Way, Buffalo, NY, 14260-1110. Tel: 716-645-8590. p. 1511

Beatty, Joshua, Libr Dir, State University of New York College at Plattsburgh, Two Draper Ave, Plattsburgh, NY, 12901. Tel: 518-564-5200. p. 1619

Beatty, Luke, Libr Dir, Illinois College, 1101 W College Ave, Jacksonville, IL, 62650-2299. Tel: 217-245-3020. p. 602

Beatty, Luke, Exec Dir, Info Res, Libr Dir, Saint Ambrose University Library, 518 W Locust St, Davenport, IA, 52803. Tel: 563-333-6241. p. 744

Beatty, Matt, Br Mgr, San Diego Public Library, Ocean Beach, 4801 Santa Monica Ave, San Diego, CA, 92107. Tel: 619-531-1532. p. 220

Beau, Michelle, Head, Bibliog Serv, Winchester Public Library, 80 Washington St, Winchester, MA, 01890. Tel: 781-721-7171. p. 1070

Beaucage-Roy, Kevin, Librn, College de l'Assomption, 270 boul l'Ange-Gardien, L'Assomption, QC, J5W 1R7, CANADA. Tel: 450-589-5621, Ext 258. p. 2715

Beauchamp, Alexis, Library Contact, Loto-Quebec, 500 Sherbrooke W, Montreal, QC, H3A 3G6, CANADA. Tel: 514-282-8000. p. 2725

Beauchamp, Darrell G, EdD, Exec Dir, Museum of Western Art, 1550 Bandera Hwy, Kerrville, TX, 78028-9547. Tel: 830-896-2553. p. 2205

Beauchamp, Davey, Br Mgr, Cabarrus County Public Library, Harrisburg Branch, 201 Sims Pkwy, Harrisburg, NC, 28075. Tel: 704-920-2080. p. 1682

Beauchamp, Jesi, District Manager, Cedar County Library District, 717 East St, Stockton, MO, 65785. Tel: 417-276-3413. p. 1282

Beauchamp, Josee, Libr Support Serv Asst, Stormont, Dundas & Glengarry County Library, Crysler Branch, 16 Third St, Crysler, ON, K0C 1G0, CANADA. Tel: 613-987-2090. p. 2638

Beauchamp, Judy, Ch, Miami Public Library, 200 N Main St, Miami, OK, 74354. Tel: 918-541-2292. p. 1853

Beauchamp, R Mitchel, Librn, Beauchamp Botanical Library, 1434 E 24th St, National City, CA, 91950-6010. Tel: 619-477-5333. p. 182

Beauchamp, Ty, Div Dir, Info Tech, Harris County Public Library, 5749 S Loop E, Houston, TX, 77033. Tel: 713-274-6600. p. 2192

Beaudoin, Anne, Acq, College de Rosemont (Cegep) Bibliotheque, 6400 16th Ave, Montreal, QC, H1X 2S9, CANADA. Tel: 514-376-1620, Ext 7265. p. 2723

Beaudoin, Cathleen C, Libr Dir, Dover Public Library, 73 Locust St, Dover, NH, 03820-3785. Tel: 603-516-6050. p. 1361

Beaudoin, Joan, Dr, Asst Prof, Wayne State University, 106 Kresge Library, Detroit, MI, 48202. Tel: 313-577-1825. p. 2787

Beaudoin, Johane, Libr Tech, Conseil Superieur de l'Education, 1175 ave Lavigerie, Bur 180, Sainte-Foy, QC, G1V 5B2, CANADA. Tel: 418-528-0608. p. 2734

Beaudoin, Shauna, Dir, Info Serv, Dir, Programs, Hydrocephalus Canada, 16 Four Seasons Pl, Ste 111, Toronto, ON, M9B 6E5, CANADA. Tel: 416-214-1056. p. 2690

Beaudry, Guylaine, Dr, Univ Librn, Concordia University Libraries, 1400 de Maisonneuve Blvd W, LB 2, Montreal, QC, H3G 1M8, CANADA. Tel: 514-848-2424, Ext 7777. p. 2723

Beaudry, Katherine, Asst Dir, East Hartford Public Library, 840 Main St, East Hartford, CT, 06108. Tel: 860-290-4339. p. 310

Beaudry, Marie-Christine, Librn, Universite du Quebec, CP 8889, Succ Centre-Ville, 1255 Rue St Denis, Locale-A-1200, Montreal, QC, H3C 3P3, CANADA. Tel: 514-987-6134. p. 2728

Beaudry, Melissa, Dir, Polytechnique Montreal Library, Campus de l'Universite de Montreal, 2500, chemin de Polytechnique, 2900, boul Edouard-Montpetit, Montreal, QC, H3T 1J4, CANADA. Tel: 514-340-4711, Ext 4652. p. 2727

Beaudry, Nicole, Director, Children's Library, Bibliotheque Publique Juive, 5151 Cote Ste Catherine, Montreal, QC, H3W 1M6, CANADA. Tel: 514-345-2627. p. 2717

Beaudry, Violet, Librn, Palliser Regional Library, Tugaske Branch, 106 Ogema St, Tugaske, SK, S0H 4B0, CANADA. Tel: 306-759-2215. p. 2743

Beaulieu, Chantal, Chef de Div, Bibliotheques de Montreal, Georges-Vanier, 2450 rue Workman, Montreal, QC, H3J 1L8, CANADA. Tel: 514-872-3067. p. 2718

Beaulieu, Chantal, Chef de Div, Bibliotheques de Montreal, Marie-Uguay, 6052 rue Monk, Montreal, QC, H4E 3H6, CANADA. Tel: 514-872-3067. p. 2719

Beaulieu, Chantal, Chef de Div, Bibliotheques de Montreal, Saint-Charles, 2333 rue Mullins, Montreal, QC, H3K 3E3, CANADA. Tel: 514-872-3067. p. 2720

Beaulieu, Chantal, Chef de Div, Bibliotheques de Montreal, Saint-Henri, 4707 rue Notre-Dame Ouest, Montreal, QC, H4C 1S9, CANADA. Tel: 514-872-3067. p. 2720

Beaulieu, Daniel, Head, Coll, Université de Saint-Boniface, 200, ave de la Cathedrale, Winnipeg, MB, R2H 0H7, CANADA. Tel: 204-235-4403. p. 2594

Beaumont, Bob, Pres, Wallingford Historical Society Inc, Library, Samuel Parsons House, 180 S Main St, Wallingford, CT, 06492. Tel: 203-294-1996. p. 342

Beauregard, Susan, Teen Serv Librn, Reading Public Library, 64 Middlesex Ave, Reading, MA, 01867-2550. Tel: 781-944-0840. p. 1049

Beausejour, Johanne, Acq & Cat, Adult Coll, Bibliothèque Raymond-Laberge, 25 Maple Blvd, Chateauguay, QC, J6J 3P7, CANADA. Tel: 450-698-3080. p. 2710

Beauvais, Cassey, Mgr, Pub Serv, Chatham-Kent Public Library, 120 Queen St, Chatham, ON, N7M 2G6, CANADA. Tel: 519-354-2940. p. 2635

Beaver, Abby, State Librn, WYLD Network, c/o Wyoming State Library, 2800 Central Ave, Cheyenne, WY, 82002-0060. Tel: 307-777-6333. p. 2777

Beaver, Abigail, State Librn, Wyoming State Library, 2800 Central Ave, Cheyenne, WY, 82002. Tel: 307-777-5913. p. 2493

Beaver, Emma, Head Librn, Pennsylvania State University, 2201 University Dr, Uniontown, PA, 15456. Tel: 724-430-4156. p. 2014

Beavers, Jefferson, Dir, Conway Public Library, 15 Main Ave, Conway, NH, 03818. Tel: 603-447-5552. p. 1360

Beavers, Melissa, Br Mgr, High Plains Library District, Lincoln Park Library, 1012 11th St, Ste B, Greeley, CO, 80631. p. 285

Beazer, Donna, Libr Mgr, Jim & Mary Kearl Library of Cardston, 25 Third Ave W, Cardston, AB, T0K 0K0, CANADA. Tel: 403-653-4775. p. 2530

Beazer, Dylan, Ref Supvr, Naval History & Heritage Command, 805 Kidder-Breese St SE, Washington Navy Yard, DC, 20374-5060. Tel: 202-433-2060. p. 382

Bebbington, Clare, Br Mgr, Atlantic County Library System, Hammonton Branch, 451 Egg Harbor Rd, Hammonton, NJ, 08037. Tel: 609-561-2264. p. 1417

Bebee, Emily, Head, Children's & Young Adult Serv, Perry County Public Library, 2328 Tell St, Tell City, IN, 47586. Tel: 812-547-2661. p. 720

Bebej, Cheryl, Youth Serv Librn, Princeton Public Library, 698 E Peru St, Princeton, IL, 61356. Tel: 815-875-1331. p. 636

Bebout, Donna, Libr Dir, La Vergne Public Library, 5063 Murfreesboro Rd, La Vergne, TN, 37086. Tel: 615-793-7303. p. 2108

Bebris, Rosemary, Libr Dir, Walker Memorial Library, 800 Main St, Westbrook, ME, 04092. Tel: 207-854-0630, Ext 4260. p. 946

Becca, Pad, Dir, College for Creative Studies Library, Manoogian Visual Resource Ctr, 301 Frederick Douglass Dr, Detroit, MI, 48202-4034. Tel: 313-664-7641. p. 1097

Bechard, Marjo, Librn, Cegep de Victoriaville, E'cole Quebecoise du Meuble et du Bois Ouvre, 765 Est Notre Dame, Victoriaville, QC, G6P 4B3, CANADA. Tel: 819-758-6401, Ext 2621. p. 2738

Bechard, Staci, Library Contact, Montana School for the Deaf & Blind Library, 3911 Central Ave, Great Falls, MT, 59405. Tel: 406-771-6051. p. 1294

Becho, Arnoldo, Dir, Mayor Joe V Sanchez Public Library, 525 S Kansas Ave, Weslaco, TX, 78596. Tel: 956-968-4533. p. 2256

Beck, Alison M, Spec Project Dir, University of Texas Libraries, Briscoe Center for American History, Sid Richard Hall, Unit 2, Rm 2106, 2300 Red River St, Austin, TX, 78712-1426. Tel: 512-495-4515. p. 2142

Beck, Allisa, Coll Mgt Librn, University of Southern Mississippi, 730 E Beach Blvd, Long Beach, MS, 39560-2698. Tel: 228-214-3468. p. 1225

Beck, Elizabeth, Cat & Syst Librn, Millsaps College, 1701 N State St, Jackson, MS, 39210. Tel: 601-974-1076. p. 1222

Beck, Erik, Head, Libr Syst, Info Tech, California State University, Sacramento, 6000 J St, Sacramento, CA, 95819-6039. Tel: 916-278-6708. p. 208

Beck, Faye, Asst Librn, Theresa Public Library, 290 Mayville St, Theresa, WI, 53091-0307. Tel: 920-488-2342. p. 2481

Beck, Jamie, Syst Adminr, High Point Public Library, 901 N Main St, High Point, NC, 27262. Tel: 336-883-3660. p. 1696

Beck, Jeannie, Coordr, Ser, Southeastern Baptist Theological Seminary Library, 114 N Wingate St, Wake Forest, NC, 27587. Tel: 919-863-2325. p. 1720

Beck, Jeff, Libr Dir, Wabash College, 301 W Wabash Ave, Crawfordsville, IN, 47933. Tel: 765-361-6346. p. 677

Beck, Kayla, Asst Librn, Youth Serv Coordr, Mineral Point Public Library, 137 High St, Ste 2, Mineral Point, WI, 53565. Tel: 608-987-2447. p. 2462

Beck, Maribeth, Br Mgr, Saint Johns County Public Library System, Bartram Trail Branch, 60 Davis Pond Blvd, Fruit Cove, FL, 32259-4390. Tel: 904-827-6961. p. 440

Beck, Melissa, Head, Cat, University of California Los Angeles Library, Hugh & Hazel Darling Law Library, 1112 Law Bldg, 385 Charles E Young Dr E, Los Angeles, CA, 90095-1458. Tel: 310-825-7826. p. 169

Beck, Michelle, Tech Serv, Archbold Community Library, 205 Stryker St, Archbold, OH, 43502-1142. Tel: 419-446-2783. p. 1746

Beck, Sandra, Libr Mgr, Sno-Isle Libraries, Mariner Library, 520 128th St SW, Ste A9 & A10, Everett, WA, 98204. Tel: 425-423-9017. p. 2370
Beck, Thomas J, Teaching & Learning Librn, Auraria Library, 1100 Lawrence St, Denver, CO, 80204-2095. Tel: 303-315-7742. p. 273
Beck, Torri, Cat, Online Serv, Toccoa Falls College, 107 Kincaid Dr, MSC 749, Toccoa Falls, GA, 30598. Tel: 706-886-7299, Ext 5300. p. 500
Beck, Tracey Rae, Exec Dir, American Swedish Historical Museum Library, 1900 Pattison Ave, Philadelphia, PA, 19145. Tel: 215-389-1776. p. 1974
Beckendorf, Andrea, Dr, Res & Instruction Librn, Luther College, 700 College Dr, Decorah, IA, 52101. Tel: 563-387-1227. p. 745
Becker, Adam, Libr Dir, Pueblo of Pojoaque Public Library, 37 Camino del Rincon, Ste 2, Santa Fe, NM, 87506-9810. Tel: 505-455-7511. p. 1476
Becker, Alexis, Archives Librn, Pub Serv Librn, Briar Cliff University, 3303 Rebecca St, Sioux City, IA, 51104. Tel: 712-279-5449. p. 782
Becker, Alexis, Dir, Dakota Wesleyan University, 1200 W University Ave, Mitchell, SD, 57301. Tel: 605-995-2617. p. 2079
Becker, Brooke, Ref Librn, University of Alabama at Birmingham, Mervyn H Sterne Library, 917 13th St S, Birmingham, AL, 35205. Tel: 205-934-6364. p. 9
Becker, Carolyn, Dir, What Cheer Public Library, 308 S Barnes St, What Cheer, IA, 50268-0008. Tel: 641-634-2859. p. 791
Becker, Carrie, Dir, New Hampton Public Library, 20 W Spring St, New Hampton, IA, 50659. Tel: 641-394-2184. p. 772
Becker, Cathy, Dir, Atkins Public Library, 480 Third Ave, Atkins, IA, 52206. Tel: 319-446-7676. p. 733
Becker, Cecelia, Ref Librn, Tech Coordr, Somers Public Library, Two Vision Blvd, Somers, CT, 06071. Tel: 860-763-3501. p. 337
Becker, Christina, Dir, Cambridge Public Library, 21 W Main St, Cambridge, NY, 12816. Tel: 518-677-2443. p. 1512
Becker, Danielle, Med Librn, Hennepin County Medical Center, Mail Code R2, 701 Park Ave, Minneapolis, MN, 55415. Tel: 612-873-2710. p. 1183
Becker, Devin, Assoc Dean, Res & Instruction, University of Idaho Library, 850 S Rayburn St, Moscow, ID, 83844. Tel: 208-885-7040. p. 526
Becker, Elizabeth, Sr Libr Asst, Moore College of Art & Design, Sarah Peter Hall, 1st Flr, 20th St & The Parkway, Philadelphia, PA, 19103-1179. Tel: 215-965-4054. p. 1983
Becker, Kristen, Dir, Libr Serv, Eastern Arizona College, 615 N Stadium Ave, Thatcher, AZ, 85552. Tel: 928-428-8308. p. 80
Becker, Laurie, Dir, Libr Mgr, Falconer Public Library, 101 W Main St, Falconer, NY, 14733. Tel: 716-665-3504. p. 1532
Becker, Leslie, Circ Supvr, Curry College, 1071 Blue Hill Ave, Milton, MA, 02186-9984. Tel: 617-333-2102. p. 1036
Becker, Lisabeth, Librn, Roswell Park Comprehensive Cancer Center, Elm & Carlton Sts, Buffalo, NY, 14263. Tel: 716-845-5966. p. 1510
Becker, Michelle, Supvr, Pub Serv, Bellingham Public Library, 210 Central Ave, Bellingham, WA, 98225. Tel: 360-778-7224. p. 2358
Becker, Rachel, Librn, University of Rochester Medical Center, Basil G Bibby Library, Eastman Dental, Rm 208, 625 Elmwood Ave, Rochester, NY, 14620. Tel: 585-275-5010. p. 1631
Becker, Sue, Br Assoc, Modoc County Library, Cedarville Branch, 460 Main St, Cedarville, CA, 96104. Tel: 530-279-2614. p. 116
Beckerman, Shari, Library Contact, Warshaw Burstein, LLP, 575 Lexington Avenue, 7th Flr, New York, NY, 10022. Tel: 212-984-7700. p. 1603
Beckert, Helen, Ref Librn, Glen Ridge Free Public Library, 240 Ridgewood Ave, Glen Ridge, NJ, 07028. Tel: 973-748-5482. p. 1405
Beckes, Michelle, Br Mgr, Tulsa City-County Library, Skiatook Branch, 316 E Rogers Blvd, Skiatook, OK, 74070. p. 1866
Beckett, Joseph, Prog Coordr, Maryland State Library for the Blind & Print Disabled, 415 Park Ave, Baltimore, MD, 21201-3603. Tel: 410-230-2424. p. 955
Beckett, Mary, Youth Serv, Edythe L Dyer Community Library, 269 Main Rd N, Hampden, ME, 04444. Tel: 207-862-3550. p. 926
Beckett, Michael, Adminr, Missouri Department of Natural Resources, 26600 Park Rd N, Lawson, MO, 64062. Tel: 816-580-3387. p. 1259
Beckett, Tameca, Ref & Access Serv Librn, Delaware State University, 1200 N Dupont Hwy, Dover, DE, 19901-2277. Tel: 302-857-7886. p. 352
Beckham, Brandon, Mgr, Libr Operations, Metropolitan Library System in Oklahoma County, Almonte Library, 2914 SW 59th St, Oklahoma City, OK, 73119-6402. p. 1857
Beckham, Sharon, Mgr, Patron Serv, Texas Tech University Health Sciences Center, 3601 Fourth St, Lubbock, TX, 79430. Tel: 806-743-2200. p. 2214
Beckhorn, Roberta, Dir, Elizabeth B Pert Library, Valois-Logan-Hector Fire House, 5736 Rte 414, Hector, NY, 14841. Tel: 607-546-2605. p. 1545
Beckley-Jackson, Laurel, Pub Serv Librn, Onslow County Public Library, 58 Doris Ave E, Jacksonville, NC, 28540. Tel: 910-455-7350, Ext 1421. p. 1697
Beckman, Amy, Asst Dir, Millington Arbela District Library, 8530 Depot St, Millington, MI, 48746. Tel: 989-871-2003. p. 1132
Beckman, Andrew, Archivist, Studebaker National Museum Archives, 201 Chapin St, South Bend, IN, 46601. Tel: 574-235-9714. p. 719
Beckman, Noah, Instruction & Ref Librn, Gallaudet University Library, 800 Florida Ave NE, Washington, DC, 20002. Tel: 202-651-1724. p. 367
Becknell, Elissah, Ref Serv Librn, Minneapolis Community & Technical College Library, Wheelock Whitney Hall, 1501 Hennepin Ave, Minneapolis, MN, 55403. Tel: 612-659-5334. p. 1184
Beckstrom, Briony, Youth Serv, Franklin Public Library, 9151 W Loomis Rd, Franklin, WI, 53132. Tel: 414-425-8214. p. 2436
Beckstrom, Matthew A, Syst Mgr, Lewis & Clark Library, 120 S Last Chance Gulch, Helena, MT, 59601. Tel: 406-447-1690. p. 1296
Beckwith, Lara, Access Serv Librn, Arapahoe Community College, 5900 S Santa Fe Dr, Littleton, CO, 80160. Tel: 303-797-5739. p. 289
Beckwith, LeeAnn, Librn Supvr, Charlotte County Library System, Punta Gorda Public, 424 W Henry St, Punta Gorda, FL, 33950. Tel: 941-833-5459. p. 438
Beckwith, Rachel, Access & Art Librn, Interim Dir, Hampshire College Library, 893 West St, Amherst, MA, 01002. Tel: 413-559-5440. p. 984
Becnel, Kim, Dr, Assoc Prof, Prog Dir, Appalachian State University, Reich College of Education, Ste 204, 151 College St, ASU Box 32086, Boone, NC, 28608. Tel: 828-262-2243. p. 2789
Becraft-Johnan, Amber, Mgr, Brown County Public Library, Fayetteville-Perry Branch, 406 N East St, Fayetteville, OH, 45118. Tel: 513-274-2665. p. 1804
Becraft-Johnan, Amber, Mgr, Brown County Public Library, Sardinia Branch, 13309 Purdy Rd, Sardinia, OH, 45171. Tel: 937-446-1565. p. 1804
Becza, Mary Lynn, Asst Dir, The Morristown & Morris Township Library, One Miller Rd, Morristown, NJ, 07960. Tel: 973-538-6161. p. 1421
Beda, Sandy, Head, Communications, Warren-Newport Public Library District, 224 N O'Plaine Rd, Gurnee, IL, 60031. Tel: 847-244-5150, Ext 3018. p. 596
Bedard, Amy T, Libr Dir, William H Miner Agricultural Research Institute, 596 Ridge Rd, Chazy, NY, 12921. Tel: 518-846-7121, Ext 149. p. 1517
Bedard, Anne Marie, Circ Serv Librn, Saint Clair County Library System, 210 McMorran Blvd, Port Huron, MI, 48060-4098. Tel: 810-987-7323. p. 1142
Bedard, Francis, Librn, Ministere de l Énergie et des Ressources naturelles du Québec, 5700 4e Ave Ouest, B-205, Quebec, QC, G1H 6R1, CANADA. Tel: 418-627-8686. p. 2731
Bedard, Kami, Mgr, Libr Serv, Pierce Atwood LLP, 254 Commercial St, Portland, ME, 04101. Tel: 207-791-1100. p. 937
Bedard, Linda, Library Contact, Standardbred Canada Library, 2150 Meadowvale Blvd, Mississauga, ON, L5N 6R6, CANADA. Tel: 905-858-3060. p. 2659
Bedard, Remi, Doc/Ref Serv, Commission d'Acces A L'Information, 525 boul Rene-Levesque Est, Bur 236, Quebec, QC, G1R 5S9, CANADA. Tel: 418-528-7741. p. 2730
Bedard, Roxanne, Librn, Chinook Regional Library, Ponteix Branch, 130 First Ave E, Ponteix, SK, S0N 1Z0, CANADA. Tel: 306-625-3353. p. 2752
Beddingfield, Connie, Asst Librn, Attalla-Etowah County Public Library, 604 N Fourth St, Attalla, AL, 35954. Tel: 256-538-9266. p. 5
Bede, Gilbert, Syst Librn, Okanagan College Library, 1000 KLO Rd, Kelowna, BC, V1Y 4X8, CANADA. Tel: 250-762-5445, Ext 4751. p. 2568
Bedel, Julianne, Dir, Medina County District Library, 210 S Broadway, Medina, OH, 44256. Tel: 330-725-0588. p. 1801
Bedell, Stephanie, Ref (Info Servs), Suffolk Public Library System, 443 W Washington St, Suffolk, VA, 23434. Tel: 757-514-7323. p. 2348
Bedenbaugh, Robin A, Marketing & Communications Coord, University of Tennessee, Knoxville, 1015 Volunteer Blvd, Knoxville, TN, 37996-1000. Tel: 865-974-4351. p. 2107
Bedetti, Kim, Archivist, Research Librn, Monmouth County Historical Association Library & Archives, 70 Court St, Freehold, NJ, 07728. Tel: 732-462-1466. p. 1404
Bedford, Cindy, Asst Br Mgr, Hartshorne Public Library, 720 Pennsylvania Ave, Hartshorne, OK, 74547. Tel: 918-297-2113. p. 1849
Bedford, Erin, Mgr, Libr Operations, Metropolitan Library System in Oklahoma County, Bethany Library, 7941 NW 23rd, Bethany, OK, 73008. p. 1857
Bedi, Param, VPres, Libr & Info Tech, Bucknell University, 220 Bertrand Library, One Dent Dr, Lewisburg, PA, 17837. Tel: 570-577-1557. p. 1955
Bedi, Shailoo, Dir, Pub Serv, University of Victoria Libraries, McPherson Library, PO Box 1800, Victoria, BC, V8W 3H5, CANADA. Tel: 250-721-8211. p. 2583
Bednar, Denise, Asst Librn, St Paul Public Library, 145 Fifth St, Saint Paul, AR, 72760. Tel: 479-677-2907. p. 109
Bednar, Leslie, Ms, Exec Dir, Illinois Heartland Library System, 6725 Goshen Rd, Edwardsville, IL, 62025. Tel: 618-656-3216, Ext 420. p. 581
Bednar, Liz, Br Head, Monterey County Free Libraries, San Lucas Branch, 54692 Teresa St, San Lucas, CA, 93954. Tel: 831-382-0414. p. 173
Bednarski, Diane, Dep Libr Dir, Carlsbad City Library, 1775 Dove Lane, Carlsbad, CA, 92011. Tel: 760-602-2010. p. 127
Bednarski, Diane Z, Exec Dir, 49-99 Cooperative Library System, c/o Southern California Library Cooperative, 254 N Lake Ave, Pasadena, CA, 91101. Tel: 626-359-6111. p. 2761
Bednarski, Diane Z, Exec Dir, Serra Cooperative Library System, c/o SCLC, 254 N Lake Ave, No 874, Pasadena, CA, 91101. Tel: 626-283-5949. p. 2762

Beiles, Karen, Br Mgr, Ottawa Public Library/Bibliothèque publique d'Ottawa, North Gower Branch, 6579 Fourth Line Rd, Ottawa, ON, K0A 2T0, CANADA. p. 2669
Beiles, Karen, Br Mgr, Ottawa Public Library/Bibliothèque publique d'Ottawa, Richmond Branch, 6240 Perth St, Ottawa, ON, K0A 2Z0, CANADA. p. 2669
Beiles, Karen, Br Mgr, Ottawa Public Library/Bibliothèque publique d'Ottawa, Ruth E Dickinson Branch, Walter Baker Sports Centre, 100 Malvern Dr, Ottawa, ON, K2J 2G5, CANADA. p. 2669
Beiles, Karen, Br Mgr, Ottawa Public Library/Bibliothèque publique d'Ottawa, Stittsville Branch, 1637 Stittsville Main St, Ottawa, ON, K2S 1A9, CANADA. p. 2669
Beilin, Ian G, Dr, Research Servs Librn, Columbia University, Butler Library, 301 Butler Library, 535 W 114th St, New York, NY, 10027. Tel: 212-854-2241. p. 1584
Beinhoff, Lisa, Managing Dir, Texas Tech University Health Sciences Center El Paso, Medical Educ Bldg, Rm 2100, 5001 El Paso Dr, El Paso, TX, 79905. Tel: 915-215-4306. p. 2174
Beinhoff, Lisa, Dr, Managing Dir, Texas Tech University Health Sciences Center El Paso, Montes-Gallo Delia Library, 170 Rick Francis Dr, El Paso, TX, 79905. Tel: 915-215-4306, 915-215-4681. p. 2174
Beiriger, Angie, Dir, Res Serv, Reed College, 3203 SE Woodstock Blvd, Portland, OR, 97202-8199. Tel: 503-777-7702. p. 1894
Beis, Tina, Director, Collections, Strategies & Services, University of Dayton Libraries, 300 College Park Dr, Dayton, OH, 45469. Tel: 937-229-4221. p. 1780
Beisler, Molly, Discovery Serv, University of Nevada-Reno, 1664 N Virginia St, Mailstop 0322, Reno, NV, 89557-0322. Tel: 775-682-5602. p. 1349
Beisner, Keith, Librn, North Carolina School of Science & Mathematics Library, Library, Instructional Technologies & Communications, 1219 Broad St, Durham, NC, 27705. Tel: 919-416-2916. p. 1686
Beiting, Sarah, Libr Dir, Waldorf University, 106 S Sixth St, Forest City, IA, 50436. Tel: 641-585-8671. p. 753
Bejune, Kate, Res & Instruction Librn, Assumption University, 500 Salisbury St, Worcester, MA, 01609. Tel: 508-767-7020. p. 1071
Bejune, Matt, Exec Dir, Worcester State University, 486 Chandler St, Worcester, MA, 01602. Tel: 508-929-8027. p. 1073
BeJune, Veronica, Head, Coll Mgt, Gale Free Library, 23 Highland St, Holden, MA, 01520. Tel: 508-210-5560. p. 1025
Bekauri, Janell, Asst Dir, Head of Colls, Discovery & Systems, Hobart & William Smith Colleges, 334 Pulteney St, Geneva, NY, 14456. Tel: 315-781-3550. p. 1538
Bekele, Araya-Yohannes, Mr, Med Librn, Chaleur Regional Hospital, 1750 Sunset Dr, Bathurst, NB, E2A 4L7, CANADA. Tel: 506-544-2446. p. 2599
Bekkattla, Richelle, Libr Tech, Horizon College & Seminary, 604 Webster St, Saskatoon, SK, S7N 3P9, CANADA. Tel: 306-374-6655, Ext 234. p. 2748
Bekker, Jennifer, Dir of Libr, Denton Public Library, 502 Oakland St, Denton, TX, 76201. Tel: 940-349-8753. p. 2170
Belair, Andrea, Spec Coll & Archives Librn, Union College, 807 Union St, Schenectady, NY, 12308. Tel: 518-388-6277. p. 1638
Belan, Teri, Asst Dir, Manhattan Public Library, 629 Poyntz Ave, Manhattan, KS, 66502. Tel: 785-776-4741. p. 823
Beland, Matthew, Univ Archivist, Drew University Library, 36 Madison Ave, Madison, NJ, 07940. Tel: 973-408-3532. p. 1414
Belanger, Anne, Prog Dir, Presque Isle District Library, 181 E Erie St, Rogers City, MI, 49779-1709. Tel: 989-734-2477. p. 1145
Belanger, Annie, Dean, Univ Libr, Grand Valley State University Libraries, One Campus Dr, Allendale, MI, 49401-9403. Tel: 616-331-3500. p. 1077
Belanger, Arthur, Mgr, Libr Syst, Yale University Library, Harvey Cushing/John Hay Whitney Medical Library, Sterling Hall of Medicine, 333 Cedar St, New Haven, CT, 06510. Tel: 203-785-6928. p. 327
Belanger, Bri, Youth Librn, Columbia Heights Public Library, 3939 Central Ave NE, Columbia Heights, MN, 55421. Tel: 763-706-3690. p. 1170
Belanger, Bri, Youth Serv Supvr, Duluth Public Library, 520 W Superior St, Duluth, MN, 55802. Tel: 218-730-4219. p. 1172
Belanger, David, Dir of Libr, Lower Merion Library System, 75 E Lancaster Ave, Ardmore, PA, 19003. Tel: 610-645-6110. p. 1907
Belanger, Esther, Mgr, Fasken Martineau DuMoulin LLP, 800 Victoria Sq, Ste 3500, Montreal, QC, H4Z 1E9, CANADA. Tel: 514-397-7400. p. 2724
Belanger, Judy, Youth Serv, Lee Public Library, Nine Mast Rd, Lee, NH, 03861. Tel: 603-659-2626. p. 1370
Belanger Morrow, Janet, Head, Res Mgt, Northeastern University Libraries, 360 Huntington Ave, Boston, MA, 02115. Tel: 617-373-4959. p. 998
Belanger, Mylene, Archivist, EXPORAIL Archives Library, The Canadian Railway Museum, 110 rue, St-Pierre, Saint Constant, QC, J5A 1G7, CANADA. Tel: 450-638-1522, Ext 237. p. 2733
Belanger, Pascal, Tech Serv, College de l'Assomption, 270 boul l'Ange-Gardien, L'Assomption, QC, J5W 1R7, CANADA. Tel: 450-589-5621, Ext 258. p. 2715
Bélanger, Pierre, Coordr, Cegep Marie-Victorin Bibliotheque, 7000 rue Marie-Victorin, Rm G-130, Montreal, QC, H1G 2J6, CANADA. Tel: 514-325-0150. p. 2721
Belarde-Lewis, Miranda, Dr, Asst Prof, University of Washington, Mary Gates Hall, Ste 370, Campus Box 352840, Seattle, WA, 98195-2840. Tel: 206-543-1794. p. 2794
Belbin, Nicole, Assoc Dir, Western New England University, 1215 Wilbraham Rd, Springfield, MA, 01119-2689. Tel: 413-782-1484. p. 1057
Belcher, Dana, Libr Dir, East Central University, 1100 E 14th St, Ada, OK, 74820. Tel: 580-559-5564. p. 1839
Belcher, Ellen, Dr, Spec Coll Librn, John Jay College of Criminal Justice, 899 Tenth Ave, New York, NY, 10019. Tel: 212-237-8238. p. 1589
Belcher, Rebecca, Access Serv Librn, Appalachian School of Law Library, 1221 Edgewater Dr, Grundy, VA, 24614-7062. Tel: 276-935-6688, Ext 1308. p. 2322
Belcher, Robin, Head Librn, Victoria Conservatory of Music Library, 900 Johnson St, Rm 113, Victoria, BC, V8V 3N4, CANADA. Tel: 250-386-5311, Ext 5001. p. 2583
Belcher, Roxanne, Br Mgr, Johnson County Library, Oak Park, 9500 Bluejacket St, Overland Park, KS, 66214. p. 830
Belcinski, Donna, Managing Librn, Greenwich Hospital, Five Perryridge Rd, Greenwich, CT, 06830. Tel: 203-863-3293. p. 314
Belden, Anne, Dep Dir, Pub Serv, Mount Prospect Public Library, Ten S Emerson St, Mount Prospect, IL, 60056. Tel: 847-253-5675. p. 621
Belden, Cynthia D, Head, Cat, Angelo State University Library, 2025 S Johnson, San Angelo, TX, 76904-5079. Tel: 325-486-6552. p. 2235
Belden, Dreanna, Asst Dean, External Relations, University of North Texas Libraries, 1155 Union Circle, No 305190, Denton, TX, 76203-5017. Tel: 940-369-8740. p. 2170
Belderis, I, Ref (Info Servs), Theosophical Library Center, 2416 N Lake Ave, Altadena, CA, 91001. Tel: 626-798-8020. p. 116
Belderis, James T, Head of Libr, Theosophical Library Center, 2416 N Lake Ave, Altadena, CA, 91001. Tel: 626-798-8020. p. 116
Belen, Linda, Children's & Prog Serv Spec, Little Falls Public Library, Eight Warren St, Little Falls, NJ, 07424. Tel: 973-256-2784. p. 1413
Belfont, Lew, Chief Opearting Officer, Pub Serv, Howard County Library System, 9411 Frederick Rd, Ellicott City, MD, 21042. Tel: 410-313-7750. p. 965
Belgard, Titus, Ser, Tech Serv, Louisiana State University at Alexandria, 8100 Hwy 71 S, Alexandria, LA, 71302. Tel: 318-473-6440. p. 879
Beliele, Laressa, PhD, Dept Chair, University of Central Oklahoma, 100 N University Dr, Edmond, OK, 73034. Tel: 405-974-5437. p. 2791
Beline, Jayne, Dir, Parsippany-Troy Hills Free Public Library, 449 Halsey Rd, Parsippany, NJ, 07054. Tel: 973-887-5150. p. 1432
Belinfante, Anne-Marie, Libr Mgr, Weller Public Library, 41 W Main St, Mohawk, NY, 13407. Tel: 315-866-2983. p. 1573
Belisle, Gisele, Chief Librn, Bibliotheque Publique de Moonbeam, 53 St-Aubin Ave, Moonbeam, ON, P0L 1V0, CANADA. Tel: 705-367-2462. p. 2660
Belisle, Nicole, Br Mgr, Greenstone Public Library, Longlac Branch, 110 Kenogami Rd, Longlac, ON, P0T 2A0, CANADA. Tel: 807-876-4515. p. 2643
Béliveau-Cantin, Éliane, Chef de Section, Bibliotheques de Montreal, Georges-Vanier, 2450 rue Workman, Montreal, QC, H3J 1L8, CANADA. Tel: 514-872-3763. p. 2718
Béliveau-Cantin, Éliane, Chef de Section, Bibliotheques de Montreal, Saint-Charles, 2333 rue Mullins, Montreal, QC, H3K 3E3, CANADA. Tel: 514 872-3763. p. 2720
Belizaire, Daphnee, Librn, HEC Montreal Library, 3000, chemin de la Cote-Sainte-Catherine, Montreal, QC, H3T 2A7, CANADA. Tel: 514-340-6220. p. 2724
Belk, Michele, Br Dir, Cedarville Public Library, 737 Pirates Way, Cedarville, AR, 72932. Tel: 479-410-1853. p. 92
Belknap, Lori, Mgr, Illinois Department of Natural Resources, 30 Ramey St, Collinsville, IL, 62234. Tel: 618-346-5160. p. 573
Bell, A, Br Supvr, Saint Lucie County Library System, Paula A Lewis Branch Library, 2950 SW Rosser Blvd, Port Saint Lucie, FL, 34953. Tel: 772-871-5470. p. 405
Bell, Abby, Tech Librn, Alaska Oil & Gas Conservation Commission Library, 333 W Seventh Ave, Ste 100, Anchorage, AK, 99501. Tel: 907-793-1225. p. 41
Bell, Aisha, Ch, Scarsdale Public Library, 54 Olmsted Rd, Scarsdale, NY, 10583. Tel: 914-722-1300. p. 1637
Bell, Alicia, Ch, Belvedere Tiburon Library, 1501 Tiburon Blvd, Tiburon, CA, 94920. Tel: 415-789-2665. p. 252
Bell, Amber, Br Tech, US Courts Library - Tenth Circuit Court of Appeals, Byron Rogers Courthouse, 1929 Stout St, Rm 430, Denver, CO, 80294. Tel: 303-844-3591. p. 277
Bell, Amber, Reader Serv Mgr, Tigard Public Library, 13500 SW Hall Blvd, Tigard, OR, 97223-8111. Tel: 503-684-6537, Ext 2812. p. 1900
Bell, Antronette, Libr Tech II, University of Mississippi Medical Center, 2500 N State St, Jackson, MS, 39216-4505. Tel: 601-984-1230. p. 1223
Bell, Aranda, Mgr, Libr Serv, Zula Bryant Wylie Public Library, 225 Cedar St, Cedar Hill, TX, 75104-2655. Tel: 972-291-7323, Ext 1313. p. 2154
Bell, Audra, Libr Dir, Elkins Public Library, 352 N Center St, Elkins, AR, 72727. Tel: 479-643-2904. p. 94
Bell, Beth, Br Mgr, Charleston County Public Library, West Ashley, 45 Windermere Blvd, Charleston, SC, 29407. Tel: 843-766-6635. p. 2050

Bell, Brian, Br Mgr, Richmond Hill Public Library, Richvale Library, 40 Pearson Ave, Richmond Hill, ON, L4C 6T7, CANADA. Tel: 905-889-2847. p. 2676

Bell, Brigette, Dir, Libr Serv, University of St Francis, 600 Taylor St, Joliet, IL, 60435. Tel: 815-740-3447. p. 603

Bell, Burnette, Ref Librn, Wake Technical Community College, Perry Health Sciences Library, Bldg C, Rm 123, 2901 Holston Lane, Raleigh, NC, 27610-2092. Tel: 919-747-0002. p. 1711

Bell, Caleb M, Exec Dir, Tyler Museum of Art Library, 1300 S Mahon, Tyler, TX, 75701. Tel: 903-595-1001. p. 2250

Bell, Candace, Branch Experience Mgr, Evansville Vanderburgh Public Library, Stringtown, 2100 Stringtown Rd, Evansville, IN, 47711. Tel: 812-428-8233. p. 682

Bell, Christina, Curator, Exec Dir, Headley-Whitney Museum Library, 4435 Old Frankfort Pike, Lexington, KY, 40510. Tel: 859-255-6653. p. 862

Bell, Christina, Humanities Librn, Bates College, 48 Campus Ave, Lewiston, ME, 04240. Tel: 207-786-8323. p. 929

Bell, Colleen, Assessment Librn, University of the Fraser Valley, 33844 King Rd, Bldg G, Abbotsford, BC, V2S 7M8, CANADA. Tel: 604-504-7441, Ext 4396. p. 2562

Bell, David, Ref Librn, Eastern Illinois University, 600 Lincoln Ave, Charleston, IL, 61920. Tel: 217-581-7547. p. 552

Bell, Emily, Dir, Bolivar County Library System, 104 S Leflore Ave, Cleveland, MS, 38732. Tel: 662-843-2774. p. 1213

Bell, Erica, Br Mgr, Union Public Library, Vauxhall Branch, 123 Hilton Ave, Vauxhall, NJ, 07088. Tel: 908-851-5451. p. 1449

Bell, Erin, Mgr, Libr Serv, Oak Point University Library, 1431 N Claremont Ave, Chicago, IL, 60622. Tel: 630-537-9790. p. 567

Bell, Ervin, Librn, Michigan Department of Corrections, 9625 Pierce Rd, Freeland, MI, 48623. Tel: 989-695-9880, Ext 2731314, p. 1108

Bell, Gladys, Peabody Librn, Hampton University, 129 William R Harvey Way, Hampton, VA, 23668. Tel: 757-727-5185. p. 2323

Bell, James, Ref Librn, Anderson University, 1100 E Fifth St, Anderson, IN, 46012-3495. Tel: 765-641-4281. p. 668

Bell, Jami, Asst Librn, Claiborne County Public Library, 1304 Old Knoxville Rd, Tazewell, TN, 37879. Tel: 423-626-5414. p. 2127

Bell, Jane, Librn, Dallas College, 5001 N MacArthur Blvd, Irving, TX, 75062. Tel: 972-273-3400. p. 2202

Bell, Janice, Sr Librn, National Endowment for the Humanities Library, NEH Library, 4th Flr, 400 Seventh St SW, Washington, DC, 20506. Tel: 202-606-8244. p. 372

Bell, Jessica, Libr Dir, MGH Institute of Health Professions Library, Charlestown Navy Yard, 38 Third Ave, 4th Flr, Charlestown, MA, 02129. Tel: 617-643-5714. p. 1009

Bell, Jody, Mgr, Carnegie Library of Pittsburgh, Squirrel Hill, 5801 Forbes Ave, Pittsburgh, PA, 15217-1601. Tel: 412-422-9650. p. 1992

Bell, Kathie, Curator, Boot Hill Museum, 500 W Wyatt Earp Blvd, Dodge City, KS, 67801. Tel: 620-227-8188. p. 804

Bell, Kathy, Dir, Nancy Carol Roberts Memorial Library, 100 Martin Luther King Jr Pkwy, Brenham, TX, 77833. Tel: 979-337-7201. p. 2150

Bell, Ken, Dir, Haysville Community Library, 210 S Hays, Haysville, KS, 67060. Tel: 316-524-5242. p. 812

Bell, Kendra, Circ Mgr, Cherokee County Public Library, 300 E Rutledge Ave, Gaffney, SC, 29340-2227. Tel: 864-487-2711. p. 2059

Bell, Kristi, Coll, Tech Serv Supvr, Carlsbad City Library, 1775 Dove Lane, Carlsbad, CA, 92011. Tel: 760-602-2029. p. 128

Bell, Lachelle, Libr Asst, South Pointe Hospital Library, 20000 Harvard Rd, Warrensville Heights, OH, 44122. Tel: 216-491-7455. p. 1828

Bell, Laurie M, Libr Dir, Pomfret Public Library, 449 Pomfret St, Pomfret, CT, 06258. Tel: 860-928-3475. p. 334

Bell, Linda, Asst Dir, Frothingham Free Library, 28 W Main St, Fonda, NY, 12068. Tel: 518-853-3016. p. 1534

Bell, Lisa, Dir, Sunfield District Library, 112 Main St, Sunfield, MI, 48890. Tel: 517-566-8065. p. 1153

Bell, Lori, Head, Youth Serv, Middleton Public Library, 7425 Hubbard Ave, Middleton, WI, 53562-3117. Tel: 608-827-7411. p. 2457

Bell, Marcia R, Dir, San Francisco Law Library, 1145 Market St, 4th Flr, San Francisco, CA, 94103. Tel: 415-554-1772. p. 227

Bell, Melleta, Sr Archivist, Sul Ross State University, PO Box C-109, Alpine, TX, 79832. Tel: 432-837-8123. p. 2133

Bell, Michael, Asst Dean, University of Tennessee at Chattanooga Library, 400 Douglas Ave, Dept 6456, Chattanooga, TN, 37403-2598. Tel: 423-425-4501. p. 2092

Bell, Regina, Dir, Atlantic County Library System, 40 Farragut Ave, Mays Landing, NJ, 08330-1750. Tel: 609-625-2776. p. 1417

Bell, Robert, IT Mgr, Hinsdale Public Library, 20 E Maple St, Hinsdale, IL, 60521. Tel: 630-986-1976. p. 600

Bell, Robert David, Curric Mat Librn, Ref Librn, Oklahoma State University - Tulsa Library, 700 N Greenwood Ave, Tulsa, OK, 74106-0702. Tel: 918-594-8136. p. 1865

Bell, Sarah, Libr Mgr, Virginia Beach Public Library, Pungo-Blackwater Library, 916 Princess Anne Rd, Virginia Beach, VA, 23457. Tel: 757-385-7790. p. 2351

Bell, Shane, Archivist, National Archives & Records Administration, 5780 Jonesboro Rd, Morrow, GA, 30260. Tel: 770-968-2100. p. 491

Bell, Steven, Assoc Univ Librn, Learning & Res Serv, Temple University Libraries, 1210 W Berks St, Philadelphia, PA, 19122-6088. Tel: 215-204-8231. p. 1986

Bell, Tara, Tech Info Spec, United States Geological Survey, Great Lakes Science Center, 1451 Green Rd, Ann Arbor, MI, 48105-2807. Tel: 734-214-7210. p. 1079

Bell, Thomas, Med Librn, Ochsner Medical Library, 1514 Jefferson Hwy, 1st Flr, New Orleans, LA, 70121-2429. Tel: 504-842-3760. p. 903

Bell, Valerie, Dir, Athens Regional Library System, 2025 Baxter St, Athens, GA, 30606-6331. Tel: 706-613-3650. p. 458

Bell-Harney, Kathy, Cat, Boyden Library, Ten Bird St, Foxborough, MA, 02035. Tel: 508-543-1245. p. 1019

Bell-Johnson, Mary Fran, Ser Spec, Longwood University, Redford & Race St, Farmville, VA, 23909. Tel: 434-395-2450. p. 2318

Bellafante, Nancy, Evening Ref Librn, Drexel University Libraries, Hagerty Library, 33rd & Market Sts, Philadelphia, PA, 19104-2875. Tel: 215-895-2750. p. 1976

Bellafiore, Ken, Dir, Freeport Memorial Library, 144 W Merrick Rd, Freeport, NY, 11520. Tel: 516-379-3274. p. 1535

Bellaire, Nancy, Dir, Monroe County Library System, 840 S Roessler St, Monroe, MI, 48161. Tel: 734-241-5770. p. 1133

Bellamy-Smith, Lisa, Acq & Cat, University of Baltimore, Law Library, Angelos Law Center, 7th thru 12th Flrs, 1401 N Charles St, Baltimore, MD, 21201. Tel: 410-837-4591. p. 957

Bellan, Jennifer, Dir, Thayer Public Library, Three Main St, Ashuelot, NH, 03441-2616. Tel: 603-329-0175. p. 1354

Bellar, Patricia, Ch Serv, Stokes Brown Public Library, 405 White St, Springfield, TN, 37172-2340. Tel: 615-384-5123. p. 2127

Bellar, Stephanie, Dean, Salem State University, Graduate School, 352 Lafayette St, Salem, MA, 01970. Tel: 978-542-6000, 978-542-7044. p. 2786

Bellavance, Tory, Library Contact, Arizona State Hospital Library, 2500 E Van Buren St, Phoenix, AZ, 85008. Tel: 602-220-6045. p. 68

Bellavia, Rand, Libr Dir, D'Youville College, 320 Porter Ave, Buffalo, NY, 14201-1084. Tel: 716-829-7616. p. 1509

Belle-Isle, Lynn, Chief Exec Officer, Hawkesbury Public Library, 550 Higginson St, Hawkesbury, ON, K6A 1H1, CANADA. Tel: 613-632-0106, Ext 2251. p. 2647

Belleau, Suzanne, Dir, Krotz Springs Municipal Public Library, 216 Park St, Krotz Springs, LA, 70570. Tel: 337-566-8190. p. 892

Bellemare, Chantale, Libr Dir, Albert-Westmorland-Kent Regional Library, Moncton Public, 644 Main St, Ste 101, Moncton, NB, E1C 1E2, CANADA. Tel: 506-869-6000. p. 2603

Bellemare, Kelly, Ch, George Holmes Bixby Memorial Library, 52 Main St, Francestown, NH, 03043-3025. Tel: 603-547-2730. p. 1364

Bellemare, Nathalie, Libr Serv Section Chief, Bibliotheques de Montreal, Pavillon Prince, 801 rue Brennan, 5e etage, Montreal, QC, H3C 0G4, CANADA. Tel: 514-872-1542. p. 2718

Bellemer, Jessica, Dir, Libr Serv, Lees-McRae College, 191 Main St W, Banner Elk, NC, 28604-9238. Tel: 828-898-8727. p. 1673

Beller, Michael, Sr Commun Libr Mgr, Contra Costa County Library, Orinda Library, 26 Orinda Way, Orinda, CA, 94563. Tel: 925-254-2184. p. 174

Bellessis, Chris, Adult Ref Librn, Pendleton Community Library, 595 E Water St, Pendleton, IN, 46064-1070. Tel: 765-778-7527. p. 713

Bellettini, Dario, Br Mgr, Coal County Public Library, 115 W Ohio St, Coalgate, OK, 74538. Tel: 580-927-3103. p. 1845

Belley, Luc-Michel, Chef de Div, Bibliotheque Publique de Chicoutimi, 155, rue Racine Est, Chicoutimi, QC, G7H 1R5, CANADA. Tel: 418-698-5350. p. 2710

Belli, Holly, Dir, Bloomfield Public Library, 90 Broad St, Bloomfield, NJ, 07003. Tel: 973-566-6200. p. 1391

Bellian, Susan, Curator, USS Bowfin Submarine Museum & Park Library, 11 Arizona Memorial Dr, Honolulu, HI, 96818-3145. Tel: 808-423-1341. p. 513

Belling, Christine, Dir, Syosset Public Library, 225 S Oyster Bay Rd, Syosset, NY, 11791-5897. Tel: 516-921-7161. p. 1648

Bellino, Leo, Dir, North Arlington Free Public Library, 210 Ridge Rd, North Arlington, NJ, 07031. Tel: 201-955-5640. p. 1429

Bellis, Amanda, Asst Dir, Interim Dir, Nevada Public Library, 631 K Ave, Nevada, IA, 50201. Tel: 515-382-2628. p. 772

Bellis, Christy, Ch, East Morgan County Library District, 500 Clayton St, Brush, CO, 80723-2110. Tel: 970-842-4596. p. 269

Belliston, Jeffrey, Assoc Univ Librn, Brigham Young University, Harold B Lee Library, 2060 HBLL, Provo, UT, 84602. Tel: 801-422-2927. p. 2269

Bellistri, Joan, Librn, Anne Arundel County Circuit Court, Seven Church Circle, Ste 303, Annapolis, MD, 21401. Tel: 410-222-1387. p. 950

Belliveau, Gerard J, Jr, Head Librn, Racquet & Tennis Club Library, 370 Park Ave, New York, NY, 10022. Tel: 212-753-9700. p. 1600

Bello, Cammie, Colls Mgr, Museum of the Cherokee People, 589 Tsali Blvd, Cherokee, NC, 28719. Tel: 828-497-3481, 828-554-0479. p. 1681

Bello, Maria, Librn, National Marine Fisheries Service, 75 Virginia Beach Dr, Miami, FL, 33149. Tel: 305-361-4229. p. 424

Bello, Maria, Librn, National Marine Fisheries Service, 3500 Delwood Beach Rd, Panama City, FL, 32408. Tel: 850-234-6541, Ext 227. p. 435

Bello, Maria, Br Mgr, Pike County Public Library, Dingman Township, 100 Bond Ct, Milford, PA, 18337. Tel: 570-686-7045. p. 1963

Bellofatto, Kim, Dir, Madison County Public Library, 1335 N Main St, Marshall, NC, 28753-6901. Tel: 828-649-3741. p. 1703
Bellofatto, Kim, Libr Dir, Madison County Public Library, Hot Springs Branch, 170 Bridge St, Hot Springs, NC, 28743. Tel: 828-649-3741. p. 1703
Bellon, Susan, Librn, Hope Library, PO Box 115, Hope, ND, 58046. Tel: 701-945-2796. p. 1736
Bellot, Cindy, Dir, Dixie County Public Library, 16328 SE Hwy 19, Cross City, FL, 32628. Tel: 352-498-1219. p. 391
Bellucci, Anthony, Acq, United States Air Force, 744 Douhet Dr, Bldg 4244, Barksdale AFB, LA, 71110. Tel: 318-456-4101. p. 881
Bellucci, Stephanie M, Dir, Cliffside Park Free Public Library, 505 Palisade Ave, Cliffside Park, NJ, 07010. Tel: 201-945-2867. p. 1396
Belluomini, Michele, Librn, Community College of Philadelphia Library, West Regional Center Learning Commons, 4725 Chestnut St, Rm 160, Philadelphia, PA, 19139. Tel: 215-299-5848. p. 1975
Belluscio, Lynne, Dir, LeRoy Historical Society Library, 23 E Main St, LeRoy, NY, 14482. Tel: 585-768-7433. p. 1562
Belly, Melannie, Computer Spec, Yakama Nation Library, 100 Spiel-Yi Loop, Toppenish, WA, 98948. Tel: 509-865-2800, Ext 6. p. 2388
Belmar, Cynthia, Librn, Houston Community College - Northwest College, Katy Campus Library, 1550 Foxlake Dr, Houston, TX, 77084-6029. Tel: 713-718-5849. p. 2194
Belmont, Michael, IT Librn, Mount Saint Mary's University, 16300 Old Emmitsburg Rd, Emmitsburg, MD, 21727. Tel: 301-447-5591. p. 965
Belniak, Theodora, Clinical Serv Librn, University at Buffalo Libraries-State University of New York, Charles B Sears Law Library, John Lord O'Brian Hall, 211 Mary Talbert Way, Buffalo, NY, 14260-1110. Tel: 716-645-8504. p. 1511
Beloungy, Julie, Libr Dir, Thorp Public Library, 401 S Conway Dr, Thorp, WI, 54771. Tel: 715-669-5953. p. 2481
Belshaw, Lisa, Develop Dir, Princeton Public Library, 65 Witherspoon St, Princeton, NJ, 08542. Tel: 609-924-9529. p. 1436
Belt, Deanna, Circ, William Rainey Harper College Library, 1200 W Algonguin Rd, Palatine, IL, 60067. Tel: 847-925-6584. p. 631
Belt, Gordon, Dir, Pub Serv, Tennessee State Library & Archives, 403 Seventh Ave N, Nashville, TN, 37243-0312. Tel: 615-741-2764. p. 2121
Belt, Robyn, Br Mgr, Wichita Public Library, Lionel Alford Regional Library, 3447 S Meridian, Wichita, KS, 67217-2151. Tel: 316-337-9119. p. 843
Belt, Robyn, Br Mgr, Wichita Public Library, Linwood Park Branch, 1901 S Kansas Ave, Wichita, KS, 67211. Tel: 316-337-9125. p. 844
Belt, Yolie, Br Librn, Chambers County Library System, Sam & Carmena Goss Memorial Branch, One John Hall Dr, Mont Belvieu, TX, 77580. Tel: 281-576-2245. p. 2134
Beltle, Karyn, Adult Serv Mgr, Manheim Township Public Library, 595 Granite Run Dr, Lancaster, PA, 17601. Tel: 717-560-6441. p. 1952
Belton, Tom, Head Archivist, Western University Libraries, Archives & Research Collections Centre, The D B Weldon Library, 1151 Richmond St, Ste 2, London, ON, N6A 3K7, CANADA. Tel: 519-661-4046. p. 2655
Beltran del Rio, Deidre, Librn, North Central Washington Libraries, Chelan Public Library, 216 N Emerson St, Chelan, WA, 98816. Tel: 509-682-5131. p. 2393
Beltran, Eric, Education Facility Admin, Illinois Department of Corrections, 4017 E 2603 Rd, Sheridan, IL, 60551. Tel: 815-496-2181. p. 646
Beltran, Maria, Law Librn, Yuma County Law Library, 250 W Second St, Yuma, AZ, 85364. Tel: 928-817-4165. p. 87
Belvadi, Melissa, Colls Librn, User Experience Librn, University of Prince Edward Island, 550 University Ave, Charlottetown, PE, C1A 4P3, CANADA. Tel: 902-566-0343. p. 2707
Belvin, Robert, Dir, New Brunswick Free Public Library, 60 Livingston Ave, New Brunswick, NJ, 08901-2597. Tel: 732-745-5721. p. 1424
Belyeu, Elizabeth, ILL Coordr, University of Dallas, 1845 E Northgate Dr, Irving, TX, 75062-4736. Tel: 972-721-5328. p. 2203
Ben, Susan, Br Mgr, Free Library of Philadelphia, Wynnefield Branch, 5325 Overbrook Ave, Philadelphia, PA, 19131-1498. Tel: 215-685-0298. p. 1980
Ben-Hur, Lisa, Computer Spec, Hebrew Union College-Jewish Institute of Religion, 3101 Clifton Ave, Cincinnati, OH, 45220-2488. Tel: 513-221-1875. p. 1761
Bena, Amanda L, Access Serv Librn, Frostburg State University, One Susan Eisel Dr, Frostburg, MD, 21532. Tel: 301-687-7012. p. 967
Benador, Marc, Cat, Metadata Serv, Boston University Libraries, Music Library, 771 Commonwealth Ave, Boston, MA, 02215. Tel: 617-353-3705. p. 993
Benanti, Jeanine, Libr Dir, West Sangamon Public Library, 112 E Illinois St, New Berlin, IL, 62670. Tel: 217-488-7733. p. 624
Benard, Paula, Asst Dir, Warren County-Vicksburg Public Library, 700 Veto St, Vicksburg, MS, 39180-3595. Tel: 601-636-6411. p. 1235
Benavides, Mina, Sr Libr Spec, Howard County Junior College, 1001 Birdwell Lane, Big Spring, TX, 79720. Tel: 432-264-5090. p. 2148
Benavides, Reba, Ch, Val Verde County Library, 300 Spring St, Del Rio, TX, 78840. Tel: 830-774-7595. p. 2169
Benavides, Roxana, Managing Librn, Brooklyn Public Library, Sunset Park, 4201 Fourth Ave, Brooklyn, NY, 11220. Tel: 718-435-3648. p. 1504
Bencini, Emery, Acq, Supvr, High Point University, One University Pkwy, High Point, NC, 27268. Tel: 336-841-9100. p. 1697
Bend, Evan, Libr Serv Mgr, Outagamie Waupaca Library System (OWLS), 225 N Oneida, Appleton, WI, 54911. Tel: 920-832-6192. p. 2420
Bender, Alex, Br Mgr, Free Library of Philadelphia, Wyoming Branch, 231 E Wyoming Ave, Philadelphia, PA, 19120-4439. Tel: 215-685-9158. p. 1980
Bender, Alyssa, Br Mgr, Stark County District Library, Sandy Valley Branch, 9754 Cleveland Ave SE, Magnolia, OH, 44643. Tel: 330-866-3366. p. 1756
Bender, Becky, Asst Librn, Humphrey Public Library, 307 Main St, Humphrey, NE, 68642. Tel: 402-923-0957. p. 1319
Bender, Eric, Librn, California State Department of Water Resources, 1416 Ninth St, Rm 1118-13, Sacramento, CA, 95814. Tel: 916-651-0822. p. 208
Bender, Jackie, Chair, Lakeland College, 2602 59 Ave, Bag 6600, Lloydminster, SK, T9V 3N7, CANADA. Tel: 780-871-5528. p. 2742
Bender, Jeana, Dir, Viola Township Library, 100 N Grice, Viola, KS, 67149. Tel: 620-584-6679. p. 841
Bender, John, IT Mgr, Naperville Public Library, 95th Street, 3015 Cedar Glade Dr, Naperville, IL, 60564. Tel: 630-961-4100, Ext 4980. p. 623
Bender, Thomas B, IV, Libr Dir, Notre Dame Seminary Graduate School of Theology, 2901 S Carrollton Ave, New Orleans, LA, 70118-4391. Tel: 504-866-7426, Ext 700. p. 903
Bender, Tina, Librn, Citronelle Memorial Library, 7855 State St, Citronelle, AL, 36522. Tel: 251-866-7319. p. 12
Benedett, Barbara, Digital Archivist, Curtis Institute of Music, 1720 Locust St, Philadelphia, PA, 19103. Tel: 215-717-3139. p. 1976
Benedetti, Allison R, Dir, University of California Los Angeles Library, Arts Library, 1400 Public Affairs Bldg, Los Angeles, CA, 90095. Tel: 310-206-8746. p. 169
Benedetti, Allison R, Dir, University of California Los Angeles Library, Powell Library, Powell Library Bldg, Los Angeles, CA, 90095. Tel: 310-825-1938. p. 169
Benedetti, Susannah, Assoc Dir, Resource Description & Mgmt, University of North Carolina Wilmington Library, 601 S College Rd, Wilmington, NC, 28403. Tel: 910-962-4243. p. 1723
Benedetto Beals, Jennifer, Dept Head, University of Tennessee, Knoxville, Special Collections, 121 Hodges Library, 1015 Volunteer Blvd, Knoxville, TN, 37996. Tel: 865-974-4480. p. 2108
Benedict, Glen, Access Serv Librn, University of the District of Columbia, Learning Resources Division, 4200 Connecticut Ave NW, Bldg 39, Level B, Washington, DC, 20008. p. 380
Benedict, Heidi, Univ Archivist, Roger Williams University Library, One Old Ferry Rd, Bristol, RI, 02809. Tel: 401-254-3049. p. 2030
Benedict, Jeanne, Dir, Henry D Moore Parrish House & Library, 22 Village Rd, Steuben, ME, 04680. Tel: 207-546-7301. p. 942
Benedict, Jenny, Libr Dir, Gloucester, Lyceum & Sawyer Free Library, Two Dale Ave, Gloucester, MA, 01930. Tel: 978-325-5500. p. 1021
Benefield, Melissa, Coll Develop, Southeast Arkansas Regional Library, 114 E Jackson St, Monticello, AR, 71655. Tel: 870-367-8584, Ext 223. p. 104
Benekin, Vanessa, Br Mgr, Jersey City Free Public Library, Lafayette, 307 Pacific Ave, Jersey City, NJ, 07304. Tel: 201-547-5017. p. 1409
Benevides, Molly, Ch, Townsend Public Library, 12 Dudley Rd, Townsend, MA, 01469. Tel: 978-597-1714. p. 1060
Benfield, Judy, Libr Mgr, Bucks County Free Library, Pennwood, 301 S Pine St, Langhorne, PA, 19047-2887. Tel: 215-757-2510. p. 1927
Bengston, Katherine, Br Mgr, Hawaii State Public Library System, Princeville Public Library, 4343 Emmalani Dr, Princeville, HI, 96722. Tel: 808-826-4310. p. 510
Benham, Jennifer, Youth & Teen Serv Librn, Prince Memorial Library, 266 Main St, Cumberland, ME, 04021-9754. Tel: 207-829-2215. p. 922
Benham, Robin, Youth Serv Librn, Fort Smith Public Library, 3201 Rogers Ave, Fort Smith, AR, 72903. Tel: 479-783-0229. p. 96
Benham, Tammie, Youth Serv Consult, Southeast Kansas Library System, 218 E Madison Ave, Iola, KS, 66749. Tel: 620-365-5136. p. 815
Benhart, Jacque, YA Librn, Indiana Free Library, Inc, 845 Philadelphia St, Indiana, PA, 15701-3907. Tel: 724-465-8841. p. 1945
Beninghove, Linda, Dir, Stevens Institute of Technology, One Castle Point Terrace, Hoboken, NJ, 07030. Tel: 201-216-5412. p. 1408
Benitez, Debra, Ch Serv, Gilpin County Public Library District, 15131 Hwy 119, Black Hawk, CO, 80422. Tel: 303-582-5777. p. 266
Benitez, Michele, Librn, Stanford Health Library, Cancer Center South Bay, 2589 Samaritan Dr, Rm 3302, San Jose, CA, 95124. Tel: 408-353-0197. p. 192
Benjamin, David R, Head, Spec Coll & Univ Archives, University of Central Florida Libraries, 12701 Pegasus Dr, Orlando, FL, 32816-8030. Tel: 407-823-2788. p. 432
Benjamin, Katie, Dr, Dir, Duke University Libraries, Divinity School Library, 407 Chapel Dr, Durham, NC, 27708. Tel: 919-660-3453. p. 1684
Benjamin, Kelly, Librn, Northwest Regional Library, Warroad Public Library, 202 Main Ave NE, Warroad, MN, 56763. Tel: 218-386-1283. p. 1205
Benjamin, Marianne, Librn, Anti-Defamation League, 605 Third Ave, New York, NY, 10158. Tel: 212-885-5844, 212-885-7823. p. 1579

Benjamin, Pamela, Exec Dir, Treasure State Academic Information & Library Services, Montana State University Library, Centennial Mall, PO Box 173320, Bozeman, MT, 59717-3320. Tel: 406-994-4432. p. 2769
Benjamins, Haley, Ref & Instrul Serv Librn, Edmonds College Library, 20000 68th Ave W, Lynnwood, WA, 98036. Tel: 425-640-1529. p. 2370
Benjaminsen, Linda, Tech Serv, Framingham Public Library, 49 Lexington St, Framingham, MA, 01702-8278. Tel: 508-879-5570, Ext 4319. p. 1019
Benko, Karen Gorss, Cat Librn, Williams College, 26 Hopkins Hall Dr, Williamstown, MA, 01267. Tel: 413-597-4322. p. 1069
Benkwitt, Allison, Head, Tech Serv, Dorothy Alling Memorial Library, 21 Library Lane, Williston, VT, 05495. Tel: 802-878-4918. p. 2299
Bennedbeak, Darel, Libr Coord, Lethbridge College, 3000 College Dr S, Lethbridge, AB, T1K 1L6, CANADA. Tel: 403-320-3352. p. 2546
Benner, Dana, Circ, George H & Ella M Rodgers Memorial Library, 194 Derry Rd, Hudson, NH, 03051. Tel: 603-886-6030. p. 1368
Benner, Diane, Br Mgr, Arundel Anne County Public Library, Michael E Busch Annapolis Library, 1410 West St, Annapolis, MD, 21401. Tel: 410-222-1750. p. 950
Benner, Ellyn, Ch, Horsham Township Library, 435 Babylon Rd, Horsham, PA, 19044-1224. Tel: 215-443-2609, Ext 206. p. 1944
Benner, Karen, Asst Dir, Lucy Robbins Welles Library, 95 Cedar St, Newington, CT, 06111. Tel: 860-665-8729. p. 330
Benner, Nancy, Br Mgr, Montgomery County Public Libraries, Connie Morella Library, 7400 Arlington Rd, Bethesda, MD, 20814. Tel: 240-773-0934. p. 974
Benner, Patrick, Dept Chair, Dir, Syst Librn, Pacific Union College, One Angwin Ave, Angwin, CA, 94508-9705. Tel: 707-965-6641. p. 116
Benner, Vickie, Youth Serv, Epsom Public Library, 1606 Dover Rd, Epsom, NH, 03234. Tel: 603-736-9920. p. 1363
Bennet, Bonnie, Cat Librn, Hinds Community College, 505 E Main St, Raymond, MS, 39154. Tel: 601-857-3355. p. 1231
Bennett, Andrew, Br Mgr, Fort Bend County Libraries, Fort Bend County Law Library, Inside the Justice Center, Rm 20714, 1422 Eugene Heimann Circle, Richmond, TX, 77469. Tel: 281-341-3718. p. 2232
Bennett, Angela, Asst Library Dir for Public Services & Branch Operations, Henrico County Public Library, 1700 N Parham Rd, Henrico, VA, 23229. Tel: 804-501-1900. p. 2325
Bennett, Angela, Prog Coordr, Kaslo & District Public Library, 413 Fourth St, Kaslo, BC, V0G 1M0, CANADA. Tel: 250-353-2942. p. 2568
Bennett, Ashley, Electronic Res Librn, Middle Georgia State University, 100 University Pkwy, Macon, GA, 31206. Tel: 478-471-2866. p. 487
Bennett, Bonnie, Chief Librn, Bassano Memorial Library, 522 Second Ave, Bassano, AB, T0J 0B0, CANADA. Tel: 403-641-4065. p. 2523
Bennett, Brittany, Librn, Palliser Regional Library, Riverhurst Branch, 324 Teck St, Riverhurst, SK, S0H 3P0, CANADA. Tel: 306-353-2130. p. 2743
Bennett, Cindy, Circ Supvr, Carroll College, 1601 N Benton Ave, Helena, MT, 59625. Tel: 406-447-4340. p. 1295
Bennett, Claudia L, Dir & Librn, California Area Public Library, 100 Wood St, California, PA, 15419. Tel: 724-938-2907. p. 1917
Bennett, David B, Syst Librn, Robert Morris University Library, 6001 University Blvd, Moon Township, PA, 15108-1189. Tel: 412-397-6870. p. 1965
Bennett, Dixon, Library Contact, Eisenhower Medical Center, 39000 Bob Hope Dr, Rancho Mirage, CA, 92270. Tel: 760-340-3911. p. 197
Bennett, Erica, Syst Librn, Fullerton College, 321 E Chapman Ave, Fullerton, CA, 92832-2095. Tel: 714-992-7375. p. 147
Bennett, Ernestine, Genealogist, Adair County Public Library, 307 Greensburg St, Columbia, KY, 42728-1488. Tel: 270-384-2472. p. 852
Bennett, Felicity, Colls Mgr, Allaire Village Inc, 4263 Atlantic Ave, Farmingdale, NJ, 07727. Tel: 732-919-3500. p. 1402
Bennett, Holly, Exec Dir, Memorial Library of Nazareth & Vicinity, 295 E Center St, Nazareth, PA, 18064. Tel: 610-759-4932. p. 1968
Bennett, Hunter, Br Mgr, Southeast Arkansas Regional Library, Dumas Branch, 120 E Choctow, Dumas, AR, 71639. Tel: 870-382-5763. p. 104
Bennett, Jackie, Dir, Bristol Area Library, 619 Old County Rd, Rte 130, Pemaquid, ME, 04458. Tel: 207-677-2115. p. 935
Bennett, Jennifer, Exec Dir, National Economic Research Associates, Inc, 360 Hamilton Ave, 10th Flr, White Plains, NY, 10601. Tel: 212-345-2993. p. 1664
Bennett, Jillian, Ch, Hudson Public Library, Three Washington St, Hudson, MA, 01749-2499. Tel: 978-568-9644. p. 1025
Bennett, Joseph W, Libr Dir, Library Company of the Baltimore Bar, 100 N Calvert St, Rm 618, Baltimore, MD, 21202-1723. Tel: 410-727-0280. p. 954
Bennett, Josh, Br Librn, Mendocino County Library District, Round Valley, 23925 Howard St, Covelo, CA, 95428. Tel: 707-983-6736. p. 254
Bennett, Karen, Interim Co-Dir, ILL, Tech Serv, Weston Public Library, 56 Norfield Rd, Weston, CT, 06883. Tel: 203-222-2665. p. 346
Bennett, Kathleen, Librn, Catlin Public Library District, 101 Mapleleaf Dr, Catlin, IL, 61817. Tel: 217-427-2550. p. 551
Bennett, Kay, Br Mgr, Smith County Public Library, Gordonsville Branch, 63 E Main St, Gordonsville, TN, 38563-0217. Tel: 615-683-8063. p. 2090
Bennett, Kelly, Head, Circ, Ferndale Area District Library, 222 E Nine Mile Rd, Ferndale, MI, 48220. Tel: 248-546-2504, Ext 697. p. 1105
Bennett, Kristin, Br Mgr, Volusia County Public Library, New Smyrna Beach Public, 1001 S Dixie Freeway, New Smyrna Beach, FL, 32168. Tel: 386-424-2910. p. 393
Bennett, Linda, Dir, Phillips-Lee-Monroe Regional Library, 702 Porter St, Helena, AR, 72342-3142. Tel: 870-338-7732. p. 98
Bennett, Linda, Ad, Belvedere Tiburon Library, 1501 Tiburon Blvd, Tiburon, CA, 94920. Tel: 415-789-2665. p. 252
Bennett, Linda, Circ, Windsor Storm Memorial Public Library District, 102 S Maple, Windsor, IL, 61957. Tel: 217-459-2498. p. 663
Bennett, Lindsey, Asst Mgr, Libr Serv, Hinton Municipal Library, 803 Switzer Dr, Hinton, AB, T7V 1V1, CANADA. Tel: 780-865-6052. p. 2543
Bennett, Marilyn, Electronic Res Librn, Outreach Librn, Montana State Library, 1515 E Sixth Ave, Helena, MT, 59620. Tel: 406-444-3115. p. 1296
Bennett, Mary, Spec Coll Librn, State Historical Society of Iowa, 402 Iowa Ave, Iowa City, IA, 52240-1806. Tel: 319-335-3938. p. 760
Bennett, Melissa, Sr Curator, Art Gallery of Hamilton, 123 King St W, Hamilton, ON, L8P 4S8, CANADA. Tel: 905-527-6610. p. 2644
Bennett, Melissa, Legislative Librn, Saskatchewan Legislative Library, 234-2405 Legislative Dr, Regina, SK, S4S 0B3, CANADA. Tel: 306-787-2276. p. 2748
Bennett, Miranda, Prog Dir, Coll, University of Houston, M D Anderson Library, 114 University Libraries, Houston, TX, 77204-2000. Tel: 713-743-9800. p. 2199
Bennett, Nancy, Electronic Res Librn, University of Wisconsin-Whitewater, 750 W Main St, Whitewater, WI, 53190-1790. Tel: 262-472-5517. p. 2488
Bennett, Pamela, Librn, Rapides Parish Library, Martin Branch, 801 W Shamrock, Pineville, LA, 71360. Tel: 318-442-7575. p. 880
Bennett, Pamela S, Dep Dir, Pub Serv Librn, United States Army, Combined Arms Research Library, US Army Command & General Staff College, Eisenhower Hall, 250 Gibbon Ave, Fort Leavenworth, KS, 66027-2314. Tel: 913-758-3058. p. 808
Bennett, Patrice, Dir, Libr Serv, Wiregrass Georgia Technical College, 667 Perry House Rd, Fitzgerald, GA, 31750. Tel: 229-468-2012. p. 478
Bennett, Regina, Circ, Satilla Regional Library, 200 S Madison Ave, Ste D, Douglas, GA, 31533. Tel: 912-384-4667. p. 476
Bennett, Sarah, Dir, Libr Serv, Foley & Hoag LLP Library, 155 Seaport Blvd, Boston, MA, 02210. Tel: 617-832-7070. p. 995
Bennett, Steve, Librn, Illinois Department of Corrections, 950 Kingshighway St, East Saint Louis, IL, 62203. Tel: 618-394-2200, Ext 407. p. 581
Bennett, Sue, Libr Dir, Waldport Public Library, 460 Hemlock St, Waldport, OR, 97394. Tel: 541-563-5880. p. 1901
Bennett, Swannee, Exec Dir, Historic Arkansas Museum Library, 200 E Third St, Little Rock, AR, 72201-1608. Tel: 501-324-9395. p. 101
Bennett, Teri, Youth Serv Librn, Rowley Public Library, 141 Main St, Rowley, MA, 01969. Tel: 978-948-2850. p. 1050
Bennett, Terrence, Bus & Econ Librn, The College of New Jersey, 2000 Pennington Rd, Ewing, NJ, 08628-1104. Tel: 609-771-2311. p. 1402
Bennett, Tina, Dir, Garland Smith Public Library, 702 W. Main, Marlow, OK, 73055. Tel: 580-658-5354. p. 1852
Bennett, Trevor, Information & Privacy Coord, Canada-Newfoundland Offshore Petroleum Board Library, West Campus Hall, Ste 7100, 240 Waterford Bridge Rd, St. John's, NL, A1E 1E2, CANADA. Tel: 709-778-1474. p. 2608
Bennett, Vivian, Head Librn, Snow Lake Community Library, 101 Poplar Ave, Snow Lake, MB, R0B 1M0, CANADA. Tel: 204-358-2322. p. 2590
Bennett, Wendy, Head, Ref, Bayport-Blue Point Public Library, 203 Blue Point Ave, Blue Point, NY, 11715-1217. Tel: 631-363-6133. p. 1495
Bennett-Copeland, Michelle, Libr Mgr, Flint River Regional Library System, Fayette County Public Library, 1821 Heritage Pkwy, Fayetteville, GA, 30214. Tel: 770-305-5426. p. 481
Bennett-Reid, Yolounda, Libr Mgr, New York Public Library - Astor, Lenox & Tilden Foundations, Hamilton Grange Branch, 503 W 145th St, New York, NY, 10031-5101. Tel: 212-926-2147. p. 1595
Bennett-Sutton, Kimberly, Learning Services, Officer, Department of Veterans Affairs, 2360 E Pershing Blvd, Cheyenne, WY, 82001. Tel: 307-778-7550. p. 2492
Bennewies, Sherri, ILL, Libr Asst, West Perth Public Library, 105 Saint Andrew St, Mitchell, ON, N0K 1N0, CANADA. Tel: 519-348-9234. p. 2659
Bennewitz, Sophie, Br Mgr, Dare County Library, 700 N Hwy 64-264, Manteo, NC, 27954. Tel: 252-473-2372. p. 1702
Bennhoff, Elizabeth, Dir, Spanish Peaks Library District, 415 Walsen Ave, Walsenburg, CO, 81089. Tel: 719-738-2774. p. 297
Bennick, Walter, Archivist, Winona County Historical Society, 160 Johnson St, Winona, MN, 55987. Tel: 507-454-2723, Ext 2. p. 1209
Bennie, Scott, Dean of Academic Services, Kettering College, 3737 Southern Blvd, Kettering, OH, 45429-1299. Tel: 937-395-8053. p. 1793
Bennin, Cheryl, Librn, Fishkill Correctional Facility Library, Bldg 13, Beacon, NY, 12508. Tel: 845-831-4800, Ext 4600. p. 1491
Benninger, Fran, Ch, Pamlico County Public Library, 603 Main St, Bayboro, NC, 28515. Tel: 252-745-3515. p. 1673

Bennison, Alana, Ch, Cyrenius H Booth Library, 25 Main St, Newtown, CT, 06470. Tel: 203-426-4533. p. 330

Beno, Julie, Br Supvr, Lincoln City Libraries, South Branch, 2675 South St, Lincoln, NE, 68502-3099. Tel: 402-441-8535. p. 1321

Benoit, Edward A, III, Dr, Assoc Prof, Louisiana State University, 267 Coates Hall, Baton Rouge, LA, 70803. Tel: 225-578-3158, 225-578-3159. p. 2785

Benoit, Greg, Libr Dir, Irondequoit Public Library, 1290 Titus Ave, Rochester, NY, 14617. Tel: 585-210-2390 ((Text)), 585-336-6060. p. 1628

Benoit, Marie-Josee, Dir, Saint Lambert Municipal Library, 490 Mercille Ave, Saint Lambert, QC, J4P 2L5, CANADA. Tel: 450-466-3910. p. 2734

Benoit, Rozalind, Asst Dir, Gilman Library, 100 Main St, Alton, NH, 03809. Tel: 603-875-2550. p. 1353

Benoit, Samantha, Asst Dir, Ayer Library, 26 E Main St, Ayer, MA, 01432. Tel: 978-772-8250. p. 987

Benolken, Julie, Acq, Instruction Librn, Inver Hills Community College Library, 2500 80th St E, Inver Grove Heights, MN, 55076-3209. Tel: 651-450-8622. p. 1179

Benoy, Eric, Coll Develop Librn, Music Librn, Ref Librn, New Orleans Baptist Theological Seminary, 4110 Seminary Pl, New Orleans, LA, 70126. Tel: 504-816-8270. p. 902

Benoy, Eric, Dir, New Orleans Baptist Theological Seminary, Martin Music Library, 4110 Seminary Pl, New Orleans, LA, 70126. Tel: 504-816-8248. p. 902

Benrubi, Deborah, Tech Serv Librn, University of San Francisco, 2130 Fulton St, San Francisco, CA, 94117-1080. Tel: 415-422-5672. p. 229

Benschop, Diane, Chief Librn/CEO, Township of Athens Public Library, Five Central St, Athens, ON, K0E 1B0, CANADA. Tel: 613-924-2048. p. 2628

Bensen, Mary Lynn, Head, Ref & Instruction, SUNY Oneonta, 108 Ravine Pkwy, Oneonta, NY, 13820. Tel: 607-436-2729. p. 1611

Bensinger, Gina, Circ, Pottsville Free Public Library, 215 W Market St, Pottsville, PA, 17901. Tel: 570-622-8105, 570-622-8880. p. 1999

Bensley, Ruth, Circ, The Morristown & Morris Township Library, One Miller Rd, Morristown, NJ, 07960. Tel: 973-538-6161. p. 1421

Benson, Anne, Librn, Yoakum County Library, 901 Ave E, Plains, TX, 79355. Tel: 806-456-8725. p. 2227

Benson, Carol, Librn, Ref (Info Servs), Oakland Community College, 739 S Washington Ave, Bldg C, Royal Oak, MI, 48067-3898. Tel: 248-246-2528. p. 1146

Benson, Catherine, Dir, Heermance Memorial Library, One Ely St, Coxsackie, NY, 12051. Tel: 518-731-8084. p. 1523

Benson, Cherese, Assoc Librn, PPG Industries, Inc, Technical Information Center, 4325 Rosanna Dr, Allison Park, PA, 15101. Tel: 412-492-5262. p. 1996

Benson, Debbie, Exec Dir, Maturango Museum, 100 E Las Flores Ave, Ridgecrest, CA, 93555. Tel: 760-375-6900. p. 200

Benson, Debbie, Circ Coordr, Henrico County Public Library, 1700 N Parham Rd, Henrico, VA, 23229. Tel: 804-501-1900. p. 2325

Benson, Denise, Head, Adult Serv, Calumet City Public Library, 660 Manistee Ave, Calumet City, IL, 60409. Tel: 708-862-6220, Ext 249. p. 548

Benson, Hope, Head, Children's Servx, Monroeville Public Library, 4000 Gateway Campus Blvd, Monroeville, PA, 15146-3381. Tel: 412-372-0500, Ext 127. p. 1965

Benson, Julie, Programming Librn, Dunbar Free Library, 401 Rte 10 S, Grantham, NH, 03753. Tel: 603-863-2172. p. 1365

Benson, Karen, Libr Dir, Gravette Public Library, 119 Main St SE, Gravette, AR, 72736-9363. Tel: 479-787-6955. p. 96

Benson, Kristina, Libr Dir, Du Quoin Public Library, 28 S Washington St, Du Quoin, IL, 62832. Tel: 618-542-5045. p. 579

Benson, Mike, Tech Mgr, Hoover Public Library, 200 Municipal Dr, Hoover, AL, 35216. Tel: 205-444-7810. p. 21

Benson, Molly, Head, Outreach, Montrose Regional Library District, 320 S Second St, Montrose, CO, 81401. Tel: 970-249-9656. p. 291

Benson, Peter, Dir, Saranac Lake Free Library, 109 Main St, Saranac Lake, NY, 12983. Tel: 518-891-4190. p. 1636

Benson, Sarah, Adult Programs Assoc, San Juan Island Library, 1010 Guard St, Friday Harbor, WA, 98250-9612. Tel: 360-378-2798. p. 2364

Benson, Steve, Fac Mgr, Upper Arlington Public Library, 2800 Tremont Rd, Columbus, OH, 43221. Tel: 614-486-9621. p. 1778

Benson, Steven, Bus Coordr, University of Southern California Libraries, Asa V Call Law Library, 699 Exposition Blvd, LAW 202, MC 0072, Los Angeles, CA, 90089-0072. Tel: 213-740-6482. p. 170

Bent, Kim, Circ Supvr, York Library Region, Fredericton Public Library, 12 Carleton St, Fredericton, NB, E3B 5P4, CANADA. Tel: 506-460-2800. p. 2602

Bente, Heather, Dir, Waterville Public Library, 115 Main St, Unit 3, Waterville, IA, 52170. Tel: 563-535-7295. p. 789

Bentle, Diaina, Youth Serv Mgr, Lompoc Public Library, 501 E North Ave, Lompoc, CA, 93436. Tel: 805-875-8788. p. 158

Bentler, Kerry, Mgr, Human Res, Lone Cone Library, 1455 Pinion St, Norwood, CO, 81423. Tel: 970-327-4833. p. 292

Bentley, Barbara J, Mgr, Cummings & Lockwood, Six Landmark Sq, Stamford, CT, 06901. Tel: 203-351-4375. p. 338

Bentley, Christopher, Head Librn, Parkland Regional Library-Manitoba, Birtle Branch, 907 Main St, Birtle, MB, R0M 0C0, CANADA. Tel: 204-842-3418. p. 2586

Bentley, Dona, Prof, User Serv Librn, University of La Verne, 2040 Third St, La Verne, CA, 91750. Tel: 909-593-3511, Ext 4305. p. 155

Bentley, Heather, Cat Librn, Webster County Public Library, 101 State Rte 132 E, Dixon, KY, 42409. Tel: 270-639-9171. p. 853

Bentley, Jason, Interim Dean, Ferris State University Library, 1010 Campus Dr, Big Rapids, MI, 49307-2279. Tel: 231-591-3500. p. 1085

Bentley, Luke, Dir, Briggs Lawrence County Public Library, 321 S Fourth St, Ironton, OH, 45638. Tel: 740-532-1124. p. 1791

Bentley, Margaret Ann, Ad, Asst Dir, Shiawassee District Library, 502 W Main St, Owosso, MI, 48867-2607. Tel: 989-725-5134. p. 1139

Bentley, Margie, Customer Serv Coordr, Brockville Public Library, 23 Buell St, Brockville, ON, K6V 5T7, CANADA. Tel: 613-342-3936. p. 2634

Bentley, Peggy, Head Librn, Letcher County Public Library District, Jenkins Public, 9543 Hwy 805, Jenkins, KY, 41537. Tel: 606-832-4101. p. 877

Bentley-Flannery, Paige, Commun Librn, Deschutes Public Library District, Sisters Branch, 110 N Cedar St, Sisters, OR, 97759. Tel: 541-617-7078. p. 1874

Benton, Elaine, Dir, Augusta Richmond County Historical Society Library, c/o Reese Library @ GRU, 2500 Walton Way, Augusta, GA, 30904-2200. Tel: 706-737-1532. p. 466

Benton, Jim, Sr Librn, Columbia County Historical Society Library, CCHS Museum & Library, Five Albany Ave, Kinderhook, NY, 12106. Tel: 518-758-9265. p. 1560

Benton, Kimshiro, Youth Serv, James Kennedy Public Library, 320 First Ave E, Dyersville, IA, 52040. Tel: 563-875-8912. p. 749

Benton, Rhoda, Br Mgr, Mendenhall Public Library, 1630 Simpson Hwy 149, Mendenhall, MS, 39114. Tel: 601-847-2181. p. 1226

Benton, Sue, Head, Technical & Collection Services & Serials, University of South Dakota, McKusick Law Library, Knudson School of Law, 414 E Clark St, Vermillion, SD, 57069-2390. Tel: 605-658-3521. p. 2084

Bents, Stephanie, Ch Serv Librn, Siouxland Libraries, 200 N Dakota Ave, Sioux Falls, SD, 57104. Tel: 605-367-8719. p. 2082

Bentz, Adam T, PhD, Dir, Libr & Archives, Historical Society of York County, York County Heritage Trust, 121 N Pershing Ave, York, PA, 17401. Tel: 717-848-1587, Ext 223. p. 2026

Bentz, Maureen, Libr Dir, Lebanon Valley College, 101 N College Ave, Annville, PA, 17003-1400. Tel: 717-867-6974. p. 1906

Bentz, Stephanie, Library Contact, Titanium Metals Corporation of America, 181 N Water St, Gate 3, Henderson, NV, 89015. Tel: 702-564-2544, Ext 396. p. 1346

Benvenuti, Irene, Educ Librn, Eagle Public Library, 100 N Stierman Way, Eagle, ID, 83616. Tel: 208-939-6814. p. 520

Benvie, Kathleen, Dir, Pembroke Public Library, 142 Center St, Pembroke, MA, 02359. Tel: 781-293-6771, Ext 26. p. 1046

Benware, Arthur, Colls Mgr, New York State Office of Parks, Recreation & Historic Preservation, 400 Jay St, Rte 22, Katonah, NY, 10536. Tel: 914-232-5651. p. 1559

Benway, Natasha, Mkt Coordr, Montgomery County Memorial Library System, 104 I-45 N, Conroe, TX, 77301-2720. Tel: 936-522-2137. p. 2159

Benz, Tonette, Libr Asst, John F Kennedy Memorial Library, 92 Hathaway St, Wallington, NJ, 07057. Tel: 973-471-1692. p. 1451

Benzel, Kathy, Asst Dir, Altoona Area Public Library, 1600 Fifth Ave, Altoona, PA, 16602-3693. Tel: 814-946-0417. p. 1905

Benzing, Matthew, Computing & Engineering Librn, Miami University Libraries, Business, Engineering, Science, & Technology Library, Laws Hall, 551 E High St, Oxford, OH, 45056. Tel: 513-529-6886. p. 1812

Bera, Barbara, Libr Asst, Central Carolina Community College, Harnett County Campus, 1075 E Cornelius Harnett Blvd, Lillington, NC, 27546. Tel: 910-814-8873. p. 1715

Berardino, Bailey, Ch Serv, West Hartford Public Library, Bishop's Corner, 15 Starkel Rd, West Hartford, CT, 06117. Tel: 860-561-8210. p. 346

Berardino, Kristin, Children's Serv Supvr, Kensington Public Library, 126 Amesbury Rd, Kensington, NH, 03833-5621. Tel: 603-772-5022. p. 1370

Berast, Chasity, Prog Head, Saskatchewan Polytechnic Library & Information Technology, 107 Fourth Ave S, Saskatoon, SK, S7K 5X2, CANADA. Tel: 306-659-3846. p. 2797

Berdini, Annalise, Digital Archivist, Princeton University, Seeley G Mudd Manuscript Library, 65 Olden St, Princeton, NJ, 08544. Tel: 609-258-3248. p. 1438

Berdish, Laura, Fac Res Serv/Ref Serv Librn, University of Michigan, Kresge Library Services, Stephen M Ross School of Business, 701 Tappan St, Ann Arbor, MI, 48109-1234. Tel: 734-763-9360. p. 1079

Bere, Laura, Interim Chief Exec Officer, Perth East Public Library, 19 Mill St E, Milverton, ON, N0K 1M0, CANADA. Tel: 519-595-8395. p. 2658

Berean, Leah, Librn, Michigan Department of Corrections, 1500 Caberfae Hwy, Manistee, MI, 49660. Tel: 231-723-8272. p. 1129

Berecka, Alan, Ref Librn, Del Mar College, 101 Baldwin Blvd, Corpus Christi, TX, 78404. Tel: 361-698-1933. p. 2160

Berent, Joanne, Ref Librn/Trainer, Gowling WLG (Canada) Library, One First Canadian Pl, 100 King St W, Ste 1600, Toronto, ON, M5X 1G5, CANADA. Tel: 416-862-5735. p. 2689

Berg, Angela, Dir, Fairbank Public Library, 212 E Main St, Fairbank, IA, 50629. Tel: 319-635-2487. p. 752

Berg, Cara, Ref Librn & Co-Coordr of User Educ, William Paterson University, 300 Pompton Rd, Wayne, NJ, 07470. Tel: 973-720-3189. p. 1452
Berg, Elaine W, Access Serv Coordr, Austin Peay State University, 601 College St, Clarksville, TN, 37044. Tel: 931-221-6405. p. 2092
Berg, Elizabeth, Coll Mgt Librn, Siouxland Libraries, 200 N Dakota Ave, Sioux Falls, SD, 57104. Tel: 605-367-8732. p. 2082
Berg, Georgia, Dir, Admin Serv, Kindred Public Library, 330 Elm St, Kindred, ND, 58051. Tel: 701-428-3456. p. 1736
Berg, Heidi, Br Mgr, Nashville Public Library, Green Hills Branch, 3701 Benham Ave, Nashville, TN, 37215. Tel: 615-862-5863. p. 2119
Berg, Janis, Dir, DeForest Area Public Library, 203 Library St, DeForest, WI, 53532. Tel: 608-846-5482. p. 2430
Berg, Jenny, Libr Dir, McMinnville Public Library, 225 NW Adams St, McMinnville, OR, 97128. Tel: 503-435-5562. p. 1886
Berg, John, Head, Circ & Ref, University of Wisconsin - Platteville, One University Plaza, Platteville, WI, 53818. Tel: 608-342-1355. p. 2470
Berg, Lynn, Asst Dir, Garrett-Evangelical Theological Seminary, 2121 Sheridan Rd, Evanston, IL, 60201. Tel: 847-866-3909. p. 586
Berg, Phillip, Exec Dir, Main Library Alliance, 16 Wing Dr, Ste 212, Cedar Knolls, NJ, 07927. Tel: 973-862-4606. p. 2770
Berg, Rebecca, Br Mgr, Chicago Public Library, Mayfair, 4400 W Lawrence Ave, Chicago, IL, 60630. Tel: 312-744-1254. p. 557
Berg, Selinda, Univ Librn, University of Windsor, 401 Sunset Ave, Windsor, ON, N9B 3P4, CANADA. Tel: 519-253-3000, Ext 3196. p. 2704
Berg, Susan, Dir, Locke Lord Bissell & Liddell LLP, 111 S Wacker Dr, Chicago, IL, 60606. Tel: 312-443-0646. p. 563
Bergdorf, Randy, Dir, Peninsula Library & Historical Society, 6105 Riverview Rd, Peninsula, OH, 44264. Tel: 330-467-7323, 330-657-2291. p. 1814
Bergdorf, Randy, Dir, Peninsula Library & Historical Society, Cuyahoga Valley Historical Museum, 1775 Main St, 2nd Flr, Peninsula, OH, 44264. Tel: 330-657-2892. p. 1814
Bergen, Jerri, Pres, American Aviation Historical Society, Flabob Airport, 4130 Mennes Ave, Bldg 56, Riverside, CA, 92509. Tel: 951-777-1332. p. 201
Bergen, Phillip, Librn, Blue Ridge Community College Library, 180 W Campus Dr, Flat Rock, NC, 28731. Tel: 828-694-1681. p. 1689
Bergen-Aurand, Brian, Dr, Dir, Libr Serv, Wor-Wic Community College, 32000 Campus Dr, Salisbury, MD, 21804. Tel: 410-334-2884, 410-334-2888. p. 977
Berger, Bernadette, Dir, IT, Jefferson County Public Library, 10200 W 20th Ave, Lakewood, CO, 80215. Tel: 303-235-5275. p. 288
Berger, Brittany, Br Mgr, Fox River Valley Public Library District, 555 Barrington Ave, East Dundee, IL, 60118-1496. Tel: 847-428-3661. p. 580
Berger, Gene, Colls Librn, Lackawanna College, 406 N Washington Ave, Scranton, PA, 18503. Tel: 570-961-1590. p. 2004
Berger, Jane A, Dir, Libr Serv, Owens Community College Library, 30335 Oregon Rd, Perrysburg, OH, 43551. Tel: 567-661-7459. p. 1815
Berger, Jessica, Asst Dir, Victoria Public Library, 302 N Main St, Victoria, TX, 77901. Tel: 361-485-3302. p. 2252
Berger, Jessica, Dir, Victoria Public Library, 302 N Main St, Victoria, TX, 77901. Tel: 361-485-3302. p. 2252
Berger, Kathleen M, Asst Librn, Info serv, Boston University Libraries, Frederic S Pardee Management Library, Boston University School of Management, 595 Commonwealth Ave, Boston, MA, 02215. Tel: 617-353-4312. p. 993
Berger, Shelly, Colls Mgr, Beth Ahabah Museum & Archives, 1109 W Franklin St, Richmond, VA, 23220. Tel: 804-353-2668. p. 2340
Berger, Shulamith Z, Curator, Spec Coll, Yeshiva University Libraries, 2520 Amsterdam Ave, New York, NY, 10033. Tel: 646-592-4107. p. 1604
Berger, Stacy, Br Mgr, Saint Louis County Library, Indian Trails Branch, 8400 Delport Dr, Saint Louis, MO, 63114-5904. Tel: 314-994-3300, Ext 3350. p. 1274
Berger, Tori, Br Mgr, Akron-Summit County Public Library, Norton Branch, 3930 S Cleveland-Massillon Rd, Norton, OH, 44203-5563. Tel: 330-825-7800. p. 1744
Berger, Zach, Br Librn, Cranston Public Library, William H Hall Free Library, 1825 Broad St, Cranston, RI, 02905-3599. Tel: 401-781-2450. p. 2031
Bergeron, Amy, Librn, McGill University Health Centre - Glen Site, 1001 Boul DeCarie, Rm B RC 0078, Montreal, QC, H4A 3J1, CANADA. Tel: 514-934-1934, Ext 35290. p. 2725
Bergeron, Dana, Br Mgr, Pointe Coupee Parish Library, Morganza Branch, 221 S Louisiana Hwy 1, Morganza, LA, 70759. Tel: 225-694-2428. p. 905
Bergeron, Denise, Libr Tech II, White Mountains Community College, 2020 Riverside Dr, Berlin, NH, 03570-3799. Tel: 603-342-3087. p. 1355
Bergeron, Devon, Libr Mgr, Timberland Regional Library, Salkum Branch, 2480 US Hwy 12, Salkum, WA, 98582. Tel: 360-985-2148. p. 2389
Bergeron, Jeffrey, Accounts Coord, Lawrence Public Library, 707 Vermont St, Lawrence, KS, 66044-2371. Tel: 785-843-3833, Ext 145. p. 819
Bergeron, Judy, Dir, Smithville Public Library, 507 Main St, Smithville, TX, 78957. Tel: 512-237-3282, Ext 6. p. 2244
Bergeron, Sherry, Br Mgr, Evangeline Parish Library, Basile Branch, 3036 Stagg Ave, Basile, LA, 70515. Tel: 337-432-6794. p. 912
Bergeron, Sue, Children's & Teen Serv Coordr, North Grenville Public Library, Norenberg Bldg, One Water St, Kemptville, ON, K0G 1J0, CANADA. Tel: 613-258-4711, Ext 5. p. 2649
Bergeron, Tangella, Br Mgr, Lafourche Parish Public Library, Bayou Blue Branch, 198 Mazerac St, Houma, LA, 70364. Tel: 985-580-0634. p. 911
Bergfeld, Emily, Ref Librn, Bernard E Witkin Alameda County Law Library, 125 Twelfth St, Oakland, CA, 94607-4912. Tel: 510-272-6486. p. 187
Berggren-Thomas, Priscilla, Dir, Phillips Free Library, 37 S Main St, Homer, NY, 13077-1323. Tel: 607-749-4616. p. 1547
Berghman, Lauren, YA Librn, Dover Town Library, 56 Dedham St, Dover, MA, 02030-2214. Tel: 508-785-8113. p. 1014
Berghman, Lauren, Tech Librn, YA Serv, Stoughton Public Library, 84 Park St, Stoughton, MA, 02072-2974. Tel: 781-344-2711. p. 1058
Berghoef, Peter, Asst Libr Dir, Abbott Library, 11 Soonipi Circle, Sunapee, NH, 03782. Tel: 603-763-5513. p. 1382
Berghorst, Dena, Dir, Edgerton Public Library, 811 First Ave W, Edgerton, MN, 56128. Tel: 507-442-7071. p. 1174
Berghuis, Shara, Libr Dir, Wray Public Library, 621 Blake St, Wray, CO, 80758. Tel: 970-332-4744. p. 299
Bergin, Jessica, Dir, Carnegie-Schadde Memorial Public Library, 230 Fourth Ave, Baraboo, WI, 53913. Tel: 608-356-6166. p. 2422
Bergjord, Judi, Outreach Serv Librn, Creighton University, Health Sciences Library-Learning Resource Center, 2770 Webster St, Omaha, NE, 68178-0210. Tel: 402-280-5199. p. 1328
Bergjord, Judith, Consortium Contact, ICON Library Consortium, c/o Clarkson College Library, 101 S 42nd St, Omaha, NE, 68131. Tel: 402-552-3387. p. 2769
Bergman, Barbara, Media Serv Librn, Minnesota State University, Mankato, 601 Maywood Ave, Mankato, MN, 56001. Tel: 507-389-5952. p. 1181
Bergmark, Margaret, Circ, Rider University, Katharine Houk Talbott Library, Franklin F Moore Library Bldg, 3rd & 4th Flrs, 2083 Lawrenceville Rd, Lawrenceville, NJ, 08648. Tel: 609-921-7100, Ext 8237. p. 1412
Bergquist, Vi, Chief Info Officer, Libr Dir, Saint Cloud Technical & Community College Library, 1520 Whitney Ct, Saint Cloud, MN, 56303-1240. Tel: 320-308-5141. p. 1198
Bergstein, Brenda Sislen, Librn, OHR Kodesh Congregation, 8300 Meadowbrook Lane, Chevy Chase, MD, 20815. Tel: 301-589-3880. p. 961
Bergstrom, Jackie, Ch Prog, Lowell Public Library, 1505 E Commercial Ave, Lowell, IN, 46356-1899. Tel: 219-696-7704. p. 704
Bergstrom, Jenne, Br Mgr, San Diego County Library, Alpine Branch, 1752 Alpine Blvd, Alpine, CA, 91901. Tel: 619-445-4221. p. 216
Bergstrom, John, Circ Librn, ILL Librn, University of Iowa Libraries, College of Law Library, 200 Boyd Law Bldg, Iowa City, IA, 52242-1166. Tel: 319-335-9015. p. 761
Bergstrom, Stefanie, Ch, Fairfield Public Library, Fairfield Woods, 1147 Fairfield Woods Rd, Fairfield, CT, 06825. Tel: 203-255-7310. p. 312
Bergstrome, Crystal, Chief Librn/CEO, Bracebridge Public Library, 94 Manitoba St, Bracebridge, ON, P1L 2B5, CANADA. Tel: 705-645-4171. p. 2632
Berhanu, Aslaku, Librn, Temple University Libraries, Blockson Afro-American Collection, Sullivan Hall, 1st Flr, 1330 W Berks St, Philadelphia, PA, 19122. Tel: 215-204-6632. p. 1986
Berhow, Samantha, Ad, Winona Public Library, 151 W Fifth St, Winona, MN, 55987. Tel: 507-452-4582. p. 1209
Berhow, Wesley, Br Mgr, Marshall County Public Library System, Calvert City, 23 Park Rd, Calvert City, KY, 42029. Tel: 270-527-9969, Ext 221. p. 849
Beringhele, Dan, Br Supvr, Berkeley Public Library, North Branch, 1170 The Alameda, Berkeley, CA, 94707. Tel: 510-981-6250. p. 121
Beristain, Connor, Library Contact, Nevada Youth Training Center Library, 100 Youth Center Rd, Elko, NV, 89801. Tel: 775-738-7182. p. 1345
Berk, Josh, Exec Dir, Bethlehem Area Public Library, 11 W Church St, Bethlehem, PA, 18018. Tel: 610-867-3761, Ext 215. p. 1911
Berkes, Elena, Dir, Libr Serv, Cameron Public Library, 304 E Third St, Cameron, TX, 76520. Tel: 254-697-2401. p. 2152
Berkoff, Nancy, Librn, St Mary Medical Center, 1050 Linden Ave, Long Beach, CA, 90813. Tel: 562-491-9295, 714-886-9067. p. 159
Berkov, Joshua, Coll Mgt Librn, North Carolina Regional Library for the Blind & Physically Handicapped, 1841 Capital Blvd, Raleigh, NC, 27635. Tel: 919-733-4376. p. 1709
Berkowitz Duff, Shari, Research Librn, Jones Day, 110 N Wacker Dr, Ste 4800, Chicago, IL, 60606. Tel: 312-782-3939. p. 562
Berkowitz, MaryGrace, Cataloger/Ref Librn, Oklahoma City Community College, 7777 S May Ave, Oklahoma City, OK, 73159. Tel: 405-682-1611, Ext 7229. p. 1858
Berkshire, Janette, Asst Librn, Glen Lake Community Library, 10115 W Front St, Empire, MI, 49630-9418. Tel: 231-326-5361. p. 1103
Berlanstein, Debra, Assoc Dir, Tufts University, Hirsh Health Sciences Library, 145 Harrison Ave, Boston, MA, 02111. Tel: 617-636-6705. p. 1034
Berlin, Valerie, ILL Librn, Licia & Mason Beekley Community Library, Ten Central Ave, New Hartford, CT, 06057. Tel: 860-379-7235. p. 325
Berlstein, Chaya, Circ Serv, Norfolk Library, Nine Greenwoods Rd E, Norfolk, CT, 06058-1320. Tel: 860-542-5075. p. 330
Berman, Ellen, Head, Adult Serv, Rockville Centre Public Library, 221 N Village Ave, Rockville Centre, NY, 11570. Tel: 516-766-6257. p. 1632
Berman, Erin, Principal Librn, Alameda County Library, 2450 Stevenson Blvd, Fremont, CA, 94538-2326. Tel: 510-745-1500. p. 143

Bermann, Carlene, Dir, Collections & Community Engagement, Saint Lawrence County Historical Association Archives, Three E Main St, Canton, NY, 13617. Tel: 315-386-8133. p. 1513
Bermann, Sue, Head, Tech Serv, Palm Beach County Library System, Palm Beach County Library Annex, 4249 Cherry Rd, West Palm Beach, FL, 33409. Tel: 561-649-5500. p. 454
Bermann, Sue, Tech Serv, Palm Beach County Library System, 3650 Summit Blvd, West Palm Beach, FL, 33406-4198. Tel: 561-233-2600. p. 454
Bermel, Elizabeth, Dir, Scarsdale Public Library, 54 Olmsted Rd, Scarsdale, NY, 10583. Tel: 914-722-1300. p. 1637
Bermeo, Anamaria, Adjunct Librn, Compton College Library, 1111 E Artesia Blvd, Compton, CA, 90221. Tel: 310-900-1600, Ext 2179. p. 132
Bermudez, Nathalia, Adult Serv, East Orange Public Library, 21 S Arlington Ave, East Orange, NJ, 07018. Tel: 973-266-5600. p. 1400
Bermudez-Lopez, Normary, Libr Tech, Department of Veterans Affairs, Library Service 142D, Ten Calle Casia, San Juan, PR, 00921-3201. Tel: 787-641-7582, Ext 12276, 787-641-7582, Ext 31905. p. 2513
Bernal, Becky, ILL, Colorado Mesa University, 1100 North Ave, Grand Junction, CO, 81501. Tel: 970-248-1844. p. 283
Bernal, Deborah, Literacy Coordr, Fresno County Public Library, 2420 Mariposa St, Fresno, CA, 93721. Tel: 559-600-7323. p. 145
Bernal, Deborah, Literacy Coordr, Fresno County Public Library, Literacy Services Center, 2420 Mariposa St, Fresno, CA, 93721. Tel: 559-600-9243. p. 146
Bernal, Eva, Youth Serv Librn, Bastrop Public Library, 1100 Church St, Bastrop, TX, 78602. Tel: 512-332-8880. p. 2144
Bernard, Amy, Ch, Iberia Parish Library, 445 E Main St, New Iberia, LA, 70560-3710. Tel: 337-364-7024, 337-364-7074. p. 900
Bernard, Brenda, Admin Officer, National Archives & Records Administration, Mid Atlantic Region (Center City Philadelphia), 14700 Townsend Rd, Philadelphia, PA, 19154. Tel: 215-305-2007. p. 1983
Bernard, Carrie, Br Mgr, Public Library of Cincinnati & Hamilton County, Miami Township, Eight N Miami Ave, Cleves, OH, 45002. Tel: 513-369-6050. p. 1763
Bernard, Halsted, Libr Dir, Tigard Public Library, 13500 SW Hall Blvd, Tigard, OR, 97223-8111. Tel: 503-684-6537, Ext 2501. p. 1900
Bernard, Jamie, Head, Youth Serv, Albion District Library, 501 S Superior St, Albion, MI, 49224. Tel: 517-629-3993. p. 1076
Bernard, Linda, Deputy Archivist, Stanford University Libraries, Hoover Institution Library & Archives, 434 Galvez Mall, Stanford, CA, 94305. Tel: 650-723-0141. p. 248
Bernard, Sara, Dir, Pittsfield Public Library, 205 N Memorial St, Pittsfield, IL, 62363-1406. Tel: 217-285-2200. p. 635
Bernard, Suzanne, Cataloger, City University of New York, 365 Fifth Ave, New York, NY, 10016-4309. Tel: 212-817-7040. p. 1582
Bernardi, Julie, Head, Circ, Reuben Hoar Library, 35 Shattuck St, Littleton, MA, 01460. Tel: 978-540-2600. p. 1029
Bernardi, Kathleen, Ch Serv, Tech Serv, Haddon Heights Public Library, 608 Station Ave, Haddon Heights, NJ, 08035-1907. Tel: 856-547-7132. p. 1406
Bernardin, Lois, Head Librn, Pinawa Public Library, Vanier Rd, Pinawa, MB, R0E 1L0, CANADA. Tel: 204-753-2496. p. 2589
Bernardis, Tim, Libr Dir, Little Big Horn College Library, 8645 S Weaver Dr, Crow Agency, MT, 59022. Tel: 406-638-3113. p. 1291
Bernardo, Al, Soc Sci Librn, North Dakota State University Libraries, 1201 Albrecht Blvd, Fargo, ND, 58108. Tel: 701-231-6534. p. 1733
Bernardo, Alfred, Program Mgr, Library Services, Jewish Hospital, 4777 E Galbraith Rd, Cincinnati, OH, 45236. Tel: 513-686-5173. p. 1761
Bernardo, David, Educ Librn, Research Librn, Providence College, One Cunningham Sq, Providence, RI, 02918. Tel: 401-865-2581. p. 2039
Bernas, Maureen, Circ Supvr, Evening Supvr, Saint Bonaventure University, 3261 W State Rd, Saint Bonaventure, NY, 14778. Tel: 716-375-2337. p. 1635
Bernat, Sabrina, Exec Dir, Winter Park Public Library, 460 E New England Ave, Winter Park, FL, 32789. Tel: 407-623-3458. p. 456
Bernath, Tina, Spec Coll & Archives Librn, Troy University, 502 University Dr, Dothan, AL, 36304. Tel: 334-983-6556, Ext 1324. p. 15
Bernau, Brent, Coll Develop Librn, University of San Diego, Katherine M & George M Pardee Jr Legal Research Center, 5998 Alcala Park, San Diego, CA, 92110-2492. Tel: 619-260-7557. p. 223
Berndt, Liz, Music Librn, Ref, Research Servs Librn, Harvard Library, Eda Kuhn Loeb Music Library, Music Bldg, Three Oxford St, Cambridge, MA, 02138. Tel: 617-495-2794. p. 1007
Berner, Mark, Branch Cluster Supvr, Fresno County Public Library, 2420 Mariposa St, Fresno, CA, 93721. Tel: 559-225-0140. p. 145
Bernhardt, Sharon, Area Res Mgr, Mid-Region, Indianapolis Public Library, 2450 N Meridian St, Indianapolis, IN, 46208. Tel: 317-275-4475. p. 694
Bernier, Diane, ILL, Ref, Cegep de Saint Felicien, 1105 boul Hamel, Saint Felicien, QC, G8K 2R8, CANADA. Tel: 418-679-5412, Ext 284. p. 2733
Bernier, Janice, Br Librn, Wapiti Regional Library, St Louis Public Library, 205 Second St, St. Louis, SK, S0J 2C0, CANADA. Tel: 306-422-8511. p. 2746
Bernier, Jennifer, Co-Librn, Connecticut Legislative Library, Legislative Office Bldg, Rm 5400, 300 Capitol Ave, Hartford, CT, 06106-1591. Tel: 860-240-8888. p. 317
Bernier, Michael G, Libr Dir, Bloomberg Industry Group Library, 1801 S Bell St, Arlington, VA, 22202. Tel: 703-341-5752. p. 2305
Bernier, Sally, Asst Dir, ILL Librn, Richards Free Library, 58 N Main St, Newport, NH, 03773. Tel: 603-863-3430. p. 1376
Berning, Juliana, Br Mgr, Mercer County District Library, Zahn-Marion Township Branch, Five E Franklin St, Chickasaw, OH, 45826. Tel: 419-925-4966. p. 1757
Bernnard, Deborah, Dir, Pub Serv, University at Albany, State University of New York, 1400 Washington Ave, Albany, NY, 12222-0001. Tel: 518-442-3561. p. 1484
Bernoudy, Angela, Br Mgr, El Dorado County Library, Georgetown Branch, 6680 Orleans St, Georgetown, CA, 95634. Tel: 530-333-4724. p. 195
Berns, Artie, Res/Emerging Tech Librn, Western New England University, 1215 Wilbraham Rd, Springfield, MA, 01119-2689. Tel: 413-782-1454. p. 1057
Berns, Artie W, Asst Law Librarian, Collection Servs, Roger Williams University, Ten Metacom Ave, Bristol, RI, 02809-5171. Tel: 401-254-4546. p. 2029
Berns, Cindy, Dir, Postville Public Library, 235 W Tilden, Postville, IA, 52162. Tel: 563-864-7600. p. 777
Bernstein, Adriana, Ad, North Brunswick Free Public Library, 880 Hermann Rd, North Brunswick, NJ, 08902. Tel: 732-246-3545. p. 1429
Bernstein, Alan, Dr, Dean of Libr, Valdosta State University, 1500 N Patterson St, Valdosta, GA, 31698-0150. Tel: 229-333-5860. p. 501
Bernstein, Beth, Libr Mgr, Seyfarth Shaw Library, 2029 Century Park E, Ste 3300, Los Angeles, CA, 90067. Tel: 310-277-7200. p. 167
Bernstein, Josh, Br Mgr, Kent District Library, Grandville Branch, 4055 Maple St SW, Grandville, MI, 49418. p. 1094
Bernstein, Kelly, Chief Exec Officer, County of Brant Public Library, 12 William St, Paris, ON, N3L 1K7, CANADA. Tel: 519-442-2433. p. 2671
Bernstein, Kelly, Pres, Ontario Library Consortium, c/o Georgina Public Library, 90 Wexford Dr, Keswick, ON, L4P 3P7, CANADA. Tel: 905-627-8662. p. 2778
Bernstein, Lee, Libr Mgr, Haynes & Boone LLP, 2323 Victory Ave, Ste 700, Dallas, TX, 75219. Tel: 214-651-5711. p. 2167
Bernstein, Michael, Librn, Dodge Correctional Institution Library, One W Lincoln St, Waupun, WI, 53963. Tel: 920-324-5577, Ext 6570. p. 2485
Bernstein, Robin R, Sr Dir for Libr Serv, Bellevue University, 1028 Bruin Blvd, Bellevue, NE, 68005. Tel: 402-557-7300. p. 1307
Bernstein, Steven, Assoc Cataloging Librn, Central Connecticut State University, 1615 Stanley St, New Britain, CT, 06050. Tel: 860-832-2079. p. 324
Bernsten, Suzanne, Web Serv Librn, Lansing Community College Library, Technology & Learning Ctr, 400 N Capitol Ave, Lansing, MI, 48933. Tel: 517-483-1644. p. 1125
Berntsen, Willow, Metadata Specialist, University of Puget Sound, 1604 N Warner St, Upper Loading Dock, Tacoma, WA, 98416. Tel: 253-879-3107. p. 2387
Bero, Margaret, Dir, Nashua Community College, 505 Amherst St, Nashua, NH, 03063-1026. Tel: 603-578-8905. p. 1374
Berowski, Alfred, Dir, Libr Serv, Herkimer College Library, 100 Reservoir Rd, Herkimer, NY, 13350. Tel: 315-866-0300, Ext 8345. p. 1546
Berra, Daniel, Asst Dir, Pflugerville Public Library, 1008 W Pfluger, Pflugerville, TX, 78660. Tel: 512-990-6375. p. 2226
Berrett, Lonnie, Ref Librn, Ennis Public Library, 115 W Brown St, Ennis, TX, 75119. Tel: 972-875-5360. p. 2175
Berrey, Holly, Asst Dir, Wood River Public Library, 326 E Ferguson Ave, Wood River, IL, 62095-2098. Tel: 618-254-4832. p. 664
Berriman, Whitney, Dir, Powhatan County Public Library, 2270 Mann Rd, Powhatan, VA, 23139-5748. Tel: 804-598-5670. p. 2338
Berringer, Rebecca, Exec Dir, Mason County Historical Society, 1687 S Lakeshore Dr, Ludington, MI, 49431. Tel: 231-843-4808. p. 1128
Berrini, Lucas, Coll Develop Librn, North Carolina Wesleyan University, 3400 N Wesleyan Blvd, Rocky Mount, NC, 27804. Tel: 252-985-5344. p. 1713
Berry, Alyssa, Tech Serv Librn, Joplin Public Library, 1901 E 20th St, Joplin, MO, 64804. Tel: 417-623-7953. p. 1253
Berry, Amy, Libr Coord, Highland Park United Methodist Church Library, 3300 Mockingbird Lane, Dallas, TX, 75205. Tel: 214-521-3111. p. 2167
Berry, Anita, Librn I, Montgomery City-County Public Library System, Governors Square Branch Library, 2885-B E South Blvd, Montgomery, AL, 36116. Tel: 334-284-7929. p. 29
Berry, Bailey, Librn for Digital Publishing, Curation & Conversion, Pepperdine University Libraries, 24255 Pacific Coast Hwy, Malibu, CA, 90263. Tel: 310-506-4252. p. 171
Berry, Brook, Dir, Wethersfield Public Library, 515 Silas Deane Hwy, Wethersfield, CT, 06109. Tel: 860-529-2665. p. 347
Berry, Carol, Patron Serv Supvr, Eagle Public Library, 100 N Stierman Way, Eagle, ID, 83616. Tel: 208-939-6814. p. 520
Berry, David, Libr Dir, Homer Public Library, 500 Hazel Ave, Homer, AK, 99603. Tel: 907-435-3151. p. 46

Berry, Diane, Dir, New York Mills Public Library, 399 Main St, New York Mills, NY, 13417. Tel: 315-736-5391. p. 1605
Berry, Evette, Mgr, Calgary Public Library, Nose Hill, 1530 Northmount Dr NW, Calgary, AB, T2L 0G6, CANADA. p. 2527
Berry, Evette, Mgr, Calgary Public Library, Signal Hill, 5994 Signal Hill Centre SW, Calgary, AB, T3H 3P8, CANADA. p. 2527
Berry, Hillary, Circ Supvr, Kalamazoo College Library, 1200 Academy St, Kalamazoo, MI, 49006-3285. Tel: 269-337-5731. p. 1121
Berry, Jane D, Asst Dir, Glenview Public Library, 1930 Glenview Rd, Glenview, IL, 60025. Tel: 847-729-7500. p. 594
Berry, Janelle, Dir, Crosby County Library, 114 W Aspen St, Crosbyton, TX, 79322. Tel: 806-675-2673. p. 2162
Berry, Jennifer, Libr Tech, New Mexico Junior College, One Thunderbird Circle, Hobbs, NM, 88240. Tel: 575-492-2870. p. 1469
Berry, Jessica R, Tech Serv Librn, Kansas City University, 1750 Independence Ave, Kansas City, MO, 64106-1453. Tel: 816-654-7265. p. 1256
Berry, Kathy, Chief Exec Officer, Head Librn, NEMI Public Library, 50 Meredith St W, Little Current, ON, P0P 1K0, CANADA. Tel: 705-368-2444. p. 2653
Berry, Lisa, Pub Serv Librn, Blessing-Rieman College of Nursing & Health Sciences, 3609 N Marx Dr, Quincy, IL, 62305. Tel: 217-228-5520, Ext 6970. p. 637
Berry, Marie, Head, Access Serv, Campbell University, 113 Main St, Buies Creek, NC, 27506. Tel: 910-893-1762. p. 1676
Berry, Mary Grace, Ad, Lucius E & Elsie C Burch Jr Library, 501 Poplar View Pkwy, Collierville, TN, 38017. Tel: 901-457-2600. p. 2094
Berry, Maya, Digital Serv Librn, Northwest Mississippi Community College, Senatobia Learning Resource Ctr, 4975 Hwy 51 N, Senatobia, MS, 38668-1701. Tel: 662-562-3278. p. 1232
Berry, Nancy, Dep Dir, Lancaster County Library, Del Webb Library at Indian Land, 7641 Charlotte Hwy, Indian Land, SC, 29707. Tel: 803-548-9260. p. 2064
Berry, Nick, Libr Dir, Witherle Memorial Library, 41 School St, Castine, ME, 04421. Tel: 207-326-4375. p. 921
Berry, Odessa, Head, Circ & Reserves, Tuskegee University, 1200 W Old Mongtomery Rd, Ford Motor Company Library, Tuskegee, AL, 36088. Tel: 334-727-8892. p. 38
Berry, Sandra S, Librn, Montgomery City-County Public Library System, Pintlala Branch Library, 255 Federal Rd, Pintlala, AL, 36043-9781. Tel: 334-281-8069. p. 30
Berry-Mason, Tomeka, Libr Mgr, Henrico County Public Library, Twin Hickory Area Library, 5001 Twin Hickory Rd, Glen Allen, VA, 23059. Tel: 804-501-1920. p. 2326
Berry-Sullivan, Samantha O, Ref Librn, Utica University, 1600 Burrstone Rd, Utica, NY, 13502-4892. Tel: 315-792-3016. p. 1656
Berryhill, Hannah, Dir, Kemper-Newton Regional Library System, 101 Peachtree St, Union, MS, 39365-2617. Tel: 601-774-9297. p. 1234
Berryhill, Kelsey, Librn, State Historical Society of Iowa, 600 E Locust, Des Moines, IA, 50319-0290. Tel: 515-281-6200. p. 747
Bersee, Hannah, Br Mgr, Wayne County Public Library, Shreve Branch, 189 W McConkey St, Shreve, OH, 44676. Tel: 330-567-2219. p. 1833
Berson, Matt, Pub Info Officer, Oakland Public Library, 125 14th St, Oakland, CA, 94612. Tel: 510-238-6932. p. 186
Berstler, Andrea, Exec Dir, Carroll County Public Library, 1100 Green Valley Rd, New Windsor, MD, 21776. Tel: 410-386-4500. p. 971
Berstler, Susan, Emerging Technologies Specialist, Harvard Library, Godfrey Lowell Cabot Science Library, Science Ctr, One Oxford St, Cambridge, MA, 02138. Tel: 617-495-5355. p. 1005
Bertalan, Benjamin, Acq, Allentown Public Library, 1210 Hamilton St, Allentown, PA, 18102. Tel: 610-820-2400. p. 1904
Bertelsen, Dana, Asst Dir, Hoard Historical Museum Library, 401 Whitewater Ave, Fort Atkinson, WI, 53538. Tel: 920-563-7769. p. 2436
Berthelette, Josee, Tech Serv, Hospital Santa Cabrini, 5655 est Saint Zotique, Montreal, QC, H1T 1P7, CANADA. Tel: 514-252-4897. p. 2724
Bertholf, Nancy, Libr Dir, Chandler Public Library, 900 Hwy 31 E, Chandler, TX, 75758. Tel: 903-849-4122. p. 2155
Bertinelli, Lina, Br Mgr, Greenville County Library System, Simpsonville Branch, 626 NE Main St, Simpsonville, SC, 29681. Tel: 864-527-9216. p. 2061
Bertino, Brenda, Libr Dir, Tellico Plains Public Library, 209 Hwy 165, Tellico Plains, TN, 37385. Tel: 423-253-7388. p. 2127
Bertke, Heather, Acq Asst, Washtenaw Community College, 4800 E Huron River Dr, Ann Arbor, MI, 48105-4800. Tel: 734-973-3402. p. 1081
Bertoia, Elizabeth, Ad, Schertz Public Library, 798 Schertz Pkwy, Schertz, TX, 78154. Tel: 210-619-1700. p. 2242
Bertoia, James, Head Librn, Sparwood Public Library, 110 Pine Ave, Sparwood, BC, V0B 2G0, CANADA. Tel: 250-425-2299. p. 2576
Bertoldi, Robert, Circ, Pub Serv, Everett Community College, 2000 Tower St, Everett, WA, 98201-1352. Tel: 425-388-9492. p. 2364
Bertolini, David, Dean, North Dakota State University Libraries, NDSU Archives/Institute For Regional Studies, NDSU West Bldg, Rm 123, 3551 7th Ave N, Fargo, ND, 58102. Tel: 701-231-8338. p. 1733
Bertram, Dorie, Dir, Pub Serv, Washington University Libraries, Law Library, Washington Univ Sch Law, Anheuser-Busch Hall, One Brookings Dr, Campus Box 1171, Saint Louis, MO, 63130. Tel: 314-935-6484. p. 1277
Bertram, Lucille, Librn, Bergen County Historical Society, 355 Main St, Rm 124, Hackensack, NJ, 07601. Tel: 201-343-9492. p. 1406
Bertram, Patrick, Libr Mgr, Florida State College at Jacksonville, Nassau Center Library & Learning Commons, 76346 William Burgess Blvd, Yulee, FL, 32097. Tel: 904-548-4467. p. 411
Bertrand, Gordon, Assoc Univ Librn, Wilfrid Laurier University Library, 75 University Ave W, Waterloo, ON, N2L 3C5, CANADA. Tel: 519-884-0710, Ext 4923. p. 2703
Bertrand, Kelly, Dir, Admin Serv, University of Guelph, 50 Stone Rd E, Guelph, ON, N1G 2W1, CANADA. Tel: 519-824-4120, Ext 53359. p. 2644
Bertrand, Shayne, Mgr, Rapides Parish Library, J L Robertson Branch, 809 Tioga High School Rd, Ball, LA, 71405. Tel: 318-640-3098. p. 880
Bertrand, Sylvie, Asst Librn, Canada Aviation & Space Museum, 11 Aviation Pkwy, Ottawa, ON, K1K 4R3, CANADA. Tel: 343-548-4368. p. 2665
Bertrand, Sylvie, Library Services, Canada Science & Technology Museum, 1865 St Laurent, Ottawa, ON, K1G 5A3, CANADA. Tel: 613-990-5015. p. 2665
Bertuca, Jeanine, Ref Librn, Alicia Salinas City of Alice Public Library, 401 E Third St, Alice, TX, 78332. Tel: 361-664-9506, 361-664-9507. p. 2132
Bertucci, Joanna, Libr Dir, Park Ridge Public Library, 20 S Prospect, Park Ridge, IL, 60068. Tel: 847-720-3203. p. 633
Beru, Tsegaye, Asst Dir, Pub Serv, Duquesne University, Center for Legal Information, 900 Locust St, Pittsburgh, PA, 15282. Tel: 412-396-4423. p. 1993
Berube, Charles, Dir, Admin Serv, Universite Laval Bibliotheque, Pavillon Jean-Charles-Bonenfant, 2345, allée des Bibliothèques, Quebec, QC, G1V 0A6, CANADA. Tel: 418-656-3344. p. 2732
Berube, Martin, Libr Dir, Cegep de La Pocatiere, 140 Fourth Ave, La Pocatiere, QC, G0R 1Z0, CANADA. Tel: 418-856-1525, Ext 2203. p. 2714
Berube, Matthew, Head, Info Serv, Jones Library, Inc, 43 Amity St, Amherst, MA, 01002-2285. Tel: 413-259-3195. p. 984
Berube, Matthew, Head, Info Serv, Jones Library, Inc, North Amherst Branch, Eight Montague Rd, Amherst, MA, 01002. Tel: 413-259-3099. p. 984
Berumen, Tina, Dir, Libr Serv, Parker University Library, 2540 Walnut Hill Lane, Dallas, TX, 75220. Tel: 214-902-3404. p. 2167
Besara, Rachel, Assoc Dean, Missouri State University, 850 S John Q Hammons Pkwy, Springfield, MO, 65807. p. 1281
Besecker, Scott, IT Support, Bradford Public Library, 138 E Main St, Bradford, OH, 45308-1108. Tel: 937-448-2612. p. 1752
Besedich, Janet, Br Mgr, Marion County Public Library, Mannington Public, 109 Clarksburg St, Mannington, WV, 26582. Tel: 304-986-2803. p. 2402
Besetzny, DeAnne, Circ Mgr, University of Saint Mary of the Lake - Mundelein Seminary, 1000 E Maple Ave, Mundelein, IL, 60060. Tel: 847-970-4820. p. 622
Beshears, Lonetta, Dir, Sunbright Public Library, 142 Melton Dr, Sunbright, TN, 37872. Tel: 423-628-2439. p. 2127
Beshers, Stacey, Ch Serv, YA Serv, Holmes Public Library, 470 Plymouth St, Halifax, MA, 02338. Tel: 781-293-2271. p. 1023
Besnoy, Amy, Sci, University of San Diego, Helen K & James S Copley Library, 5998 Alcala Park, San Diego, CA, 92110. p. 222
Beson, Kathy, Children's Serv Supvr, Menasha Public Library, 440 First St, Menasha, WI, 54952-3143. Tel: 920-967-3671. p. 2455
Beson, Svea, Info Serv Coordr, Wetaskiwin Public Library, 5002 51st Ave, Wetaskiwin, AB, T9A 0V1, CANADA. Tel: 780-361-4446. p. 2559
Bess, Bennett, Dir, Pawnee Public Library, 613 Douglas St, Pawnee, IL, 62558. Tel: 217-625-7716. p. 633
Bess, Erica, Asst Dir, Princeton Public Library, 65 Witherspoon St, Princeton, NJ, 08542. Tel: 609-924-9529. p. 1436
Bess, Peter, Asst Dir, Butler Area Public Library, 218 N McKean St, Butler, PA, 16001. Tel: 724-287-1715. p. 1917
Bess, Rebecca, Asst Libr Dir, Cranberry Public Library, Municipal Ctr, 2525 Rochester Rd, Ste 300, Cranberry Township, PA, 16066-6423. Tel: 724-776-9100, Ext 1147. p. 1924
Bess, Robbie, Librn, Calhoun County Library, Seadrift Branch, 502 S 4th St, Seadrift, TX, 77983. Tel: 361-785-4241. p. 2228
Bess, Robert, Mgr, Libr Depository, West Virginia University Libraries, 1549 University Ave, Morgantown, WV, 26506. Tel: 304-293-4040. p. 2409
Besse, Geraldine, Supvr, Morgan City Public Library, 220 Everett St, Morgan City, LA, 70380. Tel: 985-380-4646. p. 899
Besser, Brenda, Instr, Librn, Inver Hills Community College Library, 2500 80th St E, Inver Grove Heights, MN, 55076-3209. Tel: 651-450-3798. p. 1179
Bessinger, Jeff, Archivist, Lakeshore Museum Center Archives, 430 W Clay Ave, Muskegon, MI, 49440-1002. Tel: 231-722-0278. p. 1136
Bessler, Cindy, Tech Serv, Whittier College, Bonnie Bell Wardman Library, 7031 Founders Hill Rd, Whittier, CA, 90608-9984. Tel: 562-907-4247. p. 259
Best, Ann, Outreach Coordr, Menominee County Library, S319 Railroad St, Stephenson, MI, 49887. Tel: 906-753-6923. p. 1152
Best, Beverly, Librn, Arnold's Cove Public Library, Five Highliner Dr, Arnold's Cove, NL, A0B 1A0, CANADA. Tel: 709-463-8707. p. 2607

Best, Karene, Librn, Valencia College, Poinciana Campus Library, 3255 Pleasant Hill Rd, Bldg 1, Rm 331, Kissimmee, FL, 34746. Tel: 407-582-6027. p. 414

Best, Matthew, Sr Librn, Erie Community College-North, 6205 Main St, Williamsville, NY, 14221-7095. Tel: 716-220-5262. p. 1666

Best, Rae Ellen, Librn, United States House of Representatives Library, 292 Cannon House Office Bldg, Washington, DC, 20515-6612. Tel: 202-225-9000. p. 379

Best, Rickey D, Coll Develop Librn, Auburn University, 7440 East Dr, Montgomery, AL, 36117. Tel: 334-244-3200. p. 28

Best, William, Mgr, Champaign County History Museum, Cattle Bank Bldg, 102 E University Ave, Champaign, IL, 61820-4111. Tel: 217-356-1010. p. 551

Bester, Greg, Mgr, Idea Exchange, Preston, 435 King St E, Cambridge, ON, N3H 3N1, CANADA. Tel: 519-653-3632. p. 2635

Betcher, Dwayne, Pub Serv Mgr, Herrick District Library, 300 S River Ave, Holland, MI, 49423. Tel: 616-355-3712. p. 1115

Betchik, Kari, Dept Head, Tech Serv, Perry Public Library, 3753 Main St, Perry, OH, 44081-9501. Tel: 440-259-3300. p. 1815

Beth, Amy, Chief Librn, Dir, Acad Tech, Lesbian Herstory Archives, 484 14th St, Brooklyn, NY, 11215. Tel: 718-768-3953. p. 1505

Bethel, Jennifer, Branch Cluster Supvr, Fresno County Public Library, 2420 Mariposa St, Fresno, CA, 93721. Tel: 559-600-7323. p. 145

Bethke, Shawn, Chief Librn/CEO, Sioux Lookout Public Library, 21 Fifth Ave, Sioux Lookout, ON, P8T 1B3, CANADA. Tel: 807-737-3660. p. 2678

Bethke, Sherri, Head, Continuing Coll, University of Iowa Libraries, College of Law Library, 200 Boyd Law Bldg, Iowa City, IA, 52242-1166. Tel: 319-335-9041. p. 761

Bethoulle, Tina, Dir, Mackay District Library, 320 Capitol Ave, MacKay, ID, 83251. Tel: 208-588-3333. p. 524

Bethurem, Kip, Fac Mgr, Sheridan County Public Library System, 335 W Alger St, Sheridan, WY, 82801. Tel: 307-674-8585. p. 2499

Betit, Jessica, YA Librn, Gardiner Public Library, 152 Water St, Gardiner, ME, 04345. Tel: 207-582-3312. p. 926

Betlejewski, Karen, Coordr, Del Norte County Historical Society Museum Library, 577 H St, Crescent City, CA, 95531. Tel: 707-464-3922. p. 133

Betler, Sammie, Dir, Casey County Public Library, 238 Middleburg St, Liberty, KY, 42539. Tel: 606-787-9381. p. 864

Beto, Tami, Br Mgr, Pine River Public Library, 212 Park Ave, Pine River, MN, 56474. Tel: 218-587-4639. p. 1192

Beto, Tami, Libr Dir, Wells Public Library, 54 First St SW, Wells, MN, 56097-1913. Tel: 507-553-3702. p. 1207

Bettencourt-McCarthy, Aja, Instruction Librn, Oregon Institute of Technology Library, 3201 Campus Dr, Klamath Falls, OR, 97601-8801. Tel: 541-885-1772. p. 1883

Bettig, Allen, Technology Spec, Glenview Public Library, 1930 Glenview Rd, Glenview, IL, 60025. Tel: 847-729-7500. p. 594

Bettinger, Ray, Br Mgr, Calaveras County Library, Valley Springs Branch, 240 Pine St, Valley Springs, CA, 95252. Tel: 209-772-1318. p. 211

Bettinger, Sheila, Dir, Ellisburg Free Library, 12117 NY-193, Ellisburg, NY, 13636. Tel: 315-846-5087. p. 1530

Bettivia, Rhiannon, Asst Prof, Simmons University, 300 The Fenway, Boston, MA, 02115. Tel: 617-521-2800. p. 2786

Bettner, Lisa, Head Librn, Tiskilwa Public Library, 119 E Main, Tiskilwa, IL, 61368. Tel: 815-646-4511. p. 654

Betts, Jennifer, Asst Dir, Univ Archivist, Brown University, John Hay Library, 20 Prospect St, Box A, Providence, RI, 02912. Tel: 401-863-6414. p. 2037

Betts, Samantha, Coordr of Libr, Fairfield County District Library, Baltimore Branch / Griley Memorial, 205 E Market St, Baltimore, OH, 43105. Tel: 740-862-8505. p. 1794

Betts, Samantha, Coordr of Libr, Fairfield County District Library, Bremen Rushcreek Memorial Branch, 200 School St, Bremen, OH, 43107. Tel: 740-569-7246. p. 1794

Betts, Samantha, Coordr of Libr, Fairfield County District Library, Johns Memorial Branch, 116 E High St, Amanda, OH, 43102. Tel: 740-969-2785. p. 1794

Betts, Samantha, Coordr, Circ & Customer Serv, Fairfield County District Library, 219 N Broad St, Lancaster, OH, 43130-3098. Tel: 740-653-2745. p. 1794

Betts, Theresa, User Experience Librn, Henry Ford College, 5101 Evergreen Rd, Dearborn, MI, 48128-1495. Tel: 313-845-9763. p. 1096

Betty, Jan, Coordr, Ch & Youth Serv, Milanof-Schock Library, 1184 Anderson Ferry Rd, Mount Joy, PA, 17552. Tel: 717-653-1510. p. 1966

Betty, Paul, Res & Instruction Librn, Regis University, 3333 Regis Blvd, D20, Denver, CO, 80221-1099. Tel: 303-458-4030, 303-458-4031. p. 276

Betz, Carrie, Youth Serv, Saint Louis Public Library, 1301 Olive St, Saint Louis, MO, 63103. Tel: 314-539-0300. p. 1274

Betz, Clare, Head, Circ, Douglas Library of Hebron, 22 Main St, Hebron, CT, 06248. Tel: 860-228-9312, Ext 310. p. 319

Betz, Corinne, Info Serv, Lehigh Carbon Community College Library, 4750 Orchard Rd, Schnecksville, PA, 18078. Tel: 610-799-1150. p. 2003

Beulah, Shauna, Br Mgr, Talbot County Free Library, Saint Michaels Branch, 106 N Fremont St, Saint Michaels, MD, 21663. Tel: 410-745-5877. p. 964

Beutler, Joan, Mgr, Foremost Municipal Library, 103 First Ave E, Foremost, AB, T0K 0X0, CANADA. Tel: 403-867-3855. p. 2540

Bevacqua, Joanna, Coll Develop Librn, Borough of Manhattan Community College Library, 199 Chambers St, S410, New York, NY, 10007. Tel: 212-220-1446. p. 1580

Bevel, Brittny, Educ Curator, Tampa Museum of Art, 120 W Gasparilla Plaza, Tampa, FL, 33602. Tel: 813-274-8130. p. 449

Beveridge, Marguerite, Principal Librn, California Department of Justice, Attorney General's Law Library, 1300 I St, Sacramento, CA, 95814. Tel: 916-324-5312. p. 207

Beverly, Lysobey, Metadata Librn, Sacred Heart University, 5151 Park Ave, Fairfield, CT, 06825-1000. Tel: 203-365-4855. p. 312

Beverly, Terri, Circ Supvr, Saint Johns County Public Library System, Hastings Branch, 6195 S Main St, Hastings, FL, 32145. Tel: 904-827-6974. p. 440

Bevier, Amber, Librn, Nauvoo Public Library, 1270 Mulholland St, Nauvoo, IL, 62354. Tel: 217-453-2707. p. 623

Bevilacqua, Louise, Circ, Northern Essex Community College, 100 Elliott St, Haverhill, MA, 01830. Tel: 978-556-3422. p. 1024

Bevill, Sheila, Librn, Arkansas History Commission Library, One Capitol Mall, 2nd Flr, Little Rock, AR, 72201. Tel: 501-682-6900. p. 100

Bevill, Sheila, Librn, Arkansas State Archives, One Capitol Mall, Ste 215, Little Rock, AR, 72201. Tel: 501-682-6900. p. 100

Bevilocqua, Sara, Managing Librn, Pub Serv, Falmouth Public Library, 300 Main St, Falmouth, MA, 02540. Tel: 508-457-2555, Ext 2904. p. 1018

Bevins, Brian, Ref Librn, Akin Gump Strauss Hauer & Feld LLP, Robert S Strauss Tower, 2001 K St NW, Washington, DC, 20006-1037. Tel: 202-887-4000. p. 359

Bevis, Mary, Acq, Per Librn, Jacksonville State University Library, 700 Pelham Rd N, Jacksonville, AL, 36265. Tel: 256-782-5758. p. 23

Bewley, John, Assoc Librn, University at Buffalo Libraries-State University of New York, Music Library, 112 Baird Hall, Buffalo, NY, 14260-4750. Tel: 716-645-2923. p. 1511

Beyeler, Jeri Ann, Dir, Leadore Community Library, 202 S Railroad St, Leadore, ID, 83464. Tel: 208-768-2640. p. 524

Beyer, Charlotte, Instruction & Ref Librn, Rosalind Franklin University of Medicine & Science, 3333 Green Bay Rd, North Chicago, IL, 60064-3095. Tel: 847-578-8808. p. 626

Beyer, Charlotte, Libr Dir, Rosalind Franklin University of Medicine & Science, 3333 Green Bay Rd, North Chicago, IL, 60064-3095. Tel: 847-578-8808. p. 626

Beyer, Hope, Dir, Libr Serv, Del Mar College, 101 Baldwin Blvd, Corpus Christi, TX, 78404. Tel: 361-698-1382. p. 2160

Beyer, Jenna, Dir, Plum City Public Library, 611 Main St, Plum City, WI, 54761-9044. Tel: 715-647-2373. p. 2470

Beyer, Laura, Head, Circ, Matawan-Aberdeen Public Library, 165 Main St, Matawan, NJ, 07747. Tel: 732-583-9100. p. 1417

Beyer, Matthew, Libr Assoc, Union University, 1050 Union University Dr, Jackson, TN, 38305-3697. Tel: 731-661-5067. p. 2102

Beyler, Curt, Fac Mgr, Brown County Library, 515 Pine St, Green Bay, WI, 54301. Tel: 920-448-5849. p. 2438

Bezanson, Elizabeth, Libr Dir, Sprague Public Library, 76 Main St, Baltic, CT, 06330. Tel: 860-822-3012. p. 302

Bezdicek, Adam, Fac Librn, Hennepin Technical College Library, 9000 Brooklyn Blvd, Brooklyn Park, MN, 55445. Tel: 763-488-2634. p. 1166

Bezkorowajny, Carol, Automation Syst Coordr, Head, Circ & Tech Serv, Monroe Free Library, 44 Millpond Pkwy, Monroe, NY, 10950. Tel: 845-783-4411. p. 1573

Bhagat, Sudesh Angie, Acq, University of Maryland Libraries, Theodore R McKeldin Library, 7649 Library Lane, College Park, MD, 20742-7011. Tel: 301-405-9306. p. 962

Bhandari, Linda, Prog Coordr, Mamaroneck Public Library, 136 Prospect Ave, Mamaroneck, NY, 10543. Tel: 914-698-1250. p. 1568

Bharti, Neelam, Assoc Dean, Librn, Carnegie Mellon University, Mellon Institute Library, 4400 Fifth Ave, 4th Flr, Pittsburgh, PA, 15213. Tel: 412-268-7213. p. 1992

Bhat, Akhila, Br Mgr, Harris County Public Library, Maud Smith Marks Branch, 1815 Westgreen Blvd, Katy, TX, 77450. Tel: 832-927-7860. p. 2193

Bhat, Nimisha, Digital Humanities Librn, Smith College Libraries, Hillyer Art Library, Brown Fine Arts Ctr, 20 Elm St, Northampton, MA, 01063. Tel: 413-585-2941. p. 1042

Bhatnagar, Deepak, Dir, United States Department of Agriculture, 1100 Allen Toussaint Blvd, New Orleans, LA, 70124-4305. Tel: 504-286-4214. p. 904

Bhatnagar, Neera, Pub Serv, Syst Serv, McMaster University Library, Health Sciences Library, 1280 Main St W, Hamilton, ON, L8S 4K1, CANADA. Tel: 905-525-9140, Ext 23775. p. 2647

Bhatt, Anjana, Univ Librn, Florida Gulf Coast University Library, 10501 FGCU Blvd S, Fort Myers, FL, 33965. Tel: 239-590-7634. p. 403

Bhatt, Jay, Ref Librn, Drexel University Libraries, Hagerty Library, 33rd & Market Sts, Philadelphia, PA, 19104-2875. Tel: 215-895-1873. p. 1976

Bhattacharya, Rakhi, Managing Librn, Brooklyn Public Library, Midwood, 975 E 16th St, Brooklyn, NY, 11230. Tel: 718-252-0967. p. 1503

Bhatti, Sherry, Youth Serv, Menands Public Library, Four N Lyons Ave, Menands, NY, 12204. Tel: 518-463-4035. p. 1570

Bhogal, Surinder, Chief Librn, Surrey Libraries, 10350 University Dr, Surrey, BC, V3T 4B8, CANADA. Tel: 604-598-7300. p. 2577

Bhullar, Goodie, Coordr, Libr Instruction, University of Missouri-Columbia, Elmer Ellis Library, 104 Ellis Library, Columbia, MO, 65201-5149. Tel: 573-882-9163. p. 1243

Biaggi, Cali, Online Learning Librn, Doane College, 1014 Boswell Ave, Crete, NE, 68333. Tel: 402-826-8224. p. 1311

Biagi, Damian, Systems & Metadata Librn, Western New England University, 1215 Wilbraham Rd, Springfield, MA, 01119. Tel: 413-782-1635. p. 1057

Biagini, Mary Kay, Chair, University of Pittsburgh, Information Science Bldg 5th Flr, 135 N Bellefield Ave, Pittsburgh, PA, 15260. Tel: 412-624-5015. p. 2791

Biagiotti, Joseph L, Asst Dir, Head, Ref, Cadwalader, Wickersham & Taft Library, 200 Liberty St, New York, NY, 10281. Tel: 212-504-6000. p. 1580

Biala, Marcy, Mgr, Patron Serv, Westmont Public Library, 428 N Cass Ave, Westmont, IL, 60559-1502. Tel: 630-869-6150, 630-869-6160. p. 661

Bialek, Stacey, Fac Mgr, Manitowoc Public Library, 707 Quay St, Manitowoc, WI, 54220. Tel: 920-686-3000. p. 2453

Bialkowski, Mark, Tech Serv Librn, D'Youville College, 320 Porter Ave, Buffalo, NY, 14201-1084. Tel: 716 829-8106. p. 1509

Bialski, Holly, Adult Programmer, Youth Programmer, River Valley District Library, 214 S Main St, Port Byron, IL, 61275. Tel: 309-523-3440. p. 636

Bianchi, Christopher, Adult Reference & Literacy Librn, Floyd Memorial Library, 539 First St, Greenport, NY, 11944-1399. Tel: 631-477-0660. p. 1541

Bianchi, June, ILL & Ser, Cape Cod Hospital, 27 Park St, Hyannis, MA, 02601-5230. Tel: 508-862-5867. p. 1026

Bianchi, Michael, Br Mgr, Akron-Summit County Public Library, Tallmadge Branch, 90 Community Rd, Tallmadge, OH, 44278. Tel: 330-633-4345. p. 1744

Bianco, Elena, Copyright Officer, Syst & Tech Serv Librn, Skagit Valley College, 2405 E College Way, Mount Vernon, WA, 98273-5899. Tel: 360-416-7624. p. 2371

Bianco, Jane, Assoc Curator, William A Farnsworth Library at the Farnsworth Art Museum, 16 Museum St, Rockland, ME, 04841. Tel: 207-390-6012. p. 939

Bianco, Mary, Youth Serv Librn, Hyannis Public Library, 401 Main St, Hyannis, MA, 02601. Tel: 508-775-2280. p. 1026

Bias, Jason, Librn, Genesee District Library, Talking Book Center, 4195 W Pasadena Ave, Flint, MI, 48504. Tel: 810-732-1120. p. 1106

Bias, Linda, Archivist, Houston Chronicle Library, 4747 Southwest Fwy, Houston, TX, 77027. Tel: 713-362-7171. p. 2194

Bibbs, Bradley, Teen Serv Coordr, Poplar Creek Public Library District, 1405 S Park Ave, Streamwood, IL, 60107-2997. Tel: 630-837-6800. p. 652

Bibens, Hope, Dir, Archives & Spec Coll, Drake University, 2725 University Ave, Des Moines, IA, 50311. Tel: 515-271-2088. p. 746

Biby, Darren, Libr Dir, Waurika Public Library, 203 S Meridian St, Waurika, OK, 73573. Tel: 580-228-3274. p. 1868

Biccum, Connie, Youth Serv Librn, Flat Rock Public Library, 25200 Gibraltar Rd, Flat Rock, MI, 48134. Tel: 734-782-2430. p. 1105

Bicicchi, Rachel, Coordr, Educ Tech, Librn, Millikin University, 1184 W Main St, Decatur, IL, 62522. Tel: 217-424-6214. p. 576

Bickerstaff, Rhonda, Librn, New Madrid County Library, New Madrid Memorial, 431 Mill St, New Madrid, MO, 63869. Tel: 573-748-2378. p. 1266

Bickford, Jane, Br Librn, Boston Public Library, South Boston, 646 E Broadway, Boston, MA, 02127-1502. Tel: 617-268-0180. p. 992

Bickford, Keisha, Dir, Moffat County Libraries, 570 Green St, Craig, CO, 81625. Tel: 970-824-5116. p. 272

Bickford, Louella, Dir, Lawrence Public Library, 33 Lawrence Ave, Fairfield, ME, 04937. Tel: 207-453-6867. p. 924

Bickley, Tom, Assoc Librn, California State University, East Bay Library, CSU East Bay Library, 25800 Carlos Bee Blvd, Hayward, CA, 94542-3052. Tel: 510-885-7554. p. 150

Bicknell-Holmes, Tracy, Dr, Instruction & Res Serv Librn, Boise State University, 1865 Cesar Chavez Lane, Boise, ID, 83725. Tel: 208-426-1204. p. 517

Bicknese, Douglas, Regional Archives Dir, National Archives & Records Administration, 7358 S Pulaski Rd, Chicago, IL, 60629-5898. Tel: 773-948-9001. p. 565

Bidal, Carole, Br Head, West Nipissing Public Library, Verner Branch, 11790 Hwy 64, Verner, ON, P0H 2M0, CANADA. Tel: 705-594-2800. p. 2682

Bidal, Deborah, Br Head, West Nipissing Public Library, Cache Bay Branch, 55 Cache St, Cache Bay, ON, P0H 1G0, CANADA. Tel: 705-753-9393. p. 2682

Biddle, Daniel, Supvr, New York University, Stephen Chan Library of Fine Arts & Conservation Center Library, One E 78th St, New York, NY, 10075. Tel: 212-992-5854. p. 1599

Bidlack, Beth, Libr Dir, Vermont State University - Castleton, 178 Alumni Dr, Castleton, VT, 05735. Tel: 802-468-1256. p. 2281

Bidney, Marcy, Curator, Library Assoc Dir for Distinctive Collections, University of Wisconsin-Milwaukee Libraries, American Geographical Society Library, Golda Meir Library, 2311 E Hartford Ave, Milwaukee, WI, 53211. Tel: 414-229-3984, 414-229-6282. p. 2461

Bidwell, Jennifer, Ref Librn, California State Polytechnic University Library, College of Environmental Design Library, 3801 W Temple Ave, Bldg 7, Pomona, CA, 91768. Tel: 909-869-3084. p. 196

Bidwell, Mary, Dir, Henderson Free Library, 8939 New York State Rte 178, Henderson, NY, 13650. Tel: 315-938-7169. p. 1545

Bidzinski, Heather, Head, Archives & Spec Coll, University of Manitoba Libraries, Elizabeth Dafoe Library, 25 Chancellor's Circle, Winnipeg, MB, R3T 2N2, CANADA. Tel: 204-474-6350. p. 2595

Bieber, Karla, Libr Dir, A H Brown Public Library, 521 N Main St, Mobridge, SD, 57601. Tel: 605-845-2808. p. 2079

Bieck, Barbara, Spec Coll Librn, The New York Society Library, 53 E 79th St, New York, NY, 10075. Tel: 212-288-6900, Ext 242. p. 1598

Biedermann, Heather, Librn, South Central College, 1920 Lee Blvd, North Mankato, MN, 56003-2504. Tel: 507-389-7223. p. 1190

Biegun, Teresa, Electronic Info Librn, Macomb Community College Libraries, Center Campus, 44575 Garfield Rd, C-Bldg, Clinton Township, MI, 48038-1139. Tel: 586-286-2233. p. 1157

Bielser, Barb, Prog Dir, Clyde Public Library, 107 S Green St, Clyde, KS, 66938. Tel: 785-446-3563. p. 802

Bielskas, Amanda, Dir, Columbia University, Science & Engineering Library, 401 Northwest Corner Bldg, 550 W 120th St, New York, NY, 10027. Tel: 212-854-6767. p. 1583

Bielucke, Susn, Dir, Whitehall Township Public Library, 3700 Mechanicsville Rd, Whitehall, PA, 18052. Tel: 610-432-4339. p. 2021

Bier, Lisa, Interim Libr Dir, Southern Connecticut State University, 501 Crescent St, New Haven, CT, 06515. Tel: 203-392-5131. p. 326

Bierman, James, Eng Librn, University of Oklahoma Libraries, Engineering Library, 222FH, 865 Asp Ave, Norman, OK, 73019. Tel: 405-325-2941. p. 1856

Bierman, James, Interim Librn, University of Oklahoma Libraries, Youngblood Energy (Geology) Library, Youngblood Energy Library, R220, 100 E Boyd, Norman, OK, 73019. Tel: 405-325-6451. p. 1856

Bierman, Johnna, Ch Serv, Librn, Bennington Public Library, 11401 N 156th St, Bennington, NE, 68007. Tel: 402-238-2201. p. 1308

Biersner, Lisa, Dir, Janesville Public Library, 227 Main St, Janesville, IA, 50647. Tel: 319-987-2925. p. 761

Bieszka, Lynn, Br Supvr, Warren Public Library, One City Sq, Ste 100, Warren, MI, 48093-2396. Tel: 586-751-0770. p. 1157

Biette, Kim, Libr Mgr, Gem Jubilee Library, 125 Center St, Gem, AB, T0J 1M0, CANADA. Tel: 403-641-3245. p. 2540

Bigam, Joyce, Ch Serv, Cuyahoga Falls Library, 2015 Third St, Cuyahoga Falls, OH, 44221-3294. Tel: 330-928-2117. p. 1779

Bigelow, Lynne, Ch Serv, Youth Serv, Iosco-Arenac District Library, 120 W Westover St, East Tawas, MI, 48730. Tel: 989-362-2651. p. 1102

Bigelow, Nora, Curator, Peabody Historical Society & Museum, 31 Washington St, Peabody, MA, 01960-5520. Tel: 978-531-0805. p. 1045

Bigelow, Ryan, Libr Mgr, Cottonwood Public Library, 100 S Sixth St, Cottonwood, AZ, 86326. Tel: 928-340-2780. p. 59

Bigenwald, Jenny, ILL Coordr, Saint John Fisher University, 3690 East Ave, Rochester, NY, 14618-3599. Tel: 585-385-8165. p. 1630

Biger, Jackie, Assoc Prof, University of Iowa, 3087 Main Library, 125 W Washington St, Iowa City, IA, 52242-1420. Tel: 319-335-5707. p. 2785

Biggar, George, Syst Adminr, Rensselaer Libraries, Rensselaer Architecture Library, Greene Bldg 308, 3rd Flr, 110 Eighth St, Troy, NY, 12180-3590. Tel: 518-276-8310. p. 1652

Bigger, Samantha, Info Serv, Tech, Boulder City Library, 701 Adams Blvd, Boulder City, NV, 89005-2207. Tel: 702-293-1281. p. 1343

Biggerstaff, Marilyn, Librn, Nowata City-County Library, 224 S Pine St, Nowata, OK, 74048. Tel: 918-273-3363. p. 1856

Biggin-Pound, Janice, Commun Librn, Cariboo Regional District Library, Anahim Lake Branch, 2409 Whispering Pines Trailer Court, Unit 1, Hwy 20, Anahim Lake, BC, V0l 1C0, CANADA. Tel: 250-742-2056. p. 2584

Biggins, Megan, Dir, Pub Serv, Grand Rapids Public Library, 111 Library St NE, Grand Rapids, MI, 49503-3268. Tel: 616-988-5400. p. 1111

Biggins, Megan, Br Mgr, Arlington County Department of Libraries, Columbia Pike, 816 S Walter Reed Dr, Arlington, VA, 22204. Tel: 703-228-5711. p. 2305

Biggs, Ashley, Mkt, Outreach Librn, Maryland State Library for the Blind & Print Disabled, 415 Park Ave, Baltimore, MD, 21201-3603. Tel: 410-230-2424. p. 955

Biggs, Barbara, Br Mgr, Portsmouth Public Library, Wheelersburg Branch, 10745 Old Gallia Pike, Wheelersburg, OH, 45694. Tel: 740-574-6116. p. 1816

Biggs, Eric, Librn, Saint Johns River State College, Saint Augustine Campus Library, 2990 College Dr, Saint Augustine, FL, 32084. Tel: 904-808-7474. p. 434

Bigham, Denice, Co-Dir, Coyle Free Library, 102 N Main St, Chambersburg, PA, 17201. Tel: 717-263-1054. p. 1920

Bigler, Cindy, Dir, Gooding Public Library, 306 Fifth Ave W, Gooding, ID, 83330-1205. Tel: 208-934-4089. p. 521

Bigler, Julie, Circ Serv Dept Head, Hussey-Mayfield Memorial Public Library, 250 N Fifth St, Zionsville, IN, 46077-1324. Tel: 317-873-3149. p. 728

Bigler, Mariko, Library Services Asst, Arizona State University, College of Law, Arizona State University MC 9620, 111 E Taylor St, Ste 350, Phoenix, AZ, 85004. Tel: 480-965-7392. p. 69

Bignoli, Callan, Asst Dir/Tech Librn, Public Library of Brookline, 361 Washington St, Brookline, MA, 02445. Tel: 617-730-2370. p. 1003

Bigras, Lise, Br Head, West Nipissing Public Library, River Vally Branch, Seven Forget Ave, River Valley, ON, P0H 1C0, CANADA. Tel: 705-758-1186. p. 2682

Bikman, Margaret, Ref Librn, Whatcom Community College Library, Heiner Bldg, 231 W Kellogg Rd, Bellingham, WA, 98226. Tel: 360-383-3300. p. 2359

Bilal, Dania, Prof, University of Tennessee, Knoxville, 451 Communications Bldg, 1345 Circle Park Dr, Knoxville, TN, 37996-0332. Tel: 865-974-2148. p. 2792

Bilal, Waheedah, Dir, Libr Serv, Lincoln University of Missouri, 712 Lee Dr, Jefferson City, MO, 65101. Tel: 573-681-5504. p. 1252

Bilbrey, Dana, Asst Dir, Lebanon-Wilson County Library, 108 S Hatton Ave, Lebanon, TN, 37087-3590. Tel: 615-444-0632. p. 2109

Bilby, Becky, Dir, Sioux Center Public Library, 102 S Main Ave, Sioux Center, IA, 51250-1801. Tel: 712-722-2138. p. 782

Bilcowski, Lisa, Head Librn, Minnedosa Regional Library, 45 First Ave SE, Minnedosa, MB, R0J 1E0, CANADA. Tel: 204-867-2585. p. 2588

Bildz, Judith, Coll Develop, Dallas College, L Bldg, Rm L200, 3737 Motley Dr, Mesquite, TX, 75150-2033. Tel; 972-860-7176. p. 2219

Bilek, Jerry, Youth Serv Mgr, Teton County Library, 125 Virginian Lane, Jackson, WY, 83001. Tel: 307-733-2164, Ext 3163. p. 2495

Bilenkin, Veronica, Consumer Health Librn, Greenwich Hospital, Five Perryridge Rd, Greenwich, CT, 06830. Tel: 203-863-3286. p. 314

Bilka, Hazel A, Co-Dir, Bellwood-Antis Public Library, 526 Main St, Bellwood, PA, 16617-1910. Tel: 814-742-8234. p. 1910

Bilko, Kathy, Librn, Banner Health Library Services, Banner Children's at Desert, 1st Flr, 1400 S Dobson Rd, Mesa, AZ, 85202. Tel: 602-839-4353. p. 66

Bill, Leah, Asst Dir, Coal City Public Library District, 85 N Garfield St, Coal City, IL, 60416. Tel: 815-634-4552. p. 572

Biller, Lauren, Programming Librn, Cocoa Beach Public Library, 550 N Brevard Ave, Cocoa Beach, FL, 32931. Tel: 321-868-1104. p. 390

Billerbeck, Ann Rae, Asst Librn, Reinbeck Public Library, 501 Clark St, Reinbeck, IA, 50669. Tel: 319-788-2652. p. 778

Billesberger, Valerie, Archives & Rec Mgr, Mission Community Archives, 33215 Second Ave, Mission, BC, V2V 4L1, CANADA. Tel: 604-820-2621. p. 2570

Billet, Kirk-Evan, Resource Librn, Johns Hopkins University-Peabody Conservatory of Music, 21 E Mount Vernon Pl, Baltimore, MD, 21202-2397. Tel: 667-208-6659. p. 954

Billey, Amber, Metadata Librn, Syst Librn, Bard College, One Library Rd, Annandale-on-Hudson, NY, 12504. Tel: 845-758-7619. p. 1487

Billiet, Sara, Head, Youth Serv, Kewanee Public Library District, 102 S Tremont St, Kewanee, IL, 61443. Tel: 309-852-4505. p. 605

Billings, Cathy Warren, Libr Dir, South Pasadena Public Library, 1100 Oxley St, South Pasadena, CA, 91030. Tel: 626-403-7350. p. 247

Billings, J, Dir, Silver Bay Public Library, Nine Davis Dr, Silver Bay, MN, 55614-1318. Tel: 218-226-4331. p. 1204

Billings, Marilyn, Scholarly Communications Librn, University of Massachusetts Amherst Libraries, 154 Hicks Way, University of Massachusetts, Amherst, MA, 01003-9275. Tel: 413-545-6891. p. 985

Billings, Marilyn, Supvr, Haliburton County Public Library, Gooderham Branch, 1032 Gooderham St, Gooderham, ON, K0M 1R0, CANADA. Tel: 705-447-3163. p. 2644

Billings, Shane Malcolm, Ad, Charles M Bailey Public Library, 39 Bowdoin St, Winthrop, ME, 04364. Tel: 207-377-8673. p. 947

Billings, Victoria A, Tech Serv Librn, Portage County Public Library, Charles M White Library Bldg, 1001 Main St, Stevens Point, WI, 54481-2860. Tel: 715-346-1544. p. 2479

Billingsley, Jennifer, Head, Youth & Family Learning, Russell Library, 123 Broad St, Middletown, CT, 06457. Tel: 860-347-2528. p. 322

Billingsley, Jennifer, Dir, Portland Library, 20 Freestone Ave, Portland, CT, 06480. Tel: 860-342-6770. p. 334

Billingsley, Jerome, Access Serv Librn, Delta State University, Laflore Circle at Fifth Ave, Cleveland, MS, 38733-2599. Tel: 662-846-4430. p. 1214

Bilodeau, Edward, Head, Tech & Syst Serv, Carleton University Library, 1125 Colonel By Dr, Ottawa, ON, K1S 5B6, CANADA. Tel: 613-520-2600, Ext 6040. p. 2666

Bilodeau, Jordan, Ch Serv, Haddonfield Public Library, 60 Haddon Ave, Haddonfield, NJ, 08033-2422. Tel: 856-429-1304. p. 1406

Bilodeau, Nancy, Acq, Cat, Ch Serv, Bibliothèque Raymond-Laberge, 25 Maple Blvd, Chateauguay, QC, J6J 3P7, CANADA. Tel: 450-698-3080. p. 2710

Bilodeau, Nancy, Ch Serv Librn, Bibliothèque Municipale de Gatineau, Ville de Gatineau, CP 1970 Succ. Hull, Gatineau, QC, J8X 3Y9, CANADA. Tel: 819-243-2345. p. 2712

Bilsland, Mary Jane, Mgr, Edmonton Public Library, Lois Hole Library, 17650 69 Ave NW, Edmonton, AB, T5T 3X9, CANADA. Tel: 780-442-0880. p. 2536

Bilton, Karen, Ref/YA, Franklin Township Free Public Library, 485 DeMott Lane, Somerset, NJ, 08873. Tel: 732-873-8700. p. 1442

Bilyeau, Amy, Law Librn, United States Department of the Interior Library, 1849 C St NW, MS 1151, Washington, DC, 20240. Tel: 202-208-3686. p. 378

Bilz, Kelly, Govt Doc Librn, Ref Librn, Thomas More University Benedictine Library, 333 Thomas More Pkwy, Crestview Hills, KY, 41017-2599. Tel: 859-344-3615. p. 852

Bindeman, Thomas C, Syst Dir, Nioga Library System, 6575 Wheeler Rd, Lockport, NY, 14094. Tel: 716-434-6167, Ext 24. p. 1564

Binder, Carley, Libr Mgr, Blackfalds Public Library, 5302 Broadway Ave, Blackfalds, AB, T0M 0J0, CANADA. Tel: 403-885-2343. p. 2523

Binder, Natalie, Dir, Jefferson County Public Library, 375 S Water St, Monticello, FL, 32344. Tel: 850-342-0205, 850-342-0206. p. 426

Bindman, Rachel, Sr Librn, Los Angeles Public Library System, Palms-Rancho Park Branch Library, 2920 Overland Ave, Los Angeles, CA, 90064-4220. Tel: 310-840-2142. p. 165

Bineault, Marc, Dir, Bibliotheque H J Hemens, 339 Chemin Grande-Cote, Rosemere, QC, J7A 1K2, CANADA. Tel: 450-621-3500, Ext 7221. p. 2733

Binegar, Erika, Ch Serv Librn, Coralville Public Library, 1401 Fifth St, Coralville, IA, 52241. Tel: 319-248-1850. p. 742

Binette, Dennis, Asst Curator, Fall River Historical Society Museum, 451 Rock St, Fall River, MA, 02720. Tel: 508-679-1071. p. 1017

Binford, Marilyn, Bus Mgr, Ouachita Parish Public Library, 1800 Stubbs Ave, Monroe, LA, 71201. Tel: 318-327-1490. p. 898

Bing, Meagan, IT/Tech Serv Librn, Orange Beach Public Library, 26267 Canal Rd, Orange Beach, AL, 36561-3917. Tel: 251-981-2360. p. 32

Bingemann, Kira, Ref Librn, David & Joyce Milne Public Library, 1095 Main St, Williamstown, MA, 01267-2627. Tel: 413-458-5369. p. 1069

Bingham, Gina, Pub Serv Adminr, Adult Serv, New Haven Free Public Library, 133 Elm St, New Haven, CT, 06510. Tel: 203-946-8130, Ext 216. p. 326

Bingham, Ralph S, III, Exec Dir, LibraryLinkNJ, The New Jersey Library Cooperative, 44 Stelton Rd, Ste 330, Piscataway, NJ, 08854. Tel: 732-752-7720. p. 2770

Binkley, Julie, Admin Serv Coordr, Lake Villa District Library, 140 N Munn Rd, Lindenhurst, IL, 60046. Tel: 847-245-5101. p. 609

Binkley, Tim, Head, Spec Coll & Archives, Berea College, 100 Campus Dr, Berea, KY, 40404. Tel: 859-985-3267. p. 849

Binnendyk, Myra, Libr Mgr, Penhold & District Public Library, Penhold Regional Multiplex, One Waskasoo Ave, Penhold, AB, T0M 1R0, CANADA. Tel: 403-886-2636. p. 2550

Binns, Laura, Librn, Lenawee District Library, Britton Branch, 120 College Ave, Britton, MI, 49229-9705. Tel: 517-451-2860. p. 1075

Binoniemi, Amanda, Ref & Instruction Librn, Michigan Technological University, 1400 Townsend Dr, Houghton, MI, 49931-1295. Tel: 906-487-1814. p. 1116

Binsfeld, Carrie, Dir, Finance & Gen Serv, Williamsburg Regional Library, 7770 Croaker Rd, Williamsburg, VA, 23188-7064. Tel: 757-741-3407. p. 2353

Biondo, Michael, E-Resources Librn, Scholarly Communications Librn, South Dakota State University, 1300 N Campus Dr, Box 2115, Brookings, SD, 57007. Tel: 605-688-5567. p. 2074

Biorn, Wendy, Exec Dir, Carver County Historical Society Library, 555 W First St, Waconia, MN, 55387. Tel: 952-442-4234. p. 1206

Birbal, Ashley, Dir, Bayville Free Library, 34 School St, Bayville, NY, 11709. Tel: 516-628-2765. p. 1491

Birch, Paul M, Computer Serv Librn, University of Richmond, William T Muse Law Library, 203 Richmond Way, Richmond, VA, 23173. Tel: 804-289-8222. p. 2343

Birch, Rodney, Dr, Instruction & Res Serv Librn, Northwest Nazarene University, 804 E Dewey St, Nampa, ID, 83686. Tel: 208-467-8606. p. 527

Birchall, Paul, Mgr, County of Los Angeles Public Library, Avalon Library, 210 Metropole Ave, Avalon, CA, 90704. Tel: 310-510-1050. p. 135

Birckhead, Janet, Adult Serv Mgr, Long Branch Free Public Library, 328 Broadway, Long Branch, NJ, 07740. Tel: 732-222-3900. p. 1413

Bird, David, Mgr, Salt Lake County Library Services, Ruth Vine Tyler Branch, 8041 S Wood St, 55 W, Midvale, UT, 84047-7559. p. 2275

Bird, Debbie, Dir, Portage Public Library, 253 W Edgewater St, Portage, WI, 53901. Tel: 608-742-4959. p. 2470

Bird, Elaine, Dir, Support Serv, Pickering Public Library, One The Esplanade, Pickering, ON, L1V 2R6, CANADA. Tel: 905-831-6265, Ext 6231. p. 2672

Bird, Jason, Mgr, Libr Serv, Sault College Library, 443 Northern Ave, Rm H1112, Sault Ste. Marie, ON, P6B 4J3, CANADA. Tel: 705-759-2554, Ext 2711. p. 2677

Bird, Kelly, Dir, Lettie W Jensen Public Library, 278 N Main St, Amherst, WI, 54406-9101. Tel: 715-824-5510. p. 2420

Bird, Michael, Head, Pub Serv, Ref Librn, Capital University, Law School Library, 303 E Broad St, Columbus, OH, 43215. Tel: 614-236-6463. p. 1772

Bird, Nora J, PhD, Assoc Prof, Dir, Grad Studies, University of North Carolina at Greensboro, School of Education Bldg, Rm 446, 1300 Spring Garden St, Greensboro, NC, 27412. Tel: 336-256-1313. p. 2790

Bird, Rosemary, Cat, Roane State Community College Library, 276 Patton Lane, Harriman, TN, 37748-5011. Tel: 865-882-4553. p. 2100

Bird, Sean, Assoc Dean, Univ Libr, Washburn University, 1700 SW College Ave, Topeka, KS, 66621. Tel: 785-670-1550. p. 839

Birden, Andrew, Head Librn, Fort Kent Public Library, One Monument Sq, Fort Kent, ME, 04743. Tel: 207-834-3048. p. 925

Birden, Drew, Br Mgr, Free Library of Philadelphia, Falls of Schuylkill Branch, 3501 Midvale Ave, Philadelphia, PA, 19129-1633. Tel: 215-685-2093. p. 1978

Birden, Sofia, Libr Dir, Ref Librn, University of Maine at Fort Kent, 23 University Dr, Fort Kent, ME, 04743. Tel: 207-834-7525. p. 925

Birdsell, Mary, Exec Dir, Canadian Foundation for Children, Youth & the Law, 55 University Ave, 15th Flr, Toronto, ON, M5J 2H7, CANADA. Tel: 416-920-1633. p. 2687

Birdsong, Logan, Libr Asst, Caryville Public Library, 4839 Old Hwy 63, Ste 2, Caryville, TN, 37714. Tel: 423-562-1108. p. 2090

Birdsong, Natalie, Librn, Arkansas Geological Survey Library, 3815 W Roosevelt Rd, Little Rock, AR, 72204-6369. Tel: 501-683-0120, p. 100

Birely, Judy, Libr Dir, Stanwood Public Library, 202 E Broadway, Stanwood, IA, 52337. Tel: 563-942-3531. p. 784

Birgel, Carey, Exec Dir, Northampton County Historical & Genealogical Society, Sigal Museum, 342 Northampton St, Easton, PA, 18042. Tel: 610-253-1222. p. 1929

Birilli, Carolynn Clark, Curator, Historic Courthouse Museum Library, 255 N Main St, Lakeport, CA, 95453. Tel: 707-262-4552. p. 155

Birk, Cathy, Br Supvr, Boonslick Regional Library, Boonville Branch, 618 Main St, Boonville, MO, 65233. Tel: 660-827-7323. p. 1279

Birk, Holly, Pub Serv Librn, Ohio Wesleyan University, 43 Rowland Ave, Delaware, OH, 43015-2370. Tel: 740-368-3207. p. 1782

Birk, Janet, Dir, Coffey County Library, Gridley Branch, 512 Main St, Gridley, KS, 66852. Tel: 620-836-3905. p. 800

Birkeland, Paddy, Ms, Libr Mgr, Spruce View Community Library, Hwy 54, Spruce View, AB, T0M 1V0, CANADA. Tel: 403-728-0012. p. 2554

Birkenes, Richard, ILL, Langara College Library, 100 W 49th Ave, Vancouver, BC, V5Y 2Z6, CANADA. Tel: 604-323-5462. p. 2579

Birkenseer, Susan, Ref & Instruction Librn, Saint Mary's College Library, 1928 Saint Mary's Rd, Moraga, CA, 94575. Tel: 925-631-4229. p. 180

Birkett, Hayden, Br Supvr, Riverside Public Library, Orange Terrace Branch, 20010-B Orange Terrace Pkwy, Riverside, CA, 92508. Tel: 951-826-2184. p. 203

Birkett-Parker, Gloria, Librn, Wills Eye Hospital, 840 Walnut St, Philadelphia, PA, 19107. Tel: 215-928-3288. p. 1989

Birkhead, Paul, Librn, Rowan Public Library, South, 920 Kimball Rd, China Grove, NC, 28023. p. 1715

Birkholz, Alexander, Classroom Support Technician, Northwood Technical College, 1900 College Dr, Rice Lake, WI, 54868. Tel: 715-234-7082. p. 2473

Birkholz, Amelia, Br Librn, East Central Regional Library, North Branch Area Library, 6355 379th St, North Branch, MN, 55056. Tel: 651-674-8443. p. 1168

Birkholz, Tina, Ref Librn, Elgin Community College, 1700 Spartan Dr, Elgin, IL, 60123. Tel: 847-214-7337. p. 584

Birkmeyer, Carl, Media Support Serv Mgr, Baltimore County Public Library, 320 York Rd, Towson, MD, 21204-5179. Tel: 410-887-6100. p. 979

Birmingham, Laura, Asst Dir, Indian Prairie Public Library District, 401 Plainfield Rd, Darien, IL, 60561-4207. Tel: 630-887-8760. p. 575

Birmingham, Nancy, Asst Br Mgr, Johnson County Library, Central Resource, 9875 W 87th St, Overland Park, KS, 66212. p. 830

Birmingham, Sean, Head, Pub Serv, Villa Park Public Library, 305 S Ardmore Ave, Villa Park, IL, 60181-2698. Tel: 630-834-1164, Ext 109. p. 658

Birnbach, Alexandra, Commun Libr Mgr, Contra Costa County Library, Ygnacio Valley Library, 2661 Oak Grove Rd, Walnut Creek, CA, 94598. Tel: 925-938-1481. p. 175

Birnbaun, Alan, Pres, Temple Beth Israel Library, 6622 N Maroa Ave, Fresno, CA, 93704. Tel: 559-432-3600. p. 147

Birney, Kathryn, Br Mgr, Puskarich Public Library, Scio Branch, 331 W Main St, Scio, OH, 43988. Tel: 740-945-6811. p. 1754

Biro, Olivia, Prog Coordr, Bennington College, Jennings Music Library, One College Dr, Jennings Music Bldg, Bennington, VT, 05201. Tel: 802-440-4512. p. 2279

Birrer, Belinda, Children & Youth Serv Librn, Poplar Bluff Municipal Library, 318 N Main St, Poplar Bluff, MO, 63901. Tel: 573-686-8639, Ext 28. p. 1266

Birtalan, Mary, Cat, Kent State University, 6000 Frank Ave NW, North Canton, OH, 44720-7548. Tel: 330-244-3323. p. 1809

Bisaccia, Andrew, Tech Serv Librn, Derby Neck Library Association, 307 Hawthorne Ave, Derby, CT, 06418. Tel: 203-734-1492. p. 308

Bisaillon, Brigitte, Electronic Res Librn, Chicopee Public Library, 449 Front St, Chicopee, MA, 01013. Tel: 413-594-1800. p. 1011

Bisaillon, Emelie, Chief Exec Officer, West Nipissing Public Library, 225 Holditch St, Ste 107, Sturgeon Falls, ON, P2B 1T1, CANADA. Tel: 705-753-2620. p. 2682

Bisanti, Eugene, Dir, Oxford Public Library, 42 Washington Ave, Oxford, NJ, 07863-3037. Tel: 908-453-2625. p. 1431

Bisbee, Stuart, Dir, Brodhead Memorial Public Library, 1207 25th St, Brodhead, WI, 53520. Tel: 608-897-4070. p. 2425

Bisch, Steve, Circ Supvr, Washington State University Tri-Cities Library, 2770 Crimson Way, Richland, WA, 99354. Tel: 509-372-7313. p. 2375

Bischoff, Helen, Head, Pub Serv, Transylvania University Library, 300 N Broadway, Lexington, KY, 40508. Tel: 859-233-8225. p. 863

Bischoffberger, Michele, Librn, Schleicher County Public Library, 201 SW Main St, Eldorado, TX, 76936. Tel: 325-853-3767. p. 2175

Bish, Daniel, Libr Dir, Phelps Library, Eight Banta St, Ste 200, Phelps, NY, 14532. Tel: 315-548-3120. p. 1617

Bishop, Ann, Human Res Mgr, Greenville County Library System, 25 Heritage Green Pl, Greenville, SC, 29601-2034. Tel: 864-242-5000, Ext 2262. p. 2061

Bishop, Aric, Dir, Gibson Memorial Library, 200 W Howard St, Creston, IA, 50801-2339. Tel: 641-782-6507. p. 743

Bishop, Aric, Libr Dir, Osceola Public Library, 300 S Fillmore St, Osceola, IA, 50213. Tel: 641-342-2237. p. 775

Bishop, Celina, Human Res Dir, Mid-Columbia Libraries, 405 S Dayton St, Kennewick, WA, 99336. p. 2367

Bishop, Christopher, Head, Access & Discovery Serv, Agnes Scott College, 141 E College Ave, Decatur, GA, 30030-3770. Tel: 404-471-6337. p. 475

Bishop, Dorothy, Librn, Sheridan Public Library, 103 W First St, Sheridan, IN, 46069. Tel: 317-758-5201. p. 718

Bishop, Eleanor, Libr Spec, Bellingham Technical College Library, 3028 Lindbergh Ave, Bellingham, WA, 98225-1599. Tel: 360-752-8383. p. 2358

Bishop, Francesca, Commun Libr Mgr, Queens Library, Hillcrest Community Library, 187-05 Union Tpk, Flushing, NY, 11366. Tel: 718-454-2786. p. 1554

Bishop, Janet, Dean of Libr, Claremont Colleges Library, 800 Dartmouth Ave, Claremont, CA, 91711. Tel: 909-621-8014. p. 130

Bishop, Julie, Dir, Linden Public Library, 131 S Main St, Linden, IA, 50146. Tel: 641-744-2124. p. 765

Bishop, Katie, Dir, Res & Instruction Serv, University of Nebraska at Omaha, 6001 Dodge St, Omaha, NE, 68182-0237. Tel: 402-554-2992. p. 1330

Bishop, Kelsey, Libr Tech, J T Fyles Natural Resources Library, 1810 Blanshard St, Victoria, BC, V8W 9N3, CANADA. Tel: 250-952-0564. p. 2582

Bishop, Lesa, Br Librn, Reynolds County Library District, Bunker Branch, 203 N Main St, Bunker, MO, 63629. Tel: 573-689-2718. p. 1241

Bishop, Lindsey, Dir, Parke County Public Library, 106 N Market St, Rockville, IN, 47872. Tel: 765-569-5544. p. 716

Bishop, Lisa, Circ, J Sargeant Reynolds Community College Library, Parham Campus-Library & Information Services, Massey LTC, Rm 103, 1651 E Parham Rd, Richmond, VA, 23228. Tel: 804-523-5220. p. 2341

Bishop, Marlene, Head, Coll Develop, Louisiana State University Health Sciences Center, 433 Bolivar St, Box B3-1, New Orleans, LA, 70112-2223. Tel: 504-568-6109. p. 901

Bishop, Marsha, Libr Dir, Observatory Librn, National Radio Astronomy Observatory Library, 520 Edgemont Rd, Charlottesville, VA, 22903-2475. Tel: 434-296-0254. p. 2309

Bishop, Matt, Curator, Operations Mgr, Bangor Historical Society Library, 159 Union St, Bangor, ME, 04401. Tel: 207-942-1900. p. 915

Bishop, Michelle, First Year Experience Librn, State University of New York at Oswego, SUNY Oswego, 7060 State Rte 104, Oswego, NY, 13126-3514. Tel: 315-312-3564. p. 1613

Bishop, Misty, Dir, Vermillion County Public Library, 385 E Market St, Newport, IN, 47966. Tel: 765-492-3555. p. 710

Bishop, Natalie, Assoc Dean of Libr, Univ Archivist, Gardner-Webb University, 110 S Main St, Boiling Springs, NC, 28017. Tel: 704-406-3274. p. 1674

Bishop, Pearlie, Libr Mgr, Kinchafoonee Regional Library System, Terrell County Library, 913 Forrester Dr SE, Dawson, GA, 39842-2106. Tel: 229-995-2902. p. 475

Bishop, Rachel, Ref & Instrul Serv Librn, Hope College, Van Wylen Library, 53 Graves Pl, Holland, MI, 49422. Tel: 616-395-7299. p. 1115

Bishop, Robin, Dir, Lincoln Public Library, 47475 US Hwy 78, Lincoln, AL, 35096. Tel: 205-763-4080. p. 24

Bishop, Roy, Head of Libr, Public Libraries of Saginaw, Ruth Brady Wickes Library, 1713 Hess St, Saginaw, MI, 48601. Tel: 989-752-3821. p. 1147

Bishop, Sasha, Dir, Learning Res, Technical College of the Lowcountry, 921 Ribaut Rd, Beaufort, SC, 29902. Tel: 843-525-8304. p. 2047

Bishop, Shauna, Dir, Ilion Free Public Library, 78 West St, Ilion, NY, 13357-1797. Tel: 315-894-5028. p. 1550

Bishop, Shawna, Instrul Serv Librn, East Central University, 1100 E 14th St, Ada, OK, 74820. Tel: 580-559-5370. p. 1839

Bishop, Sheila K, Dir, Niceville Public Library, 206 Partin Dr N, Niceville, FL, 32578. p. 428

Bishop, Susan, Librn, Lone Oak Area Public Library, 102 Jones St, Lone Oak, TX, 75453. Tel: 903-662-4565. p. 2212

Bishop, Suzanne, Dir, Saint Helens Public Library, 375 S 18th St, Ste A, Saint Helens, OR, 97051-2022. Tel: 503-397-4544. p. 1896
Bishop, Teresa, Supv Librn, New Hanover County Public Library, Pleasure Island Branch, 1401 N Lake Park Blvd, Ste 72, Carolina Beach, NC, 28428. Tel: 910-798-6389. p. 1723
Biskin, Karen, Head, Libr Serv, Bibliotheque Publique Juive, 5151 Cote Ste Catherine, Montreal, QC, H3W 1M6, CANADA. Tel: 514-345-2627. p. 2717
Bismark, Shannon, Teen Librn, Cleveland Bradley County Public Library, 795 Church St NE, Cleveland, TN, 37311-5295. Tel: 423-472-2163. p. 2092
Biss, Catherine, Chief Exec Officer, Markham Public Library, 6031 Hwy 7, Markham, ON, L3P 3A7, CANADA. Tel: 905-513-7977, Ext 5999. p. 2656
Bissada, Nadia, Pres, Bibliotheque Baie-D'Urfe, 20551 chemin du Bord du Lac, Baie-D'Urfe, QC, H9X 1R3, CANADA. Tel: 514-457-3274. p. 2709
Bisschop, Karen, Adult Programming, Outreach Librn, Peterborough Public Library, 345 Aylmer St N, Peterborough, ON, K9H 3V7, CANADA. Tel: 705-745-5382, Ext 2352. p. 2672
Bissell, Martha, Librn, Walden Community Library, 135 Cahoon Farm Rd, West Danville, VT, 05873. Tel: 802-563-2195. p. 2298
Bissell, Michelle, Ch, Gilmore City Public Library, 308 S Gilmore St, Gilmore City, IA, 50541. Tel: 515-373-6562. p. 755
Bissett, John P, Head, Tech Serv, Washington & Lee University, Wilbur C Hall Law Library, Lewis Hall, E Denny Circle, Lexington, VA, 24450. Tel: 540-458-8546. p. 2329
Bissett, Trish, Ch Mgr, Martin Memorial Library, 159 E Market St, York, PA, 17401-1269. Tel: 717-846-5300. p. 2026
Bisson, Jacques, Head, Info Serv, Transport Canada, Civil Aviation, NAS-CRT, Rm 0135, 700 Leigh Capreol St, Dorval, QC, H4Y 1G7, CANADA. Tel: 514-633-3589. p. 2711
Bissonette, David, Librn, Central Lakes College, 501 W College Dr, Brainerd, MN, 56401. Tel: 218-855-8178. p. 1166
Bissonnette, Elaine, Libr Develop, Maine State Library, Region 1, Five Monument Sq, Portland, ME, 04101. Tel: 207-871-1766. p. 936
Bissonnette, Sheila, Dir, Pere Marquette District Library, 185 E Fourth St, Clare, MI, 48617. Tel: 989-386-7576, Ext 4. p. 1091
Bissonnette, Shelia, Dir, Harrison Community Library, 105 E Main St, Harrison, MI, 48625. Tel: 989-539-6711, Ext 6. p. 1113
Bistyga, Heather, Extn Serv, Anderson County Library, 300 N McDuffie St, Anderson, SC, 29621-5643. Tel: 864-260-4500. p. 2046
Biswas, Peyton, Libr Tech, Gowling WLG (Canada) Library, One First Canadian Pl, 100 King St W, Ste 1600, Toronto, ON, M5X 1G5, CANADA. Tel: 416-862-5735. p. 2689
Biswas, Shukla, Tech Serv, Massachusetts School of Law Library, 500 Federal St, Andover, MA, 01810. Tel: 978-681-0800. p. 985
Bitetti, Bronwen, Assoc Librn, Bard College, Center for Curatorial Studies, PO Box 5000, Annandale-on-Hudson, NY, 12504-5000. Tel: 845-752-2395. p. 1487
Bittel, Aaron, Dir, Music Librn, Wesleyan University, Music Library, 252 Church St, Middletown, CT, 06459. Tel: 860-685-3899. p. 323
Bitten, Loretta, Br Mgr, Birmingham Public Library, Powderly, 3301 Jefferson Ave SW, Birmingham, AL, 35221-1241. Tel: 205-925-6178. p. 7
Bitter, Janelle, Tech Serv & Syst Librn, Raritan Valley Community College, Theater Bldg Branchburg, 118 Lamington Rd, Somerville, NJ, 08876. Tel: 908-218-8865. p. 1442
Bitter, Janelle, Ref & Instruction, Ocean County College Library, College Dr, Toms River, NJ, 08754. Tel: 732-255-0400, Ext 2351. p. 1446
Bitters, Molly, Asst Head, Ref Serv, Eisenhower Public Library District, 4613 N Oketo Ave, Harwood Heights, IL, 60706. Tel: 708-867-7828. p. 597
Bitters, Victoria, Head, Tech Serv, Eisenhower Public Library District, 4613 N Oketo Ave, Harwood Heights, IL, 60706. Tel: 708-867-7828. p. 597
Bittinger, William, Library Contact, Garrett County Circuit Court Library, Courthouse, Rm 107B, 203 S Fourth St, Oakland, MD, 21550. Tel: 301-334-1934. p. 972
Bittman, Lana, Electronic Res & Per Librn, Fashion Institute of Technology-SUNY, Seventh Ave at 27th St, 227 W 27th St, New York, NY, 10001-5992. Tel: 212-217-4382. p. 1585
Bittner, Anne, Bibliographer, Cataloger, Northampton Community College, College Ctr, 3835 Green Pond Rd, Bethlehem, PA, 18020-7599. Tel: 610-861-3360. p. 1912
Bittner, Todd, Libr Dir, Lone Cone Library, 1455 Pinion St, Norwood, CO, 81423. Tel: 970-327-4833. p. 292
Bitunjac, Robert, Br Mgr, Chicago Public Library, Clearing, 6423 W 63rd Pl, Chicago, IL, 60638. Tel: 312-747-5657. p. 556
Bitzer, Wade, Asst Librn, Monterey County Law Library, Monterey Branch, Monterey County Courthouse, 1200 Aguajito Rd, Rm 202, Monterey, CA, 93940. Tel: 831-264-4207. p. 211
Bivens, Judy, Prog Dir, Trevecca Nazarene University, School of Education, 333 Murfreesboro Rd, Nashville, TN, 37210-2877. Tel: 615-248-1201, 615-248-1206. p. 2792
Bivens, Lynn, Head, Ref, Info Literacy, Saint Joseph's College, 278 Whites Bridge Rd, Standish, ME, 04084-5263. Tel: 207-893-7724. p. 942
Bivin, Patricia, Librn, City College, 177 Montgomery Rd, Altamonte Springs, FL, 32714. Tel: 407-831-9816. p. 383
Bivins, Hulen E, Dr, Exec Dir, Mississippi Library Commission, 3881 Eastwood Dr, Jackson, MS, 39211. Tel: 601-432-4038. p. 1222
Bivins, Joy, Dir, New York Public Library - Astor, Lenox & Tilden Foundations, Schomburg Center for Research in Black Culture, 515 Malcolm X Blvd, (135th & Malcolm X Blvd), New York, NY, 10037-1801. p. 1597
Bixler, Dawn, Pub Serv, Lee University, 260 11th St NE, Cleveland, TN, 37311. Tel: 423-614-8551. p. 2093
Biza, Jillah, Librn, St Joseph Mercy Hospital, 5301 E Huron River Dr, Rm 1712, Ann Arbor, MI, 48106. Tel: 734-712-3045. p. 1079
Bizanos, Heather, Librn & Archivist, Greene County Historical Society, 90 County Rte 42, Coxsackie, NY, 12051. Tel: 518-731-1033. p. 1523
Bizimana, Bernard, Dir, HEC Montreal Library, 3000, chemin de la Cote-Sainte-Catherine, Montreal, QC, H3T 2A7, CANADA. Tel: 514-340-6689. p. 2724
Bizonet, Rebecca, Librn, Lenawee District Library, Deerfield Branch, 170 Raisin St, Deerfield, MI, 49238-9717. Tel: 517-447-3400. p. 1075
Bizub, Johanna C, Dir, Libr Serv, Prudential Financial, Three Gateway Ctr, NJ -05-03-15, 100 Mulberry St, Newark, NJ, 07102. Tel: 973-367-3175. p. 1428
Bizzell Boyer, Kenneth, Librn, Donora Public Library, 510 Meldon Ave, Donora, PA, 15033-1333. Tel: 724-379-7940. p. 1926
Bizzell Boyer, Mark G, Libr Dir, Donora Public Library, 510 Meldon Ave, Donora, PA, 15033-1333. Tel: 724-379-7940. p. 1926
Bjarnason-stomp, Koreana, Br Librn, Southeast Regional Library, Fillmore Branch, 51 Main St, Fillmore, SK, S0G 1N0, CANADA. Tel: 306-722-3369. p. 2753
Bjartmarsdottir, Anna, Ref & Instruction, University of Alaska Anchorage, Consortium Library, 3211 Providence Dr, Anchorage, AK, 99508-8176. Tel: 907-786-1871. p. 43
Bjerke, Jill, Dir, Carnegie Regional Library, 630 Griggs Ave, Grafton, ND, 58237. Tel: 701-331-9073. p. 1734
Bjork, Johanna, Dir, Lewis-Clark State College Library, 500 Eighth Ave, Lewiston, ID, 83501. Tel: 208-792-2395. p. 524
Bjork, Karen, Head, Digital Initiatives, Portland State University Library, 1875 SW Park Ave, Portland, OR, 97201-3220. Tel: 503-725-5874. p. 1893
Bjorklund, Dana M, Asst Dir, Tech Serv Librn, Cleveland Institute of Art, 11610 Euclid Ave, Cleveland, OH, 44106. Tel: 216-421-7446. p. 1767
Bjorness, Virginia, Dept Head, Tech Serv, State Historical Society of North Dakota, North Dakota Heritage Ctr, 612 E Boulevard Ave, Bismarck, ND, 58505-0830. Tel: 701-328-2091. p. 1730
Bjornstad, Jill, Librn, Cashton Memorial Library, 720 Broadway St, Cashton, WI, 54619. Tel: 608-654-5465. p. 2427
Blabac-Myers, Carrie, Asst Head, Reader Services, Stacks & Media, State University of New York at Binghamton, Library Annex at Conklin, 400 Corporate Pkwy, Conklin, NY, 13748. Tel: 607-777-5787. p. 1494
Black, Alyssa, Br Mgr, Scottsdale Public Library, Arabian Library, 10215 E McDowell Mountain Ranch Rd, Scottsdale, AZ, 85255. p. 77
Black, Amanda, Coordr, Access Serv, University of Dayton Libraries, 300 College Park Dr, Dayton, OH, 45469. Tel: 937-229-5408. p. 1780
Black, Angela, Tech Serv Librn, Arkansas Tech University, 305 West Q St, Russellville, AR, 72801. Tel: 479-964-0558. p. 108
Black, Bessi, Br Mgr, Choctaw County Public Library, 703 E Jackson St, Hugo, OK, 74743. Tel: 580-326-5591. p. 1850
Black, Brandy, Br Mgr, Clay County Public Library System, Middleburg Clay-Hill Branch, 2245 Aster Ave, Middleburg, FL, 32068. Tel: 904-541-5855. p. 396
Black, Cathy, Libr Dir, Orena Humphreys Public Library, 13535 Tennessee Hwy 28, Whitwell, TN, 37397. Tel: 423-658-6134. p. 2130
Black, Christine, Lead Librn, Data Contracts, Board of Governors of The Federal Reserve System, Research Library, 20th & C St NW, MS 102, Washington, DC, 20551. Tel: 202-452-3333. p. 361
Black, Devin C, Dir, Tuscola Public Library, 112 E Sale St, Tuscola, IL, 61953. Tel: 217-253-3812. p. 655
Black, Donna, Coordr, Northeast Alabama Regional Medical Center, 400 E Tenth St, Anniston, AL, 36207. Tel: 256-235-5224. p. 4
Black, Felicia, Librn, Placer County Library, Auburn Branch, 350 Nevada St, Auburn, CA, 95603-3789. Tel: 530-886-4500. p. 118
Black, Heather, Asst Libr Dir, Cortland Community Library, 63 S Somonauk Rd, Cortland, IL, 60112. Tel: 815-756-7274. p. 574
Black, Jacob, Res & Instruction Librn, University of Oklahoma Libraries, University of Oklahoma College of Law, 300 Timberdell Rd, Norman, OK, 73019. Tel: 405-325-4311. p. 1856
Black, Janet, Tech Serv Technician, Southwestern Oklahoma State University, 100 Campus Dr, Weatherford, OK, 73096-3002. Tel: 580-774-3089. p. 1868
Black, Jason, Asst Dir, Libr Serv, Clay County Public Library System, 1895 Town Center Blvd, Fleming Island, FL, 32003. Tel: 904-278-3720. p. 396
Black, Joanna, Digital Archivist, Sierra Club, 2101 Webster St, Ste 1300, Oakland, CA, 94612. Tel: 415-977-5506. p. 187
Black, Judy, Asst Librn, Dixonville Community Library, PO Box 206, Dixonville, AB, T0H 1E0, CANADA. Tel: 780-971-2593. p. 2533
Black, Justine, Dir, Juniata College, 1700 Moore St, Huntingdon, PA, 16652-2119. Tel: 816-641-5349. p. 1945

Blair, Leigh, Br Mgr, Jackson County Library Services, Central Point Branch, 116 S Third St, Central Point, OR, 97502. Tel: 541-664-3228. p. 1886

Blair, Linda, Asst Librn, Lake Placid Public Library, 2471 Main St, Lake Placid, NY, 12946. Tel: 518-523-3200. p. 1561

Blair, Lynn, Dir, Southwick Public Library, 95 Feeding Hills Rd, Southwick, MA, 01077-9683. Tel: 413-569-1221. p. 1055

Blair, Patrick, Asst to the Dir, Bellarmine University, 2001 Newburg Rd, Louisville, KY, 40205-0671. p. 864

Blair, Tracy, Ch Serv, Corry Public Library, 117 W Washington St, Corry, PA, 16407. Tel: 814-664-7611. p. 1924

Blais, Carole, ILL/Doc Delivery Serv, Ref Serv, Canadian Nuclear Safety Commission Library, 280 Slater St, Ottawa, ON, K1P 1C2, CANADA. Tel: 613-995-5894. p. 2666

Blais, Julie, Dir, Centre Regional de Service aux Bibliotheque Publique de Pret Gaspesie Isle de la Madelene, 31 Rue des Ecoliers, CP 430, Cap-Chat, QC, G0J 1E0, CANADA. Tel: 418-786-5597. p. 2710

Blaisdell, Martha, Libr Serv Supvr, Moore County Library, 101 Saunders St, Carthage, NC, 28327. Tel: 910-947-5335. p. 1677

Blake, Amy, Youth Librn, Knox County Public Library, 502 N Seventh St, Vincennes, IN, 47591-2119. Tel: 812-886-4380. p. 723

Blake, Catherine, Assoc Dean, Acad Affairs, Prof, University of Illinois at Urbana-Champaign, Library & Information Science Bldg, 501 E Daniel St, Champaign, IL, 61820-6211. Tel: 217-333-3280. p. 2784

Blake, Denise, Health Sci Librn, Shenandoah University, 1460 University Dr, Winchester, VA, 22601. Tel: 540-678-4351. p. 2354

Blake, Erin, Dr, Sr Cataloger, Folger Shakespeare Library, 201 E Capitol St SE, Washington, DC, 20003-1094. Tel: 202-675-0323. p. 366

Blake, Gail, Br Mgr, Beaufort, Hyde & Martin County Regional Library, Hyde County Public, 33460 US 264, Rm 5, Engelhard, NC, 27824. Tel: 252-925-2222. p. 1720

Blake, Joni, PhD, Exec Dir, Greater Western Library Alliance, 5200 W 94th Terrace, Ste 200, Prairie Village, KS, 66027. Tel: 913-370-4422. p. 2765

Blake, Monique, Dean, Broward College, Bldg 17, 3501 SW Davie Rd, Davie, FL, 33314. Tel: 954-201-6648. p. 391

Blake, Susan LeAnn, Circ Supvr, Jacksonville Public Library, 526 E Commerce St, Jacksonville, TX, 75766. Tel: 903-586-7664. p. 2203

Blake, Vanessa, Librn, Lillooet Area Library Association, Bridge River Branch, 41 Bridge River Town Site, Shalaith, BC, V0N 3C0, CANADA. Tel: 250-259-8242. p. 2569

Blake, Virginia, Archivist, Pub Serv Librn, Wesleyan College, 4760 Forsyth Rd, Macon, GA, 31210. Tel: 478-757-5274. p. 487

Blakely, Kate, Head, Children's Servx, Bremen Public Library, 304 N Jackson St, Bremen, IN, 46506. Tel: 574-546-2849. p. 672

Blakely, Kimberly, Adult Serv, Head, Ref, Wilmington Memorial Library, 175 Middlesex Ave, Wilmington, MA, 01887-2779. Tel: 978-658-2967. p. 1070

Blakely, Missy, Dir, Mildred G Fields Memorial Library, 1075-A E Van Hook St, Milan, TN, 38358. Tel: 731-686-8268. p. 2116

Blakely, Rosetta, Circ Mgr, North Chicago Public Library, 2100 Argonne Dr, North Chicago, IL, 60064. Tel: 847-689-0125, Ext 106. p. 626

Blakeman, T J, Pres, Champaign County History Museum, Cattle Bank Bldg, 102 E University Ave, Champaign, IL, 61820-4111. Tel: 217-356-1010. p. 551

Blakemore, Teri, Tech Serv Mgr, Morley Library, 184 Phelps St, Painesville, OH, 44077-3926. Tel: 440-352-3383. p. 1812

Blakeney, Shirley, Br Mgr, Saint Joseph Public Library, East Hills Library, 502 N Woodbine Rd, Saint Joseph, MO, 64506. Tel: 816-236-2136. p. 1269

Blaker, Laura, Libr Dir, Independence Public Library, 805 First St E, Independence, IA, 50644. Tel: 319-334-2470. p. 759

Blakeslee, Carol, Youth Serv Librn, Oradell Free Public Library, 375 Kinderkamack Rd, Oradell, NJ, 07649-2122. Tel: 201-262-2613. p. 1431

Blakeslee, Julie, Pub Serv Librn, Tech Serv Librn, Ellinwood School & Community Library, 210 N Schiller Ave, Ellinwood, KS, 67526. Tel: 620-564-2306. p. 806

Blakesley, Beth, Assoc Dean of Libr, Washington State University Libraries, 100 Dairy Rd, Pullman, WA, 99164. Tel: 509-335-6134. p. 2374

Blakesley, Beth, Assoc Dean of Libr, Washington State University Libraries, Owen Science & Engineering, PO Box 643200, Pullman, WA, 99164-3200. Tel: 509-335-6134. p. 2374

Blakney, Sandi, Dir, Allen Park Public Library, 8100 Allen Rd, Allen Park, MI, 48101. Tel: 313-381-2425. p. 1077

Blalock, Beverly, Head, Circ, Presbyterian College, 211 E Maple St, Clinton, SC, 29325. Tel: 864-833-8299. p. 2052

Blalock, Jennifer, Librn, Youth & Family Serv, Chesapeake Public Library, Russell Memorial, 2808 Taylor Rd, Chesapeake, VA, 23321-2210. Tel: 757-410-7027. p. 2311

Blalock, Rebecca, Adminr, Tennessee Technological University, Graduate Studies, Dewberry Hall 306, One William L Jones Dr, Cookeville, TN, 38505. Tel: 931-372-3233. p. 2792

Blanchard, Colleen, Prog Mgr, Itasca Community Library, 500 W Irving Park Rd, Itasca, IL, 60143. Tel: 630-773-1699. p. 602

Blanchard, Edith, Dir, Charles H MacNider Museum Library, 303 Second St SE, Mason City, IA, 50401. Tel: 641-421-3666. p. 768

Blanchard, JoElla, Dir, Cantwell Community-School Library, Mile 133-5 Denali Hwy & Second Ave, Cantwell, AK, 99729. Tel: 907-768-2372. p. 43

Blanchard, Jolene, Asst Librn, Belle Plaine Community Library, 904 12th St, Belle Plaine, IA, 52208-1711. Tel: 319-444-2902. p. 734

Blanchard, Karey, Br Librn, Wilson County Public Library, Lucama Branch, 103 E Spring St, Lucama, NC, 27851. Tel: 252-239-0046. p. 1724

Blanchard, Laurie, Librn, University of Manitoba, Sister St Odilon Library, Misericordia Health Centre, Education & Resource Bldg, 691 Wolseley Ave, 1st Flr, Winnipeg, MB, R3G 1C3, CANADA. Tel: 204-788-8108. p. 2595

Blanchard, Linda, Mgr, Superior District Library, Curtis Library, N 9220 Portage Ave, Curtis, MI, 49820. Tel: 906-586-9411. p. 1149

Blanchard, Linda, Head, Coll Develop, York County Public Library, 100 Long Green Blvd, Yorktown, VA, 23693. Tel: 757-890-5104. p. 2355

Blanchard, Monica, Dr, Curator, Catholic University of America, Semitics/ICOR Library, 035 Mullen Library, 620 Michigan Ave NE, Washington, DC, 20064. Tel: 202-319-4532. p. 362

Blanchard, Ruth, Chief Exec Officer, Head Librn, Elizabethtown-Kitley Township Public Library, 4103 County Rd 29, Addison, ON, K6V 5T4, CANADA. Tel: 613-498-3338. p. 2627

Blanchard, Saige, Info Spec, Philbrook Museum of Art, 2727 S Rockford Rd, Tulsa, OK, 74114. Tel: 918-748-5359. p. 1865

Blanchard, Sandy, Head, Circ, Coe College, 1220 First Ave NE, Cedar Rapids, IA, 52402. Tel: 319-399-8595. p. 738

Blanchard, Tammi, Br Mgr, Lafourche Parish Public Library, South Lafourche Public Library, 16241 East Main St, CutOff, LA, 70345. Tel: 985-632-7140. p. 911

Blanchette, Christy, Asst Dir, Valley Cottage Free Library, 110 Rte 303, Valley Cottage, NY, 10989. Tel: 845-268-7700, Ext 155. p. 1656

Blanchette, Gaetan, Brother, Library Contact, The Abbey of Gethsemani Library, 3642 Monks Rd, Trappist, KY, 40051. Tel: 502-549-4406. p. 876

Blanchette, Hollie, Technology & Interlibrary Loan, Valemount Public Library, 1090A Main St, Valemount, BC, V0E 2Z0, CANADA. Tel: 250-566-4367. p. 2578

Blanchette, Max, Head, Adult Serv, Merrimack Public Library, 470 Daniel Webster Hwy, Merrimack, NH, 03054-3694. Tel: 603-424-5021. p. 1373

Blanck, Dag, PhD, Dr, Dir, Swenson Swedish Immigration Research Center, Augustana College, 3520 Seventh Ave, Rock Island, IL, 61201. Tel: 309-794-7204. p. 641

Blanco, Dilia, Libr Tech, San Juan Bautista City Library, 801 Second St, San Juan Bautista, CA, 95045. Tel: 831-623-4687. p. 232

Blanco, Elaine Tornes, Librn, University of Miami, 1311 Miller Dr, Coral Gables, FL, 33146. Tel: 305-284-2251. p. 390

Blanco, Marie, Mgr, Miami-Dade Public Library System, Doral Branch, 8551 NW 53rd St, Ste A107, Doral, FL, 33166. Tel: 305-716-9598. p. 423

Bland, Annette, Libr Dir, Columbia Public Library, 106 N Metter Ave, Columbia, IL, 62236-2299. Tel: 618-281-4237. p. 573

Bland, Rose, Dir, University of South Florida, Hinks & Elaine Shimberg Health Sciences Library, 12901 Bruce B Downs Blvd, MDC 31, Tampa, FL, 33612. Tel: 813-974-2390. p. 449

Bland, Sarah, Circ, Corning Public Library, 613 Pine St, Corning, AR, 72422. Tel: 870-857-3453. p. 93

Bland, Shannon, Br Mgr, Charles County Public Library, Waldorf West Branch, 10405 O'Donnell Pl, Waldorf, MD, 20603. Tel: 301-645-1395. p. 969

Blandino, Laurie, Exec Dir, Louisiana Library Network, 1201 N Third St, Ste 6-200, Baton Rouge, LA, 70802. Tel: 225-342-4253. p. 2766

Blando, Mark L, Libr Dir, Owatonna Public Library, 105 N Elm Ave, Owatonna, MN, 55060. Tel: 507-444-2460. p. 1192

Blando, Stephanie, Teen Serv Librn, Seymour Library, 161 East Ave, Brockport, NY, 14420. Tel: 585-637-1050. p. 1497

Blanford, Rita, Ref Librn, Lorain County Community College, 1005 Abbe Rd N, North Elyria, OH, 44035-1691. Tel: 440-366-7279. p. 1810

Blank, Bryan, Head, Adult Serv, Elmhurst Public Library, 125 S Prospect Ave, Elmhurst, IL, 60126-3298. Tel: 630-279-8696. p. 585

Blank, James, Mgr, Caterpillar Inc, 14009 Old Galena Rd, Mossville, IL, 61552. Tel: 309-578-6118. p. 620

Blank, Sharon L, Asst Dir, Screven-Jenkins Regional Library, 106 S Community Dr, Sylvania, GA, 30467. Tel: 912-564-7526. p. 498

Blankemeyer, Bethany, Ser & Electronic Res Librn, Duke University Libraries, 411 Chapel Dr, Durham, NC, 27708. Tel: 919-668-2955. p. 1684

Blankemeyer, Sue A, Head Librn, United States Air Force, 201 Mitchell Blvd, Bldg 223, Laughlin AFB, TX, 78843-5212. Tel: 830-298-5119. p. 2210

Blankenship, April, Br Mgr, Prairie-River Library District, Kamiah Community, 505 Main St, Kamiah, ID, 83536-9702. Tel: 208-935-0428. p. 524

Blankenship, Brandi, Libr Dir, Catoosa Public Library, 105 E Oak, Catoosa, OK, 74015. Tel: 918-266-1684. p. 1843

Blankenship, Jennifer, Med Librn, Department of Veterans Affairs, 1970 Roanoke Blvd, Salem, VA, 24153. Tel: 540-982-2463, Ext 2380. p. 2346

Blankenship, John A, Libr Dir, Humboldt Public Library, 115 S 16th Ave, Humboldt, TN, 38343-3403. Tel: 731-784-2383. p. 2101

Blankenship, Karen, Dir, Libr Serv, San Jacinto College, 8060 Spencer Hwy, Pasadena, TX, 77505. Tel: 281-476-1850. p. 2225

Blankenship, Richard, Librn, Onondaga Community College, 4585 W Seneca Tpk, Syracuse, NY, 13215-4585. Tel: 315-498-2912. p. 1649

Blankenship, Stefanie, Libr Dir, North Providence Union Free Library, 1810 Mineral Spring Ave, North Providence, RI, 02904. Tel: 401-353-5600. p. 2036

Blankenship, Tim, Br Mgr, Campbell County Public Library, Staunton River Memorial, 500 Washington St, Altavista, VA, 24517. Tel: 434-369-5140. p. 2346

Blankvoort, Antoinette, Librn, North Norfolk MacGregor Regional Library, 35 Hampton St E, MacGregor, MB, R0H 0R0, CANADA. Tel: 204-685-2796. p. 2588

Blansett, Betty, Circ, Ada Public Library, 124 S Rennie, Ada, OK, 74820. Tel: 580-436-8125. p. 1839

Blansett, Janet, Br Mgr, White County Regional Library System, El Paso Community Library, 1607 Ridge Rd, El Paso, AR, 72045. Tel: 501-796-5974. p. 110

Blanton, Beth W, Dir of Coll, University of Virginia, Charles L Brown Science & Engineering Library, Clark Hall, Charlottesville, VA, 22903-3188. Tel: 434-924-7209. p. 2310

Blanton, Beth W, Librn, University of Virginia, Astronomy, Charles L Brown Sci & Eng Library, 264 Astronomy Bldg, 530 McCormick Rd, Charlottesville, VA, 22904. Tel: 434-924-7209. p. 2310

Blanton, Brigitte, Dir, Greensboro Public Library, 219 N Church St, Greensboro, NC, 27402. Tel: 336-373-2471. p. 1692

Blanton, Jim, Dir, Roanoke County Public Library, 6303 Merriman Rd, Roanoke, VA, 24018-6496. Tel: 540-772-7507. p. 2345

Blanton-Watkins, Jackie, Coll Develop Librn, Electronic Res, Kennesaw State University Library System, 385 Cobb Ave NW, MD 1701, Kennesaw, GA, 30144. Tel: 470-578-2983. p. 483

Blaschke, Melissa, Exec Dir, Federal Library & Information Network, Library of Congress FEDLINK, Adams Bldg, Rm 217, 101 Independence Ave SE, Washington, DC, 20540-4935. Tel: 202-707-2457. p. 2763

Blasi, Alanna, Circulation & Technical Servs Supvr, Jervis Public Library Association, Inc, 613 N Washington St, Rome, NY, 13440-4296. Tel: 315-336-4570. p. 1632

Blasier, Charlotte, Ch Mgr, Rocky River Public Library, 1600 Hampton Rd, Rocky River, OH, 44116-2699. Tel: 440-895-3736. p. 1818

Blatchley, Carolyn, Exec Dir, Cumberland County Library System, 400 Bent Creek Blvd, Ste 150, Mechanicsburg, PA, 17050. Tel: 717-240-6175. p. 1960

Blatt, Jerri, Mgr, Portland Public Library, Peaks Island Branch, 129 Island Ave, Peaks Island, ME, 04108. Tel: 207-766-5540. p. 937

Blattner, Bettina, Dir, Lost Rivers District Library, 126 S Front St, Arco, ID, 83213. Tel: 208-527-8511. p. 515

Blau, Amy, Scholarly Communications Librn, Whitman College, 345 Boyer Ave, Walla Walla, WA, 99362. Tel: 509-527-4905. p. 2393

Blauer, Amber, ILL, Van Buren District Library, 200 N Phelps St, Decatur, MI, 49045. Tel: 269-423-4771. p. 1096

Blauert, Kristine, Mrs, Asst Librn, Rock Springs Public Library, 251 Railroad St, Rock Springs, WI, 53961. Tel: 608-737-1063. p. 2474

Blawat, Courtney, Adult Prog Coordr, Waterford Public Library, 101 N River St, Waterford, WI, 53185-4149. Tel: 262-534-3988, Ext 19. p. 2483

Blaylock, Marci, Fed Doc Librn, Wyoming State Library, 2800 Central Ave, Cheyenne, WY, 82002. Tel: 307-777-6955. p. 2493

Blaylock, Michelle, Libr Mgr, William Bradford Huie Library of Hartselle, 152 NW Sparkman St, Hartselle, AL, 35640. Tel: 256-773-9880. p. 20

Blaylock, Solomon, Access Serv Librn, Woodbury University Library, 7500 Glenoaks Blvd, Burbank, CA, 91510. Tel: 818-252-5200. p. 125

Blazecka, Christina, Chief Exec Officer, Cochrane Public Library, 178 Fourth Ave, Cochrane, ON, P0L 1C0, CANADA. Tel: 705-272-4178. p. 2636

Blazek, Jesse, Dir, Palos Heights Public Library, 12501 S 71st Ave, Palos Heights, IL, 60463. Tel: 708-448-1473. p. 631

Blean, Irene, Br Mgr, Hartford Public Library, Barbour, 261 Barbour St, Hartford, CT, 06120. Tel: 860-695-7400. p. 318

Bleattler, Mercedes, Head, Youth Serv, Clearwater Public Library System, 100 N Osceola Ave, Clearwater, FL, 33755. Tel: 727-562-4970. p. 388

Bleck, Betsy, Dep Libr Dir, Brookfield Public Library, 1900 N Calhoun Rd, Brookfield, WI, 53005. Tel: 262-782-4140. p. 2425

Bleck, Betsy, Dir, Oconomowoc Public Library, 200 South St, Oconomowoc, WI, 53066-5213. Tel: 262-569-2193. p. 2466

Blecker, Marian, Librn, Alamance Regional Medical Center; Div of Cone Health, 1240 Huffman Mill Rd, Burlington, NC, 27216. Tel: 336-538-7574. p. 1676

Bledsoe, Korleen, Dir, Coatesville-Clay Township Public Library, 4928 Milton St, Coatesville, IN, 46121. Tel: 765-386-2355. p. 675

Bledsoe, Rebecca, Dir, West Memphis Public Library, 213 N Avalon St, West Memphis, AR, 72301. Tel: 870-732-7590. p. 112

Bledsoe, Stephanie, Dir, Mississippi County Library District, Mitchell Memorial, 204 E Washington St, East Prairie, MO, 63845. Tel: 573-649-2131. p. 1241

Bledsoe, Stephanie R, Dir, Mississippi County Library District, 105 E Marshall St, Charleston, MO, 63834. Tel: 573-683-6748. p. 1241

Bleech, Marena, Libr Mgr, Piedmont Regional Library System, Jefferson Public Library, 100 Washington St, Jefferson, GA, 30549. Tel: 706-367-8012. p. 482

Bleecker, Jeanne, Co-Dir, Smoky Valley Library District, 73 Hadley Circle, Round Mountain, NV, 89045. Tel: 775-377-2215. p. 1351

Blees, Elissa, Law Librn, Carver County Library, Law Library, Carver County Government Ctr, 604 E Fourth St, Chaska, MN, 55318. Tel: 952-361-1564. p. 1169

Blehm, Henrietta, Dep Dir, Okeene Public Library, 215 N Main St, Okeene, OK, 73763. Tel: 580-822-3306. p. 1856

Bleich, Jackie, Br Mgr, Onondaga County Public Libraries, White Branch Branch Library, 763 Butternut St, Syracuse, NY, 13208. Tel: 315-435-3519. p. 1649

Bleiler, Marissa, Access Serv Librn, Hood College, 401 Rosemont Ave, Frederick, MD, 21701. Tel: 301-696-3909. p. 966

Blend, L, Ch Serv, North Shore Public Library, 250 Rte 25A, Shoreham, NY, 11786-9677. Tel: 631-929-4488. p. 1641

Blend, Michael, Librn, Napa County Law Library, Historic Courthouse, 825 Brown St, Rm 138, Napa, CA, 94559. Tel: 707-299-1201. p. 181

Blenke, Christina, Electronic Res Librn, Pace University, 861 Bedford Rd, Pleasantville, NY, 10570-2799. Tel: 914-773-3222. p. 1620

Blenski, Peter, Ch, Hartland Public Library, 110 E Park Ave, Hartland, WI, 53029. Tel: 262-367-3350. p. 2441

Blessing, Marilyn, Libr Dir, Brookston - Prairie Township Public Library, 111 W Second St, Brookston, IN, 47923. Tel: 765-563-6511. p. 672

Blevens, Cheryl, Ref & Instruction Librn, Indiana State University, 510 North 6 1/2 St, Terre Haute, IN, 47809. Tel: 812-237-3700. p. 720

Blevins, Alisha, Asst Dir, Luther Rice University & Seminary, 3038 Evans Mill Rd, Lithonia, GA, 30038. Tel: 770-484-1204, Ext 5756. p. 485

Blevins, Eric, Sr Mgr, Info Technology, RIT Libraries, 90 Lomb Memorial Dr, Rochester, NY, 14623-5604. Tel: 585-475-7741. p. 1629

Blevins, George, Circ, Gilpin County Public Library District, 15131 Hwy 119, Black Hawk, CO, 80422. Tel: 303-582-5777. p. 266

Blevins, Heather, Dir, Lassen Library District, 1618 Main St, Susanville, CA, 96130-4515. Tel: 530-251-8127. p. 251

Blevins, Kim, Youth Serv, Carnegie Public Library, 219 E Fourth St, East Liverpool, OH, 43920-3143. Tel: 330-385-2048, Ext 101. p. 1783

Blevins, Sandra, Librn, Scioto County Law Library, Scioto County Court House, 3rd Flr, 602 Seventh St, Portsmouth, OH, 45662. Tel: 740-355-8259. p. 1816

Blevins, William, Operations Mgr, Romeo District Library, 65821 Van Dyke, Washington, MI, 48095. Tel: 586-752-0603. p. 1157

Blewett, Daniel, Ref Librn, College of DuPage Library, 425 Fawell Blvd, Glen Ellyn, IL, 60137-6599. Tel: 630-942-2279. p. 593

Bley, Ryan, Tech Officer, Public Library of Cincinnati & Hamilton County, 800 Vine St, Cincinnati, OH, 45202-2009. Tel: 513-369-4405. p. 1761

Bleyer, Christina, PhD, Dir, Spec Coll & Archives, Trinity College Library, Watkinson Library, 300 Summit St, Hartford, CT, 06106. Tel: 860-297-2266. p. 318

Bleyl, Sarah J, Libr Dir, Lompoc Public Library, 501 E North Ave, Lompoc, CA, 93436. Tel: 805-875-8785. p. 158

Blicher, Heather, Online Learning Librn, Northern Virginia Community College Libraries, Extended Learning Institute, 3922 Pender Dr, Fairfax, VA, 22030. Tel: 703-503-6225. p. 2304

Blick, William, Circ Coordr, Electronic Res, Queensborough Community College, City University of New York, 222-05 56th Ave, Bayside, NY, 11364-1497. Tel: 718-281-5778. p. 1491

Blickenstaff, Aaron, Access Serv Mgr, Maryland Institute College of Art, 1401 W Mount Royal Ave, Baltimore, MD, 21217. Tel: 410-225-2304, 410-225-2311. p. 955

Blier, Jason, Superintendent, Quetico Provincial Park, Quetico Provincial Park, Atikokan, ON, P0T 1C0, CANADA. Tel: 807-929-2571, Ext 224. p. 2629

Bligh, Kevin, Ref Serv Librn, Ocean City Free Public Library, 1735 Simpson Ave, Ste 4, Ocean City, NJ, 08226. Tel: 609-399-2434, Ext 5226. p. 1430

Blimes, Tracy, Regional Br Mgr, Pasco County Library System, Regency Park, 9701 Little Rd, New Port Richey, FL, 34654. Tel: 727-861-3049. p. 410

Bliss, April R, Libr Dir, Dunham Public Library, 76 Main St, Whitesboro, NY, 13492. Tel: 315-736-9734. p. 1665

Bliss, Becky, Libr Spec, Maysville Community & Technical College, Montgomery Campus Library, 201 Calk Ave, Mount Sterling, KY, 40353. Tel: 859-499-6282, Ext 66525. p. 869

Bliss, Beth, Br Mgr, Atlantic County Library System, Pleasantville Branch, 33 Martin L King Jr Dr, Pleasantville, NJ, 08232. Tel: 609-641-1778. p. 1417

Bliss, Heide-Marie, Br Mgr, O'Melveny & Myers LLP, Times Square Tower, Seven Times Sq, New York, NY, 10036. Tel: 212-326-2020. p. 1599

Bliss, Peggy Renee, Asst Dir, Cataloger, Corning Public Library, 613 Pine St, Corning, AR, 72422. Tel: 870-857-3453. p. 93

Blix, Carol, Librn, Cathlamet Public Library, 115 Columbia St, Cathlamet, WA, 98612. Tel: 360-795-3254. p. 2361

Blizzard, Kara, Librn, University of Alberta, 4901 46th Ave, Camrose, AB, T4V 2R3, CANADA. Tel: 780-679-1156. p. 2530

Blluemle, Stefanie, Dir, Augustana College Library, 3435 9 1/2 Ave, Rock Island, IL, 61201-2296. Tel: 309-794-7167. p. 640

Blobaum, Paul, Ref (Info Servs), Governors State University Library, One University Pkwy, University Park, IL, 60466-0975. Tel: 708-534-4139. p. 655

Bloch, Beth, Dr, Asst Prof, University of Kentucky, 320 Little Library Bldg, Lexington, KY, 40506-0224. Tel: 859-257-8876. p. 2785

Bloch, Judith, Coop Librn, Shannon & Wilson, Inc, 400 N 34th St, Ste 100, Seattle, WA, 98103. Tel: 206-695-6821. p. 2380

Blocher, Jonathan, Team Leader, Muskegon Area District Library, Muskegon Heights Branch, 2808 Sanford St, Muskegon Heights, MI, 49444-2010. Tel: 231-739-6075. p. 1136

Block, Jessica, Asst Dir, Head, Youth Serv, Ames Free Library, 53 Main St, North Easton, MA, 02356. Tel: 508-238-2000. p. 1041

Block, Karla, Librn, Tompkins Cortland Community College Library, Baker Commons, 2nd Flr, 170 North St, Dryden, NY, 13053-8504. Tel: 607-844-8222, Ext 4360. p. 1526

Block, Kevin, Interim Dir, Syst Librn, Rowan University School of Osteopathic Medicine, Academic Ctr, One Medical Center Dr, Stratford, NJ, 08084. Tel: 856-566-6804. p. 1444

Block, Laura, Dep Dir, Operations, Laramie County Library System, 2200 Pioneer Ave, Cheyenne, WY, 82001-3610. Tel: 307-773-7223. p. 2492

Block, Ron, Br Mgr, Cuyahoga County Public Library, Brooklyn Branch, 4480 Ridge Rd, Brooklyn, OH, 44144-3353. Tel: 216-398-4600. p. 1813

Blocker, James, Librn, Georgia Department of Corrections, Office of Library Services, 3178 Mt Zion Church Rd, Pelham, GA, 31779. Tel: 229-294-2940. p. 493

Blocker, Vicki, Electronic Res Librn, Elon University, 308 N O'Kelly Ave, Elon, NC, 27244-0187. Tel: 336-278-6600. p. 1688

Blocksidge, Katie, Dir, Ohio State University LIBRARIES, Newark Campus Library, Warner Library & Student Ctr, 1179 University Dr, Newark, OH, 43055-1797. Tel: 740-366-9307. p. 1776

Blocksidge, Katie, Dir, Ohio State University LIBRARIES, William Oxley Thompson Library, 1858 Neil Ave Mall, Columbus, OH, 43210-1286. Tel: 614-292-6785. p. 1776

Blodgett, Gayle, Dir, Libr Serv, Spoon River Public Library District, 201 S Third St, Cuba, IL, 61427. Tel: 309-785-5496. p. 575

Blodgett, Gini, Archivist/Librn, American Physical Therapy Association Library, 3030 Potomac Ave, Ste 100, Alexandria, VA, 22305. Tel: 703-706-8534. p. 2303

Blodgett, Jayne, Assoc Dean of Libr, University of Northern Colorado Libraries, 1400 22nd Ave, Greeley, CO, 80631. Tel: 970-351-2671. p. 285

Bloechle, Brent, Libr Mgr, Plano Public Library System, Maribelle M Davis Library, 7501-B Independence Pkwy, Plano, TX, 75025. Tel: 972-208-8000. p. 2227

Bloedorn, Andy, Curator of Coll, Winona County Historical Society, 160 Johnson St, Winona, MN, 55987. Tel: 507-454-2723, Ext 4. p. 1209

Blomberg, Krista, Asst Dir, Rib Lake Public Library, 645 Pearl St, Rib Lake, WI, 54470. Tel: 715-427-5769. p. 2473

Blomberg, Tammie, Dir, Rib Lake Public Library, 645 Pearl St, Rib Lake, WI, 54470. Tel: 715-427-5769. p. 2473

Blomquist, Brittany, Technology & Outreach Librn, Abbott Library, 11 Soonipi Circle, Sunapee, NH, 03782. Tel: 603-763-5513. p. 1382

Blomquist, Donna, Youth Serv Librn, LaSalle Public Library, 305 Marquette St, LaSalle, IL, 61301. Tel: 815-223-2341. p. 607

Blomquist, Randall, Presv Spec, Missouri Historical Society, 225 S Skinker Blvd, Saint Louis, MO, 63105. Tel: 314-746-4500. p. 1272

Blondeau, Karen, Dir, Valencia College, Raymer Maguire Jr Learning Resources Center, West Campus, 1800 S Kirkman Rd, Orlando, FL, 32811. Tel: 407-582-1601. p. 433

Blondo, Darla, ILL Coordr, Swanton Public Library, One First St, Swanton, VT, 05488. Tel: 802-868-7656. p. 2296

Bloodworth, Liz J, Spec Coll Librn, Bradley University, Virginius H Chase Special Collections Center, 1501 W Bradley Ave, Peoria, IL, 61625. Tel: 309-677-2822. p. 634

Bloom, Hilary, Dir, Libr Serv, Squamish Public Library, 37907 Second Ave, Squamish, BC, V8B 0A7, CANADA. Tel: 604-892-3110. p. 2576

Bloom, Jenny, Libr Dir, Locust Valley Library, 170 Buckram Rd, Locust Valley, NY, 11560-1999. Tel: 516-671-1837. p. 1564

Bloom, Myra, Instruction Librn, Ref Librn, Oral Roberts University Library, 7777 S Lewis Ave, Tulsa, OK, 74171. Tel: 918-495-7174. p. 1865

Bloom, Susan, Branch Experience Mgr, Evansville Vanderburgh Public Library, Central, 200 SE Martin Luther King Jr Blvd, Evansville, IN, 47713. p. 681

Bloom, Susan, Chair, Nubanusit Library Cooperative, c/o Keene Public Library, 60 Winter St, Keene, NH, 03431. Tel: 603-757-0613. p. 2769

Bloomberg, Mike, Digital & Research Servs Librn, Augsburg University, 630 22nd Ave S, Minneapolis, MN, 55454. Tel: 612-330-1604. p. 1182

Bloomdahl, Susana, Dr, Interim Assoc Dean, Murray State University, College of Education & Human Services, 3201 Alexander Hall, Murray, KY, 42071-3309. Tel: 270-809-6471. p. 2785

Bloomenthal, Batia, Br Supvr, Public Library of Brookline, Putterham, 959 W Roxbury Pkwy, Chestnut Hill, MA, 02467. Tel: 617-730-2385. p. 1003

Bloomfield, Christopher, IT Coordr, Springfield Town Library, 43 Main St, Springfield, VT, 05156. Tel: 802-885-3108. p. 2295

Bloomfield, Pat, Librn, Clifton Public Library, 104 E Parallel, Clifton, KS, 66937. Tel: 785-455-2222. p. 802

Bloomingburg, Rachel, Evening Circ Supvr, Union University, 1050 Union University Dr, Jackson, TN, 38305-3697. Tel: 731-661-5418. p. 2102

Bloomquist, Mary Jane, Asst Prof, Govt Info Librn, Head, Govt Info, McNeese State University, 300 S Beauregard Dr, Lake Charles, LA, 70609. Tel: 337-475-5718. p. 894

Bloomstone, Ajaye, Acq Librn, Louisiana State University Libraries, Paul M Hebert Law Center, One E Campus Dr, Baton Rouge, LA, 70803-1000. Tel: 225-578-4044. p. 884

Bloor, Katie, Br Librn, Southeast Regional Library, Oungre Branch, Lyndale School, Hwy 18, Oungre, SK, S0C 1Z0, CANADA. Tel: 306-456-2662. p. 2754

Bloream, Anna, Librn, Buncombe County Public Libraries, Skyland/South Buncombe, 260 Overlook Rd, Asheville, NC, 28803. Tel: 828-250-6488. p. 1672

Bloss, Stephanie, Dir, Brookfield Public Library, 102 E Boston St, Brookfield, MO, 64628. Tel: 660-258-7439. p. 1239

Blough, Kathy, Cat Librn, Music, Saint Olaf College, Rolvaag Memorial Library, Hustad Science Library, Halvorson Music Library, 1510 Saint Olaf Ave, Northfield, MN, 55057-1097. Tel: 507-786-3794. p. 1191

Blount, Allison, Br Mgr, Meherrin Regional Library, William E Richardson Jr Memorial Library, 100 Spring St, Emporia, VA, 23847. Tel: 434-634-2539. p. 2327

Blount, Patti, Dir, Durand Public Library, 604 Seventh Ave E, Durand, WI, 54736. Tel: 715-672-8730. p. 2431

Blow, Sara, Libr Asst, Vermont Department of Libraries, 60 Washington St, Ste 2, Barre, VT, 05641. Tel: 802-636-0020. p. 2278

Blowers, Kevin, Asst Librn, Tech Serv, Bethel College, 1001 Bethel Circle, Mishawaka, IN, 46545. Tel: 574-807-7720. p. 706

Bloy, Jonathan, Head, Digital Initiatives, Edgewood College Library, 959 Edgewood College Dr, Madison, WI, 53711-1997. Tel: 608-663-3300. p. 2449

Bloyd, Alison, Dir, Thomas-Wilhite Memorial Library, 101 E Thomas, Perkins, OK, 74059. Tel: 405-547-5185. p. 1860

Blubaugh, Penny, Teen Serv Coordr, Eisenhower Public Library District, 4613 N Oketo Ave, Harwood Heights, IL, 60706. Tel: 708-867-7828. p. 597

Blue, Amy, Asst Libr Dir, Head, Adult Serv, Antioch Public Library District, 757 Main St, Antioch, IL, 60002. Tel: 847-395-0874. p. 537

Blue, Ana Rosa, Librn, Klohn Crippen Berger Ltd, 500 2955 Virtual Way, Vancouver, BC, V5M 4X6, CANADA. Tel: 604-669-3800. p. 2579

Blue, Belinda, Br Mgr, Loudoun County Public Library, Cascades Branch, 21030 Whitfield Pl, Potomac Falls, VA, 20165. Tel: 703-444-3228. p. 2328

Blue, Christal, Br Mgr, Somerset County Library System of New Jersey, North Plainfield Library, Six Rockview Ave, North Plainfield, NJ, 07060. Tel: 908-458-8435. p. 1392

Blue, Christal, Libr Dir, Hillside Public Library, John F Kennedy Plaza, 1409 Liberty Ave, Hillside, NJ, 07205. Tel: 973-923-4413. p. 1408

Blue, Jane, Librn, Davie County Public Library, Cooleemee Branch, 7796 Hwy 801 S, Cooleemee, NC, 27014. Tel: 336-284-2805. p. 1703

Blue, Jane, Libr Dir, Northumberland Public Library, Inc, 7204 Northumberland Hwy, Heathsville, VA, 22473. Tel: 804-580-5051. p. 2325

Blue, Lisa, YA Librn, Winter Park Public Library, 460 E New England Ave, Winter Park, FL, 32789. Tel: 407-623-3300. p. 456

BlueEyes, Sharon, Tech Serv Supvr, Farmington Public Library, 2101 Farmington Ave, Farmington, NM, 87401. Tel: 505-599-1274. p. 1468

Bluemer, BillieJo, Libr Dir, Rauchholz Memorial Library, 1140 N Hemlock Rd, Hemlock, MI, 48626. Tel: 989-642-8621. p. 1114

Bluestone, Karla, Coordr, Libr Instruction, Woodbury University Library, 7500 Glenoaks Blvd, Burbank, CA, 91510. Tel: 818-252-5200. p. 125

Bluford, Cameron, Tech Serv & Syst Librn, Los Medanos College Library, 2700 E Leland Rd, Pittsburg, CA, 94565. Tel: 925-473-7576. p. 195

Bluhm-Stieber, Hella, Med Librn, Santa Clara Valley Medical Center, 751 S Bascom Ave, Rm 2E063, San Jose, CA, 95128. Tel: 408-885-5654. p. 232

Blum, Cynthia, Cat, Holdrege Area Public Library, 604 East Ave, Holdrege, NE, 68949. Tel: 308-995-6556. p. 1318

Blum, Jennifer, Access Serv Supvr, Owens Community College Library, 30335 Oregon Rd, Perrysburg, OH, 43551. Tel: 567-661-7016. p. 1815

Blum Schneider, Morgan, Dir, JFCS Holocaust Center, 2245 Post St, San Francisco, CA, 94115. Tel: 415-449-3717, 415-449-3748. p. 225

Blumberg, Kristin, Dir, Little Falls Public Library, Eight Warren St, Little Falls, NJ, 07424. Tel: 973-256-2784. p. 1413

Blume, Kathy, Campus Librn, ILL, Milwaukee Area Technical College, 5555 W Highland Rd, Rm A282, Mequon, WI, 53092-1199. Tel: 262-238-2212. p. 2456

Blumhagen, Laura, Mgr, Ch Serv, University of Washington Botanic Gardens, 3501 NE 41st St, Seattle, WA, 98105. Tel: 206-543-0415. p. 2381

Blundon, Brenda, Law Librn, Department of Justice & Public Safety, East Block, Confederation Bldg, 5th Flr, 100 Prince Philip Dr, St. John's, NL, A1B 4J6, CANADA. Tel: 709-729-0285. p. 2610

Blunier, Debra, Dir, Filger Public Library, 261 E Fifth St, Minonk, IL, 61760. Tel: 309-432-2929. p. 618

Blunt, Johnnie R, Educ Librn, Youth Serv Librn, University of Northern Iowa Library, 1227 W 27th St, Cedar Falls, IA, 50613-3675. Tel: 319-273-6167. p. 737

Bluteau, Elodie, Libr Tech, Commission de Toponymie du Quebec Bibliotheque, 750, boul Charest Est, RC, Quebec, QC, G1K 9K4, CANADA. Tel: 418-643-4575. p. 2730

Blycker Koll, Beth, Circ Mgr, Salve Regina University, 100 Ochre Point Ave, Newport, RI, 02840-4192. Tel: 401-341-2330. p. 2035

Blydenburgh, Will, Principal Librn, Lee County Library System, Northwest Regional Library, 519 N Chiquita Blvd, Cape Coral, FL, 33993. Tel: 239-533-4700. p. 403

Blyth, Krista, Libr Mgr, York Library Region, Chipman Branch, Eight King St, Chipman, NB, E4A 2H3, CANADA. Tel: 506-339-5852. p. 2602

Blythe, Lois J, Coll Tech Librn, Burlington Public Library, 210 Court St, Burlington, IA, 52601. Tel: 319-753-1647. p. 736

Boal, Gillian, Conservator, Graduate Theological Union Library, 2400 Ridge Rd, Berkeley, CA, 94709-1212. Tel: 510-649-2527. p. 122

Boardman, Dale, Librn II, Colorado Department of Corrections, 12101 Hwy 61, Sterling, CO, 80751. Tel: 970-521-5010, Ext 3404. p. 296

Boardman, Dale, Librn II, Colorado Department of Corrections, Sterling Correctional Facility Library- West - East, 12101 Hwy 61, Sterling, CO, 80751. p. 296

Boatman, Christopher, Ref Librn, Westcliff University, 16735 Von Karman, Ste 100, Irvine, CA, 92606. Tel: 714-459-1171. p. 153

Boatman, Patricia, Br Mgr, Lafourche Parish Public Library, Martha Sowell Utley Memorial (Administrative Office), 314 St Mary St, Thibodaux, LA, 70301-2620. Tel: 985-447-4119. p. 911

Boatright, Christine, Dir, Libr Serv, Florida Gateway College, 149 SE College Pl, Lake City, FL, 32025-2006. Tel: 386-754-4337. p. 415

Boatright, Joshua, Dept Chair, Librn, Berkeley City College Library, 2050 Center St, Rm 131, Berkeley, CA, 94704. Tel: 510-981-2991. p. 121

Boatwright, Eulas, Syst Adminr, Willingboro Public Library, Willingboro Town Ctr, 220 Willingboro Pkwy, Willingboro, NJ, 08046. Tel: 609-877-0476, 609-877-6668. p. 1455

Boback, Karen, Library Contact, New York State Supreme Court Ninth Judicial District, 50 Market St, 2nd Flr, Poughkeepsie, NY, 12601-3203. Tel: 845-431-1859. p. 1623

Bobb, Yolanda, Head, Circ, Northwestern State University Libraries, 913 University Pkwy, Natchitoches, LA, 71497. Tel: 318-357-4477. p. 900

Bobbitt, Phyllis, Br Mgr, Wythe-Grayson Regional Library, 147 S Independence Ave, Independence, VA, 24348. Tel: 276-773-3018. p. 2326

Bobinski, Katherine, Dir, Deer Lodge Public Library, 110 Corinne Ave, Deer Lodge, TN, 37726. Tel: 423-965-0101. p. 2096

Bobish, Michael, Asst Libr Dir, East Brunswick Public Library, Two Jean Walling Civic Ctr, East Brunswick, NJ, 08816-3599. Tel: 732-390-6950. p. 1399

Bobka, Marlene S, Pres, FOI Services Inc Library, 23219 Stringtown Rd, #240, Clarksburg, MD, 20871-9363. Tel: 301-975-9400. p. 962

Bobo, Rachel, Circ, Orange Beach Public Library, 26267 Canal Rd, Orange Beach, AL, 36561-3917. Tel: 251-981-2923. p. 32

Bobrowska, Natalie, Libr Coord, Illinois College of Optometry Library, 3241 S Michigan Ave, Chicago, IL, 60616-3878. Tel: 312-949-7160. p. 562

Bobrowsky, Tammy, Coll Develop, Electronic Res Librn, Bemidji State University, 1500 Birchmont Dr NE, No 28, Bemidji, MN, 56601-2699. Tel: 218-755-4110. p. 1165

Boccia, Terri, Coll Develop Librn, Sterling & Francine Clark Art Institute Library, 225 South St, Williamstown, MA, 01267. Tel: 413-458-0437. p. 1069

Bocell, Kelley, Operations Mgr, Vinson & Elkins, Texas Tower, 845 Texas Ave, Ste 4700, Houston, TX, 77002. Tel: 713-758-2222, 713-758-2990. p. 2200

Bochicchio, Nicholas A, Jr, Admin Serv Dir, The Ferguson Library, One Public Library Plaza, Stamford, CT, 06904. Tel: 203-351-8202. p. 338

Bochin, Janet, Cataloger, California State University, Fresno, Henry Madden Library, 5200 N Barton Ave, Mail Stop ML-34, Fresno, CA, 93740-8014. Tel: 559-278-2158. p. 144

Bock, Amanda, Managing Librn, Youth Serv, Falmouth Public Library, 300 Main St, Falmouth, MA, 02540. Tel: 508-457-2555, Ext 2920. p. 1018

Bock, David, Fr, Librn, New Melleray Library, 6632 Melleray Circle, Peosta, IA, 52068. Tel: 563-588-2319, Ext 426. p. 776

Bock, Deborah, Head, Ref, Johnson Free Public Library, 274 Main St, Hackensack, NJ, 07601-5797. Tel: 201-343-4169. p. 1406

Bock, Susie, Coordr, Spec Coll, University of Southern Maine Libraries, 314 Forest Ave, Portland, ME, 04103. Tel: 207-780-4269. p. 937

Bockler, Peggy, Librn, Illinois Prairie District Public Library, Metamora Branch, 208 E Partridge St, Metamora, IL, 61548. p. 617

Bocko, Amy, Digital Projects Librn, Western Michigan University, 1903 W Michigan Ave, WMU Mail Stop 5353, Kalamazoo, MI, 49008-5353. Tel: 269-387-5150. p. 1122

Bodas, Carol, Libr Mgr, Salk Institute for Biological Studies, 10010 N Torrey Pines Rd, La Jolla, CA, 92037. Tel: 858-453-4100, Ext 1235. p. 154

Bodden, Mary Alice, Dir, Theresa Public Library, 290 Mayville St, Theresa, WI, 53091-0307. Tel: 920-488-2342. p. 2481

Boddy, Brijin, Br Mgr, Cuyahoga County Public Library, South Euclid-Lyndhurst Branch, 1876 S Green Rd, South Euclid, OH, 44121-4018. Tel: 216-382-4880. p. 1813

Bode, Barb, Co-Dir, Elgin Public Library, 503 S Second St, Elgin, NE, 68636-3222. Tel: 402-843-2460. p. 1313

Boden, Dana, Mr, ILL, University of Nebraska Medical Center, 600 S 42nd St, Omaha, NE, 68198. Tel: 402-559-3732. p. 1331

Boden, Karleen, Libr Dir, Corning City Library, 6221 Fifth St, Corning, KS, 66417-8485. Tel: 785-868-2755. p. 803

Boden, Stacey, Dir, Rossland Public Library Association, 2180 Columbia Ave, Rossland, BC, V0G 1Y0, CANADA. Tel: 250-362-7611. p. 2575

Bodenheimer, Lisa, Head, Cat, Librn, Clemson University Libraries, 116 Sigma Dr, Clemson, SC, 29631. Tel: 864-656-1769. p. 2052

Bodewes, Ted, Dir, Thomas Ford Memorial Library, 800 Chestnut St, Western Springs, IL, 60558. Tel: 708-246-0520. p. 661

Bodick, Patricia, Chief Exec Officer, Librn, Larder Lake Public Library, 69 Fourth Ave, Larder Lake, ON, P0K 1L0, CANADA. Tel: 705-643-2222. p. 2652

Bodie, Mathew, Librn, Saint Petersburg College, Tarpon Springs Campus Library, 600 Klosterman Rd, Tarpon Springs, FL, 34689. Tel: 727-712-5240. p. 438

Bodine, Gary, Librn, Snead State Community College, 102 Elder St, Boaz, AL, 35957. Tel: 256-840-4173. p. 10

Bodine, Kristen, Youth Serv Supvr, Louisville Public Library, 951 Spruce St, Louisville, CO, 80027. Tel: 303-335-4849. p. 290

Bodine, Samantha, Dir, Fobes Memorial Library, Four Maple St, Unit 9, Oakham, MA, 01068. Tel: 508-882-3372. p. 1044

Bodnar, Jeanne, Libr Coord, AdventHealth Shawnee Mission Medical Library, 9100 W 74th St, Shawnee Mission, KS, 66204. Tel: 913-676-2101. p. 836

Bodnar, Nick, Mgr, Florida State College at Jacksonville, Downtown Campus Library & Learning Commons, 101 W State St, Bldg A, Rm A-2102 & A-3040, Jacksonville, FL, 32202-3056. Tel: 904-633-8368. p. 411

Bodnar, Zachary, Archivist, American Congregational Association, 14 Beacon St, 2nd Flr, Boston, MA, 02108-9999. Tel: 617-523-0470. p. 990

Bodnar-Anderson, Christina, Libr Coord, University of California, Berkeley, Pacific Earthquake Engineering Research (PEER) Center Library - NISEE, Bldg 453, 1301 S 46th St, Richmond, CA, 94804. Tel: 510-665-3419. p. 123

Bodwell, Hope, Libr Dir, Monson Free Library, Two High St, Monson, MA, 01057-1095. Tel: 413-267-9035. p. 1036

Bodycomb, Aphrodite, Assoc Dir, Libr Admin, University of Maryland, Baltimore, Health Sciences & Human Services Library, 601 W Lombard St, Baltimore, MD, 21201. Tel: 410-706-8853. p. 957

Bodziock, Pam, Asst Dir, Teen Librn, Monroeville Public Library, 4000 Gateway Campus Blvd, Monroeville, PA, 15146-3381. Tel: 412-372-0500. p. 1964

Bodzislaw, Angela, Ch, Dir, Spooner Memorial Library, 421 High St, Spooner, WI, 54801. Tel: 715-635-2792. p. 2478

Boe, James, Dr, Dept Chair, Valley City State University, 327 E McFarland Hall, 101 College St SW, Valley City, ND, 58072-4098. Tel: 701-845-7303. p. 2790

Boe, Michael, Libr Serv Mgr, Hennepin County Library, 12601 Ridgedale Dr, Minnetonka, MN, 55305-1909. Tel: 612-543-5627. p. 1186

Boeckenstedt, Ann, Sr Serv, James Kennedy Public Library, 320 First Ave E, Dyersville, IA, 52040. Tel: 563-875-8912. p. 749

Boedigheimer, Amber, Law Librn, Linn County Law Library, 304 Broadalbin St SW, Albany, OR, 97321. p. 1871

Boehlke, Cindy, Dir, Prairie Skies Public Library District, 125 W Editor St, Ashland, IL, 62612. Tel: 217-476-3417. p. 537

Boehlke, Cindy, Dir, Prairie Skies Public Library District, Pleasant Plains Branch, 555 Buckeye Rd, Pleasant Plains, IL, 62677. Tel: 217-626-1553. p. 537

Boehlke, Cindy, Youth Serv Librn, Jacksonville Public Library, 201 W College Ave, Jacksonville, IL, 62650-2497. Tel: 217-243-5435. p. 602

Boehm, Alan, Spec Coll Librn, Middle Tennessee State University, 1611 Alumni Dr, Murfreesboro, TN, 37132. Tel: 615-904-8501. p. 2117

Boehm, Beth, Cat, Waynesburg College, 51 W College St, Waynesburg, PA, 15370. Tel: 724-852-7640. p. 2019

Boehm, Lenore, Acq Mgr, DePaul University Libraries, Vincent G Rinn Law Library, 25 E Jackson Blvd, 5th Flr, Chicago, IL, 60604-2287. Tel: 312-362-5224. p. 560

Boehm, Sarah, Dir, Bradford Public Library District, 111 S Peoria St, Bradford, IL, 61421. Tel: 309-897-8400. p. 544

Boehme, Andrea, Dir, Access Serv, Bowling Green State University Libraries, 1001 E Wooster St, Bowling Green, OH, 43403-0170. p. 1752

Boerboom, Deborah, Mgr, Rapides Parish Library, Boyce Branch, 500 A Ulster Ave, Boyce, LA, 71409. Tel: 318-793-2182. p. 880

Boerdoom, Deborah, Librn, Central Louisiana State Hospital, Distefano Memorial Library, 242 W Shamrock St, Pineville, LA, 71361. Tel: 318-484-6363. p. 905

Boerdoom, Deborah, Librn, Central Louisiana State Hospital, Forest Glen Patient's Library, 242 W Shamrock St, Pineville, LA, 71361. Tel: 318-484-6364. p. 905

Boeree-Kline, Kate, Br Mgr, Arundel Anne County Public Library, Linthicum Library, 400 Shipley Rd, Linthicum, MD, 21090. Tel: 410-222-6265. p. 950

Boersma-Scott, Chelsey, Actg Dir, Midway Public Library, 612 Sixth Ave, Midway, BC, V0H 1M0, CANADA. Tel: 250-449-2620. p. 2570

Boertmann, Mary, Dir of Circ, Hazel Park Memorial District Library, 123 E Nine Mile Rd, Hazel Park, MI, 48030. Tel: 248-542-0940, 248-546-4095. p. 1114

Boes, Kanjana, ILL Tech, Alliant International University, 10455 Pomerado Rd, San Diego, CA, 92131-1799. Tel: 858-635-4511. p. 214

Boese, Kent, Mgr, Libr Serv, Wiley Rein LLC Library, 1776 K St NW, Washington, DC, 20006. Tel: 202-719-7000. p. 381

Boeshans, Kristen, Libr Asst, La Crescent Public Library, 321 Main St, La Crescent, MN, 55947. Tel: 507-895-4047. p. 1179

Boetcher, Kerrianne, Dir, Ward County Public Library, 225 Third Ave SE, Minot, ND, 58701-4020. Tel: 701-852-5388. p. 1738

Boettcher, Bonna, Dir of Libr, Cornell University Library, Olin & Uris Libraries, 161 Ho Plaza, Ithaca, NY, 14853. Tel: 607-255-5998. p. 1552

Boettcher, Pat, Libr Mgr, Tangent Community Library, West Entrance, 1009 Railway Ave, Tangent, AB, T0H 3J0, CANADA. Tel: 780-359-2666. p. 2556

Boettger, Jennifer, Coordr, Teen Serv, Coordr, Youth Serv, North Kingstown Free Library, 100 Boone St, North Kingstown, RI, 02852-5150. Tel: 401-294-3306. p. 2036

Boettger, Rose, Acq, Lehigh Carbon Community College Library, 4750 Orchard Rd, Schnecksville, PA, 18078. Tel: 610-799-1150. p. 2003

Boettger, Vera, Co-Mgr, Bentley Municipal Library, 5014 - 49 Ave, Bentley, AB, T0C 0J0, CANADA. Tel: 403-748-4626. p. 2523

Boff, Colleen, Head Librn, Bowling Green State University Libraries, 1001 E Wooster St, Bowling Green, OH, 43403-0170. p. 1752

Boff, Colleen, Head Librn, Bowling Green State University Libraries, Curriculum Resource Center, Jerome Library, 2nd Flr, Bowling Green, OH, 43403-0178. Tel: 419-372-2956. p. 1752

Bogaert, Beth, Dir, Lenox Township Library, 58976 Main St, New Haven, MI, 48048-2685. Tel: 586-749-3430. p. 1137

Bogan, Katie, Libr Asst, Stacks Mgr, Museum of Fine Arts, Houston, 1001 Bissonnet St, Houston, TX, 77005. Tel: 713-639-7325. p. 2197

Bogan, Sharon, Libr Assoc, Desoto Parish Library, Stonewall Branch, 808 Hwy 171, Stonewall, LA, 71078. Tel: 318-925-9191. p. 896

Bogardus, Carolyn, Br Mgr, Montgomery County Public Libraries, Little Falls Library, 5501 Massachusetts Ave, Bethesda, MD, 20816. Tel: 240-773-9526. p. 974

Bogart, Debra, Tampa Campus Libr Dir, Keiser University Library System, 1500 NW 49th St, Fort Lauderdale, FL, 33309. Tel: 954-351-4035. p. 401

Bogart, Jim, Develop Mgr, Saint Louis County Library, 1640 S Lindbergh Blvd, Saint Louis, MO, 63131-3598. Tel: 314-994-3300, Ext 2156. p. 1273

Bogart, Ramona, Libr Mgr, Afton Free Library, 105A Main St, Afton, NY, 13730. Tel: 607-639-1212. p. 1481

Bogda, Neal, Digital Res Librn, Web Librn, Cardinal Stritch University Library, 6801 N Yates Rd, Milwaukee, WI, 53217. Tel: 414-410-4263. p. 2458

Bogdanov, Stan, Mgr, Library Web Technologies, Adelphi University, One South Ave, Garden City, NY, 11530. Tel: 516-877-3674. p. 1536

Bogdanowicz, Harriet, Head, Communication Serv, American Planning Association Library, 205 N Michigan Ave, Ste 1200, Chicago, IL, 60601. Tel: 312-431-9100, Ext 6353. p. 554

Bogdash, Jaime, E-Resources Specialist, Orbis Cascade Alliance, PO Box 6007, Portland, OR, 97228. Tel: 541-246-2470. p. 2773

Bogel, Gayle, Dir, Clark Memorial Library, 538 Amity Rd, Bethany, CT, 06524. Tel: 203-393-2103. p. 302

Bogel, Steven, Evening Ref Librn, Drexel University Libraries, Hagerty Library, 33rd & Market Sts, Philadelphia, PA, 19104-2875. Tel: 215-895-2750. p. 1976

Bogel, Steven, Ref Librn, Drexel University Libraries, Hahnemann Library, 245 N 15th St MS 449, Philadelphia, PA, 19102-1192. p. 1976

Boger, Jo, Br Supvr, Boonslick Regional Library, Sedalia Branch, 219 W Third St, Sedalia, MO, 65301. Tel: 660-827-7323. p. 1279

Boger, Paul, Head, Reference & Scholarly Comms, University of Mary Washington, 1801 College Ave, Fredericksburg, VA, 22401-5300. Tel: 540-654-1148. p. 2320

Bogert, Jonathan, Exec Dir, Historical & Genealogical Society of Indiana County, 621 Wayne Ave, Indiana, PA, 15701. Tel: 724-463-9600. p. 1945

Boggs, Elizabeth, Br Mgr, Harris County Public Library, Katy Branch, 5414 Franz Rd, Katy, TX, 77493. Tel: 281-391-3509. p. 2192

Boggs, Genne, Br Mgr, Anythink Libraries, Anythink Huron Street, 9417 Huron St, Thornton, CO, 80260. Tel: 303-452-7534. p. 296

Boggs, Katelyn, Libr Asst, Dandridge Memorial Library, 1235 Circle Dr, Dandridge, TN, 37725-4750. Tel: 865-397-9758. p. 2096

Boggs, Kelly, Fiscal Officer, North Canton Public Library, 185 N Main St, North Canton, OH, 44720-2595. Tel: 330-499-4712. p. 1809

Boggs, Lauren, Cataloger, Suburban Library Cooperative, 44750 Delco Blvd, Sterling Heights, MI, 48313. Tel: 586-685-5750. p. 2767

Boggs, Paula, Dir & Librn, Piedmont Public Library, One Child Ave, Piedmont, WV, 26750. Tel: 304-355-2757. p. 2412

Boggs, Stephen, Dir, Bell Memorial Public Library, 101 W Main St, Mentone, IN, 46539. Tel: 574-893-3200. p. 705

Boghozian, Tina, Access Serv, Mission College Library, 3000 Mission College Blvd, Santa Clara, CA, 95054-1897. Tel: 408-855-5165. p. 241

Bognanni, Kathy, Br Mgr, Carver County Library, Chanhassen Branch, 7711 Kerber Blvd, Chanhassen, MN, 55317. Tel: 952-227-1500. p. 1169

Bognanni, Kathy, Br Mgr, Carver County Library, Victoria Branch, 1670 Stieger Lake Lane, Victoria, MN, 55386. Tel: 952-442-3050. p. 1169

Bogner, Irene, Librn, Beverly Hospital, 309 W Beverly Blvd, Montebello, CA, 90640. Tel: 323-725-4305. p. 179

Bogniak, Sara, Events Coord, Warren County Historical Society, 210 Fourth Ave, Warren, PA, 16365. Tel: 814-723-1795. p. 2017

Bogucka, Roxanne, Liaison Librn, University of Texas Libraries, Life Science (Biology, Pharmacy), Main Bldg, 2400 Inner Campus Dr, Austin, TX, 78712. Tel: 512-495-4630. p. 2142

Bogue, Carol, Asst Librn, Danvers Township Library, 117 E Exchange St, Danvers, IL, 61732-9347. Tel: 309-963-4269. p. 575

Bogue, Mary A, Assoc Libr Dir, Tech Serv Librn, Earlham College, 801 National Rd W, Richmond, IN, 47374-4095. Tel: 765-983-1363. p. 715

Bohall, Rob, Res & Instruction Librn, George Fox University, 416 N Meridian St, Newberg, OR, 97132. Tel: 503-554-2416. p. 1888

Bohan, Rick, Sr Dir, Portland Cement Association, 5420 Old Orchard Rd, Skokie, IL, 60077-1083. Tel: 847-972-9174. p. 647

Bohannan, Kelly, Br Mgr, Clay County Public Library System, 1895 Town Center Blvd, Fleming Island, FL, 32003. Tel: 904-278-3720. p. 396

Bohannon, Chris, Colls Mgr, Dallas Historical Society, Hall of State in Fair Park, 3939 Grand Ave, Dallas, TX, 75210. Tel: 214-421-4500, Ext 117. p. 2164

Bohannon, Rachel, Mgr, Erlanger Health System Library, 975 E Third St, Chattanooga, TN, 37403. Tel: 423-778-7246. p. 2091

Bohemier, Kayleigh, Librn, Yale University Library, Astronomy, Steinbach Hall, 56 Hillhouse Ave, New Haven, CT, 06511. Tel: 203-432-3000. p. 326

Bohemier, Kayleigh, Research Support Librarian, Yale University Library, Geology, 210 Whitney Ave, Rm 328, New Haven, CT, 06511. Tel: 203-432-3157. p. 327

Bohl, Echo, Asst Br Librn, Crook County Library, Hulett Branch, 401 Sager St, Hulett, WY, 82720. Tel: 307-467-5676. p. 2499

Bohlar, Sally, Dir & Librn, Lovett Memorial Library, 302 N Main St, McLean, TX, 79057. Tel: 806-779-2851. p. 2218

Bohleke, B, Dr, Law Librn, Adams County Law Library, Court House, 117 Baltimore St, Gettysburg, PA, 17325. Tel: 717-337-9812. p. 1935

Bohling, Chris, Operations Mgr, University of Kansas Libraries, Thomas Gorton Music & Dance Library, 1530 Naismith Dr, Lawrence, KS, 66045-3102. Tel: 785-864-3397. p. 820

Bohman, Molly, Asst Librn, First Church West Hartford, 12 S Main St, West Hartford, CT, 06107. Tel: 860-232-3893. p. 345

Bohme, Carol, Libr Assoc, Colby Community College, 1255 S Range Ave, Colby, KS, 67701. Tel: 785-460-4689. p. 802

Bohn, Elise J, Libr Dir, Ferris State University, 17 Fountain St NW, Grand Rapids, MI, 49503-3002. Tel: 616-259-1123. p. 1110

Bohn, Loretta, Circ Serv Coordr, Berkeley Public Library, 1637 N Taft Ave, Berkeley, IL, 60163-1499. Tel: 708-544-6017. p. 542

Bohn, Regina, Br Librn, Sussex County Library System, E Louise Childs Memorial, 21 Stanhope Sparta Rd, Stanhope, NJ, 07874. Tel: 973-770-1000. p. 1429

Bohnenkamper, Katherine, Assoc Librn, Head, Access Serv, Drury University, 900 N Benton Ave, Springfield, MO, 65802. Tel: 417-873-7485. p. 1280

Bohnet, Denise, Dir, Sanborn Public Library, 407 Main St, Sanborn, IA, 51248. Tel: 712-930-3215. p. 780

Bohnstedt, Mark, Br Mgr, Houston County Public Library System, Nola Brantley Memorial Library, 721 Watson Blvd, Warner Robins, GA, 31093. Tel: 478-923-0128. p. 493

Bohr, Darsi, Dir, Speedway Public Library, 5633 W 25th St, Speedway, IN, 46224-3899. Tel: 317-243-8959. p. 719

Bohrer, Clara Nalli, Dir, West Bloomfield Township Public Library, 4600 Walnut Lake Rd, West Bloomfield, MI, 48323. Tel: 248-682-2120. p. 1158

Bohrer, Karen, Dir, Libr Coll, Wellesley College, 106 Central St, Wellesley, MA, 02481. Tel: 781-283-2127. p. 1064

Bohstedt, Beth, Dir, Access Services & Coll Strategies, Hamilton College, Music, McEwen Hall, 198 College Hill Rd, Clinton, NY, 13323-1299. Tel: 315-859-4485. p. 1519

Bohstedt, Beth, Dir, Res & Learning Serv, Hamilton College, 198 College Hill Rd, Clinton, NY, 13323. Tel: 315-859-4485. p. 1519

Boice, Daniel, Dir, University of Arkansas at Monticello, 1326 Hwy 52 W, Crossett, AR, 71635. Tel: 870-364-6414. p. 93

Boice, Daniel, Dir, Libr Serv, University of Arkansas-Monticello Library, 514 University Dr, Monticello, AR, 71656. Tel: 870-460-1480. p. 105

Boies, Laurie Ellen, Dir, Ruth Suckow Memorial Library, 122 Northern Ave, Earlville, IA, 52041. Tel: 563-923-5235. p. 750

Boileau, Elisabeth, Libr Tech, Lakehead University, Education Library, Bora Laskin Bldg, 1st Flr, 955 Oliver Rd, Thunder Bay, ON, P7B 5E1, CANADA. Tel: 807-343-8718. p. 2685

Boily-Bernal, Mirabelle, Mem Serv Librn, Manitoba Department of Sport, Culture & Heritage, Legislative Reading Room, 450 Broadway Ave, Rm 260, Winnipeg, MB, R3C 0V8, CANADA. Tel: 204-945-4243. p. 2593

Boisclair, Marc, Access Services Assoc, Drew University Library, 36 Madison Ave, Madison, NJ, 07940. Tel: 973-408-3486. p. 1414

Boisitz, Emma, Librn, Yeshiva University Libraries, Dr Lillian & Dr Rebecca Chutick Law Library, Benjamin N Cardozo School of Law, 55 Fifth Ave, New York, NY, 10003-4301. Tel: 212-790-0223. p. 1604

Boisvenue-Fox, Michelle, Dir, Mesa County Public Library District, 443 N Sixth St, Grand Junction, CO, 81501. Tel: 970-243-4442. p. 284

Boisvert, Mary Ellen, Circ Librn, Aldrich Public Library, Six Washington St, Barre, VT, 05641. Tel: 802-476-7550. p. 2278

Boivin, Christian, Asst Dir, Commun Relations & Mkt, Jacksonville Public Library, 303 N Laura St, Jacksonville, FL, 32202-3505. Tel: 904-630-7595. p. 411

Boivin, Sophie, Libr Asst, Bibliotheque Marie-Antoinette-Foucher, 101 Place du Cure-Labelle, Saint Jerome, QC, J7Z 1X6, CANADA. Tel: 450-432-0569. p. 2734

Boivin, Wanda, Asst Libr Mgr, Oneida Community Library, 201 Elm St, Oneida, WI, 54155. Tel: 920-869-2210. p. 2466

Bokay, Kevin Patrick, Actg Dir, United States Army, Grant Library, 1637 Flint St, Fort Carson, CO, 80913-4105. Tel: 719-526-8144. p. 280

Bokka, Rohini, Tech Serv Mgr, Naperville Public Library, 200 W Jefferson Ave, Naperville, IL, 60540-5374. Tel: 630-961-4200, Ext 6141. p. 622

Boksenbaum, Martha, Youth Serv Librn, Cranston Public Library, William H Hall Free Library, 1825 Broad St, Cranston, RI, 02905-3599. Tel: 401-781-2450. p. 2031

Bolan, Pamela, Coll, Quality Assurance Coord, Seneca College of Applied Arts & Technology, Seneca @ York, 70 The Pond Rd, North York, ON, M3J 3M6, CANADA. Tel: 416-491-5050, Ext 33055. p. 2650

Boland, Amy, Br Mgr, Trails Regional Library, Waverly Branch, 203 E Kelling, Waverly, MO, 64096. Tel: 660-493-2987. p. 1285

Boland, Caitlyn, Dir, Mars Area Public Library, 107 Grand Ave, Mars, PA, 16046. Tel: 724-625-9048. p. 1958

Boland, Susan, Assoc Dir, Pub & Res Serv, University of Cincinnati, 2540 Clifton Ave, Cincinnati, OH, 45219. Tel: 513-556-4407. p. 1764

Bolander, Amanda, Dir, Rush Copley Medical Center, 2000 Ogden Ave, Aurora, IL, 60504. Tel: 630-499-2324. p. 539

Bolce, Sarah, Resource Sharing Coord, Saint Joseph's University, Francis A Drexel Library, 5600 City Ave, Philadelphia, PA, 19131-1395. Tel: 610-660-1907. p. 1985

Bolden, Heather, Librn, New Jersey Department of Corrections, 215 Burlington Rd S, Bridgeton, NJ, 08302. Tel: 856-459-7000, Ext 8145. p. 1392

Bolden, Rachael, ILL Mgr, Supvr, User Serv, Washington & Jefferson College Library, 60 S Lincoln St, Washington, PA, 15301. Tel: 724-223-6070. p. 2018

Bolden, Yolanda, Libr Dir, Forsyth County Public Library, 660 W Fifth St, Winston-Salem, NC, 27105. Tel: 336-703-2665. p. 1724

Boldenow, Jill, Libr Dir, Ramsey County Library, 4570 N Victoria St, Shoreview, MN, 55126. Tel: 651-486-2201. p. 1203

Bolding, Charles, Librn, Correctional Service of Canada-Pacific Region, 4732 Cemetery Rd, Agassiz, BC, V0M 1A0, CANADA. Tel: 604-796-2121, Ext 4329. p. 2562

Boldt, Gabriel, Clinical Librn, London Health Sciences Centre, 800 Commissioners Rd E, London, ON, N6A 4G5, CANADA. Tel: 519-685-8500, Ext 75934. p. 2654

Boldt, Janet, Dir, Spring Lake Public Library, 1501 Third Ave, Spring Lake, NJ, 07762. Tel: 732-449-6654. p. 1444

Boldt, Kelsey, Asst Librn, Ishpeming Carnegie Public Library, 317 N Main St, Ishpeming, MI, 49849-1994. Tel: 906-486-4381. p. 1119

Bolduc, Janet, Librn, MaineGeneral Medical Center, 35 Medical Center Pkwy, Augusta, ME, 04330. Tel: 207-626-1325. p. 914

Bole, Mary, Chair, Manitoba Genealogical Society Inc Library, 1045 St James St, Unit E, Winnipeg, MB, R3H 1B1, CANADA. Tel: 204-783-9139. p. 2593

Boleen, Patricia, Acq, Ser Tech, Yukon College Library, 500 College Dr, Whitehorse, YT, Y1A 5K4, CANADA. Tel: 867-668-8870. p. 2758

Bolek, Barbara, Cat Librn, University of Michigan-Dearborn, 4901 Evergreen Rd, Dearborn, MI, 48128-2406. Tel: 313-593-5401. p. 1096

Bolen, Kelli, Youth Serv, Carroll County Library, 625 High St, Ste 102, Huntingdon, TN, 38344-3903. Tel: 731-986-1919. p. 2101

Boles, Christine, Br Mgr, Walnut Cove Public Library, 106 W Fifth St, Walnut Cove, NC, 27052. Tel: 336-591-7496. p. 1720

Boles, Jenni, Br Mgr, Huron County Library, Exeter Branch, 330 Main St, Exeter, ON, N0M 1S6, CANADA. Tel: 519-235-1890. p. 2636

Boles, Jenni, Br Mgr, Huron County Library, Hensall Branch, 108 King St, Hensall, ON, N0M 1X0, CANADA. Tel: 519-262-2445. p. 2636

Boles, Jenni, Br Mgr, Huron County Library, Kirkton Branch, c/o Kirkton-Woodham Community Ctr, 70497 Perth Rd 164, RR 1, Kirkton, ON, N0K 1K0, CANADA. Tel: 519-229-8854. p. 2636

Boley, Deborah, Br Mgr, Perry County District Library, Somerset Branch, 103 Public Sq, Somerset, OH, 43783. Tel: 740-743-1161. p. 1806

Bolger, Gina, ILL, Ref Librn, Cornerstone University, 1001 E Beltline Ave NE, Grand Rapids, MI, 49525. Tel: 616-254-1650, Ext 1245. p. 1110

Bolin, Julie, Dir, Scott & White Healthcare, 2401 S 31st, MS-AG-302, Temple, TX, 76508. Tel: 254-724-2228. p. 2247

Boling, Jeff, Ref Serv, Joint Base Pearl Harbor-Hickam Library, Bldg 595, 990 Mills Blvd, Hickam AFB, HI, 96853. Tel: 808-449-8299. p. 505

Boling, Karen, Mgr, West Georgia Regional Library, Tallapoosa Public Library, 388 Bowden St, Tallapoosa, GA, 30176. Tel: 770-574-3124. p. 470

Bolinger, Becky, Br Librn, Platte County Public Library, Guernsey Branch, 108 S Wyoming Ave, Guernsey, WY, 82214. Tel: 307-836-2816. p. 2500

Bolinger, Ruth, Libr Asst, Southwestern Community College, 1501 W Townline St, Creston, IA, 50801. Tel: 641-782-1462. p. 743

Bolitho, Stacia, Pub Serv Librn, Gardiner Public Library, 152 Water St, Gardiner, ME, 04345. Tel: 207-582-3312. p. 926

Bollar, Maggie, Ch, New Carlisle Public Library, 111 E Lake Ave, New Carlisle, OH, 45344-1418. Tel: 937-845-3601. p. 1806

Bollenbach, Katherine, Libr Asst, Belmont Public Library, 146 Main St, Belmont, NH, 03220. Tel: 603-267-8331. p. 1355

Bollenbach, Katherine, Libr Dir, Salisbury Free Library, 641 Old Turnpike Rd, Salisbury, NH, 03268. Tel: 603-648-2278. p. 1380

Bollenback, Mark, ILL, Ref Serv, Valencia College, East Campus Library, 701 N Econlockhatchee Trail, Orlando, FL, 32825. Tel: 407-582-2467. p. 432

Boller, Mary, Children's Consult, Sch Libr Consult, Talking Bks Consult, Northwest Kansas Library System, Two Washington Sq, Norton, KS, 67654-1615. Tel: 785-877-5148. p. 827

Bollerman, Matthew, Chief Exec Officer, Hauppauge Public Library, 1373 Veterans Memorial Hwy, Ste 1, Hauppauge, NY, 11788. Tel: 631-979-1600. p. 1545

Bolling, Kathy, Libr Mgr, University of Alaska Southeast, 2600 Seventh Ave, Ketchikan, AK, 99901. Tel: 907-228-4517. p. 48

Bolling, Laura, Br Supvr, Birchard Public Library of Sandusky County, Green Springs Memorial, 217 N Broadway, Green Springs, OH, 44836. Tel: 419-639-2014. p. 1786

Bollinger, Stephen, Head, Libr Syst, North Carolina Agricultural & Technical State University, 1601 E Market St, Greensboro, NC, 27411-0002. Tel: 336-285-4164. p. 1693

Bollom, Chelsea, Ad, Circ Mgr, Keene Memorial Library, 1030 N Broad St, Fremont, NE, 68025-4199. Tel: 402-727-2694. p. 1314

Bollom, Kay, Ch, Wharton County Library, 1920 N Fulton St, Wharton, TX, 77488. Tel: 979-532-8080. p. 2256

Bolm, George C, Dir, Vicksburg & Warren County Historical Society, Old Court House Museum, 1008 Cherry St, Vicksburg, MS, 39183. Tel: 601-636-0741. p. 1234

Bolser, Barbara, Ref & Instruction Librn, Black Hawk College, 26230 Black Hawk Rd, Galva, IL, 61434. Tel: 309-854-1730. p. 591

Bolster, Barbara, Ref & Instruction Librn, Black Hawk College, 6600 34th Ave, Moline, IL, 61265. Tel: 309-796-5700. p. 618

Bolster, Norma, Libr Mgr, Eaglesham Public Library, 4902 53rd Ave, Eaglesham, AB, T0H 1H0, CANADA. Tel: 780-359-3792. p. 2534

Bolt, Jonathan, Libr Assoc, Concord University, Vermillion St, Athens, WV, 24712. Tel: 304-384-5371. p. 2397

Bolt, Joy, Asst Dean, Libr, University of North Georgia, Cumming Campus Library, 300 Aquatic Circle, Cumming, GA, 30040. Tel: 678-717-3466. p. 493

Bolt, Joy, Dean of Libr, Head Librn, University of North Georgia, Dahlonega Campus Library, 82 College Circle, Dahlonega, GA, 30597. Tel: 706-864-1514. p. 493

Bolt, Joy, Dean of Libr, University of North Georgia, 3820 Mundy Mill Rd, Oakwood, GA, 30566. Tel: 678-717-3653. p. 493

Bolte, Elisha, Librn, Randall Public Library, 107 Main St, Randall, KS, 66963. Tel: 785-739-2380. p. 833

Bolthouse, Jon-Mark, Dir, Fond Du Lac Public Library, 32 Sheboygon St, Fond du Lac, WI, 54935. Tel: 920-929-7080. p. 2435

Bolton, Brigette, Br Librn, Plaquemines Parish Library, Belle Chasse Branch, 8442 Hwy 23, Belle Chasse, LA, 70037. Tel: 504-393-0449, 504-394-3570. p. 885

Bolton, Brooke, Dir, Boonville-Warrick County Public Library, 611 W Main St, Boonville, IN, 47601-1544. Tel: 812-897-1500. p. 671

Bolton, Elizabeth, Dir, Blaisdell Memorial Library, 129 Stage Rd, Nottingham, NH, 03290. Tel: 603-679-8484. p. 1377

Bolton, Janine C, Libr Supvr, NASA, 2101 NASA Pkwy, B30A/1077, Houston, TX, 77058. Tel: 281-483-4245. p. 2197

Bolton, Karen, Circ Mgr, Fremont Public Library District, 1170 N Midlothian Rd, Mundelein, IL, 60060. Tel: 847-566-8702. p. 622

Bolton, Michael, Asst Dean, Texas A&M University Libraries, 400 Spence St, College Station, TX, 77843. Tel: 979-845-5751. p. 2157

Bolton, Teresa, Dir, Operations, The Kansas City Public Library, 14 W Tenth St, Kansas City, MO, 64105. Tel: 816-701-3747. p. 1255

Bolton, Tiffany, Supvr, Middlesex County Library, Delaware Branch, 29 Young St, Delaware, ON, N0L 1E0, CANADA. Tel: 519-652-9978. p. 2682

Bolton-Bacon, Tamsin, Assoc Univ Librn, University of Windsor, 401 Sunset Ave, Windsor, ON, N9B 3P4, CANADA. Tel: 519-253-3000, Ext 3197. p. 2704

Boltz, Robin, Dr, Libr Dir, North Carolina School of Science & Mathematics Library, Library, Instructional Technologies & Communications, 1219 Broad St, Durham, NC, 27705. Tel: 919-416-2914. p. 1686

Bomba, Dana, Br Mgr, Chesterfield County Public Library, Chester Branch, 11800 Centre St, Chester, VA, 23831. Tel: 804-751-2275. p. 2312

Bomba-Lewandoski, Vickie Marie, Info Officer, The Connecticut Agricultural Experiment Station, 123 Huntington St, New Haven, CT, 06511-2000. Tel: 203-974-8447. p. 325

Bombace, Giulia, Dir, Montvale Free Public Library, 12 DePiero Dr, Ste 100, Montvale, NJ, 07645. Tel: 201-391-5090. p. 1420

Bombardo, Chris, IT Supvr, Mercer University, Walter F George School of Law, Furman Smith Law Library, 1021 Georgia Ave, Macon, GA, 31201-1001. Tel: 478-301-2182. p. 486

Bombaro, Christine, Assoc Dir, Info Literacy & Res Serv, Dickinson College, 28 N College St, Carlisle, PA, 17013-2311. Tel: 717-245-1397. p. 1919

Bomberger, Bruce, Dr, Archivist/Librn, Lebanon County Historical Society Library, 924 Cumberland St, Lebanon, PA, 17042. Tel: 717-272-1473. p. 1954

Bomhoff, Alexandra, Dir, Elkader Public Library, 130 N Main St, Elkader, IA, 52043. Tel: 563-245-1446. p. 751

Bona, Jay, Circ Coordr, Vermont State University - Lyndon, 1001 College Rd, Lyndonville, VT, 05851. p. 2288

Bonamico, Lee Aura, Ref & ILL Librn, Aldrich Public Library, Six Washington St, Barre, VT, 05641. Tel: 802-476-7550. p. 2278

Bonanno, Rosemary, Exec Dir, Vancouver Island Regional Library, 6250 Hammond Bay Rd, Nanaimo, BC, V9T 6M9, CANADA. Tel: 250-729-2313. p. 2570

Bond, Abby, Youth Serv Librn, Eastpointe Memorial Library, 15875 Oak St, Eastpointe, MI, 48021-2390. Tel: 586-445-5096. p. 1102

Bond, Cory, Br Mgr, Calcasieu Parish Public Library System, Moss Bluff, 261 Parish Rd, Lake Charles, LA, 70611. Tel: 337-721-7128. p. 894

Bond, David, Librn, Val Verde County Library, 300 Spring St, Del Rio, TX, 78840. Tel: 830-774-7595. p. 2169

Bond, Emily, Instruction & Outreach, Pub Serv, Cosumnes River College Library, 8401 Center Pkwy, Sacramento, CA, 95823. Tel: 916-691-7249. p. 208

Bond, Jared, Asst Librn, Belgrade Public Library, 124 Depot Rd, Belgrade, ME, 04917. Tel: 207-495-3508. p. 917

Bond, Jasmine, Dir, Phoenix Public Library District, 15500 Eighth Ave, Phoenix, IL, 60426. Tel: 708-596-5515. p. 635

Bond, Melody, Br Mgr, Uinta County Library, Mountain View Branch, 322 W Second St, Mountain View, WY, 82939. Tel: 307-782-3161. p. 2494

Bond, Michelle, Asst Librn, Ch, Tombigbee Regional Library System, Amory Municipal Library, 401 Second Ave N, Amory, MS, 38821-3514. Tel: 662-256-5261. p. 1235

Bond, Morgan, Res Sharing Librn, State University of New York at Oswego, SUNY Oswego, 7060 State Rte 104, Oswego, NY, 13126-3514. Tel: 315-312-3562. p. 1613

Bond, Natalie, Govt Info Librn, University of Montana Missoula, 32 Campus Dr, Missoula, MT, 59812. Tel: 406-243-6866. p. 1300

Bond, Paul, Instruction & Outreach Librn, SUNY Broome Community College, 907 Front St, Binghamton, NY, 13905-1328. Tel: 607-778-5239. p. 1494

Bond, Trevor James, Assoc Dean, Digital Initiatives, Spec Coll, Washington State University Libraries, 100 Dairy Rd, Pullman, WA, 99164. Tel: 509-335-6693. p. 2374

Bondareff, Hyla, Electronic Res Librn, Washington University Libraries, Law Library, Washington Univ Sch Law, Anheuser-Busch Hall, One Brookings Dr, Campus Box 1171, Saint Louis, MO, 63130. Tel: 314-935-6434. p. 1277

Bonde, Marie, Customer Serv Coordr, Lester Public Library, 1001 Adams St, Two Rivers, WI, 54241. Tel: 920-793-7105. p. 2482

Bondi, Diane, Asst Dir, Merrick Library, 2279 Merrick Ave, Merrick, NY, 11566. Tel: 516-377-6112, Ext 102. p. 1570

Bondi, Joseph, Instruction & Research Mgr, Broadview Public Library District, 2226 S 16th Ave, Broadview, IL, 60155. Tel: 708-345-1325, Ext 18. p. 545

Bonds, Laura, Children's Spec, Educ Spec, Cranbury Public Library, 30 Park Place W, Cranbury, NJ, 08512. Tel: 609-799-6992. p. 1397

Bondy, Christy, Asst Dir, H Leslie Perry Memorial Library, 205 Breckenridge St, Henderson, NC, 27536. Tel: 252-438-3316. p. 1695

Bondy, Christy M, Dir, Warren County Memorial Library, 119 South Front St, Warrenton, NC, 27589. Tel: 252-257-4990, Ext 1050. p. 1720

Bondy, Jennifer L, Acad Serv Officer IV, Wayne State University, 106 Kresge Library, Detroit, MI, 48202. Tel: 313-577-2523. p. 2787

Bone, Jennifer, Ref Librn, Southwestern Illinois College, 2500 Carlyle Ave, Belleville, IL, 62221. Tel: 618-235-2700, Ext 5204. p. 541

Bonell, Jo, Ms, Dir, Des Plaines Public Library, 1501 Ellinwood St, Des Plaines, IL, 60016. Tel: 847-827-5551. p. 578

Bonelli, Deborah, Dir, Libr Serv, Saint Barnabas Hospital, 4487 Third Ave, Bronx, NY, 10457-2594. Tel: 718-960-6113, Ext 6466. p. 1500

Bonen, Kim, Ad, K O Lee Aberdeen Public Library, 215 S E Fourth Ave, Aberdeen, SD, 57401. Tel: 605-626-7097. p. 2073

Bonen, Kim, Digital Res Coordr, Electronic Res, South Dakota State Library, 800 Governors Dr, Pierre, SD, 57501-2294. Tel: 605-295-3174. p. 2080

Boneno, Jennifer, Br Mgr, Forsyth County Public Library, Reynolda Manor, 2839 Fairlawn Dr, Winston-Salem, NC, 27106. Tel: 336-703-2960. p. 1725

Bonet, Maria, Electronic Res Librn, Prince George's Community College Library, 301 Largo Rd, Largo, MD, 20774-2199. Tel: 301-546-0471. p. 970

Bonet, Mary Beth, Cat, Berea College, 100 Campus Dr, Berea, KY, 40404. Tel: 859-985-3283. p. 849

Bonfield, Arthur E, Assoc Dean, Res, University of Iowa Libraries, College of Law Library, 200 Boyd Law Bldg, Iowa City, IA, 52242-1166. Tel: 319-335-9020. p. 761

Bonfield, Brett, Chief Operating Officer, Public Library of Cincinnati & Hamilton County, 800 Vine St, Cincinnati, OH, 45202-2009. Tel: 513-369-6941. p. 1761

Bonfiglio, Audra, Head, Children's Servx, Woodbury Public Library, 33 Delaware St, Woodbury, NJ, 08096. Tel: 856-845-2611. p. 1456

Bonfiglio, Bryan, Head, Digital Serv, Gloucester County Library System, 389 Wolfert Station Rd, Mullica Hill, NJ, 08062. Tel: 856-223-6017. p. 1423

Bongers, Desiree M, Dir, Ripon Public Library, 120 Jefferson St, Ripon, WI, 54971. Tel: 920-748-6160. p. 2474

Bongers, Joe, Adult Serv Supvr, Menasha Public Library, 440 First St, Menasha, WI, 54952-3143. Tel: 920-967-3696. p. 2455

Bongolo, Anna, Libr Dir, Greenfield Public Library, 412 Main St, Greenfield, MA, 01301. Tel: 413-772-1544. p. 1022

Boni, Bethyn A, Dir, New York Chiropractic College Library, 2360 State Rte 89, Seneca Falls, NY, 13148-9460. Tel: 315-568-3244. p. 1639

Bonianian, Zohreh, Libr Supvr, Rutgers University Libraries, Archibald Stevens Alexander Library, 169 College Ave, New Brunswick, NJ, 08901-1163. Tel: 848-932-6056. p. 1424

Bonifacic, Lisa, Assoc Librn, Andrew W Mellon Foundation, 140 E 62nd St, New York, NY, 10065. Tel: 212-838-8400. p. 1591

Bonifacio, Ashley, Br Supvr, Berkeley Public Library, Tarea Hall Pittman South Branch, 1901 Russell St, Berkeley, CA, 94703. Tel: 510-981-6260. p. 121

Bonilla-Madrigal, Luis, Cat, Supreme Court Library of Puerto Rico, Ave Munoz Rivera Parada 8 1/2 Puerta de Tierra, Parque Munoz Rivera, San Juan, PR, 00902. Tel: 787-723-6033, Ext 2163. p. 2514

Bonjack, Stephanie, Head Music Libr, University of Colorado Boulder, Howard B Waltz Music Library, Imig Music Bldg, 2nd Flr N, 1020 18th St, Boulder, CO, 80302. Tel: 303-492-9895. p. 268

Bonk, Neil, Head, Tech Serv, Elmhurst Public Library, 125 S Prospect Ave, Elmhurst, IL, 60126-3298. Tel: 630-279-8696. p. 585

Bonk, Sharon B, Dir, Libr Serv, Benjamin Franklin Institute of Technology, Franklin Union Bldg, Rm U108, 41 Berkeley St, Boston, MA, 02116. Tel: 617-588-1356. p. 990

Bonkowski, Andrea, Br Librn, Evergreen Regional Library, Riverton Branch, 56 Laura Ave, Riverton, MB, R0C 2R0, CANADA. Tel: 204-378-2988. p. 2587

Bonman, Trina, Assoc Dir, Marshall Public Library, 113 S Garfield Ave, Pocatello, ID, 83204. Tel: 208-232-1263. p. 529

Bonman, Trina, Treas, Library Consortium of Eastern Idaho, 110 N State, Rigby, ID, 83442-1313. Tel: 208-745-8231. p. 2764

Bonn, Maria, Assoc Prof, MSLIS & CAS Program Director, University of Illinois at Urbana-Champaign, Library & Information Science Bldg, 501 E Daniel St, Champaign, IL, 61820-6211. Tel: 217-333-3280. p. 2784

Bonneau, Annie, Tech Serv, Bibliothèque Raymond-Laberge, 25 Maple Blvd, Chateauguay, QC, J6J 3P7, CANADA. Tel: 450-698-3080. p. 2710

Bonneau, Janet, Dir, Grand Isle Free Library, Ten Hyde Rd, Grand Isle, VT, 05458. Tel: 802-372-4797. p. 2285

Bonner, Christina, Research, Learning & Assessment Librn, Web Serv Librn, Ohio Dominican University Library, 1216 Sunbury Rd, Columbus, OH, 43219. Tel: 614-251-4752. p. 1774

Bonner, Jo, Br Head, Lake County Public Library, Hobart Branch, 100 Main St, Hobart, IN, 46342-4391. Tel: 219-942-2243. p. 705

Bonner, Sarah, Dir, Libr Serv, Chowan University, One University Pl, Murfreesboro, NC, 27855. Tel: 252-398-6439. p. 1705

Bonner, Scott, Dir, Ferguson Municipal Public Library, 35 N Florissant Rd, Ferguson, MO, 63135. Tel: 314-521-4820. p. 1246

Bonnett, Polly, Dir, Mesa Public Library, 64 E First St, Mesa, AZ, 85201-6768. Tel: 480-644-3100. p. 66

Bonnette, Becky, Ch Serv Librn, Kling Memorial Library, 708 Seventh St, Grundy Center, IA, 50638-1430. Tel: 319-825-3607. p. 757

Bonney, John, Dir, Neptune Public Library, 25 Neptune Blvd, Neptune, NJ, 07753-1125. Tel: 732-775-8241. p. 1423

Bonney, Nancey, Circ & ILL, Southwest Virginia Community College Library, Russell Hall, 599 Community College Rd, Cedar Bluff, VA, 24609. Tel: 276-964-7265. p. 2309

Bonney, Pamela Fesq, Libr Dir, Winslow Public Library, 136 Halifax St, Winslow, ME, 04901. Tel: 207-872-1978. p. 946

Bonnici, Laurie, Dr, Assoc Prof, University of Alabama, 7035 Gorgas Library, Campus Box 870252, Tuscaloosa, AL, 35487-0252. Tel: 205-348-4610. p. 2781

Bonsall, Dan, Head, Digital Serv, Anderson County Library, 300 N McDuffie St, Anderson, SC, 29621-5643. Tel: 864-260-4500. p. 2046

Bonser, Julie, Ch Serv, Eastern Monroe Public Library, 1002 N Ninth St, Stroudsburg, PA, 18360. Tel: 570-421-0800. p. 2010

Bontekoe, Karen, Librn, Kaweah Delta Health Care District Library, 400 W Mineral King Ave, Visalia, CA, 93291-6263. Tel: 559-624-2000. p. 257

Bontenbal, Kevin, Ref Librn, Cuesta College Library, Hwy 1, San Luis Obispo, CA, 93401. Tel: 805-546-3117. p. 233

Bontrager, Jason, Librn, Blinn College Library, 800 Blinn Blvd, Brenham, TX, 77833. Tel: 979-830-4250. p. 2149

Bonzo, Ruth, Dir, Nephi Public Library, 21 E 100 N, Nephi, UT, 84648. Tel: 435-623-1312. p. 2267

Boodhoo, Compton, Library Computer Technology, Queensborough Community College, City University of New York, 222-05 56th Ave, Bayside, NY, 11364-1497. Tel: 718-631-6672. p. 1491

Book, Andrea, Dir, Lasalle Parish Library, 3165 N First St, Jena, LA, 71342. Tel: 318-992-5675. p. 891

Book, Ellen, Mgr, Miami-Dade Public Library System, Country Walk Branch, 15433 SW 137th Ave, Miami, FL, 33177. Tel: 786-293-4577. p. 423

Book, Ellen, Mgr, Miami-Dade Public Library System, Pinecrest Branch, 5835 SW 111 St, Pinecrest, FL, 33156. Tel: 305-668-4571. p. 424

Booker, Bera, Asst Librn, Southeastern Technical College Library, 346 Kite Rd, Swainsboro, GA, 30401. Tel: 478-289-2322. p. 498

Booker, Carolyn, Dir, Lewisville Public Library System, 1197 W Main St, Lewisville, TX, 75067. Tel: 972-219-3571. p. 2211

Booker, David, III, Commun Libr Mgr, Queens Library, Lefferts Community Library, 103-34 Lefferts Blvd, Richmond Hill, NY, 11419. Tel: 718-843-5950. p. 1555

Booker, Edward, Br Mgr, Orange County Library System, Alafaya Branch, 12000 E Colonial Dr, Orlando, FL, 32826. p. 431

Booker, Edward, Br Mgr, Orange County Library System, Herndon Branch, 4324 E Colonial Dr, Orlando, FL, 32803. p. 431

Booker, Kelly, Libr Asst, Weil, Gotshal & Manges LLP, 2001 M St NW, Ste 600, Washington, DC, 20036. Tel: 202-682-7000, 202-682-7117. p. 381

Booker, Melissa, Coll Librn, Kirbyville Public Library, 210 S Elizabeth St, Kirbyville, TX, 75956. Tel: 409-423-4653. p. 2207

Bookman, Quanah Monique, Dir, Mickey Reily Public Library, 604 S Matthews St, Corrigan, TX, 75939. Tel: 936-398-4156. p. 2161

Books, Stacy L, Dir, Lebanon Public Library, 101 S Broadway, Lebanon, OH, 45036. Tel: 513-932-2665. p. 1795

Boomhower, Daniel, Dir, Harvard Library, Dumbarton Oaks Library & Archives, 1703 32nd St NW, Washington, MA, 20007. Tel: 202-339-6400, Ext 6968. p. 1006

Boon, Belinda, Dr, Assoc Prof, Kent State University, 314 University Library, 1125 Risman Dr, Kent, OH, 44242-0001. Tel: 330-672-2782. p. 2790

Boone, Amy, Librn, Conran Memorial Library, 302 E Main St, Hayti, MO, 63851. Tel: 573-359-0599. p. 1248

Boone, Charlie, Info Tech, Spec Projects, Blauvelt Free Library, 541 Western Hwy, Blauvelt, NY, 10913. Tel: 845-359-2811. p. 1494

Boone, Jason, Circ Supvr, North Carolina Wesleyan University, 3400 N Wesleyan Blvd, Rocky Mount, NC, 27804. Tel: 252-985-5350. p. 1713

Boone, John, Health Sciences & Graduate Studies Librn, Harding University, 915 E Market St, Searcy, AR, 72149-5615. Tel: 501-279-4376. p. 109

Boone, Kimball, Libr Mgr, Virginia Beach Public Library, , 2425 Nimmo Pkwy, Judicial Ctr, Court Support Bldg 10B, Virginia Beach, VA, 23456. Tel: 757-385-6386. p. 2351

Boone, Laurie, Spec Coll Librn, Yuma County Free Library District, 2951 S 21st Dr, Yuma, AZ, 85364. Tel: 928-373-6517. p. 85

Boone, Laurie, Spec Coll Librn, Yuma County Free Library District, Heritage Branch, 350 Third Ave, Yuma, AZ, 85364. Tel: 928-373-6486. p. 86

Boone, Meg, Asst Librn, Millville Free Public Library, 169 Main St, Millville, MA, 01529. Tel: 508-883-1887. p. 1036

Boone, Nancy, Librn, Ohio School for the Deaf Library, 500 Morse Rd, Columbus, OH, 43214. Tel: 614-728-1414. p. 1774

Boone, Regina, Br Mgr, Memphis Public Library, Levi Branch, 3676 Hwy 61 S (S 3rd St), Memphis, TN, 38109-8296. Tel: 901-415-2773. p. 2113

Booth, Ann, Librn, Weber County Library System, North Branch, 475 E 2600 North, North Ogden, UT, 84414-2833. Tel: 801-782-8800. p. 2268

Booth, Barbara, Br Mgr, Richmond Public Library, Belmont Branch, 3100 Ellwood Ave, Richmond, VA, 23221. Tel: 804-646-1139. p. 2341

Booth, Brian, Libr Dir, Nashville Public Library, 114 W Church St, Nashville, NC, 27856. Tel: 252-459-2106. p. 1705

Booth, Cheryl, Dr, Assoc Dir, Reference & Research, Nova Southeastern University Libraries, Panza Maurer Law Library, Shepard Broad College of Law, Leo Goodwin Sr Bldg, 3305 College Ave, Davie, FL, 33314. Tel: 954-262-6215. p. 402

Booth, Cindy, Mgr, Oregon State Correctional Institution Library, 3405 Deer Park Dr SE, Salem, OR, 97310-3985. Tel: 503-373-7523. p. 1896

Booth, George, Law Librn II, Connecticut Judicial Branch Law Libraries, Danbury Law Library, Danbury Courthouse, 146 White St, Danbury, CT, 06810. Tel: 203-207-8625. p. 316

Booth, Germaine, Ch Serv, Massapequa Public Library, Central Avenue, 523 Central Ave, Massapequa, NY, 11758. Tel: 516-798-4607. p. 1569

Booth, H Austin, Ms, Dean, Division of Libraries, New York University, 70 Washington Sq S, New York, NY, 10012-1019. Tel: 212-998-2500. p. 1599

Booth, Judy, Libr Dir, Fullerton Public Library, 353 W Commonwealth Ave, Fullerton, CA, 92832. Tel: 714-738-6333. p. 147

Booth, Michael, Dir, North Judson-Wayne Township Public Library, 208 Keller Ave, North Judson, IN, 46366. Tel: 574-896-2841. p. 710

Booth, Sarah, Asst Dir, Montgomery County Memorial Library System, 104 I-45 N, Conroe, TX, 77301-2720. Tel: 936-788-8377, Ext 6236. p. 2159

Booth, Todd, Br Mgr, Saint Johns County Public Library System, 6670 US 1 South, Saint Augustine, FL, 32086. Tel: 904-827-6913. p. 440

Booth, Tomaz, Sr Libr Tech, Canadian Grain Commission Library, 801-303 Main St, Winnipeg, MB, R3C 3G8, CANADA. Tel: 431-337-6271. p. 2592

Booth-Moyle, Gillian, Br Mgr, Caledon Public Library, 150 Queen St S, Bolton, ON, L7E 1E3, CANADA. Tel: 905-857-1400, Ext 217. p. 2631

Boothby, Denise, Chief of Staff, Denver Public Library, Ten W 14th Ave Pkwy, Denver, CO, 80204-2731. Tel: 720-865-1111. p. 275

Boothe, Elizabeth, Info Serv Librn, Central Virginia Community College Library, Bedford Hall, Rm 3100, 3506 Wards Rd, Lynchburg, VA, 24502-2498. Tel: 434-832-7750. p. 2330

Boothe, Scott, Librn, Kaiser-Permanente Medical Center, 2425 Geary Blvd, Mezzanine M150, San Francisco, CA, 94115. Tel: 415-833-2000. p. 225

Bootman, Maggie, Dir, Mitchell County Public Library, 340 Oak St, Colorado City, TX, 79512. Tel: 325-728-3968. p. 2158

Boozer, Rhonda, Resource Sharing Coord, Clayton State University Library, 2000 Clayton State Blvd, Morrow, GA, 30260. Tel: 678-466-4325. p. 491

Boragine, Becky A, Dir, Lincoln Public Library, 145 Old River Rd, Lincoln, RI, 02865. Tel: 401-333-2422, Ext 13. p. 2034

Boras, David, Circ Serv, Blue Island Public Library, 2433 York St, Blue Island, IL, 60406-2011. Tel: 708-388-1078, Ext 15. p. 543

Borawski, Christopher, Br Mgr, Montgomery County Public Libraries, Chevy Chase Library, 8005 Connecticut Ave, Chevy Chase, MD, 20815-5997. Tel: 240-773-9581. p. 974

Borch, Robert, Asst Librn, Priest Lake Public Library, 28769 Hwy 57, Priest Lake, ID, 83856. Tel: 208-443-2454. p. 529

Borchardt, Meredith, Circ Supvr, Wartburg College Library, 100 Wartburg Blvd, Waverly, IA, 50677-0903. Tel: 319-352-8500. p. 789

Borchers, Margaret, Dir, Edith Wheeler Memorial Library, 733 Monroe Tpk, Monroe, CT, 06468. Tel: 203-452-2850. p. 323

Borchert, James, Br Librn, Siouxland Libraries, Caille Branch, 4100 Carnegie Circle, Sioux Falls, SD, 57106-2320. Tel: 605-367-8144. p. 2082

Borchert, James, Br Librn, Siouxland Libraries, Oak View Branch, 3700 E Third St, Sioux Falls, SD, 57103. Tel: 605-367-8060. p. 2082

Borchert, Theresa, Electronic Res Librn, Concordia College, 901 S Eighth St, Moorhead, MN, 56562. Tel: 218-299-3235. p. 1187

Borck, Cathy Jean, Dir, Kilbourn Public Library, 620 Elm St, Wisconsin Dells, WI, 53965. Tel: 608-254-2146. p. 2489

Bordeleau, Krista, Head, Teen Serv, Mkt, Pelham Public Library, 24 Village Green, Pelham, NH, 03076. Tel: 603-635-7581. p. 1377

Borden, Amanda, Dir, Hoover Public Library, 200 Municipal Dr, Hoover, AL, 35216. Tel: 205-444-7810. p. 21

Borden, Charmaine, Regional Librn, Nova Scotia Community College, Truro Campus Library, McCarthy Hall, 36 Arthur St, Truro, NS, B2N 1X5, CANADA. Tel: 902-893-5326. p. 2620

Borden, Dennis, Asst Dir, Drake State Community & Technical College, 3421 Meridan St N, Huntsville, AL, 35811-1544. Tel: 256-551-3120, 256-551-5218. p. 21

Borden, Margaret, Asst Dir, Falmouth Public Library, East Falmouth Branch, 310 E Falmouth Hwy, East Falmouth, MA, 02536. Tel: 508-548-6340. p. 1018

Borden, Meg, Asst Dir, Falmouth Public Library, 300 Main St, Falmouth, MA, 02540. Tel: 508-457-2555. p. 1018

Borden, Meg, Asst Dir, Falmouth Public Library, North Falmouth Branch, Six Chester St, North Falmouth, MA, 02556. Tel: 508-563-2922. p. 1018

Borden, Pam, Law Librn, Law Society of Prince Edward Island Library, 42 Water St, Charlottetown, PE, C1A 1A4, CANADA. Tel: 902-368-6099. p. 2707

Borden, Sara, Tech Serv Mgr, Logansport-Cass County Public Library, 616 E Broadway, Logansport, IN, 46947. Tel: 574-753-6383. p. 703

Borden, Tammy, Dir, Freeport District Library, 208 S State St, Freeport, MI, 49325-9759. Tel: 616-765-5181. p. 1108

Borden, Tara, Asst Dir, East Lyme Public Library, 39 Society Rd, Niantic, CT, 06357. Tel: 860-739-6926. p. 330

Border, Peggy, Libr Mgr, Fruitville Public Library, 100 Apex Rd, Sarasota, FL, 34240. Tel: 941-861-2500. p. 442

Borders, Sherryl, Dir, Jefferson County Public Law Library, Old Jail Bldg, Ste 240, 514 W Liberty St, Louisville, KY, 40202. Tel: 502-574-5943. p. 865

Borders, Susan, Dir, Darby Free Library, 1001 Main St, Darby, PA, 19023-0169. Tel: 610-586-7310. p. 1926

Borderud, Jennifer, Assoc Librn, Dir, Baylor University Libraries, Armstrong Browning Library & Museum, 710 Speight Ave, Waco, TX, 76798. Tel: 254-710-3825. p. 2253

Borelli, Alissa, Mgr, Northern Onondaga Public Library, Brewerton Branch, 5440 Bennett St, Brewerton, NY, 13029. Tel: 315-676-7484. p. 1518

Boren, Melody, Youth Serv, Amarillo Public Library, 413 E Fourth Ave, Amarillo, TX, 79101. Tel: 806-378-3054. p. 2134

Borene, Beth, Mgr, Hockessin Public Library, 1023 Valley Rd, Hockessin, DE, 19707. Tel: 302-239-5160. p. 353

Borene, Beth, Mgr, Kirkwood Library, 6000 Kirkwood Hwy, Wilmington, DE, 19808. Tel: 302-995-7663. p. 357

Borer, Ann, Librn, Douglas County District Court, Rm H07 Civic Ctr, Harney Street Level, 1819 Farnam St, Omaha, NE, 68183. Tel: 402-444-7174. p. 1328

Borezo, Patrick, Dir, Hadley Public Library, 50 Middle St, Hadley, MA, 01035. Tel: 413-584-7451. p. 1023

Borgen, Tamara, Librn, Alaska State Court Law Library, Fairbanks Branch, 101 Lacey St, Fairbanks, AK, 99701. Tel: 907-452-9241. p. 42

Borges Ocasio, Elizabeth, Ref Supvr, Nevins Memorial Library, 305 Broadway, Methuen, MA, 01844-6898. Tel: 978-686-4080. p. 1035

Borges, Stephanie, Br Supvr, Kern County Library, Eleanor N Wilson Branch, 1901 Wilson Rd, Bakersfield, CA, 93304-5612. Tel: 661-834-4044. p. 120

Borin, Jill, Head, Archives, Widener University, One University Pl, Chester, PA, 19013. Tel: 610-499-4067. p. 1921

Boring, Andrew L, Dir, Tulare County Public Law Library, County Courthouse, Rm 1, 221 S Mooney Blvd, Visalia, CA, 93291-4544. Tel: 559-636-4600. p. 257

Boring, Cody, Exec Dir, Rocky Mount Historical Association Library, 200 Hyder Hill Rd, Piney Flats, TN, 37686-4630. Tel: 423-538-7396. p. 2124

Boring, Michael, Librn, University of South Dakota, I D Weeks Library, 414 E Clark St, Vermillion, SD, 57069. Tel: 605-658-3364. p. 2084

Boris, LuAnn, Dir, Libr Serv, Walsh University, 2020 E Maple St NW, North Canton, OH, 44720-3336. Tel: 330-490-7185. p. 1809

Borisovets, Natalie, Head, Pub Serv, Rutgers University Libraries, John Cotton Dana Library, 185 University Ave, Newark, NJ, 07102. Tel: 973-353-5222. p. 1428

Borkowski, Sadie, Br Mgr, Saint Joseph County Public Library, Virginia M Tutt Branch, 2223 S Miami St, South Bend, IN, 46613. Tel: 574-282-4637. p. 719

Borland, Karin, Mgr, Libr Serv, Winnipeg Public Library, 251 Donald St, Winnipeg, MB, R3C 3P5, CANADA. Tel: 204-986-6462. p. 2596

Borman, Sherrie, Dir, Oldham County Public Library, 914 Main St, Vega, TX, 79092. Tel: 806-267-2635. p. 2251

Bormet, Noreen, Dir, Peotone Public Library District, 515 N First St, Peotone, IL, 60468. Tel: 708-258-3436. p. 635

Bornhoft, Kathy, Libr Dir, Heginbotham Library, 539 S Baxter St, Holyoke, CO, 80734. Tel: 970-854-2597. p. 286

Bornstein, Paula, Circ, Lindenhurst Memorial Library, One Lee Ave, Lindenhurst, NY, 11757-5399. Tel: 631-957-7755. p. 1563

Boroff, Cindy, Tech Serv Mgr, Danville Public Library, 319 N Vermilion St, Danville, IL, 61832. Tel: 217-477-5223, Ext 119. p. 575

Borowiec, Josselyn, Ch Serv, Corfu Free Library, Seven Maple Ave, Corfu, NY, 14036. Tel: 585-599-3321. p. 1522

Borowiec, Josselyn, Libr Mgr, Hollwedel Memorial Library, Five Woodrow Dr, Pavilion, NY, 14525. Tel: 585-584-8843. p. 1615

Borowske, Kate, Ref (Info Servs), Hamline University, Bush Memorial Library, 1536 Hewitt, Saint Paul, MN, 55104. Tel: 651-523-2375. p. 1199

Borras, Katya, Sr Mgr, Bibliotheque Publique de Pointe-Claire, 100 ave Douglas-Shand, Pointe-Claire, QC, H9R 4V1, CANADA. Tel: 514-630-1217. p. 2728

Borrell, Karen, Cat/Acq Tech, Kutztown University, 15200 Kutztown Rd, Bldg 5, Kutztown, PA, 19530. Tel: 610-683-4480. p. 1949

Borsody, Rosemarie, Pub Serv, Lee Library Association, 100 Main St, Lee, MA, 01238-1688. Tel: 413-243-0385. p. 1027

Borst, Barbara, Coll Develop Coordr, Colorado Mesa University, 1100 North Ave, Grand Junction, CO, 81501. Tel: 970-248-1872. p. 283

Bort, Kathleen, Dir, Otis Library & Museum, 48 N Main Rd, Otis, MA, 01253. Tel: 413-269-0100, Ext 117, 413-269-0109. p. 1045

Borthakur, Papari, Libr Mgr, Irricana & Rural Municipal Library, 226 Second St, Irricana, AB, T0M 1B0, CANADA. Tel: 403-935-4818. p. 2544

Bortz, Merry, Head, Tech Serv, Del Mar College, 101 Baldwin Blvd, Corpus Christi, TX, 78404. Tel: 361-698-1951. p. 2160

Boruff-Jones, Polly, Dean, Univ Libr, Oakland University Library, 100 Library Dr, Rochester, MI, 48309-4479. Tel: 248-370-2471. p. 1144

Borycz, David, Asst Univ Librn, Admin & Policy Develop, The University of Chicago Library, 1100 E 57th St, Chicago, IL, 60637-1502. Tel: 773-702-2494. p. 569

Borysiewicz, Thomas J, Ad, Bethel Public Library, 189 Greenwood Ave, Bethel, CT, 06801-2598. Tel: 203-794-8756. p. 302

Bos, Donna, Dir, Inwood Public Library, 103 S Main St, Inwood, IA, 51240. Tel: 712-753-4814. p. 760

Bosanko, Ruby, Librn, Marcus P Beebe Memorial Library, 120 Main St, Ipswich, SD, 57451. Tel: 605-426-6707. p. 2077

Bosben, Pam, Dir, Rosemary Garfoot Public Library, 2107 Julius St, Cross Plains, WI, 53528. Tel: 608-798-3881. p. 2429

Bosch, Eileen, Assoc Dean, Bowling Green State University Libraries, 1001 E Wooster St, Bowling Green, OH, 43403-0170. p. 1752

Bosch, Nigel, Asst Prof, University of Illinois at Urbana-Champaign, Library & Information Science Bldg, 501 E Daniel St, Champaign, IL, 61820-6211. Tel: 217-333-3280. p. 2784

Boschert, Lori, Br Mgr, Saint Louis County Library, Grant's View Branch, 9700 Musick Rd, Saint Louis, MO, 63123-3935. Tel: 314-994-3300, Ext 3850. p. 1274

Boschman, Suzie, Dir, Dudley Township Public Library, 105 N Sequoyah St, Satanta, KS, 67870. Tel: 620-649-2213. p. 835

Bosco, David, Circ Serv Coordr, Saint Norbert College, 400 Third St, De Pere, WI, 54115. Tel: 920-403-3293. p. 2430

Bose, Arpita, Dir, New York Presbyterian Brooklyn Methodist Hospital, Wesley House, Rm 2H, 501 Sixth St, Brooklyn, NY, 11215. Tel: 718-780-5197. p. 1505

Bose, Matthew, Asst Dir, Head, Tech Serv, Concord Public Library, 45 Green St, Concord, NH, 03301. Tel: 603-230-3686. p. 1358

Bosh, Jeffrey V, Dir, Sidley Austin LLP, 1501 K St NW, Washington, DC, 20005. Tel: 202-736-8525. p. 374

Boska, Amanda, Adult & Teen Serv, Colfax-Perry Township Public Library, 207 S Clark St, Colfax, IN, 46035. Tel: 765-324-2915. p. 675

Bosket, Jamie, Pres & Chief Exec Officer, Virginia Historical Society Library, 428 North Blvd, Richmond, VA, 23220. Tel: 804-340-1800. p. 2344

Bosky, Amanda, Adult Serv, Stoughton Public Library, 304 S Fourth St, Stoughton, WI, 53589. Tel: 608-873-6281. p. 2479

Bosler, Sarah, Pub Serv Librn, Citrus College, 1000 W Foothill Blvd, Glendora, CA, 91741-1899. Tel: 626-914-8640. p. 149

Bosley, Katie, Youth Serv, Pierson Library, 5376 Shelburne Rd, Shelburne, VT, 05482. Tel: 802-985-5124. p. 2294

Bosman, Ellen, Head, Tech Serv, New Mexico State University Library, 2911 McFie Circle, Las Cruces, NM, 88003. Tel: 575-646-1723. p. 1471

Bosman, Renee, Govt Info Librn, University of North Carolina at Chapel Hill, 208 Raleigh St, CB 3916, Chapel Hill, NC, 27515. Tel: 919-962-1053. p. 1678

Boss, Anna Maria, Head Librn, German Historical Institute Library, 1607 New Hampshire Ave NW, Washington, DC, 20009-2562. Tel: 202-387-3355. p. 368

Boss, Benjamin, Content Mgr, Scholarly Communications, Ferris State University, 17 Fountain St NW, Grand Rapids, MI, 49503-3002. Tel: 616-259-1126. p. 1110

Boss, Chelsey, Asst Dir, Adrian District Library, 143 E Maumee St, Adrian, MI, 49221-2773. Tel: 517-265-2265. p. 1075

Boss, Emily, Cat & Metadata, University of Nevada-Reno, 1664 N Virginia St, Mailstop 0322, Reno, NV, 89557-0322. Tel: 775-682-5614. p. 1349

Boss, Katherine, Librn for Journalism, Media Culture & Communications, New York University, 70 Washington Sq S, New York, NY, 10012-1019. Tel: 212-998-2666. p. 1599

Boss, Sam, Libr Dir, Vermont State University - Lyndon, 1001 College Rd, Lyndonville, VT, 05851. Tel: 802-626-6446. p. 2288

Boss, Stephen, IT Librn, University of Wyoming Libraries, 13th & Ivinson Ave, 1000 E University Ave, Laramie, WY, 82071. Tel: 307-766-4948. p. 2496

Bossaller, Jenny, Assoc Prof, University of Missouri-Columbia, 303 Townsend Hall, Columbia, MO, 65211. Tel: 573-882-4546. p. 2787

Bosse, Melanie, Chef de Section, Bibliotheques de Montreal, Saint-Pierre, 183 rue des Erables, Lachine, QC, H8R 1B1, CANADA. Tel: 514-872-5077. p. 2721

Bosse, Melanie, Chef de Section, Bibliotheques de Montreal, Saul-Bellow, 3100 rue Saint-Antoine, Lachine, QC, H8S 4B8, CANADA. Tel: 514 872-5077. p. 2721

Bost, Cathy, Libr Asst, West Georgia Technical College, Carroll Campus, 500 Technology Pkwy, Carrollton, GA, 30117. Tel: 770-836-4711. p. 502

Bostelle, Timothy, Head, Libr Info Tech, University of Washington Libraries, Tacoma Library, 1900 Commerce St, Box 358460, Tacoma, WA, 98402-3100. Tel: 253-692-4650. p. 2382

Bostic, Donna, Librn, Clark Hill PLC Library, 901 Main St, Ste 6000, Dallas, TX, 75202. Tel: 214-651-4300. p. 2163

Boston, Jaymey, Libr Dir, Gentry Public Library, 105 E Main St, Gentry, AR, 72734. Tel: 479-736-2054. p. 96

Bostwick, Dawn S, Dir, Pub Libr Serv, Nassau County Public Library System, 25 N Fourth St, Fernandina Beach, FL, 32034-4123. Tel: 904-530-6500, Ext 1. p. 395

Bostwick, Debbie, Br Mgr, Manistee County Library System, Kaleva Branch, 14618 Walta St, Kaleva, MI, 49645. Tel: 231-362-3178. p. 1129

Boswell, Allison, Youth Librn, Carnegie Evans Public Library Albia Public, 203 Benton Ave E, Albia, IA, 52531-2036. Tel: 641-932-2469. p. 729

Boswell, Catherine, Syst Serv, Antioch University New England Library, 40 Avon St, Keene, NH, 03431. Tel: 603-283-2400. p. 1369

Boswell, Catherine, Syst Adminr, Antioch University Library, 900 Dayton St, Yellow Springs, OH, 45387. Tel: 603-762-8571. p. 1835

Boswell, Tristan, Libr Dir, South Milwaukee Public Library, 1907 Tenth Ave, South Milwaukee, WI, 53172. Tel: 414-768-8195. p. 2478

Bosworth, LaKeisha, Youth Serv Coordr, Ouachita Parish Public Library, 1800 Stubbs Ave, Monroe, LA, 71201. Tel: 318-327-1490. p. 898

Boteler, Jessyka, Dir, Tonopah Library District, 167 S Central St, Tonopah, NV, 89049. Tel: 775-482-3374. p. 1351

Botello, Yolanda, Dir, Libr Serv, Mansfield Public Library, 104 S Wisteria St, Mansfield, TX, 76063. Tel: 817-728-3690. p. 2215

Botero, Cecilia, Dean of Libr, University of Mississippi, One Library Loop, University, MS, 38677. Tel: 662-915-7091. p. 1234

Botluk, Diana, Assoc Dir, Head, Pub Serv, Barry University, 6441 E Colonial Dr, Orlando, FL, 32807. Tel: 321-206-5727. p. 430

Bott, Corrie, Librn, Santa Barbara City College, 721 Cliff Dr, Santa Barbara, CA, 93109-2394. Tel: 805-730-4430. p. 240

Bott, David, Mgr, Info Tech, Network Serv, St Catharines Public Library, 54 Church St, St. Catharines, ON, L2R 7K2, CANADA. Tel: 905-688-6103. p. 2680

Bott, Erin, Libr Dir, Morgan County Library, 50 N 100 West, Morgan, UT, 84050. Tel: 801-829-3481. p. 2267

Bott, Kristen, Ref Librn, Fruitville Public Library, 100 Apex Rd, Sarasota, FL, 34240. Tel: 941-861-2500. p. 442

Bott, Natalie, Libr Dir, Moriarty Community Library, 202 S Broadway, Moriarty, NM, 87035. Tel: 505-832-2513. p. 1473

Botte, Lisa, Supvr, Tech Serv, Billerica Public Library, 15 Concord Rd, Billerica, MA, 01821. Tel: 978-671-0948, 978-671-0949. p. 989

Botti, Aldo, Ref (Info Servs), Central Arkansas Library System, 100 Rock St, Little Rock, AR, 72201-4698. Tel: 501-918-3000. p. 101

Botticelli, Jill, Archivist & Spec Coll Librn, Southwestern Baptist Theological Seminary Libraries, 2001 W Seminary Dr, Fort Worth, TX, 76115-2157. Tel: 817-923-1921, Ext 4000. p. 2180

Botticelli, Peter, Assoc Prof, Simmons University, 300 The Fenway, Boston, MA, 02115. Tel: 617-521-2800. p. 2786

Bottino, Marlane, Archivist, Old York Historical Society Research Center, 22 Shapleigh Rd, Kittery, ME, 03904. Tel: 207-361-3556. p. 929

Bottle, Ina, Libr Spec, Clemson University Libraries, Gunnin Architecture Library, 2-112 Lee Hall, Clemson University, Clemson, SC, 29634. Tel: 864-656-3933. p. 2052

Bottoms, Ary, Coordr, AV, Gardner-Webb University, 110 S Main St, Boiling Springs, NC, 28017. Tel: 704-406-4291. p. 1674

Botton, Kayla Louise, Libr Asst I, University of Georgia College of Agricultural & Environmental Sciences, 4601 Research Way, Tifton, GA, 31793. Tel: 229-386-3447. p. 500

Botts, Kathy, Ch Serv, W A Rankin Memorial Library, 502 Indiana St, Neodesha, KS, 66757. Tel: 620-325-3275. p. 826

Botts, Laura, Head, Spec Coll, Mercer University, Jack Tarver Library, 1300 Edgewood Ave, Macon, GA, 31207. Tel: 478-301-2968. p. 486

Bou-Crick, Carmen, Head, Ref & Educ Serv, University of Miami, Louis Calder Memorial Library, Miller School of Medicine, 1601 NW Tenth Ave, Miami, FL, 33136. Tel: 305-243-1967. p. 425

Bouchard, Andrea, Youth Serv Librn, North Hampton Public Library, 239 Atlantic Ave, North Hampton, NH, 03862-2341. Tel: 603-964-6326. p. 1376

Bouchard, Anja, Librn III, Outreach Coordr, Clinton-Essex-Franklin Library System, 33 Oak St, Plattsburgh, NY, 12901-2810. Tel: 518-563-5190, Ext 118. p. 1619

Bouchard, Jane A, Dir, Schroon Lake Public Library, 15 Leland Ave, Schroon Lake, NY, 12870. Tel: 518-532-7737, Ext 13. p. 1639

Bouchard, Jasmine, Res Mgr, Bibliothèque Municipale de Gatineau, Ville de Gatineau, CP 1970 Succ. Hull, Gatineau, QC, J8X 3Y9, CANADA. Tel: 819-243-2345. p. 2712

Bouchard, Kerry, Dir, Libr Syst, Texas Christian University, 2913 Lowden St, TCU Box 298400, Fort Worth, TX, 76129. Tel: 817-257-7106. p. 2181

Bouchard, Michelle, Communications, Advocacy & Outreach Serv Coordr, United States Geological Survey, Mundt Federal Bldg, 47914 252nd St, Sioux Falls, SD, 57198-0001. Tel: 605-594-2611, 605-594-6511. p. 2083

Bouchard, Steven, Librn, Julia Adams Morse Memorial Library, 105 Main St, Greene, ME, 04236. Tel: 207-946-5544. p. 926

Bouchard, Steven, Ad, Lewiston Public Library, 200 Lisbon St, Lewiston, ME, 04240. Tel: 207-513-3004. p. 929

Bouchard-Lord, Stephanie, Documentation Tech, McGill University Health Centre - Glen Site, 1001 Boul DeCarie, Rm B RC 0078, Montreal, QC, H4A 3J1, CANADA. Tel: 514-934-1934, Ext 35290. p. 2726

Bouchdoug, Mariam, Libr Tech, College LaSalle, 2000 Saint Catherine St W, 4th Flr, Montreal, QC, H3H 2T2, CANADA. Tel: 514-939-2006, Ext 4439. p. 2723

Bouche, Nicole, Exec Dir/Librn, Yale University Library, Lewis Walpole Library, 154 Main St, Farmington, CT, 06032. Tel: 860-677-2140. p. 328

Boucher, Marc, Libr Dir, Lake Superior State University, 906 Ryan Ave, Sault Sainte Marie, MI, 49783. Tel: 906-635-2815. p. 1149

Boucouvalas, Mary-Lou, Libr Dir, Louis T Graves Memorial Public Library, 18 Maine St, Kennebunkport, ME, 04046. Tel: 207-967-2778. p. 928

Boudet, Janet R, Dir, Roddenbery Memorial Library, 320 N Broad St, Cairo, GA, 39828-2109. Tel: 229-377-3632. p. 468

Boudouris, Kathryn, Outreach & Res Serv Librn, University of Virginia, Arthur J Morris Law Library, 580 Massie Rd, Charlottesville, VA, 22903-1738. Tel: 434-924-2522. p. 2310

Boudreau, Dan, Head, Reader Serv, American Antiquarian Society Library, 185 Salisbury St, Worcester, MA, 01609-1634. Tel: 508-755-5221. p. 1071

Boudreau, Joan, Asst Librn, Schroeder Public Library, 93 Main St, Keystone, IA, 52249. Tel: 319-442-3329. p. 763

Boudreau, Marianne, Libr Tech, National Theatre School of Canada Library, 5030 rue Saint-Denis, Montreal, QC, H2J 2L8, CANADA. Tel: 514-842-7954, Ext 112. p. 2727

Boudreau, Mary, Librn, Morrison, Mahoney LLP, 250 Summer St, Boston, MA, 02210. Tel: 617-439-7507. p. 997

Boudreau, Tanya, Asst Dir, Cold Lake Public Library, 5513-B 48th Ave, Cold Lake, AB, T9M 1X9, CANADA. Tel: 780-639-3967. p. 2532

Boudreau, Tanya, Librn, Cold Lake Public Library, Harbor View, 1301 Eighth Ave, Cold Lake, AB, T9M 1J7, CANADA. Tel: 780-639-3967. p. 2532

Boudreaux, April, Bus Mgr, Saint Mary Parish Library, 206 Iberia St, Franklin, LA, 70538. Tel: 337-828-1624, 337-828-1627. p. 890

Boudreaux, Jared, Dir, Mancos Public Library, 211 W First St, Mancos, CO, 81328. Tel: 970-533-7600. p. 291

Boudreaux, Tina, Financial Admin Officer, Cameron Parish Library, 512 Marshall St, Cameron, LA, 70631. Tel: 337-775-5421. p. 886

Boudrot, Christopher, Dir, Finance & Operations, Boston Athenaeum, Ten 1/2 Beacon St, Boston, MA, 02108-3777. Tel: 617-227-0270. p. 991

Boufath, Salimah, Youth Serv Libr, Chicago Ridge Public Library, 10400 S Oxford Ave, Chicago Ridge, IL, 60415. Tel: 708-423-7753. p. 571

Boughey, Karin, Head, Adult Serv, Milford Public Library, 330 Family Dr, Milford, MI, 48381-2000. Tel: 248-684-0845. p. 1132

Boughida, Karim, Dir of Libr, Stony Brook University, Marine & Atmospheric Sciences Information Center, 165 Challenger Hall, Stony Brook, NY, 11794-5000. Tel: 631-632-8679. p. 1647

Boughida, Karim B, Dean of Libr, University of Rhode Island, 15 Lippitt Rd, Kingston, RI, 02881-2011. Tel: 401-874-2666. p. 2033

Boughton, Toni, Access Serv, University of Wyoming Libraries, Library Annex, Science Complex, Dept 3254 Basement, 1000 E University Ave, Laramie, WY, 82071. Tel: 307-766-6535. p. 2497

Bouisset, Simon, Librn, Universite du Quebec en Outaouais, 283, Blvd Alexandre-Tache, CP 1250, succursale Hull, Gatineau, QC, J8X 3X7, CANADA. Tel: 819-595-3900, Ext 2373. p. 2713

Boule, Michelle, Dir, Libr Serv, Northern Wyoming Community College District - Sheridan College, Griffith Memorial Bldg, One Whitney Way, Sheridan, WY, 82801. Tel: 307-675-0220. p. 2498

Boule-Smith, Michelle, Pres, LIBRAS, Inc, c/o North Central College, 30 N Brainard St, Naperville, IL, 60540. p. 2765

Boulet, Richard, Dir, Blue Hill Public Library, Five Parker Point Rd, Blue Hill, ME, 04614. Tel: 207-374-5515, Ext 13. p. 918

Bouley, Gregg, ILL, Ref, Woburn Public Library, 36 Cummings Park, Woburn, MA, 01801. Tel: 781-933-0148. p. 1070

Boulrice, Melissa-Renee, Asst Admin, Canada Council for the Arts, 150 Elgin St, 2nd Flr, Ottawa, ON, K2P 1L4, CANADA. Tel: 613-566-4414. p. 2665

Boulrice, Theresa, Ch & Youth Librn, Libr Mgr, Millbury Public Library, 128 Elm St, Millbury, MA, 01527. Tel: 508-865-1181. p. 1035

Boulter, Rebecca, Regional Librn, Prince Edward Island Public Library Service, Summerside Rotary Library, 57 Central St, Summerside, PE, C1N 3K9, CANADA. Tel: 902-436-7323, 902-888-8370. p. 2708

Bouman, Judith, Head, Adult Serv, North Bay Public Library, 271 Worthington St E, North Bay, ON, P1B 1H1, CANADA. Tel: 705-474-4830. p. 2661

Bounds, Daria, Mgr, County of Los Angeles Public Library, Quartz Hill Library, 5040 West Ave M-2, Quartz Hill, CA, 93536-3509. Tel: 661-943-2454. p. 137

Bounds, Kat, Head, Circ Serv, Canton Public Library, 1200 S Canton Center Rd, Canton, MI, 48188-1600. Tel: 734-397-0999. p. 1088

Bounds Wilson, Jamie, Col Librn, Millsaps College, 1701 N State St, Jackson, MS, 39210. Tel: 601-974-1086. p. 1222

Bouquin, Daina, Head Librn, Center for Astrophysics Library / Harvard & Smithsonian Library, 60 Garden St, MS-56, Cambridge, MA, 02138. Tel: 617-496-5769. p. 1005

Bourdages, Lauren, Copyright & Reserves Supervisor, Wilfrid Laurier University Library, 75 University Ave W, Waterloo, ON, N2L 3C5, CANADA. Tel: 519-884-0710, Ext 4916. p. 2703

Bourdon, Jean-Philippe, Librn, Cegep de Saint-Laurent Bibliotheque, 625 Ave Sainte-Croix, Saint-Laurent, QC, H4L 3X7, CANADA. Tel: 514-747-6521, Ext 7211. p. 2735

Bourdon, Jesse G, Libr Dir, Croton Free Library, 171 Cleveland Dr, Croton-on-Hudson, NY, 10520. Tel: 914-271-6612. p. 1523

Bourdon, Nathalie, Develop Dir, National Film Board of Canada, 3155 Cote-de-Liesse Rd, Saint-Laurent, QC, H4N 2N4, CANADA. Tel: 514-496-1044. p. 2736
Bourdon-Charest, Alex, Chef de Section, Bibliotheques de Montreal, Parc-Extension, 421 rue Saint-Roch, Montreal, QC, H3N 1K2, CANADA. Tel: 514-872-7416. p. 2720
Bourg, Chris, Dr, Dir of Libr, Massachusetts Institute of Technology Libraries, Office of the Director, Bldg NE36-6101, 77 Massachusetts Ave, Cambridge, MA, 02139-4307. Tel: 617-253-5297. p. 1008
Bourgault, Jean-Daniel, Libr Mgr, Institut National de la Recherche Scientifique, 490 de la Couronne, Quebec, QC, G1K 9A9, CANADA. Tel: 418-654-2577. p. 2731
Bourgeois, Lynn, Libr Mgr, Albert-Westmorland-Kent Regional Library, Memramcook Public, 540 Centrale St, Unit 1, Memramcook, NB, E4K 3S6, CANADA. Tel: 506-758-4029. p. 2603
Bourget, Diane, Tech Serv, Cégep Garneau, 1660 blvd de l'Entente, Quebec, QC, G1S 4S3, CANADA. Tel: 418-688-8310, Ext 2290. p. 2796
Bourke, Rosanne, Acq, Circ, Cayuga County Community College, 197 Franklin St, Auburn, NY, 13021. Tel: 315-294-8596. p. 1488
Bourne, Ann, Dr, Asst Dir, University of Alabama, 7035 Gorgas Library, Campus Box 870252, Tuscaloosa, AL, 35487-0252. Tel: 205-348-4610. p. 2781
Bourne, Brandy, Univ Librn, University of North Carolina at Asheville, One University Heights, Ramsey Library, CPO 1500, Asheville, NC, 28804. Tel: 828-251-6639. p. 1673
Bourne, Ehron, Circ Supvr, Riverdale Public Library District, 208 W 144th St, Riverdale, IL, 60827-2733. Tel: 708-841-3311. p. 639
Bourne, Floyd, IT Admin, San Juan Island Library, 1010 Guard St, Friday Harbor, WA, 98250-9612. Tel: 360-378-2798. p. 2364
Bourne, Jill, Dir, San Jose Public Library, 150 E San Fernando St, San Jose, CA, 95112-3580. Tel: 408-808-2150. p. 231
Bourne, Rebecca, Asst Dir, Riverdale Public Library District, 208 W 144th St, Riverdale, IL, 60827-2733. Tel: 708-841-3311. p. 639
Bourque, Kati, Youth Serv Librn, Newbury Town Library, Zero Lunt St, Byfield, MA, 01922-1232. Tel: 978-465-0539. p. 1004
Bourque, Kevin, Dir, Boxford Town Library, Seven-A Spofford Rd, Boxford, MA, 01921. Tel: 978-887-7323. p. 1001
Bourque, Lisa, Ref (Info Servs), Lynn Public Library, Five N Common St, Lynn, MA, 01902. Tel: 781-595-0567. p. 1030
Bourque, Marianne, Dir, South English Public Library, 407 Ives St, South English, IA, 52335. Tel: 319-667-2715. p. 783
Bourque, Michelle, Mgr, Bibliotheque Municipale de Amos, 222 Front St E, Amos, QC, J9T 1H3, CANADA. Tel: 819-732-6070. p. 2709
Bourque, Michelle, Head of Libraries, Bibliotheque Municipale de Val-D'or, 600, 7e Rue, Val-d'Or, QC, J9P 3P3, CANADA. Tel: 819-874-7469, Ext 4233. p. 2738
Bourque, Sylvie, Libr Mgr, Albert-Westmorland-Kent Regional Library, Richibucto Public, 9376 Main St, Richibucto, NB, E4W 4C9, CANADA. Tel: 506-523-7851. p. 2603
Bouska, Andrew, Mgr, Ad Serv, Council Bluffs Public Library, 400 Willow Ave, Council Bluffs, IA, 51503-9042. Tel: 712-323-7553, Ext 5416. p. 742
Boutard, Guillaume, Asst Prof, Universite de Montreal, 3150, rue Jean-Brillant, bur C-2004, Montreal, QC, H3T 1N8, CANADA, Tel: 514-343-6044. p. 2797
Boutaugh, Alison, Libr Dir, Thompson Public Library, 934 Riverside Dr, North Grosvenordale, CT, 06255. Tel: 860-923-9779. p. 331
Bouthillette, Bonoit, Dir, Bibliotheque de Coaticook, Inc, 34 rue Main Est, Coaticook, QC, J1A 1N2, CANADA. Tel: 819-849-4013. p. 2711
Bouthillier, France, Assoc Prof, McGill University, 3661 Peel St, Montreal, QC, H3A 1X1, CANADA. Tel: 514-398-4204. p. 2796
Boutilier, Elizabeth, Libr Dir, Albert-Westmorland-Kent Regional Library, Riverview Public, 34 Honour House Ct, Riverview, NB, E1B 3Y9, CANADA. Tel: 506-387-2108. p. 2603
Boutin, Jay-Lynn, Mgr, Carbon Municipal Library, 310 Bruce Ave, Carbon, AB, T0M 0L0, CANADA. Tel: 403-572-3440. p. 2530
Boutwell, Kaci, Libr Dir, Flomaton Public Library, 436 Dr Van Ave, Flomaton, AL, 36441. Tel: 251-296-3552. p. 17
Boutwell, Marcie, Dean of the Library, Bethel University, 325 Cherry Ave, McKenzie, TN, 38201. Tel: 731-352-6913. p. 2111
Boutwell, Mary, Librn, Starkville-Oktibbeha County Public, Maben Branch, 831 Second Ave, Maben, MS, 39750. Tel: 662-263-5619. p. 1233
Bouwsma, Julia, Libr Dir, Webster Free Library, 22 Depot St, Kingfield, ME, 04947. Tel: 207-265-2052. p. 928
Bovee, Laura, Libr Dir, Chicopee Public Library, 449 Front St, Chicopee, MA, 01013. Tel: 413-594-1800. p. 1011
Bovee, Laura, Libr Dir, Chicopee Public Library, Fairview, 402 Britton St, Chicopee, MA, 01020. Tel: 413-533-8218. p. 1011
Boware, Theresa, Br Mgr, Akron-Summit County Public Library, Odom Boulevard Branch, 600 Vernon Odom Blvd, Akron, OH, 44307-1828. Tel: 330-434-8726. p. 1744
Bowden, Amanda, Ch, Portneuf District Library, 5210 Stuart Ave, Chubbuck, ID, 83202. Tel: 208-237-2192. p. 519
Bowden, Heather, Team Lead, Colls of Distinction Team, University of Colorado Boulder, 1720 Pleasant St, Boulder, CO, 80309. Tel: 303-492-8705. p. 267
Bowden, Laurie, Br Mgr, Burlington County Library System, Pemberton Library, 16 Broadway, Browns Mills, NJ, 08015. Tel: 609-893-8262. p. 1454
Bowden, Pat, Libr Asst, Bevill State Community College, Irma D Nicholson Library, Jasper Campus, 1411 Indiana Ave, Jasper, AL, 35501. Tel: 205-387-0511, Ext 5748. p. 17
Bowden, Ronald, Dir, Libr Serv, Northeast Texas Community College, 2886 Farm-to-Market Rd 1735, Mount Pleasant, TX, 75456. Tel: 903-434-8163. p. 2221
Bowdoin, Natalia Taylor, Coll Coordr, University of South Carolina Aiken, 471 University Pkwy, Aiken, SC, 29801. Tel: 803-641-3492. p. 2046
Bowdoin, Sally, Head, Ser, Brooklyn College Library, 2900 Bedford Ave, Brooklyn, NY, 11210. Tel: 718-951-5339. p. 1501
Bowe, Martin, Ref Serv, Garden City Public Library, 60 Seventh St, Garden City, NY, 11530. Tel: 516-742-8405. p. 1536
Bowe, Stephanie, Res Acq & Metadata Serv Librn, University of Maryland, Baltimore, Thurgood Marshall Law Library, 501 W Fayette St, Baltimore, MD, 21201-1768. Tel: 410-706-0783. p. 957
Bowen, Aaron, Instruction & Res Serv Librn, Wichita State University Libraries, 1845 Fairmount, Wichita, KS, 67260-0068. Tel: 316-978-5077. p. 844
Bowen, Anne H, Dir, Ocmulgee Regional Library System, 531 Second Ave, Eastman, GA, 31023. Tel: 478-374-4711. p. 477
Bowen, Becky, Supvr, Coll Develop, Kenton County Public Library, Administration Center, 3095 Hulbert Ave, Erlanger, KY, 41018. Tel: 859-578-7949. p. 852
Bowen, Breana, Dir, Cabell County Public Library, 455 Ninth Street Plaza, Huntington, WV, 25701. Tel: 304-528-5700. p. 2404
Bowen, Brigitte, Library Contact, Parmalat Canada, Ltd, 65 Bathurst St, London, ON, N6B 1N8, CANADA. Tel: 519-667-7769. p. 2655
Bowen, Casey, Br Mgr, Riverside County Library System, Indio Library, 200 Civic Ctr Mall, Indio, CA, 92201. Tel: 760-347-2383. p. 202
Bowen, Corinne, ILL/Circ Supvr, Madison Public Library, 39 Keep St, Madison, NJ, 07940. Tel: 973-377-0722. p. 1415
Bowen, Elizabeth, Br Mgr, Montgomery County Public Libraries, Maggie Nightingale Library, 19633 Fisher Ave, Poolesville, MD, 20837-2071. Tel: 240-773-9552. p. 974
Bowen, Eve, Librn, Hill College Library, 112 Lamar Dr, Hillsboro, TX, 76645. Tel: 254-659-7831. p. 2190
Bowen, Frances, Mgr, Libr Serv, Southern Arkansas University Tech, 6415 Spellman Rd, Camden, AR, 71701. Tel: 870-574-4518. p. 92
Bowen, Jake, Youth Serv Librn, Oak Creek Public Library, Drexel Town Sq, 8040 S Sixth St, Oak Creek, WI, 53154. Tel: 414-766-7900. p. 2465
Bowen, Jennifer, Assoc Dean, University of Rochester, River Campus Libraries, 755 Library Rd, Rochester, NY, 14627-0055. Tel: 585-275-4461. p. 1631
Bowen, Jessica, Dir, Nanuet Public Library, 149 Church St, Nanuet, NY, 10954. Tel: 845-623-4281, Ext 116. p. 1575
Bowen, Jonnica, Managing Librn, Washoe County Library System, North Valleys Library, 1075 N Hills Blvd, No 340, Reno, NV, 89506. Tel: 775-972-0281. p. 1350
Bowen, Kathy, Head, Youth Serv, Thorntown Public Library, 124 N Market St, Thorntown, IN, 46071-1144. Tel: 765-436-7348. p. 721
Bowen, Marvin, Br Mgr, Chicago Public Library, Chicago Bee, 3647 S State St, Chicago, IL, 60609. Tel: 312-747-6872. p. 556
Bowen, Patricia, Librn, Kentucky Mountain Bible College, 855 Hwy 541, Jackson, KY, 41339-9433. Tel: 606-693-5000. p. 861
Bowen, Sarah, Br Mgr, Stark County District Library, Jackson Township Branch, 7186 Fulton Dr NW, Canton, OH, 44718. Tel: 330-833-1010. p. 1755
Bowen, Sheila, Br Mgr, Wayne County Public Library, Fort Gay Public, 80 Rear Broadway, Fort Gay, WV, 25514. Tel: 304-648-5338. p. 2406
Bowen, Susan, Outreach Coordr, Person County Public Library, 319 S Main St, Roxboro, NC, 27573. Tel: 336-597-7881. p. 1714
Bowens, Lisa, Br Mgr, Clayton County Library System, Lovejoy, 1721 McDonough Rd, Hampton, GA, 30228. Tel: 770-472-8129. p. 483
Bower, Cheryl, Dir, Delton District Library, 330 N Grove St, Delton, MI, 49046. Tel: 269-623-8040. p. 1097
Bower, Linda, Circ, Eccles-Lesher Memorial Library, 673 Main St, Rimersburg, PA, 16248-4817. Tel: 814-473-3800. p. 2001
Bower, Mary McNamee, Exec Dir, Evansville Museum of Arts, History & Science Library, 411 SE Riverside Dr, Evansville, IN, 47713. Tel: 812-425-2406, Ext 230. p. 681
Bower, Pam, Cat, Circ, Kansas State University at Salina, Technology Ctr Bldg, Rm 111, 2310 Centennial Rd, Salina, KS, 67401. Tel: 785-826-2636. p. 835
Bower, Rick, Ref Librn, Johnson University, 7902 Eubanks Dr, Knoxville, TN, 37998. Tel: 865-251-2277. p. 2105
Bowers, Annie, Libr Mgr, Timberland Regional Library, Hoodsport Branch, 40 N Schoolhouse Hill Rd, Hoodsport, WA, 98548. Tel: 360-877-9339. p. 2389
Bowers, Ashley, Asst State Librn, Admin, Tennessee State Library & Archives, 403 Seventh Ave N, Nashville, TN, 37243-0312. Tel: 615-532-4628. p. 2121
Bowers, Carol L, Dean of Libr, Allen University, 1530 Harden St, Columbia, SC, 29204. Tel: 803-376-5719. p. 2053
Bowers, Ingrid, Br Mgr, Fairfax County Public Library, Chantilly Regional, 4000 Stringfellow Rd, Chantilly, VA, 20151-2628. Tel: 703-502-3883. p. 2316
Bowers, Leighton, Dir, Western Costume Co, 11041 Vanowen St, North Hollywood, CA, 91605. Tel: 818-508-2148. p. 183

Bowers, Matt, Libr Dir, Wakarusa Public Library, 124 N Elkhart St, Wakarusa, IN, 46573. Tel: 574-862-2465. p. 724

Bowers, Olivia, Adult Serv, Berkshire Athenaeum, One Wendell Ave, Pittsfield, MA, 01201-6385. Tel: 413-499-9480. p. 1046

Bowers, Robin, Br Adminr, Frederick County Public Libraries, Walkersville Branch, Two S Glade Rd, Walkersville, MD, 21793. Tel: 301-600-8200. p. 966

Bowers, Shari, Br Mgr, Dayton Metro Library, Northmont, 333 W National Rd, Englewood, OH, 45322. Tel: 937-496-8950. p. 1779

Bowers, Sharon, Dir, Wilton Public Library, 1215 Cypress, Wilton, IA, 52778. Tel: 563-732-2583. p. 792

Bowers, Stephanie, Re/Ser Librn, Pitt Community College, Clifton W Everett Bldg, 1986 Pitt Tech Rd, Winterville, NC, 28590. Tel: 252-493-7350, p. 1727

Bowers, Steven, Exec Dir, The Library Network, 41365 Vincenti Ct, Novi, MI, 48375. Tel: 248-536-3100, Ext 107. p. 2767

Bowie, Cathryn, State Law Librn, State of Oregon Law Library, Supreme Court Bldg, 1163 State St, Salem, OR, 97301. Tel: 503-986-5640. p. 1897

Bowie, Vicky, Br Mgr, Hawaii State Public Library System, Pearl City Public Library, 1138 Waimano Home Rd, Pearl City, HI, 96782. Tel: 808-453-6566. p. 510

Bowker, Elizabeth, Br Mgr, Harford County Public Library, Jarrettsville Branch, 3722 Norrisville Rd, Jarrettsville, MD, 21084. Tel: 410-692-7887. p. 959

Bowker, Jean, Libr Dir, Riverside Public Library, Ten Zurbrugg Way, Riverside, NJ, 08075. Tel: 856-461-6922. p. 1440

Bowlby, Elizabeth, Libr Dir, Clyde-Savannah Public Library, 204 Glasgow St, Clyde, NY, 14433. Tel: 315-923-7767. p. 1519

Bowlby, Joan, Mgr, San Jose Public Library, Edenvale, 101 Branham Lane E, San Jose, CA, 95111. Tel: 408-808-3036. p. 231

Bowlby, Joan, Mgr, San Jose Public Library, Santa Teresa, 290 International Circle, San Jose, CA, 95119-1132. Tel: 408-808-3068. p. 231

Bowler, Meagan, Dean, Mount Royal University Library, 4825 Mount Royal Gate SW, Calgary, AB, T3E 6K6, CANADA. Tel: 403-440-6086. p. 2528

Bowles, Kathy, Dir, Cawker City Public Library, 802 Locust, Cawker City, KS, 67430. Tel: 785-781-4925. p. 800

Bowles, Kelly, Mgr, Youth Serv, Mary Wood Weldon Memorial Library, 1530 S Green St, Glasgow, KY, 42141. Tel: 270-651-2824. p. 857

Bowles, Nancy, Br Librn, Crook County Library, Hulett Branch, 401 Sager St, Hulett, WY, 82720. Tel: 307-467-5676. p. 2499

Bowles, Vickery, Ms, City Librn, Toronto Public Library, 789 Yonge St, Toronto, ON, M4W 2G8, CANADA. Tel: 416-393-7131. p. 2693

Bowlin, Cindy, Libr Tech, Norris Public Library, 132 N Main, Rutherfordton, NC, 28139. Tel: 828-287-4981, Ext 3. p. 1714

Bowlin, Joel, Sr Librn, California Department of Corrections Library System, Wasco State Prison, 701 Scofield Ave, Wasco, CA, 93280. Tel: 661-758-8400, Ext 5477. p. 207

Bowling, Carol, Libr Mgr, Lane Public Libraries, 300 N Third St, Hamilton, OH, 45011-1629. Tel: 513-894-7156. p. 1789

Bowling Dixon, Joslyn, Dir, Newark Public Library, Five Washington St, Newark, NJ, 07101. Tel: 973-733-7784, 973-733-7800. p. 1427

Bowling, Karen, Ch Serv, Interim Dir, Smithfield Public Library, 25 N Main St, Smithfield, UT, 84335-1957. Tel: 435-563-3555. p. 2273

Bowling, Stephen, Dir, Breathitt County Public Library, 1024 College Ave, Jackson, KY, 41339. Tel: 606-666-5541. p. 860

Bowman, Ann, Sr Librn, Los Angeles Public Library System, North Hollywood Amelia Earhart Regional Library, 5211 Tujunga Ave, Los Angeles, CA, 91601. Tel: 818-766-7185. p. 165

Bowman, Betsy, Librn, Phillips-Lee-Monroe Regional Library, Lee County Library, 77 W Main St, Marianna, AR, 72360-2297. Tel: 870-295-2688. p. 98

Bowman, Brandon, Jr, Dir, Mount Clemens Public Library, 300 N Groesbeck Ave, Mount Clemens, MI, 48043. Tel: 586-469-6200. p. 1134

Bowman, Cheryl, Libr Tech, Thorold Public Library, 14 Ormond St N, Thorold, ON, L2V 1Y8, CANADA. Tel: 905-227-2581. p. 2684

Bowman, Elizabeth, Libr Dir, Santa Barbara City College, 721 Cliff Dr, Santa Barbara, CA, 93109-2394. Tel: 805-965-0581, Ext 2633. p. 240

Bowman, Jacinta, Circ, Lakeview Public Library, 1120 Woodfield Rd, Rockville Centre, NY, 11570. Tel: 516-536-3071. p. 1632

Bowman, Jackie, Asst Dir, Ch, Alice M Farr Library, 1603 L St, Aurora, NE, 68818-2132. Tel: 402-694-2272. p. 1306

Bowman, Karla, Adult Serv Mgr, Euclid Public Library, 631 E 222nd St, Euclid, OH, 44123-2091. Tel: 216-261-5300, Ext 301. p. 1785

Bowman, Kathleen, Br Mgr, Indian River County Library System, North Indian River County Library, 1001 Sebastian Blvd, CR 512, Sebastian, FL, 32958. Tel: 772-400-6360. p. 452

Bowman, Kathleen, Libr Dir, Starke County Public Library System, 152 W Culver Rd, Knox, IN, 46534-2220. Tel: 574-772-7323. p. 699

Bowman, Kristin, Ad, Bulverde-Spring Branch Library, 131 Bulverde Crossing, Bulverde, TX, 78163. Tel: 830-438-4864. p. 2151

Bowman, Lanesa, Clinical Librn, Ballad Health, 400 N State of Franklin Rd, Johnson City, TN, 37604-6094. Tel: 423-431-1691. p. 2103

Bowman, Laura, Ad, Corning Public Library, 603 Ninth St, Corning, IA, 50841-1304. Tel: 641-322-3866. p. 742

Bowman, Lee, Cataloger, Librn, Wilmington College, 120 College St, Wilmington, OH, 45177. Tel: 937-481-2394. p. 1832

Bowman, Leslie, Assoc Libr Dir, University of the Sciences in Philadelphia, 4200 Woodland Ave, Philadelphia, PA, 19104. Tel: 215-596-8964. p. 1989

Bowman, Linda, Hed, Bkmobile Dept, Kansas City, Kansas Public Library, 625 Minnesota Ave, Kansas City, KS, 66101. Tel: 913-295-8250, Ext 6500. p. 816

Bowman, Loree K, Dir & Librn, Linn County Library District No 1, 234 W Main St, Parker, KS, 66072. Tel: 913-898-4650. p. 831

Bowman, Mary, Dir, Little Wood River District Library, 16 Panther Ave, Carey, ID, 83320-5063. Tel: 208-823-4510. p. 519

Bowman, Mary Anne, Dep Dir, Saint Mary's County Library, 23630 Hayden Farm Lane, Leonardtown, MD, 20650. Tel: 301-475-2846, Ext 1015. p. 971

Bowman, Michael, Interim Dean, Portland State University Library, 1875 SW Park Ave, Portland, OR, 97201-3220. Tel: 503-725-5874. p. 1893

Bowman, Randall, Archives Librn, Elon University, 308 N O'Kelly Ave, Elon, NC, 27244-0187. Tel: 336-278-6600. p. 1688

Bowman, Rebecca, Br Mgr, Anythink Libraries, Anythink Wright Farms, 5877 E 120th Ave, Thornton, CO, 80602. Tel: 303-405-3200. p. 296

Bowman, Shannon, Research Librn, Sci, Stephen F Austin State University, 1936 North St, Nacogdoches, TX, 75962. Tel: 936-468-1528. p. 2221

Bowman, Terri, Br Mgr, Clark County Public Library, Enon Branch, 209 E Main St, Enon, OH, 45323. Tel: 937-864-2502. p. 1821

Bowman, Tim A, Pres, Westerners International Library, c/o Panhandle-Plains Historical Museum, 2503 Fourth Ave, Canyon, TX, 79015. Tel: 806-654-6920. p. 2153

Bowman, Timothy, Dr, Asst Prof, Wayne State University, 106 Kresge Library, Detroit, MI, 48202. Tel: 888-497-8754, Ext 702. p. 2787

Bowron, Ross, Health Sci Librn, Austin Peay State University, 601 College St, Clarksville, TN, 37044. Tel: 931-221-7381. p. 2092

Bowser, Erika, Website Mgr, Milton-Union Public Library, 560 S Main St, West Milton, OH, 45383. Tel: 937-698-5515. p. 1830

Bowsher, Mary, ILL, Libr Assoc, Marshall University Libraries, One John Marshall Dr, Huntington, WV, 25755-2060. Tel: 304-696-2320. p. 2405

Box, Debbie, Mgr, Saint Mary Parish Library, Centerville Branch, 9340 Hwy 182, Centerville, LA, 70522. Tel: 337-836-1717. p. 890

Box, Debbie, Dir, Cross Plains Public Library, 149 N Main St, Cross Plains, TX, 76443. Tel: 254-725-7722. p. 2162

Box, Krista, Sr Res Librn, Board of Governors of The Federal Reserve System, Research Library, 20th & C St NW, MS 102, Washington, DC, 20551. Tel: 202-452-3333. p. 361

Box, Rebecca, Br Mgr, Enoch Pratt Free Library, Patterson Park Branch, 158 N Linwood Ave, Baltimore, MD, 21224-1255. Tel: 443-984-4946. p. 953

Boxrud, Amy, Exec Dir, Norwegian-American Historical Association Archives, 1510 St Olaf Ave, Northfield, MN, 55057. Tel: 507-786-3221. p. 1191

Boyar, Ilene, Libr Asst, Norwalk Community College, 188 Richards Ave, Norwalk, CT, 06854-1655. Tel: 203-857-3319. p. 331

Boyar, Tristan, Libr Tech, University of Montana Missoula, 32 Campus Dr, Missoula, MT, 59812. Tel: 406-243-6866. p. 1300

Boyce, Crystal, Librn, Northern Virginia Community College Libraries, Media Processing Services, 8333 Little River Tpk, Annandale, VA, 22003-3796. Tel: 703-323-3095. p. 2304

Boyce, Helen E, Head, Doc Serv, University of Houston, The O'Quinn Law Library, 12 Law Library, Houston, TX, 77204-6054. Tel: 713-743-2300. p. 2199

Boycik, Stacey, Br Mgr, Cuyahoga County Public Library, Parma-Snow Branch, 2121 Snow Rd, Parma, OH, 44134-2728. Tel: 216-661-4240. p. 1813

Boyd, Ali, Br Mgr, Cuyahoga County Public Library, Warrensville Heights Branch, 4415 Northfield Rd, Warrensville Heights, OH, 44128-4603. Tel: 216-464-5280. p. 1813

Boyd, Alissa, Sr Libr Mgr, Live Oak Public Libraries, Oglethorpe Mall Branch, Seven Mall Annex, Savannah, GA, 31406. Tel: 912-921-2082. p. 496

Boyd, Angela, Educ Res Librn, San Diego Miramar College, 10440 Black Mountain Rd, San Diego, CA, 92126-2999. Tel: 619-388-7615. p. 218

Boyd, Chris, Mr, Presv Officer, Sac & Fox National Public Library & Archives, 920883 S Hwy 99, Stroud, OK, 74079-5178. Tel: 918-968-3526, Ext 2021. p. 1863

Boyd, Christopher, Asst Librn, Head, Tech Serv, Florida Gulf Coast University Library, 10501 FGCU Blvd S, Fort Myers, FL, 33965. Tel: 239-590-7640. p. 403

Boyd, Connie, Br Supvr, Mecklenburg County Public Library, Burnett Library & Learning Center, 914 Virginia Ave, Clarksville, VA, 23927. Tel: 434-374-8692. p. 2308

Boyd, Doug, Dir, Louis B Nunn Ctr for Oral Hist, University of Kentucky Libraries, Special Collections Research Center, Margaret I King Library, 179 Funkhouser Dr, Lexington, KY, 40506-0039. Tel: 859-257-9672. p. 864

Boyd, Evan, Archivist, Libr Dir, United Lutheran Seminary, 66 Seminary Ridge, Gettysburg, PA, 17325. Tel: 215-248-6330. p. 1936

Boyd, Evan, Dir, Archives, Lutheran Theological Seminary, United Lutheran Seminary, 7301 Germantown Ave, Philadelphia, PA, 19119-1794. Tel: 215-248-6330. p. 1982

Boyd, Jackie, Communications Mgr, Orland Park Public Library, 14921 Ravinia Ave, Orland Park, IL, 60462. Tel: 708-428-5205. p. 630
Boyd, Jim, Curator, Alpine County Historical Society, One School St, Markleeville, CA, 96120. Tel: 530-694-2317. p. 173
Boyd, John, Ref & ILL Librn, Bellarmine University, 2001 Newburg Rd, Louisville, KY, 40205-0671. p. 864
Boyd, Joy, Outreach Mgr, Central Kansas Library System, 1409 Williams St, Great Bend, KS, 67530-4020. Tel: 620-792-4865. p. 810
Boyd, Kate, Dir, Digital Serv, University of South Carolina, Digital Collections, Hollings Special Collections Library, 1322 Greene St, Columbia, SC, 29208. Tel: 803-777-0735. p. 2055
Boyd, Kellie, Clinical Librn, John Peter Smith Hospital, John S Marietta Memorial, 1500 S Main St, Fort Worth, TX, 76104. Tel: 817-702-5057. p. 2180
Boyd, Kimberly, Head, Res & Instruction, Brenau University, 625 Academy St, Gainesville, GA, 30501-3343. Tel: 770-534-6213. p. 480
Boyd, Mary, Circ Supvr, Ligonier Valley Library, 120 W Main St, Ligonier, PA, 15658-1243. Tel: 724-238-6451. p. 1955
Boyd, Mindy, Br Mgr, Mitchell County Public Library, 18 N Mitchell Ave, Bakersville, NC, 28705. Tel: 828-688-2511. p. 1673
Boyd, Rand, Libr Dir, Laguna College of Art & Design (LCAD), 2222 Laguna Canyon Rd, Laguna Beach, CA, 92651. Tel: 949-376-6000, Ext 225. p. 155
Boyd, Roberta, ILL, Lied Scottsbluff Public Library, 1809 Third Ave, Scottsbluff, NE, 69361-2493. Tel: 308-630-6250. p. 1335
Boyd, Sara, Librn, Central Georgia Technical College Library, I Bldg, 2nd Flr, 3300 Macon Tech Dr, Macon, GA, 31206-3628. Tel: 478-757-3549. p. 486
Boyd, Trenton, Head Librn, University of Missouri-Columbia, Zalk Veterinary Medical Library, W-218 Veterinary-Medicine Bldg, Columbia, MO, 65211. Tel: 573-882-2461. p. 1244
Boyd-Byrnes, Mary Kate, Ref Librn, Long Island University Post, 720 Northern Blvd, Brookville, NY, 11548. Tel: 516-299-4145. p. 1507
Boydston, Becky, Dir, Mount Laurel Library, 100 Walt Whitman Ave, Mount Laurel, NJ, 08054. Tel: 856-234-7319. p. 1422
Boydston, Naomi, Public Services Assoc, San Juan Island Library, 1010 Guard St, Friday Harbor, WA, 98250-9612. Tel: 360-378-2798. p. 2364
Boye, Gary, Music Librn, Appalachian State University, Music Library, 813 Rivers St, Boone, NC, 28608-2097. Tel: 828-262-2389. p. 1675
Boyer, Allison, Youth Serv, Loutit District Library, 407 Columbus Ave, Grand Haven, MI, 49417. Tel: 616-850-6912. p. 1109
Boyer, Amanda, Student Success Librn, Susquehanna University, 514 University Ave, Selinsgrove, PA, 17870-1050. Tel: 570-372-4459. p. 2005
Boyer, Christy, Access Serv Mgr, University of Wisconsin-River Falls, 410 S Third St, River Falls, WI, 54022. Tel: 715-425-3542. p. 2474
Boyer, Daniel, Head Librn, McGill University Libraries, Nahum Gelber Law Library, 3660 Peel St, Montreal, QC, H3A 1W9, CANADA. Tel: 514-398-4715, Ext 00171. p. 2726
Boyer, Jenn, Head, Adult Serv, Crandall Public Library, 251 Glen St, Glens Falls, NY, 12801-3546. Tel: 518-792-6508. p. 1539
Boyer, Jessica J, Libr Dir, Mount Saint Mary's University, 16300 Old Emmitsburg Rd, Emmitsburg, MD, 21727. Tel: 301-447-5426. p. 965
Boyer, Joyce, Dir, Altona Reading Center, 524 Devils Den Rd, Altona, NY, 12910. Tel: 518-236-7035, Ext 7. p. 1485
Boyer, Kate, Dir, Benton Harbor Public Library, 213 E Wall St, Benton Harbor, MI, 49022-4499. Tel: 269-926-6139. p. 1084
Boyer, Marie-Eve, Tech Serv, Bibliothèque Raymond-Laberge, 25 Maple Blvd, Chateauguay, QC, J6J 3P7, CANADA. Tel: 450-698-3080. p. 2710
Boyer, Monica, Youth Serv Mgr, Fox River Valley Public Library District, 555 Barrington Ave, East Dundee, IL, 60118-1496. Tel: 847-428-3661. p. 580
Boyett, Liz, Br Mgr, Marshall County Library System, Potts Camp Public, 20 S Center St, Potts Camp, MS, 38659. Tel: 601-333-7068. p. 1220
Boykin, Dianne, Acq & Ser, Charleston Southern University, 9200 University Blvd, Charleston, SC, 29406. Tel: 843-863-7925. p. 2050
Boylan, Danni, Dir, Kellogg Public Library, 16 W Market Ave, Kellogg, ID, 83837. Tel: 208-786-7231. p. 523
Boylan, Maggie, Dir, Zelienople Area Public Library, 227 S High St, Zelienople, PA, 16063. Tel: 724-452-9330. p. 2027
Boyle, Annmarie, Chair, Ref Serv & Coll Develop, Hofstra University, 123 Hofstra University, Hempstead, NY, 11549. Tel: 516 463-6529. p. 1545
Boyle, Brian, Dir, Knowledge Mgt, Kramer, Levin, Naftalis & Frankel LLP, 1177 Avenue of the Americas, New York, NY, 10036. Tel: 212-715-9321. p. 1590
Boyle, Catherine, Dir, Ref, Dir, Technology, Tredyffrin Public Library, 582 Upper Gulph Rd, Strafford, PA, 19087-2096. Tel: 610-688-7092. p. 2010
Boyle, Christina-Anne, Head, Coll Develop, Government of Canada, Federal Courts & Tax Court of Canada, Courts Administration Service-Library Services, 90 Sparks St, Ottawa, ON, K1A 0H9, CANADA. Tel: 613-947-3906. p. 2667
Boyle, Donn, Librn, Whitewood Public Library, 1201 Ash St, Whitewood, SD, 57793. Tel: 605-269-2616. p. 2085
Boyle, Katie, Libr Asst, Cowley County Community College, 131 S Third St, Arkansas City, KS, 67005. Tel: 620-441-5334. p. 796
Boyle, Kim, Br Mgr, Mexico-Audrain County Library District, Martinsburg Branch, 201 E Washington St, Martinsburg, MO, 65264. Tel: 573-492-6254. p. 1262
Boyle, Lisa, Head, Tech Serv, Starke County Public Library System, 152 W Culver Rd, Knox, IN, 46534-2220. Tel: 574-772-7323. p. 699
Boyle, Louise, Tech Serv, Ulster County Community College, 491 Cottekill Rd, Stone Ridge, NY, 12484. Tel: 845-687-5213. p. 1646
Boyle, Wendy, Librn, Stratton Public Library, 88 Main St, Stratton, ME, 04982. Tel: 207-246-4401. p. 943
Boynton, Mia, Librn, Monhegan Memorial Library, One Library Lane, Monhegan, ME, 04852. Tel: 207-295-7042. p. 932
Boysen, Alysia, Sr Librn, Siouxland Libraries, 200 N Dakota Ave, Sioux Falls, SD, 57104. Tel: 605-367-8702. p. 2082
Bozak, Nina, Curator, Rare Bks, Historic New Orleans Collection, 410 Chartres St, New Orleans, LA, 70130. Tel: 504-598-7118. p. 901
Bozarth, Sandra, Dean, Univ Libr, California State University, Bakersfield, 9001 Stockdale Hwy, 60 LIB, Bakersfield, CA, 93311. Tel: 661-654-3172. p. 119
Bozek, Iwona, Curator, Head Librn, Head, Spec Coll, Polish Museum of America Library, 984 N Milwaukee Ave, Chicago, IL, 60642. Tel: 773-384-3352, Ext 2106. p. 567
Bozeman, Miles, Circ, Reserves Mgr, Florida State University Libraries, Warren D Allen Music Library, Housewright Music Bldg, 122 N Copeland St, Tallahassee, FL, 32306. Tel: 850-644-7068. p. 447
Bracco, Caroline, Dir, San Mateo County Law Library, 710 Hamilton St, Redwood City, CA, 94063. Tel: 650-363-4913. p. 200
Braceros-Simon, Charity, Access Serv Librn, Willamette University, 900 State St, Salem, OR, 97301. Tel: 503-370-6673. p. 1897
Bracey, Renee M, Circ Serv Coordr, Siena Heights University Library, 1247 E Siena Heights Dr, Adrian, MI, 49221-1796. Tel: 517-264-7150. p. 1076
Bracher, Thomas, Libr Tech, United States Army, Basset Army Hospital Medical Library, 1060 Gaffney Rd, No 7440, Fort Wainwright, AK, 99703-7440. Tel: 907-361-5194. p. 45
Brack, Amanda, Communications Mgr, North Central Washington Libraries, Omak Public Library, 30 S Ash, Omak, WA, 98841. Tel: 509-826-1820. p. 2394
Brack, Laura, Tech Serv, Training Servs Mgr, Plainfield-Guilford Township Public Library, 1120 Stafford Rd, Plainfield, IN, 46168. Tel: 317-839-6602, Ext 2152. p. 713
Brackeen, Susan, Libr Asst, Northeast Mississippi Community College, 101 Cunningham Blvd, Booneville, MS, 38829. Tel: 662-720-7407. p. 1212
Brackett, Amanda, Bus & Human Res Mgr, Gunnison Public Library of the Gunnison County Library District, 307 N Wisconsin, Gunnison, CO, 81230-2627. Tel: 970-641-3485. p. 285
Brackey, Scott, Instrul Librn, Washburn University, 1700 SW College Ave, Topeka, KS, 66621. Tel: 785-670-2609. p. 839
Bracy, Pauletta B, Assoc Prof, North Carolina Central University, 1801 Fayetteville St, Durham, NC, 27707. Tel: 919-530-6485. p. 2790
Bradberry, Cara, Sr Librn, Collins Correctional Facility Library, Middle Rd, Collins, NY, 14034. Tel: 716-532-4588. p. 1520
Bradberry, Richard, Dr, Dir, Libr Serv, Morgan State University, 1700 E Cold Spring Lane, Baltimore, MD, 21251. Tel: 443-885-3477. p. 956
Bradbury-Carlin, Candace, Dir, Tilton Library, 75 N Main St, South Deerfield, MA, 01373. Tel: 413-665-4683. p. 1054
Bradby, Sherida, Supv Librn, Pamunkey Regional Library, 7527 Library Dr, Hanover, VA, 23069. Tel: 804-537-6211. p. 2323
Braddlee, Dr, Dean, Learning & Tech Res, Northern Virginia Community College Libraries, Goodwin Bldg, CG206, 8333 Little River Tpk, Annandale, VA, 22003. Tel: 703-323-3004. p. 2304
Bradds, Dara, City Librn, Libr Dir, Escondido Public Library, 239 S Kalmia St, Escondido, CA, 92025. Tel: 760-839-4683. p. 141
Brade, Angela, Chief Operating Officer, Support Serv, Howard County Library System, 9411 Frederick Rd, Ellicott City, MD, 21042. Tel: 410-313-7750. p. 965
Braden, Darren, Teen Serv Librn, Monterey Park Bruggemeyer Library, 318 S Ramona Ave, Monterey Park, CA, 91754-3399. Tel: 626-307-1368. p. 180
Braden, Deborah, Circ Supvr, Saint Johns County Public Library System, Anastasia Island Branch, 124 Seagrove Main St, Saint Augustine Beach, FL, 32080. Tel: 904-209-3734. p. 440
Braden, Patty, Dir, Romulus Public Library, 11121 Wayne Rd, Romulus, MI, 48174. Tel: 734-955-4516. p. 1145
Braden, Rita Jo, Dir, Wakefield Public Library, 205 Third St, Wakefield, KS, 67487. Tel: 785-461-5510. p. 841
Brader, Theresa, Asst Libr Dir, Leon Valley Public Library, 6425 Evers Rd, Leon Valley, TX, 78238-1453. Tel: 210-684-0720. p. 2211
Bradfield, Angie, Br Mgr, Spiro Public Library, 208 S Main St, Spiro, OK, 74959. Tel: 918-962-3461. p. 1862
Bradford, Barry, Dir, Tangipahoa Parish Library, 204 NE Central Ave, Amite, LA, 70422. Tel: 985-748-7559. p. 880
Bradford, Brenda Kay, Univ Archivist, Northeastern State University, 711 N Grand Ave, Tahlequah, OK, 74464-2333. Tel: 918-456-5511, Ext 3200. p. 1863

Bradford, Charlene, Br Mgr, First Regional Library, Sardis Public Library, 101 McLaurin St, Sardis, MS, 38666. Tel: 662-487-2126. p. 1220
Bradford, David, Libr Dir, Nobles County Library, 407 12th St, Worthington, MN, 56187. Tel: 507-295-5340. p. 1210
Bradford, Joanie, Mgr, Baltimore County Public Library, Catonsville Branch, 1100 Frederick Rd, Baltimore, MD, 21228. Tel: 410-887-0951. p. 979
Bradford, John, Head, Mat Serv, Villa Park Public Library, 305 S Ardmore Ave, Villa Park, IL, 60181-2698. Tel: 630-834-1164. p. 658
Bradford, Judy, Dir, United States Marine Corps, 1401 West Rd, Bldg 1220, Camp Lejeune, NC, 28547-2539. Tel: 910-451-5724. p. 1677
Bradford, Judy, Dir, United States Marine Corps, Bldg AS213-213, Bancroft St, Jacksonville, NC, 28540. Tel: 910-449-6715. p. 1698
Bradford, Kristi, Br Mgr, Pima County Public Library, Nanini, 7300 N Shannon Rd, Tucson, AZ, 85741. Tel: 520-594-5365. p. 82
Bradford, Nancy, Coll Serv Supvr, Napa County Library, 580 Coombs St, Napa, CA, 94559-3396. Tel: 707-253-4281. p. 182
Bradford, Sheila, Br Mgr, Jefferson Parish Library, Charles A Wagner Branch, 6646 Riverside Dr, Metairie, LA, 70003. Tel: 504-838-1193. p. 897
Bradford, William, Br Mgr, Cleveland Public Library, Langston Hughes, 10200 Superior Ave, Cleveland, OH, 44106. Tel: 216-623-6975. p. 1768
Bradham, Kamesha, Librn, Augusta Technical College, McDuffie Campus Library, 338 Tech Dr, Thomson, GA, 30824. Tel: 706-595-0166. p. 467
Bradley, Anne, Asst Mgr, Saint Louis County Library, Daniel Boone Branch, 300 Clarkson Rd, Ellisville, MO, 63011-2222. Tel: 314-994-3300, Ext 3100. p. 1273
Bradley, Beau, Br Adminr, Frederick County Public Libraries, Middletown Branch, 101 Prospect, Middletown, MD, 21769. Tel: 301-600-7560. p. 966
Bradley, Celena, Ch, Wichita Falls Public Library, 600 11th St, Wichita Falls, TX, 76301-4604. Tel: 940-767-0868, Ext 4244. p. 2258
Bradley, Christine, Dir, Mystic & Noank Library, Inc, 40 Library St, Mystic, CT, 06355. Tel: 860-536-7721. p. 323
Bradley, Darlene, Dir, Libr & Mus Serv, Arcadia Public Library, 20 W Duarte Rd, Arcadia, CA, 91006. Tel: 626-821-5567. p. 117
Bradley, Ellen, Libr Dir, Turner Public Library, 98 Matthews Way, Turner, ME, 04282-3930. Tel: 207-225-2030. p. 943
Bradley, Eric, Head, Ref & Instruction, Goshen College, Harold & Wilma Good Library, 1700 S Main, Goshen, IN, 46526-4794. Tel: 574-535-7424. p. 687
Bradley, Holly, Dir, Sayre Public Library, Inc, 122 S Elmer Ave, Sayre, PA, 18840. Tel: 570-888-2256. p. 2003
Bradley, James, Instruction Librn, Wilmington University Library, 320 N DuPont Hwy, New Castle, DE, 19720. Tel: 302-356-6872. p. 354
Bradley, Jeffrey, Librn, Pitkin County Library, 120 N Mill St, Aspen, CO, 81611. Tel: 970-429-1900. p. 264
Bradley, Jennifer, Head, Instrul Serv, Head, Ref & Res Serv, Creighton University, Health Sciences Library-Learning Resource Center, 2770 Webster St, Omaha, NE, 68178-0210. Tel: 402-280-4127. p. 1328
Bradley, Jeronell W, Dir of Libr, Florence-Darlington Technical College Libraries, 2715 W Lucas St, Florence, SC, 29501. Tel: 843-661-8032. p. 2059
Bradley, Jeronell W, Dir of Libr, Florence-Darlington Technical College Libraries, Segars Library Health Sciences Campus, 320 W Cheves St, Florence, SC, 29501. Tel: 843-676-8575. p. 2059
Bradley, Johnny, Libr Operations Supvr, Marshall University Libraries, One John Marshall Dr, Huntington, WV, 25755-2060. Tel: 304-696-6434. p. 2405
Bradley, Karen, Dir, Schenectady County Public Library, 99 Clinton St, Schenectady, NY, 12305-2083. Tel: 518-388-4500. p. 1638
Bradley, Kourtnee, Asst Librn, Opp Public Library, 1604 N Main St, Opp, AL, 36467. Tel: 334-493-6423. p. 32
Bradley, Lola, Head Librn, Piedmont Technical College Library, Bldg K, 2nd Flr, 620 N Emerald Rd, Greenwood, SC, 29646. Tel: 864-941-8441. p. 2063
Bradley, Michelle, Mgr, Libr Develop, Library of Michigan, 702 W Kalamazoo St, Lansing, MI, 48915. Tel: 517-373-9489. p. 1125
Bradley, Mike, Patron Serv Mgr, North Riverside Public Library District, 2400 S Des Plaines Ave, North Riverside, IL, 60546. Tel: 708-447-0869, Ext 241. p. 626
Bradley, Ruth, County Historian, Cayuga County Historian's Office, Ten Court St, Auburn, NY, 13021. Tel: 315-253-1300. p. 1489
Bradley, Ryan, Mkt Coordr, Jackson County Library Services, 205 S Central Ave, Medford, OR, 97501-2730. Tel: 541-774-8679. p. 1886
Bradley, Scott, Exec Dir, Thunder Bay Historical Museum Society, 425 Donald St E, Thunder Bay, ON, P7E 5V1, CANADA. Tel: 807-623-0801. p. 2685
Bradley, Sharon, Digital Ser & Scholarly Res Librn, Mercer University, Walter F George School of Law, Furman Smith Law Library, 1021 Georgia Ave, Macon, GA, 31201-1001. Tel: 478-301-2612. p. 486
Bradley, Sharon A, Spec Coll Librn, University of Georgia, Alexander Campbell King Law Library, 225 Herty Dr, Athens, GA, 30602-6018. Tel: 706-542-5083. p. 459
Bradley, Sue, Adult Serv, Essex Library Association, Inc, 33 West Ave, Essex, CT, 06426-1196. Tel: 860-767-1560. p. 311
Bradley, Tanya, Libr Mgr, New York Public Library - Astor, Lenox & Tilden Foundations, Soundview Branch, 660 Soundview Ave, (@ Seward Ave), Bronx, NY, 10473. Tel: 718-589-0880. p. 1597
Bradley, Tiffany, Dir, Libr & Archives, Petroleum Museum Library & Hall of Fame, 1500 Interstate 20 W, Midland, TX, 79701. Tel: 432-683-4403. p. 2220
Bradley, Tina, Libr Dir, Arkansas State University, 1600 S College St, Mountain Home, AR, 72653-5326. Tel: 870-508-6112. p. 105
Bradley, Tina, Asst Librn, Emery County Library System, Cleveland Branch, 45 W Main, Cleveland, UT, 84518. Tel: 435-653-2204. p. 2261
Bradley, Venus, Supvr, Magee Rehabilitation Hospital, 1513 Race St, 6th Flr, Philadelphia, PA, 19102. Tel: 215-587-3146. p. 1982
Bradshaw, Bernice, Br Mgr, Shreve Memorial Library, North Caddo Branch, 615 N Pine St, Vivian, LA, 71082. Tel: 318-375-3975. p. 909
Bradshaw, Beth, Head, Ref & Tech Serv, Hickory Public Library, 375 Third St NE, Hickory, NC, 28601. Tel: 828-304-0500. p. 1696
Bradshaw, Cherron, Libr Asst I, New Jersey Institute of Technology, Barbara & Leonard Littman Architecture & Design Library, 456 Weston Hall, 323 King Blvd, Newark, NJ, 07102-1982. Tel: 973-596-3083. p. 1427
Bradshaw, Connie, Head Librn, Glenwood & Souris Regional Library, 18-114 Second St S, Souris, MB, R0K 2C0, CANADA. Tel: 204-483-2757. p. 2590
Bradshaw, David O, Dir, Electronic Res Librn, Warren Wilson College, 701 Warren Wilson Rd, Swannanoa, NC, 28778. Tel: 828-771-3059. p. 1718
Bradshaw, Debra, Dir, Libr Serv, Nazarene Theological Seminary, 1700 E Meyer Blvd, Kansas City, MO, 64131. Tel: 816-268-5472. p. 1257
Bradshaw, Elizabeth, Dir, Libr Serv, Wiley University, 711 Wiley Ave, Marshall, TX, 75670. Tel: 903-927-3275. p. 2216
Bradshaw, Jaime, Asst Dir, Somerset County Library System, 11767 Beechwood St, Princess Anne, MD, 21853. Tel: 410-968-0955. p. 973
Bradshaw, Kathy, Asst Dean for Organizational Dev, Virginia Commonwealth University Libraries, 901 Park Ave, Richmond, VA, 23284. Tel: 804-828-1171. p. 2343
Bradshaw, Kayla, Circ, Green County Public Library, 112 W Court St, Greensburg, KY, 42743. Tel: 270-932-7081. p. 857
Bradshaw, Lori, Med Librn, Saint Mary's Hospital, 56 Franklin St, Waterbury, CT, 06706. Tel: 203-709-6408. p. 344
Bradshaw, Marlys, Tech Serv Mgr, Supreme Court of Ohio, 65 S Front St, 11th Flr, Columbus, OH, 43215-3431. Tel: 614-387-9661. p. 1777
Bradshaw, Sharon K, Librn, Lawrence County Law Library Association, Lawrence County Courthouse, 4th Flr Annex, 111 S Fourth St, Ironton, OH, 45638-1586. Tel: 740-533-0582. p. 1791
Bradshaw, Tracie, Electronic Res Coordr, Colorado Mesa University, 1100 North Ave, Grand Junction, CO, 81501. Tel: 970-248-1520. p. 283
Bradsher, Elizabeth, Dir, Learning Res Ctr, Chattahoochee Valley Community College, Owen Hall, 2602 College Dr, Phenix City, AL, 36869. Tel: 334-291-4978. p. 32
Bradway, Paula, Tech Serv Librn, Ely Public Library, 1595 Dows St, Ely, IA, 52227. Tel: 319-848-7616. p. 751
Brady, Abigail, Head, Adult Serv, Summit Free Public Library, 75 Maple St, Summit, NJ, 07901-9984. Tel: 908-273-0350. p. 1445
Brady, Addy, Br Mgr, Montgomery County-Norristown Public Library, Royersford Public, 200 S Fourth Ave, Royersford, PA, 19468. Tel: 610-948-7277. p. 1971
Brady, Brandy, Dir, Library Servs & Ops, Northwest Missouri State University, 800 University Dr, Maryville, MO, 64468-6001. Tel: 660-562-1193. p. 1261
Brady, Carrie, Cat Mgr, Maryland Department of Legislative Services Library, B-00 Legislative Services Bldg, 90 State Circle, Annapolis, MD, 21401. Tel: 410-946-5400. p. 951
Brady, Cathy, Dir, Wyalusing Public Library, 115 Church St, Wyalusing, PA, 18853. Tel: 570-746-1711. p. 2024
Brady, Frances, Pub Serv Librn, Adler University, 17 N Dearborn St, 15th Flr, Chicago, IL, 60602. Tel: 312-662-4230. p. 553
Brady, Jane, Sister, Per/Circ Librn, Christ the King Seminary Library, 711 Knox Rd, East Aurora, NY, 14052. Tel: 716-652-8900. p. 1527
Brady, John, Asst Dir, Res, Springfield College, 263 Alden St, Springfield, MA, 01109-3797. Tel: 413-748-3505. p. 1057
Brady, Kathryn, Librn I, Cleveland State Community College Library, 3535 Adkisson Dr, Cleveland, TN, 37312-2813. Tel: 423-473-2277, 423-478-6209. p. 2093
Brady, Kelly, Br Mgr, Washington County Public Library, New Matamoras Branch, 100 Merchant St, New Matamoras, OH, 45767. Tel: 740-865-3386. p. 1799
Brady-Vickerman, Maureen, Circ Supvr, Libr Serv Spec, Valencia College, Poinciana Campus Library, 3255 Pleasant Hill Rd, Bldg 1, Rm 331, Kissimmee, FL, 34746. Tel: 407-582-6027. p. 414
Bragdon, Marc, Ref Librn, University of New Brunswick Libraries, Five Macaulay Lane, Fredericton, NB, E3B 5H5, CANADA. Tel: 506-458-7741. p. 2601
Bragg, Chloe, Cat Librn, Cleveland Museum of Art, 11150 East Blvd, Cleveland, OH, 44106-1797. Tel: 216-707-2530. p. 1767
Bragg, Gail, Asst Admin, Law Library of Louisiana, Louisiana Supreme Court, 2nd Flr, 400 Royal St, New Orleans, LA, 70130-2104. Tel: 504-310-2411. p. 901

Bragg, Kelli, Libr Mgr, Sno-Isle Libraries, Camano Island Library, 848 N Sunrise Blvd, Camano Island, WA, 98282-8770. Tel: 360-387-5150. p. 2370

Bragg, Laura, Librn, Pouch Cove Public Library, PO Box 40, Pouch Cove, NL, A0A 3L0, CANADA. Tel: 709-335-2652. p. 2608

Bragg-Hurlburt, Lisa, Circ Librn, Libr Dir, Colfax Public Library, 613 Main St, Colfax, WI, 54730. Tel: 715-962-4334. p. 2428

Braggs, Courtney, Br Mgr, Huntsville-Madison County Public Library, Cavalry Hill Public Library, 2800 Poplar Ave, Huntsville, AL, 35816. Tel: 256-970-6313. p. 22

Brahme, Maria, Head Librn, Pepperdine University Libraries, West Los Angeles Graduate Campus Library, Howard Hughes Ctr, 6100 Center Dr, Los Angeles, CA, 90045. Tel: 310-568-5670. p. 171

Brahms, William, Br Mgr, Camden County Library System, 203 Laurel Rd, Voorhees, NJ, 08043. Tel: 856-772-1636, Ext 7308. p. 1450

Brainard, Angela, Dir, Scribner Public Library, 530 Main St, Scribner, NE, 68057. Tel: 402-664-3540. p. 1335

Brainard, Lisa, Dir of Libr, The Sage Colleges, 140 New Scotland Ave, Albany, NY, 12208. Tel: 518-292-1959. p. 1483

Braithwaite, Elaine, City Librn, Bridgeport Public Library, 925 Broad St, Bridgeport, CT, 06604. Tel: 203-576-7400. p. 303

Brake, Carly, Campus Librn, Nova Scotia Community College, Institute of Technology Library, 5685 Leeds St, Halifax, NS, B3J 3C4, CANADA. Tel: 902-491-4694. p. 2619

Brakebill, Sandra, Dir, Niota Public Library, 11 E Main St, Niota, TN, 37826. Tel: 423-568-2613. p. 2122

Braker, Elizabeth, Dr, Chief Exec Officer, Organization for Tropical Studies Library, 408 Swift Ave, Durham, NC, 27705. Tel: 919-684-5774. p. 1686

Braker-Reed, Karen, Ch Serv, Susquehanna County Historical Society & Free Library Association, 458 High School Rd, Montrose, PA, 18801. Tel: 570-278-1881. p. 1965

Brakesmith, John, Dir, Technology, Saint Louis Public Library, 1301 Olive St, Saint Louis, MO, 63103. Tel: 314-539-0300. p. 1274

Braley, Mary, Mrs, Asst Libr Dir, Davis Memorial Library, 928 Cape Rd, Limington, ME, 04049. Tel: 207-637-2422. p. 930

Bram, Debbie, Libr Dir, Congregation Shaare Emeth, 11645 Ladue Rd, Saint Louis, MO, 63141. Tel: 314-692-5308. p. 1270

Braman, Kate, Govt Doc Librn, University of Wisconsin-Whitewater, 750 W Main St, Whitewater, WI, 53190-1790. Tel: 262-472-4671. p. 2488

Bramble, Diana, Superintendent, Kings Mountain National Military Park Library, 2625 Park Rd, Blacksburg, SC, 29702. Tel: 864-936-7921. p. 2047

Bramble, John, Assoc Dir, National Network of Libraries of Medicine Region 4, Univ Utah, Spencer S Eccles Health Sci Libr, Bldg 589, 10 North 1900 East, Salt Lake City, UT, 84112-5890. Tel: 801-585-9646. p. 2776

Brambley, Jamie, Dir, Fulton County Library, 227 N First St, McConnellsburg, PA, 17233-1003. Tel: 717-485-5327. p. 1958

Bramlett, Judy, Ref (Info Servs), Chester County Library, 100 Center St, Chester, SC, 29706. Tel: 803-377-8145. p. 2052

Bramlett, Rene, Dir, Clover Public Library District, 440 N Division St, Woodhull, IL, 61490. Tel: 309-334-2680. p. 664

Bramley, Darcy, Circ Supvr, Mansfield Public Library, 255 Hope St, Mansfield, MA, 02048-2353. Tel: 508-261-7380. p. 1031

Bramman, Julie, Librn, United States Marine Corps, 1524 Sixth St, MCAGCC Box 788150, Twentynine Palms, CA, 92278-8150. Tel: 760-830-6875. p. 254

Brammer, Charissa, Dir, Res Serv, Colorado State Library, 201 E Colfax Ave, Rm 309, Denver, CO, 80203-1799. Tel: 720-648-2948. p. 274

Branagan, Sara, Br Librn, Sussex County Library System, Sussex-Wantage, 69 Rte 639, Wantage, NJ, 07461. Tel: 973-875-3940. p. 1429

Branam-Snyder, Nikki, Asst Dir, Ocoee River Regional Library, 718 George St NW, Athens, TN, 37303-2214. Tel: 423-745-5194. p. 2088

Brancato, Michele, Interim Libr Mgr, Trocaire College Library, 360 Choate Ave, Buffalo, NY, 14220-2094. Tel: 716-827-2434. p. 1510

Branch, Mariana, Dir, Kingsville Public Library, 6006 Academy St, Kingsville, OH, 44048. Tel: 440-224-0239. p. 1793

Branch, Nicole, Dean, Univ Libr Serv, Santa Clara University Library, 500 El Camino Real, Santa Clara, CA, 95053-0500. Tel: 408-554-5020. p. 242

Branch, Sharon, Br Mgr, East Providence Public Library, Riverside, 475 Bullocks Point Ave, East Providence, RI, 02915. Tel: 401-433-4877. p. 2032

Branciforte, Jessica, Head, Children's & Young Adult Serv, Essex Library Association, Inc, 33 West Ave, Essex, CT, 06426-1196. Tel: 860-767-1560. p. 311

Brand, Beth, Librn, Desert Botanical Garden Library, 1201 N Galvin Pkwy, Phoenix, AZ, 85008. Tel: 480-481-8133. p. 69

Brand, Ross, Asst Mgr, Saint Louis County Library, Prairie Commons Branch, 915 Utz Lane, Hazelwood, MO, 63042-2739. Tel: 314-994-3300, Ext 3700. p. 1274

Brandenburg, Lisa, Br Mgr, Camden County Library System, Gloucester Township-Blackwood Rotary Library, 15 S Black Horse Pike, Blackwood, NJ, 08012. Tel: 856-228-0022. p. 1450

Brander, Elisabeth, Rare Bk Librn, Washington University Libraries, Bernard Becker Medical Library, 660 S Euclid Ave, Campus Box 8132, Saint Louis, MO, 63110. Tel: 314-362-4235. p. 1277

Brandi, Holly, Tech Serv Mgr, Findlay-Hancock County District Public Library, 206 Broadway, Findlay, OH, 45840-3382. Tel: 419-422-1712. p. 1785

Brandler, Sherry, Circ Supvr, Orange Beach Public Library, 26267 Canal Rd, Orange Beach, AL, 36561-3917. Tel: 251-981-2923. p. 32

Brandolino, Diane, Asst Librn, Will County Law Library, 14 W Jefferson St, 4th Flr, Joliet, IL, 60432-4300. Tel: 815-774-7887. p. 603

Brandon, Gina, Govt Doc, Ser, University of Baltimore, Law Library, Angelos Law Center, 7th thru 12th Flrs, 1401 N Charles St, Baltimore, MD, 21201. Tel: 410-837-4582. p. 957

Brandon, William, Acq & Pub Serv Librn, Christian Brothers University, 650 East Pkwy S, Memphis, TN, 38104. Tel: 901-321-3432. p. 2112

Brandon-Smith, Lindsay, Commun Engagement Mgr, Ashland Public Library, 224 Claremont Ave, Ashland, OH, 44805. Tel: 419-289-8188. p. 1746

Brandow, Elliot, Dir, Res & Instruction Serv, Rowan University Library, 201 Mullica Hill Rd, Glassboro, NJ, 08029. Tel: 856-256-4981. p. 1405

Brandt, Catherine, Tech Serv & Circ Supvr, Menasha Public Library, 440 First St, Menasha, WI, 54952-3143. Tel: 920-967-3683. p. 2455

Brandt, D Scott, Assoc Dean, Res, Purdue University Libraries, 504 W State St, West Lafayette, IN, 47907-2058. Tel: 765-494-2889. p. 725

Brandt, John, Electronic Res Librn, ILL, California State University, Stanislaus, One University Circle, Turlock, CA, 95382. Tel: 209-664-6563. p. 253

Brandt, Kimberly, Librn, Drake Public Library, 411 Main St, Drake, ND, 58736. Tel: 701-465-3732. p. 1732

Brandt, Mary, Libr Asst, Toledo Public Library, 206 E High St, Toledo, IA, 52342-1617. Tel: 641-484-3362. p. 786

Brandt, Sophia, Libr Dir, Marcellus Free Library, 32 Maple St, Marcellus, NY, 13108. Tel: 315-673-3221. p. 1569

Brandvold, Cathy S, Dir & Librn, Valier Public Library, 400 Teton Ave, Valier, MT, 59486. Tel: 406-279-3366. p. 1303

Brandwein, Edward, Head Librn, Patterson, Belknap, Webb & Tyler LLP Library, 1133 Avenue of the Americas, New York, NY, 10036. Tel: 212-336-2000. p. 1600

Branea, Dorian, Dir, Romanian Cultural Institute, 200 E 38th St, New York, NY, 10016. Tel: 212-687-0180. p. 1601

Branham, Janie, Interim Dir, Southeastern Louisiana University, SLU Box 10896, 1211 SGA Dr, Hammond, LA, 70402. Tel: 985-549-2027, 985-549-3860. p. 890

Branham, Stephanie, Librn, Cordelia B Preston Memorial Library, 510 Orleans Ave, Orleans, NE, 68966. Tel: 308-473-3425. p. 1331

Brann, Lesley, Head, Adult Serv, Head, Circ, Colchester-East Hants Public Library, 754 Prince St, Truro, NS, B2N 1G9, CANADA. Tel: 902-895-4183. p. 2623

Brann, Marge, Librn, First United Methodist Church, Nine N Almansor St, Alhambra, CA, 91801-2699. Tel: 626-289-4258. p. 116

Brannen, Samantha, Dir, Cape Sable Historical Society Archives & Library, 2401 Hwy 3, Barrington, NS, B0W 1E0, CANADA. Tel: 902-637-2185. p. 2616

Branner, Lee, Br Mgr, Athens County Public Libraries, Chauncey Public, 29 Converse St, Chauncey, OH, 45719. Tel: 740-797-2512. p. 1805

Branning, Katharine, VPres, Libr Serv, French Institute-Alliance Francaise Library, 22 E 60th St, New York, NY, 10022-1011. Tel: 646-388-6614. p. 1586

Brannock, Cindy, Br Librn, Dobson Community Library, 113 S Crutchfield St, Dobson, NC, 27017. Tel: 336-386-8208. p. 1683

Brannock, Jennifer, Spec Coll Librn, University of Southern Mississippi Library, William David McCain Library & Archives, 118 College Dr, No 5148, Hattiesburg, MS, 39406. Tel: 601-266-4347. p. 1219

Brannon, Barbie, Br Librn, New Madrid County Library, Parma Service Center, 209 Broad, Parma, MO, 63870. p. 1266

Brannon, Christopher, Info Serv, Coeur d'Alene Public Library, 702 E Front Ave, Coeur d'Alene, ID, 83814-2373. Tel: 208-769-2315. p. 519

Brannon, Debbie, Dir, Hardin County Library, 1365 Pickwick St, Savannah, TN, 38372. Tel: 731-925-4314, 731-925-6848. p. 2125

Brannon, Page, Head, Ref & Instruction, University of Alaska Anchorage, Consortium Library, 3211 Providence Dr, Anchorage, AK, 99508-8176. Tel: 907-786-1873. p. 43

Brannon, Sian, Assoc Dean Coll Mgt, University of North Texas Libraries, 1155 Union Circle, No 305190, Denton, TX, 76203-5017. Tel: 940-891-6945. p. 2170

Branske, Eric, Asst Libr Dir, Hales Corners Library, 5885 S 116th St, Hales Corners, WI, 53130-1707. Tel: 414-529-6150. p. 2440

Branson, Cathy, Dir, Libr Serv, Hazard Community & Technical College Library, One Community College Dr, Hazard, KY, 41701. Tel: 606-487-3550. p. 858

Branson, Cathy, Dir, Libr Serv, Hazard Community & Technical College, 601 Jefferson Ave, Jackson, KY, 41339. Tel: 606-487-3550. p. 860

Branson, Colleen, Dir, Mannford Public Library, 101 Green Valley Park Rd, Mannford, OK, 74044. Tel: 918-865-2665. p. 1852

Branson, Gary, Exec Dir, Fiscal Officer, Marion Public Library, 445 E Church St, Marion, OH, 43302-4290. Tel: 740-387-0992. p. 1799

Branson, Linda, Coordr, Support Serv, Saint Petersburg Public Library, 3745 Ninth Ave N, Saint Petersburg, FL, 33713. Tel: 727-893-7318. p. 441

Branson, Pamela, Dir, Sullivan County Public Library, 109 E Second St, Milan, MO, 63556. Tel: 660-265-3911. p. 1262

Branson, Timothy, Human Res Mgr, Wayne Township Library, 80 N Sixth St, Richmond, IN, 47374. Tel: 765-966-8291, Ext 1130. p. 715

Brant, Natalie, Ref Librn, State Library of Oregon, 250 Winter St NE, Salem, OR, 97301-3950. Tel: 503-378-5007. p. 1897

Brantley, Cammie, Libr Mgr, San Antonio Public Library, Cortez, 2803 Hunter Blvd, San Antonio, TX, 78224. Tel: 210-207-9130. p. 2239

Brantley, Christine, Mkt & Communications Mgr, Virginia Beach Public Library, Municipal Ctr, Bldg 19, Rm 210, 2416 Courthouse Dr, Virginia Beach, VA, 23452. Tel: 757-385-8709. p. 2350

Brantley, Kimberly, Libr Dir, City of Wolfforth Library, 508 E Hwy 62-82, Wolfforth, TX, 79382-7001. Tel: 806-855-4150. p. 2258

Brantley, Steve, Head, Ref, Eastern Illinois University, 600 Lincoln Ave, Charleston, IL, 61920. Tel: 217-581-6072. p. 552

Brantley, Tracy, Exec Dir, Atlanta Regional Council for Higher Education, 133 Peachtree St, Ste 4925, Atlanta, GA, 30303. Tel: 404-651-2668. p. 2764

Branum, Candise, Dir, Libr Serv, Oregon College of Oriental Medicine Library, 75 NW Couch St, Portland, OR, 97209. Tel: 503-253-3443, Ext 134. p. 1893

Brashear, Pat, Asst Dir, Midland County Public Library, 301 W Missouri Ave, Midland, TX, 79701. Tel: 432-688-4321. p. 2219

Brashears, Sarah, Asst Librn, Richland Parish Library, 1410 Louisa St, Rayville, LA, 71269. Tel: 318-728-4806. p. 906

Brasley, Stephanie, Dean of Libr, California State University Dominguez Hills, 1000 E Victoria St, Carson, CA, 90747. Tel: 310-243-3700. p. 129

Brass, Margaret, Libr Adminr, Tawowikamik Public Library, PO Box 100, Pelican Narrows, SK, S0P 0E0, CANADA. Tel: 306-632-2161. p. 2744

Brassel, Beth, YA Librn, Pollard Memorial Library, 401 Merrimack St, Lowell, MA, 01852. Tel: 978-674-4120. p. 1029

Brassell, Sally, Librn, Aphne Pattillo Nixon Public Library, 401 N Nixon Ave, Nixon, TX, 78140. Tel: 830-582-1913. p. 2222

Brasseur, Dina, Libr Dir, Acushnet Public Library, 232 Middle Rd, Acushnet, MA, 02743. Tel: 508-998-0270. p. 983

Brassil, Ellen, Dir, Baystate Medical Center, 759 Chestnut St, Springfield, MA, 01199. Tel: 413-794-1866. p. 1056

Braswell, Mavour, Dean of Libr, Howard County Junior College, 1001 Birdwell Lane, Big Spring, TX, 79720. Tel: 432-264-5025. p. 2148

Braswell, Mavour, Ms, Dir, Howard County Library, 500 Main St, Big Spring, TX, 79720. Tel: 432-264-2260. p. 2148

Braswell, Toni, Actg Br Mgr, Regional Mgr, Memphis Public Library, Whitehaven Branch, 4120 Mill Branch Rd, Memphis, TN, 38116. Tel: 901-415-2781. p. 2114

Bratcher, Kathryn, Librn, Filson Historical Society Library, 1310 S Third St, Louisville, KY, 40208. Tel: 502-635-5083. p. 865

Bratcher, Perry, Librn, Northern Kentucky University, University Dr, Highland Heights, KY, 41099. Tel: 859-572-5457. p. 859

Bratnober, Carolyn, Pub Serv Librn, Columbia University, The Burke Library at Union Theological Seminary, 3041 Broadway, New York, NY, 10027. Tel: 212-851-5606. p. 1583

Bratton, Diane, Circ, Millburn Free Public Library, 200 Glen Ave, Millburn, NJ, 07041. Tel: 973-376-1006, Ext 121. p. 1419

Bratton, Karen, Research Librn, Douglas County Museum, 123 Museum Dr, Roseburg, OR, 97471. Tel: 541-957-7007. p. 1895

Bratton, Megan, Pub Relations & Mkt Mgr, Natrona County Library, 307 E Second St, Casper, WY, 82601. Tel: 307-577-7323. p. 2492

Bratzel, Kaci, Libr Asst, New Mexico State University at Grants Library, 1500 N Third St, Grants, NM, 87020. Tel: 505-287-6638. p. 1469

Braud, Cheryl, Asst Dir, Iberia Parish Library, 445 E Main St, New Iberia, LA, 70560-3710. Tel: 337-364-7024, 337-364-7074. p. 900

Braud, John, Br Mgr, Iberia Parish Library, Jeanerette Branch, 411 Kentucky St, Jeanerette, LA, 70544. Tel: 337-276-4014. p. 900

Brauer, Meghan, Libr Dir, Wilson Community Library, 265 Young St, Wilson, NY, 14172-9500. Tel: 716-751-6070. p. 1666

Brault, Charles, Dir, Chamberlin Free Public Library, 46 Main St, Greenville, NH, 03048. Tel: 603-878-1105. p. 1365

Braun, Christine, Colls Mgr, Art Gallery of Hamilton, 123 King St W, Hamilton, ON, L8P 4S8, CANADA. Tel: 905-527-6610. p. 2644

Braun, Ken, Librn, Corteva Agriscience, 8325 NW 62nd Ave, Johnston, IA, 50131. Tel: 515-535-4818. p. 762

Braun, Marcia, Librn, Houston Community College-Central College, Central Campus Library, 1300 Holman, Houston, TX, 77004. Tel: 713-718-6133. p. 2194

Braun, Matthew E, Dir, Law Libr, Saint Louis University, Vincent C Immel Law Library, 100 N Tucker Blvd, Flrs 5 & 6, Saint Louis, MO, 63101. Tel: 314-977-3449. p. 1275

Braun-McGee, Suzanne, Librn, Eiteljorg Museum of American Indians & Western Art, 500 W Washington St, Indianapolis, IN, 46204-2707. Tel: 317-275-1347. p. 691

Braund-Allen, Juli, Librn, Alaska Resources Library & Information Services ARLIS, Library Bldg, 3211 Providence Dr, Ste 111, Anchorage, AK, 99508-4614. Tel: 907-786-7666. p. 41

Braund-Allen, Juli, Ref & Instruction, University of Alaska Anchorage, Consortium Library, 3211 Providence Dr, Anchorage, AK, 99508-8176. Tel: 907-786-1871. p. 43

Braunel, Emilie, Dir, Plum Lake Public Library, 8789 Peterson St, Sayner, WI, 54560. Tel: 715-542-2020. p. 2475

Brauner, Ashley, Librn, Saint Edward Public Library, 302 Beaver St, Saint Edward, NE, 68660. Tel: 402-678-2204. p. 1334

Brautigam, Colette, Coordr, Digital Coll Serv, Lawrence University, 113 S Lawe St, Appleton, WI, 54911-5683. p. 2420

Brautigam, Faith, Dir, Kokomo-Howard County Public Library, 220 N Union St, Kokomo, IN, 46901-4614. Tel: 765-457-3242. p. 699

Brautigam, Sandra, Br Mgr, Riverside County Library System, Wildomar Library, 34303 Mission Trail, Wildomar, CA, 92595. Tel: 951-471-3855. p. 203

Braver, Adam, Prog Dir, Roger Williams University Library, One Old Ferry Rd, Bristol, RI, 02809. Tel: 401-254-3720. p. 2030

Bravi, Robyn, Tech Consult, South Central Kansas Library System, 321 N Main St, South Hutchinson, KS, 67505. Tel: 620-663-3211. p. 837

Bravo, Deyse, Dir of Libr, Southern Adventist University, 4851 Industrial Dr, Collegedale, TN, 37315. Tel: 423-236-2789. p. 2094

Bravo, Roberto, Sr Dir, Administration & Operations, Pritzker Military Museum & Library, 104 S Michigan Ave, 2nd Flr, Chicago, IL, 60603. Tel: 312-374-9333. p. 567

Brawley, Beth, Br Mgr, Wayne County Public Library, Doylestown Branch, 169 N Portage St, Doylestown, OH, 44230. Tel: 330-804-4689. p. 1833

Braxton, Tyvonnia, Br Mgr, Worcester County Library, Ocean City Branch, 10003 Coastal Hwy, Ocean City, MD, 21842. Tel: 410-524-1818. p. 978

Bray, Angela, Br Mgr, Eugene Public Library, Bethel Branch, 1990 Echo Hollow Rd, Eugene, OR, 97402-7004. p. 1878

Bray, Angela, Br Mgr, Eugene Public Library, Sheldon Branch, 1566 Coburg Rd, Eugene, OR, 97401-4802. p. 1878

Bray, Angie, Br Serv Mgr, Eugene Public Library, 100 W Tenth Ave, Eugene, OR, 97401. Tel: 541-682-5450. p. 1878

Bray, Katie, Ad, Bellingham Public Library, 210 Central Ave, Bellingham, WA, 98225. Tel: 360-778-7230. p. 2358

Braye, Cherri, Dir, Libr Res, Thunder Bay Public Library, 285 Red River Rd, Thunder Bay, ON, P7B 1A9, CANADA. Tel: 807-684-6804. p. 2685

Braysen, lisa, Exec Dir, Libr Serv, University of Houston-Downtown, One Main St, Houston, TX, 77002. Tel: 713-221-8187. p. 2199

Brayton, Spencer A, Libr Mgr, Waubonsee Community College, Collins Hall, 2nd Flr, State Rte 47 at Waubonsee Dr, Sugar Grove, IL, 60554. Tel: 630-466-2405. p. 652

Braz, Zoltan L, Jr, Libr Dir, North Brunswick Free Public Library, 880 Hermann Rd, North Brunswick, NJ, 08902. Tel: 732-246-3545. p. 1429

Brazeal, Marlene, Circ Supvr, Evangel University, 1111 N Glenstone Ave, Springfield, MO, 65802. Tel: 417-865-2815, Ext 7268. p. 1280

Brazeau, Lyne, Br Head, Alfred & Plantagenet Public Library System, Lefaivre Branch, 1963 Hotel de Ville St, Lefaivre, ON, K0B 1J0, CANADA. p. 2652

Brazeau, Lyne, Br Head, Alfred & Plantagenet Public Library System, Plantagenet Branch, 550 Albert St, Plantagenet, ON, K0B 1L0, CANADA. Tel: 613-673-2051. p. 2652

Brazeau, Lyne, Library Contact, Alfred & Plantagenet Public Library System, 1963 Hotel de ville St, Lefaivre, ON, K0B 1J0, CANADA. Tel: 613-679-4928. p. 2652

Brazer, Susan, Supv Librn, Alameda Health System Medical Library, 1411 E 31st St, Oakland, CA, 94602. Tel: 510-437-4701. p. 184

Brazil, Joanna, Youth Serv Librn, Winfield Public Library, 605 College St, Winfield, KS, 67156-3199. Tel: 620-221-4470. p. 845

Brdecka, John, Exec Dir, Hancock County Library System, 312 Hwy 90, Bay Saint Louis, MS, 39520-3595. Tel: 228-467-5282. p. 1211

Breakenridge, Susan, Asst Dean, University of Oregon Libraries, 1501 Kincaid St, Eugene, OR, 97403-1299. Tel: 541-346-3053. p. 1879

Breakfield, David, Supvr, Manatee County Public Library System, South Manatee County, 6081 26th St N, Bradenton, FL, 34207. Tel: 941-755-3892. p. 387

Breault, Liz, Dir, Abbott Memorial Library, One Church St, Dexter, ME, 04930. Tel: 207-924-7292. p. 923

Breaux, Stephanie, Dir, Whittier College, Fairchild Aerial Photography Collection, Fairchild Collection, Whittier College, Whittier, CA, 90608. Tel: 562-907-4220. p. 259

Breazile, Jerry, Bus Mgr, Nebraska Library Commission, The Atrium, 1200 N St, Ste 120, Lincoln, NE, 68508-2023. Tel: 402-471-2045. p. 1322

Brecheen, Sherry, Libr Dir, Onalaska Public Library, 372 South FM 356, Onalaska, TX, 77360. Tel: 936-646-2665. p. 2223

Brecheisen, Grady, Adult & Tech Serv Coordr, Birchard Public Library of Sandusky County, 423 Croghan St, Fremont, OH, 43420. Tel: 419-334-7101. p. 1786

Breckbill, Anita, Music Librn, University of Nebraska-Lincoln, Music Library, Westbrook Music Bldg, Rm 30, Lincoln, NE, 68588-0101. Tel: 402-472-6300. p. 1323

Breckenridge, Jessica, Archivist, St Petersburg Museum of History, 335 Second Ave NE, Saint Petersburg, FL, 33701. Tel: 727-894-1052, Ext 202. p. 441

Brecknock, Darlyne, Commun Librn, Cariboo Regional District Library, Alexis Creek Branch, 7651 Yells Rd, Alexis Creek, BC, V0L 1A0, CANADA. Tel: 250-394-4346. p. 2584

Bredberg, Leann, Dir, Andalusia Township Library, 503 W Second St, Andalusia, IL, 61232. Tel: 309-798-2542. p. 536

Bredekamp, Caroline M, Dir, Preston Public Library, One W Gillet, Preston, IA, 52069. Tel: 563-689-3581. p. 778

Bredenkamp, Paige, E-Resources & School Library Consultant, Wyoming State Library, 2800 Central Ave, Cheyenne, WY, 82002. Tel: 307-777-6331. p. 2493

Bree, Joseph D, Head, Access Serv, University of Maryland-Eastern Shore, 11868 Academic Oval, Princess Anne, MD, 21853. Tel: 410-651-6270. p. 973

Breed, Liz, Asst Dir, Jackson District Library, 244 W Michigan Ave, Jackson, MI, 49201. Tel: 517-788-4087. p. 1120

Breedlove, Marea, Dir, Locust Grove Public Library, 715 E Main St, Locust Grove, OK, 74352. Tel: 918-479-6585. p. 1852

Breen, Joanna, Exec Dir, Boothbay Harbor Memorial Library, Four Oak St, Boothbay Harbor, ME, 04538. Tel: 207-633-3112. p. 918

Breen, Kimberly, Circ Librn, Millbrook Public Library, 3650 Grandview Rd, Millbrook, AL, 36054. Tel: 334-285-6688. p. 25

Breen, Maribeth, Dir, Henry Carter Hull Library, Inc, Ten Killingworth Tpk, Clinton, CT, 06413. Tel: 860-669-2342. p. 306

Breen, Marty J, Ref & Instruction Librn, Concordia University, 7400 Augusta St, River Forest, IL, 60305-1499. Tel: 708-209-3181. p. 639

Breen, Peggy, Librn, Oregon School for the Deaf Library, 999 Locust St NE, Salem, OR, 97301-0954. Tel: 503-378-3825. p. 1896

Breen, Rachel, Libr Dir, Norwell Public Library, 64 South St, Norwell, MA, 02061-2433. Tel: 781-659-2015. p. 1043

Breeyear, Tom, Educ Spec, Ray Brook Federal Correctional Institution Library, 128 Ray Brook Rd, Ray Brook, NY, 12977. Tel: 518-897-4000, 518-897-4161. p. 1626

Breezeel, Brenda, Syst Librn, Harding University, 915 E Market St, Searcy, AR, 72149-5615. Tel: 501-279-5387. p. 109

Brehm-Heeger, Paula, Dir, Public Library of Cincinnati & Hamilton County, 800 Vine St, Cincinnati, OH, 45202-2009. Tel: 513-369-6941. p. 1761

Breidenbaugh, Andrew, Dir of Libr, Tampa-Hillsborough County Public Library System, 102 E Seventh Ave, Tampa, FL, 33602-3704. p. 448

Breitbach, Will, Dean, Libr Serv & Educ Tech, Shasta College Library, 11555 Old Oregon Trail, Redding, CA, 96003-7692. Tel: 530-242-7550. p. 198

Breithaupt, Lisa, Br Mgr, Clermont County Public Library, Goshen Branch, 6678 State Rte 132, Goshen, OH, 45122. Tel: 513-722-1221. p. 1803

Breithaupt, Richard H, Jr, Libr Dir, American Heritage Library & Museum, 600 S Central Ave, Glendale, CA, 91204-2009. Tel: 818-240-1775. p. 148

Breithut, Kathy, Youth Serv Mgr, Worcester County Library, 307 N Washington St, Snow Hill, MD, 21863. Tel: 410-632-2600. p. 978

Breitkopf, Mia, Instruction Coordr, Res Serv, Saint John Fisher University, 3690 East Ave, Rochester, NY, 14618-3599. Tel: 585-385-7399. p. 1630

Breitkreutz, Diane, Librn, Ord Township Library, 1718 M St, Ord, NE, 68862. Tel: 308-728-3012. p. 1331

Breitling, Mary, Dir, Hand County Library, 402 N Broadway, Miller, SD, 57362-1438. Tel: 605-853-3693. p. 2079

Brekhus, Rachel, Humanities Librn, University of Missouri-Columbia, Elmer Ellis Library, 104 Ellis Library, Columbia, MO, 65201-5149. Tel: 573-882-7563. p. 1243

Breland, Mary-Louise, Dir, Laurel-Jones County Library System, Inc, 530 Commerce St, Laurel, MS, 39440. Tel: 601-428-4313, Ext 101. p. 1224

Breland, Moddie, Head Librn, Ref & Instruction, Mercy College Libraries, Bronx Campus, 1200 Waters Pl, Bronx, NY, 10461. Tel: 718-678-8850. p. 1526

Breland, Moddie V, Jr, Dr, Dir of Libr, Mercy College Libraries, 555 Broadway, Dobbs Ferry, NY, 10522. Tel: 914-674-7256. p. 1526

Brelsford, Emma, Ch Serv, Boyden Library, Ten Bird St, Foxborough, MA, 02035. Tel: 508-543-1245. p. 1019

Bremer, Peter, Ref & Instruction Coordr, University of Minnesota-Morris, 600 E Fourth St, Morris, MN, 56267. Tel: 320-589-6173. p. 1189

Bremigen, Jean, Libr Operations & Pub Serv Mgr, Pennsylvania College of Technology, 999 Hagan Way, Williamsport, PA, 17701. Tel: 570-327-4523. p. 2023

Bremner, Sally, Med Ref Librn, University of Alaska Anchorage, Consortium Library, 3211 Providence Dr, Anchorage, AK, 99508-8176. Tel: 907-786-1871. p. 43

Brende, Susan, Librn, Moody County Resource Center, Colman Branch, 120 N Main Ave, Colman, SD, 57017. Tel: 605-534-3154. p. 2076

Brendle, Susie, Br Mgr, Mountain Regional Library System, Union County Public Library, 303 Hunt Martin St, Blairsville, GA, 30512. Tel: 706-745-7491. p. 504

Brendler, Beth, Assoc Teaching Prof, University of Missouri-Columbia, 303 Townsend Hall, Columbia, MO, 65211. Tel: 573-882-4546. p. 2788

Breneisen, Corey, Dir, Muncy Public Library, 108 S Main St, Muncy, PA, 17756-0119. Tel: 570-546-5014. p. 1967

Brenes-Dawsey, Joseph, Dr, Sr Librn for Assessment & Instruction, Piedmont University Library, 1021 Central Ave, Demorest, GA, 30535. Tel: 706-776-0111. p. 476

Brenion, Frederick, Sr Librn, Patton State Hospital, Patients Library, 3102 E Highland Ave, Patton, CA, 92369. Tel: 909-425-6039. p. 195

Brennan, Adam, Ref Librn, Tulsa Community College Libraries, Metro Campus, 909 S Boston Ave, Tulsa, OK, 74119-2011. Tel: 918-595-7330. p. 1866

Brennan, Amy, Coll Serv Librn, Duke University Libraries, Ford Library, 100 Fuqua Dr, Durham, NC, 27708. Tel: 919-660-7873. p. 1684

Brennan, Carolyn, Co-Dir, Kellogg-Hubbard Library, 135 Main St, Montpelier, VT, 05602. Tel: 802-223-3338. p. 2289

Brennan, Cathy, Libr Mgr, Alberta Beach Municipal Library, 4815 50 Ave, Alberta Beach, AB, T0E 0A0, CANADA. Tel: 780-924-3491. p. 2521

Brennan, David, Libr Dir, McDaniel College, 2 College Hill, Westminster, MD, 21157-4390. Tel: 410-857-2284. p. 981

Brennan, Emily, Res & Educ Informationist, Medical University of South Carolina Libraries, 171 Ashley Ave, Ste 419, Charleston, SC, 29425-0001. Tel: 843-792-9275. p. 2051

Brennan, Monica, Head, Children's Dept, Turner Free Library, Two N Main St, Randolph, MA, 02368. Tel: 781-961-0932. p. 1049

Brennan, Patti, Dir, US National Library of Medicine, 8600 Rockville Pike, Bethesda, MD, 20894. Tel: 301-594-5983. p. 2766

Brennan, Ray, Tech Librn, Cross' Mills Public Library, 4417 Old Post Rd, Charlestown, RI, 02813. Tel: 401-364-6211. p. 2030

Brennan, Ryan, Br Supvr, Public Library of Brookline, Coolidge Corner, 31 Pleasant St, Brookline, MA, 02446. Tel: 617-730-2380. p. 1003

Brennan, Ryan, Dir, Dedham Public Library, 43 Church St, Dedham, MA, 02026. Tel: 781-751-9284. p. 1014

Brennan, Theresa, Asst Librn, Stirling-Rawdon Public Library, 43 W Front St, Stirling, ON, K0K 3E0, CANADA. Tel: 613-395-2837. p. 2681

Brennecke, Adrienne, Mgr, Federal Reserve Bank of Saint Louis, One Federal Reserve Bank Plaza, Saint Louis, MO, 63102-2005. Tel: 314-444-7479. p. 1270

Brenner, Aaron, Assoc Univ Librn, Res & Learning, University of Pittsburgh Library System, 3960 Forbes Ave, Pittsburgh, PA, 15260. Tel: 412-648-3330. p. 1996

Brenner, Anji, City Librn, Mill Valley Public Library, 375 Throckmorton Ave, Mill Valley, CA, 94941. Tel: 415-389-4292, Ext 4742. p. 177

Brenner, Eric, Librn, Skyline College Library, 3300 College Dr, San Bruno, CA, 94066-1698. Tel: 650-738-4311. p. 214

Brenner, Kathleen C, Syst Tech, Stonehill College, 320 Washington St, Easton, MA, 02357. Tel: 508-565-1213. p. 1016

Brenner, Michelle, Dir, Casco Public Library, Five Leach Hill Rd, Casco, ME, 04015. Tel: 207-627-4541. p. 921

Breno, Pat, Libr Tech, Rutherford B Hayes Presidential Library & Museums, Spiegel Grove, Fremont, OH, 43420-2796. Tel: 419-332-2081. p. 1786

Brenot, Nancy, Libr Spec, Allegheny College, 520 N Main St, Meadville, PA, 16335. Tel: 814-332-3363. p. 1959

Brent, Bethaney, Librn, Breckinridge County Public Library, Cloverport Community, 301 Poplar St, Cloverport, KY, 40111. Tel: 270-788-3388, Ext 236. p. 857

Brent, Katherine, Archives Librn, ILL Librn, SUNY Cobleskill College of Agriculture & Technology, 142 Schenectady Ave, Cobleskill, NY, 12043. Tel: 518-255-5841. p. 1520

Brents, Jessica, Br Mgr, Mattie Terry Public Library, 311 N Johnson, Valliant, OK, 74764. Tel: 866-258-6157. p. 1867

Brenycz, Andrew M, Libr Asst, Seton Hall University, 400 S Orange Ave, South Orange, NJ, 07079. Tel: 973-761-9198, 973-761-9336. p. 1443

Brenza, Andrew, Dir, Free Public Library of Audubon, 239 Oakland Ave, Audubon, NJ, 08106-1598. Tel: 856-547-8686. p. 1388

Bresee, Andrea, Dir, Johnston Public Library, 210 W Tenth St, Baxter Springs, KS, 66713. Tel: 620-856-5591. p. 798

Bresett, Ardyce, Dir, Pember Library & Museum of Natural History, 33 W Main St, Granville, NY, 12832. Tel: 518-642-2525. p. 1540

Bresler, Barbara, Librn, Adath Israel Congregation, 3201 E Galbraith Rd, Cincinnati, OH, 45236. Tel: 513-793-1800. p. 1759

Bresler, Carey, Dir, Oxford Public Library, 48 S Second St, Oxford, PA, 19363-1377. Tel: 610-932-9625. p. 1973

Breslin, Jessica, Br Mgr, Cuyahoga County Public Library, Bay Village Branch, 502 Cahoon Rd, Bay Village, OH, 44140-2179. Tel: 440-871-6392. p. 1813

Bresnahan, Kimberly, Coordr, Libr Serv, Missouri Department of Corrections, 2729 Plaza Dr, Jefferson City, MO, 65109-1146. Tel: 573-526-6540. p. 1252

Bressette, Jody, Actg Chief Exec Officer, Tay Township Public Library, 715 Fourth Ave, Port McNicoll, ON, L0K 1R0, CANADA. Tel: 705-534-3511. p. 2674

Bressler, Amanda, Asst Dir, Albany Public Library, 2450 14th Ave SE, Albany, OR, 97322. Tel: 541-917-7580. p. 1871

Bressler, Jennifer Balas, Asst Dir, Pub Serv, Reading Public Library, 100 S Fifth St, Reading, PA, 19602. Tel: 610-655-6350. p. 2000

Breton, Ariane, Head of Library Systems & Colls, Lycoming College, One College Pl, Williamsport, PA, 17701. Tel: 570-321-4068. p. 2023

Breton, Maryse, Head, Client Serv, Polytechnique Montreal Library, Campus de l'Universite de Montreal, 2500, chemin de Polytechnique, 2900, boul Edouard-Montpetit, Montreal, QC, H3T 1J4, CANADA. Tel: 514-340-4711, Ext 4659. p. 2727

Bretsnyder, Shelly, Ch, Saint Charles City-County Library District, Corporate Parkway Branch, 1200 Corporate Pkwy, Wentzville, MO, 63385-4828. Tel: 636-327-4010, 636-332-8280. p. 1278
Brett, Morgan, Head, Patron Serv, Sayville Library, 88 Greene Ave, Sayville, NY, 11782. Tel: 631-589-4440. p. 1637
Brett, Pam, Br Mgr, Albemarle Regional Library, Northampton Memorial Library, 207 W Jefferson St, Jackson, NC, 27845. Tel: 252-534-3571. p. 1727
Breu, Amanda, Head, Access Serv, University of Saint Thomas, 2115 Summit Ave, Mail Box 5004, Saint Paul, MN, 55105. Tel: 651-962-5498. p. 1202
Breuer, Jennifer, Dir, Holston River Regional Library, 2700 S Roan St, Ste 435, Johnson City, TN, 37601-7587. Tel: 423-926-2951. p. 2104
Brew, Charlar, Dir, Saint Martin Parish Library, 201 Porter St, Saint Martinville, LA, 70582. Tel: 337-394-2207, Ext 223. p. 907
Brewer, Amanda J, Libr Dir, Harlan Community Library, 718 Court St, Harlan, IA, 51537. Tel: 712-755-5934. p. 757
Brewer, Amy, Libr Dir, Pawnee Public Library, 653 Illinois St, Pawnee, OK, 74058. Tel: 918-762-2138. p. 1860
Brewer, Brittany, Libr Dir, Melbourne Public Library, 603 Main St, Melbourne, IA, 50162. Tel: 641-482-3115. p. 769
Brewer, Cyndi, Ch Serv, Ottawa Library, 105 S Hickory St, Ottawa, KS, 66067. Tel: 785-242-3080. p. 829
Brewer, Debra, Br Mgr, Alleghany County Public Library, 115 Atwood St, Sparta, NC, 28675. Tel: 336-372-5573. p. 1717
Brewer, Dianne, Asst Librn, Yalobusha County Public Library System, 14432 Main St, Coffeeville, MS, 38922-2590. Tel: 662-675-8822. p. 1214
Brewer Dickman, Amanda, Dir, Beaufort County Library, 311 Scott St, Beaufort, SC, 29902. p. 2047
Brewer, Gayla C, Dir, Libr Serv, Chattanooga College Medical, Dental & Technical Careers, 5600 Brainerd Rd, Ste B38, Chattanooga, TN, 37411. Tel: 423-305-7781. p. 2091
Brewer, Janet L, Dr, Libr Dir, Anderson University, 1100 E Fifth St, Anderson, IN, 46012-3495. Tel: 765-641-4280. p. 668
Brewer, Jessica, Br Mgr, First Regional Library, Emily Jones Pointer Public Library, 104 Main St, Como, MS, 38619. Tel: 662-526-5283. p. 1220
Brewer, Johnette, Libr Spec, Central Carolina Technical College Library, 506 N Guignard Dr, Sumter, SC, 29150. Tel: 803-778-7884. p. 2071
Brewer, Julie, Assoc Univ Librn, Human Res, Assoc Univ Librn, Organizational Develop, University of Delaware Library, 181 S College Ave, Newark, DE, 19717-5267. Tel: 302-831-2965. p. 355
Brewer, Kevin, Head, Coll Mgt, Head, Resource Sharing, Utah State University, 3000 Old Main Hill, Logan, UT, 84322-3000. Tel: 435-797-3961. p. 2265
Brewer, Kit, Ms, Libr Mgr, Hampton B Allen Library, 120 S Greene St, Wadesboro, NC, 28170. Tel: 704-694-5177. p. 1719
Brewer, Meave, Ch, Frankfort Community Public Library, 208 W Clinton St, Frankfort, IN, 46041. Tel: 765-654-8746. p. 685
Brewer, Megan, Ch, Citizens Library, 55 S College St, Washington, PA, 15301. Tel: 724-222-2400. p. 2018
Brewer, Michael, Senior Info Resources Officer, University of Arizona Libraries, 1510 E University Blvd, Tucson, AZ, 85721. Tel: 520-307-2771. p. 83
Brewer, Nikki, Libr Dir, Burt Public Library, 119 Walnut St, Burt, IA, 50522. Tel: 515-924-3680. p. 736
Brewer, Patsy, Libr Dir, Waynesboro-Wayne County Library System, 1103A Mississippi Dr, Waynesboro, MS, 39367. Tel: 601-735-2268. p. 1235
Brewer, Purnell, Info Tech, Syst Adminr, Saint John the Baptist Parish Library, 2920 New Hwy 51, LaPlace, LA, 70068. Tel: 985-652-6857. p. 894
Brewer, Rick, Libr Dir, University of Kentucky Libraries, Medical Center Library, William R Willard Medical Education Bldg 298, 800 Rose St, Lexington, KY, 40536-0298. Tel: 859-323-5296. p. 864
Brewer, Sophia, Coll Develop Librn, Grand Rapids Community College, 140 Ransom NE Ave, Grand Rapids, MI, 49503. Tel: 616-234-3868. p. 1110
Brewer, Tanisha, Evening/Weekend Supvr, Judson University, 1151 N State St, Elgin, IL, 60123. Tel: 847-628-2030. p. 584
Brewer, Tracie, Libr Dir, Selma Public Library, 301 N Pollock St, Selma, NC, 27576. Tel: 919-965-8613, Ext 7001. p. 1716
Brewster, Chris, Dir, Waverly Free Library, 18 Elizabeth St, Waverly, NY, 14892. Tel: 607-565-9341. p. 1661
Brewster, Erica, Dir, Edward U Demmer Memorial Library, 6961 W School St, Three Lakes, WI, 54562. Tel: 715-546-3391. p. 2481
Brewster, Joy, Dir, Wells Village Library, Five E Wells Rd, Wells, VT, 05774-9791. Tel: 802-645-0611. p. 2297
Brewster, Mary, Dir, Bethalto Public Library District, 321 S Prairie St, Bethalto, IL, 62010-1525. Tel: 618-377-8141. p. 542
Brezina, Jason, Circ Mgr, Midwestern State University, 3410 Taft Blvd, Wichita Falls, TX, 76308-2099. Tel: 940-397-4176. p. 2257
Breznay, Ann Marie, Assoc Dean, Budget & Planning, University of Utah, J Willard Marriott Library, 295 S 1500 East, Salt Lake City, UT, 84112-0860. Tel: 801-581-3852. p. 2272
Brezovar, Debra, Libr Operations Supvr, Carroll University, 100 N East Ave, Waukesha, WI, 53186. Tel: 262-524-7307. p. 2484
Brian, Tober, Metadata Librn, Utah State Library Division, 250 N 1950 West, Ste A, Salt Lake City, UT, 84116-7901. Tel: 801-715-6752. p. 2272
Briand, Marie, Libr Coord, Cegep de Jonquiere, 2505 rue St Hubert, Jonquiere, QC, G7X 7W2, CANADA. Tel: 418-547-2191, Ext 6303. p. 2714
Briand, Mary B, Head Librn, Harris Corporation, Harris Corp, 1000 Charles J Herbert Dr, MS HTC-1N, Palm Bay, FL, 32905. p. 434
Briand, Simone, Dir, Cleveland University Chiropractic & Health Sciences, 10850 Lowell Ave, Overland Park, KS, 66210. Tel: 913-234-0814. p. 829
Brice, Cheryl, Dept Head, Adult Serv, Eastern Monroe Public Library, 1002 N Ninth St, Stroudsburg, PA, 18360. Tel: 570-421-0800. p. 2010
Brice, Donna, Circ, Manchester Community College Library, Great Path, Manchester, CT, 06040. Tel: 860-512-2878. p. 320
Brice, Kenton, Dir, University of Oklahoma Libraries, University of Oklahoma College of Law, 300 Timberdell Rd, Norman, OK, 73019. Tel: 405-325-4311. p. 1856
Brice, Michael, Commun Libr Mgr, Queens Library, Saint Albans Community Library, 191-05 Linden Blvd, Saint Albans, NY, 11412. Tel: 718-528-8196. p. 1555
Bricker, Lisa, Youth Serv, Anchorage Public Library, 3600 Denali St, Anchorage, AK, 99503. Tel: 907-343-2840. p. 42
Brickey, Sherri, Libr Dir, Brown Public Library, 93 S Main St, Northfield, VT, 05663. Tel: 802-485-4621. p. 2290
Brideau, Marthe, Chief Librn, Universite de Moncton, 18, ave Antonine-Maillet, Moncton, NB, E1A 3E9, CANADA. Tel: 506-858-4012. p. 2603
Bridgeman, Matthew, Info & Educ Librn, Rutgers University Libraries, Robert Wood Johnson Library of the Health Sciences, One Robert Wood Johnson Pl, New Brunswick, NJ, 08903. p. 1425
Bridges, Amber, Ch, Hancock County Public Library, 1210 Madison St, Hawesville, KY, 42348. Tel: 270-927-6760. p. 858
Bridges, Debbie, Cat Mgr, Stone County Library, 322 West State Hwy 248, Galena, MO, 65656. Tel: 417-357-6410. p. 1247
Bridges, Emily, Pub Serv Librn, Advocates for Youth, 1325 G St NW, Ste 980, Washington, DC, 20005. Tel: 202-419-3420, Ext 43. p. 359
Bridges, Evette, Asst Br Mgr, Ch, Atlanta-Fulton Public Library System, Fairburn Branch, 60 Valley View Dr, Fairburn, GA, 30213. Tel: 404-613-5750. p. 461
Bridges, James D, Circ Mgr, West Baton Rouge Parish Library, 830 N Alexander Ave, Port Allen, LA, 70767. Tel: 225-342-7920. p. 906
Bridges, Kevin, ILL, Gardner-Webb University, 110 S Main St, Boiling Springs, NC, 28017. Tel: 704-406-4290. p. 1674
Bridges, Petre, Mr, Libr Dir, Macon County-Tuskegee Public Library, 302 S Main St, Tuskegee, AL, 36083. Tel: 334-727-5192. p. 38
Bridges, Sherry, Br Mgr, Mid-Continent Public Library, Red Bridge Branch, 11140 Locust St, Kansas City, MO, 64131. Tel: 816-942-1780. p. 1251
Bridges, Shirley, Supvr, Libr Serv, Paris Junior College, 2400 Clarksville St, Paris, TX, 75460. Tel: 903-782-0215, 903-782-0415. p. 2225
Bridgett, Inez, Digital Serv Librn, United States Geological Survey Library, Mail Stop 150, 12201 Sunrise Valley Dr, Reston, VA, 20192. p. 2340
Bridgewater, David, Dir, Stephenson Memorial Library, 761 Forest Rd, Greenfield, NH, 03047. Tel: 603-547-2790. p. 1365
Bridgewater, Gera J, Librn, Delgado Community College, City Park Campus, Marvin E Thames Sr Learning Resource Ctr, 615 City Park Ave, Bldg 7, New Orleans, LA, 70119. Tel: 504-671-5360. p. 900
Bridwell, Joy, Libr Dir, Stone Child College, 8294 Upper Box Elder Rd, Box Elder, MT, 59521. Tel: 406-395-4875, Ext 1213. p. 1289
Briese, LeeAnn, Dir, Community Library, 24615 89th St, Salem, WI, 53168. Tel: 262-843-3348. p. 2475
Brigandi, Lisa, Librn, San Jose City College Library, LRC Bldg, 2nd & 3rd Flrs, 2100 Moorpark Ave, San Jose, CA, 95128-2799. Tel: 408-288-3775. p. 230
Brigante, Cheryl, ILS LIbrn, Metadata Librn, Stonehill College, 320 Washington St, Easton, MA, 02357. Tel: 505-565-1151. p. 1016
Brigantino, Maria, Bus Mgr, Fort Erie Public Library, 136 Gilmore Rd, Fort Erie, ON, L2A 2M1, CANADA. Tel: 905-871-2546, Ext 307. p. 2642
Brigati, Danielle, Libr Dir, Butt-Holdsworth Memorial Library, 505 Water St, Kerrville, TX, 78028. Tel: 830-257-8422. p. 2205
Briggs, Amanda, Asst Dir, Waterville Public Library, 206 White St, Waterville, NY, 13480. Tel: 315-841-4651. p. 1660
Briggs, Amanda, Librn, Petersburg Public Library, A P Hill Branch, 1237 Halifax St, Petersburg, VA, 23803. Tel: 804-733-2391. p. 2337
Briggs, Celia, Librn, Friendship Public Library, Three Main St, Friendship, ME, 04547. Tel: 207-832-5332. p. 925
Briggs, Isabelle, YA Serv, Altadena Library District, 600 E Mariposa St, Altadena, CA, 91001. Tel: 626-798-0833. p. 116
Briggs, Krista, Librn, Gouverneur Correctional Facility, 112 Scotch Settlement Rd, Gouverneur, NY, 13642. Tel: 315-287-7351. p. 1540
Briggs, Michele, Libr Dir, Underwood Memorial Library, 2006 Main St, Fayette, ME, 04349. Tel: 207-685-3778. p. 925

Briggs, Nola, Librn, Walthill Public Library, 323 Main St, Walthill, NE, 68067. Tel: 402-846-5051. p. 1340
Briggs, Rachel, Br Mgr, Clayton County Library System, Morrow Branch, 6225 Maddox Rd, Morrow, GA, 30260. Tel: 404-366-7749. p. 483
Briggs, Tonya, Br Mgr, Cleveland Public Library, Addison, 6901 Superior Ave, Cleveland, OH, 44103. Tel: 216-623-6906. p. 1768
Briggs, Tonya, Asst Dean, Cuyahoga Community College, Metropolitan Campus Library, 2900 Community College Ave, Cleveland, OH, 44115. Tel: 216-987-4296. p. 1769
Brigham, David R, Dr, Pres & Chief Exec Officer, Historical Society of Pennsylvania, 1300 Locust St, Philadelphia, PA, 19107-5699. Tel: 215-732-6200, Ext 213. p. 1981
Brigham, Doug, Shared Print Archive Network Coord, Council of Prairie & Pacific University Libraries, 150B -1711 85th St NW, Calgary, AB, T3R 1J3, CANADA. Tel: 604-827-0578. p. 2777
Brigham, Jeffrey, Libr Dir, Spellman Museum of Stamps & Postal History Library, 241 Wellesley St, Weston, MA, 02493. Tel: 781-768-8367. p. 1068
Brigham, Lois, Br Mgr, Van Buren District Library, Covert Branch, 33680 M-140 Hwy, Covert, MI, 49043. Tel: 269-764-1298. p. 1096
Bright, Donna, Chief Librn, Exec Officer, Ajax Public Library, 55 Harwood Ave S, Ajax, ON, L1S 2H8, CANADA. Tel: 905-683-4000, Ext 8825. p. 2627
Bright, Hal, Dir of the Univ Libr, A T Still University, 5850 E Still Circle, Mesa, AZ, 85206-6091. Tel: 480-219-6036. p. 66
Bright, Kawanna, Dr, Asst Prof, East Carolina University, 104B Ragsdale Hall, Greenville, NC, 27858. Tel: 252-737-1150. p. 2790
Bright, Laura, Adult Serv, Ref Librn, Harnett County Public Library, 601 S Main St, Lillington, NC, 27546-6107. Tel: 910-893-3446. p. 1700
Bright, Samantha, Libr Mgr, New York Public Library - Astor, Lenox & Tilden Foundations, Todt Hill-Westerleigh Branch, 2550 Victory Blvd, (Past Willowbrook Rd), Staten Island, NY, 10314. Tel: 718-494-1642. p. 1597
Bright, Sherry, Dir, Buchanan County Public Library, 1185 Poe Town St, Grundy, VA, 24614-9613. Tel: 276-935-5721. p. 2322
Brightly, Patricia, Chief Librn, Ch, ILL Librn, Whitneyville Library Association, Inc, Six Cross St, Whitneyville, ME, 04654. Tel: 207-255-8077. p. 946
Brightly, Renee, Asst Cat Librn, Asst Librn, Whitneyville Library Association, Inc, Six Cross St, Whitneyville, ME, 04654. Tel: 207-255-8077. p. 946
Brighton, Debra F, Libr Dir, El Segundo Public Library, 111 W Mariposa Ave, El Segundo, CA, 90245. Tel: 310-524-2730. p. 140
Brightwell, Lori, Libr Dir, Zephyrhills Public Library, 5347 Eighth St, Zephyrhills, FL, 33542. Tel: 813-780-0064. p. 456
Brigl, Ursula, Chief Librn, Cranbrook Public Library, 1212 Second St N, Cranbrook, BC, V1C 4T6, CANADA. Tel: 250-426-4063. p. 2565
Brigss, Valorie, Asst Dir, Kiowa County Public Library District, 1305 Goff St, Eads, CO, 81036. Tel: 719-438-5581. p. 278
Brikiatis, Sylvie, Libr Dir, Nesmith Library, Eight Fellows Rd, Windham, NH, 03087-1909. Tel: 603-432-7154. p. 1384
Briley, Janice, Dir, Librn, Christopher Public Library, 202 E Market St, Christopher, IL, 62822-1759. Tel: 618-724-7534. p. 571
Briley, Shaun R, Dir, Coronado Public Library, 640 Orange Ave, Coronado, CA, 92118-1526. Tel: 619-522-7390. p. 132
Brill, Kyle, Exec Dir, Lizzadro Museum of Lapidary Art Library, 1220 Kensington Rd, Oak Brook, IL, 60523. Tel: 630-833-1616. p. 627
Brillant, Bianca, Librn, Department of Veterans Affairs Medical Center, 4801 Veterans Dr, Saint Cloud, MN, 56303. Tel: 320-255-6342. p. 1196
Brillant-Giangrande, Laura, Youth Serv Librn, Bancroft Memorial Library, 50 Hopedale St, Hopedale, MA, 01747-1799. Tel: 508-634-2209. p. 1025
Brilmyer, Gracen, Asst Prof, McGill University, 3661 Peel St, Montreal, QC, H3A 1X1, CANADA. Tel: 514-398-4204. p. 2796
Brim-Jones, Shirley, Libr Asst, Rockingham County Public Library, Madison Mayodan Branch, 140 E Murphy St, Madison, NC, 27025. Tel: 336-548-6553. p. 1686
Brimeyer, Katherine, Archivist, Research Librn, Telegraph Herald Library, 801 Bluff St, Dubuque, IA, 52001. Tel: 563-588-5777. p. 749
Brimhall, Daphne, Libr Spec III, Northland Pioneer College Libraries, PO Box 610, Holbrook, AZ, 86025. Tel: 928-532-6123. p. 63
Brimmage, Beatrice, Librn, United States Army, Bldg 530, 301 C St, Yuma, AZ, 85365. Tel: 928-328-2558. p. 85
Brimmell, Andrea, District Coord, Greater Victoria Public Library, 735 Broughton St, Victoria, BC, V8W 3H2, CANADA. Tel: 250-940-4875, Ext 237. p. 2582
Brin, Lise, Head Librn, Université de Saint-Boniface, 200, ave de la Cathedrale, Winnipeg, MB, R2H 0H7, CANADA. Tel: 204-235-4403. p. 2594
Brincks, Annie, Dir, Adair Public Library, 310 Audubon, Adair, IA, 50002. Tel: 641-742-3323. p. 729
Brindle, Cassandra, Programming Librn, Oneonta Public Library, 221 Second St S, Oneonta, AL, 35121. Tel: 205-274-7641. p. 31
Brindza, Steve, Dir, Mount Sterling Public Library, 60 W Columbus St, Mount Sterling, OH, 43143. Tel: 740-869-2430. p. 1804
Bringard, Celeste, Circ Mgr, Eustis Memorial Library, 120 N Center St, Eustis, FL, 32726. Tel: 352-357-5686. p. 395
Bringman, Beth, Pub Serv Asst, Methodist Theological School, 3081 Columbus Pike, Delaware, OH, 43015. Tel: 740-362-3439. p. 1782
Brink, Carolee, Ch Serv, First United Methodist Church Library, 805 E Denman Ave, Lufkin, TX, 75901. Tel: 936-631-3233. p. 2214
Brink, Carrie, Librn, Plankinton Community Library, 404 E Davenport St, Plankinton, SD, 57368. Tel: 605-942-7600. p. 2081
Brink, Peter, Univ Archivist, Creighton University, 2500 California Plaza, Omaha, NE, 68178-0209. Tel: 402-280-2746. p. 1328
Brinker, Gary, IT Mgr, Saint Charles City-County Library District, 77 Boone Hills Dr, Saint Peters, MO, 63376. Tel: 636-441-2300. p. 1277
Brinker, Kerry, Acq, Coastal Carolina Community College, 444 Western Blvd, Jacksonville, NC, 28546. Tel: 910-938-6844. p. 1697
Brinkerhoff, Celia, Sci Librn, Kwantlen Polytechnic University Library, 12666 72nd Ave, Surrey, BC, V3W 2M8, CANADA. Tel: 604-599-3235. p. 2576
Brinkerhoff, Kathie, Libr Dir, Pershing County Library, 1125 Central Ave, Lovelock, NV, 89419. Tel: 775-273-2216. p. 1348
Brinkerhoff, Sarah, Mgr, Salt Lake County Library Services, Draper Branch, 1136 E Pioneer Rd, Draper, UT, 84020-9628. p. 2274
Brinkley, Bruce, Sr Ref Librn, Indiana Wesleyan University, 4201 S Washington St, Marion, IN, 46953. Tel: 765-677-2179. p. 704
Brinkley, Jacquelyn, Coordr, NorthNet Library System, 32 W 25th Ave, Ste 201, San Mateo, CA, 94403. Tel: 650-349-5538. p. 235
Brinkley, Joan, Dir, Goshen County Library, 2001 East A St, Torrington, WY, 82240-2898. Tel: 307-532-3411. p. 2500
Brinkley, Marlan, Jr, Libr Dir, McDowell County Public Library, 90 W Court St, Marion, NC, 28752. Tel: 828-652-3858. p. 1702
Brinkman, Bernadette, Libr Dir, Penfield Public Library, 1985 Baird Rd, Penfield, NY, 14526. Tel: 585-340-8720. p. 1616
Brinkman, Dana, Dir, Kent County Library, 156 W Fourth St, Jayton, TX, 79528. Tel: 806-237-3287. p. 2203
Brinston, Gail, Pub Serv Coordr, Sunflower County Library System, 201 Cypress Dr, Indianola, MS, 38751. Tel: 622-887-2153. p. 1220
Brintzenhofe, Rose Marie, Br Mgr, Chesterfield County Public Library, Clover Hill, 6701 Deer Run Rd, Midlothian, VA, 23112. Tel: 804-751-2275. p. 2312
Briody, Michael, Circ, Goodnow Library, 21 Concord Rd, Sudbury, MA, 01776-2383. Tel: 978-440-5535. p. 1058
Briones, Sandra, Ch, Wharton County Library, East Bernard Branch, 746 Clubside Dr, East Bernard, TX, 77435. Tel: 979-335-6142. p. 2256
Brisbin, Melissa, Assoc Dir, Livingston Public Library, Ten Robert Harp Dr, Livingston, NJ, 07039. Tel: 973-992-4600. p. 1413
Briseno, Alexandra, Sr Librn, The National Academies, Keck 439, 500 Fifth St NW, Washington, DC, 20001. Tel: 202-334-2989. p. 371
Brislin, Thomas, Fr, Library Contact, St Paul of the Cross Province, 86-45 Edgerton Blvd, Jamaica, NY, 11432-0024. Tel: 718-739-6502. p. 1556
Brison, Trina, Librn, Breeden Memorial Library & Literacy Center, 529 West Old State Rd 62, Leavenworth, IN, 47137. Tel: 812-739-4092. p. 702
Brisson, Carole, Cat Mgr, Mgr, Libr Syst, Supreme Court of Canada Library, 301 Wellington St, Ottawa, ON, K1A 0J1, CANADA. Tel: 613-947-0628. p. 2670
Brisson, Caroline, Tech Serv, Norton Rose Fulbright Canada LLP Library, One Place Ville Marie, Ste 2500, Montreal, QC, H3B 1R1, CANADA. Tel: 514-847-4701. p. 2727
Brisson, Ruth, Circ Mgr, Western Piedmont Community College, Phifer Hall, 1001 Burkemont Ave, Morganton, NC, 28655. Tel: 828-448-6195. p. 1704
Brister, Amelia, Dir, Libr Serv, Louisiana Delta Community College, 7500 Millhaven Rd, Rm 139, Monroe, LA, 71203. Tel: 318-345-9143. p. 898
Brister, Michele, Librn, Pike-Amite-Walthall Library System, Alpha Center, 414 McComb Ave, McComb, MS, 39648. Tel: 601-684-8312. p. 1226
Bristow, Rob, Dir, Georgetown Township Public Library, 1525 Baldwin St, Jenison, MI, 49428. Tel: 616-457-9620. p. 1120
Brite, Christopher, Libr Dir, Conception Abbey & Seminary Library, 37174 State Hwy VV, Conception, MO, 64433. Tel: 660-944-2863. p. 1244
Britsch, Sheri, Dir, Pleasant Grove City Library, 30 E Center St, Pleasant Grove, UT, 84062. Tel: 801-785-3950. p. 2269
Britski, April, Exec Dir, Canadian Artists' Representation, Two Daly Ave, Ste 250, Ottawa, ON, K1N 6E2, CANADA. Tel: 613-233-6161. p. 2665
Britt, Brandon, Br Mgr, Greensboro Public Library, Vance H Chavis Lifelong Learning Branch, 900 S Benbow Rd, Greensboro, NC, 27406. Tel: 336-373-5841. p. 1692
Britt, Ginger, Br Mgr, Southern Oklahoma Library System, Mary E Parker Memorial Library, 500 W Broadway, Sulphur, OK, 73086. Tel: 580-622-5807. p. 1841
Britt, James, Head, Access & Coll Serv, Duke University Libraries, J Michael Goodson Law Library, 210 Science Dr, Durham, NC, 27708. Tel: 919-613-7129. p. 1684
Britt, Savanna, ILL, Fort Meade Public Library, 75 E Broadway, Fort Meade, FL, 33841-2998. Tel: 863-285-8287. p. 402

Britt-Wernke, Lisa, Coll & Access Serv Librn, University of Cincinnati, 2540 Clifton Ave, Cincinnati, OH, 45219. Tel: 513-556-0156. p. 1764

Brittain, Helena, Br Head, Lincoln County Public Library, 306 W Main St, Lincolnton, NC, 28092. Tel: 704-735-8044. p. 1701

Brittain, Shannon, Youth Serv, Lawrence Library, 15 Main St, Pepperell, MA, 01463. Tel: 978-433-0330. p. 1046

Britten, Nancy, Circ, Neenah Public Library, 240 E Wisconsin Ave, Neenah, WI, 54956. Tel: 920-886-6315. p. 2463

Brittingham, Mary, Dir, Millsboro Public Library, 217 W State St, Millsboro, DE, 19966. Tel: 302-934-8743. p. 354

Britto, Marwin, Assoc Dean, California State University Dominguez Hills, 1000 E Victoria St, Carson, CA, 90747. Tel: 310-243-2207. p. 129

Britton, Alexis, Ch Serv, Aaron Cutler Memorial Library, 269 Charles Bancroft Hwy, Litchfield, NH, 03052. Tel: 603-424-4044. p. 1371

Britton, Caleb, Info Serv & Instrul Librn, Indiana University-Purdue University Fort Wayne, 2101 E Coliseum Blvd, Fort Wayne, IN, 46805-1499. Tel: 260-481-5759. p. 684

Britton, Jen, Librn, Southport Memorial Library, 1032 Hendricks Hill Rd, Southport, ME, 04576-3309. Tel: 207-633-2741. p. 942

Britton, Robert, Dir, Saint Jude Children's Research Hospital, 262 Danny Thomas Place, MS 306, Memphis, TN, 38105-3678. Tel: 901-595-3389. p. 2114

Britton, Scott, Assoc Univ Librn, Pub Serv, Boston College Libraries, 140 Commonwealth Ave, Chestnut Hill, MA, 02467. Tel: 617-552-3155. p. 1010

Britton, Valerie, Head, Circ, Pleasant Valley Free Library, Three Maggiacomo Lane, Pleasant Valley, NY, 12569. Tel: 845-635-8460. p. 1620

Britton-Spears, Ona, Dir, Libr Serv, Connors State College, 700 College Rd, Warner, OK, 74469-9700. Tel: 918-463-6210. p. 1868

Britton-Spears, Ona, Dir, Libr Serv, Connors State College, Muskogee Port Campus Library, 2501 N 41st St E, Muskogee, OK, 74403. Tel: 918-463-6269. p. 1868

Brnger, Gabby, Weekend Librn, Gilmanton Year-Round Library, 1385 NH Rte 140, Gilmanton Iron Works, NH, 03837. Tel: 603-364-2400. p. 1364

Brnik, Julie, Mgr, Libr Res, Hershey Public Library, 701 Cocoa Ave, Hershey, PA, 17033. Tel: 717-533-6555. p. 1943

Broad, Kathryn, Syst Librn, Oklahoma City University, School of Law Library, 2501 N Blackwelder, Oklahoma City, OK, 73106. Tel: 405-208-5271. p. 1858

Broadbent, Abigal, Archives, Tech Serv Librn, William Jewell College, 500 William Jewell College Dr, Liberty, MO, 64068. Tel: 816-415-5062. p. 1260

Broadfield, J G, Library Contact, Philadelphia Yearly Meeting of the Religious Society of Friends, 1515 Cherry St, Philadelphia, PA, 19102. Tel: 215-241-7220. p. 1984

Broadhurst, Mandy, Ch, Guntersville Public Library, 1240 O'Brig Ave, Guntersville, AL, 35976. Tel: 256-571-7595. p. 20

Broadley, Louise, Libr Mgr, Vancouver Island Regional Library, Port Alice Branch, 951 Marine Dr, Port Alice, BC, V0N 2N0, CANADA. Tel: 250-284-3554. p. 2571

Broadley, Louise, Libr Mgr, Vancouver Island Regional Library, Port Hardy Branch, 7110 Market St, Port Hardy, BC, V0N 2P0, CANADA. Tel: 250-949-6661. p. 2571

Broadley, Louise, Libr Mgr, Vancouver Island Regional Library, Port McNeill Branch, 4-1584 Broughton Blvd, Port McNeill, BC, V0N 2R0, CANADA. Tel: 250-956-3669. p. 2571

Broadley, Louise, Libr Mgr, Vancouver Island Regional Library, Sointula Branch, 280 First St, Sointula, BC, V0N 3E0, CANADA. Tel: 250-973-6493. p. 2571

Broadley, Louise, Libr Mgr, Vancouver Island Regional Library, Woss Branch, 4503B Railway Ave, Woss, BC, V0N 3P0, CANADA. Tel: 250-281-2263. p. 2572

Broadway, Melissa, Dir, Madison Public Library, 1700 Fifth St, Madison, IL, 62060. Tel: 618-876-8448. p. 612

Broady, Marcia, Dir, Selby Township Library District, 101 Depot St, De Pue, IL, 61322. Tel: 815-447-2660. p. 576

Broberg, Lori, Circ Supvr, Pierce College Library, Puyallup Campus, 1601 39th Ave SE, Puyallup, WA, 98374. Tel: 253-840-8300. p. 2368

Broch, Elana, Asst Population Res Librn, Princeton University, Donald E Stokes Library - Public & International Affairs & Population Research, Wallace Hall, Lower Flr, Princeton, NJ, 08544. Tel: 609-258-5517. p. 1438

Broch, Roz, Asst Dir, David & Joyce Milne Public Library, 1095 Main St, Williamstown, MA, 01267-2627. Tel: 413-458-5369. p. 1069

Brock, Charlene, ILL, United States Department of Health & Human Services, National Center for Health Statistics Staff Research Library, 3311 Toledo Rd, Rm 2403, Hyattsville, MD, 20782. Tel: 301-458-4775. p. 975

Brock, Darlene, Dir, Chilton Clanton Public Library, 100 First Ave, Clanton, AL, 35045. Tel: 205-755-1768. p. 12

Brock, John, Asst Dir, Operations, Lake County Public Library, 1919 W 81st Ave, Merrillville, IN, 46410-5488. Tel: 219-769-3541. p. 705

Brock, Lindsay, Dir, Libr Serv, Middlesex County Library, 34-B Frank St, Strathroy, ON, N7G 2R4, CANADA. Tel: 519-245-8237, Ext 4022. p. 2682

Brock, Lisa, Libr Operation & Coll Mgr, Palm Springs Public Library, 300 S Sunrise Way, Palm Springs, CA, 92262-7699. Tel: 760-322-8387. p. 191

Brock, Mathew, Historical Colls Mgr, Librn, Mazamas Library & Archives, 527 SE 43rd Ave, Portland, OR, 97215. Tel: 503-227-2345, Ext 2. p. 1892

Brock, Monica, Asst Librn, Johnson County Library, Kaycee Branch, 231 Ritter Ave, Kaycee, WY, 82639. Tel: 307-738-2473. p. 2491

Brock, Rebecca, Dir, Chapmanville Public Library, 740 Crowley Creek Rd, Chapmanville, WV, 25508. Tel: 304-855-3405. p. 2399

Brock, Rose, Dr, Asst Prof, Sam Houston State University, 1905 Bobby K Marks Dr, Huntsville, TX, 77340. Tel: 936-294-3158. p. 2793

Brock, Verna, Br Mgr, Collins LeRoy Leon County Public Library System, Woodville Branch, 8000 Old Woodvile Rd, Tallahassee, FL, 32305. Tel: 850-606-2925. p. 445

Brockett, Rebecca, Syst Mgr, Lois Wagner Memorial Library, 35200 Division Rd, Richmond, MI, 48062. Tel: 586-727-2665. p. 1144

Brockman, Liz, Ch Serv, North Richland Hills Public Library, 9015 Grand Ave, North Richland Hills, TX, 76180. Tel: 817-427-6818. p. 2223

Brockman, Terry, Cataloger, Marion County Public Library, 201 E Main St, Lebanon, KY, 40033-1133. Tel: 270-692-4698. p. 861

Brockman, William, Paterno Family Librn for Lit, Pennsylvania State University Libraries, George & Sherry Middlemas Arts & Humanities Library, Pennsylvania State University, W 337 Pattee Library, University Park, PA, 16802-1801. Tel: 814-865-9718. p. 2016

Brockmeyer, Carol, Dir, Daugherty Public Library District, 220 S Fifth St, Dupo, IL, 62239. Tel: 618-286-4444. p. 580

Brockmeyer, Donna, Dr, Libr Dir, Saint Thomas More College-University of Saskatchewan, 1437 College Dr, Saskatoon, SK, S7N 0W6, CANADA. Tel: 306-966-8962. p. 2749

Brodar, Maureen, Dep Dir, Shaker Heights Public Library, 16500 Van Aken Blvd, Shaker Heights, OH, 44120. Tel: 216-991-2030. p. 1820

Brodbeck-Kenney, Kirsten, Libr Dir, Driftwood Public Library, 801 SW Hwy 101, Ste 201, Lincoln City, OR, 97367-2720. Tel: 541-996-2277. p. 1885

Brodeur, Chantal, Head, Libraries Div, Bibliotheque Edmond-Archambault, 231, blvd J A Pare, Repentigny, QC, J5Z 4M6, CANADA. p. 2732

Brodeur, Chantal, Head, Libraries Div, Bibliotheque Robert-Lussier, One Place d'Evry, Repentigny, QC, J6A 8H7, CANADA. Tel: 450-470-3420. p. 2732

Brodeur, Mia, Reader Advisor, Great Lakes Talking Books, 1615 Presque Isle Ave, Marquette, MI, 49855. Tel: 906-228-7697, Ext 0. p. 1130

Brodie, Adrienne, Liaison Librn, A T Still University, 5850 E Still Circle, Mesa, AZ, 85206-6091. Tel: 480-218-6192. p. 66

Brodie, Alexis, Br Mgr, Riverside County Library System, Desert Hot Springs Library, 11691 West Dr, Desert Hot Springs, CA, 92240. Tel: 760-329-5926. p. 202

Brodin, Jared, Dir, Info Serv, American Institute for Biosocial & Medical Research Inc Library, 2800 E Madison St, Ste 202, Seattle, WA, 98112. Tel: 253-286-2888. p. 2376

Brodosi, David, Assoc Dir, Distance Learning Serv, Instrul Tech, University of South Florida Saint Petersburg, 140 Seventh Ave S, POY118, Saint Petersburg, FL, 33701-5016. Tel: 727-873-4126. p. 442

Brodrick, Anya, Instrul & Reserves Coordr, Boston University Libraries, Music Library, 771 Commonwealth Ave, Boston, MA, 02215. Tel: 617-353-3705. p. 993

Brodsky, Karen, Dir, Morris-Union Federation, 214 Main St, Chatham, NJ, 07928. Tel: 973-635-0603. p. 2770

Brodt, Barbara, Coordr, Outreach Serv, Mary Wood Weldon Memorial Library, 1530 S Green St, Glasgow, KY, 42141. Tel: 270-651-2824. p. 857

Brodt, Kristin, Mgr, ILL, Muhlenberg College, 2400 Chew St, Allentown, PA, 18104-5586. Tel: 484-664-3500. p. 1905

Brody, Adam, Dir, Libr Serv, Everglades University, Orlando Campus, 850 Trafalgar Ct, Ste 100, Maitland, FL, 32751. Tel: 407-277-0311. p. 385

Brody, Amy, Librn, New Mexico School for the Blind & Visually Impaired Library, 1900 N White Sands Blvd, Alamogordo, NM, 88310. Tel: 575-437-3505, Ext 4510. p. 1459

Brody, Eric, Research & Education Librn, Virginia Commonwealth University Libraries, Tompkins-McCaw Library for the Health Sciences, Medical College of Virginia Campus, 509 N 12th St, Richmond, VA, 23298-0582. Tel: 804-828-2004. p. 2343

Brody, Meggie, Circ, User Experience Mgr, Rochester Hills Public Library, 500 Olde Towne Rd, Rochester, MI, 48307-2043. Tel: 248-650-7162. p. 1144

Brody, Roberta, Prof, Queens College of the City University of New York, Benjamin Rosenthal Library, Rm 254, 65-30 Kissena Blvd, Flushing, NY, 11367-1597. Tel: 718-997-3790. p. 2789

Broeder, Kathleen, Head, Spec Coll & Archives, Dixie State University Library, 225 S 700 E, Saint George, UT, 84770. Tel: 435-652-7718. p. 2270

Broersma, Lorene, Ref & Local Hist Librn, Upland Public Library, 450 N Euclid Ave, Upland, CA, 91786-4732. Tel: 909-931-4200. p. 254

Brogan, Tom, Managing Librn, Brooklyn Public Library, DeKalb Branch, 790 Bushwick Ave, Brooklyn, NY, 11221. Tel: 718-455-3898. p. 1503

Brogdon, Dennise, Med Librn, Med Librn, Med Librn, Hughston Foundation Library, 6262 Veterans Pkwy, Columbus, GA, 31909-3540. Tel: 706-494-3390. p. 472

Brogdon, Patty, Libr Dir, Virginia Memorial Public Library, 100 N Main St, Virginia, IL, 62691-1364. Tel: 217-452-3846. p. 658

Broge, Harli, Sr Libr Asst, Ohio Northern University, Taggart Law Library, 525 S Main St, Ada, OH, 45810. Tel: 419-772-3058. p. 1743

Brogle, Robert, Pres, Connecticut Electric Railway Association, Inc, 58 North Rd, East Windsor, CT, 06088. Tel: 860-627-6540. p. 310

Broholm, Leah, Circ Desk Mgr, Franklin County Public Library, Westlake Branch, 84 Westalake Rd, Ste 109, Hardy, VA, 24101. Tel: 540-483-3098, Ext 2, 540-719-2383. p. 2346

Broker, Stephanie, Campus Librn, Greenville Technical College Libraries, Benson Campus Learning Commons, Bldg 301, Rm 121, 2522 Locust Hill Rd, Taylors, SC, 29687. Tel: 864-250-3010. p. 2062

Brokopp, Barbara, Circ, Hamline University, Bush Memorial Library, 1536 Hewitt, Saint Paul, MN, 55104. Tel: 651-523-2375. p. 1199

Broll, Sharon, Asst Ch, Georgetown Peabody Library, Two Maple St, Georgetown, MA, 01833. Tel: 978-352-5728. p. 1020

Broman, Elizabeth, Ref Librn, Smithsonian Libraries, Cooper-Hewitt, National Design Library, Two E 91st St, New York, DC, 10128. Tel: 212-633-8336. p. 375

Broman, Susan, Asst City Librn, Los Angeles Public Library System, 630 W Fifth St, Los Angeles, CA, 90071. Tel: 213-228-7461. p. 163

Brommer, Colleen, Libr Dir, Harlem Public Library, 37 First Ave SE, Harlem, MT, 59526. Tel: 406-353-2712. p. 1295

Brondfield, Ellen, Dir, Steptoe & Johnson Library, 1330 Connecticut Ave NW, Washington, DC, 20036. Tel: 202-429-6429. p. 376

Bronshteyn, Karen, Assoc Dir, Res/Worldwide Libr Serv, Embry-Riddle Aeronautical University, One Aerospace Blvd, Daytona Beach, FL, 32114. Tel: 386-226-6602. p. 392

Bronson, Angela, Actg Br Mgr, Toledo-Lucas County Public Library, Washington, 5560 Harvest Lane, Toledo, OH, 43623. Tel: 419-259-5330. p. 1825

Bronson, Mark C, Dir, Cheboygan Area Public Library, 100 S Bailey St, Cheboygan, MI, 49721-1661. Tel: 231-627-2381. p. 1090

Brook, Freeda, Acq Librn, Res Mgt Librn, Luther College, 700 College Dr, Decorah, IA, 52101. Tel: 563-387-2124. p. 745

Brook, Hara, Ref Librn, Highline College Library, 2400 S 240th St, MS 25-4, Des Moines, WA, 98198. Tel: 206-592-3248. p. 2363

Brook, Hara, Prog Coordr, Highline College, 2400 S 240th St, Bldg 25, Rm 416, Des Moines, WA, 98198. Tel: 206-592-3248. p. 2794

Brookbank, Elizabeth, Libr Instruction, Western Oregon University, 345 N Monmouth Ave, Monmouth, OR, 97361-1396. Tel: 503-838-8657. p. 1887

Brookbank, Shawn, Mrs, Evening Circ Supvr, Ohio State University LIBRARIES, Newark Campus Library, Warner Library & Student Ctr, 1179 University Dr, Newark, OH, 43055-1797. Tel: 740-366-9183. p. 1776

Brooke, Jean, Asst Librn, Red Rock Public Library Board, 42 Salls St, Red Rock, ON, P0T 2P0, CANADA. Tel: 807-886-2558. p. 2675

Brooke, Sandra L, Libr Dir, Henry E Huntington Library & Art Gallery, 1151 Oxford Rd, San Marino, CA, 91108. Tel: 626-405-2244. p. 235

Brookens, Glynis, Sr Librn/Youth Serv, Metuchen Public Library, 480 Middlesex Ave, Metuchen, NJ, 08840. Tel: 732-632-8526. p. 1418

Brookfield, Juliette, Coordr, Ch Serv, Librn II, Clinton-Essex-Franklin Library System, 33 Oak St, Plattsburgh, NY, 12901-2810. Tel: 518-563-5190, Ext 120. p. 1619

Brookhart, Drew, Dir, Gunnison Public Library of the Gunnison County Library District, 307 N Wisconsin, Gunnison, CO, 81230-2627. Tel: 970-641-3485. p. 285

Brookie, Janeen, Dir, Phillips County Library, Ten S Fourth St E, Malta, MT, 59538. Tel: 406-654-2407. p. 1299

Brookins, Amber, Tech Serv, Chattahoochee Valley Libraries, 3000 Macon Rd, Columbus, GA, 31906-2201. Tel: 706-243-2820. p. 471

Brookins, Joni L, Asst Dir, Cat, Warsaw Community Public Library, 310 E Main St, Warsaw, IN, 46580-2882. Tel: 574-267-6011. p. 724

Brookman, Richard, Dir, Talking Bks, Southwest Kansas Library System, Talking Books, 100 Military Ave, Ste 210, Dodge City, KS, 67801. Tel: 620-225-1231. p. 805

Brookman, Richard, Dir, Southwest Kansas Library System, 100 Military Ave, Ste 210, Dodge City, KS, 67801. Tel: 620-225-1231. p. 805

Brooks, Carla, Librn, University of Michigan-Dearborn, 4901 Evergreen Rd, Dearborn, MI, 48128-2406. Tel: 313-593-5616. p. 1096

Brooks, Caroline, Exec Dir, Roswell Museum & Art Center Library, 1011 N Richardson Ave, Roswell, NM, 88201. Tel: 575-624-6744. p. 1474

Brooks, Catherine, Librn, East Burke Community Library, 368 Rt 114, East Burke, VT, 05832. Tel: 802-626-9823. p. 2283

Brooks, Catherine, Assoc Prof, Dir, University of Arizona, Harvill Bldg, 4th Flr, 1103 E Second St, Tucson, AZ, 85721. Tel: 520-621-3565. p. 2782

Brooks, Cindy, Br Mgr, Montgomery County Library, Mount Gilead Branch, 110 W Allenton St, Mount Gilead, NC, 27306. Tel: 910-439-6651. p. 1719

Brooks, Darlene, Dir, Rhodes College, 2000 North Pkwy, Memphis, TN, 38112-1694. Tel: 901-843-3890. p. 2114

Brooks, Donna, Colls Mgr, Millis Public Library, 961 Main St, Millis, MA, 02054. Tel: 508-376-8282. p. 1036

Brooks, Doris, Librn, Missouri Department of Corrections, Potosi Correctional Center, 11593 State Hwy O, Mineral Point, MO, 63660. Tel: 573-438-6000. p. 1252

Brooks, Jan, Br Mgr, Chicago Public Library, Thurgood Marshall Branch, 7506 S Racine Ave, Chicago, IL, 60620. Tel: 312-747-5927. p. 557

Brooks, Jane, Asst Librn, Deerfield Public Library, 12 W Nelson St, Deerfield, WI, 53531-9669. Tel: 608-764-8102. p. 2430

Brooks, Jeanne M, Sr Dir, Library Ops & Dev, California State Polytechnic University Library, 3801 W Temple Ave, Bldg 15, Pomona, CA, 91768. Tel: 909-869-3074. p. 196

Brooks, Jeff, Dir, Pekin Public Library, 301 S Fourth St, Pekin, IL, 61554-4284. Tel: 309-347-7111, Ext 228. p. 634

Brooks, Jesika, Educ Tech Librn, Columbia College, 1301 Columbia College Dr, Columbia, SC, 29203-9987. Tel: 803-786-3716. p. 2053

Brooks, Jessica, Library Contact, Confluence Health - Central Washington Hospital, 1201 S Miller St, Wenatchee, WA, 98801. Tel: 509-664-3476. p. 2393

Brooks, JoAnn, Libr Dir, Lenora Public Library, 110 N Main St, Lenora, KS, 67645. Tel: 785-567-4432. p. 820

Brooks, Kaitlin, Librn, Bowman Regional Public Library, 18 E Divide St, Bowman, ND, 58623. Tel: 701-523-3797. p. 1731

Brooks, Katie, Libr Assoc, Upper Iowa University, 605 Washington St, Fayette, IA, 52142. Tel: 563-425-5261. p. 753

Brooks, Kelli, Youth Serv Dept Head, Hussey-Mayfield Memorial Public Library, 250 N Fifth St, Zionsville, IN, 46077-1324. Tel: 317-873-3149. p. 728

Brooks, Mackenzie, Digital Humanities Librn, Head, Digital Culture & Info, Washington & Lee University, University Library, 204 W Washington St, Lexington, VA, 24450-2116. Tel: 540-458-8643. p. 2329

Brooks, Martin, Br Supvr, Greater Victoria Public Library, James Bay Branch, 385 Menzies St, Victoria, BC, V8V 0C2, CANADA. Tel: 250-940-4875, Ext 684. p. 2583

Brooks, Megan, Dean of Libr, Wheaton College Library, 26 E Main St, Norton, MA, 02766-2322. Tel: 508-286-8224. p. 1043

Brooks, Michael, Librn, Temple Beth Sholom, 1809 Whitney Ave, Hamden, CT, 06517. Tel: 203-288-7748. p. 316

Brooks, Monica Garcia, Dr, Dean, Univ Libr, Marshall University Libraries, One John Marshall Dr, Huntington, WV, 25755-2060. Tel: 304-696-6474. p. 2405

Brooks, Pamela, Head, Adult Serv, Scotch Plains Public Library, 1927 Bartle Ave, Scotch Plains, NJ, 07076-1212. Tel: 908-322-5007. p. 1441

Brooks, Shannon, Dir, Libr Serv, Southern Wesleyan University, 916 Wesleyan Dr, Central, SC, 29630-9748. Tel: 864-644-5072. p. 2048

Brooks, Sharon, Evening Librn, Eastern Correctional Institution, East Library, 30420 Revells Neck Rd, Westover, MD, 21890. Tel: 410-845-4000, Ext 6227. p. 981

Brooks, Sharon D, Actg Dir, Libr Serv, Media Librn, University of Maryland-Eastern Shore, 11868 Academic Oval, Princess Anne, MD, 21853. Tel: 410-651-6275. p. 973

Brooks, Shay, Supvr, Youth Serv, Richardson Public Library, 2360 Campbell Creek Blvd, Ste 500, Richardson, TX, 75082. Tel: 972-744-4383. p. 2231

Brooks, Stacie, Co-Dir, Mooers Free Library, 25 School St, Mooers, NY, 12958. Tel: 518-236-7744. p. 1574

Brooks, Susan, Libr Asst, Hazeltine Public Library, 891 Busti-Sugar Grove Rd, Jamestown, NY, 14701. Tel: 716-487-1281. p. 1557

Brooks, Theresa, Dir, Moore Memorial Library District, 509 Main St, Hillsdale, IL, 61257. Tel: 309-658-2666. p. 599

Brooks, Tina, Electronic Serv Librn, University of Kentucky Libraries, Law Library, J David Rosenberg College of Law, 620 S Limestone St, Lexington, KY, 40506-0048. Tel: 859-257-8347. p. 863

Brooks, Tina M, Dir, Rainbow City Public Library, 3702 Rainbow Dr, Rainbow City, AL, 35906. Tel: 256-442-8477. p. 33

Brooks, Wendy, Dean, Learning Res, Media Serv, Alpena Community College, Newport Center Bldg, Rm 111, 665 Johnson St, Alpena, MI, 49707. Tel: 989-358-7249. p. 1078

Broome, Christina, Br Mgr, Lamar County Library System, Purvis Public, 122 Shelby Speights Dr, Purvis, MS, 39475. Tel: 601-794-6291. p. 1231

Broome, Kerri, Exec Dir, Lorain County Historical Society, 284 Washington Ave, Elyria, OH, 44035. Tel: 440-322-3341. p. 1784

Broome, Kyle, IT Spec, Iredell County Public Library, 201 N Tradd St, Statesville, NC, 28677. Tel: 704-878-3148. p. 1717

Broome, Melba, Libr Dir, University of the District of Columbia, Learning Resources Division, 4200 Connecticut Ave NW, Bldg 39, Level B, Washington, DC, 20008. p. 380

Broome, Susan G, Assoc Dir, Tech Serv, Spec Coll & Archives Librn, Mercer University, Jack Tarver Library, 1300 Edgewood Ave, Macon, GA, 31207. Tel: 478-301-2193. p. 486

Broomfield, Loretta, Libr Dir, Marion Carnegie Library, 206 S Market St, Marion, IL, 62959-2519. Tel: 618-993-5935. p. 613

Broomfield, Loretta, Dir, Sallie Logan Public Library, 1808 Walnut St, Murphysboro, IL, 62966. Tel: 618-684-3271. p. 622

Broomfield, Tina, Educ Serv Mgr, Rochester Regional Library Council, 3445 Winton Pl, Ste 204, Rochester, NY, 14623. Tel: 585-223-7570. p. 2771

Brooms, Thalma, Manager, Safety, Skokie Public Library, 5215 Oakton St, Skokie, IL, 60077-3680. Tel: 847-673-7774. p. 647

Brophy, Denise, Libr Mgr, Community Libraries of Providence, Wanskuck Library, 233 Veazie St, Providence, RI, 02904. Tel: 401-274-4145. p. 2038

Brophy, Julie, Coord, Ad Serv, Baltimore County Public Library, 320 York Rd, Towson, MD, 21204-5179. Tel: 410-887-6100. p. 979

Brophy, Linda, Circ & Ref, The Free Public Library of the Borough of Pompton Lakes, 333 Wanaque Ave, Pompton Lakes, NJ, 07442. Tel: 973-835-0482. p. 1435

Brosamer, Laura, Librn, HSHS Saint Mary's Hospital, 1800 E Lake Shore Dr, Decatur, IL, 62521. Tel: 217-464-2966. p. 576

Brosamer, Laura, Librn, St John's Hospital, 800 E Carpenter, Springfield, IL, 62769. Tel: 217-464-2182. p. 650

Brosard, Carmen, Libr Dir, Quemado Public Library, 19791 N Hwy 277, Quemado, TX, 78877. Tel: 830-757-1313. p. 2230

Brose, Bonnie, Librn, Logan County Libraries, West Mansfield Branch, 127 N Main St, West Mansfield, OH, 43358. Tel: 937-355-0033. p. 1750

Brose, Christopher, Computer Serv Mgr, Tiffin-Seneca Public Library, 77 Jefferson St, Tiffin, OH, 44883. Tel: 419-447-3751. p. 1823

Brose, Jacqueline, Branch Services, Ridgemont Public Library, 124 E Taylor St, Mount Victory, OH, 43340. Tel: 937-354-4445. p. 1805

Brosenne, Mary, Br Mgr, Howard County Library System, Glenwood Branch, 2350 State Rte 97, Cooksville, MD, 21723. Tel: 410-313-5575. p. 965

Brosk, Carol, Librn, Barack, Ferrazzano, Kirshbaum & Nagelberg Library, 200 W Madison St, Ste 3900, Chicago, IL, 60606. Tel: 312-984-3100. p. 555

Broskey, Lorelei A, Dir, Lehigh County Law Library, County Court House, 455 W Hamilton St, Allentown, PA, 18101-1614. Tel: 610-782-3385. p. 1905

Brosnan, Laura, Ch Serv, Salem Public Library, 370 Essex St, Salem, MA, 01970-3298. Tel: 978-744-0860. p. 1051

Brosowsky-Roth, Anne, Training & Resource Spec, Planned Parenthood of Wisconsin, Inc, 302 N Jackson St, Milwaukee, WI, 53202. p. 2461

Bross, Adrienne, Electronic Res Librn, Saint Elizabeth University, Two Convent Rd, Morristown, NJ, 07960-6989. Tel: 973-290-4253. p. 1422

Brosseau, Danielle, Librn, Harper Grey LLP Library, 3200-650 W Georgia St, Vancouver, BC, V6B 4P7, CANADA. Tel: 604-895-2861. p. 2578

Brosseau, Esther, Librn, Phillips County Library, Saco Branch, 201 B Taylor St, Saco, MT, 59261. p. 1299

Brosseau, Nora, ILL Spec, Emerson College, 120 Boylston St, Boston, MA, 02116-4624. Tel: 617-824-8668. p. 995

Brostoff, Tera, Librn/Mgr, Wilkinson Barker Knauer LLP Library, 1800 M St NW, Ste 800N, Washington, DC, 20036. Tel: 202-383-3420. p. 381

Brostuen, Lori, Dep Libr Dir, United States Naval War College Library, 686 Cushing Rd, Newport, RI, 02841-1207. Tel: 401-841-2641. p. 2035

Brothers, Rebecca, E-Resources Librn, Media Librn, Oakwood University, 7000 Adventist Blvd NW, Huntsville, AL, 35896. Tel: 256-726-7253. p. 22

Brothers, Vicky, Librn, Hepburn Library of Norfolk, One Hepburn St, Norfolk, NY, 13667. Tel: 315-384-3052. p. 1606

Brotherton, Elizabeth, Music Library Coord, Hamilton College, Music, McEwen Hall, 198 College Hill Rd, Clinton, NY, 13323-1299. Tel: 315-859-4479. p. 1519

Brotherton, Lise, Prof, College de Maisonneuve, 3800, rue Sherbrooke Est, Montreal, QC, H1X 2A2, CANADA. Tel: 514-254-7131. p. 2796

Brough, Laurie, Lead Libr Asst, Ivy Tech Community College, 815 E 60th St, Anderson, IN, 46013. Tel: 765-643-7133, Ext 2081. p. 668

Brough, Marianna, Br Coordr, Indiana University Bloomington, Neal-Marshall Black Culture Center Library, Neal-Marshall Ctr, Rm A113, 275 N Jordan, Bloomington, IN, 47405. Tel: 812-855-5932. p. 671

Broughman, Lisa Lee, Dir, Randolph College, 2500 Rivermont Ave, Lynchburg, VA, 24503. Tel: 434-947-8133. p. 2330

Broughton, Jason, Dir, Library of Congress, National Library Service for the Blind & Print Disabled, Library Collections & Services Group, 1291 Taylor St NW, Washington, DC, 20542. Tel: 202-707-5100. p. 370

Broughton, Kelly, Asst Dean for Res Serv, Ohio University Libraries, 30 Park Pl, Athens, OH, 45701. Tel: 740-593-2709. p. 1748

Brouillard, Kelly, Ref & Adult Serv Supvr, Lewisville Public Library System, 1197 W Main St, Lewisville, TX, 75067. Tel: 972-219-3758. p. 2211

Brouillette, Carole, Mgr, Coll Develop, Université du Québec à Montréal Bibliotheque, 400 rue Ste-Catherine Est, Local A-M100, Montreal, QC, H2L 2C5, CANADA. Tel: 514-987-6114. p. 2728

Brouse, Kim, Libr Mgr, South Georgia Regional Library System, Salter Hahira Branch, 220 E Main St, Hahira, GA, 31632. Tel: 229-794-3063. p. 501

Broussard, Ashley, Br Mgr, East Baton Rouge Parish Library, Baker Branch, 3501 Groom Rd, Baker, LA, 70714. Tel: 225-778-5980. p. 883

Broussard, Camille, Dir, New York Law School, 185 W Broadway, New York, NY, 10013. Tel: 212-431-2354. p. 1594

Broussard, Kersha, ILL, East Baton Rouge Parish Library, 7711 Goodwood Blvd, Baton Rouge, LA, 70806-7625. Tel: 225-231-3755. p. 882

Broussard, Linda, Br Mgr, Lafayette Public Library, 301 W Congress, Lafayette, LA, 70501-6866. Tel: 337-504-5332. p. 892

Broussard, Mike, Br Mgr, Grand Prairie Public Library System, Tony Shotwell Branch, 2750 Graham St, Grand Prairie, TX, 75050. Tel: 972-237-7540. p. 2186

Broussard, Sheila, Syst Adminr, Jasper County Public Library, 208 W Susan St, Rensselaer, IN, 47978. Tel: 219-866-5881. p. 714

Broussard, Sondra, Human Res, Onebane Law Firm APC, Park Tower Bldg, 400 E Kaliste Saloon Rd, Ste 3000, Lafayette, LA, 70508. Tel: 337-237-2660. p. 893

Brousseau, Julie, Chief Libr Officer, Centre d'acces a l'information juridique/Legal Informatin Access Center, 480 Saint-Laurent, Bur 503, Montreal, QC, H2Y 3Y7, CANADA. Tel: 514-844-2245. p. 2721

Brouwer, Amanda, Dir, Acton Public Library, 60 Old Boston Post Rd, Old Saybrook, CT, 06475-2200. Tel: 860-388-8924. p. 333

Browar, Lisa, Pres, Linda Hall Library of Science, Engineering & Technology, 5109 Cherry St, Kansas City, MO, 64110. Tel: 816-926-8745. p. 1255

Browder, Tonya, Libr Dir, Tompkins Memorial Library, 104 Courthouse Sq, Edgefield, SC, 29824. Tel: 803-637-4010. p. 2058

Brower, Alex, Dir, Info Serv, Mississippi Library Commission, 3881 Eastwood Dr, Jackson, MS, 39211. Tel: 601-432-4117. p. 1222

Brower, Dan, Dir, Cass County Public Library, 400 E Mechanic St, Harrisonville, MO, 64701. Tel: 816-380-4600. p. 1248

Brower, Eric, Pub Serv Mgr, Georgia Institute of Technology Library, 260 Fourth St NW, Atlanta, GA, 30332. Tel: 404-385-2382. p. 464

Brower, Reilly, Interim Dir, Dorr Township Library, 1804 Sunset Dr, Dorr, MI, 49323. Tel: 616-681-9678. p. 1101

Brower, Stewart, Dir, University of Oklahoma, Schusterman Ctr, 4502 E 41st St, Tulsa, OK, 74135. Tel: 918-660-3222. p. 1867

Brown, Aaron, Head, Circ Serv, Southwestern Law School, Bullock Wilshire Bldg, 1st Flr, 3050 Wilshire Blvd, Los Angeles, CA, 90010. Tel: 213-738-5771. p. 168

Brown, Alice, Mgr, Libr Serv, Shalimar Public Library, 115 Richbourg Ave, Shalimar, FL, 32579. Tel: 850-609-1515. p. 444

Brown, Alison, Teen & Adult Librn, Indianola Public Library, 207 North B St, Indianola, IA, 50125. Tel: 515-961-9418. p. 759

Brown, Alison, Lecturer, Dalhousie University, Kenneth C Rowe Management Bldg, Ste 4010, 6100 University Ave, Halifax, NS, B3H 4R2, CANADA. Tel: 902-494-3656. p. 2795

Brown, Alyssa, Asst Librn, Balsam Lake Public Library, 404 Main St, Balsam Lake, WI, 54810. Tel: 715-485-3215. p. 2422

Brown, Amanda, Circ, Pacifica Graduate Institute, 249 Lambert Rd, Carpinteria, CA, 93013. Tel: 805-969-3626, Ext 115. p. 128

Brown, Amanda, Dir, Southern Pines Public Library, 170 W Connecticut Ave, Southern Pines, NC, 28387-4819. Tel: 910-692-8235. p. 1716

Brown, Amy, Head, Metadata Creation & Mgt, Special Colls Technical Head, Boston College Libraries, Thomas P O'Neill Jr Library (Main Library), 140 Commonwealth Ave, Chestnut Hill, MA, 02467. Tel: 617-552-8124. p. 1011

Brown, Amy, Libr Mgr, Worthington Libraries, Worthington Park Library, 1389 Worthington Centre Dr, Worthington, OH, 43085. Tel: 614-807-2624. p. 1834

Brown, Angela, Tech Serv Librn, Amherst Town Library, 14 Main St, Amherst, NH, 03031. Tel: 603-673-2288. p. 1353

Brown, Angela, Head, Youth Serv, Easttown Library & Information Center, 720 First Ave, Berwyn, PA, 19312-1769. Tel: 610-644-0138. p. 1910

Brown, Anne, Dir, Walworth-Seely Public Library, 3600 Lorraine Dr, Walworth, NY, 14568. Tel: 315-986-1511. p. 1658

Brown, Ashlee, Libr Asst, Churchill County Library, 553 S Maine St, Fallon, NV, 89406-3387. Tel: 775-423-7581. p. 1345

Brown, Aubrie, Dir, Saint Paul Library, 1301 Howard Ave, Saint Paul, NE, 68873-2021. Tel: 308-754-5223. p. 1334

Brown, Barbara, Librn, Georgia Department of Corrections, Office of Library Services, 2728 Hwy 49 S, Oglethorpe, GA, 31068. Tel: 478-472-3486. p. 493

Brown, Barry, Dean of Libr, University of Montana Missoula, 32 Campus Dr, Missoula, MT, 59812. Tel: 406-243-6866. p. 1300

Brown, Belinda, Dir, Choctaw County Public Library, 124 N Academy Ave, Butler, AL, 36904. Tel: 205-459-2542. p. 10

Brown, Belinda, Asst Dir, Victor Public Library, 124 S Third St, Victor, CO, 80860. Tel: 719-689-2011. p. 297

Brown, Belva, Libr Mgr, York Library Region, Doaktown Community-School Library, 430 Main St, Doaktown, NB, E9C 1E8, CANADA. Tel: 506-365-2018. p. 2602

Brown, Ben, Dir, Harvey Mitchell Memorial Library, 151 Main St, Epping, NH, 03042. Tel: 603-679-5944, 603-734-4587. p. 1363

Brown, Beverly, Interim Dir, Oconee Regional Library, 801 Bellevue Ave, Dublin, GA, 31021. Tel: 478-272-5710. p. 477

Brown, Bly, Br Mgr, Massanutten Regional Library, North River Library, 118 Mount Crawford Ave, Bridgewater, VA, 22812. Tel: 540-434-4475, Ext 4. p. 2324

Brown, Brenda, Br Mgr, Northeast Missouri Library Service, H E Sever Memorial, 207 W Chestnut St, Kahoka, MO, 63445. Tel: 660-727-3262. p. 1254

Brown, Brenda, Dr, Acad Res Coordr, Baker College of Flint Library, 1050 W Bristol Rd, Flint, MI, 48507-5508. Tel: 810-766-4282. p. 1105

Brown, Camille, Assoc Dir, Spertus Institute of Jewish Studies, 610 S Michigan Ave, Chicago, IL, 60605. Tel: 312-322-1712. p. 568

Brown, Caris, Local Hist Librn, Helen Hall Library, 100 W Walker, League City, TX, 77573-3899. Tel: 281-554-1105. p. 2210

Brown, Carlton, Dir, Duke University Libraries, Ford Library, 100 Fuqua Dr, Durham, NC, 27708. Tel: 919-660-7871. p. 1684

Brown, Carol, Br Mgr, Crawford County Library District, Recklein Memorial, 305 N Smith St, Cuba, MO, 65453. Tel: 573-885-7324. p. 1282

Brown, Carys, Br Coordr, North Vancouver District Public Library, Capilano, 3045 Highland Blvd, North Vancouver, BC, V7R 2X4, CANADA. Tel: 604-987-4471. p. 2573

Brown, Cassandra, Dir, Heidelberg University, Ten Greenfield St, Tiffin, OH, 44883-2420. Tel: 419-448-2242. p. 1823

Brown, Ceora, Libr Dir, Performing Arts Librn, American Academy of Dramatic Arts, 6305 Yucca St, Los Angeles, CA, 90028. Tel: 323-603-5924. p. 160

Brown, Chad, Head, Pub Serv, Western Michigan University-Cooley Law School Libraries, 9445 Camden Field Pkwy, Riverview, FL, 33578. Tel: 813-419-5100, Ext 5113. p. 439

Brown, Charles E, Head, Ref, Saint Louis Mercantile Library at the University of Missouri-St Louis, Thomas Jefferson Library Bldg, One University Blvd, Saint Louis, MO, 63121-4400. Tel: 314-516-7243. p. 1274

Brown, Charlotte, Cat Librn, University of Tennessee Southern, 433 W Madison St, Pulaski, TN, 38478-2799. Tel: 931-363-9844. p. 2124

Brown, Cherie, Asst Librn, Belle Plaine Community Library, 904 12th St, Belle Plaine, IA, 52208-1711. Tel: 319-444-2902. p. 734

Brown, Cheryl, Asst Dir, Cat, Lake Blackshear Regional Library System, 307 E Lamar St, Americus, GA, 31709-3633. Tel: 229-924-8091. p. 458

Brown, Chris, Dep County Librn, Santa Clara County Library District, 1370 Dell Ave, Campbell, CA, 95032. Tel: 408-293-2326. p. 126

Brown, Chris, Ref (Info Servs), University of Denver, 2150 E Evans Ave, Denver, CO, 80208. Tel: 303-871-3441. p. 277

Brown, Chris, Commissioner, Chicago Public Library, 400 S State St, Chicago, IL, 60605. Tel: 312-747-4090. p. 555

Brown, Chris, Head of Mkt, Head, Community Engagement, Medicine Hat Public Library, 414 First St SE, Medicine Hat, AB, T1A 0A8, CANADA. Tel: 403-502-8536. p. 2548

Brown, Chris M, Commissioner, Chicago Public Library, Harold Washington Library Center, 400 S State St, Chicago, IL, 60605. Tel: 312-747-4090. p. 557

Brown, Christie, Dir, Muhlenberg Community Library, 3612 Kutztown Rd, Laureldale, PA, 19605-1842. Tel: 610-929-0589. p. 1953

Brown, Christie, Dir, Schuylkill Valley Community Library, 1310 Washington Rd, Leesport, PA, 19533-9708. Tel: 610-926-1555. p. 1954

Brown, Christine, Head, Educ Res Ctr, Bridgewater State University, Ten Shaw Rd, Bridgewater, MA, 02325. Tel: 508-531-2023. p. 1002

Brown, Christine, Dr, Head of Libr, University of Alberta, Rutherford Humanities & Social Sciences Library, 1-01 Rutherford South, Edmonton, AB, T6G 2J8, CANADA. Tel: 780-492-1405. p. 2538

Brown, Christopher, Community Hub Mgr, Hartford Public Library, Albany, 1250 Albany Ave, Hartford, CT, 06112. Tel: 860-695-7380. p. 318

Brown, Christopher, Dir, Williamsport-Washington Township Public Library, 28 E Second St, Williamsport, IN, 47993-1299. Tel: 765-762-6555. p. 726

Brown, Christopher, Asst Dir, Pella Public Library, 603 Main St, Pella, IA, 50219. Tel: 641-628-4268. p. 776

Brown, Christopher, Curator, Spec Coll, Free Library of Philadelphia, Children's Department, 1901 Vine St, Rm 22, Philadelphia, PA, 19103-1116. Tel: 215-686-5369. p. 1977

Brown, Courtney, Librn, Ohioana Library, 274 E First Ave, Ste 300, Columbus, OH, 43201. Tel: 614-466-3831. p. 1777

Brown, Courtney, Dir, Evergreen Indiana Library Consortium, Indiana State Library, 315 W Ohio St, Indianapolis, IN, 46202. Tel: 317-232-3691. p. 2765

Brown, Creston, Circ Serv, Donald W Reynolds Community Center & Library, 1515 W Main St, Durant, OK, 74701. Tel: 580-924-3486, 580-931-0231. p. 1846

Brown, Crystal, Metadata Librn, Jackson State University, 1325 J R Lynch St, Jackson, MS, 39217. Tel: 601-979-2123, 601-979-4270. p. 1222

Brown, Dany, Dir, Musee de la Civilisation - Bibliotheque du Seminaire de Quebec, 9 rue de l'Universite, Quebec, QC, G1R 5K1, CANADA. Tel: 418-643-2158, Ext 796. p. 2731

Brown, Darla, Br Mgr, Kansas City, Kansas Public Library, South Branch, 3104 Strong Ave, Kansas City, KS, 66106. Tel: 913-295-8250, Ext 3. p. 816

Brown, Dave, Cat Librn, Fullerton College, 321 E Chapman Ave, Fullerton, CA, 92832-2095. Tel: 714-992-7376. p. 147

Brown, David, Tech Serv, Alhambra Civic Center Library, 101 S First St, Alhambra, CA, 91801-3432. Tel: 626-570-5008. p. 115

Brown, David, Libr Dir, Canal Fulton Public Library, 154 Market St NE, Canal Fulton, OH, 44614-1196. Tel: 330-854-4148. p. 1754

Brown, Dawn C, Dir, Beaver City Public Library, 408 Tenth St, Beaver City, NE, 68926. Tel: 308-268-4115. p. 1307

Brown, Dawnita, Ch Serv, Ardmore Free Library, 108 Ardmore Ave, Ardmore, PA, 19003-1399. Tel: 610-642-5187. p. 1907

Brown, Deborah, Circ Supvr, La Roche University, 9000 Babcock Blvd, Pittsburgh, PA, 15237. Tel: 412-536-1063. p. 1994

Brown, Deborah, Libr Dir, Sutton County Public Library, 306 E Mulberry St, Sonora, TX, 76950-2603. Tel: 325-387-2111. p. 2244

Brown, Denise, Libr Asst I, Jackson State University, 1325 J R Lynch St, Jackson, MS, 39217. Tel: 601-979-2123, 601-979-4270. p. 1222

Brown, Derek, Dir, Info Tech, Rochester Hills Public Library, 500 Olde Towne Rd, Rochester, MI, 48307-2043. Tel: 248-650-7123. p. 1144

Brown, Diana, Admin Librn, Hinds Community College, William H Holtzdaw Library - Utica Campus, 3417 MS-18 West, Utica, MS, 39175-9599. Tel: 601-885-7035. p. 1231

Brown, Diane, Br Mgr, New Haven Free Public Library, Stetson Branch, 200 Dixwell Ave, New Haven, CT, 06511. Tel: 203-946-6786. p. 326

Brown, Donna, Asst Dir, Great Barrington Libraries, 231 Main St, Great Barrington, MA, 01230. Tel: 413-528-2403. p. 1022

Brown, Dorinda, Asst Librn, Stromsburg Public Library, 320 Central St, Stromsburg, NE, 68666. Tel: 402-764-7681. p. 1337

Brown, Dustin, Ad, Commerce Township Community Library, 180 E Commerce, Commerce Township, MI, 48382. Tel: 248-669-8101, Ext 115. p. 1093

Brown, Elizabeth, Family/Adult Programming Librn, Graves County Public Library, 601 N 17th St, Mayfield, KY, 42066. Tel: 270-247-2911. p. 868

Brown, Ellen, Dir, Mercer County Library System, 2751 Brunswick Pike, Lawrenceville, NJ, 08648-4132. Tel: 609-883-8290. p. 1411

Brown, Ellen, Sci Librn, Austin Peay State University, 601 College St, Clarksville, TN, 37044. Tel: 931-221-7741. p. 2092

Brown, Emily, Dir, Linn Grove Public Library, 110 Weaver St, Linn Grove, IA, 51033. Tel: 712-296-3919. p. 766

Brown, Emily, Coord, Research & Instruction, Bristol Community College, 777 Elsbree St, Fall River, MA, 02720. Tel: 774-357-3040. p. 1017

Brown, Erica, Br Mgr, Jacksonville Public Library, Southeast Regional, 10599 Deerwood Park Blvd, Jacksonville, FL, 32256-0507. Tel: 904-996-0325. p. 412

Brown, Erica, Librn, West Lafayette Public Library, 208 W Columbia St, West Lafayette, IN, 47906. Tel: 765-743-2261. p. 726

Brown, Erica, Libr Dir, Upper Skagit Library, 45952 Main St, Concrete, WA, 98237. Tel: 360-853-7716. p. 2362

Brown, Erin, Dir, Avalon Free Public Library, 235 32nd St, Avalon, NJ, 08202. Tel: 609-967-7155. p. 1388

Brown Evans, Sheila, Dir, Hoke County Public Library, 334 N Main St, Raeford, NC, 28376. Tel: 910-875-2502. p. 1708

Brown, Evelyn, Librn, Bolivar County Library System, Thelma Rayner Memorial Library, 201 Front St, Merigold, MS, 38759. Tel: 662-748-2105. p. 1214

Brown, Frances, Librn, Union Springs Public Library, 103 Prairie St N, Union Springs, AL, 36089. Tel: 334-738-2760. p. 39

Brown, Gail, Youth Serv Librn, Voorheesville Public Library, 51 School Rd, Voorheesville, NY, 12186. Tel: 518-765-2791. p. 1657

Brown, Galin, Access Services & Assessment Librn, Willamette University, J W Long Law Library, 245 Winter St SE, Salem, OR, 97301. Tel: 503-375-5421. p. 1897

Brown, Geoff, Sci Librn, Northeastern Illinois University, 5500 N Saint Louis Ave, Chicago, IL, 60625-4699. Tel: 773-442-4400. p. 566

Brown, Georgia, Pub Serv Librn, University of Wisconsin-Milwaukee Libraries, American Geographical Society Library, Golda Meir Library, 2311 E Hartford Ave, Milwaukee, WI, 53211. Tel: 414-229-3984, 414-229-6282. p. 2461

Brown, Gina, Asst Librn, Donald W Reynolds Community Center & Library, 1515 W Main St, Durant, OK, 74701. Tel: 580-924-3486, 580-931-0231. p. 1846

Brown, Gina M, Head, Res & Instruction, United States Naval War College Library, 686 Cushing Rd, Newport, RI, 02841-1207. Tel: 401-841-6500. p. 2035

Brown, Greg, Mkt Mgr, Barry-Lawrence Regional Library, 213 Sixth St, Monett, MO, 65708-2147. Tel: 417-235-6646. p. 1262

Brown, Hana, Librn Supvr, Charlotte County Library System, Port Charlotte Public, 2280 Aaron St, Port Charlotte, FL, 33952. Tel: 941-764-5570. p. 438

Brown, Hannah, Cat Serv Librn, Georgia Military College, 201 E Greene St, Milledgeville, GA, 31061. Tel: 478-387-4731. p. 491

Brown, Harry, Law Librn, Delaware County Libraries, Bldg 19, 340 N Middletown Rd, Media, PA, 19063-5597. Tel: 610-891-8622. p. 1961

Brown, Heather, Assoc Dean, University of Nebraska Medical Center, 600 S 42nd St, Omaha, NE, 68198. Tel: 402-559-7097. p. 1331

Brown, Holly, Libr Dir, Gilman Library, 100 Main St, Alton, NH, 03809. Tel: 603-875-2550. p. 1353

Brown, Jan, Br Librn, Pottawatomie Wabaunsee Regional Library, Eskridge Branch, 115 S Main St, Eskridge, KS, 66423. Tel: 785-449-2296. p. 834

Brown, Janice, Asst Dir, Info Syst, University of Southern California Libraries, Norris Medical Library, 2003 Zonal Ave, Los Angeles, CA, 90089-9130. Tel: 323-442-1116. , Asst Dir, Info Syst, University of Southern California Libraries, Norris Medical Library, 2003 Zonal Ave, Los Angeles, CA, 90089-9130. Tel: 323-442-1116. p. 170

Brown, Jennifer, Dir of Develop, University of California, San Diego, 9500 Gilman Dr, Mail Code 0175G, La Jolla, CA, 92093-0175. Tel: 858-822-4554. p. 154

Brown, Jennifer, Librn, Marlow Town Library, 12 Church St, Marlow, NH, 03456. Tel: 603-446-3466. p. 1373

Brown, Jennifer, Exec Dir, The Field Library, Four Nelson Ave, Peekskill, NY, 10566. Tel: 914-737-1212. p. 1616

Brown, Rachel, Libr Serv Spec, Davenport University, 6191 Kraft Ave SE, Grand Rapids, MI, 49512. Tel: 616-554-5664. p. 1110

Brown, Rachel, Dir of Educ, Adath Israel Congregation, 3201 E Galbraith Rd, Cincinnati, OH, 45236. Tel: 513-793-1800, Ext 104. p. 1759

Brown, Rachel, Chief Exec Officer, North Grenville Public Library, Norenberg Bldg, One Water St, Kemptville, ON, K0G 1J0, CANADA. Tel: 613-258-4711, Ext 6. p. 2649

Brown, Rachelle, Librn, Canada Department of Fisheries & Oceans, 1190 Westmount Rd, Sydney, NS, B1R 2J6, CANADA. Tel: 902-564-3660, Ext 1128. p. 2622

Brown, Raina, Children's Serv Supvr, Laurel County Public Library District, 120 College Park Dr, London, KY, 40741. Tel: 606-864-5759. p. 864

Brown, Rebecca, Mgr, Pub Serv, Takoma Park Maryland Library, 7505 New Hampshire Ave, Ste 205, Takoma Park, MD, 20912. Tel: 301-891-7259. p. 979

Brown, Rebecca, Circ & Outreach, Wilton Public & Gregg Free Library, Seven Forest Rd, Wilton, NH, 03086. Tel: 603-654-2581. p. 1384

Brown, Rebekkah, Libr Assoc, Marshall University Libraries, One John Marshall Dr, Huntington, WV, 25755-2060. Tel: 304-696-2320. p. 2405

Brown, Rhonda, Librn, Wilton Public Library, 1215 Cypress, Wilton, IA, 52778. Tel: 563-732-2583. p. 792

Brown, Richard, Dir, Clive Public Library, 1900 NW 114th St, Clive, IA, 50325. Tel: 515-453-2221. p. 741

Brown, Robert, Ref Librn II, Joe A Guerra Laredo Public Library, 1120 E Calton Rd, Laredo, TX, 78041. Tel: 956-795-2400. p. 2209

Brown, Robin, Head, Pub Serv, Borough of Manhattan Community College Library, 199 Chambers St, S410, New York, NY, 10007. Tel: 212-220-1445. p. 1580

Brown, Rory, Br Mgr, Chicago Public Library, Independence, 4024 N Elston Ave, Chicago, IL, 60618. Tel: 312-744-0900. p. 556

Brown, Roy, Research & Education Librn, Virginia Commonwealth University Libraries, Tompkins-McCaw Library for the Health Sciences, Medical College of Virginia Campus, 509 N 12th St, Richmond, VA, 23298-0582. Tel: 804-828-1592. p. 2343

Brown, Sandra, Librn, United States Army, 7400 Leake Ave, Rm 108, New Orleans, LA, 70118. Tel: 504-862-2559. p. 904

Brown, Sandra, Libr Dir, Mount Marty University, 1105 W Eighth St, Yankton, SD, 57078-3725. Tel: 605-668-1555. p. 2086

Brown, Sandra, Tech Serv Librn, Lee College Library, 150 Lee Dr, Baytown, TX, 77520. Tel: 281-425-6379. p. 2145

Brown, Sandra, Admin Officer, Algonquin College Library, 1385 Woodroffe Ave, Rm C350, Ottawa, ON, K2G 1V8, CANADA. Tel: 613-727-4723, Ext 5288. p. 2664

Brown, Sara, Libr Mgr, Selby Public Library, 1331 First St, Sarasota, FL, 34236. Tel: 941-861-1100. p. 443

Brown, Sarah, Libr Mgr, Wickenburg Public Library & Learning Center, 164 E Apache St, Wickenburg, AZ, 85390. Tel: 928-668-0552. p. 84

Brown, Sarah, Head, Circ, Richton Park Public Library District, 22310 Latonia Lane, Richton Park, IL, 60471. Tel: 708-481-5333. p. 638

Brown, Sarah B, Adminr, All Souls Unitarian Church, 5805 E 56th St, Indianapolis, IN, 46226-1526. Tel: 317-545-6005. p. 690

Brown, Sarah B, Dir, Mason Public Library, 200 Reading Rd, Mason, OH, 45040. Tel: 513-398-2711. p. 1800

Brown, Sarah Beth, Commun Serv, Wilmette Public Library District, 1242 Wilmette Ave, Wilmette, IL, 60091-2558. Tel: 847-256-6925. p. 663

Brown, Shannon, Exec Dir, Holy Family University Library, 9801 Frankford Ave, Philadelphia, PA, 19114. Tel: 267-341-3314. p. 1981

Brown, Sharon, Libr Dir, Macon Public Library, 210 N Rutherford St, Macon, MO, 63552. Tel: 660-385-3314. p. 1260

Brown, Shelley, Circ, University of Alberta, John Alexander Weir Memorial Law Library, Law Ctr, 111 St & 89 Ave, Edmonton, AB, T6G 2H5, CANADA. Tel: 780-492-1445. p. 2538

Brown, Sheri, Librn, Florida State College at Jacksonville, Downtown Campus Library & Learning Commons, 101 W State St, Bldg A, Rm A-2102 & A-3040, Jacksonville, FL, 32202-3056. Tel: 904-633-8414. p. 411

Brown, Sophia, Head, Youth Serv, Bellwood Public Library, 600 Bohland Ave, Bellwood, IL, 60104-1896. Tel: 708-547-7393. p. 541

Brown, Stacey, Instruction & Outreach Librn, Eckerd College, 4200 54th Ave S, Saint Petersburg, FL, 33711. Tel: 727-864-8337. p. 441

Brown, Stacy L, Regional Dir, Azalea Regional Library System, 1121 East Ave, Madison, GA, 30650. Tel: 706-342-4974, Ext 1010. p. 488

Brown, Stan, Dir, Libr Tech, Miami University Libraries, 151 S Campus Ave, Oxford, OH, 45056. Tel: 513-529-2351. p. 1811

Brown, Stella, Dir, Putnam County Library System, 601 College Rd, Palatka, FL, 32177-3873. Tel: 386-329-0126. p. 433

Brown, Stephanie, Asst City Librn, Lakeland Public Library, 100 Lake Morton Dr, Lakeland, FL, 33801-5375. Tel: 863-834-4280. p. 417

Brown, Sue, Tech Serv Mgr, Brookfield Public Library, 1900 N Calhoun Rd, Brookfield, WI, 53005. Tel: 262-782-4140. p. 2425

Brown, Susan, Circ Serv, Linn County Library District No 5, 752 Main St, Pleasanton, KS, 66075. Tel: 913-352-8554. p. 832

Brown, Susan, Asst Dir, Hadley Public Library, 50 Middle St, Hadley, MA, 01035. Tel: 413-584-7451. p. 1023

Brown, Susan, Asst Dir, Head, Adult Serv, Derry Public Library, 64 E Broadway, Derry, NH, 03038-2412. Tel: 603-432-6140. p. 1361

Brown, Susan, Dir, Chapel Hill Public Library, 100 Library Dr, Chapel Hill, NC, 27514. Tel: 919-968-2777. p. 1678

Brown, Susan, Automation Mgr, Circ Mgr, Ella M Everhard Public Library, 132 Broad St, Wadsworth, OH, 44281-1897. Tel: 330-335-2607. p. 1827

Brown, Susan M, Libr Dir, Transylvania University Library, 300 N Broadway, Lexington, KY, 40508. Tel: 859-233-8408. p. 863

Brown, Suzanne, Coll Develop, Marion County Public Library System, 2720 E Silver Springs Blvd, Ocala, FL, 34470. Tel: 352-671-8551. p. 430

Brown, Suzanne, Librn, Clearfield Public Library, 401 Broadway, Ste 200, Clearfield, IA, 50840-0028. Tel: 641-336-2939. p. 740

Brown, Sylvia, Mgr, Miami-Dade Public Library System, North Central Branch, 9590 NW 27th Ave, Miami, FL, 33147. Tel: 305-693-4541. p. 423

Brown, Sylvia, Mgr, Miami-Dade Public Library System, Opa-Locka Branch, 780 Fisherman St, Ste 140, Opa-Locka, FL, 33054. Tel: 305-688-1134. p. 424

Brown, Sylvia, Dir, Woodland Public Library, 169 Main St, Baileyville, ME, 04694. Tel: 207-427-3235. p. 915

Brown, Sylvia, Archivist, Williams College, 26 Hopkins Hall Dr, Williamstown, MA, 01267. Tel: 413-597-2596. p. 1069

Brown, Teena, Libr Tech, Grantsville City Library, 42 N Bowery St, Grantsville, UT, 84029. Tel: 435-884-1670. p. 2264

Brown, Tekolya, Admin Serv Coordr, Bensenville Community Public Library, 200 S Church Rd, Bensenville, IL, 60106. Tel: 630-766-4642. p. 541

Brown, Teresa, Circ Mgr, University of Tampa, 401 W Kennedy Blvd, Tampa, FL, 33606-1490. Tel: 813-257-3053. p. 450

Brown, Teresa, Libr Supvr, Harnett County Public Library, Coats Branch, 29 E Main St, Coats, NC, 27521. Tel: 910-230-1944. p. 1701

Brown, Terrence Neal, Dir, Libr Serv, Mid-America Baptist Theological Seminary, 2095 Appling Rd, Cordova, TN, 38016. Tel: 901-751-3007. p. 2095

Brown, Timothy, First Year Interaction Librn, Instruction Librn, Wofford College, 429 N Church St, Spartanburg, SC, 29303-3663. Tel: 864-597-4300. p. 2070

Brown, Tony, Info Tech, Bellwood Public Library, 600 Bohland Ave, Bellwood, IL, 60104-1896. Tel: 708-547-7393. p. 541

Brown, Uli, Libr Office Mgr, Newfoundland & Labrador Historical Society Library, 95 Bonaventure Ave, Ste 500, St. John's, NL, A1B 2X5, CANADA. Tel: 709-722-3191. p. 2611

Brown, Vikki, Coordr, Heartland Library Cooperative, 319 W Center Ave, Sebring, FL, 33870. Tel: 863-402-6716. p. 444

Brown, Vikki, Libr Syst Mgr, Highlands County Library, Avon Park Public Library, 100 N Museum Ave, Avon Park, FL, 33825. Tel: 863-452-3803. p. 444

Brown, Vikki, Librn, Highlands County Library, 319 W Center Ave, Sebring, FL, 33870-3109. Tel: 863-402-6716. p. 444

Brown, Wanda, Dir, Mims/Scottsmoor Public Library, 3615 Lionel Rd, Mims, FL, 32754. Tel: 321-264-5080. p. 426

Brown, Wanda, Libr Dir, Titusville Public Library, 2121 S Hopkins Ave, Titusville, FL, 32780. Tel: 321-264-5026. p. 451

Brown, Wanda, Br Mgr, Dougherty County Public Library, Southside, 2114 Habersham Rd, Albany, GA, 31705. Tel: 229-420-3260. p. 457

Brown, Wanda K, Dir, Libr Serv, Winston-Salem State University, 601 Martin Luther King Jr Dr, Winston-Salem, NC, 27110. Tel: 336-750-2446. p. 1726

Brown, Whitney, Asst Dir, Head, Ref, Mansfield Public Library, 255 Hope St, Mansfield, MA, 02048-2353. Tel: 508-261-7380. p. 1031

Brown, Yvette, Commun Librn, Cariboo Regional District Library, Lac la Hache Branch, 4787 Clark Ave, Lac la Hache, BC, V0K 1T0, CANADA. Tel: 250-396-7642. p. 2584

Brown, Yvonne, Asst Dir, Tech Serv, Lapeer District Library, 201 Village West Dr S, Lapeer, MI, 48446-1699. Tel: 810-664-9521. p. 1126

Brown-Barbier, Rebecca, Libr Mgr, New York Public Library - Astor, Lenox & Tilden Foundations, Riverdale Branch, 5540 Mosholu Ave, (@ W 256th St), Bronx, NY, 10471. Tel: 718-549-1212. p. 1597

Brown-Green, Fredriatta, Ch, Librn II, Montgomery City-County Public Library System, Juliette Hampton Morgan Memorial Library, 245 High St, Montgomery, AL, 36104. Tel: 334-240-4991. p. 29

Brown-Jackson, Jacqueline, Head, Circ, Flagler County Public Library, 2500 Palm Coast Pkwy NW, Palm Coast, FL, 32137. Tel: 386-446-6763. p. 434

Brown-Kitamura, Christine, Librn, California Department of Corrections Library System, California State Prison, Solano, 2100 Peabody Rd, Vacaville, CA, 95696. Tel: 704-451-0182, Ext 3435. p. 206

Brown-Suon, Emily, Coordr, Youth Serv, Cranston Public Library, 140 Sockanosset Cross Rd, Cranston, RI, 02920-5539. Tel: 401-943-9080. p. 2031

Brownback, Lisa, Ref (Info Servs), Cape May County Library, 30 Mechanic St, Cape May Court House, NJ, 08210. Tel: 609-463-6350. p. 1394

Browne, Diane, Tech Serv, Needham Free Public Library, 1139 Highland Ave, Needham, MA, 02494-3298. Tel: 781-455-7559, Ext 214. p. 1038

Browne, Gretchen, Dir, Plainview-Old Bethpage Public Library, 999 Old Country Rd, Plainview, NY, 11803-4995. Tel: 516-938-0077, Ext 239. p. 1618

Browne, Maggie, Dep Dir, North Kingstown Free Library, 100 Boone St, North Kingstown, RI, 02852-5150. Tel: 401-294-3306. p. 2036

Browne, Melanie, Digital Content Spec, Info Res Spec, Workplace Safety & Insurance Board, 200 Front St W, 17th Flr, Toronto, ON, M5V 3J1, CANADA. Tel: 416-344-4962. p. 2700

Brownell, Eric, Coll Develop Librn, Center for Astrophysics Library / Harvard & Smithsonian Library, 60 Garden St, MS-56, Cambridge, MA, 02138. Tel: 617-496-5769. p. 1005

Brownfield, Lindsay, Ref & Instruction Librn, University of Nebraska at Kearney, 2508 11th Ave, Kearney, NE, 68849-2240. Tel: 308-865-8853. p. 1319

Browning, Alaina, Librn, Bevill State Community College, Sumiton Campus, Bldg 1200, 1st Flr, 101 State St, Sumiton, AL, 35148. p. 17

Browning, Barbara, Ref Librn, Tech Serv Librn, Allegany College of Maryland Library, 12401 Willowbrook Rd SE, Cumberland, MD, 21502. Tel: 301-784-5240. p. 963

Browning, Doris, Libr Spec, Southeast Kentucky Community & Technical College, 700 College Rd, Cumberland, KY, 40823. Tel: 606-589-3001. p. 853

Browning, Greta, Ref Librn, Appalachian State University, William Leonard Eury Appalachian Collection, 218 College St, Boone, NC, 28608. Tel: 828-262-7974. p. 1675

Browning, Laura, Cat Librn, Eastern Florida State College, 1519 Clearlake Rd, Cocoa, FL, 32922. p. 389

Browning, Sommer, Assoc Dir, Tech Serv, Auraria Library, 1100 Lawrence St, Denver, CO, 80204-2095. Tel: 303-315-7728. p. 273

Browning, Susan, Br Mgr, Fort Bend County Libraries, Bob Lutts Fulshear Simonton Branch, 8100 FM 359 S, Fulshear, TX, 77441. Tel: 281-633-4675. p. 2232

Browning, Vicki, Adult Programming, Bath County Memorial Library, 24 W Main St, Owingsville, KY, 40360. Tel: 606-674-2531. p. 871

Browning, Wes, Info Syst Mgr, University of Texas, M D Anderson Cancer Center Research Medical Library, 1400 Pressler St, Houston, TX, 77030-3722. Tel: 713-745-1545. p. 2200

Browning-Mullis, Shannon, Exec Dir, Girl Scouts of the USA, Ten E Oglethorpe Ave, Savannah, GA, 31401. Tel: 912-233-4501. p. 495

Brownlee, Debbie, Cat Librn, Tombigbee Regional Library System, 436 Commerce St, West Point, MS, 39773-2923. Tel: 662-494-4872. p. 1235

Brownlee, Robert, Dir, AV, American University Library, 4400 Massachusetts Ave NW, Washington, DC, 20016-8046. Tel: 202-885-2297. p. 361

Brownlie, Stacey, Libr Dir, University of Maine at Augusta Libraries, 46 University Dr, Augusta, ME, 04330-9410. Tel: 207-621-3186. p. 915

Brownson, Lori, Mgr, Superior District Library, Brevort Township Community Library, 1941 W Church St, Moran, MI, 49760. p. 1149

Brownson, Lori, Ch Serv, Napoleon Public Library, 310 W Clinton St, Napoleon, OH, 43545. Tel: 419-592-2531. p. 1805

Broyles, Linda, Dir, Tech Serv, Pensacola State College, Bldg 20, 1000 College Blvd, Pensacola, FL, 32504-8998. Tel: 850-484-1107. p. 436

Brozovich, Kimberly, Dir, Tech Serv, Rock Island Public Library, 401 19th St, Rock Island, IL, 61201. Tel: 309-732-7344. p. 641

Brubaker, Jana, Interim Assoc Dean, Coll & Serv, Northern Illinois University Libraries, 217 Normal Rd, DeKalb, IL, 60115-2828. Tel: 815-753-9805. p. 577

Brubaker, Jerome P, Curator & Asst Site Dir, Old Fort Niagara Association Library & Archives, Old Fort Niagara Visitor Ctr, Fort Niagara State Park, Youngstown, NY, 14174. Tel: 716-745-7611. p. 1668

Brubaker, Kimberly, Adult Serv, Milton-Union Public Library, 560 S Main St, West Milton, OH, 45383. Tel: 937-698-5515. p. 1830

Brubaker, Sherry, Curator, Maturango Museum, 100 E Las Flores Ave, Ridgecrest, CA, 93555. Tel: 760-375-6900. p. 200

Bruce, Amy, Chairperson for Teaching & Research, Legal Info Librn & Lecturer in Law, Boston College, 885 Centre St, Newton Centre, MA, 02459. Tel: 617-552-2896. p. 1039

Bruce, Boyd, Br Supvr, Lake County Library System, Cooper Memorial Library, 2525 Oakley Seaver Dr, Clermont, FL, 34711. Tel: 352-536-2275. p. 451

Bruce, Carrie, Teen Serv, Manitowoc Public Library, 707 Quay St, Manitowoc, WI, 54220. Tel: 920-686-3000. p. 2453

Bruce, Eugene, Tec Data Librn, United States Navy, Albert T Camp Technical Library, Naval Surface Warfare Ctr IHD-Technical Library, 4171 Fowler Rd, Bldg 299, Ste 101, Indian Head, MD, 20640-5110. Tel: 301-744-4742. p. 969

Bruce, Gail, Dir, Laurel Public Library, 101 E Fourth St, Laurel, DE, 19956-1567. Tel: 302-875-3184. p. 353

Bruce, Jen, Librn, Rochester Community & Technical College, 851 30 Ave SE, Rochester, MN, 55904. Tel: 507-285-7233. p. 1194

Bruce, Paula, Asst County Librn, OC Public Libraries, 1501 E St Andrew Pl, Santa Ana, CA, 92705. Tel: 714-566-3000. p. 237

Bruce, Ranea, Youth Serv, Peotone Public Library District, 515 N First St, Peotone, IL, 60468. Tel: 708-258-3436. p. 635

Bruce, Tobi, Chief Curator, Dir, Exhibitions & Coll, Art Gallery of Hamilton, 123 King St W, Hamilton, ON, L8P 4S8, CANADA. Tel: 905-527-6610. p. 2644

Bruce, William P, Dir & Librn, John A Gupton College, 1616 Church St, Nashville, TN, 37203. Tel: 615-327-3927. p. 2118

Bruch, Courtney, Libr Dir, Northern New Mexico College, 921 Paseo de Onate, Espanola, NM, 87532. Tel: 505-747-2100. p. 1467

Bruch, Scottie, Sch Libr Coordr, South Dakota State Library, 800 Governors Dr, Pierre, SD, 57501-2294. Tel: 605-773-3131. p. 2080

Bruchis, Wanda, Exec Dir, Mid-York Library System, 1600 Lincoln Ave, Utica, NY, 13502. Tel: 315-735-8328. p. 1655

Brucker, Amy, Dir, Hamilton County Library, 102 W Ave C, Syracuse, KS, 67878. Tel: 620-384-5622. p. 838

Brucklan, Joan, Head, Adult Serv, Alexandrian Public Library, 115 W Fifth St, Mount Vernon, IN, 47620. Tel: 812-838-3286. p. 708

Bruckner, Nancy, Tech Serv Librn, Otis Library, 261 Main St, Norwich, CT, 06360. Tel: 860-889-2365. p. 332

Brudner, Benjamin, Head, Ref, Curry College, 1071 Blue Hill Ave, Milton, MA, 02186-9984. Tel: 617-333-2170. p. 1036

Brudno, Roger, Dir, Oroville Hospital, 2767 Olive Hwy, Oroville, CA, 95966. Tel: 530-554-1309. p. 190

Brudwick, Melissa, Student Success Librn, Dakota College at Bottineau Library, 105 Simrall Blvd, Bottineau, ND, 58318. Tel: 701-228-5454. p. 1731

Brueckel, Stephanie, Managing Librn, Brooklyn Public Library, Park Slope, 431 Sixth Ave, Brooklyn, NY, 11215. Tel: 718-832-1853. p. 1503

Brueckner, Amanda, Asst Dir, Youth Serv Librn, Karl Junginger Memorial Library, 625 N Monroe St, Waterloo, WI, 53594-1183. Tel: 920-478-3344. p. 2483

Brueggeman, Carol, Asst Dir, North Freedom Public Library, 105 N Maple St, North Freedom, WI, 53951. Tel: 608-522-4571. p. 2465

Brueland, Anjanae, Dep Dir, Blount County Public Library, 508 N Cusick St, Maryville, TN, 37804. Tel: 865-982-0981. p. 2111

Bruenderman, Jason, Libr Syst Mgr, Southeast Missouri State University, 929 Normal Ave, Cape Girardeau, MO, 63701. Tel: 573-986-6833. p. 1240

Bruesehoff, Sara, YA Librn, Ocean City Free Public Library, 1735 Simpson Ave, Ste 4, Ocean City, NJ, 08226. Tel: 609-399-2434, Ext 5235. p. 1430

Bruestle, Beth, Dir, McLean-Mercer Regional Library, 216 Second St, Riverdale, ND, 58565. Tel: 701-654-7652. p. 1739

Bruggeman, Jane, Dir, Coldwater Public Library, 305 W Main St, Coldwater, OH, 45828. Tel: 419-678-2431. p. 1771

Bruggenthies, Cindy, Libr Serv Coordr, Great River Regional Library, Little Falls Public Library, 108 NE Third St, Little Falls, MN, 56345-2708. Tel: 320-632-9676. p. 1197

Bruggenthies, Cindy, Libr Serv Coordr, Great River Regional Library, Swanville Library, 213 DeGraff Ave, Swanville, MN, 56382. Tel: 320-547-2346. p. 1197

Brugman, Ron, Educ Supvr, Arizona Department of Corrections, Arizona State Prison Complex - Phoenix Library, 2500 E Van Buren St, Phoenix, AZ, 85008. Tel: 602-685-3100, Ext 3758. p. 68

Bruguier, Elsa, Campus Librn, Union County College Libraries, Plainfield Campus, 232 E Second St, Plainfield, NJ, 07060-1308. Tel: 908-412-3545. p. 1398

Bruhn, Christopher, Dr, Music Librn, University of North Carolina School of the Arts Library, 1533 S Main St, Winston-Salem, NC, 27127. Tel: 336-770-3270. p. 1726

Bruley, Marie, Dr, Dean of Learning Resource Ctr, Distance Educ, Merced College, 3600 M St, Merced, CA, 95348. Tel: 209-384-6082. p. 176

Brumback, Sherilyn, Br Mgr, Bemidji Public Library, 509 America Ave NW, Bemidji, MN, 56601. Tel: 218-751-3963. p. 1164

Brumbaugh, Penny, Youth Serv Supvry Librn, Apache Junction Public Library, 1177 N Idaho Rd, Apache Junction, AZ, 85119. Tel: 480-474-8570. p. 55

Brumett, Renee, Dir, Clever Public Library, 7450 W Veterans Blvd, Clever, MO, 65631. Tel: 417-743-2277. p. 1242

Brumett, Renee, Exec Dir, Christian County Library, 1005 N Fourth Ave, Ozark, MO, 65721. Tel: 417-581-2432. p. 1265

Brumett, Renee, Electronic Res Librn, Springfield-Greene County Library District, 4653 S Campbell Ave, Springfield, MO, 65810-1723. Tel: 417-882-0714. p. 1281

Brumfield, Shamera, Youth Serv, Pearl Public Library, 2416 Old Brandon Rd, Pearl, MS, 39208-4601. Tel: 601-932-2562. p. 1229

Brumit, Melanie, Dir, Cameron J Jarvis Troup Municipal Library, 102 S Georgia, Troup, TX, 75789-2020. Tel: 903-842-3101. p. 2249

Brumley, Aaron, Coordr, Info Tech, Lawrence Public Library, 707 Vermont St, Lawrence, KS, 66044-2371. Tel: 785-843-3833, Ext 106. p. 819

Brumley, Dianne, Libr Dir, Lawrence Public Library District, 814 12th St, Lawrenceville, IL, 62439. Tel: 618-943-3016. p. 607

Brumley, Nathan, Asst Dir, Libr Serv, Livermore Public Library, 1188 S Livermore Ave, Livermore, CA, 94550. Tel: 925-373-5572. p. 157

Brummel, Steve, Asst Dir, User Engagement & Experience, Rhodes College, 2000 North Pkwy, Memphis, TN, 38112-1694. Tel: 901-843-3890. p. 2114

Brummett, Judi, Libr Mgr, Timberland Regional Library, Packwood Branch, 109 W Main St, Packwood, WA, 98361. Tel: 360-494-5111. p. 2389

Brummett, Phoebe, Librn, Morton County Library, Rolla Branch, 202 Third St, Rolla, KS, 67954. Tel: 620-593-4328. p. 806

Brun, Nathalie, Libr Dir, Albert-Westmorland-Kent Regional Library, Dieppe Public, 333 Acadie Ave, Dieppe, NB, E1A 1G9, CANADA. Tel: 506-877-7945. p. 2603

Brunal-Perry, Omaira, Assoc Prof, Spanish Doc Coll, University of Guam, Guam & Micronesia Collection, UOG Sta, Mangilao, GU, 96923. Tel: 671-735-2157, 671-735-2160. p. 2505
Brundage, Julie, Libr Mgr, Three Cities Public Library, Corner of Phillippe Ave & Park Ave, Box 89, Paradise Valley, AB, T0B 3R0, CANADA. Tel: 780-745-2277. p. 2550
Brundage, Ken, Dir, Gannon University, 619 Sassafras St, Erie, PA, 16541. Tel: 814-871-7557. p. 1931
Bruneau, Alain-Phillipe, Dir, Innovation, Science & Economic Development, 235 Queen St, 2nd Flr, W Tower, Ottawa, ON, K1A 0H5, CANADA. Tel: 343-291-1569. p. 2667
Bruneau, Jennifer, Dir, Northborough Free Library, 34 Main St, Northborough, MA, 01532-1942. Tel: 508-393-5025. p. 1043
Brunell, Luce, Dir, Admin Serv, Centre Regional de Services aux Bibliotheques Publiques de la Monteregie, 275 rue Conrad-Pelletier, La Prairie, QC, J5R 4V1, CANADA. Tel: 450-444-5433. p. 2714
Brunelle, Mary, Head, Libr Syst & Tech, Assumption University, 500 Salisbury St, Worcester, MA, 01609. Tel: 508-767-7002. p. 1071
Bruner, Christal, Libr Dir, Mexico-Audrain County Library District, 305 W Jackson St, Mexico, MO, 65265. Tel: 573-581-4939. p. 1261
Bruner, Larami, Circ Librn, Sidney Public Library, 1112 12th Ave, Sidney, NE, 69162. Tel: 308-254-3110. p. 1336
Bruner, Mia, Res & Instruction Librn, Sarah Lawrence College, One Mead Way, Bronxville, NY, 10708. Tel: 914-395-2225. p. 1500
Bruner, Rebecca, Libr Tech, Smithsonian Libraries, Hirshhorn Museum & Sculpture Garden Library, Hirshhorn Museum, 4th Flr, 700 Independence Ave SW, Washington, DC, 20560. Tel: 202-633-2775. p. 375
Bruner, Rhiannon, Electronic Res Mgr, Wesleyan College, 4760 Forsyth Rd, Macon, GA, 31210. Tel: 478-757-5202. p. 487
Bruner, Scott A, Libr Dir, Chino Valley Public Library, 1020 W Palomino Rd, Chino Valley, AZ, 86323-5500. Tel: 928-636-2687. p. 58
Brunet, Julianne, Chief Exec Officer, Welland Public Library, 50 The Boardwalk, Welland, ON, L3B 6J1, CANADA. Tel: 905-734-6210. p. 2703
Brunet, Kim, Br Mgr, Greenstone Public Library, Beardmore Branch, 285 Main St, Beardmore, ON, P0T 1G0, CANADA. Tel: 807-875-2212. p. 2643
Brunette, Peter, Libr Coord, Bay Path College, 539 Longmeadow St, Longmeadow, MA, 01106. Tel: 413-565-1376. p. 1029
Brungard, Allison, Librn, Slippery Rock University of Pennsylvania, 109 Campus Loop, Slippery Rock, PA, 16057. Tel: 724-738-2058. p. 2007
Brungard, Charlene, Dir, Jersey Shore Public Library, 110 Oliver St, Jersey Shore, PA, 17740. Tel: 570-398-9891. p. 1947
Brungardt, LeAnne, Youth Serv Supvr, Topeka & Shawnee County Public Library, 1515 SW Tenth Ave, Topeka, KS, 66604-1374. Tel: 785-580-4400. p. 839
Brungot, Ann, Dir, Berlin Public Library, 270 Main St, Berlin, NH, 03570. Tel: 603-752-5210. p. 1355
Brunick, Lisa, Pub Serv, Augustana University, 2001 S Summit Ave, Sioux Falls, SD, 57197-0001. Tel: 605-274-4921. p. 2081
Brunk, Daniel, Sr Librn, California Department of Corrections Library System, Pleasant Valley State Prison, 24863 W Jayne Ave, Coalinga, CA, 93210. Tel: 559-935-4900, Ext 6165. p. 207
Brunkow, Shirley, Dir, Milligan Public Library, 507 Main St, Milligan, NE, 68406. Tel: 402-629-4302. p. 1325
Brunner, Karen, Assoc Dir, Research, Education & Engagement, University of Saint Thomas, 2115 Summit Ave, Mail Box 5004, Saint Paul, MN, 55105. Tel: 651-962-5011. p. 1202
Brunner, Marta, Col Librn, Skidmore College, 815 N Broadway, Saratoga Springs, NY, 12866. Tel: 518-580-5506. p. 1636
Bruno, Amy, Ref Librn, Pahrump Community Library, 701 E St, Pahrump, NV, 89048. Tel: 775-727-5930. p. 1348
Bruno, Coleen, Dir, Kim Yerton Indian Action Library, 2905 Hubbard Ln, Ste C, Eureka, CA, 95501. Tel: 707-443-8401. p. 142
Bruno, James, Dir, Shedd Free Library, 46 N Main, Washington, NH, 03280. Tel: 603-495-3592. p. 1383
Bruno, Lois, Dir, Member Relations, Network of Illinois Learning Resources in Community Colleges, c/o Kishwaukee College, 21193 Malta Rd, Malta, IL, 60150. Tel: 262-287-8017. p. 2765
Bruno, Sophie, Asst Dir, Placer County Library, 145 Fulweiler Ave, Ste 150, Auburn, CA, 95603. Tel: 530-886-4550. p. 118
Bruno, Tom, Dir, Access & Tech Serv, University of Pennsylvania Libraries, Morris Arboretum Library, 100 Northwestern Ave, Philadelphia, PA, 19118-2697. Tel: 215-247-5777, Ext 115. p. 1988
Bruns, Diana, Pres, Nancy Fawcett Memorial Library, 724 Oberfelder St, Lodgepole, NE, 69149-0318. Tel: 308-483-5714. p. 1323
Bruns, Linda Spillman, Ch, Newburgh Chandler Public Library, 4111 Lakeshore Dr, Newburgh, IN, 47630-2274. Tel: 812-589-5468, Ext 308. p. 709
Bruns, Todd, Institutional Repository Librn, Eastern Illinois University, 600 Lincoln Ave, Charleston, IL, 61920. Tel: 217-581-8381. p. 552
Brunsma, Kathy, Tech Serv, Lincoln Memorial University, 6965 Cumberland Gap Pkwy, Harrogate, TN, 37752. Tel: 423-869-6221. p. 2101
Brunson, Gene, Dir, IT Dir, Berkeley County Library System, 1003 Hwy 52, Moncks Corner, SC, 29461. Tel: 843-719-4223. p. 2065
Brunson, Neal E, Dir, Afro-American Historical Society Museum Library, Jersey City Free Library - Earl A Morgan Branch, 1841 Kennedy Blvd, Jersey City, NJ, 07305. Tel: 201-547-5262. p. 1409
Brunsting, Karen, Acq & Coll Develop Librn, University Libraries, University of Memphis, 3785 Norriswood Ave, Memphis, TN, 38152. Tel: 901-678-4400. p. 2115
Brush, Barbara, Dir, Lamar Warren Law Library of Broward County, Broward County Judicial Complex, North Wing, Rm 1800, 201 SE Sixth St, Fort Lauderdale, FL, 33301. Tel: 954-831-6226. p. 402
Brusik, Susan, ILL, University of Utah, J Willard Marriott Library, 295 S 1500 East, Salt Lake City, UT, 84112-0860. Tel: 801-581-8558. p. 2272
Brussow, Michele, Head Librn, Capital Area District Libraries, 401 S Capitol Ave, Lansing, MI, 48933. Tel: 517-367-6300. p. 1124
Brust, Eric, Circuit Librn, United States Court of Appeals, 110 E Court Ave, Ste 358, Des Moines, IA, 50309. Tel: 515-284-6228. p. 747
Brust, Eric, Circuit Librn, United States Court of Appeals Library, Thomas F Eagleton US Courthouse, 111 S Tenth St, Rm 22-300, Saint Louis, MO, 63102. Tel: 314-244-2665. p. 1276
Brust, Eric W, Circuit Librn, US Court Library - Eighth Circuit, 9440 Charles Evans Whittaker US Courthouse, 400 E Ninth St, Kansas City, MO, 64106. Tel: 816-512-5790. p. 1257
Brutchen, Melissa, Dir, Ch Serv, Winchester Community Library, 125 N East St, Winchester, IN, 47394-1698. Tel: 765-584-4824. p. 727
Bruton, Ben, Ref & Instruction Librn, Minot State University, 500 University Ave W, Minot, ND, 58707. Tel: 701-858-3013. p. 1738
Bruton, Elke, Prog Mgr, Oregon State Library Talking Book & Braille Services, 250 Winter St NE, Salem, OR, 97301. Tel: 503-378-5455. p. 1896
Brutton, Lori, Librn, Valmeyer Public Library District, 300 S Cedar Bluff, Valmeyer, IL, 62295. Tel: 618-935-2626. p. 657
Bruxvoort, Barbara, Libr Serv Mgr, South San Francisco Public Library, 840 W Orange Ave, South San Francisco, CA, 94080-3125. Tel: 650-829-3860. p. 247
Bruxvoort, Diane, Dean of Libr, University of North Texas Libraries, 1155 Union Circle, No 305190, Denton, TX, 76203-5017. Tel: 940-565-2413. p. 2170
Bruzzese, Christine, Supv Librn, City of New York Department of Records & Information Services, 31 Chambers St, Rm 112, New York, NY, 10007. Tel: 212-788-8590. p. 1582
Bryan, Ashley, Access Serv Librn, Archivist, Wentworth Institute of Technology, 550 Huntington Ave, Boston, MA, 02115-5998. Tel: 617-989-4681. p. 1000
Bryan, Bonita, Coordr, Coll Serv, Emory University Libraries, Woodruff Health Sciences Center Library, 1462 Clifton Rd NE, Atlanta, GA, 30322. Tel: 404-727-8727. p. 463
Bryan, Jackie, Ref & Instrul Serv Librn, Saint Leo University, 33701 State Rd 52, Saint Leo, FL, 33574. Tel: 352-588-7437. p. 441
Bryan, Jennifer A, PhD, Head, Spec Coll & Archives, United States Naval Academy, 589 McNair Rd, Annapolis, MD, 21402-5029. Tel: 410-293-6945. p. 951
Bryan, Karla, Dr, Dir, Trinity Valley Community College Library, 100 Cardinal Dr, Athens, TX, 75751. Tel: 903-675-6229. p. 2137
Bryan, Lindsey, Mgr, Libr Operations, Metropolitan Library System in Oklahoma County, Belle Isle Library, 5501 N Villa Ave, Oklahoma City, OK, 73112-7164. p. 1857
Bryan, Michael, Libr Dir, Seminole Community Library at St Petersburg College, 9200 113th St N, Seminole, FL, 33772. Tel: 727-394-6923. p. 444
Bryan-Reeder, Emily, Asst Dir, Green Tree Public Library, Ten W Manilla Ave, 1st Flr, Pittsburgh, PA, 15220-3310. Tel: 412-921-9292. p. 1994
Bryant, Amy, Libr Dir, Earlham College, 801 National Rd W, Richmond, IN, 47374-4095. p. 715
Bryant, Ashley, Dir, Maplewood Public Library, 7550 Lohmeyer Ave, Maplewood, MO, 63143. Tel: 314-781-7323. p. 1260
Bryant, Barbara, Supvr, Circ, Whitman Public Library, 100 Webster St, Whitman, MA, 02382. Tel: 781-447-7613. p. 1069
Bryant, Ben, Med Librn, Ochsner Medical Library, 1514 Jefferson Hwy, 1st Flr, New Orleans, LA, 70121-2429. Tel: 504-842-3760. p. 903
Bryant, Clare, Tech Serv, Edmonds College Library, 20000 68th Ave W, Lynnwood, WA, 98036. Tel: 425-640-1529. p. 2370
Bryant, Gary, Circ Mgr, New River Community College, 226 Martin Hall, 5255 College Dr, Dublin, VA, 24084. Tel: 540-674-3600, Ext 4334. p. 2315
Bryant, Jacquelyn A, Librn, Community College of Philadelphia Library, Northwest Regional Center Library, 1300 W Godfrey Ave, Rm 117, Philadelphia, PA, 19141. Tel: 215-496-6019. p. 1975
Bryant, Karen, Asst Dir, Tech Serv, Calhoun County Public Library, 17731 NE Pear St, Blountstown, FL, 32424. Tel: 850-674-8773. p. 385
Bryant, Karen, Br Head, Henderson County Public Library, Etowah Branch, 101 Brickyard Rd, Etowah, NC, 28729. Tel: 828-891-6577. p. 1695
Bryant, Katherine, Asst Dir, Bloomfield Township Public Library, 1099 Lone Pine Rd, Bloomfield Township, MI, 48302-2410. Tel: 248-642-5800. p. 1086
Bryant, Katherine, Br Mgr, Nashville Public Library, Bellevue Branch, 720 Baugh Rd, Nashville, TN, 37221. Tel: 615-862-5854. p. 2119
Bryant, Kelli, Librn, Grand Saline Public Library, 201 E Pacific Ave, Grand Saline, TX, 75140. Tel: 903-962-5516. p. 2186

Bryant, Kelly, Co-Mgr, Andrews Public Library, 871 Main St, Andrews, NC, 28901. Tel: 828-321-5956. p. 1671

Bryant, Kelly, Libr Asst, Marketing & Communications Coord, Hood Theological Seminary Library, 300 Bldg, 1810 Luthern Synod Dr, Salisbury, NC, 28144. Tel: 704-636-6840. p. 1714

Bryant, Kristi, Sr Librn, Peabody Institute Library, West, 603 Lowell St, Peabody, MA, 01960. Tel: 978-535-3354, Ext 11. p. 1045

Bryant, Lauren, Web & Usability Librarian, Shoreline Community College, 16101 Greenwood Ave N, Shoreline, WA, 98133-5696. Tel: 206-533-2548. p. 2383

Bryant, Lee, Syst Adminr, Albemarle Regional Library, 303 W Tryon St, Winton, NC, 27986. Tel: 252-358-7864. p. 1727

Bryant, Llewann, Dir, Keck Memorial Library, 119 N Second St, Wapello, IA, 52653. Tel: 319-523-5261. p. 788

Bryant, Marion, Regional Libr Dir, Tennessee State Library & Archives, 403 Seventh Ave N, Nashville, TN, 37243-0312. Tel: 931-388-9282. p. 2121

Bryant, Marion K, Dir, Buffalo River Regional Library, 230 E James Campbell Blvd, Ste 108, Columbia, TN, 38401-3359. Tel: 931-380-2601. p. 2094

Bryant, Maureen, Librn, United States International Trade Commission, Law Library, 500 E St SW, Rm 614, Washington, DC, 20436. Tel: 202-205-3287. p. 379

Bryant, Megan, Librn, Pea Ridge Community Library, 801 N Curtis Ave, Pea Ridge, AR, 72751-2306. Tel: 479-451-8442. p. 107

Bryant, Melissa Lynn, Librn, Satre Memorial Library, 528 Fifth St, Milnor, ND, 58060. Tel: 701-427-5295. p. 1738

Bryant, Penny Lynn, Dir, Pecatonica Public Library District, 400 W 11th St, Pecatonica, IL, 61063. Tel: 815-239-2616. p. 633

Bryant, Rachel, Children's Spec, Camden County Library, 104 Investors Way, Units CDEF, Camden, NC, 27921. Tel: 252-331-2543. p. 1677

Bryant, Robyn, Circ Supvr, Taunton Public Library, 12 Pleasant St, Taunton, MA, 02780. Tel: 508-821-1410. p. 1059

Bryant, Sally, Assoc University Librn for Public Servs & Instruction, Pepperdine University Libraries, 24255 Pacific Coast Hwy, Malibu, CA, 90263. Tel: 310-506-4252. p. 171

Bryant, Sarah, Ref & Instruction Librn, Western Wyoming Community College, 2500 College Dr, Rock Springs, WY, 82902. Tel: 307-382-1700. p. 2498

Bryant, Sarah, Asst Prof, University of Alabama, 7035 Gorgas Library, Campus Box 870252, Tuscaloosa, AL, 35487-0252. Tel: 205-348-4610. p. 2781

Bryant, Skyla, Asst Dir, Texas Tech University Health Sciences, Harrington Library, 1400 Wallace Blvd, Amarillo, TX, 79106. Tel: 806-414-9964. p. 2214

Bryant, Teresa, Interim Dir, Samson Public Library, 200 N Johnson St, Samson, AL, 36477-2006. Tel: 334-898-7806. p. 35

Bryant, Thedis, Mrs, Asst Dir, Res Info Serv, Alabama A&M University, 4900 Meridian St N, Normal, AL, 35762. Tel: 256-372-4724. p. 31

Bryant-Smith, Kimberly, Libr Assoc, Norwalk Community College, 188 Richards Ave, Norwalk, CT, 06854-1655. Tel: 203-857-6895. p. 331

Bryars, Paula, Librn, Louisiana Economic Development Library, LaSalle Bldg, 617 N Third St, 11th Flr, Baton Rouge, LA, 70802. Tel: 225-342-3071. p. 883

Bryce, Alan L, Libr Assoc, University of New Hampshire Library, Engineering, Mathematics & Computer Science, Kingsbury Hall, 33 Academic Way, Durham, NH, 03824. Tel: 603-862-1740. p. 1362

Bryce, Shauna, Assoc University Librarian, Colls, Athabasca University, One University Dr, Athabasca, AB, T9S 3A3, CANADA. Tel: 780-675-6254. p. 2522

Bryce, Shawna, Br Mgr, Madison County Public Library, Mars Hill Branch, 25 Library St, Mars Hill, NC, 28754-9783. Tel: 828-689-5183. p. 1703

Bryden, David L, Dir, High Point University, One University Pkwy, High Point, NC, 27268. Tel: 336-841-9102. p. 1697

Bryden, Eric, ILL, Hawkeye Community College Library, 1501 E Orange Rd, Waterloo, IA, 50701-9014. Tel: 319-296-4006, Ext 1716. p. 789

Brydon, Heather, Chair, Manitoba Library Consortium, Inc, c/o Library Administration, University of Winnipeg, 515 Portage Ave, Winnipeg, MB, R3B 2E9, CANADA. Tel: 204-786-9801. p. 2777

Bryl, James, Libr Mgr, Wabamun Public Library, 5132 53rd Ave, Wabamun, AB, T0E 2K0, CANADA. Tel: 780-892-2713. p. 2558

Bryson, Asheley, Libr Mgr, Sno-Isle Libraries, Darrington Library, 1005 Cascade St, Darrington, WA, 98241. Tel: 360-436-1600. p. 2370

Bryson, Ben, Asst Dir, Marshes of Glynn Libraries, 208 Gloucester St, Brunswick, GA, 31520. Tel: 912-279-3740. p. 468

Brzeski, Laura, Br Mgr, Morgan County Public Library, Brooklyn Branch, Six E Mill St, Brooklyn, IN, 46111. Tel: 317-834-2003. p. 705

Brzeski, Laura, Br Mgr, Morgan County Public Library, Eminence Branch, Eminence Lion's Club, 11604 Walters Rd, Eminence, IN, 46125. Tel: 765-528-2117. p. 705

Brzeski, Laura, Br Mgr, Morgan County Public Library, Morgantown Branch, 79 W Washington St, Morgantown, IN, 46160. Tel: 812-597-0889. p. 705

Brzozowski, Robin, Genealogy Serv, Athol Public Library, 568 Main St, Athol, MA, 01331. Tel: 978-249-9515. p. 986

Brzozowski, Steven, Librn, Harvard Library, Harvard College Library (Headquarters), Harry Elkins Widener Memorial Library, Rm 110, Cambridge, MA, 02138. Tel: 617-495-2413. p. 1006

Bublitz, Sarah, Youth Serv, Franklin Public Library, 9151 W Loomis Rd, Franklin, WI, 53132. Tel: 414-425-8214. p. 2436

Bubnis, Alana, Ch Serv, New Cumberland Public Library, One Benjamin Plaza, New Cumberland, PA, 17070-1597. Tel: 717-774-7820. p. 1969

Bubnis, Alana, Dir, New Cumberland Public Library, One Benjamin Plaza, New Cumberland, PA, 17070-1597. Tel: 717-774-7820. p. 1969

Bucacink, Ian, Archivist, Tech Librn, American Society of Landscape Architects, 636 I St NW, Washington, DC, 20001-3736. Tel: 202-216-2354. p. 360

Bucalo, Kathy, Dir of Libraries for User Engagement & Admin Servs, Adelphi University, One South Ave, Garden City, NY, 11530. Tel: 516-877-3521. p. 1536

Bucci, Antonio, Tech Serv, Arizona Talking Book Library, 1030 N 32nd St, Phoenix, AZ, 85008. Tel: 602-255-5578. p. 69

Buccieri, Michael, Mgr, Network Serv, Tarrant County College, 828 W Harwood Rd, Hurst, TX, 76054. Tel: 817-515-6623. p. 2201

Buch, Jennifer, Dir, Huron Public Library, 333 Williams St, Huron, OH, 44839. Tel: 419-433-5009. p. 1791

Buchalter, Ann, Syst Librn, Tech Serv Librn, College of Alameda, 555 Ralph Appezzato Memorial Pkwy, Alameda, CA, 94501. Tel: 510-748-2253. p. 115

Buchanan, Ann, Libr Adminr, British Columbia Genealogical Society, 12837 76th Ave, No 211, Surrey, BC, V3W 2V3, CANADA. Tel: 604-502-9119. p. 2576

Buchanan, Bob, Librn, Auburn University, Veterinary Medical, 101 Greene Hall, Auburn, AL, 36849-5606. Tel: 334-844-1749. p. 6

Buchanan, Heidi, Assoc Dean, Western Carolina University, 176 Central Dr, Cullowhee, NC, 28723. Tel: 828-227-3408. p. 1683

Buchanan, Jennifer, Youth & Program Dir, Lawrence Public Library District, 814 12th St, Lawrenceville, IL, 62439. Tel: 618-943-3016. p. 607

Buchanan, Laura Lin, Interim Dir, Princeton Public Library, 920 Mercer St, Princeton, WV, 24740-2932. Tel: 304-487-5045. p. 2413

Buchanan, Mary, Libr Dir, Tombstone City Library, 210 S Fourth St, Tombstone, AZ, 85638. Tel: 520-457-3612. p. 80

Buchanan, Mary, Research Servs Librn, Pennsylvania Western University - Clarion, 840 Wood St, Clarion, PA, 16214. Tel: 814-393-1811. p. 1922

Buchanan, Sarah, Asst Prof, University of Missouri-Columbia, 303 Townsend Hall, Columbia, MO, 65211. Tel: 573-882-4546. p. 2787

Buchanan, Stephanie, Dir, Bucyrus Public Library, 200 E Mansfield St, Bucyrus, OH, 44820-2381. Tel: 419-562-7327, Ext 108. p. 1753

Buchen, Richard, Special Colls & Reference Librn, Pacifica Graduate Institute, 249 Lambert Rd, Carpinteria, CA, 93013. Tel: 805-969-3626, Ext 133. p. 128

Bucher, Debra, Head, Coll, Head, Discovery Serv, Vassar College Library, 124 Raymond Ave, Box 20, Poughkeepsie, NY, 12604. Tel: 845-437-7762. p. 1624

Bucher, Judy, Interim Libr Dir, Pioneer Memorial Public Library, Rte 33, Harman, WV, 26270. Tel: 304-227-4788. p. 2403

Buchman, Michele, Circ Supvr, University of California, Berkeley, Marian Koshland Bioscience, Natural Resources & Public Health Library, 2101 Valley Life Science Bldg, No 6500, Berkeley, CA, 94720-6500. Tel: 510-642-2531. p. 123

Buchman, Michele, Circ Supvr, University of California, Berkeley, Optometry & Health Sciences Library, 490 Minor Hall, Berkeley, CA, 94720-6000. Tel: 510-642-1020. p. 123

Buchmann, Rebecca, Acq & Cat, Tech Serv, Door County Library, 107 S Fourth Ave, Sturgeon Bay, WI, 54235. Tel: 920-746-7116. p. 2479

Buchsbaum, Kathy, Asst Dir, Head, Ref, Lynbrook Public Library, 56 Eldert St, Lynbrook, NY, 11563. Tel: 516-599-8630. p. 1566

Buchwald, Norman, Info Tech, Chabot College Library, 25555 Hesperian Blvd, Hayward, CA, 94545. Tel: 510-723-6993. p. 150

Buchwalter, Susan, Human Res, Wayne County Public Library, 220 W Liberty St, Wooster, OH, 44691. Tel: 330-804-4683. p. 1833

Buck, Allie, Curator, Cambria County Historical Society Library, 615 N Center St, Ebensburg, PA, 15931. Tel: 814-472-6674. p. 1929

Buck, Amber, Br Mgr, Clark County Library, Cabe Public Library, 204 E Walnut, Gurdon, AR, 71743. Tel: 870-353-2911. p. 89

Buck, Doug, Finance Mgr, Pioneer Library System, 300 Norman Ctr Ct, Norman, OK, 73072. Tel: 405-801-4505. p. 1855

Buck, Jamie, Pub Serv Coordr, Tye Preston Memorial Library, 16311 S Access Rd, Canyon Lake, TX, 78133-5301. Tel: 830-964-3744. p. 2153

Buck, Jeanne, Dir, Reed Memorial Library, 1733 Rte 6, Carmel, NY, 10512. Tel: 845-225-2439. p. 1514

Buck, Laura, Info Spec I, University of Missouri-Columbia, Zalk Veterinary Medical Library, W-218 Veterinary-Medicine Bldg, Columbia, MO, 65211. Tel: 573-882-2461. p. 1244

Buck, Linda, Site Mgr, High Plains Museum Library, 413 Norris Ave, McCook, NE, 69001. Tel: 308-345-3661. p. 1324

Buck, Mary, Br Mgr, Central Rappahannock Regional Library, William J Howell Branch, 806 Lyons Blvd, Fredericksburg, VA, 22406. Tel: 540-372-1144, Ext 7440. p. 2320

Buck, Megan, Dir, Dickinson County Library, 401 Iron Mountain St, Iron Mountain, MI, 49801-3435. Tel: 906-774-1218. p. 1118

Buck, Susannah Bingham, Ref Librn, University of Dallas, 1845 E Northgate Dr, Irving, TX, 75062-4736. Tel: 972-721-5075. p. 2203

Buck, Teresa, Head, Tech Serv, University of Mary Hardin-Baylor, 900 College St, UMHB Sta, Box 8016, Belton, TX, 76513-2599. Tel: 254-295-4640. p. 2147

Buck, Will, Campus Librn, Pellissippi State Community College, 2731 W Lamar Alexander Pkwy, Friendsville, TN, 37737. Tel: 865-981-5326. p. 2099

Buckanaga, Dan, Sr Libr Tech, Duluth Public Library, West Duluth, 5830 Grand Ave, Duluth, MN, 55807. Tel: 218-730-4280. p. 1172

Buckardt, Kate, Head, Adult Serv, Lake Forest Library, 360 E Deerpath Rd, Lake Forest, IL, 60045. Tel: 847-810-4613. p. 606

Buckborough, Karla, Chief Exec Officer, Chief Librn, The Cavan Monaghan Libraries, One Dufferin St, Millbrook, ON, L0A 1G0, CANADA. Tel: 705-932-2919. p. 2658

Buckingham, Richard, Dir, Info Res, Suffolk University, John Joseph Moakley Law Library, 120 Tremont St, 6th Flr, Boston, MA, 02108-4977. Tel: 617-573-8177. p. 1000

Buckles Harkness, Shaina, Librn, Salvador Dali Foundation Inc, One Dali Blvd, Saint Petersburg, FL, 33701. Tel: 727-623-4734. p. 441

Buckley, Angela, Ch Serv, Indian Valley Public Library, 100 E Church Ave, Telford, PA, 18969. Tel: 215-723-9109. p. 2012

Buckley, Barbara, Br Mgr, Adams County Library System, Harbaugh-Thomas Library, 50 W York St, Biglerville, PA, 17307. Tel: 717-677-6257. p. 1935

Buckley, Brandon, YA Librn, St Charles Public Library District, One S Sixth Ave, Saint Charles, IL, 60174-2105. Tel: 630-584-0076, Ext 201. p. 644

Buckley, Don, City Librn, Cerritos Library, 18025 Bloomfield Ave, Cerritos, CA, 90703. Tel: 562-916-1350. p. 129

Buckley, Emilie, Librn, Valencia College, Lake Nona Campus Library, 12350 Narcoossee Rd, Bldg 1, Rm 330, Orlando, FL, 32832. Tel: 407-582-7107. p. 433

Buckley, Eugennie, ILL Serv, Georgetown University, Dahlgren Memorial Library, Preclinical Science Bldg GM-7, 3900 Reservoir Rd NW, Washington, DC, 20007. Tel: 202-687-1448. p. 368

Buckley, Jaki, Human Res, Interim Dir, District of Columbia Public Library, 1990 K St NW, Washington, DC, 20006. Tel: 202-727-1101. p. 363

Buckley, Janet, Head, Cat, Greenwood Public Library, 310 S Meridian St, Greenwood, IN, 46143-3135. Tel: 317-881-1953. p. 688

Buckley, Keith, Head, Pub Serv, Indiana University, School of Law Library, Maurer School of Law, 211 S Indiana Ave, Bloomington, IN, 47405. Tel: 812-855-7216. p. 670

Buckley, Kimberli, Sr Commun Libr Mgr, Contra Costa County Library, Concord Library, 2900 Salvio St, Concord, CA, 94519. Tel: 925-646-5455. p. 174

Buckley, Lynell S, Mrs, Head, Ref, Louisiana Tech University, Everett St at The Columns, Ruston, LA, 71272. Tel: 318-257-3555. p. 906

Buckley, Mary Alice, Scholarly Communications Librn, Argonne National Laboratory, 9700 S Cass Ave, Bldg 240, Lemont, IL, 60439-4801. Tel: 630-252-0007. p. 608

Buckley, Matt, Head, Res & Instrul Serv, Saginaw Valley State University, 7400 Bay Rd, University Center, MI, 48710. Tel: 989-964-2844. p. 1155

Buckley, Rebecca, Dir, Rolla Free Public Library, 900 Pine St, Rolla, MO, 65401. Tel: 573-364-2604. p. 1267

Buckman, Kathie, Academic Specialist, Emporia State University, One Kellogg Circle, Campus Box 4025, Emporia, KS, 66801-4025. Tel: 620-757-9088. p. 2785

Buckman, Katrina, Br Mgr, Whatcom County Library System, North Fork Community Library, 7506 Kendall Rd, Maple Falls, WA, 98266. Tel: 360-599-2020. p. 2359

Buckman, Meghan, Library Contact, LAF Library, 120 S La Salle St, Ste 900, Chicago, IL, 60603. Tel: 312-341-1070. p. 563

Buckman, Ronnie, Youth Serv Librn, William D Weeks Memorial Library, 128 Main St, Lancaster, NH, 03584-3031. Tel: 603-788-3352. p. 1370

Buckmaster, Christine, Br Mgr, San Diego County Library, Descanso Branch, 9545 River Dr, Descanso, CA, 91916. Tel: 619-445-5279. p. 217

Buckmelter, Jason, Syst Adminr, Stetson University College of Law Library, 1401 61st St S, Gulfport, FL, 33707. Tel: 727-562-7820. p. 408

Bucknall, Tim M, Asst Dean, Colls & Info Tech, University of North Carolina at Greensboro, 320 College Ave, Greensboro, NC, 27412-0001. Tel: 336-256-1216. p. 1693

Buckner, Melinda, Librn, Mississippi Department of Corrections, PO Box 1057, Parchman, MS, 38738. Tel: 662-745-6611, Ext 3101. p. 1228

Buckson, Kate, Dir, St Charles Public Library District, One S Sixth Ave, Saint Charles, IL, 60174-2105. Tel: 630-584-0076, Ext 273. p. 644

Buckstead, Jonathan, Fac Librn, Austin Community College, Cypress Creek Campus Library, 1555 Cypress Creek Rd, 1st Flr, Rm 2121, Cedar Park, TX, 78613. Tel: 512-223-2132. p. 2137

Buckton, Rowan, Adult Serv Mgr, Asst Dir, San Juan Island Library, 1010 Guard St, Friday Harbor, WA, 98250-9612. Tel: 360-378-2798. p. 2364

Buckwalter, Heather, Acq, Ser, Creighton University, Klutznick Law Library - McGrath North Mullin & Kratz Legal Research Center, School of Law, 2500 California Plaza, Omaha, NE, 68178-0340. Tel: 402-280-5543. p. 1328

Bucky, Karen, Coll & Access Serv Librn, Ref Librn, Sterling & Francine Clark Art Institute Library, 225 South St, Williamstown, MA, 01267. Tel: 413-458-0532. p. 1069

Bucy, Mary L, Dir, Hudson Public Library, 401 Fifth St, Hudson, IA, 50643. Tel: 319-988-4217. p. 759

Budach, Jill, Librn, Hector Public Library, 126 S Main St, Hector, MN, 55342. Tel: 320-848-2841. p. 1178

Budd, Nancy, Br Librn, Wapiti Regional Library, Nipawin Public Library, 501 Second St E, Nipawin, SK, S0E 1E0, CANADA. Tel: 306-862-4867. p. 2746

Budde, Bill, Curator, Martha Canfield Memorial Free Library, 528 E Arlington Rd, Arlington, VT, 05250. Tel: 802-753-6229. p. 2277

Budde, Mitzi J, Head Librn, Prof, Virginia Theological Seminary, 3737 Seminary Rd, Alexandria, VA, 22304-5201. Tel: 703-461-1756. p. 2303

Budde, Sara, Libr Mgr, Live Oak Public Libraries, Midway-Riceboro Branch, 9397 E Oglethorpe Hwy, Midway, GA, 31320. Tel: 912-884-5742. p. 496

Budinger-Mulhearn, Rebecca, Dir, Avon Free Library, 143 Genesee St, Avon, NY, 14414. Tel: 585-226-8461. p. 1489

Budinger-Mulhearn, Rebecca, Mgr, Circ Serv, RIT Libraries, 90 Lomb Memorial Dr, Rochester, NY, 14623-5604. Tel: 585-475-7713. p. 1629

Budlong, Kristen, Librn, Bremen Library, 204 Waldoboro Rd, Bremen, ME, 04551. Tel: 207-529-5572. p. 918

Budnick, Haley, ILL, Syst Tech, Neumann University Library, One Neumann Dr, Aston, PA, 19014-1298. Tel: 610-361-5216. p. 1907

Budny, Andrew, Sr Libr Asst, Kent State University, 4314 Mahoning Ave NW, Warren, OH, 44483-1998. Tel: 330-675-8865, 330-847-0571. p. 1828

Budzynski, Abby, Adult Serv, Bloomingdale Public Library, 101 Fairfield Way, Bloomingdale, IL, 60108. Tel: 630-529-3120. p. 542

Buechler, Sam, Ms, Libr Dir, Student Success Librn, Washington State University Libraries, 14204 NE Salmon Creek Ave, Vancouver, WA, 98686. Tel: 360-546-9680. p. 2391

Bueckert, Debbie, Librn/Mgr, Fort Vermilion Community Library, 5103 River Rd, Fort Vermilion, AB, T0H 1N0, CANADA. Tel: 780-927-4279. p. 2540

Buehler, Kim, Asst Dir, Freeport District Library, 208 S State St, Freeport, MI, 49325-9759. Tel: 616-765-5181. p. 1108

Buehner, Cathy, Head, Adult Serv, Highland Township Public Library, 444 Beach Farm Circle, Highland, MI, 48357. Tel: 248-887-2218. p. 1115

Buehner, Katie, Head Librn, University of Iowa Libraries, Rita Benton Music Library, 2006 Main Library, Iowa City, IA, 52242. Tel: 319-335-3086. p. 761

Buehner, Kristen, Outreach & Prog Coordr, Mount Angel Public Library, 290 E Charles St, Mount Angel, OR, 97362. Tel: 503-845-6401. p. 1887

Buenafe, Brandy, Libr Serv Adminr, California Department of Corrections Library System, c/o The Office of Correctional Education, 1515 S St, Sacramento, CA, 95814-7243. Tel: 916-322-2803. p. 206

Buenaventura, Nenita, Adjunct Librn, Compton College Library, 1111 E Artesia Blvd, Compton, CA, 90221. Tel: 310-900-1600, Ext 2179. p. 132

Buendorf, Deni, Ch, Buckham Memorial Library, 11 Division St E, Faribault, MN, 55021-6000. Tel: 507-334-2089. p. 1175

Bueno, Cristina, Youth Programming Coord, Deerfield Public Library, 920 Waukegan Rd, Deerfield, IL, 60015. Tel: 847-945-3311. p. 577

Bueno, Yolanda, Dir, Alicia Salinas City of Alice Public Library, 401 E Third St, Alice, TX, 78332. Tel: 361-664-9506, 361-664-9507. p. 2132

Bueno-Granados, Catherine, Mgr, County of Los Angeles Public Library, Huntington Park Library, 6518 Miles Ave, Huntington Park, CA, 90255-4388. Tel: 323-583-1461. p. 136

Buerkle, Korie Jones, Libr Dir, Newberg Public Library, 503 E Hancock St, Newberg, OR, 97132. Tel: 503-554-7734. p. 1888

Bueti, Teresa, Head, Children's Servx, Chappaqua Public Library, 195 S Greeley Ave, Chappaqua, NY, 10514. Tel: 914-238-4779. p. 1516

Buettner, Debbie, Head of Br Serv, Head, Youth Serv, Lima Public Library, 650 W Market St, Lima, OH, 45801. Tel: 419-228-5113. p. 1795

Buff, Caroline, Res & Instruction Librn, Schenectady County Community College, 78 Washington Ave, Schenectady, NY, 12305. Tel: 518-381-1235. p. 1638

Buffaloe, Don, Research Librn, Pepperdine University Libraries, School of Law-Jerene Appleby Harnish Law Library, 24255 Pacific Coast Hwy, Malibu, CA, 90263. Tel: 310-506-4643. p. 171

Buffington, Sarah, Curator, Pennsylvania Historical & Museum Commission, Old Economy Village, 270 16th St, Ambridge, PA, 15003. Tel: 724-266-4500, Ext 111. p. 1906

Buffleben, Kathleen, Br Librn, Stockton-San Joaquin County Public Library, Mountain House Branch, 250 E Main St, Mountain House, CA, 95391. p. 250

Bufford, Mandrell, Head, Pub Serv, Baylor Health Sciences Library, 3302 Gaston Ave, Dallas, TX, 75246. Tel: 214-820-2377, 214-828-8151. p. 2163

Buford, Renee, Head, Circ, Pearl River County Library System, 900 Goodyear Blvd, Picayune, MS, 39466. Tel: 601-798-5081. p. 1229

Bugg, Alan, Br Mgr, San Diego Public Library, Valencia Park/Malcolm X, 5148 Market St, San Diego, CA, 92114. Tel: 619-527-3405. p. 221

Bugniazet, Judi, Dir, Shepard-Pruden Memorial Library, 106 W Water St, Edenton, NC, 27932. Tel: 252-482-4112. p. 1686

Bugniazet, Judi, Regional Dir, Pettigrew Regional Library, 201 E Third St, Plymouth, NC, 27962. Tel: 252-793-2875. p. 1708

Bugniazet, Judi, Dir, Washington County Library, 201 E Third St, Plymouth, NC, 27962. Tel: 252-793-2113. p. 1708

Bugorski, Jessica, Dir, Fanshawe College, 1001 Fanshawe College Blvd, London, ON, N5Y 5R6, CANADA. Tel: 519-452-4240. p. 2653

Buhalo, Michelle, Ref Librn, Jenkins Law Library, Ten Penn Ctr, 1801 Market St, Ste 900, Philadelphia, PA, 19103-6405. Tel: 215-574-7911. p. 1982

Buhl, Maria, Head, Ad Ref Serv, Head, Prog, Guilderland Public Library, 2228 Western Ave, Guilderland, NY, 12084. Tel: 518-456-2400, Ext 142. p. 1542

Buhn, Cindy, Digital Serv Librn, Info Serv Librn, Bracebridge Public Library, 94 Manitoba St, Bracebridge, ON, P1L 2B5, CANADA. Tel: 705-645-4171. p. 2632

Buhr, Genna, Libr Dir, Fondulac Public Library District, 400 Richland St, East Peoria, IL, 61611. Tel: 309-699-3917. p. 581

Buhr, Mary, Dir, Iroquois County Genealogical Society Library, Old Courthouse Museum, 103 W Cherry St, Watseka, IL, 60970-1524. Tel: 815-432-3730. p. 659

Bui, Kim, Dir, Phillipsburg City Library, 888 Fourth St, Phillipsburg, KS, 67661. Tel: 785-543-5325. p. 831

Buice, Dorothy, Ref Librn, Dallas International University Library, 7500 W Camp Wisdom Rd, Dallas, TX, 75236-5699. Tel: 972-708-7416. p. 2164

Buie, MacKenzie, Library Contact, Boise Art Museum Library, 670 Julia Davis Dr, Boise, ID, 83702. Tel: 208-345-8330, Ext 110. p. 516

Builta, Vicki, Dir, South Whitley Community Public Library, 201 E Front St, South Whitley, IN, 46787-1315. Tel: 260-723-5321. p. 719

Buisson, JoAnie, Head, Tech Serv, Libr Tech, Bibliotheque Municipale Marcel-Dugas, 16 rue Marechal, Saint Jacques, QC, J0K 2R0, CANADA. Tel: 450-839-3671, Ext 7682. p. 2734

Buiwit, Heather, Digital Serv Librn, Lunenburg Public Library, 1023 Massachusetts Ave, Lunenburg, MA, 01462. Tel: 978-582-4140. p. 1030

Bujalski, Eileen, Emerging Tech Librn, Albertus Magnus College, 700 Prospect St, New Haven, CT, 06511. Tel: 203-773-8594. p. 325

Buka, Andrea, Tech Serv Mgr, Preston Public Library, 389 Rt 2, Preston, CT, 06365. Tel: 860-886-1010. p. 334

Buker, Christi, Exec Dir, Pennsylvania Library Association, 220 Cumberland Pkwy, Ste 10, Mechanicsburg, PA, 17055. Tel: 717-766-7663. p. 2774

Buker, Kathleen M, Archives Chief, United States Army, Combined Arms Research Library, US Army Command & General Staff College, Eisenhower Hall, 250 Gibbon Ave, Fort Leavenworth, KS, 66027-2314. Tel: 913-758-3161. p. 808

Bukovac, Jamie, Dir, Indian Prairie Public Library District, 401 Plainfield Rd, Darien, IL, 60561-4207. Tel: 630-887-8760. p. 575

Bukrey, Sarah, Tech Serv, Stoughton Public Library, 304 S Fourth St, Stoughton, WI, 53589. Tel: 608-873-6281. p. 2479

Bukva, Rich, Br Mgr, La Porte County Public Library, Coolspring, 6925 W 400 N, Michigan City, IN, 46360. Tel: 219-879-3272. p. 700

Bulbrook, Jordan, Network Adminr, Perth County Information Network, c/o Stratford Public Library, 19 St Andrew St, Stratford, ON, N5A 1A2, CANADA. Tel: 519-271-0220. p. 2778

Bulemu, Bernard, Asst Dir, South Georgia Regional Library System, 2906 Julia Dr, Valdosta, GA, 31602. Tel: 229-333-0086. p. 501

Bulfor, Monica, Dir, LaMoille-Clarion Public Library District, 81 Main St, LaMoille, IL, 61330. Tel: 815-638-2356. p. 607

Bulgarelli, Nancy, Dir, Med Libr, Oakland University Library, 100 Library Dr, Rochester, MI, 48309-4479. Tel: 248-370-2481. p. 1144

Bulger, Jim, Mgr, Allina Health Library Services, Abbott Northwestern Hospital, 800 E 28th St, Mail Stop 11008, Minneapolis, MN, 55407. Tel: 612-863-4312. p. 1182

Bulic, Letitia, Librn, Saint Johns River State College, Saint Augustine Campus Library, 2990 College Dr, Saint Augustine, FL, 32084. Tel: 904-808-7474. p. 434

Bulick, Natalie, Metadata Librn, Indiana State University, 510 North 6 1/2 St, Terre Haute, IN, 47809. Tel: 812-237-3700. p. 720

Bull, Barry, Sr Librn, Savannah River Site, Bldg 773-A, A-1029, Aiken, SC, 29808. Tel: 803-725-0069. p. 2045

Bull, Cheryl, Br Mgr, Van Buren District Library, Bloomingdale Branch, 109 E Kalamazoo St, Bloomingdale, MI, 49026. Tel: 269-521-7601. p. 1096

Bull, Elizabeth, Libr Spec, University of Southern Maine Libraries, Lewiston-Auburn College Library, 51 Westminster St, Lewiston, ME, 04240. Tel: 207-753-6526. p. 938

Bull, Jonathan, Assoc Professor of Library Science, Dir of Coll, Valparaiso University, 1410 Chapel Dr, Valparaiso, IN, 46383-6493. Tel: 219-464-5771. p. 723

Bull, Lauren, Media Serv, Supvr, Upper Grand District School Board, 500 Victoria Rd N, Guelph, ON, N1E 6K2, CANADA. Tel: 519-822-4420, Ext 554. p. 2644

Bullard, Donna, Br Librn, Wilson County Public Library, Crocker-Stantonsburg Branch, 114 S Main St, Stantonsburg, NC, 27883. Tel: 252-238-3758. p. 1724

Bullard, Elizabeth, Br Mgr, Fort Bend County Libraries, First Colony, 2121 Austin Pkwy, Sugar Land, TX, 77479-1219. Tel: 281-238-2800. p. 2232

Bullard, Julia, Asst Prof, University of British Columbia, The Irving K Barber Learning Ctr, 1961 E Mall, Ste 470, Vancouver, BC, V6T 1Z1, CANADA. Tel: 604-822-2404. p. 2795

Bullard, Mary Kay, Dir, Rosebud County Library, Bicentennial Library of Colstrip, 419 Willow Ave, Colstrip, MT, 59323. Tel: 406-748-3040. p. 1293

Bullard, Sandy, Asst Librn, Rushville Public Library, 514 Maple Ave, Rushville, IL, 62681-1044. Tel: 217-322-3030. p. 644

Bullard, Zach, Br Mgr, Robeson County Public Library, McMillan Memorial Library, 205 E Second Ave, Red Springs, NC, 28377. Tel: 910-843-4205. p. 1702

Buller, Jessica, Librn, Glendive Public Library, Richey Public Library, 223 S Main St, Richey, MT, 59259. Tel: 406-773-5585. p. 1294

Bullington, Jeffrey, Libr Dir, Adams State University, 208 Edgemont Blvd, Alamosa, CO, 81101-2373. Tel: 719-587-7781. p. 263

Bullis, Lory, Dir, Ogden Public Library, 220 Willow St, Ogden, KS, 66517. Tel: 785-537-0351. p. 828

Bullock, Beverly, Dir, Meekins Library, Two Williams St, Williamsburg, MA, 01096. Tel: 413-268-7472. p. 1069

Bullock, Deborah, Br Mgr, Granville County Library System, Stovall Branch, 300 Main St, Stovall, NC, 27582. Tel: 919-693-5722. p. 1707

Bullock, Julie, Dir, Paige Memorial Library, 87 Petersham Rd, Hardwick, MA, 01037. Tel: 413-477-6704. p. 1023

Bullock, Kacey, Librn, Sierra College Library, 5100 Sierra College Blvd, Rocklin, CA, 95677. Tel: 916-660-7230. p. 203

Bullock, Karrie, Ref Librn, Merced College, 3600 M St, Merced, CA, 95348. Tel: 209-386-6703. p. 176

Bulman, Kim, Ch, Bellevue Public Library, 106 N Third St, Ste 1, Bellevue, IA, 52031. Tel: 563-872-4991. p. 734

Bulmer, Kathy, Libr Mgr, Boyle Public Library, 4800 Third St S, Boyle, AB, T0A 0M0, CANADA. Tel: 780-689-4161. p. 2524

Buls, Sara, Dir, Haakon County Public Library, 140 S Howard Ave, Philip, SD, 57567. Tel: 605-859-2442. p. 2080

Bultman, Anne, Adult Serv Supvr, Naperville Public Library, 200 W Jefferson Ave, Naperville, IL, 60540-5374. Tel: 630-961-4100, Ext 6106. p. 622

Bultman, Gail, Admin Dir, Debra S Fish Early Childhood Resource Library, Ten Yorkton Ct, Saint Paul, MN, 55117. Tel: 651-641-6674. p. 1199

Bumbarger, William, Conservator, Haverford College, 370 Lancaster Ave, Haverford, PA, 19041-1392. Tel: 610-896-1165. p. 1942

Bumbico, Jason, Exec Dir, Minerva Public Library, 677 Lynnwood Dr, Minerva, OH, 44657-1200. Tel: 330-868-4101. p. 1803

Bumgarner, Ada, ILL, Shelby County Libraries, 230 E North St, Sidney, OH, 45365-2785. Tel: 937-492-8354. p. 1820

Bumgarner, Ruth, Adult Serv, Pub Serv Spec, Winfield Public Library, 605 College St, Winfield, KS, 67156-3199. Tel: 620-221-4470. p. 845

Bumgarner, Steve, Libr Dir, Eagle Public Library, 100 N Stierman Way, Eagle, ID, 83616. Tel: 208-939-6814. p. 520

Bumpers, Gwen, Head, Tech Serv, Edwardsville Public Library, 112 S Kansas St, Edwardsville, IL, 62025. Tel: 618-692-7556. p. 581

Bumpus, Maria, Adult Serv, Holmes Public Library, 470 Plymouth St, Halifax, MA, 02338. Tel: 781-293-2271. p. 1023

Bumpus, Sandy, Asst Librn, Abington Public Library, 600 Gliniewicz Way, Abington, MA, 02351. Tel: 781-982-2139. p. 983

Bunas, Eric, Librn, Veterans Affairs Medical Library, 4101 Woolworth Ave, Omaha, NE, 68105. Tel: 402-995-3530. p. 1331

Bunce, Heather, Dir, Libr Serv, Great Lakes Christian College, 6211 W Willow Hwy, Lansing, MI, 48917. Tel: 517-321-0242, Ext 251. p. 1124

Bunch, Gena, Librn, Lapeer District Library, Otter Lake Branch, 6361 Detroit St, Otter Lake, MI, 48464-9104. Tel: 810-793-6300. p. 1126

Bunch, Ruby, Br Mgr, Heartland Regional Library System, Eldon Public Library, 308 E First St, Eldon, MO, 65026-1802. Tel: 573-392-6657. p. 1249

Bunck, Renee, Library Contact, Eastern Nebraska Genealogical Society Library, 1643 N Nye Ave, Fremont, NE, 68025. Tel: 402-721-4515. p. 1314

Bunde, Janet, Univ Archivist, New York University, Tamiment Library/Robert F Wagner Labor Archives, Special Collections Ctr, 70 Washington Sq S, 2nd Flr, New York, NY, 10012. Tel: 212-998-2642. p. 1599

Bundy, Allison M, Archives Assoc, Concordia College, 901 S Eighth St, Moorhead, MN, 56562. Tel: 218-299-3241. p. 1187

Bundy, Amanda, Dir, Kaibab Paiute Public Library, 250 N Pipe Springs Rd, Fredonia, AZ, 86022. Tel: 928-643-6004. p. 61

Bundy, Gene, Spec Coll Librn, Eastern New Mexico University - Portales, 1500 S Ave K, Portales, NM, 88130-7402. Tel: 575-562-2636. p. 1473

Bundy, Jennifer, Librn, Keen Mountain Correctional Center, 3402 Kennel Gap Rd, Oakwood, VA, 24631. Tel: 276-498-7411. p. 2336

Bunge, Rosalie, Acq, Normandale Community College Library, 9700 France Ave S, Bloomington, MN, 55431. Tel: 952-487-8296. p. 1166

Bunger, Ron, Dir of Libr, Richmont Graduate University, 1815 McCallie Ave, Chattanooga, TN, 37404-3026. Tel: 423-648-2410. p. 2092

Bunker, Andrea, Dir, Woburn Public Library, 36 Cummings Park, Woburn, MA, 01801. Tel: 781-933-0148. p. 1070

Bunker, Donna, Libr Dir, Chesley Memorial Library, Eight Mountain Ave, Northwood, NH, 03261. Tel: 603-942-5472. p. 1377

Bunker, Nancy, Univ Archivist, Whitworth University, 300 W Hawthorne Rd, Spokane, WA, 99251-0001. Tel: 509-777-4481. p. 2385

Bunker-Lohrenz, Jackie, Local Hist Librn, Franklin Lakes Public Library, 470 DeKorte Dr, Franklin Lakes, NJ, 07417. Tel: 201-891-2224. p. 1404

Bunn, Amy, Br Librn, Blue Ridge Regional Library, Ridgeway Branch, 900 Vista View Lane, Ridgeway, VA, 24148. Tel: 276-956-1828. p. 2332

Bunn, Gayla, Asst Dir, Hickman County Public Library, 120 W Swan St, Centerville, TN, 37033. Tel: 931-729-5130. p. 2091

Bunn, Katie, Circ Supvr, Canton Public Library, 40 Dyer Ave, Canton, CT, 06019. Tel: 860-693-5800. p. 305

Bunn, Rosemary, Libr Mgr, Flint River Regional Library System, J Joel Edwards Public Library, 7077 Hwy 19 S, Zebulon, GA, 30295. Tel: 770-567-2014. p. 481

Bunn, Silvia, Br Mgr, Chattahoochee Valley Libraries, Mildred L Terry Branch, 640 Veterans Pkwy, Columbus, GA, 31901. Tel: 706-243-2782. p. 472

Bunnelle, Jim, Acq & Coll Develop Librn, Lewis & Clark College, Aubrey R Watzek Library, 0615 SW Palatine Hill Rd, Portland, OR, 97219-7899. Tel: 503-768-7274. p. 1892

Buno, Craig, Br Mgr, Kent District Library, Walker Branch, 4293 Remembrance Rd NW, Walker, MI, 49534-7502. p. 1094

Buntin, Will, Asst Dir, University of Kentucky, 320 Little Library Bldg, Lexington, KY, 40506-0224. Tel: 859-257-8876. p. 2785

Bunting, Nancy, Libr Serv Coordr, Great River Regional Library, St Michael Public Library, 11800 Town Center Dr NE, Ste 100, Saint Michael, MN, 55376. Tel: 763-497-1998. p. 1197

Bunting, Susan, Br Mgr, Oldham County Public Library, Mahan Oldham County Public, 12505 Harmony Landing Lane, Goshen, KY, 40026. Tel: 502-228-1852. p. 861

Bunyan, Emily Cooper, Dir, Knox County Public Library, 502 N Seventh St, Vincennes, IN, 47591-2119. Tel: 812-886-4380. p. 723

Buono, Michael, Libr Dir, Deer Park Public Library, 44 Lake Ave, Deer Park, NY, 11729. Tel: 631-586-3000. p. 1524

Buote, Carol, Cat, Berkley Public Library, Two N Main St, Berkley, MA, 02779. Tel: 508-822-3329. p. 989

Bur, Grace, Head, Youth Serv, Milford Public Library, 330 Family Dr, Milford, MI, 48381-2000. Tel: 248-684-0845. p. 1132

Buran, Johanna, Br Mgr, Rochester Public Library, Maplewood, 1111 Dewey Ave, Rochester, NY, 14613. Tel: 585-428-8220. p. 1630

Buras, Steven, Libr Dir, Plymouth Public Library, 201 N Center St, Plymouth, IN, 46563. Tel: 574-936-2324. p. 714

Burbank, Danielle, Librn, San Juan College Library, 4601 College Blvd, Farmington, NM, 87402. Tel: 505-566-3100. p. 1468

Burbank, Karen, Asst Dir, Circ Mgr, Outreach Serv, Nesmith Library, Eight Fellows Rd, Windham, NH, 03087-1909. Tel: 603-432-7154. p. 1384

Burbank, Rebecca, Chief Librn, Powell River Public Library, 100-6975 Alberni St, Powell River, BC, V8A 2B8, CANADA. Tel: 604-485-4796. p. 2574

Burbante, Brandy, Cat Librn, Nicholls State University, 906 E First St, Thibodaux, LA, 70310. Tel: 985-448-4646. p. 911

Burbante, Brandy, Dir, Nicholls State University, 906 E First St, Thibodaux, LA, 70310. Tel: 985-448-4646. p. 911

Burbine, David, Library Contact, The Massachusetts Archaeological Society Research Library, 17 Jackson St, Middleborough, MA, 02346-2413. Tel: 508-947-9005. p. 1035

Burbridge, Lisa, Dir, Poteet Public Library, 126 S Fifth St, Poteet, TX, 78065. Tel: 830-742-8917. p. 2229

Burch, Alisa, Libr Dir, Harrison County Public Library, 105 N Capitol Ave, Corydon, IN, 47112. Tel: 812-738-4110, Ext 227. p. 677

Burch, Brian, Br Mgr, Akron-Summit County Public Library, Ellet Branch, 2470 E Market St, Akron, OH, 44312. Tel: 330-784-2019. p. 1744

Burch, Brian, Interim Br Mgr, Akron-Summit County Public Library, Kenmore Branch, 969 Kenmore Blvd, Akron, OH, 44314-2302. Tel: 330-745-6126. p. 1744

Burch, Katrina, Univ Archivist, University of Illinois at Springfield, One University Plaza, MS BRK-140, Springfield, IL, 62703-5407. Tel: 217-206-6520. p. 651

Burch, Leah, Commun Librn, User Experience Librn, Camas Public Library, 625 NE Fourth Ave, Camas, WA, 98607. Tel: 360-834-4692. p. 2360

Burch, Natalie, Ch, Seymour Library, 161 East Ave, Brockport, NY, 14420. Tel: 585-637-1050. p. 1497

Burch, Noelle, Commun Libr Mgr, Contra Costa County Library, Martinez Library, 740 Court St, Martinez, CA, 94553. Tel: 925-646-9900. p. 174

Burch, Paul, Br Mgr, Public Library of Cincinnati & Hamilton County, Mount Washington, 2049 Beechmont Ave, Cincinnati, OH, 45230. Tel: 513-369-6033. p. 1763

Burchard, Grace, Adult Serv, Willimantic Public Library, 905 Main St, Willimantic, CT, 06226. Tel: 860-465-3079. p. 347

Burchard, Shannon S, Head, Coll Serv, University of San Francisco, Zief Law Library, 2101 Fulton St, San Francisco, CA, 94117-1004. Tel: 415-422-6679. p. 230

Burchell, Cynthia, Ch Serv, Wells County Public Library, 200 W Washington St, Bluffton, IN, 46714-1999. Tel: 260-824-1612. p. 671

Burchett, Sue, Dir, Cantril Public Library, 104 W Third St, Cantril, IA, 52542. Tel: 319-397-2366. p. 736

Burchfield, Amy, Access & Fac Serv Librn, Cleveland State University, Cleveland-Marshall Law Library, Cleveland-Marshall College of Law, 1801 Euclid Ave, Cleveland, OH, 44115-2223. Tel: 216-687-6885. p. 1769

Burchfield, Jessie, Ms, Assoc Dean Information & Tech Services, Dir, Law Libr, University of Arkansas at Little Rock, William H Bowen School of Law / Pulaski County Law Library, 1201 McMath Ave, Little Rock, AR, 72202. Tel: 501-916-5407. p. 102

Burchfield, Lee, Mr, Dir, Louisville Free Public Library, 301 York St, Louisville, KY, 40203-2205. Tel: 502-574-1611. p. 865

Burchfield, Scarlett, Dir, Texas Health Harris Methodist Fort Worth Hospital, 1301 Pennsylvania Ave, Fort Worth, TX, 76104. Tel: 817-250-2916. p. 2181

Burchill, Maria, Head, Adult Serv, Schlow Centre Region Library, 211 S Allen St, State College, PA, 16801-4806. Tel: 814-237-6236. p. 2010

Burchstead, Christine, Cat Librn, Ref Librn, Walpole Town Library, Bridge Memorial Library, 48 Main St, Walpole, NH, 03608. Tel: 603-756-9806. p. 1383

Burchsted, Fred, Research Librn, Harvard Library, History of Science Library - Cabot Science Library, Science Ctr, Rm 371, One Oxford St, Cambridge, MA, 02138. Tel: 617-495-5355. p. 1007

Burden, Shirley, Librn, Cullman County Public Library System, Hanceville Public, 200 Commercial St SE, Hanceville, AL, 35077. Tel: 256-352-0685. p. 13

Burdett, Danny, Head, Circ, Glencoe Public Library, 320 Park Ave, Glencoe, IL, 60022. Tel: 847-835-5056. p. 593

Burdick, Faith, Ref Librn, Galesburg Public Library, 40 E Simmons St, Galesburg, IL, 61401-4591. Tel: 309-343-6118. p. 591

Burdick, Kelly, Chief Librn, Watertown Daily Times Library, 260 Washington St, Watertown, NY, 13601. Tel: 315-782-1000, Ext 2445. p. 1660

Burdick, Patricia, Head, Spec Coll, Colby College Libraries, 5100 Mayflower Hill, Waterville, ME, 04901. Tel: 207-859-5151. p. 945

Burdiss, Angela, Head, Tech Serv & Syst, Marietta College, 215 Fifth St, Marietta, OH, 45750. Tel: 740-376-4537. p. 1798

Burean, Kim, Head, Youth Serv, Oxford Public Library, 530 Pontiac St, Oxford, MI, 48371-4844. Tel: 248-628-3034. p. 1140

Bureau-Seixo, François, Chef de Section, Bibliotheques de Montreal, Marie-Uguay, 6052 rue Monk, Montreal, QC, H4E 3H6, CANADA. Tel: 514-872-2313. p. 2719

Bureau-Seixo, François, Chef de Section, Bibliotheques de Montreal, Saint-Henri, 4707 rue Notre-Dame Ouest, Montreal, QC, H4C 1S9, CANADA. Tel: 514-872-2313. p. 2720

Burel, Greg, Br Supvr, Boonslick Regional Library, Cole Camp Branch, 701 W Main St, Cole Camp, MO, 65325. Tel: 660-668-3887. p. 1279

Buretta, Kathleen R, Youth Serv Librn, Hazen Memorial Library, Three Keady Way, Shirley, MA, 01464. Tel: 978-425-2620. p. 1053

Burgamy, Pamela, Br Mgr, Chattahoochee Valley Libraries, Cusseta-Chattahoochee Public Library, 262 Broad St, Cusseta, GA, 31805. Tel: 706-989-3700. p. 472

Burgamy, Robin, Librn, McKay Library, 105 S Webster St, Augusta, MI, 49012-9601. Tel: 269-731-4000. p. 1082

Burgard, Daniel, Dir, South Central Academic Medical Libraries Consortium, c/o Lewis Library-UNTHSC, 3500 Camp Bowie Blvd, Fort Worth, TX, 76107. Tel: 817-735-2380. p. 2775

Burgard, Daniel E, Univ Librn, University of North Texas Health Science Center at Fort Worth, 955 Montgomery St, Fort Worth, TX, 76107. Tel: 817-735-2070. p. 2181

Burge, Brandon, Dir, Blairstown Public Library, 305 Locust St NW, Ste 2, Blairstown, IA, 52209. Tel: 319-454-6497. p. 735

Burge, Kelly, Br Mgr, Webster Parish Library System, Doyline Branch, 333 Main St, Doyline, LA, 71023. Tel: 318-745-3800. p. 898

Burge, Peggy, Assoc Dir, Pub Serv, University of Puget Sound, 1604 N Warner St, Upper Loading Dock, Tacoma, WA, 98416. Tel: 253-879-3512. p. 2387

Burgener, Marsha, Dir, Atwood-Hammond Public Library, 123 N Main St, Atwood, IL, 61913. Tel: 217-578-2727. p. 538

Burger, Amy, Ref & Instruction Librn, Dalton State College, 650 College Dr, Dalton, GA, 30720-3778. Tel: 706-272-4585. p. 474

Burger, Evelyn, Ref Serv, Midlands Technical College Library, 1260 Lexington Dr, West Columbia, SC, 29170-2176. Tel: 803-822-3537. p. 2072

Burger, John, Exec Dir, Association of Southeastern Research Libraries, c/o Robert W Woodruff Library, 540 Asbury Circle, Ste 316, Atlanta, GA, 30322-1006. Tel: 404-727-0137. p. 2763

Burger, Linda, Libr Tech, Harlan Community Library, 718 Court St, Harlan, IA, 51537. Tel: 712-755-5934. p. 757

Burger, Shari, Dir, Lenox Public Library, 101 N Main St, Lenox, IA, 50851. Tel: 641-333-4411. p. 765

Burgert, Lisa, Coll Develop, Librn, San Diego Mesa College Library, 7250 Mesa College Dr, San Diego, CA, 92111-4998. Tel: 619-388-2695. p. 218

Burgess, Alicia, Ch, Washington County Library System, 88 West 100 S, Saint George, UT, 84770. Tel: 435-634-5737. p. 2270
Burgess, Edwin B, Dir, United States Army, Combined Arms Research Library, US Army Command & General Staff College, Eisenhower Hall, 250 Gibbon Ave, Fort Leavenworth, KS, 66027-2314. Tel: 913-758-3001. p. 808
Burgess, Elizabeth, Director, Collections & Research, Harriet Beecher Stowe Center Research Collections, 77 Forest St, Hartford, CT, 06105-3296. Tel: 860-522-9258, Ext 313. p. 318
Burgess, Jim, Mus Spec, Manassas National Battlefield Park Library, 6511 Sudley Rd, Manassas, VA, 20109-2005. Tel: 703-361-1339. p. 2331
Burgess, John, Dr, Asst Prof, University of Alabama, 7035 Gorgas Library, Campus Box 870252, Tuscaloosa, AL, 35487-0252. Tel: 205-348-4610. p. 2781
Burgess, Kristen, Asst Dir, Research & Informatics, University of Cincinnati Libraries, Donald C Harrison Health Sciences Library, 231 Albert Sabin Way, Cincinnati, OH, 45267. Tel: 513-558-3071. p. 1765
Burgess, Lynn, Dir, Boaz Public Library, 404 Thomas Ave, Boaz, AL, 35957. Tel: 256-593-3000, 256-593-8056. p. 10
Burgess, Markesha, Librn, Holley A G State Hospital, Benjamin L Brock Medical Library, 1199 W Lantana Rd, Lantana, FL, 33462. Tel: 561-582-5666. p. 417
Burgess, Mary, Dir, Learning Serv, Camosun College, Landsdowne Campus, 3100 Foul Bay Rd, Victoria, BC, V8P 5J2, CANADA. Tel: 250-370-3604. p. 2582
Burgess, Michele, Library Contact, Vermont Veterans Home Library, 325 North St, Bennington, VT, 05201. Tel: 802-447-6520. p. 2279
Burgess, Phillip, Tech Serv Librn, Gadsden State Community College, Allen Hall, Rms 204 & 220, 1001 George Wallace Dr, Gadsden, AL, 35903. Tel: 256-549-8333. p. 18
Burgess, Robert, Digital Res Librn, Southwestern Baptist Theological Seminary Libraries, 2001 W Seminary Dr, Fort Worth, TX, 76115-2157. Tel: 817-923-1921, Ext 4000. p. 2180
Burgess, Sarena, Dir, Executive Office of the President Library, Eisenhower Executive Office Bldg, Washington, DC, 20503. Tel: 202-395-4690. p. 365
Burgess, Sherrill, Circ, Lawrence Library, 15 Main St, Pepperell, MA, 01463. Tel: 978-433-0330. p. 1046
Burgess, Sienna, User Serv Spec, Berea College, 100 Campus Dr, Berea, KY, 40404. Tel: 859-985-3364. p. 849
Burgett, Amanda, Asst Dir, ILL, Baldwin County Library Cooperative, Inc, PO Box 399, Robertsdale, AL, 36567-0399. Tel: 251-970-4010. p. 34
Burghardt, Linda, PhD, Library Contact, Holocaust Memorial & Tolerance Center of Nassau County, Welwyn Preserve, 100 Crescent Beach Rd, Glen Cove, NY, 11542. Tel: 516-571-8040, Ext 102, 516-571-8040, Ext 104. p. 1538
Burgin, Kaya, Br Mgr, Public Library of Cincinnati & Hamilton County, Avondale, 3566 Reading Rd, Cincinnati, OH, 45229. Tel: 513-369-4440. p. 1762
Burgin, Robin, Dir, Sequatchie County Public Library, 227 Cherry St, Dunlap, TN, 37327. Tel: 423-949-2357. p. 2097
Burgos, Francisco, Exec Dir, Pendle Hill Library, 338 Plush Mill Rd, Wallingford, PA, 19086. Tel: 610-566-4507. p. 2017
Burgos, Mary, Head, Tech Serv, Columbia University, Arthur W Diamond Law Library, 435 W 116th St, New York, NY, 10027. Tel: 212-854-3922. p. 1583
Burgos-Mira, Rosemary, Dir, Pub & Tech Serv, New York Institute of Technology, Northern Blvd, Old Westbury, NY, 11568. Tel: 516-686-3790. p. 1610
Burgoyne, Mary Beth, Librn, Chandler-Gilbert Community College Library, 2626 E Pecos Rd, Chandler, AZ, 85225-2499. Tel: 480-857-5100. p. 58
Burhanna, Kenneth, Dean, Kent State University Libraries, Risman Plaza, 1125 Risman Dr, Kent, OH, 44242. Tel: 330-672-2962. p. 1792
Burhop-Service, Kimberly, Dir, Library Human Resources, Duke University Libraries, 411 Chapel Dr, Durham, NC, 27708. Tel: 919-660-5937. p. 1684
Buri, Darin, Br Mgr, University of North Dakota, F D Holland Jr Geology Library, 81 Cornell St, Stop 8358, Grand Forks, ND, 58202-8358. Tel: 701-777-2408. p. 1735
Burington, Peg, Dir, Waupaca Area Public Library, 107 S Main St, Waupaca, WI, 54981-1521. Tel: 715-258-4414. p. 2485
Burk, Brandyn, Librn, Edgewood Community Library, 171 B State Rd 344, Edgewood, NM, 87015. Tel: 505-281-0138. p. 1467
Burk, Brenda, Assoc Librn, Head, Spec Coll, Clemson University Libraries, 116 Sigma Dr, Clemson, SC, 29631. Tel: 864-656-5176. p. 2052
Burk, Brenda, Head, Spec Coll, Clemson University Libraries, Special Collections & Archives, Strom Thurmond Inst Bldg, 230 Kappa St, Clemson, SC, 29634. Tel: 864-656-3214. p. 2052
Burk, Patrick, Teen Librn, Hancock County Public Library, 1210 Madison St, Hawesville, KY, 42348. Tel: 270-927-6760. p. 858
Burk, Sarah, Dir, Sheridan County Library, 801 Royal Ave, Hoxie, KS, 67740. Tel: 785-675-3102. p. 814
Burk, Teresa, Dir, ACA Library of Savannah College of Art & Design, 1600 Peachtree St NW, Atlanta, GA, 30309. Tel: 404-253-3196. p. 460
Burkard, Patti, Circ, Mahoning County Law Library, Courthouse 4th Flr, 120 Market St, Youngstown, OH, 44503-1752. Tel: 330-740-2295. p. 1835
Burkart, Stacy, Dir, Verona Public Library, 500 Silent St, Verona, WI, 53593. Tel: 608-845-7180. p. 2482
Burke, Adam, Librn, Waubonsee Community College, Collins Hall, 2nd Flr, State Rte 47 at Waubonsee Dr, Sugar Grove, IL, 60554. Tel: 630-466-2421. p. 652
Burke, Alison, Libr Asst, Yale University Library, Lillian Goldman Library Yale Law School, 127 Wall St, New Haven, CT, 06511. Tel: 203-432-1640. p. 328
Burke, Andrew, Access Serv Coordr, Harvard Library, Harvard-Yenching Library, Two Divinity Ave, Cambridge, MA, 02138. Tel: 617-495-2756. p. 1006
Burke, Annie, Dir, Wendell Public Library, 375 First Ave E, Wendell, ID, 83355. Tel: 208-536-6195. p. 532
Burke, Becky, Dir, Jesup Public Library, 721 Sixth St, Jesup, IA, 50648. Tel: 319-827-1533. p. 762
Burke, Brittany, Asst Librn, East Travis Gateway Library District, Garfield Library, 5121 Albert Brown Dr, Del Valle, TX, 78617. Tel: 512-247-7371. p. 2169
Burke, Carol, Mgr, County of Los Angeles Public Library, George Nye Jr Library, 6600 Del Amo Blvd, Lakewood, CA, 90713-2206. Tel: 562-421-8497. p. 137
Burke, Cathy, Br Mgr, Oakville Public Library, Clearview Neighbourhood, 2860 Kingsway Dr, Oakville, ON, L6J 6R3, CANADA. Tel: 905-338-4247, Ext 5906. p. 2662
Burke, Cathy, Br Mgr, Oakville Public Library, Iroquois Ridge, 1051 Glenashton Dr, Oakville, ON, L6H 6Z4, CANADA. Tel: 905-338-4247. p. 2662
Burke, Cathy, Br Mgr, Oakville Public Library, Sixteen Mile Branch, 3070 Neyagawa Blvd, Oakville, ON, L6M 4L6, CANADA. Tel: 905-338-4247, Ext 5906. p. 2662
Burke, Chris, Info Res & Serv Support Spec, Pennsylvania State University, Wilkes-Barre Commonwealth College, PO Box PSU, Lehman, PA, 18627-0217. Tel: 570-675-9212. p. 1955
Burke, Derva, Libr Dir, Meehan Memorial Lansing Public Library, 515 Main St, Lansing, IA, 52151. Tel: 563-538-4693. p. 764
Burke, Duke, Managing Librn, Yukon College Library, 500 College Dr, Whitehorse, YT, Y1A 5K4, CANADA. Tel: 867-456-8549. p. 2758
Burke, Gabe, Librn, California Department of Corrections Library System, Substance Abuse Treatment Faclity & State Prison, Corcoran, 900 Quebec Ave, Corcoran, CA, 93212. Tel: 559-992-7100. p. 207
Burke, Janet, Youth Serv Librn, Mashpee Public Library, 64 Steeple St, Mashpee, MA, 02649. Tel: 508-539-1435, Ext 3007. p. 1033
Burke, Jeanne, Sr Ref & Instruction Librn, Creighton University, Health Sciences Library-Learning Resource Center, 2770 Webster St, Omaha, NE, 68178-0210. Tel: 402-280-5143. p. 1328
Burke, John, Dir, Miami University Libraries, Gardner-Harvey Library, 4200 N University Blvd, Middletown, OH, 45042-3497. Tel: 513-727-3293. p. 1812
Burke, Joseph, Ref (Info Servs), United States Air Force, National Air & Space Intelligence Center Research Center, 4180 Watson Way, Wright-Patterson AFB, OH, 45433-5648. Tel: 937-257-3531. p. 1834
Burke, Joseph P, Dir, Altamont Free Library, 179 Main St, Altamont, NY, 12009. Tel: 518-861-7239. p. 1485
Burke, Joseph Paul Justice, III, Dr, Dir & Law Librn-in-Chief, Hon Max Rosenn Memorial Law Library, Wilkes-Barre Law & Library Association, 200 N River St, Rm 23, Wilkes-Barre, PA, 18711-1001. Tel: 570-822-6712. p. 2022
Burke, Lauri, Br Mgr, Avoyelles Parish Library, Moreauville Branch, Community Ctr, 343 Tassin St, Moreauville, LA, 71355. Tel: 318-985-2767. p. 897
Burke, Mary, Mgr, Spec Coll, Hardin-Simmons University, 2200 Hickory St, Abilene, TX, 79698. Tel: 325-670-1236. p. 2132
Burke, Raymonde, Libr Asst, Cornwall Library, 30 Pine St, Cornwall, CT, 06753. Tel: 860-672-6874. p. 306
Burke, Regina W, ILL Librn, Saint John the Baptist Parish Library, 2920 New Hwy 51, LaPlace, LA, 70068. Tel: 985-652-6857. p. 894
Burke, Renee, Dir, Elma Public Library, 710 Busti Ave, Elma, IA, 50628. Tel: 641-393-8100. p. 751
Burke, Sandra, Libr Tech, Outreach Serv Librn, Palmer Public Library, 1455 N Main St, Palmer, MA, 01069. Tel: 413-283-3330. p. 1045
Burke, Susan, PhD, Dr, Assoc Prof, Dir, University of Oklahoma, Bizzell Memorial Library, 401 W Brooks, Rm 120, Norman, OK, 73019-6032. Tel: 405-325-3921. p. 2791
Burke, Timothy, Exec Dir, Upper Hudson Library System, 28 Essex St, Albany, NY, 12206. Tel: 518-437-9880, Ext 222. p. 1484
Burke, Trudy J, Law Libr Dir/Law Librn, Madera County Law Library, County Government Ctr, 209 W Yosemite Ave, Madera, CA, 93637. Tel: 559-673-0378. p. 171
Burke-Urr, Fran, Coll Mgr, Fauquier County Public Library, 11 Winchester St, Warrenton, VA, 20186. Tel: 540-422-8500, Ext 1. p. 2351
Burkell, Jacquie, Prof, Western University, FIMS & Nursing Bldg, Rm 2020, London, ON, N6A 5B9, CANADA. Tel: 519- 661-2111, Ext 88506. p. 2796
Burkes, Tasha, Education Program Specialist, Department of Veterans Affairs, 2215 Fuller Rd, Ann Arbor, MI, 48105. Tel: 734-845-5408, p. 1078
Burkett, Harry, Br Mgr, Worcester County Library, Ocean Pines Branch, 11107 Cathell Rd, Berlin, MD, 21811. Tel: 410-208-4014. p. 978
Burkett, Jenny S, Libr Dir, United States Navy, Crew's Library, Naval Hospital, 200 Mercy Circle, Camp Pendleton, CA, 92055-5191. Tel: 760-719-3463, 760-719-4636. p. 126

Burkett, Jenny S, Libr Dir, United States Navy, Medical Library, Naval Hospital, Box 555191, Camp Pendleton, CA, 92055-5191. Tel: 760-725-1322. p. 126

Burkett, Kyle, Mgr, San Jose Public Library, Dr Roberto Cruz - Alum Rock, 3090 Alum Rock Ave, San Jose, CA, 95127. Tel: 408-808-3090. p. 231

Burkett, Kyle, Mgr, San Jose Public Library, Hillview, 1600 Hopkins Dr, San Jose, CA, 95122-1199. Tel: 408-808-3033. p. 231

Burkette, Karen, Br Mgr, Pender County Public Library, Hampstead Branch, 75 Library Dr, Hampstead, NC, 28443. Tel: 910-270-4603. p. 1676

Burkey, Ramona, Libr Dir, Russell Library, 123 Broad St, Middletown, CT, 06457. Tel: 860-347-2528. p. 322

Burkhalter, Laura, Assoc Curator, Des Moines Art Center Library, 4700 Grand Ave, Des Moines, IA, 50312. Tel: 515-277-4405. p. 745

Burkhalter, Walter, Dir, Fontana Public Library, 166 Second Ave, Fontana, WI, 53125. Tel: 262-275-5107. p. 2435

Burkhardt, Dallas, ILL Mgr, University of North Carolina at Greensboro, 320 College Ave, Greensboro, NC, 27412-0001. Tel: 336-334-5452. p. 1693

Burkhardt, Jeannette, Libr Serv Coordr, Great River Regional Library, Becker Library, 11500 Sherburne Ave, Becker, MN, 55308. Tel: 763-261-4454. p. 1196

Burkhardt, Jeannette, Libr Serv Coordr, Great River Regional Library, Big Lake Library, 790 Minnesota Ave, Ste 500, Big Lake, MN, 55309. Tel: 763-263-6445. p. 1196

Burkhardt, Joanna M, Coll Mgt, Officer, University of Rhode Island, 15 Lippitt Rd, Kingston, RI, 02881-2011. Tel: 401-874-4799. p. 2033

Burkhardt, Joanna M, Dir, University of Rhode Island, 80 Washington St, Providence, RI, 02903. Tel: 401-277-5130. p. 2041

Burkhardt, Sue Ann, Libr Mgr, Levy County Public Library System, Luther Callaway Public, 104 NE Third St, Chiefland, FL, 32626-0937. Tel: 352-493-2758. p. 387

Burkhart, Linda, Dir, Sanford Museum & Planetarium, 117 E Willow, Cherokee, IA, 51012. Tel: 712-225-3922. p. 739

Burkhart, Monica, Librn, Patton Public Library, 444 Magee Ave, Patton, PA, 16668-1210. Tel: 814-674-8231. p. 1973

Burkholder, Chris, Libr Mgr, Fairview Public Library, 10209 109th St, Fairview, AB, T0H 1L0, CANADA. Tel: 780-835-2613. p. 2539

Burkholder, Joel, Ref & Instruction Librn, Penn State University York, 1031 Edgecomb Ave, York, PA, 17403. Tel: 717-771-4024. p. 2026

Burkholder, Keely, Music Librn, Banff Centre, 107 Tunnel Mountain Dr, Banff, AB, T1L 1H5, CANADA. Tel: 403-762-6265. p. 2522

Burkholder, Kristen, PhD, Access Serv Librn, Oklahoma City University, 2501 N Blackwelder, Oklahoma City, OK, 73106. Tel: 405-208-5068. p. 1858

Burks, China, Pub Serv Librn, Lamar State College Orange Library, 410 Front St, Orange, TX, 77630-5796. Tel: 409-882-3081. p. 2224

Burks, Delena, Br Mgr, Hutchinson County Library, Fritch Branch, 205 N Cornell, Fritch, TX, 79036. Tel: 806-857-3752. p. 2149

Burks, Kris, Tech Serv Mgr, Carroll & Madison Library System, 106 Spring St, Berryville, AR, 72616. Tel: 870-423-5300. p. 91

Burks, Meredith, Librn, CHRISTUS Good Shepherd Health System, 700 E Marshall Ave, Longview, TX, 75601. Tel: 903-315-2165. p. 2213

Burks, Tina, Librn, Benton County Library System, Hickory Flat Public Library, 260 Oak St, Hickory Flat, MS, 38633. Tel: 662-333-1322. p. 1211

Burky, Abagail, Ref Librn, Ohio State University LIBRARIES, Agricultural Technical Institute Library, Halterman Hall, 1328 Dover Rd, Wooster, OH, 44691-4000. Tel: 330-287-1294. p. 1774

Burleson, Karlee, Pub Serv Librn, Lubbock Christian University Library, 5601 19th St, Lubbock, TX, 79407-2009. Tel: 806-720-7331. p. 2213

Burleson, Winslow, Asst Dir, Dir, Res, University of Arizona, Harvill Bldg, 4th Flr, 1103 E Second St, Tucson, AZ, 85721. Tel: 520-621-3565. p. 2782

Burley, Cheryl, Circ Mgr, Euclid Public Library, 631 E 222nd St, Euclid, OH, 44123-2091. Tel: 216-261-5300, Ext 501. p. 1785

Burlij, Paul, Exec Dir, Ukrainian Museum-Archives Inc, 1202 Kenilworth Ave, Cleveland, OH, 44113. Tel: 216-781-4329. p. 1770

Burlingame, Ann M, Dep Libr Dir, Wake County Public Library System, 4020 Carya Dr, Raleigh, NC, 27610-2900. Tel: 919-250-1200. p. 1710

Burlingame, Gregory, Coll, Develop Dir, Stark County District Library, 715 Market Ave N, Canton, OH, 44702. Tel: 330-458-2832. p. 1755

Burlingame, William, Pub Serv Spec, Allegheny College, 520 N Main St, Meadville, PA, 16335. Tel: 814-332-3359. p. 1959

Burlingham, Susan, Commun Librn, Cariboo Regional District Library, Forest Grove Branch, 4485 Eagle Creek Rd, Forest Grove, BC, V0K 1M0, CANADA. Tel: 250-397-2927. p. 2584

Burlison, Katie, Chief Curator, Hermann-Grima House Library, 820 Saint Louis St, New Orleans, LA, 70112. Tel: 504-274-0745. p. 901

Burmeister, Nora, Electronic Serv Librn, Online Learning Librn, Central Carolina Community College Libraries, 1105 Kelly Dr, Sanford, NC, 27330. Tel: 919-718-7435. p. 1715

Burmeister, Sarah, Dir, Grand Meadow Public Library, 125 Grand Ave E, Grand Meadow, MN, 55936. Tel: 507-754-5859. p. 1177

Burnash, Eileen, Dir, Wharton Public Library, 15 S Main St, Wharton, NJ, 07885. Tel: 973-361-1333. p. 1454

Burnell, Heather, Librn, North Central Washington Libraries, Oroville Public Library, 1276 Main St, Oroville, WA, 98844. Tel: 509-476-2662. p. 2394

Burnell Neilson, Jonathan, Dir, Libr Serv, Concordia University, 1282 Concordia Ave, Saint Paul, MN, 55104. Tel: 651-641-8237. p. 1199

Burnett, Alex, Sr Law Librn, Maine State Law & Legislative Reference Library, 43 State House Sta, Augusta, ME, 04333-0043. Tel: 207-287-1600. p. 914

Burnett, Anne E, Foreign & Intl Law Librn, University of Georgia, Alexander Campbell King Law Library, 225 Herty Dr, Athens, GA, 30602-6018. Tel: 702-542-5298. p. 459

Burnett, Elizabeth, Asst Dir, Br Mgr, Pineville-Bell County Public Library, 214 Walnut St, Pineville, KY, 40977. Tel: 606-337-3422. p. 873

Burnett, Heidi, Dir, Cultural Serv, Libr Dir, Ethel M Gordon Oakland Park Library, 1298 NE 37th St, Oakland Park, FL, 33334. Tel: 954-630-4370. p. 429

Burnett, Jenny, Dir, Seneca Falls Library, 47 Cayuga St, Seneca Falls, NY, 13148. Tel: 315-568-8265, Ext 3. p. 1640

Burnett, Jessica, Librn, NASA Headquarters Library, 300 E St SW, Rm 1W53, Washington, DC, 20546. Tel: 202-358-0168. p. 371

Burnett, Sheila, Dep Dir, Support Serv, San Diego Public Library, 330 Park Blvd, MS 17, San Diego, CA, 92101. Tel: 619-236-5800. p. 219

Burnett, Tracy, Libr Dir, Morrison & Mary Wiley Library District, 206 W Main St, Elmwood, IL, 61529. Tel: 309-742-2431. p. 585

Burnett, Vickie, Dir, Brenizer Public Library, 430 W Center Ave, Merna, NE, 68856. Tel: 308-643-2268. p. 1325

Burnette, Brandon, Govt Doc Librn, Southeastern Oklahoma State University, 425 W University, Durant, OK, 74701-0609. Tel: 580-745-2795. p. 1846

Burnette, Debbie, Ref (Info Servs), Ramsey Free Public Library, 30 Wyckoff Ave, Ramsey, NJ, 07446. Tel: 201-327-1445. p. 1438

Burnette, Jane, Librn, Carilion Roanoke Memorial Hospital, 1906 Belleview Ave, Roanoke, VA, 24014-1838. Tel: 540-981-8039. p. 2344

Burnette, Jessica, Libr Assoc I, Pub Serv, Texas A&M University-San Antonio, One University Way, San Antonio, TX, 78224. Tel: 210-784-1514. p. 2239

Burnette-Dean, Kimberly, Br Librn, Roanoke County Public Library, Vinton Branch, 300 S Pollard St, Vinton, VA, 24179. Tel: 540-857-5043. p. 2345

Burney, Doris, Head Librn, Waelder Public Library, 310 North Ave E, Waelder, TX, 78959. Tel: 830-788-7167. p. 2254

Burney, Jan, Libr Mgr, Sheep River Library, 129 Main St NW, Diamond Valley, AB, T0L 2A0, CANADA. Tel: 403-933-3278. p. 2533

Burnham, Amber, Youth Serv, Barry-Lawrence Regional Library, Monett Branch, 2200 Park St, Monett, MO, 65708. Tel: 417-235-7350. p. 1263

Burnham, Carol, Dir, Calhoun Memorial Library, 321 Moore St, Chetek, WI, 54728. Tel: 715-924-3195. p. 2427

Burnham, Kerry, Libr Dir, Salem City Library, 59 S Main St, Salem, UT, 84653. Tel: 801-423-2622. p. 2270

Burnham, Mary, Libr Dir, Tenney Memorial Library, 4886 Main St S, Newbury, VT, 05051. Tel: 802-866-5366. p. 2289

Burniston, Daniel, Libr Dir, Edith B Siegrist Vermillion Public Library, 18 Church St, Vermillion, SD, 57069-3093. Tel: 605-677-7060. p. 2084

Burnk, Patricia, Pres, Warren County Historical Society & Genealogy, 313 Mansfield St, Belvidere, NJ, 07823-1828. Tel: 908-475-4246. p. 1389

Burnley, Alesia, Dir, Lebanon-Wilson County Library, 108 S Hatton Ave, Lebanon, TN, 37087-3590. Tel: 615-444-0632. p. 2109

Burnley, Alesia, Dir, Lebanon-Wilson County Library, Mount Juliet-Wilson County Library, 2765 N Mount Juliet Rd, Mount Juliet, TN, 37122. Tel: 615-758-7051. p. 2109

Burno, LaTanya, Dir, Marple Public Library, 2599 Sproul Rd, Broomall, PA, 19008-2399. Tel: 610-356-1510. p. 1915

Burns, Alecia Danielle, Dir, Clay County Public Library, 116 Guffey St, Celina, TN, 38551-9802. Tel: 931-243-3442. p. 2090

Burns, Alei, Libr Mgr, Chattanooga Public Library, South Chattanooga, 925 W 39th St, Chattanooga, TN, 37410. Tel: 423-643-7780. p. 2091

Burns, Allison, Libr Mgr, FHI 360, 1825 Connecticut Ave NW, Washington, DC, 20009. Tel: 202-884-8000. p. 366

Burns, Amy, Med Librn, Cabarrus College Health Sciences Library, 920 Church St N, Concord, NC, 28025. Tel: 704-403-1798. p. 1682

Burns, Chris, Data & Criminology Liaison Librn, Kwantlen Polytechnic University Library, 12666 72nd Ave, Surrey, BC, V3W 2M8, CANADA. Tel: 604-599-3198. p. 2576

Burns, Christopher Sean, Dr, Asst Prof, University of Kentucky, 320 Little Library Bldg, Lexington, KY, 40506-0224. Tel: 859-257-8876. p. 2785

Burns, Cindy C, Branch & Customer Servs, Albuquerque-Bernalillo County Library System, 501 Copper Ave NW, Albuquerque, NM, 87102. p. 1459

Burns, Danielle, Dir, Oxford Public Library, 411 Ogden St, Oxford, NE, 68967. Tel: 308-824-3381. p. 1332

Burns, Diane, Librn, Bird City Public Library, 110 E Fourth St, Bird City, KS, 67731. Tel: 785-734-2203. p. 798

Burns, Dylan, Art Librn, Humanities Librn, University of Washington Libraries, Music, 113 Music Bldg, Box 353450, Seattle, WA, 98195-3450. Tel: 206-543-1159, 206-543-1168. p. 2382

Burton, Carla, Br Mgr, Atlanta-Fulton Public Library System, Ocee Branch, 5090 Abbotts Bridge Rd, Johns Creek, GA, 30005-4601. Tel: 404 613-6840, 770-360-8897. p. 461

Burton, Denise, Asst Dir, Conway County Library Headquarters, 101 W Church St, Morrilton, AR, 72110. Tel: 501-354-5204. p. 105

Burton, Jared, Librn, Mt San Antonio College Library, 1100 N Grand Ave, Walnut, CA, 91789. Tel: 909-274-4260. p. 258

Burton, Jason, Lead Librn, University of Mississippi, Science, 1031 Natural Products Ctr, University, MS, 38677. Tel: 662-915-7910. p. 1234

Burton, Jay, Dir, Southeast Regional Library System, 252 W 13th St, Wellston, OH, 45692. Tel: 740-384-2103. p. 2773

Burton, Jeannie, Dir, Benton County Library System, 247 Court St, Ashland, MS, 38603. Tel: 662-224-6400. p. 1211

Burton, Jenera, Br Coordr, Oakland Public Library, 125 14th St, Oakland, CA, 94612. Tel: 510-238-3670. p. 186

Burton, Karen, Librn, Weber County Library System, Ogden Valley Branch, 131 S 7400 East, Huntsville, UT, 84317-9309. Tel: 801-745-2220. p. 2268

Burton, Kimberly, Instruction & Ref Librn, Walden University Library, 100 Washington Ave S, Ste 900, Minneapolis, MN, 55401. p. 1186

Burton, Kristin, Br Librn, Wapiti Regional Library, Christopher Lake Public Library, District of Lakeland Bldg, Hwy 263, Christopher Lake, SK, S0J 0N0, CANADA. Tel: 306-982-4763. p. 2745

Burton, Laura, Mgr, West Georgia Regional Library, Ruth Holder Public Library, 337 Sage St, Temple, GA, 30179. Tel: 770-562-5145. p. 470

Burton, Marcia, IT Mgr, Maywood Public Library District, 121 S Fifth Ave, Maywood, IL, 60153-1307. Tel: 708-343-1847, Ext 13. p. 615

Burton, Megan, State Archivist, Kansas Historical Society, 6425 SW Sixth Ave, Topeka, KS, 66615-1099. Tel: 785-272-8681, Ext 272. p. 838

Burton, Sara, Asst Librn, Childress Public Library, 117 Ave B NE, Childress, TX, 79201-4509. Tel: 940-937-8421. p. 2155

Burton, Shonn, Adult Serv, Circ, Paterson Free Public Library, 250 Broadway, Paterson, NJ, 07501. Tel: 973-321-1223. p. 1433

Burton-Conte, Maria, Res & Instruction Librn, Felician University, 262 S Main St, Lodi, NJ, 07644. Tel: 201-559-6071. p. 1413

Burwash, Janice, Asst Dir, Burlington Public Library, 820 E Washington Ave, Burlington, WA, 98233. Tel: 360-755-0760. p. 2360

Burwell, Anna, Head, Adult Serv, Swanton Local School District Public Library, 305 Chestnut St, Swanton, OH, 43558. Tel: 419-826-2760. p. 1822

Burwell, Cathy, Asst Dir, Cape Fear Community College, 415 N Second St, Wilmington, NC, 28401-3905. Tel: 910-362-7456. p. 1722

Bury, Stephen J, Chief Librn, The Frick Collection, 945 Madison Ave at 75th St, New York, NY, 10021. Tel: 212-288-0641. p. 1586

Burychka, Heather, Ref Librn, Neumann University Library, One Neumann Dr, Aston, PA, 19014-1298. Tel: 610-361-5316. p. 1907

Burychka, Heather, Instrul Serv/Ref Librn, Gwynedd Mercy University, 1325 Sumneytown Pike, Gwynedd Valley, PA, 19437. Tel: 215-646-7300, Ext 21494. p. 1939

Busbea, Erin, Dir, Columbus-Lowndes Public Library, 314 Seventh St N, Columbus, MS, 39701. Tel: 662-329-5300. p. 1215

Busbee, Tracey, Asst Dir, Augusta-Richmond County Public Library, 823 Telfair St, Augusta, GA, 30901. Tel: 706-821-2600. p. 466

Busby, Terry, Ad, Carlsbad Public Library, 101 S Halagueno St, Carlsbad, NM, 88220. Tel: 575-885-6776. p. 1465

Busch, Barbara, Dir, United States Navy, SPAWAR Systems Center San Diego Technical Library, Code 84300, 53560 Hull St, San Diego, CA, 92152-5001. Tel: 619-553-4890. p. 222

Busch, Elizabeth, Asst to the Dir, Budget Coord, Loras College Library, 1450 Alta Vista St, Dubuque, IA, 52004-4327. Tel: 563-588-7009. p. 748

Busch, Heidi, Pub Serv Librn, University of Tennessee at Martin, Ten Wayne Fisher Dr, Martin, TN, 38238. Tel: 731-881-3078. p. 2111

Busch, Lavinia, Access Serv Librn, California Institute of the Arts, 24700 McBean Pkwy, Valencia, CA, 91355. Tel: 661-253-7885. p. 255

Buschman, Elaine, Supvr, Essex County Library, Cottam Branch, 122 Fox St, Cottam, ON, N0R 1B0, CANADA. Tel: 226-946-1529, Ext 212. p. 2641

Buschman, Elaine, Supvr, Essex County Library, Kingsville - Highline Branch, 40 Main St W, Kingsville, ON, N9Y 1H3, CANADA. Tel: 226-946-1529, Ext 270. p. 2641

Buschman, Elaine, Supvr, Essex County Library, Ruthven Branch, 1695 Elgin St, Ruthven, ON, N0P 2G0, CANADA. Tel: 226-946-1529, Ext 221. p. 2641

Buschman, John, Dean of Libr, Seton Hall University Libraries, 340 Kingsland St, Nutley, NJ, 07110. Tel: 973-761-9005. p. 1430

Buschman, John, Dean, Univ Libr, Seton Hall University Libraries, Walsh Library Bldg, 400 S Orange Ave, South Orange, NJ, 07079. Tel: 973-761-9005. p. 1443

Busekrus, Susie, Curator, Warren County Historical Society, 102 W Walton St, Warrenton, MO, 63383. Tel: 636-456-3820. p. 1285

Buser, Robin, Acq, Metadata Serv, Columbus State Community College Library, 550 E Spring St, Columbus, OH, 43215. Tel: 614-287-2469. p. 1773

Bush, Brice, Asst Dir, Head, Customer Experience, East Lansing Public Library, 950 Abbot Rd, East Lansing, MI, 48823-3105. Tel: 517-319-6939. p. 1101

Bush, Cheryl, Pub Relations Mgr, Warren-Trumbull County Public Library, 444 Mahoning Ave NW, Warren, OH, 44483. Tel: 330-399-8807. p. 1828

Bush, Dymond, Res & Instruction Librn, Bryant University, 1150 Douglas Pike, Smithfield, RI, 02917-1284. Tel: 401-232-6125. p. 2042

Bush, Emily, Instruction Librn, Nashville State Technical Community College, 120 White Bridge Rd, Nashville, TN, 37209-4515. Tel: 615-353-3559. p. 2120

Bush, Heather, Access Serv Librn, Eckerd College, 4200 54th Ave S, Saint Petersburg, FL, 33711. Tel: 727-864-8337. p. 441

Bush, Joe, Librn, North Central Correctional Facility, 313 Lanedale, Rockwell City, IA, 50579. Tel: 712-297-7521, Ext 229. p. 779

Bush, Keith, Dir, Oak Hills Christian College, 1600 Oak Hills Rd SW, Bemidji, MN, 56601-8832. Tel: 218-333-9961. p. 1165

Bush, Martha M, Libr Dir, Franklin-Springboro Public Library, 44 E Fourth St, Franklin, OH, 45005. Tel: 937-746-2665. p. 1786

Bush, Pamela, Br Librn, Fayette County Public Libraries, Mt Hope Public Library, 500 Main St, Mount Hope, WV, 25880. Tel: 304-877-3260. p. 2411

Bush, Renae, Dir, Attalla-Etowah County Public Library, 604 N Fourth St, Attalla, AL, 35954. Tel: 256-538-9266. p. 5

Bushey, Mary, Dir, Res, United States Army, Center for Army Analysis, Bldg 1839, 6001 Goethals Rd, Fort Belvoir, VA, 22060-5230. Tel: 703-806-5191. p. 2318

Bushin, Clifford, Librn, California Department of Corrections Library System, California Institution for Women, 16756 Chino-Corona Rd, Corona, CA, 92880. Tel: 909-597-1771, Ext 7303. p. 206

Bushkar, Mary, Br Mgr, Charleston County Public Library, Folly Beach Branch, 55 Center St, Folly Beach, SC, 29439. Tel: 843-588-2001. p. 2049

Bushman, Carrie, Libr Dir, Cook Memorial Library, 2006 Fourth St, La Grande, OR, 97850-2496. Tel: 541-962-1339. p. 1883

Bushman, Catherine, Asst Dir, West Haven Public Library, 300 Elm St, West Haven, CT, 06516-4692. Tel: 203-937-4233. p. 346

Bushnell, Kimberly, Librn, Middletown Springs Public Library, 39 West St, Middletown Springs, VT, 05757-4401. Tel: 802-235-2435. p. 2289

Bushnell, Tina, Br Mgr, Alachua County Library District, Library Partnership, 912 NE 16th Ave, Gainesville, FL, 32601. Tel: 352-334-0165. p. 406

Bushong, Sara A, Dean, Bowling Green State University Libraries, 1001 E Wooster St, Bowling Green, OH, 43403-0170. p. 1752

Busick, Andrea, Adult Serv, Adams Public Library System, 128 S Third St, Decatur, IN, 46733-1691. Tel: 260-724-2605. p. 678

Buskey, Amy, Br Mgr, Clermont County Public Library, New Richmond Branch, 103 River Valley Blvd, New Richmond, OH, 45157. Tel: 513-553-0570. p. 1803

Buss, Carla Wilson, Librn, University of Georgia Libraries, Curriculum Materials, 207 Aderhold Hall, 110 Carlton St, Athens, GA, 30602. Tel: 706-542-2957. p. 459

Buss, Crystal, Head, Access Serv, University of Wisconsin Oshkosh, 801 Elmwood Ave, Oshkosh, WI, 54901. Tel: 920-424-7315. p. 2467

Buss, Erica, Librn, Altadena Library District, Bob Lucas Memorial Library & Literacy Center, 2659 N Lincoln Ave, Altadena, CA, 91001-4963. Tel: 626-798-8338. p. 116

Buss, Rayla, Librn, Russell & District Regional Library, Binscarth Branch, 106 Russell St, Binscarth, MB, R0J 0G0, CANADA. Tel: 204-532-2447. p. 2589

Buss, Susan, Actg Chief Librn, New Westminster Public Library, 716 Sixth Ave, New Westminster, BC, V3M 2B3, CANADA. Tel: 604-527-4669. p. 2572

Bussart, Barbara, Head, Ref, Woonsocket Harris Public Library, 303 Clinton St, Woonsocket, RI, 02895. Tel: 401-769-9044. p. 2044

Bussell, Melba, Librn, Barton Public Library, Smackover Public, 700 N Broadway, Smackover, AR, 71762. Tel: 870-725-3741. p. 94

Bussey, Dawn A, Dir, Glen Ellyn Public Library, 400 Duane St, Glen Ellyn, IL, 60137-4508. Tel: 630-469-0879. p. 593

Bussey, Karen W, Law Libr Asst, Jefferson County Law Library, Jefferson County Court House, Ste 530, 716 Richard Arrington Jr Blvd N, Birmingham, AL, 35203. Tel: 205-325-5628. p. 8

Bussey, Tosha, Dir, Libr Serv, Atlanta Technical College, 1560 Metropolitan Pkwy SW, Atlanta, GA, 30310. Tel: 404-225-4596. p. 462

Bussinger, Deborah, Prog Coordr, Leesburg Public Library, 100 E Main St, Leesburg, FL, 34748. Tel: 352-728-9790. p. 418

Bussmann, Jeffra, Sr Asst Librn, California State University, East Bay Library, CSU East Bay Library, 25800 Carlos Bee Blvd, Hayward, CA, 94542-3052. Tel: 510-885-3780. p. 150

Busta, Heather, Acq, Northeast Iowa Community College, Calmar Campus Library, 1625 Hwy 150, Calmar, IA, 52132. Tel: 563-562-3263. p. 776

Bustamante, Stephen, Access Serv, ILL, University of Connecticut, Waterbury Regional Campus Library, 99 E Main St, Waterbury, CT, 06702. Tel: 203-236-9901. p. 340

Bustamante, Yolanda, Libr Dir, Sinton Public Library, 100 N Pirate Blvd, Sinton, TX, 78387. Tel: 361-364-4545. p. 2244

Bustillo, Monica, Libr Mgr, San Antonio Public Library, Johnston, 6307 Sun Valley, San Antonio, TX, 78237. Tel: 210-207-9240. p. 2239

Bustin, Lynne, Youth Librn, Bacon Memorial District Library, 45 Vinewood, Wyandotte, MI, 48192-5221. Tel: 734-246-8357. p. 1160

Bustos, Tom, Dir, Libr Tech, University of California, Merced Library, 5200 N Lake Rd, Merced, CA, 95343. Tel: 209-337-8710. p. 176

Butch, Barbara, Dir, Sleeper Public Library, 2236 E Main St, Ubly, MI, 48475-9726. Tel: 989-658-8901. p. 1155

Butchart, Lorraine, Tech Serv Coordr, Jackson District Library, 244 W Michigan Ave, Jackson, MI, 49201. Tel: 517-788-4087. p. 1120

Butcheck, Shannon, Head, Electronic Res, Cleveland Health Sciences Library, Allen Memorial Medical Library, 11000 Euclid Ave, Cleveland, OH, 44106-7130. Tel: 216-368-3644. p. 1766

Butcheck, Shannon, Financial Serv, Res Mgt Librn, Cleveland Health Sciences Library, Allen Memorial Medical Library, 11000 Euclid Ave, Cleveland, OH, 44106-7130. Tel: 216-368-3643. p. 1767

Butcher, Denise, Operations Mgr, Oregon City Public Library, 606 John Adams St, Oregon City, OR, 97045. Tel: 503-657-8269. p. 1890

Butcher, Lori, Circ Supvr, Bradford County Public Library, 456 W Pratt St, Starke, FL, 32091. Tel: 904-368-3911. p. 444

Butcher, Mikki, Dir, Interlibrary Loan & Course Reserve, James Madison University Libraries, 880 Madison Dr, MSC 1704, Harrisonburg, VA, 22807. Tel: 540-568-6807. p. 2324

Buteau, Shannon, Dir, Gorham Public Library, 35 Railroad St, Gorham, NH, 03581. Tel: 603-466-2525. p. 1365

Butera, Mary, Dir, South Londonderry Free Library, 15 Old School St, South Londonderry, VT, 05155. Tel: 802-824-3371. p. 2295

Buth, Karen, City Librn, Beverly Hills Public Library, 444 N Rexford Dr, Beverly Hills, CA, 90210-4877. Tel: 310-288-2220. p. 124

Buth, Karen, City Librn, Beverly Hills Public Library, Roxbury Book Nook, 471 S Roxbury Dr, Beverly Hills, CA, 90212. Tel: 310-285-6849. p. 124

Butikofer, Annette, Dir, Fayette Community Library, 104 W State St, Fayette, IA, 52142. Tel: 563-425-3344. p. 753

Butkovich, Nan, Head of Libr, Pennsylvania State University Libraries, Physical & Mathematical Sciences, 201 Davey Lab, University Park, PA, 16802-6301. Tel: 814-865-3716. p. 2016

Butler, A Hays, Head, Govt Doc & Micro, Ref & Instrul Serv Librn, Rutgers University Libraries, Camden Law Library, 217 N Fifth St, Camden, NJ, 08102-1203. Tel: 856-225-6496. p. 1394

Butler, Adior, Curator, Alan Wofsy Fine Arts Reference Library, 1109 Geary Blvd, San Francisco, CA, 94109. Tel: 415-292-6500. p. 230

Butler, Amy, Head, Acq & Electronic Res, University of North Alabama, One Harrison Plaza, Box 5028, Florence, AL, 35632-0001. Tel: 256-765-4266. p. 17

Butler, Ann, Dir, Libr & Archives, Bard College, Center for Curatorial Studies, PO Box 5000, Annandale-on-Hudson, NY, 12504-5000. Tel: 845-758-7566. p. 1487

Butler, Becky, Asst Archivist, University of Alaska Fairbanks, 1732 Tanana Dr, Fairbanks, AK, 99775. Tel: 907-474-6688. p. 45

Butler, Brian, Head Librn, Hazelton District Public Library, 4255 Government St, Hazelton, BC, V0J 1Y0, CANADA. Tel: 250-842-5961. p. 2567

Butler, Brooke, Youth Serv Librn, George F Johnson Memorial Library, 1001 Park St, Endicott, NY, 13760. Tel: 607-757-5350. p. 1531

Butler, Cathryn, Dir, Fairfax Public Law Library, 4110 Chain Bridge Rd, Rm 115, Fairfax, VA, 22030. Tel: 703-246-2170. p. 2316

Butler, Chris, Fiscal Officer, Stark County District Library, 715 Market Ave N, Canton, OH, 44702. Tel: 330-458-2690. p. 1755

Butler, Chris, Dir, In-Sight Library, 43 Jefferson Blvd, Warwick, RI, 02888-9961. Tel: 401-941-3322. p. 2043

Butler, Darilyn, Br Mgr, East Baton Rouge Parish Library, Delmont Gardens, 3351 Lorraine St, Baton Rouge, LA, 70805. Tel: 225-354-7080. p. 883

Butler, Darin, Mgr, Salt Lake County Library Services, Sandy Branch, 10100 S Petunia Way, 1450 E, Sandy, UT, 84092-4380. p. 2275

Butler, David, YA Mgr, Salem Public Library, 28 E Main St, Salem, VA, 24153. Tel: 540-375-3089. p. 2347

Butler, Donna, Br Mgr, Athens Regional Library System, Bogart Branch, 200 S Burson Ave, Bogart, GA, 30622. Tel: 770-725-9443. p. 458

Butler, Emily F, Ref Librn, Springfield Technical Community College Library, One Armory Sq, Bldg 27, Ste 1, Springfield, MA, 01105. Tel: 413-755-4532, 413-755-4845. p. 1057

Butler, Gary, Head, Patron Serv, Marion Public Library, 445 E Church St, Marion, OH, 43302-4290. Tel: 740-387-0992. p. 1799

Butler, Jason, Libr Dir, Joslin Memorial Library, 4391 Main St, Waitsfield, VT, 05673-6155. Tel: 802-496-4205. p. 2297

Butler, Jennifer, ILL, Walnut Public Library District, 101 Heaton St, Walnut, IL, 61376. Tel: 815-379-2159. p. 658

Butler, John, Assoc Univ Librn, Info Tech, University of Minnesota Libraries-Twin Cities, 499 Wilson Library, 309 19th Ave S, Minneapolis, MN, 55455. Tel: 612-624-3321. p. 1185

Butler, John, Head, Ref, Jersey City Free Public Library, 472 Jersey Ave, Jersey City, NJ, 07302-3499. Tel: 201-547-4526. p. 1409

Butler, Julia, Librn, Kinsley Public Library, 208 E Eighth St, Kinsley, KS, 67547-1422. Tel: 620-659-3341. p. 817

Butler, Kathy, Dir & Librn, Corning Public Library, 613 Pine St, Corning, AR, 72422. Tel: 870-857-3453. p. 93

Butler, Katie, Head, Circ Serv, Attleboro Public Library, 74 N Main St, Attleboro, MA, 02703. Tel: 508-222-0157. p. 986

Butler, Kelly, Head Librn, Tuscaloosa Public Library, Brown Library, 300 Bobby Miller Pkwy, Tuscaloosa, AL, 35405. Tel: 205-391-9989. p. 38

Butler, Kiki, Head, Adult Serv, Coventry Public Library, 1672 Flat River Rd, Coventry, RI, 02816. Tel: 401-822-9100. p. 2030

Butler, Kim, Libr Dir, Hamilton-Wenham Public Library, 14 Union St, South Hamilton, MA, 01982. Tel: 978-468-5577, Ext 21. p. 1055

Butler, Kimball, ILL, Pontiac Public Library, 211 E Madison St, Pontiac, IL, 61764. Tel: 815-844-7229. p. 636

Butler, Linda, Pres, Dahlgren Public Library, 401 S Third St, Dahlgren, IL, 62828. Tel: 618-736-2652. p. 575

Butler, Lisa, Dir, Spiceland Town-Township Public Library, 106 W Main St, Spiceland, IN, 47385. Tel: 765-987-7472. p. 719

Butler, Marcia, Tech Serv Mgr, Williamson County Public Library, 1314 Columbia Ave, Franklin, TN, 37064. Tel: 615-595-1241. p. 2098

Butler, Martha, Dir, Back Mountain Memorial Library, 96 Huntsville Rd, Dallas, PA, 18612. Tel: 570-675-1182. p. 1925

Butler, Mary, Br Mgr, Loudoun County Public Library, Ashburn Branch, 43316 Hay Rd, Ashburn, VA, 20147. Tel: 703-737-8100. p. 2328

Butler, Melanie, Librn, Bell Island Public Library, Provincial Bldg, 20 Bennett St, Bell Island, NL, A0A 4H0, CANADA. Tel: 709-488-2413. p. 2607

Butler, Michelle, Librn, Natrona County Library, Mark J Davis Jr Memorial - Edgerton Branch, 935 Cottonwood, Edgerton, WY, 82635. Tel: 307-437-6617. p. 2492

Butler, Scott, Librn, Peace River Bible Institute Library, 9601 100th St, Sexsmith, AB, T0H 3C0, CANADA. Tel: 780-568-3962. p. 2553

Butler, Stephanie, Librn, Bevill State Community College, Pickens County Educational Center, 491 Tuscaloosa Ave, Carrollton, AL, 35447. p. 17

Butler, Syreeta, Br Mgr, Nashville Public Library, Thompson Lane Branch, 380 Thompson Lane, Nashville, TN, 37211. Tel: 615-862-5873. p. 2120

Butler, Tabetha, Dir, Ashville Free Library, 2200 N Maple St, Ashville, NY, 14710. Tel: 716-763-9906. p. 1488

Butler, Tamara, Dir, Rumford Public Library, 56 Rumford Ave, Rumford, ME, 04276-1919. Tel: 207-364-3661. p. 939

Butler, Tamara, PhD, Exec Dir, College of Charleston, Avery Research Center for African American History & Culture, 125 Bull St, Charleston, SC, 29424. Tel: 843-953-7609. p. 2050

Butterfield, Elizabeth, Monographs & Acq Mgr, Willamette University, 900 State St, Salem, OR, 97301. Tel: 503-370-6267. p. 1897

Butterfield, Kevin, Univ Librn, University of Richmond, 261 Richmond Way, Richmond, VA, 23173. Tel: 804-289-8456. p. 2342

Butterfield, Kevin, Head, Tech Serv, College of William & Mary in Virginia, The Wolf Law Library, 613 S Henry St, Williamsburg, VA, 23187. Tel: 757-221-3255. p. 2353

Butterfield, Megan, Youth Serv Librn, Fletcher Free Library, 235 College St, Burlington, VT, 05401. Tel: 802-865-7216. p. 2281

Butterworth, Don, Dir, Coll Serv, Strategic Operations, Asbury Theological Seminary, 204 N Lexington Ave, Wilmore, KY, 40390-1199. Tel: 859-858-2100. p. 877

Button, Elizabeth M, Librn, McNeil & Foster Library, 121 Chanlon Rd, Ste G-20, New Providence, NJ, 07974. Tel: 908-219-0278. p. 1426

Button, Eric, Dep Dir, Saint Louis County Library, 1640 S Lindbergh Blvd, Saint Louis, MO, 63131-3598. Tel: 314-994-3300, Ext 3253. p. 1273

Button, Rachael, Ch, YA Librn, Decorah Public Library, 202 Winnebago St, Decorah, IA, 52101. Tel: 563-382-3717. p. 744

Buttram, Janet, Br Mgr, Botetourt County Libraries, Buchanan Branch, 19795 Main St, Buchanan, VA, 24066. Tel: 540-254-2538. p. 2344

Buttrey, Katie, Support Serv Mgr, Ashland Public Library, 224 Claremont Ave, Ashland, OH, 44805. Tel: 419-289-8188. p. 1746

Buttrey, Michael, Head, Access Serv, The College of Wooster Libraries, 1140 Beall Ave, Wooster, OH, 44691-2364. Tel: 330-263-2442. p. 1832

Butts, Kay, Asst Dir, Oneonta Public Library, 221 Second St S, Oneonta, AL, 35121. Tel: 205-274-7641. p. 31

Butts, Peter, Ch, Three Rivers Public Library, 88 N Main St, Three Rivers, MI, 49093-2137. Tel: 269-273-8666. p. 1154

Butz, Jesse, Dir, Porter County Public Library System, 103 Jefferson St, Valparaiso, IN, 46383-4820. Tel: 219-462-0524, Ext 126. p. 722

Butzel, Steve, Dir, Portsmouth Public Library, 175 Parrott Ave, Portsmouth, NH, 03801-4452. Tel: 603-427-1540. p. 1379

Buxton, Kristin, Head, Sci Libr, University of Oregon Libraries, Mathematics, 218 Fenton Hall, Eugene, OR, 97403. Tel: 541-346-2654. p. 1879

Buxton, Vicky, Dir, Forrest County General Hospital, 6051 Hwy 49 S, Hattiesburg, MS, 39402. Tel: 601-288-4214. p. 1218

Buydos, Jason, Dir, Louisville Public Library, 700 Lincoln Ave, Louisville, OH, 44641-1474. Tel: 330-875-1696. p. 1797

Buzan, Dan, Reserves, Butte College Library, Chico Center, 2320 Forest Ave, Rm 219, Chico, CA, 95928. Tel: 530-879-4366. p. 189

Buzard, Brian L, Librn, Winnebago County Law Library, 400 W State St, Rm 300, Rockford, IL, 61101. Tel: 815-319-4965. p. 642

Buzby, Juli, Librn, Sutton Public Library, 11301 N Chickaloon Way, Sutton, AK, 99674. Tel: 907-861-7640. p. 51

Buzza, Jane, Develop Officer, University of Victoria Libraries, McPherson Library, PO Box 1800, Victoria, BC, V8W 3H5, CANADA. Tel: 250-721-8211. p. 2583
Buzzard, Allison, Library Contact, Saint Elmo Public Library District, Beecher City Branch, 108 N James St, Beecher City, IL, 62414. Tel: 618-487-9400. p. 644
Buzzell, Heather, Chief Librn, Penticton Public Library, 785 Main St, Penticton, BC, V2A 5E3, CANADA. Tel: 250-770-7781. p. 2573
Buzzell, William, Library Associate Specialist, Brown University, Library Collections Annex, 10 Park Lane, Providence, RI, 02907-3124. Tel: 401-863-5722. p. 2037
Byars, David, Circ/Reserves, De Anza College, 21250 Stevens Creek Blvd, Cupertino, CA, 95014-5793. Tel: 408-864-8759. p. 133
Byce, Debbie, Br Librn, Whitewater Region Public Library, 2022 Foresters Fall Rd, Foresters Falls, ON, K0J 1V0, CANADA. Tel: 613-646-2543. p. 2642
Byerly, Jim, Electronic Res Librn, Minnesota Department of Transportation Library, 395 John Ireland Blvd, MS 155, Saint Paul, MN, 55155. Tel: 651-366-3739. p. 1200
Byerly, Tracy, Chief Programs Officer, Amigos Library Services, Inc, 4901 LBJ Freeway, Ste 150, Dallas, TX, 75244-6179. Tel: 972-340-2893. p. 2775
Byers, Dee, Chief Librn, Severn Township Public Library, 31 Coldwater Rd, Coldwater, ON, L0K 1E0, CANADA. Tel: 705-686-3601. p. 2637
Byers, Elisabeth, Dir, Prairie du Chien Memorial Library, 125 S Wacouta Ave, Prairie du Chien, WI, 53821-1632. Tel: 608-326-6211. p. 2471
Byers, Jessica, Reference & Curator Librarian, Ashland University Library, 509 College Ave, Ashland, OH, 44805. Tel: 419-289-5407. p. 1747
Byers, Luene, Asst Dir, Ch Serv, Cedar City Public Library in the Park, 303 N 100 East, Cedar City, UT, 84720. Tel: 435-586-6661. p. 2262
Byers, Ruth, Librn, Community College of Allegheny County, Allegheny Campus Library, 808 Ridge Ave, Pittsburgh, PA, 15212-6003. Tel: 412-237-2585. p. 1993
Byers, Sherree, Libr Spec, Allegheny College, 520 N Main St, Meadville, PA, 16335. Tel: 814-332-2968. p. 1959
Byke, Suzanne, Assoc Univ Librn, University of Texas at Arlington Library, 702 Planetarium Pl, Arlington, TX, 76019. Tel: 817-272-9405. p. 2136
Byland, Tom, Mgr, Appalachian State University, Music Library, 813 Rivers St, Boone, NC, 28608-2097. Tel: 828-262-2388. p. 1675
Bynoe, Vivian, Ms, Head, Ref & Instruction, Georgia Southern University, 11935 Abercorn St, Savannah, GA, 31419. Tel: 912-344-3028. p. 495
Bynog, David, Head, Acq, Rice University, 6100 Main, MS-44, Houston, TX, 77005. Tel: 713-348-4811. p. 2197
Bynum Wilmore, Kizzy, Dir, Madison Parish Library, 403 N Mulberry St, Tallulah, LA, 71282. Tel: 318-574-4308. p. 911
Byrd, Betsy, Ref Serv, Presbyterian College, 211 E Maple St, Clinton, SC, 29325. Tel: 864-833-8299. p. 2052
Byrd, Bonnie, Curator, Exec Dir, Waukesha County Historical Society & Museum, 101 W Main St, Waukesha, WI, 53186. Tel: 262-521-2859. p. 2484
Byrd, Caroline, Exec Dir, Saint Mary's University, Louis J Blume Library, One Camino Santa Maria, San Antonio, TX, 78228-8608. Tel: 210-436-3441. p. 2238
Byrd, Carrie, Ref & Instruction Librn, University of the Cumberlands, 821 Walnut St, Williamsburg, KY, 40769. Tel: 606-539-4160. p. 877
Byrd, Emily, Dir, United States Navy, 1481 D St, Bldg 3016, Norfolk, VA, 23521. Tel: 757-462-7691. p. 2336
Byrd, Jackie, Libr Office Mgr, Walnut Creek Historical Society, 2660 Ygnacio Valley Rd, Walnut Creek, CA, 94598. Tel: 925-935-7871. p. 258
Byrd, James C, Spec Projects Librn, Avery-Mitchell-Yancey Regional Library System, 289 Burnsville School Rd, Burnsville, NC, 28714. Tel: 828-682-4476. p. 1677
Byrd, Jason, Dir, Libr Serv, University of Arkansas Fort Smith, 5210 Grand Ave, Fort Smith, AR, 72904. Tel: 479-788-7200. p. 96
Byrd, Jeannie, Tech Serv Librn, Union University, 1050 Union University Dr, Jackson, TN, 38305-3697. Tel: 731-661-5339. p. 2102
Byrd, Kathleen, Br Mgr, Ouachita Parish Public Library, West Ouachita Branch, 188 Hwy 546, West Monroe, LA, 71291. Tel: 318-397-5414. p. 898
Byrd, Kathy, Br Mgr, Pine Forest Regional Library System - Headquarters, McLain Public, 106 S Church Ave, McLain, MS, 39456. Tel: 601-753-9207. p. 1232
Byrd, Lillie, Interim Libr Dir, Dolton Public Library District, 14037 Lincoln Ave, Dolton, IL, 60419-1091. Tel: 708-849-2385. p. 579
Byrd, Sharon H, Spec Coll Outreach Librn, Davidson College, 209 Ridge Rd, Davidson, NC, 28035-0001. Tel: 704-894-2331. p. 1683
Byrd, Stephen, Dir, Info Tech, Institute of Transportation Engineers, 1627 Eye St NW, Ste 600, Washington, DC, 20006. Tel: 202-785-0060, Ext 120. p. 369
Byrd, Tracie, Learning Res Ctr Coordr, Wayne County Community College District, Joseph F Young LRC Library, Eastern Campus, 5901 Conner St, Detroit, MI, 48213. Tel: 313-579-6904. p. 1100
Byrd, Wendy, Dir, Rains County Public Library, 150 Doris Briggs Pkwy, Emory, TX, 75440-3012. Tel: 903-473-5096. p. 2175
Byrge, Debra, Ch, Fentress County Public Library, 306 S Main St, Jamestown, TN, 38556-3845. Tel: 931-879-7512. p. 2103
Byrge, Kimberlee, Libr Dir, Norris Community Library, One Norris Sq, Norris, TN, 37828. Tel: 865-494-6800. p. 2123
Byrne, Andrea, Digital & Tech Serv, New York Academy of Medicine Library, 1216 Fifth Ave, New York, NY, 10029. Tel: 212-822-7274. p. 1593
Byrne, Anna, Asst Dir, Hingham Public Library, 66 Leavitt St, Hingham, MA, 02043. Tel: 781-741-1405, Ext 2604. p. 1024
Byrne, Christina A, Asst Head, University of Washington Libraries, Engineering Library, Engineering Library Bldg, Box 352170, Seattle, WA, 98195-2170. Tel: 206-685-8371. p. 2381
Byrne, Christopher, Instrul Serv Librn, Ref (Info Servs), Res, College of William & Mary in Virginia, The Wolf Law Library, 613 S Henry St, Williamsburg, VA, 23187. Tel: 757-221-3255. p. 2353
Byrne, Donna, Law Librn, Hancock Estabrook, LLP, 1800 AXA Tower One, 100 Madison St, Syracuse, NY, 13202. Tel: 315-565-4706. p. 1648
Byrne, Emily, Libr Asst, Chapman & Cutler, 320 S Canal St, 27th Flr, Chicago, IL, 60606. Tel: 312-845-3000, 312-845-3749. p. 555
Byrne, Erin, Librn, Oklahoma Library for the Blind & Physically Handicapped, 300 NE 18th St, Oklahoma City, OK, 73105. Tel: 405-521-3514. p. 1859
Byrne, Gabriella, Libr Asst, Historical & Genealogical Society of Indiana County, 621 Wayne Ave, Indiana, PA, 15701. Tel: 724-463-9600. p. 1945
Byrne, Marci, Family Dept Supvr, Rogers Memorial Library, 91 Coopers Farm Rd, Southampton, NY, 11968. Tel: 631-283-0774. p. 1643
Byrne, Michelle, Ch Serv, Williamson Public Library, 6380 Rte 21, Ste 1, Williamson, NY, 14589. Tel: 315-589-2048. p. 1665
Byrne, Patricia (Trish), Head, Ad Ref Serv, Mamaroneck Public Library, 136 Prospect Ave, Mamaroneck, NY, 10543. Tel: 914-698-1250. p. 1568
Byrne, Shane, Dir, University of Arizona Libraries, Space Imagery Center, 1629 E University Blvd, Tucson, AZ, 85721-0092. Tel: 520-621-0407. p. 84
Byrnes, Coreena, Ch Mgr, Teen Serv Mgr, Lancaster Public Library, 125 N Duke St, Lancaster, PA, 17602. Tel: 717-394-2651. p. 1951
Byrnes, Julia, Librn, Chinook Regional Library, Lafleche Branch, 157 Main St, Lafleche, SK, S0H 2K0, CANADA. Tel: 306-472-5466. p. 2752
Byrnes, Linda, Dir, Jordan Bramley Library, 15 Mechanic St, Jordan, NY, 13080. Tel: 315-689-3296. p. 1558
Byrnes, Mike, Dir, Yavapai College Library, 1100 E Sheldon St, Bldg 3, Prescott, AZ, 86301. Tel: 928-771-6124. p. 74
Byro, Amy, Dir, Hanska Community Library, 109 Broadway St, Hanska, MN, 56041. Tel: 507-439-7323. p. 1177
Byroade, Kate, Libr Dir, Cragin Memorial Library, Eight Linwood Ave, Colchester, CT, 06415. Tel: 860-537-5752. p. 306
Byron, Debby, Asst Dir, Bus Operations, Jefferson County Library, 5678 State Rd PP, High Ridge, MO, 63049-2216. Tel: 636-677-8689. p. 1248
Byrum, Amy, Asst Dir, Lebanon-Wilson County Library, Mount Juliet-Wilson County Library, 2765 N Mount Juliet Rd, Mount Juliet, TN, 37122. Tel: 615-758-7051. p. 2109
Byrum, Christin L, Dir, The Museums of Oglebay Institute Library, Oglebay Institute, The Burton Center, Wheeling, WV, 26003. Tel: 304-242-7272. p. 2417
Bystrom, Elaine, Dir, Kalama Public Library, 312 N First St, Kalama, WA, 98625. Tel: 360-673-4568. p. 2367
Bystrom, Sara, Br Mgr, Pacific Northwest College of Art, 511 NW Broadway, Portland, OR, 97209. Tel: 503-821-8966. p. 1893
Bzdel, Joanne, Br Librn, Wapiti Regional Library, Birch Hills Public Library, 126 McCallum Ave, Birch Hills, SK, S0J 0G0, CANADA. Tel: 306-749-3281. p. 2745
Caballero, Cesar, Dean & Univ Librn, California State University, San Bernardino, 5500 University Pkwy, San Bernardino, CA, 92407-2318. Tel: 909-537-5090. p. 212
Caballero, Erica, Dir, Sweetwater County-City Library, 206 Elm St, Sweetwater, TX, 79556. Tel: 325-235-4978. p. 2246
Caban-Padilla, Jeannette, Coll Develop, Librn, Inter-American University of Puerto Rico, 104 Parque Industrial Turpeaux, Rd 1, Mercedita, PR, 00715-1602. Tel: 787-284-1912, Ext 2125. p. 2512
Cabana, Mia, Head, Youth Serv, Jones Library, Inc, 43 Amity St, Amherst, MA, 01002-2285. Tel: 413-259-3219. p. 984
Cabanas-Malave, Eva, Supvry Librn, United States Army, Post Library, Bldg 518, 518 Depot Rd, Fort Buchanan, PR, 00965. Tel: 787-707-3208. p. 2510
Cabanero, Jennifer, Cat Librn, Shelton State Community College, Martin Campus, 9500 Old Greensboro Rd, Tuscaloosa, AL, 35405. Tel: 205-391-2971. p. 37
Cabaniss, Maria, Dir of the Univ Libr, Our Lady of the Lake University, 411 SW 24th St, San Antonio, TX, 78207-4689. p. 2237
Cabe, Kate, Asst Dean, Libr, Western Washington University, 516 High St, MS 9103, Bellingham, WA, 98225. Tel: 360-650-6740. p. 2358
Cabello, Juana, Head Librn, University of Puerto Rico Library System, Music Library, Rio Piedras Campus, Agustin Stahl Bldg, San Juan, PR, 00931. Tel: 787-764-0000, Ext 85930, 787-764-0000, Ext 85933. p. 2515
Cabo, Joanna, Asst Dir, Glen Cove Public Library, Four Glen Cove Ave, Glen Cove, NY, 11542-2885. Tel: 516-676-2130. p. 1538

Caissie, Tammy, Interim Dir, Levi Heywood Memorial Library, 55 W Lynde St, Gardner, MA, 01440. Tel: 978-632-5298. p. 1020
Caitlin, Pereira, Visual Res Librn, Massachusetts College of Art & Design, 621 Huntington Ave, Boston, MA, 02115-5882. Tel: 617-879-7150. p. 996
Calabrese, Nancy, Pub Serv Librn, Res Serv, Marist College, 3399 North Rd, Poughkeepsie, NY, 12601-1387. Tel: 845-575-3199. p. 1623
Calabrese, Stacie, Res Serv, VPres, American Association of Advertising Agencies, 1065 Avenue of the Americas, 16th Flr, New York, NY, 10018. Tel: 212-682-2500. p. 1578
Calametti, Jeffrey D, Dir, Libr Serv, University of Mobile, 5735 College Pkwy, Mobile, AL, 36613-2842. Tel: 251-442-2243. p. 26
Calandro, Daniel, Electronic Res Librn, Mercer County Community College Library, 1200 Old Trenton Rd, West Windsor, NJ, 08550. Tel: 609-570-3554, 609-570-3560. p. 1453
Calarco, Karen, Mgr, Libr Serv, Farella, Braun & Martel, One Bush St, Ste 900, San Francisco, CA, 94104. Tel: 415-954-4400. p. 224
Calarco, Pascal, Scholarly Communications Librn, University of Windsor, 401 Sunset Ave, Windsor, ON, N9B 3P4, CANADA. Tel: 519-253-3000, Ext 3402. p. 2704
Calaway, Barbara, Libr Dir, Pittsville Community Library, 5291 Third Ave, Pittsville, WI, 54466-0911. Tel: 715-884-6500. p. 2469
Calaycay, Ruth, Dir, Peru Library Inc, Six W Main Rd, Peru, MA, 01235-9254. Tel: 413-655-8650. p. 1046
Calbow, Marilyn, Librn, Putnam County Public Library District, McNabb Branch, 322 W Main St, McNabb, IL, 61335. Tel: 815-882-2378. p. 598
Caldara, Tara, Head, Adult Serv, Lake Villa District Library, 140 N Munn Rd, Lindenhurst, IL, 60046. Tel: 847-245-5106. p. 609
Caldarello, Beth Ann, Dr, Libr Dir, North Central Missouri College Library, Geyer Hall, 1st & 2nd Flr, 1301 Main St, Trenton, MO, 64683. Tel: 660-359-3948, Ext 1322, 660-359-3948, Ext 1325, 660-359-3948, Ext 1335. p. 1282
Caldeira, Leah, Dir, Bernice P Bishop Museum, 1525 Bernice St, Honolulu, HI, 96817. Tel: 808-848-4148. p. 505
Calder, Pat, Dir, Errol Public Library, 67 Main St, Errol, NH, 03579. Tel: 603-482-7720. p. 1363
Calderon, Barbara, Librn, School of Visual Arts Library, SVA Library West, 133/141 W 21st St, Lower Level, New York, NY, 10011. Tel: 212-592-2291. p. 1601
Calderon, Ivan I, Educ Coordr, El Paso Museum of Art, One Arts Festival Plaza, El Paso, TX, 79901. Tel: 915-212-3061. p. 2174
Calderon, Julieta, Info Serv Librn, Yuma County Free Library District, 2951 S 21st Dr, Yuma, AZ, 85364. Tel: 928-373-6498. p. 85
Calderon, Maggie, Youth Librn, Columbus Village Library, 112 W Broadway Ave, Columbus, NM, 88029. Tel: 575-531-2612. p. 1466
Calderon, Neshmayda, Readers' Advisory, State of Rhode Island, Talking Books Library, One Capitol Hill, Providence, RI, 02908-5803. Tel: 401-574-9313. p. 2041
Caldwell, Angela, Library Contact, Real Estate Board of New York, 570 Lexington Ave, 2nd Flr, New York, NY, 10022. Tel: 212-532-3100. p. 1600
Caldwell, Christine, Librn, University of California, 1156 High St, Santa Cruz, CA, 95064. Tel: 831-459-1287. p. 243
Caldwell, Heather, Technical Services & STEM Supvr, Ringwood Public Library, 30 Cannici Dr, Ringwood, NJ, 07456. Tel: 973-962-6256, Ext 121. p. 1439
Caldwell, Kathleen, Dir, Agency Public Library, 104 E Main St, Agency, IA, 52530. Tel: 641-937-6002. p. 729
Caldwell, Kristine, Youth Librn, Deborah Rawson Memorial Library, Eight River Rd, Jericho, VT, 05465. Tel: 802-899-4962. p. 2287
Caldwell, Patricia, Libr Dir, North Dakota State College of Science, 800 Sixth St N, Wahpeton, ND, 58076-0001. Tel: 701-671-2612. p. 1741
Caldwell, Rachel, Customer Experience Mgr, Operations Mgr, Conestoga College, 299 Doon Valley Dr, Kitchener, ON, N2G 4M4, CANADA. Tel: 519-748-5220, Ext 3361. p. 2651
Caldwell, Robbi, Info Serv Mgr, Brownsburg Public Library, 450 S Jefferson St, Brownsburg, IN, 46112-1310. Tel: 317-852-3167. p. 673
Caldwell, Robert, Librn, Newmarket Public Library, 438 Park Ave, Newmarket, ON, L3Y 1W1, CANADA. Tel: 905-953-5110. p. 2660
Caldwell, Waynette, Circ Librn, Colchester District Library, 203 Macomb St, Colchester, IL, 62326. Tel: 309-776-4861. p. 573
Cale, Eric M, Dir, Wichita-Sedgwick County Historical Museum Library, 204 S Main St, Wichita, KS, 67202. Tel: 316-265-9314. p. 844
Caleah, James, Performing Arts Librn, Reed College, 3203 SE Woodstock Blvd, Portland, OR, 97202-8199. Tel: 503-777-7702. p. 1894
Calease, Patricia, Asst Librn, Clarksville Public Library, 103 W Greene St, Clarksville, IA, 50619-0039. Tel: 319-278-1168. p. 740
Caleb, Peter, Dir, Manhattan School of Music, 130 Claremont Ave, New York, NY, 10027. Tel: 917-493-4511. p. 1590
Calev, Suzanne, Archivist, Pub Serv Librn, Wilkes University, 84 W South St, Wilkes-Barre, PA, 18766. Tel: 570-408-2012. p. 2023
Caley, Lynn, Bus Mgr, Lucy Robbins Welles Library, 95 Cedar St, Newington, CT, 06111. Tel: 860-665-8728. p. 330
Calfo, Pam, Dir, Plum Borough Community Library, 445 Center-New Texas Rd, Plum Borough, PA, 15239. Tel: 412-798-7323. p. 1998
Calhoun, Chip, Digital Archivist, American Institute of Physics, One Physics Ellipse, College Park, MD, 20740. Tel: 301-209-3177. p. 962
Calhoun, Christy, Archival Librn, William Carey University Libraries, 710 William Carey Pkwy, Hattiesburg, MS, 39401. Tel: 601-318-6169. p. 1219
Calhoun, Jennifer, Br Mgr, Ottawa Public Library/Bibliothèque publique d'Ottawa, Alta Vista, 2516 Alta Vista Dr, Ottawa, ON, K1V 7T1, CANADA. p. 2668
Calhoun, Jennifer, Br Mgr, Ottawa Public Library/Bibliothèque publique d'Ottawa, Elmvale Acres, Elmvale Acres Shopping Ctr, 1910 St Laurent Blvd, Ottawa, ON, K1G 1A4, CANADA. p. 2669
Calhoun, Jennifer, Br Mgr, Ottawa Public Library/Bibliothèque publique d'Ottawa, Greely Branch, 1448 Meadow Dr, Ottawa, ON, K4P 1B1, CANADA. p. 2669
Calhoun, Jennifer, Br Mgr, Ottawa Public Library/Bibliothèque publique d'Ottawa, Greenboro District Library, 363 Lorry Greenberg Dr, Ottawa, ON, K1T 3P8, CANADA. p. 2669
Calhoun, Jennifer, Br Mgr, Ottawa Public Library/Bibliothèque publique d'Ottawa, Metcalfe Branch, 2782 Eighth Line Rd, Ottawa, ON, K0A 2P0, CANADA. p. 2669
Calhoun, Jennifer, Br Mgr, Ottawa Public Library/Bibliothèque publique d'Ottawa, Osgoode Branch, 5630 Osgoode Main St, Ottawa, ON, K0A 2W0, CANADA. p. 2669
Calhoun, Jennifer, Br Mgr, Ottawa Public Library/Bibliothèque publique d'Ottawa, Vernon Branch, 8682 Bank St, Ottawa, ON, K0A 3J0, CANADA. p. 2669
Calhoun, Judy, Regional Dir, Southeast Arkansas Regional Library, 114 E Jackson St, Monticello, AR, 71655. Tel: 870-367-8584, Ext 222. p. 104
Calhoun, Marc, Cat/Ref Librn, Rhode Island School of Design Library, 15 Westminster St, Providence, RI, 02903. Tel: 401-709-5941. p. 2040
Calhoun, Margaret, Dir, Annie L Awbrey Public Library, 736 College St, Roanoke, AL, 36274-1616. Tel: 334-863-2632. p. 34
Calhoun, Margie, Asst Dir, Mobile Public Library, 701 Government St, Mobile, AL, 36602. Tel: 251-545-3552. p. 26
Calhoun, Monica, Patron Serv Supvr, Elizabethton-Carter County Public Library, 201 N Sycamore St, Elizabethton, TN, 37643. Tel: 423-547-6360. p. 2098
Calhoun, Patricia, Asst Dir, Learning Res, Sherman College of Chiropractic, 2020 Springfield Rd, Boiling Springs, SC, 29316-7251. Tel: 864-578-8770, Ext 253. p. 2048
Calhoun, Ryan, Head, YA, Bremen Public Library, 304 N Jackson St, Bremen, IN, 46506. Tel: 574-546-2849. p. 672
Calhoun, Shawn, Dean, Univ Libr, University of San Francisco, 2130 Fulton St, San Francisco, CA, 94117-1080. Tel: 415-422-2048. p. 229
Calhoun, Stephanie, Dir, Develop & Communications, Stonington Free Library, 20 High St, Stonington, CT, 06378. Tel: 860-535-0658. p. 339
Cali, Jeanine, Librn, Prince William County Law Library, Judicial Ctr, Rm 039, 9311 Lee Ave, Manassas, VA, 20110-5555. Tel: 703-792-6262. p. 2331
Calicchio, Kari, Asst Libr Dir, Dunedin Public Library, 223 Douglas Ave, Dunedin, FL, 34698. Tel: 727-298-3080, Ext 1703. p. 394
Calixte, Claudette, Ref, Miami-Dade County Law Library, County Courthouse, Rm 321A, 73 W Flagler St, Miami, FL, 33130. Tel: 305-349-7548. p. 422
Calkins, Keagan, Dir, Worthen Library, 28 Community Lane, South Hero, VT, 05486. Tel: 802-372-6209. p. 2294
Calkins-Mushrush, Genna, Co-Dir, West Custer County Library District, 209 Main St, Westcliffe, CO, 81252. Tel: 719-893-9138. p. 298
Call, Brenna, Dir, Vienna Public Library, 2300 River Rd, Vienna, WV, 26105. Tel: 304-295-7771. p. 2416
Call, Elizabeth, Univ Archivist, RIT Libraries, 90 Lomb Memorial Dr, Rochester, NY, 14623-5604. Tel: 585-475-2557. p. 1629
Call, Keith, Spec Coll Librn, Wheaton College, 510 Irving Ave, Wheaton, IL, 60187-4234. Tel: 630-752-5851. p. 662
Callaghan, Carolyn, Professional Technical Librn, Shoreline Community College, 16101 Greenwood Ave N, Shoreline, WA, 98133-5696. Tel: 206-533-2548. p. 2383
Callaghan, Chris, Head, Tech Serv, Milton Public Library, 476 Canton Ave, Milton, MA, 02186-3299. Tel: 617-698-5757. p. 1036
Callaghan, Patrick, Ref (Info Servs), Westchester Public Library, 10700 Canterbury St, Westchester, IL, 60154. Tel: 708-562-3573. p. 661
Callaghan, Richard, Dir, Bedford Free Public Library, Seven Mudge Way, Bedford, MA, 01730. Tel: 781-275-9440. p. 987
Callahan, Beth, Head, Res Support Serv, Interim Assoc Univ Librn, University of California, Davis, 100 NW Quad, Davis, CA, 95616. Tel: 530-752-8792. p. 134
Callahan, Daniel, Mgr, United States Navy, 601 Nimitz Ave, Bldg 3766, Kingsville, TX, 78363. Tel: 361-516-6449. p. 2207
Callahan, Dianne, Dir, Grand Junction Public Library, 530 Madison Ave W, Grand Junction, TN, 38039. Tel: 731-764-2716. p. 2100
Callahan, Gregory, Dir, Hyde Park Free Library, Two Main St, Hyde Park, NY, 12538. Tel: 845-229-7791. p. 1550
Callahan, Lauren, Human Res, Camden County Library System, 203 Laurel Rd, Voorhees, NJ, 08043. Tel: 856-772-1636, Ext 7347. p. 1450
Callahan, Leann, Dir, Saint Charles Parish Library, 160 W Campus Dr, Destrehan, LA, 70047. Tel: 985-764-2366. p. 888
Callahan, Regina, Coll Develop & Tech Serv Mgr, Wood Buffalo Regional Library, One CA Knight Way, Fort McMurray, AB, T9H 5C5, CANADA. Tel: 780-743-7800. p. 2540

Callais, Kati, Commun Outreach Coordr, Terrebonne Parish Library, 151 Library Dr, Houma, LA, 70360. Tel: 985-876-5861. p. 891

Callan, Doris, Dir, Pine Bush Area Library, 223-227 Maple Ave, Pine Bush, NY, 12566. Tel: 845-744-3375. p. 1618

Callanan, Ellen, Chief Librn, Sussex County Library System, 125 Morris Tpk, Newton, NJ, 07860. Tel: 973-948-3660. p. 1429

Callas, Jennie, Head, Ref & Instruction, University of Wisconsin-Parkside Library, 900 Wood Rd, Kenosha, WI, 53141. Tel: 262-595-3432. p. 2445

Callaway, Stacia, Librn, Waubonsee Community College, Collins Hall, 2nd Flr, State Rte 47 at Waubonsee Dr, Sugar Grove, IL, 60554. Tel: 630-466-2396. p. 652

Calleja, Linda, Adult Serv, Edith B Siegrist Vermillion Public Library, 18 Church St, Vermillion, SD, 57069-3093. Tel: 605-677-7060. p. 2084

Callihan, Denise, Dir, Libr Serv, PPG Industries, Inc, Technical Information Center, 4325 Rosanna Dr, Allison Park, PA, 15101. Tel: 724-325-5221. p. 1996

Callihan, Denise, Mgr, PPG Industries, Inc, Chemicals Technical Information Center, 440 College Park Dr, Monroeville, PA, 15146. Tel: 724-325-5221. p. 1996

Callihan, Janae, Head, Youth Serv, Cranberry Public Library, Municipal Ctr, 2525 Rochester Rd, Ste 300, Cranberry Township, PA, 16066-6423. Tel: 724-776-9100, Ext 1124. p. 1924

Callihan, Michelle, Libr Mgr, Sno-Isle Libraries, Granite Falls Library, 815 E Galena St, Granite Falls, WA, 98252-8472. Tel: 360-691-6087. p. 2370

Callinan, Ellen, Dir, Arnold & Porter Library, 601 Massachusetts Ave NW, Washington, DC, 20001-3743. Tel: 202-942-5000. p. 361

Callison, Camille, Univ Librn, University of the Fraser Valley, 33844 King Rd, Bldg G, Abbotsford, BC, V2S 7M8, CANADA. Tel: 604-854-4545. p. 2562

Callison, L, Circ, Massapequa Public Library, Central Avenue, 523 Central Ave, Massapequa, NY, 11758. Tel: 516-798-4607. p. 1569

Callister, Paul D, Libr Dir, University of Missouri-Kansas City Libraries, 500 E 52nd St, Kansas City, MO, 64110. Tel: 816-235-1650. p. 1258

Callow, Jennifer, Cat Librn, Missouri Western State University, 4525 Downs Dr, Saint Joseph, MO, 64507-2294. Tel: 816-271-4368. p. 1268

Calloway, Carolynne, Dir, Grand Prairie of the West Public Library District, 142 W Jackson St, Virden, IL, 62690. Tel: 217-965-3015. p. 658

Calmes, Vicky, Dir, Colby Community Library, 505 W Spence St, Colby, WI, 54421. Tel: 715-223-2000. p. 2428

Calog, Nettie-Lee, Mgr, Warrenton Community Library, 160 S Main Ave, Warrenton, OR, 97146. Tel: 503-861-8156. p. 1901

Calter, Mimi, Vice Provost & Univ Librn, Washington University Libraries, One Brookings Dr, Campus Box 1061, Saint Louis, MO, 63130-4862. Tel: 314-935-5400. p. 1276

Calunas, Marianne, Tech Serv, Oakland Community College, Library Systems, 2900 Featherstone Rd, MTEC A210, Auburn Hills, MI, 48326. Tel: 248-232-4478. p. 1082

Caluori, Rob, Chief Financial Officer, Westchester Library System, 570 Taxter Rd, Ste 400, Elmsford, NY, 10523-2337. Tel: 914-231-3207. p. 1531

Calvaruso, Marie, Dir, Libr & Res Serv, Harris, Beach PLLC, 99 Garnsey Rd, Pittsford, NY, 14534. Tel: 585-419-8800. p. 1618

Calvert, Andy, Youth Serv, Saint Johns County Public Library System, Main Branch, 1960 N Ponce de Leon Blvd, Saint Augustine, FL, 32084. Tel: 904-827-6943. p. 440

Calvert, Bea, Librn, Tulane University, A H Clifford Mathematics Research Library, 430 Gibson Hall, 6823 St Charles Ave, New Orleans, LA, 70118. Tel: 504-862-3455. p. 904

Calvert, Donna, Spec Serv Dir, West Virginia Library Commission, Culture Center, Bldg 9, 1900 Kanawha Blvd E, Charleston, WV, 25305. Tel: 304-558-4061. p. 2401

Calvert, Donna, Spec Serv Dir, Parkersburg & Wood County Public Library, Services for the Blind & Physically Handicapped, 3100 Emerson Ave, Parkersburg, WV, 26104. Tel: 304-420-4587, Ext 503. p. 2411

Calvert, Hilde M, Head, Coll Develop, Ball State University Libraries, 2000 W University Ave, Muncie, IN, 47306-1099. Tel: 765-285-8033. p. 708

Calvert, Jennie, Youth Serv, Fulton County Public Library, 320 W Seventh St, Rochester, IN, 46975-1332. Tel: 574-223-2713. p. 716

Calvin, Diane L, Head, Info Serv, Ball State University Libraries, 2000 W University Ave, Muncie, IN, 47306-1099. Tel: 765-285-3327. p. 708

Camacho, Edwin, Ref Serv, Pontifical Catholic University of Puerto Rico, Ramon Emeterio Betances St 482, Mayaguez, PR, 00680. Tel: 787-834-5151, Ext 5012. p. 2511

Camarda, Jan, Homebound Serv, Westhampton Free Library, Seven Library Ave, Westhampton Beach, NY, 11978-2697. Tel: 631-288-3335, Ext 125. p. 1664

Camargo, Teasha, Youth Serv Librn, Lincoln Public Library, 22 Church St, Lincoln, NH, 03251. Tel: 603-745-8159. p. 1370

Camarillo, Angie, Tech Serv, United States Army, 201 N Third, Walla Walla, WA, 99362-1876. Tel: 509-527-7427. p. 2392

Camarillo, Josephine, Dir, Ellensburg Public Library, 209 N Ruby St, Ellensburg, WA, 98926-3397. Tel: 509-962-7218. p. 2363

Camastro, Nick, Circ Mgr, Great Neck Library, 159 Bayview Ave, Great Neck, NY, 11023. Tel: 516-466-8055, Ext 207. p. 1540

Camehl, Shawana, Circ Supvr, South Charleston Public Library, 312 Fourth Ave, South Charleston, WV, 25303. Tel: 304-744-6561. p. 2415

Camejo, Joanne, Librn, Greenspoon Marder, 200 E Broward Blvd, Ste 1800, Fort Lauderdale, FL, 33301. Tel: 954-491-1120. p. 401

Cameron, Andrea, Res Ctr Mgr, Holland College Library Services, 140 Weymouth St, Charlottetown, PE, C1A 4Z1, CANADA. Tel: 902-853-0020. p. 2707

Cameron, Brian, Acting Head Archivist, Head, Acq, Head, Coll Serv, Ryerson University Library, 350 Victoria St, 2nd Flr, Toronto, ON, M5B 2K3, CANADA. Tel: 416-979-5000, Ext 5146. p. 2692

Cameron, Carrie, Youth Serv Librn, Hodgkins Public Library District, 6500 Wenz Ave, Hodgkins, IL, 60525. Tel: 708-579-1844. p. 600

Cameron, Deb, Ref Supvr, Greenville Public Library, 520 Sycamore St, Greenville, OH, 45331-1438. Tel: 937-548-3915. p. 1788

Cameron, Heather, Children's Coordr, Wagoner City Public Library, 302 N Main St, Wagoner, OK, 74467-3834. Tel: 918-485-2126. p. 1868

Cameron, Jessica Ford, Co-Dir, Bellwood-Antis Public Library, 526 Main St, Bellwood, PA, 16617-1910. Tel: 814-742-8234. p. 1910

Cameron, Maria, Adult Serv, Southlake Public Library, 1400 Main St, Ste 130, Southlake, TX, 76092-7640. Tel: 817-748-8243. p. 2245

Cameron, Monica, Dir, Shelbyville Public Library, 154 N Broadway St, Shelbyville, IL, 62565. Tel: 217-774-4432. p. 646

Cameron, Susan, Spec Coll Librn, Saint Francis Xavier University, 3080 Martha Dr, Antigonish, NS, B2G 2W5, CANADA. Tel: 902-867-5328. p. 2615

Cameron, Temple, Chief Exec Officer, Librn, Wollaston Public Library, 5629-A Hwy 620, Coe Hill, ON, K0L 1P0, CANADA. Tel: 613-337-5183. p. 2637

Cameron, Vannessa, Coordr, Patron Serv, Park Forest Public Library, 400 Lakewood Blvd, Park Forest, IL, 60466. Tel: 708-748-3731. p. 633

Cameron-Klugh, Druet, Bibliographer, Ref Librn, University of Iowa Libraries, College of Law Library, 200 Boyd Law Bldg, Iowa City, IA, 52242-1166. Tel: 319-335-9038. p. 761

Cameron-Vedros, Crystal, Dir, University of Kansas Medical Center, 2100 W 39th Ave, Kansas City, KS, 66160. Tel: 913-588-7166. p. 817

Camidge, Kaitlin, Dir, Epsom Public Library, 1606 Dover Rd, Epsom, NH, 03234. Tel: 603-736-9920. p. 1363

Camino, Holly, Br Mgr, Cuyahoga County Public Library, Middleburg Heights Branch, 16699 Bagley Rd, Middleburg Heights, OH, 44130. Tel: 440-234-3600. p. 1813

Cammack, Nancy, Br Mgr, Lubbock Public Library, Groves, 5520 19th St, Lubbock, TX, 79407. Tel: 806-767-3733. p. 2213

Cammarata, Paul, Head, Coll Develop, University of South Carolina, 1322 Greene St, Columbia, SC, 29208-0103. Tel: 803-777-3142. p. 2055

Cammarata, Paula, Circ/Reserves, Tufts University, Edwin Ginn Library, Mugar Bldg, 1st Flr, 160 Packard St, Medford, MA, 02155-7082. Tel: 617-627-3273. p. 1034

Cammire, Tedi, Cat, Rusk County Community Library, 418 Corbett Ave W, Ladysmith, WI, 54848-1396. Tel: 715-532-2604. p. 2447

Camona, Maricelia, Librn I, Santa Fe Springs City Library, 11700 E Telegraph Rd, Santa Fe Springs, CA, 90670-3600. Tel: 562-868-7738. p. 243

Camp, Aimee, Br Mgr, El Paso Public Library, Esperanza Acosta Moreno Regional, 12480 Pebble Hills Blvd, El Paso, TX, 79938. Tel: 915-212-0442. p. 2174

Camp, Mary, Dir, Texas Legislative Reference Library, State Capitol Bldg, 1100 N Congress Ave, Rm 2N-3, Austin, TX, 78701. Tel: 512-463-1252. p. 2140

Camp, Melody, Librn, Cullman County Public Library System, Guy Hunt Public, 60 Lions Park Rd, Holly Pond, AL, 35083. Tel: 256-796-5226. p. 13

Camp, Rebecca, Circ Mgr, Sequoyah Regional Library System, 116 Brown Industrial Pkwy, Canton, GA, 30114. Tel: 770-479-3090. p. 469

Camp-Fisher, Cindy, Br Head, Henderson County Public Library, Edneyville Branch, Two Firehouse Rd, Hendersonville, NC, 28792. Tel: 828-687-1218. p. 1695

Campagna, Sierra, Br Supvr, Berkeley Public Library, West Branch, 1125 University Ave, Berkeley, CA, 94702. Tel: 510-981-6270. p. 122

Campana, Claire, Coll Develop, Horry County Memorial Library, 1008 Fifth Ave, Conway, SC, 29526. Tel: 843-915-5285. p. 2056

Campany, Dawn, Libr Asst, Parish Public Library, Three Church St, Parish, NY, 13131. Tel: 315-625-7130. p. 1615

Campbell, Aimee, Dir, Carnegie Evans Public Library Albia Public, 203 Benton Ave E, Albia, IA, 52531-2036. Tel: 641-932-2469. p. 729

Campbell, Allison, Commun Engagement Mgr, North Vancouver District Public Library, 1277 Lynn Valley Rd, North Vancouver, BC, V7J 0A2, CANADA. Tel: 604-984-0286, 604-990-5800. p. 2573

Campbell, Amanda, Mgr, Br, Eastern Counties Regional Library, 390 Murray St, Mulgrave, NS, B0E 2G0, CANADA. Tel: 902-747-2597. p. 2621

Campbell, Amy, Librn, Montgomery City-County Public Library System, Bertha Pleasant Williams Library - Rosa L Parks Avenue Branch, 1276 Rosa L Parks Ave, Montgomery, AL, 36108. Tel: 334-240-4979. p. 30

Campbell, Amy, Ref Librn, Marshall Public Library, 113 S Garfield Ave, Pocatello, ID, 83204. Tel: 208-232-1263. p. 529
Campbell, Amy, Libr Spec, Metropolitan Community College, Blue River Library, 20301 E 78 Hwy, Independence, MO, 64057. Tel: 816-604-6642. p. 1256
Campbell, Amy, Br Mgr, Harris County Public Library, Katherine Tyra Branch @ Bear Creek, 16719 Clay Rd, Houston, TX, 77084. Tel: 832-927-5590. p. 2193
Campbell, Angela, Dir, Rock Island Public Library, 401 19th St, Rock Island, IL, 61201. Tel: 309-732-7323. p. 641
Campbell, Angela, Teen Librn, Tipp City Public Library, 11 E Main St, Tipp City, OH, 45371. Tel: 937-667-3826. p. 1823
Campbell, Ann, Access Serv Mgr, University of Miami, 4600 Rickenbacker Causeway, SLAB 160 Library, Miami, FL, 33149-1098. Tel: 305-421-4021, 305-421-4060. p. 425
Campbell, Anne, Librn II, Programming & Partnerships Coord, Groton Public Library, 52 Newtown Rd, Groton, CT, 06340. Tel: 860-441-6750. p. 314
Campbell, Annette, Librn, Naples Community Hospital, 350 Seventh St N, Naples, FL, 34102-5730. Tel: 239-436-5384. p. 427
Campbell, Brenda J, Dir, Hagerstown Jefferson Township Library, Ten W College St, Hagerstown, IN, 47346. Tel: 765-489-5632. p. 688
Campbell, Carol, Librn, St Thomas Episcopal Church Library, 231 Sunset Ave, Sunnyvale, CA, 94086-5938. Tel: 408-736-4155. p. 251
Campbell, Cathy, Ch Serv, Otsego County Library, 700 S Otsego Ave, Gaylord, MI, 49735-1723. Tel: 989-732-5841. p. 1109
Campbell, Cathy, Circ Serv Supvr, Highline College Library, 2400 S 240th St, MS 25-4, Des Moines, WA, 98198. Tel: 206-592-3234. p. 2363
Campbell, Chris, Mgr, Richland Library, Edgewood Branch, 2101 Oak St, Columbia, SC, 29204. Tel: 803-509-8355. p. 2054
Campbell, Cindy, Acq, Florida SouthWestern State College, 8099 College Pkwy SW, Bldg J-212, Fort Myers, FL, 33919. Tel: 239-489-9367. p. 403
Campbell, Cindy, Br Mgr, Massanutten Regional Library, Page Public, 100 Zerkel St, Luray, VA, 22835. Tel: 540-434-4475, Ext 5, 540-743-6867. p. 2325
Campbell, Clydeen, Sr Librn, Casey County Public Library, 238 Middleburg St, Liberty, KY, 42539. Tel: 606-787-9381. p. 864
Campbell, Corey, Youth Serv Mgr, Vespasian Warner Public Library District, 310 N Quincy, Clinton, IL, 61727. Tel: 217-935-5174. p. 572
Campbell, Cynthia, Actg Adminr, Bristol Law Library, Superior Court House, Nine Court St, Taunton, MA, 02780. Tel: 508-824-7632. p. 1059
Campbell, Daniel, Dir, United States Court of International Trade, One Federal Plaza, New York, NY, 10278. Tel: 212-264-2816. p. 1603
Campbell, Dauna, Libr Dir, Harlingen Public Library, 410 76 Dr, Harlingen, TX, 78550. Tel: 956-216-5803. p. 2188
Campbell, David, Mgr, Digital Serv & Mkt, Palos Verdes Library District, 701 Silver Spur Rd, Rolling Hills Estates, CA, 90274. Tel: 310-377-9584, Ext 284. p. 205
Campbell, DeAnn, Ch, The Community Library, 415 Spruce Ave N, Ketchum, ID, 83340. Tel: 208-726-3493. p. 523
Campbell, Deanna, Youth Serv Coordr, Gilliam County Public Library, 134 S Main St, Condon, OR, 97823. p. 1875
Campbell, Debbie, Dir, Tech Serv, Owen County Public Library, Ten S Montgomery St, Spencer, IN, 47460-1738. Tel: 812-829-3392. p. 719
Campbell, Denise, Head Librn, United States Department of Justice, One Range Rd, Quantico, VA, 22135. Tel: 703-632-3443. p. 2339
Campbell, Diana, Br Librn, Wapiti Regional Library, Shellbrook Public Library, 105 Railway Ave W, Shellbrook, SK, S0J 2E0, CANADA. Tel: 306-747-3419. p. 2746
Campbell, Diane K, Librn, Rider University, 2083 Lawrenceville Rd, Lawrenceville, NJ, 08648. p. 1411
Campbell, Dixie, Librn, Greater West Central Public Library District, Bowen Branch, 116 W Fifth St, Bowen, IL, 62316. Tel: 217-842-5573. p. 538
Campbell, Donna, Tech Serv & Syst Librn, Westminster Theological Seminary, 2960 W Church Rd, Glenside, PA, 19038. Tel: 215-935-3872. p. 1937
Campbell, Edith, Educ Librn, Ref & Instruction Librn, Indiana State University, 510 North 6 1/2 St, Terre Haute, IN, 47809. Tel: 812-237-3700. p. 720
Campbell, Emma, Circ Librn, Art Circle Public Library, Three East St, Crossville, TN, 38555. Tel: 931-484-6790. p. 2095
Campbell, Erin, Ref Librn, Tech Librn, Lloyd Library & Museum, 917 Plum St, Cincinnati, OH, 45202. Tel: 513-721-3707. p. 1761
Campbell, Eryn, Libr Mgr, National Association of Insurance Commissioners, 1100 Walnut St, Ste 1000, Kansas City, MO, 64106. Tel: 816-783-8253. p. 1256
Campbell, Gowen, ILL Mgr, Hunter College Libraries, East Bldg, 695 Park Ave, New York, NY, 10065. Tel: 212-772-4192. p. 1588
Campbell, Grant, Assoc Prof, Western University, FIMS & Nursing Bldg, Rm 2020, London, ON, N6A 5B9, CANADA. Tel: 519-661-2111, Ext 88483. p. 2796
Campbell, James, Curator, Libr Supvr, National Watch & Clock Museum, 514 Poplar St, Columbia, PA, 17512-2124. Tel: 717-684-8261. p. 1923
Campbell, Jeanette, Libr Asst, Tech Serv, Harrison Memorial Library, Ocean Ave & Lincoln St, Carmel, CA, 93921. Tel: 831-624-4629. p. 128
Campbell, Jeff, Head, Libr & Info Serv, James Madison University Libraries, 880 Madison Dr, MSC 1704, Harrisonburg, VA, 22807. Tel: 540-568-6818. p. 2324
Campbell, Jennifer, Br Mgr, Webster Parish Library System, Minden Main, 521 East & West St, Minden, LA, 71055. Tel: 318-371-3080. p. 898
Campbell, Jessi, Br Mgr, Galax-Carroll Regional Library, 610 W Stuart Dr, Galax, VA, 24333. Tel: 276-236-2351. p. 2321
Campbell, Jessie, Mgr, Calgary Public Library, Seton, 4995 Market St SE, Calgary, AB, T3M 2P9, CANADA. p. 2527
Campbell, Jessie, Mgr, Calgary Public Library, Shawnessy, South Fish Creek Complex, 333 Shawville Blvd SE, Calgary, AB, T2Y 4H3, CANADA. p. 2527
Campbell, Jessie, Libr Mgr, Southern Alberta Institute of Technology Library, 1301 16th Ave NW, Calgary, AB, T2M 0L4, CANADA. Tel: 403-210-4477. p. 2529
Campbell, Jill, Librn, Lincoln Land Community College Library, Sangamon Hall, 5250 Shepherd Rd, Springfield, IL, 62794. Tel: 217-786-2360. p. 650
Campbell, Joan, Librn/Mgr, Urban Land Institute, 2001 L St NW, Ste 200, Washington, DC, 20036. Tel: 202-624-7000, 202-624-7137. p. 380
Campbell, Joan, Colls Librn, Bowdoin College Library, 3000 College Sta, Brunswick, ME, 04011-8421. Tel: 207-725-3285. p. 919
Campbell, Joan, Head, Tech Serv, Dover Town Library, 56 Dedham St, Dover, MA, 02030-2214. Tel: 508-785-8113. p. 1014
Campbell, Jonathan, Dir, Floyd County Public Library, 161 N Arnold Ave, Prestonsburg, KY, 41653. Tel: 606-886-2981. p. 873
Campbell, Karlene, Librn, Genesis Medical Center, Illini Campus, 855 Illini Dr, Ste 102, Silvis, IL, 61282. Tel: 309-281-5110. p. 647
Campbell, Karlene, Med Librn, Genesis Health System, 1227 E Rusholme St, Davenport, IA, 52803. Tel: 563-421-2287. p. 744
Campbell, Karma, Asst Libr Dir, Catoosa Public Library, 105 E Oak, Catoosa, OK, 74015. Tel: 918-266-1684. p. 1843
Campbell, Kasey, Access Services Assoc, Drew University Library, 36 Madison Ave, Madison, NJ, 07940. Tel: 973-408-3486. p. 1414
Campbell, Kathleen, Library Contact, Country Music Hall of Fame & Museum, 222 Fifth Ave S, Nashville, TN, 37203. Tel: 615-416-2025. p. 2118
Campbell, Kathy, Ref & Instruction Librn, East Tennessee State University, Sherrod Library, Seehorn Dr & Lake St, Johnson City, TN, 37614-0204. Tel: 423-439-5629. p. 2103
Campbell, Kelly D, Dr, Dir & Assoc Dean for Info Serv, Columbia Theological Seminary, 701 S Columbia Dr, Decatur, GA, 30030. Tel: 404-687-4547. p. 475
Campbell, Kristen, Libr Mgr, Hurley Library, 48 Main St, Hurley, NY, 12443. Tel: 845-338-2092. p. 1550
Campbell, Lynne, Ch, John Curtis Free Library, 534 Hanover St, Hanover, MA, 02339. Tel: 781-826-2972. p. 1023
Campbell, Marcy, Br Mgr, Whitman County Rural Library District, Rosalia Branch, 402 S Whitman Ave, Rosalia, WA, 99170. Tel: 509-523-3109. p. 2362
Campbell, Margaret, Librn, Jackson County Library, Tuckerman Branch, 200 W Main St, Tuckerman, AR, 72473. Tel: 870-349-5336. p. 106
Campbell, Mary, Dir, Pelham Public Library, 2000 Ball Park Rd, Pelham, AL, 35124. Tel: 205-620-6418. p. 32
Campbell, Mary, Br Mgr, Cumberland County Public Library & Information Center, North Regional, 855 McArthur Rd, Fayetteville, NC, 28311-2053. p. 1688
Campbell, Mary, Libr Mgr, Sno-Isle Libraries, Oak Harbor Library, 1000 SE Regatta Dr, Oak Harbor, WA, 98277-3091. Tel: 360-675-5115. p. 2371
CampBell, Meaghann, Asst Dir, Spalding Memorial Library, 724 S Main St, Athens, PA, 18810-1010. Tel: 570-888-7117. p. 1908
Campbell, Melissa M, Dir, Plainville Public Library, 198 South St, Plainville, MA, 02762-1512. Tel: 508-695-1784. p. 1047
Campbell, Michael, Tech Asst, University of South Alabama Libraries, Doy Leale McCall Rare Book & Manuscript Library, Marx Library, 3rd Flr, Ste 300, 5901 USA Dr N, Mobile, AL, 36688. Tel: 251-341-3900. p. 27
Campbell, Michelle, Br Supvr, Guelph Public Library, Westminster Square Branch, 100-31 Farley Dr, Guelph, ON, N1L 0B7, CANADA. Tel: 519-829-4404. p. 2643
Campbell, Neil A, Assoc Prof, Assoc Univ Librn, University of Victoria Libraries, Diana M Priestly Law Library, PO Box 2300, STN CSC, Victoria, BC, V8W 3B1, CANADA. Tel: 250-721-8565. p. 2583
Campbell, Nicole, Assoc Libr Dir, Washington State University Libraries, 14204 NE Salmon Creek Ave, Vancouver, WA, 98686. Tel: 360-546-9687. p. 2391
Campbell, Pamela, Archivist, Federal Reserve Bank of Saint Louis, One Federal Reserve Bank Plaza, Saint Louis, MO, 63102-2005. Tel: 314-444-8907. p. 1270
Campbell, Rachel, Dir, Eccles-Lesher Memorial Library, 673 Main St, Rimersburg, PA, 16248-4817. Tel: 814-473-3800. p. 2001
Campbell, Rebecca, Dir, City of Tavares Public Library, 314 N New Hampshire Ave, Tavares, FL, 32778. Tel: 352-742-6204. p. 450
Campbell, Robin, Dir, Killen Public Library, 325 J C Malden Hwy, Killen, AL, 35645. Tel: 256-757-5471. p. 23
Campbell, Sarah, Asst Archivist, College of the Holy Cross, One College St, Worcester, MA, 01610. Tel: 508-793-2575. p. 1072
Campbell, Sherie, Libr Mgr, Trochu Municipal Library, 317 Main St, Trochu, AB, T0M 2C0, CANADA. Tel: 403-442-2458. p. 2557

Campbell, Sherri, ILL, Eccles-Lesher Memorial Library, 673 Main St, Rimersburg, PA, 16248-4817. Tel: 814-473-3800. p. 2001
Campbell, Stacy, Libr Dir, Rockford Public Library, 202 W Main Ave, Rockford, IA, 50468-1212. Tel: 641-756-3725. p. 779
Campbell, Stan, Head, Commun Relations, Alexandrian Public Library, 115 W Fifth St, Mount Vernon, IN, 47620. Tel: 812-838-3286. p. 708
Campbell, Steve, Libr Dir, Scenic Regional Library, 251 Union Plaza Dr, Union, MO, 63084. Tel: 636-583-0652, Ext 101. p. 1283
Campbell, Suzanne, Br Librn, Eastern Monroe Public Library, Pocono Township Branch, 112 Township Dr, Tannersville, PA, 18372. Tel: 570-629-5858. p. 2010
Campbell, Tanya E, Dir, Dayton Public Library, 22 First St NW, Dayton, IA, 50530. Tel: 515-547-2700. p. 744
Campbell, Victoria, Youth Serv Mgr, Beaverton City Library, 12375 SW Fifth St, Beaverton, OR, 97005-2883. Tel: 503-644-2197. p. 1873
Campbell, Wendy, Asst Dir, Youth Serv Librn, Bitterroot Public Library, 306 State St, Hamilton, MT, 59840. Tel: 406-363-1670. p. 1294
Campbell, Zandra, Br Mgr, Enoch Pratt Free Library, Pennsylvania Avenue Branch, 1531 W North Ave, Baltimore, MD, 21217-1735. Tel: 443-984-4939. p. 953
Campbell-Shoaf, Heidi, Dir, National Society of the Daughters of the American Revolution, Museum Reference Library, 1776 D St NW, Washington, DC, 20006. Tel: 202-879-3241. p. 373
Campeau, Kathy, Br Asst, Middlesex County Library, Dorchester Branch, 2123 Dorchester Rd, Dorchester, ON, N0L 1G0, CANADA. Tel: 519-268-3451. p. 2682
Campen, Cathy, Ch Serv, Andover Public Library, 355 Rte 6, Andover, CT, 06232. Tel: 860-742-7428. p. 301
Campion, Elizabeth, Adult Serv, Shelby Township Library, 51680 Van Dyke, Shelby Township, MI, 48316-4448. Tel: 586-739-7414. p. 1150
Campos, Denise, Br Mgr, Monterey County Free Libraries, Soledad Branch, 401 Gabilan Dr, Soledad, CA, 93960. Tel: 831-678-2430. p. 173
Campos, Jesus, Dr, Dean, Libr & Learning Support, South Texas College Library, 3201 W Pecan Blvd, McAllen, TX, 78501-6661. Tel: 956-872-2528. p. 2217
Campos, Judy, Br Mgr, Cochise County Library District, Alice Woods Sunizona Library, Ash Creek School, 6460 E Hwy 181, Pearce, AZ, 85625. Tel: 520-824-3145. p. 56
Camposagrado, Ricardo, Prog Spec, Support Serv, Rutgers University Libraries, George F Smith Library of the Health Sciences, 30 12th Ave, Newark, NJ, 07101. Tel: 973-972-5317. p. 1425
Camren, Brenda, Br Mgr, Joint Base Lewis-McChord Library System, McChord Library, 851 Lincoln Blvd, Joint Base Lewis-McChord, WA, 98438. Tel: 253-982-3454. p. 2366
Camuti, Alice, Dr, Assoc Dean, Tennessee Technological University, Graduate Studies, Dewberry Hall 306, One William L Jones Dr, Cookeville, TN, 38505. Tel: 931-372-6006. p. 2792
Canada, Dayna, Supvr, Pub Serv, Thousand Oaks Library, 1401 E Janss Rd, Thousand Oaks, CA, 91362-2199. Tel: 805-449-2660, Ext 7347. p. 252
Canaday, Renny, Br Mgr, Scenic Regional Library, Union Branch, 251 Union Plaza Dr, Union, MO, 63084. Tel: 636-583-3224. p. 1283
Canales, Joanne, Head, Tech Serv, Bronx Community College Library, 2115 University Ave, NL 252A, Bronx, NY, 10453. Tel: 718-289-5100, Ext 3616. p. 1497
Canales, Juanita, Dir, Bicentennial City-County Public Library, 809 Richards St, Ste A, Paducah, TX, 79248. Tel: 806-492-2006. p. 2224
Canas, Maurizio, Libr Mgr, University of West Los Angeles, 9800 S LaCienega Blvd, Inglewood, CA, 90301. Tel: 310-342-5253. p. 153
Cancienne, Julie, Circ Supvr, Saint Charles Parish Library, West Regional Branch, 105 Lakewood Dr, Luling, LA, 70070. Tel: 985-785-8471. p. 889
Candelaria, Diana, Pub Serv Coordr, Arlington Public Library System, Northeast, 1905 Brown Blvd, Arlington, TX, 76006. p. 2136
Candelora, Maryanne, Supervising Library Assoc, Sadie Pope Dowdell Library of South Amboy, 100 Harold G Hoffman Plaza, South Amboy, NJ, 08879. Tel: 732-721-6060. p. 1442
Candiloro, Cyndi M, Dir, Readsboro Community Library, 301 Phelps Lane, Readsboro, VT, 05350. Tel: 802-423-5460. p. 2293
Canen, Aaron, Tech Adminr, Belgrade Community Library, 106 N Broadway, Belgrade, MT, 59714. Tel: 406-388-4346. p. 1287
Canfield, Stella, Mkt & Communications Spec, University of Florida, 2725 S Binion Rd, Apopka, FL, 32703-8504. Tel: 407-410-6929, 407-884-2034, Ext 140. p. 383
Canfield-Riggs, Darcie, Ch Serv, Hutchinson Public Library, 901 N Main, Hutchinson, KS, 67501-4492. Tel: 620-663-5441. p. 814
Cangelosi, Daniel, Br Mgr, Jefferson Parish Library, Jane O'Brien Chatelain West Bank Regional, 2751 Manhattan Blvd, Harvey, LA, 70058. Tel: 504-364-2660. p. 897
Cangelosi, Katie, Head, Circ, Winnetka-Northfield Public Library District, 768 Oak St, Winnetka, IL, 60093-2515. Tel: 847-446-7220. p. 664
Cangiano, Barbara, Head, Borrower Serv, Wallingford Public Library, 200 N Main St, Wallingford, CT, 06492. Tel: 203-284-6415. p. 342
Canham, Robin, Digital Res Librn, Saskatchewan Polytechnic, 4500 Wascana Pkwy, Regina, SK, S4P 3A3, CANADA. Tel: 306-775-7409. p. 2748
Canham-Clyne, Melissa ', Dir, Hamden Public Library, 2901 Dixwell Ave, Hamden, CT, 06518-3135. Tel: 203-287-2686, Ext 1. p. 315
Cani, Lindita, Head, Ref & Libr Serv, South Orange Public Library, 65 Scotland Rd, South Orange, NJ, 07079. Tel: 973-762-0230. p. 1443
Canick, Simon, Dir, Columbia University, Arthur W Diamond Law Library, 435 W 116th St, New York, NY, 10027. Tel: 212-854-3922. p. 1583
Canino, Sarah, Music Librn, Vassar College Library, George Sherman Dickinson Music Library, 124 Raymond Ave, Box 38, Poughkeepsie, NY, 12604-0038. Tel: 845-437-7492. p. 1624
Cannady, Bernadette, Br Mgr, Wicomico Public Library, 122 S Division St, Salisbury, MD, 21801. Tel: 410-749-3612, Ext 133. p. 976
Cannady, Lori, Libr Dir, Dillon City Library, 121 S Idaho St, Dillon, MT, 59725-2500. p. 1292
Cannady, Lori, Libr Dir, Broad Valleys Federation of Libraries, 120 S Last Chance Gulch, Helena, MT, 59601-4133. Tel: 406-683-4544. p. 1295
Cannarozzi, Kathryn, Dir, Cranford Free Public Library, 224 Walnut Ave, Cranford, NJ, 07016-2931. Tel: 908-709-7272. p. 1398
Cannell, Claire, Univ Archivist, Lawrence University, 113 S Lawe St, Appleton, WI, 54911-5683. Tel: 920-832-6753. p. 2420
Canney, Kara, Dir, Cromwell Belden Public Library, 39 West St, Cromwell, CT, 06416. Tel: 860-632-3460. p. 307
Canning, Cathy, Br Asst, Cumberland Public Libraries, Springhill Miners Memorial Library, 85 Main St, Springhill, NS, B0M 1X0, CANADA. Tel: 902-597-2211. p. 2615
Canning, Heather, Dir, Dummer Public Library, 67 Hill Rd, Dummer, NH, 03588. Tel: 603-449-0995. p. 1361
Cannizzaro, Regina, Coordr, Tech Serv, County College of Morris, 214 Center Grove Rd, Randolph, NJ, 07869-2086. Tel: 973-328-5300. p. 1438
Cannon, Ann D, Ref Librn, Norfolk State University Library, 700 Park Ave, Norfolk, VA, 23504-8010. Tel: 757-823-2417. p. 2335
Cannon, Caley, Sr Libr Supvr, Glendale Library, Arts & Culture, Brand Library & Art Center, 1601 W Mountain St, Glendale, CA, 91201. Tel: 818-548-2010. p. 148
Cannon, Eliza, Librn, Texas County Library, Cabool Branch, 418 Walnut Ave, Cabool, MO, 65689. Tel: 417-962-3722. p. 1249
Cannon, Heather, Resources Librn, Syst Librn, Adler University, 17 N Dearborn St, 15th Flr, Chicago, IL, 60602. Tel: 312-662-4230. p. 553
Cannon, James, Ref Librn, Montgomery City-County Public Library System, Juliette Hampton Morgan Memorial Library, 245 High St, Montgomery, AL, 36104. Tel: 334-240-4992. p. 29
Cannon, Kelly, Scholarly Communications Librn, Muhlenberg College, 2400 Chew St, Allentown, PA, 18104-5586. Tel: 484-664-3602. p. 1905
Cannon, Kimberly, Acq Mgr, Oklahoma Christian University, 2501 E Memorial Rd, Edmond, OK, 73013. Tel: 405-425-5319. p. 1846
Cannon, Linda, Coll Develop Librn, Joplin Public Library, 1901 E 20th St, Joplin, MO, 64804. Tel: 417-623-7953. p. 1253
Cannon, Lynne, Circ, Pettee Memorial Library, 16 S Main St, Wilmington, VT, 05363. Tel: 802-464-8557. p. 2299
Cannon, Marcia, Head, Children's Servx, Abbot Public Library, Three Brook Rd, Marblehead, MA, 01945. Tel: 781-631-1481. p. 1031
Cannon, Marlene, Pub Serv Coordr, Mountain Regional Library System, 698 Miller St, Young Harris, GA, 30582. Tel: 706-379-3732. p. 503
Cannon, Rhonda, Assoc Dean of Finance, Adm & Human Resources, University of Oklahoma Libraries, 401 W Brooks St, Norman, OK, 73019. Tel: 405-325-3341. p. 1856
Cannon, Susan, Mgr, Access Serv, Saint Mary's University, 923 Robie St, Halifax, NS, B3H 3C3, CANADA. Tel: 902-420-5656. p. 2621
Cano, Marisol, Libr Mgr, Bridgeport Public Library, 2159 Tenth St, Bridgeport, TX, 76426. Tel: 940-683-3450. p. 2150
Cano-Loomis, Lisa, Commun Libr Mgr, Contra Costa County Library, Oakley Branch, 1050 Neroly Rd, Oakley, CA, 94561. Tel: 925-625-2400. p. 174
Canonaco, Gail, Mgr, Oshawa Public Library, Jess Hann Branch, Lake Vista Sq, 199 Wentworth St W, Oshawa, ON, L1J 6P4, CANADA. Tel: 905-579-6111, Ext 5860. p. 2664
Canonaco, Gail, Mgr, Oshawa Public Library, Northview, 250 Beatrice St E, Oshawa, ON, L1G 7T6, CANADA. Tel: 905-576-6040. p. 2664
Canora, Edward, Asst Dir, Head, Circ, Head, Tech Serv, Dobbs Ferry Public Library, 55 Main St, Dobbs Ferry, NY, 10522. Tel: 914-231-3055. p. 1526
Canosa-Albano, Jean, Asst Dir, Pub Serv, Springfield City Library, 220 State St, Springfield, MA, 01103. Tel: 413-263-6828, Ext 291. p. 1056
Canovan, Becky, Asst Dir, Libr Instruction & Pub Serv, University of Dubuque Library, 2000 University Ave, Dubuque, IA, 52001. Tel: 563-589-3100. p. 749
Cantelmo, Gabriella, Museum Collections Specialist, Chesapeake Bay Maritime Museum Library, 109A Mill St, Saint Michaels, MD, 21663. Tel: 410-745-4972. p. 976
Canter, Brandi, Patron Serv Supvr, Great River Regional Library, 1300 W St Germain St, Saint Cloud, MN, 56301. Tel: 320-650-2530. p. 1196
Cantin, Sylvie, Chef de Section, Bibliotheques de Montreal, Cartierville, 5900 rue De Salaberry, Montreal, QC, H4J 1J8, CANADA. Tel: 514-868-5916. p. 2718
Cantin, Sylvie, Chef de Section, Bibliotheques de Montreal, De Salaberry, 4170 rue De Salaberry, Montreal, QC, H4J 1H1, CANADA. Tel: 514-868-5916. p. 2718

Cantley, Kim, Librn, Horry County Memorial Library, Conway Branch, 801 Main St, Conway, SC, 29526. Tel: 843-915-7323. p. 2056

Cantoni, Jamie, Dir, Sherman Library Association, Rte 37 & 39, Sherman, CT, 06784. Tel: 860-354-2455. p. 336

Cantor, Emily, Head, Children's Servx, Woodbridge Town Library, Ten Newton Rd, Woodbridge, CT, 06525. Tel: 203-389-3447. p. 349

Cantor, Rachel, Br Mgr, Ocean County Library, Barnegat Branch, 112 Burr St, Barnegat, NJ, 08005. Tel: 609-698-3331. p. 1446

Cantrell, Sarah, Assoc Dir, Res & Educ, Duke University Libraries, Medical Center Library & Archives, DUMC Box 3702, Ten Searle Dr, Durham, NC, 27710-0001. Tel: 919-660-1131. p. 1684

Cantu, Brenda M, Libr Dir, Southwest Texas Junior College, 2401 Garner Field Rd, Uvalde, TX, 78801. Tel: 830-591-7254, 830-591-7367. p. 2251

Cantu, Eliamar, Librn, Starr County Public Library, 1705 N Athens St, Roma, TX, 78584. Tel: 956-849-0072. p. 2234

Cantu, Esteban, Info Technology Librarian, University of Texas at San Antonio Libraries, One UTSA Circle, San Antonio, TX, 78249-0671. Tel: 210-458-4574, 210-458-7506. p. 2240

Cantwell, Amy, Dir, Hockley County Memorial Library, 811 Austin St, Levelland, TX, 79336. Tel: 806-894-6750. p. 2211

Cantwell, Patricia, Assoc Dir, College of the Atlantic, 105 Eden St, Bar Harbor, ME, 04609-1198. Tel: 207-801-5661. p. 916

Cantwell-Cole, Kathryn, Librn, Placer County Library, Colfax Branch, Ten W Church St, Colfax, CA, 95713. Tel: 530-346-8211. p. 118

Cantwell-Jurkovic, Laureen, Head, Access Serv, Colorado Mesa University, 1100 North Ave, Grand Junction, CO, 81501. Tel: 970-248-1865. p. 283

Canty, Adrienne, Head, Knowledge Resources, J T Fyles Natural Resources Library, 1810 Blanshard St, Victoria, BC, V8W 9N3, CANADA. Tel: 250-952-0564. p. 2582

Canty-Tisdale, Jackie, Libr Asst, Sterne, Kessler, Goldstein & Fox Library, 1100 New York Ave NW, Ste 600, Washington, DC, 20005. Tel: 202-371-2600. p. 376

Canuel, Robin, Univ Librn, Lakehead University, 955 Oliver Rd, Thunder Bay, ON, P7B 5E1, CANADA. Tel: 807-343-8010, Ext 8125. p. 2685

Canzano, Deborah, Ref Librn, Orange County Community College Library, 115 South St, Middletown, NY, 10940. Tel: 845-341-4855. p. 1571

Canzano, Deborah, Ref Librn, Orange County Community College Library, Newburgh Campus, One Washington Ctr, Newburgh, NY, 12550. Tel: 845-341-9020. p. 1571

Canzonieri, Bridget, Asst Dir, Circ, Pub Serv Librn, Saint Vincent College & Seminary Library, 300 Fraser Purchase Rd, Latrobe, PA, 15650-2690. Tel: 724-805-2966. p. 1953

Cao, Wendy, Adminr, NorthNet Library System, 32 W 25th Ave, Ste 201, San Mateo, CA, 94403. Tel: 650-349-5538. p. 235

Caparas, Michael, Circ, ILL, Justice Institute of British Columbia Library, 715 McBride Blvd, New Westminster, BC, V3L 5T4, CANADA. Tel: 604-528-5598. p. 2572

Capasso, Stephanie, Dir, Manor Public Library, 44 Main St, Manor, PA, 15665. Tel: 724-864-6850. p. 1957

Capatosto, Victoria, Ref Librn, Howard University Libraries, Law Library, 2929 Van Ness St NW, Washington, DC, 20008. Tel: 202-806-8175. p. 369

Capdarest-Arest, Nicole, Head of Libr, University of California, Davis, 4610 X St, Sacramento, CA, 95817. Tel: 916-734-3529. p. 210

Capeci, James, Libr Dir, Missouri Southern State University, 3950 E Newman Rd, Joplin, MO, 64801-1595. Tel: 417-625-9806. p. 1253

Capizzo, Louise, Youth Serv Mgr, Scarborough Public Library, 48 Gorham Rd, Scarborough, ME, 04074. Tel: 207-396-6278. p. 939

Caplan, Libby, Dir, Idaho Springs Public Library, 219 14th Ave, Idaho Springs, CO, 80452. Tel: 303-567-2020. p. 286

Caples, Joann, Coll Asst, Louisiana College, 1140 College Dr, Pineville, LA, 71359. Tel: 318-487-7143. p. 905

Capley, Brent, Mgr, Miami-Dade Public Library System, Coral Gables Branch, 3443 Segovia St, Coral Gables, FL, 33134. Tel: 305-442-8706. p. 423

Capley, Bryant, Mgr, Miami-Dade Public Library System, Miami Beach Regional, 227 22nd St, Miami Beach, FL, 33139. Tel: 305-535-4219. p. 423

Capobianco, Alexandra, Library & Archives Coord, Allaire Village Inc, 4263 Atlantic Ave, Farmingdale, NJ, 07727. Tel: 732-919-3500. p. 1402

Capocchi, Cecilia, Managing Dir, Historical Society of Haute-Yamaska Library, 135 rue Principale, Granby, QC, J2G 2V1, CANADA. Tel: 450-372-4500. p. 2713

Capone, Andrea, Dir, Canton Public Library, 786 Washington St, Canton, MA, 02021. Tel: 781-821-5027. p. 1009

Capone, Mary Ann, ILL Librn, Ansonia Library, 53 S Cliff St, Ansonia, CT, 06401. Tel: 203-734-6275. p. 301

Caponis, Autherine, Dir, Prichard Public Library, 300 W Love Joy Loop, Prichard, AL, 36610. Tel: 251-452-7847. p. 33

Capote, Melody, Exec Dir, Caribbean Cultural Center Library, 120 E 125th St, New York, NY, 10035. Tel: 212-307-7420. p. 1580

Capozzella, Michele, Dir, Mahopac Public Library, 668 Rte 6, Mahopac, NY, 10541. Tel: 845-628-2009. p. 1567

Cappel, Lisa, Br Mgr, Public Library of Cincinnati & Hamilton County, Monfort Heights, 3825 W Fork Rd, Cincinnati, OH, 45247. Tel: 513-369-4472. p. 1763

Cappeta, Patricia, Children's Serv Coordr, Penn Area Library, 2001 Municipal Court, Harrison City, PA, 15636. Tel: 724-744-4414. p. 1941

Capps, Jennifer, VP, Curatorship & Exhibition, President Benjamin Harrison Research Library, 1230 N Delaware St, Indianapolis, IN, 46202. Tel: 317-631-1888. p. 697

Capps, John, Head, Ref, Bergenfield Public Library, 50 W Clinton Ave, Bergenfield, NJ, 07621-2799. Tel: 201-387-4040. p. 1390

Caprio, Katie, Libr Asst, Rensselaerville Library, 1459 County Rte 351, Rensselaerville, NY, 12147. Tel: 518-797-3949. p. 1626

Caprio, Mark J, Libr Dir, Providence College, One Cunningham Sq, Providence, RI, 02918. Tel: 401-865-1996. p. 2039

Capsuto, Stephanie M, Sci Librn, Amherst College, Keefe Science Library, Science Center, 61 Quadrangle Dr, Amherst, MA, 01002. Tel: 413-542-2076. p. 984

Capuano, Rob, Mgr, Borrower Serv, Colgate University, 13 Oak Dr, Hamilton, NY, 13346-1398. Tel: 315-228-7301. p. 1543

Capuozzo, Steve, Actg Br Mgr, Cleveland Public Library, Fulton, 3545 Fulton Rd, Cleveland, OH, 44109. Tel: 216-623-6969. p. 1768

Capurso, Judith, Asst Librn, Ref, Ulster County Community College, 491 Cottekill Rd, Stone Ridge, NY, 12484. Tel: 845-687-5213. p. 1646

Caputo, Amanda, Health Sci Librn, Sault Area Hospital, 750 Great Northern Rd, Sault Ste. Marie, ON, P6B 2A8, CANADA. Tel: 705-759-3434, Ext 4368. p. 2677

Caputo, Christina, Research & Knowledge Services Mgr, Forefront Library, 200 W Madison St, 2nd Flr, Chicago, IL, 60606. Tel: 312-578-0175. p. 561

Caputo, Corinne, Head, Tech Serv, Westminster College, Reeves Memorial Library, 501 Westminster Ave, Fulton, MO, 65251-1299. Tel: 573-592-5245. p. 1246

Caputo, Lisa, Commun Libr Mgr, Queens Library, Queensboro Hill Community Library, 60-05 Main St, Flushing, NY, 11355. Tel: 718-359-8332. p. 1555

Caputo, Liz, Coord, Ad Serv, Osterhout Free Library, 71 S Franklin St, Wilkes-Barre, PA, 18701. Tel: 570-823-0156. p. 2022

Caputo, Victor, Dir, Bryant Library, Two Paper Mill Rd, Roslyn, NY, 11576. Tel: 516-621-2240. p. 1633

Carabba, Katrina, Br Mgr, Whatcom County Library System, Deming Branch, 5044 Mount Baker Hwy, Deming, WA, 98244. Tel: 360-592-2422. p. 2359

Caradine, Mary L, Librn, Coahoma Community College, 3240 Friars Point Rd, Clarksdale, MS, 38614. Tel: 662-621-4289. p. 1213

Caradine, Tracy, Dir, Carnegie Public Library, 114 Delta Ave, Clarksdale, MS, 38614-4212. Tel: 662-624-4461. p. 1213

Caravello, A, Circ, North Shore Public Library, 250 Rte 25A, Shoreham, NY, 11786-9677. Tel: 631-929-4488. p. 1641

Carbaugh, Cassie, Head, Youth Serv, Grayslake Area Public Library District, 100 Library Lane, Grayslake, IL, 60030. Tel: 847-223-5313. p. 595

Carbiener, Megan, Outreach Supervisory Librn, Apache Junction Public Library, 1177 N Idaho Rd, Apache Junction, AZ, 85119. Tel: 480-474-5498. p. 55

Carbone, Aimee, Tech Serv, North Babylon Public Library, 815 Deer Park Ave, North Babylon, NY, 11703-3812. Tel: 631-669-4020. p. 1607

Carbone, Christopher, Mr, Libr Dir, South Brunswick Public Library, 110 Kingston Lane, Monmouth Junction, NJ, 08852. Tel: 732-329-4000, Ext 7287. p. 1419

Cardell, Katie, Br Mgr, Easton Area Public Library & District Center, Palmer Branch Library, One Weller Pl, Easton, PA, 18045. Tel: 610-258-7492. p. 1928

Cardell, Rashell, District Dir, Fremont County District Library, 420 N Bridge, Ste E, Saint Anthony, ID, 83445. Tel: 208-624-3192. p. 530

Cardell, Rashell, District Dir, Fremont County District Library, Ashton Branch, 925 Main, Ashton, ID, 83420. Tel: 208-652-7280. p. 530

Cardell, Rashell, District Dir, Fremont County District Library, Island Park Branch, 3775 Sand Crane Dr, Island Park, ID, 83429. Tel: 208-558-0991. p. 530

Cardello, Margaret, Dir, Marlborough Public Library, 35 W Main St, Marlborough, MA, 01752-5510. Tel: 508-624-6901. p. 1032

Carden, Barbara, Circ Supvr, Whitworth University, 300 W Hawthorne Rd, Spokane, WA, 99251-0001. Tel: 509-777-3767. p. 2385

Carden, Melanie, Dir, Leeds Jane Culbreth Public Library, 8104 Parkway Dr, Leeds, AL, 35094. Tel: 205-699-5962. p. 23

Carden-Berry, Sandra, Librn, Lallouise Florey McGraw Public Library, 42860 Hwy 25, Vincent, AL, 35178-6156. Tel: 205-672-2749. p. 39

Cardenas, Diana, Dir, Admin Serv, Head, Operations & Budget, Florida International University, 11200 SW Eighth St, Miami, FL, 33199. Tel: 305-348-1900. p. 421

Cardenas, Gabriel, Circ Serv Mgr, West Chicago Public Library District, 118 W Washington St, West Chicago, IL, 60185. Tel: 630-231-1552. p. 660

Cardenas, Hugo, Head, Facility Services, Bloomfield Township Public Library, 1099 Lone Pine Rd, Bloomfield Township, MI, 48302-2410. Tel: 248-642-5800. p. 1086

Cardenas, Jorge, Head Librn, Simon Fraser University - Vancouver Campus, 515 W Hastings St, Vancouver, BC, V6B 5K3, CANADA. Tel: 778-782-5050. p. 2579

Cardenas, Ricardo, Br Mgr, Anythink Libraries, Anythink Commerce City, 7185 Monaco St, Commerce City, CO, 80022. Tel: 303-287-0063. p. 296
Carder, Samantha, Appalachian Campus Librn, Chattahoochee Technical College Library, 980 S Cobb Dr, Marietta, GA, 30060. Tel: 706-253-4571. p. 488
Carder, Samantha, Librn, Library Services, Chattahoochee Technical College Library, Appalachian Campus Library, 100 Campus Dr, Jasper, GA, 30143. Tel: 770-975-4134. p. 488
Cardiff, Catherine, Br Supvr, Greater Victoria Public Library, Oak Bay, 1442 Monterey Ave, Victoria, BC, V8S 4W1, CANADA. Tel: 250-940-4875, Ext 844. p. 2583
Cardillo, Tayla, Br Librn, Cranston Public Library, Oak Lawn Branch, 230 Wilbur Ave, Cranston, RI, 02921-1046. Tel: 401-942-1787. p. 2031
Cardinal, Dawn, Libr Mgr, Paddle Prairie Public Library, Box 58, Paddle Prairie, AB, T0H 2W0, CANADA. Tel: 780-981-3100. p. 2550
Cardinal, Nancy, Ch Serv Librn, Fort Walton Beach Library, 185 Miracle Strip Pkwy SE, Fort Walton Beach, FL, 32548. Tel: 850-833-9590. p. 405
Cardon, Donna L, Dir, Highland City Library, 5400 W Civic Center Dr, Ste 2, Highland, UT, 84003. Tel: 801-772-4529. p. 2264
Cardona, Bonnie, Asst Dir, Operations, University of Texas at El Paso Library, 500 W University Ave, El Paso, TX, 79968-0582. Tel: 915-747-5686. p. 2175
Cardoso, Kristen, Libr Dir, Joseph H Plumb Memorial Library, 17 Constitution Way, Rochester, MA, 02770. Tel: 508-763-8600. p. 1049
Cardoza, Sandy, Media Spec, De Anza College, 21250 Stevens Creek Blvd, Cupertino, CA, 95014-5793. Tel: 408-864-8771. p. 133
Cardwell, Carolyn, Instrul Tech Adminr, Louisville Presbyterian Theological Seminary, 1044 Alta Vista Rd, Louisville, KY, 40205-1798. Tel: 502-895-3411, Ext 422. p. 866
Cardwell, Glenda, Dir, Rockford Public Library, 100 Main St, Rockford, AL, 35136. Tel: 256-377-4911. p. 34
Cardwell, Mary E, Librn, Roosevelt Public Library, 27 W Fulton Ave, Roosevelt, NY, 11575. Tel: 516-378-0222. p. 1633
Careaga, Greg, Head, Assessment & Planning, University of California, 1156 High St, Santa Cruz, CA, 95064. Tel: 831-459-3687. p. 243
Carek, Jacqie, Libr Mgr, Mannville Centennial Public Library, 5029 50 St, Mannville, AB, T0B 2W0, CANADA. Tel: 780-763-3611. p. 2547
Carew, Jill, Adjunct Librn, Harrisburg Area Community College, 2010 Pennsylvania Ave, York, PA, 17404. Tel: 717-801-3220. p. 2026
Carey, Diane, Asst Librn, Kennedy Free Library, 649 Second St, Kennedy, NY, 14747. Tel: 716-267-4265. p. 1559
Carey, Dianne, Ref Serv, Olympic College, 1600 Chester Ave, Bremerton, WA, 98337. Tel: 360-475-7250. p. 2360
Carey, Dylan, Technology Spec, Ronan Library District, 203 Main St SW, Ronan, MT, 59864. Tel: 406-676-3682. p. 1301
Carey, Ian, Curator, Permanent Art Coll, Indiana State University, 510 North 6 1/2 St, Terre Haute, IN, 47809. Tel: 812-237-3700. p. 720
Carey, Janice, Supvr, Canadian Centre for Occupational Health & Safety, 135 Hunter St E, Hamilton, ON, L8N 1M5, CANADA. Tel: 905-572-2981, Ext 4454. p. 2644
Carey, John, Head of Libr, Hunter College Libraries, Health Professions Library, Hunter College Brookdale Campus, 425 E 25th St, New York, NY, 10010. Tel: 212-481-5117. p. 1588
Carey, Mercedes, Budget & Coll Develop Mgr, LeRoy Collins Leon County Public Library System, 200 W Park Ave, Tallahassee, FL, 32301-7720. Tel: 850-606-2665. p. 445
Carey Nevin, Judy, Dir, Libr Serv, Ohio University-Lancaster Library, 1570 Granville Pike, Lancaster, OH, 43130-1097. Tel: 740-681-3351. p. 1794
Carey, Paula, Ref Libr, Boston University Libraries, Science & Engineering Library, 38 Cummington St, Boston, MA, 02215. Tel: 617-358-3963. p. 994
Carey, Sean, Law Librn, Connecticut Judicial Branch Law Libraries, Hartford Law Library, Hartford Courthouse, 95 Washington St, Hartford, CT, 06106. Tel: 860-548-2866. p. 316
Carey, Susan, Libr Dir, Ear Falls Public Library, Two Willow Crescent, Ear Falls, ON, P0V 1T0, CANADA. Tel: 807-222-3209. p. 2639
Carey, Teresa, Asst Dir, Circ Tech, El Reno Carnegie Library, 215 E Wade St, El Reno, OK, 73036-2753. Tel: 405-262-2409. p. 1846
Carey, Tracy, Dir, Pub Serv, Centre County Library & Historical Museum, 200 N Allegheny St, Bellefonte, PA, 16823-1601. Tel: 814-355-1516. p. 1910
Cargo, John, Tech Coordr, Iosco-Arenac District Library, 120 W Westover St, East Tawas, MI, 48730. Tel: 989-362-2651. p. 1102
Cariello, Nancy, Head, Circ, Hampton Bays Public Library, 52 Ponquogue Ave, Hampton Bays, NY, 11946. Tel: 631-728-6241. p. 1544
Cariker, Sarah, Ref Serv, Public Library of Enid & Garfield County, 120 W Maine, Enid, OK, 73701-5606. Tel: 580-234-6313. p. 1847
Carini, Peter, Col Archivist, Dartmouth College Library, Rauner Special Collections Library, 6065 Webster Hall, Hanover, NH, 03755-3519. Tel: 603-646-0538. p. 1367
Carkuff, Maria, Librn, Arizona Department of Corrections - Adult Institutions, 7125 E Juan Sanchez Blvd, San Luis, AZ, 85349. Tel: 928-627-8871. p. 76
Carl, Bonnie, Libr Dir, Milltown Public Library, 61 W Main St, Milltown, WI, 54858. Tel: 715-825-2313. p. 2457
Carla, Waldrup, Librn, Haleyville Public Library, 913 20th St, Haleyville, AL, 35565. Tel: 205-486-7450. p. 20
Carle, Daria, Ref & Instruction, University of Alaska Anchorage, Consortium Library, 3211 Providence Dr, Anchorage, AK, 99508-8176. Tel: 907-786-1871. p. 43
Carle, Heidimarie, Dir & Librn, Rensselaerville Library, 1459 County Rte 351, Rensselaerville, NY, 12147. Tel: 518-797-3949. p. 1626
Carle, Jane R, Dir, Kirtland Public Library, 9267 Chillicothe Rd, Kirtland, OH, 44094. Tel: 440-256-7323. p. 1793
Carle, Mary-Jane, Ch, Bill Memorial Library, 240 Monument St, Groton, CT, 06340. Tel: 860-445-0392. p. 314
Carle, Melissa, Dir, Info Syst, Kansas City Library Service Program, Kansas City Public Library, 14 W Tenth St, Kansas City, MO, 64105-1702. Tel: 816-701-3520. p. 2769
Carlene, Morrison, Dir, Independence County Library, 267 E Main St, Batesville, AR, 72501. Tel: 870-793-8814. p. 89
Carles, Pam, Access Serv Coordr, The University of Findlay, 1000 N Main St, Findlay, OH, 45840-3695. Tel: 419-434-4612. p. 1785
Carleton, Don, Dr, Dir, University of Texas at Austin, Briscoe Center, 3738 FM 2714, Round Top, TX, 78954-4901. Tel: 979-278-3530. p. 2234
Carleton, Don E, Dr, Exec Dir, University of Texas Libraries, Briscoe Center for American History, Sid Richard Hall, Unit 2, Rm 2106, 2300 Red River St, Austin, TX, 78712-1426. Tel: 512-495-4515. p. 2142
Carliff, Alice, Br Mgr, Stanly County Public Library, Oakboro Branch, 214 S Main St, Oakboro, NC, 28129. Tel: 704-485-4310. p. 1671
Carlile, Pamela, Br Mgr, New Braunfels Public Library, Westside Community Center, 2932 S IH 35 Frontage Rd, New Braunfels, TX, 78130. Tel: 830-221-4301. p. 2222
Carlile, Pamela, Commun Br Supvr, New Braunfels Public Library, 700 E Common St, New Braunfels, TX, 78130-5689. Tel: 830-221-4316. p. 2222
Carlin, Aaron, Asst Dir of Br, Rockford Public Library, 214 N Church St, Rockford, IL, 61101-1023. Tel: 815-965-7606. p. 642
Carlin, Aaron, Br Mgr, Rockford Public Library, Montague, 1238 S Winnebago St, Rockford, IL, 61102-2944. Tel: 815-965-7606, Ext 739. p. 642
Carlin, Anna, Instrul Tech Librn, Florida Gulf Coast University Library, 10501 FGCU Blvd S, Fort Myers, FL, 33965. Tel: 239-590-7663. p. 403
Carlin, Donna, Br Mgr, DeKalb County Public Library, Henagar Branch, 17163 Alabama Hwy 75, Henagar, AL, 35978. Tel: 256-657-1380. p. 18
Carlin, Emily, Librn, Sisters of Charity Hospital, 2157 Main St, Buffalo, NY, 14215. Tel: 716-862-1256. p. 1510
Carlin, Jane A, Libr Dir, University of Puget Sound, 1604 N Warner St, Upper Loading Dock, Tacoma, WA, 98416. Tel: 253-879-3118. p. 2387
Carlin, Jo Anne, Circ, Gilpin County Public Library District, 15131 Hwy 119, Black Hawk, CO, 80422. Tel: 303-582-5777. p. 266
Carlin, Sarah, Ref Serv Librn, YA Librn, Scott County Library System, 200 N Sixth Ave, Eldridge, IA, 52748. Tel: 563-285-4794. p. 750
Carline, Emily, Br Mgr, Iberville Parish Library, Bayou Pigeon, 36625 Hwy 75, Plaquemine, LA, 70764. Tel: 225-545-8567. p. 906
Carline, Emily, Br Mgr, Iberville Parish Library, Bayou Sorrel, 33415 Hwy 75, Plaquemine, LA, 70764. Tel: 225-659-7055. p. 906
Carlis, Julia, Sr Libr Mgr, Washington County Library, R H Stafford Branch, 8595 Central Park Pl, Woodbury, MN, 55125-9613. Tel: 651-731-1320. p. 1210
Carlis, Julia, Sr Libr Mgr, Washington County Library, Valley Branch, 380 St Croix Trail S, Lakeland, MN, 55043. Tel: 651-436-5882. p. 1210
Carlisle, John, Cataloger, Librn, Southern Union State Community College, 750 Robert St, Wadley, AL, 36276. Tel: 256-395-2211, Ext 5130. p. 39
Carlisle, Molly, Dir, Garden Home Community Library, 7475 SW Oleson Rd, Portland, OR, 97223. Tel: 503-245-9932. p. 1891
Carlisle, Pam, Outreach/Educ, Bossier Parish Libraries, History Center, 2206 Beckett St, Bossier City, LA, 71111. Tel: 318-746-7717. p. 886
Carlisle, Tara, Coll Develop Librn, Shepherd University, 301 N King St, Shepherdstown, WV, 25443. Tel: 304-876-5302. p. 2414
Carlito, Delores, Ref Librn, Instruction & Outreach, University of Alabama at Birmingham, Mervyn H Sterne Library, 917 13th St S, Birmingham, AL, 35205. Tel: 205-934-6364. p. 9
Carll, Lynette, Educ Coordr, Bradford Regional Medical Center, 116 Interstate Pkwy, Bradford, PA, 16701. Tel: 814-368-4143. p. 1914
Carlock, Barbara, Mgr, Sheridan County Public Library System, Clearmont Branch, 1254 Front St, Clearmont, WY, 82835. Tel: 307-758-4331. p. 2499
Carlock, Sherry, Asst Librn, Sallie Logan Public Library, 1808 Walnut St, Murphysboro, IL, 62966. Tel: 618-684-3271. p. 622
Carloni, Thomas, Dir, Elma Public Library, 1860 Bowen Rd, Elma, NY, 14059. Tel: 716-652-2719. p. 1530
Carlos, Andrew, Sr Asst Librn, California State University, East Bay Library, CSU East Bay Library, 25800 Carlos Bee Blvd, Hayward, CA, 94542-3052. Tel: 510-885-2303. p. 150
Carlotta, Justine, Mgr, Children's Dept, Westchester Public Library, 200 W Indiana Ave, Chesterton, IN, 46304. Tel: 219-926-7696. p. 674
Carls, Trenton, Archivist, Head Librn, Cape Ann Museum Library & Archives, 27 Pleasant St, Gloucester, MA, 01930. Tel: 978-283-0455, Ext 119. p. 1021

Carlson, Alexis, Ref/Outreach Librn, Indian River State College, 3209 Virginia Ave, Fort Pierce, FL, 34981-5599. Tel: 772-462-7194. p. 404

Carlson, Alexis, Ref/Outreach Librn, Indian River State College, Dixon Hendry Campus Library, 2229 NW Ninth Ave, Okeechobee, FL, 34972. Tel: 863-462-7194. p. 404

Carlson, Alissa, Libr Asst, Avoca Free Library, 18 N Main St, Avoca, NY, 14809. Tel: 607-566-9279. p. 1489

Carlson, Amy, Ch Serv, Granville County Library System, 210 Main St, Oxford, NC, 27565-3321. Tel: 919-693-1121. p. 1707

Carlson, Anna, Pub Serv Mgr, Granville Public Library, 217 E Broadway, Granville, OH, 43023-1398. Tel: 740-587-0196. p. 1788

Carlson, Autumn, Co-Dir, Central Plains Library System, 2727 W Second St, Ste 233, Hastings, NE, 68901. Tel: 402-462-1975. p. 1317

Carlson, Barbara L, Ch Serv, Lyme Public Library, 482 Hamburg Rd, Lyme, CT, 06371-3110. Tel: 860-434-2272. p. 320

Carlson, Catie, Libr Dir, University of Cincinnati, 4200 Clermont College Dr, Batavia, OH, 45103-1785. Tel: 513-732-5233. p. 1749

Carlson, Debra, Ch Serv, Lied Scottsbluff Public Library, 1809 Third Ave, Scottsbluff, NE, 69361-2493. Tel: 308-630-6284. p. 1335

Carlson, Elizabeth, Librn, Gardner Public Library, 114 W Third St, Wakefield, NE, 68784. Tel: 402-287-2334. p. 1339

Carlson, Erik, Libr Dir, Dobbs Ferry Public Library, 55 Main St, Dobbs Ferry, NY, 10522. Tel: 914-693-6614. p. 1526

Carlson, Frances, Libr Dir, Louisiana House of Representatives, 900 N Third St, Baton Rouge, LA, 70804. Tel: 225-342-2430. p. 883

Carlson, Gayle B, Libr Dir, East Hanover Township Free Public Library, 415 Ridgedale Ave, East Hanover, NJ, 07936. Tel: 973-888-6095. p. 1399

Carlson, Jennifer, Ch, Holliston Public Library, 752 Washington St, Holliston, MA, 01746. Tel: 508-429-0617. p. 1025

Carlson, Jennifer, Instruction & Outreach Librn, Concordia University, 1282 Concordia Ave, Saint Paul, MN, 55104. Tel: 651-641-8770. p. 1199

Carlson, Jessica, Libr Dir, Montana Bible College, 100 Discovery Dr, Bozeman, MT, 59718. Tel: 406-586-3585, Ext 25. p. 1289

Carlson, Jody, Dir, Grant County Public Library, 207 E Park Ave, Milbank, SD, 57252. Tel: 605-432-6543. p. 2079

Carlson, Jonathan, Sci Librn, Saint John's University, 2835 Abbey Plaza, Collegeville, MN, 56321. Tel: 320-363-2579. p. 1170

Carlson, Jonathan, Sci Librn, College of Saint Benedict, 37 S College Ave, Saint Joseph, MN, 56374. Tel: 320-363-2579. p. 1199

Carlson, Joshua, Youth Serv, White Plains Public Library, 100 Martine Ave, White Plains, NY, 10601. Tel: 914-422-1400. p. 1665

Carlson, Julie, Br Mgr, Cameron Parish Library, Johnson Bayou, 4586 Gulf Beach Hwy, Cameron, LA, 70631. Tel: 337-569-2892. p. 886

Carlson, Kerry, Library Instruction & Electronic Res, Suffolk County Community College, 1001 Crooked Hill Rd, Brentwood, NY, 11717. Tel: 631-851-6349. p. 1496

Carlson, Linda, Library Contact, Ballad Health, 130 W Ravine Rd, Kingsport, TN, 37660. Tel: 423-224-6870. p. 2104

Carlson, Mark, Br Mgr, Tulsa City-County Library, Charles Page Branch, 551 E Fourth St, Sand Springs, OK, 74063. p. 1866

Carlson, Mary, Med Librn, M Health Fairview Southdale Hospital, 6401 France Ave S, Edina, MN, 55435. Tel: 952-924-5005. p. 1174

Carlson, Michael, Dir, Gilpin County Public Library District, 15131 Hwy 119, Black Hawk, CO, 80422. Tel: 303-582-5777. p. 266

Carlson, Nancy, Circ Supvr, Burton Public Library, 14588 W Park St, Burton, OH, 44021. Tel: 440-834-4466. p. 1753

Carlson, Paula, Circ, Trumbull Library System, Fairchild Nichols Memorial, 1718 Huntington Tpk, Trumbull, CT, 06611. Tel: 203-452-5196. p. 342

Carlson, Robert, Br Mgr, San Francisco Public Library, Presidio Branch Library, 3150 Sacramento St, San Francisco, CA, 94115-2006. Tel: 415-355-2880. p. 228

Carlson, Susan, Libr Dir, Mason County District Library, 217 E Ludington Ave, Ludington, MI, 49431. Tel: 231-843-8465. p. 1127

Carlson, Tanya, Tech Serv, Skadden, Arps, Slate, Meagher & Flom LLP Library, 155 N Wacker Dr, Suite 2700, Chicago, IL, 60606. Tel: 312-407-0700, 312-407-0925. p. 568

Carlson-Prandini, Suzanne, Ad, Bellingham Public Library, 210 Central Ave, Bellingham, WA, 98225. Tel: 360-778-7236. p. 2358

Carlstrom, Judith, Head, Tech Serv, The State Library of Massachusetts, State House, Rm 341, 24 Beacon St, Boston, MA, 02133. Tel: 617-727-2590. p. 1000

Carlton, Hannah, Ref & Instruction Librn, Saint Ambrose University Library, 518 W Locust St, Davenport, IA, 52803. Tel: 563-333-6474. p. 744

Carlton, Pam, Ch, Missoula Public Library, 301 E Main, Missoula, MT, 59802-4799. Tel: 406-721-2665. p. 1300

Carlton, Sandra, Br Mgr, Cape May County Library, Wildwood Crest Branch, 6300 Atlantic Ave., Wildwood Crest, NJ, 08260. Tel: 609-522-0564. p. 1395

Carlucci, Kerry, Head, Tech Serv, Marlborough Public Library, 35 W Main St, Marlborough, MA, 01752-5510. Tel: 508-624-6900. p. 1032

Carmack, Dani, Res & Instruction Librn, Embry-Riddle Aeronautical University, 3700 Willow Creek Rd, Prescott, AZ, 86301-3720. Tel: 928-777-3858. p. 73

Carmack, Joyce, Libr Dir, Martin Township Public Library, 132 W Main St, Colfax, IL, 61728. Tel: 309-723-2541. p. 573

Carmack, Tony, Sr Librn, Placer County Library, Rocklin Branch, 4890 Granite Dr, Rocklin, CA, 95677. Tel: 916-624-3133. p. 118

Carman, Ben, Librn II, Plattsburgh Public Library, 19 Oak St, Plattsburgh, NY, 12901. Tel: 518-563-0921. p. 1619

Carman, Elsworth, Dir, Iowa City Public Library, 123 S Linn St, Iowa City, IA, 52240. Tel: 319-356-5241. p. 760

Carman, Sara, Librn, Pine Technical & Community College Library, 900 Fourth St SE, Pine City, MN, 55063. Tel: 320-629-5169. p. 1192

Carman, Stephanie, Dir, Elizabethtown Library Association, 8256 River St, Elizabethtown, NY, 12932. Tel: 518-873-2670. p. 1529

Carmical, Ethel, Dir, Humphreys County Public Library, 201 Pavo St, Waverly, TN, 37185-1529. Tel: 931-296-2143. p. 2129

Carmichael, Beverly, Chair, Windham Town Library, 7071 Windham Hill Rd, Windham, VT, 05359. Tel: 802-875-4874. p. 2299

Carmichael, Christine, Sr Ref & Instruction Librn, Creighton University, 2500 California Plaza, Omaha, NE, 68178-0209. Tel: 402-280-1757. p. 1328

Carmichael, Lisandra, Dr, Dean, Georgia Southern University, 11935 Abercorn St, Savannah, GA, 31419. Tel: 912-478-5116. p. 495

Carmichael, Lisandra R, Dr, Dean of Libr, Georgia Southern University, 1400 Southern Dr, Statesboro, GA, 30458. Tel: 912-478-5115. p. 497

Carmichael, Lyndsey, Archivist, Rotary Club of Slave Lake Public Library, 50 Main St SW, Slave Lake, AB, T0G 2A0, CANADA. Tel: 780-849-5250. p. 2554

Carmichael, Shelby, Dir, Libr Serv, Blue Mountain College, 201 W Main St, Blue Mountain, MS, 38610. Tel: 662-685-4771, Ext 147. p. 1212

Carmody, Steve, Regional Mgr, Libr Serv, Pierce County Library System, Fife Branch, 6622 20th St E, Fife, WA, 98424. Tel: 253-548-3323. p. 2386

Carmona, Yann, Lit Develop Assoc, French Institute-Alliance Francaise Library, 22 E 60th St, New York, NY, 10022-1011. Tel: 646-388-6639. p. 1586

Carmoney, Sheila, Librn, Axtell Public Library, 305 N Main St, Axtell, NE, 68924. Tel: 308-743-2592. p. 1306

Carner, Ashleigh, Librn, Southern Technical College, 1685 Medical Lane, Fort Myers, FL, 33907. Tel: 239-939-4766, Ext 1403. p. 404

Carner, Dorothy, Librn, University of Missouri-Columbia, Columbia Missourian Newspaper Library, School of Journalism, 315 Lee Hills Hall, Columbia, MO, 65205. Tel: 573-882-6591. p. 1243

Carner, Dorothy J, Head, Journalism Libr, University of Missouri-Columbia, Frank Lee Martin Memorial Journalism Library, 449 S Ninth St, 102 Reynolds Journalism Institute, Columbia, MO, 65211. Tel: 573-882-7502. p. 1244

Carnes, Lee Elliott, Libr Mgr, K&L Gates Law Library, Hearst Tower, 214 N Tryon St, 47th Flr, Charlotte, NC, 28202. Tel: 704-331-7553. p. 1680

Carnevale, Angelina, Ch Serv, Guilford Free Library, 67 Park St, Guilford, CT, 06437. Tel: 203-453-8282. p. 315

Carney, Erin, Info Literacy Librn, Holy Family University Library, 9801 Frankford Ave, Philadelphia, PA, 19114. Tel: 267-341-3312. p. 1981

Carney, Susan, Libr Mgr, Timberland Regional Library, Ilwaco Branch, 158 First Ave N, Ilwaco, WA, 98624. Tel: 360-642-3908. p. 2389

Carney-Smith, Jessie, PhD, Librn Emeritus, Fisk University, 1000 17th Ave N, Nashville, TN, 37208-3051. Tel: 615-329-8730. p. 2118

Carnley, Rebecca M, Mrs, Mgr, Res Serv, Balch & Bingham LLP Library, 1901 Sixth Ave N, Ste 1500, Birmingham, AL, 35203. Tel: 205-251-8100. p. 7

Carns, Paula Mae, Dr, Head, Lit & Lang Libr, University of Illinois Library at Urbana-Champaign, Literatures & Languages, 225 Main Library, MC-522, 1408 W Gregory Dr, Urbana, IL, 61801. Tel: 217-333-0076. p. 656

Caro, Susanne, Govt Info Librn, North Dakota State University Libraries, 1201 Albrecht Blvd, Fargo, ND, 58108. Tel: 701-231-8863. p. 1733

Carol, Robin, Communications Mgr, Johnson County Library, 9875 W 87th St, Overland Park, KS, 66212. Tel: 913-826-4600. p. 830

Carolan, Mary Lou, Dir, Newburgh Free Library, 124 Grand St, Newburgh, NY, 12550. Tel: 845-563-3605. p. 1606

Caroli, Carlo, Circ, A T Still University, Kirksville Campus, 800 W Jefferson St, Kirksville, MO, 63501. Tel: 660-626-2345. p. 1258

Carollo, Cheryl, Ch Serv, Currituck County Public Library, 4261 Caratoke Hwy, Barco, NC, 27917-9707. Tel: 252-453-8345. p. 1673

Caron, Josephine, Sr Librn, Long Beach Public Library, Dana, 3680 Atlantic Ave, Long Beach, CA, 90807. Tel: 562-570-1042. p. 159

Caron, Susan, Dir of Coll, Toronto Public Library, 789 Yonge St, Toronto, ON, M4W 2G8, CANADA. Tel: 416-393-7131. p. 2693

Caron, Taylor, Ms, Libr Dir, Salmo Valley Public Library, 104 Fourth St, Salmo, BC, V0G 1Z0, CANADA. Tel: 250-357-2312. p. 2575

Carpenter, Abby, Exec Dir, Florence-Lauderdale Public Library, 350 N Wood Ave, Florence, AL, 35630. Tel: 256-764-6564. p. 17

Carpenter, Ann, Youth Serv Librn, Brooks Free Library, 739 Main St, Harwich, MA, 02645. Tel: 508-430-7562. p. 1023

Carpenter, Brian, Curator, American Philosophical Society Library, 105 S Fifth St, Philadelphia, PA, 19106-3386. Tel: 215-440-3400. p. 1974

Carpenter, Charlotte, Dir, Bentleyville Public Library, 931 Main St, Bentleyville, PA, 15314-1119. Tel: 724-239-5122. p. 1910
Carpenter, Coleen, Head, Circ, Mount Kisco Public Library, 100 E Main St, Mount Kisco, NY, 10549. Tel: 914-864-0131. p. 1574
Carpenter, Diane, Library Contact, Alton Library, 516 Nicholas Ave, Alton, KS, 67623. p. 795
Carpenter, Elizabeth, Librn, Public Library of Mount Vernon & Knox County, Gambier Public, 115 Meadow Lane, Gambier, OH, 43022. Tel: 740-427-2665. p. 1805
Carpenter, Elizabeth, Mgr, Public Library of Mount Vernon & Knox County, Danville Public, 512 S Market St, Danville, OH, 43014-9609. Tel: 740-599-2665. p. 1805
Carpenter, Judy, Ch, Penfield Public Library, 1985 Baird Rd, Penfield, NY, 14526. Tel: 585-340-8720. p. 1616
Carpenter, Kathryn, Assoc Univ Librn, Health Sci Librn, University of Illinois at Chicago, MC 234, 801 S Morgan St, Chicago, IL, 60607. Tel: 312-996-8974. p. 570
Carpenter, Kathryn, Asst Univ Librn, University of Illinois at Chicago, Library of the Health Sciences, Chicago, 1750 W Polk St, Chicago, IL, 60612. Tel: 312-996-8966. p. 570
Carpenter, Laurie, Dir, Orono Public Library, 39 Pine St, Orono, ME, 04473. Tel: 207-866-5060, Ext 300. p. 934
Carpenter, Leigh, Head Librn, Bellaire Public Library, 111 S Bridge St, Bellaire, MI, 49615-9566. Tel: 231-533-8814. p. 1084
Carpenter, Lorene, Dir, Webster-Addison Public Library, 331 S Main St, Webster Springs, WV, 26288. Tel: 304-847-5764. p. 2416
Carpenter, Lorenza, Libr Asst, Imperial County Free Library, Holtville Branch, 101 E Sixth St, Holtville, CA, 92250. Tel: 760-356-2385. p. 140
Carpenter, Lynn, Dir, Lake Benton Public Library, 110 E Benton St, Lake Benton, MN, 56149. Tel: 507-368-4641, Ext 3. p. 1179
Carpenter, Mary, Support Serv Mgr, Council Bluffs Public Library, 400 Willow Ave, Council Bluffs, IA, 51503-9042. Tel: 712-323-7553, Ext 5425. p. 742
Carpenter, Mary, Regional Libr Dir, Tennessee State Library & Archives, 403 Seventh Ave N, Nashville, TN, 37243-0312. Tel: 731-587-2347. p. 2121
Carpenter, Meghan, Ch, Sylvester Memorial Wellston Public Library, 135 E Second St, Wellston, OH, 45692. Tel: 740-384-6660. p. 1829
Carpenter, Mildred, Lead Multi-Media Tech, Allan Hancock College, 800 S College Dr, Santa Maria, CA, 93455. Tel: 805-922-6966, Ext 3637. p. 243
Carpenter, Peggy, Librn, Zeigler Public Library, 102 E Maryland St, Zeigler, IL, 62999. Tel: 618-596-2041. p. 665
Carpenter, Renee, Circ Mgr, Mercer County District Library, 303 N Main St, Celina, OH, 45822. Tel: 419-586-4442. p. 1757
Carpenter, Rob, Br Mgr, Herrick District Library, North Branch, 155 Riley St, Holland, MI, 49424. Tel: 616-738-4365. p. 1115
Carpenter, Sarah, Outreach & Programming Librn, Brodhead Memorial Public Library, 1207 25th St, Brodhead, WI, 53520. Tel: 608-897-4070. p. 2425
Carpenter, Susan, Dir, Earle A Rainwater Memorial Library, 124 Ninth Ave SW, Childersburg, AL, 35044. Tel: 256-378-7239. p. 12
Carpenter, Van E, Libr Dir, South University, Nine Science Ct, Columbia, SC, 29203. Tel: 803-935-4336. p. 2055
Carr, Alan F, Assoc Dir, University of California Los Angeles Library, Louise M Darling Biomedical Library, 12-077 Ctr for the Health Sciences, Los Angeles, CA, 90095. Tel: 310-825-7263. p. 169
Carr, Allison, Academic Transitions Librn, California State University, 333 S Twin Oaks Valley Rd, San Marcos, CA, 92096. Tel: 760-750-4348. p. 234
Carr Allmon, Jennifer, Exec Dir, Catholic Archives of Texas, 6225 Hwy 290 E, Austin, TX, 78723. Tel: 512-476-6296. p. 2139
Carr, Amber, Asst Libr Dir, Missouri Southern State University, 3950 E Newman Rd, Joplin, MO, 64801-1595. Tel: 417-625-3124. p. 1253
Carr, Ashley, Asst Head Librn, Austin Community College, Highland Campus Library, 6101 Airport Blvd, 1st Flr, Rm 1325, Austin, TX, 78752. Tel: 512-223-7389. p. 2138
Carr, Barbara, Cat, Johnson C Smith University, 100 Beatties Ford Rd, Charlotte, NC, 28216. Tel: 704-371-6731, 704-371-6740. p. 1680
Carr, Barbara, Dir, Moomau Grant County Library, 18 Mountain View St, Petersburg, WV, 26847. Tel: 304-257-4122. p. 2412
Carr, Brenda, Acq Librn, United States Naval War College Library, 686 Cushing Rd, Newport, RI, 02841-1207. Tel: 401-841-6494. p. 2035
Carr, Brian, Libr Asst, C G Jung Institute of San Francisco, 2040 Gough St, San Francisco, CA, 94109. Tel: 415-771-8055, Ext 207. p. 225
Carr, Coleen, Acq, Rider University, 2083 Lawrenceville Rd, Lawrenceville, NJ, 08648. p. 1411
Carr, Dana, Br Librn, Moomau Grant County Library, Allegheny-Mountain Top, 8455 Union Hwy, Mount Storm, WV, 26739. Tel: 304-693-7504. p. 2412
Carr, Donald, Tech Learning Specialist, Virginia Peninsula Community College Library, 227C Kecoughtan Hall, 99 Thomas Nelson Dr, Hampton, VA, 23666. Tel: 757-825-6503. p. 2323
Carr, Gina, Libr Assoc, Illinois School for the Visually Impaired Library, 658 E State St, Jacksonville, IL, 62650-2130. Tel: 217-479-4471. p. 602
Carr, Gregory C, Br Mgr, Las Vegas-Clark County Library District, Summerlin Library & Performing Arts Center, 1771 Inner Circle Dr, Las Vegas, NV, 89134. Tel: 702-507-3860. p. 1347
Carr, Jean, Dir, Vernon Free Library, 567 Governor Hunt Rd, Vernon, VT, 05354. Tel: 802-257-0150. p. 2296
Carr, Jennifer, Librn, Crittenden County Library, Turrell Branch, 52 Flippo St, Turrell, AR, 72384. Tel: 870-343-4005. p. 104
Carr, John J, Dir, Brumback Library, 215 W Main St, Van Wert, OH, 45891-1695. Tel: 419-238-2168. p. 1827
Carr, Lauren, Actg Dir, Catawba Hospital, 5525 Catawba Hospital Dr, Catawba, VA, 24070. Tel: 540-375-4281. p. 2309
Carr, Lisa, Dir, Seymour Public Library District, 176-178 Genesee St, Auburn, NY, 13021. Tel: 315-252-2571. p. 1489
Carr, Marcia, Br Mgr, Door County Library, Washington Island Branch, Main & Lakeview Rds, Washington Island, WI, 54246. Tel: 920-847-2323. p. 2480
Carr, Marietta, Librn, Schenectady County Historical Society, 32 Washington Ave, Schenectady, NY, 12305. Tel: 518-374-0263, Ext 3. p. 1638
Carr, Meagan, Dir, Littleton Public Library, 92 Main St, Littleton, NH, 03561-1238. Tel: 603-444-5741. p. 1371
Carr, Meagan, Youth Serv Librn, Lancaster Public Library, 5466 Broadway, Lancaster, NY, 14086. Tel: 716-683-1120. p. 1562
Carr, Melissa, Br Librn, Mendocino County Library District, Ukiah Main Library, 105 N Main St, Ukiah, CA, 95482. Tel: 707-463-4490. p. 254
Carr, Patrick, Prog Mgr, Connecticut State College & University Library Consortium, 61 Woodland St, Hartford, CT, 06105. Tel: 860-723-0168. p. 2762
Carr, Peggy, Circ, Liberty Municipal Library, 1710 Sam Houston Ave, Liberty, TX, 77575-4741. Tel: 936-336-8901. p. 2211
Carr, Sharon, Ad, Wayne Public Library, Robert B & Mary Y Benthack Library-Senior Ctr, 410 Pearl St, Wayne, NE, 68787. Tel: 402-375-3135. p. 1340
Carr, Stella, Principal Libr Asst, Metuchen Public Library, 480 Middlesex Ave, Metuchen, NJ, 08840. Tel: 732-632-8526. p. 1418
Carr, Steven, Br Mgr, Arlington County Department of Libraries, Glencarlyn, 300 S Kensington St, Arlington, VA, 22204. Tel: 703-228-6548. p. 2305
Carr, Tracy, Dir, Libr Serv Bur, Mississippi Library Commission, 3881 Eastwood Dr, Jackson, MS, 39211. Tel: 601-432-4450. p. 1222
Carr, Vicki, Asst Librn, South Macon Public Library District, 451 W Glenn St, Macon, IL, 62544. Tel: 217-764-3356. p. 612
Carr-Payne, Ella, Res Libr Adminr, Framatome Inc, 3315 Old Forest Rd, Lynchburg, VA, 24501. Tel: 434-832-2476. p. 2330
Carr-Wiggin, Anne, Mgr, NEOS Library Consortium, 5-07 Cameron Library, University of Alberta, Edmonton, AB, T6G 2J8, CANADA. Tel: 780-492-0075. p. 2777
Carranza, Amanda, Br Supvr, Saint Lucie County Library System, 101 Melody Lane, Fort Pierce, FL, 34950-4402. Tel: 772-462-1607. p. 405
Carranza, John, Head, Library Facilities, Ela Area Public Library District, 275 Mohawk Trail, Lake Zurich, IL, 60047. Tel: 847-438-3433. p. 607
Carrasco, Rita, Mgr, Contra Costa County Library, Moraga Library, 1500 Saint Mary's Rd, Moraga, CA, 94556. Tel: 925-376-6852. p. 174
Carrasco-Vigil, Amanda, Libr Dir, Bosque Farms Public Library, 1455 W Bosque Loop, Bosque Farms, NM, 87068. Tel: 505-869-2227. p. 1464
Carrataca, Emma, Librn, Woodstock Hospital Regional Library Services, Woodstock Hospital, 310 Juliana Dr, Woodstock, ON, N4V 0A4, CANADA. Tel: 519-421-4233, Ext 2735. p. 2778
Carraway, Shawn, Syst Librn, Midlands Technical College Library, Beltline Library, 316 S Beltline Blvd, 2nd Flr, Columbia, SC, 29205. Tel: 803-738-7734. p. 2072
Carreau, Annie, Team Leader, Bibliothèque du CISSS de l'Outaouais, CISSS de l'Outaouais - Hôpital Pierre-Janet, 20 rue Pharand, Gatineau, QC, J9A 1K7, CANADA. Tel: 819-966-6050. p. 2712
Carreau, Annie, ILL, Centre Hospitalier des Vallees de l'Outaouais Bibliotheque, 116, Blvd Lionel-Emond, local C-001, Gatineau, QC, J8Y 1W7, CANADA. Tel: 819-966-6050. p. 2713
Carreiro, Mary, Asst Librn, Headingley Municipal Library, 49 Alboro St, Headingley, MB, R4J 1A3, CANADA. Tel: 204-888-5410. p. 2587
Carreon, Brittany, Libr Asst, La Marque Public Library, 1011 Bayou Rd, La Marque, TX, 77568-4195. Tel: 409-938-9270. p. 2207
Carreon, Martha, Ch Serv, El Progreso Memorial Library, 301 W Main St, Uvalde, TX, 78801. Tel: 830-278-2017. p. 2251
Carreras-Hubbard, Karen, Coordr, Libr Serv, Berkshire Community College, 1350 West St, Pittsfield, MA, 01201. Tel: 413-236-2153. p. 1046
Carrick, Greta, Dir, Palmer Public Library, 2115 Main St, Palmer, TN, 37365-9999. Tel: 931-779-5292. p. 2123
Carrico, Kent, Bus Outreach Librn, Benedictine University Library, 5700 College Rd, Lisle, IL, 60532-0900. Tel: 630-829-6055. p. 610
Carrico, Mandy, Libr Dir, Tolleson Public Library, 9555 W Van Buren St, Tolleson, AZ, 85353. Tel: 623-936-2746. p. 80
Carrier, Jean, Libr Mgr, Pikes Peak Library District, Monument Library, 1706 Lake Woodmoor Dr, Monument, CO, 80132-9074. Tel: 719-531-6333, Ext 6061. p. 271
Carrier, Jean, Libr Mgr, Pikes Peak Library District, Palmer Lake Library, 66 Lower Glenway, Palmer Lake, CO, 80133. p. 271

Carrier, Nancy, Chief Exec Officer, Head Librn, Red Rock Public Library Board, 42 Salls St, Red Rock, ON, P0T 2P0, CANADA. Tel: 807-886-2558. p. 2675

Carrier, Raymond, Chef de Div, Bibliotheques de Montreal, Benny, 6400 Ave de Monkland, Montreal, QC, H4B 1H3, CANADA. Tel: 514-868-4021. p. 2718

Carrier, Raymond, Chef de Div, Bibliotheques de Montreal, Cote-des-Neiges, 5290 chemin de la Cote-des-Neiges, Montreal, QC, H3T 1Y2, CANADA. Tel: 514-868-4021. p. 2718

Carrier, Raymond, Chef de Div, Bibliotheques de Montreal, Interculturelle, 6767 chemin de la Cote-des-Neiges, Montreal, QC, H3S 2T6, CANADA. Tel: 514-868-4021. p. 2719

Carrier, Raymond, Chef de Div, Bibliotheques de Montreal, Notre-Dame-de-Grace, 3755 rue Botrel, Montreal, QC, H4A 3G8, CANADA. Tel: 514-868-4021. p. 2720

Carrier, Sarah, Res & Instruction Librn, University of North Carolina at Chapel Hill, 208 Raleigh St, CB 3916, Chapel Hill, NC, 27515. Tel: 919-962-1053. p. 1678

Carrier, Stephanie, Librn, Englehart Public Library, 71 Fourth Ave, Englehart, ON, P0J 1H0, CANADA. Tel: 705-544-2100. p. 2640

Carrier, Terriruth, Exec Dir, Operations, Syracuse University Libraries, 222 Waverly Ave, Syracuse, NY, 13244-2010. Tel: 315-443-1187. p. 1650

Carrier, Timothy, YA Serv, Jefferson-Madison Regional Library, 201 E Market St, Charlottesville, VA, 22902-5287. Tel: 434-979-7151, Ext 6671. p. 2309

Carriere, Diane, Ref Librn, Universite de Saint-Boniface, 0140-200 Ave de la Cathedrale, Winnipeg, MB, R2H 0H7, CANADA. Tel: 204-945-4782. p. 2594

Carriere, Joyce, Br Librn, Wapiti Regional Library, Spiritwood Public Library, 200 Main St, Spiritwood, SK, S0J 2M0, CANADA. Tel: 306-883-2337. p. 2746

Carrigan, Lea, Coord, Ad Serv, Fairfield County District Library, 219 N Broad St, Lancaster, OH, 43130-3098. Tel: 740-653-2745. p. 1794

Carriker, Jennifer, Dir, Hedrick Public Library, 109 N Main St, Hedrick, IA, 52563. Tel: 641-653-2211. p. 758

Carrillo, Brenda, Head, Coll Mgt Serv, California State University, Sacramento, 6000 J St, Sacramento, CA, 95819-6039. Tel: 916-278-6708. p. 208

Carrillo Irizarry, Jose, Info Res Spec, University of the Sacred Heart, Rosales St, PO Box 12383, Santurce, PR, 00914-0383. Tel: 787-728-1515, Ext 4357. p. 2515

Carrillo-Sotomayor, Magdy, Libr Mgr, Hillsboro Public Library, Shute Park, 775 SE Tenth Ave, Hillsboro, OR, 97123. p. 1881

Carrington, Nicole, Coordr, Ch & Youth Serv, Northumberland Public Library, Inc, 7204 Northumberland Hwy, Heathsville, VA, 22473. Tel: 804-580-5051. p. 2325

Carriveau, Ane, Sr Acad Librn, University of Wisconsin-Fox Valley Library, 1478 Midway Rd, Menasha, WI, 54952-1297. Tel: 920-832-2672. p. 2455

Carriveau, Ane, Acad Librn, University of Wisconsin Oshkosh, 801 Elmwood Ave, Oshkosh, WI, 54901. Tel: 920-832-2675. p. 2467

Carriveau Storie, Monique, Dean, University of Guam, UOG Sta, Mangilao, GU, 96913. Tel: 671-735-2333. p. 2505

Carroll, Aubrey, Info Serv Mgr, Florence County Library System, 509 S Dargan St, Florence, SC, 29506. Tel: 843-662-8424. p. 2058

Carroll, Bill, Libr Dir, Marion Public Library, 1101 Sixth Ave, Marion, IA, 52302. Tel: 319-377-3412. p. 768

Carroll, Dale, Librn, Centralia College, 600 Centralia College Blvd, Centralia, WA, 98531. Tel: 360-623-8373. p. 2361

Carroll, Donna, Br Mgr, Jacksonville Public Library, Regency Square Branch, 9900 Regency Square Blvd, Jacksonville, FL, 32225-6539. Tel: 904-726-5142. p. 412

Carroll, Edward W, Sr Legal Ref Librn, Hennepin County Law Library, C-2451 Government Ctr, 300 S Sixth St, Minneapolis, MN, 55487. Tel: 612-348-8860. p. 1183

Carroll, Heather, Asst Librn, Bern Community Library, 405 Main St, Bern, KS, 66408. Tel: 785-336-3000. p. 798

Carroll, Jennifer, Coll Develop Librn, University of New Hampshire Library, 18 Library Way, Durham, NH, 03824. Tel: 603-862-4049. p. 1362

Carroll, Jessica, Asst Libr Dir, Scurry County Library, 1916 23rd St, Snyder, TX, 79549-1910. Tel: 325-573-5572. p. 2244

Carroll, Jim, Imaging Specialist, Regional Digital Imaging Ctr, The Athenaeum of Philadelphia, East Washington Sq, 219 S Sixth St, Philadelphia, PA, 19106-3794. Tel: 215-925-2688. p. 1975

Carroll, Keri, Accounts Mgr, Fox River Valley Public Library District, 555 Barrington Ave, East Dundee, IL, 60118-1496. Tel: 847-428-3661. p. 580

Carroll, Kimberley, Dep City Librn, Salem Public Library, 585 Liberty St SE, Salem, OR, 97301. Tel: 503-588-6064. p. 1897

Carroll, Kris, Asst Dir, Geauga County Public Library, 12701 Ravenwood Dr, Chardon, OH, 44024-1336. Tel: 440-286-6811. p. 1758

Carroll, Kris, Mgr, Geauga County Public Library, Bainbridge Branch, 17222 Snyder Rd, Chagrin Falls, OH, 44023. Tel: 440-543-5611. p. 1758

Carroll, Kristi, Head, Pub Serv, Montana Tech Library, 1300 W Park St, Butte, MT, 59701. Tel: 406-496-4222. p. 1290

Carroll, Laura, Br Mgr, Shreve Memorial Library, Rodessa Branch, 10093 Main St, Rodessa, LA, 71069. Tel: 318-223-4336. p. 910

Carroll, Laura, Archivist, Ohio County Public Library, 52 16th St, Wheeling, WV, 26003. Tel: 304-232-0244. p. 2417

Carroll, Laura, Asst Dir, Head, Adult Serv, Ohio County Public Library, 52 16th St, Wheeling, WV, 26003. Tel: 304-232-0244. p. 2417

Carroll, LeighAnn, Automation Spec, Lawson State Community College Library, 1100 Ninth Ave SW, Bessemer, AL, 35022. Tel: 205-929-3434, 205-929-6333. p. 6

Carroll, Leslie, Librn, Grapeland Public Library, 106 N Oak St, Grapeland, TX, 75844. Tel: 936-687-3425. p. 2186

Carroll, Lida, Youth Serv Librn, Pearle L Crawford Memorial Library, 40 Schofield Ave, Dudley, MA, 01571. Tel: 508-949-8021. p. 1015

Carroll, Melissa, Dir, East Hounsfield Free Library, 19438 State Rte 3, Watertown, NY, 13601. Tel: 315-788-0637. p. 1659

Carroll, Shelby, Sci Librn, Clemson University Libraries, 116 Sigma Dr, Clemson, SC, 29631. Tel: 864-656-3027. p. 2052

Carroll, Shirley, Br Mgr, Snyder County Libraries, Middleburg Community Library, 13 N Main St, Middleburg, PA, 17842. Tel: 570-837-5931. p. 2005

Carroll-Gavula, Macaire, Libr Dir, United States Department of Labor, 200 Constitution Ave NW, Rm N-2445, Washington, DC, 20210. Tel: 202-693-6600. p. 378

Carroll-Horacks, Beth, Head, Spec Coll, The State Library of Massachusetts, State House, Rm 341, 24 Beacon St, Boston, MA, 02133. Tel: 617-727-2595. p. 1000

Carroll-Mann, Robin, Adult Programming, Summit Free Public Library, 75 Maple St, Summit, NJ, 07901-9984. Tel: 908-273-0350. p. 1445

Carrothers, Kevin, Librn Supvr, William T Cozby Public Library, 177 N Heartz Rd, Coppell, TX, 75019. Tel: 972-304-7048. p. 2159

Carrubba, Nicole, Asst Dir, Portsmouth Free Public Library, 2658 E Main Rd, Portsmouth, RI, 02871. Tel: 401-683-9457. p. 2037

Carruth, Debra, Dr, Lecturer, Valdosta State University, Odum Library, 1500 N Patterson St, Valdosta, GA, 31698. Tel: 229-333-5657. p. 2784

Carruthers, Hilda, Librn, Iosco-Arenac District Library, Mary Johnston Memorial Library - Standish Branch, 114 N Court, Standish, MI, 48658-9416. Tel: 989-846-6611. p. 1102

Carruthers, Rachael, Patron Serv Librn, Butt-Holdsworth Memorial Library, 505 Water St, Kerrville, TX, 78028. Tel: 830-257-8422. p. 2205

Carscadden, Alexis, Exec Dir, National Louis University Library, 18 S Michigan Ave, 3rd Flr, Chicago, IL, 60603. Tel: 312-261-3645. p. 565

Carscaddon, Laura, Head, Research & Engagment, Georgia State University, 100 Decatur St SE, Atlanta, GA, 30303-3202. Tel: 404-413-2804. p. 464

Carson, Amy, Libr Coord, North Dakota State College of Science, 800 Sixth St N, Wahpeton, ND, 58076-0001. Tel: 701-671-2192. p. 1741

Carson, Curtis, Asst Librn, Saint John's Episcopal Hospital-South Shore Division, 327 Beach 19th St, Far Rockaway, NY, 11691. Tel: 718-869-7699. p. 1532

Carson, Denise, Dir, Libr Serv, Bethany College, 335 E Swensson St, Lindsborg, KS, 67456-1896. Tel: 785-227-3380, Ext 8342. p. 821

Carson, Edward, Librn, Cape May County Library, Lower Cape Branch, 2600 Bayshore Rd, Villas, NJ, 08251. Tel: 609-886-8999. p. 1395

Carson, Griar, Dir, Monroe County Public Library, 303 E Kirkwood Ave, Bloomington, IN, 47408. Tel: 812-349-3050. p. 671

Carson, Jennifer, Libr Dir, Haut-Saint-Jean Regional Library, L P Fisher Public Library, 679 Main St, Woodstock, NB, E7M 2E1, CANADA. Tel: 506-325-4777. p. 2600

Carson, Kim, Coll & Syst Coordr, Orangeville Public Library, One Mill St, Orangeville, ON, L9W 2M2, CANADA. Tel: 519-941-0610, Ext 5226. p. 2663

Carson, Pam, Librn, International Society Daughters of Utah Pioneers, 300 N Main St, Salt Lake City, UT, 84103-1699. Tel: 801-532-6479. p. 2271

Carson, Tom, Dir, W J Niederkorn Library, 316 W Grand Ave, Port Washington, WI, 53074-2293. Tel: 262-284-5031. p. 2470

Carstens, Cathy, Tech Librn, Gates Public Library, 902 Elmgrove Rd, Rochester, NY, 14624. Tel: 585-247-6446. p. 1628

Carston, Rose, Br Mgr, Watonwan County Library, Butterfield Branch, 111 Second St N, Butterfield, MN, 56120. Tel: 507-956-2361. p. 1198

Carswell, Roger L, Dir, Iola Public Library, 218 E Madison Ave, Iola, KS, 66749. Tel: 620-365-3262. p. 815

Carswell, Roger L, Dir, Southeast Kansas Library System, 218 E Madison Ave, Iola, KS, 66749. Tel: 620-365-5136. p. 815

Carter, Amber, Ad, Ardmore Public Library, 320 E St NW, Ardmore, OK, 73401. Tel: 580-223-8290. p. 1840

Carter, Amy, Ch, Cook Memorial Library, 93 Main St, Tamworth, NH, 03886. Tel: 603-323-8510. p. 1382

Carter, Andrea, Asst Mgr, Saint Louis County Library, Mid-County Branch, 7821 Maryland Ave, Saint Louis, MO, 63105-3875. Tel: 314-994-3300, Ext 3500. p. 1274

Carter, Anna, Br Mgr, Scott-Sebastian Regional Library, Mansfield Library, 200 N Sebascott Ave, Mansfield, AR, 72944. p. 97

Carter, Ben, Asst State Librn, Georgia Public Library Service, 5800 Jonesboro Rd, Morrow, GA, 30260. Tel: 404-235-7123. p. 491

Carter, Carolyn, Br Mgr, Jackson/Hinds Library System, Willie Morris Branch, 4912 Old Canton Rd, Jackson, MS, 39211-5404. Tel: 601-987-8181. p. 1221

Carter, Cathy, Libr Dir, Benzie Shores District Library, 630 Main St, Frankfort, MI, 49635. Tel: 231-352-4671. p. 1108

Carter, Chaise, Dir, Youth Serv, Hamilton East Public Library, One Library Plaza, Noblesville, IN, 46060. Tel: 317-773-1384. p. 710

Carter, Charlotte, VPres, White Haven Area Community Library, 121 Towanda St, White Haven, PA, 18661. Tel: 570-443-8776. p. 2021

Carter, Christina, Ref & Instruction, University of Alaska Anchorage, Consortium Library, 3211 Providence Dr, Anchorage, AK, 99508-8176. Tel: 907-786-1871. p. 43

Carter, Cynthia, Libr Dir, Milford Public Library, 100 West 400 S, Milford, UT, 84751. Tel: 435-387-5039. p. 2266

Carter, Debbie, Budget Off Mgr, Finance Mgr, Blackwater Regional Library, 22511 Main St, Courtland, VA, 23837. Tel: 757-653-2821. p. 2313

Carter, Deborah, Workforce Librarian, San Marcos Public Library, 625 E Hopkins, San Marcos, TX, 78666. Tel: 512-393-8200. p. 2241

Carter, Denise, Dir, Lake Whitney Public Library, 602 E Jefferson Ave, Whitney, TX, 76692. Tel: 254-694-4639. p. 2257

Carter, Destiny, Libr Dir, University of Arkansas for Medical Sciences, 300 E Sixth St, Texarkana, AR, 71854. Tel: 870-779-6053. p. 111

Carter, Dianna, Libr Mgr, Kinchafoonee Regional Library System, Calhoun County Library, 19379 E Hartford St, Edison, GA, 39846-5626. Tel: 229 835-2012. p. 475

Carter, Dianna, Libr Mgr, Kinchafoonee Regional Library System, Randolph County Library, 106 Pearl St, Cuthbert, GA, 39840-1474. Tel: 229-732-2566. p. 475

Carter, Drusilla, Libr Dir, Douglas Library of Hebron, 22 Main St, Hebron, CT, 06248. Tel: 860-228-9312. p. 319

Carter, Genevieve, Curator, Huronia Museum, 549 Little Lake Park Rd, Midland, ON, L4R 4P4, CANADA. Tel: 705-526-2844. p. 2658

Carter, Genny, Regional Dir, Hatchie River Regional Library, 63 Executive Dr, Jackson, TN, 38305. Tel: 731-668-0710. p. 2102

Carter, Genny, Regional Libr Dir, Tennessee State Library & Archives, 403 Seventh Ave N, Nashville, TN, 37243-0312. Tel: 731-668-0710. p. 2121

Carter, Greg, Dr, Libr Dir, West Plains Public Library, 750 W Broadway St, West Plains, MO, 65775. Tel: 417-256-4775. p. 1286

Carter, Gwendolyn, Dr, Librn, Mississippi Gulf Coast Community College, 2300 Hwy 90, Gautier, MS, 39553. Tel: 228-497-7715. p. 1216

Carter, Heather, Br Supvr, Smyth County Public Library, Chilhowie Public, 807 Chilhowie St, Chilhowie, VA, 24319. Tel: 276-646-3404. p. 2331

Carter, Hugh, Dir, Learning Res, Lurleen B Wallace Community College Library, 1000 Dannelly Blvd, Andalusia, AL, 36420. Tel: 334-881-2265. p. 4

Carter, J Drusilla, Dir, Pearle L Crawford Memorial Library, 40 Schofield Ave, Dudley, MA, 01571. Tel: 508-949-8021. p. 1015

Carter, Jan, Library Contact, University of California, Berkeley, Howison Philosophy Library, Moses Hall, 3rd Flr, Berkeley, CA, 94720. Tel: 510-643-2281. p. 123

Carter, Jay, Libr Dir, Conway County Library Headquarters, 101 W Church St, Morrilton, AR, 72110. Tel: 501-354-5204. p. 105

Carter, Jennifer, Br Mgr, Cecil County Public Library, Rising Sun Branch, 111 Colonial Way, Rising Sun, MD, 21911. Tel: 410-398-2706, 410-658-4025. p. 965

Carter, Joanna, Commun Liaison Librn, Plainfield-Guilford Township Public Library, 1120 Stafford Rd, Plainfield, IN, 46168. Tel: 317-839-6602, Ext 2159. p. 713

Carter, Jonah, Registrar, Owls Head Transportation Museum, 117 Museum St, Owls Head, ME, 04854. Tel: 207-594-4418. p. 935

Carter, Judith, Electronic Res Librn, Syst Librn, Carroll University, 100 N East Ave, Waukesha, WI, 53186. Tel: 262-650-4886. p. 2484

Carter, Judy, Librn, Georgia Department of Corrections, Office of Library Services, 373 Upper River Rd, Hawkinsville, GA, 31036. Tel: 478-783-6000, Ext 6102. p. 482

Carter, Julia, Cataloging & Metadata Librn, Minot State University, 500 University Ave W, Minot, ND, 58707. Tel: 701-858-3859. p. 1738

Carter, Julie, Head, User Serv, Whitman College, 345 Boyer Ave, Walla Walla, WA, 99362. Tel: 509-527-5915. p. 2393

Carter, Kathy, Assoc Univ Librn, University of Texas Rio Grande Valley, School of Medicine, 2102 Treasure Hills Blvd, Harlingen, TX, 78550. Tel: 956-296-1507. p. 2188

Carter, Kimbroe, Dr, Dir, Med Libr, Mercy Health Saint Elizabeth Health Center, 1044 Belmont Ave, Youngstown, OH, 44501-1790. Tel: 330-480-3039. p. 1835

Carter, Kirsten, Dep Dir, Supvry Archivist, National Archives & Records Administration, 4079 Albany Post Rd, Hyde Park, NY, 12538. Tel: 845-486-7770. p. 1550

Carter, Laura, Chief Librn/CEO, Kingston Frontenac Public Library, 130 Johnson St, Kingston, ON, K7L 1X8, CANADA. Tel: 613-549-8888. p. 2650

Carter, Lenora, Dir, Assumption Parish Library, 293 Napoleon Ave, Napoleonville, LA, 70390. Tel: 985-369-7070. p. 899

Carter, Linda, Dir, Metropolitan Community College, Maple Woods Library, 2601 NE Barry Rd, Kansas City, MO, 64156. Tel: 816-604-3080. p. 1256

Carter, Lisa, Dir, Hartford Hospital, Education & Resource Ctr, 3rd Flr, 560 Hudson St, Hartford, CT, 06102. Tel: 860-972-2230. p. 317

Carter, Lisa, Vice Provost & Univ Librn, University of Wisconsin-Madison, 728 State St, Madison, WI, 53706. Tel: 608-262-2600. p. 2450

Carter, Lisa R, Univ Librn & Dean of Libr, University of Michigan, 818 Hatcher Graduate Library South, 913 S University Ave, Ann Arbor, MI, 48109-1190. Tel: 734-764-0400. p. 1080

Carter, Lois, Br Mgr, Shreve Memorial Library, Means Branch, 7016 E Magnolia Lane, Ida, LA, 71044. Tel: 318-284-3416. p. 909

Carter, Lucas, Dir, Argos Public Library, 142 N Michigan St, Argos, IN, 46501. Tel: 574-892-5818. p. 668

Carter, Marie, Libr Mgr, VA Long Beach Health Care System, 5901 E Seventh St, Bldg 2, Rm 345, Long Beach, CA, 90822-5201. Tel: 562-826-8000, ext 5463. p. 159

Carter, Mariel, Col Librn, Bay De Noc Community College, 2001 N Lincoln Rd, Escanaba, MI, 49829-2511. Tel: 906-217-4055. p. 1103

Carter, Mary, Commun Serv Librn, Belmont Public Library, 336 Concord Ave, Belmont, MA, 02478-0904. Tel: 617-489-2000, 617-993-2850. p. 988

Carter, Michael K, Librn, Metropolitan Museum of Art, Cloisters Library, Fort Tryon Park, New York, NY, 10040. Tel: 212-396-5365. p. 1591

Carter, Michelle, Libr Dir, Aram Public Library, 404 E Walworth Ave, Delavan, WI, 53115-1208. Tel: 262-728-3111. p. 2431

Carter, Michelle, Br Mgr, Huron County Library, Clinton Branch, 27 Albert St, Clinton, ON, N0M 1L0, CANADA. Tel: 519-482-3673. p. 2636

Carter, Michelle, Br Mgr, Huron County Library, Zurich Branch, Ten Goshen St N, Zurich, ON, N0M 2T0, CANADA. Tel: 519-236-4965. p. 2636

Carter, Monifa, Govt Doc Librn, Ref & Ser Librn, Delaware State University, 1200 N Dupont Hwy, Dover, DE, 19901-2277. Tel: 302-857-7588. p. 352

Carter, Nicole, Res & Ref Librn, Saint Mary's University, 923 Robie St, Halifax, NS, B3H 3C3, CANADA. Tel: 902-420-5540. p. 2621

Carter, Phillip, Dir, Lamar County Library System, 144 Shelby Speights Dr, Purvis, MS, 39475. Tel: 601-794-3220. p. 1230

Carter, Phillip, Dir, Starkville-Oktibbeha County Public Library System, 326 University Dr, Starkville, MS, 39759. Tel: 662-323-2766, p. 1233

Carter, Phoebe, Assoc Dir, Weber County Library System, 2464 Jefferson Ave, Ogden, UT, 84401-2464. Tel: 801-337-2617. p. 2267

Carter, Phoebe, Librn, Weber County Library System, Southwest Branch, 2039 W 4000 S, Roy, UT, 84067. Tel: 801-773-2556. p. 2268

Carter, Robert, Head, Children's Servx, Acton Memorial Library, 486 Main St, Acton, MA, 01720. Tel: 978-929-6655. p. 983

Carter, Russell, Interim Libr Dir, Danville Public Library, 511 Patton St, Danville, VA, 24541. Tel: 434-799-5195. p. 2315

Carter, Sabrina, Dir, Frankston Depot Library, 159 W Railroad St, Frankston, TX, 75763. Tel: 903-876-4463. p. 2181

Carter, Schuyler, Libr Asst, Spec Coll, Fisk University, 1000 17th Ave N, Nashville, TN, 37208-3051. Tel: 615-329-8730. p. 2118

Carter, Sheila, Librn, Joshua School & Public Library, 907 S Broadway, Joshua, TX, 76058. Tel: 817-202-2547. p. 2204

Carter, Stacey, Librn, Lincoln Correctional Center Library, 1098 1350th St, Lincoln, IL, 62656. Tel: 217-735-5411, Ext 368. p. 609

Carter, Terrah, Mgr, Dallas Public Library, Lochwood, 11221 Lochwood Blvd, Dallas, TX, 75218. Tel: 214-670-8403. p. 2166

Carter, Tiffani, Mgr, Columbus Metropolitan Library, Barnett Branch, 3434 E Livingston Ave, Columbus, OH, 43227. p. 1772

Carter, Toni, Dir, Athens State University, 407 E Pryor St, Athens, AL, 35611. Tel: 256-216-6659. p. 5

Carter, Tonya, Libr Mgr, Texas A&M University Libraries, Business Library & Collaboration Commons, 214 Olsen Blvd, College Station, TX, 77843. Tel: 979-845-2111. p. 2157

Carter, Tonya, Ch, Lancaster Community Library, 16 Town Center Dr, Kilmarnock, VA, 22482-3830. Tel: 804-435-1729. p. 2327

Carter, Tracey, Asst Libr Dir, Venice Public Library, 325 Broadway, Venice, IL, 62090. Tel: 618-877-1330. p. 657

Carter, Vern, Cat, Tech Serv, Fresno Pacific University, 1717 S Chestnut Ave, Fresno, CA, 93702. Tel: 559-453-7124. p. 146

Carter-Bowman, Junelle, Libr Mgr, New York Public Library - Astor, Lenox & Tilden Foundations, George Bruce Branch, 518 W 125th St, New York, NY, 10027. Tel: 212-662-9727. p. 1594

Cartolano, Robert, Assoc VPres, Presv, Tech, Columbia University, Butler Library, 535 W 114th St, New York, NY, 10027. Tel: 212-854-7309. p. 1582

Carton, Debbie, Librn, Forman Public Library, 347 Main St, Forman, ND, 58032. Tel: 701-724-4032. p. 1733

Carton, Ninette, Libr Dir, Atkinson Public Library District, 109 S State, Atkinson, IL, 61235. Tel: 309-936-7606. p. 538

Carton, Ruthann, Asst Librn, Atkinson Public Library District, 109 S State, Atkinson, IL, 61235. Tel: 309-936-7606. p. 538

Cartusciello, Gina, Dir, Libr Res Serv, Cahill, Gordon & Reindel Library, 1990 K St NW, Ste 950, Washington, DC, 20006. Tel: 212-701-3541. p. 362

Cartusciello, Gina, Dir, Libr & Res Serv, Cahill, Gordon & Reindel Library, 80 Pine St, New York, NY, 10005. Tel: 212-701-3541. p. 1580

Cartwright, Jennifer, Law Librn, Charles B Swartwood Supreme Court Library, Hazelett Bldg, 1st Flr, 203-205 Lake St, Elmira, NY, 14901. Tel: 607-873-9443. p. 1531

Caruso, Arlene, Dir, Newtown Public Library, 201 Bishop Hollow Rd, Newtown Square, PA, 19073. Tel: 610-353-1022. p. 1970
Caruso, Janet, Librn, Mental Health America Library, 253 Mansion St, 2nd Flr, Poughkeepsie, NY, 12601. Tel: 845-473-2500, Ext 1325. p. 1623
Caruso, Ken, Head, Circ, Johnson Free Public Library, 274 Main St, Hackensack, NJ, 07601-5797. Tel: 201-343-4169. p. 1406
Caruso, Monica, County Librn, Watauga County Public Library, 140 Queen St, Boone, NC, 28607. Tel: 828-264-8784. p. 1675
Caruso, Yuusuf S, PhD, Librn, Columbia University, African Studies, Lehman Library, 420 W 118th St, New York, NY, 10027. Tel: 212-854-8045. p. 1582
Caruthers, Felecia, Univ Librn, Winston-Salem State University, 601 Martin Luther King Jr Dr, Winston-Salem, NC, 27110. Tel: 336-750-8867. p. 1726
Carvajal, Elena, Colls Mgr, Westbank Community Library District, 1309 Westbank Dr, Austin, TX, 78746. Tel: 512-327-3045. p. 2143
Carvalho, Kathy, Head, Circ, Westwood Public Library, 49 Park Ave, Westwood, NJ, 07675. Tel: 201-664-0583. p. 1454
Carver, Charlotte, Asst Dir, Lilly Library, 19 Meadow St, Florence, MA, 01062. Tel: 413-587-1500. p. 1019
Carver, Christy, Asst Librn, Greenbrier County Public Library, 152 Robert W McCormick Dr, Lewisburg, WV, 24901. Tel: 304-647-7568. p. 2407
Carver, Donna J, Coordr, Ref (Info Servs), Valencia College, Raymer Maguire Jr Learning Resources Center, West Campus, 1800 S Kirkman Rd, Orlando, FL, 32811. Tel: 407-582-1210. p. 433
Carver, Jan, Academic Liaison, University of Kentucky Libraries, Science & Engineering Library, 211 King Bldg, 179 Funkhouser Dr, Lexington, KY, 40506-0039. Tel: 859-257-4074. p. 864
Carver, Molly, Exec Dir, Sandusky Library, 114 W Adams St, Sandusky, OH, 44870. Tel: 419-625-3834. p. 1819
Carver, Nico, Librn, Collaborative Pojects, Center for Astrophysics Library / Harvard & Smithsonian Library, 60 Garden St, MS-56, Cambridge, MA, 02138. Tel: 617-496-5769. p. 1005
Carwile, Marti, Acq Mgr, Monmouth College, 700 E Broadway, Monmouth, IL, 61462-1963. Tel: 309-457-2191. p. 619
Cary, Paul, Conservatory Librn, Baldwin Wallace University, Riemenschneider Bach Institute, Boesel Musical Arts Bldg, Rm 160, 49 Seminary St, Berea, OH, 44017. Tel: 440-826-2044. p. 1751
Cary, Paul, Dir, Baldwin Wallace University, Jones Music Library, 49 Seminary St, Berea, OH, 44017. Tel: 440-826-2375. p. 1751
Cary, Sandra, Librn, West Hartford Library, 5133 Rte 14, West Hartford, VT, 05084. Tel: 802-295-7992. p. 2298
Carzon, Eric, Br Mgr, Montgomery County Public Libraries, Twinbrook Library, 202 Meadow Hall Dr, Rockville, MD, 20851-1551. Tel: 240-777-0249. p. 975
Casabona, Abby, Circ Asst, Maynard Public Library, 77 Nason St, Maynard, MA, 01754-2316. Tel: 978-897-1010. p. 1033
Casaccio, Ellen, Dir of Circ, Richards Memorial Library, 118 N Washington St, North Attleboro, MA, 02760. Tel: 508-699-0122. p. 1041
Casalaspi, Paul, Dir, Info Tech Serv Div, The Library of Virginia, 800 E Broad St, Richmond, VA, 23219-8000. Tel: 804-692-3500. p. 2341
Casale, Anthony, Ch, Oldsmar Public Library, 400 St Petersburg Dr E, Oldsmar, FL, 34677. Tel: 813-749-1178. p. 430
Casarez, Gabriela, Res Tech, Southwest Texas Junior College, 3101 Bob Rogers Dr, Eagle Pass, TX, 78852. Tel: 830-758-4118. p. 2172
Casari, William, Spec Coll & Archives Librn, Hostos Community College Library, Shirley J Hinds Allied Health & Science Bldg, 475 Grand Concourse, Rm A308, Bronx, NY, 10451. Tel: 718-518-4220. p. 1499
Casas, Nicholas A, Asst Librn for Teaching & Learning, Indiana University Northwest, 3400 Broadway, Gary, IN, 46408. Tel: 219-980-6806. p. 686
Casasanto, Nancy, Librn, McCook Public Library District, 8419 W 50th St, McCook, IL, 60525-3187. Tel: 708-442-1242. p. 616
Casavan, Mary, Librn, Northwest Regional Library, Red Lake Falls Public Library, 105 Champagne Ave SW, Red Lake Falls, MN, 56750. Tel: 218-253-2992. p. 1205
Cascio, Nina, Foreign & Intl Law Librn, University at Buffalo Libraries-State University of New York, Charles B Sears Law Library, John Lord O'Brian Hall, 211 Mary Talbert Way, Buffalo, NY, 14260-1110. Tel: 716-645-2633. p. 1511
Case, Angie, Sr Librn, Pierce County Library System, Gig Harbor Branch, 4424 Point Fosdick Dr NW, Gig Harbor, WA, 98335. Tel: 253-548-3305. p. 2386
Case, Beau, Dean of Libr, University of Central Florida Libraries, 12701 Pegasus Dr, Orlando, FL, 32816-8030. Tel: 407-823-2564. p. 432
Case, Beau, Dean, Univ Libr, University of Toledo, 2975 W Centennial Dr, Toledo, OH, 43606-3396. Tel: 419-530-4286. p. 1825
Case, Chris, Ms, Br Mgr, Prairie-River Library District, Winchester Community, 314 Nezperce St, Winchester, ID, 83555. Tel: 208-924-5164. p. 524
Case, Jacqueline, Libr Dir, Kellyville Public Library, 230 E Buffalo, Kellyville, OK, 74039. Tel: 918-247-3740. p. 1851
Case, Maureen, Head, Tech Serv, Upper St Clair Township Library, 1820 McLaughlin Run Rd, Upper St Clair, PA, 15241-2397. Tel: 412-835-5540. p. 2016
Case, Robyn, Tech Serv, Wright Memorial Public Library, 1776 Far Hills Ave, Oakwood, OH, 45419-2598. Tel: 937-294-7171. p. 1810
Casebier, Diane, Ref & Libr Instruction, Ser, Houston Baptist University, 7502 Fondren Rd, Houston, TX, 77074-3298. Tel: 281-649-3178. p. 2194
Casella, Darla, Ch, Abilene Public Library, Mockingbird Branch, 1326 N Mockingbird, Abilene, TX, 79603. Tel: 325-437-7323. p. 2132
Casella, Jessie, Pres, Massachusetts Health Sciences Library Network, Lamar soutter Library, UMass Medical School, 55 Lake Ave, n, Worcester, MA, 01655. Tel: 508-856-1966. p. 2766
Caserotti, Gretchen, Libr Dir, Meridian Library District, 1326 W Cherry Lane, Meridian, ID, 83642. Tel: 208-888-4451. p. 525
Caserotti, Gretchen, Exec Dir, Pierce County Library System, 3005 112th St E, Tacoma, WA, 98446-2215. Tel: 253-548-3300. p. 2386
Casey, Anne Marie, Libr Dir, Embry-Riddle Aeronautical University, One Aerospace Blvd, Daytona Beach, FL, 32114. Tel: 386-226-6593. p. 392
Casey, Anthony, Librn & Archivist, Wesleyan Church, 13300 Olio Rd, Fishers, IN, 46037. Tel: 317-774-3864. p. 682
Casey, Christopher, Pub Serv Librn, Outreach, Franklin University Library, Frasch Hall, 1st Flr, 201 S Grant Ave, Columbus, OH, 43215. Tel: 614-947-6565. p. 1773
Casey, Derrick, Libr Dir, Lincoln College, 300 Keokuk St, Lincoln, IL, 62656. Tel: 217-735-7290. p. 609
Casey, Erin, Library Contact, Missoula Public Library, Lolo Branch, Lolo School/Community Library, 11395 Hwy 93 S, Lolo, MT, 59847. Tel: 406-273-0451, Ext 211. p. 1300
Casey, Jeanette, Head of Libr, University of Wisconsin-Madison, Mills Music Library, B162 Memorial Library, 728 State St, Madison, WI, 53706. Tel: 608-263-2721. p. 2451
Casey, Jen, Asst Dir, Frankfort Community Public Library, 208 W Clinton St, Frankfort, IN, 46041. Tel: 765-654-8746. p. 685
Casey, Jessica, Dir, Farmington Public Library, 117 Academy St, Farmington, ME, 04938. Tel: 207-778-4312. p. 925
Casey, Judy F, Dir, Rogers Public Library, 711 S Dixieland Rd, Rogers, AR, 72758. Tel: 479-621-1152. p. 108
Casey, Kaela, Librn, Ventura College, 4667 Telegraph Rd, Ventura, CA, 93003. Tel: 805-289-6563. p. 255
Casey, Katherine, Asst Dean, Instruction Librn, Phillips Theological Seminary Library, 901 N Mingo Rd, Tulsa, OK, 74116. Tel: 918-270-6432. p. 1865
Casey, Kathleen, Govt Doc, Saint Louis University, Vincent C Immel Law Library, 100 N Tucker Blvd, Flrs 5 & 6, Saint Louis, MO, 63101. Tel: 314-977-2742. p. 1275
Casey, Kelsey, Libr Dir, Canterbury Public Library, One Municipal Dr, Canterbury, CT, 06331-1453. Tel: 860-546-9022. p. 305
Casey, Kelsey, Libr Dir, Plymouth Public Library, 132 South St, Plymouth, MA, 02360. Tel: 508-830-4250. p. 1047
Casey, Lynn, Br Mgr, Prince William Public Libraries, Lake Ridge Library, 2239 Old Bridge Rd, Woodbridge, VA, 22192. Tel: 703-792-5675. p. 2339
Casey, Mary, Sr Libr Tech, Whitman Public Library, 100 Webster St, Whitman, MA, 02382. Tel: 781-447-7613. p. 1069
Casey, Michael, Customer Experience Dir, Gwinnett County Public Library, 1001 Lawrenceville Hwy NW, Lawrenceville, GA, 30046-4707. Tel: 770-822-5334. p. 485
Casey, Olga, Tech Serv Librn, Troy University, 502 University Dr, Dothan, AL, 36304. Tel: 334-983-6556, Ext 1325. p. 15
Casey, Tom, Tech Dir, Public Library of Youngstown & Mahoning County, 305 Wick Ave, Youngstown, OH, 44503. Tel: 330-744-8636. p. 1835
Cash, Brenda, ILL, Southeast Kansas Library System, 218 E Madison Ave, Iola, KS, 66749. Tel: 620-365-5136. p. 815
Cash, Brenda L, Dir, Pennville Township Public Library, 195 N Union St, Pennville, IN, 47369. Tel: 260-731-3333. p. 713
Cash, Debbie, Librn, Virginia Polytechnic Institute & State University Libraries, Northern Virginia Resource Center, 7054 Haycock Rd, Falls Church, VA, 22043-2311. Tel: 703-538-8341. p. 2307
Cash, Gina, Libr Dir, Cleveland State Community College Library, 3535 Adkisson Dr, Cleveland, TN, 37312-2813. Tel: 423-473-2277, 423-478-6209. p. 2093
Cash, Greg, Asst Dir, Ref, Lewis & Clark Community College, 5800 Godfrey Rd, Godfrey, IL, 62035. Tel: 618-468-4330. p. 594
Cash, Marilyn, Libr Mgr, Central Arkansas Library System, Maumelle Branch, Ten Lake Pointe Dr, Maumelle, AR, 72113-6230. Tel: 501-851-2551. p. 101
Cash, Pam, Mgr, Dallas Public Library, Park Forest, 3421 Forest Lane, Dallas, TX, 75234-7776. Tel: 214-670-6333. p. 2166
Cashman, Liz, Head, Info Literacy & Instruction Serv, Western New England University, 1215 Wilbraham Rd, Springfield, MA, 01119. Tel: 413-782-1537. p. 1057
Cashmore, Audrey, Outreach Coordr, Hennepin County Law Library, C-2451 Government Ctr, 300 S Sixth St, Minneapolis, MN, 55487. Tel: 612-348-7961. p. 1183
Casias, Sheree, Br Mgr, Neuse Regional Library, Pink Hill Public Library, 114 W Broadway St, Pink Hill, NC, 28572. Tel: 252-568-3631. p. 1699
Casiello, Alessandra Petrino, Ch Serv, YA Serv, Weston Public Library, 56 Norfield Rd, Weston, CT, 06883. Tel: 203-222-2651. p. 346

Caskey, Kendra, Dir, Goodall City Library, 203 West A St, Ogallala, NE, 69153. Tel: 308-284-4354. p. 1327
Caskey, Nicole, Resources Librn, Clarkson College Library, 101 S 42nd St, Omaha, NE, 68131-2739. Tel: 402-552-3387. p. 1327
Casner, Regina, Dir, Mound City Library District 4, 630 Main St, Mound City, KS, 66056. Tel: 913-795-2788. p. 826
Cason, Beth, Adult Serv, Public Library of Anniston-Calhoun County, 108 E Tenth St, Anniston, AL, 36201. Tel: 256-237-8501. p. 4
Cason, Deb, Cat & Adult Serv, Okeechobee County Public Library, 206 SW 16th St, Okeechobee, FL, 34974. Tel: 863-763-3536. p. 430
Cason, Lea, Adjunct Librn, Florida State College at Jacksonville, Deerwood Center Library, 9911 Old Baymeadows Rd, Jacksonville, FL, 32256. Tel: 904-997-2562. p. 411
Cason, Meghan, Digital Resources & Reference, Los Angeles Valley College Library, 5800 Fulton Ave, Valley Glen, CA, 91401-4096. Tel: 818-778-7261. p. 255
Cason, Paul, Librn, Georgia Department of Corrections, Office of Library Services, 1153 N Liberty St, Nicholls, GA, 31554. Tel: 912-345-5058, Ext 25473. p. 493
Casper, Betty, Asst Librn, Belle Fourche Public Library, 905 Fifth Ave, Belle Fourche, SD, 57717. Tel: 605-892-4407. p. 2074
Casper, Chris, Librn, Broward College, South Campus Library LRC, Bldg 81, 7300 Pines Blvd, Pembroke Pines, FL, 33024. Tel: 954-201-8825, 954-201-8896. p. 391
Casper, Chrisynthia, Dir, Eau Claire District Library, 6528 E Main St, Eau Claire, MI, 49111. Tel: 269-461-6241. p. 1103
Casper, Dana, Grad Serv Librn, Middle Georgia State University, 100 University Pkwy, Macon, GA, 31206. Tel: 478-471-2042. p. 487
Casper, Kristine, Asst Dir, Huntington Public Library, 338 Main St, Huntington, NY, 11743. Tel: 631-427-5165, Ext 203. p. 1549
Casper, Nicole, Dir, Archives, Hist Coll Dir, Stonehill College, 320 Washington St, Easton, MA, 02357. Tel: 508-565-1396. p. 1016
Casper, Vicki, Dir, Hildreth Public Library, 248 Commercial Ave, Hildreth, NE, 68947. Tel: 308-938-3008. p. 1318
Casperson, Christine, Br Mgr, Free Library of Philadelphia, Fox Chase Branch, 501 Rhawn St, Philadelphia, PA, 19111-2504. Tel: 215-685-0547. p. 1978
Cassady, Dawn, Assoc Dir, The Urbana Free Library, 210 W Green St, Urbana, IL, 61801. Tel: 217-367-4057. p. 657
Cassano, Rocco, Asst Dir, East Meadow Public Library, 1886 Front St, East Meadow, NY, 11554-1705. Tel: 516-794-2570. p. 1528
Cassanova, Belinda, Dir, Libr Serv, Ingleside Public Library, 2775 Waco St, Ingleside, TX, 78362. Tel: 361-776-5355. p. 2202
Cassar, Zarena, Br Mgr, Brampton Library, Gore Meadows Branch, 10150 The Gore Rd, Brampton, ON, L6P 0A6, CANADA. Tel: 905-793-4636, Ext 74707. p. 2633
Cassel, Jody, Asst Librn, Danvers Township Library, 117 E Exchange St, Danvers, IL, 61732-9347. Tel: 309-963-4269. p. 575
Casselberry, Brad, Archivist, University of Wisconsin-Stevens Point, 900 Reserve St, Stevens Point, WI, 54481-1985. Tel: 715-346-2586. p. 2479
Cassell, Jessica, Br Mgr, Lafourche Parish Public Library, Gheens Branch, 153 N Leon Dr, Gheens, LA, 70355. Tel: 985-532-2288. p. 911
Cassell, Judith, Libr Dir, Seymour Community Library, 320 E Clinton Ave, Seymour, MO, 65746. Tel: 417-935-4193. p. 1279
Cassella, Teresa, Dir, Law Libr, A Max Brewer Memorial Law Library, Harry T & Harriette V Moore Justice Ctr, 2825 Judge Fran Jamieson Way, Viera, FL, 32940. Tel: 321-617-7295. p. 453
Cassels, Kathy, Librn, Pike-Amite-Walthall Library System, Crosby Branch, 106 W Pine St, Crosby, MS, 39633. Tel: 601-639-4633. p. 1226
Cassens, David, II, Libr Dir, Tri-Township Public Library District, 209 S Main St, Troy, IL, 62294. Tel: 618-667-2133. p. 654
Cassens, Treisa, Dr, Dean, Libr & Learning Res, Cypress College Library, 9200 Valley View St, Cypress, CA, 90630-5897. Tel: 714-484-7302. p. 133
Casser, Kyle, Teen & Adult Librn, Free Public Library of Monroe Township, 713 Marsha Ave, Williamstown, NJ, 08094. Tel: 856-629-1212, Ext 209. p. 1455
Casserly, Thomas, Assoc Univ Librn, Undergrad & Distance Serv, Boston University Libraries, Mugar Memorial Library, 771 Commonwealth Ave, Boston, MA, 02215. Tel: 617-353-3710. p. 993
Cassetti, Sara, Libr Tech III, MiraCosta College Library, San Elijo Campus, 3333 Manchester Ave, Bldg 100, Cardiff, CA, 92007-1516. Tel: 760-634-7877. p. 187
Cassidy, Brenda, Librn, J A Tarbell Library, 136 Forest Rd, Lyndeborough, NH, 03082. Tel: 603-654-6790. p. 1371
Cassidy, Carol, Tech Serv, Springfield Township Library, 70 Powell Rd, Springfield, PA, 19064-2446. Tel: 610-543-2113. p. 2009
Cassidy, Lisa, Head, Circ, Belmont Public Library, 336 Concord Ave, Belmont, MA, 02478-0904. Tel: 617-489-2000, 617-993-2850. p. 988
Cassidy, Lori, Instrul Design Librn, Orange Coast College Library, 2701 Fairview Rd, Costa Mesa, CA, 92626. Tel: 714-432-5885. p. 132
Cassidy, Suzanne L, Dir, Mercer University, Walter F George School of Law, Furman Smith Law Library, 1021 Georgia Ave, Macon, GA, 31201-1001. Tel: 478-301-2612. p. 486
Castanada, Shellee, Testing Ctr Coord, North Central Missouri College Library, Geyer Hall, 1st & 2nd Flr, 1301 Main St, Trenton, MO, 64683. Tel: 660-359-3948, Ext 1322, 660-359-3948, Ext 1325, 660-359-3948, Ext 1335. p. 1282
Castañeda, Elizabeth, Libr Tech II, Guerra Joe A Laredo Public Library, Lamar Bruni Vergara Inner City Branch Library, 202 W Plum St, Laredo, TX, 78041. Tel: 956-795-2400, Ext 2520. p. 2209
Castaneda-Rocha, Patricia, Dep Dir, Finance, East Chicago Public Library, 2401 E Columbus Dr, East Chicago, IN, 46312-2998. Tel: 219-397-2453. p. 680
Castano, Susana, Librn, Greenville Law Library Association, 331 S Broadway St, Greenville, OH, 45331. Tel: 937-680-0548. p. 1788
Castanon, Dorothea, Br Mgr, Corpus Christi Public Libraries, Ben F McDonald Branch, 4044 Greenwood Dr, Corpus Christi, TX, 78416. Tel: 361-826-2356. p. 2160
Castanon, Jenny, Asst Librn, Bayard Public Library, 1112 Central Ave, Bayard, NM, 88023. Tel: 575-537-6244. p. 1463
Casteel, Chandra, Libr Asst, Abraham Baldwin Agricultural College, 2802 Moore Hwy, Tifton, GA, 31793. Tel: 229-391-4990. p. 500
Casteel, Chandra, Libr Asst, Abraham Baldwin Agricultural College, Bainbridge Campus Library, 2500 E Shotwell St, Bainbridge, GA, 39819. Tel: 229-248-3795. p. 500
Casteel, Christine, Dir, Valley District Public Library, 515 Carter St, Fairview, IL, 61432. Tel: 309-778-2240. p. 588
Casteel, Shannon, Cat, Lewis-Clark State College Library, 500 Eighth Ave, Lewiston, ID, 83501. Tel: 208-792-2229. p. 524
Castel, Devin, Sr Bus Mgr, Syst Spec, Carlsbad City Library, 1775 Dove Lane, Carlsbad, CA, 92011. Tel: 760-602-2065. p. 127
Castellani, Jo Nell, Dir, Chadwick Public Library District, 110 Main St, Chadwick, IL, 61014. Tel: 815-684-5215. p. 551
Castellano, Harvey, Assoc Dir, Access Serv, Assoc Dir, Res & Instruction, University of Texas at El Paso Library, 500 W University Ave, El Paso, TX, 79968-0582. Tel: 915-747-6734. p. 2175
Castellanos, Carina, Mgr, County of Los Angeles Public Library, Lennox Library, 4359 Lennox Blvd, Lennox, CA, 90304. Tel: 310-674-0385. p. 137
Castellanos, Cleo, Dir, Clearwater Memorial Public Library, 402 Michigan Ave, Orofino, ID, 83544. Tel: 208-476-3411. p. 528
Castellanos, Nicolas O, Assoc Dir of Tech & Digital Services, Texas Southern University, 3100 Cleburne Ave, Houston, TX, 77004. Tel: 713-313-5024. p. 2198
Castelluzzo, Julie, Librn, Cooper Union for Advancement of Science & Art Library, Seven E Seventh St, New York, NY, 10003. Tel: 212-353-4186. p. 1584
Caster, Shannon, Head, Pub Serv, Cedar Mill Community Library, 1080 NW Saltzman Rd, Portland, OR, 97229-5603. Tel: 503-644-0043, Ext 105. p. 1891
Casterline, Lisa, Dir, Nokomis Public Library, 22 S Cedar St, Ste 2, Nokomis, IL, 62075. Tel: 217-563-2734. p. 625
Castilaw, Katrina, Dir, Lincoln-Lawrence-Franklin Regional Library, 100 S Jackson St, Brookhaven, MS, 39601. Tel: 601-833-3369, 601-833-5038. p. 1213
Castilla, Ana, Libr Serv Coordr, Edmonton Public Library, Calder, 12710 131 Ave NW, Edmonton, AB, T5L 2Z6, CANADA. Tel: 780-496-7093. p. 2536
Castillo, Andrea, Librn, Alexandria Library, 5005 Duke St, Alexandria, VA, 22304. Tel: 703-746-1702. p. 2302
Castillo, Jeanette, Head, Circ, Dustin Michael Sekula Memorial Library, 1906 S Closner Blvd, Edinburg, TX, 78539. Tel: 956-383-6246. p. 2173
Castillo, Krissy, Exec Dir, Santa Ynez Valley Historical Society, 3596 Sagunto St, Santa Ynez, CA, 93460. Tel: 805-688-7889. p. 245
Castillo, Martha, Libr Spec, Central New Mexico Community College Libraries, Westside Campus Library, WS1 200, 10549 Universe Blvd NW, Albuquerque, NM, 87114. Tel: 505-224-4000, Ext 52990. p. 1461
Castillo, Ruth, Libr Dir, Emory & Henry College, 30480 Armbrister Dr, Emory, VA, 24327. Tel: 276-944-6208. p. 2315
Castillo, Soledad, Mgr, County of Los Angeles Public Library, Bell Gardens Library, 7110 S Garfield Ave, Bell Gardens, CA, 90201-3244. Tel: 562-927-1309. p. 135
Castillo, Tim, Br Mgr, Chippewa River District Library, Shepherd Community Library, 257 W Wright Ave, Shepherd, MI, 48883. Tel: 989-828-6801. p. 1135
Castillo-Speed, Lillian, Head Librn, University of California, Berkeley, Ethnic Studies, 30 Stephens Hall, Berkeley, CA, 94720-2360. Tel: 510-642-3947. p. 122
Castle, Elaine, Librn, Logan County Libraries, Lakeview Branch, 130 N Main St, Lakeview, OH, 43331. Tel: 937-842-4144. p. 1750
Castle, Emma, Br Mgr, Martin County Library System, Hoke Library, 1150 NW Jack Williams Way, Jensen Beach, FL, 34957. Tel: 772-463-2870. p. 445
Castle, Heather, Br Head, Lake County Public Library, Highland Branch, 2841 Jewett St, Highland, IN, 46322-1617. Tel: 219-838-2394. p. 705
Castle, Lynn, Exec Dir, Amon Carter Museum of American Art, 3501 Camp Bowie Blvd, Fort Worth, TX, 76107-2695. Tel: 817-738-1933. p. 2179
Castle, Sara, Youth/Young Adult Librn, Pinckney Community Public Library, 125 Putnam St, Pinckney, MI, 48169. Tel: 734-878-3888. p. 1141

Castleberry, Crata, Librn, United States Court of Appeals, 600 W Capitol Ave, Rm 224, Little Rock, AR, 72201. Tel: 501-604-5215. p. 102
Castleberry, Liz, Head, Youth Serv, Comstock Township Library, 6130 King Hwy, Comstock, MI, 49041. Tel: 269-345-0136. p. 1093
Castleberry, Travis, Br Mgr, Public Library of Cincinnati & Hamilton County, Westwood, 3345 Epworth Ave, Cincinnati, OH, 45211. Tel: 513-369-4474. p. 1763
Casto, Joanna, Dir, Paden City Public Library, 114 S Fourth Ave, Paden City, WV, 26159. Tel: 304-337-9333. p. 2411
Casto, Lisa, Dir, Libr Serv, The Art Institute of Dallas, Two North Park E, 8080 Park Lane, Ste 100, Dallas, TX, 75231-5993. Tel: 469-587-1246. p. 2163
Casto, Mitch, Staff Librn, West Virginia University Institute of Technology, 405 Fayette Pike, Montgomery, WV, 25136-2436, Tel: 304-442-3230. p. 2409
Castonguay, Isabelle, Lead Librn, University of Ottawa Libraries, Health Sciences Library, Roger-Guindon Hall, Rm 1020, 451 Smyth Rd, Ottawa, ON, K1H 8M5, CANADA. Tel: 613-562-5407. p. 2670
Castor, Molly, Mkt Mgr, Outreach Mgr, Hinsdale Public Library, 20 E Maple St, Hinsdale, IL, 60521. Tel: 630-986-1976. p. 600
Castro, Arnold, Librn, Victorville City Library, 15011 Circle Dr, Victorville, CA, 92395. Tel: 760-243-1966. p. 256
Castro, Danilo, Mgr, Miami-Dade Public Library System, Virrick Park Branch, 3255 Plaza St, Coconut Grove, FL, 33133. Tel: 305-442-7872. p. 424
Castro, Eileen, Grants Coordr, Ref Librn, Galesburg Public Library, 40 E Simmons St, Galesburg, IL, 61401-4591. Tel: 309-343-6118. p. 591
Castro, Isabel, Br Mgr, Newark Public Library, Branch Brook, 235 Clifton Ave, Newark, NJ, 07104. Tel: 973-733-7760. p. 1427
Castro, Isabel, Asst Dir, West Orange Public Library, Ten Rooney Circle, West Orange, NJ, 07052. Tel: 973-736-0198. p. 1453
Castro, Victoria, Systems Access & Data Librarian, Heritage University, 3240 Fort Rd, Toppenish, WA, 98948. Tel: 509-865-8500, Ext 5421. p. 2388
Castro, Yoshira, Br Mgr, Manatee County Public Library System, Palmetto Branch, 923 Sixth St W, Palmetto, FL, 34221. Tel: 941-722-3333, p. 387
Castro-Santos, Jocelyn, Dir, Slate Memorial Library, 332 Main Rd, Gill, MA, 01376. Tel: 413-863-2591. p. 1020
Caswell, Cameron, Ref (Info Servs), Anne Arundel Community College, 101 College Pkwy, Arnold, MD, 21012-1895. Tel: 410-777-2211. p. 951
Caswell, Deena, Dir, Bushnell-Sage Library, 48 Main St, Sheffield, MA, 01257. Tel: 413-229-7004. p. 1052
Caswell, Meriah, Chief Exec Officer, Carleton Place Public Library, 101 Beckwith St, Carleton Place, ON, K7C 2T3, CANADA. Tel: 613-257-2702. p. 2635
Caswell, Thomas, Dir, Pub Serv, University of North Florida, Bldg 12-Library, One UNF Dr, Jacksonville, FL, 32224-2645. Tel: 904-620-5455. p. 413
Catahan, Margaret, Libr Coord, Saint Joseph Library, 440 S Batavia St, Orange, CA, 92868. Tel: 714-633-8121, Ext 7765. p. 189
Catalanello, Kim, Librn, Penfield Public Library, 1985 Baird Rd, Penfield, NY, 14526. Tel: 585-340-8720. p. 1616
Catalano, Lisa, Tech Serv, Flagler County Public Library, 2500 Palm Coast Pkwy NW, Palm Coast, FL, 32137. Tel: 386-446-6763. p. 434
Cataldo, Susan, Br Supvr, Hernando County Public Library System, 238 Howell Ave, Brooksville, FL, 34601. Tel: 352-754-4043. p. 387
Cataldo, Tobin, Dir, Jefferson County Library Cooperative Inc, 2100 Park Place, Birmingham, AL, 35203-2794. Tel: 205-226-3615. p. 2761
Cataldo, Willow, Br Mgr, Porter County Public Library System, Valparaiso Public, 103 Jefferson St, Valparaiso, IN, 46383-4820. Tel: 219-462-0524. p. 722
Catallo, Christine, Chief Librn, Pequot Library, 720 Pequot Ave, Southport, CT, 06890-1496. Tel: 203-259-0346. p. 338
Catano, Rachel, Libr Asst, The John W King New Hampshire Law Library, Supreme Court Bldg, One Charles Doe Dr, Concord, NH, 03301-6160. Tel: 603-271-3777. p. 1358
Cater, Lisa, Mgr, Satilla Regional Library, Willacoochee Public Library, 165 E Fleetwood Ave, Willacoochee, GA, 31650. Tel: 912-534-5252. p. 476
Cates, Jo, Libr Dir, Columbia College Chicago Library, 624 S Michigan Ave, Chicago, IL, 60605-1996. Tel: 312-369-8781. p. 559
Cates, Juana, Dir, Media Library, First Baptist Church Library, 200 E Main St, Murfreesboro, TN, 37130. Tel: 615-893-2514. p. 2117
Cates, Kristi, Teen Serv, Normal Public Library, 206 W College Ave, Normal, IL, 61761. Tel: 309-452-1757. p. 625
Cathcart, Cynthia, Dir, Conde Nast Publications Library, One World Trade Ctr, New York, NY, 10007. Tel: 212-286-2860. p. 1584
Cathcart, Shelley, Curator of Collections & Exhibits, Museum of Early Trades & Crafts Library, Nine Main St, Madison, NJ, 07940. Tel: 973-377-2982, Ext 10. p. 1415
Cathcart, Taylor, Circ, Steeleville Area Public Library District, 625 S Sparta St, Steeleville, IL, 62288-2147. Tel: 618-965-9732. p. 651
Cathel, Elke, Mgt Analyst, Glendora Public Library & Cultural Center, 140 S Glendora Ave, Glendora, CA, 91741. Tel: 626-852-4827. p. 149
Cathey, Gail, Access Serv Librn, Chestnut Hill College, 9601 Germantown Ave, Philadelphia, PA, 19118-2695. Tel: 215-248-7053. p. 1975
Cathi, Carmack, Dir of Archival Tech Serv, Tennessee State Library & Archives, 403 Seventh Ave N, Nashville, TN, 37243-0312. Tel: 615-253-3468. p. 2121
Catlett, Chelsea, Supvr, Oklahoma Department of Corrections, 19603 E Whippoorwill Ln, Atoka, OK, 74525-5560. Tel: 580-889-6651. p. 1841
Catlin, Paula, Librn, Pawnee Heights Library, 603 Elm St, Burdett, KS, 67523. Tel: 620-525-6279. p. 799
Catlyn, Stephanie, Circ Supvr, Clearwater Public Library System, Countryside, 2642 Sabal Springs Dr, Clearwater, FL, 33761. Tel: 727-562-4970. p. 389
Caton, Amy, Assoc Dir, Libr Serv, Texas A&M University at Galveston, Bldg 3010, 200 Seawolf Pkwy, Galveston, TX, 77554. Tel: 409-740-4711. p. 2183
Caton, Rebecca, Dir, Libr Serv, Midwestern University, 555 31st St, Downers Grove, IL, 60515. Tel: 630-515-6200. p. 579
Catron, Donna, Br Mgr, Muncie Public Library, John F Kennedy Branch, 1700 W McGalliard Rd, Muncie, IN, 47304. Tel: 765-741-9727. p. 709
Catron, Staci, Libr Dir, Atlanta History Center, Cherokee Garden Library, 130 W Paces Ferry Rd, Atlanta, GA, 30305. Tel: 404-814-4046. p. 462
Catto, Natalie, Libr Asst, Nova Scotia Community College, Annapolis Valley - Middleton Campus Library, 295 Commercial St, Middleton, NS, B0S 1P0, CANADA. Tel: 902-825-2930, 902-825-5481. p. 2619
Cauce, Rita, Head, Cat, Florida International University, 11200 SW Eighth St, Miami, FL, 33199. Tel: 305-348-0547. p. 421
Caudill, Amanda, Librn, Dallas College, 3030 N Dallas Ave, Lancaster, TX, 75134-3799. Tel: 972-860-8140. p. 2209
Caudill, Mitch, Campus Libr Dir, Southeast Kentucky Community & Technical College, 700 College Rd, Cumberland, KY, 40823. Tel: 606-589-3099. p. 853
Caudill, Mitchell, Campus Libr Dir, Southeast Kentucky Community & Technical College, Two Long Ave, Whitesburg, KY, 41858. Tel: 606-589-3209, 606-589-3334. p. 877
Caudill, Seth, Archivist, Librn, West Virginia State University, Campus Box L17, Institute, WV, 25112. Tel: 304-766-3023. p. 2406
Caudill, Seth D, Assoc Univ Librn, Libr Dir, Potomac State College of West Virginia University, 103 Fort Ave, Keyser, WV, 26726. Tel: 304-788-6901. p. 2406
Caudill, Tessa, Ch, Letcher County Public Library District, 220 Main St, Whitesburg, KY, 41858. Tel: 606-633-7547. p. 877
Caudle Chavira, Debra, Dir, Ellsworth Public Library, 1549 Dewitt St, Ellsworth, IA, 50075. Tel: 515-836-4852. p. 751
Caudle, Mary Anne, Libr Dir, Martin Community College Library, 1161 Kehukee Park Rd, Williamston, NC, 27892-4425. Tel: 252-789-0238. p. 1722
Caufield, Daniel, Institutional Serv Mgr, Buffalo & Erie County Public Library System, Erie County Correctional Facility, 11581 Walden Ave, Alden, NY, 14004-0300. Tel: 716-858-5578. p. 1508
Caufield, Daniel, Mgr, Buffalo & Erie County Public Library System, Erie County Holding Center, 40 Delaware Ave, Buffalo, NY, 14202-3999. Tel: 716-858-8909. p. 1508
Caughlin, Amy, Chief Exec Officer, Scugog Memorial Public Library, 231 Water St, Port Perry, ON, L9L 1A8, CANADA. Tel: 905-985-7686. p. 2674
Caughman, Jenny, Library Contact, First United Methodist Church, 1350 Oak Ridge Tpk, Oak Ridge, TN, 37830. Tel: 865-483-4357. p. 2123
Caulder, Susan Wong, Librn, United States District Court, Phillip Burton Federal Bldg, 450 Golden Gate Ave, San Francisco, CA, 94102. Tel: 415-436-8130. p. 229
Cauley, Heidi, Tech Serv, Attleboro Public Library, 74 N Main St, Attleboro, MA, 02703. Tel: 508-222-0157. p. 986
Cauley, Kate, Emerging Tech Librn, John Jay College of Criminal Justice, 899 Tenth Ave, New York, NY, 10019. Tel: 212-237-8261. p. 1589
Caulfield, Elizabeth, Librn, California Second District Court of Appeals, 300 S Spring St, Rm 3547, Los Angeles, CA, 90013. Tel: 213-830-7242. p. 160
Caulkins, Sandra, Circ Librn, Kirbyville Public Library, 210 S Elizabeth St, Kirbyville, TX, 75956. Tel: 409-423-4653. p. 2207
Cauntay, Robin, Br Mgr, Monterey County Free Libraries, King City Branch, 402 Broadway St, King City, CA, 93930. Tel: 831-385-3677. p. 172
Cause, Cheryl, Librn, Newfield Village Library & Reading Room, 637 Water St, West Newfield, ME, 04095. Tel: 207-809-7014. p. 946
Causey, Colby, Archivist, Calhoun County Museum & Cultural Center, 313 Butler St, Saint Matthews, SC, 29135. Tel: 803-874-3964. p. 2069
Causey, Enid, Archivist, Charleston Southern University, 9200 University Blvd, Charleston, SC, 29406. Tel: 843-863-7940. p. 2050
Causey, Lisa, Br Mgr, Athens County Public Libraries, Coolville Public, 26401 Main St, Coolville, OH, 45723-9059. Tel: 740-667-3354. p. 1805
Causey, Melissa, Youth Serv, Bartow Public Library, 2150 S Broadway Ave, Bartow, FL, 33830. Tel: 863-534-0131. p. 384
Caust-Ellenbogen, Celia, Assoc Curator, Swarthmore College, Friends Historical Library, 500 College Ave, Swarthmore, PA, 19081. Tel: 610-328-8496. p. 2012
Cauthen, Paul, Asst Music Librn, University of Cincinnati Libraries, College-Conservatory of Music, 600 Blegen Library, Cincinnati, OH, 45221. Tel: 513-556-1965. p. 1765

Cauthen, Robert, Libr Mgr, Wake County Public Library System, Express Library Fayetteville Street, Wake County Off Bldg, 336 Fayetteville St, Raleigh, NC, 27601. Tel: 919-856-6690. p. 1711

Cavacco, Julie, Ch, Tilton Library, 75 N Main St, South Deerfield, MA, 01373. Tel: 413-665-4683. p. 1054

Cavada, J, Libr Asst, Tiskilwa Public Library, 119 E Main, Tiskilwa, IL, 61368. Tel: 815-646-4511. p. 654

Cavaleri, Vinny, Technology Spec, Gilchrist County Public Library, 105 NE 11th Ave, Trenton, FL, 32693-3803. Tel: 352-463-3176. p. 451

Cavalier, Donald, Librn, Dixon Correctional Institute, 5568 LA-68, Jackson, LA, 70748. Tel: 225-634-1200. p. 891

Cavaliere, Ciro, Circ Mgr/ILL, Emmaus Public Library, 11 E Main St, Emmaus, PA, 18049. Tel: 610-965-9284. p. 1930

Cavaliere, Rita, Librn, Nicola Valley Institute of Technology Library, 4155 Belshaw St, Merritt, BC, V1K 1R1, CANADA. Tel: 250-378-3303. p. 2570

Cavallero, Jennifer, Libr Mgr, District of Columbia Talking Book & Braille Library, Center for Accessibility, Rm 215, 901 G St NW, Washington, DC, 20001. Tel: 202-727-2142. p. 365

Cavallo, Richard J, Chief Financial Officer, Mercer County Library System, 2751 Brunswick Pike, Lawrenceville, NJ, 08648-4132. Tel: 609-883-8298. p. 1411

Cavanagh, Joan, Assoc Univ Librn, Learning & User Services, University of Ottawa Libraries, 65 University Private, Ottawa, ON, K1N 6N5, CANADA. Tel: 613-562-5690. p. 2670

Cavanagh, Moira, Ref Librn, Thayer Public Library, 798 Washington St, Braintree, MA, 02184. Tel: 781-848-0405, Ext 4434. p. 1001

Cavanaugh, Billi-Jo, Admin Coordr, Royal Roads University Library, 2005 Sooke Rd, Victoria, BC, V9B 5Y2, CANADA. Tel: 250-391-2595. p. 2583

Cavanaugh, Daniel, Archivist, University of Virginia, Arthur J Morris Law Library, 580 Massie Rd, Charlottesville, VA, 22903-1738. Tel: 434-924-3460. p. 2310

Cavanaugh, Jason, Ref Librn, Forbush Memorial Library, 118 Main St, Westminster, MA, 01473. Tel: 978-874-7416. p. 1067

Cavanaugh, Jerome, Dr, Dir, Far Eastern Research Library, Nine First Ave NE, Plato, MN, 55370. Tel: 612-926-6887. p. 1193

Cavanaugh, Linda, Libr Dir, Clyde Public Library, 125 Oak St, Clyde, TX, 79510-4702. Tel: 325-893-5315. p. 2156

Cavanaugh, Luci, Libr Asst, Johnson County Public Library, 219 N Church St, Mountain City, TN, 37683. Tel: 423-727-6544. p. 2117

Cavazos, Leo, Librn, Houston Community College-Central College, Central Campus Library, 1300 Holman, Houston, TX, 77004. Tel: 713-718-6133. p. 2194

Cave, Laksamee Putnam, Ad, Bixby Memorial Free Library, 258 Main St, Vergennes, VT, 05491. Tel: 802-877-2211. p. 2296

Cave, Mark, Senior Historian, Historic New Orleans Collection, 410 Chartres St, New Orleans, LA, 70130. Tel: 504-5987132. p. 901

Cave-Davis, Carol, Dir, Ref, Jamaica Hospital Medical Center, Axel Bldg, 4th Flr, 8900 Van Wyck Expressway, Jamaica, NY, 11418-2832. Tel: 718-206-8450. p. 1553

Cavicchi, Jon R, IP Librn, University of New Hampshire School of Law, Two White St, Concord, NH, 03301. p. 1360

Cavill, Melissa, Circ Supvr, Cotuit Library, 871 Main St, Cotuit, MA, 02635. Tel: 508-428-8141. p. 1013

Cavin, Tina, Dir, Pub Libr Serv, Blackwell Public Library, 123 W Padon, Blackwell, OK, 74631-2805. Tel: 580-363-1809. p. 1842

Caviness, Celeste, Library Contact, Butler Hospital, 345 Blackstone Blvd, Providence, RI, 02906. Tel: 401-455-6248. p. 2037

Cawley, Betsy, Dir of Libr, Bard College, One Library Rd, Annandale-on-Hudson, NY, 12504. Tel: 845-758-6822. p. 1487

Cawley, Cindy, Mgr, Columbus Metropolitan Library, Southeast, 3980 S Hamilton Rd, Groveport, OH, 43125. p. 1773

Cawley, Kristine, Librn, Tri-City Jewish Center Library, 2215 E Kimberly Rd, Davenport, IA, 52807. Tel: 309-644-2765. p. 744

Cawley, Sarah, Exec Dir, Lewis & Clark Trail Heritage Foundation, Inc, 4201 Giant Spring Rd, Ste 2, Great Falls, MT, 59405. Tel: 406-454-1234. p. 1294

Cawthon, Amanda, Youth Serv Librn, Pflugerville Public Library, 1008 W Pfluger, Pflugerville, TX, 78660. Tel: 512-990-6375. p. 2226

Cawthorne, Jon E, Dean, Wayne State University Libraries, 5150 Gullen Mall, Ste 3100, Detroit, MI, 48202. Tel: 313-577-4020. p. 1100

Cawthorne, Jon E, Dr, Dean, Wayne State University, 106 Kresge Library, Detroit, MI, 48202. Tel: 313-577-4020. p. 2787

Cawthron, Lillie, Br Mgr, Huntsville-Madison County Public Library, R Showers Center, 4600 Blue Spring Rd, Huntsville, AL, 35810. Tel: 256-851-7492. p. 22

Caya, Aimee, Dir, Libr & Res Serv, LancasterHistory, 230 N President Ave, Lancaster, PA, 17603-3125. Tel: 717-392-4633. p. 1951

Cayouette, Veronique, Librn, Revenu Quebec Centre de documentation, 3800 rue de Marly, Secteur 5-1-10, Quebec, QC, G1X 4A5, CANADA. Tel: 418-652-5765. p. 2731

Cazares, Len, Librn, Houston Community College-Central College, Central Campus Library, 1300 Holman, Houston, TX, 77004. Tel: 713-718-6133. p. 2194

Cazares, Theresa, Mgr, County of Los Angeles Public Library, Los Nietos Library, 8511 Duchess Dr, Whittier, CA, 90606. Tel: 562-695-0708. p. 137

Cearley Hill, Gretchen, Pub Serv Mgr, Elon University, 308 N O'Kelly Ave, Elon, NC, 27244-0187. Tel: 336-278-6600. p. 1688

Cease, Jennifer, Cat, Pfeiffer University, 48380 US Hwy 52 N, Misenheimer, NC, 28109. Tel: 704-463-3351. p. 1703

Cebula, Emily, Libr Dir, Yates Community Library, 15 N Main St, Lyndonville, NY, 14098. Tel: 585-765-9041. p. 1566

Cech, Maureen, Archivist, Misericordia University, 301 Lake St, Dallas, PA, 18612-1098. Tel: 570-674-6420. p. 1925

Cech, Yvonne, Dir, The Brookfield Library, 182 Whisconier Rd, Brookfield, CT, 06804. Tel: 203-775-6241, Ext 101. p. 304

Cech, Yvonne, Dir, John C Hart Memorial Library, 1130 Main St, Shrub Oak, NY, 10588. Tel: 914-245-5262. p. 1641

Ceci, Kyle, Instruction Librn, Delta College Library, 1961 Delta Rd, University Center, MI, 48710. Tel: 989-686-9006. p. 1155

Cecil, Brad, Head Librn, Ohio University, Shannon Hall, 1st Flr, 45425 National Rd, Saint Clairsville, OH, 43950-9724. Tel: 740-699-2332. p. 1818

Cecil, Cheryl, Chair, Circ, Samford University Library, 800 Lakeshore Dr, Birmingham, AL, 35229. Tel: 205-726-2699. p. 8

Cecil, Kimberly, Br Mgr, Enlow Ruth Library of Garrett County, Accident Branch, 106 S North St, Accident, MD, 21520. Tel: 301-746-8792. p. 972

Cecil, Patricia Baudino, Librn & Archivist, University of Kansas, Department of Religious Studies, Smith Hall, Rm 109, 1300 Oread Ave, Lawrence, KS, 66045-7615. Tel: 785-864-4341. p. 819

Ceder-Ryba, Kelly, Circ Mgr, Fayette Public Library, 855 S Jefferson St, La Grange, TX, 78945. Tel: 979-968-3765. p. 2207

Cederbaum, Lisa, Ch, Mark Twain Library, 439 Redding Rd, Redding, CT, 06896. Tel: 203-938-2545. p. 334

Cegan, Sarah, Law Librn, Tehama County Law Library, 955 Main St, Ste C, Red Bluff, CA, 96080. Tel: 530-529-5033. p. 198

Celec, Michael, Libr Dir, Union Library Company of Hatborough, 243 S York Rd, Hatboro, PA, 19040. Tel: 215-672-1420. p. 1942

Celek, Maxwell, Operations & Bus Mgr, Birchard Public Library of Sandusky County, 423 Croghan St, Fremont, OH, 43420. Tel: 419-334-7101. p. 1786

Celestin, Charlotte, Br Mgr, Terrebonne Parish Library, Gibson Branch, 6400 Bayou Black Dr, Gibson, LA, 70356. Tel: 985-575-2639. p. 891

Celestine, KC, Director of Library & Academic Support, Fletcher Technical Community College Library, 1407 Hwy 311, Rm 128, Schriever, LA, 70395. Tel: 985-448-7963. p. 907

Celli, Barbara, Coordr, Italian Cultural Institute of Montreal La Bibliotheque, 1200 Dr Penfield Ave, Montreal, QC, H3A 1A9, CANADA. Tel: 514-849-3473. p. 2725

Cellini, Jacqueline, Head, Libr Serv, Mathematica Inc Library, 600 Alexander Park, Ste 100, Princeton, NJ, 08543. Tel: 609-275-2239. p. 1436

Celsie, Mary Jane, Dir, Content Prog, Richmond Hill Public Library, One Atkinson St, Richmond Hill, ON, L4C 0H5, CANADA. Tel: 905-884-9288. p. 2675

Cen, Wei, Librn, Middlesex Community College, 100 Training Hill Rd, Middletown, CT, 06457. Tel: 860-343-5834. p. 322

Cengel, Abigail, Dir, Swarthmore Public Library, Borough Hall, 121 Park Ave, Swarthmore, PA, 19081-1536. Tel: 610-543-0436, 610-543-3171. p. 2012

Censke, Julie, Dir, Colon Township Library, 128 S Blackstone Ave, Colon, MI, 49040. Tel: 269-432-3958. p. 1093

Centeno, Fatima, Mgr, Miami-Dade Public Library System, Homestead Branch, 700 N Homestead Blvd, Homestead, FL, 33030. Tel: 305-246-0168. p. 423

Centeno-Alayon, Purisima C, Librn III, University of Puerto Rico RP College of Natural Sciences Library, 17 Ave Universidad, Ste 1701, San Juan, PR, 00925-2537. Tel: 787-764-0000, Ext 88387. p. 2515

Center, Clark, Curator, University of Alabama, University Libraries, University of Alabama Campus, Capstone Dr, Tuscaloosa, AL, 35487. Tel: 205-348-0513. p. 38

Center, Joanne, Ref & Info Serv, Sr Librn, Oxnard Public Library, 251 South A St, Oxnard, CA, 93030. Tel: 805-200-5689. p. 190

Centivany, Alissa, Asst Prof, Western University, FIMS & Nursing Bldg, Rm 2020, London, ON, N6A 5B9, CANADA. Tel: 519-661-2111, Ext 88510. p. 2796

Centrella, Susan, Colls Serv Mgr, Teton County Library, 125 Virginian Lane, Jackson, WY, 83001. Tel: 307-733-2164, Ext 3104. p. 2495

Cepeda, Geraldine Amparo, Exec Dir/Librn, Guam Law Library, 141 San Ramon St, Hagatna, GU, 96910-4333. Tel: 671-477-7623. p. 2505

Cepeda, Sharon, Yout Serv Asst, Newton Public Library, 720 N Oak, Newton, KS, 67114. Tel: 316-283-2890. p. 826

Ceperich, Lee B, Dir, Dir, Spec Coll, Virginia Museum of Fine Arts Library, 200 N Arthur Ashe Blvd, Richmond, VA, 23220-4007. Tel: 804-340-1496. p. 2344

Ceppaglia, Deborah, Ref & Instruction Librn, Medaille College Library, 18 Agassiz Circle, Buffalo, NY, 14214. Tel: 716-880-2283. p. 1509

Ceravolo, Teresa, Librn, Birmingham Public Library, Southside, 1814 11th Ave S, Birmingham, AL, 35205-4808. Tel: 205-933-7776. p. 7

Cerce, Linda, Develop, New Jersey State Library, Talking Book & Braille Center, 2300 Stuyvesant Ave, Trenton, NJ, 08618. Tel: 609-406-7179, Ext 835. p. 1448

Cerise, Caitie, Libr Dir, Walton County Public Library System, Three Circle Dr, De Funiak Springs, FL, 32435-2542. Tel: 850-892-3624. p. 393

Cernich, Jennifer, Dir, Riverton Village Library, 1200 E Riverton Rd, Riverton, IL, 62561-8200. Tel: 217-629-6353. p. 639

Cerniglia, Lauren, Asst Dir, Cook Memorial Public Library District, 413 N Milwaukee Ave, Libertyville, IL, 60048-2280. Tel: 847-362-2330. p. 608

Cernik, Laura, Dir, Menands Public Library, Four N Lyons Ave, Menands, NY, 12204. Tel: 518-463-4035. p. 1570

Cernin, Shirley, Asst Librn, Belle Plaine Community Library, 904 12th St, Belle Plaine, IA, 52208-1711. Tel: 319-444-2902. p. 734

Cerqua, Russell, Bus Mgr, Cook Memorial Public Library District, 413 N Milwaukee Ave, Libertyville, IL, 60048-2280. Tel: 847-362-2330. p. 608

Cerri, Jessica, Curator, Spec Coll, Univ Archivist, Wichita State University Libraries, 1845 Fairmount, Wichita, KS, 67260-0068. Tel: 316-978-3590. p. 844

Cerul, Christa, Dir, Stanford Free Library, 6035 Rte 82, Stanfordville, NY, 12581. Tel: 845-868-1341. p. 1644

Cervantes, Melinda, County Librn, Contra Costa County Library, 777 Arnold Dr, Ste 210, Martinez, CA, 94553. Tel: 925-608-7700. p. 173

Cervantes, Michelle, Libr Dir, Round Rock Public Library, 200 E Liberty Ave, Round Rock, TX, 78664. Tel: 512-218-7010. p. 2234

Cervantes, Nallely, Br Librn, Livermore Public Library, Rincon, 725 Rincon Ave, Livermore, CA, 94550. Tel: 925-373-5540. p. 157

Cervantes, Vikki, City Librn, Porterville Public Library, 15 E Thurman Ave, 2nd Flr, Ste B, Porterville, CA, 93257. Tel: 559-782-7493, 559-784-0177. p. 197

Cervantes-Squires, Michaelene, Coll Develop, Dir, Mokena Community Public Library District, 11327 W 195th St, Mokena, IL, 60448. Tel: 708-479-9663. p. 618

Cervarich, Kate, Br Mgr, Henrico County Public Library, Gayton Branch Library, 10600 Gayton Rd, Henrico, VA, 23238. Tel: 804-501-1960. p. 2325

Cervelli, Kara, Ch Serv, Perry Public Library, 3753 Main St, Perry, OH, 44081-9501. Tel: 440-259-3300. p. 1815

Cesar, Courtney, Libr Dir, American Truck Historical Society, 10380 N Ambassador Dr, Ste 101, Kansas City, MO, 64153-1378. Tel: 816-777-0924. p. 1254

Cesena, Danielle, Ch, Glen Rock Public Library, 315 Rock Rd, Glen Rock, NJ, 07452. Tel: 201-670-3970. p. 1405

Cesnales, Lauren, Dir, New Brighton Public Library, 1021 Third Ave, New Brighton, PA, 15066-3011. Tel: 724-846-7991. p. 1968

Cessna, Barbara, Researcher, Fenton History Center, 73 Forest Ave, Jamestown, NY, 14701. Tel: 716-664-6256, Ext 104. p. 1557

Cesta, Jennifer, Pub Serv, Public Library of Steubenville & Jefferson County, 407 S Fourth St, Steubenville, OH, 43952-2942. Tel: 740-282-9782. p. 1822

Cetina, Judith G, PhD, Dr, Archivist, Cuyahoga County Archives Library, 3951 Perkins Ave, Cleveland, OH, 44114. Tel: 216-443-7250. p. 1769

Cettina, Wendy, Dir, Oceanic Free Library, 109 Avenue of Two Rivers, Rumson, NJ, 07760. Tel: 732-842-2692. p. 1441

Cetwinski, Tom, Dir, Admin Serv, University of South Florida, Tampa Campus Library, 4101 USF Apple Dr, LIB122, Tampa, FL, 33620. Tel: 813-974-4592. p. 450

Ceus, Nerolie, ILL, Ser, Palm Beach Atlantic University, 300 Pembroke Pl, West Palm Beach, FL, 33401-6503. Tel: 561-803-2226. p. 453

Cha, Teng, Prog Spec, Iredell County Public Library, 201 N Tradd St, Statesville, NC, 28677. Tel: 704-878-5448. p. 1717

Chaban, Kelsey, Commun Outreach Librn, Kwantlen Polytechnic University Library, 12666 72nd Ave, Surrey, BC, V3W 2M8, CANADA. Tel: 604-599-3236. p. 2576

Chaberek, Guna K, Dir, Mineral County Public Library, 301 Second Ave E, Superior, MT, 59872. Tel: 406-822-3563. p. 1302

Chabot, Billye, Exec Dir, The Seward House Museum, 33 South St, Auburn, NY, 13021-3929. Tel: 315-252-1283. p. 1489

Chabot, Juanita, Libr Spec, Stanford University Libraries, Branner Earth Sciences & Map Collections, Mitchell Bldg, 2nd Flr, 397 Panama Mall, Stanford, CA, 94305-2174. Tel: 650-723-2746. p. 248

Chabot, Shannon, Children & Youth Serv Librn, Fort Nelson Public Library, Municipal Sq, 5315-50th Ave S, Fort Nelson, BC, V0C 1R0, CANADA. Tel: 250-774-6777. p. 2566

Chace, Mickey, Curator, Research Librn, Mohave County Historical Society, 400 W Beale St, Kingman, AZ, 86401. Tel: 928-753-3195. p. 64

Chacon, Josephine, Mgr, Libr Serv, Trinidad State Junior College, 600 Prospect St, Trinidad, CO, 81082. Tel: 719-846-5474. p. 297

Chaddock, Heather, Exec Dir, Westchester Public Library, 200 W Indiana Ave, Chesterton, IN, 46304. Tel: 219-926-7696. p. 674

Chadwell, Donna, Dir, Corbin Public Library, 215 Roy Kidd Ave, Corbin, KY, 40701. Tel: 606-528-6366. p. 852

Chadwell, Jeff, Dir, Peterstown Public Library, 23 College Dr, Peterstown, WV, 24963. Tel: 304-753-9568. p. 2412

Chadwick, Autumn, Librn, Brownville Free Public Library, 27 Church St, Brownville, ME, 04414-3235. Tel: 207-965-8334. p. 919

Chadwick, Cindy, County Librn, Alameda County Library, 2450 Stevenson Blvd, Fremont, CA, 94538-2326. Tel: 510-745-1504. p. 143

Chadwick, Erica, Asst Dir, Suttons Bay Bingham District Library, 416 Front St, Suttons Bay, MI, 49682. Tel: 231-271-3512. p. 1153

Chadwick, Gayle, Br Librn, Lincoln County Library System, Cokeville Branch, 240 E Main St, Cokeville, WY, 83114. Tel: 307-279-3213. p. 2496

Chadwick, Kay Marie, Libr Tech II, Colorado Department of Corrections, 11363 Lockhart Rd, Delta, CO, 81416. Tel: 970-874-7614, Ext 2955. p. 273

Chadwick, Nathan, Br Mgr, Montgomery County Public Libraries, Long Branch Library, 8800 Garland Ave, Silver Spring, MD, 20901. Tel: 240-773-9526. p. 974

Chadwick, Peggy, Libr Tech, Williams Baptist University, 60 W Fulbright, Walnut Ridge, AR, 72476. Tel: 870-759-4139. p. 112

Chae, Hui Soo, Dir, Res & Develop, Teachers College, Columbia University, 525 W 120th St, New York, NY, 10027-6696. Tel: 212-678-3448. p. 1602

Chaffee, Joanne, Br Mgr, Milan-Berlin Library District, Berlin Public Library, Four E Main St, Berlin Heights, OH, 44814-9602. Tel: 419-588-2250. p. 1802

Chaffee, Sue, Libr Dir, Newfield Public Library, 198 Main St, Newfield, NY, 14867. Tel: 607-564-3594. p. 1606

Chaffey, Charlotte, Archivist, Royal Ontario Museum, 100 Queen's Park, Toronto, ON, M5S 2C6, CANADA. Tel: 416-586-8000, Ext 4033. p. 2692

Chaffin, Dena, Youth Serv Librn, Silver Falls Library District, 410 S Water St, Silverton, OR, 97381. Tel: 503-873-5173. p. 1899

Chaffin, Melanie, Mgr, Superior District Library, Engadine Library, W13920 Melville St, Engadine, MI, 49827. Tel: 906-477-6313, Ext 140. p. 1149

Chaffin, Nina, Libr Dir, Union County Public Library, 316 E Windsor St, Monroe, NC, 28112. Tel: 704-283-8184. p. 1703

Chaffin, Sharon, Br Mgr, Perry County District Library, Thornville Branch, 99 E Columbus St, Thornville, OH, 43076. Tel: 740-246-5133. p. 1806

Chaffin, Walker, Mr, Librn, K&L Gates Library, 1717 Main St, Ste 2800, Dallas, TX, 75201. Tel: 214-939-5510. p. 2167

Chafin, Sandra, Ch Serv, Mims/Scottsmoor Public Library, 3615 Lionel Rd, Mims, FL, 32754. Tel: 321-264-5080. p. 426

Chagnon, Danielle, Libr Dir, Bibliotheque et Archives Nationales du Quebec, 475 de Maisonneuve E, Montreal, QC, H2L 5C4, CANADA. Tel: 514-873-1101, Ext 3245. p. 2717

Chagnon, Nichole, Fac Librn, Austin Community College, Riverside Campus Library, 1020 Grove Blvd, 1st Flr, Rm 1108, Austin, TX, 78741. Tel: 512-223-6004. p. 2138

Chahal, Christine, Principal Advisor, Coll Dev, Polytechnique Montreal Library, Campus de l'Universite de Montreal, 2500, chemin de Polytechnique, 2900, boul Edouard-Montpetit, Montreal, QC, H3T 1J4, CANADA. Tel: 514-340-4711, Ext 7207. p. 2727

Chakmakian, Susan, Syst Librn, United States Naval War College Library, 686 Cushing Rd, Newport, RI, 02841-1207. Tel: 401-841-6492. p. 2035

Chakraborty, Moushumi, Dir, External Libr Serv, Salisbury University, 1101 Camden Ave, Salisbury, MD, 21801-6863. Tel: 410-543-6130. p. 976

Chalick, David, Librn, Collier County Public Library, Golden Gate, 2432 Lucerne Rd, Naples, FL, 34116. Tel: 239-455-1441. p. 427

Chaliff, Pamela, Dir, Rockcastle County Public Library, 60 Ford Dr, Mount Vernon, KY, 40456. Tel: 606-256-2388. p. 870

Chalker, Cynthia, Librn, Moran Public Library, 308 N Spruce St, Moran, KS, 66755. Tel: 620-237-4334. p. 826

Chalmers, Judy, Tech Serv Librn, Washoe County Law Library, 75 Courth St, Rm 101, Reno, NV, 89501. Tel: 775-328-3250. p. 1350

Chalmers, Patricia L, Asst Librn, Access Serv, University of King's College Library, 6350 Coburg Rd, Halifax, NS, B3H 2A1, CANADA. Tel: 902-422-1271. p. 2621

Chalmers, Stephen, Br Mgr, Mid-Continent Public Library, Excelsior Springs Branch, 1460 Kearney Rd, Excelsior Springs, MO, 64024. Tel: 816-630-6721. p. 1250

Chalungsooth, Apichart, Access Serv, Syst Librn, Howard Community College Library, 10901 Little Patuxent Pkwy, 2nd Flr, Columbia, MD, 21044. Tel: 443-518-4683. p. 963

Chalupa, Kira, Libr Mgr, Vegreville Centennial Library, 4709-50 St, Vegreville, AB, T9C 1R1, CANADA. Tel: 780-632-3491. p. 2558

Chamberlain, Beth, Head, Tech Serv, Touro University, 225 Eastview Dr, Central Islip, NY, 11722-4539. Tel: 631-761-7150. p. 1516

Chamberlain, Carol, Cataloger, Circ, Weeks Public Library, 36 Post Rd, Greenland, NH, 03840-2312. Tel: 603-436-8548. p. 1365

Chamberlain, Deborah, Librn, Russell Memorial Library, 4333 State Prison Hollow Rd, Monkton, VT, 05469. Tel: 802-453-4471. p. 2289

Chamberlain, Enrique, Dr, Head Librn, Dallas College, 5001 N MacArthur Blvd, Irving, TX, 75062. Tel: 972-273-3400. p. 2202

Chamberlain, Jennifer, Interim Dir, Monarch Library System, 4632 S Taylor Dr, Sheboygan, WI, 53081-1107. Tel: 920-208-4900, Ext 312. p. 2477

Chamberlain, Jennifer, Exec Dir, WiLS, 1360 Regent St, Ste 121, Madison, WI, 53715-1255. Tel: 608-205-8591. p. 2777

Chamberlain, Jennifer, Project Mgr, Wisconsin Public Library Consortium, c/o WiLS, 1360 Regent St, No 121, Madison, WI, 53713. Tel: 608-218-4480. p. 2777

Chamberlain, Jessica, Dir, Norfolk Public Library, 308 W Prospect Ave, Norfolk, NE, 68701-4138. Tel: 402-844-2100. p. 1326

Chamberlain, Marion, Circ Supvr, Seminole Community Library at St Petersburg College, 9200 113th St N, Seminole, FL, 33772. Tel: 727-394-6909. p. 444

Chamberlain, Mitchell, Circ Librn, Tennessee State University, Avon Williams Library, 330 Tenth Ave N, Nashville, TN, 37203. Tel: 615-963-7190. p. 2121

Chamberot, Robert, Chef de Section, Bibliotheques de Montreal, Cote-des-Neiges, 5290 chemin de la Cote-des-Neiges, Montreal, QC, H3T 1Y2, CANADA. Tel: 514-872-2935. p. 2718

Chamberot, Robert, Chef de Section, Bibliotheques de Montreal, Notre-Dame-de-Grace, 3755 rue Botrel, Montreal, QC, H4A 3G8, CANADA. Tel: 514-872-2935. p. 2720

Chambers, Albert, Ref Librn, Donna Public Library, 301 S Main St, Donna, TX, 78537. Tel: 956-464-2221. p. 2171

Chambers, Christina, Br Mgr, Summit County Libraries, South Branch, Breckenridge Grand Vacations Community Ctr, 103 S Harris St, Breckenridge, CO, 80424. Tel: 970-453-3544. p. 282

Chambers, Cynthia, Head, Info Mgt, St John's University Library, St Augustine Hall, 8000 Utopia Pkwy, Jamaica, NY, 11439. Tel: 718-990-1355. p. 1556

Chambers, Diane, Mgr, West Georgia Regional Library, Centralhatchee Public Library, 171 Motnomis Rd, Franklin, GA, 30217. Tel: 678-853-9047. p. 469

Chambers, Hayley, Sr Curator, Mus Coll, Ketchikan Museums, Tongass Historical Museum Research Library, 629 Dock St, Ketchikan, AK, 99901. Tel: 907-228-5708. p. 48

Chambers, Helen, Br Mgr, Polkville Public Library, 6334 Hwy 13, Morton, MS, 39117. Tel: 601-537-3116. p. 1227

Chambers, Holly, Sr Asst Librn, State University of New York College at Potsdam, Lougheed Learning Commons, 44 Pierrepont Ave, Potsdam, NY, 13676-2294. Tel: 315-267-3312. p. 1622

Chambers, Kathy, Librn, Inyo County Free Library, Lone Pine Branch, 127 Bush St, Lone Pine, CA, 93545. Tel: 760-876-5031. p. 152

Chambers, Margaret, Dir, Membership & Communications, Consortium of Academic & Research Libraries in Illinois, 1704 Interstate Dr, Champaign, IL, 61822. Tel: 217-333-2618. p. 2764

Chambers, Nicole, Educ Coordr, Anamosa State Penitentiary, 406 N High St, Anamosa, IA, 52205. Tel: 319-462-3504, Ext 2237. p. 731

Chambers, Reachell, Libr Serv Spec, Lincoln University, 1570 Baltimore Pike, Lincoln University, PA, 19352. Tel: 484-365-7358. p. 1956

Chambers, Stephanie, Dir, Fairmont Public Library, 600 F St, Fairmont, NE, 68354. Tel: 402-268-6081. p. 1314

Chambers, Sydney, Cat Librn, Gonzaga University, 502 E Boone Ave, Spokane, WA, 99258-0095. Tel: 509-313-6537. p. 2383

Chambers, Tarita, Ref Librn, Atlanta Metropolitan State College Library, 1630 Metropolitan Pkwy SW, Atlanta, GA, 30310. Tel: 404-756-4010. p. 462

Chambers, Victoria, Libr Tech, Juravinski Cancer Centre, 699 Concession St, Hamilton, ON, L8V 5C2, CANADA. Tel: 905-387-9495, Ext 65109. p. 2647

Chambliss, Darla, Syst Dir, Northwest Georgia Regional Library System, 310 Cappes St, Dalton, GA, 30720. Tel: 706-876-1360. p. 474

Chambon, Rick, Adult Serv Mgr, Mgr, Programming, Washington Carnegie Public Library, 300 W Main St, Washington, IN, 47501-2698. Tel: 812-254-4586. p. 725

Chameides, Emily, Libr Dir, Hudson Area Library, 51 N Fifth St, Hudson, NY, 12534. Tel: 518-828-1792. p. 1549

Chamness, Berry, Dir of Collection Mgmt & Discovery, Bryn Mawr College, 101 N Merion Ave, Bryn Mawr, PA, 19010-2899. Tel: 610-526-5295. p. 1916

Champ, Debra, Dir, Info Tech, Indianapolis Public Library, 2450 N Meridian St, Indianapolis, IN, 46208. Tel: 317-275-4840. p. 694

Champagne, Carol, Youth Serv Coordr, Plymouth District Library, 223 S Main St, Plymouth, MI, 48170-1687. Tel: 734-453-0750, Ext 237. p. 1141

Champagne, Guy, Prof, College de Maisonneuve, 3800, rue Sherbrooke Est, Montreal, QC, H1X 2A2, CANADA. Tel: 514-254-7131. p. 2796

Champagne, Louisa, Ref Librn, Southington Public Library & Museum, 255 Main St, Southington, CT, 06489. Tel: 860-628-0947. p. 337

Champagne, Manon, Admin Support Coordr, Cegep du Trois-Rivieres Bibliotheque, 3175 Laviolette, Trois-Rivieres, QC, G9A 5E6, CANADA. Tel: 819-376-1721, Ext 2633. p. 2738

Champagne, Sidney, Resource Sharing Coord, Maryland Institute College of Art, 1401 W Mount Royal Ave, Baltimore, MD, 21217. Tel: 410-225-2304, 410-225-2311, p. 955

Champagne, Theo, Librn, Louisiana Correctional Institute for Women Library, 15200 Scenic Hwy, Baker, LA, 70714. Tel: 225-319-2701, Ext 2703. p. 881

Champe, Nan, Dir, Pewaukee Public Library, 210 Main St, Pewaukee, WI, 53072. Tel: 262-691-5670, Ext 920. p. 2469

Champion, Jason, Educ Dir, American Watchmakers-Clockmakers Institute, 701 Enterprise Dr, Harrison, OH, 45030-1696. Tel: 513-367-9800. p. 1789

Champney, Stephanie, Dir, Mary L Wilcox Memorial Library, 2630 Main St, Whitney Point, NY, 13862. Tel: 607-692-3159. p. 1665

Chan, Allan, Law Librn, Fillmore Riley LLP, 1700-360 Main St, Winnipeg, MB, R3C 3Z3, CANADA. Tel: 204-957-8389. p. 2593

Chan, Amy, Dir, Libr, Archives & Mus, Alaska State Library, 395 Whittier St, Juneau, AK, 99801. Tel: 907-465-8718. p. 47

Chan, Anita Say, Assoc Prof, University of Illinois at Urbana-Champaign, Library & Information Science Bldg, 501 E Daniel St, Champaign, IL, 61820-6211. Tel: 217-333-3280. p. 2784

Chan, Connie, Ref (Info Servs), Alhambra Civic Center Library, 101 S First St, Alhambra, CA, 91801-3432. Tel: 626-570-5008. p. 115

Chan, Emily, Assoc Dean, Research & Scholarship, San Jose State University, One Washington Sq, San Jose, CA, 95192-0028. Tel: 408-808-2044. p. 232

Chan, Frederick, Sr Cat Librn, Washington University Libraries, Law Library, Washington Univ Sch Law, Anheuser-Busch Hall, One Brookings Dr, Campus Box 1171, Saint Louis, MO, 63130. Tel: 314-935-6415. p. 1277

Chan, Hana, Libr Mgr, University of Oregon Libraries, John E Jaqua Law Library, William W Knight Law Ctr, 2nd Flr, 1515 Agate St, Eugene, OR, 97403. Tel: 541-346-8271. p. 1879

Chan, John, Coll Develop, Online Learning Librn, Chabot College Library, 25555 Hesperian Blvd, Hayward, CA, 94545. Tel: 510-723-6778. p. 150

Chan, Lawrence, Library Computer Technology, Queensborough Community College, City University of New York, 222-05 56th Ave, Bayside, NY, 11364-1497. Tel: 718-281-5595. p. 1491

Chan, Phan Thi Ngoc, Librn, Harvard Library, Harvard-Yenching Library, Two Divinity Ave, Cambridge, MA, 02138. Tel: 617-495-2756. p. 1006

Chan, Wing, Br Mgr, San Francisco Public Library, Sunset Branch Library, 1305 18th Ave, San Francisco, CA, 94122-1807. Tel: 415-355-2808. p. 228

Chan, Yvonne, Cat/Metadata Tech, Alberta Government Library, Capital Blvd, 11th Flr, 10044 - 108 St, Edmonton, AB, T5J 5E6, CANADA. Tel: 780-427-2985. p. 2534

Chanas, Becky, Libr Tech, Lebanon Valley College, 101 N College Ave, Annville, PA, 17003-1400. Tel: 717-867-6977. p. 1906

Chandler, Christine, Curator, Putnam Museum & Science Center, 1717 W 12th St, Davenport, IA, 52804. Tel: 563-324-1933. p. 744

Chandler, Cindy, Dir, Blaine Public Library, 220 Indian Ridge Rd, Blaine, TN, 37709. Tel: 865-933-0845. p. 2088

Chandler, Cristen, Dir, Choctaw County Library, 511 S Louisville St, Ackerman, MS, 39735. Tel: 662-285-6348. p. 1211

Chandler, Dana, Univ Archivist, Tuskegee University, 1200 W Old Mongtomery Rd, Ford Motor Company Library, Tuskegee, AL, 36088. Tel: 334-727-8892. p. 39

Chandler, Donna, Bibliog Instruction Librn, Fresno City College Library, 1101 E University Ave, Fresno, CA, 93741. Tel: 559-442-4600, Ext 8150. p. 145

Chandler, Eileen, Exec Dir, Cape Libraries Automated Materials Sharing Network, 270 Communication Way, Unit 4E, Hyannis, MA, 02601. Tel: 508-790-4399. p. 2766

Chandler, Elisa, Tech Serv, The Blue Mountains Public Library, 173 Bruce St S, Thornbury, ON, N0H 2P0, CANADA. Tel: 519-599-3681. p. 2684

Chandler, Jessica, Youth Serv Librn, Perry County Public Library, 289 Black Gold Blvd, Hazard, KY, 41701. Tel: 606-436-2475, 606-436-4747. p. 858

Chandler, Michelle, Dir of Develop, Crandall Public Library, 251 Glen St, Glens Falls, NY, 12801-3546. Tel: 518-792-6508. p. 1539

Chandler, Ruby, Circ Coordr, Montgomery County Memorial Library System, 104 I-45 N, Conroe, TX, 77301-2720. Tel: 936-788-8377, Ext 6244. p. 2159

Chandler, Simone, Librn, Northeast Regional Library, Anne Spencer Cox Library, 303 N Third St, Baldwyn, MS, 38824-1517. Tel: 662-365-3305. p. 1216

Chandler, Susan, Dir, Nesbitt Memorial Library, 529 Washington St, Columbus, TX, 78934-2326. Tel: 979-732-3392. p. 2158

Chandonnet, Denise, Access Serv, University of Massachusetts Lowell Library, Lydon Library, 84 University Ave, Lowell, MA, 01854-2896. Tel: 978-934-3215. p. 1030

Chandra, Deepa, Asst Dir, Bryant Library, Two Paper Mill Rd, Roslyn, NY, 11576. Tel: 516-621-2240. p. 1633

Chandra, Yasmin, Dir, Info Serv, Dentons Canada LLP, 77 King St W, Ste 400, Toronto, ON, M5K 0A1, CANADA. Tel: 416-863-4511. p. 2688

Chandra, Yasmin, Dir, Libr Serv, Goodmans LLP Library, Bay Adelaide Ctr, 333 Bay St, Ste 3400, Toronto, ON, M5H 2S7, CANADA. Tel: 416-979-2211, Ext 6070. p. 2689

Chaney, Kathy, Br Mgr, Highland County District Library, Rocky Fork Branch, 11125 North Shore Dr, Hillsboro, OH, 45133. Tel: 937-661-6866. p. 1789

Chaney, M, Ms, Librn, Georgia Department of Corrections, Office of Library Services, 1412 Plunkett Rd, Unadilla, GA, 31091. Tel: 478-627-2000. p. 501

Chaney, Nick, YA Librn, St Charles Public Library District, One S Sixth Ave, Saint Charles, IL, 60174-2105. Tel: 630-584-0076, Ext 226. p. 644

Chaney, Raymond, Libr Asst, Estill County Public Library, 246 Main St, Irvine, KY, 40336-1026. Tel: 606-723-3030. p. 860

Chaney, Robin, Librn, Blinn College Library, 800 Blinn Blvd, Brenham, TX, 77833. Tel: 979-830-4250. p. 2149

Chaney, Shannon, Ch, Putnam County Library System, 50 E Broad St, Cookeville, TN, 38501. Tel: 931-526-2416. p. 2095

Chaney, Tina, Dir, Lebanon-Laclede County Library, 915 S Jefferson Ave, Lebanon, MO, 65536. Tel: 417-532-2148. p. 1259

Chaney, Vicki, Librn, Grant Public Library, 5379 Main St, Grant, AL, 35747. Tel: 256-728-5128. p. 19

Chaney-Blankenship, Stacey, Spec Coll Librn, Ohio Wesleyan University, 43 Rowland Ave, Delaware, OH, 43015-2370. Tel: 740-368-3288. p. 1782

Chang, Bernice, Ch Serv Librn, Bellingham Public Library, 210 Central Ave, Bellingham, WA, 98225. Tel: 360-778-7266. p. 2358

Chang, Elfie, Cat/Metadata Librn, Hood College, 401 Rosemont Ave, Frederick, MD, 21701. Tel: 301-695-3911. p. 966

Chang, Helen, Librn, Dignity Health Northridge Hospital, 18300 Roscoe Blvd, Northridge, CA, 91328. Tel: 209-467-6332. p. 184

Chang, Helen, Librn, Saint Joseph's Medical Center Library, 1800 N California St, Stockton, CA, 95204. Tel: 209-467-6332. p. 249

Chang, Hillary, Br Mgr, Hawaii State Public Library System, McCully-Moiliili Public Library, 2211 S King St, Honolulu, HI, 96826. Tel: 808-973-1099. p. 509

Chang, Hui-Fen, Head Librn, Oklahoma State University Libraries, College of Veterinary Medicine, William E Brock Memorial Library, 102 McElroy Hall, Stillwater, OK, 74078. Tel: 405-744-5281. p. 1862

Chang, Hui-Fen, Veterinary Med Librn, Oklahoma State University Libraries, Athletic Ave, 216, Stillwater, OK, 74078. Tel: 405-744-5281. p. 1862

Chang, Lena, Head, Ref, De Anza College, 21250 Stevens Creek Blvd, Cupertino, CA, 95014-5793. Tel: 408-864-8728. p. 133

Chang, Sherry, Assoc Dir, Stony Brook University, Mathematics-Physics-Astronomy, Physics Bldg C-124, Stony Brook, NY, 11794-3855. Tel: 631-632-7145. p. 1647

Chang, Shu Ching, Commun Libr Mgr, Queens Library, Briarwood Community Library, 85-12 Main St, Briarwood, NY, 11435. Tel: 718-658-1680. p. 1554

Chang, Sue, Libr Assoc, City of Palo Alto Library, College Terrace, 2300 Wellesley St, Palo Alto, CA, 94306. Tel: 650-838-2965. p. 192

Chanley, Jennifer, ILL Serv, Crawford County Public Library, 203 Indiana Ave, English, IN, 47118. Tel: 812-338-2606. p. 681

Chanse, Andrew, Exec Dir, Spokane Public Library, Station Plaza, 2nd Flr, 701 W Riverside Ave, Spokane, WA, 99201. Tel: 509-444-5300. p. 2385

Chao, Eric, Libr Relations Mgr, Statewide California Electronic Library Consortium, 617 S Olive St, Ste 1210, Los Angeles, CA, 90014. Tel: 310-775-9807. p. 2762

Chao, Gloria, Head, Tech Serv, Rutgers University Libraries, Camden Law Library, 217 N Fifth St, Camden, NJ, 08102-1203. Tel: 856-225-6457. p. 1394

Chapa, Angelica, Law Librn, Hidalgo County Law Library, Courthouse, 100 N Closner, Edinburg, TX, 78539. Tel: 956-318-2155. p. 2173

Chapa, Sonya, Libr Spec I, Okeechobee County Public Library, 206 SW 16th St, Okeechobee, FL, 34974. Tel: 863-763-3536. p. 430

Chapdelaine, Sarah, Head, Children's Servx, Leominster Public Library, 30 West St, Leominster, MA, 01453. Tel: 978-534-7522, Ext 3600. p. 1028

Chapin, Laura, Acq, Coordr, Berry College, 2277 Martha Berry Hwy, Mount Berry, GA, 30149. Tel: 706-233-4094. p. 492

Chapin, Linda, Librn, Field Library, 243 Millers Falls Rd, Northfield, MA, 01360. Tel: 413-225-3038. p. 1043

Chapin, Michele, Asst Libr Dir, Dean College, 99 Main St, Franklin, MA, 02038-1994. Tel: 508-541-1771. p. 1020

Chapin, Paul, Br Mgr, Spokane Public Library, Hillyard, 4005 N Cook Ave, Spokane, WA, 99207. p. 2385

Chapin, Paul, Br Mgr, Spokane Public Library, Indian Trail, 4909 W Barnes Rd, Spokane, WA, 99208. p. 2385

Chapkin, Joshua, Computer Serv, Valencia College, East Campus Library, 701 N Econlockhatchee Trail, Orlando, FL, 32825. Tel: 407-582-2467. p. 432

Chaplinsky, Paula, Financial Serv Adminr, Clearwater Public Library System, 100 N Osceola Ave, Clearwater, FL, 33755. Tel: 727-562-4970. p. 388

Chapman, Amanda, Dir, Davisville Free Library, 481 Davisville Rd, North Kingstown, RI, 02852. Tel: 401-884-5524. p. 2036

Chapman, Ann F, Asst Dir, Darlington County Historical Commission & Museum, 204 Hewitt St, Darlington, SC, 29532. Tel: 843-398-4710. p. 2057

Chapman, Carol, Adult Literacy Coordr, Ventura County Library, 5600 Everglades St, Ste A, Ventura, CA, 93003. Tel: 805-677-7159. p. 256

Chapman, Carolina, Dir, Sarcoxie Public Library, 508 Center St, Sarcoxie, MO, 64862. Tel: 417-548-2736. p. 1279

Chapman, Carroll, Mgr, Idea Exchange, Clemens Mill, 50 Saginaw Pkwy, Cambridge, ON, N1T 1W2, CANADA. Tel: 519-740-6294. p. 2635

Chapman, CC, Libr Assoc, Tulane University, Music & Media Library, 7001 Freret St, 6th Flr, New Orleans, LA, 70118-5682. Tel: 504-865-5642. p. 904

Chapman, Christopher, Circ Mgr, Clemson University Libraries, Gunnin Architecture Library, 2-112 Lee Hall, Clemson University, Clemson, SC, 29634. Tel: 864-656-3933. p. 2052

Chapman, Curtis, Dr, Dir, Clovis Community College Library, 417 Schepps Blvd, Clovis, NM, 88101. Tel: 575-769-4179. p. 1466

Chapman, Dan, ILL, Musser Public Library, 408 E Second St, Muscatine, IA, 52761. Tel: 563-263-3065. p. 772

Chapman, Darlene, Librn, IWK Health, 5850/5980 University Ave, Halifax, NS, B3K 6R8, CANADA. Tel: 902-470-8646. p. 2619

Chapman, Donna, Dir, Woodbury County Library, 825 Main St, Moville, IA, 51039. Tel: 712-873-3322. p. 771

Chapman, Dustin, Library Contact, McLennan County Law Library, 501 Washington, Waco, TX, 76701. Tel: 254-757-5191. p. 2253

Chapman, Eileen, Asst Dir, West Springfield Public Library, 200 Park St, West Springfield, MA, 01089. Tel: 413-736-4561, Ext 1113. p. 1066

Chapman, Gina, Cat, Gilbert Public Library, 17 N Broadway, Gilbert, MN, 55741. Tel: 218-748-2230. p. 1176

Chapman, Heidi, Dir, Frankenmuth Historical Association, 613 S Main St, Frankenmuth, MI, 48734. Tel: 989-652-9701, Ext 102. p. 1107

Chapman, Janis, Asst Librn, White Hall Township Library, 119 E Sherman St, White Hall, IL, 62092. Tel: 217-374-6014. p. 662

Chapman, Jessica, Area Mgr, Vaughan Public Libraries, Pierre Berton Resource Library, 4921 Rutherford Rd, Woodbridge, ON, L4L 1A6, CANADA. Tel: 905-653-7323. p. 2701

Chapman, Jonathan P, Librn, Minnesota Department of Corrections, 7600 - 525th St, Rush City, MN, 55069. Tel: 320-358-0400, Ext 373. p. 1195

Chapman, Julie, Supvr, Libr Instruction, Northeast Wisconsin Technical College Library, 2740 W Mason St, Green Bay, WI, 54303-4966. Tel: 920-498-5487. p. 2439

Chapman, Karena, Circ, Charles A Ransom District Library, 180 S Sherwood Ave, Plainwell, MI, 49080-1896. Tel: 269-685-8024. p. 1141

Chapman, Kimbre, Ch Serv, McMinnville Public Library, 225 NW Adams St, McMinnville, OR, 97128. Tel: 503-435-5559. p. 1886

Chapman, Kristin, Med Librn, Danbury Hospital, 24 Hospital Ave, Danbury, CT, 06810. Tel: 203-739-7035. p. 307

Chapman, Marcella, Dir, Coffey County Library, Waverly Branch, 608 Pearson, Waverly, KS, 66871-9688. Tel: 785-733-2400. p. 800

Chapman, Omar, Libr Dir, Bessemer Public Library, 400 19th St N, Bessemer, AL, 35020. Tel: 205-428-7882. p. 6

Chapman, Ophelia, Info Tech, Librn, Fayetteville State University, 1200 Murchison Rd, Fayetteville, NC, 28301-4298. Tel: 910-672-1546. p. 1689

Chapman, Paul, Coll Develop Librn, Northern Virginia Community College Libraries, Alexandria Campus, Bisdorf Bldg, Rm 232, 5000 Dawes Ave, Alexandria, VA, 22311. Tel: 703-845-5066. p. 2304

Chapman, Paul K, Dir, Vestal Public Library, 320 Vestal Pkwy E, Vestal, NY, 13850-1632. Tel: 607-754-4243. p. 1657

Chapman, Rebecca, Dir, United States Air Force, McBride Library, 81 FSS/FSDL McBride Library, 512 Larcher Blvd Bldg 2222, Keesler AFB, MS, 39534-2345. Tel: 228-377-2181. p. 1223

Chapman, Rebecca, Undergrad Law & Indigenous Outreach Librn, University at Buffalo Libraries-State University of New York, Charles B Sears Law Library, John Lord O'Brian Hall, 211 Mary Talbert Way, Buffalo, NY, 14260-1110. Tel: 716-645-3832. p. 1511

Chapman, Roberta, Br Coordr, Haldimand County Public Library, Caledonia Branch, 100 Haddington St, Unit 2, Caledonia, ON, N3W 2N4, CANADA. p. 2639

Chapman, Roberta, Br Coordr, Haldimand County Public Library, Hagersville Branch, 13 Alma St N, Hagersville, ON, N0A 1H0, CANADA. p. 2639

Chapman, Roberta, Br Coordr, Haldimand County Public Library, Jarvis Branch, Two Monson St, Jarvis, ON, N0A 1J0, CANADA. p. 2639

Chapman, Sammy, Jr, Ref Librn/Coll Develop, Purdue University, 2200 169th St, Hammond, IN, 46323. Tel: 219-989-2903. p. 689

Chapman, Sarah, Dir, Whipple Free Library, 67 Mont Vernon Rd, New Boston, NH, 03070. Tel: 603-487-3391. p. 1375

Chapman, Sharon, Head Librn, University of South Carolina Sumter, 200 Miller Rd, Sumter, SC, 29150-2498. Tel: 803-938-3810. p. 2071

Chapman, Susan Sabers, Pres, Alden-Ewell Free Library, 13280 Broadway, Alden, NY, 14004. Tel: 716-937-7082. p. 1484

Chapp, Debra, Bus Mgr, White Oak Library District, 201 W Normantown Rd, Romeoville, IL, 60446. Tel: 815-886-2030. p. 643

Chappell, Anita, Libr Mgr, Tilley District & Public Library, 148 First Ave E, Tilley, AB, T0J 3K0, CANADA. Tel: 403-377-2233, Ext 150. p. 2557

Chappell, Arlene, Dir, Delhi Public Library, 311 Franklin St, Delhi, IA, 52223. Tel: 563-922-2037. p. 745

Chappell, Leanna, Head, Youth Serv, Swanton Local School District Public Library, 305 Chestnut St, Swanton, OH, 43558. Tel: 419-826-2760. p. 1822

Chappell, Patti, Br Mgr, Cannon County Library System, Auburntown Branch Library, 73 E Main St, Auburntown, TN, 37016. Tel: 615-464-2622. p. 2130

Chappo, Debbie, Info Spec, Minot Public Library, 516 Second Ave SW, Minot, ND, 58701-3792. Tel: 701-852-0333. p. 1738

Charbonneau, Catherine, Ch, Blanding Free Public Library, 124 Bay State Rd, Rehoboth, MA, 02769. Tel: 508-252-4236. p. 1049

Charbonneau, Darline, Dir, Human Res, Yakima Valley Libraries, 102 N Third St, Yakima, WA, 98901. Tel: 509-452-8541. p. 2395

Charbonneau, Deborah, Dr, Asst Prof, Wayne State University, 106 Kresge Library, Detroit, MI, 48202. Tel: 313-577-1825. p. 2787

Charbonneau, Lisa, Coordr, Bibliotheque Municipale et Scolaire de Sutton, 19 Highland St, Sutton, QC, J0E 2K0, CANADA. Tel: 450-538-5843. p. 2737
Charbonneau, Louise, Electronic Res Librn, ILL & Serials Librn, Mohawk Valley Community College Libraries, 1101 Sherman Dr, Utica, NY, 13501-5394. Tel: 315-731-5793. p. 1655
Charette, Elizabeth, Dir, Northfield Township Area Library, 125 Barker Rd, Whitmore Lake, MI, 48189. Tel: 734-449-0066. p. 1160
Charette, Jim, Mgr, Portland Public Library, Burbank, 377 Stevens Ave, Portland, ME, 04103. Tel: 207-774-4229. p. 937
Charland, Glorea, Br Supvr, Hernando County Public Library System, East Hernando, 6457 Windemere Rd, Brooksville, FL, 34602. Tel: 352-754-4043. p. 388
Charles, Catalina, Libr Mgr, Otselic Valley Public Library, 125 County Rd 13A, Bronx, NY, 13155. Tel: 315-653-7218, Ext 4106. p. 1500
Charles, Catherine, Dir, Commun Relations, Richmond Hill Public Library, One Atkinson St, Richmond Hill, ON, L4C 0H5, CANADA. Tel: 905-884-9288. p. 2675
Charles, Cynthia J, Dr, Dir, Libr & Media Serv, Huston-Tillotson University, 900 Chicon St, Austin, TX, 78702. Tel: 512-505-3088. p. 2139
Charles, David, Asst Teaching Prof, University of Illinois at Urbana-Champaign, Library & Information Science Bldg, 501 E Daniel St, Champaign, IL, 61820-6211. Tel: 217-333-3280. p. 2784
Charles, Jane V, Fac Librn, Florida SouthWestern State College, 8099 College Pkwy SW, Bldg J-212, Fort Myers, FL, 33919. Tel: 239-489-8345. p. 403
Charles, Leslin, Instrul Design Librn, Rutgers University Libraries, James Dickson Carr Library, 75 Ave E, Piscataway, NJ, 08854-8040. Tel: 848-445-4432. p. 1424
Charles, Mario A, Librn, College of New Rochelle, Rosa Parks Campus, 144 W 125th St, New York, NY, 10027. Tel: 212-662-7500. p. 1577
Charles, Nicole, Dir, Bruce County Public Library, 1243 MacKenzie Rd, Port Elgin, ON, N0H 2C6, CANADA. Tel: 519-832-6935. p. 2673
Charles, Patrick, Dir, Gonzaga University School of Law, 721 N Cincinnati St, Spokane, WA, 99220. Tel: 509-313-3739. p. 2383
Charles, Rodger L, Libr Dir, Peabody Township Library, 214 Walnut St, Peabody, KS, 66866. Tel: 620-983-2502. p. 831
Charles-Scaringi, Kristen, Head of Borrowing & Tech Services, Poughkeepsie Public Library District, 93 Market St, Poughkeepsie, NY, 12601. Tel: 845-485-3445, Ext 3345. p. 1623
Charlesbois-Nordan, Stacy, Fac Librn, Oakland Community College, 22322 Rutland Dr, Rm A212, Southfield, MI, 48075-4793. Tel: 248-233-2826. p. 1151
Charley, Susan J, Dean of LRC, Dyersburg State Community College, 1510 Lake Rd, Dyersburg, TN, 38024. Tel: 731-286-3361. p. 2097
Charlie, Tracey A, Libr Mgr, Pueblo of San Felipe Community Library, 18 Cougar Rd, San Felipe Pueblo, NM, 87001. Tel: 505-771-9970. p. 1474
Charlson, Kim L, Dir, Perkins School for the Blind, 175 N Beacon St, Watertown, MA, 02472. Tel: 617-972-7240. p. 1062
Charlton, Joyce, Librn, Naples Public Library, 103 Walnut St, Naples, TX, 75568. Tel: 903-897-2964. p. 2221
Charlton, Sara, Dir, Tillamook County Library, 1716 Third St, Tillamook, OR, 97141. Tel: 503-842-4792. p. 1900
Charney, Brenda, Asst Dir, Mgr, Greene County Public Library, 76 E Market St, Xenia, OH, 45385-3100. Tel: 937-352-4000. p. 1834
Charney, Donna, Head Librn, Parkland Regional Library-Manitoba, Shoal Lake Branch, 418 The Drive, Shoal Lake, MB, R0J 1Z0, CANADA. Tel: 204-759-2242. p. 2587
Charpentier, Debbie, Archivist, Millicent Library, 45 Centre St, Fairhaven, MA, 02719. Tel: 508-992-5342. p. 1017
Charrier, Melanie, Br Mgr, Washington Parish Library System, Bogalusa Branch, 304 Ave F, Bogalusa, LA, 70427. Tel: 985-735-1961. p. 890
Charron, Chris, Ms, Librn, French River Public Library, 15 Dollard St, Noelville, ON, P0M 2N0, CANADA. Tel: 705-898-2965. p. 2661
Charron, Chris, Ms, Librn, French River Public Library, Alban Branch, 796 Hwy 64, Unit A, Alban, ON, P0M 1A0, CANADA. Tel: 705-857-1771. p. 2661
Charters, Megan, Dir, The Colony Public Library, 6800 Main St, The Colony, TX, 75056-1133. Tel: 972-624-3184. p. 2249
Chartier, Courtney, Dir, Columbia University, Rare Book & Manuscript, Butler Library, 6th Flr E, 535 W 114th St, New York, NY, 10027. Tel: 212-854-5590. p. 1583
Chartier, Heather, Libr Serv Coordr, Edmonton Public Library, Riverbend, 460 Riverbend Sq, Rabbit Hill Rd & Terwillegar Dr, Edmonton, AB, T6R 2X2, CANADA. Tel: 780-944-5323. p. 2537
Chartier, Terry, Exec Dir, Ottawa Library, 105 S Hickory St, Ottawa, KS, 66067. Tel: 785-242-3080. p. 829
Chartrand, Richard, Dir, East Alton Public Library District, 250 Washington Ave, East Alton, IL, 62024-1547. Tel: 618-259-0787. p. 580
Chase, Alexander, Dir, Dannemora Free Library, Village Community Ctr, 40 Emmons St, Dannemora, NY, 12929. Tel: 518-492-7005. p. 1524
Chase, Alli, Dir, Alice Baker Memorial Public Library, 820 E Main St, Eagle, WI, 53119. Tel: 262-594-2800. p. 2431
Chase, Annie, Dir, Potsdam Public Library, Civic Ctr, Ste 1, Two Park St, Potsdam, NY, 13676. Tel: 315-265-7230. p. 1622
Chase, Brian, Dir, Normal Public Library, 206 W College Ave, Normal, IL, 61761. Tel: 309-452-1757. p. 625
Chase, Brian, Exec Dir, Southwest Florida Library Network, 13120 Westlinks Tr, Unit 3, Fort Myers, FL, 33913. Tel: 239-313-6338. p. 2763
Chase, Connie, Chair, Taylor Memorial Library, 155 Main St, Hancock, MA, 01237. Tel: 413-738-5326. p. 1023
Chase, Darren, Libr Dir, SUNY Oneonta, 108 Ravine Pkwy, Oneonta, NY, 13820. Tel: 607-436-3702. p. 1611
Chase, Elizabeth, Mgr, Mat Serv, Frisco Public Library, 6101 Frisco Square Blvd, Frisco, TX, 75034-3000. Tel: 972-292-5669. p. 2182
Chase, Jessie, Coordr, Learning Commons, University of Southern Maine Libraries, Gorham Library, 120 Bailey Hall, Gorham, ME, 04038. Tel: 207-780-5346. p. 937
Chase, Liz, Sr Assoc Dir, Academic Assessment, Emerson College, 120 Boylston St, Boston, MA, 02116-4624. Tel: 617-824-8668. p. 995
Chase, Myrtle, Head Librn, Parkland Regional Library-Manitoba, Roblin Branch, 123 First Ave NW, Roblin, MB, R0L 1P0, CANADA. Tel: 204-937-2443. p. 2587
Chase, Nancy, Head, Youth Serv, Haverhill Public Library, 99 Main St, Haverhill, MA, 01830-5092. Tel: 978-373-1586, Ext 626. p. 1024
Chase, Nancy, Librn, Cove City-Craven County Public Library, 102 N Main St, Cove City, NC, 28523. Tel: 252-638-6363. p. 1683
Chase-Lauther, Deborah, Dir, Hepburn Library of Madrid, 11 Church St, Madrid, NY, 13660. Tel: 315-322-5673. p. 1567
Chase-Williams, Janet, Head Librn, Mariposa County Law Library, 4978 Tenth St, Mariposa, CA, 95338. Tel: 209-966-2140. p. 173
Chasen, Lori, Supvr, Springfield City Library, Sixteen Acres Branch, 1187 Parker St, Springfield, MA, 01129. Tel: 413-263-6858. p. 1056
Chassanoff, Alexandra, Asst Prof, North Carolina Central University, 1801 Fayetteville St, Durham, NC, 27707. Tel: 919-530-6485. p. 2790
Chasse, Emily, Br Mgr, Cape Breton Regional Library, 50 Falmouth St, Sydney, NS, B1P 6X9, CANADA. Tel: 902-562-3161. p. 2622
Chasse, Paul, Librn, US Environmental Protection Agency, 200 SW 35th St, Corvallis, OR, 97333. Tel: 541-754-4355. p. 1877
Chastellaine, Jacquie, Libr Mgr, Amisk Public Library, 5005 50 St, Amisk, AB, T0B 0B0, CANADA. Tel: 780-628-5457. p. 2522
Chatelain, Benedict, Archives Assoc, Info Assoc, Longwood University, Redford & Race St, Farmville, VA, 23909. Tel: 434-395-2448. p. 2318
Chatham, Debra, Spec, Sierra Vista Public Library, 2600 E Tacoma, Sierra Vista, AZ, 85635. Tel: 520-458-4225. p. 78
Chatham, Jessica, Br Mgr, Chesapeake Public Library, Indian River, 2320 Old Greenbrier Rd, Chesapeake, VA, 23325. Tel: 757-410-7007. p. 2311
Chatman, Ronalee, Br Mgr, Jersey City Free Public Library, Glenn D Cunningham Branch Library & Community Center, 275 Martin Luther King Jr Dr, Jersey City, NJ, 07305. Tel: 201-547-4555. p. 1409
Chatmon, Catherine, Dr, Libr Dir, Carolina University, 420 S Broad St, Winston-Salem, NC, 27101-5025. Tel: 336-714-7953. p. 1724
Chatten, Kat, Br Head, Thompson-Nicola Regional District Library System, Clinton Branch, 1506 Tingley St, Clinton, BC, V0K 1K0, CANADA. Tel: 250-459-7752. p. 2567
Chatterjee, Aneliia, Librn, Essex County College Library, 303 University Ave, Newark, NJ, 07102. Tel: 973-877-3238. p. 1426
Chatterjee, Aneliia, Librn, Essex County College Library, Branch Campus, 730 Bloomfield Ave, West Caldwell, NJ, 07006. Tel: 973-877-1883. p. 1426
Chatterley, Trish, Colls Mgr, University of Alberta, John W Scott Health Sciences Library, Walter C Mackenzie Health Sciences Ctr 2K3 28, Edmonton, AB, T6G 2R7, CANADA. Tel: 780-492-7933. p. 2538
Chatterton, Caroline, Dir, Fulton Public Library, 160 S First St, Fulton, NY, 13069. Tel: 315-592-5159. p. 1536
Chattin, Gena, Librn, Marshall University Libraries, One John Marshall Dr, Huntington, WV, 25755-2060. Tel: 304-696-2320. p. 2405
Chattin, Gena, Librn, Marshall University Libraries, South Charleston Campus Library, 100 Angus E Peyton Dr, South Charleston, WV, 25303-1600. Tel: 304-746-8900. p. 2405
Chau, Amelia, Electronic Serv Librn, Helen Hall Library, 100 W Walker, League City, TX, 77573-3899. Tel: 281-554-1111. p. 2210
Chauderlot, Fabienne, Dr, Dean, Palomar College Library, 1140 W Mission Rd, San Marcos, CA, 92069-1487. Tel: 760-744-1150, Ext 2251. p. 234
Chaudhary, Niraj, Dean of Libr, University of the Pacific Libraries, 3601 Pacific Ave, Stockton, CA, 95211. Tel: 209-932-2877. p. 250
Chaudhry, Sonia, Head, Children's Servx, Delray Beach Public Library, 100 W Atlantic Ave, Delray Beach, FL, 33444. Tel: 561-266-0194. p. 394
Chaudhuri, Lisa, Libr Dir, Le Moyne College, 1419 Salt Springs Rd, Syracuse, NY, 13214. Tel: 315-445-4321. p. 1648
Chaudron, Gerald, Dr, Head, Spec Coll, University Libraries, University of Memphis, 3785 Norriswood Ave, Memphis, TN, 38152. Tel: 901-678-8242. p. 2115
Chauvin, Candace, Bus Mgr, Terrebonne Parish Library, Dulac Branch, 200 Badou Rd, Dulac, LA, 70353. Tel: 985-563-5014. p. 891
Chauvin, Ellen, Br Mgr, Albemarle Regional Library, Sallie Harrell Jenkins Memorial Library, 302 Broad St, Aulander, NC, 27805. Tel: 252-345-4461. p. 1727

Chauvin, Harvey, Info Literacy Librn, Western New England University, 1215 Wilbraham Rd, Springfield, MA, 01119. Tel: 413-782-1533. p. 1057

Chauvin, Janet, Br Mgr, Terrebonne Parish Library, Chauvin Branch, 5500 Hwy 56, Chauvin, LA, 70344. Tel: 985-594-9771. p. 891

Chavarria, Ivonne, Asst Librn, Estancia Public Library, 601 S Tenth St, Estancia, NM, 87016. Tel: 505-384-9655. p. 1467

Chavez, Alex, Circ Mgr, Watsonville Public Library, 275 Main St, Ste 100, Watsonville, CA, 95076. Tel: 831-768-3400. p. 258

Chavez, Andrea, Asst Dir, Los Lunas Public Library, 460 Main St NE, Los Lunas, NM, 87031. Tel: 505-839-3850. p. 1472

Chavez, Ashlee, Libr Dir, Corvallis-Benton County Public Library, 645 NW Monroe Ave, Corvallis, OR, 97330. Tel: 541-766-6926. p. 1876

Chavez Buchanan, Joanne, Bus Mgr, Stickney-Forest View Public Library District, 6800 W 43rd St, Stickney, IL, 60402. Tel: 708-749-1050. p. 651

Chavez, Carlos, Libr Mgr, New York Public Library - Astor, Lenox & Tilden Foundations, Roosevelt Island Branch, 524 Main St, New York, NY, 10044-0001. Tel: 212-308-6243. p. 1597

Chavez, Fabiola, Night/Weekend Serv Coordr, University of California, Merced Library, 5200 N Lake Rd, Merced, CA, 95343. Tel: 209-201-5013. p. 177

Chavez, Gracie, Libr Asst, Alexander Memorial Library, La Salle County Library - Encinal Branch, 201 Center St, Cotulla, TX, 78014. p. 2161

Chavez, Jason, Media Res & Reserves Mgr, California State University, East Bay Library, CSU East Bay Library, 25800 Carlos Bee Blvd, Hayward, CA, 94542-3052. Tel: 510-885-2299. p. 150

Chavez, John U, Librn, Paradise Valley Community College, 18401 N 32nd St, Phoenix, AZ, 85032-1200. Tel: 602-787-7222. p. 71

Chavez, Jorge, Libr Mgr, San Antonio Public Library, Schaefer, 6322 US Hwy 87 E, San Antonio, TX, 78222. Tel: 210-207-9300. p. 2239

Chavez, Kristi, Cat & Metadata, California State University, Bakersfield, 9001 Stockdale Hwy, 60 LIB, Bakersfield, CA, 93311. Tel: 661-654-3172. p. 119

Chavez, Leeana, Dir, Rocky Ford Public Library, 400 S Tenth St, Rocky Ford, CO, 81067. Tel: 719-254-6641. p. 294

Chavez, Lillian, Librn, Mescalero Community Library, 148 Cottonwood Dr, Mescalero, NM, 88340. Tel: 575-464-5010. p. 1473

Chavez, Lyena, Head, Instruction & Outreach, Merrimack College, 315 Turnpike St, North Andover, MA, 01845. Tel: 978-837-5045. p. 1040

Chavez, N, Legal Library Coord, Two Rivers Correctional Institute, 82911 Beach Access Rd, Umatilla, OR, 97882. Tel: 541-922-2181. p. 1901

Chavez, Patricia, Res Info Spec, Library of Rush University Medical Center, Armour Academic Ctr, 600 S Paulina St, Ste 571, Chicago, IL, 60612. Tel: 312-942-2731. p. 563

Chavez, Rebecca, Librn, Central Wyoming College Library, 2660 Peck Ave, Riverton, WY, 82501. Tel: 307-855-2141. p. 2498

Chavez, Sandra, Dir, Laingsburg Public Library, 255 E Grand River, Laingsburg, MI, 48848. Tel: 517-651-6282. p. 1123

Chavez, Todd A, Dir, Acad Res, University of South Florida, Tampa Campus Library, 4101 USF Apple Dr, LIB122, Tampa, FL, 33620. Tel: 813-974-7905. p. 450

Chavez-Brumell, Luis, Dep Dir, New Haven Free Public Library, 133 Elm St, New Haven, CT, 06510. Tel: 203-946-8130, Ext 318. p. 326

Chavira, Adriana, Mgr, Delta County Libraries, Delta Public Library, 211 W Sixth St, Delta, CO, 81416. Tel: 970-874-9630. p. 286

Chavis, Joanie, Head, Engagement & Instructional Servs, Head, Res Serv, North Carolina Agricultural & Technical State University, 1601 E Market St, Greensboro, NC, 27411-0002. Tel: 336-285-4164. p. 1693

Chawla, Narinderpal, Managing Librn, Brooklyn Public Library, Flatbush, 22 Linden Blvd, Brooklyn, NY, 11226. Tel: 718-856-0813. p. 1503

Chayanuwat, Piya, Exec Dir, Library Systems, Nova Southeastern University Libraries, 3100 Ray Ferrero Jr Blvd, Fort Lauderdale, FL, 33314. Tel: 954-262-4696. p. 402

Chayes, Jennifer, Dean, University of California at Berkeley, 102 South Hall, No 4600, Berkeley, CA, 94720-4600. Tel: 510-642-1464. p. 2782

Cheairs, Jackie, Head, Ser, Tech Serv, Indiana University Northwest, 3400 Broadway, Gary, IN, 46408. Tel: 219-980-6935. p. 686

Cheatham, Brenda, Librn, Mae S Bruce Library, 13302 Sixth St, Santa Fe, TX, 77510-9148. Tel: 409-925-5540. p. 2242

Cheatham, Cheryl, Ref (Info Servs), Case Western Reserve University, School of Law Library, 11075 East Blvd, Cleveland, OH, 44106-7148. Tel: 216-368-1611. p. 1766

Cheatham, Richard, Dir, Whittier College, Media Center, 13406 Philadelphia St, Whittier, CA, 90601-4413. Tel: 562-907-4846. p. 259

Cheatwood, Mary, Dir, Mount Morris Public Library, 105 S McKendrie Ave, Mount Morris, IL, 61054. Tel: 815-734-4927. p. 620

Chebbour, Jocelyn, Libr Asst IV, University of Texas at Dallas, Callier Library, 1966 Inwood Rd, Dallas, TX, 75235. Tel: 972-883-3165. p. 2231

Chebotarev, Tanya, Curator, Bakhmeteff Archives, Columbia University, Rare Book & Manuscript, Butler Library, 6th Flr E, 535 W 114th St, New York, NY, 10027. Tel: 212-854-3986. p. 1583

Checchio, Frankie, Ref & Instruction Librn, Pennsylvania State University, 100 University Dr, Monaca, PA, 15061. Tel: 724-773-3790. p. 1964

Checkai, Peg, Libr Dir, Watertown Public Library, 100 S Water St, Watertown, WI, 53094-4320. Tel: 920-545-2322. p. 2484

Checovetes, Kaitlin, Circ Supvr, Burlington Public Library, 34 Library Lane, Burlington, CT, 06013. Tel: 860-673-3331. p. 305

Cheek, Belinda, Coordr, Access Serv, North Central College, 320 E School St, Naperville, IL, 60540. Tel: 630-637-5703. p. 623

Cheek, Jennifer, Pub Relations Mgr, Boone County Public Library, 1786 Burlington Pike, Burlington, KY, 41005. Tel: 859-342-2665. p. 850

Cheetham, Natalie, Youth Serv, Cedar Grove Free Public Library, One Municipal Plaza, Cedar Grove, NJ, 07009. Tel: 973-239-1447. p. 1395

Cheever, Clayton, Libr Dir, Morrill Memorial Library, 33 Walpole St, Norwood, MA, 02062-1206. Tel: 781-769-0200. p. 1044

Cheever, Clayton, Asst Dir, Thomas Crane Public Library, 40 Washington St, Quincy, MA, 02269-9164. Tel: 617-376-1300. p. 1048

Cheever, Lisa, Libr Dir, Blackstone Public Library, 86 Main St, Blackstone, MA, 01504. Tel: 508-883-1931. p. 990

Cheikhi, Ikram, Open Info Analyst, Alberta Government Library, Capital Blvd, 11th Flr, 10044 - 108 St, Edmonton, AB, T5J 5E6, CANADA. Tel: 780-427-2985. p. 2534

Chekijian, Berj, Dir of Finance, Armenian Museum of America, Inc, Mugar Bldg, 4th Flr, 65 Main St, Watertown, MA, 02472. Tel: 617-926-2562, Ext 111. p. 1062

Cheladyn, Amber, Adjunct Archivist, Saint Bonaventure University, 3261 W State Rd, Saint Bonaventure, NY, 14778. Tel: 716-375-2323. p. 1635

Chellino, Amy, Archives, Librn, Joliet Junior College Library, Campus Ctr (A-Bldg), 2nd Flr, 1215 Houbolt Rd, Joliet, IL, 60431. Tel: 815-280-6708. p. 603

Chemay, Connie, Head, Tech Serv, River Parishes Community College Library, 925 W Edenborne Pkwy, Rm 141, Gonzales, LA, 70737. Tel: 225-743-8550. p. 890

Chen, Anna, Head Librn, University of California Los Angeles Library, William Andrews Clark Memorial Library, 2520 Cimarron St, Los Angeles, CA, 90018. Tel: 310-794-5155. p. 169

Chen, Barbara, Doc Delivery Spec, ILL, University of Saint Francis, Pope John Paul II Ctr, 2701 Spring St, Rm 102 & 202, Fort Wayne, IN, 46808. Tel: 260-399-7700, Ext 6061. p. 685

Chen, Bin, Doc Delivery, Hopital Hotel-Dieu du CHUM, 3840 rue St-Urbain, Montreal, QC, H2W 1T8, CANADA. Tel: 514-890-8000, Ext 35867. p. 2724

Chen, Chaichin, Resource Sharing Coord, State of Rhode Island, Department of Administration, One Capitol Hill, 2nd Flr, Providence, RI, 02908. Tel: 401-574-9307. p. 2041

Chen, Dung Lam, Acq Librn, Bibliog Serv, Skidmore College, 815 N Broadway, Saratoga Springs, NY, 12866. Tel: 518-580-5502. p. 1636

Chen, Gladys, Br Head, Vancouver Public Library, West Point Grey Branch, 4566 W Tenth Ave, Vancouver, BC, V6R 2J1, CANADA. Tel: 604-665-3982. p. 2582

Chen, Gwen, Sr Librn, California Environmental Protection Agency Public Library, Department of Toxic Substances Control - Technical Reference, 1001 I St, Sacramento, CA, 95814-2828. Tel: 916-324-5898. p. 207

Chen, Hong, Br Mgr, Manchester Public Library, 586 Main St, Manchester, CT, 06040. Tel: 860-643-6892. p. 320

Chen, Hong, Librn II, Manchester Public Library, Whiton Branch, 100 N Main St, Manchester, CT, 06040. Tel: 860-643-6892. p. 321

Chen, Hsien-min, Ref Serv, New Brunswick Free Public Library, 60 Livingston Ave, New Brunswick, NJ, 08901-2597. Tel: 732-745-5108, Ext 23. p. 1424

Chen, Hsin-Liang, Chief Libr Officer, Philadelphia College of Osteopathic Medicine, 4170 City Ave, Philadelphia, PA, 19131-1694. Tel: 215-871-6475. p. 1984

Chen, Jiangping, Interim Executive Assoc Dean, Vis Prof, University of Illinois at Urbana-Champaign, Library & Information Science Bldg, 501 E Daniel St, Champaign, IL, 61820-6211. Tel: 217-333-3280. p. 2784

Chen, Jiangping, Dr, Chair, Prof, University of North Texas, 3940 N Elm St, Ste E292, Denton, TX, 76207. Tel: 940-565-2445. p. 2793

Chen, Li, Dir, Libr Syst, Kennesaw State University Library System, 385 Cobb Ave NW, MD 1701, Kennesaw, GA, 30144. Tel: 470-578-7276. p. 483

Chen, Li, Dir, Libr Syst, Kennesaw State University Library System, Lawrence V Johnson Library, 1100 S Marietta Pkwy, Marietta, GA, 30060-2896. Tel: 678-915-7467. p. 483

Chen, Mingyu, Asst Dean, Dir, Tech Serv, University of North Carolina at Pembroke, One University Dr, Pembroke, NC, 28372. Tel: 910-521-6516. p. 1707

Chen, Mingyu, Head, Metadata Serv, University of Texas at Dallas, 800 W Campbell Rd, Richardson, TX, 75080. Tel: 972-883-3534. p. 2231

Chen, Nora, Mgr, County of Los Angeles Public Library, San Dimas Library, 145 N Walnut Ave, San Dimas, CA, 91773-2603. Tel: 909-599-6738. p. 137

Chen, Sean, Head, Cat & Metadata Serv, Duke University Libraries, J Michael Goodson Law Library, 210 Science Dr, Durham, NC, 27708. Tel: 919-613-7028. p. 1684

Chen, Stacey, Acq, Stanislaus County Library, 1500 I St, Modesto, CA, 95354-1166. Tel: 209-558-7800. p. 178

Chen, Su, Head Librn, University of California Los Angeles Library, Richard C Rudolph East Asian Library, 21617 Research Library YRL, Los Angeles, CA, 90095. Tel: 310-825-1401. p. 169

Chew, Marynelle, Coll & Access Serv Librn, Brigham Young University-Hawaii, BYU-Hawaii, No 1966, 55-220 Kulanui St, Bldg 5, Laie, HI, 96762-1294. Tel: 808-675-3863. p. 514

Chi, Yu, Dr, Asst Prof, University of Kentucky, 320 Little Library Bldg, Lexington, KY, 40506-0224. Tel: 859-257-8876. p. 2785

Chianese, Scott, Dir, Hamilton Township Public Library, One Justice Samuel A Alito, Jr Way, Hamilton, NJ, 08619. Tel: 609-581-4060. p. 1407

Chianese-Lopez, Lisa, Br Mgr, Free Library of Philadelphia, Ramonita G De Rodriguez Branch, 600 W Girard Ave, Philadelphia, PA, 19123-1311. Tel: 215-686-1768. p. 1978

Chiao, Karl, Exec Dir, Dallas Historical Society, Hall of State in Fair Park, 3939 Grand Ave, Dallas, TX, 75210. Tel: 214-421-4500, Ext 102. p. 2164

Chiapperi, Elizabeth, Chief Knowledge Officer, Nixon Peabody, 70 W Madison St, Ste 5200, Chicago, IL, 60602. Tel: 312-977-4400. p. 566

Chiappone, Samantha, Br Mgr, Algonquin Area Public Library District, Eastgate Branch, 115 Eastgate Dr, Algonquin, IL, 60102. Tel: 847-658-4343. p. 536

Chiarella, Deborah, Ref Librn/Health Sci Liaison, University at Buffalo Libraries-State University of New York, Health Sciences Library, Abbott Hall, 3435 Main St, Bldg 28, Buffalo, NY, 14214-3002. Tel: 716-829-5753. p. 1510

Chiavaroli, Melissa, Ref Serv, Ad, Cumberland Public Library, 1464 Diamond Hill Rd, Cumberland, RI, 02864-5510. Tel: 401-333-2552, Ext 201. p. 2031

Chiba, Toru, Electronic Serv Librn, Fairmont State University, 1201 Locust Ave, Fairmont, WV, 26554. Tel: 304-367-4594. p. 2402

Chibnall, Dan, STEM Librarian, Drake University, 2725 University Ave, Des Moines, IA, 50311. Tel: 515-271-2112. p. 746

Chibnik, Kitty, Assoc Dir, Head, Access Serv, Columbia University, Avery Architectural & Fine Arts Library, 300 Avery Hall, 1172 Amsterdam Ave, MC 0301, New York, NY, 10027. Tel: 212-854-3506. p. 1583

Chic, Kelsey, Libr Mgr, Carmangay & District Municipal Library, 416 Grand Ave, Carmangay, AB, T0L 0N0, CANADA. Tel: 403-643-3777. p. 2530

Chick, Amanda, Circ Mgr, Palm Beach State College, 3160 PGA Blvd, Palm Beach Gardens, FL, 33410-2893. Tel: 561-207-5800. p. 434

Chickering, Chris, Tech Serv Asst, Griffin Free Public Library, 22 Hooksett Rd, Auburn, NH, 03032. Tel: 603-483-5374. p. 1354

Chicone, Andre, Archivist/Librn, Archives Provinciales des Capucins, 3650 Blvd de la Rousseliere, Montreal, QC, H1A 2X9, CANADA. Tel: 514-642-5391, Ext 345. p. 2716

Chidester, Gracie, Libr Dir, Helvetia Public Library, 4901 Pickens Rd, Helvetia, WV, 26224. Tel: 304-924-5063. p. 2404

Chidester, John K, Dir, Public Library of Mount Vernon & Knox County, 201 N Mulberry St, Mount Vernon, OH, 43050-2413. Tel: 740-392-2665. p. 1804

Chidsey, Marni, Assoc Librn, Northwest Florida State College, 100 College Blvd E, Niceville, FL, 32578. Tel: 850-729-5318. p. 428

Chien, Felicia, Br Mgr, Riverside County Library System, Eastvale Library, 7447 Scholar Way, Corona, CA, 92880-4019. Tel: 951-273-2025. p. 202

Chikwendu, Talibah, Librn, Maryland Correctional Institution-Jessup Library, 7803 House of Corrections Rd, Rte 175, Jessup, MD, 20794. Tel: 410-799-7610. p. 969

Chilcoat, Jennifer, Libr Dir, State Librn, Arkansas State Library, 900 W Capitol, Ste 100, Little Rock, AR, 72201-3108. Tel: 501-682-1526. p. 100

Childers, Bruce, Interim Dean, University of Pittsburgh, Information Science Bldg 5th Flr, 135 N Bellefield Ave, Pittsburgh, PA, 15260. Tel: 412-624-5015. p. 2791

Childers, Jessica, Libr Spec, Wytheville Community College Library, 1000 E Main St, Wytheville, VA, 24382. Tel: 276-223-4743. p. 2355

Childers, Julie, Dir, Field-Carnegie Library, 200 Walnut St, Odebolt, IA, 51458. Tel: 712-668-2718. p. 774

Childers, Kailey, Dir, Arthur Public Library, 224 S Main St, Arthur, IA, 51431. Tel: 712-367-2240. p. 732

Childers, Pam, Syst & Web Mgt Librn, Indiana Wesleyan University, 4201 S Washington St, Marion, IN, 46953. Tel: 765-677-2893. p. 704

Childers, Scott, Exec Dir, Southeast Library System (SLS), 5730 R St, Ste C1, Lincoln, NE, 68505. Tel: 531-530-3011. p. 1323

Childress, Boyd, Librn, Auburn University, The Library of Architecture, Design & Construction, Dudley Hall Commons, Auburn, AL, 36849. Tel: 334-844-1752. p. 6

Childress, Courtney, Br Mgr, Kitsap Regional Library, Bainbridge Island Branch, 1270 Madison Ave N, Bainbridge Island, WA, 98110-2747. Tel: 206-842-4162. p. 2359

Childress, Diane, Coordr of Info & Tech Res, Baker College of Allen Park Library, 4500 Enterprise Dr, Allen Park, MI, 48101. Tel: 810-766-4235. p. 1077

Childress, Diane, Coordr of Info & Tech Res, Baker College of Auburn Hills, 1500 University Dr, Auburn Hills, MI, 48326-2642. Tel: 810-766-4235. p. 1081

Childress, Diane, Coordr of Info & Tech Res, Baker College of Cadillac Library, 9600 E 13th St, Cadillac, MI, 49601-9169. Tel: 810-766-4235. p. 1088

Childress, Diane, Coordr, Info Tech, Baker College of Jackson, 2800 Springport Rd, Jackson, MI, 49202-1255. Tel: 810-766-4235. p. 1119

Childress, Diane, Coordr of Info & Tech Res, Baker College of Owosso Library, 1020 S Washington St, Owosso, MI, 48867-4400. Tel: 810-766-4235. p. 1139

Childress, Robert, IT Dir, Pueblo City-County Library District, 100 E Abriendo Ave, Pueblo, CO, 81004-4290. Tel: 719-562-5622. p. 293

Childress, Sheri, Librn, Leighton Public Library, 8740 Main St, Leighton, AL, 35646. Tel: 256-446-5380. p. 24

Childress, Stacy, Colls Mgr, Saline County Public Library, 1800 Smithers Dr, Benton, AR, 72015. Tel: 501-778-4766. p. 90

Childs, Bruce, Coordr of Info & Tech Res, Baker College of Flint Library, 1050 W Bristol Rd, Flint, MI, 48507-5508. Tel: 810-766-4239. p. 1105

Childs, Carolyn, Dir, Gunnison Civic Library, 38 W Center St, Gunnison, UT, 84634. Tel: 435-528-3104. p. 2264

Childs, Cynthia, Ref Outreach Librn, Southeastern University, 1000 Longfellow Blvd, Lakeland, FL, 33801. Tel: 863-667-5089. p. 417

Childs, Deirdre, Head, Access Serv, Drexel University Libraries, Hagerty Library, 33rd & Market Sts, Philadelphia, PA, 19104-2875. Tel: 215-895-6785. p. 1976

Childs, Deirdre, Interim Assoc Dean of Libraries, Pub Serv, West Chester University, 25 W Rosedale Ave, West Chester, PA, 19383. Tel: 610-738-0480. p. 2020

Childs, Gary, Educ Librn, Drexel University Libraries, Hahnemann Library, 245 N 15th St MS 449, Philadelphia, PA, 19102-1192. p. 1976

Childs, Mary, Curator, Exec Dir, The Sandwich Glass Museum Library, 129 Main St, Sandwich, MA, 02563. Tel: 508-888-0251. p. 1051

Childs, Miriam, Dir, Law Libr, Law Library of Louisiana, Louisiana Supreme Court, 2nd Flr, 400 Royal St, New Orleans, LA, 70130-2104. Tel: 504-310-2403. p. 901

Childs, Sarah, Dept Head, Tech Serv, Hussey-Mayfield Memorial Public Library, 250 N Fifth St, Zionsville, IN, 46077-1324. Tel: 317-873-3149. p. 728

Childs, Scott, Assoc Dean, University of Tennessee, Taylor Law Ctr, 1505 W Cumberland Ave, Knoxville, TN, 37996-1800. Tel: 865-974-6733. p. 2107

Childs-Helton, Sally, Spec Coll & Archives Librn, Butler University Libraries, 4600 Sunset Ave, Indianapolis, IN, 46208. Tel: 317-940-9265. p. 690

Chilton, Sarah, Archives, Sr Res Librn, Brookings Institution Library, 1775 Massachusetts Ave NW, Washington, DC, 20036. Tel: 202-797-6240. p. 361

Chim, Melissa, Ref Librn, General Theological Seminary, 440 West 21st St, New York, NY, 10011. Tel: 646-717-9747. p. 1586

Chiment, Clay, Librn, Ulysses Philomathic Library, 74 E Main St, Trumansburg, NY, 14886. Tel: 607-387-5623. p. 1653

Chin, Amanda, Fac Librn, Green River College, 12401 SE 320th St, Auburn, WA, 98092-3699. Tel: 253-833-9111. p. 2357

Chin, Jessie, Asst Prof, University of Illinois at Urbana-Champaign, Library & Information Science Bldg, 501 E Daniel St, Champaign, IL, 61820-6211. Tel: 217-333-3280. p. 2784

Chin, Kristen, Libr Dir, Barrington Public Library, 281 County Rd, Barrington, RI, 02806. Tel: 401-247-1920. p. 2029

Chin, Olivia, Circ Mgr, Union University, 1050 Union University Dr, Jackson, TN, 38305-3697. Tel: 731-661-6579. p. 2102

Chin, Sushan, Asst Dir, Archives & Spec Coll, Bellevue Medical Library, 462 First Ave & 27th St, 14N12, New York, NY, 10016. Tel: 212-263-8280. p. 1580

Chin, Susie, Instrul Serv Librn, Glendale Community College Library, 1500 N Verdugo Rd, Glendale, CA, 91208-2894. Tel: 818-240-1000, Ext 5581, 818-240-1000, Ext 5586. p. 148

Chin-Parker, Lucy, Commun Engagement Librn, Granville Public Library, 217 E Broadway, Granville, OH, 43023-1398. Tel: 740-587-0196. p. 1788

China, Dominique, Br Mgr, Brampton Library, Cyril Clark Branch, 20 Loafers Lake Lane, Brampton, ON, L6Z 1X9, CANADA. Tel: 905-793-4636, Ext 74403. p. 2633

Chinault, Sue, Mgr, Michigan Bureau of Services for Blind Persons - Braille & Talking Book Library, Michigan Library & Historical Ctr, 702 W Kalamazoo St, Lansing, MI, 48915-1703. Tel: 517-284-2870. p. 1125

Ching, Cathy, Dir, Libr Serv, South Central Regional Library, 160 Main St, Winkler, MB, R6W 4B4, CANADA. Tel: 204-325-5864. p. 2592

Ching, Tina, Ref (Info Servs), Seattle University, School of Law Library, Sullivan Hall, 901 12th Ave, Seattle, WA, 98122-4411. Tel: 206-398-4221. p. 2380

Chinnaswamy, Sai, Mr, Dep Div Chief, Joint World Bank-International Monetary Fund Library, 700 19th St NW, Rm HQ1-CN-650J, Washington, DC, 20431. Tel: 202-623-5995. p. 370

Chinnery, Symra, Librn, Virgin Islands Division of Libraries, Archives & Museums, 4607 Tutu Park Mall, Saint Thomas, VI, 00802. Tel: 340-774-0630. p. 2517

Chiocchi, Rose, Libr Dir, Pike County Public Library, 119 E Harford St, Milford, PA, 18337. Tel: 570-296-8211. p. 1963

Chioffe, Colleen, Libr Mgr, New York Public Library - Astor, Lenox & Tilden Foundations, New Dorp Branch, 309 New Dorp Lane, Staten Island, NY, 10306. Tel: 718-351-2977. p. 1596

Chipps, Laurie, Tech Serv Librn, Montana Historical Society, 225 N Roberts St, Helena, MT, 59601-4514. Tel: 406-444-4787. p. 1296

Chipps, Susan, Br Mgr, Washington County Public Library, Beverly Library, MacIntosh St, Beverly, OH, 45715. Tel: 740-984-4060. p. 1799

Chirgwin, Jane, Libr Dir, Rensselaer Public Library, 676 East St, Rensselaer, NY, 12144. Tel: 518-462-1193. p. 1626
Chirinos, Joel, Head, Res & Instrul Serv, University of Texas Rio Grande Valley, One W University Blvd, Brownsville, TX, 78520. Tel: 956-882-7465. p. 2150
Chirombo, Fanuel, Dr, E-Res Mgt, Head, Acq, Ser, Morgan State University, 1700 E Cold Spring Lane, Baltimore, MD, 21251. Tel: 443-885-1712. p. 956
Chisholm, Alexandria, Ref & Instruction Librn, Pennsylvania State University, Berks Campus, Tulpehocken Rd, Reading, PA, 19610. Tel: 610-396-6339. p. 2000
Chisholm, Cathy, Librn, Cape Breton University Library, 1250 Grand Lake Rd, Sydney, NS, B1P 6L2, CANADA. Tel: 902-563-1993. p. 2623
Chisholm, Faye, Pub Serv Coordr, Vancouver School of Theology, 6015 Walter Gage Rd, Vancouver, BC, V6T 1Z1, CANADA. Tel: 604-822-9382. p. 2582
Chism, Ashlee, Libr Dir, General Conference of Seventh-Day Adventists, 12501 Old Columbia Pike, Silver Spring, MD, 20904. Tel: 301-680-5020, 301-680-6495. p. 977
Chisman, Janet, Librn, Kentucky Talking Book Library, 300 Coffee Tree Rd, Frankfort, KY, 40601. Tel: 502-564-1735. p. 855
Chitow, Natasha, Head Librn, Cottage Grove Public Library, 700 E Gibbs Ave, Cottage Grove, OR, 97424. Tel: 541-942-3828. p. 1877
Chittim, David, Pres, Androscoggin Historical Society, 93 Lisbon St, Lewiston, ME, 04240. Tel: 207-784-0586. p. 929
Chitty, A Ben, Syst Coordr, Queens College, Benjamin S Rosenthal Library, 65-30 Kissena Blvd, Flushing, NY, 11367-0904. Tel: 718-997-3700. p. 1534
Chitwood, Missy, Dir, Winfield Public Library, 275 Pine Grove Rd, Winfield, TN, 37892. Tel: 423-569-9047. p. 2130
Chiu, Carlene, Tech Serv, Altadena Library District, 600 E Mariposa St, Altadena, CA, 91001. Tel: 626-798-0833. p. 116
Chiu, Philip, Reserves Streaming Coord, University of California, Riverside, 900 University Ave, Riverside, CA, 92521. Tel: 951-827-3220. p. 203
Chlebo, Dawn, Head, Circ, Milford Public Library, 330 Family Dr, Milford, MI, 48381-2000. Tel: 248-684-0845. p. 1132
Chmiel, Mary Faith, Libr Dir, Elizabeth Public Library, 11 S Broad St, Elizabeth, NJ, 07202. Tel: 908-354-6060. p. 1401
Cho, Christie, Learning Commons Coord, NHTI, Concord's Community College, 31 College Dr, Concord, NH, 03301-7425. Tel: 603-271-6484, Ext 4201. p. 1359
Cho, Eunhye, Libr Mgr, Saint Paul Municipal Library, 4802-53 St, St. Paul, AB, T0A 3A0, CANADA. Tel: 780-645-4904. p. 2555
Cho, Hyrim, Asst Prof, University of Missouri-Columbia, 303 Townsend Hall, Columbia, MO, 65211. Tel: 573-882-4546. p. 2787
Cho, J Silvia, Res Sharing Librn, City University of New York, 365 Fifth Ave, New York, NY, 10016-4309. Tel: 212-817-7045. p. 1582
Cho, Ruth, Instruction & Outreach Librn, Biola University Library, 13800 Biola Ave, La Mirada, CA, 90639. Tel: 562-944-0351, Ext 5625. p. 155
Cho, Sanghun, Librn, University of California Los Angeles Library, Richard C Rudolph East Asian Library, 21617 Research Library YRL, Los Angeles, CA, 90095. Tel: 310-825-9535. p. 169
Choate, Celeste, Exec Dir, The Urbana Free Library, 210 W Green St, Urbana, IL, 61801. Tel: 217-367-4057. p. 656
Choate, Filomena, Youth Serv, Winfield Public Library, 0S291 Winfield Rd, Winfield, IL, 60190. Tel: 630-653-7599. p. 663
Choate, Kristy, Dir, Ridgely Public Library, 134 N Main St, Ridgely, TN, 38080-1316. Tel: 731-264-5809. p. 2125
Choate, Susannah, Ref Librn, Spec Coll Librn, The John P Holt Brentwood Library, 8109 Concord Rd, Brentwood, TN, 37027. Tel: 615-371-0090, Ext 8230. p. 2089
Chodock, Ted, Instruction & Ref Librn, College of Southern Nevada, Bldg L, 1st Flr, 6375 W Charleston Blvd, Las Vegas, NV, 89146. Tel: 702-651-5509. p. 1346
Chodosch, Margery, Head, Ref, Great Neck Library, 159 Bayview Ave, Great Neck, NY, 11023. Tel: 516-466-8055, Ext 220. p. 1540
Chohan, Sundeet, Supvr, New Westminster Public Library, Queensborough, 920 Ewen Ave, New Westminster, BC, V3M 5C8, CANADA. Tel: 604-636-4450. p. 2572
Choi, Christy, Dir, Libr Serv, Alliance University, Two Washington St, New York, NY, 10004-1008. Tel: 646-378-6142. p. 1578
Choi, Helen, Cataloger, Pace University, 78 N Broadway, White Plains, NY, 10603. Tel: 914-422-4648. p. 1665
Choi, Inkyung, Asst Teaching Prof, University of Illinois at Urbana-Champaign, Library & Information Science Bldg, 501 E Daniel St, Champaign, IL, 61820-6211. Tel: 217-333-3280. p. 2784
Choi, Jenny, Dep Dir, Operations, San Jose Public Library, 150 E San Fernando St, San Jose, CA, 95112-3580. Tel: 408-808-2152. p. 231
Choi, Kahyun, Asst Prof, University of Illinois at Urbana-Champaign, Library & Information Science Bldg, 501 E Daniel St, Champaign, IL, 61820-6211. Tel: 217-333-3280. p. 2784
Choi, Lan, Ref Librn, Bloomberg Industry Group Library, 1801 S Bell St, Arlington, VA, 22202. Tel: 703-341-3313. p. 2305
Choi, Namjoo, Dr, Assoc Prof, University of Kentucky, 320 Little Library Bldg, Lexington, KY, 40506-0224. Tel: 859-257-8876. p. 2785
Choi, Nan, Supervising Librn, Children's & Teens Services, Sunnyvale Public Library, 665 W Olive Ave, Sunnyvale, CA, 94086-7622. Tel: 408-730-7300. p. 251
Choi, Sylvia, Head, Coll Mgt, School of the Art Institute of Chicago, 37 S Wabash Ave, Chicago, IL, 60603-3103. Tel: 312-899-5097. p. 568
Choi, Youngok, Dr, Chair, Catholic University of America, 620 Michigan Ave NE, Washington, DC, 20064. Tel: 202-319-5085. p. 2783
Choi, Yumi, Sr Cat Librn, Bergen County Cooperative Library System, Inc, 21-00 Route 208 S, Ste 130, Fair Lawn, NJ, 07410. Tel: 201-498-7313. p. 2770
Choi, Yunseon, Dr, Assoc Prof, Valdosta State University, Odum Library, 1500 N Patterson St, Valdosta, GA, 31698. Tel: 229-245-3725. p. 2784
Chojnacki, Denise, Ch Serv, Rhinelander District Library, 106 N Stevens St, Rhinelander, WI, 54501-3193. Tel: 715-365-1070. p. 2472
Cholach, Barb, Librn, Grassland Public Library, Hwy 63, Box 150, Grassland, AB, T0A 1V0, CANADA. Tel: 780-525-3733. p. 2541
Chomel, Suzanne, Br Mgr, Westchester Public Library, Hageman, 100 Francis St, Porter, IN, 46304. Tel: 219-926-9080. p. 675
Chomsky, Herschel, Bus Mgr, Perth Amboy Free Public Library, 196 Jefferson St, Perth Amboy, NJ, 08861. Tel: 732-826-2600. p. 1434
Chong, Douglas, Pres, Hawaii Chinese History Center Archives, 111 N King St, Rm 307, Honolulu, HI, 96817. Tel: 808-521-5948. p. 506
Chong, Simon, Syst Mgr, Newmarket Public Library, 438 Park Ave, Newmarket, ON, L3Y 1W1, CANADA. Tel: 905-953-5110. p. 2660
Chonko, Doreen, Tech Serv, Dunedin Public Library, 223 Douglas Ave, Dunedin, FL, 34698. Tel: 727-298-3080, Ext 1739. p. 394
Chontos, Viola, Ref Librn, Franciscan University of Steubenville, 1235 University Blvd, Steubenville, OH, 43952-1763. Tel: 740-283-6366. p. 1821
Choo, Robinson, Libr Assoc, American Samoa Community College Library, Malaeimi Village, Malaeimi Rd, Mapusaga, AS, 96799. p. 2503
Chorney, Alan, Br Head, Winnipeg Public Library, Transcona, One Transcona Blvd, Winnipeg, MB, R2C 5R6, CANADA. Tel: 204-330-4716. p. 2597
Chosa, Linda, Finance Mgr, Brown County Library, 515 Pine St, Green Bay, WI, 54301. Tel: 920-448-5802. p. 2438
Choudhury, Sayeed, Assoc Dean, Johns Hopkins University Libraries, The Sheridan Libraries, 3400 N Charles St, Baltimore, MD, 21218. Tel: 410-516-8325. p. 954
Chouinard, Anita, Librn, Traverse Area District Library, Talking Book Library, 610 Woodmere, Traverse City, MI, 49686. Tel: 231-932-8558. p. 1155
Chouinard, Mary, Libr Dir, Shaw Library, Mercer Community Center, 1015 Beach Hill Rd, Ste B, Mercer, ME, 04957. Tel: 207-779-3977. p. 931
Chow, Anthony, Dr, Dir, San Jose State University, Clark Hall 417, One Washington Sq, San Jose, CA, 95192-0029. Tel: 408-924-2490. p. 2782
Chow, Anthony S, PhD, Assoc Prof, University of North Carolina at Greensboro, School of Education Bldg, Rm 446, 1300 Spring Garden St, Greensboro, NC, 27412. Tel: 336-334-3477. p. 2790
Chow, Connie, Actg Dep Dir, Huntsville-Madison County Public Library, 915 Monroe St, Huntsville, AL, 35801. Tel: 256-532-5940. p. 21
Chow, Cynthia, Br Mgr, Hawaii State Public Library System, Kaneohe Public Library, 45-829 Kamehameha Hwy, Kaneohe, HI, 96744. Tel: 808-233-5676. p. 508
Chow, Judy, Librn, West Los Angeles College Library, 9000 Overland Ave, Culver City, CA, 90230. Tel: 310-287-4408. p. 133
Chow, Mei Ling, Cat Librn, Montclair State University, One Normal Ave, Montclair, NJ, 07043-1699. Tel: 973-655-4422. p. 1420
Chown, Deborah, Libr Dir, Greenfield Community College, Core Bldg, 3rd Flr, One College Dr, Greenfield, MA, 01301-9739. Tel: 413-775-1832. p. 1022
Chrey, Bonnie, Librn, Kitsap County Historical Society, 280 Fourth St, Bremerton, WA, 98337-1813. Tel: 360-479-6226. p. 2359
Chrin, Oscar, Tech Serv Librn, Culinary Institute of America, 1946 Campus Dr, Hyde Park, NY, 12538-1430. Tel: 845-451-1373. p. 1550
Chrin, Oscar, Ad, Rose Memorial Library, 79 E Main St, Stony Point, NY, 10980-1699. Tel: 845-786-2100. p. 1647
Chris, Burton, Co-Chair, Asbury First United Methodist Church, 1050 East Ave, Rochester, NY, 14607. Tel: 585-271-1050. p. 1628
Chrisinske, Julie, Head Librn, Capital Area District Libraries, Williamston Library, 3845 Vanneter Rd, Williamston, MI, 48895. Tel: 517-655-1191. p. 1124
Chrisman, Sarah, Librn, Garden Grove Public Library, 103 W Main St, Garden Grove, IA, 50103. Tel: 641-443-2172. p. 754
Christ, Marian, Asst Librn, Head Cataloger, American Philosophical Society Library, 105 S Fifth St, Philadelphia, PA, 19106-3386. Tel: 215-440-3400. p. 1974
Christakos, Melissa, Adult Serv Coordr, Chesapeake Public Library, 298 Cedar Rd, Chesapeake, VA, 23322-5512. Tel: 757-410-7135. p. 2311
Christein, Heidi, Ad, Archivist, Saint Clair Shores Public Library, 22500 11 Mile Rd, Saint Clair Shores, MI, 48081-1399. Tel: 586-771-9020. p. 1147
Christel, Mark, Librn of the Col, Grinnell College Libraries, 1111 Sixth Ave, Grinnell, IA, 50112-1770. Tel: 641-269-3350. p. 756
Christensen, Andrew, Dep Dir, Washington & Lee University, Wilbur C Hall Law Library, Lewis Hall, E Denny Circle, Lexington, VA, 24450. Tel: 540-458-8554. p. 2329

Christensen, Beth, Music Librn, Saint Olaf College, Rolvaag Memorial Library, Hustad Science Library, Halvorson Music Library, 1510 Saint Olaf Ave, Northfield, MN, 55057-1097. Tel: 507-786-3362. p. 1191

Christensen, Carla M, Dir, T O H P Burnham Public Library, 30 Martin St, Essex, MA, 01929. Tel: 978-768-7410. p. 1017

Christensen, Cecily, Ref Librn, Bellingham Public Library, 100 Blackstone St, Bellingham, MA, 02019. Tel: 508-966-1660. p. 988

Christensen, Dan, Exec Dir, Nebraska Prairie Museum, 2701 Burlington St., Holdrege, NE, 68949. Tel: 308-995-5015. p. 1318

Christensen, Dani, State Rec Mgr, Idaho State Historical Society, Idaho History Ctr, 2205 Old Penitentiary Rd, Boise, ID, 83712-8250. Tel: 208-514-2316. p. 517

Christensen, Jennifer, Tech Serv Mgr, Upper Arlington Public Library, 2800 Tremont Rd, Columbus, OH, 43221. Tel: 614-486-9621. p. 1778

Christensen, Jill, Librn, Arlington Community Library, 306 S Main St, Arlington, SD, 57212. Tel: 605-983-5741, Ext 230. p. 2074

Christensen, Kaylene, Dir, North Bingham County District Library, 197 W Locust St, Shelley, ID, 83274-1139. Tel: 208-357-7801. p. 531

Christensen, Larraine, Librn, Woodbury County Library, Cord Memorial Library, 215 Main St, Danbury, IA, 51019. Tel: 712-883-2207. p. 771

Christensen, Mark, Head, Access Serv, Simon Fraser University - Burnaby Campus, 8888 University Dr, Burnaby, BC, V5A 1S6, CANADA. Tel: 778-782-4081. p. 2564

Christensen, Mason, Archivist, Dearborn Historical Museum Library, Dearborn Historical Museum, 915 Brady St, Dearborn, MI, 48126. Tel: 313-565-3000. p. 1095

Christensen, Monique, Asst Dir, Siouxland Libraries, 200 N Dakota Ave, Sioux Falls, SD, 57104. Tel: 605-367-8723. p. 2082

Christensen, Susan, Coordr, Bldg Mgt, California State University, Fresno, Henry Madden Library, 5200 N Barton Ave, Mail Stop ML-34, Fresno, CA, 93740-8014. Tel: 559-278-5792. p. 144

Christensen, Zan, Adminr, Seattle Psychoanalytic Society & Institute, 4020 E Madison St, Ste 230, Seattle, WA, 98112. Tel: 206-328-5315. p. 2379

Christenson, Bridget, Dir, Hatch Public Library, 111 W State St, Mauston, WI, 53948-1344. Tel: 608-847-4454. p. 2455

Christenson, Gayle, Librn, Kidder County Library, 115 W Broadway Ave, Steele, ND, 58482. Tel: 701-475-2855. p. 1740

Christenson, Julie, Rare Bk Librn, Texas Christian University, 2913 Lowden St, TCU Box 298400, Fort Worth, TX, 76129. Tel: 817-257-7106. p. 2181

Christenson, Katie, Dir, Chisholm Public Library, 300 W Lake St, Chisholm, MN, 55719-1718. Tel: 218-254-7913. p. 1170

Christian, Alison, Librn, Mount Carmel Library, 100 Main St, Mount Carmel, TN, 37645-9999. Tel: 423-357-4011. p. 2117

Christian, Jessica, Libr Mgr, Aiken-Bamberg-Barnwell-Edgefield Regional Library, Aiken County, 314 Chesterfield St SW, Aiken, SC, 29801. Tel: 803-642-2020. p. 2045

Christian, Kim, Prog Spec, Kinnelon Public Library, 132 Kinnelon Rd, Kinnelon, NJ, 07405. Tel: 973-838-1321. p. 1410

Christian, Mariel, Sr Dir for Libr Serv, RTI International, 3040 E Cornwallis Rd, Research Triangle Park, NC, 27709. Tel: 919-541-6303. p. 1712

Christian, Michele, Archives & Spec Coll Librn, South Dakota State University, 1300 N Campus Dr, Box 2115, Brookings, SD, 57007. Tel: 605-688-4906. p. 2074

Christian, Patricia, Librn, Squire Patton Boggs, 2000 Huntington Ctr, 41 S High St, Columbus, OH, 43215. Tel: 614-365-2700. p. 1777

Christian, Raymond, Br Mgr, Garfield County-Panguitch City Library, Escalante Branch, 90 N 100 West, Escalante, UT, 84726. p. 2268

Christian-Whitney, Janice, Libr Supvr, Placer County Library, Foresthill Branch, 24580 Main St, Foresthill, CA, 95631. Tel: 530-367-2785. p. 118

Christians, Corey, Dir, Yavapai County Free Library District, 1971 Commerce Ctr Circle, Ste D, Prescott, AZ, 86301. Tel: 928-771-3191. p. 74

Christians, Corey, Dir, Yavapai County Free Library District, Seligman Public Library, 54170 N Floyd St, Seligman, AZ, 86337. Tel: 928-422-3633. p. 75

Christiansen, Arne, Acq, Wellesley Free Library, 530 Washington St, Wellesley, MA, 02482. Tel: 781-235-1610. p. 1064

Christiansen, Donna, Dir, Plainview Public Library, 209 N Pine St, Plainview, NE, 68769. Tel: 402-582-4507. p. 1333

Christiansen, Jeannie, Financial Mgr, Fresno County Public Library, 2420 Mariposa St, Fresno, CA, 93721. Tel: 559-600-7323. p. 145

Christiansen, Karen, Ad, Paso Robles City Library, 1000 Spring St, Paso Robles, CA, 93446-2207. Tel: 805-237-3870. p. 194

Christiansen, Nicole, Syst Librn, Northern State University, 1200 S Jay St, Aberdeen, SD, 57401. Tel: 605-626-3018. p. 2073

Christiansen, Renee, Youth Serv Mgr, Library System of Lancaster County, 1866 Colonial Village Lane, Ste 107, Lancaster, PA, 17601. Tel: 717-207-0500. p. 1952

Christiansen, Sharon, Librn, Mammoth Public Library, 125 N Clark St, Mammoth, AZ, 85618. Tel: 520-487-2026. p. 66

Christianson, Darla, Br Librn, Wapiti Regional Library, Naicam Public Library, 109 Centre St, Naicam, SK, S0K 2Z0, CANADA. Tel: 306-874-2156. p. 2746

Christianson, Erica, Exec Dir, Ela Area Public Library District, 275 Mohawk Trail, Lake Zurich, IL, 60047. Tel: 847-438-3433. p. 607

Christianson, Kimberly, Libr Tech, Per, Normandale Community College Library, 9700 France Ave S, Bloomington, MN, 55431. Tel: 952-487-8291. p. 1166

Christie, Holland, Br Mgr, Fort Vancouver Regional Library District, Battle Ground Community Library, 1207 SE Eighth Way, Battle Ground, WA, 98604. p. 2391

Christie, Holland, Br Mgr, Fort Vancouver Regional Library District, Yacolt Library Express, 105 E Yacolt Rd, Yacolt, WA, 98675. p. 2391

Christie, Julian, Libr Mgr, York Library Region, McAdam Public Library, 146 Saunders Rd, McAdam, NB, E6J 1L2, CANADA. Tel: 506-784-1403. p. 2602

Christie, Laurie, Literacy Serv, Morse Institute Library, 14 E Central St, Natick, MA, 01760. Tel: 508-647-6400, Ext 1583. p. 1037

Christie, Lisa, Ref Librn, Viterbo University, 900 Viterbo Dr, La Crosse, WI, 54601. Tel: 608-796-3268. p. 2446

Christie, Thomas, Cat/Metadata Librn, Muhlenberg College, 2400 Chew St, Allentown, PA, 18104-5586. Tel: 484-664-3575. p. 1905

Christina, Manry, Ch, Natchitoches Parish Library, 450 Second St, Natchitoches, LA, 71457-4649. Tel: 318-238-9222. p. 899

Christine, Erin, Acq Assoc, The College of Wooster Libraries, 1140 Beall Ave, Wooster, OH, 44691-2364. Tel: 330-263-2467. p. 1833

Christlieb, Kelsey, Academic Specialist, Minnesota State Community & Technical College, 1900 28th Ave S, Moorhead, MN, 56560. Tel: 218-299-6514, 218-299-6552. p. 1188

Christman, Andrea, Tech Serv & Syst Librn, Sinclair Community College Library, 444 W Third St, Dayton, OH, 45402-1460. Tel: 937-512-4513. p. 1780

Christman, Raven, Dir & Librn, Lemmon Public Library, 303 First Ave W, Lemmon, SD, 57638. Tel: 605-374-5611. p. 2078

Christman, Vanessa, Pub Serv Librn, Riverside County Law Library, 3989 Lemon St, Riverside, CA, 92501-4203. Tel: 951-368-0365. p. 201

Christmas, Erin, Libr Dir, Riverside Public Library, 3900 Mission Inn Ave, Riverside, CA, 92501. Tel: 951-826-5201. p. 203

Christoff, Suzanne, Assoc Dir, Spec Coll & Archives, United States Military Academy Library, Jefferson Hall Library & Learning Ctr, 758 Cullum Rd, West Point, NY, 10996. Tel: 845-938-8301. p. 1663

Christoffer, Angela, Br Mgr, Hancock County Library System, Waveland Public Library, 345 Coleman Ave, Waveland, MS, 39576. Tel: 228-467-9240. p. 1212

Christofferson, Kim, Br Mgr, Riverside County Library System, Temecula - Grace Mellman Library, 41000 County Center Dr, Temecula, CA, 92591. Tel: 951-296-3893. p. 202

Christofferson, Kim, Br Mgr, Santa Clarita Public Library, Valencia Library, 23743 W Valencia Blvd, Santa Clarita, CA, 91355. p. 242

Christofferson, Rolane, Dir, Prairie County Library, 309 Garfield Ave, Terry, MT, 59349. Tel: 406-635-5546. p. 1303

Christophe, Kytara, Adminr, Loan System Helping Automate Retrieval of Knowledge, State Library of Louisiana, 701 North Fourth St, Baton Rouge, LA, 70802. Tel: 225-342-4918. p. 2766

Christopher, Lynn, Librn, Hill Public Library, 30 Crescent St, Hill, NH, 03243. Tel: 603-934-9712. p. 1367

Christopherson, Gary, Access Serv Mgr, Algonquin Area Public Library District, 2600 Harnish Dr, Algonquin, IL, 60102-5900. Tel: 847-458-6060. p. 536

Christopoulos-Nutting, Suellen, Media & Digital Res Librn, New York Chiropractic College Library, 2360 State Rte 89, Seneca Falls, NY, 13148-9460. Tel: 315-568-3244. p. 1639

Christy, Dana, Regional Mgr, Yolo County Library, Arthur F Turner Community Library, 1212 Merkley Ave, West Sacramento, CA, 95691. Tel: 916-375-6464. p. 260

Christy, Jan, Tech Serv, Johnson University, 7902 Eubanks Dr, Knoxville, TN, 37998. Tel: 865-251-2277. p. 2105

Christy, Silvia D, Asst Libr Dir, Seguin Public Library, 313 W Nolte St, Seguin, TX, 78155-3217. Tel: 830-401-2426. p. 2242

Christy, Wendy, Youth Serv Mgr, Saline County Public Library, 1800 Smithers Dr, Benton, AR, 72015. Tel: 501-778-4766. p. 90

Chronopoulos, Corinne, Dir, Peterborough Town Library, Two Concord St, Peterborough, NH, 03458. Tel: 603-924-8040. p. 1378

Chroussis, Karen, Librn, Terra Alta Public Library, 701-B E State Ave, Terra Alta, WV, 26764. Tel: 304-789-2724. p. 2415

Chrystian, Annette, Librn, Holden Municipal Library, 4912-50 St, Holden, AB, T0B 2C0, CANADA. Tel: 780-688-3838. p. 2543

Chrystian, Barb, Libr Mgr, Viking Municipal Library, 5120 45 St, Viking, AB, T0B 4N0, CANADA. Tel: 780-336-4992. p. 2558

Chu, Ashley N, Univ Archivist, Taylor University, 1846 Main St, Upland, IN, 46989. Tel: 765-998-5242. p. 722

Chu, Heting, Dr, Prof, Long Island University, C W Post Campus, 720 Northern Blvd, Brookville, NY, 11548-1300. Tel: 516-299-2866, 516-299-2900. p. 2788

Chu, Mary, Librn, Population Council Library, One Dag Hammarskjold Plaza, New York, NY, 10017. Tel: 212-339-0533. p. 1600

Chu, Melanie, Dir, Lake Tahoe Community College, One College Dr, South Lake Tahoe, CA, 96150. Tel: 530-541-4660, Ext 232. p. 247

Chu, Penny, Digital Serv, Libr Tech, Alberta Government Library, Capital Blvd, 11th Flr, 10044 - 108 St, Edmonton, AB, T5J 5E6, CANADA. Tel: 780-427-2985. p. 2534

Chu, Wendy, Per, Ser, Kingsborough Community College, 2001 Oriental Blvd, Brooklyn, NY, 11235. Tel: 718-368-6564. p. 1504

Chua, Vanesa, Ch, Oxnard Public Library, 251 South A St, Oxnard, CA, 93030. Tel: 805-240-7339. p. 190
Chuah, Sally, Cat & Ref Librn, Syst, Santa Barbara City College, 721 Cliff Dr, Santa Barbara, CA, 93109-2394. Tel: 805-965-0581, Ext 2643. p. 240
Chubb, Jelain, State Archivist, Texas State Library & Archives Commission, 1201 Brazos St, Austin, TX, 78701. Tel: 512-463-5467. p. 2141
Chubet, Elizabeth, Acq, Pub Relations, Southington Public Library & Museum, 255 Main St, Southington, CT, 06489. Tel: 860-628-0947. p. 338
Chubon, Jeannine, Dir, Salina Library, 100 Belmont St, Mattydale, NY, 13211. Tel: 315-454-4524. p. 1570
Chukumah, Vincent, Ch, Atlanta-Fulton Public Library System, Dogwood Branch, 1838 Donald L Hollowell Pkwy NW, Atlanta, GA, 30318. Tel: 404-612-3900. p. 461
Chumak, Arkadij, Head of Libr, St Volodymyr's Cultural Centre, 404 Meredith Rd NE, Calgary, AB, T2E 5A6, CANADA. Tel: 403-264-3437. p. 2529
Chumas, Laura, Dir, Cresskill Public Library, 53 Union Ave, Cresskill, NJ, 07626. Tel: 201-567-3521. p. 1398
Chumbley, Lesleigh, Br Mgr, Public Library of Cincinnati & Hamilton County, Loveland Branch, 649 Loveland-Madeira Rd, Loveland, OH, 45140. Tel: 513-369-4476. p. 1762
Chun Ng, Lorraine, Med Librn, Ref, New York College of Podiatric Medicine, 53 E 124th St, New York, NY, 10035. Tel: 212-410-8020, 212-410-8142. p. 1593
Chun, Terrilyn, Dep Dir, Multnomah County Library, 919 NE 19th Ave, Ste 250, Portland, OR, 97232. Tel: 503-988-5123. p. 1892
Chung, Hai-Chin, Head, Tech Serv, Network Adminr, South Brunswick Public Library, 110 Kingston Lane, Monmouth Junction, NJ, 08852. Tel: 732-329-4000, Ext 7284. p. 1419
Chung, Hsi Hsi, Ms, Libr Dir, Metuchen Public Library, 480 Middlesex Ave, Metuchen, NJ, 08840. Tel: 732-632-8526. p. 1418
Chung, Jaeyeon Lucy, Dr, Dir, Garrett-Evangelical Theological Seminary, 2121 Sheridan Rd, Evanston, IL, 60201. Tel: 847-866-3909. p. 586
Chung, Katharine, Asst Dir, Danbury Public Library, 170 Main St, Danbury, CT, 06810. Tel: 203-797-4505. p. 307
Chung, Lynn, Instruction Librn, Compton College Library, 1111 E Artesia Blvd, Compton, CA, 90221. Tel: 310-900-1600, Ext 2179. p. 132
Chung, Talia, Univ Librn, Vice Provost, University of Ottawa Libraries, 65 University Private, Ottawa, ON, K1N 6N5, CANADA. Tel: 613-562-5880. p. 2670
Chupp, Hannah, ILL Librn, Richardson Public Library, 2360 Campbell Creek Blvd, Ste 500, Richardson, TX, 75082. Tel: 972-744-4350. p. 2231
Church, Anna, Ch, Joslin Memorial Library, 4391 Main St, Waitsfield, VT, 05673-6155. Tel: 802-496-4205. p. 2297
Church, Casady, Acq Tech, Southwestern Oklahoma State University, 100 Campus Dr, Weatherford, OK, 73096-3002. Tel: 580-774-3737. p. 1868
Church, Donna, Pub Serv Librn, Concordia Seminary Library, 801 Seminary Pl, Saint Louis, MO, 63105-3199. Tel: 314-505-7038. p. 1270
Church, Jill, Database Librn, ILL Librn, Ser Librn, D'Youville College, 320 Porter Ave, Buffalo, NY, 14201-1084. Tel: 716-829-8107. p. 1509
Church, Joanna, Librn, General Federation of Women's Clubs, 1734 N St NW, Washington, DC, 20036-2990. Tel: 202-683-2028. p. 367
Church, Joanna, Dir of Coll, Jewish Museum of Maryland, 15 Lloyd St, Baltimore, MD, 21202. Tel: 410-500-5349. p. 953
Church, Kristin, Youth Serv Librn, Blair Memorial Library, 416 N Main St, Clawson, MI, 48017-1599. Tel: 248-588-5500. p. 1091
Church, Matt, Dir, Berkley Public Library, 3155 Coolidge Hwy, Berkley, MI, 48072. Tel: 248-658-3440. p. 1084
Church, Miriam, Ref Serv, YA, Anderson County Library, 300 N McDuffie St, Anderson, SC, 29621-5643. Tel: 864-260-4500. p. 2046
Church, Rachel, Team Leader, Muskegon Area District Library, Dalton Branch, 3175 Fifth St, Twin Lake, MI, 49457-9501. Tel: 231-828-4188. p. 1136
Church, Sara, Br Mgr, Surrey Libraries, Clayton Library, 7155 187A St, Surrey, BC, V4N 6L9, CANADA. Tel: 236-598-3087. p. 2577
Church, Stacey, Dir, Norwalk Public Library, 46 W Main St, Norwalk, OH, 44857. Tel: 419-668-6063. p. 1810
Churchill, Amy, Dir, Lapeer District Library, 201 Village West Dr S, Lapeer, MI, 48446-1699. Tel: 810-664-9521. p. 1126
Churchill, Kristen, Youth Serv Librn, Caldwell Public Library, 268 Bloomfield Ave, Caldwell, NJ, 07006-5198. Tel: 973-226-2837. p. 1393
Churchill, Sara, Dr, Asst Prof, University of Nebraska at Omaha, College of Education, Roskens Hall, Omaha, NE, 68182. Tel: 402-554-3485. p. 2788
Churchill, Yelena, Libr Dir, Greenwood Public Library, 346 S Copper Ave, Greenwood, BC, V0H 1J0, CANADA. Tel: 250-445-6111. p. 2567
Churchill-Calkins, Mo, Youth Librn, Richards Free Library, 58 N Main St, Newport, NH, 03773. Tel: 603-863-3430. p. 1376
Churchouse, Martyn, Patron Serv Mgr, Oak Park Public Library, 834 Lake St, Oak Park, IL, 60301. Tel: 708-383-8200. p. 628
Churchwell, Desi Rae, Ms, Dir, Jay Johnson Public Library, 411 Main St, Quinter, KS, 67752. Tel: 785-754-2171. p. 833
Churley, Margaret, Ref Librn, River Edge Free Public Library, 685 Elm Ave, River Edge, NJ, 07661. Tel: 201-261-1663. p. 1439
Chute, Angie, Libr Dir, Trenton Public Library, 118 E Indiana, Trenton, IL, 62293. Tel: 618-224-7662. p. 654
Chute, Mary, State Librn, New Jersey State Library, 185 W State St, Trenton, NJ, 08608. Tel: 609-278-2640, Ext 101. p. 1448
Chuzmir, Dan, Libr Dir, Merrick Library, 2279 Merrick Ave, Merrick, NY, 11566. Tel: 516-377-6112. p. 1570
Ciambar, Barbara, Outreach Librn, Rochester Regional Library Council, 3445 Winton Pl, Ste 204, Rochester, NY, 14623. Tel: 585-223-7570. p. 2771
Ciambella, Christine, Dir, Libr Serv, Miller & Chevalier, 900 Sixteenth St, NW, Washington, DC, 20006. Tel: 202-626-6094. p. 371
Ciarochi, Helene, Libr Tech, Seton Hill University, One Seton Hill Dr, Greensburg, PA, 15601. Tel: 724-830-1091. p. 1938
Cicchini, Deborah, Med Librn, Ascension Saint John Hospital & Medical Center Library, 22101 Moross Rd, Detroit, MI, 48236. Tel: 313-343-3733. p. 1097
Ciccone, Michael, Chief Librn/CEO, London Public Library, 251 Dundas St, London, ON, N6A 6H9, CANADA. Tel: 519-661-4600. p. 2654
Cicconetti, Paula, Dir, Holmes County District Public Library, 3102 Glen Dr, Millersburg, OH, 44654. Tel: 330-674-5972, Ext 202. p. 1803
Cich, Keith, Librn, Fond du Lac Tribal & Community College, 2101 14th St, Cloquet, MN, 55720. Tel: 218-879-0837. p. 1170
Cichewicz, Joy, Br Mgr, Ypsilanti District Library, West Michigan Avenue, 229 W Michigan Ave, Ypsilanti, MI, 48197-5485. Tel: 734-482-4110. p. 1161
Ciciora, Irene, Youth Serv Mgr, Chicago Ridge Public Library, 10400 S Oxford Ave, Chicago Ridge, IL, 60415. Tel: 708-423-7753. p. 571
Ciejka, Patricia, Assoc VP, Academic Resources, University of Texas Medical Branch, 914 Market St, Galveston, TX, 77555. Tel: 409-772-4164. p. 2183
Ciemniewski, Christopher, Publicity & Public Servs Librn, Wallingford Public Library, 200 N Main St, Wallingford, CT, 06492. Tel: 203-284-6421. p. 343
Cierocki, Anna, Ref Librn, Tech Librn, Essex Library Association, Inc, 33 West Ave, Essex, CT, 06426-1196. Tel: 860-767-1560. p. 311
Ciesla, Carolyn, Dean, Learning Resources & Assessment, Prairie State College Library, 202 S Halsted St, Chicago Heights, IL, 60411-8200. Tel: 708-709-3552. p. 571
Ciesla, Carolyn, Libr Dir, Elmhurst University, 190 Prospect St, Elmhurst, IL, 60126. Tel: 630-617-3172. p. 585
Cieslik, Bob, Coordr, Fac & Admin Serv, Cleveland State University, Michael Schwartz Library, Rhodes Tower, Ste 501, 2121 Euclid Ave, Cleveland, OH, 44115-2214. Tel: 216-687-2256. p. 1769
Cieszynski, Jasmine, Instrul Serv Librn, Olivet Nazarene University, One University Ave, Bourbonnais, IL, 60914-2271. Tel: 815-928-5449. p. 544
Cifelli, Laura, Libr Mgr, Pub Serv, Lee County Library System, 2201 Second St, Ste 400, Fort Myers, FL, 33901. Tel: 239-533-4800. p. 403
Cifelli, Linda, Librn, Kean University, 1000 Morris Ave, Union, NJ, 07083. Tel: 908-737-4629. p. 1449
Cifferelli, Michael, Tech Serv Librn, Gateway Community College Library & Learning Commons, 20 Church St, New Haven, CT, 06510. Tel: 203-285-2052. p. 325
Cifor, Marika, Dr, Asst Prof, University of Washington, Mary Gates Hall, Ste 370, Campus Box 352840, Seattle, WA, 98195-2840. Tel: 206-543-1794. p. 2794
Cignoli, Nicole, Dir, Derby Public Library, 313 Elizabeth St, Derby, CT, 06418. Tel: 203-736-1482. p. 309
Cigrand, Carol, Libr Asst, Cascade Public Library, 310 First Ave W, Cascade, IA, 52033. Tel: 563-852-3222. p. 737
Cilenti, Jeanne, Br Mgr, Cuyahoga County Public Library, North Royalton Branch, 5071 Wallings Rd, North Royalton, OH, 44133-5120. Tel: 440-237-3800. p. 1813
Cina, Greg, Head, Research Branch, Library of the Marine Corps, Gray Research Ctr, 2040 Broadway St, Quantico, VA, 22134-5107. Tel: 703-784-4409. p. 2339
Cinnamon, Wendy, Chief Librn, Valemount Public Library, 1090A Main St, Valemount, BC, V0E 2Z0, CANADA. Tel: 250-566-4367. p. 2578
Cinnater, Nan, Lead Librn, Provincetown Public Library, 356 Commercial St, Provincetown, MA, 02657-2209. Tel: 508-487-7094, Ext 217. p. 1048
Cinquemani, Angela, Dir, Jericho Public Library, One Merry Lane, Jericho, NY, 11753. Tel: 516-935-6790. p. 1558
Cintron, Kristina, Facilities Dir, Pierce County Library System, 3005 112th St E, Tacoma, WA, 98446-2215. Tel: 253-548-3454. p. 2386
Cintron, Linnae, Head, Tech Serv, Eastern Monroe Public Library, 1002 N Ninth St, Stroudsburg, PA, 18360. Tel: 570-421-0800. p. 2010
Cintron, Reinaldo, Circ, Libr Asst, Inter-American University of Puerto Rico, 104 Parque Industrial Turpeaux, Rd 1, Mercedita, PR, 00715-1602. Tel: 787-284-1912, Ext 2287. p. 2512
Ciocco, Ronalee, Dir, Libr Serv, Washington & Jefferson College Library, 60 S Lincoln St, Washington, PA, 15301. Tel: 724-503-1001, Ext 3039. p. 2018
Cioffi, Dawn, Tech Serv, The Brookfield Library, 182 Whisconier Rd, Brookfield, CT, 06804. Tel: 203-775-6241. p. 305
Cioffi, Kristin, Fiscal Officer, Tech Mgr, Amherst Public Library, 221 Spring St, Amherst, OH, 44001. Tel: 440-988-4230. p. 1746
Cioffi, M Renata, Dir of Library Data & Budget, Sacred Heart University, 5151 Park Ave, Fairfield, CT, 06825-1000. Tel: 203-371-7702. p. 312

Ciparelli, Peter, Asst Librn, Cragin Memorial Library, Eight Linwood Ave, Colchester, CT, 06415. Tel: 860-537-5752. p. 306

Cipoletti, Anna, Learning Res Librn, Bethany College, Mary Cutlip Center for Library & Information Technology, Phillips Library Number 9, 31 E Campus Dr, Bethany, WV, 26032. Tel: 304-829-7321. p. 2398

Cipolla, Annie, Sr Librn, Los Angeles Public Library System, John C Fremont Branch Library, 6121 Melrose Ave, Los Angeles, CA, 90038-3501. Tel: 323-962-3521. p. 164

Cipparrone, Polly, Br Mgr, San Diego County Library, Del Mar Branch, 1309 Camino del Mar, Del Mar, CA, 92014-2693. Tel: 858-755-1666. p. 216

Cipriano, Debi, Cat, Lewis & Clark Community College, 5800 Godfrey Rd, Godfrey, IL, 62035. Tel: 618-468-4301. p. 594

Cira, Diane, Circ Asst, Seabrook Library, 25 Liberty Lane, Seabrook, NH, 03874-4506. Tel: 603-474-2044. p. 1381

Cirasella, Jill, Scholarly Communications Librn, City University of New York, 365 Fifth Ave, New York, NY, 10016-4309. Tel: 212-817-7046. p. 1582

Circle, Alison, Chief Cust Experience Officer, Columbus Metropolitan Library, 96 S Grant Ave, Columbus, OH, 43215-4702. Tel: 614-645-2275. p. 1772

Cirelli, Marie, Coll Access & Support Serv, Pennsylvania State University, College of Medicine, Penn State Hershey, 500 University Dr, Hershey, PA, 17033. Tel: 717-531-8640. p. 1943

Cirilo, Victor, Circ Supvr, Val Verde County Library, 300 Spring St, Del Rio, TX, 78840. Tel: 830-774-7595. p. 2169

Cirka, Lisa, Youth Serv Coordr, Brockville Public Library, 23 Buell St, Brockville, ON, K6V 5T7, CANADA. Tel: 613-342-3936. p. 2634

Cisna Mills, Jennie, Dir, Shorewood-Troy Public Library District, 650 Deerwood Dr, Shorewood, IL, 60404. Tel: 815-725-1715. p. 647

Cisneros, Mary Jane, Head Librn, Floyd County Library, 111 S Wall St, Floydada, TX, 79235. Tel: 806-983-4922. p. 2177

Cisneros, Toyya, Head Librn, Austin Community College, South Austin Campus Library, 1820 W Stassney Lane, 2nd Flr, Rm 1201, Austin, TX, 78745. Tel: 512-223-9184. p. 2138

Ciszek, Matthew P, Head Librn, Penn State Behrend, 4951 College Dr, Erie, PA, 16563-4115. Tel: 814-898-6106. p. 1932

Citizen, Angela, Head, Children's/Youth Serv, Inglewood Public Library, 101 W Manchester Blvd, Inglewood, CA, 90301-1771. Tel: 310-412-5397. p. 152

Citro, Lynda L, Librn, Charlotte County Library System, Englewood Charlotte Public, 3450 N Access Rd, Englewood, FL, 34224. Tel: 941-681-3739. p. 438

Citrola, Connie, Circ Serv, East Meadow Public Library, 1886 Front St, East Meadow, NY, 11554-1705. Tel: 516-794-2570. p. 1528

Ciurria, Andrea, Borrower & Tech Services Mgr, Bradford-West Gwillimbury Public Library, 425 Holland St W, Bradford, ON, L3Z 0J2, CANADA. Tel: 905-775-3328, Ext 6106. p. 2632

Civis, Laura, Libr Asst, Wiregrass Georgia Technical College, Lowndes Hall, 4089 Val Tech Rd, Rm 7147A, Valdosta, GA, 31602. Tel: 229-259-5177. p. 501

Cizon, Rhiannon, Exec Dir, Berrien County Historical Association Library, 313 N Cass St, Berrien Springs, MI, 49103-1038. Tel: 269-471-1202. p. 1085

Claar, Becky, Asst Dir, Ch, Bedford County Library System, 240 S Wood St, Bedford, PA, 15522. Tel: 814-623-5010. p. 1909

Claar, Rebecca, Asst Dir, Children's Librn, Bedford County Library, 240 S Wood St, Bedford, PA, 15522. Tel: 814-623-5010. p. 1909

Clabough, Kate, Dir, Loudon Public Library, 210 River Rd, Loudon, TN, 37774. Tel: 865-458-3161. p. 2109

Clague, Tracey, Libr Dir, Nassau Free Library, 18 Church St, Nassau, NY, 12123. Tel: 518-766-2715. p. 1575

Claiborne, Dawn, Dir, Scott County Public Library, 290 S Main St, Oneida, TN, 37841-2605. Tel: 423-569-8634. p. 2123

Claiborne, Mary Pomeroy, Communications Adminr, Pub Relations, Knox County Public Library System, 500 W Church Ave, Knoxville, TN, 37902. Tel: 865-215-8750. p. 2105

Clair, Crystal, Dir, Maxwell Public Library, 109 Main St, Maxwell, IA, 50161. Tel: 515-387-8780. p. 769

Clair, Traci, Dir, Carnegie Public Library, 101 W Clay, Albany, MO, 64402. Tel: 660-726-5615. p. 1237

Clair, Tracy, Youth Serv Librn, Ely Public Library, 1595 Dows St, Ely, IA, 52227. Tel: 319-848-7616. p. 751

Clairmont, Audrea, Dir, Todd County Public Library, 302 E Main St, Elkton, KY, 42220. Tel: 270-265-9071. p. 854

Clairmont-Schmidt, Cynthia, Admin Serv, Dep Dir, North Dakota State Library, Liberty Memorial Bldg, Dept 250, 604 East Blvd Ave, Bismarck, ND, 58505-0800. Tel: 701-328-4652. p. 1730

Clairoux, Natalie, Librn, Association des Bibliotheques de la Sante Affiliees a L'Universite de Montreal, c/o Health Library Univ Montreal, Pavillon Roger-Gaudry, 2900 Boul Edouard-Montpetit, 6e Etage, Salle L-623, Montreal, QC, H3C 3J7, CANADA. Tel: 514-343-6111, Ext 3585. p. 2778

Clancy, Lisa, Dir, William Jeanes Memorial Library, 4051 Joshua Rd, Lafayette Hill, PA, 19444-1400. Tel: 610-828-0441, Ext 108. p. 1950

Clancy, Lisa, Pres, Montgomery County Library & Information Network Consortium, 520 Virginia Dr, Fort Washington, PA, 19034. Tel: 610-238-0580. p. 2774

Clancy, Meg, Youth Serv, South Hadley Public Library, Two Canal St, South Hadley, MA, 01075. Tel: 413-538-5045. p. 1054

Clancy, Sarah, Fiscal Officer, Ventura County Library, 5600 Everglades St, Ste A, Ventura, CA, 93003. Tel: 805-677-7150. p. 256

Clancy, Sean, Law Libr Asst, New York Supreme Court, Cayuga County Court House, 152 Genesee St, Auburn, NY, 13021-3476. Tel: 315-237-6122. p. 1489

Clanton, Clista, Asst Dir, Strategic Serv, University of South Alabama Libraries, Biomedical Library, Biomedical Library Bldg, 5791 USA Dr N, Mobile, AL, 36688-0002. Tel: 251-460-7043. p. 27

Clanton, Kay, Dir, Washington County Library System, 341 Main St, Greenville, MS, 38701. Tel: 662-335-2331. p. 1217

Clanton-Green, Kim, Br Mgr, Las Vegas-Clark County Library District, Sahara West Library, 9600 W Sahara Ave, Las Vegas, NV, 89117. Tel: 702-507-3630. p. 1347

Clapp, Debbie, Dir, Ladoga-Clark Township Public Library, 128 E Main St, Ladoga, IN, 47954. Tel: 765-942-2456. p. 701

Clapp, Janet, Ad, Rutland Free Library, Ten Court St, Rutland, VT, 05701-4058. Tel: 802-773-1860. p. 2293

Clapp, Jessica, Libr Dir, Wilder Memorial Library, 24 Lawrence Hill Rd, Weston, VT, 05161. Tel: 802-824-4307. p. 2298

Clapp, Joyce, Libr Dir, Marceline Carnegie Library, 119 E California Ave, Marceline, MO, 64658. Tel: 660-376-3223. p. 1260

Clapp, Sharon, Digital Res Librn, Central Connecticut State University, 1615 Stanley St, New Britain, CT, 06050. Tel: 860-832-2059. p. 324

Clapper, Melissa, Br Librn, Wapiti Regional Library, Big River Public Library, 606 First St N, Big River, SK, S0J 0E0, CANADA. Tel: 306-469-2152. p. 2745

Clarage, Elizabeth, Dir, Coll Serv, Consortium of Academic & Research Libraries in Illinois, 1704 Interstate Dr, Champaign, IL, 61822. Tel: 217-300-2624. p. 2764

Claringbole, Ryan, Libr Dir, Monona Public Library, 1000 Nichols Rd, Monona, WI, 53716. Tel: 608-216-7458. p. 2462

Clark, Adam, Doc Delivery, Libr Tech, Lycoming College, One College Pl, Williamsport, PA, 17701. Tel: 570-321-4053. p. 2023

Clark, Aileen, Circ Serv, Emma S Clark Memorial Library, 120 Main St, Setauket, NY, 11733-2868. Tel: 631-941-4080, Ext 114. p. 1640

Clark, Amanda, Libr Dir, Whitworth University, 300 W Hawthorne Rd, Spokane, WA, 99251-0001. Tel: 509-777-3260. p. 2385

Clark, Angelina, Mgr, Circ Serv, Mary Wood Weldon Memorial Library, 1530 S Green St, Glasgow, KY, 42141. Tel: 270-651-2824. p. 857

Clark, Anne Hiller, Dep Dir, State of Delaware, 121 Martin Luther King Jr Blvd N, Dover, DE, 19901. Tel: 302-257-3002. p. 352

Clark, Annette, Asst Dir, Norwalk Easter Public Library, 1051 North Ave, Norwalk, IA, 50211. Tel: 515-981-0217. p. 774

Clark, Ashley, Br Mgr, East Baton Rouge Parish Library, Zachary Branch, 1900 Church St, Zachary, LA, 70791. Tel: 225-658-1880. p. 883

Clark, Becky, Libr Assoc, University of Guelph, 120 Main St E, Ridgetown, ON, N0P 2C0, CANADA. Tel: 519-674-1500, Ext 63540. p. 2676

Clark, Brenda, Librn, Revere Memorial Library, Revere Memorial Hall, Ten Main St, Isle Au Haut, ME, 04645. Tel: 207-335-5001. p. 928

Clark, Bryan, Tech Serv Librn, Illinois Central College, Kenneth L Edward Library Administration Bldgs, L312, One College Dr, East Peoria, IL, 61635-0001. Tel: 309-694-5508. p. 581

Clark, Carla, Librn, Miami Dade College, Medical Center Campus Library & Information Resource Center, 950 NW 20th St, Miami, FL, 33127. Tel: 305-237-4342. p. 422

Clark, Carmella, Br Mgr, Cherokee Regional Library System, Rossville Public, 504 McFarland Ave, Rossville, GA, 30741. Tel: 706-866-1368. p. 484

Clark, Carmen, Head, Coll Mgt, Bozeman Public Library, 626 E Main St, Bozeman, MT, 59715. Tel: 406-582-2400. p. 1289

Clark, Carol, Patron Serv Mgr, Marengo-Union Library District, 19714 E Grant Hwy, Marengo, IL, 60152. Tel: 815-568-8236. p. 613

Clark, Caroline, Librn, Pearl River Community College, Hancock Center Library, 454 Hwy 90, Ste D, Waveland, MS, 39756. Tel: 228-252-7000. p. 1230

Clark, Chris, Mkt Coordr, Eisenhower Public Library District, 4613 N Oketo Ave, Harwood Heights, IL, 60706. Tel: 708-867-7828. p. 597

Clark, Craig B, Libr Dir, Boynton Beach City Library, 115 N Federal Hwy, Boynton Beach, FL, 33435. Tel: 561-742-6390. p. 386

Clark, Cynthia, Br Mgr, Shreve Memorial Library, Hosston Branch, 15487 US Hwy 71, Hosston, LA, 71043. Tel: 318-287-3265. p. 909

Clark, Cynthia, Br Mgr, Shreve Memorial Library, Mooringsport Branch, 603 Latimer St, Mooringsport, LA, 71060. Tel: 318-996-6720. p. 909

Clark, Dana, Libr Syst Mgr, Keene State College, 229 Main St, Keene, NH, 03435-3201. Tel: 603-358-2755. p. 1369

Clark, Dennis, Chief of Research & Ref Servs Div, Library of Congress, James Madison Memorial Bldg, 101 Independence Ave SE, Washington, DC, 20540. Tel: 202-707-5000. p. 370

Clark, Donna, Dir, Libr Serv, Cisco College, 101 College Heights, Cisco, TX, 76437. Tel: 254-442-5026. p. 2155

Clark, Donna, Mgr, Ottawa Public Library/Bibliothèque publique d'Ottawa, 120 Metcalfe St, Ottawa, ON, K1P 5M2, CANADA. Tel: 613-580-2945. p. 2668

Clark, Elizabeth, Circ, Lewis & Clark Community College, 5800 Godfrey Rd, Godfrey, IL, 62035. Tel: 618-468-4313. p. 594

Clark, Ellen, Libr Dir, Society of the Cincinnati Library, 2118 Massachusetts Ave NW, Washington, DC, 20008. Tel: 202-785-2040, Ext 426. p. 376

Clark, Frances, Circ Supvr, Somers Public Library, Two Vision Blvd, Somers, CT, 06071. Tel: 860-763-3501. p. 337

Clark, George E, Librn, Harvard Library, Lamont Library-Undergraduate, Harvard Yard, Harvard University, Cambridge, MA, 02138. Tel: 617-495-2450. p. 1007

Clark, Ginny, Libr Dir, Prescott City Public Library, 174 W Third, Prescott, KS, 66767. Tel: 913-471-4593. p. 833

Clark, Heidi, Libr Mgr, Tulare Public Library, 475 North M St, Tulare, CA, 93274. Tel: 559-685-4505. p. 253

Clark, Irina, Ref & Instruction Librn, Alliant International University, 10455 Pomerado Rd, San Diego, CA, 92131-1799. Tel: 858-635-4552. p. 214

Clark, Janice, Br Mgr, Branch District Library, Algansee Branch, 580-B S Ray Quincy Rd, Quincy, MI, 49082-9530. Tel: 517-639-9830. p. 1092

Clark, Jennifer, ILL Librn, Silsby Free Public Library, 226 Main St, Charlestown, NH, 03603. Tel: 603-826-7793. p. 1357

Clark, Jessica, Mgr, Carnegie Library of Pittsburgh, Brookline, 708 Brookline Blvd, Pittsburgh, PA, 15226. Tel: 412-561-1003. p. 1991

Clark, Jill, Dir, West Union Community Library, 210 N Vine St, West Union, IA, 52175. Tel: 563-422-3103. p. 791

Clark, Jo, Circ Supvr, Reedsburg Public Library, 370 Vine St, Reedsburg, WI, 53959. Tel: 608-768-7323. p. 2472

Clark, Joan, Ref & Instruction Librn, United States Coast Guard Academy Library, 35 Mohegan Ave, New London, CT, 06320. Tel: 860-444-6421. p. 329

Clark, Joe, Head Librn, Kent State University Libraries, Performing Arts, D-004 Center for Performing Arts, 1325 Theatre Dr, Kent, OH, 44242. Tel: 330-672-1667. p. 1792

Clark, Jolene, Dir, Archives, Unity Archives, 1901 NW Blue Pkwy, Unity Village, MO, 64065-0001. Tel: 816-347-5539, 816-524-3550, Ext 2020. p. 1284

Clark, Jonathan, Cat, ILL Spec, Harrisburg Area Community College, 735 Cumberland St, Lebanon, PA, 17042. Tel: 717-780-1152. p. 1953

Clark, Judy, Asst Dir, Circ Librn, Merrill Memorial Library, 215 Main St, Yarmouth, ME, 04096. Tel: 207-846-4763. p. 947

Clark, Julia, Branch Experience Mgr, Evansville Vanderburgh Public Library, Oaklyn, 3001 Oaklyn Dr, Evansville, IN, 47711. Tel: 812-428-8234. p. 681

Clark, Karen, Dir, Logan Library, 255 N Main, Logan, UT, 84321-3914. Tel: 435-716-9130. p. 2265

Clark, Katharine, Head of Programming & Community Engagement, Beloit Public Library, 605 Eclipse Blvd, Beloit, WI, 53511. Tel: 608-364-2897. p. 2423

Clark, Kathy, Libr Dir, American Academy of Pediatrics, 345 Park Blvd, Itasca, IL, 60143. Tel: 630-626-6636. p. 602

Clark, Katie, Adult/YA Serv Librn, Winfield Public Library, 0S291 Winfield Rd, Winfield, IL, 60190. Tel: 630-653-7599. p. 663

Clark, Kayla, Dir, Clearfield County Public Library, 601 Beech St, Curwensville, PA, 16833. Tel: 814-236-0589. p. 1925

Clark, Kevin, Electronic Res, ILL, Saint Meinrad Archabbey & School of Theology, 200 Hill Dr, Saint Meinrad, IN, 47577. Tel: 812-357-6401. p. 717

Clark, Kimball, Cataloger, Harvard Library, Dumbarton Oaks Library & Archives, 1703 32nd St NW, Washington, MA, 20007. Tel: 202-339-6400, Ext 6968. p. 1006

Clark, Kristen, Operations Mgr, Mill Valley Public Library, 375 Throckmorton Ave, Mill Valley, CA, 94941. Tel: 415-389-4292, Ext 4730. p. 177

Clark, Kristen, Dir, Clarksville Public Library, 103 W Greene St, Clarksville, IA, 50619-0039. Tel: 319-278-1168. p. 740

Clark, Lana, Dir, Montrose Public Library, 200 Main St, Montrose, IA, 52639. Tel: 319-463-5532. p. 771

Clark, Laura, Dir, Thorne Bay Public Library, 120 Freeman Dr, Thorne Bay, AK, 99919. Tel: 907-828-3303. p. 52

Clark, Laurel, Libr Dir, South Kingstown Public Library, 1057 Kingstown Rd, Peace Dale, RI, 02879-2434. Tel: 401-783-4085, 401-789-1555. p. 2036

Clark, Leslie, Dir, Chestatee Regional Library System, 56 Mechanicsville Rd, Dahlonega, GA, 30533. Tel: 706-864-3668. p. 474

Clark, Lillian, Libr Dir, Aguilar Public Library, 146 W Main St, Aguilar, CO, 81020. Tel: 719-941-4426. p. 263

Clark, Linda, Circ, South Windsor Public Library, 1550 Sullivan Ave, South Windsor, CT, 06074. Tel: 860-644-1541. p. 337

Clark, Lissa, Librn, Bluefield State University, 219 Rock St, Bluefield, WV, 24701. Tel: 304-327-4564. p. 2398

Clark, Lori, Dir, Middleton Public Library, 307 Cornell St, Middleton, ID, 83644. Tel: 208-585-3931. p. 525

Clark, Lynne, Dir, River Rapids District Library, 227 E Broad St, Chesaning, MI, 48616. Tel: 989-845-3211. p. 1091

Clark, M, ILL, North Shore Public Library, 250 Rte 25A, Shoreham, NY, 11786-9677. Tel: 631-929-4488. p. 1641

Clark, Margaret, Asst Dir, Intl Legal Res, Florida State University Libraries, College of Law Library, 425 W Jefferson St, Tallahassee, FL, 32306. Tel: 850-644-9244. p. 447

Clark, Mary, Br Mgr, Chicago Public Library, Uptown, 929 W Buena Ave, Chicago, IL, 60613. Tel: 312-744-8400. p. 557

Clark, McKayla, Libr Operations Spec, Missouri Southern State University, 3950 E Newman Rd, Joplin, MO, 64801-1595. Tel: 417-625-9342. p. 1253

Clark, Mellissa, Libr Mgr, Camden County Public Library, 1410 Hwy 40 E, Kingsland, GA, 31548-9380. Tel: 912-729-3741. p. 484

Clark, Mia Y, Circ Mgr, Talbot County Free Library, 100 W Dover St, Easton, MD, 21601-2620. Tel: 410-822-1626. p. 964

Clark, Michael L, Librn, Huron County Law Library, Court House, 1st Flr, Two E Main St, Norwalk, OH, 44857. Tel: 419-351-4244. p. 1810

Clark, Midori, Libr Coord, Aurora Public Library, Mission Viejo Branch, 15324 E Hampden Circle, Aurora, CO, 80015. Tel: 303-326-8600. p. 265

Clark, Midori, Supvr, S Region Libr, Aurora Public Library, Tallyns Reach, 23911 E Arapahoe Rd, Aurora, CO, 80016. Tel: 303-627-3050. p. 265

Clark, Mikalah, Adult Serv, Ref, Page Public Library, 479 S Lake Powell Blvd, Page, AZ, 86040. Tel: 928-645-4270. p. 67

Clark, Monica, Br Mgr, Mountain Regional Library System, Fannin County Public Library, 400 W Main St, Ste 104, Blue Ridge, GA, 30513. Tel: 706-632-5263. p. 504

Clark, Monica M, Dir, Inola Public Library, 15 North Broadway, Inola, OK, 74036. Tel: 918-543-8862. p. 1850

Clark, Myeshia, Tech Serv, Hinds Community College, William H Holtzdaw Library - Utica Campus, 3417 MS-18 West, Utica, MS, 39175-9599. Tel: 601-885-7035. p. 1231

Clark, Nan, Circ, State University of New York, College of Environmental Science & Forestry, One Forestry Dr, Syracuse, NY, 13210. Tel: 315-470-6726. p. 1650

Clark, Nancy, Br Mgr, Anchorage Public Library, Chugiak-Eagle River Branch, Eagle River Town Ctr, 12001 Business Blvd, No 176, Eagle River, AK, 99577. Tel: 907-343-1530. p. 42

Clark, Nathan, Dir, Emmetsburg Public Library, 707 N Superior St, Emmetsburg, IA, 50536. Tel: 712-852-4009. p. 751

Clark, Nicole, Asst Dir, Louis B Goodall Memorial Library, 952 Main St, Sanford, ME, 04073. Tel: 207-324-4714. p. 939

Clark, Pam, Librn, Stone Memorial Library, 1101 Main St, Conneautville, PA, 16406. Tel: 814-587-2142. p. 1924

Clark, Patty, Outreach Librn, Silver Lake Library, 203 Railroad St, Silver Lake, KS, 66539. Tel: 785-582-5141. p. 836

Clark, Patty, Library Contact, Manufacturers Association of Central New York Library, 5788 Widewaters Pkwy, Syracuse, NY, 13214. Tel: 315-474-4201, Ext 10. p. 1649

Clark, Penny, Spec Coll Librn, Lamar University, 4400 Martin Luther King Jr Pkwy, Beaumont, TX, 77705. Tel: 409-880-7787. p. 2146

Clark, Phil, Br Mgr, Pioneer Library System, Newcastle Public, 705 NW Tenth St, Newcastle, OK, 73065. Tel: 405-387-5076. p. 1855

Clark, Phil, Regional Coordr, Pioneer Library System, Moore Public, 225 S Howard, Moore, OK, 73160. Tel: 405.793.5100. p. 1855

Clark, Rebecca, Br Mgr, Aurora Public Library District, Eola Road Branch, 555 S Eola Rd, Aurora, IL, 60504-8992. Tel: 630-264-3400. p. 539

Clark, Rebecca, Assoc Libr Dir, School of Visual Arts Library, 380 Second Ave, 2nd Flr, New York, NY, 10010. Tel: 212-592-2944. p. 1601

Clark, Renee Cherie, Asst Librn, University of Arkansas-Monticello Library, 514 University Dr, Monticello, AR, 71656. Tel: 870-460-1481. p. 105

Clark, Richard, Jr, Borrower Serv Librn, Palmer Public Library, 1455 N Main St, Palmer, MA, 01069. Tel: 413-283-3330. p. 1045

Clark, Sarah, Head, Br Libr, Albany Public Library, 161 Washington Ave, Albany, NY, 12210. Tel: 518-427-4300. p. 1482

Clark, Sarah, Libr Dir, Voorheesville Public Library, 51 School Rd, Voorheesville, NY, 12186. Tel: 518-765-2791. p. 1657

Clark, Sarah, Dr, Dean & Univ Librn, La Salle University, 1900 W Olney Ave, Philadelphia, PA, 19141-1199. Tel: 215-951-1286. p. 1982

Clark, Sheila, Librn, Georgia Department of Corrections, Office of Library Services, 701 Prison Blvd, Sparta, GA, 31087. Tel: 706-444-1000. p. 497

Clark, Sheila, Librn, Pub Serv, Burman University Library, 5410 Ramona Ave, Lacombe, AB, T4L 2B7, CANADA. Tel: 403-782-3381, Ext 4101. p. 2545

Clark, Stacy, Youth Serv Librn, Groton Public Library, 52 Newtown Rd, Groton, CT, 06340. Tel: 860-441-6750. p. 314

Clark, Stacy, Adult Programmer, Outreach Coordr, New London Public Library, 63 Huntington St, New London, CT, 06320. Tel: 860-447-1411, Ext 105. p. 329

Clark, Stephanie, Dean of Libr, University of West Florida, 11000 University Pkwy, Pensacola, FL, 32514-5750. Tel: 850-474-2492. p. 436

Clark, Stephen D, Head, Acq, College of William & Mary in Virginia, Earl Gregg Swem Library, One Landrum Dr, Williamsburg, VA, 23187. Tel: 757-221-3107. p. 2353

Clark, Susan, Cataloger, Ref, University of Kansas School of Medicine-Wichita, 1010 N Kansas, Wichita, KS, 67214-3199. Tel: 316-293-2629. p. 843

Clark, Susan, Br Librn, Caldwell County Public Library, Granite Falls Public, 24 S Main St, Granite Falls, NC, 28630. Tel: 828-396-7703. p. 1700

Clark, Susan, Br Librn, Caldwell County Public Library, Hudson Public, 530 Central St, Hudson, NC, 28638-1230. Tel: 828-728-4207. p. 1700

Clark, Terry, Asst Dir, Ch, Jefferson Public Library, 200 W Lincoln Way, Jefferson, IA, 50129-2185. Tel: 515-386-2835. p. 761

Clark, Tony, Pub Affairs, National Archives & Records Administration, 441 Freedom Pkwy, Atlanta, GA, 30307-1498. Tel: 404-865-7109. p. 465

Clark, Tracy, Ch Serv, Paris Public Library, 326 S Main St, Paris, TX, 75460. Tel: 903-785-8531. p. 2225

Clark, Veronica, Dir, North Adams Public Library, 74 Church St, North Adams, MA, 01247. Tel: 413-662-3133. p. 1040

Clark, Wanda, Dir, Lauderdale County Library, 120 Lafayette St, Ripley, TN, 38063. Tel: 731-635-1872. p. 2125

Clark, Wendy, Cataloger, Spring Arbor University, 106 E Main St, Spring Arbor, MI, 49283. Tel: 517-750-6437. p. 1152

Clark, Wendy, Asst Librn, Vermont Department of Libraries, 60 Washington St, Ste 2, Barre, VT, 05641. Tel: 802-636-0020. p. 2278

Clark, Yvonne, Librn, Mid-Mississippi Regional Library System, Tchula Public, 105 Mercer St, Tchula, MS, 39169-5235. Tel: 662-235-5235. p. 1224

Clark-Bridges, Robyn, Ref & ILL Librn, Mount Mercy University, 1330 Elmhurst Dr NE, Cedar Rapids, IA, 52402-4797. Tel: 319-368-6465. p. 738

Clark-Dawe, Cathryn, Libr Dir, Webster Free Public Library, 947 Battle St, Webster, NH, 03303. Tel: 603-648-2706. p. 1383

Clark-Gorey, Kenda, Legislative Librn, Legislative Library of New Brunswick, Legislative Assembly Bldg, Centre Block, 706 Queen St, Fredericton, NB, E3B 5H1, CANADA. Tel: 506-453-2338. p. 2601

Clark-Hughes, Angela, Librn, University of Miami, 4600 Rickenbacker Causeway, SLAB 160 Library, Miami, FL, 33149-1098. Tel: 305-421-4021, 305-421-4060. p. 425

Clarke, Amber, Access & Collection Services Specialist, St John's University Library, Rittenberg Law Library, 8000 Utopia Pkwy, Jamaica, NY, 11439. Tel: 718-990-6825. p. 1556

Clarke, Angela, Head, Outreach Serv, Warren-Newport Public Library District, 224 N O'Plaine Rd, Gurnee, IL, 60031. Tel: 847-244-5150, Ext 3025. p. 596

Clarke Arado, Therese, Actg Dir, Dep Dir, Research Librn, Northern Illinois University Libraries, David C Shapiro Memorial Law Library, Swen Parson Hall, 2nd Flr, Normal Rd, DeKalb, IL, 60115-2890. Tel: 815-753-9497. p. 578

Clarke, Carol, Archivist, Bryant Library, Two Paper Mill Rd, Roslyn, NY, 11576. Tel: 516-621-2240. p. 1633

Clarke, Christie, Youth Serv Librn, Gering Public Library, 1055 P St, Gering, NE, 69341. Tel: 308-436-7433. p. 1315

Clarke, Elizabeth, Assoc Librn, Res Serv, Marist College, 3399 North Rd, Poughkeepsie, NY, 12601-1387. Tel: 845-575-3199. p. 1623

Clarke, Erin, Br Mgr, Rochester Public Library, Highland, 971 South Ave, Rochester, NY, 14620. Tel: 585-428-8206. p. 1630

Clarke, Florette, Library Contact, Carter, Ledyard & Milburn Library, 28 Liberty St, 41st Flr, New York, NY, 10005. Tel: 212-238-8691. p. 1580

Clarke, Griselda, Br Mgr, Orange County Library System, Fairview Shore Branch, 902 Lee Rd, Ste 26, Orlando, FL, 32810. p. 431

Clarke, Jennie, Librn, Durham Region Law Association, 150 Bond St E, Oshawa, ON, L1G 0A2, CANADA. Tel: 905-579-9554. p. 2663

Clarke, Kim, Dir, University of Calgary Library, Bennett Jones Law Library, Murray Fraser Hall 2340, 2500 University Dr NW, Calgary, AB, T2N 1N4, CANADA. Tel: 403-220-6702. p. 2529

Clarke, Leslie, Asst Libr Dir, Ch Serv, Ocean City Free Public Library, 1735 Simpson Ave, Ste 4, Ocean City, NJ, 08226. Tel: 609-399-2434, Ext 5241. p. 1430

Clarke, Linda, Libr Dir, Chatham County Public Libraries, 197 NC Hwy 87 N, Pittsboro, NC, 27312. Tel: 919-545-8081. p. 1707

Clarke, Maggie, Ref Coordr, California State University Dominguez Hills, 1000 E Victoria St, Carson, CA, 90747. Tel: 310-243-2084. p. 129

Clarke, Margie, Acq Librn, Camosun College, Liz Ashton Campus Centre Library, 4461 Inteurban Rd, 3rd Flr, Victoria, BC, V9E 2C1, CANADA. Tel: 250-370-4533. p. 2582

Clarke, Marilyn, Librn, Bay Roberts Public Library, PO Box 610, Bay Roberts, NL, A0A 1G0, CANADA. Tel: 709-786-9629. p. 2607

Clarke, Megan, Dir, Libr Serv, Bay Mills Community College, 12214 W Lakeshore Dr, Brimley, MI, 49715-9320. Tel: 906-248-3354, Ext 8435. p. 1087

Clarke, Nels, Br Librn, Stockton-San Joaquin County Public Library, Lathrop Branch, 450 Spartan Way, Lathrop, CA, 95330. p. 250

Clarke, Samantha, Mgr, Knowledge Mgt, Center for Creative Leadership Library, One Leadership Pl, Greensboro, NC, 27410. Tel: 336-286-4083. p. 1691

Clarke, Sharon, Youth Librn, Seekonk Public Library, 410 Newman Ave, Seekonk, MA, 02771. Tel: 508-336-8230, Ext 56142. p. 1052

Clarke, Tahirah, Head, Circ, Summit Free Public Library, 75 Maple St, Summit, NJ, 07901-9984. Tel: 908-273-0350. p. 1445

Clarke, Tricia, Commun Engagement Librn, University of the District of Columbia, Learning Resources Division, 4200 Connecticut Ave NW, Bldg 39, Level B, Washington, DC, 20008. p. 380

Clarke, Virginia, Head, Circ, Acton Public Library, 60 Old Boston Post Rd, Old Saybrook, CT, 06475-2200. Tel: 860-501-5066. p. 333

Clarkin, Deirdre, Libr Dir, National Oceanic & Atmospheric Administration, 1315 East West Hwy, SSMC 3, 2nd Flr, Silver Spring, MD, 20910. Tel: 301-713-2607, Ext 157. p. 977

Clarkson, Bev, Dir, Pittsburg Public Library, 308 N Walnut, Pittsburg, KS, 66762-4732. Tel: 620-231-8110. p. 831

Clarkson, Wendy, Automation Mgr, Somerset County Library System of New Jersey, One Vogt Dr, Bridgewater, NJ, 08807-2136. Tel: 908-458-4942. p. 1392

Clary, Anita, Spec Coll Librn, Kent State University Libraries, Risman Plaza, 1125 Risman Dr, Kent, OH, 44242. Tel: 330-672-2751. p. 1792

Clary, Nanette, Fiscal Officer, Chillicothe & Ross County Public Library, 140 S Paint St, Chillicothe, OH, 45601. Tel: 740-702-4145. p. 1758

Claspell, Barbara, Dir, Nicholas P Sims Library, 515 W Main, Waxahachie, TX, 75165-3235. Tel: 972-937-2671. p. 2255

Claspy, William, Spec Coll & Univ Archives, Team Leader, Case Western Reserve University, 11055 Euclid Ave, Cleveland, OH, 44106. Tel: 216-368-3595. p. 1766

Class, Julianne, Archivist, Free Methodist Church - USA, 5235 Decatur Blvd, Indianapolis, IN, 46241. Tel: 317-244-3660. p. 692

Claus, Cindy, Law Libr Operations Mgr, University of Nevada, Las Vegas Univ Libraries, Wiener-Rogers Law Library, William S Boyd School of Law, 4505 S Maryland Pkwy, Las Vegas, NV, 89154. Tel: 702-895-2400. p. 1348

Claus, Susan, Mgr, Children's & YA, Northland Public Library, 300 Cumberland Rd, Pittsburgh, PA, 15237-5455. Tel: 412-366-8100, Ext 120. p. 1994

Clausen, Beth, Dean, Libr Serv, Metropolitan State University, 645 E Seventh St, Saint Paul, MN, 55106. Tel: 651-793-1618. p. 1200

Clausen, Keely, Dir, Oglala Lakota College, LaCreek College Center, PO Box 629, Martin, SD, 57551. Tel: 605-685-6407. p. 2077

Clausen, Leesa, Ch, Pocahontas Public Library, 14 Second Ave NW, Pocahontas, IA, 50574. Tel: 712-335-4471. p. 777

Clavell, Caroline, Librn, Kimbell Art Museum Library, 3333 Camp Bowie Blvd, Fort Worth, TX, 76107. Tel: 817-332-8451. p. 2180

Clawser, Shanna, Dir, Karl Miles Lecompte Memorial Library, 110 S Franklin, Corydon, IA, 50060-1518. Tel: 641-872-1621. p. 742

Clawson, Madilyn, Library Access & Outreach Servs Mgr, Defiance College, 201 College Pl, Defiance, OH, 43512-1667. Tel: 419-783-2414. p. 1781

Clawson, Nicole, Mgr, Youth Serv, Saint Louis County Library, 1640 S Lindbergh Blvd, Saint Louis, MO, 63131-3598. Tel: 314-994-3300, Ext 2230. p. 1273

Clawson, Stacey, Mgr, DeWitt Public Library, Cleon Collier Memorial Library, 211 Main St, Gillett, AR, 72055. Tel: 870-548-2821. p. 94

Claxton, Janice, Asst Librn, Trinity Baptist College Library, 800 Hammond Blvd, Jacksonville, FL, 32221. Tel: 904-596-2451. p. 413

Claxton, Jean, Br Mgr, Audubon Regional Library, St Helena Branch, 6108 Hwy 10, Greensburg, LA, 70441. Tel: 225-435-7135. p. 887

Claxton, Zenobia, Admin Coordr, Atlanta-Fulton Public Library System, One Margaret Mitchell Sq, Atlanta, GA, 30303-1089. Tel: 404-612-3189. p. 460

Clay, Elonda, Dir, Methodist Theological School, 3081 Columbus Pike, Delaware, OH, 43015. Tel: 740-363-1146. p. 1782

Clay, JoAnn, Br Co-Mgr, Iberia Parish Library, Lydia Branch, 4800 Freyou Rd, New Iberia, LA, 70560. Tel: 337-364-7808. p. 900

Clay, Karen, Dir, Eastern Oregon University, One University Blvd, La Grande, OR, 97850. Tel: 541-962-3792. p. 1884

Clay, Khelani, Access Serv Librn, American University, 4300 Nebraska Ave NW, Washington, DC, 20016-8182. Tel: 202-274-4441. p. 360

Clay, Nan, Libr Dir, Commerce Public Library, 1210 Park St, Commerce, TX, 75428. Tel: 903-886-6858. p. 2158

Clay Powers, Amanda, Dean, Libr Serv, Mississippi University For Women, 1200 Fifth Ave S, Columbus, MS, 39701. p. 1215

Clay, Richard, Chief Exec Officer, Pres, Filson Historical Society Library, 1310 S Third St, Louisville, KY, 40208. Tel: 502-635-5083. p. 865

Clay, Sarah, Librn, Holmes Community College, Goodman Campus, One Hill St, Goodman, MS, 39079. Tel: 662-472-9021. p. 1216

Clay, Sarah, Operations Mgr, Roberts Wesleyan College & Northeastern Seminary, 2301 Westside Dr, Rochester, NY, 14624-1997. Tel: 585-594-6816. p. 1629

Clay, Twila, Libr Mgr, Bear Point Community Library, PO Box 43, Bear Canyon, AB, T0H 0B0, CANADA. Tel: 780-595-3771. p. 2523

Clay, Wendy, Mgr, Tri-County Regional Library, Lockesburg Public Library, 112 E Main St, Lockesburg, AR, 71846. Tel: 870-289-2233. p. 106

Claybrooks, Lisa, Br Mgr, Louisville Free Public Library, Bon Air Regional, 2816 Del Rio Pl, Louisville, KY, 40220. Tel: 502-574-1795. p. 865

Claycomb, Brittany, Libr Asst, State Correctional Institution, 1120 Pike St, Huntingdon, PA, 16652. Tel: 814-643-6520. p. 1945

Clifford, Rosalind, Ref Librn, San Jacinto College South, 13735 Beamer Rd, S10, Houston, TX, 77089-6099. Tel: 281-998-6150, Ext 3306. p. 2198
Clifford, Samantha, Libr Dir, Tulsa Community College Libraries, West Campus Library, 7505 W 41st St, Tulsa, OK, 74107-8633. Tel: 918-595-8010. p. 1867
Clifford, Tom, Libr Supvr, University of Rochester, Art-Music, Rush Rhees Library, Rochester, NY, 14627. Tel: 585-275-4476. p. 1631
Clift, Carla, Dir, Libr Serv, Drake State Community & Technical College, 3421 Meridan St N, Huntsville, AL, 35811-1544. Tel: 256-551-3120, 256-551-5218. p. 21
Clifton, Cyndi, Dir, Owen County Public Library, 1370 Hwy 22 E, Owenton, KY, 40359. Tel: 502-484-3450. p. 871
Clifton, Debbie, Dir, Richards Memorial Library, 118 N Washington St, North Attleboro, MA, 02760. Tel: 508-699-0122. p. 1041
Clifton, Deborah J, PhD, Dr, Coll Curator, Lafayette Science Museum, 433 Jefferson St, Lafayette, LA, 70501-7013. Tel: 337-291-5415. p. 893
Clifton, Debra, Assoc Dir, Seekonk Public Library, 410 Newman Ave, Seekonk, MA, 02771. Tel: 508-336-8230, Ext 56101. p. 1052
Clifton, Felecia, Br Mgr, University of North Dakota, Gordon Erickson Music Library, Hughes Fine Arts Ctr 170, 3350 Campus Rd, Stop 7125, Grand Forks, ND, 58202-7125. Tel: 701-777-2817. p. 1735
Clifton, Garry, Br Mgr, Blue Ridge Regional Library, Patrick County, 116 W Blue Ridge St, Stuart, VA, 24171. Tel: 276-694-3352. p. 2332
Clifton, Jennifer, Supvr, Libr Develop, Indiana State Library, 315 W Ohio St, Indianapolis, IN, 46202. Tel: 317-232-3675. p. 692
Clifton, Shari, Bibliographer, University of Oklahoma Health Sciences Center, 1105 N Stonewall Ave, Oklahoma City, OK, 73117-1220. Tel: 405-271-2285, Ext 48752. p. 1859
Cline, Becky, Youth Serv Supvr, Belleville Public Library, 121 E Washington St, Belleville, IL, 62220. Tel: 618-234-0441. p. 541
Cline, Carrie, Dir, Neosho/Newton County Library, 201 W Spring St, Neosho, MO, 64850. Tel: 417-451-4231. p. 1264
Cline, Claire, Chief Librn/CEO, Central Manitoulin Public Libraries, 6020 Hwy 542, Mindemoya, ON, P0P 1S0, CANADA. Tel: 705-377-5334. p. 2658
Cline, Consuela, Coordr, Libr Instruction, Coordr, Ref (Info Serv), Mercer University, Jack Tarver Library, 1300 Edgewood Ave, Macon, GA, 31207. Tel: 478 301-5334. p. 486
Cline, Darlene, Br Librn, Chouteau County Library, Big Sandy Branch, 60 Johannes Ave, Big Sandy, MT, 59520. Tel: 406-378-2161. p. 1293
Cline, Ellen, Ref Librn, Curtis Laws Wilson Library, 400 W 14th St, Rolla, MO, 65409-0060. Tel: 573-341-7839. p. 1268
Cline, Ellen, Eng Librn, Phys Sci Librn, Elon University, 308 N O'Kelly Ave, Elon, NC, 27244-0187. Tel: 336-278-6600. p. 1688
Cline, Jonathan, Br Mgr, Dayton Metro Library, Electra C Doren Branch, 701 Troy St, Dayton, OH, 45404. Tel: 937-496-8928. p. 1779
Cline, Kent, Head, Coll & Access Serv, Linfield University, Portland Campus, 2900 NE 132nd Ave, Bldg 6, Portland, OR, 97230. Tel: 971-369-4173. p. 1886
Cline, Lee Ann, Archives, Cat & Tech Serv Librn, Dalton State College, 650 College Dr, Dalton, GA, 30720-3778. Tel: 706-272-4585. p. 474
Cline, Marlene, Commun Librn, Cariboo Regional District Library, Nazko Branch, 1351 Palmer Rd, Nazko, BC, V2J 3H9, CANADA. Tel: 250-249-5289. p. 2584
Cline, Suzanne, Dir, Shelby County Libraries, 230 E North St, Sidney, OH, 45365-2785. Tel: 937-492-8354, Ext 102. p. 1820
Cline, Virginia, YA Serv, Atlanta-Fulton Public Library System, Ocee Branch, 5090 Abbotts Bridge Rd, Johns Creek, GA, 30005-4601. Tel: 404 613-6840, 770-360-8897. p. 461
Cline, Wendi, Libr Asst, Tohono O'odham Community College Library, Hwy 86 Milepost 111 W, Sells, AZ, 85634. Tel: 520-383-0032. p. 78
Clinefelter, Julie, Dir, Austin Public Library, 323 Fourth Ave NE, Austin, MN, 55912-3370. Tel: 507-433-2391. p. 1164
Clinger, Melinda, Dir, Fulton County Historical Society, Inc, 37 E 375 N, Rochester, IN, 46975. Tel: 574-223-4436. p. 716
Clingman, Diane, Human Res Officer, Missouri River Regional Library, 214 Adams St, Jefferson City, MO, 65101. Tel: 573-634-2464. p. 1252
Clink, Kellian, Librn, Minnesota State University, Mankato, 601 Maywood Ave, Mankato, MN, 56001. Tel: 507-389-5952. p. 1181
Clinkscales, Angela, Admin Operations Specialist, Piedmont Technical College Library, Library Resource Center - Abbeville County Campus, 143 Hwy 72 W, Rm 07AA, Abbeville, SC, 29620. Tel: 864-446-8324. p. 2063
Clinkscales, Joyce, Media Spec, Music, Emory University Libraries, Robert W Woodruff Library, 540 Asbury Circle, Atlanta, GA, 30322-2870. Tel: 404-727-1066. p. 463
Clinton, Beth, Regional Librn, Charlottetown Library Learning Centre, 97 Queen St, Charlottetown, PE, C1A 4A9, CANADA. Tel: 902-368-4654. p. 2707
Clinton, Beth, Regional Librn, Prince Edward Island Public Library Service, Charlottetown Library Learning Centre, 100-97 Queen St, Charlottetown, PE, C1A 4A9, CANADA. Tel: 902-368-4642. p. 2708
Clinton, Esther, Supvr, Deschutes Public Library District, Bend Branch, 601 NW Wall St, Bend, OR, 97703. Tel: 541-312-1052. p. 1874
Clinton, Luke, Libr Mgr, Mount Sinai West, 1000 Tenth Ave, 2nd Flr, New York, NY, 10019. Tel: 212-523-6100. p. 1592
Clinton, Morgan, Circ Librn, Wyalusing Public Library, 115 Church St, Wyalusing, PA, 18853. Tel: 570-746-1711. p. 2024
Clive, Myndi, Ref Librn, Washoe County Law Library, 75 Courth St, Rm 101, Reno, NV, 89501. Tel: 775-328-3250. p. 1350
Clogston, Mary, Br Head, Volusia County Public Library, Orange City Public Library, 148 Albertus Way, Orange City, FL, 32763. Tel: 386-775-5270. p. 393
Clohosey, Kaitlyn, Asst Dir, Libr Serv, Felician University, 262 S Main St, Lodi, NJ, 07644. Tel: 201-559-6071. p. 1413
Cloo, Derek, Libr Serv Coordr, Clackamas Community College Library, 19600 Molalla Ave, Oregon City, OR, 97045. Tel: 503-594-3491. p. 1889
Cloonan, Ann, Dir, Bedford Free Library, 32 Village Green, Bedford, NY, 10506. Tel: 914-234-3570. p. 1491
Close, Heather, Dir, Libr Serv, Alberta Legislature Library, 216 Legislature Bldg, 10800-97 Ave NW, Edmonton, AB, T5K 2B6, CANADA. Tel: 780-427-0204. p. 2535
Clossey, Brian, Pub Serv Librn, Wake Technical Community College, Perry Health Sciences Library, Bldg C, Rm 123, 2901 Holston Lane, Raleigh, NC, 27610-2092. Tel: 919-747-0002. p. 1711
Closson, Jaymie, Dir, Kellogg Free Library, 5681 Telephone Rd Extension, Cincinnatus, NY, 13040. Tel: 607-863-4300. p. 1518
Clough, Audrey, Asst Librn, Patten-North Haverhill Library, 2885 Dartmouth College Hwy, North Haverhill, NH, 03774-4533. Tel: 603-787-2542. p. 1377
Clough, Debra, Librn, Grafton Public Library, 47 Library Rd, Grafton, NH, 03240. Tel: 603-523-7865. p. 1365
Clough, Karalea, Libr Tech, Nevada Historical Society, 1650 N Virginia St, Reno, NV, 89503. Tel: 775-688-1190, Ext 227. p. 1349
Clough, Letitia, Dir, Lovington Public Library District, 110 W State St, Lovington, IL, 61937. Tel: 217-873-4468. p. 611
Clough, Lynne, Tech Serv Librn, Wolfeboro Public Library, 259 S Main St, Wolfeboro, NH, 03894. Tel: 603-569-2428. p. 1384
Clough, Spencer, Dir, Law Libr, University of Massachusetts School of Law Library, 333 Faunce Corner Rd, North Dartmouth, MA, 02747. Tel: 508-985-1121. p. 1041
Clougherty, Leo, Head Librn, University of Iowa Libraries, Sciences, 120 Iowa Ave, Iowa City, IA, 52242-1325. Tel: 319-335-3083. p. 761
Clouse, Beverly, Br Mgr, Mohave County Library District, Kingman Library, 3269 N Burbank St, Kingman, AZ, 86401. Tel: 928-692-2665. p. 65
Clouse, Linda, Coordr, Patron Serv, ILL, Almont District Library, 213 W St Clair St, Almont, MI, 48003-8476. Tel: 810-798-3100. p. 1077
Cloutier, Bryan, Dir, Oxford Public Library, 530 Pontiac St, Oxford, MI, 48371-4844. Tel: 248-628-3034. p. 1140
Cloutier, Claudette, Assoc Univ Librn, Res & Learning, University of Calgary Library, 2500 University Dr NW, Calgary, AB, T2N 1N4, CANADA. Tel: 403-220-3447. p. 2529
Cloutier, Guillaume, Librn, College de Maisonneuve Centre des Medias, 3800 Est rue Sherbrooke E, 4th Flr, Rm D-4690, Montreal, QC, H1X 2A2, CANADA. Tel: 514-254-7131, Ext 4279. p. 2723
Cloutier, Marie Eve, Head, Children's Servx, Bibliotheque Municipale Eva-Senecal, 450 Marquette St, Sherbrooke, QC, J1H 1M4, CANADA. Tel: 819-821-5596. p. 2736
Cloutier, Marleen, Cataloging & Metadata Librn, University of Scranton, 800 Linden St, Scranton, PA, 18510-4634. Tel: 570-941-7482. p. 2005
Cloutier, Nicole Luongo, Ref Serv Supvr, Portsmouth Public Library, 175 Parrott Ave, Portsmouth, NH, 03801-4452. Tel: 603-427-1540. p. 1379
Clover-Owens, Ryan, Dir, Durland Alternatives Library, 130 Anabel Taylor Hall, Ithaca, NY, 14853-1001. Tel: 607-255-6486. p. 1552
Clowers, Kat, Interim Dir, Craven-Pamlico-Carteret Regional Library System, 400 Johnson St, New Bern, NC, 28560. Tel: 252-638-7800. p. 1706
Clowers, Katherine, County Librn, Pamlico County Public Library, 603 Main St, Bayboro, NC, 28515. Tel: 252-745-3515. p. 1673
Clowes, Mia, Head, Circ Serv, Valley Cottage Free Library, 110 Rte 303, Valley Cottage, NY, 10989. Tel: 845-268-7700, Ext 113. p. 1656
Cloyd, Joseph, ILL Librn, Pocono Mountain Public Library, Coolbaugh Township Municipal Ctr, 5500 Municipal Dr, Tobyhanna, PA, 18466. Tel: 570-894-8860. p. 2013
Clucas, Carolina, Head, Children's Dept, Wayne County Public Library, 1001 E Ash St, Goldsboro, NC, 27530. Tel: 919-735-1824, Ext 5104. p. 1691
Clunie, Simone, Cat & Syst Librn, Lincoln University, 1570 Baltimore Pike, Lincoln University, PA, 19352. Tel: 484-365-7357. p. 1956
Clute, Mary, Children & Youth Serv Librn, Alpena County Library, 211 N First St, Alpena, MI, 49707. Tel: 989-356-6188, Ext 13. p. 1078
Clutter, Pam, Dir, Marianna Community Public Library, 247 Jefferson Ave, Ste 1, Marianna, PA, 15345. Tel: 724-267-3888. p. 1958
Clymer, Annie, Outreach Coordr, Scotland County Memorial Library, 312 W Church St, Laurinburg, NC, 28352-3720. Tel: 910-276-0563. p. 1700
Clyne, Christine, Genealogy & Hist Librn, Cook Memorial Library, 93 Main St, Tamworth, NH, 03886. Tel: 603-323-8510. p. 1382
Clyne, Dawn, IT Spec, Minnesota State University, Mankato, 601 Maywood Ave, Mankato, MN, 56001. Tel: 507-389-5952. p. 1181

Cmor, Dianne, Assoc Univ Librn, Learning & Teaching, Concordia University Libraries, 1400 de Maisonneuve Blvd W, LB 2, Montreal, QC, H3G 1M8, CANADA. Tel: 514-848-2424, Ext 7693. p. 2723
Co, Hannah, Digital Serv Librn, Northwest University, 5520 108th Ave NE, Kirkland, WA, 98083. Tel: 425-889-5207. p. 2368
Co-Dyre, Adrienne, Dir of Libr, King's University College at the University of Western Ontario, 266 Epworth Ave, London, ON, N6A 2M3, CANADA. Tel: 519-433-3491, Ext 4390. p. 2653
Co-Dyre, Adrienne, Dir of Libr, Saint Peter's Seminary, 1040 Waterloo St N, London, ON, N6A 3Y1, CANADA. Tel: 519-433-3491, Ext 4390. p. 2655
Coady, Marie, Asst Dir, Tech Coordr, Holmes Public Library, 470 Plymouth St, Halifax, MA, 02338. Tel: 781-293-2271. p. 1023
Coakley, Lauren, Educ Tech Spec, Mount Aloysius College Library, 7373 Admiral Peary Hwy, Cresson, PA, 16630-1999. Tel: 814-886-6541. p. 1925
Coakley, Stephanie J, Exec Dir, Pequot Library, 720 Pequot Ave, Southport, CT, 06890-1496. Tel: 203-259-0346. p. 338
Coakley-Welch, Kevin, Law Librn, Law Library of the Massachusetts Attorney General, One Ashburton Pl, Boston, MA, 02108. Tel: 617-963-2060, 617-963-2098. p. 996
Coale, Kim, Tech Serv, Coastal Alabama Community College, Leigh Library, 220 Alco Dr, Brewton, AL, 36426. Tel: 251-809-1582. p. 6
Coalson, Jenafer, Youth Serv Librn, Pulaski County Public Library System, 60 W Third St, Pulaski, VA, 24301. Tel: 540-980-7770. p. 2339
Coalson, Marianne, Libr Mgr, Cedar Mill Community Library, Bethany Branch, 15325 NW Central Dr, Ste J-8, Portland, OR, 97229-0986. Tel: 503-617-7323, Ext 204. p. 1891
Coan, Dianne, Dir, Tech Serv, Fairfax County Public Library, 12000 Government Center Pkwy, Ste 324, Fairfax, VA, 22035-0012. Tel: 703-324-3100. p. 2316
Coates, Carolyn, Acq Librn, Eastern Connecticut State University, 83 Windham St, Willimantic, CT, 06226-2295. Tel: 860-465-5557. p. 347
Coates, Dawn, Libr Dir, Mount Pleasant Public Library, 24 E Main St, Mount Pleasant, UT, 84647-1429. Tel: 435-462-3240. p. 2267
Coates, Elizabeth, Br Operations Mgr, Kingston Frontenac Public Library, 130 Johnson St, Kingston, ON, K7L 1X8, CANADA. Tel: 613-549-8888. p. 2650
Coates, Evan, Pub Serv, Torrance Public Library, 3301 Torrance Blvd, Torrance, CA, 90503. Tel: 310-618-5950. p. 253
Coates, Evan, Pub Serv, Torrance Public Library, Isabel Henderson Branch, 4805 Emerald St, Torrance, CA, 90503-2899. Tel: 310-371-2075. p. 253
Coates, Janet, Head, Circ/ILL, Woodbury Public Library, 33 Delaware St, Woodbury, NJ, 08096. Tel: 856-845-2611. p. 1456
Coates, Joseph, Ref Mgr, University Archives, Purdue University, 2200 169th St, Hammond, IN, 46323. Tel: 219-989-2063. p. 689
Coates, Marcille, Libr Assoc, Lima Public Library, Lafayette Branch, 225 E Sugar St, Lafayette, OH, 45854. Tel: 419-649-6482. p. 1796
Coats, Meagan, Dir, Learning Res Ctr, Southeast Arkansas College, 1900 Hazel St, Pine Bluff, AR, 71603. Tel: 870-850-3124. p. 107
Cobb, Betty, Youth Serv Mgr, Johnson City Public Library, 100 W Millard St, Johnson City, TN, 37604. Tel: 423-434-4350. p. 2104
Cobb, Christopher, Libr Dir, Monterey County Law Library, 142 W Alisal St, Ste E-107, Salinas, CA, 93901. Tel: 831-755-5046. p. 211
Cobb, Christopher, Libr Dir, Monterey County Law Library, Monterey Branch, Monterey County Courthouse, 1200 Aguajito Rd, Rm 202, Monterey, CA, 93940. Tel: 831-264-4207. p. 211
Cobb, Cynthia, Dir, Riviera Beach Public Library, 600 W Blue Heron Blvd, Riviera Beach, FL, 33404-4398. Tel: 561-845-4195. p. 439
Cobb, Deborah, ILL, University of South Alabama Libraries, Marx Library, 5901 USA Drive N, Mobile, AL, 36688. Tel: 251-460-7021. p. 27
Cobb, Dennis, Librn, Arizona State Schools for the Deaf & the Blind Library, 1200 W Speedway, Tucson, AZ, 85745. Tel: 602-698-6222. p. 81
Cobb, Elizabeth, Ref Serv, Jefferson County Library, Windsor, 7479 Metropolitian Blvd, Barnhart, MO, 63012. Tel: 636-461-1914. p. 1249
Cobb, Emma, Head, Ref Serv, Verona Public Library, 500 Silent St, Verona, WI, 53593. Tel: 608-845-7180. p. 2482
Cobb, Hannah, Br Mgr, Washington County Free Library, Williamsport Memorial, 104 E Potomac St, Williamsport, MD, 21795. Tel: 301-223-7027. p. 968
Cobb, Heather M, Dir, Lamont Memorial Free Library, Five Main St, McGraw, NY, 13101. Tel: 607-836-6767. p. 1570
Cobb, Kim, Public Access Coord, Langston University, 701 Sammy Davis Jr Dr, Langston, OK, 73050. Tel: 405-466-3603. p. 1851
Cobb, Sidney, Dir, Humphreys County Library System, 105 S Hayden St, Belzoni, MS, 39038. Tel: 662-247-3606. p. 1212
Cobb, Susan, Br Mgr, Raleigh Public Library, 150 Main St, Raleigh, MS, 39153. Tel: 601-782-4277. p. 1231
Cobb, Warren, Res & Instruction Librn, University of South Carolina at Beaufort Library, Eight E Campus Dr, Bluffton, SC, 29909. Tel: 843-521-3122. p. 2048
Cobbs, Carol, Dir, Fiscal Officer, Columbiana Public Library, 332 N Middle St, Columbiana, OH, 44408. Tel: 330-482-5509. p. 1771
Coberly, William, Dir, Libr Serv, Shepherds Theological Seminary Library, 6051 Tryon Rd, Cary, NC, 27518. Tel: 919-390-1104. p. 1677
Cobham, Jude, LTA Supvr, Circ, Florida International University, 3000 NE 151st St, North Miami, FL, 33181-3600. Tel: 305-919-5797. p. 428
Coble, Carol, Librn, Texhoma Public Library, Main St, Texhoma, OK, 73949. Tel: 580-423-7150. p. 1864
Coble, Lora, Dir, Mgt Serv, Dartmouth College Library, 6025 Baker Berry Library, Rm 115, Hanover, NH, 03755-3527. Tel: 603-646-2236. p. 1366
Coburn, Jan, Sr Libr Tech, University of Kentucky Libraries, Science & Engineering Library, 211 King Bldg, 179 Funkhouser Dr, Lexington, KY, 40506-0039. Tel: 859-257-2965. p. 864
Cocariu, Dacia, Ref Librn, Brooklyn Law School Library, 250 Joralemon St, Brooklyn, NY, 11201. Tel: 718-780-7973. p. 1501
Coccia, Elizabeth, Dir, Keene Valley Library Association, 1796 Rte 73, Keene Valley, NY, 12943. Tel: 518-576-4335. p. 1559
Cocciolo, Anthony, Dean, Pratt Institute, 144 W 14th St, 6th Flr, New York, NY, 10011-7301. Tel: 212-647-7702. p. 2788
Cochran, Amy, Youth Serv, Grand Rapids Public Library, 111 Library St NE, Grand Rapids, MI, 49503-3268. Tel: 616-988-5400. p. 1111
Cochran, Beth, Sr Libr Assoc, Emmanuel University, 2261 W Main St, Franklin Springs, GA, 30639. Tel: 706-245-7226, Ext 2848. p. 480
Cochran, Christopher, Auromated Serv Adminr, Alachua County Library District, 401 E University Ave, Gainesville, FL, 32601-5453. Tel: 352-334-3995. p. 406
Cochran, Dana, Head, Info Res, Thomas Jefferson National Accelerator Facility, 12050 Jefferson Ave, ARC 126, Newport News, VA, 23606. Tel: 757-269-7244. p. 2333
Cochran, Gabrielle, Br Mgr, Kanawha County Public Library, Glasgow Branch, 129 Fourth Ave, Glasgow, WV, 25086. Tel: 304-949-2400. p. 2400
Cochran, Jennifer, Br Supvr, Barry-Lawrence Regional Library, Eagle Rock Branch, 27824 State Hwy 86, Eagle Rock, MO, 65641. Tel: 417-271-3186. p. 1263
Cochran, Jennifer, Br Supvr, Barry-Lawrence Regional Library, Shell Knob Branch, 24931 State Hwy 39, Shell Knob, MO, 65747. Tel: 417-858-3618. p. 1263
Cochran, Keith, Assoc Dir, Indiana University Bloomington, William & Gayle Cook Music Library, Simon Music Library & Recital Ctr M160, 200 S Jordan Ave, Bloomington, IN, 47405. Tel: 812-855-2974. p. 671
Cochran, Kelly, Youth Serv Mgr, Delaware County District Library, 84 E Winter St, Delaware, OH, 43015. Tel: 740-362-3861. p. 1781
Cochran, Lori, Ch, Barberton Public Library, 602 W Park Ave, Barberton, OH, 44203-2458. Tel: 330-745-1194. p. 1748
Cochran, Lori A, Dir, Powers Library, 29 Church St, Moravia, NY, 13118. Tel: 315-497-1955. p. 1574
Cochrane, Alison, Head, Teen Serv, Nevins Memorial Library, 305 Broadway, Methuen, MA, 01844-6898. Tel: 978-686-4080. p. 1035
Cochrane, Joe, Br Mgr, Sonoma County Library, Petaluma Regional Library, 100 Fairgrounds Dr, Petaluma, CA, 94952. Tel: 707-763-9801. p. 204
Cochrane, Ken, Dir, United Theological Seminary, 4501 Denlinger Rd, Dayton, OH, 45426. Tel: 937-529-2290, Ext 4239. p. 1780
Cochrane, Susan, Knowledge & Resource Mgmt Specialist, Nova Scotia Government, 1690 Hollis St, Halifax, NS, B3J 3J9, CANADA. Tel: 902-717-3603. p. 2620
Cockburn, Brian, Librn, James Madison University Libraries, Music Library, MSC 7301, Harrisonburg, VA, 22807. Tel: 540-568-6978. p. 2324
Cocker, Martha, Mgr, O'Melveny & Myers LLP, 1625 Eye St NW, Washington, DC, 20006. Tel: 202-383-5300. p. 373
Cockerham, Robyn, Dep Libr Dir, Louisiana House of Representatives, 900 N Third St, Baton Rouge, LA, 70804. Tel: 225-342-2434. p. 883
Cockfield, Holly, Dir, Harvin Clarendon County Library, 215 N Brooks St, Manning, SC, 29102. Tel: 803-435-8633. p. 2065
Cocking, Shellie, Chief, Coll & Tech Serv, San Francisco Public Library, 100 Larkin St, San Francisco, CA, 94102. Tel: 415-557-4369. p. 227
Cockrell, Michael, Head, Adult Serv, Kalamazoo Public Library, 315 S Rose St, Kalamazoo, MI, 49007-5264. Tel: 269-553-7841. p. 1121
Coco, Anne, Assoc Dir, Academy of Motion Picture Arts & Sciences, 333 S La Cienega Blvd, Beverly Hills, CA, 90211. Tel: 310-247-3000, Ext 2274. p. 124
Cocozzoli, Gary R, Libr Dir, Lawrence Technological University Library, 21000 W Ten Mile Rd, Southfield, MI, 48075-1058. Tel: 248-204-3000. p. 1151
Coddington, Gwen, Col Archivist, Spec Coll Librn, McDaniel College, 2 College Hill, Westminster, MD, 21157-4390. Tel: 410-857-2793. p. 981
Codner, Dixie, Supvr, Central Community College, 3134 W Hwy 34, Grand Island, NE, 68802. Tel: 308-398-7395, 308-398-7396. p. 1316
Codner, Jocelyn, Ref/Outreach Librn, Chatham College, Woodland Rd, Pittsburgh, PA, 15232. Tel: 412-365-1619. p. 1992
Cody, Sarah, Tech Serv Mgr, Bedford Public Library, 1323 K St, Bedford, IN, 47421. Tel: 812-275-4471. p. 669
Cody, Sheila, Head, Youth Serv, Winnetka-Northfield Public Library District, 768 Oak St, Winnetka, IL, 60093-2515. Tel: 847-446-7220. p. 664
Coe, Cheri, Col Librn, Montserrat College of Art, 23 Essex St, Beverly, MA, 01915. p. 989

Coe, Erica, Dean of Libr, Olympic College, 1600 Chester Ave, Bremerton, WA, 98337. Tel: 360-475-7250. p. 2360

Coe, Jonathan, Coordr, Pub Serv, Niagara University Library, Four Varsity Dr, Niagara University, NY, 14109. Tel: 716-286-8005. p. 1606

Coe, Linda, Librn, Florence-Darlington Technical College Libraries, Segars Library Health Sciences Campus, 320 W Cheves St, Florence, SC, 29501. Tel: 843-676-8575. p. 2059

Coe, Linda B, Librn, Florence-Darlington Technical College Libraries, 2715 W Lucas St, Florence, SC, 29501. Tel: 843-661-8034. p. 2059

Coe, Mary, Ref Librn, Fairfield Public Library, Fairfield Woods, 1147 Fairfield Woods Rd, Fairfield, CT, 06825. Tel: 203-255-7310. p. 312

Coelho, Gail, Tech Serv Supvr, Taunton Public Library, 12 Pleasant St, Taunton, MA, 02780. Tel: 508-821-1410. p. 1059

Coelho, John, Archivist, Scottish Rite Masonic Museum & Library, Inc, 33 Marrett Rd, Lexington, MA, 02421. Tel: 781-457-4116. p. 1028

Coelho, Linda, Dir, Taunton Public Library, 12 Pleasant St, Taunton, MA, 02780. Tel: 508-821-1410. p. 1059

Coen, Jamie, Digital Res Librn, La Grange College, 601 Broad St, LaGrange, GA, 30240-2999. Tel: 706-880-8312. p. 484

Coen, Julia C, Dir, Westmont Public Library, 428 N Cass Ave, Westmont, IL, 60559-1502. Tel: 630-869-6150, 630-869-6160. p. 661

Coffey, Adrianne, Dir, Nenana Public Library, 106 E Second St, Nenana, AK, 99760. Tel: 907-832-5812. p. 49

Coffey, Carol, Dir, Libr Res, Central Arkansas Library System, 100 Rock St, Little Rock, AR, 72201-4698. Tel: 501-918-3008. p. 101

Coffey, Elizabeth, Access Serv, Libr Asst, Gordon-Conwell Theological Seminary, 130 Essex St, South Hamilton, MA, 01982-2317. Tel: 978-646-4074. p. 1054

Coffey, Jennifer, Dir, Pflugerville Public Library, 1008 W Pfluger, Pflugerville, TX, 78660. Tel: 512-990-6375. p. 2226

Coffey, Shannon, Research Librn, Williams & Connolly Library, 680 Maine Ave SW, Washington, DC, 20024. Tel: 202-434-5000. p. 381

Coffin, Andrea, Communications & Consortia Mgr, WISPALS Library Consortium, c/o WiLS, 1360 Regent St, No 121, Madison, WI, 53715. Tel: 414-979-9457. p. 2777

Coffin, Carl K, Libr Dir, Colleton County Memorial Library, 600 Hampton St, Walterboro, SC, 29488-4098. Tel: 843-549-5621. p. 2072

Coffin, Linda, Br Mgr, Aiken-Bamberg-Barnwell-Edgefield Regional Library, Midland Valley, Nine Hillside Rd, Warrenville, SC, 29851. Tel: 803-593-7379. p. 2045

Coffin, Sarah, Client Serv Librn, Department of Canadian Heritage, 15 Eddy St, Gatineau, QC, J8X 4B3, CANADA. Tel: 819-953-0527. p. 2713

Coffin, Vicky, Librn, Adult Serv, Mansfield Public Library, 54 Warrenville Rd, Mansfield Center, CT, 06250. Tel: 860-423-2501. p. 321

Coffman, Amy, Libr Dir, Sutherland Public Library, 900 Second St, Sutherland, NE, 69165. Tel: 308-386-2228. p. 1337

Coffman, Carol, Asst Librn, Waveland-Brown Township Public Library, 115 E Green, Waveland, IN, 47989. Tel: 765-435-2700. p. 725

Coffman, Mary, Asst Dir, The Museums of Oglebay Institute Library, Oglebay Institute, The Burton Center, Wheeling, WV, 26003. Tel: 304-242-7272. p. 2417

Coffman, Pat, Dir, Libr Serv, Clay County Public Library System, 1895 Town Center Blvd, Fleming Island, FL, 32003. Tel: 904-278-3720. p. 396

Coffta, Michael J, Research Librn, Bloomsburg University of Pennsylvania, 400 E Second St, Bloomsburg, PA, 17815-1301. Tel: 570-389-4205. p. 1913

Coffta Sims, Kathy, Communications Dir, Onondaga County Public Libraries, The Galleries of Syracuse, 447 S Salina St, Syracuse, NY, 13202-2494. Tel: 315-435-1900. p. 1649

Cogan, Allyson, Dir, Pennsville Public Library, 190 S Broadway, Pennsville, NJ, 08070. Tel: 856-678-5473. p. 1434

Cogar, Kathy, Chief Financial Officer, Harford County Public Library, 1221-A Brass Mill Rd, Belcamp, MD, 21017-1209. Tel: 410-273-5646. p. 958

Cogdill, Robin, Asst Dir, Pub Serv, Sevier County Public Library System, 408 High St, Sevierville, TN, 37862. Tel: 865-365-1417. p. 2125

Coghill, Jeffrey G, Dir, Eastern AHEC Libr Serv/Head, Outreach Serv, East Carolina University, William E Laupus Health Sciences Library, 500 Health Sciences Dr, Greenville, NC, 27834. Tel: 252-744-2066. p. 1693

Cognata, Sarah, Libr Dir, Georgetown Peabody Library, Two Maple St, Georgetown, MA, 01833. Tel: 978-352-5728. p. 1020

Cogswell, Chrissy, Library & Learning Resource Ctr Librn, Northeastern Illinois University, El Centro Library & Learning Resource Center, 3390 N Avondale Ave, Chicago, IL, 60618. Tel: 773-442-4090. p. 566

Cogswell, James A, Dir of Libr, University of Missouri-Columbia, Elmer Ellis Library, 104 Ellis Library, Columbia, MO, 65201-5149. Tel: 573-882-4701. p. 1243

Cohan, Linda, Libr Mgr, Levy County Public Library System, AF Knotts Public, 11 56th St, Yankeetown, FL, 34498. Tel: 352-447-4212. p. 387

Cohen, Barbara, Ch, Warner Library, 121 N Broadway, Tarrytown, NY, 10591. Tel: 914-631-7734. p. 1651

Cohen, Becky, Library Contact, Linklaters, 1290 Avenue of the Americas, New York, NY, 10105. Tel: 212-424-9000. p. 1590

Cohen, Benjamin, Ch Mgr, San Francisco Public Library, Richmond/Senator Milton Marks Branch Library, 351 Ninth Ave, San Francisco, CA, 94118-2210. Tel: 415-355-5600. p. 228

Cohen, Buzzard, Coll Develop, Alan Wofsy Fine Arts Reference Library, 1109 Geary Blvd, San Francisco, CA, 94109. Tel: 415-292-6500. p. 230

Cohen, Cheryl, Sr Librn, Innovation, Science & Economic Development Canada, 50 Victoria St, Rm 309, Place du Portage Phase I, Gatineau, QC, K1A 0C9, CANADA. Tel: 873-455-5104. p. 2713

Cohen, Cynthia, Dept Chair, Los Angeles Valley College Library, 5800 Fulton Ave, Valley Glen, CA, 91401-4096. Tel: 818-947-2766. p. 255

Cohen, Dan M, Dean, Univ Libr, Northeastern University Libraries, 360 Huntington Ave, Boston, MA, 02115. Tel: 617-373-8778. p. 998

Cohen, Hananya, Librn, Maryland Correctional Institution for Women Library, 7943 Brock Bridge Rd, Jessup, MD, 20794. Tel: 410-379-3800, 410-379-3828. p. 969

Cohen, Jennifer, Teen Serv, Suffern Free Library, 210 Lafayette Ave, Suffern, NY, 10901. Tel: 845-357-1237. p. 1647

Cohen, Jeri, Head, Media Serv, Head, Teen Serv, Patchogue-Medford Library, 54-60 E Main St, Patchogue, NY, 11772. Tel: 631-654-4700. p. 1615

Cohen, John, Dir, Ogden Farmers' Library, 269 Ogden Center Rd, Spencerport, NY, 14559. Tel: 585-617-6181. p. 1643

Cohen, Joshua, Instruction & Outreach Librn, Elizabethtown College, One Alpha Dr, Elizabethtown, PA, 17022-2227. Tel: 717-361-1453. p. 1929

Cohen, Kerry, Mgr, Suwannee River Regional Library, Greenville Public Library, 1325 SW Main St, Greenville, FL, 32331. Tel: 850-948-2529. p. 419

Cohen, Madeline, Asst Dir, University of Denver, Westminster Law Library, Sturm College of Law, 2255 E Evans Ave, Denver, CO, 80208. Tel: 303-871-6252. p. 278

Cohen, Michael, Dir, Operations, Emanuel Congregation, 5959 N Sheridan Rd, Chicago, IL, 60660. Tel: 773-561-5173. p. 560

Cohen, Naomi, Ref Serv, Saint Joseph's University, Francis A Drexel Library, 5600 City Ave, Philadelphia, PA, 19131-1395. Tel: 610-660-1057. p. 1985

Cohen, Nava, Assoc Dir of Libr, Pasco-Hernando State College-North Campus, 11415 Ponce de Leon Blvd, Rm C125, Brooksville, FL, 34601-8698. Tel: 352-797-5139. p. 388

Cohen, Sandy, Mgr, Nashville Public Library, Library Service for the Deaf & Hard of Hearing, 615 Church St, Nashville, TN, 37219-2314. Tel: 615-862-5750. p. 2119

Cohen, Scott, Libr Dir, Jackson State Community College Library, 2046 North Pkwy, Jackson, TN, 38301. Tel: 731-425-2609. p. 2102

Cohen, Terri, Library Contact, Temple Judah, 3221 Lindsay Lane SE, Cedar Rapids, IA, 52403. Tel: 319-362-1261. p. 738

Cohlman Bracchi, Jennifer, Actg Head Librn, Smithsonian Libraries, Cooper-Hewitt, National Design Library, Two E 91st St, New York, DC, 10128. Tel: 212-848-8333. p. 375

Cohn, Deborah, Adminr, Archivist, Jewish Historical Society of Central Jersey Library, 222 Livingston Ave, New Brunswick, NJ, 08901. Tel: 732-249-4894. p. 1424

Cohn, Judith, Dir, Health Sci Libr, Rutgers University Libraries, George F Smith Library of the Health Sciences, 30 12th Ave, Newark, NJ, 07101. Tel: 973-972-0560. p. 1425

Cohn, Judy, Asst VP, Info Servs, Rutgers University Libraries, 169 College Ave, New Brunswick, NJ, 08901-1163. Tel: 973-972-0560. p. 1424

Cohn, Lisa, Librn, Bloomfield Public Library, 90 Broad St, Bloomfield, NJ, 07003. Tel: 973-566-6200. p. 1391

Cohn, Mary, Libr Dir, Austin Memorial Library, 220 S Bonham Ave, Cleveland, TX, 77327-4591. Tel: 281-592-3920. p. 2156

Cohn, Patricia, Sr Librn, Ch Serv, Warner Library, 121 N Broadway, Tarrytown, NY, 10591. Tel: 914-631-7734. p. 1651

Cohn, Sarah, Head, Ref, City College of the City University of New York, North Academic Ctr, 160 Convent Ave, New York, NY, 10031. Tel: 212-650-7155, 212-650-7292. p. 1581

Cohn, Suzette, Doc Delivery, ILL, National Renewable Energy Laboratory Library, 15013 Denver West Pkwy, Golden, CO, 80401-3305. Tel: 303-275-4134. p. 283

Cohn, Tom, Head, Tech Serv, Huntington Public Library, 338 Main St, Huntington, NY, 11743. Tel: 631-427-5165, Ext 270. p. 1549

Cohoe, Diane, Asst Librn, Boyne Regional Library, 15 First St SW, Carman, MB, R0G 0J0, CANADA. Tel: 204-745-3504. p. 2586

Cohrs, Mary, Dir, Bellaire City Library, 5111 Jessamine, Bellaire, TX, 77401-4498. Tel: 713-662-8160. p. 2147

Coiffe, Dorothea, Faculty Res Librn, Scholarly Communications Librn, Borough of Manhattan Community College Library, 199 Chambers St, S410, New York, NY, 10007. Tel: 212-220-1444. p. 1580

Coil, Tami, Dir, Sloan Public Library, 502 Evans St, Sloan, IA, 51055. Tel: 712-428-4200. p. 783

Coish, Theresa L, Dir, Libr Serv, Middletown Public Library, 700 W Main Rd, Middletown, RI, 02842-6391. Tel: 401-846-1573. p. 2034

Coit, Laura, Asst Librn, West Tisbury Free Public Library, 1042 State Rd, Vineyard Haven, MA, 02568. Tel: 508-693-3366. p. 1061

Coito, Bethany, Youth Serv Coordr, New Bedford Free Public Library, 613 Pleasant St, New Bedford, MA, 02740-6203. Tel: 508-991-6275. p. 1038

Coker, Betty, Librn, Eclectic Public Library, 50 Main St, Eclectic, AL, 36024. Tel: 334-639-4727. p. 15

Coker, Janea, Prog Coordr, Barry-Lawrence Regional Library, 213 Sixth St, Monett, MO, 65708-2147. Tel: 417-235-6646. p. 1262

Coker, Janea Kay, Br Supvr, Youth Serv Coordr, Barry-Lawrence Regional Library, Marionville Branch, 303 W Washington St, Marionville, MO, 65705. Tel: 417-463-2675. p. 1263

Coker, Rebecca, Librn, Hardin Northern Public Library, 153 N Main St, Dunkirk, OH, 45836-1064. Tel: 419-759-3558. p. 1783

Colacchio, Kelly, Ref Librn, New Hanover County Public Library, Northeast Regional Library, 1241 Military Cutoff Rd, Wilmington, NC, 28405. Tel: 910-798-6378. p. 1723

Colahan, Woody, Music & Performing Arts Librn, University of Denver, Music Library, Lamont School of Music, Rm 440, 2344 E Iliff Ave, Denver, CO, 80208. Tel: 303-871-6427. p. 277

Colander, Joyce, Br Mgr, Chicago Public Library, Beverly, 1962 W 95th St, Chicago, IL, 60643. Tel: 312-747-9673. p. 556

Colarosa, Dolores, Youth Serv Coordr, Baldwin Borough Public Library, 5230 Wolfe Dr, Pittsburgh, PA, 15236. Tel: 412-885-2255. p. 1990

Colbert, Gary, ILL, Ada Public Library, 124 S Rennie, Ada, OK, 74820. Tel: 580-436-8125. p. 1839

Colbert, Jason, Sr Librn, Lee County Library System, Bonita Springs Public Library, 10560 Reynolds St, Bonita Springs, FL, 34135. Tel: 239-533-4860. p. 403

Colbert, JeTaun, Br Mgr, Milwaukee Public Library, Washington Park, 2121 N Sherman Blvd, Milwaukee, WI, 53208. p. 2460

Colbert, Judy, Mgr, Richard T Liddicoat Gemological Library & Information Center, 5345 Armada Dr, Carlsbad, CA, 92008. Tel: 760-603-4046, 760-603-4068. p. 128

Colbert, Lynne, Access Serv Librn, Marian University, 3200 Cold Spring Rd, Indianapolis, IN, 46222-1997. Tel: 317-955-6090. p. 697

Colbert, Mary, VPres, Dutchess County Genealogical Society Library, Family History Ctr, LDS Church, 204 Spackenkill Rd, Poughkeepsie, NY, 12603-5135. Tel: 845-462-6909. p. 1623

Colbert, Susan, Libr Dir, Sparta Public Library, 211 W Broadway, Sparta, IL, 62286. Tel: 618-443-5014. p. 648

Colborne, Allison, Libr Dir, Museum of New Mexico, Museum of Indian Arts & Culture-Laboratory of Anthropology Library, 708 Camino Lejo, Santa Fe, NM, 87505. Tel: 505-476-1264. p. 1475

Colbourne, Shona, Librn, Victoria Public Library, Municipal Ctr, 2nd Flr, Main Rd, Rte 74, Victoria, NL, A0A 4G0, CANADA. Tel: 709-596-3682. p. 2611

Colburn, Joan, Dir, Libr Serv, Mountain Area Health Education Center, 121 Hendersonville Rd, Asheville, NC, 28803. Tel: 828-257-4438. p. 1672

Colby, Anita, Adjunct Librn, Compton College Library, 1111 E Artesia Blvd, Compton, CA, 90221. Tel: 310-900-1600, Ext 2179. p. 132

Colby, Cheryl, Librn, Silas L Griffith Memorial Library, 74 S Main St, Danby, VT, 05739. Tel: 802-293-5106. p. 2282

Colby, Heather, Info Serv Librn, Teen Serv Coordr, Homer Township Public Library District, 14320 W 151st St, Homer Glen, IL, 60491. Tel: 708-301-7908. p. 600

Colby, Julie, Dir, Colebrook Public Library, 126 Main St, Colebrook, NH, 03576. Tel: 603-237-4808. p. 1358

Colding, Linda, Dr, Head, Ref, Res & Instruction, Florida Gulf Coast University Library, 10501 FGCU Blvd S, Fort Myers, FL, 33965. Tel: 239-590-7604. p. 402

Coldren, Andrew, Dir, McCowan Memorial Library, 15 Pitman Ave, Pitman, NJ, 08071. Tel: 856-589-1656. p. 1435

Coldwell, Paula J, Libr Tech, Nova Scotia Community College, Kingstec Campus Library, 236 Belcher St, Kentville, NS, B4N 0A6, CANADA. Tel: 902-679-7380. p. 2620

Cole, Angela M, Interim Mgr, Arizona State University Libraries, Downtown Phoenix Campus, UCENT Lower Level, Ste L1-61, 411 N Central Ave, Phoenix, AZ, 85004-2115. Tel: 602-496-0300. p. 79

Cole, Brad, Dean of Libr, Utah State University, 3000 Old Main Hill, Logan, UT, 84322-3000. Tel: 435-797-2687. p. 2265

Cole, Brian, Dir, Mazomanie Free Library, 102 Brodhead St, Mazomanie, WI, 53560. Tel: 608-795-2104. p. 2455

Cole, Carmen, Bus Liaison Librn, Pennsylvania State University Libraries, William & Joan Schreyer Business Library, 309 Paterno Library, 3rd Flr, University Park, PA, 16802-1810. Tel: 814-865-6493. p. 2016

Cole, Cecelia, Acad Librn, University of Wisconsin-Eau Claire, 1800 College Dr, Rice Lake, WI, 54868-2497. Tel: 715-788-6250. p. 2473

Cole, Cody, Br Mgr, Campbell County Public Library, Timbrook Branch, 18891 Leesville Rd, Lynchburg, VA, 24501. Tel: 434-592-9551. p. 2346

Cole, Cynthia, Ref Serv, Ser, Spec Coll Librn, Rust College, 150 E Rust Ave, Holly Springs, MS, 38635. Tel: 662-252-8000, Ext 4100. p. 1220

Cole, Darla J, Libr Dir, Chelsea Public Library, 618 Pine St, Chelsea, OK, 74016-0064. Tel: 918-789-3364. p. 1843

Cole, Diana, Dir, Bowerston Public Library, 200 Main St, Bowerston, OH, 44695. Tel: 740-269-8531. p. 1752

Cole, Elizabeth, Curator of Coll, Dep Dir, Red Mill Museum Library, 56 Main St, Clinton, NJ, 08809. Tel: 908-735-4101, Ext 103. p. 1397

Cole, Erica, Libr Asst, Union University, Germantown Campus Library, 2745 Hacks Cross Rd, Germantown, TN, 38138. Tel: 901-312-1948. p. 2103

Cole, Frances, Coll Serv Librn, Chowan University, One University Pl, Murfreesboro, NC, 27855. Tel: 252-398-6592. p. 1705

Cole, Glenn, Library Contact, Transportation Association of Canada, 401-1111 Prince of Wales Dr, Ottawa, ON, K2C 3T2, CANADA. Tel: 613-736-1350, Ext 244. p. 2670

Cole, Helen, Br Asst, Cumberland Public Libraries, Oxford Library, 22 Water St, Oxford, NS, B0M 1P0, CANADA. Tel: 902-447-2440. p. 2615

Cole, Jesse, Tech Serv Coordr, Greenfield Public Library, 412 Main St, Greenfield, MA, 01301. Tel: 413-772-1544. p. 1022

Cole, Jody, Dir, Shippensburg Public Library, 73 W King St, Shippensburg, PA, 17257-1299. Tel: 717-532-4508. p. 2007

Cole, Julie A, Librn, Queen Elizabeth Hospital, 60 Riverside Dr, Charlottetown, PE, C1A 8T5, CANADA. Tel: 902-894-2371. p. 2707

Cole, Kathy, Dir, Confederated Tribes of Grand Ronde, 9615 Grand Ronde Rd, Grand Ronde, OR, 97347. Tel: 503-879-1488. p. 1880

Cole, Kelly, Cat & Proc Mgr, Greene County Public Library, 120 N 12th St, Paragould, AR, 72450. Tel: 870-236-8711. p. 107

Cole, Laura, Readers' Serv Manager, Bernardsville Public Library, One Anderson Hill Rd, Bernardsville, NJ, 07924. Tel: 908-766-0118. p. 1390

Cole, Lauren, Librn, Columbia State Community College, Williamson County Center Library, 104 Claude Yates Dr, Franklin, TN, 37064. Tel: 615-790-4406. p. 2094

Cole, Lesa, Ch Serv, Iola Public Library, 218 E Madison Ave, Iola, KS, 66749. Tel: 620-365-3262. p. 815

Cole, Lynda, Campus Library Coord, Seminole State College of Florida, 1055 AAA Dr, Heathrow, FL, 32746. Tel: 407-708-4415. p. 408

Cole, Mary, Archivist, Catholic Diocesan Archives, 525 E Mission Ave, Spokane, WA, 99202. Tel: 509-358-7336. p. 2383

Cole, Melissa, Head Librn, Capital Area District Libraries, Downtown Lansing Library, 401 S Capitol Ave, Lansing, MI, 48933. Tel: 517-367-6363. p. 1124

Cole, Melissa, Head Librn, Capital Area District Libraries, South Lansing Library, 3500 S Cedar St, Ste 108, Lansing, MI, 48910. Tel: 517-272-9840. p. 1124

Cole, Melissa S, Head Librn, Capital Area District Libraries, Foster Library, 200 N Foster Ave, Lansing, MI, 48912. Tel: 517-485-5185. p. 1124

Cole, Nikey, Program/Market Coord, Allen Parish Libraries, 320 S Sixth St, Oberlin, LA, 70655. Tel: 318-491-4543. p. 905

Cole, Pam, Br Mgr, Upper Arlington Public Library, Lane Road Branch, 1945 Lane Rd, Upper Arlington, OH, 43220. Tel: 614-459-0273. p. 1778

Cole, Peter, Chief, Learning Resources, Department of Veterans Affairs, New York Harbor Healthcare, 423 E 23rd St, New York, NY, 10010. Tel: 212-686-7500, Ext 7684. p. 1585

Cole, Rebecca, Dir, Rushford Free Library, 9012 Main St, Rushford, NY, 14777-9700. Tel: 585-437-2533. p. 1634

Cole, Sarah, Mgr, DeWitt Public Library, 205 W Maxwell St, DeWitt, AR, 72042. Tel: 870-946-1151. p. 94

Cole, Stacey, Dir, Kilgore Public Library, 301 Henderson Blvd, Kilgore, TX, 75662-2799. Tel: 903-984-1529. p. 2206

Colee, Lucinda, Libr Dir, Volusia County Public Library, 1290 Indian Lake Rd, Daytona Beach, FL, 32124. Tel: 386-248-1745. p. 392

Colegrove, Tod, Head Librn, University of Nevada-Reno, DeLaMare Library, 1664 N Virginia St, MS 262, Reno, NV, 89557-0262. Tel: 775-682-5644. p. 1349

Colegrove, Tod, PhD, Dean of Libr, Boise State University, 1865 Cesar Chavez Lane, Boise, ID, 83725. Tel: 208-426-1755. p. 517

Coleman, Betty, Libr Dir, Sterling County Public Library, 301 Main St, Sterling City, TX, 76951. Tel: 325-378-2212. p. 2246

Coleman, Bonnie, Librn, Farmington Public Library, 101 North A St, Farmington, MO, 63640. Tel: 573-756-5779. p. 1245

Coleman, Claudia A, Libr Tech, United States Army, Public Health Command Library, 5158 Blackhawk Rd, BLDG E-5158, Aberdeen Proving Ground, MD, 21010-5403. Tel: 410-436-4236. p. 949

Coleman, Dale, Interim Dean, Library & Learning Innovation, Tacoma Community College Library, Bldg 7, 6501 S 19th St, Tacoma, WA, 98466-6100. Tel: 253-460-5091. p. 2387

Coleman, Dan, Network Adminr, Juneau Public Libraries, 292 Marine Way, Juneau, AK, 99801. Tel: 907-586-5249. p. 47

Coleman, Darlene, Ser, Lehigh Carbon Community College Library, 4750 Orchard Rd, Schnecksville, PA, 18078. Tel: 610-799-1150. p. 2003

Coleman, David, Med Librn, Hawaii Pacific Health Straub Medical Center, 888 S King St, Honolulu, HI, 96813. Tel: 808-522-4471. p. 506

Coleman, Frances N, Dean of Libr, Mississippi State University, 395 Hardy Rd, Mississippi State, MS, 39762. Tel: 662-325-7668. p. 1227

Coleman, Georgia, Chief Customer Officer, Richland Library, 1431 Assembly St, Columbia, SC, 29201-3101. Tel: 803-799-9084. p. 2054

Coleman, Glenna, Youth Librn, Weathersfield Proctor Library, 5181 Rte 5, Ascutney, VT, 05030. Tel: 802-674-2863. p. 2277

Coleman, Gordon, Head, Resource Acquisition, Metadata & Mgmt, Simon Fraser University - Burnaby Campus, 8888 University Dr, Burnaby, BC, V5A 1S6, CANADA. Tel: 778-782-3916. p. 2564

Coleman, Hailee, Youth Serv, Augusta County Library, 1759 Jefferson Hwy, Fishersville, VA, 22939. Tel: 540-885-3961, 540-949-6354. p. 2318

Coleman, Jason, Asst to the Dir, New England Conservatory of Music, 255 St Butolph St, Boston, MA, 02115. Tel: 617-585-1250. p. 998

Coleman, Jennifer, Dir, Summerville Public Library, 114 Second Ave, Summerville, PA, 15864. Tel: 814-856-3169. p. 2011

Coleman, Kate, Tech Serv Mgr, Jefferson County Library, 5678 State Rd PP, High Ridge, MO, 63049-2216. Tel: 636-677-8689. p. 1248

Coleman, Kathleen, Librn, Harvard Library, Herbert Weir Smyth Classical Library, Widener, Rm E, Cambridge, MA, 02138. Tel: 617-495-4027. p. 1007

Coleman, Kim, Div Mgr, Tech Serv, High Point Public Library, 901 N Main St, High Point, NC, 27262. Tel: 336-883-3645. p. 1696

Coleman, Lynn, Academic Services, Dir of Libr, Mohawk College Library, 135 Fennell Ave W, Hamilton, ON, L9C 0E5, CANADA. p. 2647

Coleman, Nikki, Youth Engagement Coord, Park Forest Public Library, 400 Lakewood Blvd, Park Forest, IL, 60466. Tel: 708-748-3731. p. 633

Coleman, Patrick, Dir, Tarrant Public Library, 1143 Ford Ave, Tarrant, AL, 35217. Tel: 205-841-0575. p. 36

Coleman, Rebeckah, Circ Mgr, Cleveland Bradley County Public Library, 795 Church St NE, Cleveland, TN, 37311-5295. Tel: 423-472-2163. p. 2092

Coleman, Ron, Library Chief, United States Holocaust Memorial Museum Library, 100 Raoul Wallenberg Pl SW, Washington, DC, 20024. Tel: 202-479-9717. p. 379

Coleman, Rosetta, Br Mgr, Chicago Public Library, Martin Luther King Jr Branch, 3436 S King Dr, Chicago, IL, 60616. Tel: 312-747-7543. p. 556

Coleman, Selah, Outreach Coordr, University of Richmond, 261 Richmond Way, Richmond, VA, 23173. Tel: 804-289-8876. p. 2342

Coleman, Sheila, Coordr, Spec Serv, Regional Librn, State Library of Louisiana, 701 N Fourth St, Baton Rouge, LA, 70802. Tel: 225-342-4942. p. 885

Coleman, Sheila, Outreach Serv, State Library of Louisiana, 701 N Fourth St, Baton Rouge, LA, 70802-5232. Tel: 225-342-4942. p. 885

Coleman, Shirley, Asst Dir, Watonwan County Library, 125 Fifth St S, Saint James, MN, 56081. Tel: 507-375-1278. p. 1198

Coleman, Sterling, Dr, Dir, Libr Serv, Clark State Community College Library, 570 E Leffel Lane, Springfield, OH, 45505. Tel: 937-328-6023. p. 1821

Coleman, Valerie, Librn, Chaminade University of Honolulu, 3140 Waialae Ave, Honolulu, HI, 96816-1578. Tel: 808-739-4661. p. 506

Coleman, Vicki, Dean, Libr Serv, North Carolina Agricultural & Technical State University, 1601 E Market St, Greensboro, NC, 27411-0002. Tel: 336-285-4164. p. 1693

Colemere, Ilna, Archives, Historian, San Antonio Art League & Museum, 130 King William St, San Antonio, TX, 78204. Tel: 210-223-1140. p. 2238

Colemire, Alexa, Dir, Mason County Public Library, 218 E Third St, Maysville, KY, 41056. Tel: 606-564-3286. p. 868

Coles, Catherine, Mgr, Libr Serv, Lennox & Addington County Public Library, 97 Thomas St E, Napanee, ON, K7R 4B9, CANADA. Tel: 613-354-4883, Ext 3237. p. 2660

Coles, Denise, Librn, Houston Community College - Northeast College, Codwell Campus Library, 555 Community College Dr, Houston, TX, 77013-6127. Tel: 713-718-8354. p. 2194

Coles, Janet, Law Librn, Yolo County Law Library, 204 Fourth St, Ste A, Woodland, CA, 95695. Tel: 530-666-8918. p. 260

Coles, Patricia, Libr Coord, Walter & Haverfield LLP, The Tower at Erieview, Ste 3500, 1301 E Ninth St, Cleveland, OH, 44114-1821. Tel: 216-781-1212. p. 1770

Colette, Archambault, Coordr, Bibliotheque Municipale JR L'Heureux, 14 Comeau St, Maniwaki, QC, J9E 2R8, CANADA. Tel: 819-449-2738. p. 2716

Coley, Kristina, Electronic Res Librn, University of Health Sciences & Pharmacy in Saint Louis Library, One Pharmacy Pl, Saint Louis, MO, 63110. Tel: 314-446-8558. p. 1276

Colfer, Debby, Libr Mgr, Sno-Isle Libraries, Clinton Library, 4781 Deer Lake Rd, Clinton, WA, 98236-0530. Tel: 360-341-4280. p. 2370

Colford, Michael, Dir, Libr Serv, Boston Public Library, 700 Boylston St, Boston, MA, 02116. Tel: 617-859-2389. p. 991

Colgan, Karen, Br Mgr, Camden County Library District, 89 Rodeo Rd, Camdenton, MO, 65020. Tel: 573-346-5954. p. 1239

Colin, Conrad, Dr, Asst Prof, Dalhousie University, Kenneth C Rowe Management Bldg, Ste 4010, 6100 University Ave, Halifax, NS, B3H 4R2, CANADA. Tel: 902-494-8378. p. 2795

Colin, Elizabeth, Br Mgr, Mount Prospect Public Library, South Branch, 1711 W Algonquin Rd, Mount Prospect, IL, 60056. Tel: 847-590-4090. p. 621

Colin, Guadalupe, Br Mgr, Palatine Public Library District, Rand Road Branch, 1585 N Rand Rd, Palatine, IL, 60074. Tel: 847-202-1194. p. 631

Collado, Frances, Libr Mgr, New York Public Library - Astor, Lenox & Tilden Foundations, Pelham Parkway - Van Nest Library, 2147 Barnes Ave, (Near Pelham Pkwy South), Bronx, NY, 10462. Tel: 718-829-5864. p. 1596

Collard, Scott, Assoc Dean, Res, New York University, 70 Washington Sq S, New York, NY, 10012-1019. Tel: 212-992-9240. p. 1599

Coller, Kimberly, Court Adminr, Librn, Williams County Law Library Association, One Courthouse Sq, Bryan, OH, 43506. Tel: 419-636-3436. p. 1753

Collerius, Frank, Libr Mgr, New York Public Library - Astor, Lenox & Tilden Foundations, Jefferson Market Branch, 425 Avenue of the Americas, New York, NY, 10011-8454. Tel: 212-243-4334. p. 1596

Collett, Connie, Head Librn, Greene County Public Library, Yellow Springs Community Library, 415 Xenia Ave, Yellow Springs, OH, 45387-1837. Tel: 937-352-4003. p. 1835

Collett, Katherine, Archivist, Hamilton College, 198 College Hill Rd, Clinton, NY, 13323. Tel: 315-859-4471. p. 1519

Collett, Mason, Librn, Leslie County Public Library, 22065 Main St, Hyden, KY, 41749. Tel: 606-672-2460. p. 860

Colley, Lora, Librn, Little Dixie Regional Libraries, Huntsville Branch, 102 E Library St, Huntsville, MO, 65259-1125. Tel: 660-277-4518. p. 1262

Collier, Jenny, Youth Serv Mgr, Wood Dale Public Library District, 520 N Wood Dale Rd, Wood Dale, IL, 60191. Tel: 630-766-6762. p. 664

Collier, Joseph, Bus Librn, Mount Prospect Public Library, Ten S Emerson St, Mount Prospect, IL, 60056. Tel: 847-253-5675. p. 621

Collier, Karen, Acq Librn, Talbot County Free Library, 100 W Dover St, Easton, MD, 21601-2620. Tel: 410-822-1626. p. 964

Collier, Mark, Coordr, Ref & Coll, Converse College, 580 E Main St, Spartanburg, SC, 29302. Tel: 864-596-9020, 864-596-9071. p. 2069

Collier, Maureen, Serv Area Mgr, Halifax Public Libraries, 60 Alderney Dr, Dartmouth, NS, B2Y 4P8, CANADA. Tel: 902-490-5744. p. 2617

Collier, Tressy, Asst Dir, Ch, Blackstone Public Library, 86 Main St, Blackstone, MA, 01504. Tel: 508-883-1931. p. 990

Colligan, Mary Kate, Ref Librn, Louisiana State University at Eunice, 2048 Johnson Hwy, Eunice, LA, 70535. Tel: 337-550-1380. p. 889

Collings, Trevor, Dir, Audubon Regional Library, 12220 Woodville St, Clinton, LA, 70722. Tel: 225-683-8753. p. 887

Collings, Trevor, Br Mgr, Livingston Parish Library, Denham Springs - Walker Branch, 8101 US Hwy 190, Denham Springs, LA, 70726. Tel: 225-686-4140. p. 895

Collington, Jason, Librn, Tulsa World, 315 S Boulder Ave, Tulsa, OK, 74103-3401. Tel: 918-732-8182. p. 1867

Collins, Alicemarie, Ch Serv, Gladwyne Free Library, 362 Righters Mill Rd, Gladwyne, PA, 19035-1587. Tel: 610-642-3957. p. 1936

Collins, Ann, Regional Librn, Volusia County Public Library, 1290 Indian Lake Rd, Daytona Beach, FL, 32124. Tel: 386-822-6430. p. 392

Collins, Ann, Regional Librn, Volusia County Public Library, Pierson Public Library, 115 N Volusia Ave, Pierson, FL, 32180. Tel: 386-749-6930. p. 393

Collins, Beaulah, Dir, Baca County Library, Two Buttes Branch, Main St, Two Buttes, CO, 81084. p. 295

Collins, Betty, Youth Serv Mgr, Musser Public Library, 408 E Second St, Muscatine, IA, 52761. Tel: 563-263-3065, Ext 109. p. 772

Collins, Beulah, Dir, Baca County Library, 1260 Main St, Springfield, CO, 81073-1542. Tel: 719-523-6962. p. 295

Collins, Brennan, Libr Asst, University of Southern Mississippi-Gulf Coast Research Laboratory, 703 E Beach Dr, Ocean Springs, MS, 39564. Tel: 228-872-4213, 228-872-4253. p. 1228

Collins, Brian, Outreach Librn, Louisiana State University Libraries, LSU School of Veterinary Medicine Library, Skip Bertman Dr, Baton Rouge, LA, 70803-8414. Tel: 225-578-9794. p. 884

Collins, Carol, Head, Tech Serv, University of Tennessee, Taylor Law Ctr, 1505 W Cumberland Ave, Knoxville, TN, 37996-1800. Tel: 865-974-6552. p. 2107

Collins, Cathleen, Br Mgr, Big Horn County Library, Lovell Branch Library, 300 Oregon Ave, Lovell, WY, 82431. Tel: 307-548-7228. p. 2491

Collins, Cathy, Librn, Northwest Regional Library, Sulligent Public Library, 514 Elm St, Sulligent, AL, 35586-9053. Tel: 205-698-8631. p. 40

Collins, Cher, Ad, Agawam Public Library, 750 Cooper St, Agawam, MA, 01001. Tel: 413-789-1550. p. 984

Collins, Christel, Br Mgr, Hawaii State Public Library System, Manoa Public Library, 2716 Woodlawn Dr, Honolulu, HI, 96822. Tel: 808-988-0459. p. 509

Collins, Christin, Discovery Librn, Res Mgt Librn, Kennesaw State University Library System, 385 Cobb Ave NW, MD 1701, Kennesaw, GA, 30144. Tel: 470-578-4445. p. 483

Collins, Christine, Libr Dir, New Castle Public Library, 301 Wentworth Rd, New Castle, NH, 03854. Tel: 603-431-6773. p. 1375

Collins, David, Librn, Wyoming Correctional Facility, 3203 Dunbar Rd, Attica, NY, 14011. Tel: 585-591-1010. p. 1488

Collins, Dawn, Dir, Toluca Public Library, 102 N Main St, Toluca, IL, 61369. Tel: 815-452-2211. p. 654

Collins, Emily, Children's Prog, Makerspace Prog Spec, YA Serv, Patterson Library, 40 S Portage St, Westfield, NY, 14787. Tel: 716-326-2154. p. 1664

Collins, Gladys, Libr Mgr, Franklin Memorial Library, 331 W Main St, Swainsboro, GA, 30401. Tel: 478-237-7791. p. 498

Collins, Jan, Br Mgr, Winn Parish Library, Calvin Branch, 255 Second St, Calvin, LA, 71410. Tel: 318-727-9644. p. 912

Collins, Janice, Head, Ref, Head, Tech, Mandel Public Library of West Palm Beach, 411 Clematis St, West Palm Beach, FL, 33401. Tel: 561-868-7765. p. 453

Collins, Janice, Res Analyst, Dentons US LLP, 233 S Wacker Dr, Ste 5900, Chicago, IL, 60606-6361. Tel: 312-876-8000. p. 560
Collins, Jean E, Dir, Auburn Public Library, 369 Southbridge St, Auburn, MA, 01501. Tel: 508-832-7790. p. 986
Collins, Jeff, Dir, Davenport Public Library, 321 Main St, Davenport, IA, 52801-1490. Tel: 563-326-7832. p. 743
Collins, Jeff, Dep Dir, Pub Serv, Laramie County Library System, 2200 Pioneer Ave, Cheyenne, WY, 82001-3610. Tel: 307-773-7220. p. 2492
Collins, Jennifer, Circ, Morrison & Mary Wiley Library District, 206 W Main St, Elmwood, IL, 61529. Tel: 309-742-2431. p. 585
Collins, Jennifer, Budget Dir, Syracuse University Libraries, 222 Waverly Ave, Syracuse, NY, 13244-2010. Tel: 315-443-5781. p. 1650
Collins, Jessica, Dir, Plains Community Library, 500 Grand Ave, Plains, KS, 67869. Tel: 620-563-7326. p. 832
Collins, Jim, Cat, Tech Serv, The Morristown & Morris Township Library, One Miller Rd, Morristown, NJ, 07960. Tel: 973-538-6161. p. 1421
Collins, Joshua, Br Mgr, Sullivan County Public Libraries, Merom Public, 8554 W Market St, Merom, IN, 47861. Tel: 812-356-4612. p. 720
Collins, Joy, Ser, University of Southern California Libraries, Von KleinSmid Center Library, Von KleinSmid Ctr, 3518 Trousdale Pkwy, Los Angeles, CA, 90089-0182. Tel: 213-740-1770. p. 170
Collins, Judith, Libr Tech 1, Ocean County College Library, College Dr, Toms River, NJ, 08754. Tel: 732-255-0440, Ext 2151. p. 1446
Collins, Julie, Asst Head, Res Serv, Mount Prospect Public Library, Ten S Emerson St, Mount Prospect, IL, 60056. Tel: 847-253-5675. p. 621
Collins, Kathleen, Reserves Librn, John Jay College of Criminal Justice, 899 Tenth Ave, New York, NY, 10019. Tel: 212-237-8242. p. 1589
Collins, Kathleen, Ref Coordr, University of Washington Libraries, Odegaard Undergraduate Library, Box 353080, Seattle, WA, 98195-3080. Tel: 206-685-2771. p. 2382
Collins, Kathy, Dir, W G Rhea Public Library, 400 W Washington St, Paris, TN, 38242-3903. Tel: 731-642-1702. p. 2123
Collins, Katrina, Youth Serv, Neenah Public Library, 240 E Wisconsin Ave, Neenah, WI, 54956. Tel: 920-886-6330. p. 2463
Collins, Kelly, Dir, Bolton Public Library, 738 Main St, Bolton, MA, 01740. Tel: 978-779-2839. p. 990
Collins, Kent, Dir, William T Cozby Public Library, 177 N Heartz Rd, Coppell, TX, 75019. Tel: 972-304-3655. p. 2159
Collins, Kevin, Br Librn, Genesee District Library, Genesee Valley Center Library, 3293 S Linden Rd, Flint, MI, 48507. Tel: 810-732-1822. p. 1106
Collins, Lauren M, Assoc Prof of Law, Dir, Cleveland State University, Cleveland-Marshall Law Library, Cleveland-Marshall College of Law, 1801 Euclid Ave, Cleveland, OH, 44115-2223. Tel: 216-687-3547. p. 1769
Collins, Laurie, Ch, Ipswich Public Library, 25 N Main St, Ipswich, MA, 01938. Tel: 978-412-8713. p. 1026
Collins, Louise, Dir, Massachusetts Eye & Ear Infirmary Libraries, 243 Charles St, Boston, MA, 02114. Tel: 617-573-3196. p. 997
Collins, Maria, Dept Head, Acquisitions & Discovery, North Carolina State University Libraries, D H Hill Jr Library, Two Broughton Dr, Raleigh, NC, 27695. Tel: 919-515-3188. p. 1709
Collins, Mary, Dir, Town of Ulster Public Library, 860 Ulster Ave, Kingston, NY, 12401. Tel: 845-338-7881. p. 1560
Collins, Matt, Asst Librn, Lees-McRae College, 191 Main St W, Banner Elk, NC, 28604-9238. Tel: 828-898-8727. p. 1673
Collins, N, Asst Supervisor, Education, Federal Correctional Institution, 1100 River Rd, Hopewell, VA, 23860. Tel: 804-733-7881. p. 2326
Collins, Nanette, Ref Librn, Texas Southern University, Thurgood Marshall School of Law Library, 3100 Cleburne Ave, Houston, TX, 77004. Tel: 713-313-1106. p. 2199
Collins, Nora, Br Mgr, Ouachita Parish Public Library, Ouachita Valley Branch, 601 McMillian Rd, West Monroe, LA, 71291. Tel: 318-327-1470. p. 898
Collins, Pam, Dir, Musser Public Library, 408 E Second St, Muscatine, IA, 52761. Tel: 563-263-3065, Ext 104. p. 772
Collins, Patricia, Br Mgr, Gloucester County Library System, Greenwich Township Branch, 411 Swedesboro Rd, Gibbstown, NJ, 08027. Tel: 856-423-0684. p. 1423
Collins, Patty, Youth Serv Consult, Central Kansas Library System, 1409 Williams St, Great Bend, KS, 67530-4020. Tel: 620-792-4865. p. 810
Collins, Rachel, Librn, Greenwood Genetic Center Library, 106 Gregor Mendel Circle, Greenwood, SC, 29646. Tel: 864-388-1708. p. 2062
Collins, Sandra, Adminr, Lawrence County Federated Library System, 207 E North St, New Castle, PA, 16101-3691. Tel: 724-658-6659, Ext 113. p. 1968
Collins, Sandra, Dir, New Castle Public Library, 207 E North St, New Castle, PA, 16101-3691. Tel: 724-658-6659, Ext 113. p. 1969
Collins, Sandra A, Dir, Informational Serv, Byzantine Catholic Seminary of Saints Cyril & Methodius Library, 3605 Perrysville Ave, Pittsburgh, PA, 15214. Tel: 412-321-8383, Ext 23. p. 1990
Collins, Shannon, Ch Serv Librn, Upper Dublin Public Library, 520 Virginia Ave, Fort Washington, PA, 19034. Tel: 215-628-8744. p. 1933
Collins, Sheila, Dir, Harvey Public Library, 119 E Tenth St, Harvey, ND, 58341. Tel: 701-324-2156. p. 1735
Collins, Timothy, Asst Music Librn, Cataloger, Baldwin Wallace University, Jones Music Library, 49 Seminary St, Berea, OH, 44017. Tel: 440-826-2375. p. 1751
Collins, Tonie, Librn, James Bryan Creech Public Library, 206 W Hatcher St, Four Oaks, NC, 27524. Tel: 919-963-6013. p. 1690
Collins, Verlin, Dir, Ardmore Public Library, 25836 Main St, Ardmore, TN, 38449. Tel: 931-427-4883. p. 2087
Collins-Fuerbringer, Shelly, Dep Dir, L E Phillips Memorial Public Library, 400 Eau Claire St, Eau Claire, WI, 54701. Tel: 715-839-5063. p. 2432
Collinsworth, Rebecca, Archivist, Los Alamos Historical Society, 1050 Bathtub Row, Los Alamos, NM, 87544. Tel: 505-662-6272. p. 1472
Collis, Stephanie, Dir, Royal Center-Boone Township Public Library, 203 N Chicago St, Royal Center, IN, 46978. Tel: 574-643-3185. p. 717
Collister, Madison, Ch, Belen Public Library, 333 Becker Ave, Belen, NM, 87002. Tel: 505 966 2608. p. 1464
Collister, Nancy, Dir, Br Operations, Dir, Customer Serv, London Public Library, 251 Dundas St, London, ON, N6A 6H9, CANADA. Tel: 519-661-5100, Ext 5136. p. 2654
Collius, Jacklynn, Electronic Serv Librn, ECRI Institute Library, 5200 Butler Pike, Plymouth Meeting, PA, 19462. Tel: 610-825-6000, Ext 5309. p. 1998
Collogan, Jessica, Dean, Libr Serv, University of North Carolina at Pembroke, One University Dr, Pembroke, NC, 28372. Tel: 910-521-6365. p. 1707
Collopy, Peter, Spec Coll, Univ Archivist, California Institute of Technology, 1200 E California Blvd, M/C 1-43, Pasadena, CA, 91125-4300. Tel: 626-395-2702. p. 193
Colls, Limarie, Librn II, University of the Sacred Heart, Rosales St, PO Box 12383, Santurce, PR, 00914-0383. Tel: 787-728-1515, Ext 2695. p. 2515
Collum, Dale, Dir, Three Rivers Regional Library System, 176 SW Community Circle, Ste B, Mayo, FL, 32066. Tel: 386-294-3858. p. 420
Collura, Michael, Asst Dean, Cuyahoga Community College, Western Campus Library, 11000 Pleasant Valley Rd, Parma, OH, 44130-5199. Tel: 216-987-5416. p. 1769
Collura, Mike, Asst Dean for Tech, Collections & Branch Libraries, Kent State University Libraries, Risman Plaza, 1125 Risman Dr, Kent, OH, 44242. Tel: 330-672-0499. p. 1792
Collyer, Diane, Libr Mgr, Calling Lake Public Library, 2824 Central Dr, Calling Lake, AB, T0G 0K0, CANADA. Tel: 780-331-3027. p. 2529
Collyer, Diane, Libr Mgr, Wabasca Public Library, 2853 Alook Dr, Wabasca, AB, T0G 2K0, CANADA. Tel: 780-891-2203. p. 2558
Colombo, Brianne, Dir, Fairfield Public Library, 261 Hollywood Ave, Fairfield, NJ, 07004. Tel: 973-227-3575. p. 1402
Colombo, Fran, Libr Assoc, Roeliff Jansen Community Library, 9091 Rte 22, Hillsdale, NY, 12529. Tel: 518-325-4101. p. 1547
Colon, Angie E, Dir, Inter-American University of Puerto Rico - Fajardo Campus, Calle Union, Batey Central, Carretera 195, Fajardo, PR, 00738. Tel: 787-863-2390, Ext 2213. p. 2510
Colon, Jose, Interim Libr Mgr, Dauphin County Library System, McCormick Riverfront Library, 101 Walnut St, Harrisburg, PA, 17101. Tel: 717-234-4976, Ext 1115. p. 1940
Colon, Karl, Dir, Greene County Public Library, 76 E Market St, Xenia, OH, 45385-3100. Tel: 937-352-4000. p. 1834
Colon, Lizzie, Libr Dir, Inter-American University of Puerto Rico, Carretera 459, Int 463 Barrio Corrales, Sector Calero, Aguadilla, PR, 00605. Tel: 787-891-0925. p. 2509
Colonder, Lacretia, Dir, Altoona Public Library, 714 Main St, Altoona, KS, 66710. Tel: 620-568-6645. p. 796
Colorado, Monica, Br Librn, Yuma County Free Library District, Foothills Branch, 13226 E South Frontage Rd, Yuma, AZ, 85367. Tel: 928-373-6524. p. 86
Colson, Amy, Libr Mgr, Mississauga Library System, Churchill Meadows, 3801 Thomas St, Mississauga, ON, L5M 7G2, CANADA. Tel: 905-615-4735. p. 2659
Colson, Amy, Libr Mgr, Mississauga Library System, Meadowvale, 6655 Glen Erin Dr, Mississauga, ON, L5N 3L4, CANADA. Tel: 905-615-4710. p. 2659
Colson, Lenese M, Dr, Assoc Prof, Interim Dept Head, Valdosta State University, Odum Library, 1500 N Patterson St, Valdosta, GA, 31698. Tel: 229-333-5966. p. 2784
Colson, Leslie, Asst Dir, Human Res, Security & Phys Plant, Newark Public Library, Five Washington St, Newark, NJ, 07101. Tel: 973-733-7740. p. 1427
Colson, Liz, Libr Serv Supvr, Bronson Methodist Hospital, 601 John St, Box B, Kalamazoo, MI, 49007. Tel: 269-341-8627. p. 1121
Colston, Connie, YA Librn, Nicholas P Sims Library, 515 W Main, Waxahachie, TX, 75165-3235. Tel: 972-937-2671. p. 2255
Colt, Pam, Ref Librn, Pollard Memorial Library, 401 Merrimack St, Lowell, MA, 01852. Tel: 978-674-4120. p. 1029
Coltrin, Emily, Libr Dir, Hyrum Library, 50 W Main, Hyrum, UT, 84319. Tel: 435-245-6411. p. 2265
Coluccio, Kate, Dir, Carnegie Free Library of Swissvale, 1800 Monongahela Ave, Pittsburgh, PA, 15218-2312. Tel: 412-731-2300. p. 1991
Colville, Hannah, Serv Mgr, Halifax Public Libraries, Keshen Goodman Branch, 330 Lacewood Dr, Halifax, NS, B3S 0A3, CANADA. Tel: 902-490-5738. p. 2617

Colvin, Bryan, Univ Archivist, Mercyhurst University, 501 E 38th St, Erie, PA, 16546. Tel: 814-824-2295. p. 1932

Colvin, Ian, Librn, Dentons Canada LLP, 77 King St W, Ste 400, Toronto, ON, M5K 0A1, CANADA. Tel: 416-863-4511. p. 2688

Colvin, Jenny, Asst Dir, Outreach Serv, Furman University Libraries, 3300 Poinsett Hwy, Greenville, SC, 29613-4100. Tel: 864-294-3797. p. 2061

Colvin, Leona, Br Librn, Roosevelt County Library, Culbertson Public, 307 Broadway Ave, Culbertson, MT, 59218. Tel: 406-787-5275. p. 1304

Colvin, Matthew, Sr Librn, California Department of Corrections Library System, Folsom State Prison, 300 Prison Rd, Represa, CA, 95671. Tel: 831-678-3951, Ext 4549. p. 206

Colvin, Patrick, Library Contact, Pilgrim Congregational Church Library, 2310 E Fourth St, Duluth, MN, 55812. Tel: 218-724-8503. p. 1172

Colvin, Teresa, Asst Librn, Northwest-Shoals Community College, 800 George Wallace Blvd, Muscle Shoals, AL, 35661-3206. Tel: 256-331-5283. p. 31

Colvin, Teresa, Asst Librn, Northwest-Shoals Community College, 2080 College Rd, Phil Campbell, AL, 35581. Tel: 256-331-6271. p. 33

Colwell, David, Tech Serv, Inver Hills Community College Library, 2500 80th St E, Inver Grove Heights, MN, 55076-3209. Tel: 651-450-3625. p. 1179

Colwell, Priscilla, Dir, Putnam Public Library, 225 Kennedy Dr, Putnam, CT, 06260-1691. Tel: 860-963-6826. p. 334

Coly, Lisette, Pres, Parapsychology Foundation Inc, 308 Front St, Greenport, NY, 11944. Tel: 212-628-1550, 631-477-2560. p. 1542

Colyer, Pamela, Head, Cat, Head, Tech Serv, Morehead State University, 150 University Blvd, Morehead, KY, 40351. Tel: 606-783-5118. p. 869

Comanda, Bridgette, Instruction Librn, Trinity University, 125 Michigan Ave NE, Washington, DC, 20017. Tel: 202-884-9352. p. 377

Combest, Seairah, Children's Coordr, Page Public Library, 479 S Lake Powell Blvd, Page, AZ, 86040. Tel: 928-645-5802. p. 67

Combs, Chris, Exec Dir, Institute for American Indian Studies, 38 Curtis Rd, Washington, CT, 06793. Tel: 860-868-0518. p. 343

Combs, George K, Br Mgr, DeKalb County Library System, Alexandria Branch, 109 Public Sq, Alexandria, TN, 37012-2141. Tel: 615-529-4124. p. 2126

Combs, Hannah, Exec Dir, Bonner County Historical Society, 611 S Ella Ave, Sandpoint, ID, 83864. Tel: 208-263-2344. p. 530

Combs, Julie, Emerging Tech Librn, Northern Virginia Community College Libraries, Loudoun Campus, 21200 Campus Dr, Rm 200, Sterling, VA, 20164-8699. Tel: 703-948-2641. p. 2304

Combs, Rachel, Pub Serv Mgr, University of Kentucky Libraries, Science & Engineering Library, 211 King Bldg, 179 Funkhouser Dr, Lexington, KY, 40506-0039. Tel: 859-257-6217. p. 864

Combs, Robyn, Librn, Missouri Department of Corrections, Jefferson City Correctional Center, 8200 No More Victims Rd, Jefferson City, MO, 65101-4539. Tel: 573-751-3224. p. 1252

Combs, Teneia, Circ Supvr, Redford Township District Library, 25320 W Six Mile, Redford, MI, 48240. Tel: 313-531-5960. p. 1143

Combs-Stauffer, Ramona, Libr Dir, Salmon Public Library, 300 Main St, Salmon, ID, 83467-4111. Tel: 208-756-2311. p. 530

Comeau, Ariane, Libr Serv Tech, Hearst Public Library, 801 George St, Hearst, ON, P0L 1N0, CANADA. Tel: 705-372-2843. p. 2648

Comeau, Denise, Dir, Jamesburg Public Library, 229 Gatzmer Ave, Jamesburg, NJ, 08831. Tel: 732-521-0440. p. 1409

Comeau, Erin, Exec Dir, Regional Librn, Western Counties Regional Library, 405 Main St, Yarmouth, NS, B5A 1G3, CANADA. Tel: 902-742-2486. p. 2623

Comeau, George T, Curator, Canton Historical Society Library, 1400 Washington St, Canton, MA, 02021. Tel: 781-615-9040. p. 1009

Comeaux, Christy, Pub Info Officer, Calcasieu Parish Public Library System, 301 W Claude St, Lake Charles, LA, 70605-3457. Tel: 337-721-7147. p. 893

Comer, Alberta, Dean, University of Utah, J Willard Marriott Library, 295 S 1500 East, Salt Lake City, UT, 84112-0860. Tel: 801-581-8558. p. 2272

Comer, Janis, Ch Serv Librn, Indianola Public Library, 207 North B St, Indianola, IA, 50125. Tel: 515-961-9418. p. 759

Comerford, Kevin, Assoc Univ Librn for the Digital Library, University of California, Riverside, 900 University Ave, Riverside, CA, 92521. Tel: 951-827-3220. p. 203

Comerford, Kim, Colls Mgr, Glenview Public Library, 1930 Glenview Rd, Glenview, IL, 60025. Tel: 847-729-7500. p. 594

Comfort, Mike, Dir, Libr & Mus Serv, The Masonic Library & Museum of Pennsylvania, Masonic Temple, One N Broad St, Philadelphia, PA, 19107-2520. Tel: 215-988-1977. p. 1983

Comfort, Sarah, Mgr, County of Los Angeles Public Library, Angelo M Iacoboni Library, 4990 Clark Ave, Lakewood, CA, 90712-2676. Tel: 562-866-1777. p. 136

Comfort, Stacey, Youth & Teen Serv Librn, Chelsea District Library, 221 S Main St, Chelsea, MI, 48118-1267. Tel: 734-475-8732. p. 1091

Comito, Lauren, Managing Librn, Brooklyn Public Library, Leonard, 81 Devoe St, Brooklyn, NY, 11211. Tel: 718-486-6006. p. 1503

Comito, Lauren, Managing Librn, Brooklyn Public Library, Mill Basin, 2385 Ralph Ave, Brooklyn, NY, 11234. Tel: 718-241-3973. p. 1503

Comizio, Betsy, Dir, Montgomery Free Library, 133 Clinton St, Montgomery, NY, 12549. Tel: 845-457-5616. p. 1573

Commander, Patricia, Dir, Writing Ctr Dir, Hood Theological Seminary Library, 300 Bldg, 1810 Luthern Synod Dr, Salisbury, NC, 28144. Tel: 704-636-6779. p. 1714

Commons, Roland, Ref Librn, Grayson County College Library, 6101 Grayson Dr, Denison, TX, 75020-8299. Tel: 903-463-8637. p. 2170

Compoe, Stevyn, Dir, Niles District Library, 620 E Main St, Niles, MI, 49120. Tel: 269-683-8545. p. 1137

Compton, Adrienne, Asst Mgr, Marion Public Library, 4036 Maple Ave, Marion, NY, 14505. Tel: 315-926-4933. p. 1569

Compton, Dan, Libr Dir, Summit County Library, 1885 W Ute Blvd, Park City, UT, 84098. Tel: 435-615-3947. p. 2268

Compton, Emily, Dir, River Forest Public Library, 735 Lathrop Ave, River Forest, IL, 60305-1883. Tel: 708-366-5205. p. 639

Compton, Jennifer, Archivist, Head, Tech Serv, Oklahoma Christian University, 2501 E Memorial Rd, Edmond, OK, 73013. Tel: 405-425-5314. p. 1846

Compton, Lawrence, Info Spec, University of New Mexico, Bureau of Business & Economic Research Data Bank, 1919 Las Lomas NE, Albuquerque, NM, 87106. Tel: 505-277-2142. p. 1462

Compton, Linda, Pub Serv, Whatcom Community College Library, Heiner Bldg, 231 W Kellogg Rd, Bellingham, WA, 98226. Tel: 360-383-3300. p. 2359

Compton, Norm, Mgr, Access Serv, Allen County Public Library, 900 Library Plaza, Fort Wayne, IN, 46802. Tel: 260-421-1246. p. 683

Compton, Troy, Circ Serv Dept Head, San Diego State University, 5500 Campanile Dr, San Diego, CA, 92182-8050. Tel: 619-594-2184. p. 221

Compton-Dzak, Emily, Asst Libr Dir, Winnetka-Northfield Public Library District, 768 Oak St, Winnetka, IL, 60093-2515. Tel: 847-446-7220. p. 664

Comstock, Mary Ann, Br Mgr, South Kingstown Public Library, Kingston Free Branch, 2605 Kingstown Rd, Kingston, RI, 02881. Tel: 401-783-8254. p. 2037

Comstock, Mary Ann, Br Mgr, South Kingstown Public Library, Robert Beverley Hale Library, 2601 Commodore Perry Hwy, Wakefield, RI, 02879. Tel: 401-783-5386. p. 2037

Comstock, Sharon, Asst Teaching Prof, University of Illinois at Urbana-Champaign, Library & Information Science Bldg, 501 E Daniel St, Champaign, IL, 61820-6211. Tel: 217-333-3280. p. 2784

Comte, Gisele, Dir, Bibliotheque Pere Champagne, 44 Rue Rogers, Notre Dame de Lourdes, MB, R0G 1M0, CANADA. Tel: 204-248-2386. p. 2588

Conable, Ted, Br Mgr, Riverside County Library System, Cabazon Branch, 50425 Carmen Ave, Cabazon, CA, 92230. Tel: 951-849-8234. p. 201

Conard, Michelle, Dir, Head Librn, Fairfield Public Library, 300 SE Second St, Fairfield, IL, 62837. Tel: 618-842-4516. p. 587

Conarton, Stephanie, Tech Serv Coordr, Delta Township District Library, 5130 Davenport Dr, Lansing, MI, 48917-2040. Tel: 517-321-4014. p. 1124

Conatser, Donna, Dir, Fentress County Public Library, 306 S Main St, Jamestown, TN, 38556-3845. Tel: 931-879-7512. p. 2103

Conboy, Andrea, Youth Serv Librn, Hopkinton Public Library, 13 Main St, Hopkinton, MA, 01748. Tel: 508-497-9777. p. 1025

Conboy, Michael, Asst Dir, Tech Serv, Reuben Hoar Library, 35 Shattuck St, Littleton, MA, 01460. Tel: 978-540-2600. p. 1029

Conboy, Michael, Asst Dir, Milford Town Library, 80 Spruce St, Milford, MA, 01757. Tel: 508-473-2145, Ext 211. p. 1035

Concepcion, Cattleya M, Assoc Dir, Research, Assoc Dir, User Serv, Georgetown University, Georgetown Law Library (Edward Bennett Williams Library), 111 G St NW, Washington, DC, 20001. Tel: 202-662-9144. p. 368

conchas, Karina, Circ Serv, Fresno County Public Law Library, Fresno County Courthouse, Ste 600, 1100 Van Ness Ave, Fresno, CA, 93724. Tel: 559-600-2227. p. 145

Condello, Vincent, Tech Serv Asst, Moravian College & Moravian Theological Seminary, 1200 Main St, Bethlehem, PA, 18018. Tel: 610-861-1679. p. 1912

Condit, Cynthia, Head, Faculty & Access Servs, University of Arizona Libraries, Daniel F Cracchiolo Law Library, James E Rogers College of Law, 1201 E Speedway, Tucson, AZ, 85721. p. 83

Condlin, Jessica, Ref & Instruction Librn, University of Dubuque Library, 2000 University Ave, Dubuque, IA, 52001. Tel: 563-589-3100. p. 749

Condon, Christina, Head, Access Serv, Merrimack College, 315 Turnpike St, North Andover, MA, 01845. Tel: 978-837-5994. p. 1040

Condon, Dillon, Pub Serv Asst, Pepperdine University Libraries, Irvine Graduate Campus Library, Lakeshore Towers III, 18111 Von Karman Ave, Irvine, CA, 92612. Tel: 949-223-2520. p. 171

Condon, Eileen, Dean, Univ Libr, Webster University, 101 Edgar Rd, Saint Louis, MO, 63119. Tel: 314-968-7154. p. 1277

Condon, Joanne, ILL & Cat Coordr, Derby Public Library, 1600 E Walnut Grove, Derby, KS, 67037. Tel: 316-788-0760. p. 804

Condon, Lorna, Sr Curator, Libr & Archives, Historic New England, 141 Cambridge St, Boston, MA, 02114-2702. Tel: 617-227-3956. p. 996

Condon, William, Ref & Instruction Librn, Prairie State College Library, 202 S Halsted St, Chicago Heights, IL, 60411-8200. Tel: 708-709-3552. p. 571

Condra, Karina, Ref Librn, University of Denver, Westminster Law Library, Sturm College of Law, 2255 E Evans Ave, Denver, CO, 80208. Tel: 303-871-6567. p. 278

Condy, Mark, Coll Mgr, United Theological Seminary, 4501 Denlinger Rd, Dayton, OH, 45426. Tel: 937-529-2290, Ext 4239. p. 1780

Cone, Walter, Access Serv, ILL, University of South Florida, Louis de la Parte Florida Mental Health Institute Research Library, 13301 Bruce B Downs Blvd, Tampa, FL, 33612-3899. Tel: 813-974-4471. p. 449

Coney, Jo Ellen, ILL, Sr Libr Tech, Roosevelt University, Robert R McCormick Tribune Foundation Library, 1400 N Roosevelt Blvd, Schaumburg, IL, 60173. Tel: 847-619-7982. p. 567

Confer, Stephanie, Ch, Haven Public Library, 121 N Kansas Ave, Haven, KS, 67543. Tel: 620-465-3524. p. 812

Congelio, Christiana, Youth Serv Mgr, Marysville Public Library, 231 S Plum St, Marysville, OH, 43040-1596. Tel: 937-642-1876, Ext 25. p. 1800

Congelosi, Catherine, Circ, Berkshire Athenaeum, One Wendell Ave, Pittsfield, MA, 01201-6385. Tel: 413-499-9480. p. 1046

Conger, Libby, Community Engagement Coord, Northfield Township Area Library, 125 Barker Rd, Whitmore Lake, MI, 48189. Tel: 734-449-0066. p. 1160

Congiardo, Wendy, Managing Librn, Thomas B Norton Public Library, 221 W 19th Ave, Gulf Shores, AL, 36542. Tel: 251-968-1176. p. 20

Congleton, Robert, Archivist, Librn, Rider University, 2083 Lawrenceville Rd, Lawrenceville, NJ, 08648. Tel: 609-896-5248. p. 1411

Coniglio, Mary, Libr Assoc, Tech Serv, Canizaro Library at Ave Maria University, 5251 Donahue St, Ave Maria, FL, 34142. Tel: 239-280-2428. p. 384

Conkey, Adam, Curator, Ellis County Historical Society Archives, 100 W Seventh St, Hays, KS, 67601. Tel: 785-628-2624. p. 812

Conklin, Claudia, Head, Pub Serv, Mississippi College, 130 W College St, Clinton, MS, 39058. Tel: 601-925-3943. p. 1214

Conklin, Curt E, Cat, Brigham Young University, Howard W Hunter Law Library, 256 JRCB, Provo, UT, 84602-8000. Tel: 801-422-3593. p. 2269

Conklin, David, Dir, Genesee District Library, 4195 W Pasadena Ave, Flint, MI, 48504. Tel: 810-732-0110. p. 1105

Conklin, Judith, Chief Info Officer, Library of Congress, James Madison Memorial Bldg, 101 Independence Ave SE, Washington, DC, 20540. Tel: 202-707-5000. p. 370

Conlan, Brian, Libr Dir, Warren Wilson College, 701 Warren Wilson Rd, Swannanoa, NC, 28778. Tel: 828-771-3061. p. 1718

Conlan, Moira, Asst Librn, The Frederick Gunn School, 99 Green Hill Rd, Washington, CT, 06793. Tel: 860-868-7334, Ext 224. p. 343

Conley, Helen, Circ & ILL, Supvr, Pub Serv, Smyth County Public Library, 118 S Sheffey St, Marion, VA, 24354. Tel: 276-783-2323. p. 2331

Conley, Jerome, Dean & Univ Librn, Miami University Libraries, 151 S Campus Ave, Oxford, OH, 45056. Tel: 513-529-3934. p. 1811

Conley, Jessica, Dir, Pub Libr Serv, University of Tulsa Libraries, 2933 E Sixth St, Tulsa, OK, 74104-3123. Tel: 918-631-3061. p. 1867

Conley, Kathleen, Ref & Instruction Librn, Harrisburg Area Community College, One HACC Dr, Harrisburg, PA, 17110-2999. Tel: 717-780-1186. p. 1940

Conley, Marlene, Tech Serv, Hazard Community & Technical College Library, One Community College Dr, Hazard, KY, 41701. Tel: 606-487-3146. p. 858

Conley, Michael, Br Mgr, Cape May County Library, Woodbine Branch, 800 Monroe St, Woodbine, NJ, 08270. Tel: 609-861-2501. p. 1395

Conley, Peggy, Asst Librn, Golconda Public Library, 126 W Main St, Golconda, IL, 62938. Tel: 618-683-6531. p. 594

Conley, Rachel, Spec Coll Archivist, Mariners' Museum & Park Library, 100 Museum Dr, Newport News, VA, 23606-3759. Tel: 757-591-7782. p. 2333

Conley, Sean, Archives & Spec Coll Librn, Siena College, 515 Loudon Rd, Loudonville, NY, 12211. Tel: 518-783-2539. p. 1566

Conley, Stephanie, Tech Serv Librn, Herkimer College Library, 100 Reservoir Rd, Herkimer, NY, 13350. Tel: 315-866-0300, Ext 8271. p. 1546

Conley, Tamara, Ref Librn, Cardinal Stafford Library, 1300 S Steele St, Denver, CO, 80210-2526. Tel: 303-715-3146. p. 273

Conley, Teresa, Circulation Specialist Supvr, Balch Springs Library-Learning Center, 12450 Elam Rd, Balch Springs, TX, 75180. Tel: 972-913-3000. p. 2144

Conley, Theresa R, Dir, Lyme Public Library, 482 Hamburg Rd, Lyme, CT, 06371-3110. Tel: 860-434-2272. p. 320

Conley-Abrams, Ingrid, Adjunct Ref Librn, Outreach Librn, City University of New York, 365 Fifth Ave, New York, NY, 10016-4309. Tel: 212-817-7054. p. 1582

Conlin, Marie, Libr Planner, Saint Louis County Library, 1640 S Lindbergh Blvd, Saint Louis, MO, 63131-3598. Tel: 314-994-3300. p. 1273

Conlin, Pam, Librn, Harrisville Free Library, 8209 Main St, Harrisville, NY, 13648. Tel: 315-543-2577. p. 1544

Conlon, Mary, Librn, Connecticut Valley Hospital, Hallock Medical Library, Page Hall, Silver St, Middletown, CT, 06457. Tel: 860-262-5059. p. 322

Conlon, Michael, Br Mgr, Chicago Public Library, Brighton Park, 4314 S Archer Ave, Chicago, IL, 60632. Tel: 312-747-0666. p. 556

Conlon, Susan, Youth Serv Dept Head, Princeton Public Library, 65 Witherspoon St, Princeton, NJ, 08542. Tel: 609-924-9529. p. 1436

Conn, Brian, Lead Libr Tech, Tech Info Spec, Department of Veterans Affairs, One Veterans Dr, Mail Stop 142 D, Minneapolis, MN, 55417. Tel: 612-467-4200. p. 1183

Conn, Debra, Head, Children's Servx, Upper St Clair Township Library, 1820 McLaughlin Run Rd, Upper St Clair, PA, 15241-2397. Tel: 412-835-5540. p. 2016

Conn, Donia, Assoc Prof of Practice, Simmons University, 300 The Fenway, Boston, MA, 02115. Tel: 617-521-2800. p. 2786

Conn, Janet Witten, Dir, New Martinsville Public Library, 160 Washington St, New Martinsville, WV, 26155. Tel: 304-455-4545. p. 2410

Conn, Krissy, Ch, Lone Star College System, CyFair Library, 9191 Barker Cypress Rd, Cypress, TX, 77433. Tel: 281-290-3214, 281-290-3219. p. 2197

Conn, Richard, Librn, Houston Community College - Southeast College, Eastside Campus Library, 6815 Rustic St, Houston, TX, 77087. Tel: 713-718-7050. p. 2194

Connaghan, Stephen, Univ Librn, Catholic University of America, 315 Mullen Library, 620 Michigan Ave NE, Washington, DC, 20064. Tel: 202-319-5055. p. 362

Connal, Wendy, Dir, Bill Memorial Library, 240 Monument St, Groton, CT, 06340. Tel: 860-445-0392. p. 314

Connell, Jewel, Libr Dir, West Virginia University Institute of Technology, 405 Fayette Pike, Montgomery, WV, 25136-2436. Tel: 304-442-3230. p. 2409

Connell, Joanne, Librn, Eastern Florida State College, Dr Frank Elbert Williams Learning Resource Ctr, 1311 N US 1, Titusville, FL, 32796-2192. Tel: 321-433-5036. p. 451

Connell, Ruth, Dir, Access Serv, Prof, Libr Sci, Valparaiso University, 1410 Chapel Dr, Valparaiso, IN, 46383-6493. Tel: 219-464-5360. p. 723

Connell, Virginia, Coordr, Libr Instruction, Concordia College, 901 S Eighth St, Moorhead, MN, 56562. Tel: 218-299-3237. p. 1187

Connell-Connor, Carol, Dir, Suffern Free Library, 210 Lafayette Ave, Suffern, NY, 10901. Tel: 845-357-1237. p. 1647

Connelly, Adrienne, Outreach Librn, Programming Librn, Art Gallery of Ontario, 317 Dundas St W, Toronto, ON, M5T 1G4, CANADA. Tel: 416-979-6642. p. 2686

Connelly, Correy, Circ Mgr, Erie County Public Library, 160 E Front St, Erie, PA, 16507. Tel: 814-451-6908. p. 1931

Connelly, Erika, Libr Dir, Kanawha County Public Library, 123 Capitol St, Charleston, WV, 25301. Tel: 304-343-4646. p. 2400

Connelly, Frank, Ref Librn, Larchmont Public Library, 121 Larchmont Ave, Larchmont, NY, 10538. Tel: 914-834-2281. p. 1562

Connelly, Jeff, Tech Serv Librn, South Park Township Library, 2575 Brownsville Rd, South Park, PA, 15129-8527. Tel: 412-833-5585. p. 2009

Connelly, Maureen, YA Serv, John C Hart Memorial Library, 1130 Main St, Shrub Oak, NY, 10588. Tel: 914-245-5262. p. 1641

Conner, Anne, Dir, Littleton Regional Healthcare, 600 St Johnsbury Rd, Littleton, NH, 03561. Tel: 603-444-9564. p. 1371

Conner, Carolina, Dir, Obion County Public Library, 1221 E Reelfoot Ave, Union City, TN, 38261. Tel: 731-885-7000, 731-885-9411. p. 2128

Conner, Julie, Librn, Plano Public Library System, L E R Schimelpfenig Library, 5024 Custer Rd, Plano, TX, 75023. Tel: 972-769-4200. p. 2227

Conner, Karyn, Asst Librn, Spindale Public Library, 131 Tanner St, Spindale, NC, 28160. Tel: 828-286-3879. p. 1717

Conner, Patricia, Libr Dir, Petros Public Library, 208 Main St, Petros, TN, 37845. Tel: 423-324-0101. p. 2124

Conner, Patricia, Libr Dir, Wartburg Public Library, 514 Spring St, Wartburg, TN, 37887. Tel: 423-346-0201. p. 2129

Conner, Shemeka, Dir, Noxubee County Library System, 145 Dr Martin Luther King Jr Dr, Macon, MS, 39341. Tel: 662-726-5461. p. 1225

Conner, Susan, Asst Dir, Palatine Public Library District, 700 N North Ct, Palatine, IL, 60067. Tel: 847-907-3600. p. 631

Conner, Susan, Asst Dir, Head, Tech, Swampscott Public Library, 61 Burrill St, Swampscott, MA, 01907. Tel: 781-596-8867. p. 1059

Conner, Tracy, Dir, Kankakee Community College, 100 College Dr, Kankakee, IL, 60901-6505. Tel: 815-802-8400. p. 604

Conners, Michelle, Libr Dir, Kennebunk Free Library, 112 Main St, Kennebunk, ME, 04043. Tel: 207-985-2173. p. 928

Conners, Susan, Librn, Berry Creek Community Library, 116 First Ave, Cessford, AB, T0J 0P0, CANADA. p. 2531

Connery, Dianne, Dir, Pottsboro Area Public Library, 104 N Main, Pottsboro, TX, 75076. Tel: 903-786-8274. p. 2229

Conness, Erinn, Youth Serv, Paul Sawyier Public Library, 319 Wapping St, Frankfort, KY, 40601-2605. Tel: 502-352-2665. p. 856

Connick, Nicole, Dir, Minburn Public Library, 315 Baker St, Minburn, IA, 50167. Tel: 515-677-2712. p. 770

Connley, Claire, Dir, Nampa Public Library, 215 12th Ave S, Nampa, ID, 83651. Tel: 208-468-5800. p. 527

Connolly, Andrea, Youth Serv Librn, Jaffrey Public Library, 38 Main St, Jaffrey, NH, 03452-1196. Tel: 603-532-7301. p. 1369

Connolly, Christina, Resource Librn, Worcester Public Library, Great Brook Valley, 89 Tacoma St, Worcester, MA, 01605-3518. Tel: 508-799-1729. p. 1073

Connolly, Danelle, Head, Children's Servx, Valley Cottage Free Library, 110 Rte 303, Valley Cottage, NY, 10989. Tel: 845-268-7700, Ext 124. p. 1656
Connolly, Erin, Youth Serv, Leelanau Township Public Library, 119 E Nagonaba St, Northport, MI, 49670. Tel: 231-386-5131. p. 1138
Connolly, Regina, Educ Librn, Salve Regina University, 100 Ochre Point Ave, Newport, RI, 02840-4192. Tel: 401-341-2330. p. 2035
Connolly, Sarah, Youth Serv Librn, South Saint Paul Public Library, 106 Third Ave N, South Saint Paul, MN, 55075. Tel: 651-554-3244. p. 1204
Connolly, Timothy, Dir, Admin & Finance, Washington Research Library Consortium, 901 Commerce Dr, Upper Marlboro, MD, 20774. Tel: 301-390-2000. p. 2766
Connor, Christina, Instruction & Emerging Tech Librn, Ramapo College of New Jersey, 505 Ramapo Valley Rd, Mahwah, NJ, 07430-1623. Tel: 201-684-7581. p. 1415
Connor, Ellen L, Dir, Sturm Memorial Library, 130 N Bridge St, Manawa, WI, 54949-9517. Tel: 920-596-2252. p. 2453
Connor, Kate, Coordr, Med Staff Spec, Frisbie Memorial Hospital, 11 Whitehall Rd, Rochester, NH, 03867. Tel: 603-335-8419. p. 1380
Connor, Lisa, Res & Instruction Librn, Sam Houston State University, 1830 Bobby K Marks Dr, Huntsville, TX, 77340. Tel: 936-294-3527. p. 2201
Connor, Su, Librn, West Woodstock Library, Five Bungay Hill Rd, Woodstock, CT, 06281. Tel: 860-974-0376. p. 349
Connors, Andrew, Dir, The Albuquerque Museum, 2000 Mountain Rd NW, Albuquerque, NM, 87104. Tel: 505-243-7255. p. 1460
Connors, Claire, Librn, Westwood Public Library, Islington, 280 Washington St, Westwood, MA, 02090. Tel: 781-326-5914. p. 1068
Connors, Grant, Assoc Dir, Edu Servs, Georgetown University, Dahlgren Memorial Library, Preclinical Science Bldg GM-7, 3900 Reservoir Rd NW, Washington, DC, 20007. Tel: 202-687-2914. p. 368
Connors, Laura, Br Mgr, Palm Beach County Library System, West Boca Branch, 18685 State Rd 7, Boca Raton, FL, 33498. Tel: 561-470-1600. p. 454
Connors, Mary Pat, Research Librn, Oneida County Historical Center, 1608 Genesee St, Utica, NY, 13502-5425. Tel: 315-735-3642. p. 1655
Connors-Suarez, Alice, Mgr, Miami-Dade Public Library System, Tamiami Branch, 13250-52 SW Eighth St, Miami, FL, 33184. Tel: 305-223-4758. p. 424
Connot, Jessica, Youth Librn, Spring Township Library, 78C Commerce Dr, Wyomissing, PA, 19610. Tel: 610-373-9888. p. 2025
Conod, Nancy, Exec Dir, Minisink Valley Historical Society Research Archives, c/o Port Jervis Free Library, 138 Pike St, 2nd Flr, Port Jervis, NY, 12771. Tel: 845-856-2375. p. 1621
Conolly, Erin, Br Mgr, Toledo-Lucas County Public Library, Sylvania, 6749 Monroe St, Sylvania, OH, 43560. Tel: 419-882-2089. p. 1825
Cononica, Julia, Chief Librn, Department of Veterans Affairs Library, 1400 Black Horse Hill Rd, Coatesville, PA, 19320-2040. Tel: 610-384-7711, Ext 6119. p. 1923
Cononie, Virginia Alexander, Coordr of Ref Serv, Pub Serv Librn, University of South Carolina Upstate Library, 800 University Way, Spartanburg, SC, 29303. Tel: 864-503-5735. p. 2070
Conover, John, Assoc Dir, Library & Information Science, Louisiana Universities Marine Consortium, 8124 Hwy 56, Chauvin, LA, 70344. Tel: 985-851-2875. p. 887
Conrad, Alexander, Dep Libr Dir, Pinal County Library District, 92 W Butte Ave, Florence, AZ, 85132. Tel: 520-866-6457. p. 61
Conrad, Bob, Dir, Chappaqua Public Library, 195 S Greeley Ave, Chappaqua, NY, 10514. Tel: 914-238-4779, Ext 208. p. 1516
Conrad, Chris, Br Mgr, Southwest La Plata Library District, Fort Lewis Mesa Public Library, 11274 Colorado State Hwy 140, Hesperus, CO, 81326. Tel: 970-588-3331. p. 278
Conrad, Craig S, Libr Tech II, Wilmington University Library, 320 N DuPont Hwy, New Castle, DE, 19720. Tel: 302-356-6876. p. 355
Conrad, Lana, Asst Dir, Tyrone-Snyder Public Library, 1000 Pennsylvania Ave, Tyrone, PA, 16686. Tel: 814-684-1133. p. 2014
Conrad, Ramona, Libr Dir, Katahdin Public Library, 20 Library St, Island Falls, ME, 04747. p. 927
Conrad, Ruth, Br Mgr, Atlantic County Library System, Egg Harbor Township Branch, One Swift Ave, Egg Harbor Township, NJ, 08234. Tel: 609-927-8664. p. 1417
Conrad, Suzanna, Dean, Univ Libr, Towson University, 8000 York Rd, Towson, MD, 21252. Tel: 410-704-2456. p. 980
Conrath, Russ, Dr, Outreach Librn, Newberry College, 2100 College St, Newberry, SC, 29108-2197. Tel: 803-321-5229. p. 2066
Conroy, Joyce, Dr, Dir, Historian, Roscoe Free Library, 85 Highland Ave, Roscoe, NY, 12776. Tel: 607-498-5574. p. 1633
Conroy, Margaret, Dir, Daniel Boone Regional Library, 100 W Broadway, Columbia, MO, 65203. Tel: 573-443-3161. p. 1242
Conroy, Michelle, Libr Dir, Bethel Library Association, Six Broad St, Bethel, ME, 04217. Tel: 207-824-2520. p. 917
Conroy, Patricia, Head, Ref, Cicero Public Library, 5225 W Cermak Rd, Cicero, IL, 60804. Tel: 708-652-8084. p. 571
Conroy, Terrye, Asst Dir, Legal Res Instruction, University of South Carolina, Law Library, 1525 Senate St, Columbia, SC, 29208. Tel: 803-777-5942. p. 2055
Consales, Judith C, Dir, University of California Los Angeles Library, Louise M Darling Biomedical Library, 12-077 Ctr for the Health Sciences, Los Angeles, CA, 90095. Tel: 310-825-1201. p. 169
Consalvi, Carrie, Librn, Mount San Jacinto College, Menifee Valley, 800/LRC Bldg, 2nd Flr, 28237 La Piedra Rd, Menifee Valley, CA, 92584. Tel: 951-639-5456. p. 230
Considine, Michael, Dir, Info Tech, Fordham University Libraries, 441 E Fordham Rd, Bronx, NY, 10458-5151. Tel: 718-817-3570. p. 1498
Consiglio, David, Dir of Assessment, Learning Spaces & Special Projects, Bryn Mawr College, 101 N Merion Ave, Bryn Mawr, PA, 19010-2899. Tel: 610-526-6534. p. 1916
Consolatore, Lauren, Instruction Librn, Mitchell College Library, 437 Pequot Ave, New London, CT, 06320. Tel: 860-701-5486. p. 329
Constant, Marcelynn, Br Librn, Wapiti Regional Library, James Smith Public Library, Box 3848, Melfort, SK, S0E 1A0, CANADA. Tel: 306-864-2955. p. 2746
Constant, Reginald, Pub Serv, Laney College, 900 Fallon St, Oakland, CA, 94607. Tel: 510-464-3495. p. 185
Constantine, Maria, Dir, Columbus Village Library, 112 W Broadway Ave, Columbus, NM, 88029. Tel: 575-531-2612. p. 1466
Constantine, Robert, Libr Assoc, University of New Hampshire Library, Chemistry, Parsons Hall, 23 College Rd, Durham, NH, 03824-3598. Tel: 603-862-1083. p. 1362
Constantinescu, Teodora, Librn, Jewish General Hospital, Dr Henry Kravitz Library-Institute of Community & Family Psychiatry, 4333 Cote Ste Catherine Rd, Montreal, QC, H3T 1E4, CANADA. Tel: 514-340-8210, Ext 5243. p. 2725
Constantinou, Constantia, Dean of Libr, Stony Brook University, W-1502 Melville Library, John S Toll Dr, Stony Brook, NY, 11794-3300. Tel: 631-632-7100. p. 1646
Conte, Jean, Genealogist, Washington County Historical Society, 135 W Washington St, Hagerstown, MD, 21740. Tel: 301-797-8782. p. 968
Conte, Jill, Head, Humanities & Soc Sci, New York University, 70 Washington Sq S, New York, NY, 10012-1019. Tel: 212-998-2622. p. 1599
Conte, Nora S, County Librn, San Benito County Free Library, 470 Fifth St, Hollister, CA, 95023-3885. Tel: 831-636-4097. p. 151
Conteh, Alhaji, PhD, Manuscript Librn, Howard University Libraries, Moorland-Spingarn Research Center, 500 Howard Pl NW, Washington, DC, 20059. Tel: 202-806-7480. p. 369
Contelmo, Celia, Br Librn, Boston Public Library, Grove Hall, 41 Geneva Ave, Dorchester, MA, 02121-3109. Tel: 617-427-3337. p. 992
Conteraz, Victoria, Distance Learning Librn, Montana State University-Billings Library, 1500 University Dr, Billings, MT, 59101. Tel: 406-657-1691. p. 1288
Conti, Carolyn G, Librn, Gladwyne Free Library, 362 Righters Mill Rd, Gladwyne, PA, 19035-1587. Tel: 610-642-3957. p. 1936
Contin, Laura, Sr Librn, Los Angeles Public Library System, Pacoima Branch Library, 13605 Van Nuys Blvd, Pacoima, CA, 91331-3613. Tel: 818-899-5203. p. 165
Contini, Wendy, Tech Serv Mgr, Dover Public Library, 525 N Walnut St, Dover, OH, 44622. Tel: 330-343-6123. p. 1782
Contreras, Andrew, Mgr, Texas Tech University Health Sciences Center El Paso, Medical Educ Bldg, Rm 2100, 5001 El Paso Dr, El Paso, TX, 79905. Tel: 915-215-4306. p. 2174
Contreras, Fawn, Head, Youth Serv, Valley Community Library, 739 River St, Peckville, PA, 18452. Tel: 570-489-1765. p. 1974
Contreras, Jeanette, Dir, Placentia Library District, 411 E Chapman Ave, Placentia, CA, 92870. Tel: 714-528-1925, Ext 200. p. 195
Contreras, Orquidia, Br Mgr, San Diego County Library, Vista Branch, 700 Eucalyptus Ave, Vista, CA, 92084-6245. Tel: 760-643-5100. p. 218
Contreras, Rachel, Mgr, Ward County Library, Barstow Branch, Community Bldg, Barstow, TX, 79719. Tel: 432-445-5205. p. 2220
Contreras, Stacy, Circ, Lake County Public Library, 1115 Harrison Ave, Leadville, CO, 80461-3398. Tel: 719-486-0569. p. 289
Contreras, Sylvia T, Librn, Mounce, Green, Meyers, Safi, Paxon & Galatzan, 100 N Stanton, Ste 1000, El Paso, TX, 79901. Tel: 915-532-2000. p. 2174
Conventini, Antonella, Tech Serv Librn, San Mateo County Law Library, 710 Hamilton St, Redwood City, CA, 94063. Tel: 650-363-4913. p. 200
Convery, Tara, Circ Coordr, Neumann University Library, One Neumann Dr, Aston, PA, 19014-1298. Tel: 610-361-2565. p. 1907
Conville, Bryon, Dir, Learning Res, Copiah-Lincoln Community College, Simpson County Ctr, 151 Co-Lin Dr, Mendenhall, MS, 39114. Tel: 601-849-0116. p. 1226
Conway, Ellen, Asst Dir, Cataloger, Falmouth Memorial Library, Five Lunt Rd, Falmouth, ME, 04105. Tel: 207-781-2351. p. 924
Conway, Emma Rose, Dir, Clinton Township Public Library, 110 S Elm St, Waterman, IL, 60556. Tel: 815-264-3339. p. 659
Conway, Jo, Br Mgr, Brazoria County Library System, Brazoria Branch, 620 S Brooks, Brazoria, TX, 77422-9022. Tel: 979-798-2372. p. 2135
Conway, Kathleen, Archivist, Friends of Historic Boonville, 614 E Morgan, Boonville, MO, 65233. Tel: 660-882-7977. p. 1238
Conway, Marilyn, Dir, Lewis County Public Library, 27 Third St, Vanceburg, KY, 41179. Tel: 606-796-2532. p. 876
Conway, Mark, Computer Support Spec, Web Serv, University of North Dakota, Thormodsgard Law Library, 215 Centennial Dr, Grand Forks, ND, 58202. Tel: 701-777-2204. p. 1735

Conway, Martha O'Hara, Dir, University of Michigan, Special Collections Research Center, Harlan Hatcher Graduate Library South, 913 S University Ave, Ann Arbor, MI, 48109-1190. Tel: 734-647-8151. p. 1080

Conway, Michael, Library Contact, Arizona Geological Survey at University of Arizona, 1955 E Sixth St, Tucson, AZ, 85721. Tel: 520-621-2352. p. 81

Conway, Patty, Communications & Media Mgr, Henrico County Public Library, 1700 N Parham Rd, Henrico, VA, 23229. Tel: 804-501-1900. p. 2325

Conway, Robert, Circ Mgr, University of Massachusetts at Boston, 100 Morrissey Blvd, Boston, MA, 02125-3300. Tel: 617-287-5948. p. 1000

Conway, Susan, Head Librn, Free Library of Philadelphia, Art, 1901 Vine St, Rm 208, Philadelphia, PA, 19103-1116. Tel: 215-686-5403. p. 1977

Conway, Susan, Head Librn, Free Library of Philadelphia, Literature, 1901 Vine St, Rm 207, Philadelphia, PA, 19103-1116. Tel: 215-686-5402. p. 1979

Conwell, Christine, City Librn, Moorpark City Library, 699 Moorpark Ave, Moorpark, CA, 93021. Tel: 805-517-6371. p. 180

Coogan, Carrie, Dep Dir, Pub Affairs, The Kansas City Public Library, 14 W Tenth St, Kansas City, MO, 64105. Tel: 816-701-3514. p. 1255

Coogan, Carrie, Deputy Director, Public Affairs, Kansas City Public Library, Lucile H Bluford Branch, 3050 Prospect Ave, Kansas City, MO, 64128. Tel: 816-701-3482. p. 1255

Cook, Amy, Circ Mgr, Flint River Regional Library System, 800 Memorial Dr, Griffin, GA, 30223. Tel: 770-412-4770. p. 481

Cook, Beth, Librn, Broughton Hospital, 1000 S Sterling St, Morganton, NC, 28655. Tel: 828-608-4276. p. 1704

Cook, Beth, Mgr, Youth & Outreach Serv, Laramie County Library System, 2200 Pioneer Ave, Cheyenne, WY, 82001-3610. Tel: 307-773-7227. p. 2492

Cook, Betty, Br Mgr, Oconee Regional Library, Glascock County Library, 738 Railroad Ave, Gibson, GA, 30810. Tel: 706-598-9837. p. 477

Cook, C Colleen, PhD, Dean of Libr, McGill University Libraries, McLennan Library Bldg, 3459 McTavish St, Montreal, QC, H3A 0C9, CANADA. Tel: 514-398-4677. p. 2726

Cook, Chanel, Outreach Serv Mgr, Erie County Public Library, 160 E Front St, Erie, PA, 16507. Tel: 814-451-6959. p. 1931

Cook, Charles, Tech Serv, Joe Barnhart Bee County Public Library, 110 W Corpus Christi St, Beeville, TX, 78102-5604. Tel: 361-362-4901. p. 2146

Cook, Chrissy, Br Mgr, Allendale-Hampton-Jasper Regional Library, Hampton County Library, 12 Locust St, Hampton, SC, 29924. Tel: 803-943-7528. p. 2046

Cook, Claudia, Dir, Missouri River Regional Library, 214 Adams St, Jefferson City, MO, 65101. Tel: 573-634-2464. p. 1252

Cook, Dani, Assoc Univ Librn, Learning & User Experience, University of California, San Diego, 9500 Gilman Dr, Mail Code 0175G, La Jolla, CA, 92093-0175. Tel: 858-534-1278. p. 154

Cook, Danita, Outreach Serv Librn, Preble County District Library, 450 S Barron St, Eaton, OH, 45320-2402. Tel: 937-456-4250. p. 1784

Cook, Dixie, Fac Mgr, Network Coordr, Ignacio Community Library, 470 Goddard Ave, Ignacio, CO, 81137. Tel: 970-563-9287. p. 286

Cook, Elise, Libr Dir, Red Oak Public Library, 200 Lakeview Pkwy, Red Oak, TX, 75154. Tel: 469-218-1230. p. 2230

Cook, Emily, Res & Instruction Librn, Washington & Lee University, University Library, 204 W Washington St, Lexington, VA, 24450-2116. Tel: 540-458-8643. p. 2329

Cook, Erin, Dir, Knoxville Public Library, 112 E Main St, Knoxville, PA, 16928. Tel: 814-326-4448. p. 1949

Cook, Hannah, Br Mgr, Mid-Continent Public Library, Blue Springs South Branch, 2220 South Hwy 7, Blue Springs, MO, 64014. Tel: 816-229-3571. p. 1250

Cook, Hansel, Archives Librn, Saint Mary's University, 923 Robie St, Halifax, NS, B3H 3C3, CANADA. Tel: 902-420-5508. p. 2621

Cook, Hope Marie, Curric Center Librn, Eastern Connecticut State University, 83 Windham St, Willimantic, CT, 06226-2295. Tel: 860-465-4456. p. 347

Cook, Jan, ILL, Tech Serv, Lake County Library, 1425 N High St, Lakeport, CA, 95453-3800. Tel: 707-263-8817. p. 156

Cook, Jean, Ref Coordr, Sci Librn, University of West Georgia, 1601 Maple St, Carrollton, GA, 30118. Tel: 678-839-6495. p. 469

Cook, Jenn, Br Mgr, Garfield County Public Library District, New Castle Branch, 402 W Main, New Castle, CO, 81647. Tel: 970-984-2346. p. 294

Cook, Jerilee, Head, Ref, Howell Carnegie District Library, 314 W Grand River Ave, Howell, MI, 48843. Tel: 517-546-0720, Ext 104. p. 1117

Cook, Joanita, Circ Mgr, Thomas County Public Library System, 201 N Madison St, Thomasville, GA, 31792-5414. Tel: 229-225-5252. p. 499

Cook, Joette, Ch Serv, Grand Prairie Public Library System, 901 Conover Dr, Grand Prairie, TX, 75051. Tel: 972-237-5700. p. 2185

Cook, Johnny, Librn, Hampton University, Architecture, Bemis Laboratory, Rm 208, Hampton, VA, 23668. Tel: 757-727-5443. p. 2323

Cook, Julie, Info Serv Librn, University of Washington Libraries, Engineering Library, Engineering Library Bldg, Box 352170, Seattle, WA, 98195-2170. Tel: 206-543-0740. p. 2381

Cook, Kathy, Mgr, Township of Springwater Public Library, 12 Finlay Mill Rd, Midhurst, ON, L9X 0N7, CANADA. Tel: 705-737-5650. p. 2657

Cook, Kevin, Electronic Res, State Law Library of Montana, 215 N Sanders, Helena, MT, 59601-4522. Tel: 406-444-3660. p. 1297

Cook, Kimberlee, Asst Dir, Access Serv, Emporia Public Library, 110 E Sixth Ave, Emporia, KS, 66801-3960. Tel: 620-340-6462. p. 806

Cook, Kimberly, Br Serv Coordr, Central Mississippi Regional Library System, 100 Tamberline St, Brandon, MS, 39042. Tel: 601-825-0100. p. 1212

Cook, Lareyna, Circ, Hondo Public Library, 2003 Ave K, Hondo, TX, 78861-2431. Tel: 830-426-5333. p. 2190

Cook, Linda, Librn, Inclusion Alberta, 11724 Kingsway Ave, Edmonton, AB, T5G 0X5, CANADA. Tel: 780-451-3055, Ext 225. p. 2537

Cook, Lisa M, Exec Secy, Warren County Law Library Association, 500 Justice Dr, Lebanon, OH, 45036. Tel: 513-695-1309. p. 1795

Cook, Marty, Asst Librn, Central Alabama Community College, 1675 Cherokee Rd, Alexander City, AL, 35010. Tel: 256-215-4291. p. 3

Cook, Mary, Libr Dir, Allendale Township Library, 6175 Library Ln, Allendale, MI, 49401. Tel: 616-895-4178, Ext 2. p. 1077

Cook, Mary, Asst Dir, Herrick District Library, 300 S River Ave, Holland, MI, 49423. Tel: 616-355-3724. p. 1115

Cook, Matthew, Head Librarian, Library Services, Capital University, One College & Main, Columbus, OH, 43209. Tel: 614-236-6614. p. 1772

Cook, Megan, Mgr, Pub Serv, Woodstock Public Library, 445 Hunter St, Woodstock, ON, N4S 4G7, CANADA. Tel: 519-539-4801. p. 2705

Cook, Michele, Libr Coord, Coast Mountain College Library, 5331 McConnell Ave, Terrace, BC, V8G 4X2, CANADA. Tel: 250-638-5407. p. 2577

Cook, Peter, Info Syst Mgr, Falmouth Public Library, 300 Main St, Falmouth, MA, 02540. Tel: 508-457-2555, Ext 2941. p. 1018

Cook, Phyllis, Libr Asst, Smoky Valley Library District, Manhattan Branch, 555 W Mineral St, Manhattan, NV, 89022. Tel: 775-487-2326. p. 1351

Cook, Rachel, Pub Relations Mgr, Alachua County Library District, 401 E University Ave, Gainesville, FL, 32601-5453. Tel: 352-334-3909. p. 406

Cook, Rebecca, Dir, Poultney Public Library, 205 Main St, Ste 1, Poultney, VT, 05764. Tel: 802-287-5556. p. 2291

Cook, Sam, Pub Serv, Syst Librn, Library Connection, Inc, 599 Matianuck Ave, Windsor, CT, 06095-3567. Tel: 860-937-8263. p. 2763

Cook, Sarah, Mgr, Libr Serv, Hanson Bridgett LLP, 425 Market St, 26th Flr, San Francisco, CA, 94105. Tel: 415-995-5855. p. 225

Cook, Shelly, Mgr, Delaware County Library, 429 S Ninth St, Jay, OK, 74346. Tel: 918-786-0103. p. 1851

Cook, Susan, Mgr, Washington County Library, Wausau Public Library, Town Hall, 1607 Second Ave, Wausau, FL, 32463. Tel: 850-638-2532. p. 388

Cook, Tatum, Libr Asst, Ohio School for the Deaf Library, 500 Morse Rd, Columbus, OH, 43214. Tel: 614-728-1414. p. 1774

Cook, Tracy, Dir, Statewide Libr Res, Montana State Library, 1515 E Sixth Ave, Helena, MT, 59620. Tel: 406-444-3115. p. 1296

Cook, William, Libr Dir, Eastern Maine Community College Library, Katahdin Hall, 354 Hogan Rd, Bangor, ME, 04401. Tel: 207-974-4640. p. 915

Cook-Roberts, Wendy, Libr Spec I, Camp Verde Community Library, 130 N Black Bridge Rd, Camp Verde, AZ, 86322. Tel: 928-554-8385. p. 57

Cooke, Angela, Asst Dir, North Castle Public Library, 19 Whippoorwill Rd E, Armonk, NY, 10504. Tel: 914-273-3887, Option 4. p. 1488

Cooke, Carol, Health Sci Librn, University of Manitoba Libraries, Neil John Maclean Health Sciences Library, Brodie Center Atrium, Mezzanine Level, 2nd Flr, 727 McDermot Ave, Winnipeg, MB, R3E 3P5, CANADA. Tel: 204-789-3342. p. 2595

Cooke, Emily, Chair, Coll Assessment, Coll Develop Librn, Atlantic School of Theology Library, 624 Francklyn St, Halifax, NS, B3H 3B4, CANADA. Tel: 902-496-7948. p. 2618

Cooke, Harry, Dr, Dir of Libr, Gaston College, 201 Hwy 321 S, Dallas, NC, 28034-1499. Tel: 704-922-6359. p. 1683

Cooke, Harry, Dr, Dir of Libr, Gaston College, Harvey A Jonas Library, 511 S Aspen St, Lincolnton, NC, 28092. Tel: 704-748-1050. p. 1683

Cooke, James, Asst Dir, Baltimore County Public Library, 320 York Rd, Towson, MD, 21204-5179. Tel: 410-887-6100. p. 979

Cooke, Kristen, Dep Dir, Arkansas State Library, 900 W Capitol, Ste 100, Little Rock, AR, 72201-3108. Tel: 501-682-2863. p. 100

Cooke, Lisa, Libr Assoc, Lee County Library System, Talking Books Library, 1651 Lee St, Fort Myers, FL, 33901. Tel: 239-533-4780. p. 404

Cooke, Michele, Librn, Lillian Perdido Bay Library, 34081 Ickler Ave N, Lillian, AL, 36549. Tel: 251-962-4700. p. 24

Cooke, Rachel, Univ Librn, Florida Gulf Coast University Library, 10501 FGCU Blvd S, Fort Myers, FL, 33965. Tel: 239-590-7606. p. 403

Cooke, Raeshelle, Mgr, Legal Research & Education, Adams & Reese LLP, Hancock Whitney Center, 701 Poydras St, Ste 4500, New Orleans, LA, 70139. Tel: 504-581-3234. p. 900

Cooke, Rhiannon, Circ Coordr, Radford University, 101 Elm Ave SE, 5th Flr, Roanoke, VA, 24013. Tel: 540-831-1875. p. 2345

Cooková, Anna, Archives Dir, Educ Dir, American Sokol Organization Library & Archives, 9126 Ogden Ave, Brookfield, IL, 60513. Tel: 708-255-5397. p. 545
Cooks, Katrina, Dir, Libr Serv, Augusta Technical College, 3200 Augusta Tech Dr, Augusta, GA, 30906. Tel: 706-771-4161, 706-771-4162. p. 467
Cookson, Melissa, Mgr, Cat Serv, Tarleton State University Library, 201 Saint Felix, Stephenville, TX, 76401. Tel: 254-968-9339. p. 2246
Cookson, Mikaela, Librn, Gowling WLG (Canada) Library, One First Canadian Pl, 100 King St W, Ste 1600, Toronto, ON, M5X 1G5, CANADA. Tel: 416-862-5735. p. 2689
Cool, Jacques, Dir, Centre d'Animation, de Developpement et de Recherche, 1940 Est Blvd Henri Bourassa, Montreal, QC, H2B 1S2, CANADA. Tel: 514-381-8891, Ext 241. p. 2722
Cool, Marc, Libr Dir, Haut-Saint-Jean Regional Library, Monseigneur W J Conway Public, 33 rue Irene, Edmundston, NB, E3V 1B7, CANADA. Tel: 506-735-4713. p. 2600
Cooley, Abigail, Libr Dir, Everett Public Library, 2702 Hoyt Ave, Everett, WA, 98201-3556. Tel: 425-257-8022. p. 2364
Cooley, Abigail, Libr Dir, Everett Public Library, Evergreen, 9512 Evergreen Way, Everett, WA, 98204. Tel: 425-257-8260. p. 2364
Cooley, Bridget, Commun Planning Librn, Pollard Memorial Library, 401 Merrimack St, Lowell, MA, 01852. Tel: 978-674-4120. p. 1029
Cooley, Carol, Chief Exec Officer, Dir of Libr, Saskatoon Public Library, 311-23rd St E, Saskatoon, SK, S7K 0J6, CANADA. Tel: 306-975-7558. p. 2749
Cooley, Ken, Assoc Univ Librn, Info Tech, Assoc Univ Librn, Tech Serv, University of Victoria Libraries, McPherson Library, PO Box 1800, Victoria, BC, V8W 3H5, CANADA. Tel: 250-721-8211. p. 2583
Cooley, Laura, ILL, Tech Serv, Saint John's College, 1160 Camino Cruz Blanca, Santa Fe, NM, 87505. Tel: 505-984-6045. p. 1476
Cooley Nichols, Sandra, Chair, University of Memphis, 406 Ball Hall, Memphis, TN, 38152. Tel: 901-678-2365. p. 2792
Cooley, Shannon, Br Mgr, Pine Forest Regional Library System - Headquarters, Richton Public, 210 Front St, Richton, MS, 39476. Tel: 601-788-6539. p. 1232
Coolidge, Bill, Br Mgr, Sonoma County Library, Rincon Valley Library, 6959 Montecito Blvd, Santa Rosa, CA, 95409. Tel: 707-537-0162. p. 204
Coolidge, Laurie, Librn, South Suburban Genealogical & Historical Society Library, 3000 W 170th Pl, Hazel Crest, IL, 60429-1174. Tel: 708-335-3340. p. 598
Cooling, Becka, Tech Serv Librn, Glendale Community College Library, 1500 N Verdugo Rd, Glendale, CA, 91208-2894. Tel: 818-240-1000, Ext 5581, 818-240-1000, Ext 5586. p. 148
Cooling, Heidi, Branch Services, Watonwan County Library, Lewisville Branch, 129 Lewis St W, Lewisville, MN, 56060. Tel: 507-435-2781. p. 1198
Coombs, Marita, Mgr, Somerville Public Library, East, 115 Broadway, Somerville, MA, 02145. Tel: 617-623-5000, Ext 2970. p. 1054
Coombs, Matthew, VPres, Libr & Info Tech, Hartnell College, 411 Central Ave, Salinas, CA, 93901. Tel: 831-755-6700, 831-755-6872. p. 2782
Coombs-Tuller, Janet, Librn, Library of the Legal Aid Society of Westchester County, 150 Grand St, Ste 100, White Plains, NY, 10601. Tel: 914-286-3400. p. 1664
Coomes, Phylis A, ILL, Libr Asst, Labette Community College Library, 1230 S Main St, Parsons, KS, 67357. Tel: 620-820-1167. p. 831
Coon Hamilton, Katherine, Bibliog Instruction/Ref, Los Angeles City College Library, 855 N Vermont Ave, Los Angeles, CA, 90029. Tel: 323-953-4000, Ext 1396. p. 162
Coon, Kathleen, Dir, Libr & Res Serv, Montgomery, McCracken, Walker & Rhoads LLP Library, 1735 Market St, Philadelphia, PA, 19103. Tel: 215-772-7611. p. 1983
Coon, Mary, Head, Br Libr, Albany Public Library, 161 Washington Ave, Albany, NY, 12210. Tel: 518-427-4300. p. 1482
Coon, Twilla, Dir, Mount Carmel Public Library, 727 N Mulberry St, Mount Carmel, IL, 62863. Tel: 618-263-3531. p. 620
Cooney, Courtney, Libr Asst, Ref, CMU Health, CMU College of Medicine, Educ Bldg, 1632 Stone St, Saginaw, MI, 48602. Tel: 989-746-7577. p. 1146
Cooney, Courtney, Libr Asst, Ref, CMU Health, St Mary's Branch, 800 S Washington, 2nd Flr, Saginaw, MI, 48601-2551. Tel: 989-746-7577. p. 1146
Cooney, Sharon, Assoc Archivist, New York State Division for Historic Preservation, 17 Rippleton Rd, Cazenovia, NY, 13035. Tel: 315-655-3200. p. 1515
Cooper, Alecia, Librn, Kinmundy Public Library, 111 S Monroe St, Kinmundy, IL, 62854. Tel: 618-547-3250. p. 605
Cooper, Alice, Dir, Libr Serv, Lancaster Community Library, 16 Town Center Dr, Kilmarnock, VA, 22482-3830. Tel: 804-435-1729. p. 2327
Cooper, Allison, Br Mgr, East Baton Rouge Parish Library, River Center, 250 North Blvd, Baton Rouge, LA, 70802. Tel: 225-389-4967. p. 883
Cooper, Ann, Head Librn, Greene County Public Library, Fairborn Community Library, One E Main St, Fairborn, OH, 45324-4798. Tel: 937-878-9383. p. 1835
Cooper, Brent, Instruction Librn, Research Librn, Brazosport College Library, 500 College Dr, Lake Jackson, TX, 77566. Tel: 979-230-3366. p. 2208
Cooper, Bryan, Dr, Assoc Dean, Tech & Digital Serv, Florida International University, 11200 SW Eighth St, Miami, FL, 33199. Tel: 305-348-2982. p. 421
Cooper, Bryan, Dr, Assoc Dean, Florida International University, 3000 NE 151st St, North Miami, FL, 33181-3600. Tel: 305-348-5764. p. 428
Cooper, Caitlin, Coord, Collection Dev, Mgmt & Acquisitions, Librn, Delgado Community College, City Park Campus, Marvin E Thames Sr Learning Resource Ctr, 615 City Park Ave, Bldg 7, New Orleans, LA, 70119. Tel: 504-671-5317. p. 900
Cooper, Carrie Lynn, Dean, College of William & Mary in Virginia, Earl Gregg Swem Library, One Landrum Dr, Williamsburg, VA, 23187. Tel: 757-221-3050. p. 2353
Cooper Cary, Amy, Head, Archival Colls & Institutional Repository, Marquette University, 1355 W Wisconsin Ave, Milwaukee, WI, 53233. Tel: 414-288-5901. p. 2458
Cooper, Cassandra, Br Mgr, Jackson/Hinds Library System, Ella Bess Austin Library, 420 W Cunningham Ave, Terry, MS, 39170. Tel: 601-878-5336. p. 1221
Cooper, Chris, Mr, Dir, Libr Serv, Humboldt County Library, 1313 Third St, Eureka, CA, 95501-0553. Tel: 707-269-1918. p. 141
Cooper, Christina, Libr Coord, Yavapai County Free Library District, Black Canyon City Community Library, 34701 S Old Black Canyon Hwy, Black Canyon City, AZ, 85324. Tel: 623-374-5866. p. 74
Cooper, Crys, Librn, Hocking Correctional Facility Library, 16759 Snake Hollow Rd, Nelsonville, OH, 45764-9658. Tel: 740-753-1917. p. 1806
Cooper, Darla, Dir, United States Air Force, McConnell AFB, Robert J Dole Community Ctr, Education Ctr Wing, 53476 Wichita St, Bldg 412, McConnell AFB, KS, 67221. Tel: 316-759-4207. p. 824
Cooper, Deana, Bus Off Mgr, Erie County Public Library, 160 E Front St, Erie, PA, 16507. Tel: 814-451-6980. p. 1931
Cooper, Donna-Lynne, Head, Children's Servx, Englewood Public Library, 31 Engle St, Englewood, NJ, 07631. Tel: 201-568-2215, Ext 243. p. 1401
Cooper, Elizabeth, Br Mgr, Benton County Public Library, Big Sandy Branch, 12 Front St, Big Sandy, TN, 38221. Tel: 731-593-0225. p. 2090
Cooper, Gerilyn, Asst Librn, Burlington Public Library, Patterson Creek Rd S, Burlington, WV, 26710. Tel: 304-289-3690. p. 2399
Cooper, Helen, Asst Librn, West Stockbridge Public Library, 21 State Line Rd, West Stockbridge, MA, 01266. Tel: 413-232-0300, Ext 308. p. 1066
Cooper, Hope, Metadata Librn, Syst Librn, Wesley Theological Seminary Library, 4500 Massachusetts Ave NW, Washington, DC, 20016-5690. Tel: 202-885-8658. p. 381
Cooper, James, Libr Mgr, Mississauga Library System, South Common, 2233 S Millway Dr, Mississauga, ON, L5L 3H7, CANADA. Tel: 905-615-4770. p. 2659
Cooper, James, Libr Mgr, Mississauga Library System, Woodlands, 3255 Erindale Station Rd, Mississauga, ON, L5C 1Y5, CANADA. Tel: 905-615-4825. p. 2659
Cooper, Jason, Head, Tech Serv, Transylvania University Library, 300 N Broadway, Lexington, KY, 40508. Tel: 859-233-8225. p. 863
Cooper, Jean, Circ Mgr, Chesapeake Public Library, South Norfolk Memorial, 1100 Poindexter St, Chesapeake, VA, 23324-2447. Tel: 757-410-7048. p. 2311
Cooper, Jim, Dir, Salt Lake County Library Services, 8030 S 1825 W, West Jordan, UT, 84088. Tel: 801-944-7504. p. 2274
Cooper, Judie, Dir, Lake Park Public Library, 529 Park Ave, Lake Park, FL, 33403. Tel: 561-881-3330. p. 415
Cooper, Karen, Librn, Halton County Law Association, 491 Steeles Ave E, Milton, ON, L9T 1Y7, CANADA. Tel: 905-878-1272. p. 2658
Cooper, Karina, Metadata Librn, American Institute of Physics, One Physics Ellipse, College Park, MD, 20740. Tel: 301-209-3177. p. 962
Cooper, Lachelle, Tech Support, University of the District of Columbia, David A Clarke School of Law, Charles N & Hilda H M Mason Law Library, Bldg 39, Rm B-16, 4200 Connecticut Ave NW, Washington, DC, 20008. Tel: 202-274-7310. p. 380
Cooper Mack, Cathi, Coordr, Tech Serv, South Carolina State University, 300 College St NE, Orangeburg, SC, 29115. Tel: 803-536-8633. p. 2067
Cooper, Mary, Dir, Stanton County Public Library, 103 E Sherman, Johnson, KS, 67855. Tel: 620-492-2302. p. 816
Cooper, Matt, Asst Dir, Pub Serv, Ohio State University LIBRARIES, Michael E Moritz Law Library, 55 W 12th Ave, Columbus, OH, 43210-1391. Tel: 614-688-0052. p. 1776
Cooper, Matthew, Libr Dir, Cincinnati Children's Hospital, Jack H Rubinstein Library, 3430 Burnet Ave, Ste 300, Cincinnati, OH, 45229. Tel: 513-636-4626. p. 1759
Cooper, Mavet, Libr Asst, Osage City Public Library, 515 Main St, Osage City, KS, 66523. Tel: 785-528-2620, 785-528-3727. p. 828
Cooper, Michael, Br Mgr, Florence County Library System, Lake City Public Library, 221 E Main St, Lake City, SC, 29560-2113. Tel: 843-394-8071. p. 2058
Cooper, Myles, Programming Librn, Mechanics' Institute Library, 57 Post St, Ste 504, San Francisco, CA, 94104-5003. Tel: 415-393-0101. p. 226
Cooper, Rachel, Librn, Gutenberg College Library, 1883 University St, Eugene, OR, 97403. Tel: 541-683-5141. p. 1878
Cooper, Regina, Exec Dir, Springfield-Greene County Library District, 4653 S Campbell Ave, Springfield, MO, 65810-1723. Tel: 417-882-0714. p. 1281

Cooper, Robyn, Libr Asst, Conway Springs City Library, 210 W Spring St, Conway Springs, KS, 67031. Tel: 620-456-2859. p. 803
Cooper, Sarah, Circ Mgr, University of West Georgia, 1601 Maple St, Carrollton, GA, 30118. Tel: 678-839-6495. p. 469
Cooper, Stephanie, Dir, Sussex County Community College Library, One College Hill Rd, Newton, NJ, 07860. Tel: 973-300-2162. p. 1428
Cooper, Susan, Youth Serv Mgr, Wichita Falls Public Library, 600 11th St, Wichita Falls, TX, 76301-4604. Tel: 940-767-0868, Ext 4245. p. 2258
Cooper, Tara, Dir, Johnson Free Public Library, 274 Main St, Hackensack, NJ, 07601-5797. Tel: 201-343-4169. p. 1406
Cooper, Teresa, Exec Dir/Librn, Horseshoe Bend District Library, 392 Hwy 55, Horseshoe Bend, ID, 83629-9701. Tel: 208-793-2460. p. 522
Cooper, Tina, Vice President, Finance & Admin, American Indian Higher Education Consortium, 121 Oronoco St, Alexandria, VA, 22314. Tel: 703-838-0400, Ext 101. p. 2776
Cooper, Tom, Dir, Webster Groves Public Library, 301 E Lockwood Ave, Webster Groves, MO, 63119-3102. Tel: 314-961-3784. p. 1286
Cooper, Tonya, Mgr, Brown County Public Library, Mary P Shelton Branch, 200 W Grant Ave, Georgetown, OH, 45121. Tel: 937-378-3197. p. 1804
Cooper, Virginia, Dir, Rake Public Library, 123 N Main St, Rake, IA, 50465. Tel: 641-566-3388. p. 778
Cooper, William, Librn, California Department of Corrections Library System, North Kern State Prison, 2737 W Cecil Ave, Delano, CA, 93215. Tel: 661-721-2345, Ext 5224. p. 207
Cooper, Yolanda, Vice Provost, Case Western Reserve University, 11055 Euclid Ave, Cleveland, OH, 44106. Tel: 216-368-3506. p. 1766
Cooperman, Lisa, University Curator, University of the Pacific Libraries, 3601 Pacific Ave, Stockton, CA, 95211. Tel: 209-932-3254. p. 250
Coote Pack, Andrea, Br Mgr, Hancock County Library System, Pearlington Public Library, 6096 First St, Pearlington, MS, 39572. Tel: 228-533-0755. p. 1212
Copas, Amy, Asst Librn, Macon County Public Library, Red Boiling Springs Branch, 335 E Main St, Red Boiling Springs, TN, 37150. Tel: 615-699-3701. p. 2108
Cope, Angie, Cat, University of Wisconsin-Milwaukee Libraries, American Geographical Society Library, Golda Meir Library, 2311 E Hartford Ave, Milwaukee, WI, 53211. Tel: 414-229-3984, 414-229-6282. p. 2461
Cope, Charla, ILL, Marshall County Public Library System, 1003 Poplar St, Benton, KY, 42025. Tel: 270-527-9969, Ext 129. p. 848
Cope, Melanie, Dir, Armoral Tuttle Public Library, 301 N Plymouth Ave, New Plymouth, ID, 83655. Tel: 208-278-5338. p. 527
Copeland, Ann, Head, Cat & Metadata Serv, Pennsylvania State University Libraries, 510 Paterno Library, University Park, PA, 16802. Tel: 814-865-2259. p. 2015
Copeland, Anne, Asst Dir, Bassett Historical Center, 3964 Fairystone Park Hwy, Bassett, VA, 24055. Tel: 276-629-9191. p. 2306
Copeland, Clayton A, PhD, Instr, University of South Carolina, 1501 Greene St, Columbia, SC, 29208. Tel: 803-777-3858. p. 2792
Copeland, Evonda, Supvr, Scottsdale Healthcare, Dr Robert C Foreman Health Sciences Library, Scottsdale Healthcare Osborn, 7400 E Osborn Rd, Scottsdale, AZ, 85251. Tel: 480-882-4870. p. 77
Copeland, Evonda, Supvr, Scottsdale Healthcare, Health Sciences Library, 9003 E Shea Blvd, Scottsdale, AZ, 85260. Tel: 480-323-3870. p. 77
Copeland, Hall, Mr, Curator, Alabama Supreme Court & State Law Library, Heflin-Torbert Judicial Bldg, 300 Dexter Ave, Montgomery, AL, 36104. Tel: 334-229-0564. p. 28
Copeland, Marcus, Dir, Student Servs & Academic Engagement, Southern Arkansas University Tech, 6415 Spellman Rd, Camden, AR, 71701. Tel: 870-574-4518. p. 92
Copeland, Sarah, Dir, Patron Serv, University of Tennessee at Chattanooga Library, 400 Douglas Ave, Dept 6456, Chattanooga, TN, 37403-2598. Tel: 423-425-4501. p. 2092
Copeland, Teresa, Ch, Crowley Public Library, 409 Oak St, Crowley, TX, 76036. Tel: 817-297-6707, Ext 2030. p. 2162
Coplen, Wendy, Dir, Finance & Grants, South Carolina State Library, 1500 Senate St, Columbia, SC, 29201. Tel: 803-734-0436. p. 2054
Copp, Steven, Br Mgr, Ocean County Library, Beachwood Branch, 126 Beachwood Blvd, Beachwood, NJ, 08722-2810. Tel: 732-244-4573. p. 1446
Coppedge, Lyn, Homebound Serv, Bedford Public Library System, 321 N Bridge St, Bedford, VA, 24523-1924. Tel: 540-586-8911, Ext 1114. p. 2306
Coppen, David Peter, Spec Coll & Archives Librn, University of Rochester, Sibley Music Library, 27 Gibbs St, Rochester, NY, 14604-2596. Tel: 585-274-1350. p. 1631
Coppernoll, Nic, Adult Serv, Grand Rapids Public Library, 111 Library St NE, Grand Rapids, MI, 49503-3268. Tel: 616-988-5400. p. 1111
Coppersmith, Erin, Librn, Kohler Public Library, 240 School St, Kohler, WI, 53044. Tel: 920-459-2923. p. 2445
Coppin, Tamikka, Br Mgr, Free Library of Philadelphia, Overbrook Park, 7422 Haverford Ave, Philadelphia, PA, 19151-2995. Tel: 215-685-0182. p. 1979
Coppola, Gene, Dir, Palm Harbor Library, 2330 Nebraska Ave, Palm Harbor, FL, 34683. Tel: 727-784-3332, Ext 3001. p. 435
Copsey, Mark, Coll Mgt & Syst Librn, Walla Walla University Libraries, 104 S College Ave, College Place, WA, 99324-1159. Tel: 509-527-2134. p. 2362
Cora, Pamela, Head, Access Serv, Baruch College-CUNY, 151 E 25th St, Box H-0520, New York, NY, 10010-2313. Tel: 646-312-1610. p. 1580
Coraccio, Kate, Libr Dir, Westborough Public Library, 55 W Main St, Westborough, MA, 01581. Tel: 508-366-3050 ext. 5280. p. 1066
Coradin, Jose, Dir, Tech Serv, George Mason University Libraries, Law Library, 3301 N Fairfax Dr, Arlington, VA, 22201-4426. Tel: 703-993-8100. p. 2317
Corall, Dawn, Circ Serv Coordr, Penn Area Library, 2001 Municipal Court, Harrison City, PA, 15636. Tel: 724-744-4414. p. 1941
Corbett, Amanda, Dir, Beaufort, Hyde & Martin County Regional Library, Old Court House, 158 N Market St, Washington, NC, 27889. Tel: 252-946-6401. p. 1720
Corbett, Caitlin, Head, Tech Serv, Langston University, 701 Sammy Davis Jr Dr, Langston, OK, 73050. Tel: 405-466-3412. p. 1851
Corbett, Kim, Dep Dir, Jackson/Hinds Library System, 300 N State St, Jackson, MS, 39201-1705. Tel: 601-968-5825. p. 1221
Corbett, Lauren, Dir, Res Serv, Wake Forest University, 1834 Wake Forest Rd, Winston-Salem, NC, 27109. Tel: 336-758-6136. p. 1726
Corbett, Matthew, Chief Exec Officer, Bradford-West Gwillimbury Public Library, 425 Holland St W, Bradford, ON, L3Z 0J2, CANADA. Tel: 905-775-3328, Ext 6101. p. 2632
Corbett, Monica, Law Librn, Huey P Long Memorial Law Library, State Capitol, 900 N Third St, 14th Flr, Baton Rouge, LA, 70802. Tel: 225-342-2414. p. 883
Corbett, Natalee, Libr Mgr, Kelso Public Library, 351 Three Rivers Dr, Ste 1263, Kelso, WA, 98626. Tel: 360-577-3390. p. 2367
Corbett, Susan, VPres, North Carolina Biotechnology Center Life Science Intelligence, 15 T W Alexander Dr, Research Triangle Park, NC, 27709. Tel: 919-541-9366. p. 1712
Corbett, Thomas B, Syst Librn, Scarborough Public Library, 48 Gorham Rd, Scarborough, ME, 04074. Tel: 207-396-6271. p. 939
Corbin, Ashley, Government Analyst, Florida Attorney General's Law Library, Collins Bldg, 107 W Gaines St, Rm 437, Tallahassee, FL, 32399-1050. Tel: 850-414-3300. p. 446
Corbin, Jennifer, Dir, Pub Serv, Stetson University, 421 N Woodland Blvd, Unit 8418, DeLand, FL, 32723. Tel: 386-822-7178. p. 393
Corbin, Kristin, Cat, Ser, Florida Gateway College, 149 SE College Pl, Lake City, FL, 32025-2006. Tel: 386-754-4339. p. 415
Corbin, Rachel, Libr Asst, Sampson-Clinton Public Library, Roseboro Public Library, 300 W Roseboro St, Roseboro, NC, 28382. Tel: 910-525-5436. p. 1682
Corbit, Brenna, Tech Serv Librn, Reading Area Community College, 30 S Front St, Reading, PA, 19602. Tel: 610-372-4721, Ext 5033. p. 2000
Corbit, Patty Jean, Br Mgr, White County Regional Library System, Lyda Miller Public, 2609 Hwy 367 N, Bald Knob, AR, 72010. Tel: 501-724-5452. p. 110
Corbitt, Janet, Staff Librn, West Virginia Northern Community College Library, New Martinsville Campus, 141 Main St, New Martinsville, WV, 26155-1211. Tel: 304-510-8781. p. 2418
Corby, Kristen, Libr Mgr, New Orleans Public Library, Norman Mayer Library, 3001 Gentilly Blvd, New Orleans, LA, 70122. Tel: 504-596-3100. p. 903
Corchado, Angel, Ref (Info Servs), University of Puerto Rico, Sector Las Dunas, Carr 653 Km 0.8, Arecibo, PR, 00612. Tel: 787-815-0000, Ext 3175. p. 2509
Corcoran, Katie, Asst Dir, Sandusky Library, 114 W Adams St, Sandusky, OH, 44870. Tel: 419-625-3834. p. 1819
Corcoran, Mary, Libr Dir, Williams Public Library, 113 S First St, Williams, AZ, 86046. Tel: 928-635-2263. p. 84
Cordeiro, Susan, Cataloger, Somerset Public Library, 1464 County St, Somerset, MA, 02726. Tel: 508-646-2829. p. 1053
Cordell, Douglas, Ser & Electronic Res Librn, Los Angeles County Museum of Art, 5905 Wilshire Blvd, Los Angeles, CA, 90036-4597. Tel: 323-857-6531. p. 163
Cordell, Jennifer, Libr Mgr, Central Arkansas Library System, Adolphine Fletcher Terry Branch, 2015 Napa Valley Dr, Little Rock, AR, 72212. Tel: 501-228-0129. p. 101
Cordell, Ryan, Assoc Prof, University of Illinois at Urbana-Champaign, Library & Information Science Bldg, 501 E Daniel St, Champaign, IL, 61820-6211. Tel: 217-333-3280. p. 2784
Corder, Bethany, Adult Programming, Outreach Coordr, Bulverde-Spring Branch Library, 131 Bulverde Crossing, Bulverde, TX, 78163. Tel: 830-438-4864. p. 2151
Cordes, Ellen, Head, Tech Serv, Yale University Library, Lewis Walpole Library, 154 Main St, Farmington, CT, 06032. Tel: 860-677-2140. p. 328
Cordes, Mary, Asst Dir, Circ, Hayner Public Library District, 326 Belle St, Alton, IL, 62002. Tel: 618-462-0677. p. 536
Cordova, Taylor, Head, Adult Serv, West Haven Public Library, 300 Elm St, West Haven, CT, 06516-4692. Tel: 203-937-4233. p. 346
Coree, Sara, Dir, Collins Public Library, 212 Main St, Collins, IA, 50055. Tel: 641-385-2464. p. 741
Corey, Brenda, Libr Assoc I, New Hampshire State Library, Gallen State Office Park, Dolloff Bldg, 117 Pleasant St, Concord, NH, 03301-3852. Tel: 603-271-2417, 603-271-3429. p. 1359

Corey, Denise, Chief Librn, Cumberland Public Libraries, 21 Acadia St, 2nd Flr, Amherst, NS, B4H 4W3, CANADA. Tel: 902-667-2135. p. 2615
Corey, Patricia, Libr Mgr, Haut-Saint-Jean Regional Library, Plaster Rock Public-School Library, 290A Main St, Plaster Rock, NB, E7G 2C6, CANADA. Tel: 506-356-6018. p. 2600
Corgel, Colleen, Libr Supvr, Circ & Media, Las Cruces Public Libraries, 200 E Picacho Ave, Las Cruces, NM, 88001-3499. Tel: 575-541-2098. p. 1471
Corkern, Wendy, Br Mgr, Livingston Parish Library, South Branch, 23477 Louisiana Hwy 444, Livingston, LA, 70754. Tel: 225-686-4170. p. 895
Corley, Betty, Libr Dir, Odenville Public Library, 200 Alabama St, Odenville, AL, 35120. Tel: 205-629-5901. p. 31
Corley, Christopher, Dean, Libr & Learning Res, Minnesota State University, Mankato, 601 Maywood Ave, Mankato, MN, 56001. Tel: 507-389-5953. p. 1181
Corlis, Timothy, Head, Presv, Rutgers University Libraries, Special Collections & University Archives, Alexander Library, 169 College Ave, New Brunswick, NJ, 08901-1163. Tel: 848-932-6147. p. 1425
Cormier, L J, Circ Mgr, Kingston Library, 55 Franklin St, Kingston, NY, 12401. Tel: 845-331-0507. p. 1560
Cornelia, Skye, Br Mgr, Jefferson Parish Library, Rosedale, 4036 Jefferson Hwy, Jefferson, LA, 70121. Tel: 504-838-4350. p. 897
Cornelisen, Wendy, Asst State Librn, Georgia Public Library Service, 5800 Jonesboro Rd, Morrow, GA, 30260. Tel: 404-235-7122. p. 491
Cornelison, Christina, Dir, Madison County Public Library, 507 W Main St, Richmond, KY, 40475. Tel: 859-623-6704. p. 874
Cornelison, Joy, Cat, Tech Serv, Donald W Reynolds Community Center & Library, 1515 W Main St, Durant, OK, 74701. Tel: 580-924-3486, 580-931-0231. p. 1846
Cornelius, Barbara, Col Librn, Dir, Austin College, 900 N Grand Ave, Ste 6L, Sherman, TX, 75090-4402. p. 2243
Cornelius, Blaine, Youth Serv, Cherry Valley Public Library District, 755 E State St, Cherry Valley, IL, 61016-9699. Tel: 815-332-5161, Ext 26. p. 553
Cornelius, Carrie, Librn, Haskell Indian Nations University, 155 Indian Ave, Lawrence, KS, 66046-4800. Tel: 785-749-8470, Ext 211. p. 819
Cornelius, Donald, Ms Curator, Hunterdon County Historical Society, 114 Main St, Flemington, NJ, 08822. Tel: 908-782-1091. p. 1403
Cornelius, Jason, Librn, Logan Library, 255 N Main, Logan, UT, 84321-3914. Tel: 435-716-9143. p. 2265
Cornell, John, Librn, California Department of Corrections Library System, San Quentin State Prison Library, Main St, San Quentin, CA, 94964. Tel: 415-454-4160, Ext 3384. p. 207
Cornell, John, Pres, Hillsboro Community Library, 158 Elenora St, Hillsboro, NM, 88042. Tel: 575-895-3349. p. 1469
Cornell, Melanie, Head, Coll Mgt, Syst Librn, University of New Hampshire School of Law, Two White St, Concord, NH, 03301. p. 1360
Cornell, Sarah, Tech Serv Supvr, Portsmouth Public Library, 175 Parrott Ave, Portsmouth, NH, 03801-4452. Tel: 603-427-1540. p. 1379
Cornelsen, Tamara, Dir, Fairview City Library, 115 S Sixth Ave, Fairview, OK, 73737-2141. Tel: 580-227-2190. p. 1847
Cornett, Jeanna, Dir, Pineville-Bell County Public Library, 214 Walnut St, Pineville, KY, 40977. Tel: 606-248-4812. p. 873
Cornett, Robin, Br Mgr, San Bernardino County Library, Wrightwood Branch, 6011 Pine St, Wrightwood, CA, 92397-1962. Tel: 760-249-4577. p. 213
Cornette, Jackie, Br Mgr, Watauga County Public Library, Western Watauga, 1085 Old US Hwy 421, Sugar Grove, NC, 28679. Tel: 828-297-5515. p. 1675
Cornish, Brittany, Br Mgr, Saint Mary's County Library, Charlotte Hall Branch, 37600 New Market Rd, Charlotte Hall, MD, 20622. Tel: 301-884-2211. p. 971
Cornish, Cassey, Med Librn, Cayuga Medical Center at Ithaca, 101 Dates Dr, Ithaca, NY, 14850. Tel: 607-274-4226. p. 1551
Corns, Diana, Cataloger, Libr Spec, Virginia Highlands Community College Library, 100 VHCC Dr, Abingdon, VA, 24210. Tel: 276-739-2542. p. 2301
Cornwall, Daniel, Tech Coordr, Alaska State Library, 395 Whittier St, Juneau, AK, 99801. Tel: 907-465-2920. p. 47
Cornwell, Mary Margaret, Undergrad Support Librn, Kennesaw State University Library System, 385 Cobb Ave NW, MD 1701, Kennesaw, GA, 30144. Tel: 470-578-6188. p. 483
Corona, Linda, Dir, Edgewater Free Public Library, 49 Hudson Ave, Edgewater, NJ, 07020. Tel: 201-224-6144. p. 1400
Coronado, Ian, Dean of Libr, Lane Community College Library, Library-Center Bldg, 4000 E 30th Ave, Eugene, OR, 97405-0640. Tel: 541-463-5220. p. 1879
Coronado, Jennifer, Scholarly Communications Librn, Butler University Libraries, 4600 Sunset Ave, Indianapolis, IN, 46208. Tel: 317-940-9549. p. 690
Coronel, Terri Ann, Electronic Res Librn, Ithaca College Library, 953 Danby Rd, Ithaca, NY, 14850-7060. Tel: 607-274-1892. p. 1552
Corporaal, Micah, Libr Supvr, Tempe Public Library, 3500 S Rural Rd, Tempe, AZ, 85282. Tel: 480-350-5554. p. 80
Corpus, Paula, Asst Librn, Ladd Public Library District, 125 N Main St, Ladd, IL, 61329. Tel: 815-894-3254. p. 606
Corpuz, Laura, ILL Coordr, Bradley University, 1501 W Bradley Ave, Peoria, IL, 61625. Tel: 309-677-2850. p. 634
Corrado, Marie, Libr Mgr, Carnegie Museum of Natural History Library, 4400 Forbes Ave, Pittsburgh, PA, 15213-4080. Tel: 412-622-3264. p. 1992
Corral, Kristina, Children's Serv Supvr, McAllen Public Library, 4001 N 23rd St, McAllen, TX, 78504. Tel: 956-681-3000. p. 2217
Corrales, Mario, Supvr, Hawaii State Circuit Court-Second Circuit, 2145 Main St, Rm 207, Wailuku, HI, 96793. Tel: 808-244-2959. p. 514
Correa, Dale, PhD, Ms, Librn, University of Texas Libraries, Middle Eastern Library Program, 2501 Speedway, Austin, TX, 78712. Tel: 512-495-4322. p. 2143
Correa, Madlyn, Head Librn, Massachusetts Trial Court Law Libraries, Superior Courthouse, 186 S Main St, Fall River, MA, 02721. Tel: 508-491-3475. p. 1018
Correa, Mary-Alice, Circ Serv, Columbia Basin College Library, 2600 N 20th Ave, Pasco, WA, 99301. Tel: 509-542-5528. p. 2373
Correa, Sarah, Br Mgr, San Bernardino County Library, Joshua Tree Branch, 6465 Park Blvd, Joshua Tree, CA, 92252. Tel: 760-366-8615. p. 213
Corredor, Javier, Mgr, Miami-Dade Public Library System, Kendall Branch, 9101 SW 97th Ave, Miami, FL, 33176. Tel: 305-279-0520. p. 423
Corredor, Javier, Mgr, Miami-Dade Public Library System, Sunset Branch, 10855 SW 72 St, No 13-14, Miami, FL, 33173. Tel: 305-270-6368. p. 424
Corredor-Hyland, Marel, Human Res, Team Leader, Case Western Reserve University, 11055 Euclid Ave, Cleveland, OH, 44106. Tel: 216-368-2990. p. 1766
Correia, Melissa, Dir, Newark Public Library, 121 High St, Newark, NY, 14513-1492. Tel: 315-331-4370. p. 1605
Correll, Melissa, Information Literacy Coord, Arcadia University, 450 S Easton Rd, Glenside, PA, 19038. Tel: 215-572-8528. p. 1937
Corrente, Jill, Dir, Enabling Infrastructure, Douglas County Libraries, 100 S Wilcox, Castle Rock, CO, 80104. Tel: 303-688-7631. p. 270
Corrente, William, Electronic Res/Ser Librn, United States Naval War College Library, 686 Cushing Rd, Newport, RI, 02841-1207. Tel: 401-841-4345. p. 2035
Corriell, Suzanne, Librn, United States Court of Appeals, United States Courthouse, 1000 E Main St, Richmond, VA, 23219-3517. Tel: 804-916-2322. p. 2342
Corrigan, Andy, Assoc Dean, Tulane University, 7001 Freret St, New Orleans, LA, 70118-5682. Tel: 504-865-5679. p. 903
Corrigan, Ellen, Cat/Digitization Libr, Eastern Illinois University, 600 Lincoln Ave, Charleston, IL, 61920. Tel: 217-581-8456. p. 552
Corrigan, Katie, Ad, Seekonk Public Library, 410 Newman Ave, Seekonk, MA, 02771. Tel: 508-336-8230, Ext 56143. p. 1052
Corrigan-Buchen, Mary Beth, Dir, Commun Engagement, Mount Prospect Public Library, Ten S Emerson St, Mount Prospect, IL, 60056. Tel: 847-253-5675. p. 621
Corriveau, Josee, Librn, College de Rosemont (Cegep) Bibliotheque, 6400 16th Ave, Montreal, QC, H1X 2S9, CANADA. Tel: 514-376-1620, Ext 7265. p. 2723
Corscadden, Laura, Libr Dir, Fundy Library Region, Saint John Free Public Library, Central Branch, One Market Sq, Saint John, NB, E2L 4Z6, CANADA. Tel: 506-643-7236. p. 2605
Corscadden, Laura, Libr Dir, Fundy Library Region, Saint John Free Public Library, West Branch, Lancaster Mall, 621 Fairville Blvd, Saint John, NB, E2M 4X5, CANADA. Tel: 506-643-7260. p. 2605
Corsiga, Carina, Access Serv Mgr, University of Texas at Dallas, 800 W Campbell Rd, Richardson, TX, 75080. Tel: 972-883-2958. p. 2231
Corsillo, Gretchen, Dir, Rutherford Public Library, 150 Park Ave, Rutherford, NJ, 07070. Tel: 201-939-8600. p. 1441
Corso, Sarah, YA Librn, Oak Creek Public Library, Drexel Town Sq, 8040 S Sixth St, Oak Creek, WI, 53154. Tel: 414-766-7900. p. 2465
Cortez, Antony, Chief Financial Officer, Rockford Public Library, 214 N Church St, Rockford, IL, 61101-1023. Tel: 815-965-7606. p. 642
Cortez, Cassandra, Libr Dir, Lytle Public Library, 19325 W FM Rd, 2790 S, Lytle, TX, 78052. Tel: 830-709-4142. p. 2215
Cortez, Elisa, Access Serv, Loma Linda University, 11072 Anderson St, Loma Linda, CA, 92350-0001. Tel: 909-558-4581. p. 157
Cortez, Luticia, Br Mgr, Lafourche Parish Public Library, Choctaw Branch, 1887 Choctaw Rd, Thibodaux, LA, 70301. Tel: 985-633-6453. p. 911
Cortez, Maria, Asst Librn, Yoakum County / Cecil Bickley Library, 205 W Fourth St, Denver City, TX, 79323. Tel: 806-592-2754. p. 2170
Cortez, Peter, Assoc Univ Librn, Resource Management, University of Texas Rio Grande Valley, 1201 W University Blvd, Edinburg, TX, 78541-2999. Tel: 956-665-2758. p. 2173
Cortner, Callie, Dir, Miami Public Library, 200 N Main St, Miami, OK, 74354. Tel: 918-541-2292. p. 1853
Corvidae, Indigo, Curator, Rare Bks, Kalamazoo College Library, 1200 Academy St, Kalamazoo, MI, 49006-3285. Tel: 269-337-5762. p. 1121
Corwin, Rhonda, Librn, Ruth Dole Memorial Library, 121 N Burrton Ave, Burrton, KS, 67020. Tel: 620-463-7902. p. 800
Cory, Shelly, Dir, Roy R Estle Memorial Library, 1308 Walnut St, Dallas Center, IA, 50063. Tel: 515-992-3185. p. 743
Coryell, Lori, Libr Dir, Chelsea District Library, 221 S Main St, Chelsea, MI, 48118-1267. Tel: 734-475-8732, Ext 206. p. 1090

Cotter, Catherine, Assoc Dean, University of New Brunswick Libraries, Gerard V La Forest Law Library, Law School, 2nd Flr, 41 Dineen Dr, Fredericton, NB, E3B 5A3, CANADA. Tel: 506-477-3265. p. 2602

Cotter, Kerry J, Librn, Northern Virginia Community College Libraries, Woodbridge Library, Bldg WAS, Rm 230, 15200 Neabsco Mills Rd, Woodbridge, VA, 22191. Tel: 703-878-5733. p. 2304

Cotter, Teresa, Ch Serv, Port Chester-Rye Brook Public Library, One Haseco Ave, Port Chester, NY, 10573. Tel: 914-939-6710, Ext 108. p. 1620

Cotterell, Seth, Libr & Archives Asst, California Academy of Sciences Library, Golden Gate Park, 55 Music Concourse Dr, San Francisco, CA, 94118. Tel: 415-379-5487. p. 223

Cotterman, Billie, Head, Access Serv & Electronic Res, Nebraska Wesleyan University, 5000 St Paul Ave, Lincoln, NE, 68504. Tel: 402-465-2404. p. 1322

Cotterman, Paula, Br Mgr, Perry County District Library, Junction City Branch, 108 W Main St, Junction City, OH, 43748. Tel: 740-987-7646. p. 1806

Cotto, Leticia, Customer Experience Officer, Hartford Public Library, 500 Main St, Hartford, CT, 06103. Tel: 860-695-6335. p. 317

Cotton, Cyndy, Exec Dir, Osterville Village Library, 43 Wianno Ave, Osterville, MA, 02655. Tel: 508-428-5757. p. 1044

Cotton, D Page, Mr, Dir, Libr Serv, Ivy Tech Community College, 220 Dean Johnson Blvd, South Bend, IN, 46601. Tel: 574-289-7001, Ext 1125. p. 718

Cotton, Dakota, Univ Archivist, Athens State University, 407 E Pryor St, Athens, AL, 35611. Tel: 256-216-6663. p. 5

Cotton, Dustin, Br Mgr, Livingston Parish Library, Albany Springfield, 26941 Louisiana Hwy 43, Hammond, LA, 70403. Tel: 225-686-4130. p. 895

Cotton, Gregory, Dir, Cornell College, 620 Third St SW, Mount Vernon, IA, 52314-1012. Tel: 319-895-4454. p. 771

Cotton, Lisa, Library Contact, Lafayette Public Library, East Regional Library, 215 La Nueville Rd, Youngsville, LA, 70592. Tel: 337-445-3168. p. 892

Cotton, Stephanie, Dir, Mendham Township Library, Two W Main St, Brookside, NJ, 07926. Tel: 973-543-4018. p. 1393

Cottonaro, Sarah, Dir, Alsip-Merrionette Park Public Library District, 11960 S Pulaski Rd, Alsip, IL, 60803. Tel: 708-371-5666. p. 536

Cottone, Alisa, Dir, Pension Benefit Guaranty Corporation, 1200 K St NW, Ste 360, Washington, DC, 20005-4026. Tel: 202-326-4000, Ext 3091. p. 374

Cottone, Cathy, Genealogist, Lyon Township Public Library, 27005 S Milford Rd, South Lyon, MI, 48178. Tel: 248-437-8800. p. 1150

Cottoy, Fay, Ft Lauderdale Campus Libr Dir, Keiser University Library System, 1500 NW 49th St, Fort Lauderdale, FL, 33309. Tel: 954-351-4035. p. 401

Cottrell, Genevieve, Cataloger, Southern Adventist University, 4851 Industrial Dr, Collegedale, TN, 37315. Tel: 423-236-2795. p. 2094

Cottrell, Jeff, Ref (Info Servs), Parkersburg & Wood County Public Library, 3100 Emerson Ave, Parkersburg, WV, 26104-2414. Tel: 304-420-4587. p. 2411

Cottrell, Paula, Library Asst, Digital Projects, East Texas Baptist University, One Tiger Dr, Marshall, TX, 75670-1498. Tel: 903-923-2258. p. 2215

Cottrell, Stanley, Tech Serv Librn, Southern Adventist University, 4851 Industrial Dr, Collegedale, TN, 37315. Tel: 423-236-2798. p. 2094

Cottrill, Beverly, Dir, Gassaway Public Library, 536 Elk St, Gassaway, WV, 26624. Tel: 304-364-8292. p. 2403

Cottrill, Jennifer, Libr Dir, Midlothian Public Library, 14701 S Kenton Ave, Midlothian, IL, 60445-4122. Tel: 708-535-2027. p. 617

Couch, Carol, Ch, Britt Public Library, 132 Main Ave S, Britt, IA, 50423-1627. Tel: 641-843-4245. p. 736

Couch, Deb, Ch, Athens County Public Libraries, Glouster Public, 20 Toledo St, Glouster, OH, 45732. Tel: 740-767-3670. p. 1805

Couch, Marilla, Libr Dir, Mexico Free Public Library, 134 Main St, Mexico, ME, 04257. Tel: 207-364-3281. p. 931

Couch, Matt, Mgr, Omaha Public Library, 215 S 15th St, Omaha, NE, 68102-1629. Tel: 402-444-4800. p. 1329

Couch, Nena, Curator, Ohio State University LIBRARIES, Jerome Lawrence & Robert E Lee Theatre Research Institute, 1430 Lincoln Tower, 1800 Cannon Dr, Columbus, OH, 43210-1230. Tel: 614-292-6614. p. 1775

Couck, Lynn, Syst Mgr, Lenox Township Library, 58976 Main St, New Haven, MI, 48048-2685. Tel: 586-749-3430. p. 1137

Coude, Dino, Libr Mgr, Bibliotheque de Farnham, Inc, 479 rue Hotel de Ville, Farnham, QC, J2N 2H3, CANADA. Tel: 450-293-3326, Ext 268. p. 2712

Coufal, Robyn, Dir, Vernon Public Library, 4441 Peterboro St, Vernon, NY, 13476. Tel: 315-829-2463. p. 1657

Coughlin, Carol, Dir, Virginia Institute of Marine Science, College of William & Mary, 1208 Greate Rd, Gloucester Point, VA, 23062. Tel: 804-684-7114. p. 2322

Coughran, Kimberly, Libr Dir, Linda Sokol Francis Brookfield Library, 3541 Park Ave, Brookfield, IL, 60513. Tel: 708-485-6917. p. 545

Coulas, Kristen, Chief Librn, Canadian Army Command & Staff College, 317 Ontario St, Kingston, ON, K7K 7B4, CANADA. Tel: 613-541-5010, Ext 5815. p. 2650

Coulbourne, Eric, Head, Acq & Coll Develop, Yeshiva University Libraries, Dr Lillian & Dr Rebecca Chutick Law Library, Benjamin N Cardozo School of Law, 55 Fifth Ave, New York, NY, 10003-4301. Tel: 212-790-0223. p. 1604

Coulombe, Mathieu, Libr Serv Mgr, Cegep de La Pocatiere, 140 Fourth Ave, La Pocatiere, QC, G0R 1Z0, CANADA. Tel: 418-856-1525, Ext 2229. p. 2714

Coulter, Ann, Dir, Libr Serv, Southwestern Community College, 1501 W Townline St, Creston, IA, 50801. Tel: 641-782-1340. p. 743

Coulter, C, Ms, Librn, Illinois Department of Corrections, 2021 Kentville Rd, Kewanee, IL, 61443. Tel: 309-852-4601. p. 605

Coulter, Jennifer, Dir & Librn, Pound Ridge Library, 271 Westchester Ave, Pound Ridge, NY, 10576. Tel: 914-764-5085. p. 1624

Coulter, Nate, Exec Dir, Central Arkansas Library System, 100 Rock St, Little Rock, AR, 72201-4698. Tel: 501-918-3037. p. 101

Coulter, Sandy, Tech Asst, Antioch College, One Morgan Pl, Yellow Springs, OH, 45387-1694. Tel: 937-769-1240. p. 1835

Coulthard, Joanna, Dir of Libr, Georgian College, 825 Memorial Ave, Orillia, ON, L3V 6S2, CANADA. Tel: 705-329-3101. p. 2663

Council, Floyd, Regional Mgr, Saint Louis Public Library, Julia Davis Branch, 4415 Natural Bridge Rd, Saint Louis, MO, 63115. Tel: 314-383-3021. p. 1275

Council, Floyd G, Sr, Exec Dir, Birmingham Public Library, 2100 Park Pl, Birmingham, AL, 35203-2744. Tel: 205-226-3600. p. 7

Counihan, Martha, Archivist, The College of New Rochelle, 29 Castle Pl, New Rochelle, NY, 10805-2308. Tel: 914-654-5345. p. 1577

Counterman, Amanda, Librn, Monroe County Law Library, Court House, 610 Monroe St, Stroudsburg, PA, 18360. Tel: 570-517-3332. p. 2011

Counterman, Traci, Br Mgr, Branch District Library, Sherwood Branch, 118 E Sherman St, Sherwood, MI, 49089. Tel: 517-741-7976. p. 1093

Countryman, Mandy, Dir of Educ, Shodair Children's Hospital, 2755 Colonial Dr, Helena, MT, 59601. Tel: 406-444-7564. p. 1297

Counts, Peggy, Br Mgr, Massanutten Regional Library, Grottoes Branch, 601 Dogwood Ave, Grottoes, VA, 24441. Tel: 540-434-4475, Ext 3. p. 2324

Coupe, Jennifer, Area Librn, Cariboo Regional District Library, 180 N Third Ave, Ste A, Williams Lake, BC, V2G 2A4, CANADA. Tel: 250-305-2182, 250-392-3630. p. 2584

Courcelles, Michel, Librn, INRS - Institut Armand-Frappier - Bibliotheque, 531 blvd des Prairies, Laval, QC, H7V 1B7, CANADA. Tel: 450-687-5010, Ext 4265. p. 2715

Courchane, Samantha, Libr Asst, Stone Child College, 8294 Upper Box Elder Rd, Box Elder, MT, 59521. Tel: 406-395-4875, Ext 1214. p. 1289

Couri, Sarah, Br Mgr, Peoria Public Library, McClure, 315 W McClure Ave, Peoria, IL, 61604-3556. Tel: 309-497-2701. p. 634

Courier, William, Bus Mgr, Fac Mgr, Cambridge Public Library, 449 Broadway, Cambridge, MA, 02138. Tel: 617-349-4041. p. 1004

Cournoyer, Sarah, Youth Serv Librn, Beaver Dam Community Library, 311 N Spring St, Beaver Dam, WI, 53916-2043. Tel: 920-887-4631, Ext 105. p. 2423

Coursey, Darlene, Libr Asst, Monroe Public Library, 19 Plains Rd, Monroe, NH, 03771. Tel: 603-638-4736. p. 1374

Court, Alexandra, Central Servs Mgr, Div Chief, Bibliotheques de Montreal, Pavillon Prince, 801 rue Brennan, 5e etage, Montreal, QC, H3C 0G4, CANADA. Tel: 514-872-6563. p. 2718

Courtemanche, Brian, Libr Dir, Endicott College Library, 376 Hale St, Beverly, MA, 01915. Tel: 978-232-2279. p. 989

Courtney, Aida, Head, Customer & Info Serv, Parsippany-Troy Hills Free Public Library, 449 Halsey Rd, Parsippany, NJ, 07054. Tel: 973-887-5150. p. 1433

Courtney, Julia, Coll Curator, Art Complex Museum, 189 Alden St, Duxbury, MA, 02332. Tel: 781-934-6634, Ext 217. p. 1015

Courtney, Latoya, Br Mgr, San Bernardino County Library, Loma Linda Branch, 25581 Barton Rd, Loma Linda, CA, 92354-3125. Tel: 909-796-8621. p. 213

Courtney, Latoya, Interim Br Mgr, San Bernardino County Library, Sam J Racadio Library & Environmental Learning Center, 7863 Central Ave, Highland, CA, 92346-4107. Tel: 909-425-4700. p. 213

Courtney, Marian, Libr Operations Mgr, Saint Joseph's University, Francis A Drexel Library, 5600 City Ave, Philadelphia, PA, 19131-1395. Tel: 610-660-1905. p. 1985

Courtney, Ralph, Ref & Instruction, University of Alaska Anchorage, Consortium Library, 3211 Providence Dr, Anchorage, AK, 99508-8176. Tel: 907-786-1871. p. 43

Courtney, Sandy, Youth Serv Librn, Monson Free Library, Two High St, Monson, MA, 01057-1095. Tel: 413-267-3866. p. 1036

Courtney, Sarah, Ad, South Hadley Public Library, Gaylord Memorial Library, 47 College St, South Hadley, MA, 01075. Tel: 413-538-5047. p. 1054

Courtney, Sherry, Librn, Missouri Department of Corrections, Northeast Correctional Center, 13698 Airport Rd, Bowling Green, MO, 63334. Tel: 573-324-9975. p. 1252

Courtney, Stephanie, Libr Spec, Horry-Georgetown Technical College, 2050 Hwy 501 E, Conway, SC, 29526-9521. Tel: 843-349-7596. p. 2057

Courvelle, Penelope, Br Mgr, Cameron Parish Library, Hackberry Branch, 983 Main St, Hackberry, LA, 70645. Tel: 337-762-3978. p. 886

Cousar, Harnethia, Ref (Info Servs), United States Department of Health & Human Services, National Center for Health Statistics Staff Research Library, 3311 Toledo Rd, Rm 2403, Hyattsville, MD, 20782. Tel: 301-458-4775. p. 975

Cousar, Judi, ILL, York County Library, 138 E Black St, Rock Hill, SC, 29730. Tel: 803-203-9220. p. 2068

Couser, Yvette, Dir, Merrimack Public Library, 470 Daniel Webster Hwy, Merrimack, NH, 03054-3694. Tel: 603-424-5021. p. 1373

Cousin, Heather, City Librn, Torrance Public Library, 3301 Torrance Blvd, Torrance, CA, 90503. Tel: 310-618-5950. p. 253

Cousin, Heather, City Librn, Torrance Public Library, El Retiro, 126 Vista Del Parque, Redondo Beach, CA, 90277. Tel: 310-375-0922. p. 253

Cousineau, Carrie, Libr Tech, St Lawrence College Library, 2288 Parkedale Ave, Brockville, ON, K6V 5X3, CANADA. Tel: 613-345-0660, Ext 3104. p. 2634

Cousino, Nicholas, Electronic Res Librn, State University of New York, College of Technology, Upper College Dr, Alfred, NY, 14802. Tel: 607-587-4313. p. 1485

Cousins, Heather, Sr Librn, Torrance Public Library, Southeast, 23115 S Arlington Ave, Torrance, CA, 90501-5816. Tel: 310-530-5044. p. 253

Cousins, Rebekah, Curator, The Whale Museum Library, 62 First St N, Friday Harbor, WA, 98250-7973. Tel: 360-378-4710, Ext 31. p. 2364

Cousins, Wendy, Libr Dir, Case Memorial Library, 911 Stetson Rd E, Kenduskeag, ME, 04450. Tel: 207-884-8598. p. 928

Coutts, Paula, Head Librn, Tumbler Ridge Public Library, 340 Front St, Tumbler Ridge, BC, V0C 2W0, CANADA. Tel: 250-242-4778. p. 2578

Coutts, Sandie, Dir, Staff Develop, Jefferson County Public Library, 10200 W 20th Ave, Lakewood, CO, 80215. Tel: 303-275-6160. p. 288

Coutu, Amélie, Chef de Section, Bibliotheques de Montreal, Pierrefonds, 13555 Blvd Pierrefonds, Pierrefonds, QC, H9A 1A6, CANADA. Tel: 514-242-0224. p. 2720

Coutu, Amélie, Chef de Section, Bibliotheques de Montreal, William G Boll Library, 110 rue Cartier, Roxboro, QC, H8Y 1G8, CANADA. Tel: 514-242-0224. p. 2721

Couture, Daves, Libr Tech, Conseil Superieur de l'Education, 1175 ave Lavigerie, Bur 180, Sainte-Foy, QC, G1V 5B2, CANADA. Tel: 418-643-2845. p. 2734

Couture, Faye, Dir, United States Army, Fort Stewart Main Post Library, 316 Lindquist Rd, Fort Stewart, GA, 31314-5126. Tel: 912-767-2260, 912-767-2828. p. 479

Couture, Jackie, Assoc Dir, Spec Coll & Archives, Eastern Kentucky University Libraries, 103 Crabbe Library, 521 Lancaster Ave, Richmond, KY, 40475. Tel: 859-622-1792. p. 873

Couture, Juliann, Head of Libr, University of Colorado Boulder, William M White Business Library, Koelbel Bldg, 995 Regent Dr, Boulder, CO, 80309. Tel: 303-492-9716. p. 268

Covalt, Caryle, Librn, Minatare Public Library, 309 Main St, Minatare, NE, 69356. Tel: 308-783-1414. p. 1325

Cove, Jeanne, Br Mgr, Montgomery County-Norristown Public Library, Upper Perkiomen Valley, 350 Main St, Red Hill, PA, 18076. Tel: 215-679-2020. p. 1971

Covelli, Emma, Acq Mgr, Colorado School of Mines, 1400 Illinois St, Golden, CO, 80401-1887. Tel: 303-273-3698. p. 283

Covelli, Rita, Head, Adult Serv, Ridgefield Library Association Inc, 472 Main St, Ridgefield, CT, 06877-4585. Tel: 203-438-2282. p. 335

Covello, Nicola, YA Librn, Hillside Public Library, 405 N Hillside Ave, Hillside, IL, 60162-1295. Tel: 708-449-7510. p. 599

Cover, Heather, Spec Projects Librn, Homewood Public Library, 1721 Oxmoor Rd, Homewood, AL, 35209-4085. Tel: 205-332-6621. p. 21

Covert, Claudia, Spec Coll Librn, Rhode Island School of Design Library, 15 Westminster St, Providence, RI, 02903. Tel: 401-709-5927. p. 2040

Covert, Jocelyn, Librn, Halifax Public Libraries, Bedford Branch, Wardour Ctr, 15 Dartmouth Rd, Bedford, NS, B4A 3X6, CANADA. Tel: 902-490-5740. p. 2617

Covey, Matthew, Univ Librn, The Rockefeller University, Welch Hall, 1230 York Ave, RU Box 203, New York, NY, 10065. Tel: 212-327-8904. p. 1601

Covington, Julia B, Ref Librn, North Carolina Legislative Library, 500 Legislative Office Bldg, 300 N Salisbury St, Raleigh, NC, 27603-5925. Tel: 919-733-9390. p. 1709

Covington, Kenny, Br Mgr, Cherokee County Public Library, Blacksburg Branch, 201 S Rutherford St, Blacksburg, SC, 29702. Tel: 864-839-2630. p. 2059

Covington-Isidore, Omisha, Libr Mgr, New York Public Library - Astor, Lenox & Tilden Foundations, Epiphany Branch, 228 E 23rd St, (Near Second Ave), New York, NY, 10010-4672. Tel: 212-679-2645. p. 1595

Covino, Laura, Librn, Center for Modern Psychoanalytic Studies Library, 16 W Tenth St, New York, NY, 10011. Tel: 212-260-7050, Ext 15. p. 1581

Covis, Samantha, Asst Dir, Lee-Whedon Memorial Library, 620 West Ave, Medina, NY, 14103. Tel: 585-798-3430. p. 1570

Cowan, Barbara, Circ Mgr, Libr Office Mgr, Conception Abbey & Seminary Library, 37174 State Hwy VV, Conception, MO, 64433. Tel: 660-944-2803. p. 1244

Cowan, Carol, Head, Youth Serv, Glen Cove Public Library, Four Glen Cove Ave, Glen Cove, NY, 11542-2885. Tel: 516-676-2130. p. 1538

Cowan, Helen, Head, Youth Serv, Vineland Public Library, 1058 E Landis Ave, Vineland, NJ, 08360. Tel: 856-794-4244. p. 1450

Cowan, Kathy, Spec Coll Librn, Maryland Institute College of Art, 1401 W Mount Royal Ave, Baltimore, MD, 21217. Tel: 410-225-2304, 410-225-2311. p. 955

Cowan, Melinda, Ch, Eunice Public Library, 1003 Ave N, Eunice, NM, 88231. Tel: 575-394-2336. p. 1467

Cowan, Penny, Dir of Coll, University of the South, 178 Georgia Ave, Sewanee, TN, 37383-1000. Tel: 931-598-1573. p. 2126

Cowan, Travaughn, Librn, Fox College Library, 18020 Oak Park Ave, Tinley Park, IL, 60477. Tel: 708-444-4500. p. 653

Cowan-Henderson, Jennifer, Dir, Libr Develop, Dir, Libr Planning, Tennessee State Library & Archives, 403 Seventh Ave N, Nashville, TN, 37243-0312. Tel: 615-741-1923. p. 2121

Coward, Barb, Dir, Cortland Community Library, 63 S Somonauk Rd, Cortland, IL, 60112. Tel: 815-756-7274. p. 574

Coward, Danielle, Br Mgr, Lorain Public Library System, South Lorain, 2121 Homewood Dr, Lorain, OH, 44055. Tel: 440-277-5672. p. 1797

Cowart, Caitlin, Pub Relations Mgr, San Antonio Public Library, 600 Soledad, San Antonio, TX, 78205-2786. Tel: 210-207-2638. p. 2238

Cowart, Michaela, Libr Tech II, Lamar State College Orange Library, 410 Front St, Orange, TX, 77630-5796. Tel: 409-882-3952. p. 2224

Cowden, Chapel, Health Sci Librn, University of Tennessee at Chattanooga Library, 400 Douglas Ave, Dept 6456, Chattanooga, TN, 37403-2598. Tel: 423-425-4501. p. 2092

Cowden, Nancy A, Asst Dir, Tech Serv, Oklahoma City University, School of Law Library, 2501 N Blackwelder, Oklahoma City, OK, 73106. Tel: 405-208-5271. p. 1858

Cowell, Amanda, Emerging Tech Librn, The College of New Jersey, 2000 Pennington Rd, Ewing, NJ, 08628-1104. Tel: 609-771-2311. p. 1402

Cowell, Ann, Librn, Massachusetts Department of Corrections, Institutional Library at Old Colony Correctional Center, One Administration Rd, Bridgewater, MA, 02324. Tel: 508-279-6006, Ext 6803. p. 1002

Cowell, Elizabeth, Univ Librn, University of California, 1156 High St, Santa Cruz, CA, 95064. Tel: 831-459-2076. p. 243

Cowell, Fillamay, Ch, Russell County Public Library, 535 N Main St, Jamestown, KY, 42629. Tel: 270-343-7323. p. 861

Cowell, Kim, Head, Eng Libr, Pennsylvania State University Libraries, Engineering, 325 Hammond Bldg, University Park, PA, 16802. Tel: 814-865-3451. p. 2015

Cowen, Diane, Br Mgr, Santa Cruz City-County Library System, Branciforte, 230 Gault St, Santa Cruz, CA, 95062-2599. Tel: 831-427-7704. p. 243

Cowen Fletcher, Jane, Ch, South Berwick Public Library, 27 Young St, South Berwick, ME, 03908. Tel: 207-384-3308. p. 941

Cowen, Jim, Access Serv, Music Librn, University of the Arts University Libraries, Music Library, Merriam Theater, 3rd Flr, 250 S Broad St, Philadelphia, PA, 19102. Tel: 215-717-6293. p. 1988

Cowgill, Allison, Head, Ref, California State University, Fresno, Henry Madden Library, 5200 N Barton Ave, Mail Stop ML-34, Fresno, CA, 93740-8014. Tel: 559-278-1022. p. 144

Cowie, Doug, Mgr, Marine Museum of the Great Lakes at Kingston, 53 Yonge St, Kingston, ON, K7M 6G4, CANADA. Tel: 613-542-2261. p. 2650

Cowin, Christa, Br Librn, Carter County Library District, Ellsinore Branch, RR2 Box 17, Ellsinore, MO, 63937. Tel: 573-322-0015. p. 1284

Cowin, Christa, Br Librn, Carter County Library District, Grandin Branch, 201 S Plum St, Grandin, MO, 63943. Tel: 573-593-4084. p. 1284

Cowing, Jared, Syst Librn, Woodbury University Library, 7500 Glenoaks Blvd, Burbank, CA, 91510. Tel: 818-252-5200. p. 125

Cowles, Mary, Head, Children's Dept, Lapeer District Library, 201 Village West Dr S, Lapeer, MI, 48446-1699. Tel: 810-664-9521. p. 1126

Cowley, Joseph, Actg Br Mgr, Toledo-Lucas County Public Library, Locke, 703 Miami St, Toledo, OH, 43605. Tel: 419-259-5310. p. 1824

Cowling Watters, Lola, Fac Librn, Austin Community College, San Gabriel Campus, 449 San Gabriel Campus Dr, 2nd Flr, Rm 1200, Leander, TX, 78641. Tel: 512-223-2560. p. 2138

Cowser, Catherine, Asst Dir, Collier County Public Library, 2385 Orange Blossom Dr, Naples, FL, 34109. Tel: 239-593-0334. p. 427

Cox, Amanda, Network Adminr, Henry County Public Library System, 1001 Florence McGarity Blvd, McDonough, GA, 30252. Tel: 678-432-5353. p. 490

Cox, Amber, Libr Mgr, Pikes Peak Library District, Old Colorado City Library, 2418 W Pikes Peak Ave, Colorado Springs, CO, 80904. Tel: 719-531-6333, Ext 6202. p. 271

Cox, Angela, Liaison & Instruction Librn, University of Northern Iowa Library, 1227 W 27th St, Cedar Falls, IA, 50613-3675. Tel: 319-273-2839. p. 737

Cox, Anne, Br Mgr, Van Buren District Library, Lawrence Community, 212 N Paw Paw St, Lawrence, MI, 49064. Tel: 269-674-3200. p. 1096

Cox, Anne, Instruction Librn, Stephens College, 1200 E Broadway, Columbia, MO, 65215. Tel: 573-876-7181. p. 1243

Cox, Barb, Libr Mgr, Killam Municipal Library, 5017 49th Ave, Killam, AB, T0B 2L0, CANADA. Tel: 780-385-3032. p. 2544

Cox, Brooke, Dean of Libr, DePauw University, 405 S Indiana St, Greencastle, IN, 46135. Tel: 765-658-4420. p. 687

Cox, Caitlin, Dir, Alabama Institute for the Deaf & Blind, 705 South St E, Talladega, AL, 35160. Tel: 256-761-3237. p. 36
Cox, Caitlin, Libr Dir, Talladega College, 627 Battle St W, Talladega, AL, 35160. Tel: 256-761-6377. p. 36
Cox, Caitlyn, Libr Dir, South University Library, 5355 Vaughn Rd, Montgomery, AL, 36116-1120. Tel: 334-395-8891. p. 30
Cox, Christine, Dir, Church of Jesus Christ of Latter-Day Saints, Church History Library & Archives, 50 E North Temple, Salt Lake City, UT, 84150. Tel: 801-240-3603. p. 2271
Cox, Christopher, Dean of Libr, Clemson University Libraries, 116 Sigma Dr, Clemson, SC, 29631. Tel: 864-656-3027. p. 2052
Cox, Danielle, Libr Serv Spec, Sterling Heights Public Library, 40255 Dodge Park Rd, Sterling Heights, MI, 48313-4140. Tel: 586-446-2665. p. 1152
Cox, David B, II, Tech Serv Librn, University of Alaska Southeast, 11066 Auke Lake Way, BE1, Juneau, AK, 99801. Tel: 907-796-6345. p. 47
Cox, David, Dr, Dir, New Mexico Tech, 801 Leroy Pl, Socorro, NM, 87801. Tel: 575-835-5614. p. 1478
Cox, Deborah, Ref Serv, Lone Star College System, Montgomery College Library, 3200 College Park Dr, Conroe, TX, 77384. Tel: 936-273-7490. p. 2197
Cox, Donna, Dir, Virginia Department for the Blind & Vision Impaired, 395 Azalea Ave, Richmond, VA, 23227-3633. Tel: 804-371-3661. p. 2343
Cox, Dwayne, Head Archivist, Head, Spec Coll, Auburn University, Ralph Brown Draughon Library, 231 Mell St, Auburn, AL, 36849. Tel: 334-844-1707. p. 5
Cox, Halle, Dir, Kane County Law Library & Self Help Legal Center, Kane County Judicial Ctr, 2nd Flr, 37W777W IL Rte 38, Saint Charles, IL, 60175. Tel: 630-406-7126. p. 644
Cox, Hannah, Librn & Archivist, Albany Institute of History & Art, 125 Washington Ave, Albany, NY, 12210-2296. Tel: 518-463-4478. p. 1481
Cox, Heidi, Dir, McFarland Public Library, 5920 Milwaukee St, McFarland, WI, 53558-8962. Tel: 608-838-9030. p. 2455
Cox, James, Dir, Marathon Public Library, 306 W Attica St, Marathon, IA, 50565. Tel: 712-289-2200. p. 767
Cox, Jamie, Pub Serv Librn, Vincennes University, Shake Library, 1002 N First St, Vincennes, IN, 47591. Tel: 812-888-4427. p. 724
Cox, Jan, Head Librn, Indiana University, School of Dentistry Library, 1121 W Michigan St, Rm 128, Indianapolis, IN, 46202-5186. Tel: 317-274-5207. p. 693
Cox, Janet, Tech Serv Mgr, Plano Public Library System, Library Administration, 2501 Coit Rd, Plano, TX, 75075. Tel: 972-769-4291. p. 2227
Cox, Janet, Regional Supvr, Wythe-Grayson Regional Library, 147 S Independence Ave, Independence, VA, 24348. Tel: 276-773-3018. p. 2326
Cox, Jennifer, Dean, Libr & Learning Res, Chemeketa Community College Library, 4000 Lancaster Dr NE, Bldg 9, 2nd Flr, Salem, OR, 97305-1500. Tel: 503-399-5043. p. 1896
Cox, Joanna, Info Syst Librn, Harnett County Public Library, 601 S Main St, Lillington, NC, 27546-6107. Tel: 910-893-3446. p. 1700
Cox, Joseph, Fr, Cat, Saint Meinrad Archabbey & School of Theology, 200 Hill Dr, Saint Meinrad, IN, 47577. Tel: 812-357-6401. p. 717
Cox, Julia, Youth Serv Librn, Penticton Public Library, 785 Main St, Penticton, BC, V2A 5E3, CANADA. Tel: 250-770-7783. p. 2573
Cox, Kacy, Mgr, Columbus Metropolitan Library, Whitehall Branch, 4445 E Broad St, Columbus, OH, 43213. p. 1773
Cox, Kathie, Librn, Texas County Library, Summersville Branch, 480 First St, Summersville, MO, 65571. Tel: 417-932-5261. p. 1249
Cox, Kathy, Head, Tech Serv, Trails Regional Library, 432 N Holden St, Warrensburg, MO, 64093. Tel: 660-747-1699. p. 1285
Cox, Katie, Br Mgr, Gaston County Public Library, Belmont Branch, 125 Central Ave, Belmont, NC, 28012. Tel: 704-825-5426. p. 1690
Cox, Kiersten, Instr, University of South Florida, 4202 Fowler Ave, CIS 1040, Tampa, FL, 33620-7800. Tel: 813-974-3520. p. 2783
Cox, Kyle, Exec Dir, Mid-Columbia Libraries, 405 S Dayton St, Kennewick, WA, 99336. p. 2367
Cox, Laura, Mgr, Learning Serv, Arizona State University Libraries, Polytechnic Campus, Academic Ctr, Lower Level, 5988 S Backus Mall, Mesa, AZ, 85212. Tel: 480-727-1330. p. 79
Cox, Laurel, Ref Librn, Patten Free Library, 33 Summer St, Bath, ME, 04530. Tel: 207-443-5141, Ext 12. p. 916
Cox, Leana J, Interim Libr Dir, Colorado Northwestern Community College Library, 500 Kennedy Dr, CNCC-Box 29, Rangely, CO, 81648. Tel: 970-675-3334, 970-675-3576. p. 294
Cox, Lori, Dir, West Polk Public Library, 126 Polk St, Benton, TN, 37307. Tel: 423-338-4536. p. 2088
Cox, Lori, Dir, Olney Community Library & Arts Center, 807 W Hamilton St, Olney, TX, 76374. Tel: 940-564-5513. p. 2223
Cox, Lucy, Intl Law Librn, Ref Librn, Rutgers University Libraries, Camden Law Library, 217 N Fifth St, Camden, NJ, 08102-1203. Tel: 856-225-6464. p. 1394
Cox, Lynn, Dir, Libr Serv, Southeast Kentucky Community & Technical College, 700 College Rd, Cumberland, KY, 40823. Tel: 606-589-3073. p. 853
Cox, Lynn, Br Mgr, Norfolk Public Library, Van Wyck Branch, 1368 DeBree Ave, Norfolk, VA, 23517. Tel: 757-441-2844. p. 2335
Cox, Michael, Dep Dir, Whatcom County Library System, 5205 Northwest Dr, Bellingham, WA, 98226. Tel: 360-305-3600. p. 2359
Cox, Robert, Head, Spec Coll & Archives, University of Massachusetts Amherst Libraries, 154 Hicks Way, University of Massachusetts, Amherst, MA, 01003-9275. Tel: 413-545-6842. p. 985
Cox, Ryan, Dir, Berkeley Public Library, 1637 N Taft Ave, Berkeley, IL, 60163-1499. Tel: 708-544-6017. p. 542
Cox, Sarah, Pub Serv Mgr, Brescia University, 717 Frederica St, Owensboro, KY, 42301. Tel: 270-686-4212. p. 871
Cox, Shelly, Br Mgr, Annapolis Valley Regional Library, Kingston Branch, 671 Main St, Kingston, NS, B0P 1R0, CANADA. Tel: 902-765-3631. p. 2616
Cox, Stephanie, Libr Coord, Bossier Parish Community College Library, 6220 E Texas St, Bldg A, Bossier City, LA, 71111. Tel: 318-678-6224. p. 885
Cox, Stephen H, Jr, Br Librn, Smithsonian Libraries, National Zoological Park & Conservation Biology Institute Library, Nat Zoological Park, Education Bldg-Visitor Ctr, 3000 Block of Connecticut Ave NW, Washington, DC, 20008-0551. Tel: 202-633-1798. p. 376
Cox, Toni, Asst Dir, Roanoke County Public Library, 6303 Merriman Rd, Roanoke, VA, 24018-6496. Tel: 540-772-7507. p. 2345
Cox, Toni, Asst Dir, Roanoke County Public Library, Glenvar, 3917 Daugherty Rd, Salem, VA, 24153. Tel: 540-387-6163. p. 2345
Cox, Tricia, Ch, Waterford Public Library, 101 N River St, Waterford, WI, 53185-4149. Tel: 262-534-3988, Ext 13. p. 2483
Cox-Steib, Rorie, Br Adminr, Frederick County Public Libraries, Myersville Community Library, Eight Harp Pl, Myersville, MD, 21773. Tel: 301-600-8350. p. 966
Coy, Howard L, Jr, Dir, Vernon Parish Library, 1401 Nolan Trace, Leesville, LA, 71446. Tel: 337-239-2027. p. 895
Coy, Julie, Head, Metadata Serv, Visual Res Librn, Haverford College, 370 Lancaster Ave, Haverford, PA, 19041-1392. Tel: 610-896-1273. p. 1942
Coy, Lauren, Dir of Develop, Phoenixville Public Library, 183 Second Ave, Phoenixville, PA, 19460-3420. Tel: 610-933-3013, Ext 131. p. 1989
Coy, Silvia, Head, Circ, University of Saint Thomas, 3800 Montrose Blvd, Houston, TX, 77006. Tel: 713-525-2192. p. 2200
Coyan, Michael L, Dr, Exec Dir, Warren County Historical Society, 105 S Broadway, Lebanon, OH, 45036. Tel: 513-932-1817. p. 1795
Coyl, Peter, Dir, Montclair Public Library, 50 S Fullerton Ave, Montclair, NJ, 07042. Tel: 973-744-0500. p. 1420
Coyle, Jeff, E-Resources Librn, Texas Chiropractic College, 5912 Spencer Hwy, Pasadena, TX, 77505. Tel: 281-998-6049. p. 2225
Coyne, Catherine, Dir, Mansfield Public Library, 255 Hope St, Mansfield, MA, 02048-2353. Tel: 508-261-7380. p. 1031
Coyne, Mick, Dir, Technology, Massachusetts School of Law Library, 500 Federal St, Andover, MA, 01810. Tel: 978-681-0800. p. 985
Coyne, Tracy, Librn, Northwestern University Libraries, Joseph Schaffner Library, Wieboldt Hall, 2nd Flr, 339 E Chicago Ave, Chicago, IL, 60611. Tel: 312-503-6617. p. 587
Coyner, Libby, Archives Librn, Elon University, 308 N O'Kelly Ave, Elon, NC, 27244-0187. Tel: 336-278-6600. p. 1688
Cozzo, Jocelyn, Ch, Hatfield Public Library, 39 Main St, Hatfield, MA, 01038. Tel: 413-247-9097. p. 1024
Crabb, John, Libr Dir, Reformed Theological Seminary Library, 5422 Clinton Blvd, Jackson, MS, 39209. Tel: 601-923-1623. p. 1223
Crabill, Jane, Sr Librn, United States Army, Marquat Memorial Library, Bank Hall, Bldg D-3915, 3004 Ardennes St, Fort Bragg, NC, 28310-9610. Tel: 910-432-8184. p. 1689
Crabtree, Martin, Ref Librn, Mercer County Community College Library, 1200 Old Trenton Rd, West Windsor, NJ, 08550. Tel: 609-570-3545. p. 1453
Crabtree, Vanessa, Syst Librn, Cochise County Library District, Jimmie Libhart Library, 201 N Central Ave, Bowie, AZ, 85605. Tel: 520-847-2522. p. 56
Craft, Deborah, Head Librn, Citronelle Memorial Library, 7855 State St, Citronelle, AL, 36522. Tel: 251-866-7319. p. 12
Craft, Jennifer, Mgr, Community Library Network, Post Falls Branch, 821 N Spokane St, Post Falls, ID, 83854. Tel: 208-773-1506. p. 522
Craft, Julie, Asst Mgr, Big Horn County Library, Greybull Branch, 325 Greybull Ave, Greybull, WY, 82426. Tel: 307-765-2551. p. 2491
Craft, Lori, Dir, Clarendon Hills Public Library, Seven N Prospect Ave, Clarendon Hills, IL, 60514. Tel: 630-323-8188. p. 572
Craft, Matt, Mgr, Columbus Metropolitan Library, Canal Winchester Branch, 115 Franklin St, Canal Winchester, OH, 43110. p. 1772
Craft, Matt, Mgr, Columbus Metropolitan Library, Marion-Franklin Branch, 2740 Lockbourne Rd, Columbus, OH, 43207. p. 1773
Craft, Rebekah, Assoc Dir, Baldwin Public Library, 300 W Merrill St, Birmingham, MI, 48009-1483. Tel: 248-647-1700. p. 1086
Craft, Tina, Dir, Libr Serv, Ohio Christian University, 1476 Lancaster Pike, Circleville, OH, 43113. Tel: 740-477-7737. p. 1765
Craft, Tracey, Ad, Springfield Town Library, 43 Main St, Springfield, VT, 05156. Tel: 802-885-3108. p. 2295
Crafton, Sherry, Ch Serv, Circ, Greene County Public Library, 120 N 12th St, Paragould, AR, 72450. Tel: 870-236-8711. p. 107
Crafts, Amanda, Librn, Bass Harbor Memorial Library, 89 Bernard Rd, Bernard, ME, 04612. Tel: 207-244-3798. p. 917

Cragg, Dana, Librn, Petersburg Public Library, Rodof Sholom Branch, 1865 S Sycamore St, Petersburg, VA, 23805. Tel: 804-733-2393. p. 2337

Cragg, Dana, Tech Librn, Petersburg Public Library, 201 W Washington St, Petersburg, VA, 23803. Tel: 804-733-2387. p. 2337

Craig, Adam, Chief Librn/CEO, Essex County Library, 360 Fairview Ave W, Ste 101, Essex, ON, N8M 1Y3, CANADA. Tel: 519-776-5241. p. 2640

Craig, Angela, Exec Dir, Charleston County Public Library, 68 Calhoun St, Charleston, SC, 29401. Tel: 843-805-6801. p. 2048

Craig, Anne, Sr Dir, Consortium of Academic & Research Libraries in Illinois, 1704 Interstate Dr, Champaign, IL, 61822. Tel: 217-300-0375. p. 2764

Craig, Calvin, Ref Serv, Gaston College, 201 Hwy 321 S, Dallas, NC, 28034-1499. Tel: 704-922-6359. p. 1683

Craig, Cory, Ms, Librn, University of California, Davis, Physical Sciences & Engineering Library, One Shields Ave, Davis, CA, 95616. Tel: 530-752-0347. p. 134

Craig, Daza, Adult Serv, Augusta County Library, 1759 Jefferson Hwy, Fishersville, VA, 22939. Tel: 540-885-3961, 540-949-6354. p. 2318

Craig, Edward L, Jr, Ref Librn, Samford University Library, Lucille Stewart Beeson Law Library, 800 Lakeshore Dr, Birmingham, AL, 35229. Tel: 205-726-2714. p. 9

Craig, Julie, Libr Mgr, Haut-Saint-Jean Regional Library, Andrew & Laura McCain Public Library, Eight McCain St, Florenceville-Bristol, NB, E7L 3H6, CANADA. Tel: 506-392-5294. p. 2600

Craig, Kaylin, Dir, Farnam Public Library, 310 Main St, Farnam, NE, 69029. Tel: 308-569-2318. p. 1314

Craig, Linda, Circ, Gilpin County Public Library District, 15131 Hwy 119, Black Hawk, CO, 80422. Tel: 303-582-5777. p. 266

Craig, Lora L, Dir, Anchor Point Public Library, 34020 N Fork Rd, Anchor Point, AK, 99556. Tel: 907-235-5692. p. 41

Craig, Lori-Ann, Dep Dir, Harris County Robert W Hainsworth Law Library, Congress Plaza, 1019 Congress, 1st Flr, Houston, TX, 77002. Tel: 713-755-5183. p. 2191

Craig, Roberta, Med Librn, OSF Saint Anthony Medical Center, 5666 E State St, Rockford, IL, 61108-2472. Tel: 815-227-2558. p. 641

Craig, Roberta, Coordr, Munson Healthcare, Community Health Library, 550 Munson Ave, Ste 100, Traverse City, MI, 49686. Tel: 231-935-9265. p. 1154

Craig, Sandra, Dir, Wabash Valley College, 2200 College Dr, Mount Carmel, IL, 62863. Tel: 618-263-5097. p. 620

Craig, Tara, Head, Pub Serv, Columbia University, Rare Book & Manuscript, Butler Library, 6th Flr E, 535 W 114th St, New York, NY, 10027. Tel: 212-854-4051. p. 1583

Craig, Thomas B, Dir, Libr Serv, University of Texas Health Science Center at Tyler, 11937 US Hwy 271, Tyler, TX, 75708-3154. Tel: 903-877-2865. p. 2250

Craige, Danielle, Libr Serv Mgr, Somerset County Library System, 11767 Beechwood St, Princess Anne, MD, 21853. Tel: 410-651-0852. p. 973

Craigle, Valeri, Access Technologies Librn, University of Utah, S J Quinney Law Library, 332 S 1400 East, Salt Lake City, UT, 84112-0731. Tel: 801-585-5475. p. 2272

Crain, Ellen, Ref Librn, Jackson County Library, 213 Walnut St, Newport, AR, 72112. Tel: 870-523-2952. p. 106

Crain, Josh, Br Mgr, Indianapolis Public Library, Decatur, 5301 Kentucky Ave, Indianapolis, IN, 46221-6540. Tel: 317-275-4335. p. 694

Crain, Mary, Media Prod, New Jersey State Library, Talking Book & Braille Center, 2300 Stuyvesant Ave, Trenton, NJ, 08618. Tel: 609-406-7179, Ext 809. p. 1448

Craine, Susan, Circ Coordr, Milanof-Schock Library, 1184 Anderson Ferry Rd, Mount Joy, PA, 17552. Tel: 717-653-1510. p. 1966

Cramer, Heidi, Dir, Piscataway Township Free Public Library, 500 Hoes Lane, Piscataway, NJ, 08854. Tel: 732-463-1633. p. 1435

Cramer, Jane, Govt Info Spec, Brooklyn College Library, 2900 Bedford Ave, Brooklyn, NY, 11210. Tel: 718-951-5332. p. 1501

Cramer, Shanda, Libr Dir, Clay Center Carnegie Library, 706 Sixth St, Clay Center, KS, 67432. Tel: 785-632-3889. p. 802

Cramer, Tom, Assoc Univ Librn, Stanford University Libraries, 557 Escondido Mall, Stanford, CA, 94305-6063. Tel: 650-725-1064. p. 248

Cramner, Cathy, Br Librn, Community District Library, Corunna Branch, 210 E Corunna Ave, Corunna, MI, 48817. Tel: 989-743-4800. p. 1095

Cramp, Isabelle, Libr Mgr, Morinville Community Library, 10125 100th Ave, Morinville, AB, T8R 1P8, CANADA. Tel: 780-939-3292. p. 2548

Crandall, Christina, Ch, Phillipsburg Free Public Library, 200 Broubalow Way, Phillipsburg, NJ, 08865. Tel: 908-454-3712. p. 1434

Crandall, Ginette, Asst Librn, Wainwright Public Library, 921 Third Ave, Wainwright, AB, T9W 1C5, CANADA. Tel: 780-842-2673. p. 2559

Crandall, Janet, Librn, Little River Community Library, 125 Main St, Little River, KS, 67457. Tel: 620-897-6610. p. 821

Crandall, Katie, Assoc Dir, Florida State University Libraries, College of Law Library, 425 W Jefferson St, Tallahassee, FL, 32306. Tel: 850-644-4578. p. 447

Crandall, Shana, Libr Instruction, Ref, Century College Library, 3300 N Century Ave, White Bear Lake, MN, 55110. Tel: 651-779-3969. p. 1208

Crandall, Steve, Dir, Alfred University, Herrick Memorial Library, One Saxon Dr, Alfred, NY, 14802. Tel: 607-871-2987. p. 1485

Crandell, Adam, Music Librn, User Experience Coord, Haverford College, 370 Lancaster Ave, Haverford, PA, 19041-1392. Tel: 610-896-1169. p. 1942

Crane, Ashley, Res & Instruction Librn, Sam Houston State University, 1830 Bobby K Marks Dr, Huntsville, TX, 77340. Tel: 936-294-4686. p. 2201

Crane, Casandria, Dir, American Fork City Library, 64 S 100 E, American Fork, UT, 84003. Tel: 801-763-3070. p. 2261

Crane, Douglas, Dir, Palm Beach County Library System, 3650 Summit Blvd, West Palm Beach, FL, 33406-4198. Tel: 561-233-2600. p. 454

Crane, Jill, Cat, Saint Mary's University, Louis J Blume Library, One Camino Santa Maria, San Antonio, TX, 78228-8608. Tel: 210-436-3441. p. 2238

Crane, Karen, Library Contact, The Century Association Library, Seven W 43rd St, New York, NY, 10036. Tel: 212-944-0090. p. 1581

Crane, Michael, Syst Librn, United States Air Force Academy Libraries, 2354 Fairchild Dr, Ste 3A15, USAF Academy, CO, 80840-6214. Tel: 719-333-4406. p. 297

Crane, Patty, Ref Librn, Joplin Public Library, 1901 E 20th St, Joplin, MO, 64804. Tel: 417-623-7953. p. 1253

Crane, Peter, Curator, Mount Washington Observatory, 2779 White Mountain Hwy, Lower Level, North Conway, NH, 03860. Tel: 603-356-2137, Ext 203. p. 1376

Crane, Priscilla, Ref Librn, Thayer Public Library, 798 Washington St, Braintree, MA, 02184. Tel: 781-848-0405, Ext 4407. p. 1001

Crane, Rachel, Fine Arts Librn, Music Librn, Wichita State University Libraries, Music Library, 122A Ablah Library, 1845 Fairmont, Wichita, KS, 67260-0068. Tel: 316-978-5078. p. 844

Crane, Ruth, Tech Serv, Emma S Clark Memorial Library, 120 Main St, Setauket, NY, 11733-2868. Tel: 631-941-4080, Ext 122. p. 1640

Crane, Terri, Libr Asst, Plainfield Public Libraries, 22 Bean Rd, Meriden, NH, 03770. Tel: 603-469-3252. p. 1373

Crane, Vanneshia, ILL Serv, Southern Oklahoma Library System, 601 Railway Express St, Ardmore, OK, 73401. Tel: 580-223-3164. p. 1840

Craner, Cresta, Dir, Portneuf District Library, 5210 Stuart Ave, Chubbuck, ID, 83202. Tel: 208-237-2192. p. 519

Cranford, Anita, Dir, Libr Serv, First Baptist Church Library, 1000 W Friendly Ave, Greensboro, NC, 27401. Tel: 336-274-3286, Ext 229. p. 1691

Cranshaw, Moira, Youth Serv Coordr, Emily Williston Memorial Library, Nine Park St, Easthampton, MA, 01027. Tel: 413-527-1031. p. 1016

Crater, Paul, Dir, Atlanta History Center, 3101 Andrews Dr NW, Atlanta, GA, 30305. Tel: 404-814-4000, 404-814-4040. p. 462

Crater, Peggy, Circ Asst, Forsyth Technical Community College Library, 2100 Silas Creek Pkwy, Winston-Salem, NC, 27103. Tel: 336-734-7219. p. 1725

Crauderueff, Mary, Curator of Quaker Coll, Haverford College, 370 Lancaster Ave, Haverford, PA, 19041-1392. Tel: 610-896-1158. p. 1942

Craughwell-Varda, Kathy, Colls Mgr, Curator, Greenwich Historical Society, 47 Strickland Rd, Cos Cob, CT, 06807. Tel: 203-869-6899, Ext 10. p. 306

Cravedi, Eileen, Head, Access & Discovery Serv, College of the Holy Cross, One College St, Worcester, MA, 01610. Tel: 508-793-2672. p. 1072

Cravedi, Kathleen, Communications Dir, National Library of Medicine, Bldg 38, Rm 2E-17B, 8600 Rockville Pike, Bethesda, MD, 20894. Tel: 301-496-6308. p. 960

Craven, Heather, Dean of Learning Resource Ctr, County College of Morris, 214 Center Grove Rd, Randolph, NJ, 07869-2086. Tel: 973-328-5300. p. 1438

Craven, Nora, Mgr, Libr Serv, Nicolet Area Technical College, Lakeside Center, 3rd Flr, 5364 College Dr, Rhinelander, WI, 54501. Tel: 715-365-4576. p. 2472

Craven, Susan, Asst Libr Dir, Davidson County Public Library System, 602 S Main St, Lexington, NC, 27292. Tel: 336-242-2040. p. 1700

Craven, Susan, Br Mgr, Davidson County Public Library System, Denton Public, 310 W Salisbury St, Denton, NC, 27239-6944. Tel: 336-859-2215. p. 1700

Craver, Kristin, Circ Librn, Drake Public Library, 115 Drake Ave, Centerville, IA, 52544. Tel: 641-856-6676. p. 739

Crawford, Adrian, Dean, Learning Res, Bossier Parish Community College Library, 6220 E Texas St, Bldg A, Bossier City, LA, 71111. Tel: 318-678-6143. p. 885

Crawford, Anne, Adult Serv, Asst Br Mgr, Saint Johns County Public Library System, Ponte Vedra Beach Branch, 101 Library Blvd, Ponte Vedra Beach, FL, 32082. Tel: 904-827-6952. p. 440

Crawford, Brooke, Admin Serv Mgr, Arkansas State Library, 900 W Capitol, Ste 100, Little Rock, AR, 72201-3108. Tel: 501-682-2053. p. 100

Crawford, Canon, Librn, Santa Rosa Junior College, 1501 Mendocino Ave, Santa Rosa, CA, 95401. Tel: 707-527-4904. p. 245

Crawford, Carol, Melbourne Campus Libr Dir, Keiser University Library System, 1500 NW 49th St, Fort Lauderdale, FL, 33309. Tel: 954-351-4035. p. 401

Crawford, Christine, Br Mgr, Mercer County Library System, Hollowbrook Community Center, 320 Hollowbrook Dr, Trenton, NJ, 08638. Tel: 609-883-5914. p. 1411

Crawford, Claire Kennefick, Dir, Geneseo Public Library District, 805 N Chicago St, Geneseo, IL, 61254. Tel: 309-944-6452. p. 591

Crawford, Claretta, Libr Dir, United States Army, Bruce C Clarke Library Academic Services Division, Bldg 3202, 14020 MSCOE Loop, Ste 200, Fort Leonard Wood, MO, 65473-8928. Tel: 573-563-5608. p. 1246

Crawford, Erin, Interim Dir, Public Library of Enid & Garfield County, 120 W Maine, Enid, OK, 73701-5606. Tel: 580-234-6313. p. 1847

Crawford, Hilda, Circ, Coalinga-Huron Library District, 305 N Fourth St, Coalinga, CA, 93210. Tel: 559-935-1676. p. 131

Crawford, James, Dir, Lakewood Public Library, 15425 Detroit Ave, Lakewood, OH, 44107. Tel: 216-226-8275. p. 1793

Crawford, Jane, Libr Mgr, Sno-Isle Libraries, Mukilteo Library, 4675 Harbour Pointe Blvd, Mukilteo, WA, 98275-4725. Tel: 425-493-8202. p. 2371

Crawford, Jo, Librn, Joyce Public Library, 9490 W State Rd 120, Orland, IN, 46776. Tel: 260-829-6329. p. 712

Crawford, John, Asst Dir, Woodford County Library, 115 N Main St, Versailles, KY, 40383-1289. Tel: 859-873-5191. p. 876

Crawford, Joselyn, Ch Serv, Crestline Public Library, 324 N Thoman St, Crestline, OH, 44827-1410. Tel: 419-683-3909. p. 1779

Crawford, Julienne, Curator, Arkansas History Commission Library, One Capitol Mall, 2nd Flr, Little Rock, AR, 72201. Tel: 501-682-6900. p. 100

Crawford, Julienne, Curator, Arkansas State Archives, One Capitol Mall, Ste 215, Little Rock, AR, 72201. Tel: 501-682-6978. p. 100

Crawford, Kathy, Libr Asst, North Island College, 140-8950 Granville St, Port Hardy, BC, V0N 2P0, CANADA. Tel: 250-949-7912. p. 2574

Crawford, Kathyrn, Head, Access Serv, Western Colorado University, One Western Way, Gunnison, CO, 81231. Tel: 970-943-2107. p. 285

Crawford, Kimberly, Cataloger, Iredell County Public Library, 201 N Tradd St, Statesville, NC, 28677. Tel: 704-878-3147. p. 1717

Crawford, Laurie, Adult Serv, Stevens County Library, 500 S Monroe, Hugoton, KS, 67951-2639. Tel: 620-544-2301. p. 814

Crawford, Marilyn, Br Librn, Wapiti Regional Library, Marcelin Public Library, 100 First Ave, Marcelin, SK, S0J 1R0, CANADA. Tel: 306-226-2110. p. 2745

Crawford, Marjorie E, Ref Librn, Rutgers University Library for the Center for Law & Justice, 123 Washington St, Newark, NJ, 07102-3094. Tel: 973-353-3144. p. 1428

Crawford, Meghan, Tech Serv Asst, Capital University, One College & Main, Columbus, OH, 43209. Tel: 614-236-6614. p. 1772

Crawford, Michaelyn, Br Mgr, Manistee County Library System, Wellston Branch, 1273 Seaman Rd, Wellston, MI, 49689. Tel: 231-848-4013. p. 1129

Crawford, Pamela, Asst Dir, Public & Technical Servs, University of Kansas Libraries, Wheat Law Library, Green Hall, Rm 200, 1535 W 15th St, Lawrence, KS, 66045-7608. Tel: 785-864-3025. p. 820

Crawford, Stephanie, Archivist, Mattatuck Museum of the Mattatuck Historical Society, 144 W Main St, Waterbury, CT, 06702. Tel: 203-753-0381. p. 343

Crawford, Stephanie, Circuit Librn, Library of the US Courts of the Seventh Circuit, 219 S Dearborn St, Rm 1637, Chicago, IL, 60604-1769. Tel: 312-435-5660. p. 563

Crawford, Terri, Dir, Watonga Public Library, 301 N Prouty, Watonga, OK, 73772. Tel: 580-623-7748. p. 1868

Crawford, Theresa Ann, Libr Dir, Bremond Public Library & Visitors Center, 115 S Main St, Bremond, TX, 76629. Tel: 254-746-7752. p. 2149

Crawford, Virginia, Libr Dir, Alberta Genealogical Society Library & Research Centre, No 162-14315-118 Ave, Edmonton, AB, T5L 4S6, CANADA. Tel: 780-424-4429. p. 2534

Crawhorn, Denise, Br Mgr, Knox County Public Library System, Sequoyah Branch, 1140 Southgate Rd, Knoxville, TN, 37919. Tel: 865-525-1541. p. 2106

Crawley, Alison, Supvr, Halton Hills Public Library, Acton Branch, 17 River St, Acton, ON, L7J 1C2, CANADA. Tel: 905-873-2681, Ext 2551. p. 2642

Crawley, Mildred, Circ, Decatur County Library, 20 W Market St, Decaturville, TN, 38329. Tel: 731-852-3325. p. 2096

Crawley, Sandra, Librn, Birmingham Public Library, North Birmingham, 2501 31st Ave N, Birmingham, AL, 35207-4423. Tel: 205-226-4025. p. 7

Crayne, Tiffany, Tech Serv Supvr, Greenwood County Library, 600 S Main St, Greenwood, SC, 29646. Tel: 864-941-4650. p. 2062

Crea, Kathleen, Ref Librn, Henry Carter Hull Library, Inc, Ten Killingworth Tpk, Clinton, CT, 06413. Tel: 860-669-2342. p. 306

Creager, Carol, Univ Librn, Mary Baldwin University, 201 E Frederick St, Staunton, VA, 24401. Tel: 540-887-7310. p. 2347

Creager, Carol, Info Officer, Virginia Independent College & University Library Association, c/o Alison Gregory, Marymount University, 2807 N Glebe Rd, Arlington, VA, 22207. Tel: 703-284-1673. p. 2776

Creamer, Angela, Head Librn, Estancia Public Library, 601 S Tenth St, Estancia, NM, 87016. Tel: 505-384-9655. p. 1467

Creamer, Tim, Librn, Thaddeus Stevens College of Technology, 750 E King St, Lancaster, PA, 17602-3198. Tel: 717-391-3503. p. 1952

Creaser, Julie, Regional Mgr, Libr Serv, University Hospital of Northern British Columbia, Learning & Development Ctr, 1475 Edmonton St, Prince George, BC, V2M 1S2, CANADA. Tel: 250-565-2219. p. 2574

Creasong, Joy, Youth Serv Librn, Bossier Parish Libraries, 2206 Beckett St, Bossier City, LA, 71111. Tel: 318-746-1693. p. 885

Cree, Justin, Dir, Akwesasne Cultural Center Library, 321 State Rte 37, Hogansburg, NY, 13655. Tel: 518-358-2240. p. 1547

Creech, Robin, Libr Mgr, Columbus County Public Library, East Columbus Library, 103 Church Rd, Riegelwood, NC, 28456. Tel: 910-655-4157. p. 1722

Creech, Sarah, Adult Serv Coordr, Belgrade Community Library, 106 N Broadway, Belgrade, MT, 59714. Tel: 406-388-4346. p. 1287

Creech, Sue, Law Librn, United States Court of Appeals, 600 Camp St, Rm 106, New Orleans, LA, 70130. Tel: 504-310-7797. p. 904

Creede, Diane, Asst Dir for Instructional Tech, Connecticut College, 270 Mohegan Ave, New London, CT, 06320-4196. Tel: 860-439-2655. p. 328

Creef, Tama, Archivist, North Carolina Office of Archives & History, One Festival Park Blvd, Manteo, NC, 27954. Tel: 252-473-2655. p. 1702

Creek, Ashley, Dir, Libr Serv, University of Saint Mary, 4100 S Fourth St, Leavenworth, KS, 66048. Tel: 913-758-6306. p. 820

Creel, Angela, Dir, Libr Serv, Arizona Western College, 2020 S Ave 8E, Yuma, AZ, 85366. Tel: 928-344-7776. p. 85

Creelman, Kathryn, Pub Serv Coordr, Orangeville Public Library, One Mill St, Orangeville, ON, L9W 2M2, CANADA. Tel: 519-941-0610, Ext 5232. p. 2663

Creevy, Jennifer, Govt Doc Librn, Ref Serv Librn, University of Holy Cross, 4123 Woodland Dr, New Orleans, LA, 70131. Tel: 504-398-2102. p. 904

Creger, Beth Anne, Dir, Lewiston Public Library, 29 S Main St, Lewiston, UT, 84320. Tel: 435-258-5515. p. 2265

Creighton, Cheryl, Operations Mgr, Nantucket Atheneum, One India St, Nantucket, MA, 02554-3519. Tel: 508-228-1110. p. 1037

Creighton, Mary Lynn, Librn, Porter, Wright, Morris & Arthur LLP, 2020 K St, NW, Ste 600, Washington, DC, 20006. Tel: 202-778-3000. p. 374

Crelinsten, Michael, Exec Dir, Bibliotheque Publique Juive, 5151 Cote Ste Catherine, Montreal, QC, H3W 1M6, CANADA. Tel: 514-345-2627. p. 2717

Cremer, Judith, Dir, Pottawatomie Wabaunsee Regional Library, 306 N Fifth St, Saint Marys, KS, 66536-1404. Tel: 785-437-2778. p. 834

Cremonese, Rocco, User Experience Librn, Slippery Rock University of Pennsylvania, 109 Campus Loop, Slippery Rock, PA, 16057. Tel: 724-738-2058. p. 2007

Crenner, Christopher, Dr, Dir, Kansas University Medical Center, 1020-1030 Robinson Bldg, 3901 Rainbow Blvd, Kansas City, KS, 66160-7311. Tel: 913-588-7244. p. 817

Crenshaw, Annie, VPres, Butler County Historical-Genealogical Society Library, 309 Fort Dale Rd, Greenville, AL, 36037. Tel: 334-383-9564. p. 19

Crenshaw, J B, Dir, Lunenburg County Public Library System Inc, 117 S Broad St, Kenbridge, VA, 23944. Tel: 434-676-3456. p. 2327

Crenshaw, Jennifer, Br Mgr, Pickens County Library System, Central-Clemson Regional Branch, 105 Commons Way, Central, SC, 29630. Tel: 864-639-2711. p. 2058

Crenshaw, Marie, Libr Dir, Clarence Dillon Public Library, 2336 Lamington Rd, Bedminster, NJ, 07921. Tel: 908-234-2325. p. 1389

Crenshaw, Melissa, Br Mgr, Greenwood County Library, Ware Shoals Community Library, 54 S Greenwood Ave, Ware Shoals, SC, 29692. Tel: 864-377-4440. p. 2062

Cresap, Vern, Ref Librn, Thomas B Norton Public Library, 221 W 19th Ave, Gulf Shores, AL, 36542. Tel: 251-968-1176. p. 20

Cresci Callahan, Maureen, Head, Archives & Spec Coll, University of Connecticut, Archives & Special Collections, 405 Babbidge Rd, Unit 1205, Storrs, CT, 06269-1205. Tel: 860-486-3646. p. 340

Crespi, Maria, Mgr, Miami-Dade Public Library System, South Dade Regional, 10750 SW 211th St, Miami, FL, 33189. Tel: 305-233-8140. p. 424

Crespo, Hilda, VPres, Aspira Association Library, 1220 L St NW, Ste 701, Washington, DC, 20005. Tel: 202-841-0497. p. 361

Crespo, Javier, Mgr, University of Massachusetts Medical School, 55 Lake Ave N, Worcester, MA, 01655-0002. Tel: 508-856-7633. p. 1072

Crespo, Pastor, Jr, Archivist, Research Librn, Bronx County Historical Society, 3309 Bainbridge Ave, Bronx, NY, 10467. Tel: 718-881-8900, Ext 105. p. 1498

Cresswell, Samantha, Head, Circ, Elmhurst Public Library, 125 S Prospect Ave, Elmhurst, IL, 60126-3298. Tel: 630-279-8696. p. 585

Creutz, Joy, Circ Supvr, Rossford Public Library, 720 Dixie Hwy, Rossford, OH, 43460-1289. Tel: 419-666-0924. p. 1818

Creveling, Deb, Board Pres, Panorama Library, The Quinault, 1835 Circle Lane SE, Lacey, WA, 98503. Tel: 360-456-0111, Ext 4005. p. 2368

Crevelling, Sarah, Youth Serv Librn, Penn Yan Public Library, 214 Main St, Penn Yan, NY, 14527. Tel: 315-536-6114. p. 1617

Crew, Madeleine, Ref & Instruction, Sheridan College Library, 1430 Trafalgar Rd, Oakville, ON, L6H 2L1, CANADA. Tel: 905-459-7533, Ext 2574. p. 2663

Crews, Denise, PhD, Instruction Librn, Regent University Library, 1000 Regent University Dr, Virginia Beach, VA, 23464-5037. Tel: 757-352-4121. p. 2349

Crews, Gloria, Youth Serv, Shalimar Public Library, 115 Richbourg Ave, Shalimar, FL, 32579. Tel: 850-609-1515. p. 444

Crews, Meghan, Interim Dir, East Georgia State College Library, 131 College Circle, Swainsboro, GA, 30401-2699. Tel: 478-289-2087. p. 498

Crewse, Marissa, Br Mgr, Wright County Library, Laura Ingalls Wilder Library, 120 Business 60, Hwy 5, Mansfield, MO, 65804. Tel: 417-924-8068. p. 1248

Cribb, Kelly, Dir, Higgins Public Library, 201 N Main St, Higgins, TX, 79046. Tel: 806-852-2214. p. 2190

Cribbs, Jen, Ch Serv, Beaver Area Memorial Library, 100 College Ave, Beaver, PA, 15009-2794. Tel: 724-775-1132. p. 1908

Cribbs, Rhoda, Libr Mgr, Gilchrist County Public Library, 105 NE 11th Ave, Trenton, FL, 32693-3803. Tel: 352-463-3176. p. 451

Crichton, Deirdre, Chief Exec Officer, Librn, Gananoque Public Library, 100 Park St, Gananoque, ON, K7G 2Y5, CANADA. Tel: 613-382-2436. p. 2642

Crider, Bonita, Acq, Cat, Coll Develop, Houston Baptist University, 7502 Fondren Rd, Houston, TX, 77074-3298. Tel: 281-649-3179. p. 2194

Crider, Jo, Br Mgr, Aiken-Bamberg-Barnwell-Edgefield Regional Library, Williston Branch, 5121 Springfield Rd, Williston, SC, 29853-9762. Tel: 803-621-6000. p. 2045

Crighton, Lori, Librn, Palliser Regional Library, Assiniboia & District Public Library, 201 Third Ave W, Assiniboia, SK, S0H 0B0, CANADA. Tel: 306-642-3631. p. 2742

Crill, Katie, Dir, West Bonner Library District, 118 Main St, Priest River, ID, 83856-5059. Tel: 208-448-2207. p. 529

Crilley, Emily, Br Mgr, Tuscarawas County Public Library, Emma Huber Memorial Library, 356 Fifth St SW, Strasburg, OH, 44680. Tel: 330-878-5711. p. 1807

Crilly, Caitlin, Genealogy Librn, Teen Serv Librn, Ogden Farmers' Library, 269 Ogden Center Rd, Spencerport, NY, 14559. Tel: 585-617-6181, p. 1643

Crilly, Jody, Mgr, Edmonton Public Library, Clareview, 3808 139 Ave, Edmonton, AB, T5Y 3G4, CANADA. Tel: 780-495-1930. p. 2536

Crim, Victoria, Librn, California Department of Corrections Library System, Richard J Donovan Correctional Facility at Rock Mountain, 480 Alta Rd, San Diego, CA, 92179. Tel: 619-661-6500. p. 206

Criminger, Tommy, Youth Serv Mgr, Monticello-Union Township Public Library, 321 W Broadway St, Monticello, IN, 47960. Tel: 574-583-2665. p. 707

Crippen, Sheila, Curator, El Monte Museum of History Library, 3150 N Tyler Ave, El Monte, CA, 91731. Tel: 626-580-2232. p. 140

Criscione, Dan, Tech Librn, Mount Prospect Public Library, Ten S Emerson St, Mount Prospect, IL, 60056. Tel: 847-253-5675. p. 621

Crisco, Joseph, Libr Mgr, Palm Beach County Law Library, 200 W Atlantic Ave, Rm 2E-205, Delray Beach, FL, 33444. Tel: 561-274-1440. p. 394

Crisco, Karen, Br Mgr, Palm Beach County Library System, Royal Palm Beach Branch, 500 Civic Center Way, Royal Palm Beach, FL, 33411. Tel: 561-790-6030. p. 454

Crisler-Ruskey, Sarah, Libr Dir, Harrison County Library System, 12135 Old Hwy 49, Gulfport, MS, 39501. Tel: 228-539-0110. p. 1217

Crisman, Lisa, Br Mgr, Richmond Public Library, West End, 5420 Patterson Ave, Richmond, VA, 23226. Tel: 804-646-1877. p. 2342

Crissinger, John, Archivist, Ref (Info Servs), Ohio State University LIBRARIES, Newark Campus Library, Warner Library & Student Ctr, 1179 University Dr, Newark, OH, 43055-1797. Tel: 740-366-9307. p. 1776

Crissman, Crystal Sue, Libr Serv Mgr, Hollidaysburg Area Public Library, One Furnace Rd, Hollidaysburg, PA, 16648-1051. Tel: 814-695-5961. p. 1944

Crist, Annie, Ch, Beresford Public Library, 115 S Third St, Beresford, SD, 57004. Tel: 605-763-2782. p. 2074

Crist, Emily, Dir, Champlain College Library, 95 Summit St, Burlington, VT, 05401. Tel: 802-651-5827. p. 2280

Cristobal, Leggie, Librn, Nunavut Public Library Services, May Hakongak Community Library, PO Box 2106, Cambridge Bay, NU, X0B 0C0, CANADA. Tel: 867-983-2163. p. 2625

Critchfield, Ron, Dr, Exec Dir, Jessamine County Public Library, 600 S Main St, Nicholasville, KY, 40356. Tel: 859-885-3523. p. 870

Critchley, Elizabeth-Ann, Library Contact, College of the North Atlantic Library Services, St Anthony Campus, 83-93 East St, Rm 120, St. Anthony, NL, A0K 4S0, CANADA. Tel: 709-454-3559. p. 2609

Crittenden, Linda, Asst Dir, New Brunswick Free Public Library, 60 Livingston Ave, New Brunswick, NJ, 08901-2597. Tel: 732-745-5108, Ext 11. p. 1424

Croad, Patty, Asst Dir, Libr Serv, Bay Mills Community College, 12214 W Lakeshore Dr, Brimley, MI, 49715-9320. Tel: 906-248-3354, Ext 8418. p. 1087

Crocamo, Jim, Head of Libr, Columbia University, Social Work Library, School of Social Work, 2nd Flr, 1255 Amsterdam Ave, New York, NY, 10027. Tel: 2128546769. p. 1583

Crocco, Bruce, VPres, Libr Serv, OCLC Online Computer Library Center, Inc, 6565 Kilgour Pl, Dublin, OH, 43017-3395. Tel: 614-764-6000. p. 2772

Crocco, T J, ILL Tech, United States Coast Guard Academy Library, 35 Mohegan Ave, New London, CT, 06320. Tel: 860-444-8513. p. 329

Crochet, Tammie, Circ Mgr, Bossier Parish Libraries, 2206 Beckett St, Bossier City, LA, 71111. Tel: 318-746-1693. p. 885

Crocker, Daniel, Coordr, Electronic Res, Ref Librn, Emerson College, 120 Boylston St, Boston, MA, 02116-4624. Tel: 617-824-8939. p. 995

Crocker, Jane, Dir, Rowan College of New Jersey, 1400 Tanyard Rd, Sewell, NJ, 08080. Tel: 856-415-2252. p. 1442

Crocker, Jody, Dir, McCook Public Library, 802 Norris Ave, McCook, NE, 69001-3143. Tel: 308-345-1906. p. 1324

Crocker, Kimberly, Assoc Dir, Libr Serv, Covenant College, 14049 Scenic Hwy, Lookout Mountain, GA, 30750. Tel: 706-419-1430. p. 486

Crocker, Lori, Br Supvr, Duluth Public Library, 520 W Superior St, Duluth, MN, 55802. Tel: 218-730-4211. p. 1172

Crocker, Rachel, Libr Dir, Albany County Public Library, 310 S Eighth St, Laramie, WY, 82070-3969. Tel: 307-721-2580. p. 2496

Crocker, Wayne M, Dir, Petersburg Public Library, 201 W Washington St, Petersburg, VA, 23803. Tel: 804-733-2387. p. 2337

Crockett, Bridgette, Asst Libr Dir, Head, Pub Serv, Marple Public Library, 2599 Sproul Rd, Broomall, PA, 19008-2399. Tel: 610-356-1510. p. 1915

Crockett, Emily, Knowledge Management Analyst, Center for Creative Leadership Library, One Leadership Pl, Greensboro, NC, 27410. Tel: 336-286-4083. p. 1691

Crockett, John, Managing Librn, Washoe County Library System, Sierra View Library, 4001 S Virginia St, Reno, NV, 89502. Tel: 775-827-3232. p. 1350

Crockett, LaResa, Children's Coordr, Franklin Public Library, 421 12th St, Franklin, PA, 16323-0421. Tel: 814-432-5062. p. 1934

Crockett, Rebecca, Electronic Res Librn, Anna Maria College, 50 Sunset Lane, Paxton, MA, 01612-1198. Tel: 508-849-3405. p. 1045

Croff, Philip, Librn, Muskegon Area District Library, North Muskegon Walker Branch, 1522 Ruddiman Dr, North Muskegon, MI, 49445-3038. Tel: 231-744-6080. p. 1136

Crofford, Mary, Dir, Langley Public Library, 325 W Osage, Langley, OK, 74350. Tel: 918-782-4461. p. 1851

Croft Berry, Lara, Dir, Langdon Library, 328 Nimble Hill Rd, Newington, NH, 03801. Tel: 603-436-5154. p. 1376

Croft, Betty, Libr Tech, United States Navy, Naval Health Research Center, Wilkins Biomedical Library, Gate 4, Barracks Bldg 333, Rm 101, McClelland & Patterson Rds, San Diego, CA, 92152. Tel: 619-553-8426. p. 222

Croft, Janet Brennan, Assoc Univ Librn, University of Northern Iowa Library, 1227 W 27th St, Cedar Falls, IA, 50613-3675. Tel: 319-273-2812. p. 737

Croft, Jennifer, Librn, Southern Regional Technical College Library Services, Industrial Drive Campus, 361 Industrial Dr, Moultrie, GA, 31788. Tel: 229-217-4208. p. 499

Croft, Renee, Prog Mgr, Maryland State Library, 25 S Charles St, Ste 1310, Baltimore, MD, 21201. Tel: 410-713-2414. p. 955

Croft, Rosie, Univ Librn, Royal Roads University Library, 2005 Sooke Rd, Victoria, BC, V9B 5Y2, CANADA. Tel: 250-391-2699. p. 2583

Crogh, Audrey, Dir, Meadows Valley Public Library District, 400 Virginia St, New Meadows, ID, 83654. Tel: 208-347-3147. p. 527

Crognale, Amy M, Librn, Cleveland Psychoanalytic Center Library, 2460 Fairmount Blvd, Ste 312, Cleveland Heights, OH, 44106. Tel: 216-229-5959, Ext 102. p. 1771

Crohan, Catherine, Info Literacy/Instruction Coordr, Siena College, 515 Loudon Rd, Loudonville, NY, 12211. Tel: 518-782-6725. p. 1566

Croley, Betty, Circ Supvr, Whitley County Library, 285 S Third St, Williamsburg, KY, 40769. Tel: 606-549-0818. p. 877

Crolla, Vincent, Legislative Librn, Wyoming State Library, 2800 Central Ave, Cheyenne, WY, 82002. Tel: 307-777-5914. p. 2493

Cromartie, Shamella, Head, Pub Serv, Fayetteville State University, 1200 Murchison Rd, Fayetteville, NC, 28301-4298. Tel: 910-672-1750. p. 1689

Cromer, Jennifer, Librn, Lewis-Clark State College Library, 500 Eighth Ave, Lewiston, ID, 83501. Tel: 208-792-2829. p. 524

Cromi, Patricia, Managing Librn, Timken Co, 4500 Mt Pleasant Rd NW, WHQ-05, North Canton, OH, 44720. Tel: 234-262-2049. p. 1809

Cromley, Jami, Dir, Community District Library, 210 E Corunna Ave, Corunna, MI, 48817. Tel: 989-743-3287. p. 1094

Crompton, Sam, Tech Coordr, ImagineIF Libraries, 247 First Ave E, Kalispell, MT, 59901. Tel: 406-758-5820. p. 1297

Cromwell, Kara, Assoc Dir, Abilene Public Library, 209 NW Fourth, Abilene, KS, 67410-2690. Tel: 785-263-3082. p. 795

Cromwell, Verna, Tech, Cibecue Community Library, Six W Third St, Cibecue, AZ, 85911. Tel: 928-532-6240. p. 58

Cronce, Sandra L, Dir, Willingboro Public Library, Willingboro Town Ctr, 220 Willingboro Pkwy, Willingboro, NJ, 08046. Tel: 609-877-0476, 609-877-6668. p. 1455

Croneis, Karen, Assoc Dean, University of Alabama, University Libraries, University of Alabama Campus, Capstone Dr, Tuscaloosa, AL, 35487. Tel: 205-348-5569. p. 38

Cronin, Dorothy, Adult/YA Serv Librn, Crane Thomas Public Library, North Quincy Branch, 381 Hancock St, Quincy, MA, 02171. Tel: 617-376-1320, 617-376-1321. p. 1048

Cronin, Jill, Libr Dir, Greenwood Lake Public Library, 79 Waterstone Rd, Greenwood Lake, NY, 10925. Tel: 845-477-8377. p. 1542

Cronin, Kevin-Andrew, Evening & Weekend Access Serv Mgr, East Carolina University, Music Library, A J Fletcher Music Ctr, Rm A110, Greenville, NC, 27858. Tel: 252-328-1238. p. 1694

Cronin, Mary, Libr Dir, Cook Memorial Library, 93 Main St, Tamworth, NH, 03886. Tel: 603-323-8510. p. 1382
Cronin, Nick, Br Mgr, Cuyahoga County Public Library, Brook Park Branch, 6155 Engle Rd, Brook Park, OH, 44142-2105. Tel: 216-267-5250. p. 1813
Cronin, Nick, Br Mgr, Cuyahoga County Public Library, Parma Heights Branch, 6206 Pearl Rd, Parma Heights, OH, 44130-3045. Tel: 440-884-2313. p. 1813
Cronin, Susan, Ch Serv, Lynn Public Library, Five N Common St, Lynn, MA, 01902. Tel: 781-595-0567. p. 1030
Cronin, Timothy, Educ Coordr, Spring Creek Correctional Center Library, 3600 Bette Cato Rd, Seward, AK, 99664. Tel: 907-224-8143. p. 51
Cronin, Trisha, District Libr Mgr, Timberland Regional Library, 415 Tumwater Blvd SW, Tumwater, WA, 98501-5799. Tel: 360-943-5001. p. 2388
Cronise, Justin, Col Librn, Erie Community College-City Campus, 121 Ellicott St, Rm 101, Buffalo, NY, 14203. Tel: 716-851-1774. p. 1509
Cronise, Justin, Col Librn, Erie Community College-South Campus, 4041 Southwestern Blvd, Orchard Park, NY, 14127. Tel: 716-851-1775. p. 1612
Cronk, Beth, Head Librn, Cosmos Public Library, 230 Milky Way S, Cosmos, MN, 56228. Tel: 320-440-1012. p. 1171
Cronk, Beth, Head Librn, Litchfield Public Library, 216 N Marshall Ave, Litchfield, MN, 55355. Tel: 320-693-2483. p. 1180
Cronk, Bob, Dep Dir, Pub Serv, San Diego Public Library, 330 Park Blvd, MS 17, San Diego, CA, 92101. Tel: 619-236-5800. p. 219
Cronk, Elizabeth, Head Librn, Dassel Public Library, 460 Third St N, Dassel, MN, 55325. Tel: 320-275-3756. p. 1171
Cronk, Elizabeth, Head Librn, Grove City Public Library, 210 Atlantic Ave W, Grove City, MN, 56243. Tel: 320-857-2550. p. 1177
Cronk, Konnie, Curator, Registrar, Laramie Plains Museum Association Inc Library, 603 Ivinson Ave, Laramie, WY, 82070-3299. Tel: 307-742-4448. p. 2496
Cronk, Lindsay, Dean, Tulane University, 7001 Freret St, New Orleans, LA, 70118-5682. Tel: 504-865-5131. p. 903
Cronkhite, Jane, Assoc Dir, Monroe County Public Library, 303 E Kirkwood Ave, Bloomington, IN, 47408. Tel: 812-349-3050. p. 671
Crook, Don, Cataloger, Iberia Parish Library, 445 E Main St, New Iberia, LA, 70560-3710. Tel: 337-364-7024, 337-364-7074. p. 900
Crooker, Beth, Libr Dir, Mansfield Public Library, Five Main St, Temple, NH, 03084. Tel: 603-878-3100. p. 1382
Crooks, Harris, Dir, Knowledge Serv, Dir, Res Serv, Stroock & Stroock & Lavan Library, 180 Maiden Lane, New York, NY, 10038. Tel: 212-806-5700. p. 1602
Crooks, Judy, Circ & ILL, Connecticut State Library, 231 Capitol Ave, Hartford, CT, 06106. Tel: 860-704-2205. p. 317
Crooks, Laura, Dir, Alexander County Library, 77 First Ave SW, Taylorsville, NC, 28681. Tel: 828-632-4058. p. 1718
Crooks, Linda, Head, Circ, Eastern Monroe Public Library, 1002 N Ninth St, Stroudsburg, PA, 18360. Tel: 570-421-0800. p. 2010
Croos, Saran, Head, Eng Libr, University of New Brunswick Libraries, Engineering & Computer Science, Sir Edmund Head Hall, Rm C-15, 15 Dineen Dr, Fredericton, NB, E3B 5H5, CANADA. Tel: 506-458-7959. p. 2602
Cropper, Katie, Ch, Attica Public Library, 305 S Perry St, Attica, IN, 47918. Tel: 765-764-4194. p. 668
Cropper, Maureen, Electronic Res Librn, Bluegrass Community & Technical College, 221 Oswald Bldg, 470 Cooper Dr, Lexington, KY, 40506-0235. Tel: 859-246-6394. p. 862
Crosby, Jacqueline, Library Contact, Dawson Technical Institute, 3901 S State St, Chicago, IL, 60609. Tel: 773-602-5555. p. 560
Crosby, Jeanne, Cataloger, Circ Asst, Granby Free Public Library, 297 E State St, Granby, MA, 01033. Tel: 413-467-3320. p. 1021
Crosby, Jennifer, Dir, Granby Free Public Library, 297 E State St, Granby, MA, 01033. Tel: 413-467-3320. p. 1021
Crosby, Jo Ann, Br Mgr, Jackson County Library Services, White City Branch, 3143 Ave C, White City, OR, 97503-1443. Tel: 541-864-8880. p. 1886
Crosby, Kathy, Head Librn, Brooklyn Botanic Garden Library, 1000 Washington Ave, Brooklyn, NY, 11225. Tel: 718-623-7270. p. 1501
Crosby, Kathy, Asst Librn, Henryetta Public Library, 518 W Main St, Henryetta, OK, 74437. Tel: 918-652-7377. p. 1849
Crosby, Linda, Curric Librn, Research Librn, Fanshawe College, 1001 Fanshawe College Blvd, London, ON, N5Y 5R6, CANADA. Tel: 519-452-4240. p. 2653
Crosby, Lisa, Mgr, Brooks Public Library, JBS Canada Recreation Centre, 323 First St E, Brooks, AB, T1R 1C5, CANADA. Tel: 403-362-2947. p. 2524
Crosby, Luann, Assoc Librn, Northland Pioneer College Libraries, PO Box 610, Holbrook, AZ, 86025. Tel: 928-536-6222. p. 63
Crosby, Marita, Libr Mgr, Trapper Creek Public Library, 8901 E Devonshire Dr, Trapper Creek, AK, 99683. Tel: 907-861-7650. p. 52
Crosby, Paul, Mgr, FM, One Technology Way, Norwood, MA, 02062. Tel: 781-762-4300. p. 1044
Crosby, Sharon, Br Mgr, Macon County Public Library, Nantahala Community, 128 Nantahala School Rd, Topton, NC, 28781. Tel: 828-321-3020. p. 1690
Crosby, Sheila, Dep Dir, Carlsbad City Library, Library Learning Center, 3368 Eureka Pl, Carlsbad, CA, 92008. Tel: 760-931-4500. p. 128
Crosby, Yolanda, Cat, Tech Serv, South Georgia State College, 100 W College Park Dr, Douglas, GA, 31533-5098. Tel: 912-260-4323. p. 477
Crosby-Wilson, Shanna, Media Spec, Father Flanagan's Boys Home, 13727 Flanagan Blvd, Boys Town, NE, 68010. Tel: 531-355-8340. p. 1308
Crosman, Sarah, Coordr, Access Serv, Bradley University, 1501 W Bradley Ave, Peoria, IL, 61625. Tel: 309-677-2850. p. 634
Cross, Amy, Br Mgr, Manistee County Library System, Keddie Norconk Memorial Library, 12325 Virginia St, Bear Lake, MI, 49614. Tel: 231-864-2700. p. 1129
Cross, Amy Lynn, Libr Dir, Mount Carmel Library, 100 Main St, Mount Carmel, TN, 37645-9999. Tel: 423-357-4011. p. 2117
Cross, Denise, Tech Serv & Syst Librn, Quinsigamond Community College, 670 W Boylston St, Worcester, MA, 01606-2092. Tel: 508-854-4480. p. 1072
Cross, Jeanine, Libr Mgr, New York Public Library - Astor, Lenox & Tilden Foundations, Mott Haven Branch, 321 E 140th St, (@ Alexander Ave), Bronx, NY, 10454. Tel: 718-665-4878. p. 1596
Cross, Kat, Admin Serv, Consortium of College & University Media Centers, Indiana University, Franklin Hall 0009, 601 E Kirkwood Ave, Bloomington, IN, 47405-1223. Tel: 812-855-6049. p. 2765
Cross, Kiel, Communications Mgr, Palatine Public Library District, 700 N North Ct, Palatine, IL, 60067. Tel: 847-907-3600. p. 631
Cross, Mary, Librn, Meadowlark Library, 208 Main St, Lewis, KS, 67552. Tel: 620-324-5743. p. 821
Cross, Megan, Teen Librn, Willingboro Public Library, Willingboro Town Ctr, 220 Willingboro Pkwy, Willingboro, NJ, 08046. Tel: 609-877-0476, 609-877-6668. p. 1455
Cross, Naomi, Dir, Rostraver Public Library, 700 Plaza Dr, Belle Vernon, PA, 15012. Tel: 724-379-5511. p. 1909
Cross, Randall, Mgr, Libr Serv, Sachse Public Library, 3815 Sachse Rd, Ste C, Sachse, TX, 75048. Tel: 972-530-8966. p. 2235
Cross, Terry, Fac Mgr, Lakeland Library Cooperative, 4138 Three Mile Rd NW, Grand Rapids, MI, 49534-1134. Tel: 616-559-5253. p. 2767
Cross-Roen, Carol Ann, Head, Youth Serv, Medicine Hat Public Library, 414 First St SE, Medicine Hat, AB, T1A 0A8, CANADA. Tel: 403-502-8532. p. 2548
Crossed, Susan, Br Mgr, Mesa County Public Library District, Collbran Branch, 111 Main St, Collbran, CO, 81624. Tel: 970-487-3545. p. 284
Crossen, Patrick, Head, Tech Serv, Southwest Public Libraries, SPL Admin, 3359 Broadway, Grove City, OH, 43123. Tel: 614-875-6716. p. 1789
Crossen, Tami, Dir, Hudson Public Library, 100 S Beech St, Hudson, CO, 80642. Tel: 303-536-4550. p. 286
Crosser, Karen, Dir, Libr Serv, University of Arkansas for Medical Sciences, 223 E Jackson, Jonesboro, AR, 72401. Tel: 870-972-1290. p. 99
Crossley, Ruth, Asst Librn, Granisle Public Library, Two Village Sq, McDonald Ave, Granisle, BC, V0J 1W0, CANADA. Tel: 250-697-2713. p. 2567
Crossman, Jacquelyn, Librn, Pacific Islands Fisheries Science Center Library, NOAA IRC-NMFS/PIFSC/SOD/Library, 1845 Wasp Blvd, Bldg 176, Honolulu, HI, 96818. Tel: 808-725-5579. p. 512
Crossman, Paula, Dept Chair, Librn, Paradise Valley Community College, 18401 N 32nd St, Phoenix, AZ, 85032-1200. Tel: 602-787-7203. p. 71
Crosson, Helen, Exec Dir, Half Hollow Hills Community Library, Chestnut Hill School, 600 S Service Rd, Dix Hills, NY, 11746. Tel: 631-421-4530. p. 1526
Croston, Kendel, Dir, Stark County Law Library, 110 Central Plaza S, Ste 401, Canton, OH, 44702. Tel: 330-451-7380. p. 1756
Croteau, Bethany, Res Support & Instruction Librn, Bunker Hill Community College, E Bldg, 3rd Flr, Rm E300, 250 New Rutherford Ave, Boston, MA, 02129-2925. Tel: 617-936-1916. p. 994
Croteau, Ginette, Libr Supvr, University of Manitoba Libraries, Albert D Cohen Management Library, 206 Drake Ctr, 181 Freedman Crescent, Winnipeg, MB, R3T 5V4, CANADA. Tel: 204-474-6567. p. 2595
Croteau, Ginette, Libr Supvr, University of Manitoba Libraries, Architecture & Fine Arts Library, 206 Russell Bldg, 84 Curry Pl, Winnipeg, MB, R3T 2N2, CANADA. Tel: 204-474-6567. p. 2595
Croteau, Jeff, Dir, Libr & Archives, Scottish Rite Masonic Museum & Library, Inc, 33 Marrett Rd, Lexington, MA, 02421. Tel: 781-457-4125. p. 1028
Crotty, Kaitlin, Dir, Rogers State University Library, 1701 W Will Rogers Blvd, Claremore, OK, 74017-3252. Tel: 918-343-7717. p. 1844
Crouch, Megan L, Library Contact, Izard County Library, Nine Club Rd, Horseshoe Bend, AR, 72512-2717. Tel: 870-670-4318. p. 98
Crouch, Stephanie, Libr Dir, Dunkirk Public Library, 127 W Washington St, Dunkirk, IN, 47336-1218. Tel: 765-768-6872. p. 679
Croucher, Lisa, Exec Dir, Triangle Research Libraries Network, Wilson Library, CB No 3940, Chapel Hill, NC, 27514-8890. Tel: 919-962-8022. p. 2772
Crouse, Julie, Br Mgr, Forsyth County Public Library, Paddison Memorial Branch, 248 Harmon Lane, Kernersville, NC, 27284. Tel: 336-703-2930. p. 1725
Crouse, Tony, Dir, Shelton Public Library, 313 C St, Shelton, NE, 68876. Tel: 308-647-5182. p. 1336
Croushore, Renee, Head of Libr, University of Wisconsin-Madison, Steenbock Library, 550 Babcock Dr, Madison, WI, 53706. Tel: 608-262-1371, 608-262-9635. p. 2452

Crovatto, Ellen, Dir of Develop, New Canaan Library, 151 Main St, New Canaan, CT, 06840. Tel: 203-594-5025. p. 324

Crow, Alyssa, Br Mgr, Abilene Public Library, South Branch Library, 4310 Buffalo Gap Rd, No 1246, Abilene, TX, 79606. Tel: 325-698-7378. p. 2132

Crow, Amy, Mgr, County of Los Angeles Public Library, Helen Renwick Library - Claremont Branch, 208 N Harvard Ave, Claremont, CA, 91711. Tel: 909-621-4902. p. 137

Crow, Andrea, Mgr, County of Los Angeles Public Library, Paramount Library, 16254 Colorado Ave, Paramount, CA, 90723-5085. Tel: 562-630-3171. p. 137

Crow, Becky, Br Mgr, Nicholson Memorial Library System, South Garland Branch Library, 4845 Broadway Blvd, Garland, TX, 75043. Tel: 972-205-3920. p. 2184

Crow, Beth, Dir, Gilman Public Library, 106 N Main St, Gilman, IA, 50106. Tel: 641-498-2120. p. 755

Crow, Betty, Asst Libr Mgr, Bawlf Public Library, 203 Hanson St, Box 116, Bawlf, AB, T0B 0J0, CANADA. Tel: 780-373-3882. p. 2523

Crow, Lance, Educ Dir, Richmond Art Museum Library, 350 Hub Etchison Pkwy, Richmond, IN, 47374-0816. Tel: 765-966-0256. p. 715

Crow, Lynda, Br Mgr, Prairie-River Library District, Culdesac Community, 714 Main St, Culdesac, ID, 83524-7806. Tel: 208-843-5215. p. 524

Crow Sheaner, Kim, Libr Dir, Baxter County Library, 300 Library Hill, Mountain Home, AR, 72653. Tel: 870-580-0987. p. 105

Crowder, Amy, State Law Librn, Wisconsin State Law Library, 120 Martin Luther King Jr Blvd, 2nd Flr, Madison, WI, 53703. Tel: 608-261-2340. p. 2452

Crowder, Elizabeth, Librn, United States Court of Appeals, US Courts Library, 5122 Federal Bldg, 844 King St, Unit 43, Wilmington, DE, 19801. Tel: 302-573-5880, 302-573-5881. p. 358

Crowdy, Deborah, Youth Serv Mgr, Coshocton Public Library, 655 Main St, Coshocton, OH, 43812-1697. Tel: 740-622-0956. p. 1778

Crowe, Cathy, Libr Tech, Southern Union State Community College, Opelika Campus Library, 301 Lake Condy Rd, Opelika, AL, 36801. Tel: 334-745-6437, Ext 5407. p. 39

Crowe, Corinne, Asst Librn, Lake Benton Public Library, 110 E Benton St, Lake Benton, MN, 56149. Tel: 507-368-4641, Ext 3. p. 1179

Crowe, Jessica, Dir, Fayette County Memorial Library, 326 Temple Ave N, Fayette, AL, 35555. Tel: 205-932-6625. p. 17

Crowe, Kate, Rare Bks, Spec Coll Librn, University of Denver, 2150 E Evans Ave, Denver, CO, 80208. Tel: 303-871-3441. p. 277

Crowe, Lilah J, Exec Dir, Itasca County Historical Society, 201 Pokegama Ave N, Grand Rapids, MN, 55744. Tel: 218-326-6431. p. 1177

Crowe, Linda, Librn, Augustana Lutheran Church Library, 5000 E Alameda Ave, Denver, CO, 80246. Tel: 303-388-4678. p. 273

Crowe, Pam, Br Mgr, Kitsap Regional Library, Downtown Bremerton Branch, 612 Fifth St, Bremerton, WA, 98337-1416. Tel: 360-377-3955. p. 2359

Crowe, Stephanie, Assoc Dir, Academic & Research Engagement, University of North Carolina Wilmington Library, 601 S College Rd, Wilmington, NC, 28403. Tel: 910-962-7858. p. 1723

Crowell, Beverly J, Pub Serv Librn, Alfred University, Scholes Library of Ceramics, New York State College of Ceramics at Alfred University, Two Pine St, Alfred, NY, 14802-1297. Tel: 607-871-2950. p. 1485

Crowell, Brian, Electronic Res Librn, Florida Agricultural & Mechanical University Libraries, 525 Orr Dr, Tallahassee, FL, 32307-4700. Tel: 850-599-8675. p. 446

Crowell, Garrett, Circ Mgr, Rutherford County Library System, 105 W Vine St, Murfreesboro, TN, 37130-3673. Tel: 615-893-4131, Ext 116. p. 2117

Crowell, Jennifer, Libr Dir, United States Air Force, Bldg 219, 7424 N Homer Dr, 56 SVS/SVMG FL 4887, Luke AFB, AZ, 85309. Tel: 623-856-7191. p. 66

Crowell, Karen, Youth Serv Librn, Oakmont Carnegie Library, 700 Allegheny River Blvd, Oakmont, PA, 15139. Tel: 412-828-9532. p. 1972

Crowell, Nancy E, Libr Dir, Scarborough Public Library, 48 Gorham Rd, Scarborough, ME, 04074. Tel: 207-396-6266. p. 939

Crowell, Rhoda, Youth Serv Supvr, West Springfield Public Library, 200 Park St, West Springfield, MA, 01089. Tel: 413-736-4561, Ext 4. p. 1066

Crowford, Allison, Access Serv Librn, Jacksonville University, 2800 University Blvd N, Jacksonville, FL, 32211-3394. Tel: 904-256-7934. p. 413

Crowley, Brian R, Ref Librn, Benedict College Library, 1600 Harden St, Columbia, SC, 29204. Tel: 803-705-4364. p. 2053

Crowley, Michael, Chief, Music Librn, City College of the City University of New York, Music Library, Shepard Hall, Rm 160, 160 Convent Ave, New York, NY, 10031. Tel: 212-650-7120. p. 1582

Crowley, Shae, Dir, Williamsburg Community Library, 107 S Louisa, Williamsburg, KS, 66095. Tel: 785-746-5407. p. 844

Crowson, Nicole, Pub Serv Librn, Cedar Mill Community Library, Bethany Branch, 15325 NW Central Dr, Ste J-8, Portland, OR, 97229-0986. Tel: 503-617-7323. p. 1891

Crowther, Sherry, Librn, Lester B Pearson College of the Pacific, 650 Pearson College Dr, Victoria, BC, V9C 4H7, CANADA. Tel: 250-391-2411. p. 2583

Crowthers, Kim, Libr Dir, Clermont County Law Library Association, Clermont County Court House, 270 Main St, Batavia, OH, 45103. Tel: 513-732-7109. p. 1749

Croy, Betty, Tech Serv, Edmonds College Library, 20000 68th Ave W, Lynnwood, WA, 98036. Tel: 425-640-1529. p. 2370

Crozier, Charlene, Dir, Orem Public Library, 58 N State St, Orem, UT, 84057. Tel: 801-229-7050. p. 2268

Crozier, Heather, Electronic Res Librn, Ohio Northern University, 525 S Main St, Ada, OH, 45810. Tel: 419-772-2182. p. 1743

Cruce, Sarah, Dir, Rainsville Public Library, 941 Main St E, Rainsville, AL, 35986. Tel: 256-638-3311. p. 34

Cruickshank, Diane, Ref & Instruction Librn, University of the Fraser Valley, Chilliwack Campus, 45190 Caen Ave, Bldg A, Chilliwack, BC, V2R 0N3, CANADA. Tel: 604-504-7441, Ext 2268. p. 2562

Cruickshank, John W, Librn, University of Georgia Libraries, 1109 Experiment St, Griffin, GA, 30223-1797. Tel: 770-228-7238. p. 481

Cruickshank, Michael, Operations Mgr, Woodstock Public Library, 445 Hunter St, Woodstock, ON, N4S 4G7, CANADA. Tel: 519-539-4801. p. 2705

Cruise, Adele, Operations Dir, Cecil County Public Library, 301 Newark Ave, Elkton, MD, 21921-5441. Tel: 510-996-1055, Ext 104. p. 964

Crum, Janet, Dir, University of Arizona Libraries, Health Sciences Library, 1501 N Campbell Ave, Tucson, AZ, 85724. Tel: 520-626-6178. p. 83

Crum, Jennifer, Fulfillment & Front Desk Coord, Wabash College, 301 W Wabash Ave, Crawfordsville, IN, 47933. Tel: 765-361-6039. p. 677

Crumbley, Paige, Instruction Librn, ILL, Res & Ref Librn, Huntingdon College, 1500 E Fairview Ave, Montgomery, AL, 36106. Tel: 334-833-4421. p. 28

Crumit-Hancock, Lisa, Asst Dean, Libr & Acad Support Serv, Libr Dir, Defiance College, 201 College Pl, Defiance, OH, 43512-1667. Tel: 419-783-2332. p. 1781

Crumlish, Sandra, Mgr, St Jude Medical Library & Resource Center, Library & Resource Ctr, 15900 Valley View Ct, Sylmar, CA, 91342. Tel: 818-362-6822, 818-493-3101. p. 251

Crummey, Karon J, Client Serv Librn, Government of Canada, Federal Courts & Tax Court of Canada, Courts Administration Service-Library Services, 90 Sparks St, Ottawa, ON, K1A 0H9, CANADA. Tel: 613-943-0839. p. 2667

Crummy, Kelly, Ch, Bedford Free Library, 32 Village Green, Bedford, NY, 10506. Tel: 914-234-3570. p. 1491

Crump, Amy, Dir, Bellwood Public Library, 600 Bohland Ave, Bellwood, IL, 60104-1896. Tel: 708-547-7393. p. 541

Crump, Amy, Adminr, Homewood Public Library, 17917 Dixie Hwy, Homewood, IL, 60430-1703. Tel: 708-798-0121, Ext 214. p. 601

Crump, Carol, Libr Assoc, Desoto Parish Library, Pelican Branch, 145 Jackson Ave, Pelican, LA, 71063-2803. Tel: 318-755-2353. p. 896

Crump, Chrissy, Youth Librn, Enterprise Public Library, 101 E Grubbs St, Enterprise, AL, 36330. Tel: 334-347-2636. p. 15

Crump, Christi, Asst Dir, Operations, Bath County Memorial Library, Sharpsburg Branch, 7781 W Tunnel Hill Rd, Sharpsburg, KY, 40374. Tel: 606-247-2100. p. 871

Crump, Cynthia, Mgr, Libr Serv, St Clair College of Applied Arts & Technology Library, 2000 Talbot Rd W, Windsor, ON, N9A 6S4, CANADA. Tel: 519-972-2739. p. 2704

Crump, Dan, Pub Serv Librn, American River College Library, 4700 College Oak Dr, Sacramento, CA, 95841. Tel: 916-484-8455. p. 205

Crump, Kelsey, ILL Mgr, University of South Carolina Aiken, 471 University Pkwy, Aiken, SC, 29801. Tel: 803-641-3504. p. 2046

Crump, Lois, Cataloger, Bath County Memorial Library, 24 W Main St, Owingsville, KY, 40360. Tel: 606-674-2531. p. 871

Crump, Rene, Br Mgr, Gaston County Public Library, Union Road, 5800 Union Rd, Gastonia, NC, 28056. Tel: 704-852-4073. p. 1690

Crumpler, Dawn L, Collection Support Librn, United States Military Academy Library, Jefferson Hall Library & Learning Ctr, 758 Cullum Rd, West Point, NY, 10996. Tel: 845-938-8301. p. 1663

Crumpton, Michael A, Dean, Univ Libr, University of North Carolina at Greensboro, 320 College Ave, Greensboro, NC, 27412-0001. p. 1693

Crumrin, Robin A, Dean, Libr Serv, Indiana State University, 510 North 6 1/2 St, Terre Haute, IN, 47809. Tel: 812-237-3700. p. 720

Cruse, Cheryl, Syst/Tech Proc Librn, Shasta College Library, 11555 Old Oregon Trail, Redding, CA, 96003-7692. Tel: 530-242-2348. p. 198

Cruse, David, Electronic Res Librn, Adrian College, 110 S Madison St, Adrian, MI, 49221. Tel: 517-265-5161, Ext 4241. p. 1075

Crusham, Cate, Br Mgr, Public Library of Cincinnati & Hamilton County, Green Township, 6525 Bridgetown Rd, Cincinnati, OH, 45248. Tel: 513-369-6095. p. 1762

Crusham, Cate, Br Mgr, Public Library of Cincinnati & Hamilton County, Reading Branch, 8740 Reading Rd, Reading, OH, 45215. Tel: 513-369-4465. p. 1763

Cruson, Stella, Asst Librn, Lyons Public Library, 279 Eighth St, Lyons, OR, 97358-2122. Tel: 503-859-2366. p. 1885

Crutcher, Martica, Libr Spec, Humboldt County Library, McDermitt Branch, 135 Oregon Rd, McDermitt, NV, 89421. Tel: 775-532-8014. p. 1351

Crutcher, Wendy, Coll Develop Coordr, Head, Tech Serv, County of Los Angeles Public Library, 7400 E Imperial Hwy, Downey, CA, 90242-3375. Tel: 562-940-8571. p. 134

Crutchfield, Allison, Coll Serv Librn, East Central University, 1100 E 14th St, Ada, OK, 74820. Tel: 580-559-5369. p. 1839
Cruz, Alesha J, Dir, Runge Public Library, 311 N Helena St, Runge, TX, 78151. Tel: 830-239-4192. p. 2235
Cruz, Aurora, Br Adminr, Yonkers Public Library, Grinton I Will Branch, 1500 Central Park Ave, Yonkers, NY, 10710. Tel: 914-337-5963. p. 1668
Cruz, Brandon, Commun Librn, Fort Vancouver Regional Library District, The Mall Library Connection, 8700 NE Vancouver Mall Dr, Ste 285, Vancouver, WA, 98662. p. 2391
Cruz, Carlos, Multimedia/Instruction Designer, Brooklyn College Library, 2900 Bedford Ave, Brooklyn, NY, 11210. Tel: 718-951-4667. p. 1501
Cruz, Crissy, Head, Children's Servx, Dustin Michael Sekula Memorial Library, 1906 S Closner Blvd, Edinburg, TX, 78539. Tel: 956-383-6246. p. 2173
Cruz, David, Dir, Operations, Butler, Rubin, Saltarelli & Boyd LLP, 321 N Clark St, Ste 400, Chicago, IL, 60654. Tel: 312-223-1690, 312-444-9660. p. 555
Cruz, Delia, Librn III, Inter-American University of Puerto Rico, PO Box 70351, Hato Rey, PR, 00936. Tel: 787-751-1912, Ext 2031. p. 2511
Cruz, Francisco, Head, Circ, Cicero Public Library, 5225 W Cermak Rd, Cicero, IL, 60804. Tel: 708-652-8084. p. 571
Cruz, John, Mgr, Circ Serv, Stevens Institute of Technology, One Castle Point Terrace, Hoboken, NJ, 07030. Tel: 201-216-5334. p. 1408
Cruz, Noemi, Dir, Calhoun County Library, 200 W Mahan St, Port Lavaca, TX, 77979. Tel: 361-552-7323. p. 2228
Cruz, Nydia, Asst Admin, Stevens Institute of Technology, One Castle Point Terrace, Hoboken, NJ, 07030. Tel: 201-216-5200. p. 1408
Cruz, Susan R, Head Librn, Hardtner Public Library, 102 E Central, Hardtner, KS, 67057. Tel: 620-296-4586. p. 811
Cruz-Chaudhry, Isbel, Mgr, Cat & Coll Serv, Wake Forest University, Law Library, Worrell Professional Ctr, 1834 Wake Forest Rd, Winston-Salem, NC, 27109. Tel: 336-758-4520. p. 1726
Cryans, Lynda, Libr Tech, Canada Department of Justice Montreal Headquarters Library, East Tower, 9th flr, No 200 Quest boul Rene-Levesque W, Montreal, QC, H2Z 1X4, CANADA. Tel: 514-283-6674, 514-283-8739. p. 2721
Cryderman, Deb, Dir, Airdrie Public Library, 111-304 Main St SE, Airdrie, AB, T4B 3C3, CANADA. Tel: 403-948-0600. p. 2521
Cryderman, Deb, Dir, Grande Prairie Public Library, 101-9839 103 Ave, Grande Prairie, AB, T8V 6M7, CANADA. Tel: 780-532-3580. p. 2541
Crymes, Martha, Br Mgr, Morehouse Parish Library, Collinston Branch, 4620 Main St, Collinston, LA, 71229. Tel: 318-874-3531. p. 881
Cryst, Amy, Asst Br Mgr, Orange County Public Library, Wilderness, 6421 Flat Run Rd, Locust Grove, VA, 22508. Tel: 540-854-5310. p. 2336
Cubbon, Natalie, Cataloger, Oil City Library, Two Central Ave, Oil City, PA, 16301-2795. Tel: 814-678-3072. p. 1973
Cubie, David, Dir, West Orange Public Library, Ten Rooney Circle, West Orange, NJ, 07052. Tel: 973-736-0198. p. 1453
Cuccaro, Maria, District Consultant, Cambria County Library System & District Center, 248 Main St, Johnstown, PA, 15901. Tel: 814-536-5131. p. 1947
Cuccaro, Sydney, Sr Researcher, White & Case LLP, 701 13th St NW, Washington, DC, 20005-3807. Tel: 202-626-3600, 202-626-6475. p. 381
Cuccia, Kevin Dominic, Sci/Eng Librn, Louisiana Tech University, Everett St at The Columns, Ruston, LA, 71272. Tel: 318-257-3555. p. 906
Cucco, Caren, Mgr, Circ & Tech Serv, Napa County Library, American Canyon Branch, 300 Crawford Way, American Canyon, CA, 94503. Tel: 707-644-1136. p. 182
Cucksey, Elli, Head Librn, Trinity Lutheran Seminary at Capital University, 2199 E Main St, Columbus, OH, 43205. Tel: 614-236-6853. p. 1778
Cuenco, Marlene, Pub Serv Librn, Supreme Court Law Library, 417 S King St, Rm 119, Honolulu, HI, 96813. Tel: 808-539-4964. p. 512
Cuervo, Adriana, Head, Archival Colls & Servs, Rutgers University Libraries, Institute of Jazz Studies, John Cotton Dana Library, 185 University Ave, 4th Flr, Newark, NJ, 07102. Tel: 973-353-5595. p. 1428
Cuffe, Justin, Curator, Reynolds-Alberta Museum Reference Centre, 6426 40th Ave, Wetaskiwin, AB, T9A 2G1, CANADA. Tel: 780-312-2080. p. 2559
Cuffy, Tywanda L, Dir, External Relations, University of Delaware Library, 181 S College Ave, Newark, DE, 19717-5267. Tel: 302-831-2965. p. 355
Cui, Hong, Prof, University of Arizona, Harvill Bldg, 4th Flr, 1103 E Second St, Tucson, AZ, 85721, Tel: 520-621-3565. p. 2782
Culbertson, Dee, Libr Dir, Madison Public Library, 6111 Middle Ridge Rd, Madison, OH, 44057-2818. Tel: 440-428-2189. p. 1798
Cull, Samara, Chief Exec Officer, Head Librn, Armstrong Township Public Library, 35 Tenth St, Earlton, ON, P0J 1E0, CANADA. Tel: 705-563-2717. p. 2639
Cullen, Alesia, Br Mgr, Scenic Regional Library, Saint Clair Branch, 515 E Springfield Rd, Saint Clair, MO, 63077. Tel: 636-629-2546. p. 1283
Cullen, Amber, Dir of Develop, The University of Chicago Library, 1100 E 57th St, Chicago, IL, 60637-1502. Tel: 773-834-3744. p. 569
Cullen, Ann, Bus Librn, Emory University Libraries, Goizueta Business Library, 540 Asbury Circle, Atlanta, GA, 30322. Tel: 404-727-1641. p. 463
Cullen, Cindy, Dir, Dennis Public Library, Five Hall St, Dennisport, MA, 02639. Tel: 508-760-6219. p. 1014
Cullen, Emily, Curator, University of Maryland, Baltimore County, 1000 Hilltop Circle, Baltimore, MD, 21250. Tel: 410-455-2356. p. 958
Cullen, Inga, Libr Dir, Davis Public Library, 1391 Rte 123 N, Stoddard, NH, 03464. Tel: 603-446-6251. p. 1381
Cullen, Jennifer, Libr Dir, Elmwood Park Public Library, 210 Lee St, Elmwood Park, NJ, 07407. Tel: 201-796-8888. p. 1401
Cullen, Kevin, Chief Curator, Dep Dir, Wisconsin Maritime Museum, 75 Maritime Dr, Manitowoc, WI, 54220. Tel: 920-684-0218. p. 2453
Cullen, Mary Ann, Assoc Dept Head, Georgia State University, Alpharetta Campus, 3705 Brookside Pkwy, Alpharetta, GA, 30022. Tel: 678-240-6139. p. 464
Cullen, Robert, Info Res Mgr, American Association of State Highway & Transportation Officials Library, 555 12th St NW, Ste 1000, Washington, DC, 20004. Tel: 202-624-8918. p. 359
Culler, Julie, Librn, Kingsley Public Library, 220 Main St, Kingsley, IA, 51028. Tel: 712-378-2410. p. 763
Culler, Lois H, Dir, Inova Fairfax Hospital, 3300 Gallows Rd, Falls Church, VA, 22042. Tel: 703-776-3234. p. 2317
Culleton, James, Archivist, Roman Catholic Diocese of Fresno Library, 1550 N Fresno St, Fresno, CA, 93703-3788. Tel: 559-488-7400. p. 147
Culley, Sharon, Asst Librn, Lyndon Carnegie Library, 127 E Sixth, Lyndon, KS, 66451. Tel: 785-828-4520. p. 822
Culligan, Lurana, Circ, Edmonds College Library, 20000 68th Ave W, Lynnwood, WA, 98036. Tel: 425-640-1529. p. 2370
Cullings, Karen, Exec Dir, Dauphin County Library System, 101 Walnut St, Harrisburg, PA, 17101. Tel: 717-234-4961. p. 1940
Cullnane, Chris, Dir of Libr, Belhaven University, 1500 Peachtree St, Jackson, MS, 39202. Tel: 601-968-5947. p. 1221
Cullum, Marguerite, Librn, Crazy Horse Memorial Library, 12151 Avenue of the Chiefs, Crazy Horse, SD, 57730-8900. Tel: 605-673-4681, Ext 285. p. 2075
Culp, Christine, Div Dir, Pub Serv, Alachua County Library District, 401 E University Ave, Gainesville, FL, 32601-5453. Tel: 352-334-3922. p. 406
Culpepper Brookins, Lauren, Asst Dir, De Soto Trail Regional Library System, 145 E Broad St, Camilla, GA, 31730. Tel: 229-336-8372. p. 468
Culshaw, John P, Univ Librn, University of Iowa Libraries, 100 Main Library, 125 W Washington St, Iowa City, IA, 52242-1420. p. 760
Culver, Caroline, Librn, Coastal Pines Technical College, Jesup Library, 1777 W Cherry St, Jesup, GA, 31545. Tel: 912-427-1929. p. 503
Culver, Kate, Colls Mgr, Longwood University, Redford & Race St, Farmville, VA, 23909. Tel: 434-395-2438. p. 2318
Culver, Rachel, Dir, Georgetown Public Library, 123 W Pine St, Georgetown, DE, 19947. Tel: 302-856-7958. p. 353
Culwell, Charlotte, Vols Librn, Oak Grove Baptist Church Library, 2829 Oak Grove Church Rd, Carrollton, GA, 30117. Tel: 770-834-7019. p. 469
Cumbey, Susan, Dir of Collections & Exhibitions, Fort Ward Museum, 4301 W Braddock Rd, Alexandria, VA, 22304. Tel: 703-746-4848. p. 2303
Cumby, Jamie Elizabeth, Librn, Grolier Club of New York Library, 47 E 60th St, New York, NY, 10022. Tel: 212-838-6690, Ext 5. p. 1587
Cumming, Alice, Br Mgr, Stone County Library, Crane Area Branch, 201 Main St, Crane, MO, 65633. Tel: 417-723-8261. p. 1247
Cumming, Gregory, Mus Historian, National Archives & Records Administration, 18001 Yorba Linda Blvd, Yorba Linda, CA, 92886. Tel: 714-983-9120, 714-983-9320. p. 260
Cumming, Linda, Br Librn, Grand County Library District, Granby Branch, 55 Zero St, Granby, CO, 80446. Tel: 970-887-2149. p. 283
Cumming, Malia, Access Serv Asst, University of Western States Library, 8000 NE Tillamook St, Portland, OR, 97213. Tel: 503-251-5752. p. 1894
Cummings, Arlene, Librn, First Baptist Church, 395 Marion St NE, Salem, OR, 97301. Tel: 503-364-2285. p. 1896
Cummings, Brandi, Interim Dir, Kenosha County Library System, 7979 38th Ave, Kenosha, WI, 53142. Tel: 262-564-6113. p. 2444
Cummings, Brandi, Interim Dir, Kenosha Public Library, 7979 38th Ave, Kenosha, WI, 53142. Tel: 262-564-6113. p. 2444
Cummings, Brenda, Access Serv, Head, Outreach Serv, Worcester Polytechnic Institute, 100 Institute Rd, Worcester, MA, 01609-2280. Tel: 508-831-5410. p. 1073
Cummings, Ellen, Br Mgr, Tulsa City-County Library, Zarrow Regional Library, 2224 W 51st, Tulsa, OK, 74107. p. 1866
Cummings, Joel, Head, Coll Develop, Washington State University Libraries, 100 Dairy Rd, Pullman, WA, 99164. Tel: 509-335-6493. p. 2374
Cummings, Katherine, Libr Dir, Luzerne County Community College Library, 1333 S Prospect St, Nanticoke, PA, 18634-3899. Tel: 800-377-5222, Ext 7420. p. 1967
Cummings, Kathy, Br Mgr, Lincoln County Libraries, Alum Creek Public Library, 255 Midway School Rd, Alum Creek, WV, 25003. Tel: 304-756-9211. p. 2403
Cummings, Ken, Supvr, Libr Serv, Aird & Berlis LLP, Brookfield Pl, Ste 1800, 181 Bay St, Toronto, ON, M5J 2T9, CANADA. Tel: 416-863-1500. p. 2686

Cummings, Lindsay, Head of Adult & Young Adult Services, Upper Dublin Public Library, 520 Virginia Ave, Fort Washington, PA, 19034. Tel: 215-628-8744. p. 1933
Cummings, Lindy, Research Historian, Tryon Palace, 529 S Front St, New Bern, NC, 28562-5614. Tel: 252-639-3500, 252-639-3593. p. 1706
Cummings, Michael, Libr Supvr, North Carolina Justice Academy, 200 W College St, Salemburg, NC, 28385. Tel: 910-926-6016. p. 1714
Cummings, Michael D, Dir, Flat Rock Public Library, 25200 Gibraltar Rd, Flat Rock, MI, 48134. Tel: 734-782-2430. p. 1105
Cummings, Nina, Photo Archivist, Field Museum of Natural History, 1400 S DuSable Lake Shore Dr, Chicago, IL, 60605-2496. Tel: 312-665-7892. p. 561
Cummings, Rod, Automation Syst Coordr, Lincoln City Libraries, 136 S 14th St, Lincoln, NE, 68508-1899. Tel: 402-441-8522. p. 1321
Cummings-Witter, Pat, Archivist, State University of New York at Fredonia, 280 Central Ave, Fredonia, NY, 14063. Tel: 716-673-3191. p. 1535
Cummings-Young, Elaine, Dir, Bellmore Memorial Library, 2288 Bedford Ave, Bellmore, NY, 11710. Tel: 516-785-2990. p. 1492
Cummins, Ashley Copeland, Libr Dir, Russellville Public Library, 110 E Lawrence St, Russellville, AL, 35653. Tel: 256-332-1535. p. 35
Cummins, Lee Ann, Dir, Lyon County Public Library, 261 Commerce St, Eddyville, KY, 42038. Tel: 270-388-7720. p. 853
Cummins, Patti, Ref & ILL Librn, Southwest Kansas Library System, 100 Military Ave, Ste 210, Dodge City, KS, 67801. Tel: 620-225-1231, Ext 207. p. 805
Cundick, Bryce D, Dir, University of Maine at Farmington, 116 South St, Farmington, ME, 04938-1990. Tel: 207-778-7210. p. 925
Cundieff, Jackie, Adult Serv Supvr, Temple Public Library, 100 W Adams Ave, Temple, TX, 76501-7641. Tel: 254-298-5333. p. 2247
Cunetto, Stephen, Assoc Dean, Univ Libr, Mississippi State University, 395 Hardy Rd, Mississippi State, MS, 39762. Tel: 662-325-7668. p. 1227
Cunha, Linda R, Asst Dir, Westport Free Public Library, 408 Old County Rd, Westport, MA, 02790. Tel: 508-636-1100. p. 1068
Cunio, Bridget, Ref Librn, Endicott College Library, 376 Hale St, Beverly, MA, 01915. Tel: 978-232-2285. p. 989
Cunniff, Nina, Dep Chief Exec Officer, Bradford-West Gwillimbury Public Library, 425 Holland St W, Bradford, ON, L3Z 0J2, CANADA. Tel: 905-775-3328, Ext 6105. p. 2632
Cunningham, Christine, Head Librn, Homer Community Library, 500 E Second St, Homer, IL, 61849. Tel: 217-896-2121. p. 600
Cunningham, Deana, Br Mgr, Alamance County Public Libraries, May Memorial Library, 342 S Spring St, Burlington, NC, 27215. Tel: 336-229-3588. p. 1676
Cunningham, Deanna, Info Serv Assoc, Drake University, 2725 University Ave, Des Moines, IA, 50311. Tel: 515-271-3993. p. 746
Cunningham, Deborah, Circ Supvr, Stoneham Public Library, 431 Main St, Stoneham, MA, 02180. Tel: 781-438-1324. p. 1058
Cunningham, Donna, Libr Dir, Athens Municipal Library, 410 E Hargrave St, Athens, IL, 62613-9702. Tel: 217-636-8047. p. 538
Cunningham, Elora, Librn, Web Coordr, Community College of Allegheny County, Allegheny Campus Library, 808 Ridge Ave, Pittsburgh, PA, 15212-6003. Tel: 412-237-2585. p. 1993
Cunningham, Gregory, Assoc Dir, Access & Organization, The John Marshall Law School, 300 S State St, 6th Flr, Chicago, IL, 60604. Tel: 312-427-2737. p. 564
Cunningham, Gwendolyn, Sci Librn, Saint Lawrence University, Launders Science Library, Fox Hall, 23 Romoda Dr, Canton, NY, 13617. Tel: 315-229-5404. p. 1514
Cunningham, Heather, Teen Librn, Saratoga Springs Public Library, 49 Henry St, Saratoga Springs, NY, 12866. Tel: 518-584-7860, Ext 260. p. 1636
Cunningham, Helen, Asst Dir/Res Librn, University of Toronto Libraries, Gerstein Science Information Centre, Sigmund Samuel Library Bldg, Nine Kings College Circle, Toronto, ON, M5S 1A5, CANADA. Tel: 416-978-2280. p. 2699
Cunningham, Joan, Mgr, Simpson, Gumpertz & Heger, Inc Library, 480 Totten Pond Rd, Waltham, MA, 02451. Tel: 781-907-9000, Ext 9347. p. 1062
Cunningham, Katie, Tech Serv, Conway Public Library, 15 Main Ave, Conway, NH, 03818. Tel: 603-447-5552. p. 1360
Cunningham, Kay, Dir, Christian Brothers University, 650 East Pkwy S, Memphis, TN, 38104. Tel: 901-321-3432. p. 2112
Cunningham, Kelly, Br Mgr, Cabarrus County Public Library, Mt Pleasant Branch, 8556 Cook St, Mount Pleasant, NC, 28124. Tel: 704-920-2310. p. 1682
Cunningham, Kristin, Dir, Okmulgee Public Library, 218 S Okmulgee Ave, Okmulgee, OK, 74447. Tel: 918-756-1448. p. 1860
Cunningham, Kristy, Bus Librn, Austin Peay State University, 601 College St, Clarksville, TN, 37044. Tel: 931-221-7017. p. 2092
Cunningham, Leigh, Assoc Dir, Libraries & Student Success, St Lawrence College Library, Two Saint Lawrence Dr, Cornwall, ON, K6H 4Z1, CANADA. Tel: 613-544-5400, Ext 1156. p. 2637
Cunningham, Leigh, Assoc Dir of Libr, St Lawrence College Library, 100 Portsmouth Ave, Kingston, ON, K7L 5A6, CANADA. Tel: 613-544-5400, Ext 1156. p. 2651
Cunningham, Leslie, Cataloging & Govt Info Librn, Albany Law School, 80 New Scotland Ave, Albany, NY, 12208. p. 1482
Cunningham, Lisa, Ch Serv, Tech Serv, Dennis Public Library, Five Hall St, Dennisport, MA, 02639. Tel: 508-760-6219. p. 1014
Cunningham, Lynn, Art Librn, University of California, Berkeley, Art History/Classics, 308 Doe Library, Berkeley, CA, 94720-6000. Tel: 510-642-7361. p. 122
Cunningham, Marie, Sr Librn, State of Delaware, 121 Martin Luther King Jr Blvd N, Dover, DE, 19901. Tel: 302-257-3006. p. 352
Cunningham, Marie, Sr Librn, State of Delaware, Delaware Library Access Services, 121 Martin Luther King Blvd N, Dover, DE, 19901. Tel: 302-257-2713. p. 352
Cunningham, Marie, Circ Librn, Warren County-Vicksburg Public Library, 700 Veto St, Vicksburg, MS, 39180-3595. Tel: 601-636-6411. p. 1235
Cunningham, Michelle, Cataloger, Dir, Miles City Public Library, One S Tenth St, Miles City, MT, 59301. Tel: 406-234-1496. p. 1299
Cunningham, Nancy A, Dir, Acad Serv, University of South Florida, Tampa Campus Library, 4101 USF Apple Dr, LIB122, Tampa, FL, 33620. Tel: 813-974-0450. p. 450
Cunningham, Nicholas, Pub Serv Librn, Student Engagement Librn, Muhlenberg College, 2400 Chew St, Allentown, PA, 18104-5586. Tel: 484-664-3606. p. 1905
Cunningham, Nikki, Dir, Carroll County Library, 625 High St, Ste 102, Huntingdon, TN, 38344-3903. Tel: 731-986-1919. p. 2101
Cunningham, Reni, Circ Supvr, Concord Free Public Library, 129 Main St, Concord, MA, 01742. Tel: 978-318-3363. p. 1012
Cunningham, Sarah, Marketing & Social Media Mgr, Westborough Public Library, 55 W Main St, Westborough, MA, 01581. Tel: 508-366-3050. p. 1066
Cunningham, Sarah, Boards Comn Asst, North Carolina Legislative Library, 500 Legislative Office Bldg, 300 N Salisbury St, Raleigh, NC, 27603-5925. Tel: 919-733-9390. p. 1709
Cunningham, Shawn, Communications Dir, Multnomah County Library, 919 NE 19th Ave, Ste 250, Portland, OR, 97232. Tel: 503-988-5123. p. 1892
Cunningham, Susan, Cat Librn, Franciscan Missionaries of Our Lady University Library, 5414 Brittany Dr, Baton Rouge, LA, 70808. Tel: 225-526-1730. p. 883
Cunningham, Tara, Head, Coll Serv, Law Library of Louisiana, Louisiana Supreme Court, 2nd Flr, 400 Royal St, New Orleans, LA, 70130-2104. Tel: 504-310-2402. p. 901
Cunnion, Katie, Fac Librn, Green River College, 12401 SE 320th St, Auburn, WA, 98092-3699. Tel: 253-833-9111, Ext 2104. p. 2357
Cunnyngham, Beau, Dir, Lebanon Public Library, 104 E Washington St, Lebanon, IN, 46052. Tel: 765-482-3460. p. 703
Cuperus, Beth, Dir, Fulda Memorial Library, 101 Third St NE, Fulda, MN, 56131-1106. Tel: 507-425-3277. p. 1175
Cupp, Anthony, Librn, Iowa Genealogical Society Library, 628 E Grand Ave, Des Moines, IA, 50309-1924. Tel: 515-276-0287. p. 746
Curbow, Joan, Archivist, Buena Vista University Library, H W Siebens School of Business/Forum, 610 W Fourth St, Storm Lake, IA, 50588. Tel: 712-749-2094. p. 785
Curci-Gonzalez, Lucy, Exec Dir, New York Law Institute Library, 120 Broadway, Rm 932, New York, NY, 10271-0094. Tel: 212-732-8720. p. 1594
Cure, Emily, Chief of Staff, Boston Athenaeum, Ten 1/2 Beacon St, Boston, MA, 02108-3777. Tel: 617-720-7661. p. 991
Cureton, Janice, Librn, Dunklin County Library, Cardwell Branch, Main St, Cardwell, MO, 63829. Tel: 573-654-3366. p. 1258
Curle, Clint, Libr Dir, South Interlake Regional Library, 419 Main St, Stonewall, MB, R0C 2Z0, CANADA. Tel: 204-467-5767. p. 2591
Curlee, Mimi, Govt Doc, Ser, Charlotte Mecklenburg Library, 310 N Tryon St, Charlotte, NC, 28202-2176. Tel: 704-416-0100. p. 1679
Curley, Christine, Libr Dir, Southwestern College, 100 College St, Winfield, KS, 67156. Tel: 620-229-6312. p. 845
Curley, Christopher, Br Mgr, San Diego County Library, Bonita-Sunnyside Branch, 4375 Bonita Rd, Bonita, CA, 91902-2698. Tel: 619-475-3867. p. 216
Curley, Patricia, Dir, Stockton Springs Community Library, Six Station St, Stockton Springs, ME, 04981. Tel: 207-567-4147. p. 942
Curley, Sara, Dir, Bolivar-Harpers Ferry Public Library, 151 Polk St, Harpers Ferry, WV, 25425. Tel: 304-535-2301. p. 2403
Curotto, Nick, Digital Serv, Mgr, Libr Syst, Virginia Museum of Fine Arts Library, 200 N Arthur Ashe Blvd, Richmond, VA, 23220-4007. Tel: 804-340-5523. p. 2344
Curphey, Richena, Librn, Thomas Aquinas College, 10000 N Ojai Rd, Santa Paula, CA, 93060-9980. Tel: 805-525-4417. p. 245
Curran, Catherine, Mgr, Portland Public Library, Riverton, 1600 Forest Ave, Portland, ME, 04103-1399. Tel: 207-797-2915. p. 937
Curran, Jim, Br Mgr, Anchorage Public Library, Muldoon Branch, 1251 Muldoon Rd, Ste 158, Anchorage, AK, 99504. Tel: 907-343-4032. p. 42
Curran, Natalie, Dir, Phoenix Public Library, 34 Elm St, Phoenix, NY, 13135. Tel: 315-695-4355. p. 1618
Curran, Tallin, IT & Fac Mgr, Six Mile Regional Library District, Niedringhaus Bldg, 2001 Delmar Ave, Granite City, IL, 62040-4590. Tel: 618-452-6238. p. 594
Curran-Ball, Clare, Asst Dir, Tech Serv, Memorial Hall Library, 2 N Main St, Andover, MA, 01810. Tel: 978-623-8400. p. 985

Currano, Judith, Head of Libr, University of Pennsylvania Libraries, Chemistry, Chemistry Laboratories, 1973 Wing, 231 S 34th St, Philadelphia, PA, 19104-6323. Tel: 215-898-2177. p. 1988

Current, Michael, Govt Info Librn, Ref Librn, University of Wisconsin-La Crosse, 1631 Pine St, La Crosse, WI, 54601-3748. Tel: 608-785-8739. p. 2446

Currie, Gregg, Col Librn, Selkirk College Library, 301 Frank Beinder Way, Castlegar, BC, V1N 4L3, CANADA. Tel: 250-365-1263. p. 2564

Currie, Natalie, Archivist, Dir, State Librn, Oklahoma Department of Libraries, 200 NE 18th St, Oklahoma City, OK, 73105. Tel: 405-522-3215. p. 1859

Currier, Amy, Libr Tech, Colorado Mountain College, 3000 County Rd 114, Glenwood Springs, CO, 81601. Tel: 970-947-8271. p. 282

Currier, Gail, Mkt Coordr, Pub Info, Southern Oklahoma Library System, 601 Railway Express St, Ardmore, OK, 73401. Tel: 580-223-3164. p. 1840

Currier, Pat, Asst Dir, Dudley-Tucker Library, Six Epping St, Raymond, NH, 03077. Tel: 603-895-7057. p. 1379

Currier, Susan, Fac Librn, Vermont State University - Johnson, 337 College Hill, Johnson, VT, 05656. Tel: 802-635-1494. p. 2287

Curry, Alexis, Head Librn, Los Angeles County Museum of Art, 5905 Wilshire Blvd, Los Angeles, CA, 90036-4597. Tel: 323-857-6122. p. 163

Curry, Amy E, Dir, Morris County Historical Society, 68 Morris Ave, Morristown, NJ, 07960. Tel: 973-267-3465. p. 1421

Curry, Claire, Librn, National Weather Center Library, 120 David L Boren Blvd, Ste 4300, Norman, OK, 73072-7303. Tel: 405-325-1171. p. 1855

Curry, Colleen, Chief of Resources, National Park Service, Department of Interior, One Washington Pkwy, Farmington, PA, 15437. Tel: 724-329-5805. p. 1933

Curry, Diana, Info Spec, Fort Smith Public Library, 3201 Rogers Ave, Fort Smith, AR, 72903. Tel: 479-783-0229. p. 96

Curry, Esther, Asst Dir, C E Brehm Memorial Public Library District, 101 S Seventh St, Mount Vernon, IL, 62864. Tel: 618-242-6322. p. 621

Curry, Jane, Br Mgr, Wallowa County Library, Troy Branch, 66247 Redmond Grade, Enterprise, OR, 97828. Tel: 541-828-7788. p. 1878

Curry, Janice, Mgr, Tri-County Regional Library, 426 N Main St, Ste 5, Nashville, AR, 71852-2009. Tel: 870-845-2566. p. 106

Curry, JoEllyn, Librn, Illinois Prairie District Public Library, Marcella Schneider Branch, 509 Woodland Knolls Rd, Germantown Hills, IL, 61548. Tel: 309-921-5056. p. 617

Curry, Katie, Mgr, Cabell County Public Library, Guyandotte, 203 Richmond St, Huntington, WV, 25702. Tel: 304-528-5698. p. 2404

Curry, Larrie, Mrs, Chmn, Harrodsburg Historical Society, 220 S Chiles St, Harrodsburg, KY, 40330. Tel: 859-734-5985. p. 858

Curry, Melissa, Youth Serv Supvr, Leesburg Public Library, 100 E Main St, Leesburg, FL, 34748. Tel: 352-728-9790. p. 418

Curry, Missy, Libr Mgr, Green County Public Library, 112 W Court St, Greensburg, KY, 42743. Tel: 270-932-7081. p. 857

Curry, Pat, Dir, Nancy Nail Memorial Library, 124 S Pearl St, Mart, TX, 76664-1425. Tel: 254-876-2465. p. 2216

Curry, Sherry, Asst Dean, Tech Serv, University of Louisiana at Lafayette, 400 E St Mary Blvd, Lafayette, LA, 70503. Tel: 337-482-5704. p. 893

Curtin, Christina, Pub Serv Librn, Houston Community College - Northwest College, Spring Branch Campus Library, 1010 W Sam Houston Pkwy N, Houston, TX, 77043-5008. Tel: 713-718-5655. p. 2194

Curtin, Dana, Ref Librn, SUNY Broome Community College, 907 Front St, Binghamton, NY, 13905-1328. Tel: 607-778-5249. p. 1494

Curtin, Donna D, Exec Dir, Pilgrim Society, 75 Court St, Plymouth, MA, 02360. Tel: 508-746-1620. p. 1047

Curtis, Alison, Librn, Langara College Library, 100 W 49th Ave, Vancouver, BC, V5Y 2Z6, CANADA. Tel: 604-232-5465. p. 2579

Curtis, Andrea, Prog Coordr, Guelph Public Library, 100 Norfolk St, Guelph, ON, N1H 4J6, CANADA. Tel: 519-824-6220, Ext 263. p. 2643

Curtis, Anna M, Libr Dir, Eaton Rapids Area District Library, 220 S Main St, Eaton Rapids, MI, 48827-1256. Tel: 517-663-0950, Ext 401. p. 1103

Curtis, Brenda, Dir & Librn, Linn County Library District No 3, 316 E Main St, Blue Mound, KS, 66010. Tel: 913-756-2628. p. 799

Curtis, Dave, Libr Dir, Orange Public Library & History Center, 407 E Chapman Ave, Orange, CA, 92866-1509. Tel: 214-288-2474. p. 189

Curtis, Dave, Pres, Wheat Ridge Historical Society Library, 4610 Robb St, Wheat Ridge, CO, 80033. Tel: 303-421-9111. p. 298

Curtis, Debbie, Libr Mgr, South Routt Library District, Yampa Public Library, 116 Main St, Yampa, CO, 80483. Tel: 970-638-4654. p. 292

Curtis, Debbie Annette, Head, Circ & Reserves, Indiana University Northwest, 3400 Broadway, Gary, IN, 46408. Tel: 219-980-6583. p. 686

Curtis, Deborah, Libr Mgr, South Routt Library District, 227 Dodge Ave, Oak Creek, CO, 80467. Tel: 970-736-8371. p. 292

Curtis, Greg, Dept Head, Head, Content Org, University of Maine, 5729 Fogler Library, Orono, ME, 04469-5729. Tel: 207-581-1681. p. 934

Curtis, Gwen, Cat & Ref Librn, Maps Selector, University of Kentucky Libraries, Science & Engineering Library, 211 King Bldg, 179 Funkhouser Dr, Lexington, KY, 40506-0039. Tel: 859-257-1853. p. 864

Curtis, Jason, Acq Librn, University of San Diego, Katherine M & George M Pardee Jr Legal Research Center, 5998 Alcala Park, San Diego, CA, 92110-2492. Tel: 619-260-2875. p. 223

Curtis, Jeannette, Supvr, Tech Serv, Mesquite Public Library, 300 W Grubb Dr, Mesquite, TX, 75149. Tel: 972-216-6220. p. 2219

Curtis, Judy, Circ Supvr, Carpenter-Carse Library, 69 Ballards Corner Rd, Hinesburg, VT, 05461. Tel: 802-482-2878. p. 2286

Curtis, Katy, Humanities Librn, University of Puget Sound, 1604 N Warner St, Upper Loading Dock, Tacoma, WA, 98416. Tel: 253-879-3672. p. 2387

Curtis, Lori, Spec Coll & Archives Librn, Loma Linda University, 11072 Anderson St, Loma Linda, CA, 92350-0001. Tel: 909-558-4581. p. 157

Curtis, Lori, Archivist, Spec Coll Librn, Hillsdale College, 33 E College St, Hillsdale, MI, 49242. Tel: 517-607-2403. p. 1115

Curtis, Marjorie, Head, Borrower Serv, Greenfield Public Library, 412 Main St, Greenfield, MA, 01301. Tel: 413-772-1544. p. 1022

Curtis, Melissa, Info Literacy, Student Success Librn, Wartburg College Library, 100 Wartburg Blvd, Waverly, IA, 50677-0903. Tel: 319-352-8500. p. 789

Curtis, Michael, Library Contact, Peckar & Abramson, 70 Grand Ave, River Edge, NJ, 07661. Tel: 201-343-3434. p. 1439

Curtis, Robbie, Librn, Palliser Regional Library, Bethune Branch, Community Hall, 524 East St, Bethune, SK, S0G 0H0, CANADA. Tel: 306-638-3046. p. 2742

Curtis, Sandy, Dir, Hollis Public Library, PO Box 764, Craig, AK, 99921. Tel: 907-530-7112. p. 44

Curtis-Bonardi, Joyce, Libr Mgr, Bon Accord Public Library, 5025 50th Ave, Bon Accord, AB, T0A 0K0, CANADA. Tel: 780-921-2540. p. 2524

Curtiss, Janet, Coordr, Pub Serv, Saint Clair County Library System, Memphis Branch Library, 34830 Potter St, Memphis, MI, 48041. Tel: 810-392-2980. p. 1142

Curtiss, Janet, Pub Serv Coordr, Saint Clair County Library System, Burtchville Township Branch Library, 7093 Second St, Lakeport, MI, 48059. Tel: 810-385-8550. p. 1142

Curtiss, Janet, Pub Serv Coordr, Saint Clair County Library System, Marysville Branch Library, 1175 Delaware, Marysville, MI, 48040. Tel: 810-364-9493. p. 1142

Curtiss, Janet, Pub Serv Coordr, Saint Clair County Library System, Yale Branch Library, Two Jones St, Yale, MI, 48097. Tel: 810-387-2940. p. 1142

Curuso, Yuusuf, Librn, Columbia University, Global Studies, Lehman Library, International Affairs Bldg, 420 W 118th St, New York, NY, 10027. Tel: 212-854-3630. p. 1583

Curzon, Betty Ann, Br Mgr, Door County Library, Sister Bay-Liberty Grove Branch, 301 Mill Rd, Sister Bay, WI, 54234. Tel: 920-854-2721. p. 2480

Cusher, Allison, Head, Teen Serv, Grafton Public Library, 35 Grafton Common, Grafton, MA, 01519. Tel: 508-839-4649, Ext 1104. p. 1021

Cushing, Benjamin, Res & Instruction Librn, Catholic University of America, Reference & Instructional Services Division, 124 Mullen Library, 620 Michigan Ave NE, Washington, DC, 20064. Tel: 202-319-5548. p. 362

Cushing, Johannah, ILL, Libr Asst, Libby Memorial Library, 27 Staples St, Old Orchard Beach, ME, 04064. Tel: 207-934-4351. p. 934

Cushman, Robert, Chief Info Officer, State University of New York College at Brockport, 350 New Campus Dr, Brockport, NY, 14420-2997. Tel: 585-395-2032. p. 1497

Cushman, Ruth, Tech Serv, West Lafayette Public Library, 208 W Columbia St, West Lafayette, IN, 47906. Tel: 765-743-2261. p. 726

Custeau, Rene-Pierre, Librn, Cegep de Sherbrooke, 475 rue du Cegep, Sherbrooke, QC, J1E 4K1, CANADA. Tel: 819-564-6350, Ext 5231, 819-564-6350, Ext 5233. p. 2736

Custer, Angie, Dir, Carrollton Public Library, 509 S Main St, Carrollton, IL, 62016. Tel: 217-942-6715. p. 550

Custer, Cheryl, Dir, Fendrick Library, 20 N Main St, Mercersburg, PA, 17236. Tel: 717-328-9233. p. 1962

Custer, Wesley, Dir, Instrul Serv, Asbury Theological Seminary, 204 N Lexington Ave, Wilmore, KY, 40390-1199. Tel: 859-858-2100. p. 877

Cutforth, Jana, Co-Dir, Kuna Library District, 457 N Locust, Kuna, ID, 83634-1926. Tel: 208-922-1025. p. 523

Cuthbert, John, Curator, West Virginia University Libraries, 1549 University Ave, Morgantown, WV, 26506. Tel: 304-293-4040. p. 2409

Cuthbert, John, Curator, West Virginia University Libraries, West Virginia & Regional History Center, 1549 University Ave, Morgantown, WV, 26506-6069. Tel: 304-293-3536. p. 2410

Cutietta, Melanie, Librn, Yellowstone National Park, 20 Old Yellowstone Trail, Gardiner, MT, 59030. Tel: 307-344-2264. p. 1293

Cutinella, Jamie, Dir, East Williston Public Library, Two Prospect St, East Williston, NY, 11596. Tel: 516-741-1213. p. 1528

Cutinella, Stacy, Br Mgr, Anoka County Library, Mississippi, 410 Mississippi St NE, Fridley, MN, 55432. Tel: 763-324-1560. p. 1165

Cutinella, Stacy, Res & Ref Librn, Augsburg University, 630 22nd Ave S, Minneapolis, MN, 55454. Tel: 612-330-1604. p. 1182

Cutko, Kate, Dir, Bowdoinham Public Library, 13A School St, Bowdoinham, ME, 04008. Tel: 207-666-8405. p. 918

Cutler, Ethan, Digital Serv Librn, Kalamazoo College Library, 1200 Academy St, Kalamazoo, MI, 49006-3285. Tel: 269-337-7147. p. 1121

Cutright, Judith, Libr Dir, Millard Oakley Library, 107 E Main St, Livingston, TN, 38570. Tel: 931-823-1888. p. 2109

Cutter, Brian, Br Librn, Genesee District Library, Burton Memorial Library, 4012 E Atherton Rd, Burton, MI, 48519. Tel: 810-742-0674. p. 1106

Cutter, Brian, Br Librn, Genesee District Library, Linden Library, 201 N Main St, Linden, MI, 48451. Tel: 810-735-7700. p. 1106

Cutting, Brud, Info Mgt, Knolls Atomic Power Laboratory Inc, Library, 2401 River Rd, Niskayuna, NY, 12309. Tel: 518-395-6000. p. 1606

Cuturic, Visnja, Libr Asst, West Perth Public Library, 105 Saint Andrew St, Mitchell, ON, N0K 1N0, CANADA. Tel: 519-348-9234. p. 2659

Cuvelier, Amie, Supvr, Access Serv, Bastrop Public Library, 1100 Church St, Bastrop, TX, 78602. Tel: 512-332-8880. p. 2144

Cuyugan, Erica, Dir, Libr Serv, Santa Monica Public Library, 601 Santa Monica Blvd, Santa Monica, CA, 90401. Tel: 310-458-8600. p. 244

Cygert, Jennifer, Dir, Walkerton-Lincoln Township Public Library, 406 Adams St, Walkerton, IN, 46574. Tel: 574-279-0177. p. 724

Cynova, Lauren, Circ Supvr, Cape Canaveral Public Library, 201 Polk Ave, Cape Canaveral, FL, 32920-3067. Tel: 321-868-1101. p. 388

Cypert, Angela, Librn, Fox Lake Correctional Institution Library, PO Box 147, Fox Lake, WI, 53933-0147. Tel: 920-928-3151, Ext 6240. p. 2436

Cyr, Cheryl, Circ Mgr, Tigard Public Library, 13500 SW Hall Blvd, Tigard, OR, 97223-8111. Tel: 503-684-6537, Ext 2509. p. 1900

Cyr, Kat, Asst Librn, Russell Memorial Library, 4333 State Prison Hollow Rd, Monkton, VT, 05469. Tel: 802-453-4471. p. 2289

Cyr, Lyn, Dir, Port Leyden Community Library, 3145 Canal St, Port Leyden, NY, 13433. Tel: 315-348-6077. p. 1622

Cyr, Sophie-Michele, Libr Mgr, Haut-Saint-Jean Regional Library, Dr Lorne J Violette Public Library, 180 rue St-Jean, Saint Leonard, NB, E7E 2B9, CANADA. Tel: 506-423-3025. p. 2600

Cyr, Stephanie, Ad, Jacob Edwards Library, 236 Main St, Southbridge, MA, 01550-2598. Tel: 508-764-5426. p. 1055

Cyr, Vicki, Br Mgr, San Luis Obispo County Library, Shell Beach Library, 230 Leeward Ave, Shell Beach, CA, 93449. Tel: 805-773-2263. p. 234

Cyre, Heather, Head, Pub Serv, University of Washington Libraries, Bothell Campus/Cascadia College Library, University of Washington Bothell, 18225 Campus Way NE, Box 358550, Bothell, WA, 98011-8245. Tel: 425-352-5340. p. 2381

Cyrier, Lesley, Head, Adult Serv, Addison Public Library, Four Friendship Plaza, Addison, IL, 60101. Tel: 630-458-3314. p. 535

Cyrus, Abby, Mgr, Charlestown-Clark County Public Library, 51 Clark Rd, Charlestown, IN, 47111. Tel: 812-256-3337. p. 674

Cyrus, Hannah, Asst Dir, Blue Hill Public Library, Five Parker Point Rd, Blue Hill, ME, 04614. Tel: 207-374-5515, Ext 11. p. 918

Cyrus, John W, Research & Education Librn, Virginia Commonwealth University Libraries, Tompkins-McCaw Library for the Health Sciences, Medical College of Virginia Campus, 509 N 12th St, Richmond, VA, 23298-0582. Tel: 804-828-0636. p. 2343

Czaja, Pamela, Ref Librn/Distance Learning, Monroe Community College, LeRoy V Good Library, 1000 E Henrietta Rd, Rochester, NY, 14692. Tel: 585-292-2308. p. 1629

Czajkowski, Cathy, Librn, Groveton Public Library, 125 W First St, Groveton, TX, 75845. Tel: 936-642-2483. p. 2187

Czanyo, Elizabeth, Ref Librn, Canadian Medical Association, 1410 Blair Towers Place, Ste 500, Ottawa, ON, K1J 9B9, CANADA. Tel: 613-731-9331, Ext 8432. p. 2665

Czerny, Susan, Archives, Digital Projects, Kutztown University, 15200 Kutztown Rd, Bldg 5, Kutztown, PA, 19530. Tel: 610-683-4480. p. 1949

Czerwinskyj, Simon, Tech Serv Librn, Concordia University, 7400 Augusta St, River Forest, IL, 60305-1499. Tel: 708-209-3254. p. 639

D'Acunto, Samantha, Actg Head, Pub Serv, Ref Librn, The LuEsther T Mertz Library, The New York Botanical Garden, 2900 Southern Blvd, Bronx, NY, 10458-5126. Tel: 718-817-8728. p. 1499

D'Adamo, Charles, Exec Coordr, Alternative Press Center Library, 2239 Kirk Ave, Baltimore, MD, 21218. Tel: 312-451-8133. p. 951

D'Agostino, Anna, Dir, Eastern Lancaster County Library, 11 Chestnut Dr, New Holland, PA, 17557-9437. Tel: 717-354-0525. p. 1969

D'Agostino, Cindy, Dir, Dormont Public Library, 2950 W Liberty Ave, Pittsburgh, PA, 15216-2594. Tel: 412-531-8754. p. 1993

D'Agostino, Denise, Libr Asst, Seton Hall University Libraries, 340 Kingsland St, Nutley, NJ, 07110. Tel: 973-542-6969. p. 1430

D'Agostino, Erin, Access Serv Librn, North Shore Community College Library, One Ferncroft Rd, Danvers Campus Library, Danvers, MA, 01923-4093. Tel: 978-739-5523. p. 1013

D'Agostino, Erin, Access Serv Librn, North Shore Community College Library, McGee Bldg, LE127, 300 Broad St, Lynn, MA, 01901. Tel: 978-762-4000, Ext 6248. p. 1030

D'Agostino, Kristina, Research Librn, Sacred Heart University, 5151 Park Ave, Fairfield, CT, 06825-1000. Tel: 203-371-7746. p. 312

D'Agostino, Melissa A, Instrul Librn, Cecil College, One Seahawk Dr, North East, MD, 21901-1904. Tel: 443-674-1492. p. 972

D'Agostino, Rachel, Curator of Printed Bks, Library Company of Philadelphia, 1314 Locust St, Philadelphia, PA, 19107. Tel: 215-546-3181. p. 1982

D'Almeida, Diane, Coordr, Boston University Libraries, George H Beebe Communications Library, College of Communication, 640 Commonwealth Ave, Rm B31, Boston, MA, 02215. Tel: 617-353-9240. p. 993

D'Amario, Patti, Mgr, Borrower Serv, Springfield City Library, 220 State St, Springfield, MA, 01103. Tel: 413-263-6828, Ext 220. p. 1056

D'Amato, Kristin, Head, Acq, Head, Ser, Central Connecticut State University, 1615 Stanley St, New Britain, CT, 06050. Tel: 860-832-2074. p. 324

D'Amato, Tara, Asst Dir, Mastics-Moriches-Shirley Community Library, 407 William Floyd Pkwy, Shirley, NY, 11967. Tel: 631-399-1511. p. 1640

D'Ambrosio, Amber, Archives & Spec Coll Librn, Colorado Mesa University, 1100 North Ave, Grand Junction, CO, 81501. Tel: 970-248-1864. p. 283

D'Amico, Jill, Head, Info Serv, Ref, South Brunswick Public Library, 110 Kingston Lane, Monmouth Junction, NJ, 08852. Tel: 732-329-4000, Ext 7638. p. 1419

D'Amour, Heather, Assoc University Librarian, Colls, University of Calgary Library, 2500 University Dr NW, Calgary, AB, T2N 1N4, CANADA. Tel: 403-220-3591. p. 2529

D'Amours, Guillaume, Dir, College de Bois-de-Boulogne Bibliotheque, 10555, ave de Bois-de-Boulogne, Montreal, QC, H4N 1L4, CANADA. Tel: 514-332-3000, Ext 7540. p. 2722

D'Angela, Nicole, Library Contact, Presbyterian Church in Canada Archives, 50 Wynford Dr, Toronto, ON, M3C 1J7, CANADA. Tel: 416-441-1111, Ext 310. p. 2692

D'Angelo, Alyssa, Ch Serv, Cherokee County Public Library, 300 E Rutledge Ave, Gaffney, SC, 29340-2227. Tel: 864-487-2711. p. 2059

D'Angelo, Diana, Assoc Dir, Pub Serv, Suffolk University, John Joseph Moakley Law Library, 120 Tremont St, 6th Flr, Boston, MA, 02108-4977. Tel: 617-573-8177. p. 1000

D'Angelo, John, Head, Circ, Fordham University Libraries, 441 E Fordham Rd, Bronx, NY, 10458-5151. Tel: 718-817-3570. p. 1498

D'Angelo, Tonie Ann, Asst Dir, Ref Serv, Blauvelt Free Library, 541 Western Hwy, Blauvelt, NY, 10913. Tel: 845-359-2811. p. 1494

D'Arelli, Francesco, Dir, Italian Cultural Institute of Montreal La Bibliotheque, 1200 Dr Penfield Ave, Montreal, QC, H3A 1A9, CANADA. Tel: 514-849-3473. p. 2725

D'Arnaud, Judea, ILL, University of California, San Diego, 9500 Gilman Dr, Mail Code 0175G, La Jolla, CA, 92093-0175. Tel: 858-534-3011. p. 154

D'Arpa, Christine, Asst Prof, Wayne State University, 106 Kresge Library, Detroit, MI, 48202. Tel: 313-577-1825. p. 2787

D'Avanza, Mia, Dir, University of Pennsylvania Libraries, Fisher Fine Arts Library, Furness Bldg, 220 S 34th St, Philadelphia, PA, 19104-6308. Tel: 215-898-8325. p. 1988

d'Avernas, Marc, Head, Collections & Content, Mount Royal University Library, 4825 Mount Royal Gate SW, Calgary, AB, T3E 6K6, CANADA. Tel: 403-440-6287. p. 2528

D'Aveta, Laura, Syst/Electronic Res Librn, Hiram College Library, 11694 Hayden St, Hiram, OH, 44234. Tel: 330-569-5363. p. 1790

D'Avignon, Andie, Libr Dir, Springtown Public Library, 626 N Main St, Springtown, TX, 76082. Tel: 817-523-5862. p. 2245

D'Avy, Richard, Asst Admin, Val Verde County Library, 300 Spring St, Del Rio, TX, 78840. Tel: 830-774-7595. p. 2169

D'Elia, MaryEllen, Asst Dir, Ringwood Public Library, 30 Cannici Dr, Ringwood, NJ, 07456. Tel: 973-962-6256, Ext 111. p. 1439

D'Entremont, Susan, Continuing Educ Coordr, Digital Serv, Capital District Library Council, 28 Essex St, Albany, NY, 12206. Tel: 518-438-2500. p. 2770

D'Errico, Megan, Ref Librn, Proskauer Rose LLP Library, 11 Times Sq, New York, NY, 10036. Tel: 212-969-3000, 212-969-5001. p. 1600

D'Onofrio-Jones, Mellissa, Chief Exec Officer, Ontario Library Service, 1504 One Yonge St, Ste107, Toronto, ON, M5E 1E5, CANADA. Tel: 416-961-1669. p. 2691

D'Souza, Adrienne, Br Mgr, Chillicothe & Ross County Public Library, 140 S Paint St, Chillicothe, OH, 45601. Tel: 740-702-4145. p. 1758

D'Yan, Alex, Dir, Roselle Park Veterans Memorial Library, 404 Chestnut St, Roselle Park, NJ, 07204. Tel: 908-245-2456. p. 1441

Da Sylva, Lyne, Dir, Prof, Universite de Montreal, 3150, rue Jean-Brillant, bur C-2004, Montreal, QC, H3T 1N8, CANADA. Tel: 514-343-7400. p. 2797

Dabbas, Su, Dir, Gilbert Public Library, 17 N Broadway, Gilbert, MN, 55741. Tel: 218-748-2230. p. 1176

Dabbondanza, Ashley, Asst Dir, Head, Teen & Family Services, Hall Memorial Library, 93 Main St, Ellington, CT, 06029. Tel: 860-870-3160. p. 310

Dabbour, Katherine S, Assoc Dean, California State University, Northridge, 18111 Nordhoff St, Northridge, CA, 91330. Tel: 818-677-2272. p. 184

Dabiri Alaee, Valeh, Supv Librn, City of Palo Alto Library, Mitchell Park, 3700 Middlefield Rd, Palo Alto, CA, 94303. Tel: 650-838-2976. p. 192

Dabkey, Rachael, Ch Mgr, La Grange Public Library, Ten W Cossitt Ave, La Grange, IL, 60525. Tel: 708-215-3212. p. 605

Daby, Jill, Regional Medical Librn, Champlain Valley Physicians Hospital, 75 Beekman St, Plattsburgh, NY, 12901. p. 1619

Dacay, Garett, Br Mgr, North Las Vegas Library District, Alexander Library, 1755 W Alexander Rd, North Las Vegas, NV, 89032. Tel: 702-633-2880. p. 1348

Dacier, Lori, Asst Librn, Canaan Town Library, 1173 US Rte 4, Canaan, NH, 03741. Tel: 603-523-9650. p. 1356

Dack, Deborah, Dir & Librn, Culbertson Public Library, 612 Wyoming St, Culbertson, NE, 69024. Tel: 308-278-2135. p. 1311

Daddio, Jennifer, Dir, Somers Library, Rte 139 & Reis Park, Somers, NY, 10589. Tel: 914-232-5717. p. 1642

Dady, Lisa, Exec Dir, The Jackson Homestead & Museum, 527 Washington St, Newton, MA, 02458. Tel: 617-796-1450. p. 1039

Daebler, Cora, Tech Serv, United States Army, Morris J Swett Technical Library, Snow Hall 16, Bldg 730, Fort Sill, OK, 73503-5100. Tel: 580-442-4525. p. 1848

Daeschler, Ted, PhD, Dir, Libr & Archives, Academy of Natural Sciences of Drexel University, 1900 Benjamin Franklin Pkwy, Philadelphia, PA, 19103-1195. Tel: 215-299-1040. p. 1974

Daffron, Kristina, Youth Serv Librn, Russell County Public Library, 535 N Main St, Jamestown, KY, 42629. Tel: 270-343-7323. p. 861

Dafoe, Emily, User Serv Librn, Valley City State University Library, 101 College St SW, Valley City, ND, 58072-4098. Tel: 701-845-7277. p. 1740

Dafoe, Ruth, Genealogy/Local Hist Spec, Milton-Union Public Library, 560 S Main St, West Milton, OH, 45383. Tel: 937-698-5515. p. 1830

Daganaar, Mark, Dir, Johnson County Community College, 12345 College Blvd, Overland Park, KS, 66210. Tel: 913-469-3882. p. 829

Dagenais, Andree, Indexer, Librn, Centre de documentation collegiale, 1111 rue Lapierre, LaSalle, QC, H8N 2J4, CANADA. Tel: 514-364-3327, Ext 2. p. 2715

Dager, Katey, Youth Serv Librn, Simi Valley Library, 2969 Tapo Canyon Rd, Simi Valley, CA, 93063. Tel: 805-526-1735. p. 246

Dagg, Emily, Head, Youth Serv, Everett Public Library, 2702 Hoyt Ave, Everett, WA, 98201-3556. Tel: 425-257-7632. p. 2364

Dagher, Fadi, Pembroke Pines Campus Libr Dir, Keiser University Library System, 1500 NW 49th St, Fort Lauderdale, FL, 33309. Tel: 954-351-4035. p. 401

Dagley, Helen, Ref Librn, State Library of Iowa, 1112 E Grand Ave, Des Moines, IA, 50319. Tel: 515-281-3063. p. 747

Dagley, Lon, Asst Libr Dir, Computer Serv Librn, Univ Archivist, MidAmerica Nazarene University, 2030 E College Way, Olathe, KS, 66062-1899. Tel: 913-971-3566. p. 828

Dague, Angela, Dir, Garrison Public Library, 201 E Pine St, Garrison, IA, 52229. Tel: 319-477-5531. p. 754

Daguerre, Danielle, Libr Serv Coordr, Bkmobile/Outreach Serv, LeRoy Collins Leon County Public Library System, 200 W Park Ave, Tallahassee, FL, 32301-7720. Tel: 850-606-2665. p. 445

Dahl, Jeanne, Asst Librn, Genealogy Librn, Raymond A Whitwer Tilden Public Library, 202 S Center St, Tilden, NE, 68781. Tel: 402-368-5306. p. 1338

Dahl, Mark, Interim Dir, Lewis & Clark College, Aubrey R Watzek Library, 0615 SW Palatine Hill Rd, Portland, OR, 97219-7899. Tel: 503-768-7339. p. 1892

Dahl, Peggy, Libr Asst, Santa Barbara Museum of Natural History Library, 2559 Puesta del Sol Rd, Santa Barbara, CA, 93105. Tel: 805-682-4711, Ext 135. p. 240

Dahlen, Sarah, Librn, California State University - Monterey Bay, 3054 Divarty St, Seaside, CA, 93955. Tel: 831-582-4432. p. 246

Dahlgreen, MaryKay, Dir, Lincoln County Library District, 132 NE 15th St, Newport, OR, 97365. Tel: 541-265-3066. p. 1888

Dahlgren, Eva, Br Mgr, Teton County Library, Alta Branch, 50 Alta School Rd, Alta, WY, 83414. Tel: 307-353-2505. p. 2495

Dahlgren, Jodi, Libr Mgr, Wainwright Public Library, 921 Third Ave, Wainwright, AB, T9W 1C5, CANADA. Tel: 780-842-2673. p. 2559

Dahlhauser, Julie, Asst Dir, Hatchie River Regional Library, 63 Executive Dr, Jackson, TN, 38305. Tel: 731-668-0710. p. 2102

Dahlke, Lezlea, Libr Dir, Winona Public Library, 151 W Fifth St, Winona, MN, 55987. Tel: 507-452-4582. p. 1209

Dahlke, Rita, Librn, Temple Emanuel Library, 51 Grape St, Denver, CO, 80220. Tel: 303-388-4013. p. 277

Dahlman, Gavena, Dir, Richland Community College, One College Park, Decatur, IL, 62521. Tel: 217-875-7211, Ext 6303. p. 576

Dahlstrom-Ledbetter, Molly, Fac Librn, Austin Community College, Cypress Creek Campus Library, 1555 Cypress Creek Rd, 1st Flr, Rm 2121, Cedar Park, TX, 78613. Tel: 512-223-2137. p. 2137

Dahman, Sofiya, ILL Librn, University Libraries, University of Memphis, 3785 Norriswood Ave, Memphis, TN, 38152. Tel: 901-678-8223. p. 2115

Dahms-Stinson, Nancee, Youth Serv Coordr, Springfield-Greene County Library District, 4653 S Campbell Ave, Springfield, MO, 65810-1723. Tel: 417-882-0714. p. 1281

Dahmus, Jeni, Archivist, Dir, Juilliard School, 60 Lincoln Center Plaza, New York, NY, 10023-6588. Tel: 212-799-5000, Ext 265. p. 1590

Dahnke, April, Br Librn, Southeast Regional Library, Wolseley Branch, RM Office, 500 Front St, Wolseley, SK, S0G 5H0, CANADA. Tel: 306-698-2221. p. 2755

Dai, Weiqing, Commun Libr Mgr, Queens Library, Jackson Heights Community Library, 35-51 81st St, Jackson Heights, NY, 11372. Tel: 718-899-2500. p. 1554

Daigle, Ben, Dir, Info Syst & Digital Access, University of Dayton Libraries, 300 College Park Dr, Dayton, OH, 45469. Tel: 937-229-4221. p. 1780

Daigle, Christine, Dir, Acadia Parish Library, 1125 N Parkerson Ave, Crowley, LA, 70526. Tel: 337-788-1880, 337-788-1881. p. 888

Daigle, Jessie, Dir, Bibliotheques de Trois-Rivieres, 1425 Place de l'Hotel de Ville, Trois-Rivieres, QC, G9A 5L9, CANADA. Tel: 819-372-4641, Ext 4622. p. 2737

Daigle, Paula, Librn III, First Nations University of Canada, One First Nations Way, Regina, SK, S4S 7K2, CANADA. Tel: 306-790-5950, Ext 3425. p. 2746

Dail, Andrew, Ref & Instruction, Lake-Sumter State College Library, 9501 US Hwy 441, Leesburg, FL, 34788. Tel: 352-365-3527. p. 418

Dailey, Carole, Ch Serv, Shenandoah Public Library, 201 S Elm St, Shenandoah, IA, 51601. Tel: 712-246-2315. p. 781

Dailey, Dawn, Dir, Douglas County Library, 720 Fillmore St, Alexandria, MN, 56308. Tel: 320-762-3014. p. 1163

Dailey, Debbie, Chief Exec Officer, Head Librn, Bancroft Public Library, 14 Flint Ave, Bancroft, ON, K0L 1C0, CANADA. Tel: 613-332-3380. p. 2629

Dailey, Dennis, Head, Archives & Spec Coll, New Mexico State University Library, 2911 McFie Circle, Las Cruces, NM, 88003. Tel: 575-646-1508. p. 1471

Dailey, Doreen, Ad, Asst Dir, Webster Public Library, Webster Plaza, 980 Ridge Rd, Webster, NY, 14580. Tel: 585-872-7075. p. 1661

Dailey, Jackie, Media Serv, Wells County Public Library, 200 W Washington St, Bluffton, IN, 46714-1999. Tel: 260-824-1612. p. 671

Dailey, Laura, Dir, Goessel Public Library, 101 S Cedar, Goessel, KS, 67053. Tel: 620-367-8440. p. 810

Dailey, Mariko, Ref Librn, Johnson & Wales University, 801 W Trade St, Charlotte, NC, 28202. Tel: 980-598-1603. p. 1680

Dailey, Sarah, Dir, Marengo County Public Library, 210 N Shiloh St, Linden, AL, 36748. Tel: 334-295-2246. p. 24

Dailey, Shannon, Librn II, Santa Fe Springs City Library, 11700 E Telegraph Rd, Santa Fe Springs, CA, 90670-3600. Tel: 562-868-7738. p. 243

Dailey, Susan, Br Mgr, Wells County Public Library, Ossian Branch, 207 N Jefferson St, Ossian, IN, 46777. Tel: 260-622-4691. p. 671

Dailey, Veronica, Circ Supvr, Maitland Public Library, 501 S Maitland Ave, Maitland, FL, 32751-5672. Tel: 407-647-7700. p. 419

Daily, Dan, Dean of Libr, University of South Dakota, I D Weeks Library, 414 E Clark St, Vermillion, SD, 57069. Tel: 605-658-3369. p. 2084

Daily, Paula, Dir, Chrisman Public Library, 108 N Illinois St, Chrisman, IL, 61924. Tel: 217-269-3011. p. 571

Dainty, Lauren, Dir, Columbus Public Library, 205 N Kansas, Columbus, KS, 66725. Tel: 620-429-2086. p. 803

Daisey, Stephanie, Head, Prog & Outreach, Wicomico Public Library, 122 S Division St, Salisbury, MD, 21801. Tel: 410-749-3612, Ext 155. p. 976

Daiss, Debbie, Bus Mgr, Bibliomation Inc, 24 Wooster Ave, Waterbury, CT, 06708. Tel: 203-577-4070, Ext 104. p. 2762

Daix, Erin C, Dir of Assessment, University of Delaware Library, 181 S College Ave, Newark, DE, 19717-5267. Tel: 302-831-2965. p. 355

Daka, Paul, Br Mgr, Free Library of Philadelphia, Holmesburg Branch, 7810 Frankford Ave, Philadelphia, PA, 19136-3013. Tel: 215-685-8756. p. 1978

Dalby, Michael, Br Mgr, Cleveland Public Library, West Park, 3805 W 157th St, Cleveland, OH, 44111. Tel: 216-623-7102. p. 1769

Dale, Denise, Archives & Design Liaison Librn, Kwantlen Polytechnic University Library, 12666 72nd Ave, Surrey, BC, V3W 2M8, CANADA. Tel: 604-599-2999. p. 2576

Dale, Jenny, Head, Res, Outreach & Instruction, University of North Carolina at Greensboro, 320 College Ave, Greensboro, NC, 27412-0001. Tel: 336-256-0240. p. 1693

Dale, John, Pub Serv Librn, Orange Coast College Library, 2701 Fairview Rd, Costa Mesa, CA, 92626. Tel: 714-432-5885. p. 132

Dale, John, Dir, Darlington Public Library, 203 W Main St, Darlington, IN, 47940. Tel: 765-794-4813. p. 678

Dale, Ray, Dir, Big Horn County Public Library, 419 N Custer Ave, Hardin, MT, 59034. Tel: 406-665-1808. p. 1295

Dale, Rella, Cat, Avery-Mitchell-Yancey Regional Library System, 289 Burnsville School Rd, Burnsville, NC, 28714. Tel: 828-682-4476. p. 1677

Dale, Robin, Dep Librn, Library of Congress, John W Kluge Center, Library Collections & Services Group, Thomas Jefferson Bldg, LJ-120, First St SE, Washington, DC, 20540-4860. Tel: 202-707-3302. p. 370

Dale, Robin L, Assoc Librn, Libr Serv, Library of Congress, James Madison Memorial Bldg, 101 Independence Ave SE, Washington, DC, 20540. Tel: 202-707-5000. p. 370

Dalesandro, Anne, Dir, Law Libr & Assoc Prof of Law, Rutgers University Libraries, Camden Law Library, 217 N Fifth St, Camden, NJ, 08102-1203. Tel: 856-225-8182. p. 1394

Daley, Jan, Br Mgr, Saint Louis Public Library, Baden, 8448 Church Rd, Saint Louis, MO, 63147-1898. Tel: 314-388-2400. p. 1274

Daley, Lisc, Legislative Librn, Legislative Library of the Northwest Territories, Legislative Assembly Bldg, 4570 - 48th St, Yellowknife, NT, X1A 2L9, CANADA. Tel: 867-767-9132, Ext 12054. p. 2613
Daley, Marisa, Coll Mgt Librn, Sterling & Francine Clark Art Institute Library, 225 South St, Williamstown, MA, 01267. Tel: 413-458-0532. p. 1069
Daley, Patricia, Circ, Woburn Public Library, 36 Cummings Park, Woburn, MA, 01801. Tel: 781-933-0148. p. 1070
Daley, Renee, Libr Dir, Lester Public Library of Rome, 1157 Rome Center Dr, Nekoosa, WI, 54457. Tel: 715-325-8990. p. 2464
Dalfovo, Barbara, Library Contact, Istituto Italiano di Cultura, Biblioteca, 686 Park Ave, New York, NY, 10065. Tel: 212-879-4242. p. 1589
Dalius, Kathryn, Ser Spec, Bucknell University, 220 Bertrand Library, One Dent Dr, Lewisburg, PA, 17837. Tel: 570-577-1557. p. 1955
Dall, Billie, Dir, Dike Public Library, 133 E Elder, Dike, IA, 50624-9612. Tel: 319-989-2608. p. 748
Dallafior, Beverley, Library Contact, Amasa Community Library, 109 W Pine St, Amasa, MI, 49903. Tel: 906-284-9151. p. 1078
Dallair, Ann, Libr Dir, Millbury Public Library, 128 Elm St, Millbury, MA, 01527. Tel: 508-865-1181. p. 1035
Dallaire, Louis, Exec Dir, Reseau BIBLIO Abitibi-Temiscaminque-Nord-du-Quebec, 20 Quebec Ave, Rouyn-Noranda, QC, J9X 2E6, CANADA. Tel: 819-762-4305, Ext 23. p. 2733
Dallam, Linda, Librn, Mills & Petrie Memorial Library, 704 N First St, Ashton, IL, 61006. Tel: 815-453-2213. p. 538
Dallamora, Thomas, Dir, Librn, Monson Free Public Library, 35 Greenville Rd, Monson, ME, 04464-6432. Tel: 207-997-3476. p. 932
Dallas, Costis, Dr, Assoc Prof, University of Toronto, 140 St George St, Toronto, ON, M5S 3G6, CANADA. Tel: 416-978-3234. p. 2796
Dallas, Larayne, Liaison Librn, University of Texas Libraries, McKinney Engineering Library, Engineering Education & Research Center, EER 1706, 2501 Speedway, Austin, TX, 78712. Tel: 512-495-4511. p. 2143
Dallas, Pam, Librn, Tatum Community Library, 323 E Broadway, Tatum, NM, 88267. Tel: 575-398-4822. p. 1478
Dallas, Sara, Dir, Southern Adirondack Library System, 22 Whitney Pl, Saratoga Springs, NY, 12866-4596. Tel: 518-584-7300, Ext 205. p. 1636
Dalling, Laurel, Head Asst Librn, Hamer Public Library, 2450 E 2100 N, Hamer, ID, 83425. Tel: 208-662-5275. p. 521
Dalmoro, Anneliese, Librn, Hatch Ltd, 840 Seventh Ave SW, Ste 400, Calgary, AB, T2P 3G2, CANADA. Tel: 403-920-3101. p. 2528
Dalrymple, Connie, Dir, Guernsey Memorial Library, Three Court St, Norwich, NY, 13815. Tel: 607-334-4034. p. 1609
Dalrymple, Jennifer, Head, Circ, Bedford Free Public Library, Seven Mudge Way, Bedford, MA, 01730. Tel: 781-275-9440. p. 987
Dalton, Andrew I, Pres & Chief Exec Officer, Adams County Historical Society, 625 Biglerville Rd, Gettysburg, PA, 17325. Tel: 717-334-4723. p. 1935
Dalton, Dorothy, Libr Coord, Yavapai County Free Library District, Congress Public Library, 26750 Santa Fe Rd, Congress, AZ, 85332. Tel: 928-427-3945. p. 74
Dalton, Greg, Library Contact, The Commonwealth Club of California Library, 110 The Embarcadero, San Francisco, CA, 94105. Tel: 415-597-6710. p. 224
Dalton, Jolene, Asst Librn, Emery County Library System, Green River Branch, 85 S Long St, Green River, UT, 84525. Tel: 435-564-3349. p. 2262
Dalton, Lexi, Asst Librn, John Mosser Public Library District, 106 W Meek St, Abingdon, IL, 61410-1451. Tel: 309-462-3129. p. 535
Dalton, Malynda, Interim Dir, Texas A&M International University, 5201 University Blvd, Laredo, TX, 78041-1900. Tel: 956-326-2403. p. 2210
Dalton, Nicole, Librn, Ile a la Crosse Public Library, Bag Service 540, Ile a la Crosse, SK, S0M 1C0, CANADA. Tel: 306-833-3027. p. 2741
Dalton, Patricia J, Ch, Art Circle Public Library, Three East St, Crossville, TN, 38555. Tel: 931-484-6790. p. 2095
Dalton, Rebecca, Acq, Supvr, Converse College, 580 E Main St, Spartanburg, SC, 29302. Tel: 864-596-9020, 864-596-9071. p. 2069
Dalton, Steve, Head Librn, Boston College Libraries, Theology & Ministry Library, 117 Lake St, Brighton, MA, 02135. Tel: 617-552-6541. p. 1011
Dalton, Tina, Dir, Cuba Circulating Library, 39 E Main St, Cuba, NY, 14727. Tel: 585-968-1668. p. 1523
Dalusung, Joan, Asst Libr Dir, Washoe County Library System, 301 S Center St, Reno, NV, 89501-2102. p. 1350
Daly, Daphne, Br Mgr, Pima County Public Library, Murphy-Wilmot, 530 N Wilmot Rd, Tucson, AZ, 85711. Tel: 520-594-5420. p. 82
Daly, Erin, Youth Serv Coordr, Chicopee Public Library, 449 Front St, Chicopee, MA, 01013. Tel: 413-594-1800. p. 1011
Daly, Janet, Indexer, Mgr, The National Academies, Keck 439, 500 Fifth St NW, Washington, DC, 20001. Tel: 202-334-2989. p. 371
Daly, Jessica, Librn, Orlando Health, Clifford E Graese Community Health Library, 1400 S Orange Ave, Orlando, FL, 32806. Tel: 321-841-7234. p. 432
Daly, Meghan, Med Librn, American Academy of Ophthalmology Library, 655 Beach St, San Francisco, CA, 94109. Tel: 415-561-8500. p. 223
Daly, Rebecca, Head Librn, Finlandia University, 601 Quincy St, Hancock, MI, 49930. Tel: 906-487-7252. p. 1113
Daly, Tracy, Br Mgr, Onslow County Public Library, Swansboro Branch, 1460 W Corbett Ave, Swansboro, NC, 28584. Tel: 910-326-4888, Ext 141. p. 1698
Daly-Doran, Maryanne, Digital Services Reference Librn, University of Connecticut, Thomas J Meskill Law Library, 39 Elizabeth St, Hartford, CT, 06105. Tel: 860-570-5167. p. 340
Dalzin, Jennifer, Dir, Digital Initiatives & Serv, Newberry Library, 60 W Walton St, Chicago, IL, 60610-3305. Tel: 312-255-3536. p. 565
Damasco, Ione T, Assoc Dean, Engagement & Operations, University of Dayton Libraries, 300 College Park Dr, Dayton, OH, 45469. Tel: 937-229-4238. p. 1780
Damberger, Lindsey, Libr Mgr, Hughenden Public Library, Seven McKenzie Ave, Hughenden, AB, T0B 2E0, CANADA. Tel: 780-856-2435. p. 2543
Dambiinyam, Enerel, Head, Tech Serv, South Dakota State University, 1300 N Campus Dr, Box 2115, Brookings, SD, 57007. Tel: 605-688-5565. p. 2074
Dameron, Harriet, Libr Tech, Gaston College, 201 Hwy 321 S, Dallas, NC, 28034-1499. Tel: 704-922-6356. p. 1683
Dames, Christopher, Dean of Libr, University of Missouri-Saint Louis Libraries, Thomas Jefferson Library, One University Blvd, Saint Louis, MO, 63121-4400. Tel: 314-516-5060. p. 1276
Damewood, Mindy, Tech Proc Mgr, Monmouth College, 700 E Broadway, Monmouth, IL, 61462-1963. Tel: 309-457-2334. p. 619
Damiani, Catherine, Digital Serv Librn, Head, Ref, East Providence Public Library, 41 Grove Ave, East Providence, RI, 02914. Tel: 401-434-2453. p. 2032
Damiani, Catherine, Dir, Tiverton Public Library, 34 Roosevelt Ave, Tiverton, RI, 02878. Tel: 401-625-6796, Ext 6. p. 2042
Damiano, Jeanne, Br Mgr, Jackson-George Regional Library System, Vancleave Public Library, 12604 Hwy 57, Vancleave, MS, 39565. Tel: 228-826-5857. p. 1228
Damiano, Maureen, Mgr, Libr Operations, Ursinus College Library, 601 E Main St, Collegeville, PA, 19426. Tel: 610-409-3607. p. 1923
Damico, Andrew, Presv Librn, Rice University, 6100 Main, MS-44, Houston, TX, 77005. Tel: 713-348-2602. p. 2197
DaMico, Jim, Curator, Photog & Prints, Ref Librn, Cincinnati Museum Center At Union Terminal, 1301 Western Ave, Ste 2133, Cincinnati, OH, 45203. Tel: 513-287-7094. p. 1760
Damico, Rosalyn, Br Mgr, Buffalo & Erie County Public Library System, Elaine M Panty Branch Library, 820 Tonawanda St, Buffalo, NY, 14207-1448. Tel: 716-875-0562. p. 1508
Dampier, Shaina, Libr Mgr, Glatfelter Memorial Library, 101 Glenview Rd, Spring Grove, PA, 17362. Tel: 717-225-3220. p. 2009
Damptz, Rebecca, Head, Archives & Spec Coll, Decatur Public Library, 130 N Franklin St, Decatur, IL, 62523. Tel: 217-421-9711. p. 576
Damrau, Jon, Access Serv Librn, Outreach Serv Librn, Mount Saint Mary College, 330 Powell Ave, Newburgh, NY, 12550-3494. Tel: 845-569-3546. p. 1605
Damron, James, Br Mgr, Mercer County Library System, Lawrence Headquarters, 2751 Brunswick Pike, Lawrenceville, NJ, 08648. Tel: 609-882-9246. p. 1411
Damron, James, Mgr, Mercer County Library System, 2751 Brunswick Pike, Lawrenceville, NJ, 08648-4132. Tel: 609-883-8291. p. 1411
Damron, May, Dir, Toronto Public Library, 215 W Main St, Toronto, KS, 66777. Tel: 620-637-2661. p. 840
Damron, Wonda, Ref Librn, The John P Holt Brentwood Library, 8109 Concord Rd, Brentwood, TN, 37027. Tel: 615-371-0090, Ext 8130. p. 2089
Danaher, Ross W, Dir, Libr & Res Serv, The Parrott Centre, 376 Wallbridge-Loyalist Rd, Belleville, ON, K8N 5B9, CANADA. Tel: 613-969-1913, Ext 2249. p. 2631
Danak, Megan, Librn III, Saint Petersburg Public Library, Mirror Lake, 280 Fifth St N, Saint Petersburg, FL, 33701. Tel: 727-893-7268. p. 442
Danak, Megan, Librn III, Saint Petersburg Public Library, North, 861 70th Ave N, Saint Petersburg, FL, 33702. Tel: 727-892-5005. p. 442
Danak, Megan, Librn III, Saint Petersburg Public Library, West Saint Petersburg Community Library, 6700 Eighth Ave N, Saint Petersburg, FL, 33710. Tel: 727-341-7199. p. 442
Danboise, Sharon, Libr Asst, Vernon Public Library, 4441 Peterboro St, Vernon, NY, 13476. Tel: 315-829-2463. p. 1657
Danchik, Margaret J, Head, Acq, United States Naval Academy, 589 McNair Rd, Annapolis, MD, 21402-5029. Tel: 410-293-6945. p. 951
Dandekar, Anjali, Librn, Gardiner Roberts LLP Library, Bay Adelaide Centre-East Tower, 22 Adelaide St W, Ste 3600, Toronto, ON, M5H 4E3, CANADA. Tel: 416-865-6600. p. 2689
Dane, Lily, Mgr, Libr Operations, MacEwan University Library, 10700 104th Ave, Edmonton, AB, T5J 4S2, CANADA. Tel: 780-497-5850. p. 2537
Dane, Magen, Chief Librn, United States Department of the Navy, Office of Naval Intelligence Research Library, 4251 Suitland Rd, Washington, DC, 20395-5720. Tel: 301-669-3116. p. 379
Danes, Genavieve, Dir, Butler Public Library, 12808 W Hampton Ave, Butler, WI, 53007. Tel: 262-783-2535. p. 2426

Dang, Angel, Ref Librn, US International Development Finance Corp, 1100 New York Ave NW, Washington, DC, 20527. Tel: 202-336-8400. p. 380

Dang, Shannen, Libr Spec, Alhambra Civic Center Library, 101 S First St, Alhambra, CA, 91801-3432. Tel: 626-570-5008. p. 115

Danhart, Valerie, Circ, Paramus Public Library, 116 E Century Rd, Paramus, NJ, 07652. Tel: 201-599-1300. p. 1432

Daniel, Celia, Librn, Howard University Libraries, Afro-American Studies Resource Center, 500 Howard Pl NW, Rm 300, Washington, DC, 20059. Tel: 202-806-7242. p. 369

Daniel, Celia C, Head, Ref & Instruction, Howard University Libraries, 500 Howard Pl NW, Ste 203, Washington, DC, 20059. Tel: 202-806-7446. p. 369

Daniel, Cody, Librn, Northeast Regional Library, Corinth Public Library, 1023 Fillmore St, Corinth, MS, 38834. Tel: 662-287-2441. p. 1216

Daniel, Dominique, Coordr, Spec Coll, Humanities Librn, Hist & Modern Lang, Oakland University Library, 100 Library Dr, Rochester, MI, 48309-4479. Tel: 248-370-2478. p. 1144

Daniel, Donna, Tech Serv Librn, Dallas Baptist University, 3000 Mountain Creek Pkwy, Dallas, TX, 75211-9299. Tel: 214-333-5299. p. 2163

Daniel, Emy, Asst Dir, College Montmorency Bibliotheque, 475 Boul de L'Avenir, Laval, QC, H7N 5H9, CANADA. Tel: 450-975-6100, Ext 6364. p. 2715

Daniel, Heidi, Chief Exec Officer, Enoch Pratt Free Library, 400 Cathedral St, Baltimore, MD, 21201. Tel: 410-396-5430. p. 952

Daniel, Heidi, Pres & Chief Exec Officer, Maryland Interlibrary Loan Organization, c/o Enoch Pratt Free Library, 400 Cathedral St, Baltimore, MD, 21201-4484. Tel: 410-396-5498. p. 2766

Daniel, Jan, Tech Serv Librn, Greenville Technical College Libraries, Bldg 102, 506 S Pleasantburg Dr, Greenville, SC, 29607. Tel: 864-250-8320. p. 2062

Daniel, Karen, Dir, Johnson County Public Library, 444 Main St, Paintsville, KY, 41240. Tel: 606-789-4355. p. 872

Daniel, Katie, Mgr, West Georgia Regional Library, Ephesus Public Library, 200 Rogers St, Roopville, GA, 30170. Tel: 770-854-7323. p. 470

Daniel Lindsay, Beth, Instrul & Res Librn, Wabash College, 301 W Wabash Ave, Crawfordsville, IN, 47933. Tel: 765-361-6081. p. 677

Daniel Lindsay, Beth, Assoc Dir, Sweet Briar College, 134 Chapel Rd, Sweet Briar, VA, 24595. Tel: 434-381-6138. p. 2348

Daniel, Nancy L, Libr Dir, Western Piedmont Community College, Phifer Hall, 1001 Burkemont Ave, Morganton, NC, 28655. Tel: 828-448-3160. p. 1704

Daniel Walkuski, Julia, Digital Initiatives Coordr, Head Archivist, University of Michigan-Dearborn, 4901 Evergreen Rd, Dearborn, MI, 48128-2406. Tel: 313-593-5615. p. 1096

Daniel, Wanda, Mgr, Oconee Regional Library, Talking Book Center, 801 Bellevue Ave, Dublin, GA, 31021. Tel: 478-275-5382. p. 477

Daniels, Avery, Mr, Archivist, Coll Coordr, South Carolina State University, 300 College St NE, Orangeburg, SC, 29115. Tel: 803-536-8627. p. 2067

Daniels, Billie, Pub Serv Mgr, Union College, 310 College St, Campus Box D-21, Barbourville, KY, 40906-1499. Tel: 606-546-1242. p. 848

Daniels, Candy, Acq, Vermont State University - Randolph, Main St, Randolph Center, VT, 05061. Tel: 802-728-1237. p. 2292

Daniels, Caroline, Syst, Web & ILL Librn, Kwantlen Polytechnic University Library, 12666 72nd Ave, Surrey, BC, V3W 2M8, CANADA. Tel: 604-599-3036. p. 2576

Daniels, Debbie, Libr Mgr, Northwest Regional Library System, Parker Public Library, 4710 Second St, Parker, FL, 32404. Tel: 850-871-3092. p. 436

Daniels, Elizabeth, Dir, Iron Ridge Public Library, 205 Park St, Iron Ridge, WI, 53035. Tel: 920-387-3637. p. 2442

Daniels, Erin, Electronic Serv Librn, Santa Rosa Junior College, 1501 Mendocino Ave, Santa Rosa, CA, 95401. Tel: 707-527-4773. p. 245

Daniels, Heidi, Librn, Gadsen Correctional Institution Library, 6044 Greensboro Hwy, Quincy, FL, 32351-9100. Tel: 850-875-9701, Ext 2261. p. 439

Daniels, Jack, Teaching & Learning Librn, Flagler College, 44 Sevilla St, Saint Augustine, FL, 32084-4302. Tel: 904-819-6206. p. 439

Daniels, John, Computer Syst Mgr, Minneapolis Community & Technical College Library, Wheelock Whitney Hall, 1501 Hennepin Ave, Minneapolis, MN, 55403. Tel: 612-659-6284. p. 1184

Daniels, Keith, Sr Librn, University of Houston, William R Jenkins Architecture & Art Library, 122 Architecture Bldg, Houston, TX, 77204-4000. Tel: 713-743-2340. p. 2199

Daniels, Kent, Asst Dir, Bexley Public Library, 2411 E Main St, Bexley, OH, 43209. Tel: 614-545-6938. p. 1751

Daniels, LaBae, Br Mgr, Free Library of Philadelphia, Frankford Branch, 4634 Frankford Ave, Philadelphia, PA, 19124-5804. Tel: 215-685-1473. p. 1978

Daniels, LeAnne, Br Mgr, Sullivan County Public Libraries, Farmersburg Public, 102 W Main St, Farmersburg, IN, 47850. Tel: 812-696-2194. p. 720

Daniels, Lewis B, III, Dir, Westbrook Public Library, 61 Goodspeed Dr, Westbrook, CT, 06498. Tel: 860-399-6422. p. 346

Daniels, Lisa, Dir, Augusta Public Library, 1609 State St, Augusta, KS, 67010-2098. Tel: 316-775-2681. p. 797

Daniels, Marilyn, Mgr, Independence Health System Latrobe Hospital, One Mellon Way, Latrobe, PA, 15650. Tel: 724-537-1275. p. 1953

Daniels, Michelle, Libr Dir, Louisville Public Library, 217 Main St, Louisville, NE, 68037. Tel: 402-234-6265. p. 1323

Daniels, Nancy, Circ, Fiske Public Library, 110 Randall Rd, Wrentham, MA, 02093. Tel: 508-384-5440. p. 1073

Daniels, Rebecca, Libr Dir, Mercy College of Ohio Library, 2221 Madison Ave, Toledo, OH, 43604. Tel: 419-251-1821. p. 1824

Daniels, Robbie, Ms, Br Mgr, Walton County Public Library System, Freeport Public, 76 Hwy 20 W, Freeport, FL, 32439. Tel: 850-835-2040. p. 393

Daniels, Robin, Libr Mgr, Northwest Area Health Education Center Library at Boone, Watauga Medical Ctr, 336 Deerfield Rd, Boone, NC, 28607-5008. Tel: 828-262-4300. p. 1675

Daniels, Robin, Info Serv, South Dakota State University, 1300 N Campus Dr, Box 2115, Brookings, SD, 57007. Tel: 605-688-5955. p. 2074

Daniels, Sarah, Librn, Aims Community College, College Ctr, 5401 W 20th St, 7501, Greeley, CO, 80634-3002. Tel: 970-339-6458. p. 284

Daniels, Sharon, Br Librn, Wapiti Regional Library, Sturgeon Lake Public Library, 721 White Buffalo Lane, Shellbrook, SK, S0J 2E1, CANADA. Tel: 306-764-5506. p. 2746

Daniels, Stephanie, Dir, Hartford Public Library, 12 Church St, Hartford, MI, 49057. Tel: 269-588-5103. p. 1114

Daniels, Sue, Youth Serv Librn, Elm Grove Public Library, 13600 Juneau Blvd, Elm Grove, WI, 53122. Tel: 262-782-6717. p. 2434

Daniels, Tonya, Libr Tech, Hinds Community College, Nursing/Allied Health Center, 1750 Chadwick Dr, Jackson, MS, 39204-3490. Tel: 601-376-4816. p. 1231

Danielson, Tania, Dir, Res & Info Serv, Sheppard, Mullin, Richter & Hampton Library, 333 S Hope, 43rd Flr, Los Angeles, CA, 90071. Tel: 213-620-1780. p. 167

Danilow, Janet, Head Librn, Kearny Public Library, 912-A Tilbury Rd, Kearny, AZ, 85237. Tel: 520-363-5861. p. 63

Danin, Barbara, Acq, Admin Coordr, University of the Arts University Libraries, Anderson Hall, 1st Flr, 333 S Broad St, Philadelphia, PA, 19102. Tel: 215-717-6286. p. 1988

Danis, Carl, Dir, Libr Res, Sandhills Community College, 3395 Airport Rd, Pinehurst, NC, 28374. Tel: 910-695-3819. p. 1707

Danisher, Geoffrey, Head, ILL/Access Serv Librn, Sarah Lawrence College, One Mead Way, Bronxville, NY, 10708. Tel: 914-395-2474. p. 1500

Danke, Danielle, Libr Dir, Suttons Bay Bingham District Library, 416 Front St, Suttons Bay, MI, 49682. Tel: 231-271-3512. p. 1153

Dankert, Holly Stec, Access Serv, Res, School of the Art Institute of Chicago, 37 S Wabash Ave, Chicago, IL, 60603-3103. Tel: 312-899-5097. p. 568

Danko, Mary, Dir, Fletcher Free Library, 235 College St, Burlington, VT, 05401. Tel: 802-863-3403. p. 2281

Danku, Patricia, Br Librn, Wapiti Regional Library, Prairie River Public Library, Two Arras St, Prairie River, SK, S0E 1J0, CANADA. Tel: 306-889-4521. p. 2746

Dann, Lucinda, Dir, Satellite Beach Public Library, 751 Jamaica Blvd, Satellite Beach, FL, 32937. Tel: 321-779-4004. p. 443

Danneker, John, Dean of Libr, Western Washington University, 516 High St, MS 9103, Bellingham, WA, 98225. Tel: 360-650-3084. p. 2358

Dannelley, Leta J, Med Librn, CHRISTUS Spohn Health System, 600 Elizabeth St, Corpus Christi, TX, 78404. Tel: 361-902-4348. p. 2160

Dannenbaum, Claire, Ref Serv, Lane Community College Library, Library-Center Bldg, 4000 E 30th Ave, Eugene, OR, 97405-0640. Tel: 541-463-5357. p. 1879

Dannenberg, Anne, Dir, Huntington Public Library, 2156 Main Rd, Huntington, VT, 05462. Tel: 802-434-4583. p. 2286

Danner, Arystine, Br Mgr, Chicago Public Library, North Austin, 5724 W North Ave, Chicago, IL, 60639. Tel: 312-746-4233. p. 557

Danner, Charles A, Ref/Tech Support Librn, Portage County Public Library, Charles M White Library Bldg, 1001 Main St, Stevens Point, WI, 54481-2860. Tel: 715-346-1544. p. 2479

Danner, Kerri, Libr Mgr, Valleyview Municipal Library, 4804 50th Ave, Valleyview, AB, T0H 3N0, CANADA. Tel: 780-524-3033. p. 2557

Danner, Patricia, Asst Librn, Conception Abbey & Seminary Library, 37174 State Hwy VV, Conception, MO, 64433. Tel: 660-944-2882. p. 1244

Danowski, Dennis, Libr Dir, Macomb Public Library District, 235 S Lafayette St, Macomb, IL, 61455. Tel: 309-833-2714. p. 612

Danowski, Fred, Info Syst Librn, Milford Public Library, 57 New Haven Ave, Milford, CT, 06460. Tel: 203-701-4553. p. 323

Dansberger, Sarah, Archivist, Head Librn, Baltimore Museum of Art, Ten Art Museum Dr, Baltimore, MD, 21218-3898. Tel: 443-573-1780. p. 952

Dansby, Charles, Br Head, Volusia County Public Library, John H Dickerson Heritage Library, 411 S Keech St, Daytona Beach, FL, 32114. Tel: 386-239-6478. p. 393

Dansby, Claudia, Acq, University of Toledo, LaValley Law Library, Mail Stop 508, 2801 W Bancroft St, Toledo, OH, 43606-3390. Tel: 419-530-2733. p. 1825

Dansby, Cullen, Adult Serv, Benbrook Public Library, 1065 Mercedes St, Benbrook, TX, 76126. Tel: 817-249-6632. p. 2147

Dansby, David, Dir, Hickman County Public Library, 120 W Swan St, Centerville, TN, 37033. Tel: 931-729-5130. p. 2091

Daveluy, Suzanne M, City Librn, Deputy Dir, Community Serv, Stockton-San Joaquin County Public Library, 605 N El Dorado St, Stockton, CA, 95202. Tel: 209-937-8221. p. 250

Davenport, Amy, Outreach Librn, Bethel Public Library, 189 Greenwood Ave, Bethel, CT, 06801-2598. Tel: 203-794-8756. p. 302

Davenport, Cheryl, Dir, Vernon District Public Library, 115 E Main St, Vernon, MI, 48476. Tel: 989-288-6486. p. 1156

Davenport, Heather, Ch, Fort Sumner Public Library, 235 W Sumner Ave, Fort Sumner, NM, 88119. Tel: 575-355-2832. p. 1468

Davenport, Kathy, Youth Serv, Fleming County Public Library, 202 Bypass Blvd, Flemingsburg, KY, 41041-1298. Tel: 606-845-7851. p. 854

Davenport, Kim, Tech Serv Supvr, George H & Laura E Brown Library, 122 Van Norden St, Washington, NC, 27889. Tel: 252-946-4300. p. 1721

Davenport, Mina, Librn, Children's Hospital & Research Center Oakland, 747 52nd St, 4th Flr, Oakland, CA, 94609. Tel: 510-428-3448. p. 185

Davenport, Montell, Exec Law Librn, Cook County Law Library, 50 W Washington St, Rm 2900, Chicago, IL, 60602. Tel: 312-603-5423. p. 559

Davenport, Nan, Dir, Wetmore Community Library, 95 County Rd 393, Wetmore, CO, 81253. Tel: 719-784-6669. p. 298

Davenport, Sadie, Assoc Librn, California Northstate University Library, Ranch Cordova Campus, 2910 Prospect Park Dr, Rancho Cordova, CA, 95670. Tel: 916-686-7674. p. 140

Davenport, Sadie, Health Sci Librn, University of California, Davis, 4610 X St, Sacramento, CA, 95817. Tel: 916-734-3529. p. 210

Davenport, Sara, Libr Dir, Cayuga County Community College, 197 Franklin St, Auburn, NY, 13021. Tel: 315-294-8596. p. 1488

Davenport, Sara, Libr Dir, Cayuga Community College, 11 River Glenn Dr, Fulton, NY, 13069. Tel: 315-593-9319. p. 1536

Davey, Donna, Adjunct Reference & Scholarly Communication Librn, City University of New York, 365 Fifth Ave, New York, NY, 10016-4309. Tel: 212-817-7071. p. 1582

Davey, John H, Libr Mgr, Alston & Bird, LLP Library, 90 Park Ave, 12th Flr, New York, NY, 10016. Tel: 212-210-9526. p. 1578

Davey, Linda, Circ, Ref (Info Servs), Holdrege Area Public Library, 604 East Ave, Holdrege, NE, 68949. Tel: 308-995-6556. p. 1318

Daviau, Nicole, Dir, Porter Memorial Library, 87 Main St, Blandford, MA, 01008. Tel: 413-848-2853. p. 990

David, Emily, Dir, Springfield Public Library, 225 Fifth St, Springfield, OR, 97477-4697. Tel: 541-726-3766. p. 1899

David, Kenneth, Library Contact, Eastern Counties Regional Library, Petit de Grat Branch, 3435 Hwy, No 206, Petit de Grat, NS, B0E 2L0, CANADA. Tel: 902-226-3534. p. 2621

David, Meredith, Library & Academic Resource Ctr Specialist, Moberly Area Community College Library & Academic Resource Center, Columbia Campus, 601 Business Loop 70 W, Ste 216, Columbia, MO, 65203. Tel: 573-234-1067, 660-263-4100, Ext 12116. p. 1262

David, Sophie, Bibliothecaire de Liaison, Bibliotheques de Montreal, L'Ile-Bizard, 500 montee de l'Eglise, L'Ile-Bizard, QC, H9C 1G9, CANADA. Tel: 514-620-6257. p. 2719

Davide, Michael, Tech Coordr, Mid-Mississippi Regional Library System, 201 S Huntington St, Kosciusko, MS, 39090-9002. Tel: 662-289-5151. p. 1224

Davidow, Kathy, Circ Asst, Bradford Public Library, 21 S Main St, Bradford, VT, 05033. Tel: 802-222-4536. p. 2280

Davidson, Ashley, Community & Extension Servs Mgr, Hoover Public Library, 200 Municipal Dr, Hoover, AL, 35216. Tel: 205-444-7810. p. 21

Davidson, Catherine, Chief Librn, University of Ontario Institute of Technology Library, 2000 Simcoe St N, Oshawa, ON, L1H 7K4, CANADA. Tel: 905-721-3082. p. 2664

Davidson, Chris, Asst Librn, Missouri School for the Blind Library, 3815 Magnolia Ave, Saint Louis, MO, 63110. Tel: 314-633-1566. p. 1272

Davidson, Christopher, Asst Vice Chancellor, State Archivist, Georgia Archives, 5800 Jonesboro Rd, Morrow, GA, 30260. Tel: 678-364-3710. p. 491

Davidson, Jeanne, Assoc Dean, Coll, Patron Serv, Utah State University, 3000 Old Main Hill, Logan, UT, 84322-3000. Tel: 435-797-2633. p. 2265

Davidson, Jennifer, Dir, Libr Serv, Richardson Public Library, 2360 Campbell Creek Blvd, Ste 500, Richardson, TX, 75082. Tel: 972-744-4353. p. 2231

Davidson, Jenny Emery, Exec Dir, The Community Library, 415 Spruce Ave N, Ketchum, ID, 83340. Tel: 208-726-3493. p. 523

Davidson, Jill, Youth Serv Librn, Nevada County Community Library, Madelyn Helling Library, 980 Helling Way, Nevada City, CA, 95959. Tel: 530-265-7078. p. 183

Davidson, Karen, Coordr, Northeast Iowa Community College, Calmar Campus Library, 1625 Hwy 150, Calmar, IA, 52132. Tel: 563-562-3263, Ext 257. p. 776

Davidson, Kevin, Br Librn, London Public Library, R E Crouch, 550 Hamilton Rd, London, ON, N5Z 1S4, CANADA. Tel: 519-673-0111. p. 2654

Davidson, Laura, Dean of Libr, Meredith College, 3800 Hillsborough St, Raleigh, NC, 27607-5298. Tel: 919-760-8532. p. 1708

Davidson, M, Librn, Oregon State Penitentiary Library, OSP Minimum, 2809 State St, Salem, OR, 97310. Tel: 503-378-2081. p. 1896

Davidson, MacKenzie, Student Success Librn, Paul Smiths College of Arts & Sciences, 7833 New York 30, Paul Smiths, NY, 12970. Tel: 518-327-6904. p. 1615

Davidson, Martha, Dir & Librn, Thompson-Sawyer Public Library, 403 W Third St, Quanah, TX, 79252. Tel: 940-663-2654. p. 2229

Davidson, Mildred Elizabeth, Assoc Dir, Head, Pub Serv, McDaniel College, 2 College Hill, Westminster, MD, 21157-4390. Tel: 410-857-2278. p. 981

Davidson, Patricia, Dep Fiscal Officer, Tech Coordr, Upper Sandusky Community Library, 301 N Sandusky Ave, Upper Sandusky, OH, 43351-1139. Tel: 419-294-1345. p. 1826

Davidson, Paula, Librn, Greensboro Free Library, 53 Wilson St, Greensboro, VT, 05841. Tel: 802-533-2531. p. 2285

Davidson, Russell, III, Assoc Dean, Instrul Tech, University of Detroit Mercy Libraries, 4001 W McNichols Rd, Detroit, MI, 48221-3038. Tel: 313-993-1129. p. 1099

Davidson, Saleena, Principal Librn, YA, South Brunswick Public Library, 110 Kingston Lane, Monmouth Junction, NJ, 08852. Tel: 732-329-4000, Ext 7634. p. 1419

Davidson, Shaun, Br Mgr, Public Library of Cincinnati & Hamilton County, Forest Park Branch, 655 Waycross Rd, Forest Park, OH, 45240. Tel: 513-369-4478. p. 1762

Davidson, Sheryl, Ch, Abilene Public Library, 209 NW Fourth, Abilene, KS, 67410-2690. Tel: 785-263-1303. p. 795

Davidson Squibb, Sara, Head, Learning Serv, Head, Res Serv, University of California, Merced Library, 5200 N Lake Rd, Merced, CA, 95343. Tel: 209-205-8237. p. 176

Davidson, Stephanie, Dir, Willamette University, J W Long Law Library, 245 Winter St SE, Salem, OR, 97301. Tel: 503-375-5345. p. 1897

Davies, Anne, Head, Access Serv, Xavier University, 1535 Musketeer Dr, Cincinnati, OH, 45207. Tel: 513-745-4803. p. 1765

Davies, Annmarie, Head, Tech Serv, ILL, Rogers Memorial Library, 91 Coopers Farm Rd, Southampton, NY, 11968. Tel: 631-283-0774. p. 1643

Davies, April, Head, Pub Serv, Head, Tech Serv, SUNY Cobleskill College of Agriculture & Technology, 142 Schenectady Ave, Cobleskill, NY, 12043. Tel: 518-255-5841. p. 1520

Davies, Beth, Chief Librn, Burnaby Public Library, 6100 Willingdon Ave, Burnaby, BC, V5H 4N5, CANADA. Tel: 604-436-5431. p. 2563

Davies, Carra, Br Supvr, Madison Public Library, Lakeview, 2845 N Sherman Ave, Madison, WI, 53704. Tel: 608-246-4547. p. 2449

Davies, Cheryl, Adminr, Thompson Public Library, 81 Thompson Dr N, Thompson, MB, R8N 0C3, CANADA. Tel: 204-677-3717. p. 2591

Davies, Cindy L, Assoc Librn, Colls Mgr, Syst Librn, South Dakota School of Mines & Technology, 501 E Saint Joseph St, Rapid City, SD, 57701-3995. p. 2081

Davies, Elaine, Dir, Heart of the Valley Public Library, 1252 E 1500 N, Terreton, ID, 83450. Tel: 208-663-4834. p. 531

Davies, Elizabeth, Br Mgr, Burnaby Public Library, Bob Prittie Metrotown Branch, 6100 Willingdon Ave, Burnaby, BC, V5H 4N5, CANADA. Tel: 604-436-5403. p. 2563

Davies, Evan, Dr, Dir, Institute of Historical Survey Foundation Library, 3035 S Main, Las Cruces, NM, 88005-3756. Tel: 575-525-3035. p. 1470

Davies, Jennifer, Asst Libr Dir, Oak Creek Public Library, Drexel Town Sq, 8040 S Sixth St, Oak Creek, WI, 53154. Tel: 414-766-7900. p. 2465

Davies, Jeremy, Br Mgr, San Diego Public Library, Tierrasanta Branch Library, 4985 La Cuenta Dr, San Diego, CA, 92124. Tel: 858-573-1384. p. 221

Davies, Joe, Libr Dir, Burlington Public Library, 166 E Jefferson St, Burlington, WI, 53105. Tel: 262-342-1130. p. 2426

Davies, Kathy, Dir, Augusta University, 1459 Laney-Walker Blvd, Augusta, GA, 30912-0004. Tel: 706-721-9911. p. 467

Davies-Smith, Alayna, Br Mgr, Hawaii State Public Library System, Lahaina Public Library, 680 Wharf St, Lahaina, HI, 96761. Tel: 808-662-3950. p. 509

Davies-Wilson, Dennis, Libr Dir, University of New Mexico, 4000 University Dr, Los Alamos, NM, 87544. Tel: 505-662-0343. p. 1472

Davignon, Nicole, Dir, James White Memorial Library, Five Washburn Rd E, East Freetown, MA, 02717-1220. Tel: 508-763-5344. p. 1016

Davignon, Nicole, Librn, White James Memorial Library, G H Hathaway Library, Six N Main St, Assonet, MA, 02702. Tel: 508-644-2385. p. 1016

Davila Cosme, Sonia, Ref Librn, University of Puerto Rico Library, Cayey Campus, 205 Ave Antonio R Barcelo, Ste 205, Cayey, PR, 00736. Tel: 787-738-2161, Ext 2131. p. 2510

Davila, Jessica, Assoc Dean, Dir, Digital Strategies & Innovation, University of Oklahoma Libraries, 401 W Brooks St, Norman, OK, 73019. Tel: 405-325-3341. p. 1856

Davila, Rhonda, Spec Coll Librn, Daughters of the Republic of Texas Library, Bexar County Archives Bldg, 126 E Nueva, San Antonio, TX, 78204. Tel: 210-335-3006. p. 2236

Davis, Adam, Head, Outreach Serv, Palm Beach County Library System, Palm Beach County Library Annex, 4249 Cherry Rd, West Palm Beach, FL, 33409. Tel: 561-649-5500. p. 454

Davis, Adam, Syst Serv Dir, Palm Beach County Library System, 3650 Summit Blvd, West Palm Beach, FL, 33406-4198. Tel: 561-233-2600. p. 454

Davis, Alan, Eng & Math Librn, Sci & Tech Librn, West Florida Public Library, 239 N Spring St, Pensacola, FL, 32502. Tel: 850-436-5060. p. 437

Davis, Amber, Prog Coordr, Southern Illinois University Edwardsville, 601 James R Thompson Blvd, Bldg B, East Saint Louis, IL, 62201. Tel: 618-874-8719. p. 581

Davis, Amy, Dir, Myerstown Community Library, 199 N College St, Myerstown, PA, 17067. Tel: 717-866-2800. p. 1967
Davis, Angela, Ref & Instruction Librn, Penn State Behrend, 4951 College Dr, Erie, PA, 16563-4115. Tel: 814-898-6106. p. 1932
Davis, Angie, Colls Mgr, Outreach Mgr, Idaho State Historical Society, Idaho History Ctr, 2205 Old Penitentiary Rd, Boise, ID, 83712-8250. Tel: 208-488-7390. p. 517
Davis, Ann, Supvr, Ch Serv, Napa County Library, 580 Coombs St, Napa, CA, 94559-3396. Tel: 707-253-4079. p. 182
Davis, Ashley, Prog Coordr, Four Star Public Library District, 132 W South St, Mendon, IL, 62351. Tel: 217-936-2131. p. 616
Davis, Barb, Resource Acquisition & Mgmt Librn, North Dakota State University Libraries, 1201 Albrecht Blvd, Fargo, ND, 58108. Tel: 701-231-8880. p. 1733
Davis, Barbara, Youth Ref Librn, Fruitville Public Library, 100 Apex Rd, Sarasota, FL, 34240. Tel: 941-861-2500. p. 442
Davis, Bessie, Dir, Cynthiana-Harrison County Public Library, 104 N Main St, Cynthiana, KY, 41031. Tel: 859-234-4881. p. 853
Davis, Betsy, Dir, Moundridge Public Library, 220 S Christian, Moundridge, KS, 67107. Tel: 620-345-6355. p. 826
Davis, Brenda, Ref Librn, Montgomery City-County Public Library System, Juliette Hampton Morgan Memorial Library, 245 High St, Montgomery, AL, 36104. Tel: 334-240-4992. p. 29
Davis, Brenda, Br Mgr, Gary Public Library, Carter G Woodson Branch, 501 S Lake St, Gary, IN, 46403-2408. Tel: 219-938-3941. p. 686
Davis, Brenda, Asst Librn, Greene County Law Library, Court House, 3rd Flr, 45 N Detroit St, Xenia, OH, 45385. Tel: 937-562-5115. p. 1834
Davis, Brittany, Librn, United States Sentencing Commission Library, One Columbus Circle NE, Ste 2-500 S Lobby, Washington, DC, 20002-8002. Tel: 202-502-4500. p. 380
Davis, Carenado, Dean, Libr Serv, Wake Technical Community College, Bldg D, 100 Level, 9101 Fayetteville Rd, Raleigh, NC, 27603-5696. Tel: 919-866-5644. p. 1711
Davis, Carla, Dir, Mkt, Akron-Summit County Public Library, 60 S High St, Akron, OH, 44326. Tel: 330-643-9090. p. 1744
Davis, Carrie, Dir, Hawkeye Public Library, 104 S Second St, Hawkeye, IA, 52147. Tel: 563-427-5536. p. 758
Davis, Charles, Librn, Ogeechee Technical College Library, One Joe Kennedy Blvd, Statesboro, GA, 30458. Tel: 912-871-1886. p. 498
Davis, Cherie, Libr Dir, Ronceverte Public Library, 500 W Main St, Ronceverte, WV, 24970. Tel: 304-647-7400. p. 2414
Davis, Chris, Ms, Circ Supvr, Davis County Library, Clearfield/North Branch, 562 S 1000 East, Clearfield, UT, 84015. Tel: 801-451-1840. p. 2263
Davis, Christy, Dir, Silver Falls Library District, 410 S Water St, Silverton, OR, 97381. Tel: 503-873-5173. p. 1899
Davis, Cindy, Libr Dir, Spirit Lake Public Library, 702 16th St, Spirit Lake, IA, 51360. Tel: 712-336-2667. p. 784
Davis, Connie C, ILL Spec, Westminster College, S Market St, New Wilmington, PA, 16172-0001. Tel: 724-946-6000. p. 1970
Davis, Corey, Digital Preserv, Council of Prairie & Pacific University Libraries, 150B -1711 85th St NW, Calgary, AB, T3R 1J3, CANADA. Tel: 604-827-0578. p. 2777
Davis, Craig, Dir, Adult Serv, Chicago Public Library, 400 S State St, Chicago, IL, 60605. Tel: 312-747-4252. p. 555
Davis, Craig, Librn, Grand Lodge of Iowa, AF & AM, 813 First Ave SE, Cedar Rapids, IA, 52406. Tel: 319-365-1438. p. 738
Davis, Danette, Asst Dir, Seymour Public Library District, 176-178 Genesee St, Auburn, NY, 13021. Tel: 315-252-2571. p. 1489
Davis, Darnell, Building & Operations Supvr, Kankakee Public Library, 201 E Merchant St, Kankakee, IL, 60901. Tel: 815-939-4564. p. 604
Davis, Debbie, Br Librn, Roane County Public Library, Walton Public Library, Two Cunningham Lane, Walton, WV, 25286. Tel: 304-577-6071. p. 2415
Davis, Deborah, Dir, Archives & Spec Coll, Valdosta State University, 1500 N Patterson St, Valdosta, GA, 31698-0150. Tel: 229-259-7756. p. 501
Davis, Deborah, Libr Mgr, Wake County Public Library System, Middle Creek Community Library, 111 Middle Creek Park Ave, Apex, NC, 27539. Tel: 919-890-7400. p. 1711
Davis, Deedee, Digital Scholarship Servs Specialist, Indiana University, Herron Art Library, Herron School of Art & Design, 735 W New York St, Indianapolis, IN, 46202. Tel: 317-278-9439. p. 693
Davis, Dell, Dir, Pub Serv, University of the Incarnate Word, 4301 Broadway, CPO 297, San Antonio, TX, 78209-6397. Tel: 210-829-6054. p. 2240
Davis, Deniece, Acq/Cat Tech, Govt Doc, Oregon Institute of Technology Library, 3201 Campus Dr, Klamath Falls, OR, 97601-8801. Tel: 541-885-1772. p. 1883
Davis, Denise, Br Mgr, Pearl River County Library System, Poplarville Public Library, 202 W Beers St, Poplarville, MS, 39470. Tel: 601-795-8411. p. 1229
Davis, Donald, Exec Dir, Lowndes County Historical Society & Museum, 305 W Central Ave, Valdosta, GA, 31601. Tel: 229-247-4780. p. 501
Davis, Dora, Med Librn, Waukesha Memorial Hospital, 725 American Ave, Waukesha, WI, 53188. Tel: 262-928-2150. p. 2484
Davis, Elizabeth, Coll Develop Librn, Sul Ross State University, PO Box C-109, Alpine, TX, 79832. Tel: 432-837-8123. p. 2133
Davis, Emily N, Res & Instruction Librn, Texas A&M University-Commerce, 2600 S Neal St, Commerce, TX, 75428. Tel: 903-886-5720. p. 2158
Davis, Erin, Br Mgr, Latah County Library District, Juliaetta Branch, 205 Main St, Juliaetta, ID, 83535. Tel: 208-276-7071. p. 526
Davis, Erin, Access Serv Librn, Wofford College, 429 N Church St, Spartanburg, SC, 29303-3663. Tel: 864-597-4300. p. 2070
Davis, Esther, Adult Serv Coordr, Millis Public Library, 961 Main St, Millis, MA, 02054. Tel: 508-376-8282. p. 1036
Davis, Eva, Dir, Canton Public Library, 1200 S Canton Center Rd, Canton, MI, 48188-1600. Tel: 734-397-0999, Ext 1065. p. 1088
Davis, Faye, Exec Dir, Libr Dir, Collin College, 2200 W University, McKinney, TX, 75071. Tel: 972-548-6866. p. 2217
Davis, Frank, Liaison Librn, University of Kentucky Libraries, Medical Center Library, William R Willard Medical Education Bldg 298, 800 Rose St, Lexington, KY, 40536-0298. Tel: 859-323-3983. p. 864
Davis, G Kevin, Dir, Messenger Public Library of North Aurora, 113 Oak St, North Aurora, IL, 60542. Tel: 630-801-2345. p. 625
Davis, Hailey, Br Mgr, Georgetown County Library, Andrews Branch, 105 N Morgan St, Andrews, SC, 29510. Tel: 843-545-3621. p. 2060
Davis, Hugh, Dir, Albemarle Regional Library, 303 W Tryon St, Winton, NC, 27986. Tel: 252-358-7832. p. 1727
Davis, Jacqueline Z, Dir, New York Public Library - Astor, Lenox & Tilden Foundations, New York Public Library for the Performing Arts, Dorothy & Lewis B Cullman Ctr, 40 Lincoln Center Plaza, New York, NY, 10023-7498. Tel: 917-275-6975. p. 1596
Davis, Jan, Dep Dir, Grayslake Area Public Library District, 100 Library Lane, Grayslake, IL, 60030. Tel: 847-223-5313. p. 595
Davis, Janet L, Head Librn, Opp Public Library, 1604 N Main St, Opp, AL, 36467. Tel: 334-493-6423. p. 32
Davis, Jean, Intl Law Librn, Brooklyn Law School Library, 250 Joralemon St, Brooklyn, NY, 11201. Tel: 718-780-7534. p. 1501
Davis, Jeannette, Libr Mgr, San Antonio Public Library, Collins Garden, 200 N Park Blvd, San Antonio, TX, 78204. Tel: 210-207-9120. p. 2239
Davis, Jee, Assoc Univ Librn for Colls & Stewardship, Villanova University, 800 Lancaster Ave, Villanova, PA, 19085. Tel: 610-519-7821. p. 2017
Davis, Jeehyun, Univ Librn, American University Library, 4400 Massachusetts Ave NW, Washington, DC, 20016-8046. Tel: 202-885-3232. p. 361
Davis, Jeffrey, Br Mgr, San Diego Public Library, Linda Vista, 2160 Ulric St, San Diego, CA, 92111-6628. Tel: 858-573-1399. p. 219
Davis, Jenna, Dir, Hall Memorial Library, 18 Park St, Northfield, NH, 03276. Tel: 603-286-8971. p. 1377
Davis, Jennie, Librn, Vance-Granville Community College, 200 Community College Rd, Henderson, NC, 27536. Tel: 252-738-3279. p. 1695
Davis, Jeremy, Youth Serv Mgr, Hoover Public Library, 200 Municipal Dr, Hoover, AL, 35216. Tel: 205-444-7810. p. 21
Davis, Jill, Libr Dir, Hendrick Hudson Free Library, 185 Kings Ferry Rd, Montrose, NY, 10548. Tel: 914-739-5654. p. 1573
Davis, Jim, Dir, Louisiana Ctr for the Bk, State Library of Louisiana, 701 N Fourth St, Baton Rouge, LA, 70802-5232. Tel: 225-342-9714. p. 884
Davis, Jimi, Asst Libr Mgr, Lancaster Veterans Memorial Library, 1600 Veterans Memorial Pkwy, Lancaster, TX, 75134. Tel: 972-275-1415. p. 2209
Davis, Jo-Ann, Br Mgr, Pulaski County Library District, 306 Historic 66 W, Waynesville, MO, 65583. Tel: 573-774-2965. p. 1285
Davis, Joan, Br Mgr, Washington County Library System, Avon Library, 874 Riverside Rd, Avon, MS, 38723. Tel: 662-332-9346. p. 1217
Davis, Jonathon, Br Head, Lake County Public Library, Cedar Lake Branch, 10010 W 133rd Ave, Cedar Lake, IN, 46303. Tel: 219-374-7121. p. 705
Davis, Jonna, Circ, Tech Serv, Teaneck Public Library, 840 Teaneck Rd, Teaneck, NJ, 07666. Tel: 201-837-4171. p. 1445
Davis, Joseph, Head Librn, Heartland Institute, 3939 N Wilke Rd, Chicago, IL, 60004. Tel: 312-377-4000. p. 561
Davis, Joy, Head, Tech Serv, Ouachita Parish Public Library, 1800 Stubbs Ave, Monroe, LA, 71201. Tel: 318-327-1490. p. 898
Davis, Judy Ann, Res Sharing Librn, University of Washington Libraries, Gallagher Law Library, William H Gates Hall, 4000 15th Ave NE, Seattle, WA, 98195-3020. Tel: 206-543-4262. p. 2382
Davis, Julia, Dir, Kiel Public Library, 511 Third St, Kiel, WI, 53042. Tel: 920-894-7122. p. 2445
Davis, Julianna S, Tech Serv Librn, University of Mississippi, 481 Chuckie Mullins Dr, University, MS, 38677. Tel: 662-915-6832. p. 1234
Davis, Karen, Cataloger, Gardner-Webb University, 110 S Main St, Boiling Springs, NC, 28017. Tel: 704-406-4290. p. 1674
Davis, Karen, ILS Syst Mgr, Public Library of Cincinnati & Hamilton County, 800 Vine St, Cincinnati, OH, 45202-2009. Tel: 513-369-6980. p. 1761
Davis, Kate, Pub Serv Mgr, Cobourg Public Library, 200 Ontario St, Cobourg, ON, K9A 5P4, CANADA. Tel: 905-372-9271, Ext 6260. p. 2636
Davis, Kathy, Dir, Harrison Regional Library System, 50 Lester St, Columbiana, AL, 35051. Tel: 205-669-3910. p. 13

Davis, Keith, Br Mgr, San Diego County Library, Campo-Morena Village Branch, 31356 Hwy 94, Campo, CA, 91906-3112. Tel: 619-478-5945. p. 216

Davis, Kelly, Mgr, Charlestown-Clark County Public Library, New Washington Branch, 210 S Poplar St, New Washington, IN, 47162. Tel: 812-289-1142. p. 674

Davis Kendrick, Kaetrena, Dean, Libr Serv, Winthrop University, 824 Oakland Ave, Rock Hill, SC, 29733. Tel: 803-323-2131. p. 2067

Davis, Kevin, Dir, South Portland Public Library, 482 Broadway, South Portland, ME, 04106. Tel: 207-767-7660. p. 941

Davis, Kevin M, Dir, South Portland Public Library, Memorial Branch, 155 Wescott Rd, South Portland, ME, 04106. Tel: 207-775-1835. p. 941

Davis, Kim, Outreach Serv, Team Leader, Pickaway County District Public Library, 1160 N Court St, Circleville, OH, 43113-1725. Tel: 740-477-1644, Ext 230. p. 1765

Davis, Kimberly, Libr Asst, East Norwalk Improvement Association Library, 51 Van Zant St, Norwalk, CT, 06855. Tel: 203-838-0408, Ext 102. p. 331

Davis, Kristy, Cataloger, National Radio Astronomy Observatory Library, 520 Edgemont Rd, Charlottesville, VA, 22903-2475. Tel: 434-296-0254. p. 2309

Davis, Lakita, Night Supvr, North Carolina Wesleyan University, 3400 N Wesleyan Blvd, Rocky Mount, NC, 27804. Tel: 252-985-5350. p. 1713

Davis, LaTiffany, Learning Commons Librn, Kennesaw State University Library System, 385 Cobb Ave NW, MD 1701, Kennesaw, GA, 30144. Tel: 470-578-3228. p. 483

Davis, Laura, Libr Dir, Ida Long Goodman Memorial Library, 406 N Monroe, Saint John, KS, 67576. Tel: 620-549-3227. p. 834

Davis, Laurel, Curator, Spec Coll, Legal Info Librn & Lecturer in Law, Boston College, 885 Centre St, Newton Centre, MA, 02459. Tel: 617-552-4410. p. 1039

Davis, Lauren, Dir, North Branford Library Department, 1720 Foxon Rd, North Branford, CT, 06471. Tel: 203-315-6020. p. 330

Davis, Laverne, Librn, Newark Beth Israel Medical Center, 201 Lyons Ave, Newark, NJ, 07112. Tel: 973-926-7441. p. 1427

Davis, Leah, Br Supvr, Mecklenburg County Public Library, 1294 Jefferson St, Boydton, VA, 23917. Tel: 434-738-6580. p. 2308

Davis, Linda, Dir, Knightstown Public Library, Five E Main St, Knightstown, IN, 46148-1248. Tel: 765-345-5095. p. 699

Davis, Lindsay, Ref Librn, Merced College, 3600 M St, Merced, CA, 95348. Tel: 209-384-6086. p. 176

Davis, Lisa, Br Mgr, Stanly County Public Library, Norwood Branch, 207 Pee Dee Ave, Norwood, NC, 28128. Tel: 704-474-3625. p. 1671

Davis, Lisa Blanton, Dir, Cumberland County Public Library, 1539 Anderson Hwy, Cumberland, VA, 23040. Tel: 804-492-5807. p. 2314

Davis, Lori, Dir, Melcher-Dallas Public Library, 111 S Main St, Melcher-Dallas, IA, 50163. Tel: 641-947-6700. p. 769

Davis, Lou Jane, Dir, Centennial Memorial Library, 210 S Lamar St, Eastland, TX, 76448-2794. Tel: 254-629-2281. p. 2172

Davis, Luise, Coll Develop Librn, Douglas County Public Library, 1625 Library Lane, Minden, NV, 89423. Tel: 775-782-9841. p. 1348

Davis, Maggie, ILL, Menomonee Falls Public Library, W156 N8436 Pilgrim Rd, Menomonee Falls, WI, 53051. Tel: 262-532-8900. p. 2455

Davis, Mark, Br Mgr, San Diego Public Library, Oak Park, 2802 54th St, San Diego, CA, 92105. Tel: 619-527-3406. p. 220

Davis, Martha, Dir, Republic Community Library, 13 DeGregory Circle, Republic, PA, 15475. Tel: 724-246-0404. p. 2001

Davis, Marty, Ms, Libr Spec II, Louisiana Delta Community College, 7500 Millhaven Rd, Rm 139, Monroe, LA, 71203. Tel: 318-345-9140. p. 898

Davis, Mary, Bkmobile/Outreach Serv, Rochester Hills Public Library, 500 Olde Towne Rd, Rochester, MI, 48307-2043. Tel: 248-650-7152. p. 1144

Davis, Matthew, Syst Librn, Roberts Wesleyan College & Northeastern Seminary, 2301 Westside Dr, Rochester, NY, 14624-1997. Tel: 585-594-6064. p. 1629

Davis, Mattie, Circ Supvr, Chesapeake Public Library, Indian River, 2320 Old Greenbrier Rd, Chesapeake, VA, 23325. Tel: 757-410-7010. p. 2311

Davis, Melissa, Campus Librn, Pensacola State College, Warrington Campus, Bldg 3500, 5555 West Hwy 98, Pensacola, FL, 32507-1097. Tel: 850-484-2263. p. 436

Davis, Melissa, Asst Dean of Libr, Mississippi Gulf Coast Community College, 2300 Hwy 90, Gautier, MS, 39553. Tel: 228-497-7642. p. 1216

Davis, Melissa, Libr Mgr, New York Public Library - Astor, Lenox & Tilden Foundations, Bronx Library Center, 310 E Kingsbridge Rd, (At Briggs Ave), Bronx, NY, 10458. Tel: 718-579-4244. p. 1594

Davis, Melissa, Br Mgr, Public Library of Cincinnati & Hamilton County, Bond Hill, 1740 Langdon Farm Rd at Jordan Crossing, Cincinnati, OH, 45237. Tel: 513-369-4445. p. 1762

Davis, Melissa, Dir, Libr & Archives, George C Marshall Foundation Library, 340 VMI Parade, Lexington, VA, 24450. Tel: 540-463-7103, Ext 122. p. 2328

Davis, Melvin, Univ Librn, Coastal Carolina University, 376 University Blvd, Conway, SC, 29526. Tel: 843-349-2400. p. 2056

Davis, Michael, Dir, Camden County Library District, 89 Rodeo Rd, Camdenton, MO, 65020. Tel: 573-346-5954. p. 1239

Davis, Michael, Jr, Br Mgr, Arlington County Department of Libraries, Aurora Hills, 735 S 18th St, Arlington, VA, 22202. Tel: 703-228-5716. p. 2305

Davis, Mike, Libr Adminr, McAfee & Taft, Two Leadership Sq, 10th Flr, 211 N Robinson Ave, Oklahoma City, OK, 73102-7103. Tel: 405-235-9621. p. 1857

Davis, Misty, Br Mgr, Lamar County Library System, L R Boyer Memorial Library - Sumrall, 121 Poplar St, Sumrall, MS, 39482. Tel: 601-758-4711. p. 1230

Davis, Monica, Libr Dir, Stevenson Public Library, 102 W Main St, Stevenson, AL, 35772. Tel: 256-437-3008. p. 36

Davis, Nathanael, Bus Librn, Cedarville University, 251 N Main St, Cedarville, OH, 45314-0601. Tel: 937-766-7840. p. 1757

Davis, Pamela, Asst Br Mgr, Hulbert Community Library, 201 N Broadway, Hulbert, OK, 74441. Tel: 918-772-3383. p. 1850

Davis, Pat, Libr Supvr, Spokane County Library District, Argonne Library, 4322 N Argonne Rd, Spokane, WA, 99212-1868. Tel: 509-893-8260. p. 2384

Davis, Rachael-Joy, Head, User Serv, California State University, Sacramento, 6000 J St, Sacramento, CA, 95819-6039. Tel: 916-278-6708. p. 208

Davis, Rachel, Cat, ILL, Holmes County Public Library, 303 N J Harvey Etheridge St, Bonifay, FL, 32425. Tel: 850-547-3573. p. 386

Davis, Rachel, Dir, Thomas Memorial Library, Six Scott Dyer Rd, Cape Elizabeth, ME, 04107. Tel: 207-799-1720. p. 920

Davis, Robert H, Jr, Librn, Columbia University, Global Studies, Lehman Library, International Affairs Bldg, 420 W 118th St, New York, NY, 10027. Tel: 212-854-3630. p. 1583

Davis, Robert H, Jr, Librn, Columbia University, Russian, Eurasian & East European Studies, 306 International Affairs Bldg, 420 W 118th St, New York, NY, 10027. Tel: 212-854-4701. p. 1583

Davis, Roger Allen, Librn, East Central Community College, 275 E Broad St, Decatur, MS, 39327. Tel: 601-635-2111, Ext 219, 601-635-6219. p. 1216

Davis, Ron, Mgr, Info Tech, New Castle Public Library, 207 E North St, New Castle, PA, 16101-3691. Tel: 724-658-6659, Ext 130. p. 1969

Davis, Ronald W, Pub Serv Librn, Ref Serv Librn, Delaware State University, 1200 N Dupont Hwy, Dover, DE, 19901-2277. Tel: 302-857-6187. p. 352

Davis, Rose, Br Mgr, Shreve Memorial Library, Mooretown Branch, 4360 Hollywood Ave, Shreveport, LA, 71109. Tel: 318-636-5524. p. 909

Davis, Sandra, Libr Dir, Fannie Brown Booth Memorial Library, 619 Tenaha St, Center, TX, 75935. Tel: 936-598-5522. p. 2155

Davis, Sara, Asst Librn, Warren Free Public Library, 282 Main St, Warren, ME, 04864. Tel: 207-273-2900. p. 944

Davis, Sarah, Adminr, Correctional Institution for Women, PO Box 4004, Clinton, NJ, 08809-4004. Tel: 908-735-7111, Ext 3641. p. 1397

Davis, Sarah, Br Mgr, Norfolk Public Library, Barron F Black Branch, 6700 E Tanners Creek Rd, Norfolk, VA, 23513. Tel: 757-441-5806. p. 2335

Davis, Sascha, Mgr, Libr Serv, Royal Ottawa Health Care Group, 1145 Carling Ave, Ottawa, ON, K1Z 7K4, CANADA. Tel: 613-722-6521, Ext 6268. p. 2669

Davis, Scott, Dir, Fremont Public Library District, 1170 N Midlothian Rd, Mundelein, IL, 60060. Tel: 847-566-8702. p. 622

Davis, Sharon, Head Librn, Harrison County Library System, Biloxi Central Library, 580 Howard Ave, Biloxi, MS, 39530. Tel: 228-436-3095. p. 1217

Davis, Shelly, Univ Librn, Husson University, One College Circle, Bangor, ME, 04401-2999. Tel: 207-941-7187, 207-941-7188. p. 915

Davis, Stacy, Archivist, National Archives & Records Administration, 1000 Beal Ave, Ann Arbor, MI, 48109. Tel: 734-205-0563. p. 1079

Davis, Susan, Br Mgr, Carnegie Public Library, Jeffersonville Branch, Eight S Main St, Jeffersonville, OH, 43128-1063. Tel: 740-426-9292. p. 1828

Davis, Tanya, Law Librn, Law Society of New Brunswick Library, Justice Bldg, Rm 305, 427 Queen St, Fredericton, NB, E3B 1B6, CANADA. Tel: 506-453-2500. p. 2601

Davis, Tegan, Dir, Eagle Valley Library District, 600 Broadway St, Eagle, CO, 81631. Tel: 970-328-8800. p. 279

Davis, Tequila A, Libr Mgr, New York Public Library - Astor, Lenox & Tilden Foundations, Harry Belafonte 115th Street Branch, 203 W 115th St, New York, NY, 10026. Tel: 212-666-9393. p. 1594

Davis, Terri, Dir, Rapid City Public Library, 610 Quincy St, Rapid City, SD, 57701-3630. Tel: 605-394-6713. p. 2081

Davis, Theresa, Mat Mgt Mgr, Hoover Public Library, 200 Municipal Dr, Hoover, AL, 35216. Tel: 205-444-7810. p. 21

Davis, Thomas, Librn, North Carolina Supreme Court Library, 500 Justice Bldg, Two E Morgan St, Raleigh, NC, 27601-1428. Tel: 919-831-5709. p. 1710

Davis, Tiffany, Dir, Br Serv, Saint Louis Public Library, 1301 Olive St, Saint Louis, MO, 63103. Tel: 314-539-0300. p. 1274

Davis, Timur, Libr Dir, Mount Vernon Public Library, 28 S First Ave, Mount Vernon, NY, 10550. Tel: 914-668-1840. p. 1575

Davis, Tisa, Communications Mgr, Indiana Library Federation, 941 E 86th St, Ste 260, Indianapolis, IN, 46240. Tel: 317-257-2040, Ext 104. p. 2765

Davis, Traycee, Law Librn, Richland County Law Library Resources Board, 50 Park Ave E, Flr L2, Mansfield, OH, 44902. Tel: 419-774-5595. p. 1798

Davis, Troy, Dir, Media Serv, College of William & Mary in Virginia, Earl Gregg Swem Library, One Landrum Dr, Williamsburg, VA, 23187. Tel: 757-221-2643. p. 2353

Davis, Valerie, Br Mgr, Campbell County Public Library District, Newport Branch, 901 E Sixth St, Newport, KY, 41071. Tel: 859-572-5035. p. 851

Davis, Vermille, Access Services Tech, Howard University Libraries, Louis Stokes Health Sciences Library, 501 W St NW, Washington, DC, 20059. Tel: 202-884-1521. p. 369

Davis, Wanda, Director, Admin, Heartland Institute, 3939 N Wilke Rd, Chicago, IL, 60004. Tel: 312-377-4000. p. 561

Davis, Wendy, Dir, University of Arkansas - Pulaski Technical College, 3000 W Scenic Dr, North Little Rock, AR, 72118. Tel: 501-812-2272. p. 106

Davis, Yvette, Mgr, District of Columbia Public Library, Anacostia, 1800 Good Hope Rd SE, Washington, DC, 20020. Tel: 202-715-7707, 202-715-7708. p. 364

Davis-Bonner, Rutha, Dir, Hayneville-Lowndes County Public Library, 215 E Tuskeena St, Ste B, Hayneville, AL, 36040. Tel: 334-548-2686. p. 20

Davis-Driggs, Glenda, Ref Librn, Kirkwood Community College, Iowa City Campus Library, 107 Credit Center Bldg, 1816 Lower Muscatine Rd, Iowa City, IA, 52240. Tel: 319-887-3612, 319-887-3613. p. 738

Davis-Kahl, Stephanie, Dr, Univ Librn, Illinois Wesleyan University, One Ames Plaza, Bloomington, IL, 61701-7188. Tel: 309-556-3010. p. 543

Davis-Little, Carla, Librn, Monroe Public Library, 3B School St, Monroe Bridge, MA, 01350. Tel: 413-424-5272. p. 1036

Davis-Mills, Nina, Actg Music Librn, Massachusetts Institute of Technology Libraries, Lewis Music Library, Bldg 14E-109, 77 Massachusetts Ave, Cambridge, MA, 02139-4307. Tel: 617-253-5689. p. 1008

Davis-Northrup, Matilda, Tech Serv Librn, Otterbein University, 138 W Main St, Westerville, OH, 43081. Tel: 614-823-1938. p. 1830

Davis-Witherow, Leah, Curator of Hist, Colorado Springs Pioneers Museum, 215 S Tejon St, Colorado Springs, CO, 80903. Tel: 719-385-5650. p. 270

Davison, Erin, Youth Serv Librn, Norwich Public Library, 368 Main St, Norwich, VT, 05055-9453. Tel: 802-649-1184. p. 2290

Davison, Frieda, Dean of Libr, University of South Carolina Upstate Library, 800 University Way, Spartanburg, SC, 29303. Tel: 864-503-5610. p. 2070

Davison, Karissa, Head, Adult Serv, Richton Park Public Library District, 22310 Latonia Lane, Richton Park, IL, 60471. Tel: 708-481-5333. p. 638

Davison, Laura, Ch, Elizabeth Titus Memorial Library, Two W Water St, Sullivan, IL, 61951. Tel: 217-728-7221. p. 652

Davison, Laura, Asst Dir, Access, Delivery & Outreach Serv, University of Kentucky Libraries, Medical Center Library, William R Willard Medical Education Bldg 298, 800 Rose St, Lexington, KY, 40536-0298. Tel: 859-323-6138. p. 864

Davison, Olivia, Head, Media Serv, Saint Ambrose University Library, 518 W Locust St, Davenport, IA, 52803. Tel: 563-333-6242. p. 744

Davison, Raziel, Br Mgr, Santa Cruz City-County Library System, Scotts Valley Branch, 251 Kings Valley Rd, Scotts Valley, CA, 95066. Tel: 831-427-7712. p. 243

Davison, Stephen, Head, Digital Libr Develop & Syst, California Institute of Technology, 1200 E California Blvd, M/C 1-43, Pasadena, CA, 91125-4300. Tel: 626-395-6149. p. 193

Davisson, David, Info Literacy Librn, University of Tampa, 401 W Kennedy Blvd, Tampa, FL, 33606-1490. Tel: 813-257-3719. p. 450

Davitt, Jennifer, Dir, United States Securities & Exchange Commission Library, 100 F St NE, Rm 1500, Washington, DC, 20549-0002. Tel: 202-551-5450. p. 380

Daw, Lynn K, Tech Serv Librn, Monmouth College, 700 E Broadway, Monmouth, IL, 61462-1963. Tel: 309-457-2187. p. 619

Daw, Michael, Dir, Golden Gate University - Otto & Velia Butz Libraries, School of Law Library, 536 Mission St, San Francisco, CA, 94105. Tel: 415-442-6680. p. 225

Dawber, Michael, Chief Exec Officer, Librn, Rainy River Public Library, 334 Fourth St, Rainy River, ON, P0W 1L0, CANADA. Tel: 807-852-3375. p. 2675

Dawe, Ana, Interim Br Mgr, Sonoma County Library, Forestville Library, 7050 Covey Rd, Forestville, CA, 95436. Tel: 707-887-7654. p. 204

Dawe, Ana, Interim Br Mgr, Sonoma County Library, Guerneville Regional Library, 14107 Armstrong Woods Rd, Guerneville, CA, 95446. Tel: 707-869-9004. p. 204

Dawe, Ana, Interim Br Mgr, Sonoma County Library, Occidental Library, 73 Main St, Occidental, CA, 95465. Tel: 707-874-3080. p. 204

Dawe, Carol, Dir, Lakeland Library Cooperative, 4138 Three Mile Rd NW, Grand Rapids, MI, 49534-1134. Tel: 616-559-5253. p. 2767

Dawes, Trevor A, Vice Provost & May Morris Univ Librn, University of Delaware Library, 181 S College Ave, Newark, DE, 19717-5267. Tel: 302-831-2965. p. 355

Dawkins, April, Dr, Asst Prof, University of North Carolina at Greensboro, School of Education Bldg, Rm 446, 1300 Spring Garden St, Greensboro, NC, 27412. Tel: 336-334-3477. p. 2790

Dawkins, Maxine, Br Librn, Kemper-Newton Regional Library System, J Elliott McMullan Library, 300 W Church St, Newton, MS, 39345-2208. Tel: 601-683-3367. p. 1234

Dawley, Jennifer, Head, Youth Serv, Plaistow Public Library, 85 Main St, Plaistow, NH, 03865. Tel: 603-382-6011. p. 1378

Dawood, Montaha, Libr Asst, Assyrian Universal Alliance Foundation, 4343 W Touhy Ave, Lincolnwood, IL, 60712. Tel: 773-863-3575. p. 609

Dawsari, Elizabeth, Librn, The Frank Lloyd Wright Foundation, 12621 N Frank Lloyd Wright Blvd, Taliesin West, Scottsdale, AZ, 85259. Tel: 480-391-4011. p. 77

Dawson, Carolyn, Librn, Rio Hondo Public Library, 121 N Arroyo Blvd, Rio Hondo, TX, 78583. Tel: 956-748-3322. p. 2233

Dawson, Carrie E, Tech Serv Librn, Arizona Western College, 2020 S Ave 8E, Yuma, AZ, 85366. Tel: 928-317-6491. p. 85

Dawson, Grace, Regional Librn, Prince Edward Island Public Library Service, Montague Rotary Library, 53 Wood Islands Rd, Montague, PE, C0A 1R0, CANADA. Tel: 902-838-2928. p. 2708

Dawson, Jamie, Dir of Educ, Acopian Center for Conservation Learning, 410 Summer Valley Rd, Orwigsburg, PA, 17961. Tel: 570-943-3411, Ext 101. p. 1973

Dawson, Jeff, Libr Dir, Lester Public Library, 1001 Adams St, Two Rivers, WI, 54241. Tel: 920-793-7104. p. 2482

Dawson, Jeffrey, Archivist, State Historical Society of Iowa, 600 E Locust, Des Moines, IA, 50319-0290. Tel: 515-281-6200. p. 747

Dawson, Jennifer, Libr Assoc I, Citrus Research & Education Center Library, Ben Hill Griffin Jr. Citrus Hall, 700 Experiment Station Rd, Lake Alfred, FL, 33850. Tel: 863-956-5890. p. 415

Dawson, Lahoma, Br Mgr, Washington Parish Library System, Thomas, 30369 Hwy 424, Franklinton, LA, 70438. Tel: 985-848-7061. p. 890

Dawson, Leigh, Music Libr Tech, West Chester University, Presser Music Library, Wells School of Music & Performing Arts Ctr, West Chester, PA, 19383. Tel: 610-436-2379, 610-436-2430. p. 2020

Dawson, Linda, Br Mgr, Mississippi County Library System, Wilson Public, One Park St, Wilson, AR, 72395. Tel: 870-655-8414. p. 91

Dawson, Margaret, Circ, Lone Star College System, Tomball College Library, 30555 Tomball Pkwy, Tomball, TX, 77375-4036. Tel: 832-559-4206. p. 2197

Dawson, Mary Jo, Dir, Aiken-Bamberg-Barnwell-Edgefield Regional Library System, 314 Chesterfield St SW, Aiken, SC, 29801-7171. Tel: 803-642-7575. p. 2045

Dawson, Patricia, ILL/Ser & Media Coordr, Albertus Magnus College, 700 Prospect St, New Haven, CT, 06511. Tel: 203-672-6650. p. 325

Dawson, Patrick, Dir, University of Maryland, Baltimore County, 1000 Hilltop Circle, Baltimore, MD, 21250. Tel: 410-455-2356. p. 958

Dawson, Patti S, Dir, Central Lake District Library, 7900 Maple St, Central Lake, MI, 49622. Tel: 231-544-2517. p. 1089

Dawson, Peter, Pres, Canada Department of National Defence, Royal Artillery Park, Bldg No 3, 5460 Royal Artillery Court, Halifax, NS, B3J 0A8, CANADA. Tel: 902-427-0774. p. 2618

Dawson, Rhonda, Ser & Acq Tech, Alberta Government Library, Capital Blvd, 11th Flr, 10044 - 108 St, Edmonton, AB, T5J 5E6, CANADA. Tel: 780-427-2985. p. 2534

Dawson, Rose T, Exec Dir, Alexandria Library, 5005 Duke St, Alexandria, VA, 22304. Tel: 703-746-1777. p. 2302

Dawson, Sarah, Ch, Mesquite Public Library, North Branch, 2600 Oates Dr, Mesquite, TX, 75150. Tel: 972-681-0465. p. 2219

Dawson, Vicki, Libr Dir, Berkley Public Library, Two N Main St, Berkley, MA, 02779. Tel: 508-822-3329. p. 989

Dawson-Taither, Hannah, Br Mgr, Polk County Library, Fair Play Branch, 104 N Elm St, Fair Play, MO, 65649. Tel: 417-654-5013. p. 1238

Day, Adam, Computer Support Spec, Twin Falls Public Library, 201 Fourth Ave E, Twin Falls, ID, 83301-6397. Tel: 208-733-2964. p. 532

Day, Annette, Acq & Coll, Div Head, University of Nevada, Las Vegas University Libraries, 4505 S Maryland Pkwy, Box 457001, Las Vegas, NV, 89154-7001. Tel: 702-895-2738. p. 1347

Day, Billie, Circ Librn, Mercer County Library, 601 W Grant St, Princeton, MO, 64673. Tel: 660-748-3725. p. 1266

Day, Bonnie, Librn, Emery County Library System, Elmo Branch, 15 S 100 East, Elmo, UT, 84521. Tel: 435-653-2558. p. 2262

Day, Brigid, Coordr, Commun Engagement, The John P Holt Brentwood Library, 8109 Concord Rd, Brentwood, TN, 37027. Tel: 615-371-0090, Ext 8510. p. 2089

Day, Carol, Asst Librn, Kalama Public Library, 312 N First St, Kalama, WA, 98625. Tel: 360-673-4568. p. 2367

Day, Cathy, Librn, Bethel Public Library, 106 Main St, Bethel, VT, 05032. Tel: 802-234-9107. p. 2279

Day, Danielle, Youth Serv Mgr, Carnegie-Stout Public Library, 360 W 11th St, Dubuque, IA, 52001. Tel: 563-589-4138. p. 748

Day, Essy, Exec Dir, Library Center of the Ozarks, 200 S Fourth St, Branson, MO, 65616-2738. Tel: 417-334-1418. p. 1238

Day, Essy, Dir, Libr Serv, Waco-McLennan County Library System, 1717 Austin Ave, Waco, TX, 76701-1794. Tel: 254-750-5946. p. 2254

Day, Gina, Dir, Patricia Romanko Public Library, 121 N Third St, Parma, ID, 83660. Tel: 208-722-6605. p. 528

Day, Heather, Cat & Tech Serv Librn, University of Mount Olive, 646 James B Hunt Dr, Mount Olive, NC, 28365-1699. Tel: 919-299-4589. p. 1705

Day, Jane, Assoc Dir, Mgr, Pub Serv, Duke University Libraries, Ford Library, 100 Fuqua Dr, Durham, NC, 27708. Tel: 919-660-7874. p. 1684

Day, Joanne, Asst Dir, Tech Serv Librn, Albertus Magnus College, 700 Prospect St, New Haven, CT, 06511. Tel: 203-773-8511. p. 325

Day, Kevin, Libr Tech, J T Fyles Natural Resources Library, 1810 Blanshard St, Victoria, BC, V8W 9N3, CANADA. Tel: 250-952-0564. p. 2582

Day, Marie, Syst Librn, Kennesaw State University Library System, Lawrence V Johnson Library, 1100 S Marietta Pkwy, Marietta, GA, 30060-2896. Tel: 678-470-578-7276. p. 483

Day, Marlin, Br Mgr, Alachua County Library District, Newberry Branch, 110 S Seaboard Dr, Newberry, FL, 32669. Tel: 352-472-1135. p. 406

Day, Michelle, Libr Asst, Stewart Public Library, 322 Fifth Ave, Stewart, BC, V0T 1W0, CANADA. Tel: 236-749-2003. p. 2576

Day, Norma, Libr Dir, Rocky Top Public Library, 226 N Main St, Rocky Top, TN, 37769. Tel: 865-426-6762. p. 2125

Day, Ronald E, PhD, Chair, Prof, Libr Sci, Indiana University, Wells Library 001, 1320 E Tenth St, Bloomington, IN, 47405-3907. Tel: 812-855-2018. p. 2785

Day, Ross, Head of Libr, Metropolitan Museum of Art, Robert Goldwater Library, 1000 Fifth Ave, New York, NY, 10028-0198. Tel: 212-570-3707. p. 1591

Day, Ross, Acq, Metropolitan Museum of Art, Thomas J Watson Library, 1000 Fifth Ave, New York, NY, 10028-0198. Tel: 212-650-2949. p. 1592

Day, Siobahn, Asst Prof, North Carolina Central University, 1801 Fayetteville St, Durham, NC, 27707. Tel: 919-530-6485. p. 2790

Dayan, Nomi, Exec Dir, Cold Spring Harbor Whaling Museum Library, 301 Main St, Cold Spring Harbor, NY, 11724. Tel: 631-637-3418, Ext 17. p. 1520

Dayani, Katie, Mgr, Libr Serv, Children's Mercy Hospital, 2401 Gillham Rd, Kansas City, MO, 64108. Tel: 816-234-3800, 816-234-3900. p. 1254

Daynard, Kelly, Exec Dir, Farm & Food Care Ontario Library, 660 Speedvale Ave W, Unit 302, Guelph, ON, N1K 1E5, CANADA. Tel: 519-837-1326. p. 2643

Dayton, Stuart K, Media Spec, University of Nebraska Medical Center, 600 S 42nd St, Omaha, NE, 68198. Tel: 402-559-6334. p. 1331

Daza, Vilma, Commun Libr Mgr, Queens Library, Corona Community Library, 38-23 104th St, Corona, NY, 11368. Tel: 718-426-2844. p. 1554

Dazey, Megan, Libr Dir, Sweet Home Public Library, 1101 13th Ave, Sweet Home, OR, 97386. Tel: 541-367-5007. p. 1899

De Aliza, Maritxu, Campus Librn, Pacific Oaks College, 45 Eureka St, Pasadena, CA, 91103. Tel: 626-529-8451. p. 193

de Araujo, Georgia, Dir, Boyle County Public Library, 307 W Broadway, Danville, KY, 40422. Tel: 859-236-8466, 859-238-7323. p. 853

De Barra, Chelssee, Mgr, Skyline College Library, 3300 College Dr, San Bruno, CA, 94066-1698. Tel: 650-738-4311. p. 214

De Bellis, Mary, Libr Dir, La Grange Association Library, 1110 Route 55, 2nd Flr, LaGrangeville, NY, 12540. Tel: 845-452-3141. p. 1561

de Bie, Melissa, Head, Res Ctr, History Colorado, 1200 Broadway, Denver, CO, 80203. Tel: 303-866-2305. p. 276

de Bruijn, Nicole R, Tech Serv Mgr, Wilkes County Public Library, 215 Tenth St, North Wilkesboro, NC, 28659. Tel: 336-838-2818. p. 1707

De Buhan, Melanie, Prof, Cégep Garneau, 1660 blvd de l'Entente, Quebec, QC, G1S 4S3, CANADA. Tel: 418-688-8310, Ext 2290. p. 2796

de Campos Salles, Ana Elisa, Br Mgr, San Francisco Public Library, Parkside Branch Library, 1200 Taraval St, San Francisco, CA, 94116-2452. Tel: 415-355-5770. p. 228

De Caro, Sara, Spec Coll Librn & Univ Archivist, Pittsburg State University, 1605 S Joplin St, Pittsburg, KS, 66762-5889. Tel: 620-235-4883. p. 832

de Castell, Christina, Chief Librn/CEO, Vancouver Public Library, 350 W Georgia St, Vancouver, BC, V6B 6B1, CANADA. Tel: 604-331-3603. p. 2581

de Chantal Brookes, Elaine, Sister, Library Contact, Sisters, Servants of the Immaculate Heart of Mary Archives, Villa Maria House of Studies, 1140 King Rd, Immaculata, PA, 19345. Tel: 610-647-2160. p. 1945

De Fazio, Dias, Librn, Cleveland Metroparks Zoo Library, 3900 Wildlife Way, Cleveland, OH, 44109. Tel: 216-635-3333. p. 1767

de Forest, Wendy, Asst Dir, Youth Serv Librn, Richmond Free Library, 201 Bridge St, Richmond, VT, 05477. Tel: 802-434-3036. p. 2293

de Geus, Alison, Supv Librn, City of Palo Alto Library, Children's, 1276 Harriet St, Palo Alto, CA, 94301. Tel: 650-838-2960. p. 191

de Groot, Dan, Access Services Team Leader, University of the Fraser Valley, Chilliwack Campus, 45190 Caen Ave, Bldg A, Chilliwack, BC, V2R 0N3, CANADA. Tel: 604-504-7441, Ext 2468. p. 2562

De Herrera, Maria, Dir, Conejos County Library, 17703 Hwy 285, La Jara, CO, 81140. Tel: 719-274-5858. p. 287

de la Chapelle, Anne, Dir, Plattsburgh Public Library, 19 Oak St, Plattsburgh, NY, 12901. Tel: 518-563-0921. p. 1619

De la Cour, Marian A, Librn, Jordan Hospital, 275 Sandwich St, Plymouth, MA, 02360. Tel: 508-830-2157. p. 1047

De La Cruz, Aquilia, Br Librn, Chambers County Library System, Chambers County Library, 202 Cummings St, Anahuac, TX, 77514. p. 2134

de la Cruz, Maria E, Librn, Florida National University Library, 4425 W Jose Regueiro Ave, Hialeah, FL, 33012. Tel: 305-821-3333, Ext 1020. p. 408

De La Fontaine, John, Librn, Data Mgt & Integrity, Occidental College Library, 1600 Campus Rd, Los Angeles, CA, 90041. Tel: 323-259-2914. p. 167

De La Garza, Mary, Asst Dir, University of Texas Libraries, Population Research Center Library, 305 E 23rd St, Stop G1800, Austin, TX, 78712-1699. Tel: 512-471-5514. p. 2143

de la Herran, Isidro, Librn, Hallmark Cards, Inc, Business Research Library, 2501 McGee Trafficway, No 203, Kansas City, MO, 64108. Tel: 816-274-4648. p. 1255

De La Mora, Brooklyn, Libr Asst III, Parker Public Library, 1001 S Navajo Ave, Parker, AZ, 85344. Tel: 928-669-2622. p. 68

De La Rosa, Toby, Asst Libr Dir, Ellis Memorial Library, 700 W Ave A, Port Aransas, TX, 78373. Tel: 361-749-4116. p. 2228

de la Vega, Amalia, Mgr, Acq & Ser, Tech Serv, University of Miami, Louis Calder Memorial Library, Miller School of Medicine, 1601 NW Tenth Ave, Miami, FL, 33136. Tel: 305-243-6901. p. 425

De Leon, Cathy, Dir, Long Beach Public Library, 200 W Broadway, Long Beach, CA, 90802. Tel: 562-570-7500. p. 159

De Leon, Cathy, Mgr, Br Serv, Long Beach Public Library, 200 W Broadway, Long Beach, CA, 90802. Tel: 562-570-7500. p. 159

De Leon, Jo Ann, Libr Asst, Coastal Bend College, 1814 S Brahma Blvd, Rm 135A, Kingsville, TX, 78363. Tel: 361-592-1615, Ext 4084. p. 2206

De Leon, Jorge, Librn, Yale University Library, The William Robertson Coe Ornithology Library, Environmental Science Ctr, Rm 151, 21 Sachem St, New Haven, CT, 06520. Tel: 203-436-4892. p. 327

De Les Dernier, Denise, Asst Ch, Exeter Public Library, Four Chestnut St, Exeter, NH, 03833. Tel: 603-772-3101, 603-772-6036. p. 1363

de Leur, Michael, Libr Mgr, Vancouver Island Regional Library, Port Alberni Branch, 4245 Wallace St, Unit B, Port Alberni, BC, V9Y 3Y6, CANADA. Tel: 250-723-9511. p. 2571

de Leur, Michael, Libr Mgr, Vancouver Island Regional Library, Tofino Branch, 331 Main St, Tofino, BC, V0R 2Z0, CANADA. Tel: 250-725-3713. p. 2571

de Leur, Michael, Libr Mgr, Vancouver Island Regional Library, Ucluelet Branch, 500 Matterson Dr, Ucluelet, BC, V0R 3A0, CANADA. Tel: 250-726-4642. p. 2571

De Long, Sunny, Dir, Moore Public Library, 403 Fergus Ave, Moore, MT, 59464. Tel: 406-374-2364. p. 1300

De los Santos, Lynda, Pub Serv, Tarrant County College, South Campus Jenkins Garrett Library, 5301 Campus Dr, Fort Worth, TX, 76119. Tel: 817-515-4524. p. 2180

De Luise, Alexandra, Instrul Serv Librn, Queens College, Benjamin S Rosenthal Library, 65-30 Kissena Blvd, Flushing, NY, 11367-0904. Tel: 718-997-3700. p. 1534

De Pasquale, Jennifer, Libr Serv Coordr, Edmonton Public Library, Londonderry, Londonderry Mall, Ste 166, 137 Ave 66 St NW, Edmonton, AB, T5C 3C8, CANADA. Tel: 780-496-6584. p. 2536

de Perio Wittman, Jessica, Dir, Law Libr, University of Connecticut, Thomas J Meskill Law Library, 39 Elizabeth St, Hartford, CT, 06105. Tel: 860-570-5109. p. 340

De Ramus, Yolanda, Asst Dir, Admin Serv, Chief Dep, County of Los Angeles Public Library, 7400 E Imperial Hwy, Downey, CA, 90242-3375. Tel: 562-940-8406. p. 134

de Repentigny, Sylvie, Libr Mgr, Bibliotheque Municipale de Pincourt, 225 boul Pincourt, Pincourt, QC, J7W 9T2, CANADA. Tel: 514-425-1104. p. 2728

de Rochefort-Reynolds, Denise, Dir, Frank Carlson Library, 702 Broadway, Concordia, KS, 66901. Tel: 785-243-2250. p. 803

de Ruiter, Chelsea, Libr Mgr, Hythe Municipal Library, 10013 100 St, Hythe, AB, T0H 2C0, CANADA. Tel: 780-356-3014. p. 2543

De Santis, Melissa, Dir, University of Colorado Denver/ Anschutz Medical Campus, Anschutz Medical Campus, 12950 E Montview Blvd, Aurora, CO, 80045. Tel: 303-724-2152. p. 265

De Sommer-Dennis, Emilee, Asst Librn, Shilo Community Library, Bldg T114, Notre Dame Ave, Shilo, MB, R0K 2A0, CANADA. Tel: 204-765-3000, Ext 3664. p. 2590

de Varges, Jolene, Music Dir, Southern Methodist University, Hamon Arts Library, 6101 N Bishop Blvd, Dallas, TX, 75275. Tel: 214-768-1855. p. 2168

De Visser, Sarah, Libr Asst, Edwardsburgh Cardinal Public Library, Spencerville Branch, Five Henderson St, Spencerville, ON, K0E 1X0, CANADA. Tel: 613-658-5575. p. 2635

De Yurre Fatemian, Zoila, Dir, Learning Res, Miami Dade College, Wolfson Campus Library, 300 NE Second Ave, Miami, FL, 33132. Tel: 305-237-7454. p. 422

Dea, May, Library Contact, Multnomah County Library, Gregory Heights, 7921 NE Sandy Blvd, Portland, OR, 97213. p. 1892

Deacon, Douglas, Fiscal Officer, Swanton Local School District Public Library, 305 Chestnut St, Swanton, OH, 43558. Tel: 419-826-2760. p. 1822

Deacon, Heidi, Dir, Smyth Public Library, 55 High St, Candia, NH, 03034. Tel: 603-483-8245. p. 1356

Deagle, Pamela, Libr Mgr, Consort Municipal Library, 5215 50th St, Consort, AB, T0C 1B0, CANADA. Tel: 403-577-2501. p. 2532

Deahl, Jonathan, Coordr, Circ, Waterford Township Public Library, 5168 Civic Center Dr, Waterford, MI, 48329. Tel: 248-618-7678. p. 1158

Deal, Jennifer, Lead Librn, Aurora West Allis Medical Center, 8901 W Lincoln Ave, West Allis, WI, 53227-0901. Tel: 414-328-7910. p. 2486

Deal-Hansen, Terri, Libr Serv Coordr, Great River Regional Library, Royalton Library, 12 N Birch St, Royalton, MN, 56373. Tel: 320-584-8151. p. 1197

DeAlmeida, Claudia, Circ Coordr, Roger Williams University Library, Architecture, One Old Ferry Rd, Bristol, RI, 02809-2921. Tel: 401-254-3679. p. 2030

Dean, Amy, Ch Serv, Stoughton Public Library, 84 Park St, Stoughton, MA, 02072-2974. Tel: 781-344-2711. p. 1058

Dean, Annette R, Libr Dir, Charles City Public Library, 106 Milwaukee Mall, Charles City, IA, 50616-2281. Tel: 641-257-6317. p. 739

Dean, Beth, Dir, Guntersville Public Library, 1240 O'Brig Ave, Guntersville, AL, 35976. Tel: 256-571-7595. p. 20

Dean, Blue, Ms, Assoc Univ Librn, Develop, Duke University Libraries, 411 Chapel Dr, Durham, NC, 27708. Tel: 919-660-5940. p. 1684

Dean, Bridget, Circ Supvr, Jacksonville Public Library, 201 W College Ave, Jacksonville, IL, 62650-2497. Tel: 217-243-5435. p. 602

Dean, Elaine, Clinical Librn, Cincinnati Children's Hospital, Edward L Pratt Library, S9.125 ML 3012, 3333 Burnet Ave, Cincinnati, OH, 45229-3039. Tel: 513-636-4230. p. 1759

Dean, Holly, Asst Prof, Librn, Geophysical Institute, International Arctic Research Ctr, 2156 Koyukuk Dr, Fairbanks, AK, 99775. Tel: 907-474-7503. p. 45

Dean, Jennifer, Dir, Siena Heights University Library, 1247 E Siena Heights Dr, Adrian, MI, 49221-1796. Tel: 517-264-7152. p. 1076

Dean, Jennifer, Dean, Univ Librs & Instrul Tech, University of Detroit Mercy Libraries, 4001 W McNichols Rd, Detroit, MI, 48221-3038. Tel: 313-993-1071. p. 1099

Dean, Jennifer, Dr, Libr Dir, University of Michigan-Flint, 303 E Kearsley St, Flint, MI, 48502. Tel: 810-762-3018. p. 1107

Dean, Kara, Youth Serv Librn, Walpole Public Library, 143 School St, Walpole, MA, 02081. Tel: 508-660-7384. p. 1061

Dean, Larissa, Asst Libr Dir, Marion County Public Library, 321 Monroe St, Fairmont, WV, 26554-2952. Tel: 304-366-1210. p. 2402

Dean, Megan, Dir, Bethel Public Library, 189 Greenwood Ave, Bethel, CT, 06801-2598. Tel: 203-794-8756. p. 302

Dean, Naima, Br Mgr, San Francisco Public Library, Western Addition Branch Library, 1550 Scott St, San Francisco, CA, 94115-3512. Tel: 415-355-5727. p. 228

Dean, Sandra, Librn, Palliser Regional Library, Elbow Branch, 402 Minto St, Elbow, SK, S0H 1J0, CANADA. Tel: 306-854-2220. p. 2742

Dean, Tamara, Dir, Fairhope Public Library, 501 Fairhope Ave, Fairhope, AL, 36532. Tel: 251-928-7483. p. 16

Dean, Toni, Ch Serv, Librn, Congregational Church of Patchogue, 95 E Main St, Patchogue, NY, 11772. Tel: 631-475-1235. p. 1615

Deane, J, Sr Librn, Orleans Correctional Facility Library, 3531 Gaines Basin Rd, Albion, NY, 14411. Tel: 585-589-6820. p. 1484

DeAngelis, Alexandra, Asst Libr Mgr, Bucks County Historical Society, 84 S Pine St, Doylestown, PA, 18901-4999. Tel: 215-345-0210, Ext 141. p. 1927

DeAngelis, Emily, Ref & Instruction Librn, Bellevue University, 1028 Bruin Blvd, Bellevue, NE, 68005. Tel: 402-557-7278. p. 1308

DeAngelo, Karen J, Exec Dir, Montgomery County-Norristown Public Library, 1001 Powell St, Norristown, PA, 19401-3817. Tel: 610-278-5100, Ext 140. p. 1971

DeAngelus, Ramona, Dir, Libr Serv, McDowell Technical Community College Library, 54 College Dr, Marion, NC, 28752-8728. Tel: 828-652-0401. p. 1702

Deans, Dustina, Circ, Youth Serv, Lincoln County Public Libraries, 220 W Sixth St, Libby, MT, 59923-1898. Tel: 406-293-2778. p. 1298

Deans, Janet, Circ Mgr, Canal Fulton Public Library, 154 Market St NE, Canal Fulton, OH, 44614-1196. Tel: 330-854-4148. p. 1754

Deans, Mark-Jeffery, Libr Dir, University of the Virgin Islands, Two John Brewers Bay, Saint Thomas, VI, 00802. Tel: 340-693-1181. p. 2517

Dear, Beverly, Dir, Sanilac District Library, 7130 Main St, Port Sanilac, MI, 48469. Tel: 810-622-8623. p. 1143

Dearborn, Dylanne, Librn, University of Toronto Libraries, Physics Library, McLennan Physical Laboratories, 60 St George St, Rm 211C, Toronto, ON, M5S 1A7, CANADA. Tel: 416-978-5188. p. 2699

Deardorff, Julie, Dir, Coll Serv, Cedarville University, 251 N Main St, Cedarville, OH, 45314-0601. Tel: 937-766-7840. p. 1757

Dearing, Daniel, Dir, Jane B Holmes Public Library, 230 Tucker Rd, Helena, AL, 35080-7036. Tel: 205-664-8308. p. 21

Dearing, Tara, Children's Serv Coordr, East Baton Rouge Parish Library, 7711 Goodwood Blvd, Baton Rouge, LA, 70806-7625. Tel: 225-231-3760. p. 882

DeArment, Darren, Youth Serv Librn, Pottsville Free Public Library, 215 W Market St, Pottsville, PA, 17901. Tel: 570-622-8105, 570-622-8880. p. 1999

Dearmont, Dave, Dir, Res, Nebraska Department of Economic Development Library, 245 Fallbrook Blvd, Ste 002, Lincoln, NE, 68521. Tel: 402-471-3777. p. 1322

Dearness, Karin, Dir, Libr Serv, St Joseph Healthcare Centre for Mountain Health Services, 100 W Fifth St, Hamilton, ON, L8N 3K7, CANADA. Tel: 905-522-1155, Ext 36322. p. 2647

Dearness, Karin, Dir, Libr Serv, Saint Joseph's Hospital, 50 Charlton Ave E, Hamilton, ON, L8N 4A6, CANADA. Tel: 905-522-4941, Ext 33410. p. 2647

Dearth, Donna, Asst Dir, New Canaan Museum & Historical Society Library, 13 Oenoke Ridge, New Canaan, CT, 06840. Tel: 203-966-1776. p. 324

Dearth, Kim, Dir, Wonewoc Public Library, 305 Center St, Wonewoc, WI, 53968. Tel: 608-464-7625. p. 2490

Deas, Gilbert, Librn, Southern Regional Technical College Library Services, Tifton Campus, 52 Tech Dr, Tifton, GA, 31794. Tel: 229-391-2623. p. 499

Dease, Melissa, Adminr, Youth Serv, Dallas Public Library, 1515 Young St, Dallas, TX, 75201-5415. Tel: 214-670-1400. p. 2165

Dease, Nicholas, Digital Learning Librn, Pratt Institute Libraries, 200 Willoughby Ave, Brooklyn, NY, 11205-3897. Tel: 718-399-4223. p. 1506

Deason, Reagan, Dir, Albertville Public Library, 200 Jackson St, Albertville, AL, 35950. Tel: 256-891-8290. p. 3

Deatherage, Eric, Dr, Dir, Crowder College, 601 Laclede Ave, Neosho, MO, 64850. Tel: 417-455-5606. p. 1264

Deaton, Patrick, Assoc Dir, Learning Spaces & Capital Mgmt, North Carolina State University Libraries, D H Hill Jr Library, Two Broughton Dr, Raleigh, NC, 27695. Tel: 919-515-7188. p. 1709

Deatrick, Sara, Branch Lead, Circ Assoc, Harrison County Public Library, Elizabeth Branch, 5101 Main St, Ste 109, Elizabeth, IN, 47117. Tel: 812-969-2899. p. 677

Deatrick, Susan, Head, Youth Serv, Paulding County Carnegie Library, 205 S Main St, Paulding, OH, 45879-1492. Tel: 419-399-2032. p. 1814

Deaver, Brian, Librn, Dechert Law Library, 1095 Avenue of the Americas, 30th Flr, New York, NY, 10036. Tel: 212-698-3515. p. 1585

DeBalzo Green, Helen, Ref Librn, Lorain County Community College, 1005 Abbe Rd N, North Elyria, OH, 44035-1691. Tel: 440-366-7282. p. 1810

DeBell, Kyle, Access Serv Librn, Instruction Librn, Young Harris College, One College St, Young Harris, GA, 30582. Tel: 706-379-4313. p. 504

DeBenedet, Dayna, Chief Exec Officer, Leeds & the Thousand Islands Public Library, 1B Jessie St, Lansdowne, ON, K0E 1L0, CANADA. Tel: 613-659-3885. p. 2652

DeBenedet, Dayna, Libr Mgr, Confederation College Library, 1450 Nakina Dr, Thunder Bay, ON, P7C 4W1, CANADA. Tel: 807-475-6639. p. 2684

DeBenedictis, Kimberlie, Br Mgr, Akron-Summit County Public Library, Mogadore Branch, 144 S Cleveland Ave, Mogadore, OH, 44260. Tel: 330-628-9228. p. 1744

DeBernardi, Molly, Libr Dir, Reddick Public Library District, 1010 Canal St, Ottawa, IL, 61350. Tel: 815-434-0509. p. 631

DeBerry, Amber, Dir, Commun Engagement, Douglas County Libraries, 100 S Wilcox, Castle Rock, CO, 80104. Tel: 303-688-7641. p. 269

DeBiase, Andrea, Dir, Carrabassett Valley Public Library, 3209 Carrabassett Dr, Carrabassett, ME, 04947. Tel: 207-237-3535. p. 921

DeBie, Lori, Tech Serv Librn, Grand Rapids Community College, 140 Ransom NE Ave, Grand Rapids, MI, 49503. Tel: 616-234-3868. p. 1111

deBlieck, Jennifer, Libr Tech, Redeemer University, 777 Garner Rd E, Ancaster, ON, L9K 1J4, CANADA. Tel: 905-648-2131. p. 2628

Deblois, Robert, Circ, Conservatoire de Musique de Quebec Bibliotheque, 270 rue Jacques-Parizeau, Quebec, QC, G1R 5G1, CANADA. Tel: 418-643-2190, Ext 234. p. 2730

Deboer, Cindy, Sr Ref Librn, Allen Public Library, 300 N Allen Dr, Allen, TX, 75013. Tel: 214-509-4905. p. 2133

DeBolt, Dean, Spec Coll & Archives Librn, University of West Florida, 11000 University Pkwy, Pensacola, FL, 32514-5750. Tel: 850-474-2213. p. 436

DeBolt, Preston, Dir, Coloma Public Library, 155 Front St, Coloma, WI, 54930-9670. Tel: 715-228-2530. p. 2429

DeBolt, Vicki, Assoc Dir, Mercer County District Library, 303 N Main St, Celina, OH, 45822. Tel: 419-586-4442. p. 1757

DeBose, Kiri, Librn, Virginia Polytechnic Institute & State University Libraries, Veterinary Medicine, 245 Duck Pond Dr, Blacksburg, VA, 24061-0442. Tel: 540-231-0495. p. 2307

DeBose, Marvin, Br Mgr, Free Library of Philadelphia, Haverford Avenue Branch, 5543 Haverford Ave, Philadelphia, PA, 19139-1432. Tel: 215-685-1964. p. 1978

DeBoy, Kathleen, Cataloger, Dona Ana Community College, 3400 S Espina, Rm 260, Las Cruces, NM, 88003. Tel: 575-527-7555. p. 1470

Debraggio, Anne, Dir, Kirkland Town Library, 55 1/2 College St, Clinton, NY, 13323. Tel: 315-853-2038. p. 1519

Debreceni, Karen, Ch, Dunstable Free Public Library, 588 Main St, Dunstable, MA, 01827. Tel: 978-649-7830. p. 1015

Debruiel, Cherie, Br Assoc, South Central Regional Library, Miami Branch, 530 Norton Ave, Miami, MB, R0G 1H0, CANADA. Tel: 204-435-2032. p. 2592

DeBruin, Nat, Librn, Huntington Museum of Art, 2033 McCoy Rd, Huntington, WV, 25701. Tel: 304-529-2701. p. 2405

Debus, Brian, Head, Children's Servx, Emma S Clark Memorial Library, 120 Main St, Setauket, NY, 11733-2868. Tel: 631-941-4080, Ext 134. p. 1640

Debus, Casey, Libr Dir, Eastern Wyoming College Library, 3200 West C St, Torrington, WY, 82240. Tel: 307-532-8210. p. 2500

DeCampli, Cathy, Emerging Tech Librn, Haddonfield Public Library, 60 Haddon Ave, Haddonfield, NJ, 08033-2422. Tel: 856-429-1304. p. 1406

DeCara, Matthew, YA Librn, Palmer Public Library, 1455 N Main St, Palmer, MA, 01069. Tel: 413-283-3330. p. 1045

DeCardenas, Jorge, Head, Syst Admin, Stow-Munroe Falls Public Library, 3512 Darrow Rd, Stow, OH, 44224. Tel: 330-688-3295. p. 1822

DeCarlo, Jennifer A, Dir, Easton Library, 1074 State Rte 40, Greenwich, NY, 12834-9518. Tel: 518-692-2253. p. 1542

DeCaro, Jessica, Dir, Cleveland Health Sciences Library, Allen Memorial Medical Library, 11000 Euclid Ave, Cleveland, OH, 44106-7130. Tel: 216-368-3643. p. 1767

DeCaro, Jessica E, Dir, Cleveland Health Sciences Library, Allen Memorial Medical Library, 11000 Euclid Ave, Cleveland, OH, 44106-7130. Tel: 216-368-3219. p. 1766

DeCesare, Alexandra, Youth Serv Librn, Boonton Holmes Public Library, 621 Main St, Boonton, NJ, 07005. Tel: 973-334-2980. p. 1391

DeCesare, Lori, Resource Sharing Coord, Library of Rhode Island Network, One Capitol Hill, Providence, RI, 02908. Tel: 401-574-9307. p. 2774

Dechaine, Pauline, Librn, Bibliotheque Mallaig Library, 3110 First St E, Mallaig, AB, T0A 2K0, CANADA. Tel: 780-635-3858. p. 2547

deChambeau, Aimee, Dr, Dean of Libr, University of Akron, University Libraries, 315 Buchtel Mall, Akron, OH, 44325-1701. Tel: 330-972-5355. p. 1745

Dechene, Anick, Libr Mgr, Bibliotheque de St Isidore, PO Box 1168, St. Isidore, AB, T0H 3B0, CANADA. Tel: 780-624-8192. p. 2555

DeChillo, Diane, Prog Mgr, Stone Ridge Public Library, 3700 Main St, Stone Ridge, NY, 12484. Tel: 845-687-7023, Ext 108. p. 1646

Dechow, Doug, Asst Dean for Research & Data Services, Chapman University, One University Dr, Orange, CA, 92866. Tel: 714-532-7756. p. 188

DeCicco-Carey, Kyle, Libr Dir, Millicent Library, 45 Centre St, Fairhaven, MA, 02719. Tel: 508-992-5342. p. 1017

Decker, Amanda, Br Mgr, Franklin Township Free Public Library, Franklin Park Branch, 3391 Rte 27 S, Ste 101, Franklin Park, NJ, 08823. Tel: 732-873-8700, Option 5. p. 1442

Decker, Amy, Libr Asst, Sherman Free Library, 20 Church St, Port Henry, NY, 12974. Tel: 518-546-7461. p. 1621

Decker, Betty, Adult Serv Coordr, Farmington Public Library, 2101 Farmington Ave, Farmington, NM, 87401. Tel: 505-566-2203. p. 1468

Decker, Gregory, Mgr, Metadata & Digital Scholarship Servs, RIT Libraries, 90 Lomb Memorial Dr, Rochester, NY, 14623-5604. Tel: 585-475-4085. p. 1629

Decker, Hope, Dir, Wayland Free Library, 101 W Naples St, Wayland, NY, 14572. Tel: 585-728-5380. p. 1661

Decker, Jennifer, Circ/Cat Librn, Thomas-Wilhite Memorial Library, 101 E Thomas, Perkins, OK, 74059. Tel: 405-547-5185. p. 1860

Decker, John W, Archivist, Stearns History Museum, 235 33rd Ave S, Saint Cloud, MN, 56301-3752. Tel: 320-253-8424. p. 1198

Decker, Katherine, Head, Circ, Lynnfield Public Library, 18 Summer St, Lynnfield, MA, 01940-1837. Tel: 781-334-5411, 781-334-6404. p. 1031

Decker, Lauren, Ch, Kershaw County Library, 1304 Broad St, Camden, SC, 29020. Tel: 803-425-1508, Ext 3208. p. 2048

Decker, Mary Lou, Tech Serv, Kingston Library, 55 Franklin St, Kingston, NY, 12401. Tel: 845-331-0507. p. 1560

Decker, Melissa, Asst Dir, Grayson County Public Library, 163 Carroll Gibson Blvd, Leitchfield, KY, 42754-1488. Tel: 270-259-5455. p. 861

Decker, Rachel, Assoc Dir, Libr Tech Serv, Res Mgt Librn, Georgetown University, Georgetown Law Library (Edward Bennett Williams Library), 111 G St NW, Washington, DC, 20001. Tel: 202-662-9156. p. 368

Decker, Randy, Pub Serv, Red Wing Public Library, 225 East Ave, Red Wing, MN, 55066-2298. Tel: 651-385-3673. p. 1194

Decker, Shanna, Acq/Tech Serv Mgr, Boise Public Library, 715 S Capitol Blvd, Boise, ID, 83702. Tel: 208-972-8219. p. 516

Decker, Steven D, Dir, Cedar City Public Library in the Park, 303 N 100 East, Cedar City, UT, 84720. Tel: 435-586-6661. p. 2262

Decker, Vicki, Librn, Collingsworth Public Library, 711 15th St, Wellington, TX, 79095. Tel: 806-447-3183. p. 2255

Decker-Herman, Susan, Acq Librn, Bard College, One Library Rd, Annandale-on-Hudson, NY, 12504. Tel: 845-785-7617. p. 1487

DeClet, Jaime, Br Mgr, Cleveland Public Library, Jefferson, 850 Jefferson Ave, Cleveland, OH, 44113. Tel: 216-623-7004. p. 1768

Declet, Jaime, Br Mgr, Cleveland Public Library, South, 3096 Scranton Rd, Cleveland, OH, 44113. Tel: 216-623-7060. p. 1768

Declouet, Andrea, Br Librn, Plaquemines Parish Library, Belle Chasse Branch, 8442 Hwy 23, Belle Chasse, LA, 70037. Tel: 504-393-0449, 504-394-3570. p. 885

DeClue, Stephanie, Dir, Res Serv, Stinson LLP, 50 S Sixth St, Minneapolis, MN, 55402. Tel: 612-335-1500. p. 1185

DeCoster, Daisy, Dir, Saint Peter's University, 99 Glenwood Ave, Jersey City, NJ, 07306. Tel: 201-761-6461. p. 1410

DeCramer, Linda, Ch, Ripon Public Library, 120 Jefferson St, Ripon, WI, 54971. Tel: 920-748-6160. p. 2474

DeCristofaro, Christopher, Head of Digital Services, IT & Makerspace, Sachem Public Library, 150 Holbrook Rd, Holbrook, NY, 11741. Tel: 631-588-5024. p. 1547

DeCristofaro, Kimberly, Exec Dir, Connetquot Public Library, 760 Ocean Ave, Bohemia, NY, 11716. Tel: 631-567-5079. p. 1495

Dedischew, Terri, Head, Info Res, Clinton-Macomb Public Library, 40900 Romeo Plank Rd, Clinton Township, MI, 48038-2955. Tel: 586-226-5017. p. 1092

Dedmond, Arrika, Ad, Willard Library of Evansville, 21 First Ave, Evansville, IN, 47710-1294. Tel: 812-425-4309. p. 682

Dedon, Diane, Librn, Taylors Falls Public Library, 473 Bench St, Taylors Falls, MN, 55084. Tel: 651-465-6905. p. 1205

Dee, Alison, Coordr, Clarington Public Library, Newcastle Village Branch, 150 King Ave E, Newcastle, ON, L1B 1L5, CANADA. Tel: 905-987-4844. p. 2632

Dee, Connie, Br Mgr, Saint Louis County Library, Rock Road Branch, 10267 St Charles Rock Rd, Saint Ann, MO, 63074-1812. Tel: 314-994-3300, Ext 3750. p. 1274

Dee, Judi, Educ Mgr, Library of the Friends of Boerner Botanical Gardens, 9400 Boerner Dr, Hales Corners, WI, 53130. Tel: 414-525-5637. p. 2440

Dee, Kristen, Libr Dir, Berne Public Library, 166 N Sprunger St, Berne, IN, 46711-1595. Tel: 260-589-2809. p. 669

Deeds, Shawna, Asst Librn, Mabel C Fry Public Library, 1200 Lakeshore Dr, Yukon, OK, 73099. Tel: 405-354-8232. p. 1870

Deedy, Diane, Dir, Preston Public Library, 389 Rt 2, Preston, CT, 06365. Tel: 860-886-1010. p. 334

Deegan, Elizabeth, Dir, Libr & Archives, American Psychological Association, 750 First St NE, Rm 3012, Washington, DC, 20002-4242. Tel: 202-336-5645. p. 360

Deehr, Marylou, Learning Commons Mgr, Ursuline College, 2550 Lander Rd, Pepper Pike, OH, 44124-4398. Tel: 440-449-4202. p. 1815

Deeken, Lynn, Dean, Arts & Learning Res, Everett Community College, 2000 Tower St, Everett, WA, 98201-1352. Tel: 425-388-9502. p. 2363

Deeks, Linda, Dir, Sanborn-Pekin Free Library, 5884 West St, Sanborn, NY, 14132. Tel: 716-731-9933. p. 1635

Deeks, Susan, Exec Dir, Historical Society of Rockland County Library, 20 Zukor Rd, New City, NY, 10956. Tel: 845-634-9629. p. 1575

Deel, Audrey, Dir, Richwood North Union Public Library, Four E Ottawa St, Richwood, OH, 43344-1296. Tel: 740-943-3054. p. 1817

Deel, Colleen, Coll Mgt Librn, ILL Librn, Univ Archivist, Bemidji State University, 1500 Birchmont Dr NE, No 28, Bemidji, MN, 56601-2699. Tel: 218-755-3339. p. 1165

Deem, Mary, Asst Dir, Fiscal Officer, Carnegie Public Library, 219 E Fourth St, East Liverpool, OH, 43920-3143. Tel: 330-385-2048, Ext 103. p. 1783

Deeming, Kathleen, Head, Access Serv & ILL, Rosemont College Library, 1400 Montgomery Ave, Rosemont, PA, 19010-1631. Tel: 610-527-0200, Ext 2271. p. 2002

Deems, Christopher, Tech & Syst Librn, Ohio Northern University, 525 S Main St, Ada, OH, 45810. Tel: 419-772-2183. p. 1743

Deen, Mandy, Learning Tech Librn, Austin Presbyterian Theological Seminary, 100 E 27th St, Austin, TX, 78705-5797. Tel: 512-404-4874. p. 2138

Deer, Carol, Dir, Packwaukee Public Library, N3511 State St, Packwaukee, WI, 53953. Tel: 608-589-5202. p. 2468

Deer, Sarah, Evening Circ Mgr, Libr Supvr, Valparaiso University, 1410 Chapel Dr, Valparaiso, IN, 46383-6493. Tel: 219-464-5500. p. 723

Deering, Lisa, Libr Mgr, Red Earth Public Library, 115 Sandy Lane, Red Earth Creek, AB, T0G 1X0, CANADA. Tel: 780-649-3898. p. 2551

Deery, Ryan, Dir, Charlevoix Public Library, 220 W Clinton St, Charlevoix, MI, 49720. Tel: 231-237-7360. p. 1090

Dees, Clari, Asst Librn, Pittsfield Public Library, 205 N Memorial St, Pittsfield, IL, 62363-1406. Tel: 217-285-2200. p. 635

Deese, Abby Leigh Edge, Asst Library Dir, Reference & Outreach, University of Miami, 1311 Miller Dr, Coral Gables, FL, 33146. Tel: 305-284-2251. p. 390

Deets, Tracy, Ms, Librn, Beaverlodge Public Library, 406 Tenth St, Beaverlodge, AB, T0H 0C0, CANADA. Tel: 780-354-2569. p. 2523

Defazio, Anne, Br Mgr, San Diego Public Library, Mountain View-Beckwourth, 721 San Pasqual St, San Diego, CA, 92113-1839. Tel: 619-527-3404. p. 220

DeFelice, Brian, Libr Dir, Hull Public Library, Nine Main St, Hull, MA, 02045. Tel: 781-925-2295. p. 1026

DeFelice, Nathalie, Ch, Springdale Public Library, 405 S Pleasant St, Springdale, AR, 72764. Tel: 479-750-8180. p. 110

Deffenbaugh, James T, Br Librn, College of William & Mary in Virginia, Earl Gregg Swem Library, One Landrum Dr, Williamsburg, VA, 23187. Tel: 757-221-3057. p. 2353

DeFillo, Carlotta, Library Contact, Staten Island Historical Society Library, 441 Clarke Ave, Staten Island, NY, 10306. Tel: 718-351-1611, Ext 299. p. 1645

DeFino, Melissa, Head, Spec Coll Cat, Rutgers University Libraries, Special Collections & University Archives, Alexander Library, 169 College Ave, New Brunswick, NJ, 08901-1163. Tel: 848-445-5881. p. 1425

DeFoe, Richard, Librn, Nunez Community College Library, 3710 Paris Rd, Chalmette, LA, 70043. Tel: 504-278-6295, Ext 295. p. 887

DeForest, Tim, Circ Mgr, Ringling College of Art & Design, 2700 N Tamiami Trail, Sarasota, FL, 34234-5895. Tel: 941-359-7587. p. 443

DeFosse, Molly, Chief Financial Officer, Fac Mgr, Public Library of Cincinnati & Hamilton County, 800 Vine St, Cincinnati, OH, 45202-2009. Tel: 513-369-6967. p. 1761

DeFrancis Sun, Beth, Spec Coll Librn, American College of Obstetricians & Gynecologists, 409 12th St SW, Washington, DC, 20024-2188. Tel: 202-863-2518. p. 360

DeGagne, Nicolle, Librn, Gabriel Dumont Institute Library, 48 12th St E, Prince Albert, SK, S6V 1B2, CANADA. Tel: 306-922-6466. p. 2744

Degenhard, Will, Customer Serv Supvr, Naperville Public Library, Naper Boulevard, 2035 S Naper Blvd, Naperville, IL, 60565-3353. Tel: 630-961-4100, Ext 2216. p. 623

Degenhardt, Kris, Educ Adminr, New Mexico Corrections Department, 4337 NM-14, Santa Fe, NM, 87508. Tel: 505-257-8470. p. 1475

DeGeorge, Beth, Librn, Union League of Philadelphia Library, 140 S Broad St, Philadelphia, PA, 19102. Tel: 215-587-5594. p. 1987

DeGeorge, John, Mgr, Oklahoma State University Libraries, Digital Resources & Discovery Services, Edmon Low Library, Rm 215A, Stillwater, OK, 74078. Tel: 405-744-9161. p. 1862

DeGhelder, Timothy, Libr Dir, Douglas County Public Library, 1625 Library Lane, Minden, NV, 89423. Tel: 775-782-9841. p. 1348

DeGhelder, Timothy, Dir, Paris Public Library, 326 S Main St, Paris, TX, 75460. Tel: 903-785-8531. p. 2225

DeGiorgis, Amanda, Dir, Great Barrington Libraries, 231 Main St, Great Barrington, MA, 01230. Tel: 413-528-2403. p. 1022

DeGiorgis, Amanda, Libr Dir, Great Barrington Libraries, Ramsdell Public Library, 1087 Main St, Housatonic, MA, 01236-9730. Tel: 413-274-3738. p. 1022

DeGirolamo, Michael, Jr, Librn, Waterbury Republican & American Library, 389 Meadow St, Waterbury, CT, 06702. Tel: 203-574-3636, Ext 1497. p. 344

Degnan, Clare J, Exec Dir, Library of the Legal Aid Society of Westchester County, 150 Grand St, Ste 100, White Plains, NY, 10601. Tel: 914-286-3400. p. 1664

DeGraw, Theresa, Head, Circ, Tech Serv, Blauvelt Free Library, 541 Western Hwy, Blauvelt, NY, 10913. Tel: 845-359-2811. p. 1494

DeGreeve, Jacquelyn, Dir, Libr & Info Serv, Borden Ladner Gervais LLP Library, 1000 de la Gauchetiere W, Ste 900, Montreal, QC, H3B 5H4, CANADA. Tel: 514-954-3159. p. 2721

DeGreve, Luann, Assoc Univ Librn, Benedictine University Library, 5700 College Rd, Lisle, IL, 60532-0900. Tel: 630-829-6197. p. 610

DeGroat, Jennifer, Head Librn, Capital Area District Libraries, Aurelius Library, 1939 S Aurelius Rd, Mason, MI, 48854-9763. Tel: 517-628-3743. p. 1124

DeGroot, Fern, Head Librn, Parkland Regional Library-Manitoba, Bowsman Branch, 105 Patti's Way, Bowsman, MB, R0L 2H0, CANADA. Tel: 204-238-4615. p. 2586

DeGroot, Twila, Ch, Sioux Center Public Library, 102 S Main Ave, Sioux Center, IA, 51250-1801. Tel: 712-722-2138. p. 782

DeGuiseppi, Tara, Libr Dir, Bovey Public Library, 402 Second St, Bovey, MN, 55709. Tel: 218-245-1633. p. 1166

Deguzman, Thomas, Research Librn, Student Serv Librn, Santa Clara University Library, Edwin A Heafey Law Library, School of Law, 500 El Camino Real, Santa Clara, CA, 95053-0430. Tel: 408-554-5327. p. 242

Degyansky, Kathleen, Asst Dir, White Plains Public Library, 100 Martine Ave, White Plains, NY, 10601. Tel: 914-422-1400. p. 1665

DeHaan, Eric, Br Mgr, Kent District Library, Byron Township Branch, 8191 Byron Center Ave SW, Byron Center, MI, 49315. p. 1094

Deham, Lisa, Human Res Dir, Kenton County Public Library, Administration Center, 3095 Hulbert Ave, Erlanger, KY, 41018. Tel: 859-578-3604. p. 852

DeHart, Brian, Libr Coord, DePaul University Libraries, Loop Library, One E Jackson Blvd, 10th Flr, Chicago, IL, 60604. Tel: 312-362-8433. p. 560

DeHart, Liz, Liaison Librn, University of Texas Libraries, Marine Science, Marine Science Institute, 750 Channelview Dr, Port Aransas, TX, 78373-5015. Tel: 361-749-3094. p. 2142

DeHaven, Jane, Dir, Beach Haven Public Library, 219 N Beach Ave, Beach Haven, NJ, 08008. Tel: 609-492-7081. p. 1389

Dehm, Jason, Head, Tech Serv, Swanton Local School District Public Library, 305 Chestnut St, Swanton, OH, 43558. Tel: 419-826-2760. p. 1822

deHoyos, Arturo, Archivist, Scottish Rite Library, 1733 16th St NW, Washington, DC, 20009-3103. Tel: 202-777-3107. p. 374

Deifallah, Tina, Br Mgr, Montgomery County Public Libraries, Marilyn J Praisner Library, 14910 Old Columbia Pike, Burtonsville, MD, 20866. Tel: 240-773-9450. p. 975

Deignan, Sara, Supvr, Springfield City Library, Mason Square Branch, 765 State St, Springfield, MA, 01109. Tel: 413-263-6853. p. 1056

Deineh, Steven, Instruction Librn, MiraCosta College Library, One Barnard Dr, Bldg 1200, Oceanside, CA, 92056-3899. Tel: 760-795-6721. p. 187

Deines, Christine, Sr Dir, Palmer College of Chiropractic-Davenport Campus, 1000 Brady St, Davenport, IA, 52803-5287. Tel: 563-884-5442. p. 744

Deininger, Jacob, Pub Serv Librn, Cape Fear Community College, 415 N Second St, Wilmington, NC, 28401-3905. Tel: 910-362-7293. p. 1722

Deinken, Jill, Ch, Redwood Falls Public Library, 509 S Lincoln St, Redwood Falls, MN, 56283. Tel: 507-616-7420. p. 1194

Deitchman, Cory, Asst to the Dir, Greenburgh Public Library, 300 Tarrytown Rd, Elmsford, NY, 10523. Tel: 914-721-8200. p. 1531

Deitering, Anne-Marie, Interim Univ Librn, Oregon State University Libraries, 121 The Valley Library, Corvallis, OR, 97331-4501. Tel: 541-737-3331. p. 1876

Deitzer, Margaret, Local Hist Librn, Peters Township Public Library, 616 E McMurray Rd, McMurray, PA, 15317-3495. Tel: 724-941-9430. p. 1959

DeJesus, Liza, Prog Dir, Prevention First, a Division of Preferred Behavioral Health Group, Bldg B, Ste B20, 185 Hwy 36, West Long Branch, NJ, 07764. Tel: 732-663-1800, Ext 2180. p. 1453

Dejnowski, Kathy, Ch, Dir, YA Librn, Thornton Public Library, 115 E Margaret St, Thornton, IL, 60476. Tel: 708-877-2579. p. 653

DeJoice, Mary Jo, Dir, Davis & Elkins College, 100 Campus Dr, Elkins, WV, 26241. Tel: 304-637-1359. p. 2402

DeJong, Karen, Ch Serv Librn, Township of Athens Public Library, Five Central St, Athens, ON, K0E 1B0, CANADA. Tel: 613-924-2048. p. 2628

deJong, Michael, Archivist, Curator, Thunder Bay Historical Museum Society, 425 Donald St E, Thunder Bay, ON, P7E 5V1, CANADA. Tel: 807-623-0801. p. 2685

DeJong, Wynne, Librn, West Park Healthcare Centre, 82 Buttonwood Ave, Toronto, ON, M6M 2J5, CANADA. Tel: 416-243-3600, Ext 2048. p. 2700

DeJonghe, Natalie, Adult Serv Mgr, Westmont Public Library, 428 N Cass Ave, Westmont, IL, 60559-1502. Tel: 630-869-6150, 630-869-6160. p. 661

Dekara, Daniel, Info Literacy, Tuskegee University, 1200 W Old Montgomery Rd, Ford Motor Company Library, Tuskegee, AL, 36088. Tel: 334-727-8676. p. 38

Dekat, Ryann, Adult Serv, Farmers Branch Manske Library, 13613 Webb Chapel Rd, Farmers Branch, TX, 75234. Tel: 972-919-9810. p. 2176

Dekens, James, Br Mgr, Burlington Public Library, Aldershot, 550 Plains Rd E, Burlington, ON, L7T 2E3, CANADA. Tel: 905-333-9995. p. 2634

Dekens, James, Br Supvr, Burlington Public Library, Brant Hills, 2255 Brant St, Burlington, ON, L7P 5C8, CANADA. Tel: 905-335-2209. p. 2634

Dekens, James, Br Supvr, Burlington Public Library, Kilbride, Kilbride School, 6611 Panton St, Burlington, ON, L7P 0L8, CANADA. Tel: 905-335-4011. p. 2634

Dekker, Amanda, Br Mgr, Cumberland County Public Library & Information Center, Bordeaux, 3711 Village Dr, Fayetteville, NC, 28304-1530. p. 1688

Dekle, Deanne, Sr Librn, Rancho Mirage Library & Observatory, 71-100 Hwy 111, Rancho Mirage, CA, 92270. Tel: 760-341-7323. p. 198

DeKnight, Amanda, Dir, South Park Township Library, 2575 Brownsville Rd, South Park, PA, 15129-8527. Tel: 412-833-5585. p. 2009

Dekoff, Janice, Exec Dir, Chautauqua-Cattaraugus Library System, 106 W Fifth St, Jamestown, NY, 14701. Tel: 716-484-7135, Ext 228. p. 1557

Dekovich, Margaret, Br Mgr, Clinton-Macomb Public Library, South, 35679 S Gratiot Ave, Clinton Township, MI, 48035. Tel: 586-226-5071. p. 1092

Del Duca, Tracey, Librn, Interchurch Center, 475 Riverside Dr, Ste 250, New York, NY, 10115. Tel: 212-870-3804. p. 1589

Del Monaco, Tony, Dir, Finance & Fac, Hamilton Public Library, 55 York Blvd, Hamilton, ON, L8R 3K1, CANADA. Tel: 905-546-3200, Ext 3226. p. 2645

Del Rio, Jacob, Head, Adult Serv, Edwardsville Public Library, 112 S Kansas St, Edwardsville, IL, 62025. Tel: 618-692-7556. p. 581

Del Rosso, Maria, Dir, Fauquier County Public Library, 11 Winchester St, Warrenton, VA, 20186. Tel: 540-347-8750, Ext 5327. p. 2351

Del Toro, Rosemary, Coll Mgt Librn, Marquette University, 1355 W Wisconsin Ave, Milwaukee, WI, 53233. Tel: 414-288-3944. p. 2458

Del Vecchio, Kelly, Librn, Sandusky Bay Law Library Association, Inc, 247 Columbus Ave, Sandusky, OH, 44870. Tel: 419-626-4823. p. 1819

Del Vecchio, Rosemary A, Librn, New York State Office of the State Comptroller Library, 110 State St, 15th Flr, Albany, NY, 12236. Tel: 518-473-5960. p. 1483

Delacruz, Jacqueline, Children's Coordr, Lawrence Public Library, 51 Lawrence St, Lawrence, MA, 01841. Tel: 978-620-3600. p. 1027

DelaGardelle, Jody, Youth Serv, Kilbourn Public Library, 620 Elm St, Wisconsin Dells, WI, 53965. Tel: 608-254-2146. p. 2489

Delagarza, Ashley, Tech Serv Librn, University of Saint Thomas, 3800 Montrose Blvd, Houston, TX, 77006. Tel: 713-525-2192. p. 2200

DeLancey, Laura, Chair, Dept of Library Public Services, Western Kentucky University Libraries, Helm-Cravens Library Complex, 1906 College Heights Blvd, No 11067, Bowling Green, KY, 42101-1067. Tel: 270-745-3979. p. 849

DeLand, Rob, Archivist, Head Librn, Vandercook College of Music, 3140 S Federal St, Chicago, IL, 60616-3731. Tel: 312-225-6288, Ext 260. p. 570
Delaney, Ezra, Dir, Admin & Finance, Cornell University Library, 201 Olin Library, Ithaca, NY, 14853. Tel: 607-254-5257. p. 1551
Delaney, Jodi, Dir, Dolores Tillinghast Memorial Library, 234 N Fourth St, Harpers Ferry, IA, 52146. Tel: 563-586-2524. p. 757
DeLaney, Kathleen, Archivist, Ref Librn, Canisius College, 2001 Main St, Buffalo, NY, 14208-1098. Tel: 716-888-8421. p. 1509
Delaney, Lori, Dir, Libr & Res Serv, Carolina Population Center, 123 W Franklin St, Chapel Hill, NC, 27516. Tel: 919-962-6157. p. 1678
DeLaney, Matt, Libr Dir, Jesup Memorial Library, 34 Mount Desert St, Bar Harbor, ME, 04609-1727. Tel: 207-288-4245. p. 916
Delaney, Meg, Mgr, Main Libr, Toledo-Lucas County Public Library, 325 Michigan St, Toledo, OH, 43604. Tel: 419-259-5333. p. 1824
DeLangie, Jessica, Head, Tech Serv, Derry Public Library, 64 E Broadway, Derry, NH, 03038-2412. Tel: 603-432-6140. p. 1361
Delano, Karen, Asst Librn, Wiscasset Public Library, 21 High St, Wiscasset, ME, 04578-4119. Tel: 207-882-7161. p. 947
DeLano, Stacy, Libr Dir, Stillwater Public Library, 1107 S Duck St, Stillwater, OK, 74074. Tel: 405-372-3633, Ext 8124. p. 1862
Delanty, Cynthia, Br Mgr, Hawaii State Public Library System, Molokai Public Library, 15 Ala Malama Ave, Kaunakakai, HI, 96748. Tel: 808-553-1765. p. 509
Delapena, Jodi, Br Mgr, San Diego County Library, Spring Valley Branch, 836 Kempton St, Spring Valley, CA, 91977. Tel: 619-463-3006. p. 217
Delarosbil, Noemie, Libr Tech, Institut de Readaption Gingras-Lindsay-de-Montreal Bibliotheque, Lindsay Pavillon, 2nd Flr, 6363 Hudson Rd, Montreal, QC, H3S 1M9, CANADA. Tel: 514-340-2085, Ext 142270. p. 2725
Delaune, Jan, Cataloger, Harrison County Library System, 12135 Old Hwy 49, Gulfport, MS, 39501. Tel: 228-539-0110. p. 1217
DeLaurenti, Katherine, Head Librn, Johns Hopkins University-Peabody Conservatory of Music, 21 E Mount Vernon Pl, Baltimore, MD, 21202-2397. Tel: 667-208-6656. p. 954
DeLauw, Diane, Libr Mgr, Crowsnest Pass Municipal Library, 2114 127 St, Blairmore, AB, T0K 0E0, CANADA. Tel: 403-562-8393. p. 2523
Delavallade, Jaleesa, Br Mgr, East Baton Rouge Parish Library, Eden Park, 5131 Greenwell Springs Rd, Baton Rouge, LA, 70806. Tel: 225-231-3280. p. 883
DeLay, Christian, Broadband Project Mgr, Califa, 330 Townsend St, Ste 133, San Francisco, CA, 94107. Tel: 888-239-2289. p. 2761
Delcamp, Bonnie, Asst Librn, Cushman Library, 28 Church St, Bernardston, MA, 01337. Tel: 413-648-5402. p. 989
DelCegno, Gretchen, Libr Dir, Terryville Public Library, 238 Main St, Terryville, CT, 06786. Tel: 860-582-3121. p. 341
DelConte, Tammy, Br Head, Monterey County Free Libraries, Big Sur Branch, Hwy 1 at Ripplewood Resort, Big Sur, CA, 93920. Tel: 831-667-2537. p. 172
DelConte, Tammy, Br Mgr, Monterey County Free Libraries, Prunedale, 17822 Moro Rd, Salinas, CA, 93907. Tel: 831-663-2292. p. 173
Delcurla, Shay, Prof, Ref Librn, Brookdale Community College, 765 Newman Springs Rd, Lincroft, NJ, 07738-1597. Tel: 732-224-2438. p. 1412
Delehoy, Keturah, Dir, Partridge Public Library, 23 S Main St, Partridge, KS, 67566. Tel: 620-567-2467. p. 831
DeLeon, Maricela, Dir, Wauseon Public Library, 117 E Elm St, Wauseon, OH, 43567. Tel: 419-335-6626. p. 1829
DeLeon, Stephanie, Librn, CentraCare - Saint Cloud Hospital, 1406 Sixth Ave N, Saint Cloud, MN, 56303. Tel: 320-251-2700, Ext 54686. p. 1196
Delfield, Jeffrey, County Librn, Marianna Black Library, 33 Fryemont St, Bryson City, NC, 28713. Tel: 828-488-3030. p. 1675
Delgado, Anibal, Emerging Tech Librn, Daytona State College Library, Bldg 115, Rm 314, 1200 W International Speedway Blvd, Daytona Beach, FL, 32114. Tel: 386-506-3608. p. 392
Delgado, Diana, Assoc Dir, Clinical Informationist Serv, Assoc Dir, Edu Servs, Cornell University Library, Samuel J Wood Library & C V Starr Biomedical Information Center, 1300 York Ave, C115, Box 67, New York, NY, 10065-4896. Tel: 646-962-2550. p. 1552
Delgado, Jeffrey, Ref, Kingsborough Community College, 2001 Oriental Blvd, Brooklyn, NY, 11235. Tel: 718-368-5430. p. 1504
Delgado, Kaela, Libr Coord, Westminster Public Library, Irving Street, 7392 Irving St, Westminster, CO, 80030. Tel: 303-658-2309. p. 298
Delgado, Martin, Mgr, County of Los Angeles Public Library, East Los Angeles Library, 4837 E Third St, Los Angeles, CA, 90022-1601. Tel: 323-264-0155. p. 135
Delgado Ramos, Yanit, Dir, Universidad Central de Bayamon, PO Box 1725, Bayamon, PR, 00960-1725. Tel: 787-786-3030, Ext 2135. p. 2510
Delgado, Rita, Ch, David M Hunt Library, 63 Main St, Falls Village, CT, 06031. Tel: 860-824-7424. p. 312
Delgado-Player, Jodie, Chief Exec Officer, Township of Springwater Public Library, 12 Finlay Mill Rd, Midhurst, ON, L9X 0N7, CANADA. Tel: 705-737-5650. p. 2657
DeLisle, Julie, Dir, Chatham Public Library, 11 Woodbridge Ave, Chatham, NY, 12037-1399. Tel: 518-392-3666. p. 1517
Delisle, Julie, Dir, Chatham Public Library, Canaan Branch, 1647 County Rte 5, Canaan, NY, 12029-3017. Tel: 518-781-3392. p. 1517
DeLizio, Carissa, Libr Dir, Rhode Island College, 600 Mt Pleasant Ave, Providence, RI, 02908-1924. p. 2039
Dell, Dane A, Dir, Info Syst, Onondaga County Public Libraries, The Galleries of Syracuse, 447 S Salina St, Syracuse, NY, 13202-2494. Tel: 315-435-1900. p. 1649
Dell, Esther, ILL Librn, Pennsylvania State University, College of Medicine, Penn State Hershey, 500 University Dr, Hershey, PA, 17033. Tel: 717-531-8626. p. 1943
Dell, Marin, Research & Technical Servs Librn, Nova Southeastern University Libraries, Panza Maurer Law Library, Shepard Broad College of Law, Leo Goodwin Sr Bldg, 3305 College Ave, Davie, FL, 33314. Tel: 954-262-6224. p. 402
Della Barba, Maureen, Ref Asst, Thurgood Marshall State Law Library, Courts of Appeals Bldg, 361 Rowe Blvd, Annapolis, MD, 21401. Tel: 410-260-1430. p. 950
Della Marna, Jodi, Archives Librn, Cat & Per Librn, Orange Coast College Library, 2701 Fairview Rd, Costa Mesa, CA, 92626. Tel: 714-432-5885. p. 132
Della Rocca, Jared, Dir, Libr Serv, Bennington College, One College Dr, Bennington, VT, 05201-6001. Tel: 802-440-4610. p. 2279
Della Santina, Joey, Asst Dir, Belvedere Tiburon Library, 1501 Tiburon Blvd, Tiburon, CA, 94920. Tel: 415-789-2665. p. 252
Della Terza, Dave, Exec Dir, Naperville Public Library, 200 W Jefferson Ave, Naperville, IL, 60540-5374. Tel: 630-961-4100. p. 622
Dellavedova, Elizabeth Bryan, Assoc Libr Dir, Northern Virginia Community College Libraries, Annandale Campus, Goodwin Bldg (CG), 3rd Flr, 8333 Little River Tpk, Annandale, VA, 22003. Tel: 703-323-3066. p. 2304
Delli-Gatti, Barbara, Dir, Life Chiropractic College-West Library, 25001 Industrial Blvd, Hayward, CA, 94545. Tel: 510-780-4507. p. 151
Dellinger, Don, Dir, Kaltreider-Benfer Library, 147 S Charles St, Red Lion, PA, 17356. Tel: 717-244-2032. p. 2001
Dellinger, Zoe, Asst Dir, Shenandoah County Library, 514 Stoney Creek Blvd, Edinburg, VA, 22824. Tel: 540-984-8200, Ext 205. p. 2315
Dellis, Shawn, Adminr, Outreach Coordr, Pacifica Foundation, 3729 Cahuenga Blvd W, North Hollywood, CA, 91604. Tel: 818-506-1077, Ext 261. p. 183
Dellis-Quinn, Debbie, Commun Relations, Manhasset Public Library, 30 Onderdonk Ave, Manhasset, NY, 11030. Tel: 512-627-2300, Ext 150. p. 1568
Delmar, Nathan, Fac Serv Librn, Fordham University School of Law, 150 W 62nd St, New York, NY, 10023. Tel: 212-636-6903. p. 1585
Delmas, Susan, Br Librn, Jackson/Hinds Library System, Quisenberry Library, 605 E Northside Dr, Clinton, MS, 39056-5121. Tel: 601-924-5684. p. 1221
Delmonaco, Vanina, Documentation Tech, College de Montreal Bibliotheque, 1931 rue Sherbrooke Ouest, Montreal, QC, H3H 1E3, CANADA. Tel: 514-933-7397, Ext 291. p. 2723
Delneky, Akos, Dr, Dean, Learning Res, Indian River State College, 3209 Virginia Ave, Fort Pierce, FL, 34981-5599. Tel: 772-462-7590. p. 404
Delneo, Catherine, Br Mgr, San Francisco Public Library, 100 Larkin St, San Francisco, CA, 94102. Tel: 415-557-4353. p. 227
DeLoach, Charlotte, Mgr, Evans County Public Library, 701 W Main St, Claxton, GA, 30417. Tel: 912-739-1801. p. 471
Deloach, Cynthia, Br Mgr, Allendale-Hampton-Jasper Regional Library, Estill Public Library, 100 Peeples Ave, Estill, SC, 29918-4827. Tel: 803-625-4560. p. 2046
Delong, Heather, Br Librn, Tay Township Public Library, 715 Fourth Ave, Port McNicoll, ON, L0K 1R0, CANADA. Tel: 705-534-3511. p. 2674
DeLong, Kathleen, Assoc Univ Librn, University of Alberta, University Library, 5-02 Cameron Libr, Edmonton, AB, T6G 2J8, CANADA. Tel: 780-492-3790. p. 2538
DeLong, Lisa, Co-Dir, Mooers Free Library, 25 School St, Mooers, NY, 12958. Tel: 518-236-7744. p. 1574
DeLooper, John, Online Learning Librn, Web Serv Librn, Lehman College, City University of New York, 250 Bedford Park Blvd W, Bronx, NY, 10468. Tel: 718-960-8577. p. 1499
DeLooze-Klein, Emma, Dir, Adult Serv, Dir, Commun Serv, Kirkwood Public Library, 140 E Jefferson Ave, Kirkwood, MO, 63122. Tel: 314-821-5770, Ext 1025. p. 1259
Delorey, Karen, Libr Coord, MassBay Community College, Learning Resource Center, 19 Flagg Dr, Framingham, MA, 01702-5928. Tel: 508-270-4215. p. 1063
Deloria, Phil, Archivist, Little Traverse History Museum Library, 100 Depot Ct, Petoskey, MI, 49770. Tel: 231-347-2620. p. 1140
DeLorme, Brittany, Head, Children's Servx, Interim Asst Dir, Winchester Public Library, 80 Washington St, Winchester, MA, 01890. Tel: 781-721-7171. p. 1070
delos Santos, Lynda, ILL, Ref Librn, San Jacinto College South, 13735 Beamer Rd, S10, Houston, TX, 77089-6099. Tel: 281-998-6150, Ext 3306. p. 2198
DeLos, Tony, Ref Librn, Derby Public Library, 313 Elizabeth St, Derby, CT, 06418. Tel: 203-736-1482. p. 309
Delperdang, Jennifer, Br Supvr, Sioux City Public Library, Schroeder-Morningside Branch Library, 4005 Morningside Ave, Sioux City, IA, 51106-2448. Tel: 712-255-2924. p. 783
Delph, Kelly McBride, Libr Dir, Russell County Public Library, 248 W Main St, Lebanon, VA, 24266. Tel: 276-889-8044. p. 2328

Delphous, Tonya, Dir, Elk River Free Library District, 203 Main St, Elk River, ID, 83827. Tel: 208-826-3539. p. 520
DelPriore, Michele, Dir, Tivoli Free Library, 86 Broadway, Tivoli, NY, 12583. Tel: 845-757-3771. p. 1652
Delsesto, Cara, Head, Youth Serv, Coventry Public Library, 1672 Flat River Rd, Coventry, RI, 02816. Tel: 401-822-9100. p. 2030
DeLuca, Carolyn, Info Res Librn, Northwestern Health Sciences University, 2501 W 84th St, Bloomington, MN, 55431-1599. Tel: 952-885-5419. p. 1166
DeLuca, Karen, Chief Librn, Arnprior Public Library, 21 Madawaska St, Arnprior, ON, K7S 1R6, CANADA. Tel: 613-623-2279. p. 2628
DeLucia, Erin, Br Mgr, Ocean County Library, Manchester Branch, 21 Colonial Dr, Manchester, NJ, 08759. Tel: 732-657-7600. p. 1447
DeLucia, Erin, Br Mgr, Ocean County Library, Whiting Reading Center, Whiting Commons Shopping Ctr, 400 Lacey Rd, Ste 5, Whiting, NJ, 08759. Tel: 732-849-0391. p. 1447
Delury, Michael, Libr Mgr, Sno-Isle Libraries, Lynnwood Library, 19200 44th Ave W, Lynnwood, WA, 98036-5617. Tel: 425-778-2148. p. 2370
DelVecchio, Nancy, Circ Mgr, ILL, Hudson Public Library, Three Washington St, Hudson, MA, 01749-2499. Tel: 978-568-9644. p. 1025
DelVecchio, Steve, Regional Mgr, The Seattle Public Library, 1000 Fourth Ave, Seattle, WA, 98104-1109. Tel: 206-386-4636. p. 2379
deMaine, Susan, Res & Instrul Serv Librn, Indiana University, Ruth Lilly Law Library, 530 W New York St, Indianapolis, IN, 46202-3225. Tel: 317-274-3884, 317-274-4028. p. 693
Demanett, Paula, Librn, Fresno City College Library, 1101 E University Ave, Fresno, CA, 93741. Tel: 559-442-4600, Ext 8048. p. 145
Demapan, Jaylene, Asst to the Dir, Sonoma County Library, 6135 State Farm Dr, Rohnert Park, CA, 94928. Tel: 707-545-0831. p. 204
DeMaranville, Mark, Librn, Bryant Free Library, 455 Berkshire Trail, Rte 9, Cummington, MA, 01026-9610. Tel: 413-634-0109. p. 1013
DeMarce, Kim, Libr Mgr, South Central College, 1920 Lee Blvd, North Mankato, MN, 56003-2504. Tel: 507-389-7251. p. 1190
DeMarco, Adrianna, Dir, Knowledge Mgt, Stikeman Elliott, 5300 Commerce Ct W, 199 Bay St, Toronto, ON, M5L 1B9, CANADA. Tel: 416-869-5500. p. 2693
DeMarco, Cynthia, Libr Asst, Bethesda Health - Bethesda Hospital East, 2815 S Seacrest Blvd, Boynton Beach, FL, 33435-7934. Tel: 561-737-7733, Ext 85203. p. 386
DeMarco, Susan, Children's Serv Coordr, New Hanover County Public Library, 201 Chestnut St, Wilmington, NC, 28401. Tel: 910-798-6353. p. 1723
Demarest, Geralynn, Chairperson, Librn, Columbia-Greene Community College Library, 4400 Rte 23, Hudson, NY, 12534. Tel: 518-828-4181, Ext 3290. p. 1549
Demaris, Nancy, ILL, Rowan University School of Osteopathic Medicine, Academic Ctr, One Medical Center Dr, Stratford, NJ, 08084. Tel: 856-566-6808. p. 1444
DeMaris, Scott, Law Librn, Reed Smith LLP, Three Logan Sq, 1717 Arch St, Ste 3100, Philadelphia, PA, 19103. Tel: 215-851-1413, 215-851-8100. p. 1985
DeMars, Paula, Dir, Libr Serv, Leech Lake Tribal College, 6945 Little Wolf Rd NW, Cass Lake, MN, 56633. Tel: 218-335-4240. p. 1169
DeMartini, Becky, Info & Instruction Librn, Brigham Young University-Hawaii, BYU-Hawaii, No 1966, 55-220 Kulanui St, Bldg 5, Laie, HI, 96762-1294. Tel: 808-675-3946. p. 514
DeMartino, Sherrie, Br Mgr, Adams County Library System, Carroll Valley Branch, 5685 Fairfield Rd, Carroll Valley, PA, 17320. Tel: 717-642-6009. p. 1935
Demas, Chris, Dean of Libr, Northeast State Community College, 2425 Hwy 75, Blountville, TN, 37617. Tel: 423-354-2429. p. 2088
Demas, Samuel, Librn Emeritus, Carleton College, One N College St, Northfield, MN, 55057-4097. Tel: 507-222-4260. p. 1191
DeMatos, Carolann, Dir, Pub Relations, Dir, Mkt, Somerset County Library System of New Jersey, One Vogt Dr, Bridgewater, NJ, 08807-2136. Tel: 908-458-8404. p. 1392
DeMay, Derrick, Br Coordr, Oakland Public Library, 125 14th St, Oakland, CA, 94612. Tel: 510-238-3479. p. 186
DeMay, Norma, Libr Dir, Douglas Library, 108 Main St, North Canaan, CT, 06018. Tel: 860-824-7863. p. 331
Dembiec, Amanda, ILL, Nashville Public Library, 615 Church St, Nashville, TN, 37219-2314. Tel: 615-862-5780. p. 2119
Dembinski, Tracee, Libr Dir, New Virginia Public Library, 504 Book Alley, New Virginia, IA, 50210. Tel: 641-449-3614. p. 773
Dembinski, Tracee, Dir, Truro Public Library, 114 E Center St, Truro, IA, 50257. Tel: 641-765-4220. p. 787
Demby-Miller, Zandra, AV, Warren County-Vicksburg Public Library, 700 Veto St, Vicksburg, MS, 39180-3595. Tel: 601-636-6411. p. 1235
DeMeester, Kate, Libr Serv Mgr, Pima County Public Library, Santa Rosa Branch, 1075 S Tenth Ave, Tucson, AZ, 85701. Tel: 520-594-5260. p. 82
DeMeester, Kate, Br Mgr, Pima County Public Library, Joel D Valdez, 101 N Stone Ave, Tucson, AZ, 85701. Tel: 520-594-5500. p. 83
Dement, Mary, Br Librn, Reynolds County Library District, Lesterville Branch, 33285 Hwy 21, Lesterville, MO, 63654. Tel: 573-637-2532. p. 1241
Demers, Amanda, Libr Dir, Cecil College, One Seahawk Dr, North East, MD, 21901-1904. Tel: 410-287-1030. p. 972
Demers, Annette, Law Librn, University of Windsor, Paul Martin Law Library, Ron W Ianni Law Bldg, 401 Sunset Ave, Windsor, ON, N9B 3P4, CANADA. Tel: 519-253-3000, Ext 2976. p. 2704
Demers, Carole-Ann, Chief Exec Officer, Timmins Public Library, 320 Second Ave, Timmins, ON, P4N 4A8, CANADA. Tel: 705-360-2623, Ext 8519. p. 2685
Demetros, Christine, Asst Dir, Student Learning, Syracuse University College of Law Library, 228 Dineen Hall, 950 Irving Ave, Syracuse, NY, 13244-6070. Tel: 315-443-9531. p. 1650
DeMeulenaere, Christy, Dir, Ray Township Public Library, 64255 Wolcott Rd, Ray, MI, 48096. Tel: 586-749-7130. p. 1143
DeMey, Kathy, Research Librn, Calvin University & Calvin Theological Seminary, 1855 Knollcrest Circle SE, Grand Rapids, MI, 49546-4402. Tel: 616-526-6310. p. 1110
Demian, Sara, Managing Librn, Brooklyn Public Library, Clarendon, 2035 Nostrand Ave, Brooklyn, NY, 11210. Tel: 718-421-1159. p. 1502
DeMidio, Beth, Asst Dir, Libr Operations, Schenectady County Public Library, 99 Clinton St, Schenectady, NY, 12305-2083. Tel: 518-388-4500. p. 1638
DeMilia, Carl, Exec Dir, Bibliomation Inc, 24 Wooster Ave, Waterbury, CT, 06708. Tel: 203-577-4070, Ext 106. p. 2762
Deming, Ashley, Dir of Educ, Michigan Maritime Museum, 91 Michigan Ave, South Haven, MI, 49090. Tel: 269-637-9156. p. 1150
Demko, Diane, Actg Br Mgr, Scranton Public Library, Nancy Kay Holmes Branch, 1032 Green Ridge St at Wyoming Ave, Scranton, PA, 18509. Tel: 570-207-0764. p. 2005
Demopoulos, Marta, Dir, United States Air Force, Bldg 722, 842 Falcon Ave, Patrick AFB, FL, 32925-3439. Tel: 321-494-6881. p. 436
DeMoss, Lisa, Asst to the Dir, Youth Programmer, North Valley Public Library, 208 Main St, Stevensville, MT, 59870. Tel: 406-777-5061. p. 1302
Dempf, Linda, Dr, Music & Media Librn, The College of New Jersey, 2000 Pennington Rd, Ewing, NJ, 08628-1104. Tel: 609-771-2311. p. 1402
Dempsey, Cindy, Libr Asst, Coleman Public Library, 402 S Commercial Ave, Coleman, TX, 76834-4202. Tel: 325-625-3043. p. 2157
Dempsey, Georgina, Coll Develop, Midlands Technical College Library, Beltline Library, 316 S Beltline Blvd, 2nd Flr, Columbia, SC, 29205. Tel: 803-738-7626. p. 2072
Dempsey, Megan, Instrul Serv Librn, Raritan Valley Community College, Theater Bldg Branchburg, 118 Lamington Rd, Somerville, NJ, 08876. Tel: 908-218-8865. p. 1442
Dempsey, Sarah, Dir, Butler Public Library, 340 S Broadway St, Butler, IN, 46721. Tel: 260-868-2351. p. 673
Dempsey, Sean, Supvr, University of Chicago Library, John Crerar Library, 5730 S Ellis Ave, Chicago, IL, 60637. Tel: 773-702-7715. p. 569
Dempster, Sara, Head, Youth Serv, Chelmsford Public Library, 25 Boston Rd, Chelmsford, MA, 01824. Tel: 978-256-5521. p. 1010
Dempster, Sara, Head, Youth Serv, Concord Free Public Library, 129 Main St, Concord, MA, 01742. Tel: 978-318-3358. p. 1012
Demske, Nick, Interim Exec Dir, Racine Public Library, 75 Seventh St, Racine, WI, 53403. Tel: 262-636-9241. p. 2471
DeMumbrum, Virginia, Dir, White Lake Community Library, 3900 White Lake Dr, Whitehall, MI, 49461-9257. Tel: 231-894-9531. p. 1159
Denbow, Samantha, Libr Dir, Bay City Public Library, 1100 Seventh St, Bay City, TX, 77414. Tel: 979-245-6931. p. 2145
Denby, Tamara, Dir, Clinton Township Public Library, 100 Brown St, Clinton, MI, 49236. Tel: 517-456-4141. p. 1091
Denda, Kayo, Head, Educ Res Ctr, Rutgers University Libraries, Mabel Smith Douglass Library, Eight Chapel Dr, New Brunswick, NJ, 08901-8527. Tel: 848-932-5023. p. 1425
DeNero-Ackroyd, Kim, Dep Dir, Cleveland Heights-University Heights Public Library, 2345 Lee Rd, Cleveland Heights, OH, 44118-3493. Tel: 216-932-3600. p. 1771
Denes, Manuela, Commun Serv Mgr, Essex County Library, 360 Fairview Ave W, Ste 101, Essex, ON, N8M 1Y3, CANADA. Tel: 519-776-5241. p. 2640
Deng, Connie, Cat Librn, Southwestern Law School, Bullock Wilshire Bldg, 1st Flr, 3050 Wilshire Blvd, Los Angeles, CA, 90010. Tel: 213-738-5771. p. 168
Deng, Yi, PhD, Dean, Drexel University, 3675 Market St, Ste 1000, Philadelphia, PA, 19104. Tel: 215-895-2474. p. 2791
Denhalter, Meledie, Br Mgr, Davis County Library, Syracuse/Northwest Branch, 1875 S 2000 West, Syracuse, UT, 84075. Tel: 801-451-1850. p. 2263
Denham, Melissa, Libr Mgr, Thomas County Public Library System, Pavo Public Library, 3031 E Harris St, Pavo, GA, 31778. Tel: 229-859-2697. p. 499
Denham, Melissa, Youth Serv Librn, Bellingham Public Library, 100 Blackstone St, Bellingham, MA, 02019. Tel: 508-966-1660. p. 988
Denier, Kate, Br Mgr, Public Library of Cincinnati & Hamilton County, North Central, 11109 Hamilton Ave, Cincinnati, OH, 45231. Tel: 513-369-6068. p. 1763
Denis, Chris, Mrs, Br Support, Stormont, Dundas & Glengarry County Library, Long Sault Branch, 50 Milles Roches Rd (Fire Hall), Long Sault, ON, K0C 1P0, CANADA. Tel: 613-534-2605. p. 2638
Denison, Jessalynn, Dir, Andrews County Library, 109 NW First St, Andrews, TX, 79714. Tel: 432-523-9819. p. 2135

Denison, Veronica, Digital Archivist, Spec Coll Librn, Rhode Island College, 600 Mt Pleasant Ave, Providence, RI, 02908-1924. p. 2039

Denke, Jess, Outreach & Assessment Librn, Muhlenberg College, 2400 Chew St, Allentown, PA, 18104-5586. Tel: 484-664-3552. p. 1905

Denlinger, Scott, Acq, Resources Librn, Pennsylvania College of Health Sciences, 850 Greenfield Rd, Lancaster, PA, 17601. Tel: 717-947-6128. p. 1952

Denmark, Morris, Managing Librn, Brooklyn Public Library, Brower Park, 725 Saint Marks Ave, Brooklyn, NY, 11216. Tel: 718-773-7208. p. 1502

Denmark, Morris, Managing Librn, Brooklyn Public Library, Fort Hamilton, 9424 Fourth Ave, Brooklyn, NY, 11209. Tel: 718-748-6919. p. 1503

Denmark, Peter, Libr Mgr, Milk River Municipal Library, 321 Third Ave NE, Milk River, AB, T0K 1M0, CANADA. Tel: 403-647-3793. p. 2548

Dennard, Harold, AV Tech, Lawson State Community College Library, 1100 Ninth Ave SW, Bessemer, AL, 35022. Tel: 205-929-3434, 205-929-6333. p. 6

Denne, Colleen, Dir, Carnegie Library of McKeesport, 1507 Library Ave, McKeesport, PA, 15132-4796. Tel: 412-672-0625. p. 1959

Denne, Douglas, Resource Librn, University of the Ozarks, 415 N College Ave, Clarksville, AR, 72830. Tel: 479-979-1382. p. 92

Dennehy, Carol, Asst Librn, Woodsville Free Public Library, 14 School Lane, Woodsville, NH, 03785. Tel: 603-747-3483. p. 1385

Dennett, John, Circ, NHTI, Concord's Community College, 31 College Dr, Concord, NH, 03301-7425. Tel: 603-230-4028. p. 1359

Dennett, Marie, Cat Librn, United States Military Academy Library, Jefferson Hall Library & Learning Ctr, 758 Cullum Rd, West Point, NY, 10996. Tel: 845-938-8301. p. 1663

Dennie, Danielle, Head of Libr, Concordia University Libraries, Vanier Library, 7141 Sherbrooke St W, Montreal, QC, H4B 1R6, CANADA. Tel: 514-848-2424, Ext 7725. p. 2724

Dennigan, Kerry, Coordr, Griffin Hospital, 130 Division St, Derby, CT, 06418. Tel: 203-732-7399. p. 309

Dennis, Amy, Asst Dir, North Webster Community Public Library, 110 E North St, North Webster, IN, 46555. Tel: 574-834-7122. p. 711

Dennis, Bradford, Education & Human Dev Librn, Western Michigan University, 1903 W Michigan Ave, WMU Mail Stop 5353, Kalamazoo, MI, 49008-5353. Tel: 269-387-1581. p. 1122

Dennis, Carole, Youth Serv Mgr, Iredell County Public Library, 201 N Tradd St, Statesville, NC, 28677. Tel: 704-928-2414. p. 1717

Dennis, Christopher, Head, Coll Develop, Memorial University of Newfoundland, Queen Elizabeth II Library, 234 Elizabeth Ave, St. John's, NL, A1B 3Y1, CANADA. Tel: 709-737-3214. p. 2610

Dennis, Donald, Teen Serv, Georgetown County Library, Waccamaw Neck, 41 St Paul Pl, Pawleys Island, SC, 29585. Tel: 843-545-3623. p. 2060

Dennis, Gloria, Br Mgr, Atlanta-Fulton Public Library System, Cleveland Avenue Branch, 47 Cleveland Ave SW, Atlanta, GA, 30315. Tel: 404-762-4116. p. 461

Dennis Hunker, Stefanie, Interim Head Librn, Bowling Green State University Libraries, Ray & Pat Browne Popular Culture Library, Jerome Library, 4th Flr, Bowling Green, OH, 43403. Tel: 419-372-7893. p. 1752

Dennis Hunker, Stefanie, Interim Head Librn, Consortium of Popular Culture Collections in the Midwest, c/o Browne Popular Culture Library, Bowling Green State University, Bowling Green, OH, 43403-0600. Tel: 419-372-7893. p. 2772

Dennis, Jill A, Libr Dir, Dally Memorial Library, 37252 Mound St, Sardis, OH, 43946. Tel: 740-483-1288. p. 1819

Dennis, Lawrence W, Dr, Dean, Col of Communication & Info, Florida State University, College of Communication & Information, 142 Collegiate Loop, Tallahassee, FL, 32306-2100. Tel: 850-644-8741. p. 2783

Dennis, Michelle, Head, Access Serv, Hedberg Public Library, 316 S Main St, Janesville, WI, 53545. Tel: 608-758-6610. p. 2443

Dennis, Nancy, Res & Instruction Librn, Salem State University, 352 Lafayette St, Salem, MA, 01970-5353. Tel: 978-542-6218. p. 1051

Dennis, Pam, Dean of Libr, Gardner-Webb University, 110 S Main St, Boiling Springs, NC, 28017. Tel: 704-406-4298. p. 1674

Dennis, Ranell, Ch, Rock Island Public Library, 401 19th St, Rock Island, IL, 61201. Tel: 309-732-7304. p. 641

Dennis, Ryan, Chief Curator, Dir, Mississippi Museum of Art, 380 S Lamar St, Jackson, MS, 39201. Tel: 601-960-1515. p. 1223

Dennis, Stephanie, Dir, Carmi Public Library, 103 Slocumb St, Carmi, IL, 62821. Tel: 618-382-5277. p. 549

Dennis, Teresa, Dir, Middletown Fall Creek Library, 780 High St, Middletown, IN, 47356-1399. Tel: 765-354-4071. p. 706

Dennison, Anne, Librn, Perpich Center for Arts Education, 6125 Olson Memorial Hwy, Golden Valley, MN, 55422. Tel: 763-279-4170. p. 1176

Dennison, Dave, Mgr, Columbus Metropolitan Library, Reynoldsburg Branch, 1402 Brice Rd, Reynoldsburg, OH, 43068. p. 1773

Dennison, Deborah, Head, Cat, Case Western Reserve University, School of Law Library, 11075 East Blvd, Cleveland, OH, 44106-7148. Tel: 216-368-6040. p. 1766

Dennison, Donna, Hist Coll Librn, Shelby County Public Library, 57 W Broadway St, Shelbyville, IN, 46176. Tel: 317-398-7121, 317-835-2653. p. 718

Dennison, Mary, Librn, Rochester Community & Technical College, 851 30 Ave SE, Rochester, MN, 55904. Tel: 507-285-7233. p. 1194

Dennison, Staci, Chief Develop Officer, Public Library of Cincinnati & Hamilton County, 800 Vine St, Cincinnati, OH, 45202-2009. Tel: 513-369-4595. p. 1761

Denniston, Amy, Sr Res Librn, Reed Smith LLP, 1301 K St NW, Ste 1100, E Tower, Washington, DC, 20005-3317. Tel: 202-414-9200. p. 374

Denniston, Donald, Pub Serv, Student Asst Coordr, Boston University Libraries, Music Library, 771 Commonwealth Ave, Boston, MA, 02215. Tel: 617-353-3705. p. 993

Denny, Mark, Instrul Serv Mgr, Tech Serv, Sacred Heart University, 5151 Park Ave, Fairfield, CT, 06825-1000. Tel: 203-396-8278. p. 312

Denny, William, Online Learning Librn, Pennsylvania Western University - California, 250 University Ave, California, PA, 15419-1394. Tel: 724-938-4451. p. 1917

Densmore, Mari, Archivist, Skagit County Historical Museum, 501 S Fourth St, La Conner, WA, 98257. Tel: 360-466-3365. p. 2368

Denson Harrison, Aubrey, Library Contact, Haley & Aldrich Inc, Library, 465 Medford St, Ste 2200, Boston, MA, 02129. Tel: 617-886-7400. p. 995

Dent, Billie, Ad, Conrad Public Library, 114 N Main St, Conrad, IA, 50621. Tel: 641-366-2583. p. 741

Dent, Christina, Asst Dir, Emerson College, 120 Boylston St, Boston, MA, 02116-4624. Tel: 617-824-8364. p. 995

Dent, Crystal, Tech Serv Assoc, Radford University, 101 Elm Ave SE, 5th Flr, Roanoke, VA, 24013. Tel: 540-831-2272. p. 2345

Dent, Rachael, Librn, Youth & Family Serv, Chesapeake Public Library, South Norfolk Memorial, 1100 Poindexter St, Chesapeake, VA, 23324-2447. Tel: 757-926-5757. p. 2311

Dent, Valeda F, Vice Provost for Libr, Emory University Libraries, Robert W Woodruff Library, 540 Asbury Circle, Atlanta, GA, 30322-2870. Tel: 404-727-6861. p. 463

Dentan, Sarah, County Librn, Stanislaus County Library, 1500 I St, Modesto, CA, 95354-1166. Tel: 209-558-7800. p. 178

Denton, A Blake, Asst Librn, Chair, Spec Coll & Archives, Ref Serv, University of Arkansas-Monticello Library, 514 University Dr, Monticello, AR, 71656. Tel: 870-460-1581. p. 105

Denton, Alta, Ch, Curry Public Library, 94341 Third St, Gold Beach, OR, 97444. Tel: 541-247-7246. p. 1880

Denton, Eileen, Youth Serv Librn, William Jeanes Memorial Library, 4051 Joshua Rd, Lafayette Hill, PA, 19444-1400. Tel: 610-828-0441, Ext 112. p. 1950

Denton, Valerie, Br Supvr, Wellington County Library, Drayton Branch, 106 Wellington St S, Drayton, ON, N0G 1P0, CANADA. Tel: 519-638-3788. p. 2641

Denton, Valerie, Br Supvr, Wellington County Library, Palmerston Branch, 265 Bell St, Palmerston, ON, N0G 2P0, CANADA. Tel: 519-343-2142. p. 2641

Denton, William, Librn, Arts & Letters Club Library, 14 Elm St, Toronto, ON, M5G 1G7, CANADA. Tel: 416-597-0223. p. 2686

Denzer, Juan, Librn, Syracuse University Libraries, Carnegie Library, Carnegie Bldg, 130 Sims Dr, Syracuse, NY, 13244. Tel: 315-443-5537. p. 1650

Deobald, Velma, Librn, Chinook Regional Library, Morse Branch, Saskatchewan 644, Morse, SK, S0H 3C0, CANADA. Tel: 306-629-3335. p. 2752

Depa, Mark, Fac Mgr, Glenview Public Library, 1930 Glenview Rd, Glenview, IL, 60025. Tel: 847-729-7500. p. 594

DePalma, Mariel, Head, YA, Baldwin Public Library, 2385 Grand Ave, Baldwin, NY, 11510-3289. Tel: 516-223-6228. p. 1490

DeParma, Mary Jane, Br Coordr, Carnegie Library of McKeesport, White Oak Branch, McAllister Lodge, 169 Victoria Dr, White Oak, PA, 15131. Tel: 412-678-2002. p. 1959

DePatis, Jodie, Dir, Bradley Public Library District, 296 N Fulton Ave, Bradley, IL, 60915. Tel: 815-932-6245. p. 544

Depelteau, Lorraine, Admin Officer, Cegep Regional de Lanaudiere a Joliette, 20, rue Saint-Charles-Borromee Sud, Joliette, QC, J6E 4T1, CANADA. Tel: 450-759-1661. p. 2713

Depineda, Chris, Instruction Librn, Midwestern State University, 3410 Taft Blvd, Wichita Falls, TX, 76308-2099. Tel: 940-397-4172. p. 2257

Depkin, Claudia, Dir, Haverstraw King's Daughters Public Library, 10 W Ramapo Rd, Garnerville, NY, 10923. Tel: 845-786-3800. p. 1537

Depkin, Claudia, Dir, Haverstraw King's Daughters Public Library, Village Branch, 85 Main St, Haverstraw, NY, 10927. Tel: 845-429-3445. p. 1537

Depoe, Dee, Libr Mgr, Timberland Regional Library, Elma Branch, 119 N First St, Elma, WA, 98541. Tel: 360-482-3737. p. 2389

DePollo, Alison, Acq Librn, Res Sharing Librn, East Tennessee State University, Sherrod Library, Seehorn Dr & Lake St, Johnson City, TN, 37614-0204. Tel: 423-439-6998. p. 2103

DePolt, Joanna, Dr, Lecturer, University of North Carolina at Greensboro, School of Education Bldg, Rm 446, 1300 Spring Garden St, Greensboro, NC, 27412. Tel; 336-334-3477. p. 2790

DePonceau, Barbara, Libr Dir, Wilcox Public Library, 105 Clarion St, Wilcox, PA, 15870. Tel: 814-929-5639. p. 2022

Deprey, Dave, Ch, Tomah Public Library, 716 Superior Ave, Tomah, WI, 54660. Tel: 608-374-7470. p. 2481

Deprey, Nate, Libr Dir, Stewartville Public Library, 110 Second St SE, Stewartville, MN, 55976-1306. Tel: 507-533-4902. p. 1205
DePriest, Tonya, Libr Serv Mgr, Hennepin County Library, 12601 Ridgedale Dr, Minnetonka, MN, 55305-1909. Tel: 612-543-8126. p. 1186
DePriester, Margaret, Archivist, Moraga Historical Society Archives, 1500 Saint Mary's Rd, Moraga, CA, 94556-2037. Tel: 925-377-8734. p. 180
DeProsperis, Marco, Dir, Admin Serv, University of Arkansas Libraries, 365 N McIlroy Ave, Fayetteville, AR, 72701-4002. Tel: 479-575-3079. p. 95
DeQuadros, Joanne, Chief Librn, Thorold Public Library, 14 Ormond St N, Thorold, ON, L2V 1Y8, CANADA. Tel: 905-227-2581. p. 2684
Der, Lorraine, Ch, Hamilton-Wenham Public Library, 14 Union St, South Hamilton, MA, 01982. Tel: 978-468-5577, Ext 13. p. 1055
Der Mugrdechian, Barlow, Dr, Dir, California State University, Fresno, Sahatdjian Library, Armenian Studies Program, 5245 N Backer Ave PB4, Fresno, CA, 93740-8001. Tel: 559-278-2669. p. 144
Deragon, Normand T, Pres, American-French Genealogical Society Library, 78 Earle St, Woonsocket, RI, 02895. Tel: 401-765-6141. p. 2044
Derda, Roxanne, Head, Circ, Weber State University, 3921 Central Campus Dr, Dept 2901, Ogden, UT, 84408-2901. Tel: 801-626-6546. p. 2268
Deredita, Laurie, Librn, New London Maritime Society-Custom House Maritime Museum, 150 Bank St, New London, CT, 06320. Tel: 860-447-2501. p. 329
Dereka, Yelena, ILL, Glenview Public Library, 1930 Glenview Rd, Glenview, IL, 60025. Tel: 847-729-7500. p. 594
DeRemer, Nanette, Tech Serv Librn, Cedar Crest College, 100 College Dr, Allentown, PA, 18104-6196. Tel: 610-606-4666, Ext 3387. p. 1904
Dereniowski, Shauna, Ch & Youth Librn, Middlesex County Library, 34-B Frank St, Strathroy, ON, N7G 2R4, CANADA. Tel: 519-245-8237, Ext 4027. p. 2682
Derenzy, Maureen, Dir, Otsego County Library, 700 S Otsego Ave, Gaylord, MI, 49735-1723. Tel: 989-732-5841. p. 1109
DeRespino, Doris, Librn, Veterans Memorial Library, 30 Main St, Patten, ME, 04765. Tel: 207-528-2164. p. 935
Derfler, Lisa, Info Tech, Tech Serv, Camden County Library System, 203 Laurel Rd, Voorhees, NJ, 08043. Tel: 856-772-1636, Ext 7333. p. 1450
Derksen, Jim, Libr Dir, Newman Theological College Library, 10012 84 St NW, Edmonton, AB, T6A 0B2, CANADA. Tel: 780-392-2450, p. 2537
Derksen, Neil, Sr Librn, Pierce County Library System, Summit Branch, 5107 112th St E, Tacoma, WA, 98446. Tel: 253-548-3321. p. 2387
DeRocchis, Robyn, Interim Libr Dir, Burrell College of Osteopathic Medicine, 3501 Arrowhead Dr, Las Cruces, NM, 88001. Tel: 575-674-2346. p. 1470
DeRoin, Lindee, Dir, Hominy Public Library, 121 W Main, Hominy, OK, 74035. Tel: 918-885-4486. p. 1850
DeRonne, Susan, Dir, Adult Serv, Glen Ellyn Public Library, 400 Duane St, Glen Ellyn, IL, 60137-4508. Tel: 630-469-0879. p. 593
DeRosa, Antonio, Consumer Health Librn, Cornell University Library, Samuel J Wood Library & C V Starr Biomedical Information Center, 1300 York Ave, C115, Box 67, New York, NY, 10065-4896. Tel: 646-962-5727. p. 1552
DeRosa, Robin, Dr, Dir, Libr & Learning Serv, Plymouth State University, 17 High St, Plymouth, NH, 03264. Tel: 603-535-3157. p. 1378
DeRosier, Adah, Libr Dir, Highgate Library & Community Center, 17 Mill Hill Rd, Highgate Center, VT, 05459. Tel: 802-868-3970. p. 2286
DeRousse, Kim, Dir, Jamestown City Library, 311 D Walnut St, Jamestown, KS, 66948. Tel: 785-439-6258. p. 815
DeRoy, Marc-Antoine, Gen Mgr, Societe d'histoire de la Haute-Gaspesie, 5B First Ave W, Sainte-Anne-des-Monts, QC, G4V 1B4, CANADA. Tel: 418-763-7871. p. 2734
Derr, Erica, Ref Librn, Caldwell County Public Library, 120 Hospital Ave, Lenoir, NC, 28645-4454. Tel: 828-757-1270. p. 1700
Derr, Janice, Head, Acq, Eastern Illinois University, 600 Lincoln Ave, Charleston, IL, 61920. Tel: 217-581-7555. p. 552
Derr, Jenna, Cat, Warren Library Association, 205 Market St, Warren, PA, 16365. Tel: 814-723-4650. p. 2017
Derr, Suzanne, Librn, Thaddeus Stevens College of Technology, 750 E King St, Lancaster, PA, 17602-3198. Tel: 717-396-7176. p. 1952
Derrer, Linda, ILL, Massanutten Regional Library, 174 S Main St, Harrisonburg, VA, 22801. Tel: 540-434-4475, Ext 110. p. 2324
Derrick, Holly, Electronic Res Librn, Panola College, 1109 W Panola St, Carthage, TX, 75633. Tel: 903-693-2013. p. 2154
Derrick, Marlene, Med Librn, Mercy Medical Center, 1320 Mercy Dr NW, Canton, OH, 44708. Tel: 330-489-1462. p. 1755
Derrig, Stephen, Evening/Weekend Librn, Flagler College, 44 Sevilla St, Saint Augustine, FL, 32084-4302. Tel: 904-819-6206. p. 439
Derrington, Amy, Libr Dir, Singletary Memorial Library, 207 E Sixth St, Rusk, TX, 75785. Tel: 903-683-5916. p. 2235
Derrivan, Kevin, Col Librn, Bay State College Library, 31 Saint James, 2nd Flr, Boston, MA, 02116. Tel: 617-217-9449. p. 990
Derrow, Ginger, Health Sci Librn, Mercy College of Ohio Library, 2221 Madison Ave, Toledo, OH, 43604. Tel: 419-251-1327. p. 1824
Derry, Sebastian, Asst Dean, Pub Serv, Seton Hall University Libraries, Walsh Library Bldg, 400 S Orange Ave, South Orange, NJ, 07079. Tel: 973-761-2058. p. 1443
Derry, Sheryl, Operations Mgr, McMaster University Library, Health Sciences Library, 1280 Main St W, Hamilton, ON, L8S 4K1, CANADA. Tel: 905-525-9140, Ext 22320. p. 2647
Dery, Alain, Mr, Mgr, Centre de Sante et de Services Sociaux Richelieu-Yamaska, 2750 boul Laframboise, Saint-Hyacinthe, QC, J2S 4Y8, CANADA. Tel: 450-771-3333, Ext 793242. p. 2735
Dery, Sarah, Dir, Libr & Res Serv, New England Historic Genealogical Society Library, 99-101 Newbury St, Boston, MA, 02116-3007. Tel: 617-226-1233. p. 998
Derylak, Deb, Sr Librn, Pierce County Library System, Lakewood Branch, 10202 Gravelly Lake Dr SW, Lakewood, WA, 98499. Tel: 253-548-3302. p. 2386
Derylak, Deborah, Learning Res Ctr Coordr, Clover Park Technical College Library, 4500 Steilacoom Blvd SW, Bldg 15, Lakewood, WA, 98499-4098. Tel: 253-589-5544. p. 2368
Desai, Kalpana, Dir, Saint John's Episcopal Hospital-South Shore Division, 327 Beach 19th St, Far Rockaway, NY, 11691. Tel: 718-869-7699. p. 1532
Desai, Parinda, Libr Dir, Demarest Free Public Library, 90 Hardenburgh Ave, Demarest, NJ, 07627. Tel: 201-768-8714. p. 1398
Desantis, Melissa, Ch, Collingswood Public Library, 771 Haddon Ave, Collingswood, NJ, 08108. Tel: 856-858-0649. p. 1397
Desanto, Kristen, Mgr, Children's Hospital Colorado, Clinical & Research Library, 13123 E 16th Ave, B180, Aurora, CO, 80045. Tel: 720-777-6400. p. 273
DeSart, Mel, Head, Eng Libr, University of Washington Libraries, Engineering Library, Engineering Library Bldg, Box 352170, Seattle, WA, 98195-2170. Tel: 206-685-8369. p. 2381
DeSart, Mel, Head of Libr, University of Washington Libraries, Mathematics Research Library, Padelford Hall C-306, Box 354350, Seattle, WA, 98195-4350. Tel: 206-543-7296. p. 2382
Deschampe, Anna, Pub Info Officer, US National Park Service, 170 Mile Creek Rd, Grand Portage, MN, 55605. Tel: 218-475-0123. p. 1177
Deschatelets, Mary, Chief Exec Officer, Terrace Bay Public Library, 13 Selkirk Ave, Terrace Bay, ON, P0T 2W0, CANADA. Tel: 807-825-3315, Ext 234. p. 2684
Deschene-Warren, Michelle, Head, Youth Serv, Peabody Institute Library, 15 Sylvan St, Danvers, MA, 01923. Tel: 978-774-0554. p. 1013
DeSear, Courtney, Acq, Supvr, Coll Develop, Manatee County Public Library System, 1301 Barcarrota Blvd W, Bradenton, FL, 34205-7522. Tel: 941-748-5555, Ext 6333. p. 386
DeSersa, Dela, Libr Dir, Rushville Public Library, 207 Sprague St, Rushville, NE, 69360. Tel: 308-327-2740. p. 1334
Deshaies, Michele, Libr Coord, Cegep de Chicoutimi Bibliotheque, 534, rue Jacques-Cartier, Est, Chicoutimi, QC, G7H 1Z6, CANADA. Tel: 418-549-9520, Ext 2229. p. 2711
Desharnais, Judith, Coordr, Laboratoire de Sciences Judiciaires et de Medecine Legale, Ministere de la Securite Publique Edifice Wilfrid Derome, 1701 rue Parthenais, 12th Flr, Montreal, QC, H2K 3S7, CANADA. Tel: 514-873-3301, Ext 61435. p. 2725
DeShaw, Jason, Circulation & Technical Servs Supvr, Duluth Public Library, 520 W Superior St, Duluth, MN, 55802. Tel: 218-730-4200. p. 1172
DeShazo, Tracey, Youth Serv Librn, Silver Lake Library, 203 Railroad St, Silver Lake, KS, 66539. Tel: 785-582-5141. p. 836
Desierto, Mark, Mgr, Libr & Res Serv, Davis Wright Tremaine LLP, 920 Fifth Ave, Ste 3300, Seattle, WA, 98104-1610. Tel: 206-622-3150. p. 2376
Desilets, Marie, Chef de Div, Bibliotheques de Montreal, Belleville, 10400 Ave de Belleville, Montreal-Nord, QC, H1H 4Z7, CANADA. Tel: 514-328-4000, Ext 4140. p. 2718
Desilets, Marie, Chef de Div, Bibliotheques de Montreal, Henri-Bourassa, 5400 Blvd Henri-Bourassa Est, Montreal-Nord, QC, H1G 2S9, CANADA. Tel: 514-328-4000, Ext 4125 (Adult Serv), 514-328-4000, Ext 4134 (Children's Serv). p. 2718
Desilets, Marie, Chef de Div, Bibliotheques de Montreal, Maison Culturelle et Communautaire, 12002 Blvd Rolland, Montreal-Nord, QC, H1G 3W1, CANADA. Tel: 514-328-4000, Ext 5626. p. 2719
Desilets, Marie, Chef de Div, Bibliotheques de Montreal, Yves-Ryan, 4740 rue de Charleroi, Montreal-Nord, QC, H1H 1V2, CANADA. Tel: 514-328-4000, Ext 4135 (Youth), 514-328-4000, Ext 4238 (Adult). p. 2721
Desilets, Marie, Librn Spec, Institut Universitaire de Sante Mentale de Montreal, Pavilion Bedard, 3rd Flr, Rm BE-316-34, 7401 Hochelaga St, Montreal, QC, H1N 3M5, CANADA. Tel: 514-251-4000, Ext 2332. p. 2725
deSimas, Jennifer, Libr Dir, First Church West Hartford, 12 S Main St, West Hartford, CT, 06107. Tel: 860-232-3893. p. 345
Desis, Nike, YA Librn, Old Lyme, Two Library Lane, Old Lyme, CT, 06371. Tel: 860-434-1684. p. 333
Desjardin, Beth, Librn, Fletcher Memorial Library, 257 Main St, Hampton, CT, 06247. Tel: 860-455-1086. p. 316
Desjardins, Brenda, Supvr, Libr Res, Blake, Cassels & Graydon LLP, Commerce Ct W, 199 Bay St, Ste 4000, Toronto, ON, M5L 1A9, CANADA. Tel: 416-863-2650. p. 2686
Desjardins, Brian, Exec Dir, The Hangar Flight Museum, 4629 McCall Way NE, Calgary, AB, T2E 8A5, CANADA. Tel: 403-250-3752. p. 2528

Desjardins, Llia, Reader Advisor, Supvr, Talking Bk, Staunton Public Library, Talking Book Center, One Churchville Ave, Staunton, VA, 24401-3229. Tel: 540-885-6215. p. 2347

Deskins, Dreama, Coll & Tech Serv Mgr, Johnston Public Library, 6700 Merle Hay Rd, Johnston, IA, 50131-0327. Tel: 515-278-5233. p. 762

Desmarais, Fellisha, Ad, Fall River Public Library, 104 N Main St, Fall River, MA, 02720. Tel: 508-324-2700. p. 1018

DesMarais, Janis, Visual Literacy & Arts Librn, College of the Holy Cross, One College St, Worcester, MA, 01610. Tel: 508-793-2453. p. 1072

Desmareis, Maryanne, Dir, Harwich Port Library Association, 49 Lower Bank St, Harwich Port, MA, 02646. Tel: 508-432-3320. p. 1023

DeSmet, Carol, Libr Tech, Southwest Minnesota State University Library, 1501 State St, Marshall, MN, 56258. Tel: 507-537-6158. p. 1182

Desmond, Tammy, Prog Mgr, Red River College Polytechnic, School of Continuing Education, E113-2055 Notre Dame Ave, Winnipeg, MB, R3H 0J9, CANADA. Tel: 204-632-2084. p. 2795

DeSoto, Abigail, Govt Doc Librn, Louisiana Tech University, Everett St at The Columns, Ruston, LA, 71272. Tel: 318-257-3555. p. 906

DeSoto McCoy, Abigail, Dir, Res & Instruction Serv, Louisiana State University, One University Pl, Shreveport, LA, 71115. Tel: 318-797-5072. p. 907

DeSousa, Christine, Dir, Palmerton Area Library Association, 402 Delaware Ave, Palmerton, PA, 18071. Tel: 610-826-3424. p. 1973

DeSouza, Lorraine, Sr Mgr, Reed Smith LLP, 1301 K St NW, Ste 1100, E Tower, Washington, DC, 20005-3317. Tel: 202-414-9200. p. 374

Despain, Anne-Marie, Dir, Libr Serv, San Mateo County Library, Library Administration, 125 Lessingia Ct, San Mateo, CA, 94402-4000. Tel: 650-312-5245. p. 235

Despenes, Janice, Dir, Rock Creek Public Library, 2988 High St, Rock Creek, OH, 44084-9703. Tel: 440-563-3340. p. 1817

Desrocher, Alice, Archivist, Info Mgr, CSA Group, 178 Rexdale Blvd, Toronto, ON, M9W 1R3, CANADA. Tel: 416-747-4059. p. 2688

Desrochers, Nadine, Assoc Prof, Universite de Montreal, 3150, rue Jean-Brillant, bur C-2004, Montreal, QC, H3T 1N8, CANADA. Tel: 514-343-6044. p. 2797

Desrosier, Sabine, Interim Libr Mgr, New York Public Library - Astor, Lenox & Tilden Foundations, Cardinal Terence Cooke - Cathedral Library, 560 Lexington Ave, (@ E 50th St, Lower Level), New York, NY, 10022-6828. Tel: 212-752-3824. p. 1594

Desrosiers, Barbara, Circ, ILL, Hondo Public Library, 2003 Ave K, Hondo, TX, 78861-2431. Tel: 830-426-5333. p. 2190

Desselles, Arlene, Research Servs Librn, Mercer University Atlanta, 3001 Mercer University Dr, Atlanta, GA, 30341. Tel: 678-547-6283. p. 465

Destefano, Melissa, Coll Develop Librn, Mission College Library, 3000 Mission College Blvd, Santa Clara, CA, 95054-1897. Tel: 408-855-5167. p. 241

DeStefano, Shauna, Asst Dir, Libr Serv, North Haven Memorial Library, 17 Elm St, North Haven, CT, 06473. Tel: 203-239-5803. p. 331

Deter, Antony, Dir, Dixon Public Library, 221 S Hennepin Ave, Dixon, IL, 61021-3093. Tel: 815-284-7261. p. 579

Detering, Sharon, Dept Head, Ref, Perry Public Library, 3753 Main St, Perry, OH, 44081-9501. Tel: 440-259-3300. p. 1815

Dethloff, Nora, ILL Coordr, University of Houston, M D Anderson Library, 114 University Libraries, Houston, TX, 77204-2000. Tel: 713-743-9800. p. 2199

Dethloff, Nora, Program Officer for Scholarly Communication, Greater Western Library Alliance, 5200 W 94th Terrace, Ste 200, Prairie Village, KS, 66027. Tel: 913-370-4422. p. 2765

Dethman, John, Access Serv, University of Missouri-Columbia, Law Library, 203 Hulston Hall, Columbia, MO, 65211-4190. Tel: 573-884-1760. p. 1244

DeThorne, Carlen, Adult Serv, Grayslake Area Public Library District, 100 Library Lane, Grayslake, IL, 60030. Tel: 847-223-5313. p. 595

Detling, Mary, Br Mgr, Mentor Public Library, Mentor-on-the-Lake, 5642 Andrews Rd, Mentor, OH, 44060. Tel: 440-257-2512. p. 1802

Detloff, Karen, Asst Br Librn, Ref Librn, Brazoria County Library System, Lake Jackson Branch, 250 Circle Way, Lake Jackson, TX, 77566. Tel: 979-415-2590. p. 2135

Detore, Della, Libr Mgr, Sullivan Free Library, Bridgeport Branch, 8979 North Rd, Bridgeport, NY, 13030. Tel: 315-633-2253. p. 1518

Detra, Jennifer, Dir, McCoy Public Library, Gratiot Annex, 5895 Main St, Gratiot, WI, 53541. Tel: 608-965-4424, Ext 5. p. 2477

Detterbeck, Kimberly, Art Librn, State University of New York, 735 Anderson Hill Rd, Purchase, NY, 10577-1400. Tel: 914-251-6406. p. 1625

Dettinger, John, Dir, User Serv, Gettysburg College, 300 N Washington St, Gettysburg, PA, 17325. Tel: 717-337-6893. p. 1935

Dettlaff, Christine, Dir, Redlands Community College, 1300 S Country Club Rd, El Reno, OK, 73036. Tel: 405-422-1254. p. 1847

Dettling, Lisa, Ch, Rye Free Reading Room, 1061 Boston Post Rd, Rye, NY, 10580. Tel: 914-231-3162. p. 1634

Dettmer, Amy, Asst Dir, Grand Rapids Area Library, 140 NE Second St, Grand Rapids, MN, 55744. Tel: 218-327-8821. p. 1177

Dettmer, Genevieve, Supv Librn, Pierce County Library System, Milton/Edgewood Branch, 900 Meridian Ave E, Ste 29, Milton, WA, 98354. Tel: 253-548-3325. p. 2386

Dettra, Regina, Librn, Arkansas School for the Deaf Library, 2400 W Markham St, Little Rock, AR, 72205. Tel: 501-324-9515. p. 100

Detweiler, Brian, Assoc Dir, University at Buffalo Libraries-State University of New York, Charles B Sears Law Library, John Lord O'Brian Hall, 211 Mary Talbert Way, Buffalo, NY, 14260-1110. Tel: 716-645-2384. p. 1511

Detwiler, Sam, Libr Asst, Otterbein University, 138 W Main St, Westerville, OH, 43081. Tel: 614-823-1799. p. 1830

Deuble, Amy, Head, Tech Serv, Marion Public Library, 445 E Church St, Marion, OH, 43302-4290. Tel: 740-387-0992. p. 1799

Deuell, Jennifer, Br Mgr, Richmond Public Library, Hull Street, 1400 Hull St, Richmond, VA, 23224. Tel: 804-646-8699. p. 2342

Deuink, Amy, Head Librn, Pennsylvania State University, 100 University Dr, Monaca, PA, 15061. Tel: 724-773-3790. p. 1964

Deuink, Amy, Head Librn, Penn State Shenango, 177 Vine Ave, Sharon, PA, 16146. Tel: 724-983-2876. p. 2006

Deutch, Miriam, Assoc Librn, Access Serv, Brooklyn College Library, 2900 Bedford Ave, Brooklyn, NY, 11210. Tel: 718-951-5221. p. 1501

Deutsch, Dan, Exec Dir, Temple Israel Library, 477 Longwood Ave, Boston, MA, 02215. Tel: 617-566-3960. p. 1000

Deutsch, Erna, Asst Youth Librn, Brownell Library, Six Lincoln St, Essex Junction, VT, 05452-3154. Tel: 802-878-6955. p. 2284

Deutsch, Helen, Dir, University of California Los Angeles Library, William Andrews Clark Memorial Library, 2520 Cimarron St, Los Angeles, CA, 90018. Tel: 310-794-5155. p. 169

Deutsch, Molly, ILL Coordr, Tech Serv Librn, Helen Kate Furness Free Library, 100 N Providence Rd, Wallingford, PA, 19086. Tel: 610-566-9331. p. 2017

Devaney, Bob, VPres, Wallingford Historical Society Inc, Library, Samuel Parsons House, 180 S Main St, Wallingford, CT, 06492. Tel: 203-294-1996. p. 342

DeVault, Jennifer, Dir of Libr Operations, Kent District Library, Kentwood Branch, 4950 Breton SE, Kentwood, MI, 49508. p. 1094

DeVault, Nelly, Circ Mgr, Alexandria-Monroe Public Library, 117 E Church St, Alexandria, IN, 46001-2005. Tel: 765-724-2196. p. 667

deVeer, Cathy, Br Librn, Crane Thomas Public Library, North Quincy Branch, 381 Hancock St, Quincy, MA, 02171. Tel: 617-376-1320, 617-376-1321. p. 1048

Dever, Ann Marie, Ch & Youth Librn, Pocono Mountain Public Library, Coolbaugh Township Municipal Ctr, 5500 Municipal Dr, Tobyhanna, PA, 18466. Tel: 570-894-8860. p. 2013

Dever, Matt, Librn, Maine Department of Corrections, 1202 Dover Rd, Charleston, ME, 04422. Tel: 207-285-0876. p. 921

Dever, Matthew, Librn, Mountain View Correctional Facility Library, 1182 Dover Rd, Charleston, ME, 04422. Tel: 207-285-0880. p. 921

Dever, Matthew, Librn, Maine Department of Corrections, 675 Westbrook St, South Portland, ME, 04106. Tel: 207-822-2679. p. 941

Dever, Wannangwa, Tech Serv Librn, Polk County Public Library, 1289 W Mills St, Columbus, NC, 28722. Tel: 828-894-8721. p. 1682

Devereux, Chricinda, Librn, Veteran Municipal Library, 201 Lucknow St, Veteran, AB, T0C 2S0, CANADA. Tel: 403-575-3915. p. 2558

Devereux, Saint Jean, Technical Services Lead, Shoreline Community College, 16101 Greenwood Ave N, Shoreline, WA, 98133-5696. Tel: 206-533-2548. p. 2383

DeVerger, Melissa, AV Librn, Quincy Public Library, 526 Jersey St, Quincy, IL, 62301-3996. Tel: 217-223-1309, Ext 205. p. 637

Devi, Sonam, Br Mgr, San Bernardino County Library, Mentone Senior Center & Library, 1331 Opal Ave, Mentone, CA, 92359. Tel: 909-794-0327. p. 213

Devilbliss, Spencer, Syst Librn, Westminster College, 1840 S 1300 East, Salt Lake City, UT, 84105-3697. Tel: 801-832-2250. p. 2273

Devillier, Audrey, Cat, Tech Serv Adminr, Iberville Parish Library, 24605 J Gerald Berret Blvd, Plaquemine, LA, 70764. Tel: 225-687-2520, 225-687-4397. p. 906

Devine, Ana, Division Chief, Community Servs, Gail Borden Public Library District, 270 N Grove Ave, Elgin, IL, 60120-5596. Tel: 847-931-2091. p. 583

Devine, Maureen, Libr Asst, Hillview Free Library, 3717 Lake Shore Dr, Diamond Point, NY, 12824. Tel: 518-668-3012. p. 1525

Devine, Megan, Librn, State Education Resource Center Library, 175 Union St, Waterbury, CT, 06706. Tel: 860-632-1485. p. 344

Devine Mejia, Jane, Chief Librn, Vancouver Art Gallery Library, 750 Hornby St, 2nd Flr, Vancouver, BC, V6Z 2H7, CANADA. Tel: 604-662-4709. p. 2580

Devine, Noel, Mgr Fac, Rockford Public Library, 214 N Church St, Rockford, IL, 61101-1023. Tel: 815-965-7606. p. 642

DeVito, Paula, Youth Serv, East Meadow Public Library, 1886 Front St, East Meadow, NY, 11554-1705. Tel: 516-794-2570. p. 1528

Devlin, Fran, Br Mgr, Calaveras County Library, Arnold Branch, 1065 Blagen Rd, Arnold, CA, 95223. Tel: 209-795-1009. p. 211

Devlin, Krista, Youth Librn, Clarendon Hills Public Library, Seven N Prospect Ave, Clarendon Hills, IL, 60514. Tel: 630-323-8188. p. 572

Devlin, Linda, Dir, Camden County Library System, 203 Laurel Rd, Voorhees, NJ, 08043. Tel: 856-772-1636, Ext 7344. p. 1450

DeVoe, Kate, Head, Circ Serv, Tompkins County Public Library, 101 E Green St, Ithaca, NY, 14850-5613. Tel: 607-272-4557, Ext 277. p. 1553

Devoid, Melanie, Library Contact, Shelburne Public Library, 74 Village Rd, Shelburne, NH, 03581. Tel: 603-252-1851. p. 1381

DeVooght, Amy, Circ Mgr, Hendrix College, 1600 Washington Ave, Conway, AR, 72032. Tel: 501-450-1303. p. 92

Devos, Dorrene, Cat Librn, University of North Dakota, Thormodsgard Law Library, 215 Centennial Dr, Grand Forks, ND, 58202. Tel: 701-777-2204. p. 1734

DeVoss-Coca, Carissa, Exec Dir, Dodge City Public Library, 1001 N Second Ave, Dodge City, KS, 67801. Tel: 620-225-0248. p. 804

Devou, Darcel, Circ Mgr, Gray Public Library, Five Hancock St, Gray, ME, 04039. Tel: 207-657-4110. p. 926

Devoy, Diane H, Adult Serv, Waynesboro Public Library, 600 S Wayne Ave, Waynesboro, VA, 22980. Tel: 540-942-6746. p. 2352

DeVries, Cindy, Asst Dir, Gaylord Public Library, 428 Main Ave, Gaylord, MN, 55334. Tel: 507-237-2280. p. 1176

DeVries, Diane, Asst Dir, Otsego District Public Library, 401 Dix St, Otsego, MI, 49078. Tel: 269-694-9690. p. 1139

DeVries, Janet, Dir, Lime Springs Public Library, 112 W Main St, Lime Springs, IA, 52155. Tel: 563-566-2207. p. 765

Devries, Jeannette, Libr Support Serv Asst, Stormont, Dundas & Glengarry County Library, Iroquois Branch, One Dundas St & Elizabeth St, Iroquois, ON, K0E 1K0, CANADA. Tel: 613-652-4377. p. 2638

Devries, Michael, Head, Res, Beloit Public Library, 605 Eclipse Blvd, Beloit, WI, 53511. Tel: 608-364-2909. p. 2423

DeVries, Michele, Cataloger, Tech Serv, Mitchell Public Library, 221 N Duff St, Mitchell, SD, 57301. Tel: 605-995-8480. p. 2079

DeVries, Sara, Commun Relations Mgr, Herrick District Library, 300 S River Ave, Holland, MI, 49423. Tel: 616-355-3728. p. 1115

deVries, Susann, Dean, Univ Libr, Western Kentucky University Libraries, Helm-Cravens Library Complex, 1906 College Heights Blvd, No 11067, Bowling Green, KY, 42101-1067. Tel: 270-745-5055. p. 849

DeVries, Tammy, Librn, Dodge Correctional Institution Library, One W Lincoln St, Waupun, WI, 53963. Tel: 920-324-5577, Ext 6570. p. 2485

DeVries, Tiffany, Br Mgr, Fort Smith Public Library, Miller, 8701 S 28th St, Fort Smith, AR, 72908. Tel: 479-646-3945. p. 96

DeVrou, Chase, IT Spec, Mead Public Library, 710 N Eight St, Sheboygan, WI, 53081-4563. Tel: 920-459-3400, Ext 2042. p. 2476

Dew, Patricia, Libr Dir, Brunswick County Library, 109 W Moore St, Southport, NC, 28461. Tel: 910-457-6237. p. 1716

Dew, Patricia, Supv Librn, New Hanover County Public Library, Pine Valley, 3802 S College Rd, Wilmington, NC, 28412. Tel: 910-798-6328. p. 1723

Dew, Shannon, Dir, Online Library Servs, Florida State College at Jacksonville, Deerwood Center Library, 9911 Old Baymeadows Rd, Jacksonville, FL, 32256. Tel: 904-997-2562. p. 411

DeWaay, SD, Ms, Dept Chair, Librn, Clackamas Community College Library, 19600 Molalla Ave, Oregon City, OR, 97045. Tel: 503-594-6330. p. 1889

DeWall, Kim, Managing Librn, Tech Serv, Falmouth Public Library, 300 Main St, Falmouth, MA, 02540. Tel: 508-457-2555. p. 1018

DeWall, Lola, Dir, Pocahontas Public Library, 14 Second Ave NW, Pocahontas, IA, 50574. Tel: 712-335-4471. p. 777

DeWalt, Mary, Dir, Ada Community Library, 10664 W Victory Rd, Boise, ID, 83709. Tel: 208-362-0181. p. 516

Dewar, A, Librn, North Carolina Department of Adult Correction, 2821 NC Hwy 903, Maury, NC, 28554. Tel: 252-747-8101, Ext 2186. p. 1703

Dewberry, Angela, Ch Serv, Millbrook Public Library, 3650 Grandview Rd, Millbrook, AL, 36054. Tel: 334-285-6688, Ext 102. p. 25

DeWeese, Abigail, Acq Mgr, Principia College, One Maybeck Pl, Elsah, IL, 62028-9703. Tel: 618-374-5235. p. 585

DeWeese, June L, Head, Access Serv, University of Missouri-Columbia, Elmer Ellis Library, 104 Ellis Library, Columbia, MO, 65201-5149. Tel: 573-882-7315. p. 1243

Dewey, Barbara I, Dean of Univ Libr & Scholarly Communications, Pennsylvania State University Libraries, 510 Paterno Library, University Park, PA, 16802. Tel: 814-865-0401. p. 2015

Dewey Eke, Janet, Ref Librn, University of Maryland-Eastern Shore, 11868 Academic Oval, Princess Anne, MD, 21853. Tel: 410-651-7540. p. 973

Dewey, Laura, Tech Serv Supvr, Oregon Public Library, 256 Brook St, Oregon, WI, 53575. Tel: 608-835-3656. p. 2467

Dewey, Nadine, Librn, Trenton Public Library, 406 Main St, Trenton, NE, 69044. Tel: 308-334-5413. p. 1338

Dewey, Tom, Librn, Jefferson National Expansion Memorial Library, 815 Olive St, Saint Louis, MO, 63101. Tel: 314-241-1236, 314-241-1244. p. 1271

Dewing, Roberta, Dir, Kentland-Jefferson Township Public Library, 201 E Graham St, Kentland, IN, 47951-1233. Tel: 219-474-5044. p. 698

DeWinter, Marietta, Assoc Dir, Tech Serv, Barry University, 11300 NE Second Ave, Miami Shores, FL, 33161-6695. Tel: 305-899-4813. p. 426

DeWitt, Adrienne, Ref Librn, Campbell University, Norman Adrian Wiggins School of Law Library, 225 Hillsborough St, Ste 203H, Raleigh, NC, 27603. Tel: 919-865-5869. p. 1676

DeWitt, April, Br Mgr, Keyser-Mineral County Public Library, Fort Ashby Public, 57 President St, Fort Ashby, WV, 26719. Tel: 304-298-4493. p. 2406

DeWitt, Ashley, Coordr, Lecturer, University of Kentucky, 320 Little Library Bldg, Lexington, KY, 40506-0224. Tel: 859-257-8876. p. 2785

DeWitt, Cathy, Ch, Georgetown Peabody Library, Two Maple St, Georgetown, MA, 01833. Tel: 978-352-5728. p. 1020

DeWitt, Dixie D, Financial & Bus Serv Mgr, Ball State University Libraries, 2000 W University Ave, Muncie, IN, 47306-1099. Tel: 765-285-5277. p. 708

DeWitt, Gloria, Librn, Sunshine City Library, 207 Kansas St, Prairie View, KS, 67664. Tel: 785-973-2265. p. 832

DeWitt, Karen, Dir, North Carolina State University Libraries, Harrye B Lyons Design Library, 209 Brooks Hall, Campus Box 7701, Raleigh, NC, 27695-7701. Tel: 919-513-3860. p. 1710

DeWolfe, Barbara, Curator, University of Michigan, William L Clements Library, 909 S University Ave, Ann Arbor, MI, 48109-1190. Tel: 734-764-2347. p. 1079

Dexheimer, Kristine, Libr Dir, Powers Memorial Library, 115 Main St, Palmyra, WI, 53156. Tel: 262-495-4605. p. 2468

Dexter, Anne, Youth Serv Dir, Neligh Public Library, 710 Main St, Neligh, NE, 68756-1246. Tel: 402-887-5140. p. 1326

Dexter, Nadine, Chair, Consortium of Southern Biomedical Libraries, c/o Harriet F Ginsburg Health Sciences Library, 6850 Lake Nona Blvd, Orlando, FL, 32867. Tel: 407-266-1421. p. 2763

Dey, Anind K, Dr, Prof & Dean, University of Washington, Mary Gates Hall, Ste 370, Campus Box 352840, Seattle, WA, 98195-2840. Tel: 206-543-1794. p. 2794

Dey, Anita, Libr Dir, Saginaw Valley State University, 7400 Bay Rd, University Center, MI, 48710. Tel: 989-964-4236. p. 1155

Deyneka, Sasha, Librn, Durham Technical Community College, Northern Durham Center, 2401 Snow Hill Rd, Durham, NC, 27712. Tel: 919-536-7240. p. 1685

Deyo, Todd, Circ Supvr, Oceanside Public Library, Mission Branch, 3861 B Mission Ave, Oceanside, CA, 92058. Tel: 760-435-5633. p. 187

Deyoe, Nancy, Asst Dean, Tech Serv, Wichita State University Libraries, 1845 Fairmount, Wichita, KS, 67260-0068. Tel: 316-978-5140. p. 844

DeYoung, Joanna, Coordr, Acq, Lindenwood University Library, 209 S Kingshighway, Saint Charles, MO, 63301. Tel: 636-949-2250. p. 1268

DeYoung, Stephanie W, Circ Serv Mgr, Batavia Public Library District, Ten S Batavia Ave, Batavia, IL, 60510-2793. Tel: 630-879-1393. p. 540

Deyrup, Marta, Humanities Librn, Outreach Librn, Seton Hall University Libraries, Walsh Library Bldg, 400 S Orange Ave, South Orange, NJ, 07079. Tel: 973-275-2223. p. 1443

Dezarn, Olivia, Cat & Acq, Clay County Public Library, 211 Bridge St, Manchester, KY, 40962. Tel: 606-598-2617. p. 868

Dhanyamraju, Radha, Br Mgr, Edison Township Free Public Library, North Edison Branch, 777 Grove Ave, Edison, NJ, 08820. Tel: 732-548-3045. p. 1400

Dhawan, Amrita, Head, Info Serv, City College of the City University of New York, North Academic Ctr, 160 Convent Ave, New York, NY, 10031. Tel: 212-650-5763. p. 1581

Dhembe, Alexis, Electronic Res Librn, Lesley University, South Campus, 89 Brattle St, Cambridge, MA, 02138-2790. Tel: 617-349-8850. p. 1008

Dhondup, Tenzin, ILL, Fletcher Free Library, 235 College St, Burlington, VT, 05401. Tel: 802-865-7223. p. 2281

Dhyne, Paige, Sci & Outreach Librn, Furman University Libraries, 3300 Poinsett Hwy, Greenville, SC, 29613-4100. Tel: 864-294-2342. p. 2061

Dhyne, Paige, Sci Librn, Furman University Libraries, Sanders Science Library, Plyler Hall, 3300 Poinsett Hwy, Greenville, SC, 29613. Tel: 864-294-2342. p. 2061

Di Campo, Pierre, Actg Mgr, Agriculture & Agri-Food Canada, Tower 6, Flr 1, 1341 Baseline Rd, Ottawa, ON, K1A 0C5, CANADA. Tel: 613-773-1433. p. 2664

Di Campo, Pierre, Head, Libr & Info Serv, Canada Agriculture & Agri-Food Canada, 3600 Blvd Casavant W, Saint-Hyacinthe, QC, J2S 8E3, CANADA. Tel: 450-768-9618, 450-768-9619. p. 2735

Di Filippe, Adam, Dir, Holderness Library, 866 US Rte 3, Holderness, NH, 03245. Tel: 603-968-7066. p. 1368

Di Labio, Cinzia, Systems/Technical Processing Mgmt, HEC Montreal Library, 3000, chemin de la Cote-Sainte-Catherine, Montreal, QC, H3T 2A7, CANADA. Tel: 514-340-6215. p. 2724

Di Marcantonio, Rita, Mgr, Br Serv, St Catharines Public Library, 54 Church St, St. Catharines, ON, L2R 7K2, CANADA. Tel: 905-688-6103. p. 2680

Di Mento, C J, Libr Dir, Oceanside Public Library, 330 N Coast Hwy, Oceanside, CA, 92054. Tel: 760-435-5614. p. 187

Dial, Ron, Head, Ref, United States Air Force, Air University - Muir S Fairchild Research Information Center, 600 Chennault Circle, Maxwell AFB, AL, 36112-6010. Tel: 334-953-2347. p. 25

Dialysis, Peggy, Supvr, Springfield City Library, Indian Orchard Branch, 44 Oak St, Indian Orchard, MA, 01151. Tel: 413-263-6846. p. 1056

Diamand, Luana, Ref & Instruction, Lake-Sumter State College Library, 9501 US Hwy 441, Leesburg, FL, 34788. Tel: 352-365-3563, 352-365-3590. p. 418

Diamond, Beverly, Bus Mgr, German-Masontown Public Library, 104 S Main St, Masontown, PA, 15461. Tel: 724-583-7030. p. 1958

Diamond, Helen, Div Mgr, Libr & Culture, Bibliotheque de Dollard-des-Ormeaux, 12001 Blvd de Salaberry, Dollard-des-Ormeaux, QC, H9B 2A7, CANADA. Tel: 514-684-1496, Ext 422. p. 2711

Diamond, Randy, Dir, University of Missouri-Columbia, Law Library, 203 Hulston Hall, Columbia, MO, 65211-4190. Tel: 573-882-2935. p. 1244

Diamond, Timothy R, Chief Knowledge Officer, Cleveland Public Library, 325 Superior Ave, Cleveland, OH, 44114-1271. Tel: 216-623-2832. p. 1767

Diamond, Tom, Colls Librn, Louisiana State University Libraries, 295 Middleton Library, Baton Rouge, LA, 70803. Tel: 225-578-6572. p. 884

Diamond-Ortiz, Anastasia, Dir, Lorain Public Library System, 351 Sixth St, Lorain, OH, 44052. Tel: 440-244-1192. p. 1797

Dian, Margie, Br Mgr, Washington County Public Library, Mendota Branch, 2562 Mendota Rd, Mendota, VA, 24270. Tel: 276-645-2374. p. 2301

Diana, Falk, Dir, Norwin Public Library, 100 Caruthers Ln, Irwin, PA, 15642. Tel: 724-863-4700. p. 1946

Diao, Junli, Head, Cat & Ser, York College Library, 94-20 Guy R Brewer Blvd, Jamaica, NY, 11451. Tel: 718-262-2302. p. 1556

Diaz, Autumn, Cataloger, Librn, Cranbrook Academy of Art Library, 39221 Woodward Ave, Bloomfield Hills, MI, 48304. Tel: 248-645-3363. p. 1086

Diaz, Claudia C, Co-Dir, Albion College, 602 E Cass St, Albion, MI, 49224-1879. Tel: 517-629-0386. p. 1076

Diaz, Gregory, Br Mgr, Chicago Public Library, South Chicago, 9055 S Houston Ave, Chicago, IL, 60617. Tel: 312-747-8065. p. 557

Diaz, Hernan, Exec Ed, Columbia University, Latin American & Iberian Studies, 309 Lehman Library, International Affairs Bldg, 420 W 118th St, New York, NY, 10027. Tel: 212-854-1679. p. 1583

Diaz, Jennifer, Br Adminr, Frederick County Public Libraries, Brunswick Branch, 915 N Maple Ave, Brunswick, MD, 21716. Tel: 301-600-7251. p. 966

Diaz, Jessica, Dir, Ennis Public Library, 115 W Brown St, Ennis, TX, 75119. Tel: 972-875-5360. p. 2175

Diaz, Jose, Assoc Univ Librn, Access Serv, Res Serv & User Engagement Librn, Case Western Reserve University, 11055 Euclid Ave, Cleveland, OH, 44106. Tel: 216-368-6508, p. 1766

Diaz, Karen R, Dean of Libr, West Virginia University Libraries, 1549 University Ave, Morgantown, WV, 26506. Tel: 304-293-0304. p. 2409

Diaz, Kellie, Campus Librn, Seminole Community College, 2505 Lockwood Blvd, Oviedo, FL, 32765-9189. Tel: 407-971-5051. p. 433

Diaz, Ketzie, Sr Librn, Long Beach Public Library, Michelle Obama Branch, 5870 Atlantic Ave, Long Beach, CA, 90805. Tel: 562-570-1047. p. 159

Diaz, Ketzie, Mgr, Circ & Customer Serv, Palos Verdes Library District, 701 Silver Spur Rd, Rolling Hills Estates, CA, 90274. Tel: 310-377-9584, Ext 263. p. 204

Diaz, Lisa, Info Serv, Unifor Library, 115 Gordon Baker Rd, Toronto, ON, M2H 0A8, CANADA. Tel: 416-718-8481. p. 2697

Diaz Lopez, Aura, Chief Librn, Rare Bks, University of Puerto Rico Library System, Josefina Del Toro Fulladosa Collection, Rare Books & Manuscripts, Rio Piedras Campus, Jose M Lazaro Bldg, San Juan, PR, 00931. p. 2514

Diaz Lopez, Aura, Chief Librn, University of Puerto Rico Library System, Zenobia & Juan Ramon Jimenez Room, Rio Piedras Campus, Edif Jose M Lazaro, San Juan, PR, 00931. Tel: 787-764-0000, Ext 85734. p. 2515

Diaz, Lorenia, Mgr, Monroe County Public Library, Marathon Branch, 3251 Overseas Hwy, Marathon, FL, 33050. Tel: 305-743-5156. p. 414

Diaz, Mayra, Asst Dir, Pub Serv, Frisco Public Library, 6101 Frisco Square Blvd, Frisco, TX, 75034-3000. Tel: 972-292-5669. p. 2182

Diaz, Michelle, Coll Develop, Missouri Western State University, 4525 Downs Dr, Saint Joseph, MO, 64507-2294. Tel: 816-271-4368. p. 1268

Diaz, Mino, Library Contact, Izard County Library, 1007 E Main St, Melbourne, AR, 72556. Tel: 870-368-7467. p. 104

Diaz, Nancy, Dir, Hamilton Public Library, 201 N Pecan St, Hamilton, TX, 76531. Tel: 254-386-3474. p. 2187

Diaz, Nicanor, Br Cluster Mgr, Denver Public Library, Ten W 14th Ave Pkwy, Denver, CO, 80204-2731. Tel: 720-865-1111. p. 275

Diaz, Portia, Librn, Indiana University of Pennsylvania, Northpointe Regional Campus Library, Academic Bldg, 167 Northpointe Blvd, Freeport, PA, 16229. Tel: 724-294-3300. p. 1946

Diaz, Raymond, Tech Coordr, Lehman College, City University of New York, 250 Bedford Park Blvd W, Bronx, NY, 10468. Tel: 718-960-7772. p. 1499

Diaz, Rob, Access Serv Mgr, California Baptist University, 8432 Magnolia Ave, Riverside, CA, 92504. Tel: 951-343-8490. p. 201

Diaz, Shirlee, Libr Asst, Helper City Library, 19 S Main St, Helper, UT, 84526. Tel: 435-472-5601. p. 2264

Diaz, Stephanie, Ref & Instruction Librn, Penn State Behrend, 4951 College Dr, Erie, PA, 16563-4115. Tel: 814-898-6106. p. 1932

Dibarbora, Lisa, Syst Librn, Humber College, 205 Humber College Blvd, Toronto, ON, M9W 5L7, CANADA. Tel: 416-675-6622, Ext 4692. p. 2690

DiBartolo, Tammy, Coordr, Outreach Serv, Rapides Parish Library, 411 Washington St, Alexandria, LA, 71301-8338. Tel: 318-442-2483, Ext 1906. p. 880

DiBattista, Susan, Mgr, Customer Serv, Niagara Falls Public Library, 4848 Victoria Ave, Niagara Falls, ON, L2E 4C5, CANADA. Tel: 905-356-8080. p. 2660

Dibbell, Nancy, Librn, South New Berlin Free Library, 3320 State Hwy 8, South New Berlin, NY, 13843. Tel: 607-859-2420. p. 1642

Dibble, Anna, Circ Asst, ILL Spec, Houghton University, One Willard Ave, Houghton, NY, 14744. Tel: 585-567-9613. p. 1548

Dibble, Karen, Assoc Dir, Dallas County Law Library, George Allen Courts Bldg, 600 Commerce St, Rm 760, Dallas, TX, 75202-4606. Tel: 214-653-6031. p. 2164

Dibble, Mark, Interim Libr Dir, Interim Univ Librn, Texas Lutheran University, 1000 W Court St, Seguin, TX, 78155-5978. Tel: 830-372-8109. p. 2242

DiBerardino, Donna, Head, Youth Serv, Sayville Library, 88 Greene Ave, Sayville, NY, 11782. Tel: 631-589-4440. p. 1637

DiBerardino, Melissa, Digital Access & Reference Archivist, Emerson College, 120 Boylston St, Boston, MA, 02116-4624. Tel: 617-824-8338. p. 995

DiBernardo, Debbie, Head, Circ, Haverstraw King's Daughters Public Library, 10 W Ramapo Rd, Garnerville, NY, 10923. Tel: 845-786-3800. p. 1537

DiBiase, Ben, Dir, Educ Res, Florida Historical Society, 435 Brevard Ave, Cocoa, FL, 32922. Tel: 321-690-1971, Ext 211. p. 390

DiBiase, Michael, Pres & Chief Exec Officer, Rhode Island Public Expenditure Council Library, 225 Dyer St, 2nd Flr, Providence, RI, 02903. Tel: 401-521-6320. p. 2040

DiBiase, Paula, Dir, Hope Library, 374 North Rd, Hope, RI, 02831. Tel: 401-821-7910. p. 2032

Dibiasi, Dorothy, Coll Develop Serv Mgr, Pasco County Library System, 8012 Library Rd, Hudson, FL, 34667. Tel: 727-861-3020. p. 410

DiCamillo, Michael, Cat Librn, Colls Mgr, Thomas Jefferson University-East Falls, 4201 Henry Ave, Philadelphia, PA, 19144-5497. Tel: 215-951-2842. p. 1987

DiCamillo, Mickey, Librn, Atlantic Cape Community College, 5100 Black Horse Pike, Mays Landing, NJ, 08330. Tel: 609-343-4951. p. 1417

DiCarro, Christina, Digital Serv Librn, Western Connecticut State University, 181 White St, Danbury, CT, 06810. Tel: 203-837-9100. p. 307

DiCenzo, Kelly, Circ, Warwick Public Library, 600 Sandy Lane, Warwick, RI, 02889-8298. Tel: 401-739-5440, Ext 9741. p. 2043

DiChiara-Schilling, Heather, Asst Dir, Texas State Law Library, Tom C Clark Bldg, 205 W 14th St, Rm G01, Austin, TX, 78701-1614. Tel: 512-463-1722. p. 2141

Dichter, Katy, Ref Librn, Seattle Central College, 1701 Broadway, BE Rm 2101, Seattle, WA, 98122. Tel: 206-934-4098. p. 2378

DiCicco, Linda, Libr Assoc, New Jersey State Library, Department of Environmental Protection Environmental Research Library, 432 E State St, 1st Flr, Trenton, NJ, 08608. Tel: 609-940-4139. p. 1448

Dick, Laura, Dep Chief Exec Officer, Waterloo Public Library, 35 Albert St, Waterloo, ON, N2L 5E2, CANADA. Tel: 519-886-1310, Ext 110. p. 2702

Dick, Laura, Mgr, Br, Waterloo Public Library, McCormick Branch, 500 Parkside Dr, Waterloo, ON, N2L 5J4, CANADA. Tel: 519-886-1310, Ext 213. p. 2703

Dick, Lianna, Dir, Texas State Technical College, Airline Dr, Waco, TX, 76705. Tel: 254-867-2349. p. 2254

Dickens, Cheryl S, Br Mgr, Lilly Pike Sullivan Municipal Library, 103 SE Railroad St, Enfield, NC, 27823. Tel: 252-445-5203. p. 1688

Dickens, Dani, Libr Asst, Benny Gambaiani Public Library, 104 S Cherry St, Shell Rock, IA, 50670. Tel: 319-885-4345. p. 781

Dickens, Kristie, Outreach Serv Librn, Centerville-Center Township Public Library, 126 E Main St, Centerville, IN, 47330-1206. Tel: 765-855-5223. p. 674

Dickens, Meredith, Coll Develop, Jefferson-Madison Regional Library, 201 E Market St, Charlottesville, VA, 22902-5287. Tel: 434-979-7151, Ext 6671. p. 2309

Dickenson, Makenzie, Tech Serv, Mountain Empire Community College, Robb Hall, 2nd Flr, 3441 Mountain Empire Rd, Big Stone Gap, VA, 24219. Tel: 276-523-2400, Ext 267. p. 2307

Dickers, Beatrice, Library Contact, Memorial University of Newfoundland, Labrador Institute of Northern Studies Information Centre Library, Sta B, PO Box 490, Labrador, NL, A0P 1E0, CANADA. Tel: 709-896-6210. p. 2610

Dickerson, Amy, Ch, Gallatin County Public Library, 209 W Market St, Warsaw, KY, 41095. Tel: 859-567-7323. p. 876

Dickerson, Carolyn, Librn, Grundy County-Jewett Norris Library, 1331 Main St, Trenton, MO, 64683. Tel: 660-359-3577. p. 1282

Dickerson, Connie, Head, Circ, Sylvester Memorial Wellston Public Library, 135 E Second St, Wellston, OH, 45692. Tel: 740-384-6660. p. 1829

Dickerson, Constance, Br Mgr, Cleveland Heights-University Heights Public Library, Noble Neighborhood Branch, 2800 Noble Rd, Cleveland Heights, OH, 44121-2208. Tel: 216-932-3600, Ext 721. p. 1771

Dickerson, Laura, Asst Dir, Shelter Island Public Library, 37 N Ferry Rd, Shelter Island, NY, 11964. Tel: 631-749-0042. p. 1640

Dickerson, Priscilla, Cat Librn, Atlanta Technical College, 1560 Metropolitan Pkwy SW, Atlanta, GA, 30310. Tel: 404-225-4595. p. 462

Dickerson, Shirley, Dir, Stephen F Austin State University, 1936 North St, Nacogdoches, TX, 75962. Tel: 936-468-4636. p. 2221

Dickey, Tammy, Dir, Kearny County Library, 101 E Prairie, Lakin, KS, 67860. Tel: 620-355-6674. p. 818
Dickey, Wanda D, Libr Dir, Florida College, 119 N Glen Arven Ave, Temple Terrace, FL, 33617-5578. Tel: 813-988-5131, Ext 211. p. 451
Dickie, Elaine, Dir, Barrhead Public Library, 5103 53 Ave, Barrhead, AB, T7N 1N9, CANADA. Tel: 780-674-8519. p. 2522
Dickie, Julie, Library Contact, Northwest State Correctional Facility Library, 3649 Lower Newton Rd, Swanton, VT, 05488. Tel: 802-524-6771. p. 2296
Dickinson, Amy, Asst Dir, Riviera Beach Public Library, 600 W Blue Heron Blvd, Riviera Beach, FL, 33404-4398. Tel: 561-840-0155. p. 439
Dickinson, Amy, Br Mgr, Saint Mary's County Library, 23630 Hayden Farm Lane, Leonardtown, MD, 20650. Tel: 301-475-2846, Ext 1006. p. 971
Dickinson, Linda, Head, Acq, Hunter College Libraries, East Bldg, 695 Park Ave, New York, NY, 10065. Tel: 212-772-4168. p. 1588
Dickinson, Luren, Dir, Beaumont Library District, 125 E Eighth St, Beaumont, CA, 92223-2194. Tel: 951-845-1357. p. 121
Dickinson, Sarah, Research Librn, Support Serv Librn, Harvard Library, Frances Loeb Library, Harvard Graduate School of Design, 48 Quincy St, Gund Hall, Cambridge, MA, 02138. Tel: 617-495-9163. p. 1007
Dickison, Julie, Library Contact, The Ombudsman Library, 548 York St, Fredericton, NB, E3B 3R2, CANADA. Tel: 506-453-2789. p. 2601
Dickman, Alex, Br Supvr, Gaston County Public Library, Ferguson Branch, Erwin Ctr, 913 N Pryor St, Gastonia, NC, 28052. Tel: 704-868-8046. p. 1690
Dickman, Bonita, Automation Syst Librn, Head, Electronic Res, Edgewood College Library, 959 Edgewood College Dr, Madison, WI, 53711-1997. Tel: 608-663-3300. p. 2449
Dickman, Corinne, Managing Librn, Washoe County Library System, Sparks Library, 1125 12th St, Sparks, NV, 89431. Tel: 775-352-3200. p. 1351
Dickman, Ellen, Dir, Logan University/College of Chiropractic Library, 1851 Schoettler Rd, Chesterfield, MO, 63006. Tel: 636-230-1878. p. 1242
Dickman, Krista, Librn, Mercer County Law Library, Court House, Rm 206, 101 N Main St, Celina, OH, 45822. Tel: 419-584-2572. p. 1757
Dickow, Ben, Dir, Downey City Library, 11121 Brookshire Ave, Caller Box 7015, Downey, CA, 90241. Tel: 562-904-7360. p. 138
Dickson, Andrea, Dir, Wixom Public Library, 49015 Pontiac Trail, Wixom, MI, 48393-2567. Tel: 248-624-2512. p. 1160
Dickson, Jenny, Br Librn, Laurentian Hills Public Library, Chalk River Branch, 15 Main St, Chalk River, ON, K0J 1J0, CANADA. Tel: 613-589-2966. p. 2638
Dickson, Kelly, Govt Doc Librn, Legislative Library of New Brunswick, Legislative Assembly Bldg, Centre Block, 706 Queen St, Fredericton, NB, E3B 5H1, CANADA. Tel: 506-453-2338. p. 2601
Dickson, Kelly, Libr Tech, Natural Resources Canada Library, Hugh John Flemming Forestry Ctr, 1350 Regent St S, Rm 1-112, Fredericton, NB, E3B 5P7, CANADA. Tel: 506-452-3541. p. 2601
Didham, Reg, Acq Librn, Cat Librn, ILL Librn, Berklee College of Music Library, 150 Massachusetts Ave, Boston, MA, 02115. Tel: 617-747-2258. p. 990
Didham, Reginald A, Acq, Cat, The Boston Conservatory, Eight Fenway, 2nd Flr, Boston, MA, 02215-4099. Tel: 617-912-9131. p. 991
Didier, Nikki, Circ, Black Hills State University, 1200 University St, Unit 9676, Spearfish, SD, 57799-9676. Tel: 605-642-6250. p. 2083
DiDonato, James A, Exec Dir, Round Lake Area Public Library District, 906 Hart Rd, Round Lake, IL, 60073. Tel: 847-546-7060, Ext 127. p. 643
Didriksson, Sonia, Sr Ref & Instruction Librn, Suffolk University, 73 Tremont St, 2nd Flr, Boston, MA, 02108. Tel: 617-573-8535. p. 1000
Diede, Charles, Exec Dir, Community Library of DeWitt & Jamesville, 5110 Jamesville Rd, DeWitt, NY, 13078. Tel: 315-446-3578. p. 1525
Diede, Charles, Adminr, Libr Operations, Onondaga County Public Libraries, The Galleries of Syracuse, 447 S Salina St, Syracuse, NY, 13202-2494. Tel: 315-435-1900. p. 1649
Dieden, Cynthia, Adult Serv Mgr, Hinsdale Public Library, 20 E Maple St, Hinsdale, IL, 60521. Tel: 630-986-1976. p. 600
Diedrich, Jenna, Libr Dir, Galena Public Library District, 601 S Bench St, Galena, IL, 61036. Tel: 815-777-0200. p. 590
Diedrich, Norah, Chief Exec Officer, Tucson Museum of Art, 140 N Main Ave, Tucson, AZ, 85701. Tel: 520-624-2333. p. 83
Dieffenbach, Heather, Exec Dir, Lexington Public Library, 140 E Main St, Lexington, KY, 40507-1376. Tel: 859-231-5533. p. 862
Diehl, Barb, Tech Serv & Info Technology Librn, Riverdale Public Library District, 208 W 144th St, Riverdale, IL, 60827-2733. Tel: 708-841-3311. p. 639
Diehl, Dawn, Librn, Community College of Allegheny County, 1750 Clairton Rd, West Mifflin, PA, 15122-3097. Tel: 412-469-6294. p. 2021
Diehl, Heather, Library Contact, Katherine Shaw Bethea Hospital, 403 E First St, Dixon, IL, 61021. Tel: 815-285-5622. p. 578
Diehl, Jenni, Librn, Yorktown Public Library, 103 W Main, Yorktown, TX, 78164. Tel: 361-564-3232. p. 2259
Diehl, Louise, Br Librn, Wapiti Regional Library, Blaine Lake Public Library, CNR Sta, Blaine Lake, SK, S0J 0J0, CANADA. Tel: 306-497-3130. p. 2745
Diehl, Marisa, Info Literacy Librn, Pierce College Library, 6201 Winnetka Ave, Woodland Hills, CA, 91371. Tel: 818-710-4267. p. 260
Diehl, Martha, Mgr, Covington County Library System, Jane Blain Brewer Memorial, 102 S Fifth St, Mount Olive, MS, 39119. Tel: 601-797-4955. p. 1214
Diehm, Kimberly, Dir, Boulder City Library, 701 Adams Blvd, Boulder City, NV, 89005-2207. Tel: 702-293-1281. p. 1343
Diekema, Anne, Dr, Outreach Librn, Southern Utah University, 351 W University Blvd, Cedar City, UT, 84720. Tel: 435-586-5435. p. 2262
Diekman, Alyssa, Sr Librn, Lee County Library System, Riverdale Public Library, 2421 Buckingham Rd, Fort Myers, FL, 33905. Tel: 239-533-4370. p. 403
Diekmann, Florian, PhD, Head of Libr, Ohio State University LIBRARIES, Food, Agricultural & Environmental Sciences, 045 Agriculture Administration Bldg, 2120 Fyffe Rd, Columbus, OH, 43210-1066. Tel: 614-292-6125. p. 1775
DiEleuterio, Rachael, Archivist/Librn, Delaware Art Museum, 2301 Kentmere Pkwy, Wilmington, DE, 19806. Tel: 302-351-8540. p. 356
Diem, Laveta, Librn, Libr Mgr, VA Northern Indiana Healthcare Systems, 1700 E 38th St, Marion, IN, 46953. Tel: 765-674-3321. p. 705
Diemert, Susan, Tech Serv, Fairhope Public Library, 501 Fairhope Ave, Fairhope, AL, 36532. Tel: 251-928-7483. p. 16
Dienes, Susan, Exec Dir, Crete Public Library District, 1177 N Main St, Crete, IL, 60417. Tel: 708-672-8017. p. 574
Dienst, Jo, Info Literacy Librn, Alvernia University, 400 St Bernardine St, Reading, PA, 19607-1737. Tel: 610-796-8223. p. 2000
Dierckx, Karin, Ad, Champlain Library, 94 Main St E, VanKleek Hill, ON, K0B 1R0, CANADA. Tel: 613-678-2216. p. 2701
Diermier, Jamie, Head Librn, John F Kennedy University Libraries, 100 Ellinwood Way, Pleasant Hill, CA, 94523. Tel: 925-969-3100. p. 195
Diermier, Jamie, Head Librn, John F Kennedy University Libraries, Law Library, 100 Ellinwood Way, Pleasant Hill, CA, 94523-4817. Tel: 925-969-3120. p. 196
Dieterich, Gretchen, Dir, Blanchardville Public Library, 208 Mason St, Blanchardville, WI, 53506. Tel: 608-523-2055. p. 2424
Dieterle, Karen, Librn, Chinook Regional Library, Burstall Branch, 428 Martin St, Burstall, SK, S0N 0H0, CANADA. Tel: 306-679-2177. p. 2752
Dieterly, Catherine, Libr Dir, City College - Miami Library, 9250 W Flagler St, Miami, FL, 33174. Tel: 305-666-9242. p. 421
Dieterly, Catherine, Health Sci Librn, Lehigh Valley Health Network, 420 S Jackson St, Pottsville, PA, 17901. Tel: 570-621-5033. p. 1999
Dieterly, Catherine, Librn, Joseph F McCloskey School of Nursing at Lehigh Valley Hospital - Schuylkill, 700 Schuylkill Manor Rd, Pottsville, PA, 17901. Tel: 570-621-5000, 570-621-5033. p. 1999
Diethorn, Theda, Interim Dir, Fredericktown Area Public Library, 38 Water St, Fredericktown, PA, 15333. Tel: 724-377-0017. p. 1934
Dietrich, Deborah, Librn, Woodstown-Pilesgrove Public Library, 14 School Lane, Woodstown, NJ, 08098-1331. Tel: 856-769-0098. p. 1456
Dietrich, Julie D, Coordr, Libr Serv, Blessing-Rieman College of Nursing & Health Sciences, 3609 N Marx Dr, Quincy, IL, 62305. Tel: 217-228-5520, Ext 6971. p. 637
Dietrich, Lori, Dir of Develop, Lancaster Public Library, 125 N Duke St, Lancaster, PA, 17602. Tel: 717-394-2651. p. 1951
Diette, Paul, Br Coordr, Haldimand County Public Library, Dunnville Branch, 317 Chestnut St, Dunnville, ON, N1A 2H4, CANADA. p. 2639
Diette, Paul, Chief Exec Officer, Haldimand County Public Library, 317 Chestnut St, Dunnville, ON, N1A 2H4, CANADA. Tel: 289-674-0400, 905-318-5932, Ext 6111. p. 2639
Diette, Paul, Chief Exec Officer, Haldimand County Public Library, Cayuga Branch, 19 Talbot St W, Cayuga, ON, N0A 1E0, CANADA. p. 2639
Diette, Paul, Chief Exec Officer, Haldimand County Public Library, Selkirk Branch, 34 Main St W, Selkirk, ON, N0A 1P0, CANADA. p. 2639
Dietz Beyersdorf, Martha, Treas, Roger Clark Memorial Library, 40 Village Green, Pittsfield, VT, 05762. Tel: 802-746-4067. p. 2291
Dietz, Kira, Asst Dir, Spec Coll & Archives, Virginia Polytechnic Institute & State University Libraries, 560 Drillfield Dr, Blacksburg, VA, 24061. Tel: 540-231-3810. p. 2307
Dietz, Lisa, Instruction & Assessment Librn, DeSales University, 2755 Station Ave, Center Valley, PA, 18034. Tel: 610-282-1100, Ext 1443. p. 1920
Dietz, Michael, Systems Integrator II, Plainedge Public Library, 1060 Hicksville Rd, North Massapequa, NY, 11758. Tel: 516-735-4133. p. 1607
Dietz, Rick, IT Consult, California State University, Stanislaus, One University Circle, Turlock, CA, 95382. Tel: 209-667-3605. p. 253
DiFazio, Chris, Ref Librn, Free Public Library of Monroe Township, 713 Marsha Ave, Williamstown, NJ, 08094. Tel: 856-629-1212, Ext 202. p. 1455
DiFazio, Robert, Libr Dir, Dalton Free Public Library, 462 Main St, Dalton, MA, 01226. Tel: 413-684-6112. p. 1013
DiFelice, Beth, Asst Dean, Libr Dir, Arizona State University, College of Law, Arizona State University MC 9620, 111 E Taylor St, Ste 350, Phoenix, AZ, 85004. Tel: 480-965-4871. p. 69
Diffenderfer, Bridget, Librn, CAE USA, Inc Library, 4908 Tampa West Blvd, Tampa, FL, 33634. Tel: 813-885-7481, 813-887-1540. p. 448

Diffenderfer, Judy, Assoc Librn, Mgr, Res Mgt, Marist College, 3399 North Rd, Poughkeepsie, NY, 12601-1387. Tel: 845-575-3199. p. 1623
Difiore, Kristen, Supvr, East Jersey State Prison Library, 1100 Woodbridge Rd, Rahway, NJ, 07065. Tel: 732-499-5010, Ext 2695. p. 1438
Difiore, Kristen, Supvr, East Jersey State Prison Library, Law, Lock Bag R, Woodbridge Ave, Rahway, NJ, 07065. Tel: 732-499-5010, Ext 2695. p. 1438
DiFrancesco, Dominic, Community Engagement Officer, Dauphin County Library System, 101 Walnut St, Harrisburg, PA, 17101. Tel: 717-234-4961. p. 1940
DiFrancesco, Rebecca, Mgr, Ch Serv, Louisville Public Library, 700 Lincoln Ave, Louisville, OH, 44641-1474. Tel: 330-875-1696. p. 1797
DiFrancesco, Virginia, Dir, Paw Paw Public Library, 250 Moser Ave, Paw Paw, WV, 25434-9500. Tel: 304-947-7013. p. 2412
Digan, Stacey, Libr Dir, Saul Ewing LLP, 500 E Pratt St, 9th Flr, Baltimore, MD, 21202. Tel: 410-332-8832. p. 956
Digby, Todd, Chair, Information Tech, University of Florida Libraries, 1545 W University Ave, Gainesville, FL, 32611-7000. Tel: 352-273-2505. p. 407
Diggs, Jackie, Dir, Foard County Library, 110 E California St, Crowell, TX, 79227. Tel: 940-684-1250. p. 2162
Diggs, Jeannie, Librn, Riverland Community College, 1900 Eighth Ave NW, Austin, MN, 55912. Tel: 507-433-0571. p. 1164
Diggs, Valerie, Prog Coordr, Salem State University, Graduate School, 352 Lafayette St, Salem, MA, 01970. Tel: 978-542-6000, 978-542-7044. p. 2786
DiGiacomo, Daniela, Dr, Asst Prof, University of Kentucky, 320 Little Library Bldg, Lexington, KY, 40506-0224. Tel: 859-257-8876. p. 2785
DiGiacomo, Marianna, Dir, Commun Serv, Stark County District Library, 715 Market Ave N, Canton, OH, 44702. Tel: 330-458-2769. p. 1755
DiGiallonardo, Bonnie, Ref & Instruction Librn, Barry University, 11300 NE Second Ave, Miami Shores, FL, 33161-6695. Tel: 305-899-3773. p. 426
Digianantonio, DJ, Head, Ref, Head, Teen Serv, Rodman Public Library, 215 E Broadway St, Alliance, OH, 44601-2694. Tel: 330-821-2665. p. 1745
DiGilio, John, Dir, Libr Serv, Sidley Austin LLP Library, 555 W Fifth St, Ste 4000, Los Angeles, CA, 90013. Tel: 213-896-6000. p. 168
DiGiovanni, Anthony, Dir, Cataloging & Reference Services, Historical Society of Pennsylvania, 1300 Locust St, Philadelphia, PA, 19107-5699. Tel: 215-732-6200. p. 1981
DiGiulio, Emily, Libr Dir, Fairfax Community Library, 75 Hunt St, Fairfax, VT, 05454. Tel: 802-849-2420. p. 2284
DiGiustino, Elizabeth, Cataloger, Head, Tech Serv, Spec Coll Librn, Saint Vincent College & Seminary Library, 300 Fraser Purchase Rd, Latrobe, PA, 15650-2690. Tel: 724-805-2310. p. 1953
Dignan, Michael F, Dir, Paris Public Library, 37 Market Sq, South Paris, ME, 04281. Tel: 207-743-6994. p. 941
DiGregorio, Antonia, Libr Dir, State University of New York, 223 Store Hill Rd, Old Westbury, NY, 11568. Tel: 516-876-3156. p. 1610
Dike, Nnamdi, Budget Officer, Financial Serv, Kalamazoo Public Library, 315 S Rose St, Kalamazoo, MI, 49007-5264. Tel: 269-553-7856. p. 1121
Dike-Young, Ijeoma, Chief Financial Officer, Indianapolis Public Library, 2450 N Meridian St, Indianapolis, IN, 46208. Tel: 317-275-4850. p. 694
DiLandro, Daniel, Col Archivist, Head, Archives & Spec Coll, Buffalo State University of New York, 1300 Elmwood Ave, Buffalo, NY, 14222. Tel: 716-878-6308. p. 1508
Dileo, Catherine, Dir, Midland Park Memorial Library, 250 Godwin Ave, Midland Park, NJ, 07432. Tel: 201-444-2390. p. 1418
Dill, Angela, Ad, Delphi Public Library, 222 E Main St, Delphi, IN, 46923. Tel: 765-564-2929. p. 679
Dill, Debby, Dir of Libr, Howard Payne University, 1000 Fisk St, Brownwood, TX, 76801. Tel: 325-649-8602. p. 2150
Dill, Elizabeth, Dean, Univ Libr Serv, California State University, Long Beach, 1250 N Bellflower Blvd, Long Beach, CA, 90840. Tel: 562-985-2640. p. 158
Dill, Elizabeth, Dir, University of Hartford Harrison Libraries, 200 Bloomfield Ave, West Hartford, CT, 06117. Tel: 860-768-4264. p. 345
Dill, Emily A, Exec Dir, Indiana University-Purdue University, 4555 Central Ave, LC 1600, Columbus, IN, 47203. Tel: 812-314-8703. p. 676
Dill, Mike, Med Librn, Lakeland Health Care, 1234 Napier Ave, Saint Joseph, MI, 49085-2158. Tel: 269-983-8300. p. 1148
Dillane, Samantha, Br Mgr, Caledon Public Library, 150 Queen St S, Bolton, ON, L7E 1E3, CANADA. Tel: 905-857-1400, Ext 225. p. 2631
Dillard, Katie, Youth Serv Coordr, Mount Angel Public Library, 290 E Charles St, Mount Angel, OR, 97362. Tel: 503-845-6401. p. 1887
Dillard, Melissa, Librn, East Polk Public Library, 136 Main St, Ste A, Ducktown, TN, 37326. Tel: 423-496-4004. p. 2097
Dillard, Sara, Cat, Texas Christian University, 2913 Lowden St, TCU Box 298400, Fort Worth, TX, 76129. Tel: 817-257-7106. p. 2181
Dillard, Shannon, Law Libr Asst, Illinois Department of Corrections, 6665 State Rte 146E, Vienna, IL, 62995. Tel: 618-658-8331, Ext 2120. p. 657
Dillehay, Bette, Dir, Mathews Memorial Library, 251 Main St, Mathews, VA, 23109. Tel: 804-725-5747. p. 2332
Dillehunt, Tony, Mgr, Support Serv, Mission Viejo Library, 100 Civic Ctr, Mission Viejo, CA, 92691. Tel: 949-830-7100, Ext 5123. p. 177
Diller, David F, Dir, Glen Lake Community Library, 10115 W Front St, Empire, MI, 49630-9418. Tel: 231-326-5361. p. 1103
Diller, Karen R, PhD, Assoc Dean of Libr, Bellevue College, 3000 Landerholm Circle SE, Bellevue, WA, 98007. Tel: 425-564-3133. p. 2358
Dilley, Denise, Mgr, County of Los Angeles Public Library, Live Oak Library, 4153 E Live Oak Ave, Arcadia, CA, 91006-5895. Tel: 626-446-8803. p. 137
Dillinger, April, Dep Dir, Willard Library, Seven W Van Buren St, Battle Creek, MI, 49017-3009. Tel: 269-968-8166. p. 1083
Dillingham, Missy, Ch Mgr, The John P Holt Brentwood Library, 8109 Concord Rd, Brentwood, TN, 37027. Tel: 615-371-0090, Ext 8410. p. 2089
Dillon, Aimee, Br Mgr, Central Rappahannock Regional Library, Newton Branch, 22 Coles Point Rd, Hague, VA, 22469. Tel: 804-472-3820. p. 2320
Dillon, Andrew, Prof, University of Texas at Austin, 1616 Guadalupe St, Ste 5.202, Austin, TX, 78712-0390. Tel: 512-471-3821. p. 2793
Dillon, April, Dir, Hemphill County Library, 500 Main St, Canadian, TX, 79014. Tel: 806-323-5282. p. 2152
Dillon, Bernadette, Librn, Hastings Public Library, 304 Beaver St, Hastings, PA, 16646. Tel: 814-247-8231. p. 1942
Dillon, Britney K, Dir, Alvah N Belding Memorial Library, 302 E Main St, Belding, MI, 48809-1799. Tel: 616-794-1450. p. 1084
Dillon, Diana, Cataloger, Interim Dir, Sinte Gleska University Library, 1351 W Spotted Tail St, Mission, SD, 57555. Tel: 608-856-8182. p. 2079
Dillon, John, Asst Librn, Head, Tech, Saint Anselm College, 100 Saint Anselm Dr, Manchester, NH, 03102-1310. Tel: 603-641-7300. p. 1372
Dillon, Kathleen, Librn, Houston Community College - Southwest College, West Loop Center Library, 5601 West Loop S, Houston, TX, 77081-2221. Tel: 713-718-7880. p. 2195
Dillon, Mike, Cataloger, Ref Serv, Sinte Gleska University Library, 1351 W Spotted Tail St, Mission, SD, 57555. Tel: 605-856-8100, 605-856-8112. p. 2079
Dillon, Rodney, Historian, Fort Lauderdale Historical Society, 219 SW Second Ave, Fort Lauderdale, FL, 33301. Tel: 954-463-4431. p. 401
Dilts-Hill, Lynn, Mgr, Libr & Res Serv, Quarles & Brady, 411 E Wisconsin Ave, Ste 2400, Milwaukee, WI, 53202-4491. Tel: 414-277-5000. p. 2461
Dilworth, Matthew, Ref Serv Coordr, Indiana University East Campus Library, Hayes Hall, 2325 Chester Blvd, Richmond, IN, 47374. Tel: 765-973-8311. p. 715
Dimant, Tracey, Head, Operations & Budget, Massachusetts Board of Library Commissioners, 90 Canal St, Ste 500, Boston, MA, 02114. Tel: 617-725-1860. p. 996
DiMarco, Scott R, Dir, Mansfield University, Five Swan St, Mansfield, PA, 16933. Tel: 570-662-4670. p. 1957
Dimas, Aleta, Br Mgr, Sonoma County Library, Windsor Regional Library, Bldg 100, 9291 Old Redwood Hwy, Windsor, CA, 95492. Tel: 707-838-1020. p. 204
DiMassa, Michael, Dir, Yale University Library, Library Shelving Facility, 147 Leeder Hill Rd, Hamden, CT, 06518. Tel: 203-432-9140. p. 328
Dimassis, Nick, Libr Dir, Beloit Public Library, 605 Eclipse Blvd, Beloit, WI, 53511. Tel: 608-364-2917. p. 2423
DiMeo, Michelle, Dr, Libr Dir, Science History Institute Museum & Library, 315 Chestnut St, Philadelphia, PA, 19106. Tel: 215-873-8205. p. 1985
DiMichele, Donna, Libr Prog Mgr, State of Rhode Island, Department of Administration, One Capitol Hill, 2nd Flr, Providence, RI, 02908. Tel: 401-574-9303. p. 2041
Dimick, Louise, Head, Children's Servx, Addison Public Library, Four Friendship Plaza, Addison, IL, 60101. Tel: 630-543-3617. p. 535
Dimitroff, Diane, Exec Dir, Lehigh Valley Association of Independent Colleges, 1309 Main St, Bethlehem, PA, 18018. Tel: 610-625-7888. p. 2774
Dimmitt, Denise, Head, Info Serv, Kewanee Public Library District, 102 S Tremont St, Kewanee, IL, 61443. Tel: 309-852-4505. p. 605
Dimmock, Nora, Dep Univ Librn, Brown University, Ten Prospect St, Box A, Providence, RI, 02912. Tel: 401-863-2165. p. 2037
Dimond, Kathleen, Dir, Manchester District Library, 912 City Rd M-52, Manchester, MI, 48158-0540. Tel: 734-428-8045. p. 1129
DiMuzio, Michael, Youth Serv Librn, Southgate Veterans Memorial Library, 14680 Dix-Toledo Rd, Southgate, MI, 48195. Tel: 734-258-3002. p. 1152
Din, Judy, Tech Serv Mgr, United States Department of the Interior Library, 1849 C St NW, MS 1151, Washington, DC, 20240. Tel: 202-208-3402. p. 378
Dina, Yemisi, Chief Law Librn, York University Libraries, Osgoode Hall Law School Library, 92 Scholar's Walk, Keele Campus, Toronto, ON, M3J 1P3, CANADA. Tel: 416-650-8404. p. 2662
Dinallo, Antonello, Facilities Coordr, Human Res, Drexel University Libraries, Hahnemann Library, 245 N 15th St MS 449, Philadelphia, PA, 19102-1192. Tel: 215-762-7186. p. 1976
Dinan, Barb, Teen Serv Librn, Plymouth District Library, 223 S Main St, Plymouth, MI, 48170-1687. Tel: 734-453-0750, Ext 271. p. 1141
Dinan, Pamela, Admin Dir, Interlibrary Delivery Service of Pennsylvania, c/o Bucks County IU, No 22, 705 N Shady Retreat Rd, Doylestown, PA, 18901. Tel: 215-348-2940, Ext 1625. p. 2774
Dineen, Dorothy, Dir, Mexico Public Library, 3269 Main St, Mexico, NY, 13114. Tel: 315-963-3012. p. 1570

Dineiro, Matthew, Acad Librn, Music Librn, Five Towns College Library, 305 N Service Rd, Dix Hills, NY, 11746. Tel: 631-656-3187. p. 1525
Diner, Linda, ILL, Jenkintown Library, 460 York Rd, Jenkintown, PA, 19046. Tel: 215-884-0593. p. 1947
Dingel, Linda, Dir, Terril Community Library, 115 N State St, Terril, IA, 51364. Tel: 712-853-6224. p. 786
Dinges, Laurie, Asst Librn, ILL, Ness City Public Library, 113 S Iowa Ave, Ness City, KS, 67560-1992. Tel: 785-798-3415. p. 826
Dingledy, Frederick, Ref Serv, College of William & Mary in Virginia, The Wolf Law Library, 613 S Henry St, Williamsburg, VA, 23187. Tel: 757-221-3255. p. 2353
Dingley, Brenda, Dir, Coll & Access Mgt, University of Missouri-Kansas City Libraries, 800 E 51st St, Kansas City, MO, 64110. Tel: 816-235-2226. p. 1257
Dingman, Elizabeth, Ref Librn/Trainer, Gowling WLG (Canada) Library, One First Canadian Pl, 100 King St W, Ste 1600, Toronto, ON, M5X 1G5, CANADA. Tel: 416-862-5735. p. 2689
Dini, Karen, Coord, Coll Develop, Addison Public Library, Four Friendship Plaza, Addison, IL, 60101. Tel: 630-543-3617. p. 535
Dinkel, Anna, Dir, Carter Memorial Library, 405 E Huron St, Omro, WI, 54963-1405. Tel: 920-685-7016. p. 2466
Dinkins, Debora, Assoc Dean, Stetson University, 421 N Woodland Blvd, Unit 8418, DeLand, FL, 32723. Tel: 386-822-7179. p. 393
Dinkins, Julie, Mgr Digital Initiatives, Sonoma State University Library, 1801 E Cotati Ave, Rohnert Park, CA, 94928. Tel: 707-664-4077. p. 204
Dinkova-Bruun, Greti, Librn, University of Toronto Libraries, Pontifical Institute for Mediaeval Studies, St Michael's College, 113 St Joseph St, 4th Flr, Toronto, ON, M5S 1J4, CANADA. Tel: 416-926-7146. p. 2700
Dinneny, Kate, Children's/Ref Librn, Florham Park Public Library, 107 Ridgedale Ave, Florham Park, NJ, 07932. Tel: 973-377-2694. p. 1403
Dinning, Melissa, Librn, McDonald Public Library, PO Box 89, McDonald, KS, 67745-0089. Tel: 785-538-2238. p. 824
Dinsmore, Chelsea, Chair, Resource Description Servs, University of Florida Libraries, 1545 W University Ave, Gainesville, FL, 32611-7000. Tel: 352-273-0369. p. 407
Dinville, Julie, Dir, Bellevue Public Library, 1003 Lincoln Dr, Bellevue, NE, 68005. Tel: 402-293-3157. p. 1307
Dinwiddie, Janet, Librn, Elliott Lasater Maysville Public Library, 506 Williams St, Maysville, OK, 73057. Tel: 405-867-4748. p. 1852
Dion, Pascale, Circ, Institut National de la Recherche Scientifique, 490 de la Couronne, Quebec, QC, G1K 9A9, CANADA. Tel: 418-654-2577. p. 2731
Dion, Vicki, Exec Dir, Mattice-Val Cote Public Library, 189 Balmoral Ave, Mattice, ON, P0L 1T0, CANADA. Tel: 705-364-5301. p. 2657
Dionisio, Max, Dr, Actg Head, Royal Ontario Museum, 100 Queen's Park, Toronto, ON, M5S 2C6, CANADA. Tel: 416-586-5740. p. 2692
Dionne, Karen, Libr Mgr, Bibliotheque Municipale Anne-Marie-D'Amours, Centre Culturel de Trois-Pistoles, 145, rue de l'Arena, Trois-Pistoles, QC, G0L 4K0, CANADA. Tel: 418-851-2374. p. 2737
Dionne, Patrick, Dir, Bibliothèque Albert-le-Grand, Institut de pastorale des Dominicains, 2715, chemin de la Côte Ste-Catherine, Montreal, QC, H3T 1B6, CANADA. Tel: 514-731-3603, Ext 307. p. 2717
Dionne, Patrick, Librn, Institut de Formation Theologique de Montreal Bibliotheque, 2065, rue Sherbrooke Ouest, Montreal, QC, H3H 1G6, CANADA. Tel: 514-935-1169, Ext 220. p. 2725
Diorio, Geri, Asst Libr Dir, Stratford Library Association, 2203 Main St, Stratford, CT, 06615. Tel: 203-385-4160. p. 340
Diovisalvo, Dellana, Exec Dir, Tunkhannock Public Library, 220 W Tioga St, Tunkhannock, PA, 18657-6611. Tel: 570-836-1677. p. 2014
DiPadova, Sarah, Librn, Soldiers Grove Public Library, Solar Town Ctr, 102 Passive Sun Dr, Soldiers Grove, WI, 54655. Tel: 608-624-5815. p. 2478
Dipaolo, Abigail, Dir, Finance & Planning, Rutgers University Libraries, 169 College Ave, New Brunswick, NJ, 08901-1163. Tel: 848-932-5998. p. 1424
DiPaolo, Denise, Dir, Montauk Library, 871 Montauk Hwy, Montauk, NY, 11954. Tel: 631-668-3377. p. 1573
DiPaolo, Jill, Libr Dir, Lewes Public Library, 111 Adams Ave, Lewes, DE, 19958. Tel: 302-645-2733. p. 354
DiPilato, Renee, Dir, Sarasota County Library System, 1600 Ringling Blvd, 5th Flr, Sarasota, FL, 34236. Tel: 941-861-5481. p. 443
Dippel, Beth, Exec Dir, Sheboygan County Historical Research Center Library, 518 Water St, Sheboygan Falls, WI, 53085. Tel: 920-467-4667. p. 2477
Dippel, Krystina, Youth Serv Librn, Victor Farmington Library, 15 W Main, Victor, NY, 14564. Tel: 585-924-2637. p. 1657
Diptee, Jennifer, Asst Dir, Miami Dade College, Kendall Campus Library, 11011 SW 104th St, Miami, FL, 33176-3393. Tel: 305-237-0996, 305-237-2015, 305-237-2291. p. 422
Directo, Ashley, Mkt & Communications Mgr, Milton Public Library, 1010 Main St E, Milton, ON, L9T 6H7, CANADA. Tel: 905-875-2665, Ext 3295. p. 2658
Dirks, Timothy, Dir, Fargo Public Library, 102 N Third St, Fargo, ND, 58102. Tel: 701-241-1493. p. 1733
DiRusso, Richard, Coll Develop Mgr, Pima County Public Library, 101 N Stone Ave, Tucson, AZ, 85701. Tel: 520-594-5600. p. 82
DiSalvo-Harms, Phoebe, Humanities Librn, Research Servs Librn, Le Moyne College, 1419 Salt Springs Rd, Syracuse, NY, 13214. Tel: 315-445-4326. p. 1648
DiSanto, Vicki, Head, Children's Servx, Librn, Somers Library, Rte 139 & Reis Park, Somers, NY, 10589. Tel: 914-232-5717. p. 1642
Disanza, Mary, Dir, William E Dermody Free Public Library, 420 Hackensack St, Carlstadt, NJ, 07072. Tel: 201-438-8866. p. 1395
Disbro, Megan, Digital Serv Librn, Chautauqua-Cattaraugus Library System, 106 W Fifth St, Jamestown, NY, 14701. Tel: 716-484-7135, Ext 251. p. 1557
Disbro, Nancy, Dir, Andrews Dallas Township Public Library, 30 E Madison St, Andrews, IN, 46702. Tel: 260-786-3574. p. 668
Dischler, Amber, Dir, J J Hands Library, 609 Second St, Lohrville, IA, 51453. Tel: 712-465-4115. p. 766
Dischner, Sue, Br Mgr, Pines & Plains Libraries, Elbert Branch, 24489 Main St, Elbert, CO, 80106. Tel: 303-648-3533. p. 279
Dise, Justin, Digital & Archival Serv Librn, Daemen University Library, Research & Information Commons, 4380 Main St, Amherst, NY, 14226-3592. Tel: 716-839-8243. p. 1486
Disha, Kesi, Info Coordr, Canadian Environmental Law Foundation, 55 University Ave, Ste 1500, Toronto, ON, M5J 2H7, CANADA. Tel: 416-960-2284, Ext 7211. p. 2687
Dishon, Clayton D, Jr, Dep Dir, Richmond Public Library, 101 E Franklin St, Richmond, VA, 23219. Tel: 804-646-4256. p. 2341
Distance, Lynne, Ms, Br Mgr, Enoch Pratt Free Library, Southeast Anchor Library, 3601 Eastern Ave, Baltimore, MD, 21224-4109. Tel: 410-396-4401. p. 953
Distler, Larissa, Ad, Galena Public Library District, 601 S Bench St, Galena, IL, 61036. Tel: 815-777-0200. p. 590
Districh-Osiecki, Krista, Librn, Jefferson Community & Technical College, Southwest Campus Library, 1000 Community College Dr, Louisville, KY, 40272. Tel: 502-213-7222. p. 865
Ditkoff, Jennifer, Head Librn, Community College of Baltimore County, Dundalk Library, Sollers Point Rd, COMM Bldg 7200, Baltimore, MD, 21222. p. 961
Ditlow, Angie, Circ Librn, White Cloud Community Library, 1038 Wilcox Ave, White Cloud, MI, 49349. Tel: 231-689-6631. p. 1159
DiTocco, Luke, Libr Asst II, Palm Beach State College, 4200 Congress Ave, Mail Sta 17, Lake Worth, FL, 33461. Tel: 561-868-3800. p. 416
DiTomasso, Matt, Br Mgr, Mount Pleasant Public Library, 350 Bedford Rd, Pleasantville, NY, 10570. Tel: 914-769-0548. p. 1620
DiTomasso, Matt, Br Mgr, Mount Pleasant Public Library, Mount Pleasant Branch, 125 Lozza Dr, Valhalla, NY, 10595. Tel: 914-741-0276. p. 1620
Dittemore, Margaret, Librn Emeritus, Smithsonian Libraries, John Wesley Powell Library of Anthropology, Natural History Bldg, Rm 331, Tenth St & Constitution Ave NW, Washington, DC, 20560-0112. Tel: 202-633-1640. p. 376
Dittmar, Brooke, Dir, Town of Esopus Public Library, 128 Canal St, Port Ewen, NY, 12466. Tel: 845-338-5580. p. 1621
Dittmar, Dawn, Head, Teen Serv, Highland Township Public Library, 444 Beach Farm Circle, Highland, MI, 48357. Tel: 248-887-2218. p. 1115
Dittoe, Patti, Libr Mgr, Ohio State University LIBRARIES, Orton Memorial Library of Geology, 180 Orton Hall, 155 S Oval Mall, Columbus, OH, 43210. Tel: 614-292-6549. p. 1776
Dittrich, Jillian, Br Mgr, Carroll County Public Library, Taneytown Branch, Ten Grand Dr, Taneytown, MD, 21787-2421. Tel: 410-386-4510. p. 972
DiTullio, Patty, Exec Dir, Merrimack Valley Library Consortium, Four High St, Ste 175, North Andover, MA, 01845. Tel: 978-557-5409. p. 2766
Ditzler, Cindy, Univ Archivist, Northern Illinois University Libraries, 217 Normal Rd, DeKalb, IL, 60115-2828. Tel: 815-753-1094. p. 577
Ditzler, Wyatt, IT Mgr, Beloit Public Library, 605 Eclipse Blvd, Beloit, WI, 53511. Tel: 608-364-5755. p. 2423
Divack, Marcia, Adminr, Youth Serv, Atlanta-Fulton Public Library System, Kirkwood Branch, 11 Kirkwood Rd SE, Atlanta, GA, 30317. Tel: 404-613-7200. p. 461
Divack, Marcia, Asst Br Mgr, Head, Children's Servx, Atlanta-Fulton Public Library System, Ocee Branch, 5090 Abbotts Bridge Rd, Johns Creek, GA, 30005-4601. Tel: 404 613-6840, 770-360-8897. p. 461
Diver, Debbie, Libr Asst, Madison Public Library, 827 N College Ave, Huntsville, AR, 72740. Tel: 479-738-2754. p. 99
Divine, Barbara, Br Mgr, Kemper-Newton Regional Library System, Jessie Mae Everett Public Library, 306 W Broad St, Decatur, MS, 39365. Tel: 601-635-2777. p. 1234
Divis, Deborah, ILL, Ref, Nebraska Methodist College, 720 N 87th St, Omaha, NE, 68114. Tel: 402-354-7248. p. 1329
DiVittorio, M, Outreach Serv, Bellmore Memorial Library, 2288 Bedford Ave, Bellmore, NY, 11710. Tel: 516-785-2990. p. 1492
Dix, Holly, Libr Asst, Martha Canfield Memorial Free Library, 528 E Arlington Rd, Arlington, VT, 05250. Tel: 802-375-6153. p. 2277
Dix, Josephine, Libr Mgr, Lake County Library System, Minneola Schoolhouse Library, 100 S Main St, Minneola, FL, 34715. Tel: 352-432-3921, Ext 381. p. 451

Dix, Rene, Br Supvr, Birchard Public Library of Sandusky County, Woodville Branch, 101 E Main, Woodville, OH, 43469. Tel: 419-849-2744. p. 1786

Dixey, Mary, Dean, Libr Serv, Holyoke Community College Library, Donahue Bldg, 2nd Flr, 303 Homestead Ave, Holyoke, MA, 01040-1099. Tel: 413-552-2260. p. 1025

Dixon, Alison, Ch Serv, Ref (Info Servs), Washington District Library, Five Points Washington, 380 N Wilmor Rd, Washington, IL, 61571. Tel: 309-444-2241. p. 659

Dixon, Barbara, Dir, Barton Rees Pogue Memorial Library, 29 W Washington St, Upland, IN, 46989. Tel: 765-998-2971. p. 722

Dixon, Beth, Libr Asst, Fairbank Public Library, 212 E Main St, Fairbank, IA, 50629. Tel: 319-635-2487. p. 752

Dixon, Cassie, Libr Mgr, Med Librn, Cabarrus College Health Sciences Library, 920 Church St N, Concord, NC, 28025. Tel: 704-403-1798. p. 1682

Dixon, Catherine, Libr Dir, St John's College Library, 60 College Ave, Annapolis, MD, 21401. Tel: 410-626-2550. p. 951

Dixon, Celeste, Librn, US National Park Service, 1767 KS Hwy 156, Larned, KS, 67550. Tel: 620-285-6911. p. 818

Dixon, Christopher, Archives & Ref, Saint Joseph's University, Francis A Drexel Library, 5600 City Ave, Philadelphia, PA, 19131-1395. Tel: 610-660-1905. p. 1985

Dixon, Clay-Edward, Dir, Libr Serv, Graduate Theological Union Library, 2400 Ridge Rd, Berkeley, CA, 94709-1212. Tel: 510-649-2540. p. 122

Dixon, Cynthia, Librn, Southern Technical College, Tampa Campus, 3910 Riga Blvd, Tampa, FL, 33619. Tel: 813-630-4401. p. 404

Dixon, Daniela, Br Mgr, Fairfax County Public Library, Tysons-Pimmit Regional, 7584 Leesburg Pike, Falls Church, VA, 22043-2099. Tel: 703-790-8088. p. 2316

Dixon, Doreen, Electronic Rec Archivist, Drake University, 2725 University Ave, Des Moines, IA, 50311. Tel: 515-271-2933. p. 746

Dixon, Jennifer, Coll Mgt Librn, Fordham University School of Law, 150 W 62nd St, New York, NY, 10023. Tel: 212-636-6705. p. 1585

Dixon, Jennifer, Libr Mgr, Cannon Beach Library, 131 N Hemlock, Cannon Beach, OR, 97110. Tel: 503-436-1391. p. 1875

Dixon, Jill, Dean of Libr, West Chester University, 25 W Rosedale Ave, West Chester, PA, 19383. Tel: 610-436-2747. p. 2020

Dixon, Marcia, ILL, Libr Tech, Barry University, 11300 NE Second Ave, Miami Shores, FL, 33161-6695. Tel: 305-899-4050. p. 426

Dixon, Nicola, Library Contact, Troutman Pepper, 3000 Two Logan Sq, 18th & Arch Sts, Philadelphia, PA, 19103-2799. Tel: 215-981-4000. p. 1987

Dixon, Robin Miller, Br Head, NASA, Library, Bldg 21, Code 272, Greenbelt, MD, 20771. Tel: 301-286-7218. p. 967

Dixon, Rosemary, Dir, Hamer Public Library, 2450 E 2100 N, Hamer, ID, 83425. Tel: 208-662-5275. p. 521

Dixon, Sandra, Library Contact, Eastern Counties Regional Library, Canso Branch, 169 Main St, Canso, NS, B0H 1H0, CANADA. Tel: 902-366-2955. p. 2621

Dixon, Sonya, Dir, Bayard Public Library, 1112 Central Ave, Bayard, NM, 88023. Tel: 575-537-6244. p. 1463

Dixon, Steve G, Ref & Instruction Librn, SUNY Delhi, Bush Hall, 454 Delhi Dr, Delhi, NY, 13753. Tel: 607-746-4642. p. 1524

Dixon, Tiara, Br Mgr, Mid-Continent Public Library, Camden Point Branch, 401 Hardesty St, Camden Point, MO, 64018. Tel: 816-280-3384. p. 1250

Dixon, Tiara, Br Mgr, Mid-Continent Public Library, Dearborn Branch, 206 Maple Leaf Ave, Dearborn, MO, 64439. Tel: 816-450-3502. p. 1250

Dixon, Tiara, Br Mgr, Mid-Continent Public Library, Edgerton Branch, 404 Frank St, Edgerton, MO, 64444. Tel: 816-790-3569. p. 1250

Dixon, Wesley, Librn, Jones County Junior College, 900 S Court St, Ellisville, MS, 39437. Tel: 601-477-4055. p. 1216

Djokic, Mirela, Pub Serv Librn, Kwantlen Polytechnic University Library, 12666 72nd Ave, Surrey, BC, V3W 2M8, CANADA. Tel: 604-599-3389. p. 2576

Djonne, Beth, Br Mgr, San Bernardino County Library, Lewis Library & Technology Center, 8437 Sierra Ave, Fontana, CA, 92335-3892. Tel: 909-574-4500. p. 213

Djordjevic, Zorica, Librn, Hopital de L'Enfant Jesus, 1401 18e Rue, Quebec, QC, G1J 1Z4, CANADA. Tel: 418-525-4444, Ext 82132. p. 2730

Djordjevic, Zorica, Librn, Hospital du Saint-Sacrement, 1050, Chemin Sainte-Foy, Quebec, QC, G1S 4L8, CANADA. Tel: 418-525-4444, Ext 82128. p. 2731

Dlugosz, Joy, Dir of the Univ Libr, Eastern University, 1300 Eagle Rd, Saint Davids, PA, 19087-3696. Tel: 610-341-5660. p. 2002

Dmohowski, Joe, Ser Librn, Whittier College, Bonnie Bell Wardman Library, 7031 Founders Hill Rd, Whittier, CA, 90608-9984. Tel: 562-907-4246. p. 259

Doan, Georgeann, Asst Dir, Lawrenceburg Public Library District, 150 Mary St, Lawrenceburg, IN, 47025. Tel: 812-537-2775. p. 702

Doan, Janice, Dir, Canyon Area Library, 1501 Third Ave, Canyon, TX, 79015. Tel: 806-655-5015. p. 2153

Doane, Mike, Assoc Teaching Prof, University of Washington, Mary Gates Hall, Ste 370, Campus Box 352840, Seattle, WA, 98195-2840. Tel: 206-543-1794. p. 2794

Dobbins, Elizabeth, Asst Dean of Libr, Head of Research & Instruction Services, Campbell University, 113 Main St, Buies Creek, NC, 27506. Tel: 910-893-1449. p. 1676

Dobbins, Laura, Br Mgr, Montgomery-Floyd Regional Library System, Blacksburg Area Branch, 200 Miller St, Blacksburg, VA, 24060. Tel: 540-552-8246. p. 2312

Dobbins, Montie, Asst Dir, Tech Serv, Louisiana State University Health Sciences Center, 1501 Kings Hwy, Shreveport, LA, 71130. Tel: 318-675-5664. p. 908

Dobbins, Vickie, Dir, Westside Public Library, 5151 Walnut Grove Rd, Walnut Grove, AL, 35990. Tel: 205-589-6699. p. 39

Dobbins, Zhycurie, Br Mgr, Greenwood-Leflore Public Library System, Jodie Wilson Branch, 209 ½ E Martin Luther King Jr Dr, Greenwood, MS, 38930. Tel: 662-453-1761. p. 1217

Dobbs, Aaron, Scholarly Communications Librn, Shippensburg University, 1871 Old Main Dr, Shippensburg, PA, 17257. Tel: 717-477-1018. p. 2007

Dobbs, Cheryl, Dir, Greenwood Public Library, 310 S Meridian St, Greenwood, IN, 46143-3135. Tel: 317-883-4229. p. 688

Dobbs, Haylee, E-Librn, Coastal Bend College, 3800 Charco Rd, Beeville, TX, 78102. Tel: 361-354-2742. p. 2146

Dobbs, Jean, Librn, Evansville Public Library, 602 Public St, Evansville, IL, 62242. Tel: 618-853-4649. p. 587

Dobbs, Susan, Asst Dir, Anythink Libraries, 5877 E 120th Ave, Thornton, CO, 80602. Tel: 303-288-2001. p. 296

Dobda, Kathyanne, Asst Dir, Pub Serv, Cleveland State University, Michael Schwartz Library, Rhodes Tower, Ste 501, 2121 Euclid Ave, Cleveland, OH, 44115-2214. Tel: 216-875-9738. p. 1769

Dobersztyn, Paul, Pub Serv Mgr, Warrenville Public Library District, 28 W 751 Stafford Pl, Warrenville, IL, 60555. Tel: 630-393-1171. p. 659

Dobias, Dale, Dir, United Theological Seminary of the Twin Cities, 3000 Fifth St NW, New Brighton, MN, 55112-2598. Tel: 651-255-6142. p. 1190

Dobias, Dale, Dir, Minnesota Theological Library Association, Luther Seminary Library, 2375 Como Ave, Saint Paul, MN, 55108. Tel: 651-641-3447. p. 2768

Dobija, Jane, Sr Librn, Los Angeles Public Library System, Memorial Branch Library, 4625 W Olympic Blvd, Los Angeles, CA, 90019-1832. Tel: 323-938-2732. p. 164

Dobinson, Susan, Librn, First Judicial Circuit of Florida Escambia County, M C Blanchard Judicial Bldg, 190 Governmental Ctr, Pensacola, FL, 32502. Tel: 850-595-4468. p. 436

Dobra, Lisa, Librn, Youth Serv, Bethpage Public Library, 47 Powell Ave, Bethpage, NY, 11714. Tel: 516-931-3907. p. 1493

Dobrogosz, Karen, Ch Serv Librn, Avery-Mitchell-Yancey Regional Library System, 289 Burnsville School Rd, Burnsville, NC, 28714. Tel: 828-682-4476. p. 1677

Dobrovolny, Linda, Asst Dir, Tech Serv, Yankton Community Library, 515 Walnut St, Yankton, SD, 57078. Tel: 605-668-5275. p. 2086

Dobson, Guy, Dir, Tech Serv, Syst Librn, Drew University Library, 36 Madison Ave, Madison, NJ, 07940. Tel: 973-408-3486. p. 1414

Dobson, Tonya, Business Admin, Tarleton State University Library, 201 Saint Felix, Stephenville, TX, 76401. Tel: 254-968-9474. p. 2246

Docherty, Karen, Fac Chair, Libr Serv, Rio Salado College, 2323 W 14th St, Tempe, AZ, 85281. Tel: 480-517-8432. p. 79

Dockery, Crystal, Librn, Mount Carmel Library, 100 Main St, Mount Carmel, TN, 37645-9999. Tel: 423-357-4011. p. 2117

Dockery, David, III, Dr, Dir, Mississippi Department of Environmental Quality Library, 700 N State St, Jackson, MS, 39202. Tel: 601-961-5544. p. 1222

Dockery, Emory S, Jr, Dir, William O Darby Ranger Memorial Foundation Inc, 311 General Darby St, Fort Smith, AR, 72902. Tel: 479-782-3388. p. 96

Dockray, Sarah, Librn, Valencia College, Osceola Campus Library, Bldg 4, Rm 202, 1800 Denn John Lane, 6-4, Kissimmee, FL, 34744. Tel: 407-582-4156. p. 414

Dockstader, Darryll, Div Mgr, Florida Department of Transportation, Burns Bldg, 605 Suwannee St, Mail Sta 30, Tallahassee, FL, 32399. Tel: 850-414-4615. p. 446

Dockter, Sally, Asst Dir, University of North Dakota, 3051 University Ave, Stop 9000, Grand Forks, ND, 58202-9000. Tel: 701-777-2617. p. 1735

Docourneau, Emilie, Asst Map Curator, California State University, Northridge, Map Collection, University Library, Rm 26, 18111 Nordhoff St, Northridge, CA, 91330. Tel: 818-677-3465. p. 184

Doctor, Claudia, Mgr, Seminole Tribe of Florida, Willie Frank Memorial, 30901 Josie Billie Hwy, Clewiston, FL, 33440. Tel: 863-902-3200. p. 430

Doctor, David, Ref Serv, Lane Community College Library, Library-Center Bldg, 4000 E 30th Ave, Eugene, OR, 97405-0640. Tel: 541-463-5278. p. 1879

Doctor, Jenny, Dr, Head Librn, University of Cincinnati Libraries, College-Conservatory of Music, 600 Blegen Library, Cincinnati, OH, 45221. Tel: 513-556-1970. p. 1765

Docurro, Carmen, Mgr, Miami-Dade Public Library System, Miami Lakes Branch, 6699 Windmill Gate Rd, Miami Lakes, FL, 33014. Tel: 305-822-6520. p. 423

Docurro, Carmen, Mgr, Miami-Dade Public Library System, Palm Springs North Branch, 17601 NW 78th Ave, Ste 111, Hialeah, FL, 33015. Tel: 305-820-8564. p. 424

Docurro, Carmen, Mgr, Miami-Dade Public Library System, South Miami Branch, 6000 Sunset Dr, South Miami, FL, 33143. Tel: 305-667-6121. p. 424

Dodd, Anita, Access Serv, Librn, Douglas County Public Library, 301 W Webster Ave, Ava, MO, 65608. Tel: 417-683-5633. p. 1237

Dodd, Becky, Libr Dir, Wellsville City Library, 115 W Sixth St, Wellsville, KS, 66092. Tel: 785-883-2870. p. 842

Dodd, Beth, Head Librn, University of Texas Libraries, Architecture & Planning, Battle Hall 200, 302 Inner Campus Dr, S5430, Austin, TX, 78712-1413. Tel: 512-495-4620. p. 2142

Dodd Coleman, Chelsea, Dir, Bogota Public Library, 375 Larch Ave, Bogota, NJ, 07603. Tel: 201-488-7185. p. 1391

Dodd, James, Head, Tech Serv, Northeastern State University, 711 N Grand Ave, Tahlequah, OK, 74464-2333. Tel: 918-456-5511, Ext 3200. p. 1863

Dodd, Jesse, Asst Br Mgr, Chesterfield County Public Library, Bon Air, 9103 Rattlesnake Rd, Richmond, VA, 23235. Tel: 804-751-2275. p. 2312

Dodd, Sue, Archivist, Wartburg Theological Seminary, 333 Wartburg Pl, Dubuque, IA, 52003. Tel: 563-589-0320. p. 749

Dodds, Kathrin, Info Spec, Mississippi State University, Architecture, 121 Giles Hall, 889 Collegeview St, Mississippi State, MS, 39762. Tel: 662-325-2204. p. 1227

Dodge, Betty, Dir, Newport Free Library, 7390 S Main St, Newport, NY, 13416. Tel: 315-845-8533. p. 1606

Dodge, Brian, Dir, Oglala Lakota College, Wounded Knee College Center, PO Box 230, Manderson, SD, 57756. Tel: 605-867-5352. p. 2078

Dodge, Heather, Librn, Berkeley City College Library, 2050 Center St, Rm 131, Berkeley, CA, 94704. p. 121

Dodge, Lauren, Dir of Develop, Abraham Lincoln Presidential Library, 112 N Sixth St, Springfield, IL, 62701. Tel: 217-524-6358. p. 649

Dodge, Sarah, Manager, Customer Engagement, Ajax Public Library, 55 Harwood Ave S, Ajax, ON, L1S 2H8, CANADA. Tel: 905-683-4000, Ext 8802. p. 2627

Dodgson, Cathy, Sr Libr Asst, University of Wyoming Libraries, Learning Resource Center, Education Bldg 222, N 15th St & Lewis St, Laramie, WY, 82071. Tel: 307-766-2527. p. 2497

Dodin, Philippe, Head Librn, CHU Sainte-Justine Bibliothèque, 3175 Chemin de la Sainte-Catherine, Bur 5971, Montreal, QC, H3T 1C5, CANADA. Tel: 514-345-4931, Ext 4681. p. 2722

Dodington, Anne, Br Mgr, Huron County Library, Brussels Branch, 402 Turnberry St, Brussels, ON, N0G 1H0, CANADA. Tel: 519-887-6448. p. 2636

Dodington, Anne, Br Mgr, Huron County Library, Seaforth Branch, 108 Main St S, Seaforth, ON, N0K 1W0, CANADA. Tel: 519-527-1430. p. 2636

Dodson, Amy, Dir, Fox River Valley Public Library District, 555 Barrington Ave, East Dundee, IL, 60118-1496. Tel: 847-428-3661. p. 580

Dodson, Cami, Libr Dir, Sugar-Salem School Community Library, One Digger Dr, Sugar City, ID, 83448. Tel: 208-356-0271. p. 531

Dodson, Samuel, Dr, Asst Prof, University at Buffalo, The State University of New York, 534 Baldy Hall, Buffalo, NY, 14260. Tel: 716-645-2412. p. 2789

Dodson, Tom, Discovery Librn, Website Mgr, Southern Oregon University, 1250 Siskiyou Blvd, Ashland, OR, 97520. Tel: 541-552-6836. p. 1872

Doe, Douglas, Assoc Archivist, Rhode Island School of Design Library, 15 Westminster St, Providence, RI, 02903. Tel: 401-709-5922. p. 2040

Doe-Williams, Paulette, Head, Children's Servx, Willingboro Public Library, Willingboro Town Ctr, 220 Willingboro Pkwy, Willingboro, NJ, 08046. Tel: 609-877-0476, 609-877-6668. p. 1455

Doebele, Melissa, Libr Asst, University of Kansas Libraries, Wheat Law Library, Green Hall, Rm 200, 1535 W 15th St, Lawrence, KS, 66045-7608. Tel: 785-864-3025. p. 820

Doege, Marsha C, Dir, Utica Public Library, 7530 Auburn Rd, Utica, MI, 48317-5216. Tel: 586-731-4141. p. 1156

Doehrer, Zoi, Exec Dir, Rudolf Steiner Library, 351 Fairview Ave, Ste 610, Hudson, NY, 12534-1259. Tel: 518-944-7007. p. 1549

Doepp, Adrienne, Circuit Librn, Kaleida Health - Buffalo General Medical Center, Bldg D, 4th Flr, 100 High St, Buffalo, NY, 14203. Tel: 716-859-2878. p. 1509

Doerfer, Joe, Libr Asst, Interlochen Center for the Arts, Bonisteel Library - Seabury Academic Library, 4000 M-137, Interlochen, MI, 49643. Tel: 231-276-7420. p. 1118

Doerge, Janet, Br Mgr, Marin County Free Library, Novato Library, 1720 Novato Blvd, Novato, CA, 94947. Tel: 415-473-2050. p. 237

Doerhoff, Nancy, Br Mgr, Saint Louis Public Library, Machacek, 6424 Scanlan Ave, Saint Louis, MO, 63139. Tel: 314-781-2948. p. 1275

Doering, Anita T, Archives Mgr, La Crosse Public Library, 800 Main St, La Crosse, WI, 54601. Tel: 608-789-7136. p. 2446

Doering, William, Acad Librn, Systems & Metadata Librn, University of Wisconsin-La Crosse, 1631 Pine St, La Crosse, WI, 54601-3748. Tel: 608-785-8399. p. 2446

Doherty, Amanda, Libr Dir, Mount Pulaski Public Library District, 320 N Washington St, Mount Pulaski, IL, 62548. Tel: 217-792-5919. p. 621

Doherty, Ann, Dep Dir, Connecticut Judicial Branch Law Libraries, 90 Washington St, Third Flr, Hartford, CT, 06106. Tel: 860-706-5145. p. 316

Doherty, Ben, Head, Libr Instruction, University of Virginia, Arthur J Morris Law Library, 580 Massie Rd, Charlottesville, VA, 22903-1738. Tel: 434-924-7726. p. 2310

Doherty, Brian J, Dr, Dean, Univ Libr, University of Louisiana at Lafayette, 400 E St Mary Blvd, Lafayette, LA, 70503. Tel: 337-482-6396. p. 893

Doherty, Heather, Circulation & Serials Mgmt, University of New Brunswick Libraries, Gerard V La Forest Law Library, Law School, 2nd Flr, 41 Dineen Dr, Fredericton, NB, E3B 5A3, CANADA. Tel: 506-458-7982. p. 2602

Doherty, Juliette, Ad, Rye Public Library, 581 Washington Rd, Rye, NH, 03870. Tel: 603-964-8401. p. 1380

Doherty, Lisa, Libr Tech, University of Toronto Libraries, Architecture, Landscape & Design, Eberhard Zeidler Library, One Spadina Crescent, Toronto, ON, M5S 2J5, CANADA. Tel: 416-978-2649. p. 2698

Doherty, Paul, Ref Librn, Larchmont Public Library, 121 Larchmont Ave, Larchmont, NY, 10538. Tel: 914-834-2281. p. 1562

Doherty, Teresa, Interim Head, Info Services, Virginia Commonwealth University Libraries, 901 Park Ave, Richmond, VA, 23284. Tel: 804-828-8658. p. 2343

Dohnalek, Eileen, Br Mgr, Chicago Public Library, Jefferson Park, 5363 W Lawrence Ave, Chicago, IL, 60630. Tel: 312-744-1998. p. 556

Dohnalek, Richard, Br Mgr, Chicago Public Library, Lincoln Belmont, 1659 W Melrose St, Chicago, IL, 60657. Tel: 312-744-0166. p. 556

Doi, Carolyn, Liaison Librn, University of Saskatchewan Libraries, Education & Music Library, Education Bldg, Rm 2003, 28 Campus Dr, Saskatoon, SK, S7N 0X1, CANADA. Tel: 306-966-2433. p. 2750

Dojka, John, Inst Archivist, Mgr, Archives & Spec Coll, Rensselaer Libraries, Rensselaer Architecture Library, Greene Bldg 308, 3rd Flr, 110 Eighth St, Troy, NY, 12180-3590. Tel: 518-276-8310. p. 1652

Doktor, Katrina, Br Mgr, Brampton Library, South Fletcher's Branch, 500 Ray Lawson Blvd, Brampton, ON, L6Y 5B3, CANADA. Tel: 905-793-4636, Ext 74267. p. 2633

Dolan, Abby, Res & Instruction Librn, Bryant University, 1150 Douglas Pike, Smithfield, RI, 02917-1284. Tel: 401-232-6125. p. 2042

Dolan, Charles, Tech Serv Librn, Middlesex College Library, 2600 Woodbridge Ave, Edison, NJ, 08818. Tel: 732-906-4254. p. 1401

Dolan, Eileen, Tech Serv Librn, New York Law Institute Library, 120 Broadway, Rm 932, New York, NY, 10271-0094. Tel: 212-732-8720. p. 1594

Dolan, Jane, Cat, West Lafayette Public Library, 208 W Columbia St, West Lafayette, IN, 47906. Tel: 765-743-2261. p. 726

Dolan, Sarah, Fac Librn, Instruction Coordr, Quincy College, 1250 Hancock St, Rm 347, Quincy, MA, 02169. Tel: 617-405-5949. p. 1048

Dolan, Tim, Librn, Greenfield Community College, Core Bldg, 3rd Flr, One College Dr, Greenfield, MA, 01301-9739. Tel: 413-775-1872. p. 1022

Dolan-Derks, Christina, Acq, Whitworth University, 300 W Hawthorne Rd, Spokane, WA, 99251-0001. Tel: 509-777-4485. p. 2385

Dolat, Nicole, Youth Serv Librn, Bloomfield Public Library, One Tunxis Ave, Bloomfield, CT, 06002. Tel: 860-243-9721. p. 303

Dolce, Jonathan, Br Supvr, Lake County Library System, Astor County Library, 54905 Alco Rd, Astor, FL, 32102. Tel: 352-759-9913. p. 450

Dolce, Jonathan, Br Supvr, Lake County Library System, Paisley County Library, 24954 County Rd 42, Paisley, FL, 32767. Tel: 352-669-1001. p. 451

Dolde, Jenifer G, Curator & Folklife Center Dir, Chesapeake Bay Maritime Museum Library, 109A Mill St, Saint Michaels, MD, 21663. Tel: 410-745-4996. p. 976

Dole, Rana, Med Librn, Boca Raton Regional Hospital, 800 Meadows Rd, Boca Raton, FL, 33486. Tel: 561-955-4088. p. 385

Dole, Sandy, Cat, Circ, Bowling Green Public Library, 201 W Locust St, Bowling Green, MO, 63334. Tel: 573-324-5030. p. 1238

Dolen, Tom, Dir, De Anza College, 21250 Stevens Creek Blvd, Cupertino, CA, 95014-5793. Tel: 408-864-8764. p. 133

Dolence, Travis, Distance Learning & Web Librn, Minnesota State University Moorhead, 1104 Seventh Ave S, Moorhead, MN, 56563. Tel: 218-477-2922. p. 1189

Dolgos, Shannon Doutt, Br Mgr, Montgomery County Library, Star Branch, 222 S Main St, Star, NC, 27356. Tel: 910-428-2338. p. 1719

Dolin, Carol, Asst Dir, Algonquin Area Public Library District, 2600 Harnish Dr, Algonquin, IL, 60102-5900. Tel: 847-458-6060. p. 536

Dolin, Pam, Head, Ref & Instruction, United States Coast Guard Academy Library, 35 Mohegan Ave, New London, CT, 06320. Tel: 860-444-8515. p. 329

Dolinger, Elizabeth, Info Literacy Librn, Keene State College, 229 Main St, Keene, NH, 03435-3201. Tel: 603-358-2749. p. 1369

Dolinger, Lesley, Dir, Patten Free Library, 33 Summer St, Bath, ME, 04530. Tel: 207-443-5141, Ext 15. p. 916

Dolive, Mark, Dir, Libr Serv, Tarrant County College, 828 W Harwood Rd, Hurst, TX, 76054. Tel: 817-515-6637. p. 2201

Doll, Lauren, Mgr, Durham County Library, East Regional, 211 Lick Creek Lane, Durham, NC, 27703. Tel: 919-560-0128. p. 1685

Dollar, Jamie, Head, Circ, Wichita Falls Public Library, 600 11th St, Wichita Falls, TX, 76301-4604. Tel: 940-767-0868, Ext 4225. p. 2258

Dollinger, Janie, Dir, Lanark Public Library, 1118 S Broad St, Lanark, IL, 61046. Tel: 815-493-2166. p. 607

Dolly, Cesily, Br Mgr, Burlington Public Library, Patterson Creek Rd S, Burlington, WV, 26710. Tel: 304-289-3690. p. 2399

Dolman, Ann, Outreach/Pub Serv Librn, Barton College, 400 Atlantic Christian College Dr NE, Wilson, NC, 27893. Tel: 252-399-6507. p. 1723

Dolph, Stephanie, Librn, C G Jung Institute of Los Angeles, 10349 W Pico Blvd, Los Angeles, CA, 90064. Tel: 310-556-1193, Ext 229. p. 162

Dolson, Anita, Head Librn, West Union District Library, 209 W Union St, West Union, IL, 62477-0138. Tel: 217-279-3556. p. 661

Dolwick, Chris, Circ Mgr, Cleveland Health Sciences Library, Allen Memorial Medical Library, 11000 Euclid Ave, Cleveland, OH, 44106-7130. Tel: 216-368-6422. p. 1766

Dolwick, Chris, Circ Mgr, Serials & Cataloging Asst, Cleveland Health Sciences Library, Allen Memorial Medical Library, 11000 Euclid Ave, Cleveland, OH, 44106-7130. Tel: 216-368-3643. p. 1767

Doman Calkins, Adrienne, Libr Mgr, Sherwood Public Library, 22560 SW Pine St, Sherwood, OR, 97140-9019. Tel: 503-625-6688. p. 1898

Doman, Monica, Cat, Syst, Cypress College Library, 9200 Valley View St, Cypress, CA, 90630-5897. Tel: 714-484-7067. p. 133

Domann, Brent, Ref Librn, Michigan State University College of Law Library, Law College Bldg, Rm 115, 648 N Shaw Lane, East Lansing, MI, 48824-1300. Tel: 517-432-6851. p. 1102

Domann, Mary, Adult Serv, Circ Supvr, Atchison Public Library, 401 Kansas Ave, Atchison, KS, 66002. Tel: 913-367-1902, Ext 214. p. 797

Domas, Sue, Br Mgr, Monmouth County Library, Wall Township, 2700 Allaire Rd, Wall, NJ, 07719. Tel: 732-449-8877. p. 1416

Domashenko, Sergi, Govt Doc Coordr, Colgate University, 13 Oak Dr, Hamilton, NY, 13346-1398. Tel: 315-228-7508. p. 1543

Dombeck, Jenny, Found Dir, Harford County Public Library, 1221-A Brass Mill Rd, Belcamp, MD, 21017-1209. Tel: 410-273-5600, Ext 6513. p. 958

Dombowsky, Philip, Archivist, National Gallery of Canada Library & Archives, 380 Sussex Dr, Ottawa, ON, K1N 9N4, CANADA. Tel: 613-714-6000, Ext 6323. p. 2667

Dombroski, Cathy, Br Mgr, Osceola Library System, 211 E Dakin Ave, Kissimmee, FL, 34741. Tel: 407-742-8888. p. 414

Dombroski, Segrid, Libr Dir, Dundee Library, 32 Water St, Dundee, NY, 14837. Tel: 607-243-5938. p. 1527

Dombrowski, Clare, Ch Serv, Amesbury Public Library, 149 Main St, Amesbury, MA, 01913. Tel: 978-388-8148. p. 984

Dombrowski, Monica, Dir, Winnetka-Northfield Public Library District, 768 Oak St, Winnetka, IL, 60093-2515. Tel: 847-446-7220. p. 664

Domecq, Marie-Cecile, Health Sci Librn, University of Ottawa Libraries, Health Sciences Library, Roger-Guindon Hall, Rm 1020, 451 Smyth Rd, Ottawa, ON, K1H 8M5, CANADA. Tel: 613-562-5407. p. 2670

Domenech, Jennifer, Asst Dir, Pine Mountain Regional Library, 218 W Perry St, Manchester, GA, 31816. Tel: 706-846-2186. p. 488

Domine, Kay, Spec Projects, College of William & Mary in Virginia, Earl Gregg Swem Library, One Landrum Dr, Williamsburg, VA, 23187. Tel: 757-221-3091. p. 2353

Domingez, Gricel, Head, Res & Info Serv, Florida International University, 3000 NE 151st St, North Miami, FL, 33181-3600. Tel: 305-348-5719. p. 428

Domingo, Kelsey, Br Mgr, Hawaii State Public Library System, Nanakuli Public Library, 89-070 Farrington Hwy, Waianae, HI, 96792. Tel: 808-668-5844. p. 510

Domingo, Lea, Br Mgr, Hawaii State Public Library System, Kaimuki Public Library, 1041 Koko Head Ave, Honolulu, HI, 96816. Tel: 808-733-8422. p. 508

Domingue, Grant, IT Mgr, Vermilion Parish Library, 405 E Saint Victor St, Abbeville, LA, 70510-5101. Tel: 337-893-2655. p. 879

Dominguez Flores, Noraida, Assoc Prof, Interim Dir, University of Puerto Rico, Rio Piedras Campus, PO Box 21906, San Juan, PR, 00931-1906. Tel: 787-764-0000, Ext 85269. p. 2795

Dominguez Flores, Noraida, Dr, Interim Dir, University of Puerto Rico Library System, Rio Piedras Campus, San Juan, PR, 00931. Tel: 787-764-0000, Ext 5085, 787-764-0000, Ext 5086, 787-764-0000, Ext 5087. p. 2514

Dominguez, Maria, Dep Dir, Info Tech & Digital Initiatives, Phoenix Public Library, 1221 N Central Ave, Phoenix, AZ, 85004. Tel: 602-262-4636. p. 72

Dominguez, Maria, Mgr, Cobb County Public Library System, Kemp Memorial Library, 4029 Due West Rd, Marietta, GA, 30064. Tel: 770-528-2527. p. 489

Dominguez, Rachel, Mgr, Saint Mary Parish Library, Berwick Branch, 3512 Fifth St, Berwick, LA, 70342. Tel: 985-385-2943. p. 890

Dominguez, Rosa, Head Librn, Balmorhea Public Library, 102 SW Main St, Balmorhea, TX, 79718. Tel: 432-448-1697. p. 2144

Dominianni, Beth, Dir, Mark Twain Library, 439 Redding Rd, Redding, CT, 06896. Tel: 203-938-2545. p. 334

Dominicis, Eric, Dir, Miami Dade College, Kendall Campus Library, 11011 SW 104th St, Miami, FL, 33176-3393. Tel: 305-237-0996, 305-237-2015, 305-237-2291. p. 422

Dominick, Tara, Libr Dir, Treasure Valley Community College Library, 650 College Blvd, Ontario, OR, 97914-3423. Tel: 541-881-5929. p. 1889

Dominique, St Victor, Archives, Libr Tech, Spec Coll, Barry University, 11300 NE Second Ave, Miami Shores, FL, 33161-6695. Tel: 305-899-3852. p. 426

Dominquez, Daisy, Interim Chief Librn, City College of the City University of New York, North Academic Ctr, 160 Convent Ave, New York, NY, 10031. Tel: 212-650-7155, 212-650-7292. p. 1581

Dominy, Lynne, Superintendent, National Park Service, 415 Washington Ave, Bayfield, WI, 54814. Tel: 715-779-3398, Ext 1101. p. 2423

Dominy, Peggy, Ref Librn, Drexel University Libraries, Hagerty Library, 33rd & Market Sts, Philadelphia, PA, 19104-2875. Tel: 215-895-2754. p. 1976

Dommermuth, Emily, Sci/Eng Librn, University of Colorado Boulder, Gemmill Library of Engineering, Mathematics & Physics, Mathematics Bldg, Rm 135, 2300 Colorado Ave, Boulder, CO, 80309. Tel: 303-735-8365. p. 268

Dompe, Andrea, Colls Mgr, Haggin Museum, 1201 N Pershing Ave, Stockton, CA, 95203-1699. Tel: 209-940-6314. p. 249

Dompkosky, Sandy, Coordr, Department of Veterans Affairs, 1111 E End Blvd, 6th Flr, Wilkes-Barre, PA, 18711. Tel: 570-824-3521. p. 2022

Domschot, Betsy S, Librn, Consumers Energy, Legal Library, One Energy Plaza, Jackson, MI, 49201. Tel: 517-788-1088. p. 1119

Donabedian, David, Head, Access Serv, Hunter College Libraries, East Bldg, 695 Park Ave, New York, NY, 10065. Tel: 212-772-4176. p. 1588

Donadio, Lisa, ILS Adminr, Vermont Law School, 164 Chelsea St, South Royalton, VT, 05068. Tel: 802-831-1442. p. 2295

Donahoe, Jessica, Head, Cat, Webmaster, University of Wisconsin - Platteville, One University Plaza, Platteville, WI, 53818. Tel: 608-342-1348. p. 2470

Donahoo, Diana, Dir, Centralia Regional Library District, 515 E Broadway, Centralia, IL, 62801. Tel: 618-532-5222. p. 551

Donahue, Cheryl, Dir, Richard Sugden Library, Eight Pleasant St, Spencer, MA, 01562. Tel: 508-885-7513. p. 1056

Donahue, Jill, Acq & Cat Mgr, Boulder City Library, 701 Adams Blvd, Boulder City, NV, 89005-2207. Tel: 702-293-1281. p. 1343

Donahue, Lynn, Mgr, Popular Mats, Poplar Creek Public Library District, 1405 S Park Ave, Streamwood, IL, 60107-2997. Tel: 630-837-6800. p. 652

Donahue, Sandy, Librn, Northeast Regional Library, George E Allen Library, 500 W Church St, Booneville, MS, 38829-3353. Tel: 662-728-6553. p. 1215

Donald, Megan, Ref & Instruction Librn, Tulsa Community College Libraries, West Campus Library, 7505 W 41st St, Tulsa, OK, 74107-8633. Tel: 918-595-8010. p. 1867

Donald, Megan, Interim Dir, University of Tulsa Libraries, Mabee Legal Information Center, 3120 E Fourth Pl, Tulsa, OK, 74104-3189. Tel: 918-631-2404. p. 1867

Donaldson, Angela, Br Mgr, Perry County District Library, Crooksville Branch, 111 E Main St, Crooksville, OH, 43731. Tel: 740-982-4821. p. 1806

Donaldson, C, Registrar, Vancouver Holocaust Education Centre, 50-950 W 41st Ave, Vancouver, BC, V5Z 2N7, CANADA. Tel: 604-264-0499. p. 2581

Donaldson, Elizabeth, Br Mgr, Mansfield-Richland County Public Library, Crestview Branch, 1575 State Rte 96 E, Ashland, OH, 44805-9262. Tel: 419-895-0010. p. 1798

Donaldson, James, Interim Asst Dir, Montgomery County Public Libraries, 21 Maryland Ave, Ste 310, Rockville, MD, 20850. Tel: 240-777-0030. p. 974

Donaldson, Karen, Supvr, Middlesex County Library, Ilderton Branch, 40 Heritage Dr, Ilderton, ON, N0M 2A0, CANADA. Tel: 519-666-1599. p. 2682

Donaldson, Kelly, Librn, Seneca College of Applied Arts & Technology, Newnham Campus (Main), 1750 Finch Ave E, North York, ON, M2J 2X5, CANADA. Tel: 416-491-5050, Ext 26139. p. 2649

Donaldson, Kylea, Circ Supvr, Payson Public Library, 328 N McLane Rd, Payson, AZ, 85541. Tel: 928-472-5165. p. 68

Donaldson, Maplean, Assoc Dir, University of Arkansas-Pine Bluff, 1200 N University Dr, Pine Bluff, AR, 71601. Tel: 870-575-8411. p. 108

Donaldson, Nell, Acq, ILL, Chipola College Library, 3094 Indian Circle, Marianna, FL, 32446. Tel: 850-718-2273. p. 420

Donaldson, Nick, Librn, Emo Public Library, 36 Front St, Emo, ON, P0W 1E0, CANADA. Tel: 807-482-2575. p. 2640

Donaldson, Rhonda, Ref Serv Librn, Shepherd University, 301 N King St, Shepherdstown, WV, 25443. Tel: 304-876-5424. p. 2414

Donaldson, Roger, Dir, Jackson City Library, 21 Broadway St, Jackson, OH, 45640-1695. Tel: 740-286-4111. p. 1791

Donaldson, Shane, Youth Serv Mgr, Erie County Public Library, 160 E Front St, Erie, PA, 16507. Tel: 814-451-6928. p. 1931

Donaldson, Shane, Res & Ref Librn, Mercyhurst University, 501 E 38th St, Erie, PA, 16546. Tel: 814-824-2230. p. 1932

Donaldson, Thomas, Dir, United States Marine Corps, Bldg 298, Marine Corps Air Sta, Cherry Point, NC, 28533-0009. Tel: 252-466-3552. p. 1681

Donaldson, Vicki, Mgr, Suwannee River Regional Library, Madison Public Library, 378 NW College Loop, Madison, FL, 32340-1446. Tel: 850-973-6814. p. 419

Donath, Carolyn, Dir, Conrad Public Library, 15 Fourth Ave SW, Conrad, MT, 59425. Tel: 406-271-5751. p. 1291

Dorman, Mary Ellen, Actg Librn, The Belcher Memorial Library, 4452 VT Rte 107, Gaysville, VT, 05746-0144. Tel: 802-234-6608. p. 2284

Dorman, Robert, PhD, Monographs Librn, Oklahoma City University, 2501 N Blackwelder, Oklahoma City, OK, 73106. Tel: 405-208-5068. p. 1858

Dormody, Katherine, Dir, Gilford Public Library, 31 Potter Hill Rd, Gilford, NH, 03249-6803. Tel: 603-524-6042. p. 1364

Dornbaum, Robin L, Dir, Med Libr, Flushing Hospital Medical Center, 45th Ave at Parsons Blvd, Flushing, NY, 11355. Tel: 718-670-5653. p. 1533

Dorner, John, Library Contact, Normal Masonic Lodge 673, 614 E Lincoln St, Normal, IL, 61761. p. 625

Dorney, Kristi, Br Mgr, Jacksonville Public Library, Argyle Branch, 7973 Old Middleburg Rd S, Jacksonville, FL, 32222-1817. Tel: 904-573-3164. p. 412

Dorosinski, Maureen, Librn, Florida Braille & Talking Book Library, 421 Platt St, Daytona Beach, FL, 32114-2804. Tel: 386-239-6000. p. 392

Dorr, Jessica, Libr Dir, Boise Public Library, 715 S Capitol Blvd, Boise, ID, 83702. Tel: 208-972-8200. p. 516

Dorr, Jessica, Dir, LYNX! Consortium, c/o Boise Public Library, 715 S Capitol Blvd, Boise, ID, 83702-7195. Tel: 208-384-4238, 208-384-4485. p. 2764

Dorr, Marshall, Access Services Assoc, University of Nebraska at Kearney, 2508 11th Ave, Kearney, NE, 68849-2240. Tel: 308-865-8598. p. 1319

Dorris, C Scott, Assoc Dir, Research Servs, Georgetown University, Dahlgren Memorial Library, Preclinical Science Bldg GM-7, 3900 Reservoir Rd NW, Washington, DC, 20007. Tel: 202-687-2942. p. 368

Dorris, D'Ann, Librn, Geneseo Public Library, 725 Main St, Geneseo, KS, 67444-9702. Tel: 620-824-6140. p. 809

Dorris, Sonya, Dir, Carnegie Public Library of Steuben County, 322 S Wayne St, Angola, IN, 46703. Tel: 260-665-3362. p. 668

Dorscht, Melanie, Chief Exec Officer, Hilton Union Public Library, 3085 Marks St, Hilton Beach, ON, P0R 1G0, CANADA. Tel: 705-255-3520. p. 2648

Dorsey, Britta, Syst Adminr, Thorntown Public Library, 124 N Market St, Thorntown, IN, 46071-1144. Tel: 765-436-7348. p. 721

Dorsey, Chianta, Mgr, Archives & Spec Coll, University of Texas Southwestern Medical Center, 5323 Harry Hines Blvd, Dallas, TX, 75390-9049. Tel: 214-648-8991. p. 2169

Dorsey, Dewana, Br Mgr, Chicago Public Library, West Pullman, 830 W 119th St, Chicago, IL, 60628. Tel: 312-747-1425. p. 557

Dorsey, Jamie, Coll Coordr, Jacksonville Public Library, 526 E Commerce St, Jacksonville, TX, 75766. Tel: 903-586-7664. p. 2203

Dorsey, Pam, Br Mgr, Webster Parish Library System, Sarepta Branch, 24522 Hwy 371, Sarepta, LA, 71071. Tel: 318-847-4992. p. 898

Dorsey, Susan, Dir, Lenoir City Public Library, 100 W Broadway, Lenoir City, TN, 37771. Tel: 865-986-3210. p. 2109

Dorsheimer, Amy, Head, Youth Serv, Nevins Memorial Library, 305 Broadway, Methuen, MA, 01844-6898. Tel: 978-686-4080. p. 1035

Dorshimer, Mike, Network Adminr, Keystone Library Network, 2300 Vartan Way, Ste 207, Harrisburg, PA, 17110. Tel: 717-720-4208. p. 2774

Dorsky, Kait, Univ Archivist, University of North Carolina School of the Arts Library, 1533 S Main St, Winston-Salem, NC, 27127. Tel: 336-770-3270. p. 1726

Dort, Brianne, Syst Librn, Susquehanna University, 514 University Ave, Selinsgrove, PA, 17870-1050. Tel: 570-372-4322. p. 2005

Dorwaldt, Lynn, Librn, Wagner Free Institute of Science Library, 1700 W Montgomery Ave, Philadelphia, PA, 19121. Tel: 215-763-6529, Ext 12. p. 1989

Dos, DeLa, Sr Dir, Diversity, Equity & Inclusion, Association of Research Libraries, 21 Dupont Circle NW, Ste 800, Washington, DC, 20036. Tel: 202-296-2296. p. 2763

Dos Santos, Abby, Ref Librn, Caplin & Drysdale Library, One Thomas Circle, NW, Ste 1100, Washington, DC, 20005-5802. Tel: 202-862-7835. p. 362

Dos Santos, Carrie, Exec Dir, Middlesex County Public Library, 150 Grace St, Urbanna, VA, 23175. Tel: 804-758-5717. p. 2349

Dosch, Constance, Sr Librn, Los Angeles Public Library System, Lake View Terrace Branch Library, 12002 Osborne St, Los Angeles, CA, 91342. Tel: 818-890-7404. p. 164

Dose, Carrie, Dir, Jackson County Library, 311 Third St, Jackson, MN, 56143-1600. Tel: 507-847-4748. p. 1179

Doshi, Ameet, Head Librn, Princeton University, Donald E Stokes Library - Public & International Affairs & Population Research, Wallace Hall, Lower Flr, Princeton, NJ, 08544. Tel: 609-258-5455. p. 1438

Dosland, Stephanie, Dir, Wregie Memorial Library, 105 W Broadway, Oxford Junction, IA, 52323. Tel: 563-826-2450. p. 776

Doss, Sandy, Br Mgr, Southeast Arkansas Regional Library, Warren Branch, 115 W Cypress, Warren, AR, 71671. Tel: 870-226-2536. p. 105

Dossey, Sue, Dir, Coleman Public Library, 402 S Commercial Ave, Coleman, TX, 76834-4202. Tel: 325-625-3043. p. 2157

Doster-Greenleaf, Karen, Dir, Res & Instruction Serv, Kennesaw State University Library System, 385 Cobb Ave NW, MD 1701, Kennesaw, GA, 30144. Tel: 470-578-7276. p. 483

Doster-Greenleaf, Karen, Dir, Res & Instruction Serv, Kennesaw State University Library System, Lawrence V Johnson Library, 1100 S Marietta Pkwy, Marietta, GA, 30060-2896. Tel: 678-470-578-7276. p. 483

Doten, Sonya M, Librn I, Supvr, United States Environmental Protection Agency, One Sabine Island Dr, Gulf Breeze, FL, 32561-5299. Tel: 850-934-9318. p. 408

Doto, Christina, Dir, Park Ridge Public Library, 51 Park Ave, Park Ridge, NJ, 07656. Tel: 201-391-5151. p. 1432

Dotolo, Lawrence G, Dr, Pres, Virginia Tidewater Consortium for Higher Education, 4900 Powhatan Ave, Norfolk, VA, 23529. Tel: 757-683-3183. p. 2776

Dotson, Chazley, Ch, Sterling Municipal Library, Mary Elizabeth Wilbanks Ave, Baytown, TX, 77520. Tel: 281-427-7331. p. 2145

Dotson, Eloise, Librn, Lafayette Public Library, Scott Branch, 5808 W Cameron St, Scott, LA, 70583. Tel: 337-232-9321. p. 892

Dotson, Kaye, Dr, Assoc Prof, East Carolina University, 104B Ragsdale Hall, Greenville, NC, 27858. Tel: 252-328-2787. p. 2790

Dotson, Linda, Librn, New Providence Presbyterian Church, 703 W Broadway Ave, Maryville, TN, 37801. Tel: 865-983-0182. p. 2111

Dotson, Maureen, Admin Operations Specialist, Facilities Coordr, San Diego State University, 5500 Campanile Dr, San Diego, CA, 92182-8050. Tel: 619-594-4472. p. 221

Dotson, Renee, Mgr, Libr Serv, Lunar & Planetary Institute Library, 3600 Bay Area Blvd, Houston, TX, 77058-1113. Tel: 281-486-2172. p. 2197

Dotson, Tammy, Br Mgr, Jackson District Library, Concord Branch, 108 S Main St, Concord, MI, 49237. Tel: 517-905-1379. p. 1120

Dotson, Tammy, Br Mgr, Jackson District Library, Hanover Branch, 118 W Main St, Hanover, MI, 49241. Tel: 517-905-1399. p. 1120

Dotson, Tiffanie, Access Serv Librn, Huntingdon College, 1500 E Fairview Ave, Montgomery, AL, 36106. Tel: 334-833-4422. p. 28

Dotten, Rose, Chief Exec Officer, Head Librn, Shelburne Public Library, 201 Owen Sound St, Shelburne, ON, L9V 3L2, CANADA. Tel: 519-925-2168. p. 2678

Dotterer, Douglas H, Dir, Stow-Munroe Falls Public Library, 3512 Darrow Rd, Stow, OH, 44224. Tel: 330-688-3295. p. 1822

Dotto, Ashley, Libr Serv Coordr, Edmonton Public Library, Strathcona, 8331 104 St, Edmonton, AB, T6E 4E9, CANADA. Tel: 780-496-3953. p. 2537

Doty, Paul, Archives Librn, Spec Coll Librn, St Lawrence University, 23 Romoda Dr, Canton, NY, 13617. Tel: 315-229-5483. p. 1513

Doty, Rod, Librn, Charles George VA Medical Center Library, 1100 Tunnel Rd, Asheville, NC, 28805. Tel: 828-298-7911, Ext 15298. p. 1672

Doucet, Louella, Dir, Groves Public Library, 5600 W Washington St, Groves, TX, 77619. Tel: 409-962-6281. p. 2186

Doucet, Valérie, Chef de Section, Bibliotheques de Montreal, Pointe-aux-Trembles, 14001 rue Notre-Dame Est, Montreal, QC, H1A 1T9, CANADA. Tel: 514-872-0644. p. 2720

Doucet, Valérie, Chef de Section, Bibliotheques de Montreal, Riviere-des-Prairies, 9001 Blvd Perras, Montreal, QC, H1E 3J7, CANADA. Tel: 514-872-9386. p. 2720

Doucett, Elisabeth, Dir, Curtis Memorial Library, 23 Pleasant St, Brunswick, ME, 04011-2295. Tel: 207-725-5242. p. 919

Doucette, Danielle, Asst Youth Serv, Dorothy Alling Memorial Library, 21 Library Lane, Williston, VT, 05495. Tel: 802-878-4918. p. 2299

Doucette, Joanne, Assoc Dir, Massachusetts College of Pharmacy & Health Sciences, Matricaria Bldg, 2nd Flr, 179 Longwood Ave, Boston, MA, 02115. Tel: 617-732-2805. p. 997

Doucette, Patricia, Mgr, Libr Serv, Holland College Library Services, 140 Weymouth St, Charlottetown, PE, C1A 4Z1, CANADA. Tel: 902-566-9350. p. 2707

Doucette, Wendy, Grad Serv Librn, East Tennessee State University, Sherrod Library, Seehorn Dr & Lake St, Johnson City, TN, 37614-0204. Tel: 423-439-4336. p. 2103

Doucette-McLauchlin, Sarah, Dir, Rollinsford Public Library, Three Front St, Ste 2B, Rollinsford, NH, 03869. Tel: 603-516-2665. p. 1380

Doud, Beth, Ref Serv, Mims/Scottsmoor Public Library, 3615 Lionel Rd, Mims, FL, 32754. Tel: 321-264-5080. p. 426

Doud, Laurel, Librn, Fresno City College Library, 1101 E University Ave, Fresno, CA, 93741. Tel: 559-442-4600, Ext 8920. p. 145

Dougan, Kirstin, Head Librn, University of Illinois Library at Urbana-Champaign, Music & Performing Arts, 1300 Music Bldg, MC-056, 1114 W Nevada St, Urbana, IL, 61801. Tel: 217-244-4072. p. 656

Dougherty, Bobbie, Mgr, District of Columbia Public Library, Northwest One, 155 L St NW, Washington, DC, 20001. Tel: 202-939-5946. p. 364

Dougherty, Bridget, Librn, Public Library of Steubenville & Jefferson County, Toronto Branch, 607 Daniels St, Toronto, OH, 43964. Tel: 740-537-1262. p. 1822

Dougherty, Carla, Dir, Rockwell Public Library, 307 Main St E, Rockwell, IA, 50469. Tel: 641-822-3268. p. 779

Dougherty, Jane, Head, Circ Serv, Head, Tech Serv, Hazleton Area Public Library, 55 N Church St, Hazleton, PA, 18201-5893. Tel: 570-454-2961. p. 1943

Dougherty, Jay, Head, Libr Syst, University of Wisconsin-Parkside Library, 900 Wood Rd, Kenosha, WI, 53141. Tel: 262-595-3432. p. 2445

Dougherty, Kathy, Dir, Church of Jesus Christ of Latter-Day Saints, 4751 Neil Rd, Reno, NV, 89502. Tel: 775-240-5588. p. 1349

Dougherty, Kristi, Dir, Amherst Public Library, 350 John James Audubon Pkwy, Amherst, NY, 14228. Tel: 716-689-4922. p. 1486

Dougherty, Kristi, Dir, Amherst Public Library, Clearfield, 770 Hopkins Rd, Williamsville, NY, 14221. Tel: 716-688-4955. p. 1486
Dougherty, Kristi, Dir, Amherst Public Library, Eggertsville-Snyder Branch, 4622 Main St, Synder, NY, 14226. Tel: 716-839-0700. p. 1486
Dougherty, Kristi, Dir, Amherst Public Library, Williamsville, 5571 Main St, Williamsville, NY, 14221. Tel: 716-632-6176. p. 1486
Dougherty, Renee, Dir, Columbia Heights Public Library, 3939 Central Ave NE, Columbia Heights, MN, 55421. Tel: 763-706-3690. p. 1170
Dougherty, Sarah, Adminr, Saint John's Cathedral Library, 1350 Washington St, Denver, CO, 80203. Tel: 303-831-7115, Ext 7728. p. 277
Dougherty, Sarah, Dir, Beaman Community Memorial Library, 223 Main St, Beaman, IA, 50609. Tel: 641-366-2912. p. 734
Dougherty, Sharon, Interim Libr Dir, Coplay Public Library, 49 S Fifth St, Coplay, PA, 18037-1306. Tel: 610-262-7351. p. 1924
Doughty, Amanda, Libr Coord, Eastern Connecticut Health Network, 71 Haynes St, Manchester, CT, 06040-4188. Tel: 860-646-1222, Ext 2225. p. 320
Doughty, Connie, Dir, Lynn Murray Memorial Library, 625 Railroad St, Chester, WV, 26034. Tel: 304-387-1010. p. 2401
Doughty, Gretchen, Asst to the Dean of Libraries, Circ Mgr, New Orleans Baptist Theological Seminary, 4110 Seminary Pl, New Orleans, LA, 70126. Tel: 504-816-8203. p. 902
Doughty, Helen M, Librn, John Muir Health Medical Library, 1601 Ygnacio Valley Rd, Walnut Creek, CA, 94598. Tel: 925-947-5231. p. 258
Doughty, William, Colls Mgr, Bryant University, 1150 Douglas Pike, Smithfield, RI, 02917-1284. Tel: 401-232-6296. p. 2042
Douglas, Allie, Operations Mgr, Public Library InterLINK, 5489 Byrne Rd, No 158, Burnaby, BC, V5J 3J1, CANADA. Tel: 604-437-8441. p. 2777
Douglas, Cheridan, Dir, Lisle Free Library, 8998 Main St, Lisle, NY, 13797. Tel: 607-692-3115. p. 1563
Douglas Darby, Rhonda, Br Mgr, Pine Forest Regional Library System - Headquarters, William & Dolores Mauldin Library, 25 McHenry School Dr, McHenry, MS, 39561. Tel: 601-528-9465. p. 1232
Douglas, Deidra, Head, Pub Serv, River Parishes Community College Library, 925 W Edenborne Pkwy, Rm 141, Gonzales, LA, 70737. Tel: 225-743-8550. p. 890
Douglas, Jacqueline, Cat, West Hartford Public Library, 20 S Main St, West Hartford, CT, 06107-2432. Tel: 860-561-6950. p. 345
Douglas, Jennifer, Head, Tech Serv, Grand Prairie Public Library System, 901 Conover Dr, Grand Prairie, TX, 75051. Tel: 972-237-5700. p. 2185
Douglas, Jennifer, Assoc Prof, University of British Columbia, The Irving K Barber Learning Ctr, 1961 E Mall, Ste 470, Vancouver, BC, V6T 1Z1, CANADA. Tel: 604-822-2404. p. 2795
Douglas, Jessica, Asst Cataloger, East Brookfield Public Library, Memorial Town Complex, 122 Connie Mack Dr, East Brookfield, MA, 01515. Tel: 508-867-7928. p. 1015
Douglas, Julie, Br Head, Vancouver Public Library, Hastings Branch, 2674 E Hastings St, Vancouver, BC, V5K 1Z6, CANADA. Tel: 604-665-3959. p. 2581
Douglas, Karen, Librn, Department of Veterans Affairs, Southern Arizona VA Healthcare System, 3601 S Sixth Ave, Tucson, AZ, 85723. Tel: 520-792-1450, Ext 15961. p. 81
Douglas, Karen, Acq, Cincinnati State Technical & Community College, 3520 Central Pkwy, Rm 170, Cincinnati, OH, 45223-2690. Tel: 513-569-1607. p. 1760
Douglas, Laura, Spec Coll, Denton Public Library, 502 Oakland St, Denton, TX, 76201. Tel: 940-349-8749. p. 2170
Douglas, Mary, Youth Serv Coordr, LeRoy Collins Leon County Public Library System, 200 W Park Ave, Tallahassee, FL, 32301-7720. Tel: 850-606-2665. p. 445
Douglas, Meredith, Law Librn, Knox County Governmental Law Library, M-99 City County Bldg, 400 Main St, Knoxville, TN, 37902. Tel: 865-215-2368. p. 2105
Douglas, Sara, Mgr, Portage County District Library, Garrettsville Branch, 10482 South St, Garrettsville, OH, 44231. Tel: 330-527-4378. p. 1787
Douglas, Sara, Mgr, Portage County District Library, Windham Branch, 9005 Wilverne Dr, Windham, OH, 44288. Tel: 330-326-3145. p. 1788
Douglas, Scott, Library Contact, Centre for Christian Studies Library, Woodsworth House, 60 Maryland St, Winnipeg, MB, R3G 1K7, CANADA. Tel: 204-783-4490, Ext 26. p. 2593
Douglas, Sharon, Automation Coordr, Lake Agassiz Regional Library, 118 S Fifth St, Moorhead, MN, 56560-2756. Tel: 218-233-3757, Ext 138. p. 1188
Douglas-Williams, Tara, Assoc Dir, Emory University Libraries, Robert W Woodruff Library, 540 Asbury Circle, Atlanta, GA, 30322-2870. Tel: 404-727-6861. p. 463
Douglass, Johanna, Ch Serv, Edwards Public Library, 30 East St, Southampton, MA, 01073. Tel: 413-527-9480. p. 1055
Douglass, Lauren, Head, Tech, East Lansing Public Library, 950 Abbot Rd, East Lansing, MI, 48823-3105. Tel: 517-319-6882. p. 1101
Dounts, Anton, Mgr, Libr Serv, Cariboo Regional District Library, 180 N Third Ave, Ste A, Williams Lake, BC, V2G 2A4, CANADA. Tel: 250-392-3351. p. 2584
Dour, Abigail, Libr Dir, Northwest University, 5520 108th Ave NE, Kirkland, WA, 98083. Tel: 425-889-5201. p. 2368
Douthat, Ryan, Dir, Pub Serv, Dir, Spec Coll & Archives, Electronic Serv, Union Presbyterian Seminary Library, 3401 Brook Rd, Richmond, VA, 23227. Tel: 804-278-4217. p. 2342
Doutre, Robin, Circ Mgr, Michigan State University College of Law Library, Law College Bldg, Rm 115, 648 N Shaw Lane, East Lansing, MI, 48824-1300. Tel: 517-432-6869. p. 1102
Dovala, Donald, Libr Adminr, Amherst Public Library, 221 Spring St, Amherst, OH, 44001. Tel: 440-988-4230. p. 1746
Dove, Jeuron, Br Mgr, Forsyth County Public Library, Carver School Road Branch, 4915 Lansing Dr W, Winston-Salem, NC, 27105. Tel: 336-703-2910. p. 1724
Dover, Ashley, Student Success Librn, Fairmont State University, 1201 Locust Ave, Fairmont, WV, 26554. Tel: 304-367-4733. p. 2402
Dover, Emily, Br Mgr, Trion Public Library, 15 Bulldog Blvd, Trion, GA, 30753. Tel: 706-734-7594. p. 501
Dover, Michelle, Circ Mgr, Bud Werner Memorial Library, 1289 Lincoln Ave, Steamboat Springs, CO, 80487. Tel: 970-879-0240, Ext 307. p. 295
Dovico, Judy, Dir, Batavia Public Library, 902 Third St, Batavia, IA, 52533. Tel: 641-662-2317. p. 734
Dovydaitis, Amy, Head, Curric Mat Ctr, University of Central Florida Libraries, 12701 Pegasus Dr, Orlando, FL, 32816-8030. Tel: 407-823-2327. p. 432
Dow, Ericka, Supvr, Ad Serv, Manatee County Public Library System, 1301 Barcarrota Blvd W, Bradenton, FL, 34205-7522. Tel: 941-748-5555, Ext 6311. p. 386
Dow, Katie, Libr Mgr, Venice Public Library, 260 Nokomis Ave S, Venice, FL, 34285. Tel: 941-861-1350. p. 452
Dow, Katie, Ref Serv, Alexandria Library, Charles E Beatley Jr Central, 5005 Duke St, Alexandria, VA, 22304-2903. Tel: 703-746-1746. p. 2302
Dow, Marilyn, Dir, University of Detroit Mercy Libraries, School of Dentistry, Corktown Campus, 2700 Martin Luther King Jr Blvd, Detroit, MI, 48208-2576. Tel: 313-494-6900. p. 1099
Dow, Mary, Ser Librn, Morris College, 100 W College St, Sumter, SC, 29150-3599. Tel: 803-934-3230. p. 2071
Dowd, Catherine, Librn/Mgr, Ontario Provincial Police, 777 Memorial Ave, Orillia, ON, L3V 7V3, CANADA. Tel: 705-329-6886. p. 2663
Dowd, Frank, Fac Librn, Florida SouthWestern State College, 8099 College Pkwy SW, Bldg J-212, Fort Myers, FL, 33919. Tel: 239-489-9449. p. 403
Dowd, Jeffrey, Supv Law Librn, Connecticut Judicial Branch Law Libraries, 90 Washington St, Third Flr, Hartford, CT, 06106. Tel: 860-706-5145. p. 316
Dowd, Kerry, Br Mgr, Alachua County Library District, Waldo Branch, 14257 Cole St, Waldo, FL, 32694. Tel: 352-468-3298. p. 407
Dowd, Lesa, Dir, Conserv Serv, Newberry Library, 60 W Walton St, Chicago, IL, 60610-3305. Tel: 312-255-3549. p. 565
Dowd, Nathan, Libr Dir, Edgewood College Library, 959 Edgewood College Dr, Madison, WI, 53711-1997. Tel: 608-663-2837. p. 2449
Dowdell, Sue, Dir, Beacon Falls Public Library, Ten Maple Ave, Beacon Falls, CT, 06403. Tel: 203-729-1441. p. 302
Dowdell, Sue, Libr Dir, Springfield Town Library, 43 Main St, Springfield, VT, 05156. Tel: 802-885-3108. p. 2295
Dowdell, Sue, Treas, Catamount Library Network, 43 Main St, Springfield, VT, 05156. Tel: 802-885-3108. p. 2776
Dowdle, Eric, Library Contact, Acuren Group, Inc Library, 7450 18th St, Edmonton, AB, T6P 1N8, CANADA. Tel: 780-490-2438. p. 2534
Dowdy, Jackie, Access Serv Librn, Middle Tennessee State University, 1611 Alumni Dr, Murfreesboro, TN, 37132. Tel: 615-898-5104. p. 2117
Dowdy, Ona, Circ, Lynchburg Public Library, 2315 Memorial Ave, Lynchburg, VA, 24501. Tel: 434-455-6312. p. 2330
Dowdy, Robert, Circ Supvr, Little Elm Public Library, 100 W Eldorado Pkwy, Little Elm, TX, 75068. Tel: 214-975-0430. p. 2212
Dowell, Kristi, Customer Serv Mgr, Wichita Public Library, 711 W Second St, Wichita, KS, 67203. Tel: 316-261-8530. p. 843
Dowell, Trisha, Libr Dir, Charles J Rike Memorial Library, 203 Orange St, Farmersville, TX, 75442. Tel: 972-782-6681. p. 2176
Dower, Karen, Circ, Delaware Technical & Community College, 400 Stanton-Christiana Rd, Rm D 201, Newark, DE, 19713-2197. Tel: 302-453-3716. p. 355
Dower, Kellori, Dean, Santa Ana College, 1530 W 17th St, Santa Ana, CA, 92706-3398. Tel: 714-564-5600. p. 239
Dowling, Marcie, Dir, Polk County Public Library, 1289 W Mills St, Columbus, NC, 28722. Tel: 828-894-8721. p. 1682
Dowling, Shelley, Ref Serv, College of William & Mary in Virginia, The Wolf Law Library, 613 S Henry St, Williamsburg, VA, 23187. Tel: 757-221-3255. p. 2353
Dowling, Teri, Dir of Libr, California College of the Arts Libraries, 5212 Broadway, Oakland, CA, 94618. Tel: 415-703-9559. p. 185
Dowling, Teri, Dir of Libr, California College of the Arts Libraries, Simpson Library, 1111 Eighth St, San Francisco, CA, 94107. p. 185
Dowling, Thomas, Dir, Technology, Wake Forest University, 1834 Wake Forest Rd, Winston-Salem, NC, 27109. Tel: 336-758-5797. p. 1726
Downen, Rachel, Lead Librn, San Antonio Public Library, Molly Pruitt Library, 5110 Walzem Rd, San Antonio, TX, 78218. Tel: 210-650-1122. p. 2239

Downer, Diane, Dir, Gering Public Library, 1055 P St, Gering, NE, 69341. Tel: 308-436-7433. p. 1315
Downer, Maria, Dir, Butler Memorial Library, 621 Penn St, Cambridge, NE, 69022. Tel: 308-697-3836. p. 1309
Downes, Kathy, Dean of Libr, Libr Adminr, Wichita State University Libraries, 1845 Fairmount, Wichita, KS, 67260-0068. Tel: 316-978-3582. p. 844
Downes, Robin, Asst Librn, Mansfield Public Library, Five Main St, Temple, NH, 03084. Tel: 603-878-3100. p. 1382
Downey, Alison, Asst Prof, Libr Sci, Tech Serv Librn, Valparaiso University, 1410 Chapel Dr, Valparaiso, IN, 46383-6493. Tel: 219-464-6183. p. 723
Downey, Anne, Head, Conserv, American Philosophical Society Library, 105 S Fifth St, Philadelphia, PA, 19106-3386. Tel: 215-440-3400. p. 1974
Downey, Annie, Assoc Dean & Dir of Libr Serv, University of Washington Libraries, Tacoma Library, 1900 Commerce St, Box 358460, Tacoma, WA, 98402-3100. Tel: 253-692-4444. p. 2382
Downey, Greg, Assoc Dean, Prof, University of Wisconsin-Madison, Helen C White Hall, Rm 4217, 600 N Park St, Madison, WI, 53706. Tel: 608-263-2900. p. 2794
Downey, Joyce A, Coordr, University of Rhode Island, 215 S Ferry Rd, Narragansett, RI, 02882. Tel: 401-874-6161. p. 2034
Downey, Rebekkah, Sr Libr Spec, Mesa Community College Library, Red Mountain, 7110 E McKellips Rd, Mesa, AZ, 85207. Tel: 480-654-7741. p. 66
Downey, Sonja, Circ Serv Supvr, Tecumseh District Library, 215 N Ottawa St, Tecumseh, MI, 49286-1564. Tel: 517-423-2238. p. 1153
Downie, J Stephen, Assoc Dean, Res, Co-Director, HathiTrust Research Ctr, Prof, University of Illinois at Urbana-Champaign, Library & Information Science Bldg, 501 E Daniel St, Champaign, IL, 61820-6211. Tel: 217-333-3280. p. 2784
Downie, Judith A, Spec Coll Librn, California State University, 333 S Twin Oaks Valley Rd, San Marcos, CA, 92096. Tel: 760-750-4348. p. 234
Downie, Robert, Mgr, Libr Serv, Baker & Botts LLP, One Shell Plaza, 910 Louisiana St, Houston, TX, 77002. Tel: 713-229-1643. p. 2191
Downing, Heidi, Head, Tech Serv, Bedford Free Public Library, Seven Mudge Way, Bedford, MA, 01730. Tel: 781-275-9440. p. 987
Downing, Joanne, Asst Dir, Fort Bend County Libraries, 1001 Golfview Dr, Richmond, TX, 77469-5199. Tel: 281-633-4760. p. 2232
Downing, Karen, ILL, Institute for Advanced Study Libraries, One Einstein Dr, Princeton, NJ, 08540. Tel: 609-734-8000. p. 1436
Downing, Lee, Dir, Porter Memorial Library, 92 Court St, Machias, ME, 04654-2102. Tel: 207-255-3933. p. 931
Downing, Lisa, Libr Dir, Forbes Library, 20 West St, Northampton, MA, 01060-3798. Tel: 413-587-1011. p. 1042
Downing, Mary Kate, Br Mgr, Pasco County Library System, Regency Park, 9701 Little Rd, New Port Richey, FL, 34654. Tel: 727-861-3049. p. 410
Downing, Sarah, Asst Curator, Cataloger, Librn, North Carolina Office of Archives & History, One Festival Park Blvd, Manteo, NC, 27954. Tel: 252-473-2655. p. 1702
Downs, Brittany, Br Mgr, Arkansas River Valley Regional Library System, Logan County, 419 N Kennedy, Booneville, AR, 72927-3630. Tel: 479-675-2735. p. 93
Downs, Jackie, Br Mgr, Chesterfield County Public Library, Enon, 1801 Enon Church Rd, Chester, VA, 23836. Tel: 804-751-2275. p. 2312
Downs, Jackie, Br Mgr, Chesterfield County Public Library, Ettrick-Matoaca, 4501 River Rd, Petersburg, VA, 23803. Tel: 804-751-2275. p. 2312
Downs, Kathy, Cataloger, Smithfield Public Library, 25 N Main St, Smithfield, UT, 84335-1957. Tel: 435-563-3555. p. 2273
Downs, Robert, Libr Syst Spec, California State University Dominguez Hills, 1000 E Victoria St, Carson, CA, 90747. Tel: 310-243-2404. p. 129
Downs, Rondi, Librn, Grace of Christ Presbyterian Church Library, Nine S Eighth Ave, Yakima, WA, 98902. Tel: 509-248-7940. p. 2395
Dowson, Deborah, YA Serv, Groton Public Library, 99 Main St, Groton, MA, 01450. Tel: 978-448-1167, Ext 1325. p. 1022
Doyel, Wendy, Libr Dir, Woodbine Carnegie Public Library, 58 Fifth St, Woodbine, IA, 51579. Tel: 712-647-2750. p. 792
Doyle Bauer, Alexandra E, Co-Chair, Palomar College Library, 1140 W Mission Rd, San Marcos, CA, 92069-1487. Tel: 760-744-1150, Ext 2669. p. 234
Doyle, Brandie, Asst Dir, Admin Serv, Russell Library, 123 Broad St, Middletown, CT, 06457. Tel: 860-347-2528. p. 322
Doyle, Carol, Maps & Govt Info Librn, California State University, Fresno, Henry Madden Library, 5200 N Barton Ave, Mail Stop ML-34, Fresno, CA, 93740-8014. Tel: 559-278-2335. p. 144
Doyle, Cathleen, Digital Serv Mgr, Northbrook Public Library, 1201 Cedar Lane, Northbrook, IL, 60062-4581. Tel: 847-272-6224. p. 626
Doyle, Dennis, Dir, Ulster County Planning Board Library, County Office Bldg, 3rd Flr, 244 Fair St, Kingston, NY, 12402. Tel: 845-340-3340. p. 1560
Doyle, Forest, Tech Serv, Buncombe County Public Libraries, 67 Haywood St, Asheville, NC, 28801. Tel: 828-250-4700. p. 1672
Doyle, Glenda, Dir, Lee Ola Roberts Public Library, 140 W Main St, Whiteville, TN, 38075. Tel: 731-254-8834. p. 2129
Doyle, Jeannine M, Chief Operating Officer, Buffalo & Erie County Public Library System, One Lafayette Sq, Buffalo, NY, 14203-1887. Tel: 716-858-8900. p. 1507
Doyle, Jim, Ref Librn, Hoag Library, 134 S Main St, Albion, NY, 14411. Tel: 585-589-4246. p. 1484
Doyle, John, Actg Dir, National Institutes of Health Library, Ten Center Dr, Rm 1L25A, Bethesda, MD, 20892. Tel: 301-827-3839. p. 959
Doyle, John, Assoc Librn, Washington & Lee University, Wilbur C Hall Law Library, Lewis Hall, E Denny Circle, Lexington, VA, 24450. Tel: 540-458-8554. p. 2329
Doyle, Liz, Supvry Librn, United States Environmental Protection, 1200 Sixth Ave, Ste 155, MSD 1 K-03, Seattle, WA, 98101. Tel: 206-553-2134. p. 2381
Doyle, Megan, Access Serv Coordr, Rivier University, 420 S Main St, Nashua, NH, 03060-5086. Tel: 603-897-8685. p. 1375
Doyle, Mickey, Asst Dir, Ref Librn, University of Michigan-Flint, 303 E Kearsley St, Flint, MI, 48502. Tel: 810-762-3401. p. 1107
Doyle, Theresa, Asst Librn, Swayzee Public Library, 301 S Washington St, Swayzee, IN, 46986. Tel: 765-922-7526. p. 720
Doyle, Thomas, Archivist, Woburn Public Library, 36 Cummings Park, Woburn, MA, 01801. Tel: 781-933-0148. p. 1070
Doylen, Michael, Assoc Vice-Provost, Dir of Libr, University of Wisconsin-Milwaukee Libraries, 2311 E Hartford Ave, Milwaukee, WI, 53211. Tel: 414-229-4785, 414-229-6202. p. 2461
Doylen, Michael, Dir of Libr, University of Wisconsin, 400 University Dr, West Bend, WI, 53095-3619. Tel: 262-335-5206. p. 2487
Dozier, Wilene, Ref Librn, The Edward Waters College Library, 1658 Kings Rd, Jacksonville, FL, 32209-6199. Tel: 904-470-8068. p. 411
Drachaman, Debbie, Dir, The Crosswicks Library Co, 483 Main St, Crosswicks, NJ, 08515. Tel: 609-298-6271. p. 1398
Drachman, Ruth, Librn, Tinmouth Public Library, Nine MountainView Rd, Tinmouth, VT, 05773. Tel: 802-446-2498. p. 2296
Drader, Brian, Exec Dir, Manitoba Association of Playwrights, Artspace Bldg, 6th Flr, Rm 602, 100 Arthur St, Winnipeg, MB, R3B 1H3, CANADA. Tel: 204-942-8941. p. 2593
Dragga, Jack, Curator, Bedford Historical Society Library, 30 S Park St, Bedford, OH, 44146-3635. Tel: 440-232-0796. p. 1749
Drago, Keith, Ad, Dep Dir, Rockport Public Library, 485 Commercial St, Rockport, ME, 04856. Tel: 207-236-3642. p. 939
Dragoo, Melissa, Dir, Fortville-Vernon Township Public Library, 625 E Broadway, Fortville, IN, 46040-1549. Tel: 317-485-6402. p. 685
Dragos, Devra, Tech & Access Serv Dir, Nebraska Library Commission, The Atrium, 1200 N St, Ste 120, Lincoln, NE, 68508-2023. Tel: 402-471-2045. p. 1322
Drake, Alyson, Instrul Serv Librn, Fordham University School of Law, 150 W 62nd St, New York, NY, 10023. p. 1585
Drake, Cassidy, Head Librn, Big Lake Public Library, 3140 S Big Lake Rd, Big Lake, AK, 99652. Tel: 907-861-7635. p. 43
Drake, Cindy S, Curator, Head, Tech Serv, Librn, Nebraska History Library, 1500 R St, Lincoln, NE, 68508. Tel: 402-471-4786. p. 1322
Drake, Jane, Head, Children's Servx, Patchogue-Medford Library, 54-60 E Main St, Patchogue, NY, 11772. Tel: 631-654-4700. p. 1615
Drake, Lesleyanne, Archives, Coll, Orange County Regional History Center, 65 E Central Blvd, Orlando, FL, 32801. Tel: 407-836-8584. p. 432
Drake, Mike, Spec Coll, Fresno County Public Library, 2420 Mariposa St, Fresno, CA, 93721. Tel: 559-600-7323. p. 145
Drake, Robert, Asst Dir, Tech Operations, Nassau Library System, 900 Jerusalem Ave, Uniondale, NY, 11553-3039. Tel: 516-292-8920. p. 1654
Drake, Tracy, Spec Coll & Archives Librn, Reed College, 3203 SE Woodstock Blvd, Portland, OR, 97202-8199. Tel: 503-777-7702. p. 1894
Drake-Blackman, Deborah, Br Mgr, Birmingham Public Library, Pratt City Branch, 509 Dugan Ave, Birmingham, AL, 35214-5224. Tel: 205-791-4997. p. 7
Drakes, Olivia, ILL, Wenatchee Valley College, 1300 Fifth St, Wenatchee, WA, 98801. Tel: 509-682-6712. p. 2395
Draney, Rachelle, Ch, Lincoln County Library System, Alpine Branch, 243 River Circle, Alpine, WY, 83128. Tel: 307-654-7323. p. 2496
Drantch, Irene, Exec Dir, Temple Am Echad, One Saperstein Plaza, Lynbrook, NY, 11563. Tel: 516-593-4004. p. 1566
Drapa, Bree, Libr Dir, Westford Public Library, 1717 Vermont Rte 128, Westford, VT, 05494. Tel: 802-878-5639. p. 2298
Drapeau, Glenda, Librn, Freeland Holmes Library, 109 Pleasant St, Oxford, ME, 04270-4206. Tel: 207-539-4016. p. 935
Draper, Daniel, Ref Librn, US Department of Commerce, 325 Broadway, R/ESRL5, Boulder, CO, 80305-3328. Tel: 303-497-3271. p. 267
Draper, Kristen, Libr Mgr, Poudre River Public Library District, 201 Peterson St, Fort Collins, CO, 80524-2990. Tel: 970-221-6740. p. 281
Draper, Nancy, Dir, Libr Serv, Randall University, 3701 S I-35 Service Rd, Moore, OK, 73160. Tel: 405-912-9025. p. 1853
Draper, Savanna, Libr Dir, Bridgeport Public Library, 1200 Johnson Ave, Bridgeport, WV, 26330. Tel: 304-842-8248. p. 2398
Draves, Ken, Br Mgr, Poudre River Public Library District, Harmony Library, 4616 S Shields St, Fort Collins, CO, 80526-3812. Tel: 970-221-6740. p. 281
Draves, Ken, Dep Dir, Poudre River Public Library District, 201 Peterson St, Fort Collins, CO, 80524-2990. Tel: 970-221-6740. p. 281
Drawbaugh, Beth, Librn, York First Church of the Brethren Library, 2710 Kingston Rd, York, PA, 17402-3799. Tel: 717-755-0307. p. 2027

Drawe, Scott, Br Mgr, Chicago Public Library, Near North, 310 W Division St, Chicago, IL, 60610. Tel: 312-744-0991. p. 557
Drayer, Amy, Br Mgr, Athens County Public Libraries, Athens Public Library, 30 Home St, Athens, OH, 45701. Tel: 740-592-4272. p. 1805
Drayton, Quettara, Asst Br Mgr, Chesterfield County Public Library, Enon, 1801 Enon Church Rd, Chester, VA, 23836. Tel: 804-751-2275. p. 2312
Drayton, Quettara, Asst Br Mgr, Chesterfield County Public Library, Ettrick-Matoaca, 4501 River Rd, Petersburg, VA, 23803. Tel: 804-751-2275. p. 2312
Drayton, Sharea, Circ, Georgetown County Library, 405 Cleland St, Georgetown, SC, 29440-3200. Tel: 843-545-3300. p. 2060
Drazek, Michael, Libr Dir, The Free Public Library of the Borough of Pompton Lakes, 333 Wanaque Ave, Pompton Lakes, NJ, 07442. Tel: 973-835-0482. p. 1435
Dreaden, Sandra, Ref Librn, Robert L F Sikes Public Library, 1445 Commerce Dr, Crestview, FL, 32539. Tel: 850-682-4432. p. 391
Dreblow, Deanna, Libr Dir, Wolcott Community Public Library, 101 E North St, Wolcott, IN, 47995. Tel: 219-279-2695. p. 727
Drees, Kevin, Liaison Librn, Oklahoma State University Libraries, Materials Science & Engineering Division, Edmon Low Library, 3rd Flr, Stillwater, OK, 74078-1071. Tel: 405-744-9751. p. 1862
Dreesman, Lisa, Librn, Des Moines Area Community College Library, 906 N Grant Rd, Carroll, IA, 51401. Tel: 712-792-8317. p. 737
Dreimiller, Gretchen, Dir, Libr Res, Beacon College Library, 105 E Main St, Leesburg, FL, 34748. Tel: 352-638-9807. p. 418
Dreisbach, William, Tech Serv Librn, Pottsville Free Public Library, 215 W Market St, Pottsville, PA, 17901. Tel: 570-622-8105, 570-622-8880. p. 1999
Dreitlein, Karen, Head, Tech Serv, Berkeley Heights Public Library, 29 Park Ave, Berkeley Heights, NJ, 07922. Tel: 908-464-9333. p. 1390
Drennan, Elizabeth, Ch Mgr, Poplar Creek Public Library District, 1405 S Park Ave, Streamwood, IL, 60107-2997. Tel: 630-837-6800. p. 652
Drennan, Sarah, Dir, Morgan County Public Library, 105 Congress St, Berkeley Springs, WV, 25411. Tel: 304-258-3350. p. 2398
Drennan-Goin, Khristine, Sr Librn, Otisville State Correctional Facility Library, 57 Sanitorium Rd, Otisville, NY, 10963. Tel: 845-386-1490. p. 1613
Drennan-Scace, Kat, Br Mgr, Hamilton Public Library, Red Hill, 695 Queenston Rd, Hamilton, ON, L8G 1A1, CANADA. Tel: 905-546-3200, Ext 2976. p. 2646
Drepaul, Norma, Ref & Instruction Librn, Los Angeles Southwest College, Cox Bldg, 1600 W Imperial Hwy, Los Angeles, CA, 90047-4899. Tel: 323-241-5235. p. 166
Drepaul, Norma, Ref & Tech Librn, Lone Star College System, North Harris College Library, 2700 W W Thorne Dr, Houston, TX, 77073. Tel: 281-618-5491. p. 2197
Dresbach, Steve, Head, Info Tech Serv, State University of New York College, SUNY Geneseo, One College Circle, Geneseo, NY, 14454-1498. Tel: 585-245-5594. p. 1537
Drescher, Judith, Libr Dir, Molloy College, 1000 Hempstead Ave, Rockville Centre, NY, 11571. Tel: 516-323-3925. p. 1632
Dresley, Susan C, Dir, John A Volpe National Transportation Systems Center, Kendall Sq, 55 Broadway, Cambridge, MA, 02142-1093. Tel: 617-494-2117. p. 1009
Dressel, Willow, Eng Librn, Princeton University, Engineering Library, Friend Ctr, William St, Princeton, NJ, 08544. Tel: 609-258-6567. p. 1437
Dresser, Heather, Youth Serv Librn, Hooksett Public Library, 31 Mount Saint Mary's Way, Hooksett, NH, 03106-1852. Tel: 603-485-6092. p. 1368
Dresser, Lara, Dir, Williams Mullen Library, 301 Fayetteville St, Ste 1700, Raleigh, NC, 27601. Tel: 919-981-4038. p. 1712
Dresser, Leah, Adult Serv Mgr, Kendallville Public Library, 221 S Park Ave, Kendallville, IN, 46755-2248. Tel: 260-343-2010. p. 698
Dressler, Ben, Digitization Tech, Southwestern Oklahoma State University, 100 Campus Dr, Weatherford, OK, 73096-3002. Tel: 580-774-7024. p. 1868
Dressler, Emma, Dir, Fernie Heritage Library, 492 Third Ave, Fernie, BC, V0B 1M0, CANADA. Tel: 250-423-4458. p. 2566
Dressler, Mina, Br Mgr, Hickman County Public Library, East Hickman Public Library, 5009 Hwy 100, Lyles, TN, 37098. Tel: 931-670-5767. p. 2091
Drew, Eric, User Serv Librn, Halifax Public Libraries, J D Shatford Memorial, 10353 St Margaret Bay Rd, Hubbards, NS, B0J 1T0, CANADA. Tel: 902-857-9176. p. 2618
Drew, Hadiya, Dir, Summit Public Library District, 6233 S Archer Rd, Summit, IL, 60501. Tel: 708-458-1545. p. 653
Drew, Madison, Acq Assoc, Cornerstone University, 1001 E Beltline Ave NE, Grand Rapids, MI, 49525. Tel: 616-254-1650, Ext 1232. p. 1110
Drew Rather, Julia, Ref Librn, Meharry Medical College Library, 2001 Albion St, Nashville, TN, 37208. Tel: 615-327-6465. p. 2119
Drew, Robert, Digital Initiatives & Syst Librn, University of Prince Edward Island, 550 University Ave, Charlottetown, PE, C1A 4P3, CANADA. Tel: 902-566-0343. p. 2707
Drewek, Elizabeth, Youth Serv Librn, Saint Clair Shores Public Library, 22500 11 Mile Rd, Saint Clair Shores, MI, 48081-1399. Tel: 586-771-9020. p. 1147
Drewien, Lyn, Dir, Hailey Public Library, Seven W Croy St, Hailey, ID, 83333. Tel: 208-788-2036. p. 521
Drews, Tori, Libr Dir, Sherrard Public Library District, 501 Third St, Sherrard, IL, 61281. Tel: 309-593-2178. p. 646
Drey, Marian, Librn, United States Courts Library, 300 Fannin St, Rm 5012, Shreveport, LA, 71101-6305. Tel: 318-676-3230. p. 910
Dreyer, Kathleen, Chief Librn, Borough of Manhattan Community College Library, 199 Chambers St, S410, New York, NY, 10007. Tel: 212-220-1499. p. 1580
Dreyer, Katie, Youth Serv Librn, Pella Public Library, 603 Main St, Pella, IA, 50219. Tel: 641-628-4268. p. 776
Dreyer, Laurie, Br Mgr, Troy Public Library, Lansingburgh Branch, 27 114th St, Troy, NY, 12182. Tel: 518-235-5310. p. 1653
Dreyer, Rachael, Interim Head of Libr, Pennsylvania State University Libraries, Eberly Family Special Collections Library, 104 Paterno Library, University Park, PA, 16802-1808. Tel: 814-865-1793, 814-865-7931. p. 2015
Driggers, Catherine, Libr Mgr, Live Oak Public Libraries, Rincon Branch, 17th St & Hwy 21, Rincon, GA, 31326. Tel: 912-826-2222. p. 496
Drillen, Crystal, Actg County Librn, Nueces County Public Libraries, 100 Terry Shamsie Blvd, Robstown, TX, 78380. Tel: 361-387-3431. p. 2233
Drinka, Jennifer, Libr Dir, Antioch Public Library District, 757 Main St, Antioch, IL, 60002. Tel: 847-395-0874. p. 537
Drinka, Kevin, Libr Mgr, Arizona City Community Library, 13254 Sunland Gin Rd, Arizona City, AZ, 85123. Tel: 520-866-7740. p. 55
Driscoll, Carol, Asst Dir, Gutekunst Public Library, 309 Second St SE, State Center, IA, 50247-0550. Tel: 641-483-2741. p. 784
Driscoll, John, Ref Librn, YA Librn, Galesburg Public Library, 40 E Simmons St, Galesburg, IL, 61401-4591. Tel: 309-343-6118. p. 591
Driscoll, Lori, Dir, Gulf Coast State College Library, 5230 W US Hwy 98, Panama City, FL, 32401. Tel: 850-872-3893. p. 435
Driscoll, Martha J, Syst Coordr, North of Boston Library Exchange, Inc, 42A Cherry Hill Dr, Danvers, MA, 01923. Tel: 978-777-8844. p. 2767
Driskell, Mike, Exec Dir, Arlington Heights Memorial Library, 500 N Dunton Ave, Arlington Heights, IL, 60004-5966. Tel: 847-392-0100. p. 537
Driver, Anita, Dir, Jerseyville Public Library, 105 N Liberty St, Jerseyville, IL, 62052-1512. Tel: 618-498-9514. p. 603
Driver, C Berry, Jr, Librn, Southern Baptist Theological Seminary, 2825 Lexington Rd, Louisville, KY, 40280-0294. p. 866
Driver, Carol, User Serv Librn, West Kentucky Community & Technical College, 4810 Alben Barkley Dr, Paducah, KY, 42001. Tel: 270-534-3170. p. 872
Driver, Claudia, Ref Librn, Springdale Public Library, 405 S Pleasant St, Springdale, AR, 72764. Tel: 479-750-8180. p. 110
Driver, Dee, Mkt & Communications Mgr, Gwinnett County Public Library, 1001 Lawrenceville Hwy NW, Lawrenceville, GA, 30046-4707. Tel: 770-978-5154. p. 485
Driver, Jason, Br Mgr, Chicago Public Library, Legler, 115 S Pulaski Rd, Chicago, IL, 60624. Tel: 312-746-7730. p. 556
Driver, Jason, Libr Dir, Kitsap Regional Library, 1301 Sylvan Way, Bremerton, WA, 98310-3498. p. 2359
Drmacich, Jessika, Digital Archivist/Rec Mgr, Williams College, 26 Hopkins Hall Dr, Williamstown, MA, 01267. Tel: 413-597-4725. p. 1069
Drobik, Michelle, Archivist, Ohio State University LIBRARIES, Archives, 2700 Kenny Rd, Columbus, OH, 43210. Tel: 614-292-3271. p. 1774
Drobnicki, John A, Head, Acq & Coll Develop, Webmaster, York College Library, 94-20 Guy R Brewer Blvd, Jamaica, NY, 11451. Tel: 718-262-2025. p. 1556
Drockton, Lori, Asst Librn, Madill City County Library, 500 W Overton St, Madill, OK, 73446. Tel: 580-795-2749. p. 1852
Droegmiller, Elaine, Dir, Cushing Community Library, 202 Main St, Cushing, IA, 51018. Tel: 712-384-2501. p. 743
Drolet, Claire, Access Serv Librn, Delaware Valley University, 700 E Butler Ave, Doylestown, PA, 18901-2699. p. 1927
Drolet, Marie-Josee, Librn, Teluq University, 455 rue du Parvis, F015-B, Quebec, QC, G1K 9H6, CANADA. Tel: 418-657-2262, Ext 5333. p. 2732
Drolet, Nancy, Prof, Cégep Garneau, 1660 blvd de l'Entente, Quebec, QC, G1S 4S3, CANADA. Tel: 418-688-8310, Ext 2290. p. 2796
Droll, Charlotte, Dir, Libr Serv, Bloomsburg University of Pennsylvania, 400 E Second St, Bloomsburg, PA, 17815-1301. Tel: 570-389-4207. p. 1913
Drollinger, Coltyn, Youth Serv, Lester Public Library of Rome, 1157 Rome Center Dr, Nekoosa, WI, 54457. Tel: 715-325-8990. p. 2464
Drolsum, Chris, Research Servs Librn, Maryland Institute College of Art, 1401 W Mount Royal Ave, Baltimore, MD, 21217. Tel: 410-225-2304, 410-225-2311. p. 955
Drone-Silvers, Frances, Coordr, East Central Illinois Consortium, c/o CARLE Foundation Hospital, 611 W Park St, Urbana, IL, 61801. Tel: 217-383-4513. p. 2764
Dronyk, Ashleigh, Info Res Mgr, Niagara Falls Public Library, 4848 Victoria Ave, Niagara Falls, ON, L2E 4C5, CANADA. Tel: 905-356-8080. p. 2660
Droog, Alissa, Education & Social Sciences Librn, Northern Illinois University Libraries, 217 Normal Rd, DeKalb, IL, 60115-2828. Tel: 815-753-4025. p. 577

Drost, Carol, Assoc Univ Librarian for Access & Technical Services, Willamette University, 900 State St, Salem, OR, 97301. Tel: 503-370-6715. p. 1897
Drost, Jack, Syst Librn, University of Alabama in Huntsville, 4700 Holmes Ave, Huntsville, AL, 35805. Tel: 256-824-7407. p. 22
Drost, Leslie, First Year Experience Librn, Kennesaw State University Library System, 385 Cobb Ave NW, MD 1701, Kennesaw, GA, 30144. Tel: 470-578-3884. p. 483
Drotar, Sonja, Ch, Oak Bluffs Public Library, 56R School St, Oak Bluffs, MA, 02557. Tel: 568-693-9433, Ext 126. p. 1044
Drotar, Sonja, Head, Children's Dept, Shrewsbury Public Library, 609 Main St, Shrewsbury, MA, 01545. Tel: 508-841-8609. p. 1053
Drotleff, Kurt, Circ Support, Malone University, 2600 Cleveland Ave NW, Canton, OH, 44709-3308. Tel: 330-471-8215. p. 1755
Drouillard, Colette, Dr, Assoc Prof, Valdosta State University, Odum Library, 1500 N Patterson St, Valdosta, GA, 31698. Tel: 229-245-3715. p. 2784
Drow, Katie, Dir, Ventura County Law Library, 800 S Victoria Ave, Ventura, CA, 93009-2020. Tel: 805-642-8982. p. 256
Drown, Ana, Br Mgr, Grand Rapids Public Library, Madison Square, 1201 Madison SE, Grand Rapids, MI, 49507. Tel: 616-988-5411. p. 1111
Drown, Trevor, Site Supvr, Riverside County Library System, San Jacinto Library, 595 S San Jacinto Ave, Ste B, San Jacinto, CA, 92583. Tel: 951-654-8635. p. 202
Druce, Jennifer, Br Mgr, Camden County Library System, South County Regional Branch - Winslow Township, 35 Coopers Folly Rd, Atco, NJ, 08004. Tel: 856-753-2537, Ext 7404. p. 1450
Drucker, Jon, Access Serv Librn, University of the Sciences in Philadelphia, 4200 Woodland Ave, Philadelphia, PA, 19104. Tel: 215-596-8960. p. 1989
Drucker-Albert, Ellen, Head, Ref & Coll Develop, Yeshiva University Libraries, Dr Lillian & Dr Rebecca Chutick Law Library, Benjamin N Cardozo School of Law, 55 Fifth Ave, New York, NY, 10003-4301. Tel: 212-790-0223. p. 1604
Drudy, Marla, Youth/Young Adult Librn, Alma Public Library, 500 E Superior St, Alma, MI, 48801-1999. Tel: 989-463-3966, Ext 9581. p. 1077
Druga, Elizabeth, Archivist, National Archives & Records Administration, 1000 Beal Ave, Ann Arbor, MI, 48109. Tel: 734-205-0554. p. 1079
Drulia, Megen R, Acad Serv Officer III, Wayne State University, 106 Kresge Library, Detroit, MI, 48202. Tel: 313-577-8543. p. 2787
Drum, Denette, Assoc Dir, Central Community College, 4500 63rd St, Columbus, NE, 68602. Tel: 402-562-1445. p. 1310
Drumm, Karla, Head Librn, Bunnvale Public Library, Seven Bunnvale Rd, Califon, NJ, 07830. Tel: 908-638-8523, Ext 401. p. 1394
Drummond, Clara, Curator, Exhibitions Coordr, Pennsylvania State University Libraries, Eberly Family Special Collections Library, 104 Paterno Library, University Park, PA, 16802-1808. Tel: 814-865-1793, 814-865-7931. p. 2015
Drummond, Robyn, Dir, Wakulla County Public Library, 4330 Crawfordville Hwy, Crawfordville, FL, 32326. Tel: 850-926-7415. p. 391
Drummond, Valerie, Br Mgr, Fairfax County Public Library, Kings Park, 9000 Burke Lake Rd, Burke, VA, 22015-1683. Tel: 703-978-5600. p. 2316
Drury, Carol, Asst Dir, Endometriosis Association Library & Reading Room, 8585 N 76th Pl, Milwaukee, WI, 53223. Tel: 414-355-2200. p. 2458
Drury, Deborah, Chief Exec Officer, Elizabethtown Public Library, Ten S Market St, Elizabethtown, PA, 17022-2307. Tel: 717-367-7467. p. 1929
Drury, Kara, Br Mgr, Mid-Continent Public Library, Liberty Branch, 1000 Kent St, Liberty, MO, 64068. Tel: 816-781-9240. p. 1251
Drury Melsness, Leanne, Mgr, Edmonton Public Library, Heritage Valley, 2755 119A St SW, Edmonton, AB, T6W 3R3, CANADA. Tel: 780-496-8348. p. 2536
Druskovich, Amy, Local Hist Librn, Van Buren District Library, 200 N Phelps St, Decatur, MI, 49045. Tel: 269-423-4771. p. 1096
Dryden, Joyce, Librn, Lucile L Morgan Public Library, 541 Ross St, Heflin, AL, 36264. Tel: 256-463-2259. p. 20
Dryden, Nancy, Res & Instruction Librn, University of Connecticut, Jeremy Richard Library, Stamford Campus, One University Pl, Stamford, CT, 06901-2315. Tel: 203-251-8439. p. 340
Dryden, Tara, Libr Asst, Pub Serv, Adams County Public Library, West Union Public Library, 212 E Sparks St, West Union, OH, 45693. Tel: 937-544-2591. p. 1814
Drye, Sarah, Law Librn, Christian & Barton, LLP Attorneys At Law, 901 East Cary St, Ste 1800, Richmond, VA, 23219. Tel: 804-697-4100. p. 2340
Drye, Susan, Asst Dir, Admin Serv, Nashville Public Library, 615 Church St, Nashville, TN, 37219-2314. Tel: 615-880-2614. p. 2119
Drysdale, Lisa, Cat/Metadata Tech, Alberta Government Library, Capital Blvd, 11th Flr, 10044 - 108 St, Edmonton, AB, T5J 5E6, CANADA. Tel: 780-427-2985. p. 2534
Du Ruisseau, Manon, Section Head, Info Consult Serv, Polytechnique Montreal Library, Campus de l'Universite de Montreal, 2500, chemin de Polytechnique, 2900, boul Edouard-Montpetit, Montreal, QC, H3T 1J4, CANADA. Tel: 514-340-4711, Ext 7205. p. 2727
Du, Yunfei, Dr, Assoc Dean, Prof, University of North Texas, 3940 N Elm St, Ste E292, Denton, TX, 76207. Tel: 940-565-3565. p. 2793
Duan, Xiaojie, Collection Resources Librn, Xavier University of Louisiana, One Drexel Dr, New Orleans, LA, 70125-1098. Tel: 504-520-7311. p. 904
Duane, Erin, Librn, Solano Community College Library, 4000 Suisun Valley Rd, Fairfield, CA, 94534. Tel: 707-864-7000, Ext 4706. p. 142
Duangudom, Savanida, Campus Librn, Wake Technical Community College, Scott Northern Wake Library, 6600 Louisburg Rd, NF 241, Raleigh, NC, 27616. Tel: 919-532-5553. p. 1711
Duarte, Cassi, Outreach Coordr, Temple Public Library, 100 W Adams Ave, Temple, TX, 76501-7641. Tel: 254-298-5295. p. 2247
Duarte, Guillermina, Br Mgr, Chicago Public Library, Garfield Ridge, 6348 S Archer Ave, Chicago, IL, 60638. Tel: 312-747-6094. p. 556
Duball, Cheri L, Acq, Spec Projects, Washington & Jefferson College Library, 60 S Lincoln St, Washington, PA, 15301. Tel: 724-223-6104. p. 2018
Dubansky, Mindell, Conserv Librn, Metropolitan Museum of Art, Thomas J Watson Library, 1000 Fifth Ave, New York, NY, 10028-0198. Tel: 212-570-3220. p. 1592
DuBard, Melanie, Sr Res Spec, Nelson, Mullins, Riley & Scarborough, 1320 Main St, Ste 1700, Columbia, SC, 29201. Tel: 803-255-9367. p. 2053
Dubard, Melanie, Librn, Nelson, Mullins, Riley & Scarborough, 104 S Main St, Ste 900, Greenville, SC, 29601. Tel: 864-250-2300. p. 2062
Dubbelde, Nan M, Libr Mgr, Chevron Information Technology Company, Division of Chevron USA, Inc, 100 Chevron Way, Bldg 50, Rm 1212, Richmond, CA, 94802. Tel: 510-242-4755. p. 200
Dube, Noelle, Librn, Golder Associates Ltd Library, 6925 Century Avenue, Ste 100, Mississauga, ON, L5N 7K2, CANADA. Tel: 905-567-4444. p. 2659
Dube, Pam, Dir, Woodridge Public Library, Three Plaza Dr, Woodridge, IL, 60517-5014. Tel: 630-487-2549. p. 664
Dube, Sheila, Youth Serv Librn, Springvale Public Library, 443 Main St, Springvale, ME, 04083. Tel: 207-324-4624. p. 942
Dubin, David, Assoc Teaching Prof, University of Illinois at Urbana-Champaign, Library & Information Science Bldg, 501 E Daniel St, Champaign, IL, 61820-6211. Tel: 217-333-3280. p. 2784
Dubin, Susan H, Libr Consult, Sperling-Kronberg-Mack Holocaust Resource Center Library, Midbar Kodesh Temple, 1940 Pasco Verde, Henderson, NV, 89012. Tel: 702-433-0005. p. 1346
Dubnjakovic, Ana, Head Librn, University of South Carolina, Music Library, 813 Assembly St, Rm 208, Columbia, SC, 29208. Tel: 803-777-5425. p. 2055
Dubois, Alex, Curator, Litchfield Historical Society, Seven South St, Litchfield, CT, 06759-0385. Tel: 860-567-4501. p. 320
DuBois, Carolyn, Ch Serv, Abington Township Public Library, 1030 Old York Rd, Abington, PA, 19001-4594. Tel: 215-885-5180, Ext 129. p. 1903
Dubois, Justin, Supvr, University of Arkansas Libraries, Physics, 221 Physics, Fayetteville, AR, 72701. Tel: 479-575-2505. p. 95
DuBois, Larissa, Head, Ref, Duxbury Free Library, 77 Alden St, Duxbury, MA, 02332. Tel: 781-934-2721. p. 1015
DuBois, Lori, Instrul & Ref Librn, Williams College, 26 Hopkins Hall Dr, Williamstown, MA, 01267. Tel: 413-597-4614. p. 1069
Dubois, Pat, Br Mgr, Grant Parish Library, Montgomery Branch, 940 Caddo St, Montgomery, LA, 71454. Tel: 318-646-3660. p. 887
Dubois, Roger, Admin Serv Mgr, Idaho Commission for Libraries, 325 W State St, Boise, ID, 83702-6072. Tel: 208-334-2150. p. 517
Dubois, Rosemary, Br Mgr, City of San Bernardino Library Services, Paul Villasenor Branch, 525 N Mount Vernon Ave, San Bernardino, CA, 90411. Tel: 909-383-5156. p. 212
DuBois, Sharon, Mgr, Bartram Trail Regional Library, Taliaferro County, 117 Askin St, Crawfordville, GA, 30631. Tel: 706-456-2531. p. 502
Dubois, Susan, Dir, North Smithfield Public Library, 20 Main St, Slatersville, RI, 02876. Tel: 401-767-2780. p. 2041
Dubois, Yvonne, Librn, Chinook Regional Library, Glentworth Branch, Glentworth School, First Ave, Glentworth, SK, S0H 1V0, CANADA. Tel: 306-266-4804, 306-266-4940. p. 2752
Dubord, Paula, Circ, East Providence Public Library, 41 Grove Ave, East Providence, RI, 02914. Tel: 401-434-2453. p. 2032
DuBose, Debra, Head Librn, Driscoll Public Library, 202 E Hondo Ave, Devine, TX, 78016. Tel: 830-663-2993. p. 2171
DuBray, Jolene, Archive Spec, Flagler College, 44 Sevilla St, Saint Augustine, FL, 32084-4302. Tel: 904-819-6206. p. 439
Dubreuil-Moisan, Marie-Andree, Mgr, Bibliotheque Publique de Pointe-Claire, 100 ave Douglas-Shand, Pointe-Claire, QC, H9R 4V1, CANADA. Tel: 514-630-1218. p. 2728
Dubuc, Marie-Marcelle, Librn, Cegep de L'Abitibi - Temiscamingue Bibliotheque, 425 Boul du College, Rouyn-Noranda, QC, J9X 5M5, CANADA. Tel: 819-762-0931, Ext 1234. p. 2733
Ducat, Janet, Talking Bks Libr Mgr, Jacksonville Public Library, Talking Books for the Blind & Physically Handicapped, 303 N Laura St, Conference Level, Jacksonville, FL, 32202. Tel: 904-630-1999. p. 412
Ducey, Mary Ellen, Spec Coll & Archives Librn, University of Nebraska-Lincoln, 318 Love Library, 13th & R Strs, Lincoln, NE, 68588. Tel: 402-472-2526. p. 1323

Duffy, Sean, Adult Serv Mgr, Ohio County Public Library, 52 16th St, Wheeling, WV, 26003. Tel: 304-232-0244. p. 2417
Duffy, Shannon, Br Mgr, Atlanta-Fulton Public Library System, East Atlanta Branch, 400 Flat Shoals Ave SE, Atlanta, GA, 30316. Tel: 404-730-5438. p. 461
Duffy, Shannon, Libr Dir, Sutton Free Public Library, Four Uxbridge Rd, Sutton, MA, 01590. Tel: 508-865-8752. p. 1059
Dufner, Jessica, Adult Serv Mgr, Ritter Public Library, 5680 Liberty Ave, Vermilion, OH, 44089. Tel: 440-967-3798. p. 1827
Dufort, Anne-Marie, Libr Tech, Bibliotheque de Montreal-Est, 11370 rue Notre-Dame, 3rd Flr, Montreal-Est, QC, H1B 2W6, CANADA. Tel: 514-905-2144. p. 2728
Dufort, Michelle, Dir, Grafton Public Library, 204 Main St, Grafton, VT, 05146. Tel: 802-843-2404. p. 2285
Dufour, Christine, Dir, Bibliotheque Municipale de Sainte-Therese, 150 Boul du Seminaire, Sainte-Therese, QC, J7E 1Z2, CANADA. Tel: 450-434-1440, Ext 2400. p. 2734
Dufour, Christine, Assoc Prof, Universite de Montreal, 3150, rue Jean-Brillant, bur C-2004, Montreal, QC, H3T 1N8, CANADA. Tel: 514-343-6044. p. 2797
Dufresne, Catherine, Acq, Borden Ladner Gervais LLP Library, 1000 de la Gauchetiere W, Ste 900, Montreal, QC, H3B 5H4, CANADA. Tel: 514-954-3159. p. 2721
Dufresne, Manon, Librn, Centre d'Animation, de Developpement et de Recherche, 1940 Est Blvd Henri Bourassa, Montreal, QC, H2B 1S2, CANADA. Tel: 514-381-8891, Ext 246. p. 2722
Dufrey, Audrey, Librn, Ukiah Public Library, 201 Hill St, Ukiah, OR, 97880. Tel: 541-427-3735. p. 1901
Dugan, Carol Lee, Dir, Carnegie Public Library, 120 Jefferson St, Monte Vista, CO, 81144-1797. Tel: 719-852-3931. p. 291
Dugan, Kathleen, Libr Coord, Lehigh University, Linderman Library, 30 Library Dr, Bethlehem, PA, 18015. Tel: 610-758-4925. p. 1912
Dugan, Kathleen M, Chief Admin Officer, Librn, Cleveland Law Library, One W Lakeside Ave, 4th Flr, Cleveland, OH, 44113-1078. Tel: 216-861-5070. p. 1767
Dugan, Megan, Dean of Libr, Mt Hood Community College Libraries, 26000 SE Stark St, Gresham, OR, 97030. Tel: 503-491-7652. p. 1881
Dugan, Paula A, Children's Serv Supvr, Needham Free Public Library, 1139 Highland Ave, Needham, MA, 02494-3298. Tel: 781-455-7559, Ext 219. p. 1038
Dugan, Rachel, Br Mgr, Saint Martin Parish Library, Cecilia Branch, 2460 Cecilia Sr High School Hwy, Cecilia, LA, 70521. Tel: 337-667-7411. p. 907
Dugas, Corie, Exec Dir, NELLCO Law Library Consortium, Inc., 756 Madison Ave, Ste 102, Albany, NY, 12208. Tel: 518-694-3026. p. 2771
Dugas, Ginette, Info Res, Librn, Montreal City Planning Department, 303 Notre-Dame est Bureau 5A-37, Montreal, QC, H2Y 3Y8, CANADA. Tel: 514-872-4119. p. 2726
Dugas Hughes, Jill, Dir, East Greenbush Community Library, Ten Community Way, East Greenbush, NY, 12061. Tel: 518-477-7476. p. 1527
Duggal, Barbara, Librn, Ohlone College, 43600 Mission Blvd, Fremont, CA, 94539. Tel: 510-659-6160. p. 143
Duggan, Holli, Continuing Educ Coordr, Nebraska Library Commission, The Atrium, 1200 N St, Ste 120, Lincoln, NE, 68508-2023. Tel: 402-471-2694. p. 1322
Duggan, James E, Dir, Law Libr & Assoc Prof of Law, Tulane University, Law Library, Weinmann Hall, 3rd Flr, 6329 Freret St, New Orleans, LA, 70118-6231. Tel: 504-865-5952. p. 904
Duggan, Tom, Res Serv Mgr, Morrison & Foerster LLP, 4200 Republic Plaza, 370 17th St, Denver, CO, 80202. Tel: 303-592-1500. p. 276
Duggins, Brandi, Libr Dir, Spalding University Library, 853 Library Lane, Louisville, KY, 40203-9986. Tel: 502-585-7130. p. 867
DuGranrut, Emily, Archivist, Galesburg Public Library, 40 E Simmons St, Galesburg, IL, 61401-4591. Tel: 309-343-6118. p. 591
Duguay, Adam, Institutional Repository Coord, Sheridan College Library, Hazel McCallion Campus, 4180 Duke of York Blvd, Mississauga, ON, L5B 0G5, CANADA. Tel: 905-845-9430, Ext 5583. p. 2663
Duguay, Denis, Chief Admin Officer, Chapleau Public Library, 20 Pine St W, Chapleau, ON, P0M 1K0, CANADA. Tel: 705-864-0852. p. 2635
Duhon, Alice, Br Mgr, Cameron Parish Library, Lowry Branch, 454 Lowry Hwy, Lake Arthur, LA, 70549. Tel: 337-774-3030. p. 886
Duimstra, Scott, Exec Dir, Capital Area District Libraries, 401 S Capitol Ave, Lansing, MI, 48933. Tel: 517-367-6300. p. 1123
Duke, Amy, Asst Dir, Saint Charles Parish Library, 160 W Campus Dr, Destrehan, LA, 70047. Tel: 985-764-2366. p. 888
Duke, Del, Dr, Electronic Res Mgr, Instruction Librn, Libr Dir, Southern Arkansas University, 100 E University, Magnolia, AR, 71753-5000. Tel: 870-235-4171. p. 103
Duke, Fiona, Br Mgr, Indianapolis Public Library, Southport, 2630 E Stop 11 Rd, Indianapolis, IN, 46227-8899. Tel: 317-275-4517. p. 696
Duke, Heather, Dir & Librn, Oswego Public Library, 704 Fourth St, Oswego, KS, 67356. Tel: 620-795-4921. p. 829
Duke, Julie, Youth Serv Mgr, Williamson County Public Library, 1314 Columbia Ave, Franklin, TN, 37064. Tel: 615-595-1244, Ext 2. p. 2098
Dukes, Earnstein, Dean of Libr, Texas Tech University Libraries, 2802 18th St, Lubbock, TX, 79409. Tel: 806-834-1938. p. 2214
Dukes, Michelle, Ch Serv, Anderson City, Anderson, Stony Creek & Union Townships Public Library, 111 E 12th St, Anderson, IN, 46016-2701. Tel: 765-241-2448. p. 667
Dukes, Suzy, Libr Mgr, Piedmont Regional Library System, Statham Public Library, 1928 Railroad St, Statham, GA, 30666. Tel: 770-725-4785. p. 482
Dukes, Torrey, Ref Librn, North Shore Community College Library, McGee Bldg, LE127, 300 Broad St, Lynn, MA, 01901. Tel: 978-762-4000, Ext 6244. p. 1030
Dulaney, Dale, Coll Develop, Educ Res Librn, Virginia Western Community College, 3095 Colonial Ave SW, Roanoke, VA, 24015. Tel: 540-857-7438. p. 2346
Dulay, Sarah, Dir, Libr Serv, Northwestern College, 9400 S Cicero Ave, Oak Lawn, IL, 60453. Tel: 708-237-5050. p. 628
Dulepski, Deborah, Univ Librn, University of Bridgeport, 126 Park Ave, Bridgeport, CT, 06604-5620. Tel: 203-576-2388. p. 304
Dull, Claudia, Dir, Readstown Public Library, 129 W Wisconsin, Readstown, WI, 54652. Tel: 608-629-5465. p. 2472
Dull, Pam, Actg Dir, Huntingdon Valley Library, 625 Red Lion Rd, Huntingdon Valley, PA, 19006. Tel: 215-947-5138. p. 1945
Dulock, Simon, Mgr, Hewitt Public Library, 200 Patriot Ct, Hewitt, TX, 76643. Tel: 254-666-2442. p. 2189
Dulworth, Caroline, Assoc Dir, Br Mgr, Pioneer Library System, Norman Public Library Central, 225 N Webster, Norman, OK, 73069. Tel: 405-701-2600. p. 1855
Dulworth, Caroline, Dir, Br, Pioneer Library System, Noble Public, 204 N Fifth St, Noble, OK, 73068. Tel: 405-872-5713. p. 1855
Dumapay, Joanne, Librn, Gordon & Rees Scully Mansukhani, 275 Battery St, Ste 2000, San Francisco, CA, 94111. Tel: 415-986-5900. p. 225
Dumas, Janet, Ch Serv, Wheaton Public Library, 225 N Cross St, Wheaton, IL, 60187-5376. Tel: 630-868-7543. p. 662
Dumas, Sabrina, Libr Dir, Clifton Public Library, 588 Turner Ave, Clifton, AZ, 85533. Tel: 928-865-2461. p. 58
Dumas, Sabrina, County Librn, Greenlee County Library System, 122 N Hwy 75, Duncan, AZ, 85534. Tel: 928-359-2094. p. 60
Dumas, Willie Mae, Supvr, Per, University of South Carolina Aiken, 471 University Pkwy, Aiken, SC, 29801. Tel: 803-641-3284. p. 2046
Dumas Wittwer, Lindsay, Digital Archivist, Hunter College Libraries, Centro - Center for Puerto Rican Studies Library, 2180 Third Ave, Rm 121, New York, NY, 10035. Tel: 212-396-7882. p. 1588
Dumbleton, Mary, Librn, Florida State College at Jacksonville, North Campus & Learning Commons, 4501 Capper Rd, Jacksonville, FL, 32218-4499. Tel: 904-766-6717. p. 411
Dumont, Lori, Head, Circ Serv, Manchester-by-the-Sea Public Library, 15 Union St, Manchester-by-the-Sea, MA, 01944. Tel: 978-526-7711. p. 1031
Dumuhosky, Laura, Media Serv Librn, Richmond Memorial Library, 19 Ross St, Batavia, NY, 14020. Tel: 585-343-9550. p. 1491
Dunagin, Kathleen, Dir, Thompson Coburn LLP, One US Bank Plaza, Saint Louis, MO, 63101-1693. Tel: 314-552-6000. p. 1276
Dunaief, Charlotte, Libr Dir, Cornwall Public Library, 395 Hudson St, Cornwall, NY, 12518. Tel: 845-534-8282. p. 1522
Dunaway, Karen, Librn, B S Ricks Memorial Library, 310 N Main St, Yazoo City, MS, 39194. Tel: 662-746-5557. p. 1236
Dunay, Carin, Head, Access & Technical Services, Southern Maine Community College Library, Two Fort Rd, South Portland, ME, 04106. Tel: 207-741-5521. p. 941
Dunbar, Aubree, Libr Asst, Anna Maria College, 50 Sunset Lane, Paxton, MA, 01612-1198. Tel: 508-849-3405. p. 1045
Dunbar, Ian, Exec Dir, Ames Free Library, 53 Main St, North Easton, MA, 02356. Tel: 508-238-2000. p. 1041
Duncan, Alexandra, Librn/Mgr, Buncombe County Public Libraries, East Asheville, 902 Tunnel Rd, Asheville, NC, 28805. Tel: 828-250-4738. p. 1672
Duncan, Amber, Dir, Lied Public Library, 508 Iowa St, Essex, IA, 51638. Tel: 712-379-3355. p. 751
Duncan, Carol, Dir, Wisner Public Library, 1015 Ave E, Wisner, NE, 68791. Tel: 402-529-6018. p. 1341
Duncan, Cheyenne, Libr Asst, Rappahannock Community College Library, 12745 College Dr, Glenns, VA, 23149. Tel: 804-758-6710. p. 2321
Duncan, Claire, Dir, Texas Medical Association, 401 W 15th St, Austin, TX, 78701-1680. Tel: 512-370-1544. p. 2141
Duncan, Cyndi, Financial Admin Officer, Milton Public Library, 1010 Main St E, Milton, ON, L9T 6H7, CANADA. Tel: 905-875-2665, Ext 3255. p. 2658
Duncan, Diana, Tech Serv Librn, Field Museum of Natural History, 1400 S DuSable Lake Shore Dr, Chicago, IL, 60605-2496. Tel: 312-665-7892. p. 561
Duncan, Ernest, Admin Officer, Georgia State University, 100 Decatur St SE, Atlanta, GA, 30303-3202. Tel: 404-413-2713. p. 464
Duncan, Jennifer, Chair, Utah Academic Library Consortium, University of Utah, J Willard Marriott Library, 295 S 1500 E, Salt Lake City, UT, 84112-0860. Tel: 435-797-2687. p. 2776
Duncan, Jenny, Dir, Oklahoma State University, 1801 E Fourth St, Okmulgee, OK, 74447-0088. Tel: 918-293-5488. p. 1859
Duncan, Jim, Exec Dir, Colorado Library Consortium, 7400 E Arapahoe Rd, Ste 75, Centennial, CO, 80112. Tel: 303-422-1150. p. 2762
Duncan, Karlene, Libr Dir, Fort St John Public Library Association, 10015-100th Ave, Fort Saint John, BC, V1J 1Y7, CANADA. Tel: 250-785-3731. p. 2566

Duncan, Lenora, Mgr, Stone County Library, 326 W Washington St, Mountain View, AR, 72560. Tel: 870-269-3100. p. 105

Duncan, Lisa, Mgr, Sharp County Library, Williford Branch, 232 Main St, Williford, AR, 72482. Tel: 870-966-4227. p. 97

Duncan, Liza, Principal Librn, New York State Library, Cultural Education Ctr, 222 Madison Ave, Albany, NY, 12230. p. 1483

Duncan, Margo, Head, Electronic Res & Coll Develop, University of Texas at Tyler Library, 3900 University Blvd, Tyler, TX, 75799. Tel: 903-566-7174. p. 2250

Duncan, Mark, Instruction & Outreach Librn, Christian Brothers University, 650 East Pkwy S, Memphis, TN, 38104. Tel: 901-321-3432. p. 2112

Duncan, Rob, Dir, Libr & Res Serv, K&L Gates Library, The K&L Gates Ctr, 210 Sixth Ave, Pittsburgh, PA, 15222. Tel: 412-355-6311. p. 1994

Duncan, Samuel, Libr Dir, Amon Carter Museum of American Art, 3501 Camp Bowie Blvd, Fort Worth, TX, 76107-2695. Tel: 817-738-1933. p. 2179

Duncan, Sharon, Librn, Palliser Regional Library, Briercrest Branch, Community Ctr, Main St, Briercrest, SK, S0H 0K0, CANADA. Tel: 306-799-2137. p. 2742

Duncan, Sue, Libr Mgr, Alix Public Library, 4928 50th St, Alix, AB, T0C 0B0, CANADA. Tel: 403-747-3233. p. 2521

Duncan, Suzanne, Librn, Sentara College of Health Sciences, 1441 Crossways Blvd, Ste 105, Chesapeake, VA, 23320. Tel: 757-388-3693. p. 2312

Duncan, Thomasina, Libr Supvr, Paterson Free Public Library, Northside Branch, 60 Temple St, Rm 3, Paterson, NJ, 07522. Tel: 973-321-1309. p. 1433

Duncan, Todd, Libr Dir, South Charleston Public Library, 312 Fourth Ave, South Charleston, WV, 25303. Tel: 304-744-6561. p. 2415

Duncan-Kinard, Nicole, Ref, Community College of Philadelphia Library, Mint Bldg, Level 1, 1700 Spring Garden St, Philadelphia, PA, 19130. Tel: 215-751-8407. p. 1975

Dundas, Trudy, Town Librn, Manhattan Community Library, 200 W Fulton Ave, Manhattan, MT, 59741. Tel: 406-284-3341, Ext 222. p. 1299

Dundon, Kate, Supvry Archivist, University of California, 1156 High St, Santa Cruz, CA, 95064. Tel: 831-502-7587. p. 243

Dunfee, Heather, Libr Dir, Huntington Public Library, Seven E Main St, Huntington, MA, 01050. Tel: 413-512-5206. p. 1026

Dunford, Karen, Libr Mgr, Naperville Public Library, 95th Street, 3015 Cedar Glade Dr, Naperville, IL, 60564. Tel: 630-961-4100, Ext 4900. p. 623

Dungey, Danielle, Asst Br Mgr, Halifax Public Libraries, Central Library, 5440 Spring Garden Rd, Halifax, NS, B3J 1E9, CANADA. Tel: 902-490-5700. p. 2617

Dunham, Chris, Head, User Serv, Cornell University Library, Flower-Sprecher Veterinary Library, S1 201 Veterinary Education Ctr, Ithaca, NY, 14853-6401. Tel: 607-253-3512. p. 1551

Dunham, Christian D, Libr Dir, Bullard Sanford Memorial Library, 520 W Huron Ave, Vassar, MI, 48768. Tel: 989-823-2171. p. 1156

Dunham, Kassie, Faculty Coordr, Library Services, Kellogg Community College, 450 North Ave, Battle Creek, MI, 49017-3397. Tel: 269-565-2613. p. 1083

Dunham, Suzanne, Head Librn, Garfield County-Panguitch City Library, 25 S 200 East, Panguitch, UT, 84759. Tel: 435-676-2431. p. 2268

Dunham, Tina, Librn, Cleburne Public Library, 302 W Henderson St, Cleburne, TX, 76033. Tel: 817-645-0936. p. 2156

Dunham-LaGree, Carrie, Librn, Digital Literacy & Gen Educ, Drake University, 2725 University Ave, Des Moines, IA, 50311. Tel: 515-271-2175. p. 746

Dunkelberg, Todd, Dir, Deschutes Public Library District, 507 NW Wall St, Bend, OR, 97703. Tel: 541-312-1021. p. 1874

Dunkelberger, Robert A, Archivist & Spec Coll Librn, Historian, Research Librn, Bloomsburg University of Pennsylvania, 400 E Second St, Bloomsburg, PA, 17815-1301. Tel: 570-389-4205. p. 1913

Dunker, Susan, Ad, Dover Public Library, 73 Locust St, Dover, NH, 03820-3785. Tel: 603-516-6050. p. 1361

Dunkerton, David, Librn, John Van Puffelen Library of the Appalachian Bible College, 161 College Dr, Mount Hope, WV, 25880-1040. Tel: 304-877-6428. p. 2410

Dunkin, Sally, Children's Prog, Circ, Jackson County Library, 213 Walnut St, Newport, AR, 72112. Tel: 870-523-2952. p. 106

Dunkle, Jonathan, Dir, Manheim Community Library, 15 E High St, Manheim, PA, 17545-1505. Tel: 717-665-6700. p. 1957

Dunkle, Rebecca, Assoc Univ Librn, Libr Operations, University of Michigan, 818 Hatcher Graduate Library South, 913 S University Ave, Ann Arbor, MI, 48109-1190. Tel: 734-764-0400. p. 1080

Dunkleberger, Rob, Assoc VPres, Libr Info Tech, Lycoming College, One College Pl, Williamsport, PA, 17701. Tel: 570-321-4278. p. 2023

Dunklee, Chaunacey, Supervising Librn, Collection Dev & Adult Services, Sunnyvale Public Library, 665 W Olive Ave, Sunnyvale, CA, 94086-7622. Tel: 408-730-7300. p. 251

Dunkley, Cora, Dr, Assoc Prof, University of South Florida, 4202 Fowler Ave, CIS 1040, Tampa, FL, 33620-7800. Tel: 813-974-3520. p. 2783

Dunkley, Joy, Circ Librn, John Jay College of Criminal Justice, 899 Tenth Ave, New York, NY, 10019. Tel: 212-237-8239. p. 1589

Dunlany, Dan, Librn, Steward Health Care, 1350 E Market St, Warren, OH, 44482. Tel: 330-675-5704, 330-884-3476. p. 1828

Dunlap, Bryan, Tech Serv Mgr, Missouri River Regional Library, 214 Adams St, Jefferson City, MO, 65101. Tel: 573-634-2464. p. 1252

Dunlap, Ellen S, Pres, American Antiquarian Society Library, 185 Salisbury St, Worcester, MA, 01609-1634. Tel: 508-471-2161. p. 1071

Dunlap, Lanee, Asst Vice Provost, Dean of Libr, Texas A&M University-Commerce, 2600 S Neal St, Commerce, TX, 75428. Tel: 903-886-5738. p. 2158

Dunlap, Steven, Head, Tech Serv, Mechanics' Institute Library, 57 Post St, Ste 504, San Francisco, CA, 94104-5003. Tel: 415-393-0101. p. 226

Dunlavy, Lacy, Br Mgr, Garfield County Public Library District, Carbondale Branch, 320 Sopris Ave, Carbondale, CO, 81623. Tel: 970-963-2889. p. 294

Dunleavy, Christine, Head, Coll & Tech Serv, University of South Florida Saint Petersburg, 140 Seventh Ave S, POY118, Saint Petersburg, FL, 33701-5016. Tel: 727-873-4418. p. 442

Dunlop, Donna, Dir, Hopkinton Town Library, 61 Houston Dr, Contoocook, NH, 03229. Tel: 603-746-3663. p. 1360

Dunlop, Emily Jackson, Ref Spec, Northern Virginia Community College Libraries, Loudoun Campus, 21200 Campus Dr, Rm 200, Sterling, VA, 20164-8699. Tel: 703-450-2567. p. 2304

Dunlop, Jennifer, YA Librn, Lakeview Public Library, 1120 Woodfield Rd, Rockville Centre, NY, 11570. Tel: 516-536-3071. p. 1632

Dunn, Adina, Dir, Dublin Public Library, 206 W Blackjack St, Dublin, TX, 76446. Tel: 254-445-4141. p. 2171

Dunn, Adrienne, Ch Serv, Sioux City Public Library, 529 Pierce St, Sioux City, IA, 51101-1203. Tel: 712-255-2933. p. 783

Dunn, Ashley, Asst Dir, Germantown Public Library, 51 N Plum St, Germantown, OH, 45327. Tel: 937-855-4001. p. 1788

Dunn, Catherine, Assoc Dean, University of Denver, Westminster Law Library, Sturm College of Law, 2255 E Evans Ave, Denver, CO, 80208. Tel: 303-871-6494. p. 278

Dunn, Catherine, Dir, Temple University Libraries, Law Library, Charles Klein Law Bldg, 1719 N Broad St, Philadelphia, PA, 19124. Tel: 215-204-4538. p. 1986

Dunn, Christopher, Libr Serv Mgr, Niagara Falls Public Library, 4848 Victoria Ave, Niagara Falls, ON, L2E 4C5, CANADA. Tel: 905-356-8080. p. 2660

Dunn, Denise, Asst Libr Dir, First Baptist Church of Highland Park Library, James J McCord Education Bldg, Rm 200, 6801 Sheriff Rd, Landover, MD, 20785. Tel: 301-773-6655. p. 970

Dunn, Denise D, Youth Serv Librn, Scotland County Memorial Library, 312 W Church St, Laurinburg, NC, 28352-3720. Tel: 910-276-0563. p. 1700

Dunn, Eva, Dir, Bollinger County Library, 207 Mayfield Dr, Marble Hill, MO, 63764. Tel: 573-238-2713. p. 1260

Dunn, Fae, Dir, Lois Johnson Memorial Library, 406 Fifth St, Oakdale, NE, 68761. Tel: 402-843-0452. p. 1327

Dunn, Jennifer, Librn, Sebastian County Law Library, 623 Garrison Ave, Ste 418, Fort Smith, AR, 72901. Tel: 479-783-4730. p. 96

Dunn, John, Mgr, Tech Serv, St Catharines Public Library, 54 Church St, St. Catharines, ON, L2R 7K2, CANADA. Tel: 905-688-6103. p. 2680

Dunn, Kala, Res & Instruction Librn, Columbia College, 1301 Columbia College Dr, Columbia, SC, 29203-9987. Tel: 803-786-3338. p. 2053

Dunn, Karen, Librn, University of Wisconsin-Madison, Geography, Science Hall, Rm 280-B, 550 N Park St, Madison, WI, 53706. Tel: 608-262-1706. p. 2451

Dunn, Karina, Libr Dir, Vanguard College Library, 12140 103 St NW, Edmonton, AB, T5G 2J9, CANADA. Tel: 780-452-0808. p. 2538

Dunn, Karina, Libr Dir, Horizon College & Seminary, 604 Webster St, Saskatoon, SK, S7N 3P9, CANADA. Tel: 306-374-6655, Ext 234. p. 2748

Dunn, Kate, Electronic Res Librn, Alaska State Library, 395 Whittier St, Juneau, AK, 99801. Tel: 907-465-2920. p. 47

Dunn, Kathryn, Tech & Metadata Librn, Rensselaer Libraries, Rensselaer Architecture Library, Greene Bldg 308, 3rd Flr, 110 Eighth St, Troy, NY, 12180-3590. Tel: 518-276-8310. p. 1652

Dunn, Lisa, Head, Res Serv, Head, Spec Coll, Colorado School of Mines, 1400 Illinois St, Golden, CO, 80401-1887. Tel: 303-273-3698. p. 282

Dunn, Lynda, Dir, South Central Area Library, 530 Main St, Edgeley, ND, 58433. Tel: 701-493-2769. p. 1732

Dunn, Mary, Managing Archivist, Arkansas History Commission Library, One Capitol Mall, 2nd Flr, Little Rock, AR, 72201. Tel: 501-682-6900. p. 100

Dunn, Meghan, Chief Librn, United States Senate Library, SRB-15 Senate Russell Bldg, Washington, DC, 20510. Tel: 202-224-7106. p. 380

Dunn, Melanie, Coll Spec, University of Tennessee at Chattanooga Library, 400 Douglas Ave, Dept 6456, Chattanooga, TN, 37403-2598. Tel: 423-425-4501. p. 2092

Dunn, Pat, Coll Librn, Red Rocks Community College, 13300 W Sixth Ave, Lakewood, CO, 80228-1255. Tel: 303-914-6740. p. 288

Dunn, Patrick, Ref Librn, Elko-Lander-Eureka County Library System, 720 Court St, Elko, NV, 89801. Tel: 775-738-3066. p. 1344

Dunn, Peggy, Dir, Sabina Public Library, 11 E Elm St, Sabina, OH, 45169-1330. Tel: 937-584-2319. p. 1818

Dunn, Regan, Asst Librn, Sitting Bull College Library, 9299 Hwy 24, Fort Yates, ND, 58538. Tel: 701-854-8008. p. 1734
Dunn, Sam, Ms, Adult Serv Mgr, Lincoln Library, 326 S Seventh St, Springfield, IL, 62701. Tel: 217-753-4900. p. 650
Dunn, Suellen, Br Mgr, Harris County Public Library, Fairbanks Branch, 7122 N Gessner, Houston, TX, 77040. Tel: 832-927-7890. p. 2192
Dunn, Therese, Librn, Sierra Club, 2101 Webster St, Ste 1300, Oakland, CA, 94612. Tel: 415-977-5506. p. 187
Dunn, Tyler, Access Serv Librn, Palo Alto College, 1400 W Villaret St, San Antonio, TX, 78224-2499. Tel: 210-486-3560. p. 2237
Dunn-McKee, Julie, Teen Librn, Oskaloosa Public Library, 301 S Market St, Oskaloosa, IA, 52577. Tel: 641-673-0441. p. 775
Dunn-Morton, Julie, Curator, Saint Louis Mercantile Library at the University of Missouri-St Louis, Thomas Jefferson Library Bldg, One University Blvd, Saint Louis, MO, 63121-4400. Tel: 314-516-6740. p. 1274
Dunne, Elaine, Dir, Massena Public Library, 41 Glenn St, Massena, NY, 13662. Tel: 315-769-9914. p. 1569
Dunne, Jennifer, Ch Serv Librn, Moorestown Public Library, 111 W Second St, Moorestown, NJ, 08057. Tel: 856-234-0333. p. 1421
Dunnewold, Nicole, Health Librarian, University of Calgary Library, Health Sciences Library, 1450 Health Sci Ctr, 3330 Hospital Dr NW, Calgary, AB, T2N 4N1, CANADA. Tel: 403-220-7370. p. 2529
Dunnigan, Brian Leigh, Assoc Dir, University of Michigan, William L Clements Library, 909 S University Ave, Ann Arbor, MI, 48109-1190. Tel: 734-764-2347. p. 1079
Dunnigan, Virginia, Libr Dir, Saint Thomas Aquinas College, 125 Rte 340, Sparkill, NY, 10976. Tel: 845-398-4216. p. 1643
Dunning, Laurie, Librn Spec, Ventura County Library, Oak Park Library, 899 N Kanan Rd, Oak Park, CA, 91377. Tel: 818-889-2239. p. 256
Dunning, Marcy, Librn, Columbia River Maritime Museum, 1792 Marine Dr, Astoria, OR, 97103. Tel: 503-325-2323. p. 1872
Dunning, Pamela, Dir, Wiscasset Public Library, 21 High St, Wiscasset, ME, 04578-4119. Tel: 207-882-7161. p. 947
Dunning, Sue, Dir, Head Librn, Webber International University, 1201 N Scenic Hwy, Babson Park, FL, 33827. Tel: 863-638-1431, Ext 3001. p. 384
Dunphy, Sandra, Health Sci Librn, Northeastern University Libraries, 360 Huntington Ave, Boston, MA, 02115. Tel: 617-373-5322. p. 998
Dunscombe, Pamela, Head, Tech Serv, Marion County Library System, 101 East Court St, Marion, SC, 29571. Tel: 843-423-8300. p. 2065
Dunsdon, John, Dir, Leon Public Library, 200 W First St, Leon, IA, 50144. Tel: 641-446-6332. p. 765
Dunseth, Brenda, Youth Serv Dept Head, Highland Township Public Library, 444 Beach Farm Circle, Highland, MI, 48357. Tel: 248-887-2218. p. 1115
Dunstan, Tracy, Head, Ref Serv, The Nyack Library, 59 S Broadway, Nyack, NY, 10960. Tel: 845-358-3370, Ext 213. p. 1609
Dunster, Emily, Libr Tech II, Lake Washington Institute of Technology, Technology Ctr, T215, 11605 132nd Ave NE, Kirkland, WA, 98034. Tel: 425-739-8100, Ext 8320. p. 2367
Dupelle, Lisa, Dir, Human Res, Hamilton Public Library, 55 York Blvd, Hamilton, ON, L8R 3K1, CANADA. Tel: 905-546-3200, Ext 3290. p. 2645
DuPerow, Paula, Asst Prof, Librn, Cuyahoga Community College, Western Campus Library, 11000 Pleasant Valley Rd, Parma, OH, 44130-5199. Tel: 216-987-5416. p. 1769
Duperry, Robin, Libr Coord, Colby College Libraries, Bixler Art & Music Library, 5660 Mayflower Hill, Waterville, ME, 04901. Tel: 207-859-5661. p. 945
Dupeyron, Sarah, Libr Dir, Westmoreland Public Library, 33 S Village Rd, Westmoreland, NH, 03467. Tel: 603-399-7750. p. 1384
Duplaga, Jen, Archivist & Curator of Rare Bks, Hanover College, 121 Scenic Dr, Hanover, IN, 47243. Tel: 812-866-7181. p. 689
Duplain, Rene, Geography Librn, University of Ottawa Libraries, Geographic, Statistical & Government Information Centre, Morisset Hall, 3rd Flr, 65 University, Ottawa, ON, K1N 9A5, CANADA. Tel: 613-562-5211. p. 2670
Duplantis, Shelley, Ch, Desoto Parish Library, Stonewall Branch, 808 Hwy 171, Stonewall, LA, 71078. Tel: 318-925-9191. p. 896
Duplessis, Virna, Librn, College de Valleyfield, 80 rue Saint Thomas, Salaberry-de-Valleyfield, QC, J6T 4J7, CANADA. Tel: 450-373-9441, Ext 350. p. 2736
Duplissey, Aaron, Br Mgr, Loudoun County Public Library, Purcellville Branch, 220 E Main St, Purcellville, VA, 20132. Tel: 703-737-8490. p. 2328
Dupont, Christian, Burns Librn & Assoc Univ Librn, Spec Coll, Boston College Libraries, 140 Commonwealth Ave, Chestnut Hill, MA, 02467. Tel: 617-552-0105. p. 1010
Dupont, Dianne, Br Mgr, Nicholson Memorial Library System, Walnut Creek Branch Library, 3319 Edgewood Dr, Garland, TX, 75042-7118. Tel: 972-205-2587. p. 2184
DuPre, Michelle, Mgr, Richland Library, Saint Andrews Regional, 2916 Broad River Rd, Columbia, SC, 29210. Tel: 803-772-6675. p. 2054
Dupre, Zerita, Libr Assoc, Louisiana State University Health Sciences Center, School of Dentistry Library, 1100 Florida Ave, New Orleans, LA, 70119. Tel: 504-941-8158. p. 902
Dupree, Jameca, Interim Assoc Univ Librarian for Admin Services, Duke University Libraries, 411 Chapel Dr, Durham, NC, 27708. Tel: 919-660-5943. p. 1684
Dupree, Jason, Dir of Libr, Southwestern Oklahoma State University, 100 Campus Dr, Weatherford, OK, 73096-3002. Tel: 580-774-7081. p. 1868
DuPree, Nancy, Librn, Grace Presbyterian Church, 113 Hargrove Rd, Tuscaloosa, AL, 35401. Tel: 205-758-5422. p. 37
Dupuis, Elizabeth, Sr Assoc Univ Librn, University of California, Berkeley, South Hall Rd, Berkeley, CA, 94704. Tel: 510-642-6657. p. 122
Dupuis, Jennifer, Info Serv, ILL, The Parrott Centre, 376 Wallbridge-Loyalist Rd, Belleville, ON, K8N 5B9, CANADA. Tel: 613-969-1913, Ext 2249. p. 2631
Dupuis, John, Sci Librn, York University Libraries, Steacie Science & Engineering Library, 136 Campus Walk, Keele Campus, North York, ON, M3J 1P3, CANADA. Tel: 416-736-5084. p. 2662
Dupuis, Pascale, Ms, Dir, Libr & Cultural Serv, Bibliotheque de Deux-Montagnes, 200 rue Henri-Dunant, Deux-Montagnes, QC, J7R 4W6, CANADA. Tel: 450-473-2796. p. 2711
Dupuis, Peggy, Bus Mgr, Calcasieu Parish Public Library System, 301 W Claude St, Lake Charles, LA, 70605-3457. Tel: 337-721-7147. p. 893
Dupuy, Stephane, Libr Dir, Chaleur Library Region, Campbellton Centennial Library, 19 Aberdeen St, Ste 100, Campbellton, NB, E3N 2J6, CANADA. Tel: 506-753-5253. p. 2599
Duran, Arthur S, Bus Off Adminr, Yuma County Free Library District, 2951 S 21st Dr, Yuma, AZ, 85364. Tel: 928-373-6463. p. 85
Duran, Crystal, Dir, Belvedere Tiburon Library, 1501 Tiburon Blvd, Tiburon, CA, 94920. Tel: 415-789-2656. p. 252
Duran, Diana, Coordr, Access Serv, Dominican University of California, 50 Acacia Ave, San Rafael, CA, 94901-2298. Tel: 415-257-0168. p. 236
Duran, Kelly, Mgr, Jefferson County Public Library, Lakewood Library, 10200 W 20th Ave, Lakewood, CO, 80215. Tel: 303-275-6180. p. 288
Durand, Matthew, Tech Serv/Circ Assoc, Smith College Libraries, Hillyer Art Library, Brown Fine Arts Ctr, 20 Elm St, Northampton, MA, 01063. Tel: 413-585-2943. p. 1043
Durand, Paul, Supvr, Canadian War Museum, One Vimy Pl, Ottawa, ON, K1A 0M8, CANADA. Tel: 819-776-8652. p. 2666
Durand, Susan, Asst Librn, Abington Public Library, 600 Gliniewicz Way, Abington, MA, 02351. Tel: 781-982-2139. p. 983
Durant, Brandy, Circ, Mgr, Covington-Veedersburg Public Library, Veedersburg Public, 408 N Main St, Veedersburg, IN, 47987. Tel: 765-294-2808. p. 677
Durant, Jessie, Archives, Libr Coord, Museum of Art & History Library, 705 Front St, Santa Cruz, CA, 95060-4508. Tel: 831-429-1964, Ext 7019. p. 242
Durbin, Dayna, Undergrad Libr Instruction, University of North Carolina at Chapel Hill, 208 Raleigh St, CB 3916, Chapel Hill, NC, 27515. Tel: 919-962-1053. p. 1678
Durbin, Lori, Pub Serv Mgr, Greensburg-Decatur County Public Library, 1110 E Main St, Greensburg, IN, 47240. Tel: 812-663-2826. p. 688
Durbin, Mark, Head, Tech Serv, John Marshall Law School, 245 Peachtree Center Ave NE, 18th Flr, Atlanta, GA, 30303. Tel: 678-916-2662. p. 465
Durbin, Mike, Webmaster, Journal Gazette Library, 600 W Main St, Fort Wayne, IN, 46802. Tel: 260-461-8194. p. 685
DuRepos Theriault, Helene, Libr Mgr, Haut-Saint-Jean Regional Library, La Moisson Public, 206 Canada St, Saint Quentin, NB, E8A 1H1, CANADA. Tel: 506-235-1955. p. 2600
Durette, Diane, Head, Ref Serv, Lucy Robbins Welles Library, 95 Cedar St, Newington, CT, 06111. Tel: 860-665-8705. p. 330
Durgin, Brittany, Dir, Moultonborough Public Library, Four Holland St, Moultonborough, NH, 03254. Tel: 603-476-8895. p. 1374
Durham, David, Curator of Archival Coll, University of Alabama, School of Law Library, 101 Paul Bryant Dr, Tuscaloosa, AL, 35487. Tel: 205-348-5925. p. 38
Durham, Erin, Ref & Instruction Librn, University of Maryland, Baltimore County, 1000 Hilltop Circle, Baltimore, MD, 21250. Tel: 410-455-2356. p. 958
Durham, James, Dep Dir, Thurgood Marshall State Law Library, Courts of Appeals Bldg, 361 Rowe Blvd, Annapolis, MD, 21401. Tel: 410-260-1430. p. 950
Durham, Jennifer, Dir, Evans County Public Library, 701 W Main St, Claxton, GA, 30417. Tel: 912-739-1801. p. 471
Durham, Jennifer, Regional Libr Dir, Statesboro Regional Public Libraries, 124 S Main St, Statesboro, GA, 30458. Tel: 912-764-1341. p. 498
Durham, Kate, Libr Spec, Spartanburg Community College Library, Downtown Campus, Evans Academic Ctr, 2nd Flr, 220 E Kennedy St, Spartanburg, SC, 29302. Tel: 864-592-4058. p. 2069
Durham, Leslie, Dir, Elgin Community Library, 108 Thoma Dr, Elgin, OK, 73538. Tel: 580-492-6650. p. 1847
Durham, Mardi J, Ref Librn, Iredell County Public Library, 201 N Tradd St, Statesville, NC, 28677. Tel: 704-878-3109. p. 1717
Durham, Mark, Dir, Effie & Wilton Hebert Public Library, 2025 Merriman St, Port Neches, TX, 77651. Tel: 409-722-4554. p. 2228
Durham, Micajah, Res & Instruction Librn, Montreat College, 310 Gaither Circle, Montreat, NC, 28757. Tel: 828-669-8012, Ext 3505. p. 1704
Durham, Michael D, Div Dir, Admin Serv, Alachua County Library District, 401 E University Ave, Gainesville, FL, 32601-5453. Tel: 352-334-3914. p. 406
Durilin, Anna, Head Law Librn, Massachusetts Court System, 184 Main St, Worcester, MA, 01608. Tel: 508-831-2525. p. 1072

Durivage, Catherine A, Dir, Minnesota Braille & Talking Book Library, 400 NE Stinson Blvd, Minneapolis, MN, 55413. Tel: 507-384-6860. p. 1184
Durkee, Abigail, Libr Dir, Briercrest College & Seminary, 510 College Dr, Caronport, SK, S0H 0S0, CANADA. Tel: 306-756-3435. p. 2741
Durkee, Lynn, Libr Mgr, Yavapai College Library, Verde Valley Campus, 601 Black Hills Dr, Clarkdale, AZ, 86324. Tel: 928-634-6542. p. 74
Durkin, Claire Toomey, Assoc Dir, Res & Instruction, The John Marshall Law School, 300 S State St, 6th Flr, Chicago, IL, 60604. Tel: 312-427-2737. p. 564
Durkin, Debra, Circ & ILL, University of Maine at Fort Kent, 23 University Dr, Fort Kent, ME, 04743. Tel: 207-834-7526. p. 925
Durkin, Juanita, Dir, Justice Public Library District, 7641 Oak Grove Ave, Justice, IL, 60458. Tel: 708-496-1790. p. 604
Durkin, Kelly, Br Mgr, Warren County Library, Catherine Dickson Hofman Branch, Four Lambert Rd, Blairstown, NJ, 07825. p. 1389
Durkin, Tom, Soc Work & Soc Sci Librn, University of Wisconsin-Madison, Social Work Library, 236 School of Social Work, 1350 University Ave, Madison, WI, 53706. Tel: 608-263-3283, 608-263-3840. p. 2452
Durkish, Barbara, Libr Dir, Caldwell-Lake George Library, 336 Canada St, Lake George, NY, 12845-1118. Tel: 518-668-2528. p. 1561
Durler, Jolene, Libr Asst, Dodge City Community College Library, 2501 N 14th, Dodge City, KS, 67801. Tel: 620-225-1321, Ext 287, 620-227-9287. p. 804
Durman, Chris, Librn, University of Tennessee, Knoxville, George F DeVine Music Library, Natalie L Haslam Music Ctr, G04, 1741 Volunteer Blvd, Knoxville, TN, 37996-2600. Tel: 865-974-7542. p. 2107
Duro, Charlene, Br Mgr, Rodman Public Library, Branch in the Mall, 2500 W State St, Alliance, OH, 44601. Tel: 330-821-1313. p. 1746
Duroselle-Melish, Caroline, Curator, Early Modern Bks & Prints, Folger Shakespeare Library, 201 E Capitol St SE, Washington, DC, 20003-1094. Tel: 202-675-0356. p. 366
DuRoss, Anne, Interim Dir, New Hartford Public Library, Two Library Lane, New Hartford, NY, 13413-2815. Tel: 315-733-1535. p. 1576
Durov, Kelly, Youth Serv Mgr, Northbrook Public Library, 1201 Cedar Lane, Northbrook, IL, 60062-4581. Tel: 847-272-6224. p. 627
Durow, Margaret, ILL, United States Forest Service, One Gifford Pinchot Dr, Madison, WI, 53726-2398. Tel: 608-231-9200. p. 2450
Durr, Danielle, Br Mgr, Livingston Parish Library, Watson Branch, 36581 Outback Rd, Denham Springs, LA, 70706. Tel: 225-686-4180. p. 895
Durso, Patricia, Exec Adminir, Lee Memorial Library, 500 W Crescent Ave, Allendale, NJ, 07401. Tel: 201-327-4338. p. 1387
Durst, Delphine, Libr Mgr, Central Arkansas Library System, Roosevelt Thompson Branch, 38 Rahling Circle, Little Rock, AR, 72223. Tel: 501-821-3060. p. 101
Durusau, Elizabeth, Circ Assoc, Library Reserve, University of Georgia Libraries, Music, School of Music, Rm 250, 250 River Rd, Athens, GA, 30602. Tel: 706-542-2712. p. 460
Duryea, Paul, Br Mgr, Kenton County Public Library, 502 Scott Blvd, Covington, KY, 41011. Tel: 859-962-4074. p. 852
Dusek, Tari L, Dir, Thomas Township Library, 8207 Shields Dr, Saginaw, MI, 48609-4814. Tel: 989-781-3770. p. 1147
Dusenbery, Joe, IT Dir, Muskingum County Library System, 220 N Fifth St, Zanesville, OH, 43701-3587. Tel: 740-453-0391, Ext 152. p. 1836
Duskin, Jane, Librn, Hawkes Library, 100 W Eighth St, West Point, GA, 31833. Tel: 706-645-1549. p. 503
Dussault, Christi, Circ Librn, Lanpher Memorial Library, 141 Main St, Hyde Park, VT, 05655. Tel: 802-888-4628. p. 2286
Dustin, Michelle, Coordinator, Library Admin, University of Southern Maine Libraries, 314 Forest Ave, Portland, ME, 04103. Tel: 207-780-4790. p. 937
Dustman, Teresa, Circ, Wells County Public Library, 200 W Washington St, Bluffton, IN, 46714-1999. Tel: 260-824-1612. p. 671
Dusto, David, Electronic Res, Librn, Ser, Elizabeth City State University, 1704 Weeksville Rd, Elizabeth City, NC, 27909. Tel: 252-335-3432. p. 1687
Duszkiewicz, Irene A, Dir, Hempstead Public Library, 115 James A Garner Way, Hempstead, NY, 11550. Tel: 516-481-6990. p. 1545
Dutcher, Deborah, Youth & Adult Serv Librn, New Hampshire State Library, 20 Park St, Concord, NH, 03301. Tel: 603-271-2865. p. 1359
Dutka, Andrew, Archives, Broward College, Bldg 17, 3501 SW Davie Rd, Davie, FL, 33314. Tel: 954-201-6577. p. 391
Duttlinger, Beth, Dir, Lillie M Evans Library District, 207 N Walnut Ave, Princeville, IL, 61559. Tel: 309-385-4540. p. 636
Dutton, Tuya, Dir, University of Jamestown, 6070 College Lane, Jamestown, ND, 58405-0001. Tel: 701-252-3467. p. 1736
Duval, Marc, Librn, Rio Tinto Iron & Titanium Inc, 1625 Rte Marie-Victorin, Sorel-Tracy, QC, J3R 1M6, CANADA. Tel: 450-746-3160. p. 2737
Duvall, Court, Br Mgr, Greensboro Public Library, Blanche S Benjamin Branch, 1530 Benjamin Pkwy, Greensboro, NC, 27408. Tel: 336-373-7540. p. 1692
Duvall, Elizabeth, Br Supvr, Kern County Library, Kern River Valley Branch, 7054 Lake Isabella Blvd, Lake Isabella, CA, 93240-9205. Tel: 760-549-2083. p. 120
Duvall, Emilee, Dir, Ritchie County Public Library, 608 E Main St, Harrisville, WV, 26362. Tel: 304-643-2717. p. 2404
Duvall, Jamie, Mgr, Botetourt County Libraries, Eagle Rock Library, 55 Eagles Nest Dr, Eagle Rock, VA, 24085. Tel: 540-928-2800. p. 2344
Duvant, Jenny, Head, Ch, North Providence Union Free Library, 1810 Mineral Spring Ave, North Providence, RI, 02904. Tel: 401-353-5600. p. 2036
Duvernoy, Bernadette, Exec Dir, Hayner Public Library District, 326 Belle St, Alton, IL, 62002. Tel: 618-462-0677. p. 536
Dux, Linda, Ch, Fairbury Public Library, 601 Seventh St, Fairbury, NE, 68352. Tel: 402-729-2843. p. 1313
Dux-Ideus, Sherrie, Supvr, Central Community College, Hastings Campus Library, Nickolls Bldg, 550 S Technical Blvd, Hastings, NE, 68902. Tel: 402-461-2538. p. 1317
Dvorak, Diane, Cat, Circ, Mount Marty University, 1105 W Eighth St, Yankton, SD, 57078-3725. Tel: 605-668-1555. p. 2086
Dvorak, Kailey, Youth Serv Librn, Hot Springs County Library, 344 Arapahoe St, Thermopolis, WY, 82443. Tel: 307-864-3104. p. 2499
Dvorak, Karrie L, Dir/Curator, Nebraska United Methodist Historical Center Archives, Nebraska Wesleyan University, Cochrane-Woods Library, Lower Level, 5000 Saint Paul Ave, Lincoln, NE, 68504. Tel: 402-465-2175. p. 1322
Dvorak, Lisa, Librn, North Bend Public Library, 110 E 13th St, North Bend, NE, 68649. Tel: 402-652-8356. p. 1326
Dvorzak, Marie, Librn, University of Wisconsin-Madison, C K Leith Library of Geology & Geophysics, 440 Weeks Hall, 1215 W Dayton St, Madison, WI, 53706-1692. Tel: 608-262-8956. p. 2451
Dwigans-Merrit, Jacqueline, Youth Serv Librn, Delphi Public Library, 222 E Main St, Delphi, IN, 46923. Tel: 765-564-2929. p. 679
Dworkin, Rachel, Archivist, Chemung County Historical Society, Inc, 415 E Water St, Elmira, NY, 14901. Tel: 607-734-4167, Ext 207. p. 1530
Dwyer, Cara, Tech Serv Mgr, Converse County Library, 300 E Walnut St, Douglas, WY, 82633. Tel: 307-358-3644. p. 2494
Dwyer, Hayley, Br Mgr, Porter County Public Library System, Kouts Public, 101 E Daumer Rd, Kouts, IN, 46347. Tel: 219-766-2271. p. 722
Dwyer, Kathryn, Curator, Northwestern Ontario Sports Hall of Fame Library, 219 May St S, Thunder Bay, ON, P7E 1B5, CANADA. Tel: 807-622-2852. p. 2685
Dwyer, LaKeitha Bellamy, Br Mgr, Free Library of Philadelphia, Haddington Branch, 446 N 65th St, Philadelphia, PA, 19151-4003. Tel: 215-685-1970. p. 1978
Dwyer, Liz, Coordr, Commun Engagement, North Grenville Public Library, Norenberg Bldg, One Water St, Kemptville, ON, K0G 1J0, CANADA. Tel: 613-258-4711. p. 2649
Dwyer, Mary, Dep Fiscal Officer, Mansfield-Richland County Public Library, 43 W Third St, Mansfield, OH, 44902-1295. Tel: 419-521-3125. p. 1798
Dwyer, Matthew, Computer Serv, Saint Joseph's Hospital Health Center, 206 Prospect Ave, Syracuse, NY, 13203. Tel: 315-448-5053, 315-466-5040. p. 1650
Dwyer, Shawna, Exec Dir, Chilliwack Museum & Historical Society, 9291 Corbould St, Chilliwack, BC, V2P 4A6, CANADA. Tel: 604-795-5210, Ext 101. p. 2564
Dwyer, Stephanie, Ref Serv, East Meadow Public Library, 1886 Front St, East Meadow, NY, 11554-1705. Tel: 516-794-2570. p. 1528
Dy-Liacco, Kristina, Librn, Columbia University, C V Starr East Asian Library, 300 Kent Hall, MC 3901, 1140 Amsterdam Ave, New York, NY, 10027. Tel: 212-854-4318. p. 1584
Dyal, Joe, Academic Engagement Librn, Instruction Librn, Saint Norbert College, 400 Third St, De Pere, WI, 54115. Tel: 920-403-3271. p. 2430
Dyck, Maria, Libr Mgr, Vauxhall Public Library, 504 Second Ave N, Vauxhall, AB, T0K 2K0, CANADA. Tel: 403-654-2370. p. 2557
Dyck, Sabrina, Ref & Instruction Librn, Lawson State Community College Library, 3060 Wilson Rd SW, Birmingham, AL, 35221. Tel: 205-929-6333. p. 8
Dye, Damon, Tech Mgr, The Library Network, 41365 Vincenti Ct, Novi, MI, 48375. Tel: 248-536-3100. p. 2767
Dye, Joey, Mgr, Sequoyah Regional Library System, Woodstock Public, 7735 Main St, Woodstock, GA, 30188. Tel: 770-926-5859. p. 469
Dye, Randa, Br Mgr, Fremont County District Library, Island Park Branch, 3775 Sand Crane Dr, Island Park, ID, 83429. Tel: 208-558-0991. p. 530
Dyer, Ann, Dir, Eastern Washington University, 600 N Riverpoint Blvd, Rm 230, Spokane, WA, 99202. Tel: 509-358-7930. p. 2383
Dyer, Arline, Librn, Kent Hospital, 455 Toll Gate Rd, Warwick, RI, 02886. Tel: 401-274-1122, Ext 42338. p. 2043
Dyer, Brandon, Head, Children's Servx, Auburn Public Library, 49 Spring St, Auburn, ME, 04210. Tel: 207-333-6640. p. 913
Dyer, Bryan J, Dir, Head Librn, Shattuck Public Library, 101 S Main St, Shattuck, OK, 73858. Tel: 580-938-5104. p. 1861
Dyer, Celeste M, Libr Dir, Cumberland Public Library, 1464 Diamond Hill Rd, Cumberland, RI, 02864-5510. Tel: 401-333-2552, Ext 5. p. 2031
Dyer, Chloe, Dir, Chebeague Island Library, 247 South Rd, Unit 3, Chebeague Island, ME, 04017-3200. Tel: 207-846-4351. p. 921
Dyer, Cyd, Col Librn/Archivist, Simpson College, 508 North C St, Indianola, IA, 50125-1216. p. 759
Dyer, Elizabeth, Interim Dean, Libr Serv, University of New England Libraries, 11 Hills Beach Rd, Biddeford, ME, 04005. Tel: 207-602-2361. p. 917

Dyer, Elizabeth, Pub Serv Librn, University of New England Libraries, Josephine S Abplanalp Library, Portland Campus, 716 Stevens Ave, Portland, ME, 04103. Tel: 207-221-4333. p. 917

Dyer, Jennifer, Librn, Trinity Lutheran Church Library, 1904 Winnebago St, Madison, WI, 53704. Tel: 608-249-8527. p. 2450

Dyer, Lily, Access Serv Librn, Boston College, 885 Centre St, Newton Centre, MA, 02459. Tel: 617-552-8610. p. 1039

Dyer, Megan, Librn, Dallas College, 12800 Abrams Rd, Dallas, TX, 75243. Tel: 972-238-6081. p. 2164

Dyer, Michael, Maritime Curator, Old Dartmouth Historical Society, 18 Johnny Cake Hill, New Bedford, MA, 02740. Tel: 508-997-0046, Ext 137. p. 1038

Dyke, Colleen, Libr Dir, Roscommon Area District Library, 106 Lake St, Roscommon, MI, 48653. Tel: 989-281-1305. p. 1146

Dykens, Margaret, Dir, San Diego Natural History Museum, Balboa Park, 1788 El Prado, San Diego, CA, 92101. Tel: 619-232-3821. p. 219

Dykes, Andy, Br Mgr, Greenville County Library System, Berea Branch, 111 N Hwy 25 Bypass, Greenville, SC, 29617. Tel: 864-527-9201. p. 2061

Dykes, Christopher, Instrul Serv Librn, University of Houston, The O'Quinn Law Library, 12 Law Library, Houston, TX, 77204-6054. Tel: 713-743-2300. p. 2199

Dykes, Lelia, Circ Serv Coordr, Tusculum University, 60 Shiloh Rd, Greeneville, TN, 37743. Tel: 423-636-7320, Ext 5320. p. 2100

Dykgraaf, Christine, Br Mgr, Pima County Public Library, Dewhirst-Catalina, 15631 N Oracle Rd, No 199, Catalina, AZ, 85739. Tel: 520-594-5240. p. 82

Dyki, Janet, Dir, Elk Township Library, 29 E Lapeer St, Peck, MI, 48466. Tel: 810-378-5409. p. 1140

Dyki, Judy, Dir, Academic Programs, Libr Dir, Cranbrook Academy of Art Library, 39221 Woodward Ave, Bloomfield Hills, MI, 48304. Tel: 248-645-3364. p. 1086

Dykshoorn, Sharon, Libr Mgr, Western Iowa Tech Community College, 4647 Stone Ave, Sioux City, IA, 51106. Tel: 712-274-8733, Ext 1239. p. 783

Dykstra, Kathy, Ch Serv, Sturgis Public Library, 1040 Harley-Davidson Way, Ste 101, Sturgis, SD, 57785. Tel: 605-347-2624. p. 2083

Dykstra, Sharon, Supvr, Ventura County Library, Oak View Library, 555 Mahoney Ave, Oak View, CA, 93022. Tel: 805-649-1523. p. 256

Dylla, Daniel, Librn, Houston Community College - Northwest College, Katy Campus Library, 1550 Foxlake Dr, Houston, TX, 77084-6029. Tel: 713-718-5747. p. 2194

Dyment, Hugh, Educ Coordr, Yukon-Kuskokwim Correctional Center Library, 1000 Chief Eddie Hoffman Hwy, Bethel, AK, 99559. Tel: 907-543-8491. p. 43

Dymond, Jessica, Dir, Daniel Pierce Library, 328 Main St, Grahamsville, NY, 12740. Tel: 845-985-7233. p. 1540

Dynneson, Leanne, Circ Supvr, Unicoi County Public Library, 201 Nolichucky Ave, Erwin, TN, 37650. Tel: 423-743-6533. p. 2098

Dysart, Janice, Sci Librn, University of Missouri-Columbia, Elmer Ellis Library, 104 Ellis Library, Columbia, MO, 65201-5149. Tel: 573-882-1828. p. 1243

Dysart, Jennifer, Dean of Libr, Media Serv, Green River College, 12401 SE 320th St, Auburn, WA, 98092-3699. Tel: 253-833-9111, Ext 2094. p. 2357

Dyszlewski, Nicole, Head of Reference, Instruction & Engagement, Roger Williams University, Ten Metacom Ave, Bristol, RI, 02809-5171. Tel: 401-254-4546. p. 2029

Dzaugis, Andy, Sci Librn, Clark University, Science, 950 Main St, Worcester, MA, 01610. Tel: 508-793-7712. p. 1071

Dzialo, Thelma, Libr Operations Mgr, Roger Williams University Library, One Old Ferry Rd, Bristol, RI, 02809. Tel: 401-254-3063. p. 2030

Dziedzic, Ewa, Educ Librn, The College of New Jersey, 2000 Pennington Rd, Ewing, NJ, 08628-1104. Tel: 609-771-2311. p. 1402

Dzierlenga, Donna, Br Mgr, Montgomery County Memorial Library System, George & Cynthia Woods Mitchell Library, 8125 Ashlane Way, The Woodlands, TX, 77382. Tel: 936-442-7728, Ext 307. p. 2159

Dziewit, Amy, Head, Circ, Head, Reader Serv, Hamilton-Wenham Public Library, 14 Union St, South Hamilton, MA, 01982. Tel: 978-468-5577, Ext 10. p. 1055

Dziver, Sherri, Librn, Prairie Crocus Regional Library, 137 Main St, Rivers, MB, R0K 1X0, CANADA. Tel: 204-328-7613. p. 2589

Dzwir, Brooklyn, IT Mgr, Shelby County Public Library, 309 Eighth St, Shelbyville, KY, 40065. Tel: 502-633-3803. p. 874

Eachus, Amanda, Pub Serv Mgr, Hershey Public Library, 701 Cocoa Ave, Hershey, PA, 17033. Tel: 717-533-6555. p. 1943

Eaddy, Nykia, Br Mgr, Bridgeport Public Library, Newfield, 755 Central Ave, Bridgeport, CT, 06607. Tel: 203-576-7828. p. 303

Eade, Colin, Canton Campus Librn, Chattahoochee Technical College Library, 980 S Cobb Dr, Marietta, GA, 30060. Tel: 770-345-1392. p. 488

Eade, Colin M, Librn, Library Services, Chattahoochee Technical College Library, Canton Campus Library, 1645 Bluffs Pkwy, Canton, GA, 30114. Tel: 770-345-1052. p. 488

Eades, Rhiannon, Pub Info Officer, Athens Regional Library System, 2025 Baxter St, Athens, GA, 30606-6331. Tel: 706-613-3650. p. 458

Eads, Sonja R, Dir, Libr Serv, Maysville Community & Technical College, 1755 US Hwy 68, Maysville, KY, 41056. Tel: 606-759-7141, Ext 66206. p. 869

Eads, Terry, Libr Asst, Sampson-Clinton Public Library, Bryan Memorial, 302 W Weeksdale St, Newton Grove, NC, 28366. Tel: 910-594-1260. p. 1681

Eagen, Rochelle, Lead Libr Tech, San Juan Bautista City Library, 801 Second St, San Juan Bautista, CA, 95045. Tel: 831-623-4687. p. 232

Eager, Margaret, Libr Tech, Nova Scotia Community College, Strait Area Campus Library, 226 Reeves St, Port Hawkesbury, NS, B9A 2W2, CANADA. Tel: 902-625-4364. p. 2620

Eagle, Terry, Head, Tech Serv, Haverstraw King's Daughters Public Library, 10 W Ramapo Rd, Garnerville, NY, 10923. Tel: 845-786-3800. p. 1537

Eaglesham, Carolyn, Outreach Coordr, Edward U Demmer Memorial Library, 6961 W School St, Three Lakes, WI, 54562. Tel: 715-546-3391. p. 2481

Eakes, Sara G, Dir, Libr & Res Serv, Nixon Peabody LLP, 799 Ninth St NW, Ste 500, Washington, DC, 20001. Tel: 202-585-8000, Ext 8320. p. 373

Eakin, Pam, Campus Librn, Nova Scotia Community College, Akerley Campus Library, 21 Woodlawn Rd, Dartmouth, NS, B2W 2R7, CANADA. Tel: 902-491-3580. p. 2619

Eales, Barbara, Webmaster, Ventura County Library, 5600 Everglades St, Ste A, Ventura, CA, 93003. Tel: 805-218-5360. p. 256

Ealey, Brenda, Br Supvr, Lincoln City Libraries, Charles H Gere Branch, 2400 S 56th St, Lincoln, NE, 68506-3599. Tel: 402-441-8562. p. 1321

Ealy, Alvin, Asst Dir, Effingham Public Library, 200 N Third St, Effingham, IL, 62401. Tel: 217-342-2464. p. 582

Ealy, Erin, Mgr, Libr Serv, John Wood Community College Library, 1301 S 48th St, Quincy, IL, 62305. Tel: 217-641-4537. p. 637

Eames, Barbara, Assoc Dir, National Economic Research Associates, Inc, 360 Hamilton Ave, 10th Flr, White Plains, NY, 10601. Tel: 202-466-9271. p. 1664

Eames, Brenda, Librn, TIRR Memorial Hermann, 1333 Moursund St, Houston, TX, 77030. Tel: 713-797-5947, 713-799-5000 ((Main)). p. 2199

Eames, Cathy, Head Librn, Children's Hospital of Michigan, Medical Library, 3901 Beaubien Blvd, 1st Flr, Detroit, MI, 48201. Tel: 313-745-0252, 313-745-5322. p. 1097

Eames, Kathy, Head, Youth Serv, Harbor-Topky Memorial Library, 1633 Walnut Blvd, Ashtabula, OH, 44004. Tel: 440-964-9645. p. 1748

Eanes, Joel, Librn, California Department of Corrections Library System, Centinela State Prison, 2302 Brown Rd, Imperial, CA, 92251. Tel: 760-337-7900, Ext 6158. p. 206

Eannel, Lois, Dir, East Lake Community Library, 4125 East Lake Rd, Palm Harbor, FL, 34685. Tel: 727-773-2665. p. 435

Earel, Anne, Res & Instruction Librn, Augustana College Library, 3435 9 1/2 Ave, Rock Island, IL, 61201-2296. Tel: 309-794-7315. p. 641

Earl, Danielle, Librn, Saint Vladimir's Orthodox Theological Seminary Library, 575 Scarsdale Rd, Yonkers, NY, 10707-1699. Tel: 914-961-8313, Ext 365. p. 1667

Earl, Fely, Libr Mgr, Apache County Library District, Greer Memorial, 74A County Rd 1120 / Main St, Greer, AZ, 85927. Tel: 928-735-7710. p. 76

Earl, Fely, Libr Mgr, Apache County Library District, Round Valley Public, 179 S Main St, Eagar, AZ, 85925. Tel: 928-333-4694. p. 76

Earl, Gary, County Coordr, Pinellas Public Library Cooperative, 1330 Cleveland St, Clearwater, FL, 33755-5103. Tel: 727-441-8408. p. 389

Earl, Martha, Libr Dir, University of Tennessee Graduate School of Medicine, 1924 Alcoa Hwy, Box U-111, Knoxville, TN, 37920. Tel: 865-305-6616. p. 2107

Earl, Martha, Pres, Knoxville Area Health Sciences Library Consortium, UT Preston Med Libr, 1924 Alcoa Hwy, Knoxville, TN, 37920. Tel: 865-305-9525. p. 2775

Earl, Susan, Libr Dir, The John P Holt Brentwood Library, 8109 Concord Rd, Brentwood, TN, 37027. Tel: 615-371-0090, Ext 8010. p. 2089

Earle, April, Tech Serv, Farmingdale State College of New York, 2350 Broadhollow Rd, Farmingdale, NY, 11735-1021. Tel: 934-420-2040. p. 1532

Earle, Evan, Univ Archivist, Cornell University Library, Division of Rare & Manuscript Collections (Carl A Kroch Library), 2B Carl A Kroch Library, Ithaca, NY, 14853. Tel: 607-255-3530. p. 1551

Earle, Katrina, Ref & Instruction Librn, Ivy Tech Community College, 50 W Fall Creek Pkwy N Dr, Indianapolis, IN, 46208. Tel: 317-917-7993. p. 697

Earles, Andy, Library Video Operation Specialist, Marshall University Libraries, One John Marshall Dr, Huntington, WV, 25755-2060. Tel: 304-696-2320. p. 2405

Earles, Eva, Ref Librn/Instrul Serv, Carteret Community College Library, Michael J Smith Bldg, 201 College Circle, Morehead City, NC, 28557. Tel: 252-222-6213. p. 1704

Earles, Phyllis, Univ Archivist, Prairie View A&M University, L W Minor St, University Dr, Prairie View, TX, 77446-0519. Tel: 936-261-1516. p. 2229

Earll, Mary, Dir, Sibley Public Library, 406 Ninth St, Sibley, IA, 51249. Tel: 712-754-2888. p. 781

Earll, Mary Beth, ILL, Gannon University, 619 Sassafras St, Erie, PA, 16541. Tel: 814-871-7557. p. 1931

Earls, Matt, Dir, Jonathan Trumbull Library, 580 Exeter Rd, Lebanon, CT, 06249. Tel: 860-642-2020, 860-642-7763. p. 319

Earls, Stephanie, Librn, Washington State Department of Natural Resources, Natural Resources Bldg, Rm 173, 1111 Washington St SE, Olympia, WA, 98504-7007. Tel: 360-902-1473. p. 2373

Earls, Vicki, Head, Ref, Franklin Public Library, 118 Main St, Franklin, MA, 02038. Tel: 508-520-4941. p. 1020
Early, Michelle, Head, Libr Syst, Xavier University, 1535 Musketeer Dr, Cincinnati, OH, 45207. Tel: 513-745-4817. p. 1765
Earnest, Bruce, Dr, Exec Dir, Moravian Music Foundation, 457 S Church St, Winston-Salem, NC, 27101. Tel: 336-725-0651. p. 1725
Earnest, Greta, Dir, Fashion Institute of Technology-SUNY, Seventh Ave at 27th St, 227 W 27th St, New York, NY, 10001-5992. Tel: 212-217-4340. p. 1585
Earnest, Ola May, Pres, Linn County Museum & Genealogy Library, Dunlap Park, 307 E Park St, Pleasanton, KS, 66075. Tel: 913-352-8739. p. 832
Earnhart, Katie, Libr Dir, Cape Girardeau Public Library, 711 N Clark St, Cape Girardeau, MO, 63701. Tel: 573-334-5279. p. 1240
Earp, Christy, Dir, Wilkes Community College, 1328 S Collegiate Dr, 2nd Flr, Wilkesboro, NC, 28697. Tel: 336-838-6117. p. 1722
Earp, Erika, Ad, Fort Dodge Public Library, 424 Central Ave, Fort Dodge, IA, 50501. Tel: 515-573-8167, Ext 6231. p. 754
Earp, Mary Beth, Libr Tech, Hinds Community College, Rankin Library, 3805 Hwy 80 E, Pearl, MS, 39208-4295. Tel: 601-936-5538. p. 1231
Eash, Lynnell, Br Mgr, Branch District Library, Bronson Branch, 207 N Matteson St, Bronson, MI, 49028-1308. Tel: 517-369-3785. p. 1092
Easley, Juanita, Info Serv, Lee-Itawamba Library System, 219 N Madison St, Tupelo, MS, 38804-3899. Tel: 662-841-9027. p. 1233
Eason, Marcus, Managing Librn, Brooklyn Public Library, Gravesend, 303 Ave X, Brooklyn, NY, 11223. Tel: 718-382-5792. p. 1503
Eason, Melissa, Libr Serv Adminr, Sherman Public Library, 421 N Travis St, Sherman, TX, 75090. Tel: 903-892-7240. p. 2243
East, Lori, Libr Dir, Tuolumne County Genealogical Society Library, 158 Bradford St, Sonora, CA, 95370. Tel: 209-532-1317. p. 247
Easter, Hannah, Head, Teen Serv, Montrose Regional Library District, 320 S Second St, Montrose, CO, 81401. Tel: 970-249-9656. p. 291
Easter, Jennifer, Librn, Centennial College of Applied Arts & Technology, Ashtonbee Campus, 75 Ashtonbee Rd, Rm L-202, Scarborough, ON, M1L 4N4, CANADA. Tel: 416-289-5000, Ext 7000. p. 2677
Easter, Jennifer, Librn, Centennial College of Applied Arts & Technology, Morningside Campus, 755 Morningside Ave, Rm 160, Scarborough, ON, M1C 5J9, CANADA. Tel: 416-289-5000, Ext 8000. p. 2677
Easter, Johnette, Human Res Mgr, Multnomah County Library, 919 NE 19th Ave, Ste 250, Portland, OR, 97232. Tel: 503-988-5123. p. 1892
Easter, Mandy, Libr Consult, State Library of Iowa, State Capitol Bldg, 2nd Flr, 1007 E Grand Ave, Des Moines, IA, 50319. Tel: 515-281-5124. p. 747
Easterday, Mary Jane, Circ Mgr, Danville Public Library, 319 N Vermilion St, Danville, IL, 61832. Tel: 217-477-5220. p. 575
Easterly, Jane, Asst Dir, Head, Adult Serv, Galesburg Public Library, 40 E Simmons St, Galesburg, IL, 61401-4591. Tel: 309-343-6118. p. 591
Easterwood, Lori, Libr Dir, Folsom Public Library, George Murray Bldg, 411 Stafford St, Folsom, CA, 95630. Tel: 916-461-6130. p. 142
Eastham, Rosanne, Dir, Tyler County Public Library, 300 Broad St, Middlebourne, WV, 26149. Tel: 304-758-4304. p. 2408
Eastin, Amanda, Head Librn, Sutton Memorial Library, 201 S Saunders, Sutton, NE, 68979. Tel: 402-773-5259. p. 1337
Eastland, Craig, Sr Law Librn, Northeastern University School of Law Library, 416 Huntington Ave, Boston, MA, 02115. Tel: 617-373-3332. p. 999
Eastman, Garrett, Dir, Curry College, 1071 Blue Hill Ave, Milton, MA, 02186-9984. Tel: 617-333-2177. p. 1036
Eastman, Peyton, Dir, Edward Gauche Fisher Public Library, 1289 Ingleside Ave, Athens, TN, 37303. Tel: 423-745-7782. p. 2088
Easton, Bill, Instruction & Ref Librn, Monterey Peninsula College Library, 980 Fremont St, Monterey, CA, 93940. Tel: 831-645-1382. p. 179
Eastwood, Justin, Outreach Serv Librn, King University, 1350 King College Rd, Bristol, TN, 37620. Tel: 865-769-3108. p. 2090
Eaton, Denny, Per, Johnson University, 7902 Eubanks Dr, Knoxville, TN, 37998. Tel: 865-251-2277. p. 2105
Eaton, Kathleen, Prov Librn, Prince Edward Island Public Library Service, 89 Red Head Rd, Morell, PE, C0A 1S0, CANADA. Tel: 902-961-7316. p. 2708
Eaton, Mark, Electronic Res, Kingsborough Community College, 2001 Oriental Blvd, Brooklyn, NY, 11235. Tel: 718-368-6557, p. 1504
Eaton, Mike, Libr Serv Coordr, Edmonton Public Library, Clareview, 3808 139 Ave, Edmonton, AB, T5Y 3G4, CANADA. Tel: 780-496-4038. p. 2536
Eaton, Nancy, Librn, Waterford Library Association, 663 Waterford Rd, Waterford, ME, 04088. Tel: 207-583-2050. p. 944
Eaton, Patti, Asst Mgr, Ch Serv, La Grange Public Library, Ten W Cossitt Ave, La Grange, IL, 60525. Tel: 708-215-3200. p. 605
Eaton, Rebecca, Coordr, Libr Serv, Carl Sandburg College, Bldg E230, 2400 Tom L Wilson Blvd, Galesburg, IL, 61401. Tel: 309-341-5257. p. 590
Eaton, Shirley, Circ, Freed-Hardeman University, 158 E Main St, Henderson, TN, 38340-2399. Tel: 731-989-6067. p. 2101
Eaves, Shannon, Libr Dir, Taylor University, 1846 Main St, Upland, IN, 46989. Tel: 765-998-5241. p. 722
Ebanks, Donna, Circ Supvr, Plattekill Public Library, 2047 State Rte 32, Modena, NY, 12548. Tel: 845-883-7286. p. 1573
Ebarb, Patti, Br Mgr, Sabine Parish Library, Converse Branch, 108 W Port Arthur Ave, Converse, LA, 71419. Tel: 318-567-3121. p. 896
Ebbers, Laurie, Ref (Info Servs), Nobles County Library, 407 12th St, Worthington, MN, 56187. Tel: 507-295-5340. p. 1210
Ebbing, Scott, Access Serv Librn, Lincoln Land Community College Library, Sangamon Hall, 5250 Shepherd Rd, Springfield, IL, 62794. Tel: 217-786-2358. p. 650
Ebbs, Corinne, Head, Res, Westfield State University, 577 Western Ave, Westfield, MA, 01085-2580. p. 1067
Ebel, Malia, Col Librn, Colby-Sawyer College, 541 Main St, New London, NH, 03257-4648. Tel: 603-526-3375. p. 1375
Ebel-Northup, Cheryl, Dir, Wyoming Free Circulating Library, 114 S Academy St, Wyoming, NY, 14591. Tel: 585-495-6840. p. 1667
Eberhardt, Herman, Curator, National Archives & Records Administration, 4079 Albany Post Rd, Hyde Park, NY, 12538. Tel: 845-486-7770. p. 1550
Eberhardt, Ian, Mgr, Carnegie Library of Pittsburgh, Knoxville, 400 Brownsville Rd, Pittsburgh, PA, 15210-2251. Tel: 412-381-6543. p. 1991
Eberhart, George M, Librn, J Allen Hynek Center for UFO Studies, PO Box 31335, Chicago, IL, 60631. Tel: 773-271-3611. p. 561
Eberle, Alexandra L, Dir, Brooke County Public Library, 945 Main St, Wellsburg, WV, 26070. Tel: 304-737-1551. p. 2417
Eberli, Olivia, Head, Youth Serv, Westfield Athenaeum, Six Elm St, Westfield, MA, 01085-2997. Tel: 413-568-7833, Ext 102. p. 1067
Eberline, Katherine, Children's Serv Coordr, Brookings Public Library, 515 Third St, Brookings, SD, 57006. Tel: 605-692-9407. p. 2074
Eberly, Cheryl, Principal Librn, YA, Santa Ana Public Library, 26 Civic Ctr Plaza, Santa Ana, CA, 92701-4010. Tel: 714-647-5288. p. 239
Eberly, Terri, Dir, Auld Public Library, 537 N Webster St, Red Cloud, NE, 68970. Tel: 402-746-3352. p. 1334
Ebersole, Meg, Global Dir, Research Info & Intelligence, Bryan Cave Leighton Paisner LLP, One Metropolitan Sq, 211 N Broadway, Ste 3600, Saint Louis, MO, 63102-2750. Tel: 314-259-2298. p. 1269
Ebert, Amanda, Libr Mgr, High Level Municipal Library, 10601 103 St, High Level, AB, T0H 1Z0, CANADA. Tel: 780-926-2097. p. 2542
Ebert, Heather, Librn, Marion County Ohio Law Library, 258 W Center St, Marion, OH, 43302. Tel: 740-223-4170. p. 1799
Ebert, Lisa, Ad, Cardington-Lincoln Public Library, 128 E Main St, Cardington, OH, 43315. Tel: 419-864-8181. p. 1756
Ebert, Noelle, Info Resources & Instructional Librn, Southwestern Oregon Community College Library, 1988 Newmark Ave, Coos Bay, OR, 97420. Tel: 541-888-7270. p. 1876
Eblen, Lisa, Dept Head, United States Navy, Bldg 1, 4th Flr, 620 John Paul Jones Circle, Portsmouth, VA, 23708. Tel: 757-953-5383. p. 2338
Eblin, Kristi, Dir, Meigs County District Public Library, 216 W Main St, Pomeroy, OH, 45769. Tel: 740-992-5813. p. 1816
Ebnet-Desens, Rebecca, Exec Dir, Anoka County Historical Society, 2135 Third Ave N, Anoka, MN, 55303. Tel: 763-421-0600. p. 1163
Eby, Jeff, Libr Spec, Florida Department of Agriculture & Consumer Services, 1911 SW 34th St, Gainesville, FL, 32608. Tel: 352-395-4722. p. 407
Ecabert, Gayle, Exec Dir, SouthWest Ohio & Neighboring Libraries, 10250 Alliance Rd, Ste 112, Cincinnati, OH, 45242. Tel: 513-751-4423. p. 2773
Eccles, Alexa, Dir, Community Library Network, 8385 N Government Way, Hayden, ID, 83835-9280. Tel: 208-773-1506 x315. p. 522
Eccles, Alexandria C, Asst Dir, Pub Serv, McAllen Public Library, 4001 N 23rd St, McAllen, TX, 78504. Tel: 956-681-3000. p. 2217
Eccles, Kim, Asst Dean, Res Serv, Mercer University Atlanta, 3001 Mercer University Dr, Atlanta, GA, 30341. Tel: 678-547-6271. p. 465
Eccles, Sara, Dir, Olathe Public Library, 260 E Santa Fe St, Olathe, KS, 66061. Tel: 913-971-6832. p. 828
Ecer, Elif, Coll Develop Librn, Brookings Institution Library, 1775 Massachusetts Ave NW, Washington, DC, 20036. Tel: 202-797-6240. p. 361
Echelberger, Dana, Adult Serv, Newburyport Public Library, 94 State St, Newburyport, MA, 01950-6619. Tel: 978-465-4428, Ext 226. p. 1038
Echeverria, Jessica, Fac Librn, Palm Beach State College, 1977 College Dr, Mail Sta 43, Belle Glade, FL, 33430. Tel: 561-993-1150. p. 384
Echols, Kristen, Libr Asst, Washington County Public Library, McIntosh Branch, Melva Jean Daughtery Bldg, 83 Olin Rd, McIntosh, AL, 36553. Tel: 251-944-2047. p. 11
Echols, Susan, Tech Serv, Troy University, 502 University Dr, Dothan, AL, 36304. Tel: 334-983-6556, Ext 1320. p. 15
Echord, Jess G, Libr Dir, United States Air Force, 23 FSS/FSDL, 3010 Robinson Rd, Bldg 328, Moody AFB, GA, 31699-1594. Tel: 229-257-3539. p. 491
Echtenkamp, Kristin, Info Serv, South Dakota State University, 1300 N Campus Dr, Box 2115, Brookings, SD, 57007. Tel: 605-688-5958. p. 2074

Eck, Angela, Asst Dir, Bartholomew County Public Library, 536 Fifth St, Columbus, IN, 47201-6225. Tel: 812-379-1254. p. 676

Eck, Lorachelle, Circ Mgr, Rochester Public Library District, One Community Dr, Rochester, IL, 62563. Tel: 217-498-8454. p. 640

Eck, Maureen, Actg Dep Dir, Nebraska State Library, 325 State Capitol, 1445 K St, Lincoln, NE, 68509. Tel: 402-471-3189. p. 1322

Eckard, Kim, Asst Dir, Hollidaysburg Area Public Library, One Furnace Rd, Hollidaysburg, PA, 16648-1051. Tel: 814-695-5961. p. 1944

Eckel, Edward, Engineering & Natural Sciences Librn, Western Michigan University, 1903 W Michigan Ave, WMU Mail Stop 5353, Kalamazoo, MI, 49008-5353. Tel: 269-387-5140. p. 1122

Eckels, Jerice, Circ, Libr Asst, Paradise Valley Community College, 18401 N 32nd St, Phoenix, AZ, 85032-1200. Tel: 602-787-7200. p. 71

Eckerle, Mary Theresa, Dir, Marion Public Library, 600 S Washington St, Marion, IN, 46953-1992. Tel: 765-668-2900. p. 704

Eckerson, Andrea, Br Mgr, Lewis & Clark Library, East Helena Branch, 16 E Main St, East Helena, MT, 59635. Tel: 406-227-5750. p. 1296

Eckert, Barbara, Br Mgr, Monmouth County Library, Oceanport Branch, Eight Iroquios Ave, Oceanport, NJ, 07757. Tel: 732-229-2626. p. 1416

Eckert, Brendan, Ch Serv Librn, Derby Neck Library Association, 307 Hawthorne Ave, Derby, CT, 06418. Tel: 203-734-1492. p. 308

Eckert, Brent, Tech Serv Librn, Rock Valley College, 3301 N Mulford Rd, Rockford, IL, 61114. Tel: 815-921-4604. p. 641

Eckert, Jordan, Youth Serv, Waterloo-Grant Township Public Library, 300 S Wayne St, Waterloo, IN, 46793. Tel: 260-837-4491. p. 725

Eckhardt, Allison, Mgr, Outreach Serv, Springfield-Greene County Library District, Outreach Services, 4653 S Campbell, Springfield, MO, 65810-8113. Tel: 417-883-6112. p. 1281

Eckhoff, Cherie, Asst Librn, Reinbeck Public Library, 501 Clark St, Reinbeck, IA, 50669. Tel: 319-788-2652. p. 778

Eckler, Holly, Dir, Kirby Free Library of Salisbury Center, 105 Rte 29A, Salisbury Center, NY, 13454. Tel: 315-429-9006. p. 1635

Eckley, Laura, Libr Dir, Larchmont Public Library, 121 Larchmont Ave, Larchmont, NY, 10538. Tel: 914-834-2281. p. 1562

Eckmair, Leigh, Archivist, Gilbertsville Free Library, 17 Commercial St, Gilbertsville, NY, 13776. Tel: 607-783-2832. p. 1538

Eckman, Charles D, Dean, Univ Librn, University of Miami Libraries, 1300 Memorial Dr, Coral Gables, FL, 33146. Tel: 305-284-3233. p. 390

Eckman, Lynn, Dir, Capitan Public Library, 101 E Second St, Capitan, NM, 88316. Tel: 575-354-3035. p. 1464

Eckman, Paul, Board Pres, Capitan Public Library, 101 E Second St, Capitan, NM, 88316. Tel: 575-354-3035. p. 1464

Eckstadt, Christopher, Br Mgr, Walla Walla County Rural Library District, Plaza Library, 1640 Plaza Way, Walla Walla, WA, 99362. Tel: 509-525-5161. p. 2392

Economy, Linda, Asst Librn, Cavalier County Library, 600 Fifth Ave, Langdon, ND, 58249. Tel: 701-256-5353. p. 1737

Edberg, Jamie, Sch Librn, Centerville Community Library, 421 Florida, Centerville, SD, 57014. Tel: 605-563-2540. p. 2075

Eddie, Sandra, Managing Librn, Brooklyn Public Library, Arlington, 203 Arlington Ave, Brooklyn, NY, 11207. Tel: 718-277-6105. p. 1502

Eddy, Lauren, Resource Coordr, Tutoring Servs, Western Connecticut State University, 181 White St, Danbury, CT, 06810. Tel: 203-837-9100. p. 307

Eddy, Nate, Libr Dir, Winooski Memorial Library, 32E Malletts Bay Ave, Winooski, VT, 05404. Tel: 802-655-6424. p. 2299

Eddy, Paul, Br Mgr, Libr Adminr, Beaumont Public Library System, Beaumont Public, 801 Pearl St, Beaumont, TX, 77701. Tel: 409-981-5911. p. 2145

Eddy, Paul, Libr Adminr, Beaumont Public Library System, 801 Pearl St, Beaumont, TX, 77701. Tel: 409-981-5911. p. 2145

Ede-Pisano, Leah, Br Supvr, Elgin County Library, Belmont Library, 14134 Belmont Rd, Belmont, ON, N0L 1B0, CANADA. Tel: 519-644-1560. p. 2681

Ede-Pisano, Leah, Br Supvr, Elgin County Library, Springfield Library, Malahida Community Pl, 12105 Whittaker Rd, Springfield, ON, N0L 2J0, CANADA. Tel: 519-765-4515. p. 2681

Edel, Deborah, Coordr, Lesbian Herstory Archives, 484 14th St, Brooklyn, NY, 11215. Tel: 718-768-3953. p. 1505

Edelen, Edna, Technician III, Colorado Department of Corrections, 12101 Hwy 61, Sterling, CO, 80751. Tel: 970-521-5010, Ext 3404. p. 296

Edelman, David, Circ Supvr, Hastings Public Library, 227 E State St, Hastings, MI, 49058-1817. Tel: 269-945-4263. p. 1114

Edelman, Leah, Archivist, Columbia University, The Burke Library at Union Theological Seminary, 3041 Broadway, New York, NY, 10027. Tel: 212-851-5606. p. 1583

Edelson, Paul, Pres, Ocean Township Historical Museum Library, Eden Woolley House, 703 Deal Rd, Ocean, NJ, 07712. Tel: 732-531-2136. p. 1430

Eden, Veronica, Libr Mgr, West Slope Community Library, 3678 SW 78th Ave, Portland, OR, 97225-9019. Tel: 503-292-6416. p. 1895

Edens, David, Dir of Libr, Abraham Baldwin Agricultural College, 2802 Moore Hwy, Tifton, GA, 31793. Tel: 229-391-4990. p. 500

Eder, Jonathon, Mgr, The Mary Baker Eddy Library, Research & Reference Services, 210 Massachusetts Ave, P04-10, Boston, MA, 02115-3017. Tel: 617-450-7131. p. 994

Eder, Melissa, Librn, Amarillo College, 2201 S Washington, Amarillo, TX, 79109. Tel: 806-345-5582. p. 2134

Eder, Suzanne Kahn, Educ Dir, Dorothy Fish Coastal Resource Library at Wells Reserve, 342 Laudholm Farm Rd, Wells, ME, 04090. Tel: 207-646-1555, Ext 116. p. 945

Edgar, Chuck, Research Librn, Washington County Historical Society, 49 E Maiden St, Washington, PA, 15301. Tel: 724-225-6740. p. 2018

Edgar, Deonna, Teen Librn, Hyrum Library, 50 W Main, Hyrum, UT, 84319. Tel: 435-245-6411. p. 2265

Edgar, Justin, Access Serv Librn, University of California, 200 McAllister St, San Francisco, CA, 94102-4978. Tel: 415-565-4757. p. 229

Edgar, Laura, Asst Archivist, University of Puget Sound, 1604 N Warner St, Upper Loading Dock, Tacoma, WA, 98416. Tel: 253-879-6014. p. 2387

Edge, Bobby, Br Mgr, Brazoria County Library System, West Columbia Branch, 518 E Brazos, West Columbia, TX, 77486. Tel: 979-345-3394. p. 2135

Edge, Teresa, Coordr, Info Literacy, Thomas Jefferson University-East Falls, 4201 Henry Ave, Philadelphia, PA, 19144-5497. Tel: 215-951-2629. p. 1987

Edgell, Katie, Ch, Liberty Municipal Library, 1710 Sam Houston Ave, Liberty, TX, 77575-4741. Tel: 936-336-8901. p. 2211

Edgerton, Janet, Head Librn, North Carolina Museum of Natural Sciences, 11 W Jones St, Raleigh, NC, 27601. Tel: 919-707-9810. p. 1709

Edgerton, Janet G, Head Librn, North Carolina State Museum of Natural Sciences, 11 W Jones St, Raleigh, NC, 27601. Tel: 919-707-9810. p. 1709

Edinger, Elizabeth, Dir, Catholic University of America, Judge Kathryn J DuFour Law Library, 3600 John McCormack Rd NE, Washington, DC, 20064. Tel: 202-319-5228. p. 362

Edington, Becky, Dir, Clinton Public Library, 313 S Fourth St, Clinton, IN, 47842-2398. Tel: 765-832-8349. p. 675

Edington, Lynne, Librn, Marshall University Libraries, South Charleston Campus Library, 100 Angus E Peyton Dr, South Charleston, WV, 25303-1600. Tel: 304-746-8902. p. 2405

Edington, Natalie, Asst Dir, Baltimore County Public Library, 320 York Rd, Towson, MD, 21204-5179. Tel: 410-887-6100. p. 979

Edington, Sharon, Coordr, Ch Serv, Pickaway County District Public Library, 1160 N Court St, Circleville, OH, 43113-1725. Tel: 740-477-1644, Ext 228. p. 1765

Edler, Mara, Libr Dir, Gutekunst Public Library, 309 Second St SE, State Center, IA, 50247-0550. Tel: 641-483-2741. p. 784

Edlund, Apryl, Head, Tech Serv, West Bridgewater Public Library, 80 Howard St, West Bridgewater, MA, 02379-1710. Tel: 508-894-1255. p. 1065

Edminster, Bill, Asst Dir, McHenry Public Library District, 809 Front St, McHenry, IL, 60050. Tel: 815-385-0036. p. 616

Edmiston, Jan M, Tech Serv Librn, United States Merchant Marine Academy, 300 Steamboat Rd, Kings Point, NY, 11024. Tel: 516-726-5749. p. 1560

Edmond, Veyshon, Br Mgr, Chicago Public Library, Wrightwood-Ashburn, 8530 S Kedzie Ave, Chicago, IL, 60652. Tel: 312-747-2696. p. 558

Edmonds, Heather, Dir, Libr Serv, New England College of Optometry Library, 424 Beacon St, Boston, MA, 02115. Tel: 617-587-5579. p. 998

Edmonds, Kara, Interim Dir, Dimmick Memorial Library, 54 Broadway, Jim Thorpe, PA, 18229-2022. Tel: 570-325-2131. p. 1947

Edmonds, Randi, Librn, Palliser Regional Library, Avonlea Branch, 201 Main St W, Avonlea, SK, S0H 0C0, CANADA. Tel: 306-868-2076. p. 2742

Edmonds, Ryan, Libr Mgr, Gibbons Municipal Library, 5111 51 St, Gibbons, AB, T0A 1N0, CANADA. Tel: 780-923-2004. p. 2541

Edmonds, Sarah A, Assoc Libr Dir, Providence College, One Cunningham Sq, Providence, RI, 02918. Tel: 401-865-1622. p. 2039

Edmonds, Susan, Dir, Milford Town Library, 80 Spruce St, Milford, MA, 01757. Tel: 508-473-2145, Ext 210. p. 1035

Edmondson, Brenda, Br Librn, Wilson County Public Library, East Wilson Branch, 6000-C Ward Blvd, Wilson, NC, 27893-6488. Tel: 252-237-2627. p. 1724

Edmondson, Kay, ILL, Texas Christian University, 2913 Lowden St, TCU Box 298400, Fort Worth, TX, 76129. Tel: 817-257-7106. p. 2181

Edmondson, Mina, Libr Dir, Martin Memorial Library, 159 E Market St, York, PA, 17401-1269. Tel: 717-846-5300. p. 2026

Edmondson, Pam, Local History Specialist, Edgecombe County Memorial Library, 909 N Main St, Tarboro, NC, 27886. Tel: 252-823-1141. p. 1718

Edmondson, Teffany, Ch, Atlanta-Fulton Public Library System, Evelyn G Lowery Library at Southwest, 3665 Cascade Rd SW, Atlanta, GA, 30331. Tel: 404-699-6363. p. 461

Edmunds, Brock, Asst Librn, Access Serv, Boston University Libraries, Frederic S Pardee Management Library, Boston University School of Management, 595 Commonwealth Ave, Boston, MA, 02215. Tel: 617-353-4311. p. 993

Edmundson, Tony, Br Mgr, ImagineIF Libraries, Columbia Falls Branch, 130 Sixth St W, # C, Columbia Falls, MT, 59912. Tel: 406-892-5919. p. 1298

Edmunson-Morton, Tiah K, Archivist, Oregon State University Libraries, Special Collections & Archives Research Center, 121 The Valley Library, 5th Flr, Corvallis, OR, 97331. Tel: 541-737-7387. p. 1877

Edralin, Jeanine, Admin Coordinator I, Texas A&M University-San Antonio, One University Way, San Antonio, TX, 78224. Tel: 210-784-1525. p. 2239
Edrington, Kaitlynn, Libr Asst, Umpqua Community College Library, 1140 Umpqua College Rd, Roseburg, OR, 97470. Tel: 541-440-7682. p. 1895
Edson, Beth, Dir, Libr Serv, Saint Luke's Hospital, 4401 Wornall Rd, Kansas City, MO, 64111. Tel: 816-502-8704. p. 1257
Edson, Kimberly, Head, Reader Serv, Rochester Public Library, 101 Second St SE, Rochester, MN, 55904-3776. Tel: 507-328-2325. p. 1194
Edson, Kristen, Dir, Livonia Public Library, Civic Center, 32777 Five Mile Rd, Livonia, MI, 48154-3045. Tel: 734-466-2450. p. 1127
Edson, Kristen, Libr Dir, Livonia Public Library, 32777 Five Mile Rd, Livonia, MI, 48154-3045. Tel: 734-466-2491. p. 1127
Edson, Kristin, Dep Libr Dir, East Baton Rouge Parish Library, 7711 Goodwood Blvd, Baton Rouge, LA, 70806-7625. Tel: 225-231-3702. p. 882
Edstrom, Jim, Tech Serv Coordr, William Rainey Harper College Library, 1200 W Algonguin Rd, Palatine, IL, 60067. Tel: 847-925-6763. p. 631
Edstrom, Jodi, Br Mgr, Carver County Library, Chaska Branch, Three City Hall Plaza, Chaska, MN, 55318. Tel: 952-448-3886. p. 1169
Edstrom, Jodi, Libr Dir, Carver County Library, Four City Hall Plaza, Chaska, MN, 55318. Tel: 952-448-9395. p. 1169
Edwards, Alfred, Head Librn, United States Army, Center Library, Bldg 212, Corner of Ruf Ave & Novosel, Fort Rucker, AL, 36362-5000. Tel: 334-255-3885. p. 18
Edwards, Amy, Dean of Libr, Oxnard College Library, 4000 S Rose Ave, Oxnard, CA, 93033-6699. Tel: 805-986-5819. p. 190
Edwards, Angela, Dir, Beaver Public Library, 55 W Center St, Beaver, UT, 84713. Tel: 435-438-5274. p. 2261
Edwards, Beth, Librn, Mid-Mississippi Regional Library System, Winston County, 100 W Park St, Louisville, MS, 39339-3018. Tel: 662-773-3212. p. 1224
Edwards, Beverly, PhD, Lecturer, University of Oklahoma, Bizzell Memorial Library, 401 W Brooks, Rm 120, Norman, OK, 73019-6032. Tel: 405-325-3921. p. 2791
Edwards, Brenda, Libr Dir, Blue Ridge Township Public Library, 116 E Oliver St, Mansfield, IL, 61854. Tel: 217-489-9033. p. 613
Edwards, Brendan, Curator, Rare Books & Special Colls, Queen's University, W D Jordan Rare Books & Special Collections, Douglas Library, 6th Level, 2nd Flr, 93 University Ave, Kingston, ON, K7L 5C4, CANADA. Tel: 613-533-6320. p. 2651
Edwards, Brian, Libr Mgr, Alameda County Library, Fremont Library, 2400 Stevenson Blvd, Fremont, CA, 94538-2326. Tel: 510-745-1400. p. 143
Edwards, Brian, Libr Dir, Monterey Public Library, 625 Pacific St, Monterey, CA, 93940. Tel: 831-646-3933. p. 179
Edwards, Carla, Med Librn, Novant Health Presbyterian Medical Center, 200 Hawthorne Lane, Charlotte, NC, 28204-2528. Tel: 704-384-4258. p. 1680
Edwards, Chris, Head, Res Serv, University of Texas at Dallas, 800 W Campbell Rd, Richardson, TX, 75080. Tel: 972-883-2614. p. 2231
Edwards, Chris, Sr Librn, University of Texas at Dallas, Callier Library, 1966 Inwood Rd, Dallas, TX, 75235. Tel: 972-883-3165. p. 2231
Edwards, Christine, Dir, Res & Learning Serv, University of Central Oklahoma, Chambers Library, 100 N University Dr, Edmond, OK, 73034. Tel: 405-974-5199. p. 1846
Edwards, Connie, Children's/Young Adult Serv, Brigham City Library, 26 E Forest St, Brigham City, UT, 84302. Tel: 435-723-5850. p. 2261
Edwards, Dana, Assoc Librn, California State University, East Bay Library, CSU East Bay Library, 25800 Carlos Bee Blvd, Hayward, CA, 94542-3052. Tel: 510-885-3632. p. 150
Edwards, Dawn, Librn, Niles, Barton & Wilmer LLP, 111 S Calvert St, Ste 1400, Baltimore, MD, 21202. Tel: 410-783-6300. p. 956
Edwards, Dedra, Librn, Mid-Mississippi Regional Library System, Pickens Public, 309 Hwy 51, Pickens, MS, 39146. Tel: 662-468-2391. p. 1224
Edwards, Denise, Librn, Lapeer District Library, Clifford Branch, 9530 Main St, Clifford, MI, 48727. Tel: 989-761-7393. p. 1126
Edwards, Donna, Br Mgr, Neuse Regional Library, Greene County Public Library, 229-G Kingold Blvd, Snow Hill, NC, 28580. Tel: 252-747-3437. p. 1699
Edwards, Eric, ILL Librn, Illinois State Library, Gwendolyn Brooks Bldg, 300 S Second St, Springfield, IL, 62701-1796. Tel: 217-558-1928. p. 649
Edwards, Freda, Dir, Altamont Public Library, 407 Houston St, Altamont, KS, 67330. Tel: 620-784-5530. p. 795
Edwards, Ginny, Dir, Division of Legislative Services Reference Center, General Assembly Bldg, 2nd Flr, 910 Capitol St, Richmond, VA, 23219. Tel: 804-786-3591. p. 2340
Edwards, Glynn, Asst Dir, Stanford University Libraries, Mathematics & Statistics, Robin Li & Melissa Ma Science Library, 376 Lomita Dr, Stanford, CA, 94305. Tel: 650-206-0878. p. 249
Edwards, Guy P, Dir, East Islip Public Library, 381 E Main St, East Islip, NY, 11730-2896. Tel: 631-581-9200, Ext 7. p. 1528
Edwards, Jackie, Educ Coordr, United Steelworkers Library, 234 Eglinton Ave E, 8th Flr, Toronto, ON, M4P 1K7, CANADA. Tel: 416-544-5976. p. 2698
Edwards, Jean-Marc, Assoc Univ Librn, Info Tech & Syst, Concordia University Libraries, 1400 de Maisonneuve Blvd W, LB 2, Montreal, QC, H3G 1M8, CANADA. Tel: 514-848-2424, Ext 7732. p. 2723
Edwards, Jenna, Library Contact, United States Department of Agriculture, 4101 LaPorte Ave, Fort Collins, CO, 80521-2154. Tel: 970-266-6023. p. 281
Edwards, John D, Assoc Dean, Dir, Drake University, Drake Law Library, Opperman Hall, 2604 Forest Ave, Des Moines, IA, 50311. Tel: 515-271-2142. p. 746
Edwards, Jonathan, Br Mgr, Southern Oklahoma Library System, Davis Public Library, 209 E Benton Ave, Davis, OK, 73030. Tel: 580-369-2468. p. 1841
Edwards, Kamila, Library Contact, Insurance Institute of Ontario Library, 18 King St E, 6th Flr, Toronto, ON, M5C 1C4, CANADA. Tel: 416-362-8586. p. 2690
Edwards, Kathleen, Br Mgr, Centre County Library & Historical Museum, Centre Hall Area Branch, 109 W Beryl St, Centre Hall, PA, 16828. Tel: 814-364-2580. p. 1910
Edwards, Kelsey, Dir, Bladen County Public Library, 111 N Cyprus St, Elizabethtown, NC, 28337. Tel: 910-862-6990. p. 1687
Edwards, Kim, Rec Mgr, Thomas Jefferson National Accelerator Facility, 12050 Jefferson Ave, ARC 126, Newport News, VA, 23606. Tel: 757-269-7805. p. 2333
Edwards, Lane, Br Mgr, Cuyahoga County Public Library, Garfield Heights Branch, 5409 Turney Rd, Garfield Heights, OH, 44125-3203. Tel: 216-475-8178. p. 1813
Edwards, Lartoshee, Libr Asst, Desoto Parish Library, Logansport Branch, 203 Hwy 5, Logansport, LA, 71049. Tel: 318-697-2311. p. 896
Edwards, Lori, Br Librn, Giles County Public Library, Lynnville Branch, 105 Mill St, Lynnville, TN, 38472. Tel: 931-527-0707. p. 2124
Edwards, Luann, Dir, Tiffin University, 139 Miami St, Tiffin, OH, 44883-2162. Tel: 419-448-3435. p. 1823
Edwards, Margaret, Librn, Charles B Danforth Public Library, 6208 VT Rte 12, Barnard, VT, 05031. Tel: 802-234-9408. p. 2277
Edwards, Melanie, Supvr, Tech Serv, Madison Public Library, 39 Keep St, Madison, NJ, 07940. Tel: 973-377-0722. p. 1415
Edwards, Monica, Dir, Monroe County Public Library, 500 W Fourth St, Tompkinsville, KY, 42167. Tel: 270-487-5301. p. 876
Edwards, Nyala, Mgr, Northwest Georgia Regional Library System, Calhoun-Gordon County, 100 N Park Ave, Calhoun, GA, 30701. Tel: 706-624-1456. p. 474
Edwards, Ossie, Br Mgr, Onondaga County Public Libraries, Beauchamp Branch Library, 2111 S Salina St, Syracuse, NY, 13205. Tel: 315-435-3395. p. 1649
Edwards, Pamela, Assoc Librn, Pub Serv, Calcasieu Parish Public Library System, 301 W Claude St, Lake Charles, LA, 70605-3457. Tel: 337-721-7147. p. 893
Edwards, Phillip, Head Librn, Smithsonian Libraries, National Air & Space Museum Library, Steven F Udar-Hazy Center Room, 203.10 14390 Air & Space Museum Pkwy, Chantilly, DC, 20151. Tel: 703-572-4175. p. 375
Edwards, Quyen, Asst to the Dir, Portage District Library, 300 Library Lane, Portage, MI, 49002. Tel: 269-329-4544. p. 1143
Edwards, Robert, Asst City Librn, Circ Mgr, Decatur Public Library, 130 N Franklin St, Decatur, IL, 62523. Tel: 217-421-9702. p. 576
Edwards, Sandra, Asst Univ Librn, Res Serv, Rice University, 6100 Main, MS-44, Houston, TX, 77005. Tel: 713-348-2504. p. 2197
Edwards, Sean, Librn, Lakeview Public Library, 1120 Woodfield Rd, Rockville Centre, NY, 11570. Tel: 516-536-3071. p. 1631
Edwards, Sharlene, Head, Children's Servx, Piscataway Township Free Public Library, 500 Hoes Lane, Piscataway, NJ, 08854. Tel: 732-463-1633. p. 1435
Edwards, Sharon, Dir of Libr, Motlow State Community College Libraries, 6015 Ledford Mill Rd, Tullahoma, TN, 37388. Tel: 931-393-1670. p. 2128
Edwards, Sharon Kay, Br Librn, Motlow State Community College Libraries, McMinnville Center Library, 225 Cadillac Lane, McMinnville, TN, 37110. Tel: 913-668-7010, Ext 2113. p. 2128
Edwards, Shawn, Dir, Peoria Heights Public Library, 816 E Glen Ave, Peoria Heights, IL, 61616. Tel: 309-682-5578. p. 634
Edwards, Shelby, Community Archivist, University of Wisconsin-River Falls, 410 S Third St, River Falls, WI, 54022. Tel: 715-425-4633. p. 2474
Edwards, Stephanie, Exec Dir, Boston Theological Interreligious Consortium, PO Box 391069, Cambridge, MA, 02139. Tel: 207-370-5275. p. 2766
Edwards, Susan, Div Head, University of California, Berkeley, George & Mary Foster Anthropology Library, 230 Kroeber Hall, Berkeley, CA, 94720-6000. Tel: 510-643-6224. p. 123
Edwards, Susan, Div Head, University of California, Berkeley, Social Research Library, 227 Haviland Hall, Berkeley, CA, 94720-6000. Tel: 510-642-4432. p. 123
Edwards, Susan, Exec Dir, Museum of Old Newbury Library, Cushing House Museum, 98 High St, Newburyport, MA, 01950. Tel: 978-462-2681. p. 1038
Edwards, Susan, Archivist, Librn, Salem State University, 352 Lafayette St, Salem, MA, 01970-5353. Tel: 978-542-6781. p. 1051
Edwards, Susan, Asst Librn, Bayfield Carnegie Library, 37 N Broad St, Bayfield, WI, 54814. Tel: 715-779-3953. p. 2422
Edwards, Tammie, Dir, Harriman Public Library, 601 Walden St, Harriman, TN, 37748-2506. Tel: 865-882-3195. p. 2100

Edwards, Taryn, Librn, Strategic Partnerships Mgr, Mechanics' Institute Library, 57 Post St, Ste 504, San Francisco, CA, 94104-5003. Tel: 415-393-0101. p. 226
Edwards, Terrence, Librn, Ridgewater College Library, Two Century Ave SE, Hutchinson, MN, 55350. Tel: 320-222-7537. p. 1178
Edwards, Terrence B, Librn, Ridgewater College Library, 2101 15th Ave NW, Willmar, MN, 56201. Tel: 320-222-7537. p. 1208
Edwards, Terry, Br Mgr, Hunterdon County Library, North County Branch, 65 Halstead St, Clinton, NJ, 08809. Tel: 908-730-6262. p. 1403
Edwards Thomson, Michelle, Librn, Red Deer College Library, 100 College Blvd, Red Deer, AB, T4N 5H5, CANADA. Tel: 403-342-3346. p. 2551
Edwards, William, Ref Librn, University of Toronto Libraries, Pontifical Institute for Mediaeval Studies, St Michael's College, 113 St Joseph St, 4th Flr, Toronto, ON, M5S 1J4, CANADA. Tel: 416-926-1300, Ext 3423. p. 2700
Edwards-Goodson, Pamela, Br Supvr, Lake County Library System, East Lake County Library, 31340 County Rd 437, Sorrento, FL, 32776. Tel: 352-383-9980. p. 451
Edwardson, Abby, Libr Dir, Rawlins Municipal Library, 1000 E Church St, Pierre, SD, 57501. Tel: 605-773-7421. p. 2080
Edwins, Christine, Dir, Hicksville Public Library, 169 Jerusalem Ave, Hicksville, NY, 11801. Tel: 516-931-1417. p. 1546
Eells, Daniel, Adult Serv, Newton Public Library, 720 N Oak, Newton, KS, 67114. Tel: 316-283-2890. p. 826
Eels, Sharon, Br Coordr, Berkeley County Library System, 1003 Hwy 52, Moncks Corner, SC, 29461. Tel: 843-572-1376. p. 2065
Efaw, Teresa, Circ, Fairmont State University, 1201 Locust Ave, Fairmont, WV, 26554. Tel: 304-367-4733. p. 2402
Effrain, Cyndi, Sr Librn, Long Beach Public Library, Alamitos, 1836 E Third St, Long Beach, CA, 90802. Tel: 562-570-1037. p. 159
Efta, Janina, ILL, Kenai Community Library, 163 Main St Loop, Kenai, AK, 99611. Tel: 907-283-4378. p. 48
Egan, Laurel, PRN Med Librn, Logan Health Medical Library, 310 Sunnyview Lane, Kalispell, MT, 59901. Tel: 406-752-1739. p. 1298
Egan, Noelle, Electronic Res Librn, Drexel University Libraries, Hagerty Library, 33rd & Market Sts, Philadelphia, PA, 19104-2875. Tel: 215-895-2752. p. 1976
Egan, Prather, Br Mgr, Free Library of Philadelphia, Chestnut Hill Branch, 8711 Germantown Ave, Philadelphia, PA, 19118-2716. Tel: 215-685-9290. p. 1977
Egan, Siobhan, Commun Engagement Librn, Barrington Public Library, 281 County Rd, Barrington, RI, 02806. Tel: 401-247-1920. p. 2029
Egbert, Megan, District Prog Mgr, Meridian Library District, 1326 W Cherry Lane, Meridian, ID, 83642. Tel: 208-888-4451. p. 525
Ege, David, Br Mgr, San Diego Public Library, San Carlos, 7265 Jackson Dr, San Diego, CA, 92119. Tel: 619-527-3430. p. 221
Egeland, Christine, Dir, Waverly Reading Center, Main St, Saint Regis Falls, NY, 12980. Tel: 518-856-9720. p. 1635
Egeland, Sherry, Librn, Chinook Regional Library, Sceptre Branch, R M Office, 128 Kingsway St, Sceptre, SK, S0N 2H0, CANADA. Tel: 306-623-4244. p. 2752
Eger, Ernestine, Archivist, Carthage College, 2001 Alford Park Dr, Kenosha, WI, 53140-1900. Tel: 262-551-5950. p. 2444
Eger, Heather, Ref Librn, YA Serv, Altamonte Springs City Library, 281 N Maitland Ave, Altamonte Springs, FL, 32701. Tel: 407-571-8830. p. 383
Egerton, Robin, Br Dir, Mulberry Public Library, 220 N Main St, Mulberry, AR, 72947. Tel: 479-997-1226. p. 106
Egge, Amy, Ch, Rosebud County Library, Bicentennial Library of Colstrip, 419 Willow Ave, Colstrip, MT, 59323. Tel: 406-748-3040. p. 1293
Eggebraaten, Lisa, Access & Res Serv Librn, North Dakota State University Libraries, Business Learning Center, Richard H Barry Hall, Rm 22, 811 Second Ave N, Fargo, ND, 58102. Tel: 701-231-8462. p. 1733
Eggebraaten, Lisa, Access & Res Serv Librn, North Dakota State University Libraries, Klai Juba Wald Architectural Studies Library, Klai Hall, Rm 310, 711 Second Ave N, Fargo, ND, 58102. Tel: 701-231-8462. p. 1733
Egger, Christine, Dir, Dundy County Library, 102 Sixth Ave E, Benkelman, NE, 69021. Tel: 308-423-2333. p. 1308
Egger-Sider, Francine, Coordr, Tech Serv, Fiorello H LaGuardia Community College Library, 31-10 Thomson Ave, Long Island City, NY, 11101. Tel: 718-482-5423. p. 1565
Eggerman, Cora, Br Mgr, Hawaii State Public Library System, Waimanalo Public & School Library, 41-1320 Kalanianaole Hwy, Waimanalo, HI, 96795. Tel: 808-259-2610. p. 511
Eggers, Betsy K, Dir, Napoleon Public Library, 310 W Clinton St, Napoleon, OH, 43545. Tel: 419-592-2531. p. 1805
Eggert, Rose, Chief Exec Officer, Minnesota State Horticultural Society Library, 2705 Lincoln Dr, Roseville, MN, 55113. Tel: 651-643-3601. p. 1195
Eggert, Stephanie, Dir, Caledonia Public Library, 231 E Main St, Caledonia, MN, 55921-1321. Tel: 507-725-2671. p. 1167
Eggleston, Jeffrey, Adult Serv, Gilpin County Public Library District, 15131 Hwy 119, Black Hawk, CO, 80422. Tel: 303-582-5777. p. 266
Eggleston, Keith, Technology Spec, Pinson Public Library, 4509 Pinson Blvd, Pinson, AL, 35126. Tel: 205-680-9298. p. 33
Egler, Peter, Head of Libr, University of Pittsburgh, Johnstown Campus, 450 Schoolhouse Rd, Johnstown, PA, 15904. Tel: 814-269-7288. p. 1948
Ehde, Ava, Mgr, Libr Serv, Manatee County Public Library System, 1301 Barcarrota Blvd W, Bradenton, FL, 34205-7522. Tel: 941-748-5555, Ext 6301. p. 386
Ehinger, Kelly A, Dir, Adams Public Library System, 128 S Third St, Decatur, IN, 46733-1691. Tel: 260-724-2605. p. 678
Ehle, Cathie, Sr Librn, Los Angeles Public Library System, Felipe de Neve Branch Library, 2820 W Sixth St, Los Angeles, CA, 90057-3114. Tel: 213-384-7676. p. 164
Ehle, Terry, Youth Serv Coordr, Lester Public Library, 1001 Adams St, Two Rivers, WI, 54241. Tel: 920-793-7118. p. 2482
Ehlers, Katherine, Mgr, Miami-Dade Public Library System, North Shore Branch, 7501 Collins Ave, Miami Beach, FL, 33141. Tel: 305-864-5392. p. 424
Ehlers, Katherine, Mgr, Miami-Dade Public Library System, South Shore Branch, 131 Alton Rd, Miami Beach, FL, 33139. Tel: 305-535-4223. p. 424
Ehm, Marvin, Mkt, Northeast Iowa Community College, Calmar Campus Library, 1625 Hwy 150, Calmar, IA, 52132. Tel: 563-562-3263. p. 776
Ehmen, Patti, Br Mgr, Huntsville-Madison County Public Library, Bessie K Russell Branch Library, 3011 C Sparkman Dr, Huntsville, AL, 35810. Tel: 256-859-9050. p. 22
Ehn, Marcia, Dir, Pomeroy Public Library, 114 S Ontario St, Pomeroy, IA, 50575. Tel: 712-468-2311. p. 777
Ehnow, Marian, Circ, Chestnut Hill College, 9601 Germantown Ave, Philadelphia, PA, 19118-2695. Tel: 215-248-7052. p. 1975
Ehrenberg, Ann Marie, Br Mgr, Mercer County Library System, Robbinsville Branch, 42 Allentown-Robbinsville Rd, Robbinsville, NJ, 08691. Tel: 609-259-2150. p. 1411
Ehret, Carol, Head, Access/Tech Serv, Collingswood Public Library, 771 Haddon Ave, Collingswood, NJ, 08108. Tel: 856-858-0649. p. 1397
Ehret, Deborah, Br Mgr, Indianapolis Public Library, Spades Park, 1801 Nowland Ave, Indianapolis, IN, 46201-1158. Tel: 317-275-4522. p. 696
Ehrgott, Cristin, Bus Operations Mgr, West Chester University, 25 W Rosedale Ave, West Chester, PA, 19383. Tel: 610-436-2927. p. 2020
Ehrig-Burgess, Kristi, Head of Libr & Archives, Mingei International Museum, Balboa Park, 1439 El Prado, San Diego, CA, 92101. Tel: 619-704-7532. p. 215
Ehrlich, Claire, Ref & Instruction Librn, Mohawk Valley Community College Libraries, 1101 Sherman Dr, Utica, NY, 13501-5394. Tel: 315-731-5737. p. 1655
Ehrman, Deborah, Interim Exec Dir, Salt Lake City Public Library, 210 E 400 South, Salt Lake City, UT, 84111-3280. Tel: 801-524-8200. p. 2271
Ehrnst, Elizabeth, Head, Research Collections & Services, Georgia O'Keeffe Museum, 217 Johnson St, Santa Fe, NM, 87501. p. 1476
Eich, Carol, Commun Libr Mgr, Queens Library, Broad Channel Community Library, 16-26 Cross Bay Blvd, Broad Channel, NY, 11693. Tel: 718-318-4943. p. 1554
Eichelberger, Marianne, Libr Dir, Newton Public Library, 720 N Oak, Newton, KS, 67114. Tel: 316-283-2890. p. 826
Eichenlaub, Joann, Asst Dir, Libr Serv, Pennsylvania College of Technology, 999 Hagan Way, Williamsport, PA, 17701. Tel: 570-327-4523. p. 2023
Eicher, Allison, Acq Librn, Michigan State University College of Law Library, Law College Bldg, Rm 115, 648 N Shaw Lane, East Lansing, MI, 48824-1300. Tel: 517-432-6860. p. 1102
Eichholtz, Lisa, Librn, Jefferson Community & Technical College, 622 S First St, Louisville, KY, 40202. Tel: 502-213-2281. p. 865
Eichman, Kim, Librn, Palco Public Library, 309 Main St, Palco, KS, 67657. Tel: 785-737-4286. p. 830
Eichmann, David, Dr, Prof Emeritus, University of Iowa, 3087 Main Library, 125 W Washington St, Iowa City, IA, 52242-1420. Tel: 319-335-5707. p. 2785
Eichner, Kurt, Librn, Massachusetts Department of Corrections, State Hospital Library, 20 Administration Rd, Bridgewater, MA, 02324. Tel: 508-279-4500, Ext 4600. p. 1002
Eick, Kim, Fiscal Officer, Coshocton Public Library, 655 Main St, Coshocton, OH, 43812-1697. Tel: 740-622-0956. p. 1778
Eickhoff, Dennis, Dir, Hepburn Library of Colton, 84 Main St, Colton, NY, 13625. Tel: 315-262-2310. p. 1521
Eickwort, John, Network Serv, Syst Coordr, Riverhead Free Library, 330 Court St, Riverhead, NY, 11901-2885. Tel: 631-727-3228. p. 1627
Eide, Janet, Bus Mgr, The Libraries of Stevens County, 4008 Cedar St, Loon Lake, WA, 99148-9676. Tel: 509-233-3016, 509-233-9621. p. 2369
Eide, Jeff, Br Mgr, Ramsey County Library, Roseville Branch, 2180 N Hamline Ave, Roseville, MN, 55113-4241. Tel: 651-724-6061. p. 1204
Eierman, Natalie, Libr Mgr, Washington County Library, Oakdale Branch, 1010 Heron Ave N, Oakdale, MN, 55128. Tel: 651-730-0504. p. 1210
Eifert, Ron, Dir, Sikeston Public Library, 121 E North St, Sikeston, MO, 63801. Tel: 573-471-4140. p. 1279
Eifler, David, Librn, University of California, Berkeley, Environmental Design Library, 210 Wurster Hall, Berkeley, CA, 94720-6000. Tel: 510-643-7422. p. 122

Eigen, Amanda, Asst Dir, Maplewood Memorial Library, 129 Boyden Ave, Maplewood, NJ, 07040. Tel: 973-762-1688. p. 1416
Eigsti, Jennifer, Asst Dir, Admin Serv, University of Missouri-Kansas City Libraries, 800 E 51st St, Kansas City, MO, 64110. Tel: 816-235-1533. p. 1257
Eike, Betty, Cat Spec, Longwood University, Redford & Race St, Farmville, VA, 23909. Tel: 434-395-2449. p. 2318
Eilderts, Carrie, Exec Dir, Cedar Falls Historical Society Archives, 308 W Third St, Cedar Falls, IA, 50613. Tel: 319-266-5149. p. 737
Eilers, Alex, Administrator of Programs, Memphis Museum of Science & History, 3050 Central Ave, Memphis, TN, 38111. Tel: 901-636-2387. p. 2112
Eilers, Penny, Head Librn, White Hall Township Library, 119 E Sherman St, White Hall, IL, 62092. Tel: 217-374-6014. p. 662
Einoris, Jacki, Info Serv Mgr, Marengo-Union Library District, 19714 E Grant Hwy, Marengo, IL, 60152. Tel: 815-568-8236. p. 613
Einspahr, Jennifer, Dir, Arapahoe Public Library, 306 Nebraska Ave, Arapahoe, NE, 68922. Tel: 308-962-7806. p. 1305
Einstadter, Laura, County Librn, Amador County Library, 530 Sutter St, Jackson, CA, 95642. Tel: 209-223-6400. p. 153
Einstadter, Laura, County Librn, Amador County Library, Pine Grove Branch, 19889 Hwy 88, Pine Grove, CA, 95665. Tel: 209-296-3111. p. 154
Einstein, Ruth, Research Coordr, Nicollet County Historical Society, 1851 N Minnesota Ave, Saint Peter, MN, 56082. Tel: 507-934-2160. p. 1203
Einwalter, Jennifer, Libr Dir, Greenfield Public Library, 5310 W Layton Ave, Greenfield, WI, 53220. Tel: 414-321-9595. p. 2440
Einwalter, Jennifer, Libr Dir, Jack Russell Memorial Library, 100 Park Ave, Hartford, WI, 53027-1585. Tel: 262-673-8240. p. 2440
Eirenschmalz, Maggie, Librn, Truckee Meadows Community College, 7000 Dandini Blvd, Reno, NV, 89512-3999. Tel: 775-673-7011. p. 1349
Eirhart, Sheri, Outreach Serv Librn, Lamar Public Library, 102 E Parmenter St, Lamar, CO, 81052-3239. Tel: 719-336-1291. p. 289
Eisaman, Holly, Youth Serv Coordr, Annie Halenbake Ross Library, 232 W Main St, Lock Haven, PA, 17745-1241. Tel: 570-748-3321. p. 1956
Eisch, Lisa, Dir, Hancock Public Library, 114 S Main St, Hancock, WI, 54943. Tel: 715-249-5817. p. 2440
Eiseman, Jason, Emerging Tech Librn, Yale University Library, Lillian Goldman Library Yale Law School, 127 Wall St, New Haven, CT, 06511. Tel: 203-432-1600. p. 328
Eisemann, Lisa, Bks by Mail Supvr, Lake Wales Public Library, 290 Cypress Garden Lane, Lake Wales, FL, 33853. Tel: 863-679-4441. p. 416
Eisenberg, Christina, Mgr, National Business & Disability Council at the Viscardi Center, 201 IU Willets Rd, Albertson, NY, 11507. Tel: 516-465-1400. p. 1484
Eisenberg, Wendy, Branch Cluster Supvr, Fresno County Public Library, 2420 Mariposa St, Fresno, CA, 93721. Tel: 559-600-7323. p. 145
Eisenga, Diane, Dir, McBain Community Library, 107 E Maple St, McBain, MI, 49657-9672. Tel: 231-825-2197. p. 1131
Eisenhour, Cheryl, Librn, Sylvia Public Library, 121 S Main St, Sylvia, KS, 67581. Tel: 620-486-2021. p. 837
Eisenschenk, Amber, Mgr, Res, League of Minnesota Cities Library, 145 University Ave W, Saint Paul, MN, 55103-2044. Tel: 651-281-1200. p. 1200
Eisenschink, Amy, Mat Mgt Mgr, Manitowoc Public Library, 707 Quay St, Manitowoc, WI, 54220. Tel: 920-686-3000. p. 2453
Eisentrager, Deb, Dir, Dumont Community Library, 602 Second St, Dumont, IA, 50625. Tel: 641-857-3304. p. 749
Eisler, Melody Sky, Dir, Port Townsend Public Library, 1220 Lawrence St, Port Townsend, WA, 98368-6527. Tel: 360-385-3181. p. 2374
Eisley, Kathy, Circ, Milton Public Library, 541 Broadway St, Milton, PA, 17847. Tel: 570-742-7111. p. 1963
Eisloeffel, Paul J, Visual Image Curator, Nebraska History Library, 1500 R St, Lincoln, NE, 68508. Tel: 402-471-7837. p. 1322
Eister, Christine, Libr Tech, Shippensburg University, 1871 Old Main Dr, Shippensburg, PA, 17257. Tel: 717-477-1469. p. 2007
Eiten, Keith, Media Spec, Wheaton College, 510 Irving Ave, Wheaton, IL, 60187-4234. Tel: 630-752-5092. p. 662
Ek, Barbara, Libr Office Mgr, Cary Library, 107 Main St, Houlton, ME, 04730. Tel: 207-532-1302. p. 927
Ekas, Claire, Dir, Mkt, Amarillo Museum of Art Library, 2200 S Van Buren St, Amarillo, TX, 79109-2407. Tel: 806-371-5050. p. 2134
Ekey, Sarah, Instruction Librn, Metropolitan Community College, Longview Campus Library, 500 SW Longview Rd, Lee's Summit, MO, 64081-2105. Tel: 816-604-2266. p. 1256
Eklund, Dawn, Academic Specialist, Minnesota State Community & Technical College, Detroit Lakes Campus, 900 Hwy 34 E, Detroit Lakes, MN, 56501. Tel: 218-846-3769, 218-846-3772. p. 1188
Eklund, Erika, Libr Dir, Stamford Village Library, 117 Main St, Stamford, NY, 12167. Tel: 607-652-5001. p. 1644
Ekmekjian, Taline, Librn, McGill University Health Centre - Glen Site, 1001 Boul DeCarie, Rm B RC 0078, Montreal, QC, H4A 3J1, CANADA. Tel: 514-934-1934, Ext 22554. p. 2725
Ekstrom, Scott, Libr Dir, Smith Memorial Library, 21 Miller Ave, Chautauqua, NY, 14722. Tel: 716-357-6296. p. 1517
El Bashir, Joellen, Curator, Interim Chief Librn, Howard University Libraries, Moorland-Spingarn Research Center, 500 Howard Pl NW, Washington, DC, 20059. Tel: 202-806-7480. p. 369
El-Bathy, Khalil, Dir, Libr Serv, SOWELA Technical Community College Library, Arts & Humanities Bldg, 2000 Merganser St, Lake Charles, LA, 70616. Tel: 337-421-6926. p. 894
El-Warari, Deborah, Asst Dir, East Islip Public Library, 381 E Main St, East Islip, NY, 11730-2896. Tel: 631-581-9200. p. 1528
Elam, Anna, Library Colls Mgr, Museum of History & Industry, 5933 Sixth Ave S, Seattle, WA, 98108. Tel: 206-324-1126, Ext 137. p. 2377
Elam, Gary, Circ Mgr, Iredell County Public Library, 201 N Tradd St, Statesville, NC, 28677. Tel: 704-928-2405. p. 1717
Elam, Tyler, Asst Archivist, Clark County Historical Society, 117 S Fountain Ave, Springfield, OH, 45502-1207. Tel: 937-324-0657. p. 1821
Eland, Thomas, Ref Serv Librn, Minneapolis Community & Technical College Library, Wheelock Whitney Hall, 1501 Hennepin Ave, Minneapolis, MN, 55403. Tel: 612-659-6286. p. 1184
ElBashir, Joellen, Curator, Interim Chief Librn, Howard University Libraries, 500 Howard Pl NW, Ste 203, Washington, DC, 20059. Tel: 202-806-7480. p. 368
Elbe, Pamela, Archives Coll Mgr, National Museum of American Jewish Military History Collections, 1811 R St NW, Washington, DC, 20009. Tel: 202-265-6280. p. 372
Elchert, Katherine, Dir, Rice Lake Public Library, Two E Marshall St, Rice Lake, WI, 54868. Tel: 715-234-4861, Ext 1111. p. 2473
Eldana, Pam, Librn, Lighthouse Point Library, 2200 NE 38th St, Lighthouse Point, FL, 33064-3913. Tel: 954-946-6398. p. 418
Elder, Andrew, Curator, Spec Coll, Interim Univ Archivist, University of Massachusetts at Boston, 100 Morrissey Blvd, Boston, MA, 02125-3300. Tel: 617-287-5944. p. 1000
Elder, Hannah, Rights & Reproductions Librn, Massachusetts Historical Society Library, 1154 Boylston St, Boston, MA, 02215. Tel: 617-646-0542. p. 997
Elder, Jane, Ref Librn, Southern Methodist University, Bridwell Library-Perkins School of Theology, 6005 Bishop Blvd, Dallas, TX, 75205. Tel: 214-768-3483. p. 2167
Elder, Kate, Dir, Libr Serv, Colorado Mental Health Institute at Fort Logan, 3520 W Oxford Ave, Denver, CO, 80236. Tel: 303-866-7844. p. 274
Elder, Melinda, Dir, Knowledge & Res Serv, Chamberlain Hrdlicka Attorneys At Law, 1200 Smith St, Ste 1400, Houston, TX, 77002. Tel: 713-658-1818. p. 2191
Elder, Ruth E, Cataloger, Troy University Library, 309 Wallace Hall, Troy, AL, 36082. Tel: 334-670-3874. p. 37
Elder, Sue, Librn, Jamestown Public Library, 200 W Main St, Jamestown, NC, 27282. Tel: 336-454-4815. p. 1698
Elder, Zachary, Cent Libr Mgr, Chesapeake Public Library, 298 Cedar Rd, Chesapeake, VA, 23322-5512. Tel: 757-410-7110. p. 2311
Eldershaw, Tara, Librn, Halifax Public Libraries, Sackville Branch, 636 Sackville Dr, Lower Sackville, NS, B4C 2S3, CANADA. Tel: 902-865-8653. p. 2618
Eldred, Kim, Librn, Vermontville Township Library, 120 E First St, Vermontville, MI, 49096. Tel: 517-726-1362. p. 1156
Eldred, Lauren, Ch, Pollard Memorial Library, 401 Merrimack St, Lowell, MA, 01852. Tel: 978-674-4120. p. 1029
Eldred, Linda K, Dir, Springville Memorial Library, 264 Broadway St, Springville, IA, 52336. Tel: 319-854-6444. p. 784
Eldred, Wayne, Colls Mgr, Mattatuck Museum of the Mattatuck Historical Society, 144 W Main St, Waterbury, CT, 06702. Tel: 203-753-0381, Ext 112. p. 343
Eldredge, Arabella, Circ Librn, Prince Memorial Library, 266 Main St, Cumberland, ME, 04021-9754. Tel: 207-829-2215. p. 922
Eldridge, Jennifer, Dir, Longview Public Library, 222 W Cotton St, Longview, TX, 75601. Tel: 903-237-1350. p. 2213
Eldridge, Jennifer, Dir, Longview Public Library, Broughton Branch, Broughton Recreation Ctr, 801 S Martin Luther King Jr Blvd, Longview, TX, 75601. Tel: 903-237-1326. p. 2213
Eldridge, Sheryl, Ref Librn, Supv Librn, Newport Public Library, 35 NW Nye St, Newport, OR, 97365-3714. Tel: 541-265-2153. p. 1888
Elford, John, Mgr, County of Los Angeles Public Library, Lancaster Library, 601 W Lancaster Blvd, Lancaster, CA, 93534. Tel: 661-948-5029. p. 136
Elguezabal, Carmen, Dir, City of Presidio Public Library, 1200 E O'Reilly St, Presidio, TX, 79845. Tel: 432-229-3317. p. 2229
Elia, Christina, Head, Pub Serv, Head, Tech, Lansdowne Public Library, 55 S Lansdowne Ave, Lansdowne, PA, 19050-2804. Tel: 610-623-0239. p. 1953
Elias, Anne, Ref Librn, Govt Doc, Delta College Library, 1961 Delta Rd, University Center, MI, 48710. Tel: 989-686-9006. p. 1155
Elias, Lyndsi, Admin Dir, Southeast Community College, Lincoln LRC, 8800 O St, Lincoln, NE, 68520. Tel: 402-437-2586. p. 1307
Elias, Lyndsi, Dir of Libr, Southeast Community College, 4771 W Scott Rd, Beatrice, NE, 68310-7042. Tel: 402-228-8224. p. 1307
Elias, Marie Irma, Assoc Dir, Montefiore Medical Center, Moses Research Tower, 2nd Flr, 111 E 210th St, Bronx, NY, 10467. Tel: 718-920-4666. p. 1499
Elias, Victoria, Supvr, San Bernardino County Library, Baker Family Learning Center, 2818 N Macy St, Muscoy, CA, 92407. Tel: 909-887-5167. p. 212
Eliason, Victoria, Libr Asst, Sloan Public Library, 502 Evans St, Sloan, IA, 51055. Tel: 712-428-4200. p. 783

Elichko, Sarah, Soc Sci Librn, Swarthmore College, 500 College Ave, Swarthmore, PA, 19081. Tel: 610-690-5786. p. 2011
Elieff, Barbara, Ad, North Brunswick Free Public Library, 880 Hermann Rd, North Brunswick, NJ, 08902. Tel: 732-246-3545. p. 1429
Elings, Mary E, Interim Deputy Director, University of California, Berkeley, Bancroft Library, Berkeley, CA, 94720-6000. Tel: 510-642-6481. p. 122
Elizabeth, MacDonald, Dir, Libr Serv, Lindenwood University Library, 209 S Kingshighway, Saint Charles, MO, 63301. Tel: 636-949-4396. p. 1268
Elkes, Katharine, Knowledge Mmgt Officer, John Snow, Inc, 44 Farnsworth St, Boston, MA, 02210-1211. Tel: 617-482-9485. p. 999
Elkins, Helen, Dir, Rotan Public Library, 404 E Sammy Baugh Ave, Rotan, TX, 79546-3820. Tel: 325-735-3362. p. 2234
Elkins, Steve, Assoc Dir, Coll Mgt, Villanova University, Law Library, Villanova University Charles Widger School of Law, 299 N Spring Mill Rd, Villanova, PA, 19085. Tel: 610-519-7780. p. 2017
Elkins, Susan, Digital Res Librn, Sam Houston State University, 1830 Bobby K Marks Dr, Huntsville, TX, 77340. Tel: 936-294-1524. p. 2201
Ellard, Owen, Sr Dir, Libr, University of Texas Health Science Center at San Antonio Libraries, 7703 Floyd Curl Dr, MSC 7940, San Antonio, TX, 78229-3900. Tel: 210-567-2450. p. 2240
Elledge, Debra, Libr Mgr, Portland Public Library of Sumner County, 301 Portland Blvd, Portland, TN, 37148-1229. Tel: 615-325-2279. p. 2124
Ellen, Dawn, Dir, Lee County Public Library, 200 N Main St, Bishopville, SC, 29010. Tel: 803-484-5921. p. 2047
Ellenwood, Dave, Ref Librn, Seattle Central College, 1701 Broadway, BE Rm 2101, Seattle, WA, 98122. Tel: 206-934-6336. p. 2378
Eller, Aaron, Br Mgr, Saint Charles City-County Library District, Library Express @ WingHaven, 7435 Village Center Dr, O'Fallon, MO, 63368-4768. Tel: 636-561-3385. p. 1278
Eller, Aaron, Br Mgr, Saint Charles City-County Library District, Middendorf-Kredell Branch, 2750 Hwy K, O'Fallon, MO, 63368-7859. Tel: 636-272-4999, 636-978-7926. p. 1278
Eller, Chad, Digital Serv Coordr, Gaston County Public Library, 1555 E Garrison Blvd, Gastonia, NC, 28054. Tel: 704-868-2164. p. 1690
Eller, Daniel, Advanced Library Generalist, Electronic Res Mgr, Oral Roberts University Library, 7777 S Lewis Ave, Tulsa, OK, 74171. Tel: 918-495-7168. p. 1865
Eller, Nolan, Col Archivist, Wabash College, 301 W Wabash Ave, Crawfordsville, IN, 47933. Tel: 765-361-6226. p. 677
Eller, Nolan, Univ Archivist, Louisiana Tech University, Everett St at The Columns, Ruston, LA, 71272. Tel: 318-257-3555. p. 906
Eller, Sue, Supvr, Elkhart Public Library, Dunlap, 58485 E County Rd 13, Elkhart, IN, 46516. Tel: 574-875-3100. p. 680
Ellerby, Misty, Libr Assoc, Langston University, 701 Sammy Davis Jr Dr, Langston, OK, 73050. Tel: 405-466-3292. p. 1851
Ellermeyer, Robert, Ref Librn, Holy Family University Library, 9801 Frankford Ave, Philadelphia, PA, 19114. Tel: 267-341-3316. p. 1981
Elley, Christi, Libr Mgr, Daysland Public Library, 5128 50th St, Daysland, AB, T0B 1A0, CANADA. Tel: 780-781-0005. p. 2532
Ellifritt, Bill, Bus Mgr, Clarksburg-Harrison Public Library, 404 W Pike St, Clarksburg, WV, 26301. Tel: 304-627-2236. p. 2401
Elligott, Michelle, Chief Archivist, The Museum of Modern Art, 11 W 53th St, New York, NY, 10019. Tel: 212-708-9433. p. 1592
Ellinger, Emily, Teen Serv Librn, Lewes Public Library, 111 Adams Ave, Lewes, DE, 19958. Tel: 302-645-2733. p. 354
Ellington, Christy, Br Librn, Yadkin County Public Library, 233 E Main St, Yadkinville, NC, 27055. Tel: 336-679-8792. p. 1727
Ellington, Martha, Librn, Mid-Mississippi Regional Library System, Durant Public, 15338 N Jackson St, Durant, MS, 39063-3708. Tel: 662-653-3451. p. 1224
Ellinwood, Lacy, Lead Library Consultant, Mississippi Library Commission, 3881 Eastwood Dr, Jackson, MS, 39211. Tel: 601-432-4154. p. 1222
Elliot, Claire, Pub Serv Librn, Dawson College Library, 3040 Sherbrooke St W, Westmount, QC, H3Z 1A4, CANADA. Tel: 514-931-8731, Ext 1736. p. 2739
Elliot, Patrick, Tech Coordr, Barrington Public Library, 281 County Rd, Barrington, RI, 02806. Tel: 401-247-1920. p. 2029
Elliott, Amanda, Libr Tech, County of Carleton Law Library, Ottawa Court House, 2004-161 Elgin St, Ottawa, ON, K2P 2K1, CANADA. Tel: 613-233-7386, Ext 230. p. 2666
Elliott, Bonnie, Dir, Frankford Public Library, Eight Main St, Frankford, DE, 19945. Tel: 302-732-9351. p. 352
Elliott, Chad, Network Adminr, Birchard Public Library of Sandusky County, 423 Croghan St, Fremont, OH, 43420. Tel: 419-334-7101. p. 1786
Elliott, Christopher, ILL, Southeast Oklahoma Library System (SEOLS), 401 N Second St, McAlester, OK, 74501. Tel: 918-426-0456. p. 1853
Elliott, Cindy, Budget Off Mgr, Longwood University, Redford & Race St, Farmville, VA, 23909. Tel: 434-395-2440. p. 2318
Elliott, Collin, Dean, Coast Mountain College Library, 5331 McConnell Ave, Terrace, BC, V8G 4X2, CANADA. Tel: 250-638-5407. p. 2577
Elliott, Curleen, Interim Dir, Housatonic Community College Library, 900 Lafayette Blvd, Bridgeport, CT, 06604. Tel: 203-332-5179. p. 304
Elliott, Eden, Circ Supvr, Joplin Public Library, 1901 E 20th St, Joplin, MO, 64804. Tel: 417-623-7953. p. 1253
Elliott, Emily, Assoc Dean of Libr, Renton Technical College, 3000 NE Fourth St, Renton, WA, 98056. Tel: 425-235-2352, Ext 5678. p. 2375
Elliott, Emmeline, Libr Operations Mgr, South Dakota State University, 1300 N Campus Dr, Box 2115, Brookings, SD, 57007. Tel: 605-688-5564. p. 2074
Elliott, Greg, Dir, Prince Albert Public Library, 125 12th St E, Prince Albert, SK, S6V 1B7, CANADA. Tel: 306-763-8496. p. 2745
Elliott, J Eric, Archivist, Moravian Church in America, Southern Province, 457 S Church St, Winston-Salem, NC, 27101-5314. Tel: 336-722-1742. p. 1725
Elliott, Jeremy, Asst Librn, Washington County Historical Society Library, 307 E Market St, Salem, IN, 47167. Tel: 812-883-6495. p. 717
Elliott, Joan, Librn, Saskatchewan Teachers' Federation, 2311 Arlington Ave, Saskatoon, SK, S7J 2H8, CANADA. Tel: 306-373-1660. p. 2749
Elliott, John, Coll Develop Librn, Wayland Baptist University, 1900 W Seventh St, Plainview, TX, 79072-6957. Tel: 806-291-3704. p. 2227
Elliott, Kathleen, Library Contact, Cobb Institute of Archaelogy Library, Mississippi State University, Rm 206, 340 Lee Blvd, Mississippi State, MS, 39762. Tel: 662-325-3826. p. 1227
Elliott, Kathy, Asst Librn, San Diego Zoo Global Library, Beckman Ctr, 15600 San Pasqual Valley Rd, Escondido, CA, 92027. Tel: 760-747-8702, Ext 5736. p. 141
Elliott, Kelly, Librn, Lincoln County Law Association Library, Robert S K Welch Courthouse, 59 Church St, St. Catharines, ON, L2R 3C3, CANADA. Tel: 905-685-9094. p. 2679
Elliott, Michelle, Br Mgr, Public Library of Cincinnati & Hamilton County, Harrison Branch, 10398 New Haven Rd, Harrison, OH, 45030. Tel: 513-369-4442. p. 1762
Elliott, Stuart, Pres, Clay County Archives & Historical Library, 210 E Franklin St, Liberty, MO, 64068. Tel: 816-781-3611. p. 1259
Elliott, Susan N, Dir, University of Dayton School of Law, 300 College Park, Dayton, OH, 45469-2772. Tel: 937-229-2314. p. 1780
Elliott, Tamara, Head, Ref, United States Senate Library, SRB-15 Senate Russell Bldg, Washington, DC, 20510. Tel: 202-224-7106. p. 380
Elliott, Todd, Dir, Portsmouth Public Library, 601 Court St, Portsmouth, VA, 23704. Tel: 757-393-8501, Ext 6517. p. 2338
Elliott, Tracy, Dean, Univ Libr, San Jose State University, One Washington Sq, San Jose, CA, 95192-0028. Tel: 404-808-2419. p. 232
Elliott, Tracy, Dean of Libr, Florida Gulf Coast University Library, 10501 FGCU Blvd S, Fort Myers, FL, 33965. Tel: 239-590-7602. p. 402
Elliott, Tracy, Head Librn/Prog Dir II, Saint Petersburg College, Saint Petersburg-Gibbs Campus Library, 6605 Fifth Ave N, Saint Petersburg, FL, 33710. Tel: 727-341-7197. p. 438
Elliott-Coutts, Nora, Head, Children's Servx, North Bay Public Library, 271 Worthington St E, North Bay, ON, P1B 1H1, CANADA. Tel: 705-474-4830. p. 2661
Ellis, Aimee, Librn, Yukon Public Law Library, Yukon Law Courts, 2134 Second Ave, Whitehorse, YT, Y1A 2C6, CANADA. Tel: 867-667-3086. p. 2758
Ellis, Bonnie, Mgr, Crittenden County Library, Edmondson Branch, 61 Waterford St, Edmondson, AR, 72332. Tel: 870-732-9532. p. 104
Ellis, Camille, Library Information Services, Westat, Inc Library, 1600 Research Blvd, Rockville, MD, 20850. Tel: 301-251-1500. p. 976
Ellis, Carmen B, Dir, Learning Res, Brunswick Community College Library, 50 College Rd, Supply, NC, 28462. Tel: 910-755-7351. p. 1718
Ellis, Carolyn, Sr Assoc Vice Provost for Administration, University of Texas at San Antonio Libraries, One UTSA Circle, San Antonio, TX, 78249-0671. Tel: 210-458-6665. p. 2240
Ellis, David, Sr Librn, Los Angeles Public Library System, San Pedro Regional Library, 931 S Gaffey St, San Pedro, CA, 90731-3606. Tel: 310-548-7779. p. 165
Ellis, Devon, Br Mgr, Enoch Pratt Free Library, Hampden Branch, 3641 Falls Rd, Baltimore, MD, 21211-1815. Tel: 443-984-4949. p. 953
Ellis, Elizabeth, Youth Serv, Louisburg Public Library, 206 S Broadway, Louisburg, KS, 66053. Tel: 913-837-2217. p. 822
Ellis, Emily, Asst Dir, Greenwood Public Library, 310 S Meridian St, Greenwood, IN, 46143-3135. Tel: 317-883-4250. p. 688
Ellis, Jacklyn, Sr Libr Spec, Howard C Raether Library, 13625 Bishop's Dr, Brookfield, WI, 53005. Tel: 262-789-1880. p. 2425
Ellis, Jami, Ch, Circ Serv, Donald W Reynolds Community Center & Library, 1515 W Main St, Durant, OK, 74701. Tel: 580-924-3486, 580-931-0231. p. 1846
Ellis, Joyce M, Exec Dir, Minnie Stevens Piper Foundation, 1250 NE Loop 410, Ste 810, San Antonio, TX, 78209-1539. Tel: 210-525-8494. p. 2237
Ellis, Karen, Dir, AV, Dir, Libr Serv, Arkansas Northeastern College, 2501 S Division St, Blytheville, AR, 72315-5111. Tel: 870-762-1020, Ext 1234. p. 91
Ellis, Karen, Dir, Taylor Public Library, 801 Vance St, Taylor, TX, 76574. Tel: 512-352-3434, 512-365-2235. p. 2247

Ellis, Kaylan, Interim Co-Dir, Tech Serv Librn, Ohio Northern University, Taggart Law Library, 525 S Main St, Ada, OH, 45810. Tel: 419-772-2254. p. 1743

Ellis, Mark, Dir, Res & Outreach, East Tennessee State University, Sherrod Library, Seehorn Dr & Lake St, Johnson City, TN, 37614-0204. Tel: 423-439-4715. p. 2103

Ellis, Mary, Asst Mgr, Hyndman Londonderry Public Library, 161 Clarence St, Hyndman, PA, 15545. Tel: 814-842-3782. p. 1945

Ellis, Michael, Access Serv Librn, Hanover College, 121 Scenic Dr, Hanover, IN, 47243. Tel: 812-866-7169. p. 689

Ellis, Pam, Br Mgr, Annapolis Valley Regional Library, Bridgetown & Area Library, 38 Queen St, Bridgetown, NS, B0S 1C0, CANADA. Tel: 902-665-2758. p. 2616

Ellis, Rosa, Librn, Woolworth Community Library, 100 E Utah Ave, Jal, NM, 88252. Tel: 505-395-3268. p. 1470

Ellis, Rudy, Circ Coordr, Southern Oklahoma Library System, 601 Railway Express St, Ardmore, OK, 73401. Tel: 580-223-3164. p. 1840

Ellis, Sabrina, Libr Coord, Nicholson Memorial Library System, 625 Austin St, Garland, TX, 75040-6365. Tel: 972-205-2547. p. 2183

Ellis, Susan, Exec Dir, The Moravian Historical Society, 214 E Center St, Nazareth, PA, 18064. Tel: 610-759-5070. p. 1968

Ellis-Darquah, LaVentra, Interim Dir, Wayne State University Libraries, Vera P Shiffman Medical Library & Learning Resources Centers, 320 E Canfield St, Detroit, MI, 48201. Tel: 313-577-9083. p. 1100

Ellis-Dinkins, Joia, Br Mgr, Atlanta-Fulton Public Library System, Southeast Atlanta Branch - Louise Watley Library, 1463 Pryor Rd, Atlanta, GA, 30315. Tel: 404-613-5771. p. 462

Ellison, Beecher, Law Librn, Josephine County Law Library, Justice Bldg, 2nd Flr, 500 NW Sixth St, Grants Pass, OR, 97526. Tel: 541-474-5488. p. 1881

Ellison, Carol, Circ Mgr, Everett Public Library, 2702 Hoyt Ave, Everett, WA, 98201-3556. Tel: 425-257-8034. p. 2364

Ellison, Kristin, Dir of Finance, Chippewa River District Library, 301 S University Ave, Mount Pleasant, MI, 48858-2597. Tel: 989-773-3242, Ext 226. p. 1135

Ellison, Mary, Ch, Western District Library, 1111 Fourth St, Orion, IL, 61273. p. 630

Ellison, P J, Librn, Lago Vista Public Library, 5803 Thunderbird, Ste 40, Lago Vista, TX, 78645. Tel: 512-267-3868. p. 2208

Ellison, Sarah, Ref Supvr, Pearl Public Library, 2416 Old Brandon Rd, Pearl, MS, 39208-4601. Tel: 601-932-2562. p. 1229

Ellison, Virginia, Chief Operations Officer, VPres, Coll, South Carolina Historical Society Library, Addlestone Library, 3rd Flr, 205 Calhoun St, Charleston, SC, 29401. Tel: 843-723-3225, Ext 114. p. 2051

Ellisor, Pat, Ref Librn, Kirtland Community College Library, 10775 N St Helen Rd, Roscommon, MI, 48653. Tel: 989-275-5000, Ext 246. p. 1145

Ellston, Jamie, Br Mgr, Harrison County Library System, Gulfport Library, 1708 25th Ave, Gulfport, MS, 39501. Tel: 228-871-7171. p. 1217

Ellston, Melanie, Circ Mgr, Dakota County Technical College Library, 1300 145th St E, Rosemount, MN, 55068. Tel: 651-423-8366. p. 1195

Ellsworth, Adelaide, Br Spec, Bay City Public Library, Sargent Branch, 20305 FM 457, Sargent, TX, 77414. Tel: 979-476-1335. p. 2145

Ellsworth, Patty, Tech Librn, Garland Smith Public Library, 702 W. Main, Marlow, OK, 73055. Tel: 580-658-5354. p. 1852

Ellwanger, Richard, Exec Dir, Seminole Nation Museum Library, 524 S Wewoka Ave, Wewoka, OK, 74884. Tel: 405-257-5580. p. 1869

Ellzey, Michael D, Dir, National Archives & Records Administration, 18001 Yorba Linda Blvd, Yorba Linda, CA, 92886. Tel: 714-983-9120, 714-983-9320. p. 260

Elmborg, Jim, Dr, Prof, University of Alabama, 7035 Gorgas Library, Campus Box 870252, Tuscaloosa, AL, 35487-0252. Tel: 205-348-4610. p. 2781

Elmer, David, Curator, Harvard Library, Milman Parry Collection of Oral Literature, Widener, Rm C, Cambridge, MA, 02138. p. 1007

Elmore, Gillian, Mkt & Graphics Coordr, Glenwood-Lynwood Public Library District, 19901 Stony Island Ave, Lynwood, IL, 60411. Tel: 708-758-0090. p. 611

Elmore, Julie, Dir, Oakland City-Columbia Township Public Library, 210 S Main St, Oakland City, IN, 47660. Tel: 812-749-3559. p. 712

Elmore, Karen, Curator, Madera County Historical Society, 210 W Yosemite Ave, Madera, CA, 93637-3533. Tel: 559-673-0291. p. 171

Elmore, Karen, Spec Coll, University of Tennessee at Martin, Ten Wayne Fisher Dr, Martin, TN, 38238. Tel: 731-881-7094. p. 2111

Elmore, Marcus, Mkt, Ref/Outreach Librn, US Department of Commerce, 325 Broadway, R/ESRL5, Boulder, CO, 80305-3328. Tel: 303-497-3271. p. 267

Elmore, Rheena, Ms, Dir, Libr Serv, Coastal Alabama Community College, 1900 Hwy 31 S, Bay Minette, AL, 36507. Tel: 251-580-2159. p. 6

Elmore, Rheena, Ms, Dir, Libr Serv, Coastal Alabama Community College, Fairhope Learning Resources Center, 440 Fairhope Ave, Fairhope, AL, 36532. Tel: 251-580-2159, 251-990-0420. p. 6

Elmquist, Krista, Dir, Ch Serv, Spirit Lake Public Library, 702 16th St, Spirit Lake, IA, 51360. Tel: 712-336-2667. p. 784

Elnicky, Michele, Coll Spec, Librn, Utah State Historical Society, 7292 S State St, Midvale, UT, 84047. Tel: 801-245-7227. p. 2266

Eloyan, Arpine, Mgr, County of Los Angeles Public Library, Stevenson Ranch Library, 25950 The Old Road, Stevenson Ranch, CA, 91381. Tel: 661-255-2707. p. 138

Eloyan, Arpine, Ch Serv, Glendale Library, Arts & Culture, Pacific Park, 501 S Pacific Ave, Glendale, CA, 91204. Tel: 818-548-3760. p. 149

Elpern, Joanne, Doc Delivery, ILL, Western Connecticut State University, 181 White St, Danbury, CT, 06810. Tel: 203-837-9114. p. 307

Elrick, Tim, Dr, Dir, McGill University Libraries, Geographic Information Centre, Burnside Hall Bldg, 5th Flr, 805 Sherbrooke St W, Montreal, QC, H3A 2K6, CANADA. Tel: 514-398-7438. p. 2726

Elrobeh, Dede, Instruction Coordr, Ref & Coll Develop Librn, Glendale Community College - Main, 6000 W Olive Ave, Glendale, AZ, 85302. Tel: 623-845-3108. p. 61

Elrod, Melisa, Librn, R W Norton Art Gallery, 4747 Creswell Ave, Shreveport, LA, 71106. Tel: 318-865-4201. p. 908

Elrod, Rachael, Head, Educ Libr, University of Florida Libraries, 1545 W University Ave, Gainesville, FL, 32611-7000. Tel: 352-273-2627. p. 407

Elsbernd, Geri, Per, Northeast Iowa Community College, Calmar Campus Library, 1625 Hwy 150, Calmar, IA, 52132. Tel: 563-562-3263. p. 776

Elsbernd, Kay, Dir, Ossian Public Library, 123 W Main, Ossian, IA, 52161. Tel: 563-532-9461. p. 775

Elsea, Amanda, Librn, Esmeralda County Public Libraries, Goldfield Public Library, Corner of Crook & Fourth St, Goldfield, NV, 89013. Tel: 775-485-3236. p. 1351

Elsea, Margaret, Br Mgr, Sullivan County Public Library, 1655 Blountville Blvd, Blountville, TN, 37617. Tel: 423-279-2714. p. 2089

Elsener, Michael, Libr Spec, Southeast Community College, Lincoln LRC, 8800 O St, Lincoln, NE, 68520. Tel: 402-437-2589. p. 1307

Elsner, Betsy, Info & Tech Librn, Anderson University Library, 316 Boulevard, Anderson, SC, 29621. Tel: 864-231-2050. p. 2047

Elsner, Lisa, Library Spec, Circ & Technical Servs, Highland Community College Library, 2998 W Pearl City Rd, Freeport, IL, 61032-9341. Tel: 815-599-3539. p. 590

Elstro, Stephanie, Dir, Palisades Park Public Library, 257 Second St, Palisades Park, NJ, 07650. Tel: 201-585-4150. p. 1431

Elum, Hatatu, Librn, G Robert Cotton Regional Correctional Facility Library, 3500 N Elm Rd, Jackson, MI, 49201. Tel: 517-780-5000, 517-780-5172. p. 1119

Elusta, Grushenska, ILL, Broward College, Bldg 17, 3501 SW Davie Rd, Davie, FL, 33314. Tel: 954-201-6658. p. 391

Elvey, Luann, Librn, Iosco-Arenac District Library, East Tawas Branch, 760 Newman St, East Tawas, MI, 48730. Tel: 989-362-6162. p. 1102

Elvington, Joe, Br Mgr, Chesterfield County Library System, McBee Depot Library, 96 W Pine St, McBee, SC, 29101. Tel: 843-335-7515. p. 2052

Elvis-Weitzel, Tracey, Asst Dir, Horry County Memorial Library, 1008 Fifth Ave, Conway, SC, 29526. Tel: 843-915-5285. p. 2056

Elwell, Bonny Beth, Libr Dir, Camden County Historical Society, 1900 Park Blvd, Camden, NJ, 08103-3611. Tel: 856-964-3333. p. 1394

Elwell, Brent, Actg Librn, Maine Department of Corrections, Bolduc Correctional Facility Library, 516 Cushing Rd, Warren, ME, 04864. Tel: 207-273-2036. p. 944

Elwell, Joanne, Ch, Dir, Libr Serv, Newport Cultural Center, 154 Main St, Newport, ME, 04953-1139. Tel: 207-368-5074. p. 933

Elwell, Meghan, Circ Supvr, Grand Rapids Public Library, 111 Library St NE, Grand Rapids, MI, 49503-3268. Tel: 616-988-5400. p. 1111

Elwood, Marjorie, Assoc Dir, Pub Serv, High Plains Library District, 2650 W 29th St, Greeley, CO, 80631. p. 285

Elwood, Nathan, Libr Adminr, Missouri Legislative Library, State Capitol Bldg, 117A, 201 W Capital Ave, Jefferson City, MO, 65101. Tel: 573-751-4633. p. 1252

Ely, Chris, Librn, Whitewright Public Library, 200 W Grand St, Whitewright, TX, 75491. Tel: 903-364-2955. p. 2257

Ely, Steve, Ref Librn, West Texas A&M University, 110 26th St, Canyon, TX, 79016. Tel: 806-651-2230. p. 2153

Emahiser Ryder, Holly, Dir, North Baltimore Public Library, 230 N Main St, North Baltimore, OH, 45872. Tel: 419-257-3621. p. 1809

Emanuel, Kim, Ch, Hartington Public Library, 106 S Broadway, Hartington, NE, 68739. Tel: 402-254-6245. p. 1317

Emanuelson, Laura, Ref Librn, Milwaukee Area Technical College, 6665 S Howell Ave, Oak Creek, WI, 53154. p. 2465

Emard, Marie-Josee, Circ, College Jean-de-Brebeuf, 5625 rue Decelles, Montreal, QC, H3T 1W4, CANADA. Tel: 514-342-9342, Ext 5361. p. 2723

Embree, Anna, Prof, University of Alabama, 7035 Gorgas Library, Campus Box 870252, Tuscaloosa, AL, 35487-0252. Tel: 205-348-4610. p. 2781

Embrey, Theresa A R, Dir, Libr Serv, Pritzker Military Museum & Library, 104 S Michigan Ave, 2nd Flr, Chicago, IL, 60603. Tel: 312-374-9333. p. 567

Embry, Derick, Circ, Lawson State Community College Library, 3060 Wilson Rd SW, Birmingham, AL, 35221. Tel: 205-929-6333. p. 8

Embry, Stacey, Dir, Morgan County Library, 600 N Hunter, Versailles, MO, 65084-1830. Tel: 573-378-5319. p. 1284

Embser-Herbert, Elvira, Head, Pub Serv, Minnesota State Law Library, Minnesota Judicial Ctr, Rm G25, 25 Rev Dr Martin Luther King Jr Blvd, Saint Paul, MN, 55155. Tel: 651-297-7657. p. 1201

Emerick-Engle, Danielle, Librn, West Virginia School for the Deaf & Blind Library, 301 E Main St, Romney, WV, 26757. Tel: 304-822-4894, 304-822-6656. p. 2413

Emero, Shambry, Ms, Dir, DeMary Memorial Library, 417 Seventh St, Rupert, ID, 83350. Tel: 208-436-3874. p. 530

Emerson, Amy, Asst Dean, Libr & Info Serv, Asst Prof of Law, Villanova University, Law Library, Villanova University Charles Widger School of Law, 299 N Spring Mill Rd, Villanova, PA, 19085. Tel: 610-519-7023. p. 2017

Emerson, Debby, Dir, Wadsworth Library, 24 Center St, Geneseo, NY, 14454. Tel: 585-243-0440. p. 1538

Emerson, Maria, Res & Instruction Librn, Augustana College Library, 3435 9 1/2 Ave, Rock Island, IL, 61201-2296. Tel: 309-794-7823. p. 641

Emerson, Melanie, Tech Asst, Muscle Shoals Public Library, 1918 E Avalon, Muscle Shoals, AL, 35661. Tel: 256-386-9212. p. 31

Emerson, Melanie E, Dean of Libr, Spec Coll, School of the Art Institute of Chicago, 37 S Wabash Ave, Chicago, IL, 60603-3103. Tel: 312-629-9379. p. 568

Emerson, Melissa, Youth Serv Librn, Tulare Public Library, 475 North M St, Tulare, CA, 93274. Tel: 559-685-4507. p. 253

Emerson, Norah, Libr Dir, Fundy Library Region, Kennebecasis Public Library, One Landing Ct, Quispamsis, NB, E2E 4R2, CANADA. Tel: 506-849-5314. p. 2605

Emerson, Sally, Acq, Southern California Genealogical Society, 417 Irving Dr, Burbank, CA, 91504-2408. Tel: 818-843-7247. p. 125

Emerson, Steve, Dr, Libr Dir, California Baptist University, 8432 Magnolia Ave, Riverside, CA, 92504. Tel: 951-343-4228. p. 201

Emerson-Inhelder, Amy, Dir, Cheshire Public Library, 23 Depot St, Cheshire, MA, 01225. Tel: 413-743-4746. p. 1010

Emery, Amber, Ch Serv, Fargo Public Library, 102 N Third St, Fargo, ND, 58102. Tel: 701-241-1472. p. 1733

Emery, Jill, Coll Develop & Mgt Librn, Portland State University Library, 1875 SW Park Ave, Portland, OR, 97201-3220. Tel: 503-725-5874. p. 1893

Emery, Joseph, Head, Circ, Leonia Public Library, 227 Fort Lee Rd, Leonia, NJ, 07605. Tel: 201-592-5770. p. 1412

Emery, Joseph, Tech Serv, Livingston Public Library, Ten Robert Harp Dr, Livingston, NJ, 07039. Tel: 973-992-4600. p. 1413

Emery, Laura, Chief Librn, Eastern Counties Regional Library, 390 Murray St, Mulgrave, NS, B0E 2G0, CANADA. Tel: 902-747-2597. p. 2621

Emery, Leianne, Libr Dir, Sechelt Public Library, 5797 Cowrie St, Sechelt, BC, V0N 3A0, CANADA. Tel: 604-885-3260. p. 2575

Emery, Pauline, Dir, Southeast Steuben County Library, 300 Nasser Civic Center Plaza, Ste 101, Corning, NY, 14830. Tel: 607-936-3713. p. 1522

Emery, Rayeanna, Circ Desk Mgr, Perry County Public Library, 289 Black Gold Blvd, Hazard, KY, 41701. Tel: 606-436-2475, 606-436-4747. p. 858

Emery, Sharla, Commun Libr Mgr, Queens Library, Howard Beach Community Library, 92-06 156th Ave, Howard Beach, NY, 11414. Tel: 718-641-7086. p. 1554

Emesih, Stephanie, Librn, Houston Community College-Central College, Central Campus Library, 1300 Holman, Houston, TX, 77004. Tel: 713-718-6133. p. 2194

Emig, Julie, Exec Dir, McLean County Museum of History, 200 N Main, Bloomington, IL, 61701. Tel: 309-827-0428. p. 543

Emily, Bolin, Ad, Hancock County Public Library, 1210 Madison St, Hawesville, KY, 42348. Tel: 270-927-6760. p. 858

Eminhizer, Kate, Br Mgr, Pamunkey Regional Library, Mechanicsville Branch, 7461 Sherwood Crossing Pl, Mechanicsville, VA, 23111. Tel: 804-746-9615. p. 2324

Emmons, Ashlei, Libr Support Serv Asst, Blue Mountain Community College Library, 2411 NW Carden Ave, Pendleton, OR, 97801. Tel: 541-278-5915. p. 1890

Emmons, Mark, Dr, Assoc Dean, Pub Serv, University of New Mexico-University Libraries, 1900 Roma NE, Albuquerque, NM, 87131-0001. Tel: 505-277-4241. p. 1462

Emmons-Andarawis, Deborah, Curator, Exec Dir, Van Rensselear - Rankin Family Historic Cherry Hill Museum & Library, 523 1/2 S Pearl St, Albany, NY, 12202. Tel: 518-434-4791. p. 1484

Emmrich, Mary K, Libr Dir, Newton County Public Library, 9444 N 315 W, Lake Village, IN, 46349. Tel: 219-992-3490. p. 702

Emon, Danielle, Cat, Libr Tech, Tech Serv, The Parrott Centre, 376 Wallbridge-Loyalist Rd, Belleville, ON, K8N 5B9, CANADA. Tel: 613-969-1913, Ext 2183. p. 2631

Emond, James, Res & Instruction Librn, Bristol Community College, 777 Elsbree St, Fall River, MA, 02720. Tel: 774-357-2316. p. 1017

Emond-Beaulieu, Marie-Eve, Librn, Universite du Quebec a Rimouski - Service de la bibliotheque, 300 Allee des Ursulines, Rimouski, QC, G5L 3A1, CANADA. Tel: 418-833-8800, Ext 3287. p. 2732

Emons, Margaret, Libr Dir, College of Saint Mary Library, 7000 Mercy Rd, Omaha, NE, 68106-2606. Tel: 402-399-2467. p. 1327

Empey, Heather, Acq Librn, University of Northern British Columbia Library, 333 University Way, Prince George, BC, V2N 4Z9, CANADA. Tel: 250-960-6468. p. 2574

Empoliti, Rebecca, Archival Librn, Archdiocese of Hartford Pastoral Center, 467 Bloomfield Ave, Bloomfield, CT, 06002. Tel: 860-242-5573, Ext 2609. p. 303

Emrich, Priscilla E, Libr Dir, Livingston Municipal Library, 707 N Tyler Ave, Livingston, TX, 77351. Tel: 936-327-4252. p. 2212

Emrick, Sue, Ch Serv, Upper Arlington Public Library, Lane Road Branch, 1945 Lane Rd, Upper Arlington, OH, 43220. Tel: 614-459-0273. p. 1778

Emsellem, Dawn, Dir, Libr Serv, Salve Regina University, 100 Ochre Point Ave, Newport, RI, 02840-4192. Tel: 401-341-2330. p. 2035

Encarnacion, Giselle, Head, Tech Serv, Lawrence Public Library, 51 Lawrence St, Lawrence, MA, 01841. Tel: 978-620-3600. p. 1027

Encarnation, Alfred, Dir, Stratford Free Public Library, 303 Union Ave, Stratford, NJ, 08084. Tel: 856-783-0602. p. 1444

Encina, Roswell, Chief Coms Officer, Library of Congress, James Madison Memorial Bldg, 101 Independence Ave SE, Washington, DC, 20540. Tel: 202-707-5000. p. 370

Encinas, Angela, Ch Serv, ILL, City of San Bernardino Library Services, 555 W Sixth St, San Bernardino, CA, 92410-3001. Tel: 909-381-8215. p. 212

Enciso, Monica, Dir, Goddard Riverside Community Center, 26 W 84th St, New York, NY, 10024. Tel: 212-799-2369, Ext 4702. p. 1587

Encomio, Darlene, Literacy, Educ & Outreach Mgr, Martin County Library System, 2351 SE Monterey Rd, Stuart, FL, 34996. Tel: 772-219-4908. p. 444

Enderle, Emily, Libr Dir, United States Air Force, 375 FSS/FSDL, 510 Ward Dr, Scott AFB, IL, 62225-5360. Tel: 618-256-5100. p. 645

Enders, Naulayne, Dir, Kentucky Christian University, 100 Academic Pkwy, Grayson, KY, 41143. Tel: 606-474-3276. p. 857

Endres Way, Jennifer, Libr Dir, Oregon Public Library, 256 Brook St, Oregon, WI, 53575. Tel: 608-835-3656. p. 2467

Endter, Anna, Assoc Dean, Libr & Info Serv, University of Washington Libraries, Gallagher Law Library, William H Gates Hall, 4000 15th Ave NE, Seattle, WA, 98195-3020. Tel: 206-685-4084. p. 2382

Enearl, Brianna, Circ Assoc, Iowa Wesleyan University, 107 W Broad St, Mount Pleasant, IA, 52641. Tel: 319-385-6316. p. 771

Enfinger, Stephanie, Library Contact, Moultrie-Colquitt County Library, Doerun Municipal Library, 185 N Freeman St, Doerun, GA, 31744. Tel: 229-782-5507. p. 492

Eng, Catherine, Supvr, Paramus Public Library, Charles E Reid Branch, 239 W Midland Ave, Paramus, NJ, 07652. Tel: 201-444-4911. p. 1432

Eng, Mamie, Libr Dir, Henry Waldinger Memorial Library, 60 Verona Pl, Valley Stream, NY, 11582. Tel: 516-825-6422. p. 1657

Eng, Pauline, Res Serv Librn, Tyler Public Library, 201 S College Ave, Tyler, TX, 75702-7381. Tel: 903-593-7323. p. 2250

Engel, Carl, Ref Serv, Ad, Morley Library, 184 Phelps St, Painesville, OH, 44077-3926. Tel: 440-352-3383. p. 1812

Engel, Donna, Libr Mgr, Provost Municipal Library, 5035 49th St, Provost, AB, T0B 3S0, CANADA. Tel: 780-753-2801. p. 2550

Engel, Jeanne, Dir, Johnson Public Library, Seven Library Dr, Johnson, VT, 05656. Tel: 802-635-7141. p. 2287

Engel, Kathy, Dir, Henderson Public Library, 110 S Sixth St, Henderson, MN, 56044-7734. Tel: 507-248-3880. p. 1178

Engel, Kevin, Sci Librn, Grinnell College Libraries, 1111 Sixth Ave, Grinnell, IA, 50112-1770. Tel: 641-269-4234. p. 756

Engel, Regina, Asst Librn, Steinbach Bible College Library, 50 PTH 12 N, Steinbach, MB, R5G 1T4, CANADA. Tel: 204-326-6451, Ext 238. p. 2590

Engel, Tara, Dir & Head Librn, Gregory Public Library, 112 E Fifth, Gregory, SD, 57533-1463. Tel: 605-835-8531. p. 2076

Engelberg, Paul, Acquisitions & Resource Sharing Librn, Wentworth Institute of Technology, 550 Huntington Ave, Boston, MA, 02115-5998. Tel: 617-989-4887. p. 1000

Engelbrecht, Mark, Branch Lead, Charlotte Mecklenburg Library, Mountain Island Branch, 4420 Hoyt Galvin Way, Charlotte, NC, 28214. Tel: 704-416-5600. p. 1679

Engelbrecht, Michael, Tech Coordr, Charlotte Mecklenburg Library, 310 N Tryon St, Charlotte, NC, 28202-2176. Tel: 704-416-0100. p. 1679

Engelhardt, Debra, Libr Dir, Comsewogue Public Library, 170 Terryville Rd, Port Jefferson Station, NY, 11776. Tel: 631-928-1212. p. 1621

Engelking, Pamela, Librn, Elmore Public Library, 107 E Willis St, Elmore, MN, 56027. Tel: 507-943-3150. p. 1174

Engelman, Michael, Br Mgr, Mid-Continent Public Library, Antioch Branch, 6060 N Chestnut Ave, Gladstone, MO, 64119. Tel: 816-454-1306. p. 1250

Engels, Mary, Asst Librn, Milton Free Public Library, 13 Main St, Milton Mills, NH, 03852. Tel: 603-473-8535. p. 1374

Engelson, Leslie, Metadata Librn, Murray State University, 205 Waterfield Library, Dean's Office, Murray, KY, 42071-3307. Tel: 270-809-4818. p. 870

Engeman, Jeff, Circ Supvr, Edith B Siegrist Vermillion Public Library, 18 Church St, Vermillion, SD, 57069-3093. Tel: 605-677-7060. p. 2084

Engen, Maren, Asst Dir, Chouteau County Library, 1518 Main St, Fort Benton, MT, 59442. Tel: 406-622-5222. p. 1293

Enger, Kathy Brock, Exec Dir, Northern Lights Library Network, 1104 Seventh Ave S, Box 136, Moorhead, MN, 56563. Tel: 218-477-2934, p. 2768

Engerer, Stephanie, Ref/Emerging Technologies Librn, Widener University, Harrisburg Campus Law Library, 3800 Vartan Way, Harrisburg, DE, 17110. Tel: 717-541-3953. p. 358

Engert, Nick, Head, Pub Serv, Memorial & Library Association, 44 Broad St, Westerly, RI, 02891. Tel: 401-596-2877, Ext 338. p. 2044

Engeszer, Robert, Assoc Dir, Translational Res Support, Washington University Libraries, Bernard Becker Medical Library, 660 S Euclid Ave, Campus Box 8132, Saint Louis, MO, 63110. Tel: 314-362-4735. p. 1277

Enghausen, Angela, Asst Librn, Cheney's Grove Township Library, 204 S State St, Saybrook, IL, 61770. Tel: 309-475-6131. p. 645

Enghausen, Ashleigh, Libr Dir, Cheney's Grove Township Library, 204 S State St, Saybrook, IL, 61770. Tel: 309-475-6131. p. 645

England, Alyssa, Fiscal Officer, Fairfield County District Library, 219 N Broad St, Lancaster, OH, 43130-3098. Tel: 740-653-2745. p. 1794

England, Brynne, Libr Tech, McMillan Library, 1000 Sherbrooke St W, 27th Flr, Montreal, QC, H3A 3G4, CANADA. Tel: 514-987-5000. p. 2726

England, Kimberly, Librn, Angelina College Library, 3500 S First St, Lufkin, TX, 75904. Tel: 936-633-5220. p. 2214

England, Louise, Govt Doc Librn, Alberta Legislature Library, 216 Legislature Bldg, 10800-97 Ave NW, Edmonton, AB, T5K 2B6, CANADA. Tel: 780-415-4502. p. 2535

England, Margaret, Dir, Clinton County Public Library, 302 King Dr, Albany, KY, 42602. Tel: 606-387-5989. p. 847

England, Megan, Br Mgr, Jefferson-Madison Regional Library, Scottsville Branch, 330 Bird St, Scottsville, VA, 24590. Tel: 434-286-3541. p. 2309

England, Monette, Head, Circ, Flagler County Public Library, 2500 Palm Coast Pkwy NW, Palm Coast, FL, 32137. Tel: 386-446-6763. p. 434

England-Biggs, Laura, Libr Dir, Keene Memorial Library, 1030 N Broad St, Fremont, NE, 68025-4199. Tel: 402-459-2073. p. 1314

Engle, Cynthia, Exec Dir, Hawaiian Historical Society Library, 560 Kawaiahao St, Honolulu, HI, 96813. Tel: 808-537-6271. p. 511

Engle, Karen, Librn, Daly City Public Library, Bayshore, 460 Martin St, Daly City, CA, 94014. Tel: 650-991-8074. p. 134

Engle, Paul, Dir, Brockton Public Library, 304 Main St, Brockton, MA, 02301. Tel: 508-894-1400. p. 1002

Engleman, Toni, Interim Exec Dir, Jefferson County Historical Society Library, 228 Washington St, Watertown, NY, 13601. Tel: 315-782-3491. p. 1659

Engler, Lenore, Dir, Libr Serv, Ivy Tech Community College, 3501 N First Ave, Rm 141, Evansville, IN, 47710-3398. Tel: 812-429-1412. p. 682

Engler, Shanna, Br Mgr, Pines & Plains Libraries, Simla Branch, 504 Washington, Simla, CO, 80835. Tel: 719-541-2573. p. 279

English, Debi, Librn, Patten-North Haverhill Library, 2885 Dartmouth College Hwy, North Haverhill, NH, 03774-4533. Tel: 603-787-2542. p. 1377

English, Ellen, Librn, Sutter County Library, Barber, 10321 Live Oak Blvd, Live Oak, CA, 95953. Tel: 530-822-3223. p. 261

English, Ellen, Librn, Sutter County Library, Sutter Branch, 2147 California St, Sutter, CA, 95982. Tel: 530-755-0485. p. 262

English, Margaret, Librn, University of Toronto Libraries, Department of Art, Sidney Smith Hall, Rm 6032B, 100 St George St, Toronto, ON, M5S 3G3, CANADA. Tel: 416-978-5006. p. 2698

English, Margo, Dir, Owensville Carnegie Public Library, 110 S Main St, Owensville, IN, 47665. Tel: 812-724-3335. p. 712

Englot, Angela, Br Librn, Southeast Regional Library, Glenavon Branch, 311 Railway Ave, Glenavon, SK, S0G 1Y0, CANADA. Tel: 306-429-2180. p. 2753

Engsberg, Mark, Dir, Libr Serv, Emory University School of Law, 1301 Clifton Rd, Atlanta, GA, 30322. Tel: 404-727-6823. p. 463

Engstrom, Barbara, Exec Dir, Public Law Library of King County, King County Courthouse, 516 Third Ave, Ste W621, Seattle, WA, 98104. Tel: 206-477-1305. p. 2378

Engstrom, Barbara Swatt, Ref (Info Servs), Seattle University, School of Law Library, Sullivan Hall, 901 12th Ave, Seattle, WA, 98122-4411. Tel: 206-398-4221. p. 2380

Ennis, Allison, Libr Dir, Morgan County Public Library, 151 University Dr, West Liberty, KY, 41472. Tel: 606-743-4151. p. 876

Ennis, Joan, Ref Librn, Northfield Public Library, 210 Washington St, Northfield, MN, 55057. Tel: 507-645-1802. p. 1191

Ennis, Lisa, Syst Librn, University of Alabama at Birmingham, Lister Hill Library of the Health Sciences, 1700 University Blvd, Birmingham, AL, 35294-0013. Tel: 205-934-5460. p. 9

Ennis, Lisa, Libr Dir, Alabama College of Osteopathic Medicine, 445 Health Sciences Blvd, Hwy 84 E, Dothan, AL, 36303. Tel: 334-699-2266. p. 14

Ennis, Lisa, Dr, Dean of Libr, University of South Carolina Aiken, 471 University Pkwy, Aiken, SC, 29801. Tel: 803-641-3460. p. 2046

Ennis, Susan, Librn, Universal City Public Library, 100 Northview Dr, Universal City, TX, 78148-4150. Tel: 210-659-7048. p. 2250

Enniss, Stephen, Dir, University of Texas Libraries, Harry Ransom Center, 300 W 21st St, Austin, TX, 78712. Tel: 512-471-8944. p. 2143

Ennist, Kathryn, Dir, John F Kennedy Memorial Library, 92 Hathaway St, Wallington, NJ, 07057. Tel: 973-471-1692. p. 1451

Enns, Carolyn, Librn, Buset LLP, 1121 Barton St, Thunder Bay, ON, P7B 5N3, CANADA. Tel: 807-623-2500. p. 2684

Enns-Rempel, Kevin, Libr Dir, Fresno Pacific University, 1717 S Chestnut Ave, Fresno, CA, 93702. Tel: 559-453-2225. p. 146

Enoch, Larry, Dr, Sr Lecturer, University of North Texas, 3940 N Elm St, Ste E292, Denton, TX, 76207. Tel: 940-565-2445. p. 2793

Enos, Cara, Asst Dir, Burlington Public Library, 22 Sears St, Burlington, MA, 01803. Tel: 781-270-1690. p. 1004

Enos, Kelly William, Actg Dean, Los Angeles Mission College Library, 13356 Eldridge Ave, Sylmar, CA, 91342. Tel: 818-639-2221. p. 251

Enright, Angie, Ad, Thornton Public Library, 115 E Margaret St, Thornton, IL, 60476. Tel: 708-877-2579. p. 653

Enright, Marcia, Librn, Candor Free Library, Two Bank St, Candor, NY, 13743-1510. Tel: 607-659-7258. p. 1513

Enright, Zachary, Archivist, New England Osteopathic Heritage Ctr, University of New England Libraries, 11 Hills Beach Rd, Biddeford, ME, 04005. Tel: 207-602-2131. p. 917

Enriquez, Cesilia, Asst Dir, Kearny County Library, 101 E Prairie, Lakin, KS, 67860. Tel: 620-355-6674. p. 818

Enriquez, Sandy, Commun Engagement Librn, Special Colls Public Services, University of California, Riverside, Special Collections & University Archives, 900 University Ave, Riverside, CA, 92521. Tel: 951-827-3233. p. 203

Ens, Cheryl, Br Librn, Wapiti Regional Library, Gronlid Public Library, One Railway Ave, Gronlid, SK, S0E 0W0, CANADA. Tel: 306-277-4633. p. 2745

Enser, Amanda, Dir, Integrated Libr Tech Serv, Media Serv, John G Shedd Aquarium Library, 1200 S Lake Shore Dr, Chicago, IL, 60605. Tel: 312-692-3217. p. 568

Ensign, David, Dir, University of Louisville Libraries, Brandeis School of Law Library, 2301 S Third St, Louisville, KY, 40208. Tel: 502-852-6392. p. 867

Ensign, Nancy Nixon, Gallery Curator, Programmer, Patterson Library, 40 S Portage St, Westfield, NY, 14787. Tel: 716-326-2154. p. 1664

Ensing, Nicole, Archivist, Whyte Museum of the Canadian Rockies, 111 Bear St, Banff, AB, T1L 1A3, CANADA. Tel: 403-762-2291, Ext 335. p. 2522

Ensinger, Michele, Co-Dir, Pine Grove Public Library, One Main St, Pine Grove, WV, 26419. Tel: 304-889-3288. p. 2412

Ensley, J Eric, Curator, Rare Bks & Maps, University of Iowa Libraries, Special Collections & Archives, 100 Main Library, 125 W Washington St, Iowa City, IA, 52242-1420. Tel: 319-467-3253. p. 761

Enslow, Electra, Head, Res Serv, Eastern Washington University, 600 N Riverpoint Blvd, Rm 230, Spokane, WA, 99202. Tel: 509-358-7930. p. 2383

Ensor, Brandt, Asst Dir, Adams County Library System, 140 Baltimore St, Gettysburg, PA, 17325-2311. Tel: 717-334-5716. p. 1935

Ensrud, Barbara, Librn, Rhine Research Center, 2741 Campus Walk Ave, Bldg 500, Durham, NC, 27705-3707. Tel: 919-309-4600. p. 1686

Entwisle, Chris, Circ, Camden County Library System, 203 Laurel Rd, Voorhees, NJ, 08043. Tel: 856-772-1636, Ext 7309. p. 1450

Enujioke, Emmanuel, Dr, Librn, West Georgia Technical College, Coweta Campus, 200 Campus Dr, Newnan, GA, 30263. Tel: 770-755-7844. p. 502

Enyart, Lagina, Librn, Van Wert County Law Library Association, Court House, 3rd Flr, 121 Main St, Van Wert, OH, 45891. Tel: 419-238-6935. p. 1827

Enyart, Michael, Dir, University of Wisconsin-Madison, Business Library, Grainger Hall, Rm 1320, 975 University Ave, Madison, WI, 53706. Tel: 608-263-3902. p. 2451

Enz, Adam, Head, Tech Serv, Librn, Illinois College, 1101 W College Ave, Jacksonville, IL, 62650-2299. Tel: 217-245-3020. p. 602

Eouimet, Erin, Asst Dir, Newbury Town Library, Zero Lunt St, Byfield, MA, 01922-1232. Tel: 978-465-0539. p. 1004

Epling, Jimmie, Dir, Darlington County Library System, 204 N Main St, Darlington, SC, 29532. Tel: 843-398-4940. p. 2057

Eppard, Philip B, Dr, Prof, University at Albany, State University of New York, Draper 015, 135 Western Ave, Albany, NY, 12203. Tel: 518-442-5119. p. 2789

Eppenger, Cloreace, Br Mgr, Nashville Public Library, North Branch, 1001 Monroe St, Nashville, TN, 37208-2543. Tel: 615-862-5858. p. 2120

Epperson, Ellie, Youth Serv Supvr, Caldwell Public Library, 1010 Dearborn St, Caldwell, ID, 83605. Tel: 208-459-3242. p. 518

Epperson, Patrina, Circ Librn, Texas Southern University, Thurgood Marshall School of Law Library, 3100 Cleburne Ave, Houston, TX, 77004. Tel: 713-313-1011. p. 2199

Eppinger, Monica, Dir, Woodbridge Public Library, One George Frederick Plaza, Woodbridge, NJ, 07095. Tel: 732-634-4450. p. 1456

Epps, Ron, Ref & Print Res Librn, Campbell University, 113 Main St, Buies Creek, NC, 27506. Tel: 910-893-1472. p. 1676

Epstein, Barbara A, Dir, University of Pittsburgh Library System, 200 Scaife Hall, 3550 Terrace St, Pittsburgh, PA, 15261. p. 1996

Epstein, Emily, Cat Librn, University of Colorado Denver/ Anschutz Medical Campus, Anschutz Medical Campus, 12950 E Montview Blvd, Aurora, CO, 80045. Tel: 303-724-2152. p. 265

Epstein, Jessica, Campus Librn, American InterContinental University, Atlanta Campus Library, 500 Embassy Row, 6600 Peachtree-Dunwoody Rd, Atlanta, GA, 30328. Tel: 404-965-6527. p. 460

Epstein, Michael, Electronic Res, University of San Diego, Helen K & James S Copley Library, 5998 Alcala Park, San Diego, CA, 92110. p. 222

Epstein, Su, Dir, Saxton B Little Free Library, Inc, 319 Rte 87, Columbia, CT, 06237-1143. Tel: 860-228-0350. p. 306
Epstein, Susan, Syst Librn, Florida State University Libraries, Charlotte Edwards Maguire Medical Library, 1115 W Call St, Tallahassee, FL, 32306-4300. Tel: 850-644-3883. p. 447
Erbe, Evalina, Dir, South River Public Library, 55 Appleby Ave, South River, NJ, 08882-2499. Tel: 732-254-2488. p. 1444
Erbes, Scott, Dir of Coll, Speed Art Museum Library, 2035 S Third St, Louisville, KY, 40208. Tel: 502-634-2740. p. 867
Erceg, Lynn, Tech Asst III, Columbia-Greene Community College Library, 4400 Rte 23, Hudson, NY, 12534. Tel: 518-828-4181, Ext 3289. p. 1549
Erdel, Tim, Archivist, Bethel College, 1001 Bethel Circle, Mishawaka, IN, 46545. Tel: 574-807-7153. p. 706
Erdelez, Sanda, Dean, Prof, Simmons University, 300 The Fenway, Boston, MA, 02115. Tel: 617-521-2800. p. 2786
Erdman, Janet, Med Librn, M Health Fairview Ridges Hospital, 201 E Nicollet Blvd, Burnsville, MN, 55337. Tel: 952-892-2414. p. 1167
Erdman, Janet, Med Librn, M Health Fairview Southdale Hospital, 6401 France Ave S, Edina, MN, 55435. Tel: 952-924-5005. p. 1174
Erdman, Sue, Dir, Joseph T Simpson Public Library, 16 N Walnut St, Mechanicsburg, PA, 17055-3362. Tel: 717-766-0171. p. 1960
Erdmann, John, Librn, College of Marin Library, 835 College Ave, Kentfield, CA, 94904. Tel: 415-485-9656. p. 154
Erekson, Sarah, Govt Doc Librn, University of Florida Libraries, 1545 W University Ave, Gainesville, FL, 32611-7000. Tel: 352-273-2635. p. 407
Eren, Patricia D, Dir, Floral Park Public Library, 17 Caroline Pl, Floral Park, NY, 11001. Tel: 516-326-6330. p. 1533
Erenyi, Zvi, Coll Develop, Ref Librn, Yeshiva University Libraries, Mendel Gottesman Library of Hebraica-Judaica, 2520 Amsterdam Ave, New York, NY, 10033. Tel: 646-592-4190. p. 1604
Eresuma, Emily, Sr Med Librn, Primary Children's Hospital Medical Library, 81 N Mario Capecchi Dr, Salt Lake City, UT, 84113. Tel: 801-662-1391. p. 2271
Erhardt, Melissa, Dir, Chateaugay Memorial Library, Four John St, Chateaugay, NY, 12920. Tel: 518-497-0400. p. 1517
Erhart, Melanie, Br Mgr, Prince William Public Libraries, Independent Hill Library, 14418 Bristow Rd, Manassas, VA, 20112. Tel: 703-792-5668. p. 2338
Ericksen, Nikki, Libr Dir, Plains Public Library District, 108 W Railroad St, Plains, MT, 59859. Tel: 406-826-3101. p. 1301
Erickson, Abigail, Libr Assoc, North Dakota State University Libraries, Business Learning Center, Richard H Barry Hall, Rm 22, 811 Second Ave N, Fargo, ND, 58102. Tel: 701-231-8191. p. 1733
Erickson, Christine, Head, Children's Dept, Bangor Public Library, 145 Harlow St, Bangor, ME, 04401-1802. Tel: 207-947-8336. p. 915
Erickson, Cindy, Dir, Soda Springs Public Library, 149 S Main, Soda Springs, ID, 83276. Tel: 208-547-2606. p. 531
Erickson, Diana, Dir, Stratford Public Library, 816 Shakespeare, Stratford, IA, 50249. Tel: 515-838-2131. p. 785
Erickson, Doug, Dir, West Linn Public Library, 1595 Burns St, West Linn, OR, 97068. Tel: 503-742-6165. p. 1902
Erickson, Emily H, Dir & Librn, Mary Greeley Medical Center Library, 1111 Duff Ave, Ames, IA, 50010. Tel: 515-239-2154. p. 731
Erickson, Eric, Librn, United States Department of Housing & Urban Development, 451 Seventh St SW, Rm 8141, Washington, DC, 20410. Tel: 202-402-4269. p. 378
Erickson, Garrett, Mr, Dir, Libr Serv, Mead Public Library, 710 N Eight St, Sheboygan, WI, 53081-4563. Tel: 920-459-3400, Ext 2041. p. 2476
Erickson, Gary D, Dir, Libr Serv, Theological Librn, Urshan College Library, 1151 Century Tel Dr, Wentzville, MO, 63385. Tel: 314-838-8858. p. 1286
Erickson, Gwen Gosney, Quaker Archivist, Spec Coll Librn, Guilford College, 5800 W Friendly Ave, Greensboro, NC, 27410. Tel: 336-316-2264. p. 1692
Erickson, Gwendolyn Gosney, Quaker Archivist, Spec Coll Librn, Guilford College, Quaker Archives, Hege Library, 5800 W Friendly Ave, Greensboro, NC, 27410. Tel: 336-316-2264. p. 1692
Erickson, Jade, Access Serv Librn, Saint Catherine University, 2004 Randolph Ave, Saint Paul, MN, 55105. Tel: 651-690-6655. p. 1201
Erickson, Julie, Dir, Liberty County Library, 100 E First St, Chester, MT, 59522. Tel: 406-759-5445. p. 1290
Erickson, Linda, Br Librn, Wapiti Regional Library, Hudson Bay Public Library, 130 Main St, Hudson Bay, SK, S0E 0Y0, CANADA. Tel: 306-865-3110. p. 2745
Erickson, Lisa, Outreach Serv Librn, Nioga Library System, 6575 Wheeler Rd, Lockport, NY, 14094. Tel: 716-434-6167, Ext 33. p. 1564
Erickson, Lisa, Exec Dir, Huntingdon County Library, 330 Penn St, Huntingdon, PA, 16652-1487. Tel: 814-643-0200. p. 1945
Erickson, Mary Jo, Ch, Johnson Public Library, 131 E Catherine St, Darlington, WI, 53530. Tel: 608-776-4171. p. 2430
Erickson, Mirlande, Librn, North Hennepin Community College Library, 7411 85th Ave N, Brooklyn Park, MN, 55445-2298. Tel: 763-424-0737. p. 1167
Erickson, Monica, Dir, Chatfield Public Library, 314 Main St S, Chatfield, MN, 55923. Tel: 507-867-3480. p. 1169
Erickson, Nicole, Dir, Puyallup Public Library, 324 S Meridian, Puyallup, WA, 98371. Tel: 253-841-5454. p. 2375
Erickson, Norene, Dr, Assoc Prof, MacEwan University, 10700-104 Ave NW 5-306W, Edmonton, AB, T5J 4S2, CANADA. Tel: 780-633-3541. p. 2795
Erickson, Paul, Archivist, Wheaton College, 510 Irving Ave, Wheaton, IL, 60187-4234. Tel: 630-752-5102. p. 662
Erickson, Paul J, Dir, University of Michigan, William L Clements Library, 909 S University Ave, Ann Arbor, MI, 48109-1190. Tel: 734-764-2347. p. 1079
Erickson, Sandra, Librn, Stanford Health Library, Cancer Center South Bay, 2589 Samaritan Dr, Rm 3302, San Jose, CA, 95124. Tel: 408-353-0197. p. 192
Erickson, Seth, Syst Librn, Tech Serv & Automation, Traverse Des Sioux Library Cooperative, 1400 Madison Ave, Ste 622, Mankato, MN, 56001-5488. Tel: 833-837-5422. p. 1181
Erickson, Susan, Libr Dir, Virginia Wesleyan University, 5817 Wesleyan Dr, Virginia Beach, VA, 23455. Tel: 757-455-3224. p. 2351
Erickson, Tom, Dir, University of Wisconsin-Madison, Helen C White Hall, Rm 4217, 600 N Park St, Madison, WI, 53706. Tel: 608-263-2900. p. 2794
Erickson, Trina, Libr Dir, McIntosh Memorial Library, 205 S Rock Ave, Viroqua, WI, 54665. Tel: 608-637-7151. p. 2483
Ericson, Christie, E-Res Mgt, University of Alaska Anchorage, Consortium Library, 3211 Providence Dr, Anchorage, AK, 99508-8176. Tel: 907-786-1990. p. 43
Ericson, John, Br Coordr, Schaumburg Township District Library, Hoffman Estates Branch, 1550 Hassell Rd, Hoffman Estates, IL, 60169. Tel: 847-923-3456. p. 645
Ericson, Karl, Librn, Washtenaw Community College, 4800 E Huron River Dr, Ann Arbor, MI, 48105-4800. Tel: 734-973-3430. p. 1081
Ericson, Lynn, Libr Dir, Salmon Falls Library, 322 Old Alfred Rd, Hollis, ME, 04042. Tel: 207-929-3990. p. 927
Ericson, Margaret D, Art Librn, Librn, Colby College Libraries, Bixler Art & Music Library, 5660 Mayflower Hill, Waterville, ME, 04901. Tel: 207-859-5662. p. 945
Ericson, Nathan R, Dir, Wisconsin Lutheran Seminary Library, 11831 N Seminary Dr, Mequon, WI, 53092-1546. Tel: 262-242-8113. p. 2456
Ericsson, Paul, Br Mgr, Carver County Library, Norwood Young America Branch, 314 Elm St W, Norwood Young America, MN, 55397. Tel: 952-467-2665. p. 1169
Ericsson, Paul, Br Mgr, Carver County Library, Waconia Branch, 217 S Vine St, Waconia, MN, 55387. Tel: 952-442-4714. p. 1169
Ericsson, Paul, Br Mgr, Carver County Library, Watertown Branch, 309 Lewis Ave SW, Watertown, MN, 55388. Tel: 952-955-2939. p. 1169
Eriksen, Joyce, Dir, Rowan Public Library, 101 Main St, Rowan, IA, 50470. Tel: 641-853-2327. p. 780
Erikson, Marsha, Head Librn, Jewell Public Library, 216 Delaware St, Jewell, KS, 66949. Tel: 785-428-3630. p. 816
Erjavek, Edward, Dir, City of San Bernardino Library Services, 555 W Sixth St, San Bernardino, CA, 92410-3001. Tel: 909-381-8215. p. 212
Erlandson, Devin, Asst Dir, Youth Serv Librn, Allegan District Library, 331 Hubbard St, Allegan, MI, 49010. Tel: 269-673-4625. p. 1077
Erminger, Carolyn, Circ Mgr, Saint Tammany Parish Library, Slidell Branch, 555 Robert Blvd, Slidell, LA, 70458. Tel: 985-646-6470. p. 888
Ermis, Donna, Libr Dir, Falls City Public Library, 206 N Irvin, Falls City, TX, 78113. Tel: 830-254-3361. p. 2176
Ermis, Donna, Dir, Karnes County Library System, Falls City Public Library, 206 N Irvin, Falls City, TX, 78113. Tel: 830-254-3361. p. 2176
Ernat, Christine, Lead Libr Asst, Black Hawk College, 26230 Black Hawk Rd, Galva, IL, 61434. Tel: 309-854-1730. p. 591
Ernat, Marlene, Dir, Utica Public Library District, 224 Mill St, Utica, IL, 61373. Tel: 815-667-4509. p. 657
Ernest, Rebecca, Librn, Virginia Department of Transportation (VDOT) Research Library, 530 Edgemont Rd, Charlottesville, VA, 22903. Tel: 434-293-1959. p. 2310
Erni, Corinne, Chief Curator, Parrish Art Museum Library, 279 Montauk Hwy, Water Mill, NY, 11976. Tel: 631-283-2118, Ext 140. p. 1659
Ernick, Linda, Head, Info Serv, J V Fletcher Library, 50 Main St, Westford, MA, 01886-2599. Tel: 978-399-2309. p. 1067
Ernst, Ashlyn, Dir, Psychoanalytic Center of Philadelphia Library, Rockland-East Fairmount Park, 3810 Mount Pleasant Dr, Philadelphia, PA, 19121-1002. Tel: 215-235-2345. p. 1985
Ernst, Laurie, Libr Dir, Dolores County Public Library, 525 N Main St, Dove Creek, CO, 81324. Tel: 970-677-2389. p. 278
Ernst, Linda, Pub Serv Spec, Allegheny College, 520 N Main St, Meadville, PA, 16335. Tel: 814-332-3790. p. 1959
Ernst, Molly, Coll Res Mgr, Mansfield-Richland County Public Library, 43 W Third St, Mansfield, OH, 44902-1295. Tel: 419-521-3133. p. 1798
Ernst, Tony, Fr, Adminr, Old Cathedral Library, 205 Church St, Vincennes, IN, 47591-1133. Tel: 812-882-5638. p. 723
Errickson, Ben, Archivist, National Watch & Clock Museum, 514 Poplar St, Columbia, PA, 17512-2124. Tel: 717-684-8261, Ext 214. p. 1923

Errico, Lisa, Head, Res Mgt, Nassau Community College, One Education Dr, Garden City, NY, 11530-6793. Tel: 516-572-7400, 516-572-7401. p. 1537
Errington, Peggy, Dir, Orchard Park Public Library, S-4570 S Buffalo St, Orchard Park, NY, 14127. Tel: 716-662-9851. p. 1612
Ersland, Jake, Director, Archival Operations, National Archives & Records Administration, 400 W Pershing Rd, Kansas City, MO, 64108. Tel: 816-268-8014. p. 1256
Ertel, Darlene, Librn, Athenaeum of Ohio, 6616 Beechmont Ave, Cincinnati, OH, 45230-2091. Tel: 513-233-6136. p. 1759
Ertin, Donna, Head, Circ, Case Western Reserve University, School of Law Library, 11075 East Blvd, Cleveland, OH, 44106-7148. Tel: 216-368-8510. p. 1766
Ertz, Jason, Ref Librn, College of DuPage Library, 425 Fawell Blvd, Glen Ellyn, IL, 60137-6599. Tel: 630-942-3317. p. 593
Ertz, Matt, Asst Dir, University of Louisville Libraries, Dwight Anderson Music Library, 105 W Brandeis Ave, Louisville, KY, 40208. Tel: 502-852-0527. p. 867
Erven, Penny, Asst Librn, Sundridge-Strong Union Public Library, 110 Main St, Sundridge, ON, P0A 1Z0, CANADA. Tel: 705-384-7311. p. 2684
Ervin, Barbara, Br Asst, Pictou - Antigonish Regional Library, Trenton Library, 122 Main St, Trenton, NS, B0K 1X0, CANADA. Tel: 902-752-5181. p. 2622
Ervin, Chris, Head Archivist, Santa Barbara Historical Museum, 136 E De La Guerra St, Santa Barbara, CA, 93101. Tel: 805-966-1601, Ext 105. p. 240
Ervin, Seth, Chief Innovation Officer, Charlotte Mecklenburg Library, 310 N Tryon St, Charlotte, NC, 28202-2176. Tel: 704-416-0100. p. 1679
Ervin, Sherri, Head, Circ, Hammond Public Library, 564 State St, Hammond, IN, 46320-1532. Tel: 219-931-5100, Ext 328. p. 689
Ervin, Tina, Head, Children's Servx, Goshen Public Library, 601 S Fifth St, Goshen, IN, 46526. Tel: 574-537-0241. p. 687
Erwin, Gail, Librn & Archivist, San Joaquin County Historical Museum, 11793 N Micke Grove Rd, Lodi, CA, 95240. Tel: 209-331-2055. p. 157
Erwin, Lisa Jane, Mgr, Free Library of Philadelphia, Central Senior Services, 1901 Vine St, 1st Flr W, Philadelphia, PA, 19103. Tel: 215-686-5331. p. 1977
Erwin, Roseann, Librn, Los Medanos College Library, 1351 Pioneer Sq, Brentwood, CA, 94513. Tel: 925-392-9069. p. 124
Esai, Armand, Libr & Archives Mgr, Field Museum of Natural History, 1400 S DuSable Lake Shore Dr, Chicago, IL, 60605-2496. Tel: 312-665-7892. p. 561
Esai, Armand, Museum Archivist, Field Museum of Natural History, 1400 S DuSable Lake Shore Dr, Chicago, IL, 60605-2496. Tel: 312-665-7892. p. 561
Esarey, Nikki, Branch Lead, Circ Assoc, Harrison County Public Library, Palmyra Branch, 689 Haub St, Palmyra, IN, 47164. Tel: 812-364-6425. p. 677
Esaw, Corina, Br Mgr, Chesterfield County Library System, Matheson Library, 227 Huger St, Cheraw, SC, 29520. Tel: 843-537-3571. p. 2052
Esbjornson, Mary, Exec Dir, Bedford Hills Free Library, 26 Main St, Bedford Hills, NY, 10507-1832. Tel: 914-666-6472. p. 1492
Escalante, Harold, Branch Lead, Charlotte Mecklenburg Library, Myers Park Branch, 1361 Queens Rd, Charlotte, NC, 28207. Tel: 704-416-5800. p. 1679
Escalante, Maria, Dir, College of Menominee Nation Library, N 172 Hwy 47/55, Keshena, WI, 54135. Tel: 715-799-5600, Ext 3003. p. 2445
Escamilla, Mary Ann, Ref (Info Servs), Robert J Kleberg Public Library, 220 N Fourth St, Kingsville, TX, 78363. Tel: 361-592-6381. p. 2206
Eschenbrenner, Donna, Archivist, Dir, Res Serv, The History Center in Tompkins County, 110 N Tioga St, 2nd Flr, Ithaca, NY, 14850. Tel: 607-273-8284. p. 1552
Eschenfelder, Kristin, Assoc Dir, Prof, University of Wisconsin-Madison, Helen C White Hall, Rm 4217, 600 N Park St, Madison, WI, 53706. Tel: 608-263-2900. p. 2794
Escher, Maria, Mgr, District of Columbia Public Library, Francis A Gregory Neighborhood, 3660 Alabama Ave SE, Washington, DC, 20020. Tel: 202-698-6373. p. 364
Escobar, Hector, Dir, Educ & Info Delivery, University of Dayton Libraries, 300 College Park Dr, Dayton, OH, 45469. Tel: 937-229-5141. p. 1780
Escobar, Jerry, Libr Dir, Portuguese Society of America, 1100 14th St, Ste E, Modesto, CA, 95354-1030. Tel: 209-702-6364. p. 177
Escobar Nieves, Alejandro, Dir, University of the Sacred Heart, Rosales St, PO Box 12383, Santurce, PR, 00914-0383. Tel: 787-728-1515, Ext 4354. p. 2515
Escobar, Victoria, Acq, Altadena Library District, 600 E Mariposa St, Altadena, CA, 91001. Tel: 626-798-0833. p. 116
Escobedo, Franklin, Dir, Larkspur Public Library, 400 Magnolia Ave, Larkspur, CA, 94939. Tel: 415-927-5005. p. 156
Escobedo, Ramses, Br Mgr, San Francisco Public Library, Excelsior Branch Library, 4400 Mission St (at Cotter), San Francisco, CA, 94112-1927. Tel: 415-355-2868. p. 228
Escoto, Allison, Head Librn, Center for Fiction, 15 Lafayette Ave, Brooklyn, NY, 11217. Tel: 212-755-6710. p. 1504
Escoto, Cindy, Supvr, Ventura County Library, Piru Library, 3811 Center St, Piru, CA, 93040. Tel: 805-521-1753. p. 256
Escude, Andrew, Interim Exec Dir, Texas Tech University Health Sciences Center, 3601 Fourth St, Lubbock, TX, 79430. Tel: 806-743-2200. p. 2214
Eshbach, Barbara, Head Librn, Penn State University York, 1031 Edgecomb Ave, York, PA, 17403. Tel: 717-771-4023. p. 2026
Eshelman, Karen, Librn, Howard City Library, 126 S Wabash, Howard, KS, 67349. Tel: 620-374-2890. p. 814
Eshleman, Susan, Dir, Quarryville Library, 357 Buck Rd, Quarryville, PA, 17566. Tel: 717-786-1336. p. 1999
Eshleman, Tamara, Circ Mgr, Adamstown Area Library, 110 W Main St, Adamstown, PA, 19501. Tel: 717-484-4200. p. 1903
Eshun, Elizabeth, Commun Libr Mgr, Queens Library, Rosedale Community Library, 144-20 243rd St, Rosedale, NY, 11422. Tel: 718-528-8490. p. 1555
Eskin, Marcie, Librn, Beth Hillel Congregation Bnai Emunah, 3220 Big Tree Lane, Wilmette, IL, 60091. Tel: 847-256-1213, Ext 29. p. 663
Eskridge, Beverly, Circ Librn, Media Librn, Gordon State College, 419 College Dr, Barnesville, GA, 30204. Tel: 678-359-5076. p. 468
Eskridge, Honora, Libr Dir, Vanderbilt University, Sarah Shannon Stevenson Science & Engineering Library, 419 21st Ave S, Nashville, TN, 37203-2427. Tel: 615-343-2322. p. 2122
Eskritt, Julie, Libr Serv Coordr, Great River Regional Library, Rockford Public Library, 8220 Cedar St, Rockford, MN, 55373. Tel: 763-477-4216. p. 1197
Esmon, Amy, Librn, Wayne City Public Library, 102 S Main St, Wayne City, IL, 62895. Tel: 618-895-2661. p. 660
Esparo, Dorothy, Children's Serv Coordr, Clark Memorial Library, 538 Amity Rd, Bethany, CT, 06524. Tel: 203-393-2103. p. 302
Esparza, Julie, Assoc Dir, Louisiana State University Health Sciences Center, 1501 Kings Hwy, Shreveport, LA, 71130. Tel: 318-675-4179. p. 908
Espe, Lauren, Asst Dir, Beaman Memorial Public Library, Eight Newton St, West Boylston, MA, 01583. Tel: 508-835-3711. p. 1065
Espe, Michele, Dir, Fenton Public Library, 605 Maple, Fenton, IA, 50539-0217. Tel: 515-889-2333. p. 753
Espe, Sue, Libr Mgr, Saint Joseph's Hospital & Medical Center, 350 W Thomas Rd, Phoenix, AZ, 85013. Tel: 602-406-5684. p. 72
Espe, Troy, Ref & ILL Librn, University of Wisconsin-Stevens Point, 900 Reserve St, Stevens Point, WI, 54481-1985. Tel: 715-346-4443. p. 2479
Espey, Leigh, Libr Mgr, Saline County Public Library, 1800 Smithers Dr, Benton, AR, 72015. Tel: 501-778-4766. p. 90
Espinosa, Aaron, Dir, Rancho Mirage Library & Observatory, 71-100 Hwy 111, Rancho Mirage, CA, 92270. Tel: 760-341-7323. p. 198
Espinosa Cancel, Ana Maria, Libr Tech, United States Court of Appeals, Federico Degetau Federal Bldg, Rm 121, 150 Carlos Chardon St, Hato Rey, PR, 00918. Tel: 787-772-3097. p. 2511
Espinoza, Ester, Dir, Idalou Community Library, 210 Main St, Idalou, TX, 79329. Tel: 806-892-2114. p. 2202
Espinoza, Sonia, Supvr, Yakima Valley Libraries, Granger Library, 508 Sunnyside Ave, Granger, WA, 98932. Tel: 509-854-1446. p. 2395
Espinoza, Stephanie, E-Learning Librn, Lead Librn, College of Southern Nevada, Henderson Campus, 700 S College Dr, H1A, Henderson, NV, 89002. Tel: 702-651-3066. p. 1346
Espinoza, Yenni, Libr Dir, Penitas Public Library, 1111 S Main St, Penitas, TX, 78576. Tel: 956-583-5656. p. 2226
Espinoza, Yenni B, VPres, Hidalgo County Library System, c/o McAllen Memorial Library, 4001 N 3rd St, McAllen, TX, 78504. Tel: 956-583-5656. p. 2217
Espiritu, Florence, Tech Serv Librn, Diablo Valley College Library, 321 Golf Club Rd, Pleasant Hill, CA, 94523-1576. Tel: 925-969-2584. p. 195
Espitia, Sadys, Res Analyst, Weil, Gotshal & Manges LLP, 767 Fifth Ave, New York, NY, 10153. Tel: 212-310-8444. p. 1603
Esqueda, Bridget, Libr Mgr, Salem Public Library, West Salem, 395 Glen Creek Rd NW, Salem, OR, 97304. Tel: 503-588-6315. p. 1897
Essermann, Katie, Dir, Lakes Country Public Library, 15235 Hwy 32, Lakewood, WI, 54138. Tel: 715-276-9020. p. 2447
Essery, Wendy, Archives Mgr, Libr Mgr, Worcester Historical Museum, 30 Elm St, Worcester, MA, 01609. Tel: 508-753-8278, Ext 105. p. 1072
Essex, Don, Libr Dir, Washington Adventist University, 7600 Flower Ave, Takoma Park, MD, 20912-7796. Tel: 301-891-4217. p. 979
Essig, Mary, Libr Dir, West Virginia School of Osteopathic Medicine, 400 Lee St N, Lewisburg, WV, 24901. Tel: 304-647-6213. p. 2407
Esslami, Mohammed, Br Coordr, Fairfax County Public Library, 12000 Government Center Pkwy, Ste 324, Fairfax, VA, 22035-0012. Tel: 703-324-3100. p. 2316
Esslinger, Mark, Libr Dir, Wayne County Public Library, 1200 Oak St, Kenova, WV, 25530. Tel: 304-453-2462. p. 2406
Esson, Afton, Mr, Libr & Archives Mgr, Goodhue County Historical Society Library, 1166 Oak St, Red Wing, MN, 55066. Tel: 651-388-6024. p. 1194
Estabrook, Alexia, Librn, Ascension Providence Hospital, 16001 W Nine Mile Rd, Southfield, MI, 48075. Tel: 248-849-3294. p. 1151
Estabrook, Heidi, Outreach Serv Librn, Jacksonville Public Library, 201 W College Ave, Jacksonville, IL, 62650-2497. Tel: 217-243-5435. p. 602
Estelle, Andrea, Dir, Otsego District Public Library, 401 Dix St, Otsego, MI, 49078. Tel: 269-694-9690. p. 1139

Estelle, Andrea, Dir, Southwest Michigan Library Cooperative, 401 Dix St, Otsego, MI, 49078. Tel: 269-694-9690. p. 2767

Estelle-Holmer, Suzanne, Assoc Dir, Access Serv, Assoc Dir, Res & Coll, Yale University Library, Divinity School Library, 409 Prospect St, New Haven, CT, 06511. Tel: 203-432-6374. p. 327

Ester, Katie, Dir, Shelby Township Library, 51680 Van Dyke, Shelby Township, MI, 48316-4448. Tel: 586-726-2344. p. 1150

Estes, Carol Ann, Librn, Reveille United Methodist Church, 4200 Cary Street Rd, Richmond, VA, 23221. Tel: 804-359-6041, Ext 121. p. 2341

Estes, James D, Dir, Wesley Theological Seminary Library, 4500 Massachusetts Ave NW, Washington, DC, 20016-5690. Tel: 202-885-8696. p. 381

Estes, Mark E, Dir, Bernard E Witkin Alameda County Law Library, 125 Twelfth St, Oakland, CA, 94607-4912. Tel: 510-272-6481. p. 187

Estes, Rob, Head, Libr Tech, University of Washington Libraries, Bothell Campus/Cascadia College Library, University of Washington Bothell, 18225 Campus Way NE, Box 358550, Bothell, WA, 98011-8245. Tel: 425-352-5340. p. 2381

Estey, Lori, Libr Asst, Plainfield Public Libraries, 22 Bean Rd, Meriden, NH, 03770. Tel: 603-469-3252. p. 1373

Estis, Donna, Ch Serv, ILL & Distance Libr Serv Spec, Lasalle Parish Library, 3165 N First St, Jena, LA, 71342. Tel: 318-992-5675. p. 891

Estle, Kristina, Asst Dir, Bellaire Public Library, 330 32nd St, Bellaire, OH, 43906. Tel: 740-676-9421. p. 1750

Estlund, Karen, Dean of Libr, Colorado State University Libraries, Morgan Library, 1201 Center Ave Mall, Fort Collins, CO, 80523. Tel: 970-491-1838. p. 280

Estrada -Mendez, Danya, Libr Tech, Palo Verde College Library, One College Dr, Blythe, CA, 92225. Tel: 760-921-5518. p. 124

Estrada, Eugene, Sr Librn, Los Angeles Public Library System, El Sereno Branch Library, 5226 S Huntington Dr, Los Angeles, CA, 90032. Tel: 323-225-9201. p. 164

Estrada, Heather, Cat, Electronic Res Librn, Blue Mountain Community College Library, 2411 NW Carden Ave, Pendleton, OR, 97801. Tel: 541-278-5913. p. 1890

Estrada, Jose Manuel, Law Librn, Per Librn, Inter-American University of Puerto Rico, PO Box 70351, Hato Rey, PR, 00936. Tel: 787-751-1912, Ext 2064. p. 2511

Estrada, María, Librn III, Ref Serv, Inter-American University of Puerto Rico, PO Box 70351, Hato Rey, PR, 00936. Tel: 787-751-1912, Ext 2098. p. 2511

Estrada, Raquel, Coll Develop & Acq Librn, University of Texas Rio Grande Valley, One W University Blvd, Brownsville, TX, 78520. Tel: 956-882-7267. p. 2150

Estrada-Lopez, Janine, Librn, Missouri Court of Appeals Library, 1300 Oak St, Kansas City, MO, 64106-2970. Tel: 816-889-3600. p. 1256

Estrella, Debbie, Ad, Tiverton Public Library, 34 Roosevelt Ave, Tiverton, RI, 02878. Tel: 401-625-6796, Ext 5. p. 2042

Estrella, Maria, Br Mgr, Cleveland Public Library, Garden Valley, 7201 Kinsman Rd, Ste 101, Cleveland, OH, 44104. Tel: 216-623-6976. p. 1768

Estrella, Maria, Br Mgr, Cleveland Public Library, Woodland, 5806 Woodland Ave, Cleveland, OH, 44104. Tel: 216-623-7109. p. 1769

Esty, Lynn, Librn, Mary L Blood Memorial Library, 41 Brownsville-Hartland Rd, West Windsor, VT, 05037. Tel: 802-484-7205. p. 2298

Etches, Amanda, Interim Univ Librn, University of Guelph, 50 Stone Rd E, Guelph, ON, N1G 2W1, CANADA. Tel: 519-824-4120, Ext 53617. p. 2644

Ethen, Anne, Br Mgr, Wichita Public Library, Evergreen Branch, 2601 N Arkansas, Wichita, KS, 67204. Tel: 316-303-8181. p. 843

Ethen, Anne, Br Mgr, Wichita Public Library, Maya Angelou Northeast Branch, 3051 E 21st St, Wichita, KS, 67214. Tel: 316-688-9580. p. 843

Etheredge, Stacy, Libr Dir, Ref & Instruction Librn, Idaho State Law Library, 514 W Jefferson St, 2nd Flr, Boise, ID, 83702. Tel: 208-364-4558. p. 518

Etheredge, Stacy, Dir, University of Idaho Library, College of Law, 711 Rayburn St, Moscow, ID, 83844. Tel: 208-885-6521. p. 526

Etheridge, Angela, Dir, Tallahatchie County Library, 102 E Walnut St, Charleston, MS, 38921. Tel: 662-647-2638. p. 1213

Etheridge, Katie, Librn Spec, Florida DEP-Geological Survey Research Library, 3000 Commonwealth Blvd, Ste 1, Tallahassee, FL, 32303. Tel: 850-617-0316. p. 446

Etherington, Nathan, Commun Coordr, Curator, Programming, Brant Historical Society Library, 57 Charlotte St, Brantford, ON, N3T 2W6, CANADA. Tel: 519-752-2483. p. 2633

Etherton, Becky, Dir, Library District Number One, Doniphan County, 105 N Main, Troy, KS, 66087. Tel: 785-985-2597, 833-LIB-DIS1 (542-3471). p. 840

Etman, Beth, Asst Librn, Townshend Public Library, 1971 Rte 30, Townshend, VT, 05353. Tel: 802-365-4039. p. 2296

Etokana, Carole, Librn, Nunavut Public Library Services, Kugluktuk Community Library, PO Box 190, Kugluktuk, NU, X0E 0E0, CANADA. Tel: 867-982-4406. p. 2625

Etschmaier, Gale A, Dean, Univ Libr, Florida State University Libraries, Strozier Library Bldg, 116 Honors Way, Tallahassee, FL, 32306. Tel: 850-644-2706. p. 446

Etson, Lynn, Librn, Bellevue Township Library, 212 N Main St, Bellevue, MI, 49021. Tel: 269-763-3369. p. 1084

Etter, Mary J, Dir, South Windsor Public Library, 1550 Sullivan Ave, South Windsor, CT, 06074. Tel: 860-644-1541. p. 337

Ettinger, Renee, Asst Dir, Outreach Serv, Asst Dir, Res Serv, University of Wisconsin-Green Bay, 2420 Nicolet Dr, Green Bay, WI, 54311-7001. Tel: 920-465-2543. p. 2439

Etzel, Brent, Archives, Dean of the Library, Wheaton College, 510 Irving Ave, Wheaton, IL, 60187-4234. Tel: 630-752-5102. p. 662

Etzel, Matthew, Reader Serv, Allen County Public Library, 900 Library Plaza, Fort Wayne, IN, 46802. Tel: 260-421-1236. p. 683

Eubanks, Debbie, Circ Supvr, Killeen Public Library, 205 E Church Ave, Killeen, TX, 76541. Tel: 254-501-8990. p. 2206

Eubanks, Laurie, Libr Mgr, West Georgia Regional Library, Douglas County Public Library, 6810 Selman Dr, Douglasville, GA, 30134. Tel: 770-920-7125. p. 470

Eubanks, Lecia, Dir, Cherokee Regional Library System, 305 S Duke St, LaFayette, GA, 30728. Tel: 706-638-2992. p. 484

Eubanks, Toni, Dir, Barton Public Library, 100 Church St, Barton, VT, 05822. Tel: 802-525-6524. p. 2278

Eubanks, Toni, Dir, Glover Public Library, 51 Bean Hill Rd, Glover, VT, 05839. Tel: 802-525-4365. p. 2284

Eudell, Alexus, Circ Librn, Patron Serv Librn, Dominican Theological Library, 487 Michigan Ave NE, Washington, DC, 20017-1585. Tel: 202-655-4653. p. 365

Eugene, Patrick, ILL, Manatt, Phelps & Phillips LLP, 1050 Connecticut Ave NW, Ste 600, Washington, DC, 20036. Tel: 202-585-6500. p. 371

Eula, Michael, Dr, County Historian, Rec Mgt Officer, Genesee County History Department, 3837 West Main Street Rd, County Bldg 2, Batavia, NY, 14020-2021. Tel: 585-815-7904. p. 1490

Euliano, Bridget, Asst Univ Librn, George Mason University Libraries, 4348 Chesapeake River Way, Fairfax, VA, 22030. Tel: 703-993-2445. p. 2317

Euliano, John, Br Mgr, Erie County Public Library, Millcreek, 2088 Interchange Rd, Ste 280, Erie, PA, 16565-0601. Tel: 814-451-7084. p. 1931

Eustace, Jamie, City Librn, Sterling Municipal Library, Mary Elizabeth Wilbanks Ave, Baytown, TX, 77520. Tel: 281-427-7331. p. 2145

Eustis, Tammy, Asst Dir, Head Cataloger, Ref Librn, Killingworth Library Association, 301 Rte 81, Killingworth, CT, 06419. Tel: 860-663-2000. p. 319

Evangelista, Ernie, Knowledge & Info Mgmt, Federal Reserve Bank of Atlanta, 1000 Peachtree St NE, Atlanta, GA, 30309-4470. Tel: 404-498-8927. p. 463

Evanoff, Joanne, Assoc Dir, Technologies & Info Resources, Embry-Riddle Aeronautical University, 3700 Willow Creek Rd, Prescott, AZ, 86301-3720. Tel: 928-777-3802. p. 73

Evans, Alice, Bus Mgr, Northwest Kansas Library System, Two Washington Sq, Norton, KS, 67654-1615. Tel: 785-877-5148. p. 827

Evans, Anita, Library Contact, Baltimore City Department of Legislative Reference Library, City Hall, Rm 626, 100 N Holliday St, Baltimore, MD, 21202. Tel: 410-396-4730. p. 951

Evans, Anna, Dir, Camanche Public Library, 102 12th Ave, Camanche, IA, 52730. Tel: 563-259-1106. p. 736

Evans, Annamarie, Ref Librn for Adult Engagement, Jervis Public Library Association, Inc, 613 N Washington St, Rome, NY, 13440-4296. Tel: 315-336-4570. p. 1632

Evans, Annette, Dir, United States Department of the Army, CEHEC-ZL Casey Bldg, 7701 Telegraph Rd, Alexandria, VA, 22315-3860. Tel: 703-428-6388. p. 2303

Evans, Audrey, Br Mgr, Lonesome Pine Regional Library, Lee County Public, 539 Joslyn Ave, Pennington Gap, VA, 24277. Tel: 276-546-1141. p. 2355

Evans, Audrey, Br Mgr, Lonesome Pine Regional Library, Rose Hill Community, 6463 Dr Thomas Rd, Rose Hill, VA, 24281. Tel: 276-445-5329. p. 2355

Evans, Barbara, Asst Dir, Pub Serv, First Regional Library, 370 W Commerce St, Hernando, MS, 38632. Tel: 662-429-4439. p. 1219

Evans, Becka, Br Mgr, Carbon County Library System, Little Snake River Valley, 105 Second St, Baggs, WY, 82321. Tel: 307-383-7323. p. 2498

Evans, Beth, Electronic Serv, Brooklyn College Library, 2900 Bedford Ave, Brooklyn, NY, 11210. Tel: 718-758-8206. p. 1501

Evans, Betsy, Dir of Access, Instruction & Outreach, Sul Ross State University, PO Box C-109, Alpine, TX, 79832. Tel: 432-837-8123. p. 2133

Evans, Betty, Head, Cat, Sweet Briar College, 134 Chapel Rd, Sweet Briar, VA, 24595. Tel: 434-381-6138. p. 2348

Evans, Bruce, Assoc Librn, Dir of Cataloging and Metadata Services, Baylor University Libraries, Moody Memorial Library, 1312 S Third St, Waco, TX, 76798. Tel: 254-710-7863. p. 2253

Evans, Carla, Librn, Proskauer LLP Library, 1001 Pennsylvania Ave NW, Ste 600 S, Washington, DC, 20004-2533. Tel: 202-416-6823. p. 374

Evans, Celeste, Ref Librn, United States Military Academy Library, Jefferson Hall Library & Learning Ctr, 758 Cullum Rd, West Point, NY, 10996. Tel: 845-938-8301. p. 1663

Evans, Cheryl, Mgr, Columbus Metropolitan Library, Driving Park Branch, 1422 E Livingston Ave, Columbus, OH, 43205. p. 1772

Evans, Christine, Head, Circ Serv, California State University, Fresno, Henry Madden Library, 5200 N Barton Ave, Mail Stop ML-34, Fresno, CA, 93740-8014. Tel: 559-278-2403. p. 144

Evans, Colin, Commun Serv Librn, Lakeland Library Region, 1302 100 St, North Battleford, SK, S9A 0V8, CANADA. Tel: 306-445-6108. p. 2743

Evans, Craig, Lecturer, University of Illinois at Urbana-Champaign, Library & Information Science Bldg, 501 E Daniel St, Champaign, IL, 61820-6211. Tel: 217-333-3280. p. 2784

Evans, D'Arcy, Ms, Libr Mgr, Myrnam Community Library, New Myrnam School, 5105-50 St, Myrnam, AB, T0B 3K0, CANADA. Tel: 780-366-3801. p. 2549

Evans, Dana, Cat Librn, Hampton University, 129 William R Harvey Way, Hampton, VA, 23668. Tel: 757-727-5183. p. 2323

Evans, Darla, Circ Mgr, Louisville Public Library, 700 Lincoln Ave, Louisville, OH, 44641-1474. Tel: 330-875-1696. p. 1797

Evans, David, Dir of Libr, Richmont Graduate University, 1900 The Exchange SE, Bldg 100, Atlanta, GA, 30339. Tel: 404-835-6120. p. 466

Evans, David, Dr, Dean, Libr Serv, Kennesaw State University Library System, 385 Cobb Ave NW, MD 1701, Kennesaw, GA, 30144. Tel: 470-578-6194. p. 483

Evans, David, Dr, Dean, Libr Serv, Kennesaw State University Library System, Lawrence V Johnson Library, 1100 S Marietta Pkwy, Marietta, GA, 30060-2896. Tel: 678-470-578-7276. p. 483

Evans, Deanna, Youth Serv Librn, Sanibel Public Library District, 770 Dunlop Rd, Sanibel, FL, 33957. Tel: 239-472-2483. p. 442

Evans, Edward, Dr, Library Contact, University of Florida, Tropical Research & Education Center, 18905 SW 280th St, Homestead, FL, 33031. Tel: 786-217-9263. p. 409

Evans, Elizabeth, Dir, Point Park University Library, 414 Wood St, Pittsburgh, PA, 15222. Tel: 412-392-3161. p. 1995

Evans, Elizabeth, Ref, ILL & Gov Doc, Hampton University, 129 William R Harvey Way, Hampton, VA, 23668. Tel: 757-727-5371. p. 2323

Evans, Erin, Dir, Greeneville Green County Public Library, 210 N Main St, Greeneville, TN, 37745-3816. Tel: 423-638-5034. p. 2100

Evans, Gail, Dir, Dougherty County Public Library, 300 Pine Ave, Albany, GA, 31701-2533. Tel: 229-420-3200. p. 457

Evans, Gail, Asst Dir, Coll Develop, Henry County Public Library System, 1001 Florence McGarity Blvd, McDonough, GA, 30252. Tel: 678-432-5353. p. 490

Evans, Gretchen, Dir, Paw Paw District Library, 609 W Michigan Ave, Paw Paw, MI, 49079-1072. Tel: 269-657-3800. p. 1140

Evans, James, Dir, Libr Serv, Everglades University Libraries, 5002 T-REX Ave, Ste 100, Boca Raton, FL, 33431. Tel: 561-912-1211. p. 385

Evans, James, Librn, Everglades University, Tampa Campus, 5010 W Kennedy Blvd, Tampa, FL, 33609. Tel: 813-961-2837. p. 385

Evans, Janet, Assoc Dir, Pennsylvania Horticultural Society, 100 N 20th St, 1st Flr, Philadelphia, PA, 19103-1495. Tel: 215-988-8800. p. 1984

Evans, Jennifer, Info Serv Librn, North Island College, 2300 Ryan Rd, Courtenay, BC, V9N 8N6, CANADA. Tel: 250-334-5037. p. 2565

Evans, Joe, Colls Mgr, The Henry Wilson Coil Library & Museum of Freemasonry, 1111 California St, San Francisco, CA, 94108. Tel: 415-292-9141. p. 224

Evans, John E, Dr, Assoc Dean, Univ Libr, Exec Dir, University Libraries, University of Memphis, 3785 Norriswood Ave, Memphis, TN, 38152. p. 2115

Evans, Jon, Archives Chief, Chief Librn, Museum of Fine Arts, Houston, 1001 Bissonnet St, Houston, TX, 77005. Tel: 713-639-7325. p. 2197

Evans, Josephine, Managing Librn, Brooklyn Public Library, Eastern Parkway, 1044 Eastern Pkwy, Brooklyn, NY, 11213. Tel: 718-953-4225. p. 1503

Evans, Karen, Chair, Pub Serv, Indiana State University, 510 North 6 1/2 St, Terre Haute, IN, 47809. Tel: 812-237-3700. p. 720

Evans, Karen, Ch, Louisville Free Public Library, South Central Regional, 7300 Jefferson Blvd, Louisville, KY, 40219. Tel: 502-964-3515. p. 866

Evans, Kathy, Mgr, Hall County Library System, Murrayville Branch, 4796 Thompson Bridge Rd, Murrayville, GA, 30507. Tel: 770-532-3311, Ext 171. p. 480

Evans, Katrina, Dir, Columbia County Public Library, 308 NW Columbia Ave, Lake City, FL, 32055. Tel: 386-758-2101. p. 415

Evans, Keisha, Br Mgr, Greater Clarks Hill Regional Library System, Grovetown Library, 105 Old Wrightsboro Rd, Grovetown, GA, 30813. Tel: 706-868-3401. p. 478

Evans, Kelly, Bus Librn, Health Sci Librn, Eastern Washington University, 600 N Riverpoint Blvd, Rm 230, Spokane, WA, 99202. Tel: 509-358-7930. p. 2383

Evans, Kimberli, Dir, Comfort Public Library, 701 High St, Comfort, TX, 78013. Tel: 830-995-2398. p. 2158

Evans, Larry, Dir, Trenton Public Library, 406 Main St, Trenton, NE, 69044. Tel: 308-334-5413. p. 1338

Evans, Laura N, Head, Collections Mgmt, Amherst College, 61 Quadrangle Dr, Amherst, MA, 01002. p. 984

Evans, Lauren, Head, Youth Serv, J V Fletcher Library, 50 Main St, Westford, MA, 01886-2599. Tel: 978-399-2307. p. 1067

Evans, Lela, Librn, Dallas College, 801 Main St, Dallas, TX, 75202-3605. Tel: 214-860-2174. p. 2164

Evans, Lexi, Youth Librn, Doniphan-Ripley County Library, Naylor Branch, 105 Kelsey St, Naylor, MO, 63953. Tel: 573-399-2225. p. 1245

Evans, Linda, Assoc Librn, Henderson State University, 1100 Henderson St, Arkadelphia, AR, 71999-0001. Tel: 870-230-5958. p. 89

Evans, Lindy, Asst Librn, Trenton Public Library, 118 E Indiana, Trenton, IL, 62293. Tel: 618-224-7662. p. 654

Evans, Lisa, Dir, Libr Serv, Covina Public Library, 234 N Second Ave, Covina, CA, 91723-2198. Tel: 626-384-5303. p. 133

Evans, Liz, Librn, McGinnis, Lochridge, 600 Congress Ave, Ste 2100, Austin, TX, 78701. Tel: 512-495-6000. p. 2140

Evans, Lynn, Br Mgr, Lyon County Library System, Fernley Branch, 575 Silver Lace Blvd, Fernley, NV, 89408. Tel: 775-575-3366. p. 1352

Evans, Max, Assoc Prof, McGill University, 3661 Peel St, Montreal, QC, H3A 1X1, CANADA. Tel: 514-398-4204. p. 2796

Evans, Meredith, Dr, Dir, National Archives & Records Administration, 441 Freedom Pkwy, Atlanta, GA, 30307-1498. Tel: 404-865-7100. p. 465

Evans, Michael, Br Mgr, Greenville County Library System, Mauldin Branch, 800 W Butler Rd, Greenville, SC, 29607. Tel: 864-527-9204. p. 2061

Evans, Michael, Dir of Develop, Massanutten Regional Library, 174 S Main St, Harrisonburg, VA, 22801. Tel: 540-434-4475, Ext 135. p. 2324

Evans, Nancy, Pres, Dwight Library, 616 Main St, Dwight, KS, 66849. Tel: 785-482-3804. p. 805

Evans, Nancy, Dir, West Babylon Public Library, 211 Rte 109, West Babylon, NY, 11704. Tel: 631-669-5445. p. 1661

Evans, Natalie, Br Mgr, Osceola Library System, West Osceola Branch, 305 Campus St, Celebration, FL, 34747. p. 414

Evans, Patricia, Librn, Mobile County Public Law Library, Mobile Government Plaza, 205 Government St, Mobile, AL, 36644-2308. Tel: 251-574-8436. p. 26

Evans, Patricia, Mgr, Info Serv, North Grenville Public Library, Burritts Rapids Branch, One Grenville St, Burritts Rapids, ON, K0G 1B0, CANADA. Tel: 613-269-3636. p. 2649

Evans, Patricia, Mgr, Info Serv, North Grenville Public Library, Norenberg Bldg, One Water St, Kemptville, ON, K0G 1J0, CANADA. Tel: 613-258-4711. p. 2649

Evans, Paula, Dir, Dunlap Public Library, 102 S Tenth St, Dunlap, IA, 51529. Tel: 712-643-5311. p. 749

Evans, Rachel, Metadata Serv, Spec Coll Librn, University of Georgia, Alexander Campbell King Law Library, 225 Herty Dr, Athens, GA, 30602-6018. Tel: 706-542-1922. p. 459

Evans, Robin, Research Librn, Foley & Lardner LLP, 3000 K St NW, 4th Flr, Washington, DC, 20007. Tel: 202-672-5300. p. 366

Evans, Robin, Br Asst, Elko-Lander-Eureka County Library System, Eureka Branch Library, 80 S Monroe St, Eureka, NV, 89316. Tel: 775-237-5307. p. 1344

Evans, Sherry, Acq Librn, Colls Librn, Hyannis Public Library, 401 Main St, Hyannis, MA, 02601. Tel: 508-775-2280. p. 1026

Evans, Siân, Info Literacy, Instrul Design Librn, Maryland Institute College of Art, 1401 W Mount Royal Ave, Baltimore, MD, 21217. Tel: 410-225-2304, 410-225-2311. p. 955

Evans, Sonya, Libr Dir, L'Anse Area School-Public Library, 201 N Fourth St, L'Anse, MI, 49946-1499. Tel: 906-524-0334, 906-524-6213. p. 1123

Evans, Sophia L, Dir, Blanche K Werner Public Library, 203 Prospect Dr, Trinity, TX, 75862. Tel: 936-594-2087. p. 2249

Evans, Sue, Librn, Greenup County Public Library, McKell Public, 22 McKell Lane, South Shore, KY, 41175. Tel: 606-932-4478. p. 857

Evans, Taina, Coordr, Outreach Serv, Brooklyn Public Library, Services for Older Adults, 1743 86th St, Brooklyn, NY, 11214. Tel: 718-236-1760. p. 1504

Evans, Tamara, Supvr, Kings County Library, Lemoore Branch, 457 C St, Lemoore, CA, 93245. Tel: 559-924-2188. p. 150

Evans, Tamara, Supvr, Kings County Library, Stratford Branch, 20300 Main St, Stratford, CA, 93266. Tel: 559-947-3003. p. 150

Evans, Tanya, Multicultural Librn, Springdale Public Library, 405 S Pleasant St, Springdale, AR, 72764. Tel: 479-750-8180. p. 110

Evans, Trina, Br Asst, Kokomo-Howard County Public Library, Russiaville Branch, 315 Mesa Dr, Russiaville, IN, 46979. Tel: 765-883-5112. p. 700

Evans, Tristan, Archivist, Chilliwack Museum & Historical Society, 9291 Corbould St, Chilliwack, BC, V2P 4A6, CANADA. Tel: 604-795-5210, Ext 104. p. 2565

Evans, Tyler S, Head, Tech Serv, United States Air Force, Air University - Muir S Fairchild Research Information Center, 600 Chennault Circle, Maxwell AFB, AL, 36112-6010. Tel: 334-953-7691. p. 25

Evans, Veronica C, Br Mgr, Riverside County Library System, Coachella Library, 1500 Sixth St, Coachella, CA, 92236. Tel: 760-398-5148. p. 202

Evans, Walker, Libr Dir, Andrew Carnegie Free Library & Music Hall, 300 Beechwood Ave, Carnegie, PA, 15106-2699. Tel: 412-276-3456, Ext 12. p. 1919

Evans, Will, Chief Librn, Tech Serv, Boston Athenaeum, Ten 1/2 Beacon St, Boston, MA, 02108-3777. Tel: 617-227-0270. p. 991

Evans-Cullen, Heather, Libr Dir, Gibsons & District Public Library, 470 S Fletcher Rd, Gibsons, BC, V0N 1V0, CANADA. Tel: 604-886-2130. p. 2566

Evans-Perez, Kimberly, Ch Serv, Lilly Library, 19 Meadow St, Florence, MA, 01062. Tel: 413-587-1500. p. 1019

Evans-Perry, Virginia, Librn, San Bernardino Valley College Library, 701 S Mount Vernon Ave, San Bernardino, CA, 92410. Tel: 909-384-8699. p. 214

Evans-Sheppard, Denice, Exec Dir, Oyster Bay Historical Society Library, 20 Summit St, Oyster Bay, NY, 11771. Tel: 516-922-5032. p. 1614

Evavold, Kathy, Curator of Coll, Otter Tail County Historical Society, 1110 Lincoln Ave W, Fergus Falls, MN, 56537. Tel: 218-736-6038. p. 1175

Evenhaugen, Anne, Head Librn, Smithsonian Libraries, Smithsonian American Art Museum/National Portrait Gallery Library, Victor Bldg, Rm 2100, 750 Ninth St NW, Washington, DC, 20560. Tel: 202-633-8227. p. 376

Evenson, Tristyn, Head Librn, Parkland Regional Library-Manitoba, Langruth Branch, 402 Main St, Langruth, MB, R0H 0N0, CANADA. Tel: 204-445-2295. p. 2587

Evensvold, Marty, Dir, Coffeyville Community College, 400 W 11th, Coffeyville, KS, 67337-5064. Tel: 620-252-7022. p. 802

Everett, Andrea, Dir, Human Res, Allegany County Library System, 31 Washington St, Cumberland, MD, 21502. Tel: 301-777-1200. p. 963

Everett, Audra, Dir, Western Sullivan Public Library, 19 Center St, Jeffersonville, NY, 12748. Tel: 845-482-4350. p. 1558

Everett, Claudia, Pub Serv Asst, Chowan University, One University Pl, Murfreesboro, NC, 27855. Tel: 252-398-6212. p. 1705

Everett, Jenny, Mgr, Cobb County Public Library System, Kennesaw Library, 2250 Lewis St, Kennesaw, GA, 30144. Tel: 770-528-2529. p. 489

Everett, Julia B, Dir, Libr Serv, Northeast Alabama Community College, 138 Alabama Hwy 35, Rainsville, AL, 35986. Tel: 256-228-6001, Ext 2226. p. 34

Everett, Peter, Librn, Housatonic Community College Library, 900 Lafayette Blvd, Bridgeport, CT, 06604. Tel: 203-332-5074. p. 304

Everett-Hayes, Lauren, Reference & Collection Mgmt Librn, Juniata College, 1700 Moore St, Huntingdon, PA, 16652-2119. Tel: 814-641-3452. p. 1945

Everhart, Cole, Libr Dir, Towanda Public Library, 620 Highland, Towanda, KS, 67144-9042. Tel: 316-536-2464. p. 840

Everhart, Nancy, Dr, Assoc Prof, Dir, PALM Ctr, Florida State University, College of Communication & Information, 142 Collegiate Loop, Tallahassee, FL, 32306-2100. Tel: 850-644-8122. p. 2783

Everhart, Vanessa, Library Contact, Bennington Library, 300 N Nelson, Bennington, KS, 67422. Tel: 785-416-0097, 785-416-2102. p. 798

Everlove, Nora J, Librn, Rupert J Smith Law Library of Saint Lucie County, 221 S Indian River Dr, Fort Pierce, FL, 34950. Tel: 772-462-2370. p. 405

Everly, Robin, Librn, Smithsonian Libraries, Botany & Horticulture Library, Natural History Bldg, Rm W422, Tenth St & Constitution Ave NW, Washington, DC, 20560. Tel: 202-633-1685. p. 375

Everly, Robin, Librn, Smithsonian Libraries, National Museum of Natural History Library, Tenth St & Constitution Ave NW, 1st Flr, Washington, DC, 20013-0712. Tel: 202-633-1685. p. 375

Everman, Diane M, Archivist, Saul Brodsky Jewish Community Library, 12 Millstone Campus Dr, Saint Louis, MO, 63146. Tel: 314-442-3720. p. 1269

Evermon, Vandy, Tech Serv Librn, Columbia College, 1001 Rogers St, Columbia, MO, 65216. Tel: 573-875-7381. p. 1243

Evers, Linda, Youth Serv, Watauga Public Library, 7109 Whitley Rd, Watauga, TX, 76148-2024. Tel: 817-514-5864. p. 2255

Evers, Renate, Dir of Coll, Center for Jewish History, 15 W 16 St, New York, NY, 10011. Tel: 212-294-8340, 212-744-6400. p. 1580

Eversole, Amy, Ad, Perry County Public Library, 289 Black Gold Blvd, Hazard, KY, 41701. Tel: 606-436-2475, 606-436-4747. p. 858

Eversole, Rachelle J, Libr Dir, Broadwater Public Library, 251 N Starr St, Broadwater, NE, 69125. Tel: 308-262-5960. p. 1309

Everstine, Carrie, Mgr, Libr Serv, Howard Anderson Power Memorial Library, UPMC Magee-Womens Hospital, 300 Halket St, Ste 1205, Pittsburgh, PA, 15213. Tel: 412-641-4288. p. 1996

Eves, Jamie, Historian, Sr Curator, Windham Textile & History Museum, 411 Main St, Willimantic, CT, 06226. Tel: 860-456-2178. p. 347

Eves, Margaret, Mgr, Cobb County Public Library System, Lewis A Ray Library, 4500 Oakdale Rd, Smyrna, GA, 30080. Tel: 770-801-5335. p. 489

Evoy, Bradley, Library Contact, OPIRG Guelph Radical Resource Library, University of Guelph, 24 Trent Lane, Guelph, ON, N1G 2W1, CANADA. Tel: 519-824-2091. p. 2643

Evrard, Carol, Ch, Spencer County Public Library, 210 Walnut St, Rockport, IN, 47635-1398. Tel: 812-649-4866. p. 716

Ewald, Ami, Instrul Serv Librn, Lansing Community College Library, Technology & Learning Ctr, 400 N Capitol Ave, Lansing, MI, 48933. Tel: 517-483-5241. p. 1125

Ewalt, Teri, Dir, Webster Public Library, 800 Main St, Webster, SD, 57274. Tel: 605-345-3263. p. 2085

Ewbank, Ann, PhD, Dr, Assoc Prof, Montana State University, Department of Education, 215 Reid Hall, Bozeman, MT, 59717. Tel: 406-994-6786. p. 2788

Ewell, Lana, Dir, Watauga Public Library, 7109 Whitley Rd, Watauga, TX, 76148-2024. Tel: 817-514-5864. p. 2255

Ewell, Robbi, Dean, Info & Learning Tech, San Diego City College, 1313 Park Blvd, San Diego, CA, 92101. Tel: 619-388-3870. p. 216

Ewen, Bernadette, Sr Dir, Rose-Hulman Institute of Technology, 5500 Wabash Ave, Terre Haute, IN, 47803. Tel: 812-877-8200. p. 721

Ewen, Veronique, Libr Dir, Bibliotheque Ste-Anne, 16 rue de L'Eglise, Sainte Anne, MB, R5H 1H8, CANADA. Tel: 204-422-9958. p. 2590

Ewing, Carol, Head Librn, Massachusetts Trial Court, 649 High St, Ste 210, Dedham, MA, 02026-1831. Tel: 781-329-1401, Ext 2. p. 1014

Ewing, Jennifer, Seminary Library Director, San Diego Christian College & Southern California Seminary Library, c/o San Diego Christian College, 200 Riverview Pkwy, Santee, CA, 92071. Tel: 619-201-8967. p. 245

Ewing, Rick, Dir, Central Virginia Regional Library, 1303 W Third St, Farmville, VA, 23901. Tel: 434-603-6523. p. 2317

Ewing, Stacey, Chair, Library West, University of Florida Libraries, 1545 W University Ave, Gainesville, FL, 32611-7000. Tel: 352-273-2618. p. 407

Ewing, Stacey, Libr Supvr, Plattsmouth Public Library, 401 Ave A, Plattsmouth, NE, 68048. Tel: 402-296-4154. p. 1333

Exley, Piety, Libr Dir, Bristol Library, 6750 County Rd 32, Canandaigua, NY, 14424. Tel: 585-229-5862. p. 1512

Exner, Allen, Dir, Libr Serv, Capitol Technology University, 11301 Springfield Rd, Laurel, MD, 20708. Tel: 301-369-2553. p. 971

Export, Dee, Br Mgr, Madison County Library System, Flora Public Library, 144 Clark St, Flora, MS, 39071. Tel: 601-879-8835. p. 1213

Exposito, Rachel, Exec Dir, Embudo Valley Library, 217A Hwy 75, Dixon, NM, 87527. Tel: 505-579-9181. p. 1467

Exterkamp, Cynthia, Pub Serv, Richard C Sullivan Public Library of Wilton Manors, 500 NE 26th St, Wilton Manors, FL, 33305. Tel: 954-390-2195. p. 455

Eyberg, Ellen, Br Mgr, El Paso Public Library, Richard Burges Regional, 9600 Dyer St, Ste C, El Paso, TX, 79924. Tel: 915-212-0317. p. 2174

Eye, John, Dean of Libr, University of Southern Mississippi Library, 124 Golden Eagle Dr, Hattiesburg, MS, 39406. Tel: 601-266-4362. p. 1218

Eye, John, Dean, Univ Libr, University of Southern Mississippi, 730 E Beach Blvd, Long Beach, MS, 39560-2698. Tel: 228-214-3450. p. 1225

Eyeberg, Cindy, ILL, North Iowa Area Community College Library, 500 College Dr, Mason City, IA, 50401. Tel: 641-422-4232. p. 769

Eyermann, Rachel, Libr Dir, Churubusco Public Library, 116 N Mulberry St, Churubusco, IN, 46723. Tel: 260-693-6466. p. 675

Eynouf, Erica, Dean, Libr Serv, Springfield Technical Community College Library, One Armory Sq, Bldg 27, Ste 1, Springfield, MA, 01105. Tel: 413-755-4064. p. 1057

Eyring, Ardith, Adult Outreach/Prog Coordr, Harnett County Public Library, 601 S Main St, Lillington, NC, 27546-6107. Tel: 910-893-3446. p. 1700

Eystad, Nykol, Lead Librarian, Liaison & Outreach, Walden University Library, 100 Washington Ave S, Ste 900, Minneapolis, MN, 55401. p. 1186

Ezzeal, Linda, Librn, Northwest Regional Library, Weatherford Public Library, 307 Fourth Ave, Red Bay, AL, 35582. Tel: 256-356-9255. p. 40

Ezzy, Kim, Asst Librn, Cataloger, Caribou Public Library, 30 High St, Caribou, ME, 04736. Tel: 207-493-4214. p. 920

Faaborg, Sherri, Sr Sys Specialist, Maryland Institute College of Art, 1401 W Mount Royal Ave, Baltimore, MD, 21217. Tel: 410-225-2304, 410-225-2311. p. 955

Fabbi, Jennifer, Dean of Libr, California State University, 333 S Twin Oaks Valley Rd, San Marcos, CA, 92096. Tel: 760-750-4330. p. 234

Fabbro, Elaine, Dir, Libr & Scholarly Resources, Athabasca University, One University Dr, Athabasca, AB, T9S 3A3, CANADA. Tel: 780-675-6254. p. 2522

Faber, Carissa, Librn, Neponset Public Library, 201 W Commercial St, Neponset, IL, 61345. Tel: 309-594-2204. p. 623

Faber, Carolyn, Colls Librn, School of the Art Institute of Chicago, 37 S Wabash Ave, Chicago, IL, 60603-3103. Tel: 312-899-5097. p. 568

Fabian, Elvin, Circ Coordr, Lawrence Public Library, 51 Lawrence St, Lawrence, MA, 01841. Tel: 978-620-3600. p. 1027

Fabian, Todd, Libr Dir, Concord Public Library, 45 Green St, Concord, NH, 03301. Tel: 603-225-8670. p. 1358

Fabian, Todd, Library Contact, Concord Public Library, Penacook Branch, Three Merrimack St, Penacook, NH, 03303. Tel: 603-753-4441. p. 1358

Fabiano, Lisa, Circ, Ulster County Community College, 491 Cottekill Rd, Stone Ridge, NY, 12484. Tel: 845-687-5213. p. 1646

Fabiku, Adebola, Dept Head, Access Serv, North Carolina State University Libraries, D H Hill Jr Library, Two Broughton Dr, Raleigh, NC, 27695. Tel: 919-515-8263. p. 1709

Fabiszak, Dennis, Exec Dir, East Hampton Library, 159 Main St, East Hampton, NY, 11937. Tel: 631-324-0222, Ext 7. p. 1527

Fabricand-Person, Nicole, Spec, Princeton University, Marquand Library of Art & Archaeology, McCormick Hall, Princeton, NJ, 08544-0001. Tel: 609-258-3783. p. 1437

Fach, Amanda, Adminr, Rowan College of New Jersey, 1400 Tanyard Rd, Sewell, NJ, 08080. Tel: 856-415-2252. p. 1442

Facincani, Greg, Govt Doc, Tech Serv, Rhode Island State Library, State House, Rm 208, 82 Smith St, Providence, RI, 02903. Tel: 401-222-2473. p. 2041

Fack, Amanda, Outreach & Events Librn, Westchester Public Library, 200 W Indiana Ave, Chesterton, IN, 46304. Tel: 219-926-7696. p. 674

Fack, Amanda, Youth Serv, Crown Point Community Library, 122 N Main St, Crown Point, IN, 46307. Tel: 219-663-0270. p. 678

Facklam, Drew, Ms, Metadata Librn, Northeastern University Libraries, 360 Huntington Ave, Boston, MA, 02115. Tel: 617-373-7102. p. 998
Faden, Regina, PhD, Exec Dir, Historic Saint Mary's City, 18751 Hogaboom Ln, Saint Mary's City, MD, 20686. Tel: 240-895-4974. p. 976
Fader, Allison, Outreach & Inclusion Librarian, Shoreline Community College, 16101 Greenwood Ave N, Shoreline, WA, 98133-5696. Tel: 206-533-2548. p. 2383
Fader Samson, Deborah, County Librn, Mendocino County Library District, 880 N Bush St, Ukiah, CA, 95482. Tel: 707-24-2872. p. 254
Faehling, Sharon, Dir, Lincoln County Library, 63 Main St, Pioche, NV, 89043. Tel: 775-962-5244. p. 1348
Fafara, Justine, Libr Dir, Richards Free Library, 58 N Main St, Newport, NH, 03773. Tel: 603-863-3430. p. 1376
Fafara, Justine, Dir, Walpole Town Library, Bridge Memorial Library, 48 Main St, Walpole, NH, 03608. Tel: 603-756-9806. p. 1383
Fafara, Justine, Dir, Walpole Town Library, North Walpole, 70 Church St, North Walpole, NH, 03609. Tel: 603-445-5153. p. 1383
Fagan, Holly Snowden, Libr Dir, Red River Public Library, 702 E Main St, Red River, NM, 87558. Tel: 505-754-6564. p. 1473
Fagan, Mauri Guillen, Dir, Albert & Bessie Mae Kronkosky Library, 515 Main St, Bandera, TX, 78003. Tel: 830-796-4213. p. 2144
Fagan, Nick, Head, Archit Libr, Kent State University Libraries, Joseph F Morbito Architecture Library, 132 S Lincoln St, Rm 110E, Kent, OH, 44242. Tel: 330-672-1637. p. 1792
Fagan, Paula, Dir, Mercer County Library, 601 W Grant St, Princeton, MO, 64673. Tel: 660-748-3725. p. 1266
Fagan, ReLinda, Tech Info Spec, United States Navy, 1000 Kittyhawk Ave, Bldg, Rm 307A 77L, Philadelphia, PA, 19112-1403. Tel: 215-897-7078. p. 1987
Fagan, Robert, Libr Asst, Gardiner Public Library, 152 Water St, Gardiner, ME, 04345. Tel: 207-582-3312. p. 926
Fagbohunka, Bode, Mgr, United States Patent & Trademark Office, 400 Dulany St, Rm 1D58, Alexandria, VA, 22314. Tel: 571-272-3547. p. 2303
Fagen, Diane A, Archivist, Rockford University, 5050 E State St, Rockford, IL, 61108-2393. Tel: 815-226-4000, 815-226-4035. p. 642
Fagerlund, Kirsten, Cat Librn, Bergen County Cooperative Library System, Inc, 21-00 Route 208 S, Ste 130, Fair Lawn, NJ, 07410. Tel: 201-498-7306. p. 2770
Fagg, Keith, Syst Librn, Florida Agricultural & Mechanical University Libraries, 525 Orr Dr, Tallahassee, FL, 32307-4700. Tel: 850-561-2131. p. 446
Fagg, Loretta, Dir, Elwood Township Carnegie Library, 104 N State St, Ridge Farm, IL, 61870. Tel: 217-247-2820. p. 639
Fagg, Rachee, Head, Children's Servx, Head, Youth Serv, Upper Darby Township & Sellers Memorial Free Public Library, 76 S State Rd, Upper Darby, PA, 19082. Tel: 610-789-4440. p. 2016
Faggio, Angela, Br Serv Mgr, Caroline County Public Library, Federalsburg Branch, 123 Morris Ave, Federalsburg, MD, 21632. Tel: 410-754-8397. p. 964
Faggio, Angela, Br Serv Mgr, Caroline County Public Library, Greensboro Branch, 101 Cedar Lane, Greensboro, MD, 21639. Tel: 410-482-2173. p. 964
Fagnan, Deborah, Head, Children's Servx, Ridgefield Park Free Public Library, 107 Cedar St, Ridgefield Park, NJ, 07660. Tel: 201-641-0689. p. 1439
Fagnan, Vivianne, Bibliog Serv Librn, Alberta Legislature Library, 216 Legislature Bldg, 10800-97 Ave NW, Edmonton, AB, T5K 2B6, CANADA. Tel: 780-427-5893. p. 2535
Faherty, John, Exec Dir, Mercantile Library Association, 414 Walnut St, Cincinnati, OH, 45202. Tel: 513-621-0717. p. 1761
Fahey, Cathy, Res & Instruction Librn, Salem State University, 352 Lafayette St, Salem, MA, 01970-5353. Tel: 978-542-7203. p. 1051
Fahey, Sophie, Research Support Librarian, Saint Edwards University, 3001 S Congress Ave, Austin, TX, 78704-6489. Tel: 512-428-1024. p. 2140
Fahey-Flynn, Anna, Cent Libr Mgr, Boston Public Library, 700 Boylston St, Boston, MA, 02116. Tel: 617-859-2385. p. 991
Fahrencamp, Brittany, Adult Programming, Youth Serv, Hazel Mackin Community Library, 311 W Warren St, Roberts, WI, 54023. Tel: 715-749-3849. p. 2474
Faiks, Angi, Libr Dir, Macalester College, 1600 Grand Ave, Saint Paul, MN, 55105-1899. Tel: 651-696-6208. p. 1200
Failor, Jonathan, Dir, Star of the Republic Museum Library, 23200 Park Rd 12, Washington, TX, 77880. Tel: 936-878-2461, Ext 234. p. 2254
Fain, Marikit, Archives Librn, Liaison Librn, John Brown University Library, 2000 W University, Siloam Springs, AR, 72761. Tel: 479-524-7202. p. 110
Fain, Marilyn, Br Librn, McDowell Public Library, Iaeger Branch, 104 W Virginia Ave, Iaeger, WV, 24844. Tel: 304-938-3825. p. 2416
Fair, Betty, Libr Mgr, Kinchafoonee Regional Library System, Quitman County Library, 18 Kaigler Rd, Georgetown, GA, 39854. Tel: 229-334-8972. p. 475
Fairall, Elizabeth, Digital Serv Librn, Palm Beach Atlantic University, 300 Pembroke Pl, West Palm Beach, FL, 33401-6503. Tel: 561-803-2224. p. 453
Fairbairn, Allison, Clinical Librn, London Health Sciences Centre, 800 Commissioners Rd E, London, ON, N6A 4G5, CANADA. Tel: 519-685-8500, Ext 75934. p. 2654
Fairbairn, Mary, Outreach Librn, Furman University Libraries, 3300 Poinsett Hwy, Greenville, SC, 29613-4100. Tel: 864-294-3226. p. 2061
Fairbanks, Daphne, TechLab Coordr, Hope College, Van Wylen Library, 53 Graves Pl, Holland, MI, 49422. Tel: 616-395-7283. p. 1115
Fairbanks, Deb, Librn, Maltman Memorial Public Library, 910 Main St, Wood River, NE, 68883. Tel: 308-583-2349. p. 1341
Fairchild, Lynda, Libr Dir, Waller County Library, 2331 11th St, Hempstead, TX, 77445-6724. Tel: 979-826-7658. p. 2189
Fairchild, Lynda, Libr Dir, Waller County Library, Brookshire Pattison Branch, 3815 Sixth St, Brookshire, TX, 77423. Tel: 281-375-5550. p. 2189
Fairchild, Ron, Ref, Tech Librn, Woodbury Public Library, 269 Main St S, Woodbury, CT, 06798. Tel: 203-263-3502. p. 349
Fairhurst, Alice, Pres, Southern California Genealogical Society, 417 Irving Dr, Burbank, CA, 91504-2408. Tel: 818-843-7247. p. 125
Fairlie, David, Librn, Clarence Public Library, Three Town Pl, Clarence, NY, 14031. Tel: 716-741-2650. p. 1518
Fairnbairn, Allison, Libr Asst, Parkwood Institute Mental Health Care Library, 550- Wellington Rd, London, ON, N6C 5J1, CANADA. Tel: 519-455-5110. p. 2654
Fairtile, Linda, Head Music Librn, University of Richmond, 261 Richmond Way, Richmond, VA, 23173. Tel: 804-287-6849. p. 2342
Fairtile, Linda B, Dr, Head of Libr, University of Richmond, Mary Morton Parsons Music Library, Modlin Ctr for the Arts, 453 Westhampton Way, Richmond, VA, 23173. Tel: 804-287-6849. p. 2342
Faison, Colanda, Br Mgr, Sampson-Clinton Public Library, Miriam B Lamb Memorial, 144 S Church St, Garland, NC, 28441. Tel: 910-529-2441. p. 1681
Faison, Colanda, Br Mgr, Sampson-Clinton Public Library, Roseboro Public Library, 300 W Roseboro St, Roseboro, NC, 28382. Tel: 910-525-5436. p. 1682
Faison, Vernice, Librn, North Carolina Central University, Music, 1801 Fayetteville St, Durham, NC, 27707. Tel: 919-530-6220. p. 1685
Fait, Jennifer, Br Mgr, Milwaukee Public Library, Bay View, 2566 S Kinnickinnic Ave, Milwaukee, WI, 53207. p. 2460
Faithful, Brenda, Dir, Halifax County Library, 33 S Granville St, Halifax, NC, 27839. Tel: 252-583-3631. p. 1694
Faix, Allison, Instruction Coordr, Librn, Coastal Carolina University, 376 University Blvd, Conway, SC, 29526. Tel: 843-349-2511. p. 2056
Fajardo, Maria, Librn, Rainbow Lake Municipal Library, One Atco Rd, Rainbow Lake, AB, T0H 2Y0, CANADA. Tel: 780-956-3656. p. 2551
Fakoornajad, Hannah, Asst Dir, Tri-County Technical College Library, 7900 Hwy 76, Pendleton, SC, 29670. Tel: 864-646-1750. p. 2067
Falasz-Peterson, Amy, Dir, Deerfield Public Library, 920 Waukegan Rd, Deerfield, IL, 60015. Tel: 847-945-3311. p. 577
Falbel, Aaron, Head, Adult Serv, Sunderland Public Library, 20 School St, Sunderland, MA, 01375. Tel: 413-665-2642. p. 1058
Falciani Maldonado, Susan, Spec Coll & Archives Librn, Muhlenberg College, 2400 Chew St, Allentown, PA, 18104-5586. Tel: 484-664-3694. p. 1905
Falciani-White, Nancy, Libr Dir, Randolph-Macon College, 305 Henry St, Ashland, VA, 23005. Tel: 804-752-7256. p. 2306
Falcigno, Kathleen, Staff Librn, IBM Corp, 1101 Kitchawan Rd, Yorktown Heights, NY, 10598. Tel: 914-945-1415. p. 1668
Falcon, Stephanie, Librn, Fabian VanCott, 215 S State St, Ste 1200, Salt Lake City, UT, 84111-2323. Tel: 801-531-8900. p. 2271
Falcone, Andrea, Dean of Libr, Northern Kentucky University, University Dr, Highland Heights, KY, 41099. Tel: 859-572-5457. p. 859
Falcone, Edward, Interim Libr Dir, Pearl River Public Library, 75 E Central Ave, Pearl River, NY, 10965. Tel: 845-735-4084. p. 1616
Falcone, Edward, Dir, Yonkers Public Library, One Larkin Ctr, Yonkers, NY, 10701. Tel: 914-337-1500. p. 1668
Falcone, Elena, Dir, Public Innovation & Engagement, Westchester Library System, 570 Taxter Rd, Ste 400, Elmsford, NY, 10523-2337. Tel: 914-231-3240. p. 1531
Falcone, Francine, Admin Serv, Cedar Grove Free Public Library, One Municipal Plaza, Cedar Grove, NJ, 07009. Tel: 973-239-1447. p. 1395
Falconer, Patty, Ch, Dover Public Library, 73 Locust St, Dover, NH, 03820-3785. Tel: 603-516-6050. p. 1361
Falconer, Shelly, Pres & Chief Exec Officer, Art Gallery of Hamilton, 123 King St W, Hamilton, ON, L8P 4S8, CANADA. Tel: 905-527-6610. p. 2644
Faling, Andrea, Curator, Head, Ref, Nebraska History Library, 1500 R St, Lincoln, NE, 68508. Tel: 402-471-4785. p. 1322
Falk, Carrie, Dir, Shenandoah Public Library, 201 S Elm St, Shenandoah, IA, 51601. Tel: 712-246-2315. p. 781
Falk, Deborah, Head Librn, Parkland Regional Library-Manitoba, Winnipegosis Branch, 130 Second St, Winnipegosis, MB, R0L 2G0, CANADA. Tel: 204-656-4876. p. 2587
Falk, Susan, State Law Librn, Alaska State Court Law Library, 303 K St, Anchorage, AK, 99501. Tel: 907-264-0585. p. 41
Falkenstine, James, Librn, Louisville Free Public Library, Jeffersontown Branch, 10635 Watterson Trail, Jeffersontown, KY, 40299. Tel: 502-267-5713. p. 865
Falkowski, Todd, Cat Librn, Trinity College Library, 300 Summit St, Hartford, CT, 06106. Tel: 860-297-2271. p. 318

Fall, Marcia, Head, Tech Serv, Easttown Library & Information Center, 720 First Ave, Berwyn, PA, 19312-1769. Tel: 610-644-0138. p. 1910

Falla, Beth, Dir, Lied Imperial Public Library, 703 Broadway, Imperial, NE, 69033. Tel: 308-882-4754. p. 1319

Fallen, Robert, Syst Librn, Atlanta University Center, 111 James P Brawley Dr SW, Atlanta, GA, 30314. Tel: 404-978-2058. p. 462

Fallon, Linda, Ad, Beaverton City Library, 12375 SW Fifth St, Beaverton, OR, 97005-2883. Tel: 503-644-2197. p. 1873

Falls, Sarah, Univ Librn, University of North Carolina School of the Arts Library, 1533 S Main St, Winston-Salem, NC, 27127. Tel: 336-770-3270. p. 1726

Falo, Jamie, Dir, Greensburg Hempfield Area Library, 237 S Pennsylvania Ave, Greensburg, PA, 15601-3086. Tel: 724-837-5620. p. 1938

Faltermeier, Denise, Libr Spec, Spartanburg Community College Library, Peeler Academic Bldg, 1st Flr, 523 Chesnee Hwy, Gaffney, SC, 29341. Tel: 864-206-2656. p. 2060

Falvey, Jennifer, Dir, Talking Book Services, South Carolina State Library, 1500 Senate St, Columbia, SC, 29201. Tel: 803-734-8666. p. 2054

Falvey, Jennifer, Dir, South Carolina State Library, 1500 Senate St, Columbia, SC, 29201. Tel: 803-734-4611. p. 2055

Familar, Patricia B, Br Mgr, Albemarle Regional Library, Gates County Public Library, 14 Cypress Creek Dr, Gatesville, NC, 27938-9507. Tel: 252-357-0110. p. 1727

Fance, Kristin, ILL, Ref (Info Servs), Houston Baptist University, 7502 Fondren Rd, Houston, TX, 77074-3298. Tel: 281-649-3304. p. 2194

Fancher, Brooks, IT Mgr, Homewood Public Library, 1721 Oxmoor Rd, Homewood, AL, 35209-4085. Tel: 205-332-6630. p. 21

Fancher, Cathy, Ch, Dudley-Tucker Library, Six Epping St, Raymond, NH, 03077. Tel: 603-895-7057. p. 1379

Fancy, Gwen, Head of Libr, University of Pennsylvania Libraries, Jean Austin duPont Veterinary Medicine Library, New Bolton Ctr, Myrin Bldg, Ground Flr, 382 West Street Rd, Kennett Square, PA, 19348-1692. Tel: 610-925-6835. p. 1988

Fanelli, Michelle, Sr Librn, Aviation Hall of Fame & Museum Library of New Jersey, Teterboro Airport, 400 Fred Wehran Dr, Teterboro, NJ, 07608. Tel: 201-288-6344. p. 1445

Fang, Qian, Asst Dir, Libr Serv, Athens Technical College Library, 800 US Hwy 29 N, Athens, GA, 30601-1500. Tel: 706-355-5164. p. 459

Fang, Wei, Assoc Dean, Info Tech, Rutgers University Library for the Center for Law & Justice, 123 Washington St, Newark, NJ, 07102-3094. Tel: 973-353-3061. p. 1428

Fankhanel, Pam, Libr Mgr, Edberg Public Library, 48 First Ave W, Edberg, AB, T0B 1J0, CANADA. Tel: 780-678-5606. p. 2534

Fann, Lynda, Librn, Steele Public Library, 78 Hillview St, Steele, AL, 35987. Tel: 256-538-0811. p. 36

Fannin, Haley, Ref & Instruction Librn, University of Pikeville, 147 Sycamore St, Pikeville, KY, 41501-9118. Tel: 606-218-5609. p. 872

Fanning, Christopher, Lead Librn, Angelina College Library, 3500 S First St, Lufkin, TX, 75904. Tel: 936-633-5220. p. 2214

Fanshel, William, Evening/Weekend Librn, Harcum College, 750 Montgomery Ave, Bryn Mawr, PA, 19010-3476. Tel: 610-229-9311. p. 1916

Fansler, Bethany, Law Librn, Curt B Henderson Law Library, Russell A Steindam Courts Bldg, 2100 Bloomdale Rd, McKinney, TX, 75071. Tel: 972-424-1460, Ext 4255, 972-424-1460, Ext 4260. p. 2217

Fanslow, Dana, Dir, Nippersink Public Library District, 5418 Hill Rd, Richmond, IL, 60071. Tel: 815-678-4014. p. 638

Fanstill, Katie, Br Mgr, Greensboro Public Library, Kathleen Clay Edwards Family Branch, 1420 Price Park Rd, Greensboro, NC, 27410. Tel: 336-373-2923. p. 1692

Fanta, Andrea, Mkt & Communications Mgr, Nashville Public Library, 615 Church St, Nashville, TN, 37219-2314. Tel: 615-862-5800. p. 2119

Fantroy, LaGena, Librn, National Marine Fisheries Service, NMFS/SE Fisheries Science Ctr, 3209 Frederick St, Pascagoula, MS, 39568. Tel: 228-549-1617, 228-762-4591. p. 1229

Farabaugh, Dana, Dir, Jefferson Hills Public Library, 925 Old Clairton Rd, Jefferson Hills, PA, 15025. Tel: 412-655-7741. p. 1947

Farabaugh, Dede, Libr Dir, Alice Curtis Desmond & Hamilton Fish Library, 472 Rte 403, Garrison, NY, 10524. Tel: 845-424-3020. p. 1537

Farabaugh, Dede, Dir, Putnam Valley Free Library, 30 Oscawana Lake Rd, Putnam Valley, NY, 10579. Tel: 845-528-3242. p. 1625

Faraday, Christine, Chair, Nassau Community College, One Education Dr, Garden City, NY, 11530-6793. Tel: 516-572-7400, 516-572-7401. p. 1537

Farago, Sherry, Supvr, Halton Hills Public Library, Nine Church St, Georgetown, ON, L7G 2A3, CANADA. Tel: 905-873-2681. p. 2642

Farah, Reiz, Children's Serv Coordr, Beth David Congregation, 2625 SW Third Ave, Miami, FL, 33129. Tel: 305-854-3911. p. 421

Farara, Joseph, Exec Dir, Libraries Online, Inc, 100 Riverview Ctr, Ste 252, Middletown, CT, 06457. Tel: 860-347-1704. p. 2762

Fargason, Meshelle, Asst Dean, Louisiana State University Libraries, 295 Middleton Library, Baton Rouge, LA, 70803. Tel: 225-578-2217. p. 884

Farge, James, Curator, Rare Bks, University of Toronto Libraries, Pontifical Institute for Mediaeval Studies, St Michael's College, 113 St Joseph St, 4th Flr, Toronto, ON, M5S 1J4, CANADA. Tel: 416-926-7283. p. 2700

Fargo, Hailley, Student Engagement Coord, Pennsylvania State University Libraries, Library Learning Services, 216 Pattee Tower, University Park, PA, 16802-1803. Tel: 814-865-1850. p. 2015

Farid, Farrukh, Dir, Info Tech, Peninsula Library System, 32 W 25th Ave, Ste 201, Suite 201, San Mateo, CA, 94403-4000. Tel: 650-349-5538. p. 2762

Farid, Hany, Assoc Dean, University of California at Berkeley, 102 South Hall, No 4600, Berkeley, CA, 94720-4600. Tel: 510-642-1464. p. 2782

Farina-Hess, Nadra, Cat Librn, Outreach Serv, Grossmont College Library, 8800 Grossmont College Dr, El Cajon, CA, 92020-1799. Tel: 619-644-7356. p. 139

Farinacci-Gonzalez, Mariko, Mgr, County of Los Angeles Public Library, Anthony Quinn Library, 3965 Cesar E Chavez Ave, Los Angeles, CA, 90063. Tel: 323-264-7715. p. 137

Faris, Crystal, Dir, Teen Serv, The Kansas City Public Library, 14 W Tenth St, Kansas City, MO, 64105. Tel: 816-701-3513. p. 1255

Faris, Naphtali, Br Mgr, Mid-Continent Public Library, Lone Jack Branch, 211 N Bynum Rd, Lone Jack, MO, 64070. Tel: 816-697-2528. p. 1251

Faris, Theresa, Youth Serv Mgr, Round Rock Public Library, 200 E Liberty Ave, Round Rock, TX, 78664. Tel: 512-218-7000, 512-218-7001. p. 2234

Faris, Tim, Curatorial Asst, Educ Coordr, Saginaw Art Museum, 1126 N Michigan Ave, Saginaw, MI, 48602. Tel: 989-754-2491. p. 1147

Farish, Elizabeth, Chief Curator, Strawbery Banke Museum, 14 Hancock St, Portsmouth, NH, 03801. Tel: 603-422-7526. p. 1379

Fariss, Linda, Dir, Indiana University, School of Law Library, Maurer School of Law, 211 S Indiana Ave, Bloomington, IN, 47405. Tel: 812-855-9666. p. 670

Farizo, Kenneth, PhD, Dr, Asst Prof, University of New Orleans, College of Education, Rm 342, New Orleans, LA, 70148. Tel: 504-280-7063. p. 2786

Farkas, Jacky, Ch, Rossford Public Library, 720 Dixie Hwy, Rossford, OH, 43460-1289. Tel: 419-666-0924. p. 1818

Farkas, Julie, Dir, Novi Public Library, 45255 W Ten Mile Rd, Novi, MI, 48375. Tel: 248-349-0720. p. 1138

Farley, Cathy M, Dir, White County Public Library, 11 N Church St, Sparta, TN, 38583. Tel: 931-836-3613. p. 2127

Farley, Celine, Br Librn, Southeast Regional Library, Balgonie Branch, 137 Lewis St, Balgonie, SK, S0G 0E0, CANADA. Tel: 306-771-0044. p. 2753

Farley, Cindy, Chief Financial Officer, Lancaster Public Library, 125 N Duke St, Lancaster, PA, 17602. Tel: 717-394-2651, Ext 130. p. 1951

Farley, Doylenne, Br Mgr, Putnam County Library System, Monterey Branch, 401 E Commercial Ave, Monterey, TN, 38574. Tel: 931-839-2103. p. 2095

Farley, John, Sr Curator, Huntington Museum of Art, 2033 McCoy Rd, Huntington, WV, 25701. Tel: 304-529-2701. p. 2405

Farley, Mandy, Br Mgr, Huntsville-Madison County Public Library, Monrovia Public Library, 254 Allen Drake Dr, Huntsville, AL, 35806. Tel: 256-489-3392. p. 22

Farley, Marian, Dir, Libr Serv, Holy Apostles College & Seminary Library, 33 Prospect Hill Rd, Cromwell, CT, 06416-2005. Tel: 860-632-3011. p. 307

Farley, Marian D, Asst Dir, New Britain Public Library, 20 High St, New Britain, CT, 06051. Tel: 860-224-3155, Ext 114. p. 324

Farley, Nate, VPres, Association of Christian Librarians, PO Box 4, Cedarville, OH, 45314. Tel: 937-766-2255. p. 2772

Farley, Nathan, Syst Librn, University of Northwestern-St Paul, 3003 Snelling Ave N, Saint Paul, MN, 55113. Tel: 651-631-5241. p. 1202

Farley, Teresa, Ref Serv, Florida Supreme Court Library, 500 S Duval St, Tallahassee, FL, 32399-1926. Tel: 850-488-8919. p. 447

Farley, Teresa, Librn, Benton County Law Library, 559 NW Monroe Ave, Corvallis, OR, 97330. Tel: 541-766-6673. p. 1876

Farley, Tobi, Dir, Philmont Public Library, 101 Main St, Philmont, NY, 12565. Tel: 518-672-5010. p. 1617

Farlow, Justine, Pub Serv Coordr, Pulaski County Public Library System, 60 W Third St, Pulaski, VA, 24301. Tel: 540-994-2456. p. 2339

Farmer, Addalee, Prog Coordr, Otterbein Public Library, 23 E First St, Otterbein, IN, 47970. Tel: 765-583-2107. p. 712

Farmer, Austin, Br Mgr, Jackson/Hinds Library System, Raymond Public Library, 126 W Court St, Raymond, MS, 39154. Tel: 601-857-8721. p. 1221

Farmer, Bethany, ILL, Lincoln Memorial University, 6965 Cumberland Gap Pkwy, Harrogate, TN, 37752. Tel: 423-869-7079. p. 2101

Farmer, Jane, Libr Dir, Sea Bright Library, Sea Bright Beach Pavilion, 2nd Fl, 1097 Ocean Ave, Sea Bright, NJ, 07760. Tel: 732-383-8092. p. 1442

Farmer, Kate, Fac Mgr, Western Washington University, 516 High St, MS 9103, Bellingham, WA, 98225. Tel: 360-650-4994. p. 2358

Farnan, Adrienne, ILL Librn, Lebanon-Wilson County Library, Mount Juliet-Wilson County Library, 2765 N Mount Juliet Rd, Mount Juliet, TN, 37122. Tel: 615-758-7051. p. 2109

Farnan, David, Libr & Arts Dir, Boulder Public Library, 1001 Arapahoe Rd, Boulder, CO, 80302. Tel: 303-441-3100. p. 266

Farne, Stephanie, Legal Info Librn & Lecturer in Law, Boston College, 885 Centre St, Newton Centre, MA, 02459. Tel: 617-552-8607. p. 1039

Farney, Tabatha, Dir, Web Serv, University of Colorado Colorado Springs, 1420 Austin Bluffs Pkwy, Colorado Springs, CO, 80918. Tel: 719-255-3079. p. 272

Farnham, Alison, Tech Serv Librn, Wilkinson Public Library, 100 W Pacific Ave, Telluride, CO, 81435. Tel: 970-728-4519. p. 296

Farnham, Jon, Exec Dir, Philadelphia Historical Commission Library, One Parkway, 13th Flr, 1515 Arch St, Philadelphia, PA, 19102. Tel: 215-686-7660. p. 1984

Farnham, Maryann, Dir, Peru Public Library, 102 E Main St, Peru, IN, 46970-2338. Tel: 765-473-3069. p. 713

Farnham, Melodie, Libr Dir, Brevard College, One Brevard College Dr, Brevard, NC, 28712-4283. Tel: 828-641-0433. p. 1675

Farnsworth, Diana, Teen Serv Librn, Anacortes Public Library, 1220 Tenth St, Anacortes, WA, 98221-1988. Tel: 360-293-8067. p. 2357

Farnsworth, Sonja, Dir, Hamilton Public Library, 312 N Davis St, Hamilton, MO, 64644. Tel: 816-583-4832. p. 1247

Farnum, Susan, Youth Serv Mgr, Forest Park Public Library, 7555 Jackson Blvd, Forest Park, IL, 60130. Tel: 708-366-7171. p. 588

Farquahar, Jennifer, Ref Librn, Suffolk County Community College, 533 College Rd, Selden, NY, 11784-2899. Tel: 631-451-4800. p. 1639

Farquhar, Erin, Mgr, District of Columbia Public Library, Palisades, 4901 V St NW, Washington, DC, 20007. Tel: 202-282-3139. p. 364

Farr, Allison, Libr Mgr, Caroline Municipal Library, 5023 50th Ave, Caroline, AB, T0M 0M0, CANADA. Tel: 403-722-4060. p. 2530

Farr, Ann, Dir, Greenbrier County Public Library, 152 Robert W McCormick Dr, Lewisburg, WV, 24901. Tel: 304-647-7568. p. 2407

Farr, Greg, Dir, Archives & Rec Mgt, Archives of the Episcopal Church in Connecticut, The Commons, 290 Pratt St, Box 52, Meriden, CT, 06450. Tel: 203-639-3501, Ext 135. p. 321

Farragher, Kim, Libr Asst, Pomfret Public Library, 449 Pomfret St, Pomfret, CT, 06258. Tel: 860-928-3475. p. 334

Farrales, Cami, Libr Tech, United States Air Force, Bldg 25005, Hansell Ave, Yigo, GU, 96915. Tel: 671-366-4291. p. 2506

Farrar, Christi Showman, Ref Serv, YA, Woburn Public Library, 36 Cummings Park, Woburn, MA, 01801. Tel: 781-933-0148. p. 1070

Farrar, Deborah, Dir, Museum of Early Trades & Crafts Library, Nine Main St, Madison, NJ, 07940. Tel: 973-377-2982, Ext 10. p. 1415

Farrar, Judith, Archives Librn, Spec Coll Librn, University of Massachusetts Dartmouth Library, 285 Old Westport Rd, North Dartmouth, MA, 02747-2300. Tel: 508-999-8686. p. 1041

Farrar, Viola, Librn, West Fairlee Free Public Library, 894 Vt Rte 113, Unit 3, West Fairlee, VT, 05083-4405. Tel: 802-333-3502. p. 2298

Farrel, Kristin, Chief Exec Officer, Tyendinaga Township Public Library, 852 Melrose Rd, Shannonville, ON, K0K 3A0, CANADA. Tel: 613-967-0606. p. 2678

Farrell, Ben, Evening Coordr, University of Oregon Libraries, John E Jaqua Law Library, William W Knight Law Ctr, 2nd Flr, 1515 Agate St, Eugene, OR, 97403. Tel: 541-346-1658. p. 1879

Farrell, Bridget, Associate Dean for Student & Scholar Services, University of Denver, 2150 E Evans Ave, Denver, CO, 80208. Tel: 303-871-3441. p. 277

Farrell, Bridget, Ref (Info Servs), University of Denver, 2150 E Evans Ave, Denver, CO, 80208. Tel: 303-871-3441. p. 277

Farrell Clifford, Elizabeth, Dir, Florida State University Libraries, College of Law Library, 425 W Jefferson St, Tallahassee, FL, 32306. Tel: 850-644-4578. p. 447

Farrell, Emily, Head, Children's Libr, Westbury Memorial Public Library, Children's Library, 374 School St, Westbury, NY, 11590. Tel: 516-333-0176. p. 1663

Farrell, Emily, Chief Exec Officer, Brockville Public Library, 23 Buell St, Brockville, ON, K6V 5T7, CANADA. Tel: 613-342-3936. p. 2634

Farrell, Erin, Sr Librn, California Department of Corrections Library System, Avenal State Prison, One Kings Way, Avenal, CA, 93204. Tel: 559-386-0587. p. 206

Farrell, Jen, Library Services, Staff Coordr, Huron County Community Library, Six W Emerald St, Willard, OH, 44890. Tel: 419-933-8564. p. 1831

Farrell, Kathy, Chief Exec Officer, Librn, Marmora & Lake Public Library, 37 Forsyth St, Marmora, ON, K0K 2M0, CANADA. Tel: 613-472-3122. p. 2656

Farrell, Kelly, Prog Officer, Triangle Research Libraries Network, Wilson Library, CB No 3940, Chapel Hill, NC, 27514-8890. Tel: 919-962-8022. p. 2772

Farrell, Krista, Br Mgr, Jefferson-Madison Regional Library, 201 E Market St, Charlottesville, VA, 22902-5287. Tel: 434-979-7151, Ext 6671. p. 2309

Farrell, Lisa, Dir, Libr Serv, East Central College Library, 1964 Prairie Dell Rd, Union, MO, 63084. Tel: 636-584-6560. p. 1283

Farrell, Lora, Cat, Digital Serv Librn, Kansas City Art Institute Library, 4538 Warwick Blvd, Kansas City, MO, 64111. Tel: 816-802-3394. p. 1255

Farrell, Maggie, Dean, Univ Libr, University of Nevada, Las Vegas University Libraries, 4505 S Maryland Pkwy, Box 457001, Las Vegas, NV, 89154-7001. Tel: 702-895-2111. p. 1347

Farrell, Mary Anne, Head Librn, Delaware Technical & Community College, 400 Stanton-Christiana Rd, Rm D 201, Newark, DE, 19713-2197. Tel: 302-453-3716. p. 355

Farrell, Mary Anne, Pres, Tri-State College Library Cooperative, c/o Rosemont College Library, 1400 Montgomery Ave, Rosemont, PA, 19010. Tel: 610-525-0796. p. 2774

Farrell, Michael, Dir, Reformed Theological Seminary Library, 1231 Reformation Dr, Oviedo, FL, 32765. Tel: 407-278-4635. p. 433

Farrell, Robert, Information Literacy Coord, Libr Assessment Coordr, Lehman College, City University of New York, 250 Bedford Park Blvd W, Bronx, NY, 10468. Tel: 718-960-7761. p. 1499

Farrell, Sandy, Libr Dir, Hobbs Public Library, 509 N Shipp St, Hobbs, NM, 88240. Tel: 575-397-9328. p. 1469

Farrell, Sandy, Dir, Estacado Library Information Network, 509 N Shipp St, Hobbs, NM, 88240. Tel: 575-397-9328. p. 2770

Farrell, Sean, Dir, The Library of Hattiesburg, Petal, Forrest County, 329 Hardy St, Hattiesburg, MS, 39401-3496. Tel: 601-582-4461. p. 1218

Farrell, Shannon, Ref Librn, University of Minnesota Libraries-Twin Cities, Natural Resources Library, 375 Hodson Hall, 1980 Folwell Ave, Saint Paul, MN, 55108. Tel: 612-624-4799. p. 1185

Farrenkopf, Corey, Ad, Asst Dir, Sturgis Library, 3090 Main St, Barnstable, MA, 02630. Tel: 508-362-6636. p. 987

Farrens, Carly, Curator, Archives & Libr, Riley County Historical Museum, 2309 Claflin Rd, Manhattan, KS, 66502. Tel: 785-565-6490. p. 823

Farrer, Jessica, Libr Asst, Mayerthorpe Public Library, 4601 52nd St, Mayerthorpe, AB, T0E 1N0, CANADA. Tel: 780-786-2404. p. 2547

Farrier, Maureen, Br Librn, Crook County Library, Moorcroft Branch, 105 E Converse, Moorcroft, WY, 82721. Tel: 307-756-3232. p. 2499

Farrington, Cardinal, Mgr, University of Nebraska-Lincoln, Panhandle Research & Extension Center, 4502 Ave I, Scottsbluff, NE, 69361. Tel: 308-632-1230. p. 1323

Farrington, James, Head, Pub Serv, University of Rochester, Sibley Music Library, 27 Gibbs St, Rochester, NY, 14604-2596. Tel: 585-274-1350. p. 1631

Farrington, Janet, Dir, Andover Public Library, 46 Church St, Andover, ME, 04216. Tel: 207-392-4841. p. 913

Farrington, Kim, Head, Access Serv & ILL, Central Connecticut State University, 1615 Stanley St, New Britain, CT, 06050. Tel: 860-832-3403. p. 324

Farrington, Lynne, Curator, Spec Coll, University of Pennsylvania Libraries, Kislak Center for Special Collections, Rare Books & Manuscripts, 3420 Walnut St, Philadelphia, PA, 19104. Tel: 215-746-5828. p. 1988

Farris, Janell, Librn II, Port Arthur Public Library, 4615 Ninth Ave, Port Arthur, TX, 77642. Tel: 409-985-8838. p. 2228

Farris, Nick, Nashville Satellite Librn, US Court of Appeals for the Sixth Circuit Library, 540 Potter Stewart US Courthouse, 100 E Fifth St, Cincinnati, OH, 45202-3911. Tel: 615-736-7492. p. 1764

Farrow, Jessie, Br Mgr, Central Rappahannock Regional Library, Porter Branch, 2001 Parkway Blvd, Stafford, VA, 22554-3972. Tel: 540-659-4909. p. 2320

Farry, Colleen, Digital Serv Librn, University of Scranton, 800 Linden St, Scranton, PA, 18510-4634. Tel: 570-941-4831. p. 2005

Farschon, Jan, Br Assoc, Modoc County Library, Cedarville Branch, 460 Main St, Cedarville, CA, 96104. Tel: 530-279-2614. p. 116

Farstad, Sheila, Br Librn, Southeast Regional Library, Bienfait Branch, 414 Main St, Bienfait, SK, S0C 0M0, CANADA. Tel: 306-388-2995. p. 2753

Farthing, Matthew, Dir, Coll Develop, Washtenaw Community College, 4800 E Huron River Dr, Ann Arbor, MI, 48105-4800. Tel: 734-973-3470. p. 1081

Farvour, Jennifer, Dean of Student Success, Marian University, 45 S National Ave, Fond du Lac, WI, 54935-4699. Tel: 920-923-8725. p. 2435

Farwell, Beth, Assoc Librn, Dir, Baylor University Libraries, Arts & Special Collections Research Center, Moody Memorial Library, 1312 S Third St, Waco, TX, 76798. Tel: 254-710-3679. p. 2252

Farwell, Beth, Assoc Dir of Arts & Special Collections, Baylor University Libraries, Moody Memorial Library, 1312 S Third St, Waco, TX, 76798. Tel: 254-710-3679. p. 2253

Farwell, Bob, Exec Dir, Otis Library, 261 Main St, Norwich, CT, 06360. Tel: 860-889-2365. p. 332

Fasanella, Melissa, Head Librn, Greene County Public Library, Xenia Community Library, 76 E Market St, Xenia, OH, 45385-0520. Tel: 937-352-4000. p. 1835

Fascinato, Lynne, Mgr, Libr Serv, Meaford Public Library, 11 Sykes St N, Meaford, ON, N4L 1V6, CANADA. Tel: 519-538-3500. p. 2657

Fashion, Sharon M, Children's Coordr, Dep Dir, Berkeley County Library System, 1003 Hwy 52, Moncks Corner, SC, 29461. Tel: 843-719-4227. p. 2065

Fashion, Valerie, Librn, United States Army, Groninger Library, Bldg 1313, Army Transportation Ctr, Washington Blvd, Fort Eustis, VA, 23604-5107. Tel: 757-878-5017, 757-878-5583. p. 2319

Fassett, Stacie Ann, Library Contact, Gladwin County District Library, Beaverton Branch, 106 Tonkin St, Beaverton, MI, 48612. Tel: 989-435-3981. p. 1109

Fast, Karissa, Children & Teen Librn, Fort Erie Public Library, 136 Gilmore Rd, Fort Erie, ON, L2A 2M1, CANADA. Tel: 905-871-2546, Ext 306. p. 2642

Fast Wolf, Paulina, Dir, Oglala Lakota College, Oglala College Center, PO Box 19, Oglala, SD, 57764. Tel: 605-867-5780. p. 2078

Fasulo, Deb, Asst Dir, Waltham Public Library, 735 Main St, Waltham, MA, 02451. Tel: 781-314-3425. p. 1062

Fasulo, Rebecca, Dir, Corinth Free Library, 89 Main St, Corinth, NY, 12822. Tel: 518-654-6913. p. 1522

Fath, Tammy, Dir, Ashley District Library, 104 N New St, Ashley, MI, 48806. Tel: 989-847-4283, Ext 1007. p. 1081

Fattah, Vera, Br Mgr, Enoch Pratt Free Library, Reisterstown Road Branch, 6310 Reisterstown Rd, Baltimore, MD, 21215-2301. Tel: 443-984-3918. p. 953

Fattig, Karl, Syst & Digital Initiatives Librn, Bowdoin College Library, 3000 College Sta, Brunswick, ME, 04011-8421. p. 919

Fattig, Teri, Dr, Dept Chair, Libr Dir, College of Southern Idaho Library, 315 Falls Ave, Twin Falls, ID, 83301-3367. Tel: 208-732-6500. p. 531

Fattig, Teri, Dr, Dept Chair, Dir, College of Southern Idaho, Gerald R Meyerhoeffer Bldg, Main Flr, 315 Falls Ave, Twin Falls, ID, 83303. Tel: 208-732-6501. p. 2784

Faubert, Russ, Asst Dir, Libr Serv, Urshan College Library, 1151 Century Tel Dr, Wentzville, MO, 63385. Tel: 314-838-8858. p. 1286

Faubion, Susan, Libr Mgr, Timberland Regional Library, Centralia Branch, 110 S Silver St, Centralia, WA, 98531-4218. Tel: 360-736-0183. p. 2388

Faucher, Alexandra, Dir, Elkford Public Library, 816 Michel Rd, Bldg C, Elkford, BC, V0B 1H0, CANADA. Tel: 250-865-2912. p. 2566

Faucher, Linda, Libr Dir, Cary Library, 107 Main St, Houlton, ME, 04730. Tel: 207-532-1302. p. 927

Faughn, Nichelle, Dir, George Coon Public Library, 114 S Harrison St, Princeton, KY, 42445. Tel: 270-365-2884. p. 873

Faugno, Patricia, Libr Asst, Belmar Public Library, 517 Tenth Ave, Belmar, NJ, 07719. Tel: 732-681-0775. p. 1389

Faulhaber, Terri, Tech Serv Librn, Cleveland Law Library, One W Lakeside Ave, 4th Flr, Cleveland, OH, 44113-1078. Tel: 216-861-5070. p. 1767

Faulk, Cameron, Mr, Circ Spec, University of Southern Mississippi, 730 E Beach Blvd, Long Beach, MS, 39560-2698. Tel: 228-214-3414. p. 1225

Faulk, Sara, Info Serv, Mgr, LMI Library, 7940 Jones Branch Dr, Tysons Corner, VA, 22102. Tel: 703-917-7214. p. 2348

Faulkner, Brandi, Librn, Central Arizona College, San Tan Campus Learning Resource Center, 3736 E Bella Vista Rd, San Tan Valley, AZ, 85143. Tel: 480-677-7841. p. 59

Faulkner, Carole Ann, Children's Serv Coordr, Logan County Public Library, 225 Armory Dr, Russellville, KY, 42276. Tel: 270-726-6129. p. 874

Faulkner, Colby, Circ Supvr, Pearl Public Library, 2416 Old Brandon Rd, Pearl, MS, 39208-4601. Tel: 601-932-2562. p. 1229

Faulkner, Emily, Dir, DeKalb Public Library, Haish Memorial Library Bldg, 309 Oak St, DeKalb, IL, 60115-3369. Tel: 815-756-9568. p. 577

Faulkner, Jessica, Br Mgr, Enoch Pratt Free Library, Washington Village Branch, 856 Washington Blvd, Baltimore, MD, 21230. Tel: 410-396-1568. p. 953

Faulkner, Kelly, Asst Dir, Res, Stonehill College, 320 Washington St, Easton, MA, 02357. Tel: 508-565-1329. p. 1016

Faulkner, Kelly, Asst Dean, Libr Serv, Northern Essex Community College, Lawrence Campus Library, 45 Franklin St, Lawrence, MA, 01841. Tel: 978-738-7400. p. 1024

Faulkner, Tenise, Head Librn, Northwest Mississippi Community College, 5197 WE Ross Pkwy, Southaven, MS, 38671. Tel: 662-280-6164. p. 1232

Fauls-Traynor, Karen, Exec Dir, Sullivan Free Library, 101 Falls Blvd, Chittenango, NY, 13037. Tel: 315-687-6331. p. 1518

Fausnaugh, David, Dir, Pickaway County District Public Library, 1160 N Court St, Circleville, OH, 43113-1725. Tel: 740-477-1644, Ext 223. p. 1765

Faust, Aiden, Assoc Dir, Spec Coll & Archives, University of Baltimore, 1420 Maryland Ave, Baltimore, MD, 21201. Tel: 410-837-4334. p. 957

Faust, Bradley D, Asst Dean for Library Data & Discovery Solutions, Ball State University Libraries, 2000 W University Ave, Muncie, IN, 47306-1099. Tel: 765-285-8032. p. 708

Faust, David, Dr, Librn, University of Minnesota Libraries-Twin Cities, Ames Library of South Asia, S-10 Wilson Library, 309 19th Ave S, Minneapolis, MN, 55455. Tel: 612-624-5801. p. 1185

Faust, Diane, Ser Librn, Pittsburgh Theological Seminary, 616 N Highland Ave, Pittsburgh, PA, 15206. Tel: 412-924-1360. p. 1995

Faust, Jeffrey, Dir, Libr Serv, Coastal Alabama Community College, Atmore Campus Library, 2967 AL Hwy 21, Atmore, AL, 36502. Tel: 251-809-1581. p. 6

Faust, Jeffrey, Dir, Libr Serv, Coastal Alabama Community College, Leigh Library, 220 Alco Dr, Brewton, AL, 36426. Tel: 251-809-1581. p. 6

Faust, Kathy, Head, Tech Serv, Lewis & Clark College, Paul L Boley Law Library, Lewis & Clark Law School, 10015 SW Terwilliger Blvd, Portland, OR, 97219. Tel: 503-768-6776. p. 1891

Faust, Keith, Tech Librn, Lafayette College, Kirby Library of Government & Law, Kirby Hall of Civil Rights, 716 Sullivan Rd, Easton, PA, 18042-1797. Tel: 610-330-3117. p. 1928

Faust, Lindsay, Dir, Ida Rupp Public Library, 310 Madison St, Port Clinton, OH, 43452. Tel: 419-732-3212. p. 1816

Faust, Lori, Youth Serv, Warren-Trumbull County Public Library, 444 Mahoning Ave NW, Warren, OH, 44483. Tel: 330-399-8807. p. 1828

Faust, Nancy, Research Librn, Seyfarth Shaw LLP, 233 Wacker Dr, Ste 8000, Chicago, IL, 60606-6448. Tel: 312-460-5000. p. 568

Fava, Tina, Dir & Librn, Miner Memorial Library, Three 2nd NH Tpk, East Lempster, NH, 03605. Tel: 603-863-0051. p. 1362

Fava, Tina, Ch, Marlow Town Library, 12 Church St, Marlow, NH, 03456. Tel: 603-446-3466. p. 1373

Favat, Jodie, Dir, Gibbsboro Public Library, Municipal Bldg, Lower Level, 49 Kirkwood Rd, Gibbsboro, NJ, 08026. Tel: 856-783-6655, Ext 116. p. 1405

Favini, Robert, Head, Libr Advisory & Dev, Massachusetts Board of Library Commissioners, 90 Canal St, Ste 500, Boston, MA, 02114. Tel: 617-725-1860. p. 996

Favor-Dawkins, Linda, Support Serv, Piedmont Technical College Library, Library Resource Room - Edgefield County Campus, 506 Main St, Office Area, Edgefield, SC, 29824. Tel: 803-637-5388. p. 2063

Favors, Myrna, Libr Asst II, City Colleges of Chicago, Wilbur Wright College Library, 4300 N Narragansett Ave, L-200, Chicago, IL, 60634-1500. Tel: 773-481-8400. p. 559

Favreau, Jona, Admin Mgr, Upper Hudson Library System, 28 Essex St, Albany, NY, 12206. Tel: 518-437-9880. p. 1484

Favreau, Lynn, Libr Dir, Madison Public Library, 39 Keep St, Madison, NJ, 07940. Tel: 973-377-0722. p. 1415

Fawcett, Andrea, Ref Librn, Ann & Robert H Lurie Children's Hospital of Chicago, 225 E Chicago Ave, Box 12, Chicago, IL, 60611-2605. Tel: 312-227-4707. p. 564

Fawcett, Judy, ILL, Norton Public Library, One Washington Sq, Norton, KS, 67654. Tel: 785-877-2481. p. 827

Fawcett, Paula, Adult Serv Mgr, Dover Public Library, 525 N Walnut St, Dover, OH, 44622. Tel: 330-343-6123. p. 1782

Fawcett, Tonya, Dir, Libr Serv, Grace College & Grace Theological Seminary, 921 Connection Circle, Winona Lake, IN, 46590. Tel: 574-372-5100, Ext 6291. p. 727

Fawdry, Tracy, Exec Dir, Middlesex Law Association, Ground Flr, Unit N, 80 Dundas St, London, ON, N6A 6A1, CANADA. Tel: 519-679-7046. p. 2654

Fawley, Nancy, Dir, Info Serv, Dir, Instrul Serv, University of Vermont Libraries, 538 Main St, Burlington, VT, 05405-0036. Tel: 802-656-0809. p. 2281

Fay, Brenda, Associate Dean, Collection Services, Marquette University, 1355 W Wisconsin Ave, Milwaukee, WI, 53233. Tel: 414-288-7954. p. 2458

Fay, Jennifer, Assoc Dir, Pub Serv, Salt Lake County Library Services, 8030 S 1825 W, West Jordan, UT, 84088. Tel: 801-943-4636. p. 2274

Fay, Karen, Co-Dir, Addison Public Library, Six South St, Addison, NY, 14801. Tel: 607-359-3888. p. 1481

Fay, Tom, Dir, Prog & Serv, The Seattle Public Library, 1000 Fourth Ave, Seattle, WA, 98104-1109. Tel: 206-386-4636. p. 2379

Fazelian, Jaleh, Assoc Dean of Libr, University of Missouri-Saint Louis Libraries, Thomas Jefferson Library, One University Blvd, Saint Louis, MO, 63121-4400. Tel: 314-516-5060. p. 1276

Fazio, Lauren, AV Serv Librn, Tech Serv, Bryant Library, Two Paper Mill Rd, Roslyn, NY, 11576. Tel: 516-621-2240. p. 1633

Fazio, Wende, Adult Serv, Mary Meuser Memorial Library, 1803 Northampton St, Easton, PA, 18042-3183. Tel: 610-258-3040. p. 1928

Feagin, Christle, Educ Curator, Art Museum of Southeast Texas Library, 500 Main St, Beaumont, TX, 77701. Tel: 409-832-3432. p. 2145

Feagley, Jordan, Mr, Dir, Info Tech, Libr Dir, Reformed Presbyterian Theological Seminary Library, 7418 Penn Ave, Pittsburgh, PA, 15208. Tel: 412-731-6000. p. 1996

Fealy-Layer, Rachael, Ref Librn, Milwaukee Area Technical College, 5555 W Highland Rd, Rm A282, Mequon, WI, 53092-1199. Tel: 262-238-2209. p. 2456

Feanny, Deborah, Mgr, Cobb County Public Library System, Mountain View Regional Library, 3320 Sandy Plains Rd, Marietta, GA, 30066. Tel: 770-509-2725. p. 489

Fearer, Kathleen, Govt Pub Librn, Alaska State Library, 395 Whittier St, Juneau, AK, 99801. Tel: 907-465-2920. p. 47

Fearn, Andrew, Mgr, Portage County District Library, Randolph Branch, 1639 State Rte 44, Randolph, OH, 44265. Tel: 330-325-7003. p. 1787

Fearn, Andrew, Mgr, Portage County District Library, Streetsboro Branch, 8990 Kirby Lane, Streetsboro, OH, 44241-1723. Tel: 330-626-4458. p. 1788

Fearn, Bryan, Library Contact, Multnomah County Library, Gresham Branch, 385 NW Miller Ave, Gresham, OR, 97030. p. 1892

Fearn, Shelley, Juv Serv Coordr, Union County Public Library, 316 E Windsor St, Monroe, NC, 28112. Tel: 704-283-8184. p. 1703

Fearon, Brea, Youth Librn, Chillicothe Public Library District, 430 N Bradley Ave, Chillicothe, IL, 61523-1920. Tel: 309-274-2719. p. 571

Fearon, John, Dir, Mount Pleasant Public Library, 350 Bedford Rd, Pleasantville, NY, 10570. Tel: 914-769-0548, Ext 216. p. 1620

Feather, Sarah, Ch, Lincoln Public Library, Three Bedford Rd, Lincoln, MA, 01773. Tel: 781-259-8465, Ext 205. p. 1028

Featheringil, Shannon, Dir, Seneca East Public Library, 14 N Main St, Attica, OH, 44807. Tel: 419-426-8205. p. 1748

Fecho, Rachel, Ch, William Jeanes Memorial Library, 4051 Joshua Rd, Lafayette Hill, PA, 19444-1400. Tel: 610-828-0441, Ext 104. p. 1950

Fechter, Dawn, Ch Serv Librn, Inglewood Public Library, 101 W Manchester Blvd, Inglewood, CA, 90301-1771. Tel: 310-412-5397. p. 152

Fecteau, Brenda, Tech Serv, Coventry Public Library, 1672 Flat River Rd, Coventry, RI, 02816. Tel: 401-822-9100. p. 2030

Fecteau, Brenda, Librn, Adult Serv, Glocester Libraries, Harmony Library, 195 Putnam Pike, Harmony, RI, 02829. Tel: 401-949-2850. p. 2030

Fecteau, Mary, Adult Serv, Ref Librn, Brewster Ladies' Library, 1822 Main St, Brewster, MA, 02631. Tel: 508-896-3913. p. 1001

Fedden, Elizabeth, Tech Serv & Pub Serv Librn, Institute of American Indian Arts Library, 83 Avan Nu Po Rd, Santa Fe, NM, 87508. Tel: 505-424-2333. p. 1474

Fedden, Elizabeth, Acq Librn, Center for Jewish History, 15 W 16 St, New York, NY, 10011. Tel: 212-294-8340, 212-744-6400. p. 1580

Fedder, Mark, Dir, Manistee County Historical Museum, 425 River St, Manistee, MI, 49660. Tel: 231-723-5531. p. 1129

Fedder, Nicole, Librn, Clearfield County Law Library, Courthouse, 2nd Flr, Ste 228, 230 E Market St, Clearfield, PA, 16830. Tel: 814-765-2641, Ext 2096. p. 1922

Feddern, Donna, Libr Mgr, Timberland Regional Library, Shelton Branch, 710 W Alder St, Shelton, WA, 98584-2571. Tel: 360-426-1362. p. 2389

Fedders, Shari, Dir, Boyden Public Library, 609 Webb St, Boyden, IA, 51234. Tel: 712-725-2281. p. 735

Feddersen, Jeremy, Actg Chief Exec Officer, Okanagan Regional Library, 1430 KLO Rd, Kelowna, BC, V1W 3P6, CANADA. Tel: 250-860-4033, Ext 2471. p. 2568

Fedeler, Julie, ILL Supvr, Wartburg College Library, 100 Wartburg Blvd, Waverly, IA, 50677-0903. Tel: 319-352-8500. p. 789

Feder, Travis, Syst Librn, Connecticut State College & University Library Consortium, 61 Woodland St, Hartford, CT, 06105. Tel: 860-723-0273. p. 2762

Federspiel, Beverly J, Dir, Lockport Public Library, 23 East Ave, Lockport, NY, 14094. Tel: 716-433-5935. p. 1564

Federspiel, Pamela W, Dir, Shelby County Public Library, 309 Eighth St, Shelbyville, KY, 40065. Tel: 502-633-3803. p. 874

Fedorijczuk, Jaroslaw, Ref Librn, Community College of Philadelphia Library, Mint Bldg, Level 1, 1700 Spring Garden St, Philadelphia, PA, 19130. Tel: 215-751-8394. p. 1975

Fedors, Maurica, Mgr, BASF Catalysts Technical Information Center, 25 Middlesex-Essex Tpk, Iselin, NJ, 08830. Tel: 732-205-5269, 732-205-5271. p. 1409

Fedyk, Michele, Libr Dir, Fort Saskatchewan Public Library, 10011 102nd St, Fort Saskatchewan, AB, T8L 2C5, CANADA. Tel: 780-998-4288. p. 2540

Fee, Olivia, Outreach Coordr, Bonner County Historical Society, 611 S Ella Ave, Sandpoint, ID, 83864. Tel: 208-263-2344. p. 530

Fee, William T, Library Advisor for STEM, State Library of Pennsylvania, Forum Bldg, 607 South Dr, Harrisburg, PA, 17120. Tel: 717-783-7014. p. 1941

Feehan, Corinne, Ch Serv, D A Hurd Library, 41 High St, North Berwick, ME, 03906. Tel: 207-676-2215. p. 933

Feeley, Kathryn, Libr Dir, North Castle Public Library, 19 Whippoorwill Rd E, Armonk, NY, 10504. Tel: 914-273-3887, Option 5. p. 1488

Feeley, Kathryn, Dir, Mount Kisco Public Library, 100 E Main St, Mount Kisco, NY, 10549. Tel: 914-666-0935. p. 1574

Feeney, Emer Pond, Asst Dir, Fletcher Free Library, 235 College St, Burlington, VT, 05401. Tel: 802-865-7218. p. 2281

Feeney, Ina, Br Mgr, San Bernardino County Library, Big Bear Lake Branch, 41930 Garstin Dr, Big Bear Lake, CA, 92315. Tel: 909-866-5571. p. 212

Feeney, James, Jr, Head, Circ, Boston Athenaeum, Ten 1/2 Beacon St, Boston, MA, 02108-3777. Tel: 617-227-0270. p. 991

Feeney, Sylvia, Librn, US Department of Commerce, National Oceanic & Atmospheric Administration, 212 Rogers Ave, Milford, CT, 06460. Tel: 203-882-6509. p. 323

Feeney-Patten, Martha, Dir, Gleason Public Library, 22 Bedford Rd, Carlisle, MA, 01741-1857. Tel: 978-369-4898. p. 1009

Fegley, Lydia, Librn, Somerset County Historical Society, Nine Van Veghten Dr, Bridgewater, NJ, 08807. Tel: 908-218-1281. p. 1392

Fegter, Brant, Librn, Jennifer Reinke Public Library, 311 E Pearl St, Deshler, NE, 68340. Tel: 402-365-4107. p. 1312

Fehd, Darrell, Dir, Wyocena Public Library, 165 E Dodge St, Wyocena, WI, 53969. Tel: 608-429-4899. p. 2490

Fehn, Casey, YA Serv, Rogers Memorial Library, 91 Coopers Farm Rd, Southampton, NY, 11968. Tel: 631-283-0774. p. 1643

Fehr, Rebecca, Br Librn, Wapiti Regional Library, Vonda Public Library, 204 Main St, Vonda, SK, S0K 4N0, CANADA. Tel: 306-258-2035. p. 2746

Fehr, Trudy, Libr Mgr, Wrentham Public Library, 101 Carrigan Ave, Wrentham, AB, T0K 2P0, CANADA. Tel: 403-222-2485. p. 2560

Fehrer, Patricia, Supvr, Yakima Valley Libraries, Tieton Library, 418 Maple St, Tieton, WA, 98947. Tel: 509-673-2621. p. 2396

Feighery, Julie, Archivist, Head, Scholarly Communications, Subj Librn, Indiana University South Bend, 1700 Mishawaka Ave, South Bend, IN, 46615. Tel: 574-520-4410. p. 718

Feightner, Rebecca, Exec Dir, Bradford Area Public Library, 67 W Washington St, Bradford, PA, 16701-1234. Tel: 814-362-6527. p. 1914

Feikert, Eric, Cataloging & Metadata Librn, Creighton University, Health Sciences Library-Learning Resource Center, 2770 Webster St, Omaha, NE, 68178-0210. Tel: 402-280-5142. p. 1328

Feilmeyer, Kimberly, Ref (Info Servs), Hamline University, Bush Memorial Library, 1536 Hewitt, Saint Paul, MN, 55104. Tel: 651-523-2375. p. 1199

Fein, Michael T, Coordr, Libr Serv, Central Virginia Community College Library, Bedford Hall, Rm 3100, 3506 Wards Rd, Lynchburg, VA, 24502-2498. Tel: 434-832-7751. p. 2330

Feinberg, Beth, Sr Librn, Los Angeles Public Library System, Pio Pico-Koreatown Branch Library, 694 S Oxford Ave, Los Angeles, CA, 90005-2872. Tel: 213-368-7647. p. 165

Feinberg, Jennie, Head, Tech Serv, Augusta-Richmond County Public Library, 823 Telfair St, Augusta, GA, 30901. Tel: 706-821-2600. p. 466

Feinman, Rachel, Head, Cataloging & Collection Dev, Rhodes College, 2000 North Pkwy, Memphis, TN, 38112-1694. Tel: 901-843-3890. p. 2114

Feinsilber, Rebecca, Youth Serv Librn, Boynton Beach City Library, 115 N Federal Hwy, Boynton Beach, FL, 33435. Tel: 561-742-6390. p. 386

Feinsilber, Rebecca, Sr Librn, Acq, Lee County Library System, Library Processing, 881 Gunnery Rd N, Ste 2, Lehigh Acres, FL, 33971-1246. Tel: 239-533-4170. p. 403

Feis, Nathaniel, Cat & Acq, School of the Art Institute of Chicago, 37 S Wabash Ave, Chicago, IL, 60603-3103. Tel: 312-899-5097. p. 568

Fejedelem, Jake, Head Librn, Bird Island Public Library, 260 S Main St, Bird Island, MN, 55310-1226. Tel: 320-365-4640. p. 1165

Fejedelem, Jake, Head Librn, Fairfax Public Library, 101 First St SE, Fairfax, MN, 55332. Tel: 507-426-7269. p. 1174

Fejedelem, Jake, Head Librn, Olivia Public Library, 405 S Tenth St, Olivia, MN, 56277-1287. Tel: 320-523-1738. p. 1191

Fejedelem, Jake, Head Librn, Renville City Library, 221 N Main St, Renville, MN, 56284. Tel: 320-329-8193. p. 1194

Fejedelen, Jake, Head Librn, Hector Public Library, 126 S Main St, Hector, MN, 55342. Tel: 320-848-2841. p. 1178

Felchlin, Marva, Dir, Autry National Center, Autry Library, 4700 Western Heritage Way, Los Angeles, CA, 90027-1462. Tel: 323-667-2000, Ext 349. p. 160

Felde, Juliette, Libr Dir, City College Library - Fort Lauderdale, 2000 W Commercial Blvd, Ste 200, Fort Lauderdale, FL, 33309-3001. Tel: 954-492-5353. p. 401

Felde, Karen, Dir, Crooked Tree District Library, Boyne Falls Branch, 3008 Railroad St, Boyne Falls, MI, 49713. Tel: 231-549-2277. p. 1157

Felder, Doris J, Govt Doc Coordr, Ref & Info Spec, South Carolina State University, 300 College St NE, Orangeburg, SC, 29115. Tel: 803-536-8642. p. 2067

Felder, Timothy, Media Res Coordr, Orangeburg-Calhoun Technical College Library, 3250 Saint Matthews Rd NE, Orangeburg, SC, 29118. Tel: 803-535-1262. p. 2066

Felder, Tracey, Assoc Librn, Cataloging & Periodicals, Center for Jewish History, 15 W 16 St, New York, NY, 10011. Tel: 212-294-8340, 212-744-6400. p. 1580

Feldman, Annette, Dir, Louttit Library, 274 Victory Hwy, West Greenwich, RI, 02817. Tel: 401-397-3434. p. 2043

Feldman, Ellen, Access Serv, Head, Admin Serv, George Mason University Libraries, Law Library, 3301 N Fairfax Dr, Arlington, VA, 22201-4426. Tel: 703-993-8100. p. 2317

Feldman, Evelyn, Head, Coll Serv, Lakehead University, 955 Oliver Rd, Thunder Bay, ON, P7B 5E1, CANADA. Tel: 807-343-8856. p. 2685

Feldman, Genevieve, Br Mgr, San Francisco Public Library, Potrero Branch Library, 1616 20th St, San Francisco, CA, 94107-2811. Tel: 415-355-2822. p. 228

Feldman, Jennifer, Librn, Cleveland Clinic Akron General, One Akron General Ave, 2nd Flr, Rm 2202, Akron, OH, 44307. Tel: 330-344-6242. p. 1744

Feldman-Joy, Barbara, Librn, Miami Dade College, Kendall Campus Library, 11011 SW 104th St, Miami, FL, 33176-3393. Tel: 305-237-0996, 305-237-2015, 305-237-2291. p. 422

Feldmann, Christine, Mkt & Communications Mgr, Anne Arundel County Public Library, Five Harry Truman Pkwy, Annapolis, MD, 21401. Tel: 410-222-2523. p. 950

Feldt, Dennis, Dir, United States Department of Justice, 950 Pennsylvania Ave, Ste 5313, Washington, DC, 20530. Tel: 202-514-2133. p. 378

Feldt, Keith, Br Mgr, Phoenix Public Library, Harmon Library, 1325 S Fifth Ave, Phoenix, AZ, 85003. p. 72

Felice, Kayleigh, Outreach Librn, Bibliothèque Municipale de Gatineau, Ville de Gatineau, CP 1970 Succ. Hull, Gatineau, QC, J8X 3Y9, CANADA. Tel: 819-243-2345. p. 2712

Feliciano, Breanna, Ref Supvr, Napa County Library, 580 Coombs St, Napa, CA, 94559-3396. Tel: 707-265-2787. p. 182

Feliciano Garcia, Mariam, Interim Asst Dir, University of Puerto Rico Library System, Rio Piedras Campus, San Juan, PR, 00931. Tel: 787-764-0000, Ext 5085, 787-764-0000, Ext 5086, 787-764-0000, Ext 5087. p. 2514

Feliciano, Mariam, Chief Librn, University of Puerto Rico Library System, Public Administration & Periodicals Library, Rio Piedras Campus, Carmen Rivera de Alvarado Bldg, 2nd Flr, San Juan, PR, 00931. Tel: 787-764-0000, Ext 85903, 787-764-0000, Ext 85904. p. 2515

Felicie, Ada Myriam, Chief Librn, University of Puerto Rico Library System, Monserrate Santana de Pales Library, Rio Piedras Campus, Graduate School of Social Work, Beatriz Lassalle Bldg, 2nd Flr, San Juan, PR, 00931. Tel: 787-764-0000, Ext 85910. p. 2515

Felis, Edith, Head, Circ, Somers Library, Rte 139 & Reis Park, Somers, NY, 10589. Tel: 914-232-5717. p. 1642

Feliu, Vicenc, Assoc Dean, Libr Serv, Nova Southeastern University Libraries, Panza Maurer Law Library, Shepard Broad College of Law, Leo Goodwin Sr Bldg, 3305 College Ave, Davie, FL, 33314. Tel: 954-262-6100. p. 402

Feliu, Vinenc, Dir, University of the District of Columbia, David A Clarke School of Law, Charles N & Hilda H M Mason Law Library, Bldg 39, Rm B-16, 4200 Connecticut Ave NW, Washington, DC, 20008. Tel: 202-274-7354. p. 380

Felix, Brandon, Br Mgr, Albuquerque-Bernalillo County Library System, South Valley Library, 3904 Isleta SW, Albuquerque, NM, 87105. Tel: 505-877-5170. p. 1460

Felix, Michael, Libr Mgr, Mesa Community College Library, 1833 W Southern Ave, Mesa, AZ, 85202. Tel: 480-461-7677. p. 66

Felix, Michael, Libr Spec Supvr, Mesa Community College, Paul A Elsner Library, 1833 W Southern Ave, Mesa, AZ, 85202. Tel: 480-461-7686. p. 2781

Fellows, Mary, Mgr, Youth & Family Serv, Upper Hudson Library System, 28 Essex St, Albany, NY, 12206. Tel: 518-437-9880, Ext 228. p. 1484

Fellows, Sharon, Historian, Cattaraugus County Museum & Research Library, 9824 Rte 16, 1st Flr, Machias, NY, 14101. Tel: 716-353-8200. p. 1567

Fells, Matthew, Archivist, Simcoe County Archives, 1149 Hwy 26, Minesing, ON, L9X 0Z7, CANADA. Tel: 705-726-9300, Ext 1285. p. 2658

Fels, Amy, Archivist, Oshkosh Public Museum Library, 1331 Algoma Blvd, Oshkosh, WI, 54901-2799. Tel: 920-236-5799. p. 2467

Feltmann, Howard, Librn II, Monmouth Public Library, 168 S Ecols St, Monmouth, OR, 97361. Tel: 503-838-1932. p. 1887

Feltner, Kimberly, Br Mgr, Dir, Pub Serv, Branch District Library, Ten E Chicago St, Coldwater, MI, 49036-1615. Tel: 517-278-2341, Ext 123. p. 1092

Felton, Alexandra, Librn, Cochise College Library, Andrea Cracchiolo Library, Bldg 900, 901 N Colombo Ave, Sierra Vista, AZ, 85635. Tel: 520-515-5320. p. 59

Felton, Jason, Libr Syst & Applications Librn, Pacific University Libraries, 2043 College Way, Forest Grove, OR, 97116. Tel: 503-352-1407. p. 1880

Feltren, Kate, Curator, Chilliwack Museum & Historical Society, 9291 Corbould St, Chilliwack, BC, V2P 4A6, CANADA. Tel: 604-795-5210, Ext 105. p. 2565

Felts, John, Head, Coll, Head, Info Tech, Coastal Carolina University, 376 University Blvd, Conway, SC, 29526. Tel: 843-349-2400. p. 2056

Felty, Jayson, Librn, Jackson Laboratory, 600 Main St, Bar Harbor, ME, 04609-1500. Tel: 207-288-6083. p. 916

Felty, Jayson L, Dir, Libr & Info Serv, Texas Biomedical Research Institute, 8715 W Military Dr, San Antonio, TX, 78227-5301. p. 2239

Felty, Stephanie, Circ Supvr, Northern Kentucky University, Nunn Dr, Highland Heights, KY, 41099. Tel: 859-572-5715. p. 859

Felver, Richard A, Dir, Berkshire Community College, 1350 West St, Pittsfield, MA, 01201. Tel: 413-236-2151. p. 1046

Fender, Pattie, Adult Literacy Coordr, ESL Coordr, Greenwood County Library, 600 S Main St, Greenwood, SC, 29646. Tel: 864-941-3044. p. 2062

Fenderson, Evelyn, Libr Asst, Southside Virginia Community College Libraries, 109 Campus Dr, Alberta, VA, 23821. Tel: 434-949-1065. p. 2302

Fenelon, Pauline, Curator, Librn, Waseca County Historical Society, 315 Second Ave NE, Waseca, MN, 56093. Tel: 507-835-7700. p. 1207

Feng, Vivien, Librn, Langara College Library, 100 W 49th Ave, Vancouver, BC, V5Y 2Z6, CANADA. Tel: 604-323-5462. p. 2579

Feng, Yali, Librn, University of Illinois Library at Urbana-Champaign, Social Sciences, Health & Education Library, 101 Main Library, MC-522, 1408 W Gregory Dr, Urbana, IL, 61801. Tel: 217-300-6619. p. 656

Fenger, Michelle, Dir, Ronan Library District, 203 Main St SW, Ronan, MT, 59864. Tel: 406-676-3682. p. 1301

Fenimore, Jason, Ref Librn, Louis B Goodall Memorial Library, 952 Main St, Sanford, ME, 04073. Tel: 207-324-4714. p. 939

Fenn, Jessica, Instr Librn, Cumberland University, One Cumberland Sq, Lebanon, TN, 37087. Tel: 615-547-1302. p. 2108

Fenn, Joann, Ch, Montrose Public Library, 200 Main St, Montrose, IA, 52639. Tel: 319-463-5532. p. 771

Fennell, Brandi, Libr Asst, Vernonia Public Library, 701 Weed Ave, Vernonia, OR, 97064-1102. Tel: 503-429-1818. p. 1901

Fennell, Kathy, Dir of Finance, Aurora Public Library District, 101 S River St, Aurora, IL, 60506. Tel: 630-264-4118. p. 539

Fennell, Rose, Superintendent, US Department of Interior, National Park Service, Two Mark Bird Lane, Elverson, PA, 19520. Tel: 610-582-8773, Ext 240. p. 1930

Fennell, Ryan, Br Mgr, Harris County Public Library, Kingwood Branch, 4400 Bens View Lane, Kingwood, TX, 77339. Tel: 832-927-7830. p. 2193

Fennell, Sean, Dir, Commun Relations, Mkt, Muskingum County Library System, 220 N Fifth St, Zanesville, OH, 43701-3587. Tel: 740-453-0391, Ext 121. p. 1836

Fennell, Stephanie, Mgr, Durham County Library, North Regional, 221 Milton Rd, Durham, NC, 27712. Tel: 919-560-0243. p. 1685

Fennema, Audrey, Chief Librn, Fraser Lake Public Library, 228 Endako Ave, Fraser Lake, BC, V0J 1S0, CANADA. Tel: 250-699-8888. p. 2566

Fenno-Smith, Kyzyl, Assoc Librn, California State University, East Bay Library, CSU East Bay Library, 25800 Carlos Bee Blvd, Hayward, CA, 94542-3052. Tel: 510-885-2974. p. 150

Fenters, Courtney, Librn, Dillwyn Correctional Center Library, 1522 Prison Rd, Dillwyn, VA, 23936. Tel: 434-983-4200. p. 2315

Fenton, Amanda, Asst Dir, Vols Coordr, Chelsea Public Library, 16623 US 280, Chelsea, AL, 35043. Tel: 205-847-5750. p. 12

Fenton, Lori, Head, Tech Serv, Librn, Washburn University, 1700 SW College Ave, Topeka, KS, 66621. Tel: 785-670-1984. p. 839

Fenton-Stone, Christine, Libr Tech, Grey Bruce Health Services, 1800 Eighth St E, Owen Sound, ON, N4K 6M9, CANADA. Tel: 519-376-2121, Ext 2043. p. 2671

Fentress, Steve, Dir, Rochester Museum & Science Center Library, 657 East Ave, Rochester, NY, 14607. Tel: 585-271-4320, Ext 315. p. 1630

Fenwick, Bradley, Dir, Support Serv, Hutchinson Community College, 1300 N Plum St, Hutchinson, KS, 67501. Tel: 620-665-3547. p. 814

Ferber, Susan, Adult Programs, West Nyack Free Library, 65 Strawtown Rd, West Nyack, NY, 10994. Tel: 845-358-6081. p. 1662

Ferdman, Glenn, Libr Dir, Beaverton City Library, 12375 SW Fifth St, Beaverton, OR, 97005-2883. Tel: 503-644-2197. p. 1873

Ferdon, Joel, Dir, Libr Serv, Stanly Community College Library, Snyder Bldg, 141 College Dr, 1st Flr, Albemarle, NC, 28001. Tel: 704-991-0261. p. 1671

Ferdula, Tammy-Jo, Dir, United States Navy, Base Library, Naval Submarine Base New London, Bldg 164, Groton, CT, 06349. Tel: 860-694-2578, 860-694-3723. p. 315

Ferencz, Sarah, Archivist, Whitby Public Library, Whitby Archives, 405 Dundas St W, Whitby, ON, L1N 6A1, CANADA. Tel: 905-668-6531, Ext 6. p. 2704

Fereres-Moskowitz, Raquel, Project Coordr, Long Island Jewish Medical Center, Schwartz Research Bldg, 270-05 76th Ave, New Hyde Park, NY, 11040. Tel: 718-470-7356. p. 1576

Fergus, Alex, Ref Archivist, Northwest Museum of Art & Culture-Eastern Washington State Historical Society, 2316 W First Ave, Spokane, WA, 99201-1099. Tel: 509-363-5313, 509-363-5342. p. 2384

Fergus, Liz, Librn, Lenawee District Library, Clayton Branch, 3457 State St, Clayton, MI, 49235-9205. Tel: 517-445-2619. p. 1075

Ferguson, Alex, Med Librn, Covenant Health System, 3615 19th St, Lubbock, TX, 79410. Tel: 806-725-0602. p. 2213

Ferguson, Alexandra, Coll Mgt Librn, Haut-Saint-Jean Regional Library, 15 rue de l'Eglise St, Ste 102, Edmundston, NB, E3V 1J3, CANADA. Tel: 506-735-2074. p. 2600

Ferguson, Amy, Health Sci Librn, Parker University Library, 2540 Walnut Hill Lane, Dallas, TX, 75220. Tel: 972-438-6932, Ext 1846. p. 2167

Ferguson, Amy, Br Mgr, Whitman County Rural Library District, Albion Branch, 310 F St, Albion, WA, 99102. Tel: 509-338-9641. p. 2362

Ferguson, Benjamin, Tech Serv Librn, Valley City State University Library, 101 College St SW, Valley City, ND, 58072-4098. Tel: 701-845-7277. p. 1740

Ferguson, Bernice, Librn, Carnegie Regional Library, Michigan Public, PO Box 331, Michigan, ND, 58259. Tel: 701-259-2122. p. 1734

Ferguson, Cris, Asst Dean, Dir, Tech Serv, Murray State University, 205 Waterfield Library, Dean's Office, Murray, KY, 42071-3307. Tel: 270-809-5607. p. 870

Ferguson, Cristie, Dir, Libr Serv, Panola College, 1109 W Panola St, Carthage, TX, 75633. Tel: 903-693-2091. p. 2154

Ferguson, Donna, Libr Syst Adminr, Sequoyah Regional Library System, 116 Brown Industrial Pkwy, Canton, GA, 30114. Tel: 770-479-3090. p. 469

Ferguson, Frank, Head, Info & Tech, Plymouth District Library, 223 S Main St, Plymouth, MI, 48170-1687. Tel: 734-453-0750, Ext 239. p. 1141

Ferguson, Heather, Mgr, Spec Coll, San Antonio Public Library, Texana & Genealogy, 600 Soledad, San Antonio, TX, 78205-2786. Tel: 210-207-2559. p. 2239

Ferguson, Jeff, Academic Support & Services Desk Mgr, Thomas College Library, 180 W River Rd, Waterville, ME, 04901. Tel: 207-859-1204. p. 945

Ferguson, Jessame, Assoc Dir, Res & Teaching Assoc, Montgomery College Library, 51 Mannakee St, Macklin Tower, Rockville, MD, 20850. Tel: 240-567-7137. p. 973

Ferguson, Jill, Chief Exec Officer, Librn, Billings Township Public Library, 18 Upper St, Kagawong, ON, P0P 1J0, CANADA. Tel: 705-282-2944. p. 2648

Ferguson, Kathleen, Pub Serv, Ridley Township Public Library, 100 E MacDade Blvd, Folsom, PA, 19033-2592. Tel: 610-583-0593. p. 1933

Ferguson, Kristine, Access Serv Mgr, Old Lyme, Two Library Lane, Old Lyme, CT, 06371. Tel: 860-434-1684. p. 333

Ferguson, Linda, Librn, Pocahontas Public Library, 14 Second Ave NW, Pocahontas, IA, 50574. Tel: 712-335-4471. p. 777

Ferguson, Mark, Libr Dir, Saint Elizabeth University, Two Convent Rd, Morristown, NJ, 07960-6989. Tel: 973-290-4238. p. 1422

Ferguson, Michele, Ch, Mustang Public Library, 1201 N Mustang Rd, Mustang, OK, 73064. Tel: 405-376-2226. p. 1854

Ferguson, Nancy, Libr Asst, Trinity County Library, Hayfork Branch, 6641A State Hwy 3, Hayfork, CA, 96041. Tel: 530-628-5427. p. 258

Ferguson, Robin, Libr Tech, Phoenix VA Health Care System, 650 E Indian School Rd, Phoenix, AZ, 85012. Tel: 602-222-6411. p. 72
Ferguson, Sarah, Dean, Dallas College, Bldg L, 3939 Valley View Lane, Farmers Branch, TX, 75244-4997. Tel: 972-860-4854. p. 2176
Ferguson, Sean, Libr Mgr, New York Public Library - Astor, Lenox & Tilden Foundations, Chatham Square Branch, 33 E Broadway, (Near Catherine St), New York, NY, 10002-6804. Tel: 212-964-6598. p. 1595
Ferguson, Stephanie, Br Mgr, Southern Oklahoma Library System, Wilson Public Library, 1087 US Hwy 70A, Wilson, OK, 73463. Tel: 580-668-2486. p. 1841
Ferguson, Stephen, Assoc Univ Librn, External Engagement, Princeton University, One Washington Rd, Princeton, NJ, 08544-2098. Tel: 609-258-3165. p. 1437
Ferguson, Teresa, Tech Serv Mgr, Tigard Public Library, 13500 SW Hall Blvd, Tigard, OR, 97223-8111. Tel: 503-684-6537, Ext 2505. p. 1900
Ferguson, Terrye, Ch, Co-Dir, Sterling County Public Library, 301 Main St, Sterling City, TX, 76951. Tel: 325-378-2212. p. 2246
Ferguson, Vicki L, Libr Dir, Wheeler Public Library, 306 S Canadian St, Wheeler, TX, 79096. Tel: 806-826-5977. p. 2257
Ferguson, Victoria, Br Adminr, Noble County Public Library, East, 104 Ley St, Avilla, IN, 46710. Tel: 260-897-3900. p. 667
Ferguson, Victoria, Br Mgr, Kendallville Public Library, Limberlost Public Library, 164 Kelly St, Rome City, IN, 46784. Tel: 260-854-2775. p. 698
Ferguson, Yoko, Cataloging & Metadata Librn, University of the District of Columbia, Learning Resources Division, 4200 Connecticut Ave NW, Bldg 39, Level B, Washington, DC, 20008. p. 380
Ferkol, Holly, Br Mgr, Willoughby-Eastlake Public Library, Willoughby Hills Branch, 35400 Chardon Rd, Willoughby Hills, OH, 44094. Tel: 440-942-3362. p. 1783
Ferkovich, Kelly, Libr Coord, Legacy Emanuel Hospital & Health Center Library, 2801 N Gantenbein Ave, Portland, OR, 97227. Tel: 503-413-2558. p. 1891
Ferlito, Carol, Dir, Oswego Public Library, 120 E Second St, Oswego, NY, 13126. Tel: 315-341-5867. p. 1613
Fernandes, Alex, Ms, Colls Mgr, American Museum of Natural History Library, Osborn Library, 200 Central Park W, New York, NY, 10024. Tel: 212-769-5068. p. 1578
Fernandes, Susana Martins, Bibliothecaire Responsable, Bibliotheques de Montreal, Jacqueline-De Repentigny, 5955 rue Bannantyne, Verdun, QC, H4H 1H6, CANADA. Tel: 514-765-7125. p. 2719
Fernandes, Zara, Mgr, Knowledge Mgt Serv, Proskauer Rose LLP Library, 11 Times Sq, New York, NY, 10036. Tel: 212-969-3000, 212-969-5001. p. 1600
Fernandez, Elena, Head, Tech Serv, Woodbridge Town Library, Ten Newton Rd, Woodbridge, CT, 06525. Tel: 203-389-3436. p. 349
Fernandez, Emma, Instruction Librn, Stephens College, 1200 E Broadway, Columbia, MO, 65215. Tel: 573-441-5129. p. 1243
Fernandez, Jacqueline Lauren, Human & Financial Resources, Albuquerque-Bernalillo County Library System, 501 Copper Ave NW, Albuquerque, NM, 87102. Tel: 505-768-5113. p. 1460
Fernandez, Karen, Ref Librn, Highline College Library, 2400 S 240th St, MS 25-4, Des Moines, WA, 98198. Tel: 206-592-3809. p. 2363
Fernandez, Mary Anne, Library Contact, Texas Scottish Rite Hospital, 2222 Welborn St, Dallas, TX, 75219. Tel: 214-559-5000, 214-559-7573. p. 2168
Fernandez, Natalia, Multicultural Librn, Oregon State University Libraries, Special Collections & Archives Research Center, 121 The Valley Library, 5th Flr, Corvallis, OR, 97331. Tel: 541-737-3653. p. 1877
Fernandez, Robert, Coll Develop Librn, Prince George's Community College Library, 301 Largo Rd, Largo, MD, 20774-2199. Tel: 301-546-7566. p. 970
Fernandez, Stephanie, Ch, Passaic Public Library, 195 Gregory Ave, Passaic, NJ, 07055. Tel: 973-779-0474. p. 1433
Fernandez, Tina, Br Asst, Elko-Lander-Eureka County Library System, West Wendover Branch Library, 590 Camper Dr, West Wendover, NV, 89883. Tel: 775-664-2510. p. 1345
Fernandez-Baybay, Carmen, Asst Dean, Bus Mgr, University of San Francisco, 2130 Fulton St, San Francisco, CA, 94117-1080. Tel: 415-422-2035. p. 229
Fernandez-Keys, Alba, Head, Libr & Archives, Indianapolis Museum of Art at Newfields, 4000 Michigan Rd, Indianapolis, IN, 46208-3326. Tel: 317-923-1331, Ext 547. p. 693
Fernett, Laura, Br Librn, Fayette County Public Libraries, Oak Hill Branch, 611 Main St, Oak Hill, WV, 25901. Tel: 304-469-9890. p. 2411
Fernitz, Kristin, Dir, Strasburg-Heisler Library, 143 Precision Ave, Strasburg, PA, 17579. Tel: 717-687-8969. p. 2010
Ferrante, Katie, Museum & Digital Asset Archivist, Audrey & Harry Hawthorn Library & Archives at the UBC Museum of Anthropology, 6393 NW Marine Dr, Vancouver, BC, V6T 1Z2, CANADA. Tel: 604-822-4834. p. 2579
Ferrante, Michael, Head, Tech Serv, Johnson Free Public Library, 274 Main St, Hackensack, NJ, 07601-5797. Tel: 201-343-4169. p. 1406
Ferrante, Michael, Syst Librn, Franklin Township Free Public Library, 485 DeMott Lane, Somerset, NJ, 08873. Tel: 732-873-8700. p. 1442
Ferrara, Ann, Libr Office Mgr, Kinnelon Public Library, 132 Kinnelon Rd, Kinnelon, NJ, 07405. Tel: 973-838-1321. p. 1410
Ferrara, Barbara, Br Mgr, Chesterfield County Public Library, LaPrade, 9000 Hull St Rd, Richmond, VA, 23236. Tel: 804-751-2275. p. 2312
Ferrara, Connie, Ref Serv, American River College Library, 4700 College Oak Dr, Sacramento, CA, 95841. Tel: 916-484-8455. p. 205
Ferrari, Ahniwa, Mr, Assoc Dean, Libr Operations, Evergreen State College, Library Bldg, Rm 2300, 2700 Evergreen Pkwy NW, Olympia, WA, 98505-0002. Tel: 360-867-6288. p. 2372
Ferrari, Sheila, Head, Youth Serv, Maywood Public Library District, 121 S Fifth Ave, Maywood, IL, 60153-1307. Tel: 708-343-1847, Ext 24. p. 615
Ferraro, Amanda, Chief Exec Officer, Uxbridge Public Library, Nine Toronto St S, Uxbridge, ON, L9P 1P7, CANADA. Tel: 905-852-9747. p. 2701
Ferraro, Linda, YA Serv, Amityville Public Library, 19 John St, Amityville, NY, 11701. Tel: 631-264-0567. p. 1486
Ferree, Melinda, Librn, Wilcox Public Library, 107 W Sapp St, Wilcox, NE, 68982. Tel: 308-478-5510. p. 1341
Ferreira, Daniela Moutinho, Br Mgr, New Bedford Free Public Library, Casa da Saudade Branch, 58 Crapo St, New Bedford, MA, 02740. Tel: 508-991-6218. p. 1038
Ferreira, Michelle, Commun Relations, Outreach Librn, Johnson Free Public Library, 274 Main St, Hackensack, NJ, 07601-5797. Tel: 201-343-4169. p. 1406
Ferrell, Janet, Library Contact, United States Navy, General Library, Naval Support Facility-S Potomac, Strauss Ave, Bldg 620, Indian Head, MD, 20640. Tel: 301-744-4747. p. 969
Ferrell, Natalie, Dir, Trinity Valley Community College Library, Palestine Campus, 2970 Hwy 19 N, Palestine, TX, 75803. Tel: 903-723-7025. p. 2137
Ferrell, Sonja, Dir, Ottumwa Public Library, 102 W Fourth St, Ottumwa, IA, 52501. Tel: 641-682-7563, Ext 202. p. 775
Ferrell, Travis, Supvry Librn, United States Army, Bruce C Clarke Library Academic Services Division, Bldg 3202, 14020 MSCOE Loop, Ste 200, Fort Leonard Wood, MO, 65473-8928. Tel: 573-563-6111. p. 1246
Ferrero, Katie, Br Mgr, Stark County District Library, North Branch, 189 25th St NW, Canton, OH, 44709. Tel: 330-456-4356. p. 1756
Ferretti, Tara, Head of Adult & Young Adult Services, Librn, Somers Library, Rte 139 & Reis Park, Somers, NY, 10589. Tel: 914-232-5717. p. 1642
Ferri, Terry, Asst Dir, Chester Library, 250 W Main St, Chester, NJ, 07930. Tel: 908-879-7612. p. 1396
Ferrier, Brad, Digital Projects Librn, University of Iowa Libraries, Special Collections & Archives, 100 Main Library, 125 W Washington St, Iowa City, IA, 52242-1420. Tel: 319-467-0604. p. 761
Ferrier-Clarke, Tara, Libr Tech, Toronto District School Board, Three Tippett Rd, North York, ON, M3H 2V1, CANADA. Tel: 416-395-8293. p. 2661
Ferrin, Lory, Library Contact, First United Methodist Church, 1115 S Boulder Ave, Tulsa, OK, 74119-2492. Tel: 918-592-3862. p. 1864
Ferris, Deanna, Ch, Prog Coordr, Lawrence County Public Library, 102 W Main St, Louisa, KY, 41230. Tel: 606-638-4497. p. 864
Ferris, Mary, Ch Serv Librn, Wood Library Association, 134 N Main St, Canandaigua, NY, 14424-1295. Tel: 585-394-1381, Ext 304. p. 1512
Ferris, TaChalla, Instruction Librn, Goucher College Library, 1021 Dulaney Valley Rd, Baltimore, MD, 21204. Tel: 410-337-6360. p. 953
Ferris, Tom, Photo Archivist, Montana Historical Society, 225 N Roberts St, Helena, MT, 59601-4514. Tel: 406-444-2681. p. 1296
Ferriss, Jeannie, Br Mgr, Jefferson County Library System, Whitehall Community Library, 110 First St W, Whitehall, MT, 59759. Tel: 406-287-3763. p. 1289
Ferriss, Jennifer, Head, Circ, Head, Tech Serv, Saratoga Springs Public Library, 49 Henry St, Saratoga Springs, NY, 12866. Tel: 518-584-7860, Ext 242. p. 1636
Ferro, Dawn, Interim Chief Librn, Glendale Public Library, 5959 W Brown St, Glendale, AZ, 85302-1248. Tel: 623-930-3530, 623-930-3600. p. 62
Ferro, Jen, Ref Serv, Lane Community College Library, Library-Center Bldg, 4000 E 30th Ave, Eugene, OR, 97405-0640. Tel: 541-463-5825. p. 1879
Ferro, Maryann, Asst Dir, Levittown Public Library, One Bluegrass Lane, Levittown, NY, 11756-1292. Tel: 516-731-5728. p. 1562
Ferro, Pat John, Mr, Supv Librn, Clifton Public Library, 292 Piaget Ave, Clifton, NJ, 07011. Tel: 973-772-5500. p. 1397
Ferro, William, Dir, East Meadow Public Library, 1886 Front St, East Meadow, NY, 11554-1705. Tel: 516-794-2570. p. 1528
Ferro, William, Dir, Hewlett-Woodmere Public Library, 1125 Broadway, Hewlett, NY, 11557-0903. Tel: 516-374-1967. p. 1546
Ferry, Nina, Adult Serv, Tech Serv, Oak Bluffs Public Library, 56R School St, Oak Bluffs, MA, 02557. Tel: 508-693-9433, Ext 145. p. 1044
Ferullo, Donna, Assoc Dean, Acad Affairs, Purdue University Libraries, 504 W State St, West Lafayette, IN, 47907-2058. Tel: 765-494-0978. p. 725
Ferwerda, Betsy, Asst Librn, University of Minnesota Crookston, 2900 University Ave, Crookston, MN, 56716-0801. Tel: 218-281-8404. p. 1171
Feryok, Allen, Ref Librn, Monessen Public Library, 326 Donner Ave, Monessen, PA, 15062. Tel: 724-684-4750. p. 1964

Feryok, Catherine, Tech Serv, Moundsville-Marshall County Public Library, 700 Fifth St, Moundsville, WV, 26041. Tel: 304-845-6911. p. 2410
Feser, Ken, Chief Librn, Medicine Hat Public Library, 414 First St SE, Medicine Hat, AB, T1A 0A8, CANADA. Tel: 403-502-8528. p. 2548
Fester, NaKaya, Dir, Museum of the Fur Trade Library, 6321 Hwy 20, Chadron, NE, 69337. Tel: 308-432-3843. p. 1310
Fethkenher, Bethany, Circ Asst, Lancaster Bible College, Teague Learning Commons, 901 Eden Rd, Lancaster, PA, 17601-5036. Tel: 717-569-7071, Ext 5311. p. 1951
Fett, Linda, Dir, Kirkland Public Library, 513 W Main St, Kirkland, IL, 60146. Tel: 815-522-6260. p. 605
Fetterolf, Laura, Librn, Ilsley Public Library, Sarah Partridge Community, 431 E Main St, East Middlebury, VT, 05740. Tel: 802-388-7588. p. 2288
Fetters, Michael Anthony, Digital Librn, Lindenwood University Library, 209 S Kingshighway, Saint Charles, MO, 63301. Tel: 636-949-4574. p. 1268
Fetters, Val, Ch Serv, Edwin A Bemis Public Library, 6014 S Datura St, Littleton, CO, 80120-2636. Tel: 303-795-3961. p. 290
Fettig, Amy, Br Mgr, Anoka County Library, North Central, 17565 Central Ave NE, Ham Lake, MN, 55304. Tel: 763-324-1570. p. 1165
Fetzer, Rachel, Br Mgr, Rockingham County Public Library, Reidsville Branch, 204 W Morehead St, Reidsville, NC, 27320. Tel: 336-349-8476. p. 1686
Fetzer, Rachel, Supvr, Outreach Serv, Rockingham County Public Library, 527 Boone Rd, Eden, NC, 27288. Tel: 336-627-3729. p. 1686
Feuchtenberger, Paula, Dir, Hancock Community Library, 662 Sixth St, Hancock, MN, 56244-9998. Tel: 320-392-5666. p. 1177
Feuerborn, Amanda, Asst Librn, Freedom Public Library, 38 Old Portland Rd, Freedom, NH, 03836. Tel: 603-539-5176. p. 1364
Feusse, Kathy, Dir, Clearwater Public Library, 626 Main St, Clearwater, NE, 68726. Tel: 402-485-2034. p. 1310
Feustle, Maristella, Supvr, AV Serv & Coll, Southern Methodist University, Hamon Arts Library, 6101 N Bishop Blvd, Dallas, TX, 75275. Tel: 214-768-1855. p. 2168
Few, Abbe, Br Mgr, Granville County Library System, Berea Branch, 1211 Hwy 158, Berea, NC, 27565. Tel: 919-693-1231. p. 1707
Fewell, Rachel, Cent Libr Adminr, Denver Public Library, Ten W 14th Ave Pkwy, Denver, CO, 80204-2731. Tel: 720-865-1111. p. 275
Feyl, Steve, Univ Librn, Pace University Library, 15 Beekman St, New York, NY, 10038. Tel: 914-773-3233. p. 1600
Feyl, Steven, Univ Librn, Pace University, 861 Bedford Rd, Pleasantville, NY, 10570-2799. Tel: 914-773-3233. p. 1620
Feynman, Eileen, Cat, Coll Develop, Ref (Info Servs), Lindenhurst Memorial Library, One Lee Ave, Lindenhurst, NY, 11757-5399. Tel: 631-957-7755. p. 1563
Fial, Alissa, Head, Research, Teaching & Learning, Marquette University, 1355 W Wisconsin Ave, Milwaukee, WI, 53233. Tel: 414-288-3320. p. 2458
Fiala, Nathan, Dir, St Francis Public Library, 121 N Scott St, Saint Francis, KS, 67756. Tel: 785-332-3292. p. 834
Fialkovich, Jason, Youth Serv Librn, Middletown Free Library, 464 S Old Middletown Rd, Ste 3, Media, PA, 19063. Tel: 610-566-7828. p. 1961
Fiallos-Finstad, Iris, Fac Librn, Palm Beach State College, 15845 Southern Blvd, Loxahatchee, FL, 33470. Tel: 560-790-9013. p. 419
Fiamingo, Nicole, Dir, McNees, Wallace & Nurick LLC, 100 Pine St, Harrisburg, PA, 17101. Tel: 717-237-5448. p. 1940
Fiander, Janice, Serv Area Mgr, Halifax Public Libraries, 60 Alderney Dr, Dartmouth, NS, B2Y 4P8, CANADA. Tel: 902-490-5744. p. 2617
Fic, Christy, Archivist & Spec Coll Librn, Shippensburg University, 1871 Old Main Dr, Shippensburg, PA, 17257. Tel: 717-477-1516. p. 2007
Fick, Amber, Librn, Adult Serv, Siouxland Libraries, 200 N Dakota Ave, Sioux Falls, SD, 57104. Tel: 605-367-8703. p. 2082
Fick, Jodi, Dir, Siouxland Libraries, 200 N Dakota Ave, Sioux Falls, SD, 57104. Tel: 605-367-8713. p. 2082
Fick, John S, Assoc Dir, University of Missouri-Columbia, Academic Support Center Media Rental Library, 505 E Stewart Rd, Columbia, MO, 65211-2040. Tel: 573-882-3601. p. 1243
Fick, Julie, Teen Librn, Waterford Public Library, 101 N River St, Waterford, WI, 53185-4149. Tel: 262-534-3988, Ext 15. p. 2483
Fickenworth, J J, Electronic Res Librn, Horry-Georgetown Technical College, Elizabeth Mattocks Chapin Memorial Library - Grand Strand Campus, 3639 Pampas Dr, Myrtle Beach, SC, 29577. Tel: 843-477-2100. p. 2057
Fickett, Amanda, Librn, Milbridge Public Library, 18 School St, Milbridge, ME, 04658. Tel: 207-546-3066. p. 931
Fickett, Pat, Dir, Wilton Public & Gregg Free Library, Seven Forest Rd, Wilton, NH, 03086. Tel: 603-654-2581. p. 1384
Fidel, Coco Rios, Br Mgr, San Diego Public Library, Otay Mesa-Nestor, 3003 Coronado Ave, San Diego, CA, 92154. Tel: 619-424-0474. p. 220
Fidler, Evelyn, Res Mgr, Kings Landing Library, 5804 Rte 102, Prince William, NB, E6K 0A5, CANADA. Tel: 506-476-1905. p. 2604
Fiechter, Bethany, Coordr, Spec Coll & Archives, DePauw University, 405 S Indiana St, Greencastle, IN, 46135. Tel: 765-658-4420. p. 687
Fiedler, Monique, Libr Mgr, Didsbury Municipal Library, 2033 19th Ave, Didsbury, AB, T0M 0W0, CANADA. Tel: 403-335-3142. p. 2533
Fiedler, Robert, Asst Dir, Musser Public Library, 408 E Second St, Muscatine, IA, 52761. Tel: 563-263-3065, Ext 125. p. 772
Fiedor, Connie, Mgr, Sheridan County Public Library System, Tongue River Branch, 145 Coffeen St, Ranchester, WY, 82839. Tel: 307-655-9726. p. 2499
Fiegal, Allison, Services & Resources Supervisor, State University of New York Polytechnic Institute, 100 Seymour Rd, Utica, NY, 13502. Tel: 315-792-7245. p. 1655
Fiegen, Ann M, Bus Librn, California State University, 333 S Twin Oaks Valley Rd, San Marcos, CA, 92096. Tel: 760-750-4348. p. 234
Field, Chris, Mgr, Collections & Technology, Prince George Public Library, 888 Canada Games Way, Prince George, BC, V2L 5T6, CANADA. Tel: 250-563-9251, Ext 158. p. 2574
Field, Corinne, Supvr, Mid-Columbia Libraries, Othello Branch, 101 E Main St, Othello, WA, 99344. Tel: 509-488-9683. p. 2367
Field, Dawn, Librn, Texas Biomedical Research Institute, 8715 W Military Dr, San Antonio, TX, 78227-5301. p. 2239
Field, Heather, Dir, Ashaway Free Library, 15 Knight St, Ashaway, RI, 02804-1410. Tel: 401-377-2770. p. 2029
Field, Judith J, Prof in Residence, Wayne State University, 106 Kresge Library, Detroit, MI, 48202. Tel: 313-577-1825. p. 2787
Fielder-Giscombe, Rosalind, Res & Instruction Librn, Chicago State University, 9501 S Martin Luther King Jr Dr, LIB 440, Chicago, IL, 60628-1598. Tel: 773-821-2431. p. 558
Fielding, Jenny, Coordr, Libr Serv, Northern Essex Community College, Lawrence Campus Library, 45 Franklin St, Lawrence, MA, 01841. Tel: 978-738-7400. p. 1024
Fielding, Penny-Lynn, Dep Chief Exec Officer, Kitchener Public Library, 85 Queen St N, Kitchener, ON, N2H 2H1, CANADA. Tel: 519-743-0271. p. 2651
Fielding, Robin, Librn, Temple Beth El, 385 High St, Fall River, MA, 02720. Tel: 508-674-3529. p. 1018
Fields, Arleen, Archivist/Librn, Asst Dir, Methodist University, 5400 Ramsey St, Fayetteville, NC, 28311. Tel: 910-630-7123. p. 1689
Fields, Barbara, Dir, McDowell Public Library, 90 Howard St, Welch, WV, 24801. Tel: 304-436-3070. p. 2416
Fields, Brian, Dep Dir, Blanco County South Library District, 1118 Main St, Blanco, TX, 78606. Tel: 830-833-4280. p. 2148
Fields, Elizabeth, Res & Instruction Librn, Stevenson University Library, Bradley T MacDonald Learning Commons, Manning Academic Ctr S 329, 3rd Flr, 11200 Gundry Lane (Ted Herget Way), Owings Mills, MD, 21117. Tel: 443-394-9941. p. 978
Fields, Georgianna, Dir, Factoryville Public Library, 163 College Ave, Factoryville, PA, 18419. Tel: 570-945-3788. p. 1933
Fields, Janie, Librn, Sheppard Memorial Library, George Washington Carver Library, 618 W 14th Ave, Greenville, NC, 27834. Tel: 252-329-4583. p. 1694
Fields, Jason, Dir, Tipton County Public Library, 127 E Madison St, Tipton, IN, 46072. Tel: 765-675-8761. p. 722
Fields, Kristin, Librn, Farnhamville Public Library, 240 Hardin St, Farnhamville, IA, 50538. Tel: 515-544-3660. p. 753
Fields, Lucy, Cat & Acq, University of Indianapolis, 1400 E Hanna Ave, Indianapolis, IN, 46227-3697. Tel: 317-788-3268. p. 697
Fields, Natalie, Br Mgr, Public Library of Cincinnati & Hamilton County, Deer Park, 3970 E Galbraith Rd, Cincinnati, OH, 45236. Tel: 513-369-4450. p. 1762
Fields, Ruth, Adult Serv, Thomaston Public Library, 248 Main St, Thomaston, CT, 06787. Tel: 860-283-4339. p. 341
Fields, Stacey, Dir, Human Res, Howard County Library System, 9411 Frederick Rd, Ellicott City, MD, 21042. Tel: 410-313-7750. p. 965
Fields, Starla, Tech Serv, Cynthiana-Harrison County Public Library, 104 N Main St, Cynthiana, KY, 41031. Tel: 859-234-4881. p. 853
Fieth, Ken, Archivist, Nashville Public Library, 615 Church St, Nashville, TN, 37219-2314. Tel: 615-862-5800. p. 2119
Fieth, Kenneth, Archivist, Nashville Public Library, Metropolitan Government Archives, 615 Church St, 3rd Flr, Nashville, TN, 37219. Tel: 615-862-5880. p. 2120
Fifarek, Aimee, Exec Dir, Public Library of Youngstown & Mahoning County, 305 Wick Ave, Youngstown, OH, 44503. Tel: 330-744-8636. p. 1835
Fifer, Kathie, Head, Adult Serv, Warren-Newport Public Library District, 224 N O'Plaine Rd, Gurnee, IL, 60031. Tel: 847-244-5150, Ext 3002. p. 596
Fiffie, Eve, Circ Supvr, Saint Charles Parish Library, Saint Rose Branch, 90 E Club Dr, Saint Rose, LA, 70087. Tel: 504-465-0646. p. 889
Fifield, Sara, Ch Serv, Wixom Public Library, 49015 Pontiac Trail, Wixom, MI, 48393-2567. Tel: 248-624-2512. p. 1160
Figa, Jan, Dr, Dir, Libr Serv, Barry University, 11300 NE Second Ave, Miami Shores, FL, 33161-6695. Tel: 305-899-3768. p. 426
Figaratto, Andrea, Head, Circ, Oak Bluffs Public Library, 56R School St, Oak Bluffs, MA, 02557. Tel: 508-693-9433, Ext 140. p. 1044
Figaratto, Andrea, Dir, Whelden Memorial Library, 2401 Meetinghouse Way, West Barnstable, MA, 02668. Tel: 508-362-2262. p. 1065
Figart, Andrea, Libr Dir, New Port Richey Public Library, 5939 Main St, New Port Richey, FL, 34652. Tel: 727-853-1262. p. 428

Figiel-Krueger, Maria, Ref Librn, Rock Valley College, 3301 N Mulford Rd, Rockford, IL, 61114. Tel: 815-921-4606. p. 641
Figley, Joshua, Fiscal Officer, Huron County Community Library, Six W Emerald St, Willard, OH, 44890. Tel: 419-933-8564. p. 1831
Figlia, Ginny, Youth Serv Librn, Howland Public Library, 313 Main St, Beacon, NY, 12508. Tel: 845-831-1134. p. 1491
Figlioli, Catherine, Ref & Instruction Librn, Clinton Community College, 136 Clinton Point Dr, Plattsburgh, NY, 12901-5690. Tel: 518-562-4241. p. 1619
Figueira, Elda, Library Contact, City of Calgary Law Department Library, 800 Mecleod Trail SE, 12th Flr, No 8053, Calgary, AB, T2P 2M5, CANADA. Tel: 403-268-2441. p. 2528
Figuera, Jesse, Ch Serv, Buncombe County Public Libraries, 67 Haywood St, Asheville, NC, 28801. Tel: 828-250-4700. p. 1672
Figueroa, Emma, Asst Mgr, Saint Louis County Library, Grant's View Branch, 9700 Musick Rd, Saint Louis, MO, 63123-3935. Tel: 314-994-3300, Ext 3850. p. 1274
Figueroa, Ivelisse, Br Mgr, Fairfax County Public Library, John Marshall Branch, 6209 Rose Hill Dr, Alexandria, VA, 22310-6299. Tel: 703-971-0010. p. 2316
Figueroa, Mark, Dir, Libr Info Technologies & Digital Initiatives, San Diego State University, 5500 Campanile Dr, San Diego, CA, 92182-8050. Tel: 619-594-2945. p. 221
Figueroa, Miguel, Pres & Chief Exec Officer, Amigos Library Services, Inc, 4901 LBJ Freeway, Ste 150, Dallas, TX, 75244-6179. Tel: 972-340-2820. p. 2775
Figueroa, Ruben, User Experience Librn, Iliff School of Theology, 2323 E Iliff Ave, Denver, CO, 80210. Tel: 303-765-3173. p. 276
Figueroa-Ortiz, Almaluces, Chief Librn, University of Puerto Rico Library System, Caribbean & Latin American Studies Collection, Rio Piedras Campus, Jose M Lazaro Bldg, 2nd Flr, San Juan, PR, 00931. Tel: 787-764-0000, Ext 85855. p. 2514
Figueroa-Rodriguez, Sylvia, Info Spec, Librn, University of Puerto Rico RP College of Natural Sciences Library, 17 Ave Universidad, Ste 1701, San Juan, PR, 00925-2537. Tel: 787-764-0000, Ext 88395. p. 2515
Figura, Dawn, Dir, Northern Wayne Community Library, 11 Library Rd, Rt 370, Lakewood, PA, 18439. Tel: 570-798-2444. p. 1950
Fikirndi, Seyfett, Dir, United States Air Force, 425 Third Ave, Bldg 312, Sheppard AFB, TX, 76311. Tel: 940-676-6152. p. 2243
Fikkert, DiAnne, Dir, Lake View Public Library, 202 Main St, Lake View, IA, 51450. Tel: 712-657-2310. p. 764
Filander, Elina, Dir, Belle Vernon Public Library, 505 Speer St, Belle Vernon, PA, 15012-1540. Tel: 724-929-6642. p. 1909
Filapek, Joe, Assoc Exec Dir, Reaching Across Illinois Library System (RAILS), 125 Tower Dr, Burr Ridge, IL, 60527. Tel: 630-734-5132. p. 546
Filar-Williams, Beth, Head, Library Experience & Access, Oregon State University Libraries, 121 The Valley Library, Corvallis, OR, 97331-4501. Tel: 541-737-2156. p. 1876
Filatreau, Kathy, Instructional Technologist, Whittier College, Bonnie Bell Wardman Library, 7031 Founders Hill Rd, Whittier, CA, 90608-9984. Tel: 562-907-4247. p. 259
Filbert, Nathan, Instruction & Res Serv Librn, Wichita State University Libraries, 1845 Fairmount, Wichita, KS, 67260-0068. Tel: 316-978-5210. p. 844
Filbert, Nathan, Res & Instruction Librn, Wichita State University Libraries, Chemistry, 127 McKinley Hall, Wichita, KS, 67260-0051. Tel: 316-978-5210. p. 844
Filer, Phillis, Pub Serv Adminr, Alachua County Library District, 401 E University Ave, Gainesville, FL, 32601-5453. Tel: 352-334-3957. p. 406
Filer, Phillis, Pub Serv Adminr, Alachua County Library District, Newberry Branch, 110 S Seaboard Dr, Newberry, FL, 32669. Tel: 352-472-1135. p. 406
Filiatreau, Amy, Dir, Lynn University Library, 3601 N Military Trail, Boca Raton, FL, 33431-5598. Tel: 561-237-7067. p. 385
Filiatreau, Amy, Univ Librn, University of Mary Washington, 1801 College Ave, Fredericksburg, VA, 22401-5300. p. 2320
Filion, Ivan, Dir of Libr, Bibliotheques de Montreal, Pavillon Prince, 801 rue Brennan, 5e etage, Montreal, QC, H3C 0G4, CANADA. Tel: 514-872-1608. p. 2718
Filip, Dena, Br Mgr, Williams County Public Library, West Unity Branch, 109 S High St, West Unity, OH, 43570. Tel: 419-924-5237. p. 1753
Filip, Kaitlyn, Br Mgr, Jackson District Library, Henrietta Branch, 11744 Bunkerhill Rd, Pleasant Lake, MI, 49272. Tel: 517-769-6537. p. 1120
Filippone, Stephanie, Adult Serv, East Brunswick Public Library, Two Jean Walling Civic Ctr, East Brunswick, NJ, 08816-3599. Tel: 732-390-6950. p. 1399
Filkorn, Diane, Librn, Ohio Department of Rehabilitation & Correction, 5701 Burnette Rd, Leavittsburg, OH, 44430. Tel: 330-898-0820, Ext 7408. p. 1794
Filleul, Michelle, Head, Borrower Serv, Reading Public Library, 64 Middlesex Ave, Reading, MA, 01867-2550. Tel: 781-942-6702. p. 1049
Fillinger, Mike, Mgr, Res, Orrick, Herrington & Sutcliffe, 51 W 52nd St, New York, NY, 10019-6142. Tel: 212-506-5000. p. 1600
Fillion, Christine, Chef de Section, Bibliotheques de Montreal, Vieux-Saint-Laurent, 1380 rue de l'Eglise, Saint-Laurent, QC, H4L 2H2, CANADA. Tel: 514-855-6130, Ext 4726. p. 2721
Fillipitch, Jeane, Librn, Will County Law Library, 14 W Jefferson St, 4th Flr, Joliet, IL, 60432-4300. Tel: 815-774-7887. p. 603
Filson, Lea, Exec Dir, Lake County Historical Society, 415 Riverside Dr, Painesville, OH, 44077. Tel: 440-639-2945. p. 1812
Filson, Shelby, Asst Librn, Keosauqua Public Library, 608 First St, Keosauqua, IA, 52565. Tel: 319-293-3766. p. 763
Finch, Alison, Ref Librn, Mendocino College Library, 1000 Hensley Creek Rd, Ukiah, CA, 95482. Tel: 707-468-3245. p. 254
Finch, Ann, Coordr, Spec Serv, ILL, Leominster Public Library, 30 West St, Leominster, MA, 01453. Tel: 978-534-7522, Ext 3593. p. 1028
Finch, Emily, Br Supvr, Elgin County Library, Port Stanley Library, 302 Bridge St, Port Stanley, ON, N5L 1C3, CANADA. Tel: 519-782-4241. p. 2681
Finch, Emily, Br Supvr, Elgin County Library, Shedden Library-Southwold Township Library, 35921 Talbot Line, Shedden, ON, N0L 2E0, CANADA. Tel: 519-764-2081. p. 2681
Finch, Eudoxie, Br Mgr, Middle Georgia Regional Library System, Twiggs County Public Library, 109 Main St, Jeffersonville, GA, 31044. Tel: 478-945-3814. p. 487
Finch, Hollister, Librn, Youth & Family Serv, Chesapeake Public Library, Major Hillard Library, 824 Old George Washington Hwy N, Chesapeake, VA, 23323-2214. Tel: 757-410-7082. p. 2311
Finch, Jennifer, Br Mgr, Harris County Public Library, Spring Branch Memorial Branch, 930 Corbindale, Houston, TX, 77024. Tel: 832-927-5510. p. 2193
Finch, Jennifer M, Dir, Libr & Res Serv, McLane Middleton, 900 Elm St, 10th Flr, Manchester, NH, 03101. Tel: 603-628-1428. p. 1372
Finch, Kristin, Br Librn, Jackson/Hinds Library System, Evelyn Taylor Majure Library, 217 W Main St, Utica, MS, 39175-0340. Tel: 601-885-8381. p. 1221
Finch, Lisa, Librn, Alachua County Library District, Newberry Branch, 110 S Seaboard Dr, Newberry, FL, 32669. Tel: 352-472-1135. p. 406
Finch, Mary Jo, Dir, Westbank Community Library District, 1309 Westbank Dr, Austin, TX, 78746. Tel: 512-327-3045. p. 2143
Finch, Robert, Asst Dir, Rogers Public Library, 711 S Dixieland Rd, Rogers, AR, 72758. Tel: 479-621-1152. p. 108
Finch, Robert, Libr Asst, Paul D Camp Community College Library, Hobbs Suffolk Campus, 271 Kenyon Rd, Suffolk, VA, 23434. Tel: 757-925-6345. p. 2319
Finch, Shelia, Librn, Faulkner-Van Buren Regional Library System, Vilonia Branch, Three Bise St, Vilonia, AR, 72173. Tel: 501-796-8520. p. 92
Fincher, Deanne, Youth Serv Librn, Thomas B Norton Public Library, 221 W 19th Ave, Gulf Shores, AL, 36542. Tel: 251-968-1176. p. 20
Findeisen, Robin A, Syst Librn, Stevenson University Library, 1525 Greenspring Valley Rd, Stevenson, MD, 21153. Tel: 443-334-2218. p. 978
Finder, Lisa, Ser Librn, Hunter College Libraries, East Bldg, 695 Park Ave, New York, NY, 10065. Tel: 212-772-4186. p. 1588
Findlay, Karen, Br Mgr, Dayton Metro Library, West Carrollton Branch, 300 E Central Ave, West Carrollton, OH, 45449. Tel: 937-496-8962. p. 1779
Findlay, Lisa, Librn, Fredonia Public Library, 130 N Main, Fredonia, AZ, 86022. Tel: 928-643-7137. p. 61
Findorack, Catherine, YA Librn, Cyrenius H Booth Library, 25 Main St, Newtown, CT, 06470. Tel: 203-426-4533. p. 330
Findorak, Catherine, Makerspace Mrg, Teen Serv, Wilton Library Association, 137 Old Ridgefield Rd, Wilton, CT, 06897-3000. Tel: 203-762-3950. p. 348
Findra, Pat, Children's Coordr, Supv Librn, Monmouth County Library, 125 Symmes Dr, Manalapan, NJ, 07726. Tel: 732-431-7220. p. 1415
Fine, Dana, Head, Tech Serv, Princeton Public Library, 698 E Peru St, Princeton, IL, 61356. Tel: 815-875-1331. p. 636
Fine, Gary, Asst Dir, Durland Alternatives Library, 130 Anabel Taylor Hall, Ithaca, NY, 14853-1001. Tel: 607-255-6486. p. 1552
Fine, Mary Beth, Br Mgr, Atlantic County Library System, Brigantine Branch, 201 15th St S, Brigantine, NJ, 08203. Tel: 609-266-0110. p. 1417
Fine, Paula, Librn, Congregation Emanu-El B'Ne Jeshurun Library, 2020 W Brown Deer Rd, Milwaukee, WI, 53217. Tel: 414-228-7545. p. 2458
Finfrock, Ellen E, Dir, Polo Public Library District, 302 W Mason St, Polo, IL, 61064. Tel: 815-946-2713. p. 636
Finger, Chris, Libr Dir, Geneva Public Library, 244 Main St, Geneva, NY, 14456. Tel: 315-789-5303. p. 1538
Finger, Jascin Leonardo, Curator, Dep Dir, Nantucket Maria Mitchell Association, Two Vestal St, Nantucket, MA, 02554-2699. Tel: 508-228-9198. p. 1037
Fink, Catherine, Dir, North Carolina Synod of the ELCA, 1988 Lutheran Synod Dr, Salisbury, NC, 28144. Tel: 704-633-4861, Ext 9574. p. 1715
Fink, Elysse, Dir, Leonia Public Library, 227 Fort Lee Rd, Leonia, NJ, 07605. Tel: 201-592-5770. p. 1412
Fink, Katie, Pub Serv Mgr, Tech Mgr, Marshalltown Public Library, 105 W Boone St, Marshalltown, IA, 50158-4911. Tel: 641-754-5738. p. 768
Fink, Lynnea, Teen Serv, Pasadena Public Library, 1201 Jeff Ginn Memorial Dr, Pasadena, TX, 77506. Tel: 713-477-0276. p. 2225

Fink, Mark, Exec Dir, Anythink Libraries, 5877 E 120th Ave, Thornton, CO, 80602. Tel: 303-288-2001. p. 296
Fink, Norma, Dir, Attica Public Library, 305 S Perry St, Attica, IN, 47918. Tel: 765-764-4194. p. 668
Finkbeiner, Ali, Dir, Hellertown Area Library, 409 Constitution Ave, Hellertown, PA, 18055-1928. Tel: 610-838-8381. p. 1943
Finkbeiner, Mary, Libr Tech, OSF Saint Anthony Medical Center, 5666 E State St, Rockford, IL, 61108-2472. Tel: 815-227-2558. p. 641
Finkelstein, Alice, Head, Tech Serv, Hebrew Union College-Jewish Institute of Religion, 3101 Clifton Ave, Cincinnati, OH, 45220-2488. Tel: 513-487-3294. p. 1760
Finkey, Marisa, Coordr, Info Literacy, University of Wisconsin Oshkosh, 801 Elmwood Ave, Oshkosh, WI, 54901. Tel: 920-424-3436. p. 2467
Finkin, Jordan, Dr, Rare Book & Manuscript Librn, Hebrew Union College-Jewish Institute of Religion, 3101 Clifton Ave, Cincinnati, OH, 45220-2488. Tel: 513-487-3272. p. 1760
Finkin, Jordan S, Deputy Dir of Libraries, Rare Book & Manuscript Librn, Hebrew Union College-Jewish Institute of Religion, 3101 Clifton Ave, Cincinnati, OH, 45220-2488. Tel: 513-221-1875. p. 1760
Finklang, Julie, Libr Mgr, San Mateo County Library, Pacifica Sanchez Library, 1111 Terra Nova Blvd, Pacifica, CA, 94044. Tel: 650-359-3397, Ext 227. p. 235
Finklang, Julie, Libr Mgr, San Mateo County Library, Pacifica Sharp Park Library, 104 Hilton Way, Pacifica, CA, 94044. Tel: 650-355-5196, Ext 227. p. 236
Finkle, Debbie, Library Contact, Knesseth Israel Synagogue Library, 34 E Fulton St, Gloversville, NY, 12078. Tel: 518-725-0649. p. 1539
Finkle, Elizabeth, Vols Serv Coordr, Fresno County Public Library, 2420 Mariposa St, Fresno, CA, 93721. Tel: 559-600-7323. p. 145
Finkley, Kendria, Tech Serv Coordr, Scotland County Memorial Library, 312 W Church St, Laurinburg, NC, 28352-3720. Tel: 910-276-0563. p. 1700
Finlay, Jennifer, Librn, Shepard-Pruden Memorial Library, 106 W Water St, Edenton, NC, 27932. Tel: 252-482-4112. p. 1686
Finlay, Jennifer, Campus Librn, Okanagan College Library, Vernon Campus, 7000 College Way, Vernon, BC, V1B 2N5, CANADA. Tel: 250-545-7291, Ext 2249. p. 2568
Finlayson, Irene, ILL & Circ, North Country Community College Libraries, 23 Santanoni Ave, Saranac Lake, NY, 12983-2046. Tel: 518-891-2915, Ext 218. p. 1636
Finlayson, Jennifer, Libr Mgr, Timberland Regional Library, Westport Branch, 101 E Harms Ave, Westport, WA, 98595. Tel: 360-268-0521. p. 2389
Finlayson, Kathy, Libr Tech, University of Manitoba, Sister St Odilon Library, Misericordia Health Centre, Education & Resource Bldg, 691 Wolseley Ave, 1st Flr, Winnipeg, MB, R3G 1C3, CANADA. Tel: 204-788-8109. p. 2595
Finlayson, Sandy, Dir, Westminster Theological Seminary, 2960 W Church Rd, Glenside, PA, 19038. Tel: 215-572-3823. p. 1937
Finley, Daniel M, Exec Dir, Desert Caballeros Western Museum, 21 N Frontier St, Wickenburg, AZ, 85390. Tel: 928-684-2272. p. 84
Finley, Ginger, Libr Dir, McCoy Memorial Library, 130 S Washington St, McLeansboro, IL, 62859. Tel: 618-643-2125. p. 616
Finley, Molly, Libr Asst, Winchester Public Library, 203 Fourth St, Winchester, KS, 66097. Tel: 913-774-4967. p. 844
Finley, Pam, Mgr, Cobb County Public Library System, Gritters Library, 880 Shaw Park Rd, Marietta, GA, 30066. Tel: 770-528-2524. p. 489
Finley, Tami, Asst Librn, Clarence Public Library, 309 Sixth Ave, Clarence, IA, 52216. Tel: 563-452-3734. p. 740
Finley, Thomas, Mgr, Ad Serv, Frisco Public Library, 6101 Frisco Square Blvd, Frisco, TX, 75034-3000. Tel: 972-292-5669. p. 2182
Finley, Wayne, Res & Ref Librn, Northern Illinois University Libraries, 217 Normal Rd, DeKalb, IL, 60115-2828. Tel: 815-753-0991. p. 577
Finley-McGill, Jennifer, Outreach Librn, New Mexico State Library, Library for the Blind and Print Disabled, 1209 Camino Carlos Rey, Santa Fe, NM, 87507. Tel: 505-476-9773. p. 1475
Finn, Bonnie, Fine Arts Librn, College of Saint Benedict, 37 S College Ave, Saint Joseph, MN, 56374. Tel: 320-363-5513. p. 1199
Finn, Charissa, Libr Dir, Kendall Public Library, 110 E S Railroad St, Kendall, WI, 54638. Tel: 608-463-7103. p. 2444
Finn, Courtenay, Chief Curator, Orange County Museum of Art Library, 3333 Avenue of the Arts, Costa Mesa, CA, 92626. Tel: 714-780-2130. p. 132
Finn, Irja, Libr Dir, Jonathan Bourne Public Library, 19 Sandwich Rd, Bourne, MA, 02532. Tel: 508-759-0600, Ext 6103. p. 1001
Finn, Jennifer, Head, Adult Serv, East Bridgewater Public Library, 32 Union St, East Bridgewater, MA, 02333. Tel: 508-378-1616. p. 1015
Finn, John, Dir, Lewis & Clark Library, 120 S Last Chance Gulch, Helena, MT, 59601. Tel: 406-447-1690. p. 1296
Finn, Monica, Libr Mgr, Vancouver Island Regional Library, Bella Coola Branch, 450 MacKenzie St, Bella Coola, BC, V0T 1C0, CANADA. Tel: 250-799-5330. p. 2570
Finn, Monica, Libr Mgr, Vancouver Island Regional Library, South Cowichan, 310-2720 Mill Bay Rd, Mill Bay, BC, V0R 2P0, CANADA. Tel: 250-743-5436. p. 2571
Finnegan, Dianne, Coordr, Patron Serv, Head, Circ, Peters Township Public Library, 616 E McMurray Rd, McMurray, PA, 15317-3495. Tel: 724-941-9430. p. 1959
Finnegan, Karin, Libr Dir, Spotswood Public Library, 548 Main St, Spotswood, NJ, 08884. Tel: 732-251-1515. p. 1444
Finnegan, Kimberly, Dir, Panora Public Library, 102 N First St, Panora, IA, 50216. Tel: 641-755-2529. p. 776
Finnegan, Kris, Ch, Harrisville Public Library, Seven Canal St, Harrisville, NH, 03450. Tel: 603-827-2918. p. 1367
Finnegan, Kristen, Ch Serv, Libr Asst, North Adams Community Memorial Library, 110 E Main St, North Adams, MI, 49262. Tel: 517-287-4426. p. 1138
Finnegan, Kristine, Dir, Olivia Rodham Memorial Library, One Nelson Common Rd, Nelson, NH, 03457. Tel: 603-847-3214. p. 1375
Finnegan, Lisa, Acq, ILL Coordr, Loras College Library, 1450 Alta Vista St, Dubuque, IA, 52004-4327. Tel: 563-588-4969. p. 748
Finnegan-Andrews, Erin, Dir, Robert W Barlow Memorial Library, 921 Washington Ave, Iowa Falls, IA, 50126. Tel: 641-648-2872. p. 761
Finnemore, Bryan, Curator, Waterville Historical Society Library, 62 Silver St, Unit B, Waterville, ME, 04901. Tel: 207-872-9439. p. 945
Finnen, Andrea, Br Head, Thompson-Nicola Regional District Library System, Chase Branch, 614 Shuswap Ave, Chase, BC, V0E 1M0, CANADA. Tel: 250-679-3331. p. 2567
Finnerty, Sharon A, Media Res Coordr, University of Scranton, 800 Linden St, Scranton, PA, 18510-4634. Tel: 570-941-6330. p. 2005
Finney, Andy, Learning Res Coordr, North Idaho College Library, 1000 W Garden Ave, Coeur d'Alene, ID, 83814-2199. Tel: 208-769-3266. p. 520
Finney, Catherine, Acq Librn, Colls Librn, Central Oregon Community College Barber Library, 2600 NW College Way, Bend, OR, 97703. Tel: 541-383-7559. p. 1873
Finney Estrada, Tanya, Dir, Pennsauken Free Public Library, 5605 Crescent Blvd, Pennsauken, NJ, 08110. Tel: 856-665-5959. p. 1434
Finney, John, Volunteer Archivist, University of Puget Sound, 1604 N Warner St, Upper Loading Dock, Tacoma, WA, 98416. Tel: 253-879-6014. p. 2387
Finnicum, Ellen, Dir, Carroll County District Library, 70 Second St NE, Carrollton, OH, 44615. Tel: 330-627-2613. p. 1756
Finnicum, Ellen, Dir, Carroll County District Library, Malvern Branch, 710 E Porter St, Malvern, OH, 44644. Tel: 330-863-0636. p. 1756
Finnie, Jessica, Dir, Scituate Town Library, 85 Branch St, Scituate, MA, 02066. Tel: 781-545-8727. p. 1052
Finot, Erin, Adult Serv Mgr, Eugene Public Library, 100 W Tenth Ave, Eugene, OR, 97401. Tel: 541-682-5450. p. 1878
Finsel, Rishara, Libr Dir, Transylvania County Library, 212 S Gaston St, Brevard, NC, 28712. Tel: 828-884-3151. p. 1675
Finsness, Kerstin, Br Librn, East Central Regional Library, Chisago Lakes Area Public Library, 11754 302nd St, Chisago City, MN, 55013. Tel: 651-257-2817. p. 1168
Finstad, Ann, Head, Children's Servx, Glencoe Public Library, 320 Park Ave, Glencoe, IL, 60022. Tel: 847-835-5056. p. 593
Finzen, Shelly L, Dir, Tyler Public Library, 230 Tyler St N, Tyler, MN, 56178-1161. Tel: 507-247-5556. p. 1206
Fiocre, Natalie, Coll Spec, San Diego History Center, Balboa Park, 1649 El Prado, Ste 3, San Diego, CA, 92101. Tel: 616-232-6203, Ext 120. p. 218
Fiore, Carmela, Head, Tech Serv, West Nyack Free Library, 65 Strawtown Rd, West Nyack, NY, 10994. Tel: 845-358-6081. p. 1662
Fiorentino, Wesley A, Access Serv, Coordr, Libr Serv, Bunker Hill Community College, E Bldg, 3rd Flr, Rm E300, 250 New Rutherford Ave, Boston, MA, 02129-2925. Tel: 617-228-2423. p. 994
Fiori, Helen, Libr Mgr, Debevoise & Plimpton, 801 Pennsylvania Ave NW, Washington, DC, 20004. Tel: 202-383-8000. p. 363
Fiorillo, Andrea, Ad, Reading Public Library, 64 Middlesex Ave, Reading, MA, 01867-2550. Tel: 781-944-0840. p. 1049
Fiorito, Mary, Acq, Circ, ILL, New York Chiropractic College Library, 2360 State Rte 89, Seneca Falls, NY, 13148-9460. Tel: 315-568-3244. p. 1639
Fiory, Cherilyn, Dir, Upper Dublin Public Library, 520 Virginia Ave, Fort Washington, PA, 19034. Tel: 215-628-8744. p. 1933
Firchow, Heather, Youth Serv Adminr, County of Los Angeles Public Library, 7400 E Imperial Hwy, Downey, CA, 90242-3375. Tel: 562-940-8522. p. 134
Firchow, Heather, Sr Librn, Youth Serv Supvr, Torrance Public Library, 3301 Torrance Blvd, Torrance, CA, 90503. Tel: 310-618-5964. p. 253
Firchow, Nancy, Librn, California State Department of Health Services, 1515 Clay St, 16th Flr, Oakland, CA, 94612. Tel: 510-622-3200. p. 185
Firchow, Nancy, Librn, California Environmental Protection Agency Public Library, 1001 I St, 2nd Flr, Sacramento, CA, 95814. Tel: 916-327-0635. p. 207
Firestine, Scott, Libr Dir, Richmond Public Library, 101 E Franklin St, Richmond, VA, 23219. Tel: 804-646-4256. p. 2341
Firestone, Megan, Archives, Head, Spec Coll, Southwestern University, 1100 E University Ave, Georgetown, TX, 78626. Tel: 512-863-1221. p. 2184
Firestone, Michael, Dir, Bayport-Blue Point Public Library, 203 Blue Point Ave, Blue Point, NY, 11715-1217. Tel: 631-363-6133. p. 1495
Firkus, Alissa, Dir of Educ, Ryerson Nature Library, 21950 N Riverwoods Rd, Riverwoods, IL, 60015. Tel: 847-968-3320. p. 640
Firman, Lynn, Head, Circ Serv, Lake Villa District Library, 140 N Munn Rd, Lindenhurst, IL, 60046. Tel: 847-245-5107. p. 609

Firman, Peggy, Assoc Dir, University of Puget Sound, 1604 N Warner St, Upper Loading Dock, Tacoma, WA, 98416. Tel: 253-879-3615. p. 2387
Firth, Jennifer, Head, Youth Serv, Long Beach Public Library, 111 W Park Ave, Long Beach, NY, 11561-3326. Tel: 516-432-7201. p. 1565
Fisch, Ronda, Dir, Libr & Res Serv, Jones Day, 500 Grant St, Ste 4500, Pittsburgh, PA, 15219. Tel: 412-391-3939. p. 1994
Fischbuch, Trish, Libr Mgr, Oyen Municipal Library, 105 Third Ave W, Oyen, AB, T0J 2J0, CANADA. Tel: 403-664-3644, Ext 2727. p. 2550
Fischer, Adrian, Curator of Collections & Exhibits, The Bakken Museum, 3537 Zenith Ave S, Minneapolis, MN, 55416. Tel: 612-926-3878. p. 1182
Fischer, Alicia, Circ Supvr, Oregon Public Library, 256 Brook St, Oregon, WI, 53575. Tel: 608-835-3656. p. 2467
Fischer, Anita, Dir, Palmer Public Library, 520 Hanson Ave, Palmer, IA, 50571. Tel: 712-359-2296. p. 776
Fischer, Anne, Dep Exec Dir, Tech, Metropolitan Library System in Oklahoma County, 300 Park Ave, Oklahoma City, OK, 73102. Tel: 405-606-3825. p. 1857
Fischer, Bill, Ad, Free Public Library & Cultural Center of Bayonne, 697 Avenue C, Bayonne, NJ, 07002. Tel: 201-858-6970. p. 1388
Fischer, Brenda, Assoc, Libr Serv, University of Jamestown, 6070 College Lane, Jamestown, ND, 58405-0001. Tel: 701-252-3467. p. 1736
Fischer, Cheryl Kelly, Dir, Loyola Law School, 919 S Albany St, Los Angeles, CA, 90015-1211. Tel: 213-736-1197. p. 166
Fischer, Christine M, Head, Tech Serv, University of North Carolina at Greensboro, 320 College Ave, Greensboro, NC, 27412-0001. Tel: 336-256-1193. p. 1693
Fischer, Glenn, Dir, DeWitt District Library, 13101 Schavey Rd, DeWitt, MI, 48820-9008. Tel: 517-669-3156. p. 1100
Fischer, Glenn, Tech Mgr, Cromaine District Library, 3688 N Hartland Rd, Hartland, MI, 48353. Tel: 810-632-5200, Ext 110. p. 1114
Fischer, Heather, Pub Info, Monarch Library System, 4632 S Taylor Dr, Sheboygan, WI, 53081-1107. Tel: 920-208-4900. p. 2477
Fischer, Jody, Ms, Dir, Wall Lake Public Library, 116 Main St, Wall Lake, IA, 51466. Tel: 712-664-2983. p. 788
Fischer, John, Mgr, Ad Serv, Normal Public Library, 206 W College Ave, Normal, IL, 61761. Tel: 309-452-1757. p. 625
Fischer, Joshua, Archives Asst, Southwest Arkansas Regional Archives, 201 Hwy 195, Washington, AR, 71862. Tel: 870-983-2633. p. 112
Fischer, Joshua, Asst Librn, Hebrew Union College-Jewish Institute of Religion, 3101 Clifton Ave, Cincinnati, OH, 45220-2488. Tel: 513-487-3283. p. 1760
Fischer, Karen, Youth Serv Mgr, Salem Public Library, 585 Liberty St SE, Salem, OR, 97301. Tel: 503-588-6039. p. 1897
Fischer, Levi, Instrul Serv Librn, Front Range Community College, 3645 W 112th Ave, Westminster, CO, 80031. p. 298
Fischer, Mary Louise, Asst Mgr, Frances T Bourne Jacaranda Public Library, 4143 Woodmere Park Blvd, Venice, FL, 34293. Tel: 941-861-1272. p. 452
Fiscus, Allison, Br Mgr, Toledo-Lucas County Public Library, Maumee, 501 River Rd, Maumee, OH, 43537. Tel: 419-259-5360. p. 1824
Fish, Courtney, Libr Dir, Corwith Public Library, 110 NW Elm, Corwith, IA, 50430. Tel: 515-583-2536. p. 742
Fish, Katherine, Acq, University of Wisconsin-La Crosse, 1631 Pine St, La Crosse, WI, 54601-3748. Tel: 608-785-8395. p. 2446
Fish, Kenneth, Coord, Interlibrary & Consortia Lending, Dominican University of California, 50 Acacia Ave, San Rafael, CA, 94901-2298. Tel: 415-257-1340. p. 236
Fish, Maureen, Library Contact, Osceola Library, W Branch Rd & Boulder Path Rd, Waterville Valley, NH, 03215. Tel: 603-236-4730. p. 1383
Fish, Shelly, Bus Mgr, Bedford Public Library, 1323 K St, Bedford, IN, 47421. Tel: 812-275-4471. p. 669
Fisher, Adam, Dir, Collections Dev & Digital Initiatives, Maine State Library, 242 State St, Augusta, ME, 04333. Tel: 207-287-5600. p. 914
Fisher, Alex, Libr Dir, Pinckneyville Public Library, 312 S Walnut St, Pinckneyville, IL, 62274. Tel: 618-357-2410. p. 635
Fisher, Amanda, Archivist, Coll Serv, Baylor University Libraries, W R Poage Legislative Library, 201 Baylor Ave, Waco, TX, 76706. Tel: 247-710-3774. p. 2253
Fisher, Ann-Marie, Exec Dir, Congregation for Humanistic Judaism, 28611 W Twelve Mile Rd, Farmington Hills, MI, 48334. Tel: 248-477-1410. p. 1104
Fisher, Barbara, Librn, Mayer, Brown LLP, 1999 K St NW, Washington, DC, 20006-1101. Tel: 202-263-3000. p. 371
Fisher, Ben, Information Technology Coord, University of Arkansas at Little Rock, 2801 S University Ave, Little Rock, AR, 72204. Tel: 501-916-6195. p. 102
Fisher, Betsy, Libr Dir, Clark County Library, 609 Caddo St, Arkadelphia, AR, 71923. Tel: 870-246-2271. p. 89
Fisher, Brittnee, Librn, Saint Johns River State College, 5001 St Johns Ave, Palatka, FL, 32177-3897. Tel: 386-312-4153. p. 433
Fisher, Carol, Librn, Talmage Public Library, 405 Main, Talmage, NE, 68448. Tel: 402-264-3875. p. 1338
Fisher, Carol, Br Librn, Southeast Regional Library, Lumsden Branch, 50 Third Ave, Lumsden, SK, S0G 3C0, CANADA. Tel: 306-731-2665. p. 2754
Fisher, Christopher, Asst Dir, Bridgewater Library Association, 62 Main St S, Bridgewater, CT, 06752-9998. Tel: 860-354-6937. p. 304
Fisher, Corinne, Head, Children's Servx, Reading Public Library, 64 Middlesex Ave, Reading, MA, 01867-2550. Tel: 781-942-6705. p. 1049
Fisher, Dave, Tech Consult, Northwest Kansas Library System, Two Washington Sq, Norton, KS, 67654-1615. Tel: 785-877-5148. p. 827
Fisher, Dawn, Br Librn, Bedford Public Library System, Big Island Library, 1111 Schooldays Rd, Big Island, VA, 24526. Tel: 540-425-7000. p. 2306
Fisher, Delores, ILL, University of Missouri-Columbia, Elmer Ellis Library, 104 Ellis Library, Columbia, MO, 65201-5149. Tel: 573-882-1101. p. 1243
Fisher, Gwen, Librn, Palliser Regional Library, Moose Jaw Branch, 461 Langdon Crescent, Moose Jaw, SK, S6H 0X6, CANADA. Tel: 306-692-2787. p. 2742
Fisher, Heather, Head, Access Serv, Saginaw Valley State University, 7400 Bay Rd, University Center, MI, 48710. Tel: 989-964-7053. p. 1155
Fisher Isaacs, Melissa, Info Serv Coordr, Lawrence Public Library, 707 Vermont St, Lawrence, KS, 66044-2371. Tel: 785-843-3833, Ext 113. p. 819
Fisher, Jan, Dep Town Librn, Fairfield Public Library, 1080 Old Post Rd, Fairfield, CT, 06824. Tel: 203-256-3154. p. 312
Fisher, Janet, Adminr, Talking Bks, Arizona State Library, Archives & Public Records, 1901 W Madison St, Phoenix, AZ, 85009. Tel: 602-255-5578. p. 69
Fisher, Jeff, Mgr, Coll Develop, Sequoyah Regional Library System, 116 Brown Industrial Pkwy, Canton, GA, 30114. Tel: 770-479-3090. p. 469
Fisher, Johnye, Head Librn, Sevier County Library, 200 W Stillwell Ave, De Queen, AR, 71832. Tel: 870-584-4364. p. 93
Fisher, Joshua, Asst Dir, Humboldt Public Library, 115 S 16th Ave, Humboldt, TN, 38343-3403. Tel: 731-784-2383. p. 2101
Fisher, Karli, Libr Dir, Fort St James Public Library, 425 Manson St, Fort St. James, BC, V0J 1P0, CANADA. Tel: 250-996-7431. p. 2566
Fisher, Karolyn, Librn, Newtown Library Co, 114 E Centre Ave, Newtown, PA, 18940. Tel: 215-968-7659. p. 1970
Fisher, Katherine, Access Serv Librn, Evening Supvr, Drexel University Libraries, Hahnemann Library, 245 N 15th St MS 449, Philadelphia, PA, 19102-1192. Tel: 215-762-1069. p. 1976
Fisher, Kelly, Head Librn, Pub Access Librn, Eureka College, 301 E College Ave, Eureka, IL, 61530-1563. Tel: 309-467-6380. p. 585
Fisher, Kiely, Dir, Lilian S Besore Memorial Library, 305 E Baltimore St, Greencastle, PA, 17225. Tel: 717-597-7920. p. 1938
Fisher, Lindsay, Libr Spec, Ref, Clovis-Carver Public Library, 701 N Main, Clovis, NM, 88101. Tel: 505-769-7840. p. 1465
Fisher, Lori, State Librn, Maine State Library, 242 State St, Augusta, ME, 04333. Tel: 207-287-5600. p. 914
Fisher, Lori, State Librn, Maine State Library, 242 State St, Augusta, ME, 04333. Tel: 207-287-5650. p. 914
Fisher, Lori A, Dir, Baker Free Library, 509 South St, Bow, NH, 03304. Tel: 603-224-7113. p. 1355
Fisher, LuAnn, Digital Res Librn, Hagerstown Community College Library, Learning Resource Ctr, No 200B, 11400 Robinwood Dr, Hagerstown, MD, 21742-6590. Tel: 240-500-2237. p. 967
Fisher, Marcy, Supvr, Circ, Dallas Baptist University, 3000 Mountain Creek Pkwy, Dallas, TX, 75211-9299. Tel: 214-333-5320. p. 2163
Fisher, Megan, Research Librn, Banner & Witcoff, Ltd Library, 71 S Wacker Dr, Ste 3600, Chicago, IL, 60606. Tel: 312-463-5000, 312-463-5455. p. 555
Fisher, Monica, Librn Supvr, Lakeland Public Library, 100 Lake Morton Dr, Lakeland, FL, 33801-5375. Tel: 863-834-4280. p. 417
Fisher, Nanette, Finance Mgr, Anythink Libraries, 5877 E 120th Ave, Thornton, CO, 80602. Tel: 303-288-2001. p. 296
Fisher, Paul, Asst Dir, Proc Archivist, Baylor University Libraries, Texas Collection & University Archives, 1429 S Fifth St, Waco, TX, 76706. Tel: 254-710-1268. p. 2253
Fisher, Rosie, Head, Communications, Prospect Heights Public Library District, 12 N Elm St, Prospect Heights, IL, 60070-1450. Tel: 847-259-3500. p. 637
Fisher, Sabra, Circ Supvr, Davis County Library, Bountiful/South Branch, 725 S Main St, Bountiful, UT, 84010. Tel: 451-451-1760. p. 2263
Fisher, Sara, Asst to the Dir, Allen County Public Library, 900 Library Plaza, Fort Wayne, IN, 46802. Tel: 260-421-1202. p. 683
Fisher, Sharon, Coordr, Reader Serv, State University of New York at Binghamton, University Downtown Center Library Information Commons & Services, 67 Washington St, Binghamton, NY, 13902-6000. Tel: 607-777-9396. p. 1494
Fisher, Tim, Circ Supvr, NHTI, Concord's Community College, 31 College Dr, Concord, NH, 03301-7425. Tel: 603-271-6484, Ext 4338. p. 1359
Fisher, Valerie, Pub Serv Librn, New Milford Public Library, 24 Main St, New Milford, CT, 06776. Tel: 860-355-1191, Ext 203. p. 329
Fisher, Vicki, Libr Serv Coordr, Black River Falls Public Library, 222 Fillmore St, Black River Falls, WI, 54615. Tel: 715-284-4112. p. 2424
Fisher, W Martin, Mgr, Recorded Media Coll, Middle Tennessee State University, Center for Popular Music, John Bragg Media & Entertainment Bldg, Rm 140, 1301 E Main St, Murfreesboro, TN, 37132. Tel: 615-898-5509. p. 2117

Fisher-Herreman, Scarlett, Tech Serv Mgr, Topeka & Shawnee County Public Library, 1515 SW Tenth Ave, Topeka, KS, 66604-1374. Tel: 785-580-4400. p. 839
Fisher-Miller, Mary, Dir, Chatsworth Township Library, 501 E School St, Chatsworth, IL, 60921. Tel: 815-635-3004. p. 553
Fishman, Julie, Head Librn, Centers for Disease Control & Prevention, Tom Harkin Global Communications Ctr, Bldg 19, 1st Flr, MS H19, 1600 Clifton Rd NE, Atlanta, GA, 30333. Tel: 404-639-1717. p. 463
Fishman, Leslie, Sr Librn, Sullivan Correctional Facility Library, 325 Riverside Dr, Fallsburg, NY, 12733. Tel: 845-434-2080. p. 1532
Fishman, Tammy, Head Librn, California Youth Authority, N A Chaderjian Youth Correctional Facility Library, 7650 S Newcastle Rd, Stockton, CA, 95213. Tel: 209-944-6444, Ext 6755. p. 249
Fishner, Carrie, Dir, SUNY Delhi, Bush Hall, 454 Delhi Dr, Delhi, NY, 13753. Tel: 607-746-4648. p. 1524
Fisk, Jim, Interim Dir, University of New Mexico, 705 Gurley Ave, Gallup, NM, 87301. Tel: 505-863-7616. p. 1468
Fiske, Marti, Libr Dir, Keene Public Library, 60 Winter St, Keene, NH, 03431. Tel: 603-757-1842. p. 1369
Fiske, Victoria, Ch, Milton Public Library, 476 Canton Ave, Milton, MA, 02186-3299. Tel: 617-698-5757. p. 1036
Fistler, Mary, Libr Coord, Pittsburgh Technical College, 1111 McKee Rd, Pittsburgh Technical Library, Oakdale, PA, 15071. Tel: 412-809-5221. p. 1972
Fitch, Wendy, Exec Dir, Museums Association of Saskatchewan, 424 McDonald St, Regina, SK, S4N 6E1, CANADA. Tel: 306-780-9280. p. 2747
Fite, Jeraca, Ref Librn, Webster Groves Public Library, 301 E Lockwood Ave, Webster Groves, MO, 63119-3102. Tel: 314-961-3784. p. 1286
Fiterre, Jennifer, Librn, Marshall Community Health Library, 3581 Palmer Dr, Ste 101, Cameron Park, CA, 95682. Tel: 530-344-5459. p. 126
Fitol, Janet, Ch, Ansonia Library, 53 S Cliff St, Ansonia, CT, 06401. Tel: 203-734-6275. p. 301
Fitos, Athanasia, Mgr, Miami-Dade Public Library System, Kendale Lakes Branch, 15205 SW 88 St, Miami, FL, 33196. Tel: 305-388-0326. p. 423
Fitos, Athanasia, Mgr, Miami-Dade Public Library System, Lakes of the Meadow Branch, 4284 SW 152nd Ave, Miami, FL, 33185. Tel: 305-222-2149. p. 423
Fitsimmons, Gary, Dir, Libr Serv, Bryan College Library, 585 Bryan Dr, Dayton, TN, 37321. Tel: 423-775-7196. p. 2096
Fittante, Patricia J, Ch Serv, Escanaba Public Library, 400 Ludington St, Escanaba, MI, 49829. Tel: 906-789-7323. p. 1103
Fitterer, Jim, Pres, Washington Township Historical Society Library, Six Fairview Ave, Long Valley, NJ, 07853-3172. Tel: 908-876-9696. p. 1414
Fitterling, Lori A, Dir, Kansas City University, 1750 Independence Ave, Kansas City, MO, 64106-1453. Tel: 816-654-7260. p. 1256
Fitts, Lindsay, Ch Serv, Mid-Mississippi Regional Library System, 201 S Huntington St, Kosciusko, MS, 39090-9002. Tel: 662-289-5151. p. 1224
Fitts, Michael, Asst Dir, Access & Doc Delivery, University of Alabama at Birmingham, Lister Hill Library of the Health Sciences, 1700 University Blvd, Birmingham, AL, 35294-0013. Tel: 205-934-5460. p. 9
Fitz-Gerald, Kerry, Ref (Info Servs), Seattle University, School of Law Library, Sullivan Hall, 901 12th Ave, Seattle, WA, 98122-4411. Tel: 206-398-4221. p. 2380
Fitz-Gerald, Maureen, Br Mgr, Shreve Memorial Library, Cedar Grove-Line Avenue Branch, 8303 Line Ave, Shreveport, LA, 71106. Tel: 318-868-3890. p. 909
Fitzgerald, Christine, Ch, Hampton Bays Public Library, 52 Ponquogue Ave, Hampton Bays, NY, 11946. Tel: 631-728-6241. p. 1544
Fitzgerald, Constance, Sister, Archivist, Carmelite Monastery, 1318 Dulaney Valley Rd, Baltimore, MD, 21286. Tel: 410-823-7415. p. 952
Fitzgerald, Deborah R, Head, Adult Serv, Library of the Chathams, 214 Main St, Chatham, NJ, 07928. Tel: 973-635-0603. p. 1395
Fitzgerald, Edward, PhD, Exec Dir, Quincy Historical Society Library, Adams Academy Bldg, Eight Adams St, Quincy, MA, 02169. Tel: 617-773-1144. p. 1048
Fitzgerald, Elizabeth A, Exec Dir, Abington Township Public Library, 1030 Old York Rd, Abington, PA, 19001-4594. Tel: 215-885-5180, Ext 114. p. 1903
Fitzgerald, Ellen, Supvr, Ch Serv, Naperville Public Library, 200 W Jefferson Ave, Naperville, IL, 60540-5374. Tel: 630-961-4100, Ext 123. p. 622
Fitzgerald, Glynis, Dir, Operations, Black Gold Cooperative Library System, 580 Camino Mercado, Arroyo Grande, CA, 93420. Tel: 805-543-6082. p. 117
Fitzgerald, Heather, Libr Coord, Tidewater Community College, 1428 Cedar Rd, Chesapeake, VA, 23322. p. 2312
Fitzgerald, Heather, Libr Serv Coordr, Tay Township Public Library, Theo & Elaine Bernard Branch, 145 Albert St, Victoria Harbour, ON, L0K 2A0, CANADA. Tel: 705-534-3581. p. 2674
Fitzgerald, Josianne, Adult Services & Technology Librn, Moultonborough Public Library, Four Holland St, Moultonborough, NH, 03254. Tel: 603-476-8895. p. 1374
Fitzgerald, Karen, Tech Serv Coordr, Douglas County Public Library, 1625 Library Lane, Minden, NV, 89423. Tel: 775-782-9841. p. 1348
Fitzgerald, Leah, Instruction & Outreach Librn, SUNY Canton, 34 Cornell Dr, Canton, NY, 13617. Tel: 315-386-7057. p. 1514
Fitzgerald, Melissa, Br Mgr, Tacoma Public Library, Fern Hill, 765 S 84th St, Tacoma, WA, 98444. Tel: 253-341-4724. p. 2387
Fitzgerald, Melissa, Br Mgr, Tacoma Public Library, South Tacoma, 3411 S 56th St, Tacoma, WA, 98409. Tel: 253-280-2960. p. 2387
Fitzgerald, Michael, Electronic Serv Librn, University of the District of Columbia, Learning Resources Division, 4200 Connecticut Ave NW, Bldg 39, Level B, Washington, DC, 20008. p. 380
FitzGerald, Mike, Ref & Info Literacy Instruction, Los Angeles Valley College Library, 5800 Fulton Ave, Valley Glen, CA, 91401-4096. Tel: 818-778-5783. p. 255
Fitzgerald, Moira, Head, Access Serv, Yale University Library, Beinecke Rare Book & Manuscript Library, 121 Wall St, New Haven, CT, 06511. Tel: 203-432-2973. p. 327
Fitzgerald, Robert, Jr, ILL, High Point University, One University Pkwy, High Point, NC, 27268. Tel: 336-841-9102. p. 1697
Fitzgerald, Roger, Dir, Knowledge & Res Serv, Gibbons PC, One Gateway Ctr, Newark, NJ, 07102-5310. Tel: 973-596-4500. p. 1426
Fitzgibbon, Willow, Dir, Libr Serv, Fayetteville Public Library, 401 W Mountain St, Fayetteville, AR, 72701. Tel: 479-856-7000. p. 95
Fitzgibbons, Eileen, Ch Serv, Prog Coordr, Norfolk Library, Nine Greenwoods Rd E, Norfolk, CT, 06058-1320. Tel: 860-542-5075. p. 330
FitzHanso, Jessica, Head, Reader Serv, Chelmsford Public Library, 25 Boston Rd, Chelmsford, MA, 01824. Tel: 978-256-5521. p. 1010
Fitzmaurice, Tracy, County Librn, Jackson County Public Library, 310 Keener St, Sylva, NC, 28779-3241. Tel: 828-586-2016, Ext 303. p. 1718
Fitzmorris, Mona, Br Librn, Plaquemines Parish Library, Buras Branch, 35572 Hwy 11, Buras, LA, 70041. Tel: 504-564-0921, 504-564-0944. p. 885
Fitzpatrick, Geoff, IT Serv Mgr, Whatcom County Library System, 5205 Northwest Dr, Bellingham, WA, 98226. Tel: 360-305-3600. p. 2359
Fitzpatrick, Katie, Dir, Staff Develop, Tech, Upper Moreland Free Public Library, 109 Park Ave, Willow Grove, PA, 19090-3277. Tel: 215-659-0741. p. 2024
Fitzpatrick, Tara, Res & Instruction Librn, Salem State University, 352 Lafayette St, Salem, MA, 01970-5353. Tel: 978-542-6765. p. 1051
Fitzsimmons, Cathy, Coord, Corp Services, Ajax Public Library, 55 Harwood Ave S, Ajax, ON, L1S 2H8, CANADA. Tel: 905-683-4000, Ext 8821. p. 2627
Fitzsimmons, John, Ref Librn, Truckee Meadows Community College, 7000 Dandini Blvd, Reno, NV, 89512-3999. Tel: 775-674-7609. p. 1349
Fitzsimmons, Phillip, Spec Coll Librn, Univ Archivist, Southwestern Oklahoma State University, 100 Campus Dr, Weatherford, OK, 73096-3002. Tel: 580-774-3030. p. 1868
Fitzsimons, Candi, Libr Dir, Johnson Public Library, 131 E Catherine St, Darlington, WI, 53530. Tel: 608-776-4171. p. 2430
Fitzsimons, Pamela, Head, Circ, East Islip Public Library, 381 E Main St, East Islip, NY, 11730-2896. Tel: 631-581-9200. p. 1528
Fix, Trudy, Br Mgr, Fulton County Library, Hustontown Branch, 313 Pitt St, Ste B, Hustontown, PA, 17229. Tel: 717-987-3606. p. 1958
Fix, Wayne, ILL, Waupun Public Library, 123 S Forest St, Waupun, WI, 53963. Tel: 920-324-7925. p. 2485
Fjelstad, Paul, Librn, Kitsap County Law Library, 614 Division St, Port Orchard, WA, 98366. Tel: 360-337-5788. p. 2374
Flach, Barbara, Dir, Greenville Public Library, 11177 Rte 32, Greenville, NY, 12083. Tel: 518-966-8205. p. 1542
Flacks, Elena, Librn, Yuba Community College, 2088 N Beale Rd, Marysville, CA, 95901. Tel: 530-741-6755, 530-741-6756. p. 175
Flageolle, Barbara, Br Mgr, Wright County Library, Mountain Grove Branch, 206 Green Ave, Mountain Grove, MO, 65711. Tel: 417-926-4453. p. 1248
Flaherty, Corinn, Asst Dir, Salisbury Public Library, 17 Elm St, Salisbury, MA, 01952. Tel: 978-465-5071. p. 1051
Flaherty, Corinn, Libr Dir, G A R Memorial Library, 490 Main St, West Newbury, MA, 01985-1115. Tel: 978-363-1105. p. 1066
Flaherty, Dan, Dir, Oil City Library, Two Central Ave, Oil City, PA, 16301-2795. Tel: 814-678-3072. p. 1972
Flaherty, Dan, Adminr, Oil Creek District Library Center, Two Central Ave, Oil City, PA, 16301. Tel: 814-678-3071. p. 1973
Flaherty, Randi, Head, Spec Coll, Historian, University of Virginia, Arthur J Morris Law Library, 580 Massie Rd, Charlottesville, VA, 22903-1738. Tel: 434-924-6355. p. 2310
Flaherty, Susan, Librn, Maine Irish Heritage Center Library, 34 Gray St, Portland, ME, 04102. Tel: 207-210-0657. p. 936
Flahive, Jean, Libr Dir, Florence Public Library, 207 E Main St, Florence, TX, 76527-4048. Tel: 254-793-2672. p. 2176
Flahive, Ryan, Archivist, Institute of American Indian Arts Library, 83 Avan Nu Po Rd, Santa Fe, NM, 87508. Tel: 505-424-2392. p. 1474
Flaming, Vaughn, Libr Asst, Santa Clara Valley Medical Center, 751 S Bascom Ave, Rm 2E063, San Jose, CA, 95128. Tel: 408-885-5652. p. 232
Flanagan, Eugene, Dir, Library of Congress, Library Services - General & International Collections Directorate, James Madison Memorial Bldg, LM 642, 101 Independence Ave SE, Washington, DC, 20540. p. 370
Flanagan, Kathleen, Sister, Circ Coordr, Benedictine College Library, 1020 N Second St, Atchison, KS, 66002-1499. Tel: 913-360-7510. p. 797

Flanagan, Laura, Dir, Ellicottville Memorial Library, 6499 Maples Rd, Ellicottville, NY, 14731. Tel: 716-699-2842. p. 1530

Flanagan, Laura, Ref Serv, Garden City Public Library, 60 Seventh St, Garden City, NY, 11530. Tel: 516-742-8405. p. 1536

Flanagan, Maureen, Asst Dir, Ch Serv, William Fogg Library, 116 Old Rd, Eliot, ME, 03903. Tel: 207-439-9437. p. 924

Flanagan, Sarah K, Dir, Flagg-Rochelle Public Library District, 619 Fourth Ave, Rochelle, IL, 61068. Tel: 815-562-3431. p. 640

Flanagan, Shabaun, Depository Library & Procurement Coord, Indiana University South Bend, 1700 Mishawaka Ave, South Bend, IN, 46615. Tel: 574-520-4394. p. 718

Flanary, Jerry, Coord, Operations & Facilities, University of Arizona Libraries, Health Sciences Library, 1501 N Campbell Ave, Tucson, AZ, 85724. Tel: 520-626-6125. p. 83

Flanders, Cheryl, Youth Serv, Ellsworth Public Library, 20 State St, Ellsworth, ME, 04605. Tel: 207-667-6363. p. 924

Flanders, E Lorene, Exec Dir, Libr Serv, University of South Alabama Libraries, Marx Library, 5901 USA Drive N, Mobile, AL, 36688. Tel: 251-460-7021. p. 27

Flanders, Julie, Head, Strategic Collection Servs, Librn III, Mount Saint Joseph University, 5701 Delhi Rd, Cincinnati, OH, 45233-1671. Tel: 513-244-4798. p. 1761

Flanders, Kristin, Head, Tech Serv, Maywood Public Library District, 121 S Fifth Ave, Maywood, IL, 60153-1307. Tel: 708-343-1847, Ext 15. p. 615

Flanders, Mae Ella, Br Mgr, Cochise County Library District, Sunsites Community Library, 210 N Ford Rd, Pearce, AZ, 85625. Tel: 520-826-3866. p. 56

Flanders, Toni, Asst Librn, Bailey Memorial Library, 111 Moulton Ave, North Clarendon, VT, 05759-9327. Tel: 802-747-7743. p. 2290

Flanigan, Abigail, Research Librn, University of Virginia, Music, Old Cabell Hall, Charlottesville, VA, 22904. Tel: 434-924-7041. p. 2310

Flanigan, Amie, Archivist, Colls Mgr, Erie Canal Museum Research Library, 318 Erie Blvd E, Syracuse, NY, 13202. Tel: 315-471-0593. p. 1648

Flannery, Adèle, Librn, Universite du Quebec, CP 8889, Succ Centre-Ville, 1255 Rue St Denis, Locale-A-1200, Montreal, QC, H3C 3P3, CANADA. Tel: 514-987-6134. p. 2728

Flannery, Mike, Assoc Dir, Hist Coll, University of Alabama at Birmingham, Lister Hill Library of the Health Sciences, 1700 University Blvd, Birmingham, AL, 35294-0013. Tel: 205-934-5460. p. 9

Flash, Kevin, Dean, Sacramento City College, 3835 Freeport Blvd, Sacramento, CA, 95822. Tel: 916-558-2461. p. 209

Flass, Kirsten, Dir, Rush Public Library, 5977 E Henrietta Rd, Rush, NY, 14543. Tel: 585-533-1370. p. 1634

Flatley, Bob, Electronic Res, Per, Kutztown University, 15200 Kutztown Rd, Bldg 5, Kutztown, PA, 19530. Tel: 610-683-4480. p. 1949

Flatley Brennan, Patricia, Dir, National Library of Medicine, Bldg 38, Rm 2E-17B, 8600 Rockville Pike, Bethesda, MD, 20894. Tel: 301-496-6308. p. 960

Flatley, Megan, Dir, Hazel Green Public Library, 1610 Fairplay St, Hazel Green, WI, 53811. Tel: 608-854-2952. p. 2441

Flatz, Connor, Libr Dir, Saint Joseph's Seminary, 201 Seminary Ave, Yonkers, NY, 10704. Tel: 914-968-6200, Ext 8255. p. 1667

Flaxbart, David, Librn, University of Texas Libraries, Mallet Chemistry Library, Welch Hall 2132, 105 E 24th St, Austin, TX, 78713. Tel: 512-495-4600. p. 2142

Flaxbeard, Lisa M, Dir, Bennington Public Library, 11401 N 156th St, Bennington, NE, 68007. Tel: 402-238-2201. p. 1308

Flayer, Steven H, Dir, Shiawassee District Library, 502 W Main St, Owosso, MI, 48867-2607. Tel: 989-725-5134. p. 1139

Flebotte, Morrigan, Libr Mgr, Gleichen & District Library, 404 Main St, Gleichen, AB, T0J 1N0, CANADA. Tel: 403-734-2390. p. 2541

Fleckenstein, Jan, Law Libr Dir/Law Librn, Syracuse University College of Law Library, 228 Dineen Hall, 950 Irving Ave, Syracuse, NY, 13244-6070. Tel: 315-443-9571. p. 1650

Flegg, Catherine, Actg Br Mgr, Ottawa Public Library/Bibliothèque publique d'Ottawa, Beaverbrook Branch, 2500 Campeau Dr, Ottawa, ON, K2K 2W3, CANADA. p. 2668

Flegg, Catherine, Actg Br Mgr, Ottawa Public Library/Bibliothèque publique d'Ottawa, Carp Branch, 3911 Carp Rd, Ottawa, ON, K0A 1L0, CANADA. p. 2668

Flegg, Catherine, Actg Br Mgr, Ottawa Public Library/Bibliothèque publique d'Ottawa, Constance Bay Branch, 262 Len Purcell, Ottawa, ON, K0A 1L0, CANADA. p. 2668

Flegg, Catherine, Actg Br Mgr, Ottawa Public Library/Bibliothèque publique d'Ottawa, Fitzroy Harbour Branch, Fitzroy Harbour Community Ctr, 100 Clifford Campbell, Ottawa, ON, K0A 1X0, CANADA. p. 2669

Flegg, Catherine, Actg Br Mgr, Ottawa Public Library/Bibliothèque publique d'Ottawa, Hazeldean Branch, 50 Castlefrank Rd, Ottawa, ON, K2L 2N5, CANADA. p. 2669

Fleischer, Christine, Dir, Frank J Basloe Library, 245 N Main St, Herkimer, NY, 13350-1918. Tel: 315-866-1733. p. 1545

Fleischer, Constance, Research Servs Librn, University of Chicago Library, D'Angelo Law Library, 1121 E 60th St, Chicago, IL, 60637-2786. Tel: 773-702-0211. p. 570

Fleischer, Victor S, Head, Archives & Spec Coll, University of Akron, University Libraries, 315 Buchtel Mall, Akron, OH, 44325-1701. Tel: 330-972-6253. p. 1745

Fleischman, Jill, Mgr, Kershaw County Library, Bethune Public, 206 S Main St, Bethune, SC, 29009. Tel: 803-310-6006. p. 2048

Fleming, Amanda, Electronic Resource & Accessibility Librn, Linfield University, 900 SE Baker St, McMinnville, OR, 97128. Tel: 503-883-2540. p. 1885

Fleming, Bonnie Elizabeth, PhD, Music Librn, Oklahoma City University, 2501 N Blackwelder, Oklahoma City, OK, 73106. Tel: 405-208-5068. p. 1858

Fleming, Cindy, Library Contact, H O K, Inc, 3200 SW Freeway, Ste 900, Houston, TX, 77027. Tel: 713-407-7700. p. 2191

Fleming, Cindy, Educ Dir, Logan Regional Medical Center, 20 Hospital Dr, Logan, WV, 25601. Tel: 304-831-1556. p. 2407

Fleming, Corey, Dir, Paterson Free Public Library, 250 Broadway, Paterson, NJ, 07501. Tel: 973-321-1223. p. 1433

Fleming, Declan, Head, Tech Serv, University of California, San Diego, 9500 Gilman Dr, Mail Code 0175G, La Jolla, CA, 92093-0175. Tel: 858-534-1287. p. 154

Fleming, Elaine, Librn, East Mississippi Regional Library System, Stonewall Public, 801 Erwin Rd, Stonewall, MS, 39363-9610. Tel: 601-659-3080. p. 1231

Fleming, Jen, Cat & Acq, San Juan Island Library, 1010 Guard St, Friday Harbor, WA, 98250-9612. Tel: 360-378-2798. p. 2364

Fleming, Jennifer, Br Mgr, Shreve Memorial Library, West Shreveport Branch, 4380 Pines Rd, Shreveport, LA, 71119. Tel: 318-635-0883. p. 910

Fleming, Jill, Head, Circ Serv, Twin Falls Public Library, 201 Fourth Ave E, Twin Falls, ID, 83301-6397. Tel: 208-733-2964. p. 532

Fleming, Judy, Supvr, Access Serv, Glendale Community College - Main, 6000 W Olive Ave, Glendale, AZ, 85302. Tel: 623-845-3117. p. 61

Fleming, Megan, Circ Mgr, Bolivar County Library System, 104 S Leflore Ave, Cleveland, MS, 38732. Tel: 662-843-2774. p. 1213

Fleming, Nell, Librn, Wisconsin School for the Deaf, 309 W Walworth Ave, Delavan, WI, 53115. Tel: 262-728-7127, Ext 7133. p. 2431

Fleming, Rachel, Coll Librn, University of Tennessee at Chattanooga Library, 400 Douglas Ave, Dept 6456, Chattanooga, TN, 37403-2598. Tel: 423-425-4501. p. 2092

Fleming, Renee J, Librn, Santa Cruz County Law Library, 701 Ocean St, Rm 070, Santa Cruz, CA, 95060. Tel: 831-420-2205. p. 243

Fleming, Robyn, ILL, Metropolitan Museum of Art, Thomas J Watson Library, 1000 Fifth Ave, New York, NY, 10028-0198. Tel: 212-650-2225. p. 1592

Fleming, Sean, Libr Dir, Lebanon Public Libraries, Nine E Park St, Lebanon, NH, 03766. Tel: 603-448-2459. p. 1370

Fleming, Sean, Ad, Fort Erie Public Library, 136 Gilmore Rd, Fort Erie, ON, L2A 2M1, CANADA. Tel: 905-871-2546, Ext 304. p. 2642

Fleming, Shelley, Br Supvr, Elgin County Library, John Kenneth Galbraith Reference Library-Dutton Branch, 236 Shackleton St, Dutton, ON, N0L 1J0, CANADA. Tel: 519-762-2780. p. 2681

Fleming, Shelley, Br Supvr, Elgin County Library, Rodney Library, 207 Furnival Rd, Rodney, ON, N0L 2C0, CANADA. Tel: 519-785-2100. p. 2681

Fleming, Shelley, Br Supvr, Elgin County Library, West Lorne Library, 160A Main St, West Lorne, ON, N0L 2P0, CANADA. Tel: 519-768-1150. p. 2681

Fleming, Stanton, Dir, User Serv, Westminster College, S Market St, New Wilmington, PA, 16172-0001. Tel: 724-946-6000. p. 1970

Fleming, Stephen, Dir, Global Intelligence, Three Columbus Circle, New York, NY, 10019. Tel: 212-210-3983. p. 1587

Flemming, Jody, Br Mgr, Jackson County Library Services, Phoenix Branch, 510 W First St, Phoenix, OR, 97535. Tel: 541-535-7090. p. 1886

Flemmings, Tracey, Dr, Interim Pres, Barber Scotia College, 145 Cabarrus Ave W, Concord, NC, 28025. Tel: 704-789-2900. p. 1682

Flener, Becky, Librn, Bowerston Public Library, 200 Main St, Bowerston, OH, 44695. Tel: 740-269-8531. p. 1752

Flengeris, Carla L, Coordr, University of Regina, Luther College Library, 3737 Wascana Pkwy, Regina, SK, S4S 0A2, CANADA. Tel: 306-585-5030. p. 2748

Fleschner, Julius, Dean of Libr, Georgia Highlands College Libraries, 5441 Hwy 20 NE, Cartersville, GA, 30121. Tel: 678-872-8400. p. 470

Fleschner, Julius, Dean of Libr, Georgia Highlands College Libraries, 3175 Cedartown Hwy SE, Rome, GA, 30161. Tel: 706-295-6318. p. 494

Fleshman, Sandra, Prog Coordr, Rowan County Public Library, 175 Beacon Hill Dr, Morehead, KY, 40351-6031. Tel: 606-784-7137. p. 869

Fletcher, Amy, Head, Acq, Head, Tech Serv, Louis Bay 2nd Library, 345 Lafayette Ave, Hawthorne, NJ, 07506-2546. Tel: 973-427-5745, Ext 18. p. 1407

Fletcher, Anneh, Coll Spec, Ref Serv, Canadian Museum of History Library, 100 Laurier St, Gatineau, QC, K1A 0M8, CANADA. Tel: 819-776-7173. p. 2712

Fletcher, Barbara, Librn, Royal Public Library, 302 Main St, Royal, IA, 51357. Tel: 712-933-5500. p. 780

Fletcher, Brenda, Dir, Walhalla Public Library, 1010 Central Ave, Walhalla, ND, 58282-4015. Tel: 701-549-3794. p. 1741

Fletcher, Carolyn, Dir, Gruver City Library, 504 King St, Gruver, TX, 79040. Tel: 806-733-2191. p. 2187

Fletcher, Deborah, Supvr, Ventura County Library, Meiners Oaks Library, 114 N Padre Juan Ave, Meiners Oaks, CA, 93023. Tel: 805-646-4804. p. 256

Fletcher, Elizabeth, Libr Asst, Justice Institute of British Columbia Library, 715 McBride Blvd, New Westminster, BC, V3L 5T4, CANADA. Tel: 604-528-5596. p. 2572

Fletcher, Galen L, Govt Doc, Brigham Young University, Howard W Hunter Law Library, 256 JRCB, Provo, UT, 84602-8000. Tel: 801-422-3593. p. 2269

Fletcher, Karen, Br Librn, Wapiti Regional Library, Weldon Public Library, Ten First Ave, Weldon, SK, S0J 3A0, CANADA. Tel: 306-887-4466. p. 2746

Fletcher, Kathy, Ref Librn, Pub Serv, University of New Hampshire School of Law, Two White St, Concord, NH, 03301. p. 1360

Fletcher, Lauri, Digital Servs & Navigation Librn, Indiana Free Library, Inc, 845 Philadelphia St, Indiana, PA, 15701-3907. Tel: 724-465-8841. p. 1945

Fletcher, Lydia, Liaison Librn, University of Texas Libraries, Kuehne Physics-Mathematics-Astronomy Library, Robert L Moore Hall 4.200, S5441, 2515 Speedway, Austin, TX, 78713. Tel: 512-495-4610. p. 2142

Fletcher-Spear, Kristin, Br Mgr, Glendale Public Library, 5959 W Brown St, Glendale, AZ, 85302-1248. Tel: 623-930-3556. p. 62

Flett, Melissa, Dir, Wood Buffalo Regional Library, One CA Knight Way, Fort McMurray, AB, T9H 5C5, CANADA. Tel: 780-743-7800. p. 2540

Flett, Michele, Supvr, Yakima Valley Libraries, White Swan Library, 391 First St, White Swan, WA, 98952. Tel: 509-874-2060. p. 2396

Flett, Theresa, Libr Dir, St Charles Community College, 4601 Mid Rivers Mall Dr, Cottleville, MO, 63376. Tel: 636-922-8587. p. 1244

Fleure, Lynn, Pub Serv Coordr, Way Public Library, 101 E Indiana Ave, Perrysburg, OH, 43551. Tel: 419-874-3135, Ext 111. p. 1815

Fleuren-Hunter, Kristel, Ch Serv Librn, Supvr, Pictou - Antigonish Regional Library, Antigonish Town & County Library, 283 Main St, Antigonish, NS, B2G 2C3, CANADA. Tel: 902-863-4276. p. 2622

Fleurie-Wohlleb, Jodi, Librn, Groton Free Public Library, 1304 Scott Hwy, Groton, VT, 05046. Tel: 802-584-3358. p. 2285

Fleury, Carol, Ref Serv, Morris College, 100 W College St, Sumter, SC, 29150-3599. Tel: 803-934-3230. p. 2071

Fleury, Ian, Libr Tech Spec, Floyd Memorial Library, 539 First St, Greenport, NY, 11944-1399. Tel: 631-477-0660. p. 1541

Flewelling, Debra, Open Education Librn, Douglas College Library & Learning Centre, 700 Royal Ave, Rm N2100, New Westminster, BC, V3M 5Z5, CANADA. Tel: 604-527-5190. p. 2572

Flewelling, Janet, Head, Emerging & Creative Technologies, Wallingford Public Library, 200 N Main St, Wallingford, CT, 06492. Tel: 203-284-6424. p. 343

Flick, Kurt, Sr Res Librn, Consumer Technology Association (CTA), 1919 S Eads St, Arlington, VA, 22202. Tel: 703-907-7600. p. 2305

Flickner, Kevin, Tech & Ref, Columbia International University, 7435 Monticello Rd, Columbia, SC, 29203-1599. Tel: 803-807-5112. p. 2053

Fliegel, Doreen, Librn, Chinook Regional Library, Pennant Branch, 229 Standard St, Pennant, SK, S0N 1X0, CANADA. Tel: 306-626-3316. p. 2752

Fliger, Lacey, Youth Serv Librn, Mary Lib Saleh Euless Public Library, 201 N Ector Dr, Euless, TX, 76039-3595. Tel: 817-685-1480. p. 2176

Flinchbaugh, Michelle, Digital Scholarship Librn, University of Maryland, Baltimore County, 1000 Hilltop Circle, Baltimore, MD, 21250. Tel: 410-455-2356. p. 958

Flinchbaugh, Stephanie, Br Mgr, Chicago Public Library, West Town, 1625 W Chicago Ave, Chicago, IL, 60622. Tel: 312-743-0450. p. 557

Flinchum, Nathan, Pub Serv Librn, Roanoke Public Libraries, 706 S Jefferson St, Roanoke, VA, 24016-5191. Tel: 540-853-2473. p. 2345

Flinn, Sandy, Circ Supvr, LeTourneau University, 2100 S Mobberly Ave, Longview, TX, 75602-3524. Tel: 903-233-3263. p. 2213

Flint, Arlene, Asst Dir, Manteno Public Library District, Ten S Walnut St, Manteno, IL, 60950. Tel: 815-468-3323. p. 613

Flint, Debra, Libr Dir, Galway Public Library, 2112 East St, Galway, NY, 12074-2341. Tel: 518-882-6385. p. 1536

Flint, Lacey, Archivist & Curator of Res Col, Librn, The Explorers Club, 46 E 70th St, New York, NY, 10021. Tel: 212-628-8383. p. 1585

Flint, Ruth Ellen, Ref Librn, Louisville Free Public Library, Highlands-Shelby Park, 1250 Bardstown Rd, Ste 4, Louisville, KY, 40204. Tel: 502-574-1672. p. 865

Fliss, Susan, Dean of Libr, Smith College Libraries, Four Tyler Dr, Northampton, MA, 01063. Tel: 413-585-2910. p. 1042

Fliss, Susan, Dean of Libr, Smith College Libraries, Young Library, Four Tyler Dr, Northampton, MA, 01063. p. 1043

Flock, Angela, Young Adult Serv Coordr, Coeur d'Alene Public Library, 702 E Front Ave, Coeur d'Alene, ID, 83814-2373. Tel: 208-769-2315. p. 519

Flock, JoDee, Dir, Bancroft Public Library, 103 E Poplar St, Bancroft, NE, 68004. Tel: 402-648-3350. p. 1306

Flockton, Andrea, Head, Coll Develop, University of Louisiana at Lafayette, 400 E St Mary Blvd, Lafayette, LA, 70503. Tel: 337-482-6677. p. 893

Flood, Derrick, Dir, Halifax Community College Library, 100 College Dr, Weldon, NC, 27890. Tel: 252-536-7236. p. 1721

Flood, Pam, Br Mgr, Superior District Library, 541 Library Dr, Sault Sainte Marie, MI, 49783. Tel: 906-632-9331. p. 1149

Flood, Sarah, Dir, Breckinridge County Public Library, 308 Old Hwy 60, Hardinsburg, KY, 40143. Tel: 270-756-2323. p. 857

Flood, Stephanie, Libr Mgr, Avondale Public Library, Avondale Civic Center Library, 11350 W Civic Ctr Dr, Avondale, AZ, 85323. Tel: 623-333-2602. p. 55

Flood, Stephanie, Dir, Lincoln Park Public Library, 12 Boonton Tpk, Lincoln Park, NJ, 07035. Tel: 973-694-8283. p. 1412

Flood, Theresa, IT Mgr, Network Serv, East Cleveland Public Library, 14101 Euclid Ave, East Cleveland, OH, 44112-3891. Tel: 216-541-4128. p. 1783

Floor, Frank, Asst Dir, East Smithfield Public Library, 50 Esmond St, Smithfield, RI, 02917-3016. Tel: 401-231-5150, Ext 6. p. 2042

Flora, Brenda, Archivist, Amistad Research Center, Tulane University, Tilton Hall, 6823 St Charles Ave, New Orleans, LA, 70118. Tel: 504-862-3221. p. 900

Floray, Allison, Libr Dir, Emmaus Public Library, 11 E Main St, Emmaus, PA, 18049. Tel: 610-965-9284. p. 1930

Florence, Fairy, Dir, Thompson Public Library, 102 N Jackson St, Thompson, IA, 50478. Tel: 641-584-2829. p. 786

Florence-Walker, Patrice, Br Mgr, Orange County Library System, Eatonville Branch, 200 E Kennedy Blvd, Eatonville, FL, 32751. p. 431

Florenzen, Heidi, Asst Dir, Hermiston Public Library, 235 E Gladys Ave, Hermiston, OR, 97838. Tel: 541-567-2882. p. 1881

Flores, Adriana, Archivist, Spec Coll Librn, University of Puget Sound, 1604 N Warner St, Upper Loading Dock, Tacoma, WA, 98416. Tel: 253-879-2669. p. 2387

Flores, Angel, Adult & Teen Serv Mgr, Ella Johnson Memorial Public Library District, 109 S State St, Hampshire, IL, 60140. Tel: 847-683-4490. p. 596

Flores, Catalina, Br Coordr, Circ, Whitman County Rural Library District, 102 S Main St, Colfax, WA, 99111-1863. Tel: 509-397-4366. p. 2362

Flores, EvaLyn, Early Literacy Specialist, Outreach Specialist, Laramie County Library System, 2200 Pioneer Ave, Cheyenne, WY, 82001-3610. Tel: 307-773-7204. p. 2492

Flores, Griselda, Br Mgr, San Bernardino County Library, Montclair Branch, 9955 Fremont Ave, Montclair, CA, 91763. Tel: 909-624-4671. p. 213

Flores, John, Librn III, Dallas College, Bldg L, 3939 Valley View Lane, Farmers Branch, TX, 75244-4997. Tel: 972-860-4854. p. 2176

Flores, John G, Libr Dir, Dover Free Library, 22 Hollands Rd, East Dover, VT, 05341-9617. Tel: 802-348-7488. p. 2283

Flores, Kim, Br Mgr, Springfield-Greene County Library District, Library Station, 2535 N Kansas Expressway, Springfield, MO, 65803-1114. Tel: 417-865-1340. p. 1281

Flores, Noemi, Ser Librn, University of Saint Thomas, Cardinal Beran Library at Saint Mary's Seminary, 9845 Memorial Dr, Houston, TX, 77024-3498. Tel: 713-654-5774. p. 2200

Flores, Vivianna, Assoc Librn, Eloy Santa Cruz Library, 1000 N Main St, Eloy, AZ, 85131. Tel: 520-466-3814. p. 60

Flores, Xaviera, Librn & Archivist, University of California Los Angeles Library, Chicano Studies Research Center Library & Archive, 144 Haines Hall, Los Angeles, CA, 90095-1544. Tel: 310-206-6052. p. 169

Flores-Caraballo, Eliut, Prof, University of Puerto Rico, Rio Piedras Campus, PO Box 21906, San Juan, PR, 00931-1906. Tel: 787-764-0000, Ext 8521, 787-764-6199. p. 2795

Florez, Kurt, Chief Info Officer, University of Maryland, 2020 Horns Point Rd, Cambridge, MD, 21613. Tel: 410-221-2021. p. 960

Florio, Joseph, Dir, Libr Serv, Davis Polk & Wardwell LLP Library, 450 Lexington Ave, New York, NY, 10017. Tel: 212-450-4000. p. 1585

Flotten, Martha, Library Contact, Multnomah County Library, Hollywood, 4040 NE Tillamook St, Portland, OR, 97212. p. 1892

Flournoy, Ann, Dir, Keller Public Library, 640 Johnson Rd, Keller, TX, 76248. Tel: 817-743-4800. p. 2205

Flower, Ann, Asst Dir, Monterey Institute of International Studies, 425 Van Buren St, Monterey, CA, 93940. Tel: 831-647-4136. p. 179

Flower, Kenneth, Assoc Dir, Johns Hopkins University Libraries, The Sheridan Libraries, 3400 N Charles St, Baltimore, MD, 21218. Tel: 410-516-8325. p. 954

Flowers, Audrey, Dir, Meade Public Library, 104 E West Plains, Meade, KS, 67864. Tel: 620-873-2522. p. 825

Flowers, Deloris, Mgr, Tech Serv, Mary Wood Weldon Memorial Library, 1530 S Green St, Glasgow, KY, 42141. Tel: 270-651-2824. p. 857

Flowers, Jackie, Chief Exec Officer, Dir of Libr, Pickering Public Library, One The Esplanade, Pickering, ON, L1V 2R6, CANADA. Tel: 905-831-6265, Ext 6222. p. 2672

Flowers, Jamie, Libr Mgr, San Antonio Public Library, Semmes, 15060 Judson Rd, San Antonio, TX, 78247. Tel: 210-207-9110. p. 2239

Flowers, Jamon Antwain, Dir, Libr & Tech, Wright State University, 182 Andrews Hall, 7600 Lake Campus Dr, Celina, OH, 45822. Tel: 937-775-8360. p. 1757

Flowers, Marla, Exec Dir, Vigo County Historical Museum Library, 929 Wabash Ave, Terre Haute, IN, 47803. Tel: 812-235-9717. p. 721

Flowers, Nathan, Head, Syst, Librn, Francis Marion University, 4822 E Palmetto St, Florence, SC, 29506. Tel: 843-661-1306. p. 2059

Flowers, Shannon D, Librn, Rube Sessions Memorial Library, 298 Rusk Ave, Wells, TX, 75976. Tel: 936-867-4757. p. 2256

Floyd, Allison, Ref Librn, Northwest Arkansas Community College, One College Dr, Bentonville, AR, 72712. Tel: 479-619-4244. p. 91

Floyd, Debbie, Circ Supvr, Marion County Library System, 101 East Court St, Marion, SC, 29571. Tel: 843-423-8300. p. 2065

Floyd, James, Dr, Cat, Coll Develop Librn, Hardin-Simmons University, 2200 Hickory St, Abilene, TX, 79698. Tel: 325-670-1236. p. 2132

Floyd, Joni, Archivist, Howard University Libraries, Louis Stokes Health Sciences Library, 501 W St NW, Washington, DC, 20059. Tel: 202-884-1729. p. 369

Floyd, Kathryn, Cat Librn, Geneva College, 3200 College Ave, Beaver Falls, PA, 15010-3599. Tel: 724-847-6688. p. 1909

Floyd, Kristi, Admin Coordr, Pub Serv, Westbank Community Library District, 1309 Westbank Dr, Austin, TX, 78746. Tel: 512-327-3045. p. 2143

Floyd, Kristy, Tech Serv Librn, Chesapeake College, 1000 College Circle, Wye Mills, MD, 21679. Tel: 410-827-5860. p. 981

Floyd, Marilyn, Asst Pub Serv Librn, Alabama Supreme Court & State Law Library, Heflin-Torbert Judicial Bldg, 300 Dexter Ave, Montgomery, AL, 36104. Tel: 334-229-0578. p. 28

Floyd, Sherrie, Instrul Librn, Columbus Technical College Library, 928 Manchester Expressway, Columbus, GA, 31904-6577. Tel: 706-641-1680. p. 472

Fluharty, Tom, Hed, Bkmobile Dept, Head, Outreach Serv, Montgomery County-Norristown Public Library, 1001 Powell St, Norristown, PA, 19401-3817. Tel: 610-278-5100, Ext 109. p. 1971

Fluk, Louise, Coll Develop Librn, Fiorello H LaGuardia Community College Library, 31-10 Thomson Ave, Long Island City, NY, 11101. Tel: 718-482-5424. p. 1565

Flum, Judith, Bibliog Instruction Librn, Libr Coord, Contra Costa College Library, 2600 Mission Bell Dr, San Pablo, CA, 94806. Tel: 510-215-4996. p. 236

Flury, James, Mgr, Tech Serv, The Library Network, 41365 Vincenti Ct, Novi, MI, 48375. Tel: 248-536-3100. p. 2767

Flying By, Ramona, Head Librn, Dewey County Library, 712 Main, Timber Lake, SD, 57656. Tel: 605-865-3541. p. 2083

Flynn, Ally, Librn, Camosun College, Liz Ashton Campus Centre Library, 4461 Inteurban Rd, 3rd Flr, Victoria, BC, V9E 2C1, CANADA. Tel: 250-370-4994. p. 2582

Flynn, Annalise, Curator, SPACES - Saving + Preserving Arts + Cultural Environments, 725-X Woodlake Rd, Kohler, WI, 53044. Tel: 920-458-1972, Ext 70419. p. 2446

Flynn, Ashley, Exec Dir, Cambria County Library System & District Center, 248 Main St, Johnstown, PA, 15901. Tel: 814-536-5131. p. 1947

Flynn, Christie, Dean, Libr & Learning Res, Pierce College Library, Fort Steilacoom Campus/Cascade Bldg 4, 9401 Farwest Dr SW, Lakewood, WA, 98498. Tel: 253-964-6553. p. 2368

Flynn, Christine, Libr Dir, Marie Fleche Memorial Library, 49 S White Horse Pike, Berlin, NJ, 08009. Tel: 856-787-2448, Ext 5. p. 1390

Flynn, Gary, District Libr Mgr, Gateway Technical College, North Bldg, Rm N226, 400 County Rd H, Elkhorn, WI, 53121. Tel: 262-564-2640. p. 2433

Flynn, Gary, District Libr Mgr, Gateway Technical College, Academic Bldg, Rm A103, 3520 30th Ave, Kenosha, WI, 53144-1690. Tel: 262-564-2786. p. 2444

Flynn, Gary, District Libr Mgr, Gateway Technical College, Lake Bldg, Lower Level, Rm L008, 1001 S Main St, Racine, WI, 53403-1582. Tel: 262-564-2640. p. 2471

Flynn, Jennifer, Mgr, Outreach Serv, Bedford Public Library, 1323 K St, Bedford, IN, 47421. Tel: 812-275-4471. p. 669

Flynn, Jordan, Admin Mgr, Drake University, 2725 University Ave, Des Moines, IA, 50311. Tel: 515-271-1936. p. 746

Flynn, Kathie, Dir, Glen Cove Public Library, Four Glen Cove Ave, Glen Cove, NY, 11542-2885. Tel: 516-676-2130. p. 1538

Flynn, Kathleen, Sr Asst Librn, University at Albany, State University of New York, Science Library, 1400 Washington Ave, Albany, NY, 12222. Tel: 518-437-3948. p. 1484

Flynn, Kelly, Commun Relations Mgr, Genesee District Library, 4195 W Pasadena Ave, Flint, MI, 48504. Tel: 810-732-0110. p. 1105

Flynn, Larry, Computer Services Specialist, Suffolk University, John Joseph Moakley Law Library, 120 Tremont St, 6th Flr, Boston, MA, 02108-4977. Tel: 617-573-8177. p. 1000

Flynn, Mari, Assoc Dean, Keystone College, One College Green, La Plume, PA, 18440-0200. Tel: 570-945-8332. p. 1950

Flynn, Patti, Adminr, Gable & Gotwals, Inc, 1100 Oneok Plaza, 100 W Fifth St, Tulsa, OK, 74103. Tel: 918-595-4938. p. 1864

Flynn, Robbie, Asst Librn, Hebron Library, Eight Church Lane, Hebron, NH, 03241. Tel: 603-744-7998. p. 1367

Flynn, Rosemary Pleva, Librn, University of North Dakota, Energy & Environmental Research Center Library, 15 N 23rd St, Stop 9018, Grand Forks, ND, 58202-9018. Tel: 701-777-5132. p. 1735

Flynn, Thomas, Access Serv Librn, Southwest Minnesota State University Library, 1501 State St, Marshall, MN, 56258. Tel: 507-537-6788. p. 1182

Flynn, Thomas, Assoc Dir, Archives Research Learning & Outreach, Winston-Salem State University, 601 Martin Luther King Jr Dr, Winston-Salem, NC, 27110. Tel: 336-750-2426. p. 1726

Fobert, John, Electronic Res Librn, Roger Williams University Library, One Old Ferry Rd, Bristol, RI, 02809. Tel: 401-254-3374. p. 2030

Focarazzo, Marjorie, Admin Coordr, Rochester Civic Garden Center, Inc Library, Five Castle Park, Rochester, NY, 14620. Tel: 716-473-5130. p. 1629

Focht, Adria, Pres & Chief Exec Officer, Charlotte Museum of History, 3500 Shamrock Dr, Charlotte, NC, 28215. Tel: 704-568-1774. p. 1680

Focke, Amanda, Head, Spec Coll & Archives, Rice University, 6100 Main, MS-44, Houston, TX, 77005. Tel: 713-348-2124. p. 2197

Fodde-Reguer, Anna-Alexandra, Res & Instruction Librn, Haverford College, 370 Lancaster Ave, Haverford, PA, 19041-1392. Tel: 610-896-1170. p. 1942

Fogarty, Canda, Libr Dir, Dr W B Konkle Memorial Library, 384 Broad St, Montoursville, PA, 17754-2206. Tel: 570-368-1840. p. 1965

Fogarty, Kelly, Mgr, Ochsner Medical Library, 1514 Jefferson Hwy, 1st Flr, New Orleans, LA, 70121-2429. Tel: 504-842-3760. p. 903

Fogarty, Molly, Dir, Springfield City Library, 220 State St, Springfield, MA, 01103. Tel: 413-263-6828, Ext 290. p. 1056

Fogarty, Shirley, Br Mgr, Pine Mountain Regional Library, Hightower Memorial, 800 W Gordon St, Thomaston, GA, 30286-3417. Tel: 706-647-8649. p. 488

Fogarty, Stephanie, Children & Teen Librn, Madrid Public Library, 100 W Third St, Madrid, IA, 50156. Tel: 515-795-3846. p. 766

Fogel, Jaime, Ms, Dir, Libr & Archive Serv, Mote Marine Laboratory Library & Archives, 1600 Ken Thompson Pkwy, Sarasota, FL, 34236-1096. Tel: 941-388-4441, Ext 333. p. 443

Fogel, Jamie, Colls Mgr, Bok Tower Gardens, 1151 Tower Blvd, Lake Wales, FL, 33853-3412. Tel: 863-734-1227. p. 416

Fogg, Valerie, Tech Asst, American Association of Textile Chemists & Colorists Library, One Davis Dr, Research Triangle Park, NC, 27709. Tel: 919-549-3534. p. 1712

Foggatt, Stephen C, PhD, Assoc Dean, Academic Services, New Mexico Military Institute, Toles Learning Ctr, 101 W College Blvd, Roswell, NM, 88201. Tel: 575-624-8381. p. 1474

Foghino, Kimberly, Dir, Mendon Township Library, 314 W Main St, Mendon, MI, 49072. Tel: 269-496-4865. p. 1131

Fogle, Don, Info Spec, Show Low Public Library, 181 N Ninth St, Show Low, AZ, 85901. Tel: 928-532-4065. p. 78

Fogle, Laura, Dir, North Carolina State University Libraries, College of Education Media Center, DH Hill Jr Library, B404, 2 W Broughton Dr, Raleigh, NC, 27695. Tel: 919-515-3191. p. 1709

Fogle, Leroy, Ref Librn, Voorhees University, 213 Wiggins Dr, Denmark, SC, 29042. Tel: 803-780-1220. p. 2058

Fogle, Lynn, Ms, Dir, Knowledge Mgt, Ice Miller LLP, One American Sq, Ste 2900, Indianapolis, IN, 46282-0020. Tel: 317-236-2472. p. 692

Foglia, Ashley, Dir, Bradley Beach Public Library, 511 Fourth Ave, Bradley Beach, NJ, 07720. Tel: 732-776-2995. p. 1391

Fokerts, Dana, Youth Serv Mgr, Pickerington Public Library, 201 Opportunity Way, Pickerington, OH, 43147-1296. Tel: 614-837-4101, Ext 230. p. 1815

Folaron, Nancy, Asst Dir, Shiawassee District Library, Durand Memorial Branch, 700 N Saginaw St, Durand, MI, 48429-1245. Tel: 989-288-3743. p. 1140

Folck, Isabel, Archivist, Spec Coll Librn, Hollins University, 7950 E Campus Dr, Roanoke, VA, 24020. Tel: 540-362-6237. p. 2345

Folds, Dusty, Librn, Jefferson State Community College, 2601 Carson Rd, Birmingham, AL, 35215. Tel: 205-856-7786. p. 8

Folensbee-Moore, Barbara, Dir, Venable LLP Library, 750 E Pratt St, 9th Flr, Baltimore, MD, 21202. Tel: 410-244-7502. p. 958

Folensbee-Moore, Barbara, Dir, Venable LLP Library, Towson Office, 210 W Pennsylvania Ave, Ste 500, Towson, MD, 21204. Tel: 410-494-6200. p. 958

Foley, Bernadette, Head, Children's Servx, Medfield Public Library, 468 Main St, Medfield, MA, 02052-2008. Tel: 508-359-4544. p. 1033

Foley, Bernadette, Ch, Westborough Public Library, 55 W Main St, Westborough, MA, 01581. Tel: 508-366-3050. p. 1066

Foley, Brian, Librn, Mike Durfee State Prison, 1412 Wood St, Springfield, SD, 57062. Tel: 605-369-2201. p. 2083

Foley, Erin, Dir, Adams County Library, 569 N Cedar St, Ste 1, Adams, WI, 53910-9800. Tel: 608-339-4250. p. 2419

Foley, Janice, Dir, Riverside Public Library, One Burling Rd, Riverside, IL, 60546. Tel: 708-442-6366, Ext 100. p. 639

Foley, Jessica, Youth Serv, Hanson Public Library, 132 Maquan St, Hanson, MA, 02341. Tel: 781-293-2151. p. 1023

Foley, Kathryn, Dir, Chinook Regional Library, 1240 Chaplin St W, Swift Current, SK, S9H 0G8, CANADA. Tel: 306-773-3186. p. 2752

Foley, Katie, Evening & Weekend Circ Supvr, Salve Regina University, 100 Ochre Point Ave, Newport, RI, 02840-4192. Tel: 401-341-2330. p. 2035

Foley, Matt, Research Librn, Williams & Connolly Library, 680 Maine Ave SW, Washington, DC, 20024. Tel: 202-434-5308. p. 381

Foley, Shay, Dir, Metadata & Digital Strategies, Hamilton College, 198 College Hill Rd, Clinton, NY, 13323. Tel: 315-859-4487. p. 1519

Folger, Jane, Ch, Maplewood Memorial Library, Hilton, 1688 Springfield Ave, Maplewood, NJ, 07040-2923. p. 1416

Folger, Jane, Head, Children's Servx, Maplewood Memorial Library, 129 Boyden Ave, Maplewood, NJ, 07040. Tel: 973-762-1688. p. 1416

Folk, Amy, Archivist, Colls Mgr, Oysterponds Historical Society, 1555 Village Lane, Orient, NY, 11957. Tel: 631-323-2480. p. 1612

Folk, Amy, Colls Mgr, Southold Historical Society Museum Library, 54325 Main Rd, Southold, NY, 11971. Tel: 631-765-5500. p. 1643
Folken, Julie, Dir, Kothe Memorial Library, 309 Third St, Parkersburg, IA, 50665-1030. Tel: 319-346-2442. p. 776
Folkers, Karen, Dir, Armstrong Public Library, 308 Sixth St, Armstrong, IA, 50514. Tel: 712-868-3353. p. 732
Folkins, Betsy, ILL, Per, Graceland University, One University Pl, Lamoni, IA, 50140. Tel: 641-784-5483. p. 764
Follett, Kalvin, Library Contact, Christian Record Services for the Blind, 5900 S 58th St, Ste M, Lincoln, NE, 68516. Tel: 402-488-0981. p. 1321
Folmer, Fred, Dir, Library Collections, Access & Discovery, Connecticut College, 270 Mohegan Ave, New London, CT, 06320-4196. Tel: 860-439-2655. p. 328
Folse, Linda, Circ, Phillips Graduate University Library, 19900 Plummer St, Chatsworth, CA, 91311. Tel: 818-386-5640. p. 129
Folse, Stephanie, Info Tech, Texas Christian University, 2913 Lowden St, TCU Box 298400, Fort Worth, TX, 76129. Tel: 817-257-7106. p. 2181
Folsom, Danielle, ILL, Louisburg Public Library, 206 S Broadway, Louisburg, KS, 66053. Tel: 913-837-2217. p. 822
Folsom, Kristy, Dir, Manchester Public Library, 304 N Franklin St, Manchester, IA, 52057. Tel: 563-927-3719. p. 767
Foltz, Kay, Libr Operations Mgr, Ohio State University LIBRARIES, Louis Bromfield Library - Mansfield Campus, 1660 University Dr, Mansfield, OH, 44906-1599. Tel: 419-755-4324. p. 1775
Foltz, Monika, Dir & Librn, Industry Public Library, 1646 N Main St, Industry, TX, 78944. Tel: 979-357-4434. p. 2202
Fonda, Mary, Br Librn, Moss Memorial Library, 26 Anderson St, Hayesville, NC, 28904. Tel: 828-389-8401. p. 1695
Fondren, Angela, Open Educational Resources Librn, Alamo Colleges District, 1201 Kitty Hawk Rd, Universal City, TX, 78148. Tel: 210-486-5468. p. 2250
Fonfa, Raven, Ref & Info Literacy Librn, Culinary Institute of America, 1946 Campus Dr, Hyde Park, NY, 12538-1430. Tel: 845-451-1323. p. 1550
Fong, Janelle, Librn, Weintraub Tobin, 400 Capitol Mall, Ste 1100, Sacramento, CA, 95814. Tel: 916-558-6000, Ext 6094. p. 210
Fong, Kim, Libr Dir, Murray Public Library, 166 E 5300 South, Murray, UT, 84107. Tel: 801-264-2585. p. 2267
Fong, Valerie, Dean, Foothill College, 12345 El Monte Rd, Los Altos Hills, CA, 94022-4599. p. 159
Fonseca, Anthony, Archivist, Dir, College of Our Lady of the Elms, 291 Springfield St, Chicopee, MA, 01013-2839. Tel: 413-265-2280. p. 1011
Fonseca, Josee, Libr & Info Spec, NYS Small Business Development Center Research Network, Ten N Pearl St, Albany, NY, 12246. Tel: 518-944-2840. p. 1483
Fontaine, Aimee, Libr Mgr, Community Libraries of Providence, Rochambeau Library, 708 Hope St, Providence, RI, 02906. Tel: 401-272-3780. p. 2038
Fontaine, Aimee, Syst Coordr, Community Libraries of Providence, PO Box 9267, Providence, RI, 02940. Tel: 401-272-3780, Ext 4406. p. 2038
Fontaine, Jessica K, Dir, Storrowton Village Museum Library, 1305 Memorial Ave, West Springfield, MA, 01089. Tel: 413-205-5051. p. 1066
Fontaine, Julie, Dir, Bibliotheque Municipale d'Asbestos, 351 Saint Luc Blvd, Asbestos, QC, J1T 2W4, CANADA. Tel: 819-879-7171, Ext 3401. p. 2709
Fontaine, Kayla, Head, Teen Serv, Booth & Dimock Memorial Library, 1134 Main St, Coventry, CT, 06238. Tel: 860-742-7606. p. 306
Fontaine, Ray, Head, Children's Servx, Derry Public Library, 64 E Broadway, Derry, NH, 03038-2412. Tel: 603-432-6140. p. 1361
Fontane, Walt, Asst Prof, Head, Pub Serv, McNeese State University, 300 S Beauregard Dr, Lake Charles, LA, 70609. Tel: 337-475-5729. p. 894
Fontem, Nic, Tech Serv Mgr, Takoma Park Maryland Library, 7505 New Hampshire Ave, Ste 205, Takoma Park, MD, 20912. Tel: 301-891-7259. p. 979
Fonteneau-McCann, Lynne, Dir, Bennington Free Library, 101 Silver St, Bennington, VT, 05201. Tel: 802-442-9051. p. 2279
Fontenette, Edward J, Dir, University of Arkansas-Pine Bluff, 1200 N University Dr, Pine Bluff, AR, 71601. Tel: 870-575-8410. p. 108
Fontenot, Emily, Br Mgr, Evangeline Parish Library, Chataignier Branch, 111 N First St, Chataignier, LA, 70524. Tel: 337-885-2028. p. 912
Fontenot, Gigi, Br Mgr, Evangeline Parish Library, Mamou Branch, 317 Second St, Ste A, Mamou, LA, 70554. Tel: 337-468-5750. p. 912
Fontenot, Jacob, Head, ILL, Louisiana State University Libraries, 295 Middleton Library, Baton Rouge, LA, 70803. Tel: 225-578-6722. p. 884
Fontenova, Amanda, Archivist, Librn, Luzerne County Historical Society, 49 S Franklin St, Wilkes-Barre, PA, 18701. Tel: 570-823-6244, Ext 2. p. 2022
Fontno, Tiffeni, Head Librn, Boston College Libraries, Educational Resource Center, 140 Commonwealth Ave, Chestnut Hill, MA, 02467. Tel: 617-552-1172. p. 1011
Fontoura, Ana, Head of Libr, Fairleigh Dickinson University, Dickinson Hall, 140 University Plaza Dr, Hackensack, NJ, 07601. Tel: 201-692-2608. p. 1406
Fontoura, Ana, Univ Librn, Fairleigh Dickinson University, 1000 River Rd, Teaneck, NJ, 07666-1914. Tel: 201-692-2276. p. 1445
Fontoura, Ana E, Dean, The College of New Rochelle, 29 Castle Pl, New Rochelle, NY, 10805-2308. Tel: 914-654-5345. p. 1577
Fontoura, Ana Maria, Univ Librn, Fairleigh Dickinson University, 285 Madison Ave, M-LAO-03, Madison, NJ, 07940. Tel: 201-692-2276. p. 1414
Foo, Jane, Data Librn, Syst Librn, Seneca College of Applied Arts & Technology, Newnham Campus (Main), 1750 Finch Ave E, North York, ON, M2J 2X5, CANADA. Tel: 416-491-5050, Ext 22011. p. 2649
Foote, Anna, Youth & Continuing Ed Consultant, Northeast Kansas Library System, 4317 W Sixth St, Lawrence, KS, 66049. Tel: 785-838-4090. p. 819
Foote, Brenda, Head, Pub Serv, Thompson Coburn LLP, One US Bank Plaza, Saint Louis, MO, 63101-1693. Tel: 314-552-6260. p. 1276
Foote, Drake, Circ, Tech Serv, Steeleville Area Public Library District, 625 S Sparta St, Steeleville, IL, 62288-2147. Tel: 618-965-9732. p. 651
Foote, Jody A, Asst Dir, Luverne Public Library, 148 E Third St, Luverne, AL, 36049. Tel: 334-335-5326. p. 24
Foote, Sharon, Librn, Colorado Mental Health Institute of Pueblo, 1600 W 24th St, Pueblo, CO, 81003. Tel: 719-546-4197. p. 293
Footz, Valerie, Dir, Libr Serv, Alberta Government Library, Capital Blvd, 11th Flr, 10044 - 108 St, Edmonton, AB, T5J 5E6, CANADA. Tel: 780-427-2985. p. 2534
Foran, Angela, Info Mgr, Libr Serv Mgr, Administrative Tribunals Support Services of Canada, CD Howe Bldg West Tower, 6th Flr, 240 rue Sparks St 645F, Ottawa, ON, K1A 0E1, CANADA. Tel: 343-598-8514. p. 2664
Foran-Mulcahy, Katie, Head of Libr, University of Cincinnati Libraries, College of Education, Criminal Justice & Human Services Library, 400 Teachers College, Cincinnati, OH, 45221. Tel: 513-556-1758. p. 1765
Forbes, Amy, Commun Serv Librn, Cross' Mills Public Library, 4417 Old Post Rd, Charlestown, RI, 02813. Tel: 401-364-6211. p. 2030
Forbes, Carrie, Univ Librn, Southern Oregon University, 1250 Siskiyou Blvd, Ashland, OR, 97520. Tel: 541-552-6833. p. 1872
Forbes, Jordan, Fac Librn, Austin Community College, Hays Campus Library, 1200 Kohlers Crossing, 3rd Flr, Rm 1305, Kyle, TX, 78640. Tel: 512-223-1587. p. 2138
Forbes, Maggie, Exec Dir, Andrew Carnegie Free Library & Music Hall, 300 Beechwood Ave, Carnegie, PA, 15106-2699. Tel: 412-276-3456. p. 1919
Forbes, Rachel, Exec Dir, LDS - Learn. Develop. Succeed. (Learning Disabilities Society), 3292 E Broadway, Vancouver, BC, V5M 1Z8, CANADA. Tel: 604-873-8139. p. 2579
Forbes, Sean, Dir, University of Toronto Libraries, The Milt Harris Library, Joseph L Rotman School of Management, 105 St George St, South Bldg , Rm 5005, Toronto, ON, M5S 3E6, CANADA. Tel: 416-978-3421. p. 2699
Forbes, Sheldon, Supvr, Libr Serv, Otis College of Art & Design Library, 9045 Lincoln Blvd, Westchester, CA, 90045. Tel: 310-665-6930. p. 259
Forbes, Susan, Ref Librn, Kansas Historical Society, 6425 SW Sixth Ave, Topeka, KS, 66615-1099. Tel: 785-272-8681. p. 838
Forbes, Susan, Libr Dir, US Environmental Protection Agency Library, 109 T W Alexander Dr, Rm C261, Research Triangle Park, NC, 27711. Tel: 919-541-2777. p. 1712
Forbrook, Deb, Head Librn, Benson Public Library, 200 13th St N, Benson, MN, 56215-1223. Tel: 320-842-7981. p. 1165
Forbrook, Deb, Head Librn, Kerkhoven Public Library, 208 N Tenth St, Kerkhoven, MN, 56252. Tel: 320-264-2141. p. 1179
Forbus, Julie, Head Librn, Madison Public Library, 12 Old Point Ave, Madison, ME, 04950. Tel: 207-696-5626. p. 931
Force, Jenee Morgan, Metadata Serv Mgr, Berklee College of Music Library, 150 Massachusetts Ave, Boston, MA, 02115. Tel: 617-747-8684. p. 990
Force, Marilyn, Ad, Wyckoff Public Library, 200 Woodland Ave, Wyckoff, NJ, 07481. Tel: 201-891-4866. p. 1456
Force, Sallie, Br Librn, Pottawatomie Wabaunsee Regional Library, Onaga Branch, 313 Leonard St, Onaga, KS, 66521. Tel: 785-889-4531. p. 835
Forczek, Casse, Law Libr Dir/Law Librn, Lake County Law Library, 175 Third St, Lakeport, CA, 95453. Tel: 707-263-2205. p. 156
Ford, Amanda, Archivist, Dearborn Historical Museum Library, Dearborn Historical Museum, 915 Brady St, Dearborn, MI, 48126. Tel: 313-565-3000. p. 1095
Ford, Amanda, Head, Circ, Rhodes College, 2000 North Pkwy, Memphis, TN, 38112-1694. Tel: 901-843-3890. p. 2114
Ford, Amy, Br Mgr, Saint Mary's County Library, Lexington Park Branch, 21677 FDR Blvd, Lexington Park, MD, 20653. Tel: 301-863-8188, Ext 1012. p. 971
Ford, Betsy, Librn, Public Library of Steubenville & Jefferson County, Adena Branch, 167 Hanna Ave, Adena, OH, 43901-7953. Tel: 740-546-3782. p. 1822
Ford, Betsy, Librn, Public Library of Steubenville & Jefferson County, Schiappa Branch, 4141 Mall Dr, Steubenville, OH, 43952. Tel: 740-264-6166. p. 1822
Ford, Brendon, ILL Mgr, Syst Spec, Manhattan College, 4513 Manhattan College Pkwy, Riverdale, NY, 10471. Tel: 718-862-7743. p. 1627
Ford, Candy, Asst Dir, Guthrie Public Library, 201 N Division St, Guthrie, OK, 73044-3201. Tel: 405-282-0050. p. 1849

Ford, Cathy, Br Librn, Head, Circ, Claiborne Parish Library, Joe W Webb Memorial, 1919 Main St, Haynesville, LA, 71038. Tel: 318-624-0364. p. 891

Ford, Charlotte, Libr Dir, University of Montevallo, Bloch St, Montevallo, AL, 35115. Tel: 205-665-6100. p. 27

Ford, Chris, Dir, Danville Community College, 1008 S Main St, Danville, VA, 24541-4004. Tel: 434-797-8598. p. 2314

Ford, Don, Intl Law Librn, University of Iowa Libraries, College of Law Library, 200 Boyd Law Bldg, Iowa City, IA, 52242-1166. Tel: 319-335-9068. p. 761

Ford, Dylan, Librn, Barnet Public Library, 147 Church St, Barnet, VT, 05821. Tel: 802-633-4436. p. 2278

Ford, George, Br Operations Coordr, DeKalb County Public Library, Darro C Willey Administrative Offices, 3560 Kensington Rd, Decatur, GA, 30032. Tel: 404-508-7190. p. 475

Ford, Glenna, Libr Dir, Jacquelin E Opperman Memorial Library, 5790 State St, Kingston, MI, 48741. Tel: 989-683-2500. p. 1122

Ford, Janice, Govt Info Librn, Resources Librn, Ouachita Baptist University, 410 Ouachita St, OBU Box 3742, Arkadelphia, AR, 71998-0001. Tel: 870-245-5122. p. 89

Ford, Jody, Libr Dir, Stone Ridge Public Library, 3700 Main St, Stone Ridge, NY, 12484. Tel: 845-687-7023, Ext 104. p. 1646

Ford, John, Jr, Libr Mgr, Desert Research Institute, 2215 Raggio Pkwy, Reno, NV, 89512-1095. Tel: 775-674-7042. p. 1349

Ford, Judy, Electronic Res Librn, Sullivan University Library, 2222 Wendell Ave, Louisville, KY, 40205. Tel: 502-456-6773. p. 867

Ford, Judy, Supvr, Ser, Texas Tech University Health Sciences Center, 3601 Fourth St, Lubbock, TX, 79430. Tel: 806-743-2200. p. 2214

Ford, Kathleen, Mgr, University of California, Los Angeles, Instructional Media Library, Powell Library, Rm 46, Los Angeles, CA, 90095-1517. Tel: 310-825-0755. p. 168

Ford, Kayla, Dir, Sedan Public Library, 115 N Chautauqua St, Sedan, KS, 67361. Tel: 620-725-3405. p. 835

Ford, Lena, Access Serv, Circ Serv, Case Western Reserve University, Lillian & Milford Harris Library, Jack Joseph & Morton Mandel School of Applied Social Sciences, 11235 Bellflower Rd, Cleveland, OH, 44106-7164. Tel: 216-368-2302. p. 1766

Ford, Madeline, Chief Librn, Hostos Community College Library, Shirley J Hinds Allied Health & Science Bldg, 475 Grand Concourse, Rm A308, Bronx, NY, 10451. Tel: 718-518-4211. p. 1498

Ford, Maria, Dir, Tremont District Public Library, 215 S Sampson St, Tremont, IL, 61568. Tel: 309-925-5432, 309-925-5597. p. 654

Ford, Maria, Division Librn, Catholic Health Initiatives, CHI Health St Elizabeth, 555 S 70th St, Lincoln, NE, 68510. Tel: 402-219-7306. p. 1321

Ford, Maria, Med Librn, Creighton University, Health Sciences Library-Learning Resource Center, 2770 Webster St, Omaha, NE, 68178-0210. Tel: 402-280-5109. p. 1328

Ford, Maria, Main Floor Supervisor, Lebanon Public Library, 101 S Broadway, Lebanon, OH, 45036. Tel: 513-932-2665. p. 1795

Ford, Melanie, Ref Serv, Indian Valley Public Library, 100 E Church Ave, Telford, PA, 18969. Tel: 215-723-9109. p. 2012

Ford, Rachel, Res Mgt Librn, Northern Illinois University Libraries, David C Shapiro Memorial Law Library, Swen Parson Hall, 2nd Flr, Normal Rd, DeKalb, IL, 60115-2890. Tel: 815-753-2021. p. 578

Ford, Stephen, Coordr, Curric Res Ctr, Salisbury University, 1101 Camden Ave, Salisbury, MD, 21801-6863. Tel: 410-543-6130. p. 976

Ford, Stephen, Coordr, Educ Librn, Salisbury University, Dr Ernie Bond Curriculum Resource Center, Conway Hall, Rm 226, 1101 Camden Ave, Salisbury, MD, 21801. Tel: 410-677-4602. p. 976

Ford, Sue, Ch Serv Librn, New Milford Public Library, 24 Main St, New Milford, CT, 06776. Tel: 860-355-1191, Ext 205. p. 329

Forde, Barbara, Librn, Long Island Maritime Museum Library, 86 West Ave, West Sayville, NY, 11796-1908. Tel: 631-447-8679, 631-854-4974. p. 1663

Forde, Carolyn, Head, Youth Serv, T B Scott Library, 106 W First St, Merrill, WI, 54452-2398. Tel: 715-536-7191. p. 2457

Fordham, Cyndi, Executive Asst, Wood Library Association, 134 N Main St, Canandaigua, NY, 14424-1295. Tel: 585-394-1381, Ext 313. p. 1512

Fordham, Irma, Libr Dir, Dr Martin Luther King Jr Library, 955 E University Blvd, Melbourne, FL, 32920. Tel: 321-952-4511. p. 421

Fordham, Irma, Libr Dir, Melbourne Public Library, 540 E Fee Ave, Melbourne, FL, 32901. Tel: 321-952-4514. p. 421

Fordham, Sonja, Tutoring Center Dir, Writing Ctr Dir, Southern Adventist University, 4851 Industrial Dr, Collegedale, TN, 37315. Tel: 423-236-2384. p. 2094

Fording, Jennifer, Dir, Harris-Elmore Public Library, 328 Toledo St, Elmore, OH, 43416. Tel: 419-862-2482. p. 1784

Fordyce, Robyn, Med Librn, Our Lady of Lourdes Memorial Hospital Library, 169 Riverside Dr, Binghamton, NY, 13905. Tel: 607-798-5290. p. 1494

Fore, Joshua, Evening/Weekend Supvr, Drexel University Libraries, Hagerty Library, 33rd & Market Sts, Philadelphia, PA, 19104-2875. Tel: 215-895-2750. p. 1976

Fore, Tina M, Libr Tech, Department of Veterans Affairs, 17273 State Rte 104, Chillicothe, OH, 45601. Tel: 740-773-1141, Ext 17627. p. 1759

Fore, Tresa, Asst LRC Coord, Wayne County Community College District, 21000 Northline Rd, Taylor, MI, 48180. Tel: 734-374-3228. p. 1153

Fore, Trish, Regional Dir, Galax-Carroll Regional Library, 610 W Stuart Dr, Galax, VA, 24333. Tel: 276-236-2351. p. 2321

Foreback, Margaret, Libr Asst II, State Correctional Institution, Laurel Highlands Library, 5706 Glades Pike, Somerset, PA, 15501. Tel: 814-445-6501. p. 2008

Foreman, Beverly, Educ Res Assoc, Cossatot Community College of the University of Arkansas, 195 College Dr, De Queen, AR, 71832. Tel: 870-584-4471. p. 93

Foreman, Linda, Br Mgr, Desoto Parish Library, Logansport Branch, 203 Hwy 5, Logansport, LA, 71049. Tel: 318-697-2311. p. 896

Foreman, Michelle, Dr, Dean of Libr, Shippensburg University, 1871 Old Main Dr, Shippensburg, PA, 17257. Tel: 717-477-1475. p. 2007

Foreman, Pamela, Libr Dir, Virginia Union University, 1500 N Lombardy St, Richmond, VA, 23220. Tel: 804-257-5821. p. 2344

Foreman, Pamela, Pres, Richmond Academic Library Consortium, Virginia Union University, Wilder Library, 1500 N Lombardy St, Richmond, VA, 23220. Tel: 804-257-5821. p. 2776

Foreman, Randy, Ref Librn, Western Michigan University-Cooley Law School Libraries, 300 S Capitol Ave, Lansing, MI, 48933. Tel: 517-371-5140, Ext 7711. p. 1126

Foreman, Tara, Br Coordr, North Vancouver District Public Library, 1277 Lynn Valley Rd, North Vancouver, BC, V7J 0A2, CANADA. Tel: 604-984-0286, 604-990-5800. p. 2573

Forer, Anna, Librn, Temple Judea, 5500 Granada Blvd, Coral Gables, FL, 33146. Tel: 305-667-5657. p. 390

Foreshoe, Jessica, Dir, Sheffield Public Library, 123 Third St, Sheffield, IA, 50475. Tel: 641-892-4717. p. 781

Forest, Dominic, Prof, Universite de Montreal, 3150, rue Jean-Brillant, bur C-2004, Montreal, QC, H3T 1N8, CANADA. Tel: 514-343-6044. p. 2797

Foresta, Allen, Sr Librn, Teachers College, Columbia University, 525 W 120th St, New York, NY, 10027-6696. Tel: 212-678-3026. p. 1602

Forestell-Page, Meg, E-Librn, Guelph Public Library, 100 Norfolk St, Guelph, ON, N1H 4J6, CANADA. Tel: 519-824-6220, Ext 306. p. 2643

Forester, Kelsey, Sci Res & Instruction Librn, University of Georgia Libraries, Science, Boyd Graduate Studies Bldg, 210 D W Brooks Dr, Athens, GA, 30602. Tel: 706-542-0698. p. 460

Forester, Kristin, Asst to the Exec Dir, Dir, External Relations, Portland Public Library, Five Monument Sq, Portland, ME, 04101. Tel: 207-871-1700, Ext 759. p. 937

Foret, Frances, Head, Coll Mgt, Tufts University, Hirsh Health Sciences Library, 145 Harrison Ave, Boston, MA, 02111. Tel: 617-636-2448. p. 1034

Foret, Meryl, Supvr, Lafourche Parish Public Library, Raceland Branch, 177 Recreation Dr, Raceland, LA, 70394-2915. Tel: 985-537-6875. p. 911

Forget, Bruno, Libr Tech, Bibliotheque Municipale de Saint Felicien, 1209 Blvd Sacre-Coeur, Saint Felicien, QC, G8K 2R5, CANADA. Tel: 418-679-2100, Ext 2245. p. 2733

Forkenbrock, Kellee, Pub Serv Librn, North Liberty Library, 520 W Cherry St, North Liberty, IA, 52317-9797. Tel: 319-626-5701. p. 773

Forkner, Julie, Dir, Oak Ridge Public Library, 1401 Oak Ridge Tpk, Oak Ridge, TN, 37830-6224. Tel: 865-425-3455. p. 2123

Formanek, Justin, Interim Libr Dir, Blanchard-Santa Paula Library District, 119 N Eighth St, Santa Paula, CA, 93060-2709. Tel: 805-329-4114. p. 245

Formhals, Lisa, Libr Dir, Malvern Public Library, 502 Main St, Malvern, IA, 51551. Tel: 712-624-8554. p. 766

Formichella, Laurie, Head, Tech Serv, Beverly Public Library, 32 Essex St, Beverly, MA, 01915-4561. Tel: 978-921-6062. p. 989

Formsky, Stephanie, Pub Serv Mgr, St Albert Public Library, Five Saint Anne St, St. Albert, AB, T8N 3Z9, CANADA. Tel: 780-459-1530. p. 2555

Fornelli, Angela, Archivist, Dawson City Museum, 595 Fifth Ave, Dawson City, YT, Y0B 1G0, CANADA. Tel: 867-993-5291, Ext 23. p. 2757

Fornero-Green, Chalyn, Librn, Mkt, Cordova District Library, 402 Main Ave, Cordova, IL, 61242. Tel: 309-654-2330. p. 573

Forney, Annissia, Dir, Libr & Learning Serv, Lamar Community College Library & Learning Resource Center, Bowman Bldg, 2401 S Main St, Lamar, CO, 81052-3999. Tel: 719-336-1541. p. 289

Forney, Betty, Libr Asst, Highland Community College Library, 606 W Main, Highland, KS, 66035. Tel: 785-442-6054. p. 813

Forney, Marlene, Chairperson, Palomar College, 1140 W Mission Rd, San Marcos, CA, 92069-1487. Tel: 760-744-1150, Ext 2666. p. 2782

Fornwald, Emily, Educ Librn, University of British Columbia Library, Education, 2125 Main Mall, Vancouver, BC, V6T 1Z4, CANADA. Tel: 604-822-5381. p. 2580

Forquer, Vicki, Asst Dir for Res, Kankakee Public Library, 201 E Merchant St, Kankakee, IL, 60901. Tel: 815-939-4564. p. 604

Forred, Afton, Libr Dir, Harper Public Library, 708 W 14th St, Harper, KS, 67058. Tel: 620-896-2959. p. 812

Forrest, Adam, Senior VP, Operations, University of Silicon Valley, 191 Baypointe Pkwy, San Jose, CA, 95134. Tel: 408-498-5158. p. 232

Forrest, Dan, Faculty Subject Specialist, Western Kentucky University Libraries, Helm-Cravens Library Complex, 1906 College Heights Blvd, No 11067, Bowling Green, KY, 42101-1067. Tel: 270-745-6164. p. 849

Forrest, Janeane, Interim Libr Dir, Northern Baptist Theological Seminary, 410 Warrenville Rd, Ste 300, Lisle, IL, 60532. Tel: 630-620-2115. p. 610

Forrest, Jay, Asst Dean for Collections Strategy & Dev, Georgia Institute of Technology Library, 260 Fourth St NW, Atlanta, GA, 30332. Tel: 404-894-1397. p. 464

Forrest, Lisa, Libr Dir, Davidson College, 209 Ridge Rd, Davidson, NC, 28035-0001. Tel: 704-894-2331. p. 1683

Forrest, Lori, Dir, Tiptonville Public Library, 126 Tipton St, Tiptonville, TN, 38079-1133. Tel: 731-253-7391. p. 2128

Forrest, Susan, Librn, Erie County Medical Center, 462 Grider St, Buffalo, NY, 14215. Tel: 716-898-3939. p. 1509

Forrest, Tera, Youth Serv Librn, Crowell Public Library, 1890 Huntington Dr, San Marino, CA, 91108-2595. Tel: 626-300-0777. p. 234

Forshaw, Bob, IT Mgr, University of Alaska Fairbanks, 1732 Tanana Dr, Fairbanks, AK, 99775. Tel: 907-474-7921. p. 45

Forshey, Guinevere, Asst Dir, Crandall Public Library, 251 Glen St, Glens Falls, NY, 12801-3546. Tel: 518-792-6508. p. 1539

Forst, Cathy, Libr Dir, Springfield Township Library, 12000 Davisburg Rd, Davisburg, MI, 48350. Tel: 248-846-6550. p. 1095

Forst, Lacey, Dir, Caldwell Public Library, 1010 Dearborn St, Caldwell, ID, 83605. Tel: 208-459-3242. p. 518

Forsyth, Andy, Asst Dir, Ridgefield Library Association Inc, 472 Main St, Ridgefield, CT, 06877-4585. Tel: 203-438-2282. p. 335

Forsyth, Deb, Asst Librn, Southwestern Manitoba Regional Library, Pierson Library, 64 Railway Ave, Pierson, MB, R0M 1S0, CANADA. Tel: 204-634-2215. p. 2588

Forsythe, Kathy, Librn, Panorama Library, The Quinault, 1835 Circle Lane SE, Lacey, WA, 98503. Tel: 360-456-0111, Ext 4005. p. 2368

Forsythe, Linda, Head, Circ, Southern University, 167 Roosevelt Steptoe Ave, Baton Rouge, LA, 70813-0001. Tel: 225-771-4990. p. 884

Forsythe, Melissa, Library Content & Colls Specialist, Missouri Southern State University, 3950 E Newman Rd, Joplin, MO, 64801-1595. Tel: 417-625-9342. p. 1253

Fort, Cindy, Libr Tech, The Parrott Centre, 376 Wallbridge-Loyalist Rd, Belleville, ON, K8N 5B9, CANADA. Tel: 613-969-1913, Ext 2595. p. 2631

Fort, Nancy, Br Mgr, Burlington County Library System, Riverton Free Library, 306 Main St, Riverton, NJ, 08077. Tel: 856-829-2476. p. 1454

Fort, Rebecca, Acq, Archives, Dir, Libr Serv, Malone University, 2600 Cleveland Ave NW, Canton, OH, 44709-3308. Tel: 330-471-8313. p. 1755

Fort, Reginald, Commun Libr Mgr, Queens Library, South Hollis Community Library, 204-01 Hollis Ave, South Hollis, NY, 11412. Tel: 718-465-6779. p. 1555

Fort, Samantha, Tech Serv Coordr, University of California, Merced Library, 5200 N Lake Rd, Merced, CA, 95343. Tel: 209-631-0953. p. 177

Forte, Alice, Br Mgr, Mesa County Public Library District, Palisade Branch, 119 W Third St, Palisade, CO, 81526. Tel: 970-464-7557. p. 284

Forte, Andrea, Dean, University of Michigan, 4322 North Quad, 105 S State St, Ann Arbor, MI, 48109-1285. Tel: 734-763-2285. p. 2786

Forte, Christine, Univ Librn, Antioch University New England Library, 40 Avon St, Keene, NH, 03431. Tel: 603-283-2400. p. 1369

Forte, Christine, Univ Librn, Antioch University Library, 900 Dayton St, Yellow Springs, OH, 45387. Tel: 805-962-8179, Ext 5177. p. 1835

Forte, Jane, Dir, Ridgefield Public Library, 527 Morse Ave, Ridgefield, NJ, 07657. Tel: 201-941-0192, Ext 115. p. 1439

Forte, Maria, Br Librn, London Public Library, Beacock, 1280 Huron St, London, ON, N5Y 4M2, CANADA. Tel: 519-451-8140. p. 2654

Forte, Maria, Br Librn, London Public Library, W O Carson, 465 Quebec St, London, ON, N5W 3Y4, CANADA. Tel: 519-438-4287. p. 2654

Forte, Patti, Children's Prog Coordr, McCowan Memorial Library, 15 Pitman Ave, Pitman, NJ, 08071. Tel: 856-589-1656. p. 1435

Fortes, Mayra, Asst Dir, Port Chester-Rye Brook Public Library, One Haseco Ave, Port Chester, NY, 10573. Tel: 914-939-6710, Ext 111. p. 1620

Fortich, Tracey, Librn, HealthAlliance Hospital - Broadway Campus, 396 Broadway, Kingston, NY, 12401. Tel: 845-334-2786. p. 1560

Fortier, Carol, Exec Dir, Beekman Library, 11 Town Center Blvd, Hopewell Junction, NY, 12533. Tel: 845-724-3414. p. 1548

Fortier, Kady, Dir, Libr Serv, Virginia Peninsula Community College Library, 227C Kecoughtan Hall, 99 Thomas Nelson Dr, Hampton, VA, 23666. Tel: 757-825-2871. p. 2323

Fortier, Melanie, Libr Asst, Canada School of Public Service Library, Asticou Centre, 241 de la Cite-des-Jeunes Blvd, Rm 1323, Gatineau, QC, K1N 6Z2, CANADA. Tel: 819-934-7702. p. 2712

Fortier, Paula, Dep Dir, Pub Serv, Phoenix Public Library, 1221 N Central Ave, Phoenix, AZ, 85004. Tel: 602-262-4636. p. 72

Fortier, Violaine, Head of Libr, Librn, College Jean-de-Brebeuf, 5625 rue Decelles, Montreal, QC, H3T 1W4, CANADA. Tel: 514-342-9342, Ext 5374. p. 2723

Fortin, Angelica, Dir, Commun Serv, Paso Robles City Library, 1000 Spring St, Paso Robles, CA, 93446-2207. Tel: 805-237-3870. p. 194

Fortin, Genevieve, Prof, College Lionel-Groulx, 100, rue Duquet, Sainte-Therese, QC, J7E 3G6, CANADA. Tel: 450-430-3120, Ext 2407. p. 2796

Fortin, Jennifer, Chief Exec Officer, Head Librn, Blind River Public Library, Eight Woodward Ave, Blind River, ON, P0R 1B0, CANADA. Tel: 705-356-7616. p. 2631

Fortin, Mitzi, Br Head, Okanagan Regional Library, Lumby Branch, 2250 Shields Ave, Lumby, BC, V0E 2G0, CANADA. Tel: 250-547-9528. p. 2568

Fortin, Richard, Dir, Charles M Bailey Public Library, 39 Bowdoin St, Winthrop, ME, 04364. Tel: 207-377-8673. p. 947

Fortin, Thomas, Chief of Main Libr, San Francisco Public Library, 100 Larkin St, San Francisco, CA, 94102. Tel: 415-557-4200. p. 227

Fortmann, Kelly, Ref & Instruction Librn, Woodbury University Library, San Diego Campus, 2212 Main St, San Diego, CA, 92113. Tel: 619-693-4422. p. 125

Fortner, Amy, Libr Mgr, Metropolitan Community College, Penn Valley Library, 3201 SW Trafficway, Kansas City, MO, 64111-2764. Tel: 816-604-4086. p. 1256

Fortner, Jo, Sr Libr Mgr, Live Oak Public Libraries, Hinesville Branch, 236 W Memorial Dr, Hinesville, GA, 31313. Tel: 912-368-4003. p. 496

Fortner, Marolyn, Mgr, Oconee Regional Library, Harlie Fulford Memorial, 301 Elm St, Wrightsville, GA, 31096. Tel: 478-864-3940. p. 477

Fortner, Sandra, Asst Dir, New Albany-Floyd County Public Library, 180 W Spring St, New Albany, IN, 47150. Tel: 812-949-3730. p. 709

Fortney, Teresa, ILL, Oak Ridge Public Library, 1401 Oak Ridge Tpk, Oak Ridge, TN, 37830-6224. Tel: 865-425-3455. p. 2123

Forton, Alicia, Sr Assoc, National Economic Research Associates, Inc, 360 Hamilton Ave, 10th Flr, White Plains, NY, 10601. Tel: 312-573-2813. p. 1664

Fortson, Carolyn, Dean of Libr, Denmark Technical College, 113 Solomon Blatt Blvd, Denmark, SC, 29042. Tel: 803-793-5215. p. 2057

Fortson, Thomas, Librn, El Rito Public Library, 182 Placitas Rd, El Rito, NM, 87530. Tel: 575-581-4608. p. 1467

Fortwangler, Lisa, Libr Dir, Borough of Folcroft Public Library, 1725 Delmar Dr, Folcroft, PA, 19032-2002. Tel: 610-586-1690. p. 1933

Fosselman, Charles, Digital Syst & Serv Librn, Stanford University Libraries, East Asia Library, Lathrop Library Bldg, 518 Memorial Way, Stanford, CA, 94305. Tel: 650-725-3435. p. 248

Foster, Amy, Br Mgr, Boone County Public Library, Scheben Branch, 8899 US 42, Union, KY, 41091. Tel: 859-342-2665. p. 850

Foster, Amy, Access & Tech Serv Librn, Head, Coll, Montana State University Library, One Centennial Mall, Bozeman, MT, 59717. Tel: 406-994-5301. p. 1289

Foster, Ann, Youth Serv Librn, Snow Library, 67 Main St, Orleans, MA, 02653-2413. Tel: 508-240-3760. p. 1044

Foster, Brenda, Archivist, Columbus College of Art & Design, 60 Cleveland Ave, Columbus, OH, 43215. Tel: 614-222-3273. p. 1772

Foster, Dave, Facilities Dir, Public Library of Youngstown & Mahoning County, 305 Wick Ave, Youngstown, OH, 44503. Tel: 330-744-8636. p. 1835

Foster, Deborah, Access Serv, Pub Serv, Fayetteville Technical Community College, 2201 Hull Rd, Fayetteville, NC, 28303. Tel: 910-678-8257. p. 1689

Foster, Forrest, Asst Dean, North Carolina Agricultural & Technical State University, 1601 E Market St, Greensboro, NC, 27411-0002. Tel: 336-285-4164. p. 1693

Foster, Forrest C, Dir, Libr Serv, Fayetteville State University, 1200 Murchison Rd, Fayetteville, NC, 28301-4298. Tel: 910-672-1231. p. 1689

Foster, Hanna, Instrul Librn, Columbus Technical College Library, 928 Manchester Expressway, Columbus, GA, 31904-6577. Tel: 706-641-5654. p. 472

Foster, Jacqueline, Dir, Gilbertsville Free Library, 17 Commercial St, Gilbertsville, NY, 13776. Tel: 607-783-2832. p. 1538

Foster, Jennifer, Asst Libr Dir, Jesse M Smith Memorial Library, 100 Tinkham Lane, Harrisville, RI, 02830. Tel: 401-710-7800. p. 2032

Foster, Katie, Dir, Indianola Public Library, 122 N Fourth St, Indianola, NE, 69034. Tel: 308-364-9259. p. 1319

Foster, Kelli, Head, Tech Serv, Kaubisch Memorial Public Library, 205 Perry St, Fostoria, OH, 44830-2265. Tel: 419-435-2813. p. 1786

Foster, Kelly, Mkt Coordr, Manatee County Public Library System, 1301 Barcarrota Blvd W, Bradenton, FL, 34205-7522. Tel: 941-748-5555, Ext 6307. p. 386

Foster, Lesa, ILL Librn, Warren County-Vicksburg Public Library, 700 Veto St, Vicksburg, MS, 39180-3595. Tel: 601-636-6411. p. 1235

Foster, Makiba, Librn of the Col, The College of Wooster Libraries, 1140 Beall Ave, Wooster, OH, 44691-2364. Tel: 330-263-2442. p. 1832

Foster, Mary Gail, Rec Mgt Adminr, Oklahoma Department of Human Services, 200 E Hill St, Oklahoma City, OK, 73105. Tel: 405-521-2502. p. 1858

Foster, Mary Louise Irene, Dir, Libr Serv, Northeast Community College, 801 E Benjamin Ave, Norfolk, NE, 68702. Tel: 402-844-7131. p. 1326

Foster, Neale, Circ, J Sargeant Reynolds Community College Library, Downtown Campus-Library & Information Services, 700 E Jackson St, 2nd Flr, Rm 231, Richmond, VA, 23219-1543. Tel: 804-523-5211. p. 2341

Foster, Patricia, Exec Dir, Cylburn Arboretum Friends Library, 4915 Greenspring Ave, Baltimore, MD, 21209. Tel: 410-367-2217, Ext 2. p. 952

Fox, Bokshim, Bibliog Database Mgr, Cat Librn, Georgia Southwestern State University, 800 Georgia Southwestern State University Dr, Americus, GA, 31709. Tel: 229-931-2258. p. 457

Fox, Brooke, Univ Archivist, Medical University of South Carolina Libraries, 171 Ashley Ave, Ste 419, Charleston, SC, 29425-0001. Tel: 843-792-6477. p. 2051

Fox, De'Trice J, Ms, Br Mgr, Charlotte Mecklenburg Library, Sugar Creek, 4045 N Tryon St, Charlotte, NC, 28206. Tel: 704-416-7000. p. 1680

Fox, Doug, Syst Librn, University of Toronto Libraries, Victoria University, E J Pratt Library, 71 Queens Park Crescent E, Toronto, ON, M5S 1K7, CANADA. Tel: 416-585-4471. p. 2700

Fox, E Brooke, Univ Archivist, Medical University of South Carolina Libraries, Waring Historical Library, 175 Ashley Ave, Charleston, SC, 29425-0001. Tel: 843-792-6477. p. 2051

Fox, Eddie P, Br Librn, Noxubee County Library System, Vista J Daniel Memorial, 402 Residence St, Shuqualak, MS, 39361-9740. Tel: 662-793-9576. p. 1225

Fox, Elissa, Human Res, Spec, Pioneer Library System, 300 Norman Ctr Ct, Norman, OK, 73072. Tel: 405-801-4500. p. 1855

Fox, Elizabeth, Govt Doc, South Dakota State University, 1300 N Campus Dr, Box 2115, Brookings, SD, 57007. Tel: 605-688-5569. p. 2074

Fox, Emily, Dir, Switzerland County Public Library, 205 Ferry St, Vevay, IN, 47043. Tel: 812-427-3363. p. 723

Fox, Graham, Supvr, Deschutes Public Library District, Redmond Branch, 827 Deschutes Ave, Redmond, OR, 97756. Tel: 541-312-1059. p. 1874

Fox, Jana, Supvr, Mid-Columbia Libraries, Merrill's Corner, 5240 Eltopia W, Eltopia, WA, 99330. Tel: 509-546-8051. p. 2367

Fox, Jill, Dir, Mayville District Public Library, 6090 Fulton St, Mayville, MI, 48744. Tel: 989-843-6522. p. 1131

Fox, Joe, Head, Ref & Instruction, Web Serv Librn, Charleston Southern University, 9200 University Blvd, Charleston, SC, 29406. Tel: 843-863-7945. p. 2050

Fox, John, Br Mgr, Middle Georgia Regional Library System, Montezuma Public Library, 506 N Dooly St, Montezuma, GA, 31063-1308. Tel: 478-472-6095. p. 487

Fox, John, Librn, Library of the US Courts, Robert A Grant Courthouse, 204 S Main St, Rm 316, South Bend, IN, 46601. Tel: 574-246-8050. p. 718

Fox, Ken, Librn, Law Society of Saskatchewan Libraries, Saskatoon Court House, 520 Spadina Crescent E, Saskatoon, SK, S7K 3G7, CANADA. Tel: 306-933-5141. p. 2746

Fox, Kimber, Br Mgr, Dayton Metro Library, 215 E Third St, Dayton, OH, 45402. Tel: 937-463-2665. p. 1779

Fox, Lauren, Head, Youth Serv, Lynnfield Public Library, 18 Summer St, Lynnfield, MA, 01940-1837. Tel: 781-334-5411, 781-334-6404. p. 1031

Fox, Leslie, Br Mgr, Albuquerque-Bernalillo County Library System, Rudolfo Anaya North Valley Library, 7704-B Second St NW, Albuquerque, NM, 87107. Tel: 505-897-8823. p. 1460

Fox, Linda, Libr Dir, New Fairfield Free Public Library, Two Brush Hill Rd, New Fairfield, CT, 06812. Tel: 203-312-5679. p. 325

Fox, Lisa, Cat, Bolivar-Harpers Ferry Public Library, 151 Polk St, Harpers Ferry, WV, 25425. Tel: 304-535-2301. p. 2403

Fox, Lynne, Ref Librn, SCLHS Saint Joseph Hospital, 1375 E 19th Ave, 3rd Flr, Denver, CO, 80218-1191. Tel: 303-812-3625. p. 277

Fox, Megan, Asst Mgr, Youth & Outreach Serv, Youth Librn, Laramie County Library System, 2200 Pioneer Ave, Cheyenne, WY, 82001-3610. Tel: 307-773-7226. p. 2492

Fox, Patricia, Assoc Dir, Widener University, Harrisburg Campus Law Library, 3800 Vartan Way, Harrisburg, DE, 17110. Tel: 717-541-3935. p. 358

Fox, Phyllis, Instrul Serv Librn, Point Loma Nazarene University, 3900 Lomaland Dr, San Diego, CA, 92106-2899. Tel: 619-849-2312. p. 216

Fox, Rachel, Head, Children's Servx, Port Washington Public Library, One Library Dr, Port Washington, NY, 11050. Tel: 516-883-3728, Ext 1602. p. 1622

Fox, Robert E, Jr, Dean, University of Louisville Libraries, 2215 S Third St, Louisville, KY, 40208. Tel: 502-852-6745. p. 867

Fox, Robin, Educ Coordr, Exec Dir, Escondido History Center, 321 N Broadway, Escondido, CA, 92025. Tel: 760-743-8207. p. 141

Fox, Shannon Marie, Educ Curator, Operations Mgr, International Museum of Surgical Science Library, 1524 N Lake Shore Dr, Chicago, IL, 60610. Tel: 312-642-6502, Ext 3113. p. 562

Fox, Shawna, Libr Mgr, Beiseker Municipal Library, 401 Fifth St, Beiseker, AB, T0M 0G0, CANADA. Tel: 403-947-3230. p. 2523

Fox, Zac, Dir, Maury County Public Library, 211 W Eighth St, Columbia, TN, 38401. Tel: 931-375-6501. p. 2094

Foxe, Carla, Librn, Halifax Public Libraries, Dartmouth North Branch, 105 Highfield Park, Dartmouth, NS, B3A 0C2, CANADA. Tel: 902-490-5840. p. 2617

Foxenberg, Shay, Libr Dir, Shiocton Public Library, W7740 Pine St, Shiocton, WI, 54170. Tel: 920-986-3933. p. 2477

Foxx-Lupo, Tara, Br Mgr, Pima County Public Library, Martha Cooper Library, 1377 N Catalina Ave, Tucson, AZ, 85712. Tel: 520-594-5315. p. 82

Foy, Judy, Head Librn, Oklahoma Department of Corrections, Jess Dunn Leisure Library, 601 S 124th St W, Taft, OK, 74463. Tel: 918-682-7841, Ext 6544. p. 1863

Foy, Terri, Circ & ILL Mgr, Hiram College Library, 11694 Hayden St, Hiram, OH, 44234. Tel: 330-569-5489. p. 1790

Foy, Valerie, Librn, Guildhall Public Library, Rt 102 N, Guildhall, VT, 05905. Tel: 802-676-3054. p. 2285

Fraas, Julia, Library Online Learning Program Coord, Oakton College Library, 1600 E Golf Rd, Rm 1406, Des Plaines, IL, 60016. Tel: 847-635-1642, 847-635-1644. p. 578

Frackowski, Marlena, Asst Dean, The College of New Jersey, 2000 Pennington Rd, Ewing, NJ, 08628-1104. Tel: 609-771-2311. p. 1402

Fradenburgh, Robin, Assoc Dir, Tech Serv, University of Texas Libraries, Serials Acquisitions Unit, PO Box P, Austin, TX, 78713-8916. Tel: 512-495-4159. p. 2143

Frady, Teri, Chief, Research & Communications, Northeast Fisheries Science Center, 166 Water St, Woods Hole, MA, 02543-1097. Tel: 508-495-2000. p. 1071

Fragge, Melani, Br Mgr, Akron-Summit County Public Library, Springfield-Lakemore Branch, 1500 Canton Rd, Ste 360, Akron, OH, 44312. Tel: 330-643-4770. p. 1744

Fragola, Erin, Mkt, Outreach Coordr, Perkins School for the Blind, 175 N Beacon St, Watertown, MA, 02472. Tel: 617-972-7240. p. 1062

Fragola, Patricia, Head, Systems & Tech Services, University of Wisconsin-Whitewater, 750 W Main St, Whitewater, WI, 53190-1790. Tel: 262-472-5673. p. 2488

Fragoso, Veronica, Libr Spec, Venito Garcia Public Library, PO Box 837, Sells, AZ, 85634-0837. Tel: 520-383-5756. p. 78

Fraize, Robyne, Br Supvr, Marion County Public Library System, Marion Oaks Public Library, 294 Marion Oaks Lane, Ocala, FL, 34473. Tel: 352-438-2570. p. 430

Frakes, Laura, Mgr, County of Los Angeles Public Library, Culver City Julian Dixon Library, 4975 Overland Ave, Culver City, CA, 90230-4299. Tel: 310-559-1676. p. 135

Frakes, Linda, Libr Supvr, Phoenix College, 1202 W Thomas Rd, Phoenix, AZ, 85013. Tel: 602-285-7457. p. 72

Frakowski, Kimberly, Libr Spec, Belmont College, 68094 Hammond Rd, Rm 1076, Saint Clairsville, OH, 43950-9735. Tel: 740-699-3953. p. 1818

Fralick, Caitlin, Br Mgr, Hamilton Public Library, Binbrook Branch, 2641 Hwy 56, Binbrook, ON, L0R 1C0, CANADA. Tel: 905-546-3200, Ext 1022. p. 2645

Fralick, Caitlin, Br Mgr, Hamilton Public Library, Concession, 565 Concession St, Hamilton, ON, L8V 1A8, CANADA. Tel: 905-546-3415. p. 2645

Fralick, Caitlin, Br Mgr, Hamilton Public Library, Mount Hope, 3027 Homestead Dr, RR 1, Mount Hope, ON, L0R 1W0, CANADA. Tel: 905-679-6445. p. 2646

Fralick, Nathan, Archivist, Research Servs Librn, Pennsylvania Western University - Edinboro, 200 Tartan Dr, Edinboro, PA, 16444. Tel: 814-732-1542. p. 1929

Fralin, Scott, Librn, Virginia Polytechnic Institute & State University Libraries, Art & Architecture, Cowgill Hall, Rm 100, Blacksburg, VA, 24060. Tel: 540-231-3068. p. 2307

Frame, Stefanie, Dir, Foley & Lardner LLP, 555 S Flower St, Ste 3500, Los Angeles, CA, 90071-2418. Tel: 213-972-4500. p. 161

Frame, Steve, Sr Librn, Torrance Public Library, North Torrance, 3604 Artesia Blvd, Torrance, CA, 90504-3315. Tel: 310-323-7200. p. 253

Framke, Nikki, Librn, Northcentral Technical College Library, 1000 W Campus Dr, Wausau, WI, 54401. Tel: 715-803-1115. p. 2486

Frampton, Jann, Circ, Huachuca City Public Library, 506 N Gonzales Blvd, Huachuca City, AZ, 85616-9610. Tel: 520-456-1063. p. 63

Framson, Jessica, Mgr, Support & Cultural Serv, Huntington Beach Public Library System, Banning, 9281 Banning Ave, Huntington Beach, CA, 92646-8302. Tel: 714-375-5005. p. 152

France, Cynthia, Human Res Mgr, Perry County Public Library, 289 Black Gold Blvd, Hazard, KY, 41701. Tel: 606-436-2475, 606-436-4747. p. 858

France, Erik, Asst Dir, Tarrant County College, South Campus Jenkins Garrett Library, 5301 Campus Dr, Fort Worth, TX, 76119. Tel: 817-515-4524. p. 2180

France, Jane, Ch, Bala Cynwyd Memorial Library, 131 Old Lancaster Rd, Bala Cynwyd, PA, 19004-3037. Tel: 610-664-1196. p. 1908

France, Jim, Dir, South Haven Memorial Library, 314 Broadway St, South Haven, MI, 49090. Tel: 269-637-2403. p. 1150

France-Nuriddin, Roxie, Reference & Prog Specialist, Georgetown University, Bioethics Research Library, Kennedy Institute of Ethics, 37th & O St NW, Washington, DC, 20057. Tel: 202-687-3885. p. 368

Francesco, Beth, Exec Dir, National Press Club, 529 14th St NW, 13th Flr, Washington, DC, 20045. Tel: 202-662-5707. p. 373

Francetic, Brenda, Dir, Merrill District Library, 321 W Saginaw St, Merrill, MI, 48637. Tel: 989-643-7300. p. 1131

Franchois, George, Libr Dir, United States Department of the Interior Library, 1849 C St NW, MS 1151, Washington, DC, 20240. Tel: 202-208-3796. p. 378

Francini, Jeanette, Head, Coll Mgt, Lucy Robbins Welles Library, 95 Cedar St, Newington, CT, 06111. Tel: 860-665-8714. p. 330

Francis, Alison, Youth Outreach Coord, Youth Serv Librn, Poughkeepsie Public Library District, 93 Market St, Poughkeepsie, NY, 12601. Tel: 845-485-3445, Ext 3304. p. 1623

Francis, Andrea, Mgr, Pub Serv, Toledo-Lucas County Public Library, 325 Michigan St, Toledo, OH, 43604. Tel: 419-259-5200. p. 1824

Francis, Bailey, YA Serv, Lucy Robbins Welles Library, 95 Cedar St, Newington, CT, 06111. Tel: 860-665-8704. p. 330

Francis, Briana, Mgr, Jefferson County Public Library, Belmar, 555 S Alison Pkwy, Lakewood, CO, 80226. Tel: 303-403-5360. p. 288

Francis, Cindy A, Coll Develop Librn, Genesee Community College, One College Rd, Batavia, NY, 14020-9704. Tel: 585-343-0055, Ext 6126. p. 1490

Francis, Claire, Adult Serv, Libr Dir, Uinta County Library, 701 Main St, Evanston, WY, 82930. Tel: 307-783-0481. p. 2494

Francis, Frank, Supvr, Ad Serv, Inglewood Public Library, 101 W Manchester Blvd, Inglewood, CA, 90301-1771. Tel: 310-412-5397. p. 152

Francis, Genevienve, Info Tech, West Hartford Public Library, 20 S Main St, West Hartford, CT, 06107-2432. Tel: 860-561-6950. p. 345

Francis, Mary, Libr Dir, Dakota State University, 820 N Washington Ave, Madison, SD, 57042. Tel: 605-256-5203. p. 2078

Francis, Matthew, Archivist, Ohio Northern University, 525 S Main St, Ada, OH, 45810. Tel: 419-772-1925. p. 1743

Francis, Nikki, Libr Mgr, Glenwood Municipal Library, 59 Main Ave, Glenwood, AB, T0K 2R0, CANADA. Tel: 403-942-8033. p. 2541

Francis, Susan, Librn, Lapeer District Library, Columbiaville Branch, 4718 First St, Columbiaville, MI, 48421-9143. Tel: 810-793-6100. p. 1126

Francis, Wilson, Libr Mgr, New York Public Library - Astor, Lenox & Tilden Foundations, Tremont Branch, 1866 Washington Ave, (@ E 176th St), Bronx, NY, 10457. Tel: 718-299-5177. p. 1597

Francisco, Kimberly, Mgr, Libr Operations, Metropolitan Library System in Oklahoma County, Ralph Ellison Library, 2000 NE 23rd St, Oklahoma City, OK, 73111-3402. p. 1857

Francisco, Lois, Br Mgr, Clearfield County Public Library, Curwensville Public Branch Library, 601 Beech St, Curwensville, PA, 16833. Tel: 814-236-0355. p. 1925

Francisco, MaryLynn, Dir, United States Department of Defense, 7500 GEOINT Dr, Mail Stop N73, Springfield, VA, 22150-7500. Tel: 571-557-5400. p. 2347

Franciskovich, Jolene, Libr Dir, Coal City Public Library District, 85 N Garfield St, Coal City, IL, 60416. Tel: 815-634-4552. p. 572

Franck, Carol, Assoc Librn, State University of New York College at Potsdam, Lougheed Learning Commons, 44 Pierrepont Ave, Potsdam, NY, 13676-2294. Tel: 315-267-3310. p. 1622

Francka-Jones, Sarah, Br Mgr, Springfield-Greene County Library District, Ash Grove Branch, 101 E Main St, Ash Grove, MO, 65604-0248. Tel: 417-751-2933. p. 1281

Francka-Jones, Sarah, Br Mgr, Springfield-Greene County Library District, Willard Branch, East Shopping Ctr, 304 E Jackson St, Willard, MO, 65781-0517. Tel: 417-742-4258. p. 1282

Franco, Cynthia, Cataloger/Ref Librn, Southern Methodist University, DeGolyer Library of Special Collections, 6404 Robert S Hyer Lane, Dallas, TX, 75275. Tel: 214-768-3605. p. 2168

Franco, Nora, Clinical Med Librn, University of Missouri-Kansas City Libraries, Health Sciences Library, 2411 Holmes St, Kansas City, MO, 64108. Tel: 816-235-1884. p. 1258

Franco, Stephanie, Circ Serv Mgr, Teton County Library, 125 Virginian Lane, Jackson, WY, 83001. Tel: 307-733-2164, Ext 3218. p. 2495

Francoeur, Erin W, Exec Dir, Westerville Public Library, 126 S State St, Westerville, OH, 43081. Tel: 614-882-7277. p. 1830

Francois, Lucile, Libr Mgr, New York Public Library - Astor, Lenox & Tilden Foundations, Macomb's Bridge Branch, 2650 Adam Clayton Powell Jr Blvd, (Between W 152nd & 153rd Sts), New York, NY, 10039-2004. Tel: 212-281-4900. p. 1596

Francois, Natasha, Law Librn, New Hanover County Public Library, 201 Chestnut St, Wilmington, NC, 28401. Tel: 910-798-6300. p. 1723

Francomartin, Rebecca, Youth Serv Librn, Trenton Free Public Library, 120 Academy St, Trenton, NJ, 08608. Tel: 609-392-7188. p. 1448

Frandrup, Dominic, Dir, Antigo Public Library, 617 Clermont St, Antigo, WI, 54409. Tel: 715-623-3724. p. 2420

Frandsen, Wendy, Fiscal Mgr, University of Alaska Fairbanks, 1732 Tanana Dr, Fairbanks, AK, 99775. Tel: 907-474-6696. p. 45

Frangakis, Evelyn, Managing Dir, Princeton Theological Seminary Library, 25 Library Pl, Princeton, NJ, 08540. Tel: 609-497-7940. p. 1437

Frank, Andrew, Access Serv, University of Richmond, William T Muse Law Library, 203 Richmond Way, Richmond, VA, 23173. Tel: 804-289-8637. p. 2343

Frank, Anne, Dir, Wissahickon Valley Public Library, 650 Skippack Pike, Blue Bell, PA, 19422. Tel: 215-643-1320, Ext 11. p. 1914

Frank, Barbara, Br Mgr, Waco-McLennan County Library System, South Waco, 2737 S 18th St, Waco, TX, 76706. Tel: 254-750-8411. p. 2254

Frank, Becky, Asst Libr Dir, Trinity International University, 2065 Half Day Rd, Deerfield, IL, 60015-1241. Tel: 847-317-4020. p. 577

Frank, Christopher, Dir, Stafford Library, Ten Levinthal Run, Stafford Springs, CT, 06075. Tel: 860-684-2852. p. 338

Frank, Cynthia, Head of Libr, University of Maryland Libraries, Architecture Library, Bldg 145, Rm 1102, 3835 Campus Dr, College Park, MD, 20742. Tel: 301-405-6321. p. 962

Frank, Dennis, Archivist, Saint Bonaventure University, 3261 W State Rd, Saint Bonaventure, NY, 14778. Tel: 716-375-2322. p. 1635

Frank, Jean, Librn, North Central Washington Libraries, Warden Public Library, 305 S Main St, Warden, WA, 98857-9680. Tel: 509-349-2226. p. 2394

Frank, Jessica, Dir, Blount Library, Inc, Five N Main St, Franklinville, NY, 14737-1015. Tel: 716-676-5715. p. 1535

Frank, John, Sr Librn, Los Angeles Public Library System, Will & Ariel Durant Branch Library, 7140 W Sunset Blvd, Los Angeles, CA, 90046. Tel: 323-876-2741. p. 164

Frank, Karen, Librn, Chinook Regional Library, Gravelbourg Branch, Maillard Cultural Ctr, 133 Fifth Ave E, Gravelbourg, SK, S0H 1X0, CANADA. Tel: 306-648-3177. p. 2752

Frank, Marietta, Dir of Libr, Jamestown Community College, 525 Falconer St, Jamestown, NY, 14702. Tel: 716-376-1000. p. 1557

Frank, Mary Ann, Libr Dir, Peck Memorial Library, 24 Main St, Marathon, NY, 13803. Tel: 607-849-6135. p. 1568

Frank, Owen, Head Librn, Chemung County Library District, Horseheads Free Library, 405 S Main St, Horseheads, NY, 14845. Tel: 607-739-4581. p. 1530

Frank, Owen, Library Contact, Chemung County Library District, Van Etten Library, 83 Main St, Van Etten, NY, 14889. Tel: 607-589-4755. p. 1530

Frank, Patricia, Libr Dir, Ashland University Library, 509 College Ave, Ashland, OH, 44805. Tel: 419-289-5401. p. 1747

Frank, Rebecca, Dir, Volunteer State Community College Library, 1480 Nashville Pike, Gallatin, TN, 37066-3188. Tel: 615-230-3412. p. 2099

Frank, Robin, Ch Serv, Framingham Public Library, Christa Corrigan McAuliffe Branch, Ten Nicholas Rd, Framingham, MA, 01701-3469. Tel: 508-532-5636. p. 1019

Frank, Sandy, Head, Circ/ILL, Thomas Ford Memorial Library, 800 Chestnut St, Western Springs, IL, 60558. Tel: 708-246-0520. p. 661

Frank, Shoshana, Info Serv Librn, Aurora University, 315 S Gladstone Ave, Aurora, IL, 60506-4892. Tel: 630-844-5437. p. 539

Frank, Shoshana, Dir, Communications, LIBRAS, Inc, c/o North Central College, 30 N Brainard St, Naperville, IL, 60540. p. 2765

Frank, Valerie, Dir, Blaine County Library, 112 Fourth St W, Chinook, MT, 59523. Tel: 406-357-2932. p. 1291

Franke, Debra, Br Librn, London Public Library, Byron Memorial, 1295 Commissioners Rd W, London, ON, N6K 1C9, CANADA. Tel: 519-471-4000. p. 2654

Frankel, Aaron, Exec Dir, Congregation Rodfei Zedek, 5200 S Hyde Park Blvd, Chicago, IL, 60615-4213. Tel: 773-752-2770, Ext 106. p. 559

Frankel, Joe, Librn, Inyo County Free Library, Bishop Branch, 210 Academy Ave, Bishop, CA, 93514-2693. Tel: 760-873-5115. p. 152

Frankel, Kenneth, Head, Engagement & Instructional Servs, Florida Atlantic University, 777 Glades Rd, Boca Raton, FL, 33431. Tel: 561-297-0079. p. 385

Frankel, Maggie, Fac Librn, City College of San Francisco, 50 Frida Kahlo Way, 4th Flr, San Francisco, CA, 94112. Tel: 415-452-5433. p. 224

Frankel, Paul, Libr Spec, Blue Ridge Community College, One College Lane, Weyers Cave, VA, 24486. Tel: 540-453-2247. p. 2352

Frankenberger, Peggy, Info Spec, HATCH LTK, Knowledge & Information Research Centre (KIRC), 100 W Butler Ave, Ambler, PA, 19002. Tel: 215-641-8833. p. 1906

Frankenfield, Mary, Dep Dir, Mansfield-Richland County Public Library, 43 W Third St, Mansfield, OH, 44902-1295. Tel: 419-521-3127. p. 1798

Franklin, Ailesia, Bus Mgr, Anderson City, Anderson, Stony Creek & Union Townships Public Library, 111 E 12th St, Anderson, IN, 46016-2701. Tel: 765-641-2197. p. 667

Franklin, Cindy, Pub Relations, Youth Serv Librn, Cynthiana-Harrison County Public Library, 104 N Main St, Cynthiana, KY, 41031. Tel: 859-234-4881. p. 853

Franklin, Jan, Asst Dir, West Carroll Parish Library, 101 Marietta St, Oak Grove, LA, 71263. Tel: 318-428-4100. p. 905

Franklin, Jennifer, Adult Serv, Warren Library Association, 205 Market St, Warren, PA, 16365. Tel: 814-723-4650. p. 2017

Franklin, Joe, Libr Serv Mgr, St Cloud State University Library, James W Miller Learning Resource Center, 400 Sixth St S, Saint Cloud, MN, 56301. Tel: 320-308-4675. p. 1198

Franklin, Kathleen, Librn, Mount Calm Public Library, 222 Allyn Ave, Mount Calm, TX, 76673. Tel: 254-993-2761. p. 2220

Franklin, Lucy, Cat Librn, Phillips Theological Seminary Library, 901 N Mingo Rd, Tulsa, OK, 74116. Tel: 918-270-6430. p. 1865

Franklin, Mandee, Genealogy Librn, Webster County Public Library, 101 State Rte 132 E, Dixon, KY, 42409. Tel: 270-639-9171. p. 853

Franklin, Melissa, Libr Dir, Shoshoni Public Library, 216 Idaho St, Shoshoni, WY, 82649. Tel: 307-876-2777. p. 2499

Franklin, Michelle, Dir, State Fair Community College, 3201 W 16th St, Sedalia, MO, 65301. Tel: 660-530-5842. p. 1279

Franklin, Monique, Coll Develop, Ad, Fort Bend County Libraries, 1001 Golfview Dr, Richmond, TX, 77469-5199. Tel: 281-633-4764. p. 2232

Franklin, Nathan, Libr Spec, New Mexico State University at Grants Library, 1500 N Third St, Grants, NM, 87020. Tel: 505-287-6638. p. 1469

Franklin, Rachel, Ref Librn, Rockaway Township Free Public Library, 61 Mount Hope Rd, Rockaway, NJ, 07866. Tel: 973-627-2344. p. 1440

Franklin, Rachel, Br Mgr, Hawkins County Library System, Surgoinsville Public Library, 120 Old Stage Rd, Surgoinsville, TN, 37873-3145. Tel: 423-345-4805. p. 2125

Franklin, Renee, Dir, Northwest Iowa Community College Library, 603 W Park St, Sheldon, IA, 51201. Tel: 712-324-5066, Ext 116. p. 781

Franklin, Ryan, Outreach Coordr, Illinois State Library, Gwendolyn Brooks Bldg, 300 S Second St, Springfield, IL, 62701-1796. Tel: 217-785-5615. p. 649

Franklin, Sandra G, Dir, Emory University Libraries, Woodruff Health Sciences Center Library, 1462 Clifton Rd NE, Atlanta, GA, 30322. Tel: 404-727-8727. p. 463

Franklin, Sharon, Br Mgr, Boone County Public Library, Walton Branch, 21 S Main St, Walton, KY, 41094-1135. Tel: 859-342-2665. p. 850

Franklin, Shirley Ann, Libr Dir, Hepler City Library, 105 S Prairie, Hepler, KS, 66746. Tel: 620-368-4379. p. 812

Franks, James, Assoc Univ Archivist, University of Alberta, Archives, Books & Records Depository, 100 8170 50th St, Edmonton, AB, T6B 1E6, CANADA. Tel: 780-248-1304. p. 2537

Franks, Janet, Ref Librn, Saint Leo University, 33701 State Rd 52, Saint Leo, FL, 33574. Tel: 352-588-8478. p. 441

Franks, Mercedes, Dir, Judy B McDonald Public Library, 1112 North St, Nacogdoches, TX, 75961-4482. Tel: 936-559-2945. p. 2221

Franks, Patrick, Libr Assoc, Langston University, 701 Sammy Davis Jr Dr, Langston, OK, 73050. Tel: 405-466-3292. p. 1851

Frankunas, Lori, Br Mgr, Rochester Public Library, Phillis Wheatley Community, 33 Dr Samuel McCree Way, Rochester, NY, 14608. Tel: 585-428-8212. p. 1630

Franquin, Yves, VPres, Museum of Russian Culture, Inc Library, 2450 Sutter St, San Francisco, CA, 94115. Tel: 415-921-4082. p. 226

Fransen, Linda, Dir, Cottonwood County Historical Society Library, 812 Fourth Ave, Windom, MN, 56101. Tel: 507-831-1134. p. 1208

Fransen, Pattie, Librn III, Peoria Public Library, Sunrise Mountain, 21109 N 98th Ave, Peoria, AZ, 85382. Tel: 623-773-8650. p. 68

Fransler, Stephanie, Libr Asst, Milltown Public Library, 61 W Main St, Milltown, WI, 54858. Tel: 715-825-2313. p. 2457

Franssen, Brian, Br Mgr, Yuma County Free Library District, Foothills Branch, 13226 E South Frontage Rd, Yuma, AZ, 85367. Tel: 928-373-6509. p. 86

Frantes, Naomi, Head, Access & Br Serv, University of North Dakota, 3051 University Ave, Stop 9000, Grand Forks, ND, 58202-9000. Tel: 701-777-4648. p. 1735

Frantz, Jean, Library Contact, United States Air Force, 100 Kindel Dr, Ste C212, Arnold AFB, TN, 37389. Tel: 931-454-7220. p. 2087

Frantz, Melissa, Pub Serv, Iola Public Library, 218 E Madison Ave, Iola, KS, 66749. Tel: 620-365-3262. p. 815

Frantz, Melissa, Talking Bks, Southeast Kansas Library System, 218 E Madison Ave, Iola, KS, 66749. Tel: 620-365-5136. p. 815

Franz, David J, Dir, Hillsdale Free Public Library, 509 Hillsdale Ave, Hillsdale, NJ, 07642. Tel: 201-358-5072. p. 1408

Franz, Lori, ILL, Gordon College, 255 Grapevine Rd, Wenham, MA, 01984-1899. Tel: 978-867-4878. p. 1064

Franzen, Leslie, Libr Mgr, Sno-Isle Libraries, Coupeville Library, 788 NW Alexander St, Coupeville, WA, 98239. Tel: 360-678-4911. p. 2370

Franzoni, Andy, Evening Circ Supvr, Florida Southern College, 111 Lake Hollingsworth Dr, Lakeland, FL, 33801-5698. Tel: 863-616-6452. p. 417

Fraone, Kimberly, Libr Dir, Kinnelon Public Library, 132 Kinnelon Rd, Kinnelon, NJ, 07405. Tel: 973-838-1321. p. 1410

Frary, Steve, Coordr, Acq, Southeastern Baptist Theological Seminary Library, 114 N Wingate St, Wake Forest, NC, 27587. Tel: 919-863-2330. p. 1720

Fraser, Allie, Coll Mgt Librn, Critical Path Learning Center, 1233 Locust St, 2nd Flr, Philadelphia, PA, 19107. Tel: 215-985-4851. p. 1976

Fraser, Darla, Chief Exec Officer, Orangeville Public Library, One Mill St, Orangeville, ON, L9W 2M2, CANADA. Tel: 519-941-0610, Ext 5222. p. 2663

Fraser, Gary, Dir, Lima Public Library, 650 W Market St, Lima, OH, 45801. Tel: 419-228-5113. p. 1795

Fraser, Ian, Head, Ref & Instruction, University of Winnipeg Library, 515 Portage Ave, Winnipeg, MB, R3B 2E9, CANADA. Tel: 786-204-9813. p. 2596

Fraser, Jaki, Br Mgr, Annapolis Valley Regional Library, Dr Frank W Morse Memorial Library - Lawrencetown, 489 Main St, Lawrencetown, NS, B0S 1M0, CANADA. Tel: 902-584-3044. p. 2616

Fraser, Lydia, Archivist, Colls Mgr, Sandy Spring Museum, 17901 Bentley Rd, Sandy Spring, MD, 20860. Tel: 301-774-0022. p. 977

Fraser, Mary, Librn, Atikameksheng Anishinawbek Library, c/o Atikmeksheng Kendaasii-Gamik, PO Box 39, Naughton, ON, P0M 2M0, CANADA. Tel: 705-692-9901. p. 2660

Fraser, Stacey, Colls Mgr, Lexington Historical Society, 1332 Massachusetts Ave, Lexington, MA, 02420-3809. Tel: 781-862-3763. p. 1028

Fraser, Teressa, Libr Dir, Tampa-Hillsborough County Public Library System, Temple Terrace Public Library, 202 Bullard Pkwy, Temple Terrace, FL, 33617-5512. Tel: 813-506-6770. p. 449

Fraser, Victoria, Supvr, Haliburton County Public Library, Dysart Branch, 78 Maple Ave, Haliburton, ON, K0M 1S0, CANADA. Tel: 705-457-1791. p. 2644

Frasier, Robert, Syst Librn, Mercer University, Jack Tarver Library, 1300 Edgewood Ave, Macon, GA, 31207. Tel: 478-301-2027. p. 486

Frater, Jonathan, Tech Serv Librn, Metropolitan College of New York Library, 60 West St, 7th Flr, New York, NY, 10006. Tel: 212-343-1234, Ext 2001. p. 1591

Frater, Laura A, Chief Librn, Metrohealth Medical Center, 2500 MetroHealth Dr, Cleveland, OH, 44101-1998. Tel: 216-778-5623. p. 1770

Fraundorf, Valerie, Circ, Phillips Public Library, 286 Cherry St, Phillips, WI, 54555. Tel: 715-339-2868. p. 2469

Frausto, Anthony, Br Mgr, Milwaukee Public Library, Mitchell Street, 906 W Historic Mitchell St, Milwaukee, WI, 53204. p. 2460

Frawley, Joseph, Tech Serv & Syst Librn, Connecticut College, 270 Mohegan Ave, New London, CT, 06320-4196. Tel: 860-439-2655. p. 328

Frawley, Tom, Ref & Non-Fiction Serv Coordr, North Kingstown Free Library, 100 Boone St, North Kingstown, RI, 02852-5150. Tel: 401-294-3306. p. 2036

Fray, George, Head, Syst, Florida International University, 11200 SW Eighth St, Miami, FL, 33199. Tel: 305-348-2488. p. 421

Frazee, Deanna A, Dir, Killeen Public Library, 205 E Church Ave, Killeen, TX, 76541. Tel: 254-501-8995. p. 2206

Frazee, Linda, Ch Serv, Brazoria County Library System, Freeport Branch, 410 Brazosport Blvd, Freeport, TX, 77541. Tel: 979-233-3622. p. 2135

Frazer, Carrie, Youth Librn, Bath Township Public Library, 14033 Webster Rd, Bath, MI, 48808. Tel: 517-641-7111. p. 1082

Frazer, Helen, Assoc Dir, Pub Serv, University of the District of Columbia, David A Clarke School of Law, Charles N & Hilda H M Mason Law Library, Bldg 39, Rm B-16, 4200 Connecticut Ave NW, Washington, DC, 20008. Tel: 202-274-7356. p. 380

Frazer, Stuart, Dep Univ Librn, Old Dominion University Libraries, 4427 Hampton Blvd, Norfolk, VA, 23529-0256. Tel: 757-683-4143. p. 2336

Frazier, Cindy, Br Supvr, Barry-Lawrence Regional Library, Monett Branch, 2200 Park St, Monett, MO, 65708. Tel: 417-235-7350. p. 1263

Frazier, Deena, Coll Serv Librn, Boston College, 885 Centre St, Newton Centre, MA, 02459. Tel: 617-552-4409. p. 1039

Frazier, Doug, Assoc Dean, Georgia Southern University, 11935 Abercorn St, Savannah, GA, 31419. Tel: 912-344-2818. p. 495

Frazier, India, Mkt & Communications Spec, Upper Dublin Public Library, 520 Virginia Ave, Fort Washington, PA, 19034. Tel: 215-628-8744. p. 1933

Frazier, Jennifer, Librn, Kentucky State Law Library, 700 Capital Ave, Ste 200, Frankfort, KY, 40601. Tel: 502-564-4848. p. 855

Frazier, Joyce, Cataloger, Barry-Lawrence Regional Library, 213 Sixth St, Monett, MO, 65708-2147. Tel: 417-235-6646. p. 1262

Frazier, Katrina, Head, Discovery & Metadata, Nassau Community College, One Education Dr, Garden City, NY, 11530-6793. Tel: 516-572-7400, 516-572-7401. p. 1537

Frazier, Kristin, Libr Dir, Burgettstown Community Library, Two Kerr St, Burgettstown, PA, 15021-1127. Tel: 724-947-9780. p. 1916

Frazier, Mara, Asst Curator, Ohio State University LIBRARIES, Jerome Lawrence & Robert E Lee Theatre Research Institute, 1430 Lincoln Tower, 1800 Cannon Dr, Columbus, OH, 43210-1230. Tel: 614-292-6614. p. 1775

Frazier, Meg, Info Literacy/Electronic Serv Librn, Bradley University, 1501 W Bradley Ave, Peoria, IL, 61625. Tel: 309-677-2850. p. 634

Frazier, Pamela, Head, Children's Servx, Crandall Public Library, 251 Glen St, Glens Falls, NY, 12801-3546. Tel: 518-792-6508. p. 1539

Frazier, Rose, Head, Cat, Library & Learning Resource Ctr Librn, Tuskegee University, 1200 W Old Mongtomery Rd, Ford Motor Company Library, Tuskegee, AL, 36088. Tel: 334-727-8892. p. 38

Frazier, Sharon A, Br Mgr, Gary Public Library, John F Kennedy Branch, 3953 Broadway, Gary, IN, 46408-1799. Tel: 219-887-8112. p. 686

Freanch, Elyse, Br Mgr, Clermont County Public Library, Union Township, 4450 Glen Este-Withamsville Rd, Cincinnati, OH, 45245. Tel: 513-528-1744. p. 1803

Frear, Marian, Dir, Corrales Community Library, 84 W La Entrada Rd, Corrales, NM, 87048. Tel: 505-897-0733. p. 1466

Freas, Stephanie, Asst Dir, Muskingum County Library System, 220 N Fifth St, Zanesville, OH, 43701-3587. Tel: 740-453-0391. p. 1836

Frechette, Liz, Instrul Serv Librn, Ref (Info Servs), Naugatuck Valley Community College, 750 Chase Pkwy, Rm K512, Waterbury, CT, 06708. Tel: 203-575-8106. p. 344

Frechman, Paige, Librn, Earlville Library District, 205 Winthrop St, Earlville, IL, 60518. Tel: 815-246-9543. p. 580

Frecker, Sarah, Librn, Yakima Valley Libraries, Moxee Library, 255 W Seattle Ave, Moxee, WA, 98936. Tel: 509-575-8854. p. 2395

Freda, Kristin, Dir, Libr Serv, Bank Street College of Education Library, 610 W 112th St, 5th Flr, New York, NY, 10025. Tel: 212-875-4455. p. 1579

Freden, Alyssa, Tech Serv Librn, Lincoln Public Library, Three Bedford Rd, Lincoln, MA, 01773. Tel: 781-259-8465, Ext 206. p. 1028

Frederick, Connie, Br Librn, Ritchie County Public Library, Pennsboro Branch, 411 Main St, Pennsboro, WV, 26415. Tel: 304-659-2197. p. 2404

Frederick, Heather, Libr Dir, West Concord Public Library, 180 E Main St, West Concord, MN, 55985. Tel: 507-527-2031. p. 1207

Frederick, Kathleen, Libr Spec, Harrisburg Area Community College, 2010 Pennsylvania Ave, York, PA, 17404. Tel: 717-801-3220. p. 2026

Frederick, Linda, Mkt & Develop, Baltimore County Public Library, 320 York Rd, Towson, MD, 21204-5179. Tel: 410-887-6100. p. 979

Frederick, Mary, Mgr, Info Serv, Springfield City Library, 220 State St, Springfield, MA, 01103. Tel: 413-263-6828, Ext 202. p. 1056

Fredericks, Matthew D, Acad Serv Officer II, Wayne State University, 106 Kresge Library, Detroit, MI, 48202. Tel: 313-577-2446. p. 2787

Fredericks, Nancy, Libr Adminr, Pasco County Library System, 8012 Library Rd, Hudson, FL, 34667. Tel: 727-861-3020. p. 410

Frederking, Brenda, Asst Librn, Plainville Memorial Library, 200 SW First St, Plainville, KS, 67663. Tel: 785-434-2786. p. 832

Fredette, Hilary, Dir, Res Sharing, Operations Dir, West Virginia University Libraries, 1549 University Ave, Morgantown, WV, 26506. Tel: 304-293-4040. p. 2409

Fredette, Sharon, Computer Support Spec, Seekonk Public Library, 410 Newman Ave, Seekonk, MA, 02771. Tel: 508-336-8230, Ext 56150. p. 1052

Fredrich, Rorie, Assoc Dean, Research & Customer Services, Liberty University, 1971 University Blvd, Lynchburg, VA, 24515. Tel: 434-582-7572. p. 2330

Fredrickson, Jill, ILL, Spooner Memorial Library, 421 High St, Spooner, WI, 54801. Tel: 715-635-2792. p. 2478

Fredrickson, Nancy, Dir, Samuel H Wentworth Library, 35 Main St, Center Sandwich, NH, 03227. Tel: 603-284-6665. p. 1357

Freeburg, Darin, PhD, Assoc Prof, University of South Carolina, 1501 Greene St, Columbia, SC, 29208. Tel: 803-777-3858. p. 2792

Freeburg, Paulina, Dir, Plummer Public Library, 849 D St, Plummer, ID, 83851. Tel: 208-686-1812. p. 528

Freed, Jenny, Archives, Dir, Spec Coll, Earlham College, 801 National Rd W, Richmond, IN, 47374-4095. Tel: 765-983-1743. p. 715

Freed, Mark, Head, Br Libr, Saint Lucie County Library System, 101 Melody Lane, Fort Pierce, FL, 34950-4402. Tel: 772-462-1618. p. 405

Freed, Melissa, Head, Children's Servx, West Lafayette Public Library, 208 W Columbia St, West Lafayette, IN, 47906. Tel: 765-743-2261. p. 726

Freed, Rachel, Youth Serv Mgr, Wellsville Carnegie Public Library, 115 Ninth St, Wellsville, OH, 43968-1431. Tel: 330-532-1526. p. 1829

Freedle, Stephanie, Libr Mgr, Siloam Springs Public Library, 205 E Jefferson, Siloam Springs, AR, 72761. Tel: 479-524-4236. p. 110

Freedle, Stephanie, Mgr, John F Henderson Public Library, 1152 N Williams Ave, Westville, OK, 74965. Tel: 918-723-5002. p. 1869

Freedman, Howard, Dir, Jewish Community Library, 1835 Ellis St, San Francisco, CA, 94115. Tel: 415-567-3327, Ext 705. p. 225

Freedman, Jenna, Curator, Barnard College, 3009 Broadway, New York, NY, 10027-6598. Tel: 212-854-4615. p. 1579

Freedman, Phyllis D, Dr, Dir, Libr Serv, Salem University, 223 W Main St, Salem, WV, 26426. Tel: 304-326-1390. p. 2414

Freeland, Brenda, Dir, George H Stowell Free Library, 24 School St, Cornish Flat, NH, 03746. Tel: 603-543-3644. p. 1360

Freeland, Sarah, Br Mgr, Waco-McLennan County Library System, 1717 Austin Ave, Waco, TX, 76701-1794. Tel: 254-750-5958. p. 2254

Freeland, Tricia, Dir, Hoopeston Public Library, 110 N Fourth St, Hoopeston, IL, 60942-1422. Tel: 217-283-6711. p. 601

Freels, Jeanette, Mgr, County of Los Angeles Public Library, La Puente Library, 15920 E Central Ave, La Puente, CA, 91744-5499. Tel: 626-968-4613. p. 136

Freeman, Alyse, Asst to the Dean of Libraries, California State University Dominguez Hills, 1000 E Victoria St, Carson, CA, 90747. Tel: 310-243-2305. p. 129

Freeman, Beth, Libr Dir, New Carlisle Public Library, 111 E Lake Ave, New Carlisle, OH, 45344-1418. Tel: 937-845-3601. p. 1806

Freeman, Brook, Br Mgr, Free Library of Philadelphia, Welsh Road Branch, 9233 Roosevelt Blvd, Philadelphia, PA, 19114-2205. Tel: 215-685-0498. p. 1980

Freeman, Cheryl, Librn, Atchison County Library, Tarkio Branch, 405 S 11th St, Tarkio, MO, 64491. Tel: 660-736-5832. p. 1267

Freeman, Christine, Actg Br Mgr, Montgomery County Public Libraries, Olney Library, 3500 Olney-Laytonsville Rd, Olney, MD, 20832-1798. Tel: 240-773-9540. p. 975

Freeman, Christine, Br Mgr, Montgomery County Public Libraries, Noyes Library for Young Children, 10237 Carroll Pl, Kensington, MD, 20895-3361. Tel: 240-777-0105. p. 975

Freeman, Cynthia, Librn, New Providence Presbyterian Church, 703 W Broadway Ave, Maryville, TN, 37801. Tel: 865-983-0182. p. 2111

Freeman, Hannah, Ref & Tech Librn, Brooklyn Law School Library, 250 Joralemon St, Brooklyn, NY, 11201. Tel: 718-780-7927. p. 1501

Freeman, Helen, Tech Serv Librn, Gloucester, Lyceum & Sawyer Free Library, Two Dale Ave, Gloucester, MA, 01930. Tel: 978-325-5556. p. 1021

Freeman, Jennifer, Br Mgr, Rusk County Library System, McMillan Memorial Library, 401 S Commerce St, Overton, TX, 75684. Tel: 903-834-6318. p. 2189

Freeman, Kirk, Dir, Saint Charles Public Library, 113 S Lumber St, Saint Charles, IA, 50240. Tel: 641-396-2945. p. 780

Freeman, Kyri, Librn, Barstow Community College, 2700 Barstow Rd, Barstow, CA, 92311. Tel: 760-252-2411, Ext 7270. p. 120

Freeman, Michelle, Libr Mgr, Community Libraries of Providence, Knight Memorial Library, 275 Elmwood Ave, Providence, RI, 02907. Tel: 401-467-2625. p. 2038

Freeman, Rebecca T, Dir, University of South Carolina Lancaster, 476-B Hubbard Dr, Lancaster, SC, 29720. Tel: 803-313-7062. p. 2064

Freeman, Rodney, Br Mgr, Saint Louis Public Library, Walnut Park, 5760 W Florissant Ave, Saint Louis, MO, 63120. Tel: 314-383-1210. p. 1275

Freeman, Sheldon, Teen Serv, Teen Serv Librn, Helen Hall Library, 100 W Walker, League City, TX, 77573-3899. Tel: 281-554-1133. p. 2210

Freeman, Stella, Circ, Kettering College, 3737 Southern Blvd, Kettering, OH, 45429-1299. Tel: 937-395-8053, Ext 3. p. 1793

Freeman, Yvette, Br Mgr, City of San Bernardino Library Services, Dorothy Inghram Branch, 1505 W Highland Ave, San Bernardino, CA, 92411. Tel: 909-887-4494. p. 212

Freemantle, Mirka, Circ Supvr, University of Waterloo Library, Witer Learning Resource Centre, Optometry Bldg, Rm 2101, Waterloo, ON, N2L 3G1, CANADA. Tel: 519-888-4567, Ext 38875. p. 2702

Freemont, River, Assoc Archivist, Whitman College, 345 Boyer Ave, Walla Walla, WA, 99362. Tel: 509-526-4703. p. 2393

Freemyer, Vickie, Dir, Haxtun Public Library, 141 S Colorado Ave, Haxtun, CO, 80731-2711. Tel: 970-774-6106. p. 285

Freese, Jennifer, Ch Serv, Chili Public Library, 3333 Chili Ave, Rochester, NY, 14624. Tel: 585-889-2200. p. 1628

Freese, Lindsey, Dir, Kling Memorial Library, 708 Seventh St, Grundy Center, IA, 50638-1430. Tel: 319-825-3607. p. 757

Freeze, Chad, Librn, Navarro College, 3200 W Seventh Ave, Corsicana, TX, 75110-4899. Tel: 903-875-7442. p. 2161

Freeze, Thaine, Librn, Gothenburg Public Library, 1104 Lake Ave, Gothenburg, NE, 69138-1903. Tel: 308-537-2591. p. 1316

Freiboth, Susan, Circ, Phillips Public Library, 286 Cherry St, Phillips, WI, 54555. Tel: 715-339-2868. p. 2469

Freier, Ruth, Dir, Gorham Free Library, 2664 Main St, Gorham, NY, 14461. Tel: 585-526-6655. p. 1539

Freiler, Alice, Libr Dir, Harwinton Public Library, 80 Bentley Dr, Harwinton, CT, 06791. Tel: 860-485-9113. p. 319

Freilich, Jeffrey, Librn, Ivins, Philips & Barker Library, 1717 K St NW, Ste 600, Washington, DC, 20006. Tel: 202-393-7600. p. 370

Freise, Sharon, Librn, Bond Public Library, 208 S Chestnut St, Wenona, IL, 61377. Tel: 815-853-4665. p. 660

Freitag, Brian, Dir, Tahquamenon Area Library, 700 Newberry Ave, Newberry, MI, 49868. Tel: 906-293-5214. p. 1137

Freitag, JoAnne, Libr Dir, Presentation College Library, 1500 N Main, Aberdeen, SD, 57401-1299. Tel: 605-229-8546. p. 2073

Freitag, JoAnne, Continuing Educ Coordr, South Dakota State Library, 800 Governors Dr, Pierre, SD, 57501-2294. Tel: 605-773-3131. p. 2080

Freitas, Angelica, Govt Doc Librn, Ser Librn, Sarah Lawrence College, One Mead Way, Bronxville, NY, 10708. Tel: 914-395-2478. p. 1500

Frembling, Jonathan, Archivist, Ref Serv Mgr, Amon Carter Museum of American Art, 3501 Camp Bowie Blvd, Fort Worth, TX, 76107-2695. Tel: 817-738-1933. p. 2179

Fremont, Kyla, Br Librn, Wapiti Regional Library, Paddockwood Public Library, Old School Bldg, First St N, Paddockwood, SK, S0J 1Z0, CANADA. p. 2746

French, Bill, Access Serv Librn, South Louisiana Community College-Lafayette Campus, Devalcourt Bldg, 1st Flr, 1101 Bertrand Dr, Lafayette, LA, 70506. Tel: 337-521-8998. p. 893

French, Cheryl, Mgr, Bristol Public Library, 1855 Greenville Rd, Bristolville, OH, 44402-9700. Tel: 330-889-3651. p. 1753

French, Darren, Dir, Brewer Public Library, 100 S Main St, Brewer, ME, 04412. Tel: 207-989-7943. p. 918

French, Jane, Mgr, Superior District Library, Les Cheneaux Community Library, 75 E Hodeck St, Cedarville, MI, 49719. Tel: 906-484-3547. p. 1149

French, Jason, Curator of Coll, Behringer-Crawford Museum Library, 1600 Montague Rd, Devou Park, Covington, KY, 41011. Tel: 859-491-4003. p. 852

French, Jeff, Maps Librn, University of Tennessee, Knoxville, Map Collection, James D Hoskins Library, Rms 200 & 219, 1401 Cumberland Ave, Knoxville, TN, 37996. Tel: 865-974-6214. p. 2108

French, Kevin, Syst Adminr, GMILCS, Inc, 31 Mount Saint Mary's Way, Hooksett, NH, 03106. p. 2769

French, Laura, Assoc Librn, Curator, Baylor University Libraries, Armstrong Browning Library & Museum, 710 Speight Ave, Waco, TX, 76798. Tel: 254-710-4959. p. 2253

French, Leann, Dir, Geraldine E Anderson Village Library, 117 S Central Ave, Dresser, WI, 54009. Tel: 715-755-2944. p. 2431

French, Marilyn, Ref Librn, Southern University, Oliver B Spellman Law Library, Two Roosevelt Steptoe, Baton Rouge, LA, 70813. Tel: 225-771-2146. p. 884

French, Susanna, Metadata & E-Resource Management Librn, University of Connecticut, Thomas J Meskill Law Library, 39 Elizabeth St, Hartford, CT, 06105. Tel: 860-570-5009. p. 340

French, Tiana, Librn, Dentons Bingham Greenebaum LLP, 300 W Vine St, Ste 1200, Lexington, KY, 40507-1622. Tel: 859-231-8500, 859-288-4717. p. 862

French, Vanessa, Collections Strategy Librn, Butler University Libraries, 4600 Sunset Ave, Indianapolis, IN, 46208. Tel: 317-940-6491. p. 690
Frenette, Amelie, Prof, Cégep Garneau, 1660 blvd de l'Entente, Quebec, QC, G1S 4S3, CANADA. Tel: 418-688-8310, Ext 2290. p. 2796
Freng, Sarah, ILL, Black Hills State University, 1200 University St, Unit 9676, Spearfish, SD, 57799-9676. Tel: 605-642-6250. p. 2083
Frenzel, Linda, Dir, Camden Public Library, 57 Second St, Camden, NY, 13316. Tel: 315-245-1980. p. 1512
Frenzel, Phyllis, Dir, Joint Base Pearl Harbor-Hickam Library, Bldg 595, 990 Mills Blvd, Hickam AFB, HI, 96853. Tel: 808-449-8299. p. 505
Frescura, Shannon, Br Mgr, Hampton Public Library, Northampton Branch, 936 Big Bethel Rd, Hampton, VA, 23669. Tel: 757-825-4558. p. 2322
Frese, Laura, Libr Mgr, Washington County Library, Wildwood Branch, 763 Stillwater Rd, Mahtomedi, MN, 55115-2008. Tel: 651-426-2042. p. 1210
Freshly-Alspaugh, Gabby, Circ Supvr, Otterbein University, 138 W Main St, Westerville, OH, 43081. Tel: 614-823-1215. p. 1830
Freshwater, Andrew, Asst Mgr, Saint Louis County Library, Thornhill Branch, 12863 Willowyck Dr, Saint Louis, MO, 63146-3771. Tel: 314-994-3300, Ext 3900. p. 1274
Fresquez, Terry, Cat & Tech Serv Librn, Mount Saint Mary's University, 12001 Chalon Rd, Los Angeles, CA, 90049-1599. Tel: 310-954-4370. p. 166
Frethem, Renee, Br Mgr, Wadena City Library, 304 First St SW, Wadena, MN, 56482-1460. Tel: 218-631-2476. p. 1206
Fretz, Lynne, Ad, Brighton Memorial Library, 2300 Elmwood Ave, Rochester, NY, 14618. Tel: 585-784-5300. p. 1628
Fretz, Sarah, Ad, Info Serv Librn, Martin Memorial Library, 159 E Market St, York, PA, 17401-1269. Tel: 717-846-5300. p. 2026
Freudenberger, Erica, Pub Serv Consult & Outreach Coordr, Southern Adirondack Library System, 22 Whitney Pl, Saratoga Springs, NY, 12866-4596. Tel: 518-584-7300, Ext 211. p. 1636
Freudenburg, Dave, Br Supvr, Marion County Public Library System, Forest Public Library, 905 S County 314A, Ocklawaha, FL, 32179. Tel: 352-438-2540. p. 430
Freund, Laurie, Libr Develop Coordr, Bridges Library System, 741 N Grand Ave, Ste 210, Waukesha, WI, 53186. Tel: 262-896-8083. p. 2484
Freund, Peter, Tape Librn, Maharishi International University Library, 1000 N Fourth St, Fairfield, IA, 52557. Tel: 641-472-1148. p. 752
Frevert, Rhonda, Supv Librn, Des Moines Public Library, 1000 Grand Ave, Des Moines, IA, 50309. Tel: 515-283-4265. p. 745
Frevert, Rhonda J, Dir, Burlington Public Library, 210 Court St, Burlington, IA, 52601. Tel: 319-753-1647. p. 736
Frew, Heather, Asst Librn, Northwest Kansas Library System, Two Washington Sq, Norton, KS, 67654-1615. Tel: 785-877-5148. p. 827
Frew, Julie, Dir, Milford Public Library, 101 N Main St, Milford, IN, 46542. Tel: 574-658-4312. p. 706
Frew, Ken, Librn, Historical Society of Dauphin County Library, 219 S Front St, Harrisburg, PA, 17104-1619. Tel: 717-233-3462. p. 1940
Frey, Carrie, Dir, Libr Serv, Centre College of Kentucky, 600 W Walnut St, Danville, KY, 40422. Tel: 859-238-5275. p. 853
Frey, Cathy, Asst Librn, Danvers Township Library, 117 E Exchange St, Danvers, IL, 61732-9347. Tel: 309-963-4269. p. 575
Frey, Charles, Libr Dir, Munger, Tolles & Olson LLP, 350 S Grand Ave, 50th Flr, Los Angeles, CA, 90071-1560. Tel: 213-683-9100. p. 166
Frey, Emily, Br Mgr, Mercer County Library System, Hightstown Memorial, 114 Franklin St, Hightstown, NJ, 08520. Tel: 609-448-1474. p. 1411
Frey, Katie, Asst Head Librn, Center for Astrophysics Library / Harvard & Smithsonian Library, 60 Garden St, MS-56, Cambridge, MA, 02138. Tel: 617-496-5769. p. 1005
Frey, Maris, Youth Serv, Stonington Free Library, 20 High St, Stonington, CT, 06378. Tel: 860-535-0658. p. 339
Frey, Shandy, Research, Instruction & Engagement Librn, College of Coastal Georgia, One College Dr, Brunswick, GA, 31520. Tel: 912-279-5781. p. 468
Frey, Susan M, Univ Librn, Marywood University Library & Learning Commons, 2300 Adams Ave, Scranton, PA, 18509. Tel: 570-961-4707. p. 2004
Frey, Susan M, Dr, Dean of the Library, SUNY New Paltz, 300 Hawk Dr, New Paltz, NY, 12561-2493. Tel: 845-257-3700. p. 1577
Frey, Tracy, Asst Librn, Trenton Public Library, 118 E Indiana, Trenton, IL, 62293. Tel: 618-224-7662. p. 654
Freyemuth, Allison, Head Librn, Free Library of Philadelphia, Rare Book, 1901 Vine St, 3rd Flr, Philadelphia, PA, 19103-1116. Tel: 215-686-5416. p. 1979
Freyler, Andrea, Mgr, Contra Costa County Library, Brentwood Library, 104 Oak St, Brentwood, CA, 94513. Tel: 925-516-5290. p. 174
Freymiller, Peggy S, Circ, ILL, Southwest Wisconsin Library System, 1300 Industrial Dr, Ste 2, Fennimore, WI, 53809. Tel: 608-822-3393. p. 2435
Frezza, Chris, Head, Syst, Suburban Library Cooperative, 44750 Delco Blvd, Sterling Heights, MI, 48313. Tel: 586-685-5750. p. 2767
Friars, Crystal, Asst Libr Mgr, Stettler Public Library, 6202 44th Ave, 2nd Flr, Stettler, AB, T0C 2L1, CANADA. Tel: 403-742-2292. p. 2555
Fribley, Karla, Dir, Instrul Tech, Seminary Librarian, Earlham College, 801 National Rd W, Richmond, IN, 47374-4095. Tel: 765-983-1290. p. 715
Fricchione, Melanie, Ch, Memorial & Library Association, 44 Broad St, Westerly, RI, 02891. Tel: 401-596-2877, Ext 337. p. 2044
Frick, Caroline, Libr Mgr, Rabun County Public Library, 73 Jo Dotson Circle, Clayton, GA, 30525. Tel: 706-782-3731. p. 471
Frick, David, Asst Librn, Mendocino County Library District, 880 N Bush St, Ukiah, CA, 95482. Tel: 707-24-2872. p. 254
Frick, David, Asst Librn, Mendocino County Library District, Willits Branch, 390 E Commercial St, Willits, CA, 95490. Tel: 707-459-5908. p. 254
Frick, Rachel L, Exec Dir, OCLC Research Library Partnership, 6565 Kilgour Pl, Dublin, OH, 43017. Tel: 614-764-6000. p. 2772
Frick, Teresa, Tech Serv-Section Head, Orange County Public Library, 146A Madison Rd, Orange, VA, 22960. Tel: 540-672-3811. p. 2336
Fricke, Suzanne, Head of Libr, Washington State University Libraries, Animal Health Library, 170 Wegner Hall, Pullman, WA, 99164. Tel: 509-335-9556. p. 2374
Friday, Paul, Ref Librn, New Hampshire Historical Society Library, 30 Park St, Concord, NH, 03301-6384. Tel: 603-228-6688. p. 1359
Fridl, Ann, Br Mgr, Jacksonville Public Library, South Mandarin Branch, 12125 San Jose Blvd, Jacksonville, FL, 32223-2636. Tel: 904-288-6385. p. 412
Fridman, Svetlana, Libr Asst, Maimonides Medical Center, Admin Bldg, Fifth Flr, 4802 Tenth Ave, Brooklyn, NY, 11219. Tel: 718-283-7406. p. 1505
Fried, Helen, County Librn, OC Public Libraries, 1501 E St Andrew Pl, Santa Ana, CA, 92705. Tel: 714-566-3000. p. 237
Fried, Liz, Libr Dir, Norwood Public Library, 198 Summit St, Norwood, NJ, 07648. Tel: 201-768-9555. p. 1430
Fried, Regina, Mgr, Pub Relations & Mkt, Bucks County Free Library, 150 S Pine St, Doylestown, PA, 18901-4932. Tel: 215-348-0332. p. 1926
Friede, Eric, Head, Acq, Yale University Library, Beinecke Rare Book & Manuscript Library, 121 Wall St, New Haven, CT, 06511. Tel: 203-432-2975. p. 327
Friedel, Megan, Archives, University of Alaska Anchorage, Consortium Library, 3211 Providence Dr, Anchorage, AK, 99508-8176. Tel: 907-786-1871. p. 43
Friedgen-Veitch, Lori L, Ch & Youth Librn, Helen Kate Furness Free Library, 100 N Providence Rd, Wallingford, PA, 19086. Tel: 610-566-9331. p. 2017
Friedl, Eleanor, Res & Instruction Librn, Fairleigh Dickinson University, 285 Madison Ave, M-LAO-03, Madison, NJ, 07940. Tel: 973-443-8515. p. 1415
Friedlander, Kathy, Libr Assoc, Putnam Northern Westchester BOCES, 200 BOCES Dr, Yorktown Heights, NY, 10598. Tel: 914-248-2392. p. 1668
Friedlander, Suzan, Chief Curator, Exec Dir, Canajoharie Library, Two Erie Blvd, Canajoharie, NY, 13317. Tel: 518-673-2314. p. 1512
Friedler, Nadia, Teen Serv Librn, Leominster Public Library, 30 West St, Leominster, MA, 01453. Tel: 978-534-7522, Ext 3616. p. 1028
Friedli, Autumn, Supvr, Pub Serv, Topeka & Shawnee County Public Library, 1515 SW Tenth Ave, Topeka, KS, 66604-1374. Tel: 785-580-4400. p. 839
Friedman, Cheri, Exec Dir, Mondak Heritage Center, 120 Third Ave SE, Sidney, MT, 59270. Tel: 406-433-3500. p. 1302
Friedman, Deborah, Coordr, Access Serv, University of Massachusetts Lowell Library, 61 Wilder St, Lowell, MA, 01854-3098. Tel: 978-934-4572. p. 1030
Friedman, Helen, Ch Serv, North Merrick Public Library, 1691 Meadowbrook Rd, North Merrick, NY, 11566. Tel: 516-378-7474. p. 1608
Friedman, Jennifer, E-Res Mgt, Head, Acq, University of California Los Angeles Library, Hugh & Hazel Darling Law Library, 1112 Law Bldg, 385 Charles E Young Dr E, Los Angeles, CA, 90095-1458. Tel: 310-825-7826. p. 169
Friedman, Jennifer, Head, Res Serv, University of Massachusetts Amherst Libraries, 154 Hicks Way, University of Massachusetts, Amherst, MA, 01003-9275. Tel: 413-545-6890. p. 985
Friedman, Joanne, Sr Ch, Kearny Public Library, 318 Kearny Ave, Kearny, NJ, 07032. Tel: 201-998-2666. p. 1410
Friedman, Pamela, Welcome Services & Events Coord, Beth-El Synagogue, 5225 Barry St W, Saint Louis Park, MN, 55416. Tel: 952-873-7300. p. 1199
Friedman, Rebecca, Asst Librn, Princeton University, Marquand Library of Art & Archaeology, McCormick Hall, Princeton, NJ, 08544-0001. Tel: 609-258-3163. p. 1437
Friedman, Robbin, Ch, Chappaqua Public Library, 195 S Greeley Ave, Chappaqua, NY, 10514. Tel: 914-238-4779. p. 1516
Friedman, Yelena, Dir, Med Libr, Staten Island University Hospital/Northwell Health, 475 Seaview Ave, Staten Island, NY, 10305. Tel: 718-226-9545. p. 1645
Friedow, Linda, Dir, Britt Public Library, 132 Main Ave S, Britt, IA, 50423-1627. Tel: 641-843-4245. p. 736
Friedrich, Corey, Libr Dir, Chippewa River District Library, 301 S University Ave, Mount Pleasant, MI, 48858-2597. Tel: 989-773-3242, Ext 210. p. 1135
Friedrich, Pam, Asst Librn, Lake Erie College, 391 W Washington St, Painesville, OH, 44077-3309. Tel: 440-375-7402. p. 1812

Friehs, Curt, Dir, Libr Serv, Vaughn College Library, 8601 23rd Ave, Flushing, NY, 11369. Tel: 718-429-6600, Ext 184. p. 1534
Friehs, Curt, Dir, Carnegie Free Library, 1301 Seventh Ave, Beaver Falls, PA, 15010-4219. Tel: 724-846-4340. p. 1909
Friel, Cathy, Ch, Butte-Silver Bow Public Library, 226 W Broadway St, Butte, MT, 59701. Tel: 406-792-1080. p. 1290
Friend, Christina, Librn, Longton Public Library, 501 Kansas Ave, Longton, KS, 67352. Tel: 620-642-6012. p. 822
Friend, Danielle, Ch Serv, Robert J Kleberg Public Library, 220 N Fourth St, Kingsville, TX, 78363. Tel: 361-592-6381. p. 2206
Friend, Diana, Dir, Mkt & Communications, Topeka & Shawnee County Public Library, 1515 SW Tenth Ave, Topeka, KS, 66604-1374. Tel: 785-580-4400. p. 839
Friendshuh, Shelby, Libr Dir, Osceola Public Library, 102 Chieftain St, Osceola, WI, 54020. Tel: 715-294-2310. p. 2467
Fries, Elizabeth, Br Librn, Southeast Regional Library, Qu'Appelle Branch, 16 Qu'Appelle St, Qu'Appelle, SK, S0G 4A0, CANADA. Tel: 306-699-2902. p. 2754
Friese, Christine, Asst Dir, Portsmouth Public Library, 175 Parrott Ave, Portsmouth, NH, 03801-4452. Tel: 603-427-1540. p. 1379
Friesen, Paul, Assoc Librn, Canadian Mennonite University Library, 2299 Grant Ave, Winnipeg, MB, R3P 2N2, CANADA. Tel: 204-487-3300, Ext 319. p. 2593
Friesen, Rachael, Br Librn, South Central Regional Library, Altona Branch, 113-125 Centre Ave, Altona, MB, R0G 0B0, CANADA. Tel: 204-324-1503. p. 2592
Friet, Deb, Health Sci Librn, Libr Mgr, Department of Veteran Affairs, 500 E Veterans St, Tomah, WI, 54660. Tel: 608-372-3971, Ext 66267. p. 2481
Frieze, Julie, Mgr, County of Los Angeles Public Library, Westlake Village Library, 31220 Oak Crest Dr, Westlake Village, CA, 91361. Tel: 818-865-9230. p. 138
Frigge, Diane, Sr Librn, University of South Dakota, I D Weeks Library, 414 E Clark St, Vermillion, SD, 57069. Tel: 605-677-6091. p. 2084
Friginette, Marcia, Mgr, Libr Serv, Whitchurch-Stouffville Public Library, Two Park Dr, Stouffville, ON, L4A 4K1, CANADA. Tel: 905-642-7323. p. 2681
Frisbee, Steven, Dir of Libr, Mohawk Valley Community College Libraries, 1101 Sherman Dr, Utica, NY, 13501-5394. Tel: 315-792-5408. p. 1655
Frisbee, Susan Mosher, Libr Mgr, Cannon Free Library, 40 Elm St, Delhi, NY, 13753. Tel: 607-746-2662. p. 1524
Frisbie, Andrew, Coll Develop Librn, North Liberty Library, 520 W Cherry St, North Liberty, IA, 52317-9797. Tel: 319-626-5701. p. 773
Frisby, Anthony, Libr Dir, Thomas Jefferson University, 1020 Walnut St, Philadelphia, PA, 19107. Tel: 215-503-8848. p. 1986
Frisch, Laura, Libr Office Mgr, Mukwonago Community Library, 511 Division St, Mukwonago, WI, 53149-1204. Tel: 262-363-6441, Ext 4106. p. 2463
Frisch, Sheila, Sr Libr Asst/Tech Serv, Englewood Public Library, 31 Engle St, Englewood, NJ, 07631. Tel: 201-568-2215. p. 1402
Frischkorn, Mary-Ann, Circ Supvr, ILL, Malone University, 2600 Cleveland Ave NW, Canton, OH, 44709-3308. Tel: 330-471-8317. p. 1755
Frison, Carla, Dir, Linton Public Library, 101 NE First St, Linton, ND, 58552-7123. Tel: 701-254-4737. p. 1737
Frissen, Ilja, Assoc Prof, McGill University, 3661 Peel St, Montreal, QC, H3A 1X1, CANADA. Tel: 514-398-4204. p. 2796
Friszell, Claudia, Circ, Comsewogue Public Library, 170 Terryville Rd, Port Jefferson Station, NY, 11776. Tel: 631-928-1212. p. 1621
Fritchey, Carrie, Br Mgr, Heartland Regional Library System, 304 N St Louis St, Iberia, MO, 65486. Tel: 573-793-6746. p. 1249
Fritchman, Theresa, ILL, Bradford County Library System, 16093 Rte 6, Troy, PA, 16947. Tel: 570-297-2436. p. 2013
Frith, Charles, Content Serv Librn, Metadata Librn, Roanoke College, 220 High St, Salem, VA, 24153-3794. Tel: 540-375-2292. p. 2347
Fritsche, Leah, Dir, Deerfield Public Library, 12 W Nelson St, Deerfield, WI, 53531-9669. Tel: 608-764-8102. p. 2430
Fritschel, Barbara, Librn, United States Courts Library, 517 E Wisconsin Ave, Rm 516, Milwaukee, WI, 53202. Tel: 414-297-1698. p. 2461
Fritts, Jack, Univ Librn, Benedictine University Library, 5700 College Rd, Lisle, IL, 60532-0900. Tel: 630-829-6050. p. 610
Fritts, Tim, Asst Librn, Rick Warren Memorial Public Library District, 114 S Fourth St, Elkville, IL, 62932-1097. Tel: 618-568-1843. p. 584
Fritz, Jaimie, Ms, Archivist, American Kennel Club Inc Library & Archives, 101 Park Ave, 5th Flr, New York, NY, 10178. Tel: 212-696-8216. p. 1578
Fritz, Megan, Br Head, Napoleon Public Library, Florida Public, K671 County Rd 17D, Napoleon, OH, 43545-9215. Tel: 419-762-5876. p. 1805
Fritz, Natalie, Archivist, Dir of Outreach, Clark County Historical Society, 117 S Fountain Ave, Springfield, OH, 45502-1207. Tel: 937-324-0657. p. 1821
Fritzges, Vickie, Dir, Saint Edward Public Library, 302 Beaver St, Saint Edward, NE, 68660. Tel: 402-678-2204. p. 1334
Frizzell, Matt, Assessment Librn, Georgia Institute of Technology Library, 260 Fourth St NW, Atlanta, GA, 30332. Tel: 404-385-4719. p. 464
Froah, Melissa, Libr Dir, Corry Public Library, 117 W Washington St, Corry, PA, 16407. Tel: 814-664-7611. p. 1924
Froehlich, Conrad G, Dir, Martin & Osa Johnson Safari Museum, 111 N Lincoln Ave, Chanute, KS, 66720. Tel: 620-431-2730. p. 801
Froehlich, Denise, Asst Dir, Bertha Bartlett Public Library, 503 Broad St, Story City, IA, 50248-1133. Tel: 515-733-2685. p. 785
Froelich, Aaron, Bus Mgr, Kansas City, Kansas Public Library, Turner Community, 831 S 55th St, Kansas City, KS, 66106. Tel: 913-295-8250, Ext 4. p. 816
Froelich, Maggie, Ref Librn, Claremont School of Theology Library, 1325 N College Ave, Claremont, CA, 91711. Tel: 909-447-2516. p. 130
Froeliger, Rosemary, Learning Res Tech, Moraine Park Technical College Library, 700 Gould St, Beaver Dam, WI, 53916-1994. Tel: 920-887-4406. p. 2423
Froese, Vic, PhD, Libr Dir, Canadian Mennonite University Library, 2299 Grant Ave, Winnipeg, MB, R3P 2N2, CANADA. Tel: 204-487-3300, Ext 393. p. 2593
Frohlinger, Margery, Ref Librn, Englewood Public Library, 31 Engle St, Englewood, NJ, 07631. Tel: 201-568-2215. p. 1402
Frohnsdorff, Susan, Br Mgr, Charleston County Public Library, Mount Pleasant Regional, 1133 Mathis Ferry Rd, Mount Pleasant, SC, 29464. Tel: 843-849-6161. p. 2049
Frohock, Teresa, Tech Asst, Rockingham Community College, 315 Wrenn Memorial Rd, Wentworth, NC, 27375. Tel: 336-342-4261, Ext 2300. p. 1721
Froman, Darla, Mgr, Weston Public Library, Grand Rapids Branch, 17620 Bridge St, Grand Rapids, OH, 43522. Tel: 419-832-5231. p. 1831
Fromm, Patrick, Br Mgr, Montgomery County Public Libraries, Rockville Memorial Library, 21 Maryland Ave, Rockville, MD, 20850-2371. Tel: 240-777-0277. p. 975
Fromme, Gregory, Br Mgr, Enoch Pratt Free Library, Herring Run Branch, 3801 Erdman Ave, Baltimore, MD, 21213-2099. Tel: 443-984-4940. p. 953
Frommelt, Gene, Media Spec, Vernon College, 4400 College Dr, Vernon, TX, 76384. Tel: 940-552-6291, Ext 2222. p. 2252
Fromwiller, Laura, Head, Ref, Lapeer District Library, 201 Village West Dr S, Lapeer, MI, 48446-1699. Tel: 810-664-9521. p. 1126
Fromwiller, Laura, Head, Ref, Lapeer District Library, Marguerite deAngeli Branch, 921 W Nepessing St, Lapeer, MI, 48446. Tel: 810-664-6971. p. 1126
Fromwiller, Laura, Libr Dir, Brandon Township Public Library, 304 South St, Ortonville, MI, 48462. Tel: 248-627-1474. p. 1139
Fromwiller, Laura, Head, Adult Serv, Oxford Public Library, 530 Pontiac St, Oxford, MI, 48371-4844. Tel: 248-628-3034. p. 1140
Frosch, June, Assoc Libr Dir, Librn III, New Mexico Military Institute, Toles Learning Ctr, 101 W College Blvd, Roswell, NM, 88201. Tel: 575-624-8384. p. 1474
Frosina, Len, Network Serv, Comsewogue Public Library, 170 Terryville Rd, Port Jefferson Station, NY, 11776. Tel: 631-928-1212. p. 1621
Frost, Anne, Legis Spec, United States Nuclear Regulatory Commission, Law Library, 11555 Rockville Pike, Rockville, MD, 20852. Tel: 301-415-1613. p. 975
Frost, Carol, Exec Dir, NorthNet Library System, 32 W 25th Ave, Ste 201, San Mateo, CA, 94403. Tel: 650-349-5538. p. 235
Frost, Carol, Chief Exec Officer, Pacific Library Partnership (PLP), 32 W 25th Ave, Ste 201, San Mateo, CA, 94403-2273. Tel: 650-349-5538. p. 235
Frost, Carol, Exec Dir, Peninsula Library System, 32 W 25th Ave, Ste 201, Suite 201, San Mateo, CA, 94403-4000. Tel: 650-349-5538. p. 2762
Frost, Jackie, Libr Asst, Wythe-Grayson Regional Library, Fries Public, 105 W Main St, Fries, VA, 24330. Tel: 276-744-2225. p. 2326
Frost, Jean, Librn, Colorado Department of Corrections, Centennial Correctional Facility Library, PO Box 600, Canon City, CO, 81215-0600. Tel: 719-269-5546. p. 269
Frost, June, Br Mgr, San Diego County Library, Imperial Beach Branch, 810 Imperial Beach Blvd, Imperial Beach, CA, 91932-2798. Tel: 619-424-6981. p. 217
Frost, Kelly, Ref & Instruction Librn, Kalamazoo College Library, 1200 Academy St, Kalamazoo, MI, 49006-3285. Tel: 269-337-7153. p. 1121
Frost, Michele, Youth Serv - Prog, Sturgis District Library, 255 North St, Sturgis, MI, 49091. Tel: 269-659-7224. p. 1153
Frost, Sarah, Dir, Willamina Public Library, 382 NE C St, Willamina, OR, 97396. Tel: 503-876-6182. p. 1902
Frost, Sheri, Asst Dir, Stair Public Library, 228 W Main St, Morenci, MI, 49256-1421. Tel: 517-458-6510. p. 1134
Fruit, John, Head, Adult Serv, Head, Info Tech, Morris Area Public Library District, 604 Liberty St, Morris, IL, 60450. Tel: 815-942-6880. p. 619
Frumkina, Lyudmila, Libr Asst, Wyckoff Heights Medical Center, 374 Stockholm St, Brooklyn, NY, 11237. Tel: 718-963-7198. p. 1506
Frutchey, Jim, Monographic Acq Librn, Marywood University Library & Learning Commons, 2300 Adams Ave, Scranton, PA, 18509. Tel: 570-961-4707. p. 2004
Fruth, Breanne, Communications Coordr, Great River Regional Library, Elk River Library, 13020 Orono Pkwy, Elk River, MN, 55330. Tel: 763-441-1641. p. 1196
Fruth, Breanne, Communications Coordr, Great River Regional Library, Al Ringsmuth Library, 253 N Fifth Ave, Waite Park, MN, 56387-0395. Tel: 320-253-9359. p. 1197

Fruth, Breanne, Communications Coordr, Great River Regional Library, Melrose Library, 225 E First St N, Melrose, MN, 56352-1153. Tel: 320-256-3885. p. 1197

Fruth, Breanne, Communications Coordr, Great River Regional Library, Myrtle Mabee Library, 324 Washburn Ave, Belgrade, MN, 56312. Tel: 320-254-8842. p. 1197

Fruth, Breanne, Coordr, Develop & Communication, Great River Regional Library, Upsala Library, 117 Main St, Upsala, MN, 56384. Tel: 320-412-2048. p. 1197

Fruth, Breanne, Libr Serv Coordr, Great River Regional Library, Grey Eagle Community Library, 118 State St E, Grey Eagle, MN, 56336. Tel: 320-285-2505. p. 1197

Fry, Cari, Head, Youth Serv, Westland Public Library, 6123 Central City Pkwy, Westland, MI, 48185. Tel: 734-326-6123. p. 1159

Fry, Carri, Youth Serv Coordr, Derby Public Library, 1600 E Walnut Grove, Derby, KS, 67037. Tel: 316-788-0760. p. 804

Fry, Carrie, Syst Librn, Seattle Pacific University Library, 3307 Third Ave W, Seattle, WA, 98119. Tel: 206-281-2124. p. 2379

Fry, Elizabeth, Dir, Bliss Memorial Public Library, 20 S Marion St, Bloomville, OH, 44818. Tel: 419-983-4675. p. 1751

Fry, Gretchen, Dir, Martinsburg-Berkeley County Public Library, 101 W King St, Martinsburg, WV, 25401. Tel: 304-267-8088. p. 2408

Fry, Jenny, Dir, Prog & Partnerships, Surrey Libraries, 10350 University Dr, Surrey, BC, V3T 4B8, CANADA. Tel: 604-598-7300. p. 2577

Fry, Krystal, Libr Mgr, York County Library System, Village Library, 35-C N Main St, Jacobus, PA, 17407. Tel: 717-428-1034. p. 2027

Fry, Laura, Sr Curator, Thomas Gilcrease Institute of American History & Art Library, 1400 Gilcrease Museum Rd, Tulsa, OK, 74127. Tel: 918-596-2745. p. 1864

Fry, Marcus, Head, Tech Serv, Concordia University Texas Library, 11400 Concordia University Dr, Austin, TX, 78726. Tel: 512-313-5050. p. 2139

Fry, Mary B, Sr Librn, US Agency for International Development, 1300 Pennsylvania Ave NW, Rm M01-010, Washington, DC, 20523-6100. Tel: 202-712-0579. p. 377

Fry, Nick, Curator, Saint Louis Mercantile Library at the University of Missouri-St Louis, Thomas Jefferson Library Bldg, One University Blvd, Saint Louis, MO, 63121-4400. Tel: 314-516-7253. p. 1274

Fry, Peggy, Dep Univ Librn, Georgetown University, 37th & O St NW, Washington, DC, 20057-1174. Tel: 202-687-7607. p. 367

Fry, Shawn, Asst Dir, Boone County Public Library, 1786 Burlington Pike, Burlington, KY, 41005. Tel: 859-342-2665. p. 850

Fry-Matson, Ruby, Researcher, Tillamook County Pioneer Museum, 2106 Second St, Tillamook, OR, 97141. Tel: 503-842-4553. p. 1900

Frybort, Carla, Libr Dir, Leduc Public Library, Two Alexandra Park, Leduc, AB, T9E 4C4, CANADA. Tel: 780-986-2637. p. 2546

Frydenger, Kelly, Dir, Willow Branch Township Library, 330 N Eldon St, Cisco, IL, 61830. Tel: 217-669-2312. p. 572

Frye, Abby, Information Services Asst, Carl Sandburg College, Bldg E230, 2400 Tom L Wilson Blvd, Galesburg, IL, 61401. Tel: 309-341-5257. p. 590

Frye, Bettie George, Tech Serv Librn, Ashland Community & Technical College, 1400 College Dr, Ashland, KY, 41101. Tel: 606-326-2141. p. 847

Frye, Jake, Br Mgr, Lyon County Library System, Dayton Valley Branch, 321 Old Dayton Valley Rd, Dayton, NV, 89403-8902. Tel: 775-246-6212. p. 1352

Frye, Janet, Ch Serv, Herrick Memorial Library, 101 Willard Memorial Sq, Wellington, OH, 44090-1342. Tel: 440-647-2120. p. 1829

Frye, Jonathan, Sr Librn, California Youth Authority, O H Close Youth Correctional Facility Library, 7650 S Newcastle Rd, Stockton, CA, 95213-9001. Tel: 209-944-6346. p. 249

Frye, Julie Marie, Head of Libr, Indiana University Bloomington, Education Library, Wright Education 1160, 201 N Rose St, Bloomington, IN, 47405-1006. Tel: 812-856-8590. p. 671

Frye, Kristine, Dir, Service Desk, Writing Ctr Dir, Indiana University-Purdue University Fort Wayne, 2101 E Coliseum Blvd, Fort Wayne, IN, 46805-1499. Tel: 260-481-0257. p. 684

Frye, Melissa, Acq, Sandwich Public Library, 142 Main St, Sandwich, MA, 02563. Tel: 508-888-0625. p. 1052

Frye, Michael A, Univ Librn, Winston-Salem State University, 601 Martin Luther King Jr Dr, Winston-Salem, NC, 27110. Tel: 336-750-8938. p. 1726

Frye, Michelle, Circ Supvr, Seton Hill University, One Seton Hill Dr, Greensburg, PA, 15601. Tel: 724-830-1584. p. 1938

Frye, Sarah, Dept Chair, Librn, College of Marin Library, 835 College Ave, Kentfield, CA, 94904. Tel: 415-485-9656. p. 154

Frykberg, Dru, Librn, Minnesota Department of Employment & Economic Development Library, 1st National Bank Bldg, 332 Minnesota St, Ste E200, Saint Paul, MN, 55101-1351. Tel: 651-259-7188. p. 1200

Frykman, Susan, Ch Prog, Thorson Memorial Public Library, 117 Central Ave, Elbow Lake, MN, 56531. Tel: 218-685-6850. p. 1174

Frymark, Sara, Mgr, Dallas Public Library, Renner Frankford Branch, 6400 Frankford Rd, Dallas, TX, 75252-5747. Tel: 214-670-6100. p. 2166

Fu, Hengyi, Dr, Asst Prof, University of Alabama, 7035 Gorgas Library, Campus Box 870252, Tuscaloosa, AL, 35487-0252. Tel: 205-348-4610. p. 2781

Fu, Jan, Br Head, Vancouver Public Library, Renfrew Branch, 2969 E 22nd Ave, Vancouver, BC, V5M 2Y3, CANADA. Tel: 604-257-8705. p. 2582

Fu, Jennifer, Head of GIS Ctr, Florida International University, 11200 SW Eighth St, Miami, FL, 33199. Tel: 305-348-3138. p. 421

Fu, Ping, Col Librn, Whitman College, 345 Boyer Ave, Walla Walla, WA, 99362. Tel: 509-527-5193. p. 2393

Fucci, Geneva, Ch Serv, Riverdale Public Library, 93 Newark Pompton Tpk, Riverdale, NJ, 07457. Tel: 973-835-5044. p. 1440

Fucci, Lynnette, Ch, Monroe Township Public Library, Four Municipal Plaza, Monroe Township, NJ, 08831-1900. Tel: 732-521-5000, Ext 125. p. 1419

Fuchs, Caroline, Dean of Libr, St John's University Library, St Augustine Hall, 8000 Utopia Pkwy, Jamaica, NY, 11439. Tel: 718-990-5050. p. 1556

Fuchs, Lindsay, County Librn, Plumas County Library, 445 Jackson St, Quincy, CA, 95971. Tel: 530-283-6310. p. 197

Fuchs, Lindsay, County Librn, Plumas County Library, Chester Branch, 210 First Ave, Chester, CA, 96020-0429. Tel: 530-258-2742. p. 197

Fuchs, Lindsay, County Librn, Plumas County Library, Greenville Branch, Greenvill High School, 117 Grand St Rm 402, Greenville, CA, 95947. Tel: 530-283-6310. p. 197

Fuchs, Mary, Dir, Brown Memorial Library, Two Norton Pl, East Baldwin, ME, 04024. Tel: 207-787-3155. p. 923

Fuchs, Patti, Ch, Indian River County Library System, 1600 21st St, Vero Beach, FL, 32960. Tel: 772-770-5060. p. 452

Fuchs, Patti, Ch, Indian River County Library System, North Indian River County Library, 1001 Sebastian Blvd, CR 512, Sebastian, FL, 32958. Tel: 772-400-6360. p. 452

Fuchs, Susan, Ref & Instruction Librn, University of Health Sciences & Pharmacy in Saint Louis Library, One Pharmacy Pl, Saint Louis, MO, 63110. Tel: 314-446-8365. p. 1276

Fuchsen, Sarah Beth, Ch, Spencer Public Library, 21 E Third St, Spencer, IA, 51301-4131. Tel: 712-580-7290. p. 783

Fudge, Jaclyn, Children's Coordr, Ringwood Public Library, 30 Cannici Dr, Ringwood, NJ, 07456. Tel: 973-962-6256, Ext 112. p. 1439

Fuemmeler, Rosetta, Librn, Lewis Library of Glasgow, 315 Fourth St, Glasgow, MO, 65254. Tel: 660-338-2395. p. 1247

Fuentes, Claudia, Br Supvr, University of Texas Libraries, Classics Library, Waggener Hall, 2210 Speedway, Austin, TX, 78712. Tel: 512-495-4690. p. 2142

Fuentes, Janet, Mkt & Communications Mgr, Community Libraries of Providence, PO Box 9267, Providence, RI, 02940. Tel: 401-467-2700, Ext 1613. p. 2038

Fuentes, Marinilda, Media Spec, University of Puerto Rico, Sector Las Dunas, Carr 653 Km 0.8, Arecibo, PR, 00612. Tel: 787-815-0000, Ext 3150. p. 2509

Fuentes, Octavio, Asst Dean, Finance & Admin, University of Arizona Libraries, 1510 E University Blvd, Tucson, AZ, 85721. Tel: 520-621-2668. p. 83

Fuerst, Shy, Br Supvr, Kern County Library, Frazier Park Branch, 3732 Park Dr, Frazier Park, CA, 93225. Tel: 661-245-1267. p. 119

Fuerstenau, Jane E, Dir, Kenai Peninsula College Library, 156 College Rd, Soldotna, AK, 99669. Tel: 907-262-0385. p. 51

Fuertges, Daniel, Prog Coordr, Illinois Central College, S113 Banwart Library, Student Ctr, One College Dr, East Peoria, IL, 61635. Tel: 309-690-6958. p. 2784

Fugate, Edna, Dir, Libr Serv, University of Pikeville, 147 Sycamore St, Pikeville, KY, 41501. Tel: 606-218-5606. p. 872

Fugate, Edna M, Dir, Libr Serv, University of Pikeville, 147 Sycamore St, Pikeville, KY, 41501-9118. Tel: 606-218-5606. p. 872

Fugate, Tifany, Libr Dir, Butler Public Library, 100 W Atkison Ave, Butler, MO, 64730. Tel: 660-679-4321. p. 1239

Fuhrer, Hayley, Ser & Acq Supvr, Heidelberg University, Ten Greenfield St, Tiffin, OH, 44883-2420. Tel: 419-448-2098. p. 1823

Fuhrig, Katherine, Libr Dir, South Mainland Library, 7921 Ron Beatty Blvd, Micco, FL, 32976. Tel: 772-664-4066. p. 426

Fuhringer, Cheri, Libr Dir, Dutton/Teton Public Library, 22 Main St W, Dutton, MT, 59433. Tel: 406-476-3382. p. 1292

Fuhrman, Tim, Dir, Library Resources & eLearning, Big Bend Community College Library, 1800 Bldg, 7662 Chanute St NE, Moses Lake, WA, 98837. Tel: 509-793-2350. p. 2371

Fuhrmann, Dorothy, Acq, Cat, Ref, Los Angeles City College Library, 855 N Vermont Ave, Los Angeles, CA, 90029. Tel: 323-953-4000, Ext 2401. p. 162

Fuhro, Laura, Head, Children's Servx, Berkeley Heights Public Library, 29 Park Ave, Berkeley Heights, NJ, 07922. Tel: 908-464-9333. p. 1390

Fukumoto, Elaine, Mgr, County of Los Angeles Public Library, Masao W Satow Library, 14433 S Crenshaw Blvd, Gardena, CA, 90249-3142. Tel: 310-679-0638. p. 138

Fukushima, Kailey, Scholarly Comms & Copyright Librn, University Canada West, 1461 Granville St, Vancouver, BC, V6Z 0E5, CANADA. p. 2580

Fulara, Helen, Info Serv Spec, Lethbridge College, 3000 College Dr S, Lethbridge, AB, T1K 1L6, CANADA. Tel: 403-320-3352. p. 2546

Fulcher, Jenny, Circ Librn, Snow Library, 67 Main St, Orleans, MA, 02653-2413. Tel: 508-240-3760. p. 1044

Fulcher, Tammy, Adult Serv, Sheppard Memorial Library, 530 S Evans St, Greenville, NC, 27858. Tel: 252-329-4254. p. 1694

Fulcher-Anderson, Josephine, Supvr, Ferguson Library, South End, 34 Woodland Ave, Stamford, CT, 06902. Tel: 203-351-8281. p. 338

Fulco, Daniel, Curator, Washington County Museum of Fine Arts Library, 401 Museum Dr, Hagerstown, MD, 21740. Tel: 301-739-5727. p. 968

Fulford, Laurel, Librn, Orford Free Library, 2539 Rte 25A, Orford, NH, 03777. Tel: 603-353-9166. p. 1377

Fulford, Margaret, Librn, University College Library, University of Toronto, East Hall, Rm 266, 15 King's College Circle, Toronto, ON, M5S 3H7, CANADA. Tel: 416-978-4634. p. 2698

Fulkerson, Diane, Dir, State University of New York College at Brockport, 350 New Campus Dr, Brockport, NY, 14420-2997. Tel: 585-395-2140. p. 1497

Fulks, Randall, Ref Librn, Gallia County District Library, Seven Spruce St, Gallipolis, OH, 45631. Tel: 740-446-7323. p. 1787

Full, Deb, Info Res Spec, Minnesota West Community & Technical College, Canby Campus, 1011 First St W, Canby, MN, 56220. Tel: 507-223-7252. p. 1210

Fuller, Abigail, Dir, Newberry County Library System, 1100 Friend St, Newberry, SC, 29108-3416. Tel: 803-276-0854. p. 2066

Fuller, Andrea, Dir, Worthington-Jefferson Township Public Library, 26 N Commercial St, Worthington, IN, 47471-1415. Tel: 812-875-3815. p. 727

Fuller, Angela, Curatorial Asst, Taft Museum of Art Library, 316 Pike St, Cincinnati, OH, 45202-4293. Tel: 513-241-0343. p. 1763

Fuller, Ann, Head, Circ/ILL, Georgia Southern University, 11935 Abercorn St, Savannah, GA, 31419. Tel: 912-344-3006. p. 495

Fuller, Annie, Br Mgr, Saint Louis County Library, Mid-County Branch, 7821 Maryland Ave, Saint Louis, MO, 63105-3875. Tel: 314-994-3300, Ext 3500. p. 1274

Fuller, Bryan, Ref/Fed Doc Librn, Morgan State University, 1700 E Cold Spring Lane, Baltimore, MD, 21251. Tel: 443-885-1705. p. 956

Fuller, Candace L, Librn, United States Army, Patton Museum of Cavalry & Armor Emert L Davis Memorial Library, 4554 Fayette Ave, Fort Knox, KY, 40121. Tel: 502-624-6968. p. 855

Fuller, Cathy, Libr Dir, Bolivar Free Library, 390 Main St, Bolivar, NY, 14715. Tel: 585-928-2015. p. 1495

Fuller, David, Br Mgr, Alachua County Library District, High Springs Branch, 23779 W US Hwy 27, High Springs, FL, 32643. Tel: 386-454-2515. p. 406

Fuller, David, Outreach Serv Mgr, Alachua County Library District, Sheriff's Department of the Jail, 3333 NE 39th Ave, Gainesville, FL, 32609-2699. Tel: 352-334-3991. p. 406

Fuller, David, Computer Spec, Clinton-Essex-Franklin Library System, 33 Oak St, Plattsburgh, NY, 12901-2810. Tel: 518-563-5190, Ext 122. p. 1619

Fuller, Elizabeth E, Librn, The Rosenbach of the Free Library of Philadelphia, 2010 DeLancey Pl, Philadelphia, PA, 19103. Tel: 215-732-1600. p. 1985

Fuller, Heather, Libr Dir, Farmers Branch Manske Library, 13613 Webb Chapel Rd, Farmers Branch, TX, 75234. Tel: 972-919-9800. p. 2176

Fuller, Howard, Libr Dir, Whatcom Community College Library, Heiner Bldg, 231 W Kellogg Rd, Bellingham, WA, 98226. Tel: 360-383-3300. p. 2359

Fuller, Jan, Main Floor Supervisor, Lebanon Public Library, 101 S Broadway, Lebanon, OH, 45036. Tel: 513-932-2665. p. 1795

Fuller, Laura, Br Librn, Mgr, Br, Portage County Public Library, Charles M White Library Bldg, 1001 Main St, Stevens Point, WI, 54481-2860. Tel: 715-346-1544. p. 2479

Fuller, Lisa, Dir, Commun Engagement, Worthington Libraries, 820 High St, Worthington, OH, 43085. Tel: 614-807-2604. p. 1834

Fuller, Mary Jo, Librn, Lilly Endowment Library, 2801 N Meridian St, Indianapolis, IN, 46208. Tel: 317-916-7316. p. 697

Fuller, Myisha, Br Mgr, Loudoun County Public Library, Rust Branch, 380 Old Waterford Rd NW, Leesburg, VA, 20176. Tel: 703-777-0323. p. 2328

Fuller, Nancy, Librn, Currie Library, 617 N Elm St, Greensboro, NC, 27401. Tel: 336-478-4731. p. 1691

Fuller, Rachel, Director, Adult & Youth Services & Acquisitions, The Urbana Free Library, 210 W Green St, Urbana, IL, 61801. Tel: 217-367-4069. p. 657

Fuller, Sharon, Librn, Logan County Public Library, Adairville Branch, 101 Church St, Adairville, KY, 42202. Tel: 270-539-4601. p. 874

Fuller, Todd, Curator, Western Hist Coll, University of Oklahoma Libraries, Western History Collection, Western History Collection, 452 MH, 630 Parrington Oval, Norman, OK, 73019. Tel: 405-325-3678. p. 1856

Fullerton, Adam, Asst Prof, Libr Dir, Morningside University, 1501 Morningside Ave, Sioux City, IA, 51106. Tel: 712-274-5247. p. 782

Fullerton, Christina, Dir, Learning Res, Polk State College, 999 Ave H NE, Winter Haven, FL, 33881. Tel: 863-292-1040, Ext 5302. p. 455

Fullerton, Christine, Librn, Pub Serv, Chadron State College, 300 E 12th St, Chadron, NE, 69337. Tel: 308-432-7062. p. 1310

Fullerton, Crystal, Dir, Librn, Mankato City Library, 214 N High St, Ste 1, Mankato, KS, 66956-2006. Tel: 785-378-3885. p. 824

Fullerton, Rebecca M, Archivist, Appalachian Mountain Club Archives, AMC Highland Ctr at Crawford Notch, US Rte 302, Bretton Woods, NH, 03575. Tel: 603-374-8515. p. 1356

Fullhart, Tina, Dir, Grenola Public Library, 205 S Main St, Grenola, KS, 67346. Tel: 620-358-3707. p. 811

Fulling, Richard, Coll & Access Serv Librn, Barton College, 400 Atlantic Christian College Dr NE, Wilson, NC, 27893. Tel: 252-399-6504. p. 1723

Fullmer, Susan, Librn, Mount Pleasant Public Library, 24 E Main St, Mount Pleasant, UT, 84647-1429. Tel: 435-462-3240. p. 2267

Fullner, Paul, Br Mgr, Whatcom County Library System, Everson McBeath Community Library, 104 Kirsch Dr, Everson, WA, 98247. Tel: 360-966-5100. p. 2359

Fullner, Paul, Br Mgr, Whatcom County Library System, Sumas Branch, 461 Second St, Sumas, WA, 98295. Tel: 360-988-2501. p. 2359

Fulmer, Henry, Dir, University of South Carolina, South Caroliniana Library, 910 Sumter St, Columbia, SC, 29208. Tel: 803-777-3131. p. 2056

Fulmer, LeWanda, Br Mgr, Aiken-Bamberg-Barnwell-Edgefield Regional Library, Nancy Bonnette - Wagener Branch Library, 204 Park St NE, Wagener, SC, 29164. Tel: 803-291-6500. p. 2045

Fulton, Barbara, Librn, Long Ridge Library, 191 Long Ridge Rd, Danbury, CT, 06810-8463. Tel: 203-748-7520. p. 307

Fulton, Brian, Electronic Res Librn, Misericordia University, 301 Lake St, Dallas, PA, 18612-1098. Tel: 570-674-3032. p. 1925

Fulton, Brian, Libr Mgr, Scranton Times-Tribune, 149 Penn Ave, Scranton, PA, 18503. Tel: 570-348-9140. p. 2005

Fulton, Karin, ILL Librn, Flint River Regional Library System, 800 Memorial Dr, Griffin, GA, 30223. Tel: 770-412-4770. p. 481

Fulton, Kathy, Dir, Camp Wood Public Library, 106 S Nueces, Camp Wood, TX, 78833. Tel: 830-597-3208. p. 2152

Fulton, Lindsay, VPres, Libr Serv, New England Historic Genealogical Society Library, 99-101 Newbury St, Boston, MA, 02116-3007. Tel: 617-536-5740. p. 998

Fulton, Melissa, Br Mgr, Boone County Public Library, 1786 Burlington Pike, Burlington, KY, 41005. Tel: 859-342-2665. p. 850

Fulton, Molly, Cat Librn, Libr Serv Mgr, The John P Holt Brentwood Library, 8109 Concord Rd, Brentwood, TN, 37027. Tel: 615-371-0090, Ext 8220. p. 2089

Fulton, Stephanie, Assoc Dean, Libr Dir, Texas A&M University Libraries, Medical Sciences, 202 Olsen Blvd, College Station, TX, 77843. Tel: 979-845-7540. p. 2157

Fulton, Sue, Archives, Tech, Lycoming College, One College Pl, Williamsport, PA, 17701. Tel: 570-321-4333. p. 2023

Fulton, Tara Lynn, PhD, Dean, Univ Libr, University of New Hampshire Library, 18 Library Way, Durham, NH, 03824. Tel: 603-862-1506. p. 1361

Fulton-Lyne, Liz, Coordr, Libr Instruction, NorQuest College, 10215-108th St, 5th Flr, Edmonton, AB, T5J 1L6, CANADA. Tel: 708-644-6070. p. 2537

Fultz, D Elizabeth, Dir, Washington-Centerville Public Library, 111 W Spring Valley Rd, Centerville, OH, 45458. Tel: 937-610-4420. p. 1757

Fultz, Karla, Librn, Faulkner-Van Buren Regional Library System, Van Buren County, 289 Factory Rd, Clinton, AR, 72031. Tel: 501-745-2100. p. 92

Fulwider, Kathy, Librn, Northwest Kansas Heritage Center, 401 Kansas Ave, Brewster, KS, 67732. Tel: 785-694-2891. p. 799

Fung, Benjamin, Prof, McGill University, 3661 Peel St, Montreal, QC, H3A 1X1, CANADA. Tel: 514-398-4204. p. 2796

Fung, Denise, Team Leader, Burlington Public Library, New Appleby, 676 Appleby Line, Burlington, ON, L7L 5Y1, CANADA. Tel: 905-639-6373. p. 2634

Fung, Hing Choi, Librn III, New Jersey Department of Labor & Workforce Development Library, John Fitch Plaza, 4th Flr, Trenton, NJ, 08611. Tel: 609-292-2035. p. 1447

Fung, Melissa, Law Ref Librn/Foreign & Intl Spec, University of San Diego, Katherine M & George M Pardee Jr Legal Research Center, 5998 Alcala Park, San Diego, CA, 92110-2492. Tel: 619-260-4734. p. 223

Fung, Peter, Res Spec, New York Legislative Service, Inc Library, 120 Broadway, Ste 920, New York, NY, 10271. Tel: 212-962-2826, 212-962-2827, 212-962-2828. p. 1594

Fung, Sharon, Coll, Tech Serv, San Jose Public Library, 150 E San Fernando St, San Jose, CA, 95112-3580. Tel: 408-808-2468. p. 231

Funk Booher, Rachel, Youth Serv, Morristown Centennial Library, Seven Richmond St, Morrisville, VT, 05661. Tel: 802-888-3853. p. 2289

Funk, Brian, Circ, Whatcom Community College Library, Heiner Bldg, 231 W Kellogg Rd, Bellingham, WA, 98226. Tel: 360-383-3300. p. 2359

Funk, Greta, Dir, Nortonville Public Library, 407 Main St, Nortonville, KS, 66060. Tel: 913-886-2060. p. 827

Funk, John Allan, Chair, Mid Arkansas Regional Library, 202 E Third St, Malvern, AR, 72104. Tel: 501-332-5441. p. 103

Funk, Karen, Dir, Washakie County Library System, 801 Big Horn Ave, Ste 100, Worland, WY, 82401. Tel: 307-347-2231. p. 2500

Funk, Karen, Libr Dir, Washakie County Library System, Ten Sleep Branch, 200 N Fir St, Ten Sleep, WY, 82442. Tel: 307-366-2348. p. 2500

Funk, Petra, Dir, Cegep de Sherbrooke, 475 rue du Cegep, Sherbrooke, QC, J1E 4K1, CANADA. Tel: 819-564-6350, Ext 5231, 819-564-6350, Ext 5233. p. 2736

Funk, Stephanie, Adult Programming, Milanof-Schock Library, 1184 Anderson Ferry Rd, Mount Joy, PA, 17552. Tel: 717-653-1510. p. 1966

Funke, Rebecca, Dir, Libr Res, Des Moines Area Community College Library, 2006 S Ankeny Blvd, Ankeny, IA, 50023. Tel: 515-964-6317. p. 732

Funke, Rebecca, Dir, Libr Res, Des Moines Area Community College, 1125 Hancock Dr, Boone, IA, 50036-5326. Tel: 515-433-5043. p. 735
Fuqua, Deidre, Dir, Grant Parish Library, 300 Main St, Colfax, LA, 71417-1830. Tel: 318-627-9920. p. 887
Fuqua, Vicki, Ref Librn, Chappaqua Public Library, 195 S Greeley Ave, Chappaqua, NY, 10514. Tel: 914-238-4779. p. 1516
Furay, Julia, Acq, Kingsborough Community College, 2001 Oriental Blvd, Brooklyn, NY, 11235. Tel: 718-368-5971. p. 1504
Furcht, Lesliann, Librn, Mount Washington Public Library, Town Hall, 118 East St, Mount Washington, MA, 01258. Tel: 413-528-1798, 413-528-2839. p. 1037
Furcht, Lesliann, Librn, Egremont Free Library, One Buttonball Lane, South Egremont, MA, 01258. Tel: 413-528-1474. p. 1054
Furey, Donna, Ch Serv, Garden City Public Library, 60 Seventh St, Garden City, NY, 11530. Tel: 516-742-8405. p. 1536
Furgal, Tim, Libr Dir, Troy Public Library, 100 Second St, Troy, NY, 12180. Tel: 518-274-7071. p. 1653
Furguson, Carol, Mgr, Community Library Network, Spirit Lake Branch, 32575 N Fifth Ave, Spirit Lake, ID, 83869. Tel: 208-623-5353. p. 522
Furino, Anthony, Br Mgr, Cuyahoga County Public Library, Orange Branch, 31975 Chagrin Blvd, Pepper Pike, OH, 44124-5916. Tel: 216-831-4282. p. 1813
Furlong, Daniel, Librn, Yavapai County Law Library, Yavapai County Courthouse, 120 S Cortez St, Rm 112, Prescott, AZ, 86303. Tel: 928-771-3309. p. 75
Furlong, Michael, Librn, Daytona State College Library, Bldg 115, Rm 314, 1200 W International Speedway Blvd, Daytona Beach, FL, 32114. Tel: 386-506-3055. p. 392
Furness, Amy, Head of Libr & Archives, Art Gallery of Ontario, 317 Dundas St W, Toronto, ON, M5T 1G4, CANADA. Tel: 416-979-6642. p. 2686
Furnish, Rebecca, Libr Office Mgr, Christian Theological Seminary, 1000 W 42nd St, Indianapolis, IN, 46208. Tel: 317-931-2370. p. 691
Furniss, Amanda, Exec Dir, Dartmouth Heritage Museum Library, Evergreen House, 26 Newcastle St, Dartmouth, NS, B2Y 3M5, CANADA. Tel: 902-464-2916. p. 2617
Furo-Bonnstetter, Karen, Dir, Woodville Community Library, 124 Main St, Woodville, WI, 54028. Tel: 715-698-2430. p. 2490
Furr, Patty, Exec Dir, Jackson/Hinds Library System, 300 N State St, Jackson, MS, 39201-1705. Tel: 601-968-5825. p. 1221
Furrow, Stephanie, Regional Resource Librarian, York Library Region, Fredericton Public Library, 12 Carleton St, Fredericton, NB, E3B 5P4, CANADA. Tel: 506-460-2800. p. 2602
Furrows, Marie, Head, Adult Serv, Cerritos Library, 18025 Bloomfield Ave, Cerritos, CA, 90703. Tel: 562-916-1350. p. 129
Furtado, Alexandria, Head Law Librn, Commonwealth of Massachusetts - Trial Court, 72 Belmont St, Brockton, MA, 02301. Tel: 508-586-7110. p. 1002
Furtado-Chagas, Tracy, Learning Commons Coord, Bristol Community College, New Bedford Campus, 800 Purchase St, LL06, New Bedford, MA, 02740. Tel: 774-357-2831. p. 1017
Furtak, Luba, Sr Librn, Passaic Public Library, 195 Gregory Ave, Passaic, NJ, 07055. Tel: 973-779-0474. p. 1433
Furtak, Yaro, Electronic Res Librn, Passaic County Community College, One College Blvd, Paterson, NJ, 07505. Tel: 973-684-5696. p. 1433
Furukawa, Diana, Libr Dir, Millinocket Memorial Library, Five Maine Ave, Millinocket, ME, 04462. Tel: 207-723-7020. p. 931
Furuset, Cheyanne, Dir, Kansas Community Memorial Library, 107 N Front St, Kansas, IL, 61933. Tel: 217-948-5484. p. 604
Furuzawa, Shirin Eshghi, Head Librn, University of British Columbia Library, Asian, Asian Ctr, 1871 West Mall, Vancouver, BC, V6T 1Z2, CANADA. Tel: 604-822-5905. p. 2580
Fusco, Christy, Libr Dir, Uniontown Public Library, 24 Jefferson St, Uniontown, PA, 15401-3602. Tel: 724-437-1165. p. 2014
Fusich, Monica, Head, Info & Outreach Serv, California State University, Fresno, Henry Madden Library, 5200 N Barton Ave, Mail Stop ML-34, Fresno, CA, 93740-8014. Tel: 559-278-7673. p. 144
Fusik, Dolores, Librn, Satterlee, Stephens LLP, 230 Park Ave, New York, NY, 10169. Tel: 212-818-9200. p. 1601
Fussell, Sherri, Dir, Kirbyville Public Library, 210 S Elizabeth St, Kirbyville, TX, 75956. Tel: 409-423-4653. p. 2207
Fyfe, Bruce, Head, User Serv, Western University Libraries, Education Resource Centre, John George Althouse Bldg, Rm 1135, 1137 Western Rd, London, ON, N6G 1G7, CANADA. Tel: 519-661-2111, Ext 89031. p. 2655
Fyfe, Bruce, Mgr, User Serv, Western University Libraries, Allyn & Betty Taylor Library, Natural Sciences Centre, 1151 Richmond St, London, ON, N6A 5B7, CANADA. Tel: 519-661-3168. p. 2655
Fyfe, Bruce, Head, User Serv, Western University Libraries, The D B Weldon Library, 1151 Richmond St, London, ON, N6A 3K7, CANADA. Tel: 519-661-3166. p. 2656
Fyolek, Becky, Head, Youth Serv, Crystal Lake Public Library, 126 Paddock St, Crystal Lake, IL, 60014. Tel: 815-459-1687. p. 574
G'Fellers, Brenda, Br Mgr, Bristol Public Library, 1550 Volunteer Pkwy, Bristol, TN, 37620. Tel: 423-968-9663. p. 2090
Gaal, Jeffrey, Exec Dir, Jacques Marchais Museum of Tibetan Art Library, 338 Lighthouse Ave, Staten Island, NY, 10306. Tel: 718-987-3500. p. 1645
Gabaldon, Patricia, Ref Librn, Boynton Beach City Library, 115 N Federal Hwy, Boynton Beach, FL, 33435. Tel: 561-742-6390. p. 386
Gabaldon Winningham, Camila, Coll Develop, Tech Serv, Western Oregon University, 345 N Monmouth Ave, Monmouth, OR, 97361-1396. Tel: 503-838-8653. p. 1887
Gabbard, Angie, Reader Serv Librn, Grant County Public Library District, 201 Barnes Rd, Williamstown, KY, 41097-9482. Tel: 859-824-2080. p. 877
Gabbard, Paul, Br Mgr, MidPointe Library System, Monroe Branch, One Tennesse Ave, Monroe, OH, 45050. Tel: 513-360-6224. p. 1802
Gabehart, Jan, Br Mgr, Pines & Plains Libraries, Elizabeth Branch, 651 W Beverly St, Elizabeth, CO, 80107. Tel: 303-646-3416. p. 279
Gabel, Hilary, Communications Dir, Glenview Public Library, 1930 Glenview Rd, Glenview, IL, 60025. Tel: 847-729-7500. p. 594
Gabel, Jeff, Acq, Brooklyn Law School Library, 250 Joralemon St, Brooklyn, NY, 11201. Tel: 718-780-7978. p. 1501
Gabeletto, Amanda, Dir, Monongahela Area Library, 813 W Main St, Monongahela, PA, 15063. Tel: 724-258-5409. p. 1964
Gabelmann, Stephanie, Librn, Greystone Park Psychiatric Hospital, 59 Koch Ave, Morris Plains, NJ, 07950. Tel: 973-538-1800. p. 1421
Gaber, Billie, Cataloger, Head, Coll Mgt, Southington Public Library & Museum, 255 Main St, Southington, CT, 06489. Tel: 860-628-0947. p. 337
Gaber, Elaine R, Dir, Sadie Pope Dowdell Library of South Amboy, 100 Harold G Hoffman Plaza, South Amboy, NJ, 08879. Tel: 732-721-6060. p. 1442
Gabert, Kim, Libr Dir, Tyler Memorial Library, Town Hall, 157 Main St, Charlemont, MA, 01339. Tel: 413-339-4335. p. 1009
Gabert, Kim, Head, Ref & Adult Serv, Wadleigh Memorial Library, 49 Nashua St, Milford, NH, 03055. Tel: 603-249-0645. p. 1374
Gable, Anne, Dep Dir, Arlington County Department of Libraries, 1015 N Quincy St, Arlington, VA, 22201. Tel: 703-228-5981. p. 2304
Gable, Jody, Mrs, Children's Serv Coordr, Greenwood County Library, 600 S Main St, Greenwood, SC, 29646. Tel: 864-941-4659. p. 2062
Gabobe, Jamal, Media Tech, University of Washington Libraries, Tacoma Library, 1900 Commerce St, Box 358460, Tacoma, WA, 98402-3100. Tel: 253-692-4643. p. 2382
Gabridge, Tracy, Dep Dir, Massachusetts Institute of Technology Libraries, Barker Engineering, Bldg 10-500, 77 Massachusetts Ave, Cambridge, MA, 02139-4307. Tel: 617-253-8971. p. 1008
Gabridge, Tracy, Dep Dir, Massachusetts Institute of Technology Libraries, Office of the Director, Bldg NE36-6101, 77 Massachusetts Ave, Cambridge, MA, 02139-4307. Tel: 617-253-8971. p. 1008
Gabriel, Holly, Access Serv, Govt Info Librn, Southern Oregon University, 1250 Siskiyou Blvd, Ashland, OR, 97520. Tel: 541-552-6595. p. 1872
Gabriel-Smith, Mary Jane, Br Mgr, Oconee Regional Library, Treutlen County, 585 Second St, Soperton, GA, 30457. Tel: 912-529-6683. p. 477
Gabrio, Katy, Assoc Libr Dir, Macalester College, 1600 Grand Ave, Saint Paul, MN, 55105-1899. Tel: 651-696-6703. p. 1200
Gadbois, Lisa, Supvr, Youth Serv, Billerica Public Library, 15 Concord Rd, Billerica, MA, 01821. Tel: 978-671-0948, 978-671-0949. p. 989
Gadd, Pamela, Libr Asst III, Nashville State Technical Community College, 120 White Bridge Rd, Nashville, TN, 37209-4515. Tel: 615-353-3474. p. 2120
Gaddie, Sheila, Ref Librn, Lawrence Technological University Library, 21000 W Ten Mile Rd, Southfield, MI, 48075-1058. Tel: 248-204-3000. p. 1151
Gaddy, Angie, Librn, Allin Township Library, 116 W Main St, Stanford, IL, 61774. Tel: 309-379-4631. p. 651
Gadient, Kari, Tech Serv, Red Wing Public Library, 225 East Ave, Red Wing, MN, 55066-2298. Tel: 651-385-3673. p. 1194
Gadikian, Randy, Libr Dir, State University of New York at Fredonia, 280 Central Ave, Fredonia, NY, 14063. Tel: 716-673-3184. p. 1535
Gadoury, Nancy, Librn, Centre de Santé et de Services Sociaux du Nord de Lanaudière Bibliothèque, 1000 Blvd Ste-Anne, Saint Charles Borromee, QC, J6E 6J2, CANADA. Tel: 450-759-8222, Ext 2326. p. 2733
Gadrix, Vincent, Dir, Gulf Beaches Public Library, 200 Municipal Dr, Madeira Beach, FL, 33708. Tel: 727-391-2828. p. 419
Gadsby, Joanna, Ref & Instruction Librn, University of Maryland, Baltimore County, 1000 Hilltop Circle, Baltimore, MD, 21250. Tel: 410-455-2356. p. 958
Gadson, Tamika A, Financial Serv Adminr, Alachua County Library District, 401 E University Ave, Gainesville, FL, 32601-5453. Tel: 352-334-3913. p. 406
Gadzinski, Tim, Marketing Specialist, Manitowoc Public Library, 707 Quay St, Manitowoc, WI, 54220. Tel: 920-686-3000. p. 2453
Gaedecke, Gabrielle, Tech Serv, Public Health Ontario, 661 University Ave, 17th Flr, Toronto, ON, M5G 1H1, CANADA. Tel: 647-792-3179. p. 2692
Gaenzle, Jennifer, Librn, Fort Fairfield Public Library, 339 Main St, Fort Fairfield, ME, 04742-1199. Tel: 207-472-3880. p. 925
Gaertner, Holly, Ad, Lewis Egerton Smoot Memorial Library, 9533 Kings Hwy, King George, VA, 22485. Tel: 540-775-2147. p. 2327
Gaertner, Keith, Chief Financial Officer, Amigos Library Services, Inc, 4901 LBJ Freeway, Ste 150, Dallas, TX, 75244-6179. Tel: 972-340-2894. p. 2775

Galeazzo, Stephanie, Libr Dir, McKenzie County Public Library, 112 Second Ave NE, Watford City, ND, 58854. Tel: 701-444-3785. p. 1741
Galeczka, Chris, Ref Librn, Baylor University Libraries, Sheridan & John Eddie Williams Legal Research & Technology Center, 1114 S University Parks Dr, Waco, TX, 76706. Tel: 254-710-2168. p. 2253
Galentine, Tracy, Computer Spec, Indian River County Library System, North Indian River County Library, 1001 Sebastian Blvd, CR 512, Sebastian, FL, 32958. Tel: 772-400-6360. p. 452
Galiano, Monica, Children's Prog Coordr, Bloomingdale Free Public Library, Municipal Bldg, 101 Hamburg Tpk, Bloomingdale, NJ, 07403. Tel: 973-838-0077. p. 1391
Galik, Barbara A, Exec Dir, Bradley University, 1501 W Bradley Ave, Peoria, IL, 61625. Tel: 309-677-2830. p. 634
Galilova, Irina, Mrg, Admin Serv, Southeast Florida Library Information Network, Inc, Florida Atlantic University, Wimberly Library, Office 452, 777 Glades Rd, Boca Raton, FL, 33431. Tel: 561-208-0984. p. 2763
Galina, Lewandowicz, Head Librn, Cincinnati Art Museum, 953 Eden Park Dr, Cincinnati, OH, 45202-1557. Tel: 513-639-2978. p. 1759
Galindo, Becky, Head, Tech Serv, Pittsburg Public Library, 308 N Walnut, Pittsburg, KS, 66762-4732. Tel: 620-230-5563. p. 831
Galindo, Gloria, Dir, Fort Hancock ISD/Public Library, 100 School Dr, Fort Hancock, TX, 79839. Tel: 915-769-3811, Ext 1306. p. 2178
Galindo, Greta, Libr Serv Dir, Woodland Public Library, 250 First St, Woodland, CA, 95695. Tel: 530-661-5980. p. 260
Gall, Lizzie, Asst Dir, Libr Experiences, Jefferson County Public Library, 10200 W 20th Ave, Lakewood, CO, 80215. Tel: 303-275-2204. p. 288
Gall, Stacy, Mgr, Ohio Health-Riverside Methodist Hospital, 3535 Olentangy River Rd, Columbus, OH, 43214-3998. Tel: 614-566-5230. p. 1774
Gall, Stacy, Dir, Libr Serv, OhioHealth Grant Medical Center, 340 E Town St, Ste 7-200, 7th flr, Columbus, OH, 43215. Tel: 614-566-5230. p. 1777
Gall, Stacy, Pres, Ohio Health Sciences Library Association, c/o Ohio Health Riverside Methodist Hospital, 3535 Olentangy River Rd, Columbus, OH, 43214. Tel: 614-566-5740. p. 2773
Gall-Maynard, Maggie, Youth Serv, Onondaga Free Library, 4840 W Seneca Tpk, Syracuse, NY, 13215. Tel: 315-492-1727. p. 1650
Gallagher, Bonnie, Acting Assoc Dean, Academic Affairs, Dutchess Community College Library, 53 Pendell Rd, Poughkeepsie, NY, 12601-1595. Tel: 845-431-8631. p. 1622
Gallagher, Brian, Head, Access Serv, University of Rhode Island, 15 Lippitt Rd, Kingston, RI, 02881-2011. Tel: 406-874-9524. p. 2033
Gallagher, Carolyn, Ch Serv, Irvington Public Library, 12 S Astor St, Irvington, NY, 10533. Tel: 914-591-7840. p. 1550
Gallagher, Erin, Chair, Acquisitions & Collections Servs, University of Florida Libraries, 1545 W University Ave, Gainesville, FL, 32611-7000. Tel: 352-294-0449. p. 407
Gallagher, Helen, ILL Librn, Wolfeboro Public Library, 259 S Main St, Wolfeboro, NH, 03894. Tel: 603-569-2428. p. 1384
Gallagher, John, Dir, Yale University Library, Harvey Cushing/John Hay Whitney Medical Library, Sterling Hall of Medicine, 333 Cedar St, New Haven, CT, 06510. Tel: 202-785-5356. p. 327
Gallagher, Karen, Head, Circ, Westwood Public Library, 660 High St, Westwood, MA, 02090. Tel: 781-320-1049. p. 1068
Gallagher, Kathleen, Dir, Eagle Lake Public Library, 75 N Seventh St, Eagle Lake, FL, 33839-3430. Tel: 863-293-2914. p. 394
Gallagher, Kelsey, Asst Dir, Lib, Union County College Libraries, Kellogg Library, 40 W Jersey St, Elizabeth, NJ, 07202. Tel: 908-965-6075. p. 1398
Gallagher, Kelsey, Asst Dir, Union County College Libraries, 1033 Springfield Ave, Cranford, NJ, 07016. Tel: 908-709-7507. p. 1398
Gallagher, Marianne, Dir, New City Library, 198 S Main St, New City, NY, 10956. Tel: 845-634-4997. p. 1575
Gallagher, Missy M, Law Librn, Dorchester County Circuit Court, 206 High St, Cambridge, MD, 21613. Tel: 410-228-6300. p. 960
Gallagher, Paul, Assoc Dean for Resources & Digital Strategies, Western Michigan University, 1903 W Michigan Ave, WMU Mail Stop 5353, Kalamazoo, MI, 49008-5353. Tel: 269-387-5205. p. 1122
Gallagher, Sue, Cat, Albright College, 13th & Exeter Sts, Reading, PA, 19604. Tel: 610-921-7208. p. 2000
Gallagher, Terri, Ref Librn, Community College of Beaver County Library, One Campus Dr, Monaca, PA, 15061-2588. Tel: 724-480-3442. p. 1964
Gallagher-Starr, Scott, Ref & Instruction Librn, Bushnell University, 1188 Kincade, Eugene, OR, 97401. Tel: 541-684-7235. p. 1878
Gallaher, Sharon, Librn, Nanty Glo Public Library, 942 Roberts St, Nanty Glo, PA, 15943-0296. Tel: 814-749-0111. p. 1967
Gallant, Angela, Mgr, Circ Serv, Wood Buffalo Regional Library, One CA Knight Way, Fort McMurray, AB, T9H 5C5, CANADA. Tel: 780-743-7800. p. 2540
Gallant, Jean, Dir, Holmes Public Library, 470 Plymouth St, Halifax, MA, 02338. Tel: 781-293-2271. p. 1023
Gallant, Lynette, Coordr, Libr Serv, North Island College, 1685 S Dogwood St, Campbell River, BC, V9W 8C1, CANADA. Tel: 250-923-9785. p. 2564
Gallant, Lynette, Coll Develop, North Island College, 2300 Ryan Rd, Courtenay, BC, V9N 8N6, CANADA. Tel: 250-334-5097. p. 2565
Gallardo, Maricela, Circ, Mendocino College Library, 1000 Hensley Creek Rd, Ukiah, CA, 95482. Tel: 707-468-3245. p. 254
Gallardo, Meredith, Dir, Coburn Free Library, 275 Main St, Owego, NY, 13827. Tel: 607-687-3520. p. 1613
Gallardo, Veronica, Dir, Maryland National Capital Park & Planning Commission, 9118 Brandywine Rd, Clinton, MD, 20735. Tel: 301-868-1121. p. 962
Gallardo, Veronica, Colls Mgr, Operations Mgr, Casemate Museum Library, 20 Bernard Rd, Fort Monroe, VA, 23651-1004. Tel: 757-788-8064. p. 2319
Gallaway, Beth, Libr Dir, Grafton Public Library, 35 Grafton Common, Grafton, MA, 01519. Tel: 508-839-4649, Ext 1105. p. 1021
Galle-Looram, Michelle, Dir, Orangeburg Library, 20 S Greenbush Rd, Orangeburg, NY, 10962-1311. Tel: 845-359-2244. p. 1612
Gallegos, Amanda, Br Mgr, Bonneville County Library District, Westside Branch, 250 S Skyline Dr, Ste 6, Idaho Falls, ID, 83402. Tel: 208-757-6391. p. 515
Gallegos, Ana, Libr Dir, Reagan County Library, 300 Courthouse Sq, Big Lake, TX, 76932. Tel: 325-884-2854. p. 2148
Gallegos, Christopher, Br Mgr, Monterey County Free Libraries, Gonzales Branch, 851 Fifth St, Ste T, Gonzales, CA, 93926. Tel: 831-675-2209. p. 172
Gallegos, Lisa, Libr Asst, Tolleson Public Library, 9555 W Van Buren St, Tolleson, AZ, 85353. Tel: 623-936-2746. p. 80
Gallegos, Nidia, Asst Librn, Spec Coll Librn, Grant County Library, 215 E Grant Ave, Ulysses, KS, 67880. Tel: 620-356-1433. p. 840
Gallet, Marina, Head, Coll Serv, Cinematheque Quebecoise, 335 boul de Maisonneuve est, Montreal, QC, H2X 1K1, CANADA. Tel: 514-842-9768, Ext 262. p. 2722
Galley, Jenna, Ch Serv, Somerset County Library System of New Jersey, Peapack & Gladstone Public, School St, Peapack, NJ, 07977. Tel: 908-458-8440. p. 1392
Galli, Judy, Br Mgr, Calaveras County Library, Mokelumne Hill Branch, 8328 Main St, Mokelumne Hill, CA, 95245. Tel: 209-286-0507. p. 211
Galli, Lee-Ann, Teen Serv Librn, North Kingstown Free Library, 100 Boone St, North Kingstown, RI, 02852-5150. Tel: 401-294-3306. p. 2036
Galligan, Sarah E, Libr Dir, New Hampshire Historical Society Library, 30 Park St, Concord, NH, 03301-6384. Tel: 603-228-6688. p. 1359
Gallilee, Patty, Assoc Univ Librn, Coll & Scholarly Communication, Simon Fraser University - Burnaby Campus, 8888 University Dr, Burnaby, BC, V5A 1S6, CANADA. Tel: 778-782-4084. p. 2563
Gallina, Heather, Circ Mgr, Rosemary Garfoot Public Library, 2107 Julius St, Cross Plains, WI, 53528. Tel: 608-798-3881. p. 2429
Gallman, Katrina, Coordr, Piedmont Technical College Library, Library Resource Center - Newberry County Campus, 1922 Wilson Rd, Rm 200NN, Newberry, SC, 29108. Tel: 803-768-8167. p. 2063
Gallmann, Chris, Ms, Dir, Angelica Free Library, 55 W Main St, Angelica, NY, 14709. Tel: 585-466-7860. p. 1487
Gallo, Juliana, Youth Serv Librn, Baker Free Library, 509 South St, Bow, NH, 03304. Tel: 603-224-7113. p. 1355
Gallo, Samantha, Dir, Fuller Public Library, 29 School St, Hillsboro, NH, 03244. Tel: 603-464-3595. p. 1368
Gallos, Phil, Acq & Cat, North Country Community College Libraries, 23 Santanoni Ave, Saranac Lake, NY, 12983-2046. Tel: 518-891-2915, Ext 225. p. 1636
Galloway, Edward, Assoc Univ Librn, Archives & Special Colls, University of Pittsburgh Library System, 3960 Forbes Ave, Pittsburgh, PA, 15260. Tel: 412-648-5901. p. 1996
Galloway, James, Br Supvr, University of Texas Libraries, Walter Geology Library, Jackson Geological Science Bldg, 4.202, E 23rd St, Austin, TX, 78712. Tel: 512-495-4680. p. 2143
Galloway, Jeannie, Dir, Alice Lloyd College, 100 Purpose Rd, Pippa Passes, KY, 41844. Tel: 606-368-6113. p. 873
Galloway, Jennifer, ILL, Missouri Western State University, 4525 Downs Dr, Saint Joseph, MO, 64507-2294. Tel: 816-271-4368. p. 1268
Galloway, Mary Renee, Br Head, Volusia County Public Library, Hope Place Public Library, 1310 Wright St, Daytona Beach, FL, 32117. Tel: 386-258-4027. p. 393
Gallucci, Kaija, Circ, Swansea Free Public Library, 69 Main St, Swansea, MA, 02777. Tel: 508-674-9609. p. 1059
Gallucci, Kristan, Libr Asst, Cragin Memorial Library, Eight Linwood Ave, Colchester, CT, 06415. Tel: 860-537-5752. p. 306
Gallups, Shelia, Dir, Columbiana Public Library, 50 Lester St, Columbiana, AL, 35051. Tel: 205-669-5812. p. 12
Galonska, Ann, Mus Dir, Mansfield Historical Society, 954 Storrs Rd, Storrs, CT, 06268. Tel: 860-429-6575. p. 339
Galotta, Debra, Prog Serv, Stafford Library, Ten Levinthal Run, Stafford Springs, CT, 06075. Tel: 860-684-2852. p. 338
Galovich, Pamela, Campus Librn, Mohave Community College Library, Lake Havasu City Campus, 1977 W Acoma Blvd, Lake Havasu City, AZ, 86403-2999. Tel: 928-453-5809. p. 64
Galstad, Alison Ames, Dir, Coralville Public Library, 1401 Fifth St, Coralville, IA, 52241. Tel: 319-248-1850. p. 742

Galuschak, George R, Head, Adult Serv, Montvale Free Public Library, 12 DePiero Dr, Ste 100, Montvale, NJ, 07645. Tel: 201-391-5090. p. 1420
Galván, Gary, Curator, Spec Coll, Free Library of Philadelphia, Edwin A Fleisher Collection of Orchestral Music, 1901 Vine St, Rm 125, Philadelphia, PA, 19103-1116. Tel: 215-686-5313. p. 1978
Galvan, Heather, Librn, Kanopolis Public Library, 221 N Kansas, Kanopolis, KS, 67454. Tel: 785-472-3053. p. 816
Galvan, Yvonne, Tech Serv, Coalinga-Huron Library District, 305 N Fourth St, Coalinga, CA, 93210. Tel: 559-935-1676. p. 131
Galvin, Bobbi, Br Supvr, Licking County Library, Emerson R Miller Branch, 990 W Main St, Newark, OH, 43055. Tel: 740-344-2155. p. 1808
Galvin, Colleen, Asst Dir, Durango Public Library, 1900 E Third Ave, Durango, CO, 81301. Tel: 970-375-3384. p. 278
Galvin, Denis, Asst Univ Librn, Tech Serv, Rice University, 6100 Main, MS-44, Houston, TX, 77005. Tel: 713-348-3634. p. 2197
Galvin, Kathleen, Tech Serv Mgr, Elmira College, One Park Pl, Elmira, NY, 14901. Tel: 607-735-1868. p. 1530
Galvin, Rachel, Youth Serv Coordr, Sibley Public Library, 406 Ninth St, Sibley, IA, 51249. Tel: 712-754-2888. p. 781
Galway, Dan, Libr Mgr, Ponoka Jubilee Library, 5604 50 St, Ponoka, AB, T4J 1G7, CANADA. Tel: 403-783-3843. p. 2550
Galway, Mary E, Librn, Chrisman Public Library, 108 N Illinois St, Chrisman, IL, 61924. Tel: 217-269-3011. p. 571
Galyan, Abby, Youth Serv Librn, Lincoln Heritage Public Library, 105 Wallace St, Dale, IN, 47523-9267. Tel: 812-937-7170. p. 678
Galyean, Ronda, Librn, Lowgap Public Library, 9070 W Pine St, Lowgap, NC, 27024. Tel: 336-352-3000. p. 1701
Gamba, Terry, Operations Mgr, Roseland Free Public Library, 20 Roseland Ave, Roseland, NJ, 07068-1235. Tel: 973-226-8636. p. 1441
Gambill, Henry, Sr Librn, Los Angeles Public Library System, Donald Bruce Kaufman-Brentwood Branch Library, 11820 San Vicente Blvd, Los Angeles, CA, 90049-5002. Tel: 310-575-8273. p. 164
Gambino, Betsy, Dir, Strategic Initiatives, Berkeley Medical Center, 2500 Hospital Dr, Martinsburg, WV, 25401. Tel: 304-264-1246. p. 2408
Gamble, Cassie, Head Librn, Kiowa County Library, 320 S Main, Ste 120, Greensburg, KS, 67054. Tel: 620-723-1118. p. 811
Gamble, Jeanne, Libr & Archives Spec, Historic New England, 141 Cambridge St, Boston, MA, 02114-2702. Tel: 617-227-3956. p. 996
Gamble, Lydia, Head, Children's Servx, Stow-Munroe Falls Public Library, 3512 Darrow Rd, Stow, OH, 44224. Tel: 330-688-3295. p. 1822
Gamble, Lynn, Acq, Cat, College of Our Lady of the Elms, 291 Springfield St, Chicopee, MA, 01013-2839. Tel: 413-265-2280. p. 1011
Gamble, Sarah, Br Mgr, Mid-Continent Public Library, Grain Valley Branch, 101 SW Eagles Pkwy, Grain Valley, MO, 64029. Tel: 816-228-4020. p. 1250
Gamble, Theresa, Dir of Coll, Erie County Historical Society, King-Mertens Archive Bldg, 356 W 6th St, Erie, PA, 16507. Tel: 814-454-1813, Ext 30. p. 1931
Gambling, Jessica, Archivist, Los Angeles County Museum of Art, 5905 Wilshire Blvd, Los Angeles, CA, 90036-4597. Tel: 323-857-6118. p. 163
Gamboa, Tiffany, Executive Asst, Spruce Grove Public Library, 35 Fifth Ave, Spruce Grove, AB, T7X 2C5, CANADA. Tel: 780-962-4423. p. 2554
Gamertsfelder, Emily, Planning & Projects Mgr, Baltimore County Public Library, 320 York Rd, Towson, MD, 21204-5179. Tel: 410-887-6100. p. 979
Gamez Herrera, Melissa, Coll Serv, Libr Assoc II, Texas A&M University-San Antonio, One University Way, San Antonio, TX, 78224. Tel: 210-784-1505. p. 2239
Gamlin, Daniel, Mgr, Wayne State University Libraries, Purdy-Kresge Library, 5265 Cass Ave, Detroit, MI, 48202. Tel: 313-577-4042. p. 1100
Gamm, Margaret, Dir, University of Iowa Libraries, Special Collections & Archives, 100 Main Library, 125 W Washington St, Iowa City, IA, 52242-1420. Tel: 319-335-6247. p. 761
Gamma, Lynn, Archivist, United States Air Force, Historical Research Agency, AFHRA, 600 Chennault Circle, Bldg 1405, Maxwell AFB, AL, 36112-6424. Tel: 334-953-2395. p. 25
Gamman, Patrick, Superintendent, National Park Service, 900 Kennesaw Mountain Dr, Kennesaw, GA, 30152. Tel: 770-427-4686. p. 484
Gammon, Kathy, Br Mgr, Perry County Public Library, Lobelville Branch, 55 S Main St, Lobelville, TN, 37097. Tel: 931-593-3111. p. 2109
Gammon, Rachel, Libr Assoc, Massasoit Community College, Canton Campus Library, 900 Randolph St, Canton, MA, 02021. Tel: 508-588-9100, Ext 2942. p. 1003
Gampfer, Scott, Dir, Cincinnati Museum Center At Union Terminal, 1301 Western Ave, Ste 2133, Cincinnati, OH, 45203. Tel: 513-287-7084. p. 1760
Gampp, Timothy, Dir, Rowan County Public Library, 175 Beacon Hill Dr, Morehead, KY, 40351-6031. Tel: 606-784-7137. p. 869
Gamtso, Carolyn, Dir, University of New Hampshire at Manchester Library, 88 Commercial St, Manchester, NH, 03101. Tel: 603-641-4172. p. 1373
Gan, Lucy, Info Serv Librn, University of Toronto Libraries, Cheng Yu Tung East Asian Library, John P Robarts Research Library, 130 St George St, 8th Flr, Toronto, ON, M5S 1A5, CANADA. Tel: 416-978-1025. p. 2698
Gan, Ryan, Librn I, Orange Public Library & History Center, Taft Branch, 740 E Taft Ave, Orange, CA, 92865-4406. Tel: 714-288-2440. p. 189
Gan, Ryan, Syst Librn, El Camino College, 16007 S Crenshaw Blvd, Torrance, CA, 90506. Tel: 310-660-3525. p. 252
Ganbarg, Cory, Children's Serv Supvr, Naperville Public Library, Naper Boulevard, 2035 S Naper Blvd, Naperville, IL, 60565-3353. Tel: 630-961-4100, Ext 2235. p. 623
Gancarz, Anne, Commun Serv Librn, Chicopee Public Library, 449 Front St, Chicopee, MA, 01013. Tel: 413-594-1800. p. 1011
Gancos, Keli, Youth Serv Librn, Ellsworth Public Library, 20 State St, Ellsworth, ME, 04605. Tel: 207-667-6363. p. 924
Gandee, Wade, Dir, Sterling Public Library, 420 N Fifth St, Sterling, CO, 80751-3363. Tel: 970-522-2023. p. 296
Gandhi, Subash, Instrul Serv Librn, Ref Serv, Queens College, Benjamin S Rosenthal Library, 65-30 Kissena Blvd, Flushing, NY, 11367-0904. Tel: 718-997-3700. p. 1534
Gandolfo, Mark, Digital Media Tech, University of Nevada-Reno, 1664 N Virginia St, Mailstop 0322, Reno, NV, 89557-0322. Tel: 775-682-9299. p. 1349
Gandour-Rood, Eli, Sci Librn, University of Puget Sound, 1604 N Warner St, Upper Loading Dock, Tacoma, WA, 98416. Tel: 253-879-3678. p. 2387
Gandy, Brian E, Dir, Darlington County Historical Commission & Museum, 204 Hewitt St, Darlington, SC, 29532. Tel: 843-398-4710. p. 2057
Gandy, Shawna, Libr Dir, Oregon Historical Society, 1200 SW Park Ave, Portland, OR, 97205. Tel: 503-306-5265. p. 1893
Gandy, Susan, Br Mgr, Lancaster County Library, Kershaw Branch, 101 N Hampton St, Kershaw, SC, 29067. Tel: 803-283-1010. p. 2064
Gane, Gayla, Librn, Chinook Regional Library, Chaplin Branch, Second Ave Hall Complex, Chaplin, SK, S0H 0V0, CANADA. Tel: 306-395-2524. p. 2752
Ganeshram, Ramin, Exec Dir, Westport Historical Society Library, 25 Avery Pl, Westport, CT, 06880-3215. Tel: 203-222-1424, Ext 105. p. 346
Gangarossa, Dawn, Br Serv Coordr, Fort Erie Public Library, Crystal Ridge, 89 Ridge Rd S, Ridgeway, ON, L0S 1N0, CANADA. Tel: 905-871-2546 x310. p. 2642
Gange, Isaac, Circ Supvr, Davis County Library, Layton/Central Branch, 155 N Wasatch Dr, Layton, UT, 84041. Tel: 801-451-1820. p. 2263
Gangone, Lisa, Libr Asst, Middlesex Community College, 100 Training Hill Rd, Middletown, CT, 06457. Tel: 860-343-5829. p. 322
Gangone, Lucy B, Libr Dir, Leesburg Public Library, 100 E Main St, Leesburg, FL, 34748. Tel: 352-728-9790. p. 418
Gannaway, Wayne, Exec Dir, Olmsted County Historical Society, 1195 W Circle Dr SW, Rochester, MN, 55902. Tel: 507-282-9447. p. 1194
Ganne, Shanna, Exec Dir, Grand County Historical Association Library, 110 E Byers Ave, Hot Sulphur Springs, CO, 80451. Tel: 970-725-3939. p. 286
Gannod, Jenni, Libr Dir, Blair Memorial Library, 416 N Main St, Clawson, MI, 48017-1599. Tel: 248-588-5500. p. 1091
Gannon, J Violet, Exec Dir, Manchester Community Library, 138 Cemetery Ave, Rte 7A, Manchester Center, VT, 05255. Tel: 802-362-2607. p. 2288
Gannon, Michael, Chief Operating Officer, Support Serv, Prince George's County Memorial Library System, 9601 Capital Lane, Largo, MD, 20774. Tel: 301-699-3500. p. 970
Gannon, Molly, Dir, Fulton County Public Library, 312 Main St, Fulton, KY, 42041. Tel: 270-472-3439. p. 856
Gannon, Robyn, Dir, Manasquan Public Library, 55 Broad St, Manasquan, NJ, 08736. Tel: 732-223-1503. p. 1416
Gannon, Sarah, Educ Mgr, Planned Parenthood of Southern New England, 345 Whitney Ave, New Haven, CT, 06511. Tel: 203-865-5158. p. 326
Gannon, Vicky, Head, Coll Serv, Pace University, 78 N Broadway, White Plains, NY, 10603. Tel: 914-422-4369. p. 1665
Gannon-Nagle, Sarah, Chief, Libr Serv Br, United States Fish & Wildlife Service, 698 Conservation Way, Shepherdstown, WV, 25443. Tel: 304-876-7459. p. 2414
Ganong, Peggy, Tech Coordr, New Milford Public Library, 24 Main St, New Milford, CT, 06776. Tel: 860-355-1191, Ext 211. p. 329
Gansa, Alex, Dr, Pres, Museum of Russian Culture, Inc Library, 2450 Sutter St, San Francisco, CA, 94115. Tel: 415-921-4082. p. 226
Gansel, Marcy, Dir, Graham County Public Library, 414 N West St, Hill City, KS, 67642. Tel: 785-421-2722. p. 813
Ganshorn, Heather, Librn, University of Calgary Library, Gallagher Library, 170 Earth Sciences, 2500 University Dr NW, Calgary, AB, T2N 1N4, CANADA. Tel: 403-220-2611. p. 2529
Ganske, Maxine, Libr Asst III, Kansas State University Libraries, Paul Weigel Library of Architecture, Planning & Design, 323 Seaton Hall, Manhattan, KS, 66506. Tel: 785-532-5978. p. 823
Gant, Elizabeth, Libr Dir, Seagoville Public Library, 702 N Hwy 175, Seagoville, TX, 75159-1774. Tel: 972-287-7720. p. 2242
Gant, Jon, Dean, Prof, North Carolina Central University, 1801 Fayetteville St, Durham, NC, 27707. Tel: 919-530-6485. p. 2790
Gantt, John, Head, Tech Serv, Auburn University, 7440 East Dr, Montgomery, AL, 36117. Tel: 334-244-3200. p. 28

Gantt, Sean, PhD, Dir, Dolores Public Library, 1002 Railroad Ave, Dolores, CO, 81323. Tel: 970-882-4127. p. 278

Gantz, Tammy, Br Mgr, Washington County Free Library, Smithsburg Branch, 66 W Water St, Smithsburg, MD, 21783-1604. Tel: 301-824-7722. p. 968

Ganyard, Paula M, Asst Vice Chancellor, Info Tech, Library Services, University of Wisconsin-Green Bay, 2420 Nicolet Dr, Green Bay, WI, 54311-7001. p. 2439

Ganzevoort, Thomas, Instruction Librn, Columbus State University Libraries, 4225 University Ave, Columbus, GA, 31907. Tel: 706-507-8686. p. 472

Gao, Greg, Commun Libr Mgr, Queens Library, Lefrak City Community Library, 98-30 57th Ave, Corona, NY, 11368. Tel: 718-592-7677. p. 1555

Gao, Hong, Admin Librn, Hinds Community College, Nursing/Allied Health Center, 1750 Chadwick Dr, Jackson, MS, 39204-3490. Tel: 601-376-4816. p. 1231

Gao, Vera, E-Res Cat Librn, Auraria Library, 1100 Lawrence St, Denver, CO, 80204-2095. Tel: 303-315-7716. p. 273

Gaona, Antonia, Pub Serv Mgr, Boulder Public Library, 1001 Arapahoe Rd, Boulder, CO, 80302. Tel: 303-441-3100. p. 266

Gaona, Antonia, Br Mgr, Boulder Public Library, George F Reynolds Branch, 3595 Table Mesa Dr, Boulder, CO, 80305. Tel: 303-441-3120. p. 267

Gappmayer, Sam, Dir, John Michael Kohler Arts Center, 608 New York Ave, Sheboygan, WI, 53081-4507. Tel: 920-458-6144. p. 2476

Gara, Devery, Library Contact, Schenectady County Public Library, Woodlawn, Two Sanford St, Schenectady, NY, 12304. Tel: 518-386-2248. p. 1638

Garabedian, Mike, Dean of Libr, Rio Hondo College Library, 3600 Workman Mill Rd, 2nd Flr, Whittier, CA, 90601. Tel: 562-908-3417. p. 259

Garabedian, Mike, Cat Librn, Whittier College, Bonnie Bell Wardman Library, 7031 Founders Hill Rd, Whittier, CA, 90608-9984. Tel: 562-907-4247. p. 259

Garafolo, Richard M, Dir, Lenoir Community College, 231 Hwy 58 S, Kinston, NC, 28504-6836. Tel: 252-527-6223, Ext 504. p. 1699

Garay, Cynthia, Br Mgr, Big Horn County Library, Greybull Branch, 325 Greybull Ave, Greybull, WY, 82426. Tel: 307-765-2551. p. 2491

Garay, Maria, Br Mgr, Big Horn County Library, 430 West C St, Basin, WY, 82410. Tel: 307-568-2388. p. 2491

Garber, Gina J, Digital Serv Librn, Austin Peay State University, 601 College St, Clarksville, TN, 37044. Tel: 931-221-7028. p. 2092

Garber, Robert, Ref Librn, Howard Community College Library, 10901 Little Patuxent Pkwy, 2nd Flr, Columbia, MD, 21044. Tel: 443-518-1450. p. 963

Garboden, Mary, Head, Outreach Serv, Ypsilanti District Library, Superior Township, 8975 MacArthur Blvd, Ypsilanti, MI, 48198. Tel: 734-482-3747. p. 1161

Garcelon-Hart, Eva, Archivist, Henry Sheldon Museum of Vermont History, One Park St, Middlebury, VT, 05753. Tel: 802-388-2117. p. 2288

Garcia, Adolfo, Dir, Pharr Memorial Library, 121 E Cherokee St, Pharr, TX, 78577-4826. Tel: 956-402-4650. p. 2226

Garcia, Alejandra, Mgr, County of Los Angeles Public Library, East Rancho Dominguez Library, 4420 E Rose St, East Rancho Dominguez, CA, 90221-3664. Tel: 310-632-6193. p. 135

Garcia, Alex, LAII Teen/Spanish Outreach Coordr, Yuma County Free Library District, 2951 S 21st Dr, Yuma, AZ, 85364. Tel: 928-373-6481. p. 85

Garcia, Alfa J, Asst Librn, New York State Psychiatric Institute, 1051 Riverside Dr, Box 114, New York, NY, 10032. Tel: 646-774-8615. p. 1598

Garcia, Ally, Dep Dir, Pasadena Public Library, 285 E Walnut St, Pasadena, CA, 91101. Tel: 626-744-4066. p. 194

Garcia, Ally, Libr Mgr, San Mateo County Library, Atherton Library, Two Dinkelspiel Station Lane, Atherton, CA, 94027. Tel: 650-328-2422, Ext 227. p. 235

Garcia, Ally, Libr Mgr, San Mateo County Library, San Carlos Library, 610 Elm St, San Carlos, CA, 94070. Tel: 650-591-0341, Ext 227. p. 236

Garcia, Amanda, Prog Coordr, Elsa Public Library, 711 N Hidalgo St, Elsa, TX, 78543. Tel: 956-262-3061. p. 2175

Garcia, Amy, Asst Librn, Caribou Public Library, 30 High St, Caribou, ME, 04736. Tel: 207-493-4214. p. 920

Garcia, Angelica, Supvry Librn, United States Army, Sergeants Major Academy Learning Resources Center, Commandant USASMA, 11291 SGT E Churchill St, Fort Bliss, TX, 79918-8002. Tel: 915-744-8176, 915-744-8451. p. 2177

Garcia, Ashley, Syst Librn, Central Texas College, Bldg 102, 6200 W Central Texas Expressway, Killeen, TX, 76549. Tel: 254-616-3310. p. 2206

Garcia, Avelina, Supvr, Yakima Valley Libraries, Harrah Library, 21 E Pioneer St, Harrah, WA, 98933. Tel: 509-848-3458. p. 2395

Garcia, Chris, Coordr, Libr & Educ Serv, Virginia War Museum, 9285 Warwick Blvd, Newport News, VA, 23607. Tel: 757-247-8523. p. 2334

Garcia, Daniella, Librn, United States Courts Library, 2500 Tulare St, Ste 2401, Fresno, CA, 93721. Tel: 559-499-5615. p. 147

Garcia, Danny, Asst Dir, Tech Serv Librn, Belen Public Library, 333 Becker Ave, Belen, NM, 87002. Tel: 505-966-2606. p. 1464

Garcia, Darla, First Generation & First Year Librn, Linfield University, 900 SE Baker St, McMinnville, OR, 97128. Tel: 503-883-2383. p. 1885

Garcia, Diana, City Librn, Monterey Park Bruggemeyer Library, 318 S Ramona Ave, Monterey Park, CA, 91754-3399. Tel: 626-307-1418. p. 180

Garcia, Diana, Dean of Libr, American River College Library, 4700 College Oak Dr, Sacramento, CA, 95841. Tel: 916-484-8455. p. 205

Garcia, Edward, Libr Dir, Cranston Public Library, 140 Sockanosset Cross Rd, Cranston, RI, 02920-5539. Tel: 401-943-9080. p. 2031

Garcia, Esther, Librn, University of St Augustine for Health Sciences, 5010 Riverside Dr, Irving, TX, 75039. Tel: 469-498-5705. p. 2203

Garcia, Gonzalo, Co-Chair, Online Serv, Syst, Golden West College, 15744 Golden West St, Huntington Beach, CA, 92647. Tel: 714-895-8741, Ext 55250. p. 151

Garcia, Guillermo, Supvr, Glendale Library, Arts & Culture, Casa Verdugo, 1151 N Brand Blvd, Glendale, CA, 91202. Tel: 818-548-2047. p. 149

Garcia, Guillermo, Supvr, Glendale Library, Arts & Culture, Grandview, 1535 Fifth St, Glendale, CA, 91201. Tel: 818-548-2049. p. 149

Garcia, Janette, Archivist, Upper Iowa University, 605 Washington St, Fayette, IA, 52142. Tel: 563-425-5261. p. 753

Garcia, Jose, Actg Literacy Contact, Monterey Park Bruggemeyer Library, 318 S Ramona Ave, Monterey Park, CA, 91754-3399. Tel: 626-307-1251. p. 180

Garcia, Jose, Tech Serv, Lee Library Association, 100 Main St, Lee, MA, 01238-1688. Tel: 413-243-0385. p. 1027

Garcia, Jose Luis, Satellite Librn, United States Court of Appeals, Federico Degetau Federal Bldg, Rm 121, 150 Carlos Chardon St, Hato Rey, PR, 00918. Tel: 787-772-3097. p. 2511

Garcia, Jose Ramon, Pres, Pimeria Alta Historical Society, 136 N Grand Ave, Nogales, AZ, 85621. Tel: 520-287-4621. p. 67

Garcia, Joseph, Br Supvr, Riverside Public Library, Arlanza Branch, 8267 Philbin Ave, Riverside, CA, 92503. Tel: 951-826-2217. p. 203

Garcia, Karen, Ch, Palm Springs Public Library, 217 Cypress Lane, Palm Springs, FL, 33461-1698. Tel: 561-584-8350. p. 435

Garcia, Larissa, Info Literacy Librn, Northern Illinois University Libraries, 217 Normal Rd, DeKalb, IL, 60115-2828. Tel: 815-753-4822. p. 577

Garcia, Laura, Libr Mgr, Western Plains Library System, Minnie R Slief Memorial Library, 201 S Cearlock St, Cheyenne, OK, 73628. Tel: 580-497-3777. p. 1845

Garcia, Laura, Library Contact, Corpus Christi Public Libraries, Dr Clotilde P Garcia Public Library, 5930 Brockhampton, Corpus Christi, TX, 78414. Tel: 361-826-2360. p. 2160

Garcia, Laura, Library Contact, Corpus Christi Public Libraries, Janet F Harte Public Library, 2629 Waldron Rd, Corpus Christi, TX, 78418. Tel: 361-826-2310. p. 2160

Garcia, Lourdes, Librn, El Paso Community College Library, Transmountain Campus Library, 9570 Gateway Blvd N, Rm 1600, El Paso, TX, 79924. Tel: 915-831-5098. p. 2173

Garcia, Lynn, Br Mgr, Montgomery County Memorial Library System, South Regional Library, 2101 Lake Robbins Dr, The Woodlands, TX, 77380. Tel: 936-442-7727. p. 2159

Garcia, Maria Isabel, Librn, All Saints Catholic Church, 5231 Meadowcreek at Arapaho, Dallas, TX, 75248-4046. Tel: 972-778-0327. p. 2163

Garcia, Maria M, Libr Dir, Oblate School of Theology, 285 Oblate Dr, San Antonio, TX, 78216. Tel: 210-341-1366, Ext 310. p. 2237

Garcia, Maria M, Libr Dir, Donald E O'Shaughnessy Library, Oblate School of Theology, 285 Oblate Dr, San Antonio, TX, 78216-6693. Tel: 210-341-1368. p. 2237

Garcia, Mariella, Adult Serv, Librn I, Oceanside Public Library, 330 N Coast Hwy, Oceanside, CA, 92054. Tel: 760-435-5606. p. 187

Garcia, Maureen, Libr Dir, Mountain Top Library, 6093 Main St, Tannersville, NY, 12485. Tel: 518-589-5707. p. 1651

Garcia, Miguel, III, Head, Access Serv, Gateway Community College Library & Learning Commons, 20 Church St, New Haven, CT, 06510. Tel: 203-285-2059. p. 325

Garcia, Nathan, Interlibrary Serv Coordr, University of California, Merced Library, 5200 N Lake Rd, Merced, CA, 95343. Tel: 209-291-9394. p. 177

Garcia, Noemi, Libr Asst, Penitas Public Library, 1111 S Main St, Penitas, TX, 78576. Tel: 956-583-5656. p. 2226

Garcia, Olivia, Digital Serv Librn, Electronic Serv Librn, Texas A&M University-Texarkana, 7101 University Ave, Texarkana, TX, 75503. Tel: 903-223-3148. p. 2248

Garcia, Pam, Asst Dir, Waupun Public Library, 123 S Forest St, Waupun, WI, 53963. Tel: 920-324-7925. p. 2485

Garcia, Paula, Asst Librn, Haskell County Library, 300 N Ave E, Haskell, TX, 79521-5706. Tel: 940-864-2747. p. 2188

Garcia, Phillip, Managing Librn, Core Collection Books & Periodicals, Academy of Motion Picture Arts & Sciences, 333 S La Cienega Blvd, Beverly Hills, CA, 90211. Tel: 310-247-3000, Ext 2241. p. 124

Garcia, Priscilla, Librn III, Guerra Joe A Laredo Public Library, Sophie Christen McKendrick, Francisco Ochoa & Fernando A Salinas Branch, 1920 Palo Blanco St, Laredo, TX, 78046. Tel: 956-795-2400, Ext 2403. p. 2209

Garcia Rodriquez, Arleen, Lead Librn, Tech Serv, University of the Sacred Heart, Rosales St, PO Box 12383, Santurce, PR, 00914-0383. Tel: 787-728-1515, Ext 4364. p. 2515

Garcia, Rosemarie, Head, Youth Serv, River Edge Free Public Library, 685 Elm Ave, River Edge, NJ, 07661. Tel: 201-261-1663. p. 1439
Garcia, RuthAnn, Br Mgr, City of Palo Alto Library, 270 Forest Ave, Palo Alto, CA, 94301. Tel: 650-329-2562. p. 191
Garcia, RuthAnn, Br Mgr, City of Palo Alto Library, Mitchell Park, 3700 Middlefield Rd, Palo Alto, CA, 94303. p. 192
Garcia, Sarah, Br Mgr, Fairfax County Public Library, Woodrow Wilson Branch, 6101 Knollwood Dr, Falls Church, VA, 22041-1798. Tel: 703-820-8774. p. 2316
Garcia, Sharon, Librn, Pueblo de Abiquiu Library & Cultural Center, Bldg 29, County Rd 187, Abiquiu, NM, 87510. Tel: 505-685-4884. p. 1459
Garcia, Tanya, Librn, Eden Public Library, 117 Market St, Eden, TX, 76837. Tel: 325-869-7761. p. 2172
Garcia, Tiffany, Supvr, Mid-Columbia Libraries, Keewaydin Park, 405 S Dayton St, Kennewick, WA, 99336. Tel: 509-586-3156. p. 2367
Garcia, Tonya, Libr Dir, Long Branch Free Public Library, 328 Broadway, Long Branch, NJ, 07740. Tel: 732-222-3900. p. 1413
Garcia, Wess, Dep Libr Dir, Rancho Cucamonga Public Library, 12505 Cultural Center Dr, Rancho Cucamonga, CA, 91739. Tel: 909-477-2720. p. 197
Garcia, Yvette, Asst Dir, Chicago Public Library, Conrad Sulzer Regional, 4455 N Lincoln Ave, Chicago, IL, 60625. Tel: 312-744-7616. p. 557
Garcia, Zack, Libr Spec II, Teen Serv, Camp Verde Community Library, 130 N Black Bridge Rd, Camp Verde, AZ, 86322. Tel: 928-554-8390. p. 57
Garcia-Barcena, Yanira, Sr Ref Librn, University of Miami, Louis Calder Memorial Library, Miller School of Medicine, 1601 NW Tenth Ave, Miami, FL, 33136. Tel: 305-243-5439. p. 425
Garcia-Colon, Miguel, Br Mgr, Greenwich Library, Byram Shubert Branch, 21 Mead Ave, Greenwich, CT, 06830-6812. Tel: 203-531-0426. p. 314
Garcia-Ortiz, Francisco, Dr, Dir, Pub Libr Serv, Yakima Valley Libraries, 102 N Third St, Yakima, WA, 98901. Tel: 509-452-8541. p. 2395
Garcia-Rivera, Jose H, ILL & Reserves Asst, University of Puerto Rico RP College of Natural Sciences Library, 17 Ave Universidad, Ste 1701, San Juan, PR, 00925-2537. Tel: 787-764-0000, Ext 88379. p. 2515
Garczynski, Joyce, Asst Univ Librn, Develop/Communications, Towson University, 8000 York Rd, Towson, MD, 21252. Tel: 410-704-2456. p. 980
Gard, Amy C, Dir, Sterling Free Public Library, 138 N Broadway, Sterling, KS, 67579-2131. Tel: 620-278-3191. p. 837
Gard, Linda, Dir, Cobb Public Library, 109 Mifflin St, Cobb, WI, 53526. Tel: 608-623-2554. p. 2428
Gardella, Robin, Coordr, Tech Serv, Southfield Public Library, 26300 Evergreen Rd, Southfield, MI, 48076. Tel: 248-796-4340. p. 1151
Gardella, Tonya, Br Mgr, Akron-Summit County Public Library, Goodyear Branch, 60 Goodyear Blvd, Akron, OH, 44305-4487. Tel: 330-784-7522. p. 1744
Garden, Jennifer, Libr Dir, Milledgeville Public Library, 18 W Fifth St, Milledgeville, IL, 61051-9416. Tel: 815-225-7572. p. 617
Gardener, Linda C W, Dir, Melrose Public Library, 263 W Foster St, Melrose, MA, 02176. Tel: 781-665-2313. p. 1034
Gardham, Bruce, Coll Develop, Sr Librn, Supvr, Toronto Public Health Library, 277 Victoria St, 6th Flr, Toronto, ON, M5B 1W2, CANADA. Tel: 416-338-8284. p. 2693
Gardina, Colleen, Sci Res & Instruction Librn, University of Georgia Libraries, Science, Boyd Graduate Studies Bldg, 210 D W Brooks Dr, Athens, GA, 30602. Tel: 706-542-0698. p. 460
Gardiner, Daniel, Librn, Montana Masonic Library, 425 N Park Ave, Helena, MT, 59624. Tel: 406-442-7774. p. 1296
Gardiner, Kacie, Librn, Selwyn Public Library, Lakefield Branch, Eight Queen St, Bridgenorth, ON, K0L 2H0, CANADA. Tel: 705-652-8623. p. 2633
Gardiner, Kathy, Mgr, Duffield Public Library, One Main St, Duffield, AB, T0E 0N0, CANADA. Tel: 780-962-2003, Ext 270. p. 2534
Gardiner, Kathy, Libr Dir, Keephills Public Library, 15 51515 Range Rd 32A, Duffield, AB, T0E 0N0, CANADA. Tel: 780-731-3725. p. 2534
Gardiner, Kathy, Libr Mgr, Entwistle Public Library, 5232 - 50 St, Entwistle, AB, T0E 0S0, CANADA. Tel: 780-727-3811. p. 2539
Gardiner, Lori, Circ Supvr, Davis County Library, Syracuse/Northwest Branch, 1875 S 2000 West, Syracuse, UT, 84075. Tel: 801-451-1850. p. 2263
Gardiner, Sascha, Ch, Hagaman Memorial Library, 227 Main St, East Haven, CT, 06512. Tel: 203-468-3890. p. 310
Gardner, Allison, Librn, United States Navy, Naval Undersea Warfare Center Division, Newport Technical Library, 1176 Howell St, Bldg 101, Newport, RI, 02841. Tel: 401-832-4338. p. 2036
Gardner, Amanda, Youth Serv Librn, Pryor Public Library, 505 E Graham, Pryor, OK, 74361. Tel: 918-825-0777. p. 1861
Gardner, Andrew, Assoc Dir, Libraries Online, Inc, 100 Riverview Ctr, Ste 252, Middletown, CT, 06457. Tel: 860-347-1704. p. 2762
Gardner, Barb, Dir, Coulter Public Library, 111 Main St, PO Box 87, Coulter, IA, 50431-0087. Tel: 641-866-6798. p. 742
Gardner, Bonnie, Tech Librn, Lewiston City Library, 411 D St, Lewiston, ID, 83501. Tel: 208-798-2525. p. 524
Gardner, Chad, Library Contact, Canadian Wildlife Federation, 350 Michael Cowpland Dr, Kanata, ON, K2M 2W1, CANADA. Tel: 613-599-9594. p. 2648
Gardner, Chris, Br Mgr, Washington County Library System, Enterprise Branch, 393 S 200 E, Enterprise, UT, 84725. Tel: 435-878-2574. p. 2270
Gardner, Diane, Libr Mgr, Tech Serv, McLaren Flint, 401 S Ballenger Hwy, Flint, MI, 48532-3685. Tel: 810-342-2141. p. 1107
Gardner, Diane, Med Librn, McLaren Greater Lansing, 2900 Collins Rd, Lansing, MI, 48910. Tel: 517-975-6075. p. 1125
Gardner, Don, Librn, Salinas Public Library, Cesar Chavez Library, 615 Williams Rd, Salinas, CA, 93905. Tel: 831-758-7345. p. 211
Gardner, Jen, Youth Serv Mgr, Dover Public Library, 525 N Walnut St, Dover, OH, 44622. Tel: 330-343-6123. p. 1782
Gardner, Jo, Access Serv, Carrollton Public Library, 1700 N Keller Springs Rd, Carrollton, TX, 75006. Tel: 972-466-4812. p. 2153
Gardner, Justin A, Spec Coll Librn, American Printing House for the Blind, Inc, 1839 Frankfort Ave, Louisville, KY, 40206. p. 864
Gardner, Laura, Youth Serv Librn, Transylvania County Library, 212 S Gaston St, Brevard, NC, 28712. Tel: 828-884-3151. p. 1675
Gardner, Laura, Coll Develop Librn, Peterborough Public Library, 345 Aylmer St N, Peterborough, ON, K9H 3V7, CANADA. Tel: 705-745-5382, Ext 2361. p. 2672
Gardner, Lindsy, Dir, Emmet O'Neal Library, 50 Oak St, Mountain Brook, AL, 35213. Tel: 205-879-0459. p. 31
Gardner, Liz, Br Mgr, Free Library of Philadelphia, Queen Memorial Branch, 1201 S 23rd St, Philadelphia, PA, 19146-4316. Tel: 215-685-1899. p. 1979
Gardner, Lynn, Ref Librn, Southington Public Library & Museum, 255 Main St, Southington, CT, 06489. Tel: 860-628-0947. p. 337
Gardner, Marybeth, Admin Librn, Coll Develop, Chandler Public Library, 22 S Delaware, Chandler, AZ, 85225. Tel: 480-782-2816. p. 58
Gardner, Meggan, Dir, Golf Canada Library & Archives, 1333 Dorval Dr, Ste 1, Oakville, ON, L6M 4X7, CANADA. Tel: 905-849-9700, Ext 412. p. 2662
Gardner, Melissa, Exec Dir, Palatine Public Library District, 700 N North Ct, Palatine, IL, 60067. Tel: 847-907-3600. p. 631
Gardner, Melissa, Head, Circ, York County Public Library, 100 Long Green Blvd, Yorktown, VA, 23693. Tel: 757-890-5100. p. 2355
Gardner, Mellisa, Chmn, Boyle Public Library, 4800 Third St S, Boyle, AB, T0A 0M0, CANADA. Tel: 780-689-4161. p. 2524
Gardner, Morris, Mgr, Sr Librn, Atlanta-Fulton Public Library System, Auburn Avenue Research Library on African-American Culture & History, 101 Auburn Ave NE, Atlanta, GA, 30303-2503. Tel: 404-613-4001. p. 460
Gardner, Nicholas M, Staff Librn, Potomac State College of West Virginia University, 103 Fort Ave, Keyser, WV, 26726. Tel: 304-788-6901. p. 2406
Gardner, Pam, Libr Dir, Medfield Public Library, 468 Main St, Medfield, MA, 02052-2008. Tel: 508-359-4544. p. 1033
Gardner, Rebecca, Soc Sci Librn, Rutgers University Libraries, James Dickson Carr Library, 75 Ave E, Piscataway, NJ, 08854-8040. Tel: 848-445-3605. p. 1424
Gardner, Rhea, Supv Librn, Solano County Library, Dixon Public Library, 230 N First St, Dixon, CA, 95620. p. 142
Gardner, Robert, Mgr, County of Los Angeles Public Library, Artesia Library, 18801 Elaine Ave, Artesia, CA, 90701. Tel: 562-865-6614. p. 135
Gardner, Sally, Librn, Wolcott Public Library, 46 Railroad St, Wolcott, VT, 05680. Tel: 802-888-8908. p. 2299
Gardner, Susan, Archives Librn, Tech Serv Librn, Island Free Library, Nine Dodge St, Block Island, RI, 02807. Tel: 401-466-3233. p. 2029
Gardner, Tom, Br Mgr, Public Library of Cincinnati & Hamilton County, Wyoming Branch, 500 Springfield Pike, Wyoming, OH, 45215. Tel: 513-369-6014. p. 1763
Gardner, Tyler, Libr Asst, Ref, Northfield Public Library, 210 Washington St, Northfield, MN, 55057. Tel: 507-645-6606. p. 1191
Gardner, Valerie, Dir, Hampton Public Library, 4207 Victoria Blvd, Hampton, VA, 23669-4243. Tel: 757-727-1154. p. 2322
Gardner-Sheets, Hazel, Libr Dir, McDonald County Library, 808 Bailey Rd, Pineville, MO, 64856. Tel: 417-223-4489. p. 1265
Gardner-Sheets, Hazel, Libr Dir, McDonald County Library, Anne Croxdale Memorial Library, 102 N Main St, Southwest City, MO, 64863. Tel: 417-762-7323. p. 1265
Gardner-Sheets, Hazel, Libr Dir, McDonald County Library, Noel Library, 626 Johnson Rd, Noel, MO, 64854. Tel: 417-475-3223. p. 1265
Gardocki, Kathleen, Libr Asst, Alvernia University, 400 St Bernardine St, Reading, PA, 19607-1737. Tel: 610-796-8223. p. 2000
Garewal, Kevin, Assoc Dir, Coll, Assoc Dir, Libr Admin, Harvard Library, Harvard Law School Library, Langdell Hall, 1545 Massachusetts Ave, Cambridge, MA, 02138. Tel: 617-495-3416, 617-495-3455. p. 1006
Garewal, Kevin, Dean of Libr, Vice Provost, Andrew H & Janet Dayton Neilly, University of Rochester, River Campus Libraries, 755 Library Rd, Rochester, NY, 14627-0055. Tel: 585-275-4461. p. 1631
Garey, Ann, Dir, Polk Public Library, 180 N Main St, Polk, NE, 68654. Tel: 402-765-7266. p. 1333
Garey, Anna, Librn, Preble County District Library, West Elkton Branch, Town Hall, 135 N Main St, West Elkton, OH, 45070. Tel: 937-787-4873. p. 1784
Gariepy, Kenneth, PhD, Dir, University of Alberta, 7-104 Education N, University of Alberta, Edmonton, AB, T6G 2G5, CANADA. Tel: 780-492-7625. p. 2795

Gario, Michelle, Ad, Seekonk Public Library, 410 Newman Ave, Seekonk, MA, 02771. Tel: 508-336-8230, Ext 56132. p. 1052

Garity, Betty, Head, Acq, Fordham University Libraries, 441 E Fordham Rd, Bronx, NY, 10458-5151. Tel: 718-817-3570. p. 1498

Garland, Joyce M, Dir, Calais Free Library, Nine Union St, Calais, ME, 04619. Tel: 207-454-2758. p. 920

Garland, Mercy, Ch, Chappaqua Public Library, 195 S Greeley Ave, Chappaqua, NY, 10514. Tel: 914-238-4779. p. 1516

Garland, Shelly, Tech Serv Coordr, Caldwell Public Library, 1010 Dearborn St, Caldwell, ID, 83605. Tel: 208-459-3242. p. 518

Garlets, Diane, Dir, Athens Community Library, 106 E Burr Oak St, Athens, MI, 49011-9793. Tel: 269-729-4479. p. 1081

Garlick, Molly, Head, Youth Serv, Charlton Public Library, 40 Main St, Charlton, MA, 01507. Tel: 508-248-0452. p. 1010

Garloch, Betsy, Syst Librn, Gannon University, 619 Sassafras St, Erie, PA, 16541. Tel: 814-871-7557. p. 1931

Garlock, Elizabeth, Dir, Middlesex Reading Center, 1216 Rte 245, Middlesex, NY, 14507. Tel: 585-554-6945, Option 7. p. 1571

Garm, Mary, Library Systems Admin, Scranton Public Library, Lackawanna County Children's Library, 520 Vine St, Scranton, PA, 18509-3298. Tel: 570-348-3000, Ext 3015. p. 2005

Garmer, Nancy, Asst Dean, Head, User Experience, Florida Institute of Technology, 150 W University Blvd, Melbourne, FL, 32901-6988. Tel: 321-674-7542. p. 420

Garmon, Ferlandez Alando, Librn, Department of Veterans Affairs Medical Center, 2002 Holcombe Blvd, Houston, TX, 77030. Tel: 713-794-1414, Ext 27856. p. 2191

Garms, Hila, Asst Librn, Elkader Public Library, 130 N Main St, Elkader, IA, 52043. Tel: 563-245-1446. p. 751

Garnar, Martin, Dir, Amherst College, 61 Quadrangle Dr, Amherst, MA, 01002. p. 984

Garneau, Manon, Libr Asst, National Theatre School of Canada Library, 5030 rue Saint-Denis, Montreal, QC, H2J 2L8, CANADA. Tel: 514-842-7954, Ext 147. p. 2727

Garner, Anne, Libr Dir, Wayne County Public Library, 157 Rolling Hills Blvd, Monticello, KY, 42633. Tel: 606-348-8565. p. 869

Garner, Carolyn, Ref Librn, Pamunkey Regional Library, 7527 Library Dr, Hanover, VA, 23069. Tel: 804-537-6211. p. 2323

Garner, Chereeka, Librn, Valencia College, Osceola Campus Library, Bldg 4, Rm 202, 1800 Denn John Lane, 6-4, Kissimmee, FL, 34744. Tel: 407-582-4155. p. 414

Garner, Chereeka, Librn, Valencia College, Raymer Maguire Jr Learning Resources Center, West Campus, 1800 S Kirkman Rd, Orlando, FL, 32811. Tel: 407-582-1210. p. 433

Garner, Colleen, Dir & Librn, Hemingford Public Library, 812 Box Butte Ave, Hemingford, NE, 69348. Tel: 308-487-3454. p. 1318

Garner, Donna, Head, Circ, Meredith College, 3800 Hillsborough St, Raleigh, NC, 27607-5298. Tel: 919-760-8532. p. 1708

Garner, Ivy, Librn, Johns Hopkins University Libraries, Adolf Meyer Library, 600 N Wolfe St, Baltimore, MD, 21205. Tel: 410-955-5819. p. 954

Garner, Jennifer, Libr Dir, North Liberty Library, 520 W Cherry St, North Liberty, IA, 52317-9797. Tel: 319-626-5701. p. 773

Garner, Jessica, Head, Access Serv, Georgia Southern University, 1400 Southern Dr, Statesboro, GA, 30458. Tel: 912-478-5115. p. 497

Garner, Jessica, Archivist, Spec Coll Librn, Lincoln University, 1570 Baltimore Pike, Lincoln University, PA, 19352. Tel: 484-365-7370. p. 1956

Garner, Joyce, Pres, Wilson County Historical Society Museum Library, 420 N Seventh St, Fredonia, KS, 66736-1315. Tel: 620-378-3965. p. 809

Garner, Kristina, Ch, Wallingford Public Library, 200 N Main St, Wallingford, CT, 06492. Tel: 203-284-6436. p. 343

Garner, Lyn C, Libr Dir, San Jacinto College North, 5800 Uvalde Rd, Houston, TX, 77049-4599. Tel: 281-459-7116. p. 2198

Garner, Mary, Librn, Tyringham Free Public Library, 118 Main Rd, Tyringham, MA, 01264-9700. Tel: 413-243-1373. p. 1060

Garner, Michael, Dir, Libr Serv, Midway University, 512 E Stephens St, Midway, KY, 40347-1120. Tel: 859-846-5316. p. 869

Garner, Nancy, Exec Dir, Jenkins Law Library, Ten Penn Ctr, 1801 Market St, Ste 900, Philadelphia, PA, 19103-6405. Tel: 215-574-7944. p. 1982

Garner, Nicole, Librn, Brunswick Community College Library, 50 College Rd, Supply, NC, 28462. Tel: 910-755-7331. p. 1718

Garner, Sharon, Asst Dir, Peotone Public Library District, 515 N First St, Peotone, IL, 60468. Tel: 708-258-3436. p. 635

Garner, Susan, Archivist, Roman Catholic Diocese of Amarillo, 4512 NE 24th Ave, Amarillo, TX, 79107-8225. Tel: 806-383-2243, Ext 120. p. 2134

Garner, Teresa, Libr Dir, Rogersville Public Library, 74 Bank St, Rogersville, AL, 35652. Tel: 256-247-0151. p. 35

Garner, Valerie Sue, Libr Dir, Silver City Public Library, 408 Main St, Silver City, IA, 51571. Tel: 712-525-9053. p. 782

Garnett, Abigail, Managing Librn, Brooklyn Public Library, Greenpoint, 107 Norman Ave, Brooklyn, NY, 11222. Tel: 718-349-8504. p. 1503

Garnett, Ann, Ref Serv, Garden City Public Library, 60 Seventh St, Garden City, NY, 11530. Tel: 516-742-8405. p. 1536

Garnett, Meg, Spec Coll Librn, Susquehanna University, 514 University Ave, Selinsgrove, PA, 17870-1050. Tel: 570-372-4327. p. 2005

Garnsey, Beth, Librn, Oakland Community College, Woodland Hall, 7350 Cooley Lake Rd, Waterford, MI, 48327-4187. Tel: 248-942-3128. p. 1157

Garofalo, Denise A, Syst & Cat Serv Librn, Mount Saint Mary College, 330 Powell Ave, Newburgh, NY, 12550-3494. Tel: 845-569-3519. p. 1605

Garr, Darin, Librn, California Department of Corrections Library System, Valley State Prison, 21633 Ave 24, Chowchilla, CA, 93610. Tel: 559-665-6100. p. 207

Garrard, Tami, Access Serv Mgr, University of Washington Libraries, Bothell Campus/Cascadia College Library, University of Washington Bothell, 18225 Campus Way NE, Box 358550, Bothell, WA, 98011-8245. Tel: 425-352-5340. p. 2381

Garred, Erin, Br Mgr, Glendale Public Library, Foothills, 19055 N 57th Ave, Glendale, AZ, 85308. Tel: 623-930-3847. p. 62

Garren, Jonathan, Outreach & Instructional Serv Librn, Coker University, 300 E College Ave, Hartsville, SC, 29550. Tel: 843-383-8126. p. 2063

Garrera, Joseph, Exec Dir, Lehigh County Historical Society, Lehigh Valley Heritage Museum, 432 W Walnut St, Allentown, PA, 18102. Tel: 610-435-1074, Ext 19. p. 1904

Garretson, Joy, Dir, Hocutt-Ellington Memorial Library, 100 S Church St, Clayton, NC, 27520. Tel: 919-553-5542. p. 1681

Garrett, Adam, Asst Dir, Syst, University of Washington Libraries, Health Sciences Library, T-334 Health Sciences Bldg, 1959 NE Pacific St, Box 357155, Seattle, WA, 98195-7155. Tel: 206-616-4142. p. 2382

Garrett, Amy, Head, Ref Serv, Stow-Munroe Falls Public Library, 3512 Darrow Rd, Stow, OH, 44224. Tel: 330-688-3295. p. 1822

Garrett, Angela S, Libr Dir, Flora Public Library, 216 N Main St, Flora, IL, 62839-1510. Tel: 618-517-4654. p. 588

Garrett, Brenda, Youth Spec, First Regional Library, Robert C Irwin Public Library, 1285 Kenny Hill Ave, Tunica, MS, 38676. Tel: 662-363-2162. p. 1220

Garrett, Castidy, Br Mgr, Grant Parish Library, Pollock Branch, 1316 Pine St, Pollock, LA, 71467. Tel: 318-765-9616. p. 887

Garrett, Cynthia D, Libr Mgr, Josey Health Sciences Library, Prisma Health Richland, Five Richland Medical Park, Columbia, SC, 29203. Tel: 803-434-6312. p. 2053

Garrett, Jennifer, Assoc Dir, Organizational Design, Culture & Talent, North Carolina State University Libraries, D H Hill Jr Library, Two Broughton Dr, Raleigh, NC, 27695. Tel: 919-515-7188. p. 1709

Garrett, Judy, Dir, Gentry County Library, 304 N Park St, Stanberry, MO, 64489. Tel: 660-783-2335. p. 1282

Garrett, Mary Beth, Ch, Alpine Public Library, 805 W Ave E, Alpine, TX, 79830. Tel: 432-837-2621. p. 2133

Garrett, Megan, Br Mgr, Mid-Continent Public Library, Lee's Summit Branch, 150 NW Oldham Pkwy, Lee's Summit, MO, 64081. Tel: 816-524-0567. p. 1250

Garrett, Nan, Libr Dir, Perry County Public Library, 104 College Ave, Linden, TN, 37096. Tel: 931-589-5011. p. 2109

Garrett, Penny, Libr Supvr, Lake Region Community College, 379 Belmont Rd, Laconia, NH, 03246. Tel: 603-524-3207, Ext 6794. p. 1370

Garrett, Thad, Head, Coll Mgt, Librn, Cosmos Club Library, 2121 Massachusetts Ave NW, Washington, DC, 20008. Tel: 202-939-1525. p. 363

Garringer, Mimi, Law Librn, Fayette County Law Library, 110 E Court St, Washington Court House, OH, 43160-1355. Tel: 740-335-3608. p. 1828

Garris, Suzanne, Ref Librn, McElroy, Deutsch, Mulvaney & Carpenter, LLP, 1300 Mt Kemble Ave, Morristown, NJ, 07962. Tel: 973-425-8810. p. 1421

Garrison, Amanda, Pub Serv Mgr, Saline County Public Library, 1800 Smithers Dr, Benton, AR, 72015. Tel: 501-778-4766. p. 90

Garrison, Betty L, Bus Res Librn, Elon University, 308 N O'Kelly Ave, Elon, NC, 27244-0187. Tel: 336-278-6600. p. 1688

Garrison, Heather, Libr Dir, Carbondale City Library, 302 Main St, Carbondale, KS, 66414-9635. Tel: 785-836-7638. p. 800

Garrison, Jan M, Ad, Rushville Public Library, 130 W Third St, Rushville, IN, 46173-1899. Tel: 765-932-3496. p. 717

Garrison, Joshua, Dr, Assoc Prof, Dept Chair, University of Wisconsin Oshkosh College of Education & Human Services, 800 Algoma Blvd, Oshkosh, WI, 54901. Tel: 920-424-0881. p. 2794

Garrison, Julie Ann, Dean, Univ Libr, Western Michigan University, 1903 W Michigan Ave, WMU Mail Stop 5353, Kalamazoo, MI, 49008-5353. Tel: 269-387-5059. p. 1122

Garrison, Kim, Prog Dir, Christ United Methodist Church Library, 4530 A St, Lincoln, NE, 68510. Tel: 402-489-9618. p. 1321

Garrison, Margie, Librn, Havelock-Craven County Public Library, 301 Cunningham Blvd, Havelock, NC, 28532. Tel: 252-447-7509. p. 1694

Garrison, Scott, Exec Dir, Midwest Collaborative for Library Services, 1407 Rensen St, Ste 1, Lansing, MI, 48910. p. 2767

Garrison, Susan, Library Contact, Womble, Bond Dickinson, One W Fourth St, Winston-Salem, NC, 27101. Tel: 336-721-3600, 336-747-4757. p. 1726

Garrison, Susan R, Access Serv Mgr, Rice University, 6100 Main, MS-44, Houston, TX, 77005. Tel: 713-348-2573. p. 2198

Garrison, William A, Dean, University of South Florida, Tampa Campus Library, 4101 USF Apple Dr, LIB122, Tampa, FL, 33620. Tel: 813-974-1642. p. 450

Garrity, Diane, Librn, Anderson, McPharlin & Conners LLP Library, 707 Wilshire Blvd #4000, Los Angeles, CA, 90017. Tel: 213-236-1677. p. 160

Garrity, Kate, Dir, Libr Serv, Friends Free Library of Germantown, 5418 Germantown Ave, Philadelphia, PA, 19144. Tel: 215-951-2355. p. 1980

Garrity, William, Chief of Staff, Dep Univ Librn, University of California, Davis, 100 NW Quad, Davis, CA, 95616. Tel: 530-752-8792. p. 134

Garro, Lisa, Dir, Heartland Regional Library System, Vienna Branch, 315 Third St, Vienna, MO, 65582. Tel: 573-422-9866. p. 1249

Garrod, Bruce, Head Librn, University of Toronto Libraries, Mathematical Sciences, Bahen Centre for Information Technology, 40 St George St, Rm 6141, Toronto, ON, M5S 1A1, CANADA. Tel: 416-978-8624. p. 2699

Garskof, Jeremy, Asst Dean, Dir, Commun & Tech Serv, Gettysburg College, 300 N Washington St, Gettysburg, PA, 17325. Tel: 717-337-6892. p. 1935

Garsvo, Eriks, Dir, Owyhee County Historical Society, 17085 Basey St, Murphy, ID, 83650. Tel: 208-495-2319. p. 527

Garten, Tonja, Dir, Van Zandt County Sarah Norman Library, 317 First Monday Lane, Canton, TX, 75103. Tel: 903-567-4276. p. 2152

Gartler, Marc, Br Supvr, Madison Public Library, Alicia Ashman Branch, 733 N High Point Rd, Madison, WI, 53717. Tel: 608-575-9361. p. 2449

Gartler, Marc, Br Supvr, Madison Public Library, Sequoya Branch, 4340 Tokay Blvd, Madison, WI, 53711. Tel: 608-266-6385. p. 2449

Gartner, Dorothy, Librn, SNC-Lavalin, Inc Library, 455 boul Rene-Levesque ouest, Montreal, QC, H2Z 1Z3, CANADA. Tel: 514-393-1000. p. 2728

Garton, Megan, Instruction Coordr, Ref Librn, Tulane University, Law Library, Weinmann Hall, 3rd Flr, 6329 Freret St, New Orleans, LA, 70118-6231. Tel: 504-865-5941. p. 904

Garud, Meera, Instr, Sch Libr Media Prog Coordr, University of Hawaii, 2550 McCarthy Mall, Hamilton Library, Rm 002, Honolulu, HI, 96822. Tel: 808-956-7321. p. 2784

Garver, Jane, Exec Dir, Little Traverse History Museum Library, 100 Depot Ct, Petoskey, MI, 49770. Tel: 231-347-2620. p. 1140

Garvey, Kathleen, Cataloging Assoc, The College of Wooster Libraries, 1140 Beall Ave, Wooster, OH, 44691-2364. Tel: 330-263-2093. p. 1833

Garvey, Martha, Head, Children's Servx, Baldwin Public Library, 2385 Grand Ave, Baldwin, NY, 11510-3289. Tel: 516-223-6228. p. 1490

Garvey, Muriel, Med Librn, Gaylord Hospital, Jackson Pavilion Ground Flr, 50 Gaylord Farm Rd, Wallingford, CT, 06492. Tel: 203-741-3481, p. 342

Garvey, Patricia, Mgr, Brookhaven National Laboratory, Research Library, Bldg 477, Upton, NY, 11973-5000. Tel: 631-344-6062. p. 1654

Garvey, Suzanne, Dir, Seymour Public Library, 46 Church St, Seymour, CT, 06483. Tel: 203-888-3903. p. 336

Garvin, Denise, Dir, Duxbury Free Library, 77 Alden St, Duxbury, MA, 02332. Tel: 781-934-2721. p. 1015

Garvin, Tom, Dir of Facilities & Security, Mount Prospect Public Library, Ten S Emerson St, Mount Prospect, IL, 60056. Tel: 847-253-5675. p. 621

Garvin, Virginia, Dir, Whitesboro Public Library, 308 W Main, Whitesboro, TX, 76273. Tel: 903-564-5432. p. 2257

Garvin, William, Dir, Univ Archivist, Drury University, 900 N Benton Ave, Springfield, MO, 65802. Tel: 417-873-7482. p. 1280

Garwood, Susan, Exec Dir, Rice County Historical Society, 1814 Second Ave NW, Faribault, MN, 55021. Tel: 507-332-2121. p. 1175

Gary, David, Assoc Dir, Coll, American Philosophical Society Library, 105 S Fifth St, Philadelphia, PA, 19106-3386. Tel: 215-440-3400. p. 1974

Garza, Blanca, Head, Ref, Elsa Public Library, 711 N Hidalgo St, Elsa, TX, 78543. Tel: 956-262-3061. p. 2175

Garza, Cat, Libr Assoc I, Texas A&M University-San Antonio, One University Way, San Antonio, TX, 78224. Tel: 210-784-1508. p. 2239

Garza, David, Librn, Los Angeles Mission College Library, 13356 Eldridge Ave, Sylmar, CA, 91342. Tel: 818-639-2221. p. 251

Garza, Debbie, Dir, Dawson County Library, 511 N Third St, Lamesa, TX, 79331. Tel: 806-872-6502. p. 2209

Garza, Debbie, Dir, Midland County Public Library, Midland Centennial, 2503 W Loop 250 N, Midland, TX, 79705. Tel: 432-742-7400. p. 2219

Garza, Debbie, Exec Dir, Midland County Public Library, 301 W Missouri Ave, Midland, TX, 79701. Tel: 432-688-4320. p. 2219

Garza Donnolly, Taelor, Mrs, Libr Dir, H J Nugen Public Library, 103 E Main St, New London, IA, 52645. Tel: 319-367-7704. p. 772

Garza, Jackie A, Libr Dir, Martin County Library, 200 N Saint Mary, Stanton, TX, 79782. Tel: 432-756-2472. p. 2245

Garza, Janie, Bus Mgr, Fort Bend County Libraries, 1001 Golfview Dr, Richmond, TX, 77469-5199. Tel: 281-633-4778. p. 2232

Garza, Javier F, Archivist, University of Texas, M D Anderson Cancer Center Research Medical Library, 1400 Pressler St, Houston, TX, 77030-3722. Tel: 713-792-2285. p. 2200

Garza, Laura, Librn, United States Navy, Bldg 1872, Midway St, Corpus Christi, TX, 78419. Tel: 361-961-3574. p. 2161

Garza, Lila, Libr Coord, Tolleson Public Library, 9555 W Van Buren St, Tolleson, AZ, 85353. Tel: 623-936-2746. p. 80

Garza, Mary, Circ Supvr, Temple Public Library, 100 W Adams Ave, Temple, TX, 76501-7641. Tel: 254-298-5555. p. 2247

Garza, Theresa, Librn, San Antonio Public Library, Thousand Oaks, 4618 Thousand Oaks, San Antonio, TX, 78233. Tel: 210-207-9190. p. 2239

Garzano, Maureen, Adult & Teen Serv Mgr, Roselle Public Library District, 40 S Park St, Roselle, IL, 60172-2020. Tel: 630-529-1641, Ext 212. p. 643

Garzillo, Robert, Tech Serv Librn, Rhode Island School of Design Library, 15 Westminster St, Providence, RI, 02903. Tel: 401-709-5944. p. 2040

Gascon, Kathy, Asst Librn, Watkins Glen Public Library, 610 S Decatur St, Watkins Glen, NY, 14891. Tel: 607-535-2346. p. 1660

Gaskell, Carolyn, Dir of Libr, Walla Walla University Libraries, 104 S College Ave, College Place, WA, 99324-1159. Tel: 509-527-2134. p. 2362

Gaskell, Millicent, Univ Librn, Villanova University, 800 Lancaster Ave, Villanova, PA, 19085. Tel: 610-519-4290. p. 2017

Gaskell, Tamara, Libr Dir, Roeliff Jansen Community Library, 9091 Rte 22, Hillsdale, NY, 12529. Tel: 518-325-4101. p. 1547

Gaskill, Jean, Dir, Surrey Township Public Library, 105 E Michigan, Farwell, MI, 48622. Tel: 989-588-9782. p. 1104

Gaskin, Christine, Dir, Southern Methodist College, 541 Broughton St, Orangeburg, SC, 29115. Tel: 803-534-7826, Ext 106. p. 2067

Gaskin, Kathleen, Head, Ad Ref Serv, Westbury Memorial Public Library, 445 Jefferson St, Westbury, NY, 11590. Tel: 516-333-0176. p. 1663

Gaskin-Noel, Susan, Ref & Instruction Librn, Webmaster, Mercy College Libraries, 555 Broadway, Dobbs Ferry, NY, 10522. Tel: 914-674-7672. p. 1526

Gaskins, Angela, Mgr, Chesapeake Public Library, Dr Clarence V Cuffee Library, 2726 Border Rd, Chesapeake, VA, 23324-3760. Tel: 757-410-7040. p. 2311

Gaskins, Michelle, Librn, Vanceboro Public Library, 7931 Main St, Vanceboro, NC, 28586. Tel: 252-244-0571. p. 1719

Gaskins, Paul, Circ, Cañada College Library, Bldg 9, 3rd Flr, 4200 Farm Hill Blvd, Redwood City, CA, 94061-1099. p. 200

Gaskins, Shun, Libr Mgr, Hog Hammock Public Library, 1023 Hillery Ln, Sapelo Island, GA, 31327. Tel: 912-485-2291. p. 495

Gaspard, Rusty, Instruction & Ref Librn, Louisiana State University at Alexandria, 8100 Hwy 71 S, Alexandria, LA, 71302. Tel: 318-473-6443. p. 879

Gaspari Bridges, Patty, Asst Univ Librn, Coll Develop, Princeton University, One Washington Rd, Princeton, NJ, 08544-2098. Tel: 609-258-5483. p. 1437

Gasper, Ariel, Asst Librn, United States Marine Corps, Library Services, Bldg 1146, Camp Pendleton, CA, 92055. Tel: 760-725-5104, 760-725-5669. p. 126

Gasper, Johanna, Libr Tech, Minnesota Department of Corrections, 7600 - 525th St, Rush City, MN, 55069. Tel: 320-358-0400, Ext 373. p. 1195

Gasper, Leslie, Info/Res Spec, Shook, Hardy & Bacon, 2555 Grand Blvd, 3rd Flr, Kansas City, MO, 64108-2613. Tel: 816-474-6550. p. 1257

Gass, Greg, Pres, Cherry County Historical Society Archives, PO Box 284, Valentine, NE, 69201-0284. Tel: 402-376-2015. p. 1339

Gassaway, Sara, Dir, Staff Develop, Southeast Florida Library Information Network, Inc, Florida Atlantic University, Wimberly Library, Office 452, 777 Glades Rd, Boca Raton, FL, 33431. Tel: 561-208-0984. p. 2763

Gasser, Maxine, Youth Serv, Amherst County Public Library, 382 S Main St, Amherst, VA, 24521. Tel: 434-946-9488. p. 2304

Gast, Cari A, Head, Children's & Teen Curric, Howard County Library System, 9411 Frederick Rd, Ellicott City, MD, 21042. Tel: 410-313-7750. p. 965

Gast, Chris, Pub Relations, Right to Life of Michigan, 233 N Walnut St, Lansing, MI, 48933-1121. Tel: 517-487-3376. p. 1125

Gaston, Betty Jo, Librn, Saint Petersburg College, Saint Petersburg-Gibbs Campus Library, 6605 Fifth Ave N, Saint Petersburg, FL, 33710. Tel: 727-341-7179. p. 438

Gaston, Janet, Library Contact, Julie Thomas Memorial Library, 108 Main St, Morganville, KS, 67468. p. 826

Gaston, Susanna, Asst Dir, Jackson County Public Library System, 2929 Green St, Marianna, FL, 32446. Tel: 850-482-9631. p. 420

Gastonguay, Nicole, Documentation Tech, Musee national des beaux-arts du Quebec Bibliotheque, Parc des Champs-de-Bataille, Quebec, QC, G1R 5H3, CANADA. Tel: 418-644-6460. p. 2731

Gatbonton, Arielle, Libr Tech, FPInnovations, 570 Blvd St-Jean, Pointe-Claire, QC, H9R 3J9, CANADA. Tel: 514-630-4100, Option 9. p. 2729

Gateley, Steve, Librn, Southern Baptist Historical Library & Archives, 901 Commerce St, Ste 400, Nashville, TN, 37203-3630. Tel: 615-244-0344. p. 2120

Gates, Amanda, Librn, Centralia Correctional Center Library, 9330 Shattuc Rd, Centralia, IL, 62801. Tel: 618-533-4111. p. 551

Gates, Andrew, Library & Research Mgr, Tucker Ellis LLP, 950 Main Ave, Ste 1100, Cleveland, OH, 44113-7213. Tel: 216-592-5000. p. 1770

Gates, Anitra, Mgr, Tech Serv, Erie County Public Library, 160 E Front St, Erie, PA, 16507. Tel: 814-451-6919. p. 1931

Gates, Beth, Reference Dept Supervisor, Rogers Memorial Library, 91 Coopers Farm Rd, Southampton, NY, 11968. Tel: 631-283-0774. p. 1643

Gates, Christine, Libr Dir, Hamlin Public Library, 1680 Lake Rd, Hamlin, NY, 14464. Tel: 585-964-2320. p. 1543

Gates, Crystal, Dir, William F Laman Public Library, 2801 Orange St, North Little Rock, AR, 72114-2296. Tel: 501-758-1720. p. 106

Gates, Jeffery, Info Serv Librn, Cedarville University, 251 N Main St, Cedarville, OH, 45314-0601. Tel: 937-766-7840. p. 1757

Gates, Lynn, Dir, Cat, Metadata Serv, University of Colorado Colorado Springs, 1420 Austin Bluffs Pkwy, Colorado Springs, CO, 80918. Tel: 719-255-3289. p. 272

Gates, Nayru, Librn, Nunavut Public Library Services, Amitturmiut Library, PO Box 30, Igloolik, NU, X0A 0L0, CANADA. Tel: 867-934-8153. p. 2625

Gathegi, John, Dr, Prof, University of South Florida, 4202 Fowler Ave, CIS 1040, Tampa, FL, 33620-7800. Tel: 813-974-5322. p. 2783

Gathercole, Erin, Sr Librn, New Hanover County Public Library, Pine Valley, 3802 S College Rd, Wilmington, NC, 28412. Tel: 910-798-6342. p. 1723

Gathu, Evelyn, Dir, Crystal Falls District Community Library, 237 Superior Ave, Crystal Falls, MI, 49920-1331. Tel: 906-875-3344. p. 1095

Gatlabayan, Mariecris, Archivist, University of Alaska Anchorage, Consortium Library, 3211 Providence Dr, Anchorage, AK, 99508-8176. Tel: 907-786-1871. p. 43

Gatley, Randy, Br Head, Vancouver Public Library, Britannia Branch, 1661 Napier St, Vancouver, BC, V5L 4X4, CANADA. Tel: 604-665-2222. p. 2581

Gatley, Randy, Br Head, Vancouver Public Library, neca?mat ct Strathcona, 730 E Hastings St, Vancouver, BC, V6A 1V5, CANADA. Tel: 604-665-3967. p. 2582

Gatlin, Mark, Librn, Inyo County Free Library, Furnace Creek, 201 Nevares, Death Valley, CA, 92328. Tel: 760-786-2408. p. 152

Gatson, Gwen, Cataloger, Tech Asst, The Edward Waters College Library, 1658 Kings Rd, Jacksonville, FL, 32209-6199. Tel: 904-470-8083. p. 411

Gatten, Katie, Youth Serv Coordr, Mansfield-Richland County Public Library, 43 W Third St, Mansfield, OH, 44902-1295. Tel: 419-521-3148. p. 1798

Gatter, Elizabeth, Head, Cat & Coll Mgt, Wallingford Public Library, 200 N Main St, Wallingford, CT, 06492. Tel: 203-284-6427. p. 342

Gatti, Timothy, Senior Library Operations Mgr, Bryan Cave Leighton Paisner LLP, One Metropolitan Sq, 211 N Broadway, Ste 3600, Saint Louis, MO, 63102-2750. Tel: 314-259-2298. p. 1269

Gatton, Tim, Head, Ref, Oklahoma City University, School of Law Library, 2501 N Blackwelder, Oklahoma City, OK, 73106. Tel: 405-208-5271. p. 1858

Gatzek, Rosemarie, Dir, Irvington Public Library, 12 S Astor St, Irvington, NY, 10533. Tel: 914-591-7840. p. 1550

Gatzke, Heidi, Lead Librn, Muskegon Area District Library, Holton Branch, 8776 Holton Duck Lake Rd, Holton, MI, 49425. Tel: 231-821-0268. p. 1136

Gatzke, Heidi, Lead Librn, Muskegon Area District Library, Montague Branch, 8778 Ferry St, Montague, MI, 49437-1233. Tel: 231-893-2675. p. 1136

Gatzke, Jeanine, Head, Metadata Serv, Head, Tech Serv, Concordia University, 1282 Concordia Ave, Saint Paul, MN, 55104. Tel: 651-641-8242. p. 1199

Gaud, Connie, Circ Mgr, Rogers Memorial Library, 91 Coopers Farm Rd, Southampton, NY, 11968. Tel: 631-283-0774. p. 1643

Gauder, Heidi, Coordr, Instruction & Ref, University of Dayton Libraries, 300 College Park Dr, Dayton, OH, 45469. Tel: 937-229-4259. p. 1780

Gaudet, Kathleen, Outreach Librn, Legislative Library of New Brunswick, Legislative Assembly Bldg, Centre Block, 706 Queen St, Fredericton, NB, E3B 5H1, CANADA. Tel: 506-453-2338. p. 2601

Gaudet, Katina, Br Librn, Lafourche Parish Public Library, Golden Meadow Branch Biblioteca Hispana Branch, 1403 N Bayou Dr, Golden Meadow, LA, 70357-2513. Tel: 985-475-5660. p. 911

Gaudet, Lauri, Libr Asst, Gale Library, 16 S Main St, Newton, NH, 03858. Tel: 603-382-4691. p. 1376

Gaudet, Lisette, Archivist, Yarmouth County Museum & Archives, 22 Collins St, Yarmouth, NS, B5A 3C8, CANADA. Tel: 902-742-5539. p. 2624

Gaudet, Lison, Libr Mgr, Chaleur Library Region, Lamèque Public Library, 46 du Pêcheur N St, Lameque, NB, E8T 1J3, CANADA. Tel: 506-344-3262. p. 2599

Gaudette, Abigael, Dir, Swanton Public Library, One First St, Swanton, VT, 05488. Tel: 802-868-7656. p. 2296

Gaudette, Beckley, Libr Dir, Moore Free Library, 23 West St, Newfane, VT, 05345. Tel: 802-365-7948. p. 2290

Gaudette, Louise, Br Head, Timmins Public Library, C M Shields Centennial Branch, 99 Bloor Ave, South Porcupine, ON, P0N 1H0, CANADA. Tel: 705-360-2623, Ext 8590. p. 2686

Gaudin, Kytara, Head, Access Serv, State Library of Louisiana, 701 N Fourth St, Baton Rouge, LA, 70802-5232. Tel: 225-342-4920. p. 885

Gaudio-Hint, Laura, Libr Mgr, Weil, Gotshal & Manges LLP, 2001 M St NW, Ste 600, Washington, DC, 20036. Tel: 202-682-7000, 202-682-7117. p. 381

Gaudreau, Josee, Prof, Cégep Garneau, 1660 blvd de l'Entente, Quebec, QC, G1S 4S3, CANADA. Tel: 418-688-8310, Ext 2290. p. 2796

Gaudreau, Luke, Head, Libr Syst & Applications, Boston College Libraries, Thomas P O'Neill Jr Library (Main Library), 140 Commonwealth Ave, Chestnut Hill, MA, 02467. Tel: 617-552-6361. p. 1011

Gauerke, Debbie, Br Coordr, Marathon County Public Library, Edgar Branch, 224 S Third Ave, Edgar, WI, 54426. Tel: 715-352-3155. p. 2485

Gaughan, Marion, Libr Dir, Oskaloosa Public Library, 301 S Market St, Oskaloosa, IA, 52577. Tel: 641-673-0441. p. 775

Gaulrapp, Brittany, Dir, Lena Community District Library, 300 W Mason St, Lena, IL, 61048. Tel: 815-369-3180. p. 608

Gault, Anna, Tech Serv Librn, Supreme Court of Ohio, 65 S Front St, 11th Flr, Columbus, OH, 43215-3431. Tel: 614-387-9654. p. 1777

Gault, Elizabeth, Ref Librn, Lone Star College System, Tomball College Library, 30555 Tomball Pkwy, Tomball, TX, 77375-4036. Tel: 832-559-4206. p. 2197

Gault, Rachel, Librn, Southern Technical College, Sanford Campus, 2910 S Orlando Dr, Sanford, FL, 32773. Tel: 407-323-4141. p. 404

Gault, Sarah, Youth Serv Coordr, Buchanan District Library, 128 E Front St, Buchanan, MI, 49107. Tel: 269-695-3681. p. 1087

Gaus, Melissa, Circ Serv Librn, Delta Township District Library, 5130 Davenport Dr, Lansing, MI, 48917-2040. Tel: 517-321-4014. p. 1124

Gaut, Nancy, Br Mgr, Warren-Trumbull County Public Library, Brookfield Branch, 7032 Grove St, Brookfield, OH, 44403. Tel: 330-448-8134. p. 1828

Gauthier, Amélie, Libr Tech, Cegep Regional de Lanaudiere a Joliette, 20, rue Saint-Charles-Borromee Sud, Joliette, QC, J6E 4T1, CANADA. Tel: 450-759-1661. p. 2713

Gauthier, Annie, Libr Tech, Bibliotheque Municipale de Sainte-Anne-de-Bellevue, 40, rue Saint-Pierre, Sainte-Anne-de-Bellevue, QC, H9X 1Y6, CANADA. Tel: 514-457-1940. p. 2734

Gauthier, Barbara, Circ, Magee Public Library, 120 First St NW, Magee, MS, 39111. Tel: 601-849-3747. p. 1225

Gauthier, Ian, Ch, Aldrich Public Library, Six Washington St, Barre, VT, 05641. Tel: 802-476-7550. p. 2278

Gauthier, Ida, Librn, Beauval Public Library, Valley View School Library, Laliberte St, Beauval, SK, S0M 0G0, CANADA. Tel: 306-288-2022, Ext 3316. p. 2741

Gauthier, Stéphane G, Bibliothecaire Responsable, Bibliotheques de Montreal, Interculturelle, 6767 chemin de la Cote-des-Neiges, Montreal, QC, H3S 2T6, CANADA. Tel: 514-872-7367. p. 2719

Gautier, Lucienne, Head Librn, Harrison County Library System, Jerry Lawrence Memorial Library, 10391 AutoMall Pkwy, D'Iberville, MS, 39540. Tel: 228-392-2279. p. 1217

Gauvreau, Christine, LSTA Coordr, Connecticut State Library, Middletown Library Service Center, 786 S Main St, Middletown, CT, 06457. Tel: 860-704-2224. p. 317

Gauvreau, Nicole, Youth Serv, Pease Public Library, One Russell St, Plymouth, NH, 03264-1414. Tel: 603-536-2616. p. 1378

Gavaris, Eva, Campus Librn, Okanagan College Library, Penticton Campus, 583 Duncan Ave W, Penticton, BC, V2A 8E1, CANADA. Tel: 250-490-3951. p. 2568

Gavigan, Karen W, PhD, Interim Dir, University of South Carolina, 1501 Greene St, Columbia, SC, 29208. Tel: 803-777-3858. p. 2792

Gavin, Erin, Coll Asst, Science History Institute Museum & Library, 315 Chestnut St, Philadelphia, PA, 19106. Tel: 215-873-8205. p. 1985

Gavin, Jessica, Ref Librn, Trocaire College Library, 360 Choate Ave, Buffalo, NY, 14220-2094. Tel: 716-827-2434. p. 1510

Gavin, Lauren, Tech Serv, LIM College Library, 216 E 45th St, 2nd Flr, New York, NY, 10017. Tel: 646-218-4126. p. 1590

Gavin, Laurence, Dir, Fayetteville Technical Community College, 2201 Hull Rd, Fayetteville, NC, 28303. Tel: 910-678-8382. p. 1689

Gavriel, Olivia, Circ Librn, Georgetown Peabody Library, Two Maple St, Georgetown, MA, 01833. Tel: 978-352-5728. p. 1020

Gaw, Galena, Dir, South Carolina School for the Deaf & the Blind, 355 Cedar Springs Rd, Spartanburg, SC, 29302-4699. Tel: 864-577-7642, 864-585-7711. p. 2069

Gawdyda, Lori, Librn, Mercy Health Saint Elizabeth Health Center, 1044 Belmont Ave, Youngstown, OH, 44501-1790. Tel: 330-480-3589. p. 1835

Gawel, Diane, Br Supvr, Western Manitoba Regional Library, Carberry-North Cypress Branch, 115 Main St, Carberry, MB, R0K 0H0, CANADA. Tel: 204-834-3043. p. 2586

Gawletz, Cari Lynn, Libr Dir, Grand Forks & District Public Library, 7342 Fifth St, Grand Forks, BC, V0H 1H0, CANADA. Tel: 250-442-3944. p. 2566

Gawu, Helena S, Dean, Libr Serv, Lamar State College, 317 Stilwell Blvd, Port Arthur, TX, 77640. Tel: 409-984-6216. p. 2228

Gay, Brenda, Ser Librn, Montgomery County Public Library, 328 N Maysville Rd, Mount Sterling, KY, 40353. Tel: 859-498-2404. p. 870

Gay, Bruce, Dir, Waukesha Public Library, 321 Wisconsin Ave, Waukesha, WI, 53186-4713. Tel: 262-524-3681. p. 2484

Gay, Dona, Dir, Payson City Library, 66 S Main St, Payson, UT, 84651-2223. Tel: 801-465-5220. p. 2269

Gay, Jessica, Circ/Per, Outreach Serv, Gallatin County Public Library, 209 W Market St, Warsaw, KY, 41095. Tel: 859-567-2786. p. 876

Geisinger, Amy, District Consult Librn, New Castle Public Library, 207 E North St, New Castle, PA, 16101-3691. Tel: 724-658-6659, Ext 124. p. 1969
Geisinger, Christi, Circ, ILL, Manchester Community College Library, Great Path, Manchester, CT, 06040. Tel: 860-512-2880. p. 320
Geisser, Gail, Access Serv Mgr, Rhode Island School of Design Library, 15 Westminster St, Providence, RI, 02903. Tel: 401-709-5900. p. 2040
Geist, Melissa, Tech Coordr, Southeast Kansas Library System, 218 E Madison Ave, Iola, KS, 66749. Tel: 620-365-5136. p. 815
Geitz, Stefanie, Dir, Mount Hope-Funks Grove Townships Library District, 111 S Hamilton St, McLean, IL, 61754-7624. Tel: 309-874-2291. p. 616
Gelb, Stephanie, Librn, Congregation Beth Shalom, 3433 Walters Ave, Northbrook, IL, 60062-3298. Tel: 847-478-4100, Ext 13. p. 626
Geldmacher, Bonnie, Acq, Brigham Young University, Howard W Hunter Law Library, 256 JRCB, Provo, UT, 84602-8000. Tel: 801-422-3593. p. 2269
Geleskie, Bethany, Law Librn, Kent County Law Library, Kent County Courthouse, 38 The Green, Ste 100, Dover, DE, 19901. Tel: 302-674-7470. p. 352
Geller, Linda, Ref (Info Servs), Governors State University Library, One University Pkwy, University Park, IL, 60466-0975. Tel: 708-534-4136. p. 655
Gellerman, Shane, Br Librn, Boston Public Library, Jamaica Plain Branch, 30 Main St, Jamaica Plain, MA, 02130. Tel: 617-524-2053. p. 992
Gellert, Candy, Bus Mgr, Parkland Regional Library-Saskatchewan, Hwy 52 W, Yorkton, SK, S3N 3Z4, CANADA. Tel: 306-783-7022. p. 2755
Gelles, Karen, Dir, Farmingdale State College of New York, 2350 Broadhollow Rd, Farmingdale, NY, 11735-1021. Tel: 934-420-2040. p. 1532
Gellner, Brenda, Ch Serv, Parkersburg & Wood County Public Library, 3100 Emerson Ave, Parkersburg, WV, 26104-2414. Tel: 304-420-4587, Ext 510. p. 2411
Gellvear, Marla, Librn, Palliser Regional Library, Rouleau Branch, 113 Main St, Rouleau, SK, S0G 4H0, CANADA. Tel: 306-776-2322. p. 2743
Gelman, Kara, Ref Librn, Latham & Watkins, 12670 High Bluff Dr, San Diego, CA, 92130. Tel: 858-523-5400. p. 215
Gelskey, LeAnn, Prog Supvr, Idaho Commission for Libraries, 325 W State St, Boise, ID, 83702-6072. Tel: 208-639-4148. p. 517
Gembe, Joanne, Librn, North Central Washington Libraries, Leavenworth Public Library, 700 Hwy 2, Leavenworth, WA, 98826. Tel: 509-548-7923. p. 2394
Gemmell, Cynthia, Dir, Manchester-by-the-Sea Public Library, 15 Union St, Manchester-by-the-Sea, MA, 01944. Tel: 978-526-7711. p. 1031
Genack Eggli, Chelsea, Literacy Coordr, Oceanside Public Library, READS Literacy Center, 804 Pier View Way, Ste 101, Oceanside, CA, 92054. Tel: 760-435-5682. p. 187
Genardo, Patricia, Dir, National University of Health Sciences Learning Resource Center, 200 E Roosevelt Rd, Bldg C, Lombard, IL, 60148-4583. Tel: 630-889-6612. p. 611
Gendill, Patty, Libr Supvr, Westminster Public Library, Irving Street, 7392 Irving St, Westminster, CO, 80030. Tel: 303-658-2325. p. 298
Gendreau, Debrah, Circ Librn, Jacob Edwards Library, 236 Main St, Southbridge, MA, 01550-2598. Tel: 508-764-5426, Ext 103. p. 1055
Gendreau, Elizabeth, Ch, Jacob Edwards Library, 236 Main St, Southbridge, MA, 01550-2598. Tel: 508-764-5427. p. 1055
Gendron, Heather, Dir, Yale University Library, Robert B Haas Family Arts Library, Loria Ctr, 180 York St, New Haven, CT, 06511. Tel: 203-432-2642. p. 328
Gendron, Joyce, Dir, Waldron District Library, 107 N Main St, Waldron, MI, 49288. Tel: 517-286-6511. p. 1156
Generoux, Jessica, Libr Tech, Saskatchewan Indian Cultural Centre, 305-2555 Grasswood Rd E, Saskatoon, SK, S7T 0K1, CANADA. Tel: 306-244-1146. p. 2749
Genest, France, Chef de Section, Bibliotheques de Montreal, Marc-Favreau, 500 Blvd Rosemont, Montreal, QC, H2S 1Z3, CANADA. Tel: 514-872-8231. p. 2719
Genett, Johannah, Div Mgr, Res Serv, Hennepin County Library, 12601 Ridgedale Dr, Minnetonka, MN, 55305-1909. Tel: 612-543-8639. p. 1186
Geng, Zhong Ming, Electronic Res & Syst Librn, Marywood University Library & Learning Commons, 2300 Adams Ave, Scranton, PA, 18509. Tel: 570-961-4707. p. 2004
Gengler, Matthew, Head, Access Serv, Cleveland Museum of Art, 11150 East Blvd, Cleveland, OH, 44106-1797. Tel: 216-707-2530. p. 1767
Gengler, Tom, Coll, Spertus Institute of Jewish Studies, 610 S Michigan Ave, Chicago, IL, 60605. Tel: 312-322-1712. p. 568
Gennest, Tammy, Circ Chief, Rockland Memorial Library, 20 Belmont St, Rockland, MA, 02370-2232. Tel: 781-878-1236. p. 1049
Genovese, Chiara, Adult Serv, Charlotte Community Library, 226 S Bostwick St, Charlotte, MI, 48813-1801. Tel: 517-543-8859. p. 1090
Genovese, Salvatore, Dir, Walpole Public Library, 143 School St, Walpole, MA, 02081. Tel: 508-660-7334. p. 1061
Genter, Justin, Syst Coordr, Nioga Library System, 6575 Wheeler Rd, Lockport, NY, 14094. Tel: 716-434-6167, Ext 11. p. 1564
Gentile, Linda, Head, Tech Serv, Gloucester County Library System, 389 Wolfert Station Rd, Mullica Hill, NJ, 08062. Tel: 856-223-6013. p. 1423
Gentile-Jordan, Angie, Information Technologist, Central Minnesota Libraries Exchange, 570 First St SE, Saint Cloud, MN, 56304. Tel: 320-257-1933. p. 2768
Gentili, Joseph, Librn, Archbold Biological Station Library, 123 Main Dr, Venus, FL, 33960. Tel: 863-465-2571. p. 452
Gentis, Mary Lou, Br Mgr, Muncie Public Library, 2005 S High St, Muncie, IN, 47302. Tel: 765-747-8200. p. 708
Gentle, Sara, Dir, Maroa Public Library District, 305 E Garfield St, Maroa, IL, 61756. Tel: 217-794-5111. p. 614
Gentry, Jana, Mgr, West Georgia Regional Library, Buchanan-Haralson Public Library, 145 Van Wert St, Buchanan, GA, 30113. Tel: 770-646-3369. p. 469
Gentry, John C, Asst Dept Director for Operations, Henrico County Public Library, 1700 N Parham Rd, Henrico, VA, 23229. Tel: 804-501-1900. p. 2325
Gentry, Kayce, Libr Dir, La Crescent Public Library, 321 Main St, La Crescent, MN, 55947. Tel: 507-895-4047. p. 1179
Gentry, Luke, Br Mgr, Vigo County Public Library, West Terre Haute Branch, 125 N Church St, West Terre Haute, IN, 47885. Tel: 812-232-1113, Ext 3001. p. 721
Gentry, Treva, Libr Asst, Mary Gilkey City Library, 416 Ferry St, Dayton, OR, 97114-9774. Tel: 503-864-2221. p. 1877
Genuardi, Carmen, Librn, Sunnybrook Health Sciences Centre - Library Services, Holland Orthopaedic & Arthritic Centre, 43 Wellesley St E, Toronto, ON, M4Y 1H1, CANADA. Tel: 416-967-8545. p. 2693
Genz, Marcella, PhD, Dir, Charles Town Library, Inc, 200 E Washington St, Charles Town, WV, 25414. Tel: 304-725-2208. p. 2399
Geoffino, Tom, Dir, New Rochelle Public Library, One Library Plaza, New Rochelle, NY, 10801. Tel: 914-632-7879. p. 1577
Geoffrey, Maureen, Acq Librn, Chicopee Public Library, 449 Front St, Chicopee, MA, 01013. Tel: 413-594-1800. p. 1011
Georgas, Helen, Info Serv Librn, Brooklyn College Library, 2900 Bedford Ave, Brooklyn, NY, 11210. Tel: 718-758-8207. p. 1501
George, Amber, Br Librn, Sweetwater County Library System, Superior Branch Library, Three N Main, Superior, WY, 82945. Tel: 307-352-6671. p. 2495
George, Barb, Dir, Clyde Public Library, 107 S Green St, Clyde, KS, 66938. Tel: 785-446-3563. p. 802
George, Becky, Mgr, E-Serv, Georgina Public Library, Peter Gzowski Branch, 5279 Black River Rd, Sutton, ON, L0E 1R0, CANADA. Tel: 905-722-5702. p. 2649
George, Chrissy, Dir, Middlesex Public Library, 1300 Mountain Ave, Middlesex, NJ, 08846. Tel: 732-356-6602. p. 1418
George, Ciri, Dir, White City Public Library, 111 E Mackenzie, White City, KS, 66872. Tel: 785-349-5551. p. 842
George, Deborah, Dir, Libr Serv, Gwinnett Technical College Library, 5150 Sugarloaf Pkwy, Lawrenceville, GA, 30043. Tel: 770-962-7580, Ext 6650. p. 485
George, Elisia, Libr Dir, United States Army Medical Research Institute of Chemical Defense, 8350 Ricketts Point Rd, Aberdeen Proving Ground, MD, 21010. Tel: 410-436-4135. p. 949
George, Elizabeth, Young People's Librn, Walla Walla Public Library, 238 E Alder St, Walla Walla, WA, 99362. Tel: 509-524-4431. p. 2392
George, Jessica, Ch Serv, East Greenwich Free Library, 82 Peirce St, East Greenwich, RI, 02818. Tel: 401-884-9510. p. 2031
George, Jessica, Ch Serv, Youth Serv, Dorothy Alling Memorial Library, 21 Library Lane, Williston, VT, 05495. Tel: 802-878-4918. p. 2299
George, Jon, Tech Serv, River Falls Public Library, 140 Union St, River Falls, WI, 54022. Tel: 715-425-0905, Ext 3497. p. 2474
George, Julie, Dean of Libr, Eastern Kentucky University Libraries, 103 Crabbe Library, 521 Lancaster Ave, Richmond, KY, 40475. Tel: 859-622-1778. p. 873
George, Kathy, Ch, Gray Public Library, Five Hancock St, Gray, ME, 04039. Tel: 207-657-4110. p. 926
George, Kathy, Librn, Huffman Memorial United Methodist Church Library, 2802 Renick St, Saint Joseph, MO, 64507-1897. Tel: 816-232-7809. p. 1268
George, Marisa, Libr Serv Coordr, Great River Regional Library, Bryant Library, 430 Main St, Unit 1, Sauk Centre, MN, 56378. Tel: 320-352-3016. p. 1196
George, Mary, Dir, Libr Serv, Placer County Law Library, 1523 Lincoln Way, Auburn, CA, 95603. Tel: 530-557-2078. p. 118
George, Mary L, Dir, Libr Serv, Placer County Library, 145 Fulweiler Ave, Ste 150, Auburn, CA, 95603. Tel: 530-886-4550. p. 118
George, Maryjo, Libr Mgr, Wake County Public Library System, Holly Springs Community Library, 300 W Ballentine St, Holly Springs, NC, 27540. Tel: 919-577-1660. p. 1711
George, Nancy, Electronic Res Librn, Salem State University, 352 Lafayette St, Salem, MA, 01970-5353. Tel: 978-542-7182. p. 1051
George, Regina, Libr Dir, Covington-Veedersburg Public Library, 622 Fifth St, Covington, IN, 47932. Tel: 765-793-2572. p. 677
George, Regina, Libr Dir, Covington-Veedersburg Public Library, Veedersburg Public, 408 N Main St, Veedersburg, IN, 47987. Tel: 765-294-2808. p. 677

George, Sandy, Library Contact, Korn Ferry Research Library, Willis Tower, Ste 700, 233 S Wacker Dr, Chicago, IL, 60606. Tel: 312-466-1834. p. 563

George, Stephanie, Br Head, Winnipeg Public Library, St James-Assiniboia, 1910 Portage Ave, Winnipeg, MB, R3J 0J2, CANADA. Tel: 204-806-1072. p. 2596

George, Steven, Br Mgr, Jackson District Library, Eastern Branch, 3125 E Michigan Ave, Jackson, MI, 49201. Tel: 517-788-4074. p. 1120

Georgeff, Angie, Dir, Unicoi County Public Library, 201 Nolichucky Ave, Erwin, TN, 37650. Tel: 423-743-6533. p. 2098

Georger, Rachelle, Dir, The Scripps Research Institute, 10550 N Torrey Pines Rd, La Jolla, CA, 92037. Tel: 858-784-8705. p. 154

Georgetti, Michelle, Ad, Valley Community Library, 739 River St, Peckville, PA, 18452. Tel: 570-489-1765. p. 1974

Georgulis, Elise, Grad & Distance Educ, Delaware Valley University, 700 E Butler Ave, Doylestown, PA, 18901-2699. Tel: 215-489-2386. p. 1927

Gepner, Mary Kathryn, Dir, Mount Ayr Public Library, 121 W Monroe St, Mount Ayr, IA, 50854. Tel: 641-464-2159. p. 771

Geraci, Gail, Circ Supvr, Safety Harbor Public Library, 101 Second St N, Safety Harbor, FL, 34695. Tel: 727-724-1525. p. 439

Geragotelis, Mary, Dir, Scotland Public Library, 21 Brook Rd, Scotland, CT, 06264. Tel: 860-423-1492. p. 336

Gerald, Ann, Asst Dir, Bridgewater Public Library, 15 South St, Bridgewater, MA, 02324. Tel: 508-697-3331. p. 1002

Geralds, Robin, Libr Dir, Marissa Area Public Library District, 212 N Main St, Marissa, IL, 62257. Tel: 618-295-2825. p. 614

Gerami-Markham, Jenny, Br Serv Mgr, Catawba County Library, Sherrills Ford-Terrell Branch, 9154 Sherrills Ford Rd, Terrell, NC, 28682. Tel: 828-466-6827. p. 1706

Geran, Jennifer, Br Mgr, San Diego Public Library, City Heights/Weingart, 3795 Fairmount Ave, San Diego, CA, 92105. Tel: 619-641-6100. p. 219

Gerard, Gina, Head, Adult Serv, Louis Bay 2nd Library, 345 Lafayette Ave, Hawthorne, NJ, 07506-2546. Tel: 973-427-5745, Ext 19. p. 1407

Gerber, Andrew, Librn, Centrastate Healthcare System Library, 901 W Main St, Freehold, NJ, 07728. Tel: 732-294-2668. p. 1404

Gerber, Andrew, YA Librn, North Brunswick Free Public Library, 880 Hermann Rd, North Brunswick, NJ, 08902. Tel: 732-246-3545. p. 1429

Gerber, Jen, Dir, Shorewood Public Library, 3920 N Murray Ave, Shorewood, WI, 53211-2385. Tel: 414-847-2670. p. 2477

Gerdes, Catherine, Asst Univ Librn, Admin Serv, Financial Serv, University of North Carolina at Chapel Hill, 208 Raleigh St, CB 3916, Chapel Hill, NC, 27515. Tel: 919-962-1053. p. 1678

Gere, Gus, Asst Librn, Palliser Regional Library, Assiniboia & District Public Library, 201 Third Ave W, Assiniboia, SK, S0H 0B0, CANADA. Tel: 306-642-3631. p. 2742

Geremia, Cynthia, Dir, PURDUE PHARMA LP, One Stamford Forum, 201 Tresser Blvd, Stamford, CT, 06901. Tel: 203-588-7267. p. 338

Geremia, Gina Mucci, Libr Mgr, Public Library at Tellico Village, 300 Irene Lane, Loudon, TN, 37774. Tel: 865-458-5199. p. 2110

Geren, Catherine, Libr Spec II, University of Maine at Augusta, 85 Texas Ave, Belfast Hall, Bangor, ME, 04401. Tel: 207-262-7900. p. 916

Gerencser, James, Col Archivist, Dickinson College, 28 N College St, Carlisle, PA, 17013-2311. Tel: 717-245-1397. p. 1919

Gerety, Lorraine, Visual Res Curator, School of Visual Arts Library, 380 Second Ave, 2nd Flr, New York, NY, 10010. Tel: 212-592-2667. p. 1601

Gerhard, Susie, Pres, Weatherly Area Community Library, 1518 Brenkman Dr, Weatherly, PA, 18255. Tel: 570-427-5085. p. 2019

Gerhardt, Richard, Dir, Longport Public Library, 2305 Atlantic Ave, Longport, NJ, 08403. Tel: 609-487-7403. p. 1414

Gerhart, Nancy, Colls Librn, Alberta Government Library, Capital Blvd, 11th Flr, 10044 - 108 St, Edmonton, AB, T5J 5E6, CANADA. Tel: 780-427-2985. p. 2534

Gerharter, Nicholle, Asst Dir, Br Mgr, Park County Library System, 1500 Heart Mountain St, Cody, WY, 82414. Tel: 307-527-1880. p. 2493

Gerhold, Albert, Computer Ctr Mgr, Drexel University Libraries, Hahnemann Library, 245 N 15th St MS 449, Philadelphia, PA, 19102-1192. p. 1976

Gerke, Jennie, Assoc Dean, University of Colorado Boulder, 1720 Pleasant St, Boulder, CO, 80309. Tel: 303-492-8705. p. 267

Gerken, Joseph, Ref Librn, University at Buffalo Libraries-State University of New York, Charles B Sears Law Library, John Lord O'Brian Hall, 211 Mary Talbert Way, Buffalo, NY, 14260-1110. Tel: 716-645-6769. p. 1511

Gerloff, Kayla, Dir, George Public Library, 119 S Main St, George, IA, 51237. Tel: 712-475-3897. p. 755

Germain, Carol Anne, Asst Prof, University at Albany, State University of New York, Draper 015, 135 Western Ave, Albany, NY, 12203. Tel: 518-442-5258. p. 2789

Germain, Nicole Termini, Br Mgr, San Francisco Public Library, Portola Branch Library, 380 Bacon St (at Goettingen), San Francisco, CA, 94134-1526. Tel: 415-355-5660. p. 228

Germaine, Ashley, Libr Serv Dir, Duncan Public Library, 122 N Hwy 75, Duncan, AZ, 85534. Tel: 928-359-2094. p. 59

German, Elizabeth, User Serv & Instruction Design Librn, Texas A&M University Libraries, 400 Spence St, College Station, TX, 77843. Tel: 979-847-5846. p. 2157

German, Jennifer, Br Mgr, Kent District Library, Krause Memorial Branch, 140 E Bridge St, Rockford, MI, 49341. p. 1094

German, Lisa Pradt, Univ Librn & Dean of Libr, University of Minnesota Libraries-Twin Cities, 499 Wilson Library, 309 19th Ave S, Minneapolis, MN, 55455. Tel: 612-624-3321. p. 1185

Germany, Chad, Asst Librn, Saint Augustine Historical Society, Six Artillery Lane, 2nd Flr, Saint Augustine, FL, 32084. Tel: 904-825-2333. p. 440

Germar, Tia, Ref & Instruction Librn, Butte College Library, 3536 Butte Campus Dr, Oroville, CA, 95965. Tel: 530-879-4067. p. 189

Germek, George, Assoc Librn, Monmouth University Library, 400 Cedar Ave, West Long Branch, NJ, 07764. Tel: 732-571-4403. p. 1452

Germer, Jayne, E-Resources Librn, Learning Librn, Doane College, 1014 Boswell Ave, Crete, NE, 68333. Tel: 402-826-8567. p. 1311

Germon, Leah, Ch, Atlanta-Fulton Public Library System, Sandy Springs Branch, 395 Mount Vernon Hwy NE, Sandy Springs, GA, 30328. Tel: 404-612-7000. p. 461

Gernand, Bradley E, Libr Mgr, Institute for Defense Analyses Library, 4850 Mark Center Dr, Alexandria, VA, 22311. Tel: 703-845-2087. p. 2303

Gerolami, Natasha, Librn, Laurentian University Library & Archives, 935 Ramsey Lake Rd, Sudbury, ON, P3E 2C6, CANADA. Tel: 705-675-1151. p. 2683

Gerolami, Natasha, Dr, Head Librn, Huntington University, Laurentian Campus, 935 Ramsey Lake Rd, Sudbury, ON, P3E 2C6, CANADA. Tel: 705-673-4126, Ext 248. p. 2683

Gerolami, Tim, Dir, Cape Cod Community College, 2240 Iyannough Rd, West Barnstable, MA, 02668-1599. Tel: 774-330-4351. p. 1065

Gerrein, Jeff, Fac Mgr, Public Library of Cincinnati & Hamilton County, 800 Vine St, Cincinnati, OH, 45202-2009. Tel: 513-369-4515. p. 1761

Gerrish, Christine, Dir, Glen Carbon Centennial Library District, 198 S Main St, Glen Carbon, IL, 62034. Tel: 618-288-1212. p. 593

Gerrity, Caitlin, Dir, Libr Media Prog, Southern Utah University Gerald R Sherratt Library, 351 W University Blvd, Cedar City, UT, 84720. Tel: 435-586-1908. p. 2793

Gerrity, Kate, Metadata Management, Amherst College, 61 Quadrangle Dr, Amherst, MA, 01002. p. 984

Gersch, Tasha, Librn, Dolores County Public Library, 525 N Main St, Dove Creek, CO, 81324. Tel: 970-677-2389. p. 278

Gersitz, Lorraine, Libr Instruction Coordr, Ref Coordr, Cerritos College Library, 11110 Alondra Blvd, Norwalk, CA, 90650. Tel: 562-860-2451, Ext 2414. p. 184

Gerson, Kevin, Dir, Law Libr, University of California Los Angeles Library, Hugh & Hazel Darling Law Library, 1112 Law Bldg, 385 Charles E Young Dr E, Los Angeles, CA, 90095-1458. Tel: 310-825-7826. p. 169

Gerstein, Charlotte, Instruction/Ref Serv, Vermont State University - Castleton, 178 Alumni Dr, Castleton, VT, 05735. Tel: 802-468-1256. p. 2281

Gerstenecker, Ann, Circ Supvr, Holbrook Public Library, Two Plymouth St, Holbrook, MA, 02343. Tel: 781-767-3644. p. 1024

Gertsch, Karen, Asst Librn, Ned R McWherter Weakley County Library, 341 Linden St, Dresden, TN, 38225-1400. Tel: 731-364-2678. p. 2097

Gervais, Hélène, Chef de Section, Bibliotheques de Montreal, Saint-Michel, 7601 rue Francois-Perrault, Montreal, QC, H2A 3L6, CANADA. Tel: 514-872-3910. p. 2720

Gervais, Ruth, Librn, California Court of Appeal, 750 B St, Ste 300, San Diego, CA, 92101. Tel: 619-744-0760. p. 214

Gervase, Keith, Colls Mgr, New Britain Museum of American Art Library, 56 Lexington St, New Britain, CT, 06052. Tel: 860-229-0257. p. 324

Gervasio, Darcy, Actg Libr Dir, State University of New York, 735 Anderson Hill Rd, Purchase, NY, 10577-1400. Tel: 914-251-6436. p. 1625

Gervino, Mark, Head, Ref & Tech Serv, Windsor Public Library, 323 Broad St, Windsor, CT, 06095. Tel: 860-285-1920. p. 348

Gervits, Maya, Dir, New Jersey Institute of Technology, Barbara & Leonard Littman Architecture & Design Library, 456 Weston Hall, 323 King Blvd, Newark, NJ, 07102-1982. Tel: 973-596-3083. p. 1427

Gerwatowski, Kathleen, Dir, Brown, Rudnick LLP, One Financial Ctr, Boston, MA, 02111. Tel: 617-856-8213. p. 994

Geselman, Brenda, Br Librn, Carson City Public Library, Crystal Community, 221 W Lake St, Crystal, MI, 48818. Tel: 989-235-6111. p. 1089

Geshel, Dillon, Dir, Portage Lake District Library, 58 Huron St, Houghton, MI, 49931-2194. Tel: 906-482-4570. p. 1116

Gessner, Carrie, Access Services, Evening, The College of Wooster Libraries, 1140 Beall Ave, Wooster, OH, 44691-2364. Tel: 330-263-2442. p. 1833

Gest, Laura, Dir, Hartland Public Library, 110 E Park Ave, Hartland, WI, 53029. Tel: 262-367-3350. p. 2440

Getaz, Christina, Librn, Caldwell University, 120 Bloomfield Ave, Caldwell, NJ, 07006. Tel: 973-618-3337. p. 1393

Getchell, Charles, Librn, Saint Anselm College, 100 Saint Anselm Dr, Manchester, NH, 03102-1310. Tel: 603-641-7300. p. 1372

Getchell, Mary, Dir, Mkt & Communications, Pierce County Library System, 3005 112th St E, Tacoma, WA, 98446-2215. Tel: 253-548-3300. p. 2386

Geter, Karen, Ref, Virginia State University, One Hayden Dr, Petersburg, VA, 23806. Tel: 804-524-5040. p. 2337

Getsay, Heather, Acq Librn, Slippery Rock University of Pennsylvania, 109 Campus Loop, Slippery Rock, PA, 16057. Tel: 724-738-2665. p. 2007

Getselman, Anna, Exec Dir, Columbia University, Augustus C Long Health Sciences Library, 701 W 168th St, Lobby Level, New York, NY, 10032. Tel: 212-305-1406. p. 1583

Gettelman, Kathy, Br Mgr, Fremont County Library System, Dubois Branch, 202 N First St, Dubois, WY, 82513. Tel: 307-455-2992. p. 2496

Getty, Kevin, Head, Info Serv, Warren-Newport Public Library District, 224 N O'Plaine Rd, Gurnee, IL, 60031. Tel: 847-244-5150, Ext 3015. p. 596

Gettys, Abbie, Librn, Central Georgia Technical College Library, 54 Hwy 22 W, Milledgeville, GA, 31061. Tel: 478-445-2333. p. 490

Gettys, Rebecca, Assoc Dean, University of South Carolina, 1322 Greene St, Columbia, SC, 29208-0103. Tel: 803-777-3142. p. 2055

Getz, Ramona, Librn, Nickerson Public Library, 23 N Nickerson, Nickerson, KS, 67561. Tel: 620-259-3714. p. 827

Getz, Roger, Dir, Libr Serv, University of Maine at Presque Isle Library, 181 Main St, Presque Isle, ME, 04769-2888. Tel: 207-768-9595. p. 938

Gewirtz, Sarah, Soc Sci Librn, College of Saint Benedict, 37 S College Ave, Saint Joseph, MN, 56374. Tel: 320-363-5802. p. 1199

Gewissler, Laura, Coll Mgt Serv Dir, University of Vermont Libraries, 538 Main St, Burlington, VT, 05405-0036. Tel: 802-656-2024. p. 2281

Geyer, Enid, Assoc Dean, Info Res Librn, Albany Medical College, 47 New Scotland Ave, MC 63, Albany, NY, 12208. Tel: 518-262-5530. p. 1482

Geyer, Richard, Ref Librn, Adrian College, 110 S Madison St, Adrian, MI, 49221. Tel: 517-265-5161, Ext 4220. p. 1075

Ghaouti, Loubna, Dir, Universite Laval Bibliotheque, Pavillon Jean-Charles-Bonenfant, 2345, allée des Bibliothèques, Quebec, QC, G1V 0A6, CANADA. Tel: 418-656-3344. p. 2732

Gharst, Loretta, Assoc Librn, Coll & Computing Serv, Calcasieu Parish Public Library System, 301 W Claude St, Lake Charles, LA, 70605-3457. Tel: 337-721-7147. p. 893

Ghattas, Carol, Br Mgr, Rutherford County Library System, 105 W Vine St, Murfreesboro, TN, 37130-3673. Tel: 615-893-4131, Ext 119. p. 2117

Ghazar, Krista, Adult Ref Librn, Madison Heights Public Library, 240 W 13 Mile Rd, Madison Heights, MI, 48071-1894. Tel: 248-837-2850. p. 1128

Ghazarian, Ara, Curator, Armenian Cultural Foundation Library, 441 Mystic St, Arlington, MA, 02474-1108. Tel: 781-646-3090. p. 985

Ghazi, Sarah, Librn, Canadian Nuclear Safety Commission Library, 280 Slater St, Ottawa, ON, K1P 1C2, CANADA. Tel: 613-995-5894. p. 2666

Ghobrial, Amanda, Adult Serv Mgr, West Chicago Public Library District, 118 W Washington St, West Chicago, IL, 60185. Tel: 630-231-1552. p. 660

Ghorbani, Cathie, Head, Adult Serv, Cary Memorial Library, 1874 Massachusetts Ave, Lexington, MA, 02420. Tel: 781-862-6288, Ext 84411. p. 1028

Ghosh, Soumik, Syst Adminr, Virginia Polytechnic Institute & State University Libraries, 560 Drillfield Dr, Blacksburg, VA, 24061. Tel: 540-231-7022. p. 2307

Ghosh, Suchandra, Circ Supvr, City of Calabasas Library, 200 Civic Center Way, Calabasas, CA, 91302. Tel: 818-225-7616. p. 126

Ghoshal, Shyamalika, ILL, Ref Librn, United States Department of the Interior Library, 1849 C St NW, MS 1151, Washington, DC, 20240. Tel: 202-208-3309. p. 378

Giacobbe, Laura, Pub Serv Librn, New Brunswick Theological Seminary, 21 Seminary Pl, New Brunswick, NJ, 08901. Tel: 732-247-5241. p. 1424

Giaimo, Catherine L, Librn, The Masonic Library & Museum of Pennsylvania, Masonic Temple, One N Broad St, Philadelphia, PA, 19107-2520. Tel: 215-988-1933. p. 1983

Giambi, M Dina, Assoc Univ Librn, Budget & Collections, University of Delaware Library, 181 S College Ave, Newark, DE, 19717-5267. Tel: 302-831-2965. p. 355

Giampa, Kevin, Librn, United States Marine Corps, Bldg 596, Beaufort, SC, 29904. Tel: 843-228-7682. p. 2047

Giampa, Kevin, Librn, United States Marine Corps, Bldg 283, 521 Blvd DeFrance, Parris Island, SC, 29905. Tel: 843-228-1672. p. 2067

Giancaterino, Dan, Educ Serv Mgr, Jenkins Law Library, Ten Penn Ctr, 1801 Market St, Ste 900, Philadelphia, PA, 19103-6405. Tel: 215-574-7945. p. 1982

Giangreco, Tom, Govt Doc, Fordham University Libraries, 441 E Fordham Rd, Bronx, NY, 10458-5151. Tel: 718-817-3570. p. 1498

Gianlorenzo, Nancy, Br Librn, Cranston Public Library, Knightsville Branch, 1847 Cranston St, Cranston, RI, 02920-4112. Tel: 401-942-2504. p. 2031

Giannakopoulos, Thanos, Chief Librn, United Nations Dag Hammarskjöld Library, United Nations Headquarters, Rm L-105, First Ave at 42nd St, New York, NY, 10017. Tel: 212-963-0512. p. 1603

Giannitti, Aurelio, Grants Mgr, Outreach Mgr, Wicomico Public Library, 122 S Division St, Salisbury, MD, 21801. Tel: 410-749-3612, Ext 122. p. 976

Giannoumis, Karen, Library Services, Hagerstown Community College Library, Learning Resource Ctr, No 200B, 11400 Robinwood Dr, Hagerstown, MD, 21742-6590. Tel: 240-500-2237. p. 967

Giannuzzi, Mark, Mgr, San Jose Public Library, Alviso Branch, 5050 N First St, Alviso, CA, 95002. Tel: 408-263-3626. p. 231

Giannuzzi, Mark, Mgr, San Jose Public Library, Educational Park, 1772 Educational Park Dr, San Jose, CA, 95133-1703. Tel: 408-808-3073. p. 231

Gianoulis, Helen, Br Mgr, Huron County Library, Bayfield Branch, 18 Main St, Bayfield, ON, N0M 1G0, CANADA. Tel: 519-565-2886. p. 2636

Gianoulis, Helen, Br Mgr, Huron County Library, Goderich Branch, 52 Montreal St, Goderich, ON, N7A 2G4, CANADA. Tel: 519-524-9261. p. 2636

Giard, Jean-Bruno, Head of Libr & Archives, Montreal Museum of Fine Arts, 2189 Bishop St, Montreal, QC, H3G 2E8, CANADA. Tel: 514-285-1600, Ext 160, 514-285-1600, Ext 202. p. 2727

Giardi, Kirsten, Develop, Interim Asst Dir, Newark Public Library, Five Washington St, Newark, NJ, 07101. Tel: 973-424-1832. p. 1427

Giarrizzo, Ellen, Circ Mgr, Sunnyvale Public Library, 665 W Olive Ave, Sunnyvale, CA, 94086-7622. Tel: 408-730-7300. p. 251

Giarrusso, Diane, Dir, Tewksbury Public Library, 300 Chandler St, Tewksbury, MA, 01876. Tel: 978-640-4490. p. 1059

Gibbon, Cindy, Spec Project Dir, Multnomah County Library, 919 NE 19th Ave, Ste 250, Portland, OR, 97232. Tel: 503-988-5123. p. 1892

Gibbons, Barb, Librn, Palliser Regional Library, Willow Bunch Branch, Two Ave F S, Willow Bunch, SK, S0H 4K0, CANADA. Tel: 306-473-2393. p. 2743

Gibbons, Gina, Dir, Brentwood Public Library, 8765 Eulalie Ave, Brentwood, MO, 63144. Tel: 314-963-8636. p. 1239

Gibbons, Lindsay, Asst Prof, Boston University, Wheelock College of Education & Human Development, No 2 Sherborn St, Boston, MA, 02215. Tel: 617-353-3182. p. 2786

Gibbons, Susan Lynn, Vice Provost, Collections & Scholarly Communication, Yale University Library, 120 High St, New Haven, CT, 06511. Tel: 203-432-1818. p. 326

Gibbons, Susan Lynn, Vice Provost, Collections & Scholarly Communication, Yale University Library, Sterling Memorial Library, 120 High St, New Haven, CT, 06520. Tel: 203-432-1818. p. 328

Gibbons, Valerie, Makerspace Librn, Lakehead University, 955 Oliver Rd, Thunder Bay, ON, P7B 5E1, CANADA. Tel: 807-343-8205. p. 2685

Gibbons, William, Curator of Archival Coll, City College of the City University of New York, North Academic Ctr, 160 Convent Ave, New York, NY, 10031. Tel: 212-650-7602. p. 1581

Gibbs, Aaron, Asst Dir, Program Serv Librn, Morgan County Public Library, 151 University Dr, West Liberty, KY, 41472. Tel: 606-743-4151. p. 876

Gibbs, Carol, Libr Asst, Ivy Tech Community College-Northeast, 3800 N Anthony Blvd, Fort Wayne, IN, 46805-1430. Tel: 260-480-4172. p. 684

Gibbs, Daniel, Dir, Ardmore Public Library, 320 E St NW, Ardmore, OK, 73401. Tel: 580-223-8290. p. 1840

Gibbs, David, Assoc Dean, Collections & Discovery, California State University, Sacramento, 6000 J St, Sacramento, CA, 95819-6039. Tel: 916-278-6708. p. 208

Gibbs, David, Libr Dir, Gays Mills Public Library, 16381 State Hwy 131, Gays Mills, WI, 54631. Tel: 608-735-4331. p. 2436

Gibbs, Davy, Assoc Librn for Coll Dev & Info Servs, Piedmont University Library, 1021 Central Ave, Demorest, GA, 30535. Tel: 706-776-0111. p. 476

Gibbs, Denise, Library Contact, East Millinocket Public Library, 53 Main St, East Millinocket, ME, 04430. Tel: 207-746-3554. p. 924

Gibbs, George, Asst Librn, Nancy Nail Memorial Library, 124 S Pearl St, Mart, TX, 76664-1425. Tel: 254-876-2465. p. 2216

Gibbs, Keisha, Mgr, Columbus Metropolitan Library, Martin Luther King Branch, 1467 E Long St, Columbus, OH, 43203. p. 1772

Gibbs, Marilyn Y, Libr Dir, Claflin University, 400 Magnolia St, Orangeburg, SC, 29115. Tel: 803-535-5309. p. 2066

Gibbs, R Casey, Dir, Saint Edwards University, 3001 S Congress Ave, Austin, TX, 78704-6489. Tel: 512-416-5869. p. 2140

Gibbs, Robert, Libr Mgr, New York Public Library - Astor, Lenox & Tilden Foundations, St George Library Center, Five Central Ave, (Near Borough Hall), Staten Island, NY, 10301. Tel: 718-442-8560. p. 1597

Gibbs, Rylee, Tech Serv, YA Serv, Rushville Public Library, 130 W Third St, Rushville, IN, 46173-1899. Tel: 765-932-3496. p. 717

Gibbs, Tamara, Dir, Camden-Jackson Township Public Library, 183 Main St, Camden, IN, 46917. Tel: 574-686-2120. p. 674

Gibbs-Kail, Fran, Asst Dir, Head, Tech Serv, New London Public Library, 63 Huntington St, New London, CT, 06320. Tel: 860-447-1411, Ext 107. p. 329

Gibert, Ken, Br Mgr, Orange County Library System, Hiawassee Branch, 7391 W Colonial Dr, Orlando, FL, 32818. p. 431

Giblin, Paul, Head, Ref, Kelley Library, 234 Main St, Salem, NH, 03079-3190. Tel: 603-898-7064. p. 1380

Gibson, Alison, Dir, Union Township Public Library, Aberdeen Branch Library, 1730 US Rte 52, Aberdeen, OH, 45101-9302. Tel: 937-392-4871. p. 1817

Gibson, Alison J, Dir, Union Township Public Library, 27 Main St, Ripley, OH, 45167-1231. Tel: 937-392-4871. p. 1817
Gibson, Amanda, Asst Dir, Bella Vista Public Library, 11 Dickens Pl, Bella Vista, AR, 72714-4603. Tel: 479-855-1753. p. 90
Gibson, Amy, Ch Serv Librn, Killeen Public Library, 205 E Church Ave, Killeen, TX, 76541. Tel: 254-501-8990. p. 2206
Gibson, Andrew, Commun Libr Mgr, Queens Library, Pomonok Community Library, 158-21 Jewel Ave, Flushing, NY, 11365. Tel: 718-591-4343. p. 1555
Gibson, Annmarie, Libr Dir, Marshall Public Library, 214 N Lafayette, Marshall, MO, 65340. Tel: 660-886-3391, Ext 3. p. 1260
Gibson, Beverly, Ref & Instruction, Lake-Sumter State College Library, 9501 US Hwy 441, Leesburg, FL, 34788. Tel: 352-365-3563, 352-365-3590. p. 418
Gibson, Chris, Syst Librn, Lithgow Public Library, 45 Winthrop St, Augusta, ME, 04330-5599. Tel: 207-626-2415. p. 914
Gibson, Chuck, Dir, Worthington Libraries, 820 High St, Worthington, OH, 43085. Tel: 614-807-2601. p. 1833
Gibson, Cindy, Librn, Yancey County Public Library, 321 School Circle, Burnsville, NC, 28714. Tel: 828-682-2600. p. 1677
Gibson, Corey, Technology Spec, George Mason University Libraries, Law Library, 3301 N Fairfax Dr, Arlington, VA, 22201-4426. Tel: 703-993-8100. p. 2317
Gibson, Denise M, Asst Librn, Mercer University, Walter F George School of Law, Furman Smith Law Library, 1021 Georgia Ave, Macon, GA, 31201-1001. Tel: 478-301-5905. p. 486
Gibson, Donna, Exec Dir, Paul Sawyier Public Library, 319 Wapping St, Frankfort, KY, 40601-2605. Tel: 502-352-2665, Ext 200. p. 856
Gibson, Donna, Dir, Libr Serv, Memorial Sloan-Kettering Cancer Center Medical Library, Rockefeller Research Laboratories, 430 E 67th St, New York, NY, 10065. Tel: 212-639-7439. p. 1591
Gibson, Elaine, Br Mgr, Penn Hills Library, Lincoln Park Satellite, 7300 Ridgeview Ave, Pittsburgh, PA, 15235. Tel: 412-362-7729. p. 1995
Gibson, Elizabeth, Pres, Everett C Benton Library, 75 Oakley Rd, Belmont, MA, 02478-0125. Tel: 617-484-0988. p. 988
Gibson Hollow, Anna, Univ Archivist, University of Alberta, Archives, Books & Records Depository, 100 8170 50th St, Edmonton, AB, T6B 1E6, CANADA. Tel: 780-492-9942. p. 2537
Gibson, Ina, Br Mgr, San Diego Public Library, Mira Mesa, 8405 New Salem St, San Diego, CA, 92126-2398. Tel: 858-538-8165. p. 220
Gibson, Ingrid, ILL Librn, Harvard Library, Dumbarton Oaks Library & Archives, 1703 32nd St NW, Washington, MA, 20007. Tel: 202-339-6400, Ext 6968. p. 1006
Gibson, Jane, Br Head, Lake County Public Library, Griffith-Calumet Township Branch, 1215 E 45th Ave, Griffith, IN, 46319-1528. Tel: 219-838-2825. p. 705
Gibson, Jeremy, Colls Mgr, Bagaduce Music Lending Library, 49 South St, Blue Hill, ME, 04614. Tel: 207-374-5454. p. 918
Gibson, Jesse, Dir, Sandhill Regional Library System, 412 E Franklin St, Rockingham, NC, 28379. Tel: 910-997-3388. p. 1713
Gibson, Julie, Head, Circ, Crystal Lake Public Library, 126 Paddock St, Crystal Lake, IL, 60014. Tel: 815-459-1687. p. 574
Gibson, Karla, Ref (Info Servs), Wixom Public Library, 49015 Pontiac Trail, Wixom, MI, 48393-2567. Tel: 248-624-2512. p. 1160
Gibson, Kate, Br Head, Lake County Public Library, Lake Station-New Chicago Branch, 2007 Central Ave, Lake Station, IN, 46405-2061. Tel: 219-962-2409. p. 706
Gibson, Katherine, Mgr, Edmonton Public Library, Sprucewood, 11555 95 St, Edmonton, AB, T5G 1L5, CANADA. Tel: 780-496-1054. p. 2537
Gibson, Kathy, Librn, Iosco-Arenac District Library, Whittemore Branch, 483 Bullock St, Whittemore, MI, 48770-5134. Tel: 989-756-3186. p. 1102
Gibson, Ken, Dir, Univ Libr, Xavier University, 1535 Musketeer Dr, Cincinnati, OH, 45207. Tel: 513-745-4359. p. 1765
Gibson, Kimberly, Libr Dir, Haxton Memorial Library, Three N Pearl St, Oakfield, NY, 14125. Tel: 585-948-9900. p. 1609
Gibson, Lynn, Children's/Teen Coordr, Boone Area Library, 129 N Mill St, Birdsboro, PA, 19508-2340. Tel: 610-582-5666. p. 1912
Gibson, Margaret, Commun Libr Mgr, Queens Library, East Elmhurst Community Library, 95-06 Astoria Blvd, East Elmhurst, NY, 11369. Tel: 718-424-2619. p. 1554
Gibson, Marilyn, Librn, James C Poole Jr Memorial Library, 420 Prairie Ave, Eutaw, AL, 35462-1165. Tel: 205-372-9026. p. 16
Gibson, Meagan, Supvr, Acq, Tigard Public Library, 13500 SW Hall Blvd, Tigard, OR, 97223-8111. Tel: 503-684-6537, Ext 2513. p. 1900
Gibson, Melissa, Adult Serv Mgr, Scott County Public Library, 104 S Bradford Lane, Georgetown, KY, 40324-2335. Tel: 502-863-3566. p. 856
Gibson, Michael, Librn, Gadsden State Community College, Pierce C Cain Learning Resource Center, Ayers Campus, 1801 Coleman Rd, Anniston, AL, 36207. Tel: 256-835-5432. p. 18
Gibson, Michelle, Asst Dir, Youth Serv Librn, Council Grove Public Library, 829 W Main St, Council Grove, KS, 66846. Tel: 620-767-5716. p. 803
Gibson, Nancy, Soc Sci Librn, Austin Peay State University, 601 College St, Clarksville, TN, 37044. Tel: 931-221-6166. p. 2092
Gibson, Natalie, Ref Mgr, Greater Clarks Hill Regional Library System, 7022 Evans Town Center Blvd, Evans, GA, 30809. Tel: 706-447-7671. p. 478
Gibson, Penny, Ref (Info Servs), University of Alabama, School of Law Library, 101 Paul Bryant Dr, Tuscaloosa, AL, 35487. Tel: 205-348-5925. p. 38
Gibson, Rita, Access Serv Coordr, State Law Library of Montana, 215 N Sanders, Helena, MT, 59601-4522. Tel: 406-444-3660. p. 1297
Gibson, Robin, Mgr, Youth Serv, Westerville Public Library, 126 S State St, Westerville, OH, 43081. Tel: 614-882-7277. p. 1830
Gibson, Sally, Libr Dir, Missouri Western State University, 4525 Downs Dr, Saint Joseph, MO, 64507-2294. Tel: 816-271-4368. p. 1268
Gibson, Shannon, N Metro Campus Librn, Chattahoochee Technical College Library, 980 S Cobb Dr, Marietta, GA, 30060. Tel: 770-975-4054. p. 488
Gibson, Shannon, Librn, Chattahoochee Technical College Library, North Metro Campus Library, 5198 Ross Rd, Acworth, GA, 30102. Tel: 770-975-4054. p. 489
Gibson, Sherrie R, Dir, Library of Graham, 910 Cherry St, Graham, TX, 76450-3547. Tel: 940-549-0600. p. 2185
Gibson, Susan, Circ Supvr, Bellevue Public Library, 224 E Main St, Bellevue, OH, 44811-1467. Tel: 419-483-4769. p. 1750
Gibson, Tess, Head, ILL, University of Arkansas Libraries, 365 N McIlroy Ave, Fayetteville, AR, 72701-4002. Tel: 479-575-2925. p. 95
Gibson, Toby, Asst Dir, Access Serv, Library of Rush University Medical Center, Armour Academic Ctr, 600 S Paulina St, Ste 571, Chicago, IL, 60612. Tel: 312-942-5950. p. 563
Gibson, Wendy, ILL, Minnesota State University Moorhead, 1104 Seventh Ave S, Moorhead, MN, 56563. Tel: 218-477-2922. p. 1189
Gick, Julie, Librn, New York State Supreme Court, First Judicial District Civil Law Library, 60 Centre St, New York, NY, 10007. Tel: 646-386-3670. p. 1598
Gick, Natalie, Assoc Univ Librn, Admin Serv, Simon Fraser University - Burnaby Campus, 8888 University Dr, Burnaby, BC, V5A 1S6, CANADA. Tel: 778-782-3266. p. 2563
Giddens, Nancy, County Librn, Calaveras County Library, 891 Mountain Ranch Rd, San Andreas, CA, 95249. Tel: 209-754-6510. p. 211
Gideon, Angelita, Circ Supvr, San Bernardino Valley College Library, 701 S Mount Vernon Ave, San Bernardino, CA, 92410. Tel: 909-384-8567. p. 214
Giebink-Skoglind, Diane, Med Librn, ThedaCare Medical Library, 1818 N Meade, Appleton, WI, 54911-3434. Tel: 920-831-5089. p. 2420
Gielec, Linda, Libr Mgr, New Orleans Public Library, Children's Resource Center Library, 913 Napoleon Ave, New Orleans, LA, 70115-2862. Tel: 504-596-2628. p. 903
Gier, Cindy, Head, Circ, Pittsburg Public Library, 308 N Walnut, Pittsburg, KS, 66762-4732. Tel: 620-230-5512. p. 831
Gierloff, Tami, Assoc Dir, Lewis & Clark College, Paul L Boley Law Library, Lewis & Clark Law School, 10015 SW Terwilliger Blvd, Portland, OR, 97219. Tel: 503-768-6776. p. 1891
Gierymski, Christopher, Librn, Freeborn & Peters Library, 311 S Wacker Dr, Ste 3000, Chicago, IL, 60606. Tel: 312-360-6000, Ext 6425. p. 561
Giesbrecht, Don, Chief Exec Officer, Canadian Child Care Federation, 700 Industrial Ave, Ste 600, Ottawa, ON, K1G 0Y9, CANADA. Tel: 613-729-5289, Ext 220. p. 2665
Giesbrecht, JoAnne, Librn, Skagit County Law Library, Skagit County Courthouse, 205 W Kincaid, Rm 104, Mount Vernon, WA, 98273. Tel: 360-416-1290. p. 2371
Giesbrecht, Kaimi, Libr Asst, Vanderhoof Public Library, 230 Stewart St E, Vanderhoof, BC, V0J 3A0, CANADA. Tel: 250-567-4060. p. 2582
Giesbrecht, Kenneth, Mgr, Info Tech, Arkansas State Library, 900 W Capitol, Ste 100, Little Rock, AR, 72201-3108. Tel: 501-682-2053. p. 100
Giese, Ashley, Br Mgr, La Crosse County Library, Hazel Brown Leicht Memorial Library, 702 Industrial Dr, West Salem, WI, 54669-1328. Tel: 608-786-1505. p. 2441
Giese, Liz, Librn, Endeavor Health-Swedish Hospital, 5145 N California Ave, Chicago, IL, 60625. Tel: 773-878-8200, Ext 5312. p. 560
Gieselman France, Tracie D, Archivist, Missouri State University, 850 S John Q Hammons Pkwy, Springfield, MO, 65807. Tel: 417-836-4298. p. 1281
Giesking, Tammy, Br Mgr, Las Vegas-Clark County Library District, Centennial Hills Library, 6711 N Buffalo Dr, Las Vegas, NV, 89131. Tel: 702-507-6100. p. 1346
Giesler, Christy, Br Supvr, Guelph Public Library, Scottsdale Centre Branch, 650 Scottsdale Dr, Guelph, ON, N1G 3M2, CANADA. Tel: 519-829-4402. p. 2643
Giffey, Anne, Pub Serv Librn, Monmouth College, 700 E Broadway, Monmouth, IL, 61462-1963. Tel: 309-457-2190. p. 619
Giffin, Jennifer, Communications Mgr, University of Iowa Hospitals & Clinics, 8016 JCP, 200 Hawkins Dr, Iowa City, IA, 52242-1046. Tel: 319-356-2468. p. 760
Gifford, Kathleen, Libr Dir, Helen Lehmann Memorial Library, 17435 Fifth St, Montverde, FL, 34756. Tel: 407-469-3838. p. 426
Giglio, David, ILL, Tech Serv, Dover Public Library, 35 Loockerman Plaza, Dover, DE, 19901. Tel: 302-736-7030. p. 352
Gigliotti, Chandra, Assoc VP, Innovation, Learning & Effectiveness, Chesapeake College, 1000 College Circle, Wye Mills, MD, 21679. Tel: 410-827-5860. p. 981
Gigliotti, Christina, Outreach Specialist, Lawrence County Federated Library System, 207 E North St, New Castle, PA, 16101-3691. Tel: 724-658-6659, Ext 110. p. 1968
Gigov, Alex, Asst Dir/Tech Librn, Huron Public Library, 521 Dakota Ave S, Huron, SD, 57350. Tel: 605-353-8530. p. 2077

Giguere, Emily, Head, Circ, Haverhill Public Library, 99 Main St, Haverhill, MA, 01830-5092. Tel: 978-373-1586, Ext 603. p. 1024

Giknis, Mary, Dir, Cape Porpoise Library, Atlantic Hall, 173 Main St, Cape Porpoise, ME, 04014. Tel: 207-967-5668. p. 920

Gil, Eduardo, Head, Per, Montclair State University, One Normal Ave, Montclair, NJ, 07043-1699. Tel: 973-655-5286. p. 1420

Gil, Esther, Business & Economics Reference Librn, University of Denver, 2150 E Evans Ave, Denver, CO, 80208. Tel: 303-871-3441. p. 277

Gilbert, Amanda, Br Mgr, Fulton County Public Library, Aubbee, 7432 Olson Rd, Leiters Ford, IN, 46945. Tel: 574-542-4859. p. 716

Gilbert, Amy, Assoc Dir, Librn, Dominican University of California, 50 Acacia Ave, San Rafael, CA, 94901-2298. Tel: 415-257-1329. p. 236

Gilbert, Bonnie B, Dir, Vance Township Library, 107 S Main St, Fairmount, IL, 61841. Tel: 217-733-2164. p. 587

Gilbert, Bradley, Tech Serv Asst, Grand View University Library, 1350 Morton Ave, Des Moines, IA, 50316. Tel: 515-263-2936. p. 746

Gilbert, Bruce, Projects Librarian, Drake University, 2725 University Ave, Des Moines, IA, 50311. Tel: 515-271-4821. p. 746

Gilbert, Charla, Dir, Libr Serv, Vincennes University, Shake Library, 1002 N First St, Vincennes, IN, 47591. Tel: 812-888-5377. p. 724

Gilbert, Debra, Head Librn, First Regional Library, M R Dye Public Library, 2885 Goodman Rd, Horn Lake, MS, 38637. Tel: 662-393-5654. p. 1220

Gilbert, Edi, Libr Assoc, Lafayette Science Museum, 433 Jefferson St, Lafayette, LA, 70501-7013. Tel: 337-291-5544. p. 893

Gilbert, Eileen, Libr Dir, Belmont Public Library, 146 Main St, Belmont, NH, 03220. Tel: 603-267-8331. p. 1355

Gilbert, Emily, Dir, Amarillo College, 2201 S Washington, Amarillo, TX, 79109. Tel: 806-371-5403. p. 2134

Gilbert, Gabriel, Libr Asst, Vance Township Library, 107 S Main St, Fairmount, IL, 61841. Tel: 217-733-2164. p. 587

Gilbert, Jean, Library Services, Northern Oklahoma College, 1220 E Grand Ave, Tonkawa, OK, 74653-4022. Tel: 580-628-6250. p. 1864

Gilbert, Jenny, Adult Serv, Sidney Public Library, 1112 12th Ave, Sidney, NE, 69162. Tel: 308-254-3110. p. 1336

Gilbert, Kara, Head, Youth Serv, Bergenfield Public Library, 50 W Clinton Ave, Bergenfield, NJ, 07621-2799. Tel: 201-387-4040. p. 1390

Gilbert, Kathy, Ser Tech, Pierce College Library, Fort Steilacoom Campus/Cascade Bldg 4, 9401 Farwest Dr SW, Lakewood, WA, 98498. Tel: 253-964-6740. p. 2368

Gilbert, Kristine, Librn, New York Supreme Court, Three E Pulteney Sq, Bath, NY, 14810. Tel: 607-622-8190. p. 1491

Gilbert, Mary, Asst Univ Librn, Coll Mgt, Towson University, 8000 York Rd, Towson, MD, 21252. Tel: 410-704-4926. p. 980

Gilbert, Michael, Librn, Kentucky Talking Book Library, 300 Coffee Tree Rd, Frankfort, KY, 40601. Tel: 502-564-1737. p. 855

Gilbert, Nicole, Br Mgr, Jackson District Library, Napoleon Branch, 6755 S Brooklyn Rd, Napoleon, MI, 49261. Tel: 517-536-4266. p. 1120

Gilbert, Rhonda, Asst Dir, Granby Public Library, 15 N Granby Rd, Granby, CT, 06035. Tel: 860-844-5275. p. 313

Gilbert, Sandra, Circ, Iberville Parish Library, 24605 J Gerald Berret Blvd, Plaquemine, LA, 70764. Tel: 225-687-2520, 225-687-4397. p. 906

Gilbert, Savannah, Libr Dir, Chester County Public Library, 1012 E Main St, Henderson, TN, 38340-0323. Tel: 731-989-4673. p. 2101

Gilbert, Susan, Dir, Kensington Public Library, 126 Amesbury Rd, Kensington, NH, 03833-5621. Tel: 603-772-5022. p. 1370

Gilbert, Susan, Asst Librn, Gilbert Hart Library, 14 S Main St, Wallingford, VT, 05773. Tel: 802-446-2685. p. 2297

Gilbert, Todd, Br Mgr, Indianapolis Public Library, Beech Grove Branch, 1102 Main St, Beech Grove, IN, 46107. Tel: 317-275-4560. p. 694

Gilbertson, Darvy, Libr Mgr, Brownfield Community Library, 5001 Main St, Brownfield, AB, T0C 0R0, CANADA. Tel: 403-578-2247. p. 2525

Gilbertson, Mary, Head, Acq, University of Arkansas Libraries, 365 N McIlroy Ave, Fayetteville, AR, 72701-4002. Tel: 479-575-5417. p. 95

Gilchrist, Gordon, Dir, Libr Serv, Olds College Library, 4500 50th St, Olds, AB, T4H 1R6, CANADA. Tel: 403-507-7777. p. 2549

Gilchrist, Julie, Circ, ILL Librn, Derry Public Library, 64 E Broadway, Derry, NH, 03038-2412. Tel: 603-432-6140. p. 1361

Gilchrist, Pam, Bibliog Serv, Spec, Whitworth University, 300 W Hawthorne Rd, Spokane, WA, 99251-0001. Tel: 509-777-4226. p. 2385

Gildea, Catherine, Youth Serv Mgr, Cedar Mill Community Library, 1080 NW Saltzman Rd, Portland, OR, 97229-5603. Tel: 503-644-0043, Ext 125. p. 1891

Gilderson-Duwe, Jeff, Dir, Oshkosh Public Library, 106 Washington Ave, Oshkosh, WI, 54901-4985. Tel: 920-236-5201, 920-236-5205. p. 2467

Gilderson-Duwe, Jeff, Exec Dir, Winnefox Library System, 106 Washington Ave, Oshkosh, WI, 54901-4985. Tel: 920-236-5220. p. 2468

Gildone, Stephanie, Youth Serv, Conneaut Public Library, 304 Buffalo St, Conneaut, OH, 44030-2658. Tel: 440-593-1608. p. 1778

Gilera, Cheryl, Mgr, County of Los Angeles Public Library, El Monte Library, 3224 Tyler Ave, El Monte, CA, 91731-3356. Tel: 626-444-9506. p. 136

Giles, Crystal, Tech Serv Librn, Northwest Mississippi Community College, Senatobia Learning Resource Ctr, 4975 Hwy 51 N, Senatobia, MS, 38668-1701. Tel: 662-562-3278. p. 1232

Giles, David, Chief Strategy Officer, Brooklyn Public Library, Ten Grand Army Plaza, Brooklyn, NY, 11238. Tel: 718-230-2100. p. 1502

Giles, Jeffrey, Dir, Schulte Roth & Zabel LLP, 919 Third Ave, New York, NY, 10022. Tel: 212-756-2304. p. 1601

Giles, Kathy, Asst Dir, Brown Memorial Library, 53 Railroad St, Clinton, ME, 04927. Tel: 207-426-8686. p. 922

Giles, Vesta, Br Head, Thompson-Nicola Regional District Library System, Logan Lake Branch, 130 Chartrand Ave, Logan Lake, BC, V0K 1W0, CANADA. Tel: 250-523-6745. p. 2567

Giles, Wadad, Cataloger, North Carolina Central University, School of Law Library, 640 Nelson St, Durham, NC, 27707. Tel: 919-530-7177. p. 1685

Giles, Zenobia, Supvr, Circ, Manatee County Public Library System, 1301 Barcarrota Blvd W, Bradenton, FL, 34205-7522. Tel: 941-748-5555. p. 386

Gilfillian, Leah, Libr Dir, Alma M Carpenter Public Library, 300 S Ann, Sourlake, TX, 77659. Tel: 409-287-3592. p. 2244

Gilgannon, Mary, Coll Develop Coordr, Laramie County Library System, 2200 Pioneer Ave, Cheyenne, WY, 82001-3610. Tel: 307-773-5139. p. 2492

Gilgenbach, Cara, Acting University Archivist, Head, Spec Coll & Archives, Kent State University Libraries, Risman Plaza, 1125 Risman Dr, Kent, OH, 44242. Tel: 330-672-1677. p. 1792

Gilgenbach, Lisa, Ch, Barberton Public Library, 602 W Park Ave, Barberton, OH, 44203-2458. Tel: 330-745-1194. p. 1748

Gilhula, Terry, PhD, Info Serv Mgr, Knoxville-Knox County Metropolitan Planning Commission Library, City & County Bldg, Ste 403, 400 Main St, Knoxville, TN, 37902-2476. Tel: 865-215-3819. p. 2106

Giliberto, James, Librn, New York State Legislative Library, State Capitol, Rm 337, Albany, NY, 12224-0345. Tel: 518-455-2468. p. 1483

Gill, Brendon, Instrul Serv, Sierra College Library, Tahoe-Truckee Campus, 11001 College Trail, Truckee, CA, 96161. Tel: 530-550-2284. p. 203

Gill, Carole, Ch Serv, Patrick Lynch Public Library, 206 S McKenna St, Poteau, OK, 74953. Tel: 918-647-4444. p. 1860

Gill, Daphne, Asst Dir, Learning Services, Arizona State University Libraries, Hayden Library, 300 E Orange Mall Dr, Tempe, AZ, 85287. Tel: 480-965-2653. p. 79

Gill, Dragan, Ref Librn, Rhode Island College, 600 Mt Pleasant Ave, Providence, RI, 02908-1924. p. 2039

Gill, Erica, Asst Libr Dir, Haltom City Public Library, 4809 Haltom Rd, Haltom City, TX, 76117-3622. Tel: 817-222-7792. p. 2187

Gill, Harsev, Coordr, Electronic Res, Blake, Cassels & Graydon LLP, Commerce Ct W, 199 Bay St, Ste 4000, Toronto, ON, M5L 1A9, CANADA. Tel: 416-863-2650. p. 2686

Gill, James, Instruction Librn, South College, 3904 Lonas Dr, Knoxville, TN, 37909. Tel: 865-251-1832. p. 2107

Gill, Jim, Dir, Dover Public Library, 525 N Walnut St, Dover, OH, 44622. Tel: 330-343-6123. p. 1782

Gill, Linda, Br Supvr, University of Texas Libraries, Nettie Lee Benson Latin American Collection, Sid Richardson Hall, SRH 1108, 2300 Red River St, Austin, TX, 78713-8916. Tel: 512-495-4520. p. 2142

Gill, Lisa, Asst Dir, Highland Public Library, 14 Elting Pl, Highland, NY, 12528. Tel: 845-691-2275, Ext 204. p. 1546

Gill, Matt, Mgr, County of Los Angeles Public Library, West Hollywood Library, 625 N San Vicente Blvd, West Hollywood, CA, 90069-5020. Tel: 310-652-5340. p. 138

Gill, Mylynda, Archivist, Librn, College of Coastal Georgia, One College Dr, Brunswick, GA, 31520. Tel: 912-279-5782. p. 468

Gill, Mylynda, ILL Coordr, Keene State College, 229 Main St, Keene, NH, 03435-3201. Tel: 603-358-2711. p. 1369

Gill, Nita, Ad, Brookings Public Library, 515 Third St, Brookings, SD, 57006. Tel: 605-692-9407. p. 2074

Gill, Sally, Bus Mgr, Saint Tammany Parish Library, Madisonville Branch, 1123 Main St, Madisonville, LA, 70447. Tel: 985-845-4819. p. 888

Gill, Samantha, Pub Serv Librn, Hays Public Library, 1205 Main, Hays, KS, 67601-3693. Tel: 785-625-9014. p. 812

Gill, Shammi, Libr Mgr, Alameda County Library, Dublin Library, 200 Civic Plaza, Dublin, CA, 94568. Tel: 925-803-7252. p. 143

Gill, Tambra, Libr Mgr, New York Public Library - Astor, Lenox & Tilden Foundations, West Farms Branch, 2085 Honeywell Ave, (Between E 179th & 180th Sts), Bronx, NY, 10460. Tel: 718-367-5376. p. 1598

Gillahan, Donna, Asst Dir, Clay County Public Library, 211 Bridge St, Manchester, KY, 40962. Tel: 606-598-2617. p. 868

Gillanders, Heather, Librn, Tacoma Community College Library, Bldg 7, 6501 S 19th St, Tacoma, WA, 98466-6100. Tel: 253-566-5102. p. 2387

Gillane, Danny, Libr Dir, Lafayette Public Library, 301 W Congress, Lafayette, LA, 70501-6866. Tel: 337-261-5784. p. 892

Gillard, Anne, Chief Exec Officer, Chief Librn, Prescott Public Library, 360 Dibble St W, Prescott, ON, K0E 1T0, CANADA. Tel: 613-925-4340. p. 2675

Gillard, Gail, Dir, Big Horn County Library, 430 West C St, Basin, WY, 82410. Tel: 307-568-2388. p. 2491

Gillard, Sarah, Mgr, Digital & Technical Servs, George Brown College Library Learning Commons, PO Box 1015, Sta B, Toronto, ON, M5T 2T9, CANADA. Tel: 416-415-5000, Ext 8255. p. 2689

Gillean, Hannah, Br Mgr, Arkansas River Valley Regional Library System, Charleston Branch, 12 S School St, Charleston, AR, 72933-0338. Tel: 479-965-2605. p. 93

Gillen, Rose, Libr Dir, Pace University, 861 Bedford Rd, Pleasantville, NY, 10570-2799. Tel: 914-773-3382. p. 1620

Gillenwater, Amber, Asst Libr Dir, Gallia County District Library, Seven Spruce St, Gallipolis, OH, 45631. Tel: 740-446-7323. p. 1787

Gillenwater, Denise, Homebound Serv, Sheridan County Public Library System, 335 W Alger St, Sheridan, WY, 82801. Tel: 307-674-8585. p. 2499

Gilles, Lindsey, Dir, Gibson County Memorial Library, 303 S High St, Trenton, TN, 38382-2027. Tel: 731-855-1991. p. 2128

Gillespie, Donna, Dir, Crandall-Combine Community Library, 13385 FM 3039, Crandall, TX, 75114. Tel: 972-427-6120. p. 2161

Gillespie, Esther, Delivery Serv Mgr, Hayner Public Library District, 326 Belle St, Alton, IL, 62002. Tel: 618-462-0677. p. 536

Gillespie, Fawn, Ref Librn, Hagaman Memorial Library, 227 Main St, East Haven, CT, 06512. Tel: 203-468-3890. p. 310

Gillespie, Gail, Librn, Northern State Prison Library, 168 Frontage Rd, Newark, NJ, 07114-3794. Tel: 973-465-0068, Ext 4521. p. 1428

Gillespie, Hilah, Cat, Lamar Public Library, 102 E Parmenter St, Lamar, CO, 81052-3239. Tel: 719-336-1295. p. 289

Gillespie, Hollis J, Dir, Nevada State Museum, 309 S Valley View Blvd, Las Vegas, NV, 89107. Tel: 702-486-5205, 702-822-8751. p. 1347

Gillespie, Laura, Circ Serv, Allerton Public Library District, 4000 Green Apple Lane, Monticello, IL, 61856. Tel: 217-762-4676. p. 619

Gillespie, Lunden, Area Mgr, Prince George's County Memorial, Glenarden Branch, 8724 Glenarden Pkwy, Glenarden, MD, 20706-1646. Tel: 301-772-5477. p. 970

Gillespie, Lunden, Area Mgr, Prince George's County Memorial, Hillcrest Heights Branch, 2398 Iverson St, Temple Hills, MD, 20748-6850. Tel: 301-630-4900. p. 970

Gillespie, Lunden, Area Mgr, Prince George's County Memorial, Spauldings Branch, 5811 Old Silver Hill Rd, District Heights, MD, 20747-2108. Tel: 301-817-3750. p. 971

Gillespie, Stephanie, Ref Librn, Pellissippi State Community College, Hardin Valley Library, 10915 Harding Valley Rd, Knoxville, TN, 37933. Tel: 865-539-7106. p. 2106

Gillette, Allison, Libr & Archives Mgr, Shelburne Museum Library, 5555 Shelburne Rd, Shelburne, VT, 05482-7491. Tel: 802-985-3346. p. 2294

Gillette, Angela, Br Mgr, Mid-Continent Public Library, Kearney Branch, 100 S Platte-Clay Way, Kearney, MO, 64060. Tel: 816-628-5055. p. 1250

Gillette, Lynette, Dir, El Rito Public Library, 182 Placitas Rd, El Rito, NM, 87530. Tel: 575-581-4608. p. 1467

Gilley, Jennifer R, Head Librn, Pennsylvania State University, New Kensington, 3550 Seventh St Rd, Rte 780, Upper Burrell, PA, 15068-1798. Tel: 724-334-6076. p. 2016

Gilley, Terence Michael, Dir, Libr Serv, Mountain Empire Community College, Robb Hall, 2nd Flr, 3441 Mountain Empire Rd, Big Stone Gap, VA, 24219. Tel: 276-523-2400, Ext 304. p. 2307

Gillham, Kate, Dir, Dorothy Hull Library - Windsor Charter Township, 405 W Jefferson St, Dimondale, MI, 48821. Tel: 517-646-0633. p. 1101

Gilliam, Anise, Libr Asst, Goldfarb School of Nursing at Barnes-Jewish College Library, 4483 Duncan Ave, Mail Stop 90-30-697, Saint Louis, MO, 63110. Tel: 314-362-1699, 314-454-7055. p. 1271

Gilliam, Carol, Librn, Roosevelt Public Library, 27 W Fulton Ave, Roosevelt, NY, 11575. Tel: 516-378-0222. p. 1633

Gilliam, Christopher, Acq & Ser Coordr, Library of Rush University Medical Center, Armour Academic Ctr, 600 S Paulina St, Ste 571, Chicago, IL, 60612. Tel: 312-942-2107. p. 563

Gilliam, Nakeata, Cataloging & Collection Mgmt Tech, Northwest Nazarene University, 804 E Dewey St, Nampa, ID, 83686. Tel: 208-467-8616. p. 527

Gilliam, Teryn, Br Adminr, Atlanta-Fulton Public Library System, Buckhead Branch, 269 Buckhead Ave NE, Atlanta, GA, 30305. Tel: 404-814-3500. p. 461

Gilliam, Teryn D, Br Adminr, Atlanta-Fulton Public Library System, Washington Park Branch, 1116 Martin Luther King Jr Dr, Atlanta, GA, 30314. Tel: 404-612-0110. p. 462

Gillie, Ester, Dean, Regent University, 1000 Regent University Dr, Virginia Beach, VA, 23464. Tel: 757-352-4450. p. 2349

Gillie, Esther, PhD, Dean, Regent University Library, 1000 Regent University Dr, Virginia Beach, VA, 23464-5037. Tel: 757-352-4185. p. 2349

Gillie, Michelle, Coll Develop & Acq Librn, St Lawrence University, 23 Romoda Dr, Canton, NY, 13617. Tel: 315-229-5834. p. 1513

Gillie, Sarah, Dir, Okotoks Public Library, 23 Riverside Dr W, Okotoks, AB, T1S 1A6, CANADA. Tel: 403-938-2220. p. 2549

Gillies, Ron, Head Librn, Lloydminster Public Library, 5010 - 49 St, Lloydminster, AB, T9V 0K2, CANADA. Tel: 780-875-0850. p. 2547

Gillies, Scott, Assoc Univ Librn, Wilfrid Laurier University Library, 75 University Ave W, Waterloo, ON, N2L 3C5, CANADA. Tel: 519-884-0710, Ext 3117. p. 2703

Gilligan, Bryan, Head, Ref, Coal City Public Library District, 85 N Garfield St, Coal City, IL, 60416. Tel: 815-634-4552. p. 572

Gilligan, Denise, Dir of Info Resources & Assessment, Flint Hills Technical College Library, 3301 W 18th Ave, Emporia, KS, 66801. Tel: 620-341-1323. p. 807

Gillihan, Jenny, Dir, Obion River Regional Library, 542 N Lindell St, Martin, TN, 38237. Tel: 731-364-4597. p. 2110

Gillihan, Karen, Adult Serv, Dir, Goodland Public Library, 812 Broadway, Goodland, KS, 67735. Tel: 785-899-5461. p. 810

Gilliies, Scott, Assoc Dean, Mercer University Atlanta, 3001 Mercer University Dr, Atlanta, GA, 30341. Tel: 678-547-6274. p. 465

Gilliland, Kris, Dir, University of Mississippi, 481 Chuckie Mullins Dr, University, MS, 38677. Tel: 662-915-6824. p. 1234

Gillis, Arlene, Libr Asst, Bastyr University Library, 14500 Juanita Dr NE, Kenmore, WA, 98028. Tel: 425-602-3020. p. 2367

Gillis, Emma, Libr Dir, Pemberton & District Public Library, 7390A Cottonwood St, Pemberton, BC, V0N 2L0, CANADA. Tel: 604-894-6916. p. 2573

Gillis, Michelle, Libr Mgr, Elmworth Community Library, 113036 Hwy 722, Elmworth, AB, T0H 1J0, CANADA. Tel: 780-354-2930. p. 2539

Gillis, Steven A, Dir, Orange Beach Public Library, 26267 Canal Rd, Orange Beach, AL, 36561-3917. Tel: 251-981-2923. p. 32

Gillis, Theresa, Ref & Instruction, Eastern Oregon University, One University Blvd, La Grande, OR, 97850. Tel: 541-962-3605. p. 1884

Gillispie, Valerie, Univ Archivist, Duke University Libraries, 411 Chapel Dr, Durham, NC, 27708. Tel: 919-684-8929. p. 1684

Gilloon, Robyn, Libr Dir, Lynbrook Public Library, 56 Eldert St, Lynbrook, NY, 11563. Tel: 516-599-8630. p. 1566

Gills, Tina, Develop Dir, Richland Library, 1431 Assembly St, Columbia, SC, 29201-3101. Tel: 803-799-9084. p. 2054

Gillum, Holly, Dir, Ashley County Library, 211 E Lincoln St, Hamburg, AR, 71646. Tel: 870-853-2078. p. 97

Gillum, Karen, Humanities Librn, Colby College Libraries, 5100 Mayflower Hill, Waterville, ME, 04901. Tel: 207-859-5123. p. 945

Gillyard, Curlie, Ms, Libr Asst, Desoto Parish Library, 109 Crosby St, Mansfield, LA, 71052. Tel: 318-872-6100. p. 895

Gilman, Abby, Sarasota Campus Libr Dir, Keiser University Library System, 1500 NW 49th St, Fort Lauderdale, FL, 33309. Tel: 954-351-4035. p. 401

Gilman, Isaac, Dean, Univ Libr, Pacific University Libraries, 2043 College Way, Forest Grove, OR, 97116. Tel: 503-352-1401. p. 1880

Gilman Sur, Sarah, Head Librn, University of Hawaii, 45-720 Kea'ahala Rd, Kaneohe, HI, 96744. Tel: 808-235-7435. p. 513

Gilman, Susan, Head Librn, Harvard Library, Tozzer Library, 21 Divinity Ave, Cambridge, MA, 02138. Tel: 617-495-2253, 617-496-9484. p. 1007

Gilmore, Amanda, Cataloger, Material Processor, Barry-Lawrence Regional Library, 213 Sixth St, Monett, MO, 65708-2147. Tel: 417-235-6646. p. 1262

Gilmore, Brooke, Ref & Instrul Serv Librn, Mount Wachusett Community College Library, 444 Green St, Gardner, MA, 01440. Tel: 978-630-9125. p. 1020

Gilmore, Cathy, Pub Serv Dir, Upper Moreland Free Public Library, 109 Park Ave, Willow Grove, PA, 19090-3277. Tel: 215-659-0741. p. 2024

Gilmore, Julie, Tech Serv Librn, Spartanburg Community College Library, Giles Campus, 107 Community College Dr, Spartanburg, SC, 29303. Tel: 864-592-4764. p. 2069

Gilmore, Lil, Librn, The Frances Kibble Kenny Lake Public Library, Mile 5 Edgerton Hwy, Copper Center, AK, 99573. Tel: 907-822-3015. p. 44

Gilmour, Ron, Web Serv Librn, Ithaca College Library, 953 Danby Rd, Ithaca, NY, 14850-7060. Tel: 607-274-3206. p. 1552

Gilpin, Chanda, Asst Chief Librn, Wellington County Library, 190 Saint Andrews St W, Fergus, ON, N1M 1N5, CANADA. Tel: 519-787-7805. p. 2641

Gilroy, Corinne, Access Serv, Libr Operations, Mount Saint Vincent University Library & Archives, 15 Lumpkin Rd, Halifax, NS, B3M 2J6, CANADA. Tel: 902-457-6204. p. 2619

Gilroy, Heather, Libr Dir, Lost Nation Public Library, 410 Main St, Lost Nation, IA, 52254. Tel: 563-678-2114. p. 766

Gilroy, Michael, Dir, East Haddam Library System, 18 Plains Rd, Moodus, CT, 06469. Tel: 860-873-8248. p. 323

Gilson, Ashley, Libr Serv Mgr, Somerset County Library System, Crisfield Public, 100 Collins St, Crisfield, MD, 21817. Tel: 410-968-0955. p. 973

Gilson, Eric, Head, ILL, Ref & Instrul Serv Librn, Rutgers University Libraries, Camden Law Library, 217 N Fifth St, Camden, NJ, 08102-1203. Tel: 856-225-6462. p. 1394

Gilstrap, Donald A, Dean of Libr, University of Alabama, University Libraries, University of Alabama Campus, Capstone Dr, Tuscaloosa, AL, 35487. Tel: 205-348-7561. p. 38

Giltenboth, Brett, Librn, La Roche University, 9000 Babcock Blvd, Pittsburgh, PA, 15237. Tel: 412-536-1063. p. 1994

Gilton, Donna L, Dr, Prof Emerita, University of Rhode Island, Rodman Hall, 94 W Alumni Ave, Kingston, RI, 02881-0815. Tel: 401-874-2878, 401-874-2947. p. 2792

Giltrud, Marianne, Ref & Instruction Librn, Prince George's Community College Library, 301 Largo Rd, Largo, MD, 20774-2199. Tel: 301-546-0467. p. 970

Gimenez, Patricia, Libr Dir, University of Iowa Libraries, Art, 235 Art Bldg W, 141 N Riverside Dr, Iowa City, IA, 52242. Tel: 319-335-3089. p. 761
Gincley, Leslie, Mgr, Ch & Youth Serv, Frederick County Public Libraries, 110 E Patrick St, Frederick, MD, 21701. Tel: 301-600-1613. p. 966
Gindin, Kathryn, Asst Dir, Atlantic County Library System, 40 Farragut Ave, Mays Landing, NJ, 08330-1750. Tel: 609-625-2776. p. 1417
Gindlesperger, Paul, Discovery Serv, Syst Adminr, Rollins College, 1000 Holt Ave, Campus Box 2744, Winter Park, FL, 32789-2744. Tel: 407-646-1372. p. 455
Ginman, Karen, Colls Mgr, Digital Resources Mgr, Herrick District Library, 300 S River Ave, Holland, MI, 49423. Tel: 616-355-3718. p. 1115
Ginn, David S, PhD, Dir, Boston University Libraries, Alumni Medical Library, 715 Albany St L-12, Boston, MA, 02118-2394. Tel: 617-638-4232. p. 993
Ginn, Ellen, Financial Serv Adminr, Baldwin County Library Cooperative, Inc, PO Box 399, Robertsdale, AL, 36567-0399. Tel: 251-970-4010. p. 34
Ginno, Liz, Librn/Concord Campus Libr, California State University, East Bay Library, CSU East Bay Library, 25800 Carlos Bee Blvd, Hayward, CA, 94542-3052. Tel: 510-885-2969. p. 150
Gins, Paul, Fr, Archivist, Order of Servants of Mary (Servites), USA Province, 3121 W Jackson Blvd, Chicago, IL, 60612. Tel: 773-638-5800, Ext 31. p. 567
Gins, Paul, Fr, Archivist, Our Lady of Sorrows Basilica, 3121 W Jackson Blvd, Chicago, IL, 60612. Tel: 773-533-0360. p. 567
Ginsberg, Blanca, Br Mgr, San Diego County Library, Casa De Oro Branch, 9805 Campo Rd, No 180, Spring Valley, CA, 91977-1477. Tel: 619-463-3236. p. 216
Ginther, Megan, Libr Mgr, Carstairs Public Library, 1402 Scarlett Ranch Blvd, Carstairs, AB, T0M 0N0, CANADA. Tel: 403-337-3943. p. 2530
Ginther, Vicky, Ad, Fauquier County Public Library, 11 Winchester St, Warrenton, VA, 20186. Tel: 540-422-8500, Ext 1. p. 2351
Ginther, Wendy, Librn, Department of Human Services-Youth Corrections, 2200 O St, Greeley, CO, 80631-9503. Tel: 970-304-6277. p. 285
Ginzburg, Barbara, Head, Access Serv, Washburn University, School of Law Library, 1700 SW College Ave, Topeka, KS, 66621. Tel: 785-670-1087. p. 840
Ginzler, Denise, Dir, Mason Public Library, Mann House, 16 Darling Hill Rd, Mason, NH, 03048. Tel: 603-878-3867. p. 1373
Gioia, Susan, Circ Mgr, Middletown Township Public Library, 55 New Monmouth Rd, Middletown, NJ, 07748. Tel: 732-671-3700. p. 1418
Gioiosa, Dan, Customer Serv Mgr, Ajax Public Library, 55 Harwood Ave S, Ajax, ON, L1S 2H8, CANADA. Tel: 905-683-4000, Ext 8824. p. 2627
Gionet, André, Sr Info Spec, Canadian Agriculture Library-Fredericton, 850 Lincoln Rd, Fredericton, NB, E3B 4Z7, CANADA. Tel: 506-460-4446. p. 2600
Gionet, Mylene May, Libr Mgr, Chaleur Library Region, Claude LeBouthillier Public Library, 8185-2 rue Saint Paul, Bas-Caraquet, NB, E1W 6C4, CANADA. Tel: 506-726-2775. p. 2599
Giono, Angela, Head Librn, Broadwater School & Community Library, 201 N Spruce St, Townsend, MT, 59644. Tel: 406-266-5060. p. 1303
Giordano, Leah, Dir, Marathon County Public Library, 300 N First St, Wausau, WI, 54403-5405. Tel: 715-261-7200. p. 2485
Giordano, Vince, Dir, Juniata County Library, 498 Jefferson St, Mifflintown, PA, 17059-1424. Tel: 717-436-6378. p. 1963
Giorgi, Betty, Head, Adult Serv, Wilmette Public Library District, 1242 Wilmette Ave, Wilmette, IL, 60091-2558. Tel: 847-256-6936. p. 663
Giorgini, Barbra, Assoc Dean, The George Washington University, 2130 H St NW, Washington, DC, 20052. Tel: 202-994-6558. p. 367
Giotsas, Kathy, Dir, Case Memorial Library, 176 Tyler City Rd, Orange, CT, 06477-2498. Tel: 203-891-2170. p. 333
Giovinazzo, Jacqui, Circ Supvr, Iberia Parish Library, 445 E Main St, New Iberia, LA, 70560-3710. Tel: 337-364-7024, 337-364-7074. p. 900
Gipson, Barbara, Libr Asst, Gardiner Public Library, 152 Water St, Gardiner, ME, 04345. Tel: 207-582-3312. p. 926
Gipson, Brandon, Libr Dir, United States Air Force, 97 FSS/FSDL, 109 E Ave, Bldg 65, Altus Air Force Base, OK, 73523. Tel: 580-481-6302. p. 1840
Gipson, Jamie, Adminr, Rideau Lakes Public Library, Elgin/Administration Branch, 24 Halladay St, Elgin, ON, K0G 1E0, CANADA. Tel: 613-359-5315. p. 2640
Gipson, Michelle, Collection Maintenance Mgr, University of California, Riverside, 900 University Ave, Riverside, CA, 92521. Tel: 951-827-3220. p. 203
Gipson, Mindy, Br Mgr, Hawaii State Public Library System, Hanapepe Public Library, 4490 Kona Rd, Hanapepe, HI, 96716. Tel: 808-335-8418. p. 507
Giraldez, Karal, Libr Mgr, Brown County Library, Southwest Branch, 974 Ninth St, Green Bay, WI, 54304. Tel: 920-492-4910. p. 2438
Giraldez, Karla, Libr Mgr, Brown County Library, Ashwaubenon Branch, 1060 Orlando Dr, Green Bay, WI, 54304. Tel: 920-492-4913. p. 2438
Girard, Diane, Librn, Ecole de Technologie Superieure (Service de la bibliotheque), 1100 rue Notre-Dame Ouest, Montreal, QC, H3C 1K3, CANADA. Tel: 514-396-8960. p. 2724
Girard, Florence, Curator, Cloud County Historical Society Museum Library, 635 Broadway, Concordia, KS, 66901. Tel: 785-243-2866. p. 803
Girard, Mary, Dir, Dunbarton Public Library, 1004 School St, Dunbarton, NH, 03046-4816. Tel: 603-774-3546. p. 1361
Girard, Maxine, Info Literacy Librn, American International College, 1000 State St, Springfield, MA, 01109. Tel: 413-205-3225. p. 1056
Girgente, Irene, Dir, College of the Ouachitas, One College Circle, Malvern, AR, 72104. Tel: 501-337-5000. p. 103
Girod, Johnna, Ref Librn, Oklahoma State University - Tulsa Library, 700 N Greenwood Ave, Tulsa, OK, 74106-0702. Tel: 918-594-8130. p. 1865
Giroux, Claire, Coordr, Cegep de Sainte-Foy Bibliotheque, 2410 Chemin Sainte-Foy, Sainte-Foy, QC, G1V 1T3, CANADA. Tel: 418-659-6600, Ext 3714. p. 2734
Giroux, Dorothy, Librn, Lenawee District Library, Onsted Branch, 261 S Main St, Onsted, MI, 49265-9749. Tel: 517-467-2623. p. 1075
Giroux, Jeanette, Libr Tech, St Clair College, 1001 Grand Ave W, Chatham, ON, N7M 5W4, CANADA. Tel: 519-354-9100, Ext 3232, 519-354-9100, Ext 3273. p. 2636
Girsberger, Russ, Chief Librn, United States Naval School of Music, JEB Little Creek, 1420 Gator Blvd, Virginia Beach, VA, 23459-2617. Tel: 757-462-5734. p. 2350
Girton, Brittany, Libr Asst, Manhattan Christian College Library, 1415 Anderson Ave, Manhattan, KS, 66502-4081. Tel: 785-539-3571, Ext 113. p. 823
Girton, Carrie, Interim Libr Dir, University of Rio Grande, 218 N College Ave, Rio Grande, OH, 45674. Tel: 740-245-7459. p. 1817
Girven, Amy, Circ Librn, Wyalusing Public Library, 115 Church St, Wyalusing, PA, 18853. Tel: 570-746-1711. p. 2024
Gislason, Pat, Circ Assoc, San Juan Island Library, 1010 Guard St, Friday Harbor, WA, 98250-9612. Tel: 360-378-2798. p. 2364
Gisler, Antonia, Librn, Alberta School for the Deaf Library, 6240 113 St NW, Edmonton, AB, T6H 3L2, CANADA. Tel: 780-436-0465. p. 2535
Gissel, Paige, Br Mgr, Josephine Community Library District, Wolf Creek Branch, 102 Ruth Ave, Wolf Creek, OR, 97497. Tel: 541-866-2606. p. 1881
Gisselman, Gary, Librn, Marathon County Historical Society, 410 McIndoe St, Wausau, WI, 54403. Tel: 715-848-0378. p. 2485
Gissinger, Carol, Fiscal Officer, Granville Public Library, 217 E Broadway, Granville, OH, 43023-1398. Tel: 740-587-0196. p. 1788
Gitlin, Judy, Asst Librn, Tech Serv, Dominican College Library, 480 Western Hwy, Blauvelt, NY, 10913-2000. Tel: 845-848-7505. p. 1495
Gits, Carrie, Head Librn, Austin Community College, Highland Campus Library, 6101 Airport Blvd, 1st Flr, Rm 1325, Austin, TX, 78752. Tel: 512-223-7386. p. 2138
Gits, Carrie, Head Librn, Austin Community College, Rio Grande Campus Library, 1212 Rio Grande, Austin, TX, 78701. Tel: 512-223-3066. p. 2138
Gitschel, Tammie, Tech Serv Librn, Gering Public Library, 1055 P St, Gering, NE, 69341. Tel: 308-436-7433. p. 1315
Gitt, Cynthia, Ch Serv, Holdrege Area Public Library, 604 East Ave, Holdrege, NE, 68949. Tel: 308-995-6556. p. 1318
Gittemeier, Oscar, Asst Br Mgr, Ch, Atlanta-Fulton Public Library System, East Atlanta Branch, 400 Flat Shoals Ave SE, Atlanta, GA, 30316. Tel: 404-730-5438. p. 461
Gitzlaff, Brittany, Youth Serv Mgr, Waunakee Public Library, 210 N Madison St, Waunakee, WI, 53597. Tel: 608-849-4217. p. 2485
Giudice, Mary Jo, Dir of Libr, Dallas Public Library, 1515 Young St, Dallas, TX, 75201-5415. Tel: 214-670-1400. p. 2165
Giugno, Karen, Asst Dir, Ch, Acton Public Library, 60 Old Boston Post Rd, Old Saybrook, CT, 06475-2200. Tel: 860-501-5060. p. 333
Giuliani, Laura, Head, Youth Serv, Huntington Public Library, 338 Main St, Huntington, NY, 11743. Tel: 631-427-5165, Ext 230. p. 1549
Giuliani, Marisa, Access Serv Librn, Peterborough Public Library, 345 Aylmer St N, Peterborough, ON, K9H 3V7, CANADA. Tel: 705-745-5382, Ext 2351. p. 2672
Giuliano, Frederic, Gen Mgr, Université du Québec à Montréal Bibliotheque, 400 rue Ste-Catherine Est, Local A-M100, Montreal, QC, H2L 2C5, CANADA. Tel: 514-987-6114. p. 2728
Giunta, Heather, Circ Mgr, Harnett County Public Library, 601 S Main St, Lillington, NC, 27546-6107. Tel: 910-893-3446. p. 1700
Giurciullo, Kristen, Outreach & Instruction Librn, Manchester Community College Library, 1066 Front St, Manchester, NH, 03102. Tel: 603-206-8150. p. 1372
Giusti, Aidan, Paralegal, Rhode Island Office of Attorney General Library, 150 S Main St, Providence, RI, 02903. Tel: 401-274-4400. p. 2040
Giusti, Aurelia, Head Librn, Cegep Beauce Appalaches, 1055 116e rue, Saint Georges-de-Beauce, QC, G5Y 3G1, CANADA. Tel: 418-228-8896, Ext 2314. p. 2733
Giusti, Susan, Ref/Tech Serv Librn, Widener University, Harrisburg Campus Law Library, 3800 Vartan Way, Harrisburg, DE, 17110. Tel: 717-541-3929. p. 358
Givens, Rebecca, Tech Serv Librn, Covenant Theological Seminary, 478 Covenant Ln, Saint Louis, MO, 63141. Tel: 314-392-4100, 314-434-4044. p. 1270
Gjerde, Ryan, Digital Initiatives Librn, Libr Dir, Luther College, 700 College Dr, Decorah, IA, 52101. Tel: 563-387-1288. p. 745

Glab, Tracee, Library Contact, Flint Institute of Arts, 1120 E Kearsley St, Flint, MI, 48503-1915. Tel: 810-234-1695. p. 1105
Glackin, Barbara, Dean, Southeast Missouri State University, 929 Normal Ave, Cape Girardeau, MO, 63701. Tel: 573-651-2235. p. 1240
Gladis, Pam, Systems & Archives Librarian, Southwest Minnesota State University Library, 1501 State St, Marshall, MN, 56258. Tel: 507-537-6813. p. 1182
Gladstone, Donna, Chief Exec Officer, Edwardsburgh Cardinal Public Library, 618 County Rd 2, Cardinal, ON, K0E 1E0, CANADA. Tel: 613-657-3822. p. 2635
Gladstone, Donna, Chief Exec Officer, Edwardsburgh Cardinal Public Library, Spencerville Branch, Five Henderson St, Spencerville, ON, K0E 1X0, CANADA. Tel: 613-658-5575. p. 2635
Gladwin, Steve, Electronic Res Librn, Syst Librn, Lake Forest College, 555 N Sheridan Rd, Lake Forest, IL, 60045. Tel: 847-735-5065. p. 606
Glaesemann, Jodene, Br Supvr, Lincoln City Libraries, Bess Dodson Walt Branch, 6701 S 14th St, Lincoln, NE, 68512. Tel: 402-441-4460. p. 1321
Glaeser, Katie, Electronic Res Librn, University of Lynchburg, 1501 Lakeside Dr, Lynchburg, VA, 24501-3199. Tel: 434-544-8260. p. 2331
Glaettli, Lauren, Librn, United States Navy, Naval Surface Warfare Ctr, Bldg 1194, 6090 Jenkins Rd, Dahlgren, VA, 22448. Tel: 540-653-7474. p. 2314
Glascow, Jeremy, Music & Performing Arts Librn, University of North Carolina at Greensboro, Harold Schiffman Music Library, School of Music Bldg, 100 McIver St, Greensboro, NC, 27412. Tel: 336-334-5771. p. 1693
Glaser, Jody, Dir, Eagle Free Library, 3413 School St, Bliss, NY, 14024. Tel: 585-322-7701. p. 1495
Glaser, Joseph, Regional Dir, Canadian Music Centre Libaries, Ontario Region Library, 20 St Joseph St, Toronto, ON, M4Y 1J9, CANADA. Tel: 416-961-6601, Ext 007. p. 2687
Glaser, Mary, Coll/Libr Mgr, Plainfield-Guilford Township Public Library, 1120 Stafford Rd, Plainfield, IN, 46168. Tel: 317-839-6602, Ext 2147. p. 713
Glaser, Matthew, Libr Dir, Hewitt Public Library, 200 Patriot Ct, Hewitt, TX, 76643. Tel: 254-666-2442. p. 2189
Glasgow, Amanda, Libr Dir, Northwest Regional Library, Mary Wallace Cobb Memorial Library, 44425 Hwy 17, Vernon, AL, 35592. Tel: 205-695-6123. p. 40
Glasgow, Audrey, Coll Mgr, Curator, US Space & Rocket Center, One Tranquility Base, Huntsville, AL, 35805-3399. Tel: 256-721-5401, 256-721-7148. p. 22
Glasgow, Maghan, Teen Serv, Canton Public Library, 40 Dyer Ave, Canton, CT, 06019. Tel: 860-693-5800. p. 305
Glass, Amy, Ref Librn, Illinois Central College, Kenneth L Edward Library Administration Bldgs, L312, One College Dr, East Peoria, IL, 61635-0001. Tel: 309-694-5748. p. 581
Glass, Bob, Dean, Libr & Univ Librn, Piedmont University Library, 1021 Central Ave, Demorest, GA, 30535. Tel: 706-776-0111. p. 476
Glass, Christina, Ch, Upland Public Library, 450 N Euclid Ave, Upland, CA, 91786-4732. Tel: 909-931-4216. p. 254
Glass, Elizabeth, Dir, Planning, Policy & E-Serv Delivery, Toronto Public Library, 789 Yonge St, Toronto, ON, M4W 2G8, CANADA. Tel: 416-393-7131. p. 2693
Glass, Eric, Metadata Librn, Columbia University, Lehman Social Sciences Library, 300 International Affairs Bldg, 420 W 118th St, New York, NY, 10027. Tel: 212-854-3794. p. 1583
Glass, Ian, Research Librn, Institute for Wetland & Waterfowl Research Library, One Mallard Bay at Hwy 220, Stonewall, MB, R0C 2Z0, CANADA. Tel: 204-467-3276. p. 2591
Glass, Joseph, Tech Serv/Circ Librn, Notre Dame College, 4545 College Rd, South Euclid, OH, 44121. Tel: 216-373-5360. p. 1820
Glass, Lora, ILL, Ref (Info Servs), Niceville Public Library, 206 Partin Dr N, Niceville, FL, 32578. Tel: 850-279-6436, Ext 1507. p. 428
Glass, Traci, Dir, West Des Moines Public Library, 4000 Mills Civic Pkwy, West Des Moines, IA, 50265-2049. Tel: 515-222-3409. p. 791
Glass, Traci, Asst Dir, Lincoln City Libraries, 136 S 14th St, Lincoln, NE, 68508-1899. Tel: 402-441-8511. p. 1321
Glasscock, Ann, Asst Curator, Taft Museum of Art Library, 316 Pike St, Cincinnati, OH, 45202-4293. Tel: 513-241-0343. p. 1763
Glasser, Larissa Elaine, Libr Asst, Harvard Library, Arnold Arboretum Horticultural Library, 125 Arborway, Jamaica Plain, MA, 02130. Tel: 617-384-5330. p. 1005
Glassford Johnson, Barbara, Tech Serv Mgr, Bedford Public Library, 2424 Forest Ridge Dr, Bedford, TX, 76021. Tel: 817-952-2350. p. 2146
Glassman, Nancy, Asst Dir, Albert Einstein College of Medicine, Jack & Pearl Resnick Campus, 1300 Morris Park Ave, Bronx, NY, 10461-1924. Tel: 718-430-3108. p. 1497
Glassman, Paul, Dir, Cultural Serv, Scholarly Resources Librn, Yeshiva University Libraries, 2520 Amsterdam Ave, New York, NY, 10033. Tel: 646-592-4107. p. 1604
Glater, Annie, Head, Circ, Head, Tech, Marlborough Public Library, 35 W Main St, Marlborough, MA, 01752-5510. Tel: 508-624-6900. p. 1032
Glatthaar, Peggy, Head, Customer Serv, Florida Gulf Coast University Library, 10501 FGCU Blvd S, Fort Myers, FL, 33965. Tel: 239-590-1429. p. 402
Glatz, Cala, Mgr, Alexander Findley Community Library, 2883 North Rd, Findley Lake, NY, 14736. Tel: 716-769-6568. p. 1533
Glauber, Daniel, Local Hist Librn, Scarsdale Public Library, 54 Olmsted Rd, Scarsdale, NY, 10583. Tel: 914-722-1300. p. 1637
Glaude, Noah, Dir, North Olympic Library System, 2210 S Peabody St, Port Angeles, WA, 98362-6536. Tel: 360-417-8500, Ext 7717. p. 2373
Glauner, Dana, Interim Libr Dir, South Piedmont Community College, L L Polk Campus, 680 Hwy 74, Polkton, NC, 28135. Tel: 704-272-5389. p. 1708
Glaviano, Marisa, Youth Serv Coordr, Licking County Library, 101 W Main St, Newark, OH, 43055-5054. Tel: 740-349-5551. p. 1807
Glaze, Gail, Ref/Tech Serv, University of Wisconsin-Madison, Business Library, Grainger Hall, Rm 1320, 975 University Ave, Madison, WI, 53706. Tel: 608-262-4007. p. 2451
Glaze, Terrence, Educ Coordr, Alaska State Department of Corrections, 9101 Hesterberg Rd, Eagle River, AK, 99577. Tel: 907-694-9511. p. 45
Glazer, Gwen, Head of Coll Dev & User Engagement, Croton Free Library, 171 Cleveland Dr, Croton-on-Hudson, NY, 10520. Tel: 914-271-6612. p. 1523
Glazier, Rhonda, Dir, Coll Mgt, University of Colorado Colorado Springs, 1420 Austin Bluffs Pkwy, Colorado Springs, CO, 80918. Tel: 719-255-3291. p. 272
Glazier, Stacey, Libr Dir, Grafton Public Library, 47 Library Rd, Grafton, NH, 03240. Tel: 603-523-7865. p. 1365
Gleason, Crystal, Adult Services Team Leader, Niles District Library, 620 E Main St, Niles, MI, 49120. Tel: 269-683-8545. p. 1137
Gleason, Elena, Supvr, Ad Serv, Tigard Public Library, 13500 SW Hall Blvd, Tigard, OR, 97223-8111. Tel: 503-684-6537, Ext 2649. p. 1900
Gleason, James E, Dep Dir, Perkins School for the Blind, 175 N Beacon St, Watertown, MA, 02472. Tel: 617-972-7240. p. 1062
Gleason, Suzanne, Tech Serv Librn, Lindenwood University Library, 209 S Kingshighway, Saint Charles, MO, 63301. Tel: 636-949-4881. p. 1268
Gleave, Teresa, Dir, Knowledge Serv, Fasken Martineau DuMoulin LLP Library, 2900-550 Burrard St, Vancouver, BC, V6C 0A3, CANADA. Tel: 604-631-4804. p. 2578
Gleber, Jenn, Br Mgr, Mkt Mgr, Dorchester County Library, Summerville Branch, 76 Old Trolley Rd, Summerville, SC, 29485. Tel: 843-871-5075. p. 2069
Gleeson, Margaret, Supvr, Tech Serv, Nashua Public Library, Two Court St, Nashua, NH, 03060. Tel: 603-589-4624. p. 1374
Gleeson Noyes, Sarah, Librn, Surrey Memorial Hospital, 13750 96th Ave, Surrey, BC, V3V 1Z2, CANADA. Tel: 604-585-5666, Ext 774510. p. 2577
Gleiberman, Rachel, Col Archivist, Hartwick College, One Hartwick Dr, Oneonta, NY, 13820. Tel: 607-431-4450. p. 1611
Gleichauf, Carol, Ch Serv, Dodgeville Public Library, 139 S Iowa St, Dodgeville, WI, 53533. Tel: 608-935-3728. p. 2431
Gleisner, Anjie, Br Mgr, Kent District Library, Gaines Township Branch, 421 68th St SE, Grand Rapids, MI, 49548. p. 1094
Gleisner, Anjie, Regional Mgr, Kent District Library, Kelloggsville Branch, Kelloggsville High School, 4787 Division Ave S, Grand Rapids, MI, 49548. p. 1094
Gleisner, Anjie, Regional Mgr, Kent District Library, Library for the Blind & Physically Handicapped, 3350 Michael Ave SW, Wyoming, MI, 49509. Tel: 616-647-3988. p. 1094
Gleisner, Tim, Mgr, Spec Coll, Library of Michigan, 702 W Kalamazoo St, Lansing, MI, 48915. Tel: 517-373-8389. p. 1125
Gleisner, Tim, Asst State Librn, Texas State Library & Archives Commission, 1201 Brazos St, Austin, TX, 78701. Tel: 512-463-5459. p. 2141
Glena, Ellen, Teen Serv Librn, Henrietta Public Library, 625 Calkins Rd, Rochester, NY, 14623. Tel: 585-359-7092. p. 1628
Glendenning, Karin, Dir, Signal Mountain Public Library, 1114 James Blvd, Signal Mountain, TN, 37377-2509. Tel: 423-886-7323. p. 2126
Glendinning, Jo-Ann, Dir, Fruitland Park Library, 604 W Berckman St, Fruitland Park, FL, 34731. Tel: 352-360-6561. p. 405
Glendinning, Mary, Deputy Chief, NPR RAD-Research Archive & Data Strategy, 1111 N Capitol St NE, Washington, DC, 20002. p. 373
Glenn, Brianna, Dir, De Soto Public Library, 405 Walnut St, De Soto, IA, 50069. Tel: 515-834-2690. p. 744
Glenn, Eric, Director of Engagement, Dir of Organizational Dev, Virginia Polytechnic Institute & State University Libraries, 560 Drillfield Dr, Blacksburg, VA, 24061. Tel: 540-231-6170. p. 2307
Glenn, Jon, Dir, Libr Serv, Salt Lake Community College Libraries, Taylorsville Redwood Campus, 4600 S Redwood Rd, Taylorsville, UT, 84123-3145. Tel: 801-957-4905. p. 2274
Glenn, Joyce E, Library Contact, Southern University at Shreveport, Metro Campus, 610 Texas St, Shreveport, LA, 71101. Tel: 318-670-9579. p. 910
Glenn, Nancy, Librn, Chinook Regional Library, Climax Branch, 102 Main St, Climax, SK, S0N 0N0, CANADA. Tel: 306-293-2229. p. 2752
Glenn, Rachel, Libr Dir, National Institute of Standards & Technology Library, 100 Bureau Dr, Stop 2500, Gaithersburg, MD, 20899-2500. Tel: 301-975-2906. p. 967
Glenn, Sara, Youth Serv Coordr, Coralville Public Library, 1401 Fifth St, Coralville, IA, 52241. Tel: 319-248-1850. p. 742
Glenn, Taylor, Access Services Library Specialist, Blue Ridge Community College, One College Lane, Weyers Cave, VA, 24486. Tel: 540-453-2247. p. 2352

Glenn, Valerie, Head of Libr, University of Georgia Libraries, Map & Government Information, 320 S Jackson St, Athens, GA, 30602. Tel: 706-542-0664. p. 459
Glennan, Barbara, Assoc Dir, Educational Tech & Strategic Initiatives, California Western School of Law Library, 290 Cedar St, San Diego, CA, 92101. Tel: 619-525-1499. p. 215
Glennan, Kathy, Head, Spec Coll, University of Maryland Libraries, Theodore R McKeldin Library, 7649 Library Lane, College Park, MD, 20742-7011. Tel: 301-314-9046. p. 962
Glentworth, Nicole, Libr Mgr, Fraser Valley Regional Library, Agassiz Library, 7140 Cheam Ave, Agassiz, BC, V0M 1A0, CANADA. Tel: 604-792-1941. p. 2561
Glentworth, Nicole, Libr Mgr, Fraser Valley Regional Library, Boston Bar Library, 47643 Old Boston Bar Rd, Boston Bar, BC, V0K 1C0, CANADA. Tel: 604-867-8847. p. 2561
Glentworth, Nicole, Libr Mgr, Fraser Valley Regional Library, Chilliwack Library, 45860 First Ave, Chilliwack, BC, V2P 7K1, CANADA. Tel: 604-792-1941. p. 2561
Glentworth, Nicole, Libr Mgr, Fraser Valley Regional Library, Hope Library, 1005A Sixth Ave, Hope, BC, V0X 1L4, CANADA. Tel: 604-869-2313. p. 2561
Glentworth, Nicole, Libr Mgr, Fraser Valley Regional Library, Sardis Libray, 5819 Tyson Rd, Chilliwack, BC, V2R 3R6, CANADA. Tel: 604-858-5503. p. 2562
Glentworth, Nicole, Libr Mgr, Fraser Valley Regional Library, Yale Library, 65050 Albert St, Yale, BC, V0K 2S0, CANADA. Tel: 604-863-2279. p. 2562
Glentworth, Nicole, Libr Mgr, Fraser Valley Regional Library, Yarrow Library, 4670 Community St, Yarrow, BC, V2R 5E1, CANADA. Tel: 604-823-4664. p. 2562
Glick, JoEllen, Dir, Webb Shadle Memorial Library, 301 W Dallas, Pleasantville, IA, 50225. Tel: 515-848-5617. p. 777
Glick, Rita, Br Mgr, Johnson County Library, Leawood Pioneer Branch, 4700 Town Center Dr, Leawood, KS, 66211. p. 830
Glick, Shelley, Ref Librn, Briarcliff Manor Public Library, One Library Rd, Briarcliff Manor, NY, 10510. Tel: 914-941-7072. p. 1496
Glidden, Darcy, Commun Libr Mgr, Barrie Public Library, Holly Branch, 555 Essa Rd, Barrie, ON, L4N 6A9, CANADA. Tel: 705-728-1010, Ext 4310. p. 2630
Glidden, Darcy, Commun Libr Mgr, Barrie Public Library, Painswick Branch, 48 Dean Ave, Barrie, ON, L4N 0C2, CANADA. Tel: 705-728-1010, Ext 4310. p. 2630
Glidden, Kimber, Teen Prog, Teen Serv, East Bonner County Library District, 1407 Cedar St, Sandpoint, ID, 83864-2052. Tel: 208-263-6930. p. 531
Glidden, Kimber, Youth & Teen Serv, East Bonner County Library District, 1407 Cedar St, Sandpoint, ID, 83864-2052. Tel: 208-263-6930. p. 531
Gliebe, Jennifer, Dir, Perry Cook Memorial Public Library, 7406 County Rd 242, Shauck, OH, 43349. Tel: 419-362-7181. p. 1820
Glisson, Johnice, Regional Adminr, Carroll & Madison Library System, 106 Spring St, Berryville, AR, 72616. Tel: 870-423-5300. p. 91
Glisson, Lane, E-Learning Librn, Instruction Librn, Borough of Manhattan Community College Library, 199 Chambers St, S410, New York, NY, 10007. Tel: 212-220-8000, Ext 7112. p. 1580
Glisson, Mark, Asst Dir, Fac & Tech Mgr, Hooksett Public Library, 31 Mount Saint Mary's Way, Hooksett, NH, 03106-1852. Tel: 603-485-6092. p. 1368
Glogowski, Sarah, Exec Dir, Finger Lakes Library System, 1300 Dryden Rd, Ithaca, NY, 14850. Tel: 607-273-4074, Ext 222. p. 1552
Glorioso, Adora, Librn, University Hospital Elyria Medical Center, 630 E River St, Elyria, OH, 44035. Tel: 404-827-5569. p. 1785
Glorioso, Adora, Med Librn, University Hospitals St John Medical Center, 29000 Center Ridge Rd, Westlake, OH, 44145. Tel: 440-827-5569. p. 1830
Glorioso, Kimberly Koko, Sr Ref Librn, Tulane University, Law Library, Weinmann Hall, 3rd Flr, 6329 Freret St, New Orleans, LA, 70118-6231. Tel: 504-865-5902. p. 904
Glosh, Carol, Access Serv Mgr, Salem Public Library, 28 E Main St, Salem, VA, 24153. Tel: 540-375-3089. p. 2347
Glossinger, Don, Dir, Michigan City Public Library, 100 E Fourth St, Michigan City, IN, 46360-3302. Tel: 219-873-3050. p. 706
Glotfelty, Corene, Archivist, Research Servs Librn, Pennsylvania Western University - Clarion, 840 Wood St, Clarion, PA, 16214. Tel: 814-393-1805. p. 1922
Glotfelty, Olivia, Librn, UPMC Mercy Hospital of Pittsburgh, 1400 Locust St, Pittsburgh, PA, 15219. Tel: 412-232-7520. p. 1997
Glover, Alana, Outreach Coordr, Washington County Public Library, 333 W Main St, Springfield, KY, 40069. Tel: 859-336-7655. p. 875
Glover, Chris, Asst Dir, Info Tech, Central Rappahannock Regional Library, 125 Olde Greenwich Dr, Ste 160, Fredericksburg, VA, 22408. Tel: 540-372-1144, Ext 7050. p. 2319
Glover, Cindy, Ch Serv, Andover Free Library, 40 Main St, Andover, NY, 14806. Tel: 607-478-8442. p. 1487
Glover, Jeannette, Libr Serv Coordr, Spoon River College Library, 23235 N County Hwy 22, Canton, IL, 61520. Tel: 309-649-6603. p. 548
Glover, Karen, Assoc Dean for Research & Scholarly Access, Georgia Institute of Technology Library, 260 Fourth St NW, Atlanta, GA, 30332. Tel: 404-894-7116. p. 464
Glover, Shannon, Libr Coord, Northeast Georgia Health System, 743 Spring St NE, Gainesville, GA, 30501-3715. Tel: 770-219-5216. p. 480
Glover, Shatarra, Tech Serv Librn, Voorhees University, 213 Wiggins Dr, Denmark, SC, 29042. Tel: 803-780-1220. p. 2058
Glowcheski, Angela, Dep Dir, Sequoyah Regional Library System, 116 Brown Industrial Pkwy, Canton, GA, 30114. Tel: 770-479-3090, Ext 230. p. 469
Glowcheski, Angela, Br Mgr, Hall County Library System, Spout Springs Branch, 6488 Spout Springs Rd, Flowery Branch, GA, 30542. Tel: 770-532-3311, Ext 191. p. 480
Glowczewski, Joanne, Br Supvr, Boonslick Regional Library, Warsaw Branch, 102 E Jackson, Warsaw, MO, 65355. Tel: 660-438-5211. p. 1279
Gluck, Sarah, Br Mgr, Brooklyn Public Library, Borough Park, 1265 43rd St, Brooklyn, NY, 11219. Tel: 718-437-4085. p. 1502
Gluckman, Lauren, Head, Coll Serv, Ref Librn, Pennsylvania State University - Dickinson School of Law, 214 Lewis Katz Bldg, University Park, PA, 16802. Tel: 814-865-2298. p. 2015
Glueckliich, Cindy, Libr Dir, Melrose Park Public Library, 801 N Broadway, Melrose Park, IL, 60160. Tel: 708-649-7400. p. 616
Glushko, Bobby, Chief Librn, Western University Libraries, 1151 Richmond St, Ste 200, London, ON, N6A 3K7, CANADA. Tel: 519-661-2111, Ext 82740. p. 2655
Glykis, Eleni, Libr Dir, Red Bank Public Library, 84 W Front St, Red Bank, NJ, 07701. Tel: 732-842-0690. p. 1439
Glynn, Danielle, Asst Med Librn, Roswell Park Comprehensive Cancer Center, Elm & Carlton Sts, Buffalo, NY, 14263. Tel: 716-845-5966. p. 1510
Glynn, Denise, Assoc Dir for Technical Services & Processing, DePaul University Libraries, Vincent G Rinn Law Library, 25 E Jackson Blvd, 5th Flr, Chicago, IL, 60604-2287. Tel: 312-362-8176. p. 560
Glynn, John, Br Mgr, Chicago Public Library, Albany Park, 3401 W Foster Ave, Chicago, IL, 60625. Tel: 773-539-5450. p. 555
Gmiter, Chris, Mgr, Carnegie Library of Pittsburgh, East Liberty, 130 S Whitfield St, Pittsburgh, PA, 15206-3806. Tel: 412-363-8232. p. 1991
Gmiter, Chris, Dir, Upper St Clair Township Library, 1820 McLaughlin Run Rd, Upper St Clair, PA, 15241-2397. Tel: 412-835-5540. p. 2016
Gnagey, Sandra, Librn, Columbia Township Library, 6456 Center St, Unionville, MI, 48767. Tel: 989-674-2651. p. 1155
Gnagy, Maria, Adminr, Mgr, Grants & Spec Project, Yuma County Free Library District, 2951 S 21st Dr, Yuma, AZ, 85364. Tel: 928-373-6465. p. 85
Gnat, Colleen, Head, Youth Serv, Cicero Public Library, 5225 W Cermak Rd, Cicero, IL, 60804. Tel: 708-652-8084. p. 571
Gnewikow, Cindy, ILL, Tomah Public Library, 716 Superior Ave, Tomah, WI, 54660. Tel: 608-374-7470. p. 2481
Gnissios, Todd, Exec Dir, Coquitlam Public Library, 575 Poirier St, Coquitlam, BC, V3J 6A9, CANADA. Tel: 604-937-4132. p. 2565
Gnitzcavich, Nancy, Librn, Gilbert Library, Inc, 38 Main St, Northfield, CT, 06778. Tel: 860-283-8176. p. 331
Goad, Delana, Asst Dir, Fentress County Public Library, 306 S Main St, Jamestown, TN, 38556-3845. Tel: 931-879-7512. p. 2103
Gobeil, Beth, Circ/Acq, Lady Lake Public Library, 225 W Guava St, Lady Lake, FL, 32159. Tel: 352-753-2957. p. 414
Gobeli, Savannah, Libr Tech, Mount Hope-Funks Grove Townships Library District, 111 S Hamilton St, McLean, IL, 61754-7624. Tel: 309-874-2291. p. 616
Gober, Kenneth, Cat Librn, Killeen Public Library, 205 E Church Ave, Killeen, TX, 76541. Tel: 254-501-8990. p. 2206
Gobert, Tammy, Automation Archivist, Rensselaer Libraries, Rensselaer Architecture Library, Greene Bldg 308, 3rd Flr, 110 Eighth St, Troy, NY, 12180-3590. Tel: 518-276-8310. p. 1652
Gobin, Kip, Cat & Acq, University of Virginia, Arthur J Morris Law Library, 580 Massie Rd, Charlottesville, VA, 22903-1738. Tel: 434-924-3745. p. 2310
Goble, Bonnie, Libr Mgr, Fredricksen Cleve J Library, East Pennsboro, 98 S Enola Dr, Enola, PA, 17025. Tel: 717-732-4274. p. 1918
Gocker, Ivy, Libr Dir, Adirondack Experience, the Museum on Blue Mountain Lake Library, 9097 State Rte 30, Blue Mountain Lake, NY, 12812. Tel: 518-352-7311, Ext 108. p. 1495
Gockley, Jeana, Dir, Joplin Public Library, 1901 E 20th St, Joplin, MO, 64804. Tel: 417-623-7953. p. 1253
Godbee, Sara, Dir, Libr Serv, Stevenson University Library, 1525 Greenspring Valley Rd, Stevenson, MD, 21153. Tel: 443-334-2688. p. 978
Godbey, Megan, Adult Literacy Coordr, Nashville Public Library, 615 Church St, Nashville, TN, 37219-2314. Tel: 615-880-2264. p. 2119
Godbout, Gaetan, Pres, Societe Historique de la Cote-du-Sud, 100 4e Ave Painchaud, La Pocatiere, QC, G0R 1Z0, CANADA. Tel: 418-856-2104. p. 2714
Godby, Lynn, Br Mgr, Kanawha County Public Library, Nitro Public, 1700 Park Ave, Nitro, WV, 25143. Tel: 304-755-4432. p. 2400
Goddard, Debra, Librn, Rainelle Public Library, 378 Seventh St, Rainelle, WV, 25962. Tel: 304-438-3008. p. 2413
Goddard, Lisa, Div Head, Syst Coordr, Memorial University of Newfoundland, Queen Elizabeth II Library, 234 Elizabeth Ave, St. John's, NL, A1B 3Y1, CANADA. Tel: 709-737-2124. p. 2610
Godden, Laura, Spec Coll & Archives Librn, University of Wisconsin-La Crosse, 1631 Pine St, La Crosse, WI, 54601-3748. Tel: 608-785-8511. p. 2446
Godec, Anne, Br Mgr, Lorain Public Library System, Domonkas Branch, 4125 E Lake Rd, Sheffield Lake, OH, 44054. Tel: 440-949-7410. p. 1797

Godfrey, I, Acq, University of Victoria Libraries, Diana M Priestly Law Library, PO Box 2300, STN CSC, Victoria, BC, V8W 3B1, CANADA. Tel: 250-721-8565. p. 2583
Godfrey, Jessica, Libr Dir, Annie Porter Ainsworth Memorial Library, 6064 S Main St, Sandy Creek, NY, 13145. Tel: 315-387-3732. p. 1636
Godfrey, Kathleen, Circ Spec, Belgrade Community Library, 106 N Broadway, Belgrade, MT, 59714. Tel: 406-388-4346. p. 1287
Godfrey, Kelly, Youth Serv, Barry-Lawrence Regional Library, Cassville Branch, 301 W 17th St, Cassville, MO, 65625-1044. Tel: 417-847-2121. p. 1263
Godfrey, Laura, Librn, CanLearn Society, 100-1117 Macleod Trail SE, Calgary, AB, T2G 2M8, CANADA. Tel: 403-686-9300, Ext 126. p. 2528
Godfrey, Ryan, Communications & PR Mgr, Alabama Public Library Service, 6030 Monticello Dr, Montgomery, AL, 36130. Tel: 334-213-3909. p. 27
Godfrey, Sue, Res Spec, Minnesota Discovery Center, 1005 Discovery Dr, Chisholm, MN, 55719. Tel: 218-254-1229. p. 1170
Godin, Alice, Resource Sharing Coord, Vermont State University - Johnson, 337 College Hill, Johnson, VT, 05656. Tel: 802-635-1277. p. 2287
Godin, Alice, ILL Supvr, Vermont State University - Lyndon, 1001 College Rd, Lyndonville, VT, 05851. p. 2288
Godin, Alice, Vice Chair, Waterville Town Library, 850 VT Rte 109, Waterville, VT, 05492. p. 2297
Godin, Kathy, Ch, Berlin Public Library, 270 Main St, Berlin, NH, 03570. Tel: 603-752-5210. p. 1355
Godin, Sonia, Libr Mgr, Chaleur Library Region, Petit-Rocher Public Library, 702 Principale St, Office 110, Petit-Rocher, NB, E8J 1V1, CANADA. Tel: 506-542-2744. p. 2599
Godina, Tino, Supvr, Yakima Valley Libraries, Toppenish Library, One S Elm St, Toppenish, WA, 98948. Tel: 509-865-3600. p. 2396
Godino, Frank, Ad, The Field Library, Four Nelson Ave, Peekskill, NY, 10566. Tel: 914-737-1212. p. 1616
Godino, Hope, Dir, Exeter Public Library, Four Chestnut St, Exeter, NH, 03833. Tel: 603-772-3101, 603-772-6036. p. 1363
Godissart, Matt, Libr Dir, Bedford County Library System, 240 S Wood St, Bedford, PA, 15522. Tel: 814-623-5010. p. 1909
Godissart, Matt, Dir, Bedford County Library, 240 S Wood St, Bedford, PA, 15522. Tel: 814-623-5010. p. 1909
Godleski, Ashlyn, Youth Serv Librn, Haywood County Public Library, Canton Branch, 11 Pennsylvania Ave, Canton, NC, 28716. Tel: 828-648-2567. p. 1721
Godleski, Nancy, Dean, Libr Serv, University of Massachusetts Dartmouth Library, 285 Old Westport Rd, North Dartmouth, MA, 02747-2300. Tel: 508-999-8662. p. 1041
Godlesky, Jennifer, Libr Mgr, Hurley Medical Center, One Hurley Plaza, Flint, MI, 48503. Tel: 810-262-9427. p. 1106
Godsy, Samantha, Pub Serv, Auburn Public Library, 749 E Thach Ave, Auburn, AL, 36830. Tel: 334-501-3190. p. 5
Godwin, Diana, Libr Dir, Pacific Grove Public Library, 550 Central Ave, Pacific Grove, CA, 93950-2789. Tel: 831-648-5760. p. 190
Godwin, Fiona, Librn, University College of the North Libraries, Norway House Public Library, Box 880, Norway House, MB, R0B 1B0, CANADA. Tel: 204-359-6296, Ext 2446. p. 2591
Godwin, Kathryn, Youth Serv Librn, Hanson Public Library, 132 Maquan St, Hanson, MA, 02341. Tel: 781-293-2151. p. 1023
Goe, Ricki, Libr Asst, Briarcliff Manor Public Library, One Library Rd, Briarcliff Manor, NY, 10510. Tel: 914-941-7072. p. 1496
Goebel, Nancy, Diversity, Equity & Inclusion Librn, University of Alberta, 4901 46th Ave, Camrose, AB, T4V 2R3, CANADA. Tel: 780-679-1156. p. 2530
Goeden, Kerrie, Human Res & Finance Coordr, South Central Library System, 4610 S Biltmore Lane, Ste 101, Madison, WI, 53718-2153. Tel: 608-246-7972. p. 2450
Goedge, Megan, Ch Serv, Petoskey District Library, 500 E Mitchell St, Petoskey, MI, 49770. Tel: 231-758-3100. p. 1140
Goehring, Heidi, Asst Librn, Bayfield Carnegie Library, 37 N Broad St, Bayfield, WI, 54814. Tel: 715-779-3953. p. 2422
Goel, Meeta, Dean, Institutional Effectiveness, Res & Planning, Antelope Valley College Library, 3041 W Ave K, Lancaster, CA, 93536. Tel: 661-722-6300, Ext 6276. p. 156
Goeman, Ann, Head, Circ, Human Res, Charlotte Community Library, 226 S Bostwick St, Charlotte, MI, 48813-1801. Tel: 517-543-8859. p. 1090
Goenner, Dawn, Textbook Services Asst, University of Wisconsin-River Falls, 410 S Third St, River Falls, WI, 54022. Tel: 715-425-4303. p. 2474
Goeppinger, Teresa, Circ, Public Library of Mount Vernon & Knox County, 201 N Mulberry St, Mount Vernon, OH, 43050-2413. Tel: 740-392-2665. p. 1804
Goergen-Doll, Kerri, Acq, Dir, Res Sharing, Oregon State University Libraries, 121 The Valley Library, Corvallis, OR, 97331-4501. Tel: 541-737-7256. p. 1876
Goering, Kendahl, Dir, Lowden Public Library, 605 Main St, Lowden, IA, 52255. Tel: 563-941-7629. p. 766
Goertzen, Jacquie, Libr Supvr, SIAST Libraries, 1100 15th St E, Prince Albert, SK, S6V 6G1, CANADA. Tel: 306-765-1546. p. 2745
Goerz, Chris, Libr Mgr, Tomahawk Public Library, 6119 Township Rd 512, Box 69, Tomahawk, AB, T0E 2H0, CANADA. Tel: 780-339-3935. p. 2557
Goethe, Corey, Dir, Libr Serv, Mid Michigan Community College, 1375 S Clare Ave, Harrison, MI, 48625. Tel: 989-386-6617. p. 1113
Goetsch, Lori A, Dean of Libr, Kansas State University Libraries, 1117 Mid-Campus Dr N, Manhattan, KS, 66506. Tel: 785-532-3014. p. 822
Goetschius, Barbara, Sr Librn, RCS Community Library, 95 Main St, Ravena, NY, 12143. Tel: 518-756-2053. p. 1625
Goetz, Tom, Ref Serv Coordr, William Rainey Harper College Library, 1200 W Algonguin Rd, Palatine, IL, 60067. Tel: 847-925-6252. p. 631
Goff, Christina, Dir, Instruction Librn, Los Medanos College Library, 2700 E Leland Rd, Pittsburg, CA, 94565. Tel: 925-473-7571. p. 195
Goff, Emily, Dir, Pankhurst Memorial Library, Three S Jefferson Ave, Amboy, IL, 61310-1400. Tel: 815-857-3925. p. 536
Goff, Florence D, Assoc Chief Info Officer, Bryn Mawr College, 101 N Merion Ave, Bryn Mawr, PA, 19010-2899. Tel: 610-526-5275. p. 1916
Goff, Janet Lois, Exec Dir, Harvard Musical Association Library, 57A Chestnut St, Boston, MA, 02108. Tel: 617-523-2897. p. 996
Goff, Linda, Youth Serv Coordr, Lake County Library System, 418 W Alfred St, Ste C, Tavares, FL, 32778. Tel: 352-253-6169. p. 450
Goff, Renate, Dir, Caledonia Library, 3108 Main St, Caledonia, NY, 14423. Tel: 585-538-4512. p. 1511
Goff, Sarah, Librn, Great River Medical Center Library, 1221 S Gear Ave, West Burlington, IA, 52655-1679. Tel: 319-768-4075. p. 790
Goffe, Anthea, Dir, Commun Engagement, Coquitlam Public Library, 575 Poirier St, Coquitlam, BC, V3J 6A9, CANADA. Tel: 604-554-7347. p. 2565
Goffe, Anthea, Dir, Commun Engagement, Coquitlam Public Library, City Centre Branch, 1169 Pinetree Way, Coquitlam, BC, V3B 0Y1, CANADA. Tel: 604-554-7347. p. 2565
Goforth, Dustin, Br Supvr, Aurora Public Library, Central Library-Main Branch, 14949 E Alameda Pkwy, Aurora, CO, 80012. Tel: 303-739-6000. p. 264
Gogerty, Jennifer, Dir, Slater Public Library, 105 N Tama St, Slater, IA, 50244. Tel: 515-228-3558. p. 783
Goggin, Carole, Archives Asst, State Historical Society of Missouri - Rolla, University of Missouri, G-3 Curtis Laws Wilson Library, 400 W 14th St, Rolla, MO, 65409-0060. Tel: 573-341-4874. p. 1267
Goggin, Jeanne, Librn, Woodland Public Library, 169 Main St, Baileyville, ME, 04694. Tel: 207-427-3235. p. 915
Goguen, Anne Marie, Educ Mgr, Larz Anderson Auto Museum Library & Archives, Larz Anderson Park, 15 Newton St, Brookline, MA, 02445. Tel: 617-522-6547. p. 1003
Goguen, Annick, Libr Mgr, Albert-Westmorland-Kent Regional Library, Bibliotheque Publique de Rogersville, 65, rue de l'Ecole, Unit 1, Rogersville, NB, E4Y 1V4, CANADA. Tel: 506-775-2102. p. 2603
Goguen, Michele-Ann, Libr Mgr, Albert-Westmorland-Kent Regional Library, Bibliotheque Publique de Cap-Pele, 2638, Chemin Acadie, Cap-Pele, NB, E4N 1E3, CANADA. Tel: 506-577-2090. p. 2603
Goguen, Nadine, Regional Dir, Albert-Westmorland-Kent Regional Library, 644 Main St, Ste 201, Moncton, NB, E1C 1E2, CANADA. Tel: 506-869-6030. p. 2603
Goguen, Pierre, Ref Librn, Universite de Moncton, 18, ave Antonine-Maillet, Moncton, NB, E1A 3E9, CANADA. Tel: 506-858-4012. p. 2603
Goh, Charity, Libr Mgr, New York Public Library - Astor, Lenox & Tilden Foundations, Edenwald Branch, 1255 E 233rd St, (@ DeReimer Ave), Bronx, NY, 10466. Tel: 718-798-3355. p. 1595
Goheen, Rick, Asst Dean, Assoc Prof, University of Toledo, LaValley Law Library, Mail Stop 508, 2801 W Bancroft St, Toledo, OH, 43606-3390. Tel: 419-530-2733. p. 1825
Gohn, Katie, Coll Serv, Dept Head, University of Tennessee at Chattanooga Library, 400 Douglas Ave, Dept 6456, Chattanooga, TN, 37403-2598. Tel: 423-425-4501. p. 2092
Goike, Annette, Interim Dir, MacDonald Public Library, 36480 Main St, New Baltimore, MI, 48047-2509. Tel: 586-725-0273. p. 1137
Goings, Kirsten, Asst Librn, Crystal City Public Library, 736 Mississippi Ave, Crystal City, MO, 63019-1646. Tel: 636-937-7166. p. 1244
Goings, Lena, Dir, Oglala Lakota College, Pine Ridge College Center, PO Box 1052, Pine Ridge, SD, 57770. Tel: 605-867-5893. p. 2078
Goings, Sarah, Librn, Girard Public Library, 128 W Prairie Ave, Girard, KS, 66743-1498. Tel: 620-724-4317. p. 809
Golban, Zoya, Dir, New York State Supreme Court Ninth Judicial District, Ninth Judicial District, 9th Flr, 111 Dr Martin Luther King Blvd, White Plains, NY, 10601. Tel: 914-824-5660. p. 1665
Golczynski, Mike, Ch, Ionia Community Library, 126 E Main St, Ionia, MI, 48846. Tel: 616-527-3680. p. 1118
Gold, Ann, Exec Dir, Rye Historical Society, 265 Rye Beach Ave, Rye, NY, 10580. Tel: 914-967-7588. p. 1634
Gold, Ann, Libr Mgr, United States Environmental Protection, 1650 Arch St, 2nd Flr, Philadelphia, PA, 19103. Tel: 215-814-5254. p. 1987
Gold, Anna K, Univ Librn, Worcester Polytechnic Institute, 100 Institute Rd, Worcester, MA, 01609-2280. Tel: 508-831-6161. p. 1073
Gold, Debra, Copyright Librn, Health Sci Librn, Lakehead University, 955 Oliver Rd, Thunder Bay, ON, P7B 5E1, CANADA. Tel: 807-343-8129. p. 2685
Gold, Helen, Res & Instruction Librn, New College of Florida University of South Florida Sarasota Manatee, 5800 Bay Shore Rd, Sarasota, FL, 34243-2109. Tel: 941-487-4416. p. 443

Goldberg, Ed, Head, Ref Serv, Syosset Public Library, 225 S Oyster Bay Rd, Syosset, NY, 11791-5897. Tel: 516-921-7161. p. 1648

Goldberg, Elyse, Mgr, New York State Office of Parks, Recreation & Historic Preservation, 84 Liberty St, Newburgh, NY, 12550-5603. Tel: 845-562-1195. p. 1605

Goldberg, Gail, Mgr, Rapides Parish Library, J W McDonald Branch, 1075 Hwy 497, Glenmora, LA, 71433. Tel: 318-748-4848. p. 880

Goldberg, Gillian, Academic Support Librn, Spec Coll Archivist, University of the Pacific Libraries, Holt-Atherton Special Collections & Archives, 3601 Pacific Ave, Stockton, CA, 95211. Tel: 209-946-2949. p. 250

Goldberg, Susan, Dir, Elwood Public Library, 1929 Jericho Tpk, East Northport, NY, 11731. Tel: 631-499-3722. p. 1528

Goldblum, Robin, Interim Libr Mgr, New Orleans Public Library, Mid-City Library, 4140 Canal St, New Orleans, LA, 70119. Tel: 504-596-2654. p. 903

Golde, Rachelle, Head Librn, Lake Lillian Public Library, 431 Lakeview St, Lake Lillian, MN, 56253. Tel: 320-905-2152. p. 1180

Golde, Rachelle, Head Librn, Raymond Public Library, 208 Cofield St N, Raymond, MN, 56282. Tel: 320-967-4411. p. 1193

Golde, Rachelle, Head Librn, Spicer Public Library, 198 Manitoba St, Spicer, MN, 56288-9629. Tel: 320-796-5560. p. 1204

Golden, Brooke, Mgr, Libraries of Stevens County, Lakeside Community Library, 5919 Hwy 291, Ste 2, Nine Mile Falls, WA, 99026. Tel: 509-315-8339. p. 2369

Golden, Christine, Dir, Jasper-Dubois County Public Library, 1116 Main St, Jasper, IN, 47546-2899. Tel: 812-482-2712, Ext 6115. p. 697

Golden, Ginny, Commun Libr Mgr, Contra Costa County Library, Bay Point Library, 205 Pacifica Ave, Bay Point, CA, 94565. Tel: 925-458-9597. p. 174

Golden, Ginny, Commun Libr Mgr, Contra Costa County Library, Pittsburg Library, 80 Power Ave, Pittsburg, CA, 94565. Tel: 925-427-8390. p. 174

Golden, Jamie, Dir, Washington Hospital, 155 Wilson Ave, Washington, PA, 15301-3398. Tel: 724-223-3144. p. 2018

Golden, Jennifer, Asst Dir, Coastal Plain Regional Library System, 2014 Chestnut Ave, Tifton, GA, 31794. Tel: 229-386-3400. p. 500

Golden, Jocelyn, Actg Libr Dir, Lincoln City Libraries, 136 S 14th St, Lincoln, NE, 68508-1899. Tel: 402-441-8510. p. 1321

Golden, Karen, Operations Mgr, East Central Arkansas Regional Library, 410 E Merriman Ave, Wynne, AR, 72396. Tel: 870-238-3850. p. 112

Golden, Laurie, Head, Commun Relations, Canton Public Library, 1200 S Canton Center Rd, Canton, MI, 48188-1600. Tel: 734-397-0999. p. 1088

Golden, Tim, Adult Serv, Ref (Info Servs), Boyden Library, Ten Bird St, Foxborough, MA, 02035. Tel: 508-543-1245. p. 1019

Golden, Veronica, Libr Dir, Chelsea Public Library, 296 VT Rte 110, Chelsea, VT, 05038. Tel: 802-685-2188. p. 2281

Golder, Cathy J, Dir, Green Free Library, 38 N Center St, Canton, PA, 17724-1304. Tel: 570-673-5744. p. 1918

Goldfarb, Deborah, Interim Chief Exec Officer, Long Beach Jewish Community Center - The Alpert JCC, 3801 E Willow St, Long Beach, CA, 90815. Tel: 562-426-7601. p. 158

Goldfarb, Joanna, Youth Serv Consult, Ramapo Catskill Library System, 619 Rte 17M, Middletown, NY, 10940-4395. Tel: 845-343-1131, Ext 240. p. 1571

Goldin, Barbara, Dir, Edwards Public Library, 30 East St, Southampton, MA, 01073. Tel: 413-527-9480. p. 1055

Goldin, Sally, Librn, Pelham Library, Two S Valley Rd, Pelham, MA, 01002. Tel: 413-253-0657. p. 1045

Golding, Elisabeth, Archives Mgr, Florida Department of State, Division of Library & Information Services, R A Gray Bldg, 500 S Bronough St, Tallahassee, FL, 32399-0250. Tel: 850-245-6639. p. 446

Goldman, David, Mgr, Libr Serv, Choate, Hall & Stewart LLP Library, Two International Pl, Boston, MA, 02110. Tel: 617-248-5000, 617-248-5202. p. 994

Goldman, Elizabeth, Libr Serv Dir, Burbank Public Library, 110 N Glenoaks Blvd, Burbank, CA, 91502-1203. Tel: 818-238-5600. p. 125

Goldman, Helen, Cat, Auburn University, Ralph Brown Draughon Library, 231 Mell St, Auburn, AL, 36849. Tel: 334-844-0241. p. 5

Goldman, Jaime, Reference Librarian III, Nova Southeastern University Libraries, Oceanographic Campus Library, 8000 N Ocean Dr, Dania Beach, FL, 33004. Tel: 954-262-3643, 954-262-3681. p. 402

Goldman, Marcy, Head, Children's Servx, Hamden Public Library, 2901 Dixwell Ave, Hamden, CT, 06518-3135. Tel: 203-230-3770. p. 315

Goldman, Susana, Dir, Alamance County Public Libraries, 342 S Spring St, Burlington, NC, 27215. Tel: 336-229-3588. p. 1676

Goldsborough, Laura, Ch Serv Librn, La Grange Public Library, Ten W Cossitt Ave, La Grange, IL, 60525. Tel: 708-215-3200. p. 605

Goldsmith, Catherine, Librn, Starksboro Public Library, 2827 VT Rte 116, Starksboro, VT, 05487. Tel: 802-453-3732. p. 2295

Goldsmith, Cathy, Libr Dir, Fossil Public Library, 401 Main St, Fossil, OR, 97830. Tel: 541-763-2046. p. 1880

Goldsmith, David, Assoc Dir, Colls & Research Servs, North Carolina State University Libraries, D H Hill Jr Library, Two Broughton Dr, Raleigh, NC, 27695. Tel: 919-515-7188. p. 1709

Goldsmith, Kristine, Asst Dir, Pub Relations Coordr, Rossford Public Library, 720 Dixie Hwy, Rossford, OH, 43460-1289. Tel: 419-666-0924. p. 1818

Goldsmith, Norma, Vols Coordr, Kehillat Beth Israel, 1400 Coldrey Ave, Ottawa, ON, K1Z 7P9, CANADA. Tel: 613-728-3501, Ext 232. p. 2667

Goldsmith, Shelby, Admin Serv Mgr, Virginia Beach Public Library, Municipal Ctr, Bldg 19, Rm 210, 2416 Courthouse Dr, Virginia Beach, VA, 23452. Tel: 757-385-8709. p. 2350

Goldstein, Christine Wallace, Ch Serv, Woonsocket Harris Public Library, 303 Clinton St, Woonsocket, RI, 02895. Tel: 401-769-9044. p. 2044

Goldstein, Heidi, Commun Libr Mgr, Contra Costa County Library, El Cerrito Library, 6510 Stockton Ave, El Cerrito, CA, 94530. Tel: 510-526-7512. p. 174

Goldstein, Heidi, Commun Libr Mgr, Contra Costa County Library, Rodeo Community Library, 220 Pacific Ave, Rodeo, CA, 94572. Tel: 510-799-2606. p. 175

Goldstock, Kevin, Head Librn, Woodsville Free Public Library, 14 School Lane, Woodsville, NH, 03785. Tel: 603-747-3483. p. 1385

Goldtooth, Pearl, Br Mgr, Flagstaff City-Coconino County Public Library System, Tuba City Public Library, 78 Main St, Tuba City, AZ, 86045. Tel: 928-283-5856. p. 60

Goldyn, Amy, Finance Mgr, Genesee District Library, 4195 W Pasadena Ave, Flint, MI, 48504. Tel: 810-732-0110. p. 1105

Goldyn, Matthew, Dir, Mercer Area Library, 110 E Venango St, Mercer, PA, 16137-1283. Tel: 724-662-4233. p. 1962

Golemon, Larry, Exec Dir, Washington Theological Consortium, 487 Michigan Ave NE, Washington, DC, 20017-1585. Tel: 202-832-2675. p. 2763

Golian-Lui, Linda, Dr, Assoc Dean, Kennesaw State University Library System, 385 Cobb Ave NW, MD 1701, Kennesaw, GA, 30144. Tel: 470-578-6199. p. 483

Golias, Ondrej, Librn, Canadian Opera Co, 227 Front St E, Toronto, ON, M5A 1E8, CANADA. Tel: 416-363-6671. p. 2688

Golik, Valerie, Dir of Develop, Found Dir, Northland Public Library, 300 Cumberland Rd, Pittsburgh, PA, 15237-5455. Tel: 412-366-8100, Ext 104. p. 1994

Golinski-Foisy, Antonia, Dir, West Springfield Public Library, 200 Park St, West Springfield, MA, 01089. Tel: 413-736-4561, Ext 1118. p. 1066

Golisek-Nankerv, Lisa, Div Mgr, Operations, Alaska State Library, 395 Whittier St, Juneau, AK, 99801. Tel: 907-465-2920. p. 47

Golovin, Naomi, Access Serv, Kentucky Wesleyan College, 3000 Frederica St, Owensboro, KY, 42301. Tel: 270-852-3259. p. 871

Golovko, Linda, Libr Operations, Southern California Genealogical Society, 417 Irving Dr, Burbank, CA, 91504-2408. Tel: 818-843-7247. p. 125

Golston, Jenifer, Br Librn, Bedford Public Library System, Moneta/Smith Mountain Lake Library, 13641 Moneta Rd, Moneta, VA, 24121. Tel: 540-425-7004. p. 2306

Golub, Andrew J, Dean, Libr Serv, University of New England Libraries, Josephine S Abplanalp Library, Portland Campus, 716 Stevens Ave, Portland, ME, 04103. Tel: 207-602-2319. p. 917

Golz, Nancy, Ref Librn, Merced College, 3600 M St, Merced, CA, 95348. Tel: 209-386-6725. p. 176

Gomberg, Ben, Head, Br Libr, Alameda County Library, 2450 Stevenson Blvd, Fremont, CA, 94538-2326. Tel: 510-745-1500. p. 143

Gomes, Alexandra, Dep Dir, George Washington University, Paul Himmelfarb Health Sciences Library, 2300 I St NW, Washington, DC, 20037. Tel: 202-994-1825. p. 367

Gomes, Debra, Assoc Dir, Libr Systems & Tech, College of Our Lady of the Elms, 291 Springfield St, Chicopee, MA, 01013-2839. Tel: 413-265-2280. p. 1011

Gomes, Katherine, Libr Dir, Holbrook Public Library, Two Plymouth St, Holbrook, MA, 02343. Tel: 781-767-3644. p. 1024

Gomes, Nirmal, Librn, Marist College Library, 815 Varnum St NE, Washington, DC, 20017-2199. Tel: 202-529-2821, Ext 21. p. 371

Gomez, Ali, Access Serv Librn, Regis University, 3333 Regis Blvd, D20, Denver, CO, 80221-1099. Tel: 303-458-4030, 303-458-4031. p. 276

Gomez, Anahi, Dir, Friona Public Library, 109 W Seventh St, Friona, TX, 79035-2548. Tel: 806-250-3200. p. 2182

Gomez, Ann, Br Mgr, San Diego Public Library, Balboa, 4255 Mt Abernathy Ave, San Diego, CA, 92117. Tel: 858-573-1390. p. 219

Gomez, Evelyn, Ref (Info Servs), Kramer, Levin, Naftalis & Frankel LLP, 1177 Avenue of the Americas, New York, NY, 10036. Tel: 212-715-9321. p. 1590

Gomez Fultz, Norma, Dir, Rio Grande City Public Library, 591 E Third St, Rio Grande City, TX, 78582-3588. Tel: 956-487-4389. p. 2232

Gomez, Guadalupe, Br Mgr, Anaheim Public Library, Elva L Haskett Branch, 2650 W Broadway, Anaheim, CA, 92804. Tel: 714-765-5075. p. 116

Gomez, Guillermo, Librn, Haverford College, Union Music, Union Bldg, 370 W Lancaster Ave, Haverford, PA, 19041. Tel: 610-896-1169. p. 1942

Gomez, Josefina, Coll Develop Coordr, Librn, San Joaquin Delta College, 5151 Pacific Ave, Stockton, CA, 95207. Tel: 209-954-5862. p. 249

Gomez, Kathleen, Mgr, Ref & Instruction, University of St Francis, 600 Taylor St, Joliet, IL, 60435. Tel: 815-740-5061. p. 603

Gomez, Leo, Asst Dir, Fac Mgt & Develop, Miami-Dade Public Library System, 101 W Flagler St, Miami, FL, 33130-1523. Tel: 305-375-5051. p. 422

Gomez, Mary, Archives, Dir, Libr Serv, Rockingham Community College, 315 Wrenn Memorial Rd, Wentworth, NC, 27375. Tel: 336-342-4261, Ext 2320. p. 1721
Gomez, Sally, Assoc County Librn, Fresno County Public Library, 2420 Mariposa St, Fresno, CA, 93721. Tel: 559-600-7323. p. 145
Gomez, Sandra Rosa, Dir, Inter-American University of Puerto Rico, 500 Carretera Dr, John Will Harris, Bayamon, PR, 00957-6257. Tel: 787-279-7312, Ext 2149. p. 2510
Gomez, Sonia, Libr Mgr, Carnegie Public Library, 500 National Ave, Las Vegas, NM, 87701. Tel: 505-426-3304. p. 1471
Gomez Soriano, Juana, Br Mgr, Chatham County Public Libraries, Goldston Public Library, 9235 Pittsboro-Goldston Rd, Goldston, NC, 27252-0040. Tel: 919-898-4522. p. 1708
Gomez, Stefani, Libr Dir, Cedar Crest College, 100 College Dr, Allentown, PA, 18104-6196. Tel: 610-606-4666, Ext 3387. p. 1904
Gomez, Veronica, Br Mgr, Hall County Library System, Blackshear Place, 2927 Atlanta Hwy, Gainesville, GA, 30507. Tel: 770-532-3311, Ext 151. p. 480
Gomila, Magally, Libr Mgr, New York Public Library - Astor, Lenox & Tilden Foundations, Riverside Branch, 127 Amsterdam Ave, (@ W 65th St), New York, NY, 10023-6447. Tel: 212-870-1810. p. 1597
Gomm, Matthew, Dir, Goshen Public Library & Historical Society, 366 Main St, Goshen, NY, 10924. Tel: 845-294-6606. p. 1539
Gomola, Chris, Ms, Research Librn, University of North Carolina at Chapel Hill, Highway Safety Research Center, Boiling Creek Ctr, Ste 300, 730 Martin Luther King Jr Blvd, Chapel Hill, NC, 27514. Tel: 919-962-2202. p. 1678
Gomoll, Brian, Dir, East Dubuque District Library, 122 Wisconsin Ave, East Dubuque, IL, 61025-1325. Tel: 815-747-3052. p. 580
Goncalves, Aline, Info Literacy, Ref Librn, Yukon College Library, 500 College Dr, Whitehorse, YT, Y1A 5K4, CANADA. Tel: 867-668-8870. p. 2758
Goncharova, Natalya, Assoc Librn, Anoka County Law Library, 2100 Third Ave, Ste E130, Anoka, MN, 55303. Tel: 763-324-5560. p. 1163
Gondak, Elizabeth, Dir, Cogswell Free Public Library, 1999 County Rte 2, Orwell, NY, 13426. Tel: 315-298-5563. p. 1612
Gong, Regan, Br Mgr, San Francisco Public Library, Anza Branch Library, 550 37th Ave, San Francisco, CA, 94121-2691. Tel: 415-355-5717. p. 228
Gong, Xiaomei, Bus Librn, Western Connecticut State University, 181 White St, Danbury, CT, 06810. Tel: 203-837-9100. p. 307
Gong, Xiaomei, Bus Librn, Western Connecticut State University, Robert S Young Business Library, 181 White St, Danbury, CT, 06810-6885. Tel: 203-837-9139. p. 308
Gonnerman, Kasia, Head, Res & Instruction, Saint Olaf College, Rolvaag Memorial Library, Hustad Science Library, Halvorson Music Library, 1510 Saint Olaf Ave, Northfield, MN, 55057-1097. Tel: 507-786-3501. p. 1191
Gonnerman, Kasia, Dir, Cent Libr, Vanderbilt University, Central Library, 419 21st Ave S, Nashville, TN, 37203-2427. Tel: 615-322-6892. p. 2121
Gonsalves, Tosca, Electronic Res Librn, Palo Alto College, 1400 W Villaret St, San Antonio, TX, 78224-2499. Tel: 210-486-3573. p. 2237
Gontarski, Sarah, Ch, Philbrick-James Library, Four Church St, Deerfield, NH, 03037-1426. Tel: 603-463-7187. p. 1360
Gonterman, Roberta, Libr Dir, Bonaparte Public Library, 201 Washington St, Bonaparte, IA, 52620. Tel: 319-592-3677. p. 735
Gontrum, Barbara, Assoc Dean, University of Maryland, Baltimore, Thurgood Marshall Law Library, 501 W Fayette St, Baltimore, MD, 21201-1768. Tel: 410-706-7270. p. 957
Gonzales, Chris, ILL, Sheridan County Public Library System, 335 W Alger St, Sheridan, WY, 82801. Tel: 307-674-8585. p. 2499
Gonzales, Dara, Coordr, Youth Serv, Memphis Public Library, Children's Department, 3030 Poplar Ave, Memphis, TN, 38111. Tel: 901-415-2739. p. 2113
Gonzales, Garin A, Librn, California Department of Corrections Library System, Central California Women's Facility, 23370 Rd 22, Chowchilla, CA, 93610. Tel: 559-665-5531. p. 206
Gonzales, Janet, ILL, California State University, Bakersfield, 9001 Stockdale Hwy, 60 LIB, Bakersfield, CA, 93311. Tel: 661-654-2129. p. 119
Gonzales, Jason, Info Mgr, Center for Advanced Study in the Behavioral Sciences Library, 75 Alta Rd, Stanford, CA, 94305. Tel: 650-736-0100. p. 248
Gonzales, Jessie, Br Mgr, Wharton County Library, Louise Branch, 803 Third St, Louise, TX, 77455. Tel: 979-648-2018. p. 2256
Gonzales, Laura, Librn, Dallas College, 12800 Abrams Rd, Dallas, TX, 75243. Tel: 972-238-6081. p. 2164
Gonzales, Lynn, Youth Serv Librn, W T Bland Public Library, 1995 N Donnelly St, Mount Dora, FL, 32757. Tel: 352-735-7180. p. 427
Gonzales, Melissa, Head of Libr & Archives, Fine Arts Museums of San Francisco Library & Archives, Golden Gate Park, 50 Hagiwara Tea Garden Dr, San Francisco, CA, 94118. Tel: 415-750-7603. p. 225
Gonzales, Rebecca, Br Mgr, San Francisco Public Library, Bernal Heights Branch Library, 500 Cortland Ave, San Francisco, CA, 94110-5612. Tel: 415-355-2810. p. 228
Gonzales, Rhonda, Dean, Libr Serv, Colorado State University - Pueblo, 2200 Bonforte Blvd, Pueblo, CO, 81001-4901. Tel: 719-549-2361. p. 293
Gonzales, Sonia, Librn, Howard County Junior College, Southwest Collegiate Institute for the Deaf - Library, 3200 Ave C, Big Spring, TX, 79720. Tel: 432-218-4056. p. 2148
Gonzales, Tracy, Librn, Brazoria County Law Library, 111 E Locust St, Ste 315-A, Angleton, TX, 77515. Tel: 979-864-1225. p. 2135
Gonzalez, Adrian, Tech Serv Librn, Val Verde County Library, 300 Spring St, Del Rio, TX, 78840. Tel: 830-774-7595. p. 2169
Gonzalez, Amanda, Patron Serv Librn, Ref Librn, Maryland State Library for the Blind & Print Disabled, 415 Park Ave, Baltimore, MD, 21201-3603. Tel: 410-230-2424. p. 955
Gonzalez, Angela, Dir, Penn Yan Public Library, 214 Main St, Penn Yan, NY, 14527. Tel: 315-536-6114. p. 1617
Gonzalez, Anna Maria, Br Mgr, Saint Louis County Library, Natural Bridge Branch, 7606 Natural Bridge Rd, Saint Louis, MO, 63121-4905. Tel: 314-994-3300, Ext 3600. p. 1274
Gonzalez, Ashley, Libr Mgr, New York Public Library - Astor, Lenox & Tilden Foundations, Aguilar Branch, 174 E 110th St, (Between Lexington & Third Aves), New York, NY, 10029-3212. Tel: 212-534-2930. p. 1594
Gonzalez, Carina, Ad, Piscataway Township Free Public Library, 500 Hoes Lane, Piscataway, NJ, 08854. Tel: 732-463-1633. p. 1435
Gonzalez, Christine, Br Mgr, San Diego Public Library, Point Loma/Hervey, 3701 Voltaire St, San Diego, CA, 92107. Tel: 619-531-1539. p. 220
Gonzalez, Eleanor, Coordr, Info Serv, Research Coordr, A&O Shearman Library, 1101 New York Ave NW, Washington, DC, 20005. Tel: 202-683-3800. p. 359
Gonzalez, Jesse, Circ Supvr, Houston Academy of Medicine, 1133 John Freeman Blvd, No 100, Houston, TX, 77030. Tel: 713-799-7148. p. 2193
Gonzalez, Jessica, Libr Mat Proc Spec, Laredo College, West End Washington St, Laredo, TX, 78040. Tel: 956-721-5279. p. 2209
Gonzalez, Jhonnathan, Circ Supvr, Guerra Joe A Laredo Public Library, Bruni Plaza Branch Library, 1120 San Bernardo Ave, Laredo, TX, 78040. Tel: 956-795-2400, Ext 2300. p. 2209
Gonzalez, Jorge, Syst Supvr, McAllen Public Library, 4001 N 23rd St, McAllen, TX, 78504. Tel: 956-681-3000. p. 2217
Gonzalez, Joseantonio, Br Head, Monterey County Free Libraries, Pajaro Branch, 29 Bishop St, Pajaro, CA, 95076. Tel: 831-761-2545. p. 173
Gonzalez, Juli, Mgr, Dallas Public Library, Audelia Road, 10045 Audelia Rd, Dallas, TX, 75238-1999. Tel: 214-670-1350. p. 2165
Gonzalez, Kaitlyn, Libr Dir, Smith-Welch Memorial Library, 105 W Fifth St, Hearne, TX, 77859. Tel: 979-279-5191. p. 2188
Gonzalez, Kelly, Asst VPres, Libr Serv, University of Texas Southwestern Medical Center, 5323 Harry Hines Blvd, Dallas, TX, 75390-9049. Tel: 214-648-2626. p. 2169
Gonzalez, Kris, Librn, Fowler Public Library, 411 Sixth St, Fowler, CO, 81039. Tel: 719-263-4472. p. 282
Gonzalez, Linda, Dir, Tucumcari Public Library, 602 S Second, Tucumcari, NM, 88401-2899. Tel: 505-461-0295. p. 1479
Gonzalez, Margarita, Head, Ref, University of Puerto Rico, Conrado F Asenjo Library, Medical Sciences Campus, Main Bldg, Unit C, San Juan, PR, 00935. Tel: 787-751-8199, 787-758-2525, Ext 1200. p. 2514
Gonzalez, Maria, Ref & Instruction Librn, Barry University, 11300 NE Second Ave, Miami Shores, FL, 33161-6695. Tel: 305-899-3761. p. 426
Gonzalez, Maria, Libr Mgr, San Antonio Public Library, Memorial, 3222 Culebra Rd, San Antonio, TX, 78228. Tel: 210-207-9140. p. 2239
Gonzalez, Maria del C, Acq, Pontifical Catholic University, Monsignor Fremiot Torres Oliver Law Library, 2250 Blvd Luis A Ferre Aguayo, Ste 544, Ponce, PR, 00717-9997. Tel: 787-841-2000, Ext 1856. p. 2512
Gonzalez, Mario, Exec Dir, Passaic Public Library, 195 Gregory Ave, Passaic, NJ, 07055. Tel: 973-779-0474. p. 1433
Gonzalez, Milena, Mgr, Miami-Dade Public Library System, Naranja Branch, 14850 SW 280 St, Miami, FL, 33032. Tel: 305-242-2290. p. 423
Gonzalez, Millie, Dean of Libr, Framingham State University, 100 State St, Framingham, MA, 01701. Tel: 508-626-4651. p. 1019
Gonzalez, Molli, E-Learning & Instruction Librn, Brightpoint Community College Library, Midlothian Campus, Hamel Hall, Rm H202, 800 Charter Colony Pkwy, Midlothian, VA, 23114-4383. Tel: 804-594-1518. p. 2312
Gonzalez, Mona, Supvr, Mid-Columbia Libraries, Pasco Branch, 1320 W Hopkins St, Pasco, WA, 99301. Tel: 509-545-1019. p. 2367
Gonzalez, Oscar, Libr Mgr, San Antonio Public Library, Mission, 3134 Roosevelt Ave, San Antonio, TX, 78214. Tel: 210-207-2704. p. 2239
Gonzalez, Pamela, Libr Asst, Cragin Memorial Library, Eight Linwood Ave, Colchester, CT, 06415. Tel: 860-537-5752. p. 306
Gonzalez, Rebekah, Mgr, San Jose Public Library, Pearl Avenue, 4270 Pearl Ave, San Jose, CA, 95136-1899. Tel: 408-808-3053. p. 231
Gonzalez, Rebekah Bonzalez, Mgr, San Jose Public Library, Cambrian, 1780 Hillsdale Ave, San Jose, CA, 95124-3199. Tel: 408-808-3080. p. 231
Gonzalez, Roger, Libr Asst, Crane County Library, 701 S Alford St, Crane, TX, 79731-2521. Tel: 432-558-1142. p. 2161
Gonzalez, Samuel, Info Serv Librn, Amaury Veray Music Library, 951 Ave Ponce de Leon, San Juan, PR, 00907-3373. Tel: 787-751-0160, Ext 256. p. 2513

Gonzalez-Buitrago, Martha, Libr Mgr, New York Public Library - Astor, Lenox & Tilden Foundations, Kingsbridge Branch, 291 W 231st St, (@ Corlear Ave), Bronx, NY, 10463. Tel: 718-548-5656. p. 1596

Goober, Tammy, Libr Mgr, Long County Library, 270 S Main St, Ludowici, GA, 31316. Tel: 912-545-2521. p. 486

Gooch, B J, Spec Coll Librn, Transylvania University Library, 300 N Broadway, Lexington, KY, 40508. Tel: 859-233-8225. p. 863

Gooch, Donna, Ref & Ad Serv Librn, Mary Lib Saleh Euless Public Library, 201 N Ector Dr, Euless, TX, 76039-3595. Tel: 817-685-1480. p. 2176

Gooch, Mark, Discovery Serv Librn, Head, Coll Mgt, The College of Wooster Libraries, 1140 Beall Ave, Wooster, OH, 44691-2364. Tel: 330-263-2522. p. 1832

Gooch, Marquita, Libr Assoc, Atlanta-Fulton Public Library System, Auburn Avenue Research Library on African-American Culture & History, 101 Auburn Ave NE, Atlanta, GA, 30303-2503. Tel: 404-613-4001. p. 461

Gooch, Marquita, Virtual Serv Librn, Clayton County Library System, 865 Battlecreek Rd, Jonesboro, GA, 30236. Tel: 770-473-3850. p. 483

Good, Cipperly, Richard Saltonstall Jr. Curator, Maritime History, Penobscot Marine Museum, Nine Church St, Searsport, ME, 04974. Tel: 207-548-2529, Ext 212. p. 940

Good, Larisa, Head Librn, Warren County Public Library District, 62 Public Sq, Monmouth, IL, 61462. Tel: 309-734-3166. p. 619

Good, Linda, Ch, Gutekunst Public Library, 309 Second St SE, State Center, IA, 50247-0550. Tel: 641-483-2741. p. 784

Good, Mollie, Head Librn, Valdez Consortium Library, 212 Fairbanks St, Valdez, AK, 99686. Tel: 907-835-4632. p. 52

Good, Tim, Archivist, Marshall County Historical Society Library, 123 N Michigan St, Plymouth, IN, 46563. Tel: 574-936-2306. p. 714

Good-Deal, Christine, Principal, Illinois School for the Deaf, 125 Webster Ave, Jacksonville, IL, 62650. Tel: 217-479-4254. p. 602

Good-Schiff, Kathryn, Head, Adult Serv, Westfield Athenaeum, Six Elm St, Westfield, MA, 01085-2997. Tel: 413-568-7833, Ext 113. p. 1066

Goodale, Heidi, Mgr, Coll Develop, Tech Mgr, Norfolk County Public Library, 46 Colborne St S, Simcoe, ON, N3Y 4H3, CANADA. Tel: 519-426-3506, Ext 1250. p. 2678

Goodall, Carrie, Asst Dir, Ascension Parish Library, 500 Mississippi St, Donaldsonville, LA, 70346. Tel: 225-473-8052. p. 889

Goodchild, Christine, Coordr, Libr Serv, North Shore Community College Library, One Ferncroft Rd, Danvers Campus Library, Danvers, MA, 01923-4093. Tel: 978-739-5532. p. 1013

Goode, Becky, Adult & Teen Serv, Tech Mgr, Shorewood-Troy Public Library District, 650 Deerwood Dr, Shorewood, IL, 60404. Tel: 815-725-1715. p. 647

Goode, Deidre, Head, Children's Servx, Great Neck Library, 159 Bayview Ave, Great Neck, NY, 11023. Tel: 516-466-8055, Ext 210. p. 1540

Goode, Lyn, Assoc Dir, Human Resources & Admin Servs, Boston College Libraries, 140 Commonwealth Ave, Chestnut Hill, MA, 02467. Tel: 617-552-0160. p. 1010

Goode, Travis, Asst Dir, Pub Serv, University of Texas at Dallas, 800 W Campbell Rd, Richardson, TX, 75080. Tel: 972-883-2955. p. 2231

Goodeill, Phyllis, Dir, Del Norte County Library District, 190 Price Mall, Crescent City, CA, 95531-4395. Tel: 707-464-9793. p. 133

Goodell, Jon, Dir, Med Libr, Oklahoma State University - Center for Health Sciences, 1111 W 17th St, Tulsa, OK, 74107-1898. Tel: 918-562-8451. p. 1864

Goodell, Karin, Dir, Scoville Memorial Library, 38 Main St, Salisbury, CT, 06068. Tel: 860-435-2838. p. 335

Goodell, Robin, Co-Dir, Long Island Community Library, 7 Gorham Ave, Long Island, ME, 04050. Tel: 207-766-2530. p. 930

Goodemote, Jenny, Exec Dir, Wood Library Association, 134 N Main St, Canandaigua, NY, 14424-1295. Tel: 585-394-1381, Ext 306. p. 1512

Goodfellow, Rebekah, Circ, J Sargeant Reynolds Community College Library, Downtown Campus-Library & Information Services, 700 E Jackson St, 2nd Flr, Rm 231, Richmond, VA, 23219-1543. Tel: 804-523-5211. p. 2341

Goodhope, Jeanie, Media Spec, Everett Community College, 2000 Tower St, Everett, WA, 98201-1352. Tel: 425-388-9348. p. 2364

Goodhue, Stacy, Dir, Carlisle Public Library, 135 School St, Carlisle, IA, 50047-8702. Tel: 515-989-0909. p. 736

Goodier, Patti, Librn, Ponca Carnegie Library, 200 W Second St, Ponca, NE, 68770. Tel: 402-755-2739. p. 1333

Goodin, Kelly, Dir, Williamsfield Public Library, 407 Norman Dr, Williamsfield, IL, 61489. Tel: 309-639-2630. p. 663

Goodlin, Blair, Jr, Dr, Instrul Designer, Manhattan College, 4513 Manhattan College Pkwy, Riverdale, NY, 10471. Tel: 718-862-7743. p. 1627

Goodman, Amanda L, Head, Tech & User Experience, Darien Library, 1441 Post Rd, Darien, CT, 06820-5419. Tel: 203-655-1234. p. 308

Goodman, Brittney, Librn, Info Literacy Initiatives, Minnesota State University Moorhead, 1104 Seventh Ave S, Moorhead, MN, 56563. Tel: 218-477-2922. p. 1189

Goodman, Cheryl, Br Mgr, Sullivan County Public Libraries, Carlisle Public, 201 N Ledgerwood St, Carlisle, IN, 47838. Tel: 812-398-4480. p. 719

Goodman, Christie, Library Contact, Intercultural Development Research Association Library, 5815 Callaghan Rd, Ste 101, San Antonio, TX, 78228. Tel: 210-444-1710. p. 2236

Goodman, Elizabeth, Libr Dir, Gateway Community & Technical College, Urban Campus Library, 516 Madison Ave, Technology, Innovation, and Enterprise Building, Covington, KY, 41011. Tel: 859-442-4162. p. 854

Goodman, Ellen, Libr Dir, Andrew Bayne Memorial Library, 34 N Balph Ave, Bellevue, PA, 15202-3297. Tel: 412-766-7447. p. 1910

Goodman, Emily, Commun Outreach Coordr, North Kingstown Free Library, 100 Boone St, North Kingstown, RI, 02852-5150. Tel: 401-294-3306. p. 2036

Goodman, Eric B, Libr Dir, Appraisal Institute, 200 W Madison, Ste 1500, Chicago, IL, 60606. Tel: 312-335-4467. p. 554

Goodman, Gwynn, Librn, Collier County Public Library, Marco Island Branch, 210 S Heathwood Dr, Marco Island, FL, 34145. Tel: 239-394-3272. p. 427

Goodman, Jessica, Regional Mgr, Santa Cruz City-County Library System, 117 Union St, Santa Cruz, CA, 95060-3873. Tel: 831-721-7706, Ext 7612. p. 242

Goodman, Jill, Librn, Martinsville Public Library District, 120 E Cumberland St, Martinsville, IL, 62442-1000. Tel: 217-382-4113. p. 614

Goodman, Karen, Med Librn, New Hampshire Hospital, 36 Clinton St, Concord, NH, 03301-3861. Tel: 603-271-5420. p. 1359

Goodman, Kelly, Library Contact, Department of Veterans Affairs, 500 W Fort St, 531/142D, Boise, ID, 83702. Tel: 208-422-1306. p. 517

Goodman, Maggie, Dir, Johnson City Library District, 501 Nugent Ave, Johnson City, TX, 78636. Tel: 830-868-4469. p. 2204

Goodman, Mary, Br Mgr, Portsmouth Public Library, Manor, 1401 Elmhurst Lane, Portsmouth, VA, 23701. Tel: 757-465-2916. p. 2338

Goodman, Sally, Dir, Libr Serv, Coastal Carolina Community College, 444 Western Blvd, Jacksonville, NC, 28546. Tel: 910-938-6793. p. 1697

Goodnough, Alaina, Asst Dir, Berwick Public Library, 103 Old Pine Hill Rd, Berwick, ME, 03901. Tel: 207-698-5737. p. 917

Goodrich, Judith A, Exec Dir, Logan County Libraries, 220 N Main St, Bellefontaine, OH, 43311. Tel: 937-599-4189. p. 1750

Goodrich, Lana, Circ Supvr, Central College, Campus Box 6500, 812 University St, Pella, IA, 50219-1999. Tel: 641-628-5219. p. 776

Goodrich, Mona, ILL, Patrick Lynch Public Library, 206 S McKenna St, Poteau, OK, 74953. Tel: 918-647-4444. p. 1860

Goodsett, Mandi, Performing Arts & Humanities Librn, Cleveland State University, Michael Schwartz Library, Rhodes Tower, Ste 501, 2121 Euclid Ave, Cleveland, OH, 44115-2214. Tel: 216-687-2475. p. 1769

Goodson, Jennifer, Libr Dir, Fort Smith Public Library, 3201 Rogers Ave, Fort Smith, AR, 72903. Tel: 479-783-0229. p. 96

Goodson, Kymberly Anne, Dir for Spaces, Lending & Access, University of California, San Diego, 9500 Gilman Dr, Mail Code 0175G, La Jolla, CA, 92093-0175. Tel: 858-534-1271. p. 154

Goodson, Paul, Dir, Libr Serv, Pamlico Community College Library, 5049 Hwy 306 S, Grantsboro, NC, 28529. Tel: 252-249-1851, Ext 3034. p. 1691

Goodspeed, Emily, Chair, Dir, Adirondack Community College Library, Scoville Learning Ctr, 640 Bay Rd, Queensbury, NY, 12804. Tel: 518-743-2200, Ext 2351. p. 1625

Goodvin, Renee, Assoc Libr Dir, Central New Mexico Community College Libraries, 525 Buena Vista SE, Albuquerque, NM, 87106-4023. Tel: 505-224-4000, Ext 52550. p. 1460

Goodwillie, Christian, Dir, Archives & Spec Coll, Hamilton College, 198 College Hill Rd, Clinton, NY, 13323. Tel: 315-859-4447. p. 1519

Goodwillie, Karyn, Tech Serv, Parkland Regional Library-Alberta, 5404 56th Ave, Lacombe, AB, T4L 1G1, CANADA. Tel: 403-782-3850. p. 2545

Goodwin, Al, Librn, Nute High School & Library, 22 Elm St, Milton, NH, 03851. Tel: 603-652-7829. p. 1374

Goodwin, Emily, Tech Serv Librn, Norwell Public Library, 64 South St, Norwell, MA, 02061-2433. Tel: 781-659-2015. p. 1043

Goodwin, Holly, Libr Tech, SOWELA Technical Community College Library, Morgan Smith Library, Jennings Campus, 2110 N Sherman St, Jennings, LA, 70546. Tel: 337-824-4811, Ext 4656. p. 894

Goodwin, Iris, Tech Serv Librn, Oregon Institute of Technology Library, 3201 Campus Dr, Klamath Falls, OR, 97601-8801. Tel: 541-885-1965. p. 1883

Goodwin, Jennifer, Ref Librn, Alberta Legislature Library, 216 Legislature Bldg, 10800-97 Ave NW, Edmonton, AB, T5K 2B6, CANADA. Tel: 780-427-0208. p. 2535

Goodwin, Jessica, Assoc Dir, Portland Public Library, Five Monument Sq, Portland, ME, 04101. Tel: 207-871-1700, Ext 736. p. 937

Goodwin, Jessica, Librn, University of South Carolina, Peden McLeod Library, Salkehatchie East Campus, 807 Hampton St, Walterboro, SC, 29488. Tel: 843-782-8627. p. 2046

Goodwin, Lydia P, Adult Serv, Dir, William Fogg Library, 116 Old Rd, Eliot, ME, 03903. Tel: 207-439-9437. p. 924

Goodwin, Sorrel, Librn, Alaska State Library, 395 Whittier St, Juneau, AK, 99801. Tel: 907-465-2920. p. 47

Goodwin, Susan, Assoc Dean, User Serv, Texas A&M University Libraries, 400 Spence St, College Station, TX, 77843. Tel: 979-458-0138. p. 2157

Goodwyn, Donna, Head, Ref, Elmhurst University, 190 Prospect St, Elmhurst, IL, 60126. Tel: 630-617-3171. p. 585
Goodyear, Dennis, Tech Serv Supvr, Wartburg College Library, 100 Wartburg Blvd, Waverly, IA, 50677-0903. Tel: 319-352-8500. p. 789
Goof, Michael, Librn, Swedenborgian Library & Archives, 1798 Scenic Ave, Berkeley, CA, 94709. Tel: 510-849-8248. p. 122
Gookin, Lin, Asst Libr Dir, Tuolumne County Genealogical Society Library, 158 Bradford St, Sonora, CA, 95370. Tel: 209-532-1317. p. 247
Goolabsingh, David, Dir of Serv, ILL, University of Miami, Louis Calder Memorial Library, Miller School of Medicine, 1601 NW Tenth Ave, Miami, FL, 33136. Tel: 305-243-6749. p. 425
Goolishian, Nicole, Head, Tech Serv, Lynnfield Public Library, 18 Summer St, Lynnfield, MA, 01940-1837. Tel: 781-334-5411, 781-334-6404. p. 1031
Goolsby, Mary, Asst Librn, Dir, Baylor University Libraries, W R Poage Legislative Library, 201 Baylor Ave, Waco, TX, 76706. Tel: 254-710-6735. p. 2253
Goonis, Patty, YA Serv, Livonia Public Library, Carl Sandburg Branch, 30100 W Seven Mile Rd, Livonia, MI, 48152-1918. Tel: 248-893-4010. p. 1127
Goontz, Donna, Co-Dir, Pine Grove Public Library, One Main St, Pine Grove, WV, 26419. Tel: 304-889-3288. p. 2412
Goos, Norman, Librn, Atlantic County Historical Society Library, 907 Shore Rd, Somers Point, NJ, 08244. Tel: 609-927-5218. p. 1442
Goossen, Taylor, Classroom Support Technician, Northwood Technical College, 1019 S Knowles Ave, New Richmond, WI, 54017. Tel: 715-246-6561. p. 2465
Goral, Miki, Librn, University of California Los Angeles Library, Powell Library, Powell Library Bldg, Los Angeles, CA, 90095. Tel: 310-825-1938. p. 169
Gorda, Ronald, Ref Librn, Cranford Free Public Library, 224 Walnut Ave, Cranford, NJ, 07016-2931. Tel: 908-709-7272. p. 1398
Gordano, Samantha, Mgr, San Antonio Public Library, Cody, 11441 Vance Jackson, San Antonio, TX, 78230. Tel: 210-207-9100. p. 2239
Gorden, Noel, Ms, Exec Dean, Indian Hills Community College Library, 525 Grandview Ave, Ottumwa, IA, 52501. Tel: 641-683-5199. p. 775
Gorder, Erika, Archivist, Rutgers University Libraries, Special Collections & University Archives, Alexander Library, 169 College Ave, New Brunswick, NJ, 08901-1163. Tel: 848-932-6150. p. 1425
Gordillo, Colleen, Asst Dir, Coll Serv Mgr, Anderson City, Anderson, Stony Creek & Union Townships Public Library, 111 E 12th St, Anderson, IN, 46016-2701. Tel: 765-641-2455. p. 667
Gordon, Alfreda, Circ Spec, Camden County Library, 104 Investors Way, Units CDEF, Camden, NC, 27921. Tel: 252-331-2543. p. 1677
Gordon, Barbara, Dir, Cass District Library, 319 M-62 N, Cassopolis, MI, 49031. Tel: 269-216-7088, Ext 101. p. 1089
Gordon, Barbara, Ref, The Morristown & Morris Township Library, One Miller Rd, Morristown, NJ, 07960. Tel: 973-538-6161. p. 1421
Gordon, Carla Z, Dir, Provo City Library, 550 N University Ave, Provo, UT, 84601. Tel: 801-852-6650. p. 2269
Gordon, Connie, Librn, F Lee Doctor Library, 222 Main St, Agra, KS, 67621. Tel: 785-638-2444. p. 795
Gordon, Derek, Libr Serv Rep, Stark County District Library, 715 Market Ave N, Canton, OH, 44702. Tel: 330-458-2712. p. 1755
Gordon, Gayle, Mgr, Dallas Public Library, Kleberg-Rylie, 1301 Edd Rd, Dallas, TX, 75253-4010. Tel: 214-670-8471. p. 2165
Gordon, Ian, Librn III, Brock University, 1812 Sir Isaac Brock Way, St. Catharines, ON, L2S 3A1, CANADA. Tel: 905-688-5550, Ext 3727. p. 2679
Gordon, Jill, Librn, Saint Louis Zoo Library, One Government Dr, Saint Louis, MO, 63110. Tel: 314-781-0900, Ext 4554. p. 1276
Gordon, Joshua, Libr Serv Mgr, Indiana Baptist College Library, 1301 W County Line Rd, Greenwood, IN, 46142. Tel: 317-882-2345. p. 688
Gordon, Karen, Actg Dir, The Whitehall Free Library, 12 William St, Whitehall, NY, 12887. Tel: 518-499-1366. p. 1665
Gordon, Kate, Head, Admin Budget, University of Alaska Anchorage, Consortium Library, 3211 Providence Dr, Anchorage, AK, 99508-8176. Tel: 907-786-1903. p. 43
Gordon, Katie, Mgr, West Georgia Regional Library, Dog River Public Library, 6100 Georgia Hwy 5, Douglasville, GA, 30135. Tel: 770-577-5186. p. 470
Gordon, Katie, Mgr, West Georgia Regional Library, Lithia Springs Public Library, 7100 Turner Dr, Lithia Springs, GA, 30122. Tel: 770-944-5931. p. 470
Gordon, Linda, Prof, Res & Instruction Librn, University of La Verne, 2040 Third St, La Verne, CA, 91750. Tel: 909-593-3511, Ext 4305. p. 155
Gordon, Lois, Outreach Serv Librn, Mohawk Valley Library System, 858 Duanesburg Rd, Schenectady, NY, 12306. Tel: 518-355-2010. p. 1638
Gordon, Lynnea, Libr Asst, Jamaica Memorial Library, 17 Depot St, Jamaica, VT, 05343. Tel: 802-874-4901. p. 2286
Gordon, Mary, Tech Serv, Amityville Public Library, 19 John St, Amityville, NY, 11701. Tel: 631-264-0567. p. 1486
Gordon, Maurice, Br Librn, Boston Public Library, Mattapan, 1350 Blue Hill Ave, Mattapan, MA, 02126. Tel: 617-298-9218. p. 992
Gordon, Nancie Anne, Circ, Patrick Lynch Public Library, 206 S McKenna St, Poteau, OK, 74953. Tel: 918-647-4444. p. 1860
Gordon, Nicole, Br Mgr, Queens Library, Arverne Community Library, 312 Beach 54th St, Arverne, NY, 11692. Tel: 718-634-4784. p. 1554
Gordon, Nilufar, Mrs, Librn, Association for Baha'i Studies, 34 Copernicus St, Ottawa, ON, K1N 7K4, CANADA. Tel: 613-233-1903, Press 2. p. 2664
Gordon, Rebecca, Dir, Stony Creek Free Library, 37 Harrisburg Rd, Stony Creek, NY, 12878. Tel: 518-696-5911. p. 1647
Gordon, Sade, Circ Mgr, University of St Augustine for Health Sciences, 800 Douglas Rd, Coral Gables, FL, 33134. Tel: 786-725-4031. p. 391
Gordon, Sarah, Asst Dean, University of Vermont Libraries, 538 Main St, Burlington, VT, 05405-0036. Tel: 802-656-3293. p. 2281
Gordon, Tom, Pub Serv Librn, Forsyth Technical Community College Library, 2100 Silas Creek Pkwy, Winston-Salem, NC, 27103. Tel: 336-734-7219. p. 1725
Gordon, Tricia, Libr Mgr, Aiken-Bamberg-Barnwell-Edgefield Regional Library, Barnwell County, 40 Burr St, Barnwell, SC, 29812-1917. Tel: 803-259-3612. p. 2045
Gordon, Valerie, Head, Cat, University of Alabama at Birmingham, Lister Hill Library of the Health Sciences, 1700 University Blvd, Birmingham, AL, 35294-0013. Tel: 205-934-5460. p. 9
Gordon, Victor, Assoc Dir, Admin Serv, Duke University Libraries, Medical Center Library & Archives, DUMC Box 3702, Ten Searle Dr, Durham, NC, 27710-0001. Tel: 919-660-1149. p. 1684
Gore, April, Asst Dir, Cataloger, Doniphan-Ripley County Library, 207 Locust St, Doniphan, MO, 63935. Tel: 573-996-2616. p. 1245
Gore, Debby, Dir, Jordaan Memorial Library, 724 Broadway St, Larned, KS, 67550-3051. Tel: 620-285-2876. p. 818
Gore, Mark, Librn, Housatonic Community College Library, 900 Lafayette Blvd, Bridgeport, CT, 06604. Tel: 203-332-5069. p. 304
Gore, Pamela, Acq, Asst Librn, Tech Support, Gordon-Conwell Theological Seminary, 130 Essex St, South Hamilton, MA, 01982-2317. Tel: 978-646-4078. p. 1054
Gore, Robert, Visual Arts Librn, University of California Los Angeles Library, Arts Library, 1400 Public Affairs Bldg, Los Angeles, CA, 90095. Tel: 310-206-5426. p. 169
Gores, Julie, Dean, Libr & Acad Support, Madison Area Technical College, 3550 Anderson St, Rm A3000, Madison, WI, 53704. Tel: 608-246-6633. p. 2449
Gorf, Oliver, Exec Dir, German Cultural Center, Colony Sq, Plaza Level, 1197 Peachtree St NE, Atlanta, GA, 30361-2401. Tel: 404-892-2388. p. 464
Gorham, Gwen, Dir, Sheridan Public Library, 142 NW Yamhill St, Sheridan, OR, 97378. Tel: 503-843-3420. p. 1898
Gorham, Jael, Circ & Tech Serv Librn, Randall Library, 19 Crescent St, Stow, MA, 01775. Tel: 978-897-8572. p. 1058
Gorham, Luke, IT Coordr, Ref Librn, Galesburg Public Library, 40 E Simmons St, Galesburg, IL, 61401-4591. Tel: 309-343-6118. p. 591
Gorham, Ursula, Prog Dir, University of Maryland, Hornbake Library, Ground Flr, Rm 0220, 4130 Campus Dr, College Park, MD, 20742-4345. Tel: 301-405-2039. p. 2786
Gorka, Gary, Univ Librn, Dominican University of California, 50 Acacia Ave, San Rafael, CA, 94901-2298. Tel: 415-247-1301. p. 236
Gorland, Deena, Librn & Archivist, American Psychiatric Association Foundation, 800 Maine Ave SW, Ste 900, Washington, DC, 20024. Tel: 202-559-3759. p. 360
Gorman, Beck, Dir, Aledo Public Library, 201 FM 1187 N, Aledo, TX, 76008. Tel: 817-769-9443. p. 2132
Gorman, Bruce, Chief Exec Officer, Aurora Public Library, 15145 Young St, Aurora, ON, L4G 1M1, CANADA. Tel: 905-727-9494. p. 2629
Gorman, Dusty, Electronic Res Librn, University of Puget Sound, 1604 N Warner St, Upper Loading Dock, Tacoma, WA, 98416. Tel: 253-879-3617. p. 2387
Gorman, Jacque, YA Librn, Milford Town Library, 80 Spruce St, Milford, MA, 01757. Tel: 508-473-2145, Ext 223. p. 1035
Gorman, Joan, Interim Dir, Rokeby Museum, 4334 Rte 7, Ferrisburg, VT, 05456-9711. Tel: 802-877-3406. p. 2284
Gorman, Kate, Libr Dir, Dixon Homestead Library, 180 Washington Ave, Dumont, NJ, 07628. Tel: 201-384-2030. p. 1399
Gorman, Kathleen, Dir, Potter Public Library, 333 Chestnut, Potter, NE, 69156. Tel: 308-879-4345. p. 1333
Gorman, Maeleah, Asst Mgr, Springfield City Library, East Forest Park Branch, 136 Surrey Rd, Springfield, MA, 01118. Tel: 413-263-6836. p. 1056
Gorman, Michael, Govt Pub Librn, St Cloud State University Library, James W Miller Learning Resource Center, 400 Sixth St S, Saint Cloud, MN, 56301. Tel: 320-308-2028. p. 1198
Gorman, Michele, Asst Dir, Pub Serv, Fort Worth Library, 500 W Third St, Fort Worth, TX, 76102. Tel: 817-392-7323. p. 2179
Gorman, Peggy, Head, Children's Servx, Plainedge Public Library, 1060 Hicksville Rd, North Massapequa, NY, 11758. Tel: 516-735-4133. p. 1607
Gorman, Peter, Nat Librn, Canadian Music Centre Libaries, Ontario Region Library, 20 St Joseph St, Toronto, ON, M4Y 1J9, CANADA. Tel: 416-961-6601, Ext 007. p. 2687
Gorman, Taylor, Dir of Libr, Pikes Peak State College Library, 5675 S Academy Blvd, C7, Colorado Springs, CO, 80906-5498. p. 272

Gormley, John C, Res & Instruction Librn, Manhattan College, 4513 Manhattan College Pkwy, Riverdale, NY, 10471. Tel: 718-862-7743. p. 1627
Gormley, Katrina, Cat, Chippewa River District Library, 301 S University Ave, Mount Pleasant, MI, 48858-2597. Tel: 989-773-3242, Ext 221. p. 1135
Gormley, Madeline, Mgr, Edmonton Public Library, Jasper Place, 9010 156 St, Edmonton, AB, T5R 5X7, CANADA. Tel: 780-496-8362. p. 2536
Gormly, Brianna, Digital Initiatives Librn, Franklin & Marshall College, Martin Library of the Sciences, Bldg 22, 681 Williamson Way, Lancaster, PA, 17604. Tel: 717-358-4206. p. 1951
Gorney, Robert, Br Librn, Genesee District Library, Baker Park Library, G3410 S Grand Traverse, Burton, MI, 48529. Tel: 810-742-7860. p. 1106
Gornik, Laurie, ILL, Glen Ellyn Public Library, 400 Duane St, Glen Ellyn, IL, 60137-4508. Tel: 630-469-0879. p. 593
Goroski, Sarah, Head, Circ Serv, Pikes Peak State College Library, 5675 S Academy Blvd, C7, Colorado Springs, CO, 80906-5498. p. 272
Goroski, Sarah, Managing Librn, Pikes Peak State College Library, Rampart Range Campus, 11195 Hwy 83, Box R-7, Colorado Springs, CO, 80921-3602. Tel: 719-502-2440. p. 272
Gorrell, Renee, Dir, Libr & Info Serv, Goldfarb School of Nursing at Barnes-Jewish College Library, 4483 Duncan Ave, Mail Stop 90-30-697, Saint Louis, MO, 63110. Tel: 314-454-8171. p. 1270
Gorshe, Phyllis, Dir, Dunedin Public Library, 223 Douglas Ave, Dunedin, FL, 34698. Tel: 727-298-3080, Ext 1701. p. 394
Gorski, Stan, Libr Dir, Thomas Jefferson University-East Falls, 4201 Henry Ave, Philadelphia, PA, 19144-5497. Tel: 215-951-2581. p. 1987
Gorsline, Dayle, Mrs, Electronic Res, Libr Tech, The Parrott Centre, 376 Wallbridge-Loyalist Rd, Belleville, ON, K8N 5B9, CANADA. Tel: 613-969-1913, Ext 2249. p. 2631
Gorsuch, Christopher, Coll Mgt Mgr, LeRoy Collins Leon County Public Library System, 200 W Park Ave, Tallahassee, FL, 32301-7720. Tel: 850-606-2665. p. 445
Gorsuch, Jennifer, Dir, Greater West Central Public Library District, 202 Center St, Augusta, IL, 62311. Tel: 217-392-2211. p. 538
Gorton, Chris, Libr Asst, Windsor Public Library, 323 Broad St, Windsor, CT, 06095. Tel: 860-285-1913. p. 348
Gorzelsky, Stefanie, Access Serv Librn, Saint Martin's University, 5000 Abbey Way SE, Lacey, WA, 98503. Tel: 360-688-2254. p. 2368
Gosbee, Robin, Librn, Denmark Public Library, 121 E Main St, Denmark, ME, 04022. Tel: 207-452-2200. p. 923
Gosnell, Joan, Archivist, Southern Methodist University, DeGolyer Library of Special Collections, 6404 Robert S Hyer Lane, Dallas, TX, 75275. Tel: 214-768-2261. p. 2168
Goss, Amanda, Libr Dir, Moose Pass Public Library, 33657 Depot Rd, Moose Pass, AK, 99631. Tel: 907-288-3111. p. 49
Goss, Deborah, Ref Librn, Massachusetts Eye & Ear Infirmary Libraries, 243 Charles St, Boston, MA, 02114. Tel: 617-573-3196. p. 997
Goss, Harold J, Librn, University of Alabama at Birmingham, Department of Anesthesiology Library, 619 19th St S, J965, Birmingham, AL, 35249-6810. Tel: 205-975-0158. p. 9
Goss, Jillian, Teen Serv Coordr, Cumberland Public Library, 1464 Diamond Hill Rd, Cumberland, RI, 02864-5510. Tel: 401-333-2552, Ext 208. p. 2031
Goss, John, Ref Mgr, Pritzker Military Museum & Library, 104 S Michigan Ave, 2nd Flr, Chicago, IL, 60603. Tel: 312-374-9333. p. 567
Goss, Laura, Exec Dir, Adams County Library System, 140 Baltimore St, Gettysburg, PA, 17325-2311. Tel: 717-334-5716. p. 1935
Gosse, Joel, Asst Curator, Mineral Point Public Library, 137 High St, Ste 2, Mineral Point, WI, 53565. Tel: 608-987-2447. p. 2462
Gosseen, Jill, Asst Dir, Moberly Area Community College Library & Academic Resource Center, Main Bldg, 2nd Flr, 101 College Ave, Moberly, MO, 65270-1304. Tel: 660-263-4100, Ext 11210, 660-263-4100, Ext 11310. p. 1262
Gossett, J Gabriel, Head, Hacherl Research & Writing Studio, Western Washington University, 516 High St, MS 9103, Bellingham, WA, 98225. Tel: 360-650-7555. p. 2358
Gostautas, Stefanie, Technology Spec, South Central Kansas Library System, 321 N Main St, South Hutchinson, KS, 67505. Tel: 620-663-3211. p. 837
Gostin, Laura, Learning Res Coordr, Bristol Community College, Attleboro Campus, 11 Field Rd, Rm 107, Attleboro, MA, 02703. Tel: 774-357-3601. p. 1017
Gostomski, Michelle, Bus Mgr, Northern Waters Library Service, 3200 E Lakeshore Dr, Ashland, WI, 54806-2510. Tel: 715-685-1070. p. 2421
Goswami, Sukrit D, Dir, Haverford Township Free Library, 1601 Darby Rd, Havertown, PA, 19083-3798. Tel: 610-446-3082, Ext 500. p. 1942
Gotauco, Liz, Ch Serv, Cumberland Public Library, 1464 Diamond Hill Rd, Cumberland, RI, 02864-5510. Tel: 401-333-2552, Ext 125. p. 2031
Gotch, Julie, Assoc Dir, Digital Serv, Davenport University, 6191 Kraft Ave SE, Grand Rapids, MI, 49512. Tel: 616-554-5664. p. 1110
Gotkiewicz, Sharon, Head, ILL, Virginia Polytechnic Institute & State University Libraries, 560 Drillfield Dr, Blacksburg, VA, 24061. Tel: 540-231-9202. p. 2307
Goto, Rie, Librn, Hospital for Special Surgery, 535 E 70th St, 8th Flr, Rm 8W-837 West, New York, NY, 10021. Tel: 212-606-1000, 212-606-1210. p. 1588
Goto, Rie, Asst Univ Librn, The Rockefeller University, Welch Hall, 1230 York Ave, RU Box 203, New York, NY, 10065. Tel: 212-327-8980. p. 1601
Gotsch, Melissa, Mgr, Baltimore County Public Library, Pikesville Branch, 1301 Reisterstown Rd, Baltimore, MD, 21208. Tel: 410-887-1234. p. 980
Gotshall, Leigh, Librn, Kenly Public Library, 205 Edgerton St, Kenly, NC, 27542. Tel: 919-284-4217. p. 1699
Gottesman, Andrew, Coll Mgt Librn, Bucks County Community College Library, 275 Swamp Rd, Newtown, PA, 18940-0999. Tel: 215-504-8619. p. 1970
Gottfried, Beth, Outreach Mgr, Tiffin-Seneca Public Library, 77 Jefferson St, Tiffin, OH, 44883. Tel: 419-447-3751. p. 1823
Gottlieb, Jane, VPres, Libr & Info Serv, Juilliard School, 60 Lincoln Center Plaza, New York, NY, 10023-6588. Tel: 212-799-5000, Ext 265. p. 1590
Gottlieb, Laura, Librn, Temple Beth El, 7400 Telegraph Rd, Bloomfield Hills, MI, 48301-3876. Tel: 248-851-1100. p. 1086
Gottlieb, Robin, Circ Librn, Roeliff Jansen Community Library, 9091 Rte 22, Hillsdale, NY, 12529. Tel: 518-325-4101. p. 1547
Gottsch, Cathy, Adminr, Ray County Historical Society & Museum Library, 901 W Royle St, Richmond, MO, 64085. Tel: 816-776-2305. p. 1267
Gottschalk, Alice R, Circ, Libr Spec II, Camp Verde Community Library, 130 N Black Bridge Rd, Camp Verde, AZ, 86322. Tel: 928-554-8383. p. 57
Gottschalk, Mark, Dir, Libr Serv, South Plains College Library, 1401 S College Ave - Box E, Levelland, TX, 79336. Tel: 806-716-2300, 806-716-2330. p. 2211
Gottschalk, Tania, Assoc Univ Librn, Thompson Rivers University, 900 McGill Rd, Kamloops, BC, V2C 5N3, CANADA. Tel: 250-828-5000. p. 2568
Gotwals, Jennifer, Lea Archivist, Harvard Library, Arthur & Elizabeth Schlesinger Library on the History of Women in America, Three James St, Cambridge, MA, 02138-3766. Tel: 617-495-8647. p. 1007
Goudeau, Kelly, Libr Asst, Betty Foster Public Library, 405 Shaffner St, Ponder, TX, 76259. Tel: 940-479-2683. p. 2228
Goudie, Allen R, Supervisory Library Tech, United States Army, 4300 Camp Hale Rd, Fort Drum, NY, 13602. Tel: 315-772-4502. p. 1534
Goudreau, Alex, Librn, University of New Brunswick, Saint John Campus, 100 Tucker Park Rd, Saint John, NB, E2L 4L5, CANADA. Tel: 506-648-5710. p. 2605
Gough, Maggie, Dir, Manhasset Public Library, 30 Onderdonk Ave, Manhasset, NY, 11030. Tel: 516-627-2300. p. 1568
Gough, Stephanie, Actg Libr Mgr, Fundy Library Region, Campobello Public Library, Three Welshhpool St, Campobello Parish, NB, E5E 1G3, CANADA. Tel: 506-752-7082. p. 2604
Goughnour, Kelsey, Dir, East Texas Medical Center, 1000 S Beckham Ave, Tyler, TX, 75701. Tel: 903-531-8685. p. 2249
Gouin, Elisabeth, Coordr, Grand Seminaire des Saints Apotres Library, Archeveche de Sherbrooke Cathedrale, 130 rue de la Cathedrale, Sherbrooke, QC, J1H 4M1, CANADA. Tel: 819-563-9934, Ext 209. p. 2737
Gould, Amy, Head, Tech Serv, Kewanee Public Library District, 102 S Tremont St, Kewanee, IL, 61443. Tel: 309-852-4505. p. 605
Gould, Brenda Lynn, Dir, West Paris Public Library, 226 Main St, West Paris, ME, 04289. Tel: 207-674-2004. p. 946
Gould, Catherine, Head, Youth Serv, Newport Public Library, 300 Spring St, Newport, RI, 02840. Tel: 401-847-8720. p. 2035
Gould, Elyssa, Library Contact, University of Tennessee, Knoxville, Acquisitions & Continuing Resources, 1015 Volunteer Blvd, Knoxville, TN, 37996-1000. Tel: 865-974-4236. p. 2107
Gould, Gretchen B, Coll Strategist Librn, Resource Management, University of Northern Iowa Library, 1227 W 27th St, Cedar Falls, IA, 50613-3675. Tel: 319-273-6327. p. 737
Gould, Jennifer, VP, Communications, RAND Corporation Library, 1776 Main St, M1LIB, Santa Monica, CA, 90407. Tel: (310) 393-0411, ext. 6815. p. 244
Gould, Mary Ann, Librn, Temple Sholom in Broomall Library, 55 N Church Lane, Broomall, PA, 19008. Tel: 610-356-5165. p. 1915
Gould, Renee, Coll Develop Librn, Saint Leo University, 33701 State Rd 52, Saint Leo, FL, 33574. Tel: 352-588-8265. p. 441
Gould, Rhonda, Exec Dir, Walla Walla County Rural Library District, 37 Jade Ave, Walla Walla, WA, 99362. Tel: 509-527-3284. p. 2392
Gould, Tammy, Circ Supvr, Springfield Town Library, 43 Main St, Springfield, VT, 05156. Tel: 802-885-3108. p. 2295
Goulding, Charles, Libr Coord, Yavapai County Free Library District, Black Canyon City Community Library, 34701 S Old Black Canyon Hwy, Black Canyon City, AZ, 85324. Tel: 623-374-5866. p. 74
Goulet, Carol, Tech Serv, Edwards Public Library, 30 East St, Southampton, MA, 01073. Tel: 413-527-9480. p. 1055
Goulet, Gwendlyn, Chief Exec Officer, Librn, Spanish Public Library, Eight Trunk Rd, Spanish, ON, P0P 2A0, CANADA. Tel: 705-844-2555. p. 2679
Goulet, Samantha, Chief Exec Officer, Librn, McGarry Public Library, One 27th St, Virginiatown, ON, P0K 1X0, CANADA. Tel: 705-634-2312. p. 2701

Goupil, Heather, Head Librn, Capital Area District Libraries, Mason Library, 145 W Ash St, Mason, MI, 48854. Tel: 517-676-9088. p. 1124
Goupil, Mario, Prof, Cégep Garneau, 1660 blvd de l'Entente, Quebec, QC, G1S 4S3, CANADA. Tel: 418-688-8310, Ext 2290. p. 2796
Gourlay, Peter, Dir, British Columbia Legislative Library, Parliament Bldgs, Victoria, BC, V8V 1X4, CANADA. Tel: 250-387-6500. p. 2582
Gourlay, Robert, Circ, Fairhope Public Library, 501 Fairhope Ave, Fairhope, AL, 36532. Tel: 251-928-7483. p. 16
Gourley, Donald, Dir, Info Tech, Washington Research Library Consortium, 901 Commerce Dr, Upper Marlboro, MD, 20774. Tel: 301-390-2000. p. 2766
Gourley, Elizabeth, Dir of Libr, Interlochen Center for the Arts, Bonisteel Library - Seabury Academic Library, 4000 M-137, Interlochen, MI, 49643. Tel: 231-276-7420. p. 1118
Gourley, Elizabeth, Dir of Libr, Interlochen Center for the Arts, Frederick & Elizabeth Ludwig Fennell Music Library, 4000 Hwy M-137, Interlochen, MI, 49643. Tel: 231-276-7230. p. 1118
Gouthro, Daniel, Sr Research Coord, Ontario Ministry of Finance, 95 Grosvenor St, 1st Flr, Toronto, ON, M7A 1Y8, CANADA. Tel: 416-325-1204. p. 2691
Gouveia, Carl, Dir, Fairport Public Library, One Fairport Village Landing, Fairport, NY, 14450. Tel: 585-223-9091. p. 1532
Govan, Jennifer L, Sr Librn, Teachers College, Columbia University, 525 W 120th St, New York, NY, 10027-6696. Tel: 212-678-3022. p. 1602
Gove, Hope, Co-Dir, Willington Public Library, Seven Ruby Rd, Willington, CT, 06279. Tel: 860-429-3854. p. 347
Gove, Megan, Dir, Talcott Free Library, 101 E Main St, Rockton, IL, 61072. Tel: 815-624-7511. p. 642
Gover, Harvey R, Emeritus Faculty Librarian, Washington State University Tri-Cities Library, 2770 Crimson Way, Richland, WA, 99354. Tel: 509-372-7430. p. 2375
Gover, Jill, Dir, Luck Public Library, 301 S Main St, Luck, WI, 54853. Tel: 715-472-2770. p. 2448
Govin, Megan, Mgr, Archives & Spec Coll, The Museum of Modern Art, 11 W 53th St, New York, NY, 10019. Tel: 212-708-9433. p. 1592
Gow, Athol, Mgr, University of Guelph, Student Accessibility Services, University Centre, Level 2, 50 Stone Rd E, Guelph, ON, N1G 2W1, CANADA. Tel: 519-824-1420, Ext 52312. p. 2644
Gowen, Danielle, Actg Head Librn, Penn Wynne Library, 130 Overbrook Pkwy, Wynnewood, PA, 19096-3211. Tel: 610-642-7844. p. 2025
Gowen, Elise D, Librn, Pennsylvania State University Libraries, Fletcher L Byrom Earth & Mineral Sciences Library, 105 Deike Bldg, University Park, PA, 16802. Tel: 814-863-7324. p. 2015
Gowen, Jana, Electronic Res & Syst Librn, Cameron University Library, 2800 W Gore Blvd, Lawton, OK, 73505-6377. Tel: 580-581-5915. p. 1851
Gower, Donna V, Librn, Lackawanna County Law Library, Courthouse, Ground Flr, 200 N Washington Ave, Scranton, PA, 18503. Tel: 570-963-6712. p. 2004
Gower, Michael, Adminr, Info Syst, Idaho State University, 850 S Ninth Ave, Pocatello, ID, 83209. Tel: 208-282-2882. p. 528
Gower, Rena, Dir, Learning Commons, Lincoln Trail College, 11220 State Hwy 1, Robinson, IL, 62454-5707. Tel: 618-544-8657, Ext 1427. p. 640
Gowin, Ruth, Info Assoc, Longwood University, Redford & Race St, Farmville, VA, 23909. Tel: 434-395-2741. p. 2318
Gowing, Cheryl, Assoc Dean, Library Info Systems & Facilities, University of Miami Libraries, 1300 Memorial Dr, Coral Gables, FL, 33146. Tel: 305-284-3233. p. 390
Gowman, Randall, Asst Dir, Pub Serv, Gordon College, 255 Grapevine Rd, Wenham, MA, 01984-1899. Tel: 978-867-4878. p. 1064
Goyda, Ed, Libr Dir, Somerset County Library System, 11767 Beechwood St, Princess Anne, MD, 21853. Tel: 410-651-0852. p. 973
Goyette, Anne, Acq/Cat Tech, Ecole de Technologie Superieure (Service de la bibliotheque), 1100 rue Notre-Dame Ouest, Montreal, QC, H3C 1K3, CANADA. Tel: 514-396-8960. p. 2724
Goyette, Julie, Libr Dir, Rockbridge Regional Library System, 138 S Main St, Lexington, VA, 24450-2316. Tel: 540-463-4324. p. 2329
Goykin, Robert, Asst Dir, Sayville Library, 88 Greene Ave, Sayville, NY, 11782. Tel: 631-589-4440. p. 1637
Gozdz, Henry, Librn, Bergen County Law Library, Bergen County Justice Ctr, Ten Main St, 1st Flr, Hackensack, NJ, 07601. Tel: 201-527-2274. p. 1406
Grabeel, Kelsey, Asst Dir, University of Tennessee Graduate School of Medicine, 1924 Alcoa Hwy, Box U-111, Knoxville, TN, 37920. Tel: 865-305-5707. p. 2107
Grabek, Valerie, Asst Librn, Teen Serv, Cragin Memorial Library, Eight Linwood Ave, Colchester, CT, 06415. Tel: 860-537-5752. p. 306
Graber, David, Dir, Wayne State College, 1111 Main St, Wayne, NE, 68787. Tel: 402-375-7272. p. 1340
Graber, Kristina, Mgr, San Francisco Camerawork, 1011 Market St, 2nd Flr, San Francisco, CA, 94103. Tel: 415-487-1011. p. 227
Graber, Susan, Dir, Odon Winkelpleck Public Library, 202 W Main St, Odon, IN, 47562. Tel: 812-636-4949. p. 712
Grabhorn, Cody, Exec Dir, Ontario County Historical Society Library, 55 N Main St, Canandaigua, NY, 14424. Tel: 585-394-4975. p. 1512
Grace, Barbara, Ch Serv, Garden City Public Library, 60 Seventh St, Garden City, NY, 11530. Tel: 516-742-8405. p. 1536
Grace, Charla, Librn, Mid-Mississippi Regional Library System, Attala County, 201 S Huntington St, Kosciusko, MS, 39090-9002. Tel: 662-289-5141. p. 1224
Grace, Kevin, Head of Libr, Univ Archivist, University of Cincinnati Libraries, Archives & Rare Books, Blegan Library, 8th Flr, 2602 McMicken Circle, Cincinnati, OH, 45221. Tel: 513-556-1959. p. 1764
Grace, Michael, Dir, Fiske Free Library, 108 Broad St, Claremont, NH, 03743-2673. Tel: 603-542-7017. p. 1358
Grace, Shelly, Exec Dir, Prairielands Library Exchange, 109 S Fifth St, Marshall, MN, 56258. Tel: 507-532-9013. p. 2768
Grace, William, Br Mgr, Beaumont Public Library System, Tyrrell Historical, 695 Pearl St, Beaumont, TX, 77701. Tel: 409-833-2759. p. 2146
Graceffo, Mark, Librn, Saint Peter's University, Hudson Terrace, Englewood Cliffs, NJ, 07632. Tel: 201-761-7488. p. 1402
Gracenin, Daniel, Exec Dir, Mercer County Regional Planning Commission Library, 2491 Highland Rd, Hermitage, PA, 16148. Tel: 724-981-2412. p. 1943
Gracey, Lois, Circ, Kent Memorial Library, 50 N Main St, Suffield, CT, 06078-2117. Tel: 860-668-3896. p. 341
Gracy, Karen, Dr, Prof, Kent State University, 314 University Library, 1125 Risman Dr, Kent, OH, 44242-0001. Tel: 330-672-2782. p. 2790
Grad, Kimberly, Libr Dir, Abbot Public Library, Three Brook Rd, Marblehead, MA, 01945. Tel: 781-631-1481. p. 1031
Graden, Lizette, Chief Curator, Nordic Heritage Museum, Walter Johnson Memorial Library, 3014 NW 67th St, Seattle, WA, 98117. Tel: 206-789-5707. p. 2377
Grady, Eileen, Dir, Operations, Samuels Public Library, 330 E Criser Rd, Front Royal, VA, 22630. Tel: 540-635-3153. p. 2321
Grady, Fiona, Head Librn, Suffolk County Community College, 1001 Crooked Hill Rd, Brentwood, NY, 11717. Tel: 631-851-6746. p. 1496
Grady, Lee C, Sr Reference Archivist, Wisconsin Historical Society Library, 816 State St, 2nd Flr, Madison, WI, 53706. Tel: 608-264-6535. p. 2452
Grady, Mitch, Libr Dir, Livingston-Park County Public Library, 228 W Callender St, Livingston, MT, 59047. Tel: 406-222-0862. p. 1299
Graebner, Rebecca, Head, Youth Services & Education, Memorial & Library Association, 44 Broad St, Westerly, RI, 02891. Tel: 401-596-2877, Ext 317. p. 2044
Graefe, Cynthia, Librn, Athabasca Municipal Library, 4716 48th St, Athabasca, AB, T9S 2B6, CANADA. Tel: 780-675-2735. p. 2522
Graefnitz, Katie, Mgr, Medina County District Library, Seville Library, 45 Center St, Seville, OH, 44273. Tel: 330-769-2852. p. 1802
Graetz, Ken, Dean of Libr, Winona State University, 175 W Mark St, Winona, MN, 55987. Tel: 507-457-2339. p. 1209
Graf, Betty, Head, Cat, University of Waterloo Library, 200 University Ave W, Waterloo, ON, N2L 3G1, CANADA. Tel: 519-888-4567, Ext 46584. p. 2702
Graf, Jennifer, Circ Supvr, Nicholas P Sims Library, 515 W Main, Waxahachie, TX, 75165-3235. Tel: 972-937-2671. p. 2255
Graff, Matthew, Exec Dir, Skidompha Public Library, 184 Main St, Damariscotta, ME, 04543. Tel: 207-563-5513. p. 922
Graff, Michelle, Ref Librn, Supreme Court of Ohio, 65 S Front St, 11th Flr, Columbus, OH, 43215-3431. Tel: 614-387-9692. p. 1777
Graffius, Jeff, Dir, Libr Serv, Washington State Community College, 710 Colegate Dr, Marietta, OH, 45750. Tel: 740-374-8716, Ext 3108. p. 1799
Grafton, Cathy, Libr Dir, Odell Public Library District, 301 E Richard St, Odell, IL, 60460. Tel: 815-998-2012. p. 628
Grafton, Floria, Libr Mgr, New Hope Christian College, 2155 Bailey Hill Rd, Eugene, OR, 97405. Tel: 541-485-1780, Ext 3102. p. 1879
Grafton, Jennifer, Librn, Coulterville Public Library, 103 S Fourth St, Coulterville, IL, 62237. Tel: 618-758-3013. p. 574
Grafton, Karla, Dir, Libr Serv, Hartford International University Library, 77 Sherman St, Hartford, CT, 06105-2260. Tel: 860-509-9500. p. 317
Grafton, Suzanne, Tech Serv Librn, Meridian Community College, 910 Hwy 19 N, Meridian, MS, 39307. Tel: 601-484-8766. p. 1226
Gragg, Kim, Undergrad Serv Coordr, Tarleton State University Library, 201 Saint Felix, Stephenville, TX, 76401. Tel: 254-968-9246. p. 2246
Gragg, Phyllis, Assoc Dean, Libr & Info Serv, California Western School of Law Library, 290 Cedar St, San Diego, CA, 92101. Tel: 619-525-1420. p. 215
Gragg, Wendell, Supvr, Automation Serv, Bryan College Station Public Library System, 201 E 26th St, Bryan, TX, 77803-5356. Tel: 979-209-5600. p. 2151
Grah, Tammy, Admin Librn, Chester Public Library, 733 State St, Chester, IL, 62233. Tel: 618-826-3711. p. 553
Graham, Adrian, Fac Librn, Austin Community College, South Austin Campus Library, 1820 W Stassney Lane, 2nd Flr, Rm 1201, Austin, TX, 78745. Tel: 512-223-9179. p. 2138
Graham, Amy, Librn, Ohev Shalom Synagogue, Two Chester Rd, Wallingford, PA, 19086. Tel: 610-874-1465. p. 2017
Graham, Beverly, Asst Dir, Knowledge Serv, Bank of Canada, 234 Wellington St, Ottawa, ON, K1A 0G9, CANADA. Tel: 613-782-8881. p. 2664

Graham, Christopher, Tech Serv Spec, Ocean County College Library, College Dr, Toms River, NJ, 08754. Tel: 732-255-0400, Ext 4489. p. 1446
Graham, Clare, Libr Dir, Mid Arkansas Regional Library, 202 E Third St, Malvern, AR, 72104. Tel: 501-332-5441. p. 103
Graham, Cynthia, Librn, Saint Catherine University, 2004 Randolph Ave, Saint Paul, MN, 55105. Tel: 651-690-6650. p. 1201
Graham, Deborah, Dep Dir, Montgomery County Public Library, 328 N Maysville Rd, Mount Sterling, KY, 40353. Tel: 859-498-2404. p. 870
Graham, Denise, Mgr, Carnegie Library of Pittsburgh, Homewood, 7101 Hamilton Ave, Pittsburgh, PA, 15208-1052. Tel: 412-731-3080. p. 1991
Graham, Jeanette, Mgr, District of Columbia Public Library, Woodridge, 1801 Hamlin St NE, Washington, DC, 20018. Tel: 202-541-6226. p. 365
Graham, Jennifer, Dir, New Alexandria Public Library, Keystone Plaza, Rte 22, New Alexandria, PA, 15670-9703. Tel: 724-668-7747. p. 1968
Graham, Jerry, Librn, Salvation Army School for Officer Training, 201 Lafayette Ave, Suffern, NY, 10901. Tel: 845-368-7228. p. 1647
Graham, Jo Ann, Eng Librn, Tuskegee University, 1200 W Old Mongtomery Rd, Ford Motor Company Library, Tuskegee, AL, 36088. Tel: 334-727-8892. p. 38
Graham, John-Bauer, Dean, Libr Serv, Jacksonville State University Library, 700 Pelham Rd N, Jacksonville, AL, 36265. Tel: 256-782-5758. p. 23
Graham, Karen, Librn, Massachusetts Water Resources Authority Library, Two Griffin Way, Chelsea, MA, 02150. Tel: 617-305-5583, 617-305-5584. p. 1010
Graham, Karen, Dir, De Soto Public Library, 712 S Main St, De Soto, MO, 63020. Tel: 636-586-3858. p. 1245
Graham, Karen, Ref Serv, Jefferson County Library, Windsor, 7479 Metropolitian Blvd, Barnhart, MO, 63012. Tel: 636-461-1914. p. 1249
Graham, Krista, Head, Digital Libr Serv, Georgia State University, 100 Decatur St SE, Atlanta, GA, 30303-3202. Tel: 404-413-2752. p. 464
Graham, Kurt, Dr, Dir, National Archives & Records Administration, 500 W US Hwy 24, Independence, MO, 64050-1798. Tel: 816-268-8200. p. 1251
Graham, Laurel, Head of Libr, University of Pennsylvania Libraries, Leon Levy Dental Medicine Library, Evans Bldg, 240 S 40th St, Philadelphia, PA, 19104. Tel: 215-898-8978. p. 1988
Graham, Margaret, Supvr, Haliburton County Public Library, Minden Hills Branch, 176 Bobcaygeon Rd, Minden, ON, K0M 2K0, CANADA. Tel: 705-286-2491. p. 2644
Graham, Matt Patrick, Dr, Dir, Emory University Libraries, Pitts Theology Library, Candler School of Theology, 1531 Dickey Dr, Ste 560, Atlanta, GA, 30322-2810. Tel: 404-727-4166. p. 463
Graham, Michael S, Dir, Shaker Library, 707 Shaker Rd, New Gloucester, ME, 04260. Tel: 207-926-4597. p. 932
Graham, Nick, Archivist, University of North Carolina at Chapel Hill, 208 Raleigh St, CB 3916, Chapel Hill, NC, 27515. Tel: 919-962-1053. p. 1678
Graham, Pamela, PhD, Dir, Columbia University, Global Studies, Lehman Library, International Affairs Bldg, 420 W 118th St, New York, NY, 10027. Tel: 212-854-3630. p. 1583
Graham, Penny, Libr Mgr, West Feliciana Parish Library, 5114 Burnett Rd, Saint Francisville, LA, 70775-4341. Tel: 225-635-3364. p. 907
Graham, Regina, Dir, Dixie Regional Library System, 111 N Main St, Pontotoc, MS, 38863. Tel: 662-489-3961. p. 1229
Graham, Sandra, Interim Mgr, Kent District Library, Englehardt Branch, 200 N Monroe St, Lowell, MI, 49331. p. 1094
Graham, Sandy, Br Mgr, Kent District Library, Alto Branch, 6071 Linfield Ave, Alto, MI, 49302. p. 1093
Graham, Shawnetta, Librn, Phoenix Emerging Adult Career & Education (PEACE) Center, 3825 Campton Hills Rd, Saint Charles, IL, 60175. Tel: 630-584-0506. p. 644
Graham, Shawnetta, Librn, Illinois Youth Center, 30 W 200 Ferry Rd, Warrenville, IL, 60555. Tel: 630-983-6231. p. 658
Graham, Stephanie, Br Head, Winnipeg Public Library, St Vital, Six Fermor Ave, Winnipeg, MB, R2M 0Y2, CANADA. Tel: 204-806-1250. p. 2596
Graham, Stephen, Sr Mgr, The Mary Baker Eddy Library, Research & Reference Services, 210 Massachusetts Ave, P04-10, Boston, MA, 02115-3017. Tel: 617-450-7000. p. 994
Graham, Susan, Spec Coll Librn, University of Maryland, Baltimore County, 1000 Hilltop Circle, Baltimore, MD, 21250. Tel: 410-455-2356. p. 958
Graham, Susie, Asst Dir, Bienville Parish Library, 2768 Maple St, Arcadia, LA, 71001. Tel: 318-263-7410. p. 881
Graham, Suzanne R, Cat Serv Librn, University of Georgia, Alexander Campbell King Law Library, 225 Herty Dr, Athens, GA, 30602-6018. Tel: 706-542-5082. p. 459
Graham, Tauni, Circ, ILL, Reserves, Ohio State University LIBRARIES, Newark Campus Library, Warner Library & Student Ctr, 1179 University Dr, Newark, OH, 43055-1797. Tel: 740-366-9307. p. 1776
Graham, Ticee, Libr Dir, Tri-Valley Community Library, Suntrana Rd, Healy, AK, 99743. Tel: 907-683-2507. p. 46
Graham, Toby, Assoc Provost, Univ Librn, University of Georgia Libraries, 320 S Jackson St, Athens, GA, 30602-1641. Tel: 706-542-3251. p. 459
Graham, Tracey, Head, Adult Serv, Leominster Public Library, 30 West St, Leominster, MA, 01453. Tel: 978-534-7522, Ext 3598. p. 1028
Graham, Tracey, Ad, Westborough Public Library, 55 W Main St, Westborough, MA, 01581. Tel: 508-366-3050. p. 1066
Grahame, Gita, Libr Tech, Sheep River Library, 129 Main St NW, Diamond Valley, AB, T0L 2A0, CANADA. Tel: 403-933-3278. p. 2533
Grahek, David, Assoc Dir, University of Maryland, Baltimore, Thurgood Marshall Law Library, 501 W Fayette St, Baltimore, MD, 21201-1768. Tel: 410-706-2025. p. 957
Grai, Rebecca, Head, Circ, Northwood University, 4000 Whiting Dr, Midland, MI, 48640-2398. Tel: 989-837-4333. p. 1132
Gralenski, Frederick, Dir, Pembroke Library, 221 Old County Rd, Pembroke, ME, 04666. Tel: 207-726-4745. p. 935
Grallo, Jacqueline, Interim Dean of Libr, California State University - Monterey Bay, 3054 Divarty St, Seaside, CA, 93955. Tel: 831-582-3142. p. 246
Grama, Remus, Fr, Library Contact, Romanian Ethnic Arts Museum Library, 3256 Warren Rd, Cleveland, OH, 44111. Tel: 216-941-5550. p. 1770
Gramaglia, Joanne, Asst Dir, Hicksville Public Library, 169 Jerusalem Ave, Hicksville, NY, 11801. Tel: 516-931-1417. p. 1546
Gramazio, Gabrielle, Libr Asst, City College Library - Fort Lauderdale, 2000 W Commercial Blvd, Ste 200, Fort Lauderdale, FL, 33309-3001. Tel: 954-492-5353. p. 401
Gramer, Kristen, Asst Dir, Lewes Public Library, 111 Adams Ave, Lewes, DE, 19958. Tel: 302-645-2733. p. 354
Gramlich, Laura, Dir, Bacon Memorial District Library, 45 Vinewood, Wyandotte, MI, 48192-5221. Tel: 734-246-8357. p. 1160
Gramm, Christine, Br Mgr, Medina County District Library, 210 S Broadway, Medina, OH, 44256. Tel: 330-725-0588. p. 1801
Gramowski, Kari, Youth Serv Dir, Emmetsburg Public Library, 707 N Superior St, Emmetsburg, IA, 50536. Tel: 712-852-4009. p. 751
Gran, Karen, Asst Librn, Caledonia Public Library, 231 E Main St, Caledonia, MN, 55921-1321. Tel: 507-725-2671. p. 1167
Granado, Rosa, Br Mgr, High Plains Library District, Kersey Library, 413 First St, Kersey, CO, 80644. p. 285
Granados, Daniel, Mgr, County of Los Angeles Public Library, Hawthorne Library, 12700 S Grevillea Ave, Hawthorne, CA, 90250-4396. Tel: 310-679-8193. p. 136
Granados, Gwen E, Regional Archives Dir, National Archives & Records Administration, 17101 Huron St, Broomfield, CO, 80023. Tel: 303-604-4740. p. 268
Granados, Osvaldo, ILL, The Amargosa Valley Library, 1660 E Amargosa Farm Rd, Amargosa Valley, NV, 89020. Tel: 775-372-5340. p. 1343
Granath, Jack, Libr Dir, Bonner Springs City Library, 201 N Nettleton Ave, Bonner Springs, KS, 66012. Tel: 913-441-2665. p. 799
Granberry, Eugene, Law Librn, Cook County Law Library, Markham Branch, 16501 S Kedzie Pkwy, Markham, IL, 60426. Tel: 708-232-4125. p. 560
Grande, M.J., Youth Serv, Juneau Public Libraries, 292 Marine Way, Juneau, AK, 99801. Tel: 907-586-5249. p. 47
Grandgeorge, Jan, Dir, Eagle Grove Memorial Library, 101 S Cadwell Ave, Eagle Grove, IA, 50533. Tel: 515-448-4115. p. 750
Grandison, Maxine, Head, Per, Mount Vernon Public Library, 28 S First Ave, Mount Vernon, NY, 10550. Tel: 914-668-1840, Ext 206. p. 1575
Grando, Natasha, Dir, Tech Serv, Nova Southeastern University Libraries, 3100 Ray Ferrero Jr Blvd, Fort Lauderdale, FL, 33314. Tel: 954-262-4665. p. 402
Grandy, Ann, Coll Mgr, Pope County Historical Society, 809 S Lakeshore Dr, Glenwood, MN, 56334. Tel: 320-634-3293. p. 1176
Grandy, Roslyn, Librn, Ref Serv, The College of New Rochelle, 29 Castle Pl, New Rochelle, NY, 10805-2308. Tel: 914-654-5345. p. 1577
Graney, Brian, Librn & Archivist, Museum of International Folk Art, 706 Camino Lejo, Santa Fe, NM, 87505. Tel: 505-476-1210. p. 1475
Graney, Jen, Libr Dir, Cortland Free Library, 32 Church St, Cortland, NY, 13045. Tel: 607-753-1042. p. 1522
Granger, Nancy, Br Mgr, Houston County Public Library System, Centerville Branch, 206 Gunn Rd, Centerville, GA, 31028. Tel: 478-953-4500. p. 493
Granger, Nancy, Head Librn, Houston County Public Library System, Perry Branch, 1201 Washington Ave, Perry, GA, 31069. Tel: 478-987-3050. p. 493
Grangier, Sarah, Law Librn, Somerset County Circuit Court Library, Courthouse, 30512 Prince William St, Princess Anne, MD, 21853. Tel: 410-621-7581. p. 973
Granoth, Elena, Dir, Morris Public Library, Four North St, Morris, CT, 06763-1415. Tel: 860-567-7440. p. 323
Gransee, Susan, Br Mgr, Buncombe County Public Libraries, Leicester Branch, 1561 Alexander Rd, Leicester, NC, 28748. Tel: 828-250-6480. p. 1672
Granskog, Kay, Assoc Univ Librn, Syst, Tech Serv, Michigan State University Libraries, Main Library, 366 W Circle Dr, East Lansing, MI, 48824-1048. Tel: 517-884-0814. p. 1102
Grant, Betsy, Head, Cat, Head, Spec Coll, University of the South, 178 Georgia Ave, Sewanee, TN, 37383-1000. Tel: 931-598-1663. p. 2126
Grant, Casey, Outreach Librn, Tech Librn, Portland Public Library, Five Monument Sq, Portland, ME, 04101. Tel: 207-871-1700, Ext 729. p. 937

Grant, Cedric, Chief Financial Officer, Anne Arundel County Public Library, Five Harry Truman Pkwy, Annapolis, MD, 21401. Tel: 410-222-7236. p. 950

Grant, Constance, Dir, Libr Serv, Catawba College, 2300 W Innes St, Salisbury, NC, 28144-2488. Tel: 704-870-9848. p. 1714

Grant, D L, Libr Mgr, San Antonio Public Library, Carver, 3350 E Commerce St, San Antonio, TX, 78220. Tel: 210-207-9180. p. 2238

Grant, Diana, Dir, Helper City Library, 19 S Main St, Helper, UT, 84526. Tel: 435-472-5601. p. 2264

Grant, Garrett, Asst Libr Dir, Aldrich Public Library, Six Washington St, Barre, VT, 05641. Tel: 802-476-7550. p. 2278

Grant, Jerry, Dir, Res Serv, Shaker Museum & Library, 88 Shaker Museum Rd, Old Chatham, NY, 12136. Tel: 518-794-9100, Ext 211. p. 1610

Grant, Julienne, Foreign & Intl Research Specialist, Ref Librn, Loyola University Chicago Libraries, School of Law Library, Philip H Corboy Law Ctr, 25 E Pearson St, Chicago, IL, 60611. Tel: 312-915-8520. p. 564

Grant, Kate, Coordr, Harvard Library, Robbins Library of Philosophy, Emerson Hall 211, Harvard University, Dept of Philosophy, 25 Quincy St, Cambridge, MA, 02138. p. 1007

Grant, Kayla, Head, Prog, Clearwater Public Library System, 100 N Osceola Ave, Clearwater, FL, 33755. Tel: 727-562-4970. p. 388

Grant, Kristel, Librn, Chinook Regional Library, Eastend Branch, Eastend Memorial Hall, Oak Ave N, Eastend, SK, S0N 0T0, CANADA. Tel: 306-295-3788. p. 2752

Grant, Lily, Libr Mgr, Timberland Regional Library, Chehalis Branch, 400 N Market Blvd, Chehalis, WA, 98532. Tel: 360-748-3301. p. 2388

Grant, Megan, Mkt Coordr, Redford Township District Library, 25320 W Six Mile, Redford, MI, 48240. Tel: 313-531-5960. p. 1143

Grant, Michele, Pres, Norfolk Historical Society, 420 Main St, Port Dover, ON, N0A 1N0, CANADA. p. 2673

Grant, Rhett, Dir, Ada Public Library, 320 N Main St, Ada, OH, 45810-1199. Tel: 419-634-5246. p. 1743

Grant, Richard, Dir/Curator, Fort Polk Military Museum Library, 7881 Mississippi Ave, Bldg 927, Fort Polk, LA, 71459. Tel: 337-531-4840. p. 889

Grant, Ruth, Br Mgr, Pima County Public Library, Oro Valley Public Library, 1305 W Naranja Dr, Oro Valley, AZ, 85737. Tel: 520-594-5580. p. 82

Grant, Sara, Br Mgr, Surrey Libraries, Ocean Park, 12854 17th Ave, Surrey, BC, V4A 1T5, CANADA. Tel: 604-592-6911. p. 2577

Grant, Sara, Br Mgr, Surrey Libraries, Semiahmoo Library, 1815-152 St, Surrey, BC, V4A 9Y9, CANADA. Tel: 604-592-6911. p. 2577

Grant, Sarah, Librn, United States Department of Energy, 3610 Collins Ferry Rd, Morgantown, WV, 26507. Tel: 304-285-4184. p. 2409

Grant, Shanneon, Dir, La Crosse Public Library, 800 Main St, La Crosse, WI, 54601. Tel: 608-789-7100. p. 2446

Grant, Shawn, Computer Serv Mgr, Eugene Public Library, 100 W Tenth Ave, Eugene, OR, 97401. Tel: 541-682-5450. p. 1878

Grant, Sheehan, Operations Mgr, University of California, Berkeley, Jean Gray Hargrove Music Library, Berkeley, CA, 94720-6000. Tel: 510-642-2623. p. 123

Grant, Susan, Educ Tech Spec, Quincy University, 1800 College Ave, Quincy, IL, 62301-2699. Tel: 217-228-5347, Ext 3806. p. 638

Grant, Susan, Head, Access Serv, Head, Info Serv, Southern Maryland Regional Library Association, Inc, 37600 New Market Rd, Charlotte Hall, MD, 20622. Tel: 301-884-0436. p. 961

Grant, Susan, Dir, North Hampton Public Library, 239 Atlantic Ave, North Hampton, NH, 03862-2341. Tel: 603-964-6326. p. 1376

Grant, Tiffany, Info Spec, University of Cincinnati Libraries, Donald C Harrison Health Sciences Library, 231 Albert Sabin Way, Cincinnati, OH, 45267. Tel: 513-558-9153. p. 1765

Grant, TJ, Asst Dir, Colleton County Memorial Library, 600 Hampton St, Walterboro, SC, 29488-4098. Tel: 843-549-5621. p. 2072

Grant, Zachary, Interim Tech Services & Systems Librn, Clark College, Mail Stop LIB 112, 1933 Fort Vancouver Way, Vancouver, WA, 98663-3598. Tel: 360-992-2971. p. 2390

Grant-Jackson, Latrishia, Libr Asst, Desoto Parish Library, 109 Crosby St, Mansfield, LA, 71052. Tel: 318-872-6100. p. 895

Grantham, Rebecca, Tech Serv Librn, Emory & Henry College, 30480 Armbrister Dr, Emory, VA, 24327. Tel: 276-944-6208. p. 2315

Granville, Sarah, Teen Serv Librn, Barberton Public Library, 602 W Park Ave, Barberton, OH, 44203-2458. Tel: 330-745-1194. p. 1748

Grasmick, Amy, Dir, Kimball Public Library, 67 N Main St, Randolph, VT, 05060. Tel: 802-728-5073. p. 2292

Grasse, David, Ad, Ref Librn, Payson Public Library, 328 N McLane Rd, Payson, AZ, 85541. Tel: 928-472-5161. p. 68

Grassinger, Alicia, Head Librn, Parkland Regional Library-Manitoba, Rossburn Regional Library, 53 Main St N, Rossburn, MB, R0J 1V0, CANADA. Tel: 204-859-2687. p. 2587

Grasto, Jenny, Head, Resource Acquisition, Mgmt & Discovery, North Dakota State University Libraries, 1201 Albrecht Blvd, Fargo, ND, 58108. Tel: 701-231-6462. p. 1733

Grater, Peggy, Libr Dir, Leonardville City Library, 117 N Erpelding Ave, Leonardville, KS, 66449. Tel: 785-293-5606. p. 821

Grattidge, Scott, Exec Dir, Stockmen's Memorial Foundation Library, 101 RancheHouse Rd, Cochrane, AB, T4C 2K8, CANADA. Tel: 403-932-3782. p. 2531

Gratton, Korina, Library Tech, Circulation, University of the Fraser Valley, Chilliwack Campus, 45190 Caen Ave, Bldg A, Chilliwack, BC, V2R 0N3, CANADA. Tel: 604-504-7441, Ext 2431. p. 2562

Gratton-Tétreault, Noëlle, Res Mgr, Bibliothèque Municipale de Gatineau, Ville de Gatineau, CP 1970 Succ. Hull, Gatineau, QC, J8X 3Y9, CANADA. Tel: 819-243-2345. p. 2712

Gratz, Erin, Instrul Serv Librn, Orange Coast College Library, 2701 Fairview Rd, Costa Mesa, CA, 92626. Tel: 714-432-5885. p. 132

Gratz, Erin, Asst Prof, Instrul Tech Librn, Web Librn, University of La Verne, 2040 Third St, La Verne, CA, 91750. Tel: 909-593-3511, Ext 4305. p. 155

Graul, Amanda, Cat, Greenville Area Public Library, 330 Main St, Greenville, PA, 16125-2615. Tel: 724-588-5490. p. 1938

Graulich, Mary, Circ Supvr, Dexter District Library, 3255 Alpine St, Dexter, MI, 48130. Tel: 734-426-4477. p. 1100

Gravander, Laura, Ref Serv, YA, Franklin Public Library, 9151 W Loomis Rd, Franklin, WI, 53132. Tel: 414-425-8214. p. 2436

Gravel, Rachel, Head of Borrowing & Tech Services, Simsbury Public Library, 725 Hopmeadow St, Simsbury, CT, 06070. Tel: 860-658-7663. p. 336

Graveline, Jeffery, Ref Librn, University of Alabama at Birmingham, Mervyn H Sterne Library, 917 13th St S, Birmingham, AL, 35205. Tel: 205-934-6364. p. 9

Graveline, Laura, Visual Arts Librn, Dartmouth College Library, Sherman Art Library, Carpenter Hall, 25 N Main St, Hanover, NH, 03755-3570. Tel: 603-646-3831. p. 1367

Graven, Samantha, Dir, Parsons Public Library, 311 S 17th St, Parsons, KS, 67357. Tel: 620-421-5920. p. 831

Gravenor-Stacey, Betsy, Br Mgr, Worcester County Library, Snow Hill Branch, 307 N Washington St, Snow Hill, MD, 21863. Tel: 410-632-3495. p. 978

Graves, Brandy, Libr Dir, Shelby County Public Library, 57 W Broadway St, Shelbyville, IN, 46176. Tel: 317-398-7121, 317-835-2653. p. 718

Graves, Ellen, Librn, Bluffs Public Library, 110 N Bluffs St, Bluffs, IL, 62621. Tel: 217-754-3804. p. 543

Graves, Gale, Educ Mgr, Mgr, Literacy Serv, Waukegan Public Library, 128 N County St, Waukegan, IL, 60085. Tel: 847-623-2041. p. 660

Graves, Ginger, Br Mgr, Rutherford County Library System, Smyrna Public Library, 400 Enon Springs Rd W, Smyrna, TN, 37167. Tel: 615-459-4884. p. 2118

Graves, Howard, Assoc Dean, Libr Serv, Hofstra University, 123 Hofstra University, Hempstead, NY, 11549. Tel: 516 463-6429. p. 1545

Graves, Jackie, Asst Librn, Sandusky District Library, 55 E Sanilac Ave, Sandusky, MI, 48471-1146. Tel: 810-648-2644. p. 1149

Graves, Jeremiah, Access Serv Mgr, Massachusetts Institute of Technology Libraries, Barker Engineering, Bldg 10-500, 77 Massachusetts Ave, Cambridge, MA, 02139-4307. Tel: 617-253-2208. p. 1008

Graves, Kevin, Br Mgr, Gadsden Public Library, Warsham-Junkins Alabama City Genealogy Branch, 2700 W Meighan Blvd, Gadsden, AL, 35904. Tel: 256-549-4688. p. 18

Graves, Michele, Libr Dir, Eagle Mountain Library, 1650 E Stagecoach Run, Eagle Mountain, UT, 84005. Tel: 801-789-6623. p. 2263

Graves, Robert, Dr, Research Librn, Harrison County Historical Museum, 104 E Crockett St, Marshall, TX, 75670. Tel: 903-938-2680. p. 2216

Graves, Sheri, Librn, Ulysses Library Association, 401 N Main St, Ulysses, PA, 16948. Tel: 814-848-7226. p. 2014

Graves, Tess, Senior Coord, Piqua Public Library, 116 W High St, Piqua, OH, 45356. Tel: 937-773-6753. p. 1815

Gravius, Sharon, Emerging Technology Librarian, Ursuline College, 2550 Lander Rd, Pepper Pike, OH, 44124-4398. Tel: 440-449-4202. p. 1815

Gravlin, Karen, Libr Dir, Vermont Department of Libraries, 60 Washington St, Ste 2, Barre, VT, 05641. Tel: 802-636-0020. p. 2278

Gravot, Edna, Libr Asst, Valmeyer Public Library District, 300 S Cedar Bluff, Valmeyer, IL, 62295. Tel: 618-935-2626. p. 657

Gray, Angelaica, Librn, Tucumcari Public Library, 602 S Second, Tucumcari, NM, 88401-2899. Tel: 505-461-0295. p. 1479

Gray, Anita L, Dir, Libr Serv, Huntington University, 2303 College Ave, Huntington, IN, 46750. Tel: 260-359-4063. p. 690

Gray, Ashley, Coordr, University of Arkansas for Medical Sciences South Arkansas Library, 1617 N. Washington, Magnolia, AR, 71753. Tel: 870-234-7676, 870-562-2587. p. 103

Gray, B Allison, Dir, Goleta Valley Library, 500 N Fairview Ave, Goleta, CA, 93117. Tel: 805-562-5502. p. 149

Gray, Barbara, Dir, Res, New York Times, Reference Library, 620 Eighth Ave, 5th Flr, New York, NY, 10018. Tel: 212-556-7428. p. 1599

Gray, Bethany, Head, Ref, Lowell Public Library, 1505 E Commercial Ave, Lowell, IN, 46356-1899. Tel: 219-696-7704. p. 704

Gray, Brian, Coll Librn I, Case Western Reserve University, 11055 Euclid Ave, Cleveland, OH, 44106. Tel: 216-368-8685. p. 1766

Gray, Catherine, Coordr, Libr Serv, Idaho State University, University Library Center, 1784 Science Center Dr, Rm 225, Idaho Falls, ID, 83402. Tel: 208-282-7906. p. 528

Gray, Christina, Dir, Leon County Library, 207 E Saint Mary's, Centerville, TX, 75833. Tel: 903-536-3726. p. 2155

Gray, Chuck, Br Mgr, Central Rappahannock Regional Library, Snow Branch, 8740 Courthouse Rd, Spotsylvania, VA, 22553-2513. Tel: 540-507-7565. p. 2320

Gray, Dave, Dir, Hancock County Public Library, 900 W McKenzie Rd, Greenfield, IN, 46140-1741. Tel: 317-462-5141. p. 688

Gray, David, Dir, Libr Serv, Univ Archivist, University of Mary, 7500 University Dr, Bismarck, ND, 58504-9652. Tel: 701-355-8070. p. 1730

Gray, David, Dir, Learning Res, Lord Fairfax Community College, 173 Skirmisher Lane, Middletown, VA, 22645. Tel: 540-868-7154. p. 2332

Gray, David, Dir, Learning Res, Lord Fairfax Community College, Bob G Sowder Library, 6480 College St, Warrenton, VA, 20187. Tel: 540-541-1596. p. 2333

Gray, Elaine, Dir, Hinsdale County Library District, 206 Silver St, Lake City, CO, 81235. Tel: 970-944-2615. p. 288

Gray, Elizabeth, Asst County Librn, Yolo County Library, 226 Buckeye St, Woodland, CA, 95695-2600. Tel: 530-666-8084. p. 260

Gray, Gina, Mgr, Hundred Public Library, Rte 250, Hundred, WV, 26575. Tel: 304-775-5161. p. 2404

Gray, Gwen, Soc Sci Librn, University of Missouri-Columbia, Elmer Ellis Library, 104 Ellis Library, Columbia, MO, 65201-5149. Tel: 573-882-9162. p. 1243

Gray, Holly, Dir, Itawamba Community College, 602 W Hill St, Fulton, MS, 38843. Tel: 662-862-8384. p. 1216

Gray, Holly, Dir, Itawamba Community College, 2176 S Eason Blvd, Tupelo, MS, 38804. Tel: 662-620-5091. p. 1233

Gray, Isabel, Dir, Libr Serv, Camden County College Library, 200 College Dr, Blackwood, NJ, 08012. Tel: 856-227-7200, Ext 4405. p. 1390

Gray, Jerome, Interim Exec Dir, Black Heritage Library & Multicultural Center, 817 Harmon St, Findlay, OH, 45840. Tel: 419-423-4954. p. 1785

Gray, Jessica, Museum Assoc - Curator, Bureau County Historical Society Museum & Library, 109 Park Ave W, Princeton, IL, 61356-1927. Tel: 815-875-2184. p. 636

Gray, Jim, Tech Serv, Wake Technical Community College, Bldg D, 100 Level, 9101 Fayetteville Rd, Raleigh, NC, 27603-5696. Tel: 919-866-5644. p. 1711

Gray, Joanna, Ref Librn, Middlesex Community College, Academic Resources Bldg 1A, 591 Springs Rd, Bedford, MA, 01730. Tel: 781-280-3708. p. 988

Gray, Jody, Tech Serv Supvr, Horry County Memorial Library, 1008 Fifth Ave, Conway, SC, 29526. Tel: 843-915-5285. p. 2056

Gray, Jody, Head, Tech Serv, Horry County Memorial Library, Technical Services, Extension Bldg, 1603 Fourth Ave, Conway, SC, 29526. Tel: 843-915-5289. p. 2057

Gray, Johnnie, Digital Serv Librn, Christopher Newport University, One Avenue of the Arts, Newport News, VA, 23606. Tel: 757-594-7249. p. 2333

Gray, Judy, Supvr, Indiana State Library, 140 N Senate Ave, Indianapolis, IN, 46204. Tel: 317-232-3684. p. 692

Gray, Julie, Br Librn, Wapiti Regional Library, Arborfield Public Library, 201 Main St, Arborfield, SK, S0E 0A0, CANADA. p. 2745

Gray, Juliet, Interim Asst Dean, Southern Illinois University Edwardsville, Campus Box 1063, 30 Hairpin Dr, Edwardsville, IL, 62026-1063. Tel: 618-650-3429. p. 582

Gray, Kathleen, Head, Archives & Cat Div/Librn, New Mexico Highlands University, 802 National Ave, Las Vegas, NM, 87701. Tel: 505-454-3255. p. 1471

Gray, Krista Lauren, Archives, Prog Officer, University of Illinois Library at Urbana-Champaign, Illinois History & Lincoln Collections, 324 Main Library, MC-522, 1408 W Gregory Dr, Urbana, IL, 61801. Tel: 217-333-1777. p. 656

Gray, Kurtis, Dir, Campus Serv & Libr Res Ctr, Lambton College, 1457 London Rd, Sarnia, ON, N7S 6K4, CANADA. Tel: 519-542-7751, Ext 3428. p. 2676

Gray, Lauren, Asst Dir, Pike County Public Library, 1008 E Maple St, Petersburg, IN, 47567-1736. Tel: 812-354-6257. p. 713

Gray, Lauren, Head, Ref, Kansas Historical Society, 6425 SW Sixth Ave, Topeka, KS, 66615-1099. Tel: 785-272-8681. p. 838

Gray, Lauren, Research Servs Librn, Massachusetts Historical Society Library, 1154 Boylston St, Boston, MA, 02215. Tel: 617-646-0561. p. 997

Gray, Leigh, Dir, Schuyler County Library District, 108 E Jackson St, Lancaster, MO, 63548. Tel: 660-457-3731. p. 1259

Gray, Lesli, Head, Acq & Ser, State Library of Louisiana, 701 N Fourth St, Baton Rouge, LA, 70802-5232. Tel: 225-342-4937. p. 885

Gray, Linda, Libr Dir, Blinn College Library, 800 Blinn Blvd, Brenham, TX, 77833. Tel: 979-830-4250. p. 2149

Gray, Linda, Youth Serv Librn, Tyler Public Library, 201 S College Ave, Tyler, TX, 75702-7381. Tel: 903-593-7323. p. 2250

Gray, Louise, Prog Coordr, Syst Mgr, Catholic University of America, 620 Michigan Ave NE, Washington, DC, 20064. Tel: 202-319-5085. p. 2783

Gray McDonald, Dawna, Head Librn, Bette Winner Public Library, 235 Mattonnabee Ave, Gillam, MB, R0B 0L0, CANADA. Tel: 204-652-2617. p. 2587

Gray, Michael, Dir, Public Library of Steubenville & Jefferson County, 407 S Fourth St, Steubenville, OH, 43952-2942. Tel: 740-282-9782. p. 1822

Gray, Michelle, Managing Dir, Warren County Historical Society, 210 Fourth Ave, Warren, PA, 16365. Tel: 814-723-1795. p. 2017

Gray, Rachel, Dir, Van Horn Public Library, 115 SE Third St, Pine Island, MN, 55963. Tel: 507-356-8558. p. 1192

Gray, Robert, Committee Chair, Collectors Club Library, 22 E 35th St, New York, NY, 10016-3806. Tel: 212-683-0559. p. 1582

Gray, Roberta, Pub Serv Librn, University of New England Libraries, Josephine S Abplanalp Library, Portland Campus, 716 Stevens Ave, Portland, ME, 04103. Tel: 207-221-4323. p. 917

Gray, Sarah, Digital Serv Librn, Davenport University, 6191 Kraft Ave SE, Grand Rapids, MI, 49512. Tel: 616-554-5664. p. 1110

Gray, Seneca, Head, Ref, Lewis & Clark College, Paul L Boley Law Library, Lewis & Clark Law School, 10015 SW Terwilliger Blvd, Portland, OR, 97219. Tel: 503-768-6776. p. 1891

Gray, Suzanne, Women's & Gender Studies Librn, Eastern Michigan University, Administrative Office, Rm 200, 955 W Circle Dr, Ypsilanti, MI, 48197. Tel: 734-487-2517. p. 1160

Gray, Sylvia, Librn, Amelia County Historical Society Library, Jackson Bldg, 16501 Church St, Amelia, VA, 23002. Tel: 804-561-3180. p. 2304

Gray, Tammy L, Dir, Eastern Owyhee County Library, 520 Boise Ave, Grand View, ID, 83624. Tel: 208-834-2785. p. 521

Gray, Tracy, Dir, Mountain View Public Library, 585 Franklin St, Mountain View, CA, 94041-1998. Tel: 650-903-6887. p. 181

Gray-Williams, Donna, Tech Serv Mgr, Lake County Library System, 418 W Alfred St, Ste C, Tavares, FL, 32778. Tel: 352-253-6161. p. 450

Graybeal, Kathy, County Librn, Sussex County Department of Libraries, 22215 DuPont Blvd, Georgetown, DE, 19947-2809. Tel: 302-855-7890. p. 353

Graybeal, Tanya, Library Contact, Woods Rogers, PLC, Wells Fargo Tower, 10 S Jefferson St, Ste 1800, Roanoke, VA, 24011. Tel: 540-983-7623. p. 2346

Graybill, Jeremy, Mkt Dir, Multnomah County Library, 919 NE 19th Ave, Ste 250, Portland, OR, 97232. Tel: 503-988-5123. p. 1892

Grayburn, Jennifer N, Digital Scholarship Librn, Dir, Pub Serv, Union College, 807 Union St, Schenectady, NY, 12308. Tel: 518-388-6277. p. 1638

Graydon, Elisa, Spec Coll Librn, United States Coast Guard Academy Library, 35 Mohegan Ave, New London, CT, 06320. Tel: 860-444-8553. p. 329

Grayshaw, John, Br Librn, Dauphin County Library System, Madeline L Olewine Memorial Library, 2410 N Third St, Harrisburg, PA, 17110. Tel: 717-232-7286. p. 1940

Grayshaw, John, Dir, Middletown Public Library, 20 N Catherine St, Middletown, PA, 17057-1401. Tel: 717-944-6412. p. 1962

Grayson, Debra, Dir, Pub Relations, White Smith Memorial Library, 213 College Ave, Jackson, AL, 36545. Tel: 251-246-4962. p. 23

Grayson, Mary, Head, Youth Serv, Boyne District Library, 201 E Main St, Boyne City, MI, 49712. Tel: 231-582-7861. p. 1087

Grayson, Sue, Circ/ILL Librn, Hudson Valley Community College, 80 Vandenburgh Ave, Troy, NY, 12180. Tel: 518-629-7555. p. 1652

Graystone, Sean, Dir, Scottish Rite Library, 1733 16th St NW, Washington, DC, 20009-3103. Tel: 202-777-3131. p. 374

Graziade, Lisa Ann, Bus Mgr, Mount Kisco Public Library, 100 E Main St, Mount Kisco, NY, 10549. Tel: 914-864-0043. p. 1574

Grealish-Rust, Britt, Circ Librn, Dighton Public Library, 979 Somerset Ave, Dighton, MA, 02715. Tel: 508-669-6421. p. 1014

Greathouse, Caitlin, Dir, Hannibal Free Public Library, 200 S Fifth St, Hannibal, MO, 63401. Tel: 573-221-0222. p. 1247

Greathouse, Heidi, Librn, Central Arizona College, 805 S Idaho Rd, Apache Junction, AZ, 85119. Tel: 480-677-7747. p. 55

Greathouse, Michael D, Dir, Res, Illinois Appellate Court, 14th & Main Sts, Mount Vernon, IL, 62864. Tel: 618-242-6414. p. 622

Greathouse, Penny, Libr Tech, Department of Veterans Affairs North Texas Health Care System, Library Service 142D, 4500 S Lancaster Rd, Dallas, TX, 75216. Tel: 214-857-1245. p. 2166

Grebel, Alicia, Br Mgr, Pueblo City-County Library District, Frank & Marie Barkman Branch, 1300 Jerry Murphy Rd, Pueblo, CO, 81001. p. 293

Grebinar, Alex, Dir, Conant Public Library, Four Meetinghouse Hill Rd, Sterling, MA, 01564. Tel: 978-422-6409. p. 1057

Grebinoski, Jodi, Libr Dir, Virginia Public Library, 215 Fifth Ave S, Virginia, MN, 55792-2642. Tel: 218-748-7525. p. 1206

Greco, Jamie, Dir, Glacier County Library, 21 First Ave SE, Cut Bank, MT, 59427. Tel: 406-873-4572. p. 1291

Greco, Jamie, Dir, Glacier County Library, East Glacier Park Branch, Hwy Two, East Glacier Park, MT, 59434. p. 1291

Greco, Nancy, Instruction Librn, Univ Archivist, Saint John Fisher University, 3690 East Ave, Rochester, NY, 14618-3599. Tel: 585-385-8139. p. 1630

Greco, Sal, Libr Dir, South University, 9801 Belvedere Rd, Royal Palm Beach, FL, 33411-3640. Tel: 561-273-6402. p. 439

Greco, Shanda, Dir, Michigan Legislative Service Bureau Library, Boji Tower, 4th Flr, Lansing, MI, 48909. Tel: 517-373-5200. p. 1125

Greear, Cori, Pub Serv Librn, Winter Haven Public Library, 325 Ave A NW, Winter Haven, FL, 33881. Tel: 863-291-5880. p. 455

Greeley, Shawn, Municipal Video Spec, Groton Public Library, 52 Newtown Rd, Groton, CT, 06340. Tel: 860-441-6750. p. 314

Green, Alan, Head of Libr, Ohio State University LIBRARIES, Music & Dance, 166 Sullivant Hall, 1813 N High St, Columbus, OH, 43210-1307. Tel: 614-292-2319. p. 1776

Green, Alyson, Dir, Joliet Public Library, 211 E Front Ave, Joliet, MT, 59041. Tel: 406-962-3013. p. 1297
Green, Andrea, Librn, Northeast Regional Library, Belmont Public Library, 102 S Third St, Belmont, MS, 38827. Tel: 662-454-7841. p. 1215
Green, Anne-Marie, Dean, Libr & Acad Support, Kishwaukee College Library, 21193 Malta Rd, Malta, IL, 60150-9699. Tel: 815-825-9443. p. 612
Green, April, Librn, Catawba County Library, Southwest Branch, West Over Plaza, 2944 Hwy 127 S, Hickory, NC, 28602. Tel: 828-466-6818. p. 1706
Green, Audra, Outreach Mgr, Meridian Library District, 1326 W Cherry Lane, Meridian, ID, 83642. Tel: 208-888-4451. p. 525
Green, Barbara, Circ, Lake County Library, 1425 N High St, Lakeport, CA, 95453-3800. Tel: 707-263-8817. p. 156
Green, Barbara, Archives, Spec Coll, Claflin University, 400 Magnolia St, Orangeburg, SC, 29115. Tel: 803-535-5406. p. 2066
Green, Ben, Tween Librarian, Memorial & Library Association, 44 Broad St, Westerly, RI, 02891. Tel: 401-596-2877, Ext 318. p. 2044
Green, Brian, Librn, Columbia College Library, 11600 Columbia College Dr, Sonora, CA, 95370-8581. Tel: 209-588-5179. p. 246
Green, Brittany, Br Mgr, Gadsden County Public Library, Cowen Public Library, 300 Maple St, Chattahoochee, FL, 32324. Tel: 850-663-2707. p. 439
Green, Carol, Libr Mgr, Chattanooga Public Library, Eastgate, 5900 Bldg, 5705 Marlin Rd, Ste 1500, Chattanooga, TN, 37411. Tel: 423-855-2686. p. 2091
Green, Charlotte, Law Librn, Schuylkill County Law Library, Schuylkill County Courthouse, 401 N Second St, 4th Fl, Pottsville, PA, 17901. Tel: 570-628-1235. p. 1999
Green, Cheree, Staff Experience Dir, Pierce County Library System, 3005 112th St E, Tacoma, WA, 98446-2215. Tel: 253-548-3354. p. 2386
Green, Cheryl, Dir, Clay Center Public Library, 117 W Edgar St, Clay Center, NE, 68933. Tel: 402-762-3861. p. 1310
Green, Daidre, Teen Serv, Franklin Public Library, 421 12th St, Franklin, PA, 16323-0421. Tel: 814-432-5062. p. 1934
Green, Daidre, Teen Serv, Oil City Library, Two Central Ave, Oil City, PA, 16301-2795. Tel: 814-678-3072. p. 1973
Green, Deborah, Coordr, McDaniel College, 2 College Hill, Westminster, MD, 21157-4390. Tel: 410-386-4822. p. 981
Green, Denise, Sr Res Serv Librn, Cleveland Institute of Music, 11021 East Blvd, Cleveland, OH, 44106-1776. Tel: 216-791-5000, Ext 699. p. 1767
Green, Eleanor, Teen Serv, Keene Public Library, 60 Winter St, Keene, NH, 03431. Tel: 603-352-0157. p. 1369
Green, Elizabeth, Dir, Oregon Public Library District, 300 Jefferson St, Oregon, IL, 61061. Tel: 815-732-2724. p. 630
Green, Eric, Libr Consult, Southeast Kansas Library System, 218 E Madison Ave, Iola, KS, 66749. Tel: 620-365-5136. p. 815
Green, Esme, Libr Dir, Goodnow Library, 21 Concord Rd, Sudbury, MA, 01776-2383. Tel: 978-440-5515. p. 1058
Green, Gary, Dir, Fremont Public Library, 1004 W Toledo St, Fremont, IN, 46737. Tel: 260-495-7157. p. 686
Green, Heather, Chief Financial Officer, San Francisco Public Library, 100 Larkin St, San Francisco, CA, 94102. Tel: 415-347-4209. p. 227
Green, Heather, Head, Reader Serv, Historic New Orleans Collection, 410 Chartres St, New Orleans, LA, 70130. Tel: 504-598-7113. p. 901
Green, Heather, Mgr, Richland Library, John Hughes Cooper Branch, 5317 N Trenholm Rd, Columbia, SC, 29206. Tel: 803-787-3462. p. 2054
Green, Holly, Assoc Univ Librn, Pub Serv, Brigham Young University-Idaho, 525 S Center St, Rexburg, ID, 83460. Tel: 208-496-9522. p. 529
Green, James, Head, User Experience, Xavier University, 1535 Musketeer Dr, Cincinnati, OH, 45207. Tel: 513-745-1940. p. 1765
Green, James N, Librn, Library Company of Philadelphia, 1314 Locust St, Philadelphia, PA, 19107. Tel: 215-546-3181. p. 1982
Green, Janet, Head, Children's Servx, Mount Pleasant Public Library, 350 Bedford Rd, Pleasantville, NY, 10570. Tel: 914-769-0548. p. 1620
Green, Jeannette, Ref Librn, Vestal Public Library, 320 Vestal Pkwy E, Vestal, NY, 13850-1632. Tel: 607-754-4243. p. 1657
Green, Jennifer, Assoc Univ Librn, Res & Learning, The University of Chicago Library, 1100 E 57th St, Chicago, IL, 60637-1502. Tel: 773-702-8740. p. 569
Green, Jennifer, Digital Scholarship Librn, Team Leader, Case Western Reserve University, 11055 Euclid Ave, Cleveland, OH, 44106. Tel: 216-368-3756. p. 1766
Green, Jennifer, Mgr, Access Serv, Mgr, Coll Serv, Oshawa Public Library, 65 Bagot St, Oshawa, ON, L1H 1N2, CANADA. Tel: 905-579-6111, Ext 5200. p. 2664
Green, Jeremy, Libr Dir, Carroll Community College, 1601 Washington Rd, Westminster, MD, 21157-6944. Tel: 410-386-8335. p. 980
Green, Jill, Mgr, Sequoyah Regional Library System, Rose Creek Public, 4476 Towne Lake Pkwy, Woodstock, GA, 30189. Tel: 770-591-1491. p. 469
Green, Jon, Asst Dir, Archives, Stonehill College, 320 Washington St, Easton, MA, 02357. Tel: 508-565-1110. p. 1016
Green, Judy, Ref & Instruction, University of Alaska Anchorage, Consortium Library, 3211 Providence Dr, Anchorage, AK, 99508-8176. Tel: 907-786-1871. p. 43
Green, June, Br Mgr, Columbia County Public Library, Fort White Branch, 17700 SW State Rd 47, Fort White, FL, 32038. Tel: 386-497-1108. p. 415
Green, K'Lani, Br Mgr, Charleston County Public Library, John L Dart Branch, 1067 King St, Charleston, SC, 29403. Tel: 843-722-7550. p. 2049
Green, Karen, Acq, Electronic Res Librn, New England Law, 154 Stuart St, Boston, MA, 02116-5687. Tel: 617-422-7293. p. 998
Green, Kim, Cat/Circ, Chesapeake College, 1000 College Circle, Wye Mills, MD, 21679. Tel: 410-827-5860. p. 981
Green, Kisha, Br Mgr, Sheppard Memorial Library, East, 2000 Cedar Lane, Greenville, NC, 27858. Tel: 252-329-4582. p. 1694
Green, Kristin, Dir, Freeburg Area Library, 407 S Belleville, Freeburg, IL, 62243. Tel: 618-539-5454. p. 590
Green, Laura Gayle, Head of Libr, Univ Librn, Florida State University Libraries, Warren D Allen Music Library, Housewright Music Bldg, 122 N Copeland St, Tallahassee, FL, 32306. Tel: 850-644-5028. p. 447
Green, Lisa, Br Mgr, Toledo-Lucas County Public Library, Oregon, 3340 Dustin Rd, Oregon, OH, 43616. Tel: 419-259-5250. p. 1824
Green, Lynda, Circ, Siuslaw Public Library District, 1460 Ninth St, Florence, OR, 97439. Tel: 541-997-3132. p. 1879
Green, Marilyn, Cat Librn, Midlands Technical College Library, 1260 Lexington Dr, West Columbia, SC, 29170-2176. Tel: 803-822-3616. p. 2072
Green, Monique, Cat, Circ Mgr, Moultrie-Colquitt County Library, 204 Fifth St SE, Moultrie, GA, 31768. Tel: 229-985-6540. p. 492
Green, Nancy, Actg Libr Dir, Ouachita Parish Public Library, 1800 Stubbs Ave, Monroe, LA, 71201. Tel: 318-327-1490. p. 898
Green, Nancy, Head, Pub Serv, Ouachita Parish Public Library, 1800 Stubbs Ave, Monroe, LA, 71201. Tel: 318-327-1490. p. 898
Green, Nancy, Actg Dir, Trail Blazer Library System, c/o Ouachita Public Library, 1800 Stubbs Ave, Monroe, LA, 71201. Tel: 318-327-1490. p. 899
Green, Nancy J, Libr Dir, La Follette Public Library, 201 S Ninth St, La Follette, TN, 37766-3606. Tel: 423-562-5154. p. 2108
Green, Nathan, Libr Spec II, University of Maine at Augusta, 85 Texas Ave, Belfast Hall, Bangor, ME, 04401. Tel: 207-262-7900. p. 916
Green, Patricia W, Dir, Libr & Info Mgt, Aerospace Corp, 2360 E El Segundo Blvd, El Segundo, CA, 90245. Tel: 310-336-5000. p. 140
Green, Randy, Chief, Financial & Bus Officer, Pikes Peak Library District, 20 N Cascade Ave, Colorado Springs, CO, 80903. Tel: 719-531-6333. p. 271
Green, Roger, Libr & Info Spec, NYS Small Business Development Center Research Network, Ten N Pearl St, Albany, NY, 12246. Tel: 518-944-2840. p. 1483
Green, Rosemary, Grad Prog Librn, Shenandoah University, 1460 University Dr, Winchester, VA, 22601. Tel: 540-665-4634. p. 2354
Green, Sarah, Librn, Spiegel & McDiarmid LLP, 1875 Eye St NW, Ste 700, Washington, DC, 20006. Tel: 202-879-4055. p. 376
Green, Sarah, Librn, Graham Correctional Center Library, 12078 Illinois Rte 185, Hillsboro, IL, 62049. Tel: 217-532-6961. p. 599
Green, Shay, Br Mgr, Pine Bluff & Jefferson County Library System, Watson Chapel Public Library, 4120 Camden Rd, Pine Bluff, AR, 71603. Tel: 870-879-3406. p. 107
Green, Staci, Head, Libr Operations, Dickinson State University, 291 Campus Dr, Dickinson, ND, 58601. Tel: 701-483-2562. p. 1732
Green, Suellen, Sector Mgr, Massachusetts Institute of Technology, 244 Wood St, Lexington, MA, 02420-9176. Tel: 781-981-3221. p. 1028
Green, Susan, Tech Serv Mgr, Bettendorf Public Library Information Center, 2950 Learning Campus Dr, Bettendorf, IA, 52722. Tel: 593-344-4193. p. 735
Green, Susan, Dir & Librn, Jaquith Public Library, Old Schoolhouse Common, 122 School St, Rm 2, Marshfield, VT, 05658. Tel: 802-426-3581. p. 2288
Green, Tammy, ILL, University of Missouri-Columbia, Elmer Ellis Library, 104 Ellis Library, Columbia, MO, 65201-5149. Tel: 573-882-3224. p. 1243
Green, Terri, Librn, Palomino Horse Breeders of America Library, 15253 E Skelly Dr, Tulsa, OK, 74116. Tel: 918-438-1234. p. 1865
Green, Terry Ilene, Actg Dir, Florida Free Library, 56 N County Rd, Florida, MA, 01247-9614. Tel: 413-664-0153. p. 1019
Green, Valerie, Asst Dir, Head, Tech Serv, Tredyffrin Public Library, 582 Upper Gulph Rd, Strafford, PA, 19087-2096. Tel: 610-688-7092. p. 2010
Green, Virginia, Librn, Gadsden County Public Library, Havana Public Library, 203 E Fifth Ave, Havana, FL, 32333. Tel: 850-539-2844. p. 439
Green, Wanda, Asst Libr Dir, Tom Green County Library System, 33 W Beauregard, San Angelo, TX, 76903. Tel: 325-655-7321. p. 2235
Green-Puik, Sade, Youth Serv Mgr, East Brunswick Public Library, Two Jean Walling Civic Ctr, East Brunswick, NJ, 08816-3599. Tel: 732-390-6950. p. 1399
Greenacre, Debra, Libr Dir, Manistee County Library System, 95 Maple St, Manistee, MI, 49660. Tel: 231-723-2519. p. 1129
Greenawalt, Keith, Dir, Dillsburg Area Public Library, 204 Mumper Lane, Dillsburg, PA, 17019. Tel: 717-432-5613. p. 1926

Greenawalt-Johnson, Alisha, Head, Circ, Stow-Munroe Falls Public Library, 3512 Darrow Rd, Stow, OH, 44224. Tel: 330-688-3295. p. 1822

Greenbaum, David, Ref & Instruction Librn, Clayton State University Library, 2000 Clayton State Blvd, Morrow, GA, 30260. Tel: 678-466-4325. p. 491

Greenbaum, Megan, Youth Serv Librn, Gilmanton Year-Round Library, 1385 NH Rte 140, Gilmanton Iron Works, NH, 03837. Tel: 603-364-2400. p. 1364

Greenberg, Mark I, Dr, Dir, Spec & Digital Coll, Fla Studies Ctr & Holocaust & Genocide Prog, University of South Florida, Tampa Campus Library, 4101 USF Apple Dr, LIB122, Tampa, FL, 33620. Tel: 813-974-4141. p. 450

Greene, Amber, Libr Dir, Eaton Public Library, 132 Maple Ave, Eaton, CO, 80615-3441. Tel: 970-454-2189. p. 279

Greene, Anne, Exec Dir, James Prendergast Library, 509 Cherry St, Jamestown, NY, 14701. Tel: 716-484-7135. p. 1557

Greene, Beverly, Circ, Memorial University of Newfoundland, Ferriss Hodgett Library, University Dr, Corner Brook, NL, A2H 6P9, CANADA. Tel: 709-637-6267. p. 2610

Greene, Brian, Head, Access Serv, Northeastern University Libraries, 360 Huntington Ave, Boston, MA, 02115. Tel: 617-373-2401. p. 998

Greene, Brian, Libr Develop, Prog Mgr, Wyoming State Library, 2800 Central Ave, Cheyenne, WY, 82002. Tel: 307-777-6339. p. 2493

Greene, Daniel, Librn, Pres, Newberry Library, 60 W Walton St, Chicago, IL, 60610-3305. Tel: 312-255-3600. p. 565

Greene, Dawn, Cat Spec, Becket Athenaeum, Inc, 3367 Main St, Becket, MA, 01223. Tel: 413-623-5483. p. 987

Greene, Jennifer, Univ Archivist, University of Southern Indiana, 8600 University Blvd, Evansville, IN, 47712. Tel: 812-464-1832. p. 682

Greene, Jennifer, Libr Dir, Pelham Public Library, 24 Village Green, Pelham, NH, 03076. Tel: 603-635-7581. p. 1377

Greene, Katherine, Asst Dir for Res, Georgetown University, Dahlgren Memorial Library, Preclinical Science Bldg GM-7, 3900 Reservoir Rd NW, Washington, DC, 20007. Tel: 202-687-8670. p. 368

Greene, Katlin Heidgerken, Mgr, Ref Serv, Northfield Public Library, 210 Washington St, Northfield, MN, 55057. Tel: 507-645-1804. p. 1191

Greene, Linette, YA Librn, Missoula Public Library, 301 E Main, Missoula, MT, 59802-4799. Tel: 406-721-2665. p. 1300

Greene, Loretta Zwolak, Archives Dir, Providence Archives, 4800 37th Ave SW, Seattle, WA, 98126. Tel: 206-923-4010. p. 2378

Greene, Melanie, Br Mgr, Norfolk Public Library, Little Creek Branch, 7853 Tarpon Pl, Norfolk, VA, 23518. Tel: 757-441-1751. p. 2335

Greene, Michael, Ser Spec, Wake Forest University, Law Library, Worrell Professional Ctr, 1834 Wake Forest Rd, Winston-Salem, NC, 27109. Tel: 336-758-4520. p. 1726

Greene, Michelle, Cat/Circ, ILL, University of Maine at Presque Isle Library, 181 Main St, Presque Isle, ME, 04769-2888. Tel: 207-768-9593. p. 938

Greene, Nancy K, Dir, Ridgewood Public Library, 125 N Maple Ave, Ridgewood, NJ, 07450-3288. Tel: 201-670-5600. p. 1439

Greene, Octavia, Libr Asst, Philadelphia Corporation for Aging Library, Wallace Bldg, 642 N Broad St, Philadelphia, PA, 19130-3049. Tel: 215-765-9000. p. 1984

Greene, Patty, Asst Librn, Kentucky Christian University, 100 Academic Pkwy, Grayson, KY, 41143. Tel: 606-474-3241. p. 857

Greene, Richard, Libr Tech, Smithsonian Libraries, National Museum of Natural History Library, Tenth St & Constitution Ave NW, 1st Flr, Washington, DC, 20013-0712. Tel: 202-633-1672. p. 375

Greene, Roberta, Dir, Public Library for Union County, 255 Reitz Blvd, Lewisburg, PA, 17837-9211. Tel: 570-523-1172. p. 1955

Greene, Roberta, Adminr, Union County Library System, 255 Reitz Blvd, Lewisburg, PA, 17837-9211. Tel: 570-523-1172. p. 1955

Greene, Sarah, Libr Dir, Hickory Public Library, 375 Third St NE, Hickory, NC, 28601. Tel: 828-304-0500. p. 1696

Greene, Sarah, Dir, State Library of Pennsylvania, Forum Bldg, 607 South Dr, Harrisburg, PA, 17120. Tel: 717-787-5968. p. 1941

Greene Stanhope, Kate, Regional Mgr, Libr Serv, McInnes Cooper Library, 1300-1969 Upper Water St, Halifax, NS, B3J 2V1, CANADA. Tel: 902-444-8468. p. 2619

Greene, Taylor, Chair, Res & Instrul Serv, Chapman University, One University Dr, Orange, CA, 92866. Tel: 714-532-7756. p. 188

Greene, Trish, Head, Access Serv, Outreach Librn, University of Mary Washington, 1801 College Ave, Fredericksburg, VA, 22401-5300. Tel: 540-654-1758. p. 2320

Greene, Virginia, Br Mgr, Mgr Digital Initiatives, Twin Lakes Library System, Lake Sinclair, 130 Log Cabin Rd, Unit D, Milledgeville, GA, 31061. Tel: 478-452-6522. p. 491

Greenhalgh-Johnson, Mark, Libr Mgr, Dallas Public Library, 950 Main St, Dallas, OR, 97338. Tel: 503-623-2633. p. 1877

Greenhill, Josie, Colls Librn, University Club Library, One W 54th St, New York, NY, 10019. Tel: 212-572-3418. p. 1603

Greening, Carol, Br Librn, Southeast Regional Library, Rocanville Branch, 218 Ellice St, Rocanville, SK, S0A 3L0, CANADA. Tel: 306-645-2088. p. 2754

Greenlaw, Susan, Pres, Deer Isle-Stonington Historical Society Library, Archives & Museum, Rte 15A/416 Sunset Rd, Deer Isle, ME, 04627. Tel: 207-348-6400. p. 923

Greenlay, Elissa, Librn, Southwestern Manitoba Regional Library, 149 Main St, Melita, MB, R0M 1L0, CANADA. Tel: 204-522-3923. p. 2588

Greenleaf, Rene L, Dir, Hammond Public Library, 564 State St, Hammond, IN, 46320-1532. Tel: 219-931-5100, Ext 305. p. 689

Greenlee, Carmen, Humanities Librn, Media Librn, Bowdoin College Library, 3000 College Sta, Brunswick, ME, 04011-8421. Tel: 207-725-3286. p. 919

Greenlee, Pam, Dir, Libr Serv, Olivet Nazarene University, One University Ave, Bourbonnais, IL, 60914-2271. Tel: 815-939-5354. p. 544

Greenlee, Renee, Dir, Vinton Public Library, 510 Second Ave, Vinton, IA, 52349. Tel: 319-472-4208. p. 788

Greenly, Eric, Archivist, Lorain County Historical Society, 284 Washington Ave, Elyria, OH, 44035. Tel: 440-322-3341. p. 1784

Greenly Smith, Leslie, Mkt & Communications Adminr, Harford County Public Library, 1221-A Brass Mill Rd, Belcamp, MD, 21017-1209. Tel: 410-273-5707. p. 958

Greentree, Leslie, Communications Coordr, St Albert Public Library, Five Saint Anne St, St. Albert, AB, T8N 3Z9, CANADA. Tel: 780-459-1750. p. 2555

Greenwald, Cindy, Ch, Hillsdale Free Public Library, 509 Hillsdale Ave, Hillsdale, NJ, 07642. Tel: 201-358-5072. p. 1408

Greenwald, Dolores, Dir, Williamson County Public Library, 1314 Columbia Ave, Franklin, TN, 37064. Tel: 615-595-1240. p. 2098

Greenwalt, Toby, Dir, Digital Strategy & Tech Integration, Carnegie Library of Pittsburgh, 4400 Forbes Ave, Pittsburgh, PA, 15213-4007. Tel: 412-622-3114. p. 1991

Greenward, Joseph, Dir, Lane Public Libraries, 300 N Third St, Hamilton, OH, 45011-1629. Tel: 513-894-7156. p. 1789

Greenwell, Bridgett, Libr Mgr, War Public Library, 701 Berwind Lake Rd, War, WV, 24892. Tel: 304-875-4622. p. 2416

Greenwell, Michael, Libr Dir, Nelson County Public Library, 201 Cathedral Manor, Bardstown, KY, 40004-1515. Tel: 502-348-3714. p. 848

Greenwell, Stacey, Assoc Dean, Acad Affairs & Res, University of Kentucky Libraries, 401 Hilltop Ave, Lexington, KY, 40506. Tel: 859-218-1322. p. 863

Greenwood, Aleteia, Biomedical Librn, Head of Libr, University of British Columbia Library, Woodward Library, 2198 Health Sciences Mall, Vancouver, BC, V6T 1Z3, CANADA. Tel: 604-822-0689. p. 2580

Greenwood, Aleteia, Head of Libr, University of British Columbia Library, Biomedical, Gordon & Leslie Diamond Health Care Ctr, 2775 Laurel St, 2nd Flr, Vancouver, BC, V5Z 1M9, CANADA. Tel: 604-822-0689. p. 2580

Greenwood, Alexis, Br Head, Vancouver Public Library, Mount Pleasant Branch, One Kingsway, Vancouver, BC, V5T 3H7, CANADA. Tel: 604-665-3962. p. 2581

Greenwood, Anne, Libr Supvr, Placer County Library, Kings Beach Branch, 301 Secline St, Kings Beach, CA, 96143. Tel: 530-546-2021. p. 118

Greenwood, Carolee, Evening Librn, Eastern Correctional Institution, West Library, 30420 Revells Neck Rd, Westover, MD, 21890. Tel: 410-845-4000, Ext 6423. p. 981

Greenwood, Christine, Br Mgr, Madison County Library System, Canton Public Library, 102 Priestley St, Canton, MS, 39046. Tel: 601-859-3202. p. 1213

Greenwood, Linda, Ad, Glenwood Public Library, 109 N Vine St, Glenwood, IA, 51534. Tel: 712-527-5252. p. 755

Greenwood, Luna, Ch Serv Librn, Hadley Public Library, 50 Middle St, Hadley, MA, 01035. Tel: 413-584-7451. p. 1023

Greenwood Rodriguez, Honora, Ad, South Saint Paul Public Library, 106 Third Ave N, South Saint Paul, MN, 55075. Tel: 651-554-3243. p. 1204

Greer, Elektra, Dir, Nederland Community Library, 200 Hwy 72 N, Nederland, CO, 80466. Tel: 303-258-1101. p. 292

Greer, Heidi, Br Mgr, Shasta Public Libraries, Burney Branch, 37116 Main St, Burney, CA, 96013. Tel: 530-335-4317. p. 199

Greer, James A, Head Librn, Montgomery City-County Public Library System, Ramer Branch Library, 5444 State Hwy 94, Ramer, AL, 36069-5008. Tel: 334-562-3364. p. 30

Greer, Joshua, Asst Dir, Beaufort County Library, 311 Scott St, Beaufort, SC, 29902. p. 2047

Greer, Karla, Exec Dean, Dallas College, L Bldg, Rm L200, 3737 Motley Dr, Mesquite, TX, 75150-2033. Tel: 972-860-7173. p. 2219

Greer, Katie, Fine & Performing Arts Librn, Oakland University Library, 100 Library Dr, Rochester, MI, 48309-4479. Tel: 248-370-2480. p. 1144

Greer, Kelley Brianne, Librn, Erick Public Library, 200 S Sheb Wooley, Erick, OK, 73645. Tel: 580-526-3425. p. 1847

Greer, Nancy B, Librn, United States Environmental Protection National Enforcement Investigations Center, One Denver Federal Ctr, Bldg 25, Door W-2, Denver, CO, 80225. p. 277

Greer, Terri, Libr Dir, University Center of Southern Oklahoma Library, 2901 Mt Washington Rd, Ardmore, OK, 73401. Tel: 580-319-0340. p. 1841

Greer, Terri, Libr Dir, Murray State College Library, One Murray Campus St, Ste LS 101, Tishomingo, OK, 73460. Tel: 580-387-7310. p. 1864

Greges, Chrystie, Coll Develop, Outreach Librn, Northern Virginia Community College Libraries, Loudoun Campus, 21200 Campus Dr, Rm 200, Sterling, VA, 20164-8699. Tel: 703-450-2642. p. 2304

Gregg, Diane, Dr, Prog Coordr, Georgia College & State University, Campus Box 079, Milledgeville, GA, 31061. Tel: 478-445-5004, Ext 2515. p. 2783

Gregg, Raven, Tech Serv Librn, Plaistow Public Library, 85 Main St, Plaistow, NH, 03865. Tel: 603-382-6011. p. 1378

Gregg, Susan, Instruction & Ref Librn, Lead Librn, College of Southern Nevada, Cheyenne Campus, 3200 E Cheyenne Ave, Rm 201, North Las Vegas, NV, 89030. Tel: 702-651-4622. p. 1346

Gregg, Tabitha, Br Head, Volusia County Public Library, Lake Helen Public, 221 N Euclid Ave, Lake Helen, FL, 32744. Tel: 386-228-1152. p. 393

Gregoire, Marie, Pres & Chief Exec Officer, Bibliotheque et Archives Nationales du Quebec, 475 de Maisonneuve E, Montreal, QC, H2L 5C4, CANADA. Tel: 514-873-1100, Option 3. p. 2717

Gregor, Paul, Head Librn, Greene County Public Library, Jamestown Community Library, 86 Seaman Dr, Jamestown, OH, 45335. Tel: 937-352-4005. p. 1835

Gregorski, Peggy, Exec Dir, Kenosha Public Museum Library, 5500 First Ave, Kenosha, WI, 53140. Tel: 262-653-4140, 262-653-4426. p. 2445

Gregory, Alison, Univ Librn, Marymount University, 2807 N Glebe Rd, Arlington, VA, 22207-4299. Tel: 703-284-1533. p. 2305

Gregory, Alison S, Chair, Virginia Independent College & University Library Association, c/o Alison Gregory, Marymount University, 2807 N Glebe Rd, Arlington, VA, 22207. Tel: 703-284-1673. p. 2776

Gregory, Cadigan, Ms, Libr Dir, Mount Caesar Union Library, 628 Old Homestead Hwy, Swanzey, NH, 03446. Tel: 603-357-0456. p. 1382

Gregory, Curtis, Library Contact, US National Park Service, 5646 Carver Rd, Diamond, MO, 64840-8314. Tel: 417-325-4151. p. 1245

Gregory, Cynthia, Head, Electronic Res, Librn III, Mount Saint Joseph University, 5701 Delhi Rd, Cincinnati, OH, 45233-1671. Tel: 513-244-4762. p. 1761

Gregory, David, Dean, Libr Serv, Morehead State University, 150 University Blvd, Morehead, KY, 40351. Tel: 606-783-5100. p. 869

Gregory, Ed, Dir, Res, Brewers Association of Canada Library, PO Box 654, Stittsville, ON, K2S 1A7, CANADA. Tel: 613-232-9601. p. 2681

Gregory, Gwen, Assoc Dean Coll Mgt, Northern Illinois University Libraries, 217 Normal Rd, DeKalb, IL, 60115-2828. Tel: 815-753-1746. p. 577

Gregory, Jennifer, Cat Mgr, Colls Serv Mgr, Boone County Public Library, 1786 Burlington Pike, Burlington, KY, 41005. Tel: 859-342-2665. p. 850

Gregory, Jenny, Access Serv Coordr, University of Connecticut, Jeremy Richard Library, Stamford Campus, One University Pl, Stamford, CT, 06901-2315. Tel: 203-251-8518. p. 340

Gregory, Katherine, Dir, Bartram Trail Regional Library, 204 E Liberty St, Washington, GA, 30673. Tel: 706-678-7736. p. 502

Gregory, Laurel, Dir, University of Hawaii West Hawaii Center, 81-964 Halekii St, Kealakekua, HI, 96750. Tel: 808-322-4858, 808-934-2530. p. 514

Gregory, Lua, Co-Dir, University of Redlands, 1249 E Colton Ave, Redlands, CA, 92374-3755. Tel: 909-748-8022. p. 199

Gregory, Megan, Electronic Res Tech, University of Washington Libraries, Tacoma Library, 1900 Commerce St, Box 358460, Tacoma, WA, 98402-3100. Tel: 253-692-4657. p. 2382

Gregory, Megan, Br Head, Thompson-Nicola Regional District Library System, Merritt Branch, 1691 Garcia St, Merritt, BC, V1K 1B8, CANADA. Tel: 250-378-4737. p. 2567

Gregory, Patricia, PhD, Asst Dean, Research Librn, Saint Louis University, 3650 Lindell Blvd, Saint Louis, MO, 63108-3302. Tel: 314-977-3107. p. 1275

Gregory, Scott, Library Contact, Western Illinois Correctional Center Library, 2500 Rt 99 S, Mount Sterling, IL, 62353. Tel: 217-773-4441. p. 621

Gregory, Susan, Dir, Bozeman Public Library, 626 E Main St, Bozeman, MT, 59715. Tel: 406-582-2400. p. 1289

Gregory, Tammy, Br Head, Mackinaw Area Public Library, Pellston Branch, 125 N Milton St, Pellston, MI, 49769-9301. Tel: 231-539-8858. p. 1128

Gregory, Tammy, Br Asst, Elko-Lander-Eureka County Library System, Carlin Branch Library, 330 Memory Lane, Carlin, NV, 89822. Tel: 775-754-6766. p. 1344

Gregory, Vicki L, Prof, University of South Florida, 4202 Fowler Ave, CIS 1040, Tampa, FL, 33620-7800. Tel: 813-974-3520. p. 2783

Gregson, Nina, Circ Mgr, Brewster Ladies' Library, 1822 Main St, Brewster, MA, 02631. Tel: 508-896-3913. p. 1001

Gregus, Bridget, ILL Spec, Charlotte Community Library, 226 S Bostwick St, Charlotte, MI, 48813-1801. Tel: 517-543-8859. p. 1090

Greibrok, Patty, Ch Serv Librn, Albert Lea Public Library, 211 E Clark St, Albert Lea, MN, 56007. Tel: 507-377-4350. p. 1163

Greider, Julia, Tech Serv Librn, Norwich Public Library, 368 Main St, Norwich, VT, 05055-9453. Tel: 802-649-1184. p. 2290

Greifenkamp, Katie, Regional Br Operations Mgr, Public Library of Cincinnati & Hamilton County, 800 Vine St, Cincinnati, OH, 45202-2009. Tel: 513-665-3358. p. 1761

Greifenstein, Charles B, Assoc Librn, Curator of Ms, American Philosophical Society Library, 105 S Fifth St, Philadelphia, PA, 19106-3386. Tel: 215-440-3400. p. 1974

Greil, Amy, Ad, Seekonk Public Library, 410 Newman Ave, Seekonk, MA, 02771. Tel: 508-336-8230, Ext 56141. p. 1052

Greiner, Jacquie, Dir, De Soto Public Library, 111 S Houghton St, De Soto, WI, 54624. Tel: 608-648-3593. p. 2430

Greiner, Toni, Dir, Wilson Memorial Library, 109 E Washington Ave, Keota, IA, 52248. Tel: 641-636-3850. p. 763

Greis, Katie, Circ Tech, Wilson College, 1015 Philadelphia Ave, Chambersburg, PA, 17201-1285. Tel: 717-262-2008. p. 1921

Grek Martin, Jennifer, Lecturer, Dalhousie University, Kenneth C Rowe Management Bldg, Ste 4010, 6100 University Ave, Halifax, NS, B3H 4R2, CANADA. Tel: 902-494-2462. p. 2795

Grell, Krystyna, Librn, Polish Museum of America Library, 984 N Milwaukee Ave, Chicago, IL, 60642. Tel: 773-384-3352, Ext 2106. p. 567

Gremmels, Gillian, Dean of Libr, Drake University, 2725 University Ave, Des Moines, IA, 50311. Tel: 515-271-1823. p. 746

Grenfell, Jenny, Libr Mgr, Timberland Regional Library, Ocean Park Branch, 1308 256th Pl, Ocean Park, WA, 98640. Tel: 360-665-4184. p. 2389

Grenkow, Diane, Libr Dir, Jeudevine Memorial Library, 93 N Main St, Hardwick, VT, 05843. Tel: 802-472-5948. p. 2285

Grenot, Teresa, Student Success Librn, Victor Valley College Library, 18422 Bear Valley Rd, Victorville, CA, 92395-5850. Tel: 760-245-4271, Ext 2262. p. 256

Gresehover, Beverly, Assoc Dir, Resources, University of Maryland, Baltimore, Health Sciences & Human Services Library, 601 W Lombard St, Baltimore, MD, 21201. Tel: 410-706-1784. p. 957

Gresh, Ariel, Br Mgr, Harris-Elmore Public Library, Genoa Branch, 602 West St, Genoa, OH, 43430. Tel: 419-855-3380. p. 1784

Gresham, Anne, Asst Dir, Springdale Public Library, 405 S Pleasant St, Springdale, AR, 72764. Tel: 479-750-8180. p. 110

Gresham, Gabe, Children's & Prog Serv Mgr, Saint Lucie County Library System, 101 Melody Lane, Fort Pierce, FL, 34950-4402. Tel: 772-462-1615. p. 405

Gresham, Lisa, Coll Serv Mgr, Whatcom County Library System, 5205 Northwest Dr, Bellingham, WA, 98226. Tel: 360-305-3600. p. 2359

Gresham, Marilyn, ILL, Coastal Carolina Community College, 444 Western Blvd, Jacksonville, NC, 28546. Tel: 910-938-6114. p. 1697

Gress, Stephanie, Curator, Suffolk County Vanderbilt Museum Library, 180 Little Neck Rd, Centerport, NY, 17721. Tel: 631-854-5508, 631-854-5551. p. 1516

Grether, Barbara, Librn, Danville Community College, 1008 S Main St, Danville, VA, 24541-4004. Tel: 434-797-8405. p. 2314

Greufe, Sandra, Libr Serv Mgr, Ellsworth Community College, 1100 College Ave, Iowa Falls, IA, 50126-1199. Tel: 641-648-8560. p. 761

Grey, Alys, Librn, Reiss-Davis Graduate School, Vista Del Mar, 3200 Motor Ave, Los Angeles, CA, 90034. Tel: 310-204-1666, Ext 359. p. 167

Grey, April, Student Success Librn, Wofford College, 429 N Church St, Spartanburg, SC, 29303-3663. Tel: 864-597-4300. p. 2070

Grey, Jennifer, Pub Serv Coordr, Florida State College at Jacksonville, Downtown Campus Library & Learning Commons, 101 W State St, Bldg A, Rm A-2102 & A-3040, Jacksonville, FL, 32202-3056. Tel: 904-633-8368. p. 411

Grey, Mariana, Ref Librn, United States Air Force, Air Force Research Lab, Tyndall Research Site Technical Information Center, 139 Barnes Dr, Ste 2, Tyndall AFB, FL, 32403-5323. Tel: 850-283-6285. p. 451

Grey, Rosemary, Ch, Elizabeth Taber Library, Eight Spring St, Marion, MA, 02738. Tel: 508-748-1252. p. 1031

Greybill, Lisa, Adminr, Columbia Public Library, 24 S Sixth St, Columbia, PA, 17512-1599. Tel: 717-684-2255. p. 1923

Grguev, Michael, Syst Adminr, Bergen County Cooperative Library System, Inc, 21-00 Route 208 S, Ste 130, Fair Lawn, NJ, 07410. Tel: 201-498-7314. p. 2770

Gribben, Brian, Govt Doc, Spec Coll, Fort Hays State University, 502 S Campus Dr, Hays, KS, 67601. Tel: 785-628-4434. p. 812

Gribble, Joyce, Mgr, Texas A&M University Libraries, Policy Sciences & Economics, Presidential Conference Ctr, Rm 1019, 1002 George Bush Dr W, College Station, TX, 77845. Tel: 979-862-3544. p. 2157

Gribko, Daniel E, Library Contact, Whiting Forensic Institute Library, 70 O'Brien Dr, Middletown, CT, 06457. Tel: 860-262-6466. p. 323

Grice, Daisy, Adult Serv, Circ Serv Supvr, Durango Public Library, 1900 E Third Ave, Durango, CO, 81301. Tel: 970-375-3387. p. 278

Grice, Gail, Circ Supvr, Matheson Memorial Library, 101 N Wisconsin, Elkhorn, WI, 53121. Tel: 262-723-2678. p. 2433

Grice, Janet, Librn, North Kawartha Library, Woodview Branch, 66 Northeys Bay Rd, Woodview, ON, K0L 3E0, CANADA. Tel: 705-654-1071. p. 2628

Gricius, Lisa, Dir, Warsaw Public Library, 130 N Main St, Warsaw, NY, 14569. Tel: 585-786-5650. p. 1658

Griebel, Tess, Libr Mgr, Castor Municipal Library, 4905 50 Ave, Castor, AB, T0C 0X0, CANADA. Tel: 403-882-3999. p. 2531

Grieco, Susan, Br Mgr, North Castle Public Library, North White Plains Branch, Ten Clove Rd, North White Plains, NY, 10603. Tel: 914-948-6359. p. 1488

Grief, Terri, Prog Coordr, Murray State University, College of Education & Human Services, 3201 Alexander Hall, Murray, KY, 42071-3309. Tel: 270-809-2500. p. 2785

Griefhaber, Cindy, Dir, William K Kohrs Memorial Library, 501 Missouri Ave, Deer Lodge, MT, 59722-1152. Tel: 406-846-2622. p. 1291

Grieme, Trish, Asst Librn, Slayton Public Library, 2451 Broadway Ave, Slayton, MN, 56172. Tel: 507-836-8778. p. 1204

Grier, PJ, Assoc Dir, Philadelphia College of Osteopathic Medicine, 4170 City Ave, Philadelphia, PA, 19131-1694. Tel: 215-871-6470. p. 1984

Grier-Coward, Nathifa, Mgr, Knowledge Services, Fasken, Bay Adelaide Ctr, 333 Bay St, Ste 2400, Toronto, ON, M5H 2T6, CANADA. Tel: 416-865-5143. p. 2688

Griesemer, David, Librn, Webmaster, Illinois Institute of Technology, Moffett Campus, 6502 S Archer Rd, Bedford Park, IL, 60501-1957. Tel: 708-563-8160. p. 540

Griffen, Crystal, Libr Dir, Alta Vista Public Library, 203 S White Ave, Alta Vista, IA, 50603. Tel: 641-364-6009. p. 730

Griffen, Lacie, Coll Develop Mgr, Johnson County Library, 9875 W 87th St, Overland Park, KS, 66212. Tel: 913-826-4600. p. 830

Griffey, Derrick, Dir, Learning Res, Gadsden State Community College, Allen Hall, Rms 204 & 220, 1001 George Wallace Dr, Gadsden, AL, 35903. Tel: 256-549-8333. p. 18

Griffie, Lavonne, Libr Tech 1, SCLHS Saint Joseph Hospital, 1375 E 19th Ave, 3rd Flr, Denver, CO, 80218-1191. Tel: 303-812-3625. p. 277

Griffin, Allison, Dir, Raymond Village Library, Three Meadow Rd, Raymond, ME, 04071-6461. Tel: 207-655-4283. p. 938

Griffin, Anna, Dir, Centuria Public Library, 409 Fourth St, Centuria, WI, 54824-7468. Tel: 715-646-2630. p. 2427

Griffin, Brittany, Br Mgr, Latah County Library District, Bovill Branch, 310 First Ave, Bovill, ID, 83806. Tel: 208-826-3451. p. 526

Griffin, Brittany, Br Mgr, Latah County Library District, Deary Branch, 304 Second Ave, Deary, ID, 83823. Tel: 208-877-1664. p. 526

Griffin, Elizabeth, Youth Serv Librn, San Juan Island Library, 1010 Guard St, Friday Harbor, WA, 98250-9612. Tel: 360-378-2798. p. 2364

Griffin, Jeff, Dr, Dean of Libr, New Orleans Baptist Theological Seminary, 1800 Satellite Blvd NW, Duluth, GA, 30097. Tel: 470-655-6717. p. 477

Griffin, Jeff, Dr, Dean of Libr, New Orleans Baptist Theological Seminary, 4110 Seminary Pl, New Orleans, LA, 70126. Tel: 504-282-4455, Ext 8247. p. 902

Griffin, Jennifer, Access Serv Supvr, Georgia Southwestern State University, 800 Georgia Southwestern State University Dr, Americus, GA, 31709. Tel: 229-931-2266. p. 458

Griffin, Julianne, Customer Experience Dir, Douglas County Libraries, 100 S Wilcox, Castle Rock, CO, 80104. Tel: 303-688-7657. p. 269

Griffin, Kahlil, Br Mgr, Kenosha Public Library, Gilbert M Simmons Library, 711 59th Pl, Kenosha, WI, 53140-4145. p. 2445

Griffin, Kahlil, Br Mgr, Kenosha Public Library, Uptown Library, 2419 63rd St, Kenosha, WI, 53143-4331. p. 2445

Griffin, Laura, Librn, Pennsylvania Public Utility Commission Library, Commonwealth Keystone Bldg, 400 North St, Harrisburg, PA, 17120-0079. Tel: 727-772-4597. p. 1941

Griffin, Lawanza, Br Mgr, Clayton County Library System, Riverdale Branch, 420 Valley Hill Rd, Riverdale, GA, 30274. Tel: 770-472-8100. p. 483

Griffin, Leslie, Interim Libr Dir, Caldwell County Public Library, 120 Hospital Ave, Lenoir, NC, 28645-4454. Tel: 828-757-1270. p. 1700

Griffin, Liz, Libr Asst, Belmar Public Library, 517 Tenth Ave, Belmar, NJ, 07719. Tel: 732-681-0775. p. 1389

Griffin, Lois, Asst Dir, Pub Serv, Flint River Regional Library System, 800 Memorial Dr, Griffin, GA, 30223. Tel: 770-412-4770. p. 481

Griffin, Lolita, Br Mgr, Chicago Public Library, Pullman, 11001 S Indiana Ave, Chicago, IL, 60628. Tel: 312-747-2033. p. 557

Griffin, Mark, Ref Serv, Logan County Public Library, 225 Armory Dr, Russellville, KY, 42276. Tel: 270-726-6129. p. 874

Griffin, Mary, Librn, Cullman County Public Library System, Garden City Public, Municipal Bldg, 501 First Ave S, Garden City, AL, 35070. Tel: 256-352-4552. p. 13

Griffin, Mary, Br Librn, Graham County Public Library, 80 Knight St, Robbinsville, NC, 28771. Tel: 828-479-8796. p. 1713

Griffin, Mary Ann, Dir, Sunflower County Library System, 201 Cypress Dr, Indianola, MS, 38751. Tel: 622-887-2153. p. 1220

Griffin, Melinda, Librn, Sulphur Springs Public Library, 512 S Black Ave, Sulphur Springs, AR, 72768. Tel: 479-298-1291. p. 111

Griffin, Nancy L, Dir, Yale Public Library, 213 N Main, Yale, OK, 74085. Tel: 918-387-2135. p. 1869

Griffin, Paul, Sr Libr Tech, Duluth Public Library, Mount Royal, 105 Mount Royal Shopping Circle, Duluth, MN, 55803. Tel: 218-730-4290. p. 1172

Griffin, Rhonda, Dir, Gunn Memorial Public Library (Caswell County Public Library), 161 Main St E, Yanceyville, NC, 27379. Tel: 336-694-6241, Ext 1116. p. 1727

Griffin, Rhonda, Dir, Pittsylvania County Public Library, 24 Military Dr, Chatham, VA, 24531. Tel: 434-432-3271. p. 2311

Griffin, Richard, Dir, Washington County Public Library, 200 Sabin Dr, Jonesborough, TN, 37659. Tel: 423-753-1800. p. 2104

Griffin, Robin, Librn, Vernice Stoudenmire Public Library, 9905 N Main St, Wilsonville, AL, 35186. Tel: 205-669-6180. p. 40

Griffin, Ronda, Circ, Greene County Public Library, 120 N 12th St, Paragould, AR, 72450. Tel: 870-236-8711. p. 107

Griffin, Shon, Tech Serv Mgr, Poplar Bluff Municipal Library, 318 N Main St, Poplar Bluff, MO, 63901. Tel: 573-686-8639, Ext 24. p. 1266

Griffin, Stephanie, Br Mgr, Lonesome Pine Regional Library, Scott County Public, 297 W Jackson St, Gate City, VA, 24251. Tel: 276-386-3302. p. 2355

Griffin, Swalena, Asst Br Mgr, Ch, Atlanta-Fulton Public Library System, Northside Branch, 3295 Northside Pkwy NW, Atlanta, GA, 30327. Tel: 404-613-6870. p. 461

Griffin, Swalena, Br Mgr, Atlanta-Fulton Public Library System, East Roswell Branch, 2301 Holcomb Bridge Rd, Roswell, GA, 30076. Tel: 404-613-4050. p. 461

Griffin, Tracy, Dir, Brent-Centreville Public Library, 20 Library St, Centreville, AL, 35042. Tel: 205-926-4736. p. 11

Griffin, Tyler, Asst Regional Dir, York Library Region, 570 Two Nations Crossing, Ste 1, Fredericton, NB, E3A 0X9, CANADA. Tel: 506-453-5380. p. 2602

Griffing, Elizabeth, Pub Serv Librn, Chesapeake Public Library, South Norfolk Memorial, 1100 Poindexter St, Chesapeake, VA, 23324-2447. Tel: 757-410-7053. p. 2311

Griffis, Jaime, Dir, Programming, Dir, Promotion, Idea Exchange, One North Sq, Cambridge, ON, N1S 2K6, CANADA. Tel: 519-621-0460. p. 2635

Griffis, Samantha, Coordr, Libr Serv, Northern Wyoming Community College District - Gillette College, 300 W Sinclair, Gillette, WY, 82718. Tel: 307-681-6221. p. 2495

Griffis, Sarah, Sr Ref & Instruction Librn, Suffolk University, 73 Tremont St, 2nd Flr, Boston, MA, 02108. Tel: 617-573-8535. p. 1000

Griffith, Abbey, Libr Mgr, Med Librn, Kansas City University, 1750 Independence Ave, Kansas City, MO, 64106-1453. Tel: 816-654-7260. p. 1256

Griffith, Alison, Br Mgr, Saint Charles City-County Library District, McClay, 2760 McClay Rd, Saint Charles, MO, 63303-5427. Tel: 636-441-7577. p. 1278

Griffith, April, Dir, Eureka Springs Carnegie Public Library, 194 Spring St, Eureka Springs, AR, 72632. Tel: 479-253-8754. p. 94

Griffith, Cathy, Head, Access Serv, University of North Carolina at Greensboro, 320 College Ave, Greensboro, NC, 27412-0001. Tel: 336-334-5492. p. 1693

Griffith, Cathy, Asst Dir, Johnson City Public Library, 100 W Millard St, Johnson City, TN, 37604. Tel: 423-434-4463. p. 2104

Griffith, Charlotte, Libr Coord, Ref Librn, Muskegon Community College, 221 S Quarterline Rd, Muskegon, MI, 49442. Tel: 231-777-0260. p. 1136

Griffith, Jan, Ser, Hamline University, Bush Memorial Library, 1536 Hewitt, Saint Paul, MN, 55104. Tel: 651-523-2375. p. 1199

Griffith, Jason, Acq Librn, Syst, Morehead State University, 150 University Blvd, Morehead, KY, 40351. Tel: 606-783-5119. p. 869

Griffith, Kevin, Libr Adminr, Pasco County Library System, 8012 Library Rd, Hudson, FL, 34667. Tel: 727-861-3020. p. 410

Griffith, Marilyn, Dir, Haskell County Library, 300 N Ave E, Haskell, TX, 79521-5706. Tel: 940-864-2747. p. 2188

Griffith, Mary, Librn, Church of the Incarnation, 3966 McKinney Ave, Dallas, TX, 75204. Tel: 214-521-5101, Ext 2025. p. 2163

Griffith, Myrna, Dir, Woodward Public Library, 118 S Main St, Woodward, IA, 50276. Tel: 515-438-2636. p. 793

Griffith, ReBecca, Libr Serv Coordr, Southern State Community College Library, 100 Hobart Dr, Hillsboro, OH, 45133-9487. Tel: 937-393-3431, Ext 2684. p. 1790

Griffith, Sarah, Librn, United States Courts Library, 700 Stewart St, Rm 19105, Seattle, WA, 98101. Tel: 206-370-8975. p. 2381

Griffith-Kees, Julie, Cat, University of Alabama, School of Law Library, 101 Paul Bryant Dr, Tuscaloosa, AL, 35487. Tel: 205-348-5925. p. 38

Griffiths, Barbara, Bus Mgr, Wilmette Public Library District, 1242 Wilmette Ave, Wilmette, IL, 60091-2558. Tel: 847-256-6910. p. 663

Griffiths, Jasmine, Sr Librn, Data Contracts, Board of Governors of The Federal Reserve System, Research Library, 20th & C St NW, MS 102, Washington, DC, 20551. Tel: 202-452-3333. p. 361

Griffiths, Kelly Ann, Head Librn, Shelton State Community College, Martin Campus, 9500 Old Greensboro Rd, Tuscaloosa, AL, 35405. Tel: 205-391-2268. p. 37

Griffiths, Kim L, Dir, Tremonton City Library, 210 N Tremont St, Tremonton, UT, 84337-1329. Tel: 435-257-9525. p. 2274

Griffiths, Leah, Libr Tech, Law Society of Newfoundland Law Library, 196-198 Water St, St. John's, NL, A1C 5M3, CANADA. Tel: 709-753-7770. p. 2610

Griffiths, Susan, Dir, Libr Serv, North Haven Memorial Library, 17 Elm St, North Haven, CT, 06473. Tel: 203-239-5803. p. 331

Griffitts, Madison, Br Mgr, Cecil County Public Library, Port Deposit Branch, 13 S Main St, Port Deposit, MD, 21904. Tel: 410-996-6055. p. 965

Griffitts, Madison, Bus Mgr, Cecil County Public Library, Perryville Branch, 500 Coudon Blvd, Perryville, MD, 21903. Tel: 410-996-6070. p. 965

Grigas, Tracy, Libr Asst, Cragin Memorial Library, Eight Linwood Ave, Colchester, CT, 06415. Tel: 860-537-5752. p. 306

Grigg, Kathleen, Libr Mgr, Albert-Westmorland-Kent Regional Library, Port Elgin Public, 33 Moore Rd, Port Elgin, NB, E4M 2E6, CANADA. Tel: 506-538-9001. p. 2603

Griggs, Debbie, Asst Dir, Three Rivers Public Library District, 25207 W Channon Dr, Channahon, IL, 60410-5028. Tel: 815-467-6200, Ext 204. p. 552

Griggs, La Ferne D, Ref (Info Servs), Andalusia Public Library, 212 S Three Notch St, Andalusia, AL, 36420. Tel: 334-222-6612. p. 4

Griggs, Ronald, VPres, Libr & Info Serv, Kenyon College Library & Information Services, Olin & Chalmers Libraries, 103 College Dr, Gambier, OH, 43022. Tel: 740-427-5632. p. 1787

Grigsby, Alyssa, Digital Res Librn, Tech Serv Librn, Buena Vista University Library, H W Siebens School of Business/Forum, 610 W Fourth St, Storm Lake, IA, 50588. Tel: 712-749-2092. p. 784

Grigsby, Kay, Archivist, Wartburg College Library, 100 Wartburg Blvd, Waverly, IA, 50677-0903. Tel: 319-352-8500. p. 789

Grigsby, Paula, Librn, Rim Community Library, 3404 Mustang Ave, Heber, AZ, 85928. Tel: 928-535-5749. p. 63

Grill, Jen, Dep Dir, Human Res Mgr, Mentor Public Library, 8215 Mentor Ave, Mentor, OH, 44060. Tel: 440-255-8811. p. 1802

Grillo, Jeffrey, Access Serv, Assoc Dir, Res Mgt, University of Pennsylvania Libraries, Biddle Law Library, 3501 Sansom St, Philadelphia, PA, 19104. Tel: 215-898-7690. p. 1988

Grills, Lyla, Dir, Mendon Public Library, 22 N Main St, Honeoye Falls, NY, 14472. Tel: 585-624-6067. p. 1548

Grills, Lyla, YA Librn, Penfield Public Library, 1985 Baird Rd, Penfield, NY, 14526. Tel: 585-340-8720. p. 1616

Grim, Nancy, Chair, Chicago State University, Education Bldg, Rm 208, 9501 S King Dr, Chicago, IL, 60628-1598. Tel: 773-995-2598. p. 2784

Grim, Peggy, Assoc Dir, Arcanum Public Library, 101 W North St, Arcanum, OH, 45304-1185. Tel: 937-692-8484. p. 1746

Grimard, Nicole, Chief Librn, Bibliotheque Municipale Guy-Belisle Saint Eustache, 12 chemin de la Grande-Cote, Saint Eustache, QC, J7P 1AZ, CANADA. Tel: 450-974-5035. p. 2733

Grime, Rachael, Dir, Librn, Little Dixie Regional Libraries, 111 N Fourth St, Moberly, MO, 65270-1577. Tel: 660-263-4426. p. 1262

Grimes, Beth, Head, Teen Serv, Stratford Library Association, 2203 Main St, Stratford, CT, 06615. Tel: 203-385-4167. p. 340

Grimes, Cassandra, ILL, Daviess County Public Library, 2020 Frederica St, Owensboro, KY, 42301. Tel: 270-684-0211. p. 871

Grimes, Gwin, Librn, Jeff Davis County Library, 100 Memorial Sq, Fort Davis, TX, 79734. Tel: 432-426-3802. p. 2178

Grimes, Jessica, Libr Tech, University of Detroit Mercy Libraries, School of Dentistry, Corktown Campus, 2700 Martin Luther King Jr Blvd, Detroit, MI, 48208-2576. Tel: 313-494-6901. p. 1099

Grimes, Joshua, Librn, West Georgia Technical College, Douglas Campus, 4600 Timber Ridge Dr, Douglasville, GA, 30135. Tel: 770-947-7238. p. 502

Grimes, Neil, Educ Res Librn, William Paterson University, 300 Pompton Rd, Wayne, NJ, 07470. Tel: 973-720-3184. p. 1452

Grimm, Christine, Libr Dir, Montezuma Public Library, 500 E Main St, Montezuma, IA, 50171. Tel: 641-623-3417. p. 770

Grimm, Christopher, Pres, Tallmadge Historical Society Library, 12 Tallmadge Circle, Tallmadge, OH, 44278. Tel: 330-630-9760. p. 1823

Grimm, Erica, Br Mgr, Jackson District Library, Brooklyn Branch, 207 N Main St, Brooklyn, MI, 49230. Tel: 517-905-1369. p. 1120

Grimm, Heidi, Dir, Merrill Memorial Library, 215 Main St, Yarmouth, ME, 04096. Tel: 207-846-4763. p. 947

Grimm, Irene, Librn, Community College of Allegheny County, 1750 Clairton Rd, West Mifflin, PA, 15122-3097. Tel: 412-469-4322. p. 2021

Grimm, Laura, Librn, Beveridge & Diamond, PC Library, 1900 N St NW, Ste 100, Washington, DC, 20036. Tel: 202-789-6000. p. 361

Grimm, Mandy, Dir, Columbus Junction Public Library, 232 Second St, Columbus Junction, IA, 52738-1028. Tel: 319-728-7972. p. 741

Grimm, Vanessa, Libr Dir, East Adams Library District, 302 W Main Ave, Ritzville, WA, 99169. Tel: 509-659-1222. p. 2375

Grimmett, Deborah, Dir, Abington Public Library, 600 Gliniewicz Way, Abington, MA, 02351. Tel: 781-982-2139. p. 983

Grimmett, Mary Jane, Dir, Florence Public Library, 324 Main St, Florence, KS, 66851. Tel: 620-878-4649. p. 808

Grimmett, Pepper, Br Mgr, Chattahoochee Valley Libraries, Parks Memorial Public Library, 890 Wall St, Richland, GA, 31825-0112. Tel: 229-887-2103. p. 472

Grimmett, Rose, Br Mgr, Lake Blackshear Regional Library System, Byromville Public, 452 Main St, Byromville, GA, 31007-2500. Tel: 478-433-5100. p. 458

Grimminck, Cory E, Dir, Portland District Library, 334 Kent St, Portland, MI, 48875-1735. Tel: 517-647-6981. p. 1143

Grimmitt, Bea, Evening Circ Supvr, Salve Regina University, 100 Ochre Point Ave, Newport, RI, 02840-4192. Tel: 401-341-2330. p. 2035

Grimsbo, Liz, Research Librn, Simpson College, 508 North C St, Indianola, IA, 50125-1216. p. 759

Grimse, Denise, Dir, Weeks Public Library, 36 Post Rd, Greenland, NH, 03840-2312. Tel: 603-436-8548. p. 1365

Grimshaw, Carrie, Libr Dir, Nichols College, 127 Center Rd, Dudley, MA, 01571. Tel: 508-213-2334. p. 1015

Grimshaw-Haven, Kathleen, Head, Reference & Local History, Clifton Public Library, 292 Piaget Ave, Clifton, NJ, 07011. Tel: 973-772-5500. p. 1397

Grimsley, Ramona L, Digital Projects Librn, Berkeley County Library System, 1003 Hwy 52, Moncks Corner, SC, 29461. Tel: 843-719-4240. p. 2065

Grimsley, Reagan, Archives, University of Alabama in Huntsville, 4700 Holmes Ave, Huntsville, AL, 35805. Tel: 256-824-5781. p. 22

Grimwood, Karen E, Head, Curric Mat(s) Ctr, North Carolina Central University, 1801 Fayetteville St, Durham, NC, 27707-3129. Tel: 919-530-6383. p. 1685

Grinch, Stephen, Archivist, Otterbein University, 138 W Main St, Westerville, OH, 43081. Tel: 614-823-1761. p. 1830

Grindstaff, Pam, Librn, Flint-Groves Baptist Church Library, 2017 E Ozark Ave, Gastonia, NC, 28054. Tel: 704-865-4068. p. 1690

Grine, Katie, Br Mgr, Williams County Public Library, Pioneer Branch, 106 Baubice St, Pioneer, OH, 43554. Tel: 419-737-2833. p. 1753

Griner, Stuart, Br Mgr, Chicago Public Library, Chinatown, 2100 S Wentworth Ave, Chicago, IL, 60616. Tel: 312-747-8013. p. 556

Gring, Heather, Archivist, Burchfield Penney Art Center, Burchfield Penney Art Center at Buffalo State College, 1300 Elmwood Ave, Buffalo, NY, 14222. Tel: 716-878-3216, 716-878-6011. p. 1509

Grinnell, Gennett, Assoc Librn, Tech Serv, James Blackstone Memorial Library, 758 Main St, Branford, CT, 06405-3697. Tel: 203-488-1441, Ext 316. p. 303

Grinstead, Carrie, Regional Librn, Providence Saint Joseph Medical Center, 501 S Buena Vista St, Burbank, CA, 91505-4866. Tel: 818-847-3881. p. 125

Griscom, Richard, Assoc Univ Librn, University of Pennsylvania Libraries, 3420 Walnut St, Philadelphia, PA, 19104-6206. Tel: 215-898-7556. p. 1987

Grisham, Brenda L, Libr Dir, Drumright Public Library, 104 E Broadway St, Drumright, OK, 74030. Tel: 918-352-2228. p. 1845

Griswold, Barbara, Libr Spec, Copper Mountain College, 6162 Rotary Way, Joshua Tree, CA, 92252. Tel: 760-366-3791, Ext 5906. p. 154

Griswold, Nick, Libr Asst, Duncombe Public Library, 621 Prince St, Duncombe, IA, 50532. Tel: 515-543-4646. p. 749

Griswold, Patricia, Br Mgr, East Haddam Library System, Rathbun Free Memorial Library, 36 Main St, East Haddam, CT, 06423. Tel: 860-873-8210. p. 323

Griswold, Sarah, Adult Prog Coordr, Minor Memorial Library, 23 South St, Roxbury, CT, 06783. Tel: 860-350-2181. p. 335

Grizzell, Cheryl, Asst Dir, Lorain Public Library System, 351 Sixth St, Lorain, OH, 44052. Tel: 440-244-1192. p. 1797

Groccia, Margaret, Circ Supvr, John C Hart Memorial Library, 1130 Main St, Shrub Oak, NY, 10588. Tel: 914-245-5262. p. 1641

Groch, Stacie, Head, Libr Operations, West Liberty University, 208 University Dr, West Liberty, WV, 26074. Tel: 304-336-8001. p. 2417

Grochalski, John, Managing Librn, Brooklyn Public Library, McKinley Park, 6802 Fort Hamilton Pkwy, Brooklyn, NY, 11219. Tel: 718-230-2267. p. 1503

Grochowski, Paul, Eng Librn, University of Michigan, Art, Architecture & Engineering Library, Duderstadt Ctr, 2281 Bonnisteel Blvd, Ann Arbor, MI, 48109-2094. Tel: 734-647-5747. p. 1080

Groe, Laurie, Mgr, Youth Serv, Caledon Public Library, 150 Queen St S, Bolton, ON, L7E 1E3, CANADA. Tel: 905-857-1400, Ext 231. p. 2632

Groenwald, Rosemary, Head, Bibliog Serv, Head, Coll, Mount Prospect Public Library, Ten S Emerson St, Mount Prospect, IL, 60056. Tel: 847-253-5675. p. 621

Groesbeck, Veronica, Youth Serv Librn, Anamosa Public Library & Learning Center, 600 E First St, Anamosa, IA, 52205. Tel: 319-462-2183. p. 731

Groezinger, Jennifer, Ch Serv, Belleville Public Library & Information Center, 221 Washington Ave, Belleville, NJ, 07109-3189. Tel: 973-450-3434. p. 1389

Groff, Katty, Ch, Hazel M Lewis Library, 511 Third Ave, Powers, OR, 97466. Tel: 541-439-5311. p. 1895

Groft, Tammis, Exec Dir, Albany Institute of History & Art, 125 Washington Ave, Albany, NY, 12210-2296. Tel: 518-463-4478, Ext 423. p. 1481

Groholski, Vanessa, Dir, Vandergrift Public Library Association, 128C Washington Ave, Vandergrift, PA, 15690-1214. Tel: 724-568-2212. p. 2016

Grohowski, Hannah, Actg Br Mgr, Toledo-Lucas County Public Library, Holland, 1032 S McCord Rd, Holland, OH, 43528. Tel: 419-259-5240. p. 1824

Grohs, Peggy, Libr Asst, Licia & Mason Beekley Community Library, Ten Central Ave, New Hartford, CT, 06057. Tel: 860-379-7235. p. 325

Grohs, Stephanie, Librn, Napa Valley College, 1700 Bldg, 2277 Napa-Vallejo Hwy, Napa, CA, 94558. Tel: 707-256-7400. p. 182

Grohse, Malik, Ref Librn, Atlanta-Fulton Public Library System, Evelyn G Lowery Library at Southwest, 3665 Cascade Rd SW, Atlanta, GA, 30331. Tel: 404-699-6363. p. 461

Grom, Brenton, Curator, Spec Coll, Delaware Historical Society Research Library, 505 N Market St, Wilmington, DE, 19801. Tel: 302-655-7161. p. 357

Gromatzky, Steven, Libr Dir, Benedictine College Library, 1020 N Second St, Atchison, KS, 66002-1499. Tel: 913-360-7511. p. 797

Grona, Marian, Dir, Libr Serv, Vernon College, 4400 College Dr, Vernon, TX, 76384. Tel: 940-552-6291, Ext 2222. p. 2252

Grond, Greta, Libr Dir, Northwestern College, 101 Seventh St SW, Orange City, IA, 51041. Tel: 712-707-7248. p. 774

Grondin, Megan, Youth Librn, Hill Library, 1151 Parker Mountain Rd, Strafford, NH, 03884. Tel: 603-664-2800. p. 1381

Gronlund, Gregg, Br Mgr, Orange County Library System, West Oaks Branch & Genealogy Center, 1821 E Silver Star Rd, Ocoee, FL, 34761. p. 431

Grooms, Bobbie J, Dir, Marlboro County Library System, 203 Fayetteville Ave, Bennettsville, SC, 29512. Tel: 843-479-5630. p. 2047

Grooms, Carlos, Student Success Librn, Elon University, 308 N O'Kelly Ave, Elon, NC, 27244-0187. Tel: 336-278-6600. p. 1688

Grooms, Veronica, Dir, Madison County Library, 605 S May, Madisonville, TX, 77864. Tel: 936-348-6118. p. 2215

Gropp, Lori, Libr Mgr, Marshfield Clinic, 1000 N Oak Ave, Marshfield, WI, 54449. Tel: 715-389-7676. p. 2454

Grosch, Mary, Tech Asst, Kenrick-Glennon Seminary, 5200 Glennon Dr, Saint Louis, MO, 63119. Tel: 314-792-6126. p. 1271

Groscup, Peggy, Law Librn, Watt, Tieder, Hoffar & Fitzgerald, 1765 Greensboro Station Pl, Ste 1000, McLean, VA, 22102. Tel: 703-749-1019. p. 2332

Groseclose, Jennifer, Br Mgr, Wythe-Grayson Regional Library, Rural Retreat Public, 119 N Greever St, Rural Retreat, VA, 24368. Tel: 276-686-8337. p. 2326

Groseclose, Jennifer, Br Mgr, Wythe-Grayson Regional Library, Wythe County Public, 300 E Monroe St, Wytheville, VA, 24382. Tel: 276-228-4951. p. 2327

Grosenheider, Alan, Dep Univ Librn, Human Res, University of California, Santa Barbara, UCEN Rd, Bldg 525, Santa Barbara, CA, 93106-9010. Tel: 805-893-4098. p. 241

Grosh, David, Chief Librn, National Geodetic Survey Library, 1315 East West Hwy, N/NGS12, SSMC III, No 8716, Silver Spring, MD, 20910-3282. Tel: 301-713-3249. p. 977

Grosholz, Charlie, Ref Librn, YA Serv, Ventress Memorial Library, 15 Library Plaza, Marshfield, MA, 02050. Tel: 781-834-5535. p. 1032

Groshong, Sue, Librn, Seattle Children's Hospital, 4800 Sand Point Way NE, OB.8.520, Seattle, WA, 98105. Tel: 206-987-2098. p. 2378

Gross, April, Syst Adminr, Fulton County Public Library, 320 W Seventh St, Rochester, IN, 46975-1332. Tel: 574-223-2713. p. 716

Gross, Asia, Br Mgr, Saint Charles City-County Library District, Kathryn Linnemann Branch, 2323 Elm St, Saint Charles, MO, 63301. Tel: 636-723-0232, 636-946-6294. p. 1278

Gross, Asia, Br Mgr, Saint Charles City-County Library District, Library Express @ Discovery Village, 378 Shadow Pines Dr, Wentzville, MO, 63385-3745. Tel: 636-332-6476. p. 1278

Gross, Calvin, Dir, Libr Serv, Berea College, 100 Campus Dr, Berea, KY, 40404. Tel: 859-985-3364. p. 849

Gross, Claudia, Librn, Orwigsburg Area Free Public Library, 216 E Independent St, Orwigsburg, PA, 17961-2304. Tel: 570-366-1638. p. 1973

Gross, Elizabeth, Dr, Asst Prof, Sam Houston State University, 1905 Bobby K Marks Dr, Huntsville, TX, 77340. Tel: 936-294-4740. p. 2793

Gross, Jacki, Libr Dir, Seguin Public Library, 313 W Nolte St, Seguin, TX, 78155-3217. Tel: 830-401-2466. p. 2242

Gross, Joe, Dir, Charles A Ransom District Library, 180 S Sherwood Ave, Plainwell, MI, 49080-1896. Tel: 269-685-8024. p. 1141

Gross, Kayla, Pub Serv, Moundsville-Marshall County Public Library, 700 Fifth St, Moundsville, WV, 26041. Tel: 304-845-6911. p. 2410

Gross, Ken, Asst Dir, Camden Public Library, 55 Main St, Camden, ME, 04843-1703. Tel: 207-236-3440. p. 920

Gross, Linda, Ref Librn, Hagley Museum & Library, 298 Buck Rd E, Wilmington, DE, 19807. Tel: 302-658-2400. p. 357

Gross, Michelle, Br Mgr, Cumberland County Public Library & Information Center, Spring Lake Branch, 101 Laketree Blvd, Spring Lake, NC, 28390-3189. p. 1689

Gross, Pat, Br Mgr, Charleston County Public Library, McClellanville Branch, 222 Baker St, McClellanville, SC, 29458. Tel: 843-887-3699. p. 2049

Gross, Patty, Dir, Council District Library, 104 California Ave, Council, ID, 83612. Tel: 208-253-6004. p. 520

Gross, Peggy, Dir, North Carolina State University Libraries, William Rand Kenan, Jr Library of Veterinary Medicine, 1060 William Moore Dr, Campus Box 8401, Raleigh, NC, 27607. Tel: 919-513-6219. p. 1710

Gross, Stephanie, Electronic Reserves Librn, Scholarly Communications Librn, Yeshiva University Libraries, Pollack Library Landowne Bloom Collection, Wilf Campus, 2520 Amsterdam Ave, New York, NY, 10033. Tel: 646-592-4045, 646-592-4450. p. 1605

Gross, Stephen, Dir, West Central Minnesota Historical Research Center, University of Minnesota, 600 E Fourth St, Morris, MN, 56267. Tel: 320-589-6172. p. 1189

Gross, Tina, Metadata/Cat Librn, North Dakota State University Libraries, 1201 Albrecht Blvd, Fargo, ND, 58108. Tel: 701-231-9677. p. 1733

Gross, Velma, Coll Develop, Saint Mary's Public Library, 127 Center St, Saint Marys, PA, 15857. Tel: 814-834-6141. p. 2002

Grossardt, Sharon, Dir, Saint Charles Public Library, 125 W 11th St, Saint Charles, MN, 55972-1141. Tel: 507-932-3227. p. 1195

Grosse, Russell, Exec Dir, Black Cultural Centre for Nova Scotia Library, Ten Cherry Brook Rd, Cherry Brook, NS, B2Z 1A8, CANADA. Tel: 902-434-6223. p. 2616

Grossen, Virgina, Dir, McCoy Public Library, 190 N Judgement St, Shullsburg, WI, 53586. Tel: 608-965-4424, Ext 5. p. 2477

Grosshans, Maxine, Research Librn, University of Maryland, Baltimore, Thurgood Marshall Law Library, 501 W Fayette St, Baltimore, MD, 21201-1768. Tel: 410-706-0791. p. 957

Grossholz, Lori, Archives, Tech Serv, Gannon University, 619 Sassafras St, Erie, PA, 16541. Tel: 814-871-7557. p. 1931

Grossman, Amy, Head, Youth & Teen Serv, Lincolnwood Public Library District, 4000 W Pratt Ave, Lincolnwood, IL, 60712. Tel: 847-677-5277. p. 609

Grossman, Amy, Mgr, Ch Serv, River Forest Public Library, 735 Lathrop Ave, River Forest, IL, 60305-1883. Tel: 708-366-5205, Ext 315. p. 639

Grossman, Rachael, Outreach Coordr, Kellogg-Hubbard Library, 135 Main St, Montpelier, VT, 05602. Tel: 802-223-3338. p. 2289

Grosso, Brandi, Br Mgr, Atlantic County Library System, Galloway Branch, 306 E Jimmie Leeds Rd, Galloway, NJ, 08205. Tel: 609-652-2352. p. 1417

Grosso, Jill, Dir, Beecher Community Library, 660 Penfield St, Beecher, IL, 60401. Tel: 708-946-9090. p. 540

Grosso, Joseph, Commun Libr Mgr, Queens Library, Rego Park Community Library, 91-41 63rd Dr, Rego Park, NY, 11374. Tel: 718-459-5140. p. 1555

Grote, Annabel, Libr Consult, Neiswander Library of Homeopathy, 1006 W 8th Ave, Ste B, King of Prussia, PA, 19406. Tel: 800-456-7818, Ext 2251. p. 1948

Grotewold, Kimberly, Educ Librn, Texas A&M University-San Antonio, One University Way, San Antonio, TX, 78224. Tel: 210-784-1519. p. 2239

Groth, Angela, Dir, Ardsley Public Library, Nine American Legion Dr, Ardsley, NY, 10502. Tel: 914-693-6636. p. 1487

Groth, Erin, Youth Serv Librn, Washington Talking Book & Braille Library, 2021 Ninth Ave, Seattle, WA, 98121. Tel: 206-615-0400. p. 2382

Groth, Rhonda, Youth Serv Coordr, Black River Falls Public Library, 222 Fillmore St, Black River Falls, WI, 54615. Tel: 715-284-4112. p. 2424

Groth, Sandra, Libr Dir, Aurora Free Library, 370 Main St, Aurora, NY, 13026. Tel: 315-364-8074. p. 1489

Grotheer, Rachel, ILL, Holderness Library, 866 US Rte 3, Holderness, NH, 03245. Tel: 603-968-7066. p. 1368

Grothoff, Joan, Dir, Eldora Public Library, 1202 Tenth St, Eldora, IA, 50627. Tel: 641-939-2173. p. 750

Grotluschen, Heather, Dir, Ashton Public Library, 3029 Third St, Ashton, IA, 51232. Tel: 712-724-6426. p. 733

Grotophorst, Wally, Assoc Univ Librn, Digital Programs, Syst, George Mason University Libraries, 4348 Chesapeake River Way, Fairfax, VA, 22030. Tel: 703-993-9005. p. 2317

Grotto, Scott, Br Mgr, Aurora Public Library District, West Branch, 233 S Constitution Dr, Aurora, IL, 60506-0506. Tel: 630-264-3600. p. 539

Grotyohann, Susan, Ref (Info Servs), Monroe Township Public Library, Four Municipal Plaza, Monroe Township, NJ, 08831-1900. Tel: 732-521-5000, Ext 153. p. 1419

Groustra, Chelsea, Campus Library Manager, Macomb Community College Libraries, Center Campus, 44575 Garfield Rd, C-Bldg, Clinton Township, MI, 48038-1139. Tel: 586-286-2105. p. 1157

Grout, Renee, Dir, Linesville Community Public Library, 111 Penn St, Linesville, PA, 16424. Tel: 814-683-4354. p. 1956

Groux, Susan, Research Librn, Williams & Connolly Library, 680 Maine Ave SW, Washington, DC, 20024. Tel: 202-434-5000. p. 381

Grove, Amber, Librn, Boise Bible College Library, 8695 W Marigold St, Boise, ID, 83714-1220. Tel: 208-376-7731. p. 516

Grove, Cindy, Libr Dir, Rockport Public Library, 17 School St, Rockport, MA, 01966. Tel: 978-546-6934. p. 1050

Grove, Jaime, Libr Dir, Lewistown Carnegie Public Library District, 1126 N Main St, Lewistown, IL, 61542. Tel: 309-547-2860. p. 608

Grove, JoAnn, Asst Libr Dir, Lexington Public Library, 907 N Washington St, Lexington, NE, 68850. Tel: 308-324-2151. p. 1320

Grove, Nick, Br Mgr, Meridian Library District, unBound Technology Library, 722 NE Second St, Meridian, ID, 83642. Tel: 208-258-2000. p. 525

Grove, Robyn, Dir, Iola Village Library, 180 S Main St, Iola, WI, 54945-9689. Tel: 715-445-4330. p. 2442

Grove Rohrbaugh, Rachel, Archivist, Elizabethtown College, One Alpha Dr, Elizabethtown, PA, 17022-2227. Tel: 717-361-1506. p. 1929

Grover, Kay, Librn, Sargentville Library Association, 653 Reach Rd, Sargentville, ME, 04673. Tel: 207-359-8086. p. 939

Grover, Lisa, Dir, Stonington Township Public Library, 500 E North St, Stonington, IL, 62567. Tel: 217-325-3512. p. 652

Grover, Lisa, Tech Serv Librn, Bismarck State College Library, 1500 Edwards Ave, Bismarck, ND, 58501. Tel: 701-224-5450. p. 1729

Grover, Riti, Libr Dir, Farmington Community Library, 32737 W 12 Mile Rd, Farmington Hills, MI, 48334. Tel: 248-553-0300. p. 1104

Groves, Bethany, Dir, Libr Serv, Asbury University, One Macklem Dr, Wilmore, KY, 40390-1198. Tel: 859-858-3511, Ext 2269. p. 877

Groves, Chad, Dir, Instrul Serv, Olney Central College, 305 N West St, Olney, IL, 62450. Tel: 618-395-7777, Ext 2260. p. 629

Groves, Christy, Assoc Dean, Middle Tennessee State University, 1611 Alumni Dr, Murfreesboro, TN, 37132. Tel: 615-898-2652. p. 2117
Groves, Deana, Head, Tech Serv, Western Kentucky University Libraries, Helm-Cravens Library Complex, 1906 College Heights Blvd, No 11067, Bowling Green, KY, 42101-1067. Tel: 270-745-6151. p. 849
Groves, Gloria, Circ Serv Supvr, Adrian District Library, 143 E Maumee St, Adrian, MI, 49221-2773. Tel: 517-265-2265. p. 1075
Groves Hannan, Heather, Dir, Libr Serv, University of Virginia's College at Wise, One College Ave, Wise, VA, 24293. Tel: 276-328-0150. p. 2355
Groves, Nicholas T, PhD, Librn, New Gracanica Monastery, 35240 W Grant Ave, Third Lake, IL, 60046. Tel: 847-223-4300, Ext 6. p. 653
Groves, Polly, Mgr, Hyndman Londonderry Public Library, 161 Clarence St, Hyndman, PA, 15545. Tel: 814-842-3782. p. 1945
Groves, Sara, Ch, Lewiston Public Library, 200 Lisbon St, Lewiston, ME, 04240. Tel: 207-513-3004. p. 929
Groves, Sylvia P, Ser Spec, Southside Virginia Community College Libraries, 109 Campus Dr, Alberta, VA, 23821. Tel: 434-949-1065. p. 2302
Groves-Scott, Victoria, Dr, Dean, University of Central Arkansas, College of Education, PO Box 4918, Conway, AR, 72032-5001. Tel: 501-450-3177, 501-450-5497. p. 2782
Grow, Brenda, Br Mgr, Bethlehem Area Public Library, South Side, 400 Webster St, Bethlehem, PA, 18015. Tel: 610-867-7852. p. 1911
Grow, Mary, Librn, Albert Church Brown Memorial Library, 37 Main St, China, ME, 04358. Tel: 207-968-2926. p. 922
Growney, Kathryn, Dir, Tyngsborough Public Library, 25 Bryant Lane, Tyngsborough, MA, 01879-1003. Tel: 978-649-7361. p. 1060
Growney, Kathy, Dir, Griffin Free Public Library, 22 Hooksett Rd, Auburn, NH, 03032. Tel: 603-483-5374. p. 1354
Grubb, Beverly, Libr Asst, Desoto Parish Library, Stonewall Branch, 808 Hwy 171, Stonewall, LA, 71078. Tel: 318-925-9191. p. 896
Grubb, Christine, Br Mgr, Jackson County Library Services, Applegate Branch, 18484 N Applegate Rd, Applegate, OR, 97530. Tel: 541-846-7346. p. 1886
Grubb, Jason, Libr Dir, Sweetwater County Library System, 300 N First East, Green River, WY, 82935. Tel: 307-875-3615, Ext 5130. p. 2495
Grubb, Jenn, Outreach Coordr, Annie Halenbake Ross Library, 232 W Main St, Lock Haven, PA, 17745-1241. Tel: 570-748-3321. p. 1956
Grubbs, Allison, Asst Dir, Broward County Libraries Division, 100 S Andrews Ave, Fort Lauderdale, FL, 33301. Tel: 954-357-6592. p. 396
Grubbs, Amy, Br Mgr, Greenville County Library System, Travelers Rest Branch, 17 Center St, Travelers Rest, SC, 29690. Tel: 864-527-9208. p. 2062
Grubbs, Erika, Archivist, Public Library of Steubenville & Jefferson County, 407 S Fourth St, Steubenville, OH, 43952-2942. Tel: 740-264-6166. p. 1822
Grube, Dawn, Librn, Rockville Correctional Facility Library, 811 W 50 N, Rockville, IN, 47872. Tel: 765-569-3178. p. 717
Grube, Glenn, Libr Dir, Avon Free Public Library, 281 Country Club Rd, Avon, CT, 06001. Tel: 860-673-9712. p. 301
Grube, Paula, Dir, Crittenton Hospital Medical Center, 1101 W University Dr, Rochester, MI, 48307. p. 1144
Gruben, Karl, Assoc Dean, Libr & Info Serv, University of San Diego, Katherine M & George M Pardee Jr Legal Research Center, 5998 Alcala Park, San Diego, CA, 92110-2492. Tel: 619-260-6846. p. 222
Gruber, Anne Marie, Liaison & Instruction Librn, University of Northern Iowa Library, 1227 W 27th St, Cedar Falls, IA, 50613-3675. Tel: 319-273-3711. p. 737
Gruber, Elizabeth, Research Librn, Marquette Regional History Center, 145 W Spring St, Marquette, MI, 49855. Tel: 906-226-3571. p. 1130
Gruber, Karen A, Acq & Budget Mgr, Muhlenberg College, 2400 Chew St, Allentown, PA, 18104-5586. Tel: 484-664-3570. p. 1905
Gruber, Kateri, Libr Serv Coordr, Great River Regional Library, Long Prairie Library, 42 Third St N, Ste 1, Long Prairie, MN, 56347. Tel: 320-732-2332. p. 1197
Gruber, Krista, Govt Doc Librn, Suffolk County Community College, 533 College Rd, Selden, NY, 11784-2899. Tel: 631-451-4800. p. 1639
Gruber, Sam, Dir, D R Evarts Library, 80 Second St, Athens, NY, 12015. Tel: 518-945-1417. p. 1488
Gruber, Vicki, Librn, Hope Community Library, 216 N Main St, Hope, KS, 67451. Tel: 785-366-7219. p. 814
Grubich, Deb, Libr Dir, Lake Park Public Library, 905 S Market St, Lake Park, IA, 51347. Tel: 712-832-9505. p. 764
Grudecki, Susan, Mgr, Acadia Municipal Library, Warren Peers School, 103 First Ave N, Acadia Valley, AB, T0J 0A0, CANADA. Tel: 403-972-3744. p. 2521
Grudnoski, Jennifer, Commun Librn, Monroe County Library System, Dundee Branch, 144 E Main St, Dundee, MI, 48131-1202. Tel: 734-529-3310. p. 1133
Grudza, Meghan, Libr Dir, Whitehouse Community Library, Inc, 107 Bascom Rd, Whitehouse, TX, 75791-3230. Tel: 903-839-2949. p. 2257
Gruener, Maria, Asst City Librn, Watertown Regional Library, 160 Sixth St NE, Watertown, SD, 57201-2778. Tel: 605-882-6220. p. 2085
Gruenman, Marina, ILL/Circ Supvr, Saint Elizabeth University, Two Convent Rd, Morristown, NJ, 07960-6989. Tel: 973-290-4258. p. 1422
Gruentzel, Alex, Teaching & Learning Librn, Carroll University, 100 N East Ave, Waukesha, WI, 53186. Tel: 262-650-4887. p. 2484
Grugel, Chris, Instrul Tech Librn, Carthage College, 2001 Alford Park Dr, Kenosha, WI, 53140-1900. Tel: 262-551-5950. p. 2444
Grulke, Nicole, Ref, Presque Isle District Library, 181 E Erie St, Rogers City, MI, 49779-1709. Tel: 989-734-2477. p. 1145
Grullon, Guarina, Librn, Lewis-Clark State College Library, 500 Eighth Ave, Lewiston, ID, 83501. Tel: 208-792-2235. p. 524
Grumet, Lori, Libr Dir, Abilene Public Library, 202 Cedar St, Abilene, TX, 79601-5793. Tel: 325-676-6025. p. 2131
Grumman, George, Circ Supvr, The Brookfield Library, 182 Whisconier Rd, Brookfield, CT, 06804. Tel: 203-775-6241. p. 304
Grundset, Eric G, Coll Develop, Dir, National Society of the Daughters of the American Revolution, DAR Library, 1776 D St NW, Washington, DC, 20006-5303. Tel: 202-879-3229. p. 373
Grundstrom, Lynn, Dir, Fluvanna Free Library, 3532 Fluvanna Ave Ext, Jamestown, NY, 14701. Tel: 716-487-1773. p. 1557
Grunow, Gregg, Librn, Newport News Public Library System, Main Street, 110 Main St, Newport News, VA, 23601. Tel: 757-591-4858. p. 2334
Grunseth, Erica, Coordr, Pub Serv, University of Wisconsin-Green Bay, 2420 Nicolet Dr, Green Bay, WI, 54311-7001. Tel: 920-465-2304. p. 2439
Grunwald, Clarissa, Access Serv Librn, Elizabethtown College, One Alpha Dr, Elizabethtown, PA, 17022-2227. Tel: 717-361-1222. p. 1929
Grunwald, Peggy, Libr Asst, Goddard Public Library, 201 N Main St, Goddard, KS, 67052. Tel: 316-794-8771. p. 810
Grunwald, Robin, Librn, Fish & Wildlife Research Institute, 100 Eighth Ave SE, Saint Petersburg, FL, 33701-5095. Tel: 727-896-8626. p. 441
Grunwell, John, Ref/Acq, NASA, Library, Bldg 21, Code 272, Greenbelt, MD, 20771. Tel: 301-286-7218. p. 967
Grunwerg, Laura, Dir, Blauvelt Free Library, 541 Western Hwy, Blauvelt, NY, 10913. Tel: 845-359-2811. p. 1494
Grusendorf, Natasha, Librn, Millarville Community Library, 130 Millarville Rd, Millarville, AB, T0L 1K0, CANADA. Tel: 403-931-3919. p. 2548
Gruss, Mandi, Pub Serv Mgr, Tiffin-Seneca Public Library, 77 Jefferson St, Tiffin, OH, 44883. Tel: 419-447-3751. p. 1823
Grussing, Jake J, Dir, Scott County Library System, 1615 Weston Ct, Shakopee, MN, 55379. Tel: 952-496-8010. p. 1203
Gruszka, Carol, Librn, Wales Public Library, 77 Main St, Wales, MA, 01081. Tel: 413-245-9072. p. 1061
Gruszka, Enid, Br Mgr, Milwaukee Public Library, East, 2320 N Cramer St, Milwaukee, WI, 53211. p. 2460
Grutzeck, Laura, Archives & Digital Coll Librn, University of the Arts University Libraries, Anderson Hall, 1st Flr, 333 S Broad St, Philadelphia, PA, 19102. Tel: 215-717-6294. p. 1988
Grutzeck, Laura, Spec Coll Librn, Visual Res, University of the Arts University Libraries, Visual Resources & Special Collections, Anderson Hall, Mezzanine, 333 S Broad St, Philadelphia, PA, 19102. Tel: 215-717-6290. p. 1989
Grygla, Melissa, Libr Dir, Saratoga Springs Public Library, 1307 N Commerce Dr, Ste 140, Saratoga Springs, UT, 84045. Tel: 801-766-6513. p. 2273
Grynwich, Julie, Dir, New Buffalo Township Public Library, 33 N Thompson St, New Buffalo, MI, 49117. Tel: 269-469-2933. p. 1137
Grzybowski, Judy, Br Mgr, Lakewood Public Library, Madison, 13427 Madison Ave, Lakewood, OH, 44107. Tel: 216-228-7428. p. 1794
Grzybowski, Melissa, Youth Serv Librn, Pflugerville Public Library, 1008 W Pfluger, Pflugerville, TX, 78660. Tel: 512-990-6375. p. 2226
Gschwind, Deana, Dir, Graves County Public Library, 601 N 17th St, Mayfield, KY, 42066. Tel: 270-247-2911. p. 868
Gu, Wen, Libr Dir, Gloucester City Library, 50 N Railroad Ave, Gloucester City, NJ, 08030. Tel: 856-456-4181. p. 1405
Guan, Amy, Learning Res Tech, Napa Valley College, 1700 Bldg, 2277 Napa-Vallejo Hwy, Napa, CA, 94558. Tel: 707-256-7400. p. 182
Guan, Wei, Ref Serv Librn, Tech Serv Librn, Fort Lee Public Library, 320 Main St, Fort Lee, NJ, 07024. Tel: 201-592-3615. p. 1403
Guana, Maria, Asst Librn, Dilley Public Library, 231 W FM 117, Dilley, TX, 78017. Tel: 830-965-1951. p. 2171
Guaracha-Martinez, Monica, Br Head, Monterey County Free Libraries, Aromas Branch, 387 Blohm Ave, Aromas, CA, 95004. Tel: 831-726-3240. p. 172
Guarcello, Catherine, Librn, St Elizabeth's Medical Center, 736 Cambridge St, Boston, MA, 02135. Tel: 617-789-2177. p. 999
Guardado, Anthony, Head, Round Rock Libr Serv, Texas State University, 601 University Dr, San Marcos, TX, 78666-4684. Tel: 512-245-4701. p. 2241
Guardi, Margaret, Curator, Walt Whitman Birthplace Association, 246 Old Walt Whitman Rd, Huntington Station, NY, 11746. Tel: 631-427-5240. p. 1550
Guardian, Adriana, Librn, Millstadt Library District, 115 W Laurel St, Millstadt, IL, 62260. Tel: 618-476-1887. p. 618
Guarino-Kozlowicz, Liz, Br Mgr, Kent District Library, Caledonia Township Branch, 6260 92nd St SE, Caledonia, MI, 49316. p. 1094

Guartiere, Maura, Ch, Plumb Memorial Library, 65 Wooster St, Shelton, CT, 06484. Tel: 203-924-1580. p. 336
Guastavino, Catherine, Prof, McGill University, 3661 Peel St, Montreal, QC, H3A 1X1, CANADA. Tel: 514-398-4204. p. 2796
Gudenas, Jean, Coll Serv, Dir, Info Res, Medical University of South Carolina Libraries, 171 Ashley Ave, Ste 419, Charleston, SC, 29425-0001. Tel: 843-792-8309. p. 2051
Guderian, Angie, Libr Dir, New Sarepta Public Library, 5150 Centre St, New Sarepta, AB, T0B 3M0, CANADA. Tel: 780-975-7513. p. 2549
Gudmestad, Beth, Ch Serv, Loveland Public Library, 300 N Adams Ave, Loveland, CO, 80537. Tel: 970-962-2448. p. 290
Gudmundson, Crystal, Br Librn, Wapiti Regional Library, Pilger Public Library, 622 Main St, Pilger, SK, S0K 3G0, CANADA. Tel: 306-367-4809. p. 2746
Guedea Carreno, Lisa, Dir, Elkhart Public Library, 300 S Second St, Elkhart, IN, 46516-3109. p. 680
Guedea, Esther, Evening Circ Supvr, Goshen College, Harold & Wilma Good Library, 1700 S Main, Goshen, IN, 46526-4794. Tel: 574-535-7427. p. 687
Guedel, Robyn, Mgr, Ad Serv, Tuscarawas County Public Library, 121 Fair Ave NW, New Philadelphia, OH, 44663-2600. Tel: 330-364-4474. p. 1807
Guedel, Theodore, Ref & Instruction Librn, Kent State University, 6000 Frank Ave NW, North Canton, OH, 44720-7548. Tel: 330-244-3322. p. 1809
Gueffier, Elisa, Head, Youth Serv, Lake Villa District Library, 140 N Munn Rd, Lindenhurst, IL, 60046. Tel: 847-245-5112. p. 609
Guengerich, Anna Marie, Librn, University of Iowa, Blommers Measurement Resources Library, 304 Lindquist Ctr, Iowa City, IA, 52242-1587. Tel: 319-335-5416. p. 760
Gueniat, Jessica, Libr Dir, Torrington Library, 12 Daycoeton Pl, Torrington, CT, 06790. Tel: 860-489-6684. p. 342
Guenther, Jenna, Info Serv, ILL, Juneau Public Libraries, 292 Marine Way, Juneau, AK, 99801. Tel: 907-586-5249. p. 47
Guerin, Donna, Dir, Libr Serv, Gratz College, 7605 Old York Rd, Melrose Park, PA, 19027. Tel: 215-635-7300, Ext 159. p. 1962
Guerin, Susan, Tech Serv, Comsewogue Public Library, 170 Terryville Rd, Port Jefferson Station, NY, 11776. Tel: 631-928-1212. p. 1621
Guerra, Cynthia, ILL Coordr, Haddonfield Public Library, 60 Haddon Ave, Haddonfield, NJ, 08033-2422. Tel: 856-429-1304. p. 1406
Guerra, Elizabeth, Dir, Teinert Memorial Public Library, 337 N Dalton St, Bartlett, TX, 76511. Tel: 254-527-3208. p. 2144
Guerra, Juan J, Dir, Libr Serv, Brownsville Public Library System, 2600 Central Blvd, Brownsville, TX, 78520-8824. Tel: 956-548-1055, Ext 2125. p. 2150
Guerra, Leticia, Asst Br Mgr, Rio Grande City Public Library, 591 E Third St, Rio Grande City, TX, 78582-3588. Tel: 956-487-4389. p. 2232
Guerra, Michelle, Librn, Betsie Valley District Library, 14744 Thompson Ave, Thompsonville, MI, 49683. Tel: 231-378-2716. p. 1153
Guerrero, Ashley, Libr Dir, Martindale Community Library, 411 Main St, Martindale, TX, 78655. Tel: 512-357-4492. p. 2216
Guerrero, Diana, Br Supvr, Kern County Library, Delano Branch, 925 Tenth Ave, Delano, CA, 93215-2229. Tel: 661-725-1078. p. 119
Guerrero, Diana, Br Supvr, Kern County Library, Wasco Branch, 1102 Seventh St, Wasco, CA, 93280-1801. Tel: 661-758-2114. p. 120
Guerrero, Elena A, Asst Librn, Jim Hogg County Public Library, 210 N Smith Ave, Hebbronville, TX, 78361. Tel: 361-527-3421. p. 2188
Guerrero, Mary J, Librn, Imperial Valley College, 380 E Ira Aten Rd, Imperial, CA, 92251. Tel: 760-355-6382. p. 152
Guerrero, Mary Jane, County Librn, Imperial County Free Library, 1331 S Clark Rd, Bldg 24, El Centro, CA, 92243. Tel: 760-339-7100. p. 139
Guerrero, Robert, Librn, GlaxoSmithKline Pharmaceuticals, Research & Development Library, UW2322, 709 Swedeland Rd, King of Prussia, PA, 19406-2799. Tel: 610-270-6400. p. 1981
Guerrero, Robert L, Libr Mgr, Richards, Layton & Finger Library, One Rodney Square, 920 N King St, Wilmington, DE, 19801. Tel: 302-651-7775. p. 358
Guerrero, Rose, Dir, Res, Historical Society of Palm Beach County, 300 N Dixie Hwy, West Palm Beach, FL, 33401. Tel: 561-832-4164. p. 453
Guerrette, Liza, Asst Librn, ILL, Caribou Public Library, 30 High St, Caribou, ME, 04736. Tel: 207-493-4214. p. 920
Guertin, Brigid, Exec Dir, Danbury Museum & Historical Society, 43 Main St, Danbury, CT, 06810. Tel: 203-743-5200. p. 307
Guertin, Emilie, Libr Coord, Bibliotheque Municipale d'Alma, 500 rue Collard, Alma, QC, G8B 1N2, CANADA. Tel: 418-669-5140, Ext 5139. p. 2709
Guessferd, Mimi, Librn, Manchester VA Medical Center Library, 718 Smyth Rd, Manchester, NH, 03104-7004. Tel: 603-624-4366. p. 1372
Guest, Betty, Br Librn, Southeast Regional Library, Yellow Grass Branch, 213 Souris St, Yellow Grass, SK, S0G 5J0, CANADA. Tel: 306-465-2574. p. 2755
Guest, Graham, Archives, Historian, Pahkisimon Nuye?ah Library System, 118 Avro Pl, Air Ronge, SK, S0J 3G0, CANADA. Tel: 306-425-4525. p. 2741
Guest, Jane, Library Contact, Missoula Public Library, Frenchtown Branch, Frenchtown High School - School/Community Library, 17620 Frontage Rd, Frenchtown, MT, 59834. Tel: 406-626-2730. p. 1300
Guest, Raechel, Dir, Silas Bronson Library, 267 Grand St, Waterbury, CT, 06702-1981. Tel: 203-574-8205. p. 343
Guevara, Beatriz, Branch Lead, Charlotte Mecklenburg Library, Scaleybark Branch, 101 Scaleybark Rd, Charlotte, NC, 28209. Tel: 704-416-6400. p. 1680
Guevin, Peter, Educational Resource Ctr Asst, Rivier University, 420 S Main St, Nashua, NH, 03060-5086. Tel: 603-897-8463. p. 1375
Guevremont, Johanne, Dir, Bibliotheque de Beloeil, 620 rue Richelieu, Beloeil, QC, J3G 5E8, CANADA. Tel: 450-467-7872. p. 2710
Guffey, Karen M, Br Mgr, Athens County Public Libraries, Glouster Public, 20 Toledo St, Glouster, OH, 45732. Tel: 740-767-3670. p. 1805
Guggemos, Eva, Archives & Spec Coll Librn, Pacific University Libraries, 2043 College Way, Forest Grove, OR, 97116. Tel: 503-610-2721. p. 1880
Gugliotti, Lisa, Digital Syst Librn, Middlesex Community College, 100 Training Hill Rd, Middletown, CT, 06457. Tel: 860-343-5832. p. 322
Gugluizza, Barbara, Head, Ref Serv, Concord Free Public Library, 129 Main St, Concord, MA, 01742. Tel: 978-318-3347. p. 1012
Guibord, Kathy, Librn, McIntyre Memorial Library, 208 Dallas St, Dallas, WI, 54733. Tel: 715-837-1186. p. 2430
Guida, Joe, IT Serv, Sr Libr Tech, Bergen County Cooperative Library System, Inc, 21-00 Route 208 S, Ste 130, Fair Lawn, NJ, 07410. Tel: 201-498-7317. p. 2770
Guidal, Kathy, Ch Serv Librn, Floral Park Public Library, 17 Caroline Pl, Floral Park, NY, 11001. Tel: 516-326-6330. p. 1533
Guiden, Karen, Res Spec, Pillsbury Winthrop Shaw Pittman LLP, Four Embarcadero Ctr, 22nd Flr, San Francisco, CA, 94111. Tel: 415-983-1000. p. 226
Guido, Richard, Exec Dir/Librn, Salem County Historical Society, 83 Market St, Salem, NJ, 08079. Tel: 856-935-5004. p. 1441
Guidroz, Sally, Br Mgr, Lafourche Parish Public Library, Larose Branch, 305 E Fifth St, Larose, LA, 70373. Tel: 985-693-3336. p. 911
Guidry, Nancy, Br Mgr, Iberia Parish Library, St Peter Street Branch, 1111 W Saint Peter St, New Iberia, LA, 70560. Tel: 337-364-7670. p. 900
Guigli, Caron, Asst Dir, Malden Public Library, 36 Salem St, Malden, MA, 02148-5291. Tel: 781-324-0218. p. 1031
Guijarro, Nieves, Chief Exec Officer, Burk's Falls, Armour & Ryerson Union Public Library, 39 Copeland St, Burk's Falls, ON, P0A 1C0, CANADA. Tel: 705-382-3327. p. 2634
Guilbert, France, Documentation Tech, Archives Provinciales des Capucins, 3650 Blvd de la Rousseliere, Montreal, QC, H1A 2X9, CANADA. Tel: 514-642-5391, Ext 347. p. 2716
Guild, Craig, Ref & Instruction Librn, Three Rivers Community College, 574 New London Tpk, Norwich, CT, 06360-6598. Tel: 860-215-9270. p. 332
Guildroy, Jonathan, Head, Media Serv, Port Washington Public Library, One Library Dr, Port Washington, NY, 11050. Tel: 516-883-3728, Ext 1800. p. 1622
Guile, Sarah, Library Contact, Northwest Atlantic Fisheries Organization Library, 2 Morris Dr, Ste 100, Dartmouth, NS, B3B 1K8, CANADA. Tel: 902-468-5590. p. 2618
Guilford, Claudia, Librn, Roslyn Public Library, 201 S First, Roslyn, WA, 98941. Tel: 509-649-3105, Option 4. p. 2375
Guill, Kacy, County Librn, Trinity County Library, 351 Main St, Weaverville, CA, 96093. Tel: 530-623-1373. p. 258
Guillemard, Teresita, Circ, Ref (Info Servs), Pontifical Catholic University, Monsignor Fremiot Torres Oliver Law Library, 2250 Blvd Luis A Ferre Aguayo, Ste 544, Ponce, PR, 00717-9997. Tel: 787-841-2000, Ext 1850, 787-841-2000, Ext 1851. p. 2512
Guillen, Timothy, W Palm Beach Campus Libr Dir, Keiser University Library System, 1500 NW 49th St, Fort Lauderdale, FL, 33309. Tel: 954-351-4035. p. 401
Guilliams, David, Br Mgr, Chicago Public Library, Vodak-East Side, 3710 E 106th St, Chicago, IL, 60617. Tel: 312-747-5500. p. 557
Guillory, Agnes, Dir, Allen Parish Libraries, 320 S Sixth St, Oberlin, LA, 70655. Tel: 318-491-4543. p. 905
Guillory, David, Cat Librn, ILL Librn, McNeese State University, 300 S Beauregard Dr, Lake Charles, LA, 70609. Tel: 337-475-5716. p. 894
Guillou, Christian, Media & Electronic Resources Librn, Douglas College Library & Learning Centre, 700 Royal Ave, Rm N2100, New Westminster, BC, V3M 5Z5, CANADA. Tel: 604-527-5184. p. 2572
Guilmant-Smith, Gillian, Br Head, Vancouver Public Library, Champlain Heights Branch, 7110 Kerr St, Vancouver, BC, V5S 4W2, CANADA. Tel: 604-665-3955. p. 2581
Guilmant-Smith, Gillian, Br Head, Vancouver Public Library, Collingwood Branch, 2985 Kingsway, Vancouver, BC, V5R 5J4, CANADA. Tel: 604-665-3953. p. 2581
Guilmartin, Lore, Dir, Libr Serv, Sweet Briar College, 134 Chapel Rd, Sweet Briar, VA, 24595. Tel: 434-381-6138. p. 2348
Guilmette, Amy, Dep Chief Exec Officer, Pelham Public Library, 43 Pelham Town Sq, Fonthill, ON, L0S 1E0, CANADA. Tel: 905-892-6443. p. 2642
Guilmette, Dennis, Libr Dir, Tuftonboro Free Library, 221 Middle Rd, Rte 109A, Center Tuftonboro, NH, 03816. Tel: 603-569-4256. p. 1357
Guimaeres, Sabrina, Br Mgr, Ocean County Library, Jackson Branch, Two Jackson Dr, Jackson, NJ, 08527-3601. Tel: 732-928-4400. p. 1446
Guimara, Kristel, Libr Mgr, Long Lake Public Library, 1195 Main St, Long Lake, NY, 12847. Tel: 518-624-3825. p. 1565

Guimaraes, Ana, Interim Dept Chair, Pub Serv, Kennesaw State University Library System, 385 Cobb Ave NW, MD 1701, Kennesaw, GA, 30144. Tel: 470-578-7920. p. 483
Guimond, Andrea, Interim Librn, Soldiers Memorial Library, 85 Main St, Hiram, ME, 04041. Tel: 207-625-4650. p. 927
Guin, Pam, Cat, Oneonta Public Library, 221 Second St S, Oneonta, AL, 35121. Tel: 205-274-7641. p. 31
Guinan, Gina, Libr Dir, Collingdale Public Library, 823 MacDade Blvd, Collingdale, PA, 19023-1422. Tel: 610-583-2214. p. 1923
Guiney, T J, Librn, Anoka-Ramsey Community College, 11200 Mississippi Blvd NW, Coon Rapids, MN, 55433-3470. Tel: 763-433-1150. p. 1171
Guinn, Richard, Br Mgr, Pima County Public Library, Salazar-Ajo Branch, 15 W Plaza St, Ste 179, Ajo, AZ, 85321. Tel: 520-387-6075. p. 82
Guinn, Richard, Tech Serv, University of Texas, School of Public Health Library, 1200 Herman Pressler Blvd, Houston, TX, 77030-3900. Tel: 713-500-9121. p. 2200
Guinnee, Eli, State Librn, New Mexico State Library, 1209 Camino Carlos Rey, Santa Fe, NM, 87507-5166. Tel: 505-476-9700. p. 1475
Guinta, Laura, YA Serv, Garden City Public Library, 60 Seventh St, Garden City, NY, 11530. Tel: 516-742-8405. p. 1536
Guinther, Angela, Br Mgr, Cleveland Public Library, Carnegie West, 1900 Fulton Rd, Cleveland, OH, 44113. Tel: 216-623-6927. p. 1768
Guise, Janneka, Head Librn, University of Toronto Libraries, Faculty of Music Library, Edward Johnson Bldg, 80 Queens Park Crescent, Toronto, ON, M5S 2C5, CANADA. Tel: 416-978-6920. p. 2698
Guistini, Dean, Ref Librn, University of British Columbia Library, Biomedical, Gordon & Leslie Diamond Health Care Ctr, 2775 Laurel St, 2nd Flr, Vancouver, BC, V5Z 1M9, CANADA. Tel: 604-875-4111, Ext 62392. p. 2580
Guiterrez, Janella, Supvr, Yakima Valley Libraries, Mabton Library, 415 B St, Mabton, WA, 98935. Tel: 509-894-4128. p. 2395
Guitron-Rodriguez, Miguel, Br Mgr, Riverside County Library System, Mecca Library, 91-260 Ave 66, Mecca, CA, 92254. Tel: 760-396-2363. p. 202
Gulacsy, Elizabeth, Archivist, Alfred University, Scholes Library of Ceramics, New York State College of Ceramics at Alfred University, Two Pine St, Alfred, NY, 14802-1297. Tel: 607-871-2948. p. 1485
Gulas, Greg, Libr Mgr, Vancouver Island Regional Library, Courtenay Branch, 300 Sixth St, Courtenay, BC, V9N 9V9, CANADA. Tel: 250-334-3369. p. 2570
Gulas, Greg, Libr Mgr, Vancouver Island Regional Library, Union Bay Branch, 5527 Island Hwy S, Union Bay, BC, V0R 3B0, CANADA. Tel: 250-335-2433. p. 2571
Gulbraa, Krista, Libr Mgr, Phyllis Craig Legacy Library, 5011 53rd Ave, Irma, AB, T0B 2H0, CANADA. Tel: 780-754-3746. p. 2543
Gulbrandsen, Linda K, Mgr, Church of Jesus Christ of Latter-Day Saints, Family History Library, 35 N West Temple St, Salt Lake City, UT, 84150. p. 2271
Guldan, Martha, Dir, Greenback Public Library, 6889 Morganton Rd, Greenback, TN, 37742-4143. Tel: 865-856-2841. p. 2100
Gulden, Jodi, Librn, Northwest Regional Library, Godel Memorial Library, 314 E Johnson Ave, Warren, MN, 56762. Tel: 218-745-5465. p. 1205
Gulick, Cindy, Youth Serv, Barry-Lawrence Regional Library, Mount Vernon Branch, 206 W Water St, Mount Vernon, MO, 65712. Tel: 417-466-2921. p. 1263
Gulka, Josef, Circ, Herbert D Katz Center for Advanced Judaic Studies Library, 420 Walnut St, Philadelphia, PA, 19106-3703. Tel: 215-746-1290, 215-746-5154. p. 1982
Gulla, Sharon, Head, Youth Serv, Moultonborough Public Library, Four Holland St, Moultonborough, NH, 03254. Tel: 603-476-8895. p. 1374
Gullacher, Darcy, Univ Librn, Trinity Western University, 22500 University Dr, Langley, BC, V2Y 1Y1, CANADA. Tel: 604-513-2121, Ext 3905. p. 2569
Gullahorn, Kat, Pub Serv Librn, University of New Mexico, Valencia Campus, 280 La Entrada, Los Lunas, NM, 87031. Tel: 505-925-8993. p. 1463
Gullet, Jan, Ch, Briggs Lawrence County Public Library, 321 S Fourth St, Ironton, OH, 45638. Tel: 740-532-1124. p. 1791
Gullett, Elisabeth, Dir, Helen Keller Public Library, 511 N Main St, Tuscumbia, AL, 35674. Tel: 256-383-7065. p. 38
Gulley, Delores, Outreach Coordr, Conyers-Rockdale Library System, 864 Green St SW, Conyers, GA, 30012. Tel: 770-388-5040. p. 473
Gulley, Krystal, Dir, Harrisburg Public Library District, Two W Walnut St, Harrisburg, IL, 62946-1261. Tel: 618-253-7455. p. 597
Gulley, T Jane, Br Mgr, Newton County Public Library, Morocco Community Library, 205 S West St, Morocco, IN, 47963. Tel: 219-285-2664. p. 702
Gulley, Wendy S, Librn, United States Navy, Historic Ship Nautilus-Submarine Force Library & Archives, One Crystal Lake Rd, Groton, CT, 06340-2464. Tel: 860-694-3558. p. 315
Gulliford, Joyce, Dir, Forrest Public Library District, 301 S James, Forrest, IL, 61741. Tel: 815-657-8805. p. 589
Gullings, Terra, Univ Archivist, University of Texas at Tyler Library, 3900 University Blvd, Tyler, TX, 75799. Tel: 903-565-5849. p. 2250
Gullion, Robert, Libr Assoc, Desoto Parish Library, Stonewall Branch, 808 Hwy 171, Stonewall, LA, 71078. Tel: 318-925-9191. p. 896
Gulliver, Nancy, Librn, Atascadero State Hospital, Logan Patient's Library, 10333 El Camino Real, Atascadero, CA, 93422. Tel: 805-468-2520. p. 118
Gulliver, Nancy, Librn, Atascadero State Hospital, Logan Professional Library, 10333 El Camino Real, Atascadero, CA, 93422. Tel: 805-468-2491. p. 118
Gulliver, Terry, Br Asst, Cumberland Public Libraries, Advocate Library, Fundy Tides Recreation Ctr, 93 Mills Rd, Advocate Harbour, NS, B0M 1A0, CANADA. Tel: 902-392-2214. p. 2615
Gullo, Amy, Youth Serv Librn, Hillside Public Library, 405 N Hillside Ave, Hillside, IL, 60162-1295. Tel: 708-449-7510. p. 599
Gullon, Ismael, Assoc Librn, Mercer University, Walter F George School of Law, Furman Smith Law Library, 1021 Georgia Ave, Macon, GA, 31201-1001. Tel: 478-301-5904. p. 486
Gully, Matthew, Dir, East Mississippi Regional Library System, 116 Water St, Quitman, MS, 39355-2336. Tel: 601-776-3881. p. 1231
Gulnac, Donna, Dir, Access Serv, Dir, Info Serv, University of California Los Angeles Library, Hugh & Hazel Darling Law Library, 1112 Law Bldg, 385 Charles E Young Dr E, Los Angeles, CA, 90095-1458. Tel: 310-825-7826. p. 169
Gulsvig, Brent, Archivist, Pope County Historical Society, 809 S Lakeshore Dr, Glenwood, MN, 56334. Tel: 320-634-3293. p. 1176
Gum, Dennie, Ms, Librn, Arthur Johnson Memorial Library, 244 Cook Ave, Raton, NM, 87740. Tel: 575-445-9711. p. 1473
Gum, Jason, Libr Dir, Glenville State College, 100 High St, Glenville, WV, 26351. Tel: 304-462-6163. p. 2403
Gum-Fowler, Jennifer, Libr Dir, Fort Scott Public Library, 201 S National Ave, Fort Scott, KS, 66701. Tel: 620-223-2882. p. 808
Gum-Fowler, Jennifer, Libr Dir, Kincaid Community Library, 500 Fifth Ave, Kincaid, KS, 66039. Tel: 620-439-5500. p. 817
Gumb, Lindsey, Scholarly Communications Librn, Roger Williams University Library, One Old Ferry Rd, Bristol, RI, 02809. Tel: 401-243-3225. p. 2030
Gumeci, Ozlem, Tech Serv Librn, Schoolcraft College, 18600 Haggerty Rd, Livonia, MI, 48152-2696. Tel: 734-462-4437. p. 1127
Guminski, Paul, Mgr, Buffalo & Erie County Public Library System, North Park, 975 Hertel Ave, Buffalo, NY, 14216. Tel: 716-875-3748. p. 1508
Gunawan, Upi, Admin Coordr, The College of Wooster Libraries, 1140 Beall Ave, Wooster, OH, 44691-2364. Tel: 330-263-2442. p. 1833
Gunby, Matthew, Circ Librn, Meredith Public Library, 91 Main St, Meredith, NH, 03253. Tel: 603-279-4303. p. 1373
Gundel, L, Adult Ref Librn, Massapequa Public Library, Central Avenue, 523 Central Ave, Massapequa, NY, 11758. Tel: 516-798-4607. p. 1569
Gundersen, Geir, Supvry Archivist, National Archives & Records Administration, 1000 Beal Ave, Ann Arbor, MI, 48109. Tel: 734-205-0556. p. 1079
Gunderson, Christina, Dir, Learning Res Ctr, Saint Mary-of-the-Woods College, One Saint Mary of the Woods College, Saint Mary-of-the-Woods, IN, 47876. Tel: 812-535-5223. p. 717
Gunderson, Dianne, Co-Dir, Elgin Public Library, 503 S Second St, Elgin, NE, 68636-3222. Tel: 402-843-2460. p. 1313
Gunderson, Emrick, Computer Syst Mgr, Hedberg Public Library, 316 S Main St, Janesville, WI, 53545. Tel: 608-758-6599. p. 2443
Gunderson, Gayle, Dean of Libr, Colorado Christian University, 180 S Garrison St, Lakewood, CO, 80226. Tel: 303-963-3250. p. 288
Gunderson, Jan, Circ, University of North Dakota, Harley E French Library of the Health Sciences, School of Medicine & Health Sciences, 501 N Columbia Rd, Stop 9002, Grand Forks, ND, 58202-9002. Tel: 701-777-3993. p. 1734
Gunderson, Jeff, Librn, San Francisco Art Institute, 800 Chestnut St, San Francisco, CA, 94133. Tel: 415-749-4562. p. 226
Gunderson, Molly, Asst Dean, Portland State University Library, 1875 SW Park Ave, Portland, OR, 97201-3220. Tel: 503-725-5874. p. 1893
Gundlach, Sarah-Elizabeth, Curator, Louisiana State Museum, 400 Esplanade Ave, New Orleans, LA, 70116. Tel: 504-568-3660. p. 901
Gundrum, Kathleen, Exec Dir, Capital District Library Council, 28 Essex St, Albany, NY, 12206. Tel: 518-438-2500. p. 2770
Gundry, Jenifer, Exec Secy, Southeastern Pennsylvania Theological Library Association, c/o Biblical Seminary, 200 N Main St, Hatfield, PA, 19440. Tel: 609-497-7758. p. 2774
Gunkel, Tanya, Educ Mat Ctr/Instruction/Ref Librn, University of Wisconsin-Stout, 315 Tenth Ave, Menomonie, WI, 54751-0790. Tel: 715-232-1892. p. 2456
Gunn, Amy, Tech Serv Asst, Crawford County Library System, 1409 Main St, Van Buren, AR, 72956. Tel: 479-471-3226. p. 111
Gunn, Emily, Librn, Alexander College, 4805 Kingsway, Burnaby, BC, V5H 4T6, CANADA. Tel: 604-558-7369. p. 2563
Gunn, Joy, Br Mgr, Henderson District Public Libraries, Green Valley Library, 2797 N Green Valley Pkwy, Henderson, NV, 89014. Tel: 702-207-4260. p. 1346
Gunn, Maureen Elizabeth, Circ, Ref, Nunavut Arctic College, 502 Niaqungusiariaq Dr, Iqaluit, NU, X0A 0H0, CANADA. Tel: 867-979-7220. p. 2625
Gunnar, Bridgetta, Cat, Saint Mary Parish Library, 206 Iberia St, Franklin, LA, 70538. Tel: 337-828-1624, 337-828-1627. p. 890
Gunnerson, Suzanne, Head, Circ, Duxbury Free Library, 77 Alden St, Duxbury, MA, 02332. Tel: 781-934-2721. p. 1015
Gunning, Darla, Mgr, Community Library Network, 8385 N Government Way, Hayden, ID, 83835-9280. Tel: 208-772-5612. p. 522

Gunning, Nicolas, Dir, David A Howe Public Library, 155 N Main St, Wellsville, NY, 14895. Tel: 585-593-3410. p. 1661
Gunter, Joe D, Dir, East Travis Gateway Library District, 13512 Fm 812, Del Valle, TX, 78617. Tel: 512-243-1981. p. 2169
Gunter, Judy, Librn, Chinook Regional Library, Val Marie Branch, Val Marie Village Complex, 101 Centre St, Val Marie, SK, S0N 2T0, CANADA. Tel: 306-298-2133. p. 2753
Gunter, Mendy, Br Mgr, Forsyth County Public Library, Sharon Forks, 2820 Old Atlanta Rd, Cumming, GA, 30041. Tel: 770-781-9840. p. 473
Gunter, Taryn, Libr Asst, Harper Grey LLP Library, 3200-650 W Georgia St, Vancouver, BC, V6B 4P7, CANADA. Tel: 604-895-2861. p. 2579
Gunther, Alan, Libr Mgr, Community Libraries of Providence, Smith Hill Library, 31 Candace St, Providence, RI, 02908. Tel: 401-272-4140. p. 2038
Gunther, Jeri, Chief Librn, Ocean County Library, 101 Washington St, Toms River, NJ, 08753. Tel: 732-914-5415. p. 1446
Gunther-Blackman, Alison, Br Mgr, Norfolk Public Library, Park Place Branch, 620 W 29th St, Norfolk, VA, 23508. Tel: 757-664-7330. p. 2335
Gunzenhauser, Jackie, Libr Dir, Humeston Public Library, 302 Broad St, Humeston, IA, 50123. Tel: 641-877-4811. p. 759
Guo, Pipei, Info Assoc, University of Arizona Libraries, Health Sciences Library, 1501 N Campbell Ave, Tucson, AZ, 85724. Tel: 520-626-7172. p. 83
Guo, Yue, Asst Prof, University of Illinois at Urbana-Champaign, Library & Information Science Bldg, 501 E Daniel St, Champaign, IL, 61820-6211. Tel: 217-333-3280. p. 2784
Gupta, Madhu, Exec Dir, New London Public Library, 63 Huntington St, New London, CT, 06320. Tel: 860-447-1411, Ext 106. p. 329
Guptill, Christopher, Div Dean, San Joaquin Delta College, 5151 Pacific Ave, Stockton, CA, 95207. p. 249
Gupton, Erica, IT Tech, Delta Township District Library, 5130 Davenport Dr, Lansing, MI, 48917-2040. Tel: 517-321-4014. p. 1124
Guraliuc, Irene, Libr Dir, Chaleur Library Region, Monseigneur Paquet Public Library, 10A du Colisée St, Caraquet, NB, E1W 1A5, CANADA. Tel: 506-726-2681. p. 2599
Gurcke, Karl, Historian, US National Park Service, Park Headquarters, Second Ave Broadway, Skagway, AK, 99840. Tel: 907-983-9214. p. 51
Gurley, Cally, Curator, University of New England Libraries, Josephine S Abplanalp Library, Portland Campus, 716 Stevens Ave, Portland, ME, 04103. Tel: 207-221-4324. p. 918
Gurnee, Jeff, Adult Serv, Clark County Public Library, 370 S Burns Ave, Winchester, KY, 40391-1876. Tel: 859-744-5661. p. 878
Gurner, Joseph, Dir, Blackmur Memorial Library, 608 Blackmur Dr, Water Valley, MS, 38965-6070. Tel: 662-473-2444. p. 1235
Gurney, Holly, Dir, Learning Commons, Southern Maine Community College Library, Two Fort Rd, South Portland, ME, 04106. Tel: 207-741-5521. p. 941
Gurrola, Rosemary, Mgr, County of Los Angeles Public Library, Montebello Library, 1550 W Beverly Blvd, Montebello, CA, 90640-3993. Tel: 323-722-6551. p. 137
Gurt, Deborah, Interim Dir, University of South Alabama Libraries, Doy Leale McCall Rare Book & Manuscript Library, Marx Library, 3rd Flr, Ste 300, 5901 USA Dr N, Mobile, AL, 36688. Tel: 251-341-3900. p. 27
Gurthet, Andrew, Financial Serv, San Mateo County Law Library, 710 Hamilton St, Redwood City, CA, 94063. Tel: 650-363-4913. p. 200
Gurtler, Gretchen, Dir, Ghost Ranch Library, 280 Private Dr 1708, Abiquiu, NM, 87510-9601. Tel: 505-685-1000, Ext 4109. p. 1459
Gurung, Purna, Admin Serv Mgr, Rochester Public Library, 101 Second St SE, Rochester, MN, 55904-3776. Tel: 507-328-2300. p. 1194
Guscott, John, Br Mgr, Lorain Public Library System, Columbia Branch, 13824 W River Rd N, Columbia Station, OH, 44028. Tel: 440-236-8751. p. 1797
Guscott, Richard, Youth Serv Librn, Willamina Public Library, 382 NE C St, Willamina, OR, 97396. Tel: 503-876-6182. p. 1902
Guss, Erin, Br Mgr, Saint Louis Public Library, Barr, 1701 S Jefferson Ave, Saint Louis, MO, 63104. Tel: 314-771-7040. p. 1275
Gust, Samantha, Head, Acq, Niagara University Library, Four Varsity Dr, Niagara University, NY, 14109. Tel: 716-286-8031. p. 1606
Gustafson, Ashia, Dir, Brookings Public Library, 515 Third St, Brookings, SD, 57006. Tel: 605-692-9407. p. 2074
Gustafson, Elaine, Libr Instruction, Online Serv, Concordia University Wisconsin, 12800 N Lake Shore Dr, Mequon, WI, 53097-2402. Tel: 262-243-4403. p. 2456
Gustafson, Eric, Dir, Derby Public Library, 1600 E Walnut Grove, Derby, KS, 67037. Tel: 316-788-0760. p. 804
Gustafson, Jennifer, Practicum Coordr, Wayne State University, 106 Kresge Library, Detroit, MI, 48202. Tel: 313-577-1825. p. 2787
Gustafson, Melissa, Electronic Res Librn, Indiana State University, 510 North 6 1/2 St, Terre Haute, IN, 47809. Tel: 812-237-3700. p. 720
Gustafson, Robin, Head, Access & Delivery Serv, University of California, Davis, 100 NW Quad, Davis, CA, 95616. Tel: 530-752-8792. p. 134
Gustavson, Carrie, Dir, Bisbee Mining & Historical Museum, Five Copper Queen Plaza, Bisbee, AZ, 85603. Tel: 520-432-7071, Ext 2. p. 56
Gustina, Margo, Dep Dir, Southern Tier Library System, 9424 Scott Rd, Painted Post, NY, 14870-9598. Tel: 607-962-3141, Ext 205. p. 1614
Guston, Judith M, Curator, The Rosenbach of the Free Library of Philadelphia, 2010 DeLancey Pl, Philadelphia, PA, 19103. Tel: 215-732-1600. p. 1985
Gutbier, Carrie, Ch, YA Librn, Bennington Free Library, 101 Silver St, Bennington, VT, 05201. Tel: 802-442-9051. p. 2279
Gutekanst, Joe, ILL Coordr, Davidson College, 209 Ridge Rd, Davidson, NC, 28035-0001. Tel: 704-894-2331. p. 1683
Gutelius, Alexandra, Dir, Clifton Park-Halfmoon Public Library, 475 Moe Rd, Clifton Park, NY, 12065-3808. Tel: 518-371-8622. p. 1519
Gutenberger, Susie, Libr Dir, Lansing Community Library, 27 Auburn Rd, Lansing, NY, 14882. Tel: 607-533-4939. p. 1562
Guth, Karen, Staff Develop Coordr, Manitoba Developmental Centre Memorial Library, 840 Third St NE, Portage la Prairie, MB, R1N 3C6, CANADA. Tel: 204-856-4230. p. 2589
Guth, LuMarie, Bus Librn, Western Michigan University, 1903 W Michigan Ave, WMU Mail Stop 5353, Kalamazoo, MI, 49008-5353. Tel: 269-387-5153. p. 1122
Guthmiller, Christine, Dir, Kanawha Public Library, 121 N Main St, Kanawha, IA, 50447. Tel: 641-762-3595. p. 762
Guthrie, Alyce N, Exec VPres, PT Boats, Inc, 1384 Cordova Cove, Ste 2, Memphis, TN, 38138-2200. Tel: 901-755-8440. p. 2114
Guthrie, Amanda, Libr Dir, Lubbock Christian University Library, 5601 19th St, Lubbock, TX, 79407-2009. Tel: 806-720-7326. p. 2213
Guthrie, Emily, Dir, Colonial Williamsburg Foundation, 313 First St, Williamsburg, VA, 23185-4306. Tel: 757-220-7249. p. 2353
Guthrie, Katie, Interim Dir, Public Library of Johnston County & Smithfield, 305 E Market St, Smithfield, NC, 27577-3919. Tel: 919-934-8146. p. 1716
Guthrie, Lawrence Simpson, II, ILL Librn, Covington & Burling LLP, One City Ctr, 850 Tenth St, NW, Washington, DC, 20001. Tel: 202-662-6158. p. 363
Guthrie, Maggie, Dir, North Powder Library, 290 E St, North Powder, OR, 97867. Tel: 541-898-2175. p. 1889
Guthrie, Tara, Dir, Libr Serv, Central Carolina Community College Libraries, 1105 Kelly Dr, Sanford, NC, 27330. Tel: 919-718-7245. p. 1715
Guthrie-McNaughton, Isabella, Pub Serv, Tyndale University College & Seminary, 3377 Bayview Ave, Toronto, ON, M2M 3S4, CANADA. Tel: 416-226-6380. p. 2697
Guthwin, David, Libr Mgr, Metropolitan Hospital Center, 1901 First Ave & 97th St, New York, NY, 10029. Tel: 212-423-6055. p. 1591
Gutierrez, Alexandra, Mgr, Miami-Dade Public Library System, Key Biscayne Branch, 299 Crandon Blvd, Key Biscayne, FL, 33149. Tel: 305-361-6134. p. 423
Gutiérrez, Jolene, Librn, Denver Academy Library, 4400 E Iliff Ave, Denver, CO, 80222. Tel: 303-777-5870. p. 275
Gutierrez, Louise, Br Mgr, Riverside County Library System, Highgrove Library, 530 W Center St, Highgrove, CA, 92507. Tel: 951-682-1507. p. 202
Gutierrez, Manuel de la Cruz, Interim Dir, University of Pennsylvania Libraries, Biomedical Library, Johnson Pavilion, 3610 Hamilton Walk, Philadelphia, PA, 19104-6060. Tel: 215-898-5818. p. 1988
Gutierrez, Marisol, Chief Librn, University of Puerto Rico Library System, Gerardo Selles Sola Library, Rio Piedras Campus, Eugenio Maria de Hostos Bldg, Rm 211, San Juan, PR, 00931. Tel: 787-764-0000, Ext 85929. p. 2515
Gutierrez, Sandra, Admin Serv, Libr Spec, Yuma County Free Library District, 2951 S 21st Dr, Yuma, AZ, 85364. Tel: 928-373-6495. p. 85
Gutierrez, Veronica, Law Librn, Atascadero State Hospital, Logan Patient's Library, 10333 El Camino Real, Atascadero, CA, 93422. Tel: 805-468-3343. p. 118
Gutman, Ruth, Asst Librn, Milton Free Public Library, 13 Main St, Milton Mills, NH, 03852. Tel: 603-473-8535. p. 1374
Gutmann, Ted, Dir, Emma S Clark Memorial Library, 120 Main St, Setauket, NY, 11733-2868. Tel: 631-941-4080, Ext 112. p. 1640
Gutstein, Margo, Tech Serv, Simon Wiesenthal Center & Museum of Tolerance, 1399 S Roxbury Dr, 3rd Flr, Los Angeles, CA, 90035-4709. Tel: 310-772-7605. p. 168
Guttilla, Jayna Leipart, Access Serv Librn, Coll Develop Librn, Illinois Valley Community College, 815 N Orlando Smith Rd, Oglesby, IL, 61348-9692. Tel: 815-224-0387. p. 629
Guy, Criss, Digital Librn, Instruction Prog & Info Literacy Librn, Warren Wilson College, 701 Warren Wilson Rd, Swannanoa, NC, 28778. Tel: 828-771-3062. p. 1718
Guy, Curtis, Pub Serv Spec, Golden Gate University - Otto & Velia Butz Libraries, 536 Mission St, San Francisco, CA, 94105-2967. Tel: 415-442-7256. p. 225
Guy, Debbie, Supvr, Middlesex County Library, Thorndale Branch, 21790 Fairview Rd, Thorndale, ON, N0M 2P0, CANADA. Tel: 519-461-1150. p. 2682
Guy, Melissa, Dir, Librn, University of Texas Libraries, Nettie Lee Benson Latin American Collection, Sid Richardson Hall, SRH 1108, 2300 Red River St, Austin, TX, 78713-8916. Tel: 512-495-4520. p. 2142
Guy, Misty, Dir, Lovett Memorial Library, 111 N Houston St, Pampa, TX, 79065. Tel: 806-669-5780. p. 2224
Guy, Peyton, Libr Asst, Desoto Parish Library, 109 Crosby St, Mansfield, LA, 71052. Tel: 318-872-6100. p. 895

Guyan, Tracy, Asst Dir, Terrebonne Parish Library, 151 Library Dr, Houma, LA, 70360. Tel: 985-876-5861. p. 891
Guyant, Scott, Libr Tech, Montana State University-Northern, 300 13th St W, Havre, MT, 59501. Tel: 406-265-3544. p. 1295
Guyette, Frederick W, Asst Prof, Librn, Erskine College & Theological Seminary, One Depot St, Due West, SC, 29639. Tel: 864-379-8784. p. 2058
Guyette, Gizelle, Youth Serv Dir, Manchester Community Library, 138 Cemetery Ave, Rte 7A, Manchester Center, VT, 05255. Tel: 802-362-2607. p. 2288
Guyette, Gizelle, Dir, Morristown Centennial Library, Seven Richmond St, Morrisville, VT, 05661. Tel: 802-888-3853. p. 2289
Guzman, Andrew T, Interim Dean of Libr, University of Southern California Libraries, University Park Campus, 3550 Trousdale Pkwy, Los Angeles, CA, 90089. Tel: 213-740-2543. p. 169
Guzman, George, Admin Serv Mgr, Riverside Public Library, 3900 Mission Inn Ave, Riverside, CA, 92501. Tel: 951-826-5201. p. 203
Guzman, Isabel, Br Supvr, Riverside Public Library, La Sierra, 4600 La Sierra Ave, Riverside, CA, 92505-2722. Tel: 951-826-2461. p. 203
Guzman, Michelle, Head Librn, National Sporting Library & Museum, 102 The Plains Rd, Middleburg, VA, 20117. Tel: 540-687-6542, Ext 18. p. 2332
Guzman, Sonia, Circ Supvr, Deer Park Public Library, 3009 Center St, Deer Park, TX, 77536. Tel: 281-478-7208. p. 2169
Guzzo, Stacie, Br Librn, Romeo District Library, Kezar Branch, 107 Church St, Romeo, MI, 48065. Tel: 586-752-2583. p. 1157
Guzzy, Judith, Coll Develop Librn, Johnson County Community College, 12345 College Blvd, Overland Park, KS, 66210. Tel: 913-469-8500, Ext 3297. p. 829
Gwiazda, Cynthia, Commun Serv Librn, Hagaman Memorial Library, 227 Main St, East Haven, CT, 06512. Tel: 203-468-3890. p. 310
Gwilt, Kimberly, Asst Dir, Dalton Free Public Library, 462 Main St, Dalton, MA, 01226. Tel: 413-684-6112. p. 1013
Gwilt, Roberta, Assoc Dean, Access & Res Mgt, Syracuse University Libraries, 222 Waverly Ave, Syracuse, NY, 13244-2010. Tel: 315-443-9773. p. 1650
Gwinett, Lori, Actg Head, Res Serv, Georgia Southern University, 1400 Southern Dr, Statesboro, GA, 30458. Tel: 912-478-5115. p. 497
Gwinn, Christopher, Historian, Gettysburg National Military Park Library, 1195 Baltimore Pike, Ste 100, Gettysburg, PA, 17325. Tel: 717-338-4424. p. 1936
Gwinn, Sherry, Asst Librn, Summers County Public Library, 201 Temple St, Hinton, WV, 25951. Tel: 304-466-4490. p. 2404
Gwozdz, Lindsey, Asst Dean of Libr, Community College of Rhode Island, 1762 Louisquisset Pike, Lincoln, RI, 02865. Tel: 401-825-1059. p. 2033
Gwozdz, Lindsey, Asst Dean of Libr, Community College of Rhode Island, One John H Chafee Blvd, 2nd Flr, Newport, RI, 02840. Tel: 401-851-1600, 401-851-1696. p. 2034
Gwyn, Cassie, Ch, Atlanta-Fulton Public Library System, Gladys S Dennard Library at South Fulton, 4055 Flat Shoals Rd, Union City, GA, 30291-1590. Tel: 770-306-3092. p. 461
Gwyn, Cathy, Ch, Atlanta-Fulton Public Library System, West End Branch, 525 Peeples St SW, Atlanta, GA, 30310. Tel: 404-613-8000. p. 462
Gyles, Leon L, Dir, Scotland County Memorial Library, 312 W Church St, Laurinburg, NC, 28352-3720. Tel: 910-276-0563. p. 1700
Gyles, Stephanie, Sr Librn, California Department of Corrections Library System, Mule Creek State Prison, 4001 Hwy 104, Ione, CA, 95640. Tel: 209-274-4911, Ext 6510. p. 207
Gysel, Lisa D, Librn, Interior Health Library, 311 Columbia St, Kamloops, BC, V2C 2T1, CANADA. Tel: 250-314-2234. p. 2567
Gyulveszi, Jane, Dir, Bellaire Public Library, 111 S Bridge St, Bellaire, MI, 49615-9566. Tel: 231-533-8814. p. 1084
Ha, Corey, Libr Dir, State University of New York College, SUNY Geneseo, One College Circle, Geneseo, NY, 14454-1498. Tel: 585-245-5594. p. 1537
Ha, Kim T, Libr Dir, Pennington Public Library, 30 N Main St, Pennington, NJ, 08534. Tel: 609-737-0404. p. 1434
Haack, Sarah, Ref Serv Librn, Kearney Public Library, 2020 First Ave, Kearney, NE, 68847. Tel: 308-233-3282. p. 1319
Haack, Stephanie, Libr Dir, Fairfield Public Library, 412 North D St, Fairfield, NE, 68938. Tel: 402-726-2104. p. 1314
Haake, Amy, Archivist, Saint Charles County Historical Society Archives, Old Market House, 101 S Main St, Saint Charles, MO, 63301-2802. Tel: 636-946-9828. p. 1268
Haake, Katie, Ref Librn, Wyckoff Public Library, 200 Woodland Ave, Wyckoff, NJ, 07481. Tel: 201-891-4866. p. 1456
Haan, Cathy, Cataloging Assoc, Cornerstone University, 1001 E Beltline Ave NE, Grand Rapids, MI, 49525. Tel: 616-254-1650, Ext 1065. p. 1110
Haas, Anne, Art Librn, Bowdoin College Library, 3000 College Sta, Brunswick, ME, 04011-8421. p. 919
Haas, Anne, Art Librn, Bowdoin College Library, Pierce Art Library, Visual Arts Ctr, 9300 College Sta, Brunswick, ME, 04011-8493. Tel: 207-725-3690. p. 919
Haas, Cindy, Head, Children's Servx, W J Niederkorn Library, 316 W Grand Ave, Port Washington, WI, 53074-2293. Tel: 262-284-5031. p. 2470
Haas, Diane, Metadata Serv Tech, University of Oregon Libraries, John E Jaqua Law Library, William W Knight Law Ctr, 2nd Flr, 1515 Agate St, Eugene, OR, 97403. Tel: 541-346-1656. p. 1879
Haas, Janel, Dir, Way Public Library, 101 E Indiana Ave, Perrysburg, OH, 43551. Tel: 419-874-3135, Ext 102. p. 1815
Haas, Jennifer, Head, Info Serv & Res, University of Waterloo Library, Davis Centre Library, 200 University Ave W, Waterloo, ON, N2L 3G1, CANADA. Tel: 519-888-4567, Ext 37469. p. 2702
Haas, Kelly, Youth Serv, Julia Hull District Library, 100 Library Lane, Stillman Valley, IL, 61084. Tel: 815-645-8611. p. 651
Haas, Lori, Dir, Montmorency County Public Libraries, 11901 Haymeadow Rd, Atlanta, MI, 49709. Tel: 989-785-3941. p. 1081
Haas, Nicole, Adult & Tech Serv Coordr, Librn III, West Babylon Public Library, 211 Rte 109, West Babylon, NY, 11704. Tel: 631-669-5445. p. 1661
Haas, Rob, Prog Serv Dir, Williamsburg Regional Library, 7770 Croaker Rd, Williamsburg, VA, 23188-7064. Tel: 757-741-3371. p. 2353
Haase, Lynne, Br Mgr, Free Library of Philadelphia, Logan Branch, 1333 Wagner Ave, Philadelphia, PA, 19141-2916. Tel: 215-685-9156. p. 1979
Habashy, Tarek, Dr, Managing Dir, Schlumberger-Doll Research Center, One Hampshire St, Cambridge, MA, 02139. Tel: 617-768-2081. p. 1008
Habata, Michael, Cat Librn, Pierce College Library, 6201 Winnetka Ave, Woodland Hills, CA, 91371. Tel: 818-710-2834. p. 260
Haberkern, Michaela, Exec Dir, Aurora Public Library District, 101 S River St, Aurora, IL, 60506. Tel: 630-264-4100. p. 539
Haberli, Joann, Dir, Louise Adelia Read Memorial Library, 104 Read St, Hancock, NY, 13783. Tel: 607-637-2519. p. 1544
Habermacher, Caroline, Dir, Sabinal Public Library, 312 N Center St, Sabinal, TX, 78881. Tel: 830-988-2911. p. 2235
Habermahl, Susan, Children's Prog, Three Hills Municipal Library, 135 Third Ave S, Three Hills, AB, T0M 2A0, CANADA. Tel: 403-443-2360. p. 2557
Haberman, David, Co-Dir, Head, Student Serv, University of North Dakota, Thormodsgard Law Library, 215 Centennial Dr, Grand Forks, ND, 58202. Tel: 701-777-2204. p. 1734
Habib, Faten, Mrs, Ref Librn, Moorpark College Library, 7075 Campus Rd, Moorpark, CA, 93021-1695. Tel: 805-553-1472. p. 180
Hable, Liz, Br Mgr, Pulaski County Library District, Richland Library, 111 Camden Ave, Richland, MO, 65556. Tel: 573-993-4355. p. 1286
Habousha, Racheline, Dir, Albert Einstein College of Medicine, Jack & Pearl Resnick Campus, 1300 Morris Park Ave, Bronx, NY, 10461-1924. Tel: 718-430-3115. p. 1497
Hache, Nicole, Coordr, Champlain Regional College at Saint-Lambert, 900 Riverside Dr, Saint Lambert, QC, J4P 3P2, CANADA. Tel: 450-672-7360. p. 2734
Hachey, Judy, Br Mgr, Albemarle Regional Library, Elizabeth Sewell Parker Memorial Library, 213 E Main St, Murfreesboro, NC, 27855. Tel: 252-398-4494. p. 1727
Hachmeister, Gretchen, Exec Dir, Hotchkiss Library of Sharon, Inc, Ten Upper Main St, Sharon, CT, 06069. Tel: 860-364-5041. p. 336
Hack, Janie, Librn, Thompson Hine LLP, Discovery Place, 10050 Innovation Dr, Ste 400, Dayton, OH, 45342-4934. Tel: 937-443-6823. p. 1780
Hacke, Misha, Supv Librn, Pierce County Library System, Steilacoom Branch, 2950 Steilacoom Blvd, Steilacoom, WA, 98388. Tel: 253-548-3313. p. 2386
Hacker, Hannah, Archives Asst, University of Wisconsin-Green Bay, 2420 Nicolet Dr, Green Bay, WI, 54311-7001. p. 2439
Hacker, Susan, Head, Ref Serv, Willingboro Public Library, Willingboro Town Ctr, 220 Willingboro Pkwy, Willingboro, NJ, 08046. Tel: 609-877-0476, 609-877-6668. p. 1455
Hackett, Doris, Head, Circ, Mount Vernon Public Library, 28 S First Ave, Mount Vernon, NY, 10550. Tel: 914-668-1840. p. 1575
Hackett, Jill, Bus Mgr, Bernardsville Public Library, One Anderson Hill Rd, Bernardsville, NJ, 07924. Tel: 908-766-0118. p. 1390
Hackett, Loren, Med Librn, Hillcrest Hospital, 6780 Mayfield Rd, Mayfield Heights, OH, 44124. Tel: 440-312-3250. p. 1800
Hackman, Heather, Libr Dir, Nashua Public Library, 220 Brasher St, Nashua, IA, 50658. Tel: 641-435-4635. p. 772
Hackman, Maxwell, Instruction & Outreach Librn, Daytona State College Library, Bldg 115, Rm 314, 1200 W International Speedway Blvd, Daytona Beach, FL, 32114. Tel: 386-506-3521. p. 392
Hackman, Timothy, Assoc Dir, Pub Serv, University of Maryland, Baltimore County, 1000 Hilltop Circle, Baltimore, MD, 21250. Tel: 410-455-2356. p. 958
Hackney, Carrie, Head Librn, Howard University Libraries, Divinity, 2929 Van Ness St NW, 4th Flr, Washington, DC, 20017. Tel: 202-806-0768. p. 369
Hackney, Carrie M, Assoc Dir, Howard University Libraries, 500 Howard Pl NW, Ste 203, Washington, DC, 20059. Tel: 202-806-0768. p. 368
Hackney, Sharon, Head, Curric Mat(s) Ctr, Head, Media Libr, Truman State University, 100 E Normal, Kirksville, MO, 63501-4211. Tel: 660-785-7366. p. 1259
Haddad, April, Dir, Libr Serv, Justice Institute of British Columbia Library, 715 McBride Blvd, New Westminster, BC, V3L 5T4, CANADA. Tel: 604-528-5594. p. 2572
Haddad, Stephen, Electronic Res Librn, Carroll College, 1601 N Benton Ave, Helena, MT, 59625. Tel: 406-447-4340. p. 1295

Haddaway, Wade, Libr Tech, University of Washington Libraries, Tacoma Library, 1900 Commerce St, Box 358460, Tacoma, WA, 98402-3100. Tel: 253-692-5746. p. 2382
Hadden, Missy, Dir, Latt Maxcy Memorial Library, 15 N Magnolia Ave, Frostproof, FL, 33843. Tel: 863-635-7857. p. 405
Haddin, Amanda, Law Librn, Jefferson County Law Library, Jefferson County Court House, Ste 530, 716 Richard Arrington Jr Blvd N, Birmingham, AL, 35203. Tel: 205-325-5628. p. 8
Haddix, Megan, Dir, Glasgow City-County Library, 408 Third Ave S, Glasgow, MT, 59230. Tel: 406-228-2731. p. 1293
Haddock, Kristin, Libr Dir, Bartlett-Carnegie Sapulpa Public Library, 27 W Dewey Ave, Sapulpa, OK, 74066. Tel: 918-248-5978. p. 1861
Haddox, Lisa, Br Mgr, Saint Louis County Library, Weber Road Branch, 4444 Weber Rd, Saint Louis, MO, 63123-6744. Tel: 314-994-3300, Ext 3950. p. 1274
Hadeler, Kurt, Dir, Mahwah Public Library, 100 Ridge Rd, Mahwah, NJ, 07430. Tel: 201-529-7323, Ext 221. p. 1415
Hadfield, Michael, Ch Serv, Corinth Free Library, 89 Main St, Corinth, NY, 12822. Tel: 518-654-6913. p. 1522
Hadidi, Rachel, Dir, Libr Serv, Lake Dallas Public Library, 302 S Shady Shores Rd, Lake Dallas, TX, 75065-3609. Tel: 940-497-3566. p. 2208
Hadler, John, Sr Law Librn, Tenth Judicial District Supreme Court Law Library, John P Cohalan, Jr Courthouse, 400 Carleton Ave, 4th Flr, Central Islip, NY, 11722. Tel: 631-740-3961. p. 1516
Hadley, Amber, Youth Serv Coordr, Brandywine Community Library, 60 Tower Dr, Topton, PA, 19562-1301. Tel: 610-682-7115. p. 2013
Hadley, Becky, Readers' Advisor Librn, Marshall Public Library, 113 S Garfield Ave, Pocatello, ID, 83204. Tel: 208-232-1263. p. 529
Hadley, Beth, Libr Dir, Sinclairville Free Library, 15 Main St, Sinclairville, NY, 14782. Tel: 716-962-5885. p. 1641
Hadley, Diana, Libr Dir, Molalla Public Library, 201 E Fifth St, Molalla, OR, 97038. Tel: 503-829-2593. p. 1887
Hadley, Diana L, Librn, Douglas County Law Library, Justice Bldg, Rm 305, 1036 SE Douglas Ave, Roseburg, OR, 97470. Tel: 541-440-4341. p. 1895
Hadley, Elizabeth, Interim Library Coord, Rappahannock Community College Library, 12745 College Dr, Glenns, VA, 23149. Tel: 804-758-6710. p. 2321
Hadley, Elizabeth, Dir, Richmond County Public Library, Rappahannock Community College Library Ctr, 52 Campus Dr, Warsaw, VA, 22572. Tel: 804-333-6710. p. 2352
Hadley, Heather, Dep Dir, Port Moody Public Library, 100 Newport Dr, Port Moody, BC, V3H 5C3, CANADA. Tel: 604-469-4575. p. 2574
Hadley, Jay, Library Contact, Multnomah County Library, Hillsdale, 1525 SW Sunset Blvd, Portland, OR, 97239. p. 1892
Hadsell, Darlene, Cat, Indian River County Library System, 1600 21st St, Vero Beach, FL, 32960. Tel: 772-770-5060. p. 452
Haduch, Diann, Head, Children's Servx, Reuben Hoar Library, 35 Shattuck St, Littleton, MA, 01460. Tel: 978-540-2600. p. 1029
Hady, Maureen, Coordr, Tech Serv, J Sargeant Reynolds Community College Library, Goochland Campus-Library & Information Services, 1851 Dickinson Rd, Goochland, VA, 23285. Tel: 804-523-5442. p. 2341
Haessly, Lisa, Br Coordr, Marathon County Public Library, Marathon City Branch, 515 Washington St, Marathon, WI, 54448. Tel: 715-443-2775. p. 2486
Hafemeister, Richard, Dir, Operations, The Texas State Museum of Asian Cultures & Educational Center, 1809 N Chaparral, Corpus Christi, TX, 78401. Tel: 361-881-8827. p. 2161
Hafer, Amy, Dir, Hastings Public Library, 314 N Denver Ave, Hastings, NE, 68901. Tel: 402-461-2346. p. 1317
Haferkamp, Jennifer, Dir, Nineveh Public Library of Colesville Township, 3029 NY State Hwy 7, Nineveh, NY, 13813. Tel: 607-693-1858. p. 1606
Haff, Sally E, Med Librn, Memorial Healthcare System, 3501 Johnson St, Hollywood, FL, 33021. Tel: 954-265-5840. p. 409
Haffer, Michelle, Ch Serv, Webster Groves Public Library, 301 E Lockwood Ave, Webster Groves, MO, 63119-3102. Tel: 314-961-7262. p. 1286
Haffner, Michelle, Community Engagement Supvr, Richland Public Library, 955 Northgate Dr, Richland, WA, 99352. Tel: 509-942-7665. p. 2375
Hafner, Joseph, Assoc Dean, Coll Serv, McGill University Libraries, McLennan Library Bldg, 3459 McTavish St, Montreal, QC, H3A 0C9, CANADA. Tel: 514-398-4788. p. 2726
Hafner, Kay, Libr Dir, Hudson Falls Free Library, 220 Main St, Hudson Falls, NY, 12839. Tel: 518-747-6406. p. 1549
Hagan, Ashley, Spec Projects Librn, Fort Smith Public Library, 3201 Rogers Ave, Fort Smith, AR, 72903. Tel: 479-783-0229. p. 96
Hagan, Brandon, Circ Mgr, Pub Serv, Daviess County Public Library, 2020 Frederica St, Owensboro, KY, 42301. Tel: 270-684-0211. p. 871
Hagan, Judy, Dir, Atkinson Public Library, 210 W State St, Atkinson, NE, 68713. Tel: 402-925-2855. p. 1306
Hagan, Tara, Dir, Thomas University, 1501 Millpond Rd, Thomasville, GA, 31792. Tel: 229-226-1621, Ext 1107. p. 500
Hagar, Angela, ILL, Saint Francis Xavier University, 3080 Martha Dr, Antigonish, NS, B2G 2W5, CANADA. Tel: 902-867-2421. p. 2615
Hage, Anne, Adult Serv, Dir, Huntington Woods Public Library, 26415 Scotia Rd, Huntington Woods, MI, 48070. Tel: 248-543-9720. p. 1118
Hagedorn, Connie, Tech Serv Librn, Blair Public Library, 2233 Civic Dr, Blair, NE, 68008. Tel: 402-426-3617. p. 1308
Hagedorn, Jeff, Syst Mgr, Medical College of Wisconsin Libraries, Health Research Ctr, 3rd Flr, 8701 Watertown Plank Rd, Milwaukee, WI, 53226-0509. Tel: 414-955-8515. p. 2459
Hagel, Delphine, Head Librn, Sisseton Wahpeton College Library, Agency Village, PO Box 689, Sisseton, SD, 57262-0698. Tel: 605-742-1104. p. 2083
Hagelaar, David, Assoc Chief Librn, University of Toronto Libraries, John M Kelly Library, University of St Michael's College, 81 St Mary St, Toronto, ON, M5S 1J4, CANADA. Tel: 416-926-7250. p. 2699
Hagelberger, Cindy S, Ref Serv Librn, Genesee Community College, One College Rd, Batavia, NY, 14020-9704. Tel: 585-343-0055, Ext 6231. p. 1490
Hageman, Cheryl, Dir, Plainville Memorial Library, 200 SW First St, Plainville, KS, 67663. Tel: 785-434-2786. p. 832
Hagen, Geraldine, Tech Serv, United States Marine Corps, Seaside Square Library, San Onofre, Bldg 51093, Camp Pendleton, CA, 92055. Tel: 760-725-7325. p. 126
Hagen, Kimberly, Br Mgr, Chicago Public Library, Hall, 4801 S Michigan Ave, Chicago, IL, 60615. Tel: 312-747-2541. p. 556
Hagen, Lori, Ref Librn, Allegheny County Law Library, 921 City-County Bldg, 414 Grant St, Pittsburgh, PA, 15219-2543. Tel: 412-350-5353. p. 1990
Hagen, Sharon, Librn/Mgr, Enchant Community Library, 116 Center St, Enchant, AB, T0K 0V0, CANADA. Tel: 403-739-3835. p. 2539
Hagenhoff, Betty, Asst Dir, Missouri River Regional Library, 214 Adams St, Jefferson City, MO, 65101. Tel: 573-634-2464. p. 1252
Hager, Anne, Genealogy Serv, Crawford County Public Library, 203 Indiana Ave, English, IN, 47118. Tel: 812-338-2606. p. 681
Hager, Gregory M, Dir, Willard Library of Evansville, 21 First Ave, Evansville, IN, 47710-1294. Tel: 812-425-4309. p. 682
Hager, Jackson, Librn Supvr, Lakeland Public Library, 100 Lake Morton Dr, Lakeland, FL, 33801-5375. Tel: 863-834-4280. p. 417
Hager, Jackson, Librn Supvr, Lakeland Public Library, Larry R Jackson Branch, 1700 N Florida Ave, Lakeland, FL, 33805. Tel: 863-834-4288. p. 417
Hagerman, David, Librn, Elgin Mental Health Center Library, 750 S State St, Elgin, IL, 60123-7692. Tel: 847-742-1040, Ext 3437. p. 584
Hagerman, Naomi, Libr Dir, Cowen Public Library, 47 Mill St, Cowen, WV, 26206. Tel: 304-226-5332. p. 2401
Hagerman, Phyllis, Head Librn, Lockwood Public Library, 721 Main St, Lockwood, MO, 65682. Tel: 417-232-4204. p. 1260
Haggard, Matthew, Syst Instruction Librn, Nichols College, 127 Center Rd, Dudley, MA, 01571. Tel: 508-213-2437. p. 1015
Haggard, Nancy, Asst Dir, Pub Serv, Westfield Washington Public Library, 17400 Westfield Blvd, Unit A, Westfield, IN, 46074-9283. Tel: 317-896-9391. p. 726
Haggarty, Penny, Acq Librn, Thompson Rivers University, 900 McGill Rd, Kamloops, BC, V2C 5N3, CANADA. Tel: 250-828-5000. p. 2568
Haggerty, Kenneth, Dr, Coordr, Digital Initiatives, University Libraries, University of Memphis, 3785 Norriswood Ave, Memphis, TN, 38152. Tel: 901-678-4465. p. 2115
Haggerty, Lynnette, Tech Serv Librn, Ardmore Public Library, 320 E St NW, Ardmore, OK, 73401. Tel: 580-223-8290. p. 1840
Hagins, Marla, Asst Librn, Martin County Library, 200 N Saint Mary, Stanton, TX, 79782. Tel: 432-756-2472. p. 2245
Hagins, Nancy R, Librn, Freeport Area Library, 428 Market St, Freeport, PA, 16229-1122. Tel: 724-295-3616. p. 1934
Hagle-Kiper, Judy, Dir, Lee Public Library, 312 W Pacific, Gladewater, TX, 75647-2135. Tel: 903-845-2640. p. 2185
Hagman, Jess, Librn, University of Illinois Library at Urbana-Champaign, Social Sciences, Health & Education Library, 101 Main Library, MC-522, 1408 W Gregory Dr, Urbana, IL, 61801. Tel: 217-333-3005. p. 656
Hagman, Sherry, Circ Mgr, Hancock County Public Library, 1210 Madison St, Hawesville, KY, 42348. Tel: 270-927-6760. p. 858
Hagopian, David, Sr Librn, Los Angeles Public Library System, Platt Branch Library, 23600 Victory Blvd, Woodland Hills, CA, 91367. Tel: 818-340-9386. p. 165
Hagstrom, Kristi, Dir, Ord Township Library, 1718 M St, Ord, NE, 68862. Tel: 308-728-3012. p. 1331
Hague, Nomi, Asst Dir, Cross' Mills Public Library, 4417 Old Post Rd, Charlestown, RI, 02813. Tel: 401-364-6211. p. 2030
Hague, Nomi, Ch, Cranston Public Library, Auburn Branch, 396 Pontiac Ave, Cranston, RI, 02910-3322. Tel: 401-781-6116. p. 2031
Hahn, Christopher, Libr Dir, Sturgis Public Library, 1040 Harley-Davidson Way, Ste 101, Sturgis, SD, 57785. Tel: 605-347-2624. p. 2083
Hahn, Diane, Info Serv Librn, Northampton Community College, College Ctr, 3835 Green Pond Rd, Bethlehem, PA, 18020-7599. Tel: 610-861-3360. p. 1912
Hahn, Donna, Dir, Faith Memorial Library, 122 N Garrison Ave, Wallace, NE, 69169. Tel: 308-387-4537. p. 1339
Hahn, Katie, Libr Dir, Brimfield Public Library District, 111 S Galena Ave, Brimfield, IL, 61517. Tel: 309-446-9575. p. 545
Hahn, Lani, Adult Serv, Sr Librn, Haltom City Public Library, 4809 Haltom Rd, Haltom City, TX, 76117-3622. Tel: 817-222-7770. p. 2187
Hahn, Michelle, Cat, Salisbury University, 1101 Camden Ave, Salisbury, MD, 21801-6863. Tel: 410-543-6130. p. 976

Haliotis, John, Head, Tech, Round Lake Area Public Library District, 906 Hart Rd, Round Lake, IL, 60073. Tel: 847-546-7060. p. 643
Hall, Amanda, Access Serv, Georgetown University, Dahlgren Memorial Library, Preclinical Science Bldg GM-7, 3900 Reservoir Rd NW, Washington, DC, 20007. Tel: 202-687-1013. p. 368
Hall, Amanda, Interim Librn, Northwest College, 231 W Sixth St, Powell, WY, 82435. Tel: 307-754-6207. p. 2497
Hall, Amy, Librn, National Louis University Library, 18 S Michigan Ave, 3rd Flr, Chicago, IL, 60603. Tel: 312-261-3565. p. 565
Hall, Andrea, Librn, George Brown College of Applied Arts & Technology, Bldg C, 3rd Flr, Rm C330, 160 Kendal Ave, Toronto, ON, M5R 1M3, CANADA. Tel: 416-415-5000, Ext 4635. p. 2689
Hall, Angela C, Librn, Valencia College, Downtown Campus Library, Dr Phillips Academic Commons, 2nd Flr, Rm 265, 500 W Livingston St, Orlando, FL, 32801. Tel: 407-235-3720, 407-582-3504. p. 432
Hall, Angie, Librn, Susquehanna County Historical Society & Free Library Association, Hallstead-Great Bend Branch Library, 135 Franklin Ave, Hallstead, PA, 18822. Tel: 570-879-2227. p. 1965
Hall, Anne, Br Mgr, Wissahickon Valley Public Library, Ambler Branch, 209 Race St, Ambler, PA, 19002. Tel: 215-646-1072. p. 1914
Hall, Benjamin, Dir, Williamsburg County Library, 215 N Jackson, Kingstree, SC, 29556-3319. Tel: 843-355-9486. p. 2063
Hall, Bernard, Libr Asst, Duplin County Library, Rose Hill Community Memorial Library, 113 S Walnut St, Rose Hill, NC, 28458. Tel: 910-289-2490. p. 1698
Hall, Beverly, Dir, Wabasha Public Library, 168 Alleghany Ave, Wabasha, MN, 55981-1286. Tel: 651-565-3927. p. 1206
Hall, Bill, Head, Access Serv, University of San Diego, Helen K & James S Copley Library, 5998 Alcala Park, San Diego, CA, 92110. p. 222
Hall, Brenda, Interim State Librn, State Library of Iowa, 1112 E Grand Ave, Des Moines, IA, 50319. Tel: 515-281-4105. p. 747
Hall, Brenda, Interim State Librn, State Library of Iowa, State Capitol Bldg, 2nd Flr, 1007 E Grand Ave, Des Moines, IA, 50319. Tel: 515-281-5124. p. 747
Hall, Brenda, Dir of Finance, Muskegon Area District Library, 4845 Airline Rd, Unit 5, Muskegon, MI, 49444-4503. Tel: 231-737-6248. p. 1136
Hall, Bruce, Music Librn, Sam Houston State University, 1830 Bobby K Marks Dr, Huntsville, TX, 77340. Tel: 936-294-4800. p. 2201
Hall, Carol, Admin Librn, Worth Public Library District, 6917 W 111th St, Worth, IL, 60482. Tel: 708-448-2855. p. 665
Hall, Cathy, Br Mgr, Wilmington Public Library, North Wilmington, 3400 N Market St, Wilmington, DE, 19802. Tel: 302-761-4290. p. 358
Hall, Christine, Cat Librn, Cranston Public Library, 140 Sockanosset Cross Rd, Cranston, RI, 02920-5539. Tel: 401-943-9080. p. 2031
Hall, Cindy, Librn, Mount Pearl Public Library, 65 Olympic Dr, Mount Pearl, NL, A1N 5H6, CANADA. Tel: 709-368-3603. p. 2608
Hall, Danielle, Archivist, Jackson County Historical Society, 112 W Lexington Ave, Independence, MO, 64050-3700. Tel: 816-252-7454. p. 1250
Hall, Darlene, Dir, Scott County Public Library, 108 S Main St, Scottsburg, IN, 47170. Tel: 812-752-2751. p. 717
Hall, Darsi, Libr Asst, Mayerthorpe Public Library, 4601 52nd St, Mayerthorpe, AB, T0E 1N0, CANADA. Tel: 780-786-2404. p. 2547
Hall, Debbie, Chief Exec Officer, Librn, North Kawartha Library, 175 Burleigh St, Apsley, ON, K0L 1A0, CANADA. Tel: 705-656-4333. p. 2628
Hall, DeBora, Asst Librn, American Sports Medicine Institute, 833 St Vincent's Dr, Ste 205, Birmingham, AL, 35205. Tel: 205-918-2130. p. 7
Hall, Deborah, Mgr, Grants & Spec Project, Arkansas State Library, 900 W Capitol, Ste 100, Little Rock, AR, 72201-3108. Tel: 501-682-2836. p. 100
Hall, Elizabeth, Dir, Stokely Memorial Library, 383 E Broadway St, Newport, TN, 37821-3105. Tel: 423-623-3832. p. 2122
Hall, Feechi, Univ Archivist, Clayton State University Library, 2000 Clayton State Blvd, Morrow, GA, 30260. Tel: 678-466-4333. p. 491
Hall, Gayle, Libr Office Mgr, Emmaus Public Library, 11 E Main St, Emmaus, PA, 18049. Tel: 610-965-9284. p. 1930
Hall, Grace, Youth Librn, Lee-Itawamba Library System, 219 N Madison St, Tupelo, MS, 38804-3899. Tel: 662-841-9027. p. 1233
Hall, Gretchen, Libr Dir, Whitefish Township Community Library, 7247 North M Hwy 123, Paradise, MI, 49768. Tel: 906-492-3500. p. 1140
Hall, Guy, Archivist, National Archives & Records Administration, 5780 Jonesboro Rd, Morrow, GA, 30260. Tel: 770-968-2100. p. 492
Hall, Haley, Ref & Instruction, Trident Technical College, Palmer Campus Learning Resources Center, 66 Columbus St, Charleston, SC, 29403. Tel: 843-722-5539. p. 2051
Hall, Holly, Dir, Deborah Rawson Memorial Library, Eight River Rd, Jericho, VT, 05465. Tel: 802-899-4962. p. 2287
Hall, Irene, Asst Dir, Youth Serv, Witherle Memorial Library, 41 School St, Castine, ME, 04421. Tel: 207-326-4375. p. 921
Hall, Jameliya, Mgr, Miami-Dade Public Library System, Lemon City Branch, 430 NE 61st St, Miami, FL, 33137. Tel: 305-757-0662. p. 423
Hall, Jamie, Librn, Alaska Vocational Technical Center, 809 Second Ave, Seward, AK, 99664. Tel: 907-224-6114. p. 50
Hall, Jayne, Librn, Inyo County Free Library, 168 N Edwards St, Independence, CA, 93526. Tel: 760-878-0260. p. 152
Hall, Jennie, Head, Adult Serv, McPherson Public Library, 214 W Marlin, McPherson, KS, 67460-4299. Tel: 620-245-2570. p. 825
Hall, Jeremiah, Digital Tech Librn, Bard College, One Library Rd, Annandale-on-Hudson, NY, 12504. Tel: 845-785-7675. p. 1487
Hall, Jeremy, Ch, Avoca Public Library, 213 N Elm St, Avoca, IA, 51521. Tel: 712-343-6358. p. 733
Hall, Joe, Br Mgr, Snyder County Libraries, McClure Community Library, Four Library Lane, McClure, PA, 17841. Tel: 570-658-7700. p. 2005
Hall, Jolene, Librn, Independence Public Library, 175 Monmouth St, Independence, OR, 97351. Tel: 503-838-1811. p. 1882
Hall, Jon, Dir, Libr Serv, Ranger College, 1100 College Circle, Ranger, TX, 76470-3298. Tel: 254-647-1414. p. 2230
Hall, Julie, Dir, Berryville Public Library, 104 Spring St, Berryville, AR, 72616. Tel: 870-423-2323. p. 91
Hall, Karen, Head, Children's Dept, Northern Cambria Public Library, 4200 Crawford Ave, Northern Cambria, PA, 15714-1399. Tel: 814-948-8222. p. 1972
Hall, Kate, Dir, Northbrook Public Library, 1201 Cedar Lane, Northbrook, IL, 60062-4581. Tel: 847-272-6224. p. 626
Hall, Kori, Mkt & Communications Mgr, Waukesha Public Library, 321 Wisconsin Ave, Waukesha, WI, 53186-4713. Tel: 262-524-3682. p. 2484
Hall, Lareese M, Dir of Libr, Colby College Libraries, 5100 Mayflower Hill, Waterville, ME, 04901. Tel: 207-859-5117. p. 945
Hall, Larry, VP, Academic Programs, Appalachian College Association, 7216 Jewel Bell Lane, Bristol, TN, 37620. Tel: 859-986-4584. p. 2775
Hall, Leigh, Dir of Libr, Chattahoochee Technical College Library, 980 S Cobb Dr, Marietta, GA, 30060. Tel: 770-528-6461. p. 488
Hall, Lina, Dir, Oak Harbor Public Library, 147 W Main St, Oak Harbor, OH, 43449-1344. Tel: 419-898-7001. p. 1810
Hall, Lois, Asst Dir, Otis Library & Museum, 48 N Main Rd, Otis, MA, 01253. Tel: 413-269-0100, Ext 117, 413-269-0109. p. 1045
Hall, Lorene, Librn, Juvenile Correction Center Library, 2220 E 600 North, Saint Anthony, ID, 83445. Tel: 208-624-3462. p. 530
Hall, Lynn, Librn, Ohoopee Regional Library System, Jeff Davis County Public Library, 189 E Jarman St, Hazlehurst, GA, 31539. Tel: 912-375-2386. p. 502
Hall, M Todd, Dir, Libr Serv, Austin Graduate School of Theology, 7640 Guadalupe St, Austin, TX, 78752-1333. Tel: 512-476-2772. p. 2138
Hall, Margaret, Assoc Dir, Southwestern Law School, Bullock Wilshire Bldg, 1st Flr, 3050 Wilshire Blvd, Los Angeles, CA, 90010. Tel: 213-738-5771. p. 168
Hall, Micayla, Dir, Stonington Free Library, 20 High St, Stonington, CT, 06378. Tel: 860-535-0658. p. 339
Hall, Michelle, Mgr, Libr Serv, Polsinelli, 900 W 48th St Pl, Kansas City, MO, 64112. Tel: 816-753-1000. p. 1257
Hall, Michelle, Mgr, Libr Serv, Polsinelli PC, 100 S Fourth St, Ste 1000, Saint Louis, MO, 63102. Tel: 314-889-8000. p. 1272
Hall, Missy, Libr Asst, Letcher County Public Library District, Jenkins Public, 9543 Hwy 805, Jenkins, KY, 41537. Tel: 606-832-4101. p. 877
Hall, Molly, Dir, Libr Serv, Marion & Ed Hughes Public Library, 2712 Nederland Ave, Nederland, TX, 77627. Tel: 409-722-1255. p. 2222
Hall, Nicole, Ch, John G McCullough Free Library, Two Main St N, North Bennington, VT, 05257. Tel: 802-447-7121. p. 2290
Hall, Patrice, Health Sci Librn, Lenoir-Rhyne University Libraries, 625 7th Ave NE, Hickory, NC, 28601. Tel: 828-328-7236. p. 1696
Hall, Patricia, Dir, Operations, Trenton Free Public Library, 120 Academy St, Trenton, NJ, 08608. Tel: 609-392-7188. p. 1448
Hall, Rand, Head, Ref & Adult Serv, Bedford Free Public Library, Seven Mudge Way, Bedford, MA, 01730. Tel: 781-275-9440. p. 987
Hall, Roland, Br Mgr, Community Library of the Shenango Valley, Stey-Nevant Branch Library, 1000 Roemer Blvd, Farrell, PA, 16121-1899. Tel: 724-983-2714. p. 2006
Hall, Russell, Ref & Instruction Librn, Penn State Behrend, 4951 College Dr, Erie, PA, 16563-4115. Tel: 814-898-6106. p. 1932
Hall, Sabra, Libr Dir, Gaines County Library, 704 Hobbs Hwy, Seminole, TX, 79360. Tel: 432-955-1007. p. 2242
Hall, Sarah J, Exec Dir, Washington County Museum of Fine Arts Library, 401 Museum Dr, Hagerstown, MD, 21740. Tel: 301-739-5727. p. 968
Hall, Sharon, Br Librn, Siouxland Libraries, Baltic Branch, 213 St Olaf Ave, Baltic, SD, 57003. Tel: 605-529-5415. p. 2082
Hall, Sharon, Br Librn, Siouxland Libraries, Brandon Branch, 305 S Splitrock Blvd, Brandon, SD, 57005-1651. Tel: 605-582-2390. p. 2082
Hall, Sharon, Br Librn, Siouxland Libraries, Garretson Branch, 649 Main Ave, Garretson, SD, 57030. Tel: 605-594-6619. p. 2082
Hall, Sharon, Br Librn, Siouxland Libraries, Valley Springs Branch, 401 Broadway Ave, Valley Springs, SD, 57068. Tel: 605-757-6264. p. 2082
Hall Slaminski, Candace, Dir, Info Serv, Michael Best & Friedrich LLP, 790 N Water St, Ste 2500, Milwaukee, WI, 53202. Tel: 414-277-3441. p. 2459
Hall, Stephanie, Dir, West Vancouver Memorial Library, 1950 Marine Dr, West Vancouver, BC, V7V 1J8, CANADA. Tel: 604-925-7400. p. 2584

Hall, Susan, Assoc Prof, Librn, Mississippi State University, Architecture, 121 Giles Hall, 889 Collegeview St, Mississippi State, MS, 39762. Tel: 662-325-2204. p. 1227
Hall, Suzanne, Libr Dir, Leicester Public Library & Local History Museum, 1136 Main St, Leicester, MA, 01524. Tel: 508-892-7020. p. 1027
Hall, Taffey, Archivist, Dir, Southern Baptist Historical Library & Archives, 901 Commerce St, Ste 400, Nashville, TN, 37203-3630. Tel: 615-244-0344. p. 2120
Hall, Tara, Dir, Marianne Beck Memorial Library, 112 W Central Ave, Howey in the Hills, FL, 34737. Tel: 352-324-0254. p. 410
Hall, Teresa, Dir, Loyal Public Library, 214 N Main St, Loyal, WI, 54446. Tel: 715-255-8189. p. 2448
Hall, Tessa, Adult Serv Spec, Programming, Osceola Public Library, 300 S Fillmore St, Osceola, IA, 50213. Tel: 641-342-2237. p. 775
Hall, Trish, Dir, Mendham Borough Library, Ten Hilltop Rd, Mendham, NJ, 07945. Tel: 973-543-4152. p. 1418
Hall, Wendy, Br Mgr, Boulder Public Library, Carnegie Branch for Local History, 1125 Pine St, Boulder, CO, 80302-4024. Tel: 303-441-4096. p. 266
Hall, William, Libr Mgr, New York Public Library - Astor, Lenox & Tilden Foundations, Grand Central Library, 135 E 46th St, New York, NY, 10017. Tel: 212-621-0670. p. 1595
Hall, Wyolanda, Br Mgr, Shreve Memorial Library, Wallette Branch, 363 Hearne Ave, Shreveport, LA, 71103. Tel: 318-425-3630. p. 910
Hall-Bennett, Vanessa, Dir, Havana Public Library District, 201 W Adams St, Havana, IL, 62644-1321. Tel: 309-543-4701. p. 598
Hall-Louden, Janet, Bus Mgr, Aurora Public Library District, 414 Second St, Aurora, IN, 47001-1384. Tel: 812-926-0646. p. 669
Halla-Sindelar, Jennifer, Br Mgr, Saint Louis Public Library, Carondelet, 6800 Michigan Ave, Saint Louis, MO, 63111. Tel: 314-752-9224. p. 1275
Hallam, Karen, Librn, Jonesboro Public Library, 412 S Main St, Jonesboro, IL, 62952. Tel: 618-833-8121. p. 603
Hallam, Lindsay, Dir, Learning Res, Alaska Christian College, 35109 Royal Pl, Soldotna, AK, 99669. Tel: 907-260-7422. p. 51
Hallau, Lauren, Academic Services Librn, University of Saint Thomas, Charles J Keffer Library, 1000 LaSalle Ave, MOH 206, Minneapolis, MN, 55403. Tel: 651-962-4642. p. 1203
Hallberg, Betty, Br Assoc, Modoc County Library, Lookout Branch, Lookout Park, Lookout, CA, 96054. Tel: 530-294-5776. p. 116
Hallenberg, Leigh, Br Mgr, Mid-Continent Public Library, North Oak Branch, 8700 N Oak Trafficway, Kansas City, MO, 64155. Tel: 816-436-4385. p. 1251
Haller, Amber, Dir, Commun Serv, Imperial Public Library, 200 W Ninth St, Imperial, CA, 92251. Tel: 760-355-1332. p. 152
Haller, Andrea, Cat, Tech Serv, Toledo Public Library, 173 NW Seventh St, Toledo, OR, 97391. Tel: 541-336-3132. p. 1900
Hallerduff, Martinique, Chair, Inf Literacy Program Coord, Oakton College Library, 1600 E Golf Rd, Rm 1406, Des Plaines, IL, 60016. Tel: 847-635-1642, 847-635-1644. p. 578
Hallett, Dominique, Govt Doc Librn, Arkansas State University, 322 University Loop Circle, State University, AR, 72401. Tel: 870-972-3077. p. 111
Hallex, Anna, Children's/Young Adult Serv, Foley Public Library, 319 E Laurel Ave, Foley, AL, 36535. Tel: 251-943-7665. p. 17
Halley, Geeta, Asst Dir, Round Rock Public Library, 200 E Liberty Ave, Round Rock, TX, 78664. Tel: 512-218-7018. p. 2234
Halley, Susi, Asst Dir, Greenville Public Library, 520 Sycamore St, Greenville, OH, 45331-1438. Tel: 937-548-3915. p. 1788
Halley, Susie, Dir, Greenville Public Library, 520 Sycamore St, Greenville, OH, 45331-1438. Tel: 937-548-3915. p. 1788
Hallfrisch, Colleen, Metadata Librn, University of Wisconsin Oshkosh, 801 Elmwood Ave, Oshkosh, WI, 54901. Tel: 920-424-7369. p. 2467
Halliday, Annie, Libr & Archives Mgr, Bucks County Historical Society, 84 S Pine St, Doylestown, PA, 18901-4999. Tel: 215-345-0210, Ext 126. p. 1927
Halliday, Beth, Head, Children's Servx, South Orange Public Library, 65 Scotland Rd, South Orange, NJ, 07079. Tel: 973-762-0230. p. 1443
Halliday, Karen, Librn, Georgian College, One Georgian Dr, Barrie, ON, L4M 3X9, CANADA. Tel: 705-728-1968. p. 2630
Halligan, Dan, Br Operations Supvr, University of Washington Libraries, Foster Business, Paccar Hall, 1st Flr, Box 353224, Seattle, WA, 98195-3224. Tel: 206-543-4360. p. 2382
Halling, Amy, Libr Dir, Hanston City Library, 105 N Logan, Hanston, KS, 67849-9409. Tel: 620-623-2798. p. 811
Hallman, Layce, Libr Office Mgr, Levy County Public Library System, 7871 NE 90th St, Bronson, FL, 32621. Tel: 352-486-5552. p. 387
Hallmark, Norma, Dir, Allen Memorial Public Library, 121 E Blackbourn St, Hawkins, TX, 75765. Tel: 903-769-2241. p. 2188
Halloran, Jude, Dir, Highland Township Public Library, 444 Beach Farm Circle, Highland, MI, 48357. Tel: 248-887-2218, Ext 110. p. 1115
Hallowell, Susie, Sci Ref Spec, St John's River Water Management District, 4049 Reid St, Palatka, FL, 32177. Tel: 386-329-4190. p. 434
Halpern, Stefanie, Dr, Dir, Archives, YIVO Institute for Jewish Research, 15 W 16th St, New York, NY, 10011. p. 1605
Halquist, Carrie, Info Literacy Librn, User Serv Librn, Huntington University, 2303 College Ave, Huntington, IN, 46750. Tel: 260-359-4060. p. 690
Halquist, Carrie, Student Engagement Librn, Grace College & Grace Theological Seminary, 921 Connection Circle, Winona Lake, IN, 46590. Tel: 574-372-5100, Ext 6293. p. 727
Halsey, Erica, Libr Coord, Gateway Community & Technical College, 790 Thomas More Pkwy, Edgewood, KY, 41017. Tel: 859-442-4162. p. 854
Halstead, Anthony, Libr Dir, Napa County Library, 580 Coombs St, Napa, CA, 94559-3396. Tel: 707-253-4241. p. 182
Halstead, Charity, Ch, Grundy County-Jewett Norris Library, 1331 Main St, Trenton, MO, 64683. Tel: 660-359-3577. p. 1282
Halstead, Johnnie, Librn, Rick Warren Memorial Public Library District, 114 S Fourth St, Elkville, IL, 62932-1097. Tel: 618-568-1843. p. 584
Halstead, Kyle, Tech Serv, Delaware County District Library, 84 E Winter St, Delaware, OH, 43015. Tel: 740-362-3861. p. 1781
Halsted, Pat, Librn, Searcy County Library, 202 E Main St, Marshall, AR, 72650. Tel: 870-448-2420. p. 104
Halt, Jasper, Libr Mgr, Florence Community Library, 778 N Main St, Florence, AZ, 85132. Tel: 520-868-8311. p. 61
Halter, Amber, Asst Libr Dir, Spring Hill Public Library, 144 Kedron Pkwy, Spring Hill, TN, 37174. Tel: 931-486-2932. p. 2127
Halter, Cheryl, Fiscal Officer, North Baltimore Public Library, 230 N Main St, North Baltimore, OH, 45872. Tel: 419-257-3621. p. 1809
Halter, Joe, IT Coordr, Glen Ellyn Public Library, 400 Duane St, Glen Ellyn, IL, 60137-4508. Tel: 630-469-0879. p. 593
Halter, Linda, Libr Asst, Ser/Circ Coordr, Western Wyoming Community College, 2500 College Dr, Rock Springs, WY, 82902. Tel: 307-382-1703. p. 2498
Halterman, Youlanda, Digital Technology & Web Supervisor, Loyola-Notre Dame Library, Inc, 200 Winston Ave, Baltimore, MD, 21212. Tel: 410-617-6801. p. 954
Halvorsen, Alice, Libr Asst, Dennis Memorial Library Association, 1020 Old Bass River Rd, Dennis, MA, 02638. Tel: 508-385-2255. p. 1014
Halvorsen, Betsy, Libr Dir, Woodward Memorial Library, Seven Wolcott St, LeRoy, NY, 14482. Tel: 585-768-8300. p. 1562
Ham, Amanda, Br Mgr, Greater Clarks Hill Regional Library System, Harlem Branch, 145 N Louisville St, Harlem, GA, 30814. Tel: 706-650-5009. p. 478
Ham, April, Research Librn, University of San Francisco, Zief Law Library, 2101 Fulton St, San Francisco, CA, 94117-1004. Tel: 415-422-6679. p. 230
Ham, Jenny, Ref & Info Serv Librn, Pennsylvania State University - Dickinson School of Law, 214 Lewis Katz Bldg, University Park, PA, 16802. Tel: 814-863-0885. p. 2015
Hamad, Kari, Head, Children's Servx, Wallingford Public Library, 200 N Main St, Wallingford, CT, 06492. Tel: 203-284-6436. p. 342
Haman, Kristi, Mgr, Main Libr, Meridian Library District, 1326 W Cherry Lane, Meridian, ID, 83642. Tel: 208-888-4451. p. 525
Haman, Muir, Dir, Lunenburg Public Library, 1023 Massachusetts Ave, Lunenburg, MA, 01462. Tel: 978-582-4140. p. 1030
Hamann, Corinna, Head, Tech Serv, Somers Library, Rte 139 & Reis Park, Somers, NY, 10589. Tel: 914-232-5717. p. 1642
Hamann, Jeanne, Br Mgr, Free Library of Philadelphia, Charles Santore Branch, 932 S Seventh St, Philadelphia, PA, 19147-2932. Tel: 215-686-1766. p. 1980
Hambleton, Marlene, Libr Dir, Montgomery Town Library, 86 Mountain Rd, Montgomery Center, VT, 05471. Tel: 802-326-3113. p. 2289
Hambley, Douglas, Librn, Linn-Benton Community College Library, 6500 SW Pacific Blvd, Albany, OR, 97321-3799. Tel: 541-917-4470. p. 1871
Hamblin, Julie, Libr Mgr, Bowden Public Library, 2101 20th Ave, Bay # 2, Bowden, AB, T0M 0K0, CANADA. Tel: 403-224-3688. p. 2524
Hambrick, Kathe, Exec Dir, Amistad Research Center, Tulane University, Tilton Hall, 6823 St Charles Ave, New Orleans, LA, 70118. Tel: 504-862-3222. p. 900
Hambrick, Lisa, Br Mgr, White County Regional Library System, Pangburn Public, 914 Main St, Pangburn, AR, 72121. Tel: 501-728-4612. p. 110
Hambrick, Miranda, Librn, Lena Cagle Public Library, 401 Alabama Ave, Bridgeport, AL, 35740. Tel: 256-495-2259. p. 10
Hambright, Tom, Sr Librn, Monroe County Public Library, 700 Fleming St, Key West, FL, 33040. Tel: 305-292-3595. p. 414
Hamburg, Chris, Adult Serv Coordr, Lester Public Library, 1001 Adams St, Two Rivers, WI, 54241. Tel: 920-793-7113. p. 2482
Hamby, Alex, Asst Library Dir, Collections & Systemwide Programs, Henrico County Public Library, 1700 N Parham Rd, Henrico, VA, 23229. Tel: 804-501-1900. p. 2325
Hamdan, Kareemah, Libr Mgr, Henrico County Public Library, Varina Area Library, 1875 New Market Rd, Henrico, VA, 23231. Tel: 804-501-1980. p. 2326
Hamdinero, Michael, Libr Tech, Canada Department of Justice Montreal Headquarters Library, East Tower, 9th flr, No 200 Quest boul Rene-Levesque W, Montreal, QC, H2Z 1X4, CANADA. Tel: 514-283-6674, 514-283-8739. p. 2721
Hamel, Alisha, Dir, US Army Transportation Museum Library, Besson Hall, 300 Washington Blvd, Fort Eustis, VA, 23604. Tel: 757-878-1115. p. 2319
Hamelers, Rachel, Head, Pub Outreach & Info Literacy Serv, Ref Serv Librn, Muhlenberg College, 2400 Chew St, Allentown, PA, 18104-5586. Tel: 484-664-3601. p. 1905

Hamelin, Eddy, Br Mgr, Monterey County Free Libraries, Carmel Valley Branch, 65 W Carmel Valley Rd, Carmel Valley, CA, 93924. Tel: 831-659-2377. p. 172
Hamerly, Don W, Dir, Sch Libr Media Prog, Dominican University, Crown Library 300, 7900 W Division St, River Forest, IL, 60305. Tel: 708-524-6845. p. 2784
Hamersky, Steven L, Dir, Newman University, 3100 McCormick Ave, Wichita, KS, 67213. Tel: 316-942-4291, Ext 2108. p. 843
Hames, Jill, Dir, James L Hamner Public Library, 16351 Dunn St, Amelia, VA, 23002. Tel: 804-561-4559. p. 2304
Hamfeldt, Sarah, Ref (Info Servs), Jefferson-Madison Regional Library, 201 E Market St, Charlottesville, VA, 22902-5287. Tel: 434-979-7151, Ext 6671. p. 2309
Hamid, Aisha, Librn, Connecticut Clearinghouse Library, 334 Farmington Ave, Plainville, CT, 06062. Tel: 860-793-9791. p. 333
Hamidzada, Judanne, Youth Serv Coordr, Community Libraries of Providence, PO Box 9267, Providence, RI, 02940. Tel: 401-467-2700, Ext 1611. p. 2038
Hamidzadeh, Babak, Interim Dean of Libr, University of Maryland Libraries, College Park, MD, 20742. Tel: 301-405-9128. p. 962
Hamidzadeh, Babak A, Interim Dean of Libr, University of Maryland Libraries, Theodore R McKeldin Library, 7649 Library Lane, College Park, MD, 20742-7011. Tel: 301-314-9046. p. 962
Hamiel, Michelle, Chief Opearting Officer, Pub Serv, Prince George's County Memorial Library System, 9601 Capital Lane, Largo, MD, 20774. Tel: 301-699-3500. p. 970
Hamill, Lois, Univ Archivist, Northern Kentucky University, University Dr, Highland Heights, KY, 41099. Tel: 859-572-5863. p. 859
Hamilton, Amber, Circ Librn, Silver Lake Library, 203 Railroad St, Silver Lake, KS, 66539. Tel: 785-582-5141. p. 836
Hamilton, Amy, Access Serv Coordr, Franklin College, 101 Branigin Blvd, Franklin, IN, 46131-2623. Tel: 317-738-8164. p. 685
Hamilton, Andrea, Mgr, Davis, Graham & Stubbs, 1550 17th St, Ste 500, Denver, CO, 80202. Tel: 303-892-7306. p. 275
Hamilton, Andrew, Educ Librn, Health Science & Research Servs Librn, Oregon Health & Science University Library, 3181 SW Sam Jackson Park Rd, MC LIB, Portland, OR, 97239-3098. Tel: 503-494-7527. p. 1893
Hamilton, Angela, Chief Librn, University of Toronto Libraries, Scarborough UTSC Library, Academic Resource Ctr, 1265 Military Trail, Scarborough, ON, M1C 1A4, CANADA. Tel: 416-208-5174. p. 2700
Hamilton, Barbara, Mgr, Info Serv, Institute for Defense Analyses, 805 Bunn Dr, Princeton, NJ, 08540. Tel: 609-924-4600. p. 1436
Hamilton, Becky, Librn, Ninilchik Community Library, 15850 Sterling Hwy, Ninilchik, AK, 99639. Tel: 907-567-3333. p. 49
Hamilton, Blaine, Campus Librn, Mohave Community College Library, Bullhead City Campus, 3400 Hwy 95, Bullhead City, AZ, 86442-8204. Tel: 928-758-2420. p. 64
Hamilton, Brandy, Libr Mgr, Wake County Public Library System, East Regional Library, 946 Steeple Square Ct, Knightdale, NC, 27545. Tel: 919-217-5300. p. 1711
Hamilton, Cheryl, Libr Tech, Western Nebraska Community College Library, 1601 E 27th NE, Scottsbluff, NE, 69361-1899. Tel: 308-635-6040. p. 1335
Hamilton, Clifford, Dir, Leslie County Public Library, 22065 Main St, Hyden, KY, 41749. Tel: 606-672-2460. p. 860
Hamilton, Darren, Clinical Librarian Specialist, London Health Sciences Centre, 800 Commissioners Rd E, London, ON, N6A 4G5, CANADA. Tel: 519-685-8500, Ext 75934. p. 2654
Hamilton, David, Curator, Monroe County Seneca Park Zoo, 2222 St Paul St, Rochester, NY, 14621-1097. Tel: 585-753-2502. p. 1629
Hamilton, Deb, Law Librn, Pikes Peak Library District, Penrose Library, 20 N Cascade Ave, Colorado Springs, CO, 80903. Tel: 719-531-6333, Ext 6058. p. 271
Hamilton, Denise, Dir, Initiatives & Stragegies, Fort Worth Museum of Science & History Library, 1600 Gendy St, Fort Worth, TX, 76107. Tel: 817-255-9305. p. 2180
Hamilton, Donna, Dir, Orchard Public Library, 232 Windom, Orchard, NE, 68764. Tel: 402-893-4606. p. 1331
Hamilton, Elizabeth, Librn, Cades Schutte, 1000 Bishop St, Ste 1200, Honolulu, HI, 96813-4212. Tel: 808-521-9200. p. 505
Hamilton, Elna, Librn, Crook Community Library, Fourth St, Crook, CO, 80726. Tel: 970-886-2833. p. 272
Hamilton, Gina, Programming Dir, Surrey Township Public Library, 105 E Michigan, Farwell, MI, 48622. Tel: 989-588-9782. p. 1104
Hamilton, Jeanne, Dir, Bloomington Public Library, 205 E Olive St, Bloomington, IL, 61701. Tel: 309-828-6091. p. 542
Hamilton, Jennifer, Head, Instrul Serv, University of Louisiana at Lafayette, 400 E St Mary Blvd, Lafayette, LA, 70503. Tel: 337-482-1160. p. 893
Hamilton, John-Luke, Br Mgr, Chicago Public Library, Avalon, 8148 S Stony Island Ave, Chicago, IL, 60617. Tel: 312-747-5234. p. 556
Hamilton, Kelly, Dir, Hepburn Library of Hermon, 105 Main St, Hermon, NY, 13652-3100. Tel: 315-347-2285. p. 1546
Hamilton, Krystal, Youth Serv Librn, Albuquerque-Bernalillo County Library System, Central & Unser - Patrick J Baca Library, 8081 Central Ave NW, Albuquerque, NM, 87121. Tel: 505-768-4320. p. 1460
Hamilton, Leslee, Local History & Genealogy Supvr, Mississippi Valley Library District, 408 W Main St, Collinsville, IL, 62234. Tel: 618-344-1112. p. 573
Hamilton, Lillian, Libr Supvr, Paterson Free Public Library, South Paterson, 930 Main St, Paterson, NJ, 07503. Tel: 973-357-3020. p. 1433
Hamilton, Lindsay Michelle, Br Mgr, Montgomery City-County Public Library System, Hampstead Branch Library, 5251 Hampstead High St, Ste 107, Montgomery, AL, 36116. Tel: 334-625-4885. p. 29
Hamilton, Mark, Digital Serv Librn, Research Librn, Longwood University, Redford & Race St, Farmville, VA, 23909. Tel: 434-395-2443. p. 2318
Hamilton, Mary, Dir, Bradshaw H Grady Chambers County Library, Lafayette Pilot Public Library, 198 First St SE, Lafayette, AL, 36862. Tel: 334-864-0012. p. 39
Hamilton, Mary H, Dir, H Grady Bradshaw Chambers County Library, 3419 20th Ave, Valley, AL, 36854. Tel: 334-768-2161. p. 39
Hamilton, Michael, Dr, Exec Mgr, The Mary Baker Eddy Library, Research & Reference Services, 210 Massachusetts Ave, P04-10, Boston, MA, 02115-3017. Tel: 617-450-7400. p. 994
Hamilton, Mildred, Librn, Georgia Department of Corrections, Office of Library Services, 210 Longbridge Rd, Helena, GA, 31037. Tel: 229-868-7721. p. 482
Hamilton, Patricia, Br Mgr, Logansport-Cass County Public Library, Galveston Branch, 304 E Jackson, Galveston, IN, 46932. Tel: 574-699-6170. p. 703
Hamilton, Renae, Librn, Southern Technical College, Orlando Campus, 1485 Florida Mall Ave, Orlando, FL, 32809. Tel: 407-438-6000. p. 404
Hamilton, Rita, City Librn, Phoenix Public Library, 1221 N Central Ave, Phoenix, AZ, 85004. Tel: 602-262-4636. p. 72
Hamilton, Robert, Ref Librn/Coll Develop, Hobbs Public Library, 509 N Shipp St, Hobbs, NM, 88240. Tel: 575-397-9328. p. 1469
Hamilton, Sherry, Dir, Courtland Public Library, 215 College St, Courtland, AL, 35618. Tel: 256-522-8035. p. 13
Hamilton, Sionna, Young Adult Dept Manager, Westchester Public Library, 200 W Indiana Ave, Chesterton, IN, 46304. Tel: 219-926-7696. p. 675
Hamilton, Yvonne, Librn, College of New Rochelle, Co-op City Campus, 755 Co-op City Blvd, Bronx, NY, 10475. Tel: 718-320-0300, Ext 232. p. 1577
Hamlett, Rebecca, Dir, Libr Serv, William Jewell College, 500 William Jewell College Dr, Liberty, MO, 64068. Tel: 816-415-7613. p. 1260
Hamlin, Alyson, Br Mgr, Riverside County Library System, Calimesa Library, 974 Calimesa Blvd, Calimesa, CA, 92320. Tel: 909-795-9807. p. 202
Hamlin, Carl, Mgr, Cabell County Public Library, Gallaher Village, 368 Norway Ave, Huntington, WV, 25705. Tel: 304-528-5696. p. 2404
Hamlin, Jolee, Assoc Dir, Pub Serv, Sr Assoc Dir, Capital Area District Libraries, 401 S Capitol Ave, Lansing, MI, 48933. Tel: 517-367-0810. p. 1124
Hamlin, Tina, Libr Dir, Hyde County Library, 107 Commercial SE, Highmore, SD, 57345. Tel: 605-852-2514. p. 2076
Hamlin-Black, Megan, State Librn, Rhode Island State Library, State House, Rm 208, 82 Smith St, Providence, RI, 02903. Tel: 401-222-2473. p. 2040
Hamlington, Mylinh, Ch Mgr, Altadena Library District, 600 E Mariposa St, Altadena, CA, 91001. Tel: 626-798-0833. p. 116
Hamlton, Carole, Libr Office Mgr, Moses Greeley Parker Memorial Library, 28 Arlington St, Dracut, MA, 01826. Tel: 978-454-5474. p. 1015
Hamm, Jennifer, Actg Sr Librn, Los Angeles Public Library System, Fairfax Branch Library, 161 S Gardner St, Los Angeles, CA, 90036-2717. Tel: 323-936-6191. p. 164
Hamm, Kelly, Court Adminr, Carbon County Law Library, Carbon County Courthouse, Four Broadway, 2nd Flr, Jim Thorpe, PA, 18229. Tel: 570-325-3111. p. 1947
Hamm, Lara, Chief Coms Officer, Jackson Lewis LLP, 666 Third Ave, 29th Flr, New York, NY, 10017. Tel: 212-545-4000, 212-545-4033. p. 1589
Hamm, Whitney, Spec Coll Librn, Univ Archivist, Missouri Southern State University, 3950 E Newman Rd, Joplin, MO, 64801-1595. Tel: 417-625-9342. p. 1253
Hammack, Jessica, Head, Res & Instruction, Hood College, 401 Rosemont Ave, Frederick, MD, 21701. Tel: 301-696-3858. p. 966
Hammat, Angela, Med Librn, Marietta Memorial Hospital, 401 Matthew St, Marietta, OH, 45750-1699. Tel: 740-374-1455. p. 1799
Hammatt, Dawn, Dir, National Archives & Records Administration, 200 SE Fourth St, Abilene, KS, 67410-2900. Tel: 785-263-6700. p. 795
Hammatt, Dawn, Dir, National Archives & Records Administration, 1000 George Bush Dr W, College Station, TX, 77845. Tel: 979-691-4000. p. 2157
Hammer, Evan, Digital Library Admin, Montana State Library, 1515 E Sixth Ave, Helena, MT, 59620. Tel: 406-444-3115. p. 1296
Hammer, Eve, Commun Libr Mgr, Queens Library, Bay Terrace Community Library, 18-36 Bell Blvd, Bayside, NY, 11360. Tel: 718-423-7004. p. 1554
Hammer, Rachel, Coordr, Acq, Folger Shakespeare Library, 201 E Capitol St SE, Washington, DC, 20003-1094. Tel: 202-675-0384. p. 366
Hammer, Raechel, Chief Develop Officer, Library Company of Philadelphia, 1314 Locust St, Philadelphia, PA, 19107. Tel: 215-546-3181. p. 1982
Hammer, Tamara, Dir, Dickson County Public Library, 206 Henslee Dr, Dickson, TN, 37055-2020. Tel: 615-446-8293. p. 2097

Hammerquist, Leah, Mgr, Libraries of Stevens County, Colville Branch, 195 S Oak St, Colville, WA, 99114-2845. Tel: 509-684-6620. p. 2369
Hammerschmidt, Claire, Br Mgr, Camden County Library District, Sunrise Beach Branch, 14156 N State Hwy 5, Sunrise Beach, MO, 65079. Tel: 573-374-6982. p. 1239
Hammersla, Keith, Info Serv, Tech Serv Mgr, Martinsburg-Berkeley County Public Library, 101 W King St, Martinsburg, WV, 25401. Tel: 304-267-8933, Ext 4005. p. 2408
Hammes, Matt, Asst Br Mgr, Johnson County Library, Blue Valley, 9000 W 151st St, Overland Park, KS, 66221. p. 830
Hammes, Whitney, Theological Librn, Harding University, 915 E Market St, Searcy, AR, 72149-5615. Tel: 501-279-4228. p. 109
Hammett, Kevin, Terrapin Learning Commons & Student Support Serv, University of Maryland Libraries, Theodore R McKeldin Library, 7649 Library Lane, College Park, MD, 20742-7011. Tel: 301-314-9046. p. 962
Hammock, Shannon, Tech Serv, Riverside Community College District, 4800 Magnolia Ave, Riverside, CA, 92506-1299. p. 201
Hammond, Alicia, Commun Engagement Mgr, Forest Park Public Library, 7555 Jackson Blvd, Forest Park, IL, 60130. Tel: 708-366-7171. p. 588
Hammond, Andrew, Librn, Muskegon Area District Library, Egelston Branch, 5428 E Apple Ave, Muskegon, MI, 49442-3008. Tel: 231-788-6477. p. 1136
Hammond, Elizabeth D, Dean of Libr, Mercer University, Jack Tarver Library, 1300 Edgewood Ave, Macon, GA, 31207. Tel: 478-301-2960. p. 486
Hammond, Jaime, Dir, Libr Serv, Naugatuck Valley Community College, 750 Chase Pkwy, Rm K512, Waterbury, CT, 06708. Tel: 203-575-8199. p. 344
Hammond, Jason, Libr Dir, Dunkirk Public Library, 536 Central Ave, Dunkirk, NY, 14048. Tel: 716-366-2511. p. 1527
Hammond, Megan, Res Libr Adminr, Arizona State Library, Archives & Public Records, 1901 W Madison St, Phoenix, AZ, 85009. Tel: 602-926-3469. p. 69
Hammond, Paul, Exec Dir, Colorado Railroad Museum, 17155 W 44th Ave, Golden, CO, 80403-1621. Tel: 303-279-4591. p. 282
Hammond, Sharon, Librn, Department of Veterans Affairs, Patient Education Resource Center, 3601 S Sixth Ave, 7-14A, Tucson, AZ, 85723. Tel: 520-792-1450, Ext 6516. p. 81
Hammond, Sharon, Mgr, Lancaster County Library, 313 S White St, Lancaster, SC, 29720. Tel: 803-285-1502. p. 2064
Hammond, Stacie, Head, Ref Serv, Oyster Bay-East Norwich Public Library, 89 E Main St, Oyster Bay, NY, 11771. Tel: 516-922-1212. p. 1614
Hammond, Stephanie, Exec Dir, Learning Disabilites Association of Yukon, 128A Copper Rd, Whitehorse, YT, Y1A 2Z6, CANADA. Tel: 867-668-5167. p. 2758
Hammond, Wayne, Chapin Librn, Williams College, 26 Hopkins Hall Dr, Williamstown, MA, 01267. Tel: 413-597-2462. p. 1069
Hammond, Zerita, Librn, Davenport Public Library, 505 Seventh St, Davenport, WA, 99122. Tel: 509-725-4355. p. 2362
Hammonds, Robert, Tech Serv & Syst Librn, Alvernia University, 400 St Bernardine St, Reading, PA, 19607-1737. Tel: 610-796-8223. p. 2000
Hammons, Rebecca, Librn, North Branch Correctional Institution Library, 14100 McMullen Hwy, Cumberland, MD, 21502. Tel: 301-729-7602. p. 964
Hampsey, Casey, Ser & Electronic Res Librn, Iona University, 715 North Ave, New Rochelle, NY, 10801-1890. Tel: 914-633-2449. p. 1577
Hampson, Jennifer, Br Mgr, Pend Oreille County Library District, Ione Public Library, 210 Blackwell, Ste 1, Ione, WA, 99139. p. 2372
Hampson, Jennifer, Br Mgr, Pend Oreille County Library District, Metalines Community Library, Cutter Bldg, 302 Park St, Metaline Falls, WA, 99153. p. 2372
Hampson, Velva, Sr Librn, California Department of Corrections Library System, Substance Abuse Treatment Faclity & State Prison, Corcoran, 900 Quebec Ave, Corcoran, CA, 93212. Tel: 559-992-7100, Ext 5066. p. 207
Hampson, Yoonmee, Asst Libr Mgr, Bucks County Free Library, 150 S Pine St, Doylestown, PA, 18901-4932. Tel: 215-348-0332. p. 1926
Hampton, Amy, Asst Librn, Milton Free Public Library, 13 Main St, Milton Mills, NH, 03852. Tel: 603-473-8535. p. 1374
Hampton, Blossom M, Librn, United States Army, Bldg 35, One C Tree Rd, McAlester, OK, 74501. Tel: 918-420-6271, 918-420-8707. p. 1853
Hampton, Carol, Tech Asst, Arkansas Supreme Court Library, 625 Marshall St, Ste 1500, Little Rock, AR, 72201. Tel: 501-682-2147. p. 101
Hampton, Dantrea, ILL, Per/Ref Librn, Kentucky State University, 400 E Main St, Frankfort, KY, 40601-2355. Tel: 502-597-5946. p. 855
Hampton Hayes, Emily, Pub Serv Librn, Carroll Community College, 1601 Washington Rd, Westminster, MD, 21157-6944. Tel: 410-386-8342. p. 980
Hampton, Nancy, Interim Libr Dir, Xavier University of Louisiana, One Drexel Dr, New Orleans, LA, 70125-1098. Tel: 504-520-7311. p. 904
Hampton, Sheryll, Access Serv Librn, Northwest Nazarene University, 804 E Dewey St, Nampa, ID, 83686. Tel: 208-467-8357. p. 527
Hampton, T Kae, Dir, M B Noelke Jr Memorial Library, 101 S Broadway, Mertzon, TX, 76941-0766. Tel: 325-835-2704. p. 2219
Hampton, Todd, Ref & Instruction Librn, Gateway Community College Library & Learning Commons, 20 Church St, New Haven, CT, 06510. Tel: 203-285-2615. p. 325
Hampton, Valencia, Librn, Mississippi Delta Community College, GHEC Library, 2900A Hwy 1 S, Greenville, MS, 38701. Tel: 662-332-8467. p. 1227
Hamre, Troy, Ad, ILL Mgr, Bismarck Veterans Memorial Public Library, 515 N Fifth St, Bismarck, ND, 58501-4081. Tel: 701-355-1480. p. 1729
Hamrick, David, Cat, Texas Christian University, 2913 Lowden St, TCU Box 298400, Fort Worth, TX, 76129. Tel: 817-257-7106. p. 2181
Hamrick, Leah, Electronic Res Librn, Texas Christian University, 2913 Lowden St, TCU Box 298400, Fort Worth, TX, 76129. Tel: 817-257-7106. p. 2181
Hamrick, Leona, Ch, Leslie County Public Library, 22065 Main St, Hyden, KY, 41749. Tel: 606-672-2460. p. 860
Hamrick, Sharon, Tech Asst, Saint Patrick's Seminary, 320 Middlefield Rd, Menlo Park, CA, 94025. Tel: 650-289-3359. p. 175
Hamstra, Emily, Asst Dir, National Network of Libraries of Medicine Region 5, Univ of Washington, Health Sciences Bldg, Rm T230, 1959 NE Pacific St, Seattle, WA, 98195. Tel: 206-543-8262. p. 2776
Hamstra, Shaunt, Acq, California State University, East Bay Library, CSU East Bay Library, 25800 Carlos Bee Blvd, Hayward, CA, 94542-3052. Tel: 510-885-3664. p. 150
Han, Christine, Ref Librn, Westcliff University, 16735 Von Karman, Ste 100, Irvine, CA, 92606. Tel: 714-459-1177. p. 153
Han, Jiao, Tech Serv Mgr, Oakland Public Library, 125 14th St, Oakland, CA, 94612. Tel: 510-238-2217. p. 186
Han, Qiming, Syst Librn, Housatonic Community College Library, 900 Lafayette Blvd, Bridgeport, CT, 06604. Tel: 203-332-5073. p. 304
Hanan, Carol, Electronic Res Librn, Arkansas Tech University, 305 West Q St, Russellville, AR, 72801. Tel: 479-968-0288. p. 108
Hanblin, Jennifer, Ref Librn, Glenbow Museum Library, 130 Ninth Ave SE, Calgary, AB, T2G 0P3, CANADA. Tel: 403-268-4197. p. 2528
Hanchar, Dorothea, Dir, Department of Natural Resources, Government of Newfoundland & Labrador, Natural Resources Bldg, 50 Elizabeth Ave, St. John's, NL, A1B 4J6, CANADA. Tel: 709-729-3419. p. 2610
Hancock, Chantele, Dir, Richland Hills Public Library, 6724 Rena Dr, Richland Hills, TX, 76118-6297. Tel: 817-616-3760. p. 2231
Hancock, Cheryl, Libr Dir, Harney County Library, 80 West D St, Burns, OR, 97720. Tel: 541-573-6670. p. 1875
Hancock, Cynthia, Dir, DeKalb County Public Library, 504 Grand Ave NW, Fort Payne, AL, 35967. Tel: 256-845-2671. p. 18
Hancock, Don, Adminr, Southwest Research & Information Center Library, 105 Stanford SE, Albuquerque, NM, 87106-3537. Tel: 505-262-1862. p. 1462
Hancock, Kelly, Br Mgr, De Soto Trail Regional Library System, Pelham Carnegie Branch, 133 Hand Ave, Pelham, GA, 31779. Tel: 229-294-6030. p. 469
Hancock, Kim, Librn III, Team Leader, Western Memorial Regional Hospital, One Brookfield Ave, Corner Brook, NL, A2H 6J7, CANADA. Tel: 709-784-5218. p. 2608
Hancock, Kristina, Libr Mgr, Arkansas State Library for the Blind & Print Disabled, 900 W Capitol Ave, Ste 100, Little Rock, AR, 72201-3108. Tel: 501-682-1155. p. 100
Hancock, Lisa, Curator of Coll, Aspen Historical Society Archives, 620 W Bleeker St, Aspen, CO, 81611. Tel: 970-925-3721, Ext 110. p. 264
Hancock, Molly, Coordr, Youth Serv, Pollard Memorial Library, 401 Merrimack St, Lowell, MA, 01852. Tel: 978-674-4120. p. 1029
Hancock, Pat, Dir, Salem Baptist Church Library, 103 N Broad St, Salem, VA, 24153. Tel: 540-387-0416. p. 2347
Hand, Amy, Ch, Camden Public Library, 55 Main St, Camden, ME, 04843-1703. Tel: 207-236-3440. p. 920
Hand, Jill, Youth Serv Librn, Seymour Public Library District, 176-178 Genesee St, Auburn, NY, 13021. Tel: 315-252-2571. p. 1489
Hand, Katherine, Dir, Sunderland Public Library, 20 School St, Sunderland, MA, 01375. Tel: 413-665-2642. p. 1058
Hand, Kathy, Circ Librn, Suffolk County Community College, 533 College Rd, Selden, NY, 11784-2899. Tel: 631-451-4800. p. 1639
Hand, Sara, Libr Asst III, University Libraries, University of Memphis, 705 Lambuth Blvd, Jackson, TN, 38301. Tel: 731-425-1983. p. 2103
Handel, Maxx, Dir, Frances L Simek Memorial Library, 400 N Main St, Medford, WI, 54451. Tel: 715-748-1161. p. 2455
Handfield, Amy, Dir, Access Serv, Manhattan College, 4513 Manhattan College Pkwy, Riverdale, NY, 10471. Tel: 718-862-7743. p. 1627
Handis, Mike, Information Mgmt Librarian, City University of New York, 365 Fifth Ave, New York, NY, 10016-4309. Tel: 212-817-7075. p. 1582
Handrow, Margaret, Virtual Librn, Central Texas College, Bldg 102, 6200 W Central Texas Expressway, Killeen, TX, 76549. Tel: 254-526-1619. p. 2206
Hands, Africa, Dr, Asst Prof, University at Buffalo, The State University of New York, 534 Baldy Hall, Buffalo, NY, 14260. Tel: 716-645-2412. p. 2789
Hands, Africa, Dr, Asst Prof, East Carolina University, 104B Ragsdale Hall, Greenville, NC, 27858. Tel: 252-328-4389. p. 2790
Handt, Holly, ILL & Doc Delivery Coordr, Nicolet Federated Library System, 1595 Allouez Ave, Ste 4, Green Bay, WI, 54311. Tel: 920-448-4410. p. 2438

Handy, Grace, Archivist & Spec Coll Librn, Bank Street College of Education Library, 610 W 112th St, 5th Flr, New York, NY, 10025. Tel: 212-875-4455. p. 1579

Handy, Irene, Access & Tech Serv Librn, Richard Bland College Library, Commons Bldg, 11301 Johnson Rd, Petersburg, VA, 23805. Tel: 804-862-6226. p. 2337

Handy, Michele, Librn, Blue Ridge Community College Library, Transylvania County Campus, 45 Oak Park Dr, Brevard, NC, 28712. Tel: 828-694-1906. p. 1689

Hanel, Najwa, Librn, University of Southern California Libraries, Science & Engineering, Seaver Science Ctr, 920 W 37th Pl, Los Angeles, CA, 90089-0481. Tel: 213-740-4419, 213-740-8507. p. 170

Hanelt, Maggie, Asst Dir, Youth Serv, Truro Public Library, Seven Standish Way, North Truro, MA, 02652. Tel: 508-487-1125. p. 1042

Hanemaayer, Frances, Br Mgr, Burlington Public Library, Alton, 3040 Tim Dobbie Dr, Burlington, ON, L7M 0M3, CANADA. Tel: 905-639-3611 ext;1405. p. 2634

Hanemaayer, Frances, Br Mgr, Burlington Public Library, Tansley Woods, 1996 Itabashi Way, Burlington, ON, L7M 4J8, CANADA. Tel: 905-336-5583. p. 2634

Haner, Celeste, Library Contact, Arkansas Geological Survey Library, 3815 W Roosevelt Rd, Little Rock, AR, 72204-6369. Tel: 501-296-1877. p. 100

Hanes, Lindsey, Libr Dir, Garrett Memorial Library, 123 S Main, Moulton, IA, 52572. Tel: 641-642-3664. p. 771

Hanes, Michael, Dir, Cushing Public Library, 215 N Steele Ave, Cushing, OK, 74023-3319. Tel: 918-225-4188. p. 1845

Hanes-Ramos, Melanie, Access Serv & Electronic Res Librn, University of South Carolina at Beaufort Library, Eight E Campus Dr, Bluffton, SC, 29909. Tel: 843-208-8023. p. 2048

Haney, Cathy, Librn, Grandfield Public Library, 101 W Second St, Grandfield, OK, 73546-9449. Tel: 580-479-5598. p. 1848

Haney, Dana, Coordr, ILL, Libr Asst, Conway County Library Headquarters, 101 W Church St, Morrilton, AR, 72110. Tel: 501-354-5204. p. 105

Haney, David, Tech Dir, Grand Forks Public Library, 2110 Library Circle, Grand Forks, ND, 58201-6324. Tel: 701-772-8116. p. 1734

Haney, Kimberly, Circulation & Ref Support Tech, Sheridan College Library, 1430 Trafalgar Rd, Oakville, ON, L6H 2L1, CANADA. Tel: 905-845-9438, Ext 2482. p. 2663

Haney, Monica, Ch, Barberton Public Library, 602 W Park Ave, Barberton, OH, 44203-2458. Tel: 330-745-1194. p. 1748

Hanfling, Kate, Librn/Educator, Accokeek Foundation Library, 3400 Bryan Point Rd, Accokeek, MD, 20607. Tel: 301-283-2113. p. 949

Hanford, Dana, Head, Info Syst, Central Connecticut State University, 1615 Stanley St, New Britain, CT, 06050. Tel: 860-832-2058. p. 324

Hanger, Teresa, Per, Freed-Hardeman University, 158 E Main St, Henderson, TN, 38340-2399. Tel: 731-989-6067. p. 2101

Hanke-Young, Erica, Youth Serv Mgr, Six Mile Regional Library District, Niedringhaus Bldg, 2001 Delmar Ave, Granite City, IL, 62040-4590. Tel: 618-452-6238. p. 594

Hankins, Ashley, Dir, Libr Serv, Crowley's Ridge College Library & Learning Center, 100 College Dr, Paragould, AR, 72450. Tel: 870-236-6901, Ext 145. p. 107

Hankins, D, Dir, New Holstein Public Library, 2115 Washington St, New Holstein, WI, 53061-1098. Tel: 920-898-5165. p. 2464

Hankins, Darrell, Libr Mgr, Joint Base San Antonio Libraries, 3011 Harney Path, Fort Sam Houston, TX, 78234. Tel: 210-221-4387, 210-221-4702. p. 2178

Hankins, Elisha, Circ Serv Coordr, University of California, Riverside, Raymond L Orbach Science Library, 900 University Ave, Riverside, CA, 92521. Tel: 951-827-3701. p. 203

Hankins, Judith, Libr Dir, New Madrid County Library, Morehouse Service Center, 113 E Beech St, Morehouse, MO, 63868. Tel: 573-379-3583. p. 1266

Hankins-Wilk, Isabel, Librn, Wapiti Regional Library, Tisdale Community Library, 800 - 101st St, Tisdale, SK, S0E 1T0, CANADA. Tel: 306-873-4767. p. 2746

Hankinson, Carol Anne, Dir, Libr Serv, Roanoke-Chowan Community College, Jernigan Bldg-103, 109 Community College Rd, Ahoskie, NC, 27910. Tel: 252-862-1250. p. 1671

Hankinson, Jennifer, Curator, Littleton Museum Research Center, 6028 S Gallup, Littleton, CO, 80120. Tel: 303-795-3950. p. 290

Hanks, Kelly, Br Mgr, Blackduck Community Library, 72 First St SE, Blackduck, MN, 56630. Tel: 218-835-6600. p. 1165

Hanks, Marla, Court Adminr, Texas State Court of Appeals, County Courthouse, 100 W Main St, Ste 300, Eastland, TX, 76448. Tel: 254-629-2638. p. 2172

Hanks, Mary, Asst Circ Supvr, Centralia Regional Library District, 515 E Broadway, Centralia, IL, 62801. Tel: 618-532-5222. p. 551

Hanley, Andrea, Chief Curator, Wheelwright Museum of the American Indian, 704 Camino Lejo, Santa Fe, NM, 87505. Tel: 505-982-4636. p. 1477

Hanley, Ben, Head, Info Serv, Barrington Public Library, 281 County Rd, Barrington, RI, 02806. Tel: 401-247-1920. p. 2029

Hanley, Gretchen H, Libr Dir, Pascoag Public Library, 57 Church St, Pascoag, RI, 02859. Tel: 401-568-6226. p. 2036

Hanlin, Mary, Coordr, Tidewater Community College Learning Resources Center, 300 Granby St, Norfolk, VA, 23510. Tel: 757-822-1772. p. 2336

Hanlin, Renee, Ch Serv, Outreach Serv, Park County Library System, Powell Branch, 217 E Third St, Powell, WY, 82435-1903. Tel: 307-754-8828. p. 2494

Hanmann, Merrie, Asst Dir, Ahira Hall Memorial Library, 37 W Main St, Brocton, NY, 14716-9747. Tel: 716-792-9418. p. 1497

Hanna, Colleen, State Law Librn, Rhode Island State Law Library, Frank Licht Judicial Complex, 250 Benefit St, Providence, RI, 02903. Tel: 401-222-3275. p. 2040

Hanna, Hildur, Assoc Dir, Michigan State University College of Law Library, Law College Bldg, Rm 115, 648 N Shaw Lane, East Lansing, MI, 48824-1300. Tel: 517-432-6863. p. 1102

Hanna, Jane, Coms & Multimedia Engagement Mgr, Skokie Public Library, 5215 Oakton St, Skokie, IL, 60077-3680. Tel: 847-673-7774. p. 647

Hanna, Nermine, Librn, California Department of Corrections Library System, California Institution for Men, 14901 Central Ave, Chino, CA, 91710. Tel: 909-597-1821, Ext 4368. p. 206

Hannaford, Julie, Dep Chief Librn, University of Toronto Libraries, 130 St George St, Toronto, ON, M5S 1A5, CANADA. Tel: 416-978-1702. p. 2698

Hannaford, Paula, Interim Chief Librn, University of Toronto Libraries, Mississauga Library, Hazel McCallion Academic Learning Centre, Hazel McCallion Academic Learning Centre, 3359 Mississauga Rd N, Mississauga, ON, L5L 1C6, CANADA. Tel: 905-828-5236. p. 2699

Hannagan, Charlotte, Database Mgr, Website Mgr, Institute of International Finance Library, 1333 H St NW, Ste 800E, Washington, DC, 20005-4770. Tel: 202-857-3600. p. 369

Hannah, Laurie, Libr Dir, Santa Barbara County Genealogical Society, 316 Castillo St, Santa Barbara, CA, 93101-3814. Tel: 805-884-9909. p. 240

Hannah, Sonja, Sr Librn, Los Angeles Public Library System, Eagle Rock Branch Library, 5027 Caspar Ave, Los Angeles, CA, 90041-1901. Tel: 323-258-8078. p. 164

Hannan, Catalina, Librn, Historic Hudson Valley Library, 639 Bedford Rd, Tarrytown, NY, 10591. Tel: 914-366-6901. p. 1651

Hannan, Krista, Br Librn, Southeast Regional Library, Regina Beach Branch, Cultural Ctr, 133 Donovel Crescent, Regina Beach, SK, S0G 4C0, CANADA. Tel: 306-729-2062. p. 2754

Hanneman, Jody, Dir, Ettrick Public Library, 15570 School St, Ettrick, WI, 54627. Tel: 608-525-3408. p. 2434

Hanneman, Josie, Commun Librn, Deschutes Public Library District, Redmond Branch, 827 Deschutes Ave, Redmond, OR, 97756. Tel: 541-312-1088. p. 1874

Hanney, Ross, Br Mgr, Saint Joseph County Public Library, Lakeville Branch, 120 N Michigan, Lakeville, IN, 46536. Tel: 574-784-3446. p. 719

Hannon, Aline, Br Librn, Wapiti Regional Library, Debden Public Library, 3 204 Second Ave E, Debden, SK, S0J 0S0, CANADA. Tel: 306-724-2240. p. 2745

Hannon, April, Ch, East Hampton Public Library, 105 Main St, East Hampton, CT, 06424. Tel: 860-267-6621. p. 309

Hannon, Bronwyn, Acq, Hofstra University, Special Collections/Long Island Studies Institute, 032 Axinn Library, 123 Hofstra University, Hempstead, NY, 11549-1230. Tel: 516-463-6404, 516-463-6411. p. 1545

Hannon, John, Libr Serv Coordr, Great River Regional Library, Albany Public Library, 400 Railroad Ave, Albany, MN, 56307. Tel: 320-845-4843. p. 1196

Hannon, Marcia, Asst Dir, Ref Librn, Kansas Supreme Court, Kansas Judicial Ctr, 301 SW Tenth Ave, 1st Flr, Topeka, KS, 66612-1502. Tel: 785-368-7371. p. 839

Hannon, Todd L, Libr Mgr, Kaiser Permanente, 3800 N Interstate Ave, Portland, OR, 97227-1098. Tel: 503-335-2400. p. 1891

Hannon-Brobst, Kim, Ref Librn, Vermont State University - Randolph, Main St, Randolph Center, VT, 05061. Tel: 802-728-1237. p. 2292

Hannotte, Lee Ann, Br Librn, Wapiti Regional Library, St Benedict Public Library, Center St, Saint Benedict, SK, S0K 3T0, CANADA. Tel: 306-289-2072. p. 2746

Hannula, Betsy, Coll Develop, Curator, Westminster Historical Society Library, 110 Main St, Westminster, MA, 01473. Tel: 978-874-5569. p. 1067

Hannum, Mellisa, Youth Serv Librn, Nevada County Community Library, Grass Valley Library - Royce Branch, 207 Mill St, Grass Valley, CA, 95945. Tel: 530-273-4117. p. 182

Hanrahan, Chelsea, Dir, New England College, 196 Bridge St, Henniker, NH, 03242-3298. Tel: 603-428-2344. p. 1367

Hanscom, Diane, Resource Discovery & Access Librn, Husson University, One College Circle, Bangor, ME, 04401-2999. Tel: 207-941-7187, 207-941-7188. p. 915

Hansell, Jamie, Br Librn, Dauphin County Library System, William H & Marion C Alexander Family Library, 200 W Second St, Hummelstown, PA, 17036. Tel: 717-566-0949, Ext 201. p. 1940

Hansen, Alicia, Head, Research, Teaching & Learning, College of the Holy Cross, One College St, Worcester, MA, 01610. Tel: 508-793-3533. p. 1072

Hansen, Andrea, Dir, Denver Art Museum, 100 W 14th Ave Pkwy, Denver, CO, 80204. Tel: 720-913-0100. p. 275

Hansen, Bruce N, Libr Dir, Colonial Heights Public Library, 1000 Yacht Basin Dr, Colonial Heights, VA, 23834. Tel: 804-520-9384. p. 2313

Hansen, Charlie, Chief Admin Officer, Columbus Metropolitan Library, 96 S Grant Ave, Columbus, OH, 43215-4702. Tel: 614-645-2275. p. 1772

Hansen, Cheryl A, Librn, Engineering Systems Inc Library, 4215 Campus Dr, Aurora, IL, 60504-7900. Tel: 630-851-4566, Ext 1238. p. 539

Hansen, Elisa Marie, Head, Libr Serv, The John & Mable Ringling Museum of Art, 5401 Bay Shore Rd, Sarasota, FL, 34243. Tel: 941-359-5700, Ext 2701. p. 443

Hansen, Emily, Br Mgr, Fremont County District Library, 420 N Bridge, Ste E, Saint Anthony, ID, 83445. Tel: 208-624-3192. p. 530

Hansen, Eric Richard, Dir, Vicksburg District Library, 215 S Michigan Ave, Vicksburg, MI, 49097. Tel: 269-649-1648. p. 1156

Hansen, Genesis, Dir, Libr & Cultural Serv, Mission Viejo Library, 100 Civic Ctr, Mission Viejo, CA, 92691. Tel: 949-470-3076. p. 177

Hansen, Harlene, Archives Asst, Coe College, 1220 First Ave NE, Cedar Rapids, IA, 52402. Tel: 319-399-8787. p. 738

Hansen, Harry Michael, Libr Dir, Arvin A Brown Public Library, 88 Main St, Richford, VT, 05476. Tel: 802-848-3313. p. 2293

Hansen, Jean, Head, Adult & Outreach Serv, Waterford Township Public Library, 5168 Civic Center Dr, Waterford, MI, 48329. Tel: 248-618-7682. p. 1158

Hansen, Jennifer, Research Librn, Utah State Law Library, 450 S State St, W-13, Salt Lake City, UT, 84111-3101. Tel: 801-238-7990. p. 2272

Hansen, Jerry, Historian, Researcher, Laramie Plains Museum Association Inc Library, 603 Ivinson Ave, Laramie, WY, 82070-3299. Tel: 307-742-4448. p. 2496

Hansen, Jon, Dir, Virtual Serv, Kennesaw State University Library System, 385 Cobb Ave NW, MD 1701, Kennesaw, GA, 30144. Tel: 470-578-6248. p. 483

Hansen, Joni, Br Supvr, Boise Public Library, Library! at Bown Crossing, 2153 E Riverwalk Dr, Boise, ID, 83706. Tel: 208-972-8630. p. 516

Hansen, Julie, Asst Librn, Mountain Iron Public Library, 5742 Mountain Ave, Mountain Iron, MN, 55768-9636. Tel: 218-735-8625. p. 1190

Hansen, Karen, Pub Serv Mgr, Manitowoc Public Library, 707 Quay St, Manitowoc, WI, 54220. Tel: 920-686-3000. p. 2453

Hansen, Katie, Children's & Teen Serv, Warminster Township Free Library, 1076 Emma Lane, Warminster, PA, 18974. Tel: 215-672-4362. p. 2017

Hansen, Krissi, Youth Serv, Council District Library, 104 California Ave, Council, ID, 83612. Tel: 208-253-6004. p. 520

Hansen, Linda, Dir, South Plainfield Public Library, 2484 Plainfield Ave, South Plainfield, NJ, 07080. Tel: 908-754-7885. p. 1443

Hansen, Lori, Libr Serv Coordr, College of Lake County, 19351 W Washington St, Grayslake, IL, 60030. Tel: 847-543-2071. p. 595

Hansen, Mary Anne, Prof, Montana State University, Department of Education, 215 Reid Hall, Bozeman, MT, 59717. Tel: 406-994-6786. p. 2788

Hansen, Nicole, Res Sharing Librn, State Library of Kansas, 300 SW Tenth Ave, Rm 312-N, Topeka, KS, 66612-1593. Tel: 785-296-5110. p. 2765

Hansen, Roger, Curator, Alaska Masonic Library & Museum, 518 E 14th Ave, Anchorage, AK, 99501. Tel: 907-561-1477. p. 41

Hansen, Sam, Statistics Librn, University of Michigan, Shapiro Science Library, Shapiro Library Bldg, 3rd & 4th Flrs, 919 S University Ave, Ann Arbor, MI, 48109-1185. p. 1080

Hansen, Susan, Libr Mgr, New York Public Library - Astor, Lenox & Tilden Foundations, South Beach Branch, 21-25 Robin Rd, (@ Ocean Ave & Father Capodanno Blvd), Staten Island, NY, 10305. Tel: 718-816-5834. p. 1597

Hansen, Tom, Ref Librn, Tech Serv, La Marque Public Library, 1011 Bayou Rd, La Marque, TX, 77568-4195. Tel: 409-938-9270. p. 2207

Hansen, Will, Curator, Americana, Dir, Reader Serv, Newberry Library, 60 W Walton St, Chicago, IL, 60610-3305. Tel: 312-255-3527. p. 565

Hansen-Aune, Jill, Ref Serv, YA Serv, Fremont Area District Library, 104 E Main St, Fremont, MI, 49412. Tel: 231-924-3480. p. 1108

Hansen-Peterson, Jenny, Circ Mgr, Cherry Valley Public Library District, 755 E State St, Cherry Valley, IL, 61016-9699. Tel: 815-332-5161, Ext 25. p. 553

Hanset, Rebecca, Teen Librn, Sandy Public Library, 38980 Proctor Blvd, Sandy, OR, 97055-8040. Tel: 503-668-5537. p. 1898

Hansgen, Lauren, Exec Dir, Dunham Tavern Museum Library, 6709 Euclid Ave, Cleveland, OH, 44103. Tel: 216-431-1060. p. 1770

Hanshew, Jody, Govt Doc Librn, Syst & Electronic Res, Emory & Henry College, 30480 Armbrister Dr, Emory, VA, 24327. Tel: 276-944-6208. p. 2315

Hanson, Alyssa, Web Spec, Iowa City Public Library, 123 S Linn St, Iowa City, IA, 52240. Tel: 319-356-5200. p. 760

Hanson, Anastasia, Library Services Asst, University of Wisconsin-Madison, Physics Library, 4220 Chamberlin Hall, 1150 University Ave, Madison, WI, 53706. Tel: 608-262-9500. p. 2451

Hanson, Anastasia, Library Services Asst, University of Wisconsin-Madison, Stephen Cole Kleene Mathematics Library, B224 Van Vleck Hall, 480 Lincoln Dr, Madison, WI, 53706. Tel: 608-262-3596. p. 2451

Hanson, Anastasia, Library Services Asst, University of Wisconsin-Madison, Woodman Astronomical Library, 6515 Sterling Hall, 475 N Charter St, Madison, WI, 53706. Tel: 608-262-1320. p. 2452

Hanson, Ashley, Res & Instruction Librn, Connecticut College, 270 Mohegan Ave, New London, CT, 06320-4196. Tel: 860-439-2655. p. 328

Hanson, Byron, Archivist, Interlochen Center for the Arts, Bonisteel Library - Seabury Academic Library, 4000 M-137, Interlochen, MI, 49643. Tel: 231-276-7420. p. 1118

Hanson, Cammie, Br Mgr, Belmont County District Library, Bridgeport Branch, 661 Main St, Bridgeport, OH, 43912. Tel: 740-635-2563. p. 1800

Hanson, Curt, Head, Spec Coll, University of North Dakota, 3051 University Ave, Stop 9000, Grand Forks, ND, 58202-9000. Tel: 701-777-4626. p. 1735

Hanson, David, Exec Dir, Bergen County Cooperative Library System, Inc, 21-00 Route 208 S, Ste 130, Fair Lawn, NJ, 07410. Tel: 201-498-7302. p. 2769

Hanson, David B, Coll Mgt, Metadata Librn, Drake University, Drake Law Library, Opperman Hall, 2604 Forest Ave, Des Moines, IA, 50311. Tel: 515-271-2077. p. 746

Hanson, Deborah, Dir, Comanche Public Library, 311 N Austin St, Comanche, TX, 76442. Tel: 325-356-2122. p. 2158

Hanson, Ellen, Asst Librn, Lincoln Library, 222 W River Rd, Lincoln, VT, 05443. Tel: 802-453-2665. p. 2287

Hanson, Eric, Dean of Libr, California State University, Fullerton, 800 N State College Blvd, Fullerton, CA, 92831. Tel: 657-278-5430. p. 147

Hanson, Eric, Dean, Libr & Learning Support Serv, Glendale Community College Library, 1500 N Verdugo Rd, Glendale, CA, 91208-2894. Tel: 818-240-1000, Ext 5581, 818-240-1000, Ext 5586. p. 148

Hanson, Jackie, Academic & Public Services Coord, New England College, 196 Bridge St, Henniker, NH, 03242-3298. Tel: 603-428-2344. p. 1367

Hanson, Jana, Dir, Institutional Research, Assessment & Accreditation, American Indian Higher Education Consortium, 121 Oronoco St, Alexandria, VA, 22314. Tel: 703-838-0400. p. 2776

Hanson, Jenny, Sr Res Analyst, San Diego County Library, MS 070, 5560 Overland Ave, Ste 110, San Diego, CA, 92123. Tel: 858-694-2415. p. 216

Hanson, Jill, Ref Librn, Rosebud County Library, Bicentennial Library of Colstrip, 419 Willow Ave, Colstrip, MT, 59323. Tel: 406-748-3040. p. 1293

Hanson, Joanne, Library Contact, Chatham Public Library, Canaan Branch, 1647 County Rte 5, Canaan, NY, 12029-3017. Tel: 518-781-3392. p. 1517

Hanson, John, Dir, USS Liberty Memorial Public Library, 1620 11th Ave, Grafton, WI, 53024-2404. Tel: 262-375-5315. p. 2437

Hanson, Kasey, User Support Serv Coordr, University of North Dakota, Thormodsgard Law Library, 215 Centennial Dr, Grand Forks, ND, 58202. Tel: 701-777-2204. p. 1735

Hanson, Kate, Br Librn, Ch, Ridgemont Public Library, Ridgeway Branch, 109 S Main St, Ridgeway, OH, 43345. Tel: 937-363-3066. p. 1805

Hanson, Kathryn A, Dir, Graham Public Library, 1215 Main St, Union Grove, WI, 53182-1303. Tel: 262-878-2910. p. 2482

Hanson, Keith, Mgr, Columbus Metropolitan Library, Karl Road Branch, 1467 Karl Rd, Columbus, OH, 43229. p. 1772

Hanson, Kerry, Head, Pub Serv, San Joaquin College of Law Library, 901 Fifth St, Clovis, CA, 93612. Tel: 559-323-2100, Ext 121. p. 131

Hanson, Lindsay, Libr Mgr, Sno-Isle Libraries, Lake Stevens Library, 1804 Main St, Lake Stevens, WA, 98258. Tel: 425-334-1900. p. 2370

Hanson, Lora, Electronic Res Librn, A T Still University, 5850 E Still Circle, Mesa, AZ, 85206-6091. Tel: 480-219-6091. p. 66

Hanson, Maegan, Libr Dir, Buhl Public Library, 215 Broadway Ave N, Buhl, ID, 83316. Tel: 208-543-6500. p. 518

Hanson, Marianne, Asst Librn, Ch Serv, Salmo Valley Public Library, 104 Fourth St, Salmo, BC, V0G 1Z0, CANADA. Tel: 250-357-2312. p. 2575

Hanson, Mark, Libr Dir, Maranatha Baptist University, 745 W Main St, Watertown, WI, 53094. Tel: 920-206-2375. p. 2483

Hanson, Michael, Head, Tech Serv, Sam Houston State University, 1830 Bobby K Marks Dr, Huntsville, TX, 77340. Tel: 936-294-1620. p. 2201

Hanson, Robin, Head, Circ, Head, ILL, University of Alaska Anchorage, Consortium Library, 3211 Providence Dr, Anchorage, AK, 99508-8176. Tel: 907-786-1871. p. 43

Hanson, Sarena, Librn, Lapeer District Library, Elba Branch, 5508 Davison Rd, Lapeer, MI, 48446. Tel: 810-653-7200. p. 1126

Hanson, Susan, Head, Tech Serv, Westland Public Library, 6123 Central City Pkwy, Westland, MI, 48185. Tel: 734-326-6123. p. 1159

Hanson, Susanah, Libr Dir, Trinity Episcopal School for Ministry Library, 311 11th St, Ambridge, PA, 15003. Tel: 724-266-3838. p. 1906

Hanson, Theresa, Coordr, Anne Carlsen Learning Center, 701 Third St NW, Jamestown, ND, 58401-2971. Tel: 701-252-3850. p. 1736

Hantz, Kathleen, Circ & ILL, Danville Area Community College Library, 2000 E Main St, Danville, IL, 61832-5199. Tel: 217-443-8739. p. 575

Hanus, Karen, Dir, Advocate Lutheran General Hospital, 1775 Dempster St, Park Ridge, IL, 60068. Tel: 847-723-5494. p. 633

Hanus, Karen, Dir, Advocate Aurora Library, 2900 W Oklahoma Ave, Milwaukee, WI, 53215-4330. Tel: 414-649-7356. p. 2457

Hanusek, Denise, Dr, Cat, Emory University Libraries, Pitts Theology Library, Candler School of Theology, 1531 Dickey Dr, Ste 560, Atlanta, GA, 30322-2810. Tel: 404-727-4166. p. 463

Haouchine, Janet, Libr Asst, Massachusetts Trial Court, Lowell Justice Ctr, 370 Jackson St, Lowell, MA, 01852. Tel: 978-452-9301. p. 1029

Happ, Jason, Access Serv Librn, Howard University Libraries, Law Library, 2929 Van Ness St NW, Washington, DC, 20008. Tel: 202-806-8104. p. 369

Happe, Laura M, Dir, Fort Branch-Johnson Township Public Library, 107 E Locust St, Fort Branch, IN, 47648. Tel: 812-753-4212. p. 683

Happe, Tracy, Head, Adult Serv, Monroeville Public Library, 4000 Gateway Campus Blvd, Monroeville, PA, 15146-3381. Tel: 412-372-0500. p. 1964

Happel, Angie, Dir, Lamont Public Library, 616 Bush St, Lamont, IA, 50650. Tel: 563-924-3203. p. 764

Haprian, James, IT Dir, Cuyahoga County Public Library, 2111 Snow Rd, Parma, OH, 44134-2728. Tel: 216-398-1800. p. 1813

Hara, Sara, Ch, Vanderhoof Public Library, 230 Stewart St E, Vanderhoof, BC, V0J 3A0, CANADA. Tel: 250-567-4060. p. 2582

Harada, Glenda, Head, Admin Serv, California State University, Fresno, Henry Madden Library, 5200 N Barton Ave, Mail Stop ML-34, Fresno, CA, 93740-8014. Tel: 559-278-2142. p. 144

Harag, Karen, Acad Librn, Lake Superior State University, 906 Ryan Ave, Sault Sainte Marie, MI, 49783. Tel: 906-635-2862. p. 1149

Harakal, Rebecca, Libr Mgr, Vilna Municipal Library, 5431-50th St, Vilna, AB, T0A 3L0, CANADA. Tel: 780-636-2077. p. 2558

Haralson, Michele, Dir, Samford University Library, Curriculum Materials Center, Beeson Education Bldg, 800 Lakeshore Dr, Birmingham, AL, 35229. Tel: 205-726-2987. p. 9

Harant, Andrew, Dir, Cuyahoga Falls Library, 2015 Third St, Cuyahoga Falls, OH, 44221-3294. Tel: 330-928-2117. p. 1779

Harant, Andrew, Br Mgr, Cuyahoga County Public Library, North Olmsted Branch, 27403 Lorain Rd, North Olmsted, OH, 44070-4037. Tel: 440-777-6211. p. 1813

Harant, Andrew, Br Mgr, Cuyahoga County Public Library, Olmsted Falls Branch, 8100 Mapleway Dr, Olmsted Falls, OH, 44138. Tel: 440-235-1150. p. 1813

Haraughty, Melissa, Head Librn, United States Air Force, 27 SOFSS/FSDL, 107 Albright Ave, Bldg 75, Cannon AFB, NM, 88103-5211. Tel: 575-784-2786. p. 1464

Harayda, Daniel, Dir, Info Serv, Libr Dir, Massachusetts School of Law Library, 500 Federal St, Andover, MA, 01810. Tel: 978-681-0800. p. 985

Harbauer, Matt, Info Tech, YA Librn, Rossford Public Library, 720 Dixie Hwy, Rossford, OH, 43460-1289. Tel: 419-666-0924. p. 1818

Harbauer, William, Br Mgr, Toledo-Lucas County Public Library, Waterville, 800 Michigan Ave, Waterville, OH, 43566. Tel: 419-878-3055. p. 1825

Harbaugh, John, Br Mgr, Harris County Public Library, West University Branch, 6108 Auden, Houston, TX, 77005. Tel: 832-927-4590. p. 2193

Harbaugh, Melinda, Dean of Instruction, Dean, Learning Res, Lower Columbia College, 1600 Maple St, Longview, WA, 98632-3907. Tel: 360-442-2662. p. 2369

Harbec, Amélie, Div Chief, Bibliotheques de Montreal, Pavillon Prince, 801 rue Brennan, 5e etage, Montreal, QC, H3C 0G4, CANADA. Tel: 514-872-3160. p. 2718

Harber, Joy, Dir, Roann Paw Paw Township Public Library, 240 S Chippewa Rd, Roann, IN, 46974. Tel: 765-833-5231. p. 716

Harbeson, Cyndi, Dir, Clapp Memorial Library, 19 S Main St, Belchertown, MA, 01007. Tel: 413-323-0417. p. 988

Harbeson, Cynthia, Curator, Spec Coll, Jones Library, Inc, 43 Amity St, Amherst, MA, 01002-2285. Tel: 413-259-3182. p. 984

Harbine, Anna, Archives Curator, Curator, Spec Coll, Northwest Museum of Art & Culture-Eastern Washington State Historical Society, 2316 W First Ave, Spokane, WA, 99201-1099. Tel: 509-363-5313, 509-363-5342. p. 2384

Harbison, John, Dir, Research & Intelligence, Ballard, Spahr LLP Library, 1735 Market St, 51st Flr, Philadelphia, PA, 19103-7599. Tel: 215-864-8150. p. 1975

Harbison, Sarah, Mgr, Coll Mgt, Santa Cruz City-County Library System, 117 Union St, Santa Cruz, CA, 95060-3873. Tel: 831-427-7706, Ext 7616. p. 242

Harbold, Katie, Libr Asst, Hutchinson Community College, 1300 N Plum St, Hutchinson, KS, 67501. Tel: 620-665-3547. p. 814

Harbor, Amy, Libr Coord, Tippecanoe County Historical Association, 1001 South St, Lafayette, IN, 47901. Tel: 765-476-8411, Ext 2. p. 701

Harbour, Alison, Libr Dir, Medina Community Library, 13948 State Hwy 16 N, Medina, TX, 78055. Tel: 830-589-2825. p. 2218

Hard, Ryan, Tech Serv Coordr, Metropolitan Community College, Penn Valley Library, 3201 SW Trafficway, Kansas City, MO, 64111-2764. Tel: 816-604-4095. p. 1256

Hardacre, Mari, YA Serv, Allen County Public Library, 900 Library Plaza, Fort Wayne, IN, 46802. Tel: 260-421-1256. p. 683

Hardaway, Imani, Cataloging & Metadata Librn, William Paterson University, 300 Pompton Rd, Wayne, NJ, 07470. Tel: 973-720-2437. p. 1452

Hardcastle, Hilary, Dep Dir, University of California, 200 McAllister St, San Francisco, CA, 94102-4978. Tel: 415-565-4757. p. 229

Hardee, Patsy, Mgr, Leath Thomas H Memorial Library, Hamlet Public, 302 Main St, Hamlet, NC, 28345-3304. Tel: 910-582-3477. p. 1713

Hardee, Zina, Br Mgr, Granville County Library System, South, 1547 S Campus Dr, Creedmoor, NC, 27522-7381. Tel: 919-528-1752. p. 1707

Harden, Heather, Children & Teen Librn, Farmville Public Library, 4276 W Church St, Farmville, NC, 27828. Tel: 252-753-3355. p. 1688

Harden, Holly, Librn, Johns Hopkins University Libraries, Carol J Gray Nursing Information Resource Center, 525 N Wolfe St, Rm 313, Baltimore, MD, 21202. Tel: 410-955-7559. p. 954

Harden, Joan, Librn, Delaware Technical & Community College, Wilmington Campus, West Bldg, First Flr, 300 N Orange St, Wilmington, DE, 19801. Tel: 302-573-5431. p. 357

Harden, Kathy, Head, Electronic Serv, University of Mary Hardin-Baylor, 900 College St, UMHB Sta, Box 8016, Belton, TX, 76513-2599. Tel: 254-295-4161. p. 2147

Harden, Kevin, Head Librn, Averett University Library, 344 W Main St, Danville, VA, 24541-2849. Tel: 434-791-5692. p. 2314

Harden, Lynn A, Exec Dir, Brown County Public Library, 613 S High St, Mount Orab, OH, 45154. Tel: 937-444-0181. p. 1804

Harden, Robert, Dir, Sumter County Library, 111 N Harvin St, Sumter, SC, 29150. Tel: 803-773-7273. p. 2071

Hardenbrook, Joe, Assoc Dean, Research & Engagement, Marquette University, 1355 W Wisconsin Ave, Milwaukee, WI, 53233. Tel: 414-288-5979. p. 2458

Hardenbrook, Joe, Dir, Libr Serv, Carroll University, 100 N East Ave, Waukesha, WI, 53186. Tel: 262-951-3022. p. 2484

Hardenbrook, Nikki, Mrs, Tech Coordr, Stewart County Public Library, 102 Natcor Dr, Dover, TN, 37058. Tel: 931-232-3127. p. 2097

Harder, Michelle, Asst Librn, Harper Public Library, 708 W 14th St, Harper, KS, 67058. Tel: 620-896-2959. p. 812

Harder-Gissing, Laureen, Librn & Archivist, Conrad Grebel University College, 140 Westmount Rd N, Waterloo, ON, N2L 3G6, CANADA. Tel: 519-885-0220, Ext 34400. p. 2702

Harders, Denise, Co-Dir, Central Plains Library System, 2727 W Second St, Ste 233, Hastings, NE, 68901. Tel: 402-462-1975. p. 1317

Harders, Faith, Head of Libr, University of Kentucky Libraries, Design Library, 200 Pence Hall, 175 Library Dr, Lexington, KY, 40506-0041. Tel: 859-257-4305. p. 863

Harders, Stephanie, Asst Librn, Gladbrook Public Library, 301 Second St, Gladbrook, IA, 50635. Tel: 641-473-3236. p. 755

Hardesty, Joe, Libr Dir, National Society of the Sons of the American Revolution, 809 W Main St, Louisville, KY, 40202. Tel: 502-588-6138. p. 866

Hardesty, Skye, Discovery Serv, Head, Coll Develop, Georgia State University, 100 Decatur St SE, Atlanta, GA, 30303-3202. Tel: 404-413-2786. p. 464

Hardie-Belair, Erin, Libr Serv Coordr, Edmonton Public Library, Jasper Place, 9010 156 St, Edmonton, AB, T5R 5X7, CANADA. Tel: 780-496-8359. p. 2536

Hardiman, Alexis, Dir, Lake City Public Library, 110 E Washington St, Lake City, IA, 51449. Tel: 712-464-3413. p. 763

Hardiman, Elisia, Librn, Michigan Department of Corrections, Ernest C Brooks Correctional Facility Library, 2500 S Sheridan Rd, Muskegon, MI, 49444. Tel: 231-773-9200, Ext 1916. p. 1089

Hardiman, Elisia, Librn, Michigan Department of Corrections, 2400 S Sheridan Dr, Muskegon, MI, 49442. Tel: 231-773-3201, Ext 2271. p. 1136

Hardiman, Thomas, Dir, Portsmouth Athenaeum, Six-Nine Market Sq, Portsmouth, NH, 03801. Tel: 603-431-2538. p. 1378

Hardin, Evanna, Libr Dir, Arthur County Public Library, 205 Fir St, Arthur, NE, 69121. Tel: 308-764-2219. p. 1306

Hardin, Gretchen, Asst Libr Dir, Bee Cave Public Library, 4000 Galleria Pkwy, Bee Cave, TX, 78738. Tel: 512-767-6634. p. 2146

Hardin, Kyla, Dir, Human Res, Public Library of Cincinnati & Hamilton County, 800 Vine St, Cincinnati, OH, 45202-2009. Tel: 513-369-4407. p. 1761

Hardin, Nancy, Librn, Dunklin County Library, Holcomb Branch, W Main St, Holcomb, MO, 63852. Tel: 573-792-3268. p. 1258

Hardin, Sarah, Br Mgr, Southeast Arkansas Regional Library, McGehee Branch, 211 N Fourth St, McGehee, AR, 71654. Tel: 870-222-4097. p. 104

Hardin, Steve, Ref & Instruction Librn, Indiana State University, 510 North 6 1/2 St, Terre Haute, IN, 47809. Tel: 812-237-3700. p. 720

Hardina, Rhonda, Asst Librn, Britton Public Library, 759 Seventh St, Britton, SD, 57430. Tel: 605-448-2800. p. 2074

Hardina-Wilhelm, Nicole, Adult Serv, Neenah Public Library, 240 E Wisconsin Ave, Neenah, WI, 54956. Tel: 920-886-6315. p. 2463

Harding, Brian, Chief Exec Officer, Chief Librn, Greater Sudbury Public Library, 74 MacKenzie St, Sudbury, ON, P3C 4X8, CANADA. Tel: 705-673-1155. p. 2683

Harding, Julie, Dir, Libr Serv, University of Maryland, 3501 University Blvd E, Adelphi, MD, 20783. Tel: 240-684-2020. p. 949

Harding, Nicole, Youth Serv Librn, South Fayette Township Library, 515 Millers Run Rd, Morgan, PA, 15064. Tel: 412-257-8660. p. 1966

Harding, Paulette, Ref Serv Mgr, Poplar Creek Public Library District, 1405 S Park Ave, Streamwood, IL, 60107-2997. Tel: 630-837-6800. p. 652

Harding, Ronni Renee, Asst Dir, Bartley Public Library, 411 Commercial St, Bartley, NE, 69020. Tel: 308-692-3313. p. 1306

Hardison, Chase, Asst Dir, Orena Humphreys Public Library, 13535 Tennessee Hwy 28, Whitwell, TN, 37397. Tel: 423-658-6134. p. 2130

Hardison, Meghan, Outreach & Instruction Librn, Southern Maine Community College Library, Two Fort Rd, South Portland, ME, 04106. Tel: 207-741-5521. p. 941

Harmel, Daren, Dir, USDA Agricultural Research Service, 40335 County Rd GG, Akron, CO, 80720. Tel: 970-492-7771. p. 263

Harmeling, Deborah, Sister, Archivist, St Walburg Monastery Archives, 2500 Amsterdam Rd, Covington, KY, 41017. Tel: 859-331-6324. p. 852

Harmelink, Daniel, Exec Dir, Concordia Historical Institute, 804 Seminary Pl, Saint Louis, MO, 63105-3014. Tel: 314-505-7900. p. 1270

Harmer, Andrea, Dr, Prof, Kutztown University, 12 Rohrbach Library, Kutztown, PA, 19530. Tel: 610-683-4301. p. 2791

Harmer, William H, Exec Dir, The Westport Library, 20 Jesup Rd, Westport, CT, 06880. Tel: 203-291-4801. p. 347

Harmon, Carolyn, Libr Asst III, Atlanta Metropolitan State College Library, 1630 Metropolitan Pkwy SW, Atlanta, GA, 30310. Tel: 404-756-4010. p. 462

Harmon, Donald, Mgr, Ad Serv, Multimedia, Ella M Everhard Public Library, 132 Broad St, Wadsworth, OH, 44281-1897. Tel: 330-335-8253. p. 1827

Harmon, Gary, Librn, Kentucky Talking Book Library, 300 Coffee Tree Rd, Frankfort, KY, 40601. Tel: 502-564-8347. p. 855

Harmon, Katie, Acq Librn, Gardner-Webb University, 110 S Main St, Boiling Springs, NC, 28017. Tel: 704-406-4296. p. 1674

Harmon, Keta, Acq Librn, Samford University Library, Lucille Stewart Beeson Law Library, 800 Lakeshore Dr, Birmingham, AL, 35229. Tel: 205-726-2714. p. 9

Harmon, Marie, Asst Dir, Guntersville Public Library, 1240 O'Brig Ave, Guntersville, AL, 35976. Tel: 256-571-7595. p. 20

Harmon, Mary, Pub Serv Mgr, Licking County Library, 101 W Main St, Newark, OH, 43055-5054. Tel: 740-349-5521. p. 1807

Harmon, Mary A, Assoc Librn, University of Pikeville, 147 Sycamore St, Pikeville, KY, 41501-9118. Tel: 606-218-5610. p. 872

Harmon, Matt, Head, Info Tech, Marshall District Library, 124 W Green St, Marshall, MI, 49068. Tel: 269-781-7821, Ext 16. p. 1130

Harmon, Mona, Librn, J B Nickells Memorial Library, 215 S Pecan Ave, Luling, TX, 78648. Tel: 830-875-2813. p. 2214

Harmon, Paul, IT Dir, South Carolina State Library, 1500 Senate St, Columbia, SC, 29201. Tel: 803-734-8651. p. 2054

Harmon, Tracy, Law Librn, Cook County Law Library, Bridgeview Branch, 10220 S 76th Ave, Bridgeview, IL, 60455. Tel: 708-974-6201. p. 559

Harms, Brandi, Asst Dir, Toledo Public Library, 206 E High St, Toledo, IA, 52342-1617. Tel: 641-484-3362. p. 786

Harms, Lisa, Assoc Mgr, Circ & Coll, Metropolitan Museum of Art, Thomas J Watson Library, 1000 Fifth Ave, New York, NY, 10028-0198. Tel: 212-650-2344. p. 1592

Harmsen, Eric, Curatorial Specialist, Michigan Maritime Museum, 91 Michigan Ave, South Haven, MI, 49090. Tel: 269-637-9156. p. 1150

Harmsworth Dow, Joan, Librn, Regina-Qu'Appelle Health Region, Health Sciences Library-Wascana, 2180 23rd Ave, Regina, SK, S4S 0A5, CANADA. Tel: 306-766-5441. p. 2747

Harn, T, Legal Library Coord, Two Rivers Correctional Institute, 82911 Beach Access Rd, Umatilla, OR, 97882. Tel: 541-922-2181. p. 1901

Harnegie, Mary Pat, Med Librn, South Pointe Hospital Library, 20000 Harvard Rd, Warrensville Heights, OH, 44122. Tel: 216-491-7455. p. 1828

Harner, Debbie, Education Archivist, Goucher College Library, 1021 Dulaney Valley Rd, Baltimore, MD, 21204. Tel: 410-337-6360. p. 953

Harnett, Katie, Mgr, Research & Education, International Tennis Hall of Fame & Museum Library, 194 Bellevue Ave, Newport, RI, 02840. Tel: 401-849-3990, Ext 1109. p. 2034

Harney, Meghan, Dir, Lowville Free Library, 5387 Dayan St, Lowville, NY, 13367. Tel: 315-376-2131. p. 1566

Harnke, Ben, Pres, Colorado Council of Medical Librarians, PO Box 101058, Denver, CO, 80210-1058. Tel: 303-724-2124. p. 2762

Harnke, Deborah, Ref Librn, Bureau of Land Management Library, Denver Federal Ctr, Bldg 85, W-5, Denver, CO, 80225. Tel: 303-236-6650. p. 273

Harnois, Michel, Exec Dir, La Societe d'Histoire de Sherbrooke, 275, rue Dufferin, Sherbrooke, QC, J1H 4M5, CANADA. Tel: 819-821-5406. p. 2737

Harold, Andrew, Librn, Logan-Hocking County District Library, Laurelville Branch, 16240 Maple St, Laurelville, OH, 43135. Tel: 740-332-4700. p. 1796

Harold, Marlena, Youth Serv, Satellite Beach Public Library, 751 Jamaica Blvd, Satellite Beach, FL, 32937. Tel: 321-779-4004. p. 443

Haroon, Ashaki, Access Serv Supvr, Xavier University of Louisiana, One Drexel Dr, New Orleans, LA, 70125-1098. Tel: 504-520-7311. p. 904

Harp, Darcy, Programming Librn, Pub Relations Librn, Pine River Public Library District, 395 Bayfield Center Dr, Bayfield, CO, 81122. Tel: 970-884-2222. p. 266

Harp, Jessica, Br Mgr, San Bernardino County Library, Running Springs Branch, 2677 Whispering Pines Dr, Running Springs, CA, 92382. Tel: 909-867-3604. p. 213

Harp, Shea, Libr Dir, Gatesville Public Library, 111 N Eighth St, Gatesville, TX, 76528. Tel: 254-865-5367. p. 2184

Harper, Ann K, Dir, Babcock Library, 25 Pompey Hollow Rd, Ashford, CT, 06278. Tel: 860-487-4420. p. 301

Harper, Cheryl, Bus Off Mgr, The Ferguson Library, One Public Library Plaza, Stamford, CT, 06904. Tel: 203-351-8210. p. 338

Harper, Dana, Ad, Watauga Public Library, 7109 Whitley Rd, Watauga, TX, 76148-2024. Tel: 817-514-5864. p. 2255

Harper, Dorothy, Dir, Paullina Public Library, 113 S Mickley St, Paullina, IA, 51046. Tel: 712-949-3941. p. 776

Harper, Gilford, Dir, Colorado River Indian Tribes Public Library/Archives, Second Ave & Mohave Rd, Rte 1, Box 23-B, Parker, AZ, 85344. Tel: 928-669-1332. p. 67

Harper, Hannah, Mgr, Satilla Regional Library, Ambrose Public Library, 1070 Cypress St, Ambrose, GA, 31512. Tel: 912-359-2536. p. 476

Harper, James, Pub Serv Librn, Wake Forest University, 1834 Wake Forest Rd, Winston-Salem, NC, 27109. Tel: 336-758-5675. p. 1726

Harper, Jennifer, Libr Support Serv Asst, Stormont, Dundas & Glengarry County Library, Chesterville Branch, One Mill St, Chesterville, ON, K0C 1H0, CANADA. Tel: 613-448-2616. p. 2638

Harper, Jill, Info Serv Librn, Heartland Community College Library, 1500 W Raab Rd, Normal, IL, 61761. Tel: 309-268-8277. p. 625

Harper, Ketziah, Mgr, Satilla Regional Library, Broxton Public Library, 105 Church St, Broxton, GA, 31519. Tel: 912-359-3887. p. 476

Harper, Lauren, Br Librn, Bedford Public Library System, Forest Library, 15583 Forest Rd, Forest, VA, 24551. Tel: 540-425-7002. p. 2306

Harper, Linda, Dir, Hingham Public Library, 66 Leavitt St, Hingham, MA, 02043. Tel: 781-741-1405, Ext 2600. p. 1024

Harper, Lindsey, Archivist, Rec Mgt Librn, Marshall University Libraries, One John Marshall Dr, Huntington, WV, 25755-2060. Tel: 304-696-3174. p. 2405

Harper, Lu, Art Librn, University of Rochester, Charlotte Whitney Allen Library, Memorial Art Gallery, 500 University Ave, Rochester, NY, 14607. Tel: 585-276-8999. p. 1631

Harper, Lynn, Head Librn, Capital Area District Libraries, Dansville Library, 1379 E Mason St, Dansville, MI, 48819. Tel: 517-623-6511. p. 1124

Harper, Marc, Ref Librn, Universite de Moncton, 18, ave Antonine-Maillet, Moncton, NB, E1A 3E9, CANADA. Tel: 506-858-4012. p. 2603

Harper, Mary Beth, Dir, Elmhurst Public Library, 125 S Prospect Ave, Elmhurst, IL, 60126-3298. Tel: 630-279-8696. p. 585

Harper, Megan, Dr, Prof, Kent State University, 314 University Library, 1125 Risman Dr, Kent, OH, 44242-0001. Tel: 330-672-2782. p. 2790

Harper, Nancy L, Dir, White Cloud Community Library, 1038 Wilcox Ave, White Cloud, MI, 49349. Tel: 231-689-6631. p. 1159

Harper, Patti, Head, Res Support Serv, Carleton University Library, 1125 Colonel By Dr, Ottawa, ON, K1S 5B6, CANADA. Tel: 613-520-2600, Ext 8066. p. 2666

Harper, Regan, Dir, Networking & Res Sharing, Colorado State Library, 201 E Colfax Ave, Rm 309, Denver, CO, 80203-1799. Tel: 303-866-6907. p. 274

Harper, Rita, Operations Mgr, Charleston Carnegie Public Library, 712 Sixth St, Charleston, IL, 61920. Tel: 217-345-4913. p. 552

Harper, Samantha, Archivist, Buffalo Bill Historical Center, 720 Sheridan Ave, Cody, WY, 82414. Tel: 307-578-4059. p. 2493

Harper, Sarah Mae, Mgr, County of Los Angeles Public Library, Hermosa Beach Library, 550 Pier Ave, Hermosa Beach, CA, 90254-3892. Tel: 310-379-8475. p. 136

Harper, Teresa, Mgr, Eastern State Hospital, 4601 Ironbound Rd, Williamsburg, VA, 23188. Tel: 757-208-7813. p. 2353

Harpst, Chuck, Hist Coll Librn, Ref Librn, Tecumseh District Library, 215 N Ottawa St, Tecumseh, MI, 49286-1564. Tel: 517-423-2238. p. 1153

Harpster, Amy, Asst Dir, Orange Public Library & History Center, 407 E Chapman Ave, Orange, CA, 92866-1509. Tel: 714-288-2425. p. 189

Harr, Connie, Libr Mgr, Wake County Public Library System, Northeast Regional Library, 14401 Green Elm Lane, Raleigh, NC, 27614. Tel: 919-570-7166. p. 1711

Harr, Grace, Br Mgr, Shreve Memorial Library, Blanchard Branch, 344 Alexander St, Blanchard, LA, 71009. Tel: 318-929-3163. p. 908

Harral, Lisa, Dir, Blackfoot Public Library, 129 N Broadway, Blackfoot, ID, 83221-2204. Tel: 208-785-8628. p. 515

Harray, Kacie, Children's Programmer, Valemount Public Library, 1090A Main St, Valemount, BC, V0E 2Z0, CANADA. Tel: 250-566-4367. p. 2578

Harrell, Brenda M, Libr Dir, The Edward Waters College Library, 1658 Kings Rd, Jacksonville, FL, 32209-6199. Tel: 904-470-8080. p. 411

Harrell, Kendra, Libr Dir, Atlanta Public Library, 101 W Hiram St, Atlanta, TX, 75551. Tel: 903-796-2112. p. 2137

Harrell, Renee, Ref Librn, Wharton County Library, El Campo Branch, 200 W Church St, El Campo, TX, 77437. Tel: 979-543-2362. p. 2256

Harrelson, Betty, Ch Serv, Andalusia Public Library, 212 S Three Notch St, Andalusia, AL, 36420. Tel: 334-222-6612. p. 4

Harrelson, Marsha, Librn, Conway Springs City Library, 210 W Spring St, Conway Springs, KS, 67031. Tel: 620-456-2859. p. 803

Harries, Ruth, Ref & Instruction Librn, Butler Community College Library & Archives, Library 600 Bldg, 901 S Haverhill Rd, El Dorado, KS, 67042-3280. Tel: 316-323-6846. p. 805

Harrigan, Mary, Head, Ref Serv, Crown Point Community Library, 122 N Main St, Crown Point, IN, 46307. Tel: 219-663-0270. p. 678

Harriger, Sherill L, Libr Dir, Warner University, 13895 Hwy 27, Lake Wales, FL, 33859. Tel: 863-638-7674. p. 416
Harrington, Andrea, Dir, Vershire Community Library, Church-Orr House, Rte 113, Vershire, VT, 05079. Tel: 802-685-9982. p. 2297
Harrington, Brenda, Adult Prog Coordr, Belfast Free Library, 106 High St, Belfast, ME, 04915. Tel: 207-338-3884. p. 916
Harrington, Caitlin, Head, Info Access Serv, University Libraries, University of Memphis, 3785 Norriswood Ave, Memphis, TN, 38152. Tel: 901-678-8226. p. 2115
Harrington, Chris, Ref Librn, Middlesex County Library, 34-B Frank St, Strathroy, ON, N7G 2R4, CANADA. Tel: 519-245-1290. p. 2682
Harrington, Heather, Assoc Librn, Historic Deerfield Inc & Pocumtuck Valley Memorial, Six Memorial St, Deerfield, MA, 01342-9736. Tel: 413-775-7125. p. 1014
Harrington, Kathy, Libr Dir, Ferris Public Library, 301 E Tenth St, Ferris, TX, 75125. Tel: 972-904-1788. p. 2176
Harrington, Liza, Coordr, Libr Serv, Greenfield Community College, Core Bldg, 3rd Flr, One College Dr, Greenfield, MA, 01301-9739. Tel: 413-775-1836. p. 1022
Harrington, Marni, Libr Dir, University of Western Ontario, FNB 3020, London, ON, N6A 5B9, CANADA. Tel: 519-661-2111, Ext 88488. p. 2655
Harrington, Melissa, Head, Youth Serv, Huron Public Library, 333 Williams St, Huron, OH, 44839. Tel: 419-433-5009. p. 1791
Harrington, Micki, Ms, Head of Moriarty Library, Lesley University, South Campus, 89 Brattle St, Cambridge, MA, 02138-2790. Tel: 617-349-8850. p. 1008
Harrington, Rebecca, Clinical Librn, University of Tennessee Graduate School of Medicine, 1924 Alcoa Hwy, Box U-111, Knoxville, TN, 37920. Tel: 865-305-8776. p. 2107
Harrington, Richard, Law Librn, Hennepin County Law Library, C-2451 Government Ctr, 300 S Sixth St, Minneapolis, MN, 55487. Tel: 612-348-2952. p. 1183
Harrington, Ryan, Libr Dir, Mineral Area College, 5270 Flat River Rd, Park Hills, MO, 63601. Tel: 573-518-2236. p. 1265
Harrington, Sara, Archivist/Librn, Ohio University Libraries, Mahn Center for Archives & Special Collections, Vernon R Alden Library, 30 Park Pl, Fifth Flr, Athens, OH, 45701-2978. Tel: 740-593-2710. p. 1748
Harrington, Sean, Electronic Res Librn, Ref Librn, Arizona State University, College of Law, Arizona State University MC 9620, 111 E Taylor St, Ste 350, Phoenix, AZ, 85004. Tel: 480-965-4865. p. 69
Harrington, Sherre L, Dir, Berry College, 2277 Martha Berry Hwy, Mount Berry, GA, 30149. Tel: 706-236-2285. p. 492
Harrington, Steve, Circ Mgr, Gardner-Webb University, 110 S Main St, Boiling Springs, NC, 28017. Tel: 704-406-2183. p. 1674
Harrington, Wendy, Programming Librn, Hampton Falls Free Public Library, Seven Drinkwater Rd, Hampton Falls, NH, 03844. Tel: 603-926-3682. p. 1366
Harris, Adena, Asst Dir, Rossville Community Library, 407 N Main St, Rossville, KS, 66533. Tel: 785-584-6454. p. 833
Harris, Amanda, Head, Customer Serv, New Albany-Floyd County Public Library, 180 W Spring St, New Albany, IN, 47150. Tel: 812-949-3528. p. 709
Harris, Amy Houk, Asst Dean for Teaching & Learning, University of North Carolina at Greensboro, 320 College Ave, Greensboro, NC, 27412-0001. Tel: 336-256-0275. p. 1693
Harris, Angela, Regional Mgr, Dallas College, 12800 Abrams Rd, Dallas, TX, 75243. Tel: 972-238-6081. p. 2164
Harris, Arlisa, Dir, Forrest City Public Library, 421 S Washington St, Forrest City, AR, 72335-3839. Tel: 870-633-5646. p. 95
Harris, Benjamin, Univ Librn, Trinity University, One Trinity Pl, San Antonio, TX, 78212-7200. Tel: 210-999-8126. p. 2239
Harris, Beth, Ch Serv, Chester County Library, 100 Center St, Chester, SC, 29706. Tel: 803-377-8145. p. 2052
Harris, Beth R, Librn, Paier College Library, 84 Iranistan Ave, Bridgeport, CT, 06604. Tel: 203-287-3023. p. 304
Harris, Betzaida, Head, Circ, Palm Harbor Library, 2330 Nebraska Ave, Palm Harbor, FL, 34683. Tel: 727-784-3332, Ext 3011. p. 435
Harris, Beverly, Coll Develop, Ref Librn, Dillard University, 2601 Gentilly Blvd, New Orleans, LA, 70122. Tel: 504-816-4786. p. 901
Harris, Brenda, Librn, Lyons Public Library, 279 Eighth St, Lyons, OR, 97358-2122. Tel: 503-859-2366. p. 1885
Harris, Briana Rae, Dir, New England Public Library, 726 McKenzie Ave, New England, ND, 58647-7105. Tel: 701-579-4223. p. 1739
Harris, Catherine, Asst Dir, Oelwein Public Library, 201 E Charles St, Oelwein, IA, 50662-1939. Tel: 319-283-1515. p. 774
Harris, Cathy H, Br Mgr, Montgomery County Library, John C Currie Memorial Library Candor Branch, 138 S School Rd, Candor, NC, 27229. Tel: 910-974-4033. p. 1719
Harris, Chan, Acq of New Ser/Per, Anaheim Public Library, 500 W Broadway, Anaheim, CA, 92805-3699. Tel: 714-765-1840. p. 116
Harris, Chelsie, Br Mgr, San Diego County Library, La Mesa Branch, 8074 Allison Ave, La Mesa, CA, 91941-5001. Tel: 619-469-2151. p. 217
Harris, Christopher, Libr Dir, Pauline & Jane Chilton Memorial Marlin Public Library, 400 Oaks St, Marlin, TX, 76661. Tel: 254-883-6602. p. 2215
Harris, Cutrice, Head, Operations & Budget, Virginia's Academic Library Consortium, George Mason University, 4400 University Dr, Fenwick 5100, Fairfax, VA, 22030. Tel: 703-993-4654. p. 2776
Harris, Deb, Bus Mgr, Tech Serv Mgr, Forest Park Public Library, 7555 Jackson Blvd, Forest Park, IL, 60130. Tel: 708-366-7171. p. 588
Harris, Debbi, Libr Dir, Graettinger Public Library, 115 W Robins St, Graettinger, IA, 51342. Tel: 712-859-3592. p. 755
Harris, Debbie, Ch, Green County Public Library, 112 W Court St, Greensburg, KY, 42743. Tel: 270-932-7081. p. 857
Harris, Dedra, Br Mgr, Webster Parish Library System, Heflin Branch, 7041 Hwy 531, Heflin, LA, 71039. Tel: 318-371-1027. p. 898
Harris, Devon, Asst Mgr, Saint Louis County Library, Oak Bend Branch, 842 S Holmes Ave, Saint Louis, MO, 63122-6507. Tel: 314-994-3300, Ext 3650. p. 1274
Harris, Diane, Asst Librn, Hyrum Library, 50 W Main, Hyrum, UT, 84319. Tel: 435-245-6411. p. 2265
Harris, Dinah, Dir, Jackson-Madison County Library, 433 E Lafayette St, Jackson, TN, 38301. Tel: 731-425-8600. p. 2102
Harris, Emily, Asst Librn, McNairy County Libraries, Jack McConnico Memorial Library, 225 Oak Grove Rd, Selmer, TN, 38375. Tel: 731-645-5571. p. 2087
Harris, Emily, Archivist, Peace River Museum, Archives & Mackenzie Centre, 10302 99th St, Peace River, AB, T8S 1K1, CANADA. Tel: 780-624-4261. p. 2550
Harris, Essie, Br Mgr, Champaign Public Library, Douglass Branch, 504 E Grove St, Champaign, IL, 61820-3239. Tel: 217-403-2090. p. 552
Harris, Gaylee, Dir, Montgomery City Public Library, 224 N Allen St, Montgomery City, MO, 63361. Tel: 573-564-8022. p. 1263
Harris, Greg, Librn, New York State Department of Correctional Services, 1879 Davis St, Elmira, NY, 14901-1042. Tel: 607-734-3901, Ext 4600. p. 1531
Harris, Harland, Archivist, Bryan-Lang Historical Library, 311 Camden Ave, Woodbine, GA, 31569. Tel: 912-576-5841. p. 503
Harris, Harmony, Head, Children's Servx, Clinton Public Library, 313 S Fourth St, Clinton, IN, 47842-2398. Tel: 765-832-8349. p. 675
Harris, Heather, Dir, Menominee County Library, S319 Railroad St, Stephenson, MI, 49887. Tel: 906-753-6923. p. 1152
Harris, Jamey, Coordr, Tech Serv, Mansfield University, Five Swan St, Mansfield, PA, 16933. Tel: 570-662-4670. p. 1957
Harris, Jana, Librn, Joyce Public Library, 9490 W State Rd 120, Orland, IN, 46776. Tel: 260-829-6329. p. 712
Harris, Jenisa, Youth Serv Librn, Washington Public Library, 115 W Washington St, Washington, IA, 52353. Tel: 319-653-2726. p. 788
Harris, Jenny, Educ Librn, Austin Peay State University, 601 College St, Clarksville, TN, 37044. Tel: 931-221-7914. p. 2092
Harris, Jessica, Librn, Santa Rosa Junior College, 1501 Mendocino Ave, Santa Rosa, CA, 95401. Tel: 707-778-2425. p. 245
Harris, JoAnn, Librn, Marion Lawrence Memorial Library, 15 E Franklin St, Gratis, OH, 45330. Tel: 937-787-3502. p. 1788
Harris, Joanne, Ref Librn, Holmes Public Library, 470 Plymouth St, Halifax, MA, 02338. Tel: 781-293-2271. p. 1023
Harris, Johnnie, Mgr, Pine Mountain Regional Library, Butler Public, 56 W Main St, Butler, GA, 31006. Tel: 478-862-5428. p. 488
Harris, Jon, Dir, Portage County District Library, 10482 South St, Garrettsville, OH, 44231. Tel: 330-527-5082, Ext 219. p. 1787
Harris, Josh, Dir, Operations, Stark County District Library, 715 Market Ave N, Canton, OH, 44702. Tel: 330-458-2702. p. 1755
Harris, Kelly, Libr Dir, The Hampton Library, 2478 Main St, Bridgehampton, NY, 11932. Tel: 631-537-0015. p. 1496
Harris, Kelly, Dir, John Jermain Memorial Library, 201 Main St, Sag Harbor, NY, 11963. Tel: 631-725-0049, Ext 223. p. 1634
Harris, Kendra, Head Librn, United States Navy, MWR General Library, Bldg 620, 4163 N Jackson Rd, Indian Head, MD, 20640. Tel: 301-744-4850. p. 969
Harris, Kerri-Lynn, Children's & Youth Serv, Kimberly Public Library, 120 Madison St W, Kimberly, ID, 83341. Tel: 208-212-1565. p. 523
Harris, Khalisah, Librn, Spartanburg County Public Libraries, Pacolet Library, 390 W Main St, Pacolet, SC, 29372. Tel: 864-474-0421. p. 2070
Harris, Laura, Online Learning Librn, State University of New York at Oswego, SUNY Oswego, 7060 State Rte 104, Oswego, NY, 13126-3514. Tel: 315-312-3539. p. 1613
Harris, LeThesha, Interim Dir, Public Library Services, Nova Southeastern University Libraries, 3100 Ray Ferrero Jr Blvd, Fort Lauderdale, FL, 33314. Tel: 954-262-4639. p. 402
Harris, Linda, Head, Ref, University of Alabama at Birmingham, Mervyn H Sterne Library, 917 13th St S, Birmingham, AL, 35205. Tel: 205-934-6364. p. 9
Harris, Lindsay, Chief Exec Officer, Chief Librn, Woodstock Public Library, 445 Hunter St, Woodstock, ON, N4S 4G7, CANADA. Tel: 519-539-4801. p. 2705
Harris, Lindsey, Fac Mgr, Owen Sound & North Grey Union Public Library, 824 First Ave W, Owen Sound, ON, N4K 4K4, CANADA. Tel: 519-376-6623. p. 2671
Harris, Lori, Dean & Univ Librn, University of Cincinnati Libraries, PO Box 210033, Cincinnati, OH, 45221-0033. Tel: 513-556-1515. p. 1764
Harris, Lori, Asst Dir, University of Cincinnati Libraries, Donald C Harrison Health Sciences Library, 231 Albert Sabin Way, Cincinnati, OH, 45267. Tel: 513-558-0315. p. 1765

Harris, Lori-Lee, Br Librn, Southeast Regional Library, White City Branch, Community Ctr, 12 Ramm Ave, White City, SK, S4L 5B1, CANADA. Tel: 306-781-2118. p. 2755

Harris, Maggie, Head, Circ, Libr Tech, College of Southern Nevada, Henderson Campus, 700 S College Dr, H1A, Henderson, NV, 89002. Tel: 702-651-3066. p. 1346

Harris, Mallory, YA Librn, Greater Clarks Hill Regional Library System, 7022 Evans Town Center Blvd, Evans, GA, 30809. Tel: 706-863-1946. p. 478

Harris, Mandi, Youth Serv Librn, Coeur d'Alene Public Library, 702 E Front Ave, Coeur d'Alene, ID, 83814-2373. Tel: 208-769-2315. p. 519

Harris, Marie, Branch Lead, Charlotte Mecklenburg Library, Davidson Branch, 119 S Main St, Davidson, NC, 28036. Tel: 704-416-4000. p. 1679

Harris, Mary, Head Librn, Bevill State Community College, 2631 Temple Ave N, Fayette, AL, 35555. Tel: 205-932-3221, Ext 5141. p. 16

Harris, Mary, Dir & Librn, Oracle Public Library, 565 E American Ave, Oracle, AZ, 85623. Tel: 520-896-2121. p. 67

Harris, MaShonda, Br Mgr, Kansas City Public Library, Westport, 118 Westport Rd, Kansas City, MO, 64111. Tel: 816-701-3588. p. 1256

Harris, Matt, Asst Dir, Mississippi Valley Library District, Fairmont City Library Center, 4444 Collinsville Rd, Fairmont City, IL, 62201. Tel: 618-482-3966. p. 573

Harris, Megan, Circ Supvr, Sweet Briar College, 134 Chapel Rd, Sweet Briar, VA, 24595. Tel: 434-381-6308. p. 2348

Harris, Mercia, Librn, Torbay Public Library, 1339C Torbay Rd, Torbay, NL, A1K 1B2, CANADA. Tel: 709-437-6571. p. 2611

Harris, Michael, Dir, Statewide Libr Serv, Utah State University Eastern Library, 451 E & 400 N, Price, UT, 84501. Tel: 435-613-5209. p. 2269

Harris, Missy, Asst Dir, Lincoln County Library System, 519 Emerald St, Kemmerer, WY, 83101. Tel: 307-877-6961. p. 2495

Harris, Misty, News Res Librn, Express News Corp, 301 Ave E, San Antonio, TX, 78205. Tel: 210-250-3276. p. 2236

Harris, Monica, Exec Dir, Reaching Across Illinois Library System (RAILS), 125 Tower Dr, Burr Ridge, IL, 60527. Tel: 630-734-5129. p. 546

Harris, Nanci, Syst Adminr, University of Texas of the Permian Basin, 4901 E University Blvd, Odessa, TX, 79762. Tel: 432-552-2370. p. 2223

Harris, Nicole, Asst Dir, Innovative Tech Services, George Washington University, Jacob Burns Law Library, 716 20th St NW, Washington, DC, 20052. Tel: 202-994-4225. p. 367

Harris, Pam, Assoc Col Librn, Info & Res Serv, Swarthmore College, 500 College Ave, Swarthmore, PA, 19081. Tel: 610-690-2056. p. 2011

Harris, Philecia, Br Mgr, Cambridge Public Library, Central Square Branch, 45 Pearl St, Cambridge, MA, 02139. Tel: 617-349-4010. p. 1004

Harris, Rachel, Asst Dir, Operations, Frisco Public Library, 6101 Frisco Square Blvd, Frisco, TX, 75034-3000. Tel: 972-292-5669. p. 2182

Harris, Regina, Mgr, District of Columbia Public Library, Tenley-Friendship, 4450 Wisconsin Ave NW, Washington, DC, 20016. Tel: 202-727-1488. p. 364

Harris, Rob, Webmaster, Homewood Public Library, 1721 Oxmoor Rd, Homewood, AL, 35209-4085. Tel: 205-332-6631. p. 21

Harris, Robbie, Dir, McNairy County Libraries, Jack McConnico Memorial Library, 225 Oak Grove Rd, Selmer, TN, 38375. Tel: 731-645-5571. p. 2087

Harris, Robbie, Ms, Dir, McNairy County Libraries, 204 W Main St, Adamsville, TN, 38310. Tel: 731-632-3572. p. 2087

Harris, Robin, Info Serv Librn, Libr Coord, Northeastern Illinois University, Carruthers Center for Inner City Studies Library, 700 E Oakwood Blvd, Chicago, IL, 60653. Tel: 773-256-2134. p. 566

Harris, Ryan, Assoc Dean, Pub Serv, University of North Carolina at Charlotte, 9201 University City Blvd, Charlotte, NC, 28223-0001. Tel: 704-687-5892. p. 1681

Harris, Sandy, Res Spec, Tronox LLC, 3301 NW 150th St, Oklahoma City, OK, 73134. Tel: 405-775-5000. p. 1859

Harris, Sarah, Assoc Librn, National Humanities Center Library, Seven Alexander Dr, Research Triangle Park, NC, 27709. Tel: 919-549-0661. p. 1712

Harris, Sheila, Libr Dir, Enterprise Public Library, 101 E Grubbs St, Enterprise, AL, 36330. Tel: 334-347-2636. p. 15

Harris, Sherelle, Dir, Norwalk Public Library, One Belden Ave, Norwalk, CT, 06850. Tel: 203-899-2780, Ext 15123. p. 332

Harris, Shirley, Librn, Union University, Germantown Campus Library, 2745 Hacks Cross Rd, Germantown, TN, 38138. Tel: 901-312-1904. p. 2103

Harris, Stacey, Ref & Info Serv, Port Chester-Rye Brook Public Library, One Haseco Ave, Port Chester, NY, 10573. Tel: 914-939-6710. p. 1620

Harris, Steven, Dean of Libr, Northeastern Illinois University, 5500 N Saint Louis Ave, Chicago, IL, 60625-4699. Tel: 773-442-4400. p. 566

Harris, Steven R, Asst Dean, Coll & Knowledge Access Serv, University of Nevada-Reno, 1664 N Virginia St, Mailstop 0322, Reno, NV, 89557-0322. Tel: 775-682-5671. p. 1349

Harris, Suzan, Librn, Bartram Trail Regional Library, Thomson-McDuffie County, 338 Main St, Thomson, GA, 30824. Tel: 706-595-1341. p. 502

Harris, Tenisha, Br Mgr, Muncie Public Library, Connection Corner, 1824 E Cenntennial Ave, Muncie, IN, 47303. Tel: 765-747-8216. p. 708

Harris, Teresa, Dir, Access Serv, Columbia University, Access Services, Butler Library, 535 W 114th St, New York, NY, 10027. Tel: 212-854-2245. p. 1582

Harris, Teresa, Curator, Columbia University, Avery Architectural & Fine Arts Library, 300 Avery Hall, 1172 Amsterdam Ave, MC 0301, New York, NY, 10027. Tel: 212-854-6199. p. 1583

Harris, Teresa M, Dir, Columbia University, Avery Architectural & Fine Arts Library, 300 Avery Hall, 1172 Amsterdam Ave, MC 0301, New York, NY, 10027. Tel: (212) 854-3068. p. 1583

Harris, Terry, Circ, ILL, Cynthiana-Harrison County Public Library, 104 N Main St, Cynthiana, KY, 41031. Tel: 859-234-4881. p. 853

Harris, Tonia, Mgr, Libr Serv, Spartanburg Regional Medical Center, 101 E Wood St, Spartanburg, SC, 29303. Tel: 864-560-6220, 864-560-6770. p. 2070

Harris, Wade, Libr Assoc II, Texas A&M University Libraries, Business Library & Collaboration Commons, 214 Olsen Blvd, College Station, TX, 77843. Tel: 979-845-2111. p. 2157

Harris, William A, Dir, National Archives & Records Administration, 4079 Albany Post Rd, Hyde Park, NY, 12538. Tel: 845-486-1977. p. 1550

Harris, Wynn, Ref Spec, Central New Mexico Community College Libraries, 525 Buena Vista SE, Albuquerque, NM, 87106-4023. Tel: 505-224-4000, Ext 51498. p. 1460

Harrison, Amanda, Dr, Asst Prof, University of Central Missouri, Dept of Educational Technology & Library Science, Lovinger 4101, Warrensburg, MO, 64093. Tel: 660-543-4910. p. 2787

Harrison, Ann, ILL Coordr, Peterborough Town Library, Two Concord St, Peterborough, NH, 03458. Tel: 603-924-8040. p. 1378

Harrison, Anne, Theological Librn, Calvin University & Calvin Theological Seminary, 1855 Knollcrest Circle SE, Grand Rapids, MI, 49546-4402. Tel: 616-526-6121. p. 1110

Harrison, Ben, Pub Serv Librn, Lakeland College Library, 5707 College Dr, Vermilion, AB, T9X 1K5, CANADA. Tel: 780-871-5797. p. 2558

Harrison, Ben, Pub Serv Librn, Lakeland College, 2602 59 Ave, Bag 6600, Lloydminster, SK, T9V 3N7, CANADA. Tel: 780-871-5797. p. 2742

Harrison, Bill, Head, Tech Serv, Parsippany-Troy Hills Free Public Library, 449 Halsey Rd, Parsippany, NJ, 07054. Tel: 973-887-5150. p. 1433

Harrison, Bob, Distance Learning Librn, Virginia Peninsula Community College Library, 227C Kecoughtan Hall, 99 Thomas Nelson Dr, Hampton, VA, 23666. Tel: 757-825-3829. p. 2323

Harrison, C Lynne, Coordr, Tech Serv, Interim Dean, Libr Serv, Norfolk State University Library, 700 Park Ave, Norfolk, VA, 23504-8010. Tel: 757-823-9153. p. 2335

Harrison, Carol, Circ Mgr, Southern Adventist University, 4851 Industrial Dr, Collegedale, TN, 37315. Tel: 423-236-2010. p. 2094

Harrison, Carrie, Br Mgr, Morton Public Library, 16 E Fourth Ave, Morton, MS, 39117. Tel: 601-732-6288. p. 1227

Harrison, Catha, Circ, Tech Serv, Warren County Memorial Library, 119 South Front St, Warrenton, NC, 27589. Tel: 252-257-4990. p. 1720

Harrison, Chase H, Assoc Dir, Harvard Library, Harvard-MIT Data Center, CGIS Knafel Bldg, 1737 Cambridge St, Cambridge, MA, 02138. Tel: 617-495-4734. p. 1006

Harrison, Danielle, Head Librn, MPR Associates, Inc, 320 King St, Ste 400, Alexandria, VA, 22314. Tel: 703-519-0567. p. 2303

Harrison, Dorothy, Br Mgr, Athens Regional Library System, Lay Park Resource Center, Lay Park Community Ctr, 3rd Flr, 297 Hoyt St, Athens, GA, 30601. Tel: 706-613-3667. p. 458

Harrison, Fabian, Borrower Serv Librn, Colls Librn, SIAST-Saskatchewan Institute of Applied Science & Technology, 1130 Idylwyld Dr, Saskatoon, SK, S7K 3R5, CANADA. Tel: 306-659-4240. p. 2749

Harrison, Fran, Dir, Grinnell Library, 2642 E Main St, Wappingers Falls, NY, 12590. Tel: 845-297-3428, Ext 806. p. 1658

Harrison, Heather, Br Mgr, East Baton Rouge Parish Library, Central, 11260 Joor Rd, Baton Rouge, LA, 70818. Tel: 225-262-2680. p. 883

Harrison, Holly, Curator, Dep Dir, Mississippi Museum of Art, 380 S Lamar St, Jackson, MS, 39201. Tel: 601-960-1515. p. 1223

Harrison, Janet, Libr Dir, Muhlenberg County Libraries, 117 S Main St, Greenville, KY, 42345. Tel: 270-338-4760. p. 857

Harrison, Jann, Dir, Med Health Info, CHRISTUS Santa Rosa Health Care, 333 N Santa Rosa St, Ste F5626, San Antonio, TX, 78207. Tel: 210-704-3785. p. 2236

Harrison, Jasmine, Commun Libr Mgr, Queens Library, Rochdale Village Community Library, 169-09 137th Ave, Jamaica, NY, 11434. Tel: 718-723-4440. p. 1555

Harrison, Jeanne, Customer Serv Supvr, Naperville Public Library, 200 W Jefferson Ave, Naperville, IL, 60540-5374. Tel: 630-961-4100, Ext 6321. p. 622

Harrison, Julie, Asst Dir, Head, Youth Serv, Verona Public Library, 500 Silent St, Verona, WI, 53593. Tel: 608-845-7180. p. 2482

Harrison, Kate, ILL, Whatcom Community College Library, Heiner Bldg, 231 W Kellogg Rd, Bellingham, WA, 98226. Tel: 360-383-3300. p. 2359

Harrison, Laurie, Ch, Great Barrington Libraries, 231 Main St, Great Barrington, MA, 01230. Tel: 413-528-2403. p. 1022

Harrison, Linda, Br Mgr, Nashville Public Library, Edmondson Pike Branch, 5501 Edmondson Pike, Nashville, TN, 37211. Tel: 615-880-3957. p. 2119
Harrison, Linton, Br Mgr, Burnaby Public Library, Tommy Douglas Branch, 7311 Kingsway, Burnaby, BC, V5E 1G8, CANADA. Tel: 604-297-4824. p. 2563
Harrison, Lynn, Sr Asst Librn, Haldimand County Public Library, Dunnville Branch, 317 Chestnut St, Dunnville, ON, N1A 2H4, CANADA. p. 2639
Harrison, Margaret, Chief, Libr Serv, United States Army, Marquat Memorial Library, Bank Hall, Bldg D-3915, 3004 Ardennes St, Fort Bragg, NC, 28310-9610. Tel: 910-396-3958. p. 1689
Harrison, Margaret, Chief, Joint Forces Staff College, 7800 Hampton Blvd, Norfolk, VA, 23511-1702. Tel: 757-443-6400. p. 2334
Harrison, Marjorie, Dir, Calcasieu Parish Public Library System, 301 W Claude St, Lake Charles, LA, 70605-3457. Tel: 337-721-7147. p. 893
Harrison, Mary, Dir, Coloma Public Library, 151 W Center St, Coloma, MI, 49038. Tel: 269-468-3431. p. 1093
Harrison, Mary, Head, Children's Servx, Public Library for Union County, 255 Reitz Blvd, Lewisburg, PA, 17837-9211. Tel: 570-523-1172. p. 1955
Harrison, Melanie, Mkt Coordr, North Liberty Library, 520 W Cherry St, North Liberty, IA, 52317-9797. Tel: 319-626-5701. p. 773
Harrison, Pam, Libr Dir, Apache Junction Public Library, 1177 N Idaho Rd, Apache Junction, AZ, 85119. Tel: 480-474-8615. p. 55
Harrison, Priscilla, Circ Mgr, Tarrant County College, 828 W Harwood Rd, Hurst, TX, 76054. Tel: 817-515-6622. p. 2201
Harrison, Rebecca, Libr Asst, Elmer Library, 120 S Main St, Elmer, NJ, 08318. Tel: 856-358-2014. p. 1401
Harrison, Seth, Circ Supvr, Hales Corners Library, 5885 S 116th St, Hales Corners, WI, 53130-1707. Tel: 414-529-6150, Ext 13. p. 2440
Harrison, Stephanie, Dir, Patterson Library, 1167 Rte 311, Patterson, NY, 12563. Tel: 845-878-6121. p. 1615
Harrison, Stewart, Head of Libr, Defence Research & Development Canada, 1133 Sheppard Ave W, Toronto, ON, M3K 2C9, CANADA. Tel: 416-635-2070. p. 2688
Harrison, Tanja, Univ Librn, Mount Saint Vincent University Library & Archives, 15 Lumpkin Rd, Halifax, NS, B3M 2J6, CANADA. Tel: 902-457-6108. p. 2619
Harrison, Teresia, Dir, Chandler-Watts Memorial Library, 340 N Oak, Stratford, OK, 74872. Tel: 580-759-2684. p. 1863
Harrison-Cox, Lucinda, Assoc Law Librn, Roger Williams University, Ten Metacom Ave, Bristol, RI, 02809-5171. Tel: 401-254-4546. p. 2029
Harrison-Thomas, Suzanne, Asst Dir, Head, Tech Serv, Milford Public Library, 57 New Haven Ave, Milford, CT, 06460. Tel: 203-783-3290. p. 323
Harrity, Phillip, Access Serv, Archives, Point Park University Library, 414 Wood St, Pittsburgh, PA, 15222. Tel: 412-392-3171. p. 1995
Harrop, Justin, Children's Activities Dir, Hartford Public Library District, 143 W Hawthorne, Hartford, IL, 62048. Tel: 618-254-9394. p. 597
Harsha, Sonya, YA Librn, Algona Public Library, 210 N Phillips St, Algona, IA, 50511. Tel: 515-295-5476. p. 730
Harshbarger, Jess, Br Mgr, Chesterfield County Public Library, Midlothian Branch, 521 Coalfield Rd, Midlothian, VA, 23114. Tel: 804-751-2275. p. 2312
Harshbarger, Tammy, Br Mgr, Clark County Public Library, Houston, 5 W Jamestown St, South Charleston, OH, 45368. Tel: 937-462-8047. p. 1821
Harston, Julie, Circ, Ref Librn, Lipscomb University, One University Park Dr, Nashville, TN, 37204-3951. Tel: 615-966-5717. p. 2119
Hart, Amy, Libr Asst, Grafton Community Library, 2455 NY Rte 2, Grafton, NY, 12082. Tel: 518-279-0580. p. 1540
Hart, Andrew, Head, Presv, University of North Carolina at Chapel Hill, 208 Raleigh St, CB 3916, Chapel Hill, NC, 27515. Tel: 919-962-1053. p. 1678
Hart, Andrew, Ref Librn, Ohio Bureau of Worker's Compensation, 30 W Spring St, Third Flr, Columbus, OH, 43215-2256. Tel: 614-466-7388. p. 1774
Hart, Cara, Dir, Neillsville Public Library, 409 Hewett St, Neillsville, WI, 54456-1923. Tel: 715-743-2558. p. 2464
Hart, Carol Ghiorsi, Dir, Greensboro Historical Museum Archives Library, 130 Summit Ave, Greensboro, NC, 27401-3004. Tel: 336-373-2306. p. 1692
Hart, Christina, Supvr, Mid-Columbia Libraries, Basin City Branch, 50-A N Canal Blvd, Basin City, WA, 99343. Tel: 509-269-4201. p. 2367
Hart Coatsworth, Sarah, Mkt Mgr, Outreach Mgr, Chatham-Kent Public Library, 120 Queen St, Chatham, ON, N7M 2G6, CANADA. Tel: 519-354-2940. p. 2635
Hart, Cynthia, Libr Mgr, Virginia Beach Public Library, Oceanfront Area, 700 Virginia Beach Blvd, Virginia Beach, VA, 23451. Tel: 757-385-2640. p. 2351
Hart, Dana, Dir, Ilsley Public Library, 75 Main St, Middlebury, VT, 05753. Tel: 802-388-4098. p. 2288
Hart, Elizabeth, Libr Tech, California School for the Blind Library, 500 Walnut Ave, Fremont, CA, 94536. Tel: 510-794-3800, Ext 259, 510-936-5575. p. 143
Hart, Emily, Librn, Syracuse University Libraries, Carnegie Library, Carnegie Bldg, 130 Sims Dr, Syracuse, NY, 13244. Tel: 315-443-2403. p. 1650
Hart, George, Dir of Libr, University of Massachusetts Lowell Library, 61 Wilder St, Lowell, MA, 01854-3098. Tel: 978-934-4550, 978-934-4551. p. 1030
Hart, Glynis, Dir, Wilmot Public Library, 11 N Wilmot Rd, Wilmot, NH, 03287-4302. Tel: 603-526-6804. p. 1384
Hart, Haley, Head, Circ, Winchester Public Library, 80 Washington St, Winchester, MA, 01890. Tel: 781-721-7171. p. 1070
Hart, Jackie, Adult Serv Supvr, West Springfield Public Library, 200 Park St, West Springfield, MA, 01089. Tel: 413-736-4561, Ext 3. p. 1066
Hart, Jennifer, Librn, University of Chicago Library, Eckhart Library, 1118 E 58th St, Chicago, IL, 60637. Tel: 773-702-8778. p. 570
Hart, Kaeleigh, Ch Serv, Leicester Public Library & Local History Museum, 1136 Main St, Leicester, MA, 01524. Tel: 508-892-7020. p. 1027
Hart, Karen, Asst Libr Dir, Friendswood Public Library, 416 S Friendswood Dr, Friendswood, TX, 77546-3897. Tel: 281-482-7135. p. 2182
Hart, Karen, Exec Dir, Mary Ball Washington Museum & Library, Inc, 8346 Mary Ball Rd, Lancaster, VA, 22503. Tel: 804-462-7280. p. 2327
Hart, Karen C, Asst Librn, Choctaw County Public Library, 703 E Jackson St, Hugo, OK, 74743. Tel: 580-326-5591. p. 1850
Hart, Kathleen, Prog Coordr, Canterbury Public Library, One Municipal Dr, Canterbury, CT, 06331-1453. Tel: 860-546-9022. p. 305
Hart, Kerri, Dir, Garden Valley District Library, 85 Old Crouch Rd, Garden Valley, ID, 83622. Tel: 208-462-3317. p. 521
Hart, Lanette, Div Mgr, Charlotte County Library System, 2050 Forrest Nelson Blvd, Port Charlotte, FL, 33952. Tel: 941-613-3200. p. 438
Hart, Lea, District Dir, Delta County Libraries, 149 E Main St, Hotchkiss, CO, 81419. Tel: 970-399-7878. p. 286
Hart, Mary K, Dept Chair, Pub Serv, San Diego Miramar College, 10440 Black Mountain Rd, San Diego, CA, 92126-2999. Tel: 619-388-7614. p. 218
Hart, Mary Lee, Ad/Coll Develop/e-Res, Northland Public Library, 300 Cumberland Rd, Pittsburgh, PA, 15237-5455. Tel: 412-366-8100, Ext 113. p. 1994
Hart, Melanie Dawn, Br Librn, Carnegie Public Library, South Fork Branch, 0031 Mall St, South Fork, CO, 81154. Tel: 719-873-5079. p. 291
Hart, Michelle, Libr Assoc, North Dakota State College of Science, 800 Sixth St N, Wahpeton, ND, 58076-0001. Tel: 701-671-2620. p. 1741
Hart, Pat, Dir, Norton Public Library, One Washington Sq, Norton, KS, 67654. Tel: 785-877-2481. p. 827
Hart, R J, Library & Archives Paraprofessional V, Washington State University Libraries, Owen Science & Engineering, PO Box 643200, Pullman, WA, 99164-3200. Tel: 509-335-2675. p. 2374
Hart, Regina, Librn, Michael Baker International Library, 100 Airside Dr, Moon Township, PA, 15108. Tel: 724-495-4021. p. 1965
Hart, Renae, Libr Coord, Lincoln Public Library, 485 Twelve Bridges Dr, Lincoln, CA, 95648. Tel: 916-434-2410. p. 156
Hart, Sara, Librn, Darwin R Barker Library Association, Seven Day St, Fredonia, NY, 14063-1891. Tel: 716-672-8051. p. 1535
Hart, Sarah, Ref Librn, Insurance Library Association of Boston, 156 State St, 2nd Flr, Boston, MA, 02109. Tel: 617-227-2087, Ext 202. p. 996
Hart, Stephen, Tech Serv Mgr, Flint River Regional Library System, 800 Memorial Dr, Griffin, GA, 30223. Tel: 770-412-4770. p. 481
Hart, Susan, Dir, Rushford Public Library, 101 N Mill St, Rushford, MN, 55971. Tel: 507-864-7600. p. 1195
Hart, Tara, Archives Mgr, Whitney Museum of American Art, 99 Gansevoort St, New York, NY, 10014. Tel: 212-671-5335. p. 1604
Hart, Vicky, Dir, Libr Serv, Alamo Colleges District, 1201 Kitty Hawk Rd, Universal City, TX, 78148. Tel: 210-486-5461. p. 2250
Hart, Vicky, Pres, Council of Research & Academic Libraries, c/o Southwest Research Institute, 6220 Culebra Rd, San Antonio, TX, 78212. Tel: 210-486-5461. p. 2775
Harte, Jenna, Adult Serv, Evergreen Park Public Library, 9400 S Troy Ave, Evergreen Park, IL, 60805-2383. Tel: 708-422-8522. p. 587
Harte, Julie, Libr Dir, Somonauk Public Library District, 700 E LaSalle St, Somonauk, IL, 60552. Tel: 815-498-2440. p. 648
Hartel, Lynda J, Asst Dir, Ohio State University LIBRARIES, John A Prior Health Sciences Library, 376 W Tenth Ave, Columbus, OH, 43210-1240. Tel: 614-292-4892. p. 1776
Harter, Melissa, Libr Dir, Fairbanks North Star Borough Libraries, 1215 Cowles St, Fairbanks, AK, 99701. Tel: 907-459-1020. p. 45
Hartfield, Lynn, Asst Dir, Vidor Public Library, 440 E Bolivar St, Vidor, TX, 77662. Tel: 409-769-7148. p. 2252
Hartford, Brenda, Librn, Harvey Memorial Library, 771 State Hwy 150, Parkman, ME, 04443-3201. Tel: 207-876-3730. p. 935
Hartig, Elizabeth, Pub Serv Librn, Ref, Monroe County Community College, 1555 S Raisinville Rd, Monroe, MI, 48161-9047. Tel: 734-384-4204. p. 1133
Hartigan, Christine, Dir, East Rutherford Memorial Library, 143 Boiling Springs Ave, East Rutherford, NJ, 07073. Tel: 201-939-3930. p. 1400
Hartin, Linda, Circ, ILL, Morristown Centennial Library, Seven Richmond St, Morrisville, VT, 05661. Tel: 802-888-3853. p. 2289
Hartlaub, Peter, Reporter/Archives, San Francisco Chronicle Library & Archive, 901 Mission St, San Francisco, CA, 94103. p. 227
Hartle, Brooke, Dir, United States Army, 4300 Camp Hale Rd, Fort Drum, NY, 13602. Tel: 315-772-9099. p. 1534

Hartle, Rebecca, Libr Assoc II, Pub Serv, Student Asst Supvr, University of Georgia Libraries, Map & Government Information, 320 S Jackson St, Athens, GA, 30602. Tel: 706-542-0662. p. 459

Hartley, Bill, Dir, Media Serv, North Park University, Brandel Library, 5114 N Christiana Ave, Chicago, IL, 60625. Tel: 773-244-5579. p. 566

Hartley, Cody, Dir, Georgia O'Keeffe Museum, 217 Johnson St, Santa Fe, NM, 87501. p. 1476

Hartley, Jeffery, Dir, National Archives & Records Administration, 8601 Adelphi Rd, Rm 2500, College Park, MD, 20740. Tel: 301-837-1795. p. 962

Hartley, Jessica, Dir, Poquoson Public Library, 500 City Hall Ave, Poquoson, VA, 23662-1996. Tel: 757-868-3060. p. 2337

Hartley, Kathy, Asst Dir, Lewis County Public Library, 27 Third St, Vanceburg, KY, 41179. Tel: 606-796-2532. p. 876

Hartley, Katie, Instruction Librn, Gardner-Webb University, 110 S Main St, Boiling Springs, NC, 28017. Tel: 704-406-4293. p. 1674

Hartley, Natalie, Libr Asst, Bennington Public Library, 11401 N 156th St, Bennington, NE, 68007. Tel: 402-238-2201. p. 1308

Hartling, Mary, Br Asst, Cumberland Public Libraries, Pugwash Library, 10222 Durham St, Pugwash, NS, B0K 1L0, CANADA. Tel: 902-243-3331. p. 2615

Hartman, Alex, Assoc Dir, Br Mgr, Ada Community Library, Lake Hazel Branch, 10489 W Lake Hazel Rd, Boise, ID, 83709. Tel: 208-297-6700. p. 516

Hartman, Becky, Ch, Hamburg Public Library, 35 N Third St, Hamburg, PA, 19526-1502. Tel: 610-562-2843. p. 1939

Hartman, Britni, Dir, Schmaling Memorial Public Library District, 501 Tenth Ave, Fulton, IL, 61252. Tel: 815-589-2045. p. 590

Hartman, Carolyn, Dir, Cumberland Public Library, 119 Main St, Cumberland, IA, 50843-9900. Tel: 712-774-5334. p. 743

Hartman, Chrissy, Circ, Computer Serv, Massachusetts College of Art & Design, 621 Huntington Ave, Boston, MA, 02115-5882. Tel: 617-879-7150. p. 996

Hartman, David, Curator, Wyandotte County Historical Museum, 631 N 126th St, Bonner Springs, KS, 66012. Tel: 913-573-5002. p. 799

Hartman, Elizabeth, Ref Librn, John A Logan College Library, 700 Logan College Dr, Carterville, IL, 62918. Tel: 618-985-3741, Ext 8338. p. 550

Hartman, Fritz, Dir, Goshen College, Harold & Wilma Good Library, 1700 S Main, Goshen, IN, 46526-4794. Tel: 574-535-7423. p. 687

Hartman, Hanna, Archives Collections Specialist, Valparaiso University, 1410 Chapel Dr, Valparaiso, IN, 46383-6493. Tel: 219-464-5500. p. 723

Hartman, Jeffrey, Commun Relations Spec, Marketing Specialist, Chelmsford Public Library, 25 Boston Rd, Chelmsford, MA, 01824. Tel: 978-256-5521. p. 1010

Hartman, Kate, Library Operations Assoc, Northern Illinois University Libraries, David C Shapiro Memorial Law Library, Swen Parson Hall, 2nd Flr, Normal Rd, DeKalb, IL, 60115-2890. Tel: 815-753-9184. p. 578

Hartman, Lisa, Librn, Krabbenhoft Public Library, 512 Elk St, Sabula, IA, 52070. Tel: 563-687-2950. p. 780

Hartman, Lisa A, Govt Doc Coordr, Frostburg State University, One Susan Eisel Dr, Frostburg, MD, 21532. Tel: 301-687-4734. p. 967

Hartman, Mary, Exec Dir, Peabody Public Library, 1160 E State Rd 205, Columbia City, IN, 46725. Tel: 260-244-5541. p. 676

Hartman, Patricia, Libr Mgr, Bucks County Free Library, Yardley-Makefield Branch, 1080 Edgewood Rd, Yardley, PA, 19067-1648. Tel: 215-493-9020. p. 1927

Hartman, Paula, Pub Serv Librn, Wake Technical Community College, Bldg D, 100 Level, 9101 Fayetteville Rd, Raleigh, NC, 27603-5696. Tel: 919-866-5644. p. 1711

Hartman, Rachael, Mgr, Geauga County Public Library, Middlefield Branch, 16167 E High St, Middlefield, OH, 44062. Tel: 440-632-1961. p. 1758

Hartman, Robin R, Dir, Libr Serv, Hope International University, 2500 E Nutwood Ave, Fullerton, CA, 92831. Tel: 714-879-3901, Ext 1212. p. 148

Hartman, Rochelle, Dir, Lincoln Library, 326 S Seventh St, Springfield, IL, 62701. Tel: 217-753-4900. p. 650

Hartman, Rochelle, Adult Serv Mgr, La Crosse Public Library, 800 Main St, La Crosse, WI, 54601. Tel: 608-789-8191. p. 2446

Hartman, Sandy, Head, Outreach Serv, Alexandrian Public Library, 115 W Fifth St, Mount Vernon, IN, 47620. Tel: 812-838-3286. p. 708

Hartman, Sarah, Head, Tech Serv, Middleton Public Library, 7425 Hubbard Ave, Middleton, WI, 53562-3117. Tel: 608-831-5564. p. 2457

Hartman, Shawn, Librn, Outreach Serv, Chadron State College, 300 E 12th St, Chadron, NE, 69337. Tel: 308-432-7062. p. 1310

Hartmann, Anna, Youth Serv Mgr, Council Bluffs Public Library, 400 Willow Ave, Council Bluffs, IA, 51503-9042. Tel: 712-323-7553, Ext 5417. p. 742

Hartmann, Carey D, County Librn, Exec Dir, Laramie County Library System, 2200 Pioneer Ave, Cheyenne, WY, 82001-3610. Tel: 307-773-7222. p. 2492

Hartmann, James, Head, Tech, Head, User Experience, Hewlett-Woodmere Public Library, 1125 Broadway, Hewlett, NY, 11557-0903. Tel: 516-374-1967. p. 1546

Hartmann, Jody, Circ, ILL, Phillips Public Library, 286 Cherry St, Phillips, WI, 54555. Tel: 715-339-2868. p. 2469

Hartmann, Jonathan, Dir, Discovery & Integrated Syst Librn, Georgetown University, Dahlgren Memorial Library, Preclinical Science Bldg GM-7, 3900 Reservoir Rd NW, Washington, DC, 20007. Tel: 202-687-1308. p. 368

Hartog, Paul, PhD, Dr, Dir, Libr Serv, Faith Baptist Bible College & Theological Seminary, 1900 NW Fourth St, Ankeny, IA, 50023. Tel: 515-964-0601, Ext 253. p. 732

Harton, Jack, Ref Librn, Highline College Library, 2400 S 240th St, MS 25-4, Des Moines, WA, 98198. Tel: 206-592-3806. p. 2363

Hartoonian, Leslie, Mgr, Mem Serv, La Grange Public Library, Ten W Cossitt Ave, La Grange, IL, 60525. Tel: 708-215-3206. p. 605

Hartough, Margie, Br Librn, Half Hollow Hills Community Library, Melville Branch, 510 Sweet Hollow Rd, Melville, NY, 11747. Tel: 631-421-4535. p. 1526

Hartschuh, David, Network Adminr, Sheridan County Public Library System, 335 W Alger St, Sheridan, WY, 82801. Tel: 307-674-8585. p. 2499

Hartse, Merri, Head, Coll Serv, Eastern Washington University, 320 Media Lane, 100 LIB, Cheney, WA, 99004-2453. Tel: 509-359-7888. p. 2361

Hartsell, Karen, Br Mgr, Stanly County Public Library, Locust Branch, 186 Ray Kennedy Dr, Locust, NC, 28097. Tel: 704-888-0103. p. 1671

Hartsfield, Patrick, Asst Dir, Coll, Springfield College, 263 Alden St, Springfield, MA, 01109-3797. Tel: 413-748-3360. p. 1057

Hartsfield, Tammi, Dir, Caldwell Parish Library, 211 Jackson, Columbia, LA, 71418. Tel: 318-649-2259. p. 887

Hartshorn, Jenn, Youth Serv Librn, Seabrook Library, 25 Liberty Lane, Seabrook, NH, 03874-4506. Tel: 603-474-2044. p. 1381

Hartshorne, Darryl, Circ Mgr, Curtis Institute of Music, 1720 Locust St, Philadelphia, PA, 19103. Tel: 215-893-5265. p. 1976

Hartson, Melissa, Libr Serv Dir, Newport Beach Public Library, 1000 Avocado Ave, Newport Beach, CA, 92660-6301. Tel: 949-717-3800. p. 183

Hartson, Melissa, Libr Serv Dir, Newport Beach Public Library, Central Library, 1000 Avocado Ave, Newport Beach, CA, 92660-6301. p. 183

Hartung, Joel, Asst Dir, Syst, Bellevue University, 1028 Bruin Blvd, Bellevue, NE, 68005. Tel: 402-557-7317. p. 1308

Hartung, Steven, Supv Librn, Pamunkey Regional Library, 7527 Library Dr, Hanover, VA, 23069. Tel: 804-537-6211. p. 2323

Harty, Kathleen, Res & Educ Serv Librn, Sacred Heart Seminary & School of Theology, 7335 Lovers Lane Rd, Franklin, WI, 53132. Tel: 414-858-4645. p. 2436

Harty, Nathalie, Ad, Tech Librn, Ipswich Public Library, 25 N Main St, Ipswich, MA, 01938. Tel: 978-356-6648. p. 1026

Hartz, Lisa, Info Res & Serv Support Spec, Pennsylvania State University Libraries, Mary M & Bertil E Lofstrom Library, 76 University Dr, Hazleton, PA, 18202. Tel: 570-450-3127. p. 2015

Hartzell, Joann, Dir, White Sulphur Springs Public Library, 344 W Main St, White Sulphur Springs, WV, 24986. Tel: 304-536-1171. p. 2418

Hartzell, Justin, Mgr, Baltimore County Public Library, Rosedale Branch, 6105 Kenwood Ave, Baltimore, MD, 21237. Tel: 410-887-0512. p. 980

Hartzell, Lisa, Youth Serv Librn, Haywood County Public Library, 678 S Haywood St, Waynesville, NC, 28786. Tel: 828-356-2511. p. 1721

Harvancik, Alex, Dir, Horicon Public Library, 404 E Lake St, Horicon, WI, 53032-1297. Tel: 920-485-3535. p. 2441

Harvangt, Cary, Asst Dir, Edwardsville Public Library, 112 S Kansas St, Edwardsville, IL, 62025. Tel: 618-692-7556. p. 581

Harvell, Laura, Librn, United States Army, Winn Army Community Hospital Medical Library, 1061 Harman Ave, Ste 2J11B, Fort Stewart, GA, 31314-5611. Tel: 912-435-6542. p. 479

Harvey, Allison, Ch Serv, Abilene Public Library, South Branch Library, 4310 Buffalo Gap Rd, No 1246, Abilene, TX, 79606. Tel: 325-698-7565. p. 2132

Harvey, Allison, Head Librn, Centre de documentation sur l'education des adultes et la condition feminine, 469 rue Jean Talon Ouest, bureau 229, Montreal, QC, H3N 1R4, CANADA. Tel: 514-876-1180. p. 2722

Harvey, Alyssa, Head, Youth Serv, Town of Ballston Community Library, Two Lawmar Lane, Burnt Hills, NY, 12027. Tel: 518-399-8174. p. 1511

Harvey, Amber, Head, Ref, Waltham Public Library, 735 Main St, Waltham, MA, 02451. Tel: 781-314-3425. p. 1062

Harvey, Anne Marie, Br Mgr, Enoch Pratt Free Library, Waverly Branch, 400 E 33rd St, Baltimore, MD, 21218-3401. Tel: 443-984-3913. p. 953

Harvey, Diana, Dir, J Robert Jamerson Memorial Library, 157 Main St, Appomattox, VA, 24522. Tel: 434-352-5340. p. 2304

Harvey, Eric, Law Librn, Fayette County Law Library, Court House, 61 E Main St, Ste D, Uniontown, PA, 15401-3514. Tel: 724-430-1228. p. 2014

Harvey, Jacalynn, Dir, Roseville Public Library, 29777 Gratiot Ave, Roseville, MI, 48066. Tel: 586-445-5407. p. 1146

Harvey, Jamie, Research Servs Librn, Landmark College Library, 19 River Rd S, Putney, VT, 05346. Tel: 802-387-6763. p. 2292

Harvey, Jessica, Br Mgr, Norfolk Public Library, Jordan-Newby Branch at Broad Creek, 1425 Norchester Ave, Norfolk, VA, 23504. Tel: 757-664-7323. p. 2335

Harvey, Ken, Communications Dir, Sno-Isle Libraries, 7312 35th Ave NE, Marysville, WA, 98271-7417. Tel: 360-651-7030. p. 2370

Harvey, Leah, Mgr, Whitebird Community Library, 245 River St, Whitebird, ID, 83554. Tel: 208-839-2805. p. 533
Harvey, Madeline, Mgr, Alexander Graham Bell National Historic Site of Canada, 559 Chebucto St, Baddeck, NS, B0E 1B0, CANADA. Tel: 902-295-2069. p. 2616
Harvey, Mariah, Acq, Head, Electronic Res, University of Missouri-Kansas City Libraries, 800 E 51st St, Kansas City, MO, 64110. Tel: 816-235-6461. p. 1257
Harvey, Michael, Med Librn, Jonathan M Wainwright Memorial VA Medical Center Library, 77 Wainwright Dr, Walla Walla, WA, 99362. Tel: 509-525-5200, Ext 26162. p. 2392
Harvey, Michelle, Head, Archives, The Museum of Modern Art, 11 W 53th St, New York, NY, 10019. Tel: 212-708-9433. p. 1592
Harvey, Rebecca, Br Mgr, Putnam County Library, Buffalo Branch, 19209 Buffalo Rd, Buffalo, WV, 25033. Tel: 304-937-3538. p. 2405
Harvey, Renee, Librn, Thomas Gilcrease Institute of American History & Art Library, 1400 Gilcrease Museum Rd, Tulsa, OK, 74127. Tel: 918-631-6441. p. 1864
Harvey, Shane, Librn, Rock Springs Public Library, 251 Railroad St, Rock Springs, WI, 53961. Tel: 608-737-1063. p. 2474
Harvey, Steven, Exec Dir, New York Legislative Service, Inc Library, 120 Broadway, Ste 920, New York, NY, 10271. Tel: 212-962-2826, 212-962-2827, 212-962-2828. p. 1594
Harvey, Suzanne, Dir, Huachuca City Public Library, 506 N Gonzales Blvd, Huachuca City, AZ, 85616-9610. Tel: 520-456-1063. p. 63
Harvey, Vicki, Bus Mgr, Morris Area Public Library District, 604 Liberty St, Morris, IL, 60450. Tel: 815-942-6880. p. 619
Harvie, Judy, Libr Serv Dir, Norton Rose Fulbright, Devon Tower, 400 Third Ave SW, Ste 3700, Calgary, AB, T2P 4H2, CANADA. Tel: 403-921-6607. p. 2528
Harville, Kathleen, Ad, Saint Clair Shores Public Library, 22500 11 Mile Rd, Saint Clair Shores, MI, 48081-1399. Tel: 586-771-9020. p. 1147
Harvin McDonald, Mary, Libr Dir, St Andrews University, 1700 Dogwood Mile, Laurinburg, NC, 28352. Tel: 910-277-5023. p. 1700
Harwell, Kevin, Bus Librn, Pennsylvania State University Libraries, William & Joan Schreyer Business Library, 309 Paterno Library, 3rd Flr, University Park, PA, 16802-1810. Tel: 814-865-0141. p. 2016
Harwick, Marcie, Librn, Montfort Public Library, 102 E Park St, Montfort, WI, 53569. Tel: 608-943-6265. p. 2462
Harwood, Abby, Mgr, Carnegie Library of Pittsburgh, Hill District, 2177 Centre Ave, Pittsburgh, PA, 15219-6316. Tel: 412-281-3753. p. 1991
Harwood, Jon, Mr, Assoc Librn, Western Wyoming Community College, 2500 College Dr, Rock Springs, WY, 82902. Tel: 307-382-1702. p. 2498
Harwood, Silvana, Dep Dir, Dir, Technology, Coquitlam Public Library, 575 Poirier St, Coquitlam, BC, V3J 6A9, CANADA. Tel: 604-937-4131. p. 2565
Hary, Francesca, Br Mgr, Dayton Metro Library, Burkhardt, 4680 Burkhardt Ave, Dayton, OH, 45431. Tel: 937-496-8924. p. 1779
Harzan, Jan C, Exec Dir, Mutual UFO Network, Inc, 18023 Sky Park Circle, F2, Irvine, CA, 92614. Tel: 949-476-8366. p. 153
Hasekamp, Sharon, Dir, Powell Memorial Library, 951 W College St, Troy, MO, 63379. Tel: 636-462-4874. p. 1283
Haselden, Timothy, Librn, Moore Haven Correctional Facility Library, 1282 E State Rd 78, Moore Haven, FL, 33471. Tel: 863-946-2420. p. 427
Hasely, Kevin, Sr Librn, Los Angeles Public Library System, West Valley Regional Branch Library, 19036 Vanowen St, Reseda, CA, 91335. Tel: 818-345-9806. p. 166
Hasenkamp, Peggy, Dir, Axtell Public Library, 401 Maple, Axtell, KS, 66403. Tel: 785-736-2858. p. 797
Hashert, Cynthia, Assoc Dir, Digital & Scholarly Servs, Auraria Library, 1100 Lawrence St, Denver, CO, 80204-2095. Tel: 303-315-7767. p. 273
Hashimoto, Beverly, Pres, Bergen County Historical Society, 355 Main St, Rm 124, Hackensack, NJ, 07601. Tel: 201-343-9492. p. 1406
Hashimoto, Sarah, Br Mgr, Jackson District Library, Summit Branch, 104 W Bird Ave, Jackson, MI, 49203. Tel: 517-783-4030. p. 1120
Hasin, Tim, Assoc Librn, Head, Tech Serv, Molloy College, 1000 Hempstead Ave, Rockville Centre, NY, 11571. Tel: 516-323-3921. p. 1632
Haske Hare, Margaret, Dir, Cornwall Library, 30 Pine St, Cornwall, CT, 06753. Tel: 860-672-6874. p. 306
Haskell, Heather, VPres, Lyman & Merrie Wood Museum of Springfield History, 21 Edwards St, Springfield, MA, 01103. Tel: 413-263-6800, Ext 230. p. 1057
Haskell, John, Dir, Library of Congress, John W Kluge Center, Library Collections & Services Group, Thomas Jefferson Bldg, LJ-120, First St SE, Washington, DC, 20540-4860. Tel: 202-707-3302. p. 370
Haskell, Phyllis, Tech Serv Librn, Dighton Public Library, 979 Somerset Ave, Dighton, MA, 02715. Tel: 508-669-6421. p. 1014
Haskins, Bob, Libr Mgr, Canyon Lake Community Church Library, 30515 Railroad Canyon Rd, Canyon Lake, CA, 92587. Tel: 951-244-1877. p. 127
Haskins, Shari, Br Mgr, Fremont County Library System, Riverton Branch, 1330 W Park Ave, Riverton, WY, 82501. Tel: 307-856-3556. p. 2496
Haslam, Deborah, Asst Br Mgr, Duchesne Library, Roosevelt Branch, 70 W Lagoon 44-4, Roosevelt, UT, 84066-2841. Tel: 435-722-4441. p. 2262
Hasquin, Holly, Dir, Brighton Memorial Library, 110 N Main St, Brighton, IL, 62012. Tel: 618-372-8450. p. 545
Hass, Cathie, Ch, Sac City Public Library, 1001 W Main St, Sac City, IA, 50583. Tel: 712-662-7276. p. 780
Hass, V Heidi, Dir, Res Serv, The Morgan Library & Museum, 225 Madison Ave, New York, NY, 10016. Tel: 212-685-0008. p. 1592
Hassan, Louisa, Libr Spec, Ill & Tech Serv, Killeen Public Library, 205 E Church Ave, Killeen, TX, 76541. Tel: 254-501-8990. p. 2206
Hassan, Mohamed, Electronic Res, Per, William Paterson University, 300 Pompton Rd, Wayne, NJ, 07470. Tel: 973-720-2117. p. 1452
Hassan, Muhammad, Exec Dir, Kean University, 1000 Morris Ave, Union, NJ, 07083. Tel: 908-737-4629. p. 1449
Hassard, Cathy, Asst Dir, Head, Cat, Sandown Public Library, 305 Main St, Sandown, NH, 03873. Tel: 603-887-3428. p. 1380
Hassaun, Shifa, Actg Dir, Red River College Polytechnic Library, 2055 Notre Dame Ave, Winnipeg, MB, R3H 0J9, CANADA. Tel: 204-632-2528. p. 2594
Hasse, Chanteyl, Dir, Clark County Law Library, 309 S Third St, Ste 400, Las Vegas, NV, 89101. Tel: 702-455-4696. p. 1346
Hasse, Mark, Ref & Digital Librn, Washington State University Libraries, 14204 NE Salmon Creek Ave, Vancouver, WA, 98686. Tel: 360-546-9275. p. 2391
Hassefras, Jackie, Libr Tech, The Frontenac Law Association Library, Frontenac County Court House, Five Court St, Kingston, ON, K7L 2N4, CANADA. Tel: 613-542-0034. p. 2650
Hassen, Marjorie, Col Librn, Bowdoin College Library, 3000 College Sta, Brunswick, ME, 04011-8421. p. 919
Hassert, Rita, Library Colls Mgr, The Morton Arboretum, 4100 Illinois Rte 53, Lisle, IL, 60532-1293. Tel: 630-719-2429. p. 610
Hassett, Becky, Dir, Clayville Library Association, 2265 Oneida St, Clayville, NY, 13322. Tel: 315-839-5893. p. 1519
Hassman, Susan, Asst Dir, Eldora Public Library, 1202 Tenth St, Eldora, IA, 50627. Tel: 641-939-2173. p. 750
Hassouna, Hussein, Library Contact, League of Arab States, 1100 17th St NW, Ste 602, Washington, DC, 20036. Tel: 202-265-3210. p. 370
Hastie, Christina, Campus Librn, Daytona State College Library, Deland Campus Library, Bldg One, 1155 County Rd 4139, Deland, FL, 32724. Tel: 386-785-2018. p. 392
Hastings, Chelsea, Dir, Interlaken Public Library, 8390 Main St, Interlaken, NY, 14847. Tel: 607-532-4341. p. 1550
Hastings, Krista, Acq Asst, Rider University, Katharine Houk Talbott Library, Franklin F Moore Library Bldg, 3rd & 4th Flrs, 2083 Lawrenceville Rd, Lawrenceville, NJ, 08648. Tel: 609-921-7100, Ext 8336. p. 1412
Hastings, Robin, Serv Consult, Northeast Kansas Library System, 4317 W Sixth St, Lawrence, KS, 66049. Tel: 785-838-4090. p. 819
Hastings, Susan, Mgr, Idea Exchange, Hespeler, Five Tannery St E, Cambridge, ON, N3C 2C1, CANADA. Tel: 519-658-4412. p. 2635
Hastings, William, Asst Dir, Mgr, Northern Onondaga Public Library, North Syracuse, 100 Trolley Barn Lane, North Syracuse, NY, 13212. Tel: 315-458-6184. p. 1518
Hastler, Mary L, Chief Exec Officer, Harford County Public Library, 1221-A Brass Mill Rd, Belcamp, MD, 21017-1209. Tel: 410-273-5703. p. 958
Haston, Eugene, Br Mgr, Atlanta-Fulton Public Library System, Evelyn G Lowery Library at Southwest, 3665 Cascade Rd SW, Atlanta, GA, 30331. Tel: 404-699-6363. p. 461
Haston, Eugene, Br Mgr, Atlanta-Fulton Public Library System, Fairburn Branch, 60 Valley View Dr, Fairburn, GA, 30213. Tel: 404-613-5750. p. 461
Hastreiter, Michele, Dir, Humphrey Public Library, 307 Main St, Humphrey, NE, 68642. Tel: 402-923-0957. p. 1319
Hatanaka, Margaret, Libr Serv Mgr, Glendora Public Library & Cultural Center, 140 S Glendora Ave, Glendora, CA, 91741. Tel: 626-852-4862. p. 149
Hatanaka, Risa, Librn, Japan Foundation, Two Bloor St E, Ste 300, Toronto, ON, M4W 1A8, CANADA. Tel: 416-966-1600, Ext 239, 416-966-2935. p. 2690
Hatch, Beth, Dir, Upper Arlington Public Library, 2800 Tremont Rd, Columbus, OH, 43221. Tel: 614-486-9621. p. 1778
Hatch, Carey, Assoc Provost for Academic Technologies & Info Services, SUNYConnect, Office of Library & Information Services, SUNY Plaza, Albany, NY, 12246. Tel: 518-320-1477. p. 2771
Hatch, Carmella, Every Child Ready Duluth Coord, Librn II, Duluth Public Library, 520 W Superior St, Duluth, MN, 55802. Tel: 218-730-4222. p. 1172
Hatch, Cathy, Librn, Old Perlican Public Library, Town Hall, 299 Blow Me Down Dr, Old Perlican, NL, A0A 3G0, CANADA. Tel: 709-587-2028. p. 2608
Hatch, Dan, IT Mgr, Westchester Public Library, 200 W Indiana Ave, Chesterton, IN, 46304. Tel: 219-926-7696. p. 674
Hatch, Lillian, Ref Librn, United States Securities & Exchange Commission Library, 100 F St NE, Rm 1500, Washington, DC, 20549-0002. Tel: 202-551-5450. p. 380
Hatch, Roy, Libr Tech, McGlannan Health Sciences Library, Mercy Medical Ctr, 301 Saint Paul Pl, Baltimore, MD, 21202. Tel: 410-332-9189, p. 955
Hatch, Tina, Dir, Milford Public Library, 330 Family Dr, Milford, MI, 48381-2000. Tel: 248-684-0845. p. 1132

Hatchell, Sheila, Libr Dir, Minnesota Department of Transportation Library, 395 John Ireland Blvd, MS 155, Saint Paul, MN, 55155. Tel: 651-366-3733. p. 1200

Hatcher, Emily, Ref & Info Serv, Daviess County Public Library, 2020 Frederica St, Owensboro, KY, 42301. Tel: 270-684-0211. p. 871

Hatcher, Heather, Info Spec, Show Low Public Library, 181 N Ninth St, Show Low, AZ, 85901. Tel: 928-532-4075. p. 78

Hatcher, Jeanette, Spec Coll Librn, Texas A&M International University, 5201 University Blvd, Laredo, TX, 78041-1900. Tel: 956-326-2404. p. 2210

Hatcher, Jennifer, Br Mgr, Cumberland County Public Library & Information Center, Cliffdale Regional Branch, 6882 Cliffdale Rd, Fayetteville, NC, 28314-1936. p. 1688

Hatcher, Jennifer, Br Mgr, Cumberland County Public Library & Information Center, West Branch, 7469 Century Circle, Fayetteville, NC, 28306-3141. p. 1689

Hatcher, Sharon, Library Contact, Mono County Free Library, Coleville, 111591 Hwy 395, Coleville, CA, 96107. Tel: 530-495-2788. p. 172

Hatem, Christina, Director, Strategic Marketing Comms, Syracuse University Libraries, 222 Waverly Ave, Syracuse, NY, 13244-2010. Tel: 315-443-9788. p. 1650

Hatfield, Amie, Dir, Homer Public Library, 385 South St NW, Homer, OH, 43027. Tel: 740-892-2020. p. 1790

Hatfield, Jay, Regional Dir, Braille Institute Library, San Diego Center, 9635 Granite Ridge Dr, No 130, San Diego, CA, 92123. Tel: 858-452-1111. p. 160

Hatfield, Jennifer, Asst Dir, Williamson Public Library, 101 Logan St, Williamson, WV, 25661. Tel: 304-235-6029. p. 2418

Hatfield, Kathy, Mgr, Tech Serv, Wilmington College, 120 College St, Wilmington, OH, 45177. Tel: 937-481-2398. p. 1832

Hatfield, Linda, Ref & Instruction Librn, Muskingum University, Ten College Dr, New Concord, OH, 43762. Tel: 740-826-8017. p. 1806

Hatfield, Nathan, Chief of Interpretation, USDI National Park Service, PO Box 220, Nageezi, NM, 87037-0220. Tel: 505-786-7014. p. 1473

Hatfield, Teresa, Dir, Ider Public Library, 10808 Alabama Hwy 75, Ider, AL, 35981. Tel: 256-657-2170. p. 22

Hathaway, Barbara, Libr Dir, Bee Cave Public Library, 4000 Galleria Pkwy, Bee Cave, TX, 78738. Tel: 512-767-6624. p. 2146

Hathaway, Carly L, Tech Serv Mgr, Salem Public Library, 28 E Main St, Salem, VA, 24153. Tel: 540-375-3089. p. 2347

Hathaway, Clio, Supv Librn, Hayward Public Library, 835 C St, Hayward, CA, 94541. Tel: 510-881-7948. p. 150

Hathaway, Deborah, Acq, Supvr, University of Dallas, 1845 E Northgate Dr, Irving, TX, 75062-4736. Tel: 972-721-4122. p. 2203

Hathaway, Dianne, Libr Dir, Goffstown Public Library, Two High St, Goffstown, NH, 03045-1910. Tel: 603-497-2102. p. 1364

Hathaway, Janet, Interim Univ Librn, University of King's College Library, 6350 Coburg Rd, Halifax, NS, B3H 2A1, CANADA. Tel: 902-422-1271, Ext 175. p. 2621

Hathaway, Lisa, Dir, Mandel Public Library of West Palm Beach, 411 Clematis St, West Palm Beach, FL, 33401. Tel: 561-868-7700. p. 453

Hathcock, April, Dir, Scholarly Communications & Info, New York University, 70 Washington Sq S, New York, NY, 10012-1019. Tel: 212-998-2500. p. 1599

Hatheway, Holly, Head Librn, Princeton University, Marquand Library of Art & Archaeology, McCormick Hall, Princeton, NJ, 08544-0001. Tel: 609-258-5860. p. 1437

Hatley, Adam, Br Supvr, University of Texas Libraries, McKinney Engineering Library, Engineering Education & Research Center, EER 1706, 2501 Speedway, Austin, TX, 78712. Tel: 512-495-4511. p. 2143

Hatoum, Sarah, Research Librn, Cleary, Gottlieb, Steen & Hamilton LLP Library, One Liberty Plaza, New York, NY, 10006. Tel: 212-225-2000. p. 1582

Hatt, Lisa, Cat, De Anza College, 21250 Stevens Creek Blvd, Cupertino, CA, 95014-5793. Tel: 408-864-8459. p. 133

Hatter, Evan, Librn, Kentucky Talking Book Library, 300 Coffee Tree Rd, Frankfort, KY, 40601. Tel: 502-564-7885. p. 855

Hatterman, Cathy, Acq Librn, Nebraska Library Commission, The Atrium, 1200 N St, Ste 120, Lincoln, NE, 68508-2023. Tel: 402-471-4034. p. 1322

Hatton, Jason, Dir, Bartholomew County Public Library, 536 Fifth St, Columbus, IN, 47201-6225. Tel: 812-379-1251. p. 676

Hauan, Jennifer, Br Mgr, Fort Vancouver Regional Library District, Woodland Community Library, 770 Park St, Woodland, WA, 98674. p. 2391

Haubitz, Heiko, Dr, Instr, University of South Florida, 4202 Fowler Ave, CIS 1040, Tampa, FL, 33620-7800. Tel: 813-974-7650. p. 2783

Haubner, Colleen, Libr Dir, Anoka County Library, 707 County Hwy 10 Frontage Rd, Blaine, MN, 55434-2398. Tel: 763-324-1500. p. 1165

Haubrich, Danielle, Br Mgr, Burlington County Library System, Pinelands Library, 39 Allen Ave, Medford, NJ, 08055. Tel: 609-654-6113. p. 1454

Haubrich, Juliana, Circ Mgr, David & Joyce Milne Public Library, 1095 Main St, Williamstown, MA, 01267-2627. Tel: 413-458-5369. p. 1069

Hauch, Laura, Circ Mgr, Buchanan District Library, 128 E Front St, Buchanan, MI, 49107. Tel: 269-695-3681. p. 1087

Hauck, Ian, Ref Librn, Vestal Public Library, 320 Vestal Pkwy E, Vestal, NY, 13850-1632. Tel: 607-754-4243. p. 1657

Hauck, Kathryn, Br Supvr, Bruce County Public Library, Lion's Head Branch, 90 Main St, Lion's Head, ON, N0H 1W0, CANADA. Tel: 519-793-3844. p. 2673

Hauck, Kathryn, Br Supvr, Bruce County Public Library, Tobermory Branch, 22 Bay St, Tobermory, ON, N0H 2R0, CANADA. Tel: 519-596-2446. p. 2674

Hauer, Kristie, Libr Dir, Shawano County Library, 128 S Sawyer St, Shawano, WI, 54166. Tel: 715-526-3829. p. 2476

Hauf, Amy, Library Contact, Max Community Library, 215 Main St, Max, ND, 58759. Tel: 701-679-2263. p. 1737

Hauf, Marcus, Library Contact, New York Supreme Court Appellate Division, Robert Abrams Bldg for Law & Justice, State St, Albany, NY, 12223. Tel: 518-471-4713, 518-471-4777. p. 1483

Hauf-Belden, Melody, Archivist, Spec Coll Librn, Principia College, One Maybeck Pl, Elsah, IL, 62028-9703. Tel: 618-374-5238. p. 585

Haug, Keir, Br Mgr, Saint Louis County Library, Prairie Commons Branch, 915 Utz Lane, Hazelwood, MO, 63042-2739. Tel: 314-994-3300, Ext 3700. p. 1274

Haug, Sarah, Cataloger, Learning Commons Coord, Murrell Library & Commons, Missouri Valley College, 500 E College St, Marshall, MO, 65340. Tel: 660-831-4180, 660-831-4181. p. 1260

Hauge, Carol, Asst Librn, Elkader Public Library, 130 N Main St, Elkader, IA, 52043. Tel: 563-245-1446. p. 751

Hauge, Doreen, Academic Specialist, Minnesota State Community & Technical College, Detroit Lakes Campus, 900 Hwy 34 E, Detroit Lakes, MN, 56501. Tel: 218-846-3769, 218-846-3772. p. 1188

Hauge, Janet, Dir, Academic Support Services, Atlantic Cape Community College, 5100 Black Horse Pike, Mays Landing, NJ, 08330. Tel: 609-343-4937. p. 1417

Haugen, Connie, Libr Spec, Traverse Des Sioux Library Cooperative, 1400 Madison Ave, Ste 622, Mankato, MN, 56001-5488. Tel: 833-837-5422. p. 1181

Haugh, Amy, Librn, UPMC McKeesport, 1500 Fifth Ave, McKeesport, PA, 15132. Tel: 412-784-4121. p. 1959

Haugh, Amy, Dir, UPMC St Margaret, 815 Freeport Rd, Pittsburgh, PA, 15215. Tel: 412-784-4121, 412-784-4238. p. 1997

Haugh, Dana, Web Serv Librn, Yale University Library, Harvey Cushing/John Hay Whitney Medical Library, Sterling Hall of Medicine, 333 Cedar St, New Haven, CT, 06510. Tel: 203-785-3969. p. 327

Haught, Karen, Librn, College of the Muscogee Nation Library, 2170 Raven Circle, Okmulgee, OK, 74447. Tel: 918-549-2812. p. 1859

Haught, Shawn, Adminr, Judicial Branch of Arizona, Maricopa County, 101 W Jefferson St, Phoenix, AZ, 85003. Tel: 602-506-7353. p. 70

Haughton, Paul, Supvr, Columbia University, Thomas J Watson Library of Business & Economics, 130 Uris Hall, 3022 Broadway, New York, NY, 10027. Tel: 212-854-7804. p. 1584

Haun, Diana, Asst Dir, Youth Serv Librn, Hood County Public Library, 222 N Travis, Granbury, TX, 76048. Tel: 817-573-3569. p. 2185

Haupt, Benjamin, Rev, Dir, Libr Serv, Concordia Seminary Library, 801 Seminary Pl, Saint Louis, MO, 63105-3199. Tel: 314-505-7038. p. 1270

Haupt, Chris, Cat Tech, Govt Doc, ILL, Oregon Institute of Technology Library, 3201 Campus Dr, Klamath Falls, OR, 97601-8801. Tel: 541-885-1099. p. 1883

Haupt, John, Br Mgr, Sonoma County Library, Healdsburg Regional Library, 139 Piper St, Healdsburg, CA, 95448. Tel: 707-433-3772. p. 204

Hausburg, Jana, Libr Adminr, Wichita Falls Public Library, 600 11th St, Wichita Falls, TX, 76301-4604. Tel: 940-767-0868, Ext 4229. p. 2258

Hauschildt, Jennifer, Pub Serv, United States Army, Casey Memorial Library, 72nd St & 761st Tank Battalion, Bldg 3202, Fort Hood, TX, 76544-5024. Tel: 254-287-0025. p. 2178

Hauser, Alex, Librn II, Michigan State University Libraries, William C Gast Business Library, 50 Law College Bldg, 648 N Shaw Lane, East Lansing, MI, 48824. Tel: 517-355-3380. p. 1102

Hauser, Chris, Head, Access Serv, Head, Tech & Syst Serv, Weber State University, 3921 Central Campus Dr, Dept 2901, Ogden, UT, 84408-2901. Tel: 801-626-6104. p. 2268

Hauser, John R, Archivist, Thiel College, 75 College Ave, Greenville, PA, 16125-2183. Tel: 724-589-2124. p. 1939

Hauser, Marie, Libr Mgr, South Georgia Regional Library System, Miller Lakeland Branch, 18 S Valdosta Rd, Lakeland, GA, 31635. Tel: 229-482-2904. p. 501

Hauserman, Katrina, Cat Librn, Ch, Free Public Library of Monroe Township, 713 Marsha Ave, Williamstown, NJ, 08094. Tel: 856-629-1212, Ext 201. p. 1455

Hausman, Gary, Librn, Columbia University, Global Studies, Lehman Library, International Affairs Bldg, 420 W 118th St, New York, NY, 10027. Tel: 212-854-3630. p. 1583

Haval, Lori, Dir, Hillcrest Public Library, 804 Bristol, Cuba, KS, 66940. Tel: 785-729-3355. p. 804

Havard-Trepanier, Alexis, User Serv, College de Rosemont (Cegep) Bibliotheque, 6400 16th Ave, Montreal, QC, H1X 2S9, CANADA. Tel: 514-376-1620, Ext 7265. p. 2723

Havel, Peter, Dir, Oakland Public Library, Two Municipal Plaza, Oakland, NJ, 07436. Tel: 201-337-3742, Ext 7100. p. 1430

Havely, Candace, Dir, Hawkeye Community College Library, 1501 E Orange Rd, Waterloo, IA, 50701-9014. Tel: 319-296-4229. p. 788
Havemeyer, Ann, Dir, Norfolk Library, Nine Greenwoods Rd E, Norfolk, CT, 06058-1320. Tel: 860-542-5075. p. 330
Haven, Jodi, Pub Serv Librn, Petoskey District Library, 500 E Mitchell St, Petoskey, MI, 49770. Tel: 231-758-3100. p. 1140
Haven, Karen, Access & Tech Serv Librn, College of Coastal Georgia, One College Dr, Brunswick, GA, 31520. Tel: 954-279-5784. p. 468
Havener, Peggy, Dir, Albert Lea Public Library, 211 E Clark St, Albert Lea, MN, 56007. Tel: 507-377-4355. p. 1163
Havenga, Michelle, Ch, Sheridan County Public Library System, 335 W Alger St, Sheridan, WY, 82801. Tel: 307-674-8585. p. 2499
Havens, Barret, Interim Univ Librn, Woodbury University Library, 7500 Glenoaks Blvd, Burbank, CA, 91510. Tel: 818-252-5200. p. 125
Havens, Mary, Fac Librn, Austin Community College, Elgin Campus Library, 1501 W US Hwy 290, 3rd Flr, Rm 1376, Elgin, TX, 78621. Tel: 512-223-9462. p. 2138
Havens, Patricia, City Historian, Dir, Strathearn Historical Park & Museum, 137 Strathearn Pl, Simi Valley, CA, 93065-1605. Tel: 805-526-6453. p. 246
Haver, Mary-Kate, Med Librn, H Lee Moffitt Cancer Center & Research Institute, 12902 USF Magnolia Dr, Tampa, FL, 33612. Tel: 813-745-4673. p. 448
Haverkoch, Vanessa, Coll Serv Librn, Bennington College, One College Dr, Bennington, VT, 05201-6001. Tel: 802-440-4602. p. 2279
Haviland, Krista, Libr Assoc, Rutgers University Libraries, Library of Science & Medicine, 165 Bevier Rd, Piscataway, NJ, 08854-8009. Tel: 848-445-3519. p. 1425
Havill, Brad, Asst Librn, West Stockbridge Public Library, 21 State Line Rd, West Stockbridge, MA, 01266. Tel: 413-232-0300, Ext 308. p. 1066
Hawamdeh, Suliman, Dr, Prof, University of North Texas, 3940 N Elm St, Ste E292, Denton, TX, 76207. Tel: 940-565-2445. p. 2793
Hawco, Debbie, Tech Serv Librn, Department of Community Services, Government of Yukon, 1171 First Ave, Whitehorse, YT, Y1A 0G9, CANADA. Tel: 867-667-5239. p. 2757
Hawe-Ndrio, Caitlin, Br Mgr, Burlington County Library System, Bordentown Library, 18 E Union St, Bordentown, NJ, 08505. Tel: 609-298-0622. p. 1454
Hawes, Jackie, Dir, Morton Mandan Public Library, 609 W Main St, Mandan, ND, 58554. Tel: 701-667-5365. p. 1737
Hawes, Jennifer, Br Librn, Boston Public Library, North End, 25 Parmenter St, Boston, MA, 02113-2306. Tel: 617-227-8135. p. 992
Hawes, Jennifer, Br Librn, Boston Public Library, Roslindale Branch, 4246 Washington St, Roslindale, MA, 02131. Tel: 617-323-2343. p. 992
Hawk, Amanda, Pub Serv Mgr, Massachusetts Institute of Technology Libraries, Distinctive Collections, Bldg 14N-118, Hayden Library, 160 Memorial Dr, Cambridge, MA, 02139-4307. Tel: 617-253-5690. p. 1008
Hawk, Bryan, Br Mgr, Flagstaff City-Coconino County Public Library System, Forest Lakes Community Library, 417 Old Rim Rd, Forest Lakes, AZ, 85931. Tel: 928-535-9125. p. 60
Hawk, John, Head, Spec Coll & Archives, University of San Francisco, 2130 Fulton St, San Francisco, CA, 94117-1080. Tel: 415-422-2036. p. 229
Hawk, Melissa E, Libr Dir, Lehighton Area Memorial Library, 124 North St, Lehighton, PA, 18235-1589. Tel: 610-377-2750. p. 1954
Hawk, Michelle, Libr Dir, Lebanon Community Library, District Center, 125 N Seventh St, Lebanon, PA, 17046-5000. Tel: 717-273-7624. p. 1954
Hawk, Michelle, Adminr, Lebanon County Library System, 125 N Seventh St, Lebanon, PA, 17046. Tel: 717-273-7624. p. 1954
Hawker, James, Dr, Dean, South Florida State College Library, 600 W College Dr, Avon Park, FL, 33825-9356. Tel: 863-784-7306. p. 384
Hawker, Lori, Libr Dir, Scott County Library, 110 W Eighth, Scott City, KS, 67871-1599. Tel: 620-872-5341. p. 835
Hawkins, Amorette, Dir, Rangely Regional Library, 109 E Main St, Rangely, CO, 81648-2737. Tel: 970-675-8811. p. 294
Hawkins, Cheryl, Librn, Hutchins-Atwell Public Library, 300 N Denton St, Hutchins, TX, 75141-9404. Tel: 972-225-4711. p. 2201
Hawkins, Diane, Asst Dir, Hastings Public Library, 227 E State St, Hastings, MI, 49058-1817. Tel: 269-945-4263. p. 1114
Hawkins, Felita, Regional Coordr, Birmingham Public Library, 2100 Park Pl, Birmingham, AL, 35203-2744. Tel: 205-226-3600. p. 7
Hawkins, Gary, Digital Serv, Auburn University, Ralph Brown Draughon Library, 231 Mell St, Auburn, AL, 36849. Tel: 334-844-4500. p. 6
Hawkins, Jackie, ILL, Northwestern State University Libraries, 913 University Pkwy, Natchitoches, LA, 71497. Tel: 318-357-5465. p. 900
Hawkins, Jason, Research Librn, University of Maryland, Baltimore, Thurgood Marshall Law Library, 501 W Fayette St, Baltimore, MD, 21201-1768. Tel: 410-706-0735. p. 957
Hawkins, Jeffrey, IT Tech, Lassen Library District, 1618 Main St, Susanville, CA, 96130-4515. Tel: 530-251-8127. p. 251
Hawkins, Joseph, PhD, Dir, ONE National Gay & Lesbian Archives at the USC Libraries, 909 W Adams Blvd, Los Angeles, CA, 90007. Tel: 213-821-2771. p. 167
Hawkins, Kendra, Libr Coord, Tidewater Community College, 120 Campus Dr, Portsmouth, VA, 23701. p. 2338
Hawkins, Margie, Librn, Holland & Knight LLP, 200 S Orange Ave, Ste 2600, Orlando, FL, 32801. Tel: 407-244-1153. p. 431
Hawkins, Meg, Dir, Libr Serv, State College of Florida Manatee-Sarasota Libraries, 5840 26th St W, Bradenton, FL, 34207. Tel: 941-752-5305. p. 387
Hawkins, Meg, Dir, Libr Serv, State College of Florida Manatee-Sarasota Library, Lakewood Ranch Campus Learning Commons, 7131 Professional Pkwy E, Sarasota, FL, 34240. Tel: 941-363-7250. p. 387
Hawkins, Meg, Evening Ref Librn, Helen Kate Furness Free Library, 100 N Providence Rd, Wallingford, PA, 19086. Tel; 610-566-9331. p. 2017
Hawkins, Michael, Head of Libr, Kent State University Libraries, Map, McGilvrey Hall, Rm 410, 325 S Lincoln St, Kent, OH, 44242. Tel: 330-672-1663. p. 1792
Hawkins, Michelle, Asst Mgr, Saint Louis County Library, Rock Road Branch, 10267 St Charles Rock Rd, Saint Ann, MO, 63074-1812. Tel: 314-994-3300, Ext 3750. p. 1274
Hawkins, Misty, Dir, Arkansas River Valley Regional Library System, 501 N Front St, Dardanelle, AR, 72834. Tel: 479-229-4418. p. 93
Hawkins, Mollie, Libr Supvr, Placer County Library, Applegate Branch, 18018 Applegate Rd, Applegate, CA, 95703. Tel: 530-878-2721. p. 118
Hawkins, Mollie, Libr Supvr, Placer County Library, Penryn Branch, 2215 Rippey Rd, Penryn, CA, 95663. Tel: 916-663-3621. p. 118
Hawkins, Paul, Dir, South Central Kansas Library System, 321 N Main St, South Hutchinson, KS, 67505. Tel: 620-663-3211. p. 837
Hawkins, Richenda, Dept Chair, Librn, Linn-Benton Community College Library, 6500 SW Pacific Blvd, Albany, OR, 97321-3799. Tel: 541-917-4641. p. 1871
Hawkins, Sianee, IT Librn, Youth Serv Librn, Payson Public Library, 328 N McLane Rd, Payson, AZ, 85541. Tel: 928-472-5167. p. 68
Hawkins, Tammy, Librn, De Soto Trail Regional Library System, Baker County, 398 Ga Hwy 37 SW, Newton, GA, 39870. Tel: 229-734-3025. p. 468
Hawkins, Terry, Head, Reader Serv, United States Air Force, Air University - Muir S Fairchild Research Information Center, 600 Chennault Circle, Maxwell AFB, AL, 36112-6010. Tel: 334-953-2237. p. 25
Hawkins, Theresa, Dir, Edward F Owen Memorial Library, 1120 Willow Dr, Carter Lake, IA, 51510-1332. Tel: 712-347-5492. p. 737
Hawkins, Zelda, Librn, Children's Hospital Colorado, Family Health Library, 13123 E 16th Ave, Aurora, CO, 80045. Tel: 720-777-6378. p. 273
Hawley, Cathy, Dir, Susquehanna County Law Library, Court House, 31 Lake Ave, Montrose, PA, 18801. Tel: 570-278-4600. p. 1965
Hawley, Dawn, Exec Dir of Library, eLearning & Academic Support, Bellingham Technical College Library, 3028 Lindbergh Ave, Bellingham, WA, 98225-1599. Tel: 360-752-8574. p. 2358
Hawley, Heather, Libr Mgr, Legacy Emanuel Hospital & Health Center Library, 2801 N Gantenbein Ave, Portland, OR, 97227. Tel: 503-413-2558. p. 1891
Hawley, Janet, Dir, Akron Carnegie Public Library, 205 E Rochester St, Akron, IN, 46910. Tel: 574-893-4113. p. 667
Hawley, Kyle, Circ Serv, Superior Public Library, 1530 Tower Ave, Superior, WI, 54880-2532. Tel: 715-394-8860. p. 2480
Hawley, Robin, Br Mgr, San Bernardino County Library, Hesperia Branch, 9650 Seventh Ave, Hesperia, CA, 92345. Tel: 760-244-4898. p. 213
Haworth, Kerry, Dir, Info Res & Knowledge Mgt, Center for Creative Leadership Library, One Leadership Pl, Greensboro, NC, 27410. Tel: 336-286-4083. p. 1691
Hawrey, Laura, Dir, North Shore Public Library, 250 Rte 25A, Shoreham, NY, 11786-9677. Tel: 631-929-4488. p. 1641
Hawthorne, Pat, Dean, California State Polytechnic University Library, 3801 W Temple Ave, Bldg 15, Pomona, CA, 91768. Tel: 909-869-3074. p. 196
Hay, Fred J, Dr, Librn Emeritus, Appalachian State University, William Leonard Eury Appalachian Collection, 218 College St, Boone, NC, 28608. Tel: 828-262-2186. p. 1675
Hay, Kathy, Dir, Harcourt Community Library, 106 W Second St, Harcourt, IA, 50544. Tel: 515-354-5391. p. 757
Hay, Matthew, Cat, Ref Librn, Allegany College of Maryland Library, 12401 Willowbrook Rd SE, Cumberland, MD, 21502. Tel: 301-784-5366. p. 963
Hay, Ruth, Asst Dir, Lanpher Memorial Library, 141 Main St, Hyde Park, VT, 05655. Tel: 802-888-4628. p. 2286
Hay, Stuart, Head, Ref Serv, Manitoba Department of Sport, Culture & Heritage, 200 Vaughan St, Rm 100, Winnipeg, MB, R3C 1T5, CANADA. Tel: 204-945-8244. p. 2593
Hay, Tara, Info Res Coordr, Medical University of South Carolina Libraries, 171 Ashley Ave, Ste 419, Charleston, SC, 29425-0001. Tel: 843-792-2811. p. 2051
Hayashi, Junie, Pub Serv Librn, Leeward Community College Library, 96-045 Ala Ike St, Pearl City, HI, 96782. Tel: 808-455-0680. p. 514
Hayashi, Maris, Head, Coll Mgt, Florida Atlantic University, 777 Glades Rd, Boca Raton, FL, 33431. Tel: 561-297-4317. p. 385
Hayden, Alysa, Asst Dir, Peabody Institute Library, 82 Main St, Peabody, MA, 01960-5553. Tel: 951-531-0100, Ext 25. p. 1045

Hayden, Carla, Dr, Librn of Congress, Library of Congress, James Madison Memorial Bldg, 101 Independence Ave SE, Washington, DC, 20540. Tel: 202-707-5000. p. 370
Hayden, Darlene, Head Librn, Parkland Regional Library-Manitoba, St Lazare Branch, 240 Main St, St. Lazare, MB, R0M 1Y0, CANADA. Tel: 204-683-2246. p. 2587
Hayden, Jessica, Coordr, Tech Serv, Berea College, 100 Campus Dr, Berea, KY, 40404. Tel: 859-985-3268. p. 849
Hayden, John D, Libr Dir, Bonham Public Library, 305 E Fifth St, Bonham, TX, 75418. Tel: 903-583-3128. p. 2148
Hayden, Kelly, Librn, Rowan College of South Jersey, 3322 College Dr, Vineland, NJ, 08360. Tel: 856-200-4623. p. 1450
Hayden, Peggy, Asst Librn, Chappell Memorial Library & Art Gallery, 289 Babcock Ave, Chappell, NE, 69129. Tel: 308-874-2626. p. 1310
Hayden, Wally, Ref Librn, Bacon Memorial District Library, 45 Vinewood, Wyandotte, MI, 48192-5221. Tel: 734-246-8357. p. 1160
Haydon, Catherine, Branch Lead, Charlotte Mecklenburg Library, Plaza Midwood Branch, 1623 Central Ave, Charlotte, NC, 28205. Tel: 704-416-6200. p. 1680
Haydu, Steven, Library Mgr, Tech Services & Systems, Las Cruces Public Libraries, 200 E Picacho Ave, Las Cruces, NM, 88001-3499. Tel: 575-528-4043. p. 1470
Hayduke, Katie, Br Mgr, Onondaga County Public Libraries, Paine Branch Library, 113 Nichols Ave, Syracuse, NY, 13206. Tel: 315-435-5442. p. 1649
Hayek, Jennifer, Br Mgr, Chesterfield County Public Library, Central, 7051 Lucy Corr Blvd, Chesterfield, VA, 23832. p. 2312
Hayes, Alyson, Br Coordr, Southern Oklahoma Library System, 601 Railway Express St, Ardmore, OK, 73401. Tel: 580-223-3164. p. 1840
Hayes, Andrea, Dir, Roosevelt County Library, 220 Second Ave S, Wolf Point, MT, 59201-1599. Tel: 406-653-2411. p. 1304
Hayes, Annabeth, Br Mgr, Onondaga County Public Libraries, Soule Branch Library, 101 Springfield Rd, Syracuse, NY, 13214. Tel: 315-435-5320. p. 1649
Hayes, Annabeth, Libr Dir, Tully Free Library, 12 State St, Tully, NY, 13159. Tel: 315-696-8606. p. 1653
Hayes, Brieana, Libr Mgr, Thomas County Public Library System, Meigs Public Library, 3058 NE Railroad St, Meigs, GA, 31765. Tel: 229-683-3853. p. 499
Hayes, Carolyn, Head, Tech Serv, Cook County Law Library, 50 W Washington St, Rm 2900, Chicago, IL, 60602. Tel: 312-603-2433. p. 559
Hayes, Christina, Cat, Hartford Public Library District, 143 W Hawthorne, Hartford, IL, 62048. Tel: 618-254-9394. p. 597
Hayes, Cindy, Br Mgr, Jefferson County Library, Northwest, 5680 State Rd PP, High Ridge, MO, 63049. Tel: 636-677-8186. p. 1249
Hayes, Denise, Head Librn, Salem Township Public Library District, 102 N Burson St, Yates City, IL, 61572. Tel: 309-358-1678. p. 665
Hayes, Elaine Jones, Adult Serv, Asst Mgr, Spec Coll Librn, Laramie County Library System, 2200 Pioneer Ave, Cheyenne, WY, 82001-3610. Tel: 307-773-7232. p. 2492
Hayes, Emily, Global Campus Librn, Davenport University, 6191 Kraft Ave SE, Grand Rapids, MI, 49512. Tel: 616-554-5664. p. 1110
Hayes Greenhill, Kelley, Dir, Res & Info Serv, Finnegan, Henderson, Farabow, Garrett & Dunner, 901 New York Ave NW, Washington, DC, 20001-4413. Tel: 202-408-4000. p. 366
Hayes, Gregory, Dir, Holly Township Library, 1116 N Saginaw St, Holly, MI, 48442-1395. Tel: 248-634-1754. p. 1116
Hayes, Helena, Dir, Galesburg Charleston Memorial District Library, 188 E Michigan Ave, Galesburg, MI, 49053. Tel: 269-665-7839. p. 1108
Hayes, Jessica, Head, Pub Serv, Auburn University, 7440 East Dr, Montgomery, AL, 36117. Tel: 334-244-3200. p. 28
Hayes, Judith, Librn, Tuality Healthcare, Health Sciences Library, 335 SE Eighth Ave, Hillsboro, OR, 97123. Tel: 503-681-1121. p. 1881
Hayes, Judith, Libr Serv Mgr, Tuality Healthcare, Tuality Health Information Resource Center, 334 SE Eighth Ave, Hillsboro, OR, 97123-4201. Tel: 503-681-1702. p. 1882
Hayes, Kathleen, Mgr, Durham County Library, Bragtown, 3200 Dearborn Dr, Durham, NC, 27704. Tel: 919-560-0210. p. 1685
Hayes, Leslie, Libr Coord, Northeastern Oklahoma A&M College, 200 I St NE, Miami, OK, 74354. Tel: 918-540-6024. p. 1853
Hayes, Lisa, Spec Coll Librn, Charleston Library Society, 164 King St, Charleston, SC, 29401. Tel: 843-723-9912. p. 2050
Hayes, Lori, Libr Asst, Hartford Hospital, Institute of Living Medical Library, Research/Burlingame Bldg, 3rd Flr, 200 Retreat Ave, Hartford, CT, 06106. Tel: 860-545-7276. p. 317
Hayes, Lori, Libr Mgr, Piedmont Regional Library System, Braselton Library, 15 Brassie Lane, Braselton, GA, 30517. Tel: 706-654-1992. p. 482
Hayes, Marion, Libr Mgr, Department of Veterans Affairs, Medical Library 142D, 4150 Clement St, San Francisco, CA, 94121. Tel: 415-221-4810, Ext 23302. p. 224
Hayes, Maureen, Dir, Sacred Heart Academy, c/o Sacred Heart Academy, 265 Benham St, Hamden, CT, 06514. Tel: 203-288-2309. p. 316
Hayes, Melissa, Br Mgr, Barton Public Library, Harper Memorial, 301 N Myrtle, Junction City, AR, 71749. Tel: 870-924-5556. p. 94
Hayes, Natasha, Dir, Hendry County Library System, 120 W Osceola Ave, Clewiston, FL, 33440. Tel: 863-983-1493. p. 389
Hayes, Rachel K, Asst Dir, Mid-Atlantic Christian University, 715 N Poindexter St, Elizabeth City, NC, 27909-4054. Tel: 252-334-2050. p. 1687
Hayes, Rhea, Exec Dir, Wayne County Historical Society Museum Library, 21 Butternut St, Lyons, NY, 14489. Tel: 315-946-4943. p. 1566
Hayes, Rhonda, Ch, Auburndale Public Library, 100 W Bridgers Ave, Auburndale, FL, 33823. Tel: 863-965-5548. p. 383
Hayes, Sandy, Assoc Dean, Collections & Discovery, Texas A&M University-Commerce, 2600 S Neal St, Commerce, TX, 75428. Tel: 903-886-5137. p. 2158
Hayes, Scooter, Ch, New Hanover County Public Library, Pine Valley, 3802 S College Rd, Wilmington, NC, 28412. Tel: 910-798-6398. p. 1723
Hayes, Susan, Dir, Wetumpka Public Library, 212 S Main St, Wetumpka, AL, 36092. Tel: 334-567-1308. p. 39
Hayes, Teresa, Librn, Newton County Public Library, Hwy 7 S, Jasper, AR, 72641. Tel: 870-446-2983. p. 99
Hayes, Thomas, Coll Develop Librn, Rare Bks, Cleveland Health Sciences Library, Allen Memorial Medical Library, 11000 Euclid Ave, Cleveland, OH, 44106-7130. Tel: 216-368-3642. p. 1766
Hayes, Thomas, Coll Develop Librn, Engagement Librn, Cleveland Health Sciences Library, Allen Memorial Medical Library, 11000 Euclid Ave, Cleveland, OH, 44106-7130. Tel: 216-368-3642. p. 1767
Hayes, Wendy Joy, Asst Dir, Town of Chester Public Library, 6307 State Rte 9, Chestertown, NY, 12817. Tel: 518-494-5384. p. 1518
Hayes-Bohanan, Pamela, Head, Libr Instruction, Ref Librn, Bridgewater State University, Ten Shaw Rd, Bridgewater, MA, 02325. Tel: 508-531-2893. p. 1002
Hayes-Martin, Tonya, Librn, Fulton State Hospital, Patient's Library, 600 E Fifth St, Fulton, MO, 65251. Tel: 573-592-2261. p. 1246
Hayes-Martin, Tonya, Librn, Fulton State Hospital, Professional Library, 600 E Fifth St, Fulton, MO, 65251. Tel: 573-592-2261. p. 1246
Hayes-Minney, Lisa, Dir, Gilmer Public Library, 214 Walnut St, Glenville, WV, 26351. Tel: 304-462-5620. p. 2403
Hayes-Zorn, Sheryln L, Curator of Ms, Nevada Historical Society, 1650 N Virginia St, Reno, NV, 89503. Tel: 775-688-1190, Ext 227. p. 1349
Haymaker, Melissa, Br Librn, Riverside Regional Library, Perryville Branch, 800 City Park Dr, Ste A, Perryville, MO, 63775. Tel: 573-547-6508. p. 1252
Hayman, Mark, Exec Dir, Temple Beth Zion, 700 Sweet Home Rd, Buffalo, NY, 14226. Tel: 716-836-6565. p. 1510
Haymore, Teresa P, Dir, Libr Serv, Truett-McConnell University, 100 Alumni Dr, Cleveland, GA, 30528-9799. Tel: 706-865-2134, Ext 2201. p. 471
Haynes, Cindy, Librn, Talladega County Law Library, Talladega County Judicial Bldg, 148 East St N, 2nd Flr, Talladega, AL, 35160. Tel: 256-761-2110. p. 36
Haynes, Elizabeth, Head, Info Serv, Iberville Parish Library, 24605 J Gerald Berret Blvd, Plaquemine, LA, 70764. Tel: 225-687-2520, 225-687-4397. p. 906
Haynes, Frankie, Ms, Diversity & Inclusion Coord, Lawrence Public Library, 707 Vermont St, Lawrence, KS, 66044-2371. Tel: 785-843-3833, Ext 125. p. 819
Haynes, Heather, Dir, Keyser-Mineral County Public Library, 105 N Main St, Keyser, WV, 26726. Tel: 304-788-3222. p. 2406
Haynes, Jennifer, Ch, Dir, Silsby Free Public Library, 226 Main St, Charlestown, NH, 03603. Tel: 603-826-7793. p. 1357
Haynes, Joan, Dir, Leroy Pollard Memorial Library, 45 Memorial Dr, New Braintree, MA, 01531. Tel: 508-867-7650. p. 1038
Haynes, Justin, Br Mgr, White County Public Library, Helen Branch, 90 Petes Park Rd, Helen, GA, 30545. Tel: 706-878-2438. p. 471
Haynes, Richard, Dir, Harlan County Public Libraries, 107 N Third St, Harlan, KY, 40831. Tel: 606-573-5220. p. 858
Haynes, Suzanne, Ref & Instruction Librn, Tulsa Community College Libraries, Southeast Campus, 10300 E 81st St, Tulsa, OK, 74133-4513. Tel: 918-595-7704. p. 1867
Haynie, Donna, Librn, Slater Public Library, 201 N Main, Slater, MO, 65349. Tel: 660-529-3100. p. 1280
Haynie, Kate, Libr Dir, Seneca Free Library, 606 Main St, Seneca, KS, 66538. Tel: 785-336-2377. p. 836
Haynie, Steven, Br Mgr, Cuyahoga County Public Library, Maple Heights Branch, 5225 Library Lane, Maple Heights, OH, 44137-1242. Tel: 216-475-5000. p. 1813
Hayreh, Shelley, Archivist, Columbia University, Avery Architectural & Fine Arts Library, 300 Avery Hall, 1172 Amsterdam Ave, MC 0301, New York, NY, 10027. Tel: 212-854-6199. p. 1583
Hays, Beth, Ch, Ruth Culver Community Library, 540 Water St, Prairie du Sac, WI, 53578. Tel: 608-643-8318. p. 2471
Hays, Catharine, Dir, Bixby Memorial Free Library, 258 Main St, Vergennes, VT, 05491. Tel: 802-877-2211. p. 2296
Hays, Heather, Ref Librn, Bentonville Public Library, 405 S Main St, Bentonville, AR, 72712. Tel: 479-271-5976. p. 91
Hays, Laura, Mgr, Ad Serv, Carol Stream Public Library, 616 Hiawatha Dr, Carol Stream, IL, 60188. Tel: 630-653-0755. p. 549
Hays, Philip, Assessment Librn, ILL Librn, Winthrop University, 824 Oakland Ave, Rock Hill, SC, 29733. Tel: 803-323-2131. p. 2068

Hays, Sarah, Local Hist Librn, Barberton Public Library, 602 W Park Ave, Barberton, OH, 44203-2458. Tel: 330-745-1194. p. 1748

Hays, Timothy, Chief Librn, United States Army, 696 Virginia Rd, Concord, MA, 01742-2751. Tel: 978-318-8349. p. 1012

Hayse, Mark, Dr, Libr Dir, MidAmerica Nazarene University, 2030 E College Way, Olathe, KS, 66062-1899. Tel: 913-971-3485. p. 828

Hayter, Carrie, Research Servs Librn, Lowenstein Sandler LLP Library, One Lowenstein Dr, Roseland, NJ, 07068. Tel: 973-597-2500. p. 1440

Hayter, Nikki, Supv Librn, Des Moines Public Library, Franklin Avenue, 5000 Franklin Ave, Des Moines, IA, 50310. Tel: 515-283-4152. p. 746

Hayward, Craig, Syst & Digital Serv Librn, North Carolina Regional Library for the Blind & Physically Handicapped, 1841 Capital Blvd, Raleigh, NC, 27635. Tel: 919-733-4376. p. 1709

Hayward, Greg, Supvr, Tech Serv Librn, Pictou - Antigonish Regional Library, New Glasgow Library, 182 Dalhousie St, New Glasgow, NS, B2H 5E3, CANADA. Tel: 902-752-8233. p. 2622

Hayward, Karen L, Supvry Librn, United States Army, The Medal of Honor Memorial Library, 4418 Llewellyn Ave, Ste 5068, Fort George G Meade, MD, 20755-5068. Tel: 301-677-4509, 301-677-5522. p. 965

Hayward, Tracey, Mgr, ILL, Canal Fulton Public Library, 154 Market St NE, Canal Fulton, OH, 44614-1196. Tel: 330-854-4148. p. 1754

Haywood, Christy, Ch Serv, Circ, Robertson County Public Library, 207 N Main St, Mount Olivet, KY, 41064. Tel: 606-724-5746. p. 870

Haywood, Felicia, Asst Dir, Libr Serv, Middle Georgia State University, 100 University Pkwy, Macon, GA, 31206. Tel: 478-471-2867. p. 487

Hayworth, Chris, Library Contact, ISA - The International Society of Automation, 67 TW Alexander Dr, Research Triangle Park, NC, 27709. Tel: 919-549-8411. p. 1712

Hayworth, Laura, Libr Asst, Johnson County Public Library, 219 N Church St, Mountain City, TN, 37683. Tel: 423-727-6544. p. 2117

Hazel, Laurie, Dir, Cambridge Memorial Library, 225 Water St, Cambridge, IA, 50046. Tel: 515-220-4542. p. 736

Hazelden, Joanna, Br Mgr, Chicago Public Library, Edgewater, 6000 N Broadway, Chicago, IL, 60660. Tel: 312-742-1945. p. 556

Hazen, Kim, Ch, Guernsey Memorial Library, Three Court St, Norwich, NY, 13815. Tel: 607-334-4034. p. 1609

Hazen, Liza, Br Mgr, San Bernardino County Library, Adelanto Branch, 11497 Bartlett, Adelanto, CA, 92301. Tel: 760-246-5661. p. 212

Hazen, Ritza, Libr Asst, Chester County Law Library, 201 W Market St, Ste 2400, West Chester, PA, 19380-0989. Tel: 610-344-6166. p. 2020

Hazlett, Kimberly, Interim Dir, Lake Forest College, 555 N Sheridan Rd, Lake Forest, IL, 60045. Tel: 847-735-5063. p. 606

Hazzan, Linda, Dir, Communications, Dir, Programming, Toronto Public Library, 789 Yonge St, Toronto, ON, M4W 2G8, CANADA. Tel: 416-393-7131. p. 2693

He, Jingrui, MSIM Program Dir, Prof, University of Illinois at Urbana-Champaign, Library & Information Science Bldg, 501 E Daniel St, Champaign, IL, 61820-6211. Tel: 217-333-3280. p. 2784

He, Ling, Syst Librn, OCAD University, Bldg MCC, 2nd Flr, 113 McCaul St, Toronto, ON, M5T 1W1, CANADA. Tel: 416-977-6000, Ext 3703. p. 2690

He, Yan, Dean of Libr, Indiana University Kokomo Library, 2300 S Washington St, Kokomo, IN, 46902. Tel: 765-455-9265. p. 699

Heaberlin, J Charles, Archival Librn, Lexington Theological Seminary, 230 Lexington Green Circle, Ste 300, Lexington, KY, 40503. Tel: 859-280-1229. p. 863

Head, Connie, Instruction Librn, Gulf Coast State College Library, 5230 W US Hwy 98, Panama City, FL, 32401. Tel: 850-872-3893. p. 435

Head, Joanne, Br Coordr, Dep Dir, Western Counties Regional Library, 405 Main St, Yarmouth, NS, B5A 1G3, CANADA. Tel: 902-742-2486. p. 2623

Head, Karen, Supvr, Circ, Supvr, ILL, Bushnell University, 1188 Kincade, Eugene, OR, 97401. Tel: 541-684-7235. p. 1878

Head, Mary, Asst Librn, Mount Morris Public Library, 105 S McKendrie Ave, Mount Morris, IL, 61054. Tel: 815-734-4927. p. 620

Head, Tonya, Dir, Access & Strategic Initiatives, Lexington Public Library, 140 E Main St, Lexington, KY, 40507-1376. Tel: 859-231-5506. p. 862

Head, Valentino, Libr Tech, Department of Veterans Affairs, 1901 Veterans Memorial Dr, 14LIB-T, Temple, TX, 76504. Tel: 254-743-0607. p. 2247

Headlam, Elizabeth, Sr Librn, Canadian Broadcasting Corp, Radio Archives, 205 Wellington St W, Toronto, ON, M5G 3G7, CANADA. Tel: 416-205-5880. p. 2687

Headley, Heather, Libr Dir, Wayne Public Library, Robert B & Mary Y Benthack Library-Senior Ctr, 410 Pearl St, Wayne, NE, 68787. Tel: 402-375-3135. p. 1340

Headley, Ruth, Youth & Teen Serv Librn, Newberg Public Library, 503 E Hancock St, Newberg, OR, 97132. Tel: 503-537-1254. p. 1888

Headrick, Gregg, Soc Media Librn, State University of New York Downstate Health Sciences University, 395 Lenox Rd, Brooklyn, NY, 11203. Tel: 718-270-7400. p. 1506

Headrick, Laura L, Br Coordr, Marathon County Public Library, Rothschild Branch, 211 Grand Ave, Rothschild, WI, 54474-1122. Tel: 715-359-6208. p. 2486

Heady, Lisa, Asst Librn, Choctaw County Public Library, 703 E Jackson St, Hugo, OK, 74743. Tel: 580-326-5591. p. 1850

Heald, Gregory, Dir, Suffolk University, 73 Tremont St, 2nd Flr, Boston, MA, 02108. Tel: 617-573-8535. p. 1000

Healey, Lindsay, Cataloger, Ref & Instruction Librn, Des Moines Area Community College Library, 2006 S Ankeny Blvd, Ankeny, IA, 50023. Tel: 515-964-6317. p. 732

Healey, Meredith, Supvry Librn, Marine Corps Base Hawaii Libraries, Marine Corps Base Hawaii, Bldg 219, Kaneohe Bay, HI, 96863. Tel: 808-254-7624. p. 513

Healy, Christine, Circ & ILL, Southbury Public Library, 100 Poverty Rd, Southbury, CT, 06488. Tel: 203-262-0626. p. 337

Healy, Judy Pat, Sister, ILL Librn, College of Saint Mary Library, 7000 Mercy Rd, Omaha, NE, 68106-2606. Tel: 402-399-2471. p. 1327

Healy, Mary, Br Mgr, Anoka County Library, Centennial, 100 Civic Heights Circle, Circle Pines, MN, 55014. Tel: 763-324-1540. p. 1165

Healy, Shawna, Ad, Rye Public Library, 581 Washington Rd, Rye, NH, 03870. Tel: 603-964-8401. p. 1380

Heaney, Christina, Children & Teen Librn, Ref Serv, Comsewogue Public Library, 170 Terryville Rd, Port Jefferson Station, NY, 11776. Tel: 631-928-1212. p. 1621

Heans, Amy, Regional Dir, Fundy Library Region, One Market Sq, Saint John, NB, E2L 4Z6, CANADA. Tel: 506-643-7222. p. 2604

Heard, Malinda, Br Librn, Southeast Regional Library, Fort Qu'Appelle Branch, 140 Company Ave S, Fort Qu'Appelle, SK, S0G 1S0, CANADA. Tel: 306-332-6411. p. 2753

Hearn, Elise, Br Mgr, Peoria Public Library, Lakeview, 1137 W Lake Ave, Peoria, IL, 61614-5935. Tel: 309-497-2204. p. 634

Hearn, Elizabeth, Librn, Crossville Public Library, 80 Gaines St, Crossville, AL, 35962. Tel: 256-528-2628. p. 13

Hearn, Julie, Law Librn, A Max Brewer Memorial Law Library, Harry T & Harriette V Moore Justice Ctr, 2825 Judge Fran Jamieson Way, Viera, FL, 32940. Tel: 321-617-7295. p. 453

Hearn, Mike, Dir, Libr Serv, Northern Essex Community College, 100 Elliott St, Haverhill, MA, 01830. Tel: 978-556-3423. p. 1024

Hearne, Shannon, Br Supvr, Thomas H Leath Memorial Library, 412 E Franklin St, Rockingham, NC, 28379-4995. Tel: 910-895-6337. p. 1713

Hearne, Steele, Librn, Union League Club Library, 38 E 37th St, New York, NY, 10016. Tel: 212-685-3800, Ext 226. p. 1603

Hearns, Kyle, Br Supvr, Gaston County Public Library, Ferguson Branch, Erwin Ctr, 913 N Pryor St, Gastonia, NC, 28052. Tel: 704-868-8046. p. 1690

Hearst, Linda, Libr Operations, University of Missouri-Saint Louis Libraries, Thomas Jefferson Library, One University Blvd, Saint Louis, MO, 63121-4400. Tel: 314-516-5060. p. 1276

Heaster, Kim, Br Librn, Crook County Library, 414 Main St, Sundance, WY, 82729. Tel: 307-283-1006, 307-283-1008. p. 2499

Heath, Annette, Librn, Kern County Law Library, 1415 Truxtun Ave, Rm 301, Bakersfield, CA, 93301. Tel: 661-868-5320. p. 119

Heath, April, Br Assoc, Las Vegas-Clark County Library District, Moapa Valley Library, 36 N Moapa Valley Blvd, Overton, NV, 89040-0397. Tel: 702-397-2690. p. 1347

Heath, Brian, Librn, California Department of Corrections Library System, Mule Creek State Prison, 4001 Hwy 104, Ione, CA, 95640. Tel: 209-274-4911. p. 207

Heath, Clark, Ser, Henry Ford College, 5101 Evergreen Rd, Dearborn, MI, 48128-1495. Tel: 313-845-6518. p. 1096

Heath, Dale, Head, Res Serv, Mount Prospect Public Library, Ten S Emerson St, Mount Prospect, IL, 60056. Tel: 847-253-5675. p. 621

Heath, Erin, Info Serv Assoc, Sampson-Clinton Public Library, 217 Graham St, Clinton, NC, 28328. Tel: 910-592-4153. p. 1681

Heath, Gayle R, Libr Dir, Tamaqua Public Library, 30 S Railroad St, Tamaqua, PA, 18252. Tel: 570-668-4660. p. 2012

Heath, Gordon, Dr, Archives Dir, Canadian Baptist Archives, McMaster Divinity College, 1280 Main St W, Hamilton, ON, L8S 4K1, CANADA. Tel: 905-525-9140, Ext 26409. p. 2644

Heath, Janet P, Coordr, Ser, East Carolina University, William E Laupus Health Sciences Library, 500 Health Sciences Dr, Greenville, NC, 27834. Tel: 252-744-2234. p. 1693

Heath, Jeanette, Financial Serv, User Serv, Red Feather Lakes Community Library, 71 Firehouse Lane, Red Feather Lakes, CO, 80545. Tel: 970-881-2664. p. 294

Heath, Kristin, Sr Librn, Carnegie Mellon University, Hunt Library, 4909 Frew St, Pittsburgh, PA, 15213. Tel: 412-268-2444. p. 1992

Heath, Leila, Dir, Library Resources & Programs, Reaching Across Illinois Library System (RAILS), 125 Tower Dr, Burr Ridge, IL, 60527. Tel: 630-734-5119. p. 546

Heath, Margie, Adult Serv, Asst Dir, Hartley Public Library, 91 First St SE, Hartley, IA, 51346. Tel: 712-928-2080. p. 757

Heath, Phyllis, Circ, West Lafayette Public Library, 208 W Columbia St, West Lafayette, IN, 47906. Tel: 765-743-2261. p. 726

Heath, Rita, Ch Serv, Converse County Library, Glenrock Branch, 506 S Fourth St, Glenrock, WY, 82637. Tel: 307-436-2573. p. 2494

Heather, Ellen, Dir, Mitchellville Public Library, 205 Center Ave N, Mitchellville, IA, 50169. Tel: 515-967-3339. p. 770

Heatherington, Donna, Br Mgr, Greenville County Library System, Pelham Road Branch, 1508 Pelham Rd, Greenville, SC, 29615. Tel: 864-527-9206. p. 2061
Heatherington, Jordan, Libr Asst, Grassland Public Library, Hwy 63, Box 150, Grassland, AB, T0A 1V0, CANADA. Tel: 780-525-3733. p. 2541
Heatherly, Carey, Archivist, Spec Coll Librn, University of Montevallo, Bloch St, Montevallo, AL, 35115. Tel: 205-665-6107. p. 27
Heathershaw, Leslie, Dir, Oglala Lakota College, Pass Creek College Center, PO Box 630, Allen, SD, 57714. Tel: 605-455-2757. p. 2078
Heaton, Reba, Dir, Haines Borough Public Library, 111 Third Ave S, Haines, AK, 99827. Tel: 907-766-6420. p. 46
Heaton, Tony, Doc Delivery Spec, ILL, Illinois Wesleyan University, One Ames Plaza, Bloomington, IL, 61701-7188. Tel: 309-556-1040. p. 543
Heavey, Elaine, Libr Dir, Massachusetts Historical Society Library, 1154 Boylston St, Boston, MA, 02215. Tel: 617-646-0509. p. 997
Heavrin, Michael, Libr Dir, Lyons Public Library, 305 Main, Lyons, NE, 68038. Tel: 402-687-2895. p. 1324
Hebard, Jeanne, Electronic Res Librn, Babson College, 11 Babson College Dr, Babson Park, MA, 02457-0310. Tel: 781-239-6405. p. 987
Heberlie, Geri, Coordr, Search Serv, Nestle Purina Pet Care Co, One Checkerboard Sq, Saint Louis, MO, 63164. Tel: 314-982-5913. p. 1272
Hebert, Brittany, Br Mgr, Assumption Parish Library, Pierre Part Branch, 2800 Hwy 70 S, Pierre Part, LA, 70390. Tel: 985-252-4220. p. 899
Hebert, Dawn, Admin Mgr, Vermilion Parish Library, 405 E Saint Victor St, Abbeville, LA, 70510-5101. Tel: 337-893-2655. p. 879
Hebert, Francis, Librn, California Department of Corrections Library System, California State Prison, Corcoran, 4001 King Ave, Corcoran, CA, 93212. Tel: 559-992-8800, Ext 5888. p. 206
Hebert, Gina, Br Mgr, Main Libr, Terrebonne Parish Library, 151 Library Dr, Houma, LA, 70360. Tel: 985-876-5861. p. 891
Hebert, Jane, Circ Mgr, Glenside Public Library District, 25 E Fullerton Ave, Glendale Heights, IL, 60139-2697. Tel: 630-260-1550. p. 593
Hebert, Kathy, Circ Mgr, Greater Clarks Hill Regional Library System, 7022 Evans Town Center Blvd, Evans, GA, 30809. Tel: 706-447-7662. p. 478
Hebert, Lisa, Libr Dir, Grayson County College Library, 6101 Grayson Dr, Denison, TX, 75020-8299. Tel: 903-463-8637. p. 2170
Hebert, Marianne, Automation Syst Librn, Coll Develop Coordr, Syst, State University of New York College at Potsdam, Lougheed Learning Commons, 44 Pierrepont Ave, Potsdam, NY, 13676-2294. Tel: 315-267-3308. p. 1622
Hebert, Sarah, Dir, River Valley Community College, One College Pl, Claremont, NH, 03743. Tel: 603-542-7744, Ext 5465. p. 1358
Hebert, Sylvie, Libr Mgr, Albert-Westmorland-Kent Regional Library, Omer-Leger Public Library, 4556 Principale St, Ste 100, Saint-Antoine, NB, E4V 1R3, CANADA. Tel: 506-525-4028. p. 2603
Hebig, Kim, Exec Dir, Wheatland Regional Library, 806 Duchess St, Saskatoon, SK, S7K 0R3, CANADA. Tel: 306-652-5077. p. 2750
Hecht, Kathy, Circ Tech, Washington Adventist University, 7600 Flower Ave, Takoma Park, MD, 20912-7796. Tel: 301-891-4217. p. 979
Hecht, Kim, Head, Tech Serv, Worth Public Library District, 6917 W 111th St, Worth, IL, 60482. Tel: 708-448-2855. p. 665
Heck, Anne, Asst Librn, Cavalier Public Library, 200 Bjornson Dr, Cavalier, ND, 58220. Tel: 701-265-4746. p. 1731
Heck, Jessica, Acq Asst, Admin Coordr, University of Tulsa Libraries, Mabee Legal Information Center, 3120 E Fourth Pl, Tulsa, OK, 74104-3189. Tel: 918-631-2404. p. 1867
Heck, Melody, Dir, Galva Public Library District, 120 NW Third Ave, Galva, IL, 61434. Tel: 309-932-2180. p. 591
Heckel, Aleshia, Acq, Circ, Ref, Saint Meinrad Archabbey & School of Theology, 200 Hill Dr, Saint Meinrad, IN, 47577. Tel: 812-357-6401. p. 717
Hecker, Tom, Academic Liaison, University of Kentucky Libraries, Science & Engineering Library, 211 King Bldg, 179 Funkhouser Dr, Lexington, KY, 40506-0039. Tel: 859-257-8343. p. 864
Heckert, Dawn, Circ Serv, Coordr, Bldg Mgt, Haverford College, 370 Lancaster Ave, Haverford, PA, 19041-1392. Tel: 610-896-1163. p. 1942
Heckman, Ben, Mr, Libr Dir, Bexley Public Library, 2411 E Main St, Bexley, OH, 43209. Tel: 614-545-6940. p. 1751
Heckman, Heather, Dir, University of South Carolina, Moving Image Research Collections, 707 Catawba St, Columbia, SC, 29201. Tel: 803-777-6841. p. 2055
Heckman, Lucy, Head, Ref, St John's University Library, St Augustine Hall, 8000 Utopia Pkwy, Jamaica, NY, 11439. Tel: 718-990-6571. p. 1556
Heckman, Mary Ellen G, Assoc Dean, Libr Serv, Reading Area Community College, 30 S Front St, Reading, PA, 19602. Tel: 610-607-6237. p. 2000
Hector, Patricia, Dir, Saline County Public Library, 1800 Smithers Dr, Benton, AR, 72015. Tel: 501-778-4766. p. 90
Hedden, Holly H, Tech Serv, Warren County Public Library, 1225 State St, Bowling Green, KY, 42101. Tel: 270-781-4882. p. 849
Hedden, Margaret, Libr Mgr, Evans Mills Public Library, 8706 Noble St, Evans Mills, NY, 13637. Tel: 315-629-4483. p. 1532
Hedge, Jenna, Info Serv Mgr, Anderson City, Anderson, Stony Creek & Union Townships Public Library, 111 E 12th St, Anderson, IN, 46016-2701. Tel: 765-641-2456. p. 667
Hedgepeth, Sharon, Tech Serv, Gaston College, 201 Hwy 321 S, Dallas, NC, 28034-1499. Tel: 704-922-6361. p. 1683
Hedges, Ben, Head, Spec Coll & Archives, Oklahoma State University Libraries, Special Collections & University Archives, Library 204, Stillwater, OK, 74078. Tel: 405-744-6076. p. 1862
Hedges, Devon, Asst Dir, Schenectady County Public Library, 99 Clinton St, Schenectady, NY, 12305-2083. Tel: 518-388-4500. p. 1638
Hedges, Nancy, Librn, Greene County Law Library, Court House, 3rd Flr, 45 N Detroit St, Xenia, OH, 45385. Tel: 937-562-5115. p. 1834
Hedgespeth, Melanie, Dir, Salina Public Library, 301 W Elm St, Salina, KS, 67401. Tel: 785-825-4624, Ext 226. p. 835
Hedlund, Sarah, Librn & Archivist, Montgomery History, 42 W Middle Lane, Rockville, MD, 20850. Tel: 301-340-2974. p. 975
Hedquist, Pamela, Asst Archivist-Tech, Providence Archives, 4800 37th Ave SW, Seattle, WA, 98126. Tel: 509-474-2319. p. 2378
Hedstrom, Gail, Libr Dir, Thorson Memorial Public Library, 117 Central Ave, Elbow Lake, MN, 56531. Tel: 320-808-6394. p. 1174
Hedstrom, Gail, Libr Dir, Fergus Falls Public Library, 205 E Hampden, Fergus Falls, MN, 56537. Tel: 218-739-9387. p. 1175
Heeger-Brehm, Ned, Br Mgr, Public Library of Cincinnati & Hamilton County, Groesbeck, 2994 W Galbraith Rd, Cincinnati, OH, 45239. Tel: 513-369-4454. p. 1762
Heeks-Heinlein, Maria, Br Supvr, Rochester Public Library, Sully Branch, 530 Webster Ave, Rochester, NY, 14609. Tel: 585-428-8290. p. 1630
Heepe, Terri, Asst Librn, Cat, Dunbar Free Library, 401 Rte 10 S, Grantham, NH, 03753. Tel: 603-863-2172. p. 1365
Heerah, Guyatri Sharon, Law Librn, Lee County Law Library, Lee County Justice Ctr, 1700 Monroe St, Fort Myers, FL, 33901. Tel: 239-533-9195. p. 403
Heerema, Helen, Librn, Thunder Bay Law Association Library, Thunder Bay Courthouse, 2nd Flr, 125 Brodie St N, Thunder Bay, ON, P7C 0A3, CANADA. Tel: 807-344-3481. p. 2685
Heesen, Erika, Chief Exec Officer, Chief Librn, Perth & District Union Public Library, 30 Herriott St, Perth, ON, K7H 1T2, CANADA. Tel: 613-267-1224. p. 2671
Heet, Emma, Associate Dean, Collection Services, Loyola University Chicago Libraries, 1032 W Sheridan Rd, Chicago, IL, 60660. Tel: 773-508-7727. p. 563
Heffernan, Annette, Circ Mgr, Upper Arlington Public Library, 2800 Tremont Rd, Columbus, OH, 43221. Tel: 614-486-9621. p. 1778
Heffernan, Grace, Br Head, Brazoria County Library System, Lake Jackson Branch, 250 Circle Way, Lake Jackson, TX, 77566. Tel: 979-415-2590. p. 2135
Heffernan, Lorraine, Chair, Info Serv, University of Massachusetts Dartmouth Library, 285 Old Westport Rd, North Dartmouth, MA, 02747-2300. Tel: 508-999-8670. p. 1041
Heffner, Kate, Dir, Mechanicsville Public Library, 218 E First St, Mechanicsville, IA, 52306. Tel: 563-432-7135. p. 769
Heflin, Dana, Dir, Cochran County Love Memorial Library, 318 S Main St, Morton, TX, 79346-3006. Tel: 806-266-5051. p. 2220
Heflin, Shannon, Dir, Hooks Public Library, 108 W First St, Hooks, TX, 75561. Tel: 903-547-3365. p. 2191
Hefner, Lorraine, Co-Dir, Didymus Thomas Memorial Library, 9639 Main St, Remsen, NY, 13438. Tel: 315-831-5651. p. 1626
Hefner, Sheryl, Ch, Allerton Public Library, 103 S Central Ave, Allerton, IA, 50008. Tel: 641-873-4575. p. 730
Hegarty, William, Head, Ref, Larchmont Public Library, 121 Larchmont Ave, Larchmont, NY, 10538. Tel: 914-834-2281. p. 1562
Hegedus, Lorena, Dir, Hubbard Public Library, 436 W Liberty St, Hubbard, OH, 44425. Tel: 330-534-3512. p. 1790
Hegenbart, Barbara, Asst Librn, Peacham Library, 656 Bayley Hazen Rd, Peacham, VT, 05862. Tel: 802-592-3216. p. 2291
Hegerat, Elisabeth, Assoc Dir, Serv Develop, Lethbridge Public Library, 810 Fifth Ave S, Lethbridge, AB, T1J 4C4, CANADA. Tel: 403-320-4187. p. 2546
Hegge, Amanda, Dir, Whitehall Public Library, 36351 Main St, Whitehall, WI, 54773. Tel: 715-538-4107. p. 2488
Hegglund, Crystal, Bus Mgr, Converse County Library, 300 E Walnut St, Douglas, WY, 82633. Tel: 307-358-3644. p. 2494
Heggmann, Elda, Asst Prof, Kent State University, 314 University Library, 1125 Risman Dr, Kent, OH, 44242-0001. Tel: 330-672-2782. p. 2790
Heglund, Melissa, Library Contact, Northwest Technical College Library, 905 Grant Ave SE, Bemidji, MN, 56601-4907. Tel: 218-333-6633. p. 1165
Hegyes, Helene-Marie, Cataloguing & Indexing Librn, National Film Board of Canada, 1501 Bleury St, Montreal, QC, H3A 0H3, CANADA. Tel: 514-283-9045. p. 2727
Hehr, Pamela, Supvr, Tech Serv, Reading Public Library, 100 S Fifth St, Reading, PA, 19602. Tel: 610-655-6350. p. 2000
Heicher, Jeanne, Dir, Newport Public Library, 316 N Fourth St, Newport, PA, 17074-1203. Tel: 717-567-6860. p. 1970
Heichman, Linda J, Circ, Sr Librn, Los Angeles County Law Library, Mildred L Lillie Bldg, 301 W First St, Los Angeles, CA, 90012-3100. Tel: 213-785-2529. p. 162

Heldorfer, Ann Marie, Coll Develop, Youth Serv, The William K Sanford Town Library, 629 Albany Shaker Rd, Loudonville, NY, 12211-1196. Tel: 518-458-9274. p. 1565

Helfer, Olivia, Med Librn, Sisters of Charity Hospital Medical Library, 2157 Main St, 6th Flr, Buffalo, NY, 14214. Tel: 716-862-1256. p. 1510

Helfers, Amanda, Libr Spec, Wood Library-Museum of Anesthesiology, 1061 American Lane, Schaumburg, IL, 60173. Tel: 847-268-9160. p. 645

Helfrich, Sharon, Libr Dir, Robinson Township Library, 1000 Church Hill Rd, Pittsburgh, PA, 15205. Tel: 412-787-3906. p. 1996

Helfrick, Ellen, Librn, York County Library System, Collinsville Community Library, 2632 Delta Rd, Brogue, PA, 17309. Tel: 717-927-9014. p. 2026

Helgason, Kathleen, Coordr, CancerCare Manitoba, 675 McDermot Ave, Rm 1016, Winnipeg, MB, R3E 0V9, CANADA. Tel: 204-787-4279. p. 2593

Helgeson, Anna, Reader Serv Librn, Bard Graduate Center Library, 38 W 86th St, New York, NY, 10024. Tel: 212-501-3035. p. 1579

Helgeson, Charlotte, Dir, East Grand Forks Campbell Library, 422 Fourth St NW, East Grand Forks, MN, 56721. Tel: 218-773-9121. p. 1173

Helgeson, Hasleton, Commun Serv Mgr, Church of Jesus Christ of Latter-Day Saints, Family History Library, 35 N West Temple St, Salt Lake City, UT, 84150. p. 2271

Helgeson, Terry, Circ Asst, Galesville Public Library, 16787 S Main St, Galesville, WI, 54630. Tel: 608-582-2552. p. 2436

Helik, Teresa, Chief Librn, Regis College Library, 100 Wellesley St W, Toronto, ON, M5S 2Z5, CANADA. Tel: 416-922-5474, Ext 234. p. 2692

Helka, Tammi, Dir, Oakwood Public Library District, 110 E Finley, Oakwood, IL, 61858. Tel: 217-354-4777. p. 628

Hellard, Nicole, Libr Dir, Hendry County Library System, Barron Library, 461 N Main St, Labelle, FL, 33935. Tel: 863-675-0833. p. 389

Helldorfer, Ann-Marie, Youth Serv, The William K Sanford Town Library, 629 Albany Shaker Rd, Loudonville, NY, 12211-1196. Tel: 518-458-9274. p. 1565

Hellen, Sharla, Learning Res Ctr Dir, North Arkansas College Learning Resource Center, 1515 Pioneer Dr, Harrison, AR, 72601. Tel: 870-391-3560. p. 98

Hellenberg, Darlene, Asst Dir, Ferndale Area District Library, 222 E Nine Mile Rd, Ferndale, MI, 48220. Tel: 248-546-2504, Ext 691. p. 1105

Heller Cheyenne, Br Librn, Roosevelt County Library, Froid Public, 101 Second St N, Froid, MT, 59226. Tel: 406-766-2492. p. 1304

Heller, Deborah L, Asst Dean, Pace University, 78 N Broadway, White Plains, NY, 10603. Tel: 914-422-4339. p. 1665

Heller, Frederik, Managing Dir, National Association of Realtors, 430 N Michigan Ave, Chicago, IL, 60611-4087. Tel: 312-329-8577. p. 565

Heller, James, Dir, College of William & Mary in Virginia, The Wolf Law Library, 613 S Henry St, Williamsburg, VA, 23187. Tel: 757-221-3252. p. 2353

Heller, Kary, Librn, Lankenau Institute for Medical Research, 100 E Lancaster Ave, Wynnewood, PA, 19096. Tel: 484-476-2000, 484-476-2699. p. 2025

Heller, Margaret, Head, Digital Serv, DePaul University Libraries, 2350 N Kenmore, Chicago, IL, 60614. Tel: 773-325-7862, 773-325-7863. p. 560

Heller Wegner, Beth, Dir, Gladbrook Public Library, 301 Second St, Gladbrook, IA, 50635. Tel: 641-473-3236. p. 755

Heller-Tuers, Susann, Library Contact, Mill City Library, 236 SW Broadway, Mill City, OR, 97360. Tel: 503-897-6149. p. 1886

Helling, John, Dep Dir, Pub Serv, Indianapolis Public Library, 2450 N Meridian St, Indianapolis, IN, 46208. Tel: 317-275-4012. p. 694

Helling, John, Chief Impact Officer, Dep Libr Dir, Hamilton East Public Library, One Library Plaza, Noblesville, IN, 46060. Tel: 317-773-1384. p. 710

Hellman, Kate, Ad, Derby Neck Library Association, 307 Hawthorne Ave, Derby, CT, 06418. Tel: 203-734-1492. p. 308

Hellman, Kathy D, Libr Dir, Camp Verde Community Library, 130 N Black Bridge Rd, Camp Verde, AZ, 86322. Tel: 928-554-8381. p. 57

Hellmann, Kristal, Youth Serv Mgr, Plainfield-Guilford Township Public Library, 1120 Stafford Rd, Plainfield, IN, 46168. Tel: 317-839-6602, Ext 2127. p. 713

Hellmers, Nathan, Dir, William Peace University, 15 E Peace St, Raleigh, NC, 27604. Tel: 919-508-2303. p. 1712

Hellums, Dewayne, Br Mgr, Richland Public Library, 370 Scarbrough St, Richland, MS, 39218. Tel: 601-932-1846. p. 1231

Hellyer, Paul, Ref Serv, College of William & Mary in Virginia, The Wolf Law Library, 613 S Henry St, Williamsburg, VA, 23187. Tel: 757-221-3255. p. 2353

Helm, Anthony, Head, Digital Libr Tech, Dartmouth College Library, Baker-Berry Library, 6025 Baker-Berry Library, Hanover, NH, 03755-3527. Tel: 603-646-3830. p. 1366

Helm, Kelly, Archivist, Washington & Jefferson College Library, 60 S Lincoln St, Washington, PA, 15301. Tel: 724-223-6048. p. 2018

Helm, Kristen, Teen Librn, Westminster Public Library, 3705 W 112th Ave, Westminster, CO, 80031. Tel: 303-658-2624. p. 298

Helm, Sandra, Asst Librn, Chandler Public Library, 1021 Manvel Ave, Chandler, OK, 74834. Tel: 405-258-3204. p. 1843

Helman, Deborah M, Dir, University of Wisconsin-Madison, Schwerdtfeger Library, Space Science & Engineering Ctr, Rm 317, 1225 W Dayton St, Madison, WI, 53706. Tel: 608-262-7980. p. 2451

Helman, William, IT Librn, Towson University, 8000 York Rd, Towson, MD, 21252. Tel: 410-704-5748. p. 980

Helmen, Jennifer, Librn, Saint Joseph's Regional Medical Center, 5215 Holy Cross Pkwy, Mishawaka, IN, 46545-1469. Tel: 574-335-1012. p. 707

Helmer, Holly, Cat Librn, Concordia University, 800 N Columbia Ave, Seward, NE, 68434. Tel: 402-643-7254. p. 1335

Helmers, Marilyn, Dir of Develop, Andover Center for History & Culture Library, 97 Main St, Andover, MA, 01810. Tel: 978-475-2236. p. 985

Helmetsie, Elizabeth, Dir, Spencer Library, 41 N Main St, Spencer, NY, 14883-9100. Tel: 607-589-4496. p. 1643

Helmick, Sam, Commun & Access Serv Coordr, Iowa City Public Library, 123 S Linn St, Iowa City, IA, 52240. Tel: 319-887-6007. p. 760

Helmick, Samantha, Pub Serv Librn, Burlington Public Library, 210 Court St, Burlington, IA, 52601. Tel: 319-753-1647. p. 736

Helmrich, Ed, Doc Delivery Spec, Iona University, 715 North Ave, New Rochelle, NY, 10801-1890. Tel: 914-633-2351. p. 1577

Helms, Bernard, Bibliog Serv, Per/Acq Librn, Andrews University, 4190 Administration Dr, Berrien Springs, MI, 49104-1400. Tel: 269-471-3208. p. 1085

Helms, Betty Jean, Librn, Immanuel Church Library, 2414 Pennsylvania Ave, Wilmington, DE, 19806. Tel: 302-652-3121. p. 357

Helms, Caroline C, Dir, Robert Lee Brothers, Jr Memorial Library, 301 St Joseph St, Gonzales, TX, 78629. Tel: 830-672-6315. p. 2185

Helms, Judy, Ref Serv, Travis County Law Library, Ned Granger, 314 W 11th St, Ste 140, Austin, TX, 78701. Tel: 512-854-9045. p. 2141

Helmuth, Annika, Br Librn, Newport Beach Public Library, Corona del Mar Branch, 410 Marigold Ave, Corona del Mar, CA, 92625. Tel: 949-644-3075. p. 183

Helmuth, Kasia, Ad, Goodall City Library, 203 West A St, Ogallala, NE, 69153. Tel: 308-284-4354. p. 1327

Helouvry, Joanne, Librn, Stratford University, 210 S Central Ave, 2nd Flr, Baltimore, MD, 21202. Tel: 443-873-5415. p. 956

Helregel, Nicole, Liaison/Spec Librn, New York University, Courant Institute of Mathematical Sciences, Warren Weaver Hall, 251 Mercer St, 12th Flr, New York, NY, 10012-1110. Tel: 212-998-3315. p. 1599

Helsabeck, Kathleen, Exec Dir, Quincy Public Library, 526 Jersey St, Quincy, IL, 62301-3996. Tel: 217-223-1309, Ext 204. p. 637

Helsel, Daniel J, Law Librn, Mendocino County Law Library, Courthouse, Rm 307, 100 N State St, Ukiah, CA, 95482. Tel: 707-463-4201. p. 254

Helsel-Kather, Charlene, Circ Supvr, Tech Serv, Hubbard Public Library, 436 W Liberty St, Hubbard, OH, 44425. Tel: 330-534-3512. p. 1790

Helser, Madeline, Libr Dir, Jamaica Memorial Library, 17 Depot St, Jamaica, VT, 05343. Tel: 802-874-4901. p. 2286

Helser, Tracy, Research Coordr, Pillsbury Winthrop Shaw Pittman LLP, Four Embarcadero Ctr, 22nd Flr, San Francisco, CA, 94111. Tel: 415-983-1000. p. 226

Helt, James F, Librn, San Diego Model Railroad Museum, 1649 El Prado, San Diego, CA, 92101. Tel: 619-320-4912. p. 218

Helt, Tina, Chem Librn, Harvard Library, Godfrey Lowell Cabot Science Library, Science Ctr, One Oxford St, Cambridge, MA, 02138. Tel: 617-495-5355. p. 1005

Heltebridle, Beth, Br Adminr, Frederick County Public Libraries, C Burr Artz Public Library, 110 E Patrick St, Frederick, MD, 21701. Tel: 301-600-1337. p. 966

Heltne, Cindy, Libr Asst, Mayo Clinic Scottsdale Libraries, 13400 E Shea Blvd, Scottsdale, AZ, 85259. Tel: 480-301-8443. p. 77

Helton, Andrew, Dir, Kimble County Library, 208 N Tenth St, Junction, TX, 76849. Tel: 325-446-2342. p. 2204

Helton, Chad, Dir, Br, Los Angeles Public Library System, 630 W Fifth St, Los Angeles, CA, 90071. Tel: 213-228-7570. p. 163

Helton, Chad, Libr Dir, Hennepin County Library, 12601 Ridgedale Dr, Minnetonka, MN, 55305-1909. Tel: 612-543-8505. p. 1186

Helton, Erik, Campus Librn, Pepperdine University Libraries, Drescher Graduate Campus Library, 24255 Pacific Coast Hwy, Malibu, CA, 90263. Tel: 310-506-8568. p. 171

Helvling, Andrea, Br Mgr, Peoples Library, Lower Burrell, 3052 Wachter Ave, Lower Burrell, PA, 15068. Tel: 724-339-1565. p. 1970

Helwig, Laura, Libr Dir, Moose Lake Public Library, 313 Elm Ave, Moose Lake, MN, 55767. Tel: 218-485-4424. p. 1189

Helwig, Melissa, Head of Libr, Dalhousie University, W K Kellogg Health Sciences Library, Sir Charles Tupper Medical Bldg, 5850 College St, Halifax, NS, B3H 4R2, CANADA. p. 2618

Hembry, Renee, Dir, Milo Public Library, 123 Main St, Milo, IA, 50166. Tel: 641-942-6557. p. 770

Hemel, Candis, Dir, Cimarron City Library, 120 N Main, Cimarron, KS, 67835. Tel: 620-855-3808. p. 801

Hemerling, Peggy, Libr Dir, Hastings Public Library, 227 E State St, Hastings, MI, 49058-1817. Tel: 269-945-4263. p. 1114

Hemingway, Ann, Coordr, University of Ottawa Libraries, Isobel Firestone Music Library, Perez Hall, 50 University Private, Ottawa, ON, K1N 6N5, CANADA. Tel: 613-562-5209. p. 2670

Hemingway, Anne, Reserves Mgr, Massachusetts School of Law Library, 500 Federal St, Andover, MA, 01810. Tel: 978-681-0800. p. 985

Hemingway, Arielle, Syst Librn, Chippewa River District Library, 301 S University Ave, Mount Pleasant, MI, 48858-2597. Tel: 989-773-3242, Ext 220. p. 1135
Hemingway, Chrisropher, Circ Librn, Hagaman Memorial Library, 227 Main St, East Haven, CT, 06512. Tel: 203-468-3890. p. 310
Hemmasi, Harriette, Dean of Libr, Georgetown University, 37th & O St NW, Washington, DC, 20057-1174. Tel: 202-687-7607. p. 367
Hemmat, Katherine, Ch Serv, Collier County Public Library, Golden Gate, 2432 Lucerne Rd, Naples, FL, 34116. Tel: 239-455-1441. p. 427
Hemmat, Shidan, Emerging Tech Librn, University of Miami, Louis Calder Memorial Library, Miller School of Medicine, 1601 NW Tenth Ave, Miami, FL, 33136. Tel: 305-243-6424. p. 425
Hemmeke, Grace, Outreach & Events Coord, Right to Life of Michigan, 2340 Porter St SW, Grand Rapids, MI, 49519. Tel: 616-532-2300. p. 1111
Hemmelman, Brenda, Coll Serv Librn, Res & Ref Serv, South Dakota State Library, 800 Governors Dr, Pierre, SD, 57501-2294. Tel: 605-773-3131. p. 2080
Hemmerlin, Michelle, Librn, George Junior Republic Library, 233 George Junior Rd, Grove City, PA, 16127. Tel: 724-458-9330, Ext 2552. p. 1939
Hemmerling, Emily, Coordr, Libr Serv, Hutchinson Community College, 1300 N Plum St, Hutchinson, KS, 67501. Tel: 620-665-3338. p. 814
Hemming, Ashley, Ch Serv, Milford Public Library, 57 New Haven Ave, Milford, CT, 06460. Tel: 203-783-3312. p. 323
Hemming, Debbie, Mgr, Kershaw County Library, 1304 Broad St, Camden, SC, 29020. Tel: 803-425-1508, Ext 3207. p. 2048
Hemming, Laura K, Circ Librn, Wisconsin Historical Society Library, 816 State St, 2nd Flr, Madison, WI, 53706. Tel: 608-264-6535. p. 2452
Hemphill, Alisa, ILL, Houston Academy of Medicine, 1133 John Freeman Blvd, No 100, Houston, TX, 77030. Tel: 713-795-4200. p. 2193
Hempstead, Mark, ILL, Libr Tech-Mats, US Customs & Border Protection Information Resources Center, 90 K St NE, Washington, DC, 20229. Tel: 202-325-0130. p. 380
Hemsley, Nicole, Dir, Amsterdam Free Library, 28 Church St, Amsterdam, NY, 12010. Tel: 518-842-1080. p. 1486
Hemstock, Thomas, Research Instruction & Acquisitions Librn, Albany Law School, 80 New Scotland Ave, Albany, NY, 12208. p. 1482
Hendershot, Le Ann, Dir, Ohio Historical Society, 601 Second St, Marietta, OH, 45750-2122. Tel: 740-373-3750. p. 1799
Hendershott, Carmen, Ref Serv, New School, Raymond Fogelman Library, 55 W 13th St, New York, NY, 10011. Tel: 212-229-5307, Ext 3053. p. 1593
Hendershott, Liz, Pub Serv Librn, Bellingham Public Library, 210 Central Ave, Bellingham, WA, 98225. Tel: 360-778-7246. p. 2358
Henderson, Alice, Dir, Plainview Public Library, 345 First Ave NW, Plainview, MN, 55964. Tel: 507-534-3425. p. 1193
Henderson, Alynza, Head, Cat, Hanover College, 121 Scenic Dr, Hanover, IN, 47243. Tel: 812-866-7165. p. 689
Henderson, Amanda, Dir, Cosby Community Library, 3292 Cosby Hwy, Cosby, TN, 37722-0052. Tel: 423-487-5885. p. 2095
Henderson, Amy, Dir, Oxford Public Library, 110 E Sixth St, Oxford, AL, 36203. Tel: 256-831-1750. p. 32
Henderson, Annie, Head, Access Serv, East Texas Baptist University, One Tiger Dr, Marshall, TX, 75670-1498. Tel: 903-923-2264. p. 2215
Henderson, Barbara, Br Mgr, Saint Louis Public Library, Cabanne, 1106 Union Blvd, Saint Louis, MO, 63113. Tel: 314-367-0717. p. 1275
Henderson, Barbara, Librn, Fort Worth Library, Ridglea, 3628 Bernie Anderson Ave, Fort Worth, TX, 76116-5403. Tel: 817-392-6631. p. 2179
Henderson, Barbara, Librn, Fort Worth Library, Seminary South, 501 E Bolt St, Fort Worth, TX, 76110. Tel: 817-392-5490. p. 2179
Henderson, Barbara, Librn, Fort Worth Library, Southwest Regional, 4001 Library Lane, Fort Worth, TX, 76109. Tel: 817-392-5860. p. 2180
Henderson, Barbara, Librn, Fort Worth Library, Wedgwood, 3816 Kimberly Lane, Fort Worth, TX, 76133. Tel: 817-392-5480. p. 2180
Henderson, Beth, Br Mgr, Monmouth County Library, Howell Branch, 318 Old Tavern Rd, Howell, NJ, 07731. Tel: 732-938-2300. p. 1416
Henderson, Beverly, Dir, Stratton Public Library, 502 Bailey St, Stratton, NE, 69043. Tel: 308-276-2463. p. 1337
Henderson, Brooke, Art Librn, Wellesley College, Art Library, Jewett Arts Ctr, 106 Central St, Wellesley, MA, 02481. Tel: 781-283-2049. p. 1064
Henderson, Catherine, Dir, Greece Public Library, Two Vince Tofany Blvd, Greece, NY, 14612. Tel: 585-225-8951. p. 1541
Henderson, Cindy, Br Mgr, Albemarle Regional Library, Ahoskie Public Library, 210 E Church St, Ahoskie, NC, 27910. Tel: 252-332-5500. p. 1727
Henderson, Darwyn, Br Librn, Dine College, Hwy 64 & N 570, Shiprock, NM, 87420. Tel: 505-368-3346. p. 1477
Henderson, Dave, Br Librn, Mariposa County Library, Red Cloud, 10332-C Fiske Rd, Coulterville, CA, 95311. Tel: 209-878-3692. p. 173
Henderson, Deadre, Ch, Highland Park Library, 4700 Drexel Dr, Highland Park, TX, 75205-3198. Tel: 214-559-9400. p. 2190
Henderson, Dedre, Supvry Librn, United States Environmental Protection, 1595 Wynkoop St, 3rd Flr, Denver, CO, 80202-1129. Tel: 303-312-6745. p. 277
Henderson, Erin, Library Contact, Casa Grande Valley Historical Society, 110 W Florence Blvd, Casa Grande, AZ, 85122. Tel: 520-836-2223. p. 57
Henderson, Holly, Libr Mgr, Mercy Health, Van K Smith Consumer Health Information Service, 1235 E Cherokee St, Springfield, MO, 65804. Tel: 417-820-2539. p. 1280
Henderson, Holly, Mgr, Libr Serv, Mercy Health, 1235 E Cherokee St, Springfield, MO, 65804-2263. Tel: 417-820-2795. p. 1280
Henderson, Hope E, Br Mgr, Lake Blackshear Regional Library System, Dooly County, 1200 E Union St, Vienna, GA, 31092-7545. Tel: 229-268-4687. p. 458
Henderson, Janet, Mat Mgr, Lubbock Public Library, 1306 Ninth St, Lubbock, TX, 79401. Tel: 806-775-2834, 806-775-2835. p. 2213
Henderson, Jenna, Adult Collection Dev, Keene Public Library, 60 Winter St, Keene, NH, 03431. Tel: 603-352-0157. p. 1369
Henderson, Jessica, Dir, Libr Serv, East Bridgewater Public Library, 32 Union St, East Bridgewater, MA, 02333. Tel: 508-378-1616. p. 1015
Henderson, Jessica, Head, Youth Serv, Sharon Public Library, 11 N Main St, Sharon, MA, 02067-1299. Tel: 781-784-1578. p. 1052
Henderson, John, Librn, Washington & Jefferson College Library, 60 S Lincoln St, Washington, PA, 15301. Tel: 724-503-1001, Ext 3032. p. 2018
Henderson, Linda, Ch Serv, Buhl Public Library, 215 Broadway Ave N, Buhl, ID, 83316. Tel: 208-543-6500. p. 518
Henderson, Lisa, Dean, Prof, Western University, FIMS & Nursing Bldg, Rm 2020, London, ON, N6A 5B9, CANADA. Tel: 519-661-2111, Ext 84235. p. 2796
Henderson, Mantra, Dir, Mississippi Valley State University, 14000 Hwy 82 W, Itta Bena, MS, 38941. Tel: 662-254-3494. p. 1221
Henderson, Pamela, Ch, East Cleveland Public Library, 14101 Euclid Ave, East Cleveland, OH, 44112-3891. Tel: 216-541-4128. p. 1783
Henderson, Rob, Libr Serv Coordr, Edmonton Public Library, Woodcroft, 13420 114 Ave NW, Edmonton, AB, T5M 2Y5, CANADA. Tel: 780-496-6891. p. 2537
Henderson, Sarah, Dir, Monmouth College, 700 E Broadway, Monmouth, IL, 61462-1963. Tel: 309-457-2192. p. 618
Henderson, Sarah, Access Serv, Minot State University, 500 University Ave W, Minot, ND, 58707. Tel: 701-858-3201. p. 1738
Henderson, Sheila, Head Librn, Austin Community College, Round Rock Campus Library, 4400 College Park Dr, Round Rock, TX, 78665. Tel: 512-223-0116. p. 2138
Henderson, Stephanie, Pres, Kentucky Medical Library Association, University of Louisville Bldg D, Rm 110A, 500 S Preston St,, Louisville, KY, 40292. Tel: 859-323-8008. p. 2765
Henderson, Steve, Syst Librn, Cerritos Library, 18025 Bloomfield Ave, Cerritos, CA, 90703. Tel: 562-916-1350. p. 129
Henderson, Suzanne, Mgr, University of Southern California Libraries, Science & Engineering, Seaver Science Ctr, 920 W 37th Pl, Los Angeles, CA, 90089-0481. Tel: 213-740-8285. p. 170
Henderson, Tawana, Libr Spec II, Southern University at Shreveport, 3050 Martin Luther King Jr Dr, Shreveport, LA, 71107. Tel: 318-670-9392. p. 910
Henderson, Tina, Head, Circ, Hope Welty Public Library District, 100 S Madison St, Cerro Gordo, IL, 61818. Tel: 217-763-5001. p. 551
Henderson, Ty, Dir, Champaign County Library, 1060 Scioto St, Urbana, OH, 43078. Tel: 937-653-3811. p. 1826
Henderson, Veronica, Interim Dir, Alabama A&M University, 4900 Meridian St N, Normal, AL, 35762. Tel: 256-372-4712. p. 31
Henderson, Vicki, Dir, East Cheyenne County Library District, 151 S First St W, Cheyenne Wells, CO, 80810. Tel: 719-767-5138. p. 270
Henderson, Vonda, Cat, Instrul Serv Librn, Truett-McConnell University, 100 Alumni Dr, Cleveland, GA, 30528-9799. Tel: 706-865-2134, Ext 2202. p. 471
Henderson-Moore, Sheila, Libr Mgr, Live Oak Public Libraries, Port City Branch, 3501 Houlihan Ave, Savannah, GA, 31408. Tel: 912-965-0102. p. 496
Hendley, Michelle, Head, Bibliog & Digital Serv, SUNY Oneonta, 108 Ravine Pkwy, Oneonta, NY, 13820. Tel: 607-436-3341. p. 1611
Hendren, Stacey, Br Mgr, Anoka County Library, Northtown, 711 County Hwy 10 Frontage Rd, Blaine, MN, 55434. Tel: 763-324-1510. p. 1165
Hendrick, Heidi, State Data Coordr, Utah State Library Division, 250 N 1950 West, Ste A, Salt Lake City, UT, 84116-7901. Tel: 801-715-6762. p. 2272
Hendricks, Art, Soc Sci Librn, Portland State University Library, 1875 SW Park Ave, Portland, OR, 97201-3220. Tel: 503-725-5874. p. 1893
Hendricks, Catherine, Proc Archivist, University of West Georgia, 1601 Maple St, Carrollton, GA, 30118. Tel: 678-839-6495. p. 469
Hendricks, Jennifer, Ad, Franklin Lakes Public Library, 470 DeKorte Dr, Franklin Lakes, NJ, 07417. Tel: 201-891-2224. p. 1404
Hendricks, Jennifer, Mgr, Children's Dept, Canal Fulton Public Library, 154 Market St NE, Canal Fulton, OH, 44614-1196. Tel: 330-854-4148. p. 1754
Hendricks, Jonathan, Dr, Library Contact, Paleontological Research Institution Library, 1259 Trumansburg Rd, Ithaca, NY, 14850. Tel: 607-273-6623, Ext 320. p. 1553
Hendricks, Julia, Br Mgr, Greensboro Public Library, Hemphill, 2301 W Vandalia Rd, Greensboro, NC, 27407. Tel: 336-373-2925. p. 1692
Hendricks, Kath Ann, YA Librn, Marshall Public Library, 113 S Garfield Ave, Pocatello, ID, 83204. Tel: 208-232-1263. p. 529

Hendricks, Leta, Ref (Info Servs), Ohio State University LIBRARIES, Fine Arts, Wexner Ctr for the Arts, 1871 N High St, Columbus, OH, 43210. Tel: 614-292-6184. p. 1775

Hendricks, Martha, Dir, Clarksville-Montgomery County Public Library, 350 Pageant Lane, Ste 501, Clarksville, TN, 37040. Tel: 931-648-8826. p. 2092

Hendricks, Nancy, Dir, Texas State Technical College, 1902 N Loop 499, Harlingen, TX, 78550. Tel: 956-364-4708. p. 2188

Hendricks, Renee, Asst Teaching Prof, University of Illinois at Urbana-Champaign, Library & Information Science Bldg, 501 E Daniel St, Champaign, IL, 61820-6211. Tel: 217-333-3280. p. 2784

Hendricks, Richard D, Dir, Dewitt LLP, 25 W Main St, Ste 800, Madison, WI, 53703. Tel: 608-283-5504. p. 2449

Hendrickson, Beth, Cat Librn, Pittsburg State University, 1605 S Joplin St, Pittsburg, KS, 66762-5889. Tel: 620-235-4895. p. 831

Hendrickson, Gloria, Librn I, Illinois Environmental Protection Agency Library, 1021 N Grand Ave E, Springfield, IL, 62702-4072. Tel: 217-782-9691. p. 649

Hendrickson, Lois, Curator, University of Minnesota Libraries-Twin Cities, Wangensteen Historical Library of Biology & Medicine, 568 Diehl Hall, 505 Essex St SE, Minneapolis, MN, 55455. Tel: 612-626-6881. p. 1186

Hendrickson, Philip, Dir, Libr Serv, Concordia University, 800 N Columbia Ave, Seward, NE, 68434. Tel: 402-643-7254. p. 1335

Hendrickx, Cindy, Head Librn, Appleton Public Library, 322 W Schlieman Ave, Appleton, MN, 56208. Tel: 320-289-1681. p. 1164

Hendrix, Dana, Fine Arts Librn, Georgetown Public Library, 402 W Eighth St, Georgetown, TX, 78626. Tel: 512-930-3551. p. 2184

Hendrix, Dean, Vice Provost & Univ Librn, University of Texas at San Antonio Libraries, One UTSA Circle, San Antonio, TX, 78249-0671. Tel: 210-458-4574, 210-458-7506. p. 2240

Hendrix, Julie, Dir, Wolfe County Public Library, 164 KY 15 N, Campton, KY, 41301. Tel: 606-668-6571. p. 850

Hendrixson, Kathy, Dir, DeKalb County Library System, 101 S First St, Smithville, TN, 37166-1706. Tel: 615-597-4359. p. 2126

Henecke, Jennifer, Chief, Engagement Officer, Saint Joseph County Public Library, 304 S Main St, South Bend, IN, 46601. Tel: 574-282-4646. p. 718

Heney, Kathy, Library Colls & Procurement Tech, Borden Ladner Gervais LLP Library, World Exchange Plaza, 100 Queen St, Ste 1300, Ottawa, ON, K1P 1J9, CANADA. Tel: 613-237-5160. p. 2665

Heng, Sara, Electronic Info Librn, Rivier University, 420 S Main St, Nashua, NH, 03060-5086. Tel: 603-897-8683. p. 1375

Henggeler, Wilma, Asst Dir, Maryville Public Library, 509 N Main St, Maryville, MO, 64468. Tel: 660-582-5281. p. 1261

Henion, Julie, Dir, Platte County Public Library, 904 Ninth St, Wheatland, WY, 82201. Tel: 307-322-2689. p. 2500

Henke, Evelyn, Libr Mgr, Mundare Municipal Public Library, 5128 50th St, Mundare, AB, T0B 3H0, CANADA. Tel: 780-764-3929. p. 2548

Henke, Jack, Ref Librn, New Hartford Public Library, Two Library Lane, New Hartford, NY, 13413-2815. Tel: 315-733-1535. p. 1576

Henkel, Alissa, Head, Adult Serv, Head, Children's Servx, Decatur Public Library, 130 N Franklin St, Decatur, IL, 62523. Tel: 217-421-9771. p. 576

Henkel, Becky, Dir, Bayard Public Library, 509 Ave A, Bayard, NE, 69334. Tel: 308-586-1144. p. 1307

Henkel, Harold, Archives, Digital Initiatives, Head, Spec Coll, Regent University Library, 1000 Regent University Dr, Virginia Beach, VA, 23464-5037. Tel: 757-352-4198. p. 2349

Henkel, Harold, Head, Archives, Head, Digital Initiatives, Head, Spec Coll, Regent University, 1000 Regent University Dr, Virginia Beach, VA, 23464. Tel: 757-352-4198. p. 2349

Henken, Ron, Pres, Public Policy Forum, 633 W Wisconsin Ave, Ste 406, Milwaukee, WI, 53203. Tel: 414-276-8240. p. 2461

Henkin, Robert I, Dr, Chief Librn, Center for Molecular Nutrition & Sensory Disorders, 5125 MacArthur Blvd NW, Ste 20, Washington, DC, 20016. Tel: 202-364-4180. p. 362

Henkman, Doree, Sr Librn, Casey County Public Library, 238 Middleburg St, Liberty, KY, 42539. Tel: 606-787-9381. p. 864

Henley, Holly, Dir, Libr Serv, State Librn, Arizona State Library, Archives & Public Records, 1901 W Madison St, Phoenix, AZ, 85009. Tel: 602-542-6181. p. 69

Henley, Holly, Dir, State Librn, Arizona State Library, Archives & Public Records, Polly Rosenbaum Archives & History Bldg, 1901 W Madison St, Phoenix, AZ, 85009. Tel: 602-926-3720. p. 69

Henley, Kristin, Managing Dir, Center for Fiction, 15 Lafayette Ave, Brooklyn, NY, 11217. Tel: 212-755-6710. p. 1504

Henley, Tanner, Law Librn, Clark County Law Library, 309 S Third St, Ste 400, Las Vegas, NV, 89101. Tel: 702-455-4696. p. 1346

Henline, Nicole, Dir, Monroeville Public Library, 4000 Gateway Campus Blvd, Monroeville, PA, 15146-3381. Tel: 412-372-0500. p. 1964

Henn, Jayne, Br Mgr, San Diego County Library, Encinitas Branch, 540 Cornish Dr, Encinitas, CA, 92024-4599. Tel: 760-634-6451. p. 217

Henneman, Mary Lou, Librn, Boardman United Methodist Church Library, 6809 Market St, Youngstown, OH, 44512. Tel: 330-758-4527. p. 1835

Henner, Terry, Head, Outreach Serv, University of Nevada-Reno, Pennington Medical Education Bldg, 1664 N Virginia St, Reno, NV, 89557. Tel: 775-784-4625. p. 1349

Hennessey, Dennis, Librn, Community College of Allegheny County, Allegheny Campus Library, 808 Ridge Ave, Pittsburgh, PA, 15212-6003. Tel: 412-237-2585. p. 1993

Hennessey, Sara, Chief Exec Officer, Selwyn Public Library, 836 Charles St, Bridgenorth, ON, K0L 1H0, CANADA. Tel: 705-292-5065. p. 2633

Hennessy, Patti, ILL, Williams & Connolly Library, 680 Maine Ave SW, Washington, DC, 20024. Tel: 202-434-5000. p. 381

Hennessy, Thomas, Jr, Curator, Lock Museum of America, Inc Library, 230 Main St, Terryville, CT, 06786-5900. Tel: 860-589-6359. p. 341

Hennies, Tim, Dir, Libr Serv, Dinsmore & Shohl Library, 255 E Fifth St, Ste 900, Cincinnati, OH, 45202-3172. Tel: 513-977-8486. p. 1760

Hennig, Erica, Cat & Tech Serv Librn, Asheville-Buncombe Technical Community College, 340 Victoria Rd, Asheville, NC, 28801. Tel: 828-398-7574. p. 1672

Hennig, Karen, Youth Librn, Varnum Memorial Library, 194 Main St, Jeffersonville, VT, 05464. Tel: 802-644-2117. p. 2287

Henning, Amanda, Br Mgr, Delaware County District Library, Powell Branch, 460 S Liberty Rd, Powell, OH, 43065. Tel: 614-888-9160. p. 1782

Henning, Arland, Cat Librn, Jacksonville State University Library, 700 Pelham Rd N, Jacksonville, AL, 36265. Tel: 256-782-5758. p. 23

Henning, Dixie, Head, Info Tech, Houston County Public Library System, 1201 Washington Ave, Perry, GA, 31069. Tel: 478-987-3050. p. 493

Henning, Jesse, Info Mgr, Libr Mgr, Argonne National Laboratory, 9700 S Cass Ave, Bldg 240, Lemont, IL, 60439-4801. Tel: 630-252-0007. p. 608

Henning, Joanne, Assoc Univ Librn, Coll & Serv, Assoc Univ Librn, Info Serv, University of Victoria Libraries, McPherson Library, PO Box 1800, Victoria, BC, V8W 3H5, CANADA. Tel: 250-721-8211. p. 2583

Henning, Rebecca, Spec Coll Cataloger, Amherst College, 61 Quadrangle Dr, Amherst, MA, 01002. p. 984

Hennings, Kimberly, Dep Dir, L E Phillips Memorial Public Library, 400 Eau Claire St, Eau Claire, WI, 54701. Tel: 715-839-6225. p. 2432

Henningsen, Crystal, Dir, Dorchester County Public Library, 303 Gay St, Cambridge, MD, 21613. Tel: 410-228-7331. p. 960

Henningsen, Katie, Head, Res Serv, Duke University Libraries, David M Rubenstein Rare Book & Manuscript Library, 316 Perkins Library, 411 Chapel Dt, Durham, NC, 27708. Tel: 919-660-5822. p. 1685

Hennrikus, Pauline, Library Contact, Burns & Levinson, 125 High St, Boston, MA, 02110. Tel: 617-345-3000. p. 994

Henri, Janine, Archit Librn, University of California Los Angeles Library, Arts Library, 1400 Public Affairs Bldg, Los Angeles, CA, 90095. Tel: 310-206-4587. p. 169

Henrich, Sharon, Mgr, AdventHealth Tampa, 3100 E Fletcher Ave, Tampa, FL, 33613-4688. Tel: 813-615-7236. p. 448

Henrichs, Apryl, Libr Dir, Little Rock Public Library, 402 Main St, Little Rock, IA, 51243. Tel: 712-479-2298. p. 766

Henricks, Dan, IT Mgr, Essex County Library, 360 Fairview Ave W, Ste 101, Essex, ON, N8M 1Y3, CANADA. Tel: 519-776-5241. p. 2640

Henricksen-Georghiou, Heather, Adult Serv, Doc, Newburgh Free Library, 124 Grand St, Newburgh, NY, 12550. Tel: 845-563-3617. p. 1606

Henrickson, Kaia, Info Literacy Librn, University of Alaska Southeast, 11066 Auke Lake Way, BE1, Juneau, AK, 99801. Tel: 907-796-6515. p. 47

Henry, Angela, Ref Spec, Clark State Community College Library, 570 E Leffel Lane, Springfield, OH, 45505. Tel: 937-328-6016. p. 1821

Henry, Angie, Br Mgr, Evangeline Parish Library, Father Leslie T H Prescott Branch, 111 Walnut St, Pine Prairie, LA, 70576. Tel: 337-599-3179. p. 912

Henry, Anna, Br Mgr, Washington County Public Library, Barlow Branch, 8370 State Rte 339, Barlow, OH, 45712. Tel: 740-678-0103. p. 1799

Henry, Charles, IT Coordr, Northern New York Library Network, 6721 US Hwy 11, Potsdam, NY, 13676. Tel: 315-265-1119. p. 2771

Henry, Chris, Curator, EAA Library, 3000 Poberezny Rd, Oshkosh, WI, 54904. Tel: 920-426-4800. p. 2467

Henry, Chriselle, Ad, Ascension Parish Library, 500 Mississippi St, Donaldsonville, LA, 70346. Tel: 225-473-8052. p. 889

Henry, Christy, Archivist, Brandon University, 270 18th St, Brandon, MB, R7A 6A9, CANADA. p. 2585

Henry, Elaine J, Dir, Cherokee County Public Library, 310 Mary St, Centre, AL, 35960. Tel: 256-927-5838. p. 11

Henry, Geneva, Dean of Libraries & Acad Innovation, The George Washington University, 2130 H St NW, Washington, DC, 20052. Tel: 202-994-6558. p. 367

Henry, Geneva, Dean of Libr, George Washington University, Eckles Library, 2100 Foxhall Rd NW, Washington, DC, 20007. Tel: 202-242-6620. p. 367

Henry, Gwen, Commun Liaison Librn, Florida Department of Children & Families, 800 E Cypress Dr, Pembroke Pines, FL, 33025. Tel: 954-392-3000. p. 436

Henry, Jeff, Automation Syst Coordr, Four County Library System, 304 Clubhouse Rd, Vestal, NY, 13850-3713. Tel: 607-723-8236, Ext 310. p. 1657

Henry, Jennifer, Adminr, Olin Corp, 1186 Old Lower River Rd, Charleston, TN, 37310. Tel: 423-336-4347. p. 2091

Henry, Jo, Ref & Instruction Librn, Horry-Georgetown Technical College, Georgetown Campus, 4003 S Fraser St, Georgetown, SC, 29440. Tel: 843-520-1423. p. 2057

Henry, John B, III, Exec Dir, Flint Institute of Arts, 1120 E Kearsley St, Flint, MI, 48503-1915. Tel: 810-234-1695. p. 1105

Henry, Jordie W, Librn, Toledo Blade-Library, 541 N Superior St, Toledo, OH, 43660. Tel: 419-724-6185. p. 1824

Henry, Joshua, Ref Librn, Jefferson County Library, Arnold Branch, 1701 Missouri State Rd, Arnold, MO, 63010. Tel: 636-296-2204. p. 1249

Henry, Laura, Mgr, Young Readers, Palos Verdes Library District, 701 Silver Spur Rd, Rolling Hills Estates, CA, 90274. Tel: 310-377-9584, Ext 206. p. 205

Henry, Laurie, Br Mgr, Clermont County Public Library, Miami Township Branch, 5920 Buckwheat Rd, Milford, OH, 45150. Tel: 513-248-0700. p. 1803

Henry, Lisa, Dir of Libr Operations, Kirkwood Public Library, 140 E Jefferson Ave, Kirkwood, MO, 63122. Tel: 314-821-5770, Ext 1013. p. 1259

Henry, Loreen, Head, Info Literacy, University of Texas at Dallas, 800 W Campbell Rd, Richardson, TX, 75080. Tel: 972-883-2126. p. 2231

Henry, Michele, Tech Serv Coordr, Somerset County Library System, 11767 Beechwood St, Princess Anne, MD, 21853. Tel: 410-651-0852. p. 973

Henry, Priscilla B, Access Serv, Govt Doc, Florida Agricultural & Mechanical University Libraries, 525 Orr Dr, Tallahassee, FL, 32307-4700. Tel: 850-599-3370. p. 446

Henry, Robert, Libr Mgr, Levy County Public Library System, Williston Public, Ten SE First St, Williston, FL, 32696-2671. Tel: 352-528-2313. p. 387

Henry, Ryan, Coll Develop Mgr, Daviess County Public Library, 2020 Frederica St, Owensboro, KY, 42301. Tel: 270-684-0211. p. 871

Henry, Sara, Asst Libr Dir, Stickney-Forest View Public Library District, 6800 W 43rd St, Stickney, IL, 60402. Tel: 708-749-1050. p. 651

Henry, Sara, Libr Serv Mgr, Boone Daniel Regional Library, Holts Summit Public Library, 188 W Simon Blvd, Holts Summit, MO, 65043. Tel: 573-606-8770. p. 1243

Henry, Sean, Dr, Librn III, Frostburg State University, One Susan Eisel Dr, Frostburg, MD, 21532. Tel: 301-687-4888. p. 967

Henry, Stephen, Head of Libr, Music Librn, University of Maryland Libraries, Michelle Smith Performing Arts Library, 8270 Alumni Dr, College Park, MD, 20742-1630. Tel: 301-405-9217. p. 963

Henry, Sylvia, Librn, John Turgeson Public Library, 220 S Mound Ave, Belmont, WI, 53510. Tel: 608-762-5137. p. 2423

Henry, Youlanda, Dir, Florida State College at Jacksonville, Nassau Center Library & Learning Commons, 76346 William Burgess Blvd, Yulee, FL, 32097. Tel: 904-548-4467. p. 411

Henry, Youlanda, Dir, Florida State College at Jacksonville, North Campus & Learning Commons, 4501 Capper Rd, Jacksonville, FL, 32218-4499. Tel: 904-766-6717. p. 411

Henry-Gordon, Sandy, Br Mgr, Saint Lucie County Library System, Morningside Branch, 2410 Morningside Blvd, Port Saint Lucie, FL, 34952. Tel: 772-337-5632. p. 405

Hensel, Mike, Br Mgr, Dayton Metro Library, Wilmington-Stroop, 3980 Wilmington Pike, Dayton, OH, 45429. Tel: 937-496-8966. p. 1779

Hensen, Lindsey, Dir, Richfield District Library, 205 S Main St, Richfield, ID, 83349. Tel: 208-487-1242. p. 529

Henshall, Bobby, Learning Res Spec, Joe Barnhart Bee County Public Library, 110 W Corpus Christi St, Beeville, TX, 78102-5604. Tel: 361-362-4901. p. 2146

Henslee, Holli, Assoc Librn, Tech Serv Coordr, Drury University, 900 N Benton Ave, Springfield, MO, 65802. Tel: 417-873-7483. p. 1280

Hensley, Angela, Asst Dir, Lincoln County Public Library, 201 Lancaster St, Stanford, KY, 40484. Tel: 606-365-7513. p. 875

Hensley, Jenn, Pres & Chief Exec Officer, The Bakken Museum, 3537 Zenith Ave S, Minneapolis, MN, 55416. Tel: 612-926-3878. p. 1182

Hensley, Lisa, Circ, Missouri Western State University, 4525 Downs Dr, Saint Joseph, MO, 64507-2294. Tel: 816-271-4368. p. 1268

Hensley, Paula, Librn, Linda Duran Public Library, 1612 S Bethel Rd, Decatur, AL, 35603-5408. Tel: 256-584-0230. p. 14

Henson, Barbie, ILL, Pub Serv, Tech Serv, Hazard Community & Technical College, 601 Jefferson Ave, Jackson, KY, 41339. Tel: 606-666-7521. p. 860

Henson, Blair, Dir, Guymon Public Library & Arts Center, 1718 N Oklahoma St, Guymon, OK, 73942. Tel: 580-338-7330. p. 1849

Henson, Karl, Asst Dir, Libr Serv, Tech Serv, Prairie View A&M University, L W Minor St, University Dr, Prairie View, TX, 77446-0519. Tel: 936-261-1504. p. 2229

Henson, Mitch, Br Mgr, Warren County Public Library, Bob Kirby Branch, 175 Iron Skillet Ct, Bowling Green, KY, 47104. Tel: 270-781-4882, Ext 107. p. 849

Henson, Shannon, Libr Dir, Salem Free Public Library, 264 Hartford Rd, Salem, CT, 06420. Tel: 860-859-1130. p. 335

Henteleff, Carrie, Libr Serv Supvr, Arizona State University, College of Law, Arizona State University MC 9620, 111 E Taylor St, Ste 350, Phoenix, AZ, 85004. Tel: 480-965-7144. p. 69

Henthorn, Lisa, Librn, Parkersburg & Wood County Public Library, Williamstown Branch, 201 W Fifth St, Williamstown, WV, 26187. Tel: 304-375-6052. p. 2411

Henthorn, Michael, Br Mgr, Southern Oklahoma Library System, Johnston County Library, 116 W Main St, Tishomingo, OK, 73460. Tel: 580-371-3006. p. 1841

Hentkowski, Heather, Br Mgr, Presque Isle District Library, Grand Lake Branch, 18132 Lake Esau Hwy, Presque Isle, MI, 49777. p. 1145

Henton, LaKeisha, Br Mgr, Rapides Parish Library, Martin Luther King, Jr Branch, 1115 Broadway Ave, Alexandria, LA, 71301. Tel: 318-445-3912. p. 880

Hentz, Holly, Dir, Hamburg Township Library, 10411 Merrill Rd, Hamburg, MI, 48139. Tel: 810-231-1771. p. 1112

Hepburn, Peter, Head Librn, College of the Canyons Library, 26455 Rockwell Canyon Rd, Santa Clarita, CA, 91355-1899. Tel: 661-362-3854. p. 242

Hepburn, Peter, Head Librn, Santa Clarita Interlibrary Network, College of the Canyons, Valencia Campus, 26455 Rockwell Canyon Rd, Santa Clarita, CA, 91355-1899. Tel: 661-362-3758. p. 2762

Hepher, Robin, Chief Exec Officer, Chinook Arch Regional Library System, 2902 Seventh Ave N, Lethbridge, AB, T1H 5C6, CANADA. Tel: 403-380-1505. p. 2546

Hepler, Melissa, Br Mgr, Harford County Public Library, Edgewood Branch, 629 Edgewood Rd, Edgewood, MD, 21040-2607. Tel: 410-612-1600. p. 959

Hepner, Erica, Children's Serv Coordr, Shenandoah County Library, 514 Stoney Creek Blvd, Edinburg, VA, 22824. Tel: 540-984-8200. p. 2315

Hepp, David, Head, Exten Serv, Marion Public Library, 445 E Church St, Marion, OH, 43302-4290. Tel: 740-387-0992. p. 1799

Hepp, David, Head, Exten Serv, Marion Public Library, Caledonia Branch, 112 E Marion St, Caledonia, OH, 43314. Tel: 419-845-3666. p. 1799

Hepp, David, Head, Exten Serv, Marion Public Library, Henkle-Holliday Memorial, 86 S High, La Rue, OH, 43332. Tel: 740-499-3066. p. 1800

Hepp, David, Head, Exten Serv, Marion Public Library, Prospect Branch, 116 N Main, Prospect, OH, 43342. Tel: 740-494-2684. p. 1800

Heras, Elaine, Assoc Dir, Lewis & Clark College, Aubrey R Watzek Library, 0615 SW Palatine Hill Rd, Portland, OR, 97219-7899. Tel: 503-768-7277. p. 1892

Herb, Marie, Mgr, Dauphin County Library System, Northern Dauphin Library, 683 Main St, Lykens, PA, 17048. Tel: 717-523-0340. p. 1940

Herber, Mary Jane, Local Hist/Genealogy, Mgr, Spec Coll, Brown County Library, 515 Pine St, Green Bay, WI, 54301. Tel: 920-448-5815. p. 2438

Herberg, Robert, Ref (Info Servs), Alhambra Civic Center Library, 101 S First St, Alhambra, CA, 91801-3432. Tel: 626-570-5008. p. 115

Herberich, Elisa, Circ, Oyster Bay-East Norwich Public Library, 89 E Main St, Oyster Bay, NY, 11771. Tel: 516-922-1212. p. 1614

Herbert, Amanda, Ch, Franklin County Public Library District, 919 Main St, Brookville, IN, 47012. Tel: 765-647-4031. p. 673

Herbert, Barbara, Bus Librn, Georgian Court University, 900 Lakewood Ave, Lakewood, NJ, 08701-2697. Tel: 732-987-2428. p. 1410

Herbert, Candace, Ref (Info Servs), Fergus Falls Public Library, 205 E Hampden, Fergus Falls, MN, 56537. Tel: 218-739-9387. p. 1175

Herbert, Kelly, Dir, United States Army, Allen Memorial Library, Bldg 660, 7460 Colorado Ave, Fort Polk, LA, 71459-5000. Tel: 337-531-2665. p. 889

Herbert, Mark, Sr Librn, Support Serv, El Segundo Public Library, 111 W Mariposa Ave, El Segundo, CA, 90245. Tel: 310-524-2732. p. 140

Herbert, Sandra, Libr Mgr, Cremona Municipal Library, 205 First St E, Cremona, AB, T0M 0R0, CANADA. Tel: 403-637-3100. p. 2532

Herbert, Teri Lynn, Res & Educ Informationist, Medical University of South Carolina Libraries, 171 Ashley Ave, Ste 419, Charleston, SC, 29425-0001. Tel: 843-792-1370. p. 2051

Herbison, Tina, Reader Serv Mgr, Braille Institute Library, 741 N Vermont Ave, Los Angeles, CA, 90029-3514. Tel: 323-660-3880. p. 160

Herbst, Cristie, Pres, Chautauqua County Historical Society & Mcclurg Museum, Moore Park, 20 E Main St, Westfield, NY, 14787. Tel: 716-326-2977. p. 1664

Herbst, Jane, Librn, George Mercer Jr Memorial School of Theology, 65 Fourth St, Garden City, NY, 11530. Tel: 516-248-4800, Ext 139. p. 1536

Herbst, Luke, Teen Serv Mgr, Nashville Public Library, 615 Church St, Nashville, TN, 37219-2314. Tel: 615-862-5800. p. 2119

Herbst, Lynne, Circ Librn, Sherburne Memorial Library, 2998 River Rd, Killington, VT, 05751. Tel: 802-422-4251, 802-422-9765. p. 2287

Herc, Karen, Dir, Ch Serv, Adams Memorial Library, 1112 Ligonier St, Latrobe, PA, 15650. Tel: 724-539-1972. p. 1953

Herder, Melinda, Dir, Humboldt Public Library, 916 Bridge St, Humboldt, KS, 66748. Tel: 620-473-2243. p. 814

Herdina, Jessica, Libr Supvr, Riverside Public Library, 3900 Mission Inn Ave, Riverside, CA, 92501. Tel: 951-826-5201. p. 203

Herdman, Rose, Librn, Flatbush Community Library, General Delivery, Flatbush, AB, T0G 0Z0, CANADA. Tel: 780-681-3756. p. 2540

Herdt, Tim, Syst Spec, United States Air Force, 28 FSS/FSDL, 2650 Doolittle Dr, Bldg 3910, Ellsworth AFB, SD, 57706-4820. Tel: 605-385-1686, 605-385-1688. p. 2076

Herebia, Azalia, Circ Supvr, University of Saint Thomas, 3800 Montrose Blvd, Houston, TX, 77006. Tel: 713-525-2192. p. 2200

Heredia, Justine, Libr Asst, Illinois College of Optometry Library, 3241 S Michigan Ave, Chicago, IL, 60616-3878. Tel: 312-949-7149. p. 562

Herendeen, Donna, Mgr, Pub Serv, Lenhardt Library of the Chicago Botanic Garden, 1000 Lake Cook Rd, Glencoe, IL, 60022. Tel: 847-835-8201. p. 593

Heres, Simon, Mgr, Libr Info Tech, Biola University Library, 13800 Biola Ave, La Mirada, CA, 90639. Tel: 562-944-0351, Ext 5612. p. 155

Herff, Gail, Bus Mgr, Itasca Community Library, 500 W Irving Park Rd, Itasca, IL, 60143. Tel: 630-773-1699. p. 602

Herfindahl, Ingvild, Libr Dir, Dodge Center Public Library, 13 First Ave NW, Dodge Center, MN, 55927. Tel: 507-374-2275. p. 1171

Herfurth, Kathy, Dir, Alger Public Library, 100 W Wagner St, Alger, OH, 45812. Tel: 419-757-7755. p. 1745

Hering, Dawn, Dir, Strum Public Library, 114 Fifth Ave S, Strum, WI, 54770. Tel: 715-695-3848. p. 2479

Hering Howard, Susan, Law Librn, Seneca County Law Library, Seneca County Courthouse Annex, 71 S Washington St, Ste 1205, Tiffin, OH, 44883. Tel: 419-447-8126. p. 1823

Herington, Mindy, Youth Serv, Yarmouth Town Libraries, 312 Old Main St, South Yarmouth, MA, 02664. Tel: 508-760-4820, Ext 1316. p. 1055

Herley, Sam, Curator, South Dakota Oral History Center, University of South Dakota, I D Weeks Library, Rm 231, 414 E Clark St, Vermillion, SD, 57069. Tel: 605-658-3382. p. 2084

Herley, Samuel, Asst Librn, University of South Dakota, I D Weeks Library, 414 E Clark St, Vermillion, SD, 57069. Tel: 605-658-3382. p. 2084

Herlocker, Annie, Br Mgr, Nashville Public Library, Bordeaux Branch, 4000 Clarksville Pike, Nashville, TN, 37218. Tel: 615-862-5856. p. 2119

Herlocker, Annie, Br Mgr, Nashville Public Library, Richland Park Branch, 4711 Charlotte Ave, Nashville, TN, 37209. Tel: 615-862-5870. p. 2120

Herman, Allison, Asst Dir, Head, Youth Serv, Wells Public Library, 1434 Post Rd, Wells, ME, 04090-4508. Tel: 207-646-8181. p. 945

Herman, Aly, Dir, Lady Lake Public Library, 225 W Guava St, Lady Lake, FL, 32159. Tel: 352-753-2957. p. 414

Herman, Amy, Visual Res Curator, Bard College, One Library Rd, Annandale-on-Hudson, NY, 12504. Tel: 845-758-7304. p. 1487

Herman, Amy, Ref Serv, Olympic College, 1600 Chester Ave, Bremerton, WA, 98337. Tel: 360-475-7250. p. 2360

Herman, Brian, Info Ctr Analyst, Emerson Automation Solutions Information Center, 301 S First Ave, Marshalltown, IA, 50158. Tel: 641-754-2161, 641-754-3111. p. 768

Herman, Debbie, Dir, Libr Serv, Manchester Community College Library, Great Path, Manchester, CT, 06040. Tel: 860-512-2872. p. 320

Herman, Deborah, Youth Serv Librn, Oregon Public Library District, 300 Jefferson St, Oregon, IL, 61061. Tel: 815-732-2724. p. 630

Herman, Gina, Librn, Hokah Public Library, 57 Main St, Hokah, MN, 55941. Tel: 507-894-2665. p. 1178

Herman, Jason, Electronic Res Librn, Marymount Manhattan College, 221 E 71st St, New York, NY, 10021. Tel: 212-774-4804. p. 1591

Herman, Maureen, Youth Serv Librn, Free Public Library of Hasbrouck Heights, 320 Boulevard, Hasbrouck Heights, NJ, 07604. Tel: 201-288-0484, 201-288-0488. p. 1407

Herman, Shanea, Br Mgr, Williams County Public Library, Edgerton Branch, 319 N Michigan Ave, Edgerton, OH, 43517. Tel: 419-298-3230. p. 1753

Herman, Tracy, Librn/Educator, Beth Ahabah Museum & Archives, 1109 W Franklin St, Richmond, VA, 23220. Tel: 804-353-2668. p. 2340

Hermann, Janie, Adult Programming, Mgr, Princeton Public Library, 65 Witherspoon St, Princeton, NJ, 08542. Tel: 609-924-9529. p. 1436

Hermann, Suzanne, Librn, American Institute for Economic Research, 250 Division St, Great Barrington, MA, 01230-1119. Tel: 413-528-1216. p. 1021

Hermans, Caleb, Librn, North Central Washington Libraries, Soap Lake Public Library, 32 E Main St, Soap Lake, WA, 98851. Tel: 509-246-1313. p. 2394

Hermiller, Jessica, Dir, Bluffton Public Library, 145 S Main St, Bluffton, OH, 45817. Tel: 419-358-5016. p. 1751

Hermsen, Renee, Librn, Arizona Department of Corrections - Adult Institutions, 10000 S Wilmot Rd, Tucson, AZ, 85734. Tel: 520-574-0024, Ext 37919. p. 80

Hernan, Debbie, Youth Serv Mgr, Holly Township Library, 1116 N Saginaw St, Holly, MI, 48442-1395. Tel: 248-634-1754. p. 1116

Hernandez, Angelita, Access Serv, University of Maine at Presque Isle Library, 181 Main St, Presque Isle, ME, 04769-2888. Tel: 207-768-9611. p. 938

Hernandez, April, Dir, Goddard Public Library, 201 N Main St, Goddard, KS, 67052. Tel: 316-794-8771. p. 810

Hernandez, April, Libr Dir, Lincoln Library, 201 N Main St, Medicine Lodge, KS, 67104. Tel: 620-886-5746. p. 825

Hernandez, Blanca, Instruction & Outreach Librn, Erikson Institute, 451 N LaSalle St, Ste 210, Chicago, IL, 60654. Tel: 312-893-7210. p. 561

Hernandez, Bobbye, Senior Librarian, Latino Services, Newberg Public Library, 503 E Hancock St, Newberg, OR, 97132. Tel: 503-537-1266. p. 1888

Hernandez Brown, Veronica, Libr Dir, South Dennis Free Public Library, 389 Main St, South Dennis, MA, 02660. Tel: 508-394-8954. p. 1054

Hernandez, Colleen, Teen Serv Librn, Webster Public Library, Webster Plaza, 980 Ridge Rd, Webster, NY, 14580. Tel: 585-872-7075. p. 1661

Hernandez, Edenia, Libr Dir, North Miami Beach Public Library, 1601 NE 164th St, North Miami Beach, FL, 33162. Tel: 305-948-2970. p. 429

Hernandez, Eva, Tech Serv Mgr, Joe A Guerra Laredo Public Library, 1120 E Calton Rd, Laredo, TX, 78041. Tel: 956-795-2400. p. 2209

Hernandez, Eva, Cat Librn, Texas A&M International University, 5201 University Blvd, Laredo, TX, 78041-1900. Tel: 956-326-2114. p. 2210

Hernandez, Frank, Libr Tech, United States Army, Institute of Surgical Research Library, 3698 Chambers Pass, Bldg 3611, Fort Sam Houston, TX, 78234-6315. Tel: 210-539-4559. p. 2178

Hernandez, Heather, Libr Serv Spec, Chabot College Library, 25555 Hesperian Blvd, Hayward, CA, 94545. Tel: 510-723-6763. p. 150

Hernandez, Jamie, Head, Adult Serv, Watertown Public Library, 100 S Water St, Watertown, WI, 53094-4320. Tel: 920-545-2326. p. 2484

Hernandez, Jennifer, Cataloger, Interim Dir, Waterloo-Grant Township Public Library, 300 S Wayne St, Waterloo, IN, 46793. Tel: 260-837-4491. p. 725

Hernandez, Jennifer, Coordr, Outreach Serv, New Braunfels Public Library, Westside Community Center, 2932 S IH 35 Frontage Rd, New Braunfels, TX, 78130. Tel: 830-221-4301. p. 2222

Hernandez, Jose, Head, Ref, Patchogue-Medford Library, 54-60 E Main St, Patchogue, NY, 11772. Tel: 631-654-4700. p. 1615

Hernandez, Jose-Rodrigo, Br Mgr, Huntington Public Library, Huntington Station Branch, 1335 New York Ave, Huntington Station, NY, 11746. Tel: 631-421-5053, Ext 126. p. 1549

Hernandez, Katie, Instruction & Outreach Librn, Librn III, South Texas College Library, 3201 W Pecan Blvd, McAllen, TX, 78501-6661. Tel: 956-872-1983. p. 2217

Hernandez, Laura, Librn, Shasta County Public Law Library, 1880 Shasta St, Redding, CA, 96001. Tel: 530-245-6243. p. 198

Hernandez, Leticia M, Librn, Van Horn City County Library, 410 Crockett St, Van Horn, TX, 79855. Tel: 432-283-2855. p. 2251

Hernandez, Maira, Children's Spec, Outreach Serv Spec, Youth Spec, Peach Public Libraries, 315 Martin Luther King Jr Dr, Fort Valley, GA, 31030. Tel: 478-825-1640. p. 480

Hernandez, Maria, Dir, United States Air Force, 628 FSS/FSDL, 106 W McCaw St, Bldg 215, Charleston AFB, SC, 29404. Tel: 843-963-3320. p. 2051

Hernandez, Oscar, Mgr, San Jose Public Library, Biblioteca Latinoamericana Branch, 921 S First St, San Jose, CA, 95110-2939. Tel: 408-294-1237. p. 231

Hernandez, Oscar, Mgr, San Jose Public Library, East San Jose Carnegie, 1102 E Santa Clara St, San Jose, CA, 95116-2246. Tel: 408-808-3075. p. 231

Hernandez, Patricia, Br Mgr, El Paso Public Library, Dorris Van Doren Branch, 551 Redd Rd, El Paso, TX, 79912. Tel: 915-212-0440. p. 2174

Hernandez, Pedro Juan, Sr Archivist, Hunter College Libraries, Centro - Center for Puerto Rican Studies Library, 2180 Third Ave, Rm 121, New York, NY, 10035. Tel: 212-396-7877. p. 1588

Hernandez, Ramon, Br Mgr, San Francisco Public Library, Mission Branch Library, 300 Bartlett St, San Francisco, CA, 94110. Tel: 415-355-2800. p. 228

Hernandez, Robert, Circ Supvr, Florida Southern College, 111 Lake Hollingsworth Dr, Lakeland, FL, 33801-5698. Tel: 863-616-6453. p. 417

Hernandez, Rose, Br Mgr, Neuse Regional Library, La Grange Public Library, 119 E Washington St, La Grange, NC, 28551. Tel: 252-566-3722. p. 1699

Hernandez, Sandra, Dep Dir, Cheshire Public Library, 104 Main St, Cheshire, CT, 06410-2499. Tel: 203-272-2245. p. 305

Hernandez, Sandra, Tech Serv, Cheshire Public Library, 104 Main St, Cheshire, CT, 06410-2499. Tel: 203-272-2245. p. 305

Hernandez, Susan, Digital Archivist, Syst Librn, Cleveland Museum of Art, 11150 East Blvd, Cleveland, OH, 44106-1797. Tel: 216-707-2530. p. 1767

Hernandez-Chan, Julie, Mgr, County of Los Angeles Public Library, Hollydale Library, 12000 S Garfield Ave, South Gate, CA, 90280-7894. Tel: 562-634-0156. p. 136

Hernandez-Read, Erica, Head, Archives & Spec Coll, University of Northern British Columbia Library, 333 University Way, Prince George, BC, V2N 4Z9, CANADA. Tel: 250-960-6603. p. 2574

Hernden, Ken, Assoc Univ Librn, Univ Archivist, Queen's University, 101 Union St, Kingston, ON, K7L 2N9, CANADA. Tel: 613-533-6000, Ext 79267. p. 2650

Hernden, Ken, Assoc Univ Librn, Univ Archivist, Queen's University, W D Jordan Rare Books & Special Collections, Douglas Library, 6th Level, 2nd Flr, 93 University Ave, Kingston, ON, K7L 5C4, CANADA. Tel: 613-533-2839. p. 2651

Herndon, Holly, Res & Instruction Librn, University of California, 200 McAllister St, San Francisco, CA, 94102-4978. Tel: 415-565-4757. p. 229

Herndon, Joel, PhD, Head, Data & Visualization Serv, Duke University Libraries, 411 Chapel Dr, Durham, NC, 27708. Tel: 919-660-5946. p. 1684

Herndon, Kimmetha, Dean, Samford University Library, 800 Lakeshore Dr, Birmingham, AL, 35229. Tel: 205-726-2846. p. 8

Herndon, Laura, Ser Librn, Clayton State University Library, 2000 Clayton State Blvd, Morrow, GA, 30260. Tel: 678-466-4335. p. 491

Herner, Brian, Adult Serv Mgr, Palatine Public Library District, 700 N North Ct, Palatine, IL, 60067. Tel: 847-907-3600. p. 631
Hernstrom, Schuyler, Mgr, Carnegie Library of Pittsburgh, Sheraden, 720 Sherwood Ave, Pittsburgh, PA, 15204-1724. Tel: 412-331-1135. p. 1992
Herod, Darlene, Mrs, Ref (Info Servs), Virginia Baptist Historical Society & the Center for Baptist Heritage & Studies Library, 261 Richmond Way, University of Richmond, Richmond, VA, 23173. Tel: 804-289-8434. p. 2343
Herold, Elizbeth, Asst Dir, North Hampton Public Library, 239 Atlantic Ave, North Hampton, NH, 03862-2341. Tel: 603-964-6326. p. 1376
Herold, Hallie, Librn, Pocahontas County Free Libraries, Green Bank Public Library, 5683 Potomac Highlands Trail, Green Bank, WV, 24944. Tel: 304-456-4507. p. 2408
Herold, Irene M H, Dean of Libr, Univ Librn, Virginia Commonwealth University Libraries, 901 Park Ave, Richmond, VA, 23284. Tel: 804-828-1111. p. 2343
Herold, Kathy, Coordr, St Rita's Medical Center, 730 W Market St, 3rd Flr, Lima, OH, 45801-4667. Tel: 419-996-5842. p. 1796
Herold, Philip, Dir, University of Minnesota Libraries-Twin Cities, Magrath Library, 1984 Buford Ave, Saint Paul, MN, 55108. Tel: 612-624-2779. p. 1185
Herold, Tomi, Libr Dir, Highland County Public Library, 31 N Water St, Monterey, VA, 24465. Tel: 540-468-2373. p. 2333
Heron, Christine, Br Librn, Genesee District Library, Fenton-Winegarden Library, 200 E Caroline St, Fenton, MI, 48430. Tel: 810-629-7612. p. 1106
Herow, Victoria, Dir, Amenia Free Library, 3309 Rte 343, Amenia, NY, 12501. Tel: 845-373-8273. p. 1486
Herr, Jorene, Libr Dir, Bruun Memorial Public Library, 730 Third St, Humboldt, NE, 68376. Tel: 402-862-2914. p. 1319
Herr, Kristen, Dir, Lawton Public Library, 110 SW Fourth St, Lawton, OK, 73501. Tel: 580-581-3450. p. 1852
Herr, Melody, Dr, Head, Scholarly Communications, University of Arkansas Libraries, 365 N McIlroy Ave, Fayetteville, AR, 72701-4002. Tel: 479-575-4101. p. 95
Herr, Susan, Libr Dir, Bulverde-Spring Branch Library, 131 Bulverde Crossing, Bulverde, TX, 78163. Tel: 830-438-4864. p. 2151
Herrara, Norma, Librn, Dilley Public Library, 231 W FM 117, Dilley, TX, 78017. Tel: 830-965-1951. p. 2171
Herrell, Miriam, Br Mgr, Prince William Public Libraries, Bull Run Library, 8051 Ashton Ave, Manassas, VA, 20109. Tel: 703-792-4500. p. 2338
Herren, Lydia, Librn, Boston Free Library, 9475 Boston State Rd, Boston, NY, 14025-9768. Tel: 716-941-3516. p. 1496
Herrera, Angela, Ad, Clyde Public Library, 222 W Buckeye St, Clyde, OH, 43410. Tel: 419-547-7174. p. 1771
Herrera, Armando, Libr Asst, Del Mar College, Windward Campus, Barth Learning Resource Center, 4101 Old Brownsville Rd, Corpus Christi, TX, 78405. Tel: 361-698-1878. p. 2160
Herrera, Gail, Asst Dean, Tech Serv, University of Mississippi, One Library Loop, University, MS, 38677. Tel: 662-915-5674. p. 1234
Herrera, Manual, Librn, El Paso Community College Library, Transmountain Campus Library, 9570 Gateway Blvd N, Rm 1600, El Paso, TX, 79924. Tel: 915-831-5098. p. 2173
Herrera, Vanessa Kay, Asst Dir, Student Resources & Support, College of the Florida Keys, 106040 Overseas Hwy, Key Largo, FL, 33037. Tel: 305-809-3110. p. 413
Herrera, Yvette, Vols Mgr, Lodi Public Library, 201 W Locust St, Lodi, CA, 95240. Tel: 209-333-5566. p. 157
Herrero, Dora P, Libr Tech 1, University of Guam, Guam & Micronesia Collection, UOG Sta, Mangilao, GU, 96923. Tel: 671-735-2157, 671-735-2160. p. 2505
Herrick, Angie, Dir, Skowhegan Free Public Library, Nine Elm St, Skowhegan, ME, 04976. Tel: 207-474-9072. p. 940
Herrick, Arnie, Dir, Mellinger Memorial Library, 11 Division St, Morning Sun, IA, 52640. Tel: 319-868-7505. p. 771
Herrick Juarez, Adriane, Libr Dir, Park City Library, 1255 Park Ave, Park City, UT, 84060. Tel: 435-615-5605. p. 2268
Herrick, Susan, Research Librn, University of Maryland, Baltimore, Thurgood Marshall Law Library, 501 W Fayette St, Baltimore, MD, 21201-1768. Tel: 410-706-3213. p. 957
Herried-Kuhl, Autumn, Libr Dir, Necedah Community -Siegler Memorial Library, 217 Oak Grove Dr, Necedah, WI, 54646. Tel: 608-565-2253. p. 2463
Herriges, Jean, Div Mgr, San Jose Public Library, 150 E San Fernando St, San Jose, CA, 95112-3580. Tel: 408-808-2188. p. 231
Herring, Cathy, Supvr, Arkansas Department of Correction, Diagnostic Unit Library, 7500 Correction Circle, Pine Bluff, AR, 71603-1498. Tel: 870-267-6410. p. 107
Herring, Holly, Br Librn, Lewis & Clark Library, Augusta Branch, 205 Main St, Augusta, MT, 59410. Tel: 406-562-3348. p. 1296
Herring, Janet, Circ Librn, Keosauqua Public Library, 608 First St, Keosauqua, IA, 52565. Tel: 319-293-3766. p. 763
Herring, Joan, Tech Serv, Andalusia Public Library, 212 S Three Notch St, Andalusia, AL, 36420. Tel: 334-222-6612. p. 4
Herring, Lauren K, Cataloger, United States Army, Casey Memorial Library, 72nd St & 761st Tank Battalion, Bldg 3202, Fort Hood, TX, 76544-5024. Tel: 254-287-0025. p. 2178
Herring-Cole, Deidre, Electronic Maintenance Librn, Faulkner University, 5345 Atlanta Hwy, Montgomery, AL, 36109-3398. Tel: 334-386-7207. p. 28
Herring-Curtis, Pat, Br Mgr, Sabina Public Library, New Vienna Library, 97 Main St, New Vienna, OH, 45159. Tel: 937-987-4200. p. 1818
Herringa, Julie, Asst Dir, Manistee County Library System, 95 Maple St, Manistee, MI, 49660. Tel: 231-723-2519. p. 1129
Herrington, Jessica, Librn, Kentucky Department for Libraries & Archives, 300 Coffee Tree Rd, Frankfort, KY, 40601. Tel: 502-564-8300. p. 855
Herrington, Wyneth C, Bus Mgr, Calloway County Public Library, 710 Main St, Murray, KY, 42071. Tel: 270-753-2288, Ext 106. p. 870
Herrlein, Alex, Libr Office Mgr, Ref Librn, Lloyd Library & Museum, 917 Plum St, Cincinnati, OH, 45202. Tel: 513-721-3707. p. 1761
Herrlich, Katherine, Sci Librn, Northeastern University Libraries, 360 Huntington Ave, Boston, MA, 02115. Tel: 617-373-5305. p. 998
Herrmann, Becky, Libr Dir, Chelmsford Public Library, 25 Boston Rd, Chelmsford, MA, 01824. Tel: 978-256-5521. p. 1010
Herrmann, Carrie, Dir, Boone County Public Library, 1786 Burlington Pike, Burlington, KY, 41005. Tel: 859-342-2665. p. 850
Herrmann, Stephanie, Dir, Union Parish Library, 202 W Jackson St, Farmerville, LA, 71241. Tel: 318-368-9226, 318-368-9288. p. 889
Herron, Elizabeth, Librn, Lebanon VA Medical Center Library, 1700 S Lincoln Ave, Lebanon, PA, 17042-7597. Tel: 717-272-6621, Ext 4746. p. 1954
Herron, Jennifer, Librn, Michigan Department of Transportation Library, 425 W Ottawa, Lansing, MI, 48909-7550. Tel: 517-230-6103. p. 1125
Herron, John, Exec Dir, Kansas City Public Library, Lucile H Bluford Branch, 3050 Prospect Ave, Kansas City, MO, 64128. Tel: 816-701-3482. p. 1255
Herron, Lindsey, Mrs, Dir, Wood River Public Library, 326 E Ferguson Ave, Wood River, IL, 62095-2098. Tel: 618-254-4832. p. 664
Herron, Trey, Libr Tech, Pulaski Technical College, 13000 Interstate 30, Little Rock, AR, 72210. Tel: 501-812-2878. p. 102
Herrstrom, Kajsa, Resource Access Librn, Anabaptist Mennonite Biblical Seminary Library, 3003 Benham Ave, Elkhart, IN, 46517. Tel: 574-295-3726. p. 680
Hersberger, Julie, PhD, Assoc Prof, University of North Carolina at Greensboro, School of Education Bldg, Rm 446, 1300 Spring Garden St, Greensboro, NC, 27412. Tel: 336-334-3477. p. 2790
Hersey, Patricia, Asst Dir, Carroll County Public Library, 136 Court St, Carrollton, KY, 41008. Tel: 502-732-7020. p. 851
Hersh, Deborah, Ref & Ad Serv Librn, Northborough Free Library, 34 Main St, Northborough, MA, 01532-1942. Tel: 508-393-5025. p. 1043
Hersh, Tori, Principal Librn, Lee County Library System, Fort Myers Regional Library, 2450 First St, Fort Myers, FL, 33901. Tel: 239-533-4600. p. 403
Hershberger, Seth, Exec Dir, Wicomico Public Library, 122 S Division St, Salisbury, MD, 21801. Tel: 443-523-2723. p. 976
Hershfeld, Georgia, Cat, Chancellor Robert R Livingston Masonic Library of Grand Lodge, 71 W 23rd St, 14th Flr, New York, NY, 10010-4171. Tel: 212-337-6620. p. 1581
Hershman, Laure, Circ Supvr, Caldwell Public Library, 1010 Dearborn St, Caldwell, ID, 83605. Tel: 208-459-3242. p. 518
Hershorin, Jill, Archivist, Jewish Historical Society of New Jersey, 901 Rte 10 E, Whippany, NJ, 07981. Tel: 973-929-2994, 973-929-2995. p. 1455
Herskowitz, Lisa, Head, Children's Servx, Northport-East Northport Public Library, 151 Laurel Ave, Northport, NY, 11768. Tel: 631-261-6930. p. 1608
Hert, Darlene, Dir, Montana State University-Billings Library, 1500 University Dr, Billings, MT, 59101. Tel: 406-657-1655. p. 1288
Hertel, Karen, Research Librn, Colorado Parks & Wildlife, 317 W Prospect Rd, Fort Collins, CO, 80526-2097. Tel: 970-472-4353. p. 280
Hertel, Megan, Digital Res Librn, Argonne National Laboratory, 9700 S Cass Ave, Bldg 240, Lemont, IL, 60439-4801. Tel: 630-252-0007. p. 608
Hertel, Tina, Dir, Muhlenberg College, 2400 Chew St, Allentown, PA, 18104-5586. Tel: 484-664-3500. p. 1905
Hertel-Fernandez, Sarah, Libr Dir, Belding Memorial Library, 344 Main St, Ashfield, MA, 01330. Tel: 413-628-4414. p. 986
Hertle, Laura, Library Contact, New York State Office of Parks Recreation & Historic, 296 Fair St, Kingston, NY, 12401-3836. Tel: 845-338-2786. p. 1560
Hertz, Deb, Asst Dir, Laurens Public Library, 273 N Third St, Laurens, IA, 50554. Tel: 712-841-4612. p. 765
Hertz, Ian S, Asst Dir, Finance & Collections, Bus Ref Librn, Electronic Res Librn, Winston-Salem State University, 601 Martin Luther King Jr Dr, Winston-Salem, NC, 27110. Tel: 336-750-2532. p. 1726
Hertzoff, Hilary, Tech Serv Librn, Mamaroneck Public Library, 136 Prospect Ave, Mamaroneck, NY, 10543. Tel: 914-698-1250. p. 1568
Hervey, Ron, Libr Supvr, Paris Public Library, 326 S Main St, Paris, TX, 75460. Tel: 903-785-8531. p. 2225
Herweg-Samuels, Britta, Br Mgr, Albuquerque-Bernalillo County Library System, Juan Tabo Library, 3407 Juan Tabo Blvd NE, Albuquerque, NM, 87111. Tel: 505-291-6260. p. 1460

Herz, Britney, Librn, Eastern Correctional Institution, West Library, 30420 Revells Neck Rd, Westover, MD, 21890. Tel: 410-845-4000, Ext 6423. p. 981

Herz, Stephanie, Librn, Historical Society of Moorestown Library, 12 High St, Moorestown, NJ, 08057. Tel: 856-235-0353. p. 1420

Herzberg, Martha, Dir, Villisca Public Library, 204 S Third Ave, Villisca, IA, 50864. Tel: 712-826-2452. p. 787

Herzig, Stella, Ref & Instruction Librn, Saint Ambrose University Library, 518 W Locust St, Davenport, IA, 52803. Tel: 563-333-6056. p. 744

Herzinger, Sandra, Librn, Christ United Methodist Church Library, 4530 A St, Lincoln, NE, 68510. Tel: 402-489-9618. p. 1321

Herzl-Betz, Hans, Ref & Instruction Librn, Creighton University, Klutznick Law Library - McGrath North Mullin & Kratz Legal Research Center, School of Law, 2500 California Plaza, Omaha, NE, 68178-0340. Tel: 402-280-3436. p. 1328

Herzog, Brian, Asst Dir, Tuscarawas County Public Library, 121 Fair Ave NW, New Philadelphia, OH, 44663-2600. Tel: 330-364-4474. p. 1807

Herzog, Erin, Circ Supvr, Sr Librn, Oxnard Public Library, 251 South A St, Oxnard, CA, 93030. Tel: 805-200-5685. p. 190

Herzog, Fred, Computer Serv, Network Serv, Skene Memorial Library, 1017 Main St, Fleischmanns, NY, 12430. Tel: 845-254-4581. p. 1533

Herzog, Jess, Dir, Multimedia & Adult Serv, Spartanburg County Public Libraries, 151 S Church St, Spartanburg, SC, 29306. Tel: 864-596-3500. p. 2069

Herzog-Schmidt, Beth, Br Mgr, Jasper-Dubois County Public Library, 1116 Main St, Jasper, IN, 47546-2899. Tel: 812-482-2712, Ext 6111. p. 697

Hes, Shulamis, Electronic Res & Ref Librn, Yeshiva University Libraries, Pollack Library Landowne Bloom Collection, Wilf Campus, 2520 Amsterdam Ave, New York, NY, 10033. Tel: 646-592-4045, 646-592-4450. p. 1605

Heschke, Grace, Libr Serv Coordr, Great River Regional Library, Pierz Library, 117 S Main St, Pierz, MN, 56364. Tel: 320-468-6486. p. 1197

Hescht, Sonya, Dir, Libr & Info Literacy, Ohio Valley University Library, One Campus View Dr, Vienna, WV, 26105-8000. Tel: 304-865-6112, 304-865-6113. p. 2416

Heser, Steve, Dir, Milwaukee County Federated Library System, 709 N Eighth St, Milwaukee, WI, 53233-2414. Tel: 414-286-3210. p. 2459

Heskett, Jeannine, Librn, Darien Public Library, 47 Park Ave, Darien, WI, 53114-0465. Tel: 262-882-5155. p. 2430

Heskin, Susan, Libr Dir, Superior Public Library, 1530 Tower Ave, Superior, WI, 54880-2532. Tel: 715-394-8860. p. 2480

Hesler, June, Programming Librn, Larchmont Public Library, 121 Larchmont Ave, Larchmont, NY, 10538. Tel: 914-834-2281. p. 1562

Heslin, Liz, Library Contact, Westminster Presbyterian Church Library, 2040 Washington Rd, Upper St Clair, Pittsburgh, PA, 15241. Tel: 412-835-6630. p. 1997

Hespe, Marge, Dir, Keya Paha County Library, 118 Main St, Springview, NE, 68778. Tel: 402-497-2626. p. 1337

Hespel, Amanda, Libr Dir, Adams Public Library, 190 Main St, Adams, OR, 97810. Tel: 541-566-3038. p. 1871

Hess, Adam, Libr Dir, Arcadia University, 450 S Easton Rd, Glenside, PA, 19038. Tel: 215-572-2842. p. 1937

Hess, Alex, III, Librn, University of North Carolina at Chapel Hill, School of Government Knapp Library, Knapp-Sanders Bldg, CB No 3330, Chapel Hill, NC, 27599-3330. Tel: 919-962-2760. p. 1679

Hess, Amanda, Instruction Coordr, Research Coordr, Oakland University Library, 100 Library Dr, Rochester, MI, 48309-4479. Tel: 248-370-2487. p. 1144

Hess, Bettina, Spec Coll Librn, German Society of Pennsylvania, 611 Spring Garden St, Philadelphia, PA, 19123. Tel: 215-627-2332. p. 1980

Hess, Bradley, Tech Serv Librn, Concordia Theological Seminary, 6600 N Clinton St, Fort Wayne, IN, 46825. Tel: 260-452-2145. p. 684

Hess, Chris, Ms, Circ, Strasburg-Heisler Library, 143 Precision Ave, Strasburg, PA, 17579. Tel: 717-687-8969. p. 2010

Hess Cohen, Sarah, Head, Tech Serv, Univ Librn, Florida State University Libraries, Warren D Allen Music Library, Housewright Music Bldg, 122 N Copeland St, Tallahassee, FL, 32306. Tel: 850-644-4137. p. 447

Hess, Corrie, Dir, Louisiana State University Libraries, LSU School of Veterinary Medicine Library, Skip Bertman Dr, Baton Rouge, LA, 70803-8414. Tel: 225-578-9799. p. 884

Hess, Dan, Br Librn, Mendocino County Library District, Fort Bragg Branch, 499 E Laurel St, Fort Bragg, CA, 95437. Tel: 707-964-2020. p. 254

Hess, Elizabeth, Dir, Downingtown Library Co, 122 Wallace Ave, Downingtown, PA, 19335. Tel: 610-269-2741. p. 1926

Hess, Eric, Librn, Network Serv, Cleveland Law Library, One W Lakeside Ave, 4th Flr, Cleveland, OH, 44113-1078. Tel: 216-861-5070. p. 1767

Hess, Jay L, Dr, Dean, Indiana University, Ruth Lilly Medical Library, 975 W Walnut St, IB 100, Indianapolis, IN, 46202. Tel: 317-274-7182. p. 693

Hess, Jennifer, Exec Dir, Danville Public Library, 319 N Vermilion St, Danville, IL, 61832. Tel: 217-477-5223, Ext 118. p. 575

Hess, Jennifer, Mgr, Columbus Metropolitan Library, Whetstone Branch, 3909 N High St, Columbus, OH, 43214. p. 1773

Hess, Judy, Asst Librn, Franklin Ferguson Memorial Library, 410 N B St, Cripple Creek, CO, 80813. Tel: 719-689-2800. p. 272

Hess, Laura, Dir, Stanton Public Library, 1009 Jackpine St, Stanton, NE, 68779. Tel: 402-439-2230. p. 1337

Hess, Melody, Ch Serv, Fremont County District Library, Ashton Branch, 925 Main, Ashton, ID, 83420. Tel: 208-652-7280. p. 530

Hess, Mindy, Dir, Taylor Memorial Library, 402 Second St, Taylor, WI, 54659. Tel: 715-662-2310. p. 2481

Hess, Paula, Librn, Children's Hospital Los Angeles, 4650 Sunset Blvd, MS41, Los Angeles, CA, 90027. Tel: 323-361-2254, 323-361-2428. p. 161

Hess, Sharon, Library Contact, Clinton Public Library, Lyons, 105 Main Ave, Clinton, IA, 52732. Tel: 563-242-5355. p. 741

Hess, Shivon, Librn, Reedley College Library, 995 N Reed Ave, Reedley, CA, 93654. Tel: 559-638-0352. p. 200

Hess, Tamra, Dir, East Palestine Memorial Public Library, 309 N Market St, East Palestine, OH, 44413. Tel: 330-426-3778. p. 1783

Hess, Wendy, Syst Librn, Summa Health System, 55 Arch St, Ste G-3, Akron, OH, 44304. Tel: 330-375-3260. p. 1745

Hesse, Susan, Dir, Res & Info Serv, Wachtell, Lipton, Rosen & Katz, 51 W 52nd St, New York, NY, 10019. Tel: 212-403-1521. p. 1603

Hessel, Beth, Dr, Exec Dir, The Athenaeum of Philadelphia, East Washington Sq, 219 S Sixth St, Philadelphia, PA, 19106-3794. Tel: 215-925-2688. p. 1975

Hessenauer, Jean, Dir, Tydings & Rosenberg LLP, One E Pratt St, 9th Flr, Baltimore, MD, 21202. Tel: 410-752-9700, 410-752-9804. p. 957

Hessler, Eric, Archivist, Database Mgr, Rock County Historical Society, 426 N Jackson St, Janesville, WI, 53548. Tel: 608-756-4509. p. 2443

Hesson, Donna D, Mgr, Johns Hopkins University Libraries, William H Welch Medical Library, 1900 E Monument St, Baltimore, MD, 21205. Tel: 410-955-3028. p. 954

Hesson, Mike, Tech Serv, Richard C Sullivan Public Library of Wilton Manors, 500 NE 26th St, Wilton Manors, FL, 33305. Tel: 954-390-2195. p. 455

Hestand, Stephanie, Circ, Genealogy Serv, Monroe County Public Library, 500 W Fourth St, Tompkinsville, KY, 42167. Tel: 270-487-5301. p. 876

Hester, Hathaway, Archivist, National Association of Realtors, 430 N Michigan Ave, Chicago, IL, 60611-4087. Tel: 312-329-8577. p. 565

Hester, Hathaway, Archives & Rec Mgr, American Association of Nurse Anesthetists, 10275 W Higgins Rd, Ste 500, Rosemont, IL, 60018. Tel: 847-692-7050. p. 643

Hester, Keisha, Exec Dir, Broadview Public Library District, 2226 S 16th Ave, Broadview, IL, 60155. Tel: 708-345-1325, Ext 6. p. 545

Hester, Sandy, Dir, Coastal Plain Regional Library System, 2014 Chestnut Ave, Tifton, GA, 31794. Tel: 229-386-3400. p. 500

Heston, Sue, Asst Librn, Abbott Memorial Library, 15 Library St, South Pomfret, VT, 05067. Tel: 802-457-2236. p. 2295

Hetrick, Angela, Librn, Meadville Medical Center, 751 Liberty St, Meadville, PA, 16335. Tel: 814-333-5740. p. 1960

Hetterley, Chad, Tech Serv Supvr, DeSoto Public Library, 211 E Pleasant Run Rd, Ste C, DeSoto, TX, 75115. Tel: 972-230-9656. p. 2170

Hettich, Dana, Ref Librn, University of Alabama at Birmingham, Mervyn H Sterne Library, 917 13th St S, Birmingham, AL, 35205. Tel: 205-934-6364. p. 9

Hetzler, Svetha, Dir, Sun Prairie Public Library, 1350 Linnerud Dr, Sun Prairie, WI, 53590. Tel: 608-825-7323. p. 2480

Heuer, Maureen, Head, Adult Serv, West Islip Public Library, Three Higbie Lane, West Islip, NY, 11795-3999. Tel: 631-661-7080. p. 1662

Heuring, Tammy, Support Serv Mgr, Volusia County Public Library, 1290 Indian Lake Rd, Daytona Beach, FL, 32124. Tel: 386-248-1745. p. 392

Heus, Ann, Asst Librn, New Holstein Public Library, 2115 Washington St, New Holstein, WI, 53061-1098. Tel: 920-898-5165. p. 2464

Heuscher, Sally, Asst Librn, Choteau/Teton Public Library, 17 N Main Ave, Choteau, MT, 59422. Tel: 406-466-2052. p. 1291

Heusser-Ladwig, Susan, Librn, Perham Area Public Library, 225 Second Ave NE, Perham, MN, 56573-1819. Tel: 218-346-4892. p. 1192

Hevener, Stacie, Dir, Marstons Mills Public Library, 2160 Main St, Marstons Mills, MA, 02648. Tel: 508-428-5175. p. 1033

Hevey, Cheryl, Dir, Bonney Memorial Library, 36 Main St, Cornish, ME, 04020. Tel: 207-625-8083. p. 922

Hevron, Michelle, Sr Ref Librn, Virginia Museum of Fine Arts Library, 200 N Arthur Ashe Blvd, Richmond, VA, 23220-4007. Tel: 804-340-1495. p. 2344

Hewes, Paul, Actg Dir, Delaware County Historical Society, Nine W Front St, Media, PA, 19063. Tel: 610-359-0832. p. 1961

Hewes, Peggy, Librn, Baldwin Memorial Library, 33 Main St N, Wells River, VT, 05081. Tel: 802-757-2693. p. 2297

Hewett, Janice, Asst Librn, Henry Public Library, 702 Front St, Henry, IL, 61537. Tel: 309-364-2516. p. 598

Hewett, Linda, Libr Asst, Duplin County Library, Warsaw-Kornegay Library, 117 E College St, Warsaw, NC, 28398. Tel: 910-293-4664. p. 1698

Hewey, Brian, Syst Adminr, George H & Ella M Rodgers Memorial Library, 194 Derry Rd, Hudson, NH, 03051. Tel: 603-886-6030. p. 1368

Hewitt, Cindy, Interim Exec Dir, Huntsville-Madison County Public Library, 915 Monroe St, Huntsville, AL, 35801. Tel: 256-532-5940. p. 21

Hicks, Marla, Librn, Scott-Sebastian Regional Library, Sebastian County Library, 18 N Adair, Greenwood, AR, 72936. Tel: 479-996-2856. p. 97

Hicks, Mindy, Resource Librn, East Central Regional Library, 111 Dellwood St, Cambridge, MN, 55008-1588. Tel: 763-689-7390. p. 1167

Hicks, Terri K, Dir, Programs, Northern Plains Public Library, 216 W Second St, Ault, CO, 80610. Tel: 970-834-1259. p. 264

Hicks, Vanessa, Dir, Vinita Public Library, 215 W Illinois Ave, Vinita, OK, 74301. Tel: 918-256-2115. p. 1868

Hicks, Wendy, Dir, Pub Serv, Stratford Public Library, 19 Saint Andrew St, Stratford, ON, N5A 1A2, CANADA. Tel: 519-271-0220, Ext 111. p. 2682

Hickson, Ashlee, Supvry Librn, Joint Base San Antonio Libraries, 1930 George Ave, Lackland AFB, TX, 78236. Tel: 210-671-3610. p. 2208

Hickson, Rashad, Human Res Dir, South Carolina State Library, 1500 Senate St, Columbia, SC, 29201. Tel: 803-734-4612. p. 2054

Hickson-Stevenson, Pamela, Exec Dir, Akron-Summit County Public Library, 60 S High St, Akron, OH, 44326. Tel: 330-643-9100. p. 1744

Hidalgo, Ann, Dr, Acq Librn, Claremont School of Theology Library, Center for Process Studies, 1325 N College Ave, Claremont, CA, 91711-3154. Tel: 909-447-2533, 909-621-5330. p. 130

Hidalgo, Daisy, Libr Serv Supvr, Valencia College, Lake Nona Campus Library, 12350 Narcoossee Rd, Bldg 1, Rm 330, Orlando, FL, 32832. Tel: 407-582-7107. p. 433

Hidalgo, Kleo, Librn, Howard College - San Angelo Library, 3501 N US Hwy 67, San Angelo, TX, 76905. Tel: 325-481-8300, Ext 3310. p. 2236

Hidle, Mishelle, Dir, Emma Knox Kenan Public Library, 312 S Commerce St, Geneva, AL, 36340. Tel: 334-684-2459. p. 19

Hiebert, Jamaica, Head Librn, Lynn Lake Library, 503 Sherritt Ave, Lynn Lake, MB, R0B 0W0, CANADA. Tel: 204-356-2418, Ext 5. p. 2588

Hiebert, Jen, Librn, Chinook Regional Library, Vanguard Branch, Library/Musem Bldg, Dominion St, Vanguard, SK, S0N 2V0, CANADA. Tel: 306-582-7722. p. 2753

Hiers, Aubrey, Dir, Otto Bruyns Public Library of Northfield, 241 W Mill Rd, Northfield, NJ, 08225. Tel: 609-646-4476. p. 1430

Hiers, Wendy, Cat, Bartow Public Library, 2150 S Broadway Ave, Bartow, FL, 33830. Tel: 863-534-0131. p. 384

Hierta, Ebba, Libr Dir, Chilmark Free Public Library, 522 South Rd, Chilmark, MA, 02535. Tel: 508-645-3360. p. 1011

Higashida, Carol, Dr, Dean, Moorpark College Library, 7075 Campus Rd, Moorpark, CA, 93021-1695. Tel: 805-378-1450. p. 180

Higbie, Harmony, Libr Dir, Underwood Public Library, 88 Lincoln Ave, Underwood, ND, 58576. Tel: 701-442-3441. p. 1740

Higdon, Paul, Libr Dir, University of Northwestern Ohio, 13000 Student Commons Bldg, Lima, OH, 45805. Tel: 419-998-8446. p. 1796

Higel, Jesse, Mrs, Weekend Supvr, Ohio State University LIBRARIES, Newark Campus Library, Warner Library & Student Ctr, 1179 University Dr, Newark, OH, 43055-1797. Tel: 740-366-9307. p. 1776

Higeons, Dana, Acq, Head, Cat, Libr Syst Adminr, Oral Roberts University Library, 7777 S Lewis Ave, Tulsa, OK, 74171. Tel: 918-495-6885. p. 1865

Higginbotham, Cecelia, Librn, United States Army, USA MEDDAC Medical Library, Fort Polk - Bayne-Jones Army Community Hospital, 1585 Third St, Bldg 285, Fort Polk, LA, 71459-5110. Tel: 337-531-3725, 337-531-3726. p. 889

Higginbottom, Gretchen, Head, Resource Sharing, California State University, Fresno, Henry Madden Library, 5200 N Barton Ave, Mail Stop ML-34, Fresno, CA, 93740-8014. Tel: 559-278-3032. p. 144

Higginbottom, Mary, Br Operations Mgr, Genesee District Library, 4195 W Pasadena Ave, Flint, MI, 48504. Tel: 810-732-0110. p. 1105

Higginbottom, Patricia, Assoc Dir, Pub Serv, University of Alabama at Birmingham, Lister Hill Library of the Health Sciences, 1700 University Blvd, Birmingham, AL, 35294-0013. Tel: 205-934-5460. p. 9

Higgins, Brenda, Archivist, Pub Serv Librn, The Boston Conservatory, Eight Fenway, 2nd Flr, Boston, MA, 02215-4099. Tel: 617-912-9131. p. 991

Higgins, Carmen, Outreach Coordr, Westmont Public Library, 428 N Cass Ave, Westmont, IL, 60559-1502. Tel: 630-869-6150, 630-869-6160. p. 661

Higgins, Holly, Homebound Serv, Upper Sandusky Community Library, 301 N Sandusky Ave, Upper Sandusky, OH, 43351-1139. Tel: 419-294-1345. p. 1826

Higgins, Jean, Interim Dir, Wheelwright Museum of the American Indian, 704 Camino Lejo, Santa Fe, NM, 87505. Tel: 505-982-4636. p. 1477

Higgins, Joyce, Head, Circ, Catherine Schweinsberg Rood Central Library, 308 Forrest Ave, Cocoa, FL, 32922. Tel: 321-633-1792. p. 390

Higgins, Kristy, Libr Serv Coordr, Edmonton Public Library, Abbottsfield-Penny McKee Branch, 160-3210 118 Ave NW, Edmonton, AB, T5W 0Z4, CANADA. Tel: 780-496-7980. p. 2536

Higgins, Leila, Br Mgr, Orange County Library System, Windermere Branch, 530 Main St, Windermere, FL, 34786. p. 432

Higgins, Margaret, Access Serv & Syst, Librn, Asheville-Buncombe Technical Community College, 340 Victoria Rd, Asheville, NC, 28801. Tel: 828-398-7302. p. 1672

Higgins, Martha, Libr Dir, Carnegie Endowment for International Peace Library, 1779 Massachusetts Ave NW, Washington, DC, 20036. Tel: 202-939-2256. p. 362

Higgins, Mary Ellen, Libr Dir, Eveleth Public Library, 614 Pierce St, Eveleth, MN, 55734. Tel: 218-744-7499. p. 1174

Higgins, Michael, Dep Dir, Surface Transportation Board Library, 395 E St SW, Washington, DC, 20024. Tel: 202-245-0238. p. 377

Higgins, Nick, Chief Librn, Brooklyn Public Library, Ten Grand Army Plaza, Brooklyn, NY, 11238. Tel: 718-230-2100. p. 1502

Higgins, Phillips, Dir of Digital Strategy, Dir, Mkt, Richland Library, 1431 Assembly St, Columbia, SC, 29201-3101. Tel: 803-799-9084. p. 2054

Higgins, Robbie, Mrs, Dir, Houston County Public Library, 24 S Spring St, Erin, TN, 37061-4073. Tel: 931-289-3858. p. 2098

Higgins, Shana, Librn, University of Redlands, 1249 E Colton Ave, Redlands, CA, 92374-3755. Tel: 909-748-8022. p. 199

Higgins, Shannon, Br Serv Librn, Halifax Public Libraries, Tantallon Public, 3646 Hammonds Plains Rd, Upper Tantallon, NS, B3Z 1H3, CANADA. Tel: 902-826-3330. p. 2618

Higginson, Laura, Libr Mgr, Mississauga Library System, Frank McKechnie Branch, 310 Bristol Rd E, Mississauga, ON, L4Z 3V5, CANADA. Tel: 905-615-4660. p. 2659

Higginson, Laura, Libr Mgr, Mississauga Library System, Mississauga Valley, 1275 Mississauga Valley Blvd, Mississauga, ON, L5A 3R8, CANADA. Tel: 905-615-4670. p. 2659

Higgith, Carolee, Supvr, Middlesex County Library, Melbourne Branch, 6570 Longwoods Rd, Melbourne, ON, N0L 1T0, CANADA. Tel: 519-289-2405. p. 2682

Higgs, Nancy, Branch Experience Mgr, Evansville Vanderburgh Public Library, North Park, 960 Koehler Dr, Evansville, IN, 47710. Tel: 812-428-8237. p. 681

High, Andrea, Asst Librn, Canyon Area Library, 1501 Third Ave, Canyon, TX, 79015. Tel: 806-655-5015. p. 2153

High, JoAnne M, Br Mgr, Coastal Plain Regional Library System, Turner County-Victoria Evans Memorial, 605 North St, Ashburn, GA, 31714. Tel: 229-567-4027. p. 500

High, Lisa, Br Mgr, Pequea Valley Public Library, Salisbury Township Branch Library, The Family Center of Gap, 835 Houston Run Dr, Ste 220, Gap, PA, 17527. Tel: 717-442-3304. p. 1946

High, Susan, Circ Supvr, Johns Hopkins University School of Advanced International, 1740 Massachusetts Ave NW, 6th Flr, Washington, DC, 20036. Tel: 202-663-5900. p. 370

Higham, Charles, Ref Librn, Sumter County Library, 111 N Harvin St, Sumter, SC, 29150. Tel: 803-773-7273. p. 2071

Highfield, Heather, Info Tech, Liverpool Public Library, 310 Tulip St, Liverpool, NY, 13088-4997. Tel: 315-457-0310. p. 1564

Highfill, April, Dir, Prairie County Library System, 201 US Hwy 70 E, Hazen, AR, 72064. Tel: 870-255-3576. p. 98

Highfill, Laura, Branch Lead, Charlotte Mecklenburg Library, South County Regional, 5801 Rea Rd, Charlotte, NC, 28277. Tel: 704-416-6600. p. 1680

Highfill, Melissa, Dir, Westboro Public Library, N8855 Second St, Westboro, WI, 54490. Tel: 715-427-5864. p. 2487

Highsmith, Doug, Librn, California State University, East Bay Library, CSU East Bay Library, 25800 Carlos Bee Blvd, Hayward, CA, 94542-3052. Tel: 510-885-3610. p. 150

Hight, Ashlie, Systems & Discovery Librn, Texas A&M University-Commerce, 2600 S Neal St, Commerce, TX, 75428. Tel: 903-886-5385. p. 2158

Hightshoe, Lois, Sr Librn, California Department of Corrections Library System, Ironwood State Prison Library-Central Library, 19005 Wiley's Well Rd, Blythe, CA, 92225. Tel: 760-921-3000, Ext 5623. p. 207

Higley, Allie, Libr Tech, Grantsville City Library, 42 N Bowery St, Grantsville, UT, 84029. Tel: 435-884-1670. p. 2264

Higley, Brittane, Asst Librn, Oakley Free Library District, 185 E Main St, Oakley, ID, 83346. Tel: 208-862-3434. p. 528

Higo, Patricia, Archive Collection Mgmt, Assoc Librn, University of Detroit Mercy Libraries, 4001 W McNichols Rd, Detroit, MI, 48221-3038. Tel: 313-578-0435. p. 1099

Hilbert, Logan, Libr Spec, Blue Ridge Community College, One College Lane, Weyers Cave, VA, 24486. Tel: 540-453-2247. p. 2352

Hilburn, Gayle, Circ, Dundee Public Library, 202 E Main St, PO Box 1000, Dundee, FL, 33838. Tel: 863-439-9424. p. 394

Hilburn, Jessica, Exec Dir, Benson Memorial Library, 213 N Franklin St, Titusville, PA, 16354-1788. Tel: 814-827-2913. p. 2012

Hildebrand, Gerry, Libr Dir, Nora E Larabee Memorial Library, 108 N Union St, Stafford, KS, 67578-1339. Tel: 620-234-5762. p. 837

Hildebrand, Sara, Librn, Kettle Moraine Correctional Institution Library, W9071 Forest Dr, Plymouth, WI, 53073. Tel: 920-526-3244, Ext 2309. p. 2470

Hildebrand, Theresa, Patron Serv Mgr, Orland Park Public Library, 14921 Ravinia Ave, Orland Park, IL, 60462. Tel: 708-428-5109. p. 630

Hilder, Leslie, Br Coordr, Prince George Public Library, Nechako Branch, 6547 Hart Hwy, Prince George, BC, V2K 3A4, CANADA. Tel: 250-563-9251, Ext 401. p. 2574

Hilderbrand, Morna, ILL Librn, RIT Libraries, 90 Lomb Memorial Dr, Rochester, NY, 14623-5604. p. 1629

Hildreth, Brian M, Exec Dir, Southern Tier Library System, 9424 Scott Rd, Painted Post, NY, 14870-9598. Tel: 607-962-3141, Ext 207. p. 1614

Hildreth, Heather, Head, Circ, West Des Moines Public Library, 4000 Mills Civic Pkwy, West Des Moines, IA, 50265-2049. Tel: 515-222-3400. p. 791
Hildreth, Michelle, Dir, Franklin County Library, 906 N Main St, Louisburg, NC, 27549-2199. Tel: 919-496-2111. p. 1701
Hiles, Diana, Ref Librn, Mott Community College, 1401 E Court St, Flint, MI, 48503. Tel: 810-762-5661. p. 1107
Hilgar, Rosemarie, Doc Delivery, Rider University, 2083 Lawrenceville Rd, Lawrenceville, NJ, 08648. p. 1411
Hilke, Lorna, Br Mgr, Jackson County Library Services, Gold Hill Branch, 202 Dardanelles St, Gold Hill, OR, 97525-0136. Tel: 541-855-1994. p. 1886
Hilker, Dan, Dir, Lyons Public Library, 4209 Joliet Ave, Lyons, IL, 60534-1597. Tel: 708-447-3577. p. 612
Hilkert, Judy, Tech Serv Coordr, Hinds Community College, 505 E Main St, Raymond, MS, 39154. Tel: 601-857-3355. p. 1231
Hilkert, Judy, Tech Serv Coordr, Hinds Community College, McLendon Library, 505 E Main St, Raymond, MS, 39154. Tel: 601-857-3255. p. 1231
Hilkewich, Beverly, Br Librn, Wapiti Regional Library, Alvena Public Library, Business/Commerce Complex, 101 Main St, Alvena, SK, S0K 0E0, CANADA. Tel: 306-943-2003. p. 2745
Hilkin, Elizabeth, Asst Dir, Pub Serv, University of Florida Libraries, Holland Law Ctr, 309 Village Dr, Gainesville, FL, 32611. Tel: 352-273-0702. p. 408
Hill, Abby, Dir, Libr Serv, Thompson Home Public Library, 125 W Center St, Ithaca, MI, 48847. Tel: 989-875-4184. p. 1119
Hill, Alex, Librn, North Central Washington Libraries, Chelan Public Library, 216 N Emerson St, Chelan, WA, 98816. Tel: 509-682-5131. p. 2393
Hill, Allison, Mgr, Library Servs & Resource Discovery, AIDE Canada Library, 3688 Cessna Dr, Richmond, BC, V7B 1C7, CANADA. Tel: 604-207-1980, Ext 2006. p. 2575
Hill, Amanda, Br Mgr, Memphis Public Library, Randolph Branch, 3752 Given Ave, Memphis, TN, 38122. Tel: 901-415-2779. p. 2114
Hill, Amanda, Asst Dir, The Dell Dehay Law Library of Tarrant County, Tarrant County Historical Courthouse, 100 W Weatherford St, Rm 420, Fort Worth, TX, 76196-0800. Tel: 817-884-1481. p. 2179
Hill, Angela, Asst Admin, Head, Ref (Info Serv), Wichita Falls Public Library, 600 11th St, Wichita Falls, TX, 76301-4604. Tel: 940-767-0868, Ext 4233. p. 2258
Hill, Ann Marie, Asst Law Librn, Lewis County Law Library, Lewis County Courthouse, 7660 N State St, 2nd Flr, Lowville, NY, 13367. Tel: 315-376-5317. p. 1566
Hill, Autumn, Mgr, Omaha Public Library, A V Sorensen Branch, 4808 Cass St, Omaha, NE, 68132-3031. Tel: 402-444-5274. p. 1330
Hill, Autumn, Mgr, Omaha Public Library, Millard Branch, 13214 Westwood Lane, Omaha, NE, 68144-3556. Tel: 402-444-4848. p. 1330
Hill, Bettielue, Youth Serv Librn, Wilton Public & Gregg Free Library, Seven Forest Rd, Wilton, NH, 03086. Tel: 603-654-2581. p. 1384
Hill, Blake, Pub Serv Librn, YA Mgr, Converse County Library, 300 E Walnut St, Douglas, WY, 82633. Tel: 307-358-3644. p. 2494
Hill, Carleigh, Library Consortium Services Mgr, Washington Community & Technical Colleges Library Consortium, c/o Big Ben Community College, 7662 Chanute St NE, Moses Lake, WA, 98837. Tel: 509-795-0140. p. 2776
Hill, Casey, Br Mgr, Ozark Regional Library, Fredericktown Branch, 115 S Main St, Fredericktown, MO, 63645. Tel: 573-783-2120. p. 1251
Hill, Cheryl, Tech Serv Librn, Southeastern Libraries Cooperating, 2600 19th St NW, Rochester, MN, 55901-0767. Tel: 507-288-5513. p. 2768
Hill, Darnelle, Chief Exec Officer, Hornepayne Public Library, 68 Front St, Hornepayne, ON, P0M 1Z0, CANADA. Tel: 807-868-2332. p. 2648
Hill, David, Head Librn, American Numismatic Society Library, 75 Varick St, New York, NY, 10013. Tel: 212-571-4470, Ext 170. p. 1579
Hill de Santos, Carol, Ch, Moore Memorial Public Library, 1701 Ninth Ave N, Texas City, TX, 77590. Tel: 409-643-5966. p. 2248
Hill, Doss, Instrul Serv Librn, Outreach Coordr, Lycoming College, One College Pl, Williamsport, PA, 17701. Tel: 570-321-4087. p. 2023
Hill, Gary, Dep Dir, Brigham Young University, Howard W Hunter Law Library, 256 JRCB, Provo, UT, 84602-8000. Tel: 801-422-3593. p. 2269
Hill, Gayleen, Library Contact, University of Nebraska-Lincoln, Dinsdale Family Learning Commons, East Campus, 1625 N 38th St, Lincoln, NE, 68583-0717. p. 1323
Hill, Gregory, Chief Exec Officer, Indianapolis Public Library, 2450 N Meridian St, Indianapolis, IN, 46208. Tel: 317-275-4840. p. 694
Hill, Gregory, Br Mgr, Indianapolis Public Library, Lawrence, 7898 N Hague Rd, Indianapolis, IN, 46256-1754. Tel: 317-275-4463. p. 695
Hill, Gregory, Circ Librn, Livingstone College, 701 W Monroe St, Salisbury, NC, 28144. Tel: 704-216-6956. p. 1714
Hill, Heather, Assoc Prof, Chair, MLIS Prog, Western University, FIMS & Nursing Bldg, Rm 2020, London, ON, N6A 5B9, CANADA. Tel: 519-661-2111, Ext 88013. p. 2796
Hill, J B, Exec Dir, Libr Serv, University of Arkansas at Little Rock, 2801 S University Ave, Little Rock, AR, 72204. Tel: 501-916-6186. p. 102
Hill, Jacob, Ref & Instruction Librn, Elmhurst University, 190 Prospect St, Elmhurst, IL, 60126. Tel: 630-617-3168. p. 585
Hill, James, Dir, Zumbrota Public Library, 100 West Ave, Zumbrota, MN, 55992. Tel: 507-732-5211. p. 1210
Hill, James, Dir, Chillicothe & Ross County Public Library, 140 S Paint St, Chillicothe, OH, 45601. Tel: 740-702-4162. p. 1758
Hill, Janene, Dir, Jensen Memorial Library, 443 N Kearney, Minden, NE, 68959. Tel: 308-832-2648. p. 1325
Hill, Jeanne, Sister, Librn, Holy Trinity Monastery Library, 1605 S St Mary's Way, Saint David, AZ, 85630. Tel: 520-720-4642. p. 76
Hill, Jennifer, Head, Adult Serv, Head, Ref, ILL Supvr, Twin Falls Public Library, 201 Fourth Ave E, Twin Falls, ID, 83301-6397. Tel: 208-733-2964. p. 532
Hill, Jennifer, Asst Br Librn, Ref Librn, Brazoria County Library System, Angleton Branch, 401 E Cedar St, Angleton, TX, 77515-4652. Tel: 979-864-1513. p. 2135
Hill, Jennifer, Dir, Saint Cloud State University, Education Bldg A132, 720 Fourth Ave S, Saint Cloud, MN, 56301-4498. Tel: 320-308-4057. p. 2787
Hill, Jenny, Br Mgr, Brainerd Public Library, 416 S Fifth St, Brainerd, MN, 56401. Tel: 218-829-5574. p. 1166
Hill, Joan, Ref Librn, Livingstone College, 701 W Monroe St, Salisbury, NC, 28144. Tel: 704-216-6031. p. 1714
Hill, Joan, Librn, Wetumka Public Library, 202 N Main, Wetumka, OK, 74883. Tel: 405-452-3785. p. 1869
Hill, Johnny, Circ Librn, Oklahoma City Community College, 7777 S May Ave, Oklahoma City, OK, 73159. Tel: 405-682-1611, Ext 7315. p. 1858
Hill, Jon, Music Libr Mgr, Davidson College, 209 Ridge Rd, Davidson, NC, 28035-0001. Tel: 704-894-2331. p. 1683
Hill, Judy, Dir, Binger Public Library, 217 W Main, Binger, OK, 73009. Tel: 405-656-2543. p. 1842
Hill, Karen, Libr Dir, Cornelius Public Library, 1370 N Adair St, Cornelius, OR, 97113. Tel: 503-357-4093. p. 1876
Hill, Kathy, Admin Officer, Smithsonian Libraries, Natural History Bldg, Tenth St & Constitution Ave NW, Washington, DC, 20560. Tel: 202-633-1945. p. 375
Hill, Katie, Libr Dir, Orange County Public Library, 146A Madison Rd, Orange, VA, 22960. Tel: 540-661-5444. p. 2336
Hill Kepron, Emma, Assoc Dean, University of Winnipeg Library, 515 Portage Ave, Winnipeg, MB, R3B 2E9, CANADA. Tel: 204-786-9445. p. 2596
Hill, Latisha, Head, Circ, Hamtramck Public Library, 2360 Caniff St, Hamtramck, MI, 48212. Tel: 313-733-6822. p. 1113
Hill, Linda, Asst Librn, Smithton Public Library District, 109 S Main, Smithton, IL, 62285-1707. Tel: 618-233-8057. p. 648
Hill, Lizzy, Youth Serv Librn, Staunton Public Library, One Churchville Ave, Staunton, VA, 24401. Tel: 540-332-3902, Ext 4234. p. 2347
Hill, Mandy, Br Mgr, Mississippi County Library System, Manila Public, 103 N Dewey Ave, Manila, AR, 72442. Tel: 870-561-3525. p. 91
Hill, Mary, Dir, Hillsdale Community Library, 11 E Bacon St, Hillsdale, MI, 49242. Tel: 517-437-6470. p. 1115
Hill, Maureen E, Archivist, National Archives & Records Administration, 5780 Jonesboro Rd, Morrow, GA, 30260. Tel: 770-968-2100. p. 492
Hill, Meara, Head, Student Serv, University of Wyoming, 1820 E Willett Dr, Laramie. Tel: 307-766-5113. p. 2496
Hill, Megan, Dir, Tonkawa Public Library, 216 N Seventh St, Tonkawa, OK, 74653. Tel: 580-628-3366. p. 1864
Hill, Meghan, Info Res Spec, Pennsylvania State University, 2201 University Dr, Uniontown, PA, 15456. Tel: 724-430-4153. p. 2014
Hill, Michele, Circ, Libr Asst, Kaskaskia College Library, 27210 College Rd, Centralia, IL, 62801. Tel: 618-545-3130. p. 551
Hill, Myra, Ref Librn, Jefferson County Library, Arnold Branch, 1701 Missouri State Rd, Arnold, MO, 63010. Tel: 636-296-2204. p. 1249
Hill, Nanci, Dir, Hopkinton Public Library, 13 Main St, Hopkinton, MA, 01748. Tel: 508-497-9777. p. 1025
Hill, Nancy, Dir, General N B Baker Public Library, 315 Ash St, Sutherland, IA, 51058. Tel: 712-446-3839. p. 785
Hill, Nancy, Tech Serv Librn, Harrodsburg Historical Society, 220 S Chiles St, Harrodsburg, KY, 40330. Tel: 859-734-5985. p. 858
Hill, Nate, Exec Dir, Metropolitan New York Library Council, 599 11th Ave, 8th Flr, New York, NY, 10036. Tel: 212-228-2320. p. 2771
Hill, Nevenia, Public, Research & Tech Librn, Rhodes College, 2000 North Pkwy, Memphis, TN, 38112-1694. Tel: 901-843-3890. p. 2114
Hill, Penny, Branch Cluster Supvr, Fresno County Public Library, 2420 Mariposa St, Fresno, CA, 93721. Tel: 559-600-7323. p. 145
Hill, Penny, Br Supvr, Fresno County Public Library, Senior Resource Center, 2025 E Dakota Ave, Fresno, CA, 93726. Tel: 559-600-6767. p. 146
Hill, Rettina, Libr Mgr, Central Arkansas Library System, Hillary Rodham Clinton Children's Library & Learning Center, 4800 W Tenth St, Little Rock, AR, 72204. Tel: 501-978-3870. p. 101
Hill, Sandra D, Libr Dir, Villa Park Public Library, 305 S Ardmore Ave, Villa Park, IL, 60181-2698. Tel: 630-834-1164, Ext 111. p. 658
Hill, Sarah, Dir, Libr Serv, Lake Land College Library, 5001 Lake Land Blvd, Mattoon, IL, 61938. Tel: 217-234-5538. p. 615
Hill, Sharon, Circ, Panola College, 1109 W Panola St, Carthage, TX, 75633. Tel: 903-693-1155. p. 2154

Hill, Stacy, Mgr, Sequoyah Regional Library System, Pickens County Public, 100 Library Lane, Jasper, GA, 30143. Tel: 706-692-5411. p. 469

Hill, Susan H, Libr Dir, Brigham City Library, 26 E Forest St, Brigham City, UT, 84302. Tel: 435-723-5850. p. 2261

Hill, Sydney, Libr Asst, Ohio Department of Rehabilitation & Correction, 1580 State Rte 56 SW, London, OH, 43140. Tel: 740-490-6700. p. 1797

Hill, Terry B, Dep Dir, Durham County Library, 300 N Roxboro St, Durham, NC, 27701. Tel: 919-560-0164. p. 1685

Hill, Thomas E, Librn, Vassar College Library, Art Library, Taylor Hall, Rm 216, 124 Raymond Ave, Poughkeepsie, NY, 12604-0022. Tel: 845-437-5791. p. 1624

Hill, Victoria, Librn, East Polk Public Library, 136 Main St, Ste A, Ducktown, TN, 37326. Tel: 423-496-4004. p. 2097

Hill, Virginia, Libr Tech, Alameda Free Library, West End, 788 Santa Clara Ave, Alameda, CA, 94501-3334. Tel: 510-747-7767. p. 115

Hill-Festa, Lisa, Curator of Coll, Nordic Heritage Museum, Walter Johnson Memorial Library, 3014 NW 67th St, Seattle, WA, 98117. Tel: 206-789-5707, Ext 18. p. 2377

Hillanbrand, Amy, Dir, Macsherry Library, 112 Walton St, Alexandria Bay, NY, 13607. Tel: 315-482-2241. p. 1485

Hiller, Audra, Asst Librn, Canmore Public Library, 101-700 Railway Ave, Canmore, AB, T1W 1P4, CANADA. Tel: 403-678-2468. p. 2530

Hiller, Kimberli, Br Mgr, Holmes County District Public Library, Walnut Creek Branch, 4877 Olde Pump St, Walnut Creek, OH, 44687. Tel: 330-893-3464. p. 1803

Hiller, Laura, Cat Spec, Midwestern State University, 3410 Taft Blvd, Wichita Falls, TX, 76308-2099. Tel: 940-397-4168. p. 2257

Hiller, Lois, Libr Dir, Library Association of Warehouse Point, 107 Main St, East Windsor, CT, 06088. Tel: 860-623-5482. p. 310

Hilles, Stefanie, Art Librn, Humanities Librn, Miami University Libraries, Wertz Art & Architecture Library, Alumni Hall, Oxford, OH, 45056. Tel: 513-529-6650. p. 1812

Hillhouse, Sharon, Libr Mgr, Bouse Public Library, 44031 Plomosa Rd, Bouse, AZ, 85325. Tel: 928-851-1023. p. 56

Hillhouse, Sharon, Mgr, Centennial Public Library, 69725 Centennial Rd, Salome, AZ, 85348. Tel: 928-859-4271. p. 76

Hillick, Amy, Circ, Ref Librn, Orange County Community College Library, 115 South St, Middletown, NY, 10940. Tel: 845-341-4855. p. 1571

Hilligos-vilkman, Erin, Resource Management, US National Park Service, 2916 E South St, Lincoln City, IN, 47552. Tel: 812-937-4541. p. 703

Hilliker, Janet, Archivist, Norwich & District Historical Society Archives, 91 Stover St N, RR3, Norwich, ON, N0J 1P0, CANADA. Tel: 519-863-3638. p. 2662

Hilliker, Robert P, Assoc Provost of Libr Info Servs, Rowan University Library, 201 Mullica Hill Rd, Glassboro, NJ, 08029. Tel: 856-256-4988. p. 1405

Hillis, Dan, Libr Syst Coordr, Makerspace Mrg, University of Wisconsin-Eau Claire, 103 Garfield Ave, Eau Claire, WI, 54701-4932. Tel: 715-836-4961. p. 2433

Hillman, Christina, Assessment & Online Prog Librn, Saint John Fisher University, 3690 East Ave, Rochester, NY, 14618-3599. Tel: 585-385-8493. p. 1630

Hillman, Kathy, Director of Baptist Colls & Library Advancement, Baylor University Libraries, Moody Memorial Library, 1312 S Third St, Waco, TX, 76798. Tel: 254-710-6684. p. 2253

Hillman, Kristen, Br Mgr, Madison County Library System, Elsie E Jurgens Library, 397 Hwy 51 N, Ridgeland, MS, 39157. Tel: 601-856-4536. p. 1213

Hillner, Melanie, Sci Librn, University of Richmond, 261 Richmond Way, Richmond, VA, 23173. Tel: 804-289-8262. p. 2342

Hills, Marjorie, ILL, Ref Serv, Iberia Parish Library, 445 E Main St, New Iberia, LA, 70560-3710. Tel: 337-364-7024, 337-364-7074. p. 900

Hillson, William, Dir, Kensett Public Library, 214 Fifth St, Kensett, IA, 50448. Tel: 641-845-2222. p. 762

Hillson, William, Tech Librn, Manly Public Library, 127 S Grant, Manly, IA, 50456. Tel: 641-454-2982. p. 767

Hilman, Cathy, Med Librn, JFK Medical Center, Hackensack Meridian Health, 65 James St, Edison, NJ, 08818-3059. Tel: 732-321-7181. p. 1400

Hilterbrand, Lori, Program Mgr, Resource Sharing & Fulfillment, Orbis Cascade Alliance, PO Box 6007, Portland, OR, 97228. Tel: 541-246-2470. p. 2773

Hiltner, Katy, Head Librn, Hutchinson Public Library, 50 Hassan St SE, Hutchinson, MN, 55350-1881. Tel: 320-587-2368. p. 1178

Hiltner, Katy, Head Librn, Winsted Public Library, 180 Main Ave W, Winsted, MN, 55395. Tel: 320-485-3909. p. 1209

Hilton, Jane, Dir, Elwood Public Library, 306 Calvert St, Elwood, NE, 68937. Tel: 308-785-8155. p. 1313

Hilton, Thomas, Dept Head, Ref Librn, Lyndhurst Free Public Library, 355 Valley Brook Ave, Lyndhurst, NJ, 07071. Tel: 201-804-2478. p. 1414

Hiltz, Julia, Chief Librn, United States Department of Defense, Washington Headquarters Services, 1155 Defense Pentagon, Washington, DC, 20301-1155. p. 378

Hilyard, Abigail, Librn, Indiana University-Purdue University, 4555 Central Ave, LC 1600, Columbus, IN, 47203. Tel: 812-314-8703. p. 676

Hilyer, Lee, Exec Dir, University of Houston - Clear Lake, Bayou Bldg 2402, 2700 Bay Area Blvd, Houston, TX, 77058-1002. Tel: 281-283-3900. p. 2199

Hime, Laurie, Librn, Miami Dade College, Kendall Campus Library, 11011 SW 104th St, Miami, FL, 33176-3393. Tel: 305-237-0996, 305-237-2015, 305-237-2291. p. 422

Himelrick, Vicki, Librn, Hundred Public Library, Rte 250, Hundred, WV, 26575. Tel: 304-775-5161. p. 2404

Himmel, Jane, Dir, Pigeon District Library, 7236 Nitz St, Pigeon, MI, 48755. Tel: 989-453-2341. p. 1141

Himsel, Christian, Libr Dir, Concordia University Wisconsin, 12800 N Lake Shore Dr, Mequon, WI, 53097-2402. Tel: 262-243-4534. p. 2456

Himsel, Christian R, Dir, Libr Serv, Concordia University, 4090 Geddes Rd, Ann Arbor, MI, 48105-2797. Tel: 734-995-7454. p. 1078

Himshaw, Ashley, Librn, New York Academy of Art Library, 111 Franklin St, New York, NY, 10013-2911. Tel: 212-966-0300. p. 1593

Himze, Sandy, Co-Librn, Waubay Public Library, 94 N Main St, Waubay, SD, 57273. Tel: 605-947-4748. p. 2085

Hinchcliff, Marilou Z, Coordr, Cat, Bloomsburg University of Pennsylvania, 400 E Second St, Bloomsburg, PA, 17815-1301. Tel: 570-389-4205. p. 1913

Hinchee, Margaret, Libr Dir, Clovis-Carver Public Library, 701 N Main, Clovis, NM, 88101. Tel: 505-769-7840. p. 1465

Hinchen, Daniel, Tech & Syst Librn, Massachusetts Historical Society Library, 1154 Boylston St, Boston, MA, 02215. Tel: 617-646-0571. p. 997

Hinckley, Steven, Assoc Dean, Libr & Info Serv, Dir, Law Libr, Pennsylvania State University - Dickinson School of Law, 214 Lewis Katz Bldg, University Park, PA, 16802. Tel: 814-867-0390. p. 2015

Hinderliter, Alison, Curator, Modern MS, Newberry Library, 60 W Walton St, Chicago, IL, 60610-3305. Tel: 312-255-3694. p. 565

Hinderliter, Eric, Dir, Jay County Public Library, 315 N Ship St, Portland, IN, 47371. Tel: 260-726-7890. p. 714

Hinderliter, Lori, Exec Dir, Butler Area Public Library, 218 N McKean St, Butler, PA, 16001. Tel: 724-287-1715. p. 1917

Hinderliter, Lori, Adminr, Butler County Federated Library System, 218 N McKean St, Butler, PA, 16001. Tel: 724-283-1880. p. 1917

Hindle, Amy, Ch, Abington Public Library, 600 Gliniewicz Way, Abington, MA, 02351. Tel: 781-982-2139. p. 983

Hindman, Beth, Branch Experience Mgr, Evansville Vanderburgh Public Library, Red Bank, 120 S Red Bank Rd, Evansville, IN, 47712. Tel: 812-428-8205. p. 681

Hindman, Brette, Mrs, Dir, Seymour Mary E Memorial Free Library, Cassadaga Branch, 18 Maple Ave, Cassadaga, NY, 14718. Tel: 716-595-3323. p. 1646

Hinds, Stuart, Assoc Dean, Coll, University of Missouri-Kansas City Libraries, 800 E 51st St, Kansas City, MO, 64110. Tel: 816-235-1532. p. 1257

Hinds, Susan, Circ, Reserves, Auburn University, Ralph Brown Draughon Library, 231 Mell St, Auburn, AL, 36849. Tel: 334-844-1579. p. 6

Hindulak, Abby, Coll Develop Librn, Ella M Everhard Public Library, 132 Broad St, Wadsworth, OH, 44281-1897. Tel: 330-334-5761. p. 1827

Hine, Rebecca, Br Supvr, Wellington County Library, Fergus Branch, 190 St Andrew St W, Fergus, ON, N1M 1N5, CANADA. Tel: 519-843-1180. p. 2641

Hine, Rebecca, Chief Librn, Wellington County Library, 190 Saint Andrews St W, Fergus, ON, N1M 1N5, CANADA. Tel: 519-787-7805. p. 2641

Hine, Rebecca, Chief Librn, Wellington County Library, Arthur Branch, 110 Charles St E, Arthur, ON, N0G 1A0, CANADA. Tel: 519-848-3999. p. 2641

Hine, Rebecca, Chief Librn, Wellington County Library, Clifford Branch, Seven Brown St N, Clifford, ON, N0G 1M0, CANADA. Tel: 519-327-8328. p. 2641

Hine, Rebecca, Chief Librn, Wellington County Library, Harriston Branch, 88 Mill St, Harriston, ON, N0G 1Z0, CANADA. Tel: 519-338-2396. p. 2641

Hine, Rebecca, Chief Librn, Wellington County Library, Mount Forest Branch, 118 Main St N, Mount Forest, ON, N0G 2L0, CANADA. Tel: 519-323-4541. p. 2641

Hine, Rebecca, Chief Librn, Wellington County Library, Rockwood Branch, 121 Rockmosa Dr, Rockwood, ON, N0B 2K0, CANADA. Tel: 519-856-4851. p. 2641

Hineman, Lindsey, Ch Mgr, Converse County Library, 300 E Walnut St, Douglas, WY, 82633. Tel: 307-358-3644. p. 2494

Hiner, Sara, Br Dir, Settlement Music School, Germantown Library, 6128 Germantown Ave, Philadelphia, PA, 19144. Tel: 215-320-2610. p. 1986

Hines, Brandon, Libr Dir, Hays Public Library, 1205 Main, Hays, KS, 67601-3693. Tel: 785-625-9014. p. 812

Hines, Elijah, Digital Navigator Coord, Glenwood-Lynwood Public Library District, 19901 Stony Island Ave, Lynwood, IL, 60411. Tel: 708-758-0090. p. 611

Hines, Judy, LRC Supvr, Sandhills Community College, 3395 Airport Rd, Pinehurst, NC, 28374. Tel: 910-695-3890. p. 1707

Hines, Linda, Acq Tech, Wharton County Junior College, 911 Boling Hwy, Wharton, TX, 77488-3298. Tel: 979-532-6446. p. 2256

Hines, M'lyn, Dir, Libr Serv, Quinebaug Valley Community College Library, 742 Upper Maple St, Danielson, CT, 06239. Tel: 860-932-4131. p. 308

Hines, Scott, Dir, Acad Tech, Univ Librn, Palo Alto University, 1791 Arastradero Rd, Palo Alto, CA, 94304. Tel: 650-433-3808. p. 192

Hines, Tammy, Head, Coll, Head, Info Serv, Longwood University, Redford & Race St, Farmville, VA, 23909. Tel: 434-395-2444. p. 2318

Hines, Thomas Collier, Curator, Exec Dir, South Union Shaker Village, 850 Shaker Museum Rd, Auburn, KY, 42206. Tel: 270-542-4167. p. 848

Hines-Mayo, Lindsey, Br Mgr, Tangipahoa Parish Library, Independence Branch, 290 S Pine St, Independence, LA, 70443. Tel: 985-878-2970. p. 881

Hing, Valerie, Library Contact, Nogales-Santa Cruz County Public Library, Sonoita Community Library, County Complex Bldg, 3147 State Rte 83, Sonoita, AZ, 85637. Tel: 520-455-5517. p. 67

Hingst-Sims, Kristine, Asst Librn, Plainview Public Library, 209 N Pine St, Plainview, NE, 68769. Tel: 402-582-4507. p. 1333

Hiniker, Alexis, Dr, Assoc Prof, Prog Chair, University of Washington, Mary Gates Hall, Ste 370, Campus Box 352840, Seattle, WA, 98195-2840. Tel: 206-543-1794. p. 2794

Hink, Betty Jean, Dir, Greenwood Reading Center, Greenwood Town Hall, 2696 Main St, SR 248, Greenwood, NY, 14839. Tel: 607-225-4553. p. 1542

Hinkle, Deborah, Libr Dir, Uxbridge Free Public Library, 15 N Main St, Uxbridge, MA, 01569-1822. Tel: 508-278-8624. p. 1060

Hinkle, Debra, Dir, Fitchburg Public Library, 610 Main St, Fitchburg, MA, 01420-3146. Tel: 978-829-1780. p. 1019

Hinkle, Karyn, Visual & Performing Arts Librn, University of Kentucky Libraries, Lucille Little Fine Arts Library, 160 Patterson Dr, Lexington, KY, 40506-0224. Tel: 859-257-3938. p. 863

Hinkle, Kendra, Adminr, National Park Service, 121 Monument Ave, Greeneville, TN, 37743. Tel: 423-638-3551. p. 2100

Hinkley, Cindy, Ch, Charles M Bailey Public Library, 39 Bowdoin St, Winthrop, ME, 04364. Tel: 207-377-8673. p. 947

Hinkley, Heidi Lynn, Librn, Peabody Memorial Library, 162 Main St, Jonesport, ME, 04649. Tel: 207-497-3003. p. 928

Hinman, Charles R, Dir of Educ, USS Bowfin Submarine Museum & Park Library, 11 Arizona Memorial Dr, Honolulu, HI, 96818-3145. Tel: 808-423-1341. p. 513

Hinman, Laura, Head Librn, Midland University, 900 N Clarkson, Fremont, NE, 68025. Tel: 402-941-6250. p. 1315

Hinnant, Kate, Head, Communication & Instruction, University of Wisconsin-Eau Claire, 103 Garfield Ave, Eau Claire, WI, 54701-4932. Tel: 715-836-5117. p. 2433

Hinnefeld, Suzanne, Coll Develop Librn, Saint Mary's College, Notre Dame, IN, 46556-5001. Tel: 574-284-5289. p. 711

Hinrichs, Patrick, Family Serv Librn, North Las Vegas Library District, Aliante Library, 2400 Deer Springs Way, North Las Vegas, NV, 89084. Tel: 702-839-2980. p. 1348

Hinse, Dave, Dir, Info Tech, Centre d'acces a l'information juridique/Legal Informatin Access Center, 480 Saint-Laurent, Bur 503, Montreal, QC, H2Y 3Y7, CANADA. Tel: 514-844-2245. p. 2721

Hinseth, Anne, Librn, University of South Dakota, I D Weeks Library, 414 E Clark St, Vermillion, SD, 57069. Tel: 605-658-3392. p. 2084

Hinshaw, Janet, Librn, Wilson Ornithological Society, University of Michigan Museum of Zoology, 360 Varsity Dr, Ann Arbor, MI, 48108-2228. Tel: 734-764-0457. p. 1081

Hinson, Blair, Dir, Oconee County Public Library, 501 W South Broad St, Walhalla, SC, 29691. Tel: 864-638-4133. p. 2072

Hinson, Karen, Br Mgr, Bossier Parish Libraries, Henry L Aulds Memorial Branch, 3950 Wayne Ave, Bossier City, LA, 71112. Tel: 318-742-2337. p. 886

Hinton, Amy, Librn, Southeastern Baptist College, 4229 Hwy 15 N, Laurel, MS, 39440. Tel: 601-426-6346. p. 1225

Hinton, Danielle, Dir, Oscar Foss Memorial Library, 111 S Barnstead Rd, Center Barnstead, NH, 03225. Tel: 603-269-3900. p. 1357

Hinton, Elizabeth, Dir, University of Mississippi Medical Center, 2500 N State St, Jackson, MS, 39216-4505. Tel: 601-984-1239. p. 1223

Hinton, Jeshua, Ref (Info Servs), Oakwood University, 7000 Adventist Blvd NW, Huntsville, AL, 35896. Tel: 256-726-7246. p. 22

Hinton, Martha, Br Mgr, Dixie Regional Library System, Houlka Public, 113 Hwy 32 E, Houlka, MS, 38850. Tel: 662-568-2747. p. 1230

Hinton, Robert, Dir, Adult Serv, Danville Public Library, 319 N Vermilion St, Danville, IL, 61832. Tel: 217-477-5228. p. 575

Hintz, Laura, Mgr, Superior District Library, Drummond Island Library, 29934 E Court St, Drummond Island, MI, 49726. Tel: 906-493-5243. p. 1149

Hintz, Sarah, Pub Serv Mgr, Pickaway County District Public Library, Floyd E Younkin Branch, 51 Long St, Ashville, OH, 43103. Tel: 740-983-8856. p. 1765

Hintz, Sarah, Ref Coordr, Pickaway County District Public Library, 1160 N Court St, Circleville, OH, 43113-1725. Tel: 740-477-1644, Ext 227. p. 1765

Hinze, Shana, Mgr, Miami-Dade Public Library System, 101 W Flagler St, Miami, FL, 33130-1523. Tel: 305-375-2665. p. 422

Hinze, Shana, Mgr, Miami-Dade Public Library System, Civic Center Porta Kiosk, Metrorail Civic Ctr Sta, 1501 NW 12th Ave, Miami, FL, 33136. Tel: 305-324-0291. p. 423

Hipp, Amanda, Br Mgr, Irving Public Library, South Irving Library, 601 Schulze Dr, Irving, TX, 75060. Tel: 972-721-2606. p. 2202

Hipp, Caroline, Dir of Libr Experience, Richland Library, 1431 Assembly St, Columbia, SC, 29201-3101. Tel: 803-799-9084. p. 2054

Hipp, Melissa, Staff Librn, Hoisington Public Library, 169 S Walnut, Hoisington, KS, 67544. Tel: 620-653-4128. p. 813

Hipp, Tami, Asst Librn, McLean-Mercer Regional Library, 216 Second St, Riverdale, ND, 58565. Tel: 701-654-7652. p. 1739

Hippen, Sharon, Dir, Buffalo Center Public Library, 221 N Main St, Buffalo Center, IA, 50424. Tel: 641-562-2546. p. 736

Hipps, Kathy, Libr Dir, Tusculum University, 60 Shiloh Rd, Greeneville, TN, 37743. Tel: 423-636-7320, Ext 5123. p. 2100

Hipsley, Christina J, Coll Develop Librn, Electronic Res Librn, Stevenson University Library, 1525 Greenspring Valley Rd, Stevenson, MD, 21153. Tel: 443-334-2766. p. 978

Hirning, Maryanne, Dir, Clatskanie Library District, 11 Lillich St, Clatskanie, OR, 97016. Tel: 503-728-3732. p. 1875

Hirsbrunner, Terry, Libr Tech II, Palm Beach State College, 4200 Congress Ave, Mail Sta 17, Lake Worth, FL, 33461. Tel: 561-868-3800. p. 416

Hirsch, Adria, Libr Supvr, Latham & Watkins, 885 Third Ave, Ste 1000, New York, NY, 10022. Tel: 212-906-1200. p. 1590

Hirsch, Cindy, Ref Law Librn, University of Maine School of Law, 246 Deering Ave, Portland, ME, 04102. Tel: 207-780-4830. p. 937

Hirsch, Deborah, Mgr, District of Columbia Public Library, Juanita E Thornton/Shepherd Park Neighborhood Library, 7420 Georgia Ave NW, Washington, DC, 20012. Tel: 202-541-6100. p. 364

Hirsch, Gerald, Sr Assoc Dir, State Historical Society of Missouri Library, 605 Elm St, Columbia, MO, 65201. Tel: 573-884-7906. p. 1243

Hirsch, Nakita, Dir, Hope Community Library, 216 N Main St, Hope, KS, 67451. Tel: 785-366-7219. p. 814

Hirschy, Margaret, Col Librn for Educ, The University of Findlay, 1000 N Main St, Findlay, OH, 45840-3695. Tel: 419-434-4260. p. 1785

Hirsekorn, Patricia, Circ, ILL, Rowan College of New Jersey, 1400 Tanyard Rd, Sewell, NJ, 08080. Tel: 856-415-2252. p. 1442

Hiscoe, Holly, Librn, Correctional Service of Canada, Hwy 33, Bath, ON, K0H 1G0, CANADA. Tel: 613-351-8000. p. 2630

Hisel, Melissa, Libr Dir, Lafayette Public Library, 775 W Baseline Rd, Lafayette, CO, 80026. Tel: 303-665-5200. p. 288

Hishikawa, Judy, Librn, West Burke Public Library, 123 VT Rte 5A, West Burke, VT, 05871. Tel: 201-519-3633. p. 2298

Hisken, Loree, Dir, Belle Plaine City Library, 222 W Fifth Ave, Belle Plaine, KS, 67013. Tel: 620-488-3431. p. 798

Hisle, W Lee, Librn of the Col, VPres for Info Serv, Connecticut College, 270 Mohegan Ave, New London, CT, 06320-4196. Tel: 860-439-2655. p. 328

Hisle-Chaudri, Stacy, Libr Dir, Ray County Library, 215 E Lexington St, Richmond, MO, 64085-1834. Tel: 816-776-5104. p. 1267

Hissong, Rachael, Dir, Paola Free Library, 101 E Peoria, Paola, KS, 66071. Tel: 913-259-3655. p. 830

Hitchcock, Jennifer, Youth Ref Librn, Fruitville Public Library, 100 Apex Rd, Sarasota, FL, 34240. Tel: 941-861-2500. p. 442

Hitchens, Alison, Assoc Univ Librn, Res & Digital Discovery Serv, University of Waterloo Library, 200 University Ave W, Waterloo, ON, N2L 3G1, CANADA. Tel: 519-888-4567, Ext 35980. p. 2702

Hite, Jay, Tech Coordr, McCracken County Public Library, 555 Washington St, Paducah, KY, 42003. Tel: 270-442-2510. p. 872

Hitson, Brian A, Dir, United States Department of Energy, PO Box 62, Oak Ridge, TN, 37831-0062. Tel: 865-576-1188. p. 2123

Hitt, Anisa, Youth Serv, Venice Public Library, 260 Nokomis Ave S, Venice, FL, 34285. Tel: 941-861-1336. p. 452

Hitt, Kimberly, Libr Assoc, West Virginia University, 300 Campus Dr, Rm 1332, Parkersburg, WV, 26104-8647. Tel: 304-424-8260. p. 2411

Hitt, Rachel, Dir & Head Librn, Black Creek Village Library, 507 S Maple St, Black Creek, WI, 54106-9304. Tel: 920-984-3094. p. 2424

Hitt, Rachel, Dir, Brillion Public Library, 326 N Main St, Brillion, WI, 54110. Tel: 920-756-3215. p. 2425

Hittle, Elizabeth, Dir, Snyder Public Library, 203 Ash St, Snyder, NE, 68664. Tel: 402-568-2570. p. 1336

Hittner, Jackie, Libr Serv Mgr, American Association of Orthodontists, 401 N Lindbergh Blvd, Saint Louis, MO, 63141. Tel: 314-292-6542. p. 1269

Hitzelberger, Michael, Libr Asst, Volunteer State Community College Library, 1480 Nashville Pike, Gallatin, TN, 37066-3188. Tel: 615-452-8600, Ext 2173. p. 2099

Hively, Charley, Coordr, Ref & Instrul Serv, Fairmont State University, 1201 Locust Ave, Fairmont, WV, 26554. Tel: 304-367-4617. p. 2402

Hively, Deidre, Libr Spec, Northeast Iowa Community College, 8342 NICC Dr, Peosta, IA, 52068. Tel: 563-556-5110, Ext 2224. p. 776

Hix, Cindy, Children's Coordr, Bridgeport Public Library, 3399 Williamson Rd, Bridgeport, MI, 48601. Tel: 989-777-6030. p. 1087

Hixson, Kim, Exec Dir, Yakima Valley Libraries, 102 N Third St, Yakima, WA, 98901. Tel: 509-452-8541. p. 2395

Hixson, Tyler, Asst Dir, Flint Memorial Library, 147 Park St, North Reading, MA, 01864. Tel: 978-664-4942. p. 1042

Hjelle, Sue, Asst Dir, Mary J Barnett Memorial Library, 400 Grand St, Guthrie Center, IA, 50115-1439. Tel: 641-747-8110. p. 757
Hjelm, Lisa, Asst Librn, Bath Public Library, Four W Bath Rd, Bath, NH, 03740. Tel: 603-747-3372. p. 1354
Hladik, Kathy, Dir, Zadoc Long Free Library, Five Turner St, Buckfield, ME, 04220. Tel: 207-336-2171. p. 919
Hlady, Jean, Head, Adult Serv, Head, Ref Serv, Milton Public Library, 476 Canton Ave, Milton, MA, 02186-3299. Tel: 617-698-5757. p. 1036
Hlavka, Peggy, Coordr, Ser, Siena Heights University Library, 1247 E Siena Heights Dr, Adrian, MI, 49221-1796. Tel: 517-264-7153. p. 1076
Hneiny, Layal, Health Sci Librn, University of South Dakota, Wegner Health Sciences Library, Sanford School of Medicine, 1400 W 22nd St, Ste 100, Sioux Falls, SD, 57105. Tel: 605-658-1540. p. 2084
Hnizda, Sheryl, Library Contact, Memorial Presbyterian Church, 1310 Ashman St, Midland, MI, 48640. Tel: 989-835-6759. p. 1132
Ho, Jeanette, Cat Librn, Texas A&M University Libraries, 400 Spence St, College Station, TX, 77843. p. 2157
Ho, Jenny, Dir, American Federation of State, County & Municipal Employees, 1625 L St NW, Washington, DC, 20036-5687. Tel: 202-429-1215. p. 360
Ho, Maria, Tech Serv, Tyndale University College & Seminary, 3377 Bayview Ave, Toronto, ON, M2M 3S4, CANADA. Tel: 416-226-6380. p. 2697
Ho, Michael, Dir, Admin Serv, Surrey Libraries, 10350 University Dr, Surrey, BC, V3T 4B8, CANADA. Tel: 604-598-7300. p. 2577
Ho, Pui-Ching, Mgr, County of Los Angeles Public Library, Diamond Bar Library, 21800 Copley Dr, Diamond Bar, CA, 91765-2299. Tel: 909-861-4978. p. 135
Hoadley, Deborah, Dir, Merri-Hill-Rock Library Cooperative, c/o Kimball Library, Three Academy Ave, Atkinson, NH, 03811-2299. Tel: 603-887-3428. p. 2769
Hoadley, Sue A, Dir, Westerlo Public Library, 604 State Rte 143, Westerlo, NY, 12193. Tel: 518-797-3415. p. 1663
Hoag, Wendy, IT Librn, Arizona Western College, 2020 S Ave 8E, Yuma, AZ, 85366. Tel: 928-344-7718. p. 85
Hoag, William, Libr Dir, Roxbury Community College Library, Academic Bldg, Rm 211, 1234 Columbus Ave, Boston, MA, 02120-3423. Tel: 857-701-1380. p. 999
Hoagland, Matthew, Alamance County Historic Properties Commission, 215 N Graham Hopedale Rd, Burlington, NC, 27217. Tel: 336-570-4053. p. 1676
Hoaglin, LeAnn W, Librn, Elkland Area Community Library, 110 E Parkway Ave, Elkland, PA, 16920-1311. Tel: 814-258-7576. p. 1930
Hoang, Ann D, Univ Librn, New Jersey Institute of Technology, 186 Central Ave, Newark, NJ, 07103. Tel: 973-596-3206. p. 1426
Hoang, Ha, Pub Serv Adminr, Henrico County Public Library, 1700 N Parham Rd, Henrico, VA, 23229. Tel: 804-501-1900. p. 2325
Hobbs, Charles P, Syst Librn, Compton College Library, 1111 E Artesia Blvd, Compton, CA, 90221. Tel: 310-900-1600, Ext 2179. p. 132
Hobbs, Jon, Dep Dir, Des Moines Public Library, 1000 Grand Ave, Des Moines, IA, 50309. Tel: 515-283-4102. p. 745
Hobbs, Lynn, Dir, Pendleton Community Library, 595 E Water St, Pendleton, IN, 46064-1070. Tel: 765-778-7527. p. 713
Hobbs, Stephanie, Library Contact, Turkey Public Library, 602 Lyles Ave, Turkey, TX, 79261. Tel: 806-423-1033. p. 2249
Hobensack, Mindy, Dir, Greentown Public Library, 421 S Harrison St, Greentown, IN, 46936. Tel: 765-628-3534. p. 688
Hoberecht, Toni, Tech Serv Librn, University of Oklahoma, Schusterman Ctr, 4502 E 41st St, Tulsa, OK, 74135. Tel: 918-660-3231. p. 1867
Hobgood, Jill, Mkt Librn, Outreach Librn, Saint Mary's College, Notre Dame, IN, 46556-5001. Tel: 574-284-4804. p. 711
Hoblyak, April, Librn, Rural Municipality of Argyle Public Library, 627 Elizabeth Ave, Hwy 23, Baldur, MB, R0K 0B0, CANADA. Tel: 204-535-2314. p. 2585
Hobner, Kate, Asst Librn, Baltimore County Circuit Court Library, 401 Bosley Ave, Towson, MD, 21204. Tel: 410-887-3086. p. 979
Hobson, Ken, Circ Supvr, Driftwood Public Library, 801 SW Hwy 101, Ste 201, Lincoln City, OR, 97367-2720. Tel: 541-996-2277. p. 1885
Hoch, Susan, Asst Dir, Tech Serv, Rock Hill Public Library, 9811 Manchester Rd, Rock Hill, MO, 63119. Tel: 314-962-4723. p. 1267
Hochstetler, Mardi, Circ Serv, Albany Public Library, 2450 14th Ave SE, Albany, OR, 97322. Tel: 541-917-7580. p. 1871
Hochstetler, Ruth, Day Circ Mgr, Goshen College, Harold & Wilma Good Library, 1700 S Main, Goshen, IN, 46526-4794. Tel: 574-535-7427. p. 687
Hochstetter, Adam, Mgr, Columbus Metropolitan Library, Northside Branch, 1423 N High St, Columbus, OH, 43201. p. 1773
Hock, Janice, Acq Librn, Angelo State University Library, 2025 S Johnson, San Angelo, TX, 76904-5079. Tel: 325-486-6525. p. 2235
Hockemeyer, Breea, Cataloger, Surrey Township Public Library, 105 E Michigan, Farwell, MI, 48622. Tel: 989-588-9782. p. 1104
Hockenberry, Benjamin, Systems & Subscriptions Librn, Saint John Fisher University, 3690 East Ave, Rochester, NY, 14618-3599. Tel: 585-385-8382. p. 1630
Hockenberry, Laurie, Dir, Bushnell Public Library, 455 N Dean, Bushnell, IL, 61422-1299. Tel: 309-772-2060. p. 547
Hockensmith, Joshua, Interim Head of Libr, Tech Asst, University of North Carolina at Chapel Hill, Joseph Curtis Sloane Art Library, 102 Hanes Art Ctr, CB 3405, Chapel Hill, NC, 27599-3405. Tel: 919-962-2397. p. 1679
Hocker, John, Br Mgr, Watonwan County Library, Lewisville Branch, 129 Lewis St W, Lewisville, MN, 56060. Tel: 507-435-2781. p. 1198
Hocker, John, Branch Services, Watonwan County Library, Madelia Branch, 23 First St NW, Madelia, MN, 56062. Tel: 507-642-3511. p. 1198
Hocking, Kimberly, Head, Pub Serv, Institutional Archivist, Campbell University, Norman Adrian Wiggins School of Law Library, 225 Hillsborough St, Ste 203H, Raleigh, NC, 27603. Tel: 919-865-5869. p. 1676
Hocking, Linda, Archivist, Litchfield Historical Society, Seven South St, Litchfield, CT, 06759-0385. Tel: 860-567-4501. p. 320
Hodas, Daniel, Coordr, Media Serv, Harcum College, 750 Montgomery Ave, Bryn Mawr, PA, 19010-3476. Tel: 610-526-6167. p. 1916
Hodel, Mary Anne, Dir/Chief Exec Officer, Orange County Library System, 101 E Central Blvd, Orlando, FL, 32801. Tel: 407-835-7323. p. 431
Hodgdon, Brian, Asst Dir, Salem Public Library, 370 Essex St, Salem, MA, 01970-3298. Tel: 978-744-0860. p. 1051
Hodgdon, Nadine, Librn, The Hartford Library, 1587 Maple St, Hartford, VT, 05047. Tel: 802-296-2568. p. 2285
Hodge, Bob, Dir, Berlin Public Library, 23 Carter St, Berlin, MA, 01503-1219. Tel: 978-838-2812. p. 989
Hodge, Chris, Sr Library Sys Specialist, Marshall University Libraries, One John Marshall Dr, Huntington, WV, 25755-2060. Tel: 304-696-2320. p. 2405
Hodge Harris, Erika, Head Librn, Community College of Baltimore County, Essex Library, 7201 Rossville Blvd, Baltimore, MD, 21237. Tel: 443-840-1425. p. 961
Hodge, Kerry, Tech Serv Supvr, Washington State University Libraries, 14204 NE Salmon Creek Ave, Vancouver, WA, 98686. Tel: 360-546-9684. p. 2391
Hodge, Megan, Head, Teaching & Learning Serv, Virginia Commonwealth University Libraries, 901 Park Ave, Richmond, VA, 23284. Tel: 804-827-3910. p. 2343
Hodges, Alex R, Dr, Dir & Librn, Harvard Library, Monroe C Gutman Library, 6 Appian Way, Cambridge, MA, 02138. Tel: 617-495-3453. p. 1006
Hodges, Amy, Libr Dir, Scurry County Library, 1916 23rd St, Snyder, TX, 79549-1910. Tel: 325-573-5572. p. 2244
Hodges, Ann, Dir, Spec Coll, Texas Christian University, 2913 Lowden St, TCU Box 298400, Fort Worth, TX, 76129. Tel: 817-257-7106. p. 2181
Hodges, Bonnie, Pub Serv Librn, Tarrant County College, 828 W Harwood Rd, Hurst, TX, 76054. Tel: 817-515-6626. p. 2201
Hodges, Crystal, Mgr, County of Los Angeles Public Library, Compton Library, 240 W Compton Blvd, Compton, CA, 90220-3109. Tel: 310-637-0202. p. 135
Hodges, Daniel, Br Librn, Memphis Public Library, Randolph Branch, 3752 Given Ave, Memphis, TN, 38122. Tel: 901-415-2779. p. 2114
Hodges, David, Assoc Dean of Library for Digital Initiatives, Adelphi University, One South Ave, Garden City, NY, 11530. Tel: 516-877-3531. p. 1536
Hodges, Dean, Librn, Haltom City Public Library, 4809 Haltom Rd, Haltom City, TX, 76117-3622. Tel: 817-222-7758. p. 2187
Hodges, Dracine, Univ Librn & Vice Provost for Libr Affairs, Duke University Libraries, 411 Chapel Dr, Durham, NC, 27708. Tel: 919-660-5800. p. 1684
Hodges, Galen, Dir, Jonestown Community Library, 18649 FM 1431, Ste 10A, Jonestown, TX, 78645. Tel: 512-267-7511. p. 2204
Hodges, Jill, Br Mgr, Florence Public Library, 115 W Main St, Florence, MS, 39073. Tel: 601-845-6032. p. 1216
Hodges, Kimberly, Info Serv Librn, Aurora University, 315 S Gladstone Ave, Aurora, IL, 60506-4892. Tel: 630-844-5437. p. 539
Hodges, Melinda, Dir, Buda Public Library, 405 Loop St, Bldg 100, Buda, TX, 78610. Tel: 512-295-5899. p. 2151
Hodges, Ruth A, Dr, Info Serv, Interim Dean of Libr, South Carolina State University, 300 College St NE, Orangeburg, SC, 29115. Tel: 803-536-7045. p. 2067
Hodgett, Jasmine, Ch, Essex Free Library, One Browns River Rd, Essex, VT, 05451. Tel: 802-879-0313. p. 2283
Hodgson, Elena, Librn, Shelton State Community College, Martin Campus, 9500 Old Greensboro Rd, Tuscaloosa, AL, 35405. Tel: 205-391-2285. p. 37
Hodgson, Kayla, Youth & Teen Serv Librn, North Liberty Library, 520 W Cherry St, North Liberty, IA, 52317-9797. Tel: 319-626-5784. p. 773
Hodis, Haydee, Supvr, Springfield City Library, Brightwood Branch, 359 Plainfield St, Springfield, MA, 01107. Tel: 413-263-6805. p. 1056
Hodkey, Kathy, Circ Supvr, Lorain County Community College, 1005 Abbe Rd N, North Elyria, OH, 44035-1691. Tel: 440-366-7286. p. 1810
Hodkinson, Sarah, Librn, Main Line Health, Paoli Hospital, 255 W Lancaster Ave, Paoli, PA, 19301. Tel: 484-565-1409. p. 1973
Hodo, Laura, Libr Mgr, Central Arkansas Library System, Sidney S McMath Branch, 2100 John Barrow Rd, Little Rock, AR, 72204. Tel: 501-225-0066. p. 101
Hodson, Janice, Curator, National Archives & Records Administration, Columbia Point, Boston, MA, 02125. Tel: 617-514-1600. p. 997

Hoecherl, Vickie, Br Mgr, Otsego County Library, Johannesburg Branch, 10900 East M-32, Johannesburg, MI, 49751. Tel: 989-732-3928. p. 1109
Hoecker, Marcie, Library Contact, Florida Polytechnic University Library, 4700 Research Way, Lakeland, FL, 33805. Tel: 863-874-8643. p. 417
Hoefer, Stephen, Fiscal Officer, Ramapo Catskill Library System, 619 Rte 17M, Middletown, NY, 10940-4395. Tel: 845-343-1131, Ext 223. p. 1571
Hoefgen, Moriah, Head, Patron Serv, Newport Public Library, 300 Spring St, Newport, RI, 02840. Tel: 401-847-8720. p. 2035
Hoehamer, Matt, Dir, Hull Public Library, 1408 Main St, Hull, IA, 51239. Tel: 712-439-1321. p. 759
Hoehn, Ann, Dir, Hamilton North Public Library, 209 W Brinton St, Cicero, IN, 46034. Tel: 317-984-5623. p. 675
Hoek, D J, Assoc Univ Librn, Northwestern University Libraries, 1970 Campus Dr, Evanston, IL, 60208-2300. Tel: 847-491-7658. p. 586
Hoeksema, Sarah, Access Serv Mgr, Circ, Trinity Christian College, 6601 W College Dr, Palos Heights, IL, 60463. Tel: 708-239-4796. p. 632
Hoekstra, Cheryl, Dir, Alton Public Library, 605 Tenth St, Alton, IA, 51003. Tel: 712-756-4516. p. 730
Hoekstra, Elyshia, Dir, Coopersville Area District Library, 333 Ottawa St, Coopersville, MI, 49404-1243. Tel: 616-837-6809. p. 1094
Hoekstra, Tammy, Co-Dir, Ocheyedan Public Library, 874 Main St, Ocheyedan, IA, 51354. Tel: 712-758-3352. p. 774
Hoellen, Kathy, Assoc VP, Academic Services, Daytona State College Library, Bldg 115, Rm 314, 1200 W International Speedway Blvd, Daytona Beach, FL, 32114. Tel: 386-506-4430. p. 392
Hoelscher, Tim, Librn, North Central Washington Libraries, Royal City Public Library, 136 Camelia St NW, Royal City, WA, 98357. Tel: 509-346-9281. p. 2394
Hoelter, Laura, Asst Prof, Cat & Syst Librn, The College of Saint Scholastica Library, 1200 Kenwood Ave, Duluth, MN, 55811-4199. Tel: 218-723-6141. p. 1171
Hoenig, Lisa, Dir, Ypsilanti District Library, 5577 Whittaker Rd, Ypsilanti, MI, 48197. Tel: 734-879-1300. p. 1160
Hoeppner, Athena, Discovery Serv Librn, University of Central Florida Libraries, 12701 Pegasus Dr, Orlando, FL, 32816-8030. Tel: 407-823-2564. p. 432
Hoeppner, Christine, E-Resources Librn, University of Winnipeg Library, 515 Portage Ave, Winnipeg, MB, R3B 2E9, CANADA. Tel: 204-786-9759. p. 2596
Hoerner, Kristina L, Access Serv Mgr, Champaign Public Library, 200 W Green St, Champaign, IL, 61820-5193. Tel: 217-403-2000. p. 551
Hoesman, Pam, Libr Dir, Birchard Public Library of Sandusky County, 423 Croghan St, Fremont, OH, 43420. Tel: 419-334-7101. p. 1786
Hoey, Agnes, Br Librn, Canton Free Library, Eight Park St, Canton, NY, 13617. Tel: 315-386-3712. p. 1513
Hoey, Agnes, Libr Mgr, Canton Free Library, Morley Branch, 7230 County Rte 27, Canton, NY, 13617. Tel: 315-379-0066. p. 1513
Hoey, Agnes, Libr Mgr, Canton Free Library, Rensselaer Falls Branch, 212 Rensselaer St, Rensselaer Falls, NY, 13680. Tel: 315-344-4155. p. 1513
Hof-Mahoney, Kassidy, Library Liaison, Florida Agricultural & Mechanical University Libraries, Florida State University College of Engineering Library, 2525 Potsdamer St, Tallahassee, FL, 32306. Tel: 850-410-6328. p. 446
Hofer, Darlene, Libr Mgr, The Town of Fort Macleod Library, 264 24th St, Fort Macleod, AB, T0L 0Z0, CANADA. Tel: 403-553-3880. p. 2540
Hofer, Hanna, Pub Relations, Canby Public Library, 220 NE Second Ave, Canby, OR, 97013-3732. Tel: 503-266-3394. p. 1875
Hofer, Jayna, Asst Librn, Dumont Community Library, 602 Second St, Dumont, IA, 50625. Tel: 641-857-3304. p. 749
Hofer, Shannon, Circ/Acq, ILL, Mayville State University, 330 Third St NE, Mayville, ND, 58257. Tel: 701-788-4815. p. 1738
Hoff, Andrea, Univ Archivist, University of California, Riverside, Special Collections & University Archives, 900 University Ave, Riverside, CA, 92521. Tel: 951-827-3233. p. 203
Hoff, Ellen, Tech Serv Librn, Dakota State University, 820 N Washington Ave, Madison, SD, 57042. Tel: 605-256-5203. p. 2078
Hoff, Laura, Mgr, Association for Research & Enlightenment, 215 67th St, Virginia Beach, VA, 23451. Tel: 757-457-7223. p. 2349
Hoff, Linda, Library Contact, Imperial County Free Library, Calipatria Branch, 105 S Lake, Calipatria, CA, 92233. Tel: 760-348-2630. p. 140
Hoff, Lisa, Dept Chair, Onondaga Community College, 4585 W Seneca Tpk, Syracuse, NY, 13215-4585. Tel: 315-498-2340. p. 1649
Hoffarth, Kristi, Dir, Lakota City Library, 116 B Ave W, Lakota, ND, 58344. Tel: 701-247-2543. p. 1737
Hoffler, Katy, Campus Librn, Wake Technical Community College, Western Wake Library, Millpond Village, Ste 200, 3434 Kildaire Farms Rd, Cary, NC, 27518-2277. Tel: 919-866-5721. p. 1711
Hoffman, A P, Dir, Wallace Community College, 1141 Wallace Dr, Dothan, AL, 36303. Tel: 334-556-2217. p. 15
Hoffman, A P, Dir, Wallace Community College, 3235 S Eufaula Ave, Eufaula, AL, 36027-3542. Tel: 334-687-3543, Ext 4203. p. 16
Hoffman, Alexandra, Acq Librn, State University of New York, College of Technology, Upper College Dr, Alfred, NY, 14802. Tel: 607-587-4313. p. 1485
Hoffman, Alicia, Dir of Libr, Carl Albert State College, 1507 S McKenna, Poteau, OK, 74953. Tel: 918-647-1310. p. 1860
Hoffman, Alison, Database Mgt Librn, Monarch Library System, 4632 S Taylor Dr, Sheboygan, WI, 53081-1107. Tel: 920-208-4900, Ext 314. p. 2477
Hoffman, Amy, Dir, Ohio County Public Library, 503 Second St, Rising Sun, IN, 47040-1022. Tel: 812-438-2257. p. 715
Hoffman, Andrea, Colls Mgr, Wisconsin Department of Veterans Affairs, 30 W Mifflin St, Ste 300, Madison, WI, 53703. Tel: 608-800-6957. p. 2452
Hoffman, Anita, Archivist, Frederick County Historical Society, 24 E Church St, Frederick, MD, 21701. Tel: 301-663-1188. p. 966
Hoffman, Anne Marie, Head, Circ Serv, Mastics-Moriches-Shirley Community Library, 407 William Floyd Pkwy, Shirley, NY, 11967. Tel: 631-399-1511. p. 1640
Hoffman, Ashley, Interim Dir, Instrul Serv, Res, Kennesaw State University Library System, 385 Cobb Ave NW, MD 1701, Kennesaw, GA, 30144. Tel: 470-578-2735. p. 483
Hoffman, Barbara, Circ, Lehigh Carbon Community College Library, 4750 Orchard Rd, Schnecksville, PA, 18078. Tel: 610-799-1150. p. 2003
Hoffman, Brigid, Librn, South Dakota Supreme Court, 500 E Capitol Ave, Pierre, SD, 57501. Tel: 605-773-4898. p. 2081
Hoffman, Bryn, Dir, Cobleigh Public Library, 14 Depot St, Lyndonville, VT, 05851. Tel: 802-626-5475. p. 2288
Hoffman, Cheryl, Dir, Spies Public Library, 940 First St, Menominee, MI, 49858-3296. Tel: 906-863-2900. p. 1131
Hoffman, Claire, Br Mgr, Warren-Trumbull County Public Library, Liberty, 415 Churchill-Hubbard Rd, Youngstown, OH, 44505. Tel: 330-759-2589. p. 1828
Hoffman, Cyndi, Dir, Fluvanna County Public Library, 214 Commons Blvd, Palmyra, VA, 22963. Tel: 434-589-1400. p. 2336
Hoffman, Geneva, Youth Serv, Grant County Public Library District, 201 Barnes Rd, Williamstown, KY, 41097-9482. Tel: 859-824-2080. p. 877
Hoffman, Grace, Librn, Belmont County Law Library, Court House, 101 W Main St, Saint Clairsville, OH, 43950. Tel: 740-695-2121, Ext 1053. p. 1818
Hoffman, Halle, Librn, Odin, Feldman & Pittleman Library, 1775 Weihle Ave, Ste 400, Reston, VA, 20190. Tel: 703-218-2362. p. 2339
Hoffman, Jana, Ch Serv, Ledding Library of Milwaukie, 10660 SE 21st Ave, Milwaukie, OR, 97222. Tel: 503-786-7585. p. 1887
Hoffman, Katie, Ch Serv, White Cloud Community Library, 1038 Wilcox Ave, White Cloud, MI, 49349. Tel: 231-689-6631. p. 1159
Hoffman, Katie, Librn, Bedford Public Library System, 321 N Bridge St, Bedford, VA, 24523-1924. Tel: 540-586-8911, Ext 1110. p. 2306
Hoffman, Kimberly, Sci & Tech Librn, Team Leader, George Mason University Libraries, Mercer Library, Science & Technology Campus, 10900 University Blvd, MSN 4E6, Occoquan Bldg, Rm 104, Manassas, VA, 20110. Tel: 703-993-8344. p. 2317
Hoffman, Linda, Libr Dir, Alfred H Baumann Free Public Library, Seven Brophy Lane, Woodland Park, NJ, 07424-2733. Tel: 973-345-8120. p. 1456
Hoffman, Lisa, Supv Librn, Adult Serv, Bloomfield Public Library, 90 Broad St, Bloomfield, NJ, 07003. Tel: 973-566-6200. p. 1391
Hoffman, Lisa, Dir, Rochelle Park Library, 151 W Passaic St, Rochelle Park, NJ, 07662. Tel: 201-379-7128. p. 1440
Hoffman, Lynn, Dir, Operations, Somerset County Library System of New Jersey, One Vogt Dr, Bridgewater, NJ, 08807-2136. Tel: 908-458-4940. p. 1392
Hoffman, Maggie, Archivist, Jewish Museum of Maryland, 15 Lloyd St, Baltimore, MD, 21202. Tel: 410-732-6400. p. 953
Hoffman, Mallory C, Exec Dir, Exeter Community Library, 4569 Prestwick Dr, Reading, PA, 19606. Tel: 610-406-9431. p. 2000
Hoffman, Marci, Assoc Dir, University of California, Berkeley, Law, Berkley Law South Addition, 2nd Flr, 2778 Bancroff Way, Berkeley, CA, 94720. Tel: 510-642-0621. p. 123
Hoffman, Mary, Assoc State Dir for Strategic Planning & Org Development, NYS Small Business Development Center Research Network, Ten N Pearl St, Albany, NY, 12246. Tel: 518-944-2840. p. 1483
Hoffman, Meghan, Cat Librn, Boynton Beach City Library, 115 N Federal Hwy, Boynton Beach, FL, 33435. Tel: 561-742-6390. p. 386
Hoffman, Michael, Mgr, Libr Serv, Torys Law Library, 1114 Avenue of the Americas, 23 Flr, New York, NY, 10036. Tel: 212-880-6000. p. 1602
Hoffman, Michelle, Libr Dir, New Lebanon Library, 550 State Rte 20, New Lebanon, NY, 12125. Tel: 518-794-8844. p. 1576
Hoffman, Monica, Literacy Prog Mgr, Umatilla County Special Library District, 425 S Main St, Pendleton, OR, 97801. Tel: 541-612-2052. p. 1890
Hoffman, Nadine, Law Librn, University of Calgary Library, Bennett Jones Law Library, Murray Fraser Hall 2340, 2500 University Dr NW, Calgary, AB, T2N 1N4, CANADA. Tel: 403-220-8392. p. 2529

Hoffman, Nancy, Asst Dir, Robert W Barlow Memorial Library, 921 Washington Ave, Iowa Falls, IA, 50126. Tel: 641-648-2872. p. 761
Hoffman, Philip, Library Contact, Pryor, Cashman LLP, Seven Times Sq, New York, NY, 10036. Tel: 212-421-4100. p. 1600
Hoffman, Rebecca, Librn, Carnegie-Schuyler Library, 303 E Second St, Pana, IL, 62557. Tel: 217-562-2326. p. 632
Hoffman, Renee, Info Serv Librn, Saint Francis University, 106 Franciscan Way, Loretto, PA, 15940. Tel: 814-472-3152. p. 1957
Hoffman, Susan, Head, Children's Servx, Newmarket Public Library, 438 Park Ave, Newmarket, ON, L3Y 1W1, CANADA. Tel: 905-953-5110. p. 2660
Hoffman, Thom, Archivist, Oyster Bay Historical Society Library, 20 Summit St, Oyster Bay, NY, 11771. Tel: 516-922-5032. p. 1614
Hoffman, Wendy, Circ Serv Mgr, Three Rivers Public Library District, 25207 W Channon Dr, Channahon, IL, 60410-5028. Tel: 815-467-6200, Ext 305. p. 552
Hoffmann, Carla, Libr Supvr, Briercrest College & Seminary, 510 College Dr, Caronport, SK, S0H 0S0, CANADA. Tel: 306-756-3252. p. 2741
Hoffmann, Diane, Librn, Leeds Public Library, 221 Main St W, Leeds, ND, 58346. Tel: 701-466-2930. p. 1737
Hoffmann, Kathy, Library Contact, Mercy Medical Center, 250 Mercy Dr, Dubuque, IA, 52001. Tel: 563-589-8020. p. 749
Hoffmann, Lisa, Head, Circ, Keene Public Library, 60 Winter St, Keene, NH, 03431. Tel: 603-352-0157. p. 1369
Hoffmann, Thomas E, Librn, Kalmbach Media, 21027 Crossroads Circle, Waukesha, WI, 53186. Tel: 262-798-6602. p. 2484
Hoffmeier, Amy, Dir, Schleswig Public Library, 202 Cedar St, Schleswig, IA, 51461-0306. Tel: 712-676-3470. p. 781
Hoffner, Courtney, Librn, University of California Los Angeles Library, Science & Engineering Libraries, 8270 Boelter Hall, Los Angeles, CA, 90095. Tel: 310-825-0190. p. 169
Hoffpauir, Georgia V, Spec Coll, Quitman Public Library, 202 E Goode St, Quitman, TX, 75783-2533. Tel: 903-763-4191. p. 2230
Hofmann, Joanne, Librn, Chinook Regional Library, Shaunavon Branch, Grand Coteau Heritage & Cultural Ctr, 440 Centre St, Shaunavon, SK, S0N 2M0, CANADA. Tel: 306-297-3844. p. 2752
Hofmann, Katara, Outreach & Events Coord, Virginia's Academic Library Consortium, George Mason University, 4400 University Dr, Fenwick 5100, Fairfax, VA, 22030. Tel: 703-993-4654. p. 2776
Hofstee, Sharon, Librn, Christian Reformed Church Library, 100 Church Ave, New Holland, SD, 57364. Tel: 605-243-2346. p. 2080
Hofstetter, Lydia, Head Cataloger, United States Naval War College Library, 686 Cushing Rd, Newport, RI, 02841-1207. Tel: 401-841-6506. p. 2035
Hogan, Debbie, Libr Mgr, Worthington Libraries, 820 High St, Worthington, OH, 43085. Tel: 614-807-2622. p. 1834
Hogan, Debbie, Libr Mgr, Worthington Libraries, Northwest Library, 2280 Hard Rd, Columbus, OH, 43235. Tel: 614-807-2622. p. 1834
Hogan, Denise, Cataloger, Warren County-Vicksburg Public Library, 700 Veto St, Vicksburg, MS, 39180-3595. Tel: 601-636-6411. p. 1235
Hogan, Diane, Electronic Serv, Head, Ref, East Greenwich Free Library, 82 Peirce St, East Greenwich, RI, 02818. Tel: 401-884-9510. p. 2031
Hogan, Elizabeth, Head, Adult Serv, Glen Cove Public Library, Four Glen Cove Ave, Glen Cove, NY, 11542-2885. Tel: 516-676-2130. p. 1538
Hogan, Gina, Dr, Dean, Citrus College, 1000 W Foothill Blvd, Glendora, CA, 91741-1899. Tel: 626-914-8640. p. 149
Hogan, Kellye, Dir, Beene-Pearson Public Library, 208 Elm Ave, South Pittsburg, TN, 37380-1312. Tel: 423-837-6513. p. 2127
Hogan, Laura, Res & Instruction Librn, Bristol Community College, Attleboro Campus, 11 Field Rd, Rm 107, Attleboro, MA, 02703. Tel: 774-357-3809. p. 1017
Hogan, Lisa, Tech Serv Librn, Palm Beach State College, 3160 PGA Blvd, Palm Beach Gardens, FL, 33410-2893. Tel: 561-207-5800. p. 434
Hogan, Mary, Dir, Cora J Belden Library, 33 Church St, Rocky Hill, CT, 06067-1568. Tel: 860-258-7621. p. 335
Hogan, Matthew, Exec Dir, Akin Free Library, 378 Old Quaker Hill Rd, Pawling, NY, 12564-3411. Tel: 845-326-6168. p. 1616
Hogan, Michael R, Curator, Portsmouth Naval Shipyard Museum, Two High St, Portsmouth, VA, 23704. Tel: 757-393-8983, Ext 10. p. 2338
Hogan, Sarah, Libr & Archives Mgr, National Association of Realtors, 430 N Michigan Ave, Chicago, IL, 60611-4087. Tel: 312-329-8577. p. 565
Hogan, Sarah, Head, Circ, Wayland Free Public Library, Five Concord Rd, Wayland, MA, 01778. Tel: 508-358-2311. p. 1063
Hogan, Sean, Asst Dir, Access Services & Facilities, University of Baltimore, 1420 Maryland Ave, Baltimore, MD, 21201. Tel: 410-837-4283. p. 957
Hogan, Stephanie, Tech Serv, Goodnight Memorial Public Library, 203 S Main St, Franklin, KY, 42134. Tel: 270-586-8397. p. 856
Hogan, Tabitha, Dir, Winfield Public Library, 605 College St, Winfield, KS, 67156-3199. Tel: 620-221-4470. p. 845
Hogan-Vidal, Pat, Asst Prof, Libr Sci, Tech Serv Librn, Valparaiso University, 1410 Chapel Dr, Valparaiso, IN, 46383-6493. Tel: 219-464-6128. p. 723
Hogans, Debra, Library Contact, Walton County Public Library System, North Walton County - Gladys N Milton Memorial, 261 Flowersview Rd, Laurel Hill, FL, 32567. Tel: 850-834-5383. p. 393
Hogben, Ben, Mgr, Access Serv, Ithaca College Library, 953 Danby Rd, Ithaca, NY, 14850-7060. Tel: 607-274-1689. p. 1552
Hoge, Theresa, Head, Circ Serv, Whitefish Bay Public Library, 5420 N Marlborough Dr, Whitefish Bay, WI, 53217. Tel: 414-964-4380. p. 2488
Hogenboom, Janice, Admin Librn, Tech Serv/Ref Librn, Patterson Library, 40 S Portage St, Westfield, NY, 14787. Tel: 716-326-2154. p. 1664
Hogg, Charles, Mgr, Tech Serv, British Columbia Legislative Library, Parliament Bldgs, Victoria, BC, V8V 1X4, CANADA. Tel: 250-387-6505. p. 2582
Hogg, David S, Dir, Libr Serv, Phoenix Seminary Library, 7901 E Shea Blvd, Scottsdale, AZ, 85260. Tel: 602-429-4974. p. 77
Hoglund, Bethany, Dep Dir, Bellingham Public Library, 210 Central Ave, Bellingham, WA, 98225. Tel: 360-778-7263. p. 2358
Hoglund, Janna, Br Mgr, Harris County Public Library, Lone Star College-Tomball Community Library, 30555 Tomball Pkwy, Tomball, TX, 77375. Tel: 832-559-4200. p. 2193
Hogsett, Christopher, Br Mgr, Indianapolis Public Library, Pike, 6525 Zionsville Rd, Indianapolis, IN, 46268-2352. Tel: 317-275-4480. p. 696
Hogue, Amy, Libr Dir, Parma Public Library, Seven West Ave, Hilton, NY, 14468-1214. Tel: 585-392-8350. p. 1547
Hogue, Edwina, Asst Librn, East Mississippi Community College, Golden Triangle Campus Library, 8731 S Frontage Rd, Mayhew, MS, 39753. Tel: 662-243-1914. p. 1232
Hogue, Kathy, Archivist, Fresno City & County Historical Society Archives, 7160 W Kearney Blvd, Fresno, CA, 93706. Tel: 559-441-0862. p. 144
Hogue, Laurie, Asst Dir, Yorktown Public Library, 8920 W Adaline St, Yorktown, IN, 47396. Tel: 765-759-9723. p. 727
Hohenstein, Jenny, Res Serv Mgr, Jenkins Law Library, Ten Penn Ctr, 1801 Market St, Ste 900, Philadelphia, PA, 19103-6405. Tel: 215-574-7941. p. 1982
Hohertz, Cherie, Dean, Univ Libr, Res, University of Dallas, 1845 E Northgate Dr, Irving, TX, 75062-4736. Tel: 972-721-5328. p. 2203
Hohl, Cindy, Director, Policy Analysis, Kansas City Public Library, Lucile H Bluford Branch, 3050 Prospect Ave, Kansas City, MO, 64128. Tel: 816-701-3482. p. 1255
Hohl, Sukey, Exec Dir, Sublette County Libraries, 155 S Tyler Ave, Pinedale, WY, 82941. Tel: 307-367-4114. p. 2497
Hohlbein, Mary, Br Head, Mackinaw Area Public Library, Bliss Branch, 265 Sturgeon Bay Trail, Levering, MI, 49755. Tel: 231-537-2927. p. 1128
Hohlfeld, Katrina, Head, Teen Serv, Valley Cottage Free Library, 110 Rte 303, Valley Cottage, NY, 10989. Tel: 845-268-7700, Ext 136. p. 1656
Hohmeister, Cay, Dir, LeRoy Collins Leon County Public Library System, 200 W Park Ave, Tallahassee, FL, 32301-7720. Tel: 850-606-2665. p. 445
Hohner, Michael, Head, Coll, University of Winnipeg Library, 515 Portage Ave, Winnipeg, MB, R3B 2E9, CANADA. Tel: 204-786-9801. p. 2596
Hoiem, Elizabeth, Assoc Prof, University of Illinois at Urbana-Champaign, Library & Information Science Bldg, 501 E Daniel St, Champaign, IL, 61820-6211. Tel: 217-333-3280. p. 2784
Hoimes, Jaclyn, Head, Youth Serv, Parkland Community Library, 4422 Walbert Ave, Allentown, PA, 18104. Tel: 610-398-1361. p. 1905
Hoins, Denise, Dir, Sumner Public Library, 206 N Railroad St, Sumner, IA, 50674. Tel: 563-578-3324. p. 785
Hoisington, Julia, Pub Serv Librn, Baxter Memorial Library, 71 South St, Gorham, ME, 04038. Tel: 207-222-1190. p. 926
Hokanson, Ann, Exec Dir, Traverse Des Sioux Library Cooperative, 1400 Madison Ave, Ste 622, Mankato, MN, 56001-5488. Tel: 833-837-5422. p. 1181
Hoke, Tamara, Dir, Jay-Niles Memorial Library, 983 Main St, North Jay, ME, 04262. Tel: 207-645-4062. p. 933
Holberg, John, Dir, Libr Serv, Covenant College, 14049 Scenic Hwy, Lookout Mountain, GA, 30750. Tel: 706-419-1430. p. 486
Holbert, Diane, Librn, Baldwinsville Public Library, 33 E Genesee St, Baldwinsville, NY, 13027-2575. Tel: 315-635-5631. p. 1490
Holbert, Gentry L, Dir, Spring Hill College, 4000 Dauphin St, Mobile, AL, 36608. Tel: 251-380-3870. p. 26
Holbrook, Allison, Br Mgr, Cecil County Public Library, Chesapeake City Branch, 2527 Augustine Herman Hwy, Chesapeake City, MD, 21915. Tel: 410-996-1134. p. 964
Holbrook, Andrea, Libr Dir, Guilford Smith Memorial Library, 17 Main St, South Windham, CT, 06266-1121. Tel: 860-423-5159. p. 337
Holbrook, Lindsay, Br Mgr, Chicago Public Library, Jeffery Manor, 2401 E 100th St, Chicago, IL, 60617. Tel: 312-747-6479. p. 556
Holbrook, Susan, Exec Dir, Historical Association of Catawba County, 30 N College Ave, Newton, NC, 28658. Tel: 828-465-0383, Ext 304. p. 1706
Holcomb, Amy, Mgr, Learning Experience, Skokie Public Library, 5215 Oakton St, Skokie, IL, 60077-3680. Tel: 847-673-7774. p. 647
Holcomb, JoLynn, Br Mgr, Chesapeake Public Library, Russell Memorial, 2808 Taylor Rd, Chesapeake, VA, 23321-2210. Tel: 757-410-7028. p. 2311

Holcomb, Linda, Computer Lab Tech, Ivy Tech Community College-Northwest, 130 W 35th Ave, Gary, IN, 46408. Tel: 219-981-4410. p. 687
Holdaway, Loyette, Librn, Emery County Library System, Cleveland Branch, 45 W Main, Cleveland, UT, 84518. Tel: 435-653-2204. p. 2261
Holden, Christopher, Asst Music Librn, East Carolina University, Music Library, A J Fletcher Music Ctr, Rm A110, Greenville, NC, 27858. Tel: 252-328-1241. p. 1694
Holden, David, Innovations Mgr, Tech Mgr, Michigan Technological University, 1400 Townsend Dr, Houghton, MI, 49931-1295. Tel: 906-487-1482. p. 1116
Holden, Gwendolyn, Law Librn, District of Columbia Department of Corrections, 1901 D St SE, Washington, DC, 20003. Tel: 202-790-6622. p. 363
Holden, Irina, Info Literacy Librn, Outreach & Instruction Librn, University at Albany, State University of New York, Science Library, 1400 Washington Ave, Albany, NY, 12222. Tel: 518-437-3948. p. 1484
Holden, Jesse, Program Mgr, Share Content, Orbis Cascade Alliance, PO Box 6007, Portland, OR, 97228. Tel: 541-246-2470. p. 2773
Holden, Judy, Librn, Township of Sioux Narrows-Nestor Falls, Municipal Office Bldg, 5NF Airport Rd, Sioux Narrows, ON, P0X 1N0, CANADA. Tel: 807-484-2777. p. 2678
Holden, Julie, Asst Dir, Cranston Public Library, 140 Sockanosset Cross Rd, Cranston, RI, 02920-5539. Tel: 401-943-9080. p. 2031
Holden, Julie, Asst Dir, Cranston Public Library, Arlington Branch, 1064 Cranston St, Cranston, RI, 02920-7344. Tel: 401-944-1662. p. 2031
Holden, Laura, Head, Spec Coll, Anderson County Library, 300 N McDuffie St, Anderson, SC, 29621-5643. Tel: 864-260-4500. p. 2046
Holden, Lora, Dir, Ogden Rose Public Library, 103 W Main St, Ogden, IL, 61859. Tel: 217-582-2411. p. 629
Holden, Rachel, Adult Serv, ILL, Raymond Village Library, Three Meadow Rd, Raymond, ME, 04071-6461. Tel: 207-655-4283. p. 938
Holden, Rachel, Ch Serv, Rockingham County Public Library, 527 Boone Rd, Eden, NC, 27288. Tel: 336-627-1106. p. 1686
Holden, Renee, Head, Adult Serv, Auburn Hills Public Library, 3400 E Seyburn Dr, Auburn Hills, MI, 48326-2759. Tel: 248-370-9466. p. 1081
Holden, Stephanie, Ref Librn, Greenwood County Library, 600 S Main St, Greenwood, SC, 29646. Tel: 864-941-4650. p. 2062
Holder, Angela, Br Mgr, Jackson Parish Library, 614 S Polk Ave, Jonesboro, LA, 71251-3442. Tel: 318-259-5697, 318-259-5698. p. 892
Holder, Nell, Libr Assoc, Desoto Parish Library, Stonewall Branch, 808 Hwy 171, Stonewall, LA, 71078. Tel: 318-925-9191. p. 896
Holderbaum, Linda, Exec Dir, Art Center of Battle Creek Library, 265 E Emmett St, Battle Creek, MI, 49017. Tel: 269-962-9511. p. 1083
Holderby, Virginia, Coll Access, Libr Assoc, Marshall University Libraries, One John Marshall Dr, Huntington, WV, 25755-2060. Tel: 304-696-2320. p. 2405
Holderfield, Ann, Archit/Art Librn, Dir, Clemson University Libraries, Gunnin Architecture Library, 2-112 Lee Hall, Clemson University, Clemson, SC, 29634. Tel: 864-656-3933. p. 2052
Holderied, Anthony, Dir, Environmental Protection Agency Library, 109 Alexander Dr, Rm C261, Research Triangle Park, NC, 27711. Tel: 919-541-2777. p. 1712
Holderness, J B, Libr Syst Adminr, Yeshiva University Libraries, 2520 Amsterdam Ave, New York, NY, 10033. Tel: 646-592-4107. p. 1604
Hole, Heather, Prof, Simmons University, 300 The Fenway, Boston, MA, 02115. Tel: 617-521-2800. p. 2786
Holehan, Tom, Pub Relations, Stratford Library Association, 2203 Main St, Stratford, CT, 06615. Tel: 203-385-4162. p. 340
Holguin, Martha, Br Mgr, El Paso Public Library, Clardy Fox Branch, 5515 Robert Alva Ave, El Paso, TX, 79905. Tel: 915-212-0456. p. 2174
Holguin, Stacy, Ch, Balch Springs Library-Learning Center, 12450 Elam Rd, Balch Springs, TX, 75180. Tel: 972-913-3000. p. 2144
Holiday, Chip, Br Mgr, Memphis Public Library, Bartlett Branch, 5884 Stage Rd, Bartlett, TN, 38134. Tel: 901-386-8968. p. 2113
Holidman, Byron, Asst Librn, Pub Serv, Quincy University, 1800 College Ave, Quincy, IL, 62301-2699. Tel: 217-228-5348, Ext 3802. p. 638
Holifield, Linda, Exec Dir, Congregation Shalom, 7630 N Santa Monica Blvd, Milwaukee, WI, 53217. Tel: 414-352-9288. p. 2458
Holifield, Nicole, Dir, Tonganoxie Public Library, 303 S Bury St, Tonganoxie, KS, 66086. Tel: 913-845-3281. p. 838
Holiman, Irene, Libr Spec, California Botanic Garden Library, 1500 N College Ave, Claremont, CA, 91711. Tel: 909-625-8767, Ext 210. p. 130
Holinski, Tina, Commun Libr Mgr, Queens Library, North Hills Community Library, 57-04 Marathon Pkwy, Little Neck, NY, 11362. Tel: 718-225-3550. p. 1555
Holl, Scott, Genealogy Dept Mgr, History Dept Mgr, Saint Louis County Library, History & Genealogy Department, 1640 S Lindbergh Blvd, Saint Louis, MO, 63131-3598. Tel: 314-994-3300. p. 1274
Holland, Cecil, Br Mgr, Blue Ridge Regional Library, 310 E Church St, Martinsville, VA, 24112-2909. Tel: 276-403-5430. p. 2331
Holland, Chelsea, Head, Children's Servx, The Field Library, Four Nelson Ave, Peekskill, NY, 10566. Tel: 914-737-1212. p. 1616
Holland, Claudia, Libr Develop Coordr, Florida Department of State, Division of Library & Information Services, R A Gray Bldg, 500 S Bronough St, Tallahassee, FL, 32399-0250. Tel: 850-245-6622. p. 446
Holland, Douglas L, Dir, Missouri Botanical Garden, 4500 Shaw Blvd, 4th Flr, Saint Louis, MO, 63110. Tel: 314-577-0842. p. 1272
Holland, Elizabeth M, Exhibits Curator, Spec Coll, Chicago Public Library, Special Collections & Preservation Division, 400 S State St, Chicago, IL, 60605. Tel: 312-747-4883. p. 557
Holland, Emily, Student Success Librn, Mount Saint Mary's University, 16300 Old Emmitsburg Rd, Emmitsburg, MD, 21727. Tel: 301-447-5430. p. 965
Holland, Janet E, Libr Tech, Virginia State Law Library, Supreme Court Bldg, 2nd Flr, 100 N Ninth St, Richmond, VA, 23219-2335. Tel: 804-786-2075. p. 2344
Holland, Joseph, Jr, Libr Dir, New England Institute of Technology Library, One New England Tech Blvd, East Greenwich, RI, 02818-1205. Tel: 401-739-5000, Ext 3578. p. 2031
Holland, Leslie, Mgr, Libr Serv, Southern College of Optometry Library, 1245 Madison Ave, Memphis, TN, 38104. Tel: 901-722-3238. p. 2114
Holland, Lisa, Archivist, Instruction Librn, Wagner College, One Campus Rd, Staten Island, NY, 10301. Tel: 718-420-4219. p. 1645
Holland, Lissa, Asst Dir, Lancaster Public Library, 125 N Duke St, Lancaster, PA, 17602. Tel: 717-394-2651. p. 1951
Holland, Lori, Br Mgr, Kent District Library, Wyoming Branch, 3350 Michael Ave SW, Wyoming, MI, 49509. p. 1094
Holland, Marilyn, Cat, Mary Lou Johnson Hardin County District Library, 325 E Columbus St, Kenton, OH, 43326-1546. Tel: 419-673-2278. p. 1792
Holland, Mark G, Archivist, William McKinley Presidential Library & Museum, 800 McKinley Monument Dr NW, Canton, OH, 44708. Tel: 330-455-7043. p. 1755
Holland, Michael, Univ Archivist, University of Missouri-Columbia, Elmer Ellis Library, 104 Ellis Library, Columbia, MO, 65201-5149. Tel: 573-882-4602. p. 1243
Holland, R J, Librn, Coke County Library, 706 Austin St, Robert Lee, TX, 76945. Tel: 325-453-2495. p. 2233
Holland, Richard, Dir, Libr Admin Serv, Temple University Libraries, 1210 W Berks St, Philadelphia, PA, 19122-6088. Tel: 215-204-8231. p. 1986
Holland, Suzann, Dir, Monroe Public Library, 925 16th Ave, Monroe, WI, 53566-1497. Tel: 608-328-7010. p. 2462
Holland, Yasma, Dir, Kaufman County Library, 3790 S Houston St, Kaufman, TX, 75142. Tel: 972-932-6222. p. 2204
Holland, Zoe, Acad Librn, Tuzzy Consortium Library, 5421 North Star St, Barrow, AK, 99723. Tel: 907-852-1729. p. 43
Hollander, Gail, Asst Dir, Information Literacy Coord, Howard Community College Library, 10901 Little Patuxent Pkwy, 2nd Flr, Columbia, MD, 21044. Tel: 443-518-4633. p. 963
Hollar, Carla, Librn/Mgr, Buncombe County Public Libraries, Swannanoa Branch, 101 W Charleston St, Swannanoa, NC, 28778. Tel: 828-250-6486. p. 1672
Hollar, Dani, Electronic Res Librn, Northeast Ohio Medical University, 4209 State Rte 44, Rootstown, OH, 44272. Tel: 330-325-6601. p. 1818
Hollenbeak, Susan, Dir, Salmon River Public Library, 126 N Main St, Riggins, ID, 83549. Tel: 208-628-3394. p. 530
Hollenbeck, Elizabeth, Assoc Dean, Libr Serv, South Texas College Library, 3201 W Pecan Blvd, McAllen, TX, 78501-6661. Tel: 956-872-3482. p. 2217
Hollendonner, Liz, Coordr, Access Serv, Millikin University, 1184 W Main St, Decatur, IL, 62522. Tel: 217-424-6214. p. 576
Hollenquest, Charmice, Interim Libr Mgr, New York Public Library - Astor, Lenox & Tilden Foundations, Harlem Branch, Nine W 124th St, New York, NY, 10027-5699. Tel: 212-348-5620. p. 1595
Holler, Wendy, Dir, Marysville-Rye Library, 198 Overcrest Rd, Marysville, PA, 17053. Tel: 717-957-2851. p. 1958
Hollerbach, Catherine, Chief Operating Officer, Anne Arundel County Public Library, Five Harry Truman Pkwy, Annapolis, MD, 21401. Tel: 410-222-7287. p. 950
Hollerich, Mary, Dir, Augsburg University, 630 22nd Ave S, Minneapolis, MN, 55454. Tel: 612-330-1604. p. 1182
Hollerich, Mary, Asst Dean, Scholarly Res & Research Serv, Southern Methodist University, Central University Libraries, 6414 Robert S Hyer Lane, Dallas, TX, 75205. Tel: 214-768-4960. p. 2168
Hollerich, Mary, Asst Dean, Scholarly Res & Research Serv, Southern Methodist University, Fondren Library, 6414 Robert S Hyer Lane, Dallas, TX, 75205. Tel: 214-768-4960. p. 2168
Holles, Melanie, Dir, Cabarrus County Public Library, 27 Union St N, Concord, NC, 28025. Tel: 704-920-2050. p. 1682
Holles, Melanie, Libr Dir, Cabarrus County Public Library, Midland Branch, 4297 NC-24 27C, Midland, NC, 28107. Tel: 704-920-2040. p. 1682
Holley, Amber, Asst Dir, Learning Res, Jacksonville Public Library, 303 N Laura St, Jacksonville, FL, 32202-3505. Tel: 904-630-2982. p. 411
Holley, Beth, Head, Acq, University of Alabama, University Libraries, University of Alabama Campus, Capstone Dr, Tuscaloosa, AL, 35487. Tel: 205-348-1493. p. 38

Holley, Leta, Dir, Federal Election Commission, 1050 First S, NE, Washington, DC, 20463. Tel: 202-694-1100. p. 366

Holley, Margaret, Librn, Filer Public Library, 219 Main St, Filer, ID, 83328-5349. Tel: 208-326-4143. p. 520

Holley, Ralph, Libr Asst, New England College of Optometry Library, 424 Beacon St, Boston, MA, 02115. Tel: 617-587-5623. p. 998

Holley, Robert P, Dr, Prof Emeritus, Wayne State University, 106 Kresge Library, Detroit, MI, 48202. Tel: 313-577-1825. p. 2787

Holley, Shelley, Head, Lending Serv, Southington Public Library & Museum, 255 Main St, Southington, CT, 06489. Tel: 860-628-0947. p. 337

Holley, Shelley, Dir, Libr Serv, Frisco Public Library, 6101 Frisco Square Blvd, Frisco, TX, 75034-3000. Tel: 972-292-5669. p. 2182

Holliday, Chip, Mgr, Memphis Public Library, Humanities, 3030 Poplar Ave, Memphis, TN, 38111. Tel: 901-415-2726. p. 2113

Holliday, Deloice, Head of Libr, Indiana University Bloomington, Neal-Marshall Black Culture Center Library, Neal-Marshall Ctr, Rm A113, 275 N Jordan, Bloomington, IN, 47405. Tel: 812-855-4369. p. 671

Holliday, Sayer, Dir, Programming & Communications, The New York Society Library, 53 E 79th St, New York, NY, 10075. Tel: 212-288-6900, Ext 222. p. 1598

Holliday, Wendy, Dean of the Library, Weber State University, 3921 Central Campus Dr, Dept 2901, Ogden, UT, 84408-2901. Tel: 801-626-6403. p. 2268

Holliday, Winola, Br Mgr, Washington Parish Library System, Enon, 14093 Hwy 16, Franklinton, LA, 70438. Tel: 985-839-9385. p. 890

Hollinger, Noah, Dir, Ladd Public Library District, 125 N Main St, Ladd, IL, 61329. Tel: 815-894-3254. p. 606

Hollinger, Richard, Head, Spec Coll, University of Maine, 5729 Fogler Library, Orono, ME, 04469-5729. Tel: 207-581-1688. p. 934

Hollingshead, Emily, Dir, Libr Serv, Drumheller Public Library, 80 Veterans Way, Drumheller, AB, T0J 0Y4, CANADA. Tel: 403-823-1371. p. 2533

Hollingsworth, Cheryl, AV Librn, Mesquite Public Library, 300 W Grubb Dr, Mesquite, TX, 75149. Tel: 972-216-6220. p. 2219

Hollingsworth, David, Mgr, Covington County Library System, 403 S Fir Ave, Collins, MS, 39428. Tel: 601-765-4612. p. 1214

Hollingsworth, Erin, Br Mgr, Clearwater Public Library System, Countryside, 2642 Sabal Springs Dr, Clearwater, FL, 33761. Tel: 727-562-4970. p. 389

Hollingsworth, Janet, Coordr, Humber College, Lakeshore Campus Library, 3199 Lakeshore Blvd W, Toronto, ON, M8V 1K8, CANADA. Tel: 416-675-6622, Ext 3250. p. 2690

Hollingsworth, Janet L, Dir, Herrick Memorial Library, 101 Willard Memorial Sq, Wellington, OH, 44090-1342. Tel: 440-647-2120. p. 1829

Hollingsworth, Jill, Ref Librn, Georgetown University, Blommer Science Library, 302 Reiss Science Bldg, Washington, DC, 20057. Tel: 202-662-2573. p. 368

Hollis, Linda, Br Mgr, Concordia Parish Library, Clayton Branch, 31451 Hwy 15, Clayton, LA, 71326. Tel: 318-757-6460. p. 889

Hollis, Linda Sue, Libr Tech III, Colorado Department of Corrections, 12750 Hwy 96, Lane 13, Crowley, CO, 81034. Tel: 719-267-3520, Ext 3251. p. 273

Hollis, Wendy, Head, Children's Servx, Louis Bay 2nd Library, 345 Lafayette Ave, Hawthorne, NJ, 07506-2546. Tel: 973-427-5745, Ext 21. p. 1407

Hollister, Amanda, Syst Librn, SUNY Broome Community College, 907 Front St, Binghamton, NY, 13905-1328. Tel: 607-778-5609. p. 1494

Hollister, Dianne, Ref Librn, Bradley University, 1501 W Bradley Ave, Peoria, IL, 61625. Tel: 309-677-2850. p. 634

Hollmann, Katrina, Libr Dir, Verdigre Public Library, 101 E Third St, Verdigre, NE, 68783. Tel: 402-668-2677. p. 1339

Hollnagel, Michele, Ref Supvr, Davis County Library, Bountiful/South Branch, 725 S Main St, Bountiful, UT, 84010. Tel: 451-451-1760. p. 2263

Holloman, Gale, Dir, Atlanta-Fulton Public Library System, One Margaret Mitchell Sq, Atlanta, GA, 30303-1089. Tel: 404-612-3189. p. 460

Holloman, Katrina, Mgr, Dougherty County Public Library, Westtown, 2124 Waddell Ave, Albany, GA, 31707. Tel: 229-420-3280. p. 457

Hollow Horn Bear, Elsie, Secy Gen, Sinte Gleska University Library, 1351 W Spotted Tail St, Mission, SD, 57555. Tel: 605-856-8100, 605-856-8112. p. 2079

Holloway, Dawn, Libr Mgr, New York Public Library - Astor, Lenox & Tilden Foundations, Morris Park Branch, 985 Morris Park Ave, (Between Radcliff & Colden Aves), Bronx, NY, 10462. Tel: 718-931-0636. p. 1596

Holloway, Kristine, Distance Serv Librn, California State University, Bakersfield, 9001 Stockdale Hwy, 60 LIB, Bakersfield, CA, 93311. Tel: 661-654-5072. p. 119

Holloway, Sharon, Cat, Tech Serv, Benton Harbor Public Library, 213 E Wall St, Benton Harbor, MI, 49022-4499. Tel: 269-926-6139. p. 1084

Holloway, Tom, Br Mgr, York County Library, Fort Mill Public, 1818 Second Baxter Crossing, Fort Mill, SC, 29708. Tel: 803-547-4114. p. 2068

Holly, Fiona, Ref Outreach Librn, Conception Abbey & Seminary Library, 37174 State Hwy VV, Conception, MO, 64433. Tel: 660-944-2990. p. 1244

Holly, Janet S, Ref Librn, Virginia Military Institute, 345 Letcher Ave, Lexington, VA, 24450. Tel: 540-464-7296. p. 2329

Holly, Kathi, Br Coordr, New Britain Public Library, Jefferson, 140 Horseplain Rd, New Britain, CT, 06053. Tel: 860-225-4700. p. 324

Holm, Christina, Instruction Coordr, Kennesaw State University Library System, 385 Cobb Ave NW, MD 1701, Kennesaw, GA, 30144. Tel: 470-578-6197. p. 483

Holman, Deb, Support Serv Mgr, Licking County Library, 101 W Main St, Newark, OH, 43055-5054. Tel: 740-349-5504. p. 1807

Holman, Jennifer, Chief Financial Officer, Alabama Public Library Service, 6030 Monticello Dr, Montgomery, AL, 36130. Tel: 334-213-3929. p. 27

Holman, Jennifer, Electronic Res Librn, Hope College, Van Wylen Library, 53 Graves Pl, Holland, MI, 49422. Tel: 616-395-7790. p. 1115

Holman, Jessica, Dir, Negaunee Public Library, 319 W Case St, Negaunee, MI, 49866. Tel: 906-475-7700, Ext 18. p. 1137

Holman, Jos N, County Librn, Tippecanoe County Public Library, 627 South St, Lafayette, IN, 47901-1470. Tel: 765-429-0100. p. 701

Holman, Kali, Tech Serv Asst, Midwestern Baptist Theological Seminary Library, 5001 N Oak Trafficway, Kansas City, MO, 64118-4620. Tel: 816-414-3729. p. 1256

Holman, Lucy, Assoc Provost, Teaching, Learning & Library Servs, Dean of Libr, University of North Carolina Wilmington Library, 601 S College Rd, Wilmington, NC, 28403. Tel: 910-962-7703. p. 1723

Holman, Paige, Libr Dir, Hill Library, 1151 Parker Mountain Rd, Strafford, NH, 03884. Tel: 603-664-2800. p. 1381

Holman, Ruby, Br Librn, Tombigbee Regional Library System, Amory Municipal Library, 401 Second Ave N, Amory, MS, 38821-3514. Tel: 662-256-5261. p. 1235

Holman, Stephanie, Ch, Monroe County Public Library, Ellettsville Branch, 600 W Temperance St, Ellettsville, IN, 47429. Tel: 812-876-1272. p. 671

Holman, Virginia 'Gigi', Libr Mgr, Pikes Peak Library District, East Library, 5550 N Union Blvd, Colorado Springs, CO, 80918. Tel: 719-531-6333, Ext 6013. p. 271

Holmberg, James, Curator, Filson Historical Society Library, 1310 S Third St, Louisville, KY, 40208. Tel: 502-635-5083. p. 865

Holmberg, Linda, City Librn, Centerville Community Library, 421 Florida, Centerville, SD, 57014. Tel: 605-563-2540. p. 2075

Holmen, Amanda, Librn, Payette Associates, 290 Congress St, Boston, MA, 02210. Tel: 617-895-1000. p. 999

Holmen, Coreen, Br Librn, Wapiti Regional Library, Carrot River Public Library, Town Office/Library Complex, Main St, Carrot River, SK, S0E 0L0, CANADA. Tel: 306-768-2501. p. 2745

Holmen, Rita, Br Librn, Wapiti Regional Library, Choiceland Public Library, 116 First St E, Choiceland, SK, S0J 0M0, CANADA. Tel: 306-428-2216. p. 2745

Holmes, Abbie, Ref & Instruction Librn, Middle Georgia State University, 100 University Pkwy, Macon, GA, 31206. Tel: 478-471-2093. p. 487

Holmes, Amanda, Library Contact, Filion Wakely Thorup Angeletti LLP, 333 Bay St, Toronto, ON, M5H 2R2, CANADA. Tel: 416-408-3221. p. 2689

Holmes, Amelia, Libr Dir, Nantucket Historical Association, Seven Fair St, Nantucket, MA, 02554-3737. Tel: 508-228-1894, Ext 301. p. 1037

Holmes, Anna, Instruction Librn, Ref Librn, Baker University, 518 Eighth St, Baldwin City, KS, 66006. Tel: 785-594-8445. p. 797

Holmes, Carol, Library Contact, Wahta Mohawks, 2664 Meskoa Rd 38, Bala, ON, P0C 1A0, CANADA. Tel: 705-756-2354, Ext 233. p. 2629

Holmes, Christina, Br Mgr, Free Library of Philadelphia, Blanche A Nixon Library - Cobbs Creek Branch, 5800 Cobbs Creek Pkwy, Philadelphia, PA, 19143-3036. Tel: 215-685-1973. p. 1979

Holmes, Claire, Asst Univ Librn, Pub Serv, Towson University, 8000 York Rd, Towson, MD, 21252. Tel: 410-704-3795. p. 980

Holmes, Debbie, Dean, Libr Serv, College of Coastal Georgia, One College Dr, Brunswick, GA, 31520. Tel: 912-279-5787. p. 468

Holmes, Denise, Libr Dir, Banks Public Library, 42461 NW Market St, Banks, OR, 97106. Tel: 503-324-1382. p. 1873

Holmes, Elizabeth G, Head, Infrastructure & Content, United States Naval War College Library, 686 Cushing Rd, Newport, RI, 02841-1207. Tel: 401-841-4307. p. 2035

Holmes, Emily, Cat, Sheffield Public Library, 316 N Montgomery Ave, Sheffield, AL, 35660. Tel: 256-386-5633. p. 35

Holmes, Ernestine, Head, Acq, Florida Agricultural & Mechanical University Libraries, 525 Orr Dr, Tallahassee, FL, 32307-4700. Tel: 850-599-3314. p. 446

Holmes, Gabrielle, Asst Librn, Haston Free Public Library, 161 N Main St, North Brookfield, MA, 01535. Tel: 508-867-0208. p. 1041

Holmes, Haley, Adminr, Pub Serv, San Antonio Public Library, 600 Soledad, San Antonio, TX, 78205-2786. Tel: 210-207-2829. p. 2238

Holmes, Harriett, Prog Coordr, UAB Callahan Eye Hospital, 1720 University Blvd, Birmingham, AL, 35233-1895. Tel: 205-325-8507. p. 9

Holmes, Heather, Assoc Dir of Libr, National Network of Libraries of Medicine Region 2, MUSC James W Colbert Educ Ctr & Libr, 171 Ashley Ave, Ste 300, MSC 403, Charleston, SC, 29425. Tel: 843-792-0065. p. 2774

Holmes, Heather N, Assoc Dir, Medical University of South Carolina Libraries, 171 Ashley Ave, Ste 419, Charleston, SC, 29425-0001. Tel: 843-792-0065. p. 2051

Holmes, James, Head, Access Serv, Reed College, 3203 SE Woodstock Blvd, Portland, OR, 97202-8199. Tel: 503-777-7702. p. 1894

Holmes, Kim, Libr Mgr, Columbus County Public Library, Rube McCray Memorial, 301 Flemington Dr, Lake Waccamaw, NC, 28450. Tel: 910-646-4616. p. 1722
Holmes, Kristi, Dir, Northwestern University Libraries, Galter Health Sciences Library, Montgomery Ward Bldg, 303 E Chicago Ave, Chicago, IL, 60611. Tel: 312-503-8133. p. 586
Holmes, Maggie, Adult Serv, Richards Memorial Library, 118 N Washington St, North Attleboro, MA, 02760. Tel: 508-699-0122. p. 1041
Holmes, Marlia, Mgr, Contra Costa County Library, Pinole Library, 2935 Pinole Valley Rd, Pinole, CA, 94564. Tel: 510-758-2741. p. 174
Holmes, Nancy, Head, Tech Serv, Piedmont Regional Library System, 990 Washington St, Jefferson, GA, 30549-1011. Tel: 706-367-9399. p. 482
Holmes, Pamela V, Asst Dir, East Orange Public Library, 21 S Arlington Ave, East Orange, NJ, 07018. Tel: 973-266-5600. p. 1400
Holmes, Radonna, Dir, Libr Serv, Southwestern Assemblies of God University, 1200 Sycamore St, Waxahachie, TX, 75165-2342. Tel: 972-825-4761. p. 2255
Holmes, Robin, Dir, Summersville Public Library, 6201 Webster Rd, Summersville, WV, 26651. Tel: 304-872-0844. p. 2415
Holmes, Robin, Libr Asst Supvr, Region of Waterloo Library, Wellesley Branch, 1137 Henry St, Wellesley, ON, N0B 2T0, CANADA. Tel: 519-656-2001. p. 2629
Holmes, Sarah, Dir, Catoosa County Library, 108 Catoosa Circle, Ringgold, GA, 30736. Tel: 706-965-3600. p. 494
Holmes, Sarah, Music Librn, Northern Illinois University Libraries, 217 Normal Rd, DeKalb, IL, 60115-2828. Tel: 815-753-1426. p. 577
Holmes, Sarah, Music Librn, Northern Illinois University Libraries, Music, School of Music, Rm 175, DeKalb, IL, 60115. Tel: 815-753-1426. p. 578
Holmes, Sheri, Dir, Libr Serv, Ellinwood School & Community Library, 210 N Schiller Ave, Ellinwood, KS, 67526. Tel: 620-564-2306. p. 806
Holmes, Zella'Ques, Libr Dir, Montgomery City-County Public Library System, 245 High St, Montgomery, AL, 36104. Tel: 334-240-4300. p. 29
Holmes, Zella'Ques S, Head, Circ Serv, Montgomery City-County Public Library System, Juliette Hampton Morgan Memorial Library, 245 High St, Montgomery, AL, 36104. Tel: 334-240-4999. p. 29
Holmgren, Rick, Vice Pres, Assessment & Info Serv, Allegheny College, 520 N Main St, Meadville, PA, 16335. Tel: 814-332-2898. p. 1959
Holmquist, Kimberly J, Dir, Gibbon Public Library, 1050 Adams Ave, Gibbon, MN, 55335. Tel: 507-834-6640. p. 1176
Holmsley, Jennifer, Dir, Crockett County Public Library, 1201 Ave G, Ozona, TX, 76943. Tel: 325-392-3565. p. 2224
Holmstrom, Phyllis, Librn, Fayette County Historical Society Library, 100 N Walnut St, West Union, IA, 52175-1347. Tel: 563-422-5797. p. 791
Holoubek, Helga, Librn, US Environmental Protection Agency Library, 75 Hawthorne St, San Francisco, CA, 94105. Tel: 415-972-3657. p. 230
Holsapple, Jacque, Dir, Newton Public Library & Museum, 100 S Van Buren St, Newton, IL, 62448. Tel: 618-783-8141. p. 624
Holseth, Veronica, Libr Mgr, United States Air Force, 319 FSS/FSDL, 511 Holzapple St, Bldg 201, Grand Forks AFB, ND, 58205. Tel: 701-747-3046. p. 1735
Holsing, Brenda, Youth Serv Librn, Brockway Memorial Library, 10021 NE Second Ave, Miami Shores, FL, 33138. Tel: 305-758-8107. p. 426
Holsomback, Annette, Asst Dir, Pleasant Grove Public Library, 501 Park Rd, Pleasant Grove, AL, 35127. Tel: 205-744-1731. p. 33
Holsomback, Jimmy, Bus Mgr, Rapides Parish Library, 411 Washington St, Alexandria, LA, 71301-8338. Tel: 318-445-6436, Ext 1004. p. 880
Holst, Bruce, Dir, Marie Selby Botanical Gardens, 1534 Mound St, Sarasota, FL, 34236. Tel: 941-955-7553, Ext 312. p. 443
Holst, Holly, Br Mgr, Montgomery County-Norristown Public Library, Conshohocken Free Library, 301 Fayette St, Conshohocken, PA, 19428. Tel: 610-825-1656. p. 1971
Holstein, Tara, Dir, Boone-Madison Public Library, 375 Main St, Madison, WV, 25130. Tel: 304-369-7842. p. 2407
Holt, Chris, Regional Br Operations Mgr, Public Library of Cincinnati & Hamilton County, 800 Vine St, Cincinnati, OH, 45202-2009. Tel: 513-369-4417. p. 1761
Holt, Elizabeth, Dir, Marathon Public Library, 106 E Third St, Marathon, TX, 79842. Tel: 432-386-4136. p. 2215
Holt, Jamie, Evening Supvr, Spec Coll, Alice Lloyd College, 100 Purpose Rd, Pippa Passes, KY, 41844. Tel: 606-368-6112. p. 873
Holt, Janifer, Bus & Econ Librn, Eng Librn, Dartmouth College Library, Feldberg Business & Engineering Library, 6193 Murdough Ctr, Hanover, NH, 03755-3560. Tel: 603-646-2191. p. 1366
Holt, Jennifer, Curator of Coll, Will Rogers Memorial Museum Library, 1720 W Will Rogers Blvd, Claremore, OK, 74017. Tel: 918-343-8124. p. 1844
Holt, Joy, Libr Dir, Carson City Library, 900 N Roop St, Carson City, NV, 89701. Tel: 775-887-2244. p. 1343
Holt, Karen, Librn II, Roseville Public Library, 225 Taylor St, Roseville, CA, 95678-2681. Tel: 916-774-5221. p. 205
Holt, Karen, Mgr, Sandia National Laboratories, PO Box 5800, MS 0899, Albuquerque, NM, 87185-0899. Tel: 505-845-7619. p. 1462
Holt, Kate, Libr Dir, Riverdale Public Library District, 208 W 144th St, Riverdale, IL, 60827-2733. Tel: 708-841-3311. p. 639
Holt, Leslie, Res Ctr Mgr, Holland College Library Services, 140 Weymouth St, Charlottetown, PE, C1A 4Z1, CANADA. Tel: 902-566-9636. p. 2707
Holt, Linzi, Asst Libr Dir, Moore County Library System, 124 S Bliss Ave, Dumas, TX, 79029-3889. Tel: 806-935-4941. p. 2172
Holt, Margaret, Libr Asst, Bastyr University Library, 14500 Juanita Dr NE, Kenmore, WA, 98028. Tel: 425-602-3020. p. 2367
Holt, Mary, Cataloger, Hist Librn, Tulane University, Rudolph Matas Library of the Health Sciences, Tulane Health Sciences Campus, 1430 Tulane Ave, SL-86, New Orleans, LA, 70112-2699. Tel: 504-988-2062. p. 904
Holt, Ross, Dir, Randolph County Public Library, 201 Worth St, Asheboro, NC, 27203. Tel: 336-318-6800. p. 1672
Holt, Sarah, Instrul Librn, Washburn University, 1700 SW College Ave, Topeka, KS, 66621. Tel: 785-670-1982. p. 839
Holt, Susan, Tech Serv Supvr, Brentwood Public Library, 8765 Eulalie Ave, Brentwood, MO, 63144. Tel: 314-963-8632. p. 1239
Holt, Tom, Bibliog Control Mgr, California State University, East Bay Library, CSU East Bay Library, 25800 Carlos Bee Blvd, Hayward, CA, 94542-3052. Tel: 510-885-2429. p. 150
Holt, Vicky, Br Mgr, Stanislaus County Library, Riverbank Branch, 3442 Santa Fe St, Riverbank, CA, 95367-2319. Tel: 209-869-7008. p. 178
Holtgrave, Diane, Asst Librn, Breese Public Library, 530 N Third St, Breese, IL, 62230. Tel: 618-526-7361. p. 544
Holth, Coleman, Coordr, Cat & Acq, Metadata Librn, Hollins University, 7950 E Campus Dr, Roanoke, VA, 24020. Tel: 540-362-6240. p. 2345
Holthaus, Vernelle, Libr Dir, Calmar Public Library, 101 S Washington St, Calmar, IA, 52132. Tel: 563-562-3010. p. 736
Holther, Cyndi, Circ Supvr, Sturgis District Library, 255 North St, Sturgis, MI, 49091. Tel: 269-659-7224. p. 1153
Holthus, Jennifer, Libr Dir, Grant County Library, 105 E Harrison St, Hyannis, NE, 69350. Tel: 308-458-2218. p. 1319
Holtman, Dawn, ILL, Charles A Ransom District Library, 180 S Sherwood Ave, Plainwell, MI, 49080-1896. Tel: 269-685-8024. p. 1141
Holtman, Tracy, Assoc Dir, Access & Collection Servs, Tarleton State University Library, 201 Saint Felix, Stephenville, TX, 76401. Tel: 254-968-9466. p. 2246
Holtmann, Libby, Libr Dir, Plano Public Library System, Library Administration, 2501 Coit Rd, Plano, TX, 75075. Tel: 972-769-4208. p. 2227
Holtry, Cara, Dir, Libr & Archives, Cumberland County Historical Society, 21 N Pitt St, Carlisle, PA, 17013-2945. Tel: 717-249-7610. p. 1918
Holtsberry, Kathy, Br Mgr, Defiance Public Library, Sherwood Branch, 117 N Harrison St, Sherwood, OH, 43556. Tel: 419-899-4343. p. 1781
Holtz, Loretta, Ref Serv, Ad, Comsewogue Public Library, 170 Terryville Rd, Port Jefferson Station, NY, 11776. Tel: 631-928-1212. p. 1621
Holtz, Tim, Archive Spec, National Archives & Records Administration, 1000 Beal Ave, Ann Arbor, MI, 48109. Tel: 734-205-0592. p. 1079
Holtzclaw, John, Librn, National Center for State Courts Library, 300 Newport Ave, Williamsburg, VA, 23185-4147. Tel: 757-259-1823. p. 2353
Holtzman, Matthew, Librn, Monhegan Memorial Library, One Library Lane, Monhegan, ME, 04852. Tel: 207-295-7042. p. 932
Holub, Donna, Asst Librn, Schulenburg Public Library, 310 Simpson St, Schulenburg, TX, 78956. Tel: 979-743-3345. p. 2242
Holway, Joyce, Dir, Sturdivant Public Library, 514 Main St, East Machias, ME, 04630. Tel: 207-255-0070. p. 923
Holwell, Michlene D, Med Librn, Campbell County Health Library, 501 S Burma, Gillette, WY, 82716-3426. Tel: 307-399-7689, 307-688-6011. p. 2494
Holwick, Diane, Asst Dir, Fort Smith Public Library, 3201 Rogers Ave, Fort Smith, AR, 72903. Tel: 479-783-0229. p. 96
Holz, Karen, Dir, Bloomfield-Eastern Greene County Public Library, 125 S Franklin St, Bloomfield, IN, 47424. Tel: 812-384-4125. p. 670
Holzenberg, Phyllis, Assoc Librn, Cat/ILL Librn, Drury University, 900 N Benton Ave, Springfield, MO, 65802. Tel: 417-873-7487. p. 1280
Holzhauer, Kristin, Libr Dir, Pontiac Public Library, 211 E Madison St, Pontiac, IL, 61764. Tel: 815-844-7229. p. 636
Holzmann, Robert, Syst Librn, Tulsa Community College Libraries, Metro Campus, 909 S Boston Ave, Tulsa, OK, 74119-2011. Tel: 918-595-7173. p. 1866
Hom, Linda W, Head Law Librn, Middlesex Law Library, Superior Courthouse, 200 Trade Ctr, 3rd Flr, Woburn, MA, 01801. Tel: 781-939-2920. p. 1070
Homan, Joyce, Ref Supvr, Cambria County Library System & District Center, 248 Main St, Johnstown, PA, 15901. Tel: 814-536-5131. p. 1947
Homer, Jason, Exec Dir, Worcester Public Library, Three Salem Sq, Worcester, MA, 01608. Tel: 508-799-1726. p. 1073
Homer, Jason B, Libr Dir, Morse Institute Library, 14 E Central St, Natick, MA, 01760. Tel: 508-647-6520. p. 1037
Homer, Starr, Librn, Northwest Regional Library, Clyde Nix Public Library, 350 Bexar Ave W, Hamilton, AL, 35570. Tel: 205-921-4290. p. 40
Homeyer, Hannah, Youth Serv Librn, Conrad Public Library, 114 N Main St, Conrad, IA, 50621. Tel: 641-366-2583. p. 741

Homfeld, Hanna, Librn, Amarillo College, 2201 S Washington, Amarillo, TX, 79109. Tel: 806-371-5419. p. 2134

Hommel, Joyce, Exec Director, Learning Resources, Washtenaw Community College, 4800 E Huron River Dr, Ann Arbor, MI, 48105-4800. Tel: 734-973-3429. p. 1081

Hommerding, Nadia, Dr, Dir, Libr Serv, University of St Augustine for Health Sciences, 800 Douglas Rd, Coral Gables, FL, 33134. Tel: 786-725-4031. p. 391

Hommey, Britiny, Librn, Beaver County Law Library, Court House, 810 Third St, Beaver, PA, 15009. Tel: 724-770-4659. p. 1908

Homsley, Ken, Mgr, Borrower Serv, Yorba Linda Public Library, 4852 Lakeview Ave, Yorba Linda, CA, 92886. Tel: 714-777-2873. p. 261

Honaker, Laura, Br Mgr, Knox County Public Library System, Norwood Branch, 1110 Merchant Dr, Knoxville, TN, 37912. Tel: 865-688-2454. p. 2106

Hone, Rebecca, Libr Dir, Village Library of Wrightstown, 727 Penns Park Rd, Wrightstown, PA, 18940-9605. Tel: 215-598-3322. p. 2024

Honea, Roxanna, Br Mgr, Avoyelles Parish Library, Plaucheville Branch, Town Hall, 146 Gin St, Plaucheville, LA, 71362. Tel: 318-359-1016. p. 897

Honecker, Nikki, Asst Librn, ILL, Three Hills Municipal Library, 135 Third Ave S, Three Hills, AB, T0M 2A0, CANADA. Tel: 403-443-2360. p. 2557

Honey, Megan, Dir, Lyons Falls Library, 3918 High St, Lyons Falls, NY, 13368. Tel: 315-348-6180. p. 1566

Honeycutt, Erin, Ch, Moultrie-Colquitt County Library, 204 Fifth St SE, Moultrie, GA, 31768. Tel: 229-985-6540. p. 492

Honeysucker, Roblyn, Br Mgr, East Baton Rouge Parish Library, Carver, 720 Terrace St, Baton Rouge, LA, 70802. Tel: 225-389-7480. p. 883

Hong, E K, Cataloger, Society of the Cincinnati Library, 2118 Massachusetts Ave NW, Washington, DC, 20008. Tel: 202-785-2040, Ext 425. p. 376

Hong, John, Dir, Distance Learning Library Servs, Dallas Baptist University, 3000 Mountain Creek Pkwy, Dallas, TX, 75211-9299. Tel: 214-333-5225. p. 2163

Hong, Paul, Syst Mgr, Whittier College, Bonnie Bell Wardman Library, 7031 Founders Hill Rd, Whittier, CA, 90608-9984. Tel: 562-907-4247. p. 259

Hongyue, Pan, Librn, Institute Philippe Pinel de Montreal Bibliotheque, 10905 Henri Bourassa Blvd E, Montreal, QC, H1C 1H1, CANADA. Tel: 514-648-8461, Ext 557. p. 2725

Honig, Risa, V.P. for Capital Planning & Construction, The New York Public Library - Astor, Lenox & Tilden Foundations, 476 Fifth Ave, (@ 42nd St), New York, NY, 10018. Tel: 212-621-0579. p. 1594

Honker, Jeff, Libr Operations Supvr/Access Serv, ILL & Doc Delivery, University of South Florida, Hinks & Elaine Shimberg Health Sciences Library, 12901 Bruce B Downs Blvd, MDC 31, Tampa, FL, 33612. Tel: 813-974-2243. p. 449

Honores, Martha, Br Mgr, Carnegie Library of Pittsburgh, Woods Run, 1201 Woods Run Ave, Pittsburgh, PA, 15212-2335. Tel: 412-761-3730. p. 1992

Hony, Candace, Circ Supvr, Mgr, ILL, Greenwood-Leflore Public Library System, 405 W Washington St, Greenwood, MS, 38930-4297. Tel: 662-453-3634. p. 1217

Hood, Benjamin, Dir, Palmer Public Library, 1455 N Main St, Palmer, MA, 01069. Tel: 413-283-3330. p. 1045

Hood, Carolyn, Head, ILL, Gonzaga University School of Law, 721 N Cincinnati St, Spokane, WA, 99220. Tel: 509-313-5792. p. 2383

Hood, Dan, Ref/Outreach Librn, Indian River State College, Dixon Hendry Campus Library, 2229 NW Ninth Ave, Okeechobee, FL, 34972. Tel: 863-462-7587. p. 404

Hood, Heather, Asst Librn, Brook-Iroquois-Washington Public Library, 100 W Main St, Brook, IN, 47922. Tel: 219-275-2471. p. 672

Hood, Jessi, Circ Coordr, Hollins University, 7950 E Campus Dr, Roanoke, VA, 24020. Tel: 540-362-6090. p. 2345

Hood, Kelly, ILL Asst, University of Wisconsin-River Falls, 410 S Third St, River Falls, WI, 54022. Tel: 715-425-4325. p. 2474

Hood, Martha, Assoc Dir, Evaluation Assessment, University of Houston - Clear Lake, Bayou Bldg 2402, 2700 Bay Area Blvd, Houston, TX, 77058-1002. Tel: 281-283-3920. p. 2199

Hood, Matt, Libr Spec III, Texas A&M University Libraries, Business Library & Collaboration Commons, 214 Olsen Blvd, College Station, TX, 77843. Tel: 979-845-2111. p. 2157

Hood, Sarah, Ref & Instruction Librn, Santa Fe Community College Library, 6401 Richards Ave, Santa Fe, NM, 87508-4887. Tel: 505-428-1830. p. 1476

Hoody, Katie, ILL, Bethel College Library, 300 E 27th St, North Newton, KS, 67117-0531. Tel: 316-284-5361. p. 827

Hoogendoorn, Shelley, YA Librn, Rock Valley Public Library, 1531 Main St, Rock Valley, IA, 51247-1127. Tel: 712-476-5651. p. 779

Hoogeveen, Barb, Dir, Lynnville Public Library, 404 East St, Lynnville, IA, 50153. Tel: 641-527-2590. p. 766

Hoogstra, Shirley V, Pres, Council for Christian Colleges & Universities, 321 Eighth St NE, Washington, DC, 20002. Tel: 202-546-8713. p. 2763

Hook, Dave, Dep Chief Librn, Milton Public Library, 1010 Main St E, Milton, ON, L9T 6H7, CANADA. Tel: 905-875-2665, Ext 3233. p. 2658

Hook, Mary, Dir, Manistique School & Public Library, 100 N Cedar St, Manistique, MI, 49854-1293. Tel: 906-341-4316. p. 1129

Hook, Sheril, Chief Librn, University of Toronto Libraries, John M Kelly Library, University of St Michael's College, 81 St Mary St, Toronto, ON, M5S 1J4, CANADA. Tel: 416-926-7263. p. 2699

Hooke, Sarah J, Librn, Bernstein Shur Law Library, 100 Middle St, Portland, ME, 04104. Tel: 207-774-1200. p. 936

Hooker, Celia, Libr Dir, Upton County Public Library, 212 W Seventh St, McCamey, TX, 79752. Tel: 432-652-8718. p. 2217

Hooker, Celia, Dir, Rankin Public Library, 310 E Tenth St, Rankin, TX, 79778. Tel: 432-693-2881. p. 2230

Hooker, Douglas, Dir, Atlanta Regional Commission Information Center, 229 Peachtree St NE, Ste 100, Atlanta, GA, 30303. Tel: 404-463-3100. p. 462

Hooker, Rhonda, Adminr, Rockingham County Public Library, 527 Boone Rd, Eden, NC, 27288. Tel: 336-627-1106. p. 1686

Hooks, Alex, Librn, Gulfport Public Library, 5501 28th Ave S, Gulfport, FL, 33707. Tel: 727-893-1074. p. 408

Hooks, Leocadia, Interim Asst Dir, Ser Librn, Texas Southern University, 3100 Cleburne Ave, Houston, TX, 77004. Tel: 713-313-4304. p. 2198

Hoopengarner, Jacqueline, Br Mgr, Scott-Sebastian Regional Library, Hartford Library, 22 Broadway, Hartford, AR, 72938. p. 97

Hooper, Gailene, Librn, North Central Washington Libraries, Republic Public Library, 794 S Clark Ave, Republic, WA, 99166-8823. Tel: 509-775-3328. p. 2394

Hooper, J Leon, Dept Head, Woodstock Theological Center Library, Georgetown University, Lauinger Library, PO Box 571170, Washington, DC, 20057-1170. Tel: 202-687-4250. p. 381

Hooper, Lisa, Head, Media Serv, Tulane University, 7001 Freret St, New Orleans, LA, 70118-5682. Tel: 504-314-7822. p. 903

Hooper, Mary, Dir, Pleasants County Public Library, 101 Lafayette St, Saint Marys, WV, 26170. Tel: 304-684-7494. p. 2414

Hooper, Michael, Electronic Res Librn, Austin Peay State University, 601 College St, Clarksville, TN, 37044. Tel: 931-221-7092. p. 2092

Hooper, Peg, Mgr, Jefferson County Public Library, Standley Lake Library, 8485 Kipling St, Arvada, CO, 80005. Tel: 303-403-5100. p. 288

Hooper, Rachel, Actg Dir, Troy University, Montgomery Campus, 252 Montgomery St, Montgomery, AL, 36104-3425. Tel: 334-670-3269. p. 30

Hooper, Rachel, Bus Librn, Head, Pub Serv, Troy University Library, 309 Wallace Hall, Troy, AL, 36082. Tel: 334-670-3269. p. 37

Hooper, Tarasa, Head, Tech Serv, Pikes Peak State College Library, 5675 S Academy Blvd, C7, Colorado Springs, CO, 80906-5498. p. 272

Hooper-Lane, Christopher, Dir, University of Wisconsin-Madison, Ebling Library, Health Sciences Learning Ctr, 750 Highland Ave, Madison, WI, 53705. Tel: 608-262-2020. p. 2451

Hoopes, Erin, Br Mgr, Free Library of Philadelphia, Philadelphia City Institute, 1905 Locust St, Philadelphia, PA, 19103-5730. Tel: 215-685-6621. p. 1979

Hoops, Lisa, Libr Dir, Edison State Community College Library, 1973 Edison Dr, Piqua, OH, 45356. Tel: 937-778-7955. p. 1815

Hootman, Steve, Curator, Exec Dir, Rhododendron Species Foundation & Botanical Garden, 2525 S 336th St, Federal Way, WA, 98003. Tel: 253-838-4646, Ext 101. p. 2364

Hooton, Roanna, Dir, New Carlisle & Olive Township Public Library, 408 S Bray St, New Carlisle, IN, 46552. Tel: 574-654-3046. p. 709

Hoover, Ben, Assoc Dir, Pennsylvania State University, College of Medicine, Penn State Hershey, 500 University Dr, Hershey, PA, 17033. Tel: 717-531-0003, Ext 285325. p. 1943

Hoover, Benjamin, Ref Serv Coordr, Bucknell University, 220 Bertrand Library, One Dent Dr, Lewisburg, PA, 17837. Tel: 570-577-1557. p. 1955

Hoover, Cathy, Mgr, Charlestown-Clark County Public Library, Sellersburg Branch, 430 N Indiana Ave, Sellersburg, IN, 47172. Tel: 812-246-4493. p. 674

Hoover, Danise, Assoc Librn, Pub Serv, Hunter College Libraries, East Bldg, 695 Park Ave, New York, NY, 10065. Tel: 212-772-4190. p. 1588

Hoover, Douglas A, Campus Libr Dir, Pennsylvania Western University - California, 250 University Ave, California, PA, 15419-1394. Tel: 724-938-4096. p. 1917

Hoover, Kathy, Libr Dir, Spicewood Community Library, 1011 Spur 191, Spicewood, TX, 78669. Tel: 830-693-7892. p. 2245

Hoover, Susan, Res Spec, Global Intelligence, Three Columbus Circle, New York, NY, 10019. Tel: 212-210-3983. p. 1587

Hoover, Venita L, Dir, Oklahoma County Law Library, 321 Park Ave, Rm 247, Oklahoma City, OK, 73102-3695. Tel: 405-713-1353. p. 1858

Hope, Aileen, Librn, Nunavut Public Library Services, Rebecca P Idlout Library, PO Box 580, Pond Inlet, NU, X0A 0S0, CANADA. Tel: 867-899-8972. p. 2625

Hope, Anne Scott, Tech Serv Librn, National University of Health Sciences Learning Resource Center, 200 E Roosevelt Rd, Bldg C, Lombard, IL, 60148-4583. Tel: 630-889-6538. p. 611

Hope, Candace, Librn, Southern Illinois University Edwardsville, Biomedical Library, School of Dental Medicine, 2800 College Ave, Bldg 277, Alton, IL, 62002. Tel: 618-474-7274. p. 582

Hope, Chante, Res Sharing Librn, State University of New York, 223 Store Hill Rd, Old Westbury, NY, 11568. Tel: 516-876-2895. p. 1610

Hopfer, Jessie, Libr Mgr, Montgomery House Library, 20 Church St, McEwensville, PA, 17749. Tel: 570-538-1381. p. 1959

Hopkins, Alison, Exec Dir, Prov Librn, Provincial Library & Literacy Office, 409A Park St, Regina, SK, S4N 5B2, CANADA. Tel: 306-787-2972. p. 2747

Hopkins, Amy, Dir, Centralia Public Library, 210 S Jefferson St, Centralia, MO, 65240. Tel: 573-682-2036. p. 1241

Hopkins, Barry C, Interim Dir, Pub Serv Librn, Lutheran School of Theology At Chicago & McCormick Theological Seminary, 5416 S Cornell Ave, Chicago, IL, 60615. Tel: 773-256-0734. p. 564

Hopkins, Brigitte, Exec Dir, Memorial & Library Association, 44 Broad St, Westerly, RI, 02891. Tel: 401-596-2877, Ext 303. p. 2043

Hopkins, Elizabeth, Dir, Adult Serv, Lisle Library District, 777 Front St, Lisle, IL, 60532-3599. Tel: 630-971-1675. p. 610

Hopkins, Gabrielle, Ad, Chelsea District Library, 221 S Main St, Chelsea, MI, 48118-1267. Tel: 734-475-8732. p. 1090

Hopkins, Geri, Librn/eLearning Coordr, Big Bend Community College Library, 1800 Bldg, 7662 Chanute St NE, Moses Lake, WA, 98837. Tel: 509-793-2350. p. 2371

Hopkins, Jacob, Info Literacy Librn, University of the District of Columbia, Learning Resources Division, 4200 Connecticut Ave NW, Bldg 39, Level B, Washington, DC, 20008. p. 380

Hopkins, Jeri Kay, Dir, Independence Public Library, 220 E Maple, Independence, KS, 67301. Tel: 620-331-3030. p. 815

Hopkins, Jeri Kay, Dir, Columbus Public Library, 2500 14th St, Ste 2, Columbus, NE, 68601. Tel: 402-562-4204. p. 1310

Hopkins, Jessica, Br Mgr, Manistee County Library System, Arcadia Branch, 3586 Glovers Lake Rd, Arcadia, MI, 49613. Tel: 231-889-4230. p. 1129

Hopkins, Joan, Instruction Librn, Benedictine University Library, 5700 College Rd, Lisle, IL, 60532-0900. Tel: 630-829-6050. p. 610

Hopkins, Mary Catherine, Dir, Sussex County Department of Libraries, Milton Public, 121 Union St, Milton, DE, 19968. Tel: 302-684-8856. p. 353

Hopkins, Megan, Dir, Sullivan County Public Library, 1655 Blountville Blvd, Blountville, TN, 37617. Tel: 423-279-2714. p. 2089

Hopkins, Sara, Libr Dir, Brunswick Community Library, 4118 State Hwy 2, Troy, NY, 12180-9029. Tel: 518-279-4023. p. 1652

Hopkins, Shelley, Libr Dir, Illiopolis-Niantic Public Library District, Sixth & Mary Sts, Illiopolis, IL, 62539. Tel: 217-486-5561. p. 601

Hopkins, Sherry, Dir, Swaledale Public Library, 504 Main St, Swaledale, IA, 50477. Tel: 641-995-2352. p. 786

Hopkins, Tammy, Dir, Pike Library, 65 Main St, Pike, NY, 14130. Tel: 585-493-5900. p. 1618

Hopkins, Tony, Libr Mgr, Robley Rex Department of Veterans Affairs Medical Center Library, 800 Zorn Ave, Louisville, KY, 40206. Tel: 502-287-6240. p. 866

Hopkins-LaRocco, Rose, Dir, Ch Serv, La Grange Park Public Library District, 555 N LaGrange Rd, La Grange Park, IL, 60526-5644. Tel: 708-352-0100. p. 606

Hopp, LeAnn, Dir, Marion Public Library, 120 N Main St, Marion, WI, 54950. Tel: 715-754-5368. p. 2454

Hoppe, Beth, Res & Instruction Librn, Soc Sci Librn, Bowdoin College Library, 3000 College Sta, Brunswick, ME, 04011-8421. Tel: 207-725-3260. p. 919

Hoppen, Felicia, Children's Prog Mgr, Dr Grace O Doane Alden Public Library, 1012 Water St, Alden, IA, 50006. Tel: 515-859-3820. p. 730

Hoppenstedt, Aaron, Library Contact, American Council of Life Insurers Library, 101 Constitution Ave NW, Washington, DC, 20001-2133. Tel: 202-624-2000. p. 360

Hopper, Ashley, Dir, Manhattan-Elwood Public Library District, 240 Whitson St, Manhattan, IL, 60442. Tel: 815-478-3987. p. 613

Hopper, Laura, Dir, Schroeder Public Library, 93 Main St, Keystone, IA, 52249. Tel: 319-442-3329. p. 763

Hopper, Michael, Head Librn, Harvard Library, Hamilton A R Gibb Islamic Seminar Library, Widener Library, Rm Q, Harvard University, Cambridge, MA, 02138. Tel: 617-495-2437, 617-495-4310. p. 1006

Hopper, Paula, Libr Dir, Beaufort County Community College, 5337 US Hwy 264 E, Washington, NC, 27889. Tel: 252-940-6243. p. 1720

Hopper, Sarah, Libr Dir, Ontonagon Township Library, 311 N Steel St, Ontonagon, MI, 49953. Tel: 906-884-4411. p. 1139

Hopper, Shelly, Br Mgr, Trails Regional Library, Corder Branch, 221 N Lafayette, Corder, MO, 64021. Tel: 660-394-2565. p. 1285

Hopper, Tim, Pub Serv Librn, Lindsey Wilson College, 210 Lindsey Wilson St, Columbia, KY, 42728. Tel: 270-384-8251. p. 852

Hopping, David, Asst Teaching Prof, University of Illinois at Urbana-Champaign, Library & Information Science Bldg, 501 E Daniel St, Champaign, IL, 61820-6211. Tel: 217-333-3280. p. 2784

Hoppman, Andrew, Dir, Lied Public Library, 100 E Garfield St, Clarinda, IA, 51632. Tel: 712-542-2416. p. 740

Hopson, Donna, Mgr, Circ Serv, Rockford Public Library, 214 N Church St, Rockford, IL, 61101-1023. Tel: 815-965-7606. p. 642

Hopton, Mary, Fiscal Officer, Wright Memorial Public Library, 1776 Far Hills Ave, Oakwood, OH, 45419-2598. Tel: 937-294-7171. p. 1810

Hopwood, Jennifer, Training Coordr, Southern Maryland Regional Library Association, Inc, 37600 New Market Rd, Charlotte Hall, MD, 20622. Tel: 301-884-0436. p. 961

Hor, Annie, Circ & Tech Serv Coordr, Govt Doc, California State University, Stanislaus, One University Circle, Turlock, CA, 95382. Tel: 209-667-3709. p. 253

Horacek, Tamara, Res Serv, Sr Mgr, Dolby Laboratories, Inc, 1275 Market St, San Francisco, CA, 94103. Tel: 415-558-0268. p. 224

Horack, Megan, Ad, Warren County Public Library District, 62 Public Sq, Monmouth, IL, 61462. Tel: 309-734-3166. p. 619

Horan, Kate, Pres, Hidalgo County Library System, c/o McAllen Memorial Library, 4001 N 3rd St, McAllen, TX, 78504. Tel: 956-681-3008. p. 2217

Horan, Kate P, Libr Dir, McAllen Public Library, 4001 N 23rd St, McAllen, TX, 78504. Tel: 956-681-3000. p. 2217

Horant, Charlotte, Ch, Edward U Demmer Memorial Library, 6961 W School St, Three Lakes, WI, 54562. Tel: 715-546-3391. p. 2481

Horat, Linda, Circ, Southern California University of Health Sciences, 16200 E Amber Valley Dr, Whittier, CA, 90604-4098. Tel: 562-902-3368. p. 259

Horchem, Debbie, Librn, Forman Valley Public Library District, 404 1/2 S Harrison, Manito, IL, 61546. Tel: 309-968-6093. p. 613

Hord, Bill, Dir, Houston Community College - Southwest College, Stafford Campus Library, 9910 Cash Rd, Stafford, TX, 77477-4405. Tel: 713-718-7823. p. 2195

Hord, Bill, Dir, Houston Community College - Southwest College, West Loop Center Library, 5601 West Loop S, Houston, TX, 77081-2221. Tel: 713-718-7880. p. 2195

Horell, Amy, Libr Consult, Altoona Area Public Library, 1600 Fifth Ave, Altoona, PA, 16602-3693. Tel: 814-946-0417, Ext 134. p. 1905

Horgan, Caroline, Resource Sharing Coord, La Roche University, 9000 Babcock Blvd, Pittsburgh, PA, 15237. Tel: 412-536-1063. p. 1994

Horn, Amy, Circ Supvr, Hickory Public Library, 375 Third St NE, Hickory, NC, 28601. Tel: 828-304-0500. p. 1696

Horn, Bonnie, ILL Tech, Lincoln University, 1570 Baltimore Pike, Lincoln University, PA, 19352. Tel: 484-365-7356. p. 1956

Horn, Brittany, Libr Coord, Tidewater Community College, 1700 College Crescent, Virginia Beach, VA, 23453. p. 2350

Horn, Daphne, Libr Mgr, Centre for Addiction & Mental Health Library, 1025 Queen St W, Toronto, ON, M5S 2S1, CANADA. Tel: 416-535-8501, Ext 36991. p. 2688

Horn, Katherine Lee, Dir, Elma Ross Public Library, 1011 E Main St, Brownsville, TN, 38012-2652. Tel: 731-772-9534. p. 2090

Horn, Sundae, Br Mgr, Beaufort, Hyde & Martin County Regional Library, Ocracoke School & Community Library, 225 Back Rd, Ocracoke, NC, 27960. Tel: 252-928-4436. p. 1720

Horn, Theresa, Br Mgr, Saint Joseph County Public Library, German Township Branch Library, 52807 Lynnewood Ave, South Bend, IN, 46628. Tel: 574-271-5144. p. 719

Hornaday, Gayle, Asst Dir, Henderson District Public Libraries, 280 S Green Valley Pkwy, Henderson, NV, 89012. Tel: 702-492-6582. p. 1345

Hornak, Kim, Asst Librn, Marmora & Lake Public Library, 37 Forsyth St, Marmora, ON, K0K 2M0, CANADA. Tel: 613-472-3122. p. 2656

Hornbach, Ann, Br Mgr, Free Library of Philadelphia, Torresdale Branch, 3079 Holme Ave, Philadelphia, PA, 19136-1101. Tel: 215-685-0494. p. 1980

Hornbeck, Melanie, Outreach Librn, Laramie County Library System, 2200 Pioneer Ave, Cheyenne, WY, 82001-3610. Tel: 307-773-7229. p. 2492

Hornberger, Gretchen, Law Librn, Coconino County Law Library & Self-Help Center, 200 N San Francisco St, Flagstaff, AZ, 86001. Tel: 928-679-7540. p. 60

Hornberger, Julie, Head, Circ, Shorewood-Troy Public Library District, 650 Deerwood Dr, Shorewood, IL, 60404. Tel: 815-725-1715. p. 647

Hornbuckle, Delritta, Dean, Libr Serv, California State University, Fresno, Henry Madden Library, 5200 N Barton Ave, Mail Stop ML-34, Fresno, CA, 93740-8014. Tel: 559-278-2403. p. 144

Hornbuckle, Jessica, Digital Initiatives Librn, Berry College, 2277 Martha Berry Hwy, Mount Berry, GA, 30149. Tel: 706-236-1705. p. 492

Horne, Angela, Dir, University of California Los Angeles Library, Eugene & Maxine Rosenfeld Management Library, UCLA Anderson School of Management, 110 Westwood Plaza, E-301, Los Angeles, CA, 90095. Tel: 310-875-3047. p. 169

Horne, Brandy R, Instruction & Ref Librn, University of South Carolina Aiken, 471 University Pkwy, Aiken, SC, 29801. Tel: 803-641-3282. p. 2046

Horne, Cynthia, Access Serv, Circ, Librn, Elizabeth City State University, 1704 Weeksville Rd, Elizabeth City, NC, 27909. Tel: 252-335-3427. p. 1687

Horne, Jessica, Asst Chief Exec Officer, Cochrane Public Library, 178 Fourth Ave, Cochrane, ON, P0L 1C0, CANADA. Tel: 705-272-4178. p. 2636

Horne-Popp, Laura, Libr Dir, Rockhurst University, 1100 Rockhurst Rd, Kansas City, MO, 64110-2561. Tel: 816-501-4655. p. 1257

Horne-Popp, Laura, Asst Univ Librn, University of Central Missouri, 601 S Missouri, Warrensburg, MO, 64093-5020. Tel: 660-543-8639. p. 1285

Horner, Andrew, Dir, Converse Jackson Township Public Library, 108 S Jefferson St, Converse, IN, 46919. Tel: 765-395-3344. p. 677

Horner Button, Leslie, Assoc Dean, Res & Learning Serv, University of Massachusetts Amherst Libraries, 154 Hicks Way, University of Massachusetts, Amherst, MA, 01003-9275. Tel: 413-545-6845. p. 985
Horner, Karen, Libr Dir, Park County Library System, 1500 Heart Mountain St, Cody, WY, 82414. Tel: 307-527-1881. p. 2493
Horner, Kelly, Youth Serv Mgr, Guthrie Memorial Library, Two Library Pl, Hanover, PA, 17331. Tel: 717-632-5183. p. 1939
Horner, Nancy, Spec Projects, Eugene Public Library, 100 W Tenth Ave, Eugene, OR, 97401. Tel: 541-682-5450. p. 1878
Horner, Nathan, Libr Asst, Curtis Memorial Library, 116 S Main, Wheatland, IA, 52777. Tel: 563-374-1534. p. 791
Horner, Susan, Libr Mgr, Franklin-Springboro Public Library, 44 E Fourth St, Franklin, OH, 45005. Tel: 937-746-2665. p. 1786
Horner, Thad R, Actg Librn, Digital Scholarship Librn, Research Librn, Oral Roberts University Library, 7777 S Lewis Ave, Tulsa, OK, 74171. Tel: 918-495-6889. p. 1865
Horney, Rachele, Mgr, Stilwell Public Library, Five N Sixth St, Stilwell, OK, 74960. Tel: 918-696-7512. p. 1863
Hornfeck, Ben, Libr Dir, Bridgeville Public Library, 505 McMillen St, Bridgeville, PA, 15017. Tel: 412-221-3737. p. 1914
Hornfeck, Ben, Dir, South Fayette Township Library, 515 Millers Run Rd, Morgan, PA, 15064. Tel: 412-257-8660. p. 1966
Hornick, Julie, Instrul Serv Librn, Florida Southern College, 111 Lake Hollingsworth Dr, Lakeland, FL, 33801-5698. Tel: 863-680-4496. p. 417
Hornig, Cathy, Youth Serv Librn, Merrimac Public Library, 86 W Main St, Merrimac, MA, 01860. Tel: 978-346-9441. p. 1034
Horning, Allison, Libr Spec, Henderson Community College, 2660 S Green St, Henderson, KY, 42420. Tel: 270-831-9760. p. 859
Horning, Sandra, Libr Dir, Chaplin Public Library, 130 Chaplin St, Chaplin, CT, 06235-2302. Tel: 860-455-9424. p. 305
Hornsby, Jennifer, Ref & Access Serv Librn, Peabody Essex Museum, 306 Newburyport Tpk, Rowley, MA, 01969. Tel: 978-745-9500, Ext 3053. p. 1050
Hornstein, Christine, Librn, Nobles County Library, Adrian Branch, 214 Maine Ave, Adrian, MN, 56110. Tel: 507-483-2541. p. 1210
Horodyski, Tracy, Dir, Westbury Memorial Public Library, 445 Jefferson St, Westbury, NY, 11590. Tel: 516-333-0176. p. 1663
Horonic, Josip, Syst Mgr, Andrews University, 4190 Administration Dr, Berrien Springs, MI, 49104-1400. Tel: 269-471-3865. p. 1085
Horosky, Amy, Coord, Ad Serv, West Florida Public Library, 239 N Spring St, Pensacola, FL, 32502. Tel: 850-436-5060. p. 437
Horowitz, Ellie, Asst Librn, Info serv, Literacy Serv, Dominican College Library, 480 Western Hwy, Blauvelt, NY, 10913-2000. Tel: 845-848-7505. p. 1495
Horowitz, Marc David, Libr Dir, North Babylon Public Library, 815 Deer Park Ave, North Babylon, NY, 11703-3812. Tel: 631-669-4020. p. 1607
Horowitz, Sarah, Curator of Rare Bks & Ms, Head, Spec Coll, Haverford College, 370 Lancaster Ave, Haverford, PA, 19041-1392. Tel: 610-896-2948. p. 1942
Horrell, Stacie, Circ Supvr, Salem College, 626 S Church St, Winston-Salem, NC, 27101. Tel: 336-917-5419. p. 1725
Horrocks, Sherma M, Dir, Richland Township Library, 8821 Third St, Vestaburg, MI, 48891. Tel: 989-268-5044. p. 1156
Horrom, Jill, Internal Services, Libr Mgr, Lee County Library System, 2201 Second St, Ste 400, Fort Myers, FL, 33901. Tel: 239-533-4800. p. 403
Horsch, Joyce, Librn, Kansas Department of Corrections, 1737 SE Hwy 54, El Dorado, KS, 67042. Tel: 316-321-7284. p. 806
Horsch, Sonya, Librn, Andale District Library, 328 Main St, Andale, KS, 67001. Tel: 316-444-2363. p. 796
Horsley, Barb, Librn, Wessington Springs Carnegie Library, 109 W Main St, Wessington Springs, SD, 57382. Tel: 605-539-1803. p. 2085
Horsley, Jordan, Media Ctr Coordr, Marymount Manhattan College, 221 E 71st St, New York, NY, 10021. Tel: 212-774-4805. p. 1591
Horst, David, Dir, Bickelhaupt Arboretum Library, 340 S 14th St, Clinton, IA, 52732. Tel: 563-242-4771. p. 740
Horst, Jennifer, Library Contact, Fourth Presbyterian Church, 5500 River Rd, Bethesda, MD, 20816-3399. Tel: 301-320-3600. p. 959
Horst, Julie, HQ Librn, United States Court of Appeals for the Ninth Circuit Library, James R Browning Courthouse, 95 Seventh St, San Francisco, CA, 94103. Tel: 415-355-8650. p. 229
Horst, Victoria, Br Mgr, Coastal Plain Regional Library System, Tifton-Tift County Public, 245 Love Ave, Tifton, GA, 31794. Tel: 229-386-7148. p. 500
Hortemiller, Melissa, Pub Serv Librn, Southern Adventist University, 4851 Industrial Dr, Collegedale, TN, 37315. Tel: 423-236-2788. p. 2094
Hortman, Melinda, Mgr, Pine Mountain Regional Library, Reynolds Community, 208 N Winston St, Reynolds, GA, 31076. Tel: 478-847-3468. p. 488
Horton, Aliyah, Exec Dir, Maryland Pharmacists Association Library, 9115 Guilford Rd, Ste 200, Columbia, MD, 21046. Tel: 443-583-8000. p. 963
Horton, Allison, Head, Registration Serv, Mount Prospect Public Library, Ten S Emerson St, Mount Prospect, IL, 60056. Tel: 847-253-5675. p. 621
Horton, Amanda, Dir, Polk County Law Library, Courthouse, Rm 3076, 255 N Broadway, Bartow, FL, 33830. Tel: 863-534-4013. p. 384
Horton, Ashley, Br Mgr, Riverside County Library System, Valle Vista Library, 25757 Fairview Ave, Hemet, CA, 92544. Tel: 951-927-2611. p. 203
Horton, Darlene, Ad, Oxford Public Library, 110 E Sixth St, Oxford, AL, 36203. Tel: 256-831-1750. p. 32
Horton, Jennifer, Cat Asst, Oral Roberts University Library, 7777 S Lewis Ave, Tulsa, OK, 74171. Tel: 918-495-6881. p. 1865
Horton, Jenny, Libr Dir, University of Lynchburg, 1501 Lakeside Dr, Lynchburg, VA, 24501-3199. Tel: 434-544-8432. p. 2331
Horton, Johnna, Exec Dir, MnPALS, Minnesota State University, Mankato, 3022 Memorial Library, Mankato, MN, 56001. Tel: 507-389-2000. p. 2768
Horton, Julie, Coordr of Ref Serv, Greenwood County Library, 600 S Main St, Greenwood, SC, 29646. Tel: 864-941-3042. p. 2062
Horton, Lia, Online Learning Librn, University of New Hampshire at Manchester Library, 88 Commercial St, Manchester, NH, 03101. Tel: 603-641-4173. p. 1373
Horton, Mary C, Assoc Dean, Admin Serv, University of South Carolina, 1322 Greene St, Columbia, SC, 29208-0103. Tel: 803-777-3142. p. 2055
Horton, Melody, Co-Dir, Glover Spencer Memorial Library, 100 S Sixth St, Corner SE Sixth & Blakely Ave, Rush Springs, OK, 73082. Tel: 580-476-2108. p. 1861
Horton, Rachel, Cat Supvr, Laurel County Public Library District, 120 College Park Dr, London, KY, 40741. Tel: 606-864-5759. p. 864
Horton, Russell P, Res Archivist, Wisconsin Department of Veterans Affairs, 30 W Mifflin St, Ste 300, Madison, WI, 53703. Tel: 608-267-1790. p. 2452
Horton Sherman, Lisa, Dir, Edgartown Free Public Library, 26 W Tisbury Rd, Edgartown, MA, 02539. Tel: 508-627-4221. p. 1017
Horton, Stanley W, Interim Assoc Dean, Libr Serv, Grays Harbor College, 1620 Edward P Smith Dr, Aberdeen, WA, 98520. Tel: 360-538-4051. p. 2357
Horton, Suzanne, Head, Ref & Info Serv, Montgomery City-County Public Library System, Juliette Hampton Morgan Memorial Library, 245 High St, Montgomery, AL, 36104. Tel: 334-240-4992. p. 29
Horton, Tina, Librn, Chaffee Public Library, 202 Wright Ave, Chaffee, MO, 63740. Tel: 573-887-3298. p. 1241
Horton, Tyson, Syst Adminr, Williams County Public Library, 107 E High St, Bryan, OH, 43506-1702. Tel: 419-636-6734. p. 1753
Horton, Wesley, Libr Asst, Desoto Parish Library, Logansport Branch, 203 Hwy 5, Logansport, LA, 71049. Tel: 318-697-2311. p. 896
Hortt, Matthew, Exec Dir, High Plains Library District, 2650 W 29th St, Greeley, CO, 80631. p. 285
Horvath, Doreen, Libr Mgr, Bibliotheque Dentinger, 27 Central Ave SE, Falher, AB, T0H 1M0, CANADA. Tel: 780-837-2776. p. 2539
Horvath, Elizabeth, Librn, Mid-Hudson Forensic Psychiatric Center Library, 2834 Rte 17M, New Hampton, NY, 10958. Tel: 845-374-8700, Ext 3625. p. 1576
Horvath, Patricia, Assoc Dir, Lawyer Serv, Allegheny County Law Library, 921 City-County Bldg, 414 Grant St, Pittsburgh, PA, 15219-2543. Tel: 412-350-5353. p. 1990
Horvath, Patricia, Asst Dir, Tech Serv, Duquesne University, Center for Legal Information, 900 Locust St, Pittsburgh, PA, 15282. Tel: 412-396-5016. p. 1993
Horvath, Steven, Libr Mgr, New York Public Library - Astor, Lenox & Tilden Foundations, Huguenot Park Branch, 830 Huguenot Ave, (@ Dumgole Rd), Staten Island, NY, 10312. Tel: 718-984-4636. p. 1595
Horvay, Henrietta C, Curator, Pres, Goshen Historical Society Library, 21 Old Middle Rd, Goshen, CT, 06756. Tel: 860-491-9610. p. 313
Horwath, Nancy, ILL, Allentown Public Library, 1210 Hamilton St, Allentown, PA, 18102. Tel: 610-820-2400. p. 1904
Horwitz, Matthew, Libr Dir, Saint Patrick's Seminary, 320 Middlefield Rd, Menlo Park, CA, 94025. Tel: 650-289-3327. p. 175
Horwood-Benton, Laura, Commun Relations Librn, Pub Programming Librn, Portsmouth Public Library, 175 Parrott Ave, Portsmouth, NH, 03801-4452. Tel: 603-427-1540. p. 1379
Hosek-Heiar, Jamie, Coop Librn, Deere & Co Library, One John Deere Pl, Moline, IL, 61265. p. 618
Hoseth, Amy, Assoc Dean, User Services & Assessment, Colorado State University Libraries, Morgan Library, 1201 Center Ave Mall, Fort Collins, CO, 80523. Tel: 970-491-1838. p. 280
Hosford, Debbie, Librn, Catawba County Library, Saint Stephens Branch, 3225 Springs Rd, Hickory, NC, 28601-9700. Tel: 828-466-6821. p. 1706
Hosford, John, Visual Res Curator, Alfred University, Scholes Library of Ceramics, New York State College of Ceramics at Alfred University, Two Pine St, Alfred, NY, 14802-1297. p. 1485
Hosid, Sheridan, Dir, McCulloch County Library, 401 E Commerce, Brady, TX, 76825. Tel: 325-597-2617. p. 2149
Hosking, Jenn, Asst Dir, Nashua Public Library, Two Court St, Nashua, NH, 03060. Tel: 603-589-4621. p. 1374
Hoskins, Katie, Instrul Tech Librn, Pub Serv Librn, Northern Virginia Community College Libraries, Alexandria Campus, Bisdorf Bldg, Rm 232, 5000 Dawes Ave, Alexandria, VA, 22311. Tel: 703-845-6031. p. 2304

Hoskins, Nellie, Dir, Galena Public Library, 315 W Seventh St, Galena, KS, 66739-1293. Tel: 620-783-5132. p. 809
Hoskins, Susan, Exec Dir, Pipestone County Historical Society, 113 S Hiawatha, Pipestone, MN, 56164. Tel: 507-825-2563. p. 1193
Hoskins, William, Dir, Pettigrew Home & Museum Library, 131 N Duluth Ave, Sioux Falls, SD, 57104. Tel: 605-367-4210. p. 2082
Hoskinson-Dean, Mary, Asst Dir, Head, Children's Servx, Head, Teen Serv, Mark Twain Library, 439 Redding Rd, Redding, CT, 06896. Tel: 203-938-2545. p. 334
Hosler, Chris, Mr, Br Mgr, Monroe County Public Library, Ellettsville Branch, 600 W Temperance St, Ellettsville, IN, 47429. Tel: 812-876-1272. p. 671
Hosny, Hany, Access Serv Librn, Lending Serv Librn, Roanoke College, 220 High St, Salem, VA, 24153-3794. Tel: 540-375-2295. p. 2346
Hosseini-Ara, Moe, Mr, Dir, Br Operations, Toronto Public Library, 789 Yonge St, Toronto, ON, M4W 2G8, CANADA. Tel: 416-393-7131. p. 2693
Hostetler, Jennifer, Govt Doc, Ref Librn, University of Detroit Mercy School of Law, 651 E Jefferson, Detroit, MI, 48226. Tel: 313-596-9415. p. 1099
Hostetler, Kirsten, Instruction & Outreach Librn, Central Oregon Community College Barber Library, 2600 NW College Way, Bend, OR, 97703. Tel: 541-383-7560. p. 1873
Hostetler, Marna, Dir, Libr Serv, University of Southern Indiana, 8600 University Blvd, Evansville, IN, 47712. Tel: 812-464-1824. p. 682
Hostetter, Karen, Libr Mgr, York County Library System, Red Land Community Library, 70 Newberry Commons, Etters, PA, 17319. Tel: 717-938-5599. p. 2026
Hotalen, Trevor, YA Librn, New Brunswick Free Public Library, 60 Livingston Ave, New Brunswick, NJ, 08901-2597. Tel: 732-745-5108, Ext 22. p. 1424
Hotchkiss, Gina, Law Libr Asst, Medina County Law Library Association, 93 Public Sq, Medina, OH, 44256. Tel: 330-725-9744. p. 1802
Hotchkiss, Valerie, Univ Librn, Vanderbilt University, 419 21st Ave S, Nashville, TN, 37203-2427. Tel: 615-322-4782. p. 2121
Hotchner, Margaret, Adminr, Researcher, Rocktown History Genealogy & Research Library, 382 High St, Dayton, VA, 22821. Tel: 540-879-2681. p. 2315
Hotelling, Kimberly, Libr Asst, Blake Memorial Library, 676 Village Rd, East Corinth, VT, 05040. Tel: 802-439-5338. p. 2283
Hoth, Brian, Dir, Hamburg Public Library, 102 Buffalo St, Hamburg, NY, 14075-5097. Tel: 716-649-4415. p. 1543
Hott, Joann, Libr Dir, Henryetta Public Library, 518 W Main St, Henryetta, OK, 74437. Tel: 918-652-7377. p. 1849
Hottel, Zachary, Archivist, Shenandoah County Library, 514 Stoney Creek Blvd, Edinburg, VA, 22824. Tel: 540-984-8200. p. 2315
Hotz, Laurie, Youth Serv Librn, Fort Dodge Public Library, 424 Central Ave, Fort Dodge, IA, 50501. Tel: 515-573-8167, Ext 6244. p. 754
Houchens, Chris, Libr Dir, Charleston Carnegie Public Library, 712 Sixth St, Charleston, IL, 61920. Tel: 217-345-4913. p. 552
Houchens, Michele, Librn, Tech Serv Mgr, Three Rivers Public Library District, 25207 W Channon Dr, Channahon, IL, 60410-5028. Tel: 815-467-6200, Ext 208. p. 552
Houchens, Tracy, Adult Prog Coordr, Logan County Public Library, 225 Armory Dr, Russellville, KY, 42276. Tel: 270-726-6129. p. 874
Houchin, David, Spec Coll Librn, Clarksburg-Harrison Public Library, 404 W Pike St, Clarksburg, WV, 26301. Tel: 304-627-2236. p. 2401
Houck, Maureen, Ref Librn, Sandy Public Library, 38980 Proctor Blvd, Sandy, OR, 97055-8040. Tel: 503-668-5537. p. 1898
Houck, Michael, Librn, Johns Hopkins University Libraries, School of Professional Studies in Business & Education, Ten N Charles St, Baltimore, MD, 21201. Tel: 410-516-0700. p. 954
Houck, Michael, Librn, Johns Hopkins University Libraries, 6740 Alexander Bell Dr, Columbia, MD, 21040. Tel: 410-516-9700, 410-516-9709. p. 963
Houck, Shari, Librn, North Central Washington Libraries, Pateros Public Library, 174 Pateros Mall, Pateros, WA, 98846. Tel: 509-923-2298. p. 2394
Houde, Jo-Ann, Tech Serv Librn, Nesmith Library, Eight Fellows Rd, Windham, NH, 03087-1909. Tel: 603-432-7154. p. 1384
Houde, Lisa, Asst Dir, Coll Mgr, ILL Mgr, Rye Public Library, 581 Washington Rd, Rye, NH, 03870. Tel: 603-964-8401. p. 1380
Houf, Jeana, Libr Dir, Wellsville Public Library, 108 W Hudson St, Wellsville, MO, 63384. Tel: 573-684-6151. p. 1286
Houff, Alexandra, Mgr, Digital Equity & Virtual Servs, Baltimore County Public Library, 320 York Rd, Towson, MD, 21204-5179. Tel: 410-887-6100. p. 979
Houge, Meredith, Dir, Galesville Public Library, 16787 S Main St, Galesville, WI, 54630. Tel: 608-582-2552. p. 2436
Hough, Elizabeth, Mkt Mgr, Hedberg Public Library, 316 S Main St, Janesville, WI, 53545. Tel: 608-758-6607. p. 2443
Hough, Kathy, Libr Mgr, Project Coordr, Katten Muchin Rosenman LLP, 50 Rockefeller Plaza, New York, NY, 10020-1605. Tel: 312-577-8355. p. 1590
Houghton, Lynn, Regional History Curator, Western Michigan University, Zhang Legacy Collections Center, 1650 Oakland Dr, Kalamazoo, MI, 49008. Tel: 269-387-8491. p. 1122
Hougland, Mary, Dir, Jennings County Public Library, 2375 N State Hwy 3, North Vernon, IN, 47265. Tel: 812-346-2091. p. 711
Houissa, Ali, Middle East & Islamic Studies Curator, Cornell University Library, Division of Asia Collections (Carl A Kroch Library), Kroch Library, Level 1, Ithaca, NY, 14853. Tel: 607-255-8199. p. 1551
Houk, Deborah, Govt Doc & Tech Serv Librn, Libr Dir, Univ Archivist, McKendree University, 701 College Rd, Lebanon, IL, 62254-1299. Tel: 618-537-6950. p. 607
Houlberg, Amily, Dir, The Church of Jesus Christ of Latter-Day Saints, 3501 Loma Vista, Ventura, CA, 93003. Tel: 805-643-5607. p. 255
Houle, Anne, Coordr, Ch Serv, Whitchurch-Stouffville Public Library, Two Park Dr, Stouffville, ON, L4A 4K1, CANADA. Tel: 905-642-7323, Ext 5228. p. 2681
Houle, Cheryl, Librn, Westlock Municipal Library, Jarvie Public Library, Jarvie Community Ctr, Jarvie, AB, T0G 1H0, CANADA. Tel: 780-350-8160. p. 2559
Houle, Collette, Librn, Leach Public Library, 130 Park Ave, Irasburg, VT, 05845. Tel: 802-754-2526. p. 2286
Houle, Diane, Mgr, Springfield City Library, Mason Square Branch, 765 State St, Springfield, MA, 01109. Tel: 413-263-6853. p. 1056
Houle, Katia, Dir, Bibliotheque Municipale de Warwick, 181, rue Saint-Louis, Warwick, QC, J0A 1M0, CANADA. Tel: 819-358-4325. p. 2739
Houle, Louis, Coll Serv, Sr Dir, McGill University Libraries, McLennan Library Bldg, 3459 McTavish St, Montreal, QC, H3A 0C9, CANADA. Tel: 514-398-4763. p. 2726
Houle, Rebecca, Libr Tech, Northwood Technical College, 2100 Beaser Ave, Ashland, WI, 54806. Tel: 715-682-4591, Ext 3108. p. 2421
Houle, Sylviane, Librn, Cegep de Saint-Hyacinthe Bibliotheque, 3000 rue Boulle, Saint-Hyacinthe, QC, J2S 1H9, CANADA. Tel: 450-773-6800, Ext 2213. p. 2735
Houlihan Ng, Shannon, Br Mgr, Riverside County Library System, Idyllwild Library, 54401 Village Center Dr, Idyllwild, CA, 92549. Tel: 951-659-2300. p. 202
Houlne, Celina, Libr Dir, Rockingham Free Public Library, 65 Westminster St, Bellows Falls, VT, 05101. Tel: 802-463-4270. p. 2278
Hounshell, Janet, Librn, Cisco Public Library, 600 Ave G, Cisco, TX, 76437. Tel: 254-442-1020. p. 2155
Houppert, Anne Marie, Sr Librn, The National Academies of Sciences, Engineering & Medicine, 500 Fifth St NW, Keck 304, Washington, DC, 20001-2721. Tel: 202-334-2125. p. 371
Houpt, Helen, Librn, Tech Serv, UPMC Pinnacle - Harrisburg, Brady Bldg, 1st flr, 205 S Front St, Harrisburg, PA, 17101-2099. Tel: 717-657-7247. p. 1941
Houpt, Helen L, Librn, PinnacleHealth Library Services, 4300 Londonderry Rd, Harrisburg, PA, 17103. Tel: 717-657-7247. p. 1941
House, Debra, Exec Dir, Legal Aid of East Tennessee Library, 311 W Walnut St, Johnson City, TN, 37604. Tel: 423-928-8311. p. 2104
House, Elizabeth, Head, Ref (Info Serv), Wilmington College, 120 College St, Wilmington, OH, 45177. Tel: 937-481-2441. p. 1832
House, Lisa, Dir, Human Res, Vancouver Island Regional Library, 6250 Hammond Bay Rd, Nanaimo, BC, V9T 6M9, CANADA. Tel: 250-729-2335. p. 2570
House, Martin, Asst Dir, Pub Serv, Central Piedmont Community College Library, 1201 Elizabeth Ave, Charlotte, NC, 28235. Tel: 704-330-6752. p. 1679
House, Priscilla, Dir, Rutherford Library, 2000 State Rte 129, South Bristol, ME, 04568. Tel: 207-644-1882. p. 941
House, Sara, Mgr, Calgary Public Library, Fish Creek, 11161 Bonaventure Dr SE, Calgary, AB, T2J 6S1, CANADA. p. 2526
House, Sara, Mgr, Calgary Public Library, Quarry Park, 108 Quarry Park Rd SE, Calgary, AB, T2C 5R1, CANADA. p. 2527
House, Sara, Mgr, Calgary Public Library, Southwood, 924 Southland Dr SW, Calgary, AB, T2W 0J9, CANADA. p. 2527
Housel, Zachary, Cat/ILL Librn, Belmont Abbey College, 100 Belmont-Mt Holly Rd, Belmont, NC, 28012. Tel: 704-461-6748. p. 1674
Houser, Amy, Br Librn, Genesee District Library, Flint Township-McCarty Public Library, 2071 S Graham Rd, Flint, MI, 48532. Tel: 810-732-9150. p. 1106
Houser, Charlene, Bus Mgr, Rutgers University Libraries, Archibald Stevens Alexander Library, 169 College Ave, New Brunswick, NJ, 08901-1163. Tel: 848-932-5997. p. 1424
Houser, Danis, Br Mgr, Grosse Pointe Public Library, Ewald, 15175 E Jefferson, Grosse Pointe Park, MI, 48236. Tel: 313-821-8830. p. 1112
Houser, Danis, Head, Access Serv, Royal Oak Public Library, 222 E Eleven Mile Rd, Royal Oak, MI, 48067-2633. Tel: 248-246-3714. p. 1146
Houser, Jennifer, Dir, Church of the Brethren, 1451 Dundee Ave, Elgin, IL, 60120-1694. Tel: 847-429-4368. p. 583
Houser, Kay, Librn, Southeastern Community College, 4564 Chadbourne Hwy, Whiteville, NC, 28472. Tel: 910-642-7141, Ext 219. p. 1722
Houser, Maxine, Head Librn, Golconda Public Library, 126 W Main St, Golconda, IL, 62938. Tel: 618-683-6531. p. 594
Houser, Stephen, Dir, West Georgia Regional Library, 710 Rome St, Carrollton, GA, 30117. Tel: 770-830-2233, Ext 1010. p. 469
Houser, Stephen, Dir, Twin Lakes Library System, 151 S Jefferson St SE, Milledgeville, GA, 31061-3419. Tel: 478-452-0677. p. 491

Housewright, Keith, Dir, Case-Halstead Public Library, 550 Sixth St, Carlyle, IL, 62231. Tel: 618-594-5210. p. 549
Housknecht, Julie, Librn, South Carolina Commission on Higher Education Library, 1122 Lady St, Ste 300, Columbia, SC, 29201-3240. Tel: 803-737-2260. p. 2054
Houssiere, Barbara, Asst Prof, Pub Serv Librn, McNeese State University, 300 S Beauregard Dr, Lake Charles, LA, 70609. Tel: 337-475-5732. p. 894
Houston, Alan, Ref Librn, Chappaqua Public Library, 195 S Greeley Ave, Chappaqua, NY, 10514. Tel: 914-238-4779. p. 1516
Houston, Anne, Col Librn, Dir of Libr, Swarthmore College, 500 College Ave, Swarthmore, PA, 19081. Tel: 610-328-8489. p. 2011
Houston, Benjamin, Ref & Ser Librn, University of Detroit Mercy School of Law, 651 E Jefferson, Detroit, MI, 48226. Tel: 313-596-9414. p. 1099
Houston, Gypsy, Local Hist Librn, Union County Public Library, 316 E Windsor St, Monroe, NC, 28112. Tel: 704-283-8184. p. 1703
Houston, Hope, Exec Dir, Libr Serv, Bentley University, 175 Forest St, Waltham, MA, 02452-4705. Tel: 781-891-2450. p. 1061
Houston, James S, Dir, Art Circle Public Library, Three East St, Crossville, TN, 38555. Tel: 931-484-6790. p. 2095
Houston, Julie, Libr Dir, Ayer Public Library District, 208 Locust St, Delavan, IL, 61734. Tel: 309-244-8236. p. 578
Houston, Karen, Youth & Teen Serv, Niceville Public Library, 206 Partin Dr N, Niceville, FL, 32578. Tel: 850-279-6436, Ext 1514. p. 428
Houston, Karla, Librn, Lisbon Public Library, 45 School St, Lisbon, NH, 03585. Tel: 603-838-6615. p. 1370
Houston, Kim, Chief Financial Officer, Metropolitan Council for Educational Opportunity Library, 11 Roxbury St, Roxbury, MA, 02119. Tel: 617-427-1545, Ext 121. p. 1050
Houston, Monica, Dir, Human Res, Kitsap Regional Library, 1301 Sylvan Way, Bremerton, WA, 98310-3498. Tel: 360-475-9160. p. 2359
Houston, Nainsi, PhD, Libr Dir, Muskingum University, Ten College Dr, New Concord, OH, 43762. Tel: 740-826-8260. p. 1806
Houston, Sandra J, Pres, Longyear Museum Library, 1125 Boylston St, Chestnut Hill, MA, 02467. Tel: 617-278-9000. p. 1011
Hout, Erica, Dir, Boylston Public Library, 695 Main St, Boylston, MA, 01505. Tel: 508-869-2371. p. 1001
Houtler, Kris, Asst Dir, Reedsburg Public Library, 370 Vine St, Reedsburg, WI, 53959. Tel: 608-768-7323. p. 2472
Houtz, Thomas, Libr Dir, Tower-Porter Community Library, 230 E Grand Ave, Tower City, PA, 17980-1124. Tel: 717-647-4900. p. 2013
Houyoux, Eve Marie, Asst Dir, Universite du Quebec a Trois-Rivieres, Pavillon Albert-Tessier, 3351 Blvd des Forges, Trois-Rivieres, QC, G9A 5H7, CANADA. Tel: 819-376-5011, Ext 2266. p. 2738
Hovde, Anne, Access Serv, Coll Serv, University of Minnesota Duluth, 416 Library Dr, Duluth, MN, 55812. Tel: 218-726-7887. p. 1173
Hovekamp, Tina, Libr Dir, Central Oregon Community College Barber Library, 2600 NW College Way, Bend, OR, 97703. Tel: 541-383-7560. p. 1873
Hoveland, Danielle, Cat, ILL Mgr, Dakota County Technical College Library, 1300 145th St E, Rosemount, MN, 55068. Tel: 651-423-8366. p. 1195
Hovey, Mark, Mgr, Info Tech, Deschutes Public Library District, 507 NW Wall St, Bend, OR, 97703. Tel: 541-312-1043. p. 1874
Hovey, Melissa, Circ Mgr, Alma College Library, 614 W Superior St, Alma, MI, 48801. Tel: 989-463-7229. p. 1077
Hovind, Cynthia, Dir, Langlois Public Library, 48234 Hwy 101, Langlois, OR, 97450. Tel: 541-348-2066. p. 1884
Hovland, Matt, Head, Circ Serv, Bismarck Veterans Memorial Public Library, 515 N Fifth St, Bismarck, ND, 58501-4081. Tel: 701-355-1480. p. 1729
Howard, Alice, Head Librn, Prog Coordr, Ecorse Public Library, 4184 W Jefferson Ave, Ecorse, MI, 48229. Tel: 313-389-2030. p. 1103
Howard, Allison, Cat/Ref Librn, University of South Florida, Hinks & Elaine Shimberg Health Sciences Library, 12901 Bruce B Downs Blvd, MDC 31, Tampa, FL, 33612. Tel: 813-974-4752. p. 449
Howard, Amy, Ref Librn, Regis College Library, 235 Wellesley St, Weston, MA, 02493. Tel: 781-768-7300. p. 1068
Howard, Angela, Br Mgr, Jackson County Public Library, Ravenswood Branch, 323 Virginia St, Ravenswood, WV, 26164. Tel: 304-273-5343. p. 2413
Howard, Bryan, Dir, Delaware County District Library, 84 E Winter St, Delaware, OH, 43015. Tel: 740-362-3861. p. 1781
Howard, Cathy, ILL/Ref Librn, Greene County Public Library, 120 N 12th St, Paragould, AR, 72450. Tel: 870-236-8711. p. 107
Howard, Christine, Youth Serv Librn, Jasper-Dubois County Public Library, 1116 Main St, Jasper, IN, 47546-2899. Tel: 812-482-2712, Ext 6114. p. 697
Howard, Deanna, Dir, Plano Community Library District, 15 W North St, Plano, IL, 60545. Tel: 630-552-2009. p. 635
Howard, Dorinda, Tech Serv, Rochester Public Library, 65 S Main St, Rochester, NH, 03867-2707. Tel: 603-332-1428. p. 1380
Howard, Elizabeth, Dir, Texas Wesleyan University, 1201 Wesleyan St, Fort Worth, TX, 76105. Tel: 817-531-4800. p. 2181
Howard, Eric, Asst Dir, Santa Cruz City-County Library System, 117 Union St, Santa Cruz, CA, 95060-3873. Tel: 831-427-7706, Ext 7670. p. 242
Howard, Erin, Dir, Learning Serv, Camosun College, Liz Ashton Campus Centre Library, 4461 Inteurban Rd, 3rd Flr, Victoria, BC, V9E 2C1, CANADA. Tel: 250-370-3604. p. 2582
Howard, James Hope, Dir, Pahkisimon Nuye?ah Library System, 118 Avro Pl, Air Ronge, SK, S0J 3G0, CANADA. Tel: 306-425-4525. p. 2741
Howard, Janet, Dir, Carlinville Public Library, 510 N Broad St, Carlinville, IL, 62626-1019. Tel: 217-854-3505. p. 549
Howard, Jason, Librn, Forest History Society Library, 701 William Vickers Ave, Durham, NC, 27701-3162. Tel: 919-682-9319. p. 1685
Howard, Jessica, Ref Librn, Greenwood County Library, 600 S Main St, Greenwood, SC, 29646. Tel: 864-941-4650. p. 2062
Howard, Jo, Br Librn, Ch, Lincoln County Library System, LaBarge Branch, 262 Main St, LaBarge, WY, 83123. Tel: 307-386-2571. p. 2496
Howard, John, Dir, Mahomet Public Library District, 1702 E Oak St, Mahomet, IL, 61853-7427. Tel: 217-586-2611. p. 612
Howard, Judith, Br Librn, Kemper-Newton Regional Library System, Scooba Branch, 801-1099 Kemper St, Scooba, MS, 39358. Tel: 662-476-8454. p. 1234
Howard, Julie, Adult Programming, Librn, Ocean City Free Public Library, 1735 Simpson Ave, Ste 4, Ocean City, NJ, 08226. Tel: 609-399-2434, Ext 5222. p. 1430
Howard, Karen, Bus Officer, Northwestern Regional Library, 111 N Front St, 2nd Flr, Elkin, NC, 28621. Tel: 336-835-4894, Ext 1002. p. 1688
Howard, Kenneth, Librn, United States Army, Bruce C Clarke Library Academic Services Division, Bldg 3202, 14020 MSCOE Loop, Ste 200, Fort Leonard Wood, MO, 65473-8928. Tel: 573-563-5318. p. 1246
Howard, Kristina, Adult Serv, Tinley Park Public Library, 7851 Timber Dr, Tinley Park, IL, 60477-3398. Tel: 708-532-0160, Ext 1. p. 653
Howard, Kristy, Exec Dir, Consortium of College & University Media Centers, Indiana University, Franklin Hall 0009, 601 E Kirkwood Ave, Bloomington, IN, 47405-1223. Tel: 812-855-6049. p. 2765
Howard, Kyrra, Libr Dir, Pettee Memorial Library, 16 S Main St, Wilmington, VT, 05363. Tel: 802-464-8557. p. 2299
Howard, Laurie, Exec Dir, Passaic River Coalition, 330 Speedwell Ave, Morristown, NJ, 07960. Tel: 973-532-9830. p. 1422
Howard, Margaret, Br Mgr, Chesterfield County Public Library, Bon Air, 9103 Rattlesnake Rd, Richmond, VA, 23235. Tel: 804-751-2275. p. 2312
Howard, Mary, Supv Librn, Dearborn Heights City Libraries, Caroline Kennedy Library, 24590 George St, Dearborn Heights, MI, 48127. Tel: 313-791-3824. p. 1096
Howard, Michele P, Libr Dir, Traverse Area District Library, 610 Woodmere Ave, Traverse City, MI, 49686. Tel: 231-932-8500. p. 1154
Howard, Michelle, Law Libr Dir/Law Librn, Pinellas County Law Library, 324 S Ft Harrison Ave, Clearwater, FL, 33756-5165. Tel: 727-464-3411. p. 389
Howard, Mollie, Supvr, Circ, Memphis Public Library, Raleigh Branch, 3157 Powers Rd, Memphis, TN, 38128. Tel: 901-415-2778. p. 2113
Howard, Mykie, Ser/Govt Doc Librn, Morehead State University, 150 University Blvd, Morehead, KY, 40351. Tel: 606-783-5116. p. 869
Howard, Paul, Librn, Salem Health Community Health Education Center, Salem Hospital, 890 Oak St SE, Bldg D-CHEC, Salem, OR, 97301. Tel: 503-814-2432. p. 1896
Howard, Rachel, Ch, Circ Serv, Bonne Terre Memorial Library, Five SW Main St, Bonne Terre, MO, 63628. Tel: 573-358-2260. p. 1238
Howard, Rebecca, Br Mgr, Tulsa City-County Library, Martin Regional Library, 2601 S Garnett Rd, Tulsa, OK, 74129. p. 1866
Howard, Sarah, Libr Asst, Murphy Helwig Library, 111 N Page, Monona, IA, 52159. Tel: 563-539-2356. p. 770
Howard, Sheryl, Extended Day Librn, Lawson State Community College Library, 1100 Ninth Ave SW, Bessemer, AL, 35022. Tel: 205-929-3434, 205-929-6333. p. 6
Howard, Stephanie, Dir, Pickens County Library System, 304 Biltmore Rd, Easley, SC, 29640. Tel: 864-850-7077. p. 2058
Howard, Sue, Dir, Edgecombe County Memorial Library, 909 N Main St, Tarboro, NC, 27886. Tel: 252-823-1141. p. 1718
Howard, Tony, Dir, Pickerington Public Library, 201 Opportunity Way, Pickerington, OH, 43147-1296. Tel: 614-837-4101, Ext 222. p. 1815
Howard, Vivian, Dr, Assoc Prof, Dalhousie University, Kenneth C Rowe Management Bldg, Ste 4010, 6100 University Ave, Halifax, NS, B3H 4R2, CANADA. Tel: 902-494-3031. p. 2795
Howden, Norman, Dr, Asst Dean, Dallas College, 801 Main St, Dallas, TX, 75202-3605. Tel: 214-860-2176. p. 2164
Howe, Cara, Asst Dir, Archives & Spec Coll, SUNY Upstate Medical University, 766 Irving Ave, Syracuse, NY, 13210-1602. Tel: 315-464-4585. p. 1650
Howe, Carol, Sci Librn, Haverford College, 370 Lancaster Ave, Haverford, PA, 19041-1392. Tel: 610-896-1416. p. 1942
Howe, Carol, Sci, Haverford College, Astronomy, Observatory, 370 W Lancaster Ave, Haverford, PA, 19041. Tel: 610-896-1416. p. 1942
Howe, Carol, Sci, Haverford College, White Science, 370 W Lancaster Ave, Haverford, PA, 19041. Tel: 610-896-1416. p. 1942
Howe, Donna, Librn, Big Horn County Public Library, 419 N Custer Ave, Hardin, MT, 59034. Tel: 406-665-9742. p. 1295

Howe, Farrell, Mkt & Communications Mgr, Kalamazoo Public Library, 315 S Rose St, Kalamazoo, MI, 49007-5264. Tel: 269-553-7879. p. 1121

Howe, Kristi, Exec Dir, Vigo County Public Library, 680 Poplar St, Terre Haute, IN, 47807. Tel: 812-232-1113, Ext 1001. p. 721

Howe, Lindy, Asst Librn, Bayfield Carnegie Library, 37 N Broad St, Bayfield, WI, 54814. Tel: 715-779-3953. p. 2422

Howe, Nancy, Outreach Librn, Pub Relations Librn, Baldwinsville Public Library, 33 E Genesee St, Baldwinsville, NY, 13027-2575. Tel: 315-635-5631. p. 1490

Howe, Rebecca, Liaison Librn, University of Texas Health Science Center at San Antonio Libraries, 7703 Floyd Curl Dr, MSC 7940, San Antonio, TX, 78229-3900. Tel: 210-567-2450. p. 2240

Howe, Roseann, Circ, Elkins Public Library, Nine Center Rd, Canterbury, NH, 03224. Tel: 603-783-4386. p. 1356

Howe, Shannon, Circ Mgr, Valparaiso University, 1410 Chapel Dr, Valparaiso, IN, 46383-6493. Tel: 219-464-5500. p. 723

Howe, Susan, Mgr, Nottoway County Public Libraries, Crewe Branch, 414 Tyler St, Crewe, VA, 23930. Tel: 434-645-8688. p. 2314

Howelette-Leite, Susan, Libr Mgr, Timberland Regional Library, Amanda Park Branch, 6118 US Hwy 101, Amanda Park, WA, 98526. Tel: 360-288-2725. p. 2388

Howell, Angela, Libr Dir, Maricopa Library & Cultural Center, 18160 N Maya Angelou Dr, Maricopa, AZ, 85138. Tel: 520-568-2926. p. 66

Howell, Brad, Dir, Community & Staff Engagement, Hamilton East Public Library, One Library Plaza, Noblesville, IN, 46060. Tel: 317-773-1384. p. 710

Howell, Dana, Archivist, Research Librn, Monmouth County Historical Association Library & Archives, 70 Court St, Freehold, NJ, 07728. Tel: 732-462-1466. p. 1404

Howell, Dorothy, Libr Dir, Carteret County Public Library, 1702 Live Oak St, Ste 100, Beaufort, NC, 28516. Tel: 252-648-7725. p. 1673

Howell, Jared, Dir, Elkins-Randolph County Public Library, 416 Davis Ave, Elkins, WV, 26241. Tel: 304-637-0287. p. 2402

Howell, Jenny, Archivist, Youth Serv, Musser Public Library, 408 E Second St, Muscatine, IA, 52761. Tel: 563-263-3065, Ext 105. p. 772

Howell, Judy K, Dir, Big Sandy Community & Technical College, One Bert T Combs Dr, Prestonsburg, KY, 41653. Tel: 606-889-4750. p. 873

Howell, Katie, Interim Assoc Dean, Spec Coll & Univ Archives, University of North Carolina at Charlotte, 9201 University City Blvd, Charlotte, NC, 28223-0001. Tel: 704-687-1166. p. 1681

Howell, Kelly, Med Librn, HonorHealth John C Lincoln Medical Center, 250 E Dunlap Ave, Phoenix, AZ, 85020. Tel: 602-870-6328. p. 70

Howell, Lee, Knowledge Resource Coord, DLA Piper US LLP, 444 W Lake St, Ste 900, Chicago, IL, 60606-0089. Tel: 312-849-8690. p. 560

Howell, Mark E, Ref Librn, RTI International, 3040 E Cornwallis Rd, Research Triangle Park, NC, 27709. Tel: 919-541-6364. p. 1712

Howell, Max, Ms Archivist, American Institute of Physics, One Physics Ellipse, College Park, MD, 20740. Tel: 301-209-3177. p. 962

Howell, Ora Mims, Sr Librn, United States Environmental Protection, Region 4 Library, Atlanta Federal Ctr, 61 Forsyth St SW, Atlanta, GA, 30303-3104. Tel: 404-562-8125. p. 466

Howell, Polly, Ref (Info Servs), Wabash Carnegie Public Library, 188 W Hill St, Wabash, IN, 46992-3048. Tel: 260-563-2972. p. 724

Howell, Rachel, Asst Dir, East Central Regional Library, 111 Dellwood St, Cambridge, MN, 55008-1588. Tel: 763-689-7390. p. 1167

Howell, Ramona, Br Mgr, White County Regional Library System, Goff Public, 323 N Elm, Beebe, AR, 72012-3245. Tel: 501-882-3235. p. 110

Howell-Rouchka, Kelly, Libr Mgr, South Central College Library, 1225 SW Third St, Faribault, MN, 55021. Tel: 507-332-5883. p. 1175

Howes, Mary, Br Mgr, Puskarich Public Library, Clark Memorial, 102 W Main St, Freeport, OH, 43973. Tel: 740-658-3855, 740-673-0800. p. 1754

Howes-Joseph, Kate, Tech Serv Librn, Hyannis Public Library, 401 Main St, Hyannis, MA, 02601. Tel: 508-775-2280. p. 1026

Howison, Barbara, County Librn, Riverside County Library System, 5840 Mission Blvd, Riverside, CA, 92509. Tel: 951-369-3003. p. 201

Howitt-Covalt, Tammy, Dir, Bridgeport Public Library, 722 Main St, Bridgeport, NE, 69336. Tel: 308-262-0326. p. 1308

Howland, Jane, Learning Technologies Coordr, Teaching Prof, University of Missouri-Columbia, 303 Townsend Hall, Columbia, MO, 65211. Tel: 573-882-4546. p. 2788

Howland, Joan, Assoc Dean, Info Tech, University of Minnesota Libraries-Twin Cities, Law Library, 120 Mondale Hall, 229 19th Ave S, Minneapolis, MN, 55455. Tel: 612-625-4300. p. 1185

Howorth, Vasser, Head, Tech Serv, Historic New Orleans Collection, 410 Chartres St, New Orleans, LA, 70130. Tel: 504-598-7107. p. 901

Hoxie, David E, Dir, Libr Serv, Alderson-Broaddus University, 101 College Hill Dr, Philippi, WV, 26416. Tel: 304-457-6306. p. 2412

Hoxworth, Sharon, Librn, Holmes County District Public Library, Killbuck Branch, 160 W Front St, Killbuck, OH, 44637. Tel: 330-276-0882. p. 1803

Hoy, Charlotte, Librn, Elizabethtown-Kitley Township Public Library, Kitley Branch, 424 Hwy 29, Toledo, ON, K0E 1Y0, CANADA. p. 2627

Hoy, Edana, Head, Youth Serv, Bethlehem Area Public Library, 11 W Church St, Bethlehem, PA, 18018. Tel: 610-867-3761, Ext 218. p. 1911

Hoy, Lindsay, Digital Imaging Tech, School of the Art Institute of Chicago, 37 S Wabash Ave, Chicago, IL, 60603-3103. Tel: 312-899-5097. p. 568

Hoyda, Cleone, Ch, Libr Asst, Crawford Public Library, 601 Second St, Crawford, NE, 69339. Tel: 308-665-1780. p. 1311

Hoyle, Chloe, Outreach & Instruction Librn, Limestone University Library, 1115 College Dr, Gaffney, SC, 29340. Tel: 864-488-4446. p. 2060

Hoyle, Jeanne, Dir, Swans Island Educational Society, 451 Atlantic Rd, Swans Island, ME, 04685. Tel: 207-526-4330. p. 943

Hoyle, Julie, Dir, Waterboro Public Library, 187 Main St, East Waterboro, ME, 04030. Tel: 207-247-3363. p. 924

Hoyle, Kimberly, Dir, Geary Public Library, 106 W Main St, Geary, OK, 73040. Tel: 405-884-2372. p. 1848

Hoyne, Kathleen, Dir, Cabot Public Library, The Willey Bldg, 3084 Main St, Cabot, VT, 05647. Tel: 802-563-2721. p. 2281

Hoyt, Eric, Dir, University of Wisconsin-Madison, Wisconsin Center for Film & Theater Research, 816 State St, Madison, WI, 53706. Tel: 608-264-6466. p. 2452

Hozey, Melissa, Currahee Campus Librn, North Georgia Technical College Library, 1500 Hwy 197 N, Clarkesville, GA, 30523. Tel: 706-779-8104. p. 471

Hradecky, Allison, Circ Mgr, University of St Augustine for Health Sciences, 5401 La Crosse Ave, Austin, TX, 78739. Tel: 737-202-3229. p. 2141

Hradecky, Rachel, Head, Govt Doc, Head Govt Publ, Northern Illinois University Libraries, 217 Normal Rd, DeKalb, IL, 60115-2828. Tel: 815-753-9841. p. 577

Hranjec, Stephanie, Ref Serv, Monroe Community College, Damon City Campus Library, 228 E Main St, 4th Flr 4-101, Rochester, NY, 14604. Tel: 585-262-1413. p. 1629

Hren, Amy, Mem Serv Librn, Capital District Library Council, 28 Essex St, Albany, NY, 12206. Tel: 518-438-2500. p. 2770

Hren, Linda, Dir, Gnadenhutten Public Library, 160 N Walnut St, Gnadenhutten, OH, 44629. Tel: 740-254-9224. p. 1788

Hren, Richard, Info Access Librn, Info Mgr, Carthage College, 2001 Alford Park Dr, Kenosha, WI, 53140-1900. Tel: 262-551-5950. p. 2444

Hricko, Mary, PhD, Dr, Libr Dir, Kent State University, 11411 Claridon-Troy Rd, Burton, OH, 44021-9535. Tel: 440-834-3717. p. 1754

Hristov, Nathalie, Librn, University of Tennessee, Knoxville, George F DeVine Music Library, Natalie L Haslam Music Ctr, G04, 1741 Volunteer Blvd, Knoxville, TN, 37996-2600. Tel: 865-974-9893. p. 2107

Hristova, Rumyana, Cataloging & Outreach Librarian, Evangel University, 1111 N Glenstone Ave, Springfield, MO, 65802. Tel: 417-865-2815, Ext 7268. p. 1280

Hrivnak, David, Dir, Peoples Library, 880 Barnes St, New Kensington, PA, 15068. Tel: 724-339-1021, Ext 12. p. 1969

Hrivnak, Kimberley, Chief Operating Officer, Allegheny County Library Association (ACLA), 22 Wabash St, Ste 202, Pittsburgh, PA, 15220. Tel: 412-921-1123. p. 1990

Hronchek, Jessica, Ref & Instrul Serv Librn, Hope College, Van Wylen Library, 53 Graves Pl, Holland, MI, 49422. Tel: 616-395-7124. p. 1115

Hrubes, Jessica, Asst Librn, Montfort Public Library, 102 E Park St, Montfort, WI, 53569. Tel: 608-943-6265. p. 2462

Hruska, Brad, Business Services Librn, Columbus Public Library, 2500 14th St, Ste 2, Columbus, NE, 68601. Tel: 402-562-4205. p. 1311

Hruska, Kristy, Librn, Hastings Public Library, 314 N Denver Ave, Hastings, NE, 68901. Tel: 402-461-2354. p. 1317

Hrycelak, M, Dr, Archivist, Dir, Ukrainian Medical Association of North America, 2247 W Chicago Ave, Ste 206, Chicago, IL, 60622. Tel: 773-278-6262. p. 569

Hsieh, Fang-Lan, Dr, Librn, Southwestern Baptist Theological Seminary Libraries, Kathryn Sullivan Bowld Music Library, 1809 W Broadus, Rm 113, Fort Worth, TX, 76115-2157. Tel: 817-923-1921, Ext 2070. p. 2180

Hsu, Mona, Operations Librn, San Diego Christian College & Southern California Seminary Library, c/o San Diego Christian College, 200 Riverview Pkwy, Santee, CA, 92071. Tel: 619-201-8680. p. 245

Hu, Estelle, Dir, John H Stroger Jr Hospital of Cook County, 1950 W Polk St, Rm 5218, Chicago, IL, 60612. Tel: 312-864-0506. p. 569

Hu, Mei, Metadata Librn, Tennessee Technological University, 1100 N Peachtree Ave, Cookeville, TN, 38505. Tel: 931-372-3326. p. 2095

Hu, Robert H, Dir, Saint Mary's University, Sarita Kennedy East Law Library, One Camino Santa Maria, San Antonio, TX, 78228-8605. Tel: 210-431-2056. p. 2238

Hu, Sheila, ILL Librn, Pace University, 861 Bedford Rd, Pleasantville, NY, 10570-2799. Tel: 914-773-3853. p. 1620

Hu, Suxiao, Head, Coll Develop & Acq Develop, Montclair State University, One Normal Ave, Montclair, NJ, 07043-1699. Tel: 973-655-7151. p. 1420

Hu, Yasha, Commun Libr Mgr, Queens Library, Elmhurst Community Library, 86-07 Broadway, Elmhurst, NY, 11373. Tel: 718-271-1020. p. 1554

Huaman, Theresa, Cat Librn, College of the Holy Cross, One College St, Worcester, MA, 01610. Tel: 508-793-2638. p. 1072

Huang, Ali, Managing Librn, Brooklyn Public Library, Dyker, 8202 13th Ave, Brooklyn, NY, 11228. Tel: 718-748-6261. p. 1503

Huang, Chao, Libr Mgr, Mooresville Public Library, 304 S Main St, Mooresville, NC, 28115. Tel: 704-664-2927. p. 1704

Huang, Chao Qun, Br Mgr, San Francisco Public Library, Chinatown/Him Mark Lai Branch Library, 1135 Powell St, San Francisco, CA, 94108. Tel: 415-355-2888. p. 228
Huang, Daniel, Resource Acquisitions Manager, Lehigh University, Eight A E Packer Ave, Bethlehem, PA, 18015. Tel: 610-758-3035. p. 1912
Huang, Hong, Dr, Asst Prof, University of South Florida, 4202 Fowler Ave, CIS 1040, Tampa, FL, 33620-7800. Tel: 813-974-6361. p. 2783
Huang, Lisa, Supv Librn, United States Department of Veterans Affairs, 1601 SW Archer Rd, Gainesville, FL, 32608-1197. Tel: 352-548-6316. p. 407
Huang, Yun, Assoc Prof, University of Illinois at Urbana-Champaign, Library & Information Science Bldg, 501 E Daniel St, Champaign, IL, 61820-6211. Tel: 217-333-3280. p. 2784
Hubbard, Andrea, Sr Law Librn, California Department of Corrections Library System, California State Prison, Sacramento, 100 Prison Rd, Represa, CA, 95671. Tel: 916-985-8610. p. 206
Hubbard, Brian, Assoc Librn, Head, Ref & Info Serv, Westfield State University, 577 Western Ave, Westfield, MA, 01085-2580. p. 1067
Hubbard, Constance, Dir, Human Res, The Ferguson Library, One Public Library Plaza, Stamford, CT, 06904. Tel: 203-351-8203. p. 338
Hubbard, Cymber, Circ Librn, Research & Instruction Services, Mississippi College, 151 E Griffith St, Jackson, MS, 39201-1391. Tel: 601-925-7120. p. 1222
Hubbard, Danielle, Asst Librn, Western Manitoba Regional Library, 710 Rosser Ave, Unit 1, Brandon, MB, R7A 0K9, CANADA. Tel: 204-727-6648. p. 2586
Hubbard, Erica, Dir, Houston Community College-Central College, Central Campus Library, 1300 Holman, Houston, TX, 77004. Tel: 713-718-6133. p. 2194
Hubbard, Erin, Acq, The John W King New Hampshire Law Library, Supreme Court Bldg, One Charles Doe Dr, Concord, NH, 03301-6160. Tel: 603-271-3777. p. 1358
Hubbard, Mary, Asst Dir, Peterborough Town Library, Two Concord St, Peterborough, NH, 03458. Tel: 603-924-8040. p. 1378
Hubbard, Quatro, Archivist, Virginia Department of Historic Resources, 2801 Kensington Ave, Richmond, VA, 23221. Tel: 804-482-6102. p. 2343
Hubbard, Whitney, Dir, Fort Plain Free Library, 19 Willett St, Fort Plain, NY, 13339-1130. Tel: 518-993-4646. p. 1534
Hubbert, Elice, Librn, Nebraska Legislative Council, 1201 State Capitol Bldg, 1445 K St, Lincoln, NE, 68508. Tel: 402-471-2222. p. 1322
Hubble, Janelle, Mgr, Libr Serv, Ohio University-Zanesville/Zane State College, Herrold Hall, 1425 Newark Rd, Zanesville, OH, 43701. Tel: 740-588-1408. p. 1837
Hubbs, Susan, Dir, Benton County Public Library, 121 S Forrest Ave, Camden, TN, 38320-2055. Tel: 731-584-4772. p. 2090
Hubenschmidt, Holly, Head, Instruction, Liaison & Ref Serv, Webster University, 101 Edgar Rd, Saint Louis, MO, 63119. Tel: 314-968-8673. p. 1277
Huber, Jeffrey T, Dr, Dir, University of Kentucky, 320 Little Library Bldg, Lexington, KY, 40506-0224. Tel: 859-257-8876. p. 2785
Huber, Kathy, Mgr, Tulsa City-County Library, Genealogy Center, Hardesty Regional Library, 8316 E 93rd St, Tulsa, OK, 74133. Tel: 918-549-7691. p. 1866
Hubers, Barb, Dir, Thornapple Kellogg School & Community Library, 3885 Bender Rd, Middleville, MI, 49333-9273. Tel: 269-795-5434. p. 1132
Hubert, Tina, Exec Dir, Six Mile Regional Library District, Niedringhaus Bldg, 2001 Delmar Ave, Granite City, IL, 62040-4590. Tel: 618-452-6238. p. 594
Hubick, Lisa, Outreach Librn, Kwantlen Polytechnic University Library, 12666 72nd Ave, Surrey, BC, V3W 2M8, CANADA. Tel: 604-599-3404. p. 2576
Huchala, Sandra, Libr Asst, Sundre Municipal Library, 96-2 Ave NW, No 2, Sundre, AB, T0M 1X0, CANADA. Tel: 403-638-4000. p. 2556
Huchko, Gregory, Libr Mgr, New York Public Library - Astor, Lenox & Tilden Foundations, Yorkville Branch, 222 E 79th St, (Between Second & Third Aves), New York, NY, 10021-1295. Tel: 212-744-5824. p. 1598
Huck, Kelly, Librn, Taycheedah Correctional Institution Library, 751 County Rd K, Fond du Lac, WI, 54936-1947. Tel: 920-929-3800, Ext 3897. p. 2435
Huckaby, Justin, Pub Serv Librn, University of Mississippi, 481 Chuckie Mullins Dr, University, MS, 38677. Tel: 662-915-6824. p. 1234
Huckaby, Lillie, Dir, Chickasha Public Library, 527 W Iowa Ave, Chickasha, OK, 73018. Tel: 405-222-6075. p. 1844
Hucks, Allison, Librn, Horry County Memorial Library, Surfside Beach Branch, 410 Surfside Dr, Surfside Beach, SC, 29575. Tel: 843-238-5280. p. 2057
Huczel, Steven, Supvry Librn, NAS Meridian, 220 Fuller Rd, Meridian, MS, 39309. Tel: 601-679-2326. p. 1226
Hudak, Christine, Dr, Prof, Kent State University, 314 University Library, 1125 Risman Dr, Kent, OH, 44242-0001. Tel: 330-672-2782. p. 2790
Hudak, Milly, Curator, Library Contact, Winchester Historical Society Library, 265 Prospect St, Winsted, CT, 06098-1942. Tel: 860-379-8433. p. 349
Huddleston, Brian, Sr Ref Librn, Loyola University New Orleans, Loyola Law Library, School of Law, 7214 St Charles Ave, New Orleans, LA, 70118. p. 902
Huddleston, Jenn, Private Colls Archivist, Simcoe County Archives, 1149 Hwy 26, Minesing, ON, L9X 0Z7, CANADA. Tel: 705-726-9300, Ext 1295. p. 2658
Huddleston, Kate, Dir, Stones River Regional Library, 2118 E Main St, Murfreesboro, TN, 37130-4009. Tel: 615-893-3380. p. 2118
Huddlestun, Carey, Res & Instruction Librn, Kennesaw State University Library System, 385 Cobb Ave NW, MD 1701, Kennesaw, GA, 30144. Tel: 470-578-6534. p. 483
Huddy, John, Dir, Handley Regional Library System, 100 W Piccadilly St, Winchester, VA, 22601. Tel: 540-662-9041, Ext 14. p. 2354
Huderson-Poydras, Phebe, Dir, Southern University, Oliver B Spellman Law Library, Two Roosevelt Steptoe, Baton Rouge, LA, 70813. Tel: 225-771-2146. p. 884
Hudgens, Yvonne, Librn, Piedmont Technical College Library, Bldg K, 2nd Flr, 620 N Emerald Rd, Greenwood, SC, 29646. Tel: 864-941-8441. p. 2063
Hudgins, Edie, Asst Regional Librn, Haynesville Correctional Center, 421 Barnfield Rd, Haynesville, VA, 22472. Tel: 804-250-4158. p. 2325
Hudgins, Jean, Cat, Oglethorpe University, 4484 Peachtree Rd NE, Atlanta, GA, 30319. Tel: 404-364-8511. p. 465
Hudgins, Nelda B, Dir, Pickens County Cooperative Library, Service Ctr Bldg, 155 Reform St, Rm 120, Carrollton, AL, 35447. Tel: 205-367-8407. p. 11
Hudnall, Scott, Asst Librn, Coordinator, Reference Servs & Emerging Technologies, Indiana University Northwest, 3400 Broadway, Gary, IN, 46408. Tel: 219-980-6931. p. 686
Hudson, Carlyn, Librn I, New Jersey Department of Labor & Workforce Development Library, John Fitch Plaza, 4th Flr, Trenton, NJ, 08611. Tel: 609-292-2035. p. 1447
Hudson, Chris, Head Librn, Colorado Supreme Court Library, Ralph L Carr Colorado Judicial Ctr, Two E 14th Ave, Denver, CO, 80203. Tel: 720-625-5100. p. 274
Hudson, Chris, Dir, Coll Serv, Kenyon College Library & Information Services, Olin & Chalmers Libraries, 103 College Dr, Gambier, OH, 43022. p. 1787
Hudson, Clara, Adminr, Support Serv, Virginia Beach Public Library, Municipal Ctr, Bldg 19, Rm 210, 2416 Courthouse Dr, Virginia Beach, VA, 23452. Tel: 757-385-8709. p. 2350
Hudson, Cynthia, Dir, Pine Forest Regional Library System, 210 Front St, Richton, MS, 39476-1510. Tel: 601-788-6539. p. 1232
Hudson, Danene, Youth Serv Librn, Duncanville Public Library, 201 James Collins Blvd, Duncanville, TX, 75116. Tel: 972-780-5050. p. 2172
Hudson, Deborah, Bus Mgr, North Vancouver District Public Library, 1277 Lynn Valley Rd, North Vancouver, BC, V7J 0A2, CANADA. Tel: 604-984-0286, 604-990-5800. p. 2573
Hudson, Evelyn E, Ref Librn, Hazard Community & Technical College Library, One Community College Dr, Hazard, KY, 41701. Tel: 606-487-3147. p. 858
Hudson, Evelyn E, Ref & Instruction Librn, Hazard Community & Technical College, 601 Jefferson Ave, Jackson, KY, 41339. Tel: 606-666-7521. p. 860
Hudson, Homer, Br Mgr, Saint Louis Public Library, Marketplace Library, 6548 Manchester Ave, Saint Louis, MO, 63139. Tel: 314-647-0939. p. 1275
Hudson, James, Br Mgr, Chesterfield County Public Library, Meadowdale, 4301 Meadowdale Blvd, Richmond, VA, 23234. Tel: 804-751-2275. p. 2312
Hudson, Janice, Tech Serv Spec, Newberry College, 2100 College St, Newberry, SC, 29108-2197. Tel: 803-321-5229. p. 2066
Hudson, Jessica, Dir, Fairfax County Public Library, 12000 Government Center Pkwy, Ste 324, Fairfax, VA, 22035-0012. Tel: 703-324-3100. p. 2316
Hudson, Joan, Library Contact, Mosier Valley Library, 1003 Third Ave, Mosier, OR, 97040. Tel: 541-478-3409. p. 1887
Hudson, Joan, Librn, Shibley Righton LLP, 250 University Ave, Ste 700, Toronto, ON, M5H 3E5, CANADA. Tel: 416-214-5294. p. 2693
Hudson, John, Libr Asst, Morrill Public Library, 119 E Webster, Morrill, NE, 69358. Tel: 308-247-2611. p. 1325
Hudson, Jon, Electronic Res Librn, South College, Parkside Campus Library, 400 Goody's Lane, Ste 101, Knoxville, TN, 37922. Tel: 865-288-5750. p. 2107
Hudson, Karen, Libr Dir, Salt Spring Island Public Library, 129 McPhillips Ave, Salt Spring Island, BC, V8K 2T6, CANADA. Tel: 250-537-4666. p. 2575
Hudson, Kym, Sr Librn, Lee County Library System, Telephone & Virtual Reference Services, 2450 First St, Fort Myers, FL, 33901. p. 404
Hudson, Mark, Head, Tech Serv, Monroeville Public Library, 4000 Gateway Campus Blvd, Monroeville, PA, 15146-3381. Tel: 412-372-0500, Ext 113. p. 1965
Hudson, Mindy, Genealogy Serv, Jefferson County Library, Northwest, 5680 State Rd PP, High Ridge, MO, 63049. Tel: 636-677-8186. p. 1249
Hudson, Molly, Youth Serv Librn, Lewis & Clark Library, 120 S Last Chance Gulch, Helena, MT, 59601. Tel: 406-447-1690. p. 1296
Hudson, Patricia, Libr Dir, Loxley Public Library, 1001 Loxley Ave, Loxley, AL, 36551. Tel: 251-964-5695. p. 24
Hudson, Reba, Circ Mgr, Obion County Public Library, 1221 E Reelfoot Ave, Union City, TN, 38261. Tel: 731-885-7000, 731-885-9411. p. 2128
Hudson, Robert, Univ Librn, Boston University Libraries, Mugar Memorial Library, 771 Commonwealth Ave, Boston, MA, 02215. Tel: 617-353-3710. p. 993

Hughes, Jessica, Young Adult Serv Coordr, Havana Public Library District, 201 W Adams St, Havana, IL, 62644-1321. Tel: 309-543-4701. p. 598
Hughes, Kate, Head Librn, Wheatland Regional Library, Luseland Branch, 510 Grand Ave, Luseland, SK, S0L 2A0, CANADA. Tel: 306-372-4808. p. 2751
Hughes, Katherine, Training Coordr, South Central Kansas Library System, 321 N Main St, South Hutchinson, KS, 67505. Tel: 620-663-3211. p. 837
Hughes, Kathleen, Head, Cat, Metadata & Archival Serv, Montclair State University, One Normal Ave, Montclair, NJ, 07043-1699. Tel: 973-655-7077. p. 1420
Hughes, Katie, Br Mgr, Akron-Summit County Public Library, Nordonia Hills Branch, 9458 Olde Eight Rd, Northfield, OH, 44067-1952. Tel: 330-467-8595. p. 1744
Hughes, Kelly, Libr Mgr, Flint River Regional Library System, Barnesville-Lamar County Library, 401 Thomaston St, Barnesville, GA, 30204. Tel: 770-358-3270. p. 481
Hughes, Kelly, Dir, Mount Jewett Memorial Library, Seven E Main St, Mount Jewett, PA, 16740. Tel: 814-778-5588. p. 1966
Hughes, Kelly, Dir, D Brown Memorial Library, 203 N Second St, Rosebud, TX, 76570. Tel: 254-583-2328. p. 2234
Hughes, Kim, Actg Sr Librn, Los Angeles Public Library System, Pico Union Branch Library, 1030 S Alvarado St, Los Angeles, CA, 90006. Tel: 213-368-7545. p. 165
Hughes, Kristen, Circ, Wenatchee Valley College, 1300 Fifth St, Wenatchee, WA, 98801. Tel: 509-682-6710. p. 2395
Hughes, Lakisha, Res Sharing Librn, United States Army, 562 Quarters Rd, Bldg 12420, Fort Lee, VA, 23801-1705. Tel: 804-765-8170. p. 2319
Hughes, Lindsey, Youth Serv Librn, Marstons Mills Public Library, 2160 Main St, Marstons Mills, MA, 02648. Tel: 508-428-5175. p. 1033
Hughes, Lisa, Acq Librn, Colorado Mesa University, 1100 North Ave, Grand Junction, CO, 81501. Tel: 970-248-1436. p. 283
Hughes, Lisa, Cat, Libr Assoc, Marshall University Libraries, One John Marshall Dr, Huntington, WV, 25755-2060. Tel: 304-696-2320. p. 2405
Hughes, Marylou, ILL, Free Library of Springfield Township, 8900 Hawthorne Lane, Wyndmoor, PA, 19038. Tel: 215-836-5300. p. 2025
Hughes, Michael, PhD, Chief Librn, Dean, Baruch College-CUNY, 151 E 25th St, Box H-0520, New York, NY, 10010-2313. Tel: 646-312-1610. p. 1580
Hughes, Nancy B, Br Mgr, Albemarle Regional Library, Bertie County Public Library, 111 US Hwy 13/17 Bypass, Windsor, NC, 27983. Tel: 252-794-2244. p. 1727
Hughes, Nicole, Res Spec, Orrick, Herrington & Sutcliffe LLP, The Orrick Bldg, 405 Howard St, San Francisco, CA, 94105-2669. Tel: 415-773-5700. p. 226
Hughes, Patti, Dir, Lyme Free Library, 12165 Main St, Chaumont, NY, 13622-9603. Tel: 315-649-5454. p. 1517
Hughes, Rayedene, Librn, Attica City Library, 125 N Main St, Attica, KS, 67009. Tel: 620-254-7767. p. 797
Hughes, Ryan, Digital Initiatives Librn, Rochester Regional Library Council, 3445 Winton Pl, Ste 204, Rochester, NY, 14623. Tel: 585-223-7570. p. 2771
Hughes, Scott, Dir of Libr, Goodwin University, One Riverside Dr, East Hartford, CT, 06118. Tel: 860-727-6782. p. 310
Hughes, Shelley, Dir, Ch Serv, Chicago Public Library, Thomas Hughes Children's Library, 400 S State St, 2nd Flr, Chicago, IL, 60605. Tel: 312-747-4200. p. 556
Hughes, Shelley, Br Mgr, Chicago Public Library, Little Italy, 1336 W Taylor St, Chicago, IL, 60607. Tel: 312-746-5656. p. 557
Hughes, Stephen, Supvr, Circ, Tigard Public Library, 13500 SW Hall Blvd, Tigard, OR, 97223-8111. Tel: 503-684-6537, Ext 2525. p. 1900
Hughes, Susan, Libr Asst, Murrell Library & Commons, Missouri Valley College, 500 E College St, Marshall, MO, 65340. Tel: 660-831-4180, 660-831-4181. p. 1260
Hughes, Vickie, ILL, Clarion Free Library, 644 Main St, Clarion, PA, 16214. Tel: 814-226-7172. p. 1922
Hughesman, Carolyn, Data Spec, ILL, Chautauqua-Cattaraugus Library System, 106 W Fifth St, Jamestown, NY, 14701. Tel: 716-484-7135, Ext 259. p. 1557
Hughey, Amber, Dir, Bridgeport Public Library, 3399 Williamson Rd, Bridgeport, MI, 48601. Tel: 989-777-6030. p. 1087
Hughsam, Larry, Dir of Finance, Toronto Public Library, 789 Yonge St, Toronto, ON, M4W 2G8, CANADA. Tel: 416-393-7131. p. 2693
Hugie, Todd, Dir, Info Tech, Utah State University, 3000 Old Main Hill, Logan, UT, 84322-3000. Tel: 435-797-2638. p. 2265
Hugley, Lori, Br Mgr, Kokomo-Howard County Public Library, South Branch, 1755 E Center Rd, Kokomo, IN, 46902-5322. Tel: 765-453-4150. p. 700
Hugo, Brandon, Tech Serv Librn, Hillsdale College, 33 E College St, Hillsdale, MI, 49242. Tel: 517-607-2405. p. 1115
Hui, Cecilia, Syst Librn, De Anza College, 21250 Stevens Creek Blvd, Cupertino, CA, 95014-5793. Tel: 408-864-8383. p. 133
Hui, Jacqueline, Br Mgr, Chicago Public Library, Rogers Park, 6907 N Clark St, Chicago, IL, 60626. Tel: 312-744-0156. p. 557
Hui, Mimi, Dir, Free Public Library of Hasbrouck Heights, 320 Boulevard, Hasbrouck Heights, NJ, 07604. Tel: 201-288-0484, 201-288-0488. p. 1407
Huiner, Leslie, Dept Chair, Victor Valley College Library, 18422 Bear Valley Rd, Victorville, CA, 92395-5850. Tel: 760-245-4271, Ext 2262. p. 256
Huisman, Melissa Ann, Dir, Gary Byker Memorial Library, 3338 Van Buren St, Hudsonville, MI, 49426. Tel: 616-669-1255. p. 1117
Huisman, Rhonda, Dean of Libr, St Cloud State University Library, James W Miller Learning Resource Center, 400 Sixth St S, Saint Cloud, MN, 56301. Tel: 320-308-2022. p. 1198
Huizar, Daniel, Dir, Libr Serv, Rutan & Tucker Library, 18575 Jamboree Rd, 9th Flr, Irvine, CA, 92612. Tel: 714-641-5100. p. 153
Huizenga, Libby, Libr Serv Spec, Kuyper College, 3333 E Beltline Ave NE, Grand Rapids, MI, 49525. Tel: 616-988-3777. p. 1111
Hulbert, Kelly, Adult Serv, Digital Serv, Libr Adminr, County of Los Angeles Public Library, 7400 E Imperial Hwy, Downey, CA, 90242-3375. Tel: 562-940-8521. p. 134
Hulett, Carrie, Dir, Evergreen Community Library, 253 Maple St, Metamora, OH, 43540. Tel: 419-644-2771. p. 1802
Hulett, Elizabeth, Dir, Western Maryland Regional Library, 100 S Potomac St, Hagerstown, MD, 21740. Tel: 301-241-7616. p. 968
Huling, Jessica, Libr Asst, Sinclairville Free Library, 15 Main St, Sinclairville, NY, 14782. Tel: 716-962-5885. p. 1641
Huling, Nancy, Dir, Res Serv, University of Washington Libraries, Box 352900, Seattle, WA, 98195-2900. Tel: 206-685-2211. p. 2381
Hulinsky, Janet, Asst Br Librn, Pottawatomie Wabaunsee Regional Library, Onaga Branch, 313 Leonard St, Onaga, KS, 66521. Tel: 785-889-4531. p. 835
Hull, Ann, Exec Dir, Franklin County Historical Society - Kittochtinny Library, 175 E King St, Chambersburg, PA, 17201. Tel: 717-264-1667. p. 1920
Hull, Bryan E, Asst Librn, Head, Digital Production Servs, University of Utah, Spencer S Eccles Health Sciences Library, Bldg 589, 10 N 1900 E, Salt Lake City, UT, 84112-5890. Tel: 801-581-8771. p. 2272
Hull, Caitlin, Dir, Maywood Public Library, 459 Maywood Ave, Maywood, NJ, 07607-1909. Tel: 201-845-2915. p. 1417
Hull, Doug, Librn, Miller Nash Graham & Dunn LLP, 2801 Alaskan Way, Ste 300, Seattle, WA, 98121. Tel: 206-624-8300. p. 2377
Hull, Douglas, Ref Librn, Miller Nash Graham & Dunn LLP Library, 3400 US Bancorp Tower, 111 SW Fifth Ave, Portland, OR, 97204-3699. Tel: 503-205-2426. p. 1892
Hull, Jane, Librn, Mississippi State Hospital, Medical Library, Whitfield Rd, Whitfield, MS, 39193. Tel: 601-351-8000, Ext 4278. p. 1236
Hull, Jane, Librn, Mississippi State Hospital, Patient Library, Whitfield Rd, Whitfield, MS, 39193. Tel: 601-351-8000, Ext 4278. p. 1236
Hull, Kate, Head, Tech Serv, Sun Prairie Public Library, 1350 Linnerud Dr, Sun Prairie, WI, 53590. Tel: 608-825-7323. p. 2480
Hull, Kathryn, Librn, Waupun Correctional Institution Library, 200 S Madison St, Waupun, WI, 53963-2069. Tel: 920-324-5571, Ext 1503. p. 2485
Hull, Michael, Exec Dir, Southeast Oklahoma Library System (SEOLS), 401 N Second St, McAlester, OK, 74501. Tel: 918-426-0456. p. 1853
Hull, Nina, Mgr, County of Los Angeles Public Library, Agoura Hills Library, 29901 Ladyface Ct, Agoura Hills, CA, 91301. Tel: 818-889-2278. p. 135
Hull, Pat, Circ Mgr, Gaston College, Harvey A Jonas Library, 511 S Aspen St, Lincolnton, NC, 28092. Tel: 704-922-6358. p. 1683
Hull, Pat, ILL, Pub Serv Spec, Gaston College, 201 Hwy 321 S, Dallas, NC, 28034-1499. Tel: 704-922-6359. p. 1683
Hull, Sarah, Archivist/Head of Local Hist, Plainfield Public Library, 800 Park Ave, Plainfield, NJ, 07060-2594. Tel: 908-757-1111, Ext 136. p. 1435
Hull, Sharon, Head, Spec Coll, Tennessee State University, 3500 John A Merritt Blvd, Nashville, TN, 37209. Tel: 615-963-5219. p. 2121
Hull, Stacy, Librn, Northeast Regional Library, Blue Mountain Public Library, 125 S Railroad Ave, Blue Mountain, MS, 38610. Tel: 662-685-4559. p. 1215
Hull, Tracy, Dean, Texas Christian University, 2913 Lowden St, TCU Box 298400, Fort Worth, TX, 76129. Tel: 817-257-7106. p. 2181
Hull, Trish, Mgr, Salt Lake County Library Services, West Valley Branch, 2880 W 3650 S, West Valley City, UT, 84119-3743. p. 2275
Hull, Vernelle, Br Mgr, Mexico-Audrain County Library District, Farber Branch, 113 W Front St, Farber, MO, 63345. Tel: 573-249-2012. p. 1261
Hullett, Lisa, Head Librn, Wallace State College, 801 Main St NW, Hanceville, AL, 35077. Tel: 256-352-8260. p. 20
Hulley, Kathleen, Libr Mgr, Literary & Historical Society of Quebec Library, 44 Chaussee des Ecossais, Quebec, QC, G1R 4H3, CANADA. Tel: 418-694-9147, Ext 229. p. 2731
Hulme, Dale, Rev, Library Contact, Saint Olaf Lutheran Church, 2901 Emerson Ave N, Minneapolis, MN, 55411. Tel: 612-529-7726. p. 1185
Hulo, Romain, Librn, College Bart Bibliotheque, 751 cote d'Abraham, Rm D-13, Quebec, QC, G1R 1A2, CANADA. Tel: 418-522-3906. p. 2730
Hulse, Jacqueline, Co-Mgr, Andrews Public Library, 871 Main St, Andrews, NC, 28901. Tel: 828-321-5956. p. 1671
Hulse, Michelle, Dir, Fredonia Public Library, 807 Jefferson St, Fredonia, KS, 66736. Tel: 620-378-2863. p. 809

Hulsey, Sarah, Asst Libr Dir, Summit County Libraries, County Commons Bldg, 0037 Peak One Dr, Frisco, CO, 80443. Tel: 970-668-4138. p. 282

Hult, Mike, Museum Assoc - Research, Bureau County Historical Society Museum & Library, 109 Park Ave W, Princeton, IL, 61356-1927. Tel: 815-875-2184. p. 636

Hultberg, Jane, Libr Dir, College of the Atlantic, 105 Eden St, Bar Harbor, ME, 04609-1198. Tel: 207-801-5660. p. 916

Hulting, Fred, Dir, Knowledge Discovery Serv, General Mills, Inc, James Ford Bell Library & Information Services, 9000 Plymouth Ave N, Minneapolis, MN, 55427. Tel: 763-764-6460. p. 1183

Hultman, Heather, Sr Archivist, Montana Historical Society, 225 N Roberts St, Helena, MT, 59601-4514. Tel: 406-444-3668. p. 1296

Hults, Patricia, Mgr, Tech Serv, Rensselaer Libraries, Rensselaer Architecture Library, Greene Bldg 308, 3rd Flr, 110 Eighth St, Troy, NY, 12180-3590. Tel: 518-276-8310. p. 1652

Huma, Bnu, Digital Serv, Navajo County Library District, 121 W Buffalo, Holbrook, AZ, 86025. Tel: 928-241-0374. p. 63

Humbell, Todd, Dir, West Florida Public Library, 239 N Spring St, Pensacola, FL, 32502. Tel: 850-436-5060. p. 437

Humber, Alliah, Curator, Howard University Libraries, Architecture, 500 Howard Pl NW, Washington, DC, 20059. Tel: 202-806-7502. p. 369

Humber, Alliah V, Head, Acq & Ser, Howard University Libraries, 500 Howard Pl NW, Ste 203, Washington, DC, 20059. Tel: 202-884-7502. p. 368

Humberston, Margaret, Curator, Archives & Libr, Lyman & Merrie Wood Museum of Springfield History, 21 Edwards St, Springfield, MA, 01103. Tel: 413-314-6411. p. 1057

Humble, James, Dir, Anthony Cardinal Bevilacqua Theological Research Center, 100 E Wynnewood Rd, Wynnewood, PA, 19096. Tel: 610-785-6274. p. 2025

Humble, Jandy, Libr Dir, Liberty Lake Municipal Library, 23123 E Mission Ave, Liberty Lake, WA, 99019-7613. Tel: 509-435-0777. p. 2368

Humiston, Kelli, Dir, Fowler Public Library, 510 Main St, Fowler, KS, 67844. Tel: 620-646-5550. p. 808

Hummel, Diane, Librn, Richard R Smith Medical Library, 1840 Wealthy St SE, Grand Rapids, MI, 49506. Tel: 616-774-7931. p. 1111

Hummel, Diane, Mgr, Spectrum Health, A Level West Bldg, 100 Michigan St NE, Grand Rapids, MI, 49503-2560. Tel: 616-391-1655. p. 1111

Hummel, Kendra, Asst Dir, Tipton County Public Library, 127 E Madison St, Tipton, IN, 46072. Tel: 765-675-8761. p. 722

Hummel, Patty, Dir, Allison Public Library, 412 Third St, Allison, IA, 50602. Tel: 319-267-2562. p. 730

Humpal, Cathy, Libr Dir, Lawler Public Library, 412 E Grove, Lawler, IA, 52154. Tel: 563-238-2191. p. 765

Humphrey, Angie, Dir, Montpelier Public Library, 216 E Main St, Montpelier, OH, 43543-1199. Tel: 419-485-3287. p. 1804

Humphrey, Cathy, Supvr, Essex County Library, Essex Branch, 35 Gosfield Townline W, Essex, ON, N8M 0A1, CANADA. Tel: 226-946-1529, Ext 250. p. 2641

Humphrey, Cathy, Supvr, Essex County Library, Harrow Branch, 140 King St W, Harrow, ON, N0R 1G0, CANADA. Tel: 226-946-1529, Ext 260. p. 2641

Humphrey, Cathy, Supvr, Essex County Library, McGregor Branch, 9571 Walker Rd, McGregor, ON, N0R 1J0, CANADA. Tel: 226-946-1529, Ext 211. p. 2641

Humphrey, Holden, Dir, Tech Serv, Aiken-Bamberg-Barnwell-Edgefield Regional Library System, 314 Chesterfield St SW, Aiken, SC, 29801-7171. Tel: 803-642-7575. p. 2045

Humphrey, John, Libr Mgr, Texas Woman's University, 5500 Southwestern Medical Ave, Dallas, TX, 75235-7200. Tel: 214-689-6580. p. 2168

Humphrey, Josh, Dir, Kearny Public Library, 318 Kearny Ave, Kearny, NJ, 07032. Tel: 201-998-2667. p. 1410

Humphrey, Judi, Head, Circ & Reserves, Ashland University Library, 509 College Ave, Ashland, OH, 44805. Tel: 419-289-5400. p. 1747

Humphrey, Julie, Youth Serv Mgr, Omaha Public Library, 215 S 15th St, Omaha, NE, 68102-1629. Tel: 402-444-4800. p. 1329

Humphrey, Julie C, Dir, Durham Technical Community College, 1637 E Lawson St, Durham, NC, 27703. Tel: 919-536-7211, Ext 1631. p. 1685

Humphrey, Kaydene, Libr Mgr, New York Public Library - Astor, Lenox & Tilden Foundations, Kips Bay Branch, 446 Third Ave, (@ E 31st St), New York, NY, 10016-6025. Tel: 212-683-2520. p. 1596

Humphrey, Pinky, Ms, Libr Dir, Saint Maries Public Library, 822 College Ave, Saint Maries, ID, 83861. Tel: 208-245-3732. p. 530

Humphrey, Richard E, Ref Librn, Indiana University, Ruth Lilly Law Library, 530 W New York St, Indianapolis, IN, 46202-3225. Tel: 317-274-3884, 317-274-4028. p. 693

Humphrey, Rosemary, Res Sharing Librn, Kennesaw State University Library System, 385 Cobb Ave NW, MD 1701, Kennesaw, GA, 30144. Tel: 470-578-7277. p. 483

Humphrey, Tracey, Libr Support Spec, Ohio University-Zanesville/Zane State College, Herrold Hall, 1425 Newark Rd, Zanesville, OH, 43701. Tel: 740-588-1405. p. 1837

Humphreys, Carlos, Head Librn, El Paso Community College Library, Transmountain Campus Library, 9570 Gateway Blvd N, Rm 1600, El Paso, TX, 79924. Tel: 915-831-5098. p. 2173

Humphreys, Glenn, Head, Spec Coll, Chicago Public Library, Special Collections & Preservation Division, 400 S State St, Chicago, IL, 60605. Tel: 312-747-1941. p. 557

Humphreys, Jayne, Law Librn, Illinois Department of Corrections, 251 N Illinois Hwy 37, Ina, IL, 62846. Tel: 618-437-5300, Ext 467. p. 601

Humphreys, Stephanie, Libr Mgr, Magrath Public Library, 27 S Center St, Magrath, AB, T0K 1J0, CANADA. Tel: 403-758-6498. p. 2547

Humphreys, Suzanne, Chief Exec Officer, Quinte West Public Library, Seven Creswell Dr, Trenton, ON, K8V 6X5, CANADA. Tel: 613-394-3381, Ext 3315. p. 2700

Humphreys, Taylor, Access Serv Librn, Jefferson College Library, 1000 Viking Dr, Hillsboro, MO, 63050. Tel: 636-481-3174. p. 1249

Humphries, Sarah, Ch, Lincoln County Library System, 519 Emerald St, Kemmerer, WY, 83101. Tel: 307-877-6961. p. 2495

Humrickhouse, Elizabeth, Info Literacy, University of Wisconsin-La Crosse, 1631 Pine St, La Crosse, WI, 54601-3748. Tel: 608-785-8738. p. 2446

Hunasikatti, Monica, Librn, Bryant & Stratton College Library, 8141 Hull Street Rd, Richmond, VA, 23235. Tel: 804-745-2444, Ext 333. p. 2340

Hunceker, Roger, Supv Librn, Department of Veterans Affairs, 1901 Veterans Memorial Dr, 14LIB-T, Temple, TX, 76504. Tel: 254-743-0607. p. 2247

Hunchak, Taryn, Libr Serv Coordr, Edmonton Public Library, Idylwylde, 8310 88 Ave NW, Edmonton, AB, T6C 1L1, CANADA. Tel: 780-496-7279. p. 2536

Hund, June, Tech Serv Librn, Case Western Reserve University, Lillian & Milford Harris Library, Jack Joseph & Morton Mandel School of Applied Social Sciences, 11235 Bellflower Rd, Cleveland, OH, 44106-7164. Tel: 216-368-2302. p. 1766

Hundley, Cheryl, ILL Coordr, Ferrum College, 150 Wiley Dr, Ferrum, VA, 24088. Tel: 540-365-4424, 540-365-4426. p. 2318

Hunegs, Steve, Exec Dir, Jewish Community Relations Council, 12 N 12th St, Ste 480, Minneapolis, MN, 55403. Tel: 612-338-7816. p. 1184

Hunewell, Christine, Children's Prog Coordr, Gordon-Nash Library at New Hampton School, 69 Main St, New Hampton, NH, 03256. Tel: 603-677-3740. p. 1375

Hung, Kwei, Acq Librn, Howard University Libraries, Law Library, 2929 Van Ness St NW, Washington, DC, 20008. Tel: 202-806-8051. p. 369

Hungerford, Garrett, Dir, Redford Township District Library, 25320 W Six Mile, Redford, MI, 48240. Tel: 313-531-5960, Ext 100. p. 1143

Hunker, Stefanie, Digital Res Librn, Spec Coll, Bowling Green State University Libraries, 1001 E Wooster St, Bowling Green, OH, 43403-0170. p. 1752

Hunn, Debbie, ILL, Ref, Dallas Theological Seminary, 3909 Swiss Ave, Dallas, TX, 75204. Tel: 214-887-5284. p. 2166

Hunn, Marvin, Dir, Dallas Theological Seminary, 3909 Swiss Ave, Dallas, TX, 75204. Tel: 214-887-5281. p. 2166

Hunsaker, Marci, Academic Liaison, Librn, San Jose State University, One Washington Sq, San Jose, CA, 95192-0028. Tel: 408-808-2114. p. 232

Hunsaker, Theresa, Dir, Grundy County-Jewett Norris Library, 1331 Main St, Trenton, MO, 64683. Tel: 660-359-3577. p. 1282

Hunsberger, Tara, Youth Services Team Leader, Niles District Library, 620 E Main St, Niles, MI, 49120. Tel: 269-683-8545. p. 1137

Hunsicker, Jennifer, Br Mgr, Williamson County Public Library, College Grove Community, 8607 Horton Hwy, College Grove, TN, 37046. Tel: 615-368-3222. p. 2098

Hunsiker, Traci, Cat, Sallie Logan Public Library, 1808 Walnut St, Murphysboro, IL, 62966. Tel: 618-684-3271. p. 622

Hunsucker, Cassandra, Head Librn, New Bern-Craven County Public Library, 400 Johnson St, New Bern, NC, 28560-4098. Tel: 252-638-7800. p. 1706

Hunt, Andrew, Libr Dir, Cleveland Bradley County Public Library, 795 Church St NE, Cleveland, TN, 37311-5295. Tel: 423-472-2163. p. 2092

Hunt, Andrew, Exec Dir, Provincial Information & Library Resources Board, 48 St. George's Ave, Stephenville, NL, A2N 1K9, CANADA. Tel: 709-643-0900, 709-643-0902. p. 2611

Hunt, Ann, Dir, New London Public Library, 406 S Pearl St, New London, WI, 54961-1441. Tel: 920-982-8519. p. 2464

Hunt, Bud, Tech Serv Mgr, Clearview Library District, 720 Third St, Windsor, CO, 80550-5109. Tel: 970-686-5603. p. 298

Hunt, Carey, Asst Dir, Support Serv, Jackson County Library Services, 205 S Central Ave, Medford, OR, 97501-2730. Tel: 541-774-8679. p. 1886

Hunt, Chance, Assoc Teaching Prof, University of Washington, Mary Gates Hall, Ste 370, Campus Box 352840, Seattle, WA, 98195-2840. Tel: 206-543-1794. p. 2794

Hunt, Curtis, Makerspace Librn, Bacon Memorial District Library, 45 Vinewood, Wyandotte, MI, 48192-5221. Tel: 734-246-8357. p. 1160

Hunt, Cynthia, Asst Dir, Goodwin University, One Riverside Dr, East Hartford, CT, 06118. Tel: 860-913-2066. p. 310

Hunt, Deb, Assoc Libr Dir, Lancaster Bible College, Teague Learning Commons, 901 Eden Rd, Lancaster, PA, 17601-5036. Tel: 717-569-7071, Ext 5349. p. 1951

Hunt, Deborah, Libr Dir, Mechanics' Institute Library, 57 Post St, Ste 504, San Francisco, CA, 94104-5003. Tel: 415-393-0101. p. 226

Hunt, Emily, Br Mgr, Pima County Public Library, El Rio, 1390 W Speedway Blvd, Tucson, AZ, 85745. Tel: 520-594-5245. p. 82

Hunt, Fiona, Dept Chair, Langara College, 100 W 49th Ave, Vancouver, BC, V5Y 2Z6, CANADA. Tel: 604-323-5364. p. 2795
Hunt, Holly, Libr Asst, Beaver City Public Library, 408 Tenth St, Beaver City, NE, 68926. Tel: 308-268-4115. p. 1307
Hunt, Jenn, Head, Info & Reader Serv, Vernon Area Public Library District, 300 Olde Half Day Rd, Lincolnshire, IL, 60069. Tel: 847-634-3650. p. 609
Hunt, Jennifer, Dep Dir, Schaumburg Township District Library, 130 S Roselle Rd, Schaumburg, IL, 60193. Tel: 847-923-3209. p. 645
Hunt, Jennifer, Libr Dir, Berklee College of Music Library, 150 Massachusetts Ave, Boston, MA, 02115. Tel: 617-747-2258. p. 990
Hunt, Jennifer, Dir, The Boston Conservatory, Eight Fenway, 2nd Flr, Boston, MA, 02215-4099. Tel: 617-912-9131. p. 991
Hunt, Jessica, Dir, Grant Area District Library, 122 Elder St, Grant, MI, 49327. Tel: 231-834-5713, Ext 103. p. 1112
Hunt, Joanna, Head, Access Serv, Central Washington University, 400 E University Way, Ellensburg, WA, 98926-7548. Tel: 509-963-1901. p. 2363
Hunt, Joanne, Archive Researcher, Colchester Historical Society Archives, 29 Young St, Truro, NS, B2N 3W3, CANADA. Tel: 902-895-6284. p. 2623
Hunt, Judith Lin, Dr, Dean, Montclair State University, One Normal Ave, Montclair, NJ, 07043-1699. Tel: 973-655-4301. p. 1420
Hunt, Karla, Dir, Fort Sumner Public Library, 235 W Sumner Ave, Fort Sumner, NM, 88119. Tel: 575-355-2832. p. 1468
Hunt, Kathryn, Libr Mgr, Lincoln Public Library, 485 Twelve Bridges Dr, Lincoln, CA, 95648. Tel: 916-434-2410. p. 156
Hunt, Kim, Bus Mgr, McCracken County Public Library, 555 Washington St, Paducah, KY, 42003. Tel: 270-442-2510. p. 872
Hunt, Kris, Library Contact, Taylorville Correctional Center Library, 1144 Illinois Rte 29, Taylorville, IL, 62568. Tel: 217-824-4004, Ext 5802. p. 653
Hunt, Laura, Br Mgr, Johnson County Library, Central Resource, 9875 W 87th St, Overland Park, KS, 66212. p. 830
Hunt, Maria, Head, Scholarly Res, University of Utah, J Willard Marriott Library, 295 S 1500 East, Salt Lake City, UT, 84112-0860. Tel: 801-581-7741. p. 2272
Hunt, Mary Louise, Dir, Sally Ploof Hunter Memorial Library, 101 Public Works Dr, Black River, NY, 13612. Tel: 315-773-5163. p. 1494
Hunt, Melissa, Info Serv Mgr, Wayne Township Library, 80 N Sixth St, Richmond, IN, 47374. Tel: 765-966-8291, Ext 1123. p. 715
Hunt, Michele, Acq Librn, Northern Illinois University Libraries, 217 Normal Rd, DeKalb, IL, 60115-2828. Tel: 815-753-6985. p. 577
Hunt, Steve, Interim Dir, Libr & Info Serv, Santa Monica College Library, 1900 Pico Blvd, Santa Monica, CA, 90405-1628. Tel: 310-434-4334. p. 244
Hunt, Walter H, Dir, Grand Lodge of Masons in Massachusetts, 186 Tremont St, 2nd Flr, Boston, MA, 02111. Tel: 617-426-6040, Ext 4221. p. 995
Hunter, Amy, Br Mgr, Hamilton Public Library, Locke, 285 Locke St S, Hamilton, ON, L8P 4C2, CANADA. Tel: 905-546-3200, Ext 3400. p. 2646
Hunter, Amy, Br Mgr, Hamilton Public Library, Westdale, 955 King St W, Hamilton, ON, L8S 1K9, CANADA. Tel: 905-546-3456. p. 2646
Hunter, Amy B, Lit Prog Mgr, Mkt Mgr, Mercantile Library Association, 414 Walnut St, Cincinnati, OH, 45202. Tel: 513-621-0717. p. 1761
Hunter, Annisija, Info Serv, South Dakota State University, 1300 N Campus Dr, Box 2115, Brookings, SD, 57007. Tel: 605-688-5571. p. 2074
Hunter, Ben, Dean, Univ Libr, University of Idaho Library, 850 S Rayburn St, Moscow, ID, 83844. Tel: 208-885-5858. p. 526
Hunter, Cheri, Librn, Decatur Genealogical Society Library, 1255 W South Side Dr, Decatur, IL, 62521-4024. Tel: 217-429-0135. p. 576
Hunter, Cindy, Libr Mgr, Bashaw Public Library, 5020 52 St, Bashaw, AB, T0B 0H0, CANADA. Tel: 780-372-4055. p. 2522
Hunter, Clyde, Br Mgr, Chesapeake Public Library, Major Hillard Library, 824 Old George Washington Hwy N, Chesapeake, VA, 23323-2214. Tel: 757-382-1942. p. 2311
Hunter, Clyde, Jr, Br Mgr, Chesapeake Public Library, South Norfolk Memorial, 1100 Poindexter St, Chesapeake, VA, 23324-2447. Tel: 757-410-7052. p. 2311
Hunter, Covy, Br Mgr, Azalea Regional Library System, Morgan County Library, 1131 East Ave, Madison, GA, 30650. Tel: 706-342-1206. p. 488
Hunter, Dalena E, Librn, University of California, Los Angeles, Ralph J Bunche Center for African-American Studies Library & Media Center, 135 Haines Hall, Box 951545, Los Angeles, CA, 90095-1545. Tel: 310-825-6060. p. 168
Hunter, Deann, Libr Dir, Laconia Public Library, 695 Main St, Laconia, NH, 03246. Tel: 603-524-4775. p. 1370
Hunter, Debbie, Br Mgr, Dixie Regional Library System, Calhoun City Branch, 113 E Burkitt St, Calhoun City, MS, 38916. Tel: 662-628-6331. p. 1229
Hunter, Eleanor, Librn, Atlanta-Fulton Public Library System, Auburn Avenue Research Library on African-American Culture & History, 101 Auburn Ave NE, Atlanta, GA, 30303-2503. Tel: 404-730-4001, Ext 107. p. 460
Hunter, Gregory, Dr, Dir, PhD Prog, Prof, Long Island University, C W Post Campus, 720 Northern Blvd, Brookville, NY, 11548-1300. Tel: 516-299-7171. p. 2788
Hunter, Ina, Board Pres, Mehoopany Area Library, 310 Schoolhouse Hill Rd, Mehoopany, PA, 18629. Tel: 570-833-2818. p. 1962
Hunter, J Michael, Asst Univ Librn, Pub Serv, Brigham Young University, Harold B Lee Library, 2060 HBLL, Provo, UT, 84602. Tel: 801-422-2927. p. 2269
Hunter, Jan, Res, Waseca County Historical Society, 315 Second Ave NE, Waseca, MN, 56093. Tel: 507-835-7700. p. 1207
Hunter, Julie, Student Serv Librn, Western Connecticut State University, 181 White St, Danbury, CT, 06810. Tel: 203-837-9100. p. 307
Hunter, Kate, Librn, Orwell Free Library, 473 Main St, Orwell, VT, 05670. Tel: 802-948-2041. p. 2291
Hunter, Kimberly, Bibliographer, United States Air Force, Air University - Muir S Fairchild Research Information Center, 600 Chennault Circle, Maxwell AFB, AL, 36112-6010. Tel: 334-953-9811. p. 25
Hunter, Loretta, Learning Res Coordr, Wayne County Community College District, Arthur Cartwright LRC Library, Downtown Campus, 1001 W Fort St, Detroit, MI, 48226-3096. Tel: 313-496-2358. p. 1099
Hunter, Lynne, Adult Serv, ILL, Wilton Free Public Library, Six Goodspeed St, Wilton, ME, 04294. Tel: 207-645-4831. p. 946
Hunter, Mica, Ms, Dir, Bradford Memorial Library, 611 S Washington St, El Dorado, KS, 67042. Tel: 316-321-3363. p. 805
Hunter, Michael, Librn, Finger Lakes Community College, 3325 Marvin Sands Dr, Canandaigua, NY, 14424-8405. Tel: 585-785-1371. p. 1512
Hunter, Michael, Info Syst Tech, Southern West Virginia Community & Technical College, 128 College Dr, Saulsville, WV, 25876. Tel: 304-294-2006. p. 2414
Hunter, Nancy, Coordr, Acq/Metadata, Colorado State University Libraries, Morgan Library, 1201 Center Ave Mall, Fort Collins, CO, 80523. Tel: 970-491-1838. p. 280
Hunter, Paul, Evening Supvr, Drexel University Libraries, Hahnemann Library, 245 N 15th St MS 449, Philadelphia, PA, 19102-1192. p. 1976
Hunter, Sarah P, Asst Head, Music Libr, Boston University Libraries, Music Library, 771 Commonwealth Ave, Boston, MA, 02215. Tel: 617-353-3705. p. 993
Hunter, Shaunna, Libr Dir, Hampden Sydney College, 257 Via Sacra, Hampden Sydney, VA, 23943. Tel: 434-223-6193. p. 2322
Hunter, Steve, Asst Dir, Fac, Saint Louis County Library, 1640 S Lindbergh Blvd, Saint Louis, MO, 63131-3598. Tel: 314-994-3300. p. 1273
Hunter, Tim, Dir, Rowan-Cabarrus Community College, NCRC, 399 Biotechnology Lane, Kannapolis, NC, 28081. Tel: 704-216-7140. p. 1715
Hunter, Trevor, Libr Dir, The Cybrarium, 80 W Mowry Dr, Homestead, FL, 33030. Tel: 305-224-4410. p. 409
Hunter, Trevor, Dir, Manske Library, 13613 Webb Chapel, Farmers Branch, TX, 75234-3756. Tel: 972-247-2511. p. 2176
Hunter-Brodhead, Rhea, Circ, Waubonsee Community College, Collins Hall, 2nd Flr, State Rte 47 at Waubonsee Dr, Sugar Grove, IL, 60554. Tel: 630-466-2401. p. 652
Hunter-Larson, Leslie, Librn, Minnesota Pollution Control Agency Library, 520 Lafayette Rd, Saint Paul, MN, 55155-4194. Tel: 651-757-2314. p. 1201
Huntington, Debbie, Head, Cat, Head, Coll Develop, Northwestern State University Libraries, 913 University Pkwy, Natchitoches, LA, 71497. Tel: 318-357-6947. p. 900
Huntington, Lucas, Co-Dir, Franciscan Missionaries of Our Lady University Library, 5414 Brittany Dr, Baton Rouge, LA, 70808. Tel: 225-526-1730. p. 883
Huntington, Stan, Dir, Maywood Public Library District, 121 S Fifth Ave, Maywood, IL, 60153-1307. Tel: 703-343-1847, Ext 28. p. 615
Huntley, Aimee, ILL, Per, Mount Marty University, 1105 W Eighth St, Yankton, SD, 57078-3725. Tel: 605-668-1555. p. 2086
Huntley, Teresa, Br Mgr, Dayton Metro Library, Kettering-Moraine, 3496 Far Hills Ave, Kettering, OH, 45429. Tel: 937-496-8938. p. 1779
Huntsha, Lisa, Archivist, Librn, Swenson Swedish Immigration Research Center, Augustana College, 3520 Seventh Ave, Rock Island, IL, 61201. Tel: 309-794-7496. p. 641
Huntsman, Mary Taylor, Interim Dir, Libr Serv, Somerset Community College Learning Commons, Harold B Strunk Learning Resource Ctr, 808 Monticello St, Somerset, KY, 42501. Tel: 606-451-6710. p. 875
Huntsman, Rhonda, Dir, Salina Public Library, 90 W Main St, Salina, UT, 84654. Tel: 435-529-7753. p. 2270
Huntting, Sallie, Exec Dir, Marin History Museum Library, 45 Leveroni Ct, Novato, CA, 94949. Tel: 415-382-1182. p. 184
Huntzinger, Nicole, Libr Mgr, Western Plains Library System, Sentinel Public Library, 210 E Main St, Sentinel, OK, 73664. Tel: 580-393-2244. p. 1845
Huot, Marc-André, Chef de Section, Bibliotheques de Montreal, Le Prevost, 7355 Ave Christophe-Colomb, Montreal, QC, H2R 2S5, CANADA. Tel: 514-872-1525. p. 2719
Huot, Marc-Andre, Chef de Div, Bibliotheques de Montreal, Parc-Extension, 421 rue Saint-Roch, Montreal, QC, H3N 1K2, CANADA. Tel: 514-294-7810. p. 2720
Huot, Marc-Andre, Chef de Div, Bibliotheques de Montreal, Saint-Michel, 7601 rue Francois-Perrault, Montreal, QC, H2A 3L6, CANADA. Tel: 5142947810. p. 2720

Hupe, Meghan, Dir, Info & Delivery Services, Georgetown University, Dahlgren Memorial Library, Preclinical Science Bldg GM-7, 3900 Reservoir Rd NW, Washington, DC, 20007. Tel: 202-687-1173. p. 368

Hupp, Julie, Librn, Ohio Department of Rehabilitation & Correction, 15708 McConnelsville Rd, Caldwell, OH, 43724. Tel: 740-732-5188. p. 1754

Hurd, Jennifer, Br Mgr, Round Lake Library, Malta Community Center, One Bayberry Dr, Malta, NY, 12020. Tel: 518-682-2495. p. 1633

Hurd, Jennifer, Dir, Round Lake Library, 31 Wesley Ave, Round Lake, NY, 12151. Tel: 518-899-2285. p. 1633

Hurd, Kay, Dir, Almont District Library, 213 W St Clair St, Almont, MI, 48003-8476. Tel: 810-798-3100. p. 1077

Hurd, Meagan, Teen Serv, North Palm Beach Public Library, 303 Anchorage Dr, North Palm Beach, FL, 33408. Tel: 561-841-3383. p. 429

Hurlbut, Joe, Operating Syst/Network Analyst, Oregon Institute of Technology Library, 3201 Campus Dr, Klamath Falls, OR, 97601-8801. Tel: 541-885-1772. p. 1883

Hurley, Diane, Loan Serv, Supvr, South Brunswick Public Library, 110 Kingston Lane, Monmouth Junction, NJ, 08852. Tel: 732-329-4000, Ext 7295. p. 1419

Hurley, John, Computer Syst Adminr, National Archives & Records Administration, 1000 Beal Ave, Ann Arbor, MI, 48109. Tel: 734-205-0553. p. 1079

Hurley, John, ANSER Mgr & Network Adminr, Ramapo Catskill Library System, 619 Rte 17M, Middletown, NY, 10940-4395. Tel: 845-343-1131, Ext 228. p. 1571

Hurley, Mary, Dir, Mineola Memorial Library, Inc, 301 N Pacific St, Mineola, TX, 75773. Tel: 903-569-2767. p. 2220

Hurley, Nicole, Library Contact, DeGolyer & MacNaughton Library, 5001 Spring Valley Rd, Ste 800 E, Dallas, TX, 75244. Tel: 214-368-6391. p. 2166

Hurley, Susan, Dir, Oldsmar Public Library, 400 St Petersburg Dr E, Oldsmar, FL, 34677. Tel: 813-749-1178. p. 430

Hurley, Theresa, Chief Librn, Lynn Public Library, Five N Common St, Lynn, MA, 01902. Tel: 781-595-0567. p. 1030

Hurrell, Stephen, Dir, Libr Syst, Thunder Bay Public Library, 285 Red River Rd, Thunder Bay, ON, P7B 1A9, CANADA. Tel: 807-684-6807. p. 2685

Hursh, David, Head Librn, East Carolina University, Music Library, A J Fletcher Music Ctr, Rm A110, Greenville, NC, 27858. Tel: 252-328-1239. p. 1694

Hurson, Kim, Ref & Instruction Librn, Ivy Tech Community College, 50 W Fall Creek Pkwy N Dr, Indianapolis, IN, 46208. Tel: 317-917-1602. p. 697

Hurst, Chris, Syst Librn, Brandon University, 270 18th St, Brandon, MB, R7A 6A9, CANADA. Tel: 204-727-9687. p. 2585

Hurst, Emily J, Dep Dir, Head, Research & Education, Virginia Commonwealth University Libraries, Tompkins-McCaw Library for the Health Sciences, Medical College of Virginia Campus, 509 N 12th St, Richmond, VA, 23298-0582. Tel: 804-828-0626. p. 2343

Hurst, Leslie, Head, Teaching & Learning Serv, University of Washington Libraries, Bothell Campus/Cascadia College Library, University of Washington Bothell, 18225 Campus Way NE, Box 358550, Bothell, WA, 98011-8245. Tel: 425-352-5340. p. 2381

Hurst, Susan, Bus Librn, Miami University Libraries, Business, Engineering, Science, & Technology Library, Laws Hall, 551 E High St, Oxford, OH, 45056. Tel: 513-529-7204. p. 1812

Hurst, Vicki, Head Librn, Letcher County Public Library District, 220 Main St, Whitesburg, KY, 41858. Tel: 606-633-7547. p. 877

Hurt, Joseph, Coordr, Info Tech, Boyle County Public Library, 307 W Broadway, Danville, KY, 40422. Tel: 859-236-8466, 859-238-7323. p. 853

Hurt, Paul, Circ Serv Dir, Lisle Library District, 777 Front St, Lisle, IL, 60532-3599. Tel: 630-971-1675. p. 610

Hurt, Tara, Archivist, Spec Coll Librn, Eastern Connecticut State University, 83 Windham St, Willimantic, CT, 06226-2295. Tel: 860-465-5563. p. 347

Hurtado, Elizabeth, Ch, Springdale Public Library, 405 S Pleasant St, Springdale, AR, 72764. Tel: 479-750-8180. p. 110

Hurtado, Isaiah, Librn, California Department of Corrections Library System, San Quentin State Prison Library, Main St, San Quentin, CA, 94964. Tel: 415-454-1460. p. 207

Hurtado, Mary, Adult & Teen Serv, Outreach Librn, Shorewood-Troy Public Library District, 650 Deerwood Dr, Shorewood, IL, 60404. Tel: 815-725-1715. p. 647

Hurtado, Yuri, Dir, Upland Public Library, 450 N Euclid Ave, Upland, CA, 91786-4732. Tel: 909-931-4200. p. 254

Hurteau, Linda, Library Assistant V, Wesleyan University, Science Library, 265 Church St, Middletown, CT, 06459. Tel: 860-685-3728. p. 323

Hurteau, Natalie, Mgr, Ad Serv, Mgr, Outreach Serv, Upper Hudson Library System, 28 Essex St, Albany, NY, 12206. Tel: 518-437-9880, Ext 225. p. 1484

Hurteau, Natalie, Dir, Grafton Community Library, 2455 NY Rte 2, Grafton, NY, 12082. Tel: 518-279-0580. p. 1540

Hurteau, Rebecca, Librn, De Leon City County Library, 125 E Reynosa St, De Leon, TX, 76444-1862. Tel: 254-893-2417. p. 2169

Hurwitz-Lange, Yael, Dir, Innovations, Library Contact, Congregation Mishkan Tefila, 384 Harvard St, Brookline, MA, 02446. Tel: 617-332-7770. p. 1003

Husak, Belinda, Circ Mgr, Algonquin Area Public Library District, 2600 Harnish Dr, Algonquin, IL, 60102-5900. Tel: 847-458-6060. p. 536

Husband, Diane, Tech Adminr, Burch & Cracchiolo PA, 702 E Osborn Rd, Ste 200, Phoenix, AZ, 85014. Tel: 602-234-8704. p. 69

Husband, Patricia, Asst Dir, Br Serv, East Baton Rouge Parish Library, 7711 Goodwood Blvd, Baton Rouge, LA, 70806-7625. Tel: 225-231-3785. p. 882

Husbands, Nicole, Outreach Serv, Teen Librn, Indian Valley Public Library, 100 E Church Ave, Telford, PA, 18969. Tel: 215-723-9109. p. 2012

Huse, Bethany, Librn, College of Menominee Nation Library, N 172 Hwy 47/55, Keshena, WI, 54135. Tel: 715-799-5600, Ext 3003. p. 2445

Huser, Sonya, Dir, Archbold Community Library, 205 Stryker St, Archbold, OH, 43502-1142. Tel: 419-446-2783. p. 1746

Husher, Brent, Dir, Ledding Library of Milwaukie, 10660 SE 21st Ave, Milwaukie, OR, 97222. Tel: 503-786-7580. p. 1887

Huskey, Joanna, Admin Mgr, Wake Forest University, Coy C Carpenter Medical Library, Bowman Gray Center for Medical Education, 475 Vine St, Winston-Salem, NC, 27101. Tel: 336-716-4694. p. 1726

Huskey, Julie, Head, Cat, Tennessee State University, 3500 John A Merritt Blvd, Nashville, TN, 37209. Tel: 615-963-5236. p. 2121

Huskey, Lisa, Br Mgr, Sequoyah Regional Library System, 116 Brown Industrial Pkwy, Canton, GA, 30114. Tel: 770-479-3090. p. 469

Huskins Webb, Kim, Dir, United States Air Force, 4FSS/FSDL, 1520 Goodson St, Bldg 3660, Seymour Johnson AFB, NC, 27531. Tel: 919-722-5825. p. 1716

Husman, Sherri, Med Librn, Doctors Medical Center, 1441 Florida Ave, Modesto, CA, 95352. Tel: 209-576-3782. p. 177

Huss, Kelly, Libr Dir, Tri-Valley Free Public Library, 633 E Main St, Hegins, PA, 17938-9303. Tel: 570-682-8922. p. 1943

Hussain, Mohamed, Interim Dir, State University of New York Downstate Health Sciences University, 395 Lenox Rd, Brooklyn, NY, 11203. Tel: 718-270-7411. p. 1506

Husser, Katherine, Libr Dir, Tempe Public Library, 3500 S Rural Rd, Tempe, AZ, 85282. Tel: 480-350-5237. p. 80

Hussey, Julie, Asst Librn, Ref Librn, World Resources Institute, Ten G St NE, Ste 800, Washington, DC, 20002. Tel: 202-729-7601. p. 382

Hussey, Lisa, Prof, Simmons University, 300 The Fenway, Boston, MA, 02115. Tel: 617-521-2800. p. 2786

Hussey, Patrick, Head, Access Serv, Head, Outreach Serv, Lake Forest College, 555 N Sheridan Rd, Lake Forest, IL, 60045. Tel: 847-735-5061. p. 606

Hussing, Christine, Libr Dir, Mondamin Public Library, 201 Maple St, Mondamin, IA, 51557. Tel: 712-646-2888. p. 770

Husted, Heather, Fiscal Officer, Minerva Public Library, 677 Lynnwood Dr, Minerva, OH, 44657-1200. Tel: 330-868-4101. p. 1803

Husted, Sherry, Dir, Roane County Public Library, 110 Parking Plaza, Spencer, WV, 25276. Tel: 304-927-1130. p. 2415

Huston, Carla, Dir, Jean M Thomsen Memorial Library, 105 N Gershwin St, Stetsonville, WI, 54480. Tel: 715-678-2892. p. 2479

Huston, Carrie, Br Mgr, Walker Public Library, 207 Fourth St, Walker, MN, 56484. Tel: 218-547-1019. p. 1207

Huston, Celia, Dr, Librn, San Bernardino Valley College Library, 701 S Mount Vernon Ave, San Bernardino, CA, 92410. Tel: 909-384-8574. p. 214

Huston, Dawn, Dir, Dunbar Free Library, 401 Rte 10 S, Grantham, NH, 03753. Tel: 603-863-2172. p. 1365

Hutchens, James, Univ Librn, Nova Southeastern University Libraries, 3100 Ray Ferrero Jr Blvd, Fort Lauderdale, FL, 33314. Tel: 954-262-4648. p. 402

Hutchens, Karen, Librn, Eastern Health, Centre for Nursing Studies Learning Resource Centre, 100 Forest Rd, St. John's, NL, A1A 1E5, CANADA. Tel: 709-777-8189. p. 2610

Hutchens, Susan, Br Librn, East Bend Public Library, 420 Flint Hill Rd, East Bend, NC, 27018. Tel: 336-699-3890. p. 1686

Hutcheson, Rene R, Dir, Hardin County Public Library, 100 Jim Owen Dr, Elizabethtown, KY, 42701. Tel: 270-769-6337. p. 854

Hutcheson, Sandria, Librn, Missouri Department of Corrections, Southeast Correctional Center, 300 E Pedro Simmons Dr, Charleston, MO, 63834. Tel: 573-683-4409. p. 1252

Hutchings, Mary, Head Librn, Parkland Regional Library-Manitoba, Erickson Branch, 20 Main St W, Erickson, MB, R0J 0P0, CANADA. Tel: 204-636-2325. p. 2586

Hutchins, Dan, Dir, Van Buren District Library, 200 N Phelps St, Decatur, MI, 49045. Tel: 269-423-4771. p. 1096

Hutchins, Donna, Dir, Odem Public Library, 516 Voss Ave, Odem, TX, 78370. Tel: 361-368-7388. p. 2223

Hutchinson, Bailee, Pres, Association for Rural & Small Libraries, PO Box 33731, Seattle, WA, 98133. Tel: 206-453-3579. p. 2776

Hutchinson, Callie, Asst Mgr, Manatee County Public Library System, Lakewood Ranch, 16410 Rangeland Pkwy, Lakewood Ranch, FL, 34211. Tel: 941-742-4500. p. 387

Hutchinson, Cindy, Asst Librn, Macsherry Library, 112 Walton St, Alexandria Bay, NY, 13607. Tel: 315-482-2241. p. 1485

Hutchinson, Jonathan C, Archives Librn, Syst Adminr, Pfeiffer University, 48380 US Hwy 52 N, Misenheimer, NC, 28109. Tel: 704-463-3361. p. 1703

Hutchinson, Kamille, Educ Mgr, Beacon Health System, 615 N Michigan, South Bend, IN, 46601. Tel: 574-647-7997. p. 718

Hutchinson, Kathy, Asst Dir, Salem-South Lyon District Library, 9800 Pontiac Trail, South Lyon, MI, 48178-7021. Tel: 248-437-6431, Ext 207. p. 1151
Hutchinson, Linda, Supvry Librn, United States Equal Employment Opportunity Commission Library, 131 M St NE, Rm 4SW16N, Washington, DC, 20507. Tel: 202-921-3119. p. 379
Hutchinson, Lyn, Libr Dir, Topeka Genealogical Society Library, 2717 SE Indiana Ave, Topeka, KS, 66605-1440. Tel: 785-233-5762. p. 839
Hutchinson, Megan, Youth Serv Supvr, Terrebonne Parish Library, 151 Library Dr, Houma, LA, 70360. Tel: 985-876-5861. p. 891
Hutchinson, Michaela, Youth Serv Librn, George Hail Free Library, 530 Main St, Warren, RI, 02885. Tel: 401-245-7686. p. 2042
Hutchinson, William, III, YA Serv, Atlanta-Fulton Public Library System, Evelyn G Lowery Library at Southwest, 3665 Cascade Rd SW, Atlanta, GA, 30331. Tel: 404-699-6363. p. 461
Hutchison, Ann, Dir, Barberton Public Library, 602 W Park Ave, Barberton, OH, 44203-2458. Tel: 330-745-1194. p. 1748
Hutchison, Bailee, Br Mgr, Altus Public Library, 421 N Hudson, Altus, OK, 73521. Tel: 580-477-2890. p. 1839
Hutchison, Brenda, Fiscal Officer, Southeast Regional Library System, 252 W 13th St, Wellston, OH, 45692. Tel: 740-384-2103. p. 2773
Hutchison, Donna, Dir, Media Serv, First Baptist Church, 209 E South St, Longview, TX, 75601. Tel: 903-212-3309. p. 2213
Hutchison, Jaime, Supvr, Circ, Tigard Public Library, 13500 SW Hall Blvd, Tigard, OR, 97223-8111. Tel: 503-684-6537, Ext 2510. p. 1900
Hutchison, Jannine, Cat, Mid-Mississippi Regional Library System, 201 S Huntington St, Kosciusko, MS, 39090-9002. Tel: 662-289-5151. p. 1224
Hutchison, Kathleen, Libr Dir, Mississippi College, 130 W College St, Clinton, MS, 39058. Tel: 601-925-3870. p. 1214
Hutchison Koep, Deb, Chief Librn, North Vancouver City Library, 120 W 14th St, North Vancouver, BC, V7M 1N9, CANADA. Tel: 604-998-3450. p. 2572
Hutchison, Robin, Curator, Texas A&M University Libraries, Cushing Memorial Library & Archives, 400 Spencer St, College Station, TX, 77843. Tel: 979-845-1951. p. 2157
Hutson, Amiya, Br Mgr, Cleveland Public Library, Rice, 11535 Shaker Blvd, Cleveland, OH, 44120. Tel: 216-623-7046. p. 1768
Hutson, Melissa, Librn, Enfield Free Public Library, 23 Main St, Enfield, NH, 03748. Tel: 603-632-7145. p. 1363
Hutson, Regina, Br Mgr, Puckett Public Library, 118 Cemetery Rd, Puckett, MS, 39151. Tel: 601-824-0180. p. 1230
Hutt, Stephanie, Mgr, Sheridan County Public Library System, Story Branch, 20 N Piney, Story, WY, 82842. Tel: 307-683-2922. p. 2499
Hutte, Carol, Ref Librn, Chaffey College Library, 5885 Haven Ave, Rancho Cucamonga, CA, 91737-3002. Tel: 909-652-6800. p. 197
Hutter, James, Asst Dir, Port Washington Public Library, One Library Dr, Port Washington, NY, 11050. Tel: 516-883-3728, Ext 1102. p. 1622
Hutto, Cary, Ms, Dir, Archives, Historical Society of Pennsylvania, 1300 Locust St, Philadelphia, PA, 19107-5699. Tel: 215-732-6200, Ext 301. p. 1981
Hutto, Dena, Col Librn, Reed College, 3203 SE Woodstock Blvd, Portland, OR, 97202-8199. Tel: 503-777-7572. p. 1894
Hutto, Heather, Dir, Bristow Public Library, 111 W Seventh Ave, Bristow, OK, 74010-2401. Tel: 918-367-6562. p. 1842
Hutto, Michelle, Youth Serv, West Melbourne Public Library, 2755 Wingate Blvd, West Melbourne, FL, 32904. Tel: 321-952-4508. p. 453
Hutton, Cari, Dir, Phelps Public Library, 4495 Town Hall Rd, Phelps, WI, 54554. Tel: 715-545-2887. p. 2469
Hutton, Greg, Cat & Coll Librn, Okanagan College Library, 1000 KLO Rd, Kelowna, BC, V1Y 4X8, CANADA. Tel: 250-762-5445, Ext 4490. p. 2568
Hutton, Laura, Supvr, User Serv, Gonzaga University, 502 E Boone Ave, Spokane, WA, 99258-0095. Tel: 509-313-3813. p. 2383
Hutton, Sarah, Head, Undergrad Teaching & Learning Serv, University of Massachusetts Amherst Libraries, 154 Hicks Way, University of Massachusetts, Amherst, MA, 01003-9275. Tel: 413-545-6740. p. 985
Hutton, Terrie, Commun Libr Rep, Mohave County Library District, Dolan Springs Community Library, 16140 Pierce Ferry Rd, Dolan Springs, AZ, 86441. Tel: 928-767-4292. p. 64
Hutton, Theresa, Librn, Centre County Library & Historical Museum, Holt Memorial, 17 N Front St, Philipsburg, PA, 16866. Tel: 814-342-1987. p. 1910
Hutzel, Martha, Dir, Central Rappahannock Regional Library, 125 Olde Greenwich Dr, Ste 160, Fredericksburg, VA, 22408. Tel: 540-372-1144, Ext 7003. p. 2319
Huxley, Kelly L, Libr Mgr, Onoway Public Library, 4708 Lac St Anne Trail, Onoway, AB, T0E 1V0, CANADA. Tel: 780-967-2445. p. 2550
Huyck, Sharlyn S, Dir, Ovid Public Library, 206 N Main St, Ovid, MI, 48866. Tel: 989-834-5800. p. 1139
Huyen, Maluck, Ref Serv, Midlands Technical College Library, Beltline Library, 316 S Beltline Blvd, 2nd Flr, Columbia, SC, 29205. Tel: 803-738-7812. p. 2072
Huynh, Hai, Libr Asst, Tech Serv, Notre Dame de Namur University Library, 1500 Ralston Ave, Belmont, CA, 94002-1908. Tel: 650-508-3486. p. 121
Huynh, Roger, Libr Dir, Santa Clara County Law Library, 360 N First St, San Jose, CA, 95113. Tel: 408-299-3568. p. 232
Huyser, Sara, Engagement Librn, Outreach Librn, Northwestern College, 101 Seventh St SW, Orange City, IA, 51041. Tel: 712-707-7311. p. 774
Huyumba, Annette, Science Library Assoc, Butler University Libraries, Ruth Lilly Science Library, 740 W 46th St, Indianapolis, IN, 46208-3485. Tel: 317-940-9415. p. 691
Hviding, Marie, Ref (Info Servs), Salem Public Library, 370 Essex St, Salem, MA, 01970-3298. Tel: 978-744-0860. p. 1051
Hwang, Amy, Dir, Libr Serv, Electronic Res, Eastern Nazarene College, 23 E Elm Ave, Quincy, MA, 02170. Tel: 617-745-3850. p. 1048
Hwang, Anita, Tech Asst, Roosevelt University, Performing Arts Library, 430 S Michigan Ave, Rm 1111, Chicago, IL, 60605. Tel: 312-341-2136. p. 567
Hwang, Yunmi, Dir, Technology, Richmond Hill Public Library, One Atkinson St, Richmond Hill, ON, L4C 0H5, CANADA. Tel: 905-884-9288. p. 2675
Hyams, Rebecca, Syst Librn, Web Librn, Borough of Manhattan Community College Library, 199 Chambers St, S410, New York, NY, 10007. Tel: 212-220-1442. p. 1580
Hyatt, Daphne, Librn, Abington Memorial Hospital, 1200 York Rd, Abington, PA, 19001. Tel: 215-481-2096. p. 1903
Hyatt, Daphne, Dir, Coll Mgt, Thomas Jefferson University, 1020 Walnut St, Philadelphia, PA, 19107. Tel: 215-503-2829. p. 1986
Hyatt, Jason, Dir, Buncombe County Public Libraries, 67 Haywood St, Asheville, NC, 28801. Tel: 828-250-4700. p. 1672
Hybbert, Adam, Access Serv, South Dakota State University, 1300 N Campus Dr, Box 2115, Brookings, SD, 57007. Tel: 605-688-4049. p. 2074
Hybertsen, Katherine, Dir, Saddle Brook Free Public Library, 340 Mayhill St, Saddle Brook, NJ, 07663. Tel: 201-843-3287. p. 1441
Hyde, Debra, Libr Dir, Park Falls Public Library, 121 N Fourth Ave, Park Falls, WI, 54552. Tel: 715-762-3121. p. 2468
Hyde, Emily, Mgr, Superior District Library, Pickford Community Library, 230 E Main St, Pickford, MI, 49774. Tel: 906-647-1288. p. 1149
Hyde, Jennifer, Br Mgr, Riverside County Library System, Lakeside Library, 32593 Riverside Dr, Lake Elsinore, CA, 92530. Tel: 951-678-7083. p. 202
Hyde, Mary A, Sr Dir, American College of Obstetricians & Gynecologists, 409 12th St SW, Washington, DC, 20024-2188. Tel: 202-863-2518. p. 360
Hyde, Rebecca, Research Librn, Saint Louis University, 3650 Lindell Blvd, Saint Louis, MO, 63108-3302. Tel: 314-977-3106. p. 1275
Hyde, Whitney, Circ, Midland County Public Library, 301 W Missouri Ave, Midland, TX, 79701. Tel: 432-688-4320. p. 2219
Hyde-Lay, Robyn, Exec Dir, University of Alberta, Health Law Institute Library, Law Ctr, Edmonton, AB, T6G 2H5, CANADA. p. 2538
Hyden, Bill, Mgr, Public Library of Cincinnati & Hamilton County, TechCenter, South Bldg, 2nd Flr, 800 Vine St, Cincinnati, OH, 45202-2009. p. 1763
Hyder-Darlington, Louise, Dir, Harrisburg Area Community College, One HACC Dr, Harrisburg, PA, 17110-2999. Tel: 717-780-2460. p. 1940
Hyder-Darlington, Louise, Asst Dir, Library Public Services, Harrisburg Area Community College, 735 Cumberland St, Lebanon, PA, 17042. Tel: 717-780-1710. p. 1953
Hydorn, Sarah, Head, Children's Servx, Amherst Town Library, 14 Main St, Amherst, NH, 03031. Tel: 603-673-2288. p. 1353
Hyer, Cindy, Librn, Trinity College, 2430 Welbilt Blvd, Trinity, FL, 34655. Tel: 727-376-6911, Ext 343. p. 451
Hyke, Christy, Libr Assoc, Chatfield Public Library, 314 Main St S, Chatfield, MN, 55923. Tel: 507-867-3480. p. 1169
Hykel, Nancy, Librn, West Public Library, 209 W Tokio Rd, West, TX, 76691. Tel: 254-826-3070. p. 2256
Hyland, Cynthia, Dir, Acad Tech, Wilson College, 1015 Philadelphia Ave, Chambersburg, PA, 17201-1285. Tel: 717-262-2008. p. 1921
Hyland, Stephanie, Libr Office Mgr, Connecticut Society of Genealogists, Inc Library, 175 Maple St, East Hartford, CT, 06118-2364. Tel: 860-569-0002. p. 310
Hylen, Antonina, Mgr, Saint Joseph's Hospital Health Center, 206 Prospect Ave, Syracuse, NY, 13203. Tel: 315-448-5053, 315-466-5040. p. 1650
Hylen, Sandra, Dir, Ontario Public Library, 1850 Ridge Rd, Ontario, NY, 14519. Tel: 315-524-8381. p. 1611
Hylinski, Janice, Circ, Digital Serv, Monroe County Community College, 1555 S Raisinville Rd, Monroe, MI, 48161-9047. Tel: 734-384-4181. p. 1133
Hyman, Mark, Dir, Alan Wofsy Fine Arts Reference Library, 1109 Geary Blvd, San Francisco, CA, 94109. Tel: 415-292-6500. p. 230
Hymel, Melissa, Dir, Pointe Coupee Parish Library, 201 Claiborne St, New Roads, LA, 70760. Tel: 225-638-9847. p. 905
Hynes, Deborah, Libr Dir, Jackson County Public Library System, 2929 Green St, Marianna, FL, 32446. Tel: 850-482-9631. p. 420
Hynes, Donna, YA Serv, Rochester Public Library, 65 S Main St, Rochester, NH, 03867-2707. Tel: 603-332-1428. p. 1380
Hynes, Julie, Head, Children's Servx, Sumter County Library, 111 N Harvin St, Sumter, SC, 29150. Tel: 803-773-7273. p. 2071

Hynes, Theresa, Libr Tech II, College of the North Atlantic Library Services, Fred Campbell & Ron Bennett Library, Bay St George Campus - Martin Gallant Bldg, Rm 116, PO Box 5400 Stn Main, Stephenville, NL, A2N 2Z6, CANADA. Tel: 709-646-5704. p. 2609
Hynson, Chamyre, Ref & Instruction Librn, Oglethorpe University, 4484 Peachtree Rd NE, Atlanta, GA, 30319. Tel: 404-364-8511. p. 465
Hynson, Judith S, Dir, Libr & Res Serv, Jessie Ball Dupont Memorial Library, Stratford Hall, 483 Great House Rd, Stratford, VA, 22558. Tel: 804-493-1940. p. 2347
Hypher, Monica, Tech Librn, University of Toronto Libraries, Jean & Dorothy Newman Industrial Relations Library, 121 St George St, Toronto, ON, M5S 2E8, CANADA. Tel: 416-946-7003. p. 2699
Hyres, Ann Marie, Tech Serv, Northwestern Connecticut Community College Library, Park Pl E, Winsted, CT, 06098. Tel: 860-738-6479. p. 348
Hysa, Ledina, Commun Libr Mgr, Queens Library, East Flushing Community Library, 196-36 Northern Blvd, Flushing, NY, 11358. Tel: 718-357-6643. p. 1554
Hysko, Wendy, Dir, Brownell Library, Six Lincoln St, Essex Junction, VT, 05452-3154. Tel: 802-878-6955. p. 2284
Hyslop, Andrew, Acting State Archivist, California State Archives, 1020 O St, Sacramento, CA, 95814. Tel: 916-653-7715. p. 208
Hysong, Gabriele, Librn, Rolls-Royce, 450 S Meridian St, Indianapolis, IN, 46254. Tel: 317-230-4751. p. 697
Hyun, Shinae, Dir, Haworth Municipal Library, 165 Stevens Pl, Haworth, NJ, 07641. Tel: 201-384-1020. p. 1407
Hyun, Shinae, Libr Dir, Teaneck Public Library, 840 Teaneck Rd, Teaneck, NJ, 07666. Tel: 201-837-4171. p. 1445
Hyun, Timothy, Dr, Libr Dir, Faith Evangelical Seminary Library, 3504 N Pearl St, Tacoma, WA, 98407-2607. Tel: 753-752-2020, Ext 117. p. 2386
Iannino, Jill, Tech Serv, Kinnelon Public Library, 132 Kinnelon Rd, Kinnelon, NJ, 07405. Tel: 973-838-1321. p. 1410
Iannucci, Lisa, Instr Librn, Monmouth University Library, 400 Cedar Ave, West Long Branch, NJ, 07764. Tel: 732-571-7560. p. 1452
Iansavitchene, Alla, Clinical Librn, London Health Sciences Centre, 800 Commissioners Rd E, London, ON, N6A 4G5, CANADA. Tel: 519-685-8500, Ext 75934. p. 2654
Iantorno, Joanne, Head, Info Serv, Radnor Memorial Library, 114 W Wayne Ave, Wayne, PA, 19087. Tel: 610-687-1124. p. 2018
Ibach, Mark, Consulting Serv Coordr, South Central Library System, 4610 S Biltmore Lane, Ste 101, Madison, WI, 53718-2153. Tel: 608-246-5612. p. 2450
Ibarra, Katia, Coordr, Acq, Arizona State University, College of Law, Arizona State University MC 9620, 111 E Taylor St, Ste 350, Phoenix, AZ, 85004. Tel: 480-965-4877. p. 69
Ibaugh, Phila, Dir, Ransomville Free Library, 3733 Ransomville Rd, Ransomville, NY, 14131. Tel: 716-791-4073. p. 1625
Ibey, Dawn, Director, Central Library & Public Services, Vancouver Public Library, 350 W Georgia St, Vancouver, BC, V6B 6B1, CANADA. Tel: 604-331-3603. p. 2581
Ibraheem, Abiodum, Digital Initiatives, Metadata Librn, Robert Morris University Library, 6001 University Blvd, Moon Township, PA, 15108-1189. Tel: 412-397-6875. p. 1965
Icasas, Tess, Coordr, Los Angeles County Office of Education, 9300 Imperial Hwy, Downey, CA, 90242-2813. Tel: 562-922-6359. p. 139
Icaza, Mary Ellen, Exec Dir, CEO, Stark County District Library, 715 Market Ave N, Canton, OH, 44702. Tel: 330-452-0665. p. 1755
Ice, Mac, Head, Spec Coll & Archives, Abilene Christian University, 221 Brown Library, ACU Box 29208, Abilene, TX, 79699-9208. Tel: 325-674-2316. p. 2131
Ice-Davis, Danielle, Asst Librn, Paden City Public Library, 114 S Fourth Ave, Paden City, WV, 26159. Tel: 304-337-9333. p. 2411
Icenhour, Linda, Libr Dir, Johnson County Public Library, 219 N Church St, Mountain City, TN, 37683. Tel: 423-727-6544. p. 2117
Ida, Cheryl, Head, Acq, Cicero Public Library, 5225 W Cermak Rd, Cicero, IL, 60804. Tel: 708-652-8084. p. 571
Ide, April, Asst Dir, New Ulm Public Library, 17 N Broadway, New Ulm, MN, 56073-1786. Tel: 507-359-8331. p. 1190
Idehara, Karen, Br Mgr, Phoenix Public Library, Ironwood Library, 4333 E Chandler Blvd, Phoenix, AZ, 85048. p. 72
Ideson, Lindsay, Br Mgr, Jefferson-Madison Regional Library, Northside, 705 W Rio Rd, Charlottesville, VA, 22901-1466. Tel: 434-973-7893. p. 2309
Ieremia, Jessica, Dir, Sitka Public Library, 320 Harbor Dr, Sitka, AK, 99835-7553. Tel: 907-747-4020, 907-747-4021. p. 51
Iffland, Heidi, Circ Mgr, River Valley District Library, 214 S Main St, Port Byron, IL, 61275. Tel: 309-523-3440. p. 636
Iffland, Laurie, Dir, Libr Tech, Norwalk Public Library, One Belden Ave, Norwalk, CT, 06850. Tel: 203-899-2780, Ext 15114. p. 332
Ifie, Casandra L, Librn, Itawamba Community College, 2176 S Eason Blvd, Tupelo, MS, 38804. Tel: 662-620-5090. p. 1233
Igaz, Micheal, Commun Outreach Coordr, Champlain Library, 94 Main St E, VanKleek Hill, ON, K0B 1R0, CANADA. Tel: 613-678-2216. p. 2701
Iglesias, Edward, Tech & Syst Librn, Salve Regina University, 100 Ochre Point Ave, Newport, RI, 02840-4192. Tel: 401-341-2330. p. 2035
Iglesias, Edward, Head, Digital Strategies, Stephen F Austin State University, 1936 North St, Nacogdoches, TX, 75962. Tel: 936-468-1444. p. 2221
Iglesias, Estrella, Dir, Miami Dade College, North Campus Learning Resources, 11380 NW 27th Ave, Miami, FL, 33167. Tel: 305-237-1471. p. 422
Igna, Mary Ann, Curator, Dep Dir, Desert Caballeros Western Museum, 21 N Frontier St, Wickenburg, AZ, 85390. Tel: 928-684-2272. p. 84
Ignatenko, Helen, Asst Br Mgr, Fairfax County Public Library, Centreville Regional, 14200 Saint Germain Dr, Centreville, VA, 20121-2299. Tel: 703-830-2223. p. 2316
Ihde, Lisa, Asst Librn, Elkader Public Library, 130 N Main St, Elkader, IA, 52043. Tel: 563-245-1446. p. 751
Ihnat, Bertha, Ref (Info Servs), Ohio State University LIBRARIES, Archives, 2700 Kenny Rd, Columbus, OH, 43210. Tel: 614-292-2409. p. 1774
Ihnen, Amy, Dir, Chatham Area Public Library District, 600 E Spruce St, Chatham, IL, 62629. Tel: 217-483-2713. p. 553
Ikenouye, Eric, Dir, Albany Public Library, 2450 14th Ave SE, Albany, OR, 97322. Tel: 541-917-7580. p. 1871
Iksiktaaryuk, Kevin, Tech Serv, Nunavut Public Library Services, PO Box 270, Baker Lake, NU, X0C 0A0, CANADA. Tel: 867-793-3351. p. 2625
Ilagan, Iris, Mgr, County of Los Angeles Public Library, Leland R Weaver Library, 4035 Tweedy Blvd, South Gate, CA, 90280-6199. Tel: 323-567-8853. p. 138
Ilasenko, Laureen, Libr Tech, University of Detroit Mercy Libraries, 4001 W McNichols Rd, Detroit, MI, 48221-3038. Tel: 313-993-1130. p. 1099
Iles, Tessa, Supvr, Haliburton County Public Library, Highland Grove Branch, 5373 Loop Rd, Highland Grove, ON, K0L 2A0, CANADA. Tel: 705-448-2652. p. 2644
Iles, Tessa, Supvr, Haliburton County Public Library, Wilberforce Branch, 1101 Holmes Rd, Wilberforce, ON, K0L 3C0, CANADA. Tel: 705-448-2510. p. 2644
Ilgar, Guo, Head, Adult Serv, Uniondale Public Library, 400 Uniondale Ave, Uniondale, NY, 11553. Tel: 516-489-2220, Ext 208. p. 1654
Iliff, Dawnah, Bus Mgr, Southern Oklahoma Library System, 601 Railway Express St, Ardmore, OK, 73401. Tel: 580-223-3164. p. 1840
Illari, Jason, Exec Dir, Historical Society of Carroll County Library, 210 E Main St, Westminster, MD, 21157. Tel: 410-848-6494, Ext 204. p. 981
Ille, Jon, Archivist, Little Big Horn College Library, 8645 S Weaver Dr, Crow Agency, MT, 59022. Tel: 406-638-3182. p. 1291
Illis, Diane C, Dir, Northern Tier Regional Library, 4015 Dickey Rd, Gibsonia, PA, 15044-9713. Tel: 724-449-2665. p. 1936
Illis, Diane C, Dir, Northern Tier Regional Library, Pine Center, 700 Warrendale Rd, Gibsonia, PA, 15044. Tel: 724-625-5655. p. 1936
Illoabachie, Nonyem, Commun Libr Mgr, Queens Library, Whitestone Community Library, 151-10 14th Rd, Whitestone, NY, 11357. Tel: 718-767-8010. p. 1556
Illsley, Robin, Pub Serv Librn, Albert-Westmorland-Kent Regional Library, 644 Main St, Ste 201, Moncton, NB, E1C 1E2, CANADA. Tel: 506-869-6032. p. 2603
Illum, Lisa, Archivist, Libr Coord, Sheppard Pratt Health Systems, 6501 N Charles St, Baltimore, MD, 21204. Tel: 410-938-4595. p. 956
Imai, Jen, Head, Volunteer Services, Cedar Mill Community Library, 1080 NW Saltzman Rd, Portland, OR, 97229-5603. Tel: 503-644-0043, Ext 111. p. 1891
Imamura, Claire, Outreach Serv Librn, Alaska State Library, 395 Whittier St, Juneau, AK, 99801. Tel: 907-465-2920. p. 47
Imbesi, Jason, Music Librn, University of Michigan, Music Library, Earl V Moore Bldg, 3rd Flr, 1100 Baits Dr, Ann Arbor, MI, 48109-2085. Tel: 734-764-2512. p. 1080
Imfeld, Teresa, Circ Serv Mgr, ILL, Warren Wilson College, 701 Warren Wilson Rd, Swannanoa, NC, 28778. Tel: 828-771-3064. p. 1718
Imhoff, Josh, Engagement Mgr, Wayne Township Library, 80 N Sixth St, Richmond, IN, 47374. Tel: 765-966-8291, Ext 1103. p. 715
Imig, Lois, Mgr, Omaha Public Library, Florence Branch, 2920 Bondesson St, Omaha, NE, 68112-1822. Tel: 402-444-5299. p. 1330
Imler, Bonnie, Head Librn, Pennsylvania State Altoona, 3000 Ivyside Park, Altoona, PA, 16601-3760. Tel: 814-949-5255. p. 1906
Imler, Bonnie, Head Librn, Pennsylvania State University, College Pl, 113 Hiller Bldg, Du Bois, PA, 15801. Tel: 814-375-4756. p. 1927
Imparato, Martha, Spec Coll Librn, Univ Archivist, Washburn University, 1700 SW College Ave, Topeka, KS, 66621. Tel: 785-670-1981. p. 839
Imperial, Robin, Mgr, District of Columbia Public Library, Lamond Riggs, 5401 S Dakota Ave NE, Washington, DC, 20011. Tel: 202-541-6255. p. 364
Imperial, Robin, Mgr, District of Columbia Public Library, Takoma Park, 416 Cedar St NW, Washington, DC, 20012. Tel: 202-576-7252. p. 364
Imrie, Diane, Exec Dir, Northwestern Ontario Sports Hall of Fame Library, 219 May St S, Thunder Bay, ON, P7E 1B5, CANADA. Tel: 807-622-2852. p. 2685
Inaba, Guy, Educ Spec, Kapi'olani Community College Library, 4303 Diamond Head Rd, Honolulu, HI, 96816. Tel: 808-734-9206. p. 512
Inagi Ferguson, Yoko, Cat Chief, City College of the City University of New York, North Academic Ctr, 160 Convent Ave, New York, NY, 10031. Tel: 212-650-7623. p. 1581

Ince, Naomi, Br Mgr, San Diego County Library, Pine Valley Branch, 28804 Old Hwy 80, Pine Valley, CA, 91962. Tel: 619-473-8022. p. 217
Inciardi, Kristin, Dir, Libr Serv, Peirce College Library, 1420 Pine St, Philadelphia, PA, 19102. Tel: 215-670-9023. p. 1983
Inefuku, Harrison, Scholarly Publishing Servs Librn, Iowa State University Library, 302 Parks Library, 701 Morrill Rd, Ames, IA, 50011-2102. Tel: 515-294-3180. p. 731
Infante, Adele, Dir, Grafton-Midview Public Library, 983 Main St, Grafton, OH, 44044-1492. Tel: 440-926-3317. p. 1788
Infante, Lynda, Fac Librn, Austin Community College, Riverside Campus Library, 1020 Grove Blvd, 1st Flr, Rm 1108, Austin, TX, 78741. Tel: 512-223-6181. p. 2138
Ingalls, Buddy, Br Mgr, Tulsa City-County Library, Central Library, 400 Civic Ctr, Tulsa, OK, 74103. p. 1866
Ingalls, Kate, Librn, Beverly Public Library, Beverly Farms, 24 Vine St, Beverly, MA, 01915-2208. Tel: 978-921-6066. p. 989
Ingalls, Trisha, Dir, Leach Public Library, 130 Park Ave, Irasburg, VT, 05845. Tel: 802-754-2526. p. 2286
Ingegno, Megan, Circ, Franklin Township Free Public Library, 485 DeMott Lane, Somerset, NJ, 08873. Tel: 732-873-8700. p. 1442
Ingersoll, John, Libr Dir, Grantsville City Library, 42 N Bowery St, Grantsville, UT, 84029. Tel: 435-884-1670. p. 2264
Ingerson, Cheryl, Ch, Maxfield Public Library, 8 Rte 129, Loudon, NH, 03307. Tel: 603-798-5153. p. 1371
Inglada, Montserrat, Ms, Dir, Whiting Public Library, 1735 Oliver St, Whiting, IN, 46394-1794. Tel: 219-659-0269, Ext 111. p. 726
Ingle, Alicia, Librn, Gadsden State Community College, Allen Hall, Rms 204 & 220, 1001 George Wallace Dr, Gadsden, AL, 35903. Tel: 256-549-8333. p. 18
Ingley, Sarah, Circ Supvr, Santa Fe College, 3000 NW 83rd St, Bldg Y, Gainesville, FL, 32606. Tel: 352-395-5411. p. 407
Inglis, Amy, ILL, Barrington Public Library, 105 Ramsdell Lane, Barrington, NH, 03825-7469. Tel: 603-664-9715. p. 1354
Inglis, Jennifer, Dir, Lynnfield Public Library, 18 Summer St, Lynnfield, MA, 01940-1837. Tel: 781-334-5411, 781-334-6404. p. 1031
Inglis, Leslie, Electronic Res Librn, Franklin Pierce University Library, 40 University Dr, Rindge, NH, 03461-3114. Tel: 603-899-4140. p. 1379
Ingmire, Andrea, Dir, Peter White Public Library, 217 N Front St, Marquette, MI, 49855. Tel: 906-226-4303. p. 1130
Ingold, Cindy, Librn, University of Illinois Library at Urbana-Champaign, Social Sciences, Health & Education Library, 101 Main Library, MC-522, 1408 W Gregory Dr, Urbana, IL, 61801. Tel: 217-333-7998. p. 656
Ingold, Jane, Ref & Instruction Librn, Penn State Behrend, 4951 College Dr, Erie, PA, 16563-4115. Tel: 814-898-6106. p. 1932
Ingold, Stephanie, Libr Mgr, Tulsa Community College Libraries, Southeast Campus, 10300 E 81st St, Tulsa, OK, 74133-4513. Tel: 918-595-7730. p. 1867
Ingraham, Lizzie, Libr Dir, Wardsboro Free Public Library, 170 Main St, Wardsboro, VT, 05355. Tel: 802-896-6988. p. 2297
Ingram, Becky, Asst Dir, Fremont Public Library District, 1170 N Midlothian Rd, Mundelein, IL, 60060. Tel: 847-566-8702. p. 622
Ingram, Bill, Asst Dean, Dir, IT, Virginia Polytechnic Institute & State University Libraries, 560 Drillfield Dr, Blacksburg, VA, 24061. Tel: 540-231-8642. p. 2307
Ingram, Catherine E, Asst Libr Dir, Cedar Park Public Library, 550 Discovery Blvd, Cedar Park, TX, 78613. Tel: 512-401-5640. p. 2154
Ingram, Darian, Libr Tech 1, SCLHS Saint Joseph Hospital, 1375 E 19th Ave, 3rd Flr, Denver, CO, 80218-1191. Tel: 303-812-3625. p. 277
Ingram, James, Libr Asst, George F Johnson Memorial Library, 1001 Park St, Endicott, NY, 13760. Tel: 607-757-5350. p. 1531
Ingram, Kim, Dir, Southampton Free Library, 947 Street Rd, Southampton, PA, 18966. Tel: 215-322-1415. p. 2009
Ingram, Laurie, Youth Serv, Jerseyville Public Library, 105 N Liberty St, Jerseyville, IL, 62052-1512. Tel: 618-498-9514. p. 603
Ingram, Libby, Assoc Dir, Libr Operations, University of Arkansas for Medical Sciences Library, 4301 W Markham St, Library No 586, Little Rock, AR, 72205. Tel: 501-686-6732. p. 102
Ingram, Lisa, Br Mgr, Memphis Public Library, Poplar-White Station Branch, 5094 Poplar, Memphis, TN, 38117-7629. Tel: 901-415-2777. p. 2113
Ingram, Nadia, YA Serv, Selby Public Library, 1331 First St, Sarasota, FL, 34236. Tel: 941-861-1100. p. 443
Ingram, Pam, Library Contact, Stone Mattheis Xenopoulos & Brew, PC Library, 1025 Thomas Jefferson St NW, Ste 800 W, Washington, DC, 20007-5201. Tel: 202-342-0800. p. 376
Iniguez, Maria, Library Contact, Colusa County Free Library, Maxwell Branch, 34 Oak St, Maxwell, CA, 95955. Tel: 530-438-2250. p. 131
Inman, Alana, Mgr, Texas State Library & Archives Commission, Sam Houston Regional Library & Research Center, 650 FM 1011, Liberty, TX, 77575. Tel: 936-336-8821. p. 2141
Inman, Christine, Dir, Madison Public Library, 110 S First St, Madison, KS, 66860. Tel: 620-437-2634. p. 822
Inman, Mallory, Youth & Teen Serv Librn, Norwalk Easter Public Library, 1051 North Ave, Norwalk, IA, 50211. Tel: 515-981-0217. p. 774
Inman, Phillip, Dir, Jacob Sears Memorial Library, 23 Center St, East Dennis, MA, 02641. Tel: 508-385-8151. p. 1015
Inman, Ruth A, Chairperson, Res Mgt Librn, City Colleges of Chicago, Kennedy-King College Library, 6403 S Halsted, Chicago, IL, 60621. Tel: 773-602-5449. p. 558
Innerd, Charlotte, Head, Coll & Acq, Wilfrid Laurier University Library, 75 University Ave W, Waterloo, ON, N2L 3C5, CANADA. Tel: 519-884-0710, Ext 2073. p. 2703
Innes, Alexis, Head, Children's Servx, Louis B Goodall Memorial Library, 952 Main St, Sanford, ME, 04073. Tel: 207-324-4714. p. 939
Innes, Genevieve, Education Children's Librn, The College of New Jersey, 2000 Pennington Rd, Ewing, NJ, 08628-1104. Tel: 609-771-2311. p. 1402
Innes, Jane Ellen, Libr Dir, Jefferson County Library District, 241 SE Seventh St, Madras, OR, 97741. Tel: 541-475-3351. p. 1885
Innes, John, Gen Mgr, Lambton County Library, 787 Broadway St, Wyoming, ON, N0N 1T0, CANADA. Tel: 519-845-0801. p. 2705
Inniger, Alyssa, Dir, Libr Serv, Bethany Lutheran College Memorial Library, 700 Luther Dr, Mankato, MN, 56001-4490. Tel: 507-344-7000. p. 1181
Innocent, Kassandre, Libr Mgr, New York Public Library - Astor, Lenox & Tilden Foundations, Fort Washington Branch, 535 W 179th St, (Between St Nicholas & Audubon Aves), New York, NY, 10033-5799. Tel: 212-927-3533. p. 1595
Ino, Darla, Dir, White County Regional Library System, Ewing P Pyeatt Bldg, 113 E Pleasure Ave, Searcy, AR, 72143. Tel: 501-268-2449, 501-279-2870. p. 109
Insalaco, Robin, Archives Librn, Tyler Junior College, 1327 S Baxter St, Tyler, TX, 75701. Tel: 903-510-2549. p. 2249
Insidioso, Barb, Br Mgr, Van Buren District Library, Gobles Branch, 105 E Main St, Gobles, MI, 49055. Tel: 269-628-4537. p. 1096
Insley, Diane, Libr Dir, San Marcos Public Library, 625 E Hopkins, San Marcos, TX, 78666. Tel: 512-393-8200. p. 2241
Interiano, Luis, Ad, West Baton Rouge Parish Library, 830 N Alexander Ave, Port Allen, LA, 70767. Tel: 225-342-7920. p. 906
Interlante, Lindsey, Exec Dir, Five Colleges of Ohio, Oberlin College, 173 W Lorain St, Rm 208, Oberlin, OH, 44074. Tel: 440-775-5500. p. 2772
Intravia, Toni, Circ, Massapequa Public Library, Bar Harbour Bldg, 40 Harbor Lane, Massapequa Park, NY, 11762. Tel: 516-799-0770. p. 1569
Inyamah, Deborah C, Chief Librn, United States Consumer Product Safety Commission Library, 4330 East W Hwy, Rm 519, Bethesda, MD, 20814. Tel: 301-504-7570. p. 960
Inzerilla, Tina, Librn, Las Positas College Library, 3000 Campus Hill Dr, Livermore, CA, 94551. Tel: 925-424-1150. p. 156
Ioanid, Aurora S, Dir, Coll Mgt, Monmouth University Library, 400 Cedar Ave, West Long Branch, NJ, 07764. Tel: 732-571-5364. p. 1452
Iocca, Dawn, Br Mgr, Jackson District Library, Spring Arbor Branch, 113 E Main St, Spring Arbor, MI, 49283. Tel: 517-750-2030. p. 1120
Iodice, Anthony, Mgr of Faculty Library Services & Digital Colls, Iona University, 715 North Ave, New Rochelle, NY, 10801-1890. Tel: 914-633-2347. p. 1577
Ioselev, Boris, Managing Librn, Brooklyn Public Library, Coney Island, 1901 Mermaid Ave, Brooklyn, NY, 11224. Tel: 718-265-3220. p. 1502
Iovino, Anthony, Asst Dir, Oceanside Library, 30 Davison Ave, Oceanside, NY, 11572-2299. Tel: 516-766-2360, Ext 340. p. 1609
Ip, Lina, Cat, College of Mount Saint Vincent, 6301 Riverdale Ave, Bronx, NY, 10471-1046. Tel: 718-405-3394. p. 1498
Ip, Phillip, Electronic Serv, United States Department of the Army, CEHEC-ZL Casey Bldg, 7701 Telegraph Rd, Alexandria, VA, 22315-3860. Tel: 703-428-6388. p. 2303
Ippoliti, Cinthya, Dir, Auraria Library, 1100 Lawrence St, Denver, CO, 80204-2095. Tel: 303-315-7763. p. 273
Ippolito, Rachel, Br Mgr, Rock Island Public Library, Watts-Midtown, 2715 30th St, Rock Island, IL, 61201. Tel: 309-732-7343. p. 641
Iqbal, Saadia, Reference & Scholarly Servs Librn, St John's University Library, Rittenberg Law Library, 8000 Utopia Pkwy, Jamaica, NY, 11439. Tel: 718-990-1578. p. 1556
Iraci, Kim, Dir, Williamson Public Library, 6380 Rte 21, Ste 1, Williamson, NY, 14589. Tel: 315-589-2048. p. 1665
Ireland, Ashley, Dean, Murray State University, 205 Waterfield Library, Dean's Office, Murray, KY, 42071-3307. Tel: 270-809-5604. p. 870
Ireland, Molly, ILL, Pitkin County Library, 120 N Mill St, Aspen, CO, 81611. Tel: 970-429-1900. p. 264
Ireland, Tracy, Libr Mgr, High Prairie Municipal Library, 4723 53rd Ave, High Prairie, AB, T0G 1E0, CANADA. Tel: 780-523-3838. p. 2543
Ireland-Bilodeau, Katrina, Ch Serv Librn, Northborough Free Library, 34 Main St, Northborough, MA, 01532-1942. Tel: 508-393-5025. p. 1043
Irion, Maile, Libr Dir, Sally Stretch Keen Memorial Library, 94 Main St, Vincentown, NJ, 08088. Tel: 609-859-3598. p. 1449
Irish, Elizabeth, Educ & Outreach Librn, Albany Medical College, 47 New Scotland Ave, MC 63, Albany, NY, 12208. Tel: 518-262-4980. p. 1482
Irizarry Oliveras, Omayra, Mrs, Ref Librn, Pontifical Catholic University of Puerto Rico, Ramon Emeterio Betances St 482, Mayaguez, PR, 00680. Tel: 787-834-5151, Ext 5010. p. 2511
Irizarry-Roman, Noelia, Research Librn, Orange County Regional History Center, 65 E Central Blvd, Orlando, FL, 32801. Tel: 407-836-8581. p. 432
Irmscher, Laura, Dir, West Hartford Public Library, 20 S Main St, West Hartford, CT, 06107-2432. Tel: 860-561-6950. p. 345

Irons, Lynda R, Res & Instrul Serv Librn, Pacific University Libraries, 2043 College Way, Forest Grove, OR, 97116. Tel: 503-352-1409. p. 1880
Irvin, Brenda, Circ Assoc, Louisiana State University Libraries, LSU School of Veterinary Medicine Library, Skip Bertman Dr, Baton Rouge, LA, 70803-8414. Tel: 225-578-9800. p. 884
Irvin, Lauren, Ref Librn, Point Park University Library, 414 Wood St, Pittsburgh, PA, 15222. Tel: 412-392-3162. p. 1995
Irvin, Sally, Law Librn, Wake Forest University, Law Library, Worrell Professional Ctr, 1834 Wake Forest Rd, Winston-Salem, NC, 27109. Tel: 336-758-4520. p. 1726
Irvin, Susan, Mgr, Cobb County Public Library System, Vinings Library, 4290 Paces Ferry Rd, Atlanta, GA, 30339. Tel: 770-801-5330. p. 489
Irvin, Tyler, Coordr, Tech Support, Librn, Southeastern Libraries Cooperating, 2600 19th St NW, Rochester, MN, 55901-0767. Tel: 507-288-5513. p. 2768
Irvin, Vanessa, Dr, Asst Prof, University of Hawaii, 2550 McCarthy Mall, Hamilton Library, Rm 002, Honolulu, HI, 96822. Tel: 808-956-7321. p. 2784
Irvine, Angela, Head, Coll Serv, Xavier University, 1535 Musketeer Dr, Cincinnati, OH, 45207. Tel: 513-745-4804. p. 1765
Irvine, Glenn, Supvr, Parkland Regional Library-Manitoba, Dauphin Branch, 504 Main St N, Dauphin, MB, R7N 1C9, CANADA. Tel: 204-638-6410. p. 2586
Irving, Catherine, Libr Spec, Saint Francis Xavier University, Marie Michael Library, Coady International Institute, Antigonish, NS, B2G 2W5, CANADA. Tel: 902-867-3964. p. 2616
Irving, Jamie, Dir, Stewart Free Library, Eight Levi Stewart Dr, Corinna, ME, 04928. Tel: 207-278-2454. p. 922
Irwin, Connie, Chairperson, Hartland Public Library, 61 Center St, Rte 20, West Hartland, CT, 06091. Tel: 860-238-4400. p. 346
Irwin, Gail J, Libr Dir, Ainsworth Public Library, 445 N Main St, Ainsworth, NE, 69210. Tel: 402-387-2032. p. 1305
Irwin, Karla, Archivist, Officer, Pew Charitable Trusts Library, 901 E St NW, 5th Flr, Washington, DC, 20004. Tel: 215-575-4731. p. 374
Irwin, Katherine M, Dean, Univ Libr, Central Michigan University, 250 E Preston St, Mount Pleasant, MI, 48859. Tel: 989-774-6420. p. 1134
Irwin, Ken, Web Serv Librn, Miami University Libraries, Business, Engineering, Science, & Technology Library, Laws Hall, 551 E High St, Oxford, OH, 45056. Tel: 513-529-6886. p. 1812
Irwin, Lee, Br Supvr, Yuma County Free Library District, Wellton Branch, 28790 San Jose Ave, Wellton, AZ, 85356. Tel: 928-373-6552. p. 86
Irwin, Lisa, Librn, Youth Rehabilitation & Treatment Center Library, 2802 30th Ave, Kearney, NE, 68845. Tel: 308-865-5313, Ext 287. p. 1319
Irwin, Rebekah, Dir, Spec Coll & Archives, Middlebury College, 110 Storrs Ave, Middlebury, VT, 05753. Tel: 802-443-3028. p. 2288
Irwin, Sandy, Libr Dir, Royal Oak Public Library, 222 E Eleven Mile Rd, Royal Oak, MI, 48067-2633. Tel: 248-246-3710. p. 1146
Irwin, Susan, Univ Archivist, Willamette University, 900 State St, Salem, OR, 97301. Tel: 503-370-6764. p. 1897
Irwin, Susan K, Asst Dir, Williams County Public Library, 107 E High St, Bryan, OH, 43506-1702. Tel: 419-636-6734. p. 1753
Irwin, Tracy, Dir, Exhibitions & Coll, Dossin Great Lakes Museum, 100 Strand Dr on Belle Isle, Detroit, MI, 48207. Tel: 313-821-2661, 313-833-1805. p. 1098
Irwin-Smiler, Kate, Govt Doc Librn, Ref Librn, Wake Forest University, Law Library, Worrell Professional Ctr, 1834 Wake Forest Rd, Winston-Salem, NC, 27109. Tel: 336-758-4520. p. 1726
Isaac, Gayle, Law Librn, Whatcom County Law Library, Courthouse, Ste B-03, 311 Grand Ave, Bellingham, WA, 98225. Tel: 360-778-5790. p. 2359
Isaac, LaMeane, Managing Librn, Brooklyn Public Library, Macon, 361 Lewis Ave, Brooklyn, NY, 11233. Tel: 718-573-5606. p. 1503
Isaacs, Sarah, Librn, Illinois Early Intervention Clearinghouse, Univ of Illinois-Urbana-Champaign, Children's Research Ctr, 51 Gerty Dr, Champaign, IL, 61820-7469. Tel: 217-333-1386. p. 552
Isaacson, Mary Beth, Regional Br Mgr, Pasco County Library System, Centennial Park, 5740 Moog Rd, Holiday, FL, 34690. Tel: 727-834-3204. p. 410
Isaacson, Mary Beth, Regional Br Mgr, Pasco County Library System, South Holiday Branch, 4649 Mile Stretch Rd, Holiday, FL, 34690. Tel: 727-834-3331. p. 410
Isaak, Jon, Dir, Canadian Conference of Mennonite Brethren Churches, 1310 Taylor Ave, Winnipeg, MB, R3M 3Z6, CANADA. Tel: 204-669-6575, Ext 695. p. 2592
Isaia, Matt, Electronic Res Librn, University of Saint Mary of the Lake - Mundelein Seminary, 1000 E Maple Ave, Mundelein, IL, 60060. Tel: 847-970-8945. p. 622
Isbell, Anne M, Dir, Lake Blackshear Regional Library System, 307 E Lamar St, Americus, GA, 31709-3633. Tel: 229-924-8091. p. 458
Isbell, Becky, Dir, Brownwood Community Library Association, 600 Carnegie St, Brownwood, TX, 76801-7038. Tel: 325-646-0155. p. 2150
Isbell, Becky, Dir, Brownwood Community Library Association, Genealogy & Local History, 213 S Broadway, Brownwood, TX, 76801. Tel: 325-646-6006. p. 2150
Isbell, Carleigh, Archives Specialist, Museum of York County, 210 E Jefferson St, York, SC, 29745. Tel: 803-329-2121. p. 2072
Isbell, Linda, Asst Librn, Crosby County Library, Ralls Branch, 813 Main St, Ralls, TX, 79357. Tel: 806-253-2755. p. 2162
Isbell, Melinda, Head, Research Services & Instruction, Abilene Christian University, 221 Brown Library, ACU Box 29208, Abilene, TX, 79699-9208. Tel: 325-674-2316. p. 2131
Iscrupe, Shirley G, Archivist, Ligonier Valley Library, 120 W Main St, Ligonier, PA, 15658-1243. Tel: 724-238-6451. p. 1955
Isdell, Brian, Br Mgr, Free Library of Philadelphia, Lawncrest Branch, 6098 Rising Sun Ave, Philadelphia, PA, 19111-6009. Tel: 215-685-0549. p. 1979
Isenhower, DeAnn, Cat Spec, Missouri Southern State University, 3950 E Newman Rd, Joplin, MO, 64801-1595. Tel: 417-625-9342. p. 1253
Iserman, Ali, Dir, Mediapolis Public Library, 128 N Orchard St, Mediapolis, IA, 52637. Tel: 319-394-3895. p. 769
Isgrigg, Daniel, Dir, Holy Spirit Res Ctr, Oral Roberts University Library, Holy Spirit Research Center, 7777 S Lewis Ave, Tulsa, OK, 74171. Tel: 918-495-6899. p. 1865
Isgrigg, Daniel, PhD, Dir, Archives, Dir, Holy Spirit Res Ctr, Oral Roberts University Library, 7777 S Lewis Ave, Tulsa, OK, 74171. Tel: 918-495-6899. p. 1865
Ishee, Jenifer, Spec Coll Librn, Connecticut College, 270 Mohegan Ave, New London, CT, 06320-4196. Tel: 860-439-2655. p. 328
Ishibashi, Jane, Circ Librn, Fullerton College, 321 E Chapman Ave, Fullerton, CA, 92832-2095. Tel: 714-992-7378. p. 147
Isicson, Robin, Chief of Strategic Analysis & Business Systems, San Diego County Library, MS 070, 5560 Overland Ave, Ste 110, San Diego, CA, 92123. Tel: 858-694-2415. p. 216
Iskenderian, Marguerite, Music Cataloger, Brooklyn College Library, 2900 Bedford Ave, Brooklyn, NY, 11210. Tel: 718-951-5347. p. 1501
Isleb, Karyn, Head, Youth Serv, Manchester City Library, 405 Pine St, Manchester, NH, 03104-6199. Tel: 603-624-6550. p. 1372
Isler, Melinda, Spec Coll Librn, University Archives, Ferris State University Library, 1010 Campus Dr, Big Rapids, MI, 49307-2279. Tel: 231-591-3500. p. 1085
Isley, Cary, Sr Cat Librn, Tulsa Community College Libraries, Metro Campus, 909 S Boston Ave, Tulsa, OK, 74119-2011. Tel: 918-595-7177. p. 1866
Isley, Jesse, Children's Serv Coordr, Charlotte Mecklenburg Library, 310 N Tryon St, Charlotte, NC, 28202-2176. Tel: 704-416-0100. p. 1679
Ismail, Lizah, Dir, Limestone University Library, 1115 College Dr, Gaffney, SC, 29340. Tel: 864-488-4610. p. 2060
Ison, Robin, Dir, Mercer County Public Library, 109 W Lexington St, Harrodsburg, KY, 40330-1542. Tel: 859-734-3680. p. 858
Isopo, Michelle, Ad, Schuylerville Public Library, 52 Ferry St, Schuylerville, NY, 12871. Tel: 518-695-6641. p. 1639
Ispahany, Rafat, Coll Develop Librn, Tenafly Public Library, 100 Riveredge Rd, Tenafly, NJ, 07670-1962. Tel: 201-568-8680. p. 1445
Israel, Matthew, Exec Dir, American Camellia Society Library, 100 Massee Lane, Fort Valley, GA, 31030-6974. Tel: 478-967-2358. p. 479
Isser, Wendy, Chief Librn, Department of Veterans Affairs, Bldg 12, 1st Flr, 79 Middleville Rd, Mail Code 142D, Northport, NY, 11768. Tel: 631-261-4400, Ext 2966. p. 1608
Istance-Curtis, LaTrice, Ref Librn, Coppin State College, 2500 W North Ave, Baltimore, MD, 21216-3698. Tel: 410-951-3400. p. 952
Isuster, Marcela Y, Liaison Librn, McGill University Libraries, Education Curriculum Resources Centre, 3700 McTavish St, 1st Flr, Montreal, QC, H3A 1Y2, CANADA. Tel: 514-398-5726. p. 2726
Itkonen, Saara, Libr Dir, Creston Valley Public Library, 531-16th Ave S, Creston, BC, V0B 1G5, CANADA. Tel: 250-428-4141. p. 2565
Ito, Fusako, Cataloger, Librn, Bowie State University, 14000 Jericho Park Rd, Bowie, MD, 20715. Tel: 301-860-3867. p. 960
Itria, Amanda, Pub Relations & Prog Coordr, Sterling Heights Public Library, 40255 Dodge Park Rd, Sterling Heights, MI, 48313-4140. Tel: 586-446-2665. p. 1152
Iturrey, Mike, Asst Dir, Miami-Dade Public Library System, 101 W Flagler St, Miami, FL, 33130-1523. Tel: 305-375-5044. p. 422
Itzin, Anne-Marie, Asst Dir, Northern Waters Library Service, 3200 E Lakeshore Dr, Ashland, WI, 54806-2510. Tel: 715-685-1072. p. 2421
Itzin, Anne-Marie, Syst & Cat Serv Librn, Northland College, 1411 Ellis Ave, Ashland, WI, 54806-3999. Tel: 715-682-1559. p. 2421
Ivaldi, Janet, Head, Adult Serv, Head, Circ, Mark Twain Library, 439 Redding Rd, Redding, CT, 06896. Tel: 203-938-2545. p. 334
Ivanick, Peter, Head, Libr Syst, Drexel University Libraries, Hagerty Library, 33rd & Market Sts, Philadelphia, PA, 19104-2875. Tel: 215-895-2090. p. 1976
Ivarra, Lulu, Libr Coord, Tri-Community Library, 6910 Hwy 80, Prairie Lea, TX, 78661. Tel: 512-488-2328, Ext 4. p. 2229
Ivers, Brenda, Bkmobile/Outreach Serv, Transylvania County Library, 212 S Gaston St, Brevard, NC, 28712. Tel: 828-884-3151. p. 1675
Ivers, Kimberley, Asst Libr Dir, Southborough Library, 25 Main St, Southborough, MA, 01772. Tel: 508-485-5031. p. 1055
Ivers, Lynda, Librn, Byron Public Library, 119 Kansas Ave, Byron, NE, 68325. Tel: 402-236-8752. p. 1309
Iverson, Sandy, Univ Librn, Saint Francis Xavier University, 3080 Martha Dr, Antigonish, NS, B2G 2W5, CANADA. Tel: 902-867-3931. p. 2615
Ives, Leigh, Libr Asst III, Washburn University, School of Law Library, 1700 SW College Ave, Topeka, KS, 66621. Tel: 785-670-1777. p. 840

Ives, Nikole, Dir, Pulaski Public Library, 4917 N Jefferson St, Pulaski, NY, 13142. Tel: 315-298-2717. p. 1624

Ivester, DeAun, Dir, Elk City Carnegie Library, 221 W Broadway, Elk City, OK, 73644. Tel: 580-225-0136. p. 1847

Ivey, Ann, Dir, Eustis Memorial Library, 120 N Center St, Eustis, FL, 32726. Tel: 352-357-5686. p. 395

Ivey, Darren L, Libr Dir, Barton Community College Library, 245 NE 30 Rd, Great Bend, KS, 67530. Tel: 620-792-9365. p. 810

Ivey, David, Dir, Logansport-Cass County Public Library, 616 E Broadway, Logansport, IN, 46947. Tel: 574-753-6383. p. 703

Ivey, Jennifer, Br Mgr, Athens Regional Library System, Madison County Branch, 1315 Hwy 98 W, Danielsville, GA, 30633. Tel: 706-795-5597. p. 458

Ivey, Joshua C, Coordr, Learning Commons, Medical University of South Carolina Libraries, 171 Ashley Ave, Ste 419, Charleston, SC, 29425-0001. Tel: 843-792-6306. p. 2051

Ivey, Rebecca, Mgr, Denton Public Library, North Branch, 3020 N Locust St, Denton, TX, 76209. p. 2170

Ivey, Wilson, Libr Serv Coordr, Chipola College Library, 3094 Indian Circle, Marianna, FL, 32446. Tel: 850-718-2372. p. 420

Ivie, Derek, Youth Serv Librn, Suffolk Cooperative Library System, 627 N Sunrise Service Rd, Bellport, NY, 11713. Tel: 631-286-1600. p. 1492

Ivins, Hanna, Br Librn, Moore County Library System, Britain Memorial Library, 118 E Fifth St, Sunray, TX, 79086-0180. Tel: 806-948-5501. p. 2172

Ivory, CJ, Instruction Librn, University of West Georgia, 1601 Maple St, Carrollton, GA, 30118. Tel: 678-839-6495. p. 469

Ivy, Adrienne, Circ Mgr, Saint Tammany Parish Library, Causeway Branch, 3457 Hwy 190, Mandeville, LA, 70471. Tel: 985-626-9779. p. 888

Ivy, Estelle, Br Mgr, Dixie Regional Library System, Okolona Carnegie Branch, 321 Main St, Okolona, MS, 38860. Tel: 662-447-2401. p. 1230

Ivy, Krista, Faculty Chair, Instructional Support, Crafton Hills College Library, 11711 Sand Canyon Rd, Yucaipa, CA, 92399. Tel: 909-389-3321. p. 262

Ivy, Lance, Dir of Libr Operations, Central Arkansas Library System, 100 Rock St, Little Rock, AR, 72201-4698. Tel: 501-918-3000. p. 101

Ivy, Priscilla, Ref Librn, Tombigbee Regional Library System, 436 Commerce St, West Point, MS, 39773-2923. Tel: 662-494-4872. p. 1235

Ivy, Priscilla, Head Librn, Tombigbee Regional Library System, Mathiston Public Library, 298 Scott Ave, Mathiston, MS, 39752. Tel: 662-263-4772. p. 1236

Ivy, Priscilla, Head Librn, Tombigbee Regional Library System, Webster County Public Library, 445 W Fox Ave, Eupora, MS, 39744. Tel: 662-258-7515. p. 1236

Iwachiw, Alex, Tech Serv Librn, Bank Street College of Education Library, 610 W 112th St, 5th Flr, New York, NY, 10025. Tel: 212-875-4455. p. 1579

Iwala-Olufarati, Cecilia, Head Librn, Grambling State University, 403 Main St, Grambling, LA, 71245-2761. Tel: 318-274-7367. p. 890

Iwami, Russell, Ref Librn, National University of Health Sciences Learning Resource Center, 200 E Roosevelt Rd, Bldg C, Lombard, IL, 60148-4583. Tel: 630-889-6612. p. 611

Iwan, Martha, Head, Adult Serv, Mount Kisco Public Library, 100 E Main St, Mount Kisco, NY, 10549. Tel: 914-864-0136. p. 1574

Iwanchuk, Andre, Bus Liaison Librn, Kwantlen Polytechnic University Library, 12666 72nd Ave, Surrey, BC, V3W 2M8, CANADA. Tel: 604-599-3486. p. 2576

Iwanec, Peter, Br Mgr, Chicago Public Library, Oriole Park, 7454 W Balmoral Ave, Chicago, IL, 60656. Tel: 312-744-1965. p. 557

Iweha, Chris, Assoc Dir, Pub Serv, Morgan State University, 1700 E Cold Spring Lane, Baltimore, MD, 21251. Tel: 443-885-3478. p. 956

Iyengar, Kaushalya, Dir, Town Hall Library, N 76 W 31429 Hwy VV, North Lake, WI, 53064. Tel: 262-966-2933. p. 2465

Iyer, Hemalata, Dr, Assoc Prof, University at Albany, State University of New York, Draper 015, 135 Western Ave, Albany, NY, 12203. Tel: 518-442-5116. p. 2789

Izaryk, Jamie, Dean of Academic Services, Bridgton Academy Learning Commons, 11 Academy Lane, North Bridgton, ME, 04057. Tel: 207-647-2121. p. 933

Izatt, James, Librn, Worcester Public Library, Worcester Talking Book Library, Three Salem Sq, Worcester, MA, 01608-2015. Tel: 508-799-1655, 508-799-1730. p. 1073

Izquierdo, Tammy, Co-Mgr, Bentley Municipal Library, 5014 - 49 Ave, Bentley, AB, T0C 0J0, CANADA. Tel: 403-748-4626. p. 2523

Izzi, Beverly, Youth Serv Coordr, Calvert Library, 850 Costley Way, Prince Frederick, MD, 20678. Tel: 301-855-1862, 410-535-0291. p. 972

Jablonski, Edward R, Chief Operating Officer, Library of Congress, James Madison Memorial Bldg, 101 Independence Ave SE, Washington, DC, 20540. Tel: 202-707-5000. p. 370

Jabrocki, Aly, State Archivist, Colorado Division of State Archives & Public Records, 1313 Sherman St, Ste 122, Denver, CO, 80203. Tel: 303-866-2358, 303-866-4900. p. 274

Jacalone, Judy, Dir, Topinabee Public Library, 1576 N Straits Hwy, Topinabee, MI, 49791. Tel: 231-238-7514. p. 1154

Jacavone, Jared, Librn, Tyrrell County Public Library, 414 Main St, Columbia, NC, 27925. Tel: 252-796-3771. p. 1682

Jacius, Doreen, Dir, East Granby Public Library, 24 Center St, East Granby, CT, 06026. Tel: 860-653-3002. p. 309

Jaciw, Kim, ILL, Department of Veterans Affairs, Lyons Campus Medical Library, 151 Knollcroft Rd, Lyons, NJ, 07939. Tel: 908-647-0180, Ext 4545, 973-676-1000. p. 1414

Jack, Chantalle, Librn, Vancouver Coastal Health, 231 E 15th St, North Vancouver, BC, V7L 2L7, CANADA. Tel: 604-984-5844, 604-988-3131. p. 2573

Jack, Chantalle, Prov Libr Leader, BC Cancer Library, 675 W Tenth Ave, Vancouver, BC, V5Z 1L3, CANADA. Tel: 604-675-8004. p. 2578

Jack, Debbie, Exec Dir, Parkland Community Library, 4422 Walbert Ave, Allentown, PA, 18104. Tel: 610-398-1361. p. 1905

Jack, Eumont, Librn, Gordon, Arata, Montgomery, Barnett, McCollam, Duplantis & Eagan, LLC, 201 Saint Charles Ave, Ste 4000, New Orleans, LA, 70170. Tel: 504-582-1111. p. 901

Jack, Samuel, Ad, Newton Public Library, 720 N Oak, Newton, KS, 67114. Tel: 316-283-2890. p. 826

Jackel, Marsha, Coll Mgt, Govt Doc, Graceland University, One University Pl, Lamoni, IA, 50140. p. 764

Jackiw, Michael, Mgr, Info Tech, Indian Trails Public Library District, 355 S Schoenbeck Rd, Wheeling, IL, 60090. Tel: 847-459-4100. p. 662

Jackman, Ashley, Br Mgr, Yuma County Free Library District, Heritage Branch, 350 Third Ave, Yuma, AZ, 85364. Tel: 928-373-6531. p. 86

Jackman, Christine, Library Contact, View Royal Reading Centre, 266 Island Hwy, Victoria, BC, V9B 1G5, CANADA. Tel: 250-479-2723. p. 2583

Jackman, Kara, Archivist & Spec Coll Librn, Boston University Libraries, School of Theology Library, 745 Commonwealth Ave, 2nd Flr, Boston, MA, 02215. Tel: 617-353-3034. p. 993

Jacks, Amber, Librn, Caldwell Community College & Technical Institute, 2855 Hickory Blvd, Hudson, NC, 28638. Tel: 828-726-2312. p. 1697

Jackson, Alicia, Adult Serv Mgr, Chicago Ridge Public Library, 10400 S Oxford Ave, Chicago Ridge, IL, 60415. Tel: 708-423-7753. p. 571

Jackson, Alyce, Libr Dir, Chillicothe Public Library District, 430 N Bradley Ave, Chillicothe, IL, 61523-1920. Tel: 309-274-2719. p. 571

Jackson, Amanda, Dir, Chesapeake Public Library, 298 Cedar Rd, Chesapeake, VA, 23322-5512. Tel: 757-410-7102. p. 2311

Jackson, Andrayah, Br Mgr, Riverside County Library System, Lake Tamarisk Library, 43-880 Lake Tamarisk Dr, Desert Center, CA, 92239. Tel: 760-227-3273. p. 202

Jackson, Andrew, Librn, United States Courts Library, 515 Rusk Ave, Rm 6311, Houston, TX, 77002. Tel: 713-250-5696. p. 2199

Jackson, Anna, Community Outreach, Warsaw Community Public Library, 310 E Main St, Warsaw, IN, 46580-2882. Tel: 574-267-6011. p. 724

Jackson, Arlyne Ann, Head of Libr, Boston University Libraries, Frederic S Pardee Management Library, Boston University School of Management, 595 Commonwealth Ave, Boston, MA, 02215. Tel: 617-353-4310. p. 993

Jackson, Athena, Dean, Univ Libr, University of Houston, M D Anderson Library, 114 University Libraries, Houston, TX, 77204-2000. Tel: 713-743-9800. p. 2199

Jackson, Austin, Dir, Wymore Public Library, 116 W F St, Wymore, NE, 68466. Tel: 402-645-3787. p. 1341

Jackson, Beatheia, Info Serv, Pasquotank County Library, 100 E Colonial Ave, Elizabeth City, NC, 27909. Tel: 252-335-2473. p. 1687

Jackson, Betty Ann, Br Mgr, Columbia County Library, Taylor Public Library, 101 Pope St, Taylor, AR, 71861. Tel: 870-694-2051. p. 103

Jackson, Brenda, Acq Librn, Alcorn State University, 1000 ASU Dr, Alcorn State, MS, 39096-7500. Tel: 601-877-6354. p. 1211

Jackson, Carion, Web Serv Mgr, University of Texas at Dallas, 800 W Campbell Rd, Richardson, TX, 75080. Tel: 972-883-2923. p. 2231

Jackson, Carleton L, Head, Nonprint Media Serv, University of Maryland Libraries, R Lee Hornbake Library, 0300 Hornbake Library Bldg, North Wing, College Park, MD, 20742-7011. Tel: 301-405-9226. p. 962

Jackson, Carol, Br Mgr, Ramsey County Library, Shoreview Branch, 4560 N Victoria St, Shoreview, MN, 55126. Tel: 651-724-6006. p. 1204

Jackson, Casanna, Libr Dir, Jacksonville University, 2800 University Blvd N, Jacksonville, FL, 32211-3394. Tel: 904-256-7277. p. 413

Jackson, Courtney, Circ Asst, Ball State University Libraries, Education, Music & Media Library, Bracken Library BL-106, Muncie, IN, 47306. Tel: 765-285-3439. p. 708

Jackson, Craig, Coll Mgt Librn, Mechanics' Institute Library, 57 Post St, Ste 504, San Francisco, CA, 94104-5003. Tel: 415-393-0101. p. 226

Jackson, Cristen, Br Librn, Genesee District Library, Flushing Area Library, 120 N Maple St, Flushing, MI, 48433. Tel: 810-659-9755. p. 1106

Jackson, Crystal, Ch, Fairview City Library, 115 S Sixth Ave, Fairview, OK, 73737-2141. Tel: 580-227-2190. p. 1847

Jackson, Darlene, Librn, Galeton Public Library, Five Park Ln, Galeton, PA, 16922. Tel: 814-435-2321. p. 1934

Jackson, Darlene, Dep Dir, Charleston County Public Library, 68 Calhoun St, Charleston, SC, 29401. Tel: 843-805-6801. p. 2048

Jackson, David, Asst Librn, Reformed Theological Seminary Library, 5422 Clinton Blvd, Jackson, MS, 39209. Tel: 601-923-1622. p. 1223

Jackson, Dawn, Libr Dir, Santa Maria Public Library, 421 S McClelland St, Santa Maria, CA, 93454-5116. Tel: 805 925-0994, Ext 2319. p. 243

Jackson, Deanna, Bus Mgr, Allen Parish Libraries, 320 S Sixth St, Oberlin, LA, 70655. Tel: 318-491-4543. p. 905

Jackson, Deborah, Regional Mgr, Cobb County Public Library System, Mountain View Regional Library, 3320 Sandy Plains Rd, Marietta, GA, 30066. Tel: 770-509-2725. p. 489

Jackson, Delilah, Dir, Washington Municipal Library, 418 N Main St, Washington, LA, 70589. Tel: 337-826-7336. p. 912

Jackson, Gerald D, Head Librn, Calhoun Community College, Huntsville Campus Library, 102-B Wynn Dr NW, Huntsville, AL, 35805. Tel: 256-890-4771. p. 14

Jackson, Greta, Br Mgr, Bladen County Public Library, Clarkton Public, 10413 N College St, Clarkton, NC, 28433. Tel: 910-647-3661. p. 1687

Jackson, Gwendolyn, Br Mgr, Greater Clarks Hill Regional Library System, Burke County Library, 130 Hwy 24 S, Waynesboro, GA, 30830. Tel: 706-554-3277. p. 478

Jackson, Gwendolyn, Br Mgr, Greater Clarks Hill Regional Library System, Midville Branch, 149 Trout St, Midville, GA, 30441. Tel: 478-589-7825. p. 478

Jackson, Hayley, Col Archivist, Luther College, 700 College Dr, Decorah, IA, 52101. Tel: 563-387-1725. p. 745

Jackson, Heather, Area Mgr, Prince George's County Memorial, Bladensburg Branch, 4820 Annapolis Rd, Bladensburg, MD, 20710-1250. Tel: 301-927-4916. p. 970

Jackson, Heather, Area Mgr, Prince George's County Memorial, Hyattsville Branch, 6502 America Blvd, Hyattsville, MD, 20782. Tel: 301-985-4690. p. 970

Jackson, Heather, Area Mgr, Prince George's County Memorial, Mount Rainier Branch, 3409 Rhode Island Ave, Mount Rainier, MD, 20712-2073. Tel: 301-864-8937. p. 971

Jackson, Heather, Area Mgr, Prince George's County Memorial, New Carrollton Branch, 7414 Riverdale Rd, New Carrollton, MD, 20784-3799. Tel: 301-459-6900. p. 971

Jackson, Holly, Library Contact, Springbank Township Library, 100 E Second St, Allen, NE, 68710. Tel: 402-635-2594. p. 1305

Jackson, James, Librn, Georgia Department of Corrections, Office of Library Services, 1000 Indian Springs Dr, Forsyth, GA, 31029. Tel: 478-994-7512. p. 479

Jackson, Jeffrey, City Librn, Sausalito Public Library, 420 Litho St, Sausalito, CA, 94965. Tel: 415-289-4121. p. 246

Jackson, Jennifer, Pub Serv, Tarrant County College, South Campus Jenkins Garrett Library, 5301 Campus Dr, Fort Worth, TX, 76119. Tel: 817-515-4524. p. 2180

Jackson, Jenny, Libr Dir, Marquette Heights Public Library, 715 Lincoln Rd, Marquette Heights, IL, 61554. Tel: 309-382-3778. p. 614

Jackson, Joe, Librn, Winona State University, 175 W Mark St, Winona, MN, 55987. Tel: 507-457-5152. p. 1209

Jackson, John, Dir, Foley Public Library, 319 E Laurel Ave, Foley, AL, 36535. Tel: 251-943-7665. p. 17

Jackson, John A, Exec Dir, Campbell County Public Library System, 2101 S 4-J Rd, Gillette, WY, 82718. Tel: 307-687-0009. p. 2494

Jackson, Johnny, Dir, Central State University, 1400 Brush Row Rd, Wilberforce, OH, 45384. Tel: 937-376-6106. p. 1831

Jackson, Joy, Asst Dir, Blanche K Werner Public Library, 203 Prospect Dr, Trinity, TX, 75862. Tel: 936-594-2087. p. 2249

Jackson, Julie, Supvr, Youth Serv, Saint Charles City-County Library District, Kathryn Linnemann Branch, 2323 Elm St, Saint Charles, MO, 63301. Tel: 636-723-0232, 636-946-6294. p. 1278

Jackson, Julie, Curator, Western Development Museum, 2935 Melville St, Saskatoon, SK, S7J 5A6, CANADA. Tel: 306-934-1400, Ext 230. p. 2750

Jackson, Kathryn, Br Mgr, Clay County Public Library System, Keystone Heights Branch, 175 Oriole St, Keystone Heights, FL, 32656. Tel: 352-473-4286. p. 396

Jackson, Katie, Asst Dir, Pub Serv, Dothan Houston County Library System, 445 N Oates St, Dothan, AL, 36303. Tel: 334-793-9767. p. 14

Jackson, Kim, Library Contact, Vance-Granville Community College, Warren Campus, 210 W Ridgeway St, Warrenton, NC, 27589-1838. Tel: 252-738-3686. p. 1695

Jackson, Kimberly, Pub Serv Mgr, Jeffersonville Township Public Library, 211 E Court Ave, Jeffersonville, IN, 47130. Tel: 812-285-5630. p. 698

Jackson, LaShonna L, Libr Asst, Southwest Tennessee Community College, Burt Bornblum, 5983 Macon Cove, Memphis, TN, 38134. Tel: 901-333-4105. p. 2115

Jackson, LaTavius, Ref Librn, State of Mississippi Judiciary, Carroll Gartin Justice Bldg, 450 High St, Jackson, MS, 39201. Tel: 601-359-3672. p. 1223

Jackson, Latrishia, Mgr, Desoto Parish Library, Pelican Branch, 145 Jackson Ave, Pelican, LA, 71063-2803. Tel: 318-755-2353. p. 896

Jackson, Lisa, Coll Develop Officer, Pasadena Public Library, 1201 Jeff Ginn Memorial Dr, Pasadena, TX, 77506. Tel: 713-477-0276. p. 2225

Jackson, Lori, Head, Ref, Kenora Public Library, 24 Main St S, Kenora, ON, P9N 1S7, CANADA. Tel: 807-467-2081. p. 2649

Jackson, Lorin, Exec Dir, National Network of Libraries of Medicine Region 2, MUSC James W Colbert Educ Ctr & Libr, 171 Ashley Ave, Ste 300, MSC 403, Charleston, SC, 29425. Tel: 267-648-6170. p. 2774

Jackson, Lydia, Interim Dean of Libr, Southern Illinois University Edwardsville, Campus Box 1063, 30 Hairpin Dr, Edwardsville, IL, 62026-1063. Tel: 618-650-2712. p. 582

Jackson, Mark, Dir, Bloomfield College Library, Media Center, 80 Oakland Ave, Bloomfield, NJ, 07003. Tel: 973-748-9000, Ext 1370. p. 1391

Jackson, Mark, Interim Dir, Bloomfield College Library, Liberty St & Oakland Ave, Bloomfield, NJ, 07003. Tel: 973-748-9000, Ext 1332. p. 1391

Jackson, Marta-Kate, Mgr, Youth & Teen Serv, Cromaine District Library, 3688 N Hartland Rd, Hartland, MI, 48353. Tel: 810-632-5200, Ext 114. p. 1114

Jackson, Mary, Res & Instruction Librn, Milligan College, 200 Blowers Blvd, Milligan College, TN, 37682. Tel: 423-461-8697. p. 2116

Jackson, Mary Beth, Ch Serv, Merriam-Gilbert Public Library, Three W Main St, West Brookfield, MA, 01585. Tel: 508-867-1410. p. 1065

Jackson, Monica, Mgr, Sno-Isle Libraries, Arlington Library, 135 N Washington Ave, Arlington, WA, 98223-1422. Tel: 360-435-3033. p. 2370

Jackson, Morris, Librn, Jones Day, 325 John H McConnell Blvd, Ste 600, Columbus, OH, 43215-2673. Tel: 614-469-3939. p. 1773

Jackson, Muriel, Head of Libr, Middle Georgia Regional Library System, Genealogical & Historical Room & Georgia Archives, 1180 Washington Ave, Macon, GA, 31201-1790. Tel: 478-744-0821. p. 487

Jackson, Neal, Coordr, Upper Mississippi River Conservation Committee Library, Murphy Library, UWLC, 1631 Pine St, La Crosse, WI, 54601. Tel: 608-783-8405, 618-579-3129. p. 2446

Jackson, Needra, Tech Serv, University of Missouri-Columbia, Law Library, 203 Hulston Hall, Columbia, MO, 65211-4190. Tel: 573-882-9675. p. 1244

Jackson, Neil, Libr Serv Coordr, Edmonton Public Library, Highlands, 6710 118 Ave NW, Edmonton, AB, T5B 0P3, CANADA. Tel: 780-495-9872. p. 2536

Jackson, Nicholas, Asst Dir, Head, Adult Serv, Pequannock Township Public Library, 477 Newark Pompton Tpk, Pompton Plains, NJ, 07444. Tel: 973-835-7460. p. 1436

Jackson, Pamela, Info Literacy, San Diego State University, 5500 Campanile Dr, San Diego, CA, 92182-8050. Tel: 619-594-3809. p. 221

Jackson, Petrina, Exec Dir, Harvard Library, Arthur & Elizabeth Schlesinger Library on the History of Women in America, Three James St, Cambridge, MA, 02138-3766. Tel: 617-495-8647. p. 1007

Jackson, Rachael, Per & Govt Doc Librn, West Virginia State University, Campus Box L17, Institute, WV, 25112. Tel: 304-766-5222. p. 2406

Jackson, Renee, Asst Librn, Annawan-Alba Township Library, 200 N Meadow Lane, Ste 2, Annawan, IL, 61234-7607. Tel: 309-935-6483. p. 537

Jackson, Ron, Ref Librn, United States Army, John L Throckmorton Library, IMSE-BRG-MWR-L Bldg 1-3346, Randolph St, Fort Bragg, NC, 28310-5000. Tel: 910-396-2665. p. 1689

Jackson, Sandy, Sister, Asst Dir, Las Vegas FamilySearch Genealogy Library, 509 S Ninth St, Las Vegas, NV, 89101. Tel: 702-382-9695. p. 1347

Jackson, Scott, Asst Dean, Facilities & Systems, University of North Texas Libraries, 1155 Union Circle, No 305190, Denton, TX, 76203-5017. Tel: 940-565-3024. p. 2170

Jackson, Selma, ILL, Libr Tech, David D Acker Library & Knowledge Repository, 9820 Belvoir Rd, Bldg 270, Fort Belvoir, VA, 22060. Tel: 703-805-2293. p. 2318

Jackson, Shaakira, Libr Asst, The National Academies, Keck 439, 500 Fifth St NW, Washington, DC, 20001. Tel: 202-334-2989. p. 371

Jackson, Sharlyn, Librn, Idaho School for the Deaf & Blind Library, 1450 Main St, Gooding, ID, 83330. Tel: 208-934-1052. p. 521

Jackson, Wanda Lynn, Dir, Brewton Public Library, 206 W Jackson St, Brewton, AL, 36426. Tel: 251-867-4626. p. 10

Jackson-Darling, Andi, Syst/Tech Serv, Merrill Memorial Library, 215 Main St, Yarmouth, ME, 04096. Tel: 207-846-4763. p. 947

Jackson-Roberts, Stacey, Exec Dir, Utah Pride Center Library, 210 East 400 S, Salt Lake City, UT, 84111. Tel: 801-539-8000, Ext 1010. p. 2272

Jackson-Sarden, Lonya, Br Mgr, Azalea Regional Library System, Greene County Library, 610 S Main St, Greensboro, GA, 30642. Tel: 706-453-7276. p. 488

Jackson-Sow, Tasha, Br Mgr, First Regional Library, Robert C Irwin Public Library, 1285 Kenny Hill Ave, Tunica, MS, 38676. Tel: 662-363-2162. p. 1220

Jacob, Brooke, Br Mgr, Ocean County Library, Berkeley Branch, 30 Station Rd, Bayville, NJ, 08721-2198. Tel: 732-269-2144. p. 1446

Jacob, Craig, Libr Mgr, New York Public Library - Astor, Lenox & Tilden Foundations, Francis Martin Branch, 2150 University Ave, (@ 181st St), Bronx, NY, 10453. Tel: 718-295-5287. p. 1596

Jacob, Hollie, Librn, Hamilton Memorial Library, 195 Rte 20, Chester, MA, 01011. Tel: 413-354-7808. p. 1010

Jacob, Johanne, Head Librn, Bibliotheque Municipale de Saint-Jean-sur-Richelieu, 180, rue Laurier, Saint-Jean-Sur-Richelieu, QC, J3B 7B2, CANADA. Tel: 450-357-2111, Ext 2112. p. 2735

Jacob, John, Archivist, Washington & Lee University, Wilbur C Hall Law Library, Lewis Hall, E Denny Circle, Lexington, VA, 24450. Tel: 540-458-8969. p. 2329

Jacob, Paula, Catalog Tech Services, ILL, Outreach Serv, Karl Junginger Memorial Library, 625 N Monroe St, Waterloo, WI, 53594-1183. Tel: 920-478-3344. p. 2483
Jacob, Susan, Libr Mgr, Saint Lucie County Library System, 101 Melody Lane, Fort Pierce, FL, 34950-4402. Tel: 772-462-1615. p. 405
Jacobi, Kristin M, Head, Cat, Eastern Connecticut State University, 83 Windham St, Willimantic, CT, 06226-2295. Tel: 860-465-4508. p. 347
Jacobine, Alison, Libr Dir, Hershey Public Library, 701 Cocoa Ave, Hershey, PA, 17033. Tel: 717-533-6555, Ext 3715. p. 1943
Jacobs, Alyson, Br Librn, Community District Library, Byron Branch, 312 W Maple St, Byron, MI, 48418. Tel: 810-266-4620, Ext 312. p. 1095
Jacobs, Anita, Libr Supvr, Seneca Nation Libraries, 830 Broad St, Salamanca, NY, 14779. Tel: 716-945-3157. p. 1635
Jacobs, Barb, Children's Serv Supvr, North Suburban Library District, 6340 N Second St, Loves Park, IL, 61111. Tel: 815-633-4247. p. 611
Jacobs, Brenda, Libr Asst, Camanche Public Library, 102 12th Ave, Camanche, IA, 52730. Tel: 563-259-1106. p. 736
Jacobs, Carolyn, Dr, Head, Ref, Lone Star College System, North Harris College Library, 2700 W W Thorne Dr, Houston, TX, 77073. Tel: 281-618-5487. p. 2197
Jacobs, Christine, Interim Superintendent, National Park Service, 100 Lady Bird Lane, Johnson City, TX, 78636. Tel: 830-868-7128. p. 2204
Jacobs, Danny, Libr Mgr, Albert-Westmorland-Kent Regional Library, Petitcodiac Public, Six Kay St, Ste 101, Petitcodiac, NB, E4Z 4K6, CANADA. Tel: 506-756-3144. p. 2603
Jacobs, Donna, Libr Supvr, Moore Haven Correctional Facility Library, 1282 E State Rd 78, Moore Haven, FL, 33471. Tel: 863-946-2420. p. 427
Jacobs, Elizabeth, Asst Dir, Bismarck Veterans Memorial Public Library, 515 N Fifth St, Bismarck, ND, 58501-4081. Tel: 701-355-1480. p. 1729
Jacobs, Helen, Librn, Valerie Merrick Memorial Library, PO Box 479, Fort Totten, ND, 58335-0479. Tel: 701-766-1353. p. 1733
Jacobs, Indre, Dir, Archives, Lithuanian Research & Studies Center, Inc, 5620 S Claremont Ave, Chicago, IL, 60636-1039. Tel: 773-434-4545. p. 563
Jacobs, Jennifer, Strategic Marketing Librn, Kennesaw State University Library System, 385 Cobb Ave NW, MD 1701, Kennesaw, GA, 30144. Tel: 470-578-3167. p. 483
Jacobs, Julia, Circ Serv Mgr, Longmont Public Library, 409 Fourth Ave, Longmont, CO, 80501-6006. Tel: 303-651-8470. p. 290
Jacobs, Krista, Dir, Seneca Nation Libraries, 830 Broad St, Salamanca, NY, 14779. Tel: 716-945-3157. p. 1635
Jacobs, Leslie, Asst Dir, Clermont County Public Library, 5920 Buckwheat Rd, Milford, OH, 45150. Tel: 513-732-2736. p. 1802
Jacobs, Lisa, Dir, Suffolk Cooperative Library System, Long Island Talking Book Library, 627 N Sunrise Service Rd, Bellport, NY, 11713. Tel: 631 924-6400 x275. p. 1492
Jacobs, Lisa, Dir, Longwood Public Library, 800 Middle Country Rd, Middle Island, NY, 11953. Tel: 631-924-6400. p. 1571
Jacobs, Mark, Exec Dir, Washington Research Library Consortium, 901 Commerce Dr, Upper Marlboro, MD, 20774. Tel: 301-390-2000. p. 2766
Jacobs, Sarah, Asst Librn, Racquet & Tennis Club Library, 370 Park Ave, New York, NY, 10022. Tel: 212-753-9700. p. 1600
Jacobs, Theresa, Libr Serv Coordr, Great River Regional Library, Delano Library, 160 Railroad Ave E, Delano, MN, 55328. Tel: 763-972-3467. p. 1196
Jacobs, Thomas, Coll Mgt, Tech Serv Librn, Denver Seminary, 6399 S Santa Fe Dr, Littleton, CO, 80120. Tel: 303-762-6962. p. 290
Jacobs, Virginia, Tech Serv Librn, Alaska State Library, 395 Whittier St, Juneau, AK, 99801. Tel: 907-465-2920. p. 47
Jacobsen, Aurora, Ref & Instruction Librn, Winona State University, 175 W Mark St, Winona, MN, 55987. Tel: 507-457-5147. p. 1209
Jacobsen, Bunny, Cat, Principal Libr Asst, Deptford Free Public Library, 670 Ward Dr, Deptford, NJ, 08096. Tel: 856-848-9149. p. 1399
Jacobsen, Linda, Librn, McIntyre Memorial Library, 208 Dallas St, Dallas, WI, 54733. Tel: 715-837-1186. p. 2430
Jacobsen, Michael, Dir, Zion-Benton Public Library District, 2400 Gabriel Ave, Zion, IL, 60099. Tel: 847-872-4680. p. 665
Jacobsen, Michele, Br Mgr, Bridgeport Public Library, Black Rock, 2705 Fairfield Ave, Bridgeport, CT, 06605. Tel: 203-576-7025. p. 303
Jacobsen, Mikael, Dir, Lake Villa District Library, 140 N Munn Rd, Lindenhurst, IL, 60046. Tel: 847-245-5100. p. 609
Jacobsma, Kelly, Dir, Hope College, Van Wylen Library, 53 Graves Pl, Holland, MI, 49422. Tel: 616-395-7790. p. 1115
Jacobson, Courtney, Activities Coord, North Dakota Veterans Home Library, 1600 Veterans Dr, Lisbon, ND, 58054. Tel: 701-683-6534, 701-683-6548. p. 1737
Jacobson, Eva, Circ Supvr, Los Alamos County Library System, 2400 Central Ave, Los Alamos, NM, 87544. Tel: 505-662-8240. p. 1472
Jacobson, Joanne, Ch Serv Spec, Metuchen Public Library, 480 Middlesex Ave, Metuchen, NJ, 08840. Tel: 732-632-8526. p. 1418
Jacobson, Karen, Br Asst, Marathon County Public Library, Hatley Branch, 435 Curtis Ave, Hatley, WI, 54440. Tel: 715-446-3537. p. 2486
Jacobson, Krista, Pub Serv, Northwestern Health Sciences University, 2501 W 84th St, Bloomington, MN, 55431-1599. Tel: 952-885-5463. p. 1166
Jacobson, Kristen, Coll Mgt, Libr Asst, University of La Verne, 320 E D St, Ontario, CA, 91764. Tel: 909-460-2066. p. 188
Jacobson, Kristen, Asst Dir, Westchester Public Library, 10700 Canterbury St, Westchester, IL, 60154. Tel: 708-562-3573. p. 661
Jacobson, Kristen, Ref Serv, Ch, Westchester Public Library, 10700 Canterbury St, Westchester, IL, 60154. Tel: 708-562-3573. p. 661
Jacobson, Lynn, Bibliog Syst & Access Mgr, Jacksonville Public Library, 303 N Laura St, Jacksonville, FL, 32202-3505. Tel: 904-630-1318. p. 411
Jacobson, Pamela, Dir, Rowley Public Library, 141 Main St, Rowley, MA, 01969. Tel: 978-948-2850. p. 1050
Jacobson, Terra, Dean, Moraine Valley Community College Library, 9000 W College Pkwy, Palos Hills, IL, 60465. Tel: 708-974-5467. p. 632
Jacobus, Seth Aaron, Libr Dir, George F Johnson Memorial Library, 1001 Park St, Endicott, NY, 13760. Tel: 607-757-5350. p. 1531
Jacoby, Beth, Content Dev, York College of Pennsylvania, 441 Country Club Rd, York, PA, 17403-3651. Tel: 717-815-1950. p. 2026
Jacoby, Kelly, Youth Librn, Schuylkill Valley Community Library, 1310 Washington Rd, Leesport, PA, 19533-9708. Tel: 610-926-1555. p. 1954
Jacoby Murphy, Sally, Dir, Fred & Harriett Taylor Memorial Library, 21 William St, Hammondsport, NY, 14840. Tel: 607-569-2045. p. 1544
Jacoby, Robert, Sr Legal Res Librn, University of Toledo, LaValley Law Library, Mail Stop 508, 2801 W Bancroft St, Toledo, OH, 43606-3390. Tel: 419-530-2733. p. 1825
Jacome, Michael, Br Mgr, San Bernardino County Library, Yucca Valley Branch, 57098 Twentynine Palms Hwy, Yucca Valley, CA, 92284. Tel: 760-228-5455. p. 214
Jacot, Jaclyn, Dean of Extended Learning, Spokane Community College/Community Colleges of Spokane Library, MS 2160, 1810 N Greene St, Spokane, WA, 99217-5399. Tel: 509-533-7055. p. 2384
Jacox, Corinne, Cat, Ref Librn, Creighton University, Klutznick Law Library - McGrath North Mullin & Kratz Legal Research Center, School of Law, 2500 California Plaza, Omaha, NE, 68178-0340. Tel: 402-280-2283. p. 1328
Jacquot, Maureen, Librn, Missouri Court of Appeals, One Old Post Office Sq, Rm 304, 815 Olive St, Saint Louis, MO, 63101. Tel: 314-539-4300. p. 1272
Jacula, Mark, Pres, Durham Region Law Association, 150 Bond St E, Oshawa, ON, L1G 0A2, CANADA. Tel: 905-579-9554. p. 2663
Jadlos, Melissa, Dir, Saint John Fisher University, 3690 East Ave, Rochester, NY, 14618-3599. Tel: 585-385-8165. p. 1630
Jaeck, Sarah, Actg Mgr, Washoe County Library System, Duncan-Traner Community Library, 1650 Carville Dr, Reno, NV, 89512. Tel: 775-333-5134. p. 1350
Jaeger, Bret, Dir, Waupun Public Library, 123 S Forest St, Waupun, WI, 53963. Tel: 920-324-7925. p. 2485
Jaeger, John, Asst Librn, Johnson University, 7902 Eubanks Dr, Knoxville, TN, 37998. Tel: 865-251-2275. p. 2105
Jaehn, Tomas, Dir, University of New Mexico-University Libraries, 1900 Roma NE, Albuquerque, NM, 87131-0001. Tel: 505-277-7107. p. 1462
Jaehn, Tomas, Curator, Museum of New Mexico, Palace of the Governors-Fray Angelico Chavez History Library, 120 Washington Ave, Santa Fe, NM, 87501. Tel: 505-476-5090. p. 1475
Jaen, Ulysses, Dir, Law Libr, Ave Maria School of Law Library, 1025 Commons Circle, Naples, FL, 34119. Tel: 239-687-5501. p. 427
Jaffe, Frances, Sr Librn, Los Angeles Public Library System, Ascot Branch Library, 120 W Florence Ave, Los Angeles, CA, 90003. Tel: 323-759-4817. p. 163
Jaffe, Marina, Circ Coordr, Maryville College, 502 E Lamar Alexander Pkwy, Maryville, TN, 37804-5907. Tel: 865-981-8099. p. 2111
Jaffe, Rachel, Digital Content Librn, Metadata Librn, University of California, 1156 High St, Santa Cruz, CA, 95064. Tel: 831-502-7291. p. 243
Jaffe, Violet, Dir of Libr, Art Institute of Chicago, 111 S Michigan Ave, Chicago, IL, 60603. Tel: 312-443-3666. p. 554
Jaffy, Marc, Acq Librn, Franklin University Library, Frasch Hall, 1st Flr, 201 S Grant Ave, Columbus, OH, 43215. Tel: 614-947-6561. p. 1773
Jager, Teresa, Br Mgr, Wayne County Public Library, Dalton Branch, 127 S Church St, Dalton, OH, 44618. Tel: 330-828-8486. p. 1833
Jaggers, Kate, Dir, Highland Park Public Library, 31 N Fifth Ave, Highland Park, NJ, 08904. Tel: 732-572-2750. p. 1408
Jagos, Maureen, Dir, Chester Public Library, 1784 Kings Hwy, Chester, NY, 10918. Tel: 845-469-4252. p. 1517
Jaguszewski, Janice, Assoc Univ Librn, Dir, University of Minnesota Libraries-Twin Cities, Bio-Medical Library, Diehl Hall, 505 Essex St SE, Minneapolis, MN, 55455. Tel: 612-626-7039. p. 1185
Jahannes, Naftal, Interim Libr Supvr, Live Oak Public Libraries, Tybee Island Branch, 403 Butler Ave, Tybee Island, GA, 31328. Tel: 912-786-7733. p. 496
Jahlas, LuAnn, Dir, Brooklyn Public Library, 306 Jackson St, Brooklyn, IA, 52211. Tel: 641-522-9272. p. 736
Jahn, Anthony, State Archivist, State Historical Society of Iowa, 600 E Locust, Des Moines, IA, 50319-0290. Tel: 515-281-4895. p. 747
Jahng, Iris, Ref Librn, University of Massachusetts at Boston, 100 Morrissey Blvd, Boston, MA, 02125-3300. Tel: 617-287-5754. p. 1000

Jahnke, Elizabeth, Libr Dir, Grandview Library, 500 W Main St, Grandview, WA, 98930-1398. Tel: 509-882-7036. p. 2365
Jahnke, Jessica, Dir, Howard Whittemore Memorial Library, 243 Church St, Naugatuck, CT, 06770-4198. Tel: 203-729-4591. p. 324
Jaime, Crystal, Libr Dir, Sunland Park Community Library, 984 McNutt Rd, Sunland Park, NM, 88063-9039. Tel: 575-874-0873. p. 1478
Jain, Meena, Dir, Ashland Public Library, 66 Front St, Ashland, MA, 01721. Tel: 508-881-0134. p. 986
Jain, Sheila, Libr Dir, Morris Plains Library, 77 Glenbrook Rd, Morris Plains, NJ, 07950. Tel: 973-538-2599. p. 1421
Jakacki, Lesley, Youth Serv, McHenry Public Library District, 809 Front St, McHenry, IL, 60050. Tel: 815-385-0036. p. 616
Jakobitz, Jonathan, Br Mgr, Whatcom County Library System, Blaine Branch, 610 Third St, Blaine, WA, 98230. Tel: 360-305-3637. p. 2359
Jakubow, Alexander, Empirical Res Analyst, Duke University Libraries, J Michael Goodson Law Library, 210 Science Dr, Durham, NC, 27708. Tel: 919-613-8560. p. 1684
Jakus, Florence, Br Mgr, Las Vegas-Clark County Library District, West Charleston Library, 6301 W Charleston Blvd, Las Vegas, NV, 89146-1124. Tel: 702-507-3940. p. 1347
Jallah, Bebe, Br Mgr, Greensboro Public Library, McGirt-Horton, 2501 Phillips Ave, Greensboro, NC, 27405. Tel: 336-373-5810. p. 1692
Jalowka, Claudia, Supv Law Librn, Connecticut Judicial Branch Law Libraries, 90 Washington St, Third Flr, Hartford, CT, 06106. Tel: 860-706-5145. p. 316
Jambor, Urszula, Libr Mgr, Vaughan Public Libraries, Kleinburg Library, 10341 Islington Ave N, Kleinburg, ON, L0J 1C0, CANADA. Tel: 905-653-7323. p. 2701
Jambor, Urszula, Libr Mgr, Vaughan Public Libraries, Mackenzie Health Vaughan Library, 3200 Major Mackenzie Dr W, Vaughan, ON, L6A 4Z3, CANADA. Tel: 905-653-7323, Ext 4616. p. 2701
Jambrone, Vanessa, Head, Circ, Jericho Public Library, One Merry Lane, Jericho, NY, 11753. Tel: 516-935-6790. p. 1558
James, Alicia, Access Serv Spec, Outreach Serv Spec, Bellevue University, 1028 Bruin Blvd, Bellevue, NE, 68005. Tel: 402-557-7309. p. 1308
James, Ann, Tech Serv Librn, Troutman Sanders LLP, 1001 Haxall Point, 15th Flr, Richmond, VA, 23219. Tel: 804-697-1200. p. 2342
James, Art, Board Pres, Historical Society of Ocean Grove, 50 Pitman Ave, Ocean Grove, NJ, 07756. Tel: 732-774-1869. p. 1431
James, Betty, Librn, Briggs Lawrence County Public Library, Proctorsville Branch, 410 Elizabeth St, Proctorville, OH, 45669. Tel: 740-886-6697. p. 1791
James, Beverly, Exec Dir, Greenville County Library System, 25 Heritage Green Pl, Greenville, SC, 29601-2034. Tel: 864-527-9231. p. 2061
James, Cathy, Dir, Northeast Missouri Library Service, 207 W Chestnut St, Kahoka, MO, 63445-1489. Tel: 660-727-2327. p. 1254
James, Chris, Law Librn, Muskogee Law Library Association, Muskogee County Court House, 220 State St, Muskogee, OK, 74401. Tel: 918-348-1415. p. 1854
James, Cody, Dir, University of Montana, 32 Campus Dr, Missoula, MT, 59812. Tel: 406-243-6808. p. 1300
James, Dale, Dr, Chief Exec Officer, Rob & Bessie Welder Wildlife Foundation Library, 10429 Welder Wildlife, Hwy 77 N, Sinton, TX, 78387. Tel: 361-364-2643. p. 2244
James, Dean, Head, Ser, University of Mississippi Medical Center, 2500 N State St, Jackson, MS, 39216-4505. Tel: 601-984-1277. p. 1223
James, Debra, Libr Tech, Buena Vista Correctional Complex Library, 15125 Hwys 24 & 285, Buena Vista, CO, 81211. Tel: 719-395-7363. p. 269
James, Debra, Library Contact, Colorado Department of Corrections, 5125 Hwy 24 & 285, Buena Vista, CO, 81211. Tel: 719-395-2404, Ext 7354. p. 269
James, Delane, Dir, Buckham Memorial Library, 11 Division St E, Faribault, MN, 55021-6000. Tel: 507-334-2089. p. 1175
James, Donna V, Dir, Valley City State University, 327 E McFarland Hall, 101 College St SW, Valley City, ND, 58072-4098. Tel: 701-845-7303. p. 2790
James, Gayle, Libr Dir, Stewart B Lang Memorial Library, 2577 E Main St, Cato, NY, 13033. Tel: 315-626-2101. p. 1514
James, Heather, Interim Dean, Gonzaga University, 502 E Boone Ave, Spokane, WA, 99258-0095. Tel: 509-313-6533. p. 2383
James, Janet, Libr Mgr, Fried, Frank, Harris, Shriver & Jacobson LLP, 801 17th St NW, Ste 600, Washington, DC, 20006. Tel: 202-639-7000. p. 367
James, Jo-Lynn, Coll Develop & Automation Serv Librn, Florence-Lauderdale Public Library, 350 N Wood Ave, Florence, AL, 35630. Tel: 256-764-6564. p. 17
James, Joyce, Asst Dir, Bollinger County Library, 207 Mayfield Dr, Marble Hill, MO, 63764. Tel: 573-238-2713. p. 1260
James, Julie, Instruction & Ref Librn, Walden University Library, 100 Washington Ave S, Ste 900, Minneapolis, MN, 55401. p. 1186
James, Kim, Libr Dir, Tinton Falls Public Library, 664 Tinton Ave, Tinton Falls, NJ, 07724. Tel: 732-542-3110. p. 1446
James, Lance, Chief Develop Officer, Pikes Peak Library District, 20 N Cascade Ave, Colorado Springs, CO, 80903. Tel: 719-531-6333, Ext 6890. p. 271
James, Luanne, Grant & Assessment Coord, York County Library, 138 E Black St, Rock Hill, SC, 29730. Tel: 803-981-5838. p. 2068
James, Mary, Libr Dir, George McCone Memorial County Library, 1101 C Ave, Circle, MT, 59215. Tel: 406-485-2350. p. 1291
James, Maureen, Collections Management Coord, University of Arkansas at Little Rock, 2801 S University Ave, Little Rock, AR, 72204. Tel: 501-916-6180. p. 102
James, Meaghan, Libr Dir, Paul Pratt Memorial Library, 35 Ripley Rd, Cohasset, MA, 02025. Tel: 781-383-1348. p. 1012
James, Meredith, Br Coordr, Sheppard Memorial Library, Margaret Little Blount (Bethel) Library, 201 Ives St, Bethel, NC, 27812. Tel: 252-825-0782. p. 1694
James, Rebecca, Asst Dir, Youth Serv, Clayton County Library System, 865 Battlecreek Rd, Jonesboro, GA, 30236. Tel: 770-473-3850. p. 483
James, Robert, Assoc Libr Dir, Nash Community College Library, 522 N Old Carriage Rd, Rocky Mount, NC, 27804-9441. Tel: 252-451-8308. p. 1713
James, Sarah, Customer Serv Mgr, Georgina Public Library, Pefferlaw Branch, 76 Petes Lane, Pefferlaw, ON, L0E 1N0, CANADA. Tel: 705-437-1514. p. 2649
James, Scott, Archivist, Arts & Letters Club Library, 14 Elm St, Toronto, ON, M5G 1G7, CANADA. Tel: 416-597-0223. p. 2686
James, Seth, Libr Dir, Nappanee Public Library, 157 N Main St, Nappanee, IN, 46550. Tel: 574-773-7919. p. 709
James, Stephanie, Pub Serv Librn, Penticton Public Library, 785 Main St, Penticton, BC, V2A 5E3, CANADA. Tel: 250-770-7786. p. 2573
James, Susan, Prog Spec, Harnett County Public Library, Dunn Public, 110 E Divine St, Dunn, NC, 28334. Tel: 910-892-2899. p. 1701
James, Trina, Br Mgr, Jasper-Dubois County Public Library, Ferdinand Branch, 112 E 16th St, Ferdinand, IN, 47542. Tel: 812-367-1671, Ext 5111. p. 698
James-Jenkin, Connie, Coll Develop Librn, Electronic Res, Ref, Illinois Mathematics & Science Academy, 1500 Sullivan Rd, Aurora, IL, 60506-1000. Tel: 630-907-5920. p. 539
James-Vigil, Allyson, Ref Spec, Central New Mexico Community College Libraries, Montoya Campus Library, 4700 Morris St NE, RB 101, Albuquerque, NM, 87111. Tel: 505-224-4000, Ext 51342. p. 1461
Jameson, Jodi, Nursing Librn, University of Toledo, Mulford Library Bldg, 4th Flr, 3025 Library Circle, Toledo, OH, 43614-8000. Tel: 419-383-4225. p. 1825
Jamez, Alice, Librn, Correctional Reception Center Library, 11271 State Rte 762, Orient, OH, 43146. Tel: 614-877-2441. p. 1810
Jamieson, Anne, Asst Mgr, Adult Serv, Deerfield Public Library, 920 Waukegan Rd, Deerfield, IL, 60015. Tel: 847-945-3311. p. 577
Jamieson, BJ, Ref, Spec Coll, Belfast Free Library, 106 High St, Belfast, ME, 04915. Tel: 207-338-3884. p. 916
Jamieson, Heather, Librn, Selwyn Public Library, 836 Charles St, Bridgenorth, ON, K0L 1H0, CANADA. Tel: 705-292-5065. p. 2633
Jamieson, Steve, Libr Dir, Covenant Theological Seminary, 478 Covenant Ln, Saint Louis, MO, 63141. Tel: 314-392-4100, 314-434-4044. p. 1270
Jamison, Joanie, Dir, Colo Public Library, 309 Main St, Colo, IA, 50056. Tel: 641-377-2900. p. 741
Jamison, Laura, Coll Mgr, Maricopa County Library District, 2700 N Central Ave, Ste 700, Phoenix, AZ, 85004. Tel: 602-652-3000. p. 70
Jan, Emily, Photo Editor, San Francisco Chronicle Library & Archive, 901 Mission St, San Francisco, CA, 94103. p. 227
Jancay, Lindsey, Dir of Coll, Historic Bethlehem Partnership Library, 459 Old York Rd, Bethlehem, PA, 18018-5802. Tel: 610-882-0450, Ext 63. p. 1911
Janci, Kristen, District Administrator, Libr Dir, B F Jones Memorial Library, 663 Franklin Ave, Aliquippa, PA, 15001-3736. Tel: 724-375-2900. p. 1904
Janes, Judy, Dir, University of California, Davis, Mabie Law Library, King Hall, 400 Mrak Hall Dr, Davis, CA, 95616. Tel: 530-752-3328. p. 134
Janes, Lisa, Circ Supvr, Union Presbyterian Seminary Library, 3401 Brook Rd, Richmond, VA, 23227. Tel: 804-278-4335. p. 2342
Janes, Sara, Univ Archivist, Lakehead University, 955 Oliver Rd, Thunder Bay, ON, P7B 5E1, CANADA. Tel: 807-252-8010, Ext 8272. p. 2685
Janetvilay, Boutsaba, Acq & Metadata Serv Librn, California State University, Fresno, Henry Madden Library, 5200 N Barton Ave, Mail Stop ML-34, Fresno, CA, 93740-8014. Tel: 559-278-2403. p. 144
Janice, Hebbard, Librn, Baca County Library, Walsh Branch, 400 N Colorado St, Walsh, CO, 81090. Tel: 719-324-5349. p. 295
Janicki, Sandra L, Ref Librn, Indiana University of Pennsylvania, 431 S 11th St, Rm 203, Indiana, PA, 15705-1096. Tel: 724-357-2330. p. 1946
Janie, Barnett, Libr Dir, Wagoner City Public Library, 302 N Main St, Wagoner, OK, 74467-3834. Tel: 918-485-2126. p. 1868
Janis, Sharon, Asst Dir, Oglala Lakota College, Three Mile Creek Rd, Kyle, SD, 57752. Tel: 605-455-6067. p. 2077
Janke, Donna, Circ Mgr, Cromaine District Library, 3688 N Hartland Rd, Hartland, MI, 48353. Tel: 810-632-5200, Ext 101. p. 1114
Janke, Karen, Libr Dir, Erikson Institute, 451 N LaSalle St, Ste 210, Chicago, IL, 60654. Tel: 312-893-7210. p. 561
Janke, Robert, Interim Chief Librn, University of British Columbia Library, Okanagan Library, 3333 University Way, Kelowna, BC, V1V 1V7, CANADA. Tel: 250-807-9107. p. 2580

Janko, Denise, Dir, Beaver County Pioneer Library, 201 Douglas St, Beaver, OK, 73932. Tel: 580-625-3076. p. 1842
Jankovic, Sandra, Librn, North-West Regional Library, Benito Branch, 140 Main St, Benito, MB, R0L 0C0, CANADA. Tel: 204-539-2446. p. 2591
Jankowski, Pam, Dir, Literacy & Learning, Cuyahoga County Public Library, 2111 Snow Rd, Parma, OH, 44134-2728. Tel: 216-398-1800. p. 1813
Janning, Nicholas, Dir, Urbandale Public Library, 3520 86th St, Urbandale, IA, 50322. Tel: 515-278-3945. p. 787
Janoski, Jay, Asst Dir, Westhampton Free Library, Seven Library Ave, Westhampton Beach, NY, 11978-2697. Tel: 631-288-3335, Ext 120. p. 1664
Janota, Claudine, County Librn, Goliad County Library, 320 S Commercial St, Goliad, TX, 77963. Tel: 361-645-2291. p. 2185
Jans, Desirée, Br Mgr, Colchester-East Hants Public Library, Tatamagouche Branch, 170 Main St, Tatamagouche, NS, B0N 2J0, CANADA. Tel: 902-657-3064. p. 2623
Jans, Kathy, Libr Mgr, South Georgia Regional Library System, Mae Wisenbaker McMullen Memorial Southside Library, 527 Griffin Ave, Valdosta, GA, 31601-6343. Tel: 229-253-8313. p. 501
Jansen, Adam, State Archivist, Hawaii State Archives, Iolani Palace Grounds, 364 S King St, Honolulu, HI, 96813. Tel: 808-586-0329. p. 506
Jansen, Angela, Law Librn, Dinsmore & Shohl Library, 255 E Fifth St, Ste 900, Cincinnati, OH, 45202-3172. Tel: 513-977-8486. p. 1760
Jansen, Harold, Interim Univ Librn, University of Lethbridge Library, 4401 University Dr, Lethbridge, AB, T1K 3M4, CANADA. Tel: 403-329-2261, 403-329-2263. p. 2546
Jansen, Jean, Youth Serv Mgr, Villa Park Public Library, 305 S Ardmore Ave, Villa Park, IL, 60181-2698. Tel: 630-834-1164. p. 658
Jansen, Lloyd, Dep Dir, Charles County Public Library, Two Garrett Ave, La Plata, MD, 20646. Tel: 301-934-9001. p. 969
Jansen, Mike, City Librn, Woodburn Public Library, 280 Garfield St, Woodburn, OR, 97071. Tel: 503-982-5252. p. 1902
Jansen, Ruth, Head, Youth Serv, Dexter District Library, 3255 Alpine St, Dexter, MI, 48130. Tel: 734-426-4477. p. 1100
Janssen, Amber, Instruction & Assessment Librn, The California Maritime Academy Library, 200 Maritime Academy Dr, Vallejo, CA, 94590. Tel: 707-654-1093. p. 255
Jantz, Julie, Librn, Odessa Public Library, 21 E First Ave, Odessa, WA, 99159. Tel: 509-982-2903. p. 2372
Jantzi, Leanna, Head Librn, Simon Fraser University - Fraser Campus, Central City, Podium 3, 250-13450 102 Ave, Surrey, BC, V3T 0A3, CANADA. Tel: 778-782-7417. p. 2577
Janyk, Roën, Web Serv Librn, Okanagan College Library, 1000 KLO Rd, Kelowna, BC, V1Y 4X8, CANADA. Tel: 250-762-5445, Ext 4660. p. 2568
Janz, Jodi, Libr Asst, Sundre Municipal Library, 96-2 Ave NW, No 2, Sundre, AB, T0M 1X0, CANADA. Tel: 403-638-4000. p. 2556
Janzen, Deborah, Support Serv Mgr, Fresno County Public Library, 2420 Mariposa St, Fresno, CA, 93721. Tel: 559-600-7323. p. 145
Janzen, Grant, Coordr, Alberta Law Libraries - Lethbridge, Courthouse, 320-Four St S, Lethbridge, AB, T1J 1Z8, CANADA. Tel: 403-381-5161. p. 2546
Janzen, Rhiannon, Ch, Hillsboro Public Library, 120 E Grand Ave, Hillsboro, KS, 67063. Tel: 620-947-3827. p. 813
Janzen, Shirley, Commun Librn, Cariboo Regional District Library, Horsefly Branch, 5779 Walters Dr, Horsefly, BC, V0L 1L0, CANADA. Tel: 250-620-3345. p. 2584
Jaquith, Matthew, Prog Coordr, Springfield City Library, 220 State St, Springfield, MA, 01103. Tel: 413-263-6828, Ext 221. p. 1056
Jaramillo, Jessica, Br Mgr, San Francisco Public Library, West Portal Branch Library, 190 Lenox Way, San Francisco, CA, 94127-1113. Tel: 415-355-2886. p. 228
Jarboe, Sarah, Digital Serv, Ref Librn, Bellarmine University, 2001 Newburg Rd, Louisville, KY, 40205-0671. Tel: 502-272-8315. p. 864
Jardine, Dawn, Libr Dir, Red Hook Public Library, 7444 S Broadway, Red Hook, NY, 12571. Tel: 845-758-3241. p. 1626
Jardine, Spencer, Coordr, Instruction, Idaho State University, 850 S Ninth Ave, Pocatello, ID, 83209. Tel: 208-282-5609. p. 528
Jarecki, Kacper, Commun Libr Mgr, Queens Library, Cambria Heights Community Library, 218-13 Linden Blvd, Cambria Heights, NY, 11411. Tel: 718-528-3535. p. 1554
Jarell, Sloane, Libr Dir, Madison Library, 1895 Village Rd, Madison, NH, 03849. Tel: 603-367-8545. p. 1371
Jargaille, Dominic, Libr Mgr, Ministère de l'Emploi et de la Solidarité sociale, Marie-Guyart Bldg, RC, 700 rue Jacques-Parizeau, Quebec, QC, G1R 5E5, CANADA. Tel: 418-643-1515. p. 2731
Jarman, Julie, Dir, Staunton Public Library, 306 W Main St, Staunton, IL, 62088. Tel: 618-635-3852. p. 651
Jarman, Shonna, Asst Dir, Elko-Lander-Eureka County Library System, Wells Branch Library, 208 Baker St, Wells, NV, 89835. Tel: 775-752-3856. p. 1344
Jaroch, Diane, Adult Serv, Asst Dir, Ref (Info Servs), Irvin L Young Memorial Library, 431 W Center St, Whitewater, WI, 53190. Tel: 262-473-0530. p. 2488
Jaros, Dawn, Assoc Dir, Library Conservation, Academy of Motion Picture Arts & Sciences, 333 S La Cienega Blvd, Beverly Hills, CA, 90211. Tel: 310-247-3025. p. 124
Jarrell, Elizabeth, Asst Dir, East Morgan County Library District, 500 Clayton St, Brush, CO, 80723-2110. Tel: 970-842-4596. p. 269
Jarrell, Holly, Librn, Tech Serv, Azalea Regional Library System, 1121 East Ave, Madison, GA, 30650. Tel: 706-342-4974, Ext 1018. p. 488
Jarrell, Lisa, Head of Libr, Ball State University Libraries, Education, Music & Media Library, Bracken Library BL-106, Muncie, IN, 47306. Tel: 765-285-5333. p. 708
Jarrell, Suzanne, Chief Exec Officer, Head Librn, Wawa Public Library, 40 Broadway Ave, Wawa, ON, P0S 1K0, CANADA. Tel: 705-856-2244. p. 2703
Jarrells, Aaron, Br Mgr, Pulaski County Public Library System, Charles & Ona B Free Memorial, 300 Giles Ave, Dublin, VA, 24084. Tel: 540-674-2856. p. 2339
Jarrett, Gina, Coordr, Acq, Wake Forest University, Law Library, Worrell Professional Ctr, 1834 Wake Forest Rd, Winston-Salem, NC, 27109. Tel: 336-758-4520. p. 1726
Jarrett, Peggy, Coll Develop Coordr, University of Washington Libraries, Gallagher Law Library, William H Gates Hall, 4000 15th Ave NE, Seattle, WA, 98195-3020. Tel: 206-543-1941. p. 2382
Jarrett, Shannon, Dep Dir, National Archives & Records Administration, 2313 Red River St, Austin, TX, 78705. Tel: 512-721-0200. p. 2140
Jarrimillo, Jazzlyn, Libr Assoc, New Mexico Military Institute, Toles Learning Ctr, 101 W College Blvd, Roswell, NM, 88201. Tel: 575-624-8385. p. 1474
Jarry, Marie, Dir, Pub Serv, Hartford Public Library, 500 Main St, Hartford, CT, 06103. Tel: 860-695-6300. p. 317
Jarson, Jennifer, Head Librn, Pennsylvania State Lehigh Valley Library, 2809 E Saucon Valley Rd, Center Valley, PA, 18034-8447. Tel: 610-285-5119. p. 1920
Jarvi, Eliza, Head, Youth Serv, Lake Bluff Public Library, 123 E Scranton Ave, Lake Bluff, IL, 60044. Tel: 847-234-2540. p. 606
Jarvie, Calla, Dir, Rock County Community Library, 201 W Main, Luverne, MN, 56156. Tel: 507-449-5040. p. 1180
Jarvis, Allen, Libr Mgr, Central Arkansas Library System, Max Milam Branch, 609 Aplin Ave, Perryville, AR, 72126. Tel: 501-889-2554. p. 101
Jarvis, Anne, Univ Librn, Princeton University, One Washington Rd, Princeton, NJ, 08544-2098. Tel: 609-258-3170. p. 1437
Jarvis, BettyJo, Regional Libr Dir, Tennessee State Library & Archives, 403 Seventh Ave N, Nashville, TN, 37243-0312. Tel: 615-893-3380. p. 2121
Jarvis, Edward, Dir, Western Philatelic Library, 3004 Spring St, Redwood City, CA, 94063. Tel: 650-306-9150. p. 200
Jarvis, Helen, Ref Tech, Gowling WLG (Canada) Library, One First Canadian Pl, 100 King St W, Ste 1600, Toronto, ON, M5X 1G5, CANADA. Tel: 416-862-5735. p. 2689
Jarvis, Kathleen, Librn, Jerome Public Library, 600 Clark St, Jerome, AZ, 86331. Tel: 928-639-0574. p. 63
Jarvis, Madeline, Dir, Two Harbors Public Library, 320 Waterfront Dr, Two Harbors, MN, 55616. Tel: 218-834-3148. p. 1206
Jarzabski, Karen, Youth Serv, Highland Park Public Library, 31 N Fifth Ave, Highland Park, NJ, 08904. Tel: 732-572-2750. p. 1408
Jarzemsky, Timothy, Dir, Bloomingdale Public Library, 101 Fairfield Way, Bloomingdale, IL, 60108. Tel: 630-529-3120. p. 542
Jarzombek, Scott, Town Librn, Fairfield Public Library, 1080 Old Post Rd, Fairfield, CT, 06824. Tel: 203-256-3158. p. 312
Jarzombek, Scott, Exec Dir, Albany Public Library, 161 Washington Ave, Albany, NY, 12210. Tel: 518-427-4300. p. 1482
Jasinski, Kate, Head, Children's Servx, Scituate Town Library, 85 Branch St, Scituate, MA, 02066. Tel: 781-545-8727. p. 1052
Jasken, Laura, Academic Specialist, Minnesota State Community & Technical College, Fergus Falls Campus, 1414 College Way, Fergus Falls, MN, 56537-1000. Tel: 218-736-1650. p. 1188
Jaskowski, Selma K, Asst Dir, Info Tech & Digital Initiatives, University of Central Florida Libraries, 12701 Pegasus Dr, Orlando, FL, 32816-8030. Tel: 407-823-5444. p. 432
Jason, Darryl, Sr VPres, Tobacco Merchants Association of the United States, 1121 Situs Ct, Ste 370, Raleigh, NC, 27606. Tel: 919-917-7449. p. 1710
Jasper, Darnice, Br Mgr, Arundel Anne County Public Library, Maryland City at Russett Library, 3501 Russett Common, Laurel, MD, 20724. Tel: 410-222-1070. p. 950
Jass-Mahoney, Kimberly, Adminr, Library Contact, Willet Hauser Architectural Glass Library, 1685 Wilke Dr, Winona, MN, 55987. p. 1209
Jasso, Elyssa, Library Services, Tech Serv, Lunar & Planetary Institute Library, 3600 Bay Area Blvd, Houston, TX, 77058-1113. Tel: 281-486-2172. p. 2197
Jastrab, Marcey, Instruction & Assessment Librn, STEM Librarian, McDaniel College, 2 College Hill, Westminster, MD, 21157-4390. Tel: 410-857-2283. p. 981
Jastrzebski, Nicole, Head, Patron Serv, Huntington Public Library, 338 Main St, Huntington, NY, 11743. Tel: 631-427-5165, Ext 255. p. 1549
Jasulavic, Samantha, Head, Circ, Case Memorial Library, 176 Tyler City Rd, Orange, CT, 06477-2498. Tel: 203-891-2170. p. 333
Jatulis, Viltis A, Librn Emeritus, Thomas Aquinas College, 10000 N Ojai Rd, Santa Paula, CA, 93060-9980. Tel: 805-525-4417. p. 245
Jauquet, Tricia, Tech Serv Librn, Purdue University Northwest, Library-Student-Faculty Bldg, 2nd Flr, 1401 S US Hwy 421, Westville, IN, 46391. Tel: 219-785-5234. p. 726

Jaworski, Mary, Dir, Port Austin Township Library, 114 Railroad St, Port Austin, MI, 48467. Tel: 989-738-7212. p. 1142
Jax, John, Coll Develop Librn, Interim Dir, University of Wisconsin-La Crosse, 1631 Pine St, La Crosse, WI, 54601-3748. Tel: 608-785-8567. p. 2446
Jay, Dela Cruz, Commun Libr Mgr, Queens Library, Seaside Community Library, 116-15 Rockaway Beach Blvd, Rockaway Park, NY, 11694. Tel: 718-634-1876. p. 1555
Jay, Dianne, Librn, Paxton Public Library, 110 N Oak St, Paxton, NE, 69155. Tel: 308-239-4763. p. 1332
Jay, Marjorie, Dir, Libr & Res Serv, Greenberg Glusker LLP Library, 1900 Avenue of the Stars, Ste 2100, Los Angeles, CA, 90067. Tel: 310-785-6853. p. 162
Jaycox, Emily, Librn, Missouri Historical Society, 225 S Skinker Blvd, Saint Louis, MO, 63105. Tel: 314-746-4500. p. 1272
Jayko, Holli, Libr Dir, Adams Free Library, 92 Park St, Adams, MA, 01220. Tel: 413-743-8345. p. 983
Jayne, Esther, Head Cataloger, Shenandoah County Library, 514 Stoney Creek Blvd, Edinburg, VA, 22824. Tel: 540-984-8200. p. 2315
Jayne, Trever, Dir, Adel Public Library, 303 S Tenth St, Adel, IA, 50003-1797. Tel: 515-993-3512. p. 729
Jayne, Zina, Libr Mgr, Elsie Quirk Public Library of Englewood, 100 W Dearborn St, Englewood, FL, 34223. Tel: 941-861-1200. p. 395
Jazwinski, Linda, Admin Coordr, New Tecumseth Public Library, 17 Victoria St E, Alliston, ON, L9R 1V6, CANADA. Tel: 705-435-0250. p. 2627
Jazynka, Jennifer, Mgr, Omaha Public Library, Milton R Abrahams Branch, 5111 N 90th St, Omaha, NE, 68134-2829. Tel: 402-444-6284. p. 1329
Jeakins, Kathy, Bus Mgr, Bloomington Public Library, 205 E Olive St, Bloomington, IL, 61701. Tel: 309-828-6091. p. 542
Jean, Donna, Librn, Cissna Park Community Library District, 511 N Second St, Cissna Park, IL, 60924. Tel: 815-457-2452. p. 572
Jean-Pierre, Peguy, Head, Libr Operations, Columbia University, Lehman Social Sciences Library, 300 International Affairs Bldg, 420 W 118th St, New York, NY, 10027. Tel: 212-854-3794. p. 1583
Jedine, Monica, Br Mgr, Kansas City Public Library, Southeast, 6242 Swope Pkwy, Kansas City, MO, 64130. Tel: 816-701-3582. p. 1255
Jedlicka, Jamie, Cat, University of Georgia Libraries, Special Collections, Richard B Russell Bldg, 300 S Hull St, Athens, GA, 30602. Tel: 706-542-7123. p. 460
Jedlinski, Joann, Ch Serv, Indian River County Library System, North Indian River County Library, 1001 Sebastian Blvd, CR 512, Sebastian, FL, 32958. Tel: 772-400-6360. p. 452
Jeep, Lanie, Librn, Texas County Library, Cabool Branch, 418 Walnut Ave, Cabool, MO, 65689. Tel: 417-962-3722. p. 1249
Jefferds, Carrie, Dir, Belmont Literary & Historical Society Free Library, Two Willets Ave, Belmont, NY, 14813. Tel: 585-268-5308. p. 1492
Jefferies, Alvina, Circ Mgr, York County Library, 138 E Black St, Rock Hill, SC, 29730. Tel: 803-981-5873. p. 2068
Jefferies, Marie, ILL, Lexington County Public Library System, 5440 Augusta Rd, Lexington, SC, 29072. Tel: 803-785-2600. p. 2064
Jefferies, Tommy, Executive Asst, Kitsap Regional Library, 1301 Sylvan Way, Bremerton, WA, 98310-3498. p. 2359
Jeffers, Christine, Asst Dir, Pawtucket Public Library, 13 Summer St, Pawtucket, RI, 02860. Tel: 401-725-3714. p. 2036
Jeffers, Jennifer, Coll & Electronic Res Librn, Spalding University Library, 853 Library Lane, Louisville, KY, 40203-9986. Tel: 502-585-7130. p. 867
Jeffers, Michelle, Chief, Community Partnerships, San Francisco Public Library, 100 Larkin St, San Francisco, CA, 94102. Tel: 415-557-4277. p. 227
Jefferson, Katie, Interim Dir, University of Nevada-Reno, Pennington Medical Education Bldg, 1664 N Virginia St, Reno, NV, 89557. Tel: 775-784-4625. p. 1349
Jefferson, Lila, Acq, University of Louisiana at Monroe Library, 700 University Ave, Monroe, LA, 71209-0720. Tel: 318-342-1053. p. 899
Jefferson, Marli, Libr Mgr, Des Moines Public Library, Forest Avenue, 1326 Forest Ave, Des Moines, IA, 50314. Tel: 515-283-4152. p. 745
Jefferson, Richard, Librn, Oak Grove Lutheran Church, 7045 Lyndale Ave S, Richfield, MN, 55423. Tel: 612-869-4917. p. 1194
Jefferson, Rodney, Asst Dir, Finance & Develop, Newark Public Library, Five Washington St, Newark, NJ, 07101. Tel: 973-733-4842. p. 1427
Jefferson, Sharon, Br Mgr, Cleveland Public Library, Glenville, 11900 St Clair Ave, Cleveland, OH, 44108. Tel: 216-623-6983. p. 1768
Jefferson-Stratton, Kimberly, Libr Mgr, New York Public Library - Astor, Lenox & Tilden Foundations, Melrose Branch, 910 Morris Ave, (@ E 162nd St), Bronx, NY, 10451. Tel: 718-588-0110. p. 1596
Jeffery, Darren, Dep Libr Serv Dir, Thousand Oaks Library, 1401 E Janss Rd, Thousand Oaks, CA, 91362-2199. Tel: 805-449-2660, Ext 7225. p. 252
Jeffery, Melinda, Career Dev, Mkt Mgr, Hobart Institute of Welding Technology, 400 Trade Sq E, Troy, OH, 45373-2400. Tel: 937-332-5603. p. 1825
Jeffery, Steve, Eng Librn, North Dakota State University Libraries, 1201 Albrecht Blvd, Fargo, ND, 58108. Tel: 701-231-5912. p. 1733
Jeffery, Susan, Head Librn, Greene County Public Library, Winters-Bellbrook Community Library, 57 W Franklin St, Bellbrook, OH, 45305-1904. Tel: 937-352-4004. p. 1835
Jeffrey, Douglas, Sr Librn, California Department of Corrections Library System, San Quentin State Prison Library, Main St, San Quentin, CA, 94964. Tel: 415-454-1460, Ext 6135. p. 207
Jeffrey, Jamey, IT Mgr, Laurel County Public Library District, 120 College Park Dr, London, KY, 40741. Tel: 606-864-5759. p. 864
Jeffrey, Megan Hughes, Youth Serv Librn, Middlesborough-Bell County Public Library, 126 S 20th St, Middlesboro, KY, 40965. Tel: 606-248-4812. p. 869
Jeffrey, Penny, Dir, Oconto Public Library, 43352 Rd 780, Oconto, NE, 68860. Tel: 308-858-4920. p. 1327
Jeffreys, Nikida, Evening Library Specialist, Elon University, 308 N O'Kelly Ave, Elon, NC, 27244-0187. Tel: 336-278-6600. p. 1688
Jeffries, Brandon, Br Mgr, Queens Library, Queens Library for Teens, 2002 Cornaga Ave, Far Rockaway, NY, 11691. Tel: 718-471-2573. p. 1555
Jeffries, Carrie, Dir of Circ, Glen Ellyn Public Library, 400 Duane St, Glen Ellyn, IL, 60137-4508. Tel: 630-469-0879. p. 593
Jeffries, Freddie, AV, Ref Serv, Rust College, 150 E Rust Ave, Holly Springs, MS, 38635. Tel: 662-252-8000, Ext 4100. p. 1220
Jeffries, Lisa, Circ & ILL, Chillicothe Public Library District, 430 N Bradley Ave, Chillicothe, IL, 61523-1920. Tel: 309-274-2719. p. 571
Jeffries, Sarah, Circ & ILL Mgr, Shelby County Public Library, 309 Eighth St, Shelbyville, KY, 40065. Tel: 502-633-3803. p. 874
Jeffries, Scott, Libr Dir, Research Librn, Dallas Baptist University, 3000 Mountain Creek Pkwy, Dallas, TX, 75211-9299. Tel: 214-333-5320. p. 2163
Jeffries, William, Exec Dir, Braille Circulating Library For The Blind Inc, 2700 Stuart Ave, Richmond, VA, 23220. Tel: 804-359-3743. p. 2340
Jeffs, Kay, Asst Librn, Emery County Library System, Huntington Branch, 92 S Main, Huntington, UT, 84528. Tel: 435-687-9590. p. 2262
Jekot-Graham, Samantha, Head, Patron Serv, Hennepin County Library, 12601 Ridgedale Dr, Minnetonka, MN, 55305-1909. Tel: 612-543-5919. p. 1186
Jelar Elwell, Sandy, Dir, Tech Serv, Cleveland Public Library, 325 Superior Ave, Cleveland, OH, 44114-1271. Tel: 216-623-2817. p. 1767
Jelen, Andrew, Acq Librn, Head, Coll Develop, Wichita Falls Public Library, 600 11th St, Wichita Falls, TX, 76301-4604. Tel: 940-767-0868, Ext 4228. p. 2258
Jelley, Rachael, Ref Librn, Youth Serv, Grinnell Library, 2642 E Main St, Wappingers Falls, NY, 12590. Tel: 845-297-3428. p. 1658
Jellies, Kayla, Br Mgr, Van Buren District Library, Antwerp Sunshine Branch, 24823 Front Ave, Mattawan, MI, 49071. Tel: 269-668-2534. p. 1096
Jellison, Ashley, Dir, United States Air Force, 42 Ash Ave, Langley AFB, VA, 23665. Tel: 757-764-2906. p. 2327
Jemison, Keith, Br Mgr, Tulsa City-County Library, Rudisill Regional Library, 1520 N Hartford, Tulsa, OK, 74106. p. 1866
Jemison, Lefloris, Asst Librn, Wallace Community College, 3000 Earl Goodwin Pkwy, Selma, AL, 36701. Tel: 334-876-9344, 334-876-9345. p. 35
Jencks, Molly, Cat, New England Institute of Technology Library, One New England Tech Blvd, East Greenwich, RI, 02818-1205. Tel: 401-739-5000, Ext 3474. p. 2031
Jencks, Thom, Performing Arts Librn, Roosevelt University, Performing Arts Library, 430 S Michigan Ave, Rm 1111, Chicago, IL, 60605. Tel: 312-341-3648. p. 567
Jencks, Thom, Music Librn, Xavier University of Louisiana, One Drexel Dr, New Orleans, LA, 70125-1098. Tel: 504-520-7311. p. 904
Jenes, Eric, Libr Serv Librn, Tompkins Cortland Community College Library, Baker Commons, 2nd Flr, 170 North St, Dryden, NY, 13053-8504. Tel: 607-844-8222, Ext 4360. p. 1526
Jeng, Ling, Dr, Dir, Prof, Texas Woman's University, Stoddard Hall, Rm 404, 304 Administration Dr, Denton, TX, 76201. Tel: 940-898-2602. p. 2793
Jenkin, Camila, Outreach Librn, El Camino College, 16007 S Crenshaw Blvd, Torrance, CA, 90506. Tel: 310-660-3525. p. 252
Jenkins, Anne, Dir, Amity Public Library, 307 Trade St, Amity, OR, 97101. Tel: 503-835-8181. p. 1872
Jenkins, Austin, Br Mgr, Athens Regional Library System, Oglethorpe County Branch, 858 Athens Rd, Hwy 78, Lexington, GA, 30648. Tel: 706-743-8817. p. 458
Jenkins, Cristi, Sr Librn, California Department of Corrections Library System, High Desert State Prison, 475-750 Rice Canyon Rd, Susanville, CA, 96127. Tel: 530-251-5100, Ext 6750. p. 207
Jenkins, Dana S, Dir, South Jefferson Public Library, 49 Church St, Summit Point, WV, 25446. Tel: 304-725-6227. p. 2415
Jenkins, Dawn, Libr Dir, Old Bridge Public Library, One Old Bridge Plaza, Old Bridge, NJ, 08857-2498. Tel: 732-721-5600, Ext 5014. p. 1431
Jenkins, Devon, Asst Dir, David M Hunt Library, 63 Main St, Falls Village, CT, 06031. Tel: 860-824-7424. p. 312
Jenkins, Emily, Ch, North Haven Memorial Library, 17 Elm St, North Haven, CT, 06473. Tel: 203-239-5803. p. 331
Jenkins, Eric, Libr Spec, Daytona State College Library, Deland Campus Library, Bldg One, 1155 County Rd 4139, Deland, FL, 32724. Tel: 386-785-2099. p. 392
Jenkins, Itaski, Circ & ILL, Trident Technical College, Main Campus Learning Resources Center, LR-M, PO Box 118067, Charleston, SC, 29423-8067. Tel: 843-574-6089. p. 2051

Jenkins, James, Computer Serv, North Babylon Public Library, 815 Deer Park Ave, North Babylon, NY, 11703-3812. Tel: 631-669-4020. p. 1607

Jenkins, Jane, Libr Dir, Green Hills Public Library District, 10331 S Interlochen Dr, Palos Hills, IL, 60465. Tel: 708-598-8446, Ext 111. p. 632

Jenkins, Jeff, Pub Serv, Polk County Public Library, Saluda Branch, 44 W Main St, Saluda, NC, 28773. Tel: 828-749-2117. p. 1682

Jenkins, Julia-Ann, Head Librn, Montgomery City-County Public Library System, E L Lowder Regional Branch Library, 2590 Bell Rd, Montgomery, AL, 36117. Tel: 334-244-5717. p. 29

Jenkins, Julia-Ann, Head Librn, Montgomery City-County Public Library System, Governors Square Branch Library, 2885-B E South Blvd, Montgomery, AL, 36116. Tel: 334-284-7929. p. 29

Jenkins, Marty, Head, Content Acquisition & Magmt, Wright State University Libraries, 126 Dunbar Library, 3640 Colonel Glenn Hwy, Dayton, OH, 45435-0001. Tel: 937-775-4983. p. 1781

Jenkins, Mary, Ch, Carnegie Public Library, 114 Delta Ave, Clarksdale, MS, 38614-4212. Tel: 662-624-4461. p. 1213

Jenkins, Melody, Adult Serv, Moultrie-Colquitt County Library, 204 Fifth St SE, Moultrie, GA, 31768. Tel: 229-985-6540. p. 492

Jenkins, Pam, Youth Serv Supvr, New Bern-Craven County Public Library, 400 Johnson St, New Bern, NC, 28560-4098. Tel: 252-638-7800. p. 1706

Jenkins, Pamela, Asst Libr Dir, Youth Serv Mgr, Curtis Memorial Library, 23 Pleasant St, Brunswick, ME, 04011-2295. Tel: 207-725-5242. p. 919

Jenkins, Patty, Librn, Crittenden County Library, Crawfordsville Branch, 5444 Main St, Crawfordsville, AR, 72327. Tel: 870-823-5204. p. 104

Jenkins, Paul, Univ Librn, Franklin Pierce University Library, 40 University Dr, Rindge, NH, 03461-3114. Tel: 603-899-4142. p. 1379

Jenkins, Peter, Law Librn II, Connecticut Judicial Branch Law Libraries, New London Law Library, New London Courthouse, 70 Huntington St, New London, CT, 06320. Tel: 860-442-7561. p. 316

Jenkins, Peyton, Asst Dir, Faulkner University, 5345 Atlanta Hwy, Montgomery, AL, 36109-3398. Tel: 334-386-7207. p. 28

Jenkins, Sandra, Instr, University of Central Missouri, Dept of Educational Technology & Library Science, Lovinger 4101, Warrensburg, MO, 64093. Tel: 660-543-4150. p. 2787

Jenkins, Sandy, Libr Dir, Burns Public Library, 104 N Washington St, Burns, KS, 66840. Tel: 620-726-5717. p. 800

Jenkins, Sharon, Dr, Libr Dir, New Mexico State University at Alamogordo, 2400 N Scenic Dr, Alamogordo, NM, 88310. Tel: 575-439-3806. p. 1459

Jenkins, Trish, Br Mgr, San Diego Public Library, Rancho Bernardo, 17110 Bernardo Center Dr, San Diego, CA, 92128. Tel: 858-538-8163. p. 220

Jenkins, Yvonne, Libr Dir, Randolph Public Library, 130 Durand Rd, Randolph, NH, 03593. Tel: 603-466-5408. p. 1379

Jenkinson, Victor, Syst Librn, University of South Carolina, School of Medicine Library, Bldg 101, 6311 Garners Ferry Rd, Columbia, SC, 29209. Tel: 803-216-3200. p. 2056

Jenne, Shawn, Librn, Santiam Correctional Institution Library, 4005 Aumsville Hwy SE, Salem, OR, 97317. Tel: 503-378-3024. p. 1897

Jenner, Anne, Archives Dir, North Park University, Brandel Library, 5114 N Christiana Ave, Chicago, IL, 60625. Tel: 773-244-6224. p. 566

Jenner, Anne, Archivist, North Park University, Swedish-American Archives of Greater Chicago, 3225 W Foster Ave, Chicago, IL, 60625. Tel: 773-244-6224. p. 566

Jenner, Stephanie, Vols Coordr, Rapid City Public Library, 610 Quincy St, Rapid City, SD, 57701-3630. Tel: 605-394-6139. p. 2081

Jennerich, Christina, Dir, Marlboro Free Library, 1251 Rte 9W, Marlboro, NY, 12542. Tel: 845-236-7272. p. 1569

Jenness, Adrienne, Circ Librn, Ref Librn, Drexel University Libraries, Queen Lane Library, 2900 Queen Lane, Philadelphia, PA, 19129. Tel: 215-991-8740. p. 1976

Jenness, Jennifer, Dir, Libr Serv, Valley City State University Library, 101 College St SW, Valley City, ND, 58072-4098. Tel: 701-845-7277. p. 1740

Jennette, Sarah, Syst/Electronic Serv Librn, Clinton Community College, 136 Clinton Point Dr, Plattsburgh, NY, 12901-5690. Tel: 518-562-4241. p. 1619

Jennette, Sharon, Cat, Rare Bks, Freed-Hardeman University, 158 E Main St, Henderson, TN, 38340-2399. Tel: 731-989-6067. p. 2101

Jennings, Anita, Dir, Newport News Public Library System, Law Library, 2501 Washington Ave, Newport News, VA, 23607. Tel: 757-926-8678. p. 2334

Jennings, Anita, Libr Adminr, Newport News Public Library System, 700 Town Center Dr, Ste 300, Newport News, VA, 23606. Tel: 757-926-1350. p. 2334

Jennings, Anita N, Librn IV, Newport News Public Library System, Pearl Bailey Branch, 2510 Wickham Ave, Newport News, VA, 23607. Tel: 757-247-8677. p. 2334

Jennings, Beth M, Dir, Widener University, Harrisburg Campus Law Library, 3800 Vartan Way, Harrisburg, DE, 17110. Tel: 302-477-2111. p. 358

Jennings, Beth M, Dir, Widener University, School of Law Library, 4601 Concord Pike, Wilmington, DE, 19803. Tel: 302-477-2111. p. 358

Jennings, Brenda, Librn, Missouri Department of Corrections, Maryville Treatment Center, 30227 US Hwy 136, Maryville, MO, 64468-8353. Tel: 660-582-6542. p. 1252

Jennings, Brian, Head, Adult Serv, New City Library, 198 S Main St, New City, NY, 10956. Tel: 845-634-4997. p. 1575

Jennings, Donald W, Brother, Dir, Church of Jesus Christ of Latter-Day Saints, Boca Raton Family History Center, 1530 W Camino Real, Boca Raton, UT, 33486. Tel: 561-395-6644. p. 2271

Jennings, Eric, Assoc Univ Librn, University of Northern Iowa Library, 1227 W 27th St, Cedar Falls, IA, 50613-3675. Tel: 319-273-7403. p. 737

Jennings, Heather, Br Mgr, Knox County Public Library System, Powell Branch, 330 W Emory Rd, Knoxville, TN, 37849. Tel: 865-947-6210. p. 2106

Jennings, John, Acq, Syst Tech, Pierce College Library, Puyallup Campus, 1601 39th Ave SE, Puyallup, WA, 98374. Tel: 253-840-8309. p. 2368

Jennings, Karen, Dir, Libr Serv, MedStar Harbor Hospital, S Main Bldg, Rm 112, 3001 S Hanover St, Baltimore, MD, 21225-1290. Tel: 410-554-2817. p. 955

Jennings, Karen, Dir, Libr Serv, Medstar Union Memorial Hospital, 201 E University Pkwy, Baltimore, MD, 21218. Tel: 410-554-2817. p. 956

Jennings, Karlene N, Dir, Libr Develop, College of William & Mary in Virginia, Earl Gregg Swem Library, One Landrum Dr, Williamsburg, VA, 23187. Tel: 757-221-7779. p. 2353

Jennings, Linda, Assoc Librn, Wilkinsburg Public Library, Eastridge, 1900 Graham Blvd, Pittsburgh, PA, 15235. Tel: 412-342-0056. p. 1997

Jennings, Mariann, Dir, Prospect Park Free Library, 720 Maryland Ave, Prospect Park, PA, 19076. Tel: 610-532-4643. p. 1999

Jennings, Marie, YA Serv, United States Navy, Base Library, Naval Submarine Base New London, Bldg 164, Groton, CT, 06349. Tel: 860-694-2578, 860-694-3723. p. 315

Jennings, Maureen, Head, Spec Coll, Harvard Library, Andover-Harvard Theological Library, Divinity School, 45 Francis Ave, Cambridge, MA, 02138. Tel: 617-495-5788. p. 1005

Jennings, Pat, Library Contact, First United Methodist Church, Epworth Library & Susannah Wesley Media Center, 419 NE First St, Gainesville, FL, 32601. Tel: 352-372-8523. p. 407

Jennings, Sharon, Dir, Beatty Library District, 400 N Fourth St, Beatty, NV, 89003. Tel: 775-553-2257. p. 1343

Jennings, Susan L, Dean, Chattanooga State Community College, 4501 Amnicola Hwy, Chattanooga, TN, 37406-1097. Tel: 423-697-2576. p. 2091

Jenrich, Andrew, Dir, Taft Public Library, 29 North Ave, Mendon, MA, 01756. Tel: 508-473-3259. p. 1034

Jensen, Andrea, Coll Mgr, ILL, Northern Virginia Community College Libraries, Medical Education Campus, 6699 Springfield Center Dr, Rm 341, Springfield, VA, 22150. Tel: 703-822-6683. p. 2304

Jensen, Collista, Dir, Lordsburg-Hidalgo Library, 208 E Third St, Lordsburg, NM, 88045. Tel: 575-542-9646. p. 1471

Jensen, Deanna, Libr Tech-ILLO, Wellington County Library, 190 Saint Andrews St W, Fergus, ON, N1M 1N5, CANADA. Tel: 519-846-0918. p. 2641

Jensen, Denise, Ch Serv, Normal Memorial Library, 301 N Eagle St, Fayette, OH, 43521. Tel: 419-237-2115. p. 1785

Jensen, Diane, Librn, William Peace University, 15 E Peace St, Raleigh, NC, 27604. Tel: 919-508-2305. p. 1712

Jensen, Donna, Libr Dir, Trenton Veterans Memorial Library, 2790 Westfield Rd, Trenton, MI, 48183-2482. Tel: 734-676-9777. p. 1155

Jensen, Faye, Chief Exec Officer, South Carolina Historical Society Library, Addlestone Library, 3rd Flr, 205 Calhoun St, Charleston, SC, 29401. Tel: 843-723-3225, Ext 110. p. 2051

Jensen, Jaron, Librn, Utah Department of Corrections, 255 E 300 N, Gunnison, UT, 84634. Tel: 435-528-6000. p. 2264

Jensen, John, Acq Librn, University of the District of Columbia, David A Clarke School of Law, Charles N & Hilda H M Mason Law Library, Bldg 39, Rm B-16, 4200 Connecticut Ave NW, Washington, DC, 20008. Tel: 202-274-5214. p. 380

Jensen, Karen, Coll Develop Officer, University of Alaska Fairbanks, 1732 Tanana Dr, Fairbanks, AK, 99775. Tel: 907-474-6695. p. 45

Jensen, Karen, Dir, James Blackstone Memorial Library, 758 Main St, Branford, CT, 06405-3697. Tel: 203-488-1441, Ext 312. p. 303

Jensen, Kim, Sch Librn, Petroleum County Community Library, 305 S Broadway, Winnett, MT, 59087. Tel: 406-429-2451. p. 1304

Jensen, Lindsay, Br Mgr, Nashville Public Library, Hadley Park Branch, 1039 28th Ave N, Nashville, TN, 37208. Tel: 615-862-5865. p. 2119

Jensen, Michelle, Br Librn, Southeast Regional Library, Redvers Branch, 23B Railway Ave, Redvers, SK, S0C 2H0, CANADA. Tel: 306-452-3255. p. 2754

Jensen, Pamela, Librn, Wayne Presbyterian Church Library, 125 E Lancaster Ave, Wayne, PA, 19087. Tel: 610-688-8700. p. 2019

Jensen, Patricia, Ad, Putnam Public Library, 225 Kennedy Dr, Putnam, CT, 06260-1691. Tel: 860-963-6826. p. 334

Jensen, Robert, Reference & Distance Services Librn, Wayland Baptist University, 1900 W Seventh St, Plainview, TX, 79072-6957. Tel: 806-291-3700. p. 2227
Jensen, Roxanne, Asst Libr Dir, Br Librn, Emery County Library System, 115 N 100 E, Castle Dale, UT, 84513. Tel: 435-381-2554. p. 2261
Jensen, Sandra, Dir, United States Marine Corps, Library Services, Bldg 1146, Camp Pendleton, CA, 92055. Tel: 760-725-5104, 760-725-5669. p. 126
Jensen, Shannon, Dir, Evansdale Public Library, 123 N Evans Rd, Evansdale, IA, 50707. Tel: 319-232-5367. p. 752
Jensen, Sharla, Dir, Homedale Public Library, 121 W Owyhee, Homedale, ID, 83628. Tel: 208-337-4228. p. 522
Jensen, Teresa, Dir, Libr & Info Tech, Northfield Public Library, 210 Washington St, Northfield, MN, 55057. Tel: 507-645-1801. p. 1191
Jensen, Valerie, Dean of Libr, Mission College Library, 3000 Mission College Blvd, Santa Clara, CA, 95054-1897. Tel: 408-855-5464. p. 241
Jensen, Valerie, County Librn, Chambers County Library System, 202 Cummings St, Anahuac, TX, 77514. Tel: 409-267-2550. p. 2134
Jenson, Linda, Dir, Libr Serv, Tarrant County College, South Campus Jenkins Garrett Library, 5301 Campus Dr, Fort Worth, TX, 76119. Tel: 817-515-4524. p. 2180
Jenson, Patria, Dir, Rembrandt Public Library, Main St & Broadway, Rembrandt, IA, 50576. Tel: 712-286-6801. p. 778
Jeong, Wooseob, Dean, Emporia State University, 1200 Commercial St, Box 4051, Emporia, KS, 66801. Tel: 620-341-5207. p. 807
Jeong, Wooseob, Dean, Emporia State University, One Kellogg Circle, Campus Box 4025, Emporia, KS, 66801-4025. Tel: 800-552-4770, Ext 5203. p. 2785
Jerabek, Ann, Head, ILL, Sam Houston State University, 1830 Bobby K Marks Dr, Huntsville, TX, 77340. Tel: 936-294-3528. p. 2201
Jeremiah, Jacob, Dean of Libr, Oakton College Library, 1600 E Golf Rd, Rm 1406, Des Plaines, IL, 60016. Tel: 847-635-1642, 847-635-1644. p. 578
Jeremiah, Jacob, Asst Dean of Libr, Oakton Community College Library, 7701 N Lincoln Ave, Rm A200, Skokie, IL, 60076-2895. p. 647
Jernigan, Doug, Libr Dir, Meridian Community College, 910 Hwy 19 N, Meridian, MS, 39307. Tel: 601-484-8762. p. 1226
Jernigan, Kristen, E-Learning & Instruction Librn, Polk State College, Lakeland Campus Library, 3425 Winter Lake Rd, Sta 62, Lakeland, FL, 33803. Tel: 863-297-1042. p. 455
Jernigan, Leanne, Syst Coordr, Tech Serv, High Point University, One University Pkwy, High Point, NC, 27268. Tel: 336-841-9152. p. 1697
Jerow, Elizabeth, Libr Dir, Milwaukee School of Engineering, 500 E Kilbourn Ave, Milwaukee, WI, 53202. Tel: 414-277-7180. p. 2460
Jersey, Terri, Ch, Hendrick Hudson Free Library, 185 Kings Ferry Rd, Montrose, NY, 10548. Tel: 914-739-5654. p. 1573
Jesernik, Jeanne, Ad, La Grange Public Library, Ten W Cossitt Ave, La Grange, IL, 60525. Tel: 708-215-3200. p. 605
Jeske, Kathy, Lead Research Asst, Sheboygan County Historical Research Center Library, 518 Water St, Sheboygan Falls, WI, 53085. Tel: 920-467-4667. p. 2477
Jeske, Michelle, City Librn, Denver Public Library, Ten W 14th Ave Pkwy, Denver, CO, 80204-2731. Tel: 720-865-1111. p. 275
Jespersen, Pamela, Adult Serv, Crook County Library, Moorcroft Branch, 105 E Converse, Moorcroft, WY, 82721. Tel: 307-756-3232. p. 2499
Jesse, Sarah, Dir, Academy Art Museum, 106 South St, Easton, MD, 21601. Tel: 410-822-2787. p. 964
Jessee, Hazel, Br Mgr, Lonesome Pine Regional Library, Wise County Public, 124 Library Rd SW, Wise, VA, 24293. Tel: 276-328-8061. p. 2355
Jessee, Leeann, Libr Dir, Adair County Public Library, 307 Greensburg St, Columbia, KY, 42728-1488. Tel: 270-384-2472. p. 852
Jessen, John, City Librn & Exec Dir, New Haven Free Public Library, 133 Elm St, New Haven, CT, 06510. Tel: 203-946-8124. p. 326
Jesseph, May, Librn, Rochester Community & Technical College, 851 30 Ave SE, Rochester, MN, 55904. Tel: 507-285-7233. p. 1194
Jessie, Pamela, Librn, Birmingham Public Library, Woodlawn, 5709 First Ave N, Birmingham, AL, 35212-1603. Tel: 205-595-2001. p. 8
Jessie, Ronnie, Adminr, Dallas Public Library, 1515 Young St, Dallas, TX, 75201-5415. Tel: 214-670-1400. p. 2165
Jessing, Alli, Events & Seminars Mgr, Howard County Library System, 9411 Frederick Rd, Ellicott City, MD, 21042. Tel: 410-313-7750. p. 965
Jessop, Lauren, Asst to the Dir, Sussex County Community College Library, One College Hill Rd, Newton, NJ, 07860. Tel: 973-300-2162. p. 1428
Jessop, Lauren, Chief Exec Officer, Barrie Public Library, 60 Worsley St, Barrie, ON, L4M 1L6, CANADA. Tel: 705-728-1010, Ext 2100. p. 2630
Jessup, Joan, Br Mgr, Calaveras County Library, West Point Branch, 54 Bald Mountain Rd, West Point, CA, 95255. Tel: 209-293-7020. p. 211
Jessup, Rhonda, Chief Librn/CEO, Whitby Public Library, 405 Dundas St W, Whitby, ON, L1N 6A1, CANADA. Tel: 905-668-6531. p. 2703
Jester, Ashley, Co-Dir, Marine Biological Laboratory, McLean MS 8, 360 Woods Hole Rd, Woods Hole, MA, 02543. Tel: 508-289-3557. p. 1071
Jeter, Ann H, Librn, Jackson Walker LLP, Bank of America Plaza, 901 Main St, Ste 6000, Dallas, TX, 75202. Tel: 214-953-6038. p. 2167
Jeter, Kelli, Senior Asst Dir, Benson Public Library, 300 S Huachuca St, Benson, AZ, 85602-6650. Tel: 520-586-9535. p. 56
Jett, Allen, Tech Serv, Cape May County Library, 30 Mechanic St, Cape May Court House, NJ, 08210. Tel: 609-463-6350. p. 1394
Jett, Clarke, Librn, California Department of Corrections Library System, Central California Women's Facility, 23370 Rd 22, Chowchilla, CA, 93610. Tel: 559-665-5531. p. 206
Jett, Heather, Librn, Mayo Clinic Health System, 700 West Ave S, La Crosse, WI, 54601. Tel: 608-785-0940, Ext 2685. p. 2446
Jewel, Shannon, Br Mgr, Calaveras County Library, Copperopolis Branch, Lake Tulloch Plaza, 3505 Spangler Lane, Ste 106, Copperopolis, CA, 95228. Tel: 209-785-0920. p. 211
Jewell, Cynthia, Br Mgr, Williams County Public Library, Edon Branch, 103 N Michigan St, Edon, OH, 43518. Tel: 419-272-2839. p. 1753
Jewell, Debbie, Coord, Academic Support Services, Arkansas State University, 7648 Victory Blvd, Newport, AR, 72112-8912. Tel: 870-512-7862. p. 106
Jewell, Jenna, Librn, Lake Area Technical Institute Library, 1201 Arrow Ave, Rm 210, Watertown, SD, 57201. Tel: 605-882-5284, Ext 231. p. 2085
Jewell, Robert, Pres, Brookgreen Gardens Library, 1931 Brookgreen Dr, Murrells Inlet, SC, 29576. Tel: 843-235-6000. p. 2066
Jewett, Carol, Librn, Community College of Philadelphia Library, Northeast Regional Center Learning Commons, 12901 Townsend Rd, Rm 127, Philadelphia, PA, 19154. Tel: 215-972-6270. p. 1975
Jewett, Cynthia, Libr Dir, James A Tuttle Library, 45 Main St, Antrim, NH, 03440-3906. Tel: 603-588-6786. p. 1354
Jewett, Mary, Library Contact, Lakes Environmental Association, Bradley Lakes Center, 230 Main St, Bridgton, ME, 04009. Tel: 207-647-8580. p. 918
Jewett, Rebecca K, Spec Coll Coordr, Ohio State University LIBRARIES, Jerome Lawrence & Robert E Lee Theatre Research Institute, 1430 Lincoln Tower, 1800 Cannon Dr, Columbus, OH, 43210-1230. Tel: 614-292-6614. p. 1775
Jewitt, Sarah, Sr Mgr, Human Res, Kitchener Public Library, 85 Queen St N, Kitchener, ON, N2H 2H1, CANADA. Tel: 519-743-0271. p. 2651
Jewkes, Becky, Asst Librn, Emery County Library System, Ferron Branch, 55 N 200 West, Ferron, UT, 84523. Tel: 435-384-2637. p. 2262
Jewsbury, Kathy, Dir, Hawn Memorial Library, 220 John St, Clayton, NY, 13624-1107. Tel: 315-686-3762. p. 1518
Jezek, Lorrie, Br Mgr, Lawrenceburg Public Library District, North Dearborn Branch, 25969 Dole Rd, West Harrison, IN, 47060. Tel: 812-637-0777. p. 702
Jezik, Katie, Cat & Syst Librn, Hudson Valley Community College, 80 Vandenburgh Ave, Troy, NY, 12180. Tel: 518-629-7395. p. 1652
Jhagroo, Pansey, Circ Supvr, Indian River County Library System, 1600 21st St, Vero Beach, FL, 32960. Tel: 772-770-5060. p. 452
Jia, Die, Bus & Tech Mgr, Allen County Public Library, 900 Library Plaza, Fort Wayne, IN, 46802. Tel: 260-421-1200. p. 683
Jia, Peijun Jeffrey, Reserves & Syst Librn, Queensborough Community College, City University of New York, 222-05 56th Ave, Bayside, NY, 11364-1497. Tel: 718-281-5594. p. 1491
Jiang, Jane, Dir of Libr, Union County College Libraries, 1033 Springfield Ave, Cranford, NJ, 07016. Tel: 908-709-7623. p. 1398
Jiang, Shali Y, Med Librn, American Red Cross Holland Laboratory, 15601 Crabbs Branch Way, Rockville, MD, 20855-2743. Tel: 240-314-3453. p. 973
Jimarez-Howard, Josie, Community Engagement Coord, El Paso Museum of Art, One Arts Festival Plaza, El Paso, TX, 79901. Tel: 915-212-3061. p. 2174
Jimenez, Allison, Dir, Libr Serv, Rochester College, 800 W Avon Rd, Rochester Hills, MI, 48307. Tel: 248-218-2268. p. 1145
Jiménez, Carmen, Librn, Amaury Veray Music Library, 951 Ave Ponce de Leon, San Juan, PR, 00907-3373. Tel: 787 751-0160, Ext 284. p. 2513
Jimenez, Janie, Librn, Big Springs Public Library, 400 Pine St, Big Springs, NE, 69122. Tel: 308-889-3482. p. 1308
Jimenez, Jennifer, Reference & Electronic Resources Librn, Del Mar College, 101 Baldwin Blvd, Corpus Christi, TX, 78404. Tel: 361-698-1977. p. 2160
Jimenez, Jimmy, Libr Mgr, San Antonio Public Library, Bazan, 2200 W Commerce St, San Antonio, TX, 78207. Tel: 210-207-9160. p. 2238
Jimenez, Megan, Access Serv Supvr, Glendale Community College - North, Bldg GCN B (Beshbito), 5727 W Happy Valley Rd, Glendale, AZ, 85310. p. 62
Jimenez, Michael, County Librn, San Bernardino County Library, 777 E Rialto Ave, San Bernardino, CA, 92415-0035. Tel: 909-387-2220. p. 212
Jimenez, Valerie, Libr Operations Coordr, Manhattan College, 4513 Manhattan College Pkwy, Riverdale, NY, 10471. Tel: 718-862-7743. p. 1627
Jimerson, Jeanne, Br Mgr, Hall County Library System, 127 Main St NW, Gainesville, GA, 30501-3699. Tel: 770-532-3311, Ext 107. p. 480
Jin, David, Dir, Libr Serv, Baltimore City Community College, 2901 Liberty Heights Ave, Baltimore, MD, 21215. Tel: 410-462-8400. p. 951

Jin, Joleen, Library Contact, Missoula Public Library, Big Sky Branch, Big Sky High School, 3100 South Ave W, Missoula, MT, 59804. Tel: 406-728-2400, Ext 8605. p. 1300
Jin, Tao, Assoc Prof, Louisiana State University, 267 Coates Hall, Baton Rouge, LA, 70803. Tel: 225-578-3158, 225-578-3159. p. 2785
Jinks, Mary L, Dir, Tech Serv, University of the Incarnate Word, 4301 Broadway, CPO 297, San Antonio, TX, 78209-6397. Tel: 210-829-3839. p. 2240
Jipson, Hayley, ILL, Youth Serv Librn, Cary Library, 107 Main St, Houlton, ME, 04730. Tel: 207-532-1302. p. 927
Jirik, Kate, Libr Res Spec, San Diego Zoo Global Library, Beckman Ctr, 15600 San Pasqual Valley Rd, Escondido, CA, 92027. Tel: 760-747-8702, Ext 5735. p. 141
Jiron, Nadine, Dir, Grants Public Library, 1101 N First St, Grants, NM, 87020-2526. Tel: 505-972-0310. p. 1468
Jo, Clifford, Finance & Bus Dir, Pierce County Library System, 3005 112th St E, Tacoma, WA, 98446-2215. Tel: 253-548-3453. p. 2386
Jo, Phill, Circ, University of Oklahoma Health Sciences Center, 1105 N Stonewall Ave, Oklahoma City, OK, 73117-1220. Tel: 405-271-2285, Ext 48751. p. 1859
Joachim, Anthony, Ref Librn & Co-Coordr of User Educ, William Paterson University, 300 Pompton Rd, Wayne, NJ, 07470. Tel: 973-720-3665. p. 1452
Joachim, Danielle, Br Mgr, Jefferson Parish Library, Lakeshore, 1100 W Esplanade, Metairie, LA, 70005. Tel: 504-838-4375. p. 897
Job, Eric Jon, IT Mgr, Johnson City Public Library, 100 W Millard St, Johnson City, TN, 37604. Tel: 423-434-4468. p. 2104
Jobe, Alexandra, Deputy Legislative Librn, Nevada Legislative Counsel Bureau, 401 S Carson St, Carson City, NV, 89701-4747. Tel: 775-684-6827. p. 1344
Jobe, Janita, Asst Dean, Admin Serv, University of Nevada-Reno, 1664 N Virginia St, Mailstop 0322, Reno, NV, 89557-0322. Tel: 775-682-5688. p. 1349
Jobe-Ganucheau, Cassie, Dir, Louisiana State University at Eunice, 2048 Johnson Hwy, Eunice, LA, 70535. Tel: 337-550-1380. p. 889
Jobin-Picard, Anne, Head, Tech Serv, Librn II, Clinton-Essex-Franklin Library System, 33 Oak St, Plattsburgh, NY, 12901-2810. Tel: 518-563-5190, Ext 114. p. 1619
Joblinske, Charlotte, Librn, Stratton Public Library, 331 New York Ave, Stratton, CO, 80836. Tel: 719-348-5922. p. 296
Jochimsen, Jenny, Dir, Abbotsford Public Library, 203 N First St, Abbotsford, WI, 54405. Tel: 715-223-3920. p. 2419
Jochman, Leslie, Dir, Plymouth Public Library, 130 Division St, Plymouth, WI, 53073. Tel: 920-892-4416. p. 2470
Jochum, Nathan, Dir, Perry County Public Library, 2328 Tell St, Tell City, IN, 47586. Tel: 812-547-2661. p. 720
Jocson Porter, Alyssa, Ref Librn, Seattle Central College, 1701 Broadway, BE Rm 2101, Seattle, WA, 98122. Tel: 206-934-4483. p. 2378
Jocson-Singh, Joan, Head, Tech Serv, Lehman College, City University of New York, 250 Bedford Park Blvd W, Bronx, NY, 10468. Tel: 718-960-8428. p. 1499
Jodari, Tiyebeh, Acq & Cat, Tech Serv, Butte College Library, 3536 Butte Campus Dr, Oroville, CA, 95965. Tel: 530-879-4022. p. 189
Jodon, Kris, Librn, Chapelwood United Methodist Church, 11140 Greenbay St, Houston, TX, 77024. Tel: 713-465-3467, Ext 127. p. 2191
Joffrion, Elizabeth, Dir, Archives & Spec Coll, Western Washington University, 516 High St, MS 9103, Bellingham, WA, 98225. Tel: 360-650-3283. p. 2358
Johannesen, Ester, Libr Dir, Wall Community Library, 407 Main St, Wall, SD, 57790. Tel: 605-279-2929. p. 2085
Johannigmeier, Rachel, Dir, Prog & Youth Serv, Kirkwood Public Library, 140 E Jefferson Ave, Kirkwood, MO, 63122. Tel: 314-821-5770, Ext 1011. p. 1259
Johansen, Krista, Libr Mgr, Albert-Westmorland-Kent Regional Library, Dorchester Public, 3516 Cape Rd, Dorchester, NB, E4K 2X5, CANADA. Tel: 506-379-3032. p. 2603
Johansen, Peggy, Dir, Mamakating Library, 128 Sullivan St, Wurtsboro, NY, 12790. Tel: 845-888-8004. p. 1667
Johanson, Melissa M, Libr Dir, Steamboat Rock Public Library, 511 Market St, Steamboat Rock, IA, 50672. Tel: 641-868-2300. p. 784
Johanson, Mirja, Tech Serv, Perrot Memorial Library, 90 Sound Beach Ave, Old Greenwich, CT, 06870. Tel: 203-637-1066. p. 332
John, Bonny, Dir, Boscawen Public Library, 116 N Main St, Boscawen, NH, 03303-1123. Tel: 603-753-8576. p. 1355
John, Karen F, Supvr, Seneca Nation Libraries, Cattaraugus Branch, Three Thomas Indian School Dr, Irving, NY, 14081-9505. Tel: 716-532-9449. p. 1635
John, Melanie, Librn, Hinds Community College, 505 E Main St, Raymond, MS, 39154. Tel: 601-857-3355. p. 1231
John, Sheela, Med Librn, McLaren Oakland, 50 N Perry St, Pontiac, MI, 48342-2217. Tel: 248-338-5000, Ext 5204. p. 1141
John, Tambe-Tysha, Managing Librn, Brooklyn Public Library, New Utrecht, 1743 86th St, Brooklyn, NY, 11214. Tel: 718-236-4086. p. 1503
John, Tessymol, Ref Librn, Bronxville Public Library, 201 Pondfield Rd, Bronxville, NY, 10708. Tel: 914-337-7680. p. 1500
John-Williams, Melissa, Head, Circ, YA Serv, Somerset County Library System of New Jersey, Peapack & Gladstone Public, School St, Peapack, NJ, 07977. Tel: 908-458-8440. p. 1392
Johncola, Leah, Coordr, Ch Serv, Cambria County Library System & District Center, 248 Main St, Johnstown, PA, 15901. Tel: 814-536-5131. p. 1947
Johndro, Kelly, Asst Librn, Robert A Frost Memorial Library, 42 Main St, Limestone, ME, 04750. Tel: 207-325-4706. p. 929
Johner, Patricia, Metadata Services Librn, Pennsylvania Western University - Clarion, 840 Wood St, Clarion, PA, 16214. Tel: 814-393-2178. p. 1922
Johns, Amber, Libr Dir, Petersham Memorial Library, 23 Common St, Petersham, MA, 01366. Tel: 978-724-3405. p. 1046
Johns, Darcy, Librn, Halifax Public Libraries, Cole Harbour Branch, 51 Forest Hills Pkwy, Cole Harbour, NS, B2W 6C6, CANADA. Tel: 902-490-3820. p. 2617
Johns, Dinorah Marie, Mgr, Seminole Tribe of Florida, 5658 E Village St, Okeechobee, FL, 34974. Tel: 863-763-4236. p. 430
Johns, Heather, Dir, Black Watch Memorial Library, 99 Montcalm St, Ticonderoga, NY, 12883. Tel: 518-585-7380. p. 1651
Johns, Jennifer, Curator, Ruthmere Museum, 302 E Beardsley Ave, Elkhart, IN, 46514. Tel: 574-264-0330. p. 680
Johns, Mischa, Archivist, Spec Coll, Putnam County Library System, 601 College Rd, Palatka, FL, 32177-3873. Tel: 386-329-0126. p. 433
Johns, Stacy, Supv Librn, Newport Public Library, 35 NW Nye St, Newport, OR, 97365-3714. Tel: 541-265-2153. p. 1888
Johns, Susan, Asst Dir, Belle Center Free Public Library, 103 S Elizabeth St, Belle Center, OH, 43310. Tel: 937-464-3611. p. 1750
Johns, Warren, Cat Librn, Loma Linda University, 11072 Anderson St, Loma Linda, CA, 92350-0001. Tel: 909-558-4581. p. 157
Johns-Masten, Kathryn, Spec Coll Librn, Syst Librn, State University of New York at Oswego, SUNY Oswego, 7060 State Rte 104, Oswego, NY, 13126-3514. Tel: 315-312-3553. p. 1613
Johns-Smith, Susan, Syst Coordr, Pittsburg State University, 1605 S Joplin St, Pittsburg, KS, 66762-5889. Tel: 620-235-4115. p. 832
Johnson, Aaron, Dir, Kingwood Public Library, 205 W Main St, Kingwood, WV, 26537-1418. Tel: 304-329-1499. p. 2406
Johnson, Abby, Coll Develop, New Albany-Floyd County Public Library, 180 W Spring St, New Albany, IN, 47150. Tel: 812-944-8464. p. 709
Johnson, Adam, Ref Librn, Valencia College, 850 W Morse Blvd, Winter Park, FL, 32789. Tel: 407-582-6019. p. 456
Johnson, Adrienne, Libr Mgr, New Orleans Public Library, Alvar Library, 913 Alvar St, New Orleans, LA, 70117-5409. Tel: 504-596-2667. p. 903
Johnson, Adrienne M, Asst Dir, Wilmington University Library, 320 N DuPont Hwy, New Castle, DE, 19720. Tel: 302-669-6607. p. 354
Johnson, Aileen, Br Mgr, Montgomery County-Norristown Public Library, Perkiomen Valley, 290 Second St, Schwenksville, PA, 19473. Tel: 610-287-8360. p. 1971
Johnson, Aisha, Assoc Dean for Academic Affairs & Outreach, Georgia Institute of Technology Library, 260 Fourth St NW, Atlanta, GA, 30332. Tel: 404-894-1390. p. 464
Johnson, Ajay, Adult Serv, Williams County Public Library, 107 E High St, Bryan, OH, 43506-1702. Tel: 419-636-6734. p. 1753
Johnson, Alexis Bard, Curator, ONE National Gay & Lesbian Archives at the USC Libraries, 909 W Adams Blvd, Los Angeles, CA, 90007. Tel: 213-821-2771. p. 167
Johnson, Alice, Asst Librn, Cat, Gallatin County Public Library, 209 W Market St, Warsaw, KY, 41095. Tel: 859-567-7323. p. 876
Johnson, Alice, Dr, Dean, Learning Res, San Antonio College, 1819 N Main Ave, San Antonio, TX, 78212. Tel: 210-486-0554. p. 2238
Johnson, Alisha, Librn, Birmingham Public Library, Ensley Branch, 1201 25th St, Ensley, AL, 35218-1944. Tel: 205-785-2625. p. 7
Johnson, Allison, Cataloger, State Historical Society of Iowa, 600 E Locust, Des Moines, IA, 50319-0290. Tel: 515-281-6200. p. 747
Johnson, Allison, Cat, Metadata Librn, State Historical Society of Iowa, 402 Iowa Ave, Iowa City, IA, 52240-1806. Tel: 319-335-3936. p. 760
Johnson, Ally, Libr Mgr, Manning Municipal & District Library, 407 Main St, Manning, AB, T0H 2M0, CANADA. Tel: 780-836-3054. p. 2547
Johnson, Amanda, Libr Tech, Northland Community & Technical College Library, 2022 Central Ave NE, East Grand Forks, MN, 56721. Tel: 218-793-2435. p. 1173
Johnson, Amber L, Libr Operations Coordr, Chickasaw Public Library, 224 Grant St, Chickasaw, AL, 36611. Tel: 251-452-6465. p. 12
Johnson, Amy, State Librn, State Library of Florida, The Capitol, Rm 701, Tallahassee, FL, 32399. Tel: 850-245-6612. p. 447
Johnson, Amy, Asst Librn, Susquehanna County Historical Society & Free Library Association, 458 High School Rd, Montrose, PA, 18801. Tel: 570-278-1881. p. 1965
Johnson, Amy L, State Librn, Florida Department of State, Division of Library & Information Services, R A Gray Bldg, 500 S Bronough St, Tallahassee, FL, 32399-0250. Tel: 850-245-6603. p. 446
Johnson, Analise, Academic Services Librn, Davenport University, 6191 Kraft Ave SE, Grand Rapids, MI, 49512. Tel: 616-554-5664. p. 1110
Johnson, Andrea, Teen Librn, Mount Prospect Public Library, Ten S Emerson St, Mount Prospect, IL, 60056. Tel: 847-253-5675. p. 621
Johnson, Andrea, Br Mgr, Saint Louis County Library, Jamestown Bluffs Branch, 4153 N Hwy 67, Florissant, MO, 63034-2825. Tel: 314-994-3300, Ext 3400. p. 1274

Johnson, Andrew, Circ Mgr, ILL Mgr, Tech Serv Mgr, Rockford University, 5050 E State St, Rockford, IL, 61108-2393. Tel: 815-226-4000, 815-226-4035. p. 642
Johnson, Andy, Asst Dir, Pub Serv, University of Virginia's College at Wise, One College Ave, Wise, VA, 24293. Tel: 276-328-0150. p. 2355
Johnson, Angela, Libr Asst, Five Rivers Public Library, 301 Walnut St, Parsons, WV, 26287. Tel: 304-478-3880. p. 2411
Johnson, Anne Marie, Presv, Charles A Weyerhaeuser Memorial Museum, 2151 Lindbergh Dr S, Little Falls, MN, 56345. Tel: 320-632-4007. p. 1180
Johnson, Ashley, Youth Serv Librn, Allendale Township Library, 6175 Library Ln, Allendale, MI, 49401. Tel: 616-895-4178, Ext 3. p. 1077
Johnson, Bernadette J, Head Ref/Govt Doc Librn, Francis Marion University, 4822 E Palmetto St, Florence, SC, 29506. Tel: 843-661-1313. p. 2059
Johnson, Beth, Med Librn, Norton Healthcare, 200 E Chestnut St, Louisville, KY, 40202. Tel: 502-629-8125. p. 866
Johnson, Beth, Dir of Libr Operations, Radford University, 925 E Main St, Radford, VA, 24142. Tel: 540-831-6648. p. 2339
Johnson, Bethanne, Asst Dir, Southwest Public Libraries, SPL Admin, 3359 Broadway, Grove City, OH, 43123. Tel: 614-875-6716. p. 1789
Johnson, Bradley, Circ Mgr, Lebanon-Laclede County Library, 915 S Jefferson Ave, Lebanon, MO, 65536. Tel: 417-532-2148. p. 1259
Johnson, Brenda, Librn, Cullman County Public Library System, Tom Bevill Public, Colony Education Complex, 151 Byars Rd, Hanceville, AL, 35077. Tel: 256-287-1573. p. 13
Johnson, Brent, Ref Serv, Widener University, Harrisburg Campus Law Library, 3800 Vartan Way, Harrisburg, DE, 17110. Tel: 717-541-3984. p. 358
Johnson, Brittney, Libr Instruction, Saint Edwards University, 3001 S Congress Ave, Austin, TX, 78704-6489. Tel: 512-448-8479. p. 2140
Johnson, Brook, Metadata Library Assoc, Cornerstone University, 1001 E Beltline Ave NE, Grand Rapids, MI, 49525. Tel: 616-254-1650, Ext 1358. p. 1110
Johnson, Byron, Circ Coordr, Duluth Public Library, 520 W Superior St, Duluth, MN, 55802. Tel: 218-730-4242. p. 1172
Johnson, Caitlin, Libr Dir, Schuylerville Public Library, 52 Ferry St, Schuylerville, NY, 12871. Tel: 518-695-6641. p. 1639
Johnson, Candice, Librn, Penfield Public Library, 1985 Baird Rd, Penfield, NY, 14526. Tel: 585-340-8720. p. 1616
Johnson, Candy, ILL Supvr, Emporia State University, 1200 Commercial St, Box 4051, Emporia, KS, 66801. Tel: 620-341-5207. p. 807
Johnson, Carol, Teen & Technology Librn, Delphi Public Library, 222 E Main St, Delphi, IN, 46923. Tel: 765-564-2929. p. 679
Johnson, Carol, Br Mgr, Onondaga County Public Libraries, Hazard Branch Library, 1620 W Genesee St, Syracuse, NY, 13204. Tel: 315-435-5326. p. 1649
Johnson, Carol, Br Mgr, Onondaga County Public Libraries, Petit Branch Library, 105 Victoria Pl, Syracuse, NY, 13210. Tel: 315-435-3636. p. 1649
Johnson, Carol, Circ Tech, Alberta Government Library, Capital Blvd, 11th Flr, 10044 - 108 St, Edmonton, AB, T5J 5E6, CANADA. Tel: 780-427-2985. p. 2534
Johnson, Carolina, Circ, ILL, Nashotah House, 2777 Mission Rd, Nashotah, WI, 53058-9793. Tel: 262-646-6536. p. 2463
Johnson, Carolyn A, Music Librn, Connecticut College, Greer Music Library, 270 Mohegan Ave, Box 5234, New London, CT, 06320-4196. Tel: 860-439-2711. p. 329
Johnson, Carrie, Exec Dir, Winona County Historical Society, 160 Johnson St, Winona, MN, 55987. Tel: 507-454-2723, Ext 1. p. 1209
Johnson, Catherine R, Assoc Dir, User Serv, United States Naval Academy, 589 McNair Rd, Annapolis, MD, 21402-5029. Tel: 410-293-6945. p. 951
Johnson, Cathy, Adult Serv Coordr, Berkeley Public Library, 1637 N Taft Ave, Berkeley, IL, 60163-1499. Tel: 708-544-6017. p. 542
Johnson, Cathy, Dir, Silsbee Public Library, 295 N Fourth St, Silsbee, TX, 77656. Tel: 409-385-4831. p. 2244
Johnson, Charmaine, Sr Librn, Atlanta-Fulton Public Library System, Auburn Avenue Research Library on African-American Culture & History, 101 Auburn Ave NE, Atlanta, GA, 30303-2503. Tel: 407-730-4001, Ext 104. p. 460
Johnson, Chaundra, Dir, Libr Div, State Librn, Utah State Library Division, 250 N 1950 West, Ste A, Salt Lake City, UT, 84116-7901. Tel: 801-715-6777. p. 2272
Johnson, Chelton, Libr Tech 1, Howard University Libraries, Social Work, 601 Howard Pl NW, Rm 200, Washington, DC, 20059. Tel: 202-806-4735. p. 369
Johnson, Chrissy, Bus Mgr, Lebanon Public Library, 104 E Washington St, Lebanon, IN, 46052. Tel: 765-482-3460. p. 703
Johnson, Christina, Circ, Muscle Shoals Public Library, 1918 E Avalon, Muscle Shoals, AL, 35661. Tel: 256-386-9212. p. 31
Johnson, Christine, Br Supvr, Aurora Public Library, Hoffman Library, 1298 Peoria St, Aurora, CO, 80011. Tel: 303-739-1572. p. 264
Johnson, Christine, Dir, Waterford Public Library, 49 Rope Ferry Rd, Waterford, CT, 06385. Tel: 860-444-5805. p. 344
Johnson, Christine, Librn, Roxborough Memorial Hospital, 5800 Ridge Ave, Philadelphia, PA, 19128. Tel: 215-487-4345. p. 1985
Johnson, Clinton, Recreation Coord, Putnamville Correctional Facility, 1946 W US 40, Greencastle, IN, 46135-9275. Tel: 765-653-8441, Ext 466. p. 688
Johnson, Connie, Dir, Logan Public Library, 121 E Sixth St, Logan, IA, 51546. Tel: 712-644-2551. p. 766
Johnson, Craig, Media Serv, Augustana University, 2001 S Summit Ave, Sioux Falls, SD, 57197-0001. Tel: 605-274-4921. p. 2081
Johnson, Cristy, Br Supvr, Kern County Library, Boron Branch, 26967 20 Mule Team Rd, Boron, CA, 93516-1550. Tel: 760-762-5606. p. 119
Johnson, Cristy, Br Supvr, Kern County Library, California City Branch, 9507 California City Blvd, California City, CA, 93505-2280. Tel: 760-373-4757. p. 119
Johnson, Cristy, Br Supvr, Kern County Library, Mojave Branch, 15555 O St, Mojave, CA, 93501. Tel: 661-824-2243. p. 120
Johnson, Crystal, Library Contact, Third District Appellate Court Library, 1004 Columbus St, Ottawa, IL, 61350. Tel: 815-434-5050. p. 631
Johnson, Crystal, Mgr, Richland Library, Blythewood Branch, 218 McNulty Rd, Blythewood, SC, 29016. Tel: 803-691-9806. p. 2054
Johnson, Crystal, Distance Learning Librn, Webmaster, Tusculum University, 60 Shiloh Rd, Greeneville, TN, 37743. Tel: 423-636-7320, Ext 5801. p. 2100
Johnson, Cynthia, Br Head, Napoleon Public Library, McClure Community, 110 Cross St, McClure, OH, 43534-0035. Tel: 419-748-8922. p. 1805
Johnson, D'Lynn, Youth Serv Dept Head, Bristol Public Library, 1855 Greenville Rd, Bristolville, OH, 44402-9700. Tel: 330-889-3651. p. 1753
Johnson, Dan, Head Librn, University of South Carolina, 465 James Brandt Blvd, Allendale, SC, 29810. Tel: 803-812-7353. p. 2046
Johnson, Daniel, Digital Preservation Librn, University of Iowa Libraries, Special Collections & Archives, 100 Main Library, 125 W Washington St, Iowa City, IA, 52242-1420. Tel: 319-335-5242. p. 761
Johnson, Daphney, Actg Mgr, Memphis Public Library, Raleigh Branch, 3157 Powers Rd, Memphis, TN, 38128. Tel: 901-415-2778. p. 2113
Johnson, Darlyne, Dir, Ontario Community Library, 388 SW Second Ave, Ontario, OR, 97914. Tel: 541-889-6371. p. 1889
Johnson, David, Exec Dir, Fayetteville Public Library, 401 W Mountain St, Fayetteville, AR, 72701. Tel: 479-856-7100. p. 95
Johnson, Deborah, Mgr, Lafayette County Public Library, 120 NE Crawford St, Mayo, FL, 32066. Tel: 386-294-1021. p. 420
Johnson, Debra E, Br Mgr, Free Library of Philadelphia, Nicetown-Tioga Branch, 3720 N Broad St, Philadelphia, PA, 19140-3608. Tel: 215-685-9790. p. 1979
Johnson, Dee, II, Dir, Central Community College, 4500 63rd St, Columbus, NE, 68602. Tel: 402-562-1202. p. 1310
Johnson, Demi, Dir, Humboldt Public Library, 30 Sixth St N, Humboldt, IA, 50548. Tel: 515-332-1925. p. 759
Johnson, Derek, Assoc Dir, National Network of Libraries of Medicine Region 6, Univ of Iowa Hardin Libr for Health Sci, 600 Newton Rd, Iowa City, IA, 52242-1098. Tel: 319-335-4997. p. 2765
Johnson, Diane, Sr Librn, California Department of Corrections Library System, Valley State Prison, 21633 Ave 24, Chowchilla, CA, 93610. Tel: 559-665-6100, Ext 6066. p. 207
Johnson, Diane, Interim Dir, Martin Curtis Hendersonville Public Library, 140 Saundersville Rd, Hendersonville, TN, 37075-3525. Tel: 615-824-0656. p. 2101
Johnson, Diane M, Tech Serv, Kauai Community College, 3-1901 Kaumualii Hwy, Lihue, HI, 96766. Tel: 808-245-8240. p. 514
Johnson, Donna, Cat, Leicester Public Library & Local History Museum, 1136 Main St, Leicester, MA, 01524. Tel: 508-892-7020. p. 1027
Johnson, Donna, Dir, Mabel Public Library, 110 E Newburg Ave, Mabel, MN, 55954. Tel: 507-493-5336. p. 1181
Johnson, Donna, Librn, Tombigbee Regional Library System, Hamilton Public Library, Hwy 45 S, Hamilton, MS, 39746. Tel: 601-343-8962. p. 1235
Johnson, Dorothy, Circ Mgr, Hackley Public Library, 316 W Webster Ave, Muskegon, MI, 49440. Tel: 231-722-8024. p. 1135
Johnson, Doug, Archive Spec, University of California Los Angeles Library, Chicano Studies Research Center Library & Archive, 144 Haines Hall, Los Angeles, CA, 90095-1544. Tel: 310-206-6052. p. 169
Johnson, Elizabeth, Operations Mgr, Omaha Public Library, 215 S 15th St, Omaha, NE, 68102-1629. Tel: 402-444-4800. p. 1329
Johnson, Elizabeth, Spec Projects Coordr/Vols Coordr, The John P Holt Brentwood Library, 8109 Concord Rd, Brentwood, TN, 37027. Tel: 615-371-0090, Ext 8860. p. 2089
Johnson, Elizabeth Benson, Head, Access & Coll Serv, University of Minnesota Duluth, 416 Library Dr, Duluth, MN, 55812. Tel: 218-726-6561. p. 1173
Johnson, Elvernoy, State Librn, The State Library of Massachusetts, State House, Rm 341, 24 Beacon St, Boston, MA, 02133. Tel: 617-727-2592. p. 1000
Johnson, Emily, Asst Archivist, Virginia Museum of Fine Arts Library, 200 N Arthur Ashe Blvd, Richmond, VA, 23220-4007. Tel: 804-340-1495. p. 2344
Johnson, Eric, Head, Innovative Media, Virginia Commonwealth University Libraries, 901 Park Ave, Richmond, VA, 23284. Tel: 804-828-2802. p. 2343
Johnson, Erika, Associate Dean, Collection Services, University of San Francisco, 2130 Fulton St, San Francisco, CA, 94117-1080. Tel: 415-422-6417. p. 229

Johnson, Erika M, Head of Libr, University of North Dakota, Harley E French Library of the Health Sciences, School of Medicine & Health Sciences, 501 N Columbia Rd, Stop 9002, Grand Forks, ND, 58202-9002. Tel: 701-777-3993. p. 1734

Johnson, Erin L, Rec Mgr, Sr Archivist, Angelo State University Library, 2025 S Johnson, San Angelo, TX, 76904-5079. Tel: 325-486-6553. p. 2235

Johnson, Eva, Dir, Grove United Methodist Church Library, 490 W Boot Rd, West Chester, PA, 19380. Tel: 610-696-2663. p. 2020

Johnson, Garth, Curator, Everson Museum of Art Library, 401 Harrison St, Syracuse, NY, 13202. Tel: 315-474-6064, Ext 309. p. 1648

Johnson, Gary Lynn, Dir, Shelby County Law Library, 140 Adams Ave, Ste 334, Memphis, TN, 38103. Tel: 901-618-3990. p. 2114

Johnson, Gay, Dir, Piggott Public Library, 361 W Main, Piggott, AR, 72454. Tel: 870-598-3666. p. 107

Johnson, Greg, Ref & Info Serv Coordr, Webmaster, Sumter County Library, 111 N Harvin St, Sumter, SC, 29150. Tel: 803-773-7273. p. 2071

Johnson, Hayley, Adult Serv, Shorewood Public Library, 3920 N Murray Ave, Shorewood, WI, 53211-2385. Tel: 414-847-2670. p. 2477

Johnson, Heather, Dir, William B Ogden Free Library, 42 Gardiner Pl, Walton, NY, 13856. Tel: 607-865-5929. p. 1658

Johnson, Heidi, Asst Prof, Info Literacy, Instruction Librn, The College of Saint Scholastica Library, 1200 Kenwood Ave, Duluth, MN, 55811-4199. Tel: 218-723-6488. p. 1171

Johnson, Holly, Adult Prog Coordr, Br Mgr, Granby Public Library, 15 N Granby Rd, Granby, CT, 06035. Tel: 860-844-5275. p. 313

Johnson, Holly, Adult Programming, Br Mgr, Granby Public Library, F H Cossitt Library, 388 N Granby Rd, North Granby, CT, 06060. Tel: 860-653-8958. p. 313

Johnson, Ivan G, Mat Develop Coordr, Braille Institute Library, 741 N Vermont Ave, Los Angeles, CA, 90029-3514. Tel: 323-663-1111, Ext 1388. p. 160

Johnson, Jackee, ILS Adminr, Northern Waters Library Service, 3200 E Lakeshore Dr, Ashland, WI, 54806-2510. Tel: 715-685-1073. p. 2421

Johnson, Jacob, Dir, Webb City Public Library, 101 S Liberty St, Webb City, MO, 64870. Tel: 417-673-4326. p. 1286

Johnson, Jacqueline, Mgr, Henry County Public Library System, Cochran Public Library, 174 Burke St, Stockbridge, GA, 30281. Tel: 678-432-5353, Ext 7. p. 490

Johnson, Jacqueline, Univ Archivist, Miami University Libraries, Walter Havighurst Special Collections & University Archives, 321 King Library, Western College Memorial Archives, Oxford, OH, 45056. Tel: 513-529-6720. p. 1812

Johnson, James R, Librn, VA Pittsburgh Healthcare System, Medical Library Heinz Division, 1010 Delafield Rd, Pittsburgh, PA, 15215. Tel: 412-784-3747. p. 1997

Johnson, Jamie, Dir, Kiowa Public Library, 123 N Seventh St, Kiowa, KS, 67070. Tel: 620-825-4630. p. 817

Johnson, Jan, Br Assoc, Las Vegas-Clark County Library District, Moapa Town Library, 1340 E Hwy 168, Moapa, NV, 89025. Tel: 702-864-2438. p. 1347

Johnson, Janet, Dept Head, Tech Serv, Fulton County Public Library, 320 W Seventh St, Rochester, IN, 46975-1332. Tel: 574-223-2713. p. 716

Johnson, Janet, Tech Serv Supvr, Holbrook Public Library, Two Plymouth St, Holbrook, MA, 02343. Tel: 781-767-3644. p. 1024

Johnson, Jason, Br Mgr, Commun Engagement Mgr, Spokane Public Library, Station Plaza, 2nd Flr, 701 W Riverside Ave, Spokane, WA, 99201. Tel: 509-444-5334. p. 2385

Johnson, Jean, Librn, Stanford Health Library, 211 Quarry Rd, Ste 201, Palo Alto, CA, 94304. Tel: 650-725-8400. p. 192

Johnson, Jean, Circ Serv Coordr, Clark Memorial Library, 538 Amity Rd, Bethany, CT, 06524. Tel: 203-393-2103. p. 302

Johnson, Jenelle, Diversity Serv Librn, University of Pittsburgh at Bradford, 300 Campus Dr, Bradford, PA, 16701. Tel: 814-362-7618. p. 1914

Johnson, Jennifer, Ref Librn, Springdale Public Library, 405 S Pleasant St, Springdale, AR, 72764. Tel: 479-750-8180. p. 110

Johnson, Jennifer, Asst Librn, Dailey Memorial Library, 101 Junior High Dr, Derby, VT, 05829. Tel: 802-766-5063. p. 2283

Johnson, Jennifer, Libr Dir, Hitchcock Memorial Museum & Library, 1252 Rte 100, Westfield, VT, 05874. Tel: 802-744-8258. p. 2298

Johnson, Jenny, Maps Librn, University of Illinois Library at Urbana-Champaign, Geology Virtual Library, 1301 W Springfield Ave, Urbana, IL, 61801. Tel: 217-333-3855. p. 656

Johnson, Jenny Marie, Head of Libr, University of Illinois Library at Urbana-Champaign, Map Library, 418 Main Library, Mc-522, 1408 W Gregory Dr, Urbana, IL, 61801. Tel: 217-333-3855. p. 656

Johnson, Jill, Br Mgr, Fairfax County Public Library, Burke Centre Library, 5935 Freds Oak Rd, Burke, VA, 22015-2599. Tel: 703-249-1520. p. 2316

Johnson, Jim, Circ Asst, SRI International, Life Sciences Library, 333 Ravenswood Ave, Menlo Park, CA, 94025. Tel: 650-859-3549. p. 176

Johnson, Jo Anne, Librn, Krotz Springs Municipal Public Library, 216 Park St, Krotz Springs, LA, 70570. Tel: 337-566-8190. p. 892

Johnson, Joan, Librn, Tyndall Public Library, 110 W 17th Ave, Tyndall, SD, 57066. Tel: 605-589-3266. p. 2083

Johnson, Joan, Libr Dir, Milwaukee Public Library, 814 W Wisconsin Ave, Milwaukee, WI, 53233-2309. Tel: 414-286-3000. p. 2459

Johnson, Joanne, Librn, Huntington Woods Public Library, 26415 Scotia Rd, Huntington Woods, MI, 48070. Tel: 248-543-9720. p. 1118

Johnson, John, Head, Ref, ILL Librn, Keene Public Library, 60 Winter St, Keene, NH, 03431. Tel: 603-352-0157. p. 1369

Johnson, Josephine, Tech Serv Assoc, Indiana University South Bend, 1700 Mishawaka Ave, South Bend, IN, 46615. Tel: 574-520-4318. p. 718

Johnson, Josh, Coordr, Pendleton District Historical, Recreational & Tourism Commission, 125 E Queen St, Pendleton, SC, 29670. Tel: 864-646-3782. p. 2067

Johnson, Josh, Dep Dir, Davis County Library, 133 S Main St, Farmington, UT, 84025. Tel: 801-451-3030. p. 2263

Johnson, Judy, Dir, Colonial Library, 160 Main St, Richburg, NY, 14774. Tel: 585-928-2694. p. 1627

Johnson, Judy, Ref Librn, Clark State Community College Library, 570 E Leffel Lane, Springfield, OH, 45505. Tel: 937-328-6022. p. 1821

Johnson, Julia, Govt Doc, Ref Serv, University of Southern California Libraries, Von KleinSmid Center Library, Von KleinSmid Ctr, 3518 Trousdale Pkwy, Los Angeles, CA, 90089-0182. Tel: 213-740-9377. p. 170

Johnson, Julia, Br Supvr, Rockingham County Public Library, Stoneville Branch, 201 E Main St, Stoneville, NC, 27048. Tel: 336-573-9040. p. 1686

Johnson, Julie, Br Mgr, Enoch Pratt Free Library, Roland Park Branch, 5108 Roland Ave, Baltimore, MD, 21210-2132. Tel: 443-984-3911. p. 953

Johnson, Julie, Br Mgr, Annapolis Valley Regional Library, Kentville Branch, 440 Main St, Kentville, NS, B4N 1K8, CANADA. Tel: 902-679-2544. p. 2616

Johnson, Justine, Sr Librn, User Serv, Metuchen Public Library, 480 Middlesex Ave, Metuchen, NJ, 08840. Tel: 732-632-8526. p. 1418

Johnson, Karen, Dir, Bridgeville Public Library, 600 S Cannon St, Bridgeville, DE, 19933. Tel: 302-337-7401. p. 351

Johnson, Karen, Asst Librn, Boynton Public Library, 27 Boynton Rd, Templeton, MA, 01468-1412. Tel: 978-939-5582. p. 1059

Johnson, Karen J, Librn, United States Courts Library, Walter E Hoffman US Courthouse, 600 Granby St, Rm 319, Norfolk, VA, 23510. Tel: 757-222-7044. p. 2336

Johnson, Karla, Asst Librn, Willamina Public Library, 382 NE C St, Willamina, OR, 97396. Tel: 503-876-6182. p. 1902

Johnson, Kate, Access Serv Librn, Mount Mercy University, 1330 Elmhurst Dr NE, Cedar Rapids, IA, 52402-4797. Tel: 319-368-6465. p. 738

Johnson, Kate, Instrul Design Librn, Outreach Librn, Saint Mary's University of Minnesota, 700 Terrace Heights, No 26, Winona, MN, 55987-1399. Tel: 507-457-1511. p. 1209

Johnson, Kate, Librn, University of Toronto Libraries, Innis College Library, Two Sussex Ave, 2nd Flr, Toronto, ON, M5S 1J5, CANADA. Tel: 416-978-4497. p. 2699

Johnson, Katherine, Librn, University of Wisconsin-Madison, Schwerdtfeger Library, Space Science & Engineering Ctr, Rm 317, 1225 W Dayton St, Madison, WI, 53706. Tel: 608-262-0987. p. 2451

Johnson, Kathryn, Br Mgr, San Diego Public Library, Allied Gardens/Benjamin, 5188 Zion Ave, San Diego, CA, 92120. Tel: 619-533-3970. p. 219

Johnson, Kathryn, Dir, Hamilton Public Library, 861 Broadway St, Hamilton, IL, 62341. Tel: 217-847-2219. p. 596

Johnson, Kathy, Mgr, Alaska Department of Natural Resources, Public Information Center, 550 W Seventh Ave, Ste 1260, Anchorage, AK, 99501. Tel: 907-269-8400. p. 41

Johnson, Katie, Head, Outreach Serv, Twin Falls Public Library, 201 Fourth Ave E, Twin Falls, ID, 83301-6397. Tel: 208-733-2964. p. 532

Johnson, Katrina, Interim Dir, Louis Bennett Public Library, 148 Court Ave, Weston, WV, 26452. Tel: 304-269-5151. p. 2417

Johnson, Kay, Head, Coll & Tech Serv, Radford University, 925 E Main St, Radford, VA, 24142. Tel: 540-831-5703. p. 2339

Johnson, Kelli, Dr, Assoc Dean, Univ Libr, Marshall University Libraries, One John Marshall Dr, Huntington, WV, 25755-2060. Tel: 304-696-6567. p. 2405

Johnson, Kelly, Acad Librn, University of Wisconsin-Fox Valley Library, 1478 Midway Rd, Menasha, WI, 54952-1297. Tel: 920-832-2672. p. 2455

Johnson, Kelly, Acad Librn, University of Wisconsin Oshkosh, 801 Elmwood Ave, Oshkosh, WI, 54901. Tel: 920-832-5337. p. 2467

Johnson, Ken, Ref & Instrul Serv Librn, Saint Olaf College, Rolvaag Memorial Library, Hustad Science Library, Halvorson Music Library, 1510 Saint Olaf Ave, Northfield, MN, 55057-1097. Tel: 507-786-3793. p. 1191

Johnson, Kerry, Digitization Projects Mgr, Tyler Junior College, 1327 S Baxter St, Tyler, TX, 75701. Tel: 903-510-2309. p. 2250

Johnson, Kim, Librn, Trinity Bay North Public Library, PO Box 69, Catalina, NL, A0C 1J0, CANADA. Tel: 709-469-3045. p. 2607

Johnson, Kimberly, Chief Exec Officer, Dir, Tulsa City-County Library, 400 Civic Ctr, Tulsa, OK, 74103. Tel: 918-549-7323. p. 1865

Johnson, Kira, Libr Asst, Coastal Pines Technical College, Alma Learning Resource Center, 101 W 17th St, Rm 1106, Alma, GA, 31510. Tel: 912-632-0951. p. 503

Johnson, Kris, Head, Learning & Research Servs, Montana State University Library, One Centennial Mall, Bozeman, MT, 59717. Tel: 406-994-7708. p. 1289

Johnson, Samantha, Dir, Cadott Community Library, 331 N Main St, Cadott, WI, 54727. Tel: 715-289-4950. p. 2426
Johnson, Sandi, Head, Circ, Benton County Public Library, 102 N Van Buren Ave, Fowler, IN, 47944. Tel: 765-884-1720. p. 685
Johnson, Sara, Dir, Woodbury Public Library, 23 Smith Clove Rd, Central Valley, NY, 10917. Tel: 845-928-2114. p. 1516
Johnson, Sara, Libr Dir, Woodbury Public Library, 16 County Rte 105, Highland Mills, NY, 10930. Tel: 845-928-6162. p. 1546
Johnson, Sarah, Head, Coll Mgt, Eastern Illinois University, 600 Lincoln Ave, Charleston, IL, 61920. Tel: 217-581-7551. p. 552
Johnson, Sarah, Cat, Metadata Serv, Emporia State University, 1200 Commercial St, Box 4051, Emporia, KS, 66801. Tel: 620-341-5719. p. 807
Johnson, Sarah, Curator, Exec Dir, Cahoon Museum of American Art, 4676 Falmouth Rd, Cotuit, MA, 02635. Tel: 508-428-7581. p. 1013
Johnson, Sarah, Libr Dir, Geneva Public Library, 1043 G St, Geneva, NE, 68361. Tel: 402-759-3416. p. 1315
Johnson Schmitz, Erin, Dir of Coll, Colorado Railroad Museum, 17155 W 44th Ave, Golden, CO, 80403-1621. Tel: 303-279-4591. p. 282
Johnson, Shannon, Libr Dir, Indiana University-Purdue University Fort Wayne, 2101 E Coliseum Blvd, Fort Wayne, IN, 46805-1499. Tel: 260-481-6502. p. 684
Johnson, Sharron, Archives, Records Librn, North Carolina School of Science & Mathematics Library, Library, Instructional Technologies & Communications, 1219 Broad St, Durham, NC, 27705. Tel: 919-416-2657. p. 1686
Johnson, Sheila Grant, Dean of Libr, Oklahoma State University Libraries, Athletic Ave, 216, Stillwater, OK, 74078. Tel: 405-744-9775. p. 1862
Johnson, Sherry, Adult Serv, Highland Park Public Library, 31 N Fifth Ave, Highland Park, NJ, 08904. Tel: 732-572-2750. p. 1408
Johnson, Sidnye, Archives, Spec Coll Librn, West Texas A&M University, 110 26th St, Canyon, TX, 79016. Tel: 806-651-2209. p. 2153
Johnson, Stacey, Libr Mgr, Chino Valley Public Library, 1020 W Palomino Rd, Chino Valley, AZ, 86323-5500. Tel: 928-636-2687. p. 58
Johnson, Stan, Mgr, Access Serv, University of North Dakota, 3051 University Ave, Stop 9000, Grand Forks, ND, 58202-9000. Tel: 701-777-2617. p. 1735
Johnson, Stef, Dir, Butte-Silver Bow Public Library, 226 W Broadway St, Butte, MT, 59701. Tel: 406-792-1080. p. 1290
Johnson, Stephanie, Librn, Pensacola State College, Bldg 20, 1000 College Blvd, Pensacola, FL, 32504-8998. Tel: 850-484-2091. p. 436
Johnson, Stephanie, Dir, Kitchigami Regional Library, 310 Second St N, Pine River, MN, 56474. Tel: 218-587-2171. p. 1192
Johnson, Stephanie, Br Mgr, Sampson-Clinton Public Library, 217 Graham St, Clinton, NC, 28328. Tel: 910-592-4153. p. 1681
Johnson, Stephanie, Teen/Tech Librnb, Union County Public Library, 316 E Windsor St, Monroe, NC, 28112. Tel: 704-283-8184. p. 1703
Johnson, Stephanie, Dir, Devon Public Library, 101, 17 Athabasca Ave, Devon, AB, T9G 1G5, CANADA. Tel: 780-987-3720. p. 2533
Johnson, Stephen, Dir, Harrison County Law Library, 1801 23rd Ave, Gulfport, MS, 39501. Tel: 228-865-4004, 228-865-4068. p. 1217
Johnson, Stephen, Business & Distance Education Librn, University of South Dakota, I D Weeks Library, 414 E Clark St, Vermillion, SD, 57069. Tel: 605-658-3387. p. 2084
Johnson, Steve, Ch, Oakley Public Library, 700 W Third St, Oakley, KS, 67748. Tel: 785-671-4776. p. 828
Johnson, Susan, Libr Supvr, Paterson Free Public Library, Totowa Branch, 405 Union Ave, Paterson, NJ, 07502. Tel: 973-942-7198. p. 1433
Johnson, Susan, Librn, Cornwall Free Public Library, 2629 Rte 30, Cornwall, VT, 05753-9340. Tel: 802-462-3615. p. 2282
Johnson, Suzanne, Ref (Info Servs), Valencia College, Raymer Maguire Jr Learning Resources Center, West Campus, 1800 S Kirkman Rd, Orlando, FL, 32811. Tel: 407-582-1210. p. 433
Johnson, Suzanne, Librn, Sesser Public Library, 303 W Franklin St, Sesser, IL, 62884. Tel: 618-625-6566. p. 646
Johnson, Suzanne, Youth Serv Librn, George F Johnson Memorial Library, 1001 Park St, Endicott, NY, 13760. Tel: 607-757-5350. p. 1531
Johnson, Sylvia, Circ Supvr, Chesapeake Public Library, Greenbrier, 1214 Volvo Pkwy, Chesapeake, VA, 23320-7600. Tel: 757-410-7070. p. 2311
Johnson, Tabitha, Br Mgr, Tuscarawas County Public Library, Tuscarawas Branch, 209 S Main St, Tuscarawas, OH, 44682. Tel: 740-922-2748. p. 1807
Johnson, Tally, Br Mgr, Chester County Library, Great Falls Branch, 39 Calhoun St, Great Falls, SC, 29055. Tel: 803-482-2149. p. 2052
Johnson, Tamara, Mgr, Ch Serv, Patrick Henry School District Public Library, 208 N East Ave, Deshler, OH, 43516. Tel: 419-278-3616. p. 1782
Johnson, Tammie, Dir, Paoli Public Library, 100 W Water St, Paoli, IN, 47454. Tel: 812-723-3841. p. 713
Johnson, Tammy, Dir, Tech Serv, Columbia Theological Seminary, 701 S Columbia Dr, Decatur, GA, 30030. Tel: 404-687-4612. p. 475
Johnson, Tanika, Br Mgr, Bossier Parish Libraries, Plain Dealing Branch, 208 E Mary Lee St, Plain Dealing, LA, 71064. Tel: 318-326-4233. p. 886
Johnson, Tanya, Ref Librn, University of Connecticut, Thomas J Meskill Law Library, 39 Elizabeth St, Hartford, CT, 06105. Tel: 860-570-5072. p. 340
Johnson, Tanya, Prog Coordr, Mercer County Correction Center Library, 640 S Broad St, Trenton, NJ, 08650. Tel: 609-989-6901, Ext 2282. p. 1447
Johnson, Tara, Dir, Lanesboro Public Library, 202 Parkway Ave S, Lanesboro, MN, 55949. Tel: 507-467-2649. p. 1180
Johnson Tate, Twila, Pub Serv Librn, Walla Walla Public Library, 238 E Alder St, Walla Walla, WA, 99362. Tel: 509-524-4443. p. 2392
Johnson, Tawanda, Mgr, District of Columbia Public Library, William O Lockridge/Bellevue, 115 Atlantic St SW, Washington, DC, 20032. Tel: 202-243-1185. p. 364
Johnson, Tawney, Br Librn, Southeast Regional Library, Lampman Branch, 302 Main St, Lampman, SK, S0C 1N0, CANADA. Tel: 306-487-2202. p. 2754
Johnson, Teresa, Dir, Libr Planning, Res Libr Dir, New Brunswick Public Library Service (NBPLS), 570 Two Nations Crossing, Ste 2, Fredericton, NB, E3A 0X9, CANADA. Tel: 506-453-2354. p. 2601
Johnson, Terri, Admin Mgr, The Citadel, 171 Moultrie St, Charleston, SC, 29409-6140. p. 2050
Johnson, Terry, Ch, Jonathan Bourne Public Library, 19 Sandwich Rd, Bourne, MA, 02532. Tel: 508-759-0600, Ext 6106. p. 1001
Johnson, Tim, Br Mgr, San Bernardino County Library, Phelan Memorial Library, 9800 Clovis Rd, Phelan, CA, 92371. Tel: 760-868-3053. p. 213
Johnson, Timmi, Health Sci Librn, University of South Dakota, I D Weeks Library, 414 E Clark St, Vermillion, SD, 57069. Tel: 605-658-3389. p. 2084
Johnson, Timothy, Assoc Librn, Curator, University of Minnesota Libraries-Twin Cities, Archives & Special Collections, Elmer L Andersen Library, 222 21st Ave S, Ste 111, Minneapolis, MN, 55455. Tel: 612-624-7469. p. 1185
Johnson, Timothy, Libr Mgr, San Antonio Public Library, Igo, 13330 Kyle Seale Pkwy, San Antonio, TX, 78249. Tel: 210-207-9080. p. 2239
Johnson, Tina, Coordr, Libr Serv, Jackson-Madison County General Hospital, 620 Skyline Dr, Jackson, TN, 38301. Tel: 731-541-6023. p. 2102
Johnson, Tonja, Dir, Madison County Library System, 102 Priestley St, Canton, MS, 39046. p. 1213
Johnson, Tonya, Libr Mgr, Live Oak Public Libraries, Forest City Branch, 1501 Stiles Ave, Savannah, GA, 31415. Tel: 912-651-0942. p. 496
Johnson, Troy, Dir, Creighton University, Klutznick Law Library - McGrath North Mullin & Kratz Legal Research Center, School of Law, 2500 California Plaza, Omaha, NE, 68178-0340. Tel: 402-280-2832. p. 1328
Johnson, Tyler, Acad Librn, Donnelly College, 608 N 18th St, Kansas City, KS, 66102. Tel: 913-621-8735. p. 816
Johnson, Tyler, Research, Learning & Assessment Librn, Rockhurst University, 1100 Rockhurst Rd, Kansas City, MO, 64110-2561. Tel: 816-501-4142. p. 1257
Johnson, Valerie, Supvr, ILL, Montgomery County-Norristown Public Library, 1001 Powell St, Norristown, PA, 19401-3817. Tel: 610-278-5100, Ext 121. p. 1971
Johnson, Valerie, Ch Mgr, Pauline Haass Public Library, N64 W23820 Main St, Sussex, WI, 53089-3120. Tel: 262-246-5182. p. 2481
Johnson, Valerie Mattair, Dir, McBride Memorial Library, 500 N Market St, Berwick, PA, 18603. Tel: 570-752-2241, Ext 212. p. 1910
Johnson Varney, Suzanne, Dir, Libr Serv, Tech Serv Librn, Shawnee State University, 940 Second St, Portsmouth, OH, 45662-4344. Tel: 740-351-3255. p. 1816
Johnson, Virginia, Dir, John Curtis Free Library, 534 Hanover St, Hanover, MA, 02339. Tel: 781-826-2972. p. 1023
Johnson, Virginia, Adult Serv Supvr, Ref Supvr, Taunton Public Library, 12 Pleasant St, Taunton, MA, 02780. Tel: 508-821-1410. p. 1059
Johnson, Walt, Mgr, Monroe County Public Library, Islamorada Branch, 81830 Overseas Hwy, Islamorada, FL, 33036. Tel: 305-664-4645. p. 414
Johnson, Walt, Librn, Pendleton County Library, 256 N Main St, Franklin, WV, 26807. Tel: 304-358-7038. p. 2402
Johnson, Wendell, Humanities & Soc Sci Librn, Northern Illinois University Libraries, 217 Normal Rd, DeKalb, IL, 60115-2828. Tel: 815-753-1634. p. 577
Johnson, Wendy, Dir, Carroll Public Library, 118 E Fifth St, Carroll, IA, 51401. Tel: 712-792-3432. p. 737
Johnson, Wendy, Dir, HF & Maude E Marchant Memorial Library, 1110 Main St, Scranton, IA, 51462. Tel: 712-652-3453. p. 781
Johnson, Wendy, Dir, Libr Serv, River Parishes Community College Library, 925 W Edenborne Pkwy, Rm 141, Gonzales, LA, 70737. Tel: 225-743-8550. p. 890
Johnson, Wesley, IT Tech, Libr Assoc, Daviess County Public Library, 2020 Frederica St, Owensboro, KY, 42301. Tel: 270-684-0211. p. 871
Johnson, Wesleyann, Librn, Center Line Public Library, 7345 Weingartz St, Center Line, MI, 48015-1462. Tel: 586-758-8274. p. 1089
Johnson, Will, Br Mgr, Enoch Pratt Free Library, Northwood Branch, 4420 Loch Raven Blvd, Baltimore, MD, 21218-1553. Tel: 443-984-3910. p. 953
Johnson, William, Ref Serv, Monroe Community College, Damon City Campus Library, 228 E Main St, 4th Flr 4-101, Rochester, NY, 14604. Tel: 585-262-1413. p. 1629
Johnson, Winnie, Br Mgr, Dayton Metro Library, Madden Hills, 2542 Germantown St, Dayton, OH, 45408. Tel: 937-496-8942. p. 1779

Johnson, Winnie, Br Mgr, Dayton Metro Library, Westwood, 3207 Hoover Ave, Dayton, OH, 45407. Tel: 937-496-8964. p. 1779
Johnson-Bignotti, Darlene, Ref Librn, Oakland Community College, 739 S Washington Ave, Bldg C, Royal Oak, MI, 48067-3898. Tel: 248-246-2526. p. 1146
Johnson-Fuller, Lyra, Asst Librn, Heath Public Library, One E Main St, Heath, MA, 01346. Tel: 413-337-4934, Ext 7. p. 1024
Johnson-Houston, Debbie Delafoisse, Assoc Prof, Dir, McNeese State University, 300 S Beauregard Dr, Lake Charles, LA, 70609. Tel: 337-475-5716. p. 894
Johnson-Renvall, Poppy, Dir of Libr, Central New Mexico Community College Libraries, 525 Buena Vista SE, Albuquerque, NM, 87106-4023. Tel: 505-224-4435. p. 1460
Johnson-Saylor, Megan, Digital Scholarship Librn, Univ Archivist, Concordia University, 1282 Concordia Ave, Saint Paul, MN, 55104. Tel: 651-641-8244. p. 1199
Johnson-Spence, Jennifer, Dir, Cooke County Library, 200 S Weaver St, Gainesville, TX, 76240-4731. Tel: 940-668-5530. p. 2182
Johnson-Taylor, Sabrina, Dr, Assoc Dean, Passaic County Community College, One College Blvd, Paterson, NJ, 07505. Tel: 973-684-5877. p. 1433
Johnson-Williams, Jessica, Br Mgr, Jackson/Hinds Library System, Lois A Flagg Library, 105 Williamson Ave, Edwards, MS, 39066. Tel: 601-852-2230. p. 1221
Johnsrud, Karin, Asst Librn, Res Serv, Supreme Court of the United States Library, One First St NE, Washington, DC, 20543. Tel: 202-479-3037. p. 376
Johnston, Amy, Head, Children's Servx, Sachem Public Library, 150 Holbrook Rd, Holbrook, NY, 11741. Tel: 631-588-5024. p. 1547
Johnston, Andrea, Librn, Alberta College of Arts, 1407 14th Ave NW, Calgary, AB, T2N 4R3, CANADA. Tel: 403-284-7667. p. 2525
Johnston, Andrew, Archivist, Spec Coll Coordr, Winthrop University, 824 Oakland Ave, Rock Hill, SC, 29733. Tel: 803-323-2302. p. 2068
Johnston, Ann, Tech Serv Librn, North Idaho College Library, 1000 W Garden Ave, Coeur d'Alene, ID, 83814-2199. Tel: 208-769-3240. p. 520
Johnston, Ann, Curric Librn, Informatics Librn, Olivet Nazarene University, One University Ave, Bourbonnais, IL, 60914-2271. Tel: 815-939-5061. p. 544
Johnston, Bruce, Syst Librn, Eastern Connecticut State University, 83 Windham St, Willimantic, CT, 06226-2295. Tel: 860-465-5552. p. 347
Johnston, Cassie, Circ Librn, Silver Lake Library, 203 Railroad St, Silver Lake, KS, 66539. Tel: 785-582-5141. p. 836
Johnston, Chris, Br Mgr, Charleston County Public Library, James Island, 1248 Camp Rd, Charleston, SC, 29412. Tel: 843-795-6679. p. 2049
Johnston, Chris, Mgr, Dorchester County Library, 506 N Parler Ave, Saint George, SC, 29477. Tel: 843-563-9189. p. 2069
Johnston, Courtenay, Libr Dir, Pouce Coupe Public Library, 5010-52 Ave, Pouce Coupe, BC, V0C 2C0, CANADA. Tel: 250-786-5765. p. 2574
Johnston, Courtney, Head, Ref, Instruction Librn, Arapahoe Community College, 5900 S Santa Fe Dr, Littleton, CO, 80160. p. 289
Johnston, Dave, Head, Access Serv, University of Windsor, 401 Sunset Ave, Windsor, ON, N9B 3P4, CANADA. Tel: 519-253-3000, Ext 3208. p. 2704
Johnston, Diana, Dir, Herbert Wescoat Memorial Library, 120 N Market St, McArthur, OH, 45651-1218. Tel: 740-596-5691. p. 1801
Johnston, Elizabeth, Dir, Sherborn Library, Four Sanger St, Sherborn, MA, 01770-1499. Tel: 508-653-0770. p. 1053
Johnston, Ellen, Tech Serv, Caldwell University, 120 Bloomfield Ave, Caldwell, NJ, 07006. Tel: 973-618-3502. p. 1393
Johnston, Glenn T, Dr, Historian, Univ Archivist, Stevenson University Library, 1525 Greenspring Valley Rd, Stevenson, MD, 21153. Tel: 443-334-2196. p. 978
Johnston, Grace, Librn, Kaiser-Permanente Medical Center, 17234 Valley Rd, Fontana, CA, 92335. Tel: 909-427-5086. p. 142
Johnston, Hailey, Curator, Wellington County Museum & Archives, 0536 Wellington Rd 18, RR 1, Fergus, ON, N1M 2W3, CANADA. Tel: 519-846-0916, Ext 5225. p. 2641
Johnston, Jeff, Br Mgr, Knox County Public Library System, Burlington Branch, 4614 Asheville Hwy, Knoxville, TN, 37914. Tel: 865-525-5431. p. 2105
Johnston, Jolie, Librn, Lake Region State College, 1801 College Dr N, Devils Lake, ND, 58301. Tel: 701-662-1533. p. 1731
Johnston, Justin, Managing Librn, Lakeridge Health, One Hospital Ct, Oshawa, ON, L1G 2B9, CANADA. Tel: 905-576-8711, Ext 33754. p. 2663
Johnston, Kathryn, Libr Mgr, Fox Valley Technical College, 1825 N Bluemound Dr, Rm G113, Appleton, WI, 54912. Tel: 920-735-5653. p. 2420
Johnston, Keith, Librn, Nunavut Public Library Services, Iqaluit Centennial Library, PO Box 189A, Iqaluit, NU, X0A 0H0, CANADA. Tel: 867-975-5595. p. 2625
Johnston, Kendra, Ref & Instruction, Jewish General Hospital, 3755 Cote Ste Catherine Rd, Rm 200, Montreal, QC, H3T 1E2, CANADA. Tel: 514-340-8222, Ext 22453. p. 2725
Johnston, Layla, Dir, East Longmeadow Public Library, 60 Center Sq, East Longmeadow, MA, 01028-2459. Tel: 413-525-5400. p. 1016
Johnston, Lindsay, Pub Serv Mgr, University of Alberta, Rutherford Humanities & Social Sciences Library, 1-01 Rutherford South, Edmonton, AB, T6G 2J8, CANADA. Tel: 780-492-0598. p. 2538
Johnston, Lisa N, Dir, Libr Serv, Eckerd College, 4200 54th Ave S, Saint Petersburg, FL, 33711. Tel: 727-864-8337. p. 441
Johnston, Michelle, Librn, Miles Davison Library, 517 Teath Ave SW, Ste 900, Calgary, AB, T2R 0A8, CANADA. Tel: 403-298-0325. p. 2528
Johnston, Nathalie, Libr Dir, Klamath County Library Services District, 126 S Third St, Klamath Falls, OR, 97601-6394. Tel: 541-882-8894, Ext 26. p. 1882
Johnston, Penny, Dir, Marion Lawrence Memorial Library, 15 E Franklin St, Gratis, OH, 45330. Tel: 937-787-3502. p. 1788
Johnston, Sarah, Syst & Web Develop Librn, Saint Olaf College, Rolvaag Memorial Library, Hustad Science Library, Halvorson Music Library, 1510 Saint Olaf Ave, Northfield, MN, 55057-1097. Tel: 507-786-3771. p. 1191
Johnston, Stephanie, Digital Serv Librn, Lynchburg Public Library, 2315 Memorial Ave, Lynchburg, VA, 24501. Tel: 434-455-6309. p. 2330
Johnston, Tina, Librn/Teen & Tween Serv, Bonne Terre Memorial Library, Five SW Main St, Bonne Terre, MO, 63628. Tel: 573-358-2260. p. 1238
Johnston-Green, Dustin, Interim Co-Dir, Ref Librn, Ohio Northern University, Taggart Law Library, 525 S Main St, Ada, OH, 45810. Tel: 419-772-2255. p. 1743
Johnston-Marius, Jennifer, Dir, Rockville Public Library, 52 Union St, Vernon, CT, 06066-3155. Tel: 860-875-5892. p. 342
Johnstonbaugh, Jeff, Dir, Priestley Forsyth Memorial Library, 100 King St, Northumberland, PA, 17857-1670. Tel: 570-473-8201. p. 1972
Johnstone, Brian, Syst Librn, Bucks County Community College Library, 275 Swamp Rd, Newtown, PA, 18940-0999. Tel: 215-504-8554. p. 1970
Johnstone, Tessa, Librn, North Carolina Office of Archives & History, North Carolina Maritime Museum, Charles R McNeill Maritime Library, 315 Front St, Beaufort, NC, 28516. Tel: 252-504-7740. p. 1702
Johnting, Wendell, Cat & Govt Doc Librn, Indiana University, Ruth Lilly Law Library, 530 W New York St, Indianapolis, IN, 46202-3225. Tel: 317-274-3884, 317-274-4028. p. 693
Joiner, Marcellaus, Genealogy Serv, High Point Public Library, 901 N Main St, High Point, NC, 27262. Tel: 336-883-3637. p. 1696
Joines, Shay, Pub Serv Asst, Panola College, 1109 W Panola St, Carthage, TX, 75633. Tel: 903-693-2052. p. 2154
Jojola, Geraldine, Dir, Cochiti Pueblo Community Library, 245 Cochiti St, Cochiti Pueblo, NM, 87072. Tel: 505-465-3118. p. 1466
Jolicoeur, Catherine, Librn, Conservatoire de Musique de Montreal Bibliotheque, 4750 Ave Henri-Julien, 3rd Flr, Montreal, QC, H2T 2C8, CANADA. Tel: 514 873-4031, Ext 261. p. 2724
Jolin, Josiane, Libr Mgr, York Library Region, Harvey Community Library, 2055 Rte 3, Harvey Station, NB, E6K 1L1, CANADA. Tel: 506-366-2206. p. 2602
Jolivette, Rachael, Coordr, University of Saint Thomas, Archbishop Ireland Memorial Library, 2260 Summit Ave, Mail Stop IRL, Saint Paul, MN, 55105. Tel: 651-962-5450. p. 1202
Jolley, Daniel, Syst Librn, Gardner-Webb University, 110 S Main St, Boiling Springs, NC, 28017. Tel: 704-406-2109. p. 1674
Jolley, Laura, Asst Director, Manuscripts, State Historical Society of Missouri Library, 605 Elm St, Columbia, MO, 65201. Tel: 573-882-1187. p. 1243
Jolley, Tina, Head, Circ, Napa County Library, 580 Coombs St, Napa, CA, 94559-3396. Tel: 707-253-4072. p. 182
Jolliff, Julie, Dir, Union County Public Library, Two E Seminary St, Liberty, IN, 47353-1398. Tel: 765-458-5355, 765-458-6227. p. 703
Jolliffe, Louise, Circ Mgr, Orono Public Library, 39 Pine St, Orono, ME, 04473. Tel: 207-866-5060. p. 934
Jolly, Becky, Libr Tech, Hinds Community College, Vicksburg Campus, 755 Hwy 27, Vicksburg, MS, 39180-8699. Tel: 601-629-6846. p. 1231
Jolly, Craig, Acq, Archives, Saint John's College, 1160 Camino Cruz Blanca, Santa Fe, NM, 87505. Tel: 505-984-6043. p. 1476
Jolly, Dana, Dir, Larue County Public Library, 215 Lincoln Dr, Hodgenville, KY, 42748. Tel: 270-358-3851. p. 859
Jolly, Katie, Br Mgr, Terrebonne Parish Library, Montegut Branch, 1135 Hwy 55, Montegut, LA, 70377. Tel: 985-594-4390. p. 891
Jolly, Violet, Ch, Borough of Folcroft Public Library, 1725 Delmar Dr, Folcroft, PA, 19032-2002. Tel: 610-586-2720. p. 1933
Joly, Robert, Dir, Saint Johnsbury Athenaeum, 1171 Main St, Saint Johnsbury, VT, 05819-2289. Tel: 802-748-8291. p. 2294
Jonas, James, Instrul Serv, Libr Mgr, University of Wisconsin-Madison, MERIT Library (Media, Education Resources & Information Technology), 368 Teacher Education Bldg, 225 N Mills St, Madison, WI, 53706. Tel: 608-263-4934. p. 2451
Jones, Abagail, Access Services Admin, Antioch University Library, 900 Dayton St, Yellow Springs, OH, 45387. Tel: 603-283-2402. p. 1835
Jones, Abby, Access Serv, Antioch University New England Library, 40 Avon St, Keene, NH, 03431. Tel: 603-283-2400. p. 1369
Jones, Al, Jr, Dr, Prof, East Carolina University, 104B Ragsdale Hall, Greenville, NC, 27858. Tel: 252-328-6803. p. 2790
Jones, Alicia Granby, Ref Librn, Southern Illinois University Carbondale, Law Library, Lesar Law Bldg Mailcode 6803, 1150 Douglas Dr, Carbondale, IL, 62901. Tel: 618-453-8780. p. 549

Jones, Allison, Mgr, Saint Mary Parish Library, West End, 100 Charenton Rd, Baldwin, LA, 70514. Tel: 337-923-6205. p. 890

Jones, Amanda, Dir, Norwood Public Library, One Morton St, Norwood, NY, 13668-1100. Tel: 315-353-6692. p. 1609

Jones, Amanda, Br Mgr, Loudoun County Public Library, Sterling Branch, 22330 S Sterling Blvd, Ste A117, Sterling, VA, 20164. Tel: 571-258-3309. p. 2328

Jones, Ami, Youth Serv Librn, Alamogordo Public Library, 920 Oregon Ave, Alamogordo, NM, 88310. Tel: 575-439-4140. p. 1459

Jones, Amy, Libr Dir, Osceola Library System, 211 E Dakin Ave, Kissimmee, FL, 34741. Tel: 407-742-8888. p. 414

Jones, Amy, Libr Asst, Williamsburg Community Library, 107 S Louisa, Williamsburg, KS, 66095. Tel: 785-746-5407. p. 844

Jones, Anaya, Accessibility & Online Learning Librn, Northeastern University Libraries, 360 Huntington Ave, Boston, MA, 02115. Tel: 617-373-8778. p. 998

Jones, Angela, Sr Librn/Youth Serv, Mary Lib Saleh Euless Public Library, 201 N Ector Dr, Euless, TX, 76039-3595. Tel: 817-685-1480. p. 2176

Jones, Angie, Dir, Saint Clair County Library, 115 Chestnut St, Osceola, MO, 64776. Tel: 417-646-2214. p. 1265

Jones, Angie, Dir, Saint Clair County Library, Lowry City Branch, 406 Fourth St, Lowry City, MO, 64763. Tel: 417-644-2255. p. 1265

Jones, Ann, Vols Librn, Saint John's Cathedral Library, 1350 Washington St, Denver, CO, 80203. Tel: 303-831-7115, Ext 7728. p. 277

Jones, April, Children's Programmer, Burlington Public Library, 34 Library Lane, Burlington, CT, 06013. Tel: 860-673-3331. p. 305

Jones, Audrey, Acq, Virginia State University, One Hayden Dr, Petersburg, VA, 23806. Tel: 804-524-1030. p. 2337

Jones, Avis, Libr Mgr, Wake County Public Library System, Southgate Community Library, 1601-14 Cross Link Rd, Raleigh, NC, 27610. Tel: 919-856-6598. p. 1711

Jones, Barbara, Govt Doc Librn, ILL, Dalton State College, 650 College Dr, Dalton, GA, 30720-3778. Tel: 706-272-4585. p. 474

Jones, Barbara, Libr Assoc, Desoto Parish Library, Pelican Branch, 145 Jackson Ave, Pelican, LA, 71063-2803. Tel: 318-755-2353. p. 896

Jones, Beth, Mkt Librn, Programming Librn, Southwest Georgia Regional Library, 301 S Monroe St, Bainbridge, GA, 39819. Tel: 229-248-2665. p. 467

Jones, Bethany, Dir, Dandridge Memorial Library, 1235 Circle Dr, Dandridge, TN, 37725-4750. Tel: 865-397-9758. p. 2096

Jones, Bobbie, Br Mgr, Washington Parish Library System, Franklinton Branch, 825 Free St, Franklinton, LA, 70438. Tel: 985-839-7805. p. 890

Jones, Brenda, Ref Serv Librn, Glendale Community College Library, 1500 N Verdugo Rd, Glendale, CA, 91208-2894. Tel: 818-240-1000, Ext 5581, 818-240-1000, Ext 5586. p. 148

Jones, Brenda, Tech Serv, Albemarle Regional Library, 303 W Tryon St, Winton, NC, 27986. Tel: 252-358-7854. p. 1727

Jones Bressler, Toni, Dir, Morton County Library, 410 Kansas Ave, Elkhart, KS, 67950. Tel: 620-697-2025. p. 806

Jones, Caity, Head, Circ, Bedford Public Library, Three Meetinghouse Rd, Bedford, NH, 03110. Tel: 603-472-2300. p. 1354

Jones, Carol, Dir, Jonesboro Public Library, 124 E Fourth St, Jonesboro, IN, 46938-1105. Tel: 765-677-9080. p. 698

Jones, Carol, Syst Adminr, Pennsylvania Western University - California, 250 University Ave, California, PA, 15419-1394. Tel: 724-938-5772. p. 1917

Jones, Carol Elizabeth, Youth Serv Mgr, Rockbridge Regional Library System, 138 S Main St, Lexington, VA, 24450-2316. Tel: 540-463-4324. p. 2329

Jones, Cassie, Libr Mgr, Live Oak Public Libraries, Carnegie Branch, 537 E Henry St, Savannah, GA, 31401. Tel: 912-651-1973. p. 496

Jones, Cassie, Br Mgr, Morgan County Public Library, Monrovia Branch, 145 S Chestnut St, Monrovia, IN, 46157. Tel: 317-996-4307. p. 705

Jones, Cathy, Music Librn, University of California, Santa Barbara, Arts Library, UCSB Library, Santa Barbara, CA, 93106-9010. Tel: 805-893-2850. p. 241

Jones, Charlene, Librn, Virden Public Library, 209 Church St, Virden, NM, 88045. Tel: 575-358-2544. p. 1479

Jones, Charles E, Tombros Librn for Classics & Humanities, Pennsylvania State University Libraries, George & Sherry Middlemas Arts & Humanities Library, Pennsylvania State University, W 337 Pattee Library, University Park, PA, 16802-1801. Tel: 814-867-4872. p. 2016

Jones, Chelsea, Dir, Socorro Public Library, 401 Park St, Socorro, NM, 87801. Tel: 575-835-1114. p. 1478

Jones, Chris, Col Archivist & Spec Coll Librn, Grinnell College Libraries, 1111 Sixth Ave, Grinnell, IA, 50112-1770. Tel: 641-269-3364. p. 756

Jones, Christina, Br Librn, Boston Public Library, South End, 685 Tremont St, Boston, MA, 02118. Tel: 617-536-8241. p. 992

Jones, Christine, Dep Dir, Fairfax County Public Library, 12000 Government Center Pkwy, Ste 324, Fairfax, VA, 22035-0012. Tel: 703-324-3100. p. 2316

Jones, Craig, Youth Engagement Coord, Rapides Parish Library, Westside Regional, 5416 Provine Pl, Alexandria, LA, 71303. Tel: 318-442-2483, Ext 1904. p. 880

Jones, Cyndi, ILL & Ser, West Baton Rouge Parish Library, 830 N Alexander Ave, Port Allen, LA, 70767. Tel: 225-342-7920. p. 906

Jones, Cynthia, Librn, Law Library of Louisiana, Louisiana Supreme Court, 2nd Flr, 400 Royal St, New Orleans, LA, 70130-2104. Tel: 504-310-2406. p. 901

Jones, Cynthia, Dir, Lucas County Law Library, Lucas County Family Court Ctr, 905 Jackson St, Toledo, OH, 43604-5512. Tel: 419-213-4747. p. 1824

Jones, Cynthia E, Regional Br Mgr, Saint Louis Public Library, Carpenter, 3309 S Grand Blvd, Saint Louis, MO, 63118. Tel: 314-772-6586. p. 1275

Jones, D R, Dir, Law Libr, The University of Memphis, One N Front St, Memphis, TN, 38103. Tel: 901-678-3244. p. 2115

Jones, Darren, Dir, Maple Springs Baptist Bible College & Seminary Library, 4130 Belt Rd, Capitol Heights, MD, 20743. Tel: 301-736-3631. p. 960

Jones, David L, Cataloger, University of Alberta, William C Wonders Map Collection, 1-55 Cameron Library, Edmonton, AB, T6G 2J8, CANADA. Tel: 780-492-3433. p. 2538

Jones, Dawn R, Archivist, United States Army, 705 Washington Blvd, Rm 56, Fort Eustis, VA, 23604. Tel: 757-501-7138. p. 2319

Jones, Debbie, Dir, Henry County Library, , 105 W Benton St, Windsor, MO, 65360. Tel: 660-647-2298. p. 1242

Jones, Debbie, Libr Dir, Henry County Library, 123 E Green St, Clinton, MO, 64735. Tel: 660-885-2612. p. 1242

Jones, Donna, Bus Mgr, Thomas County Public Library System, 201 N Madison St, Thomasville, GA, 31792-5414. Tel: 229-225-5252. p. 499

Jones, Donna, Youth Serv Coordr, Duplin County Library, 107 Bowden Dr, Kenansville, NC, 28349. Tel: 910-296-2117. p. 1698

Jones, Doris, Asst Librn, Horse Cave Free Public Library, 111 Higbee St, Horse Cave, KY, 42749-1110. Tel: 270-786-1130. p. 860

Jones, Dustin, Youth Serv Dept Head, Shelby County Public Library, 57 W Broadway St, Shelbyville, IN, 46176. Tel: 317-398-7121, 317-835-2653. p. 718

Jones, Ed, Assoc Dir, Assessment & Tech Serv, National University Library, 9393 Lightwave Ave, San Diego, CA, 92123-1447. Tel: 858-541-7920. p. 215

Jones, Elizabeth, Asst Dean, Dir, Patron Serv, University of North Carolina at Pembroke, One University Dr, Pembroke, NC, 28372. Tel: 910-521-6516. p. 1707

Jones, Ellen, Ref Librn, University of Iowa Libraries, College of Law Library, 200 Boyd Law Bldg, Iowa City, IA, 52242-1166. Tel: 319-335-6829. p. 761

Jones, Emily, Br Mgr, Hightower Sara Regional Library, Rockmart Branch, Bldg 201, 316 N Piedmont Ave, Rockmart, GA, 30153-2402. Tel: 770-684-3022. p. 495

Jones, Emily, Archivist, Delta State University, Laflore Circle at Fifth Ave, Cleveland, MS, 38733-2599. Tel: 662-846-4781. p. 1214

Jones, Emily, Res & Educ Informationist, Medical University of South Carolina Libraries, 171 Ashley Ave, Ste 419, Charleston, SC, 29425-0001. Tel: 843-792-3364. p. 2051

Jones, Emma, Asst Librn, University of St Augustine for Health Sciences, 700 Windy Point Dr, San Marcos, CA, 92069. Tel: 760-410-5398. p. 234

Jones, Erica, Libr Asst, Wilmington University Library, 320 N DuPont Hwy, New Castle, DE, 19720. Tel: 302-356-6873. p. 355

Jones, Erin, Br Mgr, Scottsdale Public Library, 3839 N Drinkwater Blvd, Scottsdale, AZ, 85251-4467. Tel: 480-312-6225. p. 77

Jones, Faith, Libr Dir, Columbia College Library, 438 Terminal Ave, Vancouver, BC, V6A 0C1, CANADA. Tel: 604-683-8360, Ext 253. p. 2578

Jones, Faye, Dir, University of Illinois Library at Urbana-Champaign, Law, 142 Law Bldg, MC-594, 504 E Pennsylvia Ave, Champaign, IL, 61820. Tel: 217-265-4524. p. 656

Jones, Glenda, Libr Dir, White Pine Public Library, 1708 Main St, White Pine, TN, 37890. Tel: 865-674-6313. p. 2129

Jones, Gwendolyn, Tech Serv, Rust College, 150 E Rust Ave, Holly Springs, MS, 38635. Tel: 662-252-8000, Ext 4100. p. 1220

Jones, Hannah, Acq Tech, Utah State Library Division, 250 N 1950 West, Ste A, Salt Lake City, UT, 84116-7901. Tel: 801-715-6777. p. 2272

Jones, Hannah O, Instructional Support Programs, Alabama State University, College of Education, Ralph Abernathy Hall, 915 S Jackson St, Montgomery, AL, 36104. Tel: 334-229-6829. p. 2781

Jones, Heather, Asst Librn, Southwestern Manitoba Regional Library, 149 Main St, Melita, MB, R0M 1L0, CANADA. Tel: 204-522-3923. p. 2588

Jones, Holly, Br Mgr, Davidson County Public Library System, West Davidson Public, 246 Tyro School Rd, Lexington, NC, 27295-6006. Tel: 336-853-4800. p. 1700

Jones, Hunter, Ref Serv, Belleville Public Library & Information Center, 221 Washington Ave, Belleville, NJ, 07109-3189. Tel: 973-450-3434. p. 1389

Jones, Ida, Dr, Univ Archivist, Morgan State University, 1700 E Cold Spring Lane, Baltimore, MD, 21251. Tel: 443-885-4294. p. 956

Jones, Irene, Asst Dir, Berrien Springs Community Library, 215 W Union St, Berrien Springs, MI, 49103-1077. Tel: 269-471-7074. p. 1085

Jones, Jabari, Br Mgr, Dallas Public Library, Skyline, 6006 Everglade Rd, Dallas, TX, 75227-2799. Tel: 214-670-0938. p. 2166

Jones, Jacqueline L, Assoc Dean, Learning Res, Baton Rouge Community College, 201 Community College Dr, Baton Rouge, LA, 70806. Tel: 225-216-8170. p. 882

Jones, Jamie, Br Mgr, Peoria Public Library, North Branch, 3001 W Grand Pkwy, Peoria, IL, 61615. Tel: 309-497-2110. p. 634

Jones, Jane, Dir, Radium Hot Springs Public Library, 4863 Stanley St, Radium Hot Springs, BC, V0A 1M0, CANADA. Tel: 250-347-2434. p. 2575

Jones, Janice, Dir, Yates Center Public Library, 218 N Main, Yates Center, KS, 66783. Tel: 620-625-3341. p. 845

Jones, Janice, Dir, Constantine Township Library, 165 Canaris St, Constantine, MI, 49042-1015. Tel: 269-435-7957. p. 1094

Jones, Janice, Dir, Maury County Public Library, Mount Pleasant Branch, 200 Hay Long Ave, Mount Pleasant, TN, 38474. Tel: 931-379-3752. p. 2095

Jones, Jarian, Mgr, Henry County Public Library System, Locust Grove Public Library, 115 Martin Luther King Jr Blvd, Locust Grove, GA, 30248. Tel: 678-432-5353, Ext 4. p. 490

Jones, Jarrod, Librn, Polk State College, 999 Ave H NE, Winter Haven, FL, 33881. Tel: 863-297-1040. p. 455

Jones, Jennifer, Librn, Savannah Technical College, 100 Technology Dr, Hinesville, GA, 31313. Tel: 912-408-3024, Ext 6017. p. 482

Jones, Jennifer, Br Mgr, Harford County Public Library, Aberdeen Branch, 21 Franklin St, Aberdeen, MD, 21001-2495. Tel: 410-273-5608. p. 958

Jones, Jennifer, Libr Dir, Mattapoisett Free Public Library, Seven Barstow St, Mattapoisett, MA, 02739-0475. Tel: 508-758-4171. p. 1033

Jones, Jennifer, Assoc Exec Dir, Minnesota Historical Society, 345 Kellogg Blvd W, Saint Paul, MN, 55102. Tel: 651-259-3300. p. 1201

Jones, Jennifer, Librn, Department of Veterans Affairs, 2101 N Elm St, Fargo, ND, 58102. p. 1732

Jones, Jennifer, Chief Exec Officer, Peterborough Public Library, 345 Aylmer St N, Peterborough, ON, K9H 3V7, CANADA. Tel: 705-745-5382, Ext 2370. p. 2672

Jones, Jennifer, Pres, Toronto Pub Libr Found, Toronto Public Library, 789 Yonge St, Toronto, ON, M4W 2G8, CANADA. Tel: 416-393-7131. p. 2693

Jones, Jeremy, Br Mgr, Rieger Memorial Library, 116 N Broadway, Haskell, OK, 74436. Tel: 918-482-3614. p. 1849

Jones, Jessi, Cat Librn, Coll Develop Librn, Iliff School of Theology, 2323 E Iliff Ave, Denver, CO, 80210. Tel: 303-765-3174. p. 276

Jones, Jessica, Dir, Takoma Park Maryland Library, 7505 New Hampshire Ave, Ste 205, Takoma Park, MD, 20912. Tel: 301-891-7259. p. 979

Jones, Jessica, Youth Serv Librn, Boulder City Library, 701 Adams Blvd, Boulder City, NV, 89005-2207. Tel: 702-293-1281. p. 1343

Jones, Jessica, Br Mgr, Bryan College Station Public Library System, Larry J Ringer Library, 1818 Harvey Mitchell Pkwy S, College Station, TX, 77840. Tel: 979-764-3416. p. 2151

Jones, Jessica, Libr Asst, Fairfield Library Association, Inc, 350 W Main, Fairfield, TX, 75840. Tel: 903-389-3574. p. 2176

Jones, Jessimi, Exec Dir, Springfield Museum of Art Library, 107 Cliff Park Rd, Springfield, OH, 45504. Tel: 937-325-4673. p. 1821

Jones, Joel, Dep Dir, Libr Serv, Kansas City Public Library, Lucile H Bluford Branch, 3050 Prospect Ave, Kansas City, MO, 64128. Tel: 816-701-3482. p. 1255

Jones, Joel, Dep Dir, Libr Serv, The Kansas City Public Library, 14 W Tenth St, Kansas City, MO, 64105. Tel: 816-701-3504. p. 1255

Jones, Jon, Dir, Libr Serv, Baptist Bible College & Theological Seminary, 730 E Kearney St, Springfield, MO, 65803. Tel: 417-268-6048. p. 1280

Jones, Judith, Circ Supvr, ILL, Tech Serv Asst, Keuka College, 141 Central Ave, Keuka Park, NY, 14478. Tel: 315-279-5340. p. 1559

Jones, Judy, Br Mgr, Toledo-Lucas County Public Library, Heatherdowns, 3265 Glanzman Rd, Toledo, OH, 43614. Tel: 419-259-5270. p. 1824

Jones, Judy, Head, Youth Serv, USS Liberty Memorial Public Library, 1620 11th Ave, Grafton, WI, 53024-2404. Tel: 262-375-5315. p. 2437

Jones, Julia, Asst Librn, Rosebud County Library, 201 N Ninth Ave, Forsyth, MT, 59327. Tel: 406-346-7561. p. 1293

Jones, Julia D, ILL, Bath County Memorial Library, 24 W Main St, Owingsville, KY, 40360. Tel: 606-674-2531. p. 871

Jones, Karen, Librn, Iva Jane Peek Public Library, 121 N Main St, Decatur, AR, 72722. Tel: 479-752-7323. p. 93

Jones, Karen, Coll Serv Librn, Lewiston Public Library, 200 Lisbon St, Lewiston, ME, 04240. Tel: 207-513-3004. p. 929

Jones, Karen, Circ, Jefferson County Library, Northwest, 5680 State Rd PP, High Ridge, MO, 63049. Tel: 636-677-8186. p. 1249

Jones, Karen, Circ Tech, Clovis Community College Library, 417 Schepps Blvd, Clovis, NM, 88101. Tel: 575-769-4148. p. 1466

Jones, Karla, Head, Ref, Southern Connecticut State University, 501 Crescent St, New Haven, CT, 06515. Tel: 203-392-5762. p. 326

Jones, Karla, Exec Dir, Bernice Bienenstock Furniture Library, 1009 N Main St, High Point, NC, 27262. Tel: 336-883-4011. p. 1696

Jones, Karyn, Ref Librn, San Jacinto College North, 5800 Uvalde Rd, Houston, TX, 77049-4599. Tel: 281-998-6150, Ext 7359. p. 2198

Jones, Katherine, Ref Librn, Central College, Campus Box 6500, 812 University St, Pella, IA, 50219-1999. Tel: 641-628-5220. p. 776

Jones, Kathy, Br Mgr, Nelson County Public Library, New Haven Branch, 318 Center St, New Haven, KY, 40051. Tel: 502-549-6735. p. 848

Jones, Kathy, Head, Circ, Locust Valley Library, 170 Buckram Rd, Locust Valley, NY, 11560-1999. Tel: 516-671-1837. p. 1564

Jones, Kay, Tech Serv Librn, Foothill College, 12345 El Monte Rd, Los Altos Hills, CA, 94022-4599. Tel: 650-949-7602. p. 159

Jones, Kelly, Mgr, Richland Library, Ballentine Branch, 1200 Dutch Fork Rd, Irmo, SC, 29063. Tel: 803-781-5026. p. 2054

Jones, Kelsey, Dir, Anna Porter Public Library, 158 Proffitt Rd, Gatlinburg, TN, 37738. Tel: 865-436-5588. p. 2099

Jones, Ken, Research Coordr, Baltimore Museum of Industry, 1415 Key Hwy, 2nd Flr, Baltimore, MD, 21230. Tel: 410-727-4808, Ext 112. p. 952

Jones, Kendra, Dep Dir, Timberland Regional Library, 415 Tumwater Blvd SW, Tumwater, WA, 98501-5799. Tel: 360-943-5001. p. 2388

Jones, Kenny, Coordr, College Medical Center, 2776 Pacific Ave, Long Beach, CA, 90806. Tel: 562-997-2181. p. 158

Jones, Kevin, Head Cataloger, Librn, Alternative Press Center Library, 2239 Kirk Ave, Baltimore, MD, 21218. Tel: 312-451-8133. p. 951

Jones, Kim, Circ Supvr, Springdale Public Library, 405 S Pleasant St, Springdale, AR, 72764. Tel: 479-750-8180. p. 110

Jones, Kimberly, Mgr, Richland Library, Eastover Branch, 608 Main St, Eastover, SC, 29044. Tel: 803-353-8584. p. 2054

Jones, Koala, Circ Librn, Claremont School of Theology Library, 1325 N College Ave, Claremont, CA, 91711. Tel: 909-447-2510. p. 130

Jones, Koala, Circ Librn, Claremont School of Theology Library, Center for Process Studies, 1325 N College Ave, Claremont, CA, 91711-3154. Tel: 909-447-2533, 909-621-5330. p. 130

Jones, Kristine M, Dir, Libr Serv, Louisburg College, 501 N Main St, Louisburg, NC, 27549-7704. Tel: 919-497-3269. p. 1701

Jones, LaShawn, Libr Dir, Purdue University, 2200 169th St, Hammond, IN, 46323. Tel: 219-989-2138. p. 689

Jones, LaShawn, Dir of the Univ Libr, Purdue University Northwest, Library-Student-Faculty Bldg, 2nd Flr, 1401 S US Hwy 421, Westville, IN, 46391. Tel: 219-989-2138. p. 726

Jones, Laura, Dir, Duplin County Library, 107 Bowden Dr, Kenansville, NC, 28349. Tel: 910-296-2117. p. 1698

Jones, Laura, Dir, Duplin County Library, Warsaw-Kornegay Library, 117 E College St, Warsaw, NC, 28398. Tel: 910-293-4664. p. 1698

Jones, Laura, Libr Asst, Duplin County Library, Emily S Hill Library, 106 Park Circle Dr, Faison, NC, 28341. Tel: 910-267-0601. p. 1698

Jones, Laura, Youth Serv Spec, Jefferson County Library District, 241 SE Seventh St, Madras, OR, 97741. Tel: 541-475-3351. p. 1885

Jones, Lee, Dir, Waterville Public Library, 129 E Commercial St, Waterville, KS, 66548. Tel: 785-363-6014. p. 841

Jones, Leigh, Ref Librn, Samford University Library, Lucille Stewart Beeson Law Library, 800 Lakeshore Dr, Birmingham, AL, 35229. Tel: 205-726-2714. p. 9

Jones, Lenisa, Br Mgr, Marshall County Public Library System, 1003 Poplar St, Benton, KY, 42025. Tel: 270-527-9969, Ext 131. p. 848

Jones, Linda, Mgr, District of Columbia Public Library, Georgetown, 3260 R St NW, Washington, DC, 20007. Tel: 202-727-0232. p. 364

Jones, Linda, Libr Dir, Won Institute of Graduate Studies Library, 800 Jacksonville Rd, Warminster, PA, 18974. Tel: 215-884-8942. p. 2017

Jones, Linda, Educ Librn, Dixie State University Library, 225 S 700 E, Saint George, UT, 84770. Tel: 435-879-4243. p. 2270

Jones, Lisa, Dir, Grayson County Public Library, 163 Carroll Gibson Blvd, Leitchfield, KY, 42754-1488. Tel: 270-259-5455. p. 861

Jones, Lisa, Coordr, Piedmont Community College, 1715 College Dr, Roxboro, NC, 27573. Tel: 336-599-1181, Ext 2247. p. 1714

Jones, Lisa, Coordr, Piedmont Community College, Caswell Learning Commons, 331 Piedmont Dr, Yanceyville, NC, 27379. Tel: 336-694-5707, Ext 8072. p. 1714

Jones, Lisa R, Head, Libr Tech, University of Southern Mississippi Library, 124 Golden Eagle Dr, Hattiesburg, MS, 39406. Tel: 601-266-4244. p. 1218

Jones, Lizbeth A, Cat Librn, Spec Coll, United States Air Force Academy Libraries, 2354 Fairchild Dr, Ste 3A15, USAF Academy, CO, 80840-6214. Tel: 719-333-4406. p. 297

Jones, Lois, Libr Dir, Massanutten Regional Library, 174 S Main St, Harrisonburg, VA, 22801. Tel: 540-434-4475, Ext 128. p. 2324

Jones, Lonnie, Head, Circ Serv, Homewood Public Library, 1721 Oxmoor Rd, Homewood, AL, 35209-4085. Tel: 205-332-6600. p. 21

Jones, Lonnie, Head, Circ Serv, Homewood Public Library, 1721 Oxmoor Rd, Homewood, AL, 35209-4085. Tel: 205-332-6611. p. 21

Jones, Lynette, Info Serv, Carrollton Public Library, 1700 N Keller Springs Rd, Carrollton, TX, 75006. Tel: 972-466-4814. p. 2153

Jones, Lynette, Br Mgr, Carrollton Public Library, Hebron & Josey Branch, 4220 N Josey Lane, Carrollton, TX, 75010. p. 2154

Jones, Lynn M, Libr Mgr, Brantley County Library, 14046 Cleveland St E, Nahunta, GA, 31553-9470. Tel: 912-462-5454. p. 492

Jones, Madi, Circ Mgr, Westminster College, 1840 S 1300 East, Salt Lake City, UT, 84105-3697. Tel: 801-832-2250. p. 2273

Jones, Marcie, Sr Librn, Los Angeles Public Library System, Washington Irving Branch Library, 4117 W Washington Blvd, Los Angeles, CA, 90018-1053. Tel: 323-734-6303. p. 165

Jones, Margaret Faye, Dean, Learning Res, Nashville State Technical Community College, 120 White Bridge Rd, Nashville, TN, 37209-4515. Tel: 615-353-3440. p. 2120

Jones, Margarette, Librn, Dallas College, 801 Main St, Dallas, TX, 75202-3605. Tel: 214-860-2174. p. 2164

Jones, Marilyn, Br Mgr, Knox County Public Library System, Farragut Branch, 417 N Campbell Station Rd, Farragut, TN, 37934. Tel: 865-777-1750. p. 2106

Jones, Mary, Br Mgr, Chicago Public Library, Brainerd, 1350 W 89th St, Chicago, IL, 60620. Tel: 312-747-6291. p. 556

Jones, Mary, Br Mgr, Saint Martin Parish Library, Parks Branch, 1012 Martin St, Parks, LA, 70582. Tel: 337-342-2690. p. 907

Jones, Mary Lynne, Ch Serv, Marion County Sub-District Library, 212 S Main St, Palmyra, MO, 63461. Tel: 573-769-2830. p. 1265

Jones, Maya N, Br Head, Birmingham Public Library, West End, 1348 Tuscaloosa Ave SW, Birmingham, AL, 35211-1948. Tel: 205-226-4089. p. 8

Jones, Megan, Area Mgr, Prince George's County Memorial, Largo-Kettering, 9601 Capital Lane, Largo, MD, 20774. Tel: 301-336-4044. p. 971

Jones, Megan, Area Mgr, Prince George's County Memorial, South Bowie Branch, 15301 Hall Rd, Bowie, MD, 20721. Tel: 301-850-0475. p. 971

Jones, Megan, Area Mgr, Prince George's County Memorial, Upper Marlboro Branch, 14730 Main St, Upper Marlboro, MD, 20772-3053. Tel: 301-627-9330. p. 971

Jones, Melanie, Engagement Librn, Ref Serv, Lakeland University, W3718 South Dr, Plymouth, WI, 53073. Tel: 920-565-1038, Ext 2418. p. 2470

Jones, Melissa, Learning Commons Librn, Wilmington University Library, 320 N DuPont Hwy, New Castle, DE, 19720. Tel: 302-356-8610. p. 355

Jones, Melissa, Cat, Libr Asst, Georgia Highlands College Libraries, 3175 Cedartown Hwy SE, Rome, GA, 30161. Tel: 706-295-6318. p. 494

Jones, Michelle, Head, Ref Serv, Columbus State University Libraries, 4225 University Ave, Columbus, GA, 31907. Tel: 706-507-8688. p. 472

Jones, Mike, Spec Serv Mgr, Chillicothe & Ross County Public Library, 140 S Paint St, Chillicothe, OH, 45601. Tel: 740-702-4145. p. 1758

Jones Miner, Kate, District Supervisor, Stormont, Dundas & Glengarry County Library, Finch Branch, 17 George St, Finch, ON, K0C 1K0, CANADA. Tel: 613-984-2807. p. 2638

Jones Miner, Kate, Libr Support Serv Asst, Stormont, Dundas & Glengarry County Library, Morrisburg Branch, 34 Ottawa St, Morrisburg, ON, K0C 1X0, CANADA. Tel: 613-543-3384. p. 2638

Jones, Misty, Libr Dir, San Diego Public Library, 330 Park Blvd, MS 17, San Diego, CA, 92101. Tel: 619-236-5870. p. 219

Jones, Molly, Dir, Libr & Info Tech, Cincinnati College of Mortuary Science Library, 645 W North Bend Rd, Cincinnati, OH, 45224-1428. Tel: 513-761-2020. p. 1759

Jones, Monica, Chief Operating Officer, Library Contact, Bexar County Medical Society, 4334 N Loop 1604 W, Ste 200, San Antonio, TX, 78249-3485. Tel: 210-301-4391. p. 2236

Jones, Nancy, Asst Librn, Lewis Public Library & Heritage Center, 412 W Main, Lewis, IA, 51544. Tel: 712-769-2228. p. 765

Jones, Naomi, Dir, Greenwood-Leflore Public Library System, 405 W Washington St, Greenwood, MS, 38930-4297. Tel: 662-453-3634. p. 1217

Jones, Nelia, Librn, Barton Public Library, Strong Public, 246 Second Ave, Strong, AR, 71765. Tel: 870-797-2165. p. 94

Jones, Noel, Head, Access Serv, University of North Carolina at Asheville, One University Heights, Ramsey Library, CPO 1500, Asheville, NC, 28804. Tel: 828-251-6249. p. 1673

Jones, Olivia, Special Programs & Instruction Librn, Salve Regina University, 100 Ochre Point Ave, Newport, RI, 02840-4192. Tel: 401-341-2330. p. 2035

Jones, Olivia, Librn, Parkersburg & Wood County Public Library, South Parkersburg, 1807 Blizzard Dr, Parkersburg, WV, 26101. Tel: 304-428-7041. p. 2411

Jones, Phil, Librn, Hobe Sound Bible College Library, 11298 SE Gomez Ave, Hobe Sound, FL, 33455-3378. Tel: 772-545-1400. p. 409

Jones, Phil, Assoc Dir, Bus Serv, Northern New York Library Network, 6721 US Hwy 11, Potsdam, NY, 13676. Tel: 315-265-1119, Ext 17. p. 2771

Jones, Philip J, Dir, Fine Arts Libraryy, University of Arkansas Libraries, 365 N McIlroy Ave, Fayetteville, AR, 72701-4002. Tel: 479-575-3081. p. 95

Jones, Phillip, Coordr of Res Serv, Humanities Librn, Grinnell College Libraries, 1111 Sixth Ave, Grinnell, IA, 50112-1770. Tel: 641-269-3355. p. 756

Jones, Phillip J, Head of Libr, University of Arkansas Libraries, Fine Arts, 104 Fine Arts Bldg, Fayetteville, AR, 72701. Tel: 479-575-3081. p. 95

Jones Priggel, Tonya, Librn, Campbell Foundation Library, 1211 Union Ave, Ste 510, Memphis, TN, 38104. Tel: 901-759-3271. p. 2112

Jones, Rane, Dir, Pima Public Library, 50 S 200 West, Pima, AZ, 85543. Tel: 928-485-2822. p. 73

Jones, Reynor, Br Mgr, Hampton Public Library, Willow Oaks Branch, Willow Oaks Village Sq, 227 Fox Hill Rd, Hampton, VA, 23669. Tel: 757-850-5114. p. 2323

Jones, Rhiannon, Bus Librn, University of Calgary Library, Business Library, Haskayne School of Business, 2500 University Dr NW, Scurfield Hall 301, Calgary, AB, T2N 1N4, CANADA. Tel: 403-220-4410. p. 2529

Jones, Rhonda, Circ Librn, Bartlett-Carnegie Sapulpa Public Library, 27 W Dewey Ave, Sapulpa, OK, 74066. Tel: 918-224-5624. p. 1861

Jones, Ronald, Electronic Serv/Ref Librn, University of Cincinnati, 2540 Clifton Ave, Cincinnati, OH, 45219. Tel: 513-556-0158. p. 1764

Jones, Rotina, Mgr, Dallas Public Library, Highland Hills, 6200 Bonnie View Rd, Dallas, TX, 75241. Tel: 214-670-0987. p. 2165

Jones, Ryan, Assoc Law Librn, Maine State Law & Legislative Reference Library, 43 State House Sta, Augusta, ME, 04333-0043. Tel: 207-287-1600. p. 914

Jones, Sam, Ref, Amarillo Public Library, 413 E Fourth Ave, Amarillo, TX, 79101. Tel: 806-378-3054. p. 2134

Jones, Sandra, Dr, Dean, Western Baptist Bible College Memorial Library, 2525 E 27th St, Kansas City, MO, 64130. Tel: 816-842-4195. p. 1258

Jones, Sara, State Librn, Washington State Library, Point Plaza East, 6880 Capitol Blvd, Tumwater, WA, 98501. Tel: 360-704-5200. p. 2390

Jones, Sarah, Acq, Elizabethtown Community & Technical College Library, 600 College Street Rd, Elizabethtown, KY, 42701. Tel: 270-706-8812. p. 854

Jones, Sarah, Head, Tech Serv, Northwest Missouri State University, 800 University Dr, Maryville, MO, 64468-6001. Tel: 660-562-1193. p. 1261

Jones, Sarah, Dir, Carlsbad Public Library, 101 S Halagueno St, Carlsbad, NM, 88220. Tel: 575-885-6776. p. 1465

Jones, Sarah, Head Librn, Redfield Carnegie Library, Five E Fifth Ave, Redfield, SD, 57469. Tel: 605-472-4555. p. 2081

Jones, Sarah, User Serv Librn, Dallas Baptist University, 3000 Mountain Creek Pkwy, Dallas, TX, 75211-9299. Tel: 214-333-5220. p. 2163

Jones, Sarah, Librn, Selwyn Public Library, Ennismore Branch, c/o Ennismore Post Office, 551 Ennis Rd, Ennismore, ON, K0L 1T0, CANADA. Tel: 705-292-8022. p. 2633

Jones, Savannah, Dir, Webster Parish Library System, 521 East & West St, Minden, LA, 71055. Tel: 318-371-3080, Ext 140. p. 897

Jones, Scott, Circ Supvr, Clovis-Carver Public Library, 701 N Main, Clovis, NM, 88101. Tel: 505-769-7840. p. 1465

Jones, Scott, Chief Exec Officer, Laurentian Hills Public Library, RR1 - 34465 Hwy 17, Deep River, ON, K0J 1P0, CANADA. Tel: 613-584-2714. p. 2638

Jones, Sean, Communications Spec, Wichita Public Library, 711 W Second St, Wichita, KS, 67203. Tel: 316-261-8524. p. 843

Jones, Shanell, Actg Br Mgr, Cleveland Public Library, Martin Luther King Jr, 1962 Stokes Blvd, Cleveland, OH, 44106. Tel: 216-623-7018. p. 1768

Jones, Shannon, Circ Supvr, Mill Valley Public Library, 375 Throckmorton Ave, Mill Valley, CA, 94941. Tel: 415-389-4292, Ext 4737. p. 177

Jones, Shannon, Dir, National Network of Libraries of Medicine Region 2, MUSC James W Colbert Educ Ctr & Libr, 171 Ashley Ave, Ste 300, MSC 403, Charleston, SC, 29425. Tel: 843-792-8839. p. 2774

Jones, Shannon D, Dir of Libr, Medical University of South Carolina Libraries, 171 Ashley Ave, Ste 419, Charleston, SC, 29425-0001. Tel: 843-792-8839. p. 2051

Jones, Shelly, Librn, Greater West Central Public Library District, Golden Branch, 309 Quincy St, Golden, IL, 62339. Tel: 217-696-2428. p. 538

Jones, Sheritha, Chief Librn, Omaha World-Herald Library, 1314 Douglas St, Ste 600, Omaha, NE, 68102. Tel: 402-444-1000. p. 1330

Jones, Sheryl, Libr Asst, Rayburn Correctional Center Library, 27268 Hwy 21 N, Angie, LA, 70426. Tel: 985-661-6300. p. 881

Jones, Sonya, Curator, Robert McLaughlin Gallery Library, Civic Centre, 72 Queen St, Oshawa, ON, L1H 3Z3, CANADA. Tel: 905-576-3000, Ext 110. p. 2663

Jones, Stacey, Br Mgr, North Madison County Public Library System, Frankton Community Library, 102 S Church St, Frankton, IN, 46044. Tel: 765-551-4140. p. 680

Jones, Stephanie, Syst Librn, New Port Richey Public Library, 5939 Main St, New Port Richey, FL, 34652. Tel: 727-853-1273. p. 428

Jones, Stephanie, Asst Dir, Libr Communications, Memphis Public Library & Information Center, 3030 Poplar Ave, Memphis, TN, 38111. Tel: 901-415-2847. p. 2112

Jones, Stephen, IT Serv Mgr, University of Maryland, Baltimore County, 1000 Hilltop Circle, Baltimore, MD, 21250. Tel: 410-455-2356. p. 958

Jones, Steve, Archives Mgr, Digital Coll Mgr, Southeastern Baptist Theological Seminary Library, 114 N Wingate St, Wake Forest, NC, 27587. Tel: 919-863-2220. p. 1720

Jones, Susan, Mgr, Main Libr, Long Beach Public Library, 200 W Broadway, Long Beach, CA, 90802. Tel: 562-570-7500. p. 159

Jones, Susan, Tech Serv Librn, University of New Brunswick Libraries, Gerard V La Forest Law Library, Law School, 2nd Flr, 41 Dineen Dr, Fredericton, NB, E3B 5A3, CANADA. Tel: 506-447-3267. p. 2602

Jones, Tami, Br Mgr, Briggs Lawrence County Public Library, Chesapeake Branch, 11054 County Rd 1, Cheseapeake, OH, 45619. Tel: 740-867-3390. p. 1791

Jones, Tammy, Dir, Badger Public Library, 211 First Ave SE, Badger, IA, 50516. Tel: 515-545-4793. p. 733

Jones, Tammy, Dir, Martin County Public Library, 180 E Main St, Inez, KY, 41224. Tel: 606-298-7766. p. 860

Jones, Tammy, Coordr, Tech Serv & Automation, Central Mississippi Regional Library System, 100 Tamberline St, Brandon, MS, 39042. Tel: 601-825-0100. p. 1212

Jones, Tanya, Supvr, Coll Develop, Gaston County Public Library, 1555 E Garrison Blvd, Gastonia, NC, 28054. Tel: 704-868-2164. p. 1690

Jones, Teresa, Cataloger, New River Community College, 226 Martin Hall, 5255 College Dr, Dublin, VA, 24084. Tel: 540-674-3600, Ext 4297. p. 2315

Jones, Terry, Asst Librn, Jonesboro Public Library, 124 E Fourth St, Jonesboro, IN, 46938-1105. Tel: 765-677-9080. p. 698

Jones, Thai, Lehman Curator, Am Hist, Columbia University, Rare Book & Manuscript, Butler Library, 6th Flr E, 535 W 114th St, New York, NY, 10027. Tel: 212-854-9616. p. 1583

Jones, Theresa, Dir, Horse Cave Free Public Library, 111 Higbee St, Horse Cave, KY, 42749-1110. Tel: 270-786-1130. p. 860

Jones, Thomas, Br Mgr, Memphis Public Library, History, 3030 Poplar Ave, Memphis, TN, 38111. Tel: 901-415-2742. p. 2113

Jones, Tianne, Br Mgr, Otsego County Library, Vanderbilt Branch, 8170 Mill St, Vanderbilt, MI, 49795. Tel: 989-983-3600. p. 1109

Jones, Todd, Br Mgr, Johnson County Public Library, Trafalgar Branch, 424 Tower St, Trafalgar, IN, 46181. Tel: 317-878-9560. p. 686

Jones, Tony, Dir, Henry County Public Library, 172 Eminence Terrace, Eminence, KY, 40019-1146. Tel: 502-845-5682. p. 854

Jones, Trevor, Br Mgr, San Diego Public Library, Scripps Miramar Ranch, 10301 Scripps Lake Dr, San Diego, CA, 92131-1026. Tel: 858-538-8158. p. 221

Jones, Victor T, Jr, Spec Coll Librn, New Bern-Craven County Public Library, 400 Johnson St, New Bern, NC, 28560-4098. Tel: 252-638-7800. p. 1706

Jones, Wilma L, Chief Librn, College of Staten Island Library, 2800 Victory Blvd, Staten Island, NY, 10314-6609. Tel: 718-982-4001. p. 1644

Jones Woodruff, Kimberly, Dir, Instrul Design, Manhattan College, 4513 Manhattan College Pkwy, Riverdale, NY, 10471. Tel: 718-862-7743. p. 1627

Jones, Yolanda, Dr, Dir, Florida Agricultural & Mechanical University, 201 Beggs Ave, Orlando, FL, 32801. Tel: 407-254-3231. p. 431

Jones, Zachary, Commun Engagement Librn, Haywood County Public Library, 678 S Haywood St, Waynesville, NC, 28786. Tel: 828-356-2502. p. 1721

Jones-Martel, Sierra, Mgr, Serv Delivery, North Grenville Public Library, Norenberg Bldg, One Water St, Kemptville, ON, K0G 1J0, CANADA. Tel: 613-258-4711. p. 2649

Jones-Rhoades, Melinda, Head, Children's Servx, Galesburg Public Library, 40 E Simmons St, Galesburg, IL, 61401-4591. Tel: 309-343-6118. p. 591

Jonkel, Elizabeth, Asst Dir, Missoula Public Library, 301 E Main, Missoula, MT, 59802-4799. Tel: 406-721-2665. p. 1300

Joo, Soohyung, Dr, Asst Prof, University of Kentucky, 320 Little Library Bldg, Lexington, KY, 40506-0224. Tel: 859-257-8876. p. 2785

Joosse, Trudy, Circ, Calmar Public Library, 4705 50th Ave, Calmar, AB, T0C 0V0, CANADA. Tel: 780-985-3472. p. 2529

Joost, Jamie, Dir, Red Bud Public Library, 925 S Main St, Red Bud, IL, 62278. Tel: 618-282-2255. p. 638

Jordan, Alyse, Dr, Head of Research, Engagement & Learning Services, Lamar University, 4400 Martin Luther King Jr Pkwy, Beaumont, TX, 77705. Tel: 409-880-8131. p. 2146

Jordan, Alysse, Dir, Council on Foreign Relations Library, 58 E 68th St, New York, NY, 10065. Tel: 212-434-9400. p. 1584

Jordan, Angela, Adult Serv Mgr, Teton County Library, 125 Virginian Lane, Jackson, WY, 83001. Tel: 307-733-2164, Ext 3258. p. 2495

Jordan, C, Ms, Librn, North Carolina Department of Correction, 527 Commerce Dr, Elizabeth City, NC, 27906. Tel: 252-331-4881. p. 1687

Jordan, Chiterria, Libr Asst, Graham County Public Library, 414 N West St, Hill City, KS, 67642. Tel: 785-421-2722. p. 813

Jordan, Courtney, Libr Supvr, Bluegrass Community & Technical College, 221 Oswald Bldg, 470 Cooper Dr, Lexington, KY, 40506-0235. Tel: 859-246-6380. p. 862

Jordan, DeAnn, Learning Res Ctr Coordr, Columbia College Hollywood, 1111 S Broadway, Los Angeles, CA, 90015. Tel: 818-345-8414. p. 161

Jordan, Jackie, Dir, Marengo Public Library, 235 E Hilton St, Marengo, IA, 52301. Tel: 319-741-3825. p. 768

Jordan, Jacqueline, Br Mgr, Greater Clarks Hill Regional Library System, Sardis County Library, 750 Charles Perry Ave, Sardis, GA, 30456. Tel: 478-569-4866. p. 478

Jordan, Jessica, Tech Serv Librn, Cape Cod Community College, 2240 Iyannough Rd, West Barnstable, MA, 02668-1599. Tel: 774-330-4617. p. 1065

Jordan, Jessica, Chair, Libr Serv, Slippery Rock University of Pennsylvania, 109 Campus Loop, Slippery Rock, PA, 16057. Tel: 724-738-2663. p. 2007

Jordan, Katherine, Br Librn, East Central Regional Library, Mora Public Library, 200 W Maple Ave, Mora, MN, 55051. Tel: 320-679-2642. p. 1168

Jordan, Kendra, Mgr, District of Columbia Public Library, Parklands-Turner Community, 1547 Alabama Ave SE, Washington, DC, 20032. Tel: 202-645-4532. p. 364

Jordan, Lachelle, Br Mgr, Azalea Regional Library System, Eatonton-Putnam County Library, 309 N Madison Ave, Eatonton, GA, 31024. Tel: 706-485-6768. p. 488

Jordan, Louis, Assoc Librn, Hesburgh Libraries, 221 Hesburgh Library, University of Notre Dame, Notre Dame, IN, 46556. Tel: 574-631-5252. p. 711

Jordan, Mark, Assoc Univ Librn, Digital Strat, Simon Fraser University - Burnaby Campus, 8888 University Dr, Burnaby, BC, V5A 1S6, CANADA. Tel: 778-782-5753. p. 2563

Jordan, Mary, Tech Serv, Elizabeth City State University, 1704 Weeksville Rd, Elizabeth City, NC, 27909. Tel: 252-335-8515. p. 1687

Jordan, Mary, Head, Youth Serv, Hazleton Area Public Library, 55 N Church St, Hazleton, PA, 18201-5893. Tel: 570-454-2961. p. 1943

Jordan, Matthew, Dir, Clinch River Regional Library, 130 N Main St, Ste 2, Clinton, TN, 37716-3693. Tel: 865-220-4000. p. 2093

Jordan, Matthew, Regional Libr Dir, Tennessee State Library & Archives, 403 Seventh Ave N, Nashville, TN, 37243-0312. Tel: 865-457-0931. p. 2121

Jordan, Melissa, Legal Librarian, Officer, Pew Charitable Trusts Library, 901 E St NW, 5th Flr, Washington, DC, 20004. Tel: 202-540-6611. p. 374

Jordan, Natalie, Acq Asst, University of Saint Mary of the Lake - Mundelein Seminary, 1000 E Maple Ave, Mundelein, IL, 60060. Tel: 847-970-4894. p. 622

Jordan, Roberta, Outreach & Instruction Librn, Patten Free Library, 33 Summer St, Bath, ME, 04530. Tel: 207-443-5141, Ext 25. p. 916

Jordan, Sara, Ref & Instruction Librn, Georgia Military College, 201 E Greene St, Milledgeville, GA, 31061. Tel: 478-387-4733. p. 491

Jordan, Tina, Librn, Lanier Technical College, 408 Hwy 9 N, Rm 201, Dawsonville, GA, 30534. Tel: 678-513-5221. p. 475

Jordan-Makely, Chelsea, Libr Dir, Griswold Memorial Library, 12 Main St, Colrain, MA, 01340. Tel: 413-624-3619. p. 1012

Jordan-Makely, Chelsea, Support Serv Librn, Tech Librn, Whistler Public Library, 4329 Main St, Whistler, BC, V8E 1B2, CANADA. Tel: 604-935-8433. p. 2584

Jordebrek, Jennifer, Asst Dir, North Liberty Library, 520 W Cherry St, North Liberty, IA, 52317-9797. Tel: 319-626-5701. p. 773

Jordon, Donna, Br Supvry Clerk, Rutherford County Library System, Eagleville Bicentennial Branch, 317 Old Hwy 99, Eagleville, TN, 37060. Tel: 615-274-2626. p. 2117

Jordon, Linda, Librn, Wilkes Memorial Library, 300 NW Sixth St, Hubbard, TX, 76648. Tel: 254-576-2527. p. 2201

Jordy, Janet, Br Mgr, Calcasieu Parish Public Library System, DeQuincy Branch, 102 W Harrison St, DeQuincy, LA, 70633. Tel: 337-721-7087. p. 893

Jordy, Janet, Br Mgr, Calcasieu Parish Public Library System, Starks Branch, 113 S HWY 109, Starks, LA, 70661-4362. Tel: 337-721-7107. p. 894

Jorge, Barbara, Fac Librn, Austin Community College, Hays Campus Library, 1200 Kohlers Crossing, 3rd Flr, Rm 1305, Kyle, TX, 78640. Tel: 512-223-1586. p. 2138

Jorge, Lucila, Libr Asst, Ser, Inter-American University of Puerto Rico, 104 Parque Industrial Turpeaux, Rd 1, Mercedita, PR, 00715-1602. Tel: 787-284-1912, Ext 2170. p. 2512

Jorgensen, Anne, Mgr, Access Serv, Bentley University, 175 Forest St, Waltham, MA, 02452-4705. Tel: 781-891-2168. p. 1061

Jorgensen, Barbara, Br Mgr, Fort Vancouver Regional Library District, Three Creeks Community Library, 800-C NE Tenney Rd, Vancouver, WA, 98685. Tel: 360-906-5000. p. 2391

Jorgensen, Diane, Dir, Ringsted Public Library, Eight W Maple St, Ringsted, IA, 50578. Tel: 712-866-0878. p. 779

Jorgensen, Janis, Mgr, The Naval Institute, 291 Wood Rd, Annapolis, MD, 21402-5035. Tel: 410-295-1022. p. 951

Jorgensen, John, Head, Circ, Head, Digital Planning, Rutgers University Libraries, Camden Law Library, 217 N Fifth St, Camden, NJ, 08102-1203. Tel: 856-225-6460. p. 1394

Jorgensen, Kaitlyn, Librn, Lincoln County Library, Alamo Branch, 121 Joshua Tree St, Alamo, NV, 89001. Tel: 775-725-3343. p. 1349

Jorgensen, Kerrilynn, Head, Teen Serv, Mastics-Moriches-Shirley Community Library, 407 William Floyd Pkwy, Shirley, NY, 11967. Tel: 631-399-1511. p. 1640

Jorgensen, Kristopher, Br Mgr, San Diego County Library, Fallbrook Branch, 124 S Mission Rd, Fallbrook, CA, 92028. Tel: 760-731-4650. p. 217

Jorgensen, Laurie, Library & Information Technologist, Pine Technical & Community College Library, 900 Fourth St SE, Pine City, MN, 55063. Tel: 320-629-5145. p. 1192

Jorgensen, Sibyl, Libr Dir, Thornton Public Library, 412 Main St, Thornton, IA, 50479. Tel: 641-998-2261, 641-998-2416. p. 786

Jorgensen, Susan, Br Mgr, Chicago Public Library, Portage-Cragin, 5108 W Belmont Ave, Chicago, IL, 60641. Tel: 312-744-0152. p. 557

Jorgensen-Price, Trudy, Mgr, Salt Lake County Library Services, Alta Reading Room, Alta Community Ctr, 10351 E Hwy 210, Alta, UT, 84121. p. 2274

Jorgenson, Jane, Br Supvr, Madison Public Library, Hawthorne Branch, 2707 E Washington Ave, Madison, WI, 53704. Tel: 608-246-4548. p. 2449

Jorgenson, Jane, Br Supvr, Madison Public Library, Pinney Branch, 516 Cottage Grove Rd, Madison, WI, 53716. Tel: 608-224-7100. p. 2449

Joris, Courtney, Supvr, Middlesex County Library, Glencoe Branch, 123 McKellar St, Glencoe, ON, N0L 1M0, CANADA. Tel: 519-287-2735. p. 2682

Jorns, Dixie, Br Mgr, Door County Library, Egg Harbor Branch, 7860 Hwy 42, Egg Harbor, WI, 54209. Tel: 920-868-2664. p. 2479

Jorstad, Cynthia, Librn, Northland Community & Technical College Library, 1101 Hwy One E, Thief River Falls, MN, 56701. Tel: 218-683-8757. p. 1205

Joseph, Cathy, Br Mgr, Augusta-Richmond County Public Library, Diamond Lakes, 101 Diamond Lakes Way, Hephzibah, GA, 30815. Tel: 706-772-2432. p. 466

Joseph, Claire, Dir, Mount Sinai South Nassau, One Healthy Way, Oceanside, NY, 11572. Tel: 516-632-3452. p. 1609

Joseph, Elizabeth, Adult/Info Serv Coordr, The Ferguson Library, One Public Library Plaza, Stamford, CT, 06904. Tel: 203-351-8224. p. 338

Joseph, Elizabeth, Asst Dir, New Rochelle Public Library, One Library Plaza, New Rochelle, NY, 10801. Tel: 914-813-3732. p. 1577

Joseph, Jennifer, Ref & Instruction Librn, Geneva College, 3200 College Ave, Beaver Falls, PA, 15010-3599. Tel: 724-847-6563. p. 1909

Joseph, Joslyn, Libr Mgr, Prescott Valley Public Library, 7401 E Skoog Blvd, Prescott Valley, AZ, 86314. Tel: 928-759-3040. p. 75

Joseph, Judy, Head, Adult Serv, Finkelstein Memorial Library, 24 Chestnut St, Spring Valley, NY, 10977. Tel: 845-352-5700, Ext 293. p. 1644

Joseph, Maria, Mgr, Carnegie Library of Pittsburgh, West End, 47 Wabash St, Pittsburgh, PA, 15220-5422. Tel: 412-921-1717. p. 1992

Joseph, Meagan, Mgr, Borrower Serv, Bryant University, 1150 Douglas Pike, Smithfield, RI, 02917-1284. Tel: 401-232-6125. p. 2042

Joseph, Michael, Rare Bk Librn, Rutgers University Libraries, Special Collections & University Archives, Alexander Library, 169 College Ave, New Brunswick, NJ, 08901-1163. Tel: 848-932-6163. p. 1425

Joseph, Michiko, Ms, Interim Libr Dir, University of Hawaii - West Oahu Library, 91-1001 Farrington Hwy, Kapolei, HI, 96707. Tel: 808-689-2700. p. 514

Joseph, Mildred, Dir, Houston Community College - Northeast College, Codwell Campus Library, 555 Community College Dr, Houston, TX, 77013-6127. Tel: 713-718-8354. p. 2194

Joseph, Mildred, Dir, Houston Community College - Northeast College, North Forest Campus Library, 7525 Tidwell Rd, Houston, TX, 77016-4413. Tel: 713-635-0427. p. 2194

Joseph, Monique, Libr Dir, Wilkinson County Library System, 489 Main St, Woodville, MS, 39669. Tel: 601-888-6712. p. 1236

Joseph-Johnson, Paula, Mgr, Libr Operations, Metropolitan Library System in Oklahoma County, Jones Library, 9295 Willa Way, Jones, OK, 73049. p. 1857

Joseph-Johnson, Paula, Mgr, Libr Operations, Metropolitan Library System in Oklahoma County, Luther Library, 310 NE Third St, Luther, OK, 73054-9999. p. 1857

Joseph-Johnson, Paula, Mgr, Libr Operations, Metropolitan Library System in Oklahoma County, Nicoma Park Library, 2240 Overholser Dr, Nicoma Park, OK, 73066. p. 1857

Josephides, Analu, Ref & Instruction Librn, El Camino College, 16007 S Crenshaw Blvd, Torrance, CA, 90506. Tel: 310-660-3525. p. 252

Josephs, Ann-Marie, Commun Libr Mgr, Queens Library, Glendale Community Library, 78-60 73rd Pl, Glendale, NY, 11385. Tel: 718-821-4980. p. 1554

Joshi, Keren, Ch Serv, Wilmette Public Library District, 1242 Wilmette Ave, Wilmette, IL, 60091-2558. Tel: 847-256-6940. p. 663

Joslin, Jennifer, Librn, Pacific Institution/Regional Treatment Centre Library, 33344 King Rd, Abbotsford, BC, V2S 4P4, CANADA. Tel: 604-870-7700. p. 2562

Joslin, Lanora, Librn, Gladys Johnson Ritchie Public Library, 626 W College St, Jacksboro, TX, 76458-1655. Tel: 940-567-2240. p. 2203

Josue, Perla, Asst Dir, Williamsburg Public Library, 300 W State St, Williamsburg, IA, 52361. Tel: 319-668-1195. p. 792

Jott, Jacqueline, Br Mgr, Shreve Memorial Library, Hamilton/South Caddo Branch, 2111 Bert Kouns Industrial Loop, Shreveport, LA, 71118. Tel: 318-687-6824. p. 909

Joudrey, Daniel, Prof, Simmons University, 300 The Fenway, Boston, MA, 02115. Tel: 617-521-2800. p. 2786

Joven, Robert, Univ Librn, Quinnipiac University, 275 Mount Carmel Ave, Hamden, CT, 06518. Tel: 203-582-8634. p. 316

Jow, Brie, Digital Serv, Outreach Librn, Utica Public Library, 303 Genesee St, Utica, NY, 13501. Tel: 315-735-2279. p. 1656

Joy, Abbie, Acq & Ser Librn, Rivier University, 420 S Main St, Nashua, NH, 03060-5086. Tel: 603-897-8535. p. 1375

Joy, Dylan, Archivist, University of Texas Libraries, Nettie Lee Benson Latin American Collection, Sid Richardson Hall, SRH 1108, 2300 Red River St, Austin, TX, 78713-8916. Tel: 512-495-4520. p. 2142

Joy, Sheila, Archivist, Cataloger, United Lutheran Seminary, 66 Seminary Ridge, Gettysburg, PA, 17325. Tel: 717-339-1317. p. 1936

Joy, Shelley, Team Lead, Finance, University of Colorado Boulder, 1720 Pleasant St, Boulder, CO, 80309. Tel: 303-492-8705. p. 267

Joy, Traci, Libr Dir, Hartland Public Library, 153 US Rte 5, Hartland, VT, 05048. Tel: 802-436-2473. p. 2286

Joyal, Jan, Librn, Bibliotheque Saint Claude Library, 50 First St, Saint Claude, MB, R0G 1Z0, CANADA. Tel: 204-379-2524. p. 2590

Joyal, Paula, Bus & Finance Mgr, Lynn Public Library, Five N Common St, Lynn, MA, 01902. Tel: 781-595-0567. p. 1030

Joyaux, Aimee, Assoc Dean, Learning Res, Assoc Dean, Acad, Richard Bland College Library, Commons Bldg, 11301 Johnson Rd, Petersburg, VA, 23805. Tel: 804-862-6150. p. 2337

Joyce, Amy, Librn, Bryant & Stratton Business College, 110 Broadway, Buffalo, NY, 14203. Tel: 716-884-9120, Ext 261. p. 1507

Joyce, Kelly, Dir, Hanover College, 121 Scenic Dr, Hanover, IN, 47243. Tel: 812-866-7160. p. 689

Joyce, Marie, Head, Youth Serv, Township of Washington Public Library, 144 Woodfield Rd, Washington Township, NJ, 07676. Tel: 201-664-4586. p. 1451

Joyce, Olga, Dir, Menaul Historical Library of the Southwest, 301 Menaul Blvd NE, Albuquerque, NM, 87107. Tel: 505-343-7480. p. 1461

Joyce, Patricia, Dir, Pittston Memorial Library, 47 Broad St, Pittston, PA, 18640. Tel: 570-654-9565. p. 1997

Joyce, Steve, Dir, Gillespie Public Library, 201 W Chestnut, Gillespie, IL, 62033. Tel: 217-839-3614. p. 592

Joye, Jennifer, Cat Supvr, Hardin-Simmons University, 2200 Hickory St, Abilene, TX, 79698. Tel: 325-670-1236. p. 2132

Joyner, Larry, Financial Serv, Albemarle Regional Library, 303 W Tryon St, Winton, NC, 27986. Tel: 252-358-7834. p. 1727

Joyner, Linda, Outreach Specialist, Edgecombe County Memorial Library, 909 N Main St, Tarboro, NC, 27886. Tel: 252-823-1141. p. 1718

Joyner, Scott, Operations Mgr, LeRoy Collins Leon County Public Library System, 200 W Park Ave, Tallahassee, FL, 32301-7720. Tel: 850-606-2665. p. 445

Joyner, Stephanie, Exec Dir, Pinal County Historical Society, Inc Library, 715 S Main St, Florence, AZ, 85132. Tel: 520-868-4382. p. 61

Joyner, Susanna, Librn, Augusta Technical College, Burke Campus Library, 216 Hwy 24 S, Waynesboro, GA, 30830. Tel: 706-437-6805. p. 467

Joyner, Susanna, Libr Dir, United States Army, Woodworth Consolidated Library/Fort Gordon Post Library, 549 Rice Rd, Bldg 33500, Fort Gordon, GA, 30905-5081. Tel: 706-791-7323. p. 479

Jozwiak, John, Fac Mgr, White Oak Library District, 201 W Normantown Rd, Romeoville, IL, 60446. Tel: 815-886-2030. p. 643

Jozwiak, Kathleen, Br Mgr, Willoughby-Eastlake Public Library, Willowick Branch, 263 E 305th St, Willowick, OH, 44095. Tel: 440-943-4151. p. 1783

Ju, Boryung, Dr, Prof, Louisiana State University, 267 Coates Hall, Baton Rouge, LA, 70803. Tel: 225-578-3158, 225-578-3159. p. 2785

Ju, Eunkyoung, Ad, Metuchen Public Library, 480 Middlesex Ave, Metuchen, NJ, 08840. Tel: 732-632-8526. p. 1418

Ju, Ji Hae, Head, Access Serv, Princeton Public Library, 65 Witherspoon St, Princeton, NJ, 08542. Tel: 609-924-9529. p. 1436

Juarez, Elia, Teen Serv Mgr, Yuma County Free Library District, 2951 S 21st Dr, Yuma, AZ, 85364. Tel: 928-373-6487. p. 85

Juárez-Ponce, María, Puerto Rican Coll Librn, Inter-American University of Puerto Rico, San German Campus, Ave Inter-American University, Rd 102, K 30 6, San German, PR, 00683-9801. Tel: 787-264-1912, Ext 7536. p. 2512

Juarez-Wall, Ursula, Br Mgr, Prince William Public Libraries, Nokesville Library, 12993 Fitzwater Dr, Nokesville, VA, 20181. Tel: 703-792-5665. p. 2339

Jubera, Anne, Mgr, Columbus Metropolitan Library, Shepard Branch, 850 N Nelson Rd, Columbus, OH, 43219. p. 1773

Juchems, Jane, Dir, Plainfield Public Library, 723 Main St, Plainfield, IA, 50666. Tel: 319-276-4461. p. 777

Judd, Jerry, Librn, Nash Community College Library, 522 N Old Carriage Rd, Rocky Mount, NC, 27804-9441. Tel: 252-451-8210. p. 1713

Judd, Rebecca, Dir, Bellingham Public Library, 210 Central Ave, Bellingham, WA, 98225. Tel: 360-778-7221. p. 2358

Jude, Amanda, Br Mgr, Madera County Library, Madera Ranchos Branch, 37398 Berkshire Dr, Madera, CA, 93636. Tel: 559-645-1214. p. 171

Judice, Charlene, Circ Supvr, Iberia Parish Library, 445 E Main St, New Iberia, LA, 70560-3710. Tel: 337-364-7024, 337-364-7074. p. 900

Judith, Lihosit, Head, Pub Serv, University of San Diego, Katherine M & George M Pardee Jr Legal Research Center, 5998 Alcala Park, San Diego, CA, 92110-2492. Tel: 619-260-4766. p. 223

Judy, Christine, Br Librn, Southeast Regional Library, Broadview Branch, 515 Main St, Broadview, SK, S0G 0K0, CANADA. Tel: 306-696-2414. p. 2753

Judy, Deborah, Colls Librn, Thurgood Marshall State Law Library, Courts of Appeals Bldg, 361 Rowe Blvd, Annapolis, MD, 21401. Tel: 410-260-1430. p. 950

Jueneman, Donna, Librn, Hanover Public Library, 205 Jackson St, Hanover, KS, 66945-8874. Tel: 785-337-2424. p. 811

Juenemann, Megan, Librn, Oregon Research Institute Library, 3800 Sports Way, Springfield, OR, 97477. Tel: 541-484-2123. p. 1899

Juergens, Aleta, Librn, Missouri Department of Corrections, Ozark Correctional Center, 929 Honor Camp Lane, Fordland, MO, 65652-9700. Tel: 417-767-4491. p. 1252

Juergensmeyer, Fran, Colls Mgr, Waukegan Public Library, 128 N County St, Waukegan, IL, 60085. Tel: 847-623-2041. p. 660

Juge, Lori, Br Serv Coordr, East Baton Rouge Parish Library, 7711 Goodwood Blvd, Baton Rouge, LA, 70806-7625. Tel: 225-231-3780. p. 882

Juhala, Traci, Head, Youth Serv, Bismarck Veterans Memorial Public Library, 515 N Fifth St, Bismarck, ND, 58501-4081. Tel: 701-355-1480. p. 1729

Juhl, Beth, Web Serv Librn, University of Arkansas Libraries, 365 N McIlroy Ave, Fayetteville, AR, 72701-4002. Tel: 479-575-4665. p. 95
Juhlin, Lori, Dir, Hawarden Public Library, 803 Tenth St, Hawarden, IA, 51023. Tel: 712-551-2244. p. 758
Jui, Doris, Head, Info Resource Ctr, University of Miami Libraries, Judi Prokop Newman Information Resource Center, University of Miami, Miami Herbert Business School, Coral Gables, FL, 33124-6520. Tel: 305-284-6516. p. 391
Juilfs, Melissa, Libr Dir, Syracuse Public Library, 480 Fifth St, Syracuse, NE, 68446. Tel: 402-269-2336. p. 1337
Juk, Michael, Asst Librn, Saint Tikhon's Orthodox Theological Seminary, St Tikhon's Rd, South Canaan, PA, 18459. Tel: 570-561-1818, Ext 8. p. 2008
Julagay, Janelle, Librn, University of Redlands, 1249 E Colton Ave, Redlands, CA, 92374-3755. Tel: 909-748-8022. p. 199
Julian, Alicia, Head, Res Serv, Williams & Connolly Library, 680 Maine Ave SW, Washington, DC, 20024. Tel: 202-434-5000. p. 381
Julian, Barbara, Libr Asst, Wheeling Jesuit University, 316 Washington Ave, Wheeling, WV, 26003-6295. Tel: 304-243-2226. p. 2418
Julian, Reese, Head, Coll & Access Serv, Westminster College, 1840 S 1300 East, Salt Lake City, UT, 84105-3697. Tel: 801-832-2250. p. 2273
Julian, Renaine, Dir, Florida State University Libraries, Paul A M Dirac Science Library, 110 N Woodward Ave, Tallahassee, FL, 32301. Tel: 850-644-5534. p. 447
Julian, Stephanie, Actg Librn, Bad River Public Tribal Library, 72682 Maple St, Odanah, WI, 54861. Tel: 715-682-7111, Ext 1530. p. 2466
Julian-Milas, Sharon, Dir, Pleasant Hills Public Library, 302 Old Clairton Rd, Pleasant Hills, PA, 15236-4399. Tel: 412-655-2424. p. 1997
Juliani, Jan, Cat, Digital Projects Librn, Southern Oregon University, 1250 Siskiyou Blvd, Ashland, OR, 97520. Tel: 541-552-6839. p. 1872
Juliano, Kathleen, Dir of Coll, Electronic Res Librn, Drew University Library, 36 Madison Ave, Madison, NJ, 07940. Tel: 973-408-3478. p. 1414
Juliano, Liana, Info Res Mgr, Paul Hastings LLP, 515 S Flower, 25th Flr, Los Angeles, CA, 90071. Tel: 213-683-6000. p. 167
Julien, Heidi, Dr, Prof, University at Buffalo, The State University of New York, 534 Baldy Hall, Buffalo, NY, 14260. Tel: 716-645-2412. p. 2789
Julien, Laura, Mgr, Brockville Public Library, 23 Buell St, Brockville, ON, K6V 5T7, CANADA. Tel: 613-342-3936. p. 2634
Julien, Marc, Libr Mgr, College de Limoilou-Campus de Charlesbourg, 7600 Third Ave E, Charlesbourg, QC, G1H 7L4, CANADA. Tel: 418-647-6600, Ext 3713. p. 2710
Julien-Hayes, Lisa, Head, Children's Servx, Swampscott Public Library, 61 Burrill St, Swampscott, MA, 01907. Tel: 781-596-8867. p. 1059
Julius, Carole A, Dir, Carver Public Library, Two Meadowbrook Way, Carver, MA, 02330. Tel: 508-866-3415. p. 1009
Julius, Rachel, Liaison Librn, Art Center College of Design, 1700 Lida St, Pasadena, CA, 91103. Tel: 626-396-2233. p. 192
Julson, Ginny, Dir, Boyceville Public Library, 903 Main St, Boyceville, WI, 54725-9595. Tel: 715-643-2106. p. 2425
Julson, Marci, ILL, Minot Public Library, 516 Second Ave SW, Minot, ND, 58701-3792. Tel: 701-852-1045. p. 1738
Jumonville, Judy, Dir, Capital City Press, 10705 Rieger Rd, Baton Rouge, LA, 70809. p. 882
Jump, Joan, Cataloger, Librn III, New Mexico Military Institute, Toles Learning Ctr, 101 W College Blvd, Roswell, NM, 88201. Tel: 575-624-8383. p. 1474
Jump, Sean, Dir, Libr Serv, Union College, 310 College St, Campus Box D-21, Barbourville, KY, 40906-1499. Tel: 606-546-1246. p. 848
Jung, Heidi, Teen Librn, Gates Public Library, 902 Elmgrove Rd, Rochester, NY, 14624. Tel: 585-247-6446. p. 1628
Jung, Jennifer, Br Mgr, Saint Charles City-County Library District, Augusta Branch, 198 Jackson St, Augusta, MO, 63332-1772. Tel: 636-228-4855. p. 1278
Jung, Jennifer, Br Mgr, Saint Charles City-County Library District, Boone's Trail Branch, Ten Fiddlecreek Ridge Rd, New Melle, MO, 63365. Tel: 636-398-6200. p. 1278
Jung, Jennifer, Br Mgr, Saint Charles City-County Library District, Portage Des Sioux Branch, 1825 Commonfield Rd, Portage des Sioux, MO, 63373. Tel: 636-753-3070. p. 1278
Jung, Jennifer, Br Mgr, Saint Charles City-County Library District, Spencer Road Branch, 427 Spencer Rd, Saint Peters, MO, 63376. Tel: 636-441-0522, 636-447-2320. p. 1278
Jung, Karen, Coord, Research & Instruction, Music & Res Librn, Bowdoin College Library, 3000 College Sta, Brunswick, ME, 04011-8421. p. 919
Jung, Karen, Coord, Research & Instruction, Music Librn, Bowdoin College Library, Beckwith Music Library, Gibson Hall, 1st Flr, 9201 College Sta, Brunswick, ME, 04011. Tel: 207-725-3311. p. 919
Jung, Kathy, Br Mgr, San Diego County Library, Rancho Santa Fe Branch, 17040 Avenida de Acacias, Rancho Santa Fe, CA, 92067. Tel: 858-756-2512. p. 217
Jung, Lucien, Libr Tech, United States Courts Library, 517 E Wisconsin Ave, Rm 516, Milwaukee, WI, 53202. Tel: 414-297-1698. p. 2461
Jung, Mike, Mgr, Electronic Res, Saint Mary's College Library, 1928 Saint Mary's Rd, Moraga, CA, 94575. Tel: 925-631-4229. p. 180
Jung, Rebecca, Adult Ref Librn, Teen Librn, Belvedere Tiburon Library, 1501 Tiburon Blvd, Tiburon, CA, 94920. Tel: 415-789-2665. p. 252
Jung, Yong Ju, Asst Prof, University of Oklahoma, Bizzell Memorial Library, 401 W Brooks, Rm 120, Norman, OK, 73019-6032. Tel: 405-325-3921. p. 2791
Jung-Mathews, Anne, Library Discipline Coord, Plymouth State University, 17 High St, Plymouth, NH, 03264. Tel: 603-535-2833. p. 1378
Jungerberg, Pamela, Acq, Ser Librn, Monterey Institute of International Studies, 425 Van Buren St, Monterey, CA, 93940. Tel: 831-647-4136. p. 179
Junius, Adrianne, Youth Serv Mgr, Hall County Library System, 127 Main St NW, Gainesville, GA, 30501-3699. Tel: 770-532-3311, Ext 126. p. 480
Junker, Dawn, Branch Services, Watonwan County Library, Darfur Branch, 200 Adrian St, Darfur, MN, 56022. Tel: 507-877-5010. p. 1198
Junkin, Marieke, South Area Libr Coord, Kawartha Lakes Public Library, 190 Kent St W, Lower Level, Lindsay, ON, K9V 2Y6, CANADA. Tel: 705-324-9411, Ext 1265. p. 2652
Jurecek, Lisa, District Librn, Salinas Alicia City of Alice Public Library, Orange Grove School & Public Library, 505 S Dibrell St, Orange Grove, TX, 78372. Tel: 361-384-2330, Ext 505, 361-384-2461. p. 2133
Jurecki, Hanna, Supvr, Ad Serv, Richardson Public Library, 2360 Campbell Creek Blvd, Ste 500, Richardson, TX, 75082. Tel: 972-744-4377. p. 2231
Jurgens, Julie, Asst Head, Youth Serv, Mount Prospect Public Library, Ten S Emerson St, Mount Prospect, IL, 60056. Tel: 847-253-5675. p. 621
Jurgensen, Jamie, Dir, Wellesley Free Library, 530 Washington St, Wellesley, MA, 02482. Tel: 781-235-1610. p. 1064
Jurgensen, Jamie, Dir, Wellesley Free Library, Fells Branch, 308 Weston Rd, Wellesley, MA, 02482. Tel: 781-235-1610, Ext 1129. p. 1064
Juriew, Dana, Libr Dir, Spring Hill Public Library, 144 Kedron Pkwy, Spring Hill, TN, 37174. Tel: 931-486-2932. p. 2127
Jurkins, Jacquelyn, Law Librn, Multnomah Law Library, County Courthouse, 4th Flr, 1021 SW Fourth Ave, Portland, OR, 97204. Tel: 503-988-3394. p. 1893
Jurnak, Matt, Librn, State Correctional Institution, 11 Fairview Dr, Waymart, PA, 18472. Tel: 570-488-5811, Ext 3459. p. 2018
Jurnak, Matthew, Asst Librn, State Correctional Institution, 660 State Rte 11, Hunlock Creek, PA, 18621. Tel: 570-735-8754. p. 1944
Jurss, Stephanie, Youth Serv Librn, South Milwaukee Public Library, 1907 Tenth Ave, South Milwaukee, WI, 53172. Tel: 414-768-8195. p. 2478
Jurusik, Christina, Librn, East Mississippi Community College, 1512 Kemper St, Scooba, MS, 39358. Tel: 662-476-5054. p. 1232
Jurusik, Christina, Pub Serv Librn, University of Mississippi, 481 Chuckie Mullins Dr, University, MS, 38677. Tel: 662-915-6824. p. 1234
Jury, Elainie, Student Success & Outreach Librn, Juniata College, 1700 Moore St, Huntingdon, PA, 16652-2119. Tel: 814-641-3449. p. 1945
Jusino, Ann, Librn, St John's University, Staten Island Campus, 300 Howard Ave, Staten Island, NY, 10301. Tel: 718-390-4359. p. 1645
Jusino, Arleyn D, Asst Librn, Pontifical Catholic University, Encarnacion Valdes Library, 2250 Avenida Las Americas, Ste 509, Ponce, PR, 00717-0777. Tel: 787-841-2000, Ext 1801, 787-841-2000, Ext 1802. p. 2512
Juskiewicz, Scott, Dir, Montana Tech Library, 1300 W Park St, Butte, MT, 59701. Tel: 406-496-4284. p. 1290
Jusseaume, Rebecca, Dir, Slater Library & Fanning Annex, 26 Main St, Jewett City, CT, 06351. Tel: 860-376-0024. p. 319
Just, Melissa, Dean, Univ Libr, University of Saskatchewan Libraries, Three Campus Dr, Saskatoon, SK, S7N 5A4, CANADA. Tel: 306-966-6094. p. 2750
Justice, Ellen, Librn, Mountain Area Health Education Center, 121 Hendersonville Rd, Asheville, NC, 28803. Tel: 828-257-4446. p. 1672
Justice, Michael, Campus Libr Dir, Southeast Kentucky Community & Technical College, Administration Bldg, 100 College Rd, Middlesboro, KY, 40965. Tel: 606-248-0442. p. 869
Justice, Mike, Campus Libr Dir, Southeast Kentucky Community & Technical College, 700 College Rd, Cumberland, KY, 40823. Tel: 606-589-3099. p. 853
Justis, Lisa S, Librn, East Mississippi Community College, Golden Triangle Campus Library, 8731 S Frontage Rd, Mayhew, MS, 39753. Tel: 662-243-1914. p. 1232
Justus, Myra, Circ Coordr, Cincinnati State Technical & Community College, 3520 Central Pkwy, Rm 170, Cincinnati, OH, 45223-2690. Tel: 513-569-4690. p. 1760
Jutkiewicz, Richard, Head Librn, Manor College, 700 Fox Chase Rd, Jenkintown, PA, 19046-3399. Tel: 215-885-5752. p. 1947
Juve, Nicole, Agr Sci Librn, North Dakota State University Libraries, 1201 Albrecht Blvd, Fargo, ND, 58108. Tel: 701-231-8879. p. 1733
Kaai, Wanjiku, Pub Serv Librn, Lakeland College Library, 5707 College Dr, Vermilion, AB, T9X 1K5, CANADA. Tel: 780-853-8731. p. 2558
Kaane, Sophia, Dr, Dir, University of Texas of the Permian Basin, 4901 E University Blvd, Odessa, TX, 79762. Tel: 432-552-2370. p. 2223
Kaas, Mary Ellen, Dir, Libr Serv, McElroy, Deutsch, Mulvaney & Carpenter, LLP, 1300 Mt Kemble Ave, Morristown, NJ, 07962. Tel: 973-425-8810. p. 1421

Kaback, Susann, Ch, Deptford Free Public Library, 670 Ward Dr, Deptford, NJ, 08096. Tel: 856-848-9149. p. 1399

Kabore, Yann, Librn, University of Alberta, Bibliotheque Saint-Jean, 8406 rue Marie-Anne Gaboury (91 St), Edmonton, AB, T6C 4G9, CANADA. Tel: 780-465-8711. p. 2537

Kaceli, Stephanie S, Dir, Cairn University, 200 Manor Ave, Langhorne, PA, 19047. Tel: 215-702-4370. p. 1952

Kachan, Asa, Chief Librn/CEO, Halifax Public Libraries, 60 Alderney Dr, Dartmouth, NS, B2Y 4P8, CANADA. Tel: 902-490-5868. p. 2617

Kachelries, Kathy, Asst Dir, Mineral County Library, 110 First St, Hawthorne, NV, 89415. Tel: 775-945-2778. p. 1345

Kaczmarek, Joanne, Interim Archivist, University of Illinois Library at Urbana-Champaign, University Archives, 146 Main Library, MC-522, 1408 W Gregory Dr, Urbana, IL, 61801. Tel: 217-333-0798. p. 656

Kaczmarek, Karen, Libr Tech, Ridgewater College Library, Two Century Ave SE, Hutchinson, MN, 55350. Tel: 320-234-8566. p. 1178

Kaczmarek, Michele, Librn, Environmental Protection Agency, 2000 Traverwood Dr, Ann Arbor, MI, 48105. Tel: 734-214-4311. p. 1079

Kaczor, Sue, Assoc Librn, Ref Librn, University at Albany, State University of New York, Science Library, 1400 Washington Ave, Albany, NY, 12222. Tel: 518-437-3948. p. 1484

Kaczorowski, Thomas, Mgr, Syst & Tech, Fordham University School of Law, 150 W 62nd St, New York, NY, 10023. Tel: 212-636-6907. p. 1585

Kaczynski, Pamela, Mgr, Ref & Tech Serv, South Kingstown Public Library, 1057 Kingstown Rd, Peace Dale, RI, 02879-2434. Tel: 401-783-4085, 401-789-1555. p. 2036

Kadam, Stephanie, Exec Dir, Stratford Historical Society Library, 967 Academy Hill, Stratford, CT, 06615. Tel: 203-378-0630. p. 340

Kadavy, Rita, Br Mgr, High Plains Library District, Riverside Library & Cultural Center, 3700 Golden St, Evans, CO, 80620. p. 285

Kading, Sue, Ch Serv, Benton Harbor Public Library, 213 E Wall St, Benton Harbor, MI, 49022-4499. Tel: 269-926-6139. p. 1084

Kadouri, Soukaina, Libr Coord, College O'Sullivan Library, 1191 de la Montagne, Montreal, QC, H3G 1Z2, CANADA. Tel: 514-866-4622, Ext 117. p. 2723

Kadzie, Mark, Mgr, Info Tech, Skokie Public Library, 5215 Oakton St, Skokie, IL, 60077-3680. Tel: 847-673-7774. p. 647

Kaempfer, Bridget, Head, Administration, Prospect Heights Public Library District, 12 N Elm St, Prospect Heights, IL, 60070-1450. Tel: 847-259-3500. p. 637

Kaeser, Michaeleen, Dir, Hillsboro Public Library, 100 W Commercial St, Hillsboro, IA, 52630. Tel: 319-253-4000. p. 758

Kaeser, Rick, ILL Coordr, Webster University, 101 Edgar Rd, Saint Louis, MO, 63119. Tel: 314-968-5994. p. 1277

Kaetz, Anna, Digital Strategy & Metadata Librn, University of Alabama at Birmingham, Reynolds-Finley Historical Library, Lister Hill Library of the Health Sciences, 1700 University Blvd, 3rd Flr, Birmingham, AL, 35233. Tel: 205-934-4475. p. 9

Kafasis, Beth Anne, Operations Adminr, Cranbury Public Library, 30 Park Place W, Cranbury, NJ, 08512. Tel: 609-799-6992. p. 1397

Kafer, Diane, Dir, Grand Junction Public Library, 106 E Main St, Grand Junction, IA, 50107. Tel: 515-738-2506. p. 755

Kafferlin, Mary, Libr Spec, University of Pittsburgh at Bradford, 300 Campus Dr, Bradford, PA, 16701. Tel: 814-362-7616. p. 1914

Kagen, Jeff, Library Contact, Madison-Old Bridge Township Historical Society, 4216 Route 516, Matawan, NJ, 07747-7032. Tel: 732-566-2108. p. 1416

Kahelin, Donna, Tech Serv Asst, Florida Southern College, 111 Lake Hollingsworth Dr, Lakeland, FL, 33801-5698. Tel: 863-680-4470. p. 417

Kahili-Heede, Melissa, Info Serv & Instrul Librn, John A Burns School of Medicine, 651 Ilalo St, MEB 101, Honolulu, HI, 96813. Tel: 808-692-0825. p. 512

Kahili-Heede, Melissa, Chair, Hawaii-Pacific Chapter of the Medical Library Association, Health Sciences Library, 651 Ilalo St MEB, Honolulu, HI, 96813. Tel: 808-692-0810. p. 2764

Kahl, Chad, Data Serv Librn, Illinois State University, Campus Box 8900, 201 N School St, Normal, IL, 61790. Tel: 309-438-3451. p. 625

Kahlden, Cindy, Libr Dir, Weimar Public Library, One Jackson Sq, Weimar, TX, 78962-2019. Tel: 979-725-6608. p. 2255

Kahler, David, Syst Librn, Pittsylvania County Public Library, 24 Military Dr, Chatham, VA, 24531. Tel: 434-432-3271. p. 2311

Kahlert, Karen, Br Mgr, Neuse Regional Library, Maysville Public Library, 601 Seventh St, Maysville, NC, 28555. Tel: 910-743-3796. p. 1699

Kahly, Jenna, Dir, West Fargo Public Library, 215 Third Street E, West Fargo, ND, 58078. Tel: 701-515-5200. p. 1741

Kahmann, Glenn, Libr Mgr, College of Lake County, 19351 W Washington St, Grayslake, IL, 60030. Tel: 847-543-2438. p. 595

Kahnhauser, Joan, Head, Adult Serv, Emma S Clark Memorial Library, 120 Main St, Setauket, NY, 11733-2868. Tel: 631-941-4080, Ext 116. p. 1640

Kahny, Donna, Dir, Osmond Public Library, 412 N State St, Osmond, NE, 68765. Tel: 402-748-3382. p. 1331

Kaida, Nancy, Ref Librn, Tech Serv Librn, Northwest Vista College, Redbud Learning Ctr, 3535 N Ellison Dr, San Antonio, TX, 78251. Tel: 210-486-4571. p. 2237

Kail, Roma, Head, Reader Serv, University of Toronto Libraries, Victoria University, E J Pratt Library, 71 Queens Park Crescent E, Toronto, ON, M5S 1K7, CANADA. Tel: 416-585-4471. p. 2700

Kaimal, Swapna, Ad, Smyrna Public Library, 100 Village Green Circle, Smyrna, GA, 30080-3478. Tel: 770-431-2860. p. 497

Kain, Peggy, Electronic Res Librn, University of Alabama at Birmingham, Mervyn H Sterne Library, 917 13th St S, Birmingham, AL, 35205. Tel: 205-934-9939. p. 9

Kaip, Sarah, Ref & Instruction Librn, South Puget Sound Community College Library, 2011 Mottman Rd SW, Olympia, WA, 98512. Tel: 360-596-5271. p. 2373

Kairis, Rob, Interim Asst Dean, Libr Dir, Kent State University Libraries, Risman Plaza, 1125 Risman Dr, Kent, OH, 44242. Tel: 330-244-3326. p. 1792

Kairis, Rob, Libr Dir, Kent State University, 6000 Frank Ave NW, North Canton, OH, 44720-7548. Tel: 330-244-3326. p. 1809

Kairush, Beth, Asst Dir, Frank Sarris Public Library, 36 N Jefferson Ave, Canonsburg, PA, 15317. Tel: 724-745-1308. p. 1918

Kaiser, Amanda, Tech Serv Mgr, St Charles Public Library District, One S Sixth Ave, Saint Charles, IL, 60174-2105. Tel: 630-584-0076, Ext 237. p. 644

Kaiser, Blanka, ILL, Alberta Government Library, Capital Blvd, 11th Flr, 10044 - 108 St, Edmonton, AB, T5J 5E6, CANADA. Tel: 780-427-2985. p. 2534

Kaiser, Josephine, Tech Serv, Whiting Public Library, 1735 Oliver St, Whiting, IN, 46394-1794. Tel: 219-473-4700, Ext 115. p. 726

Kaiser, Louella, Dir, WaKeeney Public Library, 610 Russell Ave, WaKeeney, KS, 67672. Tel: 785-743-2960. p. 841

Kaiser, Marcy, Dir, Lepper Public Library, 303 E Lincoln Way, Lisbon, OH, 44432-1400. Tel: 330-424-3117. p. 1796

Kaiser, Patricia, Asst Admin, Hudson Valley Community College, 80 Vandenburgh Ave, Troy, NY, 12180. Tel: 518-629-7333. p. 1652

Kaiser, Sandy, Youth Serv Coordr, Rutherford County Library System, Smyrna Public Library, 400 Enon Springs Rd W, Smyrna, TN, 37167. Tel: 615-459-4884. p. 2118

Kaiserski, Tom, Actg Chief, Montana Department of Commerce, 301 S Park Ave, Helena, MT, 59620. Tel: 406-841-2870. p. 1296

Kaitfors, Stephanie, Ad, Grace Balloch Memorial Library, 625 N Fifth St, Spearfish, SD, 57783. Tel: 605-642-1330. p. 2083

Kajatt, Jenny, Sr Librn, Helen B Hoffman Plantation Library, 501 N Fig Tree Lane, Plantation, FL, 33317. Tel: 954-797-2140. p. 438

Kajiwara, Robert M, Head Librn, Kauai Community College, 3-1901 Kaumualii Hwy, Lihue, HI, 96766. Tel: 808-245-8233. p. 514

Kakeh, Kariann, Communications Librn, Tech, Capital District Library Council, 28 Essex St, Albany, NY, 12206. Tel: 518-438-2500. p. 2770

Kakuske, Tina, Dir, Door County Library, 107 S Fourth Ave, Sturgeon Bay, WI, 54235. Tel: 920-743-6578. p. 2479

Kalat, Mary, Libr Tech, Michigan Department of Corrections, 1790 E Parnall Rd, Jackson, MI, 49201. Tel: 517-780-6004. p. 1120

Kalata, Tomasz, Archivist/Librn, Jozef Pilsudski Institute of America Library, 138 Greenpoint Ave, Brooklyn, NY, 11222. Tel: 212-505-9077. p. 1506

Kalavaza, Gwen, Asst Libr Mgr, Los Alamos County Library System, 2400 Central Ave, Los Alamos, NM, 87544. Tel: 505-662-8240. p. 1472

Kalavazqa, Gwen, Libr Mgr, Los Alamos County Library System, 2400 Central Ave, Los Alamos, NM, 87544. Tel: 505-662-8240. p. 1472

Kalb, Rosalind, Dir, National Multiple Sclerosis Society, 733 Third Ave, New York, NY, 10017. Tel: 212-463-7787. p. 1592

Kalchthaler, Ingrid, Youth Serv Coordr, Shaler North Hills Library, 1822 Mount Royal Blvd, Glenshaw, PA, 15116. Tel: 412-486-0211. p. 1937

Kaldan, Janina, Mgr, Morristown Medical Center, Leonard B Kahn Pavilion, Level B, 100 Madison Ave, Morristown, NJ, 07960. Tel: 973-971-8926. p. 1422

Kalet, Joseph, Dir, Fresno County Public Law Library, Fresno County Courthouse, Ste 600, 1100 Van Ness Ave, Fresno, CA, 93724. Tel: 559-600-2227. p. 145

Kalet, Joseph, Librn, San Luis Obispo County Law Library, County Government Ctr, Rm 125, 1050 Monterey St, San Luis Obispo, CA, 93408. Tel: 805-781-5855. p. 233

Kaletski-Maisel, Grace, Learning & Info Literacy Librn, Stetson University, 421 N Woodland Blvd, Unit 8418, DeLand, FL, 32723. Tel: 386-822-7190. p. 393

Kaleva, Debbie, Campus Librn, Nova Scotia Community College, Pictou Campus Library, 39 Acadia Ave, Stellarton, NS, B0K 1S0, CANADA. Tel: 902-755-7201. p. 2620

Kalfatovic, Martin, Assoc Dir, Digital Serv, Smithsonian Libraries, Natural History Bldg, Tenth St & Constitution Ave NW, Washington, DC, 20560. Tel: 202-633-1705. p. 375

Kalickstein, Edie, Head, Prog, Long Beach Public Library, 111 W Park Ave, Long Beach, NY, 11561-3326. Tel: 516-432-7201. p. 1565

Kalim, Geraldine, Instrul Serv, Ref, University of Baltimore, Law Library, Angelos Law Center, 7th thru 12th Flrs, 1401 N Charles St, Baltimore, MD, 21201. Tel: 410-837-4597. p. 957

Kalim, Geraldine, Fac Serv Librn, Ref, George Mason University Libraries, Law Library, 3301 N Fairfax Dr, Arlington, VA, 22201-4426. Tel: 703-993-8100. p. 2317

Kalin, Amelia, Dir, Valley Cottage Free Library, 110 Rte 303, Valley Cottage, NY, 10989. Tel: 845-268-7700, Ext 151. p. 1656

Kalin, Kathryn, Ser, Tech Serv, North Shore Public Library, 250 Rte 25A, Shoreham, NY, 11786-9677. Tel: 631-929-4488. p. 1641

Kalina, Kris, Ms, Med Librn, Conemaugh Memorial Medical Center, 1086 Franklin St, Johnstown, PA, 15905. Tel: 814-534-9413. p. 1947

Kalinka, George, Head, Adult/Teen Serv, Woodridge Public Library, Three Plaza Dr, Woodridge, IL, 60517-5014. Tel: 630-487-2554. p. 664

Kaliris, Michael, Res Serv Mgr, The Valentine, 1015 E Clay St, Richmond, VA, 23219-1590. Tel: 804-649-0711, Ext 342. p. 2343

Kaliss, Leigh, Outreach & Vols Coordr, Lancaster Public Library, 125 N Duke St, Lancaster, PA, 17602. Tel: 717-394-2651, Ext 101. p. 1951

Kalke, Ayla, Librn, Charles Evans Community Library, 299 Antoski Dr, Galena, AK, 99741. Tel: 907-656-1883, Ext 127. p. 46

Kalker, Felicia, Libr Instruction, Grossmont College Library, 8800 Grossmont College Dr, El Cajon, CA, 92020-1799. Tel: 619-644-7553. p. 139

Kallas, Michelle, Ch Serv, Uinta County Library, 701 Main St, Evanston, WY, 82930. Tel: 307-789-1329. p. 2494

Kallas, Nick, Exec Dir, Illinois Railway Museum, 7000 Olson Rd, Union, IL, 60180. Tel: 815-923-2020. p. 655

Kallay, Jean, Libr Dir, Bridgewater Library Association, 62 Main St S, Bridgewater, CT, 06752-9998. Tel: 860-354-6937. p. 304

Kallies, James, Sr Librn, Mohawk Correctional Facility Library, 6514 Rte 26, Rome, NY, 13442. Tel: 315-339-5232. p. 1632

Kallio, Jamie, Pub Serv Mgr, Midlothian Public Library, 14701 S Kenton Ave, Midlothian, IL, 60445-4122. Tel: 708-535-2027. p. 617

Kallista, Fay, Instructional & Student Engagement Librn, Chicago School of Professional Psychology Library, 325 N Wells St, 6th Flr, Chicago, IL, 60654. Tel: 312-467-2374. p. 558

Kallunki, Sandy, Cent Libr Mgr, Brown County Library, 515 Pine St, Green Bay, WI, 54301. Tel: 920-448-5830. p. 2438

Kallusky, Barb, Head, Pub Serv, Interim Co-Dir, Hamline University, School of Law Library, 1536 Hewitt Ave, Saint Paul, MN, 55104. Tel: 651-523-2131. p. 1199

Kalman, Jay, Dir, Putnam County Public Library District, 214 N Fourth St, Hennepin, IL, 61327. Tel: 815-925-7020. p. 598

Kalman, Sharon, Ch Serv, Paramus Public Library, 116 E Century Rd, Paramus, NJ, 07652. Tel: 201-599-1300. p. 1432

Kalmar, Miriam, Dir, Ch Serv, Stephen Wise Free Synagogue, 30 W 68th St, New York, NY, 10023. Tel: 212-877-4050, Ext 265. p. 1604

Kalonde, Gilbert, Dr, Assoc Prof, Curriculum & Instruction Program Leader, Montana State University, Department of Education, 215 Reid Hall, Bozeman, MT, 59717. Tel: 406-994-6786. p. 2788

Kalota, Emily, Teen Serv Librn, Hagaman Memorial Library, 227 Main St, East Haven, CT, 06512. Tel: 203-468-3890. p. 310

Kaloudis, Stacey, Ch Serv, Oyster Bay-East Norwich Public Library, 89 E Main St, Oyster Bay, NY, 11771. Tel: 516-922-1212. p. 1614

Kalsbeek, Katherine, Head Librn, University of British Columbia Library, Rare Books & Special Collections, Irving K Barber Learning Ctr, 1961 East Mall, Vancouver, BC, V6T 1Z1, CANADA. Tel: 604-822-2819. p. 2580

Kalstrom, Pat, Dir, Ekalaka Public Library, 105 Main St, Ekalaka, MT, 59324. Tel: 406-775-6336. p. 1292

Kaltwang, Michael, Dir, Chesterfield County Library System, 119 W Main St, Chesterfield, SC, 29709-1512. Tel: 843-623-7489. p. 2052

Kalupa, Chris, Ms, Libr Dir, Patron Serv, Berlin Public Library, 121 W Park Ave, Berlin, WI, 54923. Tel: 920-361-5420. p. 2424

Kaluzny, Kate, Photo Archivist, Virginia Museum of Fine Arts Library, 200 N Arthur Ashe Blvd, Richmond, VA, 23220-4007. Tel: 804-340-1495. p. 2344

Kalvoda, Laura, Libr Assoc, Bismarck State College Library, 1500 Edwards Ave, Bismarck, ND, 58501. Tel: 701-224-5483. p. 1729

Kalyan, Sulekha, Coll Develop, Head of Acq Serv, Librn, Seton Hall University Libraries, Walsh Library Bldg, 400 S Orange Ave, South Orange, NJ, 07079. Tel: 973-761-9438. p. 1443

Kam, D Vanessa, Univ Librn, Emily Carr University of Art & Design, 520 E First Ave, Vancouver, BC, V5T 0H2, CANADA. Tel: 604-844-3840. p. 2578

Kamalich, Michelle, Libr Tech, Woodrow Wilson International Center for Scholars Library, 1300 Pennsylvania Ave NW, Washington, DC, 20004-3027. Tel: 202-691-4150. p. 381

Kamau, Josephine, Sr Librn, California Department of Corrections Library System, North Kern State Prison, 2737 W Cecil Ave, Delano, CA, 93215. Tel: 661-721-2345, Ext 5260. p. 207

Kamber, Mike, Mgr, Info Tech, Laramie County Library System, 2200 Pioneer Ave, Cheyenne, WY, 82001-3610. Tel: 307-773-7234. p. 2492

Kambestad, Janae, Librn, Butte County Library, Chico Branch, 1108 Sherman Ave, Chico, CA, 95926-3575. Tel: 530-891-2762. p. 190

Kambitsch, Timothy, Exec Dir, Dayton Metro Library, 215 E Third St, Dayton, OH, 45402. Tel: 937-463-2665. p. 1779

Kamecke, Debra, Dir, Cairo Public Library, 15 Railroad Ave, Cairo, NY, 12413. Tel: 518-622-9864. p. 1511

Kamensky, Jane, Dir, Harvard Library, Arthur & Elizabeth Schlesinger Library on the History of Women in America, Three James St, Cambridge, MA, 02138-3766. Tel: 617-495-8647. p. 1007

Kamer, Jessica, Br Mgr, Portsmouth Public Library, Vernal G Riffe Branch, 3850 Rhodes Ave, New Boston, OH, 45662. Tel: 740-456-4412. p. 1816

Kamerei, Zary, Dir, University of Rochester, Physics-Optics-Astronomy Library - River Campus, 374 Bausch & Lomb Hall, Rochester, NY, 14627-0171. Tel: 585-275-4469. p. 1631

Kamerer, Janet, Lead Librn, Toulon Public Library District, 617 E Jefferson St, Toulon, IL, 61483. Tel: 309-286-5791. p. 654

Kamffer, Grace, Acq Librn, ILL Librn, The Master's University, 21726 W Placerita Canyon Rd, Santa Clarita, CA, 91321-1200. Tel: 661-259-3540. p. 242

Kamibayashi, Sara, Br Mgr, Hawaii State Public Library System, Naalehu Public Library, 95-5669 Mamalahoa Hwy, Naalehu, HI, 96772. Tel: 808-939-2442. p. 510

Kamilos, Charlie, Librn, George Fox University, Portland Center Library, Hampton Plaza, 12753 SW 68th Ave, Portland, OR, 97223. Tel: 503-554-6131. p. 1888

Kamimura, Tomoyo, Sr Dir, Japan Society, 333 E 47th St, New York, NY, 10017. Tel: 212-715-1269. p. 1589

Kamin, Rachel, Librn, North Suburban Synagogue Beth El, 1175 Sheridan Rd, Highland Park, IL, 60035. Tel: 847-432-8900, Ext 242. p. 599

Kaminiski, Michelle, Ch Serv, South Windsor Public Library, 1550 Sullivan Ave, South Windsor, CT, 06074. Tel: 860-644-1541. p. 337

Kaminski, Carla, Circ Supvr, Hope College, Van Wylen Library, 53 Graves Pl, Holland, MI, 49422. Tel: 616-395-7889. p. 1115

Kaminski, Christopher, Libr Asst, Yale University Library, Mathematics, Leet Oliver Memorial Hall, 12 Hillhouse Ave, New Haven, CT, 06511. Tel: 203-432-4179. p. 328

Kaminski, Michele, Ch, Granby Public Library, 15 N Granby Rd, Granby, CT, 06035. Tel: 860-844-5284. p. 313

Kaminski, Toni Ann, Librn, YA Serv, Shelter Rock Public Library, 165 Searingtown Rd, Albertson, NY, 11507. Tel: 516-248-7343. p. 1484

Kaminsky, Anne-Marie, Mgr, Libr Serv, Lawrence & Memorial Hospital, 365 Montauk Ave, New London, CT, 06320. Tel: 860-442-0711, Ext 2238. p. 329

Kaminsky, Anne-Marie, Libr Mgr, Westerly Hospital, 25 Wells St, Westerly, RI, 02891. Tel: 860-442-0711, Ext 2238. p. 2044

Kammer, Dan, Dir, Stephens College, 1200 E Broadway, Columbia, MO, 65215. Tel: 573-876-7273. p. 1243

Kammer, Jenna, Dr, Assoc Prof, Prog Coordr, University of Central Missouri, Dept of Educational Technology & Library Science, Lovinger 4101, Warrensburg, MO, 64093. Tel: 660-543-4910. p. 2787

Kammer, Julianne, Dir, Lois Wagner Memorial Library, 35200 Division Rd, Richmond, MI, 48062. Tel: 586-727-2665. p. 1144

Kammer, Sarah, Head of Public, Faculty & Student Servs, University of South Dakota, McKusick Law Library, Knudson School of Law, 414 E Clark St, Vermillion, SD, 57069-2390. Tel: 605-658-3522. p. 2084

Kammerdiner, Paul, Govt Doc Librn, Ferris State University Library, 1010 Campus Dr, Big Rapids, MI, 49307-2279. Tel: 231-591-3500. p. 1085

Kammerer, James, State Publ Librn, Montana State Library, 1515 E Sixth Ave, Helena, MT, 59620. Tel: 406-444-5432. p. 1296

Kammerer, Judith, Libr Mgr, William O Owen Medical Library, Saint Agnes Medical Ctr, 1303 E Herndon Ave, Fresno, CA, 93720. Tel: 559-450-3322. p. 147

Kammerman, Amy, Dir, Watkins College of Art & Design Library, 2298 Rosa L Parks Blvd, Nashville, TN, 37228. Tel: 615-383-4848. p. 2122

Kammeyer, Scott, Network Adminr, Pataskala Public Library, 101 S Vine St, Pataskala, OH, 43062. Tel: 740-927-9986. p. 1814

Kamoche, Njambi, Dean, William Rainey Harper College Library, 1200 W Algonguin Rd, Palatine, IL, 60067. Tel: 847-925-6584. p. 631

Kamoe, Marilyn, Pres, Library Consortium of Eastern Idaho, 110 N State, Rigby, ID, 83442-1313. Tel: 208-745-8231. p. 2764

Kamoe, Marilynn, Dir, Rigby City Library, 110 N State St, Rigby, ID, 83442. Tel: 208-745-8231. p. 529

Kamper, Kris, Library Contact, Holland Hospital, 602 Michigan Ave, 3rd Flr, Holland, MI, 49423. Tel: 616-392-5141, 616-494-4145. p. 1115

Kamphuis, Melissa, Libr Mgr, Worsley & District Public Library, Worsley Central School, 216 Alberta Ave, Worsley, AB, T0H 3W0, CANADA. Tel: 780-685-3842. p. 2560

Kamran, Sheeba, Cataloger, Alberta Teachers' Association Library, 11010 142 St, Edmonton, AB, T5N 2R1, CANADA. Tel: 780-447-9400. p. 2535

Kamtman, Jeremiah, Librn/Head, Cat, Manhattan School of Music, 130 Claremont Ave, New York, NY, 10027. Tel: 917-493-4511. p. 1590

Kamula, Jamie, Br Mgr, Idea Exchange, One North Sq, Cambridge, ON, N1S 2K6, CANADA. Tel: 519-621-0460. p. 2635

Kanaan, Jessica, Libr Supvr, Celina Public Library, 142 N Ohio St, Celina, TX, 75009. Tel: 972-382-8655. p. 2155

Kanabar, Dina, Head, Automation & Tech Serv, Head, Syst, J V Fletcher Library, 50 Main St, Westford, MA, 01886-2599. Tel: 978-399-2308. p. 1067

Kanal-Scott, Borany, Libr Tech, Harrisburg Area Community College, One HACC Dr, Harrisburg, PA, 17110-2999. Tel: 717-780-1795. p. 1940

Kande, Oumy, Library Contact, Maryland Department of Planning Library, 301 W Preston St, Rm 1101, Baltimore, MD, 21201-2365. Tel: 410-767-4500. p. 955

Kane, Andrea, Tech Serv Librn, Stillwater Public Library, 1107 S Duck St, Stillwater, OK, 74074. Tel: 405-372-3633, Ext 8121. p. 1862

Kane, Aviva, Dir, Franklin Square Public Library, 19 Lincoln Rd, Franklin Square, NY, 11010. Tel: 516-488-3444. p. 1535

Kane, Beth, Libr Dir, Norway Memorial Library, 258 Main St, Norway, ME, 04268. Tel: 207-743-5309. p. 933

Kane, Cynthia, Dir of Assessment, Emporia State University, 1200 Commercial St, Box 4051, Emporia, KS, 66801. Tel: 620-341-5480. p. 807

Kane, Heidi, Ch, Wilbraham Public Library, 25 Crane Park Dr, Wilbraham, MA, 01095-1799. Tel: 413-596-6141. p. 1069

Kane, Julie, Coll Strategist Librn, Washington & Lee University, University Library, 204 W Washington St, Lexington, VA, 24450-2116. Tel: 540-458-8643. p. 2329

Kane, Laura, Access Serv Mgr, Elmira College, One Park Pl, Elmira, NY, 14901. Tel: 607-735-1195. p. 1530

Kane, Laura, Asst Dir, Info Serv, University of South Carolina, School of Medicine Library, Bldg 101, 6311 Garners Ferry Rd, Columbia, SC, 29209. Tel: 803-216-3200. p. 2056

Kane, Mary, Dir, Katonah Village Library, 26 Bedford Rd, Katonah, NY, 10536-2121. Tel: 914-232-3508. p. 1559

Kane, Matthew, Librn, Our Lady of Guadalupe Seminary Library, 7880 W Denton Rd, Denton, NE, 68339. Tel: 402-797-7700. p. 1312

Kane, Melissa A, Dir, Cascade Public Library, 310 First Ave W, Cascade, IA, 52033. Tel: 563-852-3222. p. 737

Kane, Molly, Head, Library Systems & Building Ops, Upper Dublin Public Library, 520 Virginia Ave, Fort Washington, PA, 19034. Tel: 215-628-8744. p. 1933

Kane, Rebecca, Colls Mgr, Summit County Libraries, County Commons Bldg, 0037 Peak One Dr, Frisco, CO, 80443. Tel: 970-668-4138. p. 282

Kane, Sue, Mgr, County of Los Angeles Public Library, Alondra Library, 11949 Alondra Blvd, Norwalk, CA, 90650-7108. Tel: 562-868-7771. p. 135

Kane, Sue, Mgr, County of Los Angeles Public Library, Norwalk Library, 12350 Imperial Hwy, Norwalk, CA, 90650-3199. Tel: 562-868-0775. p. 137

Kane, Tricia, Dir, Scott County Library System, 200 N Sixth Ave, Eldridge, IA, 52748. Tel: 563-285-4794. p. 750

Kane, Tricia, Dir, Scott County Library System, Walcott Branch, 207 S Main St, Walcott, IA, 52773. Tel: 563-284-6612. p. 751

Kaneshiro, Kellie, Biomedical Librn, Indiana University, Ruth Lilly Medical Library, 975 W Walnut St, IB 100, Indianapolis, IN, 46202. Tel: 317-274-1612. p. 693

Kang, Connie, Libr Tech, Ministry of the Attorney General, Superior Law Courts, 800 Smithe St, Vancouver, BC, V6Z 2E1, CANADA. Tel: 604-660-2799. p. 2579

Kang, Lili, Librn, Paradise Valley Community College, 18401 N 32nd St, Phoenix, AZ, 85032-1200. Tel: 602-787-7209. p. 71

Kang, Mikyung, Librn, Harvard Library, Harvard-Yenching Library, Two Divinity Ave, Cambridge, MA, 02138. Tel: 617-495-2756. p. 1006

Kani, Justin, Bus Librn, Weber State University, 3921 Central Campus Dr, Dept 2901, Ogden, UT, 84408-2901. Tel: 801-626-8662. p. 2268

Kanne, Lynn, Dean, Seattle Central College, 1701 Broadway, BE Rm 2101, Seattle, WA, 98122. Tel: 206-934-4072. p. 2378

Kanne, Lynn, Dean, Libr & Learning Res, South Seattle Community College, 6000 16th Ave SW, Seattle, WA, 98106-1499. Tel: 206-764-5395. p. 2380

Kanno, Faith, Dir, Library of the Marine Corps, Gray Research Ctr, 2040 Broadway St, Quantico, VA, 22134-5107. Tel: 703-784-4409. p. 2339

Kanth, Gayathri, Mrs, Interim Dir, City of Palo Alto Library, 270 Forest Ave, Palo Alto, CA, 94301. Tel: 650-329-2668. p. 191

Kantor, Sarah, Studio Librarian, University of Tennessee at Chattanooga Library, 400 Douglas Ave, Dept 6456, Chattanooga, TN, 37403-2598. Tel: 423-425-4501. p. 2092

Kanyo, Jennifer, Senior Dir, Museums & Education, Midland County Historical Society, 1801 W St Andrews Rd, Midland, MI, 48640. Tel: 989-631-5930, Ext 1306. p. 1132

Kapeller, Colleen, Br Librn, Wapiti Regional Library, Mistatim Public Library, Old School Bldg, Railway Ave, Mistatim, SK, S0E 1B0, CANADA. Tel: 306-889-2008. p. 2746

Kapetanov, Marko, Asst Librn, New Gracanica Monastery, 35240 W Grant Ave, Third Lake, IL, 60046. Tel: 847-223-4300, Ext 6. p. 653

Kaplan, Amy, Ch, Teen Librn, Briarcliff Manor Public Library, One Library Rd, Briarcliff Manor, NY, 10510. Tel: 914-941-7072. p. 1496

Kaplan, Janie, Dir, Northern Westchester Hospital, Wallace Pavilion, 1st Flr, 400 E Main St, Mount Kisco, NY, 10549-0802. Tel: 914-666-1259. p. 1574

Kaplan, Mark, Br Mgr, Chicago Public Library, Bezazian, 1226 W Ainslie St, Chicago, IL, 60640. Tel: 312-744-0019. p. 556

Kaplan, Richard, Dean, Libr & Learning Res, Dir of Libr, Massachusetts College of Pharmacy & Health Sciences, Matricaria Bldg, 2nd Flr, 179 Longwood Ave, Boston, MA, 02115. Tel: 617-732-2808. p. 997

Kapoor, Kanta, Interim Chief Librn, Mgr, Support Serv, Milton Public Library, 1010 Main St E, Milton, ON, L9T 6H7, CANADA. Tel: 905-875-2665, Ext 3259. p. 2658

Kapoun, Jim, Libr Dir, York College of Pennsylvania, 441 Country Club Rd, York, PA, 17403-3651. Tel: 717-815-1353. p. 2026

Kappanadze, Margaret, Libr Dir, Elmira College, One Park Pl, Elmira, NY, 14901. Tel: 607-735-1867. p. 1530

Kapranos, Aubrey, Tech Serv Librn, Lamar State College Orange Library, 410 Front St, Orange, TX, 77630-5796. Tel: 409-882-3953. p. 2224

Kaps, Thomas, Operations Mgr, Stanislaus County Library, 1500 I St, Modesto, CA, 95354-1166. Tel: 209-558-7800. p. 178

Kapsos, Leigh, Libr Dir, Grapevine Public Library, 1201 Municipal Way, Grapevine, TX, 76051. Tel: 817-410-3405. p. 2186

Kapteyn, Paula, Access Serv Mgr, California State University, East Bay Library, CSU East Bay Library, 25800 Carlos Bee Blvd, Hayward, CA, 94542-3052. Tel: 510-885-4905. p. 150

Kapture, Lawrence, Head, Adult Serv, Portage District Library, 300 Library Lane, Portage, MI, 49002. Tel: 269-329-4542, Ext 710. p. 1143

Kapungu, Priscilla, Libr Spec, Gateway Community & Technical College, Boone Campus Library, 500 Technology Way, Rm B09, Florence, KY, 41042. Tel: 859-442-1682. p. 854

Karageorge, Elizabeth, Adult Serv, Cumberland Public Library, 1464 Diamond Hill Rd, Cumberland, RI, 02864-5510. Tel: 401-333-2552. p. 2031

Karain, Catherine, Access Serv Tech-Reserves, Washtenaw Community College, 4800 E Huron River Dr, Ann Arbor, MI, 48105-4800. Tel: 734-477-8709. p. 1081

Karam, Nicole, Ser, Community College of Philadelphia Library, Mint Bldg, Level 1, 1700 Spring Garden St, Philadelphia, PA, 19130. Tel: 215-751-8388. p. 1975

Karami, Amir, PhD, Asst Prof, University of South Carolina, 1501 Greene St, Columbia, SC, 29208. Tel: 803-777-3858. p. 2792

Karampelas, Gabrielle, Dir, Communications & Develop, Stanford University Libraries, 557 Escondido Mall, Stanford, CA, 94305-6063. Tel: 650-725-1064. p. 248

Karas, Heather, Librn, Saint Mary's School for the Deaf Library, 2253 Main St, Buffalo, NY, 14214. Tel: 716-834-7200, Ext 152. p. 1510

Karas, Laura, Pub Serv Librn, University of South Carolina Upstate Library, 800 University Way, Spartanburg, SC, 29303. Tel: 864-503-5637. p. 2070

Karas, Sue, Emerging Technologies Adminr, Naperville Public Library, 95th Street, 3015 Cedar Glade Dr, Naperville, IL, 60564. Tel: 630-961-4100, Ext 4981. p. 623

Karass, Alan C, Dean, Libr Serv, Columbus State University Libraries, 4225 University Ave, Columbus, GA, 31907. Tel: 706-507-8670. p. 472

Kardin, Dorrie, Ch Serv, Woburn Public Library, 36 Cummings Park, Woburn, MA, 01801. Tel: 781-933-0148. p. 1070

Karel, Thomas A, Assoc Librn, Coll Mgt, Franklin & Marshall College, 450 College Ave, Lancaster, PA, 17604. Tel: 717-358-3845. p. 1950

Karels, Robert, Electronic Res Librn, University of Wisconsin Oshkosh, 801 Elmwood Ave, Oshkosh, WI, 54901. Tel: 920-424-0371. p. 2467

Karen, Daniel, Director, Admin, ProConsort, 118 N Bedford Rd, Ste 100, Mount Kisco, NY, 10549. p. 2771

Karen, Hayward, Librn, SSG Paul D Savanuck Memorial Library, Defense Information School (DINFOS), 6500 Mapes Rd, Ste 5620, Fort George G Meade, MD, 20755-5620. Tel: 301-677-4692. p. 965

Karen, Merritt, Librn, Public Library of Steubenville & Jefferson County, Tiltonsville Branch, 702 Walden Ave, Tiltonsville, OH, 43963. Tel: 740-859-5163. p. 1822

Kargut, Sigrid, Liaison Librn, Kwantlen Polytechnic University Library, 12666 72nd Ave, Surrey, BC, V3W 2M8, CANADA. Tel: 604-599-2378. p. 2576

Karhoff, Brent, Pres, Knox County Historical Society & Museum Library, 408 E Lafayette St, Edina, MO, 63537. p. 1245

Karim, Kim, Libr Serv Spec, Libr Tech, Lycoming College, One College Pl, Williamsport, PA, 17701. Tel: 570-321-4123. p. 2023

Karim, Lisa, Dir, Simsbury Public Library, 725 Hopmeadow St, Simsbury, CT, 06070. Tel: 860-658-7663. p. 336

Karim, Parveen, Asst Dir, Carroll Public Library, 118 E Fifth St, Carroll, IA, 51401. Tel: 712-792-3432. p. 737

Karim-Cooper, Farah, Dr, Dir, Folger Shakespeare Library, 201 E Capitol St SE, Washington, DC, 20003-1094. Tel: 202-544-4600. p. 366

Karki, Maya, Circ Mgr, George Mason University Libraries, Law Library, 3301 N Fairfax Dr, Arlington, VA, 22201-4426. Tel: 703-993-8100. p. 2317

Karkoff, Liz, Ch Serv, Harrison Public Library, West Harrison Branch, Two E Madison St, West Harrison, NY, 10604. Tel: 914-948-2092. p. 1544

Karl, Trina, Libr Dir, Canton Public Library, 403 Lewis St, Canton, MO, 63435. Tel: 573-288-5279. p. 1240

Karl-Johnson, Gabriella, Librn, Princeton University, Architecture Library, Architecture Bldg, 2nd Flr, S-204, Princeton, NJ, 08544. Tel: 609-258-3128. p. 1437

Karle, Lisa, Circ, Saint Mary's College, Notre Dame, IN, 46556-5001. Tel: 574-284-5396. p. 711

Karlin, Dorrie, Br Mgr, Concord Free Public Library, Fowler Memorial, 1322 Main St, Concord, MA, 01742. Tel: 978-318-3350. p. 1012

Karlin, Ron, Bibliog Instr, Electronic Res, College of the Canyons Library, 26455 Rockwell Canyon Rd, Santa Clarita, CA, 91355-1899. Tel: 661-362-3358. p. 242

Karlin, Tricia, Coll, Tech Mgr, Lawrence Public Library, 707 Vermont St, Lawrence, KS, 66044-2371. Tel: 785-843-3833, Ext 109. p. 819

Karlinchak, Stephen, Head Librn, Pittsburgh Post Gazette, 358 N Shore Dr, Pittsburgh, PA, 15212. Tel: 412-263-2585. p. 1995

Karlovski, Alex, Librn, Newmarket Public Library, 438 Park Ave, Newmarket, ON, L3Y 1W1, CANADA. Tel: 905-953-5110. p. 2660
Karlovsky, Victoria, Adult Services Outreach Assoc, Deerfield Public Library, 920 Waukegan Rd, Deerfield, IL, 60015. Tel: 847-945-3311. p. 577
Karlsberger, Mindy, Br Mgr, Flagstaff City-Coconino County Public Library System, Grand Canyon-Tusayan Community Library, 11 Navajo St, Grand Canyon, AZ, 86023. Tel: 928-638-2718. p. 60
Karlson, Rochel, Dir, Glenwood City Public Library, 217 W Oak St, Glenwood City, WI, 54013-8554. Tel: 715-265-7443. p. 2437
Karlson, Steve, Br Librn, East Central Regional Library, Princeton Area Library, 100 Fourth Ave S, Princeton, MN, 55371. Tel: 763-389-3753. p. 1168
Karlson, Steve, Br Librn, East Central Regional Library, Wyoming Area Giese Memorial Library, 26855 Forest Blvd, Wyoming, MN, 55092. Tel: 651-462-9001. p. 1168
Karn, Amy, Dir, Spencer Stuart Library, 353 N Clark, Ste 2400, Chicago, IL, 60654. Tel: 312-822-0088. p. 568
Karnes, Cara, Br Mgr, Athens Regional Library System, Oconee County-Watkinsville Branch, 1080 Experiment Station Rd, Watkinsville, GA, 30677. Tel: 706-769-3951. p. 458
Karnes, Kimberly, Dir, Saint Elmo Public Library District, 311 W Cumberland Rd, Saint Elmo, IL, 62458. Tel: 618-829-5544. p. 644
Karnes, Sarah J, Dir, Libr Develop & Networking, Texas State Library & Archives Commission, 1201 Brazos St, Austin, TX, 78701. Tel: 545-651-2463. p. 2141
Karnib, Nidaa, Head, Archives & Patient Info, Donald Berman Maimonides, 5795 Caldwell Ave, Montreal, QC, H4W 1W3, CANADA. Tel: 514-483-2121, Ext 2299. p. 2717
Karnik, Shilpa, Dir, Strategic Projects & Applied Info Tech, St John's University Library, St Augustine Hall, 8000 Utopia Pkwy, Jamaica, NY, 11439. Tel: 718-990-5819. p. 1556
Karno, Valerie, Assoc Prof, Prog Dir, University of Rhode Island, Rodman Hall, 94 W Alumni Ave, Kingston, RI, 02881-0815. Tel: 401-874-2878, 401-874-2947. p. 2792
Karns, Denise, Dir, Norris City Memorial Public Library District, 603 S Division St, Norris City, IL, 62869. Tel: 618-378-3713. p. 625
Karp, Kari, Teen Serv, West Hartford Public Library, 20 S Main St, West Hartford, CT, 06107-2432. Tel: 860-561-6950. p. 345
Karp, Susan, Libr Asst, Woodstock Theological Center Library, Georgetown University, Lauinger Library, PO Box 571170, Washington, DC, 20057-1170. Tel: 202-687-7513. p. 381
Karpen, Pat, Asst Librn, Caribou Public Library, 30 High St, Caribou, ME, 04736. Tel: 207-493-4214. p. 920
Karpinski, Robert D, Assoc VP for Academic & Library Affairs, DePaul University Libraries, 2350 N Kenmore, Chicago, IL, 60614. Tel: 773-325-7862, 773-325-7863. p. 560
Karpinski, Sarah, Libr Asst, Lyme Public Library, 482 Hamburg Rd, Lyme, CT, 06371-3110. Tel: 860-434-2272. p. 320
Karpowich, Karen, Exec Dir, English-Speaking Union, 144 E 39th St, New York, NY, 10016. Tel: 212-818-1200, Ext 222. p. 1585
Karpuk, Susan, Librn, Rocky Hill Historical Society Library, 785 Old Main St, Rocky Hill, CT, 06067. Tel: 860-563-6704. p. 335
Karr, Anne, Asst Dir, Boulder City Library, 701 Adams Blvd, Boulder City, NV, 89005-2207. Tel: 702-293-1281. p. 1343
Karr, Clifton, Librn, Mount Olive Correctional Complex Library, One Mountainside Way, Mount Olive, WV, 25185. Tel: 304-442-7213. p. 2410
Karr, Elizabeth, Libr Mgr, San Mateo County Library, Millbrae Library, One Library Ave, Millbrae, CA, 94030. Tel: 650-697-7607, Ext 227. p. 235
Karr, Enid, Sr Res Librn, Boston College Libraries, Catherine B O'Connor Library, Weston Observatory, 381 Concord Rd, Weston, MA, 02193-1340. Tel: 617-552-4477. p. 1011
Karr Gerlich, Bella, Dean of Libr, Curtis Laws Wilson Library, 400 W 14th St, Rolla, MO, 65409-0060. Tel: 573-341-4118. p. 1268
Karr, Holly, Librn, Itawamba Community College, 602 W Hill St, Fulton, MS, 38843. Tel: 662-862-8378. p. 1216
Karr, Kelly, Br Mgr, Grand Rapids Public Library, West Leonard Branch, 1017 Leonard St NW, Grand Rapids, MI, 49504. Tel: 616-988-5416. p. 1111
Karr Schmidt, Suzanne, Curator of Rare Bks & Ms, Newberry Library, 60 W Walton St, Chicago, IL, 60610-3305. Tel: 312-255-3645. p. 565
Karr, Tamara, Dir & Librn, Andrews University, Architectural Resource Center, 8435 E Campus Circle Dr, Berrien Springs, MI, 49104-0450. Tel: 269-471-3027. p. 1085
Karren, Susan, Dir, National Archives & Records Administration, 6125 Sand Point Way NE, Seattle, WA, 98115-7999. Tel: 206-336-5141. p. 2377
Karshmer, Elana, Bibliog Instr, Head, Ref Serv, Florida International University, 11200 SW Eighth St, Miami, FL, 33199. Tel: 305-348-1843. p. 421
Karshner, Beth, Dir, Belle Center Free Public Library, 103 S Elizabeth St, Belle Center, OH, 43310. Tel: 937-464-3611. p. 1750
Karsjens, Alexis, Dir, Aplington Legion Memorial Library, 929 Parrot St, Aplington, IA, 50604. Tel: 319-347-2432. p. 732
Karstadt, Bruce N, Chief Exec Officer, Pres, American Swedish Institute, 2600 Park Ave, Minneapolis, MN, 55407. Tel: 612-871-4907. p. 1182
Karsten, Eileen, Cat & Acq, Lake Forest College, 555 N Sheridan Rd, Lake Forest, IL, 60045. Tel: 847-735-5066. p. 606
Karsten, Michael, ILL Coordr, Lake Forest College, 555 N Sheridan Rd, Lake Forest, IL, 60045. Tel: 847-735-5062. p. 606
Kasacavage, Karen, Dir, Woodford County Library, 115 N Main St, Versailles, KY, 40383-1289. Tel: 859-873-5191. p. 876
Kasak, Laura, Br Mgr, Saint Louis County Library, Daniel Boone Branch, 300 Clarkson Rd, Ellisville, MO, 63011-2222. Tel: 314-994-3300, Ext 3100. p. 1273
Kasbohm, Kristine E, Libr Dir, Canisius College, 2001 Main St, Buffalo, NY, 14208-1098. Tel: 716-888-8410. p. 1509
Kaseem, Kimberly, Research Librn, Sullivan & Cromwell LLP, 1700 New York Ave NW, Ste 700, Washington, DC, 20006-5215. Tel: 202-956-7500. p. 376
Kaser, Gretchen, Dir, Worth Pinkham Memorial Library, 91 Warren Ave, Ho-Ho-Kus, NJ, 07423. Tel: 201-445-8078. p. 1408
Kash, Stephany, Librn, Oklahoma Department of Corrections, Dr Eddie Warrior Leisure Library, 400 N Oak St, Taft, OK, 74463. Tel: 918-683-8365. p. 1863
Kashman, Joyce, Librn, Department of Community Services, Government of Yukon, 1171 First Ave, Whitehorse, YT, Y1A 0G9, CANADA. Tel: 867-332-0970. p. 2757
Kasianovitz, Kris, Libr Dir, University of California, Berkeley, Institute of Governmental Studies, 109 Philosophy Hall, Ground Flr, Berkeley, CA, 94720-2370. Tel: 510-643-6429. p. 123
Kasindorf, Deborah, Exec Dir, Evanston History Center Library & Archives, 225 Greenwood St, Evanston, IL, 60201. Tel: 847-475-3410. p. 586
Kaskey, Sid, Res Asst, Stearns, Weaver, Miller, Weissler, Alhadeff & Sitterson, 2200 Museum Tower, 150 W Flagler St, Miami, FL, 33130. Tel: 305-789-3250. p. 425
Kasmier, Martha, Ch Serv, Bolivar-Harpers Ferry Public Library, 151 Polk St, Harpers Ferry, WV, 25425. Tel: 304-535-2301. p. 2403
Kasper, Barbara, Dr, Librn, Miami Correctional Facility, Phase II Library, 3038 W 850 S, Bunker Hill, IN, 46914. Tel: 765-689-8920. p. 673
Kasperek, Sheila M, Electronic Serv, Ref, Mansfield University, Five Swan St, Mansfield, PA, 16933. Tel: 570-662-4675. p. 1957
Kasperick, Carrie, Youth Serv Librn, Monmouth Public Library, 168 S Ecols St, Monmouth, OR, 97361. Tel: 503-838-1932. p. 1887
Kassebaum, Judy, Asst Librn, Hebron Secrest Library, 146 N Fourth St, Hebron, NE, 68370. Tel: 402-768-6701. p. 1318
Kassel, Karen, Libr Asst, Bacon Free Library, 58 Eliot St, Natick, MA, 01760. Tel: 508-653-6730. p. 1037
Kassel, Urszula, Libr Serv Spec, Davenport University, 6191 Kraft Ave SE, Grand Rapids, MI, 49512. Tel: 616-554-5664. p. 1110
Kassian, Jo Anne, Colls Mgr, Belen Public Library, 333 Becker Ave, Belen, NM, 87002. Tel: 505 966 2605. p. 1464
Kasten, Rebecca, Head, Youth Serv, Concord Public Library, 45 Green St, Concord, NH, 03301. Tel: 603-230-3688. p. 1358
Kastens, Grace, Librn, Atwood Public Library, 102 S Sixth St, Atwood, KS, 67730-1998. Tel: 785-626-3805. p. 797
Kastigar, Amy, Dir, Ohio County Public Library, 52 16th St, Wheeling, WV, 26003. Tel: 304-232-0244. p. 2417
Kasum, Luba, Campus Librn, Coast Mountain College Library, 5331 McConnell Ave, Terrace, BC, V8G 4X2, CANADA. Tel: 250-638-5407. p. 2577
Kaszyski, Melissa, Br Mgr, Chicago Public Library, Dunning, 7455 W Cornelia Ave, Chicago, IL, 60634. Tel: 312-743-0480. p. 556
Kaszyski, Melissa, Br Mgr, Chicago Public Library, Galewood-Mont Clare, 6871 W Belden Ave, Chicago, IL, 60707. Tel: 312-746-0165. p. 556
Katafiasz, Carl, Head, Adult Serv, Livonia Public Library, Civic Center, 32777 Five Mile Rd, Livonia, MI, 48154-3045. Tel: 734-466-2450. p. 1127
Katerberg, William, Dr, Curator of Archives, Calvin University & Calvin Theological Seminary, 1855 Knollcrest Circle SE, Grand Rapids, MI, 49546-4402. Tel: 616-526-6916. p. 1110
Kathleen, Campana, Asst Prof, Kent State University, 314 University Library, 1125 Risman Dr, Kent, OH, 44242-0001. Tel: 330-672-2782. p. 2790
Kathleen, Slocum, Accessible Library Services Mgr, South Dakota State Library, 800 Governors Dr, Pierre, SD, 57501-2294. Tel: 605-773-3131. p. 2080
Katouzian, Azar, Adult Serv, Principal Librn, Escondido Public Library, 239 S Kalmia St, Escondido, CA, 92025. Tel: 760-839-4839. p. 141
Katsioloudis, Petros, Chair, Old Dominion University, Darden College of Education, Education Bldg-4101-A, 4301 Hampton Blvd, Norfolk, VA, 23529. Tel: 757-683-4305. p. 2794
Katsion, Jason, Adult & Teen Serv Mgr, Fox River Valley Public Library District, 555 Barrington Ave, East Dundee, IL, 60118-1496. Tel: 847-428-3661. p. 580
Katsune, Joanna, Librn, Temple Beth El, Congegation Sons of Israel & David, 70 Orchard Ave, Providence, RI, 02906. Tel: 401-331-6070. p. 2041
Kattelman, Beth, Assoc Curator, Ohio State University LIBRARIES, Jerome Lawrence & Robert E Lee Theatre Research Institute, 1430 Lincoln Tower, 1800 Cannon Dr, Columbus, OH, 43210-1230. Tel: 614-292-6614. p. 1775
Katten, Beth, Librn, Emanuel Synagogue Library, 160 Mohegan Dr, West Hartford, CT, 06117. Tel: 860-236-1275, Ext 124. p. 345
Katterjohn, Brandi, Dir, Arkansas State University Mid-South, Donald W Reynolds Ctr, 2000 W Broadway, West Memphis, AR, 72301-3829. Tel: 870-733-6769. p. 112

Katz, Charna, Dir, Bolsters Mills Village Library, 659 Bolsters Mills Rd, Harrison, ME, 04040-6827. Tel: 207-583-6421. p. 927
Katz, Linda, Exec Dir, Temple Sinai Library, 50 Sewall Ave, Brookline, MA, 02446. Tel: 617-277-5888. p. 1003
Katz, Linda M, Assoc Dir, Health Sci Libr, Drexel University Libraries, Hahnemann Library, 245 N 15th St MS 449, Philadelphia, PA, 19102-1192. Tel: 215-762-7632. p. 1976
Katz, Liza, Ref Librn, Center for Brooklyn History, 128 Pierrepont St, Brooklyn, NY, 11201. Tel: 347-381-3708, 718-222-4111. p. 1504
Katz, Nicole, Archivist, Librn II, New Mexico Military Institute, Toles Learning Ctr, 101 W College Blvd, Roswell, NM, 88201. Tel: 575-624-8382. p. 1474
Katz, Sarah, Librn, Louisiana House of Representatives, 900 N Third St, Baton Rouge, LA, 70804. Tel: 225-342-5129. p. 883
Katzen, Krista, Asst Dir, Oswego Public Library District, Oswego Campus, 32 W Jefferson St, Oswego, IL, 60543. Tel: 630-978-1037. p. 630
Katzenberger, William, Librn, Patuxent Institution Library, 7555 Waterloo Rd, Jessup, MD, 20794. Tel: 410-799-3400, Ext 4226. p. 969
Katzin, Sheryl, Assoc Dir, Coll, District of Columbia Public Library, 1990 K St NW, Washington, DC, 20006. Tel: 202-727-1101. p. 363
Katzman, Dexter, Libr Mgr, San Antonio Public Library, Guerra, 7978 W Military Dr, San Antonio, TX, 78227. Tel: 210-207-9070. p. 2239
Kauczka, Beth, Adult Serv, Portland Library, 20 Freestone Ave, Portland, CT, 06480. Tel: 860-342-6770. p. 334
Kauffman, Becky J, Curator, Craft Memorial Library, 600 Commerce St, Bluefield, WV, 24701. Tel: 304-325-3943. p. 2398
Kauffman, Bethany, Libr Asst, Desoto Parish Library, 109 Crosby St, Mansfield, LA, 71052. Tel: 318-872-6100. p. 895
Kauffman, Kenneth, Cat Spec, Rider University, Katharine Houk Talbott Library, Franklin F Moore Library Bldg, 3rd & 4th Flrs, 2083 Lawrenceville Rd, Lawrenceville, NJ, 08648. Tel: 609-921-7100, Ext 8338. p. 1412
Kauffman, Laura C, Ch, Exeter Community Library, 4569 Prestwick Dr, Reading, PA, 19606. Tel: 610-406-9431. p. 2000
Kauffman, Linda, Librn, Iosco-Arenac District Library, Au Gres Community, 230 N MacKinaw, Au Gres, MI, 48703. Tel: 989-876-8818. p. 1102
Kauffman, Lucine, Library Visits Coord, Richmond Memorial Library, 19 Ross St, Batavia, NY, 14020. Tel: 585-343-9550. p. 1491
Kauffman, Shelli, Head, Adult Serv, Bremen Public Library, 304 N Jackson St, Bremen, IN, 46506. Tel: 574-546-2849. p. 672
Kauffmann, Brianne, Librn, Mohall Public Library, 115 W Main, Mohall, ND, 58761. Tel: 701-756-7242. p. 1738
Kaufman, Amy, Head Law Librn, Queen's University, Lederman Law Library, Law Bldg, 128 Union St, Kingston, ON, K7L 3N6, CANADA. Tel: 613-533-2843. p. 2651
Kaufman, Cate, Libr Serv Dir, Illinois Central College, Kenneth L Edward Library Administration Bldgs, L312, One College Dr, East Peoria, IL, 61635-0001. Tel: 309-694-8504. p. 581
Kaufman, Karla C, Chief, Corporal Michael J Crescenz VA Medical Center, 3900 Woodland Ave, Philadelphia, PA, 19104. Tel: 215-823-5860. p. 1975
Kaufman, Kimberly, Acq/Ser Librn, Geneva College, 3200 College Ave, Beaver Falls, PA, 15010-3599. Tel: 724-847-6563. p. 1909
Kaufman, LeAnn L, Libr Dir, Freeman Public Library, 322 S Main St, Freeman, SD, 57029. Tel: 605-925-7003. p. 2076
Kaufman, Pamela, Law Librn II, Connecticut Judicial Branch Law Libraries, Stamford Law Library, Stamford Courthouse, 123 Hoyt St, Stamford, CT, 06905. Tel: 203-965-5377. p. 316
Kaufmann, Chris, Tech Serv, Yarmouth Town Libraries, 312 Old Main St, South Yarmouth, MA, 02664. Tel: 508-760-4820, Ext 1315. p. 1055
Kaufmann, Linda, Library Contact, Del Norte County Library District, Smith River Branch, 241 First St, Smith River, CA, 95567. Tel: 707-487-8048. p. 133
Kaufmann, Shoshana, Assoc Librn, Queens College, Benjamin S Rosenthal Library, 65-30 Kissena Blvd, Flushing, NY, 11367-0904. Tel: 718-997-3700. p. 1533
Kaufmann, Thomas, Spec Coll, Tuskegee University, 1200 W Old Mongtomery Rd, Ford Motor Company Library, Tuskegee, AL, 36088. Tel: 334-727-8890. p. 38
Kaul, Judy, Electronic Res, Case Western Reserve University, School of Law Library, 11075 East Blvd, Cleveland, OH, 44106-7148. Tel: 216-368-8570. p. 1766
Kaune, Elisabeth, Head, Cataloging & Metadata, Marquette University, 1355 W Wisconsin Ave, Milwaukee, WI, 53233. Tel: 414-288-3671. p. 2458
Kaus, Nancy, Libr Asst, Hillsboro Public Library, 819 High Ave, Hillsboro, WI, 54634. Tel: 608-489-2192. p. 2441
Kaus, Virginia, Ch, Rawlins Municipal Library, 1000 E Church St, Pierre, SD, 57501. Tel: 605-773-7421. p. 2080
Kautzman, Amy, Dean, Univ Libr, California State University, Sacramento, 6000 J St, Sacramento, CA, 95819-6039. Tel: 916-278-6708. p. 208
Kauwenberg-Marsnik, Adam, Cat, Chair, Normandale Community College Library, 9700 France Ave S, Bloomington, MN, 55431. Tel: 952-487-8297. p. 1166
Kavaler, Ethan Matt, Dir, University of Toronto Libraries, Victoria University, Centre for Reformation & Renaissance Studies, Victoria University, E J Pratt Library, Rm 301, 71 Queen's Park Crescent E, Toronto, ON, M5S 1K7, CANADA. Tel: 416-585-4461. p. 2700
Kavanaugh, Kris, Associate VP, Admin, Finance & Human Resources, Columbia University, Butler Library, 535 W 114th St, New York, NY, 10027. Tel: 212-854-7309. p. 1582
Kavanaugh, Michelle, Head, Res Ctr, Indiana Chamber of Commerce, 115 W Washington St S, Ste 850, Indianapolis, IN, 46204-3497. Tel: 317-264-3110. p. 692
Kavanaugh, Tammy, Libr Asst, Renison University College Library, 240 Westmount Rd N, Waterloo, ON, N2L 3G4, CANADA. Tel: 519-884-4404, Ext 28646. p. 2702
Kavich, Ted, Div Dir, Admin Serv, Fairfax County Public Library, 12000 Government Center Pkwy, Ste 324, Fairfax, VA, 22035-0012. Tel: 703-324-3100. p. 2316
Kawahara, Lani, Br Mgr, Hawaii State Public Library System, Kapaa Public Library, 4-1464 Kuhio Hwy, Kapaa, HI, 96746. Tel: 808-821-4422. p. 508
Kawooya, Dick, PhD, Assoc Prof, University of South Carolina, 1501 Greene St, Columbia, SC, 29208. Tel: 803-777-3858. p. 2792
Kay, Alaine, Ref & Instruction Librn, Muskingum University, Ten College Dr, New Concord, OH, 43762. Tel: 740-826-8157. p. 1806
Kay, Amy, Br Mgr, Lennox & Addington County Public Library, Amherstview Branch, 322 Amherst Dr, Amherstview, ON, K7N 1S9, CANADA. Tel: 613-389-6006. p. 2660
Kay, Jean, Ref Librn, Historical Society of Quincy & Adams County Library, 425 S 12th St, Quincy, IL, 62301. Tel: 217-222-1835. p. 637
Kay, Michelle, Head Librn, Goethe-Institut Toronto Library, North Tower, 100 University Ave, Ste 201, Toronto, ON, M5J 1V6, CANADA. Tel: 416-593-5257, Ext 208. p. 2689
Kayacan, Laura, Ad, Door County Library, 107 S Fourth Ave, Sturgeon Bay, WI, 54235. Tel: 920-746-7121. p. 2479
Kayacan, Laura, Adult Serv, Door County Library, Sturgeon Bay Branch, 107 S Fourth Ave, Sturgeon Bay, WI, 54235. p. 2480
Kaye, Darcy, Info Literacy/Instrul Tech Librn, Iona University, 715 North Ave, New Rochelle, NY, 10801-1890. Tel: 914-633-2227. p. 1577
Kaye, Dina, Head, Coll, University of Wisconsin-Parkside Library, 900 Wood Rd, Kenosha, WI, 53141. Tel: 262-595-3432. p. 2445
Kayler, Grant, Pub Serv, University of Alberta, John Alexander Weir Memorial Law Library, Law Ctr, 111 St & 89 Ave, Edmonton, AB, T6G 2H5, CANADA. Tel: 780-492-3371. p. 2538
Kaylo, Susen, Asst Librn, Prescott Public Library, 360 Dibble St W, Prescott, ON, K0E 1T0, CANADA. Tel: 613-925-4340. p. 2675
Kaylor, Jane, Ref Serv Supvr, Gaston County Public Library, 1555 E Garrison Blvd, Gastonia, NC, 28054. Tel: 704-868-2164. p. 1690
Kays, Jeannie, Dir, Libr Serv, Palm Springs Public Library, 300 S Sunrise Way, Palm Springs, CA, 92262-7699. Tel: 760-322-7323. p. 191
Kays, Maureen T, Dir, Bond, Schoeneck & King, PLLC, One Lincoln Ctr, 110 W Fayette St, Syracuse, NY, 13202-1355. Tel: 315-218-8000. p. 1648
Kayworth, Billie, Libr Asst, Webber International University, 1201 N Scenic Hwy, Babson Park, FL, 33827. Tel: 863-638-1431, Ext 3001. p. 384
Kazakoff-Lane, Carmen, Scholarly Communications Librn, Brandon University, 270 18th St, Brandon, MB, R7A 6A9, CANADA. Tel: 204-727-7483. p. 2585
Kazalia, John, Ad, Southwest Public Libraries, Westland Area Library, 4740 W Broad St, Columbus, OH, 43228. Tel: 614-878-1301. p. 1789
Kazen, Caryl, Chief Librn, Department of Veterans Affairs, Central Office Library, 810 Vermont Ave NW, Washington, DC, 20420. Tel: 202-273-8523. p. 363
Kazin, Jeff, Access Serv Mgr, Keene State College, 229 Main St, Keene, NH, 03435-3201. Tel: 603-358-2782. p. 1369
Kazlauskas, Kate, Ref/Info Tech Serv Librn, Ames Free Library, 53 Main St, North Easton, MA, 02356. Tel: 508-238-2000. p. 1041
Kazmer, Melissa, Asst Dir, Head, Adult Serv, Neenah Public Library, 240 E Wisconsin Ave, Neenah, WI, 54956. Tel: 920-886-6315. p. 2463
Kazzi, Karen, ILL, Ridgefield Library Association Inc, 472 Main St, Ridgefield, CT, 06877-4585. Tel: 203-438-2282. p. 335
Keach, Jennifer, Coord of Organizational Learning & Dev, James Madison University Libraries, 880 Madison Dr, MSC 1704, Harrisonburg, VA, 22807. Tel: 540-568-8749. p. 2324
Keagle, Jennifer, Coll Develop, Louisburg Public Library, 206 S Broadway, Louisburg, KS, 66053. Tel: 913-837-2217. p. 822
Keagle, Matthew, Curator, Fort Ticonderoga Museum, 30 Fort Ti Rd, Ticonderoga, NY, 12883. Tel: 518-585-2821. p. 1651
Kealoha, Carole, Sr Librn, Los Angeles Public Library System, Mar Vista Branch Library, 12006 Venice Blvd, Los Angeles, CA, 90066-3810. Tel: 310-390-3454. p. 164
Keammer, Mackenzie, Ch Serv, Fort Scott Public Library, 201 S National Ave, Fort Scott, KS, 66701. Tel: 620-223-2882. p. 808
Kean, Emily, Educ Librn, Res, University of Cincinnati Libraries, Donald C Harrison Health Sciences Library, 231 Albert Sabin Way, Cincinnati, OH, 45267. Tel: 513-558-3849. p. 1765
Keane, Amy, Exec Dir, Hawley Library, 103 Main Ave, Hawley, PA, 18428-1325. Tel: 570-226-4620. p. 1942
Keane, Edward, Serials/Database Coor, Long Island University, One University Plaza, Brooklyn, NY, 11201. Tel: 718-780-4513. p. 1505

Keane, Ellen, Head, Access Serv, University of Massachusetts Lowell Library, 61 Wilder St, Lowell, MA, 01854-3098. Tel: 978-934-4594. p. 1030
Keane, Ellen, Head, Access Serv, University of Massachusetts Lowell Library, Lydon Library, 84 University Ave, Lowell, MA, 01854-2896. Tel: 978-934-3203. p. 1030
Keane, Georgette, Archives Curator, American Irish Historical Society Library, 991 Fifth Ave, New York, NY, 10028. Tel: 212-288-2263. p. 1578
Keane, Katie, Coll Develop & Tech Serv Mgr, Manheim Township Public Library, 595 Granite Run Dr, Lancaster, PA, 17601. Tel: 717-560-6441. p. 1952
Keane, Patrice, Exec Dir, American Society for Psychical Research Inc Library & Archives, Five W 73rd St, New York, NY, 10023. Tel: 212-799-5050. p. 1579
Keaney, Allison, Interim Assoc Dir, Stonehill College, 320 Washington St, Easton, MA, 02357. Tel: 508-565-1289. p. 1016
Kearney, Anne M, Ad, Peninsula Library & Historical Society, 6105 Riverview Rd, Peninsula, OH, 44264. Tel: 330-467-7323, 330-657-2291. p. 1814
Kearney, Diane, Lead Med Librn, Northern Virginia Community College Libraries, Medical Education Campus, 6699 Springfield Center Dr, Rm 341, Springfield, VA, 22150. Tel: 703-822-6681. p. 2304
Kearney, Janet, Foreign & Intl Law Librn, Fordham University School of Law, 150 W 62nd St, New York, NY, 10023. Tel: 212-636-6913. p. 1585
Kearney, Jennifer, Cataloger, ILL, Florida College, 119 N Glen Arven Ave, Temple Terrace, FL, 33617-5578. Tel: 813-988-5131, Ext 210. p. 451
Kearney, Maureen, Br Mgr, Pima County Public Library, Southwest, 6855 S Mark Rd, Tucson, AZ, 85757. Tel: 520-594-5270. p. 83
Kearney, Richard, Ref/Electronic Serv Librn, William Paterson University, 300 Pompton Rd, Wayne, NJ, 07470. Tel: 973-720-2165. p. 1452
Kearney, Susan, Dir, Lakota Public Library, 204 Third St, Lakota, IA, 50451-7084. Tel: 515-886-2312. p. 764
Kearns, Andrew, Assoc Dean, University of South Carolina Upstate Library, University Center of Greenville Library, 225 S Pleasantburg Dr, Greenville, SC, 29607-2544. Tel: 864-503-5615. p. 2070
Kearns, Andrew, Dr, Coord of Distributed Educ, Open Educ Sources, University of South Carolina Upstate Library, 800 University Way, Spartanburg, SC, 29303. Tel: 864-503-5403. p. 2070
Kearns, Heather, Mkt Coordr, Lawrence Public Library, 707 Vermont St, Lawrence, KS, 66044-2371. Tel: 785-843-3833, Ext 123. p. 819
Kearns, Jane, Dir, Dorothy Alling Memorial Library, 21 Library Lane, Williston, VT, 05495. Tel: 802-878-4918. p. 2299
Kearns, Mary, Ad, Libr Dir, Castleton Free Library, 638 Main St, Castleton, VT, 05735. Tel: 802-468-5574. p. 2281
Kearns, Mary Ann, IT Spec, Pollard Memorial Library, 401 Merrimack St, Lowell, MA, 01852. Tel: 978-674-4120. p. 1029
Kearns, Trish, Head, Cat, College of William & Mary in Virginia, Earl Gregg Swem Library, One Landrum Dr, Williamsburg, VA, 23187. Tel: 757-221-1940. p. 2353
Kearns Williams, Penny, Dir, Coatesville Area Public Library, 501 E Lincoln Hwy, Coatesville, PA, 19320-3413. Tel: 610-384-4115. p. 1923
Kearny, Andrea, Br Mgr, Free Library of Philadelphia, Wadsworth Avenue Branch, 1500 Wadsworth Ave, Philadelphia, PA, 19150-1699. Tel: 215-685-9293. p. 1980
Keary, Lianne, Libr Dir, Hebron Library, Eight Church Lane, Hebron, NH, 03241. Tel: 603-744-7998. p. 1367
Keating, Carleigh, Youth Serv Librn, Franklin Public Library, 118 Main St, Franklin, MA, 02038. Tel: 508-520-4941. p. 1020
Keating, Catherine, Digital Serv Mgr, Maitland Public Library, 501 S Maitland Ave, Maitland, FL, 32751-5672. Tel: 407-647-7700. p. 419
Keating, Kevin, Ref & Instruction, University of Alaska Anchorage, Consortium Library, 3211 Providence Dr, Anchorage, AK, 99508-8176. Tel: 907-786-1871. p. 43
Keating, Margaret, Br Mgr, Bronson Silas Library, Bunker Hill, 192 Bunker Hill Ave, Waterbury, CT, 06708. Tel: 203-574-8240. p. 343
Keating, Tara Treharn, Library Contact, Trumbull County Law Library, 120 High St NW, Warren, OH, 44481. Tel: 330-675-2525. p. 1828
Keating, Wendy, Chief Exec Officer, Hastings Highlands Public Library, 33011 Hwy 62 N, Maynooth, ON, K0L 2S0, CANADA. Tel: 613-338-2262. p. 2657
Keaton, Bernice, Library Contact, Florida Auditor General Library, Claude Pepper Bldg, Rm G-74, 111 W Madison St, Tallahassee, FL, 32399-1450. Tel: 850-412-2722. p. 446
Keaton, Kate, Br Mgr, Sonoma County Library, Central Santa Rosa Library, 211 E St, Santa Rosa, CA, 95404. Tel: 707-308-3020. p. 204
Keaton, Kate, Br Mgr, Sonoma County Library, Roseland Community Library, 470 Sebastopol Rd, Santa Rosa, CA, 95407. Tel: 707-755-2029. p. 204
Keaton, Lace, Dir, Newton County Library System, 7116 Floyd St NE, Covington, GA, 30014. Tel: 770-787-3231. p. 473
Keba, Michelle, Ref Librn, Palm Beach Atlantic University, 300 Pembroke Pl, West Palm Beach, FL, 33401-6503. Tel: 561-803-2230. p. 453
Kebaili, Melissa, Dir, Ponca Carnegie Library, 200 W Second St, Ponca, NE, 68770. Tel: 402-755-2739. p. 1333
Kebetz, Lori, Librn, Montgomery County Public Libraries, Montgomery County Correctional Facility, 22880 Whelan Lane, Boyds, MD, 20841. Tel: 240-773-9914. p. 974
Keck, Carol, Tech Serv Librn, Guilford Technical Community College, 601 E Main St, Jamestown, NC, 27282. Tel: 336-334-4822, Ext 50259. p. 1698
Keck, Jackie, Dir, Caseyville Public Library District, 419 S Second St, Caseyville, IL, 62232. Tel: 618-345-5848. p. 551
Keck, Tyler, Libr Asst, Train Collectors Association, 300 Paradise Lane, Ronks, PA, 17572. Tel: 717-687-8623, Ext 108. p. 2002
Kee, Karen, Head, Circ, Glenview Public Library, 1930 Glenview Rd, Glenview, IL, 60025. Tel: 847-729-7500. p. 594
Keefe, Sue, Dir, Sussex County Department of Libraries, South Coastal Public Library, 43 Kent Ave, Bethany Beach, DE, 19930. Tel: 302-539-5231. p. 353
Keefe, Tom, Ref Librn, Loyola University Chicago Libraries, School of Law Library, Philip H Corboy Law Ctr, 25 E Pearson St, Chicago, IL, 60611. Tel: 312-915-8516. p. 564
Keegan, Melissa, Head, Ref, Ela Area Public Library District, 275 Mohawk Trail, Lake Zurich, IL, 60047. Tel: 847-438-3433. p. 607
Keegan, Melissa, Co-Dir, Peru Public Library, 1409 11th St, Peru, IL, 61354. Tel: 815-223-0229. p. 635
Keegan, Paula, Br Mgr, Bridgeport Public Library, North, 3455 Madison Ave, Bridgeport, CT, 06606. Tel: 203-576-7003. p. 303
Keehbler, James, Dir, Hunterdon County Library, 314 State Rte 12, Bldg 3, Flemington, NJ, 08822. Tel: 908-788-1444. p. 1403
Keehn, Carl, Dir, North Carolina Regional Library for the Blind & Physically Handicapped, 1841 Capital Blvd, Raleigh, NC, 27635. Tel: 919-733-4376. p. 1709
Keehr, Karen, Curator for Photog, Nebraska History Library, 1500 R St, Lincoln, NE, 68508. Tel: 402-471-4750. p. 1322
Keel, Connie, Dir, Memorial Hospital at Gulfport, 4500 13th St, Gulfport, MS, 39501. Tel: 228-865-3157. p. 1218
Keele, Benjamin, Res & Instrul Serv Librn, Indiana University, Ruth Lilly Law Library, 530 W New York St, Indianapolis, IN, 46202-3225. Tel: 317-274-3884, 317-274-4028. p. 693
Keeler, Justin, Interim Exec Dir, Fort Vancouver Regional Library District, Bldg 1, Ste 100, 16821 SE McGillivray Blvd, Vancouver, WA, 98683. Tel: 360-906-5000. p. 2391
Keeler, Rachel, Libr Dir, Tye Preston Memorial Library, 16311 S Access Rd, Canyon Lake, TX, 78133-5301. Tel: 830-964-3744. p. 2153
Keeler, Thomas, Patient Educ Librn, Department of Veterans Affairs, One Veterans Dr, Mail Stop 142 D, Minneapolis, MN, 55417. Tel: 612-467-4200. p. 1183
Keeler, Thomas, Patient Educ Librn, Department of Veterans Affairs, Patient Education Library, One Veterans Dr,Mail Stop 142D1, Minneapolis, MN, 55417. Tel: 612-467-4212. p. 1183
Keeler, William, Archivist/Librn, Registrar, Rochester Historical Society Library, 1100 University Ave, Rochester, NY, 14607. Tel: 585-623-8285. p. 1630
Keelin, Russell W, Asst Librn, Hillsboro City Library, 118 S Waco St, Hillsboro, TX, 76645. Tel: 254-582-7385. p. 2190
Keeling, MaryAnn, Law Librn, US Customs & Border Protection Information Resources Center, 90 K St NE, Washington, DC, 20229. Tel: 202-325-0130. p. 380
Keen, Dominic, Libr Mgr, Lompoc Public Library, 501 E North Ave, Lompoc, CA, 93436. Tel: 805-875-8789. p. 158
Keen, Jennifer, Asst Dir, Ref, YA Librn, Holliston Public Library, 752 Washington St, Holliston, MA, 01746. Tel: 508-429-0617. p. 1025
Keen, Sarah, Univ Archivist, University of Iowa Libraries, Special Collections & Archives, 100 Main Library, 125 W Washington St, Iowa City, IA, 52242-1420. Tel: 319-467-1725. p. 761
Keen, Sarah, Head, Spec Coll, Univ Archivist, Colgate University, 13 Oak Dr, Hamilton, NY, 13346-1398. Tel: 315-228-7305. p. 1543
Keenan, Kathleen, Libr Dir, Stevens Memorial Library, 345 Main St, North Andover, MA, 01845. Tel: 978-688-9505, Ext 42021. p. 1040
Keenan, Linda, Chief Exec Officer, Penetanguishene Public Library, 24 Simcoe St, Penetanguishene, ON, L9M 1R6, CANADA. Tel: 705-549-7164. p. 2671
Keenan, Shane, Archivist/Librn, Lebanon County Historical Society Library, 924 Cumberland St, Lebanon, PA, 17042. Tel: 717-272-1473. p. 1954
Keene, Betsy, Curator, National Park Service, Department of Interior, One Washington Pkwy, Farmington, PA, 15437. Tel: 814-886-6135. p. 1933
Keene, Deborah, Assoc Dean, Libr Tech, George Mason University Libraries, Law Library, 3301 N Fairfax Dr, Arlington, VA, 22201-4426. Tel: 703-993-8110. p. 2317
Keene, Kara, Dir, West Hurley Public Library, 42 Clover St, West Hurley, NY, 12491. Tel: 845-679-6405. p. 1662
Keener, Erin, Br Mgr, Grand Rapids Public Library, Van Belkum Branch, 1563 Plainfield Ave NE, Grand Rapids, MI, 49505. Tel: 616-988-5410. p. 1111
Keener, Molly, Dir, Scholarly Communications, Dir, Digital Initiatives, Wake Forest University, 1834 Wake Forest Rd, Winston-Salem, NC, 27109. Tel: 336-758-5829. p. 1726
Keeney, Charlotte Kay, Dir, Pulaski County Public Library, 304 S Main St, Somerset, KY, 42501. Tel: 606-679-8401. p. 875
Keeney, Hannah, Archivist, Fresno Pacific University, 1717 S Chestnut Ave, Fresno, CA, 93702. Tel: 559-453-3437. p. 146
Keeney, Mary Ellen, Ch Serv, Ridley Park Public Library, 107 E Ward St, Ridley Park, PA, 19078. Tel: 610-583-7207. p. 2001

Keeping, Dianne, Univ Librn, Memorial University of Newfoundland, Queen Elizabeth II Library, 234 Elizabeth Ave, St. John's, NL, A1B 3Y1, CANADA. Tel: 709-737-7428. p. 2610

Keer, Gretchen, Sr Asst Librn, California State University, East Bay Library, CSU East Bay Library, 25800 Carlos Bee Blvd, Hayward, CA, 94542-3052. Tel: 510-885-2968. p. 150

Keeran, Amber, Libr Dir, The Lanier Library Association, 72 Chestnut St, Tryon, NC, 28782. Tel: 828-859-9535. p. 1719

Keeran, Peggy, Arts & Humanities Reference Librn, University of Denver, 2150 E Evans Ave, Denver, CO, 80208. Tel: 303-871-3441. p. 277

Keery, Carolyn, Dir, Hinckley, Allen & Snyder LLP, 100 Westminster St, Ste 1500, Providence, RI, 02903. Tel: 617-378-4380. p. 2038

Keesee, Marianne, Libr Asst, Trinity County Library, Trinity Center Branch, Scott Museum Bldg, 540-B Airport Rd, Trinity Center, CA, 96091. Tel: 530-266-3242. p. 258

Keesler, Lenoir C, Jr, Chief Exec Officer, Charlotte Mecklenburg Library, 310 N Tryon St, Charlotte, NC, 28202-2176. Tel: 704-416-0100. p. 1679

Keesler, Toni, Librn, Preble County District Library, Camden, 104 S Main St, Eaton, OH, 45311. Tel: 937-452-3142. p. 1784

Keetch, Jean, Libr Mgr, Rimbey Municipal Library, 4938 50th Ave, Rimbey, AB, T0C 2J0, CANADA. Tel: 403-843-2841. p. 2552

Keevan, Deanna, Ch Serv, Libr Tech, Georgetown Peabody Library, Two Maple St, Georgetown, MA, 01833. Tel: 978-352-5728. p. 1020

Keeven, Katie, Br Mgr, Saint Louis County Library, Cliff Cave Branch, 5430 Telegraph Rd, Saint Louis, MO, 63129. Tel: 314-994-3300, Ext 3050. p. 1273

Keever, Kaitlyn, Br Librn, Brazoria County Library System, Pearland Branch, 3522 Liberty Dr, Pearland, TX, 77581. Tel: 281-485-4876. p. 2135

Keever, Kaitlyn, Electronic Res Librn, University of Saint Thomas, 3800 Montrose Blvd, Houston, TX, 77006. Tel: 713-525-2175. p. 2200

Keevy, Lindsay, Fac Librn, Lower Columbia College, 1600 Maple St, Longview, WA, 98632-3907. Tel: 360-442-2667. p. 2369

Kegel, Sara, IT Coordr, Great Falls Public Library, 301 Second Ave N, Great Falls, MT, 59401-2593. Tel: 406-453-0181, Ext 230. p. 1294

Kegin, Morgan, ILL Spec, Oklahoma City University, 2501 N Blackwelder, Oklahoma City, OK, 73106. Tel: 405-208-5068. p. 1858

Kegler, Lydia, PhD, Dir, Bloomsburg Public Library, 225 Market St, Bloomsburg, PA, 17815-1726. Tel: 570-784-0883. p. 1913

Kegley, Arlene, Libr Dir, Daniels County Free Library, 203 Timmons St, Scobey, MT, 59263. Tel: 406-487-5502. p. 1302

Kehl, Robbie, Adult Serv Coordr, Coshocton Public Library, 655 Main St, Coshocton, OH, 43812-1697. Tel: 740-622-0956. p. 1778

Kehler, Kristen, Librn, Keethanow Public Library, PO Box 70, Stanley Mission, SK, S0J 1G0, CANADA. Tel: 306-635-2104. p. 2751

Kehn, Jana, Adult Serv, Lied Scottsbluff Public Library, 1809 Third Ave, Scottsbluff, NE, 69361-2493. Tel: 308-630-6250. p. 1335

Kehoe, Jillian, Libr Dir, State University of New York Maritime College, Six Pennyfield Ave, Fort Schuyler, Bronx, NY, 10465. Tel: 718-409-7231. p. 1500

Kehoe, Jillian, ILL, Ref (Info Servs), The College of New Rochelle, 29 Castle Pl, New Rochelle, NY, 10805-2308. Tel: 914-654-5419. p. 1577

Kehoe, Michelle, Exec Dir, Montgomery County Library & Information Network Consortium, 520 Virginia Dr, Fort Washington, PA, 19034. Tel: 610-238-0580. p. 2774

Kehoe, Robbyn, Dir, Atglen Public Library, 413 Valley Ave, Atglen, PA, 19310-1402. Tel: 610-593-6848. p. 1907

Kehoe, Susan, Head, Circ/ILL, Sandown Public Library, 305 Main St, Sandown, NH, 03873. Tel: 603-887-3428. p. 1380

Kehoe-Robinson, Colleen, Dir, Libr Serv, James Sprunt Community College, Boyette Bldg, 133 James Sprunt Dr, Kenansville, NC, 28349. Tel: 910-275-6332. p. 1699

Keif, Mary Beth, Circ Supvr, Hingham Public Library, 66 Leavitt St, Hingham, MA, 02043. Tel: 781-741-1405, Ext 1402. p. 1024

Keifenheim, Michele, Circ & ILL Coordr, Marian University, 45 S National Ave, Fond du Lac, WI, 54935-4699. Tel: 920-923-7641. p. 2435

Keifer, Anessa, Youth Serv Librn, Belmont County District Library, 20 James Wright Pl, Martins Ferry, OH, 43935. Tel: 740-633-0314. p. 1800

Keil, Sarah, Electronic Res & Syst Librn, Trevecca Nazarene University, 333 Murfreesboro Rd, Nashville, TN, 37210. Tel: 615-248-1353, p. 2121

Keil, Trina, Coordr, Yavapai County Free Library District, Bagdad Public Library, 700 Palo Verde, Bldg C, Bagdad, AZ, 86321. Tel: 928-633-2325. p. 74

Keiling, Vivien, Colls Mgr, Barrie Public Library, 60 Worsley St, Barrie, ON, L4M 1L6, CANADA. Tel: 705-728-1010, Ext 2420. p. 2630

Keillor, Jo, Dir, Greenville Public Library, 414 W Main St, Greenville, IL, 62246-1615. Tel: 618-664-3115. p. 596

Keim, Adam, Graduate & Faculty Services Coord, Tarleton State University Library, 201 Saint Felix, Stephenville, TX, 76401. Tel: 254-968-9246. p. 2246

Keinsley, Jason, Agr Librn, University of Kentucky Libraries, Agricultural Information Center, N24 Agricultural Science Bldg N, 1100 Nicholasville Rd, Lexington, KY, 40546-0091. Tel: 859-218-1523. p. 863

Keiper, Christina, Assoc Dir, The Library of Hattiesburg, Petal, Forrest County, 329 Hardy St, Hattiesburg, MS, 39401-3496. Tel: 601-582-4461. p. 1218

Keiper, Jan, Libr Dir, Frenchboro Library, 21 High St, Frenchboro, ME, 04635. p. 925

Keipp, Lisa, Libr Dir, Marie Ellison Memorial Library, 480 S Hwy 107, Del Rio, TN, 37727-9625. Tel: 423-487-5929. p. 2096

Keir, Courtney A, Dir, Rockwell Falls Public Library, 19 Main St, Lake Luzerne, NY, 12846. Tel: 518-696-3423. p. 1561

Keirsey, Sandra, Instr, Pub Serv Librn, McNeese State University, 300 S Beauregard Dr, Lake Charles, LA, 70609. Tel: 337-475-5740. p. 894

Keiser, Jerry, Dir, Seaford District Library, 600 N Market St Extended, Seaford, DE, 19973. Tel: 302-629-2524. p. 356

Keisha, Parks, Youth Serv Librn, Cleveland Bradley County Public Library, 795 Church St NE, Cleveland, TN, 37311-5295. Tel: 423-472-2163. p. 2092

Keisling, Bruce L, Assoc Dean & Dir, University of Louisville Libraries, William F Ekstrom Library, Belknap Campus, 2215 S Third St, Louisville, KY, 40208. Tel: 502-852-6745. p. 867

Keissling, Marie, YA Serv, Free Library of Springfield Township, 8900 Hawthorne Lane, Wyndmoor, PA, 19038. Tel: 215-836-5300. p. 2025

Keister, Patricia, Br Mgr, Orange County Public Library, Gordonsville Branch, 319 N Main St, Gordonsville, VA, 22942. Tel: 540-832-0712. p. 2336

Keith, Bob, Data Coordr, Libr Support Serv, New Jersey State Library, 185 W State St, Trenton, NJ, 08608. Tel: 609-278-2640, Ext 192. p. 1448

Keith, Ellen, Chief Librn, Dir of Res & Access, Chicago History Museum, 1601 N Clark St, Chicago, IL, 60614-6099. Tel: 312-799-2030. p. 555

Keith, Hilary, City Librn, Santa Clara City Library, 2635 Homestead Rd, Santa Clara, CA, 95051. Tel: 408-615-2900. p. 241

Keith, Latrina, Cat, Albert Einstein College of Medicine, Jack & Pearl Resnick Campus, 1300 Morris Park Ave, Bronx, NY, 10461-1924. Tel: 718-430-3114. p. 1497

Keith, Lesa, Dir, Justin Community Library, 408 Pafford St, Justin, TX, 76247-9442. Tel: 940-648-2541, Ext 6. p. 2204

Keith, Lisa, Adult Serv, Gardendale - Martha Moore Public Library, 995 Mt Olive Rd, Gardendale, AL, 35071. Tel: 205-631-6639. p. 19

Keith, Pauline, Asst Librn, Waterboro Public Library, 187 Main St, East Waterboro, ME, 04030. Tel: 207-247-3363. p. 924

Keith, Samantha, Ch, Ottumwa Public Library, 102 W Fourth St, Ottumwa, IA, 52501. Tel: 641-682-7563, Ext 210. p. 775

Keith, Tammy, Head, Coll Mgt, Kokomo-Howard County Public Library, 220 N Union St, Kokomo, IN, 46901-4614. Tel: 765-457-3242. p. 699

Keith, Vicki, ILL Spec, Prairie Lakes Library System (PLLS), 29134 Evergreen Dr, Ste 600, Waterford, WI, 53185. Tel: 262-514-4500, Ext 64. p. 2483

Keith, Wayne, Mobile Media Servs, Franklin County Public Library, 355 Franklin St, Rocky Mount, VA, 24151. Tel: 540-483-3098. p. 2346

Kelbley, Sarah, Fiscal Officer, Bliss Memorial Public Library, 20 S Marion St, Bloomville, OH, 44818. Tel: 419-983-4675. p. 1751

Kelderhouse, Jack, Tech Mgr, Joliet Public Library, 150 N Ottawa St, Joliet, IL, 60432. Tel: 815-740-2660. p. 603

Kelderhouse, Kim, Exec Dir, Leelanau Historical Society, 203 E Cedar St, Leland, MI, 49654. Tel: 231-256-7475. p. 1126

Kelehan, Martha, Asst Dir, Tufts University, 35 Professors Row, Medford, MA, 02155-5816. Tel: 617-627-3345. p. 1034

Keleher, Jackie, Dir, Libr Serv, Schenectady County Community College, 78 Washington Ave, Schenectady, NY, 12305. Tel: 518-381-1235. p. 1638

Kelemen, Eva, Libr Dir, Kaslo & District Public Library, 413 Fourth St, Kaslo, BC, V0G 1M0, CANADA. Tel: 250-353-2942. p. 2568

Kelien, Becky, Br Mgr, Jeffersonville Township Public Library, 211 E Court Ave, Jeffersonville, IN, 47130. Tel: 812-285-5630. p. 698

Kelien, Becky, Br Mgr, Jeffersonville Township Public Library, Clarksville Branch, 1312 Eastern Blvd, Clarksville, IN, 47129-1704. Tel: 812-285-5640, p. 698

Kellar, Debbie, ILL, Kennett Library, 216 E State St, Kennett Square, PA, 19348-3112. Tel: 610-444-2702. p. 1948

Kellar, Ed, Asst Dir, Jennings County Public Library, 2375 N State Hwy 3, North Vernon, IN, 47265. Tel: 812-346-2091. p. 711

Kelleher, Angie, Access Serv Librn, Alma College Library, 614 W Superior St, Alma, MI, 48801. Tel: 989-463-7345. p. 1077

Kelleher, Laura, Br Mgr, Louisville Free Public Library, Crescent Hill, 2762 Frankfort Ave, Louisville, KY, 40206. Tel: 502-574-1793. p. 865

Kelleher, Nikole, Circ Supvr, Ventress Memorial Library, 15 Library Plaza, Marshfield, MA, 02050. Tel: 781-834-5535. p. 1032

Kelleher, Sharon, Dir, Flint Memorial Library, 147 Park St, North Reading, MA, 01864. Tel: 978-664-4942. p. 1042

Kellen, Chris, Head, Syst, Carnegie Mellon University, Hunt Library, 4909 Frew St, Pittsburgh, PA, 15213. Tel: 412-268-2444. p. 1992

Kellen, Laura, Outreach Librn, California State Library, Braille & Talking Book Library, 900 N St, Sacramento, CA, 95814. Tel: 916-654-0640. p. 208

Keller, Anne, Teen Serv Librn, Tecumseh District Library, 215 N Ottawa St, Tecumseh, MI, 49286-1564. Tel: 517-423-2238. p. 1153

Kelly, David, Brother, Dir, Saint Vincent College & Seminary Library, 300 Fraser Purchase Rd, Latrobe, PA, 15650-2690. Tel: 724-805-2966. p. 1953

Kelly, Dean, Mgr, Support Serv, Fraser Valley Regional Library, 34589 Delair Rd, Abbotsford, BC, V2S 5Y1, CANADA. Tel: 604-859-7141. p. 2561

Kelly, Donna, Br Mgr, Lorain Public Library System, Avon Branch, 37485 Harvest Dr, Avon, OH, 44011-2812. Tel: 440-934-4743. p. 1797

Kelly, Elizabeth, Teen Serv, Southbury Public Library, 100 Poverty Rd, Southbury, CT, 06488. Tel: 203-262-0626. p. 337

Kelly Fischer, Cheryl, Head, Instruction Serv, Ref Librn, University of California Los Angeles Library, Hugh & Hazel Darling Law Library, 1112 Law Bldg, 385 Charles E Young Dr E, Los Angeles, CA, 90095-1458. Tel: 310-825-7826. p. 169

Kelly, Helen, Chief Exec Officer, Idea Exchange, One North Sq, Cambridge, ON, N1S 2K6, CANADA. Tel: 519-621-0460. p. 2635

Kelly, Hilary, Libr Tech, Cambrian College Library, 1400 Barrydowne Rd, 3rd Flr, Rm 3021, Sudbury, ON, P3A 3V8, CANADA. Tel: 705-524-7333. p. 2682

Kelly, James, Dir, Frederick County Public Libraries, 110 E Patrick St, Frederick, MD, 21701. Tel: 301-600-1613. p. 966

Kelly, James R, Cat, Amherst College, 61 Quadrangle Dr, Amherst, MA, 01002. p. 984

Kelly, Jane, Coordr, Williams County Public Library, 107 E High St, Bryan, OH, 43506-1702. Tel: 419-636-6734. p. 1753

Kelly, Janice, Exec Dir, NN/LM SE/ARMLS, University of Maryland, Baltimore, Health Sciences & Human Services Library, 601 W Lombard St, Baltimore, MD, 21201. Tel: 410-706-2855. p. 957

Kelly, Jessica, Libr Tech, St Paul's Hospital of Saskatoon, 1702 20th St W, Saskatoon, SK, S7M 0Z9, CANADA. Tel: 306-655-5224. p. 2749

Kelly, Joanne, Dir, Town of Inlet Public Library, 168 N Rte 28, Inlet, NY, 13360. Tel: 315-357-6494. p. 1550

Kelly, Justin, IT & Fac Mgr, Joplin Public Library, 1901 E 20th St, Joplin, MO, 64804. Tel: 417-623-7953. p. 1253

Kelly, Kim, Librn, Provincial Information & Library Resources Board, Arts & Culture Ctr, 125 Allandale Rd, St. John's, NL, A1B 3A3, CANADA. Tel: 709-737-3418. p. 2611

Kelly, Kyle, Tech Serv Librn, New England Law, 154 Stuart St, Boston, MA, 02116-5687. Tel: 617-422-7214. p. 998

Kelly, Leslie, Exec Dir, Academic Support Services, University of Maine at Fort Kent, 23 University Dr, Fort Kent, ME, 04743. Tel: 207-834-7522. p. 925

Kelly, Linda, Asst Dir, Mat, Forsyth County Public Library, 585 Dahlonega St, Cumming, GA, 30040-2109. Tel: 770-781-9840. p. 473

Kelly, Lisa, Dir, Info Serv, Nebraska Library Commission, The Atrium, 1200 N St, Ste 120, Lincoln, NE, 68508-2023. Tel: 402-471-4015. p. 1322

Kelly, Lori, Dir, Libr Serv, Mississauga Library System, 301 Burnhamthorpe Rd W, Mississauga, ON, L5B 3Y3, CANADA. Tel: 905-615-3500. p. 2659

Kelly, Madeline, Local Hist Librn, Berkshire Athenaeum, One Wendell Ave, Pittsfield, MA, 01201-6385. Tel: 413-499-9480. p. 1046

Kelly, Madeline, Dir of Coll, Western Washington University, 516 High St, MS 9103, Bellingham, WA, 98225. Tel: 360-650-4320. p. 2358

Kelly, Margaret, Br Librn, Boston Public Library, East Boston, 365 Bremen St, East Boston, MA, 02128. Tel: 617-569-0271. p. 992

Kelly, Marie, Ch Serv, Rochester Public Library, 65 S Main St, Rochester, NH, 03867-2707. Tel: 603-332-1428. p. 1380

Kelly, Mark, Lead Reference Services Librn, Pacifica Graduate Institute, 249 Lambert Rd, Carpinteria, CA, 93013. Tel: 805-969-3626, Ext 115. p. 128

Kelly, Martin, Digital Coll Librn, Colby College Libraries, 5100 Mayflower Hill, Waterville, ME, 04901. Tel: 207-859-5162. p. 945

Kelly, Meghan, Assoc Dean, Laramie County Community College, 1400 E College Dr, Cheyenne, WY, 82007-3204. Tel: 307-778-1201. p. 2492

Kelly, Melissa, Libr Dir, Lake Oswego Public Library, 706 Fourth St, Lake Oswego, OR, 97034-2399. Tel: 503-697-6584. p. 1884

Kelly, Michelle, Circ Supvr, Lyndhurst Free Public Library, 355 Valley Brook Ave, Lyndhurst, NJ, 07071. Tel: 201-804-2478. p. 1414

Kelly, Mike, Head, Archives & Spec Coll, Amherst College, 61 Quadrangle Dr, Amherst, MA, 01002. p. 984

Kelly, Mindy, Med Libr Tech, Scripps Mercy Hospital Medical Library, 4077 Fifth Ave, MER-36, San Diego, CA, 92103-2180. Tel: 619-260-7024. p. 221

Kelly, Nadine, Br Mgr, Ohoopee Regional Library System, Montgomery County Public Library, 215 S Railroad Ave, Mount Vernon, GA, 30445. Tel: 912-583-2780. p. 502

Kelly, Nancy, Cat, Head, Tech Serv, Ventress Memorial Library, 15 Library Plaza, Marshfield, MA, 02050. Tel: 781-834-5535. p. 1032

Kelly, Nina, Libr Tech, Niagara Health System, 1200 Fourth Ave, St. Catharines, ON, L2S 0A9, CANADA. Tel: 905-378-4647, Ext 44354. p. 2679

Kelly, Patricia, Head, Ref Serv, Lynnfield Public Library, 18 Summer St, Lynnfield, MA, 01940-1837. Tel: 781-334-5411, 781-334-6404. p. 1031

Kelly, Paula, Dir, Whitehall Public Library, 100 Borough Park Dr, Pittsburgh, PA, 15236. Tel: 412-882-6622. p. 1997

Kelly, Rachel, Asst Dir, Sr Librn, Jefferson Township Public Library, 1031 Weldon Rd, Oak Ridge, NJ, 07438. Tel: 973-208-6244, Ext 202. p. 1430

Kelly, Rene, IT Dir, Delaware County Libraries, Bldg 19, 340 N Middletown Rd, Media, PA, 19063-5597. Tel: 610-891-8622. p. 1961

Kelly, Savannah, Res & Instruction Librn, University of Mississippi, One Library Loop, University, MS, 38677. Tel: 662-915-5877. p. 1234

Kelly, Sharon, Dir, Berwick Public Library, 103 Old Pine Hill Rd, Berwick, ME, 03901. Tel: 207-698-5737. p. 917

Kelly, Sharon Lynn, Dir of Libr, South Georgia State College, 100 W College Park Dr, Douglas, GA, 31533-5098. Tel: 912-260-4323. p. 477

Kelly, Sharon Lynn, Dir of Libr, South Georgia State College, 2001 S Georgia Pkwy, Waycross, GA, 31503. Tel: 912-260-4324. p. 503

Kelly, Sierra, Br Mgr, Mid-Continent Public Library, Blue Springs North Branch, 850 NW Hunter Dr, Blue Springs, MO, 64015. Tel: 816-224-8772. p. 1250

Kelly, Susan, Br Mgr, Palm Beach County Library System, Lantana Road Branch, 4020 Lantana Rd, Lake Worth, FL, 33462. Tel: 561-304-4500. p. 454

Kelly, Tracey, Asst Dir, First Parish Church of Norwell, 24 West St, Norwell, MA, 02061. Tel: 781-659-7100. p. 1043

Kelly, Vickie, Br Mgr, Sevier County Public Library System, 408 High St, Sevierville, TN, 37862. Tel: 865-453-3532. p. 2125

Kelly, William, Digital Pedagogy, Scholarship Librn, Guilford College, 5800 W Friendly Ave, Greensboro, NC, 27410. Tel: 336-316-2040. p. 1692

Kelly-Johnson, Kristina, Dir, Somerset Public Library, 208 Hud St, Somerset, WI, 54025. Tel: 715-247-5228. p. 2478

Kelly-Rheaume, Paule, Librn, McGill University Health Centre - Glen Site, 1001 Boul DeCarie, Rm B RC 0078, Montreal, QC, H4A 3J1, CANADA. Tel: 514-934-1934, Ext 32593. p. 2726

Kelly-Rheaume, Paule, Librn, Montreal Neurological Institute Hospital Library, 3801 University St, Rm 285, Montreal, QC, H3A 2B4, CANADA. Tel: 514-398-1980. p. 2727

Kelm, Bill, Syst Librn, Willamette University, 900 State St, Salem, OR, 97301. Tel: 503-375-5332. p. 1897

Kelmelis, Jessica, Libr Dir, Tolland Public Library, 22 Clubhouse Rd, Tolland, MA, 01034. Tel: 413-258-4201, 413-258-4794, Ext 109. p. 1059

Kelmelis, Judy, Digital Serv Coordr, Librn II, Groton Public Library, 52 Newtown Rd, Groton, CT, 06340. Tel: 860-441-6750. p. 314

Kelsall-Dempsey, Julie, Dir, Highland Public Library, 14 Elting Pl, Highland, NY, 12528. Tel: 845-691-2275. p. 1546

Kelsch, Laurel A, Dir, Grande Cache Municipal Library, 10601 Shand Ave, Grande Cache, AB, T0E 0Y0, CANADA. Tel: 780-827-2081. p. 2541

Kelsea, Elizabeth, Asst Librn, Bartlett Public Library, 1313 US Rte 302, Bartlett, NH, 03812. Tel: 603-374-2755. p. 1354

Kelsey, David, Outreach Serv Librn, St Charles Public Library District, One S Sixth Ave, Saint Charles, IL, 60174-2105. Tel: 630-584-0076, Ext 219. p. 644

Kelsey, Elizabeth, Research Coordr, St Claire Regional Medical Center Library, 222 Medical Circle, Morehead, KY, 40351. Tel: 606-783-6500. p. 870

Kelsey, Laura, Instrul Serv Librn, Indiana Wesleyan University, 4201 S Washington St, Marion, IN, 46953. Tel: 765-677-2403. p. 704

Kelshian, Robert, Dir, Access Serv, American University Library, 4400 Massachusetts Ave NW, Washington, DC, 20016-8046. Tel: 202-885-3232. p. 361

Kelso, Craig, State Rec Mgr, Texas State Library & Archives Commission, 1201 Brazos St, Austin, TX, 78701. Tel: 512-463-5474. p. 2141

Kelso, Julia, Dir, Vista Grande Public Library, 14 Avenida Torreon, Santa Fe, NM, 87508-9199. Tel: 505-466-7323. p. 1477

Kelson, Paul, Librn, Mount Pleasant Public Library, 24 E Main St, Mount Pleasant, UT, 84647-1429. Tel: 435-462-3240. p. 2267

Kelton, Andrew, Dir, Arlington Public Library, 321 W Main St, Arlington, MN, 55307. Tel: 507-964-2490. p. 1164

Kelton, Andrew, Libr Dir, Dyckman Free Library, 345 W Main St, Sleepy Eye, MN, 56085-1331. Tel: 507-794-7655. p. 1204

Kelton, Kathleen, Circ Serv Mgr, Mission Viejo Library, 100 Civic Ctr, Mission Viejo, CA, 92691. Tel: 949-830-7100, Ext 5130. p. 177

Kemball, Jen, Asst Librn, Bibliothèque Allard Regional Library, 104086 PTH 11, Saint Georges, MB, R0E 1V0, CANADA. Tel: 204-367-8443. p. 2590

Kemen, Shannon, Research & Instruction Services, University of Cincinnati, 2540 Clifton Ave, Cincinnati, OH, 45219. Tel: 513-556-6407. p. 1764

Kemmerling, Annie, Dir, Neighborhood Servs, Denver Public Library, Ten W 14th Ave Pkwy, Denver, CO, 80204-2731. Tel: 720-865-1111. p. 275

Kemp, Angie, Head, Archives & Spec Coll, University of Mary Washington, 1801 College Ave, Fredericksburg, VA, 22401-5300. Tel: 540-654-1756. p. 2320

Kemp, Audrey, Br Mgr, Uinta County Library, Lyman Branch, 129 S Franklin St, Lyman, WY, 82937. Tel: 307-787-6556. p. 2494

Kemp, Bill, Librn, McLean County Museum of History, 200 N Main, Bloomington, IL, 61701. Tel: 309-827-0428. p. 543

Kennedy, Peggy, Librn, Uxbridge Public Library, Zephyr Branch, 13000 Concession 39, Zephyr, ON, L0E 1T0, CANADA. Tel: 905-473-2375. p. 2701

Kennedy, Sara, Br Mgr, Delaware County District Library, Orange Branch, 7171 Gooding Blvd, Delaware, OH, 43015. Tel: 740-549-2665. p. 1781

Kennedy Stephens, Myka, Librn, Lancaster Theological Seminary Library, 555 W James St, Lancaster, PA, 17603-9967. Tel: 717-290-8704. p. 1951

Kennedy, Sylvia, Ch, Mendenhall Public Library, 1630 Simpson Hwy 149, Mendenhall, MS, 39114. Tel: 601-847-2181. p. 1226

Kennedy, Tonya, Librn, New Market Public Library, 407 Main St, New Market, IA, 51646. Tel: 712-585-3467. p. 772

Kennedy, William, Librn, University of Redlands, 1249 E Colton Ave, Redlands, CA, 92374-3755. Tel: 909-748-8022. p. 199

Kennedy-Brunner, Kathy, Br Mgr, Public Library of Cincinnati & Hamilton County, Madeira Branch, 7200 Miami Ave, Madeira, OH, 45243. Tel: 513-369-6028. p. 1762

Kennedy-Grant, Alex, Supvr, New York University, Courant Institute of Mathematical Sciences, Warren Weaver Hall, 251 Mercer St, 12th Flr, New York, NY, 10012-1110. Tel: 212-998-3312. p. 1599

Kennedy-Witthar, Shawna, Dir, West Texas A&M University, 110 26th St, Canyon, TX, 79016. Tel: 806-651-2227. p. 2153

Kenner, Gil, Librn, Virginia Department of Transportation (VDOT) Research Library, 530 Edgemont Rd, Charlottesville, VA, 22903. Tel: 434-293-1926. p. 2310

Kennerly, John F, Assoc Dean of Libr, Erskine College & Theological Seminary, One Depot St, Due West, SC, 29639. Tel: 864-379-8788. p. 2058

Kennett, Dorothy, Library Contact, Second Presbyterian Church, 404 N Prairie St, Bloomington, IL, 61701. Tel: 309-828-6297. p. 543

Kennett, Julie, Circ Supvr, Greenville Public Library, 520 Sycamore St, Greenville, OH, 45331-1438. Tel: 937-548-3915. p. 1788

Kennett, Marilyn, Dir, Drake Community Library, 930 Park St, Grinnell, IA, 50112-2016. Tel: 641-236-2661. p. 756

Kenney, Ashley, Supvr, Pub Serv, Fitchburg Public Library, 610 Main St, Fitchburg, MA, 01420-3146. Tel: 978-829-1780. p. 1019

Kenney, Brian, Dir, White Plains Public Library, 100 Martine Ave, White Plains, NY, 10601. Tel: 914-422-1406. p. 1665

Kenney, Kyleen, Br Mgr, Chicago Public Library, Hegewisch, 3048 E 130th St, Chicago, IL, 60633. Tel: 312-747-0046. p. 556

Kenney, Leah, Head, Youth & Teen Serv, Royal Oak Public Library, 222 E Eleven Mile Rd, Royal Oak, MI, 48067-2633. Tel: 248-246-3731. p. 1146

Kenney, Tina, Circ, Silver Falls Library District, 410 S Water St, Silverton, OR, 97381. Tel: 503-873-5173. p. 1899

Kennon, Pamela, Br Supvr, Auglaize County Libraries, Edward R & Minnie D White Memorial Library, 108 E Wapakoneta St, Waynesfield, OH, 45896. Tel: 419-568-5851. p. 1828

Kenny, Anne, ILL Mgr, Boston College Libraries, Thomas P O'Neill Jr Library (Main Library), 140 Commonwealth Ave, Chestnut Hill, MA, 02467. Tel: 617-552-6937. p. 1011

Kenny, Gary, Librn, Sargent & Lundy, LLC, 55 E Monroe St, 24F60, Chicago, IL, 60603. Tel: 312-269-3525. p. 567

Kenny, Kathleen, Br Mgr, Monmouth County Library, West Long Branch, 95 Poplar Ave, West Long Branch, NJ, 07764. Tel: 732-222-5993. p. 1416

Kenny, Pat, Ref & Tech Librn, Glocester Libraries, Harmony Library, 195 Putnam Pike, Harmony, RI, 02829. Tel: 401-949-2850. p. 2030

Kenny, Tim, Libr Mgr, John Peter Smith Hospital, John S Marietta Memorial, 1500 S Main St, Fort Worth, TX, 76104. Tel: 817-702-5057. p. 2180

Keno, Sandy, Librn, Providence Sacred Heart Medical Center, 101 W Eighth Ave, Spokane, WA, 99204. Tel: 509-474-3094. p. 2384

Kensinger-Klopfer, Margaret, Br Mgr, San Luis Obispo County Library, Arroyo Grande Library, 800 W Branch St, Arroyo Grande, CA, 93420. Tel: 805-473-7165. p. 233

Kent, Alyson, Br Mgr, Lincoln County Public Library, Florence Soule Shanklin Memorial, 7837 Fairfield Forest Rd, Denver, NC, 28037. Tel: 704-483-3589. p. 1701

Kent, Amber, Libr Mgr, Casa Grande Public Library, 449 N Drylake St, Casa Grande, AZ, 85222. Tel: 520-421-8710. p. 57

Kent, Amber, Mgr, Casa Grande Public Library, Vista Grande Library, 1556 N Arizola Rd, Casa Grande, AZ, 85122. Tel: 520-421-8652. p. 57

Kent, April, Assoc Libr Dir, New Mexico Highlands University, 802 National Ave, Las Vegas, NM, 87701. Tel: 505-454-3139. p. 1471

Kent, Ethan, VPres, Project for Public Spaces, Inc, 419 Lafayette St, 7th Flr, New York, NY, 10003. Tel: 212-620-5660. p. 1600

Kent, Fred, Pres, Project for Public Spaces, Inc, 419 Lafayette St, 7th Flr, New York, NY, 10003. Tel: 212-620-5660. p. 1600

Kent, Gordon, Br Librn, Fayette County Public Libraries, Montgomery Branch, 507 Ferry St, Montgomery, WV, 25136. Tel: 304-442-5665. p. 2411

Kent, Julie, Dir, Erie City Public Library, 204 S Butler, Erie, KS, 66733-1349. Tel: 620-244-5119. p. 807

Kent, Kathy, Dir, Oneida County Library, 31 N 100 W, Malad City, ID, 83252-1234. Tel: 208-766-2229. p. 525

Kent, Mary, Acq, Tulsa Community College Libraries, Metro Campus, 909 S Boston Ave, Tulsa, OK, 74119-2011. Tel: 918-595-7175. p. 1866

Kent, Melinda, Librn, Sundridge-Strong Union Public Library, 110 Main St, Sundridge, ON, P0A 1Z0, CANADA. Tel: 705-384-7311. p. 2684

Kent, Nicole, Ref Librn, YA Librn, Henry Carter Hull Library, Inc, Ten Killingworth Tpk, Clinton, CT, 06413. Tel: 860-669-2342. p. 306

Kent, Nicole, Ref Librn, Teen Serv Librn, Southington Public Library & Museum, 255 Main St, Southington, CT, 06489. Tel: 860-628-0947. p. 338

Kent, Suzanne D, Adult Serv, Harper Woods Public Library, 19601 Harper, Harper Woods, MI, 48225. Tel: 313-343-2575. p. 1113

Kenton, Linda M, Town Librn, San Anselmo Public Library, 110 Tunstead Ave, San Anselmo, CA, 94960-2617. Tel: 415-258-4656. p. 212

Kenworthy, Steve, Dir, Clinton-Essex-Franklin Library System, 33 Oak St, Plattsburgh, NY, 12901-2810. Tel: 518-563-5190, Ext 111. p. 1619

Kenworthy, Wendy, Libr Asst, Dodge Center Public Library, 13 First Ave NW, Dodge Center, MN, 55927. Tel: 507-374-2275. p. 1171

Kenyon, Aimee, Librn, Otis Community Library, 122 S Main St, Otis, KS, 67565. Tel: 785-387-2287. p. 829

Kenyon, Bethany, Access Serv Librn, University of New England Libraries, Josephine S Abplanalp Library, Portland Campus, 716 Stevens Ave, Portland, ME, 04103. Tel: 207-221-4325. p. 917

Kenyon, Deborah, Libr Tech, Tri-County Community College, 21 Campus Circle, Murphy, NC, 28906. Tel: 828-835-4218, 828-837-6810. p. 1705

Kenyon, Thomas, Ref Librn, Tech Librn, Hudson Public Library, Three Washington St, Hudson, MA, 01749-2499. Tel: 978-568-9644. p. 1025

Kenzie, Monica, Archit/Art Librn, New Jersey Institute of Technology, Barbara & Leonard Littman Architecture & Design Library, 456 Weston Hall, 323 King Blvd, Newark, NJ, 07102-1982. Tel: 973-596-3083. p. 1427

Keogh, John, Br Mgr, Johnson County Library, Edgerton Branch, 319 E Nelson St, Edgerton, KS, 66021. p. 830

Keogh, John, Br Mgr, Johnson County Library, Gardner Branch, 137 E Shawnee St, Gardner, KS, 66030. p. 830

Keogh, John, Br Mgr, Johnson County Library, Spring Hill Branch, 109 S Webster St, Spring Hill, KS, 66083. p. 830

Keogh, Kristina, Dean of Libr, University of South Florida Saint Petersburg, 140 Seventh Ave S, POY118, Saint Petersburg, FL, 33701-5016. Tel: 727-873-4400. p. 442

Keogh, Patricia, Acq Librn, Head, Cat, Long Island University, One University Plaza, Brooklyn, NY, 11201. Tel: 718-780-4513. p. 1505

Keon, Dan, Dir, Human Res, Toronto Public Library, 789 Yonge St, Toronto, ON, M4W 2G8, CANADA. Tel: 416-393-7131. p. 2693

Keough, Anne, Br Mgr, Chicago Public Library, Blackstone, 4904 S Lake Park Ave, Chicago, IL, 60615. Tel: 312-747-0511. p. 556

Keough, Brian, Head, Spec Coll & Archives, University at Albany, State University of New York, 1400 Washington Ave, Albany, NY, 12222-0001. Tel: 518-437-3931. p. 1484

Keough, Nancy, Br Mgr, Martin County Library System, 2351 SE Monterey Rd, Stuart, FL, 34996. Tel: 772-221-1402. p. 444

Kepich, Jacey, Access Serv Coordr, Asst Music Librn, Interlochen Center for the Arts, Frederick & Elizabeth Ludwig Fennell Music Library, 4000 Hwy M-137, Interlochen, MI, 49643. Tel: 231-276-7230. p. 1118

Kepler, Christy, Head, Youth Serv, Oswego Public Library District, Oswego Campus, 32 W Jefferson St, Oswego, IL, 60543. Tel: 630-554-3150. p. 630

Kepner, Linda Tiernan, Tech Serv Librn, Peterborough Town Library, Two Concord St, Peterborough, NH, 03458. Tel: 603-924-8040. p. 1378

Kepple, Todd, Mgr, Klamath County Museum & Baldwin Hotel Museum, 1451 Main St, Klamath Falls, OR, 97601. Tel: 541-883-4208. p. 1883

Kerby, Erin, Veterinary Med Librn, University of Illinois Library at Urbana-Champaign, Veterinary Medicine, 1257 Veterinary Med Basic Science Bldg, 2001 S Lincoln Ave, Urbana, IL, 61802. Tel: 217-244-1295. p. 656

Kerby, Ramona N, Dr, Coordr, Prof, McDaniel College, Graduate Studies, Two College Hill, Westminster, MD, 21157-4390. Tel: 410-857-2507. p. 2786

Kercheck, Diane, Interim Libr Mgr, Milwaukee Area Technical College, 700 W State St, Milwaukee, WI, 53233-1443. Tel: 414-297-7030. p. 2459

Kercher, Rachel, Ch, Leach Public Library, 417 Second Ave N, Wahpeton, ND, 58075. Tel: 701-642-5732. p. 1741

Kerckhove, Kelly, Coll Develop, Mkt Coordr, Dunlap Public Library District, 302 S First St, Dunlap, IL, 61525. Tel: 309-243-5716. p. 580

Kerecman, Linda, Med Librn, Northern Light Eastern Maine Medical Center, 489 State St, Bangor, ME, 04401. Tel: 207-973-8228. p. 915

Kerestes, Sharon, Curric Center Librn, Cedarville University, 251 N Main St, Cedarville, OH, 45314-0601. Tel: 937-766-7840. p. 1757

Keresztury, Barbara, Ad, Southgate Veterans Memorial Library, 14680 Dix-Toledo Rd, Southgate, MI, 48195. Tel: 734-258-3002. p. 1152

Kerfien, Penny, Dir, Ogdensburg Public Library, 312 Washington St, Ogdensburg, NY, 13669-1518. Tel: 315-393-4325. p. 1610

Keris, Holly, Chief Curator, Cummer Museum of Art & Gardens Library, 829 Riverside Ave, Jacksonville, FL, 32204. Tel: 904-356-6857. p. 411

Kerkvliet, Deb, Cat, Hamline University, Bush Memorial Library, 1536 Hewitt, Saint Paul, MN, 55104. Tel: 651-523-2375. p. 1199

Kern, Alex, Asst Librn, Stanislaus County Law Library, 1101 13th St, Modesto, CA, 95354. Tel: 209-558-7759. p. 178

Kern, Brian, Assoc Dir of Libr, Allegheny College, 520 N Main St, Meadville, PA, 16335. Tel: 814-332-3792. p. 1959

Kern, Linda, Dean, Libr Serv, Brenau University, 625 Academy St, Gainesville, GA, 30501-3343. Tel: 770-534-6113. p. 480

Kern, Lisa, Library Contact, College Church in Wheaton Library, 332 E Seminary Ave, Wheaton, IL, 60187. Tel: 630-668-0878, Ext 138. p. 661

Kern, Lisa, Br Mgr, Fairfax County Public Library, Oakton Library, 10304 Lynnhaven Pl, Oakton, VA, 22124-1785. Tel: 703-242-4020. p. 2316

Kern, Lucy, Librn, Pennsylvania German Cultural Heritage Center, 15155 Kutztown Rd, Kutztown, PA, 19530. Tel: 484-646-4165. p. 1950

Kern, Thomas D, Dir, Wauconda Area Public Library District, 801 N Main St, Wauconda, IL, 60084. Tel: 847-526-6225, Ext 209. p. 659

Kerner, Susie, Librn, Tecumseh Public Library, 170 Branch St, Tecumseh, NE, 68450. Tel: 402-335-2060. p. 1338

Kernohan-Berning, Erin, Br Serv Librn, Dep Chief Exec Officer, Haliburton County Public Library, Administrative Ctr, 78 Maple Ave, Haliburton, ON, K0M 1S0, CANADA. Tel: 705-457-2241. p. 2644

Kerns, Cindi, Librn, Mosaic Life Care, 5325 Faraon St, Saint Joseph, MO, 64506. Tel: 816-271-6075. p. 1268

Kerns, Halie, Access Serv Librn, SUNY Canton, 34 Cornell Dr, Canton, NY, 13617. Tel: 315-386-7056. p. 1514

Kerns, Julie, Mgr, Outreach Serv, Westerville Public Library, 126 S State St, Westerville, OH, 43081. Tel: 614-882-7277. p. 1830

Kerns, Karen, Dir, Bowling Green Public Library, 201 W Locust St, Bowling Green, MO, 63334. Tel: 573-324-5030. p. 1238

Kerns, Kathy, Curator, Educ Res, Head of Libr, Stanford University Libraries, Cubberley Education Library, Education Bldg, Rm 202-205, 485 Lasuen Mall, Stanford, CA, 94305-3097. Tel: 650-996-0592. p. 248

Kerns, Katie, Br Mgr, Martin County Library System, Elisabeth Lahti Library, 15200 SW Adams Ave, Indiantown, FL, 34956. Tel: 772-597-4200. p. 445

Kerns, Resa, Assoc Law Librn, University of Missouri-Columbia, Law Library, 203 Hulston Hall, Columbia, MO, 65211-4190. Tel: 573-882-5108. p. 1244

Kerns, Rick, Head, Tech Serv & Electronic Res, Creighton University, 2500 California Plaza, Omaha, NE, 68178-0209. Tel: 402-280-2228. p. 1328

Kerns, Stephanie, Dir, Dartmouth College Library, Dana Biomedical Library, HB 6168, 37 Dewey Field Rd, 3rd Flr, Hanover, NH, 03755-1417. Tel: 603-650-1668. p. 1366

Kerr, Alecia, Ref & Instruction Librn, City Colleges of Chicago, Kennedy-King College Library, 6403 S Halsted, Chicago, IL, 60621. Tel: 773-602-5449. p. 558

Kerr, Alecia, Libr Dir, La Roche University, 9000 Babcock Blvd, Pittsburgh, PA, 15237. Tel: 412-536-1063. p. 1994

Kerr, Barbara E, Dir, Medford Public Library, 200 Boston Ave, Ste G-350, Medford, MA, 02155. Tel: 781-395-7950. p. 1033

Kerr Dodds, Katie, Asst Dean, Pepperdine University Libraries, School of Law-Jerene Appleby Harnish Law Library, 24255 Pacific Coast Hwy, Malibu, CA, 90263. Tel: 310-506-4643. p. 171

Kerr, Jessica A, Libr Dir, Woodstock Public Library District, Five Library Lane, Woodstock, NY, 12498. Tel: 845-679-2213. p. 1667

Kerr, Joanna Aiton, Dir, Diocesan Synod of Fredericton, 23 Dineen Dr, Fredericton, NB, E3B 5H1, CANADA. Tel: 506-429-2450. p. 2600

Kerr, Joanna Aiton, Dir, Provincial Archives of New Brunswick, 23 Dineen Dr, Fredericton, NB, E3B 5A3, CANADA. Tel: 506-453-2122. p. 2601

Kerr, John Eddie, Librn, Wellington Law Association Library, Court House, 74 Woolwich St, Guelph, ON, N1H 3T9, CANADA. Tel: 519-763-6365. p. 2644

Kerr, Karalee, Asst Dir, Grimes Public Library, 200 N James, Grimes, IA, 50111. Tel: 515-986-3551. p. 756

Kerr, Marla, Circ Serv, Sioux City Public Library, 529 Pierce St, Sioux City, IA, 51101-1203. Tel: 712-255-2933. p. 783

Kerr, Nancy, Dir, L E Phillips Memorial Public Library, 400 Eau Claire St, Eau Claire, WI, 54701. Tel: 715-839-1648, 715-839-5004. p. 2432

Kerr, Perian P, Librn, Starkville-Oktibbeha County Public, Sturgis Public Library, 2732 Hwy 12 W, Sturgis, MS, 39769. Tel: 662-465-7493. p. 1233

Kerr, Shanni, Teen Librn, Ionia Community Library, 126 E Main St, Ionia, MI, 48846. Tel: 616-527-3680. p. 1118

Kerrick, Beth, Ch, Marshall County Public Library System, 1003 Poplar St, Benton, KY, 42025. Tel: 270-527-9969, Ext 126. p. 848

Kerrigan, Beth, Ch Serv, Memorial Hall Library, 2 N Main St, Andover, MA, 01810. Tel: 978-623-8400. p. 985

Kerrigan, Dana J, Ms, Col Librn, Director of Library & Academic Support, Valley Forge Military Academy & College, 1001 Eagle Rd, Wayne, PA, 19087-3695. Tel: 610-989-1359, 610-989-1364. p. 2019

Kersey, Cheryl, Dir, Three Oaks Township Public Library, Three N Elm St, Three Oaks, MI, 49128-1303. Tel: 269-756-5621. p. 1153

Kersey, Jeff, Readers' Advisory, Arkansas State Library for the Blind & Print Disabled, 900 W Capitol Ave, Ste 100, Little Rock, AR, 72201-3108. Tel: 501-682-2856. p. 100

Kershaw, Alicia, Dir, J C Wheeler Public Library, 1576 S Main St, Martin, MI, 49070-9728. Tel: 269-672-7875. p. 1131

Kershaw, Cheryl, Librn, Township Library of Silver Creek, 309 Vine St, Silver Creek, NE, 68663. Tel: 308-773-2594. p. 1336

Kershaw, Mariko, Tech Serv Librn, University of Hawaii, 45-720 Kea'ahala Rd, Kaneohe, HI, 96744. Tel: 808-235-7439. p. 513

Kershner, Mary, Asst Dir, Whiting Public Library, 1735 Oliver St, Whiting, IN, 46394-1794. Tel: 219-659-0269, Ext 112. p. 726

Kershner, Seth, Librn, Northwestern Connecticut Community College Library, Park Pl E, Winsted, CT, 06098. Tel: 860-738-6481. p. 348

Kersten, Nicholas J, Dir of Educ, Seventh Day Baptist Historical Library & Archives, 3120 Kennedy Rd, Janesville, WI, 53545-0225. Tel: 608-752-5055. p. 2443

Kerstens, Elizabeth Kelley, Exec Dir, Plymouth Historical Museum Archives, 155 S Main St, Plymouth, MI, 48170-1635. Tel: 734-455-8940, Ext 3. p. 1141

Kersting, Dulce, Exec Dir, Latah County Historical Society Library, 327 E Second St, Moscow, ID, 83843. Tel: 208-882-1004. p. 526

Kersting-Lark, Dulce, Head, Spec Coll & Archives, University of Idaho Library, 850 S Rayburn St, Moscow, ID, 83844. Tel: 208-885-1309. p. 526

Kerth, Michael, IT Supvr, Carnegie-Stout Public Library, 360 W 11th St, Dubuque, IA, 52001. Tel: 563-589-4229. p. 748

Kerul, Linda, Br Mgr, Toledo-Lucas County Public Library, Reynolds Corners, 4833 Dorr St, Toledo, OH, 43615. Tel: 419-259-5320. p. 1824

Kervin, Jillian, Exec Dir, Waterville Public Library, 206 White St, Waterville, NY, 13480. Tel: 315-841-4651. p. 1660

Kerwin, Hannah, Br Mgr, Somerset County Library System of New Jersey, Watchung Public, 12 Stirling Rd, Watchung, NJ, 07069. Tel: 908-458-8455. p. 1393

Kerwin, Jackie, Dir, Silverton Public Library, 1117 Reese, Silverton, CO, 81433. Tel: 970-387-5770. p. 295

Kerzner, Carrie, Librn, Congregation Mishkan Israel Library, 785 Ridge Rd, Hamden, CT, 06517. Tel: 203-288-3877. p. 315

Kesey, Heather, Librn, Emma Humphrey Library, 150 A St E, Vale, OR, 97918-1345. Tel: 541-473-3902. p. 1901

Keslar, Joseph, Libr Mgr, Res, Tech, Montgomery, McCracken, Walker & Rhoads LLP Library, 1735 Market St, Philadelphia, PA, 19103. Tel: 215-772-7611. p. 1983

Kessel Szpiszar, Jodi, Dir, Johnson Creek Public Library, 125 Lincoln St, Johnson Creek, WI, 53038. Tel: 920-699-3741. p. 2443

Kessenger, Holland, Supvry Librn, Marine Corps Recruit Depot Library, 3800 Chosin Ave, Bldg 7 W, San Diego, CA, 92140-5196. Tel: 619-524-1849. p. 215

Kessler, Danielle, Archivist, Cataloger & Acq, College of Saint Mary Library, 7000 Mercy Rd, Omaha, NE, 68106-2606. Tel: 402-399-2464. p. 1327

Kessler, Evelyn, E-Resources & Content Discovery Librn, University of the Pacific Libraries, 3601 Pacific Ave, Stockton, CA, 95211. Tel: 209-946-3016. p. 250

Kessler, Jane, Dir of Coll, University at Albany, State University of New York, 1400 Washington Ave, Albany, NY, 12222-0001. Tel: 518-442-3830. p. 1484

Kessler, K Eva, Research Services Admin, Gordon Feinblatt LLC, 1001 Fleet St, Ste 700, Baltimore, MD, 21202. Tel: 410-576-4251. p. 953

Kessler Lee, Gina, Head, Teaching & Research Services, Saint Mary's College Library, 1928 Saint Mary's Rd, Moraga, CA, 94575. Tel: 925-631-4229. p. 180

Kessler, Nicole, Dir, Lincoln Park Public Library, 1381 Southfield Rd, Lincoln Park, MI, 48146. Tel: 313-381-0374. p. 1127

Kestel, Suzanne, Ch, Perry Public Library, 1101 Willis Ave, Perry, IA, 50220. Tel: 515-465-3569. p. 777

Kesten, Robert, Exec Dir, Stonewall National Museum, Archives & Library, 1300 E Sunrise Blvd, Fort Lauderdale, FL, 33304. Tel: 954-763-8565. p. 402

Kester, Denise, Ch, Corning Public Library, 603 Ninth St, Corning, IA, 50841-1304. Tel: 641-322-3866. p. 742

Kesterson, Cathy, Head, Tech Serv, Delphi Public Library, 222 E Main St, Delphi, IN, 46923. Tel: 765-564-2929. p. 679

Kesterson, Colleen, Librn, Missoula Public Library, Swan Valley Community, 6811 Hwy 83, Condon, MT, 59826. Tel: 406-754-2521. p. 1300

Kestler, Ulrike, Pub Serv Librn, Kwantlen Polytechnic University Library, 12666 72nd Ave, Surrey, BC, V3W 2M8, CANADA. Tel: 604-599-3199. p. 2576

Kestner, Tonia, Exec Dir, Bristol Public Library, 701 Goode St, Bristol, VA, 24201. Tel: 276-645-8782. p. 2308

Ketcham, Maria, Dept Head, Detroit Institute of Arts, 5200 Woodward Ave, Detroit, MI, 48202. Tel: 313-833-3460. p. 1097

Ketchan, Steve, Br Mgr, West Bloomfield Township Public Library, Westacres, 7321 Commerce Rd, West Bloomfield, MI, 48324. Tel: 248-232-2401. p. 1159

Ketchu, Karen, Dir, Madison Valley Public Library, 210 Main St, Ennis, MT, 59729. Tel: 406-682-7244. p. 1292

Ketchum, David, Head, Access Serv, University of Oregon Libraries, 1501 Kincaid St, Eugene, OR, 97403-1299. Tel: 541-346-3053. p. 1879

Ketchum, William, Ref Librn, University of La Verne, 320 E D St, Ontario, CA, 91764. Tel: 909-460-2063. p. 188

Ketelsen, Leanne, Dir, Morley Public Library, 507 Vine St, Morley, IA, 52312. Tel: 319-489-9271. p. 771

Ketelsen, Leanne M, Dir, Olin Public Library, 301 Parkway St, Olin, IA, 52320. Tel: 319-484-2944. p. 774

Ketelsen, Wendy, Asst Librn, Lied Lincoln Township Library, 603 E Norris St, Wausa, NE, 68786. Tel: 402-586-2454. p. 1340

Ketola, Jessica, Dir, Meagher County City Library, 205 SW Garfield, White Sulphur Springs, MT, 59645. Tel: 406-547-2250. p. 1304

Kettel, James, Supvr, Genealogy Serv, Boyd County Public Library, 1740 Central Ave, Ashland, KY, 41101. Tel: 606-329-0090. p. 847

Kettells, Betcinda, Dir, St Pete Beach Public Library, 365 73rd Ave, Saint Pete Beach, FL, 33706-1996. Tel: 727-363-9238. p. 441

Kettering, Laura, Mgr, Medina County District Library, Buckeye Library, 6625 Wolff Rd, Medina, OH, 44256-6211. Tel: 330-725-4415. p. 1801

Ketterman, Beth, Interim Dir, East Carolina University, William E Laupus Health Sciences Library, 500 Health Sciences Dr, Greenville, NC, 27834. Tel: 252-744-2219. p. 1693

Kettler, Pamela, Dir, Valley Park Library, 320 Benton St, Valley Park, MO, 63088. Tel: 636-225-5608. p. 1284

Kettles, Michelle, Libr Mgr, Bonanza Municipal Library, PO Box 53, Bonanza, AB, T0H 0K0, CANADA. Tel: 780-353-3067. p. 2524

Kettling Law, Elys, Res & Info Serv Librn, The College of Wooster Libraries, 1140 Beall Ave, Wooster, OH, 44691-2364. Tel: 330-263-2443. p. 1833

Ketzer, Amy, Librn, Mid-Arkansas Regional Library, Fohrell Public Library, 186 Dallas 208, Sparkman, AR, 71763. Tel: 870-678-2561. p. 103

Keuneke, Beth, Coord, Ad Serv, St Marys Community Public Library, 140 S Chestnut St, Saint Marys, OH, 45885. Tel: 419-394-7471. p. 1819

Kevil, Tim, Dean of Libr, Navarro College, 3200 W Seventh Ave, Corsicana, TX, 75110-4899. Tel: 903-875-7442. p. 2161

Keville, Kathi, Dir, American Herb Association Library, PO Box 1673, Nevada City, CA, 95959. Tel: 530-274-3140. p. 182

Kevin, Bourque, Head Librn, Newburyport Public Library, 94 State St, Newburyport, MA, 01950-6619. Tel: 978-465-4428. p. 1038

Kevlahan, Christopher, Br Head, Vancouver Public Library, Oakridge Branch, 6184 Ash St, Vancouver, BC, V5Z 3G9, CANADA. Tel: 604-665-3980. p. 2582

Key, Delissa, Head, Circ, Washington County Free Library, 100 S Potomac St, Hagerstown, MD, 21740. Tel: 301-739-3250. p. 968

Key, Nyisha, Br Mgr, Coastal Plain Regional Library System, Cook County, 213 E Second St, Adel, GA, 31620. Tel: 229-896-3652. p. 500

Keyes, Charles, Instrul Serv, Fiorello H LaGuardia Community College Library, 31-10 Thomson Ave, Long Island City, NY, 11101. Tel: 718-482-6018. p. 1565

Keyes, Christopher, Circ Serv, Norfolk Library, Nine Greenwoods Rd E, Norfolk, CT, 06058-1320. Tel: 860-542-5075. p. 330

Keyes, Christy, Dir, Lighthouse Point Library, 2200 NE 38th St, Lighthouse Point, FL, 33064-3913. Tel: 954-946-6398. p. 418

Keyes, Kelli, Youth Serv Librn, Columbus Public Library, 2500 14th St, Ste 2, Columbus, NE, 68601. Tel: 402-562-4203. p. 1311

Keyes, Linda, Librn, Spokane Community College/Community Colleges of Spokane Library, MS 2160, 1810 N Greene St, Spokane, WA, 99217-5399. Tel: 509-533-7653. p. 2384

Keyes, Patricia, Asst Dir, Oakley Public Library, 700 W Third St, Oakley, KS, 67748. Tel: 785-671-4776. p. 828

Keyes-Kaplafka, Laura, Dir, Ref Serv, Dunlap Public Library District, 302 S First St, Dunlap, IL, 61525. Tel: 309-243-5716. p. 580

Keys, Daphene, Librn, Houston Community College - Southwest College, Missouri City (Sienna) Campus, 5855 Sienna Springs Way, Missouri City, TX, 77459. Tel: 713-718-2942. p. 2195

Keyser, Jessica, Dir, Grosse Pointe Public Library, Ten Kercheval Ave, Grosse Pointe Farms, MI, 48236-3602. Tel: 313-343-2074. p. 1112

Keyser, Marcia, Instrul Serv Librn, Drake University, 2725 University Ave, Des Moines, IA, 50311. Tel: 515-271-3989. p. 746

Khachikian, Angela, Circ, Libr Tech, Glendale Community College Library, 1500 N Verdugo Rd, Glendale, CA, 91208-2894. Tel: 818-240-1000, Ext 5581, 818-240-1000, Ext 5586. p. 148

Khader, Majed, Dr, Assoc Univ Librn, Dir, Marshall University Libraries, Morrow Library, Third Ave, Huntington, WV, 25755. Tel: 304-696-3121. p. 2405

Khajadourian, Tamar, Librn, Ref, Los Angeles Harbor College, 1111 Figueroa Pl, Wilmington, CA, 90744. Tel: 310-233-4482. p. 260

Khamouna, Mo, Libr Spec, Nebraska College of Technical Agriculture Library, 404 E Seventh St, Curtis, NE, 69025. Tel: 308-367-5213. p. 1312

Khamphavong, Megan, Librn, Sentara RMH Medical Center, 2010 Health Campus Dr, Harrisonburg, VA, 22801-3293. Tel: 540-689-1777. p. 2325

Khamphavong, Megan, Librn, Southwestern Virginia Health Information Librarians, Sentara RMH Virginia Funkhouser Health Sciences Library, 2010 Health Campus Drive, Harrisonburg, VA, 22801. Tel: 540-689-1772. p. 2776

Khan, A K, Asst Dean, Finance & Admin, University of North Texas Libraries, 1155 Union Circle, No 305190, Denton, TX, 76203-5017. Tel: 940-369-8165. p. 2170

Khan, Caren, Circulation/Account Servs, Farmers Branch Manske Library, 13613 Webb Chapel Rd, Farmers Branch, TX, 75234. Tel: 972-919-9830. p. 2176

Khan, Caren, Circ Supvr, Manske Library, 13613 Webb Chapel, Farmers Branch, TX, 75234-3756. Tel: 972-247-2511. p. 2176

Khan, Hammad, Dir, Libr Serv, Columbus College of Art & Design, 60 Cleveland Ave, Columbus, OH, 43215. Tel: 614-222-3273. p. 1772

Khan, Karim, Dir, Montgomery-Floyd Regional Library System, 125 Sheltman St, Christiansburg, VA, 24073. Tel: 540-382-6965. p. 2312

Khan, Margaret, Dir, Booth & Dimock Memorial Library, 1134 Main St, Coventry, CT, 06238. Tel: 860-742-7606. p. 306

Khan, Omar, Dir, Ridgefield Park Free Public Library, 107 Cedar St, Ridgefield Park, NJ, 07660. Tel: 201-641-0689. p. 1439

Khan, Sahar, Health Sci Librn, University of Bridgeport, 126 Park Ave, Bridgeport, CT, 06604-5620. Tel: 203-576-4745. p. 304

Khan, Star, Outreach Coordr, Driftwood Public Library, 801 SW Hwy 101, Ste 201, Lincoln City, OR, 97367-2720. Tel: 541-996-2277. p. 1885

Khan, Urooj, ILL, William Paterson University, 300 Pompton Rd, Wayne, NJ, 07470. Tel: 973-720-2541. p. 1452

Khanzhina, Yelena, Librn, Pennsylvania Joint State Government Commission Library, 108 Finance Bldg, Rm G-16, Harrisburg, PA, 17120. Tel: 717-787-6851. p. 1941

Khasrowpour, Shahrzad, Acq & Cat, Coordr, Chapman University, One University Dr, Orange, CA, 92866. Tel: 714-532-7756. p. 188

Khatri, Cindy, Pub Relations Mgr, Downers Grove Public Library, 1050 Curtiss St, Downers Grove, IL, 60515. Tel: 630-960-1200, Ext 4296. p. 579

Khatun, Taslima, Libr Spec, Northern Virginia Community College Libraries, Woodbridge Library, Bldg WAS, Rm 230, 15200 Neabsco Mills Rd, Woodbridge, VA, 22191. Tel: 703-878-5733. p. 2304

Khawam, Heidi, Dir, Gowanda Free Library, 56 W Main St, Gowanda, NY, 14070-1390. Tel: 716-532-3451. p. 1540

Khebzou, Dustin, Adminr, Alcohol Research Group Library, 6001 Shellmound St, Ste 450, Emeryville, CA, 94608. Tel: 510-898-5800. p. 140

Khil, Jan, Librn, Hawaii School for the Deaf & Blind Library, Bldg E, 3440 Leahi Ave, Honolulu, HI, 96815. Tel: 808-307-6900. p. 506

Khipple, Lucia, Asst Libr Dir, Dir, Youth Serv, Rolling Meadows Library, 3110 Martin Lane, Rolling Meadows, IL, 60008. Tel: 847-259-6050. p. 642

Khokhlov, Semyon, Res & Instruction Librn, Haverford College, 370 Lancaster Ave, Haverford, PA, 19041-1392. Tel: 610-896-2976. p. 1942

Khongphatthana, Phinh, Tech Mgr, Canal Fulton Public Library, 154 Market St NE, Canal Fulton, OH, 44614-1196. Tel: 330-854-4148. p. 1754

Khoury, Jennifer, Communications Coordr, Derry Public Library, 64 E Broadway, Derry, NH, 03038-2412. Tel: 603-432-6140. p. 1361

Kia, Fatemeh Salehian, Asst Professor of Teaching, University of British Columbia, The Irving K Barber Learning Ctr, 1961 E Mall, Ste 470, Vancouver, BC, V6T 1Z1, CANADA. Tel: 604-822-2404. p. 2795

Kiang, Agnes, Law Librn, United States Court of Appeals for the Armed Forces Library, 450 E St NW, Washington, DC, 20442-0001. Tel: 202-761-1466. p. 377

Kibirige, Harry, Prof, Queens College of the City University of New York, Benjamin Rosenthal Library, Rm 254, 65-30 Kissena Blvd, Flushing, NY, 11367-1597. Tel: 718-997-3790. p. 2789

Kibler, Chris, Libr Dir, Tredyffrin Public Library, 582 Upper Gulph Rd, Strafford, PA, 19087-2096. Tel: 610-688-7092. p. 2010

Kibler, M Robin, Head, Coll Mgt, Williams College, 26 Hopkins Hall Dr, Williamstown, MA, 01267. Tel: 413-597-3047. p. 1069

Kiburn, Lena, Dir, Framingham Public Library, 49 Lexington St, Framingham, MA, 01702-8278. Tel: 508-532-5570. p. 1019

Kicinski, Joy, Br Mgr, Free Library of Philadelphia, Greater Olney Branch, 5501 N Fifth St, Philadelphia, PA, 19120-2805. Tel: 215-685-2846. p. 1978

Kickles, Christine, Ref Librn, College of DuPage Library, 425 Fawell Blvd, Glen Ellyn, IL, 60137-6599. Tel: 630-942-2313. p. 593

Kidd, Alyce, Br Supvr, Franklin County Library, Bunn Branch, 610 Main St, Bunn, NC, 27508. Tel: 919-496-6764. p. 1701

Kidd, Alyce, Br Supvr, Franklin County Library, Franklinton Branch, Nine W Mason St, Franklinton, NC, 27525. Tel: 919-494-2736. p. 1701

Kidd, Alyce, Br Supvr, Franklin County Library, Youngsville Branch, 218 US 1A Hwy S, Youngsville, NC, 27596. Tel: 919-556-1612. p. 1701

Kidd, Betty, Br Mgr, Mobile Public Library, Virginia Dillard Smith/Toulminville Branch, 601 Stanton Rd, Mobile, AL, 36617-2209. Tel: 251-438-7075. p. 26

Kidd, Creed, Libr Dir, Red Feather Lakes Community Library, 71 Firehouse Lane, Red Feather Lakes, CO, 80545. Tel: 970-881-2664. p. 294

Kidd, Jenn, Reader Advisor, Staunton Public Library, Talking Book Center, One Churchville Ave, Staunton, VA, 24401-3229. Tel: 540-885-6215. p. 2347

Kidd, Kevin, Dean, Bridgewater State University, Ten Shaw Rd, Bridgewater, MA, 02325. Tel: 508-531-1392. p. 1002

Kiddell, Dawn, Chief Librn/CEO, Cornwall Public Library, 45 Second St E, Cornwall, ON, K6H 1Y2, CANADA. Tel: 613-932-4796. p. 2637
Kidder, Rebecca, Br Mgr, Saline County Public Library, 1800 Smithers Dr, Benton, AR, 72015. Tel: 501-778-4766. p. 90
Kidder, Rebecca, Br Mgr, Saline County Public Library, Mabel Boswell Memorial Library - Bryant, 201 Pricket Rd, Bryant, AR, 72022. Tel: 501-847-2166. p. 90
Kidney, Shannon, Ref (Info Servs), Teen Serv, Pender County Public Library, 103 S Cowan St, Burgaw, NC, 28425. Tel: 910-259-1234. p. 1676
Kidwell, Barbara, Readers' Advisory, West Virginia Schools for the Deaf & the Blind Library, 301 E Main St, Romney, WV, 26757. Tel: 304-822-4894. p. 2414
Kidwell, Eric A, Dir, Libr Serv, Huntingdon College, 1500 E Fairview Ave, Montgomery, AL, 36106. Tel: 334-833-4421. p. 28
Kiebuzinski, Ksenya, Dr, Head of Libr, University of Toronto Libraries, Petro Jacyk Central & East European Resource Centre, Robarts Library, 130 St George St,3rd Flr, Rm 3008, Toronto, ON, M5S 1A5, CANADA. Tel: 416-978-4826. p. 2699
Kiedaisch, Christa, Head, Children's Servx, Booth & Dimock Memorial Library, 1134 Main St, Coventry, CT, 06238. Tel: 860-742-7606. p. 306
Kiedrowski, Cathy, Dir, Pub Libr Serv, Idea Exchange, One North Sq, Cambridge, ON, N1S 2K6, CANADA. Tel: 519-621-0460. p. 2635
Kiefer, Jessica, Head, Children's Servx, Greensburg Hempfield Area Library, 237 S Pennsylvania Ave, Greensburg, PA, 15601-3086. Tel: 724-837-5620. p. 1938
Kiehl, Gregg, Libr Dir, Tompkins Cortland Community College Library, Baker Commons, 2nd Flr, 170 North St, Dryden, NY, 13053-8504. Tel: 607-844-8222, Ext 4360. p. 1526
Kiekhaefer, Katie, Head, Youth Serv, Whitefish Bay Public Library, 5420 N Marlborough Dr, Whitefish Bay, WI, 53217. Tel: 414-964-4380. p. 2488
Kiel, Ashlee B, Dir, Highland Community Library, 330 Schoolhouse Rd, Johnstown, PA, 15904-2924. Tel: 814-266-5610. p. 1948
Kiel, Diana, Coll Develop, Coordr, Tech Serv, Iona University, 715 North Ave, New Rochelle, NY, 10801-1890. Tel: 914-633-2417. p. 1577
Kiel, Mike, Interim Head, Ref & Instruction, University of Baltimore, 1420 Maryland Ave, Baltimore, MD, 21201. Tel: 410-837-4236. p. 957
Kielar, Donna, Librn, Clark Hill PLC, 500 Woodward Ave, Ste 3500, Detroit, MI, 48226-3435. Tel: 313-965-8277. p. 1097
Kielley, Liz Y, Metadata & Discovery Librn, Messiah University, One University Ave, Ste 3002, Mechanicsburg, PA, 17055. Tel: 717-691-6006, Ext 3850. p. 1960
Kiely, Daniel, Dept Chair, Diablo Valley College Library, 321 Golf Club Rd, Pleasant Hill, CA, 94523-1576. Tel: 925-969-2583. p. 195
Kien, Adrian, Ref Librn, Montana Tech Library, 1300 W Park St, Butte, MT, 59701. Tel: 406-496-4286. p. 1290
Kienenberger, Karen, Libr Mgr, Timberland Regional Library, McCleary Branch, 121 S Fourth St, McCleary, WA, 98557. Tel: 360-495-3368. p. 2389
Kienzle, Caroline, Dir, Apalachicola Margaret Key Library, 80 12th St, Apalachicola, FL, 32320. Tel: 850-653-8436. p. 383
Kieren, Robert, Dep Dir, Prescott Valley Public Library, 7401 E Skoog Blvd, Prescott Valley, AZ, 86314. Tel: 928-759-3040. p. 75
Kierkosza, Lubomira, Commun Libr Mgr, Queens Library, Broadway Community Library, 40-20 Broadway, Long Island City, NY, 11103. Tel: 718-721-2462. p. 1554
Kieron-Sanchez, Wendy, Head, Classified Library, United States Naval War College Library, 686 Cushing Rd, Newport, RI, 02841-1207. Tel: 401-841-6504. p. 2035
Kierons, Mary, Chair, Kootenay Library Federation, PO Box 3125, Castlegar, BC, V1N 3H4, CANADA. Tel: 250-608-4490. p. 2564
Kierpiec, Rhonda, Br Mgr, Colleton County Memorial Library, Cottageville Branch Library, 72 Salley Ackerman Dr, Cottageville, SC, 29435. Tel: 843-835-5621. p. 2072
Kiesinger, Karson, Ref Librn, Bennington Free Library, 101 Silver St, Bennington, VT, 05201. Tel: 802-442-9051. p. 2279
Kiesling, Linda, Libr Asst, Central Baptist Theological Seminary Library, 6601 Monticello Rd, Shawnee, KS, 66226-3513. Tel: 913-667-5733. p. 836
Kietzman, Kim, Dir, Altoona Public Library, 700 Eighth St SW, Altoona, IA, 50009. Tel: 515-967-3881. p. 730
Kievit-Mason, Barbara A, Archivist, Sam Houston State University, 1830 Bobby K Marks Dr, Huntsville, TX, 77340. Tel: 936-294-3699. p. 2201
Kifflie, Scott, Adult Serv Mgr, Menomonee Falls Public Library, W156 N8436 Pilgrim Rd, Menomonee Falls, WI, 53051. Tel: 262-532-8900. p. 2455
Kiger, David, Librn, Emmanuel Christian Seminary Library, One Walker Dr, Johnson City, TN, 37601. Tel: 423-461-1541. p. 2104
Kiger, David, Dir of Libr, Theological Librn, Milligan College, 200 Blowers Blvd, Milligan College, TN, 37682. Tel: 423-461-1541. p. 2116
Kight, Dawn, Dean of Libr, Southern University, 167 Roosevelt Steptoe Ave, Baton Rouge, LA, 70813-0001. Tel: 225-771-4990. p. 884
Kight, Stephen, Asst Dir, Pub Serv, Forsyth County Public Library, 585 Dahlonega St, Cumming, GA, 30040-2109. Tel: 770-781-9840. p. 473
Kiiskinen, Kim, Ref Serv, River Falls Public Library, 140 Union St, River Falls, WI, 54022. Tel: 715-425-0905, Ext 664. p. 2474
Kilberg, Jackie, Tech Asst, Wake Technical Community College, Western Wake Library, Millpond Village, Ste 200, 3434 Kildaire Farms Rd, Cary, NC, 27518-2277. Tel: 919-866-5701. p. 1711
Kilbert, Linda, Br Mgr, Johnson County Public Library, White River Library, 1664 Library Blvd, Greenwood, IN, 46142. Tel: 317-885-1330. p. 686
Kilbourne, Hugh, Dir, Rimrock Foundation Library, 1231 N 29th St, Billings, MT, 59101. Tel: 406-248-3175. p. 1288
Kilbrun, Jennifer, Children's Mgr, Jackson-Madison County Library, 433 E Lafayette St, Jackson, TN, 38301. Tel: 731-425-8600. p. 2102
Kilburn, Lisa, Dir, Libr Serv, Southern Regional Area Health Education Center, 1601 Owen Dr, Fayetteville, NC, 28304. Tel: 910-678-7222. p. 1689
Kilby, Cynthia, Libr Dir, Pine Mountain Regional Library, 218 W Perry St, Manchester, GA, 31816. Tel: 706-846-2186. p. 488
Kilday, Michele Squier, Dir, Phenix City-Russell County Library, 1501 17th Ave, Phenix City, AL, 36867. Tel: 334-297-1139. p. 33
Kilduff, Deirdre, Coordr, Acq, Palm Beach Atlantic University, 300 Pembroke Pl, West Palm Beach, FL, 33401-6503. Tel: 561-803-2229. p. 453
Kile, Wendy, Exec Dir, Found, Kitsap Regional Library, 1301 Sylvan Way, Bremerton, WA, 98310-3498. Tel: 360-405-9115. p. 2359
Kileen, Darcie, Adult Serv, W J Niederkorn Library, 316 W Grand Ave, Port Washington, WI, 53074-2293. Tel: 262-284-5031. p. 2470
Kiley, Jason, Syst Adminr, Central Michigan University, 250 E Preston St, Mount Pleasant, MI, 48859. Tel: 989-774-4291. p. 1134
Kiley, Michelle, Asst Br Mgr, Youth Serv, Saint Johns County Public Library System, Hastings Branch, 6195 S Main St, Hastings, FL, 32145. Tel: 904-827-6976. p. 440
Kilfoil, Sarah, Regional Dir, York Library Region, 570 Two Nations Crossing, Ste 1, Fredericton, NB, E3A 0X9, CANADA. Tel: 506-444-2601. p. 2602
Kilgallen, Caitlin, Libr Dir, School of Visual Arts Library, 380 Second Ave, 2nd Flr, New York, NY, 10010. Tel: 212-592-2663. p. 1601
Kilgore, Aaron, Tech Serv Librn, Hillsdale College, 33 E College St, Hillsdale, MI, 49242. Tel: 517-607-2402. p. 1115
Kilgore, Clay, Exec Dir, Washington County Historical Society, 49 E Maiden St, Washington, PA, 15301. Tel: 724-225-6740. p. 2018
Kilgour, Alicia, Chief Exec Officer, Niagara Falls Public Library, 4848 Victoria Ave, Niagara Falls, ON, L2E 4C5, CANADA. Tel: 905-356-8080. p. 2660
Kilham, Jessica, Assoc Dir, National Network of Libraries of Medicine Region 7, Univ of Massachusetts Chan Med Sch, Lamar Soutter Libr, 55 Lake Ave N, Rm S4-241, Worcester, MA, 01655. Tel: 508-856-6099. p. 2767
Kilheffer, Lisa, Circ, Strasburg-Heisler Library, 143 Precision Ave, Strasburg, PA, 17579. Tel: 717-687-8969. p. 2010
Kilicoglu, Halil, Assoc Prof, University of Illinois at Urbana-Champaign, Library & Information Science Bldg, 501 E Daniel St, Champaign, IL, 61820-6211. Tel: 217-333-3280. p. 2784
Kilkenny, Amy, Curator, Dir, Archives & Spec Coll, Wadsworth Atheneum Museum of Art, 600 Main St, Hartford, CT, 06103. Tel: 860-838-4116. p. 318
Killebrew, Rachel, Libr Dir, Community of Christ Library, The Temple, 201 S River, Independence, MO, 64050. Tel: 816-833-1000, Ext 2399. p. 1249
Killebrew, Sheila, Libr Dir, Davidson County Public Library System, 602 S Main St, Lexington, NC, 27292. Tel: 336-242-2040. p. 1700
Killian, Lara, Librn/Educator, Capital Health/Nova Scotia Hospital, Hugh Bell Bldg, Rm 200, 300 Pleasant St, Dartmouth, NS, B2Y 3Z9, CANADA. Tel: 902-464-3144. p. 2617
Killian, Tessa, Exec Dir, Southeastern New York Library Resources Council, 21 S Elting Corners Rd, Highland, NY, 12528-2805. Tel: 845-883-9065. p. 2771
Killingsworth, Amanda, Librn, Vernice Stoudenmire Public Library, 9905 N Main St, Wilsonville, AL, 35186. Tel: 205-669-6180. p. 40
Killins, Allison, Sr Librn, Ontario Ministry of Natural Resources & Forestry, North Tower, 1st Flr, 300 Water St, Peterborough, ON, K9J 3C7, CANADA. Tel: 705-755-1888. p. 2672
Killough, Angel, Asst Dir, Br Mgr, Hopkins County-Madisonville Public Library, Dawson Springs Branch, 103 W Ramsey St, Dawson Springs, KY, 42408-1738. Tel: 270-797-8990. p. 868
Killough, Eric, Libr Dir, Pratt Public Library, 401 S Jackson St, Pratt, KS, 67124. Tel: 620-672-3041. p. 832
Kilmarx, Beth, Asst Dean of Libr, Assessment & Develop, Indiana University of Pennsylvania, 431 S 11th St, Rm 203, Indiana, PA, 15705-1096. Tel: 724-357-2330. p. 1946
Kilmarx, Beth T, Assoc Dean, Dir, Texas A&M University Libraries, Cushing Memorial Library & Archives, 400 Spencer St, College Station, TX, 77843. Tel: 979-845-1951. p. 2157
Kilmer, Kevin, Br Supvr, Elkhart Public Library, 300 S Second St, Elkhart, IN, 46516-3109. p. 680
Kilmon, Joan, Br Mgr, Calvert Library, Twin Beaches Branch, 3819 Harbor Rd, Chesapeake Beach, MD, 20732. Tel: 410-257-2411. p. 973
Kilpatrick, Alan, Co-Dir, Librn, Law Society of Saskatchewan Libraries, Court House, 2425 Victoria Ave, 2nd Flr, Regina, SK, S4P 3M3, CANADA. Tel: 306-569-8020. p. 2746
Kilpatrick, Darlene, Programming Serv, User Serv, Red Feather Lakes Community Library, 71 Firehouse Lane, Red Feather Lakes, CO, 80545. Tel: 970-881-2664. p. 294
Kilsby, M, Curator, Barkerville Historic Town Library & Archives, 14301 Hwy 26 E, Barkerville, BC, V0K 1B0, CANADA. Tel: 250-994-3332, Ext 35. p. 2563

Kilzer, Rebekah, Emerging Tech Librn, Drexel University Libraries, Hagerty Library, 33rd & Market Sts, Philadelphia, PA, 19104-2875. Tel: 215-895-6783. p. 1976

Kim, Andrew, Exec Dir, Glencoe Public Library, 320 Park Ave, Glencoe, IL, 60022. Tel: 847-835-5056. p. 593

Kim, Angela R, Dir, Louis Latzer Memorial Public Library, 1001 Ninth St, Highland, IL, 62249. Tel: 618-654-5066. p. 599

Kim, Bohyun, Assoc Univ Librn, Info Tech, University of Michigan, 818 Hatcher Graduate Library South, 913 S University Ave, Ann Arbor, MI, 48109-1190. Tel: 734-764-0400. p. 1080

Kim, Bohyun, Ms, Assoc Dir, Libr Applications & Knowledge Sys, University of Maryland, Baltimore, Health Sciences & Human Services Library, 601 W Lombard St, Baltimore, MD, 21201. Tel: 410-706-0405. p. 957

Kim, Daniel, Librn, Korean Cultural Center Library, 5505 Wilshire Blvd, Los Angeles, CA, 90036. Tel: 323-936-7141. p. 162

Kim, Hak Joon, Dr, Chairperson, Prof, Southern Connecticut State University, 501 Crescent St, New Haven, CT, 06515. Tel: 203-392-5703. p. 2783

Kim, Hana, Dir, University of Toronto Libraries, Cheng Yu Tung East Asian Library, John P Robarts Research Library, 130 St George St, 8th Flr, Toronto, ON, M5S 1A5, CANADA. Tel: 416-987-7690. p. 2698

Kim, Hyesoon H, Tech Serv Librn, United States Army, Van Noy Library, 5966 12th St, Bldg 1024, Fort Belvoir, VA, 22060-5554. Tel: 703-806-0093. p. 2319

Kim, Hyun (Leah), Dir, Tech Serv, Kennesaw State University Library System, 385 Cobb Ave NW, MD 1701, Kennesaw, GA, 30144. Tel: 470-578-6660. p. 483

Kim, Jane, Librn, United States Courts Library, 255 E Temple St, Rm 680, Los Angeles, CA, 90012. Tel: 213-894-8900. p. 168

Kim, Jeannie, Head, Ref (Info Serv), Southampton Free Library, 947 Street Rd, Southampton, PA, 18966. Tel: 215-322-1415. p. 2009

Kim, Jenna, Dir, Los Angeles County Harbor UCLA Medical Center, 1000 W Carson St, Torrance, CA, 90509-2910. Tel: 424-306-6100. p. 252

Kim, Jeonghyun Annie, Dr, Assoc Prof, University of North Texas, 3940 N Elm St, Ste E292, Denton, TX, 76207. Tel: 940-565-2445. p. 2793

Kim, Joy, Dep Dir, Cambridge Public Library, 449 Broadway, Cambridge, MA, 02138. Tel: 617-349-4041. p. 1004

Kim, Julia, Librn, Los Angeles County Museum of Art, Robert Gore Rifkind Center for German Expressionist Studies, 5905 Wilshire Blvd, Los Angeles, CA, 90036. Tel: 323-857-4752, 323-857-6165. p. 163

Kim, Kiwon, Asst Librn, Cresskill Public Library, 53 Union Ave, Cresskill, NJ, 07626. Tel: 201-567-3521. p. 1398

Kim, Kungwha, Tech Serv Mgr, Lamar State College Orange Library, 410 Front St, Orange, TX, 77630-5796. Tel: 409-882-3080. p. 2224

Kim, Kyung-Sun, Dir, Prof, University of Wisconsin-Madison, Helen C White Hall, Rm 4217, 600 N Park St, Madison, WI, 53706. Tel: 608-263-2900. p. 2794

Kim, Lia, Libr Tech, Lakeland College Library, 5707 College Dr, Vermilion, AB, T9X 1K5, CANADA. Tel: 780-853-8465. p. 2558

Kim, Mi-Seon, Information Literacy Coord, Sci Librn, Queensborough Community College, City University of New York, 222-05 56th Ave, Bayside, NY, 11364-1497. Tel: 718-281-5721. p. 1491

Kim, Michael, Br Mgr, Atlanta-Fulton Public Library System, Sandy Springs Branch, 395 Mount Vernon Hwy NE, Sandy Springs, GA, 30328. Tel: 404-612-7000. p. 461

Kim, Patricia, Coordr, Librn, Algonquin College Library, Pembroke Campus, One College Way, Rm 145, Pembroke, ON, K8A 0C8, CANADA. Tel: 613-735-4700, Ext 2779. p. 2664

Kim, Rebekah, Head Librn, California Academy of Sciences Library, Golden Gate Park, 55 Music Concourse Dr, San Francisco, CA, 94118. Tel: 415-379-5487. p. 223

Kim, Richard T, Syst & Emerging Tech Librn, Yeshiva University Libraries, Dr Lillian & Dr Rebecca Chutick Law Library, Benjamin N Cardozo School of Law, 55 Fifth Ave, New York, NY, 10003-4301. Tel: 212-790-0223. p. 1604

Kim, Yanghee, Acq Librn, West Valley Community College Library, 14000 Fruitvale Ave, Saratoga, CA, 95070-5698. Tel: 408-741-2484. p. 245

Kim, Yong-Mi, PhD, Dr, Assoc Prof, University of Oklahoma, Bizzell Memorial Library, 401 W Brooks, Rm 120, Norman, OK, 73019-6032. Tel: 918-660-3364. p. 2791

Kim, Youshin, Commun Libr Mgr, Queens Library, Glen Oaks Community Library, 256-04 Union Tpk, Glen Oaks, NY, 11004. Tel: 718-831-8636. p. 1554

Kim-Prieto, Dennis, Ref Librn, Rutgers University Library for the Center for Law & Justice, 123 Washington St, Newark, NJ, 07102-3094. Tel: 973-353-3037. p. 1428

Kimball, Anna, Archives Supvr, Ref Supvr, Belleville Public Library, 121 E Washington St, Belleville, IL, 62220. Tel: 618-234-0441. p. 541

Kimball, Gregg, Dir, Pub Serv & Outreach, The Library of Virginia, 800 E Broad St, Richmond, VA, 23219-8000. Tel: 804-692-3500. p. 2341

Kimball, Janice, Operations Mgr, University of California, Berkeley, Institute for Research on Labor & Employment Library, 2521 Channing Way, MC 5555, Berkeley, CA, 94720-5555. Tel: 510-642-1705. p. 123

Kimball, Lesley, Dir, Wiggin Memorial Library, Ten Bunker Hill Ave, Stratham, NH, 03885. Tel: 603-772-4346. p. 1381

Kimball, Linda, Br Librn, Southeast Regional Library, Carnduff Branch, Carnduff Education Complex, 506 Anderson Ave, Carnduff, SK, S0C 0S0, CANADA. Tel: 306-482-3255. p. 2753

Kimball, Melanie, Assoc Prof, Simmons University, 300 The Fenway, Boston, MA, 02115. Tel: 617-521-2800. p. 2786

Kimball, Susan, Head, Access Serv, Librn, Amherst College, 61 Quadrangle Dr, Amherst, MA, 01002. p. 984

Kimberley, Kelly, Head, Borrowing & Lending Services, Ryerson University Library, 350 Victoria St, 2nd Flr, Toronto, ON, M5B 2K3, CANADA. Tel: 416-979-5000, Ext 4833. p. 2692

Kimbrell, Katie, Tech Info Spec, United States Department of Labor, 1301 Airport Rd, Beaver, WV, 25813. Tel: 304-256-3266. p. 2397

Kimbro, Clare, Ref Librn, Meharry Medical College Library, 2001 Albion St, Nashville, TN, 37208. Tel: 615-327-6454. p. 2119

Kimbro, Wendy, Br Mgr, Alamance County Public Libraries, Graham Public Library, 211 S Main St, Graham, NC, 27253. Tel: 336-570-6730. p. 1676

Kimbrough, Ashley, Ch Serv, Gardendale - Martha Moore Public Library, 995 Mt Olive Rd, Gardendale, AL, 35071. Tel: 205-631-6639. p. 19

Kimbrough, Julie, Interim Dir, University of North Carolina at Chapel Hill, Kathrine R Everett Law Library, UNC Law Library, 160 Ridge Rd, CB 3385, Chapel Hill, NC, 27599-3385. Tel: 919-962-1191. p. 1678

Kimbrough, Marie, Ch, Dripping Springs Community Library, 501 Sportsplex Dr, Dripping Springs, TX, 78620. Tel: 512-858-7825. p. 2171

Kime, Caitlin, Libr Media Prog Dir, Southern Utah University, 351 W University Blvd, Cedar City, UT, 84720. Tel: 435-586-1908. p. 2262

Kimerer, Marika, Circ Mgr, King University, 1350 King College Rd, Bristol, TN, 37620. Tel: 423-652-4790. p. 2090

Kimm, Julie, Dir, Shellsburg Public Library, 110 Main St, Shellsburg, IA, 52332. Tel: 319-436-2112. p. 781

Kimmel, Sarah, Project Coordr, Charlotte AHEC Library, Medical Education Bldg, 1000 Blythe Blvd, Charlotte, NC, 28203-5812. Tel: 704-355-3129. p. 1679

Kimmel, Sue, Assoc Prof, Prog Dir, Old Dominion University, Darden College of Education, Education Bldg-4101-A, 4301 Hampton Blvd, Norfolk, VA, 23529. Tel: 757-683-4305. p. 2794

Kimmitt, Joanna Messer, Coordr, User Serv, California State University Dominguez Hills, 1000 E Victoria St, Carson, CA, 90747. Tel: 310-243-2088. p. 129

Kimmons, Dan, Ref Librn, Arizona State University, College of Law, Arizona State University MC 9620, 111 E Taylor St, Ste 350, Phoenix, AZ, 85004. Tel: 480-965-4860. p. 69

Kimok, Debra, Spec Coll Librn, State University of New York College at Plattsburgh, Two Draper Ave, Plattsburgh, NY, 12901. Tel: 518-564-5206. p. 1619

Kimok, William, Rec Mgr, Univ Archivist, Ohio University Libraries, Mahn Center for Archives & Special Collections, Vernon R Alden Library, 30 Park Pl, Fifth Flr, Athens, OH, 45701-2978. Tel: 740-593-2712. p. 1748

Kimura, Daryl, Libr Mgr, Duchess & District Public Library, 256A Louise Ave, Duchess, AB, T0J 0Z0, CANADA. Tel: 403-378-4369. p. 2534

Kimura, Sherise, Head, Electronic Resources & Systems, University of San Francisco, 2130 Fulton St, San Francisco, CA, 94117-1080. Tel: 415-422-5379. p. 229

Kimzey, Judy, Libr Dir, Van Alstyne Public Library, 151 W Cooper St, Van Alstyne, TX, 75495. Tel: 903-482-5991. p. 2251

Kin, Ostap, Archivist, Shevchenko Scientific Society Inc, 63 Fourth Ave, New York, NY, 10003. Tel: 212-254-5130. p. 1602

Kinahan-Ockay, Mary, Col Archivist, Saint Peter's University, 99 Glenwood Ave, Jersey City, NJ, 07306. Tel: 201-761-6462. p. 1410

Kinder, Greg, Br Mgr, Glendale Public Library, Velma Teague Branch, 7010 N 58th Ave, Glendale, AZ, 85301. Tel: 623-930-3441. p. 62

Kinder, Sean, Humanities & Soc Sci Librn, Western Kentucky University Libraries, Helm-Cravens Library Complex, 1906 College Heights Blvd, No 11067, Bowling Green, KY, 42101-1067. Tel: 270-745-6339. p. 849

Kindle, A, Libr Asst, Tiskilwa Public Library, 119 E Main, Tiskilwa, IL, 61368. Tel: 815-646-4511. p. 654

Kindness, Kathy, Librn, Saint Peter's Hospital College of Nursing, Marian Hall, Rm 111, 714 New Scotland Ave, Albany, NY, 12208. Tel: 518-268-5036, 518-525-1490. p. 1483

Kindness, Kathy, Libr Supvr, Samaritan Hospital School of Nursing, 1300 Massachusetts Ave, Troy, NY, 12180. Tel: 518-268-5000, 518-268-5035. p. 1653

Kindon, Rebecca, Asst Dir, Customer Serv, SUNY Upstate Medical University, 766 Irving Ave, Syracuse, NY, 13210-1602. Tel: 315-464-7193. p. 1650

Kindred, Janis, Libr Dir, Anadarko Community Library, 215 W Broadway, Anadarko, OK, 73005. Tel: 405-247-7351. p. 1840

Kindreich, Ruth, Archives, Tech, United States Air Force Academy Libraries, 2354 Fairchild Dr, Ste 3A15, USAF Academy, CO, 80840-6214. Tel: 719-333-4406. p. 297

Kindt, Clare, Coll Develop & Tech Serv Mgr, Brown County Library, 515 Pine St, Green Bay, WI, 54301. Tel: 920-448-5801. p. 2438

Kiner, Renee, Pub Serv Librn, University of Pittsburgh at Greensburg, Greensburg Campus, 150 Finoli Dr, Greensburg, PA, 15601-5804. Tel: 724-836-7914. p. 1938

King, Abraham, Br Mgr, Washington County Library System, Santa Clara Branch, 1099 N Lava Flow Dr, Saint George, UT, 84770. Tel: 435-256-6327. p. 2270
King, Albert C, Ms Curator, Rutgers University Libraries, Special Collections & University Archives, Alexander Library, 169 College Ave, New Brunswick, NJ, 08901-1163. Tel: 848-932-6153. p. 1425
King, Alex, Pub Serv Librn, Upper Moreland Free Public Library, 109 Park Ave, Willow Grove, PA, 19090-3277. Tel: 215-659-0741. p. 2024
King, Amanda, Librn, Colorado Joint Legislative Library, State Capitol Bldg, Rm 048, 200 E Colfax Ave, Denver, CO, 80203-1784. Tel: 303-866-4011. p. 274
King, Angelynn, Head Librn, Delaware Technical & Community College, 21179 College Dr, Georgetown, DE, 19947. Tel: 302-259-6199. p. 353
King, Angie, Dir, Arkoma Public Library, 1101 Main St, Arkoma, OK, 74901. Tel: 918-875-3971. p. 1841
King, Ann, Asst Librn, Ladd Public Library District, 125 N Main St, Ladd, IL, 61329. Tel: 815-894-3254. p. 606
King, Annie Lee, YA Librn, Shrewsbury Public Library, 609 Main St, Shrewsbury, MA, 01545. Tel: 508-841-8609. p. 1053
King, April, Youth Serv, Gnadenhutten Public Library, 160 N Walnut St, Gnadenhutten, OH, 44629. Tel: 740-254-9224. p. 1788
King, Ashley, Children's Serv Coordr, St Albert Public Library, Five Saint Anne St, St. Albert, AB, T8N 3Z9, CANADA. Tel: 780-459-1530. p. 2555
King, Barbara, Ref Serv Librn, Saint Clair County Library System, 210 McMorran Blvd, Port Huron, MI, 48060-4098. Tel: 810-987-7323. p. 1142
King, Bethni, Ch, Georgetown Public Library, 402 W Eighth St, Georgetown, TX, 78626. Tel: 512-930-3551. p. 2184
King, Bettina, Dep Libr Dir, Lawton Public Library, 110 SW Fourth St, Lawton, OK, 73501. Tel: 580-581-3450. p. 1852
King, Beverly, Spec Serv, Bonne Terre Memorial Library, Five SW Main St, Bonne Terre, MO, 63628. Tel: 573-358-2260. p. 1238
King, Breanna, Dir, Dora Bee Woodyard Memorial Library, 411 Mulberry St, Elizabeth, WV, 26143. Tel: 304-275-4295. p. 2402
King, Bruni, Librn, Palliser Regional Library, Imperial Branch, 310 Royal St, Imperial, SK, S0G 2J0, CANADA. Tel: 306-963-2272. p. 2742
King, Bryan, IT Spec, Grand Forks Public Library, 2110 Library Circle, Grand Forks, ND, 58201-6324. Tel: 701-772-8116. p. 1734
King, Catherine, ILL Asst, Cleveland Health Sciences Library, Allen Memorial Medical Library, 11000 Euclid Ave, Cleveland, OH, 44106-7130. Tel: 216-368-3643. p. 1767
King, Christina, Assoc Librn, National University of Natural Medicine Library, 49 S Porter St, Portland, OR, 97201. Tel: 503-552-1542. p. 1893
King, Christopher, Asst Prof, Dir, Law Libr, Appalachian School of Law Library, 1221 Edgewater Dr, Grundy, VA, 24614-7062. Tel: 276-935-6688, Ext 1308. p. 2322
King, Colleen, Teen Librn, Memorial & Library Association, 44 Broad St, Westerly, RI, 02891. Tel: 401-596-2877, Ext 301. p. 2044
King, Connie, Br Mgr, Barton County Library, Happy & Mary Curless Library - Liberal Branch, 201 S Main St, Liberal, MO, 64762-9315. Tel: 417-843-5791. p. 1259
King, Cornelia S, Chief of Ref, Library Company of Philadelphia, 1314 Locust St, Philadelphia, PA, 19107. Tel: 215-546-3181. p. 1982
King, Cynthia E, County Libr Dir, Upshur County Library, 702 W Tyler St, Gilmer, TX, 75644. Tel: 903-843-5001. p. 2184
King, Danielle, Br Chief, Orange County Library System, 101 E Central Blvd, Orlando, FL, 32801. Tel: 407-835-7323. p. 431
King, Danielle, Asst Librn, Mullan Public Library, 117 Hunter Ave, Mullan, ID, 83846. Tel: 208-744-1220. p. 527
King, David, Digital Serv Dir, Topeka & Shawnee County Public Library, 1515 SW Tenth Ave, Topeka, KS, 66604-1374. Tel: 785-580-4400. p. 839
King, Dee, Librn, Skidaway Institute of Oceanography Library, Ten Ocean Science Circle, Savannah, GA, 31411-1011. Tel: 912-598-2474. p. 496
King, Diana, Librn, University of California Los Angeles Library, Arts Library, 1400 Public Affairs Bldg, Los Angeles, CA, 90095. Tel: 310-206-4823. p. 169
King, Donald, Dept Chair, Prof, Chadron State College, 1000 Main St, Chadron, NE, 69337. Tel: 308-432-6271. p. 2788
King, Dwight, Assoc Dir, Res & Instruction, University of Notre Dame, 2345 Biolchini Hall of Law, Notre Dame, IN, 46556-4640. Tel: 574-631-7024. p. 711
King, Emily, Syst Librn, College of Southern Nevada, Bldg L, 1st Flr, 6375 W Charleston Blvd, Las Vegas, NV, 89146. Tel: 702-651-7511. p. 1346
King, Emily, Libr Mgr, Fundy Library Region, Saint John Free Public Library, East Branch, 55 McDonald St, Saint John, NB, E2J 0C7, CANADA. Tel: 506-643-7250. p. 2605
King, Evelyn, Interim Head Librn, Pub Serv Librn, Stillman College, 3601 Stillman Blvd, Tuscaloosa, AL, 35401. Tel: 205-349-4240, Ext 8850. p. 37
King, Hannah, Fiscal Officer, Athens County Public Libraries, 95 W Washington, Nelsonville, OH, 45764-1177. Tel: 740-753-2118. p. 1805
King, Heather, Chief Exec Officer, Norfolk County Public Library, 46 Colborne St S, Simcoe, ON, N3Y 4H3, CANADA. Tel: 519-426-3506 x1253. p. 2678
King, Hunter, Music Libr Tech, West Chester University, Presser Music Library, Wells School of Music & Performing Arts Ctr, West Chester, PA, 19383. Tel: 610-436-2379, 610-436-2430. p. 2020
King, Jan, Circ Coordr, Coordr, Ser, Taylor University, 1846 Main St, Upland, IN, 46989. Tel: 765-998-5522. p. 722
King, Jason L, PhD, Exec Dir, Center for American Archeology, 100 Broadway, Kampsville, IL, 62053. Tel: 618-653-4316. p. 604
King, Jennifer, Tech Serv Librn, Longview Public Library, 1600 Louisiana St, Longview, WA, 98632-2993. Tel: 360-442-5324. p. 2369
King, Julie, Br Mgr, Middle Georgia Regional Library System, Jones County Public Library, 146 Railroad Ave, Gray, GA, 31032. Tel: 478-986-6626. p. 487
King, Justin, Youth Serv Librn, Hernando County Public Library System, 238 Howell Ave, Brooksville, FL, 34601. Tel: 352-754-4043. p. 387
King, Kathy, Librn, Chinook Regional Library, Stewart Valley Branch, Senior Ctr, 20 Charles St, Stewart Valley, SK, S0N 2P0, CANADA. p. 2752
King, Katie, Ref & Instruction Librn, Oklahoma City Community College, 7777 S May Ave, Oklahoma City, OK, 73159. Tel: 405-682-1611, Ext 7643. p. 1858
King, Kevin, Br Head, Circ Serv, Kalamazoo Public Library, 315 S Rose St, Kalamazoo, MI, 49007-5264. Tel: 269-553-7881. p. 1121
King, Kevin A R, Libr Dir, East Lansing Public Library, 950 Abbot Rd, East Lansing, MI, 48823-3105. Tel: 517-319-6913. p. 1101
King, Kresta L, Dir, Okeechobee County Public Library, 206 SW 16th St, Okeechobee, FL, 34974. Tel: 863-763-3536. p. 430
King, Kristy, Youth Serv Mgr, Unicoi County Public Library, 201 Nolichucky Ave, Erwin, TN, 37650. Tel: 423-743-6533. p. 2098
King, Laura, Br Coordr, Pemberville Public Library, Stony Ridge Branch, 5805 Fremont Pike, Stony Ridge, OH, 43463. Tel: 419-837-5948. p. 1814
King, Linda, Asst Br Mgr, Johnson County Library, Central Resource, 9875 W 87th St, Overland Park, KS, 66212. p. 830
King, Linda, Dir, Garland Public Library, 86 W Factory St, Garland, UT, 84312. Tel: 435-257-3118, Ext 1005. p. 2264
King, Lindsay, Head Librn, Stanford University Libraries, Bowes Art & Architecture Library, McMurtry Bldg, 2nd Flr, 355 Roth Way, Stanford, CA, 94305. Tel: 650-723-3408. p. 248
King, Liz, Dir, Solon Public Library, 320 W Main St, Solon, IA, 52333-9504. Tel: 319-624-2678. p. 783
King, Liz, Assoc Dir, Rensselaer Libraries, Rensselaer Architecture Library, Greene Bldg 308, 3rd Flr, 110 Eighth St, Troy, NY, 12180-3590. Tel: 518-276-8310. p. 1652
King, Lyzzie, Br Mgr, Campbell County Public Library, 684 Village Hwy, Lower Level, Rustburg, VA, 24588. Tel: 434-332-9560. p. 2346
King, Manuel, Dir, Beals Memorial Library, 50 Pleasant St, Winchendon, MA, 01475. Tel: 978-297-0300. p. 1070
King, Maria, Libr Asst, Bacon Free Library, 58 Eliot St, Natick, MA, 01760. Tel: 508-653-6730. p. 1037
King, Marianne, Librn, Michael Donovan Library, 655 Topsail Rd, St. John's, NL, A1E 2E3, CANADA. Tel: 709-737-2621. p. 2610
King, Mary, Dir, Plainfield Public Libraries, 22 Bean Rd, Meriden, NH, 03770. Tel: 603-469-3252. p. 1373
King, Mary, Dir, Plainfield Public Libraries, Philip Read Memorial Library, 1088 Rte 12A, Plainfield, NH, 03781. Tel: 603-675-6866. p. 1373
King, Mary Beth, Libr Asst, Thornton Public Library, 1884 NH Rte 175, Thornton, NH, 03285. Tel: 603-726-8981. p. 1382
King, Melanie Starr, Dir, Shamrock Community Library, 712 N Main St, Shamrock, TX, 79079. Tel: 806-256-3921. p. 2243
King, Michael, Customer Experience Supervisor, Douglas County Libraries, Highlands Ranch Branch, 9292 S Ridgeline Blvd, Highlands Ranch, CO, 80129. Tel: 303-791-7323. p. 270
King, Mindy, Libr Dir, University of Wisconsin-Stevens Point, 900 Reserve St, Stevens Point, WI, 54481-1985. Tel: 715-346-2321. p. 2479
King, Nathaniel, Dean of Libr, Nevada State University, 1300 Nevada State Dr, Henderson, NV, 89002. Tel: 702-992-2806. p. 1346
King, Nichole, Commun Librn, Santa Clara County Library District, Campbell Express Library, Campbell Community Ctr, One W Campbell Ave, Bldg E, Rm 46, Campbell, CA, 95008. Tel: 408-866-1991. p. 127
King, Pambanisha, Doc Delivery, Auburn University, Ralph Brown Draughon Library, 231 Mell St, Auburn, AL, 36849. Tel: 334-844-4500. p. 6
King, Patricia, Dep Dir, Rockland Public Library, 80 Union St, Rockland, ME, 04841. Tel: 207-594-0310. p. 939
King, Patricia, Libr Dir, Stansbury Park Library, One Country Club Dr, Stansbury Park, UT, 84074. Tel: 435-882-6188. p. 2273
King, Priscilla, Libr Asst, Adams Free Library, Two N Main St, Adams, NY, 13605. Tel: 315-232-2265. p. 1481
King, Rachel, Librn/Br Mgr, Allen County Public Library, New Haven Branch, 648 Green St, New Haven, IN, 46774. Tel: 260-421-1345. p. 683
King, Robby, Circ, ILL, Libr Support Spec, Athens State University, 407 E Pryor St, Athens, AL, 35611. Tel: 256-216-6662. p. 5

King, Robert, Librn, Los Angeles Trade Technical College Library, 400 W Washington Blvd, Los Angeles, CA, 90015. Tel: 213-763-3958. p. 166
King, Ruth, Librn, Milwaukee Public Museum, 800 W Wells St, Milwaukee, WI, 53233. Tel: 414-278-2728. p. 2460
King, Sam, Ad, Trail & District Public Library, 1505 Bay Ave, Trail, BC, V1R 4B2, CANADA. Tel: 250-364-1731. p. 2577
King, Sandra, Mgr, Dallas Public Library, Bookmarks-NorthPark Center, 8687 N Central Expressway, Ste 154, Dallas, TX, 75225. Tel: 214-671-1381. p. 2165
King, Sandra, Br Mgr, Dallas Public Library, Polk-Wisdom, 7151 Library Lane, Dallas, TX, 75232-3899. Tel: 214-670-1947. p. 2166
King, Sara, Br Mgr, San Diego Public Library, College-Rolando, 6600 Montezuma Rd, San Diego, CA, 92115-2828. Tel: 619-533-3902. p. 219
King, Stephanie, Pub Serv Librn, Illinois Valley Community College, 815 N Orlando Smith Rd, Oglesby, IL, 61348-9692. Tel: 815-224-0306. p. 629
King, Stephanie, Ch, Nelson County Public Library, 201 Cathedral Manor, Bardstown, KY, 40004-1515. Tel: 502-348-3714. p. 848
King, Stephanie, Circ Mgr, Greenville Area Public Library, 330 Main St, Greenville, PA, 16125-2615. Tel: 724-588-5490. p. 1938
King, Susan, Libr Mgr, Thomas County Public Library System, Gladys H Clark Memorial Library, 1060 NE Railroad St, Ochlocknee, GA, 31773. Tel: 229-574-5884. p. 499
King, Susan, Coordr, Youth Serv, Fort Bend County Libraries, 1001 Golfview Dr, Richmond, TX, 77469-5199. Tel: 281-633-4762. p. 2232
King, Tamara M, Chief Equity & Engagement Officer, Richland Library, 1431 Assembly St, Columbia, SC, 29201-3101. Tel: 803-799-9084. p. 2054
King, Taryn, Tech Serv, Citizens Library, 55 S College St, Washington, PA, 15301. Tel: 724-222-2400. p. 2018
King, Teresa, Br Mgr, Putnam County Library, Poca Branch, 2858 Charleston Rd, Poca, WV, 25159. Tel: 304-755-3241. p. 2406
King, Thomas, ILL, Fried, Frank, Harris, Shriver & Jacobson LLP, 801 17th St NW, Ste 600, Washington, DC, 20006. Tel: 202-639-7000. p. 367
King, Tina, Br Mgr, Evangeline Parish Library, Turkey Creek, 13951 Veterans Memorial Hwy, Turkey Creek, LA, 70586. Tel: 337-461-2304. p. 912
King-Mills, Charlotte, Br Mgr, San Diego County Library, Lemon Grove Branch, 3001 School Lane, Lemon Grove, CA, 91945. Tel: 619-463-9819. p. 217
Kingdon, Beth, Dir, Marcus Public Library, 106 N Locust St, Marcus, IA, 51035. Tel: 712-376-2328. p. 767
Kingen, Kyle, Circ Supvr, Supvr, Pub Serv, Indiana University, Herron Art Library, Herron School of Art & Design, 735 W New York St, Indianapolis, IN, 46202. Tel: 317-278-2576. p. 693
Kingman Rice, Jamie, Director, Collections & Research, Maine Historical Society, 489 Congress St, Portland, ME, 04101. Tel: 207-774-1822. p. 936
Kingrey-Edwards, Kelly, Librn, Blinn College Library, 800 Blinn Blvd, Brenham, TX, 77833. Tel: 979-830-4250. p. 2149
Kingsbury, Christine, Libr Dir, Bandon Public Library, 1204 11th St SW, Bandon, OR, 97411. Tel: 541-347-3221. p. 1873
Kingsbury, Kalekona, Circ Serv Mgr, Leeward Community College Library, 96-045 Ala Ike St, Pearl City, HI, 96782. Tel: 808-455-0209. p. 514
Kingsbury, Maria, Teaching & Learning Librn, Southwest Minnesota State University Library, 1501 State St, Marshall, MN, 56258. Tel: 507-537-6165. p. 1182
Kingsland, Jane, Ref Librn, County College of Morris, 214 Center Grove Rd, Randolph, NJ, 07869-2086. Tel: 973-328-5300. p. 1438
Kingsland, Valarie, Dir, Seward Community Library & Museum, 239 Sixth Ave, Seward, AK, 99664. Tel: 907-224-4082. p. 50
Kingsley, Candace, Br Mgr, Henderson District Public Libraries, James I Gibson Library, 100 W Lake Mead Pkwy, Henderson, NV, 89015. Tel: 702-565-8402. p. 1345
Kingsley, Orson, Head, Archives & Spec Coll, Bridgewater State University, Ten Shaw Rd, Bridgewater, MA, 02325. Tel: 508-531-1389. p. 1002
Kingstad, Dawn, Dir, Glendive Public Library, 200 S Kendrick Ave, Glendive, MT, 59330. Tel: 406-377-3633. p. 1294
Kingston, Kathryn, Mgr, Info Serv, PricewaterhouseCoopers, PwC Tower, 18 York St, Ste 2600, Toronto, ON, M5J 0B2, CANADA. Tel: 416-814-5890. p. 2692
Kingwill, Britta, Asst Librn, Carleton A Friday Memorial Library, 155 E First St, New Richmond, WI, 54017. Tel: 715-243-0431. p. 2465
Kingyens, Penny, Librn, Brighton Public Library, Codrington Branch, 2992 County Rd 30, Codrington, ON, K0K 1R0, CANADA. Tel: 613-475-5628. p. 2633
Kininger, Dennis, Ref Librn, Dunham Public Library, 76 Main St, Whitesboro, NY, 13492. Tel: 315-736-9734. p. 1665
Kinkade, Heather, Dir, Waterford Public Library, 101 N River St, Waterford, WI, 53185-4149. Tel: 262-534-3988. p. 2483
Kinkelaar, Niki, Access Serv Supvr, Judson University, 1151 N State St, Elgin, IL, 60123. Tel: 847-628-2030. p. 584
Kinley, Gloria, Librn, Lakeland Regional Library, Cartwright Branch, 483 Veteran Dr, Cartwright, MB, R0K 0L0, CANADA. Tel: 204-529-2261. p. 2587
Kinnaman, Allen Jon, Dir, The James E Nichols Memorial Library, 35 Plymouth St, Center Harbor, NH, 03226-3341. Tel: 603-253-6950. p. 1357
Kinnaman, Tracey, Dir, Hot Springs County Library, 344 Arapahoe St, Thermopolis, WY, 82443. Tel: 307-864-3104. p. 2499
Kinnamon, Michele, Libr Dir, Estacada Public Library, 825 NW Wade St, Estacada, OR, 97023. Tel: 503-630-8273. p. 1878
Kinney, Gabrielle, Coordr, Prog, Ref (Info Servs), Utica Public Library, 303 Genesee St, Utica, NY, 13501. Tel: 315-735-2279. p. 1656
Kinney, Juanita, Br Mgr, Muskingum County Library System, Roseville Branch, 41 N Main, Roseville, OH, 43777. Tel: 740-697-0237. p. 1837
Kinney, Katie, Writing Center Coord, Covenant Theological Seminary, 478 Covenant Ln, Saint Louis, MO, 63141. Tel: 314-392-4100, 314-434-4044. p. 1270
Kinney, Kayla, Dir, James Lowe Log Cabin Library, 403 E Monroe St, Crescent, OK, 73028. Tel: 405-310-8200, Ext 6. p. 1845
Kinney, Margaret, Br Mgr, Cleveland Heights-University Heights Public Library, Coventry Village Branch, 1925 Coventry Rd, Cleveland Heights, OH, 44118-2001. Tel: 216-321-3400. p. 1771
Kinney, Megan, Fac Librn, City College of San Francisco, 50 Frida Kahlo Way, 4th Flr, San Francisco, CA, 94112. Tel: 415-452-5433. p. 224
Kinney, Scott, Dir, Mobile Public Library, 701 Government St, Mobile, AL, 36602. Tel: 251-545-3570. p. 26
Kinney, Scott, Dir/Chief Exec Officer, Evansville Vanderburgh Public Library, 200 SE Martin Luther King Jr Blvd, Evansville, IN, 47713-1604. Tel: 812-428-8200. p. 681
Kinniff, Jenny, Head, Archives & Spec Coll, Loyola-Notre Dame Library, Inc, 200 Winston Ave, Baltimore, MD, 21212. Tel: 410-617-6801. p. 954
Kinnin, Wade, Instruction & Outreach Librn, Howard Payne University, 1000 Fisk St, Brownwood, TX, 76801. Tel: 325-649-8095. p. 2150
Kinnon, Rachel, Jail & Re-Entry Services Mgr, San Francisco Public Library, 100 Larkin St, San Francisco, CA, 94102. Tel: 415-557-4400. p. 227
Kinoshita, Silke, Sr Librn, Long Beach Public Library, Bret Harte Branch, 1595 W Willow St, Long Beach, CA, 90810. Tel: 562-570-1044. p. 159
Kinsey, Jackie, Br Mgr, San Luis Obispo County Library, Atascadero Library, 6555 Capistrano Ave, Atascadero, CA, 93422. Tel: 805-461-6164. p. 234
Kinsler, Stephanie, Dir, Millington Public Library, 4858 Navy Rd, Millington, TN, 38053. Tel: 901-872-1585. p. 2116
Kinslow, Brenda, Dir, Colfax-Perry Township Public Library, 207 S Clark St, Colfax, IN, 46035. Tel: 765-324-2915, Ext 100. p. 675
Kinton, Meaghan, Head, Circ, Lucius Beebe Memorial Library, 345 Main St, Wakefield, MA, 01880-5093. Tel: 781-246-6334. p. 1061
Kinyatti, Njoki, Chief Librn, Dept Chair, York College Library, 94-20 Guy R Brewer Blvd, Jamaica, NY, 11451. Tel: 718-262-2034. p. 1556
Kinzie, Karen, Circ Supvr, Salem Public Library, 585 Liberty St SE, Salem, OR, 97301. Tel: 503-588-6090. p. 1897
Kinzie, Sandy, Libr Dir, Fleming Community Library, 506 N Fremont Ave, Fleming, CO, 80728. Tel: 970-265-2022, Ext 326. p. 280
Kinzounza, Raymond, Br Mgr, Nashville Public Library, Mary & Charles W Pruitt Branch Library & Learning Center, 117 Charles E Davis Blvd, Nashville, TN, 37210. Tel: 615-862-5985. p. 2120
Kiorpes, Karen E, Head, Presv, University at Albany, State University of New York, Science Library, 1400 Washington Ave, Albany, NY, 12222. Tel: 518-437-3948. p. 1484
Kipfer, Kelly, Chief Exec Officer, Waterloo Public Library, 35 Albert St, Waterloo, ON, N2L 5E2, CANADA. Tel: 519-886-1310, Ext 123. p. 2702
Kipfer, Terri, Dir, Rolfe Public Library, 319 Garfield St, Rolfe, IA, 50581-1118. Tel: 712-848-3143. p. 779
Kipling, Mary, Head, Cat, Peters Township Public Library, 616 E McMurray Rd, McMurray, PA, 15317-3495. Tel: 724-941-9430. p. 1959
Kipnes, Ian R, Acq & Budget Control Librn, California Western School of Law Library, 290 Cedar St, San Diego, CA, 92101. Tel: 619-515-1512. p. 215
Kipp, Carey, Youth Serv Librn, Carnegie-Schadde Memorial Public Library, 230 Fourth Ave, Baraboo, WI, 53913. Tel: 608-356-6166. p. 2422
Kipp, Jessica, Br Librn, London Public Library, Masonville, 30 North Centre Rd, London, ON, N5X 3W1, CANADA. Tel: 519-660-4646. p. 2654
Kipp, Merida, Libr Adminr, Yakama Nation Library, 100 Spiel-Yi Loop, Toppenish, WA, 98948. Tel: 509-865-2800, Ext 6. p. 2388
Kipp, Sara, Libr Dir, Stillwater Public Library, 662 Hudson Ave, Stillwater, NY, 12170. Tel: 518-664-6255. p. 1646
Kippenbrock, Rae Ann, Dir, Lincoln Heritage Public Library, 105 Wallace St, Dale, IN, 47523-9267. Tel: 812-937-7170. p. 678
Kirby, Alexander, Info Literacy & eLearning Librn, Pennsylvania Highlands Community College Library, 101 Community College Way, Johnstown, PA, 15904. Tel: 814-262-6484. p. 1948
Kirby, Ari, ILL, Mgr, Access Serv, Whitman College, 345 Boyer Ave, Walla Walla, WA, 99362. Tel: 509-527-5191. p. 2393

Kirby, Chris, Ref Librn, Ilsley Public Library, 75 Main St, Middlebury, VT, 05753. Tel: 802-388-4095. p. 2288

Kirby, Jason, Archivist, The Library at Birmingham Botanical Gardens, 2612 Lane Park Rd, Birmingham, AL, 35223. Tel: 205-414-3967. p. 8

Kirby, Joseph, Librn, Jackson County Law Library, 226 E Main St, Jackson, OH, 45640-1764. Tel: 740-286-5460. p. 1792

Kirby, Karla, Youth Serv - Prog, Rapides Parish Library, Westside Regional, 5416 Provine Pl, Alexandria, LA, 71303. Tel: 318-442-2483, Ext 1904. p. 880

Kirby, Katrina, Libr Asst, Cragin Memorial Library, Eight Linwood Ave, Colchester, CT, 06415. Tel: 860-537-5752. p. 306

Kirby, Lari, Libr Supvr, Citrus College, 1000 W Foothill Blvd, Glendora, CA, 91741-1899. Tel: 626-914-8640. p. 149

Kirby, Martha, Coordr, Drexel University Libraries, Queen Lane Library, 2900 Queen Lane, Philadelphia, PA, 19129. Tel: 215-991-8740. p. 1976

Kirby, Matt, Dir, Falling Water River Regional Library, 208 E Minnear St, Cookeville, TN, 38501-3949. Tel: 931-526-4016. p. 2095

Kirby, Matthew, Regional Libr Dir, Tennessee State Library & Archives, 403 Seventh Ave N, Nashville, TN, 37243-0312. Tel: 931-526-4016. p. 2121

Kirby, Michael, Head Librn, Dakota County Technical College Library, 1300 145th St E, Rosemount, MN, 55068. Tel: 651-423-8366. p. 1195

Kirby, Michael, Librn, Institutional Repository, Kingsborough Community College, 2001 Oriental Blvd, Brooklyn, NY, 11235. Tel: 718-368-5429. p. 1504

Kirby, Nicole, Libr Assoc/Acq Section, New Mexico Highlands University, 802 National Ave, Las Vegas, NM, 87701. Tel: 505-454-3336. p. 1471

Kirby, Paulette, Libr Dir, Monroe County Public Library, 303 South St, Union, WV, 24983. Tel: 304-772-3038. p. 2416

Kirchartz, Melanie, Resource Sharing Coord, Point Park University Library, 414 Wood St, Pittsburgh, PA, 15222. Tel: 412-392-3165. p. 1995

Kirchgesler, Kristen J, Ref & Instrul Serv Librn, Case Western Reserve University, Lillian & Milford Harris Library, Jack Joseph & Morton Mandel School of Applied Social Sciences, 11235 Bellflower Rd, Cleveland, OH, 44106-7164. Tel: 216-368-2302. p. 1766

Kirchhoefer, Angela, Librn, Chester Mental Health Center, 1315 Lehmen Dr, Chester, IL, 62233. Tel: 618-826-4571, Ext 10178. p. 553

Kirchhoff, Debra, Br Mgr, Trails Regional Library, Concordia Branch, 813 S Main, Concordia, MO, 64020. Tel: 660-463-2277. p. 1285

Kirchmeier, Michael, Exec Dir, Jackson County Historical Society Library, 307 N Hwy 86, Lakefield, MN, 56150. Tel: 507-662-5505. p. 1180

Kirchner, Joy, Dean of Libr, York University Libraries, 4700 Keele St, North York, ON, M3J 1P3, CANADA. Tel: 416-736-5150, Ext 55150, 416-736-5601. p. 2661

Kirchner, Kathie, Circ Supvr, Milford Town Library, 80 Spruce St, Milford, MA, 01757. Tel: 508-473-2145, Ext 218. p. 1035

Kirchner, Renee, Youth Serv Supvr, Lewisville Public Library System, 1197 W Main St, Lewisville, TX, 75067. Tel: 972-219-3691. p. 2211

Kirchner, Terry, Exec Dir, Westchester Library System, 570 Taxter Rd, Ste 400, Elmsford, NY, 10523-2337. Tel: 914-231-3223. p. 1531

Kirchofer, Jason, Adult Serv Supvry Librn, Apache Junction Public Library, 1177 N Idaho Rd, Apache Junction, AZ, 85119. Tel: 480-474-8503. p. 55

Kirchoff, Jason, Libr Serv Coordr, Great River Regional Library, Cold Spring Library, 27 Red River Rd S, Cold Spring, MN, 56320. Tel: 320-685-8281. p. 1196

Kirchoff, Jason, Libr Serv Coordr, Great River Regional Library, Richmond Library, 63 Hall Ave SW, Richmond, MN, 56368-8108. Tel: 320-597-3739. p. 1197

Kirchoff, Lori, Tech Serv, Campbell County Public Library System, 2101 S 4-J Rd, Gillette, WY, 82718. Tel: 307-687-0009. p. 2494

Kirchoffer, Joyce, Br Librn, Clearwater Public Library System, Beach, 69 Bay Esplanade, Clearwater, FL, 33767. Tel: 727-562-4970. p. 389

Kiriakova, Maria, Assoc Librn, Tech Serv, John Jay College of Criminal Justice, 899 Tenth Ave, New York, NY, 10019. Tel: 212-237-8260. p. 1589

Kirk, Christi Anne, Librn, Woodruff, Spradlin & Smart Library, 555 Anton Blvd, Ste 1200, Costa Mesa, CA, 92626. Tel: 714-558-7000. p. 133

Kirk, Jen, Govt Doc Librn, Utah State University, 3000 Old Main Hill, Logan, UT, 84322-3000. Tel: 435-797-8033. p. 2265

Kirk, Julie, Dir, New Castle Public Library, 424 Delaware St, New Castle, DE, 19720. Tel: 302-328-1995. p. 354

Kirk, Kaitlin, Libr Asst, Northern Lakes College Library, 1201 Main St SE, Slave Lake, AB, T0G 2A3, CANADA. Tel: 780-849-8670. p. 2554

Kirk, Katie, Ch Serv, Gary Byker Memorial Library, 3338 Van Buren St, Hudsonville, MI, 49426. Tel: 616-669-1255. p. 1117

Kirk, Kristen, Youth Serv Mgr, Wayne Township Library, 80 N Sixth St, Richmond, IN, 47374. Tel: 765-966-8291, Ext 1127. p. 715

Kirk, Maresa, Circ Mgr, Eugene Public Library, 100 W Tenth Ave, Eugene, OR, 97401. Tel: 541-682-5450. p. 1878

Kirk, Mary, Coordr, Tech Serv, Libr Syst Coordr, Rose State College, 6420 SE 15th St, Midwest City, OK, 73110. Tel: 405-736-0268. p. 1853

Kirk, Mike, Dir, Galion Public Library, 123 N Market St, Galion, OH, 44833. Tel: 419-468-3203. p. 1787

Kirk, Rachel, Collection Assessment Librarian, Middle Tennessee State University, 1611 Alumni Dr, Murfreesboro, TN, 37132. Tel: 615-904-8518. p. 2117

Kirk, Simone, Br Mgr, Southeast Arkansas Regional Library, Star City Branch, 200 E Wiley, Star City, AR, 71667. Tel: 870-628-4711. p. 105

Kirkbride, Kathy, Br Mgr, Muskingum County Library System, Duncan Falls-Philo Branch, 222 Main St, Duncan Falls, OH, 43734. Tel: 740-674-7100. p. 1837

Kirkbright, Cheryl, Br Mgr, Simpson Kate Love Morgan County Library, Chesterhill Branch, 7520 Marion St, Chesterhill, OH, 43728. Tel: 740-554-7104. p. 1801

Kirkby, Charlotte, Library Services, Supvr, Educational Testing Service, Turnbull Hall, Mail Stop 01-R, 660 Rosedale Rd, Princeton, NJ, 08541. Tel: 609-734-1148. p. 1436

Kirkelie, Marilyn, Libr Coord, Riley County Kansas Genealogical Society Library, 2005 Claflin Rd, Manhattan, KS, 66502-3415. Tel: 785-565-6495. p. 823

Kirkes, Sharon, Br Mgr, Jacksonville Public Library, Maxville Branch, 8375 Maxville Rd, Jacksonville, FL, 32234-2748. Tel: 904-289-7563. p. 412

Kirkes, Sharon, Br Mgr, Jacksonville Public Library, West Regional, 1425 Chaffee Rd S, Jacksonville, FL, 32221-1119. Tel: 904-693-1448. p. 412

Kirkham, Darla, Asst Librn, Rushville Public Library, 514 Maple Ave, Rushville, IL, 62681-1044. Tel: 217-322-3030. p. 644

Kirking-Russo, Allyson, Asst Dir, Ottumwa Public Library, 102 W Fourth St, Ottumwa, IA, 52501. Tel: 641-682-7563, Ext 203. p. 775

Kirkland, Carolyn, Circ, Holmes County Public Library, 303 N J Harvey Etheridge St, Bonifay, FL, 32425. Tel: 850-547-3573. p. 386

Kirkland, Laura, Cat, Stetson University, 421 N Woodland Blvd, Unit 8418, DeLand, FL, 32723. Tel: 386-822-4027. p. 393

Kirkland, Luke, Libr Dir, Ayer Library, 26 E Main St, Ayer, MA, 01432. Tel: 978-772-8250. p. 987

Kirkland, Sandra, Asst Dir, Taylor Library, 49 E Derry Rd, East Derry, NH, 03041. Tel: 603-432-7186. p. 1362

Kirkley, Chris, Br Mgr, Shreve Memorial Library, 424 Texas St, Shreveport, LA, 71101. Tel: 318-226-5897. p. 908

Kirkpatrick, Ann, Libr Asst, Volunteer State Community College Library, 1480 Nashville Pike, Gallatin, TN, 37066-3188. Tel: 615-452-8600, Ext 2750. p. 2099

Kirkpatrick, Geoffrey, Dir, Bethlehem Public Library, 451 Delaware Ave, Delmar, NY, 12054-3042. Tel: 518-439-9314. p. 1525

Kirkpatrick, Keri, Media Spec, De Anza College, 21250 Stevens Creek Blvd, Cupertino, CA, 95014-5793. Tel: 408-864-8581. p. 133

Kirkpatrick, Kristie, Dir, Whitman County Rural Library District, 102 S Main St, Colfax, WA, 99111-1863. Tel: 509-397-4366. p. 2362

Kirkpatrick, Nancy S, Dean of Libr, Florida International University, 3000 NE 151st St, North Miami, FL, 33181-3600. Tel: 305-919-5726. p. 428

Kirkpatrick, Sarah, Dir, Campus Engagement, Dir, Learning Res Ctr, Southern Illinois University Edwardsville, 601 James R Thompson Blvd, Bldg B, East Saint Louis, IL, 62201. Tel: 618-482-8366. p. 581

Kirkwood, Jonathan, Archivist, Sloan Museum Archives, 1221 E Kearsley St, Flint, MI, 48503. Tel: 810-237-3421. p. 1107

Kirkwood, Kae Hirschy, Archivist, Geneva College, 3200 College Ave, Beaver Falls, PA, 15010-3599. Tel: 724-847-6694. p. 1909

Kirkwood, Laurie, Dir, Beaver Falls Library, 9607 Lewis St, Beaver Falls, NY, 13305. Tel: 315-346-6216. p. 1491

Kiron, Arthur, Dr, Curator, Herbert D Katz Center for Advanced Judaic Studies Library, 420 Walnut St, Philadelphia, PA, 19106-3703. Tel: 215-746-1290, 215-746-5154. p. 1982

Kirsch, Breanne, Univ Librn, Briar Cliff University, 3303 Rebecca St, Sioux City, IA, 51104. Tel: 712-279-5451. p. 782

Kirsch, Deb, Dir, Temple Isaiah, 945 Risa Rd, Lafayette, CA, 94549. Tel: 925-283-8575. p. 155

Kirschner, Jessica, Coordr, Digital Initiatives, Virginia's Academic Library Consortium, George Mason University, 4400 University Dr, Fenwick 5100, Fairfax, VA, 22030. Tel: 703-993-4654. p. 2776

Kirschner, Kate, Ch, Programming Librn, Horicon Public Library, 404 E Lake St, Horicon, WI, 53032-1297. Tel: 920-485-3535. p. 2441

Kirschner, Matt, Head, Children's Dept, South Brunswick Public Library, 110 Kingston Lane, Monmouth Junction, NJ, 08852. Tel: 732-329-4000, Ext 7344. p. 1419

Kirsop, Ron, Exec Dir, OWWL Library System, 2557 State Rte 21, Canandaigua, NY, 14424. Tel: 585-394-8260, Ext 1103. p. 1512

Kirsten, Holly, Head, Outreach Serv, Info Serv, Chesterfield Township Library, 50560 Patricia Ave, Chesterfield, MI, 48051-3804. Tel: 586-598-4900. p. 1091

Kirts, Keith, Br Mgr, Wallowa County Library, Imnaha Branch, Imnaha Hwy, Imnaha, OR, 97842. Tel: 541-577-2308. p. 1878

Kirven, Melissa, Asst Librn, Lee County Public Library, 200 N Main St, Bishopville, SC, 29010. Tel: 803-484-5921. p. 2047

Kirwan, Kim, Mgr, Cabell County Public Library, Salt Rock Branch, 138 Madison Creek Rd, Salt Rock, WV, 25559. Tel: 304-733-2186. p. 2404

Kisbany, Jennifer, Libr Dir, Deckerville Public Library, 3542 N Main St, Deckerville, MI, 48427. Tel: 810-376-8015. p. 1096

Kiscaden, Elizabeth, Univ Librn, Creighton University, 2500 California Plaza, Omaha, NE, 68178-0209. Tel: 402-280-5129. p. 1328

Kiser, Beverly, Libr Asst, Pub Serv, Adams County Public Library, 157 High St, Peebles, OH, 45660. Tel: 937-587-2085. p. 1814
Kiser, Paula, Digital Scholarship Librn, Washington & Lee University, University Library, 204 W Washington St, Lexington, VA, 24450-2116. Tel: 540-458-8643. p. 2329
Kiser, Teresa, Dir, Public Library of Anniston-Calhoun County, 108 E Tenth St, Anniston, AL, 36201. Tel: 256-237-8501. p. 4
Kish, Adam, Br Mgr, Butte-Silver Bow Public Library, South Branch, Butte Plaza Mall, 3100 Harrison Ave, Butte, MT, 59701. Tel: 406-792-1080, Ext 6400. p. 1290
Kish, Anne, Electronic Res Librn, Montana Tech Library, 1300 W Park St, Butte, MT, 59701. Tel: 406-496-4839. p. 1290
Kish, Anne, Dir, University of Montana Western, 710 S Atlantic St, Dillon, MT, 59725. Tel: 406-683-7494. p. 1292
Kish, Liz, Br Librn, Genesee District Library, 4195 W Pasadena Ave, Flint, MI, 48504. Tel: 810-732-0110. p. 1105
Kish, Steven, Ref Librn, Lawrence Technological University Library, 21000 W Ten Mile Rd, Southfield, MI, 48075-1058. Tel: 248-204-3000. p. 1151
Kishel, Hans, Head, User Serv, University of Wisconsin-Eau Claire, 103 Garfield Ave, Eau Claire, WI, 54701-4932. Tel: 715-836-2959. p. 2433
Kisko, Jocelyne, Libr Mgr, Rockyford Municipal Library, Community Ctr, 412 Serviceberry Trail, Rockyford, AB, T0J 2R0, CANADA. Tel: 403-533-3964. p. 2552
Kisler, Yelena, Libr Dir, Cameron County Public Library, 27 W Fourth St, Emporium, PA, 15834. Tel: 814-486-8011. p. 1930
Kisner, Diane, Br Mgr, Enlow Ruth Library of Garrett County, Kitzmiller Branch, 288 W Main St, Kitzmiller, MD, 21538. Tel: 301-334-8091. p. 972
Kison, Lori, Spec Coll Coordr, Western Michigan University, Zhang Legacy Collections Center, 1650 Oakland Dr, Kalamazoo, MI, 49008. Tel: 269-387-5240. p. 1122
Kispert, Miranda, Sci Librn, Weber State University, 3921 Central Campus Dr, Dept 2901, Ogden, UT, 84408-2901. Tel: 801-626-6093. p. 2268
Kissel, Kelly, Librn, Evansville State Hospital, Patient Library, 3400 Lincoln Ave, Evansville, IN, 47714. Tel: 812-469-6800, Ext 4215. p. 681
Kissinger, Ann, Ch Serv, Wauwatosa Public Library, 7635 W North Ave, Wauwatosa, WI, 53213-1718. Tel: 414-471-8484. p. 2486
Kissinger, John, Libr Mgr, College of Coastal Georgia, Camden Center Learning Resources Center, 8001 Lakes Blvd, Kingsland, GA, 31548. Tel: 912-510-3332. p. 468
Kissling, Alison, Research Librn, Cincinnati Children's Hospital, Edward L Pratt Library, S9.125 ML 3012, 3333 Burnet Ave, Cincinnati, OH, 45229-3039. Tel: 513-636-4230. p. 1759
Kister, Mark, Circ, Pub Serv, Ref Serv, Shelby County Libraries, 230 E North St, Sidney, OH, 45365-2785. Tel: 937-492-8354. p. 1820
Kistler, Eric, Libr Dir, Charleston Southern University, 9200 University Blvd, Charleston, SC, 29406. Tel: 843-863-7938. p. 2050
Kistner, Laura, ILL Tech, Pub Serv, US Department of Commerce, 325 Broadway, R/ESRL5, Boulder, CO, 80305-3328. Tel: 303-497-3271. p. 267
Kiszka, Victoria, Tech & Technical Serv Librn, Avon Free Public Library, 281 Country Club Rd, Avon, CT, 06001. Tel: 860-673-9712. p. 301
Kiszka, Victoria, Teen Librn, Burlington Public Library, 34 Library Lane, Burlington, CT, 06013. Tel: 860-673-3331. p. 305
Kitchel, JoAnn, Children's Dir, Daland Memorial Library, Five N Main St, Mont Vernon, NH, 03057. Tel: 603-673-7888. p. 1374
Kitchel, Peggy, Asst Dir, Grosse Pointe Public Library, Ten Kercheval Ave, Grosse Pointe Farms, MI, 48236-3602. Tel: 313-343-2074. p. 1112
Kitchell, Catherine A, Ref Librn, Bloomberg Industry Group Library, 1801 S Bell St, Arlington, VA, 22202. Tel: 703-341-3311. p. 2305
Kitchen, Jeremy, Br Mgr, Chicago Public Library, Richard J Daley-Bridgeport Branch, 3400 S Halsted St, Chicago, IL, 60608. Tel: 312-747-8990. p. 556
Kitchen, Kelley, Chief Financial Officer, Saint Joseph County Public Library, 304 S Main St, South Bend, IN, 46601. Tel: 574-282-4646. p. 718
Kitchens, Rhonda, Librn, Big Bend Community College Library, 1800 Bldg, 7662 Chanute St NE, Moses Lake, WA, 98837. Tel: 509-793-2350. p. 2371
Kitchens, Savannah, Dir, Parnell Memorial Library, 277 Park Dr, Montevallo, AL, 35115-3882. Tel: 205-665-9207. p. 27
Kitchin, Shari, Br Mgr, Juneau Public Libraries, Mendenhall Valley, 3025 Dimond Park Loop, Juneau, AK, 99801. Tel: 907-789-0125. p. 47
Kitchin, Shari, Circ, Juneau Public Libraries, 292 Marine Way, Juneau, AK, 99801. Tel: 907-586-5249. p. 47
Kite, Kate, Asst Dir, Br Mgr, Six Mile Regional Library District, Niedringhaus Bldg, 2001 Delmar Ave, Granite City, IL, 62040-4590. Tel: 618-452-6238. p. 594
Kite, Meredith, Coll Archivist, University of Iowa Libraries, Special Collections & Archives, 100 Main Library, 125 W Washington St, Iowa City, IA, 52242-1420. Tel: 319-335-5921. p. 761
Kitlas, Marilyn, Ref & Ad Serv Librn, Canterbury Public Library, One Municipal Dr, Canterbury, CT, 06331-1453. Tel: 860-546-9022. p. 305
Kittler, Christine A, ILL, Libr Tech, Miami VA Healthcare System, 1201 NW 16th St, Miami, FL, 33125-1693. Tel: 305-575-3187. p. 424
Kittleson, Ken, Dir, Norwalk Public Library, 101 Railroad St, Norwalk, WI, 54648. Tel: 608-823-7473. p. 2465
Kittmer, Sarah, Librn, Providence Care Mental Health Services, 752 King St W, Kingston, ON, K7L 4X3, CANADA. Tel: 613-546-1101, Ext 5745. p. 2650
Kittrell, Sarah, Coll Develop Mgr, Wichita Public Library, 711 W Second St, Wichita, KS, 67203. Tel: 316-261-8580. p. 843
Kitts, Royce, Dir, Liberal Memorial Library, 519 N Kansas, Liberal, KS, 67901-3345. Tel: 620-626-0180. p. 821
Kivilahti, Stephanie, Sr Asst Librn, Red Rock Public Library Board, 42 Salls St, Red Rock, ON, P0T 2P0, CANADA. Tel: 807-886-2558. p. 2675
Kiyoshk Ross, Jeff, Coordr, University of Toronto Libraries, First Nations House Library, Bordon Bldg N, 563 Spadina Ave, 3rd Flr, Toronto, ON, M5S 1A5, CANADA. Tel: 416-978-0413. p. 2698
Kiyotake, Cynthia, Libr Mgr, Arapahoe Library District, Davies Library, 303 Third Ave, Deer Trail, CO, 80105. Tel: 303-769-4310. p. 279
Kiyotake, Cynthia, Libr Mgr, Arapahoe Library District, Kelver Public Library, 404 E Front St, Byers, CO, 80103. Tel: 303-822-9392. p. 279
Kiyotake, Cynthia, Libr Mgr, Arapahoe Library District, Sheridan Public Library, 3425 W Oxford Ave, Sheridan, CO, 80236. p. 279
Kizziar, Brenda, Dir, Ward County Library, 409 S Dwight, Monahans, TX, 79756. Tel: 432-943-3332. p. 2220
Kjaer, Sigrid K, Dr, Ref & Circ Librn, Duke University Libraries, Divinity School Library, 407 Chapel Dr, Durham, NC, 27708. Tel: 919-660-3453. p. 1684
Kjelgren, Roger, Dr, Dir, University of Florida, 2725 S Binion Rd, Apopka, FL, 32703-8504. Tel: 407-884-2035. p. 383
Kjos, Katherine, Libr Asst, National Endowment for Democracy Library, 1201 Pennsylvania Ave NW, Ste 1100, Washington, DC, 20004. Tel: 202-378-9700. p. 372
Klaahssen, Brenda, Asst Dir, Sheldon Public Library, 925 Fourth Ave, Sheldon, IA, 51201. Tel: 712-324-2442. p. 781
Klaas, Tyler, Br Mgr, Riverside County Library System, Perris Library, 163 E San Jacinto, Perris, CA, 92570. Tel: 951-657-2358. p. 202
Klaassen, Brenda, Dir, Hospers Public Library, 213 Main St, Hospers, IA, 51238. Tel: 712-752-8400. p. 758
Klaene, Robin, Dir, Pub Relations, Kenton County Public Library, Administration Center, 3095 Hulbert Ave, Erlanger, KY, 41018. Tel: 859-578-3608. p. 852
Klager, Kathy, Dir, Pauline Haass Public Library, N64 W23820 Main St, Sussex, WI, 53089-3120. Tel: 262-246-5180. p. 2481
Klaic, Irena, Head Librn, Austin Community College, Riverside Campus Library, 1020 Grove Blvd, 1st Flr, Rm 1108, Austin, TX, 78741. Tel: 512-223-6603. p. 2138
Klaich, Mitchell, Dir, Jenner & Block Library, 353 N Clark St, Ste 4300, Chicago, IL, 60654. Tel: 312-222-9350. p. 562
Klain, Laura, Dir, Hollis Social Library, Two Monument Sq, Hollis, NH, 03049. Tel: 603-465-7721. p. 1368
Klaiss, Angela, Mgr, Bettsville Public Library, 233 State St, Bettsville, OH, 44815-9999. Tel: 419-986-5198. p. 1751
Klang, Jennifer, Head, Ref Serv, United States Department of the Interior Library, 1849 C St NW, MS 1151, Washington, DC, 20240. Tel: 202-208-3396. p. 378
Klang, Keith, Libr Dir, Port Washington Public Library, One Library Dr, Port Washington, NY, 11050. Tel: 516-883-3728, Ext 1101. p. 1622
Klapes, Jeffrey M, Head, Info Serv, Lucius Beebe Memorial Library, 345 Main St, Wakefield, MA, 01880-5093. Tel: 781-246-6334. p. 1061
Klapper, Andrea, Dir, Montello Public Library, 128 Lake Ct, Montello, WI, 53949-9204. Tel: 608-297-7544. p. 2462
Klapperich, Barb, Dir, Stacyville Public Library, 106 N Broad St, Stacyville, IA, 50476. Tel: 641-710-2531. p. 784
Klapperstuck, Karen, Virtual Br Mgr, Virtual Ref, Monroe Township Public Library, Four Municipal Plaza, Monroe Township, NJ, 08831-1900. Tel: 732-521-5000, Ext 105. p. 1419
Klar, Josh, Archivist, Norfolk County Archives, 109 Norfolk St S, Simcoe, ON, N3Y 2W3, CANADA. Tel: 519-426-1583. p. 2678
Klare, Diane, Assoc Dean & Dir, United States Air Force Academy Libraries, 2354 Fairchild Dr, Ste 3A15, USAF Academy, CO, 80840-6214. Tel: 719-333-4406. p. 297
Klassen, Maecyn, Library Tech, Circulation, University of the Fraser Valley, Chilliwack Campus, 45190 Caen Ave, Bldg A, Chilliwack, BC, V2R 0N3, CANADA. Tel: 604-504-7441, Ext 2472. p. 2562
Klassen, Randall, Br Librn, South Central Regional Library, Winkler Branch, 160 Main St, Winkler, MB, R6W 0M3, CANADA. Tel: 204-325-7174. p. 2592
Klassen, Tim, Head of Libr, Cameron Science & Technology Library, University of Alberta, Science & Technology Library (Cameron), Edmonton, AB, T6G 2J8, CANADA. Tel: 780-492-7918. p. 2535
Klassen, Tim, Actg Head Librn, University of Alberta, Science & Technology Library, Cameron Library, Edmonton, AB, T6G 2J8, CANADA. Tel: 780-492-7918. p. 2538
Klasson, Cailey, Br Mgr, Windsor Public Library, Wilson, 365 Windsor Ave, Windsor, CT, 06095-4550. Tel: 860-247-8960. p. 348
Klasson, Cailey, Ref Librn, Windsor Public Library, 323 Broad St, Windsor, CT, 06095. Tel: 860-285-1919. p. 348

Klasson, Cailey, Ch, Gulfport Public Library, 5501 28th Ave S, Gulfport, FL, 33707. Tel: 727-893-1134. p. 408

Klatt, Carolyn, Assoc Dir, Library & Info Services, Memorial Health University Medical Center, 1250 E 66 St, Savannah, GA, 31404. Tel: 912-721-8230. p. 496

Klaus, Alex, Head, Youth Serv, Durham Public Library, Seven Maple Ave, Durham, CT, 06422. Tel: 860-349-9544. p. 309

Klawiter, Audrey, Adminr, Lyons Public Library, 4209 Joliet Ave, Lyons, IL, 60534-1597. Tel: 708-447-3577. p. 612

Klawitter, Michael, Archivist, Ref Librn, Grand Rapids Community College, 140 Ransom NE Ave, Grand Rapids, MI, 49503. Tel: 616-234-3868. p. 1110

Klayton, Daniel, Librn, North Central Washington Libraries, Tonasket Public Library, 209 A Whitcomb Ave, Tonasket, WA, 98855-8818. Tel: 509-486-2366. p. 2394

Kleback, Cynthia, Mgr, Baltimore County Public Library, Perry Hall Branch, 9685 Honeygo Blvd, Baltimore, MD, 21128. Tel: 410-887-5195. p. 980

Klebanoff, Abbe, Br Mgr, Free Library of Philadelphia, Fumo Family Branch, 2437 S Broad St, Philadelphia, PA, 19148-3508. Tel: 215-685-1757. p. 1978

Kleber, Beth, Archivist, School of Visual Arts Library, 380 Second Ave, 2nd Flr, New York, NY, 10010. Tel: 212-592-2636. p. 1601

Klecha, Mary Lou, Access Serv Librn, MacDonald Public Library, 36480 Main St, New Baltimore, MI, 48047-2509. Tel: 586-725-0273. p. 1137

Kleckner Keefe, Karen, Exec Dir, Hinsdale Public Library, 20 E Maple St, Hinsdale, IL, 60521. Tel: 630-986-1976. p. 600

Klee, Rosita, Cat Librn, Dine College, One Circle Dr, Rte 12, Tsaile, AZ, 86556. Tel: 928-724-6757. p. 80

Klee, Shaun, Ad, Tech Serv Librn, Grand Island Public Library, 1124 W Second St, Grand Island, NE, 68801. Tel: 308-385-5333. p. 1316

Kleespies, Gavin, Exec Dir, Gore Place Society, Inc Library, 52 Gore St, Waltham, MA, 02453. Tel: 781-894-2798. p. 1062

Kleiber, Linda, Circ Supvr, Chesapeake Public Library, Dr Clarence V Cuffee Library, 2726 Border Rd, Chesapeake, VA, 23324-3760. Tel: 757-410-7043. p. 2311

Kleiman, Allan M, Dir, Edison Township Free Public Library, 340 Plainfield Ave, Edison, NJ, 08817. Tel: 732-287-2298. p. 1400

Kleimann, Joyce, Dir, Genevieve Miller Hitchcock Public Library, 8005 Barry Ave, Hitchcock, TX, 77563. Tel: 409-986-7814. p. 2190

Klein, Adaire, Dir, Simon Wiesenthal Center & Museum of Tolerance, 1399 S Roxbury Dr, 3rd Flr, Los Angeles, CA, 90035-4709. Tel: 310-772-7605. p. 168

Klein, Alan, Dir, Tech Serv, Juilliard School, 60 Lincoln Center Plaza, New York, NY, 10023-6588. Tel: 212-799-5000, Ext 265. p. 1590

Klein, Arnie, Video Librn, Ohio Bureau of Worker's Compensation, 30 W Spring St, Third Flr, Columbus, OH, 43215-2256. Tel: 614-466-7388. p. 1774

Klein, Eric, Dr, Dean, Learning Res, Grossmont College Library, 8800 Grossmont College Dr, El Cajon, CA, 92020-1799. Tel: 619-644-7356. p. 139

Klein, Gaale, Asst Librn, Shedd-Porter Memorial Library, Two Main St, Alstead, NH, 03602. Tel: 603-835-6661. p. 1353

Klein, Gary, Management & Economics Librn, Willamette University, 900 State St, Salem, OR, 97301. Tel: 503-370-6743. p. 1897

Klein Hewett, Megan, Ad, Ames Public Library, 515 Douglas Ave, Ames, IA, 50010. Tel: 515-239-5646. p. 731

Klein, Imani, Dir, Samuel W Smith Memorial Public Library, 201 E Maple St, Port Allegany, PA, 16743. Tel: 814-642-9210. p. 1998

Klein, Janeene, Dir, Remsen Public Library, 211 Fulton St, Remsen, IA, 51050. Tel: 712-786-2911. p. 778

Klein, Janette, Univ Librn, University of Central Missouri, 601 S Missouri, Warrensburg, MO, 64093-5020. Tel: 660-543-4140. p. 1285

Klein, Joette, Asst Dir, Libr Serv, Jefferson College Library, 1000 Viking Dr, Hillsboro, MO, 63050. Tel: 636-481-3161. p. 1249

Klein, Joseph, Librn, Roanoke Public Libraries, Law Library, City of Roanoke Courthouse, 315 Church Ave SW, Ste B, Roanoke, VA, 24016. Tel: 540-853-2268. p. 2345

Klein, Karyl, Archivist, Cardinal Stafford Library, Archives of the Catholic Archdiocese of Denver, 1300 S Steele St, Denver, CO, 80210. Tel: 303-715-3144. p. 273

Klein, Miles, Law Librn, Lancaster County Law Library, 50 N Duke St, Lancaster, PA, 17602. Tel: 717-299-8090. p. 1951

Klein, Nancy, Curator, National Scouting Museum, Philmont Scout Ranch, 17 Deer Run Rd, Cimarron, NM, 87714. Tel: 575-376-2281, Ext 1271. p. 1465

Klein, Peggy, Access Serv Spec, Info Serv Spec, Nicolet Area Technical College, Lakeside Center, 3rd Flr, 5364 College Dr, Rhinelander, WI, 54501. Tel: 715-365-4606. p. 2472

Klein, Rebecca, Pub Serv Librn, Newton Public Library, 100 N Third Ave W, Newton, IA, 50208. Tel: 641-792-4108. p. 773

Klein, Sandra, Acq/Coll Develop Librn, University of Notre Dame, 2345 Biolchini Hall of Law, Notre Dame, IN, 46556-4640. Tel: 574-631-8447. p. 712

Klein, Sarah, Libr Spec, Ashland Community & Technical College, Technology Drive Campus Library, 902 Technology Dr, Grayson, KY, 41143. Tel: 606-326-2450. p. 847

Klein, Sarah, Library Contact, Westmoreland Reading Center, 50 Station Rd, Westmoreland, NY, 13490. Tel: 315-853-8001, Ext 5. p. 1664

Klein, Stephen, Digital Serv Librn, City University of New York, 365 Fifth Ave, New York, NY, 10016-4309. Tel: 212-817-7074. p. 1582

Klein-Ezell, Colleen, Dept Head, Southeastern Louisiana University, 1300 N General Pershing St, Hammond, LA, 70402. Tel: 985-549-2221. p. 2786

Kleinberg, Julia, Mgr, Libr Serv, Allan Memorial Institute of Psychiatry, Royal Victoria Hospital, 1025 Pine Ave W, Montreal, QC, H3A 1A1, CANADA. Tel: 514-934-1934, Ext 34528. p. 2716

Kleinberg, Julia, Team Leader, Jewish General Hospital, 3755 Cote Ste Catherine Rd, Rm 200, Montreal, QC, H3T 1E2, CANADA. Tel: 514-340-8222, Ext 22391. p. 2725

Kleiner, Donna, Acq Librn, NASA Ames Research Center, Technical Library, Bldg 202, Mail Stop 202-3, Moffett Field, CA, 94035-1000. Tel: 650-604-6325. p. 178

Kleinert, Lisa, Ad, Garden City Public Library, 31735 Maplewood St, Garden City, MI, 48135. Tel: 734-793-1830. p. 1108

Kleinert, Marcia, Researcher, Warren County Historical Society, 210 Fourth Ave, Warren, PA, 16365. Tel: 814-723-1795. p. 2017

Kleinknecht, Joan O, Librn, Scottish Rite Library, 1733 16th St NW, Washington, DC, 20009-3103. Tel: 202-777-3139. p. 374

Kleinmann, Lisa, Dir, Ch Serv, Youth Serv Dir, Durham Public Library, 49 Madbury Rd, Durham, NH, 03824. Tel: 603-868-6699. p. 1361

Kleinschmidt, Patty, Ch, Norton Public Library, One Washington Sq, Norton, KS, 67654. Tel: 785-877-2481. p. 827

Kleinsorge, Judy, Ch Serv, Pioneer Memorial Library, 375 W Fourth St, Colby, KS, 67701-2197. Tel: 785-460-4470. p. 802

Kleist, Karen, Libr Assoc, University of Wisconsin, 400 University Dr, West Bend, WI, 53095-3619. Tel: 262-808-4141. p. 2487

Kleiva, Sarah, Commun Engagement Mgr, Orland Park Public Library, 14921 Ravinia Ave, Orland Park, IL, 60462. Tel: 708-428-5114. p. 630

Klem, Megan, Dir of Preservation, Landmark Society of Western New York, Inc, Five Castle Park, Rochester, NY, 14620. Tel: 585-537-5958. p. 1628

Kleman, Amy, Principal Librn, Youth Serv, Oceanside Public Library, 330 N Coast Hwy, Oceanside, CA, 92054. Tel: 760-435-5583. p. 187

Klemann, Sara, Dir, Walter E Olson Memorial Library, 203 N Main St, Eagle River, WI, 54521. Tel: 715-479-8070. p. 2432

Klemas, Irene, Br Mgr, Free Library of Philadelphia, West Oak Lane Branch, 2000 Washington Lane, Philadelphia, PA, 19138-1344. Tel: 215-685-2843. p. 1980

Klemm, Jotisa H, Dir, Libr Serv, Tarrant County College, Bldg ESED 1200, 2100 Southeast Pkwy, Arlington, TX, 76018. Tel: 817-515-3082. p. 2136

Klemm, Lacey, Assoc Dir, Reference & Adult Services, East Chicago Public Library, 2401 E Columbus Dr, East Chicago, IN, 46312-2998. Tel: 219-397-2453. p. 680

Klemm, Marlene, Ch, Frances L Simek Memorial Library, 400 N Main St, Medford, WI, 54451. Tel: 715-748-2505. p. 2455

Klemme Eliceiri, Rebecca, Cataloger, St Charles Community College, 4601 Mid Rivers Mall Dr, Cottleville, MO, 63376. Tel: 636-922-8620. p. 1244

Klemme, Rhonda, Cataloger, Mayville Public Library, 111 N Main St, Mayville, WI, 53050. Tel: 920-387-7910. p. 2455

Klemmt, Mary Tuke, Librn, David D Acker Library & Knowledge Repository, 9820 Belvoir Rd, Bldg 270, Fort Belvoir, VA, 22060. Tel: 703-805-5253. p. 2318

Klemp-Skirvin, Kaitlin, Res Serv Mgr, Warner, Norcross & Judd, LLP Library, 1500 Warner Bldg, 150 Ottawa Ave NW, Grand Rapids, MI, 49503. Tel: 616-752-2000. p. 1112

Klempnauer, Christi, Admin Coordr, Baylor University Libraries, Armstrong Browning Library & Museum, 710 Speight Ave, Waco, TX, 76798. Tel: 254-710-4968. p. 2253

Klemundt, Mary, Cat/Ref Librn, Elgin Community College, 1700 Spartan Dr, Elgin, IL, 60123. Tel: 847-214-7337. p. 584

Klenke, Laura, Tech Serv, Sanger Public Library, 501 Bolivar St, Sanger, TX, 76266. Tel: 940-458-3257. p. 2241

Klenklen, Andrew, Coll Develop Librn, Wesley Theological Seminary Library, 4500 Massachusetts Ave NW, Washington, DC, 20016-5690. Tel: 202-885-8692. p. 381

Klepitsch, Heather, Libr Dir, OSF Saint Anthony Medical Center, 5666 E State St, Rockford, IL, 61108-2472. Tel: 815-227-2558. p. 641

Klesta, Maria, Creative Learning Mgr, Carson City Library, 900 N Roop St, Carson City, NV, 89701. Tel: 775-283-7593. p. 1343

Kleszcz, Emily, Head, Circ, Dearborn Heights City Libraries, Caroline Kennedy Library, 24590 George St, Dearborn Heights, MI, 48127. Tel: 313-791-3805. p. 1096

Klezli, Caroline, Asst Librn, Monroe County Public Library, 303 South St, Union, WV, 24983. Tel: 304-772-3038. p. 2416

Klich, Jerilyn, Human Res Mgr, Genesee District Library, 4195 W Pasadena Ave, Flint, MI, 48504. Tel: 810-732-0110. p. 1105

Klieman, Janet, Librn, United States Army, Lane Medical Library - Evans Army Community Hospital, 1650 Cochrane Circle, Fort Carson, CO, 80913-4604. Tel: 719-526-7285. p. 280

Klien, Christy, Dir, Portage District Library, 300 Library Lane, Portage, MI, 49002. Tel: 269-329-4544. p. 1143

Klima, John, Tech Mgr, Waukesha Public Library, 321 Wisconsin Ave, Waukesha, WI, 53186-4713. Tel: 262-524-3688. p. 2484

Klimack, Mary, Asst Dir, Sand Lake Town Library, 8428 Miller Hill Rd, Averill Park, NY, 12018. Tel: 518-674-5050. p. 1489

Klimack, Mary, Librn, North Greenbush Public Library, 141 Main Ave, Wynantskill, NY, 12198. Tel: 518-283-0303. p. 1667

Klimasara, Blake, Librn, El Paso Community College Library, Jenna Welch & Laura Bush Community Library, Northwest Campus, 6701 S Desert Rd, Rm L100, El Paso, TX, 79932. Tel: 915-831-8889. p. 2173

Klimek, Dean, Community Outreach, Tech Librn, Cranbury Public Library, 30 Park Place W, Cranbury, NJ, 08512. Tel: 609-799-6992. p. 1397

Klimek, Marsha, Librn, Utica Public Library District, 224 Mill St, Utica, IL, 61373. Tel: 815-667-4509. p. 657

Klimiades, Mario Nick, Dir, Heard Museum, 2301 N Central Ave, Phoenix, AZ, 85004-1323. Tel: 602-252-8840. p. 70

Klimowicz, Judith, Asst Dir, Ch, Cranford Free Public Library, 224 Walnut Ave, Cranford, NJ, 07016-2931. Tel: 908-709-7272. p. 1398

Klimusko, Christine, Bus Mgr, Glenview Public Library, 1930 Glenview Rd, Glenview, IL, 60025. Tel: 847-729-7500. p. 594

Kline, Barbara, Dir, Spring Township Library, 78C Commerce Dr, Wyomissing, PA, 19610. Tel: 610-373-9888. p. 2025

Kline, Jill, Outreach Librn, Pub Serv, Union College Library, 3800 S 48th St, Lincoln, NE, 68506-4386. Tel: 402-486-2600, Ext 2149. p. 1323

Kline, Kathy D, Dir, Extn Serv, North Trails Public Library, 1553 W Sunbury Rd, West Sunbury, PA, 16061-1211. Tel: 724-476-1006. p. 2021

Kline, Kelly, Dir, Selbyville Public Library, 11 Main & McCabe Sts, Selbyville, DE, 19975. Tel: 302-436-8195. p. 356

Kline, Kristyn, Asst Dir, Denver Public Library, 100 Washington St, Denver, IA, 50622. Tel: 319-984-5140. p. 745

Kline, Pauline, Librn, Winkler County Library, Wink Branch, 207 Roy Orbison Dr, Wink, TX, 79789. Tel: 432-527-3691. p. 2205

Kline, Samantha, Mgr, County of Los Angeles Public Library, Wiseburn Library, 5335 W 135th St, Hawthorne, CA, 90250-4948. Tel: 310-643-8880. p. 138

Kline, Teresa, Dir, Fennville District Library, 400 W Main St, Fennville, MI, 49408. Tel: 269-561-5050. p. 1104

Kline, Teresa, Bus Mgr, Tenn-Share, PO Box 691, Alcoa, TN, 37701. Tel: 615-669-8670. p. 2775

Kline, Vickie, Syst, York College of Pennsylvania, 441 Country Club Rd, York, PA, 17403-3651. Tel: 717-815-1459. p. 2026

Kline-Millard, Patricia, Head, Info Serv, Bedford Public Library, Three Meetinghouse Rd, Bedford, NH, 03110. Tel: 603-472-2300. p. 1354

Klinepeter, Pamela, Dir, Libr Serv, Ashland Community & Technical College, 1400 College Dr, Ashland, KY, 41101. Tel: 606-326-2254. p. 847

Klinepeter, Pamela, Libr Dir, Ashland Community & Technical College, Technology Drive Campus Library, 902 Technology Dr, Grayson, KY, 41143. Tel: 606-326-2450. p. 847

Klinetobe, Mary, Asst Librn, Neligh Public Library, 710 Main St, Neligh, NE, 68756-1246. Tel: 402-887-5140. p. 1326

Kling, Ann, Libr Dir, Clearview Library District, 720 Third St, Windsor, CO, 80550-5109. Tel: 970-686-5603, Ext 302. p. 298

Kling, Anne, Archives Mgr, Cincinnati Museum Center At Union Terminal, 1301 Western Ave, Ste 2133, Cincinnati, OH, 45203. Tel: 513-287-7066. p. 1760

Kling, Dale, Librn, Pauline & Jane Chilton Memorial Marlin Public Library, 400 Oaks St, Marlin, TX, 76661. Tel: 254-883-6602. p. 2215

Klingbeil, Joshua, IT Dir, Wisconsin Valley Library Service, 300 N First St, Wausau, WI, 54403. Tel: 715-261-7252. p. 2777

Klinge, Peggy, Acq Mgr, McDaniel College, 2 College Hill, Westminster, MD, 21157-4390. Tel: 410-857-2285. p. 981

Klinger, Esther, Librn, Snyder County Historical Society, Inc Library, 30 E Market St, Middleburg, PA, 17842-1017. Tel: 570-837-6191. p. 1962

Klinger, Norene, Dir, Lied Carroll Public Library, 506 Main St, Carroll, NE, 68723. Tel: 402-585-4768. p. 1309

Klinger, Suzanne, Head, Ref Serv, University of Washington Libraries, Tacoma Library, 1900 Commerce St, Box 358460, Tacoma, WA, 98402-3100. Tel: 253-692-4443. p. 2382

Klinkel, Lydia, Dir, Ionia Community Library, 101 W Iowa St, Ionia, IA, 50645. Tel: 641-394-4803. p. 760

Klinker, Diane, Dir, Stilwell Public library, 107 W Maple, New Sharon, IA, 50207. Tel: 641-637-4049. p. 773

Klipsch, Pamela R, Dir, Jefferson County Library, 5678 State Rd PP, High Ridge, MO, 63049-2216. Tel: 636-677-8689. p. 1248

Kliss, Courtney, Asst Dir, New Buffalo Township Public Library, 33 N Thompson St, New Buffalo, MI, 49117. Tel: 269-469-2933. p. 1137

Klitzke, Carol, Dir, Carlton County Historical Society, 406 Cloquet Ave, Cloquet, MN, 55720. Tel: 218-879-1938. p. 1170

Kloberdanz, Micah, Br Mgr, Dougherty County Public Library, Tallulah Massey Branch, 2004 Stratford Dr, Albany, GA, 31705. Tel: 229-420-3250. p. 457

Kloc, Leah, Libr Dir, Sayreville Public Library, 1050 Washington Rd, Parlin, NJ, 08859. Tel: 732-727-0212, Ext 113. p. 1432

Klocek, Angela, Tech Serv Librn, Saint Clair County Library System, 210 McMorran Blvd, Port Huron, MI, 48060-4098. Tel: 810-987-7323. p. 1142

Klocek, Paula, Dir, Aurora Town Public Library, 550 Main St, East Aurora, NY, 14052. Tel: 716-652-4440. p. 1527

Klockars, Jeremy, Libr Supvr, Dartmouth College Library, Matthews-Fuller Health Sciences Library, One Medical Center Dr, HB 7300, Lebanon, NH, 03756-0001. Tel: 603-650-5273. p. 1366

Klocksien, Sam, Exec Dir, Isanti County Historical Society, 33525 Flanders St NE, Cambridge, MN, 55008. Tel: 763-689-4229. p. 1168

Klod, Meital, Res Serv, VPres, Info Res, BCA Research Group Library, 1002 Sherbrooke St W, Ste 1600, Montreal, QC, H3A 3L6, CANADA. p. 2717

Kloeckner, Megan, Dir, Eager Free Public Library, 39 W Main St, Evansville, WI, 53536. Tel: 608-882-2260, 608-882-2275. p. 2434

Kloeppel, Chris, Dir, Howard County Public Library, 201 S Main St, Fayette, MO, 65248. Tel: 660-248-3348. p. 1245

Kloepper, Cindy, ILL, Atchison Public Library, 401 Kansas Ave, Atchison, KS, 66002. Tel: 913-367-1902. p. 797

Kloetzer, Beth, Mgr, Claymont Public Library, 400 Lenape Way, Claymont, DE, 19703. Tel: 302-798-4164. p. 351

Klonicki, Emily, Asst Dir, Main Libr, Rockford Public Library, 214 N Church St, Rockford, IL, 61101-1023. Tel: 815-987-6673. p. 642

Klopotek, Stephanie, Programming Serv, Youth Serv, Adams County Library, 569 N Cedar St, Ste 1, Adams, WI, 53910-9800. Tel: 608-339-4250. p. 2419

Kloppenborg, David, Librn, Vols Coordr, Missouri Veterans' Home Library, 1600 S Hickory, Mount Vernon, MO, 65712. Tel: 417-466-7103. p. 1263

Klopper, Susan, Bus Librn, Emory University Libraries, Robert W Woodruff Library, 540 Asbury Circle, Atlanta, GA, 30322-2870. Tel: 404-727-0177. p. 463

Klopper, Susan, Exec Dir, Emory University Libraries, Goizueta Business Library, 540 Asbury Circle, Atlanta, GA, 30322. Tel: 404-727-1641. p. 463

Klos, Joanna, Asst Dir, Wood Dale Public Library District, 520 N Wood Dale Rd, Wood Dale, IL, 60191. Tel: 630-766-6762. p. 664

Kloss, Louise, Database Coordr, Morley Library, 184 Phelps St, Painesville, OH, 44077-3926. Tel: 440-352-3383. p. 1812

Klostermann, Teresa, Libr Serv Mgr, Marshalltown Community College, 3700 S Center St, Marshalltown, IA, 50158. Tel: 641-844-5690. p. 768

Klotzbucher, Enza, Ref & ILL Librn, Widener University, School of Law Library, 4601 Concord Pike, Wilmington, DE, 19803. Tel: 302-477-2292. p. 358

Klubek, Peter, Ref Librn, Baton Rouge Community College, 201 Community College Dr, Baton Rouge, LA, 70806. Tel: 225-216-8505. p. 882

Kluever, Joanna, Dir, Julia Hull District Library, 100 Library Lane, Stillman Valley, IL, 61084. Tel: 815-645-8611. p. 651

Kluge, Kimberly, Asst Dir, Youth Serv, Kewaskum Public Library, 206 First St, Kewaskum, WI, 53040-8929. Tel: 262-626-4312. p. 2445

Klukosky, Lisa, Libr Supvr, Arizona Department of Corrections - Adult Institutions, 10000 S Wilmot Rd, Tucson, AZ, 85734. Tel: 520-574-0024, Ext 37919. p. 80

Klump, Holly, ILL Coordr, Rivier University, 420 S Main St, Nashua, NH, 03060-5086. Tel: 603-897-8255. p. 1375

Klump, Jennifer, Pub Serv Librn, Environmental Protection Agency, 2000 Traverwood Dr, Ann Arbor, MI, 48105. Tel: 734-214-4311. p. 1079

Klundt, Lynn, Librn, Northern State University, 1200 S Jay St, Aberdeen, SD, 57401. Tel: 605-626-3018. p. 2073

Klusmeyer, Hannah, Dir, Wautoma Public Library, 410 W Main St, Wautoma, WI, 54982-5415. Tel: 920-787-2988. p. 2486

Klyn, Andrea, Electronic Res Coordr, Soc Sci Librn, University of Puget Sound, 1604 N Warner St, Upper Loading Dock, Tacoma, WA, 98416. Tel: 253-879-2875. p. 2387

Kmak, Katrina, Youth Serv Librn, Park City Library, 1255 Park Ave, Park City, UT, 84060. Tel: 415-615-5603. p. 2268

Kmetz, Tom, Coordr, Head, Res & Instrul Serv, Morehead State University, 150 University Blvd, Morehead, KY, 40351. Tel: 606-783-5111. p. 869

Kmiecik, Lexy, Br Mgr, Cleveland Public Library, Hough, 1566 Crawford Rd, Cleveland, OH, 44106. Tel: 216-623-6997. p. 1768

Knaack, Vicki, Dir, Correctionville Public Library, 532 Driftwood, Correctionville, IA, 51016. Tel: 712-342-4203. p. 742

Knab, Sheryl, Exec Dir, Western New York Library Resources Council, Airport Commerce Park E, 495 Genesee St, Ste 170, Cheektowaga, NY, 14225. Tel: 716-633-0705. p. 2771

Knaff, Diane, Cat, Preble County District Library, 450 S Barron St, Eaton, OH, 45320-2402. Tel: 937-456-4250. p. 1784

Knape, Kenneth, Br Mgr, Cleveland Public Library, Eastman, 11602 Lorain Ave, Cleveland, OH, 44111. Tel: 216-623-6955. p. 1768

Knapik, Bonnie, Head, Ch, Woodbury Public Library, 269 Main St S, Woodbury, CT, 06798. Tel: 203-263-3502. p. 349

Knapik, Elizabeth, Dir, Instrul Serv, Sacred Heart University, 5151 Park Ave, Fairfield, CT, 06825-1000. Tel: 203-365-4816. p. 312

Knapp, Alice, Pres, The Ferguson Library, One Public Library Plaza, Stamford, CT, 06904. Tel: 203-351-8201. p. 338

Knapp, James, Br Serv Supvr, Dearborn Public Library, 16301 Michigan Ave, Dearborn, MI, 48126. Tel: 313-943-2330. p. 1095

Knapp, Jean, Head Librn, Bala Cynwyd Memorial Library, 131 Old Lancaster Rd, Bala Cynwyd, PA, 19004-3037. Tel: 610-664-1196. p. 1908

Knapp, Jeff A, Foster Communications Librn, Pennsylvania State University Libraries, William & Joan Schreyer Business Library, 309 Paterno Library, 3rd Flr, University Park, PA, 16802-1810. Tel: 814-867-6501. p. 2016
Knapp, Jessica, Dir, Libr Serv, Indian Hills Community College Library, 525 Grandview Ave, Ottumwa, IA, 52501. Tel: 641-683-5199. p. 775
Knapp, Kaley, Librn, Tuscarawas County Law Library Association, 125 E High Ave, New Philadelphia, OH, 44663. Tel: 330-365-3224. p. 1807
Knapp, Kay, ILL Spec, Bucknell University, 220 Bertrand Library, One Dent Dr, Lewisburg, PA, 17837. Tel: 570-577-1557. p. 1955
Knapp, Kelli, Dir, Warren Library Association, 205 Market St, Warren, PA, 16365. Tel: 814-723-4650. p. 2017
Knapp, Laura, Mgr, Knowledge Mgt Serv, Ontario Securities Commission Library, 20 W Queen St, 20th Flr, Toronto, ON, M5H 3S8, CANADA. Tel: 416-593-2303. p. 2691
Knapp, Liz, Br Mgr, Kent District Library, Tyrone Township Branch, 43 S Main St, Kent City, MI, 49330. p. 1094
Knapp, Michele, Law Ref Librn, University of San Diego, Katherine M & George M Pardee Jr Legal Research Center, 5998 Alcala Park, San Diego, CA, 92110-2492. Tel: 619-260-4532. p. 223
Knapp, Molly, Ref & Educ Librn, Tulane University, Rudolph Matas Library of the Health Sciences, Tulane Health Sciences Campus, 1430 Tulane Ave, SL-86, New Orleans, LA, 70112-2699. Tel: 504-988-5155. p. 904
Knapp, Monika L, Dir, Helen B Hoffman Plantation Library, 501 N Fig Tree Lane, Plantation, FL, 33317. Tel: 954-797-2140. p. 438
Knapp, Patricia, Br Mgr, Hartford Public Library, Camp Field, 30 Campfield Ave, Hartford, CT, 06114. Tel: 860-695-7440. p. 318
Knapp, Stephen J, Exec Dir, Canadian Copper & Brass Development Association Library, 65 Overlea Blvd, Ste 210, Toronto, ON, M4H 1P1, CANADA. Tel: 416-391-5599. p. 2687
Knapp, Tracey, Br Supvr, Bruce County Public Library, Cargill Branch, 1012 Greenock Brant, Cargill, ON, N0G 1J0, CANADA. Tel: 519-366-9990. p. 2673
Knapp, Tracey, Br Supvr, Bruce County Public Library, Walkerton Branch, 253 Durham St E, Walkerton, ON, N0G 2V0, CANADA. Tel: 519-881-3240. p. 2674
Knapp, Wendy, Assoc Dir, Indiana State Library, 315 W Ohio St, Indianapolis, IN, 46202. Tel: 317-232-3675. p. 692
Knapp, Wendy, State Librn, State Library of Ohio, 274 E First Ave, Ste 100, Columbus, OH, 43201. Tel: 614-644-7061. p. 1777
Knasiak, Lisa, Dir, Chicago Heights Public Library, 25 W 15th St, Chicago Heights, IL, 60411-3488. Tel: 708-754-0323. p. 571
Knatt, Zachary, ILL, Howard University Libraries, Law Library, 2929 Van Ness St NW, Washington, DC, 20008. Tel: 202-806-8203. p. 369
Knecht, Elaine, Dir, Info Res, Barclay Damon, LLP, 200 Delaware Ave., Buffalo, NY, 14203. Tel: 716-856-5500. p. 1507
Knecht, Louis, Ref & Instruction Librn, Univ Archivist, Dominican University of California, 50 Acacia Ave, San Rafael, CA, 94901-2298. Tel: 415-458-3728. p. 236
Knecht, Michael, Dir, Libr Serv, Henderson Community College, 2660 S Green St, Henderson, KY, 42420. Tel: 270-831-9761. p. 859
Knecht, Thomas, Dir, Parkesburg Free Library, 105 West St, Parkesburg, PA, 19365-1499. Tel: 610-857-5165. p. 1973
Knechtel, Jennifer, Admin Mgr, Wilfrid Laurier University Library, 75 University Ave W, Waterloo, ON, N2L 3C5, CANADA. Tel: 519-884-0710, Ext 3642. p. 2703
Kneedler, Corey, ILL, Coffeyville Public Library, 311 W Tenth St, Coffeyville, KS, 67337. Tel: 620-251-1370. p. 802
Kneisler, Kelly, Interim Dir, Weyauwega Public Library, 301 S Mill St, Weyauwega, WI, 54983. Tel: 920-867-3742. p. 2487
Knepp, Amy R, Dir, Oscoda County Library, 430 W Eighth St, Mio, MI, 48647. Tel: 989-826-3613. p. 1132
Knepper, Pixie, Ch, Clay Center Carnegie Library, 706 Sixth St, Clay Center, KS, 67432. Tel: 785-632-3889. p. 802
Knepper, Robert, Coordr, Info Tech, Cleveland Bradley County Public Library, 795 Church St NE, Cleveland, TN, 37311-5295. Tel: 423-472-2163. p. 2092
Knezic, Kristina, Dir, Berrien Springs Community Library, 215 W Union St, Berrien Springs, MI, 49103-1077. Tel: 269-471-7074. p. 1085
Knickman, Ellie, Ref Librn, Delaware County Community College Library, 901 S Media Line Rd, Media, PA, 19063-1094. Tel: 610-359-5133. p. 1961
Knieling, Matt, Ad, Putnam County Library System, 50 E Broad St, Cookeville, TN, 38501. Tel: 931-526-2416. p. 2095
Knies, Michael, Spec Coll Librn, Univ Archivist, University of Scranton, 800 Linden St, Scranton, PA, 18510-4634. Tel: 570-941-6341. p. 2005
Knievel, Jennifer, Team Lead, Researcher & Colls Engagement Team, University of Colorado Boulder, 1720 Pleasant St, Boulder, CO, 80309. Tel: 303-492-8705. p. 267
Knight, Allen, Br Librn, Boston Public Library, Roxbury Branch, 149 Dudley St, Roxbury, MA, 02119. Tel: 617-442-6186. p. 992
Knight, Allen, Interim Librn, Boston Public Library, Parker Hill, 1497 Tremont St, Roxbury, MA, 02120. Tel: 617-427-3820. p. 992
Knight, Allison, Br Mgr, MidPointe Library System, Liberty Township Branch, 7100 Foundry Row, Ste S-234, Liberty Township, OH, 45069. Tel: 513-318-1580. p. 1802
Knight, Carley, Ref Librn, Jacksonville State University Library, 700 Pelham Rd N, Jacksonville, AL, 36265. Tel: 256-782-5758. p. 23
Knight, Carolyne, Dir, Bledsoe County Public Library, 478 Cumberland Ave, Pikeville, TN, 37367. Tel: 423-447-2817. p. 2124
Knight, Cecilia, Librn, Shawnee Community College Library, 8364 Shawnee College Rd, Ullin, IL, 62992. Tel: 618-634-3271. p. 655
Knight, Colleen, Dir, Polk County Library, 1690 W Broadway St, Bolivar, MO, 65613. Tel: 417-326-4531. p. 1238
Knight, Delana, Librn, Syst Serv Dir, Northeast Georgia Regional Library System, 204 Ellison St, Ste F, Clarkesville, GA, 30523. Tel: 706-754-0416. p. 471
Knight, Elaine, Librn, First United Methodist Church Library, 211 N School St, Normal, IL, 61761. Tel: 309-452-2096. p. 625
Knight, Erin, Libr Mgr, National Institute of Environmental Health Sciences Library, 111 TW Alexander Dr, Bldg 101, Research Triangle Park, NC, 27709. Tel: 984-287-3609. p. 1712
Knight, J David, Librn, Virginia State Law Library, Supreme Court Bldg, 2nd Flr, 100 N Ninth St, Richmond, VA, 23219-2335. Tel: 804-786-2075. p. 2344
Knight, Janice, Br Librn, Boston Public Library, Codman Square, 690 Washington St, Dorchester, MA, 02124. Tel: 617-436-8214. p. 992
Knight, Janice, Asst Librn, Charleston Library Society, 164 King St, Charleston, SC, 29401. Tel: 843-723-9912. p. 2050
Knight, Jennifer, Cat, Southeast Arkansas Regional Library, 114 E Jackson St, Monticello, AR, 71655. Tel: 870-367-8584, Ext 224. p. 104
Knight, Jessica, Asst Librn, Hale County Public Library, 1103 Main St, Greensboro, AL, 36744. Tel: 334-624-3409. p. 19
Knight, Jo Ann, Librn, United States Army, Morris J Swett Technical Library, Snow Hall 16, Bldg 730, Fort Sill, OK, 73503-5100. Tel: 580-442-4525. p. 1848
Knight, Joanne E, Sr Ref Librn, United States Army, Combined Arms Research Library, US Army Command & General Staff College, Eisenhower Hall, 250 Gibbon Ave, Fort Leavenworth, KS, 66027-2314. Tel: 913-758-3001. p. 808
Knight, Jonathan, Br Mgr, Clark County Public Library, Park Branch, 1119 Bechtle Ave, Springfield, OH, 45504. Tel: 937-322-2498. p. 1821
Knight, Judy, Dir, Libr Serv, Princeton HealthCare System, One Plainsboro Rd, Plainsboro, NJ, 08536. Tel: 609-853-6799. p. 1435
Knight, Kimberly, Asst Dir, Chesapeake Public Library, 298 Cedar Rd, Chesapeake, VA, 23322-5512. Tel: 757-410-7110. p. 2311
Knight, Merrie, Librn, Mississippi Delta Community College, Greenwood Library, 207 W Park Ave, Greenwood, MS, 38930. Tel: 662-453-7377. p. 1227
Knight, Rose, Bus Mgr, Eastern Washington University, 320 Media Lane, 100 LIB, Cheney, WA, 99004-2453. Tel: 509-359-2306. p. 2361
Knight, Sandra, Library Contact, Amity Township Public Library, 604 E Main St, Cornell, IL, 61319. Tel: 815-358-2231, 815-510-0406. p. 574
Knight, Shandra, Libr Dir, National Jewish Health, 1400 Jackson St, Denver, CO, 80206. Tel: 303-398-1483. p. 276
Knight, Sherry, Libr Adminr, Mary Lib Saleh Euless Public Library, 201 N Ector Dr, Euless, TX, 76039-3595. Tel: 817-685-1482. p. 2175
Knight, Shirley, Govt Doc Librn, Instruction Librn, Ramapo College of New Jersey, 505 Ramapo Valley Rd, Mahwah, NJ, 07430-1623. Tel: 201-684-7315. p. 1415
Knight, Simon, Mgr, Intertek Testing Services, 1500 Brigantine Dr, Coquitlam, BC, V3K 7C1, CANADA. Tel: 604-520-3321. p. 2565
Knight, Susan, Dir, Franklin County Public Library District, 919 Main St, Brookville, IN, 47012. Tel: 765-647-4031. p. 673
Knight, Susan, Dir, Franklin County Public Library District, Laurel Public Library, 200 N Clay St, Laurel, IN, 47024. Tel: 765-698-2582. p. 673
Knight, Tim F, Head, Tech Serv, York University Libraries, Osgoode Hall Law School Library, 92 Scholar's Walk, Keele Campus, Toronto, ON, M3J 1P3, CANADA. Tel: 416-650-8403. p. 2662
Knight, Tina, Br Supvr, Marion County Public Library System, Freedom Public Library, 5870 SW 95 St, Ocala, FL, 34476. Tel: 352-438-2580. p. 430
Knight, Twyla, Libr Supvr, Region of Waterloo Library, New Hamburg Branch, 145 Huron St, New Hamburg, ON, N3A 1K1, CANADA. Tel: 519-662-1112. p. 2629
Knight, Valerie, Distance Learning Librn, Wayne State College, 1111 Main St, Wayne, NE, 68787. Tel: 402-375-7443. p. 1340
Knight, Victoria, Dir, Libr Serv, Westminster College, Reeves Memorial Library, 501 Westminster Ave, Fulton, MO, 65251-1299. Tel: 573-592-5245. p. 1246
Knight-Davis, Stacey, Head, Tech Serv, Eastern Illinois University, 600 Lincoln Ave, Charleston, IL, 61920. Tel: 217-581-7549. p. 552
Knights, Angie, Librn, Augusta Township Public Library, 4500 County Rd 15, RR 2, Brockville, ON, K6V 5T2, CANADA. Tel: 613-926-2449. p. 2633
Knihnitski, Tracey, Br Librn, Wapiti Regional Library, Hudson Bay Public Library, 130 Main St, Hudson Bay, SK, S0E 0Y0, CANADA. Tel: 306-865-3110. p. 2745
Knipe Bledsoe, Anne, Head of Instruction, Colorado Mesa University, 1100 North Ave, Grand Junction, CO, 81501. Tel: 970-248-1805. p. 283

Knipes, Melissa, Youth Serv Librn, Sherburne Memorial Library, 2998 River Rd, Killington, VT, 05751. Tel: 802-422-4251, 802-422-9765. p. 2287

Knipfel, Suzy, Asst Dir, Hampton Public Library, Four Federal St S, Hampton, IA, 50441-1934. Tel: 641-456-4451. p. 757

Knipstein, Lorraine, Br Mgr, Lubbock Public Library, Godeke, 5034 Frankford Ave, Lubbock, TX, 79424. Tel: 806-775-3362. p. 2213

Knisely, Jane, Libr Dir, Claysburg Area Public Library, 957 Bedford St, Claysburg, PA, 16625. Tel: 814-239-2782. p. 1922

Knisely, Jennifer, Exec Dir, Altoona Area Public Library, 1600 Fifth Ave, Altoona, PA, 16602-3693. Tel: 814-946-0417, Ext 122. p. 1905

Knisely, Susan, Online Serv Librn, Nebraska Library Commission, The Atrium, 1200 N St, Ste 120, Lincoln, NE, 68508-2023. Tel: 402-471-3849. p. 1322

Knisley, Emilia, Mgr, Libr Serv, Chatfield College Library, 20918 State Rte 251, Saint Martin, OH, 45118. Tel: 513-875-3344. p. 1819

Knispel, Todd, Coordr, Libr Serv, Neosho County Community College, 800 W 14th St, Chanute, KS, 66720-2699. Tel: 620-432-0384, Ext 246. p. 801

Knobel, Sara L, Dir, Groton Public Library, 112 E Cortland St, Groton, NY, 13073. Tel: 607-898-5055. p. 1542

Knobloch, Elaine, Libr Asst, Valmeyer Public Library District, 300 S Cedar Bluff, Valmeyer, IL, 62295. Tel: 618-935-2626. p. 657

Knop, Kay, Circ Mgr, Enterprise Public Library, 101 E Grubbs St, Enterprise, AL, 36330. Tel: 334-347-2636. p. 15

Knop, Paula, Librn, Saint John's Lutheran Church Library, 512 N Wilhelm Ave, Ellinwood, KS, 67526. Tel: 620-564-2044. p. 806

Knopf, Keith S, Dir, Libr Serv, Kegler Brown Hill + Ritter, 65 E State St, Ste 1800, Columbus, OH, 43215. Tel: 614-255-5502. p. 1773

Knopp, Stefanie, Coll Develop, Newton Public Library, 720 N Oak, Newton, KS, 67114. Tel: 316-283-2890. p. 826

Knorr, Ian, Operations Dir, Downers Grove Public Library, 1050 Curtiss St, Downers Grove, IL, 60515. Tel: 630-960-1200, Ext 4244. p. 579

Knorr, Rick, Dir of Finance, Spokane County Library District, 4322 N Argonne Rd, Spokane, WA, 99212. Tel: 509-893-8200. p. 2384

Knoth, Kathleen, Libr Dir, University of New Mexico, Taos Campus, 115 Civic Plaza Dr, Taos, NM, 87571. Tel: 575-737-6243. p. 1463

Knott, Angelina, Library Contact, New York State Supreme Court Library, Greene County Courthouse, 320 Main St, Catskill, NY, 12414. Tel: 518-625-3197. p. 1515

Knott, Chelsea, Dir of Development I, Georgia Institute of Technology Library, 260 Fourth St NW, Atlanta, GA, 30332. Tel: 404-894-4500. p. 464

Knott, Cheryl, Prof, University of Arizona, Harvill Bldg, 4th Flr, 1103 E Second St, Tucson, AZ, 85721. Tel: 520-621-3565. p. 2782

Knott, Christopher, Assoc Dean for the Law Library, Wake Forest University, Law Library, Worrell Professional Ctr, 1834 Wake Forest Rd, Winston-Salem, NC, 27109. Tel: 336-758-5927. p. 1726

Knott, Dana, Libr Dir, Columbus State Community College Library, 550 E Spring St, Columbus, OH, 43215. Tel: 614-287-2461. p. 1773

Knott, Diane, Dir, Coggon Public Library, 202 E Main St, Coggon, IA, 52218. Tel: 319-435-2542. p. 741

Knott, Matthew, Head, Children's Servx, Morris Area Public Library District, 604 Liberty St, Morris, IL, 60450. Tel: 815-942-6880. p. 619

Knott, Teresa L, Assoc Dean of Libr, Libr Dir, Virginia Commonwealth University Libraries, 901 Park Ave, Richmond, VA, 23284. Tel: 804-828-0634. p. 2343

Knotts, Carolyn, Dir, McLouth Public Library, 215 S Union, McLouth, KS, 66054. Tel: 913-796-2225. p. 824

Knotz, Archan, Br Asst, Cumberland Public Libraries, Pugwash Library, 10222 Durham St, Pugwash, NS, B0K 1L0, CANADA. Tel: 902-243-3331. p. 2615

Knouf, Sherry, Dir, Downs Carnegie Library, 504 S Morgan, Downs, KS, 67437-2019. Tel: 785-454-3821. p. 805

Knouse, Tracey, Libr Mgr, San Antonio Public Library, Tobin, 4134 Harry Wurzbach, San Antonio, TX, 78209. Tel: 210-207-9040. p. 2239

Knowles, Catherine, Librn, Shawano County Library, Mattoon Branch, 311 Slate Ave, Mattoon, WI, 54450-0266. Tel: 715-489-3333. p. 2476

Knowles, Christine, Br Supvr, Marion County Public Library System, Reddick Public Library, 15150 NW Gainsville Rd, Reddick, FL, 32686-3221. Tel: 352-438-2566. p. 430

Knowling, Ron, Mgr, Nunavut Public Library Services, PO Box 270, Baker Lake, NU, X0C 0A0, CANADA. Tel: 867-793-3353. p. 2625

Knowlton, Kandace, Libr Dir, Chester Public Library, Three Chester St, Jct 121 & 102, Chester, NH, 03036. Tel: 603-887-3404. p. 1357

Knowlton, Leah, Youth Serv Librn, Hampton Falls Free Public Library, Seven Drinkwater Rd, Hampton Falls, NH, 03844. Tel: 603-926-3682. p. 1366

Knox, Brenda Christine, Dir, Donnellson Public Library, 411 Main, Donnellson, IA, 52625. Tel: 319-835-5545. p. 748

Knox, Emily, Assoc Prof, University of Illinois at Urbana-Champaign, Library & Information Science Bldg, 501 E Daniel St, Champaign, IL, 61820-6211. Tel: 217-333-3280. p. 2784

Knox, Floyd, Dir, Jackson Parish Library, 614 S Polk Ave, Jonesboro, LA, 71251-3442. Tel: 318-259-5697, 318-259-5698. p. 892

Knox, Glynis, Circ Serv, Conway Public Library, 15 Main Ave, Conway, NH, 03818. Tel: 603-447-5552. p. 1360

Knox, Kelsey, Archivist, Spec Coll & Univ Archives, Pepperdine University Libraries, 24255 Pacific Coast Hwy, Malibu, CA, 90263. Tel: 310-506-4252. p. 171

Knox, Kyle, Publicity Coord & Web Mgr, Ohio County Public Library, 52 16th St, Wheeling, WV, 26003. Tel: 304-232-0244. p. 2417

Knox, Margaret, Librn III, Dallas College, 4849 W Illinois, Dallas, TX, 75211-6599. Tel: 214-860-8669. p. 2164

Knox, Nicole, Mgr, Cobb County Public Library System, Acworth Library, 4569 Dallas St, Acworth, GA, 30101. Tel: 770-917-5165. p. 489

Knox, Sheryl Cormicle, Tech Dir, Capital Area District Libraries, 401 S Capitol Ave, Lansing, MI, 48933. Tel: 517-367-6347. p. 1124

Knox-Stutsman, Esther, Operations Mgr, Mamie Doud Eisenhower Public Library, Three Community Park Rd, Broomfield, CO, 80020. Tel: 720-887-2328. p. 268

Knuckey, Donna, Dir, Winter Public Library, 5129 N Main St, Winter, WI, 54896. Tel: 715-266-2144. p. 2489

Knueven, Joe, Dir, Wilmington Public Library of Clinton County, 268 N South St, Wilmington, OH, 45177-1696. Tel: 937-382-2417. p. 1832

Knueven, Joe, Vice Chair, Consortium of Ohio Libraries, 1500 W Lane Ave, Columbus, OH, 43221. Tel: 614-484-1061. p. 2772

Knupp, Linda, Dir, North Central Kansas Libraries System, 629 Poyntz Ave, Manhattan, KS, 66502. Tel: 785-776-4741, Ext 101. p. 823

Knuth, Patricia E, Syst Adminr, United States Army, Combined Arms Research Library, US Army Command & General Staff College, Eisenhower Hall, 250 Gibbon Ave, Fort Leavenworth, KS, 66027-2314. Tel: 913-758-3019. p. 808

Knutson, Esther, Children's & Teen Serv Coordr, Larchwood Public Library, 1020 Broadway, Larchwood, IA, 51241. Tel: 712-477-2583. p. 764

Knutson Strack, Amy, Communications Dir, Mount Prospect Public Library, Ten S Emerson St, Mount Prospect, IL, 60056. Tel: 847-253-5675. p. 621

Knutzen, Matthew, Dir, New York Public Library - Astor, Lenox & Tilden Foundations, Stephen A Schwarzman Building, 476 Fifth Ave, (42nd St & Fifth Ave), New York, NY, 10018. p. 1597

Ko, Kristen, Access Serv, Bergen Community College, 400 Paramus Rd, Paramus, NJ, 07652-1595. Tel: 201-879-8920. p. 1432

Kobayashi, Chris, Librn, United States Army, 181 Chapplear Rd, Bldg 650, Fort Shafter, HI, 96858. Tel: 808-438-9521. p. 505

Kobayashi, Jill, Librn, RCS Community Library, 95 Main St, Ravena, NY, 12143. Tel: 518-756-2053. p. 1625

Kobialka, Kris, Archivist, Institutional Records Mgr, Boston Architectural College, 320 Newbury St, Boston, MA, 02115. Tel: 617-585-0133. p. 991

Kobierski, Alison, Mgr, Spec Coll, The Mary Baker Eddy Library, Research & Reference Services, 210 Massachusetts Ave, P04-10, Boston, MA, 02115-3017. Tel: 617-450-7907. p. 994

Koblizek, Laura, Libr Adminr, Albert Wisner Public Library, One McFarland Dr, Warwick, NY, 10990-3585. Tel: 845-986-1047. p. 1659

Kobrin, Lisa, Head, Ref (Info Serv), Alamance County Public Libraries, May Memorial Library, 342 S Spring St, Burlington, NC, 27215. Tel: 336-229-3588. p. 1676

Kobritz, Barbara, Instrul Serv Librn, Tompkins Cortland Community College Library, Baker Commons, 2nd Flr, 170 North St, Dryden, NY, 13053-8504. Tel: 607-844-8222, Ext 4362. p. 1526

Kobulsky, Milan, Dir, St Andrew's Abbey, 10510 Buckeye Rd, Cleveland, OH, 44104. Tel: 216-721-5300, Ext 294. p. 1770

Koca, Kathy, Cataloger, Children's Prog, Cedar County Library District, John D Smith/Eldorado Springs Branch, 808 S Main, El Dorado Springs, MO, 64744. Tel: 417-876-4827. p. 1282

Koch, Anna, Libr Mgr, San Mateo County Library, Foster City Library, 1000 E Hillsdale Blvd, Foster City, CA, 94404. Tel: 650-574-4842, Ext 227. p. 235

Koch, Barry, Mgr, Public Relations, Blauvelt Free Library, 541 Western Hwy, Blauvelt, NY, 10913. Tel: 845-359-2811. p. 1494

Koch, Cathy, Mgr, Satilla Regional Library, Pearson Public Library, 56 E Bullard Ave, Pearson, GA, 31642. Tel: 912-422-3500. p. 476

Koch, Christina, Asst Librn, Thompson-Hickman Free County Library, 217 Idaho St, Virginia City, MT, 59755. Tel: 406-843-5346. p. 1303

Koch, Deb, Adminr, Cherokee Mental Health Institute, 1251 W Cedar Loop, Cherokee, IA, 51012. Tel: 712-225-2594. p. 739

Koch, Joann, Cataloger, Cragin Memorial Library, Eight Linwood Ave, Colchester, CT, 06415. Tel: 860-537-5752. p. 306

Koch, Kate, Libr Mgr, Lomond Community Library, Two Railway Ave N, Lomond, AB, T0L 1G0, CANADA. Tel: 403-792-3934. p. 2547

Koch, Katherine, Head of Libr, University of Alberta, Herbert T Coutts Education & Physical Education Library, Educations Bldg, Edmonton, AB, T6G 2G5, CANADA. Tel: 780-492-1460. p. 2538

Koch, Mary, Dir, Gothenburg Public Library, 1104 Lake Ave, Gothenburg, NE, 69138-1903. Tel: 308-537-2591. p. 1316

Koch, PJ, ILL, Saint Louis University, Medical Center Library, 1402 S Grand Blvd, Saint Louis, MO, 63104. Tel: 314-977-8806. p. 1276

Koch, Ramona, Librn, Eustis Public Library, 108 N Morton St, Eustis, NE, 69028. Tel: 308-486-2651. p. 1313

Koch, Siobhan L, Dir, Denville Free Public Library, 121 Diamond Spring Rd, Denville, NJ, 07834. Tel: 973-627-6555. p. 1399

Koch, Teri, Coord, Serials, Acquisitions, & Electronic Resources, Drake University, 2725 University Ave, Des Moines, IA, 50311. Tel: 515-271-2941. p. 746
Koch, Tori, Asst Dir, Billings Public Library, 510 N Broadway, Billings, MT, 59101. Tel: 406-657-8295. p. 1288
Kochan, Carol, Head of Doc Delivery, Head, Resource Sharing, Utah State University, 3000 Old Main Hill, Logan, UT, 84322-3000. Tel: 435-797-2676. p. 2265
Kochendorfer, John, Dr, Dir, Atmospheric Turbulence & Diffusion Division Library, NOAA Air Resources Laboratory, 465 S Illinois Ave, Oak Ridge, TN, 37830. Tel: 865-220-1740. p. 2123
Kocher, Bruce, Libr Dir, Missouri Valley Public Library, 420 E Huron St, Missouri Valley, IA, 51555. Tel: 712-642-4111. p. 770
Kochik, Lisa, Head, Youth Serv, Newburgh Free Library, 124 Grand St, Newburgh, NY, 12550. Tel: 845-563-3616. p. 1606
Kociolek, Megan, Dir, Clark Public Library, 303 Westfield Ave, Clark, NJ, 07066. Tel: 732-388-5999. p. 1396
Kocis, Rachel, Libr Dir, Sherman Public Library District, 2100 E Andrew Rd, Sherman, IL, 62684-9676. Tel: 217-496-2496. p. 646
Kocken, Greg, Archivist, Head, Spec Coll, University of Wisconsin-Eau Claire, 103 Garfield Ave, Eau Claire, WI, 54701-4932. Tel: 715-834-3873. p. 2433
Kocman, Mary, Mgr, Tech Serv, Palos Verdes Library District, 701 Silver Spur Rd, Rolling Hills Estates, CA, 90274. Tel: 310-377-9584, Ext 242. p. 205
Kocour, Bruce G, Dean, Libr Serv, Carson-Newman University, 1634 Russell Ave, Jefferson City, TN, 37760. Tel: 865-471-3336. p. 2103
Kocovsky, Jill, Asst Librn, Neuschafer Community Library, 317 Wolf River Dr, Fremont, WI, 54940. Tel: 920-446-2474. p. 2436
Kocur, Kevin, ILL Coordr, University of Scranton, 800 Linden St, Scranton, PA, 18510-4634. Tel: 570-941-4003. p. 2005
Koczan, Sarah, Info Res & Serv Support Spec, ILL, Penn State Behrend, 4951 College Dr, Erie, PA, 16563-4115. Tel: 814-898-6106. p. 1932
Kodama, Alva, Res Support Spec, Kapi'olani Community College Library, 4303 Diamond Head Rd, Honolulu, HI, 96816. Tel: 808-734-9217. p. 512
Koehler, Robert, Chief Librn, Meriter Hospital, 202 S Park St, Madison, WI, 53715. Tel: 608-417-6234. p. 2450
Koehler, Sarah, Br Mgr, Madera County Library, North Fork Branch, 32908 Rd 222, North Fork, CA, 93643. Tel: 559-877-2387. p. 171
Koehn Frey, Sarah, Dir, Saguache Public Library, 702 Pitkin Ave, Saguache, CO, 81149. Tel: 719-655-2551. p. 295
Koehn, Michael, Dir of Libr Operations, Columbia University, Augustus C Long Health Sciences Library, 701 W 168th St, Lobby Level, New York, NY, 10032. Tel: 212-305-9216. p. 1583
Koehn, Sara, Libr Dir, Haskell Township Library, 300 Easy St, Sublette, KS, 67877. Tel: 620-675-2771. p. 837
Koehn, Tim, Librn, Mississippi Gulf Coast Community College, 2300 Hwy 90, Gautier, MS, 39553. Tel: 228-497-7716. p. 1216
Koehne, Julie, Syst Librn, Hamilton County Law Library, Hamilton County Court House, 1000 Main St, Rm 601, Cincinnati, OH, 45202. Tel: 513-946-5300. p. 1760
Koelzer, Emily, Archivist, Outreach Librn, Aquinas College, 1700 Fulton St E, Grand Rapids, MI, 49506. Tel: 616-632-2040. p. 1109
Koen, Diane, Assoc Dir, Planning & Res, McGill University Libraries, McLennan Library Bldg, 3459 McTavish St, Montreal, QC, H3A 0C9, CANADA. Tel: 514-398-2149. p. 2726
Koeneke, Heather, Dir, Auburn Memorial Library, 1810 Courthouse Ave, Auburn, NE, 68305-2323. Tel: 402-274-4023. p. 1306
Koenig, Jerissa, Early Literacy Librn, Outreach Librn, L E Phillips Memorial Public Library, 400 Eau Claire St, Eau Claire, WI, 54701. Tel: 715-839-5016. p. 2432
Koenig, Jessica, Dir, Island Park Public Library, 176 Long Beach Rd, Island Park, NY, 11558. Tel: 516-432-0122. p. 1550
Koenig, Rachel A, Research & Education Librn, Virginia Commonwealth University Libraries, Tompkins-McCaw Library for the Health Sciences, Medical College of Virginia Campus, 509 N 12th St, Richmond, VA, 23298-0582. Tel: 804-828-1150. p. 2343
Koenig, Timothy, Pres, Bull Shoals Library, 1218 Central Blvd, Bull Shoals, AR, 72619. Tel: 870-445-4265. p. 91
Koenig, Virginia, Br Mgr, Brazoria County Library System, Clute Branch, 215 N Shanks, Clute, TX, 77531-4122. Tel: 979-265-4582. p. 2135
Koenigs, Lee, Ms, Dir, Libby Memorial Library, 27 Staples St, Old Orchard Beach, ME, 04064. Tel: 207-934-4351. p. 934
Koenigs, Mary Jane, Sister, ILL Librn, Tech Serv Librn, Briar Cliff University, 3303 Rebecca St, Sioux City, IA, 51104. Tel: 712-279-5535. p. 782
Koenigsfeld, Julie, Librn, Missouri Department of Corrections, Algoa Correctional Center, 8501 No More Victims Rd, Jefferson City, MO, 65101-4567. Tel: 573-751-3911, Ext 640. p. 1252
Koep, Mark, Br Head, Vancouver Public Library, Kitsilano Branch, 2425 MacDonald St, Vancouver, BC, V6K 3Y9, CANADA. Tel: 604-665-3976. p. 2581
Koerber, Carrie, Ch, Augusta-Richmond County Public Library, 823 Telfair St, Augusta, GA, 30901. Tel: 706-821-2600. p. 466
Koertge, Jenny, Research Librn, Crowell & Moring LLP, NBC Tower, 455 N Cityfront Plaza Dr, Ste 3600, Chicago, IL, 60611-5599. Tel: 312-840-3160. p. 560
Koerting, Gayla, Curator, State Archivist, Nebraska History Library, 1500 R St, Lincoln, NE, 68508. Tel: 402-471-4783. p. 1322
Koester, Amy, Dir, Pub Serv, Skokie Public Library, 5215 Oakton St, Skokie, IL, 60077-3680. Tel: 847-673-7774. p. 647
Koffman, Lori, Library Contact, Park Avenue Synagogue Library, 50 E 87th St, New York, NY, 10128. Tel: 212-369-2600. p. 1600
Kofoed, Jennifer, Br Mgr, Converse County Library, Glenrock Branch, 506 S Fourth St, Glenrock, WY, 82637. Tel: 307-436-2573. p. 2494
Kofoid, Emily, Dir, Graves-Hume Public Library District, 1401 W Main St, Mendota, IL, 61342. Tel: 815-538-5142. p. 616
Koford, Amelia, Interim Head of Public Services, Texas Lutheran University, 1000 W Court St, Seguin, TX, 78155-5978. Tel: 830-372-8138. p. 2242
Koh, HyunSeung, Assessment Librn, Liaison & Instruction Librn, University of Northern Iowa Library, 1227 W 27th St, Cedar Falls, IA, 50613-3675. Tel: 319-273-2837. p. 737
Koh, Kyungwon, Assoc Prof, Dir, Champaign-Urbana (CU) Community Fab Lab, University of Illinois at Urbana-Champaign, Library & Information Science Bldg, 501 E Daniel St, Champaign, IL, 61820-6211. Tel: 217-333-3280. p. 2784
Kohl, Allan, Libr Instruction, Visual Res Librn, Minneapolis College of Art & Design Library, 2501 Stevens Ave, Minneapolis, MN, 55404. Tel: 612-874-3781. p. 1184
Kohl, Janelle M, Librn, Frank B Koller Memorial Library, 5761 Hwy 51, Manitowish Waters, WI, 54545. Tel: 715-543-2700. p. 2453
Kohl, Laura, Dir, Libr Serv, Bryant University, 1150 Douglas Pike, Smithfield, RI, 02917-1284. Tel: 401-232-6125. p. 2042
Kohl, Mardell, Dir, Meadow Grove Public Library, 205 Main St, Meadow Grove, NE, 68752. Tel: 402-634-2266. p. 1324
Kohl, Parker, Asst Mgr, International Museum of Surgical Science Library, 1524 N Lake Shore Dr, Chicago, IL, 60610. Tel: 312-642-6502. p. 562
Kohl, Sharon, Libr Mgr, New Orleans Public Library, Rosa F Keller Library & Community Center, 4300 S Broad Ave, New Orleans, LA, 70125. Tel: 504-596-2660. p. 903
Kohlbeck, Audrey, Br Coordr, Marathon County Public Library, Spencer Branch, 105 Park St, Spencer, WI, 54479. Tel: 715-659-3996. p. 2486
Kohlbrecher, Roslyn, Pharm Librn, University of Connecticut, Pharmacy Library, Pharmacy/Biology Bldg, 2nd Flr, 69 N Eagleville Rd, Rm 228, Storrs, CT, 06269-3092. Tel: 860-486-2218. p. 340
Kohlenberg, Sally, Head, Circ, Huntington Woods Public Library, 26415 Scotia Rd, Huntington Woods, MI, 48070. Tel: 248-543-9720. p. 1118
Kohler, Lynn, Pub Relations, Voorheesville Public Library, 51 School Rd, Voorheesville, NY, 12186. Tel: 518-765-2791. p. 1657
Kohles, Tara, Dir, Central Islip Public Library, 33 Hawthorne Ave, Central Islip, NY, 11722. Tel: 631-234-9333. p. 1516
Kohn, Geraldine, Librn, Georgia Department of Corrections, Office of Library Services, 200 Gulfstream Rd, Garden City, GA, 31418. Tel: 912-965-6209. p. 481
Kohn, Rebecca, Sr Librn, City of Palo Alto Library, Rinconda Library, 1213 Newell Rd, Palo Alto, CA, 94303. Tel: 650-838-2951. p. 192
Koivisto, Sara, Libr Serv Coordr, Great River Regional Library, Cokato Library, 175 Fourth St W, Cokato, MN, 55321. Tel: 320-286-5760. p. 1196
Koivisto, Sara, Libr Serv Coordr, Great River Regional Library, Howard Lake Library, 617 Sixth Ave, Howard Lake, MN, 55349-5644. Tel: 320-543-2020. p. 1197
Kojsza, Abigail, Mgr, Cabell County Public Library, Cox Landing Branch, 793 Cox Landing Rd, Lesage, WV, 25537. Tel: 304-733-3022. p. 2404
Kokocinski, Cynthia, Libr Tech, United States Courts Library, Edward J Schwartz US Courthouse, 221 W Broadway, Rm 3185, San Diego, CA, 92101. Tel: 619-557-5387. p. 222
Kokot, Barbara, Ref Librn, Scarsdale Public Library, 54 Olmsted Rd, Scarsdale, NY, 10583. Tel: 914-722-1300. p. 1637
Kokus, Marcia, Info Serv Librn, Saint Francis University, 106 Franciscan Way, Loretto, PA, 15940. Tel: 814-472-3161. p. 1957
Kolakowski, Chris, Dir, Wisconsin Department of Veterans Affairs, 30 W Mifflin St, Ste 300, Madison, WI, 53703. Tel: 608-267-1790. p. 2452
Kolb, Daniel, Dr, Dir, Saint Meinrad Archabbey & School of Theology, 200 Hill Dr, Saint Meinrad, IN, 47577. Tel: 812-357-6401. p. 717
Kolb, Erin, Ad, Asotin County Library, 417 Sycamore St, Clarkston, WA, 99403-2666. Tel: 509-758-5454, Ext 105. p. 2361
Kolb, Jackie, Commun Serv Coordr, Seymour Public Library District, 176-178 Genesee St, Auburn, NY, 13021. Tel: 315-252-2571. p. 1489
Kolb, Jane, Librn, Illinois Prairie District Public Library, Benson Branch, 420 E Front St, Benson, IL, 61516. Tel: 309-394-2542. p. 617
Kolb, Shelley, Dir, Hillsboro Public Library, 214 School St, Hillsboro, IL, 62049-1547. Tel: 217-532-3055. p. 599
Kolbe, Elizabeth, Lakeland Campus Libr Dir, Keiser University Library System, 1500 NW 49th St, Fort Lauderdale, FL, 33309. Tel: 954-351-4035. p. 401
Kolbeck, Cathy, Dir, Algoma Public Library, 406 Fremont St, Algoma, WI, 54201. Tel: 920-487-2295. p. 2419
Kolber, Eric N, Librn, United States Army, 1776 Niagara St, Buffalo, NY, 14201-3199. Tel: 716-879-4178. p. 1510

Kolda, Sarah, Dir, Libr Serv, Holy Cross College, 54515 State Rd 933 N, Notre Dame, IN, 46556-0308. Tel: 574-239-8361. p. 711

Kolderup, Davin, Br Mgr, Johnson County Public Library, Clark Pleasant Library, 530 Tracy Rd, Ste 250, New Whiteland, IN, 46184-9699. Tel: 317-535-6206. p. 686

Kolendo, Joanna, Electronic Res Librn, Chicago State University, 9501 S Martin Luther King Jr Dr, LIB 440, Chicago, IL, 60628-1598. Tel: 773-995-2542. p. 558

Kolesar, Jennifer, Br Mgr, Pickens County Library System, Village Branch, 124 N Catherine St, Pickens, SC, 29671. Tel: 864-898-5747. p. 2058

Kolesar, Jenny, Bus Mgr, Hendrick Hudson Free Library, 185 Kings Ferry Rd, Montrose, NY, 10548. Tel: 914-739-5654. p. 1574

Kolias, Jane, Libr Mgr, New Hampshire Audubon, McLane Center, 84 Silk Farm Rd, Concord, NH, 03301-8311. Tel: 603-224-9909, Ext 310. p. 1359

Kolisch, Frances, Librn, Mineral County Regional Library, 450 Corfair Dr, Creede, CO, 81130. Tel: 719-300-1452. p. 272

Kolk, Sarah, Head, Ref & Instruction, Calvin University & Calvin Theological Seminary, 1855 Knollcrest Circle SE, Grand Rapids, MI, 49546-4402. Tel: 616-526-6014. p. 1110

Koll, Dorothy, Libr Dir, Acorn Public Library District, 15624 S Central Ave, Oak Forest, IL, 60452-3204. Tel: 708-687-3700. p. 627

Kollar, Jamie, Youth Serv Librn, Waynesboro Public Library, 600 S Wayne Ave, Waynesboro, VA, 22980. Tel: 540-942-6746. p. 2352

Koller, Leslie, Asst Br Mgr, Dorchester County Library, Summerville Branch, 76 Old Trolley Rd, Summerville, SC, 29485. Tel: 843-871-5075. p. 2069

Kolleth, Mike, Exec Dir, Saginaw Art Museum, 1126 N Michigan Ave, Saginaw, MI, 48602. Tel: 989-754-2491. p. 1147

Kollie, Ellen, Br Mgr, Mansfield-Richland County Public Library, Plymouth Branch, 29 W Broadway, Plymouth, OH, 44865. Tel: 419-687-5655. p. 1798

Kolman, Matthew, Libr Dir, Doris Padgett Public Library, 402 Tower Pl, Sunnyvale, TX, 75182-9278. Tel: 972-226-4491. p. 2246

Kologi, Annette, Dir, Wallace Public Library, 415 River St, Wallace, ID, 83873. Tel: 208-752-4571. p. 532

Kolonay, Brittany, Emerging Tech Librn, University of the District of Columbia, David A Clarke School of Law, Charles N & Hilda H M Mason Law Library, Bldg 39, Rm B-16, 4200 Connecticut Ave NW, Washington, DC, 20008. Tel: 202-274-7310. p. 380

Kolosh, Alaina, Mgr, Libr & Info Serv, National Safety Council Library, 1121 Spring Lake Dr, Itasca, IL, 60143. Tel: 630-285-2199. p. 602

Kolosionek, Diane, Librn, Cleveland State University, Michael Schwartz Library, Rhodes Tower, Ste 501, 2121 Euclid Ave, Cleveland, OH, 44115-2214. Tel: 216-802-3358. p. 1769

Koltes, Megan, Pub Serv Librn, Hamline University, School of Law Library, 1536 Hewitt Ave, Saint Paul, MN, 55104. Tel: 651-523-2379. p. 1199

Kolupailo, Nikki, Program Dir, Comms & Engagement, University of California, San Diego, 9500 Gilman Dr, Mail Code 0175G, La Jolla, CA, 92093-0175. Tel: 858-534-0667. p. 154

Kolupailo, Nikki, Prog Dir, University of California, San Diego, Special Collections & Archives, UCSD Libraries 0175S, 9500 Gilman Dr, La Jolla, CA, 92093-0175. Tel: 858-534-2533. p. 155

Kolvenbach, Julia, Commun Libr Rep, Mohave County Library District, Meadview Community Library, 149 E Meadview Blvd, Meadview, AZ, 86444. Tel: 928-564-2535. p. 65

Komala, Elaina, Libr Dir, Fox River Grove Public Library District, 407 Lincoln Ave, Fox River Grove, IL, 60021-1406. Tel: 847-639-2274. p. 589

Koman, Cynthia, Ref Librn, Hudson Valley Community College, 80 Vandenburgh Ave, Troy, NY, 12180. Tel: 518-629-7360. p. 1652

Koman, Jana, Mgr, Baltimore County Public Library, Reisterstown Branch, 21 Cockeys Mill Rd, Reisterstown, MD, 21136-1285. Tel: 410-887-1165. p. 980

Komanecki, Bill, Librn, Saint Francis Medical Center College of Nursing, 511 NE Greenleaf St, Peoria, IL, 61603. Tel: 309-655-2180. p. 634

Komara, Edward, Music Librn, State University of New York College at Potsdam, Julia E Crane Memorial Library, Crane School of Music, Schuette Hall, 44 Pierrepont Ave, Potsdam, NY, 13676-2294. Tel: 315-267-3227. p. 1622

Kometer, Trisha, Librn & Archivist, Charleston Library Society, 164 King St, Charleston, SC, 29401. Tel: 843-723-9912. p. 2050

Kominiarek, Martina, Chief Exec Officer, Bucks County Free Library, 150 S Pine St, Doylestown, PA, 18901-4932. Tel: 215-348-0332, Ext 1101. p. 1926

Kominowski, James, Archives, Spec Coll, University of Manitoba Libraries, Elizabeth Dafoe Library, 25 Chancellor's Circle, Winnipeg, MB, R3T 2N2, CANADA. Tel: 204-474-9681. p. 2595

Komm, Kami, Dir, Germantown Public Library District, 403 Munster St, Germantown, IL, 62245. Tel: 618-523-4820. p. 592

Komornik, Emily, Metadata & Discovery Librn, Sacred Heart University, 5151 Park Ave, Fairfield, CT, 06825-1000. Tel: 203-371-7749. p. 312

Komorowski, Louis, Ref Ctr Mgr, Monroe County Library System, Ellis Library & Reference Center, 3700 S Custer Rd, Monroe, MI, 48161-9716. Tel: 734-241-5277. p. 1133

Komorowski, Walter, Head, Libr Syst, Williams College, 26 Hopkins Hall Dr, Williamstown, MA, 01267. Tel: 413-597-2084. p. 1069

Koncewicz, Alexandra, Adult Prog Coordr, Carpenter-Carse Library, 69 Ballards Corner Rd, Hinesburg, VT, 05461. Tel: 802-482-2878. p. 2286

Konczey, Tiffany L, Acq Librn, United States Army, Combined Arms Research Library, US Army Command & General Staff College, Eisenhower Hall, 250 Gibbon Ave, Fort Leavenworth, KS, 66027-2314. Tel: 913-758-3013. p. 808

Koné, David, Libr Serv Section Chief, Bibliotheques de Montreal, Pavillon Prince, 801 rue Brennan, 5e etage, Montreal, QC, H3C 0G4, CANADA. Tel: 514-872-6308. p. 2718

Konecny, Kathy, Br Mgr, Pima County Public Library, Joyner-Green Valley, 601 N La Canada Dr, Green Valley, AZ, 85614. Tel: 520-594-5295. p. 82

Kong, Fanying, Mgr, Libr Serv, Federal Reserve Bank of Dallas Library, 2200 N Pearl St, Dallas, TX, 75201. Tel: 214-922-6000, Ext 5182. p. 2166

Kong, Martin, Syst Librn, Chicago State University, 9501 S Martin Luther King Jr Dr, LIB 440, Chicago, IL, 60628-1598. Tel: 773-995-3908. p. 558

Kong, Richard, Exec Dir, Skokie Public Library, 5215 Oakton St, Skokie, IL, 60077-3680. Tel: 847-673-7774. p. 647

Kongchum, Laddawan, Supvr, Ser, Baton Rouge Community College, 201 Community College Dr, Baton Rouge, LA, 70806. Tel: 225-216-8017. p. 882

Konieczko, Sue, Access Serv, Columbia International University, 7435 Monticello Rd, Columbia, SC, 29203-1599. Tel: 803-807-5105. p. 2053

Konigsberg, Ruth Davis, Ref Librn, Vineyard Haven Public Library, 200 Main St, Vineyard Haven, MA, 02568. Tel: 508-696-4211, Ext 115. p. 1060

Konkel, Mary S, Head, Tech Serv, College of DuPage Library, 425 Fawell Blvd, Glen Ellyn, IL, 60137-6599. Tel: 630-942-2662. p. 593

Konn, Karen, Librn, Readington Township Library, 255 Main St, Whitehouse Station, NJ, 08889. Tel: 908-534-4421. p. 1455

Konold, Micky, Dir, Student & Public Outreach, Sandhills Community College, 3395 Airport Rd, Pinehurst, NC, 28374. Tel: 910-695-3817. p. 1707

Konovalske, Katy, Circ Coordr, Bonner Springs City Library, 201 N Nettleton Ave, Bonner Springs, KS, 66012. Tel: 913-441-2665. p. 799

Konstan, Ellen, Librn, Mount Zion Temple, 1300 Summit Ave, Saint Paul, MN, 55105. Tel: 651-698-3881. p. 1201

Kontic, Paola, Libr Mgr, Hamilton Wentworth Catholic District School Board, 44 Hunt St, Hamilton, ON, L8R 3R1, CANADA. Tel: 905-525-2930. p. 2646

Kontrovitz, Eileen R, Head, Info Tech, Ouachita Parish Public Library, 1800 Stubbs Ave, Monroe, LA, 71201. Tel: 318-327-1490. p. 898

Konyari, Alexander, Mgr, Budget & Fac, Concordia University Libraries, 1400 de Maisonneuve Blvd W, LB 2, Montreal, QC, H3G 1M8, CANADA. Tel: 514-848-2424, Ext 7761. p. 2723

Konze, Caitlyn, Info Serv Mgr, Viterbo University, 900 Viterbo Dr, La Crosse, WI, 54601. Tel: 608-796-3267. p. 2446

Koo, Sungji, Law Librn, Blume, Forte, Fried, Zerres & Molinari, PC, One Main St, Chatham, NJ, 07928. Tel: 973-635-5400, Ext 189. p. 1395

Kooiker, Diane, Libr Dir, Herrick District Library, 300 S River Ave, Holland, MI, 49423. Tel: 616-355-3100. p. 1115

Koon, Donna, Mgr, Suwannee River Regional Library, Branford Public Library, 703 NW Suwannee Ave, Branford, FL, 32008-3279. Tel: 386-935-1556. p. 419

Kooner, Kal, Mgr, Intertek Testing Services, 1500 Brigantine Dr, Coquitlam, BC, V3K 7C1, CANADA. Tel: 604-520-3321. p. 2565

Koons, Laura, Dir, Manson Public Library, 1312 10th Ave, Manson, IA, 50563. Tel: 712-469-3986. p. 767

Koonts, Russell, Dir, Archives & Digital Initiatives, Duke University Libraries, Medical Center Library & Archives, DUMC Box 3702, Ten Searle Dr, Durham, NC, 27710-0001. Tel: 919-383-2501. p. 1684

Koontz, Carol, Dir, Hardy County Public Library, 102 N Main St, Moorefield, WV, 26836. Tel: 304-538-6560. p. 2409

Koontz, Chuck, Syst Librn, Biola University Library, 13800 Biola Ave, La Mirada, CA, 90639. Tel: 562-944-0351 Ext 5611. p. 155

Koontz, Cindy, Dir, Timrod Literary & Library Association, 217 Central Ave, Summerville, SC, 29483. Tel: 843-871-4600. p. 2071

Koop, Katie, Br Mgr, Summit County Libraries, North Branch, 651 Center Circle, Silverthorne, CO, 80498. Tel: 970-468-4280. p. 282

Koopmans-de Bruijn, Ria, Head, Pub Serv, Librn, Columbia University, C V Starr East Asian Library, 300 Kent Hall, MC 3901, 1140 Amsterdam Ave, New York, NY, 10027. Tel: 212-854-4318. p. 1584

Kopchick, Rachel, Pub Serv Adminr, Virginia Beach Public Library, Municipal Ctr, Bldg 19, Rm 210, 2416 Courthouse Dr, Virginia Beach, VA, 23452. Tel: 757-385-8709. p. 2350

Kopecky, Linda, Assoc Dean, Univ Libr, University of Nevada-Reno, Lake Tahoe Prim Library, 999 Tahoe Blvd, Incline Village, NV, 89451. Tel: 775-881-7501. p. 1349

Kopecky, Melissa, Dir, South Orange Public Library, 65 Scotland Rd, South Orange, NJ, 07079. Tel: 973-762-0230. p. 1443

Kopecky, Susannah, Fac Librn, Allan Hancock College, 800 S College Dr, Santa Maria, CA, 93455. Tel: 805-922-6966, Ext 3453. p. 243

Kopel, Tina, Libr Office Mgr, Kingsborough Community College, 2001 Oriental Blvd, Brooklyn, NY, 11235. Tel: 718-368-5632. p. 1504

Koperski, Lynn, Librn, Kutak Rock LLP, The Omaha Bldg, 1650 Farnam St, Omaha, NE, 68102-2103. Tel: 402-346-6000. p. 1329
Kopetski, Anita, Res Spec, Marshall County Historical Society Library, 123 N Michigan St, Plymouth, IN, 46563. Tel: 574-936-2306. p. 714
Kopetsky, Brian, Dir, Menasha Public Library, 440 First St, Menasha, WI, 54952-3143. Tel: 920-967-3690. p. 2455
Koplen, Kelly, Br Supvr, Waseca-Le Sueur Regional Library, Janesville Public, 102 W Second St, Janesville, MN, 56048-3009. Tel: 507-234-6605. p. 1207
Kopp, Dana, Med Librn, The Learning Center, 500 W Broadway, Missoula, MT, 59802. Tel: 406-329-5711. p. 1300
Kopp, Melinda, Br Librn, Stockton-San Joaquin County Public Library, Ripon Branch, 333 W Main St, Ripon, CA, 95336. p. 250
Kopp, Nicole, Teen Serv, Whitman County Rural Library District, 102 S Main St, Colfax, WA, 99111-1863. Tel: 509-397-4366. p. 2362
Koppang, Diana, Dir, Research & Competitive Intel, Neal, Gerber & Eisenberg LLP, Two N La Salle St, Ste 1700, Chicago, IL, 60602-3801. Tel: 312-269-8000. p. 565
Koppe, Karen, Dir, Letts Public Library, 125 E Iowa St, Letts, IA, 52754. Tel: 319-726-5121. p. 765
Kopriva, Rayna, Librn, Gove City Library, 301 Sherman, Gove, KS, 67736. Tel: 785-938-2242. p. 810
Kopsa, Lyndsey, Dir, Hennessey Public Library, 525 S Main, Hennessey, OK, 73742. Tel: 405-853-2073. p. 1849
Kopteros, Michelle, Librn, East-West University Library, 816 S Michigan Ave, Chicago, IL, 60605. Tel: 312-939-0111, Ext 3503. p. 560
Korah, Abraham, Libr Dir, Colorado Mountain College, 3000 County Rd 114, Glenwood Springs, CO, 81601. Tel: 970-947-8271. p. 282
Korbelak, Rosemarie, Dir, Belmar Public Library, 517 Tenth Ave, Belmar, NJ, 07719. Tel: 732-681-0775. p. 1389
Korczak, Nancy, Dep Dir, Fountaindale Public Library District, 300 W Briarcliff Rd, Bolingbrook, IL, 60440. Tel: 630-759-2102. p. 543
Kordas, Marianne, Dir, Andrews University, Music Materials Center, Hamel Hall 110, 8495 University Blvd, Berrien Springs, MI, 49104. Tel: 269-471-3114. p. 1085
Korejko, Caroline, Librn, North Hero Public Library, 3195 US Rte 2, North Hero, VT, 05474. Tel: 802-372-5458. p. 2290
Koren, Linette, Mgr, Electronic Res, RIT Libraries, 90 Lomb Memorial Dr, Rochester, NY, 14623-5604. Tel: 585-475-6123. p. 1629
Korenowsky, Christopher, Pub Serv Dir, Somerset County Library System of New Jersey, One Vogt Dr, Bridgewater, NJ, 08807-2136. Tel: 908-458-4931. p. 1392
Korga, Iwona, Archivist, Jozef Pilsudski Institute of America Library, 138 Greenpoint Ave, Brooklyn, NY, 11222. Tel: 212-505-9077. p. 1506
Koritansky, Gale, Div Chief, Br Serv, Arlington County Department of Libraries, 1015 N Quincy St, Arlington, VA, 22201. Tel: 703-228-6334. p. 2305
Korklan, Michael, Libr Dir, Metropolitan Community College, Penn Valley Library, 3201 SW Trafficway, Kansas City, MO, 64111-2764. Tel: 816-759-4090. p. 1256
Korn, Jennifer, Br Mgr, Public Library of Cincinnati & Hamilton County, Pleasant Ridge, 6233 Montgomery Rd, Cincinnati, OH, 45213. Tel: 513-369-4488. p. 1763
Kornblau, Amy, Interim Dean, Florida Atlantic University, 777 Glades Rd, Boca Raton, FL, 33431. Tel: 561-297-3789. p. 385
Kornblau, Amy, Interim Dean, Florida Atlantic University, 5353 Parkside Dr, Jupiter, FL, 33458. Tel: 561-799-8530. p. 413
Kornkven, Kelly, Dir, Libr Serv, Mayville State University, 330 Third St NE, Mayville, ND, 58257. Tel: 701-788-4816. p. 1738
Kornkven, Kelly, Dir, Mayville State University, 330 Third St NE, Mayville, ND, 58257-1299. Tel: 701-788-4816. p. 2790
Korpieski, Amy, Ref Librn, Clark State Community College Library, 570 E Leffel Lane, Springfield, OH, 45505. Tel: 937-328-6022. p. 1821
Korsmo, Nicole, Dir, Northwood City Library, 206 Main St, Northwood, ND, 58267. p. 1739
Korstvedt, Paula, Dir, Princeton Public Library, Two Town Hall Dr, Princeton, MA, 01541. Tel: 978-464-2115. p. 1048
Kortbein, Karen, Br Librn, Marinette County Library System, Wausaukee Public Library, 703 Main St, Ste 3, Wausaukee, WI, 54177. Tel: 715-856-5995. p. 2454
Korth, Tamela, Ch, Plainview Public Library, 209 N Pine St, Plainview, NE, 68769. Tel: 402-582-4507. p. 1333
Kosakoff, Wendy, Outreach Librn, Pub Serv Librn, Yeshiva University Libraries, Pollack Library Landowne Bloom Collection, Wilf Campus, 2520 Amsterdam Ave, New York, NY, 10033. Tel: 646-592-4045, 646-592-4450. p. 1605
Kosakowski, John, Tech Serv Coordr, Landmark College Library, 19 River Rd S, Putney, VT, 05346. Tel: 802-387-1648. p. 2292
Koschik, Douglas, Dir, Baldwin Public Library, 300 W Merrill St, Birmingham, MI, 48009-1483. Tel: 248-647-1700. p. 1086
Koscielniak, Kim, Law Librn, Library of Michigan, 702 W Kalamazoo St, Lansing, MI, 48915. Tel: 517-373-4697. p. 1125
Koscielniak, Kimberly, Law Librn, Library of Michigan, 702 W Kalamazoo St, Lansing, MI, 48909. Tel: 517-373-0630. p. 1125
Koscielski, Roberta, Dep Dir, Peoria Public Library, 107 NE Monroe St, Peoria, IL, 61602-1070. Tel: 309-497-2186. p. 634
Kosecki, Stan, Dep Dir, United States Department of Agriculture, 10301 Baltimore Ave, Beltsville, MD, 20705-2351. Tel: 301-504-5755. p. 959
Koshelek, Miranda, Mgr, Edmonton Public Library, Abbottsfield-Penny McKee Branch, 160-3210 118 Ave NW, Edmonton, AB, T5W 0Z4, CANADA. Tel: 780-496-6298. p. 2536
Kosior, Kate, Libr Dir, Clifton Community Library, 7171 Rte 3, Cranberry Lake, NY, 12927. Tel: 315-848-3256. p. 1523
Kosior, Susan, Sr Librn, New York State Department of Correctional Services, 3595 State School Rd, Albion, NY, 14411. Tel: 585-589-5511, Ext 4600. p. 1484
Kositch, Margaret, Dir, Libr Tech, Fairfax County Public Library, 12000 Government Center Pkwy, Ste 324, Fairfax, VA, 22035-0012. Tel: 703-324-3100. p. 2316
Koskela, Heidi, Campus Library Manager, Macomb Community College Libraries, 14500 E 12 Mile Rd, J-Bldg, Warren, MI, 48088-3896. Tel: 586-445-7880. p. 1157
Koski, Justin, Exec Dir, US National Ski Hall of Fame, 610 Palms Ave, Ishpeming, MI, 49849. Tel: 906-485-6323. p. 1119
Koski, Lisa, Br Mgr, Washington District Library, Sunnyland Branch, 16 Washington Plaza, Washington, IL, 61571. Tel: 309-745-3023. p. 659
Kosmowski, Andrew J, Brother, Librn, North American Center for Marianist Studies Library, Chaminade Ctr, 4435 E Patterson Rd, Dayton, OH, 45430-1083. Tel: 937-429-2521. p. 1780
Kosrow, Lauren, Dr, Chairperson, Fac Librn, Triton College Library, Bldg A, Rm 200, 2000 Fifth Ave, River Grove, IL, 60171. Tel: 708-456-0300, Ext 3478. p. 639
Koste, Jodi, Interim Head, University Archives, Virginia Commonwealth University Libraries, 901 Park Ave, Richmond, VA, 23284. Tel: 804-828-9898. p. 2343
Kostecka, Lindsay, Co-Dir, Table Rock Public Library, 511 Luzerne St, Table Rock, NE, 68447. p. 1338
Kostecki, Keith, Acq Asst, School of the Art Institute of Chicago, 37 S Wabash Ave, Chicago, IL, 60603-3103. Tel: 312-899-5097. p. 568
Koster, Holly, Br Head, Lake County Public Library, Saint John Branch, 9450 Wicker Dr, Saint John, IN, 46373-9646. Tel: 219-365-5379. p. 706
Kostin, Sarah, Youth Serv, Bud Werner Memorial Library, 1289 Lincoln Ave, Steamboat Springs, CO, 80487. Tel: 970-879-0240, Ext 314. p. 295
Koszalka, Michael, Dir, West Allis Public Library, 7421 W National Ave, West Allis, WI, 53214-4699. Tel: 414-302-8503. p. 2487
Koszalka, Rachel, Asst Dir, Coffeyville Public Library, 311 W Tenth St, Coffeyville, KS, 67337. Tel: 620-251-1370. p. 802
Kotei, Rachel, Sr Libr Tech, Saskatoon Theological Union Library, 1121 College Dr, Saskatoon, SK, S7N 0W3, CANADA. Tel: 639-398-5561. p. 2749
Koteles, Colin, Web Serv Mgr, College of DuPage Library, 425 Fawell Blvd, Glen Ellyn, IL, 60137-6599. Tel: 630-942-2923. p. 593
Kothe, Lisa, Libr Dir, Safety Harbor Public Library, 101 Second St N, Safety Harbor, FL, 34695. Tel: 727-724-1525. p. 439
Kotheimer, Paul, Sr Librn, University of Illinois Library at Urbana-Champaign, University Laboratory High School Library, 1212 W Springfield Ave, MC-254, Urbana, IL, 61801. Tel: 217-333-1589. p. 656
Kothmann, Sandy, Librn, Menard Public Library, 100 E Mission St, Menard, TX, 76859. Tel: 325-396-2717. p. 2218
Kotila, Kayla, Admin Librn, Sr Res Librn, Schiff, Hardin LLP Library, 233 S Wacker Dr, Ste 7100, Chicago, IL, 60606. Tel: 312-258-5500. p. 568
Kott, Linda, Info Serv, South Dakota State University, 1300 N Campus Dr, Box 2115, Brookings, SD, 57007. Tel: 605-688-5957. p. 2074
Kott, Michael, Assoc Dean, Morton College Library, 3801 S Central Ave, Cicero, IL, 60804. Tel: 708-656-8000, Ext 2208. p. 571
Kotula, Victoria, Head of Children's & Family Services, Floyd Memorial Library, 539 First St, Greenport, NY, 11944-1399. Tel: 631-477-0660. p. 1541
Kotyk, Susannah, Libr Mgr, Thorsby Municipal Library, 4901 - 48 Ave, Thorsby, AB, T0C 2P0, CANADA. Tel: 780-789-3808. p. 2556
Kotzas, Leslie, Dir, Keyport Free Public Library, 109 Broad St, Keyport, NJ, 07735. Tel: 732-264-0543. p. 1410
Kotzas, Leslie, Head, Youth Serv, Matawan-Aberdeen Public Library, 165 Main St, Matawan, NJ, 07747. Tel: 732-583-9100. p. 1417
Kouns, Liz, ILL & Ser, Kentucky Christian University, 100 Academic Pkwy, Grayson, KY, 41143. Tel: 606-474-3292. p. 857
Kource, Pamela, Div Mgr, Cumberland County Public Library & Information Center, 300 Maiden Lane, Fayetteville, NC, 28301-5032. Tel: 910-483-7727. p. 1688
Koury, Regina, Dir, Rutgers University Libraries, Paul Robeson Library, 300 N Fourth St, Camden, NJ, 08102-1404. Tel: 856-225-2848, 856-225-6034. p. 1394
Kovach, Annie, Br Mgr, Harford County Public Library, Bel Air Branch, 100 E Pennsylvania Ave, Bel Air, MD, 21014-3799. Tel: 410-638-3151. p. 959
Kovach, Patti, Customer Serv Mgr, Brownsburg Public Library, 450 S Jefferson St, Brownsburg, IN, 46112-1310. Tel: 317-852-3167. p. 673
Kovacs, Danielle, Curator of Coll, University of Massachusetts Amherst Libraries, 154 Hicks Way, University of Massachusetts, Amherst, MA, 01003-9275. Tel: 413-545-2784. p. 985
Kovacs, Dawn, Dep Dir, Head, Tech Serv, Wheaton Public Library, 225 N Cross St, Wheaton, IL, 60187-5376. Tel: 630-668-1374. p. 662
Kovacs, Laszlo, Librn, American Hungarian Library & Historical Society, 215 E 82nd St, New York, NY, 10028. Tel: 646-340-4172. p. 1578

Kovacs, Michelle, Br Mgr, Montgomery County Memorial Library System, R F Meador Branch, 709 W Montgomery, Willis, TX, 77378. Tel: 936-442-7740. p. 2159
Kovalcik, Justin, Dir, Libr Info Tech, California State University, Northridge, 18111 Nordhoff St, Northridge, CA, 91330. Tel: 818-677-4549. p. 184
Kovalevskiy, Chelsea, Br Serv Librn, Cherokee Regional Library System, 305 S Duke St, LaFayette, GA, 30728. Tel: 706-638-8311. p. 484
Kovalsky, Erin, Coordr, Access Serv, State University of New York at Oswego, SUNY Oswego, 7060 State Rte 104, Oswego, NY, 13126-3514. Tel: 315-312-3554. p. 1613
Kovalsky, Erin J, Principal Law Librn, New York State Unified Court System, Onondaga County Courthouse, 401 Montgomery St, Syracuse, NY, 13202. Tel: 315-671-1150. p. 1649
Kovar, Matt, Dir, Sump Memorial Library, 222 N Jefferson St, Papillion, NE, 68046. Tel: 402-597-2042. p. 1332
Kovarik, Jennifer, Coll Mgr, Vesterheim Norwegian-American Museum, 502 W Water St, Decorah, IA, 52101. Tel: 563-382-9681. p. 745
Kovarik, Rochelle, Librn, Park River Public Library, 605 Sixth St W, Park River, ND, 58270. Tel: 701-284-6116. p. 1739
Kovash, Jaylene, ILL Librn, Dickinson Area Public Library, Billings County Resource Center, PO Box 307, Medora, ND, 58645-0307. Tel: 701-623-4604. p. 1732
Kowal, Kimberly, Assoc Univ Librn, Digital Initiatives & Serv, Boston College Libraries, 140 Commonwealth Ave, Chestnut Hill, MA, 02467. Tel: 617-552-0841. p. 1010
Kowal, Ronnie, Br Mgr, Broward College, North Campus Library LRC, 1100 Coconut Creek Blvd, Coconut Creek, FL, 33066. Tel: 954-201-2600. p. 391
Kowalcze, Amanda, Dir, Frankfort Public Library District, 21119 S Pfeiffer Rd, Frankfort, IL, 60423-8699. Tel: 815-469-2423. p. 589
Kowalik, Steven, Head Librn, Art Slide Libr, Hunter College Libraries, East Bldg, 695 Park Ave, New York, NY, 10065. Tel: 212-772-5054. p. 1588
Kowalski, Beth, Exec Dir, Neville Public Museum of Brown County Library, 210 Museum Pl, Green Bay, WI, 54303. Tel: 920-448-7848. p. 2438
Kowalski, Meghan, Ref Outreach Librn, University of the District of Columbia, Learning Resources Division, 4200 Connecticut Ave NW, Bldg 39, Level B, Washington, DC, 20008. p. 380
Kowalski, Nicholas, Coll Develop Librn, University of Saint Thomas, 3800 Montrose Blvd, Houston, TX, 77006. Tel: 713-525-2182. p. 2200
Kowalski, Sherry, Interim Dir, Broome County Public Library, 185 Court St, Binghamton, NY, 13901. Tel: 607-778-6400. p. 1493
Kowalski, Susan Finch, Supv Libr Asst, John F Kennedy Memorial Library, 92 Hathaway St, Wallington, NJ, 07057. Tel: 973-471-1692. p. 1451
Kownslar, Edward, Assoc Dir, Texas A&M University-Corpus Christi, Mary & Jeff Bell Library, 6300 Ocean Dr, Corpus Christi, TX, 78412-5501. Tel: 361-825-2643. p. 2161
Kownslar, Edward, Head, Res & Instrul Serv, Stephen F Austin State University, 1936 North St, Nacogdoches, TX, 75962. Tel: 936-468-1459. p. 2221
Kowpak, Joyce, Managing Librn, Brooklyn Public Library, Red Hook Interim Library, 362 Van Brunt St, Brooklyn, NY, 11231. Tel: 718-935-0203. p. 1503
Koz, Olga, Dr, Graduate Education Librn, Kennesaw State University Library System, 385 Cobb Ave NW, MD 1701, Kennesaw, GA, 30144. Tel: 470-578-6004. p. 483
Koza, John, Coordr, Tech Serv, North Shore Community College Library, One Ferncroft Rd, Danvers Campus Library, Danvers, MA, 01923-4093. Tel: 978-739-5413. p. 1013
Koza, John, Coordr, Tech Serv, North Shore Community College Library, McGee Bldg, LE127, 300 Broad St, Lynn, MA, 01901. Tel: 978-739-5413. p. 1030
Kozakowski, Judith, Human Res Mgr, The Library Network, 41365 Vincenti Ct, Novi, MI, 48375. Tel: 248-536-3100. p. 2767
Kozal, Kim, Adult Serv Coordr, Northfield Township Area Library, 125 Barker Rd, Whitmore Lake, MI, 48189. Tel: 734-449-0066. p. 1160
Kozel-La Ha, Sheree, Exec Dir, Homer Township Public Library District, 14320 W 151st St, Homer Glen, IL, 60491. Tel: 708-301-7908. p. 600
Kozelou, Jennifer, Br Mgr, Kenosha Public Library, Northside Library, 1500 27th Ave, Kenosha, WI, 53140-4679. p. 2445
Kozloff, Julianna, Librn, Nebraska Department of Correctional Services, 3216 W Van Dorn St, Lincoln, NE, 68522. Tel: 402-471-2861. p. 1321
Kozlowski, Elizabeth, Libr Dir, White House Public Library, 105 B College St, White House, TN, 37188. Tel: 615-672-0239. p. 2129
Kozman, Eileen, Librn, Genealogical Society of Linn County Iowa, 813 First Ave SE, Cedar Rapids, IA, 52401. Tel: 319-369-0022. p. 738
Kozol, Jill, Head, Support Serv, Lower Providence Community Library, 50 Parklane Dr, Eagleville, PA, 19403-1171. Tel: 610-666-6640. p. 1928
Kozyra-Kocikowska, Katarzyna, Admin Officer, Events Coord, Canadian Association of Research Libraries, 309 Cooper St, Ste 203, Ottawa, ON, K2P 0G5, CANADA. Tel: 613-482-9344, Ext 103. p. 2778
Kraatz, Carolyn, Dir, Carnegie Library of Ballinger, 204 N Eighth St, Ballinger, TX, 76821. Tel: 325-365-3616. p. 2144
Krabbe, Gordon, Chief Operating Officer, Enoch Pratt Free Library, 400 Cathedral St, Baltimore, MD, 21201. Tel: 410-396-5430. p. 952
Krabill, Britta, Head, Adult Serv, DeKalb Public Library, Haish Memorial Library Bldg, 309 Oak St, DeKalb, IL, 60115-3369. Tel: 815-756-9568. p. 577
Krack, Hazel, Librn, Cando Community Library, 502 Main St, Cando, ND, 58324. Tel: 701-968-4549. p. 1731
Kracke, Russell, Archives Mgr, Mgr, Tech Serv, Oakton College Library, 1600 E Golf Rd, Rm 1406, Des Plaines, IL, 60016. Tel: 847-635-1642, 847-635-1644. p. 578
Kraemer, Amy, Head, Youth & Community Servs, Keene Public Library, 60 Winter St, Keene, NH, 03431. Tel: 603-352-0157. p. 1369
Kraemer, Bridget, Dir, Westville-New Durham Township Public Library, 153 Main St, Westville, IN, 46391. Tel: 219-785-2015. p. 726
Kraemer, David, Librn, Jewish Theological Seminary Library, 3080 Broadway, New York, NY, 10027. Tel: 212-678-8844. p. 1589
Kraemer, Kelly, Bus Librn, Saint John's University, 2835 Abbey Plaza, Collegeville, MN, 56321. Tel: 320-363-2601. p. 1170
Kraepel, Kathryn, Head, Tech Serv, Springfield Township Library, 12000 Davisburg Rd, Davisburg, MI, 48350. Tel: 248-846-6552. p. 1095
Kraft, Brian, Tech Serv Mgr, Washington County Library, 8595 Central Park Pl, Woodbury, MN, 55125-9453. Tel: 651-275-8500. p. 1209
Kraft, Cheryl, Adult Serv, Neenah Public Library, 240 E Wisconsin Ave, Neenah, WI, 54956. Tel: 920-886-6315. p. 2463
Kraft, Michelle, Dir, Cleveland Clinic Library Services, 9500 Euclid Ave, NA30, Cleveland, OH, 44195-5243. Tel: 216-445-7338. p. 1766
Kraft, Steven, Chief Exec Officer, Guelph Public Library, 100 Norfolk St, Guelph, ON, N1H 4J6, CANADA. Tel: 519-824-6220, Ext 224. p. 2643
Krahn, Amy, Libr Dir, St Francis Public Library, 4230 S Nicholson Ave, Saint Francis, WI, 53235. Tel: 414-481-7323. p. 2475
Krajewski, Beth, Res & Instruction Librn, Colby-Sawyer College, 541 Main St, New London, NH, 03257-4648. Tel: 603-526-3799. p. 1375
Krajewski, Rex, Dir, Libr & Learning Res, North Shore Community College Library, One Ferncroft Rd, Danvers Campus Library, Danvers, MA, 01923-4093. Tel: 978-462-5524. p. 1013
Krajewski, Rex, Dir, Libr & Learning Res, North Shore Community College Library, McGee Bldg, LE127, 300 Broad St, Lynn, MA, 01901. Tel: 978-462-5524. p. 1030
Krakovec, Beverly Jean, Asst Dir, Br Mgr, White Oak Library District, 201 W Normantown Rd, Romeoville, IL, 60446. Tel: 815-552-4225. p. 643
Krakow, Anne, Dir, Libr Serv, Saint Joseph's University, Francis A Drexel Library, 5600 City Ave, Philadelphia, PA, 19131-1395. Tel: 610-660-1905. p. 1985
Krakow, Anne, Libr Dir, University of the Sciences in Philadelphia, 4200 Woodland Ave, Philadelphia, PA, 19104. Tel: 215-596-8960. p. 1989
Krakow, Anne Z, Dir, Saint Joseph's University, Campbell Library, Mandeville Hall, 5600 City Ave, Philadelphia, PA, 19131. Tel: 610-660-1195. p. 1985
Kral, Jennifer, Librn, Capital Health Regional Medical Center, 750 Brunswick Ave, Trenton, NJ, 08638. Tel: 609-394-6065. p. 1447
Kralicek, Mary, Librn, Hunter Public Library, 109 E First St, Hunter, KS, 67452. Tel: 785-592-3010. p. 814
Kralik, Casey, Br Mgr, Omaha Public Library, Bess Johnson Elkhorn Library, 2100 Reading Plaza, Elkhorn, NE, 68022. Tel: 402-289-4367. p. 1330
Kralik, Casey, Ms, Mgr, Omaha Public Library, W Clarke Swanson Branch, 9101 W Dodge Rd, Omaha, NE, 68114-3305. Tel: 402-444-4852. p. 1330
Krall, Susan, Syst Librn, Elizabethtown College, One Alpha Dr, Elizabethtown, PA, 17022-2227. Tel: 717-361-1457. p. 1929
Kraly, Laura J, Head, Adult/Teen Serv, Bloomfield Township Public Library, 1099 Lone Pine Rd, Bloomfield Township, MI, 48302-2410. Tel: 248-642-5800. p. 1086
Kraly, Sam, Chief Fiscal Officer, Worthington Libraries, 820 High St, Worthington, OH, 43085. Tel: 614-807-2609. p. 1834
Kramber, Malynda, Librn, Garrison Public Library, 32 S Main St, Garrison, ND, 58540. Tel: 701-463-7336. p. 1734
Kramer, Alta, Doc Delivery Mgr, ILL Mgr, University of Nebraska at Kearney, 2508 11th Ave, Kearney, NE, 68849-2240. Tel: 308-865-8594. p. 1319
Kramer, Amanda, Asst Dir, Research & Tech Services, Loyola-Notre Dame Library, Inc, 200 Winston Ave, Baltimore, MD, 21212. Tel: 410-617-6801. p. 954
Kramer, Andy, Ref & Instruction, Southeastern Oklahoma State University, 425 W University, Durant, OK, 74701-0609. Tel: 580-745-2934. p. 1846
Kramer, Andy, Head, Access Serv, University of Wisconsin-Whitewater, 750 W Main St, Whitewater, WI, 53190-1790. Tel: 262-472-1022. p. 2488
Kramer, Becky, Instrul & Ref Librn, Colorado Mountain College, 3000 County Rd 114, Glenwood Springs, CO, 81601. Tel: 970-947-8271. p. 282
Kramer, Charlene, Librn, Sasktel Corporate Library, 2121 Saskatchewan Dr, 12th Flr, Regina, SK, S4P 3Y2, CANADA. Tel: 306-777-2899. p. 2748
Kramer, Deeann, Dir, York Township Public Library, 1005 W Main St, Thomson, IL, 61285. Tel: 815-259-2480. p. 653
Kramer, Gabe, Dir, Nebraska Library Commission, The Atrium, 1200 N St, Ste 120, Lincoln, NE, 68508-2023. Tel: 402-471-4038. p. 1322

Kramer, Gabe, Talking Bk/Braille Serv Dir, Nebraska Library Commission, The Atrium, 1200 N St, Ste 120, Lincoln, NE, 68508-2023. Tel: 402-471-6242. p. 1322

Kramer, Jacquie, Libr Dir, Washington County Library, 8595 Central Park Pl, Woodbury, MN, 55125-9453. Tel: 651-275-8500. p. 1209

Kramer, Jamie, Libr Mgr, Bay County Historical Society, 321 Washington Ave, Bay City, MI, 48708. Tel: 989-893-5733. p. 1083

Kramer, Janine, Libr Asst, Isabelle Hunt Memorial Public Library, 6124 N Randall Pl, Pine, AZ, 85544. Tel: 928-476-3678. p. 73

Kramer, Jean, Tech Serv, Minnesota State University Moorhead, 1104 Seventh Ave S, Moorhead, MN, 56563. Tel: 218-477-2922. p. 1189

Kramer, Jen, Librn, Iris Swedlund School & Public Library, 101 W Fourth St, Velva, ND, 58790-7045. Tel: 701-338-2022. p. 1740

Kramer, Jodi, Academic Specialist, Minnesota State Community & Technical College, Fergus Falls Campus, 1414 College Way, Fergus Falls, MN, 56537-1000. Tel: 218-736-1650. p. 1188

Kramer, Karen, Mgr, Somerville Public Library, West, 40 College Ave, Somerville, MA, 02144. Tel: 617-623-5000, Ext 2975. p. 1054

Kramer, Kathleen, Libr Dir, Harrison Village Library, Four Front St, Harrison, ME, 04040. Tel: 207-583-2970. p. 927

Kramer, Kathryn Marie, Mgr, C M Russell Museum Library, 400 13th St N, Great Falls, MT, 59401. Tel: 406-727-8787, Ext 336. p. 1294

Kramer, Kim, Librn, Knapp, Petersen & Clarke, 550 N Brand Blvd, Ste 1500, Glendale, CA, 91203-1922. Tel: 818-547-5000. p. 149

Kramer, Linda M, Libr Dir, Martin Luther College Library, 1995 Luther Ct, New Ulm, MN, 56073-3965. Tel: 507-354-8221, Ext 296. p. 1190

Kramer, Maria, Div Mgr, Redwood City Public Library, 1044 Middlefield Rd, Redwood City, CA, 94063-1868. Tel: 650-780-7018. p. 200

Kramer, Maria, Libr Mgr, Alamosa Public Library, 300 Hunt Ave, Alamosa, CO, 81101. Tel: 719-587-2543. p. 263

Kramer, Melissa, Dir of Client Engagement & Planning, Bryn Mawr College, 101 N Merion Ave, Bryn Mawr, PA, 19010-2899. Tel: 610-527-5287. p. 1916

Kramer, Nadena, Dir, Cochranton Area Public Library, 107 W Pine St, Cochranton, PA, 16314. Tel: 814-425-3996. p. 1923

Kramer, Nicole, Commun Serv, Memorial Hall Library, 2 N Main St, Andover, MA, 01810. Tel: 978-623-8400. p. 985

Kramer, Nicole, Asst Dir, Ref Serv, Dennis Public Library, Five Hall St, Dennisport, MA, 02639. Tel: 508-760-6219. p. 1014

Kramer, Susan, Dir, Cole Memorial Library, 789 Hammett Rd, Enfield, ME, 04493-4347. Tel: 207-732-4270. p. 924

Kramschuster, Kate, Interim Libr Dir, University of Wisconsin-Stout, 315 Tenth Ave, Menomonie, WI, 54751-0790. Tel: 715-232-4071. p. 2456

Kranefeld, Laura, Head, Cat & Circ, Lansdowne Public Library, 55 S Lansdowne Ave, Lansdowne, PA, 19050-2804. Tel: 610-623-0239. p. 1953

Krantz, Bonny, Teen Serv Librn, Northborough Free Library, 34 Main St, Northborough, MA, 01532-1942. Tel: 508-393-5025. p. 1043

Krantz, Kevin B, Adminr, Lafayette Science Museum, 433 Jefferson St, Lafayette, LA, 70501-7013. Tel: 337-291-5544. p. 893

Kranz, Barbara, Dir, Gaylord Public Library, 428 Main Ave, Gaylord, MN, 55334. Tel: 507-237-2280. p. 1176

Kranz, David, Dir, Southwest Wisconsin Library System, 1300 Industrial Dr, Ste 2, Fennimore, WI, 53809. Tel: 608-822-3393. p. 2434

Kranz, LuAnn, Tech Serv Librn, DeForest Area Public Library, 203 Library St, DeForest, WI, 53532. Tel: 608-846-5482. p. 2430

Krapohl, Robert, Libr Dir, Lyon College, 2300 Highland Rd, Batesville, AR, 72501-3699. Tel: 870-307-7206. p. 89

Krasner, Stephanie, Librn, Temple Israel of New Rochelle, 1000 Pinebrook Blvd, New Rochelle, NY, 10804. Tel: 914-636-1204. p. 1577

Krasnesky, Lori, ILL Spec, Mercyhurst University, 501 E 38th St, Erie, PA, 16546. Tel: 814-824-2234. p. 1932

Krasulski, Michael, Access Serv, Dept Chair, Community College of Philadelphia Library, Mint Bldg, Level 1, 1700 Spring Garden St, Philadelphia, PA, 19130. Tel: 215-751-8397. p. 1975

Kratochvil, Catherine, Head, Access Serv, North Dakota State University Libraries, 1201 Albrecht Blvd, Fargo, ND, 58108. Tel: 701-231-8915. p. 1733

Kratz, Terence, Web Serv Librn, Carroll College, 1601 N Benton Ave, Helena, MT, 59625. Tel: 406-447-5450. p. 1295

Kraus, Aniza, Curator, Ukrainian Museum-Archives Inc, 1202 Kenilworth Ave, Cleveland, OH, 44113. Tel: 216-781-4329. p. 1770

Kraus, Jan, Dir, Aspirus Health, 333 Pine Ridge Blvd, Wausau, WI, 54401. Tel: 715-847-2184. p. 2485

Kraus, Joanna, Dir, Colwich Community Library, 432 W Colwich Ave, Colwich, KS, 67030. Tel: 316-796-1521. p. 803

Kraus, Kate, Br Mgr, Public Library of Cincinnati & Hamilton County, Saint Bernard, Ten McClelland Ave, Cincinnati, OH, 45217. Tel: 513-369-4462. p. 1763

Kraus, Kim, Libr Assoc, North Iowa Area Community College Library, 500 College Dr, Mason City, IA, 50401. Tel: 641-422-4232. p. 769

Kraus, Laura, Youth Serv Librn, Bulverde-Spring Branch Library, 131 Bulverde Crossing, Bulverde, TX, 78163. Tel: 830-438-4864. p. 2151

Kraus, Leah, Asst Dir, Fayetteville Free Library, 300 Orchard St, Fayetteville, NY, 13066-1386. Tel: 315-637-6374. p. 1533

Krause, Allie, Dir, Hortonville Public Library, 531 N Nash St, Hortonville, WI, 54944. Tel: 920-779-4279. p. 2442

Krause, Danielle, Circ Serv Coordr, Sachem Public Library, 150 Holbrook Rd, Holbrook, NY, 11741. Tel: 631-588-5024. p. 1547

Krause, Edward, Fr, Dir, Catholic Central Verein of America, 3835 Westminster Pl, Saint Louis, MO, 63108. Tel: 314-371-1653. p. 1269

Krause, Joanne, Libr Asst, Wabasso Public Library, 1248 Oak St, Wabasso, MN, 56293. Tel: 507-342-5279. p. 1206

Krause, Margaret, Librn, Old Salem Museums & Gardens, Frank L Horton Museum Ctr, 924 S Main St, Winston-Salem, NC, 27101. Tel: 336-721-7300, 336-721-7365. p. 1725

Krause, Rebecca, Dir, Children & YA, Phoenixville Public Library, 183 Second Ave, Phoenixville, PA, 19460-3420. Tel: 610-933-3013, Ext 127. p. 1989

Krause Riley, Erin, Adult Serv Coordr, Scottsdale Public Library, 3839 N Drinkwater Blvd, Scottsdale, AZ, 85251-4467. Tel: 480-312-7323. p. 77

Krause, Sarah, Electronic Res Librn, Trinity Christian College, 6601 W College Dr, Palos Heights, IL, 60463. Tel: 708-239-4841. p. 632

Krause-Blaha, Kate, Youth Services Lead, New Berlin Public Library, 15105 Library Lane, New Berlin, WI, 53151. Tel: 262-785-4980. p. 2464

Kraushaar, Shannon, Adult Ref, Washington County Free Library, 100 S Potomac St, Hagerstown, MD, 21740. Tel: 301-739-3250. p. 968

Krauspe, Claudia, Interim Exec Dir, Helen M Plum Memorial Public Library District, 110 W Maple St, Lombard, IL, 60148-2594. Tel: 630-627-0316. p. 611

Krautheim, Anne, Dir, Borough of Totowa Public Library, 537 Totowa Rd, Totowa, NJ, 07512-1699. Tel: 973-790-3265, Ext 10. p. 1447

Krautwirth, Rina, Res & Instruction Librn, Yeshiva University Libraries, Hedi Steinberg Library, 245 Lexington Ave, New York, NY, 10016. Tel: 646-592-4980. p. 1605

Kravitz, Ashley, Bus Officer, University at Buffalo Libraries-State University of New York, Lockwood Memorial Library, 235 Lockwood Library, North Campus, Buffalo, NY, 14260-2200. Tel: 716-645-2814. p. 1511

Kravitz, Ashley, Bus Officer, University at Buffalo Libraries-State University of New York, Oscar A Silverman Library, University at Buffalo, 116 Capen Hall, Buffalo, NY, 14260-1672. Tel: 716-645-1328. p. 1511

Kravitz, Merryl, Dean, Evergreen Valley College Library, 3095 Yerba Buena Rd, San Jose, CA, 95135. Tel: 408-270-6433. p. 230

Krawczyk, Richard, Br Mgr, Free Library of Philadelphia, Katharine Drexel Branch, 11099 Knights Rd, Philadelphia, PA, 19154-3516. Tel: 215-685-9383. p. 1978

Kraynak, Dan, Librn, Hemenway & Barnes, 75 State St, 16th Flr, Boston, MA, 02109. Tel: 617-227-7940. p. 996

Krebeck, Aaron, Libr Dir, User Serv, Washington Research Library Consortium, 901 Commerce Dr, Upper Marlboro, MD, 20774. Tel: 301-390-2000. p. 2766

Krebel, Linda, Librn, Red Bud Public Library, 925 S Main St, Red Bud, IL, 62278. Tel: 618-282-2255. p. 638

Krebs, Bettina, Info Technician, PricewaterhouseCoopers, PwC Tower, 18 York St, Ste 2600, Toronto, ON, M5J 0B2, CANADA. Tel: 416-814-5890. p. 2692

Krebs-Smith, Beth, Dir, Edgerton Public Library, 101 Albion St, Edgerton, WI, 53534-1836. Tel: 608-884-4511. p. 2433

Kreger, Linda, Asst Dean, Bus Mgr, Oakland University Library, 100 Library Dr, Rochester, MI, 48309-4479. Tel: 248-370-2488. p. 1144

Kreher, Jan, Circ, C E Brehm Memorial Public Library District, 101 S Seventh St, Mount Vernon, IL, 62864. Tel: 618-242-6322. p. 621

Krehnke, Sarah, Librn, Bruning Public Library, 117 E Main St, Bruning, NE, 68322. Tel: 402-353-4610. p. 1309

Kreiden, Chris, Libr Dir, Saint Helena Public Library, 1492 Library Lane, Saint Helena, CA, 94574-1143. Tel: 707-963-5244. p. 210

Kreidler, Kristine, Teen Librn, Boynton Beach City Library, 115 N Federal Hwy, Boynton Beach, FL, 33435. Tel: 561-742-6390. p. 386

Kreiger, Tanis, Pub Serv Mgr, Rensselaer Libraries, Rensselaer Architecture Library, Greene Bldg 308, 3rd Flr, 110 Eighth St, Troy, NY, 12180-3590. Tel: 518-276-8310. p. 1652

Kreilick, Amy, Librn, Mgr, Terra State Community College Library, General Technologies Bldg, B301, 2830 Napoleon Rd, Fremont, OH, 43420-9670. Tel: 419-559-2121. p. 1787

Krein, Marissa, Assessment Librn, Instruction Coordr, Loras College Library, 1450 Alta Vista St, Dubuque, IA, 52004-4327. Tel: 563-588-7917. p. 748

Kreiner, Jennifer, Dir, Lyons Township District Library, 240 E Bridge St, Lyons, MI, 48851. Tel: 989-855-3414. p. 1128

Kreiner, Mary Beth, Librn, Cranbrook Academy of Art Library, 39221 Woodward Ave, Bloomfield Hills, MI, 48304. Tel: 248-645-3477. p. 1086

Kreiner, Patricia, Libr Asst, Bullard Sanford Memorial Library, 520 W Huron Ave, Vassar, MI, 48768. Tel: 989-823-2171. p. 1156

Kreis, Esther, Commun Librn, Cariboo Regional District Library, Big Lake Branch, 4056 Lakeview Rd, Big Lake, BC, V0L 1G0, CANADA. Tel: 250-243-2355. p. 2584

Kreis, Lori, Dir, Kewaskum Public Library, 206 First St, Kewaskum, WI, 53040-8929. Tel: 262-626-4312. p. 2445

Kreiser, Nancy, Dep County Librn, Pub Serv, Contra Costa County Library, 777 Arnold Dr, Ste 210, Martinez, CA, 94553. Tel: 925-608-7700. p. 173

Kreisler, Elizabeth, Dir, Mansfield Free Public Library, 71 N Main St, Mansfield, PA, 16933. Tel: 570-662-3850. p. 1957

Kreitler, Wanda, Librn, Missouri Department of Corrections, Farmington Correctional Center, 1012 W Columbia St, Farmington, MO, 63640-2902. Tel: 573-218-7100. p. 1252

Krejsa, Debby, Mgr, Elyria Public Library System, Keystone-LaGrange Branch, 133 E Commerce Dr, LaGrange, OH, 44050. Tel: 440-322-0119. p. 1784

Krekovich, Gale, Head, Youth Serv, Calumet City Public Library, 660 Manistee Ave, Calumet City, IL, 60409. Tel: 708-862-6220, Ext 233. p. 548

Krembs, Sarah, Asst Librn, Frank B Koller Memorial Library, 5761 Hwy 51, Manitowish Waters, WI, 54545. Tel: 715-543-2700. p. 2453

Kremer, Amanda, Br Mgr, Heartland Regional Library System, Vienna Branch, 315 Third St, Vienna, MO, 65582. Tel: 573-422-9866. p. 1249

Kremer, Cynthia, Tech Serv Librn, Joliet Junior College Library, Campus Ctr (A-Bldg), 2nd Flr, 1215 Houbolt Rd, Joliet, IL, 60431. Tel: 815-729-6604. p. 603

Kremer, Gary R, Dr, Exec Dir, State Historical Society of Missouri Library, 605 Elm St, Columbia, MO, 65201. Tel: 573-882-1187. p. 1243

Kremer, Jacalyn, Dean of Libr, Fitchburg State University, 160 Pearl St, Fitchburg, MA, 01420. Tel: 978-665-3196. p. 1019

Kremer, Joyce, Libr Asst, Cascade Public Library, 310 First Ave W, Cascade, IA, 52033. Tel: 563-852-3222. p. 737

Kremer, Lori, Ref Serv, Alhambra Civic Center Library, 101 S First St, Alhambra, CA, 91801-3432. Tel: 626-570-5008. p. 115

Kremer, Ulla, Libr Office Mgr, Spec Events Coordr, Museum of Darien Library, 45 Old Kings Hwy N, Darien, CT, 06820. Tel: 203-655-9233. p. 308

Kremers, Katherine, Librn, Martin County Library System, Martin County Law Library, 2351 SE Monterey Rd, Stuart, FL, 34996. Tel: 772-221-1427. p. 445

Krempasky, Frances, Electronic Res Librn, Lansing Community College Library, Technology & Learning Ctr, 400 N Capitol Ave, Lansing, MI, 48933. Tel: 517-483-1651. p. 1125

Kren, MaryBeth, Info Coordr, Robert Wood Johnson Foundation, 50 College Rd E, Princeton, NJ, 08540. Tel: 609-627-5895. p. 1436

Kreneck, Thomas, Dr, Archivist, Spec Coll Librn, Texas A&M University-Corpus Christi, Mary & Jeff Bell Library, 6300 Ocean Dr, Corpus Christi, TX, 78412-5501. Tel: 361-825-2643. p. 2161

Krenz, Bonnie, Dir, Griggs County Public Library, 902 Burrell Ave, Cooperstown, ND, 58425. Tel: 701-797-2214. p. 1731

Kreps, Dennis, Dir, Bridgman Public Library, 4460 Lake St, Bridgman, MI, 49106-9510. Tel: 269-465-3663. p. 1087

Kresh, Diane, Dir, Arlington County Department of Libraries, 1015 N Quincy St, Arlington, VA, 22201. Tel: 703-228-3348, 703-228-5990. p. 2304

Kresh, Karen, Librn, Unalaska Public Library, 64 Eleanor Dr, Unalaska, AK, 99685. Tel: 907-581-5060. p. 52

Kresich, Anton, Sr Res Spec, Clausen Miller Research Services, Ten S LaSalle St, 16th Flr, Chicago, IL, 60603-1098. Tel: 312-606-7887. p. 559

Kressler, Tara, Br Mgr, Public Library of Cincinnati & Hamilton County, Symmes Township, 11850 E Enyart Rd, Loveland, OH, 45140. Tel: 513-369-6001. p. 1763

Krest, Rachel, Develop Dir, University of Arkansas Libraries, 365 N McIlroy Ave, Fayetteville, AR, 72701-4002. Tel: 479-575-4101. p. 95

Krettler, Kandice, Head, Circ, Outreach Serv, Villa Park Public Library, 305 S Ardmore Ave, Villa Park, IL, 60181-2698. Tel: 630-834-1164. p. 658

Kretzmer, Denise, Collection Maintenance Asst, Shepherd University, 301 N King St, Shepherdstown, WV, 25443. Tel: 304-876-5379. p. 2414

Kreuger, William, Asst Librn, Grand Lodge of Iowa, AF & AM, 813 First Ave SE, Cedar Rapids, IA, 52406. Tel: 319-365-1438. p. 738

Kreun, Julie, Adult Programming, Sioux Center Public Library, 102 S Main Ave, Sioux Center, IA, 51250-1801. Tel: 712-722-2138. p. 782

Kreutzer-Hodson, Teresa, Curator, Hastings Museum of Natural & Cultural History Library, 1330 N Burlington Ave, Hastings, NE, 68901. Tel: 402-461-2399, 402-461-4629. p. 1317

Krewski, Greg, Librn, Golder Associates, Ltd, 2920 Virtual Way, Vancouver, BC, V5M 0C4, CANADA. Tel: 604-298-6623, Ext 2697. p. 2578

Kreymer, Oleg, Syst Librn, Metropolitan Museum of Art, Thomas J Watson Library, 1000 Fifth Ave, New York, NY, 10028-0198. Tel: 212-650-2438. p. 1592

Kriaski, Susan, Cat, Union University, 1050 Union University Dr, Jackson, TN, 38305-3697. Tel: 731-661-5426. p. 2102

Kriberney, Karen, Libr Asst, ILL, University of Western States Library, 8000 NE Tillamook St, Portland, OR, 97213. Tel: 503-251-5752. p. 1894

Krick, Robert, Historian, National Park Service, 3215 E Broad St, Richmond, VA, 23223. Tel: 804-226-1981. p. 2341

Krieb, Dennis, Dir, Lewis & Clark Community College, 5800 Godfrey Rd, Godfrey, IL, 62035. Tel: 618-468-4300. p. 594

Kriegh, David, Head, Coll Mgt, Saint Mary's College Library, 1928 Saint Mary's Rd, Moraga, CA, 94575. Tel: 925-631-4229. p. 180

Krienke, Nicole, Libr Dir, Muir Library, 36 Main St N, Winnebago, MN, 56098. Tel: 507-893-3196. p. 1209

Kriesberg, Adam, Asst Prof, Simmons University, 300 The Fenway, Boston, MA, 02115. Tel: 617-521-2800. p. 2786

Kriese, Clay, Dir, Weare Public Library, Ten Paige Memorial Lane, Weare, NH, 03281. Tel: 603-529-2044. p. 1383

Krige, Ansie, Mgr, Cobb County Public Library System, East Cobb Library, 4880 Lower Roswell Rd, Marietta, GA, 30068. Tel: 770-509-2730. p. 489

Krill, Molly, Youth Serv Mgr, Ventura County Library, 5600 Everglades St, Ste A, Ventura, CA, 93003. Tel: 805-677-7150. p. 256

Krings, Adrianne, Supvr, Computer Serv, Northland Public Library, 300 Cumberland Rd, Pittsburgh, PA, 15237-5455. Tel: 412-366-8100, Ext 144. p. 1994

Krinke, Sonia, Acq, Libr Instruction, Century College Library, 3300 N Century Ave, White Bear Lake, MN, 55110. Tel: 651-773-1762. p. 1208

Krippel, Beth, Br Mgr, Harris County Public Library, Atascocita Branch, 19520 Pinehurst Trail Dr, Humble, TX, 77346. Tel: 832-927-5560. p. 2192

Kripps, Stephanie, Br Head, Vancouver Public Library, Terry Salman Branch, 4575 Clancy Loranger Way, Vancouver, BC, V5Y 2M4, CANADA. Tel: 604-665-3964. p. 2582

Krisellen, Maloney, Univ Librn, Rutgers University Libraries, 169 College Ave, New Brunswick, NJ, 08901-1163. Tel: 848-932-7505. p. 1424

Krishnaswami, Julie, Assoc Law Librn, Res & Instruction Librn, Yale University Library, Lillian Goldman Library Yale Law School, 127 Wall St, New Haven, CT, 06511. Tel: 203-432-7934. p. 328

Krishnaswamy, Vidya, Libr Dir, Collin College, 9700 Wade Blvd, Frisco, TX, 75035. Tel: 972-377-1575. p. 2182

Krishnaswamy, Vidya, Dir, Libr Serv, Dallas College, 3030 N Dallas Ave, Lancaster, TX, 75134-3799. Tel: 972-860-8140. p. 2209

Krisko, Janet, ILL, George F Johnson Memorial Library, 1001 Park St, Endicott, NY, 13760. Tel: 607-757-5350. p. 1531

Kriskovich, Tony, Tech Support, Technology Spec, Northern Waters Library Service, 3200 E Lakeshore Dr, Ashland, WI, 54806-2510. Tel: 715-685-1076. p. 2421

Krispli, Suzanna, Dir, Hampton Community Library, 3101 McCully Rd, Allison Park, PA, 15101. Tel: 412-684-1098. p. 1905

Kriss, Greg, Curator, Canton Historical Society Library, 11 Front St, Collinsville, CT, 06019. Tel: 860-693-2793. p. 306

Krissel, Kara, Library Liaison, Devereux, 444 Devereux Dr, Villanova, PA, 19085. Tel: 610-542-3051. p. 2016

Krist, Matthew, Br Mgr, Putnam County Library System, Baxter Branch, 101 Elmore Tower Rd, Baxter, TN, 38544. Tel: 931-858-1888. p. 2095

Kristek, Breana, Ch Serv, Friench Simpson Memorial Library, 705 E Fourth St, Hallettsville, TX, 77964-2828. Tel: 361-798-3243. p. 2187

Kristek, Penny, Asst Dir, Friench Simpson Memorial Library, 705 E Fourth St, Hallettsville, TX, 77964-2828. Tel: 361-798-3243. p. 2187

Kristensen, Andrew, Ad, Hartland Public Library, 110 E Park Ave, Hartland, WI, 53029. Tel: 262-367-3350. p. 2440

Kristine, John, Ref Librn, Franciscan University of Steubenville, 1235 University Blvd, Steubenville, OH, 43952-1763. Tel: 740-283-6366. p. 1821

Kristof, Cynthia, Head, Copyright & Scholarly Communication, Kent State University Libraries, Risman Plaza, 1125 Risman Dr, Kent, OH, 44242. Tel: 330-672-1641. p. 1792

Kristoff, Deborah, Dir, Lowell Public Library, 1505 E Commercial Ave, Lowell, IN, 46356-1899. Tel: 219-696-7704. p. 704

Krivicky, Mary Ann, Law Librn II, Connecticut Judicial Branch Law Libraries, Bridgeport Law Library, Bridgeport Courthouse, 1061 Main St, Bridgeport, CT, 06604. Tel: 203-579-7244. p. 316

Krivopal, Erica, Br Mgr, Teen Serv Librn, Piscataway Township Free Public Library, Johanna W Westergard Library, 20 Murray Ave, Piscataway, NJ, 08854. Tel: 732-752-1166. p. 1435

Krivoshey, Myanne, Communications & Admin Coord, Harvard Library, Monroe C Gutman Library, 6 Appian Way, Cambridge, MA, 02138. Tel: 617-495-3453. p. 1006

Krizanik, Shawn, Branch Lead, Charlotte Mecklenburg Library, Independence Regional, 6000 Conference Dr, Charlotte, NC, 28212. Tel: 704-416-4800. p. 1679

Krizek, Kathleen, Br Mgr, Jacksonville Public Library, Brentwood Branch, 3725 Pearl St, Jacksonville, FL, 32206-6401. Tel: 904-630-0924. p. 412

Krmpotich, Michelle, Asst Dir, Sweetwater County Library System, 300 N First East, Green River, WY, 82935. Tel: 307-875-3615. p. 2495

Krmpotich, Michelle, Libr Mgr, Sweetwater County Library System, White Mountain Library, 2935 Sweetwater Dr, Rock Springs, WY, 82901. Tel: 307-362-2665, Ext 3120. p. 2495

Kroeckel, Carol, Librn, Little Dixie Regional Libraries, Madison Branch, 113 E Broadway, Madison, MO, 65263. Tel: 660-291-3695. p. 1262

Kroeger Vuyk, Mary, Librn, Cincinnati Psychoanalytic Institute, 3001 Highland Ave, Cincinnati, OH, 45219. Tel: 513-961-8886, Ext 2. p. 1760

Kroehler, Beth, Asst Dir, Muncie Public Library, 2005 S High St, Muncie, IN, 47302. Tel: 765-747-8200. p. 708

Kroeker Boggs, Chrystie, Libr Dir, Jake Epp Library, 255 Elmdale Dr, Steinbach, MB, R5G 1N6, CANADA. Tel: 204-326-6841. p. 2590

Kroeker, Emily, Libr Dir, Prairie College, 330 Fourth Ave N, Three Hills, AB, T0M 2N0, CANADA. Tel: 403-443-5511, Ext 553. p. 2557

Kroening-Skime, Trina, Prog Dir, Wisconsin Secure Program Facility Library, 1101 Morrison Dr, Boscobel, WI, 53805. Tel: 608-375-5656, Ext 3105. p. 2425

Krogh, Jamie, Archive Spec, Longwood University, Redford & Race St, Farmville, VA, 23909. Tel: 434-395-2432. p. 2318

Kroh, Ryan, Head, Tech Serv, North Dakota State Library, Liberty Memorial Bldg, Dept 250, 604 East Blvd Ave, Bismarck, ND, 58505-0800. Tel: 701-328-2492. p. 1730

Krohn, Suzanne, Libr Asst, Philbrick-James Library, Four Church St, Deerfield, NH, 03037-1426. Tel: 603-463-7187. p. 1360

Krohnen, Michael, Librn, Krishnamurti Foundation of America, 1098 McAndrew Rd, Ojai, CA, 93023. Tel: 805-746-2171. p. 188

Krol, Rosemary, Libr Dir, Hampstead Public Library, Nine Mary E Clark Dr, Hampstead, NH, 03841. Tel: 603-329-6411. p. 1366

Krolak, David, Dir, Phillipsburg Free Public Library, 200 Broubalow Way, Phillipsburg, NJ, 08865. Tel: 908-454-3712. p. 1434

Kroll, Kim Adele, Dir, Libr Serv, Lena Armstrong Public Library, 301 E First Ave, Belton, TX, 76513. Tel: 254-933-5830. p. 2147

Kroll, Lisa, Br Mgr, Henrico County Public Library, Glen Allen Branch Library, 10501 Staples Mill Rd, Glen Allen, VA, 23060. Tel: 804-501-1950. p. 2325

Krom, Joyce, Youth Serv Librn, Huntington Woods Public Library, 26415 Scotia Rd, Huntington Woods, MI, 48070. Tel: 248-543-9720. p. 1118

Kromann, Sonja, Librn, Marine Mammal Laboratory Library, Bldg 4, Rm 2030, 7600 Sand Point Way NE, Seattle, WA, 98115-6349. Tel: 206-526-4013. p. 2376

Kromer, Laura, Dir, Ref, Missouri State Library, James C Kirkpatrick State Information Ctr, 600 W Main St, Jefferson City, MO, 65101. Tel: 573-751-2862. p. 1253

Kromer, Vickie, Children's Prog, Driftwood Public Library, 801 SW Hwy 101, Ste 201, Lincoln City, OR, 97367-2720. Tel: 541-996-2277. p. 1885

Kromm, Kay, Dir, Reeseville Public Library, 216 S Main St, Reeseville, WI, 53579. Tel: 920-927-7390. p. 2472

Kronebusch, Jean, Evening/Weekend Supvr, Libr Asst, University of Providence Library, 1301 20th St S, Great Falls, MT, 59405-4948. Tel: 406-791-5316. p. 1294

Kronebusch, Kathy, Br Supvr, Waseca-Le Sueur Regional Library, New Richland Public, 119 S Broadway Ave, New Richland, MN, 56072. Tel: 507-465-3708. p. 1207

Kronemer, Seth, Archivist, Howard University Libraries, Law Library, 2929 Van Ness St NW, Washington, DC, 20008. Tel: 202-806-8304. p. 369

Kronen, Steven, Librn, Miami Dade College, Kendall Campus Library, 11011 SW 104th St, Miami, FL, 33176-3393. Tel: 305-237-0996, 305-237-2015, 305-237-2291. p. 422

Kronenberg, Karen, Electronic Serv Librn, Ref, South Texas College of Law Houston, 1303 San Jacinto St, Houston, TX, 77002-7006. Tel: 713-646-1725. p. 2198

Kronenburg, John, IT Coordr, Nicolet Federated Library System, 1595 Allouez Ave, Ste 4, Green Bay, WI, 54311. Tel: 920-448-4410. p. 2439

Kronewitter, Barbara, Coll Develop, Washington County Free Library, 100 S Potomac St, Hagerstown, MD, 21740. Tel: 301-739-3250. p. 968

Kronwall, Dennis, Dir, Westfir City Library, 47441 Westoak Rd, Westfir, OR, 97492. Tel: 541-782-3733. p. 1902

Kroon, Linda, Dir, University of Iowa, Sojourner Truth Library, 130 N Madison, Iowa City, IA, 52242. Tel: 319-335-1486. p. 760

Krooswyk, Michelle, Libr Dir, New Lenox Public Library District, 120 Veterans Pkwy, New Lenox, IL, 60451. Tel: 815-485-2605. p. 624

Kropf, Valerie, Business & Legal Research Analyst, DLA Piper US LLP, 444 W Lake St, Ste 900, Chicago, IL, 60606-0089. Tel: 312-984-5703. p. 560

Kropninski, Sherry, Libr Tech II, North Island College, 3699 Roger St, Port Alberni, BC, V9Y 8E3, CANADA. Tel: 250-724-8717. p. 2573

Kropp, Lisa, Dir, Lindenhurst Memorial Library, One Lee Ave, Lindenhurst, NY, 11757-5399. Tel: 631-957-7755. p. 1563

Krossner, Laura, Electronic Res Mgr, Drake University, 2725 University Ave, Des Moines, IA, 50311. Tel: 515-271-2475. p. 746

Krubner, Lance, Head, Literacy, Englewood Public Library, 31 Engle St, Englewood, NJ, 07631. Tel: 201-568-2215. p. 1401

Krueer, Michael, Info Syst Mgr, Santa Clara County Library District, 1370 Dell Ave, Campbell, CA, 95032. Tel: 408-293-2326, Ext 3051. p. 126

Kruegel, Leslie, Ref (Info Servs), Maurice M Pine Free Public Library, 10-01 Fair Lawn Ave, Fair Lawn, NJ, 07410. Tel: 201-796-3400. p. 1402

Krueger, Amy, Libr Mgr, Support Serv, Lee County Library System, 2201 Second St, Ste 400, Fort Myers, FL, 33901. Tel: 239-533-4800. p. 403

Krueger, Barbara, Libr Dir, Deer Park Public Library, 112 Front St W, Deer Park, WI, 54007. Tel: 715-269-5464. p. 2430

Krueger, Bonnie, Cat Librn, Sr Ref Librn, Owatonna Public Library, 105 N Elm Ave, Owatonna, MN, 55060. Tel: 507-444-2460. p. 1192

Krueger, Bruce, Archives, Tech, State Historical Society of Iowa, 600 E Locust, Des Moines, IA, 50319-0290. Tel: 515-281-6200. p. 747

Krueger, Heidi, Dir, Patron Serv, Lake Forest Library, 360 E Deerpath Rd, Lake Forest, IL, 60045. Tel: 847-810-4611. p. 606

Krueger, Karla, Assoc Prof, Prog Coordr, University of Northern Iowa, Schindler 107, University of Northern Iowa, Cedar Falls, IA, 50614-0612. Tel: 319-273-7241. p. 2785

Krueger, Lura, Asst Dir, Blandinsville-Hire District Library, 130 S Main St, Blandinsville, IL, 61420. Tel: 309-652-3166. p. 542

Krueger, Mandie, Br Librn, East Central Regional Library, McGregor Public Library, 111 E Center Ave, McGregor, MN, 55760. Tel: 218-768-3305. p. 1168

Krueger, Miranda, Circ, Corning Public Library, 613 Pine St, Corning, AR, 72422. Tel: 870-857-3453. p. 93

Krueger, Mitzi, Head Law Librn, Massachusetts Trial Court Law Libraries, First District Court House, 3195 Main St, Barnstable, MA, 02630. Tel: 508-362-8539. p. 987

Krueger, Sheila, Dir, Casselton Public Library, 702 First St N, Casselton, ND, 58012. Tel: 701-347-4861, Ext 13. p. 1731

Krueger, Sperry, Sr Res Analyst, North Carolina Biotechnology Center Life Science Intelligence, 15 T W Alexander Dr, Research Triangle Park, NC, 27709. Tel: 919-541-9366. p. 1712

Krueger, Suzanne, Commun Librn, Monroe County Library System, Ida Branch, 3016 Lewis Ave, Ida, MI, 48140. Tel: 734-269-2191. p. 1134

Krueger, Virginia, Communications Coordr, Chelsea District Library, 221 S Main St, Chelsea, MI, 48118-1267. Tel: 734-475-8732. p. 1091

Kruempel, DeAnn, Ch, Missouri Valley Public Library, 420 E Huron St, Missouri Valley, IA, 51555. Tel: 712-642-4111. p. 770

Kruer, June, Dir, Charlestown-Clark County Public Library, 51 Clark Rd, Charlestown, IN, 47111. Tel: 812-256-3337. p. 674

Krug, Amy, Digital Res Librn, Howard Community College Library, 10901 Little Patuxent Pkwy, 2nd Flr, Columbia, MD, 21044. Tel: 443-518-4788. p. 963

Krug, Emily, Instrul Serv Librn, King University, 1350 King College Rd, Bristol, TN, 37620. Tel: 423-652-6301. p. 2090

Krug, Gretchen, Br Mgr, Clinton-Macomb Public Library, North, 16800 24 Mile Rd, Macomb Township, MI, 48042. Tel: 586-226-5081. p. 1092

Krug, Janene, Ch, Dir, Norma Anders Public Library, 320 Main St, Dysart, IA, 52224. Tel: 319-476-5210. p. 749

Kruger, Dawn, Dir, Clarkia District Library, 377 Poplar St, Clarkia, ID, 83812. Tel: 208-245-2908. p. 519

Kruger, Jodi, Dir, Ref, Dir, Res Serv, University of California Los Angeles Library, Hugh & Hazel Darling Law Library, 1112 Law Bldg, 385 Charles E Young Dr E, Los Angeles, CA, 90095-1458. Tel: 310-825-7826. p. 169

Kruger, Jodi, Circuit Librn, United States Court of Appeals for the Ninth Circuit Library, James R Browning Courthouse, 95 Seventh St, San Francisco, CA, 94103. Tel: 415-355-8650. p. 229

Kruger, Kathy, Circ & ILL, Jamaica Hospital Medical Center, Axel Bldg, 4th Flr, 8900 Van Wyck Expressway, Jamaica, NY, 11418-2832. Tel: 718-206-8450. p. 1553

Kruger, Mandie, Librn II, East Central Regional Library, Aitkin Public Library, 110 First Ave NE, Aitkin, MN, 56431-1319. Tel: 218-927-2339. p. 1168

Kruidenier, David, Med Librn, Virtua Health System, Voorhees Division, 100 Bowman Dr, Medical Library, Garden Level Rm GD550, Voorhees, NJ, 08043. Tel: 856-247-3207. p. 1450

Kruk, Pauline A, Librn, Connecticut Valley Hospital, Hallock Medical Library, Page Hall, Silver St, Middletown, CT, 06457. Tel: 860-262-5059. p. 322

Krukowski, Susan, Librn, Terrell County Public Library, Courthouse Sq, 109 Hackberry, Sanderson, TX, 79848. Tel: 432-345-2294. p. 2241

Krulikowski, Laura, Librn, Indiana University of Pennsylvania, Harold S Orendorff Library, 101 Cogswell Hall, 422 S 11th St, Indiana, PA, 15705-1071. Tel: 724-357-2892. p. 1946

Krull, Kathleen, Br Dir, Settlement Music School, Willow Grove Branch Library, 318 Davisville Rd, Willow Grove, PA, 19090. Tel: 215-320-2630. p. 1986

Krull, Rob C, Dir, Libr Serv, Palm Beach State College, 4200 Congress Ave, Mail Sta 17, Lake Worth, FL, 33461. Tel: 561-868-3800. p. 416

Krum-Howe, Kamey, Dir, Cedar Springs Public Library, 107 N Main St, Cedar Springs, MI, 49319. Tel: 616-696-1910. p. 1089

Krumnow, Stacy G, Libr Mgr, Piedmont Regional Library System, Banks County Public Library, 226 Hwy 51 S, Homer, GA, 30547. Tel: 706-677-3164. p. 482

Krumton, Linda, Br Mgr, Mesa County Public Library District, Gateway Branch, 42700 Hwy 141, Gateway, CO, 81522. Tel: 970-931-2428. p. 284

Krumwiede, Elly, Supv Librn, Pierce County Library System, Anderson Island Library, 11319 Yoman Rd, Anderson Island, WA, 98303. Tel: 253-548-3536. p. 2386

Krupicka-Smith, Antonia, Libr Dir, Council Bluffs Public Library, 400 Willow Ave, Council Bluffs, IA, 51503-9042. Tel: 712-323-7553, Ext 5423. p. 742

Krupko, Mykola, Mgr, Centre Hospitalier Universitaire du Sherbrooke, 580 rue Bowen Sud, Piece 1110, Sherbrooke, QC, J1G 2E8, CANADA. Tel: 819-346-1110, Ext 21126. p. 2736

Krupp, Edwin C, Dr, Dir, Griffith Observatory Library, 2800 E Observatory Rd, Los Angeles, CA, 90027. Tel: 213-473-0800. p. 162

Krupp, Joanne, Libr Board of Trustees Pres, Ozark County Volunteer Library, 200 Elm St, Gainesville, MO, 65655. Tel: 417-679-4442. p. 1247

Kruppa, Gail, Archivist, Assoc Dir, Torrington Historical Society, 192 Main St, Torrington, CT, 06790. Tel: 860-482-8260. p. 342

Kruppa, Jessica, Metadata & Discovery Librn, University of California, Riverside, 900 University Ave, Riverside, CA, 92521. Tel: 951-827-3220. p. 203

Kruse, Carrie, Dir, University of Wisconsin-Madison, College (Undergraduate) Library, Helen C White Hall, 600 N Park St, Madison, WI, 53706. Tel: 608-262-3245. p. 2451

Kruse, David, Librn, New Windsor Public Library District, 412 Main St, New Windsor, IL, 61465. Tel: 309-667-2515. p. 624

Kruse, Donna S, Dir, Morton-James Public Library, 923 First Corso, Nebraska City, NE, 68410. Tel: 402-873-5609. p. 1325

Kruse, Emma, Public, Research & Tech Specialist, Rhodes College, 2000 North Pkwy, Memphis, TN, 38112-1694. Tel: 901-843-3890. p. 2114

Kruse, Mary, Asst Dir, Pataskala Public Library, 101 S Vine St, Pataskala, OH, 43062. Tel: 740-927-9986. p. 1814

Krushell, Cathy, Supvr, Ventura County Library, Fillmore Library, 502 Second St, Fillmore, CA, 93015. Tel: 805-524-3355. p. 256

Krusling, James, Univ Librn, Golden Gate University - Otto & Velia Butz Libraries, 536 Mission St, San Francisco, CA, 94105-2967. Tel: 415-442-7248. p. 225

Kruthoffer, Betsy, Cataloger, Rare Bk Librn, Lloyd Library & Museum, 917 Plum St, Cincinnati, OH, 45202. Tel: 513-721-3707. p. 1761

Kruy, Martha, Assessment Librn, Ref & Instruction, Central Connecticut State University, 1615 Stanley St, New Britain, CT, 06050. Tel: 860-832-2063. p. 324

Kry, Tracey, Archivist, Emerging Technology Librarian, Western New England University, 1215 Wilbraham Rd, Springfield, MA, 01119. Tel: 413-782-1514. p. 1057

Krzanowski, Robert, Asst Libr Dir, Carroll Community College, 1601 Washington Rd, Westminster, MD, 21157-6944. Tel: 410-386-8337. p. 980

Krzanowski, Roseanne, Dir, Pharm Librn, University of Saint Joseph, 1678 Asylum Ave, West Hartford, CT, 06117-2791. Tel: 860-231-5647. p. 345

Krzysko, Nina, Br Mgr, Howard County Library System, Central Branch, 10375 Little Patuxent Pkwy, Columbia, MD, 21044-3499. Tel: 410-313-7800. p. 965

Ksa, Lauren, Ref Librn, High Point University, One University Pkwy, High Point, NC, 27268. Tel: 336-841-9068. p. 1697

Kub, Danielle, Dir, Hooper Public Library, 128 N Main St, Hooper, NE, 68031. Tel: 402-654-3833. p. 1318

Kubancsek, Holly, Circ Mgr, Johnson County Public Library, Clark Pleasant Library, 530 Tracy Rd, Ste 250, New Whiteland, IN, 46184-9699. Tel: 317-535-6206. p. 686

Kubash, Emily, Dir, Comstock Township Library, 6130 King Hwy, Comstock, MI, 49041. Tel: 269-345-0136. p. 1093

Kubelka, Joseph, Dir, Whitecourt & District Public Library, 5201 49th St, Whitecourt, AB, T7S 1N3, CANADA. Tel: 780-778-2900. p. 2559

Kubeny, Ali, Ch Serv Librn, Bellingham Public Library, 210 Central Ave, Bellingham, WA, 98225. Tel: 360-778-7241. p. 2358

Kubiak, Michelle L, Tech Serv Mgr, Cabell County Public Library, 455 Ninth Street Plaza, Huntington, WV, 25701. Tel: 304-528-5700. p. 2404

Kubic, Craig, Dr, Dean of Libr, Southwestern Baptist Theological Seminary Libraries, 2001 W Seminary Dr, Fort Worth, TX, 76115-2157. Tel: 817-923-1921, Ext 4000. p. 2180

Kubik, Adam, Head, Res Mgt, Clayton State University Library, 2000 Clayton State Blvd, Morrow, GA, 30260. Tel: 678-466-4337. p. 491

Kubishta, Annette, Dir, Helix Public Library, 119 Columbia St, Helix, OR, 97835. Tel: 541-457-6130. p. 1881

Kubosumi, Rachel, Youth Serv Librn, Mesquite Public Library, 300 W Grubb Dr, Mesquite, TX, 75149. Tel: 972-216-6220. p. 2219

Kubrick, Ella, Circ Supvr, Casa Grande Public Library, 449 N Drylake St, Casa Grande, AZ, 85222. Tel: 520-421-8710. p. 57

Kuchan, Barbara, Dir, Health Sci Libr, Temple University Libraries, 1210 W Berks St, Philadelphia, PA, 19122-6088. Tel: 215-204-8231. p. 1986

Kuchan, Barbara, Dir, Temple University Libraries, Ginsburg Health Sciences Library, 3500 N Broad St, Philadelphia, PA, 19140. Tel: 215-707-2402. p. 1986

Kucharski, Christine, Ref Librn, SUNY Upstate Medical University, 766 Irving Ave, Syracuse, NY, 13210-1602. Tel: 315-464-7191. p. 1650

Kucharski, Kathleen, Acq Librn, United States Air Force Academy Libraries, 2354 Fairchild Dr, Ste 3A15, USAF Academy, CO, 80840-6214. Tel: 719-333-4406. p. 297

Kucher, Sue Ann, Dir, Reedsburg Public Library, 370 Vine St, Reedsburg, WI, 53959. Tel: 608-768-7323. p. 2472

Kuchesky, Anicia, Dir, Libr Serv, Laboure College, 303 Adams St, Milton, MA, 02186. Tel: 613-322-3513. p. 1036

Kuchi, Triveni, Instrul Serv Librn, Soc Sci Librn, Rutgers University Libraries, James Dickson Carr Library, 75 Ave E, Piscataway, NJ, 08854-8040. Tel: 848-445-5733. p. 1424

Kuchieski, Ann, Head, Circ & Ref, Clapp Memorial Library, 19 S Main St, Belchertown, MA, 01007. Tel: 413-323-0417. p. 988

Kuchinski, Hope, Br Librn, Eastern Monroe Public Library, Smithfields Branch, 5200 Milford Rd, East Stroudsburg, PA, 18302. Tel: 570-223-1881. p. 2011

Kuchinsky, Scott, Adult Literacy Coordr, Plainfield Public Library, 800 Park Ave, Plainfield, NJ, 07060-2594. Tel: 908-757-1111, Ext 120. p. 1435

Kuchmay, Laura, Ad, Middletown Free Library, 464 S Old Middletown Rd, Ste 3, Media, PA, 19063. Tel: 610-566-7828. p. 1961

Kuchta, Julie, Mgr, Carnegie Library of Pittsburgh, Carrick, 1811 Brownsville Rd, Pittsburgh, PA, 15210-3907. Tel: 412-882-3897. p. 1991

Kuchta, Peter, Dir, Jefferson Carnegie Library, 301 W Lafayette, Jefferson, TX, 75657. Tel: 903-665-8911. p. 2203

Kucsma, Jason, Dir, Fiscal Officer, Toledo-Lucas County Public Library, 325 Michigan St, Toledo, OH, 43604. Tel: 419-259-5200. p. 1824

Kuczma, Michelle, Dir, Libr Serv, Buchalter Nemer, 1000 Wilshire Blvd, Ste 1500, Los Angeles, CA, 90017. Tel: 213-891-0700. p. 160

Kuden, Jodee, Acq, Head, Coll Develop, University of Alaska Anchorage, Consortium Library, 3211 Providence Dr, Anchorage, AK, 99508-8176. Tel: 907-786-1875. p. 43

Kudo, Yoko, Metadata & Media Cataloging Librn, University of California, Riverside, 900 University Ave, Riverside, CA, 92521. Tel: 951-827-3220. p. 203

Kudrna, Kelly, Libr Dir, Stanley Public Library, 116 Main St, Stanley, ND, 58784-4051. Tel: 701-628-2223. p. 1740

Kuechler, Maria, Head Librn, Jaffe Raitt Heuer & Weiss, 27777 Franklin Rd, Ste 2500, Southfield, MI, 48034-8214. Tel: 248-351-3000. p. 1151

Kuehl, Debra, Ch Serv, Smiths Falls Public Library, 81 Beckwith St N, Smiths Falls, ON, K7A 2B9, CANADA. Tel: 613-283-2911. p. 2678

Kuehl, Heidi Frostestad, Foreign, Comparative & Intl Law Librn, Northwestern University Libraries, Pritzker Legal Research Center, 375 E Chicago Ave, Chicago, IL, 60611. Tel: 312-503-4725. p. 587

Kuehl, Kristin, Libr Mgr, New York Public Library - Astor, Lenox & Tilden Foundations, Ottendorfer Branch, 135 Second Ave, New York, NY, 10003-8304. Tel: 212-674-0947. p. 1596

Kuehn, Bobbie, Libr Mgr, Brown County Library, Denmark Branch, 450 N Wall St, Denmark, WI, 54208. Tel: 920-863-6613. p. 2438

Kuehn, Bobbie, Libr Mgr, Brown County Library, East Branch, 2255 Main St, Green Bay, WI, 54302-3743. Tel: 920-391-4600. p. 2438

Kuehn, Mandi, Dir, Morgan Public Library, 210 Vernon Ave, Morgan, MN, 56266. Tel: 507-249-3153. p. 1189

Kuehn, Mary, Librn, Harrie P Woodson Memorial Library, 704 W Hwy 21, Caldwell, TX, 77836-1129. Tel: 979-567-4111. p. 2152

Kuennen, Bradley, Veterinary Med Librn, Iowa State University Library, Veterinary Medical Library, 2280 College of Veterinary Medicine, Ames, IA, 50011. Tel: 515-294-2225. p. 731

Kuffel, Kayla, Head, Circ, Galesburg Public Library, 40 E Simmons St, Galesburg, IL, 61401-4591. Tel: 309-343-6118. p. 591

Kugelmeyer, Kara, Head, Res & Instruction, Sci Librn, Colby College Libraries, Olin Science Library, 5790 Mayflower Hill, Waterville, ME, 04901-4799. Tel: 207-859-5791. p. 945

Kuglitsch, Rebecca, Team Lead, Branches & Servs, University of Colorado Boulder, 1720 Pleasant St, Boulder, CO, 80309. Tel: 303-492-8705. p. 267

Kuharski, Shawn, Ms, Info Officer, Manitoba Agriculture, Food & Rural Initiatives, 810 Phillips St, Portage la Prairie, MB, R1N 3J9, CANADA. Tel: 204-239-3150. p. 2589

Kuheim, Heidi, Admin Mgr, San Juan Island Library, 1010 Guard St, Friday Harbor, WA, 98250-9612. Tel: 360-378-2798. p. 2364

Kuhl, Brandy, Libr Dir, San Francisco Botanical Garden Society at Strybing Arboretum, 1199 Ninth Ave, San Francisco, CA, 94122-2384. Tel: 415-661-1316, Ext 403. p. 226

Kuhl, Jason, Dir, Saint Charles City-County Library District, 77 Boone Hills Dr, Saint Peters, MO, 63376. Tel: 636-441-2300. p. 1277

Kuhles, Renee, Fac Librn, Austin Community College, South Austin Campus Library, 1820 W Stassney Lane, 2nd Flr, Rm 1201, Austin, TX, 78745. Tel: 512-223-9185. p. 2138

Kuhlman, Cindy, Library Contact, Athens First United Methodist Church Library, 327 N Lumpkin St, Athens, GA, 30601. Tel: 706-543-1442. p. 458

Kuhlmann, John, Acad Librn, University of Wisconsin-Green Bay, Marinette Campus Library, 750 W Bay Shore St, Marinette, WI, 54143-4253. Tel: 715-735-4306. p. 2439

Kuhlmann, Meghann, Instruction & Res Serv Librn, Wichita State University Libraries, 1845 Fairmount, Wichita, KS, 67260-0068. Tel: 316-978-5075. p. 844

Kuhn, Dennis, Supv Libr Asst, Sadie Pope Dowdell Library of South Amboy, 100 Harold G Hoffman Plaza, South Amboy, NJ, 08879. Tel: 732-721-6060. p. 1442

Kuhn, Eric, Mgr, Bear Library, 101 Governor's Pl, Bear, DE, 19701. Tel: 302-838-3300. p. 351

Kuhn, Germaine, Cat, ILL, Northeast Iowa Community College, Calmar Campus Library, 1625 Hwy 150, Calmar, IA, 52132. Tel: 563-562-3263, Ext 253. p. 776

Kuhn, Jim, Assoc Dir & Hobby Found Librn, University of Texas Libraries, Harry Ransom Center, 300 W 21st St, Austin, TX, 78712. Tel: 512-471-8944. p. 2143

Kuhn, Ruth, Dir, Spillville Public Library, 201 Oak St, Spillville, IA, 52168. Tel: 563-562-3723. p. 784

Kuhn-Schnell, Tamara, Dean, Lincoln Land Community College Library, Sangamon Hall, 5250 Shepherd Rd, Springfield, IL, 62794. Tel: 217-786-2353. p. 650

Kuhns, Carol, Dir, Blairsville Public Library, 113 N Walnut St, Blairsville, PA, 15717-1348. Tel: 724-459-6077. p. 1913

Kuhr, Lauren, Ref Librn, Rossford Public Library, 720 Dixie Hwy, Rossford, OH, 43460-1289. Tel: 419-666-0924. p. 1818

Kuiken, Alison, Operations Supvr, Bellingham Public Library, 210 Central Ave, Bellingham, WA, 98225. Tel: 360-778-7238. p. 2358

Kuilema, Amy D, Ch, Forbush Memorial Library, 118 Main St, Westminster, MA, 01473. Tel: 978-874-7416. p. 1067

Kuiper, Rhonda, Fac Mgr, Tech Serv Coordr, Westbank Community Library District, 1309 Westbank Dr, Austin, TX, 78746. Tel: 512-327-3045. p. 2143

Kuiper, Rhonda, Libr Mgr, Round Rock Public Library, 200 E Liberty Ave, Round Rock, TX, 78664. Tel: 512-218-7000, 512-218-7001. p. 2234

Kuipers, Anne, State Publ Librn, Wyoming State Library, 2800 Central Ave, Cheyenne, WY, 82002. Tel: 307-777-7281. p. 2493

Kujawa, Christine, Dir, Bismarck Veterans Memorial Public Library, 515 N Fifth St, Bismarck, ND, 58501-4081. Tel: 701-355-1480. p. 1729

Kujawa, Louis, Br Mgr, Chicago Public Library, Mabel Manning Branch, Six S Hoyne Ave, Chicago, IL, 60612. Tel: 312-746-6800. p. 557

Kujawski, Erika, Mgr, Publications & Communications, The Royal Society of Canada Library, Walter House, 282 Somerset St W, Ottawa, ON, K2P 0J6, CANADA. Tel: 613-991-6990. p. 2670

Kuklov, Danila, Develop Dir, ProConsort, 118 N Bedford Rd, Ste 100, Mount Kisco, NY, 10549. p. 2771

Kulchychi, Audrey, Chief Exec Officer, Collingwood Public Library, 55 Ste. Marie St, Collingwood, ON, L9Y 0W6, CANADA. Tel: 705-445-1571. p. 2637

Kulczak, Deb, Head, Tech Serv, University of Arkansas Libraries, 365 N McIlroy Ave, Fayetteville, AR, 72701-4002. Tel: 479-575-4811. p. 95

Kulikowski, Leah, Libr Dir, Helen Kate Furness Free Library, 100 N Providence Rd, Wallingford, PA, 19086. Tel: 610-566-9331. p. 2017

Kulis, Margaret, Adult Serv Mgr, Fremont Public Library District, 1170 N Midlothian Rd, Mundelein, IL, 60060. Tel: 847-566-8702. p. 622

Kulman, Ruth, Librn, Brown City District Library, 4222 Main St, Brown City, MI, 48416. Tel: 810-346-2511. p. 1087

Kulp, Andrew, Info Literacy & Ref Librn, Shenandoah University, 1460 University Dr, Winchester, VA, 22601. Tel: 540-665-5444. p. 2354

Kulp, Nicole, E-Res & Ser Librn, Salisbury University, 1101 Camden Ave, Salisbury, MD, 21801-6863. Tel: 410-543-6130. p. 976

Kulpa, Kathryn, Asst Admin, Fall River Public Library, 104 N Main St, Fall River, MA, 02720. Tel: 508-324-2700. p. 1018

Kulzy, Maryellen, Ch Serv, Librn, Lyndhurst Free Public Library, 355 Valley Brook Ave, Lyndhurst, NJ, 07071. Tel: 201-804-2478. p. 1414

Kumagai, Gillian, Librn, Stanford Health Library, Stanford Comprehensive Cancer Center, 875 Blake Wilbur Dr, Stanford, CA, 94305. Tel: 650-736-1960. p. 192

Kumar, Beth, Head, Ref Serv, Graduate Theological Union Library, 2400 Ridge Rd, Berkeley, CA, 94709-1212. Tel: 510-649-2504. p. 122

Kumar, Sangeeta, Librn, South Suburban College Library, 15800 S State St, Rm 1249, South Holland, IL, 60473-1200. Tel: 708-596-2000, Ext 2574. p. 648

Kumar, Shireen, Librn, Loeb & Loeb LLP, 345 Park Ave, New York, NY, 10154. Tel: 212-407-4000, 212-407-4961. p. 1590

Kumasi, Kafi, Dr, Asst Prof, Wayne State University, 106 Kresge Library, Detroit, MI, 48202. Tel: 313-577-1825. p. 2787

Kumer, Anne, Team Leader, Tech Serv, Case Western Reserve University, 11055 Euclid Ave, Cleveland, OH, 44106. Tel: 216-368-3515. p. 1766

Kummer, Steve, Admin Mgr, Central Kansas Library System, 1409 Williams St, Great Bend, KS, 67530-4020. Tel: 620-792-4865. p. 810

Kuna, Monica, Dir, Libr Serv, Bucks County Community College Library, 275 Swamp Rd, Newtown, PA, 18940-0999. Tel: 215-968-8003. p. 1970

Kuncio, Madeline, Librn, Minnesota Department of Transportation Library, 395 John Ireland Blvd, MS 155, Saint Paul, MN, 55155. Tel: 651-366-3749. p. 1200

Kundert-Cameron, Elizabeth, Head, Archives & Spec Coll, Whyte Museum of the Canadian Rockies, 111 Bear St, Banff, AB, T1L 1A3, CANADA. Tel: 403-762-2291, Ext 335. p. 2522

Kundinger, Stacy, Libr Dir, Lester Public Library of Arpin, 8091 County Rd E, Arpin, WI, 54410. Tel: 715-652-2273. p. 2421

Kundu, Pubali, Asst Dir, River Valley District Library, 214 S Main St, Port Byron, IL, 61275. Tel: 309-523-3440. p. 636

Kuni, Kayla, Assoc Dir of Libr, Pasco-Hernando State College-Spring Hill, 450 Beverly Ct, Bldg C, Spring Hill, FL, 34606. Tel: 352-340-4829. p. 444

Kunicki, Patty, Dir, Friends Memorial Public Library, 230 Chase St, Kane, PA, 16735. Tel: 814-837-7010. p. 1948

Kunkel, Ashlee, Dir, Team Librn, Milton Public Library, 430 E High St, Milton, WI, 53563. Tel: 608-868-7462. p. 2457

Kunkel, Robbie, Ms, Dean, Libr Serv, Clovis Community College Library, 417 Schepps Blvd, Clovis, NM, 88101. Tel: 575-769-4080. p. 1466

Kunkle, Dan R, Exec Dir, Wildlife Information Center, 8844 Paint Mill Rd, Slatington, PA, 18080. Tel: 610-760-8889. p. 2007

Kunkle, Kathleene, Indexer, Alternative Press Center Library, 2239 Kirk Ave, Baltimore, MD, 21218. Tel: 312-451-8133. p. 951

Kuno, Phyllis, Dir, Libr Serv, Trinity Bible College, 50 Sixth Ave S, Ellendale, ND, 58436-7150. Tel: 701-349-5407, 701-349-5409. p. 1732

Kunsch, Kelly, Ref (Info Servs), Seattle University, School of Law Library, Sullivan Hall, 901 12th Ave, Seattle, WA, 98122-4411. Tel: 206-398-4221. p. 2380

Kunst, Kari, Supvr, Youth Serv, Tigard Public Library, 13500 SW Hall Blvd, Tigard, OR, 97223-8111. Tel: 503-684-6537, Ext 2503. p. 1900

Kuntz, Betty, Br Librn, Southeast Regional Library, Vibank Branch, 101 Second Ave, Vibank, SK, S0G 4Y0, CANADA. Tel: 306-762-2270. p. 2755

Kuntz, Bliss, Instrul Librn, Libr Dir, Res, Union College Library, 3800 S 48th St, Lincoln, NE, 68506-4386. Tel: 402-486-2600, Ext 150. p. 1323

Kuntz, Christina, Br Mgr, Carroll County Public Library, Westminster Branch, 50 E Main St, Westminster, MD, 21157-5097. Tel: 410-386-4490. p. 972

Kuntz, J, Libr Asst, Nissen Public Library, 217 W Fifth St, Saint Ansgar, IA, 50472. Tel: 641-713-2218. p. 780

Kuntz, Jennifer, Librn, United States Army, Womack Army Medical Center, Medical Library, WAMC Stop A, 2817 Reilly Rd, Fort Bragg, NC, 28310-7301. Tel: 910-907-7323. p. 1690

Kuntz, Jerry, Electronic Res Consult, Ramapo Catskill Library System, 619 Rte 17M, Middletown, NY, 10940-4395. Tel: 845-343-1131, Ext 246. p. 1571

Kuntz, Marsha, Dir, Nissen Public Library, 217 W Fifth St, Saint Ansgar, IA, 50472. Tel: 641-713-2218. p. 780

Kuntz, Robert, Mgr, Info Tech, Web Librn, Carroll County Public Library, 1100 Green Valley Rd, New Windsor, MD, 21776. Tel: 410-386-4500. p. 971

Kunz, Karen, Info Syst Librn, Oregon Institute of Technology Library, 3201 Campus Dr, Klamath Falls, OR, 97601-8801. Tel: 541-885-1769. p. 1883

Kunz, LeAnn, Asst Dir, Tech Serv Librn, Washington Public Library, 115 W Washington St, Washington, IA, 52353. Tel: 319-653-2726. p. 788

Kunze, Elizabeth, Ref & Instruction Librn, Saint Ambrose University Library, 518 W Locust St, Davenport, IA, 52803. Tel: 563-333-6035. p. 744

Kunze, Janice, Libr Assoc, Keewatin Public Library, 125 W Third Ave, Keewatin, MN, 55753. Tel: 218-778-6377. p. 1179

Kunzler, Carol, Instruction & Outreach Librn, Snow College, 141 E Center St, Ephraim, UT, 84627. Tel: 435-283-7363. p. 2263

Kuo, Andrew, Circ Serv Librn, Libr Coord, Contra Costa College Library, 2600 Mission Bell Dr, San Pablo, CA, 94806. Tel: 510-215-4997. p. 236

Kuo, Ann, Libr Operations Supvr, Douglas College Library & Learning Centre, Coquitlam Campus, 1250 Pinetree Way, Rm A1040, Coquitlam, BC, V3B 7X3, CANADA. Tel: 604-777-6136. p. 2572

Kuonen, Cheryl, Exec Dir, Mentor Public Library, 8215 Mentor Ave, Mentor, OH, 44060. Tel: 440-255-8811. p. 1802

Kupas, David, Library Instruction & Info Literacy Coord, University of Pittsburgh, Johnstown Campus, 450 Schoolhouse Rd, Johnstown, PA, 15904. Tel: 814-269-1983. p. 1948

Kupersmith, Peter, Libr Dir, Delaware Valley University, 700 E Butler Ave, Doylestown, PA, 18901-2699. p. 1927

Kuppens, Mother Lucia, Librn, Abbey of Regina Laudis Library, 273 Flanders Rd, Bethlehem, CT, 06751. Tel: 203-266-7727. p. 302

Kuraogo, Franck, Libr Asst, Savannah Technical College, 5717 White Bluff Rd, Savannah, GA, 31405-5521. Tel: 912-443-4780. p. 496

Kurdock, Donna, Teen Serv Librn, Franklin Lakes Public Library, 470 DeKorte Dr, Franklin Lakes, NJ, 07417. Tel: 201-891-2224. p. 1404

Kurhan, Scott, Pub Serv Librn, Chesapeake Public Library, Indian River, 2320 Old Greenbrier Rd, Chesapeake, VA, 23325. Tel: 757-410-7008. p. 2311

Kuric, Keith, Libr Dir, North Webster Community Public Library, 110 E North St, North Webster, IN, 46555. Tel: 574-834-7122. p. 711

Kurlansky, Amy, Ref Librn, Hamilton County Law Library, Hamilton County Court House, 1000 Main St, Rm 601, Cincinnati, OH, 45202. Tel: 513-946-5300. p. 1760

Kurpiel, Sarah, Emerging Tech Librn, Benedictine University Library, 5700 College Rd, Lisle, IL, 60532-0900. Tel: 630-829-6050. p. 610

Kurtenbach, Julie, Libr Dir, Piper City Public Library District, 39 W Main, Piper City, IL, 60959. Tel: 815-686-9234. p. 635

Kurth, Stephany, ILL, Agnes Scott College, 141 E College Ave, Decatur, GA, 30030-3770. p. 475

Kurth-Christensen, Emily, Youth Serv Librn, Harlan Community Library, 718 Court St, Harlan, IA, 51537. Tel: 712-755-5934. p. 757

Kurtz, Becky, Dir, Wheatland Township Library, 207 Michigan Ave, Remus, MI, 49340. Tel: 989-967-8271. p. 1144

Kurtz, Courtney, Br Mgr, Ross Annie Halenbake Library, Friendship Community Library, 127 Main St, Beech Creek, PA, 16822. Tel: 570-962-2048. p. 1956

Kurtz, Tony, Univ Archivist & Rec Mgr, Western Washington University, 516 High St, MS 9103, Bellingham, WA, 98225. Tel: 360-650-3114. p. 2358

Kuryliw, Ken, Librn, Gaynor Family Regional Library, 806 Manitoba Ave, Selkirk, MB, R1A 2H4, CANADA. Tel: 204-482-3522. p. 2590

Kurzmann, Susan, Archivist, Ref & Instruction Librn, Ramapo College of New Jersey, 505 Ramapo Valley Rd, Mahwah, NJ, 07430-1623. Tel: 201-684-7199. p. 1415

Kurzum, Narmin, Med Librn, HackensackUMC Mountainside, One Bay Ave, Montclair, NJ, 07042-4898. Tel: 973-429-6240, 973-429-6245. p. 1420

Kus, Karen, Exec Dir, Associated Colleges of the Saint Lawrence Valley, SUNY Potsdam, 288 Van Housen Extension, Potsdam, NY, 13676. Tel: 315-267-3331. p. 2770

Kusant, Theresa, Library Contact, Comstock Township Library, 119 W Main St, Comstock, NE, 68828. p. 1311

Kushmeder, Michele, Exec Dir, Hazleton Area Public Library, 55 N Church St, Hazleton, PA, 18201-5893. Tel: 570-454-2961. p. 1943

Kushner, Els, Br Head, Vancouver Public Library, Firehall Branch, 1455 W Tenth Ave, Vancouver, BC, V6H 1J8, CANADA. Tel: 604-665-3970. p. 2581

Kushner, Scott, Libr Dir, LaFayette Public Library, Town Commons, 2577 Rte 11 N, LaFayette, NY, 13084. Tel: 315-677-3782. p. 1561

Kushnerick, Heather, Archivist & Spec Coll Librn, South Texas College of Law Houston, 1303 San Jacinto St, Houston, TX, 77002-7006. Tel: 713-646-1720. p. 2198

Kuskie, Jeff, Electronic Res Mgr, University of Nebraska at Omaha, 6001 Dodge St, Omaha, NE, 68182-0237. Tel: 402-554-2363. p. 1330

Kusmik, Rachel, Research Servs Librn, Jones Day, 901 Lakeside Ave, Cleveland, OH, 44114. Tel: 216-586-3939. p. 1770

Kustanovich, Alex, Instruction Librn, Tech Serv, St Francis College Library, 180 Remsen St, Brooklyn, NY, 11201. Tel: 718-489-5206. p. 1506

Kuster, Richard, Libr Dir, LaGrange County Public Library, 203 W Spring St, LaGrange, IN, 46761-1845. Tel: 260-463-2841. p. 701

Kuster, Toni, Br Mgr, La Porte County Public Library, Hanna Branch, 108 E West St, Hanna, IN, 46340. Tel: 219-797-4735. p. 700

Kutaka, Aileen, Chief Librn, Walt Disney Imagineering, 1401 Flower St, Glendale, CA, 91201. Tel: 818-544-6594. p. 149

Kutan, Seline, Dir, Mkt & Communications, Surrey Libraries, 10350 University Dr, Surrey, BC, V3T 4B8, CANADA. Tel: 604-598-7300. p. 2577

Kutsi, Holly, Circ, Gilbert Public Library, 17 N Broadway, Gilbert, MN, 55741. Tel: 218-748-2230. p. 1176

Kutsunis, Maggie, Youth Serv Mgr, Fremont Public Library District, 1170 N Midlothian Rd, Mundelein, IL, 60060. Tel: 847-566-8702. p. 622

Kutulas, Nan, Ref (Info Servs), United States Army, Marquat Memorial Library, Bank Hall, Bldg D-3915, 3004 Ardennes St, Fort Bragg, NC, 28310-9610. Tel: 910-432-8920. p. 1689

Kutzli-Armstrong, Sara, Tech Librn, The Frances Banta Waggoner Community Library, 505 Tenth St, DeWitt, IA, 52742-1335. Tel: 563-659-5523. p. 747

Kuykendall, Karrah, Dir, Adult Serv, Rock Island Public Library, 401 19th St, Rock Island, IL, 61201. Tel: 309-732-7345. p. 641

Kuzama, Susan, Interim Vice Chancellor, Academic Affairs, Kapi'olani Community College Library, 4303 Diamond Head Rd, Honolulu, HI, 96816. Tel: 808-734-9155. p. 512

Kuzmina, Elena, Coordr, Coll Serv, E-Res Coordr, Vancouver Community College, 250 W Pender St, Vancouver, BC, V6B 1S9, CANADA. Tel: 604-871-7000, Ext 8346. p. 2581

Kuzyk, Rachelle, Admin Librn, Chandler Public Library, Basha, 5990 S Val Vista Dr, Chandler, AZ, 85249. Tel: 480-782-2856. p. 58

Kuzyk, Rachelle, Mgr, Libr Serv, Wetaskiwin Public Library, 5002 51st Ave, Wetaskiwin, AB, T9A 0V1, CANADA. Tel: 780-361-4446. p. 2559

Kvaracein, Kim, Dir, Warren Public Library, 934 Main St, Warren, MA, 01083-0937. Tel: 413-436-7690. p. 1062

Kvasnicka, Kara, Br Librn, Genesee District Library, Grand Blanc-McFarlen Library, 515 Perry Rd, Grand Blanc, MI, 48439. Tel: 810-694-5310. p. 1106

Kvenild, Cassandra, Assoc Dean, University of Wyoming Libraries, 13th & Ivinson Ave, 1000 E University Ave, Laramie, WY, 82071. Tel: 307-766-3859. p. 2496

Kvet, Bryan, Adjunct Librn, Kent State University Libraries, Fashion, Rockwell Hall, Rm 131, 515 Hilltop Dr, Kent, OH, 44242. Tel: 330-672-9500. p. 1792

Kviklys, Danguole, Fac Res Serv/Ref Serv Librn, University of Michigan, Kresge Library Services, Stephen M Ross School of Business, 701 Tappan St, Ann Arbor, MI, 48109-1234. Tel: 734-764-8424. p. 1079

Kwak, Aneta, Pub Serv Librn, University of Toronto Libraries, New College - D G Ivey Library, 20 Willcocks St, Toronto, ON, M5S 1C6, CANADA. Tel: 416-978-2493. p. 2699

Kwakkel, Erik, Prof, University of British Columbia, The Irving K Barber Learning Ctr, 1961 E Mall, Ste 470, Vancouver, BC, V6T 1Z1, CANADA. Tel: 604-822-2404. p. 2795

Kwan, Billy, Dir, New York School of Interior Design Library, 170 E 70th St, New York, NY, 10021. Tel: 212-452-4171. p. 1598

Kwasitsu, Lishi, PhD, Dir, Libr Serv, Warner Pacific University, 2219 SE 68th Ave, Portland, OR, 97215. Tel: 503-517-1102. p. 1894

Kwasnicki, Amy, Evening/Weekend Ref Librn, Drexel University Libraries, Hagerty Library, 33rd & Market Sts, Philadelphia, PA, 19104-2875. Tel: 215-895-2750. p. 1976

Kwasniewski, Terri, Library Contact, Geauga County Historical Society, 14653 E Park St, Burton, OH, 44021. Tel: 440-834-1492. p. 1753

Kwembe, Azungwe, Tech Serv & Acq Librn/Coordr, Chicago State University, 9501 S Martin Luther King Jr Dr, LIB 440, Chicago, IL, 60628-1598. Tel: 995-821-2848. p. 558

Kwiat, Chris, Libr Mgr, American Academy of Pediatrics, 345 Park Blvd, Itasca, IL, 60143. Tel: 630-626-6635. p. 602

Kwiatkowski, Barbara, Libr Mgr, San Antonio Public Library, Parman, 20735 Wilderness Oak, San Antonio, TX, 78258. Tel: 210-207-2703. p. 2239

Kwiatkowski, Karyn L, Cat & Acq, Carlow University, 3333 Fifth Ave, Pittsburgh, PA, 15213. Tel: 412-578-6143. p. 1990

Kwiatkowski, Kathleen, Head, Adult Serv, Orion Township Public Library, 825 Joslyn Rd, Lake Orion, MI, 48362. Tel: 248-693-3000, Ext 412. p. 1123

Kwik, Phillip, Asst Dir, Troy Public Library, 510 W Big Beaver Rd, Troy, MI, 48084-5289. Tel: 248-524-3538. p. 1155

Kwok, Holly, Br Mgr, Hawaii State Public Library System, Aina Haina Public Library, 5246 Kalanianaole Hwy, Honolulu, HI, 96821. Tel: 808-377-2456. p. 507

Kwon, Rosa, Br Mgr, San Diego Public Library, Serra Mesa-Kearny Mesa, 9005 Aero Dr, San Diego, CA, 92123. Tel: 858-573-1396. p. 221

Kwong, Bella, Med Librn, Los Angeles County-University of Southern California Medical Center, Medical Center, Inpatient Tower -3K111, 2053 Marengo St, Los Angeles, CA, 90033. Tel: 323-409-7006. p. 163

Kwong, Vincci, Director, Research & Learning, Indiana University South Bend, 1700 Mishawaka Ave, South Bend, IN, 46615. Tel: 574-520-4444. p. 718

Kydd, Sandra, Asst Dir, Circ Supvr, Pease Public Library, One Russell St, Plymouth, NH, 03264-1414. Tel: 603-536-2616. p. 1378

Kye, Kwang, Dir, Commun & Tech Serv, Kitsap Regional Library, 1301 Sylvan Way, Bremerton, WA, 98310-3498. Tel: 360-405-9139. p. 2359

Kyhn, Joy, Libr Dir, Ravenna Public Library, 324 Milan Ave, Ravenna, NE, 68869. Tel: 308-452-4213. p. 1334

Kyle, Cathy, Youth Serv Mgr, Chili Public Library, 3333 Chili Ave, Rochester, NY, 14624. Tel: 585-889-2200. p. 1628

Kyle, Cathy, Br Mgr, Rochester Public Library, Lyell, 956 Lyell Ave, Rochester, NY, 14606. Tel: 585-428-8218. p. 1630

Kyle, Sabrina, Dir, Sistersville Public Library, 518 Wells St, Sistersville, WV, 26175. Tel: 304-652-6701. p. 2415

Kyle, Todd, Chief Exec Officer, Newmarket Public Library, 438 Park Ave, Newmarket, ON, L3Y 1W1, CANADA. Tel: 905-953-5110. p. 2660

Kyprios, Linda, Exec Dir, Collin College, 2800 E Spring Creek Pkwy, Plano, TX, 75074. Tel: 972-881-5726. p. 2227

Kyqykalyu, Kena, Ch Serv, Norwood Public Library, 198 Summit St, Norwood, NJ, 07648. Tel: 201-768-9555. p. 1430

Kyriakis, Demetri, Asst Dir, Needham Free Public Library, 1139 Highland Ave, Needham, MA, 02494-3298. Tel: 781-455-7559, Ext 203. p. 1038

Kyriakis, Demetri, Asst Dir, Wellesley Free Library, 530 Washington St, Wellesley, MA, 02482. Tel: 781-235-1610, Ext 1107. p. 1064

Kyrie, Sarah, Dir, Argyle Public Library, 401 E Milwaukee St, Argyle, WI, 53504. Tel: 608-543-3193. p. 2421

Kyrios, Terry, Dir, Salisbury Public Library, 17 Elm St, Salisbury, MA, 01952. Tel: 978-465-5071. p. 1051

L'eplattenier, Chad, Br Mgr, Nashville Public Library, Old Hickory Branch, 1010 Jones St, Old Hickory, TN, 37138. Tel: 615-862-5869. p. 2120

L'Helgouach, Véronique, Bibliothecaire Responsable, Bibliotheques de Montreal, Rosemont, 3131 Blvd Rosemont, Montreal, QC, H1Y 1M4, CANADA. Tel: 514-872-4735. p. 2720

L'Heureux, Angele, Librn, Federation des Medecins Specialistes du Quebec Bibliotheque, Two Complexe Desjardins, Ste 3000, Montreal, QC, H5B 1G8, CANADA. Tel: 514-350-5000. p. 2724

L'Hommedieu, Ann Marie, Mgr, New York State Department of Health, Wadsworth Ctr-NYS Department of Health, Empire State Plaza, Albany, NY, 12237. Tel: 518-474-3623. p. 1483

La Belle, Anne, Coordr, Ref & Electronic Serv, Hudson Valley Community College, 80 Vandenburgh Ave, Troy, NY, 12180. Tel: 518-629-7384. p. 1652

La Chapelle, Jennifer, Chief Exec Officer, Clearview Public Library, 269 Regina St, Stayner, ON, L0M 1S0, CANADA. Tel: 705-428-3595. p. 2681

La Chapelle, Jennifer, Chief Exec Officer, Clearview Public Library, New Lowell Branch, 5237 Simcoe County Rd 9, New Lowell, ON, L0M 1N0, CANADA. Tel: 705-424-6288. p. 2681

La Grave, Alana, Libr Asst, West Perth Public Library, 105 Saint Andrew St, Mitchell, ON, N0K 1N0, CANADA. Tel: 519-348-9234. p. 2659

La, Mibong, Head Librn, Passaic County Community College, One College Blvd, Paterson, NJ, 07505. Tel: 973-684-5885. p. 1433

La Riviere, Marguerite, Dir, Kegoayah Kozga Public Library, Richard Foster Bldg, 100 W Seventh Ave, Nome, AK, 99762. Tel: 907-443-6628. p. 49

La Rocque, Harvey, Libr Tech, Turtle Mountain Community College Library, PO Box 340, Belcourt, ND, 58316-0340. Tel: 701-477-7854, Ext 2082. p. 1729

La Rue, Karen, Children & Youth Serv Librn, Chesterfield Public Library, 524 Rte 63, Chesterfield, NH, 03443-0158. Tel: 603-363-4621. p. 1357

La Valle, Dawn, Dir, Libr Develop, Connecticut State Library, 231 Capitol Ave, Hartford, CT, 06106. Tel: 860-757-6665. p. 317

Lacy, David, Dir, Libr Info Tech, Head, Knowledge Mgt, Temple University Libraries, 1210 W Berks St, Philadelphia, PA, 19122-6088. Tel: 215-204-8231. p. 1986
Lacy, Heather, Circ Mgr, Haddonfield Public Library, 60 Haddon Ave, Haddonfield, NJ, 08033-2422. Tel: 856-429-1304. p. 1406
Lacy, Samantha, Ref Librn, Security Public Library, 715 Aspen Dr, Security, CO, 80911-1807. Tel: 719-391-3191. p. 295
Ladd, Amanda, Dir, DeRuyter Free Library, 735 Utica St, DeRuyter, NY, 13052-9613. Tel: 315-852-6262. p. 1525
Ladd, Deborah, Ad, Webster Groves Public Library, 301 E Lockwood Ave, Webster Groves, MO, 63119-3102. Tel: 314-961-3784. p. 1286
Ladd, Lisa, Dir, Buck Memorial Library, 47 Main St, Bucksport, ME, 04416. Tel: 207-469-2650. p. 920
Ladd, Marcus, Instruction Librn, Morgan State University, 1700 E Cold Spring Lane, Baltimore, MD, 21251. Tel: 443-885-1706. p. 956
Ladd, Margaret, Librn, Piermont Public Library, 130 Rte 10, Piermont, NH, 03779. Tel: 603-272-4967. p. 1378
Ladd, Nancy, Libr Dir, Pillsbury Free Library, 18 E Main St, Warner, NH, 03278. Tel: 603-456-2289. p. 1383
Ladeau, Todd, ILL Librn, Wheeler Memorial Library, 49 E Main St, Orange, MA, 01364-1267. Tel: 978-544-2495. p. 1044
Ladejobi, Dele, Dept Head, Long Beach City College, 4901 E Carson St, Long Beach, CA, 90808. Tel: 562-938-4581. p. 158
Ladewig, Aimee, Dir, Bellville Public Library, 12 W Palm St, Bellville, TX, 77418. Tel: 979-865-3731. p. 2147
Ladick, Jason, Asst Dir, Connetquot Public Library, 760 Ocean Ave, Bohemia, NY, 11716. Tel: 631-567-5079. p. 1495
Ladika, Tina, Ch Serv, South Kingstown Public Library, 1057 Kingstown Rd, Peace Dale, RI, 02879-2434. Tel: 401-783-4085, 401-789-1555. p. 2036
Ladley, Amber, Br Librn, South Hadley Public Library, Two Canal St, South Hadley, MA, 01075. Tel: 413-538-5045. p. 1054
Ladnier, Pat, Children's Serv Team Leader, The John P Holt Brentwood Library, 8109 Concord Rd, Brentwood, TN, 37027. Tel: 615-371-0090. p. 2089
LaDonna, Viola, Dir, Julia Crowder McClellan Memorial Library, 15 W 14th St, Mounds, OK, 74047. Tel: 918-827-3949. p. 1854
Laduke, Rolande Lagacé, Mrs, Archivist, Missisquoi Historical Society, Two River St, Stanbridge East, QC, J0J 2H0, CANADA. Tel: 450-248-3153. p. 2737
Ladyman, Sarah, Ch, Doniphan-Ripley County Library, 207 Locust St, Doniphan, MO, 63935. Tel: 573-996-2616. p. 1245
Laepple, Anny, Asst Dir, Delaware County Libraries, Bldg 19, 340 N Middletown Rd, Media, PA, 19063-5597. Tel: 610-891-8622. p. 1961
Laessig, Joell, Dir, Wakefield Public Library, 401 Hancock St, Wakefield, MI, 49968. Tel: 906-229-5236. p. 1156
Lafave, Amy, Libr Dir, Lenox Library Association, 18 Main St, Lenox, MA, 01240. Tel: 413-637-0197. p. 1027
Lafazan, Bonnie, Libr Dir, Berkeley College, Woodbridge Campus, 430 Rahway Ave, Woodbridge, NJ, 07095. Tel: 732-750-1800, Ext 2200. p. 1456
Lafferty, Robert, Asst Dir, Data Mgr, Mat Mgr, Broadview Public Library District, 2226 S 16th Ave, Broadview, IL, 60155. Tel: 708-345-1325, Ext 14. p. 545
Lafferty, Sheila, Archivist, Watertown History Museum Library, 401 Main St, Watertown, CT, 06795. Tel: 860-274-1050. p. 344
Lafferty, Wilma, Librn, Tri-County Regional Library, Tollette Public Library, 205 Town Hall Dr, Tollette, AR, 71851. Tel: 870-287-7166. p. 106
Laffond, Debra, Ch, Lunenburg Public Library, 1023 Massachusetts Ave, Lunenburg, MA, 01462. Tel: 978-582-4140. p. 1030
LaFlamme, Stephanie, Br Mgr, Washington County Public Library, Glade Spring Branch, 305 N Glade St, Glade Spring, VA, 24340. Tel: 276-429-5626. p. 2301
Laflen, Delores, Dir, Greenleaf Public Library, 408 Commercial St, Greenleaf, KS, 66943. Tel: 785-747-7232. p. 811
LaFleshe, Laura, Dir, Community, Connections & Content, Barrie Public Library, 60 Worsley St, Barrie, ON, L4M 1L6, CANADA. Tel: 705-728-1010, Ext 2400. p. 2630
LaFleur, LeRoy, Assoc Dir, Tufts University, Edwin Ginn Library, Mugar Bldg, 1st Flr, 160 Packard St, Medford, MA, 02155-7082. Tel: 617-627-2974. p. 1034
Laflower, Danelle D, Res Asst, Harvard Library, Harvard Forest Library, 324 N Main St, Petersham, MA, 01366. Tel: 978-724-3302, Ext 229. p. 1006
Lafon, Kara, Supvr, Pub Serv, Assemblies of God Theological Seminary, 1435 N Glenstone Ave, Springfield, MO, 65802-2131. Tel: 417-268-1058. p. 1280
LaFond, Christine, Dir, Clear Lake Public Library, 350 Fourth Ave, Clear Lake, WI, 54005. Tel: 715-263-2802. p. 2428
Lafond, Vincent, Librn, Canadian War Museum, One Vimy Pl, Ottawa, ON, K1A 0M8, CANADA. Tel: 819-776-8652. p. 2666
LaFontain, Darbie, Children's & Youth Serv, Duncan Public Library, 2211 N Hwy 81, Duncan, OK, 73533. Tel: 580-255-0636. p. 1845
Lafontaine, Joanne, Sr Librn, New York State Department of Correctional Services, One Correction Way, Ogdensburg, NY, 13669-2288. Tel: 315-393-0281, Ext 4600. p. 1610
Lafontaine, Nicole, Chief Librn, St Charles Public Library, 22 St Anne, Rm 216-217, Saint Charles, ON, P0M 2W0, CANADA. Tel: 705-867-5332. p. 2676
LaForge, Elise, Dir, Avon Public Library, 280 W Main St, Avon, MA, 02322. Tel: 508-583-0378. p. 987
LaFortune, Christina, Library Contact, Florida Today Newspaper Library, One Gannett Plaza, Melbourne, FL, 32940. Tel: 321-242-3500. p. 420
Lafortune, Olivier, ILL, Hopital Maisonneuve-Rosemont, 5415 boul de l'Assomption, Montreal, QC, H1T 2M4, CANADA. Tel: 514-252-3463. p. 2724
LaFountain, Lisa, Interim Dir, Baldwin City Library, 800 Seventh St, Baldwin City, KS, 66006. Tel: 785-594-3411. p. 797
Laframboise, Cynthia, State Archivist, Nevada State Library, Archives & Public Records, 100 N Stewart St, Carson City, NV, 89701-4285. Tel: 775-684-3310, 775-684-3360. p. 1344
LaFrance, Barbie, Coll Mgr, Librn, Springfield Art Association, 700 N Fourth St, Springfield, IL, 62702. Tel: 217-523-2631. p. 650
LaFrance, Cecilia, Dir, Buena Vista Public Library, 131 Linderman Ave, Buena Vista, CO, 81211. Tel: 719-395-8700. p. 269
LaFrance, Danielle, Br Head, Vancouver Public Library, Carnegie Branch, 401 Main St, Vancouver, BC, V6A 2T7, CANADA. Tel: 604-665-3010. p. 2581
LaFrance, Denise, Ref Librn, Dover Public Library, 73 Locust St, Dover, NH, 03820-3785. Tel: 603-516-6050. p. 1361
LaFrance, Janet, Exec Dir, La Societe Historique de Saint-Boniface Bibliotheque, Centre du patrimoine, 340 Provencher Blvd, Saint Boniface, MB, R2H 0G7, CANADA. Tel: 204-233-4888. p. 2589
Lafreniere, Cheryl, Chief Exec Officer, Teck Centennial Library, Ten Kirkland St E, Kirkland Lake, ON, P2N 1P1, CANADA. Tel: 705-567-7966. p. 2651
LaFreniere, Dan, Librn, Beaver Island District Library, 26400 Donegal Bay Rd, Beaver Island, MI, 49782. Tel: 231-448-2701. p. 1083
LaFreniere, Jacqueline, Dir, Beaver Island District Library, 26400 Donegal Bay Rd, Beaver Island, MI, 49782. Tel: 231-448-2701. p. 1083
LaFromboise, Aaron, Dir, Libr Serv, Blackfeet Community College, 504 SE Boundary St, Browning, MT, 59417. Tel: 406-338-5441. p. 1290
Lagano, Michael, Br Mgr, Clark County Public Library, Southern Village, 1123 Sunset Ave, Springfield, OH, 45505. Tel: 937-322-2226. p. 1821
Laganosky, Jessica, Br Mgr, Adams County Library System, Jean Barnett Trone Memorial Library of East Berlin, 105 Locust St, East Berlin, PA, 17316. Tel: 717-259-9000. p. 1935
Lagasse, Haley, Dir, North Bend Public Library, 1800 Sherman Ave, North Bend, OR, 97459. Tel: 541-756-0400. p. 1889
LaGasse, Jamie, Mgr, Great Neck Library, 159 Bayview Ave, Great Neck, NY, 11023. Tel: 516-466-8055, Ext 216. p. 1540
Lage, Katie, Head Librn, San Jose State University, College of Science, 8272 Moss Landing Rd, Moss Landing, CA, 95039. Tel: 831-771-4414. p. 181
LaGenesa, Ross, Libr Dir, Wellington Public Library, 3800 Wilson Ave, Wellington, CO, 80549. Tel: 970-568-3040. p. 297
Lager, Darla, Ch, Owatonna Public Library, 105 N Elm Ave, Owatonna, MN, 55060. Tel: 507-444-2460. p. 1192
Lager, Mark, Support Serv Mgr, Ventura County Library, 5600 Everglades St, Ste A, Ventura, CA, 93003. Tel: 805-677-7150. p. 256
Lagerman, Susan, Communications & Libr Prog Mgr, Brown County Library, 515 Pine St, Green Bay, WI, 54301. Tel: 920-448-5806. p. 2438
Lagermann, Patty, Ch Serv, Jefferson County Library, Windsor, 7479 Metropolitian Blvd, Barnhart, MO, 63012. Tel: 636-461-1914. p. 1249
Lagerstrom, Kate, Ad, La Grange Public Library, Ten W Cossitt Ave, La Grange, IL, 60525. Tel: 708-215-3200. p. 605
Lagios, Melina, Youth Serv Mgr, San Juan Island Library, 1010 Guard St, Friday Harbor, WA, 98250-9612. Tel: 360-378-2798. p. 2364
LaGore, Sara, Librn, First Baptist Church Library, 300 Saint Francis St, Kennett, MO, 63857. Tel: 573-888-4689. p. 1258
Lagos, Carol, Libr Dir, Malverne Public Library, 61 Saint Thomas Pl, Malverne, NY, 11565. Tel: 516-599-0750. p. 1567
Lagos, Ronald, User Services Admin, Washburn University, School of Law Library, 1700 SW College Ave, Topeka, KS, 66621. Tel: 785-670-1782. p. 840
LaGoy, Herb, Cat Librn, Coordr, Tech Serv, Utica University, 1600 Burrstone Rd, Utica, NY, 13502-4892. Tel: 315-792-3217. p. 1656
Lague, Holly, Dir, Latham Memorial Library, 16 Library Lane, Thetford, VT, 05074. Tel: 802-785-4361. p. 2296
LaGue, Mary D, Registrar, Taubman Museum of Art, 110 Salem Ave SE, Roanoke, VA, 24011. Tel: 540-342-5760. p. 2346
Lagumina, Ann, Br Mgr, Las Vegas-Clark County Library District, Whitney Library, 5175 E Tropicana Ave, Las Vegas, NV, 89122. Tel: 702-507-4010. p. 1347
Lah, Harry, Acq & Ser Librn, University of Arkansas at Little Rock, William H Bowen School of Law / Pulaski County Law Library, 1201 McMath Ave, Little Rock, AR, 72202. Tel: 501-916-5505. p. 102
Lahaie, Gabrielle, Chief Exec Officer, Mattawa Public Library, 370 Pine St, Mattawa, ON, P0H 1V0, CANADA. Tel: 249-996-0080. p. 2657
Lahey, Cynde, Dir, Info Serv, Norwalk Public Library, One Belden Ave, Norwalk, CT, 06850. Tel: 203-899-2780, Ext 15133. p. 332

Lahlum, Kirsten, Librn, United States Army, 72 Lyme Rd, Hanover, NH, 03755-1290. Tel: 603-646-4779. p. 1367

Lahmon, Jo, Regional Mgr, Cobb County Public Library System, South Cobb Regional Library, 805 Clay Rd, Mableton, GA, 30126. Tel: 678-398-5828. p. 489

Lahr, Wayne, Libr Mgr, Bucks County Free Library, Samuel Pierce Branch, 491 Arthur Ave, Perkasie, PA, 18944-1033. Tel: 215-257-9718. p. 1927

Lahs-Gonzales, Olivia, Exec Dir, San Francisco Camerawork, 1011 Market St, 2nd Flr, San Francisco, CA, 94103. Tel: 415-487-1011. p. 227

Lahti, Cree, Dir, Pocahontas County Free Libraries, 500 Eighth St, Marlinton, WV, 24954-1227. Tel: 304-799-6000. p. 2408

Lai, Diane, Coll, Div Head, Info & Tech Serv, City of Palo Alto Library, 270 Forest Ave, Palo Alto, CA, 94301. Tel: 650-329-2517. p. 191

Lai, Diane, Archivist, Mechanics' Institute Library, 57 Post St, Ste 504, San Francisco, CA, 94104-5003. Tel: 415-393-0101. p. 226

Lai, Francesco, Head of Libr, Environment Canada Library, 867 Lakeshore Rd, Burlington, ON, L7S 1A1, CANADA. Tel: 905-336-4982. p. 2634

Lai, Raissa, Head, Circ, Bethpage Public Library, 47 Powell Ave, Bethpage, NY, 11714. Tel: 516-931-3907. p. 1493

Lai, Weiliang, Dir, West New York Public Library, 425 60th St, West New York, NJ, 07093-2211. Tel: 201-295-5135. p. 1453

Laick, Jacqueline, Syst Librn, Washington & Jefferson College Library, 60 S Lincoln St, Washington, PA, 15301. Tel: 724-223-6539. p. 2018

Laico, Lisa, Dir, Albert Wisner Public Library, One McFarland Dr, Warwick, NY, 10990-3585. Tel: 845-986-1047. p. 1659

Laidley, Emily, Ch Serv, Burlington Public Library, 166 E Jefferson St, Burlington, WI, 53105. Tel: 262-342-1130. p. 2426

Laidman, Melissa, Instruction Librn, Pub Serv, Hilbert College, 5200 S Park Ave, Hamburg, NY, 14075. Tel: 716-649-7900, Ext 245. p. 1543

Laing, Carol, Libr Mgr, Wake County Public Library System, North Regional Library, 7009 Harps Mill Rd, Raleigh, NC, 27615. Tel: 919-870-4000. p. 1711

Laing, Kate, Coll Develop, Bard College, One Library Rd, Annandale-on-Hudson, NY, 12504. Tel: 845-758-7312. p. 1487

Laing, Ken, Instrul Serv Librn, Selkirk College Library, 301 Frank Beinder Way, Castlegar, BC, V1N 4L3, CANADA. Tel: 250-365-1382. p. 2564

Laing, Stefana, Dr, Librn, Southwestern Baptist Theological Seminary Libraries, Houston Campus Library, 4105 Broadway St, Houston, TX, 77087. Tel: 713-634-0011, Ext 225. p. 2180

Laing, Sue, Head, Circ, Crandall Public Library, 251 Glen St, Glens Falls, NY, 12801-3546. Tel: 518-792-6508. p. 1539

Laing-Kobe, Elizabeth, Libr Mgr, Alice Melnyk Public Library, 5009 Diefenbaker (50th) Ave, Two Hills, AB, T0B 4K0, CANADA. Tel: 780-657-3553. p. 2557

Lainhart, Ben, Dir, Your Home Public Library, 107 Main St, Johnson City, NY, 13790. Tel: 607-797-4816. p. 1558

Laino, Tim, Fac Mgr, Syst Mgr, Ella M Everhard Public Library, 132 Broad St, Wadsworth, OH, 44281-1897. Tel: 330-335-2600. p. 1827

Lair, Chris, Br Mgr, Tulsa City-County Library, Pratt, 3219 S 113th West Ave, Sand Springs, OK, 74063. p. 1866

Laird, Brenda, Dir, Clark County Library, 21 E Main St, Dubois, ID, 83423. Tel: 208-374-5267. p. 520

Laird, Cathryn, Br Mgr, Manatee County Public Library System, Braden River, 4915 53rd Ave E, Bradenton, FL, 34203. Tel: 941-727-6079. p. 387

Laird, Katie, Teen Serv Coordr, Upland Public Library, 450 N Euclid Ave, Upland, CA, 91786-4732. Tel: 909-931-4214. p. 254

Laitinen, James, Head, Coll Develop, Okanagan Regional Library, 1430 KLO Rd, Kelowna, BC, V1W 3P6, CANADA. Tel: 250-860-4033. p. 2568

Lajaunie, Terry, Mr, Asst Dir, Lamar County Library System, 144 Shelby Speights Dr, Purvis, MS, 39475. Tel: 601-794-3222. p. 1230

Lajoie, Eviava Weinraub, Vice Provost for Libr, University at Buffalo Libraries-State University of New York, 433 Capen Hall, Buffalo, NY, 14260-1625. Tel: 716-645-2965. p. 1510

Lajoie, Paul, Pres, French-Canadian Genealogical Society of Connecticut, Inc Library, 53 Tolland Green, Tolland, CT, 06084. Tel: 860-872-2597. p. 341

Lajoie, Paul, ILL Access & Serv Mgr/Evening, Fashion Institute of Technology-SUNY, Seventh Ave at 27th St, 227 W 27th St, New York, NY, 10001-5992. Tel: 212-217-4362. p. 1585

LaJuett, Brittani, Teen Librn, Roswell P Flower Memorial Library, 229 Washington St, Watertown, NY, 13601-3388. Tel: 315-785-7705. p. 1659

Lakatos, Holly, Librn, California Court of Appeal, Third Appellate District, Mosk Library & Courts Bldg, Ste 501, 914 Capitol Mall, Sacramento, CA, 95814. Tel: 916-654-0209. p. 205

Lake, Anna, Youth Serv Librn, Vestal Public Library, 320 Vestal Pkwy E, Vestal, NY, 13850-1632. Tel: 607-754-4243. p. 1657

Lake, Elaine, Dir, Oshkosh Public Library, 307 W First St, Oshkosh, NE, 69154. Tel: 308-772-4554. p. 1331

Lake, Jacque, Dir, Winfield Public Library, 112 W Ash, Winfield, IA, 52659-9511. Tel: 319-257-3247. p. 792

Lake, Leslie, Mgr, Dallas Public Library, Lakewood, 6121 Worth St, Dallas, TX, 75214-4497. Tel: 214-670-1376. p. 2165

Lake, Rebecca, Br Asst, Elko-Lander-Eureka County Library System, Battle Mountain Branch Library, 625 S Broad St, Battle Mountain, NV, 89820. Tel: 775-635-2534. p. 1344

Lake-Farm, Naomi, Exec Dir, Maui Historical Society, 2375 A Main St, Wailuku, HI, 96793. Tel: 808-244-3326. p. 514

Lakes, Mary Ellen, Dir, Brown Memorial Library, 101 S Commerce St, Lewisburg, OH, 45338. Tel: 937-962-2377. p. 1795

Lalancette, Christian, Archivist, Le Seminaire Saint-Joseph de Trois-Rivieres, 858 rue Laviolette, local 221, Trois-Rivieres, QC, G9A 5S3, CANADA. Tel: 819-376-4459, Ext 135. p. 2738

Lalande, Valerie, Dir, Res Serv, Universite Sainte-Anne, 1695 Hwy 1, Church Point, NS, B0W 1M0, CANADA. Tel: 902-769-2114, Ext 7196. p. 2617

Lalli, Moninder, Ms, Liaison Librn, Simon Fraser University - Vancouver Campus, 515 W Hastings St, Vancouver, BC, V6B 5K3, CANADA. Tel: 778-782-5050. p. 2579

Lalli, Patricia, Ch, Joshua Hyde Public Library, 306 Main St, Sturbridge, MA, 01566-1242. Tel: 508-347-2512. p. 1058

Lalli, Robert, Ref (Info Servs), Utica Public Library, 303 Genesee St, Utica, NY, 13501. Tel: 315-735-2279. p. 1656

Lalonde, Daniel, Dir, Bibliotheque Commemorative Desautels, 603 rue Claude-De Ramezay, Marieville, QC, J3M 1J7, CANADA. Tel: 450-460-4444, Ext 272. p. 2716

LaLonde, Kristin, Mgr, MidMichigan Medical Center, 4005 Orchard Dr, Midland, MI, 48670. Tel: 989-839-3262. p. 1132

Lalonde, Mylene, Doc Librn, Teluq University, 455 rue du Parvis, F015-B, Quebec, QC, G1K 9H6, CANADA. Tel: 418-657-2262, Ext 2057. p. 2732

LaLuzerne, Angie, Exec Dir, Milwaukee Academy of Medicine Library, 8701 Watertown Plank Rd, Milwaukee, WI, 53226. Tel: 414-456-8249. p. 2459

LaLuzerne, Tony, Cat Librn, University of Wisconsin-Green Bay, 2420 Nicolet Dr, Green Bay, WI, 54311-7001. Tel: 920-465-2964. p. 2439

Lalwani, Leena, Eng Librn, University of Michigan, Art, Architecture & Engineering Library, Duderstadt Ctr, 2281 Bonnisteel Blvd, Ann Arbor, MI, 48109-2094. Tel: 734-647-5747. p. 1080

Lam, Ali, Library Contact, Pierce, Goodwin, Alexander & Linville Library, 3131 Briarpark, Ste 200, Houston, TX, 77042. Tel: 713-622-1444. p. 2197

Lam, Henry, Info Spec, Sunnybrook Health Sciences Centre - Library Services, Sunnybrook Library Services, 2075 Bayview Ave, Rm EG-29, Toronto, ON, M4N 3M5, CANADA. Tel: 416-480-6100, Ext 2562. p. 2693

Lam, Kwan-Yau, Pub Serv, City Colleges of Chicago, Harry S Truman College - Cosgrove Library, 1145 W Wilson Ave, Chicago, IL, 60640-5691. Tel: 773-907-4869. p. 559

Lam, Priscilla, Executive Asst, Pasadena Public Library, 1201 Jeff Ginn Memorial Dr, Pasadena, TX, 77506. Tel: 713-477-0276. p. 2225

Lam, Tracy, Acq, De Anza College, 21250 Stevens Creek Blvd, Cupertino, CA, 95014-5793. Tel: 408-864-8439. p. 133

Lam, Yvonne, Ser & Acq Tech, Justice Institute of British Columbia Library, 715 McBride Blvd, New Westminster, BC, V3L 5T4, CANADA. Tel: 604-528-5599. p. 2572

LaMarca, Diana, Head, Children's Dept, John Jermain Memorial Library, 201 Main St, Sag Harbor, NY, 11963. Tel: 631-725-0049, Ext 231. p. 1634

LaMarche, Sherry, Per, Hudson Valley Community College, 80 Vandenburgh Ave, Troy, NY, 12180. Tel: 518-629-7322. p. 1652

Lamarre, Chantal, Dir, Acq, Centre d'acces a l'information juridique/Legal Informatin Access Center, 480 Saint-Laurent, Bur 503, Montreal, QC, H2Y 3Y7, CANADA. Tel: 514-844-2245. p. 2721

Lamb, Amanda, Ch Mgr, Newberg Public Library, 503 E Hancock St, Newberg, OR, 97132. Tel: 503-554-7735. p. 1888

Lamb, Brianna, Br Mgr, Arkansas River Valley Regional Library System, Franklin County, 407 W Market St, Ozark, AR, 72949-2727. Tel: 479-667-2724. p. 93

Lamb, Brianna, Youth Serv Librn, Haston Free Public Library, 161 N Main St, North Brookfield, MA, 01535. Tel: 508-867-0208. p. 1041

Lamb, Diane, Librn, LandMark Communications, 200 E Market St, Greensboro, NC, 27401-2910. Tel: 336-373-7169. p. 1692

Lamb, Elizabeth, Br Coordr, Motlow State Community College Libraries, Fayetteville Center Library, 1802 Winchester Hwy, Fayetteville, TN, 37334. Tel: 931-438-0028. p. 2128

Lamb, Holly Ward, Dir, Howell Carnegie District Library, 314 W Grand River Ave, Howell, MI, 48843. Tel: 517-546-0720, Ext 112. p. 1117

Lamb, Jonas, Pub Serv Librn, University of Alaska Southeast, 11066 Auke Lake Way, BE1, Juneau, AK, 99801. Tel: 907-796-6440. p. 47

Lamb, Rebecca, Ad, Waynesboro Public Library, 600 S Wayne Ave, Waynesboro, VA, 22980. Tel: 540-942-6746. p. 2352

Lamb, Sheila, Libr Asst, Sampson-Clinton Public Library, 217 Graham St, Clinton, NC, 28328. Tel: 910-592-4153. p. 1681

Lamb, Susan, Principal Librn, Ref, Santa Monica Public Library, 601 Santa Monica Blvd, Santa Monica, CA, 90401. Tel: 310-458-8600. p. 244

Lamb, Terri, Librn, Rumberger Kirk, 300 S Orange Ave, Ste 1400, Orlando, FL, 32801. Tel: 407-872-7300. p. 432

Lamb, Tom, Head, Spec Coll & Archives, Carleton College, One N College St, Northfield, MN, 55057-4097. Tel: 507-222-7015. p. 1191

Lamb, William, Libr Dir, Mountain Home Public Library, 790 N Tenth E, Mountain Home, ID, 83647. Tel: 208-587-4716. p. 527

Lamb-Garcia, Bethany, Library Contact, Nogales-Santa Cruz County Public Library, Tubac Community Library, 50 Bridge Rd, Tubac, AZ, 85646. Tel: 520-398-9814. p. 67

Lambdin, Lynne, Head, Libr Syst, Northern Michigan University, 1401 Presque Isle Ave, Marquette, MI, 49855-5376. Tel: 906-227-2149. p. 1130

Lambdin, Lynne, Electronic Res Librn, Delta State University, Laflore Circle at Fifth Ave, Cleveland, MS, 38733-2599. Tel: 662-846-4456. p. 1214

Lambert, Damian, Libr Mgr, New Orleans Public Library, Nix Library, 1401 S Carrollton Ave, New Orleans, LA, 70118-2809. Tel: 504-596-2630. p. 903

Lambert, Deborah, Dir, Coll Mgt, Indianapolis Public Library, 2450 N Meridian St, Indianapolis, IN, 46208. Tel: 317-275-4721. p. 694

Lambert, Donna, Libr Dir, Vassalboro Public Library, 930 Bog Rd, East Vassalboro, ME, 04935. Tel: 207-923-3233. p. 924

Lambert, Frank, Dr, Asst Prof, Prog Coordr, Middle Tennessee State University, 1301 E Main St, Box 91, Murfreesboro, TN, 37132. Tel: 615-898-5378. p. 2792

Lambert, Greg, Dir, Knowledge Serv, Jackson Walker LLP, 100 Congress Ave, Ste 1100, Austin, TX, 78701-4099. Tel: 512-236-2000. p. 2139

Lambert, Greg, Dir, Libr & Res Serv, Jackson Walker LLP, Bank of America Plaza, 901 Main St, Ste 6000, Dallas, TX, 75202. Tel: 214-953-6038. p. 2167

Lambert, Greg, Chief Knowledge Officer, Jackson Walker LLP, 1401 McKinney, Ste 1900, Houston, TX, 77010. Tel: 713-752-4357. p. 2196

Lambert, Jamie, Dep Dir, Laurens County Library, Clinton Public, 107 Jacobs Hwy, Ste A, Clinton, SC, 29325. Tel: 864-833-1853. p. 2064

Lambert, Jan, Libr Serv Mgr, Mid Arkansas Regional Library, 202 E Third St, Malvern, AR, 72104. Tel: 501-332-5441. p. 103

Lambert, Kathleen, Cat, Tech Serv Supvr, Twin Falls Public Library, 201 Fourth Ave E, Twin Falls, ID, 83301-6397. Tel: 208-733-2964. p. 532

Lambert, Kim, Head, Children's & Teen Serv, Flint Memorial Library, 147 Park St, North Reading, MA, 01864. Tel: 978-664-4942. p. 1042

Lambert, Margo, Ch, Weyauwega Public Library, 301 S Mill St, Weyauwega, WI, 54983. Tel: 920-867-3742. p. 2487

Lambert, Mark, Library Contact, Texas General Land Office, Stephen F Austin Bldg, 1700 N Congress Ave, Austin, TX, 78701. Tel: 512-463-5260. p. 2140

Lambert, Mechelle, Dir, Van Horne Public Library, 114 Main St, Van Horne, IA, 52346. Tel: 319-228-8744. p. 787

Lambert, Michael, City Librn, San Francisco Public Library, 100 Larkin St, San Francisco, CA, 94102. Tel: 415-557-4400. p. 227

Lambert, Nicole, Libr Mgr, Wake County Public Library System, Southeast Regional Library, 908 Seventh Ave, Garner, NC, 27529. Tel: 919-662-2250. p. 1711

Lambert, Robert, Libr Mgr, Wake County Public Library System, Village Regional Library, 1930 Clark Ave, Raleigh, NC, 27605. Tel: 919-856-6710. p. 1711

Lambert, Robert, Pres, York County Library System, 159 E Market St, 3rd Flr, York, PA, 17401. p. 2026

Lambert, Robyn, Circ & Tech Serv Coordr, Culver-Stockton College, One College Hill, Canton, MO, 63435. Tel: 573-288-6640. p. 1240

Lambert, Samantha, Libr Dir, German-Masontown Public Library, 104 S Main St, Masontown, PA, 15461. Tel: 724-583-7030. p. 1958

Lambert, Stephanie, Br Librn, Reynolds County Library District, Ellington Branch, 130 S Main, Ellington, MO, 63638. Tel: 573-663-7289. p. 1241

Lambert, Tamatha, Dir, Middle Georgia State University, 100 University Pkwy, Macon, GA, 31206. Tel: 478-471-2865. p. 487

Lambousy, Greg, Dir of Coll, Louisiana State Museum, New Orleans Jazz Club Collection, Old US Mint, 400 Esplanade Ave, New Orleans, LA, 70176. Tel: 504-568-6968. p. 901

Lambright, Donovan, Automation Librn, Southeastern Libraries Cooperating, 2600 19th St NW, Rochester, MN, 55901-0767. Tel: 507-288-5513. p. 2768

Lambropoulos, Mary, Libr Mgr, York Library Region, Minto Public Library, 420 Pleasant Dr, Unit 2, Minto, NB, E4B 2T3, CANADA. Tel: 506-327-3220. p. 2602

Lambson, Steven, Sr Res Librn, University of Missouri-Columbia, Law Library, 203 Hulston Hall, Columbia, MO, 65211-4190. Tel: 573-882-6464. p. 1244

LaMee, James, Coordr, Libr Support for Distance Educ, Pub Serv Librn, University of South Carolina Upstate Library, 800 University Way, Spartanburg, SC, 29303. Tel: 864-503-5991. p. 2070

LaMee, James, Pub Serv Librn, University of South Carolina Upstate Library, University Center of Greenville Library, 225 S Pleasantburg Dr, Greenville, SC, 29607-2544. Tel: 864-503-5991. p. 2070

Lamie, Patty, Br Mgr, Washington County Public Library, Hayters Gap, 7720 Hayters Gap Rd, Abingdon, VA, 24210. Tel: 276-944-4442. p. 2301

Lamkin, Charles, Br Mgr, Saint Louis Public Library, Charing Cross, 356 N Skinker Blvd, Saint Louis, MO, 63130. Tel: 314-726-2653. p. 1275

Lamm, Kelly, Br Mgr, Lexington Public Library, Eastside, 3000 Blake James Dr, Lexington, KY, 40509. p. 862

Lamm, Kelly, Commun Librn, Fort Vancouver Regional Library District, Vancouver Community Library (Main Library), 901 C St, Vancouver, WA, 98660. p. 2391

Lamm, Spenser, Dir, Consortia Library Systems, Five Colleges of Ohio, Oberlin College, 173 W Lorain St, Rm 208, Oberlin, OH, 44074. Tel: 440-775-5500. p. 2772

Lammers, Deborah, Libr Mgr, Henrico County Public Library, Tuckahoe Area Library, 1901 Starling Dr, Henrico, VA, 23229-4564. Tel: 804-501-1910. p. 2326

Lammers, Glenda, Asst Libr Serv Mgr, Manatee County Public Library System, 1301 Barcarrota Blvd W, Bradenton, FL, 34205-7522. Tel: 941-748-5555, Ext 6325. p. 386

Lammott, Vignette-Noelle, Head Librn, Magnolia Library & Community Center, One Lexington Ave, Gloucester, MA, 01930. Tel: 978-335-8475. p. 1021

Lammrish, Beth, Br Mgr, Clermont County Public Library, Amelia Branch, 58 Maple St, Amelia, OH, 45102. Tel: 513-752-5580. p. 1803

Lamont, Laura, Library Contact, US Environmental Protection Agency, 11201 Renner Blvd, Lenexa, KS, 66219. Tel: 913-551-7979. p. 820

Lamont, Loraine, Tech Serv Mgr, Shaker Heights Public Library, 16500 Van Aken Blvd, Shaker Heights, OH, 44120. Tel: 216-991-2030. p. 1820

Lamont, Sharon, Dir, Organizational Serv, University of Waterloo Library, 200 University Ave W, Waterloo, ON, N2L 3G1, CANADA. Tel: 519-888-4567, Ext 33519. p. 2702

Lamontagne, Karine, Head of Libr, Ecole Nationale d'Administration Publique Bibliotheque, Montreal Campus, 4750 Ave Henri-Julien, 3e etage, Montreal, QC, H2T 3E5, CANADA. Tel: 514-849-3989. p. 2730

Lamontagne, Karine, Librn, Ecole Nationale d'Administration Publique Bibliotheque, 555 Blvd Charest Est, 2e etage, Quebec, QC, G1K 9E5, CANADA. Tel: 418-641-3000. p. 2730

Lamontagne, Nancie, Coordr of Libr, College Edouard-Montpetit Bibliotheque, 945 Chemin de Chambly, Longueuil, QC, J4H 3M6, CANADA. Tel: 450-679-2631, Ext 6047. p. 2716

Lamoreaux, Kellie, Libr Asst, Umatilla Public Library, 700 Sixth St, Umatilla, OR, 97882-9507. Tel: 541-922-5704. p. 1901

Lamoreaux, Valarie, Asst Dir, Leavenworth Public Library, 417 Spruce St, Leavenworth, KS, 66048. Tel: 913-682-5666. p. 820

Lamothe, Alain, Librn, Laurentian University Library & Archives, 935 Ramsey Lake Rd, Sudbury, ON, P3E 2C6, CANADA. Tel: 705-675-1151, Ext 3304. p. 2683

Lamothe, Joanne, Dir, Sandwich Public Library, 142 Main St, Sandwich, MA, 02563. Tel: 508-888-0625. p. 1052

Lamoureux, Isabelle, Librn, Simone de Beauvoir Library, Concordia Univ, Simone de Beauvoir Inst, ER-630, 2155 Guy St, 6th Flr, Montreal, QC, H3G 1M8, CANADA. Tel: 514-848-2424, Ext 2377. p. 2727

Lamoureux, Renee, ILL/Doc Delivery Serv, Essentia Institute of Rural Health, Essentia Health St Mary's Medical Center, 407 E Third St, Duluth, MN, 55805-1984. Tel: 218-786-4396. p. 1172

Lampe, Cliff, Assoc Dean, Acad Affairs, University of Michigan, 4322 North Quad, 105 S State St, Ann Arbor, MI, 48109-1285. Tel: 734-763-2285. p. 2786

Lampert, Don, Libr Asst, Gays Mills Public Library, 16381 State Hwy 131, Gays Mills, WI, 54631. Tel: 608-735-4331. p. 2436

Lamphere, Carly, Sci Librn, Reed College, 3203 SE Woodstock Blvd, Portland, OR, 97202-8199. Tel: 503-777-7702. p. 1894

Lamphere, Dawn, Dir, Margaret Reaney Memorial Library, 19 Kingsbury Ave, Saint Johnsville, NY, 13452. Tel: 518-568-7822. p. 1635

Lamping, Sarah, Librn, Luther Luckett Correctional Complex Library, 1612 Dawkins Rd, La Grange, KY, 40031. Tel: 502-222-0363, Ext 3580. p. 861

Lamy, Mary Anne, Coordr, Border Regional Library, 312 Seventh Ave, Virden, MB, R0M 2C0, CANADA. Tel: 204-748-3862. p. 2592

LaNae, Kristy, Dir, Adams County Library, 103 N Sixth St, Hettinger, ND, 58639. Tel: 701-567-2741. p. 1736

Lancaster, Cathy, Youth Serv Coordr, Library of Michigan, 702 W Kalamazoo St, Lansing, MI, 48915. Tel: 517-373-8129. p. 1125

Lancaster, Gail, Librn, Saint Petersburg College, Saint Petersburg-Gibbs Campus Library, 6605 Fifth Ave N, Saint Petersburg, FL, 33710. Tel: 727-341-4793. p. 438

Lancaster, Haley, Asst Librn, Carnegie Evans Public Library Albia Public, 203 Benton Ave E, Albia, IA, 52531-2036. Tel: 641-932-2469. p. 729

Lancaster, William, IT Spec, Louisiana Tech University, Everett St at The Columns, Ruston, LA, 71272. Tel: 318-257-3555. p. 906

Lance, Lisa, Head Librn, Sam T Wilson Public Library, 11968 Walker St, Arlington, TN, 38002. Tel: 901-867-1954. p. 2087

Lancellotta, Bill, Asst Dir, Memorial & Library Association, 44 Broad St, Westerly, RI, 02891. Tel: 401-596-2877, Ext 328. p. 2043

Lanciault, Sarah, Librn, Third District Court of Appeals, 2001 SW 117th Ave, Miami, FL, 33175. Tel: 305-229-3200. p. 425

Land, Caroline, Mgr, Edmonton Public Library, Capilano, 9915 67 St NW, Edmonton, AB, T6A 0H2, CANADA. Tel: 780-496-7022. p. 2536

Land, Cate, Customer Serv Supvr, Northumberland Public Library, Inc, 7204 Northumberland Hwy, Heathsville, VA, 22473. Tel: 804-580-5051. p. 2325

Land, Crystal, Ref Librn, Wichita Falls Public Library, 600 11th St, Wichita Falls, TX, 76301-4604. Tel: 940-767-0868, Ext 4232. p. 2258

Land, Elizabeth, Libr Mgr, York County Public Library, Yorktown Branch, 8500 George Washington Memorial Hwy, Yorktown, VA, 23692. Tel: 757-890-3378. p. 2355

Land, Erica, Develop Mgr, Saint Charles City-County Library District, 77 Boone Hills Dr, Saint Peters, MO, 63376. Tel: 636-441-2300. p. 1277

Landa, Keith, Dir, Teaching, Learning & Tech Ctr, State University of New York, 735 Anderson Hill Rd, Purchase, NY, 10577-1400. Tel: 914-251-6440. p. 1625

Landaker, Bonnie, Libr Mgr, Brownvale Community Library, Box 407, Grimshaw, AB, T0H 1W0, CANADA. Tel: 780-618-6216. p. 2542

Landauer, Almy, Libr Dir, Waterbury Public Library, 28 N Main St, Ste 2, Waterbury, VT, 05676. Tel: 802-244-7036. p. 2297

Landavazo, Jim, Librn, Ohlone College, 43600 Mission Blvd, Fremont, CA, 94539. Tel: 510-659-6163. p. 143

Landeau, Bill, Mgr, Br, Tillamook County Library, 1716 Third St, Tillamook, OR, 97141. Tel: 503-842-4792. p. 1900

Lander, Beth, Managing Dir, Philadelphia Area Consortium of Special Collections Libraries, c/o The Library Company, 1300 Locust St, Philadelphia, PA, 19107. Tel: 501-295-4215. p. 2774

Landers, Autumn, Ch, Harnett County Public Library, 601 S Main St, Lillington, NC, 27546-6107. Tel: 910-893-3446. p. 1700

Landeryou, Sarah, Dir, Wilkinson Public Library, 100 W Pacific Ave, Telluride, CO, 81435. Tel: 970-728-4519. p. 296

Landes, Dianna, Dir, Lakehills Area Library, 7200 FM 1283, Lakehills, TX, 78063. Tel: 830-510-2777. p. 2208

Landes, Jordan, Curator, Swarthmore College, Friends Historical Library, 500 College Ave, Swarthmore, PA, 19081. Tel: 610-328-8496. p. 2012

Landesberg, Elise, Head, Ref, Teen Librn, Hendrick Hudson Free Library, 185 Kings Ferry Rd, Montrose, NY, 10548. Tel: 914-739-5654. p. 1573

Landi, Debbie Lee, Col Archivist & Rec Mgt Coordr, Davidson College, 209 Ridge Rd, Davidson, NC, 28035-0001. Tel: 704-894-2331. p. 1683

Landin, Kinsey, Br Mgr, Mansfield-Richland County Public Library, Madison Branch, 1395 Grace St, Mansfield, OH, 44905. Tel: 419-589-7050. p. 1798

Landis, Amanda E, Coll Mgt, Libr Tech, Smithsonian Libraries, Museum Support Center Library, Smithsonian Museum Support Center, Rm C-2000, 4210 Silver Hill Rd, Suitland, DC, 20746-2863. Tel: 301-238-1027. p. 375

Landis, J J, Dir, Libr & Learning Res, Thaddeus Stevens College of Technology, 750 E King St, Lancaster, PA, 17602-3198. Tel: 717-299-7753. p. 1952

Landis, Larry A, Dir, Archives & Spec Coll, Oregon State University Libraries, Special Collections & Archives Research Center, 121 The Valley Library, 5th Flr, Corvallis, OR, 97331. Tel: 541-737-0540. p. 1877

Landis, Sian, Librn, Selkirk College Library, 301 Frank Beinder Way, Castlegar, BC, V1N 4L3, CANADA. Tel: 250-365-1339. p. 2564

Landolt, Dana, Librn, Berlin Township Library, 201 Veterans Ave, West Berlin, NJ, 08091. Tel: 856-767-0439. p. 1452

Landolt, Kris, Dir, Livermore Public Library, 402 Fifth St, Livermore, IA, 50558. Tel: 515-379-2078. p. 766

Landon, Cory, Mr, Ch, Adair County Public Library, One Library Lane, Kirksville, MO, 63501. Tel: 660-665-6038. p. 1258

Landon, Laura, Research & Teaching Librn, Mount Allison University Libraries & Archives, 49 York St, Sackville, NB, E4L 1C6, CANADA. Tel: 506-364-2572. p. 2604

Landon, Patricia, Mus Spec, Pinellas County Government, 11909 125th St N, Largo, FL, 33774. Tel: 727-582-2128. p. 418

Landreth, Richard, Dir, Lincoln County Library System, 519 Emerald St, Kemmerer, WY, 83101. Tel: 307-877-6961. p. 2495

Landriault, Michelle, Libr Asst, Prescott & Russell Law Association, 1027 Queen St, L'Orignal, ON, K0B 1K0, CANADA. Tel: 613-675-2424. p. 2656

Landrum, Maria, Libr Mgr, New Orleans Public Library, Central City Library, 2405 Jackson Ave, Bldg C, Rm 235, New Orleans, LA, 70113. Tel: 504-596-3110. p. 903

Landry, Abbie, Dir of Libr, Northwestern State University Libraries, 913 University Pkwy, Natchitoches, LA, 71497. Tel: 318-357-4477. p. 900

Landry, Adam, Pub Serv Mgr, San Marcos Public Library, 625 E Hopkins, San Marcos, TX, 78666. Tel: 512-393-8200. p. 2241

Landry, Caroline, Actg Br Mgr, Assumption Parish Library, Bayou L'ourse Branch, 1214 Hwy 662, Morgan City, LA, 70380. Tel: 985-631-3200. p. 899

Landry, Kathleen, Br Mgr, Saint Martin Parish Library, 201 Porter St, Saint Martinville, LA, 70582. Tel: 337-394-2207, Ext 223. p. 907

Landry, Kathy, Commun Librn, Cariboo Regional District Library, Wells Branch, 4269 Saunders Ave, Wells, BC, V0K 2R0, CANADA. Tel: 250-994-3424. p. 2584

Landry, Lou Ella, Br Mgr, Vermilion Parish Library, Maurice Branch, 8901 Maurice Ave, Maurice, LA, 70555. Tel: 337-893-5583. p. 879

Landry, Tara, Pres, Canadian Health Libraries Association, 468 Queen St E, Ste LL-02, Toronto, ON, M5A 1T7, CANADA. Tel: 416-646-1600. p. 2778

Landry, Yolanda, Head, ILL, University of Louisiana at Lafayette, 400 E St Mary Blvd, Lafayette, LA, 70503. Tel: 337-482-1612. p. 893

Landt, Heidi, Dir, Farmersburg Public Library, 208 S Main St, Farmersburg, IA, 52047. Tel: 563-536-2229. p. 753

Landt, Heidi, Dir, Murphy Helwig Library, 111 N Page, Monona, IA, 52159. Tel: 563-539-2356. p. 770

Landuis, Travis, Youth Librn, Nevada Public Library, 631 K Ave, Nevada, IA, 50201. Tel: 515-382-2628. p. 772

Landy, Lorraine, Asst Librn, Saul Brodsky Jewish Community Library, 12 Millstone Campus Dr, Saint Louis, MO, 63146. Tel: 314-442-3720. p. 1269

Lane, Angela, Financial Mgr, Human Res Mgr, Superior District Library, 541 Library Dr, Sault Sainte Marie, MI, 49783. Tel: 906-632-9331. p. 1149

Lane, Beverly S, Libr Dir, Pontifical College Josephinum, 7625 N High St, Columbus, OH, 43235-1498. Tel: 614-985-2295. p. 1777

Lane, Bill, Mgr, Info Tech, Public Library of Cincinnati & Hamilton County, 800 Vine St, Cincinnati, OH, 45202-2009. Tel: 513-369-6948. p. 1761

Lane, Brenda, Operations Dir, Timberland Regional Library, 415 Tumwater Blvd SW, Tumwater, WA, 98501-5799. Tel: 360-943-5001. p. 2388

Lane, Eileen, Br Librn, Wapiti Regional Library, White Fox Public Library, 301 Elinor St, White Fox, SK, S0J 3B0, CANADA. Tel: 306-276-5800. p. 2746

Lane, Elizabeth, Libr Dir, Bloomfield Public Library, One Tunxis Ave, Bloomfield, CT, 06002. Tel: 860-243-9721. p. 303

Lane, Em, Br Mgr, Pima County Public Library, Wheeler Taft Abbett Sr Library, 7800 N Schisler Dr, Tucson, AZ, 85743. Tel: 520-594-5200. p. 82

Lane, Helen T, Emerging Tech Librn, Fashion Institute of Technology-SUNY, Seventh Ave at 27th St, 227 W 27th St, New York, NY, 10001-5992. Tel: 212-217-4407. p. 1585

Lane, Ian, Govt Info Spec, Federal Maritime Commission Library, 800 N Capitol St NW, Rm 1085, Washington, DC, 20573. Tel: 202-523-5762. p. 366

Lane, Judy, Br Mgr, Carteret County Public Library, Western Carteret, 230 Taylor Notion Rd, Cape Carteret, NC, 28584. Tel: 252-648-7728. p. 1674

Lane, Judy, Asst Librn, Law Society of New Brunswick Library, Justice Bldg, Rm 305, 427 Queen St, Fredericton, NB, E3B 1B6, CANADA. Tel: 506-453-2500. p. 2601

Lane, Julianne, Libr Dir, Dickinson Public Library, 4411 Hwy 3, Dickinson, TX, 77539. Tel: 281-534-3812. p. 2171

Lane, Julie, Dir, Vermillion Public Library, 102 1/2 Main St, Vermillion, KS, 66544. Tel: 785-382-6227. p. 841

Lane, Julie, Chief Exec Officer, Librn, Deseronto Public Library, 358 Main St, Deseronto, ON, K0K 1X0, CANADA. Tel: 613-396-2744. p. 2639

Lane, Kristen C, Circ, North Babylon Public Library, 815 Deer Park Ave, North Babylon, NY, 11703-3812. Tel: 631-669-4020. p. 1607

Lane, Lauren, Br Mgr, San Bernardino County Library, Crestline Branch, 24105 Lake Gregory Dr, Crestline, CA, 92325-1087. Tel: 909-338-3294. p. 213

Lane, Lisa, Br Mgr, Lancaster Public Library, Lancaster Public Library West - Mountville Branch, 120 College Ave, Mountville, PA, 17554. Tel: 717-285-3231. p. 1951

Lane, Nicole, Br Librn, Livonia Public Library, Carl Sandburg Branch, 30100 W Seven Mile Rd, Livonia, MI, 48152-1918. Tel: 248-893-4010. p. 1127

Lane, Nicole, Br Librn, Livonia Public Library, Vest Pocket, 15128 Farmington Rd, Livonia, MI, 48154-5417. Tel: 734-466-2559. p. 1127

Lane, Nicole, Dir, Gardiner Library, 133 Farmer's Tpk, Gardiner, NY, 12525-5517. Tel: 845-255-1255. p. 1537

Lane, Rebekah, Library Contact, University of South Carolina, Educational Films, Thomas Cooper Library, Level 3, Main Level, Columbia, SC, 29208. Tel: 803-777-2858. p. 2055

Lane, Tiffany, Library Contact, United States Army, 11 Hap Arnold Blvd, Tobyhanna, PA, 18466. Tel: 570-615-8150. p. 2013

Lane, Todd Allen, Chief Librn, Bridgeport Hospital, 267 Grant St, Bridgeport, CT, 06610-2870. Tel: 203-384-3615. p. 303

Laney, Kelly, Ms, Librn, Birmingham Public Library, Springville Road, 1224 Springville Rd, Birmingham, AL, 35215-7512. Tel: 205-226-4081. p. 8

Lanford, Teresa, Br Mgr, Greenville County Library System, Augusta Road Branch, 100 Lydia St, Greenville, SC, 29605. Tel: 864-527-9205. p. 2061

Lang, Albert, Archivist, Spec Coll, Carson-Newman University, 1634 Russell Ave, Jefferson City, TN, 37760. Tel: 865-471-3542. p. 2103

Lang, Andrew, Pres, Greater Philadelphia Law Library Association, PO Box 335, Philadelphia, PA, 19105. p. 2774

Lang, David W, Librn, Dechert LLP, 1900 K St NW, Washington, DC, 20006-1110. Tel: 202-261-7909. p. 363

Lang, Dorothy, Libr Dir, Town & County Public Library, 45 N Midway St, Clayton, AL, 36016. Tel: 334-775-3506. p. 12

Lang, Erica, Head Ref Librn, Hempstead Public Library, 115 James A Garner Way, Hempstead, NY, 11550. Tel: 516-481-6990. p. 1545
Lang, Karla, Ref, Spec Coll, Palestine Public Library, 2000 S Loop 256, Ste 42, Palestine, TX, 75801-5932. Tel: 903-729-4121. p. 2224
Lang, Karla, Dir, Big Bend Village Library, W230 S9185 Nevins St, Big Bend, WI, 53103. Tel: 262-662-3571. p. 2424
Lang, Kemberly AM, Archivist, Libr Mgr, OCLC Library, Archive & Museum, 6565 Kilgour Pl, Dublin, OH, 43017. p. 1782
Lang, Michael, Dir, Kansas State Library, One Kellogg Circle, Emporia, KS, 66801. Tel: 620-341-6287. p. 807
Lang, Robin, Instrul Serv Librn, Point Loma Nazarene University, 3900 Lomaland Dr, San Diego, CA, 92106-2899. Tel: 619-849-2312. p. 216
Lang, Sharon, Dir, Comfrey Area Library, 306 Brown St W, Comfrey, MN, 56019-1167. Tel: 507-877-6600. p. 1170
Lang-Clouse, Mary Paige, Dir, Ethelbert B Crawford Public Library, 479 Broadway, Monticello, NY, 12701. Tel: 845-794-4660. p. 1573
Langan, James, Pub Serv Librn, University of Pittsburgh, Johnstown Campus, 450 Schoolhouse Rd, Johnstown, PA, 15904. Tel: 814-769-7298. p. 1948
Langan, Kate, Engagement Librn, Western Michigan University, 1903 W Michigan Ave, WMU Mail Stop 5353, Kalamazoo, MI, 49008-5353. Tel: 269-387-5823. p. 1122
Langan, Pam, Librn, Nunavut Public Library Services, May Hakongak Community Library, PO Box 2106, Cambridge Bay, NU, X0B 0C0, CANADA. Tel: 867-983-2163. p. 2625
Langdon, Amanda, Access Serv Librn, Distance Educ Librn, Adams State University, 208 Edgemont Blvd, Alamosa, CO, 81101-2373. Tel: 719-587-7781. p. 263
Langdon, Hedy, Librn, Phillips Public Library, 96 Main St, Phillips, ME, 04966. Tel: 207-639-2665. p. 935
Langdon, Rachelle, Programming Spec, Pub Relations, Edith B Siegrist Vermillion Public Library, 18 Church St, Vermillion, SD, 57069-3093. Tel: 605-677-7060. p. 2084
Lange, Astrid, Supvr, Toronto Star Newspapers Ltd Library, Eight Spadina Ave, Toronto, ON, M5V 0S8, CANADA. Tel: 416-869-4491. p. 2697
Lange, Chris, Libr Dir, Sidley, Austin LLP, 787 Seventh Ave, 23rd Flr, New York, NY, 10019. Tel: 212-839-5300. p. 1602
Lange, Diana, Dir, Rolla Public Library, 14 SE First St, Rolla, ND, 58367. Tel: 701-477-3849. p. 1739
Lange, Eleanor, Head Librn, Interlochen Center for the Arts, Frederick & Elizabeth Ludwig Fennell Music Library, 4000 Hwy M-137, Interlochen, MI, 49643. Tel: 231-276-7230. p. 1118
Lange, Kenny, Library Contact, Czech Heritage Museum & Genealogy Center Library, 119 W French Ave, Temple, TX, 76501. Tel: 254-899-2935. p. 2247
Lange, Linda, Libr Asst, Foley & Lardner, 777 E Wisconsin Ave, Milwaukee, WI, 53202-5306. Tel: 414-271-2400. p. 2458
Lange, Samantha, Librn, Paradise Valley Community College, 18401 N 32nd St, Phoenix, AZ, 85032-1200. Tel: 602-787-6692. p. 71
Lange, Thomas, Dir, Somesville Library Association, 1116 Main St, Mount Desert, ME, 04660. Tel: 207-244-7404. p. 932
Langebartels, Shirley, Librn, South Milwaukee Public Library, 1907 Tenth Ave, South Milwaukee, WI, 53172. Tel: 414-768-8195. p. 2478
Langel, Julia, Librn, Midwest Historical & Genealogical Society, Inc Library, 1203 N Main St, Wichita, KS, 67203. Tel: 316-264-3611. p. 843
Langenberg, Ashley, Libr Dir, Clarence Public Library, 309 Sixth Ave, Clarence, IA, 52216. Tel: 563-452-3734. p. 740
Langer, Carissa, Dir, Prescott Public Library, 800 Borner St N, Prescott, WI, 54021. Tel: 715-262-5555. p. 2471
Langer, Christian, User Serv Librn, Tennessee State University, Avon Williams Library, 330 Tenth Ave N, Nashville, TN, 37203. Tel: 615-963-7187. p. 2121
Langer Thomson, Lois, Exec Dir, Sno-Isle Libraries, 7312 35th Ave NE, Marysville, WA, 98271-7417. Tel: 360-651-7001. p. 2370
Langer-Liblick, Stephanie, Dir, Tappan-Spaulding Memorial Library, Six Rock St, Newark Valley, NY, 13811. Tel: 607-642-9960. p. 1605
Langerman, Joanne, Patron Serv Librn, Southern Maine Community College Library, Two Fort Rd, South Portland, ME, 04106. Tel: 207-741-5521. p. 941
Langevin, Tammy, Chief Exec Officer, Librn, Manitouwadge Public Library, Community Ctr, Two Manitou Rd, Manitouwadge, ON, P0T 2C0, CANADA. Tel: 807-826-3913. p. 2656
Langfitt, Leann, Dir, Primghar Public Library, 320 First St NE, Primghar, IA, 51245. Tel: 712-957-8981. p. 778
Langford, Claudia, Pres, San Antonio Art League & Museum, 130 King William St, San Antonio, TX, 78204. Tel: 210-223-1140. p. 2238
Langford, Donna, Exec Dir, Beloit Historical Society, Lincoln Ctr, 845 Hackett St, Beloit, WI, 53511. Tel: 608-365-7835. p. 2423
Langford, Joel C, Libr Dir, Reinhardt University, 7300 Reinhardt Circle, Waleska, GA, 30183. Tel: 770-720-5585. p. 502
Langford, Lari, Dir, Info Serv, Head, User Serv, University of Toronto Libraries, Robarts Library, 130 St George St, Toronto, ON, M5S 1A5, CANADA. Tel: 416-978-2898. p. 2700
Langford, Nell, Br Mgr, Rusk County Library System, Mount Enterprise Public Library, 201 NW Second St, Mount Enterprise, TX, 75681. Tel: 903-822-3532. p. 2189
Langford, Russ, Univ Librn, Global University Library, 1211 S Glenstone Ave, Springfield, MO, 65804. Tel: 417-862-9533, Ext 2012. p. 1280
Langford, Shawnda, Asst Dir, Ch Serv, Holmes County Public Library, 303 N J Harvey Etheridge St, Bonifay, FL, 32425. Tel: 850-547-3573. p. 386
Langford, Tessa, Curator, US National Park Service, 1001 E Fifth St, Vancouver, WA, 98661. Tel: 360-816-6244. p. 2391
Langhans, Eliza, Dir, Hatfield Public Library, 39 Main St, Hatfield, MA, 01038. Tel: 413-247-9097. p. 1024
Langhart, Nick, Dir, Forbush Memorial Library, 118 Main St, Westminster, MA, 01473. Tel: 978-874-7416. p. 1067
Langhorne, Detre, Librn, Uniontown Public Library, PO Box 637, Uniontown, AL, 36786-0637. Tel: 334-628-6681. p. 39
Langhorst, Michael, Br Librn, Wapiti Regional Library, Humboldt Reid-Thompson Public Library, 705 Main St, Humboldt, SK, S0K 2A0, CANADA. Tel: 306-682-2034. p. 2745
Langhurst, Vanessa, Supvr, Multimedia Support Ctr/Circ, Columbus State Community College Library, 550 E Spring St, Columbus, OH, 43215. Tel: 614-287-2899. p. 1773
Langis, Monique, Libr Mgr, Albert-Westmorland-Kent Regional Library, Bibliotheque Publique Gerald-Leblanc de Bouctouche, 84 boul Irving, Unite 100, Bouctouche, NB, E4S 3L4, CANADA. Tel: 506-743-7263. p. 2603
Langlais, Kris, Mgr, Free Library of Philadelphia, Field Teen Center, 1901 Vine St, Ground Flr, Philadelphia, PA, 19103. Tel: 215-686-5395. p. 1978
Langland, Laurie, Univ Archivist, Dakota Wesleyan University, 1200 W University Ave, Mitchell, SD, 57301. Tel: 605-995-2134. p. 2079
Langley, Anne, Dean, Univ Libr Serv, University of Connecticut, 369 Fairfield Rd, Storrs, CT, 06269-1005. p. 339
Langley, Kaija, Dir of Develop, Massachusetts Institute of Technology Libraries, Office of the Director, Bldg NE36-6101, 77 Massachusetts Ave, Cambridge, MA, 02139-4307. Tel: 617-452-2123. p. 1008
Langley, Leslie, Br Mgr, Patrick Lynch Public Library, 206 S McKenna St, Poteau, OK, 74953. Tel: 918-647-4444. p. 1860
Langley, Nicole, Dir, Winchester Public Library, 80 Washington St, Winchester, MA, 01890. Tel: 781-721-7171. p. 1070
Langley, Paula, Head, Circ, University of Maryland, Baltimore County, 1000 Hilltop Circle, Baltimore, MD, 21250. Tel: 410-455-2356. p. 958
Langlois, Ann, ILS Manager, Lakeland Library Cooperative, 4138 Three Mile Rd NW, Grand Rapids, MI, 49534-1134. Tel: 616-559-5253. p. 2767
Langlois, Irene, Br Head, Maplewood Memorial Library, Hilton, 1688 Springfield Ave, Maplewood, NJ, 07040-2923. p. 1416
Langlois, Sharon, Librn, Southern Technical College, Sanford Campus, 2910 S Orlando Dr, Sanford, FL, 32773. Tel: 407-323-4141. p. 404
Langlois, Suzanne, Pres, Literacy Project, St Clair County Literacy Project, 210 McMorran Blvd, Port Huron, MI, 48060. Tel: 810-987-7323, Ext 156. p. 1142
Langloss, Mary, Ch Serv, Illiopolis-Niantic Public Library District, Sixth & Mary Sts, Illiopolis, IL, 62539. Tel: 217-486-5561. p. 601
Langman, Erin, Ref & Info Serv Librn, Saskatchewan Polytechnic, 4500 Wascana Pkwy, Regina, SK, S4P 3A3, CANADA. Tel: 306-775-7411. p. 2748
Langstaff, Anna L, Dir, Beverly Public Library, 32 Essex St, Beverly, MA, 01915-4561. Tel: 978-921-6062. p. 989
Langston, Barbara, Libr Dir, Courtland Community Library, 403 Main St, Courtland, KS, 66939. Tel: 785-374-4260. p. 804
Langston, Barbara, Libr Dir, Formoso Public Library, 108 Main St, Formoso, KS, 66942. Tel: 785-794-2424. p. 808
Langston, Janine, Dep Dir, Birmingham Public Library, 2100 Park Pl, Birmingham, AL, 35203-2744. Tel: 205-226-3600. p. 7
Langston, Janine, Regional Mgr, Birmingham Public Library, Five Points West, 4812 Avenue W, Birmingham, AL, 35208-4726. Tel: 205-226-4013. p. 7
Langston, Marc, Res, Instruction & Outreach Librn, California State University, Chico, 400 W First St, Chico, CA, 95929-0295. Tel: 530-898-4587. p. 129
Langston, Robyn, Head Librn, Ludington Public Library, Five S Bryn Mawr Ave, Bryn Mawr, PA, 19010-3471. Tel: 610-525-1776. p. 1916
Langton, Beth, Librn, Hahn, Loeser & Parks, 200 Public Sq, Ste 2800, Cleveland, OH, 44114. Tel: 216-621-0150. p. 1770
Langton, Sherri, Cataloger, Libr Syst Spec, Northwestern College, 101 Seventh St SW, Orange City, IA, 51041. Tel: 712-707-7236. p. 774
Langum, Connie, Historian, National Park Service, Wilson's Creek National Battlefield, 6424 W Farm Rd 182, Republic, MO, 65738-9514. Tel: 417-732-2662, Ext 225. p. 1266
Langworthy, Sara, Assoc Prof, University of Iowa, 3087 Main Library, 125 W Washington St, Iowa City, IA, 52242-1420. Tel: 319-335-5707. p. 2785
Lanham, Mary, Coordr, Prog, Anderson County Library, 300 N McDuffie St, Anderson, SC, 29621-5643. Tel: 864-260-4500. p. 2046
Lanier, Jami, Library Contact, Cape Hatteras National Seashore, 1401 National Park Dr, Manteo, NC, 27954-9708. Tel: 252-473-2111, Ext 9021. p. 1702
Lanier, Jill, Tech Serv, O'Melveny & Myers LLP, Times Square Tower, Seven Times Sq, New York, NY, 10036. Tel: 212-326-2022. p. 1599

Lanier, Lisa, Dir, Libr Serv, Ogeechee Technical College Library, One Joe Kennedy Blvd, Statesboro, GA, 30458. Tel: 912-871-1886. p. 498

Lank, Heather, Parliamentary Librarian, Library of Parliament, Branches & Information Service, 125 Sparks St, Ottawa, ON, K1A 0A6, CANADA. Tel: 613-992-4793. p. 2667

Lank-Jones, Molly, Dir, Sherman & Ruth Weiss Community Library, 10788 State Hwy 77 W, Hayward, WI, 54843. Tel: 715-634-2161. p. 2441

Lankes, R David, Prof, University of Texas at Austin, 1616 Guadalupe St, Ste 5.202, Austin, TX, 78712-0390. Tel: 512-471-3821. p. 2793

Lann, Jennifer, Dir, Libr Serv, Landmark College Library, 19 River Rd S, Putney, VT, 05346. Tel: 802-387-1648. p. 2292

Lannen, Donna, Information Technology Assoc, Susquehanna Health Medical Library, Williamsport Regional Medical Ctr, 700 High St, 3rd Flr, Williamsport, PA, 17701. Tel: 570-321-2266. p. 2024

Lanning, Scott W, Assessment Librn, Data Mgt, Southern Utah University, 351 W University Blvd, Cedar City, UT, 84720. Tel: 435-865-8156. p. 2262

Lannon, Amber, Univ Librn, Carleton University Library, 1125 Colonel By Dr, Ottawa, ON, K1S 5B6, CANADA. Tel: 613-520-2600, Ext 8189. p. 2666

Lannon, Amy, Dir, Reading Public Library, 64 Middlesex Ave, Reading, MA, 01867-2550. Tel: 781-942-6711. p. 1049

Lanphear, Emily, Librn, Inyo County Free Library, Bishop Branch, 210 Academy Ave, Bishop, CA, 93514-2693. Tel: 760-873-5115. p. 152

Lanphear, Lara, Dir, Lied Winside Public Library, 417 Main St, Winside, NE, 68790. Tel: 402-286-1122. p. 1341

Lanphier, Connie, Dir, Utopia Memorial Library, 800 Main St, Utopia, TX, 78884. Tel: 830-966-3448. p. 2250

Lansdell, Susan, Mgr, Tri-County Regional Library, Winthrop Public Library, 720 High St, Winthrop, AR, 71866. Tel: 870-381-7580. p. 106

Lansdown, Erica, Sr Librn, Long Beach Public Library, Burnett, 560 E Hill St, Long Beach, CA, 90806. Tel: 562-570-1041. p. 159

Lansinger-Pierce, Casey, Pub Serv Mgr, Clearview Library District, 720 Third St, Windsor, CO, 80550-5109. Tel: 970-686-5603. p. 298

Lanspery, Darren, Dir, Plattekill Public Library, 2047 State Rte 32, Modena, NY, 12548. Tel: 845-883-7286. p. 1573

Lanter, Jenna, Dir, Lang Memorial Library, 2405 Ave F, Wilson, KS, 67490. Tel: 785-658-3648. p. 844

Lanter, Julia, Asst Dir, Exeter Public Library, Four Chestnut St, Exeter, NH, 03833. Tel: 603-772-3101, 603-772-6036. p. 1363

Lanteri, Sabine, Liaison Librn, Sr Asst Librn, University of Delaware Library, Chemistry, Brown Laboratory, Rm 202, 181 S College Ave, Newark, DE, 19717. Tel: 302-831-6945. p. 355

Lanthier, Deb, Head Librn, Canby Public Library, 110 Oscar Ave N, Canby, MN, 56220-1332. Tel: 507-223-5738. p. 1168

Lanthier, Deb, Head Librn, Dawson Public Library, 676 Pine St, Dawson, MN, 56232. Tel: 320-769-2069. p. 1171

Lanthier, Deb, Head Librn, Madison Public Library, 401 Sixth Ave, Madison, MN, 56256-1236. Tel: 320-598-7938. p. 1181

Lantz, Betsy, Exec Dir, Northeast Ohio Regional Library System, 1737 Georgetown Rd, Ste B, Hudson, OH, 44236. Tel: 330-655-0531, Ext 101. p. 2772

Lanucha, Crystal, Cataloger, Chicopee Public Library, 449 Front St, Chicopee, MA, 01013. Tel: 413-594-1800. p. 1011

Lanxon, Robert, Ref Serv, Ledding Library of Milwaukie, 10660 SE 21st Ave, Milwaukie, OR, 97222. Tel: 503-786-7580. p. 1887

Lanxon, Sue, Librn, Sheffield Public Library, 136 E Cook St, Sheffield, IL, 61361. Tel: 815-454-2628. p. 646

Lao-Scott, Christopher, Sr Librn, The National Academies of Sciences, Engineering & Medicine, 500 Fifth St NW, Keck 304, Washington, DC, 20001-2721. Tel: 202-334-2125. p. 371

LaPaz, James, Head, Libr Operations, Waukesha Public Library, 321 Wisconsin Ave, Waukesha, WI, 53186-4713. Tel: 262-522-7280. p. 2484

LaPean, Jessica, Youth Serv Coordr, Carleton A Friday Memorial Library, 155 E First St, New Richmond, WI, 54017. Tel: 715-243-0431. p. 2465

LaPenn, Ronna, Tech Serv, Whipple Free Library, 67 Mont Vernon Rd, New Boston, NH, 03070. Tel: 603-487-3391. p. 1375

LaPenotiere, Beth, Sr Adminr, Pub Serv, Harford County Public Library, 1221-A Brass Mill Rd, Belcamp, MD, 21017-1209. Tel: 410-273-5706. p. 958

Laper, Eugene, ILL, Lehman College, City University of New York, 250 Bedford Park Blvd W, Bronx, NY, 10468. Tel: 718-960-8577. p. 1499

LaPerla, Susan, Dir, Pub Serv, The Ferguson Library, One Public Library Plaza, Stamford, CT, 06904. Tel: 203-964-1000. p. 338

LaPerriere, Jenny, Br Cluster Mgr, Denver Public Library, Ten W 14th Ave Pkwy, Denver, CO, 80204-2731. Tel: 720-865-1111. p. 275

LaPerriere, Renee, Spec Coll Librn, Joe A Guerra Laredo Public Library, 1120 E Calton Rd, Laredo, TX, 78041. Tel: 956-795-2400. p. 2209

Laphen, Mary Kate, Chief Exec Officer, Librn, Merrickville Public Library, 446 Main St W, Merrickville, ON, K0G 1N0, CANADA. Tel: 613-269-3326. p. 2657

Lapidow, Amy, Circ Librn, Res & Instruction Librn, Tufts University, Hirsh Health Sciences Library, 145 Harrison Ave, Boston, MA, 02111. Tel: 617-636-6705. p. 1034

Lapierre, Diane, Exec Dir, Poudre River Public Library District, 201 Peterson St, Fort Collins, CO, 80524-2990. Tel: 970-221-6670. p. 281

LaPierre, Emily, Ch, Vineyard Haven Public Library, 200 Main St, Vineyard Haven, MA, 02568. Tel: 508-696-4211, Ext 114. p. 1060

LaPierre, Karen, Dir, Hoisington Public Library, 169 S Walnut, Hoisington, KS, 67544. Tel: 620-653-4128. p. 813

Lapierre, MacKenna, Asst Librn, Greensboro Free Library, 53 Wilson St, Greensboro, VT, 05841. Tel: 802-533-2531. p. 2285

LaPierre, Suzanne S, Librn, Fairfax County Public Library, 12000 Government Center Pkwy, Ste 324, Fairfax, VA, 22035-0012. Tel: 703-324-3100. p. 2316

Lapis, Susan, Asst Dir, Yavapai County Free Library District, 1971 Commerce Ctr Circle, Ste D, Prescott, AZ, 86301. Tel: 928-771-3191. p. 74

Laplante, Anne, Archivist, Coordr, Musee de la Civilisation - Bibliotheque du Seminaire de Quebec, 9 rue de l'Universite, Quebec, QC, G1R 5K1, CANADA. Tel: 418-643-2158, Ext 796. p. 2731

Laplante, Audrey, Assoc Prof, Universite de Montreal, 3150, rue Jean-Brillant, bur C-2004, Montreal, QC, H3T 1N8, CANADA. Tel: 514-343-6044. p. 2797

Laplante, Catherine, Acq, National Gallery of Canada Library & Archives, 380 Sussex Dr, Ottawa, ON, K1N 9N4, CANADA. Tel: 613-714-6000, Ext 6323. p. 2667

Laplante, Élise, Documentation Tech, Cegep de Granby, 235 Saint Jacques St, Granby, QC, J2G 3N1, CANADA. Tel: 450-372-6614, Ext 1204. p. 2713

Laplante, Isabelle, Head Librn, Centre de documentation collegiale, 1111 rue Lapierre, LaSalle, QC, H8N 2J4, CANADA. Tel: 514-364-3327, Ext 1. p. 2715

LaPlante, Jane, Dir, Minot State University, 500 University Ave W, Minot, ND, 58707. Tel: 701-858-3857. p. 1738

LaPlante, Kim, Mgr, Res Libr Serv, Northeast Wisconsin Technical College Library, 2740 W Mason St, Green Bay, WI, 54303-4966. Tel: 920-498-5487. p. 2439

Laplante, Melissa, Dir, Libr Serv, White Mountains Community College, 2020 Riverside Dr, Berlin, NH, 03570-3799. Tel: 603-342-3086. p. 1355

Lapo, Jasmine, Circ Serv Mgr, St Charles Public Library District, One S Sixth Ave, Saint Charles, IL, 60174-2105. Tel: 630-584-0076, Ext 257. p. 644

LaPointe, Amy, Dir, Amherst Town Library, 14 Main St, Amherst, NH, 03031. Tel: 603-673-2288. p. 1353

Lapointe, Jean-Michel, Librn, Universite du Quebec, CP 8889, Succ Centre-Ville, 1255 Rue St Denis, Locale-A-1200, Montreal, QC, H3C 3P3, CANADA. Tel: 514-987-6134. p. 2728

Lapointe, Lois, Asst Librn, Whitingham Free Public Library, 2948 Vt Rte 100, Jacksonville, VT, 05342. Tel: 802-368-7506. p. 2286

Lapointe, Louis-Philippe, ILL, Ministere de l Énergie et des Ressources naturelles du Québec, 5700 4e Ave Ouest, B-205, Quebec, QC, G1H 6R1, CANADA. Tel: 418-627-8686. p. 2731

Laporte, Betty Ann, Libr Mgr, Rich Valley Public Library, RR 1, Gunn, AB, T0E 1A0, CANADA. Tel: 780-967-3525. p. 2542

LaPorte, Josh, Ref & Access Serv Librn, St John's University Library, Rittenberg Law Library, 8000 Utopia Pkwy, Jamaica, NY, 11439. Tel: 718-990-6826. p. 1556

LaPorte, Michelle, Dir, Libr & Res Serv, Lerners LLP Library, 85 Dufferin Ave, London, ON, N6A 4G4, CANADA. Tel: 519-640-6355. p. 2654

LaPorte, Peter, Exec Dir, St Mary's County Historical Society, 41680 Tudor Pl, Leonardtown, MD, 20650. Tel: 301-475-2467. p. 971

Lapp, Kari, Commun Engagement Mgr, Saline County Public Library, 1800 Smithers Dr, Benton, AR, 72015. Tel: 501-778-4766. p. 90

Lappin, Amy, Dep Dir, Lebanon Public Libraries, Nine E Park St, Lebanon, NH, 03766. Tel: 603-448-2459. p. 1370

Laprade, Athena, Cataloger, Elko-Lander-Eureka County Library System, 720 Court St, Elko, NV, 89801. Tel: 775-738-3066. p. 1344

Laprade, Michelle, Asst Librn, Bracken Memorial Library, 57 Academy Rd, Woodstock, CT, 06281. Tel: 860-928-0046. p. 349

LaPratt, Linda, Librn, Charlotte County Library, Phenix Branch, Charlotte St, Phenix, VA, 23959. Tel: 434-542-4654. p. 2309

LaPrelle, Robert H, Pres & Chief Exec Officer, Museum of the American Railroad Library, 6455 Page St, Frisco, TX, 75034. Tel: 214-428-0101. p. 2182

Laramie, Shawn, Libr Asst, John F Kennedy University Libraries, 100 Ellinwood Way, Pleasant Hill, CA, 94523. Tel: 925-969-3100. p. 195

Laramie, Susan, Librn, Laconia Public Library, Lakeport (Ossian Wilbur Goss Reading Room), 188 Elm St, Laconia, NH, 03246. Tel: 603-524-3808. p. 1370

Lard, Lesley, Teen/YA Librn, Bonner Springs City Library, 201 N Nettleton Ave, Bonner Springs, KS, 66012. Tel: 913-441-2665. p. 799

Lareau, Kristina, Head, Children's Servx, Ridgefield Library Association Inc, 472 Main St, Ridgefield, CT, 06877-4585. Tel: 203-438-2282. p. 335

Large, Cathy, Librn, Salt River Project Library, 1600 N Priest Dr, Tempe, AZ, 85281-1213. Tel: 602-236-2259. p. 79

Largen, Sarah, Asst Regional Dir, Galax-Carroll Regional Library, 610 W Stuart Dr, Galax, VA, 24333. Tel: 276-236-2351. p. 2321

Largo, Lora, Librn, South Mountain Community College Library, 7050 S 24th St, Phoenix, AZ, 85042-5806. Tel: 602-243-8345. p. 73
Larios, Christina, Mgr, County of Los Angeles Public Library, Baldwin Park Library, 4181 Baldwin Park Blvd, Baldwin Park, CA, 91706-3203. Tel: 626-962-6947. p. 135
Larison, Brittanie, Librn, Long Island Community Library, 359 Washington Ave, Long Island, KS, 67647. Tel: 785-854-7474. p. 822
Larivière, Vincent, Prof, Universite de Montreal, 3150, rue Jean-Brillant, bur C-2004, Montreal, QC, H3T 1N8, CANADA. Tel: 514-343-6044. p. 2797
Larke, Julia, Br Librn, Mendocino County Library District, Coast Community, 225 Main St, Point Arena, CA, 95468. Tel: 707-882-3114. p. 254
Larkin, Carol, Programming, Walnut Public Library District, 101 Heaton St, Walnut, IL, 61376. Tel: 815-379-2159. p. 658
Larkin, Kathleen, Dep Librn, Prince Rupert Library, 101 Sixth Ave W, Prince Rupert, BC, V8J 1Y9, CANADA. Tel: 250-627-1345. p. 2574
Larkin, Mary Jo, Dean of Libr, Chestnut Hill College, 9601 Germantown Ave, Philadelphia, PA, 19118-2695. Tel: 215-248-7055. p. 1975
Larkin, Vincent Chip, Instruction & Assessment Librn, North Carolina Wesleyan University, 3400 N Wesleyan Blvd, Rocky Mount, NC, 27804. Tel: 252-985-5233. p. 1713
Larko, Jillian, Cat, New Castle Public Library, 207 E North St, New Castle, PA, 16101-3691. Tel: 724-658-6650, Ext 125. p. 1969
Larmarche, Jenna, District Supervisor, Stormont, Dundas & Glengarry County Library, Winchester Branch, 547 St Lawrence St, Winchester, ON, K0C 2K0, CANADA. Tel: 613-774-2612. p. 2638
LaRocca, Amy, Head, Ad Ref Serv, Suffern Free Library, 210 Lafayette Ave, Suffern, NY, 10901. Tel: 845-357-1237. p. 1647
LaRocca, Kelly, Dir, Saint Tammany Parish Library, 1112 W 21st Ave, Covington, LA, 70433. Tel: 985-871-1219. p. 887
LaRocca-Fels, Karen, Libr Dir, Ossining Public Library, 53 Croton Ave, Ossining, NY, 10562. Tel: 914-941-2416. p. 1613
Laroche, Kate-Lynne, Exec Dir, Rhode Island Jewish Historical Association Library, 401 Elmgrove Ave, Providence, RI, 02906. Tel: 401-331-1360. p. 2040
Laroche, Veronica, Dir, Northampton Area Public Library, 1615 Laubach Ave, Northampton, PA, 18067-1597. Tel: 610-262-7537. p. 1972
Laroche, Veronique, Libr Tech, Canada Agriculture & Agri-Food Canada, 3600 Blvd Casavant W, Saint-Hyacinthe, QC, J2S 8E3, CANADA. Tel: 450-768-9618, 450-768-9619. p. 2735
Larochelle, Grace, Mgr, Springfield City Library, East Forest Park Branch, 136 Surrey Rd, Springfield, MA, 01118. Tel: 413-263-6836. p. 1056
Larochelle, Grace, Mgr, Springfield City Library, Forest Park Branch, 380 Belmont Ave, Springfield, MA, 01108. Tel: 413-263-6843. p. 1056
LaRochelle, Stephen, Dir, Kennebec Valley Community College, 92 Western Ave, Fairfield, ME, 04937-1367. Tel: 207-453-5004. p. 924
LaRock, Tami, Dir, Goodwin Library, 422 Main St, Farmington, NH, 03835-1519. Tel: 603-755-2944. p. 1363
Larocque, Jessica, Head, Children's Servx, York Library Region, Fredericton Public Library, 12 Carleton St, Fredericton, NB, E3B 5P4, CANADA. Tel: 506-460-2800. p. 2602
Larocque, Jessica, Pub Serv Librn, York Library Region, 570 Two Nations Crossing, Ste 1, Fredericton, NB, E3A 0X9, CANADA. Tel: 506-453-5380. p. 2602
Larocque, Rebecca, Head, Info Serv, North Bay Public Library, 271 Worthington St E, North Bay, ON, P1B 1H1, CANADA. Tel: 705-474-4830. p. 2661
LaRonge-Mohr, Connie, Br Librn, Southeast Regional Library, Pilot Butte Branch, Recreation Complex, Third St & Second Ave, Pilot Butte, SK, S0G 3Z0, CANADA. Tel: 306-781-3403. p. 2754
LaRose, Debbie, Circ, The William K Sanford Town Library, 629 Albany Shaker Rd, Loudonville, NY, 12211-1196. Tel: 518-458-9274. p. 1565
LaRose, Leslie, Dir, Augusta Memorial Public Library, 113 N Stone St, Augusta, WI, 54722-6000. Tel: 715-286-2070. p. 2421
LaRose, Michele Dill, Access Serv Librn, ILL Librn, Vermont Law School, 164 Chelsea St, South Royalton, VT, 05068. Tel: 802-831-1403. p. 2295
LaRose, Suzanna, Sr Ref Librn, Gowling WLG (Canada) Library, One First Canadian Pl, 100 King St W, Ste 1600, Toronto, ON, M5X 1G5, CANADA. Tel: 416-862-5735. p. 2689
LaRosee, Nan, Libr Mgr, Forsyth County Public Library, 660 W Fifth St, Winston-Salem, NC, 27105. Tel: 336-703-2665. p. 1724
LaRoux, Christopher, Dir, Warwick Public Library, 600 Sandy Lane, Warwick, RI, 02889-8298. Tel: 401-739-5440, Ext 9760. p. 2043
Larrabee, MaryPat, Dir, Saint Albans Free Library, 11 Maiden Lane, Saint Albans, VT, 05478. Tel: 802-524-1507. p. 2293
Larribeau, Lisa, Acq, United States Court of Appeals for the Ninth Circuit Library, James R Browning Courthouse, 95 Seventh St, San Francisco, CA, 94103. Tel: 415-355-8650. p. 229
Larrier, Larissa, Managing Librn, Brooklyn Public Library, East Flatbush, 9612 Church Ave, Brooklyn, NY, 11212. Tel: 718-922-0927. p. 1503
Larrinaga, Jennifer, Info & Tech Serv Librn, Little Falls Public Library, Eight Warren St, Little Falls, NJ, 07424. Tel: 973-256-2784. p. 1413
Larrington, Jane, Fac Serv & Outreach Librn, Law Ref Librn, University of San Diego, Katherine M & George M Pardee Jr Legal Research Center, 5998 Alcala Park, San Diego, CA, 92110-2492. Tel: 619-260-4752. p. 223
Larrington, Jane, Dir, University of Oregon Libraries, John E Jaqua Law Library, William W Knight Law Ctr, 2nd Flr, 1515 Agate St, Eugene, OR, 97403. Tel: 541-346-0278. p. 1879
Larrondo, Silvia, Access Serv Librn, Benedictine University Library, 5700 College Rd, Lisle, IL, 60532-0900. Tel: 630-829-6050. p. 610
Larrow, Heather, Librn, Great Meadow Correctional Facility Library, 11739 State Rte 22, Comstock, NY, 12821. Tel: 518-639-5516. p. 1521
Larrow, Heather, Sr Librn, Washington Correctional Facility Library, 72 Lock Eleven Lane, Comstock, NY, 12821. Tel: 518-639-4486. p. 1521
Larry, Judy, Dir, Philippi Public Library, 91 S Main St, Philippi, WV, 26416. Tel: 304-457-3495. p. 2412
Larry, Rosalind, Head, Circ, Folger Shakespeare Library, 201 E Capitol St SE, Washington, DC, 20003-1094. Tel: 202-675-0310. p. 366
Larsen, Alison, Ser Mgt, Siena College, 515 Loudon Rd, Loudonville, NY, 12211. Tel: 518-782-6765. p. 1566
Larsen, Amy, Librn, North Central Washington Libraries, Waterville Public Library, 107 W Locust St, Waterville, WA, 98858. Tel: 509-745-8354. p. 2394
Larsen, Andrea, Children's Spec, Brazoria County Library System, Lake Jackson Branch, 250 Circle Way, Lake Jackson, TX, 77566. Tel: 979-415-2590. p. 2135
Larsen, Carole, Br Librn, Dir, Emery County Library System, Orangeville Branch, 125 S Main, Orangeville, UT, 84537. Tel: 435-748-2726. p. 2262
Larsen, Kate, Libr Dir, Tacoma Public Library, 1102 Tacoma Ave S, Tacoma, WA, 98402. Tel: 253-280-2823. p. 2387
Larsen, Kim, Teen Librn, Larchmont Public Library, 121 Larchmont Ave, Larchmont, NY, 10538. Tel: 914-834-2281. p. 1562
Larsen, Mary, Supvr, User Serv, University of Saint Francis, Pope John Paul II Ctr, 2701 Spring St, Rm 102 & 202, Fort Wayne, IN, 46808. Tel: 260-399-7700, Ext 6069. p. 685
Larsen, Raymond, Head, Computer Serv, Rogers Memorial Library, 91 Coopers Farm Rd, Southampton, NY, 11968. Tel: 631-283-0774. p. 1643
Larsen, Siri, Librn, Lincoln County Public Libraries, Eureka Branch, 318 Dewey Ave, Eureka, MT, 59917. Tel: 406-296-2613. p. 1299
Larsen, Sonja, Asst Librn, Fletcher Memorial Library, 257 Main St, Hampton, CT, 06247. Tel: 860-455-1086. p. 316
Larson, Alonna, Lead Libr Tech, Navajo County Library District, 121 W Buffalo, Holbrook, AZ, 86025. Tel: 928-524-4745. p. 63
Larson, Amanda, Open Education Librn, Pennsylvania State University Libraries, Library Learning Services, 216 Pattee Tower, University Park, PA, 16802-1803. Tel: 814-863-3305. p. 2015
Larson, Ann, Asst Dir, Sherman & Ruth Weiss Community Library, 10788 State Hwy 77 W, Hayward, WI, 54843. Tel: 715-634-2161. p. 2441
Larson, Annie, Humanities Librn, College of Saint Benedict, 37 S College Ave, Saint Joseph, MN, 56374. Tel: 320-363-2127. p. 1199
Larson, Bob, Dep Dir, Kandiyohi County Historical Society, 610 NE Hwy 71, Willmar, MN, 56201. Tel: 320-235-1881. p. 1208
Larson, Brittany, Dir, Muskego Public Library, S73 W16663 Janesville Rd, Muskego, WI, 53150. Tel: 262-971-2100. p. 2463
Larson, Christine, Dir, Buckeye Public Library System, 310 N Sixth St, Buckeye, AZ, 85326. Tel: 623-349-6300. p. 57
Larson, Craig, Librn, North Hennepin Community College Library, 7411 85th Ave N, Brooklyn Park, MN, 55445-2298. Tel: 763-424-0733. p. 1167
Larson, Donna, Br Librn, East Central Regional Library, Rush City Public Library, 240 W Fourth St, Rush City, MN, 55069. Tel: 320-358-3948. p. 1168
Larson, Georgeann, Cat, Metadata Specialist, Michigan Technological University, 1400 Townsend Dr, Houghton, MI, 49931-1295. Tel: 906-487-1443. p. 1116
Larson, Inga C, Curator, North Andover Historical Society Library, 153 Academy Rd, North Andover, MA, 01845. Tel: 978-686-4035. p. 1040
Larson, James, Br Mgr, Palm Beach County Library System, Okeechobee Boulevard Branch, 5689 Okeechobee Blvd, West Palm Beach, FL, 33417. Tel: 561-233-1880. p. 454
Larson, Julie, Ch, Humboldt Public Library, 30 Sixth St N, Humboldt, IA, 50548. Tel: 515-332-1925. p. 759
Larson, Kendall, Coll Mgt & Digital Initiatives, Winona State University, 175 W Mark St, Winona, MN, 55987. Tel: 507-457-5367. p. 1209
Larson, Kristine, Libr Dir, Waukee Public Library, 950 S Warrior Lane, Waukee, IA, 50263. Tel: 515-978-7944. p. 789
Larson, Laurie, Human Res Coordr, Addison Public Library, Four Friendship Plaza, Addison, IL, 60101. Tel: 630-458-3308. p. 535
Larson, Lizzy, Br Mgr, Lincoln County Library System, Star Valley Branch, 261 Washington, Afton, WY, 83110. Tel: 307-885-3158. p. 2496
Larson, Mary, Assoc Dean, Spec Coll, Oklahoma State University Libraries, Athletic Ave, 216, Stillwater, OK, 74078. Tel: 405-744-6588. p. 1862
Larson, Pam, Asst Librn, ILL, Chester Public Library, 21 W Main St, Chester, CT, 06412. Tel: 860-526-0018. p. 306
Larson, Peggy, Archivist, Librn, Arizona-Sonora Desert Museum Library, 2021 N Kinney Rd, Tucson, AZ, 85743. Tel: 520-883-1380. p. 81

Larson, Reid, Asst Dir, Cat & Metadata, Scholarly Communications & Res Serv Librn, Hamilton College, 198 College Hill Rd, Clinton, NY, 13323. Tel: 315-859-4480. p. 1519
Larson, Sandy, Dir, Roundup Community Library, 526 Sixth Ave W, Roundup, MT, 59072. Tel: 406-323-1802. p. 1301
Larson, Scott, Librn, Beveridge & Diamond, PC Library, 1900 N St NW, Ste 100, Washington, DC, 20036. Tel: 202-789-6000. p. 361
Larson, Sharon, Circ Serv Supvr, Community Library, 24615 89th St, Salem, WI, 53168. Tel: 262-843-3348. p. 2475
Larson, Shawn, PhD, Curator of Res Serv, The Whale Museum Library, 62 First St N, Friday Harbor, WA, 98250-7973. Tel: 360-378-4710, Ext 31. p. 2364
Larson, Stacie, Libr Dir, Maitland Public Library, 501 S Maitland Ave, Maitland, FL, 32751-5672. Tel: 407-647-7700. p. 419
Larson, Susan, Dir, Milton Public Library, 39 Bombadier Rd, Milton, VT, 05468. Tel: 802-893-4644. p. 2289
Larson, Vaughn, Librn, Utah State University, Ann Carroll Moore Children's Library, 6700 Old Main Hill, Logan, UT, 84322. Tel: 435-797-3093. p. 2265
Larson, Victoria, Dir, Empire State Development Library, 625 Broadway, 8th Flr, Albany, NY, 12245. Tel: 518-292-5100. p. 1482
LaRue, Erica, Libr Asst, Thaddeus Stevens College of Technology, 750 E King St, Lancaster, PA, 17602-3198. Tel: 717-391-3502. p. 1952
LaRue, Jamie, Exec Dir, Garfield County Public Library District, 207 East Ave, Rifle, CO, 81650. Tel: 970-625-4270. p. 294
LaRue, Karen, Librn, Townshend Public Library, 1971 Rte 30, Townshend, VT, 05353. Tel: 802-365-4039. p. 2296
LaRue, Linda, Mgr, Cabell County Public Library, Barboursville Branch, 749 Central Ave, Barboursville, WV, 25504. Tel: 304-736-4621. p. 2404
LaScala, Gina, Ad, Millbury Public Library, 128 Elm St, Millbury, MA, 01527. Tel: 508-865-1181. p. 1035
Lascar, Claudia, Ref Librn, City College of the City University of New York, Science-Engineering, Marshak Bldg, Rm J29, 160 Convent Ave, New York, NY, 10031. Tel: 212-650-6826. p. 1582
Lasco, Judy, Mgr, Geauga County Public Library, Chardon Branch, 110 E Park St, Chardon, OH, 44024. Tel: 440-285-7601. p. 1758
Lasell, Jennifer, Circ & Reserves Supvr, Butte College Library, 3536 Butte Campus Dr, Oroville, CA, 95965. Tel: 530-879-4060. p. 189
Laseman, Jennifer, Head, Teen Serv, Fairfield Public Library, 1080 Old Post Rd, Fairfield, CT, 06824. Tel: 203-256-3155. p. 312
Lash, Anna, Dir, West Routt Library District, 201 E Jefferson Ave, Hayden, CO, 81639. Tel: 970-276-3777. p. 285
Lash, Jeff, Libr Dir & Theol Librn, Cornerstone University, 1001 E Beltline Ave NE, Grand Rapids, MI, 49525. Tel: 616-254-1650, Ext 1451. p. 1110
Lasha, Suzanne, Dir, Canon City Public Library, 516 Macon Ave, Canon City, CO, 81212-3380. Tel: 719-269-9020. p. 269
Lashbrook, Brian, Info Tech, Daviess County Public Library, 2020 Frederica St, Owensboro, KY, 42301. Tel: 270-684-0211. p. 871
Lashbrook, Ian, Digital Serv Mgr, Orland Park Public Library, 14921 Ravinia Ave, Orland Park, IL, 60462. Tel: 708-428-5167. p. 630
Lashbrook, Shannon, Digital Serv Librn, United States Courts Library, Prince Kuhio Federal Bldg & US Courthouse, 300 Ala Moana Blvd C-341, Honolulu, HI, 96850. Tel: 808-541-1797. p. 513
Lasher, Marie A, Librn, Magdalen College of the Liberal Arts, 511 Kearsarge Mountain Rd, Warner, NH, 03278. Tel: 603-456-2656. p. 1383
Lashley, Eric, Exec Dir, Partners Library Action Network, 5806 Mesa Dr, Ste 375, Austin, TX, 78731. Tel: 512-583-0704. p. 2775
Lashley, Pat, Br Mgr, Spencer County Public Library, Parker Branch, 925 N County Rd 900W, Hatfield, IN, 47617. Tel: 812-359-4030. p. 716
Lashway, Colleen, Br Mgr, Hawaii State Public Library System, Hawaii Kai Public Library, 249 Lunalilo Home Rd, Honolulu, HI, 96825. Tel: 808-397-5833. p. 507
Lasiewski, Erik, Libr Supvr, California School for the Deaf Library, 3044 Horace St, Riverside, CA, 92506. Tel: 951-248-7700, Ext 4138. p. 201
Laskaris, Lisa, Head, Ref/IT, Rockaway Township Free Public Library, 61 Mount Hope Rd, Rockaway, NJ, 07866. Tel: 973-627-2344. p. 1440
Lasker, Polly, Ref Librn, Smithsonian Libraries, National Museum of Natural History Library, Tenth St & Constitution Ave NW, 1st Flr, Washington, DC, 20013-0712. Tel: 202-633-1702. p. 375
Laskin, Miriam, Dr, Instruction & Ref Librn, Hostos Community College Library, Shirley J Hinds Allied Health & Science Bldg, 475 Grand Concourse, Rm A308, Bronx, NY, 10451. Tel: 718-518-4207. p. 1499
Laskowski, Cas, Head, Research, Data & Instruction, University of Arizona Libraries, Daniel F Cracchiolo Law Library, James E Rogers College of Law, 1201 E Speedway, Tucson, AZ, 85721. p. 83
Laskowski, Michael, Archivist, The Masonic Library & Museum of Pennsylvania, Masonic Temple, One N Broad St, Philadelphia, PA, 19107-2520. Tel: 215-988-1933. p. 1983
Lasky, Kate, Dir, Josephine Community Library District, 200 NW C St, Grants Pass, OR, 97526-2094. Tel: 541-476-0571. p. 1880
Lasky, Robin, Head, Circ, Free Public Library of Hasbrouck Heights, 320 Boulevard, Hasbrouck Heights, NJ, 07604. Tel: 201-288-0484, 201-288-0488. p. 1407
Lasley, Noah, Univ Archivist, University of Tennessee at Chattanooga Library, 400 Douglas Ave, Dept 6456, Chattanooga, TN, 37403-2598. Tel: 423-425-4501. p. 2092
Lasley, Patricia, Research Coordr, Mount Sinai Hospital Medical Center, California Ave at 15th St, Chicago, IL, 60608. Tel: 773-257-6558. p. 565
Lasnick, Karen, Regional Mgr, Library & Research Services, Bryan Cave Leighton Paisner LLP, 120 Broadway, Ste 300, Santa Monica, CA, 90401-2386. Tel: 310-576-2100. p. 244
Laspee, Laura, Libr Mgr, Northwest Regional Library System, Panama City Beach Public Library, 12500 Hutchison Blvd, Panama City Beach, FL, 32407. Tel: 850-233-5055. p. 435
Lassen, Christie P, Dir, Communications, Partnerships, Howard County Library System, 9411 Frederick Rd, Ellicott City, MD, 21042. Tel: 410-313-7750. p. 965
Lassen, Karen, Br Mgr, Las Vegas-Clark County Library District, Laughlin Library, 2840S Needles Hwy, Laughlin, NV, 89029. Tel: 702-507-4070. p. 1347
Lassiter, Brynne, Libr Dir, Silver Lake Library, 203 Railroad St, Silver Lake, KS, 66539. Tel: 785-582-5141. p. 836
Lassiter, Hope, Dir, Atmore Public Library, 700 E Church St, Atmore, AL, 36502. Tel: 251-368-5234. p. 5
Lassiter, John, Dir, Libr Serv, Georgia Northwestern Technical College, Bldg H, Rm 156 & 148, One Maurice Culberson Dr, Rome, GA, 30161. Tel: 706-295-6845. p. 494
Lassiter, Keith, Libr Dir, Wingate University, 110 Church ST, Wingate, NC, 28174. Tel: 704-233-8089. p. 1724
Lasson-Hull, Lori, Libr Mgr, Marshes of Glynn Libraries, 208 Gloucester St, Brunswick, GA, 31520. Tel: 912-279-3740. p. 468
Lasswell, Kelsey, Libr Dir, Bunker Hill Public Library District, 220 E Warren St, Bunker Hill, IL, 62014. Tel: 618-585-4736. p. 545
Laster, Emma, Ch, Atlanta-Fulton Public Library System, Adamsville-Collier Heights Branch, 3424 Martin Luther King Jr Dr, Atlanta, GA, 30331. Tel: 404-699-4206. p. 460
Lastra, Sarai, Vice Chancellor of Info Serv, Universidad del Turabo, Rd 189 Km 3.3, Gurabo, PR, 00778. Tel: 787-743-7979, Ext 4501. p. 2511
Latalladi, Portia, Br Mgr, Chicago Public Library, Toman, 2708 S Pulaski Rd, Chicago, IL, 60623. Tel: 312-745-1660. p. 557
Latan, Graciela, Info Officer, ILL, Toronto Public Health Library, 277 Victoria St, 6th Flr, Toronto, ON, M5B 1W2, CANADA. Tel: 416-338-7862. p. 2693
Lateef, Tasneem, Br Mgr, Fort Bend County Libraries, Sugar Land Branch, 550 Eldridge Rd, Sugar Land, TX, 77478. Tel: 281-238-2140. p. 2232
Later, Sarah, Dir, Anderson City, Anderson, Stony Creek & Union Townships Public Library, 111 E 12th St, Anderson, IN, 46016-2701. Tel: 765-641-2456. p. 667
Latham, Bethany, Electronic Res Librn, Jacksonville State University Library, 700 Pelham Rd N, Jacksonville, AL, 36265. Tel: 256-782-5758. p. 23
Latham, Katie, Dir, Coll Mgt, Wisconsin Historical Society Library, 816 State St, 2nd Flr, Madison, WI, 53706. Tel: 608-264-6535. p. 2452
Latham, Lana, Dir, San Juan County Public Library, Blanding Branch, 25 W 300 South, Blanding, UT, 84511-3829. Tel: 435-678-2335. p. 2266
Latham, Laurie, Br Mgr, Blackwater Regional Library, Agnes Taylor Gray Branch, 125 Bank St, Waverly, VA, 23890-3235. Tel: 804-834-2192. p. 2313
Latham, Laurie, Br Mgr, Blackwater Regional Library, Troxler Memorial, 100 Wilson Ave, Wakefield, VA, 23888. Tel: 757-899-6500. p. 2313
Latham, Lizzie, Head, Youth Serv, Leonia Public Library, 227 Fort Lee Rd, Leonia, NJ, 07605. Tel: 201-592-5770. p. 1412
Latham, Matthew, Dir, Ramsey Free Public Library, 30 Wyckoff Ave, Ramsey, NJ, 07446. Tel: 201-327-1445. p. 1438
Latham, William, Librn, University of Miami, 1311 Miller Dr, Coral Gables, FL, 33146. Tel: 305-284-2251. p. 390
Lathrop, Ben, Br Mgr, Public Library of Cincinnati & Hamilton County, Hyde Park, 2747 Erie Ave, Cincinnati, OH, 45208. Tel: 513-369-4456. p. 1762
Lathrop, Ben, Mgr, Public Library of Cincinnati & Hamilton County, Information & Reference, South Bldg, 2nd Flr, 800 Vine St, Cincinnati, OH, 45202-2009. Tel: 513-369-6900. p. 1762
Lathrop, Beth, Librn, The Strong Museum, One Manhattan Sq, Rochester, NY, 14607. Tel: 585-263-2700, 585-410-6349. p. 1630
Lathrop, Emily, Circ Assoc, Mid-America Christian University, 3500 SW 119th St, Oklahoma City, OK, 73170-9797. Tel: 405-692-3168. p. 1858
Lathrop, Sue, Dir, Lamar Public Library, 102 E Parmenter St, Lamar, CO, 81052-3239. Tel: 719-336-1293. p. 289
Lathroum, Veronica, Br Mgr, Arundel Anne County Public Library, Mountain Road Library, 4730 Mountain Rd, Pasadena, MD, 21122. Tel: 410-222-6699. p. 950
Latimer, Carlos, Dir, East Cleveland Public Library, 14101 Euclid Ave, East Cleveland, OH, 44112-3891. Tel: 216-541-4128. p. 1783
Latimer, Julie, Chief Exec Officer, Kapuskasing Public Library, 24 Mundy Ave, Kapuskasing, ON, P5N 1P9, CANADA. Tel: 705-335-3363. p. 2648
Latimer, Tracy, Br Mgr, Hawaii State Public Library System, Kihei Public Library, 35 Waimahaihai St, Kihei, HI, 96753. Tel: 808-875-6833. p. 508

Latorraca, Ellen, Ref & Instruction Librn, University of Wisconsin-Whitewater, 750 W Main St, Whitewater, WI, 53190-1790. Tel: 262-472-5525. p. 2488
Latour, Brian, Mgr, Northwest Georgia Regional Library System, Chatsworth-Murray County, 706 Old Dalton Ellijay Rd, Chatsworth, GA, 30705. Tel: 706-695-4200. p. 474
Latour, John, Art Librn, Concordia University Libraries, Faculty of Fine Arts Slide Library, 1395 Rene Levesque Blvd W, Montreal, QC, H3G 2M5, CANADA. Tel: 514-848-2424, Ext 7811. p. 2723
Latour, Terry, Dr, Campus Libr Dir, Pennsylvania Western University - Clarion, 840 Wood St, Clarion, PA, 16214. Tel: 814-393-1931. p. 1922
LaTronica, Starr, Libr Dir, Brooks Memorial Library, 224 Main St, Brattleboro, VT, 05301. Tel: 802-254-5290. p. 2280
Latsis, Dimitrios, Dr, Asst Prof, University of Alabama, 7035 Gorgas Library, Campus Box 870252, Tuscaloosa, AL, 35487-0252. Tel: 205-348-4610. p. 2781
Latta, Leslie, Exec Dir, Provincial Archives of Alberta, Reference Library, 8555 Roper Rd, Edmonton, AB, T6E 5W1, CANADA. Tel: 780-427-1750. p. 2537
Lattanzi, Melissa, Continuing Educ Coordr, Northeast Ohio Regional Library System, 1737 Georgetown Rd, Ste B, Hudson, OH, 44236. Tel: 330-655-0531, Ext 103. p. 2772
Lattinville, Ann, Head, Adult Serv, Scituate Town Library, 85 Branch St, Scituate, MA, 02066. Tel: 781-545-8727. p. 1052
Latto, Steve, Librn, Arizona Department of Corrections - Adult Institutions, 26700 S Hwy 85, Buckeye, AZ, 85326. Tel: 623-386-6160. p. 57
Latulippe, Tina, Cat, Tech Serv, College Merici - Bibliotheque, 755 Grande Allée Ouest, Quebec, QC, G1S 1C1, CANADA. Tel: 418-683-2104, Ext 2249. p. 2730
Laturnus, Tracy, Libr Mgr, Redcliff Public Library, 131 Main St S, Redcliff, AB, T0J 2P0, CANADA. Tel: 403-548-3335. p. 2552
Latzel, Teresa, Librn, Rankin Public Library, Midkiff Public, 12701 N FM 2401, Midkiff, TX, 79755. Tel: 432-535-2311. p. 2230
Lau, Christie, Dir, Carlock Public Library District, 202 E Washington, Carlock, IL, 61725. Tel: 309-376-5651. p. 549
Lau, Kevin, Mgr, Instrul Tech, Harvard Library, Frances Loeb Library, Harvard Graduate School of Design, 48 Quincy St, Gund Hall, Cambridge, MA, 02138. Tel: 617-495-9163. p. 1007
Lau, Tammy, Spec Coll Librn, California State University, Fresno, Henry Madden Library, 5200 N Barton Ave, Mail Stop ML-34, Fresno, CA, 93740-8014. Tel: 559-278-2595. p. 144
Lau, Tracy, ILL, Orlando Health, 1400 S Orange Ave, Orlando, FL, 32806. Tel: 321-841-5454. p. 432
Lauber, Jeanne, Librn, Jessup Correctional Institute, 7803 House of Corrections Rd, Jessup, MD, 20794. Tel: 410-540-6412, 410-799-7610. p. 969
Lauber, Jeremy, Reader Serv Librn, United States Merchant Marine Academy, 300 Steamboat Rd, Kings Point, NY, 11024. Tel: 516-726-5751. p. 1560
Laubner, Nathaniel, Chief Librn, United States Air Force, Wright-Patterson Air Force Base Library FL2300, 88 MSG/SVMG, Bldg 1226, 5435 Hemlock St, Wright-Patterson AFB, OH, 45433-5420. Tel: 937-257-4340, 937-257-4815. p. 1834
Laubner, Nathaniel, Libr Mgr, San Antonio Public Library, Westfall, 6111 Rosedale Ct, San Antonio, TX, 78201. Tel: 210-207-9220. p. 2239
Lauck, Jennifer, Dir, Bloomfield Public Library, 121 S Broadway, Bloomfield, NE, 68718. Tel: 402-373-4588. p. 1308
Laucks, Stacy, Youth Serv Coordr, Fleetwood Area Public Library, 110 W Arch St, Ste 209, Fleetwood, PA, 19522-1301. Tel: 610-944-0146. p. 1933
Laudeman, Crystal, Archivist, Midland County Historical Society, 1801 W St Andrews Rd, Midland, MI, 48640. Tel: 989-631-5930, Ext 1306. p. 1132
Laudenslager, Georgia, Ref & Res Initiative, Pennsylvania College of Technology, 999 Hagan Way, Williamsport, PA, 17701. Tel: 570-327-4523. p. 2023
Lauder, Amy, Coll Develop Mgr, Carson City Library, 900 N Roop St, Carson City, NV, 89701. Tel: 775-283-7599. p. 1343
Lauder, Tracey, Asst Dean, Libr Admin, University of New Hampshire Library, 18 Library Way, Durham, NH, 03824. Tel: 603-862-3041. p. 1361
Lauderdale, Sarah, Head, Ref, Hamilton-Wenham Public Library, 14 Union St, South Hamilton, MA, 01982. Tel: 978-468-5577, Ext 19. p. 1055
Lauer, Anna, Librn, Cuyahoga Community College, Eastern Campus Library, 4250 Richmond Rd, Highland Hills, OH, 44122-6195. Tel: 216-987-2091. p. 1769
Lauer, Heather, Res & Instruction Librn, Marshall University Libraries, One John Marshall Dr, Huntington, WV, 25755-2060. Tel: 304-746-8906. p. 2405
Lauer, Heather, Res & Instruction Librn, Marshall University Libraries, South Charleston Campus Library, 100 Angus E Peyton Dr, South Charleston, WV, 25303-1600. Tel: 304-746-8906. p. 2405
Laughlin, Gregory, Bus Mgr, Goshen Public Library, 601 S Fifth St, Goshen, IN, 46526. Tel: 574-534-3699. p. 687
Laughlin, Gregory K, Dir, Samford University Library, Lucille Stewart Beeson Law Library, 800 Lakeshore Dr, Birmingham, AL, 35229. Tel: 205-726-2714. p. 9
Laughlin, Jean A, Librn, Mifflin County Historical Society Library & Museum, One W Market St, Lewistown, PA, 17044-1746. Tel: 717-242-1022. p. 1955
Laughlin, Kate, Exec Dir, Association for Rural & Small Libraries, PO Box 33731, Seattle, WA, 98133. Tel: 206-453-3579. p. 2776
Laughlin, Marcia, Dir, Barryton Public Library, 198 Northern Ave, Barryton, MI, 49305. Tel: 989-382-5288. p. 1082
Laughlin, Michelle, Br Librn, Preble County District Library, West Alexandria Branch, 16 N Main St, West Alexandria, OH, 45381. Tel: 937-533-4095. p. 1784
Laughlin, Nicole, Operations Supvr, University of Nebraska-Lincoln, Engineering Library, Nebraska Hall, Rm W204, 900 N 16 St, Lincoln, NE, 68588-0516. Tel: 402-472-3411. p. 1323
Laughlin, Nicole, Operations Supvr, University of Nebraska-Lincoln, Geology Library, Bessey Hall, Rm 10, City Campus 0344, Lincoln, NE, 68588-0344. Tel: 402-472-2653. p. 1323
Laughlin, Nicole, Operations Supvr, University of Nebraska-Lincoln, Mathematics Library, 14 Avery Hall, Lincoln, NE, 68588-0129. Tel: 402-472-6919. p. 1323
Laughlin, Patricia, Dir, Hales Corners Library, 5885 S 116th St, Hales Corners, WI, 53130-1707. Tel: 414-529-6150, Ext 20. p. 2440
Laughlin, Riva, Ref Librn, Haynes & Boone LLP, 2323 Victory Ave, Ste 700, Dallas, TX, 75219. Tel: 214-651-5711. p. 2167
Laughlin, Tania, Dir, Crystal City Public Library, 736 Mississippi Ave, Crystal City, MO, 63019-1646. Tel: 636-937-7166. p. 1244
Laughmiller, Sarah, Libr Asst, William Bradford Huie Library of Hartselle, 152 NW Sparkman St, Hartselle, AL, 35640. Tel: 256-773-9880. p. 20
Laughtin-Dunker, Kristin, Chair, Scholarly Communications, Chapman University, One University Dr, Orange, CA, 92866. Tel: 714-532-7756. p. 188
Laukhuf, Valerie, Youth Serv, Putnam County District Library, The Educational Service Ctr, 136 Putnam Pkwy, Ottawa, OH, 45875-1471. Tel: 419-523-3747. p. 1811
Lauko, Nichole, Dir, Millstadt Library District, 115 W Laurel St, Millstadt, IL, 62260. Tel: 618-476-1887. p. 618
Laumas, Lauren, Research & Distance Services Librn, Asbury University, One Macklem Dr, Wilmore, KY, 40390-1198. Tel: 859-858-3511, Ext 2467. p. 878
Laurence, Rebecca, Ch Serv, Chino Valley Public Library, 1020 W Palomino Rd, Chino Valley, AZ, 86323-5500. Tel: 928-636-9115. p. 58
Laurens, Duffy, Asst Librn, Knoxville Public Library, 112 E Main St, Knoxville, PA, 16928. Tel: 814-326-4448. p. 1949
Laurente, Kathy, Cataloger, South Puget Sound Community College Library, 2011 Mottman Rd SW, Olympia, WA, 98512. Tel: 360-596-5271. p. 2373
Laurich, Robert, Actg Chief, Tech Serv, City College of the City University of New York, North Academic Ctr, 160 Convent Ave, New York, NY, 10031. Tel: 212-650-7153. p. 1581
Lauricio, Ariel, ILL, California State University, Bakersfield, 9001 Stockdale Hwy, 60 LIB, Bakersfield, CA, 93311. Tel: 661-664-3189. p. 119
Laurie, Stacey, Br Mgr, Arkansas River Valley Regional Library System, Yell County, 904 Atlanta St, Danville, AR, 72833. Tel: 479-495-2911. p. 93
Laurino, Stephanie, Br Mgr, Monmouth County Library, Colts Neck Branch, One Winthrop Dr, Colts Neck, NJ, 07722. Tel: 732-431-5656. p. 1416
Lauritsen, Aimee, Pub Serv Mgr, Utah State University Eastern Library, 451 E & 400 N, Price, UT, 84501. Tel: 435-613-5646. p. 2269
Lauritzen, Brenda, Ref Librn, County of Carleton Law Library, Ottawa Court House, 2004-161 Elgin St, Ottawa, ON, K2P 2K1, CANADA. Tel: 613-233-7386, Ext 222. p. 2666
Laursen, Henrik, Br Mgr, Palm Beach County Library System, Jupiter Branch, 705 N Military Trail, Jupiter, FL, 33458. Tel: 561-744-2301. p. 454
Laursen, Henrik, Br Mgr, Palm Beach County Library System, Tequesta Branch, 461 Old Dixie Hwy N, Tequesta, FL, 33469. Tel: 561-746-5970. p. 454
Laursen, Janet, Librn, Aurelia Public Library, 232 Main St, Aurelia, IA, 51005. Tel: 712-434-5330. p. 733
Lauseng, Deborah, Regional Head Librn, University of Illinois at Chicago, Library of the Health Sciences, Peoria, One Illinois Dr, Peoria, IL, 61605. Tel: 309-671-8490. p. 570
Laut, Christopher, Dir, Libr Serv, Sullivan & Worcester, LLP, One Post Office Sq, Boston, MA, 02109. Tel: 617-338-2800. p. 1000
Lauth, Evangeline, Dir, Coalfield Public Library, 112 Jerry Jones Rd, Coalfield, TN, 37719. Tel: 865-435-4275. p. 2093
Lautzenheiser, Jennifer, Dir, Middle Georgia Regional Library System, 1180 Washington Ave, Macon, GA, 31201-1790. Tel: 478-744-0850. p. 486
Lauver, Bonnie, Asst Libr Dir, Blackwater Regional Library, 22511 Main St, Courtland, VA, 23837. Tel: 757-653-2821. p. 2313
Lauzar, Kate, Exec Dir, Peninsula Temple Beth El Library, 1700 Alameda de Las Pulgas, San Mateo, CA, 94403. Tel: 650-341-7701. p. 235
Lauzon, Alissa, Head, Youth Serv, Cary Memorial Library, 1874 Massachusetts Ave, Lexington, MA, 02420. Tel: 781-862-6288, Ext 84431. p. 1028
Lauzon-Albert, Angèle, Librn, Bibliotheque Publique de Moonbeam, 53 St-Aubin Ave, Moonbeam, ON, P0L 1V0, CANADA. Tel: 705-367-2462. p. 2660
Lavail, Georgette, Regional Dir, Chaleur Library Region, 113A Roseberry St, Campbellton, NB, E3N 2G6, CANADA. Tel: 506-789-6599. p. 2599

Lavalle, Heather, Br Librn, London Public Library, Sherwood Forest, Sherwood Forest Mall, 1225 Wonderland Rd N, #32, London, ON, N6G 2V9, CANADA. Tel: 519-473-9965. p. 2654

LaValle, Liliana, Digital Learning Librn, University of Wisconsin-Eau Claire, 103 Garfield Ave, Eau Claire, WI, 54701-4932. Tel: 715-836-4897. p. 2433

Lavallee, Alexandra, Head of Libr, Bibliotheque du Cegep Limoilou, 1300 Eighth Ave, Quebec, QC, G1J 5L5, CANADA. Tel: 418-647-6600, Ext 6884. p. 2729

LaVallee, Connie, Children's Serv Coordr, Lebanon Public Library, 101 S Broadway, Lebanon, OH, 45036. Tel: 513-932-2665. p. 1795

Lavallee, Julie, Ref Serv, Norton Rose Fulbright Canada LLP Library, One Place Ville Marie, Ste 2500, Montreal, QC, H3B 1R1, CANADA. Tel: 514-847-4701. p. 2727

Lavallee, Marie-Christine, Chef de Div, Bibliotheques de Montreal, Mordecai-Richler, 5434 Ave du Parc, Montreal, QC, H2V 4G7, CANADA. Tel: 514-248-0488. p. 2720

Lavallée, Marie-Christine, Chef de Div, Bibliotheques de Montreal, Plateau-Mont-Royal, 465 Ave du Mont-Royal E, Montreal, QC, H2J 1W3, CANADA. Tel: 514-248-0488. p. 2720

Lavallee, Steven, Syst Adminr, United States Air Force, 596 Fourth St, Bldg 224, Holloman AFB, NM, 88330-8038. Tel: 575-572-3939. p. 1469

Lavallee-Welch, Catherine, Univ Librn, Bishop's University, 2600 College St, Sherbrooke, QC, J1M 1Z7, CANADA. Tel: 819-822-9600, Ext 2483. p. 2736

LaVanish, Kris, Libr Dir, Milton Public Library, 541 Broadway St, Milton, PA, 17847. Tel: 570-742-7111. p. 1963

LaVanway, Dawn, Libr Dir, Jordan Valley District Library, One Library Lane, East Jordan, MI, 49727. Tel: 231-536-7131. p. 1101

Lavender, Beth, Ref Serv, Ad, Smiths Falls Public Library, 81 Beckwith St N, Smiths Falls, ON, K7A 2B9, CANADA. Tel: 613-283-2911. p. 2678

Lavender, Graham, Assoc Librn, Michener Institute of Education at UHN, 222 Saint Patrick St, 2nd Flr, Toronto, ON, M5T 1V4, CANADA. Tel: 416-596-3123. p. 2690

Lavender, Stacey, Spec Coll Librn, Ohio University Libraries, Mahn Center for Archives & Special Collections, Vernon R Alden Library, 30 Park Pl, Fifth Flr, Athens, OH, 45701-2978. Tel: 740-593-2710. p. 1748

Laver, Tara, Sr Archivist, Nelson-Atkins Museum of Art, Bloch Bldg, 2nd Flr, 4525 Oak St, Kansas City, MO, 64111. Tel: 816-751-1354. p. 1257

Laverdure, Helene, Curator, Dir, Archives, Bibliotheque et Archives Nationales du Quebec, 475 de Maisonneuve E, Montreal, QC, H2L 5C4, CANADA. Tel: 514-873-1101, Ext 6408. p. 2717

Laverdure, Paul, Dir, Libr & Archives, University of Sudbury Library, 935 Ramsey Lake Rd, Sudbury, ON, P3E 2C6, CANADA. Tel: 705-673-5661, Ext 208. p. 2683

Lavergne, Yvonne, Interim Libr Dir, Evangeline Parish Library, 916 W Main St, Ville Platte, LA, 70586. Tel: 337-363-1369. p. 911

Laverty, Lori, Dir, South Hampton Public Library, 3-1 Hilldale Ave, South Hampton, NH, 03827. Tel: 603-394-7319. p. 1381

LaVigna, Ashley, Exec Dir, Koochiching County Historical Museum Library, 214 Sixth Ave, International Falls, MN, 56649. Tel: 218-283-4316. p. 1178

Lavigne, Lucy, Br Head, Chatham-Kent Public Library, Blenheim Branch, 16 George St, Blenheim, ON, N0P 1A0, CANADA. Tel: 519-676-3174. p. 2635

Lavigne, Lucy, Br Head, Chatham-Kent Public Library, Merlin Branch, 13 Aberdeen St, Merlin, ON, N0P 1W0, CANADA. Tel: 519-689-4944. p. 2636

LaVille, Joa, Youth Serv Mgr, Marshalltown Public Library, 105 W Boone St, Marshalltown, IA, 50158-4911. Tel: 641-754-5738. p. 768

Lavin, Lucianne, Dr, Coll, Res Serv, Institute for American Indian Studies, 38 Curtis Rd, Washington, CT, 06793. Tel: 860-868-0518. p. 343

Lavin, Skye, Adult Serv Mgr, Forest Park Public Library, 7555 Jackson Blvd, Forest Park, IL, 60130. Tel: 708-366-7171. p. 588

Lavinghouse, Shapan, Asst Dir, Learning Commons, Glen Oaks Community College Learning Commons, 62249 Shimmel Rd, Centreville, MI, 49032-9719. Tel: 269-294-4372. p. 1090

LaVista, Susan, Libr Dir, Hampton Bays Public Library, 52 Ponquogue Ave, Hampton Bays, NY, 11946. Tel: 631-728-6241. p. 1544

LaVoe-Dohn, Rachael, Chief Librn, Hq, Ocean County Library, 101 Washington St, Toms River, NJ, 08753. Tel: 732-914-5403. p. 1446

LaVoice, Kelly, Dir, Vanderbilt University, Walker Management Library, Owen Graduate School of Management, 401 21st Ave S, Nashville, TN, 37203. Tel: 615-343-4182. p. 2122

Lavoie, Ellen, Head, Children's Servx, Greenfield Public Library, 412 Main St, Greenfield, MA, 01301. Tel: 413-772-1544. p. 1022

Lavoie, Lynn, Librn, Halifax Public Libraries, Alderney Gate Branch, 60 Alderney Dr, Dartmouth, NS, B2Y 4P8, CANADA. Tel: 902-490-5745, 902-490-5748. p. 2617

LaVoie, Michelle, Dir, Olean Public Library, 134 N Second St, Olean, NY, 14760. Tel: 716-372-0200. p. 1611

Lavoie, Murielle, Adminr, Institut Universitaire en Sante Mentale, 2601 rue de la Canardiere, Quebec, QC, G1J 2G3, CANADA. Tel: 418-663-5300. p. 2731

Lavoie, Raphael, Head Librn, Bibliothèque Municipale de Gatineau, Ville de Gatineau, CP 1970 Succ. Hull, Gatineau, QC, J8X 3Y9, CANADA. Tel: 819-243-2345. p. 2712

LaVold, Monica, Youth Serv, River Falls Public Library, 140 Union St, River Falls, WI, 54022. Tel: 715-425-0905, Ext 3484. p. 2474

Lavvorn, Rae, Br Mgr, York County Library, Lake Wylie Public, 185 Blucher Circle, Lake Wylie, SC, 29710. Tel: 803-831-7774. p. 2068

Law, Cindy, Br Mgr, Middle Georgia Regional Library System, Oglethorpe Public Library, 115 Chatham St, Oglethorpe, GA, 31068. Tel: 478-472-7116. p. 487

Law, J W, Head, Circ, Bala Cynwyd Memorial Library, 131 Old Lancaster Rd, Bala Cynwyd, PA, 19004-3037. Tel: 610-664-1196. p. 1908

Law, Krista, Libr Adminr, Lakeland Regional Library, 318 Williams Ave, Killarney, MB, R0K 1G0, CANADA. Tel: 204-523-4949. p. 2587

Law-Tefft, Colleen, Libr Mgr, Sherburne Public Library, Two E State St, Sherburne, NY, 13460. Tel: 607-674-4242. p. 1640

Lawler, Martha, Dir of Coll, Louisiana State University, One University Pl, Shreveport, LA, 71115. Tel: 318-798-4163. p. 907

Lawler, Terry, Br Mgr, Phoenix Public Library, Cholla Library, 10050 Metro Pkwy E, Phoenix, AZ, 85051. p. 72

Lawless, Lisa, Br Librn, Danbury Public Library, 1007 N Main St, Danbury, NC, 27016. Tel: 336-593-2419. p. 1683

Lawless, Lisa, Librn, North Central Washington Libraries, Cashmere Public Library, 300 Woodring St, Cashmere, WA, 98815-1061. Tel: 509-782-3314. p. 2393

Lawley, Rodney, Govt Doc Librn, Soc Sci Librn, Troy University Library, 309 Wallace Hall, Troy, AL, 36082. Tel: 334-670-3198. p. 37

Lawlor, Chrissy, Dir, Olive Free Library Association, 4033 Rte 28A, West Shokan, NY, 12494. Tel: 845-657-2482. p. 1663

Lawrence, Alexis, Ad, Wood Library Association, 134 N Main St, Canandaigua, NY, 14424-1295. Tel: 585-394-1381, Ext 314. p. 1512

Lawrence, Ayla, Libr Asst II, Ivy Tech Community College of Indiana, One Ivy Tech Dr, Logansport, IN, 46947. Tel: 574-753-5101, Ext 2234. p. 703

Lawrence, Betty, Dir, Suwannee River Regional Library, 1848 Ohio Ave S, Live Oak, FL, 32064-4517. Tel: 386-362-2317. p. 419

Lawrence, Cecelia C, Dir, North Platte Public Library, 120 W Fourth St, North Platte, NE, 69101-3993. Tel: 308-535-8036. p. 1327

Lawrence, Clinton, Asst Dir, Operations, Dallas Public Library, 1515 Young St, Dallas, TX, 75201-5415. Tel: 214-670-1400. p. 2165

Lawrence, Dan, Dir, Libr Serv, Community College of Aurora, 16000 E Centretech Pkwy, Aurora, CO, 80011. Tel: 303-360-4736. p. 265

Lawrence, Deirdre E, Principal Librn, Brooklyn Museum, Libraries & Archives, 200 Eastern Pkwy, Brooklyn, NY, 11238. Tel: 718-501-6307. p. 1501

Lawrence, Erin, Dir, Culver-Union Township Public Library, 107 N Main St, Culver, IN, 4651-1595. Tel: 574-842-2941. p. 678

Lawrence, Evonne Kelly, Dir, Learning Commons, Loyola University New Orleans, 6363 Saint Charles Ave, New Orleans, LA, 70118. Tel: 504-864-7111. p. 902

Lawrence, Huston, Librn, East-West University Library, 816 S Michigan Ave, Chicago, IL, 60605. Tel: 312-939-0111, Ext 3502. p. 560

Lawrence, Janna, Dir, University of Iowa Libraries, Hardin Library for the Health Sciences, 600 Newton Rd, Iowa City, IA, 52242. Tel: 319-335-9871. p. 761

Lawrence, John, Asst Dir, Spec Coll, East Carolina University, J Y Joyner Library, E Fifth St, Greenville, NC, 27858-4353. Tel: 252-328-4088. p. 1693

Lawrence, Kathy, Head, Circ Serv, Glocester Libraries, 1137 Putnam Pike, Chepachet, RI, 02814. Tel: 401-568-6077. p. 2030

Lawrence, LaVonna, Librn, Florence Township Public Library, 1350 Hornberger Ave, Roebling, NJ, 08554. Tel: 609-499-0143. p. 1440

Lawrence, Lisa, Librn, Franklin County Library, 100 Main St, Mount Vernon, TX, 75457. Tel: 903-537-4916. p. 2221

Lawrence, Mark, Dir, National Archives & Records Administration, 2313 Red River St, Austin, TX, 78705. Tel: 512-721-0157. p. 2140

Lawrence, Merrin, Librn, Sprague Public Library, 119 W Second St, Sprague, WA, 99032. Tel: 509-257-2662. p. 2385

Lawrence, Michele, Librn, Perquimans County Library, 514 S Church St, Hertford, NC, 27944. Tel: 252-426-5319. p. 1695

Lawrence, Thomas A, Libr Dir, Poughkeepsie Public Library District, 93 Market St, Poughkeepsie, NY, 12601. Tel: 845-485-3445. p. 1623

Lawrence, Troy, Interim Mgr, San Antonio Public Library, McCreless, 1023 Ada St, San Antonio, TX, 78223. Tel: 210-207-9170. p. 2239

Lawrenz, Jessica, Br Mgr, Kansas City, Kansas Public Library, Mr & Mrs F L Schlagle Library, 4051 West Dr, Kansas City, KS, 66109. Tel: 913-295-8250, Ext 2. p. 816

Lawrimore, Erin, University Archivist & Engagement Coord, University of North Carolina at Greensboro, 320 College Ave, Greensboro, NC, 27412-0001. Tel: 336-256-4038. p. 1693

Lawry, Beth, Adult Serv Mgr, Shaler North Hills Library, 1822 Mount Royal Blvd, Glenshaw, PA, 15116. Tel: 412-486-0211. p. 1937

Laws, Emily, Libr Dir, Oscar Grady Public Library, 151 S Main St, Saukville, WI, 53080. Tel: 262-284-6022. p. 2475

Laws, Paige, Dir, East Arkansas Community College, 1700 Newcastle Rd, Forrest City, AR, 72335. Tel: 870-633-4480, Ext 322. p. 95

Lawson, Anne, Br Serv Supvr, Madison County Public Library, Berea Branch, 319 Chestnut St, Berea, KY, 40403. Tel: 859-986-7112. p. 874

Lawson, Connie, Circ Mgr, Demopolis Public Library, 211 E Washington, Demopolis, AL, 36732. Tel: 334-289-1595. p. 14
Lawson, Deb, Libr Dir, Hayes Center Public Library, 407 Troth St, Hayes Center, NE, 69032. Tel: 308-286-3411. p. 1318
Lawson, Debra, Dir, Spencer County Public Library, 168 Taylorsville Rd, Taylorsville, KY, 40071. Tel: 502-477-8137. p. 875
Lawson, Donna, Adult Serv, Barry-Lawrence Regional Library, Cassville Branch, 301 W 17th St, Cassville, MO, 65625-1044. Tel: 417-847-2121. p. 1263
Lawson, Emma, Coordr, Coll Serv, E-Res & Journals, Langara College Library, 100 W 49th Ave, Vancouver, BC, V5Y 2Z6, CANADA. Tel: 604-232-5464. p. 2579
Lawson, Gerry, Mgr, Oral History Language Lab, Audrey & Harry Hawthorn Library & Archives at the UBC Museum of Anthropology, 6393 NW Marine Dr, Vancouver, BC, V6T 1Z2, CANADA. Tel: 604-822-4834. p. 2579
Lawson, Harla, Br Mgr, Delaware County District Library, Ostrander Branch, 75 N Fourth St, Ostrander, OH, 43061. Tel: 740-666-1410. p. 1782
Lawson, Jennifer, Teen Librn, Grandview Heights Public Library, 1685 W First Ave, Columbus, OH, 43212. Tel: 614-486-2951. p. 1773
Lawson, Joseph, Asst Dir, Pub Serv, University of Michigan, Law Library, 801 Monroe St, Ann Arbor, MI, 48109-1210. Tel: 734-763-9452. p. 1080
Lawson, Joseph, Dir, Harris County Robert W Hainsworth Law Library, Congress Plaza, 1019 Congress, 1st Flr, Houston, TX, 77002. Tel: 713-755-5183. p. 2191
Lawson, Keith, Dr, Asst Prof, Dalhousie University, Kenneth C Rowe Management Bldg, Ste 4010, 6100 University Ave, Halifax, NS, B3H 4R2, CANADA. Tel: 902-494-6123. p. 2795
Lawson, Kristen, Actg Dir, Youth Serv Mgr, Roselle Public Library District, 40 S Park St, Roselle, IL, 60172-2020. Tel: 630-529-1641, Ext 221. p. 643
Lawson, Laura, Librn, Mid-Mississippi Regional Library System, Lexington Public, 208 Tchula St, Lexington, MS, 39095-3134. Tel: 662-834-2571. p. 1224
Lawson, Martha, Librn, Bolivar County Library System, Rosedale Public Library, 702 Front St, Rosedale, MS, 38769. Tel: 662-759-6332. p. 1214
Lawson, Melissa E, Coordr, Access Serv, Ref Librn, Utica University, 1600 Burrstone Rd, Utica, NY, 13502-4892. Tel: 315-792-3537. p. 1656
Lawson, Michele B, Actg Dir, Middlesborough-Bell County Public Library, 126 S 20th St, Middlesboro, KY, 40965. Tel: 606-248-4812. p. 869
Lawson, Nicole, Assoc Dean, Academic Support Servs, California State University, Sacramento, 6000 J St, Sacramento, CA, 95819-6039. Tel: 916-278-6708. p. 208
Lawson, Rhea, PhD, Dr, Exec Dir, Houston Public Library, 500 McKinney Ave, Houston, TX, 77002-2534. Tel: 832-393-1313. p. 2195
Lawson, Rose, Acq & Ser, Kenrick-Glennon Seminary, 5200 Glennon Dr, Saint Louis, MO, 63119. Tel: 314-792-6131. p. 1271
Lawson, Steve, Interim Libr Dir, Colorado College, 1021 N Cascade Ave, Colorado Springs, CO, 80903-3252. Tel: 719-389-6662. p. 270
Lawson, Tyler, Librn, CGH Medical Center, 100 E LeFevre Rd, Sterling, IL, 61081-1278. Tel: 815-625-0400. p. 651
Lawton, Catherine, Head, Pub Serv, Memorial University of Newfoundland, Dr C R Barrett Library (Marine Institute), 155 Ridge Rd, St. John's, NL, A1C 5R3, CANADA. Tel: 709-778-0662. p. 2610
Lawton, Kelley, Head Librn, Duke University Libraries, William R Perkins Lilly Library, 1348 Campus Dr, Campus Box 90725, Durham, NC, 27708-0725. Tel: 919-660-5995. p. 1684
Lawton, Kelley, Head, East Campus Libr, Duke University Libraries, 411 Chapel Dr, Durham, NC, 27708. Tel: 919-660-5990. p. 1684
Lawton, LaRoi, Head, Learning Serv, Bronx Community College Library, 2115 University Ave, NL 252A, Bronx, NY, 10453. Tel: 718-289-5348. p. 1497
Lawton, Sherri, Law Librn, Rock Island County Law Library, Rock Island County Courthouse, 3rd Flr, Ste 304, 1317 Third Ave, Rock Island, IL, 61201. Tel: 309-558-3259, 309-786-4451, Ext 3259. p. 641
Lawton, Theresa, Ch, Tekamah Public Library, 204 S 13th St, Tekamah, NE, 68061. Tel: 402-374-2453. p. 1338
Lawver, Denise, Libr Dir, Wahoo Public Library, 637 N Maple St, Wahoo, NE, 68066-1673. Tel: 402-443-3871. p. 1339
Laxminarayan, Ishwar, Exec Dir, Lake Forest Library, 360 E Deerpath Rd, Lake Forest, IL, 60045. Tel: 847-810-4602. p. 606
Laxton, Julie, Human Res Dir, Capital Area District Libraries, 401 S Capitol Ave, Lansing, MI, 48933. Tel: 517-367-6349. p. 1124
Lay, Ashley, Circ Supvr, Saint Charles Parish Library, 160 W Campus Dr, Destrehan, LA, 70047. Tel: 985-764-2366. p. 888
Lay, Christalene, Libr Serv Coordr, Edmonton Public Library, Heritage Valley, 2755 119A St SW, Edmonton, AB, T6W 3R3, CANADA. Tel: 780-496-8338. p. 2536
Lay, Christalene, Libr Serv Coordr, Edmonton Public Library, Whitemud Crossing, 145 Whitemud Crossing Shopping Ctr, 4211 106 St, Edmonton, AB, T6J 6L7, CANADA. Tel: 780-496-8338. p. 2537
Lay, Debra, Exec Dir, Desert Foothills Library, 38443 N School House Rd, Cave Creek, AZ, 85331. Tel: 480-488-2286. p. 57
Lay, Jasmine, Libr Tech, Seneca Nation Libraries, Cattaraugus Branch, Three Thomas Indian School Dr, Irving, NY, 14081-9505. Tel: 716-532-9449. p. 1635
Lay, Jennie, Adult Serv Coordr, Bud Werner Memorial Library, 1289 Lincoln Ave, Steamboat Springs, CO, 80487. Tel: 970-879-0240, Ext 317. p. 295
Lay, Tracy Elizabeth, Lead Librn, United States Army, Dugway Proving Ground, TEDT-DPW-DMA, MS No 4, Dugway, UT, 84022-5004. Tel: 435-831-5009. p. 2263
Layden, Diona, Spec Coll Librn, Fisk University, 1000 17th Ave N, Nashville, TN, 37208-3051. Tel: 615-329-8730. p. 2118
Layer, Kathy, Cataloging & Metadata Librn, Western New England University, 1215 Wilbraham Rd, Springfield, MA, 01119-2689. Tel: 413-782-1309. p. 1057
Layne, Meredith, Libr Dir, Odell Public Library, 307 S Madison St, Morrison, IL, 61270. Tel: 815-772-7323. p. 619
Laytham, Jenne, Asst Dir, Basehor Community Library District 2, 1400 158th St, Basehor, KS, 66007. Tel: 913-724-2828. p. 798
Laytham, Melissa, Asst Dir, Colls & Access Services, Loyola-Notre Dame Library, Inc, 200 Winston Ave, Baltimore, MD, 21212. Tel: 410-617-6801. p. 954
Layton, Elizabeth, Access Serv Librn, Nicholls State University, 906 E First St, Thibodaux, LA, 70310. Tel: 985-448-4646. p. 911
Layton, Karina, Librn, Chinook Regional Library, Central Butte Branch, 271 Butte St, Central Butte, SK, S0H 0T0, CANADA. Tel: 306-796-4660. p. 2752
Layton, Meredith, Tech Serv, Tech Serv Librn, Webmaster, Helen Hall Library, 100 W Walker, League City, TX, 77573-3899. Tel: 281-554-1127. p. 2210
Lazar, Allyson, Coll, Res, Sr Mgr, The Mary Baker Eddy Library, Research & Reference Services, 210 Massachusetts Ave, P04-10, Boston, MA, 02115-3017. Tel: 617-450-7000. p. 994
Lazarenko, Rebecca, Pub Serv Librn, Thorold Public Library, 14 Ormond St N, Thorold, ON, L2V 1Y8, CANADA. Tel: 905-227-2581. p. 2684
Lazaris, Christine, Libr Dir, Geneva Public Library District, 127 James St, Geneva, IL, 60134. Tel: 630-232-0780, Ext 302. p. 592
Lazarri, Susan, Br Mgr, Newark Public Library, Van Buren, 140 Van Buren St, Newark, NJ, 07105. Tel: 973-733-7750. p. 1428
Lazidis, Jennifer, Librn, Elmwood Park Public Library, 210 Lee St, Elmwood Park, NJ, 07407. Tel: 201-796-8888. p. 1401
Lazzarino, Christy, Ch, Free Library of Northampton Township, 25 Upper Holland Rd, Richboro, PA, 18954-1514. Tel: 215-357-3050. p. 2001
Lazzaro, Althea, Ref Librn, Seattle Central College, 1701 Broadway, BE Rm 2101, Seattle, WA, 98122. Tel: 206-934-4071. p. 2378
Lazzerini, Edward J, Dir, Indiana University, Sinor Research Institute for Inner Asian Studies, Indiana University, Goodbody Hall 144, 1011 E Third St, Bloomington, IN, 47405-7005. Tel: 812-855-1605, 812-855-9510. p. 670
Le, Avery, Dir, Gwinnett County Judicial Circuit, Justice & Adminisration Ctr, Lower Level, 75 Langley Dr, Lawrenceville, GA, 30046. Tel: 770-822-8571. p. 485
Le, Binh, Asst Dir, Info Syst, County of Los Angeles Public Library, 7400 E Imperial Hwy, Downey, CA, 90242-3375. Tel: 562-940-8418. p. 134
Le, Binh P, Ref & Instruction Librn, Pennsylvania State University, 1600 Woodland Rd, Abington, PA, 19001. Tel: 215-881-7426. p. 1903
Le Blanc, Anne, Coordr, Bibliothèque Laurent-Michel-Vacher, 9155 rue St-Hubert, Montreal, QC, H2M 1Y8, CANADA. Tel: 514-389-5921, Ext 2240. p. 2717
Le, Button, Circ Supvr, University of Washington Libraries, Tateuchi East Asia Library, 322 Gowen Hall, Box 353527, Seattle, WA, 98195-3527. Tel: 206-543-4490. p. 2382
Le Cavalier-Parant, Marjorie, Actg Chief, Bibliotheque de Dorval, 1401 Chemin du Bord du Lac, Dorval, QC, H9S 2E5, CANADA. Tel: 514-633-4170. p. 2711
Le Faive, Rosemary, Digital Infrastructure, Discovery Librn, University of Prince Edward Island, 550 University Ave, Charlottetown, PE, C1A 4P3, CANADA. Tel: 902-566-0343. p. 2707
Le, Julie, Library Contact, Metropolitan Museum of Art, The Irene Lewisohn Costume Reference Library, Costume Institute, 1000 Fifth Ave, New York, NY, 10028. Tel: 212-396-5233, 212-650-2723. p. 1591
Le, Loan, Tech Serv, United States District Court, Phillip Burton Federal Bldg, 450 Golden Gate Ave, San Francisco, CA, 94102. Tel: 415-436-8130. p. 229
Le, Marianne, Coll Develop, Pub Serv, Everett Community College, 2000 Tower St, Everett, WA, 98201-1352. Tel: 425-388-9351. p. 2364
Lê, Mê-Linh, Actg Head, Health Sci Libr, University of Manitoba Libraries, Neil John Maclean Health Sciences Library, Brodie Center Atrium, Mezzanine Level, 2nd Flr, 727 McDermot Ave, Winnipeg, MB, R3E 3P5, CANADA. Tel: 204-228-6775. p. 2595
Le, Megan, Libr Mgr, University of Southern Mississippi-Gulf Coast Research Laboratory, 703 E Beach Dr, Ocean Springs, MS, 39564. Tel: 228-872-4213, 228-872-4253. p. 1228
Le, Richard, Br Mgr, San Francisco Public Library, North Beach Branch Library, 2000 Mason St, San Francisco, CA, 94133-2337. Tel: 415-355-5626. p. 228
Le, Thuy, Acq, Hopital Hotel-Dieu du CHUM, 3840 rue St-Urbain, Montreal, QC, H2W 1T8, CANADA. Tel: 514-890-8000, Ext 35867. p. 2724
Lea, Jason, Commun Engagement Mgr, Mentor Public Library, 8215 Mentor Ave, Mentor, OH, 44060. Tel: 440-255-8811. p. 1802

Leach, Barbara, Coordr, Info Tech, Cumberland County Library System, 400 Bent Creek Blvd, Ste 150, Mechanicsburg, PA, 17050. Tel: 717-240-6175. p. 1960
Leach, Brian, Coordr, Tech Support, Harvard Library, Godfrey Lowell Cabot Science Library, Science Ctr, One Oxford St, Cambridge, MA, 02138. Tel: 617-495-5355. p. 1005
Leach, Bruce A, Head, Sci Libr, Ohio State University LIBRARIES, Biological Sciences & Pharmacy, 102 Riffe Bldg, 496 W 12th Ave, Columbus, OH, 43210-1214. Tel: 614-292-1744. p. 1775
Leach, Cheri, Dir, Chappell Memorial Library & Art Gallery, 289 Babcock Ave, Chappell, NE, 69129. Tel: 308-874-2626. p. 1310
Leach, Cynthia J, Pub Serv Librn, Rowan County Public Library, 175 Beacon Hill Dr, Morehead, KY, 40351-6031. Tel: 606-784-7137. p. 869
Leach, Dakota, Br Mgr, Autauga Prattville Public Library, Billingsley Public, 2021 Office St, Billingsley, AL, 36006. Tel: 205-755-9809. p. 33
Leach, Deanna, Br Mgr, Saint Thomas Library, 30 School House Rd, Saint Thomas, PA, 17252-9650. Tel: 717-369-4716. p. 2003
Leach, Erin, Cat, University of Georgia Libraries, Special Collections, Richard B Russell Bldg, 300 S Hull St, Athens, GA, 30602. Tel: 706-542-7123. p. 460
Leach, Gillian, Exec Dir, Pioneer Historical Society of Bedford County Inc, 6441 Lincoln Hwy, Bedford, PA, 15522. Tel: 814-623-2011. p. 1909
Leach, Guy, Librn III, University of Georgia Libraries, Music, School of Music, Rm 250, 250 River Rd, Athens, GA, 30602. Tel: 706-542-2712. p. 460
Leach, Laura, Med Librn, Charlotte AHEC Library, Medical Education Bldg, 1000 Blythe Blvd, Charlotte, NC, 28203-5812. Tel: 704-355-3129. p. 1679
Leach, Leslie Corey, Mgr, Skadden, Arps, Slate, Meagher & Flom LLP, One Rodney Sq, 7th Flr, 920 N King St, Wilmington, DE, 19801. Tel: 302-651-3224. p. 358
Leach, Martha, Librn, Halifax County Library, Scotland Neck Memorial, 1600 Main St, Scotland Neck, NC, 27874-1438. Tel: 252-826-5578. p. 1694
Leach, Michael, Assoc Dir of Research, Instruction & Collection Resources, Harvard Library, Godfrey Lowell Cabot Science Library, Science Ctr, One Oxford St, Cambridge, MA, 02138. Tel: 617-495-5355. p. 1005
Leach, Nile, Admin Coordr, Naropa University Library, 2130 Arapahoe Ave, Boulder, CO, 80302. Tel: 303-546-3507. p. 267
Leach, Sandy, Libr Mgr, Cadillac-Wexford Public Library, Tustin Branch, 310 S Neilson St, Tustin, MI, 49688. Tel: 231-829-3012. p. 1088
Leach, Sandy, Assoc Dir, Lenoir-Rhyne University, 4201 N Main St, Columbia, SC, 29203. Tel: 803-461-3220, 803-461-3269. p. 2053
Leacock, Kathryn H, Dir of Coll, Buffalo Museum of Science, 1020 Humboldt Pkwy, Buffalo, NY, 14211. Tel: 716-896-5200. p. 1508
Leader, Kathy M, Admin Mgr, Lancaster Public Library, 125 N Duke St, Lancaster, PA, 17602. Tel: 717-394-2651, Ext 102. p. 1951
Leady, Sara, Head, ILL, Head, Per, Anderson County Library, 300 N McDuffie St, Anderson, SC, 29621-5643. Tel: 864-260-4500. p. 2046
Leaf, Brian, Exec Dir, National Network of Libraries of Medicine Region 3, UNT Health Sci Ctr, Gibson D Lewis Health Sci Libr, 3500 Camp Bowie Blvd, Rm 110, Fort Worth, TX, 76107. Tel: 817-735-2169. p. 2775
Leahy, Beth, Writing Ctr Dir, University of Tennessee at Chattanooga Library, 400 Douglas Ave, Dept 6456, Chattanooga, TN, 37403-2598. Tel: 423-425-4501. p. 2092
Leahy, Germaine, Head, Ref, George Washington University, Jacob Burns Law Library, 716 20th St NW, Washington, DC, 20052. Tel: 202-994-8551. p. 367
Leal, Adria, Librn, Miami Dade College, Wolfson Campus Library, 300 NE Second Ave, Miami, FL, 33132. Tel: 305-237-3449. p. 422
Leal, Mary, Dir, Libr Serv, Coalinga-Huron Library District, 305 N Fourth St, Coalinga, CA, 93210. Tel: 559-935-1676. p. 131
Leali, Sharon, Youth Serv, Jackson City Library, 21 Broadway St, Jackson, OH, 45640-1695. Tel: 740-286-4111. p. 1791
Leaman, Amy, Libr Dir, Rudd Public Library, 308 Chickasaw St, Rudd, IA, 50471. Tel: 641-395-2385. p. 780
Leanio, Dan, Circ Coordr, Minneapolis College of Art & Design Library, 2501 Stevens Ave, Minneapolis, MN, 55404. Tel: 612-874-3791. p. 1184
Leap, Steven, Librn, United States Army, Moncrief Army Hospital Medical Library, 4500 Stuart St, Fort Jackson, SC, 29207-5720. Tel: 803-751-2149. p. 2059
Leaper, Shannon, Dir, Libr Serv, Northwestern Oklahoma State University, 709 Oklahoma Blvd, Alva, OK, 73717. Tel: 580-327-8574. p. 1840
Lear, Bernadette A, Ref Librn, Pennsylvania State University-Harrisburg Library, 351 Olmsted Dr, Middletown, PA, 17057-4850. Tel: 717-948-6360. p. 1963
Lear, Bryon, Libr Dir, Moline Public Library, 3210 41st St, Moline, IL, 61265. Tel: 309-524-2442. p. 618
Lear, Jayne, Exec Dir, Libraries of Foster, 184 Howard Hill Rd, Foster, RI, 02825. Tel: 401-397-4801. p. 2032
Lear, Jayne, Exec Dir, Libraries of Foster, Tyler Free Library, 81A Moosup Valley Rd, Foster, RI, 02825. Tel: 401-397-7930. p. 2032
Lear, Michael, Rare Bk Librn, State Library of Pennsylvania, Forum Bldg, 607 South Dr, Harrisburg, PA, 17120. Tel: 717-783-5982. p. 1941
Lear, Paul, Mgr, New York State Office of Parks, Recreation & Historic Preservation, One E Fourth St, Oswego, NY, 13126. Tel: 315-343-4711. p. 1613
Learned, Elizabeth Peck, Dean, Univ Libr Serv, Roger Williams University Library, One Old Ferry Rd, Bristol, RI, 02809. Tel: 401-254-3625. p. 2029
Leary, Brandee, Dir, Winslow Public Library, 420 W Gilmore St, Winslow, AZ, 86047. Tel: 928-289-4982. p. 85
Leary, Deborah, Head, Circ, Closter Public Library, 280 High St, Closter, NJ, 07624-1898. Tel: 201-768-4197. p. 1397
Leas, Cathy, Dir, Montpelier Harrison Township Public Library, 301 S Main St, Montpelier, IN, 47359. Tel: 765-728-5969. p. 707
Leathe, Agnes, Head Law Librn, Massachusetts Trial Court, 649 High St, Ste 210, Dedham, MA, 02026-1831. Tel: 781-329-1401, Ext 2. p. 1014
Leather, Anne, Mgr, Libr Serv, Jones Day, 2727 N Harwood St, Dallas, TX, 75201-1515. Tel: 214-969-4823. p. 2167
Leatherman, Carrie, Soc Sci Librn, Western Michigan University, 1903 W Michigan Ave, WMU Mail Stop 5353, Kalamazoo, MI, 49008-5353. Tel: 269-387-5142. p. 1122
Leathers, Emilee, ILL Asst, Saint Leo University, 33701 State Rd 52, Saint Leo, FL, 33574. Tel: 352-588-8328. p. 441
Leathorn, Jeanette, Dir, Ogemaw District Library, 107 W Main St, Rose City, MI, 48654. Tel: 989-685-3300. p. 1146
Leathorn, Jeanette, Dir, Ogemaw District Library, Ogemaw East, 200 Washington, Prescott, MI, 48756. Tel: 989-873-5807. p. 1146
Leavens, Dorothy, Ch, Greene Public Library, 231 W Traer St, Greene, IA, 50636-9406. Tel: 641-816-5642. p. 756
Leaver, Elizabeth, Circ Asst, Maynard Public Library, 77 Nason St, Maynard, MA, 01754-2316. Tel: 978-897-1010. p. 1033
Leavitt, Carolynn, Br Assoc, Las Vegas-Clark County Library District, Bunkerville Library, Ten W Virgin St, Bunkerville, NV, 89007. Tel: 702-346-5238. p. 1346
Leavitt, John, Librn, Washington County Community College Library, One College Dr, Calais, ME, 04619. Tel: 207-454-1051. p. 920
Leavy, Claire, Dir, Lee County Public Library, 245 Walnut Ave S, Leesburg, GA, 31763-4367. Tel: 229-759-2369. p. 485
Leavy, Katrine, Librn, Allen University, 1530 Harden St, Columbia, SC, 29204. Tel: 803-376-5719. p. 2053
LeBaron, Tonya, Br Mgr, Winn Parish Library, Dodson Branch, 206 E Gresham, Dodson, LA, 71422. Tel: 318-628-2821. p. 912
Lebeau, Nicole, Fac Mgr, Martin County Library System, 2351 SE Monterey Rd, Stuart, FL, 34996. Tel: 772-221-1404. p. 444
Lebensart, Lynlee, Br Mgr, Palm Beach County Library System, Glades Road Branch, 20701 95th Ave S, Boca Raton, FL, 33434. Tel: 561-482-4554. p. 454
Lebish, Alan, Dir, Facilities, Kennesaw State University Library System, 385 Cobb Ave NW, MD 1701, Kennesaw, GA, 30144. Tel: 470-578-6192. p. 483
Lebish, Alan, Libr Dir, Kennesaw State University Library System, Lawrence V Johnson Library, 1100 S Marietta Pkwy, Marietta, GA, 30060-2896. Tel: 678-470-578-7276. p. 483
Lebita, Edzen, Tech Asst, Lenhardt Library of the Chicago Botanic Garden, 1000 Lake Cook Rd, Glencoe, IL, 60022. Tel: 847-835-8201. p. 593
LeBlanc, Allen, Coord, Research & Instruction, Louisiana State University Libraries, 295 Middleton Library, Baton Rouge, LA, 70803. Tel: 225-578-2738. p. 884
LeBlanc, Angelle, Br Mgr, Acadia Parish Library, Estherwood Branch, 116 N LeBlanc St, Estherwood, LA, 70534. Tel: 337-785-1090. p. 888
LeBlanc, Anne, Library Contact, Eastern Counties Regional Library, Coady & Tompkins Memorial, 7972 Cabot Trail Rd, Margaree Forks, NS, B0E 2A0, CANADA. Tel: 902-248-2821. p. 2621
LeBlanc, Claire, Ref Serv, Ad, Oldsmar Public Library, 400 St Petersburg Dr E, Oldsmar, FL, 34677. Tel: 813-749-1178. p. 430
LeBlanc, Eileen, Accounts Mgr, Grafton Public Library, 35 Grafton Common, Grafton, MA, 01519. Tel: 508-839-4649, Ext 1109. p. 1021
LeBlanc, Francois J, Documentation Tech, Universite de Moncton, Centre d'études Acadiennes, Champlain Library (MCH), 415 ave de l'Universite, Moncton, NB, E1A 3E9, CANADA. Tel: 506-858-4085. p. 2604
Leblanc, Gabrielle, Libr Mgr, Albert-Westmorland-Kent Regional Library, Shediac Public, 290 Main St, Unit 100, Shediac, NB, E4P 2E3, CANADA. Tel: 506-532-7014. p. 2603
LeBlanc, Helene, Govt Info Librn, Political Science Librarian, Wilfrid Laurier University Library, 75 University Ave W, Waterloo, ON, N2L 3C5, CANADA. Tel: 519-884-0710, Ext 3743. p. 2703
LeBlanc, Jenny, Asst Librn, Mackenzie Public Library, 400 Skeena Dr, Mackenzie, BC, V0J 2C0, CANADA. Tel: 250-997-6343. p. 2569
LeBlanc, Jeremie, Chief Librn, Saint Paul University Library, Guides Hall, 1st Flr, 223 Main St, Ottawa, ON, K1S 1C4, CANADA. Tel: 613-236-1393, Ext 2220. p. 2670
Leblanc, Josh, Ch, Wallingford Public Library, 200 N Main St, Wallingford, CT, 06492. Tel: 203-284-6436. p. 343
LeBlanc, Katie, Customer Serv Mgr, Clinton-Macomb Public Library, 40900 Romeo Plank Rd, Clinton Township, MI, 48038-2955. Tel: 586-226-5024. p. 1092
LeBlanc, Lee, Dir, Libr Serv, Dir, Technology, San Antonio College, 1819 N Main Ave, San Antonio, TX, 78212. Tel: 210-486-0554. p. 2238

LeBlanc, Linda, Instruction Librn, Fitchburg State University, 160 Pearl St, Fitchburg, MA, 01420. Tel: 978-665-3062. p. 1019

LeBlanc, Michele, Librn, Universite de Moncton, Bibliotheque de droit Michel-Bastarche, Pavillon Adrein-J Cormier (MAC), 409 ave de l'Universite, Moncton, NB, E1A 3E9, CANADA. Tel: 506-858-4776. p. 2604

LeBlanc, Norma, Chief Exec Officer, Librn, Thessalon Public Library, 187 Main St, Thessalon, ON, P0R 1L0, CANADA. Tel: 705-842-2306. p. 2684

LeBlanc, Patrice, Br Supvr, Vermilion Parish Library, Erath Branch, 111 W Edwards St, Erath, LA, 70533-4027. Tel: 337-937-5628. p. 879

LeBlanc, Trish, Campus Librn, Nova Scotia Community College, Annapolis Valley - Lawrencetown Campus Library, 50 Elliot Rd, RR 1, Lawrencetown, NS, B0S 1M0, CANADA. Tel: 902-584-2102. p. 2619

LeBlanc, Zoe, Asst Prof, University of Illinois at Urbana-Champaign, Library & Information Science Bldg, 501 E Daniel St, Champaign, IL, 61820-6211. Tel: 217-333-3280. p. 2784

Lebo, Barb, Ch, Thorntown Public Library, 124 N Market St, Thorntown, IN, 46071-1144. Tel: 765-436-7348. p. 721

Leboeuf, Becky, Youth Serv Librn, Delta Township District Library, 5130 Davenport Dr, Lansing, MI, 48917-2040. Tel: 517-321-4014. p. 1124

LeBoeuf, Magan, Br Mgr, Terrebonne Parish Library, Bayou Dularge, 837 Bayou Dularge Rd, Houma, LA, 70363. Tel: 985-851-1752. p. 891

LeBoeuf, Mary Cosper, Dir, Terrebonne Parish Library, 151 Library Dr, Houma, LA, 70360. Tel: 985-876-5861. p. 891

Lebron, Gretchen, Libr Spec Supvr, Paradise Valley Community College, 18401 N 32nd St, Phoenix, AZ, 85032-1200. Tel: 602-787-7207. p. 71

Lebron, Stephanie, Br Mgr, Ozark Regional Library, Viburnum Branch, City Hall Missouri Ave, Viburnum, MO, 65566. Tel: 573-244-5986. p. 1251

Leca, Benedict, PhD, Exec Dir, Redwood Library & Athenaeum, 50 Bellevue Ave, Newport, RI, 02840. Tel: 401-847-0292. p. 2035

Lecavalier, Jessica, Chef de Section, Bibliotheques de Montreal, Langelier, 6473 rue Sherbrooke Est, Montreal, QC, H1N 1C5, CANADA. Tel: 514-872-1529. p. 2719

Lechan, Arianna, Asst Prof of Practice, Simmons University, 300 The Fenway, Boston, MA, 02115. Tel: 617-521-2800. p. 2786

Lechene, Nancy, Libr Dir, Carrolltown Public Library, 140 E Carroll St, Carrolltown, PA, 15722. Tel: 814-344-6300. p. 1919

Leck, Karen, Dir, Las Animas - Bent County Public Library, 306 Fifth St, Las Animas, CO, 81054. Tel: 719-456-0111. p. 289

Leckie, Sarah, Archivist, Spec Coll Librn, Presbyterian College, 211 E Maple St, Clinton, SC, 29325. Tel: 864-833-8525. p. 2052

LeClair, Alex, Mr, Dir, Lodi Woman's Club Public Library, 130 Lodi St, Lodi, WI, 53555. Tel: 608-592-4130. p. 2448

LeClair, JoAnne, Per, Herkimer College Library, 100 Reservoir Rd, Herkimer, NY, 13350. Tel: 315-866-0300, Ext 8335. p. 1546

LeClair, Susan, Dir, Elkins Public Library, Nine Center Rd, Canterbury, NH, 03224. Tel: 603-783-4386. p. 1356

Leclerc, Andréanne, Chef de Div, Bibliotheques de Montreal, Le Prevost, 7355 Ave Christophe-Colomb, Montreal, QC, H2R 2S5, CANADA. Tel: 514-868-3444. p. 2719

Leclerc, Manon, Coordr, Institut de la Statistique du Quebec, 200 Chemin Ste Foy, 3e etage, Quebec, QC, G1R 5T4, CANADA. Tel: 418-691-2401. p. 2731

LeCompte, Rachel, Ref Supvr, Terrebonne Parish Library, 151 Library Dr, Houma, LA, 70360. Tel: 985-876-5861. p. 891

Lecoq, Sophie, Chef de Section, Bibliotheques de Montreal, Pierrefonds, 13555 Blvd Pierrefonds, Pierrefonds, QC, H9A 1A6, CANADA. Tel: 514-295-2540. p. 2720

Lecoq, Sophie, Chef de Section, Bibliotheques de Montreal, William G Boll Library, 110 rue Cartier, Roxboro, QC, H8Y 1G8, CANADA. Tel: 514-295-2540. p. 2721

Lecoq, Sophie, Asst Dir, Chambre des Notaires du Quebec, 1801 Ave McGill College, Bur 600, Montreal, QC, H3A 0A7, CANADA. Tel: 514-879-1793, Ext 5043. p. 2722

Ledbetter, Janna, Tech, Shackelford County Library, 402 N Second St, Albany, TX, 76430. Tel: 325-762-2672. p. 2132

Ledbetter, Krista, Dir, Morgan County Public Library, 110 S Jefferson St, Martinsville, IN, 46151. Tel: 765-342-3451. p. 705

Ledbetter, Terri Beth, Acq, Ithaca College Library, 953 Danby Rd, Ithaca, NY, 14850-7060. Tel: 607-274-3206. p. 1553

Ledden, Stacie, Dir, Strategic Initiatives, Anythink Libraries, 5877 E 120th Ave, Thornton, CO, 80602. Tel: 303-288-2001. p. 296

Leddy, Colleen, Dir, Stair Public Library, 228 W Main St, Morenci, MI, 49256-1421. Tel: 517-458-6510. p. 1134

LeDee, Mikel, Music Resources Supervisor, Louisiana State University Libraries, Carter Music Resources Center, 295 Middleton Library, Rm 202, Baton Rouge, LA, 70803-3300. Tel: 225-578-4674. p. 884

Ledermann, Molly, Librn, Washtenaw Community College, 4800 E Huron River Dr, Ann Arbor, MI, 48105-4800. Tel: 734-973-3313. p. 1081

Ledford, Anne, Ch Serv, Teen Serv, Boulder Public Library, 1001 Arapahoe Rd, Boulder, CO, 80302. Tel: 303-441-3100. p. 266

Ledford, Barbara, Asst Br Mgr, Louisville Free Public Library, Crescent Hill, 2762 Frankfort Ave, Louisville, KY, 40206. Tel: 502-574-1793. p. 865

Ledford, Brandie, Dir, Crittenden County Public Library, 204 W Carlisle St, Marion, KY, 42064-1727. Tel: 270-965-3354. p. 868

Ledford, Darlene, Br Librn, Carson County Public Library, Skellytown Branch, 500 Chamberlain, Skellytown, TX, 79080. Tel: 806-848-2551. p. 2225

Ledford, Lesa, Adult Serv, Estill County Public Library, 246 Main St, Irvine, KY, 40336-1026. Tel: 606-723-3030. p. 860

Ledgerwood, Georgeanna, Med Librn, Krohn Memorial Library, Fourth & Walnut St, Lebanon, PA, 17042. Tel: 717-270-7826. p. 1953

Ledin, Marcia, Tech Serv Mgr, East Central Regional Library, 111 Dellwood St, Cambridge, MN, 55008-1588. Tel: 763-689-7390. p. 1167

Ledingham, Lori, Pub Serv Coordr, Meaford Public Library, 11 Sykes St N, Meaford, ON, N4L 1V6, CANADA. Tel: 519-538-3500. p. 2657

Ledley, MacKenzie Inez, Dir, Pulaski County Public Library, 121 S Riverside Dr, Winamac, IN, 46996-1596. Tel: 574-946-3432. p. 727

LeDonne, Anna, Coordr, Acq, Coordr, Tech Serv, Murrysville Community Library, 4130 Sardis Rd, Murrysville, PA, 15668. Tel: 724-327-1102. p. 1967

Ledvina, Holly, Syst Librn, College of Lake County, 19351 W Washington St, Grayslake, IL, 60030. Tel: 847-543-2071. p. 595

Ledwith, Lisa, Asst Law Librn, Commonwealth of Massachusetts - Trial Court, 72 Belmont St, Brockton, MA, 02301. Tel: 508-586-7110. p. 1002

Lee, Alex, Acq, Cat/Circ, IT Supvr, The Ferguson Library, One Public Library Plaza, Stamford, CT, 06904. Tel: 203-351-8260. p. 338

Lee, Amy, Br Mgr, Brandon Public Library, 1475 W Government St, Brandon, MS, 39042. Tel: 601-825-2672. p. 1212

Lee, Angela, Health Sci Librn, Pacific University Libraries, 2043 College Way, Forest Grove, OR, 97116. Tel: 503-352-7208. p. 1880

Lee, Angela, Health Sci Librn, Pacific University Libraries, Hillsboro Campus, 222 SE Eighth Ave, Hillsboro, OR, 97123. Tel: 503-352-7331. p. 1880

Lee, Arnescia, Circ Mgr, Mid Arkansas Regional Library, 202 E Third St, Malvern, AR, 72104. Tel: 501-332-5441. p. 103

Lee, Audrey, Br Mgr, Washington County Library System, Leland Library, 107 N Broad St, Leland, MS, 38756. Tel: 601-686-7353. p. 1217

Lee, Becky, Br Supvr, Greater Victoria Public Library, Nellie McClung Branch, 3950 Cedar Hill Rd, Victoria, BC, V8P 3Z9, CANADA. Tel: 250-940-4875, Ext 824. p. 2583

Lee, Bertus, Law Librn, United States Nuclear Regulatory Commission, Law Library, 11555 Rockville Pike, Rockville, MD, 20852. Tel: 301-415-1526. p. 975

Lee, Betsy, Dir, Bedford Historical Society Library, 30 S Park St, Bedford, OH, 44146-3635. Tel: 440-232-0796. p. 1749

Lee, Carla, Dep Librn, University of Virginia, Charles L Brown Science & Engineering Library, Clark Hall, Charlottesville, VA, 22903-3188. Tel: 434-924-7209. p. 2310

Lee, Carla H, Dep Dir, University of Virginia, 160 McCormick Rd, Charlottesville, VA, 22903. Tel: 434-924-3021. p. 2310

Lee, Carla H, Dir, University of Virginia, Astronomy, Charles L Brown Sci & Eng Library, 264 Astronomy Bldg, 530 McCormick Rd, Charlottesville, VA, 22904. Tel: 434-243-2390. p. 2310

Lee, Carrie, Libr Mgr, Wake County Public Library System, Eva Perry Regional Library, 2100 Shepherd's Vineyard Dr, Apex, NC, 27502. Tel: 919-387-2100. p. 1711

Lee, Catherine, Dean, Cape Fear Community College, 415 N Second St, Wilmington, NC, 28401-3905. Tel: 910-362-7030. p. 1722

Lee, Cheryl, Br Mgr, Santa Clara City Library, Northside Branch, 695 Moreland Way, Santa Clara, CA, 95054. Tel: 408-615-5500. p. 242

Lee, Chu Chin, Commun Libr Mgr, Queens Library, Bayside Community Library, 214-20 Northern Blvd, Bayside, NY, 11361. Tel: 718-229-1834. p. 1554

Lee, Daniel, Libr Mgr, Chandler Public Library, 22 S Delaware, Chandler, AZ, 85225. Tel: 480-782-2813. p. 58

Lee, Danielle, Br Mgr, Pasco County Library System, New River, 34043 State Rd 54, Zephyrhills, FL, 33543. Tel: 813-788-6375. p. 410

Lee, David, Library Contact, Multnomah County Library, Rockwood, 17917 SE Stark St, Portland, OR, 97233. p. 1892

Lee, David, Library Contact, Multnomah County Library, Woodstock, 6008 SE 49th Ave, Portland, OR, 97206. p. 1893

Lee, Desiree, Mgr, County of Los Angeles Public Library, Rowland Heights Library, 1850 Nogales St, Rowland Heights, CA, 91748. Tel: 626-912-5348. p. 137

Lee, Diann, Dir, Evergreen Public Library, 119 Cemetery Ave, Evergreen, AL, 36401. Tel: 251-578-2670. p. 16

Lee, Elizabeth, Youth Serv Mgr, Wilkes County Public Library, 215 Tenth St, North Wilkesboro, NC, 28659. Tel: 336-838-2818. p. 1707

Lee, Gail, Librn, Deaconess Midtown Hospital, 600 Mary St, Evansville, IN, 47747. Tel: 812-450-3385. p. 681

Lee, Ginny, Librn, Iroquois County Genealogical Society Library, Old Courthouse Museum, 103 W Cherry St, Watseka, IL, 60970-1524. Tel: 815-432-3730. p. 659

Lee, Hanna, Youth Serv Coordr, First Regional Library, 370 W Commerce St, Hernando, MS, 38632. Tel: 662-429-4439. p. 1219

Lee, Heath, Regional Libr Dir, Mountain Regional Library System, 698 Miller St, Young Harris, GA, 30582. Tel: 706-379-3732. p. 503

Lee, Heather, Ref (Info Servs), Tech Librn, Nicholas P Sims Library, 515 W Main, Waxahachie, TX, 75165-3235. Tel: 972-937-2671. p. 2255

Lee, Heather, Area Librn, Cariboo Regional District Library, Quesnel Branch, 101 410 Kinchant St, Quesnel, BC, V2J 7J5, CANADA. Tel: 250-992-7912. p. 2584

Lee, Hee Jung, Dir of Libr, Museum of Fine Arts, Boston, 465 Huntington Ave, Boston, MA, 02115. Tel: 617-369-3385. p. 997

Lee, Helen L, Mrs, Dir & Librn, Mary Berry Brown Memorial Library, 1318 Hinton Waters Ave, Midland City, AL, 36350. Tel: 334-983-1191. p. 25

Lee, Hindishe, Ref & Instruction Librn, Yeshiva University Libraries, Hedi Steinberg Library, 245 Lexington Ave, New York, NY, 10016. Tel: 646-592-4980. p. 1605

Lee, Hyoungbae, Librn, Princeton University, East Asian Library, 33 Frist Campus Ctr, Rm 317, Princeton, NJ, 08544. Tel: 609-258-0417. p. 1437

Lee, Iris M, Head, Access Serv, George Washington University, Jacob Burns Law Library, 716 20th St NW, Washington, DC, 20052. Tel: 202-994-2733. p. 367

Lee, James, Br Mgr, Santa Cruz City-County Library System, Downtown, 224 Church St, Santa Cruz, CA, 95060-3873. Tel: 831-427-7707. p. 242

Lee, Jennifer, Electronic Res Coordr, University of Arizona Libraries, Health Sciences Library, 1501 N Campbell Ave, Tucson, AZ, 85724. Tel: 520-626-6125. p. 83

Lee, Jennifer, Site Supvr, Albuquerque-Bernalillo County Library System, Alamosa Library, 6900 Gonzales Rd SW, Albuquerque, NM, 87105. Tel: 505-836-0684. p. 1460

Lee, Jennifer, Librn, University of Calgary Library, Gallagher Library, 170 Earth Sciences, 2500 University Dr NW, Calgary, AB, T2N 1N4, CANADA. Tel: 403-220-3726. p. 2529

Lee, Jennifer B, Curator, Performing Arts & Exhibitions, Columbia University, Rare Book & Manuscript, Butler Library, 6th Flr E, 535 W 114th St, New York, NY, 10027. Tel: 212-854-4048. p. 1583

Lee, Jeong, Head Librn, San Francisco Conservatory of Music Library, 50 Oak St, San Francisco, CA, 94102. Tel: 415-503-6213, 415-503-6256. p. 227

Lee, Jessica, Br Mgr, Burnaby Public Library, McGill Branch, 4595 Albert St, Burnaby, BC, V5C 2G6, CANADA. Tel: 604-297-4813. p. 2563

Lee, Jin Ha, Dr, Assoc Prof, University of Washington, Mary Gates Hall, Ste 370, Campus Box 352840, Seattle, WA, 98195-2840. Tel: 206-543-1794. p. 2794

Lee, Joanne, Head, Ref Serv, Goodnow Library, 21 Concord Rd, Sudbury, MA, 01776-2383. Tel: 978-440-5524. p. 1058

Lee, Jonathon, Cat, Chair, Ref Serv, Los Angeles Harbor College, 1111 Figueroa Pl, Wilmington, CA, 90744. Tel: 310-233-4475. p. 260

Lee, Juan Tomas, Libr Dir, Wasatch County Library, 465 E 1200 S, Heber City, UT, 84032-3943. Tel: 435-654-1511. p. 2264

Lee, Judy, Univ Programs Teaching Librn, University of California, Riverside, 900 University Ave, Riverside, CA, 92521. Tel: 951-827-3220. p. 203

Lee, Judy, Dir, Maimonides Medical Center, Admin Bldg, Fifth Flr, 4802 Tenth Ave, Brooklyn, NY, 11219. Tel: 718-283-7406. p. 1505

Lee, Julie, Youth Serv Mgr, Manitowoc Public Library, 707 Quay St, Manitowoc, WI, 54220. Tel: 920-686-3000. p. 2453

Lee, Ken, Librn, West Los Angeles College Library, 9000 Overland Ave, Culver City, CA, 90230. Tel: 310-287-4402. p. 133

Lee, Kevin, Dir, Banning Library District, 21 W Nicolet St, Banning, CA, 92220. Tel: 951-849-3192. p. 120

Lee, Kirby, Head, Coll Serv, Newport Public Library, 300 Spring St, Newport, RI, 02840. Tel: 401-847-8720. p. 2035

Lee, Kirsten, Ref Librn, Fordham University Libraries, Quinn Library at Lincoln Center, 140 W 62nd St, New York, NY, 10023. Tel: 212-636-6050. p. 1498

Lee, Lateshe, Libr Mgr, New York Public Library - Astor, Lenox & Tilden Foundations, Muhlenberg Branch, 209 W 23rd St, (Near Seventh Ave), New York, NY, 10011-2379. Tel: 212-924-1585. p. 1596

Lee, Laurie, Dir, Titonka Public Library, 136 Main St N, Titonka, IA, 50480. Tel: 515-928-2509. p. 786

Lee, Leslie A, Asst Dir, Admin, George Washington University, Jacob Burns Law Library, 716 20th St NW, Washington, DC, 20052. Tel: 202-994-2385. p. 367

Lee, Levada, Cat, Pontiac Public Library, 211 E Madison St, Pontiac, IL, 61764. Tel: 815-844-7229. p. 636

Lee, Lillian, Circ Supvr, University of California, Berkeley, George & Mary Foster Anthropology Library, 230 Kroeber Hall, Berkeley, CA, 94720-6000. Tel: 510-642-2419. p. 123

Lee, Linda, Head Librn, Parkland Regional Library-Manitoba, Eriksdale Public Library, Nine Main St, Eriksdale, MB, R0C 0W0, CANADA. Tel: 204-739-2668. p. 2586

Lee, Lorrie, Resource Specialist, Gilchrist County Public Library, 105 NE 11th Ave, Trenton, FL, 32693-3803. Tel: 352-463-3176. p. 451

Lee, Mandy, Res & Instrul Serv Librn, Illinois Institute of Technology, Chicago-Kent College of Law Library, 565 W Adams St, 9th Flr, Chicago, IL, 60661. Tel: 312-906-5600. p. 562

Lee, Mark, Libr Serv Mgr, Carnegie Library of Pittsburgh, Library for the Blind & Physically Handicapped, Leonard C Staisey Bldg, 4724 Baum Blvd, Pittsburgh, PA, 15213-1321. Tel: 412-687-2440. p. 1991

Lee, Mark K, Dir, Libr Serv, Wayne Community College, 3000 Wayne Memorial Dr, Goldsboro, NC, 27534. Tel: 919-739-6891. p. 1690

Lee, Marsha M, Res & Instruction Librn, University of Connecticut, Hartford Campus, Uconn Library at Hartford Public Library, 500 Main St, Hartford, CT, 06103. Tel: 959-200-3466. p. 340

Lee, Megan, Libr Dir, Fred A Vaught Memorial Public Library, 211 White Oak St, Hartsville, TN, 37074. Tel: 615-374-3677. p. 2101

Lee, Merilee, Dir, Hoard Historical Museum Library, 401 Whitewater Ave, Fort Atkinson, WI, 53538. Tel: 920-563-7769. p. 2436

Lee, Michelle, Circ Mgr, Fletcher Free Library, 235 College St, Burlington, VT, 05401. Tel: 802-863-3403. p. 2281

Lee, Nicholas, Dir of Finance, King County Library System, 960 Newport Way NW, Issaquah, WA, 98027. Tel: 425-462-9600. p. 2365

Lee, Norman, Staff Librn, Hopewell Public Library, 13 E Broad St, Hopewell, NJ, 08525. Tel: 609-466-1625. p. 1409

Lee Rafuse, Rachel, Br Mgr, Mid-Continent Public Library, Platte City Branch, 2702 NW Prairie View Rd, Platte City, MO, 64079. Tel: 816-858-2322. p. 1251

Lee Rafuse, Rachel, Br Mgr, Mid-Continent Public Library, Weston Branch, 18204 Library Dr, Weston, MO, 64098. Tel: 816-640-2874. p. 1251

Lee, Randall, Exec Dir, Valley Library Consortium, 3210 Davenport Ave, Saginaw, MI, 48602-3495. Tel: 898-497-0925, Ext 5. p. 2768

Lee, Rhonda, Br Mgr, Q B Boydstun Library, 201 E South Ave, Fort Gibson, OK, 74434. Tel: 918-478-3587. p. 1848

Lee, Robert, Dir, Mount Sinai Services-Queens Hospital Center Affiliation, 82-68 164th St, Jamaica, NY, 11432. Tel: 718-883-4019. p. 1553

Lee, Roberta, Br Mgr, Josephine Community Library District, Illinois Valley, 209 W Palmer St, Cave Junction, OR, 97523. Tel: 541-592-4778. p. 1880

Lee, Salina, Assoc Dir, Electronic Resources & Tech, California Institute of Integral Studies, 1453 Mission St, 2nd Flr, San Francisco, CA, 94103. Tel: 415-575-6183. p. 224

Lee, Samantha, Head, Ref Serv, Enfield Public Library, 104 Middle Rd, Enfield, CT, 06082. Tel: 860-763-7510. p. 311

Lee, Samantha, Library Contact, Newfoundland & Labrador Teachers' Association Library, Three Kenmount Rd, St. John's, NL, A1B 1W1, CANADA. Tel: 709-726-3223. p. 2611

Lee, Sandra, Librn II, Fermi National Accelerator Laboratory, Kirk & Wilson Sts, Batavia, IL, 60510. Tel: 630-840-3401. p. 540

Lee, Sandra, Chair, SAIT Polytechnic, School of Information Communication Technologies, 1301 - 16 Ave NW, Calgary, AB, T2M 0L4, CANADA. Tel: 403-284-7231, 403-284-8897. p. 2795

Lee, Sara, Libr Dir, Central City Public Library, 1604 15th Ave, Central City, NE, 68826. Tel: 308-946-2512. p. 1309

Lee, Scott, Info Competency Librn, Antelope Valley College Library, 3041 W Ave K, Lancaster, CA, 93536. Tel: 661-722-6300, Ext 6276. p. 156

Lee, Seong Heon, Tech & Syst Librn, Chapman University Fowler School of Law, One University Dr, Orange, CA, 92866. p. 188

Lee, Shari, PhD, Assoc Prof, St John's University, Saint Augustine Hall, Rm 408A, 8000 Utopia Pkwy, Jamaica, NY, 11439. Tel: 718-990-1451. p. 2789

Lee, Sharon, Br Mgr, Kitsap Regional Library, Poulsbo Branch, 700 NE Lincoln Rd, Poulsbo, WA, 98370-7688. Tel: 360-779-2915. p. 2360

Lee, Sherman, Ref Librn, Kings County Library, 401 N Douty St, Hanford, CA, 93230. Tel: 559-582-0261. p. 150

Lee, Sherman, Supvr, Kings County Library, Avenal Branch, 501 E King St, Avenal, CA, 93204. Tel: 559-386-5741. p. 150

Lee, Sherman, Supvr, Kings County Library, Corcoran Branch, 1001-A Chittenden Ave, Corcoran, CA, 93212. Tel: 559-992-3314. p. 150

Lee, Sherman, Supvr, Kings County Library, Kettleman City Branch, 104 Becky Pease St, Kettleman City, CA, 93239. Tel: 559-386-9804. p. 150

Lee, Slaven, Dir, Missoula Public Library, 301 E Main, Missoula, MT, 59802-4799. Tel: 406-721-2665. p. 1300

Lee, Stacey, Cat, Metadata Librn, Brandon University, 270 18th St, Brandon, MB, R7A 6A9, CANADA. Tel: 204-727-7384. p. 2585

Lee, Stephanie, Commun Relations Coordr, Iberia Parish Library, 445 E Main St, New Iberia, LA, 70560-3710. Tel: 337-364-7024, 337-364-7074. p. 900

Lee, Suki, Br Mgr, Howard County Library System, East Columbia, 6600 Cradlerock Way, Columbia, MD, 21045-4912. Tel: 410-313-7700. p. 965

Lee, Susan, Actg Circuit Librn, United States Court of Appeals, John Joseph Moakley US Courthouse, Ste 9400, One Courthouse Way, Boston, MA, 02210. Tel: 617-748-9044. p. 1000

Lee, Susan M, E-Resources Librn, Sr Librn, Ref, University of Providence Library, 1301 20th St S, Great Falls, MT, 59405-4948. Tel: 406-791-5315. p. 1294

Lee, Tameka, Ms, Communications Dir, Pub Relations, Central Arkansas Library System, 100 Rock St, Little Rock, AR, 72201-4698. Tel: 501-918-3000. p. 101

Lee, Teresa, E-Resources Librn, Ref, Golden Gate University - Otto & Velia Butz Libraries, 536 Mission St, San Francisco, CA, 94105-2967. Tel: 415-442-7242. p. 225

Lee, Vanessa, Libr Tech, Copyright, The Parrott Centre, 376 Wallbridge-Loyalist Rd, Belleville, ON, K8N 5B9, CANADA. Tel: 613-969-1913, Ext 2249. p. 2631

Lee, Vija, Libr Assoc, Lima Public Library, Spencerville Branch, 2489 Wisher Dr, Spencerville, OH, 45887. Tel: 419-647-4307. p. 1796

Lee, Wendy, Mgr, County of Los Angeles Public Library, Gardena Mayme Dear Library, 1731 W Gardena Blvd, Gardena, CA, 90247-4726. Tel: 310-323-6363. p. 136

Lee, Young, Librn, Rio Hondo College Library, 3600 Workman Mill Rd, 2nd Flr, Whittier, CA, 90601. Tel: 562-908-3379. p. 259

Lee, Zemirah, Sr Librn, Bastyr University Library, 14500 Juanita Dr NE, Kenmore, WA, 98028. Tel: 425-602-3020. p. 2367

Lee-Jones, Jessie, Dir, Platteville Public Library, 225 W Main St, Platteville, WI, 53818. Tel: 608-348-7441, Ext 5. p. 2469

Leedberg, Kristina, Asst Dir, J V Fletcher Library, 50 Main St, Westford, MA, 01886-2599. Tel: 978-399-2311. p. 1067

Leeds, Jackie, Head, Circ, Ocean City Free Public Library, 1735 Simpson Ave, Ste 4, Ocean City, NJ, 08226. Tel: 609-399-2434. p. 1430

Leedy, James, Archivist, Librn, Bluefield State University, 219 Rock St, Bluefield, WV, 24701. Tel: 304-327-4053. p. 2398

Leeker, John, Dir, Libr & Archives, Meadville Lombard Theological School, 180 N Wabash Ave, Ste 625, Chicago, IL, 60601. Tel: 312-546-6483. p. 564

Leeman, Sarah, Librn, National Louis University Library, 18 S Michigan Ave, 3rd Flr, Chicago, IL, 60603. Tel: 312-261-3439. p. 565

Leeney-Panagrossi, Anne, Dir, Albertus Magnus College, 700 Prospect St, New Haven, CT, 06511. Tel: 203-773-8511. p. 325

Leeper, Heidi, Dir, Mount Pleasant Free Public Library, 120 S Church St, Mount Pleasant, PA, 15666-1879. Tel: 724-547-3850. p. 1966

Leeport, Cassy, Libr Mgr, University of Wisconsin-Madison, School of Library & Information Studies Library, 4191 Helen C White Hall, 600 N Park St, Madison, WI, 53706. Tel: 608-890-4860. p. 2451

Leerhoff, Stacey, Ch, Charles City Public Library, 106 Milwaukee Mall, Charles City, IA, 50616-2281. Tel: 641-257-6319. p. 739

Lees, Christine, Circ Mgr, Downers Grove Public Library, 1050 Curtiss St, Downers Grove, IL, 60515. Tel: 630-960-1200, Ext 4264. p. 579

Leeson, Denise, Br Mgr, Forsyth County Public Library, 585 Dahlonega St, Cumming, GA, 30040-2109. Tel: 770-781-9840. p. 473

Leestma, Emily, Ch, Van Buren District Library, 200 N Phelps St, Decatur, MI, 49045. Tel: 269-423-4771. p. 1096

LeFeber, Lindsey, Ref & Instruction Librn, College of Lake County, 19351 W Washington St, Grayslake, IL, 60030. Tel: 847-543-2071. p. 595

Lefebvre, Ann, Exec Dir, South Carolina AHEC, One S Park Circle, Ste 203, Charleston, SC, 29407. Tel: 843-792-4431. p. 2775

Lefebvre, Brigitte, Chef de Div, Bibliotheques de Montreal, La Petite-Patrie, 6707 Ave de Lorimier, Montreal, QC, H2G 2P8, CANADA. Tel: 514-868-3880. p. 2719

Lefebvre, Brigitte, Chef de Div, Bibliotheques de Montreal, Marc-Favreau, 500 Blvd Rosemont, Montreal, QC, H2S 1Z3, CANADA. Tel: 514-868-3880. p. 2719

Lefebvre, Brigitte, Chef de Div, Bibliotheques de Montreal, Rosemont, 3131 Blvd Rosemont, Montreal, QC, H1Y 1M4, CANADA. Tel: 514-868-3880. p. 2720

Lefebvre, Gaye, Dir, Libr Serv, Davies, Ward, Phillips & Vineberg, 155 Wellington St W, Toronto, ON, M5V 3J7, CANADA. Tel: 416-863-5533. p. 2688

Lefebvre, Melanie, Dir, Calumet Public Library, City Hall, 932 Gary St, Calumet, MN, 55716. Tel: 218-247-3108. p. 1167

Lefebvre, Melanie, Mgr, Translation Bureau Documentation Centre, 70 Cremazie St, 8th Flr, Gatineau, QC, K1A 0S5, CANADA. Tel: 613-294-7569. p. 2713

Lefebvre, Miriam, Dir, Libr Serv, Bibliotheque Municipale de Rouyn-Noranda, 201 Ave Dallaire, Rouyn-Noranda, QC, J9X 4T5, CANADA. Tel: 819-762-0944. p. 2733

Lefebvre, Niki, PhD, Dir, Natick Historical Society, 58 Eliot St, Natick, MA, 01760. Tel: 508-647-4841. p. 1037

LeFever, Alan, Dir, Baptist General Convention of Texas, 209 N Eighth St, Waco, TX, 76701. Tel: 254-754-9446. p. 2252

LeFevre, Catherine, Dir, Clarella Hackett Johnson Public Library, E9311 County Rd I, Sand Creek, WI, 54765. Tel: 715-658-1269. p. 2475

LeFevre, Kat, Mgr, Jefferson County Public Library, Conifer Public, 10441 Hwy 73, Conifer, CO, 80433. Tel: 303-403-5128. p. 288

LeFevre, Kit, Pub Serv Librn, Hutchinson Community College, 1300 N Plum St, Hutchinson, KS, 67501. Tel: 620-665-3548. p. 814

Leffel, Leandra, Br Mgr, Muskingum County Library System, South Branch, 2530 Maysville Pike, South Zanesville, OH, 43701. Tel: 740-454-1511. p. 1837

Leffler, Jennifer, Tech Serv Mgr, University of Northern Colorado Libraries, 1400 22nd Ave, Greeley, CO, 80631. Tel: 970-351-1543. p. 285

Leffler, Mary, Libr Dir, Logan-Hocking County District Library, 230 E Main St, Logan, OH, 43138. Tel: 740-385-2348. p. 1796

Leffler, Pamela, Exec Dir, Morton Grove Public Library, 6140 Lincoln Ave, Morton Grove, IL, 60053-2989. Tel: 847-965-4220. p. 620

Lefkowitz, Dale, Ms, Librn, Kings County Law Library, Kings County Govt Ctr, Bldg 4, 1400 W Lacey Blvd, Hanford, CA, 93230. Tel: 559-852-4430. p. 149

Lefkowitz, Kathleen, Br Mgr, Cleveland Public Library, Walz, 7910 Detroit Ave, Cleveland, OH, 44102. Tel: 216-623-7095. p. 1769

Lefler, Amy, Asst Librn, Gordon City Library, 101 W Fifth St, Gordon, NE, 69343. Tel: 308-282-1198. p. 1315

Lefner, John, Chief Exec Officer, Hyde Collection Library, 161 Warren St, Glens Falls, NY, 12801. Tel: 518-792-1761. p. 1539

LeFort, Margarita, Circ, Hornepayne Public Library, 68 Front St, Hornepayne, ON, P0M 1Z0, CANADA. Tel: 807-868-2332. p. 2648

Leforte, Jackie, Librn, Southwestern Manitoba Regional Library, Napinka Branch, 57 Souris St, Napinka, MB, R0M 1N0, CANADA. p. 2588

Lefrak, Paul, Mgr, Miami-Dade Public Library System, Arcola Lakes Branch, 8240 NW 7 Ave, Miami, FL, 33150. Tel: 305-694-2707. p. 423

Lefrak, Paul, Mgr, Miami-Dade Public Library System, Northeast Dade - Aventura Branch, 2930 Aventura Blvd, Miami, FL, 33180. Tel: 305-931-5512. p. 424

Lefrancois, Emilie, Dir, University de Moncton, 165 Hebert Blvd, Edmundston, NB, E3V 2S8, CANADA. Tel: 506-737-5266. p. 2600

LeFrancois, Mark, Chief, Res Mgt, National Park Service, 105 S Ripley St, Mountainair, NM, 87036. Tel: 505-847-2585. p. 1473

Leftokwitz, Ilene, Adult Serv, ILL, Ref (Info Servs), Denville Free Public Library, 121 Diamond Spring Rd, Denville, NJ, 07834. Tel: 973-627-6555. p. 1399

Legacy, Melissa, Dir, Libr Serv, Vancouver Island Regional Library, 6250 Hammond Bay Rd, Nanaimo, BC, V9T 6M9, CANADA. Tel: 250-753-1154, Ext 240. p. 2570

Legaspi, Lizeth, Libr Mgr, Camarena Memorial Library, 850 Encinas Ave, Calexico, CA, 92231. Tel: 760-768-2170. p. 126

Legault, Daniel, Chief Admin Officer, University of Ottawa Libraries, 65 University Private, Ottawa, ON, K1N 6N5, CANADA. Tel: 613-562-5800, Ext 3646. p. 2670

Legault, Maryse, Dir, Info Res, Universite Laval Bibliotheque, Pavillon Jean-Charles-Bonenfant, 2345, allée des Bibliothèques, Quebec, QC, G1V 0A6, CANADA. Tel: 418-656-3344. p. 2732

Legault-Venne, Ariane, Head of Libr, Cegep du Vieux Montreal Library, 255 Ontario St E, Montreal, QC, H2X 1X6, CANADA. Tel: 514-982-3437, Ext 2210. p. 2721

Leger, Lori, Regional Mgr, Libr Serv, Horizon Health Network, 135 MacBeath Ave, Moncton, NB, E1C 6Z8, CANADA. Tel: 506-870-2546. p. 2603

Legg, Andrea, Dir, North Canton Public Library, 185 N Main St, North Canton, OH, 44720-2595. Tel: 330-499-4712, Ext 315. p. 1809

Legg, Janet, ILL Librn, Clay Center Carnegie Library, 706 Sixth St, Clay Center, KS, 67432. Tel: 785-632-3889. p. 802

Leggate, Angela R, Librn, Killdeer Public Library, 101 High St NW, Killdeer, ND, 58640-0579. Tel: 701-764-5870. p. 1736

Legge, Kim, Br Mgr, Colchester-East Hants Public Library, Mount Uniacke Branch, 555 Hwy One, Mount Uniacke, NS, B0N 1Z0, CANADA. Tel: 902-866-0124. p. 2623

Leggett, David, Coordr, Nicola Valley Institute of Technology Library, 4155 Belshaw St, Merritt, BC, V1K 1R1, CANADA. Tel: 250-378-3303. p. 2570

Lego, Amy, Dir, Rock Falls Public Library District, 1007 Seventh Ave, Rock Falls, IL, 61071. Tel: 815-626-3958. p. 640

LeGree, Juannetta, Head, Access Serv, State University of New York Downstate Health Sciences University, 395 Lenox Rd, Brooklyn, NY, 11203. Tel: 718-270-7400. p. 1506

LeGrow, Jane, Registrar, Lyman Allyn Art Museum Library, 625 Williams St, New London, CT, 06320-4130. Tel: 860-443-2545, Ext 126. p. 328

LeGrow, Maryanne, Libr Dir, French-Canadian Genealogical Society of Connecticut, Inc Library, 53 Tolland Green, Tolland, CT, 06084. Tel: 860-872-2597. p. 341

Lehi, Judy, Acq, Supvr, Circ Supvr, Dakota Wesleyan University, 1200 W University Ave, Mitchell, SD, 57301. Tel: 605-995-2894. p. 2079

Lehigh, Kristin, Br Mgr, Riverside County Library System, Cathedral City Library, 33520 Date Palm Dr, Cathedral City, CA, 92234. Tel: 760-328-4262. p. 202

Lehman, Ashley, Head, Youth Serv, Orion Township Public Library, 825 Joslyn Rd, Lake Orion, MI, 48362. Tel: 248-693-3000, Ext 421. p. 1123

Lehman, Eben, Dir, Libr & Archives, Forest History Society Library, 701 William Vickers Ave, Durham, NC, 27701-3162. Tel: 919-682-9319. p. 1685

Lehman, Ellen, Dir, Finance & Fac, Idea Exchange, One North Sq, Cambridge, ON, N1S 2K6, CANADA. Tel: 519-621-0460. p. 2635

Lehman, Kaitlin, Dir, Bethel-Tulpehocken Public Library, 8601 Lancaster Ave, Bethel, PA, 19507. Tel: 717-933-4060. p. 1911

Lehman, Kathleen, Mgr, Circ Serv, Fayetteville Public Library, 401 W Mountain St, Fayetteville, AR, 72701. Tel: 479-856-7000. p. 95

Lehman, Lauryn, Res & Instruction Librn, Augustana College Library, 3435 9 1/2 Ave, Rock Island, IL, 61201-2296. Tel: 309-794-7494. p. 641

Lehman, Melissa, Librn, Edna Ralston Public Library, 116 1/2 Towner Ave, Larimore, ND, 58251. Tel: 701-343-2181. p. 1737

Lehman, Patti, Libr Dir, Antlers Public Library, 104 SE Second St, Antlers, OK, 74523-4000. Tel: 580-298-5649. p. 1840

Lehman, Sarah, Br Mgr, Rochester Public Library, Lincoln, 851 Joseph Ave, Rochester, NY, 14621. Tel: 585-428-8210. p. 1630

Lehman, Sonja, Dir, Indiana University, Herron Art Library, Herron School of Art & Design, 735 W New York St, Indianapolis, IN, 46202. Tel: 317-278-9417. p. 693

Lehman, William, Library Contact, Temple Emanu-El, 2100 Highland Ave, Birmingham, AL, 35205. Tel: 205-933-8037, Ext 238. p. 9

Lehmann, Anne, Assoc Dir, New York Public Library - Astor, Lenox & Tilden Foundations, Science, Industry & Business Library, 188 Madison Ave, (34th St & Madison Ave), New York, NY, 10016-4314. p. 1597

Lehmann, Bronna, Dir, Belleville Public Library, 130 S Vine St, Belleville, WI, 53508-9102. Tel: 608-424-1812. p. 2423

Lehmann, Marie, ILL & Distance Libr Serv Spec, Athol Public Library, 568 Main St, Athol, MA, 01331. Tel: 978-249-9515. p. 986

Lehmann, Sarah, Pub Serv Librn, American River College Library, 4700 College Oak Dr, Sacramento, CA, 95841. Tel: 916-484-8455. p. 205

Lehner, Grace, Dir, Archives, Mus Spec, Evanston History Center Library & Archives, 225 Greenwood St, Evanston, IL, 60201. Tel: 847-475-3410. p. 586

Lehner, John, Assoc Dean, Personnel Planning & Syst, University of Houston, M D Anderson Library, 114 University Libraries, Houston, TX, 77204-2000. Tel: 713-743-9800. p. 2199

Lehner, Laura, Head, Youth Serv, Hudson Library & Historical Society, 96 Library St, Hudson, OH, 44236-5122. Tel: 330-653-6658. p. 1790

Lehnerz, Greta, Bus Mgr, Human Res Officer, Natrona County Library, 307 E Second St, Casper, WY, 82601. Tel: 307-577-7323. p. 2492

Lehr, Brenda, Dir, New Baden Public Library, 210 N First St, New Baden, IL, 62265. Tel: 618-588-4554. p. 623

Lehr, Lore, Youth Serv Librn, Southwest Public Libraries, SPL Admin, 3359 Broadway, Grove City, OH, 43123. Tel: 614-875-6716. p. 1789

Lehr, Marcia Gold, Fac Serv Librn, Northwestern University Libraries, Pritzker Legal Research Center, 375 E Chicago Ave, Chicago, IL, 60611. Tel: 312-503-4356. p. 587

Lehu, Peter, Regional Librn, Free Library of Philadelphia, Northeast Regional, 2228 Cottman Ave, Philadelphia, PA, 19149-1297. Tel: 215-685-0522. p. 1979

Leibengood, Beth, Dir, Clyde Public Library, 222 W Buckeye St, Clyde, OH, 43410. Tel: 419-547-7174. p. 1771

Leibiger, Carol, Information Literacy Coord, University of South Dakota, I D Weeks Library, 414 E Clark St, Vermillion, SD, 57069. Tel: 605-658-3383. p. 2084

Leifeld, Jennifer, Vols Librn, Petersburg Public Library, 103 S Second St, Petersburg, NE, 68652. Tel: 402-386-5755. p. 1332

Leifheit, Carolyn, Head, Adult Serv, Oswego Public Library District, Oswego Campus, 32 W Jefferson St, Oswego, IL, 60543. Tel: 630-554-3150. p. 630

Leigh, Arianne, Br Mgr, San Diego Public Library, North Clairemont, 4616 Clairemont Dr, San Diego, CA, 92117. Tel: 858-581-9931. p. 220

Leigh, Chelsea, Libr Mgr, Hollis Public Library, W Broadway & Second St, Hollis, OK, 73550. Tel: 580-688-2744. p. 1850

Leigh, Kathryn, Head, Access Serv, University of Massachusetts Amherst Libraries, 154 Hicks Way, University of Massachusetts, Amherst, MA, 01003-9275. Tel: 413-577-0175. p. 985

Leighton, Ann, Asst Dir, Br Mgr, Ruth Enlow Library of Garrett County, Six N Second St, Oakland, MD, 21550. Tel: 301-334-3996. p. 972

Leighton, John, Managing Librn, Brooklyn Public Library, Carroll Gardens, 396 Clinton St, Brooklyn, NY, 11231. Tel: 718-596-6972. p. 1502

Leighton, Kristy, Ch, Franklin Public Library, 310 Central St, Franklin, NH, 03235. Tel: 603-934-2911. p. 1364

Leighton, Mark, Res Serv Spec, George Mason University Libraries, Law Library, 3301 N Fairfax Dr, Arlington, VA, 22201-4426. Tel: 703-993-8100. p. 2317

Leighton, Vernon, E-Resources & Systems Team, Winona State University, 175 W Mark St, Winona, MN, 55987. Tel: 507-457-5148. p. 1209

Leija, Letty, Dir, Dustin Michael Sekula Memorial Library, 1906 S Closner Blvd, Edinburg, TX, 78539. Tel: 956-383-6246. p. 2173

Leik, Susan, Libr Mgr, Thomas County Public Library System, Coolidge Public Library, 1029 E Verbena Ave, Coolidge, GA, 31738. Tel: 229-346-3463. p. 499

Leinaweaver, Chad, Dir, The Morristown & Morris Township Library, One Miller Rd, Morristown, NJ, 07960. Tel: 973-538-6161. p. 1421

Leinaweaver, Chad, Libr Dir, Morristown & Morris Township Library, Caroline Rose Foster, North Jersey History & Genealogy Center, One Miller Rd, Morristown, NJ, 07960. Tel: 973-538-3473. p. 1421

Leines, Michelle, Asst Dir, Benzonia Public Library, 891 Michigan Ave, Benzonia, MI, 49616-9784. Tel: 231-882-4111. p. 1084

Leinhos, Lisa, Ref, Orange Beach Public Library, 26267 Canal Rd, Orange Beach, AL, 36561-3917. Tel: 251-981-8179. p. 32

Leininger, Michele, Libr Dir, Marshall-Lyon County Library, 201 C St, Marshall, MN, 56258. Tel: 507-537-6183. p. 1182

Leisba, Indira, Libr Asst, North Shore Community College Library, McGee Bldg, LE127, 300 Broad St, Lynn, MA, 01901. Tel: 978-762-4000, Ext 6611. p. 1030

Leisenring, Rick, Curator, Glenn H Curtiss Museum of Local History, 8419 State Rte 54, Hammondsport, NY, 14840-0326. Tel: 607-569-2160. p. 1544

Leiser, Amy, Exec Dir, Monroe County Historical Association, 900 Main St, Stroudsburg, PA, 18360-1604. Tel: 570-421-7703. p. 2011

Leiss, Sara, Operations Mgr, Sioux City Public Library, 529 Pierce St, Sioux City, IA, 51101-1203. Tel: 712-255-2933. p. 783

Leister, Meg, Circ Supvr, Thomas Jefferson University-East Falls, 4201 Henry Ave, Philadelphia, PA, 19144-5497. Tel: 215-951-2841. p. 1987

Leistner, Kerstein, Head, Reference & Access Servs, Pepperdine University Libraries, School of Law-Jerene Appleby Harnish Law Library, 24255 Pacific Coast Hwy, Malibu, CA, 90263. Tel: 310-506-7342. p. 171

Leitch, Alex, Tech Serv, Kendallville Public Library, 221 S Park Ave, Kendallville, IN, 46755-2248. Tel: 260-343-2010. p. 698

Leite, Manny, Dir, Holliston Public Library, 752 Washington St, Holliston, MA, 01746. Tel: 508-429-0617. p. 1025

Leiter, Richard, Dir, University of Nebraska-Lincoln, Marvin & Virginia Schmid Law Library, 1875 N 42nd St, Lincoln, NE, 68583. Tel: 402-472-5737. p. 1323

Leith, Kristina, Librn, St Joseph Township Public Library, 1240 Richard St, Richards Landing, ON, P0R 1J0, CANADA. Tel: 705-246-2353. p. 2675

Leiting, Peggy, Dir, Lied Randolph Public Library, 111 N Douglas St, Randolph, NE, 68771-5510. Tel: 402-337-0046. p. 1334

Leitko, Betsey, Youth Serv Coordr, Tye Preston Memorial Library, 16311 S Access Rd, Canyon Lake, TX, 78133-5301. Tel: 830-964-3744. p. 2153

Leitle, Kathy, Assoc Dep Dir, Saint Louis Public Library, 1301 Olive St, Saint Louis, MO, 63103. Tel: 314-539-0300. p. 1274

Leitner, Kate, Br Mgr, Louisville Free Public Library, Jeffersontown Branch, 10635 Watterson Trail, Jeffersontown, KY, 40299. Tel: 502-267-5713. p. 865

Leitner-Marshall, Rebekah, Circ Spec, Ref Spec, Northern Virginia Community College Libraries, Manassas Campus, Colgan Hall, Rm 129, 10950 Campus Dr, Manassas, VA, 20109. Tel: 703-368-1079. p. 2304

LeJeune, Lisa, Br Mgr, Acadia Parish Library, Mermentau Branch, 107 Second St, Mermentau, LA, 70556. Tel: 318-824-0690. p. 888

LeJeune, Lisa, Br Mgr, Acadia Parish Library, Morse Branch, 209 S Jules Ave, Morse, LA, 70559. Tel: 337-783-0784. p. 888

Lejeune, Marie, Libr Dir, Rochester Public Library, 65 S Main St, Rochester, NH, 03867-2707. Tel: 603-332-1428. p. 1380

Leland, Christopher, Asst Libr Dir, Meredith Public Library, 91 Main St, Meredith, NH, 03253. Tel: 603-279-4303. p. 1373

Leland, Harriott Cheves, Research Historian, Huguenot Society of South Carolina Library, 138 Logan St, Charleston, SC, 29401. Tel: 843-723-3235. p. 2051

Lele, Pradeep, Dir, Lone Star College System, North Harris College Library, 2700 W W Thorne Dr, Houston, TX, 77073. Tel: 281-618-5497. p. 2197

LeLoup, Amanda, Cat, Covington-Veedersburg Public Library, 622 Fifth St, Covington, IN, 47932. Tel: 765-793-2572. p. 677

Lema, Mary Ann, Dir, Prairie Trails Public Library District, 8449 S Moody, Burbank, IL, 60459-2525. Tel: 708-430-3688. p. 546

Lemaire, Deanna, Br Mgr, Davis Jefferson Parish Library, Lake Arthur Branch, 600 Fourth St, Lake Arthur, LA, 70549. Tel: 337-774-3661. p. 892

Lemar, Jessie, Research & Knowledge Manager, Skadden, Arps, Slate, Meagher & Flom LLP Library, 155 N Wacker Dr, Suite 2700, Chicago, IL, 60606. Tel: 312-407-0700, 312-407-0925. p. 568

Lemar, Tyler, Branch Experience Mgr, Evansville Vanderburgh Public Library, McCollough Branch, 5115 Washington Ave, Evansville, IN, 47715. Tel: 812-428-8236. p. 681

LeMaster, Megan, Dir, Res & Develop, Harris County Public Library, 5749 S Loop E, Houston, TX, 77033. Tel: 713-274-6600. p. 2192

LeMaster, Rochelle, Librn, Cleveland Metroparks Zoo Library, 3900 Wildlife Way, Cleveland, OH, 44109. Tel: 216-635-3333. p. 1767

Lemaster, Tammy, Outreach Coordr, Lawrence County Public Library, 102 W Main St, Louisa, KY, 41230. Tel: 606-638-4497. p. 864

Lemay, Anne, Youth Serv, Franklin Township Free Public Library, 485 DeMott Lane, Somerset, NJ, 08873. Tel: 732-873-8700. p. 1442

Lemay, Annick, Chef de Div, Bibliotheque Municipale, 51, rue Jeannotte, Vaudreuil-Dorion, QC, J7V 6E6, CANADA. Tel: 450-455-3371, Ext 6. p. 2738

Lemay, Annie, Documentation Tech, CIUSSS de la Mauricie et du Centre du Quebec, 5 rue des Hospitalieres, Victoriaville, QC, G6P 6N2, CANADA. Tel: 819-357-2030, Ext 2185. p. 2739

Lemay, Bruno, Dir, Canadian Heritage Information Network, 1030 Innes Rd, Ottawa, ON, K1B 4S7, CANADA. Tel: 613-998-3721. p. 2778

Lemay, Denise, Team Leader, Bibliotheques de Trois-Rivieres, Bibliotheque Aline-Piche, 5575 boul Jean-XXIII, Trois-Rivieres, QC, G8Z 4A8, CANADA. Tel: 819-374-6525. p. 2738

LeMay, Emily, Libr Mgr, Community Libraries of Providence, South Providence Library, 441 Prairie Ave, Providence, RI, 02905. Tel: 401-467-2619. p. 2038

Lemay, Yvon, Assoc Prof, Universite de Montreal, 3150, rue Jean-Brillant, bur C-2004, Montreal, QC, H3T 1N8, CANADA. Tel: 514-343-6044. p. 2797

Lemberg, Richard, Brother, Ref & Instruction Librn, Saint Mary's College Library, 1928 Saint Mary's Rd, Moraga, CA, 94575. Tel: 925-631-4229. p. 180

Lembke, Roberta, Dir, Libr & Info Serv, Saint Olaf College, Rolvaag Memorial Library, Hustad Science Library, Halvorson Music Library, 1510 Saint Olaf Ave, Northfield, MN, 55057-1097. Tel: 507-786-3097. p. 1191

Lemerande, Cindy, Dir, Wabeno Public Library, 4556 N Branch St, Wabeno, WI, 54566. Tel: 715-473-4131. p. 2483

Lemerande, Cynthia, Dir, Edith Evans Community Library, 5216 Forest Ave, Laona, WI, 54541. Tel: 715-674-4751. p. 2448

Lemhouse, McKenzie, Asst Librn, University of South Carolina Lancaster, 476-B Hubbard Dr, Lancaster, SC, 29720. Tel: 803-313-7061. p. 2064

Lemhouse, Sherri, Dir, Brownsville Community Library, 146 Spaulding Ave, Brownsville, OR, 97327. Tel: 541-466-5454. p. 1875

Lemieux, Diane, Librn, Ministry of the Attorney General, Superior Law Courts, 800 Smithe St, Vancouver, BC, V6Z 2E1, CANADA. Tel: 604-660-2799. p. 2579

Lemieux, Dominique, Dir, Bibliotheque Gabrielle Roy, Maison de la Litterature, 40 rue Sainte-Stanislas, Quebec, QC, G1R 4H1, CANADA. Tel: 418-641-6788, Ext 7780. p. 2730

LeMieux, Mary, Asst Librn, Morristown Centennial Library, Seven Richmond St, Morrisville, VT, 05661. Tel: 802-888-3853. p. 2289

Lemieux, Shawn, Dir, New York State Library, Cultural Education Ctr, 222 Madison Ave, Albany, NY, 12230. Tel: 518-474-5935. p. 1483

Lemieux, Victoria, Prof, University of British Columbia, The Irving K Barber Learning Ctr, 1961 E Mall, Ste 470, Vancouver, BC, V6T 1Z1, CANADA. Tel: 604-822-2404. p. 2795

LeMin Lee, Jill, Librn, The Athenaeum of Philadelphia, East Washington Sq, 219 S Sixth St, Philadelphia, PA, 19106-3794. Tel: 215-925-2688. p. 1975

Lemire, Arnie, Head, Adult Serv, New Britain Public Library, 20 High St, New Britain, CT, 06051. Tel: 860-224-3155, Ext 140. p. 324

Lemire, Carly, Assoc Librn, Youth Serv, James Blackstone Memorial Library, 758 Main St, Branford, CT, 06405-3697. Tel: 203-488-1441, Ext 322. p. 303

Lemire, Michele, Ch, East Longmeadow Public Library, 60 Center Sq, East Longmeadow, MA, 01028-2459. Tel: 413-525-5400. p. 1016

Lemire-Johnston, Kate, Ch, Naples Public Library, 940 Roosevelt Trail, Naples, ME, 04055. Tel: 207-693-6841. p. 932

Lemke, Karen, Libr Dir, Rochester Public Library, 101 Second St SE, Rochester, MN, 55904-3776. Tel: 507-328-2343. p. 1194

Lemke, Susan K, Spec Coll & Archives Librn, US Department of Defense, Fort McNair, Marshall Hall, Washington, DC, 20319-5066. Tel: 202-685-3957. p. 378

Lemma, Mengistu, Acq Asst, ILL Spec, Union Presbyterian Seminary Library, 3401 Brook Rd, Richmond, VA, 23227. Tel: 804-278-4337. p. 2342

Lemmer, Catherine, Head, Info Serv, Indiana University, Ruth Lilly Law Library, 530 W New York St, Indianapolis, IN, 46202-3225. Tel: 317-274-3884, 317-274-4028. p. 693

Lemmon, Anna, Librn, Echo Public Library, 20 S Bonanza St, Echo, OR, 97826. Tel: 541-376-6038. p. 1878

LeMmon, Kim, Dir, Elsinore Town Library, 15 E 200 N, Elsinore, UT, 84724. Tel: 435-527-4345. p. 2263

Lemmon, Lauren, Adult Serv Mgr, Info Serv Mgr, Marysville Public Library, 231 S Plum St, Marysville, OH, 43040-1596. Tel: 937-642-1876, Ext 32. p. 1800

Lemmons, David, Libr Mgr, George Washington University, Eckles Library, 2100 Foxhall Rd NW, Washington, DC, 20007. Tel: 202-242-6621. p. 367

Lemon, Diedre, Exec Dir, Kansas Heritage Center Library, 1000 N Second Ave, Dodge City, KS, 67801. Tel: 620-227-1616. p. 805

Lemon, Erick T, Dir, Digital Strategies & Innovation, Medical University of South Carolina Libraries, 171 Ashley Ave, Ste 419, Charleston, SC, 29425-0001. Tel: 843-792-7672. p. 2051

Lemon, Shanda, E-Res & Ser Librn, Virginia Union University, 1500 N Lombardy St, Richmond, VA, 23220. Tel: 804-278-4120. p. 2344

Lemon, Susan, Libr Asst, Woodward Public Library, 118 S Main St, Woodward, IA, 50276. Tel: 515-438-2636. p. 793

Lemons, Rebecca, Dir, Huntington City-Township Public Library, 255 W Park Dr, Huntington, IN, 46750. Tel: 260-356-0824. p. 690

Lempges, Lisa, Regional Coordr, Pioneer Library System, McLoud Public, 133 N Main, McLoud, OK, 74851. Tel: 405-788-4132. p. 1855

Lempges, Lisa, Regional Coordr, Pioneer Library System, Southwest Oklahoma City Public Library, 2201 SW 134th St, Oklahoma City, OK, 73170. Tel: 405-979-2200. p. 1855

Lempinen-Leedy, Nance, Interim Libr Dir, Santa Fe College, 3000 NW 83rd St, Bldg Y, Gainesville, FL, 32606. Tel: 352-395-5256. p. 407

Lemyre, Elizabeth, Head Librn, Bibliotheque de Beaconsfield, 303 Beaconsfield Blvd, Beaconsfield, QC, H9W 4A7, CANADA. Tel: 514-428-4400, Ext 4474. p. 2710

Lena, Melissa, Prog Mgr, Virtual Academic Library Environment, VALE/NJEdge, 625 Broad St, Ste 260, Newark, NJ, 07102-4418. Tel: 855-832-3343. p. 2770

Lenaghan, Andrew, Libr Dir, Lewis University Library, One University Pkwy, Romeoville, IL, 60446. Tel: 815-836-5300. p. 642

Lenahen, Kathy, Circ, Free Library of Springfield Township, 8900 Hawthorne Lane, Wyndmoor, PA, 19038. Tel: 215-836-5300. p. 2025

Lenamon, Michelle, Librn, McGinley Memorial Public Library, 317 S Main St, McGregor, TX, 76657. Tel: 254-840-3732. p. 2217

Lenart, Bartlomie, Asst Librn, University of Calgary Library, Doucette Library of Teaching Resources, 370 Education Block, 2500 University Dr NW, Calgary, AB, T2N 1N4, CANADA. Tel: 403-220-5637. p. 2529

Lencinas, Soledad, Ms, Pub Serv Librn, University of Hawaii - West Oahu Library, 91-1001 Farrington Hwy, Kapolei, HI, 96707. Tel: 808-689-2700. p. 514

Lendis, Raychel, Br Assoc, Las Vegas-Clark County Library District, Mount Charleston Library, 75 Ski Chalet Pl, HCR 38, Box 269, Las Vegas, NV, 89124. Tel: 702-872-5585. p. 1347

Lendrum, Linda, Br Librn, Sable-Spanish Riversi Public Library, Webbwood Branch, 16 Main St, Webbwood, ON, P0P 1P0, CANADA. Tel: 705-869-4147. p. 2657

Lendved, Kristine, Dir, Forest Lodge Library, 13450 County Hwy M, Cable, WI, 54821. Tel: 715-798-3189. p. 2426

Lener, Edward, Assoc Dir, Coll Mgt, Virginia Polytechnic Institute & State University Libraries, 560 Drillfield Dr, Blacksburg, VA, 24061. Tel: 540-231-9249. p. 2307

Lenhoff, Carla, Librn, Guernsey County Law Library, Guernsey County Court House, 801 Wheeling Ave, Rm D 301, Cambridge, OH, 43725. Tel: 740-432-9258. p. 1754

Lenkow, Tanya, Circ Supvr, Kinnelon Public Library, 132 Kinnelon Rd, Kinnelon, NJ, 07405. Tel: 973-838-1321. p. 1410

Lennen-Stanton, Tara, Dir, Long Beach Public Library, 111 W Park Ave, Long Beach, NY, 11561-3326. Tel: 516-432-7201. p. 1565

Lennertz, Lora, Data Serv Librn, University of Arkansas Libraries, 365 N McIlroy Ave, Fayetteville, AR, 72701-4002. Tel: 479-575-5545. p. 95

Lenney-Wallace, Dorian, Ch Serv, Ogdensburg Public Library, 312 Washington St, Ogdensburg, NY, 13669-1518. Tel: 315-393-4325. p. 1610

Lenning, Abigail, Asst Dir, Corona Public Library, 650 S Main St, Corona, CA, 92882. Tel: 951-279-3728. p. 132

Lennon, Diana, Head, Adult Serv, Ossining Public Library, 53 Croton Ave, Ossining, NY, 10562. Tel: 914-941-2416. p. 1613

Lennon, Kelli, Head, Circ/ILL, Plaistow Public Library, 85 Main St, Plaistow, NH, 03865. Tel: 603-382-6011. p. 1378

Lennox, Allison, Mgr, Canadian Broadcasting Corp, Radio Archives, 205 Wellington St W, Toronto, ON, M5G 3G7, CANADA. Tel: 416-205-5880. p. 2687

Lenoir, Alice, Head Librn, Bibliotheque Municipale de Saint-Fabien de Panet, 199B, rue Bilodeau, Saint-Fabian de Panet, QC, G0R 2J0, CANADA. Tel: 418-249-4471, Ext 2. p. 2735

Lenon, Mary Ann, Libr Dir, Morton Township Library, 110 S James, Mecosta, MI, 49332-9334. Tel: 231-972-8315, Ext 203. p. 1131

Lenox, Lori, Librn, Camden County College Library, 200 College Dr, Blackwood, NJ, 08012. Tel: 856-227-7200, Ext 4407. p. 1390

Lenser, Jane, Exec Dir, Cherry Valley Public Library District, 755 E State St, Cherry Valley, IL, 61016-9699. Tel: 815-332-5161. p. 553

Lensing, Edythe, Librn, Pike-Amite-Walthall Library System, Magnolia Branch, 230 S Cherry St, Magnolia, MS, 39652. Tel: 601-783-6565. p. 1226

Lenski, Scott, Head, Adult Serv, Whitefish Bay Public Library, 5420 N Marlborough Dr, Whitefish Bay, WI, 53217. Tel: 414-964-4380. p. 2488

Lenstra, Noah, Dr, Asst Prof, University of North Carolina at Greensboro, School of Education Bldg, Rm 446, 1300 Spring Garden St, Greensboro, NC, 27412. Tel: 336-334-3477. p. 2790

Lenstra, Rachel, Archivist, Youth Serv Librn, Galena Public Library District, 601 S Bench St, Galena, IL, 61036. Tel: 815-777-0200. p. 590

Lent, Alex, Dir, Peabody Institute Library, 15 Sylvan St, Danvers, MA, 01923. Tel: 978-774-0554. p. 1013

Lent, Alexander, Dir, Leominster Public Library, 30 West St, Leominster, MA, 01453. Tel: 978-534-7522, Ext 3505. p. 1028

Lent, Amy, Dir, Cliff Island Library, 119 Sunset Ave, Cliff Island, ME, 04019. p. 922

Lent, Cassidy, Libr Dir, National Baseball Hall of Fame & Museum, Inc, 25 Main St, Cooperstown, NY, 13326. Tel: 607-547-0330, 607-547-0335. p. 1521

Lentes, Taryn, Youth Serv Coordr, Athens County Public Libraries, 95 W Washington, Nelsonville, OH, 45764-1177. Tel: 740-592-4272. p. 1805

Lentz, Harris, Librn, Crittenden County Library, Horseshoe Branch, 3181 Horseshoe Circle, Hughes, AR, 72348. Tel: 870-339-3862. p. 104

Lentz, Jennifer, Head, Coll, Ref Librn, University of California Los Angeles Library, Hugh & Hazel Darling Law Library, 1112 Law Bldg, 385 Charles E Young Dr E, Los Angeles, CA, 90095-1458. Tel: 310-825-7826. p. 169

Lentz Rowe, Crystal, Dep State Librn, Washington State Library, Point Plaza East, 6880 Capitol Blvd, Tumwater, WA, 98501. Tel: 360-704-5200. p. 2390

Lentz, Tim, Librn, Hastings Public Library, 314 N Denver Ave, Hastings, NE, 68901. Tel: 402-461-2373. p. 1318

Lenville, Jean, Assoc Dean of Libr, University of Scranton, 800 Linden St, Scranton, PA, 18510-4634. Tel: 570-941-4009. p. 2005

Lenz, Angela, Circ, Watonwan County Library, Butterfield Branch, 111 Second St N, Butterfield, MN, 56120. Tel: 507-956-2361. p. 1198

Lenz, Bobbie, Br Librn, Sweetwater County Library System, Wamsutter Branch Library, 230 Tierney, Lot 44, Wamsutter, WY, 82336. Tel: 307-324-9121. p. 2495

Lenz Muente, Tamera, Assoc Librn, Taft Museum of Art Library, 316 Pike St, Cincinnati, OH, 45202-4293. Tel: 513-352-5136. p. 1763

Lenz, Nicole, Supvr, Circ, Cambria County Library System & District Center, 248 Main St, Johnstown, PA, 15901. Tel: 814-536-5131. p. 1947
Lenze, James B, Libr Dir, Garden City Public Library, 31735 Maplewood St, Garden City, MI, 48135. Tel: 734-793-1830. p. 1108
Leo, Diane, Librn, Mendes & Mount, LLP, 750 Seventh Ave, New York, NY, 10019-6829. Tel: 212-261-8000, 212-261-8338. p. 1591
Leo-Jameson, Rhiannon, Dir, NorthEast-Millerton Library, 75 Main St, Millerton, NY, 12546. Tel: 518-789-3340. p. 1572
Leoffelholtz, Erica, Asst Dir, New Glarus Public Library, 319 Second St, New Glarus, WI, 53574. Tel: 608-527-2003. p. 2464
Leon, Andrea, Circ & ILL Mgr, Washburn University, 1700 SW College Ave, Topeka, KS, 66621. Tel: 785-670-2485. p. 839
Leon, Carl, Circ, Spec Serv, Hondo Public Library, 2003 Ave K, Hondo, TX, 78861-2431. Tel: 830-426-5333. p. 2190
Leon, Claudia, Br Mgr, Phoenix Public Library, Desert Sage Library, 7602 W Encanto Blvd, Phoenix, AZ, 85035. p. 72
Leon, Dena, Library Contact, Hubbs-Sea World Research Institute, 2595 Ingraham St, San Diego, CA, 92109. Tel: 619-226-3870. p. 215
Leon, Laurie, Head, Circ, Dixon Homestead Library, 180 Washington Ave, Dumont, NJ, 07628. Tel: 201-384-2030. p. 1399
Leon, Liz, Coll Develop, Northern Virginia Community College Libraries, Manassas Campus, Colgan Hall, Rm 129, 10950 Campus Dr, Manassas, VA, 20109. Tel: 703-257-6639. p. 2304
Leon Nogueras, Aixa, Interim Dir, Spec Coll Librn, University of Puerto Rico Library, Cayey Campus, 205 Ave Antonio R Barcelo, Ste 205, Cayey, PR, 00736. Tel: 787-738-2161, Ext 2226. p. 2510
Leon, Pedro, Br Mgr, Chicago Public Library, Back of the Yards, 2111 W 47th St, Chicago, IL, 60609. Tel: 312-747-9595. p. 556
Leon Santos, Yolianna, Librn, Inter-American University of Puerto Rico - Fajardo Campus, Calle Union, Batey Central, Carretera 195, Fajardo, PR, 00738. Tel: 787-863-2390, Ext 2322. p. 2510
Leonard, Anne, Interim Chief Librn, New York City College of Technology, 300 Jay St, Brooklyn, NY, 11201. p. 1505
Leonard, Ashley Jane, Librn, Calgary Health Region, Fisher Bldg, Rm 4EE11, 7007 14th St SW, Calgary, AB, T2V 1P9, CANADA. Tel: 403-943-3373. p. 2526
Leonard, Dana J, Mrs, Libr Dir, Earl Park-Richland Township Public Library, 102 E Fifth St, Earl Park, IN, 47942-8700. Tel: 219-474-6932. p. 680
Leonard, Elizabeth, Libr Dir, Drew University Library, 36 Madison Ave, Madison, NJ, 07940. Tel: 973-408-3322. p. 1414
Leonard, Elizabeth, Asst Dean, Info Tech, Res Acq & Description, Seton Hall University Libraries, Walsh Library Bldg, 400 S Orange Ave, South Orange, NJ, 07079. Tel: 973-761-9445. p. 1443
Leonard, Glenda, Br Mgr, Alexander County Library, Bethlehem, 45 Rink Dam Rd, Hickory, NC, 28601. Tel: 828-495-8753. p. 1719
Leonard, James, Dir, University of Alabama, School of Law Library, 101 Paul Bryant Dr, Tuscaloosa, AL, 35487. Tel: 205-348-5925. p. 38
Leonard, John, Librn, Chicago Institute for Psychoanalysis, 122 S Michigan Ave, Ste 1300, Chicago, IL, 60603. Tel: 312-897-1419, 312-922-7474. p. 555
Leonard, Judith, Libr Asst, Lyme Public Library, 482 Hamburg Rd, Lyme, CT, 06371-3110. Tel: 860-434-2272. p. 320
Leonard, Julie, Assoc Prof, University of Iowa, 3087 Main Library, 125 W Washington St, Iowa City, IA, 52242-1420. Tel: 319-335-5707. p. 2785
Leonard, Laura, Dir, Wyckoff Public Library, 200 Woodland Ave, Wyckoff, NJ, 07481. Tel: 201-891-4866. p. 1456
Leonard, Laura, Dir, Twinsburg Public Library, 10050 Ravenna Rd, Twinsburg, OH, 44087. Tel: 330-425-4268, Ext 5. p. 1826
Leonard, Linda, Br Supvr, Vermilion Parish Library, Kaplan Branch, 815 N Cushing Ave, Kaplan, LA, 70548-2614. Tel: 337-643-7209. p. 879
Leonard, Lori, Libr Asst, Bridgeport Public Library, 722 Main St, Bridgeport, NE, 69336. Tel: 308-262-0326. p. 1308
Leonard, Mona, Support Serv, Department of Veterans Affairs, 2121 North Ave, Grand Junction, CO, 81501-6428. Tel: 970-242-0731. p. 284
Leonard, Owen, Web Developer, Athens County Public Libraries, 95 W Washington, Nelsonville, OH, 45764-1177. Tel: 740-753-2118. p. 1805
Leonard, Peter, Exec Dir, Cedar Mill Community Library, 1080 NW Saltzman Rd, Portland, OR, 97229-5603. Tel: 503-644-0043. p. 1891
Leonardi, Sarah, Asst Dir, Amherst Town Library, 14 Main St, Amherst, NH, 03031. Tel: 603-673-2288. p. 1353
Leonardo, Cathy, Board Pres, Cascade Foothills Library, 39095 Dexter Rd, Dexter, OR, 97431. Tel: 541-744-1289. p. 1877
Leonards, Shani, Br Supvr, Berkeley Public Library, Claremont Branch, 2940 Benvenue Ave, Berkeley, CA, 94705. Tel: 510-981-6280. p. 121
Leone, Corinne, Dir, Libr Serv, New York State Department of Correctional Services, Harriman State Campus, 1220 Washington Ave, Albany, NY, 12226-2050. Tel: 518-485-7109. p. 1482
Leone, Gina, Dir & Librn, Scott Township Public Library, 301 Lindsay Rd, Scott Township, PA, 15106-4206. Tel: 412-429-5380. p. 2004
Leone, Nicole, Dir of Advan, University of Missouri-Kansas City Libraries, 800 E 51st St, Kansas City, MO, 64110. Tel: 816-235-5828. p. 1257
Leonetti, John, Ref/Instruction/Tech Serv Librn, Naugatuck Valley Community College, 750 Chase Pkwy, Rm K512, Waterbury, CT, 06708. Tel: 203-575-8021. p. 344
Leong, Gail, Libr Tech, Providence Sacred Heart Medical Center, 101 W Eighth Ave, Spokane, WA, 99204. Tel: 509-474-3094. p. 2384
Leong, Kelly, Head, Ref, Fordham University School of Law, 150 W 62nd St, New York, NY, 10023. Tel: 212-636-6915. p. 1585
Leong, Kelly, Assoc Dean, Libr Serv, Dir, Law Libr, Yeshiva University Libraries, Dr Lillian & Dr Rebecca Chutick Law Library, Benjamin N Cardozo School of Law, 55 Fifth Ave, New York, NY, 10003-4301. Tel: 212-790-0223. p. 1604
Leonhardt, Beverly, Ref (Info Servs), Warren Library Association, 205 Market St, Warren, PA, 16365. Tel: 814-723-4650. p. 2017
Leonhardt, Stacey, Br Mgr, Chestatee Regional Library System, Dawson County Library, 342 Allen St, Dawsonville, GA, 30534. Tel: 706-344-3690, Ext 21. p. 474
Leoni, Amy, Dir, Franciscan University of Steubenville, 1235 University Blvd, Steubenville, OH, 43952-1763. Tel: 740-283-6366. p. 1821
Leopard, Kayla, Circ Mgr, Mgr, Ser, Piedmont Technical College Library, Bldg K, 2nd Flr, 620 N Emerald Rd, Greenwood, SC, 29646. Tel: 864-941-8441. p. 2063
Leopold, Alan, Dir, Coll Serv, Newberry Library, 60 W Walton St, Chicago, IL, 60610-3305. Tel: 312-255-3629. p. 565
Leopold-Bunucci, Rebecca, Br Mgr, Ocean County Library, Lacey Branch, Ten E Lacey Rd, Forked River, NJ, 08731-3626. Tel: 609-693-8566. p. 1446
Leos, Tina, Ch, Circ, Hondo Public Library, 2003 Ave K, Hondo, TX, 78861-2431. Tel: 830-426-5333. p. 2190
Lepage, Amelie, Libr Tech, Cegep Regional de Lanaudiere a Joliette, 20, rue Saint-Charles-Borromee Sud, Joliette, QC, J6E 4T1, CANADA. Tel: 450-759-1661. p. 2713
LePage, Anne, Tech Serv & Syst Librn, Mount Allison University Libraries & Archives, 49 York St, Sackville, NB, E4L 1C6, CANADA. Tel: 506-364-2691. p. 2604
LePage, Sharon, Librn, Chaminade University of Honolulu, 3140 Waialae Ave, Honolulu, HI, 96816-1578. Tel: 808-739-4263. p. 506
Lepanto, Lauren, Br Librn, Boston Public Library, West End, 151 Cambridge St, Boston, MA, 02114. Tel: 617-523-3957. p. 993
Lepore, Darcy, Libr Dir, Langley-Adams Library, 185 Main St, Groveland, MA, 01834-1314. Tel: 978-372-1732. p. 1022
Lepore, Julie, Dir, North Scituate Public Library, 606 W Greenville Rd, North Scituate, RI, 02857. Tel: 401-647-5133. p. 2036
Lepore, Lisa, Dir, Libr Serv, Braille Institute Library, 741 N Vermont Ave, Los Angeles, CA, 90029-3514. Tel: 323-660-3880. p. 160
LePors, Teresa, Coordr, Libr Res, Coord, Scholarly Services, Elon University, 308 N O'Kelly Ave, Elon, NC, 27244-0187. Tel: 336-278-6600. p. 1688
Leprohon, Marie-Eve, Chef de Section, Bibliotheques de Montreal, Hochelaga, 1870 rue Davidson, Montreal, QC, H1W 2Y6, CANADA. Tel: 514-872-6733. p. 2719
Leprohon, Marie-Ève, Chef de Section, Bibliotheques de Montreal, Maisonneuve, 4120 rue Ontario Est, Montreal, QC, H1V 1J9, CANADA. Tel: 514-872-6733. p. 2719
Lerch, Dan, Syst Librn, Penticton Public Library, 785 Main St, Penticton, BC, V2A 5E3, CANADA. Tel: 250-770-7785. p. 2573
Lerch, Maureen, Libr Dir, University of Akron Libraries, 1901 Smucker Rd, Orrville, OH, 44667. Tel: 330-972-8789. p. 1811
Lerczak, Nicki, Instrul Serv Librn, Genesee Community College, One College Rd, Batavia, NY, 14020-9704. Tel: 585-343-0055, Ext 6418. p. 1490
Lerdal, John, Dir, Pleasant Hill Public Library, 5151 Maple Dr, Pleasant Hill, IA, 50327-8456. Tel: 515-266-7815. p. 777
Lerg, Katherine, Dir, Human Res, Indianapolis Public Library, 2450 N Meridian St, Indianapolis, IN, 46208. Tel: 317-275-4806. p. 694
Lerma, Valerie, Acq, Coll Develop, Judicial Branch of Arizona, Maricopa County, 101 W Jefferson St, Phoenix, AZ, 85003. Tel: 602-506-1647. p. 70
Lerman, Maria, Head, Ref, Bala Cynwyd Memorial Library, 131 Old Lancaster Rd, Bala Cynwyd, PA, 19004-3037. Tel: 610-664-1196. p. 1908
Lerner, Brittney, Asst Libr Dir, H J Nugen Public Library, 103 E Main St, New London, IA, 52645. Tel: 319-367-7704. p. 772
Leroux, Coralee, Scholarly Resources Librn, Scholarly Services Librn, Trent University, 1600 West Bank Dr, Peterborough, ON, K9J 7B8, CANADA. Tel: 705-748-1011, Ext 7196. p. 2672
Leroux, Eric, Assoc Prof, Universite de Montreal, 3150, rue Jean-Brillant, bur C-2004, Montreal, QC, H3T 1N8, CANADA. Tel: 514-343-6044. p. 2797
Leroux, Jeanne, Chief Exec Officer, Nation Municipality Public Library, 4531 Ste-Catherine St, St. Isidore, ON, K0C 2B0, CANADA. Tel: 613-524-2252. p. 2680
Leroux, Jeanne, Chief Exec Officer, Nation Municipality Public Library, Limoges Branch, 205 Limoges Rd, Limoges, ON, K0A 2M0, CANADA. Tel: 613-443-1630. p. 2680
Leroux, Jeanne, Chief Exec Officer, Nation Municipality Public Library, St Albert Branch, St Albert Community Centre, 201 Principale St, Saint Albert, ON, K0A 3C0, CANADA. Tel: 613-987-2143. p. 2680
Leroux, John, Mgr of Collections & Exhibitions, Beaverbrook Art Gallery Library, 703 Queen St, Fredericton, NB, E3B 1C4, CANADA. Tel: 506-458-2028. p. 2600

Lerum, Traci, Circ Serv Librn, DeForest Area Public Library, 203 Library St, DeForest, WI, 53532. Tel: 608-846-5482. p. 2430

Lesage, Yves, Team Leader, Bibliotheques de Trois-Rivieres, Bibliotheque Maurice-Loranger, 70 rue Pare, Trois-Rivieres, QC, G8T 6V8, CANADA. Tel: 819-378-8206. p. 2738

Lescallett, Trinity, Adult Programming Mgr, Tiffin-Seneca Public Library, 77 Jefferson St, Tiffin, OH, 44883. Tel: 419-447-3751. p. 1823

Lesch, Jacqueline, Co-Chair, Digital Assets Librn, Riverside Community College District, 4800 Magnolia Ave, Riverside, CA, 92506-1299. p. 201

Lesellier, Graziella, Libr Asst, Bacon Free Library, 58 Eliot St, Natick, MA, 01760. Tel: 508-653-6730. p. 1037

Leseman, Bethany, Dir, Carlton Area Public Library, 310 Chestnut Ave, Carlton, MN, 55718. Tel: 218-384-3322. p. 1169

Lesesne, Teri, Dr, Prof, Sam Houston State University, 1905 Bobby K Marks Dr, Huntsville, TX, 77340. Tel: 936-294-3673. p. 2793

Lesh, Nancy, Ref Serv, University of Alaska Anchorage, Consortium Library, 3211 Providence Dr, Anchorage, AK, 99508-8176. Tel: 907-786-1871. p. 43

Lesher, Marcella, Per, Saint Mary's University, Louis J Blume Library, One Camino Santa Maria, San Antonio, TX, 78228-8608. Tel: 210-436-3441. p. 2238

Lesher, Pete, Chief Curator, Chesapeake Bay Maritime Museum Library, 109A Mill St, Saint Michaels, MD, 21663. Tel: 410-745-4971. p. 976

Leshock, Chris, Cataloger, Boston Architectural College, 320 Newbury St, Boston, MA, 02115. Tel: 617-585-0155. p. 991

Lesinski, Lisa, Head, Children's Servx, Barrington Public Library, 281 County Rd, Barrington, RI, 02806. Tel: 401-247-1920. p. 2029

Lesko, Kelly, Dir, Westville Public Library, 1035 Broadway, Westville, NJ, 08093. Tel: 856-456-0357. p. 1454

Leskovar, Fran, Evening Supvr, University of Puget Sound, 1604 N Warner St, Upper Loading Dock, Tacoma, WA, 98416. Tel: 253-879-2664. p. 2387

Lesky, Lynne, Dir, Alanson Area Public Library, 7631 Burr Ave, Hwy 31, Alanson, MI, 49706. Tel: 231-548-5465. p. 1076

Lesley, Kimberly, Dir, Moore College of Art & Design, Sarah Peter Hall, 1st Flr, 20th St & The Parkway, Philadelphia, PA, 19103-1179. Tel: 215-965-4054. p. 1983

Leslie, Danica, Sr Dir, Tech Operations Mgr, University of Oklahoma Libraries, 401 W Brooks St, Norman, OK, 73019. Tel: 405-325-3341. p. 1856

Leslie, Hugh, Libr Mgr, Talkeetna Public Library, 24645 S Talkeetna Spur Rd, Talkeetna, AK, 99676. Tel: 907-861-7868. p. 51

Leslie, Jared, Dir, Foundation for Blind Children Library & Media Center, 1234 E Northern Ave, Phoenix, AZ, 85020. Tel: 602-678-5810, 602-678-5816. p. 69

Leslie, Su, Libr Dir, St Croix Falls Public Library, 230 S Washington St, Saint Croix Falls, WI, 54024. Tel: 715-483-1777. p. 2475

Lesniak, Hannah, Support Serv Librn, Wixom Public Library, 49015 Pontiac Trail, Wixom, MI, 48393-2567. Tel: 248-624-2512. p. 1160

Lesniak, Michelle, Dir, South Butler Community Library, 240 W Main St, Saxonburg, PA, 16056. Tel: 724-352-4810. p. 2003

Lesniaski, David, PhD, Assoc Prof, Saint Catherine University, 2004 Randolph Ave, Mailstop No 4125, Saint Paul, MN, 55105. Tel: 651-690-6802. p. 2787

Lessard, Jared, Br Mgr, Calcasieu Parish Public Library System, Fontenot Memorial, 1402 Center St, Vinton, LA, 70668. Tel: 337-721-7095. p. 893

Lessard, Renald, Archivist, Archives nationales a Quebec, Pavillon Louis Jacques Casault, Campus de l'Universite Laval, 1055 ave du Seminaire, Quebec, QC, G1V 5C8, CANADA. Tel: 418-643-8904. p. 2729

Lesser, Lauren, Acad Res Coordr, Juniata College, 1700 Moore St, Huntingdon, PA, 16652-2119. Tel: 814-641-3150. p. 1945

Lessner, Pamela, Librn, City Colleges of Chicago, Richard J Daley College Library, 7500 S Pulaski Rd, Chicago, IL, 60652-1200. Tel: 773-838-7667. p. 558

Lesso, Elizabeth, Access Serv Coordr, University of Saint Joseph, 1678 Asylum Ave, West Hartford, CT, 06117-2791. Tel: 860-232-4571. p. 345

Lester, Anne, Mgr, Salem Free Public Library, 112 W Broadway, Salem, NJ, 08079-1302. Tel: 856-935-0526, Ext 11. p. 1441

Lester, Carole, Library Contact, Mono County Free Library, June Lake, 90 W Granite Ave, June Lake, CA, 93529. Tel: 760-648-7284. p. 172

Lester, Cynthia, Br Mgr, Robeson County Public Library, Gilbert Patterson Memorial, 210 N Florence St, Maxton, NC, 28364. Tel: 910-844-3884. p. 1702

Lester, Denise, Ch, Westwood Public Library, 49 Park Ave, Westwood, NJ, 07675. Tel: 201-664-0583. p. 1454

Lester, Denita, Libr Mgr, Muscle Shoals Public Library, 1918 E Avalon, Muscle Shoals, AL, 35661. Tel: 256-386-9212. p. 31

Lester, Diane, Br Coordr, Washington County Public Library, 205 Oak Hill St, Abingdon, VA, 24210. Tel: 276-676-6222, 276-676-6233. p. 2301

Lester, Janice, Ref & Educ Librn, Long Island Jewish Medical Center, Schwartz Research Bldg, 270-05 76th Ave, New Hyde Park, NY, 11040. Tel: 718-470-7071. p. 1576

Lester, Jennifer, Dir, Ansonia Library, 53 S Cliff St, Ansonia, CT, 06401. Tel: 203-734-6275. p. 301

Lester, Jess, Br Librn, Sussex County Library System, Franklin Branch, 103 Main St, Franklin, NJ, 07416. Tel: 973-827-6555. p. 1429

Lester, Sarah, Dir, Maplewood Memorial Library, 129 Boyden Ave, Maplewood, NJ, 07040. Tel: 973-762-1688. p. 1416

Lester, Stephen, Tech Serv, Center for Health, Environment & Justice, 7139 Shreve Rd, Falls Church, VA, 22046. Tel: 703-237-2249. p. 2317

Lestini, Paula, Assoc Librn, Wheeling Jesuit University, 316 Washington Ave, Wheeling, WV, 26003-6295. Tel: 304-243-2226. p. 2418

Letarte, Marie, Dir, Bigelow Free Public Library, 54 Walnut St, Clinton, MA, 01510. Tel: 978-365-4160. p. 1012

Letch, Haley, Ch, Stirling-Rawdon Public Library, 43 W Front St, Stirling, ON, K0K 3E0, CANADA. Tel: 613-395-2837. p. 2681

LeTellier, Lise, Libr Dir, Granville Public Library, Two Granby Rd, Granville, MA, 01034-9539. Tel: 413-357-8531. p. 1021

Leto, Susan, Head, Circ, Grafton Public Library, 35 Grafton Common, Grafton, MA, 01519. Tel: 508-839-4649, Ext 1108. p. 1021

Letohic, Amanda, Actg Dir, Fallsburg Library Inc, 12 Railroad Plaza, South Fallsburg, NY, 12779. Tel: 845-436-6067. p. 1642

Letourneau, Kelly, Asst Dir, Circ Desk Supvr, Edgecombe County Memorial Library, 909 N Main St, Tarboro, NC, 27886. Tel: 252-823-1141. p. 1718

Letriz, Joseph, Electronic Systems Librn, University of Dubuque Library, 2000 University Ave, Dubuque, IA, 52001. Tel: 563-589-3100. p. 749

Letson, Terri, Mgr, Wayne County Public Library, Clifton Branch, 192 Main St, Clifton, TN, 38425. Tel: 931-676-3678. p. 2129

Lett, Rosalind, Dir, Libr Serv, Clayton County Library System, 865 Battlecreek Rd, Jonesboro, GA, 30236. Tel: 770-473-3850. p. 483

Lettieri, Robin, Dir, Port Chester-Rye Brook Public Library, One Haseco Ave, Port Chester, NY, 10573. Tel: 914-939-6710, Ext 114. p. 1620

Lettner, Amanda, Metadata Librn, Tech Serv Librn, Lenhardt Library of the Chicago Botanic Garden, 1000 Lake Cook Rd, Glencoe, IL, 60022. Tel: 847-835-8201. p. 593

Lettre, Marie-Josée, Libr Tech, Institut de Technologie Agroalimentaire, Campus La Pocatière, 401 rue Poire, local 202, La Pocatiere, QC, G0R 1Z0, CANADA. Tel: 418-856-1110, Ext 1279. p. 2714

Letts, Debra, Br Mgr, Cadillac-Wexford Public Library, Manton Branch, 404 W Main St, Manton, MI, 49663. Tel: 231-824-3584. p. 1088

Letzerich, Tracy, Br Mgr, Lynchburg Public Library, 2315 Memorial Ave, Lynchburg, VA, 24501. Tel: 434-455-3817. p. 2330

Letzerich, Tracy, Br Mgr, Lynchburg Public Library, Downtown, 900 Church St, Lynchburg, VA, 24504. Tel: 434-455-3817. p. 2330

Leuci, Lena, Coll Asst, Westminster College, America's National Churchill Museum, 501 Westminster Ave, Fulton, MO, 65251-1299. Tel: 573-592-5369. p. 1246

Leuck, Lisa, Dir, Elgin Public Library, 214 Main St, Elgin, IA, 52141. Tel: 563-426-5313. p. 751

Leung, Dorothy, Archivist, Mgr, Res Libr Serv, Stanford University Libraries, SLAC National Accelerator Laboratory Research Library, Computer Bldg 50, 2575 Sand Hill Rd, MS82, Menlo Park, CA, 94025-7090. Tel: 650-926-2411. p. 249

Leung, Maggie, Teen Serv Librn, The Field Library, Four Nelson Ave, Peekskill, NY, 10566. Tel: 914-737-1212. p. 1616

Leuszler, Lexy, Lit Prog Mgr, Eugene O'Neill Theater Center, 305 Great Neck Rd, Waterford, CT, 06385. Tel: 860-443-5378, Ext 227. p. 344

Leuzinger, Julie A, Head, Learning Serv, University of North Texas Libraries, 1155 Union Circle, No 305190, Denton, TX, 76203-5017. Tel: 940-565-3980. p. 2170

Leven, Bozena, Exec Dir, Polish Institute of Arts & Sciences in America, Inc, 208 E 30th St, New York, NY, 10016. Tel: 212-686-4164. p. 1600

Leven, Jane, Br Mgr, Camden County Library System, Riletta L Cream Ferry Avenue Branch, 852 Ferry Ave, Camden, NJ, 08104. Tel: 856-342-9789. p. 1450

Leven, Stuart, Chairperson, Western Philatelic Library, 3004 Spring St, Redwood City, CA, 94063. Tel: 650-306-9150. p. 200

Levenback, Karen L, Archivist/Librn, Franciscan Monastery Library, 1400 Quincy St NE, Washington, DC, 20017. Tel: 202-734-3866. p. 366

Levenhagen, Denise, Dir, Central City Public Library, 137 Fourth St N, Ste 2, Central City, IA, 52214. Tel: 319-438-6685. p. 739

Levenson, Helen, Coll Develop Librn, Oakland University Library, 100 Library Dr, Rochester, MI, 48309-4479. Tel: 248-370-2497. p. 1144

Lever, Victoria, Dir, Babylon Public Library, 24 S Carll Ave, Babylon, NY, 11702. Tel: 631-669-1624. p. 1489

Levergood, Barbara, Res & Instruction Librn, Bowdoin College Library, 3000 College Sta, Brunswick, ME, 04011-8421. p. 919

Leveridge, Jennifer, Mgr, Libr Serv, Newmarket Public Library, 438 Park Ave, Newmarket, ON, L3Y 1W1, CANADA. Tel: 905-953-5110. p. 2660

Levers, Carol, Libr Dir, Kansas City, Kansas Public Library, 625 Minnesota Ave, Kansas City, KS, 66101. Tel: 913-295-8250, Ext 6420. p. 816

Levesen, Stephanie, Tech Serv, Skagit Valley College, 2405 E College Way, Mount Vernon, WA, 98273-5899. Tel: 360-416-7850. p. 2371

Levesque, Gisele, Supvr, Essex County Library, Stoney Point Branch, 6690 Tecumseh Rd, Stoney Point, ON, N0R 1N0, CANADA. Tel: 226-946-1529, Ext 232. p. 2641

Lévesque, Isabelle-Annie, Dir, Universite du Quebec a Rimouski - Service de la bibliotheque, 300 Allee des Ursulines, Rimouski, QC, G5L 3A1, CANADA. Tel: 418-723-1986, Ext 1470. p. 2732

Levesque, Jacques Francois, Dir, Bibliotheque Municipale, 855 Place de l'Île-des-Moulins, Terrebonne, QC, J6W 4N7, CANADA. Tel: 450-961-2001, Ext 1252. p. 2737
Levesque, Justin, Asst Dir, Tracy Memorial Library, 304 Main St, New London, NH, 03257-7813. Tel: 603-526-4656. p. 1376
LeVesque, Maureen, Circ Supvr, Carleton A Friday Memorial Library, 155 E First St, New Richmond, WI, 54017. Tel: 715-243-0431. p. 2465
Levetzow, Maria, Asst Dir, Bettendorf Public Library Information Center, 2950 Learning Campus Dr, Bettendorf, IA, 52722. Tel: 563-344-4191. p. 734
Levi, Garren, Head, Circ, Valley Community Library, 739 River St, Peckville, PA, 18452. Tel: 570-489-1765. p. 1974
Levin, Ingrid, Colls Librn, Electronic Res, Salve Regina University, 100 Ochre Point Ave, Newport, RI, 02840-4192. Tel: 401-341-2330. p. 2035
Levin, Jocelyn, Head, Youth & Teen Serv, Lyon Township Public Library, 27005 S Milford Rd, South Lyon, MI, 48178. Tel: 248-437-8800. p. 1150
Levin, John, Access Serv Librn, SIT Graduate Institute/SIT Study Abroad, One Kipling Rd, Brattleboro, VT, 05302. Tel: 802-258-3533. p. 2280
Levin, Nancy S, Dir, Cleveland Heights-University Heights Public Library, 2345 Lee Rd, Cleveland Heights, OH, 44118-3493. Tel: 216-932-3600, Ext 1240. p. 1771
Levin, Sandra J, Exec Dir, Los Angeles County Law Library, Mildred L Lillie Bldg, 301 W First St, Los Angeles, CA, 90012-3100. Tel: 213-785-2529. p. 162
Levine, Addie, Librn, Jewish Community Center of Metropolitan Detroit, 6600 W Maple Rd, West Bloomfield, MI, 48322. Tel: 248-432-5546. p. 1158
Levine, Amy, Dir, Rockland Public Library, 80 Union St, Rockland, ME, 04841. Tel: 207-594-0310. p. 939
Levine, Beth, Head Librn, Fred Hutchinson Cancer Research Center, 1100 Fairview Ave N, B1-010, Seattle, WA, 98109. Tel: 206-667-4314. p. 2376
Levine, Christine, Dir, United States Air Force, 509 FSS/FSDL, 511 Spirit Blvd, Whiteman AFB, MO, 65305-5019. Tel: 660-687-5614, 660-687-5791. p. 1286
Levine, Dennis, Automation Serv, Broward College, Bldg 17, 3501 SW Davie Rd, Davie, FL, 33314. Tel: 954-201-6648. p. 391
Levine, Janice, Paulding Campus Librn, Chattahoochee Technical College Library, 980 S Cobb Dr, Marietta, GA, 30060. Tel: 770-443-3632. p. 488
Levine, Janice, Librn, Library Services, Chattahoochee Technical College Library, Paulding Campus Library, 400 Nathan Dean Blvd, Dallas, GA, 30132. Tel: 770-443-3632. p. 489
Levine, Jodi, Dir, Pelham Library, Two S Valley Rd, Pelham, MA, 01002. Tel: 413-253-0657. p. 1045
Levine, Joshua, Librn, Yeshiva University Libraries, Dr Lillian & Dr Rebecca Chutick Law Library, Benjamin N Cardozo School of Law, 55 Fifth Ave, New York, NY, 10003-4301. Tel: 212-790-0223. p. 1604
Levine, Kendra, Libr Dir, University of California, Berkeley, 412 McLaughlin Hall, MC 1720, Berkeley, CA, 94720-1720. Tel: 510-643-3348. p. 123
Levine Knies, Jennie, Head Librn, Pennsylvania State University, Wilkes-Barre Commonwealth College, PO Box PSU, Lehman, PA, 18627-0217. Tel: 570-963-2632. p. 1955
Levine, Maureen, Cataloger, Ansonia Library, 53 S Cliff St, Ansonia, CT, 06401. Tel: 203-734-6275. p. 301
Levine, Peter, Libr Mgr, New York Public Library - Astor, Lenox & Tilden Foundations, Port Richmond Branch, 75 Bennett St, (@ Heberton Ave), Staten Island, NY, 10302. Tel: 718-442-0158. p. 1596
Levine, Sarah, Asst Dir, Archives & Libr, Meadville Lombard Theological School, 180 N Wabash Ave, Ste 625, Chicago, IL, 60601. Tel: 312-445-9434. p. 564
Levine, Stephanie, Adult Serv Coordr, Emily Williston Memorial Library, Nine Park St, Easthampton, MA, 01027. Tel: 413-527-1031. p. 1016
Levine, Sue, Librn, Fernbank Science Center Library, 156 Heaton Park Dr NE, Atlanta, GA, 30307-1398. Tel: 678-874-7116. p. 464
Levine-Clark, Michael, Dean & Dir, Libr Serv, University of Denver, 2150 E Evans Ave, Denver, CO, 80208. Tel: 303-871-3441. p. 277
Leving, Ella, Librn, Halifax Public Libraries, Captain William Spry Branch, 16 Sussex St, Halifax, NS, B3R 1N9, CANADA. Tel: 902-490-5818. p. 2617
Levings, Katy, Access Serv Librn, Oklahoma Panhandle State University, 409 W Sewell, Goodwell, OK, 73939. Tel: 580-349-1547. p. 1848
Levingston, Errin, Head, Ref, State Library of Louisiana, 701 N Fourth St, Baton Rouge, LA, 70802-5232. Tel: 225-219-4912. p. 885
Levins, James, Br Librn, Boston Public Library, Charlestown Branch, 179 Main St, Charlestown, MA, 02129. Tel: 617-242-1248. p. 992
Levinson, Carrie, Outreach Librn, Ref Serv, New York Academy of Medicine Library, 1216 Fifth Ave, New York, NY, 10029. Tel: 212-822-7292. p. 1593
Levinson, Tiki, Libr Dir, Delta Community Library, 2291 Deborah St, Delta Junction, AK, 99737. Tel: 907-895-4102. p. 44
Levis, Joseph, Dir, College of Mount Saint Vincent, 6301 Riverdale Ave, Bronx, NY, 10471-1046. Tel: 718-405-3394. p. 1498
Levitin-Breyette, Christine, Dir, Champlain Memorial Library, 148 Elm St, Champlain, NY, 12919-5317. Tel: 518-298-8620. p. 1516
Levitt, Christine, Cat, Mount Wachusett Community College Library, 444 Green St, Gardner, MA, 01440. Tel: 978-630-9125. p. 1020
Levitt, Lisa, Acq Tech, University of Oregon Libraries, John E Jaqua Law Library, William W Knight Law Ctr, 2nd Flr, 1515 Agate St, Eugene, OR, 97403. Tel: 541-346-3802. p. 1879
Levor, L Ruth, Assoc Dir, University of San Diego, Katherine M & George M Pardee Jr Legal Research Center, 5998 Alcala Park, San Diego, CA, 92110-2492. Tel: 619-260-4604. p. 222
Levy, Belinda, Br Mgr, Russell County Public Library, Honaker Community Library, Ten Library Dr, Honaker, VA, 24260. Tel: 276-873-6600. p. 2328
Levy, Jamie, Microfilm Tech, Simcoe County Archives, 1149 Hwy 26, Minesing, ON, L9X 0Z7, CANADA. Tel: 705-726-9300, Ext 1289. p. 2658
Levy, Jason, Mgr, Libr Serv, Acadia University, 50 Acadia St, Wolfville, NS, B4P 2R6, CANADA. Tel: 902-670-9139. p. 2623
Levy, Johanne, Law Librn, Hawkins, Delafield & Wood, Seven World Trade Center, 250 Greenwich St, New York, NY, 10007. Tel: 212-820-9300, 212-820-9444. p. 1587
Levy, Joy, Exec Dir, Ontario Camps Association Library, 70 Martin Ross Ave., Toronto, ON, M3J 2L4, CANADA. Tel: 416-485-0425. p. 2691
Levy, June, Dir, Adventist Health Glendale, 1509 Wilson Terrace, Glendale, CA, 91206. Tel: 818-409-8034. p. 148
Levy, June, Libr Dir, White Memorial Medical Center, North Bldg, Basement, 1720 Cesar E Chavez Ave, Los Angeles, CA, 90033. Tel: 323-260-5715. p. 170
Levy, Laura, Ref Librn, Montclair State University, One Normal Ave, Montclair, NJ, 07043-1699. Tel: 973-655-7148. p. 1420
Levy, Michael, Assoc Dir, University of California, Berkeley, Law, Berkley Law South Addition, 2nd Flr, 2778 Bancroft Way, Berkeley, CA, 94720. Tel: 510-642-0621. p. 123
Levy, Paul, Managing Librn, Brooklyn Public Library, Brownsville, 61 Glenmore Ave, Brooklyn, NY, 11212. Tel: 718-498-9721. p. 1502
Levy, Randi, Head, Children's Libr, The New York Society Library, 53 E 79th St, New York, NY, 10075. Tel: 212-288-6900, Ext 216. p. 1598
Levy, Sarah, Access Serv Librn, Rockland Community College Library, 145 College Rd, Suffern, NY, 10901. Tel: 845-574-4472. p. 1647
Levy, Victoria W, Librn, Virginia State Law Library, Supreme Court Bldg, 2nd Flr, 100 N Ninth St, Richmond, VA, 23219-2335. Tel: 804-786-2075. p. 2344
Lew, Ken, AV Coll, Franklin Lakes Public Library, 470 DeKorte Dr, Franklin Lakes, NJ, 07417. Tel: 201-891-2224. p. 1404
Lew, Shirley, Dean, Library, Teaching & Learning Servs, Vancouver Community College, 250 W Pender St, Vancouver, BC, V6B 1S9, CANADA. Tel: 608-871-7000, Ext 7007. p. 2581
Lewallen, John, Head Librn, Sedgwick County Law Library, 225 N Market St, Ste 210, Wichita, KS, 67202-2023. Tel: 316-263-2251, Ext 120. p. 843
Lewanbowski, Daniel, Librn, Buffalo & Erie County Public Library System, Dudley, 2010 S Park Ave, Buffalo, NY, 14220-1894. Tel: 716-823-1854. p. 1508
Lewandoski, Jane, Info & Educ Librn, Saint Clair County Community College Library, 323 Erie St, Port Huron, MI, 48060. Tel: 810-989-5640. p. 1142
Lewandowski, Kat, Adminr, Thomas Ford Memorial Library, 800 Chestnut St, Western Springs, IL, 60558. Tel: 708-246-0520. p. 661
Lewin, Livia, Libr Supvr, Placer County Library, Tahoe City Branch, 740 N Lake Blvd, Tahoe City, CA, 96145. Tel: 530-583-3382. p. 118
Lewis, Aislinn, Youth Serv Librn, Rutland Free Public Library, 280 Main St, Rutland, MA, 01543. Tel: 508-886-4108, Option 5. p. 1050
Lewis, Alana, Libr Dir, Paine College, 1235 15th St, Augusta, GA, 30901-3105. Tel: 708-821-8361. p. 467
Lewis, Amy, Info Literacy Librn, Alamo Colleges District, 1201 Kitty Hawk Rd, Universal City, TX, 78148. Tel: 210-486-5465. p. 2250
Lewis, Angela, Br Mgr, Belmont County District Library, Bethesda Branch, 112 N Main St, Bethesda, OH, 43719. Tel: 740-484-4532. p. 1800
Lewis, Audrey, Curator, Brandywine Conservancy, Inc, One Hoffman's Mill Rd, Chadds Ford, PA, 19317. Tel: 610-388-2700. p. 1920
Lewis, Beth A, Dir, Libr Serv, Talbot Research Library & Media Services, 333 Cottman Ave, 3rd Flr, Philadelphia, PA, 19111-2497. Tel: 215-728-2710. p. 1986
Lewis, Blake, Cat, Circ, Libr Tech, Chabot College Library, 25555 Hesperian Blvd, Hayward, CA, 94545. Tel: 510-723-7113. p. 150
Lewis, Brandi, Dir, Constableville Village Library, 3158 Main St, Constableville, NY, 13325. Tel: 315-397-2801. p. 1521
Lewis, Carol, Mgr, Chester County Library, 100 Center St, Chester, SC, 29706. Tel: 803-377-8145. p. 2052
Lewis, Christopher, Dir, Multimedia Coll & Serv, American University Library, 4400 Massachusetts Ave NW, Washington, DC, 20016-8046. Tel: 202-885-3257. p. 361
Lewis, Christopher, Libr Spec II, Southern University in New Orleans, 6400 Press Dr, New Orleans, LA, 70126. Tel: 504-286-5225. p. 903
Lewis, Cindy, Ch, Barclay Public Library District, 220 S Main St, Warrensburg, IL, 62573-9657. Tel: 217-672-3621. p. 658

Lewis, Clayton D, Head, Reader Serv, University of Michigan, William L Clements Library, 909 S University Ave, Ann Arbor, MI, 48109-1190. Tel: 734-764-2347. p. 1079

Lewis, Clementine, Head, ILL, Fiorello H LaGuardia Community College Library, 31-10 Thomson Ave, Long Island City, NY, 11101. Tel: 718-482-5421. p. 1565

Lewis, Connie, Asst Dir, Ref Serv, Hardin County Library, 1365 Pickwick St, Savannah, TN, 38372. Tel: 731-925-4314, 731-925-6848. p. 2125

Lewis, Cynthia Patterson, Dir, King Library & Archives, 449 Auburn Ave NE, Atlanta, GA, 30312. Tel: 404-526-8986. p. 465

Lewis, Dan, Interim Libr Dir, Capital Community College, 950 Main St, Hartford, CT, 06103-1207. Tel: 860-906-5020. p. 316

Lewis, Daniel, Purchasing & Accounting Mgr, Mount Saint Mary's University, 16300 Old Emmitsburg Rd, Emmitsburg, MD, 21727. Tel: 301-447-5253. p. 965

Lewis, Dawn, Br Mgr, Kent District Library, East Grand Rapids Branch, 746 Lakeside Dr SE, East Grand Rapids, MI, 49506. p. 1094

Lewis, Debbie, Head Cataloger, Sylvester Memorial Wellston Public Library, 135 E Second St, Wellston, OH, 45692. Tel: 740-384-6660. p. 1829

Lewis, Debra, Br Mgr, Iberville Parish Library, Maringouin Branch, 77175 Ridgewood Dr, Maringouin, LA, 70757. Tel: 225-625-2743. p. 906

Lewis, Derrick, Info Spec, United States Department of Transportation, National Highway Traffic Safety Administration-Technical Information Services, NPO-411, 1200 New Jersey Ave SE, Washington, DC, 20590. Tel: 202-366-2588. p. 379

Lewis, Dory, Coordr, Automation & Tech Serv, Pollard Memorial Library, 401 Merrimack St, Lowell, MA, 01852. Tel: 978-674-4120. p. 1029

Lewis, Elise C, PhD, Instr, University of South Carolina, 1501 Greene St, Columbia, SC, 29208. Tel: 803-777-3858. p. 2792

Lewis, Erin, Adult Serv, Circ Librn, Melrose Public Library, 263 W Foster St, Melrose, MA, 02176. Tel: 781-665-2313. p. 1034

Lewis, Forrest, Dir, North Las Vegas Library District, 2250 Las Vegas Blvd, Ste 133, North Las Vegas, NV, 89030. Tel: 702-633-1070. p. 1348

Lewis, Francene, Cat Librn, Head, Coll, Calvin University & Calvin Theological Seminary, 1855 Knollcrest Circle SE, Grand Rapids, MI, 49546-4402. Tel: 616-526-6308. p. 1110

Lewis, Gabrielle, Dir, Seyfarth Shaw LLP, 233 Wacker Dr, Ste 8000, Chicago, IL, 60606-6448. Tel: 312-460-5000. p. 568

Lewis, Gabrielle, Libr Mgr, Seyfarth & Shaw New York Library, 620 Eighth Ave, Flr 32, New York, NY, 10018-1405. Tel: 212-218-5500. p. 1602

Lewis, Gina, Dir, Alburgh Public Library, 128 S Main St, Alburg, VT, 05440. Tel: 802-796-6077. p. 2277

Lewis, Ginny, Div Mgr, Res Serv, High Point Public Library, 901 N Main St, High Point, NC, 27262. Tel: 336-883-3643. p. 1696

Lewis, Heidi, Mgr, Boise Public Library, 715 S Capitol Blvd, Boise, ID, 83702. Tel: 208-972-8200. p. 516

Lewis, Ian G, Archives Librn, St John's University Library, St Augustine Hall, 8000 Utopia Pkwy, Jamaica, NY, 11439. Tel: 718-990-6682. p. 1556

Lewis, Iveta, Mgr, Health Sci Libr & Archives, Holland Bloorview Kids Rehabilitaion Hospital, 150 Kilgour Rd, Toronto, ON, M4G 1R8, CANADA. Tel: 416-425-6220, Ext 3517. p. 2689

Lewis, James, Dept Head, Morristown & Morris Township Library, Caroline Rose Foster, North Jersey History & Genealogy Center, One Miller Rd, Morristown, NJ, 07960. Tel: 973-538-3473. p. 1421

Lewis, James, Genealogy Librn, The Morristown & Morris Township Library, One Miller Rd, Morristown, NJ, 07960. Tel: 973-538-6161. p. 1421

Lewis, James, Historian, Forest History Society Library, 701 William Vickers Ave, Durham, NC, 27701-3162. Tel: 919-682-9319. p. 1685

Lewis, Janice Steed, Academic Services, Dir, East Carolina University, J Y Joyner Library, E Fifth St, Greenville, NC, 27858-4353. Tel: 252-328-2267. p. 1693

Lewis, Jean M, Librn, Mercy Health, 1235 E Cherokee St, Springfield, MO, 65804-2263. Tel: 417-820-2795. p. 1280

Lewis, Jeff, Br Mgr, Washington County Library System, Springdale Branch, 126 Lion Blvd, Springdale, UT, 84767. Tel: 435-772-3676. p. 2270

Lewis, Jennifer, Librn, Hamlin Memorial Library & Museum, 16 Hannibal Hamlin Dr, South Paris, ME, 04281. Tel: 207-743-2980. p. 941

Lewis, Jenny, Br Mgr, Lexington Public Library, Northside, 1733 Russell Cave Rd, Lexington, KY, 40505. p. 862

Lewis, Jocelyn, Head Librn, Indiana Academy of Science, Indiana State Library, 140 N Senate Ave, Indianapolis, IN, 46204. Tel: 317-232-3686. p. 692

Lewis, Jocelyn, Cat, Indiana State Library, 315 W Ohio St, Indianapolis, IN, 46202. Tel: 317-232-3675. p. 692

Lewis, Jodi, Br Librn, London Public Library, Jalna, 1119 Jalna Blvd, London, ON, N6E 3B3, CANADA. Tel: 519-685-6465. p. 2654

Lewis, Karen, Conserv Librn, Res, Oregon Zoo Animal Management Library, 4001 SW Canyon Rd, Portland, OR, 97221. Tel: 503-226-1561. p. 1893

Lewis, Karla, Assoc Dean, Southeastern Illinois College, 3575 College Rd, Harrisburg, IL, 62946. Tel: 618-252-5400, Ext 2261, 618-252-5400, Ext 2326. p. 597

Lewis, Kate, Librn, Artexte Information Centre, Two Saint-Catherine St Est, Rm 301, Montreal, QC, H2X 1K4, CANADA. Tel: 514-874-0049. p. 2716

Lewis, Kelsey E, Ref Librn, North Carolina Legislative Library, 500 Legislative Office Bldg, 300 N Salisbury St, Raleigh, NC, 27603-5925. Tel: 919-733-9390. p. 1709

Lewis, Ken, Dr, Dir, Child Custody Research Library, PO Box 202, Glenside, PA, 19038-0202. Tel: 215-576-0177. p. 1937

Lewis, Krista, Archivist, Olmsted County Historical Society, 1195 W Circle Dr SW, Rochester, MN, 55902. Tel: 507-282-9447. p. 1194

Lewis, Layna, Br Librn, Brazoria County Library System, Danbury Branch, 1702 N Main St, Danbury, TX, 77534. Tel: 979-922-1905. p. 2135

Lewis, Layna L, Br Head, Brazoria County Library System, Angleton Branch, 401 E Cedar St, Angleton, TX, 77515-4652. Tel: 979-864-1519. p. 2135

Lewis, Letoria, Instruction & Outreach Librn, University of North Carolina at Pembroke, One University Dr, Pembroke, NC, 28372. Tel: 910-521-6516. p. 1707

Lewis, Linda, Mgr, Colorado Department of Corrections, Fremont Correctional Facility Library, US Hwy 50, Evans Blvd, Canon City, CO, 81215. Tel: 719-269-5002, Ext 3566. p. 269

Lewis, Linda, Br Mgr, Garfield County Public Library District, Silt Branch, 680 Home Ave, Silt, CO, 81652. Tel: 970-876-5500. p. 294

Lewis, Lori, Asst Circ Mgr, Branch Services, Readers' Advisor Librn, Laramie County Library System, 2200 Pioneer Ave, Cheyenne, WY, 82001-3610. Tel: 307-773-7211. p. 2492

Lewis, Lynn, Mgr, Dallas Public Library, Skillman Southwestern, 5707 Skillman St, Dallas, TX, 75206. Tel: 214-670-6078. p. 2166

Lewis, Marguerite, Mgr, Info Serv, Innovation, Science & Economic Development, 235 Queen St, 2nd Flr, W Tower, Ottawa, ON, K1A 0H5, CANADA. Tel: 343-291-3033. p. 2667

Lewis, Mark, Bus Mgr, Kern County Library, 701 Truxtun Ave, Bakersfield, CA, 93301. Tel: 661-868-0700. p. 119

Lewis, Mary Ann, Libr Dir, Barrett Paradise Friendly Library, 6500 Rte 191, Cresco, PA, 18326. Tel: 570-595-7171. p. 1925

Lewis, Melinda, Dir, Johnsonburg Public Library, 520 Market St, Johnsonburg, PA, 15845. Tel: 814-965-4110. p. 1947

Lewis, Meredith, Ref Librn, Durham Technical Community College, Orange County Campus, 525 College Park Rd, Hillsborough, NC, 27278. Tel: 919-536-7238. p. 1685

Lewis, Michael, Libr Dir, James Memorial Library, 300 W Scioto St, Saint James, MO, 65559. Tel: 573-265-7211. p. 1268

Lewis, Michelle, Patron Experience Supvr, Hennepin County Library, Brooklyn Park, 8500 W Broadway Ave, Brooklyn Park, MN, 55445. Tel: 612-543-6229. p. 1186

Lewis, Mike, Dir, Human Res, Edmonton Public Library, Seven Sir Winston Churchill Sq, Edmonton, AB, T5J 2V4, CANADA. Tel: 780-496-7066. p. 2536

Lewis, Nancy, Head, Ref (Info Serv), University of Maine, 5729 Fogler Library, Orono, ME, 04469-5729. Tel: 207-581-3613. p. 934

Lewis, Peter, Tech Serv, Crown Point Community Library, 122 N Main St, Crown Point, IN, 46307. Tel: 219-663-0270. p. 678

Lewis, Richard, Libr Dir, Prescott College Library, 220 Grove Ave, Prescott, AZ, 86301. Tel: 928-350-1300. p. 73

Lewis, Rita, Ch Serv, Centralia Regional Library District, 515 E Broadway, Centralia, IL, 62801. Tel: 618-532-5222. p. 551

Lewis, Roxanne, Mgr, Northeast Missouri Library Service, Lewistown Branch, 219 W Main St, Lewistown, MO, 63452. Tel: 513-215-2601. p. 1254

Lewis, S Miles, Audio Production Admini, Texas State Library & Archives Commission, 1201 Brazos St, Austin, TX, 78701. Tel: 512-463-5458. p. 2141

Lewis, Sabrina, Dir, Avoca Public Library, 213 N Elm St, Avoca, IA, 51521. Tel: 712-343-6358. p. 733

Lewis, Sadina, Br Mgr, Horry County Memorial Library, Little River Branch, Ralph H Ellis County Complex Bldg, 107 Hwy 57 N, Little River, SC, 29566. Tel: 843-399-5541. p. 2056

Lewis, Sandy, Head Librn, Tech Serv, Palmer College of Chiropractic-Davenport Campus, 1000 Brady St, Davenport, IA, 52803-5287. Tel: 563-884-5641. p. 744

Lewis, Sara, Libr Dir, Houston Public Library, 3150 14th St, Houston, BC, V0J 1Z0, CANADA. Tel: 250-845-2256. p. 2567

Lewis, Sheri, Dir, University of Chicago Library, D'Angelo Law Library, 1121 E 60th St, Chicago, IL, 60637-2786. Tel: 773-702-9614. p. 570

Lewis, Stacey, Reader Serv Mgr, Texas State Library & Archives Commission, 1201 Brazos St, Austin, TX, 78701. Tel: 512-463-5458. p. 2141

Lewis, Sydney, Br Mgr, Crawford County Library District, Steelville City Branch, 210 S Fourth St, Steelville, MO, 65565. Tel: 573-775-2338. p. 1282

Lewis, Terri, Resource Serv Mgr, Boulder Public Library, 1001 Arapahoe Rd, Boulder, CO, 80302. Tel: 303-441-3100. p. 266

Lewis, Theresa A, Librn, Alden Balch Memorial Library, 24 E Main St, Lunenburg, VT, 05906. Tel: 802-892-5365. p. 2288

Lewis, Tiffany, Head, Children's Servx, Eisenhower Public Library District, 4613 N Oketo Ave, Harwood Heights, IL, 60706. Tel: 708-867-2298. p. 597

Lieggi, Tori, Coordr, Access Serv, Instrul Serv Librn, Lycoming College, One College Pl, Williamsport, PA, 17701. Tel: 570-321-4053. p. 2023
Lien, Charlene, Br Librn, Siouxland Libraries, Crooks Branch, 900 N West Ave, Crooks, SD, 57020-6402. Tel: 605-367-6384. p. 2082
Lien, Mardene, Dir, Joice Public Library, 303 Keerl St, Joice, IA, 50446. Tel: 641-588-3330. p. 762
Lien, Sharlene, Br Librn, Siouxland Libraries, Colton Branch, 402 S Dakota Ave, Colton, SD, 57018. Tel: 605-446-3519. p. 2082
Lien, Sharlene, Br Librn, Siouxland Libraries, Hartford Branch, 119 N Main Ave, Ste A, Hartford, SD, 57033. Tel: 605-367-6380. p. 2082
Lien, Sharlene, Br Librn, Siouxland Libraries, Humboldt Branch, 201 S Main St, Humboldt, SD, 57035. Tel: 605-363-3361. p. 2082
Lienemann, Stacy, Syst Dir, Waseca-Le Sueur Regional Library, 408 N State St, Waseca, MN, 56093. Tel: 507-835-2910. p. 1207
Liesman, Vanda, Ch, Vermillion County Public Library, 385 E Market St, Newport, IN, 47966. Tel: 765-492-3555. p. 710
Liestman, Daniel, Libr Dir, Ref Librn, Heritage University, 3240 Fort Rd, Toppenish, WA, 98948. Tel: 509-865-8520, Ext 5420. p. 2388
Liethen, Miriam, Electronic Serv Librn, Grace College & Grace Theological Seminary, 921 Connection Circle, Winona Lake, IN, 46590. Tel: 574-372-5100, Ext 6292. p. 727
Lietzan, Caitlin, Dir, Libr Serv, Williams & Connolly Library, 680 Maine Ave SW, Washington, DC, 20024. Tel: 202-434-5306. p. 381
Lietzau, Zeth, Dir, Coll & Tech, Denver Public Library, Ten W 14th Ave Pkwy, Denver, CO, 80204-2731. Tel: 720-865-1111. p. 275
Liford, Ashley, Commun Librn, Monroe County Library System, Summerfield-Petersburg Branch, 60 E Center St, Petersburg, MI, 49270. Tel: 734-279-1025. p. 1134
Light, Carolyn, Br Mgr, Raleigh County Public Library, Shady Spring Branch, 440 Flat Top Rd, Shady Spring, WV, 25918. Tel: 304-763-2681. p. 2397
Light, Phoenix, Mgr, Henry County Public Library System, Fairview Public Library, 28 Austin Rd, Stockbridge, GA, 30281. Tel: 770-389-6277. p. 490
Lightell, Peggy, Br Librn, Plaquemines Parish Library, Port Sulphur Branch, 139 Civic Dr, Port Sulphur, LA, 70083. Tel: 504-564-3681, 504-564-3682. p. 885
Lightfoot Cooper, Donna, Head, Circ, The Nyack Library, 59 S Broadway, Nyack, NY, 10960. Tel: 845-358-3370, Ext 212. p. 1609
Lightfoot, Kevin, Coll Librn, Resource Management, McLennan Community College Library, 1400 College Dr, Waco, TX, 76708-1498. Tel: 254-299-8389. p. 2253
Lightfoot, Rebecca, Br Librn, Newport Beach Public Library, Mariners Branch, 1300 Irvine Ave, Newport Beach, CA, 92660. Tel: 949-717-3838. p. 183
Lightfoot, Sandra, Librn, Addie Davis Memorial Library, 301 N Fourth St, Mountain View, OK, 73062. Tel: 580-347-2397. p. 1854
Lightfoot, Susan, Dir, Carrollton Public Library, One N Folger St, Carrollton, MO, 64633. Tel: 660-542-0183. p. 1240
Lightfoot-Horine, Sue, Dir, Livingston County Library, 450 Locust St, Chillicothe, MO, 64601-2597. Tel: 660-646-0547. p. 1242
Lighthart, Matthew, Libr Mgr, Virginia Beach Public Library, Great Neck Area, 1251 Bayne Dr, Virginia Beach, VA, 23454. Tel: 757-385-2606. p. 2350
Lightman, Lorissa, ESL Coordr, Ref Librn, River Vale Free Public Library, 412 Rivervale Rd, River Vale, NJ, 07675. Tel: 201-391-2323. p. 1440
Liimatainen, Susan, Asst Dir, Rutland Free Public Library, 280 Main St, Rutland, MA, 01543. Tel: 508-886-4108, Option 5. p. 1050
Liittschwager, Lisa, Dir, Dr Grace O Doane Alden Public Library, 1012 Water St, Alden, IA, 50006. Tel: 515-859-3820. p. 730
Likins, Rose M, Libr Dir, Smyth County Public Library, 118 S Sheffey St, Marion, VA, 24354. Tel: 276-783-2323. p. 2331
Liles, Becky, Br Mgr, Briggs Lawrence County Public Library, Symmes Valley Branch, 14778 State Rte 141, Willow Wood, OH, 45696. Tel: 740-643-2086. p. 1791
Lilien-Harper, Amy, Children's Mgr, Wilton Library Association, 137 Old Ridgefield Rd, Wilton, CT, 06897-3000. Tel: 203-762-3950. p. 347
Liljequist, Karen, Sr Mgr, Research & Instruction Servs, RIT Libraries, 90 Lomb Memorial Dr, Rochester, NY, 14623-5604. Tel: 585-475-2559. p. 1629
Lill, Jonathan, Head, Metadata Serv, Head, Syst, The Museum of Modern Art, 11 W 53th St, New York, NY, 10019. Tel: 212-708-9433. p. 1592
Lill, Kris, Librn/Br Mgr, Allen County Public Library, Aboite, 5630 Coventry Lane, Fort Wayne, IN, 46804. Tel: 260-421-1310. p. 683
Lilla, Neva, Youth Serv Mgr, New Castle Public Library, 207 E North St, New Castle, PA, 16101-3691. Tel: 724-658-6659, Ext 106. p. 1969
Lillard, Justin, Libr Dir, University of Arkansas Community College at Morrilton, 1537 University Blvd, Morrilton, AR, 72110. Tel: 501-977-2092. p. 105
Lillard, Linda, Dr, Dept Chair, Pennsylvania Western University - Clarion, 840 Wood St, Clarion, PA, 16214. Tel: 814-393-2271. p. 2791
Lillegard, Jeanne M, Dir, Judith Basin County Free Library, 93 Third St N, Stanford, MT, 59479. Tel: 406-566-2277, Ext 123. p. 1302
Lillegard, Kirsten, Evening Supvr, University of Dubuque Library, 2000 University Ave, Dubuque, IA, 52001. Tel: 563-589-3100. p. 749
Lillie, Amber, Mgr, Support Serv, Prescott Public Library, 215 E Goodwin St, Prescott, AZ, 86303. Tel: 928-777-1504. p. 73
Lilly, Jessica, Br Mgr, Harris County Public Library, Northwest Branch Library, 11355 Regency Green Dr, Cypress, TX, 77429. Tel: 832-927-5460. p. 2193
Lilyquist, Lisa, City Librn, Lakeland Public Library, 100 Lake Morton Dr, Lakeland, FL, 33801-5375. Tel: 863-834-4280. p. 417
Lim, Betty, Asst Librn, United States Courts Library, 700 Stewart St, Rm 19105, Seattle, WA, 98101. Tel: 206-370-8975. p. 2381
Lim, Robyn, Br Mgr, Atlanta-Fulton Public Library System, Peachtree Branch, 1315 Peachtree St NE, Atlanta, GA, 30309. Tel: 404-885-7830. p. 461
Lim, Sook, PhD, Assoc Prof, Saint Catherine University, 2004 Randolph Ave, Mailstop No 4125, Saint Paul, MN, 55105. Tel: 651-690-6802. p. 2787
Lim-Lovatt, Holly, Adult Prog & Serv, Leduc Public Library, Two Alexandra Park, Leduc, AB, T9E 4C4, CANADA. Tel: 780-986-2637. p. 2546
Lima, Marie-Ève, Chef de Section, Bibliotheques de Montreal, Frontenac, 2550 rue Ontario Est, Montreal, QC, H2K 1W7, CANADA. Tel: 514-872-7889. p. 2718
Lima, Robin A, Head, Circ, United States Naval War College Library, 686 Cushing Rd, Newport, RI, 02841-1207. Tel: 401-841-6508. p. 2035
Limacher, Michael, Media Spec, Illinois Wesleyan University, One Ames Plaza, Bloomington, IL, 61701-7188. Tel: 309-556-3323. p. 543
Limb, Melanie, Libr Dir, Rich County Library, 55 N Main St, Randolph, UT, 84064. Tel: 435-793-2122. p. 2270
Limer, Michael, Dir, Guernsey County District Public Library, 800 Steubenville Ave, Cambridge, OH, 43725-2385. Tel: 740-432-5946. p. 1754
Limoges, Diane, Dir, Eastern Township Public Library, 206 W Main St, Crofton, NE, 68730. Tel: 402-388-4915. p. 1311
Limon, Melissa, Libr Operations Supvr, El Centro Public Library, 1198 N Imperial Ave, El Centro, CA, 92243. Tel: 760-337-4565. p. 139
Limpitlaw, Amy, Head Librn, Boston University Libraries, School of Theology Library, 745 Commonwealth Ave, 2nd Flr, Boston, MA, 02215. Tel: 617-353-3034. p. 993
Lin, Emily S, Head, Digital Assets, University of California, Merced Library, 5200 N Lake Rd, Merced, CA, 95343. Tel: 209-658-7146. p. 176
Lin Hanick, Silvia, First Year Experience Librn, Fiorello H LaGuardia Community College Library, 31-10 Thomson Ave, Long Island City, NY, 11101. Tel: 718-482-5421. p. 1565
Lin, Hsiu-Ling, Ser Tech, Oregon Institute of Technology Library, 3201 Campus Dr, Klamath Falls, OR, 97601-8801. Tel: 541-885-1772. p. 1883
Lin, James K, Cat, Harvard Library, Harvard-Yenching Library, Two Divinity Ave, Cambridge, MA, 02138. Tel: 617-495-2756. p. 1006
Lin, Mingzhi, Acq of Monographs & Journals, Acq of New Ser/Per, Far Eastern Research Library, Nine First Ave NE, Plato, MN, 55370. Tel: 612-926-6887. p. 1193
Lin, Rebecca, Acq & Cat, Tech Serv, Door County Library, 107 S Fourth Ave, Sturgeon Bay, WI, 54235. Tel: 920-746-2491. p. 2479
Lin, Tony, Librn, Irvine Valley College Library, 5500 Irvine Center Dr, Irvine, CA, 92618-4399. Tel: 949-451-5761. p. 153
Lin, Yongtao, Ms, Librn, Natural Resources Canada Library, 3303 33rd St NW, 2nd Flr, Calgary, AB, T2L 2A7, CANADA. Tel: 403-292-7165. p. 2528
Lin, Yu-Hung, Syst & Tech Serv Librn, Saint Thomas Aquinas College, 125 Rte 340, Sparkill, NY, 10976. Tel: 845-398-4222. p. 1643
Linacre, Emily, Circulation Lead, Altoona Public Library, 700 Eighth St SW, Altoona, IA, 50009. Tel: 515-967-3881. p. 730
Linam, Alisha, Dir, Libr Serv, Coastal Alabama Community College, H Pat Lindsay Library, 251 College St, Gilbertown, AL, 36908. Tel: 334-843-4427. p. 6
Linam, Alisha, Dir, Libr Serv, Coastal Alabama Community College, John Dennis Forte Library, 2800 S Alabama Ave, Monroeville, AL, 36460. Tel: 251-575-8271. p. 6
Linam, Alisha, Dir, Libr Serv, Coastal Alabama Community College, Kathryn Tucker Windham Library & Museum, 30755 Hwy 43, Thomasville, AL, 36784-2519. Tel: 334-637-3147. p. 6
Linan, Robert, Pub Serv Coordr, Arlington Public Library System, Woodland West, 2837 W Park Row Dr, Arlington, TX, 76013. p. 2136
Linares, Debra, Co-Dir, Willington Public Library, Seven Ruby Rd, Willington, CT, 06279. Tel: 860-429-3854. p. 347
Linck, Nancy, Dir, Barnes Reading Room, 640 Main St, Everest, KS, 66424. Tel: 785-548-7733. p. 807
Lincke-Fisseler, Brenda, Dir, Friench Simpson Memorial Library, 705 E Fourth St, Hallettsville, TX, 77964-2828. Tel: 361-798-3243. p. 2187
Lincoln, Ashley, Br Mgr, Summit County Libraries, County Commons Bldg, 0037 Peak One Dr, Frisco, CO, 80443. Tel: 970-668-4138. p. 282
Lincoln, Elizabeth, Dir, Minnesota Legislative Reference Library, 645 State Office Bldg, 100 Rev Dr Martin Luther King Jr Blvd, Saint Paul, MN, 55155-1050. Tel: 651-296-0594. p. 1201
Lincoln, Gerald, Tech Dir, Lancaster Bible College, Teague Learning Commons, 901 Eden Rd, Lancaster, PA, 17601-5036. Tel: 717-569-7071, Ext 5362. p. 1951
Lincoln, Nancy, Circ, Weston Public Library, 56 Norfield Rd, Weston, CT, 06883. Tel: 203-222-2664. p. 346

Lincoln, Patty, Dir, Strawberry Point Public Library, 401 Commercial St, Strawberry Point, IA, 52076. Tel: 563-933-4340. p. 785

Lincoln, Timothy D, Dir, Austin Presbyterian Theological Seminary, 100 E 27th St, Austin, TX, 78705-5797. Tel: 512-404-4873. p. 2138

Lind, Doug, Dir, Law Libr, Southern Illinois University Carbondale, Law Library, Lesar Law Bldg Mailcode 6803, 1150 Douglas Dr, Carbondale, IL, 62901. Tel: 618-453-8713. p. 549

Lind, Nicole, Librn III, Mesa Public Library, Mesa Express Library, 2055 S Power Rd, Ste 1031, Mesa, AZ, 85209. Tel: 480-644-3300. p. 67

Lind, Werner, Co-Director, Library Services, Librn, Bluefield University, 3000 College Ave, Bluefield, VA, 24605. Tel: 276-326-4267. p. 2307

Lind-Sinanian, Gary, Coll Curator, Armenian Museum of America, Inc, Mugar Bldg, 4th Flr, 65 Main St, Watertown, MA, 02472. Tel: 617-926-2562, Ext 111. p. 1062

Lind-Sinanian, Susan, Curator, Armenian Museum of America, Inc, Mugar Bldg, 4th Flr, 65 Main St, Watertown, MA, 02472. Tel: 617-926-2562, Ext 111. p. 1062

Linda, Avellar, Dir, Develop & Communications, The Ferguson Library, One Public Library Plaza, Stamford, CT, 06904. Tel: 203-351-8208. p. 338

Linda, Crouch, Libr Asst II, Dyersburg State Community College, 1510 Lake Rd, Dyersburg, TN, 38024. Tel: 731-286-3223. p. 2097

Lindahl, Susan, Access Serv, Assoc Dir, Cat, University of Wisconsin-Stout, 315 Tenth Ave, Menomonie, WI, 54751-0790. Tel: 715-232-1184. p. 2456

Lindau, Rebecka, Head Librn, University of Cincinnati Libraries, Classics, 417 Blegen Library, Cincinnati, OH, 45221. Tel: 513-556-1315. p. 1764

Lindberg, Amber, Dir, Finance & Fac, Denver Public Library, Ten W 14th Ave Pkwy, Denver, CO, 80204-2731. Tel: 720-865-1111. p. 275

Lindblom, Sarah, Archivist/Librn, Dean College, 99 Main St, Franklin, MA, 02038-1994. Tel: 508-541-1771. p. 1020

Lindbloom, Mary-Carol, Exec Dir, South Central Regional Library Council, Clinton Hall, 108 N Cayuga St, Ithaca, NY, 14850. Tel: 607-273-9106. p. 2771

Linde-Moriarty, Katrina, Libr Dir, Monticello Public Library, 512 E Lake Ave, Monticello, WI, 53570-9658. Tel: 608-938-4011. p. 2462

Lindell, Ann, Head, Archit & Fine Arts Libr, University of Florida Libraries, 1545 W University Ave, Gainesville, FL, 32611-7000. Tel: 352-273-2805. p. 407

Lindell, Cheryl, Br Mgr, Watonwan County Library, Madelia Branch, 23 First St NW, Madelia, MN, 56062. Tel: 507-642-3511. p. 1198

Lindell, Lisa, Cat, South Dakota State University, 1300 N Campus Dr, Box 2115, Brookings, SD, 57007. Tel: 605-688-5561. p. 2074

Lindem, Margaret, Head of Libr, University of Pennsylvania Libraries, Steven W Atwood Veterinary Medicine Library, Vernon & Shirley Hill Pavilion, 380 S University Ave, Philadelphia, PA, 19104-4539. Tel: 215-898-8874. p. 1988

Lindemann, Ruth, Dr, Cat & Tech Serv Librn, Danville Area Community College Library, 2000 E Main St, Danville, IL, 61832-5199. Tel: 217-443-8735. p. 575

Lindemuth, Gay, Supvr, Yakima Valley Libraries, Zillah Library, 109 Seventh St, Zillah, WA, 98953. Tel: 509-829-6707. p. 2396

Linden, Amanda, Libr Mgr, Aikins Law, 360 Main St, 30th Flr, Winnipeg, MB, R3C 4G1, CANADA. Tel: 204-957-0050. p. 2592

Linden, Danielle, Libr Mgr, Saint Joseph Hospital & Childrens Hospital of Orange County, 1100 W Stewart Dr, Orange, CA, 92868. Tel: 714-771-8291. p. 189

Lindenbaum, Mitchell, Librn, California Department of Corrections, Fifth St & Western, Norco, CA, 92860. Tel: 951-737-2683, Ext 4202. p. 183

Lindenfield, Ellen, Regional Mgr, Broward County Libraries Division, 100 S Andrews Ave, Fort Lauderdale, FL, 33301. Tel: 954-201-8834. p. 396

Lindenmuth, Janet, Ref/Electronic Serv Librn, Widener University, School of Law Library, 4601 Concord Pike, Wilmington, DE, 19803. Tel: 302-477-2245. p. 358

Linder, Christina, Asst Dir, Greenburgh Public Library, 300 Tarrytown Rd, Elmsford, NY, 10523. Tel: 914-721-8200. p. 1531

Linder, Lynda, Assoc Dir, Central Christian College of Kansas, 1200 S Main, McPherson, KS, 67460. Tel: 620-241-0723, Ext 359. p. 824

Linder, Samuel, Youth Serv, Balsam Lake Public Library, 404 Main St, Balsam Lake, WI, 54810. Tel: 715-485-3215. p. 2422

Linder, Victoria, Libr Serv Coordr, Cleveland Community College, 137 S Post Rd, Shelby, NC, 28152. Tel: 704-669-4024. p. 1716

Linderman, Eric, Dep Dir, Willoughby-Eastlake Public Library, 35150 Lakeshore Blvd, Eastlake, OH, 44095. Tel: 440-943-2203. p. 1783

Lindgren, Kathy, Acq Spec, University of St Francis, 600 Taylor St, Joliet, IL, 60435. Tel: 815-740-5041. p. 603

Lindh, Mary Kay, Librn, Marquette Community Library, 121 N Washington, Marquette, KS, 67464-0389. Tel: 785-546-2561. p. 824

Lindley, Elizabeth A, Mgr, Tech Serv, Oakland Community College, Library Systems, 2900 Featherstone Rd, MTEC A210, Auburn Hills, MI, 48326. Tel: 248-232-4478. p. 1082

Lindner, Alley, Instruction & Learning Librn, Spalding University Library, 853 Library Lane, Louisville, KY, 40203-9986. Tel: 502-585-7130. p. 867

Lindner, Shawna, Youth Serv Librn, Kearney Public Library, 2020 First Ave, Kearney, NE, 68847. Tel: 308-233-3284. p. 1319

Lindquist, Heidi, Interim Dir, The Art Center of Waco Library, 101 S Third St, Waco, TX, 76701. Tel: 254-752-4371. p. 2252

Lindquist, Tanya, Librn, California Department of Corrections Library System, California State Prison, Sacramento, 100 Prison Rd, Represa, CA, 95671. Tel: 916-985-8610, Ext 6605. p. 206

Lindquist, Thea, Exec Dir, Ctr for Research Data & Digital Schol (CRDDS), University of Colorado Boulder, 1720 Pleasant St, Boulder, CO, 80309. Tel: 303-492-8705. p. 267

Lindquist, Virginia, Dir, Lied Lincoln Township Library, 603 E Norris St, Wausa, NE, 68786. Tel: 402-586-2454. p. 1340

Lindquist, Zachary, Night Circulation Mgr, Midwestern State University, 3410 Taft Blvd, Wichita Falls, TX, 76308-2099. Tel: 940-397-4837. p. 2257

Lindroos, Tamara, Libr Dir, Mullan Public Library, 117 Hunter Ave, Mullan, ID, 83846. Tel: 208-744-1220. p. 527

Lindsay, Amanda, Ref Librn, United States Air Force, Wright-Patterson Air Force Base Library FL2300, 88 MSG/SVMG, Bldg 1226, 5435 Hemlock St, Wright-Patterson AFB, OH, 45433-5420. Tel: 937-257-4340, 937-257-4815. p. 1834

Lindsay, Beth, Libr Operations Mgr, Saint Petersburg Public Library, 3745 Ninth Ave N, Saint Petersburg, FL, 33713. Tel: 727-892-5003. p. 441

Lindsay, J Michael, Head, Coll & Access Serv, University of Tennessee Graduate School of Medicine, 1924 Alcoa Hwy, Box U-111, Knoxville, TN, 37920. Tel: 865-305-9528. p. 2107

Lindsay, Lisa, Pub Serv Mgr, Fresno County Public Library, 2420 Mariposa St, Fresno, CA, 93721. Tel: 559-600-7323. p. 145

Lindsay, Nina, Assoc Dir, Oakland Public Library, 125 14th St, Oakland, CA, 94612. Tel: 510-228-6706. p. 186

Lindsay, Sheila, Dir, Perry County Public Library, 289 Black Gold Blvd, Hazard, KY, 41701. Tel: 606-436-2475, 606-436-4747. p. 858

Lindsey, Ann Marie, Head, Mat Proc, Glen Ellyn Public Library, 400 Duane St, Glen Ellyn, IL, 60137-4508. Tel: 630-469-0879. p. 593

Lindsey, Blake, Mr, Evening/Weekend Supvr, University of California, Berkeley, Mathematics-Statistics, 100 Evans Hall, No 6000, Berkeley, CA, 94720-6000. Tel: 510-642-3381. p. 123

Lindsey, Dan, Libr Dir, Ozarka College, 218 College Dr, Melbourne, AR, 72556-8708. Tel: 870-368-7371. p. 104

Lindsey, Kristi, Dir, Penrose Community Library District, 35 Seventh Ave, Penrose, CO, 81240-0318. Tel: 719-372-6017. p. 292

Lindsey, Laura, Youth Serv, Grayson County Public Library, 163 Carroll Gibson Blvd, Leitchfield, KY, 42754-1488. Tel: 270-259-5455. p. 861

Lindsey, Leslie, Mgr, Premier Health, Miami Valley Hospital, One Wyoming St, Dayton, OH, 45409. Tel: 937-208-2617. p. 1780

Lindsey, Robert, Interim Dean, Libr Serv, Pittsburg State University, 1605 S Joplin St, Pittsburg, KS, 66762-5889. Tel: 620-235-4878. p. 831

Lindsey, Robert, Pub Serv Librn, Pittsburg State University, 1605 S Joplin St, Pittsburg, KS, 66762-5889. Tel: 620-235-4887. p. 831

Lindsey, Ronald, Libr Tech, Smithsonian Libraries, National Museum of Natural History Library, Tenth St & Constitution Ave NW, 1st Flr, Washington, DC, 20013-0712. Tel: 202-633-1673. p. 375

Lindsey, Ronald, Libr Tech, Smithsonian Libraries, John Wesley Powell Library of Anthropology, Natural History Bldg, Rm 331, Tenth St & Constitution Ave NW, Washington, DC, 20560-0112. Tel: 202-633-1640. p. 376

Lindskold, Heather, County Coordr, Blair County Library System, 1600 Fifth Ave, Altoona, PA, 16601. Tel: 814-946-0417, Ext 132. p. 1906

Lindstrom, Elaine, Br Mgr, Dayton Metro Library, Brookville Branch, 120 Blue Pride Dr, Brookville, OH, 45309. Tel: 937-496-8922. p. 1779

Lindstrom, Jane, Dir, Duncombe Public Library, 621 Prince St, Duncombe, IA, 50532. Tel: 515-543-4646. p. 749

Lindstrom, Margaret, Head, Tech Serv, Arcadia Public Library, 20 W Duarte Rd, Arcadia, CA, 91006. Tel: 626-821-5574. p. 117

Lindstrom, Margaret, Libr Consult, Highland Park Presbyterian Church, 3821 University Blvd, Dallas, TX, 75205. Tel: 214-525-4277. p. 2167

Lindstrom, Zhenya, Dean, MiraCosta College Library, One Barnard Dr, Bldg 1200, Oceanside, CA, 92056-3899. Tel: 760-795-6678. p. 187

Lindt, Jim, Mgr, Tech Serv, Wood Dale Public Library District, 520 N Wood Dale Rd, Wood Dale, IL, 60191. Tel: 630-766-6762. p. 664

Line, Faith, Interim Libr Dir, Abbeville County Library System, 1407 N Main St, Abbeville, SC, 29620. Tel: 864-459-4009. p. 2045

Line, Faith A, Dir, Anderson County Library, 300 N McDuffie St, Anderson, SC, 29621-5643. Tel: 864-260-4500. p. 2046

Lineberry, Krystal, Dir, McCracken Public Library, 303 Main St, McCracken, KS, 67556. Tel: 785-394-2444. p. 824

Linehan, Kelly, Dir, Waltham Public Library, 735 Main St, Waltham, MA, 02451. Tel: 781-314-3425. p. 1062

Liner, Russell, Head, Pub Serv, Augusta-Richmond County Public Library, 823 Telfair St, Augusta, GA, 30901. Tel: 706-821-2600. p. 466

Lingenfelter, Mike, Webmaster, Bellwood-Antis Public Library, 526 Main St, Bellwood, PA, 16617-1910. Tel: 814-742-8234. p. 1910

Lingle, Jane, Head, Support Serv, Oldsmar Public Library, 400 St Petersburg Dr E, Oldsmar, FL, 34677. Tel: 813-749-1178. p. 430

Lingle, Victoria, Dir, North Versailles Public Library, 1401 Greensburg Ave, North Versailles, PA, 15227. Tel: 412-823-2222. p. 1971

Lingner, May, Dir, Cheatham County Public Library, 188 County Services Dr, Ste 200, Ashland City, TN, 37015-1726. Tel: 615-792-4828. p. 2088
Lininger, Cindy, Dir, Bussey Community Library, 401 Merrill St, Bussey, IA, 50044. Tel: 641-944-5994. p. 736
Lininger, Jill, Libr Dir, Oak Creek Public Library, Drexel Town Sq, 8040 S Sixth St, Oak Creek, WI, 53154. Tel: 414-766-7900. p. 2465
Linitz, Karen Storin, Assoc Dean, Learning Res, Emmanuel College, 400 The Fenway, Boston, MA, 02115. Tel: 617-975-9324. p. 995
Link, Alissa, Head, STEM, Northeastern University Libraries, 360 Huntington Ave, Boston, MA, 02115. Tel: 617-373-2458. p. 998
Link, Ashley, Libr Dir, Melbourne Beach Public Library, 324 Ocean Ave, Melbourne Beach, FL, 32951. Tel: 321-956-5642. p. 421
Link, Cathy, Mgr, Ch & Youth Serv, Frederick County Public Libraries, 110 E Patrick St, Frederick, MD, 21701. Tel: 301-600-1613. p. 966
Link, Cindy, Library Contact, Rockford Institute Library, 928 N Main St, Rockford, IL, 61103. Tel: 815-964-5053. p. 641
Link, Forrest, Acq, The College of New Jersey, 2000 Pennington Rd, Ewing, NJ, 08628-1104. Tel: 609-771-2311. p. 1402
Link, Jennifer, Libr Dir, Ebensburg Cambria Public Library, 225 W Highland Ave, Ebensburg, PA, 15931. Tel: 814-472-7957. p. 1929
Link, Ruth, Interim Mgr, Durham County Library, Southwest, 3605 Shannon Rd, Durham, NC, 27707. Tel: 919-560-8590. p. 1685
Link, Tiffany, Research Librn, Maine Historical Society, 489 Congress St, Portland, ME, 04101. Tel: 207-774-1822. p. 936
Linke, Erika, Principal Librn, Carnegie Mellon University, Hunt Library, 4909 Frew St, Pittsburgh, PA, 15213. Tel: 412-268-7800. p. 1992
Linker, Maureen, Dir, University of Michigan-Dearborn, 4901 Evergreen Rd, Dearborn, MI, 48128-2406. Tel: 313-593-5545. p. 1096
Linkewich, Bernice, Libr Serv Coordr, Edmonton Public Library, Sprucewood, 11555 95 St, Edmonton, AB, T5G 1L5, CANADA. Tel: 780-496-7043. p. 2537
Linkey, Emily, Libr Dir, Payson Public Library, 328 N McLane Rd, Payson, AZ, 85541. Tel: 928-472-5160. p. 68
Linko, Marjorie, Dir, Liberty Public Library, 189 N Main St, Liberty, NY, 12754-1828. Tel: 845-292-6070. p. 1563
Linn, Jenn, Dir, Tech Serv Librn, Niagara County Community College, 3111 Saunders Settlement Rd, Sanborn, NY, 14132. Tel: 716-614-6787. p. 1635
Linn, Rachel, Libr Mgr, West Georgia Regional Library, 710 Rome St, Carrollton, GA, 30117. Tel: 770-836-6711. p. 469
Linn, Rachel, Mgr, West Georgia Regional Library, Villa Rica Public Library, 869 Dallas Hwy, Villa Rica, GA, 30180. Tel: 770-459-7012. p. 470
Linney, Amy, Asst Dir, Adel Public Library, 303 S Tenth St, Adel, IA, 50003-1797. Tel: 515-993-3512. p. 729
Linscott, Kristin, Coordr of Develop, Plano Public Library System, Library Administration, 2501 Coit Rd, Plano, TX, 75075. Tel: 972-769-4211. p. 2227
Linsday, Shannon, Dir, Princeton Public Library, 124 S Hart St, Princeton, IN, 47670. Tel: 812-385-4464. p. 714
Linsday, Sharon, Br Supvr, Warren Public Library, Maybelle Burnette Branch, 23345 Van Dyke Ave, Warren, MI, 48089. Tel: 586-353-0579. p. 1157
Linskey-Deegan, Mara, Assoc Curator, Charles H MacNider Museum Library, 303 Second St SE, Mason City, IA, 50401. Tel: 641-421-3666. p. 768
Lintelmann, Susan, Ms Curator, United States Military Academy Library, Jefferson Hall Library & Learning Ctr, 758 Cullum Rd, West Point, NY, 10996. Tel: 845-938-8301. p. 1663
Linthicum, Som, Dir, Tri-County Technical College Library, 7900 Hwy 76, Pendleton, SC, 29670. Tel: 864-646-1750. p. 2067
Lintner, Lisa, Dir, Johnson County Public Library, 49 E Monroe St, Franklin, IN, 46131. p. 686
Linton, Anne, Dir, George Washington University, Paul Himmelfarb Health Sciences Library, 2300 I St NW, Washington, DC, 20037. Tel: 202-994-1826. p. 367
Linton, Barbara, Ref Librn, Borough of Manhattan Community College Library, 199 Chambers St, S410, New York, NY, 10007. Tel: 212-220-1448. p. 1580
Linton, Janice, Liaison Librn, University of Manitoba Libraries, Neil John Maclean Health Sciences Library, Brodie Center Atrium, Mezzanine Level, 2nd Flr, 727 McDermot Ave, Winnipeg, MB, R3E 3P5, CANADA. Tel: 204-789-3342. p. 2595
Linton, Joyelle, Br Mgr, Northwest Regional Library System, Charles Whitehead Wewahitchka Public Library, 314 North Second St, Wewahitchka, FL, 32465. Tel: 850-639-2419. p. 436
Linton, Walter, Libr Asst, New York Academy of Medicine Library, 1216 Fifth Ave, New York, NY, 10029. Tel: 212-822-7362. p. 1593
Lintott, Crystal, Librn, Eastern Irrigation District, 550 Industrial Rd W, Brooks, AB, T1R 1B2, CANADA. Tel: 403-362-1400. p. 2524
Lintz, Laura, Ch, Henrietta Public Library, 625 Calkins Rd, Rochester, NY, 14623. Tel: 585-359-7092. p. 1628
Linvill, Anne, Interim Dean, Libr Serv, Menlo College, 1000 El Camino Real, Atherton, CA, 94027. Tel: 650-543-3826. p. 118
Linz, Robert, Assoc Dir, Head, Pub Serv, University of Colorado Boulder, William A Wise Law Library, Wolf Law Bldg, 2nd Flr, 2450 Kittredge Loop Dr, Boulder, CO, 80309-0402. Tel: 303-492-2504. p. 268
Linz, Robert, Assoc Dir, University of Oklahoma Libraries, University of Oklahoma College of Law, 300 Timberdell Rd, Norman, OK, 73019. Tel: 405-325-4311. p. 1856
Linzner, Erika, User Serv Librn, Madison Area Technical College, 3550 Anderson St, Rm A3000, Madison, WI, 53704. Tel: 608-246-6659. p. 2449
Lipcan, Dan, Ann C Pingree, Dir of the Phillips Library, Peabody Essex Museum, 306 Newburyport Tpk, Rowley, MA, 01969. Tel: 978-542-1536. p. 1050
Lipford, Amy, Asst Dir for Res, Florida State University Libraries, College of Law Library, 425 W Jefferson St, Tallahassee, FL, 32306. Tel: 850-644-4578. p. 447
Lipinski, Ann Marie, Curator, Harvard Library, Nieman Foundation-Bill Kovach Collection of Contemporary Journalism Library, One Francis Ave, Cambridge, MA, 02138. Tel: 617-496-8870. p. 1007
Lipinski, Eileen, Libr Mgr, Municipal Research Library, Zeidler Municipal Bldg, Rm B-2, 841 N Broadway, Milwaukee, WI, 53202-3567. Tel: 414-286-8818. p. 2460
Lipinski, Heather, Ad, Warminster Township Free Library, 1076 Emma Lane, Warminster, PA, 18974. Tel: 215-672-4362. p. 2017
Lipinsky, Barry, Libr Supvr, Rutgers University Libraries, James Dickson Carr Library, 75 Ave E, Piscataway, NJ, 08854-8040. Tel: 848-445-3838. p. 1424
Lipke, Laura, Liaison Librn, A T Still University, Kirksville Campus, 800 W Jefferson St, Kirksville, MO, 63501. Tel: 660-626-2345. p. 1258
Lipker, Peggy, Librn, Superior Public Library, 449 N Kansas, Superior, NE, 68978-1852. Tel: 402-879-4200. p. 1337
Lipman, Penny, Librn, Royal Canadian Military Institute Library, 426 University Ave, Toronto, ON, M5G 1S9, CANADA. Tel: 416-597-0286, Ext 128. p. 2692
Lipp, Barbara, Br Mgr, Annapolis Valley Regional Library, Berwick & District Library, 236 Commercial St, Berwick, NS, B0P 1E0, CANADA. Tel: 902-538-4030. p. 2616
Lipp, Colleen, Chief Librn/CEO, Caledon Public Library, 150 Queen St S, Bolton, ON, L7E 1E3, CANADA. Tel: 905-857-1400, Ext 215. p. 2631
Lipp-Accord, Darcy, Dep Dir, Albany County Public Library, 310 S Eighth St, Laramie, WY, 82070-3969. Tel: 307-721-2580. p. 2496
Lippard, Rodney, Libr Dir, University of Central Arkansas, 201 Donaghey Ave, Conway, AR, 72035. Tel: 501-450-3174. p. 93
Lippert, Andrew, Special Colls Processing Archivist, University of California, Riverside, Special Collections & University Archives, 900 University Ave, Riverside, CA, 92521. Tel: 951-827-3233. p. 203
Lippert, Jennifer, Educ Serv Coordr, Thiel College, 75 College Ave, Greenville, PA, 16125-2183. Tel: 724-589-2124. p. 1939
Lippert, Minetta, Youth Serv Librn, Dwight Foster Public Library, 209 Merchants Ave, Fort Atkinson, WI, 53538-2049. Tel: 920-563-7790. p. 2436
Lippincott, Aura, Instrul Designer, Western Connecticut State University, 181 White St, Danbury, CT, 06810. Tel: 203-837-9100. p. 307
Lippincott, Bertram, III, Librn, Newport Historical Society Library, 82 Touro St, Newport, RI, 02840. Tel: 401-846-0813, Ext 106. p. 2034
Lippincott, Kate, Br Mgr, Manatee County Public Library System, Rocky Bluff, 7016 US Hwy 301 N, Ellenton, FL, 34222. Tel: 941-723-4821. p. 387
Lippo, Amy, Librn, Northeast State Community College, 2425 Hwy 75, Blountville, TN, 37617. Tel: 423-354-2429. p. 2088
Lippold, Karen, Head, Info Serv, Ref (Info Servs), Memorial University of Newfoundland, Queen Elizabeth II Library, 234 Elizabeth Ave, St. John's, NL, A1B 3Y1, CANADA. Tel: 709-737-7428. p. 2610
Lipscomb, Barney, Dir, Botanical Research Institute of Texas Library, 1700 University Dr, Fort Worth, TX, 76107. Tel: 817-332-4441, 817-463-4102. p. 2179
Lipscomb, Georgia, Librn, Sardis City Public Library, 1310 Church St, Sardis City, AL, 35956-2200. Tel: 256-593-5634. p. 35
Lipscomb, Pam, Mgr, Miami University Libraries, Southwest Ohio Regional Depository, 4200 N University Blvd, Middletown, OH, 45042-3458. Tel: 513-727-3474. p. 1812
Lipscomb, Pamela, Librn, Arent Fox PLLC Library, 1717 K St NW, Washington, DC, 20006. Tel: 202-857-6000. p. 361
Lipscomb, Trina, Libr Asst, Navajo Nation Library, 1/4 Mile N US Hwy 163, Kayenta, AZ, 86033. Tel: 928-697-5563. p. 63
Lipsey, Kim, Educ Coordr, Washington University Libraries, Bernard Becker Medical Library, 660 S Euclid Ave, Campus Box 8132, Saint Louis, MO, 63110. Tel: 314-362-4733. p. 1277
Lipsey, Sarah, Div Mgr, Coll Develop, Arkansas State Library, 900 W Capitol, Ste 100, Little Rock, AR, 72201-3108. Tel: 501-682-2840. p. 100
Lipski, Annie, Libr Asst, Aurora West Allis Medical Center, 8901 W Lincoln Ave, West Allis, WI, 53227-0901. Tel: 414-328-7910. p. 2486
Lipski, Jacqueline, Br Mgr, Porter County Public Library System, Hebron Public, 201 W Sigler St, Hebron, IN, 46341. Tel: 219-996-3684. p. 722
Lipsky, Melinda Lee M, Exec Dir, Pottstown Regional Public Library, 500 E High St, Pottstown, PA, 19464-5656. Tel: 610-970-6551. p. 1998

Lipstreu, Tiffany, Dir, Otterbein University, 138 W Main St, Westerville, OH, 43081. Tel: 614-823-1414. p. 1830

Liptak, Deborah, Develop Dir, Public Library of Youngstown & Mahoning County, 305 Wick Ave, Youngstown, OH, 44503. Tel: 330-744-8636. p. 1835

Liptak, Kelly, Head, Children's Servx, Head, Youth Serv, Dorothy Bramlage Public Library, 230 W Seventh St, Junction City, KS, 66441-3097. Tel: 785-238-4311. p. 816

Liptak, Rachel, Br Mgr, Florence County Library System, Baker Memorial Timmonsville Public Library, 298 W Smith St, Timmonsville, SC, 29161. Tel: 843-346-2941. p. 2058

Lipton, Faith, Asst Libr Mgr, Fruitville Public Library, 100 Apex Rd, Sarasota, FL, 34240. Tel: 941-861-2500. p. 442

Liranzo, Angelo, Regional Br Mgr, Pasco County Library System, Hugh Embry Branch, 14215 Fourth St, Dade City, FL, 33523. Tel: 352-567-3576. p. 410

Liranzo, Angelo, Regional Br Mgr, Pasco County Library System, New River, 34043 State Rd 54, Zephyrhills, FL, 33543. Tel: 813-788-6375. p. 410

Lirette, Sandra, Br Mgr, Lafourche Parish Public Library, Thibodaux Branch, 705 W Fifth St, Thibodaux, LA, 70301. Tel: 985-447-4119. p. 911

Lirones, Margaret, Sr Librn, California Department of Corrections Library System, California State Prison, Corcoran, 4001 King Ave, Corcoran, CA, 93212. Tel: 559-992-8800, Ext 5888. p. 206

Lisa, David, Assoc Dir, Camden County Library System, 203 Laurel Rd, Voorhees, NJ, 08043. Tel: 856-772-1636, Ext 7338. p. 1450

Lisa, Veronica, Librn, Department of Veterans Affairs, Lyons Campus Medical Library, 151 Knollcroft Rd, Lyons, NJ, 07939. Tel: 908-647-0180, Ext 4545, 973-676-1000. p. 1414

Lisa, Veronica Marie, Med Librn, Department of Veterans Affairs Medical Center Library, 385 Tremont Ave, East Orange, NJ, 07018-1095. Tel: 973-676-1000, Ext 1962. p. 1400

Lisefski, Alice, Librn, Hazleton Area Public Library, Nuremberg Branch, Mahanoy St, Nuremberg, PA, 18241. Tel: 570-384-4101. p. 1943

Lisenbee, Diana, Supvry Librn, Joint Base San Antonio Libraries, Bldg 598, Fifth St E, Randolph AFB, TX, 78150. Tel: 210-652-5578. p. 2230

Lishia, Kimberly, Br Mgr, Enlow Ruth Library of Garrett County, Grantsville Branch, 102 Parkview Dr, Grantsville, MD, 21536. Tel: 301-895-5298. p. 972

Liskey, Patty, Tech Serv Mgr, Massanutten Regional Library, 174 S Main St, Harrisonburg, VA, 22801. Tel: 540-434-4475, Ext 119. p. 2324

Liskiewicz, Lisa M, Law Libr Asst, Herkimer County Law Library, 301 N Washington St, Ste 5511, Herkimer, NY, 13350-1299. Tel: 315-614-3404. p. 1546

Lisowski, Loretta, Br Mgr, Gloucester County Library System, Glassboro Branch, Two Center St, Glassboro, NJ, 08028. Tel: 856-881-0001. p. 1423

List, Beth, Dir, Libr Serv, Lee County Library, 107 Hawkins Ave, Sanford, NC, 27330. Tel: 919-718-4665. p. 1715

List, Beth, Dir, Libr Serv, Lee County Library, Broadway Branch, 206 S Main St, Broadway, NC, 27505. Tel: 919-258-6513. p. 1715

List, Edith, Dir, Principia College, One Maybeck Pl, Elsah, IL, 62028-9703. Tel: 618-374-5235. p. 585

Lister Blitman, Terry, Exec Dir, Long Island Maritime Museum Library, 86 West Ave, West Sayville, NY, 11796-1908. Tel: 631-447-8679, 631-854-4974. p. 1663

Lister, Ginny, Librn, Barry Public Library, 880 Bainbridge St, Barry, IL, 62312. Tel: 217-335-2149. p. 540

Listle, John, Br Mgr, Antigo Public Library, White Lake Branch, White Lake Village Hall, 615 School St, White Lake, WI, 54491. Tel: 715-882-8525. p. 2420

Liston, Karen, Per Asst, Rochester College, 800 W Avon Rd, Rochester Hills, MI, 48307. Tel: 248-218-2260. p. 1145

Liston, Michele, Br Mgr, Enlow Ruth Library of Garrett County, Friendsville Branch, 315 Chestnut St, Friendsville, MD, 21531. Tel: 301-746-5663. p. 972

Liston, Samuel, Principal Librn, Support Servs, Oceanside Public Library, 330 N Coast Hwy, Oceanside, CA, 92054. Tel: 760-435-5628. p. 187

Liszcynskyj, Halyna, Dir, Libr Serv, Faxton Saint Luke's Healthcare, 1656 Champlin Ave, Utica, NY, 13502. Tel: 315-624-6059. p. 1655

Liszczynski, Halyna, Dir, Libr Serv, Saint Elizabeth Medical Center, 2215 Genesee St, Utica, NY, 13501. Tel: 315-798-8209. p. 1655

Litchfield, Perry, Dir of Finance, Dir, Human Res, Charleston County Public Library, 68 Calhoun St, Charleston, SC, 29401. Tel: 843-805-6801. p. 2048

Literati, Marcia, Asst Dir, Tenafly Public Library, 100 Riveredge Rd, Tenafly, NJ, 07670-1962. Tel: 201-568-8680. p. 1445

Litjens, Marcie, Dir, Center Moriches Free Public Library, 235 Main St, Center Moriches, NY, 11934. Tel: 631-878-0940. p. 1515

Litke, Amy, Head, Children's Servx, New Britain Public Library, 20 High St, New Britain, CT, 06051. Tel: 860-224-3155, Ext 117. p. 324

Litke, Donna, Prog Coordr, Great Neck Library, 159 Bayview Ave, Great Neck, NY, 11023. Tel: 516-466-8055, Ext 254. p. 1540

Litos, Marta, Asst Dir, DeWitt District Library, 13101 Schavey Rd, DeWitt, MI, 48820-9008. Tel: 517-669-3156. p. 1100

Litsey, Ryan, Assoc Dean, Librn, Texas Tech University Libraries, 2802 18th St, Lubbock, TX, 79409. Tel: 806-834-1156. p. 2214

Littell, Missy, Libr Serv Mgr, North Canton Public Library, 185 N Main St, North Canton, OH, 44720-2595. Tel: 330-499-4712. p. 1809

Litten, Anna, Dir of Libr, Public Library of Arlington, 700 Massachusetts Ave, Arlington, MA, 02476. Tel: 781-316-3200, 781-316-3233. p. 985

Litten, Anna, Librn, Public Library of Arlington, Edith M Fox Branch Library, 175 Massachusetts Ave, Arlington, MA, 02474. Tel: 781-316-3196. p. 986

Litten, Anna, Commun Relations Coordr, Morse Institute Library, 14 E Central St, Natick, MA, 01760. Tel: 508-647-6524. p. 1037

Little, Brandi, Libr Dir, Barnesville Hutton Memorial Library, 308 E Main St, Barnesville, OH, 43713-1410. Tel: 740-425-1651. p. 1749

Little, Chris, Stacks Mgr, University of Kentucky Libraries, Lucille Little Fine Arts Library, 160 Patterson Dr, Lexington, KY, 40506-0224. Tel: 859-257-4604. p. 863

Little, Dena, Libr Dir, Wayne Township Library, 80 N Sixth St, Richmond, IN, 47374. Tel: 765-966-8291, Ext 1101. p. 715

Little, Dylan, Br Mgr, Mid-Continent Public Library, Blue Ridge Branch, 9253 Blue Ridge Blvd, Kansas City, MO, 64138. Tel: 816-761-3382. p. 1250

Little, Elaine, Librn, Chinook Regional Library, Hazlet Branch, 105 Main St, Hazlet, SK, S0N 1E0, CANADA. Tel: 306-678-2155. p. 2752

Little, Ellen, Circ Supvr, Pittsburgh Theological Seminary, 616 N Highland Ave, Pittsburgh, PA, 15206. Tel: 412-924-1355. p. 1995

Little, Jane, Mgr, Human Res, Barrie Public Library, 60 Worsley St, Barrie, ON, L4M 1L6, CANADA. Tel: 705-728-1010, Ext 2120. p. 2630

Little, Jennifer, Librn, Spartanburg County Public Libraries, Inman Library, 50 Mill St, Inman, SC, 29349. Tel: 864-472-8363. p. 2070

Little, Jessica, Libr Dir, Saint Louis Public Library, 312 Michigan Ave, Saint Louis, MI, 48880. Tel: 989-681-5141. p. 1148

Little, Lara B, Libr Dir, Ref & ILL Librn, Pfeiffer University, 48380 US Hwy 52 N, Misenheimer, NC, 28109. Tel: 704-463-3350. p. 1703

Little, Laura, Actg Libr Dir, Chaleur Library Region, Bathurst Public Library, 150 St George St , Ste 1, Bathurst, NB, E2A 1B5, CANADA. Tel: 506-548-0706. p. 2599

Little, Melissa, Circ Mgr, Beaverton City Library, 12375 SW Fifth St, Beaverton, OR, 97005-2883. Tel: 503-644-2197. p. 1873

Little, Nancy, Info Literacy Librn, American International College, 1000 State St, Springfield, MA, 01109. Tel: 413-205-3225. p. 1056

Little, Patricia, Librn, Whitman Memorial Library, 28 S Main St, Bryant Pond, ME, 04219. Tel: 207-665-2505. p. 919

Little, Sabrina, Finance Mgr, Dougherty County Public Library, 300 Pine Ave, Albany, GA, 31701-2533. Tel: 229-420-3200. p. 457

Little, Sandy, Dir, La Harpe Carnegie Public Library District, 209 E Main St, La Harpe, IL, 61450. Tel: 217-659-7729. p. 606

Little Taylor, Raemona, Br Mgr, Marin County Free Library, Bolinas Library, 14 Wharf Rd, Bolinas, CA, 94924. Tel: 415-868-1171. p. 237

Little Taylor, Raemona, Br Mgr, Marin County Free Library, Inverness Library, 15 Park Ave, Inverness, CA, 94937. Tel: 415-669-1288. p. 237

Little Taylor, Raemona, Br Mgr, Marin County Free Library, Point Reyes Library, 11431 State Rte 1, Point Reyes Station, CA, 94956. Tel: 415-663-8375. p. 237

Little Taylor, Raemona, Br Mgr, Marin County Free Library, Stinson Beach Library, 3521 Shoreline Hwy, Stinson Beach, CA, 94970. Tel: 415-868-0252. p. 237

Littlefield, Barbara, Head, Youth Serv, Glenview Public Library, 1930 Glenview Rd, Glenview, IL, 60025. Tel: 847-729-7500. p. 594

Littlefield, Erica, Head, Youth Serv, Twin Falls Public Library, 201 Fourth Ave E, Twin Falls, ID, 83301-6397. Tel: 208-733-2964. p. 532

Littlefield, Jane, Librn, Clackamas Community College Library, 19600 Molalla Ave, Oregon City, OR, 97045. Tel: 503-594-3474. p. 1889

Littlefield, Lori, Librn, Ocean Park Memorial Library, 11 Temple Ave, Ocean Park, ME, 04063. Tel: 207-934-1853. p. 934

Littlefield, Yesenia, Libr Supvr, Riverside Public Library, SPC Jesus D Duran Eastside Library, 4033-C Chicago Ave, Riverside, CA, 92507. Tel: 951-826-2235. p. 203

Littlejohn, Timothy, Br Mgr, Hawaii State Public Library System, Waialua Public Library, 67-068 Kealohanui St, Waialua, HI, 96791. Tel: 808-637-8286. p. 511

LittleLight, Angie, Ch, Big Horn County Public Library, 419 N Custer Ave, Hardin, MT, 59034. Tel: 406-665-1808. p. 1295

Littler, Sheila, Customer Experience Mgr, Mgr, Serv Delivery, Prince George Public Library, 888 Canada Games Way, Prince George, BC, V2L 5T6, CANADA. Tel: 250-563-9251, Ext 143. p. 2574

Littlestar, Trudy, Dir, Haven Public Library, 121 N Kansas Ave, Haven, KS, 67543. Tel: 620-465-3524. p. 812

Littletree, Sandy, Dr, Assoc Teaching Prof, University of Washington, Mary Gates Hall, Ste 370, Campus Box 352840, Seattle, WA, 98195-2840. Tel: 206-543-1794. p. 2794

Littrel, Sharon, Librn, Davenport Public Library, 109 N Maple Ave, Davenport, NE, 68335. Tel: 402-364-2147. p. 1312

Litwack, Helen, Coll Develop, Ref Librn, New England Law, 154 Stuart St, Boston, MA, 02116-5687. Tel: 617-422-7436. p. 998

Litwak, Kenneth, Dr, Ref & Instruction Librn, Gateway Seminary Library, 3210 E Gausti Rd, Ontario, CA, 91761-8642. Tel: 909-687-1800. p. 188

Liu, Chang, Dir, Loudoun County Public Library, Admin Offices, 102 North St NW, Ste A, Leesburg, VA, 20176. Tel: 703-777-0368. p. 2328
Liu, Frank Y, Dir, Duquesne University, Center for Legal Information, 900 Locust St, Pittsburgh, PA, 15282. Tel: 412-396-5018. p. 1993
Liu, Hannah, Librn, Elling Eide Center, 8000 S Tamiami Trail, Sarasota, FL, 34231. Tel: 941-921-4304. p. 442
Liu, Hongru, Libr Tech II, First Nations University of Canada, Saskatoon Campus Library, 229 Fourth Ave S, Rm 302, Saskatoon, SK, S7K 4K3, CANADA. Tel: 306-931-1800, Ext 5430. p. 2746
Liu, James, Librn, Stanford Health Library, Stanford Hospital, Stanford Hospital, 500 Pasteur Dr, Palo Alto, CA, 94305. Tel: 650-725-8100. p. 192
Liu, James, Network & Systems Manager, Brooklyn College Library, 2900 Bedford Ave, Brooklyn, NY, 11210. Tel: 718-951-4868. p. 1501
Liu, Jiang, Commun Libr Mgr, Queens Library, Woodhaven Community Library, 85-41 Forest Pkwy, Woodhaven, NY, 11421. Tel: 718-849-1010. p. 1556
Liu, Jiqun, Asst Prof, University of Oklahoma, Bizzell Memorial Library, 401 W Brooks, Rm 120, Norman, OK, 73019-6032. Tel: 405-325-3921. p. 2791
Liu, Shang, Asst Dept Head, Bibliog Serv, Coll, Mount Prospect Public Library, Ten S Emerson St, Mount Prospect, IL, 60056. Tel: 847-253-5675. p. 621
Liu, Weilee, Ref (Info Servs), Teaneck Public Library, 840 Teaneck Rd, Teaneck, NJ, 07666. Tel: 201-837-4171. p. 1445
Liu, Yabin, Head, Info Tech, Addison Public Library, Four Friendship Plaza, Addison, IL, 60101. Tel: 630-458-3350. p. 535
Liu, Yan Quan, Dr, Prof, Southern Connecticut State University, 501 Crescent St, New Haven, CT, 06515. Tel: 203-392-5763. p. 2783
Liu, Yaoyao, Asst Prof, University of Illinois at Urbana-Champaign, Library & Information Science Bldg, 501 E Daniel St, Champaign, IL, 61820-6211. Tel: 217-333-3280. p. 2784
Liu, Yi, Cataloger, Library Connection, Inc, 599 Matianuck Ave, Windsor, CT, 06095-3567. Tel: 860-937-8263. p. 2763
Liu-DeVizio, Joan, Tech Serv, Bergen Community College, 400 Paramus Rd, Paramus, NJ, 07652-1595. Tel: 201-447-7653. p. 1432
Liudahl, Su, Dir, Lane Library District, 64 W Oregon Ave, Creswell, OR, 97426. Tel: 541-895-3053. p. 1877
Lively, Jeanie, Dir, Salado Public Library, 1151 N Main St, Salado, TX, 76571. Tel: 254-947-9191. p. 2235
Livergood, Ryan, Exec Dir, Warren-Newport Public Library District, 224 N O'Plaine Rd, Gurnee, IL, 60031. Tel: 847-244-5150, Ext 3008. p. 596
Livesay, Kami, Libr Dir, Tracy City Public Library, 50 Main St, Tracy City, TN, 37387. Tel: 931-592-9714. p. 2128
Livick, Rebecca, Br Librn, Marinette County Library System, Goodman Library Station, One Falcon Crest, Goodman, WI, 54125. Tel: 715-336-2575. p. 2453
Livick, Rebecca, Br Librn, Marinette County Library System, Niagara Public Library, 1029 Roosevelt Rd, Niagara, WI, 54151-1205. Tel: 715-251-3236. p. 2454
Livingston, Anne, Tech Serv, Wenatchee Valley College, 1300 Fifth St, Wenatchee, WA, 98801. Tel: 509-682-6710. p. 2395
Livingston, Bevonna, Libr Mgr, Woking Municipal Library, 5245 51st St, No 10, Woking, AB, T0H 3V0, CANADA. Tel: 780-774-3932. p. 2560
Livingston, Jami, Libr Dir, Adair County Public Library, One Library Lane, Kirksville, MO, 63501. Tel: 660-665-6038. p. 1258
Livingston, Kattie, Adult Serv Mgr, Charleston Carnegie Public Library, 712 Sixth St, Charleston, IL, 61920. Tel: 217-345-4913. p. 552
Livingston, Sarah, Ad, Huntington Memorial Library, 62 Chestnut St, Oneonta, NY, 13820-2498. Tel: 607-432-1980. p. 1611
Livingston, Shaney T, Libr Dir, Alachua County Library District, 401 E University Ave, Gainesville, FL, 32601-5453. Tel: 352-334-3900. p. 406
Livoti, Vincent, Dir of Libr, Massasoit Community College, One Massasoit Blvd, Brockton, MA, 02302. Tel: 508-588-9100, Ext 1941. p. 1003
Lixey, Carrie, Dir, Yorba Linda Public Library, 4852 Lakeview Ave, Yorba Linda, CA, 92886. Tel: 714-777-2466. p. 261
Llewellyn, Lisa, Br Mgr, San Bernardino County Library, Grand Terrace Branch, 22795 Barton Rd, Grand Terrace, CA, 92313. Tel: 909-783-0147. p. 213
Llewellyn, Muriel, Br Mgr, Collins LeRoy Leon County Public Library System, Northeast Branch, The Bruce J Host Center, 5513 Thomasville Rd, Tallahassee, FL, 32309. Tel: 850-606-2800. p. 445
Llewllyn, Janet, Asst Librn, Nanty Glo Public Library, 942 Roberts St, Nanty Glo, PA, 15943-0296. Tel: 814-749-0111. p. 1967
Llort, Valentine, Ch, Rancho Mirage Library & Observatory, 71-100 Hwy 111, Rancho Mirage, CA, 92270. Tel: 760-341-7323. p. 198
Lloyd, Beth, Fiscal Officer, Oak Hill Public Library, 226 South Front St, Oak Hill, OH, 45656. Tel: 740-682-6457. p. 1810
Lloyd, Billie, Librn, Pond Creek City Library, 105 S Second St, Pond Creek, OK, 73766. Tel: 580-532-6319. p. 1860
Lloyd, Courtney, Mgr, Dallas Public Library, Forest Green, 9015 Forest Lane, Dallas, TX, 75243-4114. Tel: 214-670-1335. p. 2165
Lloyd, Dawn, Acq Asst, Oklahoma Panhandle State University, 409 W Sewell, Goodwell, OK, 73939. Tel: 580-349-1548. p. 1848
Lloyd, Debbie, Librn, Delaware Technical & Community College, 100 Campus Dr, Dover, DE, 19904. Tel: 302-857-1060. p. 352
Lloyd, Derek, Dir, Middletown Free Library, 464 S Old Middletown Rd, Ste 3, Media, PA, 19063. Tel: 610-566-7828. p. 1961
Lloyd, Elizabeth, Libr Dir, United States Army, Redstone Scientific Information Center, Bldg 4484, Martin Rd, Redstone Arsenal, AL, 35898-5000. Tel: 256-876-9309. p. 34
Lloyd, Emily, Children's Prog Librn, Northfield Public Library, 210 Washington St, Northfield, MN, 55057. Tel: 507-645-6606. p. 1191
Lloyd, Erika, Learning Res Tech, Moraine Park Technical College Library, 235 N National Ave, Fond du Lac, WI, 54936. Tel: 920-929-2470. p. 2435
Lloyd, Erin, Ch, Knox Public Library, 305 N Main St, Knox, PA, 16232. Tel: 814-797-1054. p. 1949
Lloyd, Jennifer, Assoc Dir, Louisiana State University Health Sciences Center, 433 Bolivar St, Box B3-1, New Orleans, LA, 70112-2223. Tel: 504-568-5550. p. 901
Lloyd, Kristi, Libr Tech, Colorado Department of Corrections, Arrowhead Correctional Center Library, US Hwy 50, Evans Blvd, Canon City, CO, 81215. Tel: 719-269-5601, Ext 3923. p. 269
Lloyd, Linda, Dir, Clarion Public Library, 302 N Main St, Clarion, IA, 50525. Tel: 515-532-3673. p. 740
Lloyd, Matthew, Adminr, Curator, Norwich & District Historical Society Archives, 91 Stover St N, RR3, Norwich, ON, N0J 1P0, CANADA. Tel: 519-863-3638. p. 2662
Lloyd, Mckenna, Dir, Floyd County Historical Society Museum Library, 500 Gilbert St, Charles City, IA, 50616-2738. Tel: 641-228-1099. p. 739
Lloyd, Melissa, Asst Dir, Valley City Barnes County Public Library, 410 N Central Ave, Valley City, ND, 58072-2949. Tel: 701-845-3821. p. 1740
Lloyd, Rosa, Circ Serv Mgr, Indian Trails Public Library District, 355 S Schoenbeck Rd, Wheeling, IL, 60090. Tel: 847-459-4100. p. 662
Lloyd, Scott, Dir, Libr Serv, Mount Saint Joseph University, 5701 Delhi Rd, Cincinnati, OH, 45233-1671. Tel: 513-244-4347. p. 1761
Lloyd, Simon, Archives & Spec Coll Librn, University of Prince Edward Island, 550 University Ave, Charlottetown, PE, C1A 4P3, CANADA. Tel: 902-566-0343. p. 2707
Lloyd, Valerie, Dir, Madison Library District, 73 N Center St, Rexburg, ID, 83440. Tel: 208-356-341, Ext 10. p. 529
Lo, Mei Kiu, Cat & Syst Librn, University of Richmond, William T Muse Law Library, 203 Richmond Way, Richmond, VA, 23173. Tel: 804-289-8226. p. 2343
Lo, Mei Ling, Research Librn, Sci Librn, Rutgers University Libraries, Mathematical Sciences & Physics Library, Hill Ctr for Mathematical Sciences, 110 Frelinghuysen Rd, Piscataway, NJ, 08854-8019. Tel: 848-445-5914. p. 1425
Lo, Rira, Interim Dir, Brookdale Community College, 765 Newman Springs Rd, Lincroft, NJ, 07738-1597. Tel: 732-224-2706. p. 1412
Loaiza, Matthew, Teen Serv Librn, San Antonio Public Library, Teen Services, 600 Soledad, San Antonio, TX, 78205-2786. Tel: 210-207-2678. p. 2239
Loar, Amy, Asst Dir, Texas Grants Resource Center, 1191 Navasota St, Austin, TX, 78702. Tel: 512-475-7373. p. 2140
Lobdell, Claire, Archivist, Distance Learning Librn, Greenfield Community College, Core Bldg, 3rd Flr, One College Dr, Greenfield, MA, 01301-9739. Tel: 413-775-1834. p. 1022
Lobdell, Keri, Dean of Libr & Instrul Serv, Columbia Basin College Library, 2600 N 20th Ave, Pasco, WA, 99301. Tel: 509-544-4422. p. 2373
Lobert, Alyson, Libr Dir, Commerce Township Community Library, 180 E Commerce, Commerce Township, MI, 48382. Tel: 248-669-8101, Ext 101. p. 1093
Lobner, Jessica, Dir, Levi E Coe Library, 414 Main St, Middlefield, CT, 06455-1207. Tel: 860-349-3857. p. 321
Lobo, Tania, Tech Serv Team Leader, Bibliotheque H J Hemens, 339 Chemin Grande-Cote, Rosemere, QC, J7A 1K2, CANADA. Tel: 450-621-3500, Ext 7221. p. 2733
Lobrano, Kristi, Syst Librn, Franklin University Library, Frasch Hall, 1st Flr, 201 S Grant Ave, Columbus, OH, 43215. Tel: 614-947-6223. p. 1773
LoCascio, Heidi, Br Mgr, San Luis Obispo County Library, Nipomo Library, 918 W Tefft, Nipomo, CA, 93444. Tel: 805-929-3994. p. 234
Locastro, Cheryl, Head, Children's Servx, Bloomfield Public Library, 90 Broad St, Bloomfield, NJ, 07003. Tel: 973-566-6200. p. 1391
Loch, Amy, Dir, Wyandotte County Historical Museum, 631 N 126th St, Bonner Springs, KS, 66012. Tel: 913-573-5002. p. 799
Loch, Sarah, YA Librn, Springdale Public Library, 405 S Pleasant St, Springdale, AR, 72764. Tel: 479-750-8180. p. 110
Lochner, Penny, Serials & Database Librarian, Muhlenberg College, 2400 Chew St, Allentown, PA, 18104-5586. Tel: 484-664-3561. p. 1905
Lochtefeld, Abigail, Acad Librn, Asst Prof, Southern Utah University, 351 W University Blvd, Cedar City, UT, 84720. Tel: 435-586-7952. p. 2262
Lochtefeld, Eric, Info Tech, Mercer County District Library, 303 N Main St, Celina, OH, 45822. Tel: 419-586-4442. p. 1757
Lock, John, Youth Serv Librn, Meredith Public Library, 91 Main St, Meredith, NH, 03253. Tel: 603-279-4303. p. 1373
Lock, Mary Beth, Assoc Dean, Wake Forest University, 1834 Wake Forest Rd, Winston-Salem, NC, 27109. Tel: 336-758-6140. p. 1726
Lockard, Angela, Ch, Metropolis Public Library, 317 Metropolis St, Metropolis, IL, 62960. Tel: 618-524-4312. p. 617

Lockard, Anne, Metadata Librn, Metadata Serv, Cleveland Institute of Music, 11021 East Blvd, Cleveland, OH, 44106-1776. Tel: 216-791-5000, Ext 215. p. 1767
Lockard, Patricia, Genealogy Serv, ILL, Metropolis Public Library, 317 Metropolis St, Metropolis, IL, 62960. Tel: 618-524-4312. p. 617
Lockard-Ellis, Morgan, Br Mgr, Campbell County Public Library District, Philip N Carrico Branch, 1000 Highland Ave, Fort Thomas, KY, 41075. Tel: 859-572-5033. p. 851
Locke, Carolyn, Librn, Reed Free Library, Eight Village Rd, Surry, NH, 03431. Tel: 603-352-1761. p. 1382
Locke, Claudia, Br Mgr, Libr Spec, Huntington Beach Public Library System, Oak View, 17251 Oak Lane, Huntington Beach, CA, 92648. Tel: 714-375-5068. p. 152
Locke, David, Circ Supvr, University of Virginia's College at Wise, One College Ave, Wise, VA, 24293. Tel: 276-328-0150. p. 2355
Locke, Elizabeth, Br Mgr, Palm Beach County Library System, Hagen Ranch Road Branch, 14350 Hagen Ranch Rd, Delray Beach, FL, 33446. Tel: 561-894-7500. p. 454
Locke, James, Libr Tech, Saddleback College, 28000 Marguerite Pkwy, Mission Viejo, CA, 92692. Tel: 949-582-4241. p. 177
Locke, Jennifer, Libr Assoc, Maine State Law & Legislative Reference Library, 43 State House Sta, Augusta, ME, 04333-0043. Tel: 207-287-1600. p. 914
Locke, Jennifer, Librn, Milford Public Library, 40 Frenchtown Rd, Milford, NJ, 08848. Tel: 908-995-4072. p. 1419
Locke, Neal, Rev, Library Contact, First Presbyterian Church Library, 1340 Murchison St, El Paso, TX, 79902. Tel: 915-533-7551. p. 2174
Locke, Robin, Asst Dir, Drumheller Public Library, 80 Veterans Way, Drumheller, AB, T0J 0Y4, CANADA. Tel: 403-823-1371. p. 2533
Locker, Monica, Assessment Librn, Teaching & Learning Librn, College of the Holy Cross, One College St, Worcester, MA, 01610. Tel: 508-793-3473. p. 1072
Locker, Motti, Exec Dir, Abe & Esther Tenenbaum Library, c/o Congregation Augudath Achim, Nine Lee Blvd, Savannah, GA, 31405. Tel: 912-352-4737. p. 497
Lockett, Rose, Dir, Libr Serv, Coahoma Community College, 3240 Friars Point Rd, Clarksdale, MS, 38614. Tel: 662-621-4287. p. 1213
Lockett, Sonya, Librn, University of Arkansas-Pine Bluff, Human Sciences, Mail Slot 4971, Pine Bluff, AR, 71601. Tel: 870-575-8423. p. 108
Lockhart, Andrew, Div Mgr, Bell Island Public Library, Provincial Bldg, 20 Bennett St, Bell Island, NL, A0A 4H0, CANADA. Tel: 709-488-2413. p. 2607
Lockhart, Andrew, Div Mgr, Brigus Public Library, Seven S St, Brigus, NL, A0A 1K0, CANADA. Tel: 709-528-3156. p. 2607
Lockhart, Andrew, Div Mgr, Trinity Bay North Public Library, PO Box 69, Catalina, NL, A0C 1J0, CANADA. Tel: 709-469-3045. p. 2607
Lockhart, Andrew, Div Mgr, Harbour Grace Public Library, 106 Harvey St, Harbour Grace, NL, A0A 2M0, CANADA. Tel: 709-596-3894. p. 2608
Lockhart, Andrew, Div Mgr, Pouch Cove Public Library, PO Box 40, Pouch Cove, NL, A0A 3L0, CANADA. Tel: 709-335-2652. p. 2608
Lockhart, Andrew, Div Mgr, St Lawrence Public Library, PO Box 366, St. Lawrence, NL, A0E 2V0, CANADA. Tel: 709-873-2650. p. 2611
Lockhart, Andrew, Div Mgr, Trepassey Public Library, Molloy's Rd, Trepassey, NL, A0A 4B0, CANADA. Tel: 709-737-3909. p. 2611
Lockhart, Bernice, Asst Librn, Armstrong Township Public Library, 35 Tenth St, Earlton, ON, P0J 1E0, CANADA. Tel: 705-563-2717. p. 2639
Lockhart, David, Ref, Tech Serv, Richards Memorial Library, 118 N Washington St, North Attleboro, MA, 02760. Tel: 508-699-0122. p. 1041
Lockhart, Sallie, Mgr, Technology & Contracts, Dallas Public Library, 1515 Young St, Dallas, TX, 75201-5415. Tel: 214-670-1400. p. 2165
Lockhart, Trevor, Br Head, Winnipeg Public Library, Louis Riel Branch, 1168 Dakota St, Winnipeg, MB, R2N 3T8, CANADA. Tel: 204-986-4571. p. 2596
Lockhart, William M, Jr, Libr Spec III, Southern University, Oliver B Spellman Law Library, Two Roosevelt Steptoe, Baton Rouge, LA, 70813. Tel: 225-771-2146. p. 884
Locklear, Octavia, Br Mgr, Robeson County Public Library, Donald A Bonner Public Library, 113 E Main St, Rowland, NC, 28383. Tel: 910-422-3996. p. 1702
Lockwood, Barbara, City Librn, City of Calabasas Library, 200 Civic Center Way, Calabasas, CA, 91302. Tel: 818-225-7616. p. 126
Lockwood, Jamie, Dir, Manteno Public Library District, Ten S Walnut St, Manteno, IL, 60950. Tel: 815-468-3323. p. 613
Lockwood, Katie, Metadata Librn, Syst Librn, University of Western States Library, 8000 NE Tillamook St, Portland, OR, 97213. Tel: 503-251-5752. p. 1894
Lockwood, Michelle, Adult Serv Coordr, Parlin Ingersoll Public Library, 205 W Chestnut St, Canton, IL, 61520. Tel: 309-647-0328. p. 548
Lockwood, Sandra, Librn, Laceyville Public Library, 453 Main St, Laceyville, PA, 18623. Tel: 570-869-1958. p. 1950
Lockyer, Vicki, Librn, St Lawrence Public Library, PO Box 366, St. Lawrence, NL, A0E 2V0, CANADA. Tel: 709-873-2650. p. 2611
Lococo, David, Pres & Chief Exec Officer, Katzen International Inc Library, 2300 Wall St, Ste K, Cincinnati, OH, 45212-2789. Tel: 513-351-7500. p. 1761
Lodge, Sandra, Fiscal Officer, Licking County Library, 101 W Main St, Newark, OH, 43055-5054. Tel: 740-349-5505. p. 1807
Lodico, Sally, Automation Syst Mgr, Knox County Public Library System, 500 W Church Ave, Knoxville, TN, 37902. Tel: 865-215-8750. p. 2105
LoDolce, Adriana, Asst Dir, Islip Public Library, 71 Monell Ave, Islip, NY, 11751. Tel: 631-581-5933. p. 1551
Lodwick, David, Asst Dir, Admin & Syst, Cleveland State University, Michael Schwartz Library, Rhodes Tower, Ste 501, 2121 Euclid Ave, Cleveland, OH, 44115-2214. Tel: 216-687-2475. p. 1769
Loebach, Jeri, Ch Serv, Richard A Mautino Memorial Library, 215 E Cleveland St, Spring Valley, IL, 61362. Tel: 815-663-4741. p. 649
Loeffel, Jennifer, Dir, Franklin Public Library, 9151 W Loomis Rd, Franklin, WI, 53132. Tel: 414-427-7545. p. 2436
Loeffel, Pete, Dir, Wauwatosa Public Library, 7635 W North Ave, Wauwatosa, WI, 53213-1718. Tel: 414-471-8484. p. 2486
Loeffelbein, Aaron, Librn, North Central Washington Libraries, Ephrata Public Library, 45 Alder NW, Ephrata, WA, 98823-1663. Tel: 509-754-3971. p. 2393
Loeffler, Norma, Mrs, Genealogist, Stewart County Public Library, 102 Natcor Dr, Dover, TN, 37058. Tel: 931-232-3127. p. 2097
Loehr, Heather, Info Serv, Hanover College, 121 Scenic Dr, Hanover, IN, 47243. Tel: 812-866-7170. p. 689
Loehr, Shannon, ILL, Bon Accord Public Library, 5025 50th Ave, Bon Accord, AB, T0A 0K0, CANADA. Tel: 780-921-2540. p. 2524
Loendorf, Siobhan, Asst Dir, Catawba County Library, 115 West C St, Newton, NC, 28658. Tel: 828-465-8292. p. 1706
Loeper, Lindsey, Archivist, University of Maryland, Baltimore County, 1000 Hilltop Circle, Baltimore, MD, 21250. Tel: 410-455-2356. p. 958
Loesch, Martha, Head, Tech Serv, Seton Hall University Libraries, Walsh Library Bldg, 400 S Orange Ave, South Orange, NJ, 07079. Tel: 973-761-9296. p. 1443
Loew, Janet S, Communications & Pub Relations Dir, Public Library of Youngstown & Mahoning County, 305 Wick Ave, Youngstown, OH, 44503. Tel: 330-744-8636. p. 1835
Loewen, Cheryl, Dir, Moore Memorial Public Library, 1701 Ninth Ave N, Texas City, TX, 77590. Tel: 409-643-5974. p. 2248
Loewen, Hannah, Dir, Libr Serv, Providence University College & Seminary, Ten College Crescent, Otterburne, MB, R0A 1G0, CANADA. Tel: 204-433-7488. p. 2588
Loffredo, Nicole, Librn, Montgomery Area Public Library, One S Main St, Montgomery, PA, 17752-1150. Tel: 570-547-6212. p. 1965
Lofthus, Andy, Info Serv Librn, Western Seminary, 5511 SE Hawthorne Blvd, Portland, OR, 97215-3367. Tel: 503-517-1842. p. 1895
Loftin, Zelda, Asst Librn, Oak Grove Baptist Church Library, 2829 Oak Grove Church Rd, Carrollton, GA, 30117. Tel: 770-834-7019. p. 469
Loftis, Ben, Libr Dir, Cherokee County Public Library, 300 E Rutledge Ave, Gaffney, SC, 29340-2227. Tel: 864-487-2711. p. 2059
Loftis, Charissa, Coll Develop, Ref Librn, Wayne State College, 1111 Main St, Wayne, NE, 68787. Tel: 402-375-7729. p. 1340
Loftis, Lauren, Archivist & Spec Coll Librn, Pacific Lutheran University, 12180 Park Ave S, Tacoma, WA, 98447-0001. Tel: 253-535-7500. p. 2386
Loftis-Culp, Cynthia, Libr Serv Dir, Hernando County Public Library System, 238 Howell Ave, Brooksville, FL, 34601. Tel: 352-754-4043. p. 387
Loftus, Danielle, Fine Arts & Technology Librn, University of South Dakota, I D Weeks Library, 414 E Clark St, Vermillion, SD, 57069. Tel: 605-658-3386. p. 2084
Loftus, Robert, Syst Librn, Baldwinsville Public Library, 33 E Genesee St, Baldwinsville, NY, 13027-2575. Tel: 315-635-5631. p. 1490
Loftus, Sydney, Exec Dir, Madison County Historical Society Library, 435 Main St, Oneida, NY, 13421. Tel: 315-363-4136. p. 1611
Loga, Timothy, Dir, IT, Mount Prospect Public Library, Ten S Emerson St, Mount Prospect, IL, 60056. Tel: 847-253-5675. p. 621
Logan, Ayaba, Res & Educ Informationist, Medical University of South Carolina Libraries, 171 Ashley Ave, Ste 419, Charleston, SC, 29425-0001. Tel: 843-792-4213. p. 2051
Logan, Chuck, Librn, United States Navy, Naval Undersea Warfare Center Division, Newport Technical Library, 1176 Howell St, Bldg 101, Newport, RI, 02841. Tel: 401-832-4338. p. 2036
Logan, Doris, Tech Serv, Los Alamos County Library System, 2400 Central Ave, Los Alamos, NM, 87544. Tel: 505-662-8240. p. 1472
Logan, Heather, Dir, Cundy's Harbor Library, 935 Cundy's Harbor Rd, Harpswell, ME, 04079-4511. Tel: 207-725-1461. p. 927
Logan, Illyanna, Asst Libr Dir, Peters Township Public Library, 616 E McMurray Rd, McMurray, PA, 15317-3495. Tel: 724-941-9430. p. 1959
Logan, Nancy, Dir, Andover Public Library, 142 W Main St, Andover, OH, 44003-9318. Tel: 440-293-6792. p. 1746
Logan, Norma, Literacy Coordr, Morrill Memorial Library, 33 Walpole St, Norwood, MA, 02062-1206. Tel: 781-769-0200. p. 1044
Logan, Winnie, Libr Dir, New Castle-Henry County Public Library, 376 S 15th St, New Castle, IN, 47362-3205. Tel: 765-529-0362. p. 709
Logan-Walker, Tracy, Dir, Cadillac-Wexford Public Library, 411 S Lake St, Cadillac, MI, 49601. Tel: 231-775-6541. p. 1088
Loggins, Laura, Youth Serv Coordr, Rutherford County Library System, 105 W Vine St, Murfreesboro, TN, 37130-3673. Tel: 615-893-4131, Ext 114. p. 2117

Loghry, Evelyn, Adminr, Coin Public Library, 115 Main St, Coin, IA, 51636. Tel: 712-583-3684. p. 741

Logie, Diann, Br Mgr, Pueblo City-County Library District, Patrick A Lucero Library, 1315 E Seven St, Pueblo, CO, 81001. p. 293

Logsden, Kara, Lecturer, University of Iowa, 3087 Main Library, 125 W Washington St, Iowa City, IA, 52242-1420. Tel: 319-335-5707. p. 2785

Logsdon, Jennifer, Libr Dir, Hood County Public Library, 222 N Travis, Granbury, TX, 76048. Tel: 817-573-3569. p. 2185

Logsdon, Mary, Dir, Ames Public Library, 515 Douglas Ave, Ames, IA, 50010. Tel: 515-239-5646. p. 731

Logsdon, Stephen, Head Archivist, Washington University Libraries, Bernard Becker Medical Library, 660 S Euclid Ave, Campus Box 8132, Saint Louis, MO, 63110. Tel: 314-362-4239. p. 1277

Logsdon, Vicki, Dir, Hart County Public Library, 500 E Union St, Munfordville, KY, 42765. Tel: 270-524-1953. p. 870

Loguda-Summers, Debra, 3D Print Service Mgr, Pub Serv Mgr, A T Still University, Kirksville Campus, 800 W Jefferson St, Kirksville, MO, 63501. Tel: 660-626-2645. p. 1258

Logue, Carla, ILL, Ref Librn, Motlow State Community College Libraries, 6015 Ledford Mill Rd, Tullahoma, TN, 37388. Tel: 931-393-1670. p. 2128

Logue, Joseph, Libr Dir, Newport Public Library, 300 Spring St, Newport, RI, 02840. Tel: 401-847-8720, Ext 102. p. 2035

Logue, Sara, Interim Univ Archivist, Princeton University, Seeley G Mudd Manuscript Library, 65 Olden St, Princeton, NJ, 08544. Tel: 609-258-6345. p. 1438

Logue, Tim, Accounts Coord, Chapel Hill Public Library, 100 Library Dr, Chapel Hill, NC, 27514. Tel: 919-968-2777. p. 1678

LohGuan, Hilda, Dir, Alhambra Civic Center Library, 101 S First St, Alhambra, CA, 91801-3432. Tel: 626-570-5008. p. 115

Lohmann, Kathi, Info Spec, Exponent, 149 Commonwealth Dr, Menlo Park, CA, 94025. Tel: 650-688-7155, 650-688-7163. p. 175

Lohmeier, Kerry, Assoc Dean, Libr & Info Serv, University of Akron, University Libraries, School of Law Library, 150 University Ave, Akron, OH, 44325. Tel: 330-972-7330. p. 1745

Lohnes, Julie, Curator of Art & Exhibitions, Union College, 807 Union St, Schenectady, NY, 12308. Tel: 518-388-6277. p. 1638

Lohoefener, Sharon, ILL, Ref (Info Servs), North Platte Public Library, 120 W Fourth St, North Platte, NE, 69101-3993. Tel: 308-535-8036. p. 1327

Lohr, Diane, Ref & Coll Develop Librn, Trident Technical College, Main Campus Learning Resources Center, LR-M, PO Box 118067, Charleston, SC, 29423-8067. Tel: 843-574-6089. p. 2051

Lohr, Linda, Curator, University at Buffalo Libraries-State University of New York, Health Sciences Library, Abbott Hall, 3435 Main St, Bldg 28, Buffalo, NY, 14214-3002. Tel: 716-829-5737. p. 1510

Lohr, Penelope, Br Mgr, Western Sullivan Public Library, Tusten-Cochecton Branch, 198 Bridge St, Narrowsburg, NY, 12764-6402. Tel: 845-252-3360. p. 1558

Loiederman, Gabriel, Librn, California Department of Corrections Library System, San Quentin State Prison Library, Main St, San Quentin, CA, 94964. Tel: 415-454-1460. p. 207

Loigman, Andrea, Head, Access & Delivery Serv, Duke University Libraries, 411 Chapel Dr, Durham, NC, 27708. Tel: 919-660-5872. p. 1684

Lointier, Cecile, Chef de Section, Bibliotheques de Montreal, Pere-Ambroise, 2093 rue de la Visitation, Montreal, QC, H2L 3C9, CANADA. Tel: 514-872-9541. p. 2720

Loiselle, Sophie, Libr Mgr, Bibliotheque Gabrielle Roy, Bibliotheque Etienne-Parent, 3515 rue Clemenceau, Quebec, QC, G1C 7R5, CANADA. Tel: 418-641-6110. p. 2729

Loizou, Mary Jane, ILL, New England Conservatory of Music, 255 St Butolph St, Boston, MA, 02115. Tel: 617-585-1248. p. 998

Lojek, Meg, Libr Dir, McCall Public Library, 218 E Park St, McCall, ID, 83638. Tel: 208-634-5522. p. 525

Lokken, Beth, Youth Serv, Door County Library, 107 S Fourth Ave, Sturgeon Bay, WI, 54235. Tel: 920-746-7119. p. 2479

Lokken, Beth, Ch Serv, YA Serv, Door County Library, Sturgeon Bay Branch, 107 S Fourth Ave, Sturgeon Bay, WI, 54235. p. 2480

Lollis, John, Syst, White Plains Public Library, 100 Martine Ave, White Plains, NY, 10601. Tel: 914-422-1400. p. 1665

Lomaki, Tammy, Librn, St Lawrence Supreme Court, Courthouse, 2nd Flr, Rm 281, 48 Court St,, Canton, NY, 13617. Tel: 315-379-2279. p. 1513

Loman, Hope, Children's Serv Supvr, Rowan Public Library, 201 W Fisher St, Salisbury, NC, 28144-4935. Tel: 704-216-8228, 980-432-8670. p. 1715

Lomanto, Susan, Cat, Quitman Public Library, 202 E Goode St, Quitman, TX, 75783-2533. Tel: 903-763-4191. p. 2230

Lomas, Theresa, Admin Coordr, Cent Libr Serv, Winnipeg Public Library, Millennium, 251 Donald St, Winnipeg, MB, R3C 3P5, CANADA. Tel: 204-986-6440. p. 2596

Lomax, Denise W, Head of Libr, Federal Bureau of Prisons Library, Bldg 400, 3rd Flr, 320 First St NW, Washington, DC, 20534. Tel: 202-307-3029. p. 365

Lomax, Edward C, PhD, Assoc Ref Librn, West Virginia State University, Campus Box L17, Institute, WV, 25112. Tel: 304-766-3162. p. 2406

Lombard, Emmett, Outreach Librn, Gannon University, 619 Sassafras St, Erie, PA, 16541. Tel: 814-871-7557. p. 1931

Lombard, Lauren, Br Mgr, Blackwater Regional Library, Windsor Public, 18 Duke St, Windsor, VA, 23487. Tel: 757-242-3046. p. 2313

Lombardi, Roberto, Dir, Facilities, San Francisco Public Library, 100 Larkin St, San Francisco, CA, 94102. Tel: 415-557-4245. p. 227

Lombardo, Donna, Dir, Libr & Res Serv, Wilmer Cutler Pickering Hale & Dorr LLP Library, 2100 Pennsylvania Ave NW, Washington, DC, 20037. Tel: 202-663-6000. p. 381

Lombardo, Donna, Dir, Libr & Res Serv, WilmerHale Library, 60 State St, Boston, MA, 02109. Tel: 617-526-6000. p. 1001

Lombardo, Julie, Head, Circ, Woodridge Public Library, Three Plaza Dr, Woodridge, IL, 60517-5014. Tel: 630-487-2542. p. 664

Lombardo, Sandra, Mgr, Baltimore County Public Library, White Marsh Branch, 8133 Sandpiper Circle, Baltimore, MD, 21236-4973. Tel: 410-887-5097. p. 980

Lomedico, Kris, Br Mgr, Whatcom County Library System, Point Roberts Branch, 1431 Gulf Rd, Point Roberts, WA, 98281. Tel: 360-945-6545. p. 2359

Lomeli, Connie, Circ, Amarillo Public Library, 413 E Fourth Ave, Amarillo, TX, 79101. Tel: 806-378-3054. p. 2134

Lomison, Sharon, Asst Dir, Ref Serv Supvr, Billerica Public Library, 15 Concord Rd, Billerica, MA, 01821. Tel: 978-671-0948, 978-671-0949. p. 989

Lonberger, Chelsey, Dir, Lackawanna Public Library, 560 Ridge Rd, Lackawanna, NY, 14218. Tel: 716-823-0630. p. 1561

London, Diana, Librn, Iosco-Arenac District Library, Robert J Parks Library - Oscoda Branch, 6010 N Skeel Ave, Oscoda, MI, 48750. Tel: 989-739-9581. p. 1102

London, Linda, Events & Outreach, Librn, Res, Oklahoma State University - Center for Health Sciences, 1111 W 17th St, Tulsa, OK, 74107-1898. Tel: 918-561-8466. p. 1864

London, Michelle, Interim Tech Serv Mgr, Highland Park Public Library, 494 Laurel Ave, Highland Park, IL, 60035-2690. Tel: 847-432-0216. p. 599

Lonergan, Anne, Librn, Beebe Healthcare, Margaret H Rollins Nursing School Library, 424 Savannah Rd, Lewes, DE, 19958. Tel: 302-645-3100, Ext 5667. p. 353

Lonergan, Harriet, Br Mgr, Eastern Shore Public Library, Island Library, 4077 Main St, Chincoteague, VA, 23336. Tel: 757-336-3460. p. 2301

Lonergan, James L, Dir, Massachusetts Board of Library Commissioners, 90 Canal St, Ste 500, Boston, MA, 02114. Tel: 617-725-1860. p. 996

Lonergan, Karen, Dir, Cordova District Library, 402 Main Ave, Cordova, IL, 61242. Tel: 309-654-2330. p. 573

Long, Alison, Librn, Outreach Serv, Haltom City Public Library, 4809 Haltom Rd, Haltom City, TX, 76117-3622. Tel: 817-222-7768. p. 2187

Long, Allison, Dir, Pearisburg Public Library, 209 Fort Branch Rd, Pearisburg, VA, 24134. Tel: 540-921-2556. p. 2337

Long, Amy, Mat Selection & Acq, Public Library of Cincinnati & Hamilton County, 800 Vine St, Cincinnati, OH, 45202-2009. Tel: 513-369-6952. p. 1761

Long, Ann, Acq/Ser Supvr, Transylvania University Library, 300 N Broadway, Lexington, KY, 40508. Tel: 859-233-8225. p. 863

Long, Beth, Librn, Mono County Free Library, Lee Vining, 51710 Hwy 395, Lee Vining, CA, 93541. Tel: 760-647-6123. p. 172

Long, Casey, Head of Research & Instruction Services, Agnes Scott College, 141 E College Ave, Decatur, GA, 30030-3770. Tel: 404-471-6343. p. 475

Long, Chris, Team Lead, Resource Description Servs Team, University of Colorado Boulder, 1720 Pleasant St, Boulder, CO, 80309. Tel: 303-492-8705. p. 267

Long, Chris, Libr Dir, Plain City Public Library, 305 W Main St, Plain City, OH, 43064-1148. Tel: 614-873-4912, Ext 123. p. 1816

Long, Chris Evan, Cat Librn, Indiana University, Ruth Lilly Law Library, 530 W New York St, Indianapolis, IN, 46202-3225. Tel: 317-274-3884, 317-274-4028. p. 693

Long, Christian, Circ Librn, Millbrook Public Library, 3650 Grandview Rd, Millbrook, AL, 36054. Tel: 334-285-6688. p. 25

Long, Creston, Dir, Salisbury University, Edward H Nabb Research Center for Delmarva History & Culture, Guerrieri Academic Commons, 4th Flr, Rm 430, 1101 Camden Ave, Salisbury, MD, 21801. Tel: 410-548-2154. p. 976

Long, Cynthia, Dir, Glenolden Library, 211 S Llanwellyn Ave, Glenolden, PA, 19036. Tel: 610-583-1010. p. 1937

Long, Dallas, Dean of Libr, Illinois State University, Campus Box 8900, 201 N School St, Normal, IL, 61790. Tel: 309-438-3451. p. 625

Long, Deb, Adult & Teen Serv Mgr, Louisville Public Library, 700 Lincoln Ave, Louisville, OH, 44641-1474. Tel: 330-875-1696. p. 1797

Long, Diana, Dir, Altamonte Springs City Library, 281 N Maitland Ave, Altamonte Springs, FL, 32701. Tel: 407-571-8830. p. 383

Long, Dorothy, Circ Supvr, Portland Public Library of Sumner County, 301 Portland Blvd, Portland, TN, 37148-1229. Tel: 615-325-2279. p. 2124

Long, Elisabeth, Assoc Univ Librn for IT & Digital Scholarship, The University of Chicago Library, 1100 E 57th St, Chicago, IL, 60637-1502. Tel: 773-702-3732. p. 569

Long, Emilee, Libr Mgr, Woodbine Public Library, 103 E Eight St, Woodbine, GA, 31569. Tel: 912-559-2391. p. 503

Long, Helen, Chief Exec Officer, Dying With Dignity Canada Library, 802-55 Eglinton Ave E, Toronto, ON, M4P 1G8, CANADA. Tel: 416-486-3998. p. 2688

Long, Hope, Libr Dir, The Library at Birmingham Botanical Gardens, 2612 Lane Park Rd, Birmingham, AL, 35223. Tel: 205-414-3931. p. 8

Long, Jennifer, Ref Librn, University of Alabama at Birmingham, Mervyn H Sterne Library, 917 13th St S, Birmingham, AL, 35205. Tel: 205-934-6364. p. 9

Long, Jennifer, Dir, Easton Area Public Library & District Center, 515 Church St, Easton, PA, 18042-3587. Tel: 610-258-2917, Ext 310. p. 1928

Long, Jessica, Pub Serv Librn, Miami University Libraries, Gardner-Harvey Library, 4200 N University Blvd, Middletown, OH, 45042-3497. Tel: 513-727-3222. p. 1812

Long, Jessica, Coll Curator, Providence Archives, 4800 37th Ave SW, Seattle, WA, 98126. Tel: 509-474-2321. p. 2378

Long, Jessie, Asst Dir, Head, Circ, White Cloud Community Library, 1038 Wilcox Ave, White Cloud, MI, 49349. Tel: 231-689-6631. p. 1159

Long, John, Asst Dir, Independence Public Library, 220 E Maple, Independence, KS, 67301. Tel: 620-331-3030. p. 815

Long, Julie, Asst Dir, Slater Public Library, 105 N Tama St, Slater, IA, 50244. Tel: 515-228-3558. p. 783

Long, Karen, Libr Asst, Virginia Memorial Public Library, 100 N Main St, Virginia, IL, 62691-1364. Tel: 217-452-3846. p. 658

Long, Katherine, Fiscal Officer, Wayne County Public Library, 220 W Liberty St, Wooster, OH, 44691. Tel: 330-804-4680. p. 1833

Long, Kendra, Archivist, Assoc Univ Librn, University of the Fraser Valley, 33844 King Rd, Bldg G, Abbotsford, BC, V2S 7M8, CANADA. Tel: 604-504-7441, Ext 4243. p. 2562

Long, Kenn, Libr Res Spec, Marshall University Libraries, One John Marshall Dr, Huntington, WV, 25755-2060. Tel: 304-746-8904. p. 2405

Long, Kenn, Libr Res Spec, Marshall University Libraries, South Charleston Campus Library, 100 Angus E Peyton Dr, South Charleston, WV, 25303-1600. Tel: 304-746-8904. p. 2405

Long, Mike, Asst Dir, Holbrook Public Library, Two Plymouth St, Holbrook, MA, 02343. Tel: 781-767-3644. p. 1024

Long, Mindy, Dir, Ida Public Library, 320 N State St, Belvidere, IL, 61008-3299. Tel: 815-544-3838. p. 541

Long, Pam, Info Support Coord, United States Military Academy Library, Jefferson Hall Library & Learning Ctr, 758 Cullum Rd, West Point, NY, 10996. Tel: 845-938-8301. p. 1663

Long, Paula, Circ Librn, Stillwater Public Library, 1107 S Duck St, Stillwater, OK, 74074. Tel: 405-372-3633, Ext 8114. p. 1862

Long, Robert, IT Coordr, Talbot County Free Library, 100 W Dover St, Easton, MD, 21601-2620. Tel: 410-822-1626. p. 964

Long, Sandy, Dir, Whittemore Public Library, 405 Fourth St, Whittemore, IA, 50598. Tel: 515-884-2680. p. 792

Long, Savannah, Digital Serv, Ref, University of Baltimore, Law Library, Angelos Law Center, 7th thru 12th Flrs, 1401 N Charles St, Baltimore, MD, 21201. Tel: 410-837-4583. p. 957

Long, Sharon, Asst Dir, Syosset Public Library, 225 S Oyster Bay Rd, Syosset, NY, 11791-5897. Tel: 516-921-7161. p. 1648

Long, Shawn, Dir, Sainte Genevieve County Library, 21388 Hwy 32, Sainte Genevieve, MO, 63670. Tel: 573-883-3358. p. 1278

Long, Sherri, Sr Libr Assoc, Bowling Green State University Libraries, 1001 E Wooster St, Bowling Green, OH, 43403-0170. p. 1752

Long, Terri, Librn, Dunklin County Library, Senath Branch, 108 N Main St, Senath, MO, 63876. Tel: 573-738-2363. p. 1258

Long, Timbra, Dir, Weiser Public Library, 628 E First St, Weiser, ID, 83672-2241. Tel: 208-549-1243. p. 532

Long, Vickie, WISCAT User Support, Wisconsin Department of Public Instruction, Resources for Libraries & Lifelong Learning, 2109 S Stoughton Rd, Madison, WI, 53716-2899. Tel: 608-224-5394. p. 2452

Long-Taylor, Tara, Actg Dir, Faculty Res Librn, Texas Southern University, Thurgood Marshall School of Law Library, 3100 Cleburne Ave, Houston, TX, 77004. Tel: 713-313-4470. p. 2199

Longacre, Glenn, Archivist, National Archives & Records Administration, 7358 S Pulaski Rd, Chicago, IL, 60629-5898. Tel: 773-948-9001. p. 565

Longacre, Kathleen, Adult Serv Supvr, Naperville Public Library, Naper Boulevard, 2035 S Naper Blvd, Naperville, IL, 60565-3353. Tel: 630-961-4100, Ext 2232. p. 623

Longair, Barbara, Customer Serv Coordr, Lethbridge Public Library, 810 Fifth Ave S, Lethbridge, AB, T1J 4C4, CANADA. Tel: 403-380-7318. p. 2546

Longbottom, Lauren, Ch Serv, Ridley Township Public Library, 100 E MacDade Blvd, Folsom, PA, 19033-2592. Tel: 610-583-0593. p. 1933

Longchamp, Mary, Librn, Whiteford, Taylor & Preston, LLP, Seven St Paul St, Ste 1500, Baltimore, MD, 21202-1636. Tel: 410-347-8700. p. 958

Longhi, Melissa, Acq & Ser Spec, City University of New York, 365 Fifth Ave, New York, NY, 10016-4309. Tel: 212-817-7079. p. 1582

Longhorn, Cecili, Libr Dir, Stanfield Public Library, 180 W Coe Ave, Stanfield, OR, 97875. Tel: 541-449-1254. p. 1899

Longley, Dani, Dir, Naples Public Library, 940 Roosevelt Trail, Naples, ME, 04055. Tel: 207-693-6841. p. 932

Longman, Ellen, Dir, Hamburg Public Library, 1301 Main St, Hamburg, IA, 51640. Tel: 712-382-1395. p. 757

Longo, Sandy, Exec Dir, Lackawanna County Library System, 520 Vine St, Scranton, PA, 18509-3298. Tel: 570-348-3003. p. 2004

Longo, Timothy, Dir, Grayslake Area Public Library District, 100 Library Lane, Grayslake, IL, 60030. Tel: 847-223-5313. p. 595

Longo-Salvador, Estela, Ref, West New York Public Library, 425 60th St, West New York, NJ, 07093-2211. Tel: 201-295-5135. p. 1453

Longon, Jennifer, Libr Asst, New Brunswick Museum Archives & Research Library, 277 Douglas Ave, Saint John, NB, E2K 1E5, CANADA. Tel: 506-643-2322. p. 2605

Longpre, Nicole, Syst Librn, Bellevue College, 3000 Landerholm Circle SE, Bellevue, WA, 98007. Tel: 425-564-3071. p. 2358

Lonnberg, Thomas R, Curator of Hist, Evansville Museum of Arts, History & Science Library, 411 SE Riverside Dr, Evansville, IN, 47713. Tel: 812-425-2406, Ext 225. p. 681

Lonon, Edyta, Circ, Libr Spec, Harrisburg Area Community College, One HACC Dr, Harrisburg, PA, 17110-2999. Tel: 717-780-1772. p. 1940

Lonon, Vanessa Wallace, Access Serv Mgr, Memorial Health University Medical Center, 1250 E 66 St, Savannah, GA, 31404. Tel: 912-721-8230. p. 496

Lont, Tami, Youth Serv Librn, Waupun Public Library, 123 S Forest St, Waupun, WI, 53963. Tel: 920-324-7925. p. 2485

Loo, Alicia, Dir, Supreme Court of Canada Library, 301 Wellington St, Ottawa, ON, K1A 0J1, CANADA. Tel: 613-996-7996. p. 2670

Looby, Amelia B, Interim Head of Libr, Dartmouth College Library, Feldberg Business & Engineering Library, 6193 Murdough Ctr, Hanover, NH, 03755-3560. Tel: 603-646-2191. p. 1366

Look, Erin, Head, Youth Serv, Auburn Hills Public Library, 3400 E Seyburn Dr, Auburn Hills, MI, 48326-2759. Tel: 248-370-9466. p. 1081

Loomis, Diane, Dir, Tuxedo Park Library, 227 Rte 17, Tuxedo Park, NY, 10987. Tel: 845-351-2207. p. 1654

Loomis, Evonne, Acq Librn, Northampton Community College, College Ctr, 3835 Green Pond Rd, Bethlehem, PA, 18020-7599. Tel: 610-861-3360. p. 1912

Loomis, James, Fac Librn, Austin Community College, Riverside Campus Library, 1020 Grove Blvd, 1st Flr, Rm 1108, Austin, TX, 78741. Tel: 512-223-6134. p. 2138

Loomis, Lucy E, Libr Dir, Sturgis Library, 3090 Main St, Barnstable, MA, 02630. Tel: 508-362-8448. p. 987

Loomis, Nick, Asst Librn, Dir, Info Tech, Pere Marquette District Library, 185 E Fourth St, Clare, MI, 48617. Tel: 989-386-7576, Ext 5. p. 1091

Loomis, Nick, Asst Dir, Harrison Community Library, 105 E Main St, Harrison, MI, 48625. Tel: 989-539-6711, Ext 5. p. 1113

Loop, Jackie, Ref, Idaho National Laboratory Research Library, 2251 North Blvd, MS 2300, Idaho Falls, ID, 83415. Tel: 208-526-1185. p. 523

Loper, Kimberly, Exec Dir, University of Miami, Louis Calder Memorial Library, Miller School of Medicine, 1601 NW Tenth Ave, Miami, FL, 33136. Tel: 305-243-6424. p. 425

Lopes, Claudia, Coordr, Access Serv, University of Connecticut, Hartford Campus, Uconn Library at Hartford Public Library, 500 Main St, Hartford, CT, 06103. Tel: 959-200-3462. p. 340

Lopetrone, Yvonne, Homebound Delivery Coordr, Westland Public Library, 6123 Central City Pkwy, Westland, MI, 48185. Tel: 734-326-6123. p. 1159

Lopez, Alex, Prog Coordr, Purchasing, Big Bend Community College Library, 1800 Bldg, 7662 Chanute St NE, Moses Lake, WA, 98837. Tel: 509-793-2350. p. 2371

Lopez, Allen, Colls Librn, University of Texas, M D Anderson Cancer Center Research Medical Library, 1400 Pressler St, Houston, TX, 77030-3722. Tel: 713-792-2729. p. 2200

Lopez, Andrew, Res & Instruction Librn, Connecticut College, 270 Mohegan Ave, New London, CT, 06320-4196. Tel: 860-439-2655. p. 328

Lopez, Andrew, Research & Support Librn, Connecticut College, Greer Music Library, 270 Mohegan Ave, Box 5234, New London, CT, 06320-4196. Tel: 860-439-2711. p. 329

Lopez, Catherine, Ref Librn, Central New Mexico Community College Libraries, Montoya Campus Library, 4700 Morris St NE, RB 101, Albuquerque, NM, 87111. Tel: 505-224-4000, Ext 53768. p. 1461

Lopez, Christina, Law Librn, Pitblado Law Library, 2500-360 Main St, Winnipeg, MB, R3C 4H6, CANADA. Tel: 204-956-0560, Ext 373. p. 2594

Lopez, Clara, Br Mgr, Harris County Public Library, South Houston Branch, 607 Ave A, South Houston, TX, 77587. Tel: 832-927-5530. p. 2193

Lopez, Cynthia, Libr Dir, Manti Public Library, Two S Main St, Manti, UT, 84642. Tel: 435-835-2201. p. 2266

Lopez, Danitza, Libr Dir, Nogales-Santa Cruz County Public Library, 518 N Grand Ave, Nogales, AZ, 85621. Tel: 520-285-5717. p. 67

Lopez, David, Sr Librn, Santa Ana Public Library, 26 Civic Ctr Plaza, Santa Ana, CA, 92701-4010. Tel: 714-647-5250. p. 239

Lopez, Debi, Librn, El Paso Community College Library, 919 Hunter St, Rm C200, El Paso, TX, 79915. Tel: 915-831-2442. p. 2173

Lopez, Debi, Pres, Border Regional Library Association, PO Box 5342, El Paso, TX, 79954-5342. Tel: 915-491-6173. p. 2775

Lopez, Diana, Br Mgr, Marin County Free Library, Marin City Library, 164 Donahue St, Marin City, CA, 94965. Tel: 415-332-6158, 415-332-6159. p. 237

Lopez, Diana, Chief Archivist, County Librn, Yolo County Library, 226 Buckeye St, Woodland, CA, 95695-2600. Tel: 530-666-8005. p. 260
Lopez, Diana, County Librn, Yolo County Library, Yolo Branch, 37750 Sacramento St, Yolo, CA, 95697. Tel: 530-666-8005. p. 260
Lopez, Dolores, Mgr, Seminole Tribe of Florida, Diane Yzaguirre Memorial Library, 295 Stockade Rd, Immokalee, FL, 34142. Tel: 239-867-8305. p. 430
Lopez, Doris, Bus Support Unit Supvr, South Florida Water Management District, 3301 Gun Club Rd, West Palm Beach, FL, 33406. Tel: 561-686-8800. p. 454
Lopez, Edwardo, Br Mgr, McAllen Public Library, Lark Branch, 2601 Lark Ave, McAllen, TX, 78504. Tel: 956-681-3102. p. 2217
Lopez, Elizabeth, Librn, Imperial County Law Library, El Centro Courthouse Lower Level, 939 W Main St, El Centro, CA, 92243. Tel: 760-482-2271. p. 140
Lopez, Elizabeth, Library Mgr, Access, Hillsboro Public Library, 2850 NE Brookwood Pkwy, Hillsboro, OR, 97124. Tel: 503-615-6500. p. 1881
Lopez, Emme, Liaison Librn, University of Texas Health Science Center at San Antonio Libraries, 7703 Floyd Curl Dr, MSC 7940, San Antonio, TX, 78229-3900. Tel: 210-567-2450. p. 2240
Lopez, Fran, Libr Tech, Santa Fe Community College Library, 6401 Richards Ave, Santa Fe, NM, 87508-4887. Tel: 505-428-1213. p. 1476
Lopez, Gabriella, Dept Chair, Los Angeles Trade Technical College Library, 400 W Washington Blvd, Los Angeles, CA, 90015. Tel: 213-763-3958. p. 166
Lopez, Gertie, Coordr, San Xavier Learning Center Library, 1960 W Walk Lane, Tucson, AZ, 85746. Tel: 520-807-8620. p. 83
Lopez, Greta, Tech Librn, Sandia National Laboratories, 7011 East Ave, Livermore, CA, 94550. Tel: 925-294-1085. p. 157
Lopez, Ignayra, Libr Mgr, New York Public Library - Astor, Lenox & Tilden Foundations, Belmont Branch & Enrico Fermi Cultural Center, 610 E 186th St, (@ Hughes Ave), Bronx, NY, 10458. Tel: 718-933-6410. p. 1594
Lopez, Ignayra, Head, Children's Servx, Ossining Public Library, 53 Croton Ave, Ossining, NY, 10562. Tel: 914-941-2416. p. 1613
Lopez, Jackie, Regional Br Mgr, Lafayette Public Library, North Regional Branch, 5101 N University Ave, Carencro, LA, 70520. Tel: 337-896-6323. p. 892
Lopez, Jesse, Librn, Phoenix Art Museum, 1625 N Central Ave, Phoenix, AZ, 85004-1685. Tel: 602-257-2136. p. 71
Lopez, Jesse, Adult Serv Mgr, Altadena Library District, 600 E Mariposa St, Altadena, CA, 91001. Tel: 626-798-0833. p. 116
Lopez, Jessica, Dir, Ch Serv, Spartanburg County Public Libraries, 151 S Church St, Spartanburg, SC, 29306. Tel: 864-596-3500. p. 2069
Lopez, Lesbia, Br Mgr, Duval County-San Diego Public Library, Freer Branch, 608 Carolyn St, Freer, TX, 78357. Tel: 361-394-5350. p. 2241
Lopez, Livia, Dir, Catholic University of America, Oliveira Lima Library, 22 Mullen Library, 620 Michigan Ave NE, Washington, DC, 20064. Tel: 202-319-5059. p. 362
Lopez, Lizette, Head, Acq, University of Puerto Rico, Law School Library, Avenidas Ponce de Leon & Gandara, San Juan, PR, 00931. Tel: 787-999-9703. p. 2514
Lopez, Maria, Libr Tech, Texas State Technical College, 300 Homer K Taylor Dr, Sweetwater, TX, 79556. Tel: 325-235-7406. p. 2246
Lopez, Mary, Adult Serv Mgr, Hamilton Township Public Library, One Justice Samuel A Alito, Jr Way, Hamilton, NJ, 08619. Tel: 609-581-4060. p. 1407
Lopez, Mary, Br Mgr, Milwaukee Public Library, Atkinson, 1960 W Atkinson Ave, Milwaukee, WI, 53209. p. 2460
Lopez, Monica, Coll Develop & Acq Librn, Cerritos College Library, 11110 Alondra Blvd, Norwalk, CA, 90650. Tel: 562-860-2451, Ext 2434. p. 184
Lopez, Natalie, Librn, Crafton Hills College Library, 11711 Sand Canyon Rd, Yucaipa, CA, 92399. Tel: 909-389-3321. p. 262
Lopez, Pablo, Mgr, Miami-Dade Public Library System, California Club Branch, 700 Ives Dairy Rd, Miami, FL, 33179. Tel: 305-770-3161, p. 423
Lopez, Pablo, Mgr, Miami-Dade Public Library System, West Kendall Regional, 10201 Hammocks Blvd, Miami, FL, 33196. Tel: 305-385-7135. p. 424
Lopez, Patricia, Principal Librn, Adult Serv, Santa Ana Public Library, 26 Civic Ctr Plaza, Santa Ana, CA, 92701-4010. Tel: 714-647-5325. p. 239
Lopez, Raul, Assoc Dir, Res & Info Serv, Weil, Gotshal & Manges LLP, 767 Fifth Ave, New York, NY, 10153. Tel: 212-310-8445. p. 1603
Lopez, Regina, Dir, Christian Life College Library, 9023 West Lane, Stockton, CA, 95210. Tel: 209-476-7840. p. 249
Lopez, Rosa, Libr Asst, Salk Institute for Biological Studies, 10010 N Torrey Pines Rd, La Jolla, CA, 92037. Tel: 858-453-4100, Ext 1235. p. 154
Lopez, Sandra, Head, Outreach Serv, Round Lake Area Public Library District, 906 Hart Rd, Round Lake, IL, 60073. Tel: 847-546-7060, Ext 122. p. 643
Lopez, Sergio, Ref Serv Coordr, Mt Hood Community College Libraries, 26000 SE Stark St, Gresham, OR, 97030. Tel: 503-491-7694. p. 1881
Lopez, Shannon, Executive Asst, Union-Tribune Publishing Co Library, 600 B St, Ste 1201, San Diego, CA, 92101. Tel: 619-299-3131. p. 222
López, Sigfredo, Digitization Coordr, Tech Coordr, Amaury Veray Music Library, 951 Ave Ponce de Leon, San Juan, PR, 00907-3373. Tel: 787-751-0160, Ext 279. p. 2513
Lopez, Tracey, Dir, Emanuel Medical Center Library, 825 Delbon Ave, Turlock, CA, 95382. Tel: 209-667-4200, Ext 2899. p. 254
Lopez, Virginia, Librn, Church of the Holy Faith, Episcopal, 311 E Palace Ave, Santa Fe, NM, 87501. Tel: 505-982-4447, Ext 113. p. 1474
Lopez, Yesenia, Br Coordr, Lake County Library, Middletown Branch, 21256 Washington St, Middletown, CA, 95461. Tel: 707-987-3674. p. 156
Lopez-Duran, Jocelyn, Libr Tech, Outreach Serv, Alamosa Public Library, 300 Hunt Ave, Alamosa, CO, 81101. Tel: 719-589-6592. p. 263
Lopez-Fitzsimmons, Bernadette M, Res & Instruction Librn, Manhattan College, 4513 Manhattan College Pkwy, Riverdale, NY, 10471. Tel: 718-862-7743. p. 1627
Lopiccolo, Claire, Dir, Romeo District Library, 65821 Van Dyke, Washington, MI, 48095. Tel: 586-752-0603. p. 1157
LoPinto, Leonard, Dir, Paramus Public Library, 116 E Century Rd, Paramus, NJ, 07652. Tel: 201-599-1300. p. 1432
LoPresti, Karla, Libr Asst, Sugar Grove Free Library, 22 Harmon St, Sugar Grove, PA, 16350. Tel: 814-489-7872. p. 2011
Loprinzo, Gina, Dir, Brewster Public Library, 79 Main St, Brewster, NY, 10509. Tel: 845-279-6421. p. 1496
Loranc, Lisa, Libr Dir, Brazoria County Library System, 912 N Velasco, Angleton, TX, 77515. Tel: 979-864-1505. p. 2135
Lord, Ada, Library Contact, Eastern Louisiana Mental Health Systems, Chapman Memorial Library, 4502 Hwy 951, Jackson, LA, 70748. Tel: 225-634-0560. p. 891
Lord, Douglas C, Dir, Cyrenius H Booth Library, 25 Main St, Newtown, CT, 06470. Tel: 203-426-4533. p. 330
Lord, Evelyn, Head Librn, Laney College, 900 Fallon St, Oakland, CA, 94607. Tel: 510-464-3495. p. 185
Lord, Kim, Asst Dir, Kent Memorial Library, 50 N Main St, Suffield, CT, 06078-2117. Tel: 860-668-3896. p. 341
Lord, Michelle, Br Mgr, Dare County Library, Hatteras Branch, 57709 N C Hwy 12, Hatteras, NC, 27943. Tel: 252-986-2385. p. 1702
Lord, Phil, Br Mgr, Howard County Library System, Elkridge Branch + DIY Education Center, 6540 Washington Blvd, Elkridge, MD, 21075. Tel: 410-313-5077. p. 965
Loree, Sara, Libr Mgr, Saint Luke's Health System Libraries, 190 E Bannock St, Boise, ID, 83712-6297. Tel: 208-381-2276. p. 518
Lorence, David H, Dir, National Tropical Botanical Garden Library, 3530 Papalina Rd, Kalaheo, HI, 96741. Tel: 808-332-7324. p. 513
Lorente Rial, Maite, Youth Serv Librn, Sitka Public Library, 320 Harbor Dr, Sitka, AK, 99835-7553. Tel: 907-747-4022. p. 51
Lorenz, Christine, Law Librn, Butler County Law Library, Courthouse, 124 W Diamond St, Rm 303, Butler, PA, 16001. Tel: 724-284-5206. p. 1917
Lorenz, Steve, Libr Mgr, Bucks County Free Library, Levittown Branch, 7311 New Falls Rd, Levittown, PA, 19055-1006. Tel: 215-949-2324. p. 1927
Lorenzen, Kayla, Libr Mgr, Pincher Creek & District Municipal Library, 899 Main St, Box 2020, Pincher Creek, AB, T0K 1W0, CANADA. Tel: 403-627-3813. p. 2550
Lorenzetti, Diane, Dir, University of Calgary Library, Gallagher Library, 170 Earth Sciences, 2500 University Dr NW, Calgary, AB, T2N 1N4, CANADA. Tel: 403-220-6858. p. 2529
Lorenzetti, Diane, Dir, University of Calgary Library, Health Sciences Library, 1450 Health Sci Ctr, 3330 Hospital Dr NW, Calgary, AB, T2N 4N1, CANADA. Tel: 403-220-6858. p. 2529
Lorenzetti, Michael, Fac Mgr, Fox River Valley Public Library District, 555 Barrington Ave, East Dundee, IL, 60118-1496. Tel: 847-428-3661. p. 580
Lorenzi, Lara, Exec Dir, Phoenixville Public Library, 183 Second Ave, Phoenixville, PA, 19460-3420. Tel: 610-933-3013, Ext 123. p. 1989
Lorenzo, Anita, Dir, Jasonville Public Library, 611 W Main St, Jasonville, IN, 47438-0105. Tel: 812-665-2025. p. 697
Lorenzo, Cynthia, Tech Asst, Kane County Law Library & Self Help Legal Center, Kane County Judicial Ctr, 2nd Flr, 37W777W IL Rte 38, Saint Charles, IL, 60175. Tel: 630-406-7126. p. 644
Loria, Adele, Asst Dir, Pauline Haass Public Library, N64 W23820 Main St, Sussex, WI, 53089-3120. Tel: 262-246-5181. p. 2481
Lorimer, Katherine, Libr Dir, Goethe-Institut New York, 30 Irving Pl, New York, NY, 10003. Tel: 212-439-8700, Ext 2. p. 1587
Loring, Carrie, Adult Serv, George H & Ella M Rodgers Memorial Library, 194 Derry Rd, Hudson, NH, 03051. Tel: 603-886-6030. p. 1368
Lorraine, Jackie, Assoc Univ Librn, Washington University Libraries, One Brookings Dr, Campus Box 1061, Saint Louis, MO, 63130-4862. Tel: 314-935-5400. p. 1276
Lorson, Amy, Ref Librn, Indiana Wesleyan University, 4201 S Washington St, Marion, IN, 46953. Tel: 502-261-5019. p. 704
LoRusso, Jo-Ann, Libr Dir, Middlebury Public Library, 30 Crest Rd, Middlebury, CT, 06762. Tel: 203-758-2634. p. 321
Lorusso, Pegeen, Access Serv Librn, ILL Spec, Albany Law School, 80 New Scotland Ave, Albany, NY, 12208. p. 1482
LoSchiavo, Linda, Dir of Libr, Fordham University Libraries, 441 E Fordham Rd, Bronx, NY, 10458-5151. Tel: 718-817-3570. p. 1498
LoSchiavo, Linda, Dir of Libr, Fordham University Libraries, Quinn Library at Lincoln Center, 140 W 62nd St, New York, NY, 10023. Tel: 718-817-3570. p. 1498

Loscutoff, Leah, Head, Archives & Spec Coll, Stevens Institute of Technology, One Castle Point Terrace, Hoboken, NJ, 07030. Tel: 201-216-5416. p. 1408

Loseth, Amy, Head Librn, California Department of Conservation, 801 K St, Sacramento, CA, 95814-3532. Tel: 916-327-1850. p. 205

Losey, Debra A, Librn, United States Department of Commerce, NOAA Fisheries, 8901 La Jolla Shores Dr, La Jolla, CA, 92037-1509. Tel: 858-546-7196. p. 154

Losey, Doug, Dir, Hillside Public Library, 405 N Hillside Ave, Hillside, IL, 60162-1295. Tel: 708-449-7510. p. 599

Losey, Jenny, Libr Dir, Hudson Area Public Library District, 104 Pearl St, Hudson, IL, 61748. Tel: 309-726-1103. p. 601

Losick, Merill, Res Analyst, Weil, Gotshal & Manges LLP, 767 Fifth Ave, New York, NY, 10153. Tel: 212-310-8213. p. 1603

Losinski, Patrick, Chief Exec Officer, Columbus Metropolitan Library, 96 S Grant Ave, Columbus, OH, 43215-4702. Tel: 614-645-2275. p. 1772

Loss, Lori, Asst Dir, Cleve J Fredricksen Library, 100 N 19th St, Camp Hill, PA, 17011-3900. Tel: 717-761-3900, Ext 222. p. 1918

Lothian, Cathy, Br Mgr, Annapolis Valley Regional Library, Windsor Regional Library, 195 Albert St, Windsor, NS, B0N 2T0, CANADA. Tel: 902-798-5424. p. 2616

Lotito, Amanda, YA Serv, Lindenhurst Memorial Library, One Lee Ave, Lindenhurst, NY, 11757-5399. Tel: 631-957-7755. p. 1563

Lotspeich, Catherine, ILL, Randolph College, 2500 Rivermont Ave, Lynchburg, VA, 24503. Tel: 434-947-8133. p. 2330

Lott, Sila, Dir, Libr Serv, Tallahassee Community College Library, 444 Appleyard Dr, Tallahassee, FL, 32304-2895. Tel: 850-201-8376. p. 447

Lott, Stephanie, Circ Supvr, Commun Outreach Librn, Duncanville Public Library, 201 James Collins Blvd, Duncanville, TX, 75116. Tel: 972-780-5050. p. 2172

Lott, Sue, Acq, Greenwood-Leflore Public Library System, 405 W Washington St, Greenwood, MS, 38930-4297. Tel: 662-453-3634. p. 1217

Lotter, Jacob, Asst Dir, Cumberland Public Library, 1464 Diamond Hill Rd, Cumberland, RI, 02864-5510. Tel: 401-333-2552, Ext 128. p. 2031

Lotts, Megan, Art Librn, Rutgers University Libraries, Art Library, Voorhees Hall, 71 Hamilton St, New Brunswick, NJ, 08901-1248. Tel: 848-932-7189. p. 1424

Lotz, Marsha, Ref (Info Servs), Matteson Area Public Library District, 801 S School St, Matteson, IL, 60443-1897. Tel: 708-748-4431. p. 615

Loucks, Jesse, Dir, Hurst Public Library, 901 Precinct Line Rd, Hurst, TX, 76053. Tel: 817-788-7300. p. 2201

Loucks, Katie, Programming Librn, Killeen Public Library, 205 E Church Ave, Killeen, TX, 76541. Tel: 254-501-7882. p. 2206

Loucks, Lindsey, Libr Asst, McPherson College, 1600 E Euclid St, McPherson, KS, 67460. Tel: 620-242-0487. p. 824

Louden, Gretchen, Ref Librn, Stockton-San Joaquin County Public Library, 605 N El Dorado St, Stockton, CA, 95202. Tel: 209-937-8221. p. 250

Louderback, Pamela, Dr, Dir, Northeastern State University, Broken Arrow Campus Library, 3100 E New Orleans St, Broken Arrow, OK, 74014. Tel: 918-449-6453. p. 1863

Loudon, Lumi, Law Librn, Yakima County Law Library, 18 E Lincoln Ave, Yakima, WA, 98901. Tel: 509-574-2692. p. 2395

Loudy, Barbara, Circ Serv, Kankakee Community College, 100 College Dr, Kankakee, IL, 60901-6505. Tel: 815-802-8404. p. 604

Lough, Carly, Acq, Historical Society of Western Pennsylvania, 1212 Smallman St, Pittsburgh, PA, 15222. Tel: 412-454-6367. p. 1994

Lougheed, Brett, Digital Coll Curator, Univ Archivist, University of Winnipeg Library, 515 Portage Ave, Winnipeg, MB, R3B 2E9, CANADA. Tel: 204-786-9801. p. 2596

Loughlin, Becki, Br Mgr, High Plains Library District, Carbon Valley Regional Library, Seven Park Ave, Firestone, CO, 80504. p. 285

Loughran, Maria, Technology & Innovation Coord, Memorial & Library Association, 44 Broad St, Westerly, RI, 02891. Tel: 401-596-2877, Ext 311. p. 2044

Louis, Doug, Mgr, University of Kansas - Kansas Geological Survey, 4150 W Monroe St, Wichita, KS, 67209. Tel: 316-943-2343, Ext 203. p. 843

Louis-Jacques, Lyonette, Foreign & Intl Law Librn, University of Chicago Library, D'Angelo Law Library, 1121 E 60th St, Chicago, IL, 60637-2786. Tel: 773-702-9612. p. 570

Louise, Judy, Br Mgr, Bloomfield-Eastern Greene County Public Library, Eastern, 11453 East St, Rd 54, Bloomfield, IN, 47424. Tel: 812-825-2677. p. 670

Loum, Anthony, Managing Librn, Brooklyn Public Library, Mapleton, 1702 60th St, Brooklyn, NY, 11204. Tel: 718-256-2117. p. 1503

Lourentzou, Ismini, Asst Prof, University of Illinois at Urbana-Champaign, Library & Information Science Bldg, 501 E Daniel St, Champaign, IL, 61820-6211. Tel: 217-333-3280. p. 2784

Loutsch, Brooke, Children & Teen Librn, Akron Public Library, 350 Reed St, Akron, IA, 51001. Tel: 712-568-2601. p. 729

Louvierre, Aimee, Librn, Princeton Public Library, 101 Dr Donnie Jones Blvd, Princeton, NC, 27569. Tel: 919-936-9996. p. 1708

Lovan, Seng, Sr Commun Libr Mgr, Contra Costa County Library, Danville Library, 400 Front St, Danville, CA, 94526. Tel: 925-314-3750. p. 174

Lovasz, Elena, Outreach Serv Librn, Lasalle Parish Library, 3165 N First St, Jena, LA, 71342. Tel: 318-992-5675. p. 891

Lovasz, Kelli, Dir, North Branch Township Library, 3714 Huron St, North Branch, MI, 48461-8117. Tel: 810-688-2282. p. 1138

Lovato, Barbara, Dr, Dir, University of New Mexico, Valencia Campus, 280 La Entrada, Los Lunas, NM, 87031. Tel: 505-925-8991. p. 1463

Lovato, Sarah, Prog Coordr, Utah School for the Deaf & Blind, 742 Harrison Blvd, Ogden, UT, 84404. Tel: 801-629-4817. p. 2267

Lovato, Sarah, Prog Coordr, Utah School for the Deaf & Blind, Educational Resource Center - Salt Lake Extension, 1655 E 3300 South, Salt Lake City, UT, 84106. Tel: 801-629-4795. p. 2267

Lovchik, Jennifer, Teen Serv Librn, Bellingham Public Library, 210 Central Ave, Bellingham, WA, 98225. Tel: 360-778-7231. p. 2358

Love, Alex, Fac & Tech Mgr, Warren County Public Library, 1225 State St, Bowling Green, KY, 42101. Tel: 270-781-4882. p. 849

Love, Anita, Asst Dir, Trails Regional Library, 432 N Holden St, Warrensburg, MO, 64093. Tel: 660-747-1699. p. 1285

Love, Bathsheba, Circ Serv Coordr, Murrell Library & Commons, Missouri Valley College, 500 E College St, Marshall, MO, 65340. Tel: 660-831-4180, 660-831-4181. p. 1260

Love, Ben, Dir, Port Byron Library, 12 Sponable Dr, Port Byron, NY, 13140. Tel: 315-776-5694. p. 1620

Love, Brandolyn, Dr, Dir, Williamsburg Technical College Library, 601 MLK Jr Ave, Kingstree, SC, 29556. Tel: 843-355-4131. p. 2063

Love, Carina, Div Chair, Tech Serv Librn, Cuesta College Library, Hwy 1, San Luis Obispo, CA, 93401. Tel: 805-546-3159. p. 233

Love, Carol, Dir, Camden Township Library, 119 S Main St, Camden, MI, 49232. Tel: 517-368-5554. p. 1088

Love, Ciardi, Br Mgr, First Regional Library, Sam Lapidus Memorial Public Library, 108 Missouri Ave, Crenshaw, MS, 38621. Tel: 662-382-7479. p. 1220

Love, Ciardi, Youth Spec, First Regional Library, Sardis Public Library, 101 McLaurin St, Sardis, MS, 38666. Tel: 662-487-2126. p. 1220

Love, Lacey, Libr Dir, Peters Township Public Library, 616 E McMurray Rd, McMurray, PA, 15317-3495. Tel: 724-941-9430. p. 1959

Love, Laurie, Circ Mgr, Wilkes County Public Library, 215 Tenth St, North Wilkesboro, NC, 28659. Tel: 336-838-2818. p. 1706

Love, Mike, Dir, Media & End User Services, Carthage College, 2001 Alford Park Dr, Kenosha, WI, 53140-1900. Tel: 262-551-5950. p. 2444

Love, Pat, Nursing Librn, Linfield University, 900 SE Baker St, McMinnville, OR, 97128. Tel: 503-883-2262. p. 1885

Love, Pat, Dir, Linfield University, Portland Campus, 2900 NE 132nd Ave, Bldg 6, Portland, OR, 97230. Tel: 503-883-2262. p. 1886

Love, Patricia, Libr Dir, Pioneer Pacific College Library, 4145 SW Watson Ave, Ste 300, Beaverton, OR, 97005. Tel: 503-682-1862. p. 1873

Love, Rebekah, Instruction Librn, Student Success Librn, Kellogg Community College, 450 North Ave, Battle Creek, MI, 49017-3397. Tel: 269-565-7882. p. 1083

Love, Scott, Regional Mgr, Yolo County Library, Mary L Stephens-Davis Branch Library, 315 E 14th St, Davis, CA, 95616. Tel: 530-666-8005. p. 260

Love, Teresa, Fiscal Officer, Bowerston Public Library, 200 Main St, Bowerston, OH, 44695. Tel: 740-269-8531. p. 1752

Love, Toni, Asst Ch, Choctaw County Public Library, 703 E Jackson St, Hugo, OK, 74743. Tel: 580-326-5591. p. 1850

Love, Tyler, Archivist, Libr Mgr, National Park Service Independence National Historical Park, Merchants Exchange Bldg, 3rd Flr, 143 S Third St, Philadelphia, PA, 19106. Tel: 215-597-2069. p. 1983

Love-Corum, Sandra, Br Mgr, Gaston County Public Library, Bessemer City Branch, 207 N 12th St, Bessemer City, NC, 28016. Tel: 704-629-3321. p. 1690

Lovegrove Thomson, Michelle, Sr Mgr, Toronto International Film Festival Inc, TIFF Bell Lightbox, 350 King St W, Toronto, ON, M5V 3X5, CANADA. Tel: 416-599-8433. p. 2693

Lovejoy, Michelle, Librn, Delta City Library, 76 N 200 W, Delta, UT, 84624-9424. Tel: 435-864-4945. p. 2262

Lovejoy, Suzanne Eggleston, Ref & Instruction Librn, Yale University Library, Irving S Gilmore Music Library, 120 High St, New Haven, CT, 06520. Tel: 203-432-0492. p. 327

Lovejoy, Tim, IT Spec, Pine River Public Library District, 395 Bayfield Center Dr, Bayfield, CO, 81122. Tel: 970-884-2222. p. 266

Lovelace, Christine, Head, Archives & Spec Coll, University of New Brunswick Libraries, Five Macaulay Lane, Fredericton, NB, E3B 5H5, CANADA. Tel: 506-447-3263. p. 2601

Lovelace, J D, Br Mgr, Nashville Public Library, Goodlettsville Branch, 205 Rivergate Pkwy, Goodlettsville, TN, 37072. Tel: 615-862-5862. p. 2119

Lovelace, Kacy, Research & Student Success Librn, Marshall University Libraries, One John Marshall Dr, Huntington, WV, 25755-2060. Tel: 304-606-6226. p. 2405

Loveland, Bill, Libr Dir, Sherrill-Kenwood Free Library, 543 Sherrill Rd, Sherrill, NY, 13461-1263. Tel: 315-363-5980. p. 1640

Loveland, Erin, Libr Supvr, Artesia Public Library, 205 W Quay Ave, Artesia, NM, 88210. Tel: 575-746-4252. p. 1463

Loveless, Deborah, Br Mgr, Sullivan County Public Libraries, Dugger Public, 8007 E Main St, Dugger, IN, 47848. Tel: 812-648-2822. p. 720

Loveless, Janet W, Asst Dir, Nassau County Public Library System, 25 N Fourth St, Fernandina Beach, FL, 32034-4123. Tel: 904-530-6500, Ext 1. p. 395

Loveless, Shadow J, Librn, Stella Community Library, 224 N Main St, Stella, NE, 68442. Tel: 402-245-8190. p. 1337
Lovell, Amy, Mgr, Database Syst/Cat, Duquesne University, Center for Legal Information, 900 Locust St, Pittsburgh, PA, 15282. Tel: 412-396-6292. p. 1993
Lovell, Angela, Br Supvr, South Central Regional Library, Manitou Branch, 418 Main St, Manitou, MB, R0G 1G0, CANADA. Tel: 204-242-3134. p. 2592
Lovell, Chris, Syst, Palm Beach Atlantic University, 300 Pembroke Pl, West Palm Beach, FL, 33401-6503. Tel: 561-803-2221. p. 454
Lovell, Mary, Librn, Seymour Public Library District, 176-178 Genesee St, Auburn, NY, 13021. Tel: 315-252-2571. p. 1489
Lovell, Rita, Dir, Alpine County Library, 270 Laramie St, Markleeville, CA, 96120. Tel: 530-694-2120. p. 173
Loveman, Marcia, Coll Develop, ILL, Ref (Info Servs), Lake Wales Public Library, 290 Cypress Garden Lane, Lake Wales, FL, 33853. Tel: 863-678-4004. p. 416
Loveridge, Lucy, Ch Serv, Framingham Public Library, 49 Lexington St, Framingham, MA, 01702-8278. Tel: 508-879-5570, Ext 4336. p. 1019
Lovesey, Anthony, Automation Spec, Legislative Library of New Brunswick, Legislative Assembly Bldg, Centre Block, 706 Queen St, Fredericton, NB, E3B 5H1, CANADA. Tel: 506-453-2338. p. 2601
Lovett, Martha, Acq, Supvr, Hardin-Simmons University, 2200 Hickory St, Abilene, TX, 79698. Tel: 325-670-1236. p. 2132
Lovett, Rachael, Dir, Dublin Public Library, 1114 Main St, Dublin, NH, 03444. Tel: 603-563-8658. p. 1361
Lovett-Graff, Sharon, Pub Serv Adminr, New Haven Free Public Library, 133 Elm St, New Haven, CT, 06510. Tel: 203-946-7091. p. 326
Lovett-Graff, Sharon, Children's & YA Librn, Castleton Free Library, 638 Main St, Castleton, VT, 05735. Tel: 802-468-5574. p. 2281
Loving, Caitlin, Asst Dir, Bedford Public Library, Three Meetinghouse Rd, Bedford, NH, 03110. Tel: 603-472-2300. p. 1354
Loving, Kris, Br Mgr, Calaveras County Library, Murphys Branch, 480 Park Lane, Murphys, CA, 95247. Tel: 209-728-3036. p. 211
Lovitt, James, Bibliog Instr, College of New Caledonia Library, 3330 22nd Ave, Prince George, BC, V2N 1P8, CANADA. Tel: 250-561-5811, 250-562-2131, Ext 5298. p. 2574
Lovsin, Darcye, Ref & Instruction Librn, Justice Institute of British Columbia Library, 715 McBride Blvd, New Westminster, BC, V3L 5T4, CANADA. Tel: 604-528-5592. p. 2572
Low, Cynthia, Dir of Coll, Honolulu Museum of Art, 900 S Beretania St, Honolulu, HI, 96814-1495. Tel: 808-532-8754. p. 512
Low, Janet, Cat, Orem Public Library, 58 N State St, Orem, UT, 84057. Tel: 801-229-7050. p. 2268
Low, Keith, Supvr, Teck Resources Limited, 3300-550 Burrard St, Vancouver, BC, V6C 0B3, CANADA. Tel: 604-699-4263. p. 2579
Lowder, Claudia, Libr Tech, Grantsville City Library, 42 N Bowery St, Grantsville, UT, 84029. Tel: 435-884-1670. p. 2264
Lowder, David, Head, Syst, Georgia Southern University, 1400 Southern Dr, Statesboro, GA, 30458. Tel: 912-478-0161. p. 497
Lowder, Matthew, Br Mgr, Cecil County Public Library, North East Branch, 485 Mauldin Ave, North East, MD, 21901. Tel: 410-996-6269. p. 965
Lowder, Michael, Libr Dir, Southwestern Christian University Library, Springer Learning Center, 7210 NW 39th Expressway, Bethany, OK, 73008. Tel: 405-789-7661, Ext 2221. p. 1842
Lowe, Anna, Media & Technical Services Specialist, Indiana Wesleyan University, 4201 S Washington St, Marion, IN, 46953. Tel: 765-677-2982. p. 704
Lowe, Annie, Circ Supvr, Killeen Public Library, 205 E Church Ave, Killeen, TX, 76541. Tel: 254-501-8990. p. 2206
Lowe, Carrie Beth, Dir, Johnson University, 7902 Eubanks Dr, Knoxville, TN, 37998. Tel: 865-251-2277. p. 2105
Lowe, Cherokee, Br Mgr, Hulbert Community Library, 201 N Broadway, Hulbert, OK, 74441. Tel: 918-772-3383. p. 1850
Lowe, Cherokee, Mgr, Kansas Public Library, 200 W Tulsa Ave, Kansas, OK, 74347. Tel: 918-868-5257. p. 1851
Lowe, David, Computer Serv, University of Alabama, School of Law Library, 101 Paul Bryant Dr, Tuscaloosa, AL, 35487. Tel: 205-348-5925. p. 38
Lowe, Heather, Adminr, Adult Serv, Dallas Public Library, 1515 Young St, Dallas, TX, 75201-5415. Tel: 214-670-1400. p. 2165
Lowe, KT, Asst Librarian, Instruction & Outreach, Indiana University East Campus Library, Hayes Hall, 2325 Chester Blvd, Richmond, IN, 47374. Tel: 765-973-8434. p. 715
Lowe, Marisa, Br Mgr, San Diego County Library, Poway Branch, 13137 Poway Rd, Poway, CA, 92064-4687. Tel: 858-513-2900. p. 217
Lowe, Michele, Libr Mgr, Southwest Public Libraries, Westland Area Library, 4740 W Broad St, Columbus, OH, 43228. Tel: 614-878-1301. p. 1789
Lowe, Randall A, Acq, Coll Develop & Ser, Frostburg State University, One Susan Eisel Dr, Frostburg, MD, 21532. Tel: 301-687-4313. p. 967
Lowe, Rebecca, Adult Prog Coordr, Develop Dir, Lewes Public Library, 111 Adams Ave, Lewes, DE, 19958. Tel: 302-645-2733. p. 354
Lowe, Rebecca, Br Mgr, Prince William Public Libraries, Central Library, 8601 Mathis Ave, Manassas, VA, 20110. Tel: 703-792-8385. p. 2338
Lowe, Rita, Br Coordr, Wayne County Public Library, 220 W Liberty St, Wooster, OH, 44691. Tel: 330-804-4698. p. 1833
Lowe, Roberta, Syst Librn, Bridgewater College, 402 E College St, Bridgewater, VA, 22812. Tel: 540-828-5740. p. 2308
Lowe, Shelley, Asst Dir, Franklin County Library District, 109 S First E, Preston, ID, 83263. Tel: 208-852-0175. p. 529
Lowe, Zach, Circulation Lead, Libr Spec, Des Moines Area Community College Library, 2006 S Ankeny Blvd, Ankeny, IA, 50023. Tel: 515-964-6317. p. 732
Lowe-Wincentsen, Dawn, Librn, Oregon Institute of Technology Library, 3201 Campus Dr, Klamath Falls, OR, 97601-8801. Tel: 503-821-1258. p. 1883
Lowe-Wincentsen, Dawn, Exec Director, Learning Resources, Shoreline Community College, 16101 Greenwood Ave N, Shoreline, WA, 98133-5696. Tel: 206-533-2548. p. 2383
Lowell, Emily, Mgr, San Jose Public Library, Calabazas, 1230 S Blaney Ave, San Jose, CA, 95129-3799. Tel: 408-808-3066. p. 231
Lowell, Emily, Mgr, San Jose Public Library, West Valley, 1243 San Tomas Aquino Rd, San Jose, CA, 95117-3399. Tel: 408-244-4747. p. 232
Lowell, Eric, Finance Mgr, IT Mgr, Timberland Regional Library, 415 Tumwater Blvd SW, Tumwater, WA, 98501-5799. Tel: 360-943-5001. p. 2388
Lowenberg, Susan, Interim Dean, California Institute of the Arts, 24700 McBean Pkwy, Valencia, CA, 91355. Tel: 661-253-7885. p. 255
Lowenstein, Robyn, Bus Mgr, Human Res Adminr, Plymouth District Library, 223 S Main St, Plymouth, MI, 48170-1687. Tel: 734-453-0750, Ext 215. p. 1141
Lower, Brenda, Br Mgr, Davis County Library, Centerville Branch, 45 S 400 West, Centerville, UT, 84014. Tel: 801-451-1775. p. 2263
Lower, Fran, Libr Dir, Moweaqua Public Library, 600 N Putnam St, Moweaqua, IL, 62550. Tel: 217-768-4700. p. 622
Lowers, Kathy, Senior Info Assoc, University of Arizona Libraries, Health Sciences Library, 1501 N Campbell Ave, Tucson, AZ, 85724. Tel: 520-626-6142. p. 83
Lowery, Anne, Dir, New London Public Library, 67 S Main St, New London, OH, 44851-1137. Tel: 419-929-3981. p. 1806
Lowery, Lesley, Program Mgr, Tech Services, Orbis Cascade Alliance, PO Box 6007, Portland, OR, 97228. Tel: 541-246-2470. p. 2773
Lowery, Lori, Libr Syst Mgr, Lee County Library System, 2201 Second St, Ste 400, Fort Myers, FL, 33901. Tel: 239-533-4800. p. 403
Lowery, Renee, Asst Dir, Owatonna Public Library, 105 N Elm Ave, Owatonna, MN, 55060. Tel: 507-444-2460. p. 1192
Lowery, Tina, Br Supvr, Greater Victoria Public Library, Central Saanich, 1209 Clarke Rd, Victoria, BC, V8M 1P8, CANADA. Tel: 250-940-4875, Ext 724. p. 2583
Lowery, Tina, Br Supvr, Greater Victoria Public Library, Goudy Branch, 119-755 Goldstream Ave, Victoria, BC, V9B 0H9, CANADA. Tel: 250-940-4875, Ext 784. p. 2583
Lowery, Tina, Br Supvr, Greater Victoria Public Library, Langford Heritage Branch, 102-1314 Lakepoint Way, Victoria, BC, V9B 0S2, CANADA. Tel: 250-940-4875, Ext 884. p. 2583
Lowman, Jessica, Archivist, Digital Preservation Librn, Marshall University Libraries, One John Marshall Dr, Huntington, WV, 25755-2060. Tel: 304-696-3098. p. 2405
Lowman, Sara, Vice Provost & Univ Librn, Rice University, 6100 Main, MS-44, Houston, TX, 77005. Tel: 713-348-5113. p. 2197
Lowman Sheppard, Lisa, Libr Tech, Department of Veterans Affairs Medical Center Library, 385 Tremont Ave, East Orange, NJ, 07018-1095. Tel: 908-647-0180, Ext 4545, 973-676-1000, Ext 1969. p. 1400
Lowrey, Lizzy, Head, Youth Serv, North Shore Library, 6800 N Port Washington Rd, Glendale, WI, 53217. Tel: 414-351-3461. p. 2437
Lowry, Catherine, Libr Supvr, Spokane County Library District, Cheney Library, 610 First St, Cheney, WA, 99004-1688. Tel: 509-893-8280. p. 2384
Lowry, Christina, Law Librn, Tech Librn, University of Kentucky Libraries, Law Library, J David Rosenberg College of Law, 620 S Limestone St, Lexington, KY, 40506-0048. Tel: 859-257-8686. p. 863
Lowry, James, Asst Prof, Queens College of the City University of New York, Benjamin Rosenthal Library, Rm 254, 65-30 Kissena Blvd, Flushing, NY, 11367-1597. Tel: 718-997-3790. p. 2789
Lowry, Kim, Br Mgr, Chesterfield County Library System, Pageland Community Library, 109 W Blakeney St, Pageland, SC, 29728. Tel: 843-672-6930. p. 2052
Lowry, Marcus, Br Mgr, Ramsey County Library, Mounds View Branch, 2576 Mounds View Blvd, Mounds View, MN, 55112-4032. Tel: 651-724-6097. p. 1203
Loyd, James, Dir, Libr Serv, Calhoun Community College, Hwy 31 N, Decatur, AL, 35609. Tel: 256-306-2774. p. 14
Lozano, Eva, Librn, Crosby County Library, Ralls Branch, 813 Main St, Ralls, TX, 79357. Tel: 806-253-2755. p. 2162
Lozauskas, Eric, Dir, Info Tech, Bergen County Cooperative Library System, Inc, 21-00 Route 208 S, Ste 130, Fair Lawn, NJ, 07410. Tel: 201-498-7309. p. 2769
Lozauskas, Eric, Exec Dir, Sharing & Technology Enhancing Local Library Access, 27 Mayfield Ave, Edison, NJ, 08837. Tel: 732-750-2525. p. 2770
Lozito, Debora, Dir, Libr Serv, Edythe L Dyer Community Library, 269 Main Rd N, Hampden, ME, 04444. Tel: 207-862-3550. p. 926
Lu, Cindy, Head, Coll Serv, University of Mary Washington, 1801 College Ave, Fredericksburg, VA, 22401-5300. Tel: 540-654-1762. p. 2320

Lu, Jennifer, Libr Adminr, J T Fyles Natural Resources Library, 1810 Blanshard St, Victoria, BC, V8W 9N3, CANADA. Tel: 250-952-0564. p. 2582

Lu, Kun, PhD, Dr, Assoc Prof, University of Oklahoma, Bizzell Memorial Library, 401 W Brooks, Rm 120, Norman, OK, 73019-6032. Tel: 405-325-3921. p. 2791

Lu, Mei-Chen, Dir, Libr Serv, Dance Notation Bureau Library, 178 E 109th St, No 5, New York, NY, 10029. Tel: 212-571-7011. p. 1584

Lu, Nelson, Commun Libr Mgr, Queens Library, 89-11 Merrick Blvd, Jamaica, NY, 11432. Tel: 718-990-0700. p. 1553

Luayon, Jennifer, Access Serv, San Jose Public Library, 150 E San Fernando St, San Jose, CA, 95112-3580. Tel: 408-808-2325. p. 231

Luba, Glenn, Dir, Cheektowaga Public Library, 1030 Losson Rd, Cheektowaga, NY, 14227. Tel: 716-668-4991. p. 1517

Luba, Glenn, Dir, Cheektowaga Public Library, Anna Reinstein Memorial, 2580 Harlem Rd, Cheektowaga, NY, 14225. Tel: 716-892-8089. p. 1517

Lubansky, Marcia, Supv Librn, Tech Serv, Bernards Township Library, 32 S Maple Ave, Basking Ridge, NJ, 07920-1216. Tel: 908-204-3031. p. 1388

Lubbers, Chad, Br Mgr, Dakota County Library System, Burnhaven Library, 1101 W County Rd 42, Burnsville, MN, 55306. Tel: 952-891-0300. p. 1173

Lubbers, Susan, Pub & Outreach Serv Librn, Minnesota Braille & Talking Book Library, 400 NE Stinson Blvd, Minneapolis, MN, 55413. Tel: 507-384-6862. p. 1184

Lubberstedt-Arjes, Ketta, Dir, Kendall Young Library, 1201 Willson Ave, Webster City, IA, 50595-2294. Tel: 515-832-9100. p. 790

Lubeck, Mary Beth, Bus Mgr, Rye Free Reading Room, 1061 Boston Post Rd, Rye, NY, 10580. Tel: 914-231-3164. p. 1634

Lubenow, Janis, Library Services, UP Health System - Marquette, 850 W Baraga Ave, Marquette, MI, 49855. Tel: 906-449-3346. p. 1130

Lubert, Renee, Librn, State Correctional Institution, 1120 Pike St, Huntingdon, PA, 16652. Tel: 814-643-6520. p. 1945

Lubert, RoseAnn, Dir, Girard Free Library, 105 E Prospect St, Girard, OH, 44420. Tel: 330-545-2508. p. 1788

Lubetski, Edith, Head Librn, Yeshiva University Libraries, Hedi Steinberg Library, 245 Lexington Ave, New York, NY, 10016. Tel: 646-592-4980. p. 1605

Lubick, Marcia, Computer Support Spec, Montana Tech Library, 1300 W Park St, Butte, MT, 59701. Tel: 406-496-4287. p. 1290

Lubienecki, Teresa, Dir, Christ the King Seminary Library, 711 Knox Rd, East Aurora, NY, 14052. Tel: 716-655-7098. p. 1527

Lubin, Rebecca, Head, Br Libr, Albany Public Library, 161 Washington Ave, Albany, NY, 12210. Tel: 518-427-4300. p. 1482

Lubin-Tyler, Phyllis, Mgr, Pearl S Buck Birthplace Foundation, 8129 Seneca Trail, Rte 219, Hillsboro, WV, 24946. Tel: 304-653-4430. p. 2404

Lubkeman, Lynn, Archivist, Wisconsin Conference United Methodist Church, 750 Windsor St, Sun Prairie, WI, 53590. Tel: 608-837-7320. p. 2480

Lubker, Irene M, Res & Educ Informationist, Medical University of South Carolina Libraries, 171 Ashley Ave, Ste 419, Charleston, SC, 29425-0001. Tel: 843-792-7648. p. 2051

Lubkowski, Carol, Music Librn, Wellesley College, Music Library, Jewett Arts Ctr, Rm 208, 106 Central St, Wellesley, MA, 02481-8203. Tel: 781-283-2076. p. 1064

Lubrin, Lisa, Supvr, Virgin Islands Division of Libraries, Archives & Museums, Vitraco Mall, 3012 Golden Rock, Christiansted, VI, 00820. Tel: 340-718-2250. p. 2517

Lucadamo, Amy, Col Archivist, Gettysburg College, 300 N Washington St, Gettysburg, PA, 17325. Tel: 717-337-7006. p. 1935

Lucareli, Christa, Dir, Farmingdale Public Library, 116 Merritts Rd, Farmingdale, NY, 11735. Tel: 516-249-9090, Ext 226. p. 1532

Lucarelli, Tony, Adult Serv, Indian Prairie Public Library District, 401 Plainfield Rd, Darien, IL, 60561-4207. Tel: 630-887-8760. p. 575

Lucas, Ann, Libr Spec, University of Pittsburgh at Titusville, 504 E Main St, Titusville, PA, 16354. Tel: 814-827-4439. p. 2013

Lucas, Aurea, Br Mgr, Adams Memorial Library, Caldwell Memorial Library, 982 N Chestnut St Extension, Derry, PA, 15627. Tel: 724-694-5765. p. 1953

Lucas, Chela, Br Mgr, San Francisco Public Library, Golden Gate Valley Branch Library, 1801 Green St, San Francisco, CA, 94123-4921. Tel: 415-355-5666. p. 228

Lucas, Cynthia R, Dir, Law Librn, Spokane County Law Library, Spokane County Courthouse, 2nd Flr, 1116 W Broadway, Spokane, WA, 99260. Tel: 509-477-3680. p. 2384

Lucas, Greg, State Librn, California State Library, 900 N St, Sacramento, CA, 95814. Tel: 916-323-9843. p. 208

Lucas, Jody, Co-Dir, Luther Area Public Library, 115 State St, Luther, MI, 49656. Tel: 231-797-8006. p. 1128

Lucas, Kara, Outreach Serv Librn, Front Range Community College, 3645 W 112th Ave, Westminster, CO, 80031. p. 298

Lucas, Leandrea, Regional Br Mgr, Saint Louis Public Library, Schlafly, 225 N Euclid Ave, Saint Louis, MO, 63108. Tel: 314-367-4120. p. 1275

Lucas, Marcy, Dir, Finch Memorial Public Library, 205 N Walnut St, Arnold, NE, 69120. Tel: 308-848-2219. p. 1306

Lucas, Mary Lea, Exec Dir, Clarion County Historical Society, 18 Grant St, Clarion, PA, 16214. Tel: 814-226-4450. p. 1922

Lucas, Missy, Ch, Harrison County Library System, Jerry Lawrence Memorial Library, 10391 AutoMall Pkwy, D'Iberville, MS, 39540. Tel: 228-392-2279. p. 1217

Lucas, Teresa, Libr Dir, Coquille Public Library, 105 N Birch St, Coquille, OR, 97423-1299. Tel: 541-396-2166. p. 1876

Lucas, Teresa, Asst Dir, North Bend Public Library, 1800 Sherman Ave, North Bend, OR, 97459. Tel: 541-756-0400. p. 1889

Lucas, Terri, Ms, Librn, Missouri Department of Corrections, Moberly Correctional Center, 5201 S Morley, Moberly, MO, 65270. Tel: 660-263-3778. p. 1252

Lucas, Terry Z, Libr Dir, Shelter Island Public Library, 37 N Ferry Rd, Shelter Island, NY, 11964. Tel: 631-749-0042. p. 1640

Lucas, Wesley, Pres, Health Sciences Library Association of Louisiana, c/o National World War II Museum Library, 945 New Orleans, Shreveport, LA, 70130. Tel: 501-528-1944, Ext 469. p. 2766

Lucas-Alieri, Debra, Res & Instruction Librn, D'Youville College, 320 Porter Ave, Buffalo, NY, 14201-1084. Tel: 716-829-7764. p. 1509

Lucas-Youmans, Tasha, Dr, Chief Librn, Dean of Libr, Bethune-Cookman University, 640 Mary McLeod Bethune Blvd, Daytona Beach, FL, 32114. Tel: 368-481-2181. p. 392

Lucchesi, Liz, Assoc Librn, North Las Vegas Library District, 2250 Las Vegas Blvd, Ste 133, North Las Vegas, NV, 89030. Tel: 702-633-1070. p. 1348

Luce, Jessica, Br Mgr, Toledo-Lucas County Public Library, Point Place, 2727 117th St, Toledo, OH, 43611. Tel: 419-259-5390. p. 1824

Luce, Kitty, Instruction & Outreach Librn, The California Maritime Academy Library, 200 Maritime Academy Dr, Vallejo, CA, 94590. Tel: 707-654-1769. p. 255

Luce, Stephanie, Colls Mgr, National Museum of Racing & Hall of Fame, 191 Union Ave, 2nd Flr, Saratoga Springs, NY, 12866. Tel: 518-584-0400, Ext 117. p. 1636

Lucero, Manuel, IV, Exec Dir, Museum of Indigenous People, 147 N Arizona St, Prescott, AZ, 86301. Tel: 928-445-1230. p. 73

Lucero, Tana, Librn II, Youth Serv Coordr, Duluth Public Library, 520 W Superior St, Duluth, MN, 55802. Tel: 218-730-4217. p. 1172

Lucey, Jennifer M, Mgr, Ref Serv, Res Serv, International Foundation of Employee Benefit Plans, 18700 W Bluemound Rd, Brookfield, WI, 53045-2936. Tel: 262-786-6710, Ext 5. p. 2425

Lucey, Judith, Sr Archivist, New England Historic Genealogical Society Library, 99-101 Newbury St, Boston, MA, 02116-3007. Tel: 617-226-1223. p. 998

Lucey, Teresa, Circ, Salem Public Library, 370 Essex St, Salem, MA, 01970-3298. Tel: 978-744-0860. p. 1051

Luchars, Susan, Assessment Librn, Resource Dev Librn, Sacred Heart University, 5151 Park Ave, Fairfield, CT, 06825-1000. Tel: 203-371-7701. p. 312

Luchs, Mandy L, Libr Dir, Sewickley Township Public Library, 201 Highland Ave, Herminie, PA, 15637. Tel: 724-446-9940. p. 1943

Luchsinger, Claudine, Adult Programs, Western Sullivan Public Library, 19 Center St, Jeffersonville, NY, 12748. Tel: 845-482-4350. p. 1558

Lucia, Joe, Dean of Libr, Temple University Libraries, 1210 W Berks St, Philadelphia, PA, 19122-6088. Tel: 215-204-8231. p. 1986

Lucio, Nettie, Circ Mgr, Saint Mary's University, Louis J Blume Library, One Camino Santa Maria, San Antonio, TX, 78228-8608. Tel: 210-436-3441. p. 2238

Lucius, Eric, Mgr, Medina County District Library, Highland Library, 4160 Ridge Rd, Medina, OH, 44256-8618. Tel: 330-239-2674, 330-278-4271. p. 1801

Lucius, Sam, Ch, Wiggin Memorial Library, Ten Bunker Hill Ave, Stratham, NH, 03885. Tel: 603-772-4346. p. 1381

Luck, Andrew, Asst Dir, Elizabeth Public Library, 11 S Broad St, Elizabeth, NJ, 07202. Tel: 908-354-6060. p. 1401

Luck, Andrew, Asst Dir, Hoboken Public Library, 500 Park Ave, Hoboken, NJ, 07030. Tel: 201-420-2346, Ext 5101. p. 1408

Luck, Barbara, Asst Dir, ILL, Morton County Library, 410 Kansas Ave, Elkhart, KS, 67950. Tel: 620-697-2025. p. 806

Luck, Cheryl, Br Mgr, Akron-Summit County Public Library, Portage Lakes Branch, 4261 Manchester Rd, Akron, OH, 44319-2659. Tel: 330-644-7050. p. 1744

Luck, Jennifer, Coordr, Circ, Chesapeake Public Library, 298 Cedar Rd, Chesapeake, VA, 23322-5512. Tel: 757-410-7155. p. 2311

Luck, Rebecca, Dir, Libr Serv, Stormont, Dundas & Glengarry County Library, 26 Pitt St, Ste 106, Cornwall, ON, K6J 3P2, CANADA. Tel: 613-936-8777, Ext 211. p. 2637

Lucken, Pamela S, Head, Ref, University of Miami, 1311 Miller Dr, Coral Gables, FL, 33146. Tel: 305-284-2251. p. 390

Luckett, Rosemary, Interim Br Mgr, Jackson/Hinds Library System, Fannie Lou Hamer Library, 3450 Albermarle Rd, Jackson, MS, 39213-6507. Tel: 601-362-3012. p. 1221

Luckie, Caren Zentner, Research Attorney, Jackson Walker LLP, 1401 McKinney, Ste 1900, Houston, TX, 77010. Tel: 713-752-4479. p. 2196

Luckstead, Jon, Fac Librn, Austin Community College, Highland Campus Library, 6101 Airport Blvd, 1st Flr, Rm 1325, Austin, TX, 78752. Tel: 512-223-7388. p. 2138

Lucy, John, Dr, Dir, Trinity Baptist College Library, 800 Hammond Blvd, Jacksonville, FL, 32221. Tel: 904-596-2451. p. 413

Ludascher, Bertram, Dir, Ctr, Informatics Research in Science & Scholarship, Prof, University of Illinois at Urbana-Champaign, Library & Information Science Bldg, 501 E Daniel St, Champaign, IL, 61820-6211. Tel: 217-333-3280. p. 2784

Luddy, Jean, ILL, Rockville Public Library, 52 Union St, Vernon, CT, 06066-3155. Tel: 860-875-5892. p. 342

Ludemann, Nellie, Exec Dir, Seneca Falls Historical Society Library, 55 Cayuga St, Seneca Falls, NY, 13148. Tel: 315-568-8412. p. 1639

Luderitz, Marygrace, Libr Dir, Long Hill Township Public Library, 917 Valley Rd, Gillette, NJ, 07933. Tel: 908-647-2088. p. 1405

Ludington, Colleen, Br Supvr, Hernando County Public Library System, Spring Hill Branch, 9220 Spring Hill Dr, Spring Hill, FL, 34608. Tel: 352-754-4043. p. 388

Ludlam, Jean, Mgr, Calgary Public Library, Bowness, 6532 Bowness Rd NW, Calgary, AB, T3B 0E9, CANADA. p. 2526

Ludlam, Jean, Mgr, Calgary Public Library, Crowfoot, 8665 Nose Hill Dr NW, Calgary, AB, T3G 5T3, CANADA. p. 2526

Ludlam, Jean, Mgr, Calgary Public Library, Rocky Ridge, 11300 Rocky Ridge Rd NW, Calgary, AB, T3G 5H3, CANADA. p. 2527

Ludlow, Heather, Info Serv Librn, Nova Scotia Legislative Library, Province House, 2nd Flr, Halifax, NS, B3J 2P8, CANADA. Tel: 902-424-5932. p. 2620

Ludolf, Anya, Dir, Kendalia Public Library, 2610-B Hwy 473, Kendalia, TX, 78027. Tel: 830-336-2002. p. 2205

Ludovico, Carrie, Bus Librn, University of Richmond, 261 Richmond Way, Richmond, VA, 23173. Tel: 804-287-6647. p. 2342

Ludwig, Bobbi-Jean, Asst Cat Librn, Carthage College, 2001 Alford Park Dr, Kenosha, WI, 53140-1900. Tel: 262-551-5950. p. 2444

Ludwig, Dianne, Adult Serv Mgr, Freeport Public Library, 100 E Douglas St, Freeport, IL, 61032. Tel: 815-233-3000, Ext 221. p. 590

Ludwig, Jennifer, Dir, Patron Serv, Mishawaka-Penn-Harris Public Library, 209 Lincolnway E, Mishawaka, IN, 46544. Tel: 574-259-5277, Ext 1103. p. 706

Ludwig, Kathleen, Law Librn, Massachusetts Trial Court Law Libraries, Court House, 43 Hope St, Greenfield, MA, 01301. Tel: 413-775-7482. p. 1022

Ludwig, Marie, Dir, United States Air Force, Mitchell Memorial Library-Travis Air Force Base Library, 60 FSS/FSDL, 510 Travis Ave, Travis AFB, CA, 94535-2168. Tel: 707-424-4940. p. 253

Ludwig, Vicky, Coll Develop Librn, Ref Coordr, Western New England University, 1215 Wilbraham Rd, Springfield, MA, 01119. Tel: 413-796-2265. p. 1057

Ludwigsen, Jewel, Sr Librn, California Department of Corrections Library System, California Correctional Institution, 24900 Hwy 202, Tehachapi, CA, 93561. Tel: 916-985-2561, Ext 4236. p. 206

Luebke, Kate, Billing & Tech Serv Coordr, Aquinas College, 1700 Fulton St E, Grand Rapids, MI, 49506. Tel: 616-632-2125. p. 1109

Luebrecht, Brandy, Libr Asst, Bowling Green Public Library, 201 W Locust St, Bowling Green, MO, 63334. Tel: 573-324-5030. p. 1238

Lueg, Christopher, Prof, University of Illinois at Urbana-Champaign, Library & Information Science Bldg, 501 E Daniel St, Champaign, IL, 61820-6211. Tel: 217-333-3280. p. 2784

Luetkemeyer, Jennifer, Dr, Asst Prof, Appalachian State University, Reich College of Education, Ste 204, 151 College St, ASU Box 32086, Boone, NC, 28608. Tel: 828-262-2243. p. 2789

Luey, Scott, Chief Exec Officer, Port Colborne Public Library, 310 King St, Port Colborne, ON, L3K 4H1, CANADA. Tel: 905-834-6512. p. 2673

Lugar, Beth, Youth Serv Mgr, Charleston Carnegie Public Library, 712 Sixth St, Charleston, IL, 61920. Tel: 217-345-4913. p. 552

Lugo, Aide, Librn, Arizona Department of Corrections - Adult Institutions, 7125 E Juan Sanchez Blvd, San Luis, AZ, 85349. Tel: 928-627-8871. p. 76

Lugo, Angie, Dir, Ethel L Whipple Memorial Library, 402 W Ocean Blvd, Los Fresnos, TX, 78566. Tel: 956-233-5330. p. 2213

Lugo, Maribel, Libr Mgr, New York Public Library - Astor, Lenox & Tilden Foundations, Wakefield Branch, 4100 Lowerre Pl, Bronx, NY, 10466. Tel: 718-652-4663. p. 1598

Luhring, Olivia, Interim Dir, Williams Public Library, 216 Main St, Williams, IA, 50271. Tel: 515-854-2643. p. 792

Luhrs, Jennifer, Libr Supvr, University of Tennessee Graduate School of Medicine, 1924 Alcoa Hwy, Box U-111, Knoxville, TN, 37920. Tel: 865-305-7340. p. 2107

Luini, Christina, Asst Librn, United States District Court, Phillip Burton Federal Bldg, 450 Golden Gate Ave, San Francisco, CA, 94102. Tel: 415-436-8130. p. 229

Luinstra, David, Director, Student Learning, Sir Sandford Fleming College of Applied Arts & Technology, 599 Brealey Dr, Peterborough, ON, K9J 7B1, CANADA. Tel: 705-749-5530, Ext 1516. p. 2672

Luiz, Laura, Ref Librn, Bakersfield College, 1801 Panorama Dr, Bakersfield, CA, 93305-1298. Tel: 661-395-4461. p. 119

Luizzi, Jacqueline M, Med Librn, United States Army, Medical Mall, 2nd Flr, 9040 Jackson Ave, Tacoma, WA, 98431. Tel: 253-968-0118. p. 2387

Lujan, Audrey, City Librn, Anaheim Public Library, 500 W Broadway, Anaheim, CA, 92805-3699. Tel: 714-765-1880. p. 116

Lujan, Kimberly, Executive Asst, Shasta Public Libraries, 1100 Parkview Ave, Redding, CA, 96001. Tel: 530-245-7250. p. 198

Lujan, Nathaniel, Librn, Pueblo of Isleta Library, 950 Moonlight Dr SW, Albuquerque, NM, 87105. Tel: 505-869-9808. p. 1461

Lukban, Francis, Evening Mgr, Mount Saint Mary's University, 16300 Old Emmitsburg Rd, Emmitsburg, MD, 21727. Tel: 301-447-5245. p. 965

Luke, Erica, Exec Dir, South County History Center, 2636 Kingstown Rd, Kingston, RI, 02881. Tel: 401-783-1328. p. 2033

Luke, Lisa, Librn, Sea Girt Library, Railroad Station at the Plaza, Sea Girt, NJ, 08750. Tel: 732-449-1099. p. 1442

Luke, Sharon, Asst Dir, Gentry County Library, 304 N Park St, Stanberry, MO, 64489. Tel: 660-783-2335. p. 1282

Luke, Terri, Asst Dir, Br Serv, Nashville Public Library, 615 Church St, Nashville, TN, 37219-2314. Tel: 615-862-5761. p. 2119

Luker, Laverne, Circ Librn, Tombigbee Regional Library System, Evans Memorial Library, 105 N Long St, Aberdeen, MS, 39730. Tel: 662-369-4601. p. 1235

Lukert, Wendy, Pub Serv Librn, Blair Public Library, 2233 Civic Dr, Blair, NE, 68008. Tel: 402-426-3617. p. 1308

Lukitsch, Robert, Dir, Support Serv, Northland Public Library, 300 Cumberland Rd, Pittsburgh, PA, 15237-5455. Tel: 412-366-8100, Ext 106. p. 1994

Lukose, David, Br Mgr, Fort Bend County Libraries, University Branch, 14010 University Blvd, Sugar Land, TX, 77479. Tel: 281-633-5100. p. 2232

Lukow, John, Cataloger, Fort Myers Beach Public Library, 2755 Estero Blvd, Fort Myers Beach, FL, 33931. Tel: 239-765-8162. p. 404

Luksa, Jennifer, Dir, Libr Serv, Misericordia University, 301 Lake St, Dallas, PA, 18612-1098. Tel: 570-674-6231. p. 1925

Luksa, Jennifer, Dir, Libr & Learning Commons, Alvernia University, 400 St Bernardine St, Reading, PA, 19607-1737. Tel: 610-796-8223. p. 2000

Lum, Kaimi Rose, Asst Libr Dir, Snow Library, 67 Main St, Orleans, MA, 02653-2413. Tel: 508-240-3760. p. 1044

Lumpkin, Dee, Syst/Ref Librn, William Carey University Libraries, 710 William Carey Pkwy, Hattiesburg, MS, 39401. Tel: 601-318-6169. p. 1219

Lumpkin, Lisa J, Libr Asst, Southwest Tennessee Community College, Burt Bornblum, 5983 Macon Cove, Memphis, TN, 38134. Tel: 901-333-4437. p. 2115

Lumpkin, Margaret, Librn, Tallassee Community Library, 99 Freeman Ave, Tallassee, AL, 36078. Tel: 334-283-2732. p. 36

Luna, Amanda, Br Librn, Stockton-San Joaquin County Public Library, Arnold Rue Branch, 5758 Lorraine Ave, Stockton, CA, 95210. p. 250

Luna, Amanda, Br Librn, Stockton-San Joaquin County Public Library, Van Buskirk Miro Branch, Van Buskirk Community Ctr, 734 Houston Ave, Stockton, CA, 95206. p. 250

Luna, Amanda, Br Mgr, Stockton-San Joaquin County Public Library, Stribley Micro Branch, 1760 E Sonora St, Stockton, CA, 95205. p. 250

Luna, Carlos, Circ, Cañada College Library, Bldg 9, 3rd Flr, 4200 Farm Hill Blvd, Redwood City, CA, 94061-1099. p. 200

Luna, Ezequiel, Circ Mgr, Nampa Public Library, 215 12th Ave S, Nampa, ID, 83651. Tel: 208-468-5801. p. 527

Luna Hedges, Charlene, Dir, Frankfort City Library, 104 E Second St, Frankfort, KS, 66427. Tel: 785-292-4320. p. 809

Luna, Marisa, Libr Spec, Arrowhead Regional Medical Center Library, 400 N Pepper Ave, Colton, CA, 92324-1819. Tel: 909-580-1308. p. 131

Luna, Tiffany, Youth Serv Librn, Hopkinsville-Christian County Public Library, 1101 Bethel St, Hopkinsville, KY, 42240. Tel: 270-887-4262, Ext 116. p. 860

Luna-Golya, Gregory, Library Contact, National Park Service, 1207 Emery Hwy, Macon, GA, 31217. Tel: 478-752-8257, Ext 224. p. 487

Luna-Lamas, Sonia, Assoc Dir, Head, Tech Serv, Saint Thomas University Library, Alex A Hanna Law Library, 16401 NW 37th Ave, Miami Gardens, FL, 33054. Tel: 305-623-2387. p. 425

Lund, Bill, Assoc Univ Librn for I.T., Brigham Young University, Harold B Lee Library, 2060 HBLL, Provo, UT, 84602. Tel: 801-422-2927. p. 2269

Lund, Christopher, Law Librn, NYS Supreme Court Library - Binghamton, Broome County Courthouse, First Flr, 92 Court St, Binghamton, NY, 13901-3301. Tel: 607-240-5786. p. 1494

Lund, Cynthia Wales, Spec Coll Librn, Saint Olaf College, Howard V & Edna H Hong Kierkegaard Library, 1510 Saint Olaf Ave, Northfield, MN, 55057-1097. Tel: 507-646-3846. p. 1191

Lund, Daniel, Curator of Coll, Elmhurst Historical Museum, 120 E Park Ave, Elmhurst, IL, 60126. Tel: 630-530-3322. p. 585

Lund, Dean, Mgr, Provincial Archives of New Brunswick, 23 Dineen Dr, Fredericton, NB, E3B 5A3, CANADA. Tel: 506-453-2122. p. 2601

Lund, Heidi, Librn, Veteran Affairs Canada Library, 125 Maple Hills Ave, Charlottetown, PE, C1C 0B6, CANADA. Tel: 782-377-1025. p. 2707

Lund, James, Dir, Libr Serv, Westminster Seminary California Library, 1725 Bear Valley Pkwy, Escondido, CA, 92027. Tel: 760-480-8474. p. 141

Lund, Jennifer, Ad, Redford Township District Library, 25320 W Six Mile, Redford, MI, 48240. Tel: 313-531-5960. p. 1143

Lutkenhaus, Rebecca, Ref & Instruction Librn, Drake University, Drake Law Library, Opperman Hall, 2604 Forest Ave, Des Moines, IA, 50311. Tel: 515-271-3189. p. 746

Lutner, Mark, Dir, Info Tech Serv, Williamsburg Regional Library, 7770 Croaker Rd, Williamsburg, VA, 23188-7064. Tel: 757-741-3329. p. 2353

Luton, Lee, Acq, Tech Serv, Niceville Public Library, 206 Partin Dr N, Niceville, FL, 32578. Tel: 850-279-6436, Ext 1508. p. 428

Luton, Sue, Br Librn, Grand County Library District, Juniper Library at Grand Lake, 316 Garfield St, Grand Lake, CO, 80447. Tel: 970-627-8353. p. 283

Lutris, Jennifer, Librn, Housatonic Community College Library, 900 Lafayette Blvd, Bridgeport, CT, 06604. Tel: 203-332-5075. p. 304

Lutsy, Joseph, Libr Assoc, Glenville State College, 100 High St, Glenville, WV, 26351. Tel: 304-462-6162. p. 2403

Luttmann, Georgene, Tech Serv Coordr, North Kingstown Free Library, 100 Boone St, North Kingstown, RI, 02852-5150. Tel: 401-294-3306. p. 2036

Luttrell, Joy, Mgr, Rapides Parish Library, Hineston Branch, 1810 Hwy 121, Hineston, LA, 71438. Tel: 318-793-8461. p. 880

Luttrell, Sara, Cat Librn, Tech Serv Librn, Brooks Memorial Library, 224 Main St, Brattleboro, VT, 05301. Tel: 802-254-5290. p. 2280

Luttrell-Jimenez, Cara, Outreach Serv Librn, Carroll County Public Library, 136 Court St, Carrollton, KY, 41008. Tel: 502-732-7020. p. 851

Lutz, Allison, Dir, Turtle Lake Public Library, 301 Maple St S, Turtle Lake, WI, 54889. Tel: 715-986-4618. p. 2482

Lutz, Christine A, Head, Pub Serv, NJ Regional Studies Librn, Rutgers University Libraries, Special Collections & University Archives, Alexander Library, 169 College Ave, New Brunswick, NJ, 08901-1163. Tel: 848-932-6148. p. 1425

Lutz, James, Dir, Admin Serv, Texas Christian University, 2913 Lowden St, TCU Box 298400, Fort Worth, TX, 76129. Tel: 817-257-7106. p. 2181

Lutz, Loree, Ch Serv, McCord Memorial Library, 32 W Main St, North East, PA, 16428. Tel: 814-725-4057. p. 1971

Lutz, Sarah L, Dir, Ralpho Township Public Library, 206 S Market St, Elysburg, PA, 17824. Tel: 570-672-9449. p. 1930

Lutz, Sue, Libr Tech, Colorado Department of Corrections, Youth Offender Services, PO Box 35010, Pueblo, CO, 81003. Tel: 719-544-4800, Ext 3507. p. 293

Lutz, Valerie-Anne, Head, MS Processing, American Philosophical Society Library, 105 S Fifth St, Philadelphia, PA, 19106-3386. Tel: 215-440-3400. p. 1974

Lutze, Johnnie, Librn, Inyo County Free Library, Tecopa Branch, 408 Tecopa Hot Springs Rd, Tecopa, CA, 92389. Tel: 760-852-4171. p. 152

Lutzel, John, Pub Serv Librn, Owensboro Community & Technical College Library, Learning Resource Ctr Bldg, 1st Flr, 4800 New Hartford Rd, Owensboro, KY, 42303. Tel: 270-686-4574. p. 871

Lutzke, Amy, Asst Dir, Ref, Dwight Foster Public Library, 209 Merchants Ave, Fort Atkinson, WI, 53538-2049. Tel: 920-563-7790. p. 2436

Luu, Amy, Mgr, County of Los Angeles Public Library, Willowbrook Library, 11737 Wilmington Ave, Los Angeles, CA, 90059. Tel: 323-564-5698. p. 138

Luu, Xinh, Foreign, Comparative & Intl Law Librn, University of Virginia, Arthur J Morris Law Library, 580 Massie Rd, Charlottesville, VA, 22903-1738. Tel: 434-924-3970. p. 2310

Lux, Martha, Tech Serv Librn, Oak Ridge Public Library, 1401 Oak Ridge Tpk, Oak Ridge, TN, 37830-6224. Tel: 865-425-3455. p. 2123

Luy, Kristine, Dir, Early Public Library, 107 Main St, Early, IA, 50535-5010. Tel: 712-273-5334. p. 750

Luzeniecki, Anne, Asst Dir, Helen M Plum Memorial Public Library District, 110 W Maple St, Lombard, IL, 60148-2594. Tel: 630-627-0316. p. 611

Luzius, Jeff, Dr, Dir, United States Air Force, Air University - Muir S Fairchild Research Information Center, 600 Chennault Circle, Maxwell AFB, AL, 36112-6010. Tel: 334-953-2606. p. 25

Ly, Amara, Research Coordr, Historical Society of Long Beach, 4260 Atlantic Ave, Long Beach, CA, 90807. Tel: 562-424-2220. p. 158

Ly, Pearl, Dr, Dean, Palomar College, 1140 W Mission Rd, San Marcos, CA, 92069-1487. Tel: 760-744-1150, Ext 2666. p. 2782

Lybarger, Lowell, Dr, Music & Media Librn, Arkansas Tech University, 305 West Q St, Russellville, AR, 72801. Tel: 479-964-0584. p. 108

Lybbert, Anna, Librn, Tallahassee Campus, Keiser University Library System, 1500 NW 49th St, Fort Lauderdale, FL, 33309. Tel: 954-351-4035. p. 401

Lydia, Laurie, Librn, Libr Serv Mgr, Rowan Public Library, 201 W Fisher St, Salisbury, NC, 28144-4935. Tel: 704-216-8228, 980-432-8670. p. 1715

Lydon, Carla, Exec Dir, East Central Regional Library, 111 Dellwood St, Cambridge, MN, 55008-1588. Tel: 763-689-7390. p. 1167

Lydon, Christopher, Pres, Sedgwick Library Association, 45 Main St, Sedgwick, ME, 04676. p. 940

Lydston, Melissa, Research Librn, Support Serv, New England College of Optometry Library, 424 Beacon St, Boston, MA, 02115. Tel: 617-587-5657. p. 998

Lyhane, Janice, Libr Dir, Marysville Public Library, 1009 Broadway, Marysville, KS, 66508. Tel: 785-562-2491. p. 824

Lyhne, Tamara, Head, Children's Servx, Fairfield Public Library, 1080 Old Post Rd, Fairfield, CT, 06824. Tel: 203-256-3155. p. 312

Lyhne-Nielsen, Stefan, Dir, Trumbull Library System, 33 Quality St, Trumbull, CT, 06611. Tel: 203-452-5197. p. 342

Lykansion, Danny, Head, Ref, Chelmsford Public Library, 25 Boston Rd, Chelmsford, MA, 01824. Tel: 978-256-5521. p. 1010

Lykansion, Danny, Asst Dir, Head, Emerging Tech & Serv, Pelham Public Library, 24 Village Green, Pelham, NH, 03076. Tel: 603-635-7581. p. 1377

Lykens, Maggie, Librn, Mount Aloysius College Library, 7373 Admiral Peary Hwy, Cresson, PA, 16630-1999. Tel: 814-886-6445. p. 1925

Lykins, Forrest, Br Mgr, Cleveland Public Library, Rockport, 4421 W 140th St, Cleveland, OH, 44135. Tel: 216-623-7053. p. 1768

Lykins, Shelby, Libr Operations Mgr, Asbury University, One Macklem Dr, Wilmore, KY, 40390-1198. Tel: 859-858-3511, Ext 2126. p. 878

Lykow, Jean, Res Ctr Mgr, Holland College Library Services, 140 Weymouth St, Charlottetown, PE, C1A 4Z1, CANADA. Tel: 902-888-6738. p. 2707

Lykowski, Judi, Communications Mgr, Mishawaka-Penn-Harris Public Library, 209 Lincolnway E, Mishawaka, IN, 46544. Tel: 574-259-5277, Ext 1107. p. 706

Lyle, Anna, Dir, Forsyth County Public Library, 585 Dahlonega St, Cumming, GA, 30040-2109. Tel: 770-781-9840. p. 473

Lyle, Beth, Br Mgr, Pioneer Library System, Tecumseh Public, 114 N Broadway, Tecumseh, OK, 74873. Tel: 405-598-5955. p. 1856

Lyle, Kristen, Ref (Info Servs), Mansfield Public Library, 255 Hope St, Mansfield, MA, 02048-2353. Tel: 508-261-7380. p. 1031

Lyle, Suzi, Dir, Selover Public Library, 31 State Rte 95, Chesterville, OH, 43317. Tel: 419-768-3431. p. 1758

Lyles, Denise, Supvr, Ferguson Library, Harry Bennett Branch, 115 Vine Rd, Stamford, CT, 06905. Tel: 203-351-8290. p. 338

Lyles, Julie, Dir, Archives, Southern Nazarene University, 4115 N College Ave, Bethany, OK, 73008. Tel: 405-491-8124. p. 1842

Lyles, Kaitlyn, Research Librn, United States Equal Employment Opportunity Commission Library, 131 M St NE, Rm 4SW16N, Washington, DC, 20507. Tel: 202-921-3119. p. 379

Lyme, Dionne, Libr Serv Mgr, Piedmont Columbus Regional - Midtown, Educational Tower, 4th Flr, 710 Center St, Columbus, GA, 31901. Tel: 706-571-1178, 706-571-1179. p. 472

Lynam, Rebekah, Br Mgr, Pioneer Library System, Purcell Public, 919 N Ninth, Purcell, OK, 73080. Tel: 405-527-5546. p. 1855

Lynaugh, Nicole, Dir, Cedar Grove Public Library, 131 Van Altena Ave, Cedar Grove, WI, 53013. Tel: 920-668-6834. p. 2427

Lynce, CJ, Asst Dir, Westlake Porter Public Library, 27333 Center Ridge Rd, Westlake, OH, 44145-3925. Tel: 440-871-2600. p. 1830

Lynch, Andrea, Scholarly Communications Librn, City of Hope, 1500 E Duarte Rd, Duarte, CA, 91010. Tel: 626-301-8497. p. 139

Lynch, Bernadette, Libr Spec, Harrisburg Area Community College, 1641 Old Philadelphia Pike, Lancaster, PA, 17602. Tel: 717-358-2986. p. 1951

Lynch, Elizabeth, Head, Teen Serv, Addison Public Library, Four Friendship Plaza, Addison, IL, 60101. Tel: 630-543-3617. p. 535

Lynch, Eric, Tech Serv Librn, Baker University, 518 Eighth St, Baldwin City, KS, 66006. Tel: 785-594-4582. p. 797

Lynch, Erin, Ch, Wallingford Public Library, 200 N Main St, Wallingford, CT, 06492. Tel: 203-284-6436. p. 343

Lynch, James, Archivist, Bethel College Library, Mennonite Library & Archives, 300 E 27th St, North Newton, KS, 67117-0531. Tel: 316-284-5304. p. 827

Lynch, Jennifer, Dir, Mountain Lakes Public Library, Nine Elm Rd, Mountain Lakes, NJ, 07046-1316. Tel: 973-334-5095. p. 1423

Lynch, Jenny, Historian, Info Serv Mgr, United States Postal Service Library, 475 L'Enfant Plaza SW, Rm 11800, Washington, DC, 20260-1540. Tel: 202-268-2074. p. 379

Lynch, Katherine, Webmaster, Drexel University Libraries, Hagerty Library, 33rd & Market Sts, Philadelphia, PA, 19104-2875. Tel: 215-895-1344. p. 1976

Lynch, Kathleen, Libr Dir, Bangor Public Library, 39 S Main St, Bangor, PA, 18013-2690. Tel: 610-588-4136. p. 1908

Lynch, Kathy, Libr Asst, Oil City Library, Two Central Ave, Oil City, PA, 16301-2795. Tel: 814-678-3072. p. 1973

Lynch, Kimberly, Archives, Caldwell University, 120 Bloomfield Ave, Caldwell, NJ, 07006. Tel: 973-618-3337. p. 1393

Lynch, Lisa, Libr Dir, Carnegie-Schuyler Library, 303 E Second St, Pana, IL, 62557. Tel: 217-562-2326. p. 632

Lynch, Liz, Regional Libr Dir, Lake Agassiz Regional Library, 118 S Fifth St, Moorhead, MN, 56560-2756. Tel: 218-233-3757, Ext 127. p. 1188

Lynch, Mary, City Librn, Ventura County Library, Ojai Library, 111 E Ojai Ave, Ojai, CA, 93023. Tel: 805-646-1639. p. 256

Lynch, Meghan E, Br Mgr, Chester County Library & District Center, Henrietta Hankin Branch, 215 Windgate Dr, Chester Springs, PA, 19425. Tel: 610-344-5604. p. 1932

Lynch, Michael J, Dir, Law Libr, John Marshall Law School, 245 Peachtree Center Ave NE, 18th Flr, Atlanta, GA, 30303. Tel: 678-916-2661. p. 465

Lynch, Nicole, Libr Mgr, Bucks County Free Library, Bensalem Branch, 3700 Hulmeville Rd, Bensalem, PA, 19020-4491. Tel: 215-638-2030. p. 1927
Lynch, Nicole, Asst Dir, Cheltenham Township Library System, East Cheltenham Free Library, Rowland Community Ctr, 400 Myrtle Ave, Cheltenham, PA, 19012-2038. Tel: 215-379-2077. p. 1937
Lynch, Shannon, Librn, United States Courts for the Ninth Circuit Library, Bruce R Thompson US Courthouse & Fed Bldg, 400 S Virginia St, Rm 705, Reno, NV, 89501. Tel: 775-686-5776. p. 1349
Lynch, Sheryl, Br Mgr, Hawaii State Public Library System, Waianae Public Library, 85-625 Farrington Hwy, Waianae, HI, 96792. Tel: 808-697-7868. p. 511
Lynch, Susan, Syst Librn, The LuEsther T Mertz Library, The New York Botanical Garden, 2900 Southern Blvd, Bronx, NY, 10458-5126. Tel: 718-817-8536. p. 1499
Lynch, Terry R, Librn, California State Court of Appeal, 3389 12th St, Riverside, CA, 92501. Tel: 951-782-2485. p. 201
Lynch, Theresa, Coll, Wake County Public Library System, 4020 Carya Dr, Raleigh, NC, 27610-2900. Tel: 919-250-1200. p. 1710
Lynch, Tim, Media Serv, Per, The Morristown & Morris Township Library, One Miller Rd, Morristown, NJ, 07960. Tel: 973-538-6161. p. 1421
Lynch, Vickie, Libr Asst, Cragin Memorial Library, Eight Linwood Ave, Colchester, CT, 06415. Tel: 860-537-5752. p. 306
Lyne, Bridget, Head, Circ, Demarest Free Public Library, 90 Hardenburgh Ave, Demarest, NJ, 07627. Tel: 201-768-8714. p. 1398
Lynip, Kathryn, Libr Dir, Mamie Doud Eisenhower Public Library, Three Community Park Rd, Broomfield, CO, 80020. Tel: 720-887-2368. p. 268
Lynn, Beth, Ch Serv, Pub Serv, YA Serv, Thomas Beaver Free Library, 317 Ferry St, Danville, PA, 17821-1939. Tel: 570-275-4180. p. 1925
Lynn, Beth, Coll Develop Coordr, Union University, 1050 Union University Dr, Jackson, TN, 38305-3697. Tel: 731-661-5416. p. 2102
Lynn, Holly, Head, Pub Serv, Huron Public Library, 333 Williams St, Huron, OH, 44839. Tel: 419-433-5009. p. 1791
Lynn, Jessie, Co-Dir, Kellogg-Hubbard Library, 135 Main St, Montpelier, VT, 05602. Tel: 802-223-3338. p. 2289
Lynn, Kim, Asst Dir, Circ, Memorial Hall Library, 2 N Main St, Andover, MA, 01810. Tel: 978-623-8400. p. 985
Lynn, Rebecca, Br Mgr, San Diego County Library, San Marcos Branch, Two Civic Center Dr, San Marcos, CA, 92069-2949. Tel: 760-891-3000. p. 217
Lynn, Tiffany, Dir, Victor Public Library, 710 Second St, Victor, IA, 52347. Tel: 319-647-3646. p. 787
Lynn, Valerie A, Head Librn, Pennsylvania State University Libraries, Mary M & Bertil E Lofstrom Library, 76 University Dr, Hazleton, PA, 18202. Tel: 570-450-3172. p. 2015
Lynott, Shana, Asst Dir, Learning Librn, Webster Public Library, Webster Plaza, 980 Ridge Rd, Webster, NY, 14580. Tel: 585-872-7075. p. 1661
Lyon, Christina, Libr Dir, Caestecker Public Library, 518 Hill St, Green Lake, WI, 54941-8828. Tel: 920-294-3572. p. 2439
Lyon, Darlene, Media Spec, Ridge Technical College Library, 7700 State Rd 544, Winter Haven, FL, 33881. Tel: 863-419-3060, Ext 52738. p. 455
Lyon, Jennifer, Med Librn, Children's Mercy Hospital, 2401 Gillham Rd, Kansas City, MO, 64108. Tel: 816-302-8255. p. 1254
Lyon, Meghan, Head, Tech Serv, Duke University Libraries, David M Rubenstein Rare Book & Manuscript Library, 316 Perkins Library, 411 Chapel Dt, Durham, NC, 27708. Tel: 919-660-5822. p. 1685
Lyon, Wendy, Tech Serv Mgr, Akin, Gump, Strauss, Hauer & Feld LLP, 1700 Pacific Ave, Ste 4100, Dallas, TX, 75201-4624. Tel: 214-969-4628. p. 2162
Lyons, Amy, Interim Dir, University at Buffalo Libraries-State University of New York, Health Sciences Library, Abbott Hall, 3435 Main St, Bldg 28, Buffalo, NY, 14214-3002. Tel: 716-829-5719. p. 1510
Lyons, Audrey, Libr Asst, Alberta Innovates, Vegreville Branch, Hwy 16A 75th St, Vegreville, AB, T9C 1T4, CANADA. Tel: 780-632-8417. p. 2535
Lyons, Catherine, Asst Librn, Bristol Area Library, 619 Old County Rd, Rte 130, Pemaquid, ME, 04458. Tel: 207-677-2115. p. 935
Lyons, Chari, Dir, Carnegie Library of Homestead, 510 E Tenth Ave, Munhall, PA, 15120. Tel: 412-462-3444. p. 1967
Lyons, Charles F, Libr Dir, Buffalo State University of New York, 1300 Elmwood Ave, Buffalo, NY, 14222. Tel: 716-878-3026. p. 1508
Lyons, Curtis, Dir, Cornell University Library, Martin P Catherwood Industrial & Labor Relations Library, 229 Ives Hall, Tower Rd, Ithaca, NY, 14853. Tel: 607-255-2277. p. 1551
Lyons, Debbie, Operations Mgr, McCreary County Public Library District, Six N Main St, Whitley City, KY, 42653. Tel: 606-376-8738. p. 877
Lyons, Diane, Ch, McCook Public Library, 802 Norris Ave, McCook, NE, 69001-3143. Tel: 308-345-1906. p. 1324
Lyons, Eric, Lead Children's Programmer, Missouri River Regional Library, 214 Adams St, Jefferson City, MO, 65101. Tel: 573-634-2464. p. 1253
Lyons, Jeff, Media Generalist II, New Hampshire Corrections Facility for Women Library, 42 Perimeter Rd, Concord, NH, 03301. Tel: 603-271-0892. p. 1359
Lyons, Kate, IT Librn, Hostos Community College Library, Shirley J Hinds Allied Health & Science Bldg, 475 Grand Concourse, Rm A308, Bronx, NY, 10451. Tel: 718-518-4213. p. 1499
Lyons, Kevin, Circ Coordr, Grand Rapids Community College, 140 Ransom NE Ave, Grand Rapids, MI, 49503. Tel: 616-234-3868. p. 1111
Lyons, Lauretta, Head, Ref, Programming Librn, Guilford Free Library, 67 Park St, Guilford, CT, 06437. Tel: 203-453-8282. p. 315
Lyons, Renee, Prog Coordr, East Tennessee State University, Dept Curriculum & Instruction, Warf-Pickel Hall, PO Box 70684, Johnson City, TN, 37614-1709. Tel: 423-439-7845. p. 2792
Lyons, Susan, Govt Doc Librn, Rutgers University Library for the Center for Law & Justice, 123 Washington St, Newark, NJ, 07102-3094. Tel: 973-353-3121. p. 1428
Lyons, Susan, Dir, Eastern Monroe Public Library, 1002 N Ninth St, Stroudsburg, PA, 18360. Tel: 570-421-0800, Ext 304. p. 2010
Lyons, Therese, Pub Serv Mgr, Waukesha Public Library, 321 Wisconsin Ave, Waukesha, WI, 53186-4713. Tel: 262-524-3903. p. 2484
Lyons, Tori, Cataloger, Librn, Logan University/College of Chiropractic Library, 1851 Schoettler Rd, Chesterfield, MO, 63006. Tel: 636-230-1783. p. 1242
Lyons, Tori, Acq, Lead Librn, Saint Louis Community College, Instructional Resources, 11333 Big Bend Rd, Saint Louis, MO, 63122. Tel: 314-984-7297. p. 1273
Lyons-MacFarlane, Nicole, Acq, Cat, ILL/Doc Delivery Serv, University of New Brunswick Libraries, Gerard V La Forest Law Library, Law School, 2nd Flr, 41 Dineen Dr, Fredericton, NB, E3B 5A3, CANADA. Tel: 506-458-7978. p. 2602
Lysiak, Lori, Ref Librn, Pennsylvania State Altoona, 3000 Ivyside Park, Altoona, PA, 16601-3760. Tel: 814-949-5255. p. 1906
Lysiak, Stefanie, Librn, Roxbury Correctional Institution Library, 18701 Roxbury Rd, Hagerstown, MD, 21746. Tel: 240-420-3000, Ext 5290. p. 968
Lysyj, Michael, Mgr, Technology & Collections, Sault Ste Marie Public Library, 50 East St, Sault Ste. Marie, ON, P6A 3C3, CANADA. Tel: 705-759-5245. p. 2677
Lyter, Emily, Admin Dir, Good Shepherd Rehabilitation Library, 850 S Fifth St, Allentown, PA, 18103. Tel: 610-776-3220. p. 1904
Lytle, AmyJo, Br Head, Jasper-Dubois County Public Library, Birdseye Branch, 100 S State Rd 145, Birdseye, IN, 47513. Tel: 812-389-1030. p. 697
Lytle, Cindy, Librn, Schulenburg Public Library, 310 Simpson St, Schulenburg, TX, 78956. Tel: 979-743-3345. p. 2242
Lytle, Debra, Dir, Anson Public Library, 1137 12th St, Anson, TX, 79501. Tel: 325-823-2711. p. 2135
Lytle, Marian, Dir, Mooresville Public Library, 304 S Main St, Mooresville, NC, 28115. Tel: 704-664-2927. p. 1704
Lytle, Roane, Dir, Williamsburg Public Library, 511 W Second St, Williamsburg, PA, 16693. Tel: 814-832-3367. p. 2023
Lyubechansky, Alexander, Clinical Librn, University of Nevada-Reno, Pennington Medical Education Bldg, 1664 N Virginia St, Reno, NV, 89557. Tel: 775-784-4625. p. 1349
Lyubimov, Andrei, Libr Mgr, Holy Trinity Orthodox Seminary, 1407 Robinson Rd, Jordanville, NY, 13361-0036. Tel: 315-858-0945. p. 1558
Ma, Chunwei, Syst Librn, Jersey Shore University Medical Center, 1945 Route 33, Neptune, NJ, 07753. Tel: 732-776-4636. p. 1423
Ma, Evelyn, Ref Librn, Yale University Library, Lillian Goldman Library Yale Law School, 127 Wall St, New Haven, CT, 06511. Tel: 203-432-7120. p. 328
Ma, Hong, Head, Libr Syst, Loyola University Chicago Libraries, 1032 W Sheridan Rd, Chicago, IL, 60660. Tel: 773-508-2590. p. 563
Ma, Jiaqi, Asst Prof, University of Illinois at Urbana-Champaign, Library & Information Science Bldg, 501 E Daniel St, Champaign, IL, 61820-6211. Tel: 217-333-3280. p. 2784
Ma, Richard, Librn, Displays & Media Acquisitions, MiraCosta College Library, One Barnard Dr, Bldg 1200, Oceanside, CA, 92056-3899. Tel: 760-795-6851. p. 187
Ma, Wai Yi, Ref (Info Servs), University of Guam, Guam & Micronesia Collection, UOG Sta, Mangilao, GU, 96923. Tel: 671-735-2157, 671-735-2160. p. 2505
Ma, Wei, Electronic Res Librn, California State University Dominguez Hills, 1000 E Victoria St, Carson, CA, 90747. Tel: 310-243-2085. p. 129
Ma, Xiao-He, Librn, Harvard Library, Harvard-Yenching Library, Two Divinity Ave, Cambridge, MA, 02138. Tel: 617-495-2756. p. 1006
Ma, Yan, Prof, University of Rhode Island, Rodman Hall, 94 W Alumni Ave, Kingston, RI, 02881-0815. Tel: 401-874-2878, 401-874-2947. p. 2792
Maahs, Timothy, Exec Dir, Rock County Historical Society, 426 N Jackson St, Janesville, WI, 53548. Tel: 608-756-4509. p. 2443
Maas, Gwenn, Br Mgr, Henry Patrick School District Public Library, Malinta Branch, 204 N Henry St, Malinta, OH, 43535. Tel: 419-256-7223. p. 1782
Maassen, Orlyn, Dir, Bode Public Library, 114 Humboldt Ave, Bode, IA, 50519. Tel: 515-379-1258. p. 735
Mabe, Michael R, Libr Dir, Chesterfield County Public Library, 9501 Lori Rd, Chesterfield, VA, 23832. Tel: 804-751-2275. p. 2312
Mabe, Sebrina, Archives, Genealogy Serv, Surry Community College, R Bldg, 630 S Main St, Dobson, NC, 27017. Tel: 336-386-3459. p. 1683
Maben, Michael, Cat Librn, Indiana University, School of Law Library, Maurer School of Law, 211 S Indiana Ave, Bloomington, IN, 47405. Tel: 812-855-1882. p. 670

Mabie, Arlene, Dir & Librn, Hawkins Area Library, 709 Main St, Hawkins, WI, 54530-9557. Tel: 715-585-2311. p. 2441
Mabry, Holly, Librn, Louisiana Public Library, 121 N Third St, Louisiana, MO, 63353. Tel: 573-754-4491. p. 1260
Mabry, Holly, Digital Scholarship Librn, User Experience Librn, Gardner-Webb University, 110 S Main St, Boiling Springs, NC, 28017. Tel: 704-406-2184. p. 1674
Mabry, Lesa, ILL, Ser, Concordia University, 800 N Columbia Ave, Seward, NE, 68434. Tel: 402-643-7254. p. 1335
Mac, Lily, Librn, Gowling WLG (Canada) Library, One First Canadian Pl, 100 King St W, Ste 1600, Toronto, ON, M5X 1G5, CANADA. Tel: 416-862-5735. p. 2689
Macalaster, Gretul, Youth Serv Librn, Portsmouth Public Library, 175 Parrott Ave, Portsmouth, NH, 03801-4452. Tel: 603-766-1742. p. 1379
MacAndrew, Kathleen, Cataloging, Metadata & Archives Librn, Roger Williams University, Ten Metacom Ave, Bristol, RI, 02809-5171. Tel: 401-254-4546. p. 2029
MacArthur, Caroline, Dir, Southold Free Library, 53705 Main Rd, Southold, NY, 11971. Tel: 631-765-2077. p. 1643
Macasek, Joe, Pres, Canal Society of New Jersey, 35 Waterview Blvd, Ste 103, Parsippany, NJ, 07054. Tel: 973-292-2755. p. 1432
Macaulay, Jennifer, Assoc Dir, Info Syst, Interim Dir, Stonehill College, 320 Washington St, Easton, MA, 02357. Tel: 508-565-1238. p. 1016
Macaulay, Jennifer, Circ Serv Coordr, Southwestern Oklahoma State University, 100 Campus Dr, Weatherford, OK, 73096-3002. Tel: 580-774-3031. p. 1868
Macaulay, Mary K, Librn, Polsinelli PC, 100 S Fourth St, Ste 1000, Saint Louis, MO, 63102. Tel: 314-889-8000. p. 1272
MacBain, Christina, Ref Serv Coordr, Simcoe County Archives, 1149 Hwy 26, Minesing, ON, L9X 0Z7, CANADA. Tel: 705-726-9300, Ext 1292. p. 2658
MacCall, Meg, Curator, Free Library of Philadelphia, Map Collection, 1901 Vine St, Rm 201, Philadelphia, PA, 19103. Tel: 215-686-5397. p. 1979
MacCall, Melinda, Mgr, District of Columbia Public Library, Southwest, 425 M St SW, Washington, DC, 20024. Tel: 202-724-4752. p. 364
MacCall, Steven L, Dr, Assoc Prof, University of Alabama, 7035 Gorgas Library, Campus Box 870252, Tuscaloosa, AL, 35487-0252. Tel: 205-348-4610. p. 2781
MacDiarmid, Jeslyn, Ch, Churchill County Library, 553 S Maine St, Fallon, NV, 89406-3387. Tel: 775-423-7581. p. 1345
MacDonald, Ann Terese, Libr Tech, Atlantic Provinces Special Education Authority Library, 102-7071 Bayers Rd, Halifax, NS, B3L 2C2, CANADA. Tel: 902-423-8094. p. 2618
MacDonald, Anna T, Head, Ser & Media, Northwestern State University Libraries, 913 University Pkwy, Natchitoches, LA, 71497. Tel: 318-357-4407. p. 900
MacDonald, Bertrum, Dr, Prof, Dalhousie University, Kenneth C Rowe Management Bldg, Ste 4010, 6100 University Ave, Halifax, NS, B3H 4R2, CANADA. Tel: 902-494-2472. p. 2795
MacDonald, Bonney, Chmn, Westerners International Library, c/o Panhandle-Plains Historical Museum, 2503 Fourth Ave, Canyon, TX, 79015. Tel: 806-654-6920. p. 2153
MacDonald, Carolyn, Principal Librn, Lee County Library System, Lakes Regional Library, 15290 Bass Rd, Fort Myers, FL, 33919. Tel: 239-533-4000. p. 403
MacDonald, Cathy, Libr Mgr, Albert-Westmorland-Kent Regional Library, Salisbury Public, 3215 Main St, Salisbury, NB, E4J 2K7, CANADA. Tel: 506-372-3240. p. 2603
MacDonald, Joann, Ch Asst, Cragin Memorial Library, Eight Linwood Ave, Colchester, CT, 06415. Tel: 860-537-5752. p. 306
MacDonald, Karen, Ad, Eastham Public Library, 190 Samoset Rd, Eastham, MA, 02642. Tel: 508-240-5950. p. 1016
MacDonald, Karen, Asst Dir, Beaver City Public Library, 408 Tenth St, Beaver City, NE, 68926. Tel: 308-268-4115. p. 1307
MacDonald, Kathy, Head, Info Serv & Res, University of Waterloo Library, 200 University Ave W, Waterloo, ON, N2L 3G1, CANADA. Tel: 519-888-4567, Ext 33312. p. 2702
MacDonald, Kayla, Asst Libr Dir, Chetwynd Public Library, 5012 46th St, Chetwynd, BC, V0C 1J0, CANADA. Tel: 250-788-2559. p. 2564
Macdonald, Kerry, Librn, University of Manitoba, Seven Oaks General Hospital Library, 2300 McPhillips St, Winnipeg, MB, R2V 3M3, CANADA. Tel: 204-632-3107. p. 2595
MacDonald, Lauren, Dean of Libr, Saint Mary's College Library, 1928 Saint Mary's Rd, Moraga, CA, 94575. Tel: 925-631-4229. p. 180
MacDonald, Lisa, Tech Serv, Sturgis Library, 3090 Main St, Barnstable, MA, 02630. Tel: 508-362-6636. p. 987
Macdonald, Logan, Dir, Technology, Anythink Libraries, 5877 E 120th Ave, Thornton, CO, 80602. Tel: 303-288-2001. p. 296
MacDonald, Loryl, Assoc Chief Librn, University of Toronto Libraries, Thomas Fisher Rare Books Library, 120 St George St, 2nd flr, Toronto, ON, M5S 1A5, CANADA. Tel: 416-978-7656. p. 2699
MacDonald, Mary, Head, Instrul Serv, University of Rhode Island, 15 Lippitt Rd, Kingston, RI, 02881-2011. Tel: 401-874-4635. p. 2033
MacDonald, Matthew, Chief Exec Officer, Sault Ste Marie Public Library, 50 East St, Sault Ste. Marie, ON, P6A 3C3, CANADA. Tel: 705-759-5246. p. 2677
MacDonald, Nicole, Libr Tech, Nova Scotia Community College, Marconi Campus Library, 1240 Grand Lake Rd, Sydney, NS, B1P 6J7, CANADA. Tel: 902-563-2102. p. 2620
MacDonald, Norm, Curator, Ossining Historical Society Museum, 196 Croton Ave, Ossining, NY, 10562. Tel: 914-941-0001. p. 1612
Macdonald, Peregrine, Res & Instruction Librn, Bryant University, 1150 Douglas Pike, Smithfield, RI, 02917-1284. Tel: 401-232-6125. p. 2042
MacDonald, Pippin, Res & Instruction Librn, Antioch University New England Library, 40 Avon St, Keene, NH, 03431. Tel: 603-283-2400. p. 1369
MacDonald, Randall M, Libr Dir, Florida Southern College, 111 Lake Hollingsworth Dr, Lakeland, FL, 33801-5698. Tel: 863-680-4165. p. 417
MacDonald, Rose, Libr Tech, Holland College Library Services, 140 Weymouth St, Charlottetown, PE, C1A 4Z1, CANADA. Tel: 902-894-6837. p. 2707
MacDonald, Scott, Exec Dir, Tioga County Historical Society Museum, 110 Front St, Owego, NY, 13827. Tel: 607-687-2460. p. 1614
MacDonald, Susan, Asst Dir, Children's Librn, Weeks Public Library, 36 Post Rd, Greenland, NH, 03840-2312. Tel: 603-436-8548. p. 1365
MacDonald, Sydney, Bkmobile/Outreach Serv, Libr Asst, Lake Wales Public Library, 290 Cypress Garden Lane, Lake Wales, FL, 33853. Tel: 863-678-4004, Ext 230. p. 416
MacDonald, Theresa, Asst Regional Dir, Coll Librn, Cape Breton Regional Library, 50 Falmouth St, Sydney, NS, B1P 6X9, CANADA. Tel: 902-562-3279. p. 2622
MacDonald, Yvonne, Dir, Dentons Canada LLP, 77 King St W, Ste 400, Toronto, ON, M5K 0A1, CANADA. Tel: 416-863-4511. p. 2688
MacDonald-Nason, Marsha, Libr Mgr, Haut-Saint-Jean Regional Library, Dr Walter Chestnut Public Library, 395 Main St, Unit 1, Hartland, NB, E7P 2N3, CANADA. Tel: 506-375-4876. p. 2600
MacDonnell, Karen, Dr, Dir, College of Physicians & Surgeons, 300-669 Howe St, Vancouver, BC, V6C 0B4, CANADA. Tel: 604-733-6671. p. 2578
MacDougall, Diane, Exec Dir, Schizophrenia Society of Nova Scotia Resources, 5571 Cunard St, Unit 101, Halifax, NS, B3K 1C5, CANADA. Tel: 902-465-2601. p. 2621
Macdougall, Melissa, Dir, Llano County Library System, Lake Shore Library, 7346 Ranch Rd 261, Buchanan Dam, TX, 78609. Tel: 325-379-1174. p. 2212
MacDougall, PJ, Librn, University of Toronto Libraries, Massey College, Robertson Davies Library, Massey College, Four Devonshire Pl, Toronto, ON, M5S 2E1, CANADA. Tel: 416-978-2893. p. 2698
MacDougall, Susan, Libr Mgr, Keg River Community Library, A-243009 Township Rd 1014, Keg River, AB, T0H 2M0, CANADA. Tel: 780-538-4656. p. 2544
MacDowell, Sheila A, Librn, Los Angeles Mission College Library, 13356 Eldridge Ave, Sylmar, CA, 91342. Tel: 818-639-2221. p. 251
MacEachern, Lana, Libr Tech, Aberdeen Hospital, 835 E River Rd, New Glasgow, NS, B2H 3S6, CANADA. Tel: 902-759-1786. p. 2621
Macechak, Jeffrey, Educ Dir, Burlington County Historical Society, 457 High St, Burlington, NJ, 08016-4514. Tel: 609-386-4773, 609-386-4896. p. 1393
Macek, Susan, Libr Found Dir, La Conner Regional Library, 520 Morris St, La Conner, WA, 98257. Tel: 360-466-3352. p. 2368
Macera, Kim, Mgr, Oriskany Public Library, 621 Utica St, Oriskany, NY, 13424. Tel: 315-736-2532. p. 1612
MacFarlane, Andrew, Librn, Saint Johns River State College, Orange Park Center Library, 283 College Dr, Orange Park, FL, 32065-6751. Tel: 904-276-6751. p. 434
MacFarlane, Carol, Copyright Librn, Research Librn, British Columbia College of Nurses & Midwives, 900 - 200 Granville St, Vancouver, BC, V6C 1S4, CANADA. Tel: 604-742-6244. p. 2578
MacFarlane, Carrie, Dir, Res & Instruction Serv, Middlebury College, 110 Storrs Ave, Middlebury, VT, 05753. Tel: 802-443-5018. p. 2288
Macfarlane, Carrie M, Librn, Middlebury College, Armstrong Library, McCardell Bicentennial Hall, Middlebury, VT, 05753. Tel: 802-443-5018. p. 2289
MacFarlane, Erin, Customer Experience Adminr, Maricopa County Library District, 2700 N Central Ave, Ste 700, Phoenix, AZ, 85004. Tel: 602-652-3000. p. 70
MacFarline, Kati, Res & Instruction Librn, Rivier University, 420 S Main St, Nashua, NH, 03060-5086. Tel: 603-897-8673. p. 1375
MacFate, Ann C, Dir, Needham Free Public Library, 1139 Highland Ave, Needham, MA, 02494-3298. Tel: 781-455-7559, Ext 202. p. 1038
Macfie, Mandy, Asst Librn, Conrad Grebel University College, 140 Westmount Rd N, Waterloo, ON, N2L 3G6, CANADA. Tel: 519-885-0220, Ext 34400. p. 2702
MacGillivary, Karen, Dir, Laura E Richards Library, 863 Five Islands Rd, Georgetown, ME, 04548. Tel: 207-371-9995. p. 926
MacGillivray, Katie-Scarlett, Chief Exec Officer, Brock Township Public Library, 401 Simcoe St, Beaverton, ON, L0K 1A0, CANADA. Tel: 249-702-2255. p. 2631
MacGillivray, Katie-Scarlett, Libr Mgr, Mississauga Library System, Clarkson, 2475 Truscott Dr, Mississauga, ON, L5J 2B3, CANADA. Tel: 905-615-4840. p. 2659
MacGillivray, Katie-Scarlett, Libr Mgr, Mississauga Library System, Lorne Park, 1474 Truscott Dr, Mississauga, ON, L5J 1Z2, CANADA. Tel: 905-615-4845. p. 2659

MacGillivray, Katie-Scarlett, Libr Mgr, Mississauga Library System, Sheridan, 2225 Erin Mills Pkwy, Mississauga, ON, L5K 1T9, CANADA. Tel: 905-615-4815. p. 2659

MacGougan, Alice, Supv Librn, Newport Public Library, 35 NW Nye St, Newport, OR, 97365-3714. Tel: 541-265-2153. p. 1888

MacGregor, Alona, Head Librn, TEi-Library Services, LLC, 3455 S 500 W, South Salt Lake, UT, 84115-4234. Tel: 801-262-2332. p. 2273

MacGregor, Anne, Libr Mgr, Apache County Library District, Alpine Public, 17 County Rd 2061, Alpine, AZ, 85920. Tel: 928-339-4925. p. 76

MacGregor, Dave, Head, Circ, W J Niederkorn Library, 316 W Grand Ave, Port Washington, WI, 53074-2293. Tel: 262-284-5031. p. 2470

MacGregor, Ilonna, Librn, TEi-Library Services, LLC, 3455 S 500 W, South Salt Lake, UT, 84115-4234. Tel: 801-262-2332. p. 2273

MacGregor, Leslie, Dir, GEP Dodge Library, Two Main St, Bennington, NH, 03442. Tel: 603-588-6585. p. 1355

MacGregor, Ray, Dir, Santa Barbara County Law Library, 312 E Cook St, Santa Maria, CA, 93454. Tel: 805-346-7548. p. 243

MacGregor, Raymond, Dir, McMahon Law Library of Santa Barbara County, County Court House, 1100 Anacapa St, 2nd Flr, Santa Barbara, CA, 93101. Tel: 805-568-2296. p. 240

MacGuire, Mary Jane, Archives Coordr, Research Servs Librn, Landmark College Library, 19 River Rd S, Putney, VT, 05346. Tel: 802-387-6755. p. 2292

Machacek, Monika, Chief Exec Officer, Clarington Public Library, 163 Church St, Bowmanville, ON, L1C 1T7, CANADA. Tel: 905-623-7322 x2727. p. 2632

Machado, Julie, Libr Mgr, Washoe County Library System, Spanish Springs Library, 7100A Pyramid Lake Hwy, Sparks, NV, 89436-6669. Tel: 775-424-1800. p. 1350

Machalik, Samantha, Curator, Racine Heritage Museum, 701 S Main St, Racine, WI, 53403-1211. Tel: 262-636-3926. p. 2471

Macheak, Carol, Research & Scholarly Communication Coord, University of Arkansas at Little Rock, 2801 S University Ave, Little Rock, AR, 72204. Tel: 501-916-6181. p. 102

MacHenry, David, Libr Dir, Licia & Mason Beekley Community Library, Ten Central Ave, New Hartford, CT, 06057. Tel: 860-379-7235. p. 325

Machetta, Becky, Libr Mgr, Alameda County Library, Centerville Library, 3801 Nicolet Ave, Fremont, CA, 94536-3409. Tel: 510-795-2629. p. 143

Machetta, Becky, Libr Mgr, Alameda County Library, Irvington Library, 41825 Greenpark Dr, Fremont, CA, 94538-4084. Tel: 510-608-1170. p. 143

Machetta, Becky, Libr Mgr, Alameda County Library, Niles Library, 150 I St, Fremont, CA, 94538. Tel: 510-284-0695. p. 143

Machin, Kathryn, Electronic Res, Per, Farmingdale State College of New York, 2350 Broadhollow Rd, Farmingdale, NY, 11735-1021. Tel: 934-420-2040. p. 1532

Machlan, Rhonda, Res Sharing Spec, State Library of Kansas, State Capitol Bldg, Rm 312-N, 300 SW Tenth Ave, Topeka, KS, 66612. Tel: 785-296-3296. p. 839

Machno, Lisa, Br Mgr, Tech Librn, Secaucus Public Library, Katherine Steffens Annex, 1007 Riverside Station Blvd, Secaucus, NJ, 07094. Tel: 201-330-2083, Ext 4050. p. 1442

Machones, Sherry, Dir, Northern Waters Library Service, 3200 E Lakeshore Dr, Ashland, WI, 54806-2510. Tel: 715-682-2365. p. 2421

Machovec, George, Exec Dir, Colorado Alliance of Research Libraries, 3801 E Florida Ave, Ste 515, Denver, CO, 80210. Tel: 303-759-3399, Ext 101. p. 2762

Machum, Ashley, Head, Youth Serv, Okanagan Regional Library, 1430 KLO Rd, Kelowna, BC, V1W 3P6, CANADA. Tel: 250-860-4033. p. 2568

Macias-Mendez, Angie, Mgr, County of Los Angeles Public Library, South El Monte Library, 1430 N Central Ave, South El Monte, CA, 91733-3302. Tel: 626-443-4158. p. 138

Macinnis, Madonna, Library Contact, Eastern Counties Regional Library, Alexander Doyle Public Library, Dalbrae Academy, 11156 Rte 19, Mabou, NS, B0E 1X0, CANADA. Tel: 902-945-2257. p. 2621

Macintyre, Sarah, Br Mgr, Ottawa Public Library/Bibliothèque publique d'Ottawa, Blackburn Hamlet, 199 Glen Park Dr, Ottawa, ON, K1B 5B8, CANADA. p. 2668

Macintyre, Sarah, Br Mgr, Ottawa Public Library/Bibliothèque publique d'Ottawa, Cumberland Branch, 1599 Tenth Line Rd, Ottawa, ON, K1E 3E8, CANADA. p. 2668

MacIsaac, Emily, Instrul Librn, Holland College Library Services, 140 Weymouth St, Charlottetown, PE, C1A 4Z1, CANADA. Tel: 902-566-9308. p. 2707

Mack, Betsy, Dir, Prospect Free Library, 915 Trenton Falls St, Prospect, NY, 13435. Tel: 315-896-2736. p. 1624

Mack, Cheryl, Info Spec, Air Force Research Laboratory, Munitions Directorate Technical Library, 203 W Eglin Blvd, Ste 300, Eglin AFB, FL, 32542-6843. Tel: 850-882-5586. p. 394

Mack, Cheryl, Dir, Air Force Research Laboratory, Technical Library, 203 W Eglin Blvd, Ste 300, Eglin AFB, FL, 32542-6843. Tel: 850-882-6849. p. 395

Mack, Cindy J, Dir, Brighton District Library, 100 Library Dr, Brighton, MI, 48116. Tel: 810-229-6571, Ext 203. p. 1087

Mack, Diana, Libr Mgr, Metro Kalyn Community Library, 5017-49 St, Bag 250, Bruderheim, AB, T0B 0S0, CANADA. Tel: 780-796-3032. p. 2525

Mack, Kari, Dir, Libr Serv, Ulster County Community College, 491 Cottekill Rd, Stone Ridge, NY, 12484. Tel: 845-687-5213. p. 1646

Mack, Kathleen, Librn, Orchard Park Public Library, S-4570 S Buffalo St, Orchard Park, NY, 14127. Tel: 716-662-9851. p. 1612

Mack, Mary Jo, Dir, John A Stahl Library, 330 N Colfax St, West Point, NE, 68788. Tel: 402-372-3831. p. 1340

Mack, Precious, Tech Serv Librn, Teen Serv Librn, Verona Public Library, 17 Gould St, Verona, NJ, 07044-1928. Tel: 973-857-4848. p. 1449

Mack, Roxanne, Dir, Copiah-Jefferson Regional Library System, 223 S Extension St, Hazlehurst, MS, 39083-3339. Tel: 601-894-1681. p. 1219

Mack, Shenita, Br Mgr, Chicago Public Library, Bessie Coleman Branch, 731 E 63rd St, Chicago, IL, 60637. Tel: 312-747-7760. p. 556

Mack, Shenita, Div Chief, Chicago Public Library, General Information Services Division, 400 S State St, Chicago, IL, 60605. Tel: 312-747-4472. p. 556

Mackavoy, Michael, Mgr, County of Los Angeles Public Library, Lomita Library, 24200 Narbonne Ave, Lomita, CA, 90717-1188. Tel: 310-539-4515. p. 137

MacKay, Camilla, Dir, Res & Instruction Serv, Scholarly Communications Librn, Bryn Mawr College, Rhys Carpenter Library for Art, Archaeology & Cities, 101 N Merion Ave, Bryn Mawr, PA, 19104-2899. Tel: 610-526-7910. p. 1916

Mackay, Lyn, Br Mgr, Kenora Public Library, Keewatin Branch, 221 Main St, Keewatin, ON, P0X 1C0, CANADA. Tel: 807-547-2145. p. 2649

Macke, Lisa, Dir, Creighton Public Library, 701 State St, Creighton, NE, 68729-4000. Tel: 402-358-5115. p. 1311

MacKellar, Laurie, Librn, Tech Serv, Elizabethtown Community & Technical College Library, 600 College Street Rd, Elizabethtown, KY, 42701. Tel: 270-706-8812. p. 854

Macken, Megan, Interim Dir, Libr Serv, Oklahoma State University-Oklahoma City Library, 900 N Portland, Oklahoma City, OK, 73107. Tel: 405-945-3251. p. 1859

Macken, Susan, Dir, Oelwein Public Library, 201 E Charles St, Oelwein, IA, 50662-1939. Tel: 319-283-1515. p. 774

MacKenzie, Alaina, Head, Acq & Ser, University of King's College Library, 6350 Coburg Rd, Halifax, NS, B3H 2A1, CANADA. Tel: 902-422-1271. p. 2621

MacKenzie, Allison, Dir, Fayette Public Library, 855 S Jefferson St, La Grange, TX, 78945. Tel: 979-968-3765. p. 2207

Mackenzie, Caley, Ch, Parsons Memorial Library, 27 Saco Rd, Alfred, ME, 04002. Tel: 207-324-2001. p. 913

MacKenzie, Dena, Librn, Wapiti Regional Library, Star City Public Library, 400 Fourth St, Star City, SK, S0E 1P0, CANADA. Tel: 306-863-4364. p. 2746

MacKenzie, Emily, Head Librn, McGill University Libraries, Macdonald Campus Library, Barton Bldg, 21111 Lakeshore Rd, Sainte-Anne-de-Bellevue, QC, H9X 3V9, CANADA. Tel: 514-398-7876. p. 2726

MacKenzie, James, Dir, Scholarly Technologies, University of New Brunswick Libraries, Five Macaulay Lane, Fredericton, NB, E3B 5H5, CANADA. Tel: 506-259-2774. p. 2601

MacKenzie, Jason, Libr Tech II, College of the North Atlantic Library Services, Ridge Road Campus Library, 153 Ridge Rd, Rm 111, St. John's, NL, A1C 6L8, CANADA. Tel: 709-793-3305. p. 2609

MacKenzie, Kathleen, Archivist, Saint Francis Xavier University, 3080 Martha Dr, Antigonish, NS, B2G 2W5, CANADA. Tel: 902-867-2201. p. 2615

Mackenzie, Kris, Sr Libr Asst, Sausalito Public Library, 420 Litho St, Sausalito, CA, 94965. Tel: 415-289-4100, Ext 503. p. 246

MacKenzie, Marjorie, Coll Develop, Fac Librn, Green River College, 12401 SE 320th St, Auburn, WA, 98092-3699. Tel: 253-833-9111, Ext 2101. p. 2357

Mackes, Dawn, Br Mgr, Worcester County Library, Pocomoke City Branch, 301 Market St, Pocomoke City, MD, 21851. Tel: 410-957-0878. p. 978

Mackey, Barbara, Admin Assoc, Texas A&M University-Texarkana, 7101 University Ave, Texarkana, TX, 75503. Tel: 903-223-3092. p. 2248

Mackey, Jill A, County Librn, Crook County Library, 414 Main St, Sundance, WY, 82729. Tel: 307-283-1006, 307-283-1008. p. 2499

Mackey, Michele, Circ, Libr Tech, Department of Veterans Affairs, One Veterans Dr, Mail Stop 142 D, Minneapolis, MN, 55417. Tel: 612-467-4200. p. 1183

Mackey, Tonja, Dr, Dir, Libr Serv, Texarkana College, 1024 Tucker St, Texarkana, TX, 75501. Tel: 903-832-3215. p. 2248

MacKichan, Mark, Br Head, Vancouver Public Library, Joe Fortes Branch, 870 Denman St, Vancouver, BC, V6G 2L8, CANADA. Tel: 604-665-3972. p. 2581

Mackie, Adam, Ref Librn, University of Connecticut, Thomas J Meskill Law Library, 39 Elizabeth St, Hartford, CT, 06105. Tel: 860-570-5071. p. 340

Mackie, Paula, Br Mgr, Huron County Library, Alice Munro Public Library, 281 Edward St, Wingham, ON, N0G 2W0, CANADA. Tel: 519-357-3312. p. 2636

Mackie, Paula, Br Mgr, Huron County Library, Blyth Branch, 392 Queen St, Blyth, ON, N0M 1H0, CANADA. Tel: 519-523-4400. p. 2636

Mackie, Paula, Br Mgr, Huron County Library, Howick Branch, 45088 Harriston Rd, RR 1, Gorrie, ON, N0G 1X0, CANADA. Tel: 519-335-6899. p. 2636

MacKie-Mason, Jeffrey, Univ Librn, University of California, Berkeley, South Hall Rd, Berkeley, CA, 94704. Tel: 510-642-6657. p. 122

MacKillop, Clare, Br Supvr, Cape Breton Regional Library, Dominion Public, 78 Commercial St, Unit A, Dominion, NS, B1G 1B4, CANADA. Tel: 902-562-3279. p. 2622

MacKillop, Clare, Br Supvr, Cape Breton Regional Library, Florence Public, 676 Bras d'or Florence Rd, Florence, NS, B1Y 1E4, CANADA. Tel: 902-736-7583. p. 2622

MacKillop, Clare, Br Supvr, Cape Breton Regional Library, Main-a-Dieu Public, 2886 Louisbourg-Main-a-Dieu Rd, Main-a-Dieu, NS, B1C 1X5, CANADA. Tel: 902-562-3279. p. 2622

MacKillop, Clare, Br Supvr, Cape Breton Regional Library, Martha Hollett Memorial, One Fraser Ave, Sydney Mines, NS, B1V 2B8, CANADA. Tel: 902-736-3219. p. 2622

MacKillop, Clare, Br Supvr, Cape Breton Regional Library, New Waterford Branch, 3390 Plummer Ave, New Waterford, NS, B1H 4K4, CANADA. Tel: 902-862-2892. p. 2622

MacKillop, Clare, Br Supvr, Cape Breton Regional Library, Tompkins Memorial, Tompkins Pl, 2249 Sydney Rd, Unit 3, Reserve Mines, NS, B1E 1J9, CANADA. Tel: 902-562-3279. p. 2622

MacKillop, Clare, Br Supvr, Cape Breton Regional Library, W W Lewis Memorial, Ten Upper Warren St, Louisbourg, NS, B1C 1M6, CANADA. Tel: 902-733-3608. p. 2622

MacKillop, Clare, Br Supvr, Cape Breton Regional Library, Wilfred Oram Centennial, 309 Commercial St, North Sydney, NS, B2A 1B9, CANADA. Tel: 902-794-3272. p. 2622

MacKinney, Lisa, Dir, Hall County Library System, 127 Main St NW, Gainesville, GA, 30501-3699. Tel: 770-532-3311. p. 480

MacKinnon, Christy, Sr Dir, Libr & Info Serv, Bennett Jones LLP Library, 4500 Bankers Hall E, 855 Second St SW, Calgary, AB, T2P 4K7, CANADA. Tel: 403-298-3165. p. 2526

MacKinnon, Keith, Regional Resource Librarian, Fundy Library Region, One Market Sq, Saint John, NB, E2L 4Z6, CANADA. Tel: 506-643-7222. p. 2604

MacKinnon, Paula, Exec Dir, Califa, 330 Townsend St, Ste 133, San Francisco, CA, 94107. Tel: 888-239-2289. p. 2761

MacKintosh, Pamela, Econ Librn, University of Michigan, Sumner & Laura Foster Library, 265 Lorch Hall, Ann Arbor, MI, 48109-1220. Tel: 734-763-6609. p. 1079

MacKintosh, Pamela J, Coord, Libr Coll, University of Michigan, Shapiro Undergraduate Library, 919 S University Ave, Ann Arbor, MI, 48109-1185. Tel: 734-764-7490. p. 1080

Macklin, Alexis, Assoc Dean, Wayne State University Libraries, 5150 Gullen Mall, Ste 3100, Detroit, MI, 48202. Tel: 313-577-4176. p. 1100

Macklin, Alexis, Dir, Carlow University, 3333 Fifth Ave, Pittsburgh, PA, 15213. Tel: 412-578-6139. p. 1990

Macklin, Tiffany, Circ, Soc Media Coordr, Tech, Warren County Memorial Library, 119 South Front St, Warrenton, NC, 27589. Tel: 252-257-4990. p. 1720

MacLaren, Audra, Tech Librn, Oliver Wolcott Library, 160 South St, Litchfield, CT, 06759-0187. Tel: 860-567-8030. p. 320

MacLaren, Audra, Dir, Gunn Memorial Library, Inc, Five Wykeham Rd, Washington, CT, 06793-1308. Tel: 860-868-7586. p. 343

MacLaughlin, Rhoda M, Dir, Libr Serv, Cowley County Community College, 131 S Third St, Arkansas City, KS, 67005. Tel: 620-441-5334. p. 796

Maclay, Susan, Interim Exec Dir, Hermann-Grima House Library, 820 Saint Louis St, New Orleans, LA, 70112. Tel: 504-274-0750. p. 901

MacLean, Barbara, ILL, Cape Breton Regional Library, 50 Falmouth St, Sydney, NS, B1P 6X9, CANADA. Tel: 902-562-3279. p. 2622

Maclean, Lauren, Col Archivist, Head, Ref, Sarah Lawrence College, One Mead Way, Bronxville, NY, 10708. Tel: 914-395-2480. p. 1500

MacLean, Robert, Dir, Libr Serv, Weymouth Public Libraries, Fogg Library, One Columbian St, South Weymouth, MA, 02190. Tel: 781-340-5002. p. 1068

MacLean, Robert, Dir, Weymouth Public Libraries, 46 Broad St, Weymouth, MA, 02188. Tel: 781-338-5994. p. 1068

MacLehose, Stew, Assoc Dean, Digital Serv Librn, Syst Librn, University of New England Libraries, 11 Hills Beach Rd, Biddeford, ME, 04005. Tel: 207-221-4535. p. 917

MacLennan, Darren, Tech Serv Librn, SOWELA Technical Community College Library, Arts & Humanities Bldg, 2000 Merganser St, Lake Charles, LA, 70616. Tel: 337-421-6927. p. 894

Maclennan, Paul, Librn, Chabot College Library, 25555 Hesperian Blvd, Hayward, CA, 94545. p. 150

MacLeod, Jenn, Youth Serv Librn, Hampstead Public Library, Nine Mary E Clark Dr, Hampstead, NH, 03841. Tel: 603-329-6411. p. 1366

MacLeod, Kristin, Head, Circ, Acton Memorial Library, 486 Main St, Acton, MA, 01720. Tel: 978-929-6655. p. 983

MacLeod, Kristin, Mgr, West Acton Citizen's Library, 21 Windsor Ave, West Acton, MA, 01720. Tel: 978-929-6654. p. 1065

MacLeod, Melissa, Ch & Youth Librn, Carver Public Library, Two Meadowbrook Way, Carver, MA, 02330. Tel: 508-866-3415. p. 1009

Maclure, Amanda, YA Librn, Bellingham Public Library, 100 Blackstone St, Bellingham, MA, 02019. Tel: 508-966-1660. p. 988

Macmann, Carol, Br Mgr, Dayton Metro Library, New Lebanon Branch, 715 W Main St, New Lebanon, OH, 45345. Tel: 937-496-8948. p. 1779

MacMaster, Carolann, Libr Dir, East Brookfield Public Library, Memorial Town Complex, 122 Connie Mack Dr, East Brookfield, MA, 01515. Tel: 508-867-7928. p. 1015

MacMaster, Marian, Libr Tech, Metrowest Medical Center - Framingham Union Hospital, 115 Lincoln St, Framingham, MA, 01702. Tel: 508-383-1590. p. 1020

MacMurray, Kat, Librn, Bryn Mawr Presbyterian Church, 625 Montgomery Ave, Bryn Mawr, PA, 19010-3599. Tel: 610-525-2821. p. 1916

MacNamara, Ilona, Exhibits Librn, Ref Librn, Saint Peter's University, 99 Glenwood Ave, Jersey City, NJ, 07306. Tel: 201-761-6465. p. 1410

MacNaughton, Ellen, Clinical Librn, Surgery, Hartford Hospital, Education & Resource Ctr, 3rd Flr, 560 Hudson St, Hartford, CT, 06102. Tel: 860-545-2424. p. 317

MacNeal, Sarah, Digital Serv Librn, Info Serv Librn, Bracebridge Public Library, 94 Manitoba St, Bracebridge, ON, P1L 2B5, CANADA. Tel: 705-645-4171. p. 2632

MacNeil, Elizabeth, Dir, Rockland Memorial Library, 20 Belmont St, Rockland, MA, 02370-2232. Tel: 781-878-1236. p. 1049

MacNeil, Elizabeth, Ref Librn, Rockland Memorial Library, 20 Belmont St, Rockland, MA, 02370-2232. Tel: 781-878-1236. p. 1049

MacNeill, Sarah, Dir, Wells County Public Library, 200 W Washington St, Bluffton, IN, 46714-1999. Tel: 260-824-1612. p. 671

Macom, Hallie, Research Librn, Southern Nazarene University, 4115 N College Ave, Bethany, OK, 73008. Tel: 405-491-6350. p. 1842

Macomber, Nancy, Acq, Govt Doc, Queens College, Benjamin S Rosenthal Library, 65-30 Kissena Blvd, Flushing, NY, 11367-0904. Tel: 718-997-3700. p. 1534

Macon, Annie, Libr Tech, Clapp Memorial Library, 19 S Main St, Belchertown, MA, 01007. Tel: 413-323-0417. p. 988

Macon, Shelley, Dir, Dadeville Public Library, 205 N West St, Dadeville, AL, 36853. Tel: 256-825-7820. p. 13

Macoviak, Jason, Libr Mgr, Copper Queen Library, Six Main St, Bisbee, AZ, 85603. Tel: 520-432-4232. p. 56

MacPherson, Carlie, Sr Librn, Greenberg Families Library, 21 Nadolny Sachs PR, Ottawa, ON, K2A 1R9, CANADA. Tel: 613-798-9818, Ext 245. p. 2667

Macrae, Mairi, Pub Prog Librn, Department of Community Services, Government of Yukon, 1171 First Ave, Whitehorse, YT, Y1A 0G9, CANADA. Tel: 867-667-5239. p. 2757

Macri, Margaret, Br Mgr, Cambridge Public Library, Collins Branch, 64 Aberdeen Ave, Cambridge, MA, 02138. Tel: 617-349-4021. p. 1004

Macris, Jamie, Head, Children's Dept, North Canton Public Library, 185 N Main St, North Canton, OH, 44720-2595. Tel: 330-499-4712. p. 1809

MacTaggart, Mary, Mgr, County of Los Angeles Public Library, Lake Los Angeles Library, 16921 E Ave O, Ste A, Palmdale, CA, 93591. Tel: 661-264-0593. p. 136

MacTavish, Shannon, Libr Tech, Horizon Health Network, 135 MacBeath Ave, Moncton, NB, E1C 6Z8, CANADA. Tel: 506-857-5447. p. 2603

Macul, Mary, Head, Cat, Bowdoin College Library, 3000 College Sta, Brunswick, ME, 04011-8421. p. 919

Maculey, Deb, Circ, Morton Township Library, 110 S James, Mecosta, MI, 49332-9334. Tel: 231-972-8315. p. 1131

MacVaugh, Morgan, Public Service Specialist II, Susquehanna University, 514 University Ave, Selinsgrove, PA, 17870-1050. Tel: 570-372-4317. p. 2006

Macvittie, Matt, Colls Mgr, Curator, Antique Boat Museum, 750 Mary St, Clayton, NY, 13624. Tel: 315-686-4104. p. 1518

MacWaters, Cristi, ILL & Reserves Coordr, Colorado State University Libraries, Morgan Library, 1201 Center Ave Mall, Fort Collins, CO, 80523. Tel: 970-491-1838. p. 281

MacWatters, Kelly, Ref Serv, Siena College, 515 Loudon Rd, Loudonville, NY, 12211. Tel: 518-783-2588. p. 1566

MacWhinnie, Laurie, Ref (Info Servs), University of Maine at Farmington, 116 South St, Farmington, ME, 04938-1990. Tel: 207-778-7210. p. 925

MacWithey, Brian, Libr Dir, Pioneer Memorial Library, 115 W Main St, Fredericksburg, TX, 78624. Tel: 830-997-6513. p. 2182

Macy, Katharine, Interim Assoc Dean, Indiana University-Indianapolis, 755 W Michigan St, Indianapolis, IN, 46202-5195. Tel: 317-274-3532. p. 693

Madansingh, Kamini, Br Head, Winnipeg Public Library, Pembina Trail, 2724 Pembina Hwy, Winnipeg, MB, R3T 2H7, CANADA. Tel: 204-986-4378. p. 2596

Madar, Lisa, Circulation Student Supvr, Libr Asst III, Pennsylvania Western University - California, 250 University Ave, California, PA, 15419-1394. Tel: 724-938-4095. p. 1917

Madayag, Christine, Br Mgr, Hawaii State Public Library System, Waipahu Public Library, 94-275 Mokuola St, Waipahu, HI, 96797. Tel: 808-675-0358. p. 511

Maddalena, Robin, Dir, Libr Serv, Assumption University, 500 Salisbury St, Worcester, MA, 01609. Tel: 508-767-7272. p. 1071

Madden, April, Tech Asst, Prairie State College Library, 202 S Halsted St, Chicago Heights, IL, 60411-8200. Tel: 708-709-3552. p. 571

Madden, Heidi, PhD, Head, Intl & Area Studies, Duke University Libraries, 411 Chapel Dr, Durham, NC, 27708. Tel: 919-660-5984. p. 1684

Madden, Julie, Librn, Gibbs Library, 40 Old Union Rd, Washington, ME, 04574. Tel: 207-845-2663. p. 944

Magness, Maria, Youth Serv Librn, Ethel M Gordon Oakland Park Library, 1298 NE 37th St, Oakland Park, FL, 33334. Tel: 954-630-4372. p. 429

Magno, Rita, Dir, Alma Public Library, 312 N Main St, Alma, WI, 54610. Tel: 608-685-3823. p. 2419

Magno, Rita, Dir, Baldwin Public Library, 400 Cedar St, Baldwin, WI, 54002. Tel: 715-684-3813. p. 2422

Magno, Val, Libr Spec, Fox Valley Technical College, 1825 N Bluemound Dr, Rm G113, Appleton, WI, 54912. Tel: 920-735-5771. p. 2420

Magnoni, Dianna, Assoc Univ Librn, Rutgers University Libraries, Archibald Stevens Alexander Library, 169 College Ave, New Brunswick, NJ, 08901-1163. Tel: 848-932-7851. p. 1424

Magnotta, Michelle, Circ, Mamaroneck Public Library, 136 Prospect Ave, Mamaroneck, NY, 10543. Tel: 914-698-1250. p. 1568

Magnus, Carolyn B, Dir, Portsmouth Free Public Library, 2658 E Main Rd, Portsmouth, RI, 02871. Tel: 401-683-9457. p. 2037

Magnus, Julie, Br Mgr, Marin County Free Library, Corte Madera Library, 707 Meadowsweet Dr, Corte Madera, CA, 94925-1717. Tel: 415-924-3515, 415-924-4844. p. 237

Magnus, Sawyer, Univ Archivist, Texas A&M University-Commerce, 2600 S Neal St, Commerce, TX, 75428. Tel: 903-886-5433. p. 2158

Magnuson, Matthew, Librn, West Hills Community College, 300 Cherry Lane, Coalinga, CA, 93210. Tel: 559-934-2403. p. 131

Magparangalan, Shawnee, ILL Coordr, Saint Louis University, 3650 Lindell Blvd, Saint Louis, MO, 63108-3302. Tel: 314-977-3087. p. 1275

Magpuri, Glenn, Libr Supvr, San Diego Miramar College, 10440 Black Mountain Rd, San Diego, CA, 92126-2999. Tel: 619-388-7310, 619-388-7610. p. 218

Maguire, Jean, Libr Dir, Maynard Public Library, 77 Nason St, Maynard, MA, 01754-2316. Tel: 978-897-1010. p. 1033

Maguire, Mary, Dir, Libr Serv, World Resources Institute, Ten G St NE, Ste 800, Washington, DC, 20002. Tel: 202-729-7602. p. 382

Maguire, Peter, Libr Mgr, Vancouver Island Regional Library, Port Renfrew Branch, 6638 Deering Rd, Port Renfrew, BC, V0S 1K0, CANADA. Tel: 250-647-5423. p. 2571

Maguire, Peter, Libr Mgr, Vancouver Island Regional Library, Sooke Branch, 6671 Wadams Way, Sooke, BC, V9Z 0A4, CANADA. Tel: 250-642-3022. p. 2571

Maguire, Rebecca, Br Mgr, Onondaga County Public Libraries, Mundy Branch Library, 1204 S Geddes St, Syracuse, NY, 13204. Tel: 315-435-3797. p. 1649

Mahadeo, Vidya, Admin Assoc, University of Toronto Libraries, Gerstein Science Information Centre, Sigmund Samuel Library Bldg, Nine Kings College Circle, Toronto, ON, M5S 1A5, CANADA. Tel: 416-978-6434. p. 2699

Mahaffy, Ian, IT Mgr, Tipp City Public Library, 11 E Main St, Tipp City, OH, 45371. Tel: 937-667-3826. p. 1823

Mahaffy, Mardi, Head, Teaching & Learning Serv, University of Missouri-Kansas City Libraries, 800 E 51st St, Kansas City, MO, 64110. Tel: 816-235-1537. p. 1257

Mahan, Kim, Exec Dir, Amarillo Museum of Art Library, 2200 S Van Buren St, Amarillo, TX, 79109-2407. Tel: 806-371-5050. p. 2134

Mahana, Sherry, Circ, Texas Chiropractic College, 5912 Spencer Hwy, Pasadena, TX, 77505. Tel: 281-998-6049. p. 2225

Mahar, Karen, Dir, Ocean City Free Public Library, 1735 Simpson Ave, Ste 4, Ocean City, NJ, 08226. Tel: 609-399-2434. p. 1430

Mahar, Kim, Asst Dir, Head, Ref, Olean Public Library, 134 N Second St, Olean, NY, 14760. Tel: 716-372-0200. p. 1611

Maharjan, Tara, Proc Archivist, Rutgers University Libraries, Special Collections & University Archives, Alexander Library, 169 College Ave, New Brunswick, NJ, 08901-1163. Tel: 848-932-6158. p. 1425

Maher, Diane, Spec Coll & Archives Librn, University of San Diego, Helen K & James S Copley Library, 5998 Alcala Park, San Diego, CA, 92110. p. 222

Maher, Donna, Acad Librn, Ref & Instruction, University of Maine at Augusta Libraries, 46 University Dr, Augusta, ME, 04330-9410. Tel: 207-621-3161. p. 915

Maher, Pamela, Dir, Universite Sainte-Anne, 1695 Hwy 1, Church Point, NS, B0W 1M0, CANADA. Tel: 902-769-2114, Ext 7161. p. 2617

Maher, Stephanie, Youth Serv Librn, Palmer Public Library, 1455 N Main St, Palmer, MA, 01069. Tel: 413-283-3330. p. 1045

Mahitab, Frank, Dir, Libr Serv, Fort Valley State University, 1005 State University Dr, Fort Valley, GA, 31030-4313. Tel: 478-825-6753. p. 479

Mahle, Whittney, Head, Youth Serv, Marion Public Library, 445 E Church St, Marion, OH, 43302-4290. Tel: 740-387-0992. p. 1799

Mahmoud, Ibtisam, Libr Dir, Montreal General Hospital, 1650 Cedar Ave, Rm E6-157, Montreal, QC, H3G 1A4, CANADA. Tel: 514-934-1934, Ext 43057. p. 2726

Mahmoud, Zahir M, Dir, Waynesboro Public Library, 600 S Wayne Ave, Waynesboro, VA, 22980. Tel: 540-942-6746. p. 2352

Mahn, Lindsey, Cat, Librn I, Groton Public Library, 52 Newtown Rd, Groton, CT, 06340. Tel: 860-441-6750. p. 314

Mahnken, Jennifer, Assoc Dir, Br Serv, Johnson County Library, 9875 W 87th St, Overland Park, KS, 66212. Tel: 913-826-4706. p. 830

Mahnken, Sherry, Ref Librn, Curtis Laws Wilson Library, 400 W 14th St, Rolla, MO, 65409-0060. Tel: 573-341-7843. p. 1268

Mahofski, John Paul, Librn, Eastern Correctional Institution, East Library, 30420 Revells Neck Rd, Westover, MD, 21890. Tel: 410-845-4000, Ext 6227. p. 981

Mahon, Linda, Mgr, Community Library Network, Rathdrum Branch, 16320 Hwy 41, Rathdrum, ID, 83858. Tel: 208-687-1029. p. 522

Mahon, Penny, Ref/Media Serv Librn, Kansas City Kansas Community College Library, 7250 State Ave, Kansas City, KS, 66112. Tel: 913-288-7650. p. 816

Mahoney, Amanda, Chief Curator, Cleveland Health Sciences Library, Dittrick Medical History Center, 11000 Euclid Ave, Cleveland, OH, 44106-7130. Tel: 216-368-6391. p. 1767

Mahoney, Barb, Coordr, Learning Commons, Red Deer College Library, 100 College Blvd, Red Deer, AB, T4N 5H5, CANADA. Tel: 403-342-3575. p. 2551

Mahoney, Betsy, Asst Dir, Six Mile Regional Library District, Niedringhaus Bldg, 2001 Delmar Ave, Granite City, IL, 62040-4590. Tel: 618-452-6238. p. 594

Mahoney, Betsy, Mgr, Six Mile Regional Library District, Johnson Road Branch, 2145 Johnson Rd, Granite City, IL, 62040. Tel: 618-452-6238, Ext 785. p. 595

Mahoney, Brenda, Coordr, Librn, Algonquin College Library, 1385 Woodroffe Ave, Rm C350, Ottawa, ON, K2G 1V8, CANADA. Tel: 613-727-4723, Ext 5284. p. 2664

Mahoney, Jessica, Asst Dir, Info Literacy Librn, Franklin College, 101 Branigin Blvd, Franklin, IN, 46131-2623. Tel: 317-738-8164. p. 685

Mahoney, Jill, Ref Librn, William Woods University, One University Ave, Fulton, MO, 65251. p. 1246

Mahoney, Kathleen, Dir, Mashpee Public Library, 64 Steeple St, Mashpee, MA, 02649. Tel: 508-539-1435, Ext 3010. p. 1033

Mahoney, Sarah, Librn, Muskegon Area District Library, Blind & Physically Handicapped Library, 4845 Airline Rd, Unit 5, Muskegon, MI, 49444. Tel: 231-737-6310. p. 1136

Mahoney, Scott, Libr Supvr, Metropolitan Community College Library, Elkhorn Valley Campus, 829 N 204 St, Omaha, NE, 68022. Tel: 531-622-1206. p. 1329

Mahoney-Ayres, Brenda, Dir, Weston County Library System, 23 W Main St, Newcastle, WY, 82701. Tel: 307-746-2206. p. 2497

Mahoski, Samantha, Archivist, Curator, Rensselaer County Historical Society & Hart Cluett Museum, 57 Second St, Troy, NY, 12180. Tel: 518-272-7232. p. 1652

Mai, Brent, Dean of Libr, University of North Florida, Bldg 12-Library, One UNF Dr, Jacksonville, FL, 32224-2645. Tel: 904-620-2615. p. 413

Mai, Resa, Dir, Morris Area Public Library District, 604 Liberty St, Morris, IL, 60450. Tel: 815-942-6880. p. 619

Maier, Jill, Libr Mgr, Water Valley Public Library, PO Box 250, Water Valley, AB, T0M 2E0, CANADA. Tel: 403-637-3899. p. 2559

Maier, John, Head, Tech Serv, Pratt Institute Libraries, 200 Willoughby Ave, Brooklyn, NY, 11205-3897. Tel: 718-636-3659. p. 1506

Maier, Karen, Tech Serv, Presentation College Library, 1500 N Main, Aberdeen, SD, 57401-1299. Tel: 605-229-8498. p. 2073

Maier-O'Shea, Katie, Bibliog Instr, Coll Mgt, Head, Ref, North Park University, Brandel Library, 5114 N Christiana Ave, Chicago, IL, 60625. Tel: 773-244-5582. p. 566

Maike, Amy, Cat, White Cloud Community Library, 1038 Wilcox Ave, White Cloud, MI, 49349. Tel: 231-689-6631. p. 1159

Mailcoat, Galen, Tech Serv Librn, Snow Library, 67 Main St, Orleans, MA, 02653-2413. Tel: 508-240-3760. p. 1044

Mailhot, Marie-Claude, Asst Dir, Universite Laval Bibliotheque, Pavillon Jean-Charles-Bonenfant, 2345, allée des Bibliothèques, Quebec, QC, G1V 0A6, CANADA. Tel: 418-656-3344. p. 2732

Maille, Bonnie, Archives & Spec Coll Librn, Cat Librn, Tech Serv Librn, Oklahoma Panhandle State University, 409 W Sewell, Goodwell, OK, 73939. Tel: 580-349-1546. p. 1848

Mailloux, Sarah, Librn, Casper College, 125 College Dr, Casper, WY, 82601. Tel: 307-268-2269. p. 2491

Maine, Gracie, Ad, Jennings County Public Library, 2375 N State Hwy 3, North Vernon, IN, 47265. Tel: 812-346-2091. p. 711

Mainella, Elizabeth S, Adminr, Micro, Wesleyan University, 252 Church St, Middletown, CT, 06459. Tel: 860-685-3827. p. 322

Mainville, Carol, Br Head, Alfred & Plantagenet Public Library System, Curran Branch, 791 Mill St Box 29, Curran, ON, K0B 1C0, CANADA. Tel: 613-673-2072. p. 2652

Mainville, Diane, Chief Librn, Bibliotheque Publique de Fermont, 100 Place Daviault, Fermont, QC, G0G 1J0, CANADA. Tel: 418-287-3227. p. 2712

Maiorani, Stacia, Educ & First-Year Program Librn, Saint John Fisher University, 3690 East Ave, Rochester, NY, 14618-3599. Tel: 585-385-8140. p. 1630

Mairn, Chad, Info Serv Librn, Saint Petersburg College, Saint Petersburg-Gibbs Campus Library, 6605 Fifth Ave N, Saint Petersburg, FL, 33710. Tel: 727-341-7188. p. 438

Maisch, Stacey, Dir, New Providence Memorial Library, 377 Elkwood Ave, New Providence, NJ, 07974. Tel: 908-665-0311. p. 1426

Maisey, Elizabeth, Head, Spec Coll, Head, Tech Serv, Interim Archivist, Assumption University, 500 Salisbury St, Worcester, MA, 01609. Tel: 508-767-7384. p. 1071

Maisfehlt, Lillian, Information Literacy Coord, Gateway Community College Library & Learning Commons, 20 Church St, New Haven, CT, 06510. Tel: 203-285-2054. p. 325

Malinka, Helen, Libr Dir, Berlin-Peck Memorial Library, 234 Kensington Rd, Berlin, CT, 06037. Tel: 860-828-7131. p. 302
Malinka, Helen, Libr Dir, East Berlin Library Association, 80 Main St, East Berlin, CT, 06023. Tel: 860-828-3123. p. 309
Malinovsky, Michelle, Librn, Onondaga Community College, 4585 W Seneca Tpk, Syracuse, NY, 13215-4585. Tel: 315-498-2347. p. 1649
Malinowski, Ramona, Br Mgr, Henry Patrick School District Public Library, Hamler Branch, 230 Randolph St, Hamler, OH, 43524. Tel: 419-274-3821. p. 1782
Maliska, Jossie, Dir, Palm Springs Public Library, 217 Cypress Lane, Palm Springs, FL, 33461-1698. Tel: 561-584-8350. p. 435
Malland, Kathy, Ref Serv/e-Res, Ser, Concordia University Wisconsin, 12800 N Lake Shore Dr, Mequon, WI, 53097-2402. Tel: 262-243-4330. p. 2456
Mallen, Kevin, Interim Libr Dir, Yuba County Library, 303 Second St, Marysville, CA, 95901-6099. Tel: 530-749-7380. p. 175
Mallery, Mary, Chief Librn, Exec Dir, Brooklyn College Library, 2900 Bedford Ave, Brooklyn, NY, 11210. Tel: 718-951-5335. p. 1501
Malles, Evelyn, Head, Youth Serv, Winter Park Public Library, 460 E New England Ave, Winter Park, FL, 32789. Tel: 407-623-3300, Ext 115. p. 456
Mallette, Ginette, Lead Librn, Greater Sudbury Public Library, Capreol Public Library-Frank R Mazzuca Branch, Citizen Service Ctr, Nine Morin St, Capreol, ON, P0M 1H0, CANADA. Tel: 705-688-3958. p. 2683
Mallette, Ginette, Lead Librn, Greater Sudbury Public Library, Valley East Public Library, Citizen Service Ctr, 4100 Elmview Dr, Hanmer, ON, P3P 1J7, CANADA. Tel: 705-688-3961. p. 2683
Malley, Annie, Libr Mgr, San Mateo County Library, Half Moon Bay Library, 620 Correas St, Half Moon Bay, CA, 94019. Tel: 650-726-2316, Ext 227. p. 235
Malley, Peggy, Dir, Ludden Memorial Library, 42 Main St, Dixfield, ME, 04224. Tel: 207-562-8838. p. 923
Mallias, Leo, Libr Dir, Bowling Green State University, One University Dr, 2nd Flr, Huron, OH, 44839-9791. Tel: 419-372-0681. p. 1791
Mallinak, Melissa, Dir, Loudonville Public Library, 122 E Main St, Loudonville, OH, 44842. Tel: 419-994-5531. p. 1797
Mallon, Melissa, Dir, Vanderbilt University, Peabody Library, 230 Appleton Pl, PBM 135, Nashville, TN, 37203. Tel: 615-322-3147. p. 2122
Mallory, Jimmy, Writing Center Coord, United Theological Seminary, 4501 Denlinger Rd, Dayton, OH, 45426. Tel: 937-529-2290, Ext 4239. p. 1780
Mallory, Patrick, Supvr, Libr Serv, Saint Louis Community College, Meramec Campus Library, 11333 Big Bend Rd, Saint Louis, MO, 63122-5720. Tel: 314-984-7615. p. 1273
Mallory, Sara, Libr Dir, Hagaman Memorial Library, 227 Main St, East Haven, CT, 06512. Tel: 203-468-3893. p. 310
Mallory, William, Br Mgr, San Diego Public Library, Clairemont, 2920 Burgener Blvd, San Diego, CA, 92110-1027. Tel: 858-581-9935. p. 219
Mallow, Erin, Team Leader, Chillicothe & Ross County Public Library, 140 S Paint St, Chillicothe, OH, 45601. Tel: 740-702-4145. p. 1758
Malloy, Molly, Ch Serv, Miles City Public Library, One S Tenth St, Miles City, MT, 59301. Tel: 406-234-1496. p. 1299
Mally, Darrel, Library Contact, Multnomah County Library, Midland, 805 SE 122nd Ave, Portland, OR, 97233. p. 1892
Mally, Darrel, Operations Mgr, Libraries in Clackamas County, 1810 Red Soils Ct, Ste 110, Oregon City, OR, 97045. Tel: 503-723-4853. p. 2773
Malm, Amy, Assoc Dean, Univ Libr Serv, Gallaudet University Library, 800 Florida Ave NE, Washington, DC, 20002. Tel: 202-651-5217. p. 367
Malmberg, Sherry, Libr Mgr, Arrowwood Municipal Library, 22 Centre St, Arrowwood, AB, T0L 0B0, CANADA. Tel: 403-534-3932. p. 2522
Malmgren, Linda, Br Mgr, Door County Library, Ephraim Branch, 9996 Water St, Ephraim, WI, 54211. Tel: 920-854-2014. p. 2479
Malmon, Sandi-Jo, Coll Develop Librn, Harvard Library, Eda Kuhn Loeb Music Library, Music Bldg, Three Oxford St, Cambridge, MA, 02138. Tel: 617-495-2794. p. 1007
Malmquist, Deidre, Dir, Stanhope Public Library, 600 Main St, Stanhope, IA, 50246. Tel: 515-826-3211. p. 784
Malmquist, Katherine, Br Mgr, Cuyahoga County Public Library, Chagrin Falls Branch, 100 E Orange St, Chagrin Falls, OH, 44022-2735. Tel: 440-247-3556. p. 1813
Malmquist, Katherine, Br Mgr, Cuyahoga County Public Library, Gates Mills Branch, 1491 Chagrin River Rd, Gates Mills, OH, 44040-9703. Tel: 440-423-4808. p. 1813
Malmros, Stephanie, Dir of Coll, Res, University of Texas Libraries, Briscoe Center for American History, Sid Richard Hall, Unit 2, Rm 2106, 2300 Red River St, Austin, TX, 78712-1426. Tel: 512-495-4515. p. 2142
Malmsten, Pamela, Treas, Upper Peninsula Region of Library Cooperation, Inc, 1615 Presque Isle Ave, Marquette, MI, 49855. Tel: 906-228-7697. p. 2767
Malmstrom, Hannah, Tech Serv Mgr, River Valley District Library, 214 S Main St, Port Byron, IL, 61275. Tel: 309-523-3440. p. 636
Malnack, Beau, Bus Mgr, University of Nebraska at Omaha, 6001 Dodge St, Omaha, NE, 68182-0237. Tel: 402-554-2916. p. 1330
Malnar, Jakki, Hist Librn, Bacon Memorial District Library, 45 Vinewood, Wyandotte, MI, 48192-5221. Tel: 734-246-8357. p. 1160
Malnekoff, Elyse, Head, Circ Serv, Comstock Township Library, 6130 King Hwy, Comstock, MI, 49041. Tel: 269-345-0136. p. 1093
Malone, David, Dean of Libr, Calvin University & Calvin Theological Seminary, 1855 Knollcrest Circle SE, Grand Rapids, MI, 49546-4402. Tel: 616-526-6072. p. 1110
Malone, Denyce, Br Mgr, Indianapolis Public Library, Michigan Road, 6201 N Michigan Rd, Indianapolis, IN, 46268. Tel: 317-275-4375. p. 696
Malone, Derek, Assoc Prof, Univ Librn, University of North Alabama, One Harrison Plaza, Box 5028, Florence, AL, 35632-0001. Tel: 256-765-4241. p. 17
Malone, Jen, Archivist, Historical Society of Long Beach, 4260 Atlantic Ave, Long Beach, CA, 90807. Tel: 562-424-2220. p. 158
Malone, Judith, Br Mgr, Houston County Public Library System, 1201 Washington Ave, Perry, GA, 31069. Tel: 478-987-3050. p. 493
Malone, Kren, Dir, Libr Serv, Los Angeles Public Library System, 630 W Fifth St, Los Angeles, CA, 90071. Tel: 213-228-7470. p. 163
Malone, Marita, Pub Serv, Website Mgr, Rowan University School of Osteopathic Medicine, Academic Ctr, One Medical Center Dr, Stratford, NJ, 08084. Tel: 856-566-6992. p. 1444
Malone, Marita, Ad, Sally Stretch Keen Memorial Library, 94 Main St, Vincentown, NJ, 08088. Tel: 609-859-3598. p. 1449
Malone, Pamela, Dean, Ivy Tech Community College, 8000 S Education Dr, Terre Haute, IN, 47802. Tel: 812-298-2305. p. 721
Malone, Vicki, Librn, Noonday Community Library, 16662 CR 196, Tyler, TX, 75703. Tel: 903-939-0540. p. 2249
Maloney, Ann, Librn, Youth & Family Serv, Chesapeake Public Library, Indian River, 2320 Old Greenbrier Rd, Chesapeake, VA, 23325. Tel: 757-410-7009. p. 2311
Maloney, Christine, Br Mgr, Ocean County Library, Island Heights Branch, 121 Central Ave, Island Heights, NJ, 08732. Tel: 732-270-6266. p. 1446
Maloney, Dave, Librn, Millville Free Public Library, 169 Main St, Millville, MA, 01529. Tel: 508-883-1887. p. 1036
Maloney, Heather, Dir, Sr Assoc Librn, University of Cincinnati, 9555 Plainfield Rd, Muntz 113, Cincinnati, OH, 45236. Tel: 513-936-1541. p. 1764
Maloney, Kelly, Dir, Mary L Cook Public Library, 381 Old Stage Rd, Waynesville, OH, 45068. Tel: 513-897-4826. p. 1829
Maloney, Michelle, Academic Support Librn, University of the Pacific Libraries, 3601 Pacific Ave, Stockton, CA, 95211. Tel: 209-946-3171. p. 250
Maloney, Patrick, Sr Librn, California Department of Corrections Library System, California Men's Colony-East, Colony Dr, Hwy 1, San Luis Obispo, CA, 93409. Tel: 805-547-7185. p. 206
Malosh, Dan, Syst & Digital Serv Librn, Minnesota Braille & Talking Book Library, 400 NE Stinson Blvd, Minneapolis, MN, 55413. Tel: 507-384-6869. p. 1184
Malott, Alice, Dir, Pickaway County Law Library Association, 207 S Court St, Pickaway County Courthouse, Circleville, OH, 43113. Tel: 740-474-8376. p. 1766
Maloy, Frances J, Col Librn, Union College, 807 Union St, Schenectady, NY, 12308. Tel: 518-388-6739. p. 1638
Malski, Sue, Library Contact, Alcona County Library System, Lincoln Branch, 330 Traverse Bay Rd, Lincoln, MI, 48742-0115. Tel: 989-569-8177. p. 1113
Maltese, Michael, Br Mgr, Pike-Amite-Walthall Library System, Liberty Branch, 196 Clinic Dr, Liberty, MS, 39654. Tel: 601-657-8781. p. 1226
Malthaner, Ann, Pub Relations & Mkt Mgr, Stow-Munroe Falls Public Library, 3512 Darrow Rd, Stow, OH, 44224. Tel: 330-688-3295. p. 1822
Malveaux, Herbert, Mgr, District of Columbia Public Library, Cleveland Park, 3310 Connecticut Ave NW, Washington, DC, 20008. Tel: 202-282-3080. p. 364
Malveaux, Herbert, Chief, Neighborhood Libr Serv, Enoch Pratt Free Library, 400 Cathedral St, Baltimore, MD, 21201. Tel: 410-396-5430. p. 952
Malysa, Amy, Mgr, Youth Serv, Alsip-Merrionette Park Public Library District, 11960 S Pulaski Rd, Alsip, IL, 60803. Tel: 708-371-5666. p. 536
Mammone, Sandra, Br Supvr, Whitby Public Library, Brooklin Branch, Eight Vipond Rd, Brooklin, ON, L1M 1B3, CANADA. Tel: 905-655-3191. p. 2703
Mamo, Elizabeth, Libr Dir, Libraries at Rochester Regional Health, 1425 Portland Ave, Rochester, NY, 14621. Tel: 585-922-4743. p. 1628
Manahan, Becky, Asst Dir, YA Librn, Saint Albans Free Library, 11 Maiden Lane, Saint Albans, VT, 05478. Tel: 802-524-1507. p. 2293
Manahan, Meg, Assoc Dir, Coll Mgt, University of Saint Thomas, 2115 Summit Ave, Mail Box 5004, Saint Paul, MN, 55105. Tel: 651-962-5016. p. 1202
Manalli, Susan, Head, Tech Serv, Anderson County Library, 300 N McDuffie St, Anderson, SC, 29621-5643. Tel: 864-260-4500. p. 2046
Manasco, Brenna, Dir, Orange Public Library, 220 N Fifth St, Orange, TX, 77630. Tel: 409-883-1086. p. 2224
Manax, Lisa, Children's Coordr, London Public Library, Children's, 251 Dundas St, London, ON, N6A 6H9, CANADA. p. 2654
Manci, Catherine, Librn, Georgia Institute of Technology, Architecture Core Collection, 260 Fourth St NW, 1st Flr, Atlanta, GA, 30332. Tel: 404-894-4586. p. 464
Mancillas, Suzanne, Br Mgr, El Paso Public Library, Armijo, 620 E Seventh Ave, El Paso, TX, 79901. Tel: 915-212-0369. p. 2174

Mancini, Abigail, Res & Instruction Librn, Lesley University, South Campus, 89 Brattle St, Cambridge, MA, 02138-2790. Tel: 617-349-8850. p. 1008

Mancini, Andrea, Youth Serv Librn, Groton Public Library, 52 Newtown Rd, Groton, CT, 06340. Tel: 860-441-6750. p. 314

Mancini, Laura, Libr Dir, Northville District Library, 212 W Cady St, Northville, MI, 48167. Tel: 248-349-3020, Ext 206. p. 1138

Mancuso, Andrew, Presv, Team Leader, Case Western Reserve University, 11055 Euclid Ave, Cleveland, OH, 44106. Tel: 216-368-3465. p. 1766

Mancuso, Ellen, Head, Ref Serv, Boynton Beach City Library, 115 N Federal Hwy, Boynton Beach, FL, 33435. Tel: 561-742-6390. p. 386

Mancuso, Mark, Sr Librn, Lexington County Public Library System, 5440 Augusta Rd, Lexington, SC, 29072. Tel: 803-785-2673. p. 2064

Mand, Karen E, Librn & Archivist, Saint Norbert Abbey, 1016 N Broadway, De Pere, WI, 54115-2697. Tel: 920-337-4354. p. 2430

Mandal, Julie, Br Mgr, Brampton Library, Chinguacousy Branch, Brampton Civic Ctr, 150 Central Park Dr, Brampton, ON, L6T 1B4, CANADA. Tel: 905-793-4636, Ext 74120. p. 2633

Mandanayake, Anne, Adult Serv, Kinnelon Public Library, 132 Kinnelon Rd, Kinnelon, NJ, 07405. Tel: 973-838-1321. p. 1410

Mandani, Aurelia, Coordr, Coll Serv, US Department of Commerce, 325 Broadway, R/ESRL5, Boulder, CO, 80305-3328. Tel: 303-497-3271. p. 267

Mandara, Keisha, Access Serv, Joliet Public Library, 150 N Ottawa St, Joliet, IL, 60432. Tel: 815-740-2660. p. 603

Mandel, Anne, Coordr, Ch Serv, Spec Serv Librn, Clinton-Macomb Public Library, Macomb Library for the Blind & Print Disabled, 40900 Romeo Plank Rd, Clinton Township, MI, 48038-2955. Tel: 586-286-1580. p. 1092

Mandel, Mary, Asst Librn, John Rogers Memorial Public Library, 703 Second St, Dodge, NE, 68633. Tel: 402-693-2512. p. 1312

Mandel, Rachel, Ch, The Field Library, Four Nelson Ave, Peekskill, NY, 10566. Tel: 914-737-1212. p. 1616

Mandelblatt, Bertie, Curator, Brown University, John Carter Brown Library, Brown University, 94 George St, Providence, RI, 02906. Tel: 401-863-2725. p. 2037

Mandelstam, Yael, Assoc Librn, Tech Serv, Fordham University School of Law, 150 W 62nd St, New York, NY, 10023. Tel: 212-636-7971. p. 1585

Mandera, Iwona, Librn, Vancouver Premier College, 103-5300 No 3 Rd, Richmond, BC, V6X 2X9, CANADA. Tel: 604-730-1628. p. 2575

Mandeville-Gamble, Steven, Univ Librn, University of California, Riverside, 900 University Ave, Riverside, CA, 92521. Tel: 951-827-3220. p. 203

Mandiloff, Christine, Ref Librn, State Law Library of Montana, 215 N Sanders, Helena, MT, 59601-4522. Tel: 406-444-3660. p. 1297

Mandity, Edward, Asst Dir, Inf and Instructional Tech Librn, Marian University, 3200 Cold Spring Rd, Indianapolis, IN, 46222-1997. Tel: 317-955-6090. p. 697

Mandl, Kama, Acq & Cat, Asst Librn, Talking Bks, Northwest Kansas Library System, Two Washington Sq, Norton, KS, 67654-1615. Tel: 785-877-5148. p. 827

Mandler, Caroline, Exec Dir, Wilton Library Association, 137 Old Ridgefield Rd, Wilton, CT, 06897-3000. Tel: 203-762-3950. p. 347

Mandrell, Jocelyn, Dir, Olton Area Library, 701 Main St, Olton, TX, 79064. Tel: 806-285-7772. p. 2223

Maner, Mary Lin, Syst Dir, Greater Clarks Hill Regional Library System, 7022 Evans Town Center Blvd, Evans, GA, 30809. Tel: 706-863-1946. p. 478

Maner, Sarah, Mgr, Richland Library, Southeast Regional, 7421 Garners Ferry Rd, Columbia, SC, 29209. Tel: 803-776-0855. p. 2054

Maness, Chris, Cataloger, Jerseyville Public Library, 105 N Liberty St, Jerseyville, IL, 62052-1512. Tel: 618-498-9514. p. 603

Mangan, Lori, Libr Dir, North Kansas City Public Library, 2251 Howell St, North Kansas City, MO, 64116. Tel: 816-221-3360. p. 1264

Mangan, Susan, Dir, Ellenville Public Library & Museum, 40 Center St, Ellenville, NY, 12428-1396. Tel: 845-647-5530. p. 1529

Mangano, Anne, Coordr, Coll Serv, Iowa City Public Library, 123 S Linn St, Iowa City, IA, 52240. Tel: 319-887-6034. p. 760

Mangels, Andrew, Dir, Westlake Porter Public Library, 27333 Center Ridge Rd, Westlake, OH, 44145-3925. Tel: 440-871-2600. p. 1830

Manget, Debbie, Librn, Georgia Piedmont Technical College, Bldg B, Rm 109, 16200 Alcovy Rd, Covington, GA, 30014. Tel: 770-786-9522, Ext 3212, 770-786-9522, Ext 3233. p. 473

Mangin, Alicia, Libr Mgr, Des Moines Public Library, East Side, 2559 Hubbell Ave, Des Moines, IA, 50317. Tel: 515-283-4152. p. 745

Mangin, Alicia, Youth Serv Librn, Hiawatha Public Library, 150 W Willman St, Hiawatha, IA, 52233. Tel: 319-393-1414. p. 758

Mangold, Morgan, Head, Tech Serv, University of Mary Washington, 1801 College Ave, Fredericksburg, VA, 22401-5300. Tel: 540-654-1740. p. 2320

Mangrum, April, Libr Mgr, Gallatin Public Library, 123 E Main St, Gallatin, TN, 37066-2509. Tel: 615-452-1722. p. 2099

Mangrum, Suzanne, Acq Librn, Middle Tennessee State University, 1611 Alumni Dr, Murfreesboro, TN, 37132. Tel: 615-904-8517. p. 2117

Mangum, Laura, Teaching Instructor, East Carolina University, 104B Ragsdale Hall, Greenville, NC, 27858. Tel: 252-328-6391. p. 2790

Mangum, Marian, Librn, Emery County Library System, Emery Branch, 100 North Ctr, Emery, UT, 84522. Tel: 435-286-2474. p. 2262

Mangus, Kristen, Circ Mgr, Saint Johns County Public Library System, 6670 US 1 South, Saint Augustine, FL, 32086. Tel: 904-827-6916. p. 440

Mangus, Linda, Asst Mgr, Big Horn County Library, Lovell Branch Library, 300 Oregon Ave, Lovell, WY, 82431. Tel: 307-548-7228. p. 2491

Mani, Nandita S, PhD, Dean of Libr, University of Massachusetts Amherst Libraries, 154 Hicks Way, University of Massachusetts, Amherst, MA, 01003-9275. Tel: 413-545-2623. p. 985

Mani, Nandita S, PhD, Assoc Univ Librn, Dir, Health Sci Libr, University of North Carolina at Chapel Hill, Health Sciences, 355 S Columbia St, CB 7585, Chapel Hill, NC, 27599. Tel: 919-962-0800. p. 1678

Mania, Tracey, Librn, Kentucky Talking Book Library, 300 Coffee Tree Rd, Frankfort, KY, 40601. Tel: 502-564-1736. p. 856

Manier, Daniel, Dir, Technology, University of Notre Dame, 2345 Biolchini Hall of Law, Notre Dame, IN, 46556-4640. Tel: 574-631-3939. p. 711

Manigbas, Maria, Mgr, County of Los Angeles Public Library, Manhattan Beach Library, 1320 Highland Ave, Manhattan Beach, CA, 90266-4789. Tel: 310-545-8595. p. 137

Manildi, Donald, Curator, Intl Piano Archives at Maryland, University of Maryland Libraries, Michelle Smith Performing Arts Library, 8270 Alumni Dr, College Park, MD, 20742-1630. Tel: 301-405-9224. p. 963

Manion, Amy, Dir, Libr Serv, Waukesha County Technical College Library, 800 Main St, Pewaukee, WI, 53072. Tel: 262-691-5316. p. 2469

Manion, Margaret, Ref Librn, University of Massachusetts Lowell Library, Lydon Library, 84 University Ave, Lowell, MA, 01854-2896. Tel: 978-934-3211. p. 1030

Manion, Nani, Regional Librn, Free Library of Philadelphia, Lucien E Blackwell West Philadelphia Regional, 125 S 52nd St, Philadelphia, PA, 19139-3408. Tel: 215-685-7431. p. 1977

Manker, Robin, Regional Librn, Free Library of Philadelphia, Joseph E Coleman Northwest Regional, 68 W Chelten Ave, Philadelphia, PA, 19144-2795. Tel: 215-685-2151. p. 1978

Manko-Cliff, Diane, Bibliog Serv Librn, Davenport University, 6191 Kraft Ave SE, Grand Rapids, MI, 49512. Tel: 616-554-5664. p. 1110

Manley, Ellen, Head Librn, Becket Athenaeum, Inc, 3367 Main St, Becket, MA, 01223. Tel: 413-623-5483. p. 987

Manley, Laura, PhD, Ref/Tech Serv Librn, Monroe County Community College, 1555 S Raisinville Rd, Monroe, MI, 48161-9047. Tel: 734-384-4244. p. 1133

Manley, Sarah, Ch Serv, Upper Arlington Public Library, Miller Park Branch, 1901 Arlington Ave, Upper Arlington, OH, 43212. Tel: 614-488-5710. p. 1778

Mann, Becky, Dir, Gainesville Public Library, Ten Church St, Silver Springs, NY, 14550. Tel: 585-493-2970. p. 1641

Mann, Elisa, Ref Tech, Scappoose Public Library, 52469 SE Second St, Scappoose, OR, 97056. Tel: 503-543-7123. p. 1898

Mann, Erika, Dir, Digital Initiatives, Tech & Scholarship, Indiana University-Purdue University Fort Wayne, 2101 E Coliseum Blvd, Fort Wayne, IN, 46805-1499. Tel: 260-481-5404. p. 684

Mann, Jesse, Theological Librn, Drew University Library, 36 Madison Ave, Madison, NJ, 07940. Tel: 973-408-3472. p. 1414

Mann, Jessie, Librn, Mid-Mississippi Regional Library System, Duck Hill Public, 127 N State St, Duck Hill, MS, 38925-9287. Tel: 662-565-2391. p. 1224

Mann, Jessie, Dir, Beulah Public Library, Beulah City Hall, 120 Central Ave N, Beulah, ND, 58523. Tel: 701-873-2884. p. 1729

Mann, Karen, Br Mgr, Saint Joseph County Public Library, LaSalle Branch, 3232 W Ardmore Trail, South Bend, IN, 46628. Tel: 574-282-4633. p. 719

Mann, Kathryn, Coordr, ILL, University of Kansas School of Medicine-Wichita, 1010 N Kansas, Wichita, KS, 67214-3199. Tel: 316-293-2629. p. 843

Mann, Laverne, Dir, Cherry Hill Public Library, 1100 Kings Hwy N, Cherry Hill, NJ, 08034. Tel: 856-667-0300. p. 1395

Mann, Linda, Cataloger, Cedar County Library District, John D Smith/Eldorado Springs Branch, 808 S Main, El Dorado Springs, MO, 64744. Tel: 417-876-4827. p. 1282

Mann, Lisa, Law Librn, Northampton County Law Library, 669 Washington St, Easton, PA, 18042-7411. Tel: 610-829-6751. p. 1929

Mann, Mary, Archives Librn, Cooper Union for Advancement of Science & Art Library, Seven E Seventh St, New York, NY, 10003. Tel: 212-353-4186. p. 1584

Mann, Melissa, Dir, Pennsylvania Historical & Museum Commission, 202 Museum Lane, Titusville, PA, 16354-8902. Tel: 814-827-2797. p. 2013

Mann, Montie, Bookmobile Assistant, Circ Asst, Tech Serv, Baldwin County Library Cooperative, Inc, PO Box 399, Robertsdale, AL, 36567-0399. Tel: 251-970-4010. p. 34

Mann, Morgan, Commun Relations, Libr Asst, Door County Library, 107 S Fourth Ave, Sturgeon Bay, WI, 54235. Tel: 920-746-7122. p. 2479

Mann, Paige, Co-Dir, University of Redlands, 1249 E Colton Ave, Redlands, CA, 92374-3755. Tel: 909-748-8022. p. 199

Mann, Pamela, Br Mgr, Washington County Free Library, Hancock War Memorial, 231 Hancock Veterans Pkwy, Hancock, MD, 21750. Tel: 301-678-5300. p. 968

Mann, Pamela, Info Literacy/Instruction Coordr, Ref & Instruction Librn, Saint Mary's College of Maryland Library, 47645 College Dr, Saint Mary's City, MD, 20686-3001. Tel: 240-895-4285. p. 976

Mann, Sanjeet, Librn, University of Redlands, 1249 E Colton Ave, Redlands, CA, 92374-3755. Tel: 909-748-8022. p. 199

Mann, Sheryl, Librn, Spartanburg County Public Libraries, Cyrill Westside Library, 525 Oak Grove Rd, Spartanburg, SC, 29301. Tel: 864-574-6815. p. 2070

Mann, Susan, Asst Dir, Pell City Library, 1000 Bruce Etheredge Pkwy, Ste 100, Pell City, AL, 35128. Tel: 205-884-1015. p. 32

Mann, Susan S, Dir, Hillsboro City Library, 118 S Waco St, Hillsboro, TX, 76645. Tel: 254-582-7385. p. 2190

Mann, Valerie, ILL, Bethlehem Area Public Library, 11 W Church St, Bethlehem, PA, 18018. Tel: 610-867-3761, Ext 233. p. 1911

Manna, Chris, Mr, Libr Dir, Kennett Library, 216 E State St, Kennett Square, PA, 19348-3112. Tel: 610-444-2702. p. 1948

Manners, Jane, Ch Serv, Pequot Library, 720 Pequot Ave, Southport, CT, 06890-1496. Tel: 203-259-0346. p. 338

Manners, Lisa, Regional Mgr, Broward County Libraries Division, 100 S Andrews Ave, Fort Lauderdale, FL, 33301. Tel: 954-357-7444. p. 396

Mannheim, Michael, Health Sci Librn, Western New England University, 1215 Wilbraham Rd, Springfield, MA, 01119. Tel: 413-782-1534. p. 1057

Manninen, Lauren, Digital Serv Librn, Virginia Institute of Marine Science, College of William & Mary, 1208 Greate Rd, Gloucester Point, VA, 23062. Tel: 804-684-7114. p. 2322

Manning, Angelia, Libr Asst, H J Nugen Public Library, 103 E Main St, New London, IA, 52645. Tel: 319-367-7704. p. 772

Manning, Ashley, Ref Librn/Genealogy, Ottumwa Public Library, 102 W Fourth St, Ottumwa, IA, 52501. Tel: 641-682-7563, Ext 205. p. 775

Manning, Brian, Libr Dir, Appomattox Regional Library System, 209 E Cawson St, Hopewell, VA, 23860. Tel: 804-458-6329, Ext 2501. p. 2326

Manning, Brian, Curator, Reynolds-Alberta Museum Reference Centre, 6426 40th Ave, Wetaskiwin, AB, T9A 2G1, CANADA. Tel: 780-312-2080. p. 2559

Manning, Carolyn, Dir, Wimberley Village Library, 400 Farm to Market Rd 2325, Wimberley, TX, 78676. Tel: 512-847-2188. p. 2258

Manning, Catreva, Archivist, Grout Museum of History & Science, 503 South St, Waterloo, IA, 50701. Tel: 319-234-6357. p. 788

Manning, Christine, Head, Adult Serv, Topsfield Town Library, One S Common St, Topsfield, MA, 01983. Tel: 978-887-1528. p. 1060

Manning, Colleen C, Dir, South Texas College of Law Houston, 1303 San Jacinto St, Houston, TX, 77002-7006. Tel: 713-646-1729. p. 2198

Manning, Dorothy, Dir, Jourdanton Community Library, 1101 Campbell Ave, Jourdanton, TX, 78026. Tel: 830-769-3087. p. 2204

Manning, Elaine, Cat Asst, University of Detroit Mercy School of Law, 651 E Jefferson, Detroit, MI, 48226. Tel: 313-596-0246. p. 1099

Manning, Elizabeth, Asst Dir, Ref Librn, Prince Memorial Library, 266 Main St, Cumberland, ME, 04021-9754. Tel: 207-829-2215. p. 922

Manning, Elizabeth, Head, Circ, Pollard Memorial Library, 401 Merrimack St, Lowell, MA, 01852. Tel: 978-674-4120. p. 1029

Manning, Jay, Tech Mgr, Jefferson County Library, 5678 State Rd PP, High Ridge, MO, 63049-2216. Tel: 636-677-8689. p. 1248

Manning, Jeremiah, Res & Electronic Serv Librn, Katten Muchin Rosenman LLP, 50 Rockefeller Plaza, New York, NY, 10020-1605. Tel: 212-940-7027. p. 1590

Manning, Karen, Engagement & Inclusion Librarian, Georgia Institute of Technology Library, 260 Fourth St NW, Atlanta, GA, 30332. Tel: 404-894-3591. p. 464

Manning, Kathy, Circ, Slippery Rock University of Pennsylvania, 109 Campus Loop, Slippery Rock, PA, 16057. Tel: 724-738-2058. p. 2007

Manning, Kim, Dir, Hampton Public Library, Four Federal St S, Hampton, IA, 50441-1934. Tel: 641-456-4451. p. 757

Manning, Montie, Dir, Plainfield-Guilford Township Public Library, 1120 Stafford Rd, Plainfield, IN, 46168. Tel: 317-839-6602, Ext 2111. p. 713

Manning, Pat, Neighborhood Serv Mgr, Akron-Summit County Public Library, 60 S High St, Akron, OH, 44326. Tel: 330-643-9082. p. 1744

Mannino, Gary, YA Serv, Massapequa Public Library, Bar Harbour Bldg, 40 Harbor Lane, Massapequa Park, NY, 11762. Tel: 516-799-0770. p. 1569

Mannino, Tegan, Tech Serv Librn, Clapp Memorial Library, 19 S Main St, Belchertown, MA, 01007. Tel: 413-323-0417. p. 988

Mannion, Gail, Head, Lending Serv, Windsor Public Library, 323 Broad St, Windsor, CT, 06095. Tel: 860-285-1923. p. 348

Mannion, Hillary, Archivist, Colorado Springs Pioneers Museum, 215 S Tejon St, Colorado Springs, CO, 80903. Tel: 719-385-5650. p. 270

Mannisto, Mari, Chief Exec Officer, Greenstone Public Library, 405 Second St W, Geraldton, ON, P0T 1M0, CANADA. Tel: 807-854-1490. p. 2642

Mannix, Christine, Instruction Librn, Columbus College of Art & Design, 60 Cleveland Ave, Columbus, OH, 43215. Tel: 614-222-3273. p. 1772

Mannozzi, Joseph, Coordr, Putnam Northern Westchester BOCES, 200 BOCES Dr, Yorktown Heights, NY, 10598. Tel: 914-248-2392. p. 1668

Manny, Karoline, Instruction & Assessment Librn, Ref Librn, Centre College of Kentucky, 600 W Walnut St, Danville, KY, 40422. Tel: 859-238-5272. p. 853

Manochio, Janet, Libr Mgr, Union Beach Memorial Library, 810 Union Ave, Union Beach, NJ, 07735. Tel: 732-264-3792. p. 1449

Manogue, Jessica, Asst Dir, Youth Serv Librn, Jack Russell Memorial Library, 100 Park Ave, Hartford, WI, 53027-1585. Tel: 262-673-8240. p. 2440

Manohar, Vidya, Head, Tech Serv, Morris County Library, 30 E Hanover Ave, Whippany, NJ, 07981. Tel: 973-285-6955. p. 1455

Manoharan, Sharmini, Customer Experience Mgr, Facilities Servs, Coquitlam Public Library, 575 Poirier St, Coquitlam, BC, V3J 6A9, CANADA. Tel: 604-554-7332. p. 2565

Manoharan, Sharmini, Customer Experience Mgr, Facilities Servs, Coquitlam Public Library, City Centre Branch, 1169 Pinetree Way, Coquitlam, BC, V3B 0Y1, CANADA. Tel: 604-554-7332. p. 2565

Manor, Belinda, Dir, Sarah A Munsil Free Library, 5139 Rte 11, Ellenburg Depot, NY, 12935. Tel: 518-594-7314. p. 1529

Manriquez, Julio, Libr Tech, Camarena Memorial Library, 850 Encinas Ave, Calexico, CA, 92231. Tel: 760-768-2170. p. 126

Mansayon, Christopher, Ref & Info Serv, Western Oregon University, 345 N Monmouth Ave, Monmouth, OR, 97361-1396. Tel: 503-838-8441. p. 1887

Mansfield, Clarissa, Library Communications Mgr, Western Washington University, 516 High St, MS 9103, Bellingham, WA, 98225. Tel: 360-650-3052. p. 2358

Mansfield, Tara, Dir, Salem Public Library, 370 Essex St, Salem, MA, 01970-3298. Tel: 978-744-0860. p. 1051

Mansfield-Egans, Cheryl, Ref (Info Servs), Lone Star College System, Montgomery College Library, 3200 College Park Dr, Conroe, TX, 77384. Tel: 936-273-7393. p. 2197

Manson, Veronica, Dir, Italian Cultural Institute Library, 496 Huron St, Toronto, ON, M5R 2R3, CANADA. Tel: 416-921-3802. p. 2690

Manson-Reese, Amy, Br Librn, Boston Public Library, Faneuil, 419 Faneuil St, Brighton, MA, 02135. Tel: 617-782-6705. p. 992

Mansur, Helen, Tech Serv, Northern Essex Community College, 100 Elliott St, Haverhill, MA, 01830. Tel: 978-556-3425. p. 1024

Mantei, Sheri, Asst Librn, Wilson County Public Libraries, 1103 Fourth St, Floresville, TX, 78114. Tel: 830-393-7361. p. 2177

Manteuffel, Louise J, Dir, Warren Public Library, 15 Sackett Hill Rd, Warren, CT, 06754. Tel: 860-868-2195. p. 343

Manthe, Marie, Librn, Kansas Department of Transportation Library, Eisenhower Bldg, 4th Flr, 700 SW Harrison St, Topeka, KS, 66603-3745. Tel: 785-291-3854. p. 838

Mantrone, Tracey, Managing Librn, Brooklyn Public Library, Clinton Hill, 380 Washington Ave, Brooklyn, NY, 11238. Tel: 718-398-8713. p. 1502

Mantzakides, Thomas, Circ Librn, Morton College Library, 3801 S Central Ave, Cicero, IL, 60804. Tel: 708-656-8000, Ext 2321. p. 571

Manuel, Steve, Exec Dir, New London County Historical Society Library, 11 Blinman St, New London, CT, 06320. Tel: 860-443-1209. p. 329

Manvell, Arthur, Honorary Librn, Royal Canadian Military Institute Library, 426 University Ave, Toronto, ON, M5G 1S9, CANADA. Tel: 416-597-0286, Ext 128. p. 2692

Manyik, Jeremy, Dir, Koshare Indian Museum Library, 115 W 18th St, La Junta, CO, 81050. Tel: 719-384-4411. p. 287

Manzella, Morgan, Asst Dir, Head, Ref, Marlborough Public Library, 35 W Main St, Marlborough, MA, 01752-5510. Tel: 508-624-6900. p. 1032

Manzella, Patricia A, Sr Librn, Newport News Public Library System, Virgil I Grissom Branch, 366 DeShazor Dr, Newport News, VA, 23608. Tel: 757-369-3190. p. 2334

Manzer, Constance, Dir, Springfield Memorial Library, 665 Main St, Springfield, NE, 68059. Tel: 402-253-2797. p. 1337

Maounis, Nikki, Dir, Camden Public Library, 55 Main St, Camden, ME, 04843-1703. Tel: 207-236-3440. p. 920

Maparyan, Layli, Dr, Exec Dir, Wellesley College, Wellesley Centers for Women, Cheever House, Rm 107, 106 Central St, Wellesley, MA, 02481. Tel: 781-283-2503. p. 1064

Mapes, Jennifer, Asst Librn, Northwest Kansas Library System, Two Washington Sq, Norton, KS, 67654-1615. Tel: 785-877-5148. p. 827

Maple, Amanda, Music Librn, Pennsylvania State University Libraries, George & Sherry Middlemas Arts & Humanities Library, Pennsylvania State University, W 337 Pattee Library, University Park, PA, 16802-1801. Tel: 814-863-1401. p. 2016

Maple, Connie, ILL Mgr, Oklahoma Christian University, 2501 E Memorial Rd, Edmond, OK, 73013. Tel: 405-425-5312. p. 1846

Maples, Kim, Adult Serv, Nanuet Public Library, 149 Church St, Nanuet, NY, 10954. Tel: 845-623-4281, Ext 127. p. 1575

Maples, Vickey, Adult Serv, Barry-Lawrence Regional Library, Aurora Branch, 202 Jefferson, Aurora, MO, 65605. Tel: 417-678-2036. p. 1263

Mapleton, Ruth, Libr Dir, Dorcas Library, 28 Main St, Prospect Harbor, ME, 04669. Tel: 207-963-4027. p. 938

Mapleton, Ruth, Libr Dir, Winter Harbor Public Library, 18 Chapel Lane, Winter Harbor, ME, 04693. Tel: 207-963-7556. p. 947

Mapp, Kate, Ad, Park City Library, 1255 Park Ave, Park City, UT, 84060. Tel: 435-615-5602. p. 2268

Maquera, Wendy, Libr Asst, Bent Northrop Memorial Library, 164 Park St, Fairfield, VT, 05455. Tel: 802-827-3945. p. 2284

Mar, Anne, Asst Archivist, Occidental College Library, 1600 Campus Rd, Los Angeles, CA, 90041. p. 167
Maracle, Kelsi, Children's Serv Coordr, Midland Public Library, 320 King St, Midland, ON, L4R 3M6, CANADA. Tel: 705-526-4216. p. 2658
Maraffino, Ashley, Head, Tech Serv, Valley Cottage Free Library, 110 Rte 303, Valley Cottage, NY, 10989. Tel: 845-268-7700, Ext 142. p. 1656
Marallo, Julie, Dir, Tenafly Public Library, 100 Riveredge Rd, Tenafly, NJ, 07670-1962. Tel: 201-568-8680. p. 1445
Maranell, Syrena, Ad, Willmar Public Library, 410 Fifth St SW, Willmar, MN, 56201-3298. Tel: 320-235-3162, Ext 16. p. 1208
Marangelli, Becky, Archives Specialist, Ball State University Libraries, Archives & Special Collections, Bracken Library, Rm 210, Muncie, IN, 47306-0161. Tel: 765-285-5078. p. 708
Maranto, Robert, Mgr, Baltimore County Public Library, Arbutus Branch, 855 Sulphur Spring Rd, Baltimore, MD, 21227. Tel: 410-887-1451. p. 979
Maranville, Angela, Dir, Knowledge Access & Resource Mgmt, West Virginia University Libraries, 1549 University Ave, Morgantown, WV, 26506. Tel: 304-293-4040. p. 2409
Marasco, Emily, Asst Dir, Silver Lake Library, 203 Railroad St, Silver Lake, KS, 66539. Tel: 785-582-5141. p. 836
Maratita, Bergitt, Asst Librn, Joeten-Kiyu Public Library, Antonio C Atalig Memorial Public Library (Rota Public), PO Box 537, Rota, MP, 96951. Tel: 670-532-7328. p. 2507
Marbella, Fidencio, Dir, Westchester Public Library, 10700 Canterbury St, Westchester, IL, 60154. Tel: 708-562-3573. p. 661
Marble, Lawrence, Dir, Auburn Hills Public Library, 3400 E Seyburn Dr, Auburn Hills, MI, 48326-2759. Tel: 248-370-9466. p. 1081
Marble, Neta, Librn, Floyd County Library, Lockney Branch, 124 S Main, Lockney, TX, 79241. Tel: 806-652-3561. p. 2177
Marby, Lauren, Info Res Librn, Outreach Librn, Cornell University Library, Flower-Sprecher Veterinary Library, S1 201 Veterinary Education Ctr, Ithaca, NY, 14853-6401. Tel: 607-253-3510. p. 1551
Marcano, Nashieli, Graduate Bus Librn, Humanities & Soc Sci Librn, Kennesaw State University Library System, 385 Cobb Ave NW, MD 1701, Kennesaw, GA, 30144. Tel: 470-578-2791. p. 483
Marcantel, Jerome, Asst Prof, Info Res Librn, McNeese State University, 300 S Beauregard Dr, Lake Charles, LA, 70609. Tel: 337-475-5728. p. 894
Marcell, Grace, Br Mgr, Iberville Parish Library, East Iberville, 5715 Monticello St, Saint Gabriel, LA, 70776. Tel: 225-642-8380. p. 906
March, Debra, Dean, Libr Serv, Young Harris College, One College St, Young Harris, GA, 30582. Tel: 706-379-4313. p. 504
March, Gregory, Maps & Govt Info Librn, University of Tennessee, Knoxville, Map Collection, James D Hoskins Library, Rms 200 & 219, 1401 Cumberland Ave, Knoxville, TN, 37996. Tel: 865-974-6214. p. 2108
March, Mollee, Asst Dir, Learning Res, Morgan Community College Library, 920 Barlow Rd, Fort Morgan, CO, 80701-4399. Tel: 970-542-3186. p. 282
Marchand, Claire, Regional Dir, Canadian Music Centre Libaries, Quebec Regional Library, 1085 Cote du Beaver Hall, Montreal, ON, H2Z 1S5, CANADA. Tel: 514-866-3477. p. 2687
Marchand, Dot, Supvr, Essex County Library, Amherstburg Branch, 232 Sandwich St S, Amherstburg, ON, N9V 2A4, CANADA. Tel: 226-946-1549, Ext 240. p. 2641
Marchand, Melinda, Dir, Knowledge Serv, Emerson Hospital Medical Library, 133 Old Rd to Nine Acre Corner, Concord, MA, 01742. Tel: 978-287-3090. p. 1012
Marchand, Mike, Tech Serv Librn, Kearney Public Library, 2020 First Ave, Kearney, NE, 68847. Tel: 308-233-3285. p. 1319
Marchand, Simone, Librn, Dorion Public Library, 170 Dorion Loop Rd, Dorion, ON, P0T 1K0, CANADA. Tel: 807-857-2289. p. 2639
Marchese, Meghan, Ref & Instruction, Farmingdale State College of New York, 2350 Broadhollow Rd, Farmingdale, NY, 11735-1021. Tel: 934-420-2040. p. 1532
Marchese, Shannon, Libr Dir, Wantagh Public Library, 3285 Park Ave, Wantagh, NY, 11793. Tel: 516-221-1200. p. 1658
Marchetti, Denise, Ch, Wyckoff Public Library, 200 Woodland Ave, Wyckoff, NJ, 07481. Tel: 201-891-4866. p. 1456
Marchionini, Gary, Dr, Dean, University of North Carolina at Chapel Hill, Manning Hall, 216 Lenoir Dr, Campus Box 3360, Chapel Hill, NC, 27599-3360. Tel: 919-962-8366. p. 2790
Marcia, Hargett, Librn, Copeland Public Library, 109 Santa Fe St, Copeland, KS, 67837. Tel: 620-668-5559. p. 803
Marciano, Gina, Circ Mgr, North Providence Union Free Library, 1810 Mineral Spring Ave, North Providence, RI, 02904. Tel: 401-353-5600. p. 2036
Marciano, John B, Pub Affairs, United States Navy, Naval Health Research Center, Wilkins Biomedical Library, Gate 4, Barracks Bldg 333, Rm 101, McClelland & Patterson Rds, San Diego, CA, 92152. Tel: 619-553-8426. p. 222
Marconnet, Donna, User Experience Librn, Madison Area Technical College, 3550 Anderson St, Rm A3000, Madison, WI, 53704. Tel: 608-243-4085. p. 2449
Marcotte, Ray, Ref/Info Tech Serv Librn, Windham Public Library, 217 Windham Center Rd, Windham, ME, 04062. Tel: 207-892-1908. p. 946
Marcotte, Roland, Asst Libr Mgr, Venice Public Library, 260 Nokomis Ave S, Venice, FL, 34285. Tel: 941-861-1336. p. 452
Marcoux, Cyndee, Libr Dir, Ventress Memorial Library, 15 Library Plaza, Marshfield, MA, 02050. Tel: 781-834-5535. p. 1032
Marcoux, Helene, Library Contact, Bibliothèque du CIUSSS du Saguenay-Lac-Saint-Jean, 305 rue Saint Vallier, CP 5006, Chicoutimi, QC, G7H 5H6, CANADA. Tel: 418-541-1234, Ext 2496. p. 2710
Marcoux-Fortier, Jean-Philippe, Librn, Bibliotheque Gabrielle Roy, Maison de la Litterature, 40 rue Sainte-Stanislas, Quebec, QC, G1R 4H1, CANADA. Tel: 418-641-6788, Ext 7814. p. 2730
Marcum, Bobbi, Br Librn, Mingo County Library, Kermit Branch, 103 Main St, Kermit, WV, 25674. Tel: 304-393-4553. p. 2402
Marcum, Lesa, Dir, Owsley County Public Library, 185 Hwy 11, Booneville, KY, 41314. Tel: 606-593-5700. p. 849
Marcum, Steven, Librn, Spencer Township Library, 110 Main St, Spencer, NE, 68777. Tel: 402-589-1131. p. 1336
Marcus, Charles, Fac Serv Librn, University of California, 200 McAllister St, San Francisco, CA, 94102-4978. Tel: 415-565-4757. p. 229
Marcus, Irene, Ref & ILL Librn, Tarpon Springs Public Library, 138 E Lemon St, Tarpon Springs, FL, 34689. Tel: 727-943-4922. p. 450
Marcus, Rebecca, Digital Services & Research Librn, Bryant University, 1150 Douglas Pike, Smithfield, RI, 02917-1284. Tel: 401-232-6295. p. 2042
Marcus, Ronald, Librn, Stamford History Center (Historical Society), 1508 High Ridge Rd, Stamford, CT, 06903-4107. Tel: 203-329-1183. p. 339
Marcus, Shelley, Ref Librn, Chaffey College Library, 5885 Haven Ave, Rancho Cucamonga, CA, 91737-3002. Tel: 909-652-7451. p. 197
Marcy, Margaret, Dir, Tyson Library, 325 W Tyson St, Versailles, IN, 47042. Tel: 812-689-5894. p. 723
Marder, Olga, Actg Head, Tech Serv, Head, Conserv & Presv, The LuEsther T Mertz Library, The New York Botanical Garden, 2900 Southern Blvd, Bronx, NY, 10458-5126. Tel: 718-817-8746. p. 1499
Mardis, Lori, Research Librn, Northwest Missouri State University, 800 University Dr, Maryville, MO, 64468-6001. Tel: 660-562-1193. p. 1261
Mardis, Marcia, Dr, Asst Prof, Assoc Dir, PALM Ctr, Florida State University, College of Communication & Information, 142 Collegiate Loop, Tallahassee, FL, 32306-2100. Tel: 850-644-3392. p. 2783
Maree, Becca, Adult Serv Supvr, Bourbonnais Public Library District, 250 W John Casey Rd, Bourbonnais, IL, 60914. Tel: 815-933-1727. p. 544
Marek, Kate, Dir, Dominican University, Crown Library 300, 7900 W Division St, River Forest, IL, 60305. Tel: 708-524-6648. p. 2784
Mares, Vickie, Br Mgr, Huntsville-Madison County Public Library, Tillman D Hill Public Library, 131 Knowledge Dr, Hazel Green, AL, 35750. Tel: 256-828-9529. p. 22
Mareska, John, Library Contact, Alabama Department of Conservation & Natural Resources, Two North Iberville Dr, Dauphin Island, AL, 36528. Tel: 251-861-2882. p. 14
Marfione, Kathleen, Coordr, Circ, North Tonawanda Public Library, 505 Meadow Dr, North Tonawanda, NY, 14120. Tel: 716-693-4132. p. 1608
Margarida, Danielle, Youth Serv Coordr, State of Rhode Island, Department of Administration, One Capitol Hill, 2nd Flr, Providence, RI, 02908. Tel: 401-574-9309. p. 2041
Marger, Dena, Librn, Lydia Taft Pratt Library, 150 West St, West Dummerston, VT, 05357. Tel: 802-258-9878. p. 2298
Margheim, Jonathan, Outreach Librn, New Braunfels Public Library, 700 E Common St, New Braunfels, TX, 78130-5689. Tel: 830-221-4318. p. 2222
Margolin, Stephanie, Instrul Design Librn, Hunter College Libraries, East Bldg, 695 Park Ave, New York, NY, 10065. Tel: 212-772-4172. p. 1588
Margolis, Caroline, Head, Adult Serv, Head, Circ, Swampscott Public Library, 61 Burrill St, Swampscott, MA, 01907. Tel: 781-596-8867. p. 1059
Margolis, Deborah, Librn, Michigan State University Libraries, Area Studies, Main Library, 366 W Circle Dr, East Lansing, MI, 48824. Tel: 517-884-6392. p. 1102
Margulies, Max, Supvr, Ser, Thomas Jefferson University-East Falls, 4201 Henry Ave, Philadelphia, PA, 19144-5497. Tel: 215-951-5342. p. 1987
Mariacher, Sara, Br Mgr, Cooper-Siegel Community Library, Sharpsburg Community Library, 1212 Main St, Pittsburgh, PA, 15215. Tel: 412-781-0783. p. 1993
Marich, Shannon, Libr Mgr, Stoel Rives LLP, 760 SW Ninth Ave, Ste 3000, Portland, OR, 97205. Tel: 503-294-9576. p. 1894
Marier, Dominic, Dir, Bibliotheque Publique de La Malbaie, 395 rue Saint-Etienne, La Malbaie, QC, G5A 1S8, CANADA. Tel: 418-665-3747, Ext 5283. p. 2714
Marin, Luz, Libr Mgr, New York Public Library - Astor, Lenox & Tilden Foundations, Westchester Square Branch, 2521 Glebe Ave, Bronx, NY, 10461. Tel: 718-863-0436. p. 1598
Marin, Mara, Dir, Uniondale Public Library, 400 Uniondale Ave, Uniondale, NY, 11553. Tel: 516-489-2220. p. 1654
Marin, Michael, Dean, University of New Brunswick Libraries, Gerard V La Forest Law Library, Law School, 2nd Flr, 41 Dineen Dr, Fredericton, NB, E3B 5A3, CANADA. Tel: 506-453-4627. p. 2602

Marinaccio, Melanie, Law Libr Asst, Berks County Law Library, Courthouse, 10th Flr, 633 Court St, Reading, PA, 19601-4302. Tel: 610-478-3370. p. 2000
Marinaro, Mallory, Head, Patron Services, Ossining Public Library, 53 Croton Ave, Ossining, NY, 10562. Tel: 914-941-2416, p. 1613
Marine, Louisa, Dean, Libr & Learning Res, Macomb Community College Libraries, 14500 E 12 Mile Rd, J-Bldg, Warren, MI, 48088-3896. Tel: 586-447-8652. p. 1157
Marinello, Vita, Adult Serv Mgr, Upper Arlington Public Library, 2800 Tremont Rd, Columbus, OH, 43221. Tel: 614-486-9621. p. 1778
Mariner, Matthew, Digital Coll Mgr, Auraria Library, 1100 Lawrence St, Denver, CO, 80204-2095. Tel: 303-315-7776. p. 273
Mariner, Matthew, Supvr, University of Rochester, Carlson Science & Engineering Library, 160 Trustee Rd, Rochester, NY, 14627-0236. Tel: 585-275-4488. p. 1631
Mariner, Vincent, Dep Dir, Health Sciences Libraries Consortium, 3600 Market St, Ste 550, Philadelphia, PA, 19104-2646. Tel: 215-222-1532. p. 2774
Marines, Annette, Librn, University of California, 1156 High St, Santa Cruz, CA, 95064. Tel: 831-459-3255. p. 243
Maring, Marvel, Mgr, Metropolitan Community College Library, South Omaha Campus, 2808 Q St, Omaha, NE, 68107. Tel: 531-622-4506. p. 1329
Maring, Marvel, Mgr, Omaha Public Library, South Omaha Library, 2808 Q St, Omaha, NE, 68107-2828. Tel: 402-444-4850. p. 1330
Marini, Tom, Dir, University of Virginia, Darden Graduate School of Business-Camp Library, Darden Student Services Bldg, 1st & 2nd Flrs, 100 Darden Blvd, Charlottesville, VA, 22903. Tel: 434-924-7271. p. 2310
Marino, Carly, Spec Coll & Archives Librn, Humboldt State University Library, One Harpst St, Arcata, CA, 95521-8299. Tel: 707-826-4955. p. 117
Marino, Daniel, Researcher, Rye Historical Society, 265 Rye Beach Ave, Rye, NY, 10580. Tel: 914-967-7588. p. 1634
Marino, Gordon, Curator, Saint Olaf College, Howard V & Edna H Hong Kierkegaard Library, 1510 Saint Olaf Ave, Northfield, MN, 55057-1097. Tel: 507-646-3609. p. 1191
Marino, Jennifer, Head, Youth Serv, Rockville Centre Public Library, 221 N Village Ave, Rockville Centre, NY, 11570. Tel: 516-766-6257. p. 1632
Marino, Mark, Coll Develop Librn, Tech Serv Supvr, State College of Florida Manatee-Sarasota Libraries, 5840 26th St W, Bradenton, FL, 34207. Tel: 941-752-5317. p. 387
Marino, Nora, Asst Mgr, Saint Louis County Library, Cliff Cave Branch, 5430 Telegraph Rd, Saint Louis, MO, 63129. Tel: 314-994-3300, Ext 3050. p. 1273
Marino, Sarah, Librn, Yellowstone National Park, 20 Old Yellowstone Trail, Gardiner, MT, 59030. Tel: 307-344-2264. p. 1293
Marinos, Lisa, Asst Dir, Germantown Community Library, 1925 Exeter Rd, Germantown, TN, 38138. Tel: 901-757-7323. p. 2099
Marinus, Marilyn, Sr Libr Asst, Pemberton & District Public Library, 7390A Cottonwood St, Pemberton, BC, V0N 2L0, CANADA. Tel: 604-894-6916. p. 2573
Marion, Joy, Librn, United States Army, 18511 Highlander Medics St, Fort Bliss, TX, 79918. Tel: 915-569-3277, 915-742-8783. p. 2177
Marion, Laura, Dir & Librn, Missaukee District Library, 210 S Canal St, Lake City, MI, 49651. Tel: 231-839-2166. p. 1123
Mariscotti, David, Br Mgr, Free Library of Philadelphia, Thomas F Donatucci Sr Branch, 1935 Shunk St, Philadelphia, PA, 19145-4234. Tel: 215-685-1755. p. 1978
Marissa, Garza, Library Campus Asst, Del Mar College, Windward Campus, Barth Learning Resource Center, 4101 Old Brownsville Rd, Corpus Christi, TX, 78405. Tel: 361-698-1753. p. 2160
Marjorana, Ellen, Asst to the Dir, Manhasset Public Library, 30 Onderdonk Ave, Manhasset, NY, 11030. Tel: 516 627-2300, Ext 345. p. 1568
Mark, Amanda, Dir, Libr Serv, Lee Library Association, 100 Main St, Lee, MA, 01238-1688. Tel: 413-243-0385. p. 1027
Mark, Janice, Circ Supvr, South Kingstown Public Library, 1057 Kingstown Rd, Peace Dale, RI, 02879-2434. Tel: 401-783-4085, 401-789-1555. p. 2036
Markel, Fenix, Libr Dir, Parker Public Library, 1001 S Navajo Ave, Parker, AZ, 85344. Tel: 928-669-2622. p. 68
Markel-Joyet, Estelle, Asst Head, Cat, American Philosophical Society Library, 105 S Fifth St, Philadelphia, PA, 19106-3386. Tel: 215-440-3400. p. 1974
Markert, Jean, Dir, La Conner Regional Library, 520 Morris St, La Conner, WA, 98257. Tel: 360-466-3352. p. 2368
Markey, Alice, Dir, Meridian-Lauderdale County Public Library, 2517 7th St, Meridian, MS, 39301. Tel: 601-486-2261. p. 1226
Markey, Alice, Br Mgr, Lamar County Library System, Oak Grove Public, 4958 Old Hwy 11, Hattiesburg, MS, 39402. Tel: 601-296-1620. p. 1230
Markey, Tierney, Library Contact, Canadian International Trade Tribunal Library, 333 Laurier Ave W, 15th Flr, Ottawa, ON, K1A 0G7, CANADA. Tel: 613-990-2452. p. 2665
Markgraf, Jill, Dir, University of Wisconsin-Eau Claire, 103 Garfield Ave, Eau Claire, WI, 54701-4932. Tel: 715-836-4827. p. 2433
Markgren, Susanne, Dir, Tech Serv, Manhattan College, 4513 Manhattan College Pkwy, Riverdale, NY, 10471. Tel: 718-862-7743. p. 1627
Markham, Barbara, Fac Librn, Florida State College at Jacksonville, Deerwood Center Library, 9911 Old Baymeadows Rd, Jacksonville, FL, 32256. Tel: 904-997-2562. p. 411
Markham, Nicole, Coll Curator, International Tennis Hall of Fame & Museum Library, 194 Bellevue Ave, Newport, RI, 02840. Tel: 401-849-3990. p. 2034
Markham, Stephanie, Teen Serv Librn, Jervis Public Library Association, Inc, 613 N Washington St, Rome, NY, 13440-4296. Tel: 315-336-4570. p. 1632
Markham, Vicki, Circ, Oostburg Public Library, 213 N Eighth St, Oostburg, WI, 53070. Tel: 920-564-2934. p. 2467
Markin, Doug, Librn, United States Army, Fort Detrick Post Library, Fort Detrick, 1520 Freedman Dr, Frederick, MD, 21702. Tel: 301-619-7519. p. 967
Markinson, Andrea, Director of EPIC, State University of New York Downstate Health Sciences University, 395 Lenox Rd, Brooklyn, NY, 11203. Tel: 718-270-7400. p. 1506
Markland, Cara, Library Contact, The American Society for Nondestructive Testing Library & Archive, 1711 Arlingate Lane, Columbus, OH, 43228. Tel: 614-274-6003. p. 1771
Markland, Mary, Librn, Oregon State University, 2030 SE Marine Science Dr, Newport, OR, 97365. Tel: 541-867-0108. p. 1889
Markland, Penny, Br Librn, Wapiti Regional Library, Melfort Public Library, 106 Crawford Ave W, Melfort, SK, S0E 1A0, CANADA. Tel: 306-752-2022. p. 2745
Markle, Latricia, Youth Serv Librn, Tenafly Public Library, 100 Riveredge Rd, Tenafly, NJ, 07670-1962. Tel: 201-568-8680. p. 1445
Markley, Andi, Libr Mgr, Puget Sound Regional Council, 1011 Western Ave, Ste 500, Seattle, WA, 98104. Tel: 206-464-7532. p. 2378
Markley, Chris, Ms, Mgr, Kingsport Public Library & Archives, 400 Broad St, Kingsport, TN, 37660-4292. Tel: 423-229-9388. p. 2104
Markman, Rebecca, Librn, Fashion Institute of Design & Merchandising Library, 17590 Gillette Ave, Irvine, CA, 92614. Tel: 949-851-6200. p. 153
Markosyan, Kristine, Supvr, Glendale Library, Arts & Culture, Library Connection @ Adams Square, 1100 E Chevy Chase Dr, Glendale, CA, 91205. Tel: 818-548-3833. p. 149
Markosyan, Kristine, Supvr, Glendale Library, Arts & Culture, Pacific Park, 501 S Pacific Ave, Glendale, CA, 91204. Tel: 818-548-3760. p. 149
Markovich, Becky, Circ Serv Coordr, Albion College, 602 E Cass St, Albion, MI, 49224-1879. p. 1076
Markowski, Jeanne, IT Dir, Hazel Park Memorial District Library, 123 E Nine Mile Rd, Hazel Park, MI, 48030. Tel: 248-542-0940, 248-546-4095. p. 1114
Marks, Alexis Braun, Archivist, Eastern Michigan University, Administrative Office, Rm 200, 955 W Circle Dr, Ypsilanti, MI, 48197. Tel: 734-487-2594. p. 1160
Marks, David, Dean, Libr Serv, Bergen Community College, 400 Paramus Rd, Paramus, NJ, 07652-1595. Tel: 201-447-7970. p. 1432
Marks, Jeanette, Managing Librn, Bay County Library System, Sage Branch Library, 100 E Midland St, Bay City, MI, 48706. Tel: 989-892-8555. p. 1083
Marks, Jennifer, Librn, Cockrell Hill Public Library, 4125 W Clarendon, Dallas, TX, 75211. Tel: 214-330-9935. p. 2163
Marks, Lisa, Dir, Mayo Clinic Scottsdale Libraries, 13400 E Shea Blvd, Scottsdale, AZ, 85259. Tel: 480-301-8443. p. 77
Marks, Megan, Assoc Libr Dir, Margaret R Grundy Memorial Library, 680 Radcliffe St, Bristol, PA, 19007-5199. Tel: 215-788-7891. p. 1915
Marks, Sara, Ref Librn, University of Massachusetts Lowell Library, 61 Wilder St, Lowell, MA, 01854-3098. Tel: 978-934-4581. p. 1030
Marksbury, Nancy, Digital Initiatives & Syst Librn, Stetson University, 421 N Woodland Blvd, Unit 8418, DeLand, FL, 32723. Tel: 386-822-7928. p. 393
Marksbury, Nancy, Dr, Digital Literacy & Services Librn, Keuka College, 141 Central Ave, Keuka Park, NY, 14478. Tel: 315-279-5269. p. 1559
Markum, Emily, Librn, US Courts Library - Tenth Circuit Court of Appeals, 2305 US Courthouse, 200 NW Fourth St, Oklahoma City, OK, 73102. Tel: 405-609-5463. p. 1859
Markus, Amy, Dir, Hancock Town Library, 25 Main St, Hancock, NH, 03449. Tel: 603-525-4411. p. 1366
Markus, Jennifer, Librn, Laramie County Community College, 1400 E College Dr, Cheyenne, WY, 82007-3204. Tel: 307-778-1204. p. 2492
Markvicka, Linda, Librn, North Loup Township Library, 112 South B St, North Loup, NE, 68859. Tel: 308-496-4230. p. 1326
Markwalter, Mary, Dir, Mason City Public Library, 225 Second St SE, Mason City, IA, 50401. Tel: 641-421-3668. p. 768
Marlane, Laura, Exec Dir, Omaha Public Library, 215 S 15th St, Omaha, NE, 68102-1629. Tel: 402-444-4800. p. 1329
Marlar-Gearhart, Kristin, Exec Dir, Bellevue Public Library, 117 E Pine St, Bellevue, ID, 83313. Tel: 208-788-4503. p. 515
Marlatt, Greta, Outreach & Coll Develop Mgr, Naval Postgraduate School, 411 Dyer Rd, Monterey, CA, 93943. Tel: 831-656-3500. p. 179
Marlatt, Laurel, Dir, Fullerton Public Library, 903 Broadway, Fullerton, NE, 68638. Tel: 308-536-2382. p. 1315
Marlatt, Tom, Tech Serv & Automation, Carnegie Public Library, 219 E Fourth St, East Liverpool, OH, 43920-3143. Tel: 330-385-2048, Ext 108. p. 1783

Marler, Janet, Dir, Marion City Library, 101 Library St, Marion, KS, 66861. Tel: 620-382-2442. p. 824

Marlin, Mike, Dir, California State Library, Braille & Talking Book Library, 900 N St, Sacramento, CA, 95814. Tel: 916-654-0640. p. 208

Marlin, Natalie, Machine & Outreach Servs, Reader Serv, Arkansas State Library for the Blind & Print Disabled, 900 W Capitol Ave, Ste 100, Little Rock, AR, 72201-3108. Tel: 501-682-2858. p. 100

Marlin, Velvet, Circ Supvr, ILL, Pierce College Library, Fort Steilacoom Campus/Cascade Bldg 4, 9401 Farwest Dr SW, Lakewood, WA, 98498. Tel: 253-964-6547. p. 2368

Marlow, Bobbi, Youth Serv Librn, Ruthven Public Library, 1301 Gowrie St, Ruthven, IA, 51358. Tel: 712-837-4820. p. 780

Marlow, Cecilia Ann, Libr Dir, Cromaine District Library, 3688 N Hartland Rd, Hartland, MI, 48353. Tel: 810-632-5200, Ext 105. p. 1114

Marlow, Meme, Dir, Worch Memorial Public Library, 790 S Center St, Versailles, OH, 45380. Tel: 937-526-3416. p. 1827

Marlowe, Claudia, Tech Serv Librn, San Francisco Art Institute, 800 Chestnut St, San Francisco, CA, 94133. Tel: 415-749-4562. p. 226

Marmor, Dawn, Br Serv Adminr & Initiatives, Onondaga County Public Libraries, The Galleries of Syracuse, 447 S Salina St, Syracuse, NY, 13202-2494. Tel: 315-435-1900. p. 1649

Marnell, Tamara, Discovery Serv Librn, ILS LIbrn, Central Oregon Community College Barber Library, 2600 NW College Way, Bend, OR, 97703. Tel: 541-383-7560. p. 1873

Marnell, Tamara, Program Mgr, Systems, Orbis Cascade Alliance, PO Box 6007, Portland, OR, 97228. Tel: 541-246-2470. p. 2773

Marney, Katie, Dr, Libr Dir, Culver-Stockton College, One College Hill, Canton, MO, 63435. Tel: 573-288-6478. p. 1240

Marolt, Melissa, Dir, Perry County District Library, 117 S Jackson St, New Lexington, OH, 43764-1382. Tel: 740-342-4194. p. 1806

Marple, Anita, Br Mgr, Libr Dir, Fremont County Library System, 451 N Second St, Lander, WY, 82520. Tel: 307-332-5194. p. 2496

Marquardt, Cheryl, Library Contact, Waseca-Le Sueur Regional Library, Waldorf Branch, 109 Main St N, Waldorf, MN, 56091. Tel: 507-239-2248. p. 1207

Marquardt, Ingrid, Librn, The Library of the French Cultural Center Alliance Francaise of Boston, 53 Marlborough St, Boston, MA, 02116-2099. Tel: 617-912-0400, Ext 419. p. 996

Marquardt, Jennifer, Head, Youth Serv, Acorn Public Library District, 15624 S Central Ave, Oak Forest, IL, 60452-3204. Tel: 708-687-3700. p. 627

Marques, Silas, Info Literacy, Off-Campus Librn, Andrews University, 4190 Administration Dr, Berrien Springs, MI, 49104-1400. Tel: 269-471-6263. p. 1085

Marquet, Cynthia, Librn, The Historical Society of the Cocalico Valley Library, 237 W Main St, Ephrata, PA, 17522. Tel: 717-733-1616. p. 1931

Marquez, Dianne, Actg Libr Dir, Dean, New Mexico Junior College, One Thunderbird Circle, Hobbs, NM, 88240. Tel: 575-492-2841. p. 1469

Marquez, Marina, Actg Br Mgr, Cleveland Public Library, East 131st Street, 3830 E 131st St, Cleveland, OH, 44120. Tel: 216-623-6941. p. 1768

Marquez, Onnica F, Archivist, Saint Ambrose University Library, 518 W Locust St, Davenport, IA, 52803. Tel: 563-333-5868. p. 744

Marquez, Peggy, Br Mgr, Bienville Parish Library, Saline Branch, 1434 Fourth St, Saline, LA, 71070. Tel: 318-576-8990. p. 881

Marquis, Colleen, Archivist, University of Michigan-Flint, 303 E Kearsley St, Flint, MI, 48502. Tel: 810-762-3402. p. 1107

Marquis, Nickie, Libr Dir, Skaneateles Library Association, 49 E Genesee St, Skaneateles, NY, 13152. Tel: 315-685-5135. p. 1641

Marr, Jenny, Libr Dir, Ferndale Area District Library, 222 E Nine Mile Rd, Ferndale, MI, 48220. Tel: 248-547-6000. p. 1105

Marr, Nathan, Librn, Ogden Murphy Wallace Attorneys, 901 Fifth Ave, Ste 3500, Seattle, WA, 98164. Tel: 206-447-7000. p. 2377

Marra, Christina, Ms, Dir, Oceanside Library, 30 Davison Ave, Oceanside, NY, 11572-2299. Tel: 516-766-2360, Ext 308. p. 1609

Marra, Kelly, Youth Serv Librn, MacDonald Public Library, 36480 Main St, New Baltimore, MI, 48047-2509. Tel: 586-725-0273. p. 1137

Marra, Rose, Dir, University of Missouri-Columbia, 303 Townsend Hall, Columbia, MO, 65211. Tel: 573-882-4546. p. 2787

Marrapodi, Elisabeth, Libr Dir, Trinitas Regional Medical Center, 225 Williamson St, Elizabeth, NJ, 07207. Tel: 908-994-5488. p. 1401

Marredeth, Gail, Librn, Cleveland State University, Michael Schwartz Library, Rhodes Tower, Ste 501, 2121 Euclid Ave, Cleveland, OH, 44115-2214. Tel: 216-687-2291. p. 1769

Marrero, Yirah, Spanish Serv Spec, Jefferson County Library District, 241 SE Seventh St, Madras, OR, 97741. Tel: 541-475-3351. p. 1885

Marrin, Sara, Tech Serv Librn, Virginia Union University, 1500 N Lombardy St, Richmond, VA, 23220. Tel: 804-257-5823. p. 2344

Marris, Mike, Dir, C W Clark Memorial Library, 160 N Main St, Oriskany Falls, NY, 13425. Tel: 315-821-7850. p. 1612

Marrocolla, Anthony, Mgr, Ad Serv, Programming, New Canaan Library, 151 Main St, New Canaan, CT, 06840. Tel: 203-594-5010. p. 324

Marrocolla, Elisabeth, Dep Dir, Darien Library, 1441 Post Rd, Darien, CT, 06820-5419. Tel: 203-669-5263. p. 308

Marroquin, Israel, Sr Librn, Oceanside Public Library, John Landes Community Center, 2855 Cedar Rd, Oceanside, CA, 92056. Tel: 760-435-5587. p. 187

Marroquin, Israel, Sr Librn, Oceanside Public Library, Mission Branch, 3861 B Mission Ave, Oceanside, CA, 92058. Tel: 760-435-5587. p. 187

Marroquin, Marco, Dir, Live Oak County Library, 402 N Houston St, George West, TX, 78022. Tel: 361-449-1124. p. 2184

Marroquin, Marco, Dir, Live Oak County Library, Three Rivers, 102 Leroy St, Three Rivers, TX, 78071. Tel: 361-786-3037. p. 2184

Marrotta, Jenna, Children's Mgr, Charlotte Mecklenburg Library, ImaginOn: The Joe & Joan Martin Center, 300 E Seventh St, Charlotte, NC, 28202. Tel: 704-416-4600. p. 1679

Marrow, Larry, Exec Dir, Beth El Ner Tamid Library, 715 Paxon Hollow Rd, Broomall, PA, 19008-9998. Tel: 610-356-8700. p. 1915

Marrs, Margaret, Dir, Rockwood Public Library, 117 N Front St, Rockwood, TN, 37854-2320. Tel: 865-354-1281. p. 2125

Marrs-Smith, Dianne, Br Mgr, Whatcom County Library System, Lynden Branch, 216 Fourth St, Lynden, WA, 98264. Tel: 360-354-4883. p. 2359

Marsala, Penny, Dir, Park Nicollet Methodist Hospital, 6600 Excelsior Blvd, Ste 101, Saint Louis Park, MN, 55426. Tel: 952-993-5451. p. 1199

Marsala, Rita, Head, Pub Serv, Western Michigan University-Cooley Law School Libraries, 300 S Capitol Ave, Lansing, MI, 48933. Tel: 517-371-5140, Ext 3301. p. 1126

Marschall, Katherine, Systems & Metadata Librn, Saint Mary's College, Notre Dame, IN, 46556-5001. Tel: 574-284-4438. p. 711

Marsden, Brandy, Ad, Warren Township Public Library, 210 Burnett Ave, Warren, IL, 61087. Tel: 815-745-2076. p. 658

Marsee, Patsy, Asst Dir, Marion County Public Library System, 2720 E Silver Springs Blvd, Ocala, FL, 34470. Tel: 352-671-8551. p. 430

Marsh, Audrey, Br Mgr, Lakeland Library Region, Meadow Lake Branch, 320 Centre St, Meadow Lake, SK, S9X 1V8, CANADA. Tel: 306-236-5396. p. 2744

Marsh, Becky, Dir, Tech Serv, Holmes County Public Library, 303 N J Harvey Etheridge St, Bonifay, FL, 32425. Tel: 850-547-3573. p. 385

Marsh, Beth, Br Mgr, Pittsylvania County Public Library, Mt Hermon Branch Library, 4058 Franklin Tpk, Danville, VA, 24540. Tel: 434-835-0326. p. 2311

Marsh, Brenda, Dir, Lilly-Washington Public Library, 101 Memorial Dr, Ste 2, Lilly, PA, 15938-1118. Tel: 814-886-7543. p. 1956

Marsh, Carrie, Dir, Central Michigan University, Clarke Historical Library, 250 E Preston, Mount Pleasant, MI, 48859. Tel: 989-774-3965. p. 1135

Marsh, Christopher, Librn, Bibliotheque Baie-D'Urfe, 20551 chemin du Bord du Lac, Baie-D'Urfe, QC, H9X 1R3, CANADA. Tel: 514-457-3274. p. 2709

Marsh, Darlene, Tech Serv Librn, Summit County Library, 1885 W Ute Blvd, Park City, UT, 84098. Tel: 435-615-3901. p. 2268

Marsh, Denyse, Ch, Toledo Public Library, 173 NW Seventh St, Toledo, OR, 97391. Tel: 541-336-3132. p. 1900

Marsh, Erin, Archivist, New Orleans Baptist Theological Seminary, 4110 Seminary Pl, New Orleans, LA, 70126. Tel: 504-816-8020. p. 902

Marsh, Erin, Asst Dir, Youth Serv, Charles A Ransom District Library, 180 S Sherwood Ave, Plainwell, MI, 49080-1896. Tel: 269-685-8024. p. 1141

Marsh, Katherine, Development Asst, Bagaduce Music Lending Library, 49 South St, Blue Hill, ME, 04614. Tel: 207-374-5454. p. 918

Marsh, Kevin, Dir, Copperas Cove Public Library, 501 S Main St, Copperas Cove, TX, 76522. Tel: 254-547-3826. p. 2160

Marsh, Kitty, Librn, Davis Jefferson Parish Library, Elton Branch, 813 Main St, Elton, LA, 70532. Tel: 318-584-2640. p. 892

Marsh, Lucas, Interim Dir, Marshall Memorial Library, 110 S Diamond St, Deming, NM, 88030. Tel: 575-546-9202. p. 1467

Marsh, Maura, Dir, Coon Rapids Public Library, 123 Third Ave, Coon Rapids, IA, 50058-1601. Tel: 712-999-5410. p. 742

Marsh, Nicole Y, Head Librn, Lincoln University Library, 401 15th St, Oakland, CA, 94612. Tel: 510-379-4048. p. 185

Marsh, Patty, Dir, Bellevue Public Library, 224 E Main St, Bellevue, OH, 44811-1467. Tel: 419-483-8526. p. 1750

Marsh, Thomas, Dir, Johnson County Law Library, Courthouse, Rm 101, 150 W Santa Fe St, Olathe, KS, 66061. Tel: 913-715-4154. p. 828

Marshak, Suzanna, Sr Librn, California Department of Corrections Library System, California Medical Facility, 1600 California Dr, Vacaville, CA, 95696. Tel: 707-448-6841. p. 206

Marshall, Andrew, Head Librn, Pennsylvania State University, Greater Allegheny, 4000 University Dr, McKeesport, PA, 15132-7698. Tel: 412-675-9119. p. 1959

Marshall, Brenda, Asst Dir, Pine River Public Library District, 395 Bayfield Center Dr, Bayfield, CO, 81122. Tel: 970-884-2222. p. 266

Marshall, Bridget, Mgr, Howard Public Library, 3607 County Rte 70A, Hornell, NY, 14843. Tel: 607-566-2412. p. 1548

Marshall, Charmetria, Mgr, County of Los Angeles Public Library, Chet Holifield Library, 1060 S Greenwood Ave, Montebello, CA, 90640-6030. Tel: 323-728-0421. p. 136

Marshall, Christina, Br Mgr, Somerset County Library System, Ewell Branch, 4005 Smith Island Rd, Ewell, MD, 21824. Tel: 410-425-5141. p. 973

Marshall, Courtney, Cat, Eastern New Mexico University - Portales, 1500 S Ave K, Portales, NM, 88130-7402. Tel: 575-562-2622. p. 1473

Marshall, Courtney, Access Serv Spec, Virginia Peninsula Community College Library, 227C Kecoughtan Hall, 99 Thomas Nelson Dr, Hampton, VA, 23666. Tel: 757-825-4064. p. 2323

Marshall, Darlene, Libr Dir, Libr Syst Adminr, Mengle Memorial Library, 324 Main St, Brockway, PA, 15824-0324. Tel: 814-265-8245. p. 1915

Marshall, Derek, Coordr, Mississippi State University, Veterinary Medicine, 240 Wise Center Dr, Mississippi State, MS, 39762. Tel: 662-325-1114. p. 1227

Marshall, Elizabeth, Dir, Western University Libraries, C B Johnston Library, Richard Ivey Bldg, Rm 1250, 1255 Western Rd, London, ON, N6G 0N1, CANADA. Tel: 519-661-2111, Ext 84842. p. 2655

Marshall, Frances, Archives & Spec Coll Librn, Shepherd University, 301 N King St, Shepherdstown, WV, 25443. Tel: 304-876-5417. p. 2414

Marshall, Heidi, Head, Archives & Spec Coll, Columbia College Chicago Library, 624 S Michigan Ave, Chicago, IL, 60605-1996. Tel: 312-369-8689. p. 559

Marshall, James, Ref & Instruction, Ocean County College Library, College Dr, Toms River, NJ, 08754. Tel: 732-255-0400, Ext 2248. p. 1446

Marshall, Jean, Instruction Librn, Washburn University, 1700 SW College Ave, Topeka, KS, 66621. Tel: 785-670-1276. p. 839

Marshall, Jeffrey, Dir, Spec Coll, University of Vermont Libraries, 538 Main St, Burlington, VT, 05405-0036. Tel: 802-656-2596. p. 2281

Marshall, Jennifer, Colls Mgr, Pioneer Library System, 300 Norman Ctr Ct, Norman, OK, 73072. Tel: 405-801-4500. p. 1855

Marshall, Jessie W, Nonprofit Res Librn, Supvr, Pub Serv, Memphis Public Library, Business/Sciences, 3030 Poplar Ave, Memphis, TN, 38111. Tel: 901-415-2734. p. 2113

Marshall, Karen, Libr Asst, Nova Scotia Community College, Akerley Campus Library, 21 Woodlawn Rd, Dartmouth, NS, B2W 2R7, CANADA. Tel: 902-491-4968. p. 2619

Marshall, Kate, Asst Dir, Hamilton North Public Library, 209 W Brinton St, Cicero, IN, 46034. Tel: 317-984-5623. p. 675

Marshall, Kate, Br Mgr, Hamilton North Public Library, Atlanta Branch, 100 S Walnut St, Atlanta, IN, 46031. Tel: 317-984-5623. p. 675

Marshall, Keith A, PhD, Exec Dir, Big Ten Academic Alliance, 1819 S Neil St, Ste D, Champaign, IL, 61820-7271. Tel: 217-244-5756. p. 2764

Marshall, Kyle, Mgr, Edmonton Public Library, Calder, 12710 131 Ave NW, Edmonton, AB, T5L 2Z6, CANADA. Tel: 780-496-6285. p. 2536

Marshall, Laurie, Pres, The Heritage Museum & Cultural Center, 601 Main St, Saint Joseph, MI, 49085. Tel: 269-983-1191. p. 1148

Marshall, Lily, Libr Dir, Pittsburg-Camp County Public Library, 613 Quitman St, Pittsburg, TX, 75686-1035. Tel: 903-856-3302. p. 2226

Marshall, Linda, Exec Dir, Nichols House Museum, 55 Mount Vernon St, Boston, MA, 02108. Tel: 617-227-6993. p. 998

Marshall, Lisa, Librn III, College of the North Atlantic Library Services, Bay St George, Library Learning Commons, DSB Fowlow Bldg, 432 Massachusetts Dr, Stephenville, NL, A2N 2Z6, CANADA. Tel: 709-643-7752. p. 2609

Marshall, Nancy, Librn, Massachusetts General Hospital, Warren Library, 55 Fruit St, Boston, MA, 02114-2622. Tel: 617-726-2253. p. 997

Marshall, Nancy, Info Serv, South Dakota State University, 1300 N Campus Dr, Box 2115, Brookings, SD, 57007. Tel: 605-688-5093. p. 2074

Marshall, Natalie, Acq Librn, Exec Dir, Flint River Regional Library System, 800 Memorial Dr, Griffin, GA, 30223. Tel: 770-412-4770. p. 481

Marshall, Nekesha, Children's & Teen Serv, Manager, Family Services, Long Branch Free Public Library, 328 Broadway, Long Branch, NJ, 07740. Tel: 732-222-3900. p. 1413

Marshall, Patrick, Dir, Wareham Free Library, 59 Marion Rd, Wareham, MA, 02571. Tel: 508-295-2343, Ext 1010. p. 1062

Marshall, Robbie, Asst Dir, Brainerd Memorial Library, 920 Saybrook Rd, Haddam, CT, 06438. Tel: 860-345-2204. p. 315

Marshall, Robert, Assoc Dir, University of Alabama, School of Law Library, 101 Paul Bryant Dr, Tuscaloosa, AL, 35487. Tel: 205-348-5925. p. 38

Marshall, Sarah, Libr Dir, Kent Library Association, 32 N Main St, Kent, CT, 06757. Tel: 860-927-3761. p. 319

Marshall, Sarah, Mgr, Mat Serv, Midlothian Public Library, 14701 S Kenton Ave, Midlothian, IL, 60445-4122. Tel: 708-535-2027. p. 617

Marshall, Sibyl, Head of Research & Instruction Services, University of Tennessee, Taylor Law Ctr, 1505 W Cumberland Ave, Knoxville, TN, 37996-1800. Tel: 865-974-7419. p. 2107

Marshall, Sue, Ch, Rumford Public Library, 56 Rumford Ave, Rumford, ME, 04276-1919. Tel: 207-364-3661. p. 939

Marsilla, Grace, Coll Develop, Amityville Public Library, 19 John St, Amityville, NY, 11701. Tel: 631-264-0567. p. 1486

Marsola, Randy, Principal Tech Librn, South Brunswick Public Library, 110 Kingston Lane, Monmouth Junction, NJ, 08852. Tel: 732-329-4000, Ext 7636. p. 1419

Marson, Barbara M, Dr, Asst Prof, Prog Coordr, East Carolina University, 104B Ragsdale Hall, Greenville, NC, 27858. Tel: 252-328-2345. p. 2790

Marsteller, Matthew, Assoc Dean for Faculty, Principal Librn, Carnegie Mellon University, Sorrells Engineering & Science Library, 4400 Wean Hall, Pittsburgh, PA, 15213. Tel: 412-268-7217. p. 1992

Marsters, Roger, Dr, Curator, Maritime Museum of the Atlantic, 1675 Lower Water St, Halifax, NS, B3J 1S3, CANADA. Tel: 902-424-6442. p. 2619

Marston, Julie, Head, Adult Serv, Pelham Public Library, 24 Village Green, Pelham, NH, 03076. Tel: 603-635-7581. p. 1377

Marston, Lisa, Br Coordr, Leeds & the Thousand Islands Public Library, Lyndhurst Branch, 426 Lyndhurst Rd, Lyndhurst, ON, K0E 1N0, CANADA. Tel: 613-928-2277. p. 2652

Marszalek, Chris, Dep Dir, Memphis Public Library & Information Center, 3030 Poplar Ave, Memphis, TN, 38111. Tel: 901-415-2700. p. 2112

Mart, Susan Nevelow, Dir, University of Colorado Boulder, William A Wise Law Library, Wolf Law Bldg, 2nd Flr, 2450 Kittredge Loop Dr, Boulder, CO, 80309-0402. Tel: 303-492-1233. p. 268

Martalla, Alaynna, ILL Asst, Trinity University, One Trinity Pl, San Antonio, TX, 78212-7200. Tel: 210-999-8126. p. 2239

Martel, Diane, Br Tech, Monroe County Library System, Robert A Vivian Branch, 2664 Vivian Rd, Monroe, MI, 48162-9212. Tel: 734-241-1430. p. 1134

Martel, Eleanor, Head, Ref & Info Serv, Flint Memorial Library, 147 Park St, North Reading, MA, 01864. Tel: 978-664-4942. p. 1042

Martel, Marie D, Asst Prof, Universite de Montreal, 3150, rue Jean-Brillant, bur C-2004, Montreal, QC, H3T 1N8, CANADA. Tel: 514-343-6044. p. 2797

Martel, Robert, Instruction Librn, Atlantic School of Theology Library, 624 Francklyn St, Halifax, NS, B3H 3B4, CANADA. Tel: 902-420-1669. p. 2618

Martel, Susan, Circ Librn, Pellissippi State Community College, Hardin Valley Library, 10915 Harding Valley Rd, Knoxville, TN, 37933. Tel: 865-539-7047. p. 2106

Martel, Sylvain, Coordr, Cegep Trois-Rivieres, 3500 rue De Courval, Trois-Rivieres, QC, G9A 5E6, CANADA. Tel: 819-376-1721, Ext 2824. p. 2796

Martell, Suzanne, Staff Librn, Brooks Free Library, 739 Main St, Harwich, MA, 02645. Tel: 508-430-7562. p. 1023

Marten, Carrie, Electronic Res Librn, State University of New York, 735 Anderson Hill Rd, Purchase, NY, 10577-1400. Tel: 914-251-6400. p. 1625

Martens, Judy, Br Mgr, Garfield County Public Library District, Rifle Branch, 207 East Ave, Rifle, CO, 81650. Tel: 970-625-3471. p. 294

Martens, Kathryn I, Dir, Crystal Lake Public Library, 126 Paddock St, Crystal Lake, IL, 60014. Tel: 815-459-1687. p. 574

Martens, Marianne, Dr, Assoc Prof, Kent State University, 314 University Library, 1125 Risman Dr, Kent, OH, 44242-0001. Tel: 330-672-2782. p. 2790

Martens, Selena, Chief Exec Officer, Parry Sound Public Library, 29 Mary St, Parry Sound, ON, P2A 1E3, CANADA. Tel: 705-746-9601. p. 2671

Martic, Mirjana, Librn, Loto-Quebec, 500 Sherbrooke W, Montreal, QC, H3A 3G6, CANADA. Tel: 514-282-8000. p. 2725

Martilla, Deb, Librn, Alamo Colleges District, 1201 Kitty Hawk Rd, Universal City, TX, 78148. Tel: 210-486-5388. p. 2250

Martin, Aileen, Cat Serv Librn, Patrick Henry Community College, 645 Patriot Ave, Martinsville, VA, 24115. Tel: 276-656-0439. p. 2332

Martin, Alicia, Br Mgr, Phoenix Public Library, Juniper Library, 1825 W Union Hills Dr, Phoenix, AZ, 85027. p. 72

Martin, Andrew, Chief Librn, National Labor Relations Board Library, 1015 Half St SE, Ste 6038, Washington, DC, 20570-0001. Tel: 202-273-3720. p. 372

Martin, Anisa, Coll Develop, Southwestern Assemblies of God University, 1200 Sycamore St, Waxahachie, TX, 75165-2342. Tel: 972-825-4761. p. 2255

Martin, Anita, Libr Assoc, Atlanta-Fulton Public Library System, Auburn Avenue Research Library on African-American Culture & History, 101 Auburn Ave NE, Atlanta, GA, 30303-2503. Tel: 404-613-4001. p. 460

Martin, Annette, Dir & Librn, Tripoli Public Library, 101 Fourth Ave SW, Tripoli, IA, 50676. Tel: 319-882-4807. p. 787

Martin, Anthony, Libr Mgr, Vancouver Island Regional Library, Gabriola Island Branch, Folklife Village, 5-575 North Rd, Gabriola Island, BC, V0R 1X3, CANADA. Tel: 250-247-7878. p. 2570

Martin, Anthony, Libr Mgr, Vancouver Island Regional Library, Nanaimo Harbourfront Branch, 90 Commercial St, Nanaimo, BC, V9R 5G4, CANADA. Tel: 250-753-1154. p. 2571

Martin, Ashley, Youth Serv Librn, Havre Hill County Library, 402 Third St, Havre, MT, 59501. Tel: 406-265-2123. p. 1295

Martin, Barbara, Librn, Tanana Community-School Library, 89 Front St, Tanana, AK, 99777. Tel: 907-366-7211. p. 51

Martin, Basil, Dr, Research Servs Librn, Pennsylvania Western University - Clarion, 840 Wood St, Clarion, PA, 16214. Tel: 814-393-2303. p. 1922

Martin, Betty, Dep Dir, Octavia Fellin Public Library, 115 W Hill Ave, Gallup, NM, 87301. Tel: 505-863-1291, Ext 14017. p. 1468

Martin, Bob, Acq Librn, Molloy College, 1000 Hempstead Ave, Rockville Centre, NY, 11571. Tel: 516-323-3922. p. 1632

Martin, Brandon, Syst Librn, Northeastern State University, Broken Arrow Campus Library, 3100 E New Orleans St, Broken Arrow, OK, 74014. Tel: 918-449-6459. p. 1863

Martin, Brenan, Ch, Ozark Dale County Library, Inc, 416 James St, Ozark, AL, 36360. Tel: 334-774-2399, 334-774-5480. p. 32

Martin, Brian, Libr Mgr, Central Arkansas Library System, Dee Brown Library, 6325 Baseline Rd, Little Rock, AR, 72209-4810. Tel: 501-568-7494. p. 101
Martin, Chase, Br Mgr, Indianapolis Public Library, College Avenue, 4180 N College Ave, Indianapolis, IN, 46205. Tel: 317-275-4325. p. 694
Martin, Cheryl, Librn, United States Army Corps of Engineers, 109 Saint Joseph St, Mobile, AL, 36602. Tel: 251-690-3182. p. 26
Martin, Cheryl, Br Mgr, Margaret Welch Memorial Library, 5051 State Hwy 84, Longville, MN, 56655. Tel: 218-363-2710. p. 1180
Martin, Chris, Head, Access Serv, Loyola University Chicago Libraries, Elizabeth M Cudahy Memorial Library, 1032 W Sheridan Rd, Chicago, IL, 60660. Tel: 773-508-2636. p. 563
Martin, Christina, Libr Mgr, Mauney Memorial Library, 100 S Piedmont Ave, Kings Mountain, NC, 28086. Tel: 704-739-2371. p. 1699
Martin, Christy, Circ, Greene County Public Library, 120 N 12th St, Paragould, AR, 72450. Tel: 870-236-8711. p. 107
Martin, Colleen, Research Librn, Office of the Auditor General of Canada, West Tower, 240 Sparks St, 11th Flr, Ottawa, ON, K1A 0G6, CANADA. Tel: 613-952-0213. p. 2668
Martin, Crystle, Dr, Dean of Libr, El Camino College, 16007 S Crenshaw Blvd, Torrance, CA, 90506. Tel: 310-660-3525. p. 252
Martin, Cynthia, Chief Exec Officer, Head Librn, Champlain Library, 94 Main St E, VanKleek Hill, ON, K0B 1R0, CANADA. Tel: 613-678-2216. p. 2701
Martin, Dawna, Br Mgr, Carbon County Library System, Encampment Branch, 202 Rankin St, Encampment, WY, 82325. Tel: 307-327-5775. p. 2498
Martin, Deanna, Libr Tech, Seward County Community College Library, 1801 N Kansas, Liberal, KS, 67901. Tel: 620-417-1165. p. 821
Martin, Debbie, Tech Serv, New Braunfels Public Library, 700 E Common St, New Braunfels, TX, 78130-5689. Tel: 830-221-4313. p. 2222
Martin, Deborah, Info Res & Serv Support Spec, Penn State University York, 1031 Edgecomb Ave, York, PA, 17403. Tel: 717-777-4198. p. 2026
Martin, Debra, Supvr, Tech Serv, Northland Public Library, 300 Cumberland Rd, Pittsburgh, PA, 15237-5455. Tel: 412-366-8100, Ext 166. p. 1994
Martin, Diane, Head Librn, Metropolitan Community College, Longview Campus Library, 500 SW Longview Rd, Lee's Summit, MO, 64081-2105. Tel: 816-604-2080. p. 1256
Martin, Donald, Digital Res Librn, Southern Adventist University, 4851 Industrial Dr, Collegedale, TN, 37315. Tel: 423-236-2788. p. 2094
Martin, Elaine, Chief Admin Officer, Dir, Harvard Library, Francis A Countway Library of Medicine, Ten Shattuck St, Boston, MA, 02115. Tel: 617-432-2136. p. 1005
Martin, Elise, Librn, Cegep Riviere du-Loup-Bibliotheque, 80 rue Frontenac, Riviere-du-Loup, QC, G5R 1R1, CANADA. Tel: 418-862-6903, Ext 2579. p. 2732
Martin, Emily, Asst Librn, New Gloucester Public Library, 379 Intervale Rd, New Gloucester, ME, 04260. Tel: 207-926-4840. p. 932
Martin, Emma, Librn, Millstadt Library District, 115 W Laurel St, Millstadt, IL, 62260. Tel: 618-476-1887. p. 618
Martin, Erika, Dir, Libr Serv, Western Manitoba Regional Library, 710 Rosser Ave, Unit 1, Brandon, MB, R7A 0K9, CANADA. Tel: 204-727-6648. p. 2586
Martin, Greg, Ad, Wilsonville Public Library, 8200 SW Wilsonville Rd, Wilsonville, OR, 97070. Tel: 503-570-1595. p. 1902
Martin, Gregory, Digital Commons Dir, Cedarville University, 251 N Main St, Cedarville, OH, 45314-0601. Tel: 937-766-7840. p. 1757
Martin, Heather, Ref Librn, University of Alabama at Birmingham, Mervyn H Sterne Library, 917 13th St S, Birmingham, AL, 35205. Tel: 205-934-6364. p. 9
Martin, Heather, Dir, Libr Serv, Providence Willamette Falls Medical Center, 1500 Division St, Oregon City, OR, 97045. Tel: 503-650-6757. p. 1890
Martin, Heather, Dir, Providence Saint Vincent Hospital & Medical Center, 9205 SW Barnes Rd, Portland, OR, 97225. Tel: 503-216-2257. p. 1894
Martin, Heidi, Youth Serv Librn, Tipp City Public Library, 11 E Main St, Tipp City, OH, 45371. Tel: 937-667-3826. p. 1823
Martin, Jack, Exec Dir, Providence Public Library, 150 Empire St, Providence, RI, 02903-3283. Tel: 401-455-8000. p. 2039
Martin, Jane, Libr Dir, Winter Haven Public Library, 325 Ave A NW, Winter Haven, FL, 33881. Tel: 863-291-5880. p. 455
Martin, Janelle, Head, Fiction Serv, Lapeer District Library, 201 Village West Dr S, Lapeer, MI, 48446-1699. Tel: 810-664-9521. p. 1126
Martin, Janelle, Head, Fiction Serv, Lapeer District Library, Marguerite deAngeli Branch, 921 W Nepessing St, Lapeer, MI, 48446. Tel: 810-664-6971. p. 1126
Martin, Jef, Mgr, San Antonio Public Library, Maverick, 8700 Mystic Park, San Antonio, TX, 78254. Tel: 210-207-9060. p. 2239
Martin, Jeffrey, Libr Mgr, Lee-Itawamba Library System, Pratt Memorial Library, 210 W Cedar St, Fulton, MS, 38843. Tel: 662-862-4926. p. 1234
Martin, Jennifer, Librn, University of Arizona Libraries, Health Sciences Library, 1501 N Campbell Ave, Tucson, AZ, 85724. Tel: 520-626-3381. p. 83
Martin, Jennifer, Head, Adult Serv, Chicago Heights Public Library, 25 W 15th St, Chicago Heights, IL, 60411-3488. Tel: 708-754-0323. p. 571
Martin, Jennifer, Head, Cat, Salisbury University, 1101 Camden Ave, Salisbury, MD, 21801-6863. Tel: 410-543-6130. p. 976
Martin, Jenny, Libr Assoc, Law Library of Louisiana, Louisiana Supreme Court, 2nd Flr, 400 Royal St, New Orleans, LA, 70130-2104. Tel: 504-310-2401. p. 901
Martin, Jessica, Libr Asst, Mendon Library, 15 N Main St, Mendon, UT, 84325. Tel: 435-774-2200. p. 2266
Martin, Jim, Assoc Librn, University of Arizona Libraries, Albert B Weaver Science-Engineering Library, 744 N Highland, Bldg 54, Tucson, AZ, 85721. Tel: 520-621-6384. p. 84
Martin, John, Dir, Loutit District Library, 407 Columbus Ave, Grand Haven, MI, 49417. Tel: 616-850-6912. p. 1109
Martin, Julia, Dir, Instruction & Ref, University of Toledo, 2975 W Centennial Dr, Toledo, OH, 43606-3396. Tel: 419-530-2492. p. 1825
Martin, Julie, Asst Tech Serv Librn, ILL, Decatur Public Library, 130 N Franklin St, Decatur, IL, 62523. Tel: 217-424-2900. p. 576
Martin, Kaelyn, Circ Librn, Mineral Point Public Library, 137 High St, Ste 2, Mineral Point, WI, 53565. Tel: 608-987-2447. p. 2462
Martin, Karen, Librn, Faulkner-Van Buren Regional Library System, Damascus Branch, 17379 US 65, Damascus, AR, 72039. Tel: 501-335-8142. p. 92
Martin, Karen, Archivist, Huntington Historical Society, 209 Main St, Huntington, NY, 11743. Tel: 631-427-7045, Ext 406. p. 1549
Martin, Katie, Library Contact, Lafayette Public Library, Milton Branch, Cedar Village Shopping Ctr, 108 W Milton Ave, Milton, LA, 70558. Tel: 337-856-5261. p. 892
Martin, Kenna, Dir, Butler County Public Library, 116 W Ohio St, Morgantown, KY, 42261. Tel: 270-526-4722. p. 870
Martin, Kim, Br Mgr, Blue Ridge Regional Library, Collinsville Branch, 2540 Virginia Ave, Collinsville, VA, 24078. Tel: 276-647-1112. p. 2332
Martin, Kimber, Dir, Libr Serv, North Pike District Library, 119 S Corey St, Griggsville, IL, 62340. Tel: 217-833-2633. p. 596
Martin, Kimberly, Cat Librn, Gonzaga University School of Law, 721 N Cincinnati St, Spokane, WA, 99220. Tel: 509-313-5792. p. 2383
Martin, Kimberly A, Dir, Maple Park Public Library District, 302 Willow St, Maple Park, IL, 60151. Tel: 815-827-3362. p. 613
Martin, Kristin E, Dir, Tech Serv, The University of Chicago Library, 1100 E 57th St, Chicago, IL, 60637-1502. Tel: 773-702-8740. p. 569
Martin, L J, Outreach Coordr, Youth Serv Consult, Chautauqua-Cattaraugus Library System, 106 W Fifth St, Jamestown, NY, 14701. Tel: 716-664-6675, Ext 243. p. 1557
Martin, LaRuth, Computer Lab Mgr, Ref Librn, Webmaster, Montgomery City-County Public Library System, Juliette Hampton Morgan Memorial Library, 245 High St, Montgomery, AL, 36104. Tel: 334-240-4994. p. 29
Martin, Laura, Dep Dir, Res, Oklahoma Historical Society-Museum of the Western Prairie, 1100 Memorial Dr, Altus, OK, 73521. Tel: 580-482-1044. p. 1839
Martin, Laura, Dep Dir, Oklahoma Historical Society, Oklahoma History Ctr, 800 Nazih Zuhdi Dr, Oklahoma City, OK, 73105. Tel: 402-522-5225. p. 1859
Martin, Laura, Head Librn, Zion Mennonite Church & Public Library, 149 Cherry Lane, Souderton, PA, 18964. Tel: 215-723-3592. p. 2008
Martin, Laura, Mgr Community Develop & Prog, Niagara Falls Public Library, 4848 Victoria Ave, Niagara Falls, ON, L2E 4C5, CANADA. Tel: 905-356-8080. p. 2660
Martin, Lisa, Ch, Madison Public Library, 209 E Center St, Madison, SD, 57042. Tel: 605-256-7525. p. 2078
Martin, Lisa, Libr Spec, Howard College - San Angelo Library, 3501 N US Hwy 67, San Angelo, TX, 76905. Tel: 325-481-8300, Ext 3310. p. 2236
Martin, Lora, Dir, Heuvelton Free Library, 57 State St, Heuvelton, NY, 13654. Tel: 315-344-6550. p. 1546
Martin, Lori D, Dir, Res, Bradley LLP, One Federal Pl, 1819 Fifth Ave N, Birmingham, AL, 35203. Tel: 205-521-8000. p. 8
Martin, Lyn, Spec Coll Librn, Willard Library of Evansville, 21 First Ave, Evansville, IN, 47710-1294. Tel: 812-425-4309. p. 682
Martin, Lynn, ILL, Springfield College, 263 Alden St, Springfield, MA, 01109-3797. Tel: 413-748-3315. p. 1057
Martin, Maggie, Info Coordr, West Des Moines Public Library, 4000 Mills Civic Pkwy, West Des Moines, IA, 50265-2049. Tel: 515-222-3407. p. 791
Martin, Mari, Dir, British Columbia Ministry of Education, 620 Superior St, 5th Flr, Victoria, BC, V8V 1V2, CANADA. Tel: 250-356-1791. p. 2582
Martin, Marianne, AV, Colonial Williamsburg Foundation, 313 First St, Williamsburg, VA, 23185-4306. Tel: 757-565-8542. p. 2353
Martin, Marla, Programming Librn, Teen & Adult Librn, Woodbury Public Library, 269 Main St S, Woodbury, CT, 06798. Tel: 203-263-3502. p. 349
Martin, Mary, Dir, Wanaque Public Library, 616 Ringwood Ave, Wanaque, NJ, 07465. Tel: 973-839-4434. p. 1451
Martin, Mat, Provincial Archivist, Rare Book Curator, Oblate School of Theology, 285 Oblate Dr, San Antonio, TX, 78216. Tel: 210-477-0913. p. 2237
Martin, Meg, Br Mgr, US Courts Library - Tenth Circuit Court of Appeals, Byron Rogers Courthouse, 1929 Stout St, Rm 430, Denver, CO, 80294. Tel: 303-844-3591. p. 277

Martin, Meg, Br Mgr, United States Courts, 624 US Courthouse, 500 State Ave, Kansas City, KS, 66101. Tel: 913-735-2497. p. 817

Martin, Melba, Librn, Houston Community College - Northwest College, Spring Branch Campus Library, 1010 W Sam Houston Pkwy N, Houston, TX, 77043-5008. Tel: 713-718-5656. p. 2194

Martin, Melinda, Librn, Spokane Community College/Community Colleges of Spokane Library, MS 2160, 1810 N Greene St, Spokane, WA, 99217-5399. Tel: 509-533-8822. p. 2384

Martin, Melissa, Br Mgr, San Diego Public Library, University Community, 4155 Governor Dr, San Diego, CA, 92122. Tel: 858-552-1655. p. 221

Martin, Melissa, Access Serv Coordr, William Woods University, One University Ave, Fulton, MO, 65251. p. 1246

Martin, Michael, Supvr, Yakima Valley Libraries, Selah Public Library, 106 S Second St, Selah, WA, 98942. Tel: 509-698-7345. p. 2396

Martin, Michelle, Librn, Calhoun County Library, Port O'Connor Branch, 506 W Main St, Port O'Connor, TX, 77982. Tel: 361-983-4365. p. 2228

Martin, Michelle H, Dr, Cleary Prof of Ch & Youth Serv, Prog Chair, University of Washington, Mary Gates Hall, Ste 370, Campus Box 352840, Seattle, WA, 98195-2840. Tel: 206-543-1794. p. 2794

Martin, Mies, Ser & Electronic Res Librn, Aquinas College, 1700 Fulton St E, Grand Rapids, MI, 49506. Tel: 616-632-2133. p. 1109

Martin, Nancy, Head, Circ, Rutherford Public Library, 150 Park Ave, Rutherford, NJ, 07070. Tel: 201-939-8600. p. 1441

Martin, Nancy, Circ, Calmar Public Library, 4705 50th Ave, Calmar, AB, T0C 0V0, CANADA. Tel: 780-985-3472. p. 2529

Martin, Natasha, City Librn, Roseville Public Library, 225 Taylor St, Roseville, CA, 95678-2681. Tel: 916-774-5221. p. 205

Martin, Nathalie, District Prog Mgr, Libr Serv Section Chief, Bibliotheques de Montreal, Pavillon Prince, 801 rue Brennan, 5e etage, Montreal, QC, H3C 0G4, CANADA. Tel: 514-872-2449. p. 2718

Martin, Nina, Libr Mgr, Plano Public Library System, Christopher A Parr Library, 6200 Windhaven Pkwy, Plano, TX, 75093. Tel: 972-769-4300. p. 2227

Martin, Pam, Interim Mgr, Rapides Parish Library, Westside Regional, 5416 Provine Pl, Alexandria, LA, 71303. Tel: 318-442-2483. p. 880

Martin, Pamela, Instruction & User Serv Librn, University of Idaho Library, 850 S Rayburn St, Moscow, ID, 83844. Tel: 208-885-6534. p. 526

Martin, Pamela, Br Mgr, Rapides Parish Library, Libuse Branch, 6375 Hwy 28 E, Pineville, LA, 71360. Tel: 318-443-7259. p. 880

Martin, Pamela, Head, Ref Serv, Washington State University Libraries, 100 Dairy Rd, Pullman, WA, 99164. Tel: 509-335-9671. p. 2374

Martin, Patches, Ch, Oak Hill Public Library, 226 South Front St, Oak Hill, OH, 45656. Tel: 740-682-6457. p. 1810

Martin, Patricia, Tech Serv Mgr, Georgetown University, Bioethics Research Library, Kennedy Institute of Ethics, 37th & O St NW, Washington, DC, 20057. Tel: 202-687-3885. p. 368

Martin, Rebecca Y, Sr Assoc Dir, Scholarly Coms & Colls, Harvard Library, Monroe C Gutman Library, 6 Appian Way, Cambridge, MA, 02138. Tel: 617-495-3453. p. 1006

Martin, Renee, Patron Serv Mgr, Marysville Public Library, Raymond Branch, 21698 Main St, Raymond, OH, 43067. Tel: 937-642-1876, Ext 26. p. 1800

Martin, Ricky, Dr, Principal, John H Lilley Correctional Center, 407971 Hwy 62E, Boley, OK, 74829. Tel: 918-667-3381. p. 1842

Martin, Rob, Br Mgr, Reading Public Library, Northwest, 901 Schuylkill Ave, Reading, PA, 19601. Tel: 610-655-6360. p. 2001

Martin, Rosa L, Mgr, Paine College, 1235 15th St, Augusta, GA, 30901-3105. Tel: 706-821-8365. p. 467

Martin, Ruby, Dir, Lane County Library, 144 South Lane, Dighton, KS, 67839. Tel: 620-397-2808. p. 804

Martin, Russell, Pub Serv Librn, Rockingham Community College, 315 Wrenn Memorial Rd, Wentworth, NC, 27375. Tel: 336-342-4261, Ext 2315. p. 1721

Martin, Russell, Dir, Southern Methodist University, DeGolyer Library of Special Collections, 6404 Robert S Hyer Lane, Dallas, TX, 75275. Tel: 214-768-3234. p. 2168

Martin, Samantha, Colls Librn, Research Librn, Washington & Jefferson College Library, 60 S Lincoln St, Washington, PA, 15301. Tel: 724-503-1001, Ext 3127. p. 2018

Martin, Scott T, Tech Librn, Flint River Regional Library System, 800 Memorial Dr, Griffin, GA, 30223. Tel: 770-412-4770. p. 481

Martin, Shirley, Librn, Rapid City Regional Library, 425 Third Ave, Rapid City, MB, R0K 1W0, CANADA. Tel: 204-826-2732. p. 2589

Martin, Susan, Chair, Collection Dev & Mgmt, Middle Tennessee State University, 1611 Alumni Dr, Murfreesboro, TN, 37132. Tel: 615-898-2819. p. 2117

Martin, Tamie, Dir, West Baton Rouge Parish Library, 830 N Alexander Ave, Port Allen, LA, 70767. Tel: 225-342-7920. p. 906

Martin, Tammy, Libr Asst, Green Forest Public Library, 206 E Main St, Green Forest, AR, 72638-2627. Tel: 870-438-6700. p. 97

Martin, Tatyana, Library Contact, Eastern Shore Hospital Center, 5262 Woods Rd, Cambridge, MD, 21613-3796. Tel: 410-221-2388. p. 960

Martin, Terrence, Librn, Wilson Community College Library, 902 Herring Ave, Wilson, NC, 27893. Tel: 252-246-1235. p. 1724

Martin, Valerie, Libr Supvr, Artesia Historical Museum & Art Center, 505 W Richardson Ave, Artesia, NM, 88210. Tel: 575-748-2390. p. 1463

Martin, Vanessa, Libr Dir, Greensburg-Decatur County Public Library, 1110 E Main St, Greensburg, IN, 47240. Tel: 812-663-2826. p. 688

Martin, Victoria, Librn, Palliser Regional Library, Davidson Branch, 314 Washington Ave, Davidson, SK, S0G 1A0, CANADA. Tel: 306-567-2022. p. 2742

Martin-Diaz, Pamela, Librn/Br Mgr, Allen County Public Library, Shawnee, 5600 Noll Ave, Fort Wayne, IN, 46806. Tel: 260-421-1355. p. 683

Martin-Woodard, Katie, Tech Serv, Pierson Library, 5376 Shelburne Rd, Shelburne, VT, 05482. Tel: 802-985-5124. p. 2294

Martindale, Elizabeth, Youth Serv, Parlin Ingersoll Public Library, 205 W Chestnut St, Canton, IL, 61520. Tel: 309-647-0328. p. 548

Martindale, Jaime, Librn, University of Wisconsin-Madison, Arthur H Robinson Map Library, 310 Science Hall, 550 N Park St, Madison, WI, 53706-1491. Tel: 608-262-1471. p. 2451

Martineau, Elizabeth, Exec Dir, Los Alamos Historical Society, 1050 Bathtub Row, Los Alamos, NM, 87544. Tel: 505-662-6272. p. 1472

Martinelli, Patricia, Curator, Vineland Historical & Antiquarian Society, 108 S Seventh St, Vineland, NJ, 08360-4607. Tel: 856-691-1111. p. 1450

Martinez, Adrianna, Ref Librn, Seattle Central College, 1701 Broadway, BE Rm 2101, Seattle, WA, 98122. Tel: 206-934-4946. p. 2378

Martinez, Alicia, Principal Librn, Tech Serv, Watsonville Public Library, 275 Main St, Ste 100, Watsonville, CA, 95076. Tel: 831-768-3400. p. 258

Martinez, Andres, Libr Supvr, Rutgers University Libraries, Media Center, Douglass Library, Eight Chapel Dr, New Brunswick, NJ, 08901. Tel: 848-932-5006. p. 1425

Martinez, Andrew, Archivist, Rhode Island School of Design Library, 15 Westminster St, Providence, RI, 02903. Tel: 401-709-5920. p. 2040

Martinez, Annalea, Tech Serv Supvr, Caldwell Public Library, 1010 Dearborn St, Caldwell, ID, 83605. Tel: 208-459-3242. p. 518

Martinez, Annette, Br Mgr, Anythink Libraries, Anythink Perl Mack, 7611 Hilltop Circle, Denver, CO, 80221. Tel: 303-428-3576. p. 296

Martinez, April, Asst Dir, Tarrant County College, 828 W Harwood Rd, Hurst, TX, 76054. Tel: 817-515-6232. p. 2201

Martinez, Aurora, Dir, Morley Library, 184 Phelps St, Painesville, OH, 44077-3926. Tel: 440-352-3383. p. 1812

Martinez, Bertha, Dir, Libr Serv, Dr Eugene Clark Library, 217 S Main St, Lockhart, TX, 78644-2742. Tel: 512-398-3223, Ext 284. p. 2212

Martinez, Brenda, Bus Off Mgr, New Castle-Henry County Public Library, 376 S 15th St, New Castle, IN, 47362-3205. Tel: 765-529-0362. p. 709

Martinez, Carla, Dr, Dean of Libr, Golden West College, 15744 Golden West St, Huntington Beach, CA, 92647. Tel: 714-895-8741. p. 151

Martinez, Carmen, Dir, San Xavier Learning Center Library, 1960 W Walk Lane, Tucson, AZ, 85746. Tel: 520-807-8620. p. 83

Martinez, Carmen, Interim Dir, Notre Dame de Namur University Library, 1500 Ralston Ave, Belmont, CA, 94002-1908. Tel: 650-508-3748. p. 121

Martinez, Cesar, Tech, Westbank Community Library District, 1309 Westbank Dr, Austin, TX, 78746. Tel: 512-327-3045. p. 2143

Martinez, Christina, Assoc Dean, University of Colorado Colorado Springs, 1420 Austin Bluffs Pkwy, Colorado Springs, CO, 80918. Tel: 719-255-3287. p. 272

Martinez, Clarissa, Libr Asst, Nogales-Santa Cruz County Public Library, Rio Rico Library, 275 Rio Rico Dr, Rio Rico, AZ, 85648. Tel: 520-281-8067. p. 67

Martinez, Claudia, Sr Librn, Los Angeles Public Library System, Westchester-Loyola Village Branch Library, 7114 W Manchester Ave, Los Angeles, CA, 90045-3509. Tel: 310-348-1096. p. 166

Martinez, Elsie, Adult Serv Coordr, Zion-Benton Public Library District, 2400 Gabriel Ave, Zion, IL, 60099. Tel: 847-872-4680. p. 665

Martinez, Erika, Dir, Commun Engagement, Dir, Communications, Denver Public Library, Ten W 14th Ave Pkwy, Denver, CO, 80204-2731. Tel: 720-865-1111. p. 275

Martinez, Erma Jean, Br Mgr, Sabine Parish Library, Zwolle Branch, 2218 Port Arthur St, Zwolle, LA, 71486. Tel: 318-645-6955. p. 896

Martinez, Gabriela, Head, Ref Serv, Pikes Peak State College Library, 5675 S Academy Blvd, C7, Colorado Springs, CO, 80906-5498. p. 272

Martinez, Josh, Admin Assoc, City of Palo Alto Library, Downtown, 270 Forest Ave, Palo Alto, CA, 94301. Tel: 650-329-2501. p. 192

Martinez, Karen Lee, Senior Outreach Librn, Northwest Area Health Education Center, Catawba Valley Medical Ctr, 810 Fairgrove Church Rd, Hickory, NC, 28602. Tel: 828-326-3482. p. 1696

Martinez, Kelsy, Res Support & Instruction Librn, Bunker Hill Community College, E Bldg, 3rd Flr, Rm E300, 250 New Rutherford Ave, Boston, MA, 02129-2925. Tel: 617-228-2211. p. 994

Martinez, Leslie, Br Asst, Elko-Lander-Eureka County Library System, Jackpot Branch Library, 2301 Progressive Rd, Jackpot, NV, 89825. Tel: 775-755-2356. p. 1344

Martinez, Lisa, Br Mgr, Osceola Library System, Buenaventura Lakes Branch, 405 Buenaventura Blvd, Kissimmee, FL, 34743. Tel: 407-742-8888. p. 414

Martinez, Luis, Libr Supvr, City of Commerce Public Library, Bristow Library, 1466 S McDonnell Ave, Commerce, CA, 90040. Tel: 323-887-4492. p. 132
Martinez, Lydia E, Asst Librn, Circ, Universidad del Turabo, Rd 189 Km 3.3, Gurabo, PR, 00778. Tel: 787-743-7979, Ext 4501. p. 2511
Martinez, Lyndsey, Head Librn, Austin County Library System, 6730 Railroad St, Wallis, TX, 77485. Tel: 979-478-6813. p. 2254
Martinez, Manuel, Libr Mgr, New York Public Library - Astor, Lenox & Tilden Foundations, Allerton Branch, 2740 Barnes Ave, (Between Allerton & Arnow Aves), Bronx, NY, 10467. Tel: 718-881-4240. p. 1594
Martinez, Maria, Dir, Libr & Media Serv, Eastern Oklahoma State College, Bill H Hill Library Bldg, 2nd & 3rd Flrs, 1301 W Main St, Wilburton, OK, 74578. Tel: 918-465-1711. p. 1869
Martinez, Marisa, Librn, California Department of Corrections Library System, Correctional Training Facility, Soledad Prison Rd, Hwy 101 N, Soledad, CA, 93960. Tel: 831-678-3951, Ext 5872. p. 206
Martinez, Martin, Library Contact, Assumption Seminary Library, 2600 W Woodlawn, San Antonio, TX, 78228. Tel: 210-734-5137. p. 2236
Martinez, Mary, Dir & Librn, Moise Memorial Library, 208 S Fifth St, Santa Rosa, NM, 88435-2329. Tel: 575-472-3101. p. 1477
Martinez, Matthias, Fr, Ser Librn, Saint Vincent College & Seminary Library, 300 Fraser Purchase Rd, Latrobe, PA, 15650-2690. Tel: 724-805-2966. p. 1953
Martinez, Maura, Access & Discovery Librn, US Customs & Border Protection Information Resources Center, 90 K St NE, Washington, DC, 20229. Tel: 202-325-0130. p. 380
Martinez, Melissa, Library Contact, Duval County-San Diego Public Library, 315 S Dr E E Dunlap St, San Diego, TX, 78384. Tel: 361-279-6244. p. 2240
Martinez, Mike, Jr, Ref (Info Servs), Saint Mary's University, Sarita Kennedy East Law Library, One Camino Santa Maria, San Antonio, TX, 78228-8605. Tel: 210-436-3435, Ext 1374. p. 2238
Martinez, Myriam, Librn, Cat, Universidad del Turabo, Rd 189 Km 3.3, Gurabo, PR, 00778. Tel: 787-743-7979, Ext 4501. p. 2511
Martinez Nazario, Manuel, Chief Librn, University of Puerto Rico Library System, Circulation & Reserve Collection, Rio Piedras Campus, Jose M Lazaro Bldg, 2nd Flr, San Juan, PR, 00931. Tel: 787-764-0000, Ext 85540. p. 2514
Martinez Nazario, Manuel, Chief Librn, University of Puerto Rico Library System, Documents & Maps Collection, Rio Piedras Campus, Jose M Lazaro Bldg, 2nd Flr, San Juan, PR, 00931. Tel: 787-764-0000, Ext 85725. p. 2514
Martinez, Nora G, Libr Dir, Alexander Memorial Library, 201 S Center St, Cotulla, TX, 78014-2255. Tel: 830-879-2601. p. 2161
Martinez, Norma, Dir, El Paso Public Library, 501 N Oregon St, El Paso, TX, 79901. Tel: 915-212-3200. p. 2174
Martinez, Patty, Libr Tech-Mats, Alamosa Public Library, 300 Hunt Ave, Alamosa, CO, 81101. Tel: 719-587-2542. p. 263
Martinez, Paul, Archivist, Cat Librn, Montclair State University, One Normal Ave, Montclair, NJ, 07043-1699. Tel: 973-655-3465. p. 1420
Martinez, Pilar, Chief Exec Officer, Edmonton Public Library, Seven Sir Winston Churchill Sq, Edmonton, AB, T5J 2V4, CANADA. Tel: 780-496-7050. p. 2536
Martinez, Rachel, Libr Operations Mgr, Edgewood Community Library, 171 B State Rd 344, Edgewood, NM, 87015. Tel: 505-281-0138. p. 1467
Martinez Reyes, Michelle, Marketing Specialist, Greenspoon Marder, 200 E Broward Blvd, Ste 1800, Fort Lauderdale, FL, 33301. Tel: 954-491-1120. p. 401
Martinez, Rob, Ft Myers Campus Libr Dir, Keiser University Library System, 1500 NW 49th St, Fort Lauderdale, FL, 33309. Tel: 954-351-4035. p. 401
Martinez Rodriguez, Johana, Librn, Universidad Ana G Mendez, Calle 190, Esquina 220 Bo Sabana Abajo, Carolina, PR, 00983. Tel: 787-257-7373, Ext 2504. p. 2510
Martinez, Sara, Br Mgr, Tulsa City-County Library, Nathan Hale Library, 6038 E 23rd St, Tulsa, OK, 74114. p. 1866
Martinez, Shan, Head, Tech Serv & Govt Doc, Abilene Christian University, 221 Brown Library, ACU Box 29208, Abilene, TX, 79699-9208. Tel: 325-674-2316. p. 2131
Martinez, Stephanie, Br Mgr, Phoenix Public Library, Mesquite Library, 4525 E Paradise Village Pkwy N, Phoenix, AZ, 85032. p. 72
Martinez, Sylvia, Admin Coordr, Texas A&M University-Kingsville, 1050 University Blvd, MSC 197, Kingsville, TX, 78363. Tel: 361-593-4029. p. 2206
Martinez, Tammy, Automation Syst Coordr, Cat, Pontifical Catholic University, Monsignor Fremiot Torres Oliver Law Library, 2250 Blvd Luis A Ferre Aguayo, Ste 544, Ponce, PR, 00717-9997. Tel: 787-841-2000, Ext 1858. p. 2512
Martinez, Teresa, Dir, Learning Res, Baptist University of the Americas, 7838 Barlite Blvd, San Antonio, TX, 78224-1364. Tel: 210-924-4338, Ext 230. p. 2236
Martinez, Theresa, Circ Asst, Wharton County Junior College, 911 Boling Hwy, Wharton, TX, 77488-3298. Tel: 979-532-6953. p. 2256
Martinez Wormser, Jennifer, Dir & Librn, Claremont Colleges Library, Ella Strong Denison Library, Scripps College, 1090 N Columbia Ave, Claremont, CA, 91711. Tel: 909-621-8973. p. 130
Martinez, Yvonne, Dir, Eleanor Daggett Public Library, 299 W Fourth St, Chama, NM, 87520-0786. Tel: 575-756-2184. p. 1465
Martinez-Garcia, Federico, Dir, Access Serv, University of Colorado Colorado Springs, 1420 Austin Bluffs Pkwy, Colorado Springs, CO, 80918. Tel: 719-255-3908. p. 272
Martinkus, Margaret, Curator, Ref, Princeton Public Library, 698 E Peru St, Princeton, IL, 61356. Tel: 815-875-1331. p. 636
Martino, Bill, Dir, Clark County Public Library, 201 S Fountain Ave, Springfield, OH, 45506. Tel: 937-323-9751. p. 1821
Martino, Elizabeth, ILL, Stetson University, 421 N Woodland Blvd, Unit 8418, DeLand, FL, 32723. Tel: 386-822-4034. p. 393
Martino, Lauren, Mgr, Spec Coll, Galveston County Library System, 2310 Sealy Ave, Galveston, TX, 77550. Tel: 409-763-8854, Ext 117. p. 2183
Martino, Marie, Syst & Cat Librn, Moraine Valley Community College Library, 9000 W College Pkwy, Palos Hills, IL, 60465. Tel: 708-974-5709. p. 632
Martino, Nancy, Chief Librn, Department of Veterans Affairs, 1601 Brenner Ave, Salisbury, NC, 28144. Tel: 704-638-9000, Ext 14064. p. 1714
Martino, Sharon, Dir, Librn, Carnegie Free Library, 299 S Pittsburgh St, Connellsville, PA, 15425. Tel: 724-628-1380. p. 1924
Martins, Michael, Curator, Fall River Historical Society Museum, 451 Rock St, Fall River, MA, 02720. Tel: 508-679-1071. p. 1017
Martins, Rachel, Library Tech Support Specialist, Northern Lakes College Library, 64 Mission St, Grouard, AB, T0G 1C0, CANADA. Tel: 780-751-3275. p. 2542
Martinsen, Dan, Dir, McLennan Community College Library, 1400 College Dr, Waco, TX, 76708-1498. Tel: 254-299-8333. p. 2253
Martinson, Doris, Archives Mgr, Archivist, Knox County Public Library System, 500 W Church Ave, Knoxville, TN, 37902. Tel: 865-215-8750. p. 2105
Martinson, Melissa, Support Librn, Alamosa Public Library, 300 Hunt Ave, Alamosa, CO, 81101. Tel: 719-587-2541. p. 263
Martinson, Trevor, Digital Initiatives, North Dakota State Library, Liberty Memorial Bldg, Dept 250, 604 East Blvd Ave, Bismarck, ND, 58505-0800. Tel: 701-328-4629. p. 1730
Martison, Trevor, Librn, Sanford Health, 622 Ave A East, Bismarck, ND, 58501. Tel: 701-323-5390, 701-323-5392. p. 1730
Marto, Ned, Access Serv Mgr, School of the Art Institute of Chicago, 37 S Wabash Ave, Chicago, IL, 60603-3103. Tel: 312-899-5097. p. 568
Martocello, Anthony, Network & Syst Adminr, Northport-East Northport Public Library, 151 Laurel Ave, Northport, NY, 11768. Tel: 631-261-6930. p. 1608
Marton, Maureen, Librn, St Pete Beach Public Library, 365 73rd Ave, Saint Pete Beach, FL, 33706-1996. Tel: 727-363-9238. p. 441
Martorano, Jill, Pub Serv Mgr, Glenside Public Library District, 25 E Fullerton Ave, Glendale Heights, IL, 60139-2697. Tel: 630-260-1550. p. 593
Martucci, Kathleen, Chief Operating Officer, Helen Hayes Hospital, Rte 9 W, West Haverstraw, NY, 10993. Tel: 845-786-4201. p. 1662
Martynyshyn, Jenny, Admin Coordr, Stephen Leacock Memorial Museum Library, 50 Museum Dr, Orillia, ON, L3V 6K5, CANADA. Tel: 705-329-1908. p. 2663
Martz, Rusty, Pres, New Year Shooters & Mummers Museum Library, 1100 S Second St, Philadelphia, PA, 19147. Tel: 215-336-3050. p. 1983
Martz, Shaunna, Br Mgr, Kent District Library, Alpine Township Branch, 5255 Alpine Ave NW, Comstock Park, MI, 49321. p. 1093
Marushin, James, Curator, Martin County Historical Society, Inc, 304 E Blue Earth Ave, Fairmont, MN, 56031. Tel: 507-235-5178. p. 1174
Maruskin, John, Chair, Bryant Free Library, 455 Berkshire Trail, Rte 9, Cummington, MA, 01026-9610. Tel: 413-634-0109. p. 1013
Marvan, Nancy, Bus Off Mgr, Hinsdale Public Library, 20 E Maple St, Hinsdale, IL, 60521. Tel: 630-986-1976. p. 600
Marvel, Patricia, User Services Library Asst, Cleveland Health Sciences Library, Allen Memorial Medical Library, 11000 Euclid Ave, Cleveland, OH, 44106-7130. Tel: 216-368-3643. p. 1767
Marvin, Beth M, Mgr, Portville Free Library, Two N Main St, Portville, NY, 14770. Tel: 716-933-8441. p. 1622
Marvin, Carolyn, Research Librn, Portsmouth Athenaeum, Six-Nine Market Sq, Portsmouth, NH, 03801. Tel: 603-431-2538. p. 1379
Marvin, Marilyn, Asst Dir, Operations, Fort Worth Library, 500 W Third St, Fort Worth, TX, 76102. Tel: 817-392-7323. p. 2179
Marvin, Matt, Fac Mgr, Lewes Public Library, 111 Adams Ave, Lewes, DE, 19958. Tel: 302-645-2733. p. 354
Marvin, Thomas, ILL, Dutchess Community College Library, 53 Pendell Rd, Poughkeepsie, NY, 12601-1595. Tel: 845-431-8630. p. 1622
Marx, Anthony W, Dr, Pres, The New York Public Library - Astor, Lenox & Tilden Foundations, 476 Fifth Ave, (@ 42nd St), New York, NY, 10018. Tel: 212-930-0736. p. 1594
Marx, Mary Ann, Libr Mgr, New Orleans Public Library, Algiers Regional Library, 3014 Holiday Dr, New Orleans, LA, 70131. Tel: 504-596-2641. p. 902
Marx, Richard, ILL, Iosco-Arenac District Library, 120 W Westover St, East Tawas, MI, 48730. Tel: 989-362-2651. p. 1102
Marx, Sonja, Librn, Dillingham Public Library, 306 D St W, Dillingham, AK, 99576. Tel: 907-842-5610. p. 44
Marx, Tyi-Kimya, Rare Bk Librn, Spec Coll, College of Physicians of Philadelphia, 19 S 22nd St, Philadelphia, PA, 19103. Tel: 215-399-2301. p. 1975

Mary, Martha, Br Mgr, Sabine Parish Library, Pleasant Hill Branch, 8434 Bridges St, Pleasant Hill, LA, 71065. Tel: 318-796-2595. p. 896

Marzluft, Jeffrey, Librn, University of Hawaii, 310 Kaahumanu Ave, Kahului, HI, 96732. Tel: 808-984-3233, 808-984-3715. p. 513

Marzlust, Jeffrey, Dir of Libr, Quincy College, 1250 Hancock St, Rm 347, Quincy, MA, 02169. Tel: 617-405-5949. p. 1048

Marzolf, Maggi, Archivist, Baltimore Museum of Industry, 1415 Key Hwy, 2nd Flr, Baltimore, MD, 21230. Tel: 410-727-4808, Ext 112. p. 952

Marzolla, Mary K, Assoc Dir, Widener University, School of Law Library, 4601 Concord Pike, Wilmington, DE, 19803. Tel: 302-477-2157. p. 358

Marzullo, Keith, Dr, Dean, University of Maryland, Hornbake Library, Ground Flr, Rm 0220, 4130 Campus Dr, College Park, MD, 20742-4345. Tel: 301-405-2039. p. 2786

Mas, Sabine, Assoc Prof, Universite de Montreal, 3150, rue Jean-Brillant, bur C-2004, Montreal, QC, H3T 1N8, CANADA. Tel: 514-343-6044. p. 2797

Masar, Vicki, Asst Dir, John C Fremont Library District, 130 Church Ave, Florence, CO, 81226. Tel: 719-784-4649, Ext 1. p. 280

Masarof, Louise, Librn, American Folk Art Museum, Collection & Education Ctr, 47-29 32nd Pl, Long Island City, NY, 11101. Tel: 646-856-8917. p. 1565

Mascareañas, Sandra, ILL, Nogales-Santa Cruz County Public Library, 518 N Grand Ave, Nogales, AZ, 85621. Tel: 520-285-5717, Ext 0241. p. 67

Mascia, Regina, Dir, West Hempstead Public Library, 500 Hempstead Ave, West Hempstead, NY, 11552. Tel: 516-481-6591. p. 1662

Mascia, Sara, Curator, Exec Dir, Historical Society Serving Sleepy Hollow & Tarrytown, One Grove St, Tarrytown, NY, 10591. Tel: 914-631-8374. p. 1651

Masek, Amy, Access Serv Librn, Clarkson College Library, 101 S 42nd St, Omaha, NE, 68131-2739. Tel: 402-552-3387. p. 1327

Masek, Amy, Exec Secy, ICON Library Consortium, c/o Clarkson College Library, 101 S 42nd St, Omaha, NE, 68131. Tel: 402-552-3387. p. 2769

Maseles, Judy Siebert, Librn, University of Missouri-Columbia, Engineering Library & Technology Commons, W2001 Lafferre Hall, Columbia, MO, 65211. Tel: 573-882-2715. p. 1243

Masengale, Margaret, Librn, Northwest Regional Library, MCHS Community Library, 8115 US Hwy 43, Guin, AL, 35563. Tel: 205-468-2544. p. 40

Mash, David, PhD, Assoc Dir, Libr Serv, Lander University, 320 Stanley Ave, Greenwood, SC, 29649. Tel: 864-388-8046. p. 2062

Masiello, Chris, Librn, Rhode Island School for the Deaf Library, One Corliss Park, Providence, RI, 02908. Tel: 401-222-3525. p. 2040

Masiello, Jen, Br Mgr, Phoenix Public Library, Desert Broom Library, 29710 N Cave Creek Rd, Cave Creek, AZ, 85331. p. 72

Masimini, Dulani, Pres of Board, Forest Hill Public Library, 6962 Forest Hill Dr, Forest Hill, TX, 76140. Tel: 817-551-5354. p. 2177

Masinton, Anthony, Libr Dir, La Veta Regional Library District, 310 S Main St, La Veta, CO, 81055. Tel: 719-742-3572. p. 287

Maske, Miriam, Dir, E-Learning & Assessment, Eastern New Mexico University - Ruidoso, 709 Mechem Dr, Ruidoso, NM, 88345. Tel: 575-315-1136. p. 1474

Maslow, Linda, Librn, Supreme Court of the United States Library, One First St NE, Washington, DC, 20543. Tel: 202-479-3037. p. 376

Maslowski, Monika K, Head, Virtual Branch, Library of the Marine Corps, Gray Research Ctr, 2040 Broadway St, Quantico, VA, 22134-5107. Tel: 703-784-4409. p. 2339

Mason, Amy, Libr Mgr, Wake County Public Library System, Zebulon Community Library, 1000 Dogwood Ave, Zebulon, NC, 27597. Tel: 919-404-3610. p. 1711

Mason, Angie, Libr Asst, ILL, The College of Saint Scholastica Library, 1200 Kenwood Ave, Duluth, MN, 55811-4199. Tel: 218-723-6140. p. 1172

Mason, Annamaria, Libr Mgr, New York Public Library - Astor, Lenox & Tilden Foundations, Great Kills Branch, 56 Giffords Lane, (@ Margaret St), Staten Island, NY, 10308. Tel: 718-984-6670. p. 1595

Mason, Betty J, Literacy Coordr, Ref & Ad Serv Librn, San Benito County Free Library, 470 Fifth St, Hollister, CA, 95023-3885. Tel: 831-636-4107. p. 151

Mason, Carla, Libr Dir, El Centro Public Library, 1198 N Imperial Ave, El Centro, CA, 92243. Tel: 760-337-4565. p. 139

Mason, Carla, Libr Dir, El Centro Public Library, El Centro Community Center, 375 S First St, El Centro, CA, 92243. Tel: 760-336-8977. p. 139

Mason, Carrie, Libr Dir, Town of Johnsburg Library, 219 Main St, North Creek, NY, 12853. Tel: 518-251-4343. p. 1607

Mason, Casey, Dir, Youth Serv, Hartley Public Library, 91 First St SE, Hartley, IA, 51346. Tel: 712-928-2080. p. 757

Mason, Cathy, Br Mgr, Kanawha County Public Library, Sissonville, One Tinney Lane, Charleston, WV, 25312. Tel: 304-984-2244. p. 2400

Mason, Clitha, Ms, Libr Assoc, Bowling Green State University, One University Dr, 2nd Flr, Huron, OH, 44839-9791. Tel: 419-372-0652. p. 1791

Mason, Donna, Asst Dir, Emmetsburg Public Library, 707 N Superior St, Emmetsburg, IA, 50536. Tel: 712-852-4009. p. 751

Mason, Elizabeth, Libr Tech, Long Beach Memorial/Miller Children's Hospital Long Beach, 2801 Atlantic Ave, Long Beach, CA, 90806. Tel: 562-933-3841. p. 158

Mason, Gail, Serv Mgr, Coll Develop & Reading Serv, Santa Clara County Library District, 1370 Dell Ave, Campbell, CA, 95032. Tel: 408-293-2326. p. 127

Mason, Herman, Libr Dir, Voorhees University, 213 Wiggins Dr, Denmark, SC, 29042. Tel: 803-780-1229. p. 2058

Mason, Jamie L, Dir, Rocky River Public Library, 1600 Hampton Rd, Rocky River, OH, 44116-2699. Tel: 440-895-3716. p. 1818

Mason, Jennifer, Principal, Cantwell Community-School Library, Mile 133-5 Denali Hwy & Second Ave, Cantwell, AK, 99729. Tel: 907-768-2372. p. 43

Mason, Jill Marie, Assoc Dir, Head, Libr Syst & Tech, Albion College, 602 E Cass St, Albion, MI, 49224-1879. Tel: 517-629-0270. p. 1076

Mason, John, Archives Librn, Dodge City Public Library, 1001 N Second Ave, Dodge City, KS, 67801. Tel: 620-225-0248. p. 804

Mason, Julie, Librn, Fraser Health Authority, 3935 Kincaid St, Burnaby, BC, V5G 2X6, CANADA. Tel: 604-412-6255. p. 2563

Mason, Karen, Evening Supvr, Slippery Rock University of Pennsylvania, 109 Campus Loop, Slippery Rock, PA, 16057. Tel: 724-738-2058. p. 2007

Mason, Katelyn, Children's Prog Coordr, Nashville Public Library, 219 E Elm St, Nashville, IL, 62263. Tel: 618-327-3827. p. 623

Mason, Kimara, Ch, Atlanta-Fulton Public Library System, College Park Branch, 3647 Main St, College Park, GA, 30337. Tel: 404-762-4060. p. 461

Mason, Krista, Libr Dir, Apollo Memorial Library, 219 N Pennsylvania Ave, Apollo, PA, 15613. Tel: 724-478-4214. p. 1907

Mason, Laura, Asst Regional Dir, Albert-Westmorland-Kent Regional Library, 644 Main St, Ste 201, Moncton, NB, E1C 1E2, CANADA. Tel: 506-869-6032. p. 2603

Mason, Leslie, Prog Coordr, Virginia Tidewater Consortium for Higher Education, 4900 Powhatan Ave, Norfolk, VA, 23529. Tel: 757-683-3183. p. 2776

Mason, Marissa, Librn, New York State Court of Appeals Library, 20 Eagle St, Albany, NY, 12207. Tel: 518-455-7700, 518-455-7770. p. 1482

Mason, Marsia, Asst Dir, Beach Haven Public Library, 219 N Beach Ave, Beach Haven, NJ, 08008. Tel: 609-492-7081. p. 1389

Mason, Meg, Spec Coll, Univ Archivist, Syracuse University Libraries, 222 Waverly Ave, Syracuse, NY, 13244-2010. Tel: 315-443-8380. p. 1650

Mason, Melissa, Exec Dir, Millvale Community Library, 213 Grant Ave, Millvale, PA, 15209. Tel: 412-822-7081. p. 1963

Mason, Monica, Tech Librn, Owens Community College Library, 30335 Oregon Rd, Perrysburg, OH, 43551. Tel: 567-661-7015. p. 1815

Mason, Ruth, Br Mgr, Pope County Library System, Hector Branch, 11600 State Rd 27, Hector, AR, 72843. Tel: 479-284-0907. p. 109

Mass, Hayley, Young Adult Programming, Lowell Public Library, 1505 E Commercial Ave, Lowell, IN, 46356-1899. Tel: 219-696-7704. p. 704

Mass, James, Head, Property Mgmt & Security, Newport Public Library, 300 Spring St, Newport, RI, 02840. Tel: 401-847-8720. p. 2035

Massa, Mary Beth, Library Contact, Colusa County Free Library, Princeton Branch, 232 Prince St, Princeton, CA, 95970. Tel: 530-439-2235. p. 131

Masschaele, Brian, Dir, Cultural Serv, Dir, Commun Serv, Elgin County Library, County Administration Bldg, 450 Sunset Dr, St. Thomas, ON, N5R 5V1, CANADA. Tel: 519-631-1460, Ext 148. p. 2680

Masse, Nathalie, Library Contact, Waterloo Public Library, 650 Rue de la Cour, Waterloo, QC, J0E 2N0, CANADA. Tel: 450-539-2268. p. 2739

Massero, Michelle, Br Mgr, Tacoma Public Library, Kobetich, 212 Brown's Point Blvd NE, Tacoma, WA, 98422. Tel: 253-280-2920. p. 2387

Massero, Michelle, Br Mgr, Tacoma Public Library, Mottet Branch, 3523 East G St, Tacoma, WA, 98404. Tel: 253-280-2950. p. 2387

Massetti, Kristen, Br Librn, Enfield Public Library, 104 Middle Rd, Enfield, CT, 06082. Tel: 860-763-7510. p. 311

Massetti, Kristen, Br Librn, Enfield Public Library, Pearl Street, 159 Pearl St, Enfield, CT, 06082. Tel: 860-253-6433. p. 311

Massey, Cyn, Librn, Spartanburg County Public Libraries, Woodruff Library, 270 E Hayne St, Woodruff, SC, 29388. Tel: 864-476-8770. p. 2070

Massey, Julie, Asst Dir, Kurth Memorial Library, 706 S Raguet St, Lufkin, TX, 75904. Tel: 936-630-0560. p. 2214

Massey, Kevin, Br Mgr, Pope County Library System, 116 E Third St, Russellville, AR, 72801. Tel: 479-968-4368. p. 109

Massey, Kim, Extn Serv Librn, Fayette County Public Libraries, 531 Summit St, Oak Hill, WV, 25901. Tel: 304-465-0121, 304-465-5664. p. 2410

Massey, Melanie, Dir, Libr Serv, Baker University, 518 Eighth St, Baldwin City, KS, 66006. Tel: 785-594-8389. p. 797

Massey, Susan, Head, Discovery Serv, University of North Florida, Bldg 12-Library, One UNF Dr, Jacksonville, FL, 32224-2645. Tel: 904-620-2615. p. 413

Massie, Natosha, Dir, Garnet A Wilson Public Library of Pike County, 207 N Market St, Waverly, OH, 45690-1176. Tel: 740-947-4921. p. 1829

Massie, Rhonda, Mkt, Bloomington Public Library, 205 E Olive St, Bloomington, IL, 61701. Tel: 309-828-6091. p. 543

Masson, Catherine, Br Tech, Monroe County Library System, Maybee Branch, 9060 Raisin St, Maybee, MI, 48159. Tel: 734-587-3680. p. 1134

Mathys, Eileen, Dir, Croghan Free Library, 9794 State Rte 812, Croghan, NY, 13327. Tel: 315-346-6521. p. 1523
Matias, Lizandra, Br Mgr, Hartford Public Library, Dwight Branch, Seven New Park Ave, Hartford, CT, 06106. Tel: 860-695-7460. p. 318
Matin, Faria, Asst Libr Dir, Mansfield Public Library, 104 S Wisteria St, Mansfield, TX, 76063. Tel: 817-728-3690. p. 2215
Matisko, Jody, Libr Tech 1, New Hampshire State Library, Gallen State Office Park, Dolloff Bldg, 117 Pleasant St, Concord, NH, 03301-3852. Tel: 603-271-2417, 603-271-3429. p. 1359
Matlin, Erin, Libr Dir, Amesbury Public Library, 149 Main St, Amesbury, MA, 01913. Tel: 978-388-8148. p. 984
Matook, Meika, Head Librn, Johnson & Wales University Library, Harborside Library, Friedman Ctr, 321 Harborside Blvd, Providence, RI, 02905. Tel: 401-598-1466. p. 2039
Matos, Ana Rosa, Cataloger, Librn, Inter-American University of Puerto Rico, 104 Parque Industrial Turpeaux, Rd 1, Mercedita, PR, 00715-1602. Tel: 787-284-1912, Ext 2520. p. 2512
Matos, Chris, Dir, George Hail Free Library, 530 Main St, Warren, RI, 02885. Tel: 401-245-7686. p. 2042
Matos, Jorge, Ref Serv, Hostos Community College Library, Shirley J Hinds Allied Health & Science Bldg, 475 Grand Concourse, Rm A308, Bronx, NY, 10451. Tel: 718-518-4149. p. 1499
Matott, Susan, Asst Dir, Ch, Pillsbury Free Library, 18 E Main St, Warner, NH, 03278. Tel: 603-456-2289. p. 1383
Matowski, Lizzie, Adult & Teen Serv Mgr, Downers Grove Public Library, 1050 Curtiss St, Downers Grove, IL, 60515. Tel: 630-960-1200, Ext 4247. p. 579
Matson, Christine, Ref & Instruction Librn, Guam Community College, One Sesame St, Mangilao, GU, 96921. Tel: 671-735-0231. p. 2505
Matson, Elizabeth, Head, Youth Serv, Hedberg Public Library, 316 S Main St, Janesville, WI, 53545. Tel: 608-758-6584. p. 2443
Matson, Madeline, Adult Prog Coordr, Missouri River Regional Library, 214 Adams St, Jefferson City, MO, 65101. Tel: 573-634-2464. p. 1252
Matsook, Donna, Interim Dir, Rochester Public Library, 252 Adams St, Rochester, PA, 15074-2137. Tel: 724-774-7783. p. 2002
Matsuda, Shavonn, Librn, University of Hawaii, 310 Kaahumanu Ave, Kahului, HI, 96732. Tel: 808-984-3233, 808-984-3715. p. 513
Matsumoto, Lisa Anne, Librn, Hawaii State Hospital, 45-710 Keaahala Rd, Kaneohe, HI, 96744-3528. Tel: 808-236-8201. p. 513
Matsunaga, Sachiko, Dr, Dean, Acad Affairs, Learning Support & Res, Hartnell College, 411 Central Ave, Salinas, CA, 93901. Tel: 831-755-6700, 831-755-6872. p. 2782
Matsuoka, Nobue, Music & Performing Arts Librn, American University Library, Music Library, Katzen Arts Ctr, Rm 150, 4400 Massachusetts Ave NW, Washington, DC, 20016-8046. Tel: 202-885-3465. p. 361
Matsushima Chiu, Ann, Soc Sci Librn, Reed College, 3203 SE Woodstock Blvd, Portland, OR, 97202-8199. Tel: 503-777-7702. p. 1894
Matsushita, Karl K, Dir, Japanese American National Library, 1619 Sutter St, San Francisco, CA, 94109. Tel: 415-567-5006. p. 225
Matte, David, Adminr, State Archivist, Idaho State Historical Society, Idaho History Ctr, 2205 Old Penitentiary Rd, Boise, ID, 83712-8250. Tel: 208-514-2328. p. 517
Matte, Katharine, Info Spec, Chartered Professional Accountants of Canada, 277 Wellington St W, Toronto, ON, M5V 3H2, CANADA. Tel: 416-204-3227. p. 2688
Matte, Lisa M, Dir, Jervis Public Library Association, Inc, 613 N Washington St, Rome, NY, 13440-4296. Tel: 315-336-4570. p. 1632
Matte, Melina, Br Head, Township of Russell Public Library, Embrun Branch, 1215 St Augustin St, Embrun, ON, K0A 1W1, CANADA. Tel: 613-443-3636. p. 2676
Mattes, Karen, Head, Mat Mgt, Morse Institute Library, 14 E Central St, Natick, MA, 01760. Tel: 508-647-6400, Ext 1534. p. 1037
Matteson, Joy, Univ Librn, Benedictine University Library, Mesa Campus Library, 225 E Main St, Mesa, IL, 85201. Tel: 630-829-6060. p. 610
Matteucci, Kristen B, Ref Librn, Jenkins Law Library, Ten Penn Ctr, 1801 Market St, Ste 900, Philadelphia, PA, 19103-6405. Tel: 215 574-7930. p. 1982
Matthes, Nancy, Med Librn, Mary Washington Hospital, 1001 Sam Perry Blvd, Fredericksburg, VA, 22401-4453. Tel: 540-741-1598. p. 2320
Matthew, Amy, Br Mgr, Carroll County District Library, Malvern Branch, 710 E Porter St, Malvern, OH, 44644. Tel: 330-863-0636. p. 1756
Matthew, Curtis, Head, Circ & Reserves, City University of New York, 365 Fifth Ave, New York, NY, 10016-4309. Tel: 212-817-7050. p. 1582
Matthew, Judy, Head, Per, William Paterson University, 300 Pompton Rd, Wayne, NJ, 07470. Tel: 973-720-2346. p. 1452
Matthew, Nicole, Dir, Valley Head Public Library, 25369 Seneca Trail, Valley Head, WV, 26294. Tel: 304-339-6071. p. 2416
Matthew, Steven, Asst Dir, Support Serv, Florida Atlantic University, 777 Glades Rd, Boca Raton, FL, 33431. Tel: 561-297-4027. p. 385
Matthewman, Anne, Head Librn, Dalhousie University, Sir James Dunn Law Library, 6061 University Ave, Halifax, NS, B3H 4R2, CANADA. Tel: 902-494-2124. p. 2618
Matthews, Allison Paige, Educ & Ref Librn, South East Area Health Education Center Medical Library, 2131 S 17th St, Wilmington, NC, 28401. Tel: 910-343-2180. p. 1723
Matthews, Amy, Br Mgr, Greensboro Public Library, Glenwood Community Library, 1901 W Florida St, Greensboro, NC, 27403. Tel: 336-297-5000. p. 1692
Matthews, Angela, Libr Dir, Craig Public Library, 504 Third St, Craig, AK, 99921. Tel: 907-826-3281. p. 44
Matthews, Anna, Br Coordr, Mesa Public Library, Dobson Ranch Branch, 2425 S Dobson Rd, Mesa, AZ, 85202. Tel: 480-644-3444. p. 66
Matthews, Ashley, Bus Mgr, Bellwood Public Library, 600 Bohland Ave, Bellwood, IL, 60104-1896. Tel: 708-547-7393. p. 541
Matthews, Barbara, Circ Supvr, Memphis Public Library, Poplar-White Station Branch, 5094 Poplar, Memphis, TN, 38117-7629. Tel: 901-415-2777. p. 2113
Matthews, Cheryl, Ch, Dobbs Ferry Public Library, 55 Main St, Dobbs Ferry, NY, 10522. Tel: 914-693-6615. p. 1526
Matthews, Cynthia, Dir, Westmoreland Public Library, 2305 Epperson Springs Rd, Westmoreland, TN, 37186. Tel: 615-644-2026. p. 2129
Matthews, Dawn, Br Mgr, Saint Joseph County Public Library, Centre Township Branch, 1150 E Kern Rd, South Bend, IN, 46614. Tel: 574-251-3700. p. 719
Matthews, Diana, Ref Librn, Santa Fe College, 3000 NW 83rd St, Bldg Y, Gainesville, FL, 32606. Tel: 352-395-5408. p. 407
Matthews, Dusty, Adult Serv Supvr, Leesburg Public Library, 100 E Main St, Leesburg, FL, 34748. Tel: 352-728-9790. p. 418
Matthews, Emilee, Interim Head of Libr, University of Illinois Library at Urbana-Champaign, Architecture & Art Library, 208 Architecture Bldg, 608 E Lorado Taft Dr, Urbana, IL, 61801. Tel: 217-244-3960. p. 655
Matthews, Jacqueline, Br Mgr, Louisville Free Public Library, Portland, 3305 Northwestern Pkwy, Louisville, KY, 40212. Tel: 502-574-1744. p. 866
Matthews, Joe, Info Spec, University of New Mexico, 4000 University Dr, Los Alamos, NM, 87544. Tel: 505-662-0343. p. 1472
Matthews, Kelsey, Cat, Webmaster, Athol Public Library, 568 Main St, Athol, MA, 01331. Tel: 978-249-9515. p. 986
Matthews, Kim, City Librn, New Town City Library, 307 S Main St, New Town, ND, 58763. Tel: 701-627-4846. p. 1739
Matthews, Kimberly, Dir of Libr, Monroe County Public Library, 700 Fleming St, Key West, FL, 33040. Tel: 305-292-3595. p. 413
Matthews, Laura, Br Mgr, Greenwich Library, Cos Cob Branch, Five Sinawoy Rd, Cos Cob, CT, 06807-2701. Tel: 203-622-6883. p. 314
Matthews, Leah K, Exec Dir, Distance Education Accrediting Commission, 1101 17th St NW, Ste 808, Washington, DC, 20036. Tel: 202-234-5100, Ext 101. p. 363
Matthews, Letitia M, Libr Tech, United States Army, Public Health Command Library, 5158 Blackhawk Rd, BLDG E-5158, Aberdeen Proving Ground, MD, 21010-5403. Tel: 410-436-4236. p. 949
Matthews, Londa, Br Mgr, Audubon Regional Library, Jackson Branch, 3312 College St, Jackson, LA, 70748. Tel: 225-634-7408. p. 887
Matthews, Melinda, ILL Librn, University of Louisiana at Monroe Library, 700 University Ave, Monroe, LA, 71209-0720. Tel: 318-342-1063. p. 899
Matthews, Michael E, Head, Access Serv, Northwestern State University Libraries, 913 University Pkwy, Natchitoches, LA, 71497. Tel: 318-357-4466. p. 900
Matthews, Nicole, Coordr, Prog, Nicholas P Sims Library, 515 W Main, Waxahachie, TX, 75165-3235. Tel: 972-937-2671. p. 2255
Matthews, Robert, Instruction Coordr, Hudson Valley Community College, 80 Vandenburgh Ave, Troy, NY, 12180. Tel: 518-629-7392. p. 1652
Matthews, Rose, Human Res Dir, New Orleans Public Library, 219 Loyola Ave, New Orleans, LA, 70112-2044. Tel: 504-529-7323, 504-596-2570. p. 902
Matthews, Sarah, Ch Serv, Wadsworth Library, 24 Center St, Geneseo, NY, 14454. Tel: 585-243-0440. p. 1538
Matthews, Sarah, Head, Adult Serv, Bismarck Veterans Memorial Public Library, 515 N Fifth St, Bismarck, ND, 58501-4081. Tel: 701-355-1480. p. 1729
Matthews, Sasha, Libr Mgr, Virginia Beach Public Library, Meyera E Oberndorf Central Library, 4100 Virginia Beach Blvd, Virginia Beach, VA, 23452. Tel: 757-385-0150. p. 2351
Matthews, Sherry, Dir, Town of Lake Pleasant Public Library, 2864 State Hwy 8, Lake Pleasant, NY, 12108. Tel: 518-548-4411, p. 1561
Matthews, Susan, Libr Dir, Salida Regional Library, 405 E St, Salida, CO, 81201. Tel: 719-539-4826. p. 295
Matthews, Terry, Libr Tech, Nova Scotia Community College, Akerley Campus Library, 21 Woodlawn Rd, Dartmouth, NS, B2W 2R7, CANADA. Tel: 902-491-4968. p. 2619
Matthies, Brad, Assoc Dean, Libr Serv, Gonzaga University, 502 E Boone Ave, Spokane, WA, 99258-0095. Tel: 509-313-6533. p. 2383
Matthies, Margo, Dir, Walnut Public Library, 224 Antique City Dr, Walnut, IA, 51577. Tel: 712-784-3533. p. 788
Matthys Bennett, Emily, Dir, Oxford Public Library, 201 E Smith St, Oxford, IN, 47971. Tel: 765-385-2177. p. 712
Mattice, Hazel, Librn, La Moure School & Public Library, 105 Sixth Ave SE, La Moure, ND, 58458. Tel: 701-883-5396. p. 1737
Matticks, Rebecca, Dir, Res, Stuhr Museum, 3133 W Hwy 34, Grand Island, NE, 68801-7280. Tel: 308-381-5316. p. 1316
Matticks, Rebecca, Dir, Hastings Museum of Natural & Cultural History Library, 1330 N Burlington Ave, Hastings, NE, 68901. Tel: 402-461-2399, 402-461-4629. p. 1317

Mattimoe, Jean, Ref & Coll Develop Librn, University of Idaho Library, College of Law, 711 Rayburn St, Moscow, ID, 83844. Tel: 208-885-2162. p. 526

Mattingly, Donita, Youth Serv Mgr, Washington Carnegie Public Library, 300 W Main St, Washington, IN, 47501-2698. Tel: 812-254-4586. p. 725

Mattingly, Sue, Librn, Little Dixie Regional Libraries, Dulany Memorial, 101 N Main, Paris, MO, 65275-1398. Tel: 660-327-4707. p. 1262

Mattingly, Virginia, Head, Pub Serv Div/Librn, New Mexico Highlands University, 802 National Ave, Las Vegas, NM, 87701. Tel: 505-454-3237. p. 1471

Mattis, George, Coordr, Libr Serv, Wytheville Community College Library, 1000 E Main St, Wytheville, VA, 24382. Tel: 276-223-4744. p. 2355

Mattix, Carine, Head, Libr Syst, Tech Serv, Regent University Library, 1000 Regent University Dr, Virginia Beach, VA, 23464-5037. Tel: 757-352-4824. p. 2349

Mattix, Carine, Head, Tech Serv, Regent University, 1000 Regent University Dr, Virginia Beach, VA, 23464. Tel: 757-352-4824. p. 2349

Mattix, Jena, Br Mgr, Indianapolis Public Library, Glendale, Glendale Town Ctr, 6101 N Keystone Ave, Indianapolis, IN, 46220. Tel: 317-275-4410. p. 695

Mattke, Ryan, Head of Libr, Maps Librn, University of Minnesota Libraries-Twin Cities, John R Borchert Map Library, S-76 Wilson Library, 309 19th Ave S, Minneapolis, MN, 55455. Tel: 612-624-4549. p. 1185

Mattmann, Carla, Libr Tech, Gateway Technical College, Academic Bldg, Rm A103, 3520 30th Ave, Kenosha, WI, 53144-1690. Tel: 262-564-2786. p. 2444

Mattox, Gayle, Librn, Sargent Township Library, 506 Main St, Sargent, NE, 68874. Tel: 308-527-4241. p. 1334

Mattox, Stephanie, Cat & Coll Librn, San Juan Island Library, 1010 Guard St, Friday Harbor, WA, 98250-9612. Tel: 360-378-2798. p. 2364

Mattsen, Rebecca A, Head, Fac Serv, Pennsylvania State University - Dickinson School of Law, 214 Lewis Katz Bldg, University Park, PA, 16802. Tel: 814-867-2239. p. 2015

Mattson, Bonnie, Dir, Lisbon Public Library, 409 Forest St, Lisbon, ND, 58054. Tel: 701-683-5174. p. 1737

Mattson, Ingrid, Libr Dir, Orcas Island Library District, 500 Rose St, Eastsound, WA, 98245. Tel: 360-376-4985. p. 2363

Mattson, Rick, Br Mgr, Public Library of Cincinnati & Hamilton County, Elmwood Place, 6120 Vine St, Cincinnati, OH, 45216. Tel: 513-369-4452. p. 1762

Mattson, Stuart, Libr Coord, Yavapai County Free Library District, Mayer Public Library, 10004 Wicks Ave, Mayer, AZ, 86333. Tel: 928-632-7370. p. 75

Matty, Robin, Dir, West Newton Public Library, 124 N Water St, West Newton, PA, 15089. Tel: 724-633-0798. p. 2021

Matucheski, Michele, Librn, Mercy Medical Center, 500 S Oakwood Rd, Oshkosh, WI, 54904. Tel: 920-223-0340. p. 2467

Matucheski, Michele, Med Librn, Fox River Valley Area Library Consortium, c/o Ascension Mercy Hospital Library, 500 S Oakwood Rd, Oshkosh, WI, 54901. Tel: 920-223-0340. p. 2777

Matulewicz, Carolynn, Dir, Peninsula Public Library, 280 Central Ave, Lawrence, NY, 11559. Tel: 516-239-3262, Ext 214. p. 1562

Matulis, Nick, Dir, Arvilla E Diver Memorial Library, 136 Main St, Schaghticoke, NY, 12154. Tel: 518-753-4344. p. 1637

Matura, Andrea, Librn, Collectors Club Library, 22 E 35th St, New York, NY, 10016-3806. Tel: 212-683-0559. p. 1582

Maturi, Donna G, Dir of Libr, Middlesex Community College, Federal Bldg, E Merrimack St, Lowell, MA, 01852. Tel: 978-656-3005. p. 1029

Matusiak, Krystyna, Assoc Prof, University of Denver, Morgridge College of Education, Katherine A Ruffatto Hall, 1999 E Evans Ave, Denver, CO, 80208. Tel: 303-871-6163. p. 2783

Matusinec, Jane, Circ Supvr, Muskego Public Library, S73 W16663 Janesville Rd, Muskego, WI, 53150. Tel: 262-971-2100. p. 2463

Matuszak, Mary E, Dir, Libr Serv, New York County District Attorney's Office Library, One Hogan Pl, New York, NY, 10013. Tel: 212-335-4292. p. 1593

Matuszewski, Michael, Asst Dir, Massapequa Public Library, Bar Harbour Bldg, 40 Harbor Lane, Massapequa Park, NY, 11762. Tel: 516-799-0770. p. 1569

Matute, Caryl, Actg Chief, Branch Library Officer, The New York Public Library - Astor, Lenox & Tilden Foundations, 476 Fifth Ave, (@ 42nd St), New York, NY, 10018. Tel: 917-229-9503. p. 1594

Matute, Caryl, Interim Chief Librn, New York Public Library - Astor, Lenox & Tilden Foundations, Mid-Manhattan Library, 476 Fifth Ave, (at 42nd St), New York, NY, 10016-0122. Tel: 212-340-0863. p. 1596

Matveyeva, Susan, Institutional Repository Librn, Wichita State University Libraries, 1845 Fairmount, Wichita, KS, 67260-0068. Tel: 316-978-5139. p. 844

Matyi, Angela, Archivist, Dudley Observatory Library, 15 Nott Terrace Heights, Schenectady, NY, 12308. Tel: 518-382-7890, Ext 239. p. 1637

Matz, Daniel, Dir, Clarksburg Town Library, 711 W Cross Rd, Clarksburg, MA, 01247. Tel: 413-664-6050. p. 1012

Matzel, Heather, Exec Dir, Fayetteville Free Library, 300 Orchard St, Fayetteville, NY, 13066-1386. Tel: 315-637-6374. p. 1533

Matzen, George, Dir, Webermeier Memorial Library, 617 Second St, Milford, NE, 68405. Tel: 402-761-2937. p. 1325

Maubourquette, Stacy, Resources & Licensing Mgr, Northeastern University Libraries, 360 Huntington Ave, Boston, MA, 02115. Tel: 617-373-4974. p. 998

Mauchley, Daniel, County Libr Dir, Duchesne Library, 130 S Center St, Duchesne, UT, 84021. Tel: 435-738-2800. p. 2262

Maudlin, Lori, Commun Libr Rep, Mohave County Library District, Golden Valley Community Library, 3417 N Verde Rd, Golden Valley, AZ, 86413-0671. Tel: 928-565-2989. p. 65

Mauer, Peg, Libr Dir, Tupper Lake Public Library, 41 Lake St, Tupper Lake, NY, 12986. Tel: 518-359-9421. p. 1653

Mauerhoff, Petra, Chief Exec Officer, Shortgrass Library System, 2375-Tenth Ave SW, Medicine Hat, AB, T1A 8G2, CANADA. Tel: 403-529-0550, Ext 101. p. 2548

Maugle, Nicole, Dir of Libr, Montgomery County Community College, 340 DeKalb Pike, Blue Bell, PA, 19422-0796. Tel: 215-641-6593. p. 1913

Mauldan, Sarah, Dir, Smith, Gambrell & Russell, Prominade II, 1230 Peachtree St NE, Ste 3100, Atlanta, GA, 30309. Tel: 404-815-3538. p. 466

Mauldin-Ware, Alicia, Curator of Archives, United States Military Academy Library, Jefferson Hall Library & Learning Ctr, 758 Cullum Rd, West Point, NY, 10996. Tel: 845-938-8301. p. 1663

Mauler, Ginger, Br Operations Mgr, Appomattox Regional Library System, 209 E Cawson St, Hopewell, VA, 23860. Tel: 804-458-6329, Ext 2014. p. 2326

Mauney, Tina, Br Mgr, Pelahatchie Public Library, 718 Second St, Pelahatchie, MS, 39145. Tel: 601-854-8764. p. 1229

Maupin, Rita, Dir, Calhoun County Public Library, 17731 NE Pear St, Blountstown, FL, 32424. Tel: 850-674-8773. p. 385

Maura, Tina, Supvr, Coll Develop, Mandel Public Library of West Palm Beach, 411 Clematis St, West Palm Beach, FL, 33401. Tel: 561-868-7765. p. 453

Maurel, Dominique, Assoc Prof, Universite de Montreal, 3150, rue Jean-Brillant, bur C-2004, Montreal, QC, H3T 1N8, CANADA. Tel: 514-343-6044. p. 2797

Maurer, Bud, Dir, Duval County Law Library, 501 W Adams St, Rm 2291, Jacksonville, FL, 32202. Tel: 904-255-1150. p. 411

Maurer, Margaret, Head, Cat, Kent State University Libraries, Risman Plaza, 1125 Risman Dr, Kent, OH, 44242. Tel: 330-672-1702. p. 1792

Maurer, Mary, Health Res Ctr Coordr, Northeastern Vermont Regional Hospital, 1315 Hospital Dr, Saint Johnsbury, VT, 05819. Tel: 802-748-7501. p. 2294

Maurer, Megan, Asst Dir, Scenic Regional Library, 251 Union Plaza Dr, Union, MO, 63084. Tel: 636-583-0652, Ext 102. p. 1283

Mauro, Clare, Ref Librn, Torys LLP Library, 79 Wellington St W, Ste 3000, Toronto, ON, M5K 1N2, CANADA. Tel: 416-945-7737. p. 2697

Maury, Julia, Actg Libr Dir, Chaleur Library Region, Monseigneur Robichaud Public Library, 855 Principale St, Local 3, Beresford, NB, E8K 1T3, CANADA. Tel: 506-542-2704. p. 2599

Maust, Kelly, Interim Campus Librarian, University Libraries, University of Memphis, 705 Lambuth Blvd, Jackson, TN, 38301. Tel: 731-425-7351. p. 2103

Mausteller, Bill, Ref Serv, Norwin Public Library, 100 Caruthers Ln, Irwin, PA, 15642. Tel: 724-863-4700. p. 1946

Maute, Yvonne, Ref & ILL Librn, New River Community College, 226 Martin Hall, 5255 College Dr, Dublin, VA, 24084. Tel: 540-674-3600, Ext 4331. p. 2315

Mautino, Sara, Archit Librn, Oklahoma State University Libraries, Athletic Ave, 216, Stillwater, OK, 74078. Tel: 405-744-6034. p. 1862

Mautino, Sara, Librn, Oklahoma State University Libraries, Cunningham Architecture Library, School of Architecture Bldg, Rm 160, Stillwater, OK, 74078. Tel: 405-744-6047. p. 1862

Mautino, Tiffany, Br Mgr, Manatee County Public Library System, Lakewood Ranch, 16410 Rangeland Pkwy, Lakewood Ranch, FL, 34211. Tel: 941-742-4500. p. 387

Mavian, Anne, Br Mgr, Charlotte Mecklenburg Library, Mint Hill Branch, 6840 Matthews-Mint Hill Rd, Mint Hill, NC, 28227. Tel: 704-416-5200. p. 1679

Mavity, Donna, Librn, Southern Regional Technical College Library Services, Cairo Campus, 1550 Hwy 84 W, Cairo, GA, 39828. Tel: 229-378-2906. p. 499

Maw, Mary, Mgr, Communications, Mgr, Community Dev, Caledon Public Library, 150 Queen St S, Bolton, ON, L7E 1E3, CANADA. Tel: 905-857-1400, Ext 228. p. 2631

Mawhinney, David, Univ Archivist, Mount Allison University Libraries & Archives, 49 York St, Sackville, NB, E4L 1C6, CANADA. Tel: 506-364-2563. p. 2604

Mawhinney, Suzanne, Dir, University of San Francisco, Zief Law Library, 2101 Fulton St, San Francisco, CA, 94117-1004. Tel: 415-422-6679. p. 230

Maxell, Alison, Dir, Public Servs & Outreach, Research & Innovation, Maine State Library, 242 State St, Augusta, ME, 04333. Tel: 207-287-5600. p. 914

Maxey, Cindy, Dir, Rose Hill Public Library, 306 N Rose Hill Rd, Rose Hill, KS, 67133. Tel: 316-776-3013. p. 833

Maxey, Cindy, Head, Adult Serv, Shaker Heights Public Library, 16500 Van Aken Blvd, Shaker Heights, OH, 44120. Tel: 216-991-2030. p. 1820

Maxey-Harris, Charlene, Assoc Dean, University of Nebraska-Lincoln, 318 Love Library, 13th & R Strs, Lincoln, NE, 68588. Tel: 402-472-2526. p. 1323

Maxfield-Ontko, Pamela, Librn, Holmes County Law Library, Courthouse, Ste 204, One E Jackson St, Millersburg, OH, 44654. Tel: 330-763-2956. p. 1803
Maxham, Judy, Ref Serv, Amherst County Public Library, 382 S Main St, Amherst, VA, 24521. Tel: 434-946-9488. p. 2304
Maxheimer, Thomas, Commun Libr Mgr, Queens Library, Ridgewood Community Library, 20-12 Madison St, Ridgewood, NY, 11385. Tel: 718-821-4770. p. 1555
Maxson, Adele, Campus Librn, Mohave Community College Library, Kingman Campus, 1971 Jagerson Ave, Kingman, AZ, 86401. Tel: 928-757-0802. p. 64
Maxson, Rachel, Liaison & Instruction Librn, John Brown University Library, 2000 W University, Siloam Springs, AR, 72761. Tel: 479-524-7202. p. 110
Maxted, Lawrence, Librn, Gannon University, 619 Sassafras St, Erie, PA, 16541. Tel: 814-871-7557. p. 1931
Maxwell, Alison, Dir, Kemmerer Library Harding Township, 19 Blue Mill Rd, New Vernon, NJ, 07976. Tel: 973-267-2665. p. 1426
Maxwell, Amber, Youth Serv Librn, Three Rivers Public Library District, 25207 W Channon Dr, Channahon, IL, 60410-5028. Tel: 815-467-6200, Ext 308. p. 552
Maxwell, Anita, Dir, Ketchikan Museums, Tongass Historical Museum Research Library, 629 Dock St, Ketchikan, AK, 99901. Tel: 907-225-5600. p. 48
Maxwell, Caitlan, Digital & Electronic Resources Librn, Shoreline Community College, 16101 Greenwood Ave N, Shoreline, WA, 98133-5696. Tel: 206-533-2548. p. 2383
Maxwell, Carla, Asst Mgr, Saint Louis County Library, Indian Trails Branch, 8400 Delport Dr, Saint Louis, MO, 63114-5904. Tel: 314-994-3300, Ext 3350. p. 1274
Maxwell, Carol, Librn, Public Utility Commission of Texas Library, 1701 N Congress, 7th Flr, Austin, TX, 78701. Tel: 512-936-7075. p. 2140
Maxwell, Connie, Mgr, Dallas Public Library, Preston Royal Branch, 5626 Royal Lane, Dallas, TX, 75229-5599. Tel: 214-670-7128. p. 2166
Maxwell, Cynthia, Libr Dir, Streator Public Library, 130 S Park St, Streator, IL, 61364. Tel: 815-672-2729. p. 652
Maxwell, Cynthia S, Libr Dir, Kewanee Public Library District, 102 S Tremont St, Kewanee, IL, 61443. Tel: 309-852-4505. p. 605
Maxwell, Jada, Asst Dir, Thayer Public Library, 798 Washington St, Braintree, MA, 02184. Tel: 781-848-0405. p. 1001
Maxwell, Judy R, Dir, Law Librn, Delaware County Law Library, 101 N Sandusky St, Delaware, OH, 43015. Tel: 749-833-2545. p. 1782
Maxwell, Lon, Br Mgr, Williamson County Public Library, Bethesda, 4905 Bethesda Rd, Thompson's Station, TN, 37179-9231. Tel: 615-790-1887. p. 2098
Maxwell, Nancy, AV, Per, Henrietta Public Library, 625 Calkins Rd, Rochester, NY, 14623. Tel: 585-359-7092. p. 1628
Maxwell, Nancy, Genealogy Librn II, Grapevine Public Library, 1201 Municipal Way, Grapevine, TX, 76051. Tel: 817-410-3429. p. 2186
Maxwell, Noel, Libr Dir, Alaska Bible College Library, 248 E Elmwood Ave, Palmer, AK, 99645. Tel: 907-745-3201. p. 49
Maxwell, Rebekah, Assoc Dir, Libr Operations, University of South Carolina, Law Library, 1525 Senate St, Columbia, SC, 29208. Tel: 803-777-5942. p. 2055
Maxymuk, John, Head, Pub Serv, Ref Serv, Rutgers University Libraries, Paul Robeson Library, 300 N Fourth St, Camden, NJ, 08102-1404. Tel: 856-225-2848, 856-225-6034. p. 1394
May, Allison, Br Mgr, Fort Branch-Johnson Township Public Library, Haubstadt Public Library, 101 W Gibson St, Haubstadt, IN, 47639. Tel: 812-768-6005. p. 683
May, Amy B, Dir, Elizabeth Garnsey Delavan Library, 8484 S Main St, Lodi, NY, 14860. Tel: 607-582-6218. p. 1565
May, Caleb, Dir, Libr Serv, Manhattan Christian College Library, 1415 Anderson Ave, Manhattan, KS, 66502-4081. Tel: 785-539-3571, Ext 113. p. 823
May, Charles, Ref Librn, Nashville State Technical Community College, 120 White Bridge Rd, Nashville, TN, 37209-4515. Tel: 615-353-3554. p. 2120
May, Chris, Dir, Mansfield-Richland County Public Library, 43 W Third St, Mansfield, OH, 44902-1295. Tel: 419-521-3100. p. 1798
May, Francine, Assoc Dean, Collections & Metadata, Mount Royal University Library, 4825 Mount Royal Gate SW, Calgary, AB, T3E 6K6, CANADA. Tel: 403-440-6128. p. 2528
May, George, Mgr, County of Los Angeles Public Library, La Verne Library, 3640 D St, La Verne, CA, 91750-3572. Tel: 909-596-1934. p. 136
May, Jackie, Cat/ILL Spec, Jefferson County Library District, 241 SE Seventh St, Madras, OR, 97741. Tel: 541-475-3351. p. 1885
May, Jenifer, Libr Dir, Secaucus Public Library, 1379 Paterson Plank Rd, Secaucus, NJ, 07094. Tel: 201-330-2084, Ext 4011. p. 1442
May, Joyce, Adult Prog & Serv, East Providence Public Library, 41 Grove Ave, East Providence, RI, 02914. Tel: 401-434-2453. p. 2032
May, Joyce, Dir, East Providence Public Library, 41 Grove Ave, East Providence, RI, 02914. Tel: 401-434-2453. p. 2032
May, Kari, Libr Dir, Jackson County Library Services, 205 S Central Ave, Medford, OR, 97501-2730. Tel: 541-774-8679. p. 1886
May, Linda, Exec Dir, Alexander Hamilton Memorial Free Library, 45 E Main St, Waynesboro, PA, 17268-1691. Tel: 717-762-3335. p. 2019
May, Mardell, Dir, Maquon Public Library District, 210 Main St, Maquon, IL, 61458. Tel: 309-875-3573. p. 613
May, Melissa, Sr Res Libr Mgr, National Recreation & Park Association, 22377 Belmont Ridge Rd, Ashburn, VA, 20148. Tel: 703-858-2151. p. 2306
May, Michelle, Dir, Oglala Lakota College, Three Mile Creek Rd, Kyle, SD, 57752. Tel: 605-455-6064. p. 2077
May, Patricia, Dir, Saint Joseph's Regional Medical Center, Xavier Bldg, 4th Flr, 703 Main St, Paterson, NJ, 07503. Tel: 973-754-3590. p. 1433
May, Sandra, Br Mgr, Augusta-Richmond County Public Library, Wallace Branch, 1237 Laney-Walker Blvd, Augusta, GA, 30901. Tel: 706-722-6275. p. 467
May, Sherri, Dir, Brownstown Public Library, 120 E Spring St, Brownstown, IN, 47220. Tel: 812-358-2853. p. 673
May, Yvette, Mgr, Baltimore County Public Library, Essex Branch, 1110 Eastern Blvd, Baltimore, MD, 21221. Tel: 410-887-0295. p. 979
Mayall, Courtney, Youth Serv, Chickasha Public Library, 527 W Iowa Ave, Chickasha, OK, 73018. Tel: 405-222-6075. p. 1844
Mayberry, Charles, Exec Dir, Panhandle Library Access Network, Five Miracle Strip Loop, Ste 8, Panama City Beach, FL, 32407-8410. Tel: 850-233-9051. p. 2763
Mayberry, Melissa, Head, Adult Serv, Morton Grove Public Library, 6140 Lincoln Ave, Morton Grove, IL, 60053-2989. Tel: 847-965-4220. p. 620
Mayberry, Rebecca, Adult Serv, Barry-Lawrence Regional Library, Pierce City Branch, 101 N Walnut St, Pierce City, MO, 65723. Tel: 417-476-5110. p. 1263
Maycumber, Morgan, Circ Supvr, The Master's Seminary Library, 13248 Roscoe Blvd, Sun Valley, CA, 91352. Tel: 818-909-5545. p. 251
Mayelian, Lara, Br Mgr, Sonoma County Library, Northwest Santa Rosa Library, 150 Coddingtown Ctr, Santa Rosa, CA, 95401. Tel: 707-546-2265. p. 204
Mayer, Ashley, Mrs, Supvry Librn, United States Air Force, 2518 Central Ave, Bldg 3310, Eielson AFB, AK, 99702. Tel: 907-377-3174. p. 45
Mayer, Jen, Head, Res Serv, University of Northern Colorado Libraries, 1400 22nd Ave, Greeley, CO, 80631. Tel: 970-351-1531. p. 285
Mayer, Jennifer, Br Mgr, Saint Tammany Parish Library, Mandeville Branch, 844 Girod St, Mandeville, LA, 70448. Tel: 985-626-4293. p. 888
Mayer, Jordan, Dir, Herbert F Tyler Memorial Library, 821 N Shawnee, Dewey, OK, 74029. Tel: 918-534-2106. p. 1845
Mayer, Josephine, Br Mgr, Monmouth County Library, Allentown Branch, 16 S Main St, Allentown, NJ, 08501. Tel: 609-259-7565. p. 1415
Mayer, Melissa, Circ Supvr, Lake Wales Public Library, 290 Cypress Garden Lane, Lake Wales, FL, 33853. Tel: 863-678-4004. p. 416
Mayer, Reeca, Br Dir, Alma Public Library, 624 Fayetteville Ave, Alma, AR, 72921. Tel: 479-632-4140. p. 89
Mayer, Rita, Mgr, Miami-Dade Public Library System, Miami Springs Branch, 401 Westward Dr, Miami Springs, FL, 33166. Tel: 305-805-3811. p. 423
Mayer, Tess, Dir, Libr Serv, Berkeley Public Library, 2090 Kittredge St, Berkeley, CA, 94704-1427. Tel: 510-981-6100. p. 121
Mayer, Tina, Libr Dir, Mount Arlington Public Library, 333 Howard Blvd, Mount Arlington, NJ, 07856-1196. Tel: 973-398-1516. p. 1422
Mayer, Will, Distance Educ, E-Resources Librn, Lee College Library, 150 Lee Dr, Baytown, TX, 77520. Tel: 281-425-4512. p. 2145
Mayers-Twist, Emily, Research & Technical Servs Librn, Nova Southeastern University Libraries, Panza Maurer Law Library, Shepard Broad College of Law, Leo Goodwin Sr Bldg, 3305 College Ave, Davie, FL, 33314. Tel: 954-262-6223. p. 402
Mayes, Elisabeth, Ch, Oxford Public Library, 110 E Sixth St, Oxford, AL, 36203. Tel: 256-831-1750. p. 32
Mayes, Michele Coleman, VPres/Gen Counsel, The New York Public Library - Astor, Lenox & Tilden Foundations, 476 Fifth Ave, (@ 42nd St), New York, NY, 10018. Tel: 212-642-0115. p. 1594
Mayfield, Lacy, Librn, Petersburg Public Library, 1614 Main St, Petersburg, TX, 79250. Tel: 806-667-3657. p. 2226
Mayfield, Margaret, Head Librn, Hartnell College, 411 Central Ave, Salinas, CA, 93901. Tel: 831-755-6700, 831-755-6872. p. 2782
Mayfield Mullen, Jana, Info Literacy Librn, Libr Dir, Westmont College, 955 La Paz Rd, Santa Barbara, CA, 93108. Tel: 805-565-6147. p. 241
Mayfield, Patricia Lynn, Jacksonville Campus Libr Dir, Keiser University Library System, 1500 NW 49th St, Fort Lauderdale, FL, 33309. Tel: 954-351-4035. p. 401
Mayfield, Sandra, Head, Circ, Warren County-Vicksburg Public Library, 700 Veto St, Vicksburg, MS, 39180-3595. Tel: 601-636-6411. p. 1235
Mayginnes, Teresa, Tech Serv Librn, Butler Community College Library & Archives, Library 600 Bldg, 901 S Haverhill Rd, El Dorado, KS, 67042-3280. Tel: 316-323-6842. p. 805
Mayhew, Gwen, Head, Coll Access, Centre Canadien d'Architecture/Canadian Centre for Architecture, 1920 rue Baile, Montreal, QC, H3H 2S6, CANADA. Tel: 514-939-7000. p. 2721
Mayhew, Heath, Pub Serv Librn, Spec Coll Librn, Columbia University, Arthur W Diamond Law Library, 435 W 116th St, New York, NY, 10027. Tel: 212-854-3922. p. 1583
Mayle, Robin, Circ, Taylor County Public Library, 200 Beech St, Grafton, WV, 26354. Tel: 304-265-6121. p. 2403
Maymi-Sugrañes, Héctor, Dr, Dean of Libr, Western Illinois University, One University Circle, Macomb, IL, 61455. Tel: 309-298-2762. p. 612

Maynard, Adele, Asst Librn, Central City Public Library, 1604 15th Ave, Central City, NE, 68826. Tel: 308-946-2512. p. 1309
Maynard, Aubrey, Librn, Allen Oakwood Correctional Institution Library, 2338 N West St, Lima, OH, 45801. Tel: 419-224-8000. p. 1795
Maynard, Cara, Asst Librn, Mount Airy Public Library, 145 Rockford St, Mount Airy, NC, 27030-4759. Tel: 336-789-5108. p. 1705
Maynard, Clara, Br Mgr, Harris County Public Library, Barbara Bush Branch at Cypress Creek, 6817 Cypresswood Dr, Spring, TX, 77379. Tel: 832-927-7800. p. 2192
Maynard, Daniel, Bus Librn, Campbell University, 113 Main St, Buies Creek, NC, 27506. Tel: 910-893-7930. p. 1676
Maynard, Debbie, Libr Dir, Pequannock Township Public Library, 477 Newark Pompton Tpk, Pompton Plains, NJ, 07444. Tel: 973-835-7460. p. 1436
Maynard, Elizabeth, Librn, RCS Community Library, 95 Main St, Ravena, NY, 12143. Tel: 518-756-2053. p. 1625
Maynard, Jeremy, Pub Serv Librn, Hardin-Simmons University, 2200 Hickory St, Abilene, TX, 79698. Tel: 325-670-1236. p. 2132
Maynard, Jillian, Ref & Instruction Librn, Central Connecticut State University, 1615 Stanley St, New Britain, CT, 06050. Tel: 860-832-2068. p. 324
Maynard, Jocelyn, Managing Librn, Brooklyn Public Library, Stone Avenue, 581 Mother Gaston Blvd, Brooklyn, NY, 11212. Tel: 718-485-8347. p. 1504
Maynard, Kimberly, Dir, Southern West Virginia Community & Technical College, Dempsey Branch Rd, Mount Gay, WV, 25637. Tel: 304-896-7345. p. 2410
Maynard, Kimberly, Dir of Libr, Southern West Virginia Community & Technical College, 1601 Armory Dr, Williamson, WV, 25661. Tel: 304-236-7616. p. 2418
Maynard, Krista, Libr Adminr, Jolys Regional Library, 505 Herbert Ave N, Saint Pierre Jolys, MB, R0A 1V0, CANADA. Tel: 204-433-7729. p. 2590
Maynard, Larry, Supvr, N Region Libr, Aurora Public Library, Martin Luther King Jr Library, 9898 E Colfax Ave, Aurora, CO, 80010. Tel: 303-739-1940. p. 265
Maynard, Quinn, Asst Dir, Shelby Area District Library, 189 Maple St, Shelby, MI, 49455-1134. Tel: 231-861-4565. p. 1150
Maynard, Shannon, Admin & Outreach Coordr, Hardin-Simmons University, 2200 Hickory St, Abilene, TX, 79698. Tel: 325-670-1236. p. 2132
Maynes, Warren, Ser Librn, Alberta Legislature Library, 216 Legislature Bldg, 10800-97 Ave NW, Edmonton, AB, T5K 2B6, CANADA. Tel: 780-427-0201. p. 2535
Maynor, Cecilie, Dir, Red River Regional Library, 1753A Alpine Dr, Clarksville, TN, 37040-6729. Tel: 931-645-9531. p. 2092
Maynor, Cecilie, Regional Libr Dir, Tennessee State Library & Archives, 403 Seventh Ave N, Nashville, TN, 37243-0312. Tel: 615-741-2764. p. 2121
Mayo, Alexa, Assoc Dir, Serv, Pub Serv, University of Maryland, Baltimore, Health Sciences & Human Services Library, 601 W Lombard St, Baltimore, MD, 21201. Tel: 410-706-1316. p. 957
Mayo, Douglas, Assoc Librn, Colonial Williamsburg Foundation, 313 First St, Williamsburg, VA, 23185-4306. Tel: 757-565-8521. p. 2353
Mayo, Julia, Librn, Marjorie Mews Public Library, 12 Highland Dr, St. John's, NL, A1A 3C4, CANADA. Tel: 709-737-3020. p. 2611
Mayo, Justin, Dir, Washington County Public Library, 615 Fifth St, Marietta, OH, 45750-1973. Tel: 740-373-1057. p. 1799
Mayo, Kim, Lecturer, North Carolina Central University, 1801 Fayetteville St, Durham, NC, 27707. Tel: 919-530-6485. p. 2790
Mayo, Lynn, Res & Electronic Resources Librn, Hamilton College, 198 College Hill Rd, Clinton, NY, 13323. Tel: 315-859-4746. p. 1519
Mayo, Martha, Dir, Spec Coll, University of Massachusetts Lowell Library, Center for Lowell History, Patrick J Mogan Cultural Ctr, 40 French St, Lowell, MA, 01852. Tel: 978-934-4998. p. 1030
Mayo, Renotta, Asst Dir, Henderson County, 121 S Prairieville, Athens, TX, 75751. Tel: 903-677-7295. p. 2137
Mayotte, Jenna, Libr Dir, Falmouth Memorial Library, Five Lunt Rd, Falmouth, ME, 04105. Tel: 207-781-2351. p. 924
Maypother-Marini, Deborah, Head, Youth Serv, Bigelow Free Public Library, 54 Walnut St, Clinton, MA, 01510. Tel: 978-365-4160. p. 1012
Mays, Alan, Libr Operations Supvr, Pennsylvania State University-Harrisburg Library, 351 Olmsted Dr, Middletown, PA, 17057-4850. Tel: 717-948-6070. p. 1963
Mays, Brenda, Ser, Mercer University, Jack Tarver Library, 1300 Edgewood Ave, Macon, GA, 31207. Tel: 478-301-2966. p. 486
Mays, Lauren, Dir, Flanagan Public Library District, 124 S Main St, Flanagan, IL, 61740. Tel: 815-796-2212. p. 588
Mays, Regina, Assessment Librn, University of Tennessee, Knoxville, 1015 Volunteer Blvd, Knoxville, TN, 37996-1000. Tel: 865-974-4351. p. 2107
Mays, Tammy, Br Mgr, Milwaukee Public Library, Center Street, 2727 W Fond du Lac Ave, Milwaukee, WI, 53210. p. 2460
Mayton, Matthew, Archivist, Arkansas State University, 322 University Loop Circle, State University, AR, 72401. Tel: 870-972-3077. p. 111
Mayville, Gretchen, Head, Circ, Springfield Township Library, 12000 Davisburg Rd, Davisburg, MI, 48350. Tel: 248-846-6550. p. 1095
Mazak, Thom, Prog & Youth Coordr, Lady Lake Public Library, 225 W Guava St, Lady Lake, FL, 32159. Tel: 352-753-2957. p. 414
Mazanec, Mary B, Dir, Res Serv, Library of Congress, James Madison Memorial Bldg, 101 Independence Ave SE, Washington, DC, 20540. Tel: 202-707-5000. p. 370
Mazel, Norah, Dir, Res Serv, Instrul Serv, University of Colorado Colorado Springs, 1420 Austin Bluffs Pkwy, Colorado Springs, CO, 80918. Tel: 719-255-3175. p. 272
Mazelin, Janelle, Exec Dir, Association of Christian Librarians, PO Box 4, Cedarville, OH, 45314. Tel: 937-766-2255. p. 2772
Mazenc, Janine, Br Librn, Southeast Regional Library, Radville Branch, 420 Floren St, Radville, SK, S0C 2G0, CANADA. Tel: 306-869-2742. p. 2754
Maziar, Lucy, Libr Dir, United States Coast Guard Academy Library, 35 Mohegan Ave, New London, CT, 06320. Tel: 860-444-8510. p. 329
Maziarz, Jean, Libr Dir, Richard Salter Storrs Library, 693 Longmeadow St, Longmeadow, MA, 01106. Tel: 413-565-4181. p. 1029
Mazour, Ruth, Ref Serv, Logan County Public Library, 225 Armory Dr, Russellville, KY, 42276. Tel: 270-726-6129. p. 874
Mazovec, Donna, Head, Ref & Adult Serv, Huntington Public Library, 338 Main St, Huntington, NY, 11743. Tel: 631-427-5165, Ext 250. p. 1549
Mazower, David, Bibliographer, National Yiddish Book Center, Harry & Jeanette Weinberg Bldg, 1021 West St, Amherst, MA, 01002-3375. Tel: 413-256-4900. p. 985
Mazur, Lynn, Youth Serv, Somerset County Library System of New Jersey, Watchung Public, 12 Stirling Rd, Watchung, NJ, 07069. Tel: 908-458-8455. p. 1393
Mazur, Sarah, Ref Librn, Bossier Parish Community College Library, 6220 E Texas St, Bldg A, Bossier City, LA, 71111. Tel: 318-678-6077. p. 885
Mazur, Sarah, Dir, Resource Mgmt & Discovery, Louisiana State University, One University Pl, Shreveport, LA, 71115. Tel: 318-797-5070. p. 907
Mazur, Stacy, Dir, Prince Memorial Library, 266 Main St, Cumberland, ME, 04021-9754. Tel: 207-829-2215. p. 922
Mazure, Emily, Librn, Mountain Area Health Education Center, 121 Hendersonville Rd, Asheville, NC, 28803. Tel: 828-257-4441. p. 1672
Mazure, Sharon, Interim Dir, Ref & ILL Librn, Fairmont State University, 1201 Locust Ave, Fairmont, WV, 26554. Tel: 304-367-4622. p. 2402
Mazure, Vicki, Dir, Harbor Beach Area District Library, 105 N Huron Ave, Harbor Beach, MI, 48441. Tel: 989-479-3417. p. 1113
Mazza, Thomas, Librn, Onondaga Community College, 4585 W Seneca Tpk, Syracuse, NY, 13215-4585. Tel: 315-498-2708. p. 1649
Mazzariello, Kerra, Libr Assoc, Hilbert College, 5200 S Park Ave, Hamburg, NY, 14075. Tel: 716-926-8913. p. 1543
Mazzio, Louis J, Chief Info Officer, Post & Schell, PC, Four Penn Ctr, 1600 JFK Blvd, Philadelphia, PA, 19103-2808. Tel: 215-587-1498. p. 1984
Mazzoli, Casey, Pub Serv Librn, Otterbein University, 138 W Main St, Westerville, OH, 43081. Tel: 614-823-1366. p. 1830
Mazzone, Lois, Br Mgr, Warwick Public Library, Apponaug, 3267 Post Rd, Warwick, RI, 02886. Tel: 401-739-6411. p. 2043
Mazzoni, Emily, Teen Serv Librn, Monroe Township Public Library, Four Municipal Plaza, Monroe Township, NJ, 08831-1900. Tel: 732-521-5000. p. 1419
Mbugua, Wambui, Dr, Ref Librn, Borough of Manhattan Community College Library, 199 Chambers St, S410, New York, NY, 10007. Tel: 212-220-1447. p. 1580
Mbyirukira, Stella, ILL, Tech Serv, Oakwood University, 7000 Adventist Blvd NW, Huntsville, AL, 35896. Tel: 256-726-8389. p. 22
McAdam, Stephanie, Dir, Cedar Vale Memorial Library, 608 Cedar St, Cedar Vale, KS, 67024. Tel: 620-758-2598. p. 800
McAdams, A'ndrea, Dir, Librn, City of Sundown Library, 201 E Fifth St, Sundown, TX, 79372. Tel: 806-214-3099. p. 2246
McAdams, Candy, Libr Dir, Ned R McWherter Weakley County Library, 341 Linden St, Dresden, TN, 38225-1400. Tel: 731-364-2678. p. 2097
McAdams, Ella, Dir, Snowflake-Taylor Public Library, 418 S Fourth W, Snowflake, AZ, 85937. Tel: 928-536-7103, Ext 245. p. 78
McAdams, Lauren Wade, Ref Librn, Baton Rouge Community College, 201 Community College Dr, Baton Rouge, LA, 70806. Tel: 225-216-8552. p. 882
McAdams, Natalie, Libr Dir, Temple Public Library, 100 W Adams Ave, Temple, TX, 76501-7641. Tel: 254-298-5555. p. 2247
McAdoo, Monty, Dr, Student Success & Assessment Librn, Pennsylvania Western University - Edinboro, 200 Tartan Dr, Edinboro, PA, 16444. Tel: 814-732-2273. p. 1929
McAfee, Travis, Asst Dir, Way Public Library, 101 E Indiana Ave, Perrysburg, OH, 43551. Tel: 419-874-3135, Ext 108. p. 1815
McAleese, James, Senior Adjunct Faculty Librn, Adelphi University, 179 Livingston St, Brooklyn, NY, 11201. Tel: 212-965-8365. p. 1500
McAlister, George, Libr Dir, North Idaho College Library, 1000 W Garden Ave, Coeur d'Alene, ID, 83814-2199. Tel: 208-769-3393. p. 519
McAlister, Jenna, ILL Librn, Canaan Town Library, 1173 US Rte 4, Canaan, NH, 03741. Tel: 603-523-9650. p. 1356
McAlister, Leah, Access Serv Mgr, Southeast Missouri State University, 929 Normal Ave, Cape Girardeau, MO, 63701. Tel: 573-986-7308. p. 1240

McAlister, Lori, Br Mgr, Montgomery County Public Library, Camargo Branch, 4406 Camargo Rd, Mount Sterling, KY, 40353. Tel: 859-499-4244. p. 870

McAlister, Mia, Asst Mgr, Dillon County Library, 600 E Main St, Dillon, SC, 29536. Tel: 843-774-0330. p. 2058

McAlister, Rick, Circ Coordr, Saint John Fisher University, 3690 East Ave, Rochester, NY, 14618-3599. Tel: 585-385-8165. p. 1630

McAllen, Ann, Adult Prog Coordr, Whatcom County Library System, 5205 Northwest Dr, Bellingham, WA, 98226. Tel: 360-305-3600. p. 2359

McAllister, Janet, Dir, Rochester Public Library District, One Community Dr, Rochester, IL, 62563. Tel: 217-498-8454. p. 640

McAllister, Lara, Ad, Halifax Public Libraries, Woodlawn Public, 31 Eisener Blvd, Dartmouth, NS, B2W 0J1, CANADA. Tel: 902-490-2636. p. 2618

McAllister, Nadine, Library Associate Specialist, Brown University, Library Collections Annex, 10 Park Lane, Providence, RI, 02907-3124. Tel: 401-863-5722. p. 2037

McAllister, Sandra, Br Mgr, Southeast Arkansas Regional Library, Lake Village Branch, 108 Church St, Lake Village, AR, 71653. Tel: 870-265-6116. p. 104

McAllister, Tim, Res Spec, Kirkland & Ellis LLP Library, 655 15th St NW, Ste 1200, Washington, DC, 20005-5793. Tel: 202-879-5113. p. 370

McAlorum, Andrew, Head, Digital Initiatives, University of Waterloo Library, 200 University Ave W, Waterloo, ON, N2L 3G1, CANADA. Tel: 519-888-4567, Ext 39127. p. 2702

McAlpine, Jo, Librn, Palliser Regional Library, Craik Branch, 611 First Ave, Craik, SK, S0G 0V0, CANADA. Tel: 306-734-2388. p. 2742

McAlpine, Michael, Librn, Res Officer, Siskind, Cromarty, Ivey & Dowler, 680 Waterloo St, London, ON, N6A 3V8, CANADA. Tel: 519-672-2121. p. 2655

McAmmond, Sharon, Pub Serv Coordr, Leduc Public Library, Two Alexandra Park, Leduc, AB, T9E 4C4, CANADA. Tel: 780-986-2637. p. 2546

McAnally, Patti, Dir, H Leslie Perry Memorial Library, 205 Breckenridge St, Henderson, NC, 27536. Tel: 252-438-3316. p. 1695

McAnaney, Dana, ILL, Cape May County Library, 30 Mechanic St, Cape May Court House, NJ, 08210. Tel: 609-463-6350. p. 1394

McAnany, Annmarie, Libr Dir, Sloatsburg Public Library, One Liberty Rock Rd, Sloatsburg, NY, 10974-2392. Tel: 845-753-2001. p. 1641

McAndie, Joy, Circ, Eastern Oregon University, One University Blvd, La Grande, OR, 97850. Tel: 541-962-3671. p. 1884

McAndrew, Phillip, Br Mgr, Williamson County Public Library, Fairview Branch, 2240 Fairview Blvd, Fairview, TN, 37062. Tel: 615-224-6087. p. 2098

McAndrew, Tina, Dir, Randall Library, 19 Crescent St, Stow, MA, 01775. Tel: 978-897-8572. p. 1058

McAndrew-Taylor, Marie, Head, Ref, Head, YA, Stevens Memorial Library, 345 Main St, North Andover, MA, 01845. Tel: 978-688-9505. p. 1040

McAndrews, Jenna, Libr Dir, Deptford Free Public Library, 670 Ward Dr, Deptford, NJ, 08096. Tel: 856-848-9149. p. 1399

McAnneny, Eileen, Pres, Massachusetts Taxpayers Foundation Library, 333 Washington St, Ste 853, Boston, MA, 02108. Tel: 617-720-1000. p. 997

McAnulty, Kaitlyn, Br Mgr, Dothan Houston County Library System, Westgate Branch, 535 Recreation Rd, Dothan, AL, 36303. Tel: 334-699-2950. p. 15

McAphee, Sylvia, Ser, University of Alabama at Birmingham, Lister Hill Library of the Health Sciences, 1700 University Blvd, Birmingham, AL, 35294-0013. Tel: 205-934-5460. p. 9

McArdell, Carol, Asst Dir, Circ & Tech Serv Librn, Pitkin County Library, 120 N Mill St, Aspen, CO, 81611. Tel: 970-429-1900. p. 264

McArdle, Janice, Youth Serv Librn, Granby Free Public Library, 297 E State St, Granby, MA, 01033. Tel: 413-467-3320. p. 1021

McArdle, Karen, Libr Asst, University of Wisconsin-Green Bay, Sheboygan Campus Library, One University Dr, Sheboygan, WI, 53081-4789. Tel: 920-459-6625. p. 2439

McArdle Rojo, Christine, Libr Dir, La Crosse County Library, Administration Ctr, 121 W Legion St, Holmen, WI, 54636. Tel: 608-526-4198. p. 2441

McArthur, Erin, Distance Educ Librn, University of Wisconsin Oshkosh, 801 Elmwood Ave, Oshkosh, WI, 54901. Tel: 920-424-1361. p. 2467

McArthur, Michael, Asst Dir, Access & Collection, Foreign & Intl Law Ref Librn, Duke University Libraries, J Michael Goodson Law Library, 210 Science Dr, Durham, NC, 27708. Tel: 919-613-7118. p. 1684

McArthur, Rebecca, Lead Librn, Greater Sudbury Public Library, New Sudbury Public Library, 1346 Lasalle Blvd, Sudbury, ON, P3A 1Z6, CANADA. Tel: 705-688-3952. p. 2683

McArthur, Rebecca, Lead Librn, Greater Sudbury Public Library, South End Public Library, 1991 Regent St, Sudbury, ON, P3E 5V3, CANADA. Tel: 705-688-3950. p. 2683

McArthur, Riley, Teen Librn/Ref, Wyckoff Public Library, 200 Woodland Ave, Wyckoff, NJ, 07481. Tel: 201-891-4866. p. 1456

McAskill, Bill, Librn, George Brown College of Applied Arts & Technology, Bldg C, 3rd Flr, Rm C330, 160 Kendal Ave, Toronto, ON, M5R 1M3, CANADA. Tel: 416-415-5000, Ext 3702. p. 2689

McAtee, Brian P, Librn, Southeastern Community College Library, 1500 W Agency Rd, Rm 171, West Burlington, IA, 52655. Tel: 319-752-2731, Ext 5091. p. 790

McAteer, Mary Beth, Lead Librn, Virginia Mason Medical Center Library, Central Pavillion, 1100 Ninth Ave, H11-JLC, Seattle, WA, 98101. Tel: 206-223-6733. p. 2377

McAuliffe, Carol, Head, Map & Imagery Libr, University of Florida Libraries, 1545 W University Ave, Gainesville, FL, 32611-7000. Tel: 352-273-2825. p. 407

McAuliffe, Carol, Interim Chair, Special & Area Studies Colls, University of Florida Libraries, 1545 W University Ave, Gainesville, FL, 32611-7000. Tel: 352-273-2828. p. 407

McAuliffe, Lois, Ch Serv, Ashland Public Library, 66 Front St, Ashland, MA, 01721. Tel: 508-881-0134. p. 986

McAvoy, Erica, Dir, Lexington Historical Society, 1332 Massachusetts Ave, Lexington, MA, 02420-3809. Tel: 781-862-1703. p. 1028

McAvoy, Joleen, Librn, Sherman Public Library, Nine Church St, Sherman, ME, 04776. Tel: 207-365-4882. p. 940

McBaer, Neena, Ch Serv, Pawling Free Library, 11 Broad St, Pawling, NY, 12564. Tel: 845-855-3444. p. 1616

McBain, Lea, Dir, Newbury Public Library, 933 Rte 103, Newbury, NH, 03255. Tel: 603-763-5803. p. 1376

McBeath, Suzanne, Coop Librn, Metro Vancouver Library, 4515 Central Blvd, Mailroom 11th Flr, Burnaby, BC, V5H 0C6, CANADA. Tel: 604-432-6335. p. 2563

McBee, Dana, Asst Dir, Support Serv, Austin Public Library, 710 W Cesar Chavez St, Austin, TX, 78701. Tel: 512-974-7400. p. 2138

McBee, Joe David, Ser Librn, University of the South, 178 Georgia Ave, Sewanee, TN, 37383-1000. Tel: 931-598-1574. p. 2126

McBeth, Becky, Dir, Lyons Public Library, 201 W Main St, Lyons, KS, 67554. Tel: 620-257-2961. p. 822

McBeth, Glen, Instrul Tech Librn, Washburn University, School of Law Library, 1700 SW College Ave, Topeka, KS, 66621. Tel: 785-670-1778. p. 840

McBeth, Leverne, Librn, Spartanburg County Public Libraries, Middle Tyger Library, 170 Groce Rd, Lyman, SC, 29365. Tel: 864-439-4759. p. 2070

McBrayer, Laura Wiegand, Assoc Dean of Libr, University of North Carolina Wilmington Library, 601 S College Rd, Wilmington, NC, 28403. Tel: 910-962-4232. p. 1723

McBride, Jennifer, Regional Mgr, Kaiser Permanente Northwest Regional Libraries, Kaiser Sunnyside Medical Ctr, 10180 SE Sunnyside Rd - Health Sciences Library, Clackamas, OR, 97015. Tel: 503-571-4293. p. 1875

McBride, Jernine, Assoc Dir, Develop, University of California, Riverside, 900 University Ave, Riverside, CA, 92521. Tel: 951-827-3220. p. 203

McBride, Kathleen, Libr Operations Mgr, Crown College, 8700 College View Dr, Saint Bonifacius, MN, 55375-9002. Tel: 952-446-4241. p. 1195

McBride, Kathryn, Asst Dir, Obion River Regional Library, 542 N Lindell St, Martin, TN, 38237. Tel: 731-364-4597. p. 2110

McBride, Kelly, Dir, Blue Earth County Library System, 100 E Main St, Mankato, MN, 56001. Tel: 507-304-4001. p. 1181

McBride, Kelly, Dir, Blue Earth County Library System, Lake Crystal Public Library, 100 Robinson St, Lake Crystal, MN, 56055. Tel: 507-726-2726. p. 1181

McBride, Kelly, Dir, Blue Earth County Library System, Mapleton Branch, 104 First Ave, Mapleton, MN, 56065. Tel: 507-524-3513. p. 1181

McBride, Malinda, Libr Coord, State Fair Community College, 3201 W 16th St, Sedalia, MO, 65301. Tel: 660-530-5842. p. 1279

McBride, Mark, Dir, Monroe Community College, LeRoy V Good Library, 1000 E Henrietta Rd, Rochester, NY, 14692. Tel: 585-292-2321, p. 1629

McBride, Noreen, Asst Dir, Youth Serv Librn, East Palestine Memorial Public Library, 309 N Market St, East Palestine, OH, 44413. Tel: 330-426-3778. p. 1783

McBride, Susan, Supv Librn, Pierce County Library System, DuPont Branch, 1540 Wilmington Dr, DuPont, WA, 98327. Tel: 253-548-3326. p. 2386

McBride, Thomas D, Fac Mgr, Lewis Baach Kaufmann Middlemiss PLLC Library, 1899 Pennsylvania Ave NW, Ste 600, Washington, DC, 20006. Tel: 202-833-8900. p. 370

McBrien, Angela, Colls Mgr, Andover Center for History & Culture Library, 97 Main St, Andover, MA, 01810. Tel: 978-475-2236. p. 985

McBrien, Johanna, Dir, Dedham Historical Society, 612 High St, Dedham, MA, 02026. Tel: 781-326-1385. p. 1014

McBryant, Sarah, ILL Coordr, Tech Serv, God's Bible School & College Library, 507 Ringgold St, Cincinnati, OH, 45202. Tel: 513-721-7944, Ext 5113. p. 1760

McBurney, Marlene, Librn, Palliser Regional Library, Coronach Branch, 111A Centre St, Coronach, SK, S0H 0Z0, CANADA. Tel: 306-267-3260. p. 2742

McBurnie, Ann, Mgr, Libr Res, Kwantlen Polytechnic University Library, 12666 72nd Ave, Surrey, BC, V3W 2M8, CANADA. Tel: 604-599-3415. p. 2576

McCabe, Emily, Teen Serv, Edwin A Bemis Public Library, 6014 S Datura St, Littleton, CO, 80120-2636. Tel: 303-795-3961. p. 290

McCabe, Kevin, Br Mgr, Atlantic County Library System, Somers Point Branch, 801 Shore Rd, Somers Point, NJ, 08244. Tel: 609-927-7113. p. 1417

McCafferty, Bridgit, Dir of the Univ Libr, Texas A&M University Central Texas, 1001 Leadership Pl, Killeen, TX, 76549. Tel: 254-519-5798, p. 2206

McCaffery, Damien, Electronic Res Librn, Thomas Jefferson University-East Falls, 4201 Henry Ave, Philadelphia, PA, 19144-5497. Tel: 215-951-2674. p. 1987
McCaffery, Damien, Dir, Solomon Wright Library, 97 Main St, Pownal, VT, 05261. Tel: 802-823-5400. p. 2292
McCaffery, Michael, Dir, Libr Serv, Dearborn Heights City Libraries, Caroline Kennedy Library, 24590 George St, Dearborn Heights, MI, 48127. Tel: 313-791-3800. p. 1096
McCaffrey, Aurora, Dir, Essex County Historical Society / Adirondack History Museum, 7590 Court St, Elizabethtown, NY, 12932. Tel: 518-873-6466. p. 1529
McCaffrey, Colin, Classics Librn, Yale University Library, Classics, Phelps Hall, 344 College St, 5th Flr, New Haven, CT, 06511. Tel: 203-432-8239. p. 327
McCaffrey, Erin, Dean of Libr, Regis University, 3333 Regis Blvd, D20, Denver, CO, 80221-1099. Tel: 303-458-4030, 303-458-4031. p. 276
McCagg, Kelly, Libr Dir, Burnham Memorial Library, 898 Main St, Colchester, VT, 05446. Tel: 802-264-5660. p. 2282
McCahey, Neely, Dir, Sachem Public Library, 150 Holbrook Rd, Holbrook, NY, 11741. Tel: 631-588-5024. p. 1547
McCaig, Daphne, Head, Circ, Mid-America Baptist Theological Seminary, 2095 Appling Rd, Cordova, TN, 38016. Tel: 901-751-3007. p. 2095
McCain, Deborah V, Librn, Res Assoc, University of Mississippi, Science, 1031 Natural Products Ctr, University, MS, 38677. Tel: 662-915-7381. p. 1234
McCain, Gretchen T, Br Librn, Cataloger, Yalobusha County Public Library System, Oakland Public Library, 324 Holly St, Oakland, MS, 38948. Tel: 662-623-8651. p. 1214
McCain, James, Br Mgr, Free Library of Philadelphia, Cecil B Moore Branch, 2320 W Cecil B Moore Ave, Philadelphia, PA, 19121-2927. Tel: 215-685-2766. p. 1979
McCain, Laura, Head Librn, Northwest Mississippi Community College, 1310 Belk Dr, Oxford, MS, 38655. Tel: 662-238-7953. p. 1228
McCaleb, Erica, Libr Mgr, Timberland Regional Library, Yelm Branch, 210 Prairie Park St, Yelm, WA, 98597. Tel: 360-458-3374. p. 2390
McCalister, Bridgid, Asst Dir, Statesboro Regional Public Libraries, 124 S Main St, Statesboro, GA, 30458. Tel: 912-764-1341. p. 498
McCall, Bob, Br Mgr, Polk County Public Library, Saluda Branch, 44 W Main St, Saluda, NC, 28773. Tel: 828-749-2117. p. 1682
McCall, Jennifer, Dir, Chapman Public Library, 402 N Marshall, Chapman, KS, 67431. Tel: 785-922-6548. p. 801
McCall, Kevin, Librn, Squire Patton & Boggs LLP, 2550 M St NW, Washington, DC, 20037. Tel: 202-457-6000. p. 376
McCall, Les, Curator, Pendleton District Historical, Recreational & Tourism Commission, 125 E Queen St, Pendleton, SC, 29670. Tel: 864-646-3782. p. 2067
McCall, Lesa, Computer Lab Mgr, Wilson County Public Libraries, 1103 Fourth St, Floresville, TX, 78114. Tel: 830-393-7361. p. 2177
McCall, Robin, Dr, Ref Librn, Union Presbyterian Seminary Library, 3401 Brook Rd, Richmond, VA, 23227. Tel: 804-278-4310. p. 2342
McCallister, Chris, Adult Serv, Otterbein Public Library, 23 E First St, Otterbein, IN, 47970. Tel: 765-583-2107. p. 712
McCallister, Kelly, Dean of Libr, Tennessee Technological University, 1100 N Peachtree Ave, Cookeville, TN, 38505. Tel: 931-372-3884. p. 2095
McCallon, Mark, Dr, Assoc Dean, Libr & Info Serv, Abilene Christian University, 221 Brown Library, ACU Box 29208, Abilene, TX, 79699-9208. Tel: 325-674-2316. p. 2131
McCallum, Anna, Libr Tech, Teen Librn, Horicon Public Library, 404 E Lake St, Horicon, WI, 53032-1297. Tel: 920-485-3535. p. 2441
McCallum, Kriston, Adult Serv Mgr, Algonquin Area Public Library District, 2600 Harnish Dr, Algonquin, IL, 60102-5900. Tel: 847-458-6060. p. 536
McCallum, Melanie, Br Mgr, San Francisco Public Library, Mission Bay Branch Library, 960 Fourth St, San Francisco, CA, 94158-1628. Tel: 415-355-2838. p. 228
McCallum, Sheila, Ad, Youth Serv Librn, Bloomfield Public Library, P Faith McMahon Wintonbury Library, 1015 Blue Hills Ave, Bloomfield, CT, 06002. Tel: 860-242-0041. p. 303
McCallum, Vivian, User Serv Librn, Cleveland Health Sciences Library, Allen Memorial Medical Library, 11000 Euclid Ave, Cleveland, OH, 44106-7130. Tel: 216-368-1396. p. 1766
McCallum, Vivian, User Serv Librn, Cleveland Health Sciences Library, Allen Memorial Medical Library, 11000 Euclid Ave, Cleveland, OH, 44106-7130. Tel: 216-368-3643. p. 1767
McCamant, Jane, Instrul & Res Librn, Maine Maritime Academy, Pleasant St, Box C-1, Castine, ME, 04420. Tel: 207-326-2262. p. 921
McCambridge, Sara, Asst Dir, Homer Township Public Library District, 14320 W 151st St, Homer Glen, IL, 60491. Tel: 708-301-7908. p. 600
McCammond-Watts, Heather, Dir, Youth Serv, Glen Ellyn Public Library, 400 Duane St, Glen Ellyn, IL, 60137-4508. Tel: 630-469-0879. p. 593
McCan, Cindy, Dir, Richland Public Library, 100 E Main St, Richland, IA, 52585. Tel: 319-456-6541. p. 779
McCann, Christy, Co-Dir, West Warren Library, 2370 Main St, West Warren, MA, 01092. Tel: 413-436-9892. p. 1066
McCann, Elva, Librn, Rideau Lakes Public Library, Newboro Branch, Ten Brock St, Newboro, ON, K0G 1P0, CANADA. Tel: 613-272-0241. p. 2640
McCann, Jett, Dir, Sr Assoc Dean, Georgetown University, Dahlgren Memorial Library, Preclinical Science Bldg GM-7, 3900 Reservoir Rd NW, Washington, DC, 20007. Tel: 202-687-1448. p. 368
McCann, John, Head, Ref, Albertus Magnus College, 700 Prospect St, New Haven, CT, 06511. Tel: 203-773-8511. p. 325
McCann, Julie, Br Mgr, Toledo-Lucas County Public Library, Birmingham, 203 Paine Ave, Toledo, OH, 43605. Tel: 419-259-5210. p. 1824
McCann, Maggie, Co-Dir, Franciscan Missionaries of Our Lady University Library, 5414 Brittany Dr, Baton Rouge, LA, 70808. Tel: 225-526-1783. p. 883
McCann, Paul, Libr Dir, Dexter District Library, 3255 Alpine St, Dexter, MI, 48130. Tel: 734-426-4477. p. 1100
McCann, Shawn, Bus Librn, Web Serv Librn, Oakland University Library, 100 Library Dr, Rochester, MI, 48309-4479. Tel: 248-370-2456. p. 1144
McCann, Siobhan, Ref Serv, Perry Public Library, 3753 Main St, Perry, OH, 44081-9501. Tel: 440-259-3300. p. 1815
McCann, Valerie S, Librn, United States Navy, Naval Operational Medicine Institute Library, 340 Hulse Rd, Pensacola, FL, 32508-1089. Tel: 850-452-2256. p. 436
McCanna, Terran, Prog Mgr, Public Information Network for Electronic Services, Georgia Public Library Service, 2872 Woodcock Blvd, Ste 250, Atlanta, GA, 30341. Tel: 404-235-7138. p. 2764
McCardel, Tiffany, Access Serv, Tech Serv Asst, Thomas University, 1501 Millpond Rd, Thomasville, GA, 31792. Tel: 229-227-6959. p. 500
McCardell, Paul, Research Librn, Tribune Publishing, 501 N Calvert St, Baltimore, MD, 21202-3604. Tel: 410-332-6933. p. 957
McCarley, Amy, Dir, Karnes City Public Library, 302 S Panna Maria Ave, Karnes City, TX, 78118. Tel: 830-780-2539. p. 2204
McCarn, Samantha, Br Mgr, Chesterfield County Library System, 119 W Main St, Chesterfield, SC, 29709-1512. Tel: 843-623-7489. p. 2052
McCarrell, Kyle, Exec Dir, Libr Serv, McHenry County College Library, 8900 US Hwy 14, Crystal Lake, IL, 60012-2738. Tel: 815-455-8695. p. 574
McCarrell, Kyle, Libr Dir, Trinity Christian College, 6601 W College Dr, Palos Heights, IL, 60463. Tel: 708-239-4797. p. 632
McCarrey, Rosemary, Librn, Sidney Community Library, 217 S David, Sidney, IL, 61877. Tel: 217-688-2332. p. 647
McCarrier, Eileen, Asst Mgr, Research Services, Pillsbury Winthrop Shaw Pittman LLP, 7900 Tysons One Pl, Ste 500, McLean, VA, 22102. Tel: 703-770-7742. p. 2332
McCarroll, Colleen, Law Librn, Cook County Law Library, Skokie Branch, 5600 Old Orchard Rd, Skokie, IL, 60077. Tel: 847-470-7298. p. 560
McCarron, Carol, Co-Dir, Anna Field Fernald Library, 35 S Main St, Detroit, ME, 04929-3252. Tel: 207-257-4488. p. 923
McCarron, Heather, Actg Br Supvr, Bruce County Public Library, Sauble Beach, 27 Community Centre Dr, Sauble Beach, ON, N0H 2G0, CANADA. Tel: 519-422-1283. p. 2674
McCarron, Heather, Br Supvr, Bruce County Public Library, Wiarton Branch, 578 Brown St, Wiarton, ON, N0H 2T0, CANADA. Tel: 519-534-2602. p. 2674
McCarthy, Andrew, Coordr, Libr Serv, Bunker Hill Community College, E Bldg, 3rd Flr, Rm E300, 250 New Rutherford Ave, Boston, MA, 02129-2925. Tel: 617-228-2323. p. 994
McCarthy, Bailee, Asst Librn, Red Bud Public Library, 925 S Main St, Red Bud, IL, 62278. Tel: 618-282-2255. p. 638
McCarthy, Cliff, Archivist, Lyman & Merrie Wood Museum of Springfield History, 21 Edwards St, Springfield, MA, 01103. Tel: 413-263-6800, Ext 308. p. 1057
McCarthy, Daniel, Libr Dir, Searsmont Town Library, 37 Main St S, Searsmont, ME, 04973. Tel: 207-342-5549. p. 940
McCarthy, Diana, Commun Librn, Okanagan Regional Library, Falkland Branch, 5771 Hwy 97, Falkland, BC, V0E 1W0, CANADA. Tel: 250-379-2705, Ext 1811. p. 2568
McCarthy Eger, Karen, Libr Dir, South Berwick Public Library, 27 Young St, South Berwick, ME, 03908. Tel: 207-384-3308. p. 941
McCarthy, Jamie, Br Mgr, Burnaby Public Library, Cameron Branch, 9523 Cameron St, Burnaby, BC, V3J 1L6, CANADA. Tel: 604-297-4445. p. 2563
McCarthy, Jean, Dir, Robert L F Sikes Public Library, 1445 Commerce Dr, Crestview, FL, 32539. Tel: 850-682-4432. p. 391
McCarthy, Jessi, Ad, Ref Librn, Hopkinton Public Library, 13 Main St, Hopkinton, MA, 01748. Tel: 508-497-9777. p. 1025
McCarthy, Kevin, Libr Dir, Perrot Memorial Library, 90 Sound Beach Ave, Old Greenwich, CT, 06870. Tel: 203-637-1066. p. 332
McCarthy, Lissa, Circ Supvr, Schoolcraft College, 18600 Haggerty Rd, Livonia, MI, 48152-2696. Tel: 734-462-5326. p. 1127
McCarthy, Meredith, Br Mgr, Jefferson County Library, Arnold Branch, 1701 Missouri State Rd, Arnold, MO, 63010. Tel: 636-296-2204. p. 1249
McCarthy, Michael, Assoc Librn, New York Law School, 185 W Broadway, New York, NY, 10013. Tel: 212-431-2332. p. 1594
McCarthy, Patrick, Assoc Dean, San Diego State University, 5500 Campanile Dr, San Diego, CA, 92182-8050. Tel: 619-594-6728. p. 221
McCarthy, Patrick, Dir, Saint Louis University, Medical Center Library, 1402 S Grand Blvd, Saint Louis, MO, 63104. Tel: 314-977-8800. p. 1276

McCarthy, Sandy, Librn, Washtenaw Community College, 4800 E Huron River Dr, Ann Arbor, MI, 48105-4800. Tel: 734-677-5293. p. 1081
McCarthy, Siobhan, Ref Librn, Montclair State University, One Normal Ave, Montclair, NJ, 07043-1699. Tel: 973-655-7146. p. 1420
McCarthy, Tia, Assoc Dir, Vermont College of Fine Arts, Vermont College of Fine Arts Library, 36 College St, Montpelier, VT, 05602. Tel: 802-828-8512. p. 2289
McCarthy, Virginia, Res, Waseca County Historical Society, 315 Second Ave NE, Waseca, MN, 56093. Tel: 507-835-7700. p. 1207
McCarthy-Perkins, Deanna, Br Mgr, West Florida Public Library, Century Branch, 7991 N Century Blvd, Century, FL, 32535. Tel: 850-256-6217. p. 437
McCartin, Lee, Librn, Newport Cultural Center, 154 Main St, Newport, ME, 04953-1139. Tel: 207-368-5074. p. 933
McCartin, Leona, Librn, Simpson Memorial Library, Eight Plymouth Rd, Carmel, ME, 04419. Tel: 207-848-7145. p. 921
McCartney, Leslie, Curator, Oral Hist, University of Alaska Fairbanks, 1732 Tanana Dr, Fairbanks, AK, 99775. Tel: 907-474-7737. p. 45
McCartney, Lisa, Mkt, Pub Relations Coordr, Chippewa River District Library, 301 S University Ave, Mount Pleasant, MI, 48858-2597. Tel: 989-773-3242, Ext 212. p. 1135
McCartney, Peggy, Libr Asst, Pub Serv, Adams County Public Library, Manchester Public Library, 401 Pike St, Manchester, OH, 45144. Tel: 937-549-3359. p. 1814
McCarty, Brian, Libr Asst, Desoto Parish Library, 109 Crosby St, Mansfield, LA, 71052. Tel: 318-872-6100. p. 895
McCarty, Gerald, Director of Student Success, Monroe County Community College, 1555 S Raisinville Rd, Monroe, MI, 48161-9047. Tel: 734-384-4183. p. 1133
McCarty, Jarrod, Commun Engagement Mgr, Daviess County Public Library, 2020 Frederica St, Owensboro, KY, 42301. Tel: 270-684-0211. p. 871
McCarty, Patrick, Br Mgr, Jackson/Hinds Library System, R G Bolden/Anna Bell-Moore Library, 1444 Wiggins Rd, Jackson, MS, 39209-4430. Tel: 601-922-6076. p. 1221
McCarty, Wayne, Librn, Auburndale Public Library, 100 W Bridgers Ave, Auburndale, FL, 33823. Tel: 863-965-5548. p. 383
McCarty-Daniels, Nick, Dir, Burlington Public Library, 321 14th St, Burlington, CO, 80807. Tel: 719-346-8109. p. 269
McCarville, Maria, Dir, Public Libraries of Saginaw, 505 Janes Ave, Saginaw, MI, 48607. Tel: 989-755-0904. p. 1147
McCary, Amy, ILL, Gadsden Public Library, 254 S College St, Gadsden, AL, 35901. Tel: 256-549-4699. p. 18
McCaskill, Katie, Mgr, Novanet, 120 Western Pkwy, No 202, Bedford, NS, B4B 0V2, CANADA. p. 2778
McCaskill, Sherri, Libr Tech, Colorado State University Libraries, Veterinary Teaching Hospital, 300 West Drake Rd, Fort Collins, CO, 80523-1620. Tel: 970-297-1213. p. 281
McCasland, Terri, Libr Dir, Swisher County Library, 127 SW Second St, Tulia, TX, 79088. Tel: 806-995-3447. p. 2249
McCaughan, Nadine, Br Head, Winnipeg Public Library, Charleswood, 6-4910 Roblin Blvd, Winnipeg, MB, R3R 0G7, CANADA. Tel: 204-806-1119. p. 2596
McCaughtry, Dottie, Librn, Pullman & Comley, 90 State House Sq, Flr 13, Hartford, CT, 06103-3711. Tel: 860-424-4300. p. 318
McCaughtry, Michele, Libr Dir, Kasson Public Library, 607 First St NW, Kasson, MN, 55944. Tel: 507-634-7615. p. 1179
McCaughtry, Michele, Librn, Rochester Community & Technical College, 851 30 Ave SE, Rochester, MN, 55904. Tel: 507-285-7233. p. 1194
McCauley, Angela, Dir, Harnett County Public Library, 601 S Main St, Lillington, NC, 27546-6107. Tel: 910-893-3446. p. 1700
McCauley, Angela, Dir, Harnett County Public Library, Anderson Creek Public, 914 Anderson Creek School Rd, Bunn Level, NC, 28323. Tel: 910-814-4012. p. 1701
McCauley, Diantha, Dir, Augusta County Library, 1759 Jefferson Hwy, Fishersville, VA, 22939. Tel: 540-885-3961, 540-949-6354. p. 2318
McCauley, Lauren, Program Librn, Rehoboth Beach Public Library, 226 Rehoboth Ave, Rehoboth Beach, DE, 19971-2134. Tel: 302-227-8044, Ext 109. p. 356
McCauley, Maria, Dir of Libr, Cambridge Public Library, 449 Broadway, Cambridge, MA, 02138. Tel: 617-349-4041. p. 1004
McCauley, Ryan, Br Mgr, East Providence Public Library, Fuller, 260 Dover Ave, East Providence, RI, 02914. Tel: 401-228-3903. p. 2032
McCauley, Travis, Head, System Servs & Operations, University of the Pacific Libraries, 3601 Pacific Ave, Stockton, CA, 95211. Tel: 209-946-2188. p. 250
McCaulla, Sandra, Circ, Ref, Elizabeth Jones Library, 1050 Fairfield Ave, Grenada, MS, 38901. Tel: 662-226-2072. p. 1217
McCaulley, Rochelle, Dir, Trails Regional Library, 432 N Holden St, Warrensburg, MO, 64093. Tel: 660-747-1699. p. 1285
McCaully, Rochelle, Asst Libr Dir, Kansas City, Kansas Public Library, 625 Minnesota Ave, Kansas City, KS, 66101. Tel: 913-295-8250, Ext 6020. p. 816
McCawley, Patrick, Dir, Archives & Rec Mgt, South Carolina Department of Archives & History, 8301 Parklane Rd, Columbia, SC, 29223. Tel: 803-896-6104. p. 2054
McChesney, Catherine, Librn, Huntington Free Library, Nine Westchester Sq, Bronx, NY, 10461-3513. Tel: 718-829-7770. p. 1499
McChesney, Dave, Libr Dir, New England Air Museum, 36 Perimeter Rd, Windsor Locks, CT, 06096. Tel: 860-623-3305. p. 348
McClachrie, Therese, Dir, Riverdale Public Library, 93 Newark Pompton Tpk, Riverdale, NJ, 07457. Tel: 973-835-5044. p. 1440
McClain, Barbara, Mgr, Suwannee River Regional Library, Jennings Public Library, 1322 Plum St, Jennings, FL, 32053-2221. Tel: 386-938-1143. p. 419
McClain, Carrie, Chief Equity, Diversity & Inclusion Officer, Tulsa City-County Library, 400 Civic Ctr, Tulsa, OK, 74103. Tel: 918-549-7323. p. 1866
McClain, Charlene, Head, Circ, Tennessee Technological University, 1100 N Peachtree Ave, Cookeville, TN, 38505. Tel: 931-372-3326. p. 2095
McClain, Dawn, Head, Tech Serv, Clarksburg-Harrison Public Library, 404 W Pike St, Clarksburg, WV, 26301. Tel: 304-627-2236. p. 2401
McClain, Greg, Br Mgr, Chicago Public Library, Kelly, 6151 S Normal Blvd, Chicago, IL, 60621. Tel: 312-747-8418. p. 556
McClain, Janet, Libr Asst, Beaver City Public Library, 408 Tenth St, Beaver City, NE, 68926. Tel: 308-268-4115. p. 1307
McClain, Liz, Head, Adult Serv, Glencoe Public Library, 320 Park Ave, Glencoe, IL, 60022. Tel: 847-835-5056. p. 593
McClain, Matt, Assoc Dir, Prog, Outreach & Ref, Salt Lake County Library Services, 8030 S 1825 W, West Jordan, UT, 84088. Tel: 801-944-7513. p. 2274
McClain, Sarah, Dir, State Law Library of Montana, 215 N Sanders, Helena, MT, 59601-4522. Tel: 406-444-3660. p. 1297
McClain, Tasha, Dir, Learning Res, Northwest Florida State College, 100 College Blvd E, Niceville, FL, 32578. Tel: 850-729-5318. p. 428
McClain, Tom, Asst Dir for Instructional Tech, Juniata College, 1700 Moore St, Huntingdon, PA, 16652-2119. Tel: 814-641-5348. p. 1945
McClain, Tonya, AV, Kokomo-Howard County Public Library, 220 N Union St, Kokomo, IN, 46901-4614. Tel: 765-457-3242. p. 700
McClanahan, Debbie, Dir, Union County Public District Library, 126 S Morgan St, Morganfield, KY, 42437. Tel: 270-389-1696. p. 870
McClane, Tyler, Circ Mgr, Coeur d'Alene Public Library, 702 E Front Ave, Coeur d'Alene, ID, 83814-2373. Tel: 208-769-2315. p. 519
McClard, Ruth, Libr Mgr, Talihina Public Library, 900 Second St, Talihina, OK, 74571. Tel: 918-567-2002. p. 1864
McClary, Rebecca, Prog Dir, Metropolitan State Hospital Library, Enhancement Services, 11401 Bloomfield Ave, Norwalk, CA, 90650. Tel: 562-521-1349. p. 184
McClary, Tiffany, Dir, Communications, Dir, Mkt, New Jersey State Library, 185 W State St, Trenton, NJ, 08608. Tel: 609-278-2640, Ext 122. p. 1448
McClaskie, Tara, Dir, Hurt-Battelle Memorial Library of West Jefferson, 270 Lily Chapel Rd, West Jefferson, OH, 43162-1202. Tel: 614-879-8448. p. 1829
McClay, Doug, Sch of Nursing Librn, Walla Walla University Libraries, 104 S College Ave, College Place, WA, 99324-1159. Tel: 503-527-2124. p. 2362
McClay, Greg, Dir, Winthrop Public Library & Museum, Two Metcalf Sq, Winthrop, MA, 02152-3157. Tel: 617-846-1703. p. 1070
McCleary, Kimberly, Br Librn, Boston Public Library, Fields Corner, 1520 Dorchester Ave, Dorchester, MA, 02122. Tel: 617-436-2155. p. 992
McClelland, Jean, Asst Librn, University of Arizona Libraries, Health Sciences Library, 1501 N Campbell Ave, Tucson, AZ, 85724. Tel: 520-626-7508. p. 83
McClelland, Lynn, Ref Librn, University of California Los Angeles Library, Hugh & Hazel Darling Law Library, 1112 Law Bldg, 385 Charles E Young Dr E, Los Angeles, CA, 90095-1458. Tel: 310-825-7826. p. 169
McClelland, Marilyn, Customer Serv Mgr, Waukegan Public Library, 128 N County St, Waukegan, IL, 60085. Tel: 847-623-2041. p. 660
McClelland, Matt, Libr Dir, Putnam County Public Library, 103 E Poplar St, Greencastle, IN, 46135. Tel: 765-653-2755. p. 688
McClelland, Megan, Youth Serv Dir, Centerville Public Library, 585 Main St, Centerville, MA, 02632. Tel: 508-790-6220. p. 1009
McClelland, Montoya, Head, Pub Serv, Franciscan University of Steubenville, 1235 University Blvd, Steubenville, OH, 43952-1763. Tel: 740-283-6366. p. 1821
McClendon, Carolyn, Br Mgr, Orange County Library System, South Trail Branch, 4600 S Orange Blossom Trail, Orlando, FL, 32839. p. 431
McClenney, Elizabeth G, Dir, Roanoke College, 220 High St, Salem, VA, 24153-3794. Tel: 540-375-2508. p. 2346
McClenny, Shelby, Supvr, ILL, Dallas Baptist University, 3000 Mountain Creek Pkwy, Dallas, TX, 75211-9299. Tel: 214-333-5320. p. 2163
McClenon, Marca, Ch Serv, John C Hart Memorial Library, 1130 Main St, Shrub Oak, NY, 10588. Tel: 914-245-5262. p. 1641
McCleskey, Sarah, Coll Serv, Dir, Film & Media Library, Head, Res, Hofstra University, 123 Hofstra University, Hempstead, NY, 11549. Tel: 516-463-5076. p. 1545
McClesky, Gerri, Br Mgr, Hancock County Library System, East Hancock Public Library, 4545 Shepherd Sq, Diamondhead, MS, 39525. Tel: 228-255-4800. p. 1212
McClintock, Kathryn, Outreach & Coll Develop Mgr, Boston Architectural College, 320 Newbury St, Boston, MA, 02115. Tel: 617-585-0155. p. 991
McClintock, Sue, Libr Dir, Carver Memorial Library, 12 Union St, Searsport, ME, 04974. Tel: 207-548-2303. p. 940

McClintock, Sue, Dir, Vose Library, 392 Common Rd, Union, ME, 04862-4249. Tel: 207-785-4733. p. 943
McClish, Donna, Tech Info Spec, National Endowment for the Humanities Library, NEH Library, 4th Flr, 400 Seventh St SW, Washington, DC, 20506. Tel: 202-606-8244. p. 372
McClory, Margie, Head, Children's Servx, Beverly Public Library, 32 Essex St, Beverly, MA, 01915-4561. Tel: 978-921-6062. p. 989
McCloskey, James M, Libr Dir, Wilmington University Library, 320 N DuPont Hwy, New Castle, DE, 19720. Tel: 302-356-6880. p. 354
McCloskey, Jamie, Br Mgr, Cecil County Public Library, Elkton Center Library, 301 Newark Ave, Elkton, MD, 21921. Tel: 410-996-5600. p. 965
McCloud, Jacquelyn, Digital Content Serv/Ref Librn, Cleveland State University, Cleveland-Marshall Law Library, Cleveland-Marshall College of Law, 1801 Euclid Ave, Cleveland, OH, 44115-2223. Tel: 216-523-7364. p. 1769
McCloud, LaCreasha, ILL, Charlotte Mecklenburg Library, 310 N Tryon St, Charlotte, NC, 28202-2176. Tel: 704-416-0100. p. 1679
McCloy, Donna, Asst Librn, Educ Librn, Ref (Info Servs), Southern Arkansas University, 100 E University, Magnolia, AR, 71753-5000. Tel: 870-235-4178. p. 103
McCloy, Jessie, Libr Spec, Southeast Community College, Milford LRC, Eicher Technical Center, 600 State St, Milford, NE, 68405. Tel: 402-761-8245. p. 1307
McCloy, Keenon, Dir of Libr, Memphis Public Library & Information Center, 3030 Poplar Ave, Memphis, TN, 38111. Tel: 901-415-2700. p. 2112
McCloy, Kennon, Dir, Memphis Public Library, East Shelby Branch, 7200 E Shelby Dr, Memphis, TN, 38125. Tel: 901-415-2767. p. 2113
McClung, Carol, Dir, Rupert Public Library, 124 Greenbrier St, Rupert, WV, 25984. Tel: 304-392-6158. p. 2414
McClung, Eunice, Dir, Mounds Public Library, 418 First St, Mounds, IL, 62964. Tel: 618-745-6610. p. 620
McClung, Laura, Ref Librn, Goodland Public Library, 812 Broadway, Goodland, KS, 67735. Tel: 785-899-5461. p. 810
McClure, Caroline, Asst Librn, Blue Mountain College, 201 W Main St, Blue Mountain, MS, 38610. Tel: 662-685-4771, Ext 147. p. 1212
McClure, Charles, Dr, Dir, Info Inst, Prof, Florida State University, College of Communication & Information, 142 Collegiate Loop, Tallahassee, FL, 32306-2100. Tel: 850-644-8109. p. 2783
McClure, Dan, Libr Dir, Clatsop Community College-Learning Resource Center, 1680 Lexington, Astoria, OR, 97103. Tel: 503-388-2460. p. 1872
McClure, David, Dir, Friends University, 2100 W University Ave, Wichita, KS, 67213-3397. Tel: 316-295-5880. p. 842
McClure, Goldie, Librn, Pocahontas County Free Libraries, Hillsboro Public Library, 54 Third St, Hillsboro, WV, 24946. Tel: 304-653-4936. p. 2408
McClure, John, Dir, Libr & Res Serv, Virginia Historical Society Library, 428 North Blvd, Richmond, VA, 23220. Tel: 804-340-1800. p. 2344
McClure, Kathy, Exec Dir, Eva K Bowlby Public Library, 311 N West St, Waynesburg, PA, 15370-1238. Tel: 724-727-9776, Ext 15. p. 2019
McClure, Kathy, Exec Dir, Greene County Library System, 311 N West St, Waynesburg, PA, 15370. Tel: 724-627-9776, Ext 410. p. 2019
McClure, Lisa, Dir, Linden Free Public Library, 31 E Henry St, Linden, NJ, 07036. Tel: 908-298-3830. p. 1412
McClure, Randle, Chief Officer, Libr Syst Analyst, San Francisco Public Library, 100 Larkin St, San Francisco, CA, 94102. Tel: 415-509-1514. p. 227
McClure, Rita, Asst Dir, Meridian Community College, 910 Hwy 19 N, Meridian, MS, 39307. Tel: 601-484-8761. p. 1226
McClure, Robert, Libr Dir, Niton Library, 5307 50th St, Niton Junction, AB, T7E 5A1, CANADA. Tel: 780-795-2474. p. 2549
McClure, Robert, Dir, Stony Plain Public Library, 5216 50 St, Stony Plain, AB, T7Z 0N5, CANADA. Tel: 780-963-5440. p. 2555
McClure, Ted, Librn, Grand Canyon National Park Research Library, Park Headquarters Bldg, 20 S Entrance Rd, Grand Canyon, AZ, 86023. Tel: 928-638-7768. p. 62
McClure, Virginia, Libr Dir, Anchorage Public Library, 3600 Denali St, Anchorage, AK, 99503. Tel: 907-343-2892. p. 42
McClurg, Caitlin, Librn, University of Calgary Library, Gallagher Library, 170 Earth Sciences, 2500 University Dr NW, Calgary, AB, T2N 1N4, CANADA. Tel: 403-220-5319. p. 2529
McClurkan, Carolyn, Archivist, Kitsap County Historical Society, 280 Fourth St, Bremerton, WA, 98337-1813. Tel: 360-479-6226. p. 2359
McCluskey, Donna, Librn, Isaac F Umberhine Library, 86 Main St, Richmond, ME, 04357. Tel: 207-737-2770. p. 938
McCluskey, Holly H, Curator, The Museums of Oglebay Institute Library, Oglebay Institute, The Burton Center, Wheeling, WV, 26003. Tel: 304-242-7272. p. 2417
McCluskey, Melanie, Tech Serv, California Baptist University, 8432 Magnolia Ave, Riverside, CA, 92504. Tel: 951-343-4353. p. 201
McCluskey, Renee, Br Mgr, Webster Parish Library System, Willie & Mary Mack Memorial Branch, 1000 S Arkansas St, Springhill, LA, 71075. Tel: 318-539-4117. p. 898
McCole, Joanne, Access Serv, Lending Servs, Swarthmore College, Cornell Science & Engineering, 500 College Ave, Swarthmore, PA, 19081. Tel: 610-328-8267. p. 2012
McColgan, Katherine, Mrg, Admin & Prog, Canadian Association of Research Libraries, 309 Cooper St, Ste 203, Ottawa, ON, K2P 0G5, CANADA. Tel: 613-482-9344, Ext 102. p. 2778
McColl, Lisa, Cat/Metadata Librn, Lehigh University, Eight A E Packer Ave, Bethlehem, PA, 18015. Tel: 610-758-2639. p. 1912
McColl, Ron, Spec Coll Librn, West Chester University, 25 W Rosedale Ave, West Chester, PA, 19383. Tel: 610-436-3456. p. 2020
McColl, Terrie, Dir, New Milford Public Library, 200 Dahlia Ave, New Milford, NJ, 07646. Tel: 201-262-1221. p. 1425
McColley, Allyn, Pub Serv Librn, Buckham Memorial Library, 11 Division St E, Faribault, MN, 55021-6000. Tel: 507-334-2089. p. 1175
McColloch, Mary, Dir, Dexter Public Library, 724 Marshall St, Dexter, IA, 50070. Tel: 515-789-4490. p. 748
McCollough, Calista, YA Librn, Mason City Public Library, 225 Second St SE, Mason City, IA, 50401. Tel: 641-421-3668. p. 768
McCollough, Paige, Youth Serv, Barry-Lawrence Regional Library, Monett Branch, 2200 Park St, Monett, MO, 65708. Tel: 417-235-7350. p. 1263
McCollum, Cristine M, Info Spec, Federal Reserve Bank of Philadelphia, 100 N Sixth St, 4th Flr, Philadelphia, PA, 19106. Tel: 215-574-6540. p. 1977
McCollum, Julie, Material Processor, Barry-Lawrence Regional Library, 213 Sixth St, Monett, MO, 65708-2147. Tel: 417-235-6646. p. 1262
McComas, Stephanie, Admin Support Coordr, Interim Dir, London Public Library, 20 E First St, London, OH, 43140. Tel: 740-852-9543. p. 1796
McComb, Helen, Dir, Harriette Person Memorial Library, 606 Market St, Port Gibson, MS, 39150. Tel: 601-437-5202. p. 1230
McCombs, Gillian, Dean & Dir, Southern Methodist University, Central University Libraries, 6414 Robert S Hyer Lane, Dallas, TX, 75205. Tel: 214-768-2401. p. 2168
McCombs, Gillian, Dean & Dir, Southern Methodist University, Fondren Library, 6414 Robert S Hyer Lane, Dallas, TX, 75205. Tel: 214-768-2401. p. 2168
McCombs, W Douglas, PhD, Chief Curator, Albany Institute of History & Art, 125 Washington Ave, Albany, NY, 12210-2296. Tel: 518-463-4478, Ext 428. p. 1481
McConchie, Corinne, Mgr Fac, North Vancouver District Public Library, 1277 Lynn Valley Rd, North Vancouver, BC, V7J 0A2, CANADA. Tel: 604-984-0286, 604-990-5800. p. 2573
McCone, Gary, Head, Libr & Info Serv, American Indian Higher Education Consortium, 121 Oronoco St, Alexandria, VA, 22314. Tel: 410-707-9307. p. 2776
McConnaughy, Roz, Asst Dir, Educ & Outreach, University of South Carolina, School of Medicine Library, Bldg 101, 6311 Garners Ferry Rd, Columbia, SC, 29209. Tel: 803-216-3200. p. 2056
McConnel, Jon, Head, Coll Mgt & Digital Serv, Bellingham Public Library, 210 Central Ave, Bellingham, WA, 98225. Tel: 360-778-7227. p. 2358
McConnell, Barb, Libr Mgr, Lougheed Public Library, 5004 50 St, Lougheed, AB, T0B 2V0, CANADA. Tel: 780-386-2498. p. 2547
McConnell, Barb, Libr Mgr, Sedgewick & District Municipal Library, 5011 51st Ave, Sedgewick, AB, T0B 4C0, CANADA. Tel: 780-384-3003. p. 2553
McConnell, Beth, Br Mgr, Stone County Library, Blue Eye Branch, 138 State Hwy EE, Blue Eye, MO, 65611. Tel: 417-357-6510. p. 1247
McConnell, Cara, Libr Dir, Johnston Community College Library, Learning Resource Ctr, Bldg E, 245 College Rd, Smithfield, NC, 27577. Tel: 919-464-2254. p. 1716
McConnell, Elaine, Curator, Rare Bks, United States Military Academy Library, Jefferson Hall Library & Learning Ctr, 758 Cullum Rd, West Point, NY, 10996. Tel: 845-938-8301. p. 1663
McConnell, Emily, Br Mgr, White County Public Library, Ten Colonial Dr, Cleveland, GA, 30528. Tel: 706-865-5572. p. 471
McConnell, James, Library Contact, Albert C Wagner Youth Correctional Facility Library, 500 Ward Ave, Bordentown, NJ, 08505-2928. Tel: 609-298-0500. p. 1391
McConnell, Jill, Exec Dir, Cooper-Siegel Community Library, 403 Fox Chapel Rd, Pittsburgh, PA, 15238. Tel: 412-828-9520. p. 1993
McConnell, Jim, Librn, Garden State Youth Correctional Facility Library, 55 Hogback Rd, Crosswicks, NJ, 08515. Tel: 609-298-6300, Ext 2225. p. 1398
McConnell, John, ILL/Tech Serv Librn, Northeast Georgia Regional Library System, 204 Ellison St, Ste F, Clarkesville, GA, 30523. Tel: 706-754-0416. p. 471
McConnell, Kathrin L, Dir, United States Department of Health & Human Services, FDA Library, WO2, Rm 3302, 10903 New Hampshire Ave, Silver Spring, MD, 20993. Tel: 301-796-2387. p. 975
McConnell, Laura, Dir, East Morgan County Library District, 500 Clayton St, Brush, CO, 80723-2110. Tel: 970-842-4596. p. 269
McConnell, Laurie, Sr Librn, California Department of Corrections Library System, California Institution for Women, 16756 Chino-Corona Rd, Corona, CA, 92880. Tel: 909-597-1771, Ext 6488. p. 206
McConnell, Linda, Dir, Rodman Public Library, 12509 School St, Rodman, NY, 13682. Tel: 315-232-4167. p. 1632
McConnell, Patti, Br Mgr, Calvert Library, Southern Branch, 13920 HG Trueman Rd, Solomons, MD, 20688. Tel: 410-326-5289. p. 973
McConnell, Penny, Dir, Danville Area Community College Library, 2000 E Main St, Danville, IL, 61832-5199. Tel: 217-443-8739. p. 575

McConnell, Sherri, Head Librn, Capital Area District Libraries, Stockbridge Library, 200 Wood St, Stockbridge, MI, 49285. Tel: 517-851-7810. p. 1124
McConnell, Sue, Ch, Southeast Steuben County Library, 300 Nasser Civic Center Plaza, Ste 101, Corning, NY, 14830. Tel: 607-936-3713, Ext 503. p. 1522
McConnell, Susan, ILL Mgr, Hayner Public Library District, 326 Belle St, Alton, IL, 62002. Tel: 618-462-0677. p. 536
McCook, Kathleen de la Pena, Distinguished Univ Prof, University of South Florida, 4202 Fowler Ave, CIS 1040, Tampa, FL, 33620-7800. Tel: 813-974-3520. p. 2783
McCool, Jennifer, Libr Spec, Bellingham Technical College Library, 3028 Lindbergh Ave, Bellingham, WA, 98225-1599. Tel: 360-752-8382. p. 2358
McCool, Marissa, Studio Dir, Minnesota Braille & Talking Book Library, 400 NE Stinson Blvd, Minneapolis, MN, 55413. Tel: 507-384-6861. p. 1184
McCoole, Rob, Dir, Guilford Free Library, 67 Park St, Guilford, CT, 06437. Tel: 203-453-8282. p. 315
McCord, Helen, Dir, Kimberly Public Library, 120 Madison St W, Kimberly, ID, 83341. Tel: 208-423-4262. p. 523
McCord, Sarah, Data Librn, Informatics Librn, Research Librn, Massachusetts College of Pharmacy & Health Sciences, Matricaria Bldg, 2nd Flr, 179 Longwood Ave, Boston, MA, 02115. Tel: 617-735-1439. p. 997
McCord, Suzanne, Asst Law Librn, Washington County Law Library, One S Main St, Ste G004, Washington, PA, 15301. Tel: 724-250-4026. p. 2018
McCord, Tasha, YA Serv, Clark County Public Library, 370 S Burns Ave, Winchester, KY, 40391-1876. Tel: 859-744-5661. p. 878
McCorkell, Megan, Dir, Mkt & Communications, Enoch Pratt Free Library, 400 Cathedral St, Baltimore, MD, 21201. Tel: 410-396-5430. p. 952
McCorkhill, Joy, Libr Dir, Jefferson Public Library, 178 Meadows Rd, Jefferson, NH, 03583. Tel: 603-586-7791. p. 1369
McCorkhill, Tom, Dir, Twin Mountain Public Library, 92 School St, Carrol, NH, 03595. Tel: 603-846-5818. p. 1356
McCorkhill, Tom, Librn, Stratford Public Library, 74 Main St, North Stratford, NH, 03590. Tel: 603-922-9016. p. 1377
McCorkindale, Rebecca, Asst Dir, Gretna Public Library, 736 South St, Gretna, NE, 68028. Tel: 402-332-4480. p. 1316
McCormack, Edward, Assoc Dean, University of Southern Mississippi, 730 E Beach Blvd, Long Beach, MS, 39560-2698. Tel: 228-214-3466. p. 1225
McCormack, Jennifer, Dir, Nashua Public Library, Two Court St, Nashua, NH, 03060. Tel: 603-589-4620. p. 1374
McCormack, Kristen, Dir, Palestine Public Library District, 201 S Washington St, Palestine, IL, 62451. Tel: 618-586-5317. p. 631
McCormack, Lauren, Curator, Marblehead Museum & Historical Society Library, 170 Washington St, Marblehead, MA, 01945-3340. Tel: 781-631-1069. p. 1031
McCormack, Linda, Dir, Rock Rapids Public Library, 102 S Greene St, Rock Rapids, IA, 51246. Tel: 712-472-3541. p. 779
McCormack, Patricia, Librn, Trepassey Public Library, Molloy's Rd, Trepassey, NL, A0A 4B0, CANADA. Tel: 709-438-2224. p. 2611
McCormack, Sarah, Libr Dir, Banff Public Library, 101 Bear St, Banff, AB, T1L 1H3, CANADA. Tel: 403-762-2661. p. 2522
McCormick, Agnes, Librn, Nottoway County Public Libraries, Burkeville Branch, 114 S Agnew, Burkeville, VA, 23922. Tel: 434-767-5555. p. 2314
McCormick, Bryan J, Dir, Hedberg Public Library, 316 S Main St, Janesville, WI, 53545. Tel: 608-758-6594. p. 2443
McCormick, Gary, Learning Commons Librn, Bishop's University, 2600 College St, Sherbrooke, QC, J1M 1Z7, CANADA. Tel: 819-822-9600, Ext 2800. p. 2736
McCormick, Greg, Dir, Illinois State Library, Gwendolyn Brooks Bldg, 300 S Second St, Springfield, IL, 62701-1796. Tel: 217-782-3504. p. 649
McCormick, Greg, Dir, Illinois Library & Information Network, c/o Illinois State Library, Gwendolyn Brooks Bldg, 300 S Second St, Springfield, IL, 62701-1796. Tel: 217-782-3504. p. 2764
McCormick, Jonathan, Dr, Dir, Libr Serv, Gateway Seminary Library, 3210 E Gausti Rd, Ontario, CA, 91761-8642. Tel: 909-687-1482. p. 188
McCormick, Kathleen, Assoc Dean, Spec Coll, Florida State University Libraries, Strozier Library Bldg, 116 Honors Way, Tallahassee, FL, 32306. Tel: 850-644-2706. p. 446
McCormick, Lisa, Dir, Schreiner University, 2100 Memorial Blvd, Kerrville, TX, 78028-5697. Tel: 830-792-7312. p. 2205
McCormick, Lynn, Ch, Tuolumne County Public Library, 480 Greenley Rd, Sonora, CA, 95370-5956. Tel: 209-533-5507. p. 247
McCormick, Margaret, Dir, Woods Hole Public Library, 581 Woods Hole Rd, Woods Hole, MA, 02543. Tel: 508-548-8961. p. 1071
McCormick McDonald, Lynn, Dir, Saint Petersburg College, 7200 66th St N, Pinellas Park, FL, 33781. Tel: 727-341-7183. p. 437
McCormick, Mick, Info Tech, Harrison County Library System, 12135 Old Hwy 49, Gulfport, MS, 39501. Tel: 228-539-0110. p. 1217
McCormick, Monica, Assoc Univ Librn, Publishing Preservation, Research & Digital Access, University of Delaware Library, 181 S College Ave, Newark, DE, 19717-5267. Tel: 302-831-2965. p. 355
McCormick, Patricia, Dep Chief Librn, Eastern Counties Regional Library, 390 Murray St, Mulgrave, NS, B0E 2G0, CANADA. Tel: 902-747-2597. p. 2621
McCormick, Ryan, Patron Serv Supvr, Great River Regional Library, 1300 W St Germain St, Saint Cloud, MN, 56301. Tel: 320-650-2527. p. 1196
McCormick, Ryan, Patron Serv Supvr, Great River Regional Library, Saint Cloud Public Library, 1300 W Saint Germain St, Saint Cloud, MN, 56301. Tel: 320-650-2500. p. 1197
McCormick, Sara, Br Mgr, Scott-Sebastian Regional Library, Lavaca Library, 100 S Davis, Lavaca, AR, 72941. p. 97
McCormick, Tracey, Head, Pub Serv, University of Wyoming, 1820 E Willett Dr, Laramie. Tel: 307-766-5120. p. 2496
McCourry, Maurine, Libr Dir, Hillsdale College, 33 E College St, Hillsdale, MI, 49242. Tel: 517-610-2401. p. 1115
McCowan, Trina, Libr Mgr, Florida State College at Jacksonville, South Campus Library & Learning Commons, 11901 Beach Blvd, Jacksonville, FL, 32246-6624. Tel: 904-646-2174. p. 411
McCowan, Trina, Dir, Libr Serv, Flagler College, 44 Sevilla St, Saint Augustine, FL, 32084-4302. Tel: 904-819-6206. p. 439
McCown, Alice, Cataloger, Columbus Technical College Library, 928 Manchester Expressway, Columbus, GA, 31904-6577. Tel: 706-649-1444. p. 472
McCown, Paula, Doc Delivery, IU Ball Memorial Hospital, 2401 W University Ave, Muncie, IN, 47303-3499. Tel: 765-741-1959. p. 708
McCoy, Chandra, Dir, Libr & Mus Serv, Fort Morgan Public Library, 414 Main St, Fort Morgan, CO, 80701. Tel: 970-542-4006. p. 282
McCoy, Erin, Coordr, Pub Serv & Instruction, Massasoit Community College, One Massasoit Blvd, Brockton, MA, 02302. Tel: 508-588-9100, Ext 1941. p. 1003
McCoy, Ginette, Librn, Ontario Office of the Fire Marshal & Emergency Management, 2284 Nursery Rd, Midhurst, ON, L9X 1N8, CANADA. Tel: 705-571-1560. p. 2657
McCoy, Henry, Media Coordr, Chattahoochee Valley Libraries, 3000 Macon Rd, Columbus, GA, 31906-2201. Tel: 706-243-2669. p. 471
McCoy, Kelsey, Youth Serv Coordr, Germantown Public Library, 51 N Plum St, Germantown, OH, 45327. Tel: 937-855-4001. p. 1788
McCoy, Kendall, Adult Serv, Community Library of the Shenango Valley, 11 N Sharpsville Ave, Sharon, PA, 16146. Tel: 724-981-4360. p. 2006
McCoy, Michael, Adult Serv, Hastings-on-Hudson Public Library, Seven Maple Ave, Hastings-on-Hudson, NY, 10706. Tel: 914-478-3307. p. 1544
McCoy, Nancy, Dir, Educ & Pub Serv, National Archives & Records Administration, Columbia Point, Boston, MA, 02125. Tel: 617-514-1600. p. 997
McCoy, Ramona, Librn, Oregon Research Institute Library, 3800 Sports Way, Springfield, OR, 97477. Tel: 541-484-2123. p. 1899
McCoy, Samantha, Dir, West Caldwell Public Library, 30 Clinton Rd, West Caldwell, NJ, 07006. Tel: 973-226-5441. p. 1452
McCoy, Shelly L, Assoc Univ Librn, Planning & Fac, Communications Librn, University of Delaware Library, 181 S College Ave, Newark, DE, 19717-5267. Tel: 302-831-2965. p. 355
McCoy, Stephanie, Night Supvr, Res Spec, University of Detroit Mercy School of Law, 651 E Jefferson, Detroit, MI, 48226. Tel: 313-596-0241. p. 1099
McCracken, Jan, Dir, Akron Public Library, 302 Main Ave, Akron, CO, 80720-1437. Tel: 970-345-6818. p. 263
McCracken, Vivian, Librn, Mount Carmel Area Public Library, 30 S Oak St, Mount Carmel, PA, 17851-2185. Tel: 570-339-0703. p. 1966
Mccrae, Tiffany, Libr Mgr, New York Public Library - Astor, Lenox & Tilden Foundations, City Island Branch, 320 City Island Ave, (Between Bay & Fordham Sts), Bronx, NY, 10464. Tel: 718-885-1703. p. 1595
McCraly, Sarah, Circ, Geneva College, 3200 College Ave, Beaver Falls, PA, 15010-3599. Tel: 724-847-6563. p. 1909
McCrary, Martha M, Head, Syst, United States Air Force, Air University - Muir S Fairchild Research Information Center, 600 Chennault Circle, Maxwell AFB, AL, 36112-6010. Tel: 334-953-2474. p. 25
McCraw, Beverly, Librn, Spencer Public Library, 300 Fourth St, Spencer, NC, 28159. Tel: 704-636-9072. p. 1717
McCray, Benita, Managing Librn, Brooklyn Public Library, Spring Creek, 12143 Flatlands Ave, Brooklyn, NY, 11207. Tel: 718-257-6571. p. 1504
McCray, Natalie, Asst Dir, Pima Public Library, 50 S 200 West, Pima, AZ, 85543. Tel: 928-485-2822. p. 73
McCray, Nicole, Dir, Rock Valley Public Library, 1531 Main St, Rock Valley, IA, 51247-1127. Tel: 712-476-5651. p. 779
McCray Pearson, Joyce A, Assoc Dean, Washington University Libraries, Law Library, Washington Univ Sch Law, Anheuser-Busch Hall, One Brookings Dr, Campus Box 1171, Saint Louis, MO, 63130. Tel: 314-935-2929. p. 1277
McCrea, Briynne, Dir, Columbia Township Library, 6456 Center St, Unionville, MI, 48767. Tel: 989-674-2651. p. 1155
McCrea, Brynne, Libr Dir, Bad Axe Area District Library, 200 S Hanselman St, Bad Axe, MI, 48413. Tel: 989-269-8538. p. 1082
McCreary, Karl R, Archivist, Oregon State University Libraries, Special Collections & Archives Research Center, 121 The Valley Library, 5th Flr, Corvallis, OR, 97331. Tel: 541-737-0539. p. 1877

McDermott, Monica, Ref Librn, Pollard Memorial Library, 401 Merrimack St, Lowell, MA, 01852. Tel: 978-674-4120. p. 1029
McDevitt, Jeannette, Asst Librn, Carnegie Mellon University, Hunt Institute for Botanical Documentation, 4909 Frew St, Pittsburgh, PA, 15213. Tel: 412-268-7301. p. 1992
McDevitt, Jennifer, Libr Dir, Camrose Public Library, 4710-50th Ave, Camrose, AB, T4V 0R8, CANADA. Tel: 780-672-4214. p. 2529
McDevitt, Theresa R, Govt Info/Ref Librn, Indiana University of Pennsylvania, 431 S 11th St, Rm 203, Indiana, PA, 15705-1096. Tel: 724-357-2330. p. 1946
McDonald, Alvin, Dir, Guilford Memorial Library, Four Library St, Guilford, ME, 04443. Tel: 207-876-4547. p. 926
McDonald, Amy, Court Adminr, Allegany County Circuit Court, Allegany County Circuit Courthouse, 30 Washington St, Cumberland, MD, 21502. Tel: 301-777-5925. p. 963
McDonald, Amy, Libr Dir, Western Allegheny Community Library, 181 Bateman Rd, Oakdale, PA, 15071-3906. Tel: 724-695-8150. p. 1972
McDonald, Beckie, Mgr, Oshawa Public Library, Delpark, 1661 Harmony Rd N, Oshawa, ON, L1H 7K5, CANADA. Tel: 905-436-5461. p. 2664
McDonald, Beth, Project Archivist, ONE National Gay & Lesbian Archives at the USC Libraries, 909 W Adams Blvd, Los Angeles, CA, 90007. Tel: 213-821-2771. p. 167
McDonald, Brenda, Dir, Cent Serv, Saint Louis Public Library, Central Library, 1301 Olive St, Saint Louis, MO, 63103. Tel: 314-241-2288. p. 1275
McDonald, Brian, Asst Archivist, Spec Coll Librn, Adelphi University, One South Ave, Garden City, NY, 11530. Tel: 516-877-3818. p. 1536
McDonald, Carrie, Acq Librn, Nelson County Public Library, 201 Cathedral Manor, Bardstown, KY, 40004-1515. Tel: 502-348-3714. p. 848
McDonald, Casey, Dir, Oswayo Valley Memorial Library, 103 N Pleasant St, Shinglehouse, PA, 16748. Tel: 814-697-6691. p. 2007
McDonald, Catherine, Dir, Lucius Beebe Memorial Library, 345 Main St, Wakefield, MA, 01880-5093. Tel: 781-246-6334. p. 1061
McDonald, Cynthia, Branch Lead, Charlotte Mecklenburg Library, Matthews Branch, 230 Matthews Station St, Matthews, NC, 28105. Tel: 704-416-5000. p. 1679
McDonald, Danielle, Chief Exec Officer, Ottawa Public Library/Bibliothèque publique d'Ottawa, 120 Metcalfe St, Ottawa, ON, K1P 5M2, CANADA. Tel: 613-580-2945. p. 2668
McDonald, David, Legislative Librn, Nova Scotia Legislative Library, Province House, 2nd Flr, Halifax, NS, B3J 2P8, CANADA. Tel: 902-424-5932. p. 2620
McDonald, Debbie, Library Contact, American Graduate University Library, 733 N Dodsworth Ave, Covina, CA, 91724. Tel: 626-966-4576, Ext 1001. p. 133
McDonald, Deirdre, Head, Res Serv, Texas A&M University-San Antonio, One University Way, San Antonio, TX, 78224. Tel: 210-784-1503. p. 2239
McDonald, Ellen, Ref (Info Servs), Tufts University, Edwin Ginn Library, Mugar Bldg, 1st Flr, 160 Packard St, Medford, MA, 02155-7082. Tel: 617-627-3858. p. 1034
McDonald, Eva, Librn, Centennial College of Applied Arts & Technology, Progress Campus, 941 Progress Ave, L3-06, Scarborough, ON, M1G 3T8, CANADA. Tel: 416-289-5000, Ext 5400. p. 2677
McDonald, Gail, Ref Librn, Fordham University School of Law, 150 W 62nd St, New York, NY, 10023. Tel: 212-636-7005. p. 1585
McDonald, Geoffrey, Tech Info Spec, US Department of the Interior, Bureau of Reclamation, 2800 Cottage Way, Rm W-1825, Sacramento, CA, 95825-1898. Tel: 916-978-5593. p. 210
McDonald, Ginger R, Librn, Northpoint Bible College Library, 320 S Main St, Haverhill, MA, 01835. p. 1024
McDonald, Jami, Br Mgr, Tazewell County Public Library, Richlands Branch, 102 Suffolk Ave, Richlands, VA, 24641-2435. Tel: 276-964-5282. p. 2348
McDonald, Janet, Librn, Middle Haddam Public Library, Two Knowles Landing, Middle Haddam, CT, 06456. Tel: 860-267-9093. p. 321
McDonald, Jill, Librn, Memorial Public Library of the Borough of Alexandria, 313 Main St, Alexandria, PA, 16611. Tel: 814-669-4313. p. 1904
McDonald, John M, Dir of Libr Operations, Saint Xavier University, 3700 W 103rd St, Chicago, IL, 60655-3105. Tel: 773-298-3352. p. 567
McDonald, Julieta Lumbria, Coordr, Libr Serv, New Brunswick College of Craft & Design Library, 457 Queen St, Fredericton, NB, E3B 5H1, CANADA. Tel: 506-453-5938. p. 2601
McDonald, Kathy, Librn, Superior Public Library, Joan Salmen Memorial, Village Hall, 9240 E Main St, Solon Springs, WI, 54873. Tel: 715-378-4452. p. 2480
McDonald, Krista, Dir, Miami University Libraries, Rentschler Library, 1601 University Blvd, Hamilton, OH, 45011. Tel: 513-785-3235. p. 1812
McDonald, Lacy, Libr Mgr, Hayner Public Library District, Genealogy & Local History, 401 State St, Alton, IL, 62002-6113. p. 536
McDonald, Lea Ann, Head, Youth Serv, Harrison Memorial Library, Ocean Ave & Lincoln St, Carmel, CA, 93921. Tel: 831-624-4664. p. 128
McDonald, Mike, Communications Dir, Mendocino Art Center Library, 45200 Little Lake St, Mendocino, CA, 95460. Tel: 707-937-5818. p. 175
McDonald, Mike, Dir, Franklin Ferguson Memorial Library, 410 N B St, Cripple Creek, CO, 80813. Tel: 719-689-2800. p. 272
McDonald, Mike, Syst Dir, Northeast Kansas Library System, 4317 W Sixth St, Lawrence, KS, 66049. Tel: 785-838-4090. p. 819
McDonald, Paula, Mgr, Circ Serv, Mgr, ILL, Quinsigamond Community College, 670 W Boylston St, Worcester, MA, 01606-2092. Tel: 508-854-4366. p. 1072
McDonald, Robert H, Dean, Univ Libr, Senior Vice Provost Online Ed, University of Colorado Boulder, 1720 Pleasant St, Boulder, CO, 80309. Tel: 303-492-8705. p. 267
McDonald, Shaun, Br Mgr, Amarillo Public Library, North Branch, 1500 NE 24th St, Amarillo, TX, 79107. Tel: 806-381-7931. p. 2134
McDonald, Terrence J, Dir, University of Michigan, Bentley Historical Library, 1150 Beal Ave, Ann Arbor, MI, 48109-2113. Tel: 734-764-3482. p. 1079
McDonald, Tim, Dir, Libr & Info Serv, Pasadena Public Library, 285 E Walnut St, Pasadena, CA, 91101. Tel: 626-744-4066. p. 194
McDonald, Tim, Dir, Pasadena Public Library, 1201 Jeff Ginn Memorial Dr, Pasadena, TX, 77506. Tel: 713-477-0276. p. 2225
McDonald, Timothy, Br Mgr, Las Vegas-Clark County Library District, Sunrise Library, 5400 Harris Ave, Las Vegas, NV, 89110. Tel: 702-507-3900. p. 1347
McDonnell, Andrew, Projects Officer, University of Wisconsin-Madison, Nieman Grant Journalism Reading Room, 2130 Vilas Hall, 821 University Ave, Madison, WI, 53706. Tel: 608-263-3387. p. 2451
McDonnell, Joellyn, Circ/Customer Serv Mgr, The Frances Banta Waggoner Community Library, 505 Tenth St, DeWitt, IA, 52742-1335. Tel: 563-659-5523. p. 747
McDonnell, Peter, Circ & Syst Librn, Dept Chair, Bemidji State University, 1500 Birchmont Dr NE, No 28, Bemidji, MN, 56601-2699. Tel: 218-755-2967. p. 1165
McDonnell, Ryan, Dir, Grandview Heights Public Library, 1685 W First Ave, Columbus, OH, 43212. Tel: 614-486-2951. p. 1773
McDonnell, Scott, Head, Circ, Easttown Library & Information Center, 720 First Ave, Berwyn, PA, 19312-1769. Tel: 610-644-0138. p. 1910
McDonough, Anne, Coord, Ad Serv, Vineyard Haven Public Library, 200 Main St, Vineyard Haven, MA, 02568. Tel: 508-696-4211, Ext 116. p. 1061
McDonough, Collette, Libr Mgr, Kettering Foundation Library, 200 Commons Rd, Dayton, OH, 45459. Tel: 937-434-7300. p. 1780
McDonough, Darren, Dir, Oberlin Public Library, 65 S Main St, Oberlin, OH, 44074-1626. Tel: 440-775-4790. p. 1810
McDonough, Douglas, Dir, Manchester Public Library, 586 Main St, Manchester, CT, 06040. Tel: 860-643-2471. p. 320
McDonough, Gracie, Instruction & Ref Librn, College of Southern Nevada, Henderson Campus, 700 S College Dr, H1A, Henderson, NV, 89002. Tel: 702-651-3066. p. 1346
McDonough, Kevin, Head, Youth Serv, Gale Free Library, 23 Highland St, Holden, MA, 01520. Tel: 508-210-5560. p. 1025
McDonough, Kevin, Ref/Electronic Res Librn, Northern Michigan University, 1401 Presque Isle Ave, Marquette, MI, 49855-5376. Tel: 906-227-2118. p. 1130
McDonough, Timothy, Dir, Waterford Public Library, 117 Third St, Waterford, NY, 12188. Tel: 518-237-0891. p. 1659
McDougal, Brittany, Dir, Oxford Free Public Library, 339 Main St, Oxford, MA, 01540. Tel: 508-987-6003. p. 1045
McDougal, Terri, Head, Children's Servx, Kanawha County Public Library, 123 Capitol St, Charleston, WV, 25301. Tel: 304-343-4646. p. 2400
McDougall, Lynnda, Libr Asst, Smithers Public Library, 3817 Alfred Ave, Smithers, BC, V0J 2N0, CANADA. Tel: 250-847-3043. p. 2576
McDougall, Nancy, Ch, Camanche Public Library, 102 12th Ave, Camanche, IA, 52730. Tel: 563-259-1106. p. 736
McDougall, Pauline, Dir, Melvin Public Library, 232 Main St, Melvin, IA, 51350. Tel: 712-736-2107. p. 769
McDowell, Bernadette, City Librn, Ventura County Library, Ray D Prueter Library, 510 Park Ave, Port Hueneme, CA, 93041. Tel: 805-486-5460. p. 256
McDowell, Bette, Ad, Pflugerville Public Library, 1008 W Pfluger, Pflugerville, TX, 78660. Tel: 512-990-6375. p. 2226
McDowell, Bobbi, Ch Serv, Ligonier Valley Library, 120 W Main St, Ligonier, PA, 15658-1243. Tel: 724-238-6451. p. 1955
McDowell, Dustin, Adult Serv, Orange Beach Public Library, 26267 Canal Rd, Orange Beach, AL, 36561-3917. Tel: 251-981-2923. p. 32
McDowell, Jamie, Librn, Buncombe County Public Libraries, Fairview Branch, One Taylor Rd, Fairview, NC, 28730. Tel: 828-250-6484. p. 1672
McDowell, Kate, Assoc Prof, University of Illinois at Urbana-Champaign, Library & Information Science Bldg, 501 E Daniel St, Champaign, IL, 61820-6211. Tel: 217-333-3280. p. 2784
McDowell, Kelli, Br Mgr, Tulsa City-County Library, South Broken Arrow, 3600 S Chestnut, Broken Arrow, OK, 74011. p. 1866
McDowell, Kelly, Libr Mgr, Hardisty Public Library, 5027 - 50 St, Hardisty, AB, T0B 1V0, CANADA. Tel: 780-888-3947. p. 2542
McDowell, Lorena, Dir, E C Weber Fraser Public Library, 16330 East 14 Mile Rd, Fraser, MI, 48026-2034. Tel: 586-293-2055. p. 1108
McDowell, Marilyn, Youth Serv Librn, Jeudevine Memorial Library, 93 N Main St, Hardwick, VT, 05843. Tel: 802-472-5948. p. 2285
McDowell, Teri, Dir, Coudersport Public Library, 502 Park Ave, Coudersport, PA, 16915-1672. Tel: 814-274-9382. p. 1924

McEachern, Felisha, Circ, Old Bridge Public Library, One Old Bridge Plaza, Old Bridge, NJ, 08857-2498. Tel: 732-721-5600, Ext 5012. p. 1431

McEachern, Joe, Library Contact, Sunbury Shores Arts & Nature Centre, Inc Library, 139 Water St, Saint Andrews, NB, E5B 1A7, CANADA. Tel: 506-529-3386. p. 2604

McEachern, Maria, ILL, Ref Librn, Center for Astrophysics Library / Harvard & Smithsonian Library, 60 Garden St, MS-56, Cambridge, MA, 02138. Tel: 617-496-5769. p. 1005

McEachern, Mark, Dir, Torrington Historical Society, 192 Main St, Torrington, CT, 06790. Tel: 860-482-8260. p. 342

McElderry, Stuart, Dean, Las Positas College Library, 3000 Campus Hill Dr, Livermore, CA, 94551. Tel: 925-424-1150. p. 156

McElfresh, Heather, Access Serv Coordr, Athens County Public Libraries, 95 W Washington, Nelsonville, OH, 45764-1177. Tel: 740-753-2118. p. 1805

McElhaney, Julie, Br Mgr, Licking County Library, Mary E Babcock Branch, 320 N Main St, Johnstown, OH, 43031. Tel: 740-967-2982. p. 1808

McElhinney, Kathleen, Metadata/Cat Librn, University of South Dakota, I D Weeks Library, 414 E Clark St, Vermillion, SD, 57069. Tel: 605-658-3367. p. 2084

McElmurray, Anna, Evening Libr Asst, Columbia International University, 7435 Monticello Rd, Columbia, SC, 29203-1599. Tel: 803-807-5158. p. 2053

McElprang, Merideth, Libr Dir, Lewisville Legacy Library, 3453 E 480 N, Lewisville, ID, 83431. Tel: 208-754-8608. p. 524

McElroy, Emily, Dean, University of Nebraska Medical Center, 600 S 42nd St, Omaha, NE, 68198. Tel: 402-559-7078. p. 1331

McElroy-Clark, Debby, Asst Dir, Support Serv, Memphis Public Library & Information Center, 3030 Poplar Ave, Memphis, TN, 38111. Tel: 901-415-2700. p. 2113

McElveen, Rodney, Dir, Satilla Regional Library, 200 S Madison Ave, Ste D, Douglas, GA, 31533. Tel: 912-384-4667. p. 476

McElyea, Bill, Media Equipment Technician, Ball State University Libraries, Education, Music & Media Library, Bracken Library BL-106, Muncie, IN, 47306. Tel: 765-285-5340. p. 708

McEneely, Katie Rose, Electronic Res Librn, Rosalind Franklin University of Medicine & Science, 3333 Green Bay Rd, North Chicago, IL, 60064-3095. Tel: 847-578-8808. p. 626

McEnery, Nancy, Librn, Napa Valley College, 1700 Bldg, 2277 Napa-Vallejo Hwy, Napa, CA, 94558. Tel: 707-256-7430. p. 182

McEnroe, Nancy, Ref Serv, Bernard E Witkin Alameda County Law Library, 125 Twelfth St, Oakland, CA, 94607-4912. Tel: 510-208-4830. p. 187

McEntee, Heather, Libr Dir, Bossier Parish Libraries, 2206 Beckett St, Bossier City, LA, 71111. Tel: 318-746-1693. p. 885

McEvoy, Stephanie, Adult/Info Serv Coordr, Asst Dir, Riverhead Free Library, 330 Court St, Riverhead, NY, 11901-2885. Tel: 631-727-3228. p. 1627

McEvoy, Tina, Asst Dir, Dir, Adult Serv, Lawrence Library, 15 Main St, Pepperell, MA, 01463. Tel: 978-433-0330. p. 1046

McEwen, Jeanna, Asst Dir, Oxford Public Library, 110 E Sixth St, Oxford, AL, 36203. Tel: 256-831-1750. p. 32

McFadden, Ben, Tech, Wake County Public Library System, 4020 Carya Dr, Raleigh, NC, 27610-2900. Tel: 919-250-1200. p. 1710

McFadden, Brianna, Acq, Archives, Western Oregon University, 345 N Monmouth Ave, Monmouth, OR, 97361-1396. Tel: 503-838-8883. p. 1887

McFadden, Carol, Ch Serv, Patten Free Library, 33 Summer St, Bath, ME, 04530. Tel: 207-443-5141, Ext 17. p. 916

McFadden, David, Sr Ref Librn, Southwestern Law School, Bullock Wilshire Bldg, 1st Flr, 3050 Wilshire Blvd, Los Angeles, CA, 90010. Tel: 213-738-5771. p. 168

McFadden, Diane, Ad, Atlantic Public Library, 507 Poplar St, Atlantic, IA, 50022. Tel: 712-243-5466. p. 733

McFadden, Jacqueline, Head, Govt Info, Winthrop University, 824 Oakland Ave, Rock Hill, SC, 29733. Tel: 803-323-2322. p. 2068

McFadden, Katie, Head, Adult Serv, Stratford Library Association, 2203 Main St, Stratford, CT, 06615. Tel: 203-385-4160. p. 340

McFadden, Laurie, Sr Dir, Berkeley College, 44 Rifle Camp Rd, Woodland Park, NJ, 07424. Tel: 973-278-5400, Ext 1230. p. 1456

McFadden, Laurie, Access Serv, Archivist, Alfred University, Herrick Memorial Library, One Saxon Dr, Alfred, NY, 14802. Tel: 607-871-2385. p. 1485

McFadden, Laurie, Sr Dir, Berkeley College, Three E 43rd St, 7th Flr, New York, NY, 10017. Tel: 212-986-4343, Ext 4232. p. 1580

McFadden, Laurie, Dir, Berkeley College, 99 Church St, White Plains, NY, 10601. Tel: 914-694-1122, Ext 3371. p. 1664

McFadden, Rae, Youth Serv, Great Falls Public Library, 301 Second Ave N, Great Falls, MT, 59401-2593. Tel: 406-453-0349, Ext 215. p. 1294

McFadden, Robert, Asst Librn, Pub Serv, Asst Librn, Ref, Gordon-Conwell Theological Seminary, 130 Essex St, South Hamilton, MA, 01982-2317. Tel: 978-646-4074. p. 1054

McFadden, Sue, Assoc Librn, Research & Scholarly Comm, Indiana University East Campus Library, Hayes Hall, 2325 Chester Blvd, Richmond, IN, 47374. Tel: 765-973-8325. p. 715

McFadden, Sue Jones, Bus Liaison Librn, Louisiana Tech University, Everett St at The Columns, Ruston, LA, 71272. Tel: 318-257-3555. p. 906

McFadden-Keesling, Allison, Librn, Oakland Community College, Woodland Hall, 7350 Cooley Lake Rd, Waterford, MI, 48327-4187. Tel: 248-942-3127. p. 1157

McFadzen, Amanda, Libr Asst, Kingswood University, 248 Main St, Sussex, NB, E4E 1R3, CANADA. Tel: 506-432-4417. p. 2605

McFall, Lauren, Emerging Tech Librn, MiraCosta College Library, One Barnard Dr, Bldg 1200, Oceanside, CA, 92056-3899. Tel: 760-634-7836. p. 187

McFall, Lauren, Emerging Tech Librn, MiraCosta College Library, San Elijo Campus, 3333 Manchester Ave, Bldg 100, Cardiff, CA, 92007-1516. Tel: 760-634-7850. p. 187

McFall, Lisa, Metadata Librn, Hamilton College, 198 College Hill Rd, Clinton, NY, 13323. Tel: 315-859-4788. p. 1519

McFarland, Clare, Libr Dir, Norman Williams Public Library, Ten The Green, Woodstock, VT, 05091. Tel: 802-457-2295. p. 2300

McFarland, Erica, Asst Dir, Ivy Tech Community College, 50 W Fall Creek Pkwy N Dr, Indianapolis, IN, 46208. Tel: 317-917-7178. p. 697

McFarland, Marielle, Libr Dir, University of Arkansas at Hope-Texarkana, 2500 S Main St, Hope, AR, 71801. Tel: 870-722-8251. p. 98

McFarland, Melissa, Asst Librn, Austin County Library System, 6730 Railroad St, Wallis, TX, 77485. Tel: 979-478-6813. p. 2254

McFarlane, Dothlyn, Head Librn, Coaldale Public Library, 2014 18th St, Coaldale, AB, T1M 1N1, CANADA. Tel: 403-345-1340. p. 2531

McFarling, Pat, Dir, Kentucky Wesleyan College, 3000 Frederica St, Owensboro, KY, 42301. Tel: 270-852-3259. p. 871

McFate, Sheri, Dir, Toledo Public Library, 206 E High St, Toledo, IA, 52342-1617. Tel: 641-484-3362. p. 786

McFerron, Terice, Tech Serv, Indiana University of Pennsylvania, Harold S Orendorff Library, 101 Cogswell Hall, 422 S 11th St, Indiana, PA, 15705-1071. Tel: 724-357-2892. p. 1946

McGaha, Jim, Libr Dir, Jamestown Public Library, 200 W Main St, Jamestown, NC, 27282. Tel: 336-454-4815. p. 1698

McGarity, Ashlee, Library Services, Western Nevada Community College, Fallon Campus Beck Library, Virgil Getto Bldg, 160 Campus Way, Fallon, NV, 89406. Tel: 775-445-3392. p. 1344

McGarrity, Gayna, Asst Br Supvr, Region of Waterloo Library, Linwood Branch, 5279 Ament Line, Linwood, ON, N0B 2A0, CANADA. Tel: 519-698-2700. p. 2629

McGarrity, Patricia, Libr Support Serv Asst, Arkansas State University Mid-South, Donald W Reynolds Ctr, 2000 W Broadway, West Memphis, AR, 72301-3829. Tel: 870-733-6768. p. 112

McGarvey, Marycatherine, Dir, Free Library of Springfield Township, 8900 Hawthorne Lane, Wyndmoor, PA, 19038. Tel: 215-836-5300. p. 2024

McGarvey, Nancy, Asst Dir & Syst Librn, Gwynedd Mercy University, 1325 Sumneytown Pike, Gwynedd Valley, PA, 19437. Tel: 215-646-7300, Ext 21493. p. 1939

McGarvey, Sasha, Youth Librn, Jaquith Public Library, Old Schoolhouse Common, 122 School St, Rm 2, Marshfield, VT, 05658. Tel: 802-426-3581. p. 2288

McGarvey, Sean, Libr Adminr, Pasco County Library System, 8012 Library Rd, Hudson, FL, 34667. Tel: 727-861-3020. p. 410

McGary, Barbara, Exec Dir, Lycoming County Library System, 19 E Fourth St, Williamsport, PA, 17701. Tel: 570-326-0536. p. 2023

McGary, Barbara S, Dir, James V Brown Library of Williamsport & Lycoming County, 19 E Fourth St, Williamsport, PA, 17701. Tel: 570-326-0536. p. 2023

McGaughey, Amberlee, Ch, Erie County Public Library, 160 E Front St, Erie, PA, 16507. Tel: 814-451-6900. p. 1931

McGaughey, Elizabeth, Assoc Dir, Cedars-Sinai Medical Center, South Tower Plaza, Rm 2815, 8700 Beverly Blvd, Los Angeles, CA, 90048. Tel: 310-423-3751. p. 161

McGaw, Lauren, Head, Access Serv, University of Winnipeg Library, 515 Portage Ave, Winnipeg, MB, R3B 2E9, CANADA. Tel: 204-786-9801. p. 2596

McGeary, Melissa, Asst Dir, Atlantic City Free Public Library, William K Cheatham Bldg, One N Tennessee Ave, Atlantic City, NJ, 08401. Tel: 609-345-2269, Ext 3075. p. 1388

McGeary, Melissa, Library Contact, Atlantic City Free Public Library, Richmond Avenue Branch, 4115 Ventnor Ave, Atlantic City, NJ, 08401. Tel: 609-345-2269, Ext 3075. p. 1388

McGeary, Tim, Assoc Univ Librn, Info Tech, Duke University Libraries, 411 Chapel Dr, Durham, NC, 27708. Tel: 919-660-5800. p. 1684

McGeath, Kerry, Mr, Managing Dir, DeSoto Public Library, 211 E Pleasant Run Rd, Ste C, DeSoto, TX, 75115. Tel: 972-230-9656. p. 2170

McGee, Angela, Media Spec, Indiana State Prison Library, One Park Row, Michigan City, IN, 46360. Tel: 219-874-7258. p. 706

McGee, Diane P, ILL, Harrison County Library System, 12135 Old Hwy 49, Gulfport, MS, 39501. Tel: 228-539-0110. p. 1217

McGee, Jessica, Libr Dir, Red Wing Public Library, 225 East Ave, Red Wing, MN, 55066-2298. Tel: 651-385-5105. p. 1194

McGee, Loralei T, Med Librn, North Mississippi Health Services, 830 S Gloster St, Tupelo, MS, 38801. Tel: 662-377-4399. p. 1234

McGee, Mandy N, Head, Adult Serv, Elmwood Park Public Library, One Conti Pkwy, Elmwood Park, IL, 60707. Tel: 708-395-1240. p. 585

McGee, Melinda, Br Mgr, Highland County District Library, Leesburg Branch, 240 E Main St, Leesburg, OH, 45135. Tel: 937-780-7295. p. 1789

McGee, Pat, Asst Dir, Cap Projects & Fac Serv, County of Los Angeles Public Library, 7400 E Imperial Hwy, Downey, CA, 90242-3375. Tel: 562-940-4145. p. 134

McGee, Rachel, Assoc Dir, Univ Libr, Saint Mary's University of Minnesota, Twin Cities Campus Library, LaSalle Hall, Rm 108, 2500 Park Ave, Minneapolis, MN, 55404. Tel: 612-728-5172. p. 1209

McGee, Rachel, Libr Dir, Saint Mary's University of Minnesota, 700 Terrace Heights, No 26, Winona, MN, 55987-1399. Tel: 612-728-5172. p. 1209

McGee, Sharon, Head, Archives & Spec Coll, Records Librn, Kentucky State University, 400 E Main St, Frankfort, KY, 40601-2355. Tel: 502-597-6824. p. 855

McGee, Sherry, Ref Librn, Truckee Meadows Community College, 7000 Dandini Blvd, Reno, NV, 89512-3999. Tel: 775-673-8261. p. 1349

McGee, Tina, Librn, Bolivar County Library System, Benoit Public Library, 109 W Preston St, Benoit, MS, 38725. Tel: 662-742-3112. p. 1214

McGeein, Marion, Mrs, Exec Dir, Brant Historical Society Library, 57 Charlotte St, Brantford, ON, N3T 2W6, CANADA. Tel: 519-752-2483. p. 2633

McGehee, Jacqueline, Dr, Libr Dir, Arkansas Baptist College, 1600 Martin Luther King Dr, Little Rock, AR, 72202. Tel: 501-420-1252. p. 100

McGeorge, Jennifer, Asst Dir, Peabody Institute Library, 15 Sylvan St, Danvers, MA, 01923. Tel: 978-774-0554. p. 1013

McGhee, Christopher, Dir, Stoughton Public Library, 84 Park St, Stoughton, MA, 02072-2974. Tel: 781-344-2711. p. 1058

McGhee, Ralph, Br Mgr, Knox County Public Library System, Mascot Branch, 1927 Library Rd, Mascot, TN, 37806. Tel: 865-933-2620. p. 2106

McGhee, Shenise, Librn, University of Arkansas-Pine Bluff, Fine Arts, Art Department, Mail Slot 4925, Pine Bluff, AR, 71601. Tel: 870-575-8896. p. 108

McGhee, Shenise, Librn, University of Arkansas-Pine Bluff, Nursing Lab, 1200 University Dr, Mail Slot 4973, Pine Bluff, AR, 71611. Tel: 870-575-8896. p. 108

McGibbon, Marcia, Managing Librn, Brooklyn Public Library, Marcy, 617 DeKalb Ave, Brooklyn, NY, 11216. Tel: 718-935-0032. p. 1503

McGiffin, Ginger, ILL Supvr, Libr Tech, Pennsylvania Western University - Clarion, 840 Wood St, Clarion, PA, 16214. Tel: 814-393-2343. p. 1922

McGilberry, Nicole, Mgr, Tri-County Regional Library, Mineral Springs Public Library, 310 E Runnels, Mineral Springs, AR, 71851. Tel: 870-287-7162. p. 106

McGill, Jeff, Mem Serv Librn, New Port Richey Public Library, 5939 Main St, New Port Richey, FL, 34652. Tel: 727-853-1265. p. 428

McGill, Sarah, Acad Librn, Aultman Hospital, Aultman Education Ctr, C2-230, 2600 Seventh St SW, Canton, OH, 44710-1799. Tel: 330-363-3471. p. 1755

McGill, Sean, Br Mgr, Fort Vancouver Regional Library District, Ridgefield Community Library, 228 Simons St, Ridgefield, WA, 98642. p. 2391

McGill, Shellie, Libr Dir, Bartlesville Public Library, 600 S Johnstone, Bartlesville, OK, 74003. Tel: 918-338-4161. p. 1841

McGillicuddy, Madigan, Youth/Young Adult Librn, Atlanta-Fulton Public Library System, Joan P Gardner Library, 980 Ponce de Leon Ave NE, Atlanta, GA, 30306. Tel: 404-885-7820. p. 461

McGillis, Louise, Ref Serv, Memorial University of Newfoundland, Ferriss Hodgett Library, University Dr, Corner Brook, NL, A2H 6P9, CANADA. Tel: 709-637-6200, Ext 6122. p. 2610

McGillivray, Anne, Cataloger, Tech Serv, University of Toronto Libraries, Knox College Caven Library, Knox College, 59 St George St, Toronto, ON, M5S 2E6, CANADA. Tel: 416-978-6719. p. 2699

McGinley, Allen, Dir, Westfield Memorial Library, 550 E Broad St, Westfield, NJ, 07090. Tel: 908-789-4090. p. 1454

McGinley, Gina, Br Librn, New Madrid County Library, , 303 S Main St, Gideon, MO, 63848. Tel: 573-379-3583. p. 1266

McGinley, Tiffany, Br Librn, New Madrid County Library, Risco Service Center, 210 Missouri St, Risco, MO, 63874. p. 1266

McGinn, Suzanne, Executive Asst, Saint Paul Public Library, 90 W Fourth St, Saint Paul, MN, 55102-1668. Tel: 651-266-7000. p. 1202

McGinnes, Teresa, Cataloger, Computer Tech, Bedford County Library, 240 S Wood St, Bedford, PA, 15522. Tel: 814-623-5010. p. 1909

McGinness, Mike, Exec Dir, Oakland County Pioneer & Historical Society, 405 Cesar E Chavez Ave, Pontiac, MI, 48342-1068. Tel: 248-338-6732. p. 1142

McGinnis, Colin, Adult Serv Mgr, McMillan Memorial Library, 490 E Grand Ave, Wisconsin Rapids, WI, 54494-4898. Tel: 715-422-5126. p. 2489

McGinnis, Daniel, Syst Librn, University of Texas Rio Grande Valley, 1201 W University Blvd, Edinburg, TX, 78541-2999. Tel: 956-665-2878. p. 2173

McGinnis, Julia F, Archivist, Institutional Repository Librn, Spec Projects Librn, Pennsylvania Western University - California, 250 University Ave, California, PA, 15419-1394. Tel: 724-938-5472. p. 1917

McGinnis, Lynn, Mgr, Cabell County Public Library, Milton Branch, 1140 Smith St, Milton, WV, 25541. Tel: 304-743-6711. p. 2404

McGinnis, Marianne, Dir & Librn, Charlotte Public Library, Eight Couser Blvd, Charlotte, TX, 78011. Tel: 830-277-1212. p. 2155

McGinnis, Marie, Dir, Eckstein Memorial Library, 1034 E Dewey St, Cassville, WI, 53806. Tel: 608-725-5838. p. 2427

McGinnis, Penny, Tech Serv Mgr, University of Cincinnati, 4200 Clermont College Dr, Batavia, OH, 45103-1785. Tel: 513-732-5206. p. 1749

McGinnis, Rosanna, Libr Dir, Opelika Public Library, 1100 Glenn St, Opelika, AL, 36801. Tel: 334-705-5380. p. 31

McGinnis, Susan, Librn, Kentucky Talking Book Library, 300 Coffee Tree Rd, Frankfort, KY, 40601. Tel: 502-782-3640. p. 856

McGinnis, Vicki, Supv Librn, United States Navy, Bldg 3107, 1050 Remount Rd, Charleston, SC, 29406-3515. Tel: 843-794-0074. p. 2051

McGinty, Molly, Br Mgr, Harris County Public Library, Crosby Edith Fae Cook Cole Branch, 135 Hare Rd, Crosby, TX, 77532. Tel: 832-927-7790. p. 2192

McGittigan, Anne, Circ Coordr, Lone Star College System, Kingwood College Library, 20000 Kingwood Dr, Kingwood, TX, 77339. Tel: 281-312-1691. p. 2197

McGivern, Kate, Ref (Info Servs), Bergen Community College, 400 Paramus Rd, Paramus, NJ, 07652-1595. Tel: 201-447-7980. p. 1432

Mcgivney, Jessica, Access Serv, Farmingdale State College of New York, 2350 Broadhollow Rd, Farmingdale, NY, 11735-1021. Tel: 934-420-2040. p. 1532

McGivney, Peter, Ref Librn, Howland Public Library, 313 Main St, Beacon, NY, 12508. Tel: 845-831-1134. p. 1491

McGlothlin, Lori, ILL Coordr, Wagoner City Public Library, 302 N Main St, Wagoner, OK, 74467-3834. Tel: 918-485-2126. p. 1868

McGlynn, Kelly, Knowledge Serv Analyst, Skadden, Arps, Slate, Meagher & Flom LLP, 1440 New York Ave NW, Washington, DC, 20005. Tel: 202-371-7000. p. 375

McGohan, Amy, Assoc Libr Dir, Electronic Res Librn, Harding University, 915 E Market St, Searcy, AR, 72149-5615. Tel: 501-279-5334. p. 109

McGoldrick, Nancy, Circ, Manhasset Public Library, 30 Onderdonk Ave, Manhasset, NY, 11030. Tel: 516-627-2300, Ext 106. p. 1568

McGonagle, Terry, Media Coordr, Whittier College, Bonnie Bell Wardman Library, 7031 Founders Hill Rd, Whittier, CA, 90608-9984. Tel: 562-907-4247. p. 259

McGonegal, Patrick, Webmaster, Juneau Public Libraries, 292 Marine Way, Juneau, AK, 99801. Tel: 907-586-5249. p. 47

McGonigle, Katie, Youth Serv, Richard Salter Storrs Library, 693 Longmeadow St, Longmeadow, MA, 01106. Tel: 413-565-4181. p. 1029

McGough, Sara, Mgr, Mobile Public Library, 701 Government St, Mobile, AL, 36602. Tel: 251-340-1532. p. 26

McGovern, Chrissie, Br Mgr, Gaston County Public Library, Dallas Branch, 105 S Holland St, Dallas, NC, 28034. Tel: 704-922-3621. p. 1690

McGovern, Dorothy, Interim Head, Circ, St John's University Library, St Augustine Hall, 8000 Utopia Pkwy, Jamaica, NY, 11439. Tel: 718-990-6142. p. 1556

McGovern, Elizabeth, Head, Children's Servx, Westwood Public Library, 660 High St, Westwood, MA, 02090. Tel: 781-320-1043. p. 1068

McGovern, Elizabeth, Libr Dir, Westwood Public Library, 660 High St, Westwood, MA, 02090. Tel: 781-326-7562. p. 1068

McGovern, Elizabeth, Head Librn, Cheltenham Township Library System, Elkins Park Free Library, 563 E Church Rd, Elkins Park, PA, 19027-2499. Tel: 215-635-5000. p. 1937

McGovern, Kim, Acq, Harrisburg Area Community College, 735 Cumberland St, Lebanon, PA, 17042. Tel: 717-780-2465. p. 1953

McGovern, Ryan, Supvr, Pub Serv, Eckerd College, 4200 54th Ave S, Saint Petersburg, FL, 33711. Tel: 727-864-8337. p. 441

McGowan, Angie, Libr Mgr, Russell County Public Library, 535 N Main St, Jamestown, KY, 42629. Tel: 270-343-7323. p. 861

McGowan, Anna Therese, Chief, User Serv Br, United States Nuclear Regulatory Commission, Technical Library, 11545 Rockville Pike, T2C8, Rockville, MD, 20852-2738. Tel: 301-415-6239, 301-415-7204. p. 976

McGowan, Beth, Rare Bks & Spec Coll Librn, Northern Illinois University Libraries, 217 Normal Rd, DeKalb, IL, 60115-2828. Tel: 815-753-1947. p. 577

McGowan, Christina, Librn, Frenchman's Bay Library, 1776 US Hwy, No 1, Sullivan, ME, 04664. Tel: 207-422-2307. p. 943

McGowan, Edwin, Dir, Bear Mountain Trailside Museums Library, Bear Mountain State Park, Bear Mountain, NY, 10911. Tel: 845-786-2701, Ext 263. p. 1491

McGowan, Gloria, Libr Mgr, Thelma Fanning Memorial Library, 1907 21 Ave, Nanton, AB, T0L 1R0, CANADA. Tel: 403-646-5535. p. 2549

McGowan, Harleigh, Marketing & Teen Librarian, San Marcos Public Library, 625 E Hopkins, San Marcos, TX, 78666. Tel: 512-393-8200. p. 2241

McGowan, Katie, Libr Dir, Harcum College, 750 Montgomery Ave, Bryn Mawr, PA, 19010-3476. Tel: 610-526-6062. p. 1916

McGowan, Meredith, Actg Sr Librn, Los Angeles Public Library System, Sherman Oaks Martin Pollard Branch Library, 14245 Moorpark St, Sherman Oaks, CA, 91423-2722. Tel: 818-205-9716. p. 165

McGowan, Patrick, Dir, Hubbard Memorial Library, 24 Center St, Ludlow, MA, 01056-2795. Tel: 413-583-3408. p. 1030

McGowan, Sunny, Libr Mgr, Scripps Mercy Hospital Medical Library, 4077 Fifth Ave, MER-36, San Diego, CA, 92103-2180. Tel: 619-260-7024. p. 221

McGowen, Steve, Assoc Dir/Librn, Denison Public Library, 300 W Gandy St, Denison, TX, 75020-3153. Tel: 903-465-1797. p. 2170

McGrail, Joseph R, Circ/Ser, Libr Asst, ILL, Cardinal Stafford Library, 1300 S Steele St, Denver, CO, 80210-2526. Tel: 303-715-3228. p. 273

McGrail, Kathleen, Dir, Upper Saddle River Public Library, 245 Lake St, Upper Saddle River, NJ, 07458. Tel: 201-327-2583. p. 1449

McGraner, Vic, Syst Coordr, Aiken-Bamberg-Barnwell-Edgefield Regional Library System, 314 Chesterfield St SW, Aiken, SC, 29801-7171. Tel: 803-642-7575. p. 2045

McGrath, Catherine, Libr Assoc, Hilbert College, 5200 S Park Ave, Hamburg, NY, 14075. Tel: 716-926-8913. p. 1543

McGrath, Cheryl, Exec Dir, Emerson College, 120 Boylston St, Boston, MA, 02116-4624. Tel: 617-824-8668. p. 995

McGrath, Courtney, Asst Dir, Ida Rupp Public Library, 310 Madison St, Port Clinton, OH, 43452. Tel: 419-732-3212. p. 1816

McGrath, Frances, Ch Serv, Willimantic Public Library, 905 Main St, Willimantic, CT, 06226. Tel: 860-465-3082. p. 347

McGrath, Jen, Teen Librn, Westborough Public Library, 55 W Main St, Westborough, MA, 01581. Tel: 508-366-3050. p. 1066

McGrath, Jessica, Br Dir, Settlement Music School, 416 Queen St, Philadelphia, PA, 19147. Tel: 215-320-2601. p. 1986

McGrath, Karen, Curator, Kelley House Museum, Inc, 45007 Albion St, Mendocino, CA, 95460. Tel: 707-937-5791. p. 175

McGrath, Karen, Br Librn, Cranston Public Library, Auburn Branch, 396 Pontiac Ave, Cranston, RI, 02910-3322. Tel: 401-781-6116. p. 2031

McGrath, Laura, Dep Dir, Skokie Public Library, 5215 Oakton St, Skokie, IL, 60077-3680. Tel: 847-673-7774. p. 647

McGrath, Margaret, Librn, Plymouth Public Library, Manomet Branch, 12 Strand Ave, Plymouth, MA, 02360. Tel: 508-830-4185. p. 1047

McGrath, Mary, Ch Serv, Massapequa Public Library, Bar Harbour Bldg, 40 Harbor Lane, Massapequa Park, NY, 11762. Tel: 516-799-0770. p. 1569

McGrath, Renee, Youth Serv Mgr, Nassau Library System, 900 Jerusalem Ave, Uniondale, NY, 11553-3039. Tel: 516-292-8920. p. 1654

McGrath, Sharon, Librn, St Brides Public Library, Council Bldg, Main Rd, General Delivery, St. Bride's, NL, A0B 1E0, CANADA. Tel: 709-337-2360. p. 2608

McGrath, Sharon, Library Contact, Eastern Counties Regional Library, St Peter's Branch, 10036 Grenville St, Unit C, St. Peter's, NS, B0E 3B0, CANADA. Tel: 902-535-2465. p. 2621

McGraw, Amy, Asst Dir, Independence Public Library, 805 First St E, Independence, IA, 50644. Tel: 319-334-2470. p. 759

McGraw, John, Dir, Faulkner-Van Buren Regional Library System, 1900 Tyler St, Conway, AR, 72034. Tel: 501-327-7482. p. 92

McGraw, Paula, Cat/ILL Spec, Tech Serv, Fleming County Public Library, 202 Bypass Blvd, Flemingsburg, KY, 41041-1298. Tel: 606-845-7851. p. 854

McGray, Bobbie, Mgr, Satilla Regional Library, Nicholls Public Library, 108 N Liberty St, Nicholls, GA, 31554. Tel: 912-345-2534. p. 476

McGreal, Amanda, Asst Dir, Manchester Public Library, 304 N Franklin St, Manchester, IA, 52057. Tel: 563-927-3719. p. 767

McGregor, Annette, Br Mgr, Dixie Regional Library System, Pontotoc County Library, 111 N Main St, Pontotoc, MS, 38863. p. 1230

McGregor, Michele, Dir, Garden Plain Community Library, 421 W Ave B, Garden Plain, KS, 67050. Tel: 316-535-2990. p. 809

McGregor, Shannon, Libr Dir, Montezuma Township Library, 309 N Aztec, Montezuma, KS, 67867. Tel: 620-846-7032. p. 825

McGregor, Tiffany, Dir, Neumann University Library, One Neumann Dr, Aston, PA, 19014-1298. Tel: 610-361-2487. p. 1907

McGrew, Kevin, Asst Prof, Libr Dir, The College of Saint Scholastica Library, 1200 Kenwood Ave, Duluth, MN, 55811-4199. Tel: 218-723-6198. p. 1171

McGrew, Susan, Librn, Mahoning County Law Library, Courthouse 4th Flr, 120 Market St, Youngstown, OH, 44503-1752. Tel: 330-740-2295. p. 1835

McGroary, Barbara, Ref Librn, United States Army, Redstone Arsenal Family & MWR Library, 3323 Redeye Rd, Redstone Arsenal, AL, 35898. Tel: 256-876-4741. p. 34

McGuckin, Briana, Ref & Instruction Librn, Central Connecticut State University, 1615 Stanley St, New Britain, CT, 06050. Tel: 860-832-2055. p. 324

McGuffie, Raeshawn, Asst Dir, Tech Serv, Hampton University, 129 William R Harvey Way, Hampton, VA, 23668. Tel: 757-727-6803. p. 2323

McGuigan, Ciaran, Asst Dir, Newport Public Library, 316 N Fourth St, Newport, PA, 17074-1203. Tel: 717-567-6860. p. 1970

McGuigan, Glenn, Head Librn, Pennsylvania State University-Harrisburg Library, 351 Olmsted Dr, Middletown, PA, 17057-4850. Tel: 717-948-6078. p. 1963

McGuigan, Julia, Dir, Bloomfield Public Library, 23 E McClure St, New Bloomfield, PA, 17068. Tel: 717-582-7426. p. 1968

McGuigan, Niamh, Head, Ref Serv, Loyola University Chicago Libraries, Elizabeth M Cudahy Memorial Library, 1032 W Sheridan Rd, Chicago, IL, 60660. Tel: 773-508-2637. p. 563

McGuill, Tina, Libr Dir, Dennis M O'Connor Public Library, 815 S Commerce St, Refugio, TX, 78377. Tel: 361-526-2608. p. 2231

McGuire, Amy, Exec Dir, Saint Joseph County Law Library, Court House, 101 S Main St, South Bend, IN, 46601. Tel: 574-245-6753. p. 718

McGuire, Britni, Mgr, Info Serv, Arkansas State Library, 900 W Capitol, Ste 100, Little Rock, AR, 72201-3108. Tel: 501-682-2864. p. 100

McGuire, Catherine, Head, Ref & Outreach, Thurgood Marshall State Law Library, Courts of Appeals Bldg, 361 Rowe Blvd, Annapolis, MD, 21401. Tel: 410-260-1430. p. 950

McGuire, Darwin, Tech Serv Mgr, Genesee District Library, 4195 W Pasadena Ave, Flint, MI, 48504. Tel: 810-732-0110. p. 1105

McGuire, Dennis, Asst Dir, Columbia College Chicago Library, 624 S Michigan Ave, Chicago, IL, 60605-1996. Tel: 312-369-7434. p. 559

McGuire, Eva, Dir, Craft Memorial Library, 600 Commerce St, Bluefield, WV, 24701. Tel: 304-325-3943. p. 2398

McGuire, Jessica, Dir, Russell Public Library, 126 E Sixth St, Russell, KS, 67665. Tel: 785-483-2742. p. 834

McGuire, Kara, Asst Dir, Circ, ILL, Daemen University Library, Research & Information Commons, 4380 Main St, Amherst, NY, 14226-3592. Tel: 716-839-8243. p. 1486

McGuire, KellyAnne, Outreach Librn, Bard College at Simon's Rock, 84 Alford Rd, Great Barrington, MA, 01230. Tel: 413-528-7356. p. 1022

McGuire, Mariah, Ch Serv, Outreach Serv Librn, Saint Helena Public Library, 1492 Library Lane, Saint Helena, CA, 94574-1143. Tel: 707-963-5244. p. 210

McGuire, Michael C, Electronic Res Mgr, Colby College Libraries, 5100 Mayflower Hill, Waterville, ME, 04901. Tel: 207-859-5161. p. 945

McGuire, Micheal, Libr Dir, Clearwater Campus, Keiser University Library System, 1500 NW 49th St, Fort Lauderdale, FL, 33309. Tel: 954-351-4035. p. 401

McGuire, Molly, Digital Strategies Librarian, Oakland University Library, 100 Library Dr, Rochester, MI, 48309-4479. Tel: 248-370-2457. p. 1144

McGuire, Nancy Ruth, Instrul Serv Librn, Bob Jones University, 1700 Wade Hampton Blvd, Greenville, SC, 29614. Tel: 864-370-1800, Ext 6025. p. 2060

McGuire, Nicole, Dr, Educ Spec, Union Hospital, 1606 N Seventh St, Terre Haute, IN, 47804. Tel: 812-238-7641. p. 721

McGuire, Noreen, Asst Univ Librn, Coll Mgt, Pace University, 861 Bedford Rd, Pleasantville, NY, 10570-2799. Tel: 914-773-3815. p. 1620

McGuire, Patrick, Educ Curator, Elkhart County Historical Society Museum, Inc, 304 W Vistula St, Bristol, IN, 46507. Tel: 574-848-4322. p. 672

McGuire, Rachel, Mgr, Libr Serv, West Virginia School of Osteopathic Medicine, 400 Lee St N, Lewisburg, WV, 24901. Tel: 304-647-6261. p. 2407

McGuire, Ruth, Dir, University of Northwestern-St Paul, 3003 Snelling Ave N, Saint Paul, MN, 55113. Tel: 651-631-5241. p. 1202

McGuire, Sarah, Br Mgr, Allegany County Library System, South Cumberland Library, 100 Seymour St, Cumberland, MD, 21502. Tel: 301-724-1607. p. 964

McGuire, Shannon, Supvr, Essex County Library, Tecumseh - Cada Branch, 13675 St Gregory's Rd, Tecumseh, ON, N8N 3E4, CANADA. Tel: 226-946-1529, Ext 230. p. 2641

McGuire, Waller, Exec Dir, Saint Louis Public Library, 1301 Olive St, Saint Louis, MO, 63103. Tel: 314-539-0300. p. 1274

McGuirk, Heather, Head, YA, Sunderland Public Library, 20 School St, Sunderland, MA, 01375. Tel: 413-665-2642. p. 1058

McGurk, Pat, Chief Librn, Elliot Lake Public Library, Pearson Plaza, 40 Hillside Dr S, Elliot Lake, ON, P5A 1M7, CANADA. Tel: 705-848-2287, Ext 2800. p. 2640

McGurr, Melanie, Dr, Assoc Dean, Technical Servs & Faculty, University of Akron, University Libraries, 315 Buchtel Mall, Akron, OH, 44325-1701. Tel: 330-972-5390. p. 1745

McHale, Chris, Access Serv Librn, Fiorello H LaGuardia Community College Library, 31-10 Thomson Ave, Long Island City, NY, 11101. Tel: 718-482-5441. p. 1565

McHale, Mark, Adult Serv Mgr, Strathcona County Library, 401 Festival Lane, Sherwood Park, AB, T8A 5P7, CANADA. Tel: 780-410-8600. p. 2553

McHaney, Melba, Br Spec, Coalinga-Huron Library District, Huron Branch, 36050 O St, Huron, CA, 93234. Tel: 559-945-2284. p. 131

McHarg, Mary Ann, Mgr, Carnegie Library of Pittsburgh, Hazelwood, 5006 Second Ave, Pittsburgh, PA, 15207-1674. Tel: 412-421-2517. p. 1991

McHargh, Hugh, Dir, Corning Museum of Glass, Five Museum Way, Corning, NY, 14830. Tel: 607-438-5300. p. 1522

McHenry, Melissa, Media Librn, Gates Public Library, 902 Elmgrove Rd, Rochester, NY, 14624. Tel: 585-247-6446. p. 1628

McHenry, Michael, Dir, Res, Vinson & Elkins, Texas Tower, 845 Texas Ave, Ste 4700, Houston, TX, 77002. Tel: 713-758-2222, 713-758-2990. p. 2200

McHenry, Ruth, Librn, The Frances Kibble Kenny Lake Public Library, Mile 5 Edgerton Hwy, Copper Center, AK, 99573. Tel: 907-822-3015. p. 44

McHenry, Shelly, Mgr, William Sharpe Jr Hospital, 936 Sharpe Hospital Rd, Weston, WV, 26452. Tel: 304-269-1210, Ext 37148. p. 2417

McHenry, Wendie, Asst Univ Librn, University of Victoria Libraries, McPherson Library, PO Box 1800, Victoria, BC, V8W 3H5, CANADA. Tel: 250-721-8211. p. 2583

McHenry, William, Colls Librn, Bard College at Simon's Rock, 84 Alford Rd, Great Barrington, MA, 01230. Tel: 413-528-7370. p. 1022

McHone-Chase, Sarah, Dir, Univ Libr, Aurora University, 315 S Gladstone Ave, Aurora, IL, 60506-4892. Tel: 630-844-5443. p. 539
McHone-Chase, Sarah, Head, User Serv, Northern Illinois University Libraries, 217 Normal Rd, DeKalb, IL, 60115-2828. Tel: 815-753-9860. p. 577
McHose, Ashley, Library Servs Lead, Lakeshore Technical College Library, 1290 North Ave, Cleveland, WI, 53015. Tel: 920-693-1311. p. 2428
McHose, Ashley, Circ Mgr, Brown County Library, 515 Pine St, Green Bay, WI, 54301. Tel: 920-448-5825. p. 2438
McHugh, Brenda, Asst Head Librn, Ch, Saint Peter Public Library, 601 S Washington Ave, Saint Peter, MN, 56082. Tel: 507-934-7420. p. 1203
McHugh, David, BadgerLink Coordr, Wisconsin Department of Public Instruction, Resources for Libraries & Lifelong Learning, 2109 S Stoughton Rd, Madison, WI, 53716-2899. Tel: 608-224-5389. p. 2452
McHugh, Donna, Circ, ILL, Suffolk County Community College, 1001 Crooked Hill Rd, Brentwood, NY, 11717. Tel: 631-851-6507. p. 1496
McHugh, James, Tech Operations Mgr, Nassau Library System, 900 Jerusalem Ave, Uniondale, NY, 11553-3039. Tel: 516-292-8920. p. 1654
McHugh, Mary, Circ, Libr Tech, Georgetown Peabody Library, Two Maple St, Georgetown, MA, 01833. Tel: 978-352-5728. p. 1020
McHugh, Valisa, Br Mgr, Amarillo Public Library, Southwest Branch, 6801 W 45th St, Amarillo, TX, 79109. Tel: 806-359-2094. p. 2134
McIlhenney, Joseph, Dir, Milanof-Schock Library, 1184 Anderson Ferry Rd, Mount Joy, PA, 17552. Tel: 717-653-1510. p. 1966
McIllece, Emily, Libr Dir, Nebraska Methodist College, 720 N 87th St, Omaha, NE, 68114. Tel: 402-354-7246. p. 1329
McIlvain, Caitlyn, Librn, Nebraska Department of Corrections, 1107 Recharge Rd, York, NE, 68467-8003. Tel: 402-362-3317. p. 1341
McIlvaine, Patty, Board Pres, Pine Public Library, 16720 Pine Valley Rd, Pine Grove, CO, 80470. Tel: 303-838-6093. p. 292
McInerney, Claire, Assoc Prof, Rutgers, The State University of New Jersey, Four Huntington St, New Brunswick, NJ, 08901-1071. Tel: 848-932-7500. p. 2788
McInerney, Maura, Curator, Foothills Art Center, 809 15th St, Golden, CO, 80401. Tel: 303-279-3922. p. 283
McInnes, John, Head, Fiction/AV/Teen Serv, Mount Prospect Public Library, Ten S Emerson St, Mount Prospect, IL, 60056. Tel: 847-253-5675. p. 621
McInnes, Robert, Archives & Spec Coll Librn, Westminster Theological Seminary, 2960 W Church Rd, Glenside, PA, 19038. Tel: 215-572-3856. p. 1937
McInnis, Wendy, Campus Librn, Nova Scotia Community College, Pictou Campus Library, 39 Acadia Ave, Stellarton, NS, B0K 1S0, CANADA. Tel: 902-755-7201. p. 2620
McIntire, Joy, Br Serv Coordr, Central Rappahannock Regional Library, 125 Olde Greenwich Dr, Ste 160, Fredericksburg, VA, 22408. Tel: 540-372-1144, Ext 7005. p. 2319
McIntosh, Christine, Dir, Bethel Park Public Library, 5100 W Library Ave, Bethel Park, PA, 15102. Tel: 412-835-2207. p. 1911
McIntosh, Debra, Col Archivist, Millsaps College, 1701 N State St, Jackson, MS, 39210. Tel: 601-974-1077. p. 1222
McIntosh, Jennifer, Assoc Dean of Libr, College of DuPage Library, 425 Fawell Blvd, Glen Ellyn, IL, 60137-6599. Tel: 630-942-2353. p. 593
McIntosh, Megan, Tech Serv Librn, Bellevue University, 1028 Bruin Blvd, Bellevue, NE, 68005. Tel: 402-557-7305. p. 1308
McIntosh, Wendy, Dir, Lincoln Library, 222 W River Rd, Lincoln, VT, 05443. Tel: 802-453-2665. p. 2287
McIntyre, Beth, Dir, Piedmont Regional Library System, 990 Washington St, Jefferson, GA, 30549-1011. Tel: 706-367-9399. p. 482
McIntyre, Deirdre, Br Supvr, Licking County Library, Hebron Branch, 934 W Main St, Hebron, OH, 43025. Tel: 740-928-3923. p. 1808
McIntyre, Ethan, Dir, Beardstown Houston Memorial Library, 13 Boulevard Rd, Beardstown, IL, 62618-8119. Tel: 217-323-4204. p. 540
McIntyre, John, Coordr, Tonkon Torp LLP, 888 SW Fifth Ave, Ste 1600, Portland, OR, 97204. Tel: 503-221-1440. p. 1894
McIntyre, Maryanne, Ad, Sally Stretch Keen Memorial Library, 94 Main St, Vincentown, NJ, 08088. Tel: 609-859-3598. p. 1449
McIntyre, Michelle, Dir, Roaring Spring Community Library, 320 E Main St, Roaring Spring, PA, 16673-1009. Tel: 814-224-2994. p. 2002
McIntyre, Paula, Coll Develop Librn, Jacksonville University, 2800 University Blvd N, Jacksonville, FL, 32211-3394. Tel: 904-256-7265. p. 413
McIntyre, Sarah, Dir, Sandy Public Library, 38980 Proctor Blvd, Sandy, OR, 97055-8040. Tel: 503-489-2168. p. 1898
McIntyre, Sarah, Libr Dir, Hoodland Library, 24525 E Welches Rd, Welches, OR, 97067. Tel: 503-622-3460. p. 1901
Mcintyre, Sarah, Br Mgr, Ottawa Public Library/Bibliothèque publique d'Ottawa, North Gloucester, 2036 Ogilvie Rd, Ottawa, ON, K1J 7N8, CANADA. p. 2669
Mcintyre, Sarah, Br Mgr, Ottawa Public Library/Bibliothèque publique d'Ottawa, Orleans Branch, 1705 Orleans Blvd, Ottawa, ON, K1C 4W2, CANADA. p. 2669
McIntyre, Susie, Libr Dir, Great Falls Public Library, 301 Second Ave N, Great Falls, MT, 59401-2593. Tel: 406-453-0181, Ext 216. p. 1294
McIntyre, Tamara, Br Mgr, Georgetown County Library, Waccamaw Neck, 41 St Paul Pl, Pawleys Island, SC, 29585. Tel: 843-545-3623. p. 2060
McInvaill, Dwight, Dir, Georgetown County Library, 405 Cleland St, Georgetown, SC, 29440-3200. Tel: 843-545-3304. p. 2060
McKain, Joshua Van Kirk, Col Librn, Libr Dir, Fisher College Library, 118 Beacon St, Boston, MA, 02116. Tel: 617-236-8875. p. 995
McKay, Amanda D, Dir, Effingham Public Library, 200 N Third St, Effingham, IL, 62401. Tel: 217-342-2464. p. 582
McKay, Celeste, Ch Mgr, River Valley District Library, 214 S Main St, Port Byron, IL, 61275. Tel: 309-523-3440. p. 636
McKay, Elizabeth, Youth Serv Coordr, The Ferguson Library, One Public Library Plaza, Stamford, CT, 06904. Tel: 203-964-1000. p. 338
McKay, Kat, Br Mgr, Wilmington Public Library of Clinton County, Clinton-Massie Branch, 2556 Lebanon Rd, Clarksville, OH, 45113. Tel: 937-289-1079. p. 1832
McKay, Kathy, Dir, Jackson County Public Library, 412 Fourth St, Walden, CO, 80480. Tel: 970-723-4602. p. 297
McKay, Marilyn, Librn, Collier County Public Library, East Naples Branch, 8787 E Tamiami Trail, Naples, FL, 34113. Tel: 239-775-5592. p. 427
McKay, Myrna, Dir, Steele Public Library, 108 E Main St, Steele, MO, 63877-1528. Tel: 573-695-3561. p. 1282
McKay, Nancy, Head, Teen Serv, Byron Public Library District, 100 S Washington St, Byron, IL, 61010. Tel: 815-234-5107. p. 547
McKay, Nellie, Libr Dir, United States Department of Energy, 1450 Queen Ave SW, Albany, OR, 97321-2198. Tel: 541-967-5864. p. 1871
McKay, Rebecca, Dean of Libr, University of Texas at Tyler Library, 3900 University Blvd, Tyler, TX, 75799. Tel: 903-566-7342. p. 2250
McKay, Richard, Dir, San Jacinto College South, 13735 Beamer Rd, S10, Houston, TX, 77089-6099. Tel: 281-922-3416. p. 2198
McKay, Tiana, Libr Office Coord, Milton-Union Public Library, 560 S Main St, West Milton, OH, 45383. Tel: 937-698-5515. p. 1830
McKean, Alana, Curator, Starhill Forest Arboretum Library, 12000 Boy Scout Trail, Petersburg, IL, 62675. Tel: 217-632-3685. p. 635
McKean, Kelly, Commun Librn, Santa Clara County Library District, Milpitas Public, 160 N Main St, Milpitas, CA, 95035. Tel: 408-262-1171. p. 127
McKeane, Sean, Colls Mgr, Nova Scotia Museum Library, 1747 Summer St, 3rd Flr, Halifax, NS, B3H 3A6, CANADA. Tel: 902-424-6453. p. 2621
McKechnie, Sue, ILL, Jefferson Public Library, 321 S Main St, Jefferson, WI, 53549-1772. Tel: 920-674-7733. p. 2443
McKee, Alison, Dep County Librn, Support Serv, Contra Costa County Library, 777 Arnold Dr, Ste 210, Martinez, CA, 94553. Tel: 925-608-7700. p. 174
McKee, Kerry, Dir, Access Serv, Icahn School of Medicine at Mount Sinai, One Gustave L Levy Pl, New York, NY, 10029. Tel: 212-241-7791. p. 1588
McKee, Laurie, Ref/Tech Serv Librn, Little Elm Public Library, 100 W Eldorado Pkwy, Little Elm, TX, 75068. Tel: 214-975-0430. p. 2212
McKee, William, Br Mgr, Jefferson Parish Library, Gretna Branch, 102 Willow Dr, Gretna, LA, 70053. Tel: 504-364-2716. p. 897
McKeel, Rene, Access Serv Mgr, Pub Serv Mgr, Wingate University, 110 Church ST, Wingate, NC, 28174. Tel: 704-233-8089. p. 1724
McKeeman, Carolyn, Br Supvr, Bruce County Public Library, Mildmay-Carrick Branch, 51 Elora St, Mildmay, ON, N0G 2J0, CANADA. Tel: 519-367-2814. p. 2673
McKeeman, Carolyn, Br Supvr, Bruce County Public Library, Teeswater Branch, Two Clinton St, Teeswater, ON, N0G 2S0, CANADA. Tel: 519-392-6801. p. 2674
Mckeich, Cynthia, Libr Dir, Humber College, 205 Humber College Blvd, Toronto, ON, M9W 5L7, CANADA. Tel: 416-675-5079. p. 2690
McKeigue, Elizabeth, Dean of Libr, Salem State University, 352 Lafayette St, Salem, MA, 01970-5353. Tel: 978-542-6230. p. 1051
McKeithan, Maggie, Dir, Spring Lake District Library, 123 E Exchange St, Spring Lake, MI, 49456. Tel: 616-846-5770. p. 1152
McKelvy, Dina, Dir, Medical Education, MaineHealth, 22 Bramhall St, 5th Flr, Portland, ME, 04102. Tel: 207-662-2202. p. 936
McKenna, Anne, Distance Educ, Kauai Community College, 3-1901 Kaumualii Hwy, Lihue, HI, 96766. Tel: 808-245-8374. p. 514
McKenna, Bradley, Tech Librn, Wilmington Memorial Library, 175 Middlesex Ave, Wilmington, MA, 01887-2779. Tel: 978-658-2967. p. 1070
McKenna, Donna, Dir, Williston Park Public Library, 494 Willis Ave, Williston Park, NY, 11596. Tel: 516-742-1820. p. 1666
McKenna, Frank J, Dir, Seaford Public Library, 2234 Jackson Ave, Seaford, NY, 11783. Tel: 516-221-1334. p. 1639
McKenna, Gilda, ILL Supvr, Mercy College Libraries, 555 Broadway, Dobbs Ferry, NY, 10522. Tel: 914-674-7580. p. 1526
McKenna, Jane, Head Librn, College of Alameda, 555 Ralph Appezzato Memorial Pkwy, Alameda, CA, 94501. Tel: 510-748-2366. p. 115
McKenna, Julia, Circ Serv Mgr, Jacksonville University, 2800 University Blvd N, Jacksonville, FL, 32211-3394. Tel: 904-256-7944. p. 413
McKenna, Julie, Dep Dir, Regina Public Library, Library Directors Office, 2311 12th Ave, Regina, SK, S4P 0N3, CANADA. Tel: 306-777-6099. p. 2747
McKenna, Shana, Archivist, Isabella Stewart Gardner Museum Library, 25 Evans Way, Boston, MA, 02115. Tel: 617-264-6003, 617-566-1401. p. 995

McKenna, Stephanie, Circ Supvr, Horsham Township Library, 435 Babylon Rd, Horsham, PA, 19044-1224. Tel: 215-443-2609, Ext 207. p. 1944
McKenna, Susan, Dir, Operations, Quogue Library, Four Midland St, Quogue, NY, 11959. Tel: 631-653-4224. p. 1625
McKennerney, Christina, Legal Info Librn, Liberty Mutual, 175 Berkeley St, 7th Flr, Boston, MA, 02116-5066. Tel: 617-357-9500. p. 996
McKenney, Lisa, Dir, Admin Serv, Allegany County Library System, 31 Washington St, Cumberland, MD, 21502. Tel: 301-777-1200. p. 963
McKenney, Susan, ILL, Libr Asst II, Nassau County Public Library System, Bryceville Branch, 7280 Motes Rd, Bryceville, FL, 32009. p. 395
McKennon, Ayanna, Community Engagement Coord, Russell Library, 123 Broad St, Middletown, CT, 06457. Tel: 860-347-2528. p. 322
McKennon, Ed, Ref & Instruction Librn, Glendale Community College - Main, 6000 W Olive Ave, Glendale, AZ, 85302. Tel: 623-845-3195. p. 61
McKensie, Marjorie, Adminr, Dauphin County Library System, East Shore Area Library, 4501 Ethel St, Harrisburg, PA, 17109. Tel: 717-652-9380, Ext 1015. p. 1940
McKenzie, Ann, Commun Serv Mgr, Mgr, Ch Serv, St Catharines Public Library, 54 Church St, St. Catharines, ON, L2R 7K2, CANADA. Tel: 905-688-6103. p. 2680
McKenzie, Carrie, Chief Exec Officer, Head Librn, Carlow-Mayo Public Library, c/o Hermon Public School, 124 Fort Stewart Rd, Bancroft, ON, K0L 1C0, CANADA. Tel: 613-332-2544. p. 2629
McKenzie, Christi, Dir, Rossville Community Library, 407 N Main St, Rossville, KS, 66533. Tel: 785-584-6454. p. 833
McKenzie, Daniel, Library Systems Admin, Tyler Junior College, 1327 S Baxter St, Tyler, TX, 75701. Tel: 903-510-2501. p. 2249
McKenzie, Darlene, Head, Ref, Reed Memorial Library, 167 E Main St, Ravenna, OH, 44266-3197. Tel: 330-296-2827, Ext 201. p. 1817
McKenzie, Jen, Ch, Craftsbury Public Library, 12 Church St, Craftsbury Common, VT, 05827. Tel: 802-586-9683. p. 2282
Mckenzie, Joseph, Libr Dir, Martha Liebert Public Library, 124 Calle Malinche, Bernalillo, NM, 87004. Tel: 505-867-1440. p. 1464
McKenzie, Melanie, Dir, Eastham Public Library, 190 Samoset Rd, Eastham, MA, 02642. Tel: 508-240-5950. p. 1016
McKenzie, Michele, Fac Librn, City College of San Francisco, 50 Frida Kahlo Way, 4th Flr, San Francisco, CA, 94112. Tel: 415-452-5433. p. 224
McKenzie, Niketha, First Year Experience Librn, Howard University Libraries, 500 Howard Pl NW, Ste 203, Washington, DC, 20059. Tel: 202-806-7301. p. 369
McKenzie, Pam, Prof, Western University, FIMS & Nursing Bldg, Rm 2020, London, ON, N6A 5B9, CANADA. Tel: 519-661-2111, Ext 88514. p. 2796
McKenzie, Roberta, Asst Dir, Burns Lake Public Library, 585 Government St, Burns Lake, BC, V0J 1E0, CANADA. Tel: 250-692-3192. p. 2564
McKenzie, Tara, Head, Youth Serv, Conway Public Library, 15 Main Ave, Conway, NH, 03818. Tel: 603-447-5552. p. 1360
McKenzie-Hicks, Joanne, Legal Research Specialist, Burnet, Duckworth & Palmer, LLP, 2400, 525-Eighth Ave SW, Calgary, AB, T2P 1G1, CANADA. Tel: 403-260-0100. p. 2526
McKeon Armstrong, Maureen, Br Mgr, Hamden Public Library, Whitneyville, 125 Carleton St, Hamden, CT, 06517. Tel: 203-287-2677. p. 315
McKeon, Cindy, Library Contact, Schenectady County Public Library, Quaker Street, 133 Bull St, Delanson, NY, 12053. Tel: 518-895-2719. p. 1638
McKeown, Kristy, Mgr, Libr Serv, Trent University, 1600 West Bank Dr, Peterborough, ON, K9J 7B8, CANADA. Tel: 705-748-1011, Ext 7195. p. 2672
McKeown, Linda, Bus Mgr, Evergreen Park Public Library, 9400 S Troy Ave, Evergreen Park, IL, 60805-2383. Tel: 708-422-8522. p. 587
McKeown, Terri, Fiscal Officer, Grandview Heights Public Library, 1685 W First Ave, Columbus, OH, 43212. Tel: 614-486-2951. p. 1773
McKerlie, Karen, Dir, Modeste Bedient Memorial Library, 3699 State Rte 54A, Branchport, NY, 14418. Tel: 315-595-2899. p. 1496
McKernan, Ro, Copyright Librn, Whatcom Community College Library, Heiner Bldg, 231 W Kellogg Rd, Bellingham, WA, 98226. Tel: 360-383-3300. p. 2359
McKerrall, Cheryl, Libr Mgr, Pigeon Lake Public Library, 603 Second Ave, Ma-Me-O Beach, AB, T0C 1X0, CANADA. Tel: 780-586-3778. p. 2547
McKewin, Kelly, Asst Dir, Rosemary Garfoot Public Library, 2107 Julius St, Cross Plains, WI, 53528. Tel: 608-798-3881. p. 2429
McKibben-Nee, Elizabeth, Br Librn, Nassau County Public Library System, Callahan Branch, 450077 State Rd 200, Callahan, FL, 32011-3767. Tel: 904-530-6533. p. 395
McKibbens, Tangela, Mgr, Henry County Public Library System, Fortson Public Library, 61 McDonough St, Hampton, GA, 30228. Tel: 770-288-7233. p. 490
McKilligan, Fatima, Asst Librn, Houston Public Library, 3150 14th St, Houston, BC, V0J 1Z0, CANADA. Tel: 250-845-2256. p. 2567
McKillop, Mary, Circ Tech, Ellsworth Public Library, 20 State St, Ellsworth, ME, 04605. Tel: 207-667-6363. p. 924
McKim, Tasha, Asst Dir, Moberly Area Community College Library & Academic Resource Center, Kirksville Campus, 2105 E Normal St, Kirksville, MO, 63501. Tel: 660-263-4100, Ext 15013, 660-665-0345. p. 1262
McKinley, Brenda B, Dir, Ridgefield Library Association Inc, 472 Main St, Ridgefield, CT, 06877-4585. Tel: 203-438-2282. p. 335
McKinley, Jennifer, Asst Dir, Morgan County Public Library, 110 S Jefferson St, Martinsville, IN, 46151. Tel: 765-342-3451. p. 705
McKinley, Joyce, Circ Supvr, ILL, Thomas More University Benedictine Library, 333 Thomas More Pkwy, Crestview Hills, KY, 41017-2599. Tel: 859-344-3300. p. 852
McKinley, Joyce, Br Mgr, Evon A Ford Public Library, 208 Spring St, Taylorsville, MS, 39168. Tel: 601-785-4361. p. 1233
McKinley, Sara, Br Mgr, Muncie Public Library, Carnegie Library, 301 E Jackson St, Muncie, IN, 47305. Tel: 765-747-8208. p. 708
McKinnell, Jennifer, Dir, McMaster University Library, Health Sciences Library, 1280 Main St W, Hamilton, ON, L8S 4K1, CANADA. Tel: 905-525-9140, Ext 24381. p. 2647
McKinney, Anya, Dir, Libr Serv, South College, 3904 Lonas Dr, Knoxville, TN, 37909. Tel: 865-251-1832. p. 2107
McKinney, Anya, Dir, Libr Serv, South College, Parkside Campus Library, 400 Goody's Lane, Ste 101, Knoxville, TN, 37922. Tel: 865-288-5750. p. 2107
McKinney, April, Tech Serv, Cochise County Library District, 100 Clawson Ave, Bisbee, AZ, 85603. Tel: 520-432-8930. p. 56
McKinney, Cami, Integrated Resources Prog Mgr, National Park Service, Alpine Loop, Hwy 92, American Fork, UT, 84003. Tel: 801-756-5239. p. 2261
McKinney, Elizabeth, Prog Dir, Public Information Network for Electronic Services, Georgia Public Library Service, 2872 Woodcock Blvd, Ste 250, Atlanta, GA, 30341. Tel: 404-235-7141. p. 2764
McKinney, Genette, Librn, Northeast Regional Library, Chalybeate Public Library, 2501-A Hwy 354, Walnut, MS, 38683-9762. Tel: 662-223-6768. p. 1216
McKinney, James, Pub Serv Mgr, Southwestern Baptist Theological Seminary Libraries, 2001 W Seminary Dr, Fort Worth, TX, 76115-2157. Tel: 817-923-1921, Ext 4000. p. 2180
McKinney, Janet, Electronic Res, Shook, Hardy & Bacon, 2555 Grand Blvd, 3rd Flr, Kansas City, MO, 64108-2613. Tel: 816-474-6550. p. 1257
McKinney, Joyce, Dir, Wyoming County Public Library, 19 Park St, Pineville, WV, 24874. Tel: 304-732-6228. p. 2412
McKinney, Lori, Dir, Nucla Public Library, 544 Main St, Nucla, CO, 81424. Tel: 970-864-2166. p. 292
McKinney, Lorraine, Acq, Supvr, Connecticut College, 270 Mohegan Ave, New London, CT, 06320-4196. Tel: 860-439-2655. p. 328
McKinney, Lyn, Br Mgr, Fairfax County Public Library, Lorton Branch, 9520 Richmond Hwy, Lorton, VA, 22079-2124. Tel: 703-339-7385. p. 2316
McKinney, Mary, Br Mgr, Pima County Public Library, Miller-Golf Links, 9640 E Golf Links Rd, Tucson, AZ, 85730. Tel: 520-594-5355. p. 82
McKinney, Michelle, Ref, Sr Assoc Librn, Web Serv, University of Cincinnati, 9555 Plainfield Rd, Muntz 113, Cincinnati, OH, 45236. Tel: 513-936-1546. p. 1764
McKinney, Rebekah J, Dir, Libr Serv, Missouri State University-West Plains, 304 W Trish Knight St, West Plains, MO, 65775. Tel: 417-255-7945. p. 1286
McKinney, Susan Dawn, Librn, St Joseph Township-Swearingen Memorial Library, 201 N Third St, Saint Joseph, IL, 61873. Tel: 217-469-2159. p. 644
McKinney, Tammy, Head Librn, Pike County Public Library, 1008 E Maple St, Petersburg, IN, 47567-1736. Tel: 812-354-6257. p. 713
McKinney, Taylor, Coordr, Outreach & Virtual Union Catalog, Arkansas State Library, 900 W Capitol, Ste 100, Little Rock, AR, 72201-3108. Tel: 501-682-2867. p. 100
McKinney, Tom, Dr, Dir, Learning Res, Angelina College Library, 3500 S First St, Lufkin, TX, 75904. Tel: 936-633-5220. p. 2214
McKinnie, Linda, Libr Mgr, Timberland Regional Library, Tenino Branch, 172 Central Ave W, Tenino, WA, 98589. Tel: 360-264-2369. p. 2389
McKinnon, Chris, Acq, University of New England Libraries, Josephine S Abplanalp Library, Portland Campus, 716 Stevens Ave, Portland, ME, 04103. Tel: 207-221-4327. p. 918
McKinnon, Karen, Libr Dir, Leighton Township Public Library, 4451 12th St, Moline, MI, 49335. Tel: 616-877-4143. p. 1133
McKinzie, Steve, Asst Librn, Westminster Theological Seminary, 2960 W Church Rd, Glenside, PA, 19038. Tel: 215-572-3821. p. 1937
McKissack, Sally, Br Mgr, Saint Tammany Parish Library, Causeway Branch, 3457 Hwy 190, Mandeville, LA, 70471. Tel: 985-626-9779. p. 888
McKittrick, Allison, Campus Librn, Pellissippi State Community College, Strawberry Plains ERC, 7201 Strawberry Plains Pike, Knoxville, TN, 37914. Tel: 865-225-2322. p. 2107
McKiver, Sandra, Branch Lead, Live Oak Public Libraries, W W Law Branch, 909 E Bolton St, Savannah, GA, 31401. Tel: 912-644-5903. p. 496
McKnight, Ashley, Librn II, College of the North Atlantic Library Services, Happy Valley-Goose Bay Campus, 219 Hamilton River Rd, Happy Valley-Goose Bay, NL, A0P 1E0, CANADA. Tel: 709-896-6772. p. 2609
McKnight, Colleen, Dir, Libr Serv, Frederick Community College, 7932 Opossumtown Pike, Frederick, MD, 21702. Tel: 301-846-2444, p. 966
McKnight, Marshall, Librn, State of New Jersey - Department of Banking & Insurance Library, 20 W State St, Trenton, NJ, 08608-1206. Tel: 609-292-5064, 609-292-7272. p. 1448

McKowen, Alycia, Dir, Saint Ignace Public Library, 110 W Spruce St, Saint Ignace, MI, 49781-1649. Tel: 906-643-8318. p. 1148

McKoy, Faith, Cat, Allentown Public Library, 1210 Hamilton St, Allentown, PA, 18102. Tel: 610-820-2400. p. 1904

McLachlan, Kim, Libr Asst, Fowler Public Library, 510 Main St, Fowler, KS, 67844. Tel: 620-646-5550. p. 808

McLagan, Michelle A, Dir, Hepburn Library of Lisbon, 6899 County Rte 10, Lisbon, NY, 13658-4242. Tel: 315-393-0111. p. 1563

McLain, Amber, Dir, Patmos Library, 2445 Riley St, Hudsonville, MI, 49426. Tel: 616-896-9798. p. 1117

McLain, Amber, Mgr, Mem Serv, Lakeland Library Cooperative, 4138 Three Mile Rd NW, Grand Rapids, MI, 49534-1134. Tel: 616-559-5253. p. 2767

McLain, Guy, Dir, Westfield Athenaeum, Six Elm St, Westfield, MA, 01085-2997. Tel: 413-568-7833. p. 1066

Mclain, Holly, Adult Serv, Louisburg Public Library, 206 S Broadway, Louisburg, KS, 66053. Tel: 913-837-2217. p. 822

McLain, Jenna, Educ Adminr, Southwestern Vermont Health Care, 100 Hospital Dr, Bennington, VT, 05201. Tel: 802-447-5120. p. 2279

McLain, Rebecca, Exec Dir, Oneida County Historical Center, 1608 Genesee St, Utica, NY, 13502-5425. Tel: 315-735-3642. p. 1655

McLamb, Jessica, ILL, Escanaba Public Library, 400 Ludington St, Escanaba, MI, 49829. Tel: 906-789-7323. p. 1103

McLandress, Cathy, Br Librn, London Public Library, Cherryhill, 301 Oxford St W, London, ON, N6H 1S6, CANADA. Tel: 519-439-6456. p. 2654

McLane, Curren, Dir, Azle Memorial Library, 333 W Main St, Azle, TX, 76020. Tel: 817-444-7216, Ext 207. p. 2144

McLaren, Amanda, Dir, Benzonia Public Library, 891 Michigan Ave, Benzonia, MI, 49616-9784. Tel: 231-882-4111. p. 1084

McLaren, Margot, Tech Serv Librn, Westcliff University, 16735 Von Karman, Ste 100, Irvine, CA, 92606. Tel: 714-459-1178. p. 153

McLaren, Margot, Tech Serv Librn, Riverside County Law Library, 3989 Lemon St, Riverside, CA, 92501-4203. Tel: 951-368-0362. p. 201

Mclary, Pat, Br Mgr, Grosse Pointe Public Library, Woods, 20680 Mack Ave, Grosse Pointe Woods, MI, 48236. Tel: 313-343-2072. p. 1112

McLaughlin, Amanda, Br Mgr, Riverside County Library System, Canyon Lake Library, 31516 Railroad Canyon Rd, Canyon Lake, CA, 92587. Tel: 951-244-9181. p. 202

McLaughlin, Andrew E, Acq & Coll, Coordr, Libr Serv, Bunker Hill Community College, E Bldg, 3rd Flr, Rm E300, 250 New Rutherford Ave, Boston, MA, 02129-2925. Tel: 617-936-1959. p. 994

McLaughlin, Ann, Coordr, Concordia University Libraries, Counselling & Development, Career Resource Centre, Henry F Hall Bldg, 1455 de Maisonneuve Blvd W, H-440, Montreal, QC, H3G 1M8, CANADA. Tel: 514-848-2424, Ext 3556. p. 2723

McLaughlin, Courtenay, Ch Serv, White House Public Library, 105 B College St, White House, TN, 37188. Tel: 615-672-0239. p. 2129

McLaughlin, Dan, Libr Tech, Department of Veterans Affairs, 2121 North Ave, Grand Junction, CO, 81501-6428. Tel: 970-242-0731. p. 284

McLaughlin, Daniel, Res Analyst, Weil, Gotshal & Manges LLP, 767 Fifth Ave, New York, NY, 10153. Tel: 212-310-8444. p. 1603

McLaughlin, Hélène, Mgr, Universite de Moncton, Bibliotheque du Campus de Shippagan, 218 Blvd J-D-Gauthier, Shippagan, NB, E8S 1P6, CANADA. Tel: 506-336-3418, 506-336-3420. p. 2604

McLaughlin, Jackie, Libr Dir, Marienville Area Library, 106 Pine St, Marienville, PA, 16239. Tel: 814-927-8552. p. 1958

McLaughlin, Karen, Dir, Academic Support Services, Davenport University, 6191 Kraft Ave SE, Grand Rapids, MI, 49512. Tel: 616-554-5664. p. 1110

McLaughlin, Kassie, E-Resources Librn, Rockhurst University, 1100 Rockhurst Rd, Kansas City, MO, 64110-2561. Tel: 816-501-4161. p. 1257

McLaughlin, Katy, Supvr, Mid-Columbia Libraries, Prosser Branch, 902 Seventh St, Prosser, WA, 99350. Tel: 509-786-2533. p. 2367

McLaughlin, Kevin, Librn, Department of Veterans Affairs, 142D/JC, 915 N Grand Blvd, Saint Louis, MO, 63106. Tel: 314-289-6421. p. 1270

McLaughlin, Kevin, Dr, Libr Dir, Cleveland Institute of Music, 11021 East Blvd, Cleveland, OH, 44106-1776. Tel: 216-795-3181. p. 1767

McLaughlin, Kim, Ch, Libby Memorial Library, 27 Staples St, Old Orchard Beach, ME, 04064. Tel: 207-934-4351. p. 934

McLaughlin, Lauren, Assoc Dir, Coll Mgt, Ref, Wilton Library Association, 137 Old Ridgefield Rd, Wilton, CT, 06897-3000. Tel: 203-762-3950. p. 347

McLaughlin, Lauren, Ref & Ad Serv Librn, Eustis Memorial Library, 120 N Center St, Eustis, FL, 32726. Tel: 352-357-5686. p. 395

McLaughlin, LaVerne, Dir, Libr Serv, Albany State University, 504 College Dr, Albany, GA, 31705. Tel: 229-500-3468. p. 457

McLaughlin, Laverne, Dr, Dir, Univ Libr, Albany State University, Bldg G, 2400 Gillionville Rd, Albany, GA, 31707. Tel: 229-500-3468. p. 457

McLaughlin, Louise, Info Spec, Woman's Hospital, 100 Woman's Way, Baton Rouge, LA, 70817. Tel: 225-924-8462. p. 885

McLaughlin, Maria, Head, Children's Servx, Lansdowne Public Library, 55 S Lansdowne Ave, Lansdowne, PA, 19050-2804. Tel: 610-623-0239. p. 1953

McLaughlin, Megan, Dir, Lima Public Library, 1872 Genesee St, Lima, NY, 14485. Tel: 585-582-1311. p. 1563

McLaughlin, Michael, Fac/Safety Serv Adminr, Alachua County Library District, 401 E University Ave, Gainesville, FL, 32601-5453. Tel: 352-334-3915. p. 406

McLaurin, Debbie, Acq Asst, Bank Street College of Education Library, 610 W 112th St, 5th Flr, New York, NY, 10025. Tel: 212-875-4455. p. 1579

McLaurin, Dianne, Br Mgr, Forest Public Library, 210 S Raleigh St, Forest, MS, 39074. Tel: 601-469-1481. p. 1216

McLaurin, Dougald, Ref Coordr, Southeastern Baptist Theological Seminary Library, 114 N Wingate St, Wake Forest, NC, 27587. Tel: 919-863-2204. p. 1720

McLean, Debbie, Asst Librn, Avery County Morrison Public Library, 150 Library Pl, Newland, NC, 28657. Tel: 828-733-9393. p. 1706

McLean, Jamie N, Libr Dir, Groesbeck Maffett Public Library, 601 W Yeagua St, Groesbeck, TX, 76642-1658. Tel: 254-729-3667. p. 2186

McLean, Jennifer, Asst Librn, Tech Serv, North Carolina Supreme Court Library, 500 Justice Bldg, Two E Morgan St, Raleigh, NC, 27601-1428. Tel: 919-831-5902. p. 1710

McLean Johnson, Paulette, Dean of Libr, Andrews University, 4190 Administration Dr, Berrien Springs, MI, 49104-1400. Tel: 269-471-3264. p. 1085

McLean, Keith, Head, Adult Serv, Medicine Hat Public Library, 414 First St SE, Medicine Hat, AB, T1A 0A8, CANADA. Tel: 403-502-8531. p. 2548

McLean, Monica, Med Librn, Germanna Community College, Stafford Campus Library, 124 Old Potomac Church Rd, Stafford, VA, 22554. Tel: 540-891-3015. p. 2320

McLean, Rachel, Dir, Learning Res, Tri-County Community College, 21 Campus Circle, Murphy, NC, 28906. Tel: 828-835-4218, 828-837-6810. p. 1705

McLean, Robin, Adminr, Montgomery County Planning Commission Library, One Montgomery Plaza, 425 Swede St, Norristown, PA, 19401. Tel: 610-278-3722. p. 1971

McLeland, Coutenay, Head, Digital Projects, Head, Presv, University of North Florida, Bldg 12-Library, One UNF Dr, Jacksonville, FL, 32224-2645. Tel: 904-620-2615. p. 413

McLellan, Amanda, Asst Dir, Tech Operations, Discovery Serv, East Carolina University, J Y Joyner Library, E Fifth St, Greenville, NC, 27858-4353. Tel: 252-328-2780. p. 1693

McLellan, Andrea, Coll Serv, Tech Serv, McMaster University Library, Health Sciences Library, 1280 Main St W, Hamilton, ON, L8S 4K1, CANADA. Tel: 905-525-9140, Ext 24169. p. 2647

McLemore, Carolyn, Br Mgr, Webster Parish Library System, Cotton Valley Branch, 21241 Hwy 371, Cotton Valley, LA, 71018. Tel: 318-832-4290. p. 897

McLemore, Laura, Dr, Curator, Louisiana State University, One University Pl, Shreveport, LA, 71115. Tel: 318-797-5378. p. 907

McLendon, Shelly, Mgr, Catahoula Parish Library, 300 Bushley St, Harrisonburg, LA, 71340. Tel: 318-744-5271. p. 891

McLennan, Stacy, Coll Curator, Doon Heritage Crossroads Library, Ten Huron Rd, Kitchener, ON, N2P 2R7, CANADA. Tel: 519-748-1914, Ext 3268. p. 2651

McLeod, Andrew, Curator, The Moravian Historical Society, 214 E Center St, Nazareth, PA, 18064. Tel: 610-759-5070. p. 1968

McLeod, Eliza, Sr Info Officer, The World Bank Group Library, 1818 H St NW, MSN MC-C3-220, Washington, DC, 20433. Tel: 202-473-2000. p. 382

McLeod, Krista I, Dir, Nevins Memorial Library, 305 Broadway, Methuen, MA, 01844-6898. Tel: 978-686-4080. p. 1035

McLeod, Patricia, Dir, David & Joyce Milne Public Library, 1095 Main St, Williamstown, MA, 01267-2627. Tel: 413-458-5369. p. 1069

McLeod, Rob, Libr Mgr, Trent University, Durham Greater Toronto Area Campus Library & Learning Centre, 55 Thornton Rd S, Ste 102, Oshawa, ON, L1J 5Y1, CANADA. Tel: 905-435-5102, Ext 5064. p. 2672

Mcleod, Terra, Br Mgr, Jackson County Library Services, Medford Branch, 205 S Central Ave, Medford, OR, 97501. Tel: 541-774-8689. p. 1886

McLeod, Terra, Br Mgr, Fort Vancouver Regional Library District, Goldendale Community Library, 131 W Burgen St, Goldendale, WA, 98620. Tel: 509-773-4487. p. 2391

McLeod, William, Mgr, Info Serv, The National Academies, Keck 439, 500 Fifth St NW, Washington, DC, 20001. Tel: 202-334-2989. p. 371

McLonis, Kris, Assoc Librn, Cataloging & Database Mgmt, University of Detroit Mercy Libraries, 4001 W McNichols Rd, Detroit, MI, 48221-3038. Tel: 313-578-0457. p. 1099

McLoughlin, Fran, Youth Serv Librn, Eastham Public Library, 190 Samoset Rd, Eastham, MA, 02642. Tel: 508-240-5950. p. 1016

McMahan, Carla, Dean of Libr, North Greenville University, 100 Donnan Blvd, Tigerville, SC, 29688. Tel: 864-977-7091. p. 2071

McMahon, Cathy, Br Mgr, Mohave County Library District, Bullhead City Branch, 1170 Hancock Rd, Bullhead City, AZ, 86442. Tel: 928-758-0714. p. 64

McMahon, David, Teen & Adult Librn, Woodbury Public Library, 33 Delaware St, Woodbury, NJ, 08096. Tel: 856-845-2611. p. 1456

McMahon, Denise, Br Mgr, Collier County Public Library, South Regional Branch, 8065 Lely Cutural Pkwy, Naples, FL, 34113. Tel: 239-252-7542. p. 427
McMahon, Elisabeth, Communications, Advocacy & Outreach Serv Coordr, Grand Prairie Public Library System, 901 Conover Dr, Grand Prairie, TX, 75051. Tel: 972-237-5700. p. 2185
McMahon, Kevin, Mgr, Southern California Institute of Architecture, 960 E Third St, Los Angeles, CA, 90013. Tel: 213-613-5323. p. 168
McMahon, Kevin, Access Serv Mgr, Simmons College of Kentucky Library, 1000 S Fourth St, Louisville, KY, 40203. Tel: 502-776-1443, Ext 5117. p. 866
McMahon, Martha, Head Librn, Sinai Temple, 10400 Wilshire Blvd, Los Angeles, CA, 90024. Tel: 310-474-1518, 310-481-3218. p. 168
McMahon, Natalie, Dir, Southwest Mississippi Community College, 1156 College Dr, Summit, MS, 39666. Tel: 601-276-2004. p. 1233
McMahon, Penny, Head, Tech Serv, Round Lake Area Public Library District, 906 Hart Rd, Round Lake, IL, 60073. Tel: 847-546-7060, Ext 116. p. 643
McMahon, Sara, Head Law Librn, Massachusetts Trial Court, Courthouse, 99 Main St, Ste 1, Northampton, MA, 01060. Tel: 413-586-2297. p. 1042
McMahon, Shannen, Commun Librn, Monroe County Library System, Erie Branch, 2065 Erie Rd, Erie, MI, 48133-9757. Tel: 734-848-4420. p. 1133
McMahon, Shannen, Commun Librn, Monroe County Library System, Rasey Memorial, 4349 Oak St, Luna Pier, MI, 48157-4572. Tel: 734-848-4572. p. 1134
McMahon, Sheila, Exec Dir, United Native Friendship Centre, 516 Portage Ave, Fort Frances, ON, P9A 3N1, CANADA. Tel: 807-274-8541. p. 2642
McMahon, Zach, Access Serv Librn, Northeastern Illinois University, 5500 N Saint Louis Ave, Chicago, IL, 60625-4699. Tel: 773-442-4400. p. 566
McMain, Kat, Acq, Bellarmine University, 2001 Newburg Rd, Louisville, KY, 40205-0671. p. 864
McManus, Blyth, Museum Curator, National Park Service, 142 W Potomac St, Williamsport, MD, 21795. Tel: 301-739-4200. p. 981
McManus, Dede, Tech Serv Librn, Rockport Public Library, 17 School St, Rockport, MA, 01966. Tel: 978-546-6934. p. 1050
McManus, Dylan, Asst Dir, Wasco County Library District, 722 Court St, The Dalles, OR, 97058. Tel: 541-296-2815. p. 1899
McManus, Heidi, Asst Dir, Utica Public Library, 303 Genesee St, Utica, NY, 13501. Tel: 315-735-2279. p. 1656
McManus, Maureen, YA Librn, Bedford Free Library, 32 Village Green, Bedford, NY, 10506. Tel: 914-234-3570. p. 1491
McManus, Molly, Br Chief, United States Army, 3909 Halls Ferry Rd, Vicksburg, MS, 39180-6199. Tel: 601-634-2355. p. 1234
McMaster, Beverly A, Librn, United States Army, Martin Army Community Hospital Medical Library, Bldg 9200, Rm 010 MCXB-IL, 7950 Martin Loop, Fort Benning, GA, 31905-5637. Tel: 706-544-3533. p. 479
McMaster, Julie, Archivist, Toledo Museum of Art Reference Library, 2445 Monroe St, Toledo, OH, 43620. Tel: 419-255-8000. p. 1825
McMeeking, Trixie L, Libr Dir, Homer Public Library, 141 W Main St, Homer, MI, 49245. Tel: 517-568-3450. p. 1116
McMeen, Dawn, Librn, Scott County Library System, Princeton Branch, 328 River Dr, Princeton, IA, 52768. Tel: 563-289-4282. p. 751
McMillan, Alice, Ref Librn, Orange Public Library, 348 Main St, Orange, NJ, 07050. Tel: 973-786-3988. p. 1431
McMillan, Anthony, Dir, Lone Star College System, Kingwood College Library, 20000 Kingwood Dr, Kingwood, TX, 77339. Tel: 281-290-5997. p. 2197
McMillan, Brian, Dir, Western University Libraries, Music Library, Talbot College, Rm 234, 1151 Richmond St, London, ON, N6A 3K7, CANADA. Tel: 519-661-2111, Ext 85334. p. 2655
McMillan, Carolyn, Br Librn, Southeast Regional Library, Kennedy Branch, 235 Scott St, Kennedy, SK, S0G 2R0, CANADA. Tel: 306-538-2020. p. 2753
McMillan, Cathy, Adminr, El Dorado County Law Library, 550 Main St, Ste A, Placerville, CA, 95667. Tel: 530-626-1932. p. 195
McMillan, David, Librn, Bacone College, 2299 Old Bacone Rd, Muskogee, OK, 74403. Tel: 918-685-0814. p. 1854
McMillan, David, Dir, Libr Serv, Bluefield State University, 219 Rock St, Bluefield, WV, 24701. Tel: 304-327-4050. p. 2398
McMillan, Fiona, Acq Librn, Claremont School of Theology Library, 1325 N College Ave, Claremont, CA, 91711. Tel: 909-447-2518. p. 130
McMillan, Gail, Dir, Scholarly Communications, Virginia Polytechnic Institute & State University Libraries, 560 Drillfield Dr, Blacksburg, VA, 24061. Tel: 540-231-9252. p. 2307
McMillan, Mary, Digital Res Librn, El Camino College, 16007 S Crenshaw Blvd, Torrance, CA, 90506. Tel: 310-660-3525. p. 252
McMillan, Tim, Br Head, Vancouver Public Library, Kerrisdale Branch, 2112 W 42nd Ave, Vancouver, BC, V6M 2B6, CANADA. Tel: 604-665-3974. p. 2581
McMillen, Dawn, Sr Libr Assoc III/Libr Serv, Municipal Technical Advisory Service, 1610 University Ave, Knoxville, TN, 37921-6741. Tel: 865-974-8970. p. 2106
McMillen, Jessica M, Head, Digital & Web Serv, West Virginia University Libraries, 1549 University Ave, Morgantown, WV, 26506. Tel: 304-293-4040. p. 2409
McMillen, Kate, Br Mgr, San Luis Obispo County Library, Oceano Library, 1551 17th St, Oceano, CA, 93445. Tel: 805-474-7478. p. 234
McMillen, Tara, Bus Planning Officer, West Virginia University Libraries, 1549 University Ave, Morgantown, WV, 26506. Tel: 304-293-4040. p. 2409
McMillian, Morgan, Libr Dir, Lake Travis Community Library, 1938 Lohmans Crossing, Austin, TX, 78734. Tel: 512-263-2885. p. 2139
McMillin, James, Assoc Dir, Southern Methodist University, Bridwell Library-Perkins School of Theology, 6005 Bishop Blvd, Dallas, TX, 75205. Tel: 214-768-3483. p. 2167
McMillion, Anne E, Dir, Libr Serv, New River Community & Technical College, 129 Courtney Dr, Lewisburg, WV, 24901. Tel: 304-647-6575. p. 2407
McMinn, Howard, Assoc Dir, Talking Bks & Braille Serv, Illinois State Library, Talking Book & Braille Service, Gwendolyn Brooks Bldg, 300 S Second St, Springfield, IL, 62701-1796. Tel: 217-785-0022. p. 649
McMonagle, Nicole, Libr Dir, University of Science & Arts of Oklahoma, 1901 S 17th St, Chickasha, OK, 73018. Tel: 405-574-1341. p. 1844
Mcmonigle, Paul J, Eng Librn, Pennsylvania State University Libraries, Engineering, 325 Hammond Bldg, University Park, PA, 16802. Tel: 814-865-7005. p. 2015
McMullan, Lauren, Head Librn, Kalamazoo Institute of Arts, 314 S Park St, Kalamazoo, MI, 49007. Tel: 269-349-7775, Ext 3166. p. 1121
McMullen, Amanda, Pres & Chief Exec Officer, Old Dartmouth Historical Society, 18 Johnny Cake Hill, New Bedford, MA, 02740. Tel: 508-997-0046, Ext 134. p. 1038
McMullen, Amy, Libr Dir, Cavendish Fletcher Community Library, 573 Main St, Proctorsville, VT, 05153. Tel: 802-226-7503. p. 2292
McMullen, Anthony, Libr Dir, Pennsylvania Western University - Edinboro, 200 Tartan Dr, Edinboro, PA, 16444. Tel: 814-732-1070. p. 1929
McMullen, Cecelia, Libr Supvr, Spokane County Library District, Medical Lake Library, 321 E Herb, Medical Lake, WA, 99022. Tel: 509-893-8330. p. 2384
McMullen, Derek, Mgr of Digital Imaging, Otis College of Art & Design Library, 9045 Lincoln Blvd, Westchester, CA, 90045. Tel: 310-665-6930. p. 259
McMullen, Heather, Assoc Univ Librn, Queen's University, 101 Union St, Kingston, ON, K7L 2N9, CANADA. Tel: 613-533-6000, Ext 79293. p. 2650
McMullen, Karen, Head, Access Serv, University of South Carolina, School of Medicine Library, Bldg 101, 6311 Garners Ferry Rd, Columbia, SC, 29209. Tel: 803-216-3200. p. 2056
McMullen, Ken, Rev, Libr Dir, Reformed Theological Seminary Library, 2101 Carmel Rd, Charlotte, NC, 28226. Tel: 704-688-4229. p. 1681
McMullen, Maribeth, Asst Dir, Quarryville Library, 357 Buck Rd, Quarryville, PA, 17566. Tel: 717-786-1336. p. 1999
McMullen, Rosalie, Ch Serv, Norton Public Library, One Washington Sq, Norton, KS, 67654. Tel: 785-877-2481. p. 827
McMullen, Shiloh, Dir, Van Buren Public Library, 115 S First St, Van Buren, IN, 46991. Tel: 765-934-2171. p. 723
McMullen, Susan, Res Serv & User Engagement Librn, Roger Williams University Library, One Old Ferry Rd, Bristol, RI, 02809. Tel: 401-254-3086. p. 2030
McMullen-Smith, Kerrie, Dir, Riverhead Free Library, 330 Court St, Riverhead, NY, 11901-2885. Tel: 631-727-3228. p. 1627
McMullin, Ashley, Assoc Univ Librn, DePaul University Libraries, 2350 N Kenmore, Chicago, IL, 60614. Tel: 773-325-7862, 773-325-7863. p. 560
McMullin, Deidre, Br Mgr, ImagineIF Libraries, Bigfork Branch, 525 Electric Ave, Bigfork, MT, 59911. Tel: 406-837-6976. p. 1298
McMunn, Chase, Asst Dir, San Luis Obispo County Library, 995 Palm St, San Luis Obispo, CA, 93403. Tel: 805-781-5990. p. 233
McMunn, Chase, Libr Dir, Orion Township Public Library, 825 Joslyn Rd, Lake Orion, MI, 48362. Tel: 248-693-3000, Ext 430. p. 1123
McMunn, Chase, Libr Dir, Orion Township Public Library, Orion Center Branch, 1335 Joslyn Rd, Lake Orion, MI, 48360. Tel: 248-693-6840. p. 1123
McMunn-Tetangco, Elizabeth, Instruction & Res Serv Librn, University of California, Merced Library, 5200 N Lake Rd, Merced, CA, 95343. Tel: 209-631-8359. p. 176
McMurdo, Thomas, Asst State Librn, Collaborative Libraries of Vermont, Vermont Dept of Libraries, 60 Washington St, Ste 2, Barre, VT, 05641. Tel: 802-636-0040. p. 2776
McMurdo, Tom, Interim State Librn, State of Vermont Department of Libraries, 60 Washington St, Ste 2, Barre, VT, 05641. Tel: 802-636-0040. p. 2278
McMurrin, David, Asst Dir, Barbara S Ponce Public Library, 7770 52nd St, Pinellas Park, FL, 33781. Tel: 727-369-0679. p. 437
McMurry, Nan, Head, Coll Develop, University of Georgia Libraries, 320 S Jackson St, Athens, GA, 30602-1641. Tel: 706-542-8474. p. 459
McNabb, Cynthia, Dep Dir, King County Library System, 960 Newport Way NW, Issaquah, WA, 98027. Tel: 425-462-9600. p. 2365
McNair, Kate, Teen Librn, Johnson County Library, 9875 W 87th St, Overland Park, KS, 66212. Tel: 913-826-4600. p. 830

McNally, Amy, Libr Serv Mgr, Hennepin County Library, 12601 Ridgedale Dr, Minnetonka, MN, 55305-1909. Tel: 612-543-8513. p. 1186

McNally, Dorothy, Asst Librn, Wewoka Public Library, 118 W Fifth St, Wewoka, OK, 74884. Tel: 405-257-3225. p. 1869

McNally, Michael, PhD, Assoc Prof, University of Alberta, 7-104 Education N, University of Alberta, Edmonton, AB, T6G 2G5, CANADA. Tel: 780-492-7625. p. 2795

McNally, Thomas, Dean of Libr, University of South Carolina, 1322 Greene St, Columbia, SC, 29208-0103. Tel: 803-777-3142. p. 2055

McNamara, Barbara, Dir, Memorial Hall Library, 2 N Main St, Andover, MA, 01810. Tel: 978-623-8400. p. 985

McNamara, Catherine, Br Mgr, Arundel Anne County Public Library, Glen Burnie Library, 1010 Eastway, Glen Burnie, MD, 21061. Tel: 410-222-6270. p. 950

McNamara, Connor, Tech Coordr, Auburn Hills Public Library, 3400 E Seyburn Dr, Auburn Hills, MI, 48326-2759. Tel: 248-370-9466. p. 1081

McNamara, Jan, Tech Serv, Anna Maria College, 50 Sunset Lane, Paxton, MA, 01612-1198. Tel: 508-849-3321. p. 1045

Mcnamara, Kym, Family Serv Librn, Youth Serv Librn, Gunnison Public Library of the Gunnison County Library District, 307 N Wisconsin, Gunnison, CO, 81230-2627. Tel: 970-641-3485. p. 285

McNamara, Laurence, Supv Libr Dir, Mercer County Library System, 2751 Brunswick Pike, Lawrenceville, NJ, 08648-4132. Tel: 609-883-6450. p. 1411

McNamara, Linda, Dir, Parish Public Library, Three Church St, Parish, NY, 13131. Tel: 315-625-7130. p. 1615

McNamara, Paul, Dir, Abbeville Memorial Library, 301 Kirkland St, Abbeville, AL, 36310. Tel: 334-585-2818. p. 3

McNames, Sarah, Library Contact, Huron County Law Library, 250 E Huron Ave, 2nd Flr, Bad Axe, MI, 48413. Tel: 989-269-7112. p. 1082

McNaughton, John A, Dir, Grand Rapids Public Library, 111 Library St NE, Grand Rapids, MI, 49503-3268. Tel: 616-988-5402, Ext 5431. p. 1111

McNaughton, Kim, Dir, Grace M Pickens Public Library, 209 E Ninth St, Holdenville, OK, 74848. Tel: 405-379-3245. p. 1850

McNeal, Joanna, Br Mgr, Aurora Public Library, 14949 E Alameda Pkwy, Aurora, CO, 80012. Tel: 303-739-6600. p. 264

McNeal, Joanna, Br Mgr, Aurora Public Library, Central Library-Main Branch, 14949 E Alameda Pkwy, Aurora, CO, 80012. Tel: 303-739-6000. p. 264

McNeal, Joanna, Br Mgr, High Plains Library District, Erie Community Library, 400 Powers St, Erie, CO, 80516. p. 285

McNeal, Marielle, Librn, Department of Veterans Affairs, PO Box 5000-142D, Hines, IL, 60141-5142. Tel: 708-202-2000, Ext 28222. p. 600

McNeall, Carolyn, Asst Dir, Dulany Memorial Library, 501 S Broadway, Salisbury, MO, 65281. Tel: 660-388-5712. p. 1278

McNeely, Ann Marie, Dean, Western Piedmont Community College, Phifer Hall, 1001 Burkemont Ave, Morganton, NC, 28655. Tel: 828-448-6195. p. 1704

McNeely, Gary, Dir, Kinchafoonee Regional Library System, 913 Forrester Dr SE, Dawson, GA, 39842-2106. Tel: 229-995-6331. p. 474

McNeely, Gary, Dir, Kinchafoonee Regional Library System, Terrell County Library, 913 Forrester Dr SE, Dawson, GA, 39842-2106. Tel: 229-995-2902. p. 475

McNeely, Joseph C, Instruction Librn, Midwestern State University, 3410 Taft Blvd, Wichita Falls, TX, 76308-2099. Tel: 940-397-4091. p. 2257

McNeer, Lena, Br Mgr, Alachua County Library District, Cone Park Branch, 2801 E University Ave, Gainesville, FL, 32641. Tel: 352-334-0720. p. 406

McNeese, Audrey, Library Contact, Fairmont First Baptist Church, 416 S Main St, Fairmont, NC, 28340. Tel: 910-628-0626. p. 1688

McNeese, Audrey, Br Mgr, Robeson County Public Library, Hector MacLean Public Library, 106 S Main St, Fairmont, NC, 28340. Tel: 910-628-9331. p. 1702

McNeil, Beth, Dean of Libr, Purdue University Libraries, 504 W State St, West Lafayette, IN, 47907-2058. Tel: 765-494-2900. p. 725

McNeil, Brandy, Deputy Dir, Branch Programs & Servs, The New York Public Library - Astor, Lenox & Tilden Foundations, 476 Fifth Ave, (@ 42nd St), New York, NY, 10018. Tel: 212-275-6975. p. 1594

McNeil, Eileen, Dir, Patron Serv, Grandview Heights Public Library, 1685 W First Ave, Columbus, OH, 43212. Tel: 614-486-2951. p. 1773

McNeil, Jennifer, Library Asst, Children's, Grafton Public Library, 35 Grafton Common, Grafton, MA, 01519. Tel: 508-839-4649, Ext 1103. p. 1021

McNeil, Julie, Dep Dir, Pub Serv, Jacksonville Public Library, 303 N Laura St, Jacksonville, FL, 32202-3505. Tel: 904-630-2665. p. 411

McNeil, Manni, Head, Adult Serv, Lower Providence Community Library, 50 Parklane Dr, Eagleville, PA, 19403-1171. Tel: 610-666-6640. p. 1928

McNeil, Marie, Librn, East Mississippi Regional Library System, Bay Springs Municipal, 2747 Hwy 15, Bay Springs, MS, 39422. Tel: 601-764-2291. p. 1231

McNeil, Spencer, Br Mgr, Highland County District Library, Greenfield Branch, 1125 Jefferson St, Greenfield, OH, 45123. Tel: 937-981-3772. p. 1789

McNeil, Yvonnada, Ref Serv, American College of Obstetricians & Gynecologists, 409 12th St SW, Washington, DC, 20024-2188. Tel: 202-863-2518. p. 360

McNeil-Capers, Kim, Dir, Commun Engagement, Queens Library, 89-11 Merrick Blvd, Jamaica, NY, 11432. Tel: 718-990-0700. p. 1553

McNeill, Dale, Asst Dir, Pub Serv, San Antonio Public Library, 600 Soledad, San Antonio, TX, 78205-2786. Tel: 210-207-2502. p. 2238

McNeilly, Samantha, Archives & Spec Coll Librn, Libr Instruction Coordr, Auburn University, 7440 East Dr, Montgomery, AL, 36117. Tel: 334-244-3200. p. 28

McNeley, Denise, Operations & Outreach Mgr, Boise Public Library, 715 S Capitol Blvd, Boise, ID, 83702. Tel: 208-972-8210. p. 516

McNelly, Steve, Dir, Goodland & Grant Township Public Library, 111 S Newton St, Goodland, IN, 47948. Tel: 219-297-4431. p. 687

McNenly, Jennifer, Sr Dir, Knowledge Services & Infrastructure, Fasken, Bay Adelaide Ctr, 333 Bay St, Ste 2400, Toronto, ON, M5H 2T6, CANADA. Tel: 416-865-5143. p. 2688

McNew, Juvette, Head, ILL, California State University, San Bernardino, 5500 University Pkwy, San Bernardino, CA, 92407-2318. Tel: 909-537-5090. p. 212

McNicol, Katy, Assoc Librn, Development & Outreach, James Blackstone Memorial Library, 758 Main St, Branford, CT, 06405-3697. Tel: 203-488-1441, Ext 313. p. 303

McNicol, Nancy, Assoc Dir, Hamden Public Library, 2901 Dixwell Ave, Hamden, CT, 06518-3135. Tel: 203-287-2686, Ext 2. p. 315

McNiel, Courtney, Dir, Hempstead County Library, 500 S Elm St, Hope, AR, 71801. Tel: 870-777-4564. p. 98

McNiel, Denise, Interim Dir, Columbia County Library, 2057 N Jackson St, Magnolia, AR, 71753. Tel: 870-234-1991. p. 103

McNiff, Lindsay, Lecturer, Dalhousie University, Kenneth C Rowe Management Bldg, Ste 4010, 6100 University Ave, Halifax, NS, B3H 4R2, CANADA. Tel: 902-494-3656. p. 2795

McNulty, Diane R, Exec Dir, Cary Area Public Library District, 1606 Three Oaks Rd, Cary, IL, 60013-1637. Tel: 847-639-4210, Ext 224. p. 550

McNulty, Emily, Br Mgr, Reading Public Library, Southeast, 1426 Perkiomen Ave, Reading, PA, 19602-2136. Tel: 610-655-6362. p. 2001

McNulty, Margaret, Asst Dir, Woonsocket Harris Public Library, 303 Clinton St, Woonsocket, RI, 02895. Tel: 401-767-4126. p. 2044

McNulty, Philip, Exec Dir, Minuteman Library Network, Ten Strathmore Rd, Natick, MA, 01760-2419. Tel: 508-655-8008. p. 2767

McNutt, Dunstan, Ref & Instruction Librn, University of Tennessee at Chattanooga Library, 400 Douglas Ave, Dept 6456, Chattanooga, TN, 37403-2598. Tel: 423-425-4501. p. 2092

McNutt, Karen, Dir, Richville Library, 743 Richville Rd, Standish, ME, 04084. Tel: 207-776-4698. p. 942

McNutt, Megan, Br Asst, Cumberland Public Libraries, Oxford Library, 22 Water St, Oxford, NS, B0M 1P0, CANADA. Tel: 902-447-2440. p. 2615

McOwen, Denise, Youth Spec, First Regional Library, Hernando Public Library, 370 W Commerce St, Hernando, MS, 38632. Tel: 662-429-4439. p. 1220

McPartland, Gail, Dep County Librn, Pub Serv, Contra Costa County Library, 777 Arnold Dr, Ste 210, Martinez, CA, 94553. Tel: 925-608-7700. p. 174

McPartlin, Jeanine, Mgr, Libr Serv, Windels Marx Lane & Mittendorf, LLP Library, 156 W 56th St, New York, NY, 10019. Tel: 212-237-1157. p. 1604

McPhail, Bill, Librn, Royalton Public Library District, 305 S Dean St, Royalton, IL, 62983. Tel: 618-984-4463. p. 644

McPhail, Rachel, Libr Dir, Huntsville Public Library, 1219 13th St, Huntsville, TX, 77340. Tel: 736-291-5470. p. 2201

McPhaul, Adrienne, Asst Dean, Mississippi Gulf Coast Community College, 2226 Switzer Rd, Gulfport, MS, 39507. Tel: 228-895-2514. p. 1218

McPhee, Casey, Libr Dir, Largo Public Library, 120 Central Park Dr, Largo, FL, 33771. Tel: 727-587-6715. p. 417

McPheeters, Karen, Libr Dir, Farmington Public Library, 2101 Farmington Ave, Farmington, NM, 87401. Tel: 505-599-1275. p. 1468

McPherson, Bruce, Dir, West Yellowstone Public Library, 23 N Dunraven St, West Yellowstone, MT, 59758. Tel: 406-646-9017. p. 1304

McPherson, Chandra, Dir, Heritage Public Library, 7791 Invicta Lane, New Kent, VA, 23124. Tel: 804-966-2480. p. 2333

McPherson, Laura, County Librn, Ashe County Public Library, 148 Library Dr, West Jefferson, NC, 28694. Tel: 336-846-2041. p. 1722

McPherson, Melissa, Br Mgr, Willard Library, Helen Warner Branch, 36 Minges Creek Pl, Battle Creek, MI, 49015. p. 1083

McPherson, Patricia, Info Literacy Librn, Instrul Design Librn, Stonehill College, 320 Washington St, Easton, MA, 02357. Tel: 508-565-1844. p. 1016

McPherson, Ruth, Librn, First United Methodist Church Library, 500 E Colorado Blvd, Pasadena, CA, 91101. Tel: 626-796-0157. p. 193

McPherson, Tanya, Adminr, State University of New York Downstate Health Sciences University, 395 Lenox Rd, Brooklyn, NY, 11203. Tel: 718-270-7400. p. 1506

McPhillips, Dan, Head, Ref Serv, Eisenhower Public Library District, 4613 N Oketo Ave, Harwood Heights, IL, 60706. Tel: 708-867-2299. p. 597

McPhillips, Peggy, Adminr, Board Pres, Norfolk Historical Society, Fort Norfolk, 810 Front St, Norfolk, VA, 23508. Tel: 757-754-2004. p. 2335

Meakin, William, Dir, Lisbon Library Department, 28 Main St, Lisbon Falls, ME, 04252-0028. Tel: 207-353-6564. p. 930

Mealey, Nathan, Access & Delivery Librn, CTW Library Consortium, Wesleyan University, Olin Memorial Library, 252 Church St, Middletown, CT, 06459. Tel: 860-685-3887. p. 2762

Meals, Catherine, Ref & Assessment Librn, University of the District of Columbia, Learning Resources Division, 4200 Connecticut Ave NW, Bldg 39, Level B, Washington, DC, 20008. p. 380

Mealy, Brian O, Coord, Library Experience, Floyd Memorial Library, 539 First St, Greenport, NY, 11944-1399. Tel: 631-477-0660. p. 1541

Meaney, Amy, Curator, University of South Carolina, Moving Image Research Collections, 707 Catawba St, Columbia, SC, 29201. Tel: 803-777-6841. p. 2055

Meaney, Dorothy, Dir, Tufts University, 35 Professors Row, Medford, MA, 02155-5816. Tel: 617-627-3345. p. 1034

Meaney-Ryer, Shannon, Head, Access Serv, Saint Mary's College Library, 1928 Saint Mary's Rd, Moraga, CA, 94575. Tel: 925-631-4229. p. 180

Means, Latasha, Tech Serv Coordr, University of California, Merced Library, 5200 N Lake Rd, Merced, CA, 95343. Tel: 209-631-8042. p. 177

Meany, Kathy, Admin Serv, Contra Costa County Public Law Library, 1020 Ward St, 1st Flr, Martinez, CA, 94553-1360. Tel: 925-646-2783. p. 175

Mears, Kim, Health Sci Librn, Scholarly Communications Librn, University of Prince Edward Island, 550 University Ave, Charlottetown, PE, C1A 4P3, CANADA. Tel: 902-566-0343. p. 2707

Mears, Michelle, Libr Dir, Rolling Hills Consolidated Library, 1912 N Belt Hwy, Saint Joseph, MO, 64506. Tel: 816-232-5479. p. 1268

Mears, Michelle, Dir, Rolling Hills Consolidated Library, Savannah, 514 W Main St, Savannah, MO, 64485-1670. Tel: 816-324-4569. p. 1269

Mecagni, Giordana, Head, Archives & Spec Coll, Northeastern University Libraries, 360 Huntington Ave, Boston, MA, 02115. Tel: 617-373-8318. p. 998

Mecham, Linda, Dir, Jerome Public Library, 100 First Ave E, Jerome, ID, 83338-2302. Tel: 208-324-5427. p. 523

Mecklenburg, Frank, Dr, Chief Archivist, Dir, Res, Center for Jewish History, 15 W 16 St, New York, NY, 10011. Tel: 212-294-8340, 212-744-6400. p. 1580

Meckley, Andrea, ILL Supvr, University of Mary Washington, 1801 College Ave, Fredericksburg, VA, 22401-5300. Tel: 540-654-1750. p. 2320

Meckley, Mary, Libr Dir, W A Rankin Memorial Library, 502 Indiana St, Neodesha, KS, 66757. Tel: 620-325-3275. p. 826

Medaille, Ann, Res Serv, University of Nevada-Reno, 1664 N Virginia St, Mailstop 0322, Reno, NV, 89557-0322. Tel: 775-682-5600. p. 1349

Medal, Carole, Chief Exec Officer, Gail Borden Public Library District, 270 N Grove Ave, Elgin, IL, 60120-5596. Tel: 847-429-4699. p. 583

Meddaugh, Jim, Asst Librn, Piermont Public Library, 130 Rte 10, Piermont, NH, 03779. Tel: 603-272-4967. p. 1378

Medeiros, Norm, Assoc Librn, Coordr, Coll Mgt & Metadata Serv, Haverford College, 370 Lancaster Ave, Haverford, PA, 19041-1392. Tel: 610-896-1173. p. 1942

Medema, Jessica, Circ, Ser, Tech Asst, University of South Alabama Libraries, Health Information Resource Center, USA Medical Center, 2451 Fillingim St, Mobile, AL, 36617. Tel: 251-471-7855. p. 27

Medeot, Catherine, Head, Coll Serv, Manhattanville University Library, 2900 Purchase St, Purchase, NY, 10577. Tel: 914-323-5275. p. 1624

Mediati, Linda, Br Mgr, Hawaii State Public Library System, Liliha Public Library, 1515 Liliha St, Honolulu, HI, 96817. Tel: 808-587-7577. p. 509

Medin, Karin, Access Serv Librn, Framingham State University, 100 State St, Framingham, MA, 01701. Tel: 508-626-4027. p. 1019

Medina, Carlos, Info Spec, Exponent, 149 Commonwealth Dr, Menlo Park, CA, 94025. Tel: 650-688-7155, 650-688-7163. p. 175

Medina, Gary, Pub Access Librn, El Camino College, 16007 S Crenshaw Blvd, Torrance, CA, 90506. Tel: 310-660-3525. p. 252

Medina, Helen, Libr Dir, Buena Park Library District, 7150 La Palma Ave, Buena Park, CA, 90620-2547. Tel: 714-826-4100. p. 124

Medina, Jose, Director, IT & Telecom, Universidad del Turabo, Rd 189 Km 3.3, Gurabo, PR, 00778. Tel: 787-743-7979, Ext 4501. p. 2511

Medina, Kaitlin, Circ Mgr, Hartwick College, One Hartwick Dr, Oneonta, NY, 13820. Tel: 607-431-4455. p. 1611

Medina, Maiko, Info Syst Mgr, Chesapeake Public Library, 298 Cedar Rd, Chesapeake, VA, 23322-5512. Tel: 757-410-7170. p. 2311

Medina, Norma, Access & Circ Serv Librn, Lone Star College System, Montgomery College Library, 3200 College Park Dr, Conroe, TX, 77384. Tel: 936-273-7494. p. 2197

Medina, Ronnie, Circ Supvr, Adams State University, 208 Edgemont Blvd, Alamosa, CO, 81101-2373. Tel: 719-587-7781. p. 263

Medina, Sisi, Br Mgr, Harris County Public Library, Galena Park Branch, 1500 Keene St, Galena Park, TX, 77547. Tel: 832-927-5470. p. 2192

Medina-Ortiz, Norma, Br Mgr, Seminole County Public Library System, East Branch, 310 Division St, Oviedo, FL, 32765. Tel: 407-665-1560. p. 388

Medina-Ortiz, Norma, Br Mgr, Seminole County Public Library System, North Branch, 150 N Palmetto Ave, Sanford, FL, 32771. Tel: 407-665-1620. p. 388

Medjo-Me-Zengue, Mary A, Libr Dir, Addison Public Library, Four Friendship Plaza, Addison, IL, 60101. Tel: 630-458-3300. p. 535

Medlar, Andrew, Pres & Dir, Carnegie Library of Pittsburgh, 4400 Forbes Ave, Pittsburgh, PA, 15213-4007. Tel: 412-622-3114. p. 1991

Medley, Erin, Mgr, Red Clay State Historic Area Library, 1140 Red Clay Park Rd SW, Cleveland, TN, 37311. Tel: 423-478-0339. p. 2093

Medlin, Brenda, Acq, Mercer University, Jack Tarver Library, 1300 Edgewood Ave, Macon, GA, 31207. Tel: 478-301-2505. p. 486

Medlin, Brian, Tech Serv Mgr, McCracken County Public Library, 555 Washington St, Paducah, KY, 42003. Tel: 270-442-2510. p. 872

Medlock, Nicole, Libr Dir, Esmeralda County Public Libraries, Fish Lake Library, Hwy 264 Bluebird Lane, Dyer, NV, 89010. Tel: 775-937-2215. p. 1351

Medlock, Stanford, Facilities Supvr, Natchitoches Parish Library, 450 Second St, Natchitoches, LA, 71457-4649. Tel: 318-238-9226. p. 899

Medlock, Teresa, Dir, Zenda Public Library, 215 N Main, Zenda, KS, 67159. Tel: 620-243-5791. p. 845

Medows, Kevin, ILS Adminr, Mount Prospect Public Library, Ten S Emerson St, Mount Prospect, IL, 60056. Tel: 847-253-5675. p. 621

Medrano, Cloe, Registrar, Roswell Museum & Art Center Library, 1011 N Richardson Ave, Roswell, NM, 88201. Tel: 575-624-6744. p. 1474

Medrow, Elaine, Mgr, Creative & Graphic Assets, Chelsea District Library, 221 S Main St, Chelsea, MI, 48118-1267. Tel: 734-475-8732. p. 1091

Medsker-Nedderman, Susan, Librn, First Presbyterian Church Library, 621 N Lincoln, Hastings, NE, 68901. Tel: 402-984-3545. p. 1317

Medved, Jenn, Campus Librn, Milwaukee Area Technical College, 6665 S Howell Ave, Oak Creek, WI, 53154. Tel: 414-571-4604. p. 2465

Medves, Gian, Chief Law Librn, University of Toronto Libraries, Bora Laskin Law Library, Flavelle House, 78 Queen's Park Crescent, Toronto, ON, M5S 2C5, CANADA. Tel: 416-978-5537. p. 2699

Medzalabanleth, Valérie, Chef de Section, Bibliotheques de Montreal, Saint-Leonard, 8420 Blvd Lacordaire, Saint-Leonard, QC, H1R 3G5, CANADA. Tel: 514-328-8500, Ext 8594. p. 2720

Meece, Ashley, Youth Serv Mgr, Tiffin-Seneca Public Library, 77 Jefferson St, Tiffin, OH, 44883. Tel: 419-447-3751. p. 1823

Meece, James H, Dep Librn, New York City Law Department, 100 Church St, Rm 6-310, New York, NY, 10007. Tel: 212-788-0858. p. 1593

Meece, Mary Beth, Br Mgr, Louisville Free Public Library, Iroquois, 601 W Woodlawn Ave, Louisville, KY, 40215. Tel: 502-574-1720. p. 865

Meegan, Aidan, Dir, SIAST Libraries, 1100 15th St E, Prince Albert, SK, S6V 6G1, CANADA. Tel: 306-765-1550. p. 2745

Meegan, Aidan, Libr Dir, Saskatchewan Polytechnic, 4500 Wascana Pkwy, Regina, SK, S4P 3A3, CANADA. Tel: 306-775-7936. p. 2748

Meehan, Caroline, Librn, Science History Institute Museum & Library, 315 Chestnut St, Philadelphia, PA, 19106. Tel: 215-873-8205. p. 1985

Meehan Obermiller, Mary, Libr Dir, Crown College, 8700 College View Dr, Saint Bonifacius, MN, 55375-9002. Tel: 952-446-4241. p. 1195

Meehan, Rebecca, Asst Dir, Woburn Public Library, 36 Cummings Park, Woburn, MA, 01801. Tel: 781-933-0148. p. 1070

Meehan, Rebecca, Dr, Assoc Prof, Kent State University, 314 University Library, 1125 Risman Dr, Kent, OH, 44242-0001. Tel: 330-672-2782. p. 2790

Meek, Melanie, Libr Assoc, Vandalia Correctional Center Library, Rte 51 N, Vandalia, IL, 62471. Tel: 618-283-4170. p. 657

Meek, Vicki, Br Mgr, Putnam County Library, Hurricane Branch, 410 Midland Trail, Hurricane, WV, 25526. Tel: 304-562-6711. p. 2406

Meeks, David, Mgr, Springfield City Library, Brightwood Branch, 359 Plainfield St, Springfield, MA, 01107. Tel: 413-263-6805. p. 1056

Meeks, David, Mgr, Springfield City Library, Indian Orchard Branch, 44 Oak St, Indian Orchard, MA, 01151. Tel: 413-263-6846. p. 1056

Meeks, David, Mgr, Springfield City Library, Library Express at Pine Point, 204 Boston Post Rd, Springfield, MA, 01109. Tel: 413-263-6855. p. 1056

Meeks, Diane, Mgr, Oconee Regional Library, Washington County, 314 S Harris St, Sandersville, GA, 31082-2669. Tel: 478-552-7466. p. 477

Meeks, Donna, Dir, Mishawaka-Penn-Harris Public Library, 209 Lincolnway E, Mishawaka, IN, 46544. Tel: 574-259-5277, Ext 1101. p. 706

Meeks, Elizabeth, Mgr, Br, Redwood City Public Library, 1044 Middlefield Rd, Redwood City, CA, 94063-1868. Tel: 650-780-5740. p. 200

Meeks, Kim K, Interim Dir, Mercer University, School of Medicine, Medical Library & LRC, 1550 College St, Macon, GA, 31207. Tel: 478-301-2519. p. 486

Meeks, Robin, Ms, Dir, Halls Public Library, 110 N Church St, Halls, TN, 38040. Tel: 731-836-5302. p. 2100

Meeks, Stephen, Libr Coord, Georgia Northwestern Technical College, Bldg H, Rm 156 & 148, One Maurice Culberson Dr, Rome, GA, 30161. Tel: 706-295-6263. p. 494

Meen, Donna, Dir, Libr Serv, University of Alberta, Saint Joseph's College Library, 11325 89th Ave NW, Edmonton, AB, T6G 2J5, CANADA. Tel: 780-492-7681, Ext 238. p. 2538

Meerians, Patti, Br Mgr, Hawaii State Public Library System, Kailua Public Library, 239 Kuulei Rd, Kailua, HI, 96734. Tel: 808-266-9911. p. 508

Meers-Ernst, Shawna, Br Mgr, Clarkesville-Habersham County Library, 178 E Green St, Clarkesville, GA, 30523. Tel: 706-754-4413. p. 470

Meeske, Susan, Libr Dir, Old Tappan Free Public Library, 56 Russell Ave, Old Tappan, NJ, 07675. Tel: 201-664-3499. p. 1431

Meetz, Marilyn, Br Mgr, Putnam County Library System, Interlachen Public Library, 133 N County Rd 315, Interlachen, FL, 32148. Tel: 386-684-1600. p. 433

Meeusen, Fritz, Info Tech, Utica Public Library, 303 Genesee St, Utica, NY, 13501. Tel: 315-735-2279. p. 1656

Meger, Drew, Head, Circ Serv, Peabody Institute Library, 15 Sylvan St, Danvers, MA, 01923. Tel: 978-774-0554. p. 1013

Meger, Jennifer, Mgr, Res Serv, Goulston & Storrs PC, 400 Atlantic Ave, Boston, MA, 02110. Tel: 617-482-1776. p. 995

Meggers, Beth, Dir, Libr Serv, Fallon County Library, Six W Fallon Ave, Baker, MT, 59313. Tel: 406-778-7160. p. 1287

Megginson, Liz, Youth Serv Coordr, Thomasville Public Library, 1401 Mosley Dr, Thomasville, AL, 36784. Tel: 334-636-5343. p. 37

Meglio, Linda, YA Serv, Harborfields Public Library, 31 Broadway, Greenlawn, NY, 11740. Tel: 631-757-4200. p. 1541

Mehaffey, Angela, Res Sharing Mgr, University of West Georgia, 1601 Maple St, Carrollton, GA, 30118. Tel: 678-839-6495. p. 469

Meharg, Karen, Ref & Instruction Librn, Charleston Southern University, 9200 University Blvd, Charleston, SC, 29406. Tel: 843-863-7937. p. 2050

Mehlhause, Kellie, Librn, Sanford Virtual Library, 1711 S University Dr, Fargo, ND, 58103. Tel: 701-417-4917. p. 1733

Mehlhorn, Saskia, Dir, Knowledge Resources, Norton Rose Fulbright, Frost Tower, 111 W Houston St, Ste 1800, San Antonio, TX, 78205. Tel: 210-224-5575. p. 2237

Mehlin, Tracy, IT Librn, University of Washington Botanic Gardens, 3501 NE 41st St, Seattle, WA, 98105. Tel: 206-543-0415. p. 2381

Mehling, Matt, Br Supvr, Wood County District Public Library, Walbridge Branch, 108 N Main St, Walbridge, OH, 43465. Tel: 419-666-9900. p. 1752

Mehling, Rebecca, Librn, Ohio State University LIBRARIES, Philip B Hardymon Medical Library, 1492 E Broad St, Columbus, OH, 43205. Tel: 614-257-3248. p. 1775

Mehmel, Angela, Br Head, Winnipeg Public Library, River Heights, 1520 Corydon Ave, Winnipeg, MB, R3N 0J6, CANADA. Tel: 204-986-5450. p. 2596

Mehra, Bharat, Dr, Prof, University of Alabama, 7035 Gorgas Library, Campus Box 870252, Tuscaloosa, AL, 35487-0252. Tel: 205-348-4610. p. 2781

Mehrer, Susanne, Dean of Libr, Dartmouth College Library, 6025 Baker Berry Library, Rm 115, Hanover, NH, 03755-3527. Tel: 603-646-2236. p. 1366

Mehta, Diptiben, Head, Ref Serv, Bridgewater State University, Ten Shaw Rd, Bridgewater, MA, 02325. Tel: 508-531-1742. p. 1002

Mehta, Mamta, Librn, Lakeview Public Library, 1120 Woodfield Rd, Rockville Centre, NY, 11570. Tel: 516-536-3071. p. 1631

Mehu, Carole, Libr Serv Mgr, Norton Rose Fulbright Canada LLP Library, One Place Ville Marie, Ste 2500, Montreal, QC, H3B 1R1, CANADA. Tel: 514-847-4701. p. 2727

Meicher, Donna, Reserves Mgr, Tech Serv Asst, University of Wisconsin-Madison, MERIT Library (Media, Education Resources & Information Technology), 368 Teacher Education Bldg, 225 N Mills St, Madison, WI, 53706. Tel: 608-263-5797. p. 2451

Meier, BreAnne, Marketing Specialist, North Dakota State Library, Liberty Memorial Bldg, Dept 250, 604 East Blvd Ave, Bismarck, ND, 58505-0800. Tel: 701-328-4656. p. 1730

Meier, Janelle, Cat, Walla Walla Community College Library, 500 Tausick Way, Walla Walla, WA, 99362-9267. Tel: 509-527-4297. p. 2392

Meier, John J, Head, STEM for Engagement & Outreach, Pennsylvania State University Libraries, Physical & Mathematical Sciences, 201 Davey Lab, University Park, PA, 16802-6301. Tel: 814-867-1448. p. 2016

Meier, Veronica, Libr Dir, Peru State College Library, 600 Hoyt St, Peru, NE, 68421. Tel: 402-872-2311. p. 1332

Meighan, Joanna, Libr Dir, Hampton Falls Free Public Library, Seven Drinkwater Rd, Hampton Falls, NH, 03844. Tel: 603-926-3682. p. 1366

Meija, Melissa, Br Mgr, Monterey County Free Libraries, Marina Branch, 190 Seaside Circle, Marina, CA, 93933. Tel: 831-883-7507. p. 172

Meijer-Kline, Karen, Scholarly Communications Librn, Kwantlen Polytechnic University Library, 12666 72nd Ave, Surrey, BC, V3W 2M8, CANADA. Tel: 604-599-2978. p. 2576

Meiklejohn, Harriet, Tech Serv Librn, Santa Fe Community College Library, 6401 Richards Ave, Santa Fe, NM, 87508-4887. Tel: 505-428-1287. p. 1476

Meilaender, Marion, Coordr, Ser, Albion College, 602 E Cass St, Albion, MI, 49224-1879. p. 1076

Meilleur, Sarah, Chief Exec Officer, Calgary Public Library, 800 Third St SE, Level 4, Calgary, AB, T2G 2E7, CANADA. Tel: 403-260-2600. p. 2526

Mein, Dina, Dr, Univ Librn, Kettering University Library, 1700 W University Ave, Flint, MI, 48504. Tel: 810-762-7814. p. 1107

Meindl, Patricia, Chem Librn, University of Toronto Libraries, A D Allen Chemistry Library, Lash Miller Laboratories, Rm 480, 80 St George St, Toronto, ON, M5S 3H6, CANADA. Tel: 416-978-3587. p. 2698

Meiners, Tina, Head, Youth Serv, Montrose Regional Library District, 320 S Second St, Montrose, CO, 81401. Tel: 970-249-9656. p. 291

Meisch, Lisa, Archivist, Curator, Texas State Library & Archives Commission, Sam Houston Regional Library & Research Center, 650 FM 1011, Liberty, TX, 77575. Tel: 936-336-8821. p. 2141

Meisel, Gloria, Coll Develop Librn, Outreach Librn, SUNY Westchester Community College, 75 Grasslands Rd, Valhalla, NY, 10595. Tel: 914-785-6968. p. 1656

Meisel, Joseph, Univ Librn, Brown University, Ten Prospect St, Box A, Providence, RI, 02912. Tel: 401-863-2165. p. 2037

Meister, Lynn, Asst Librn, Muscoda Public Library, 400 N Wisconsin Ave, Muscoda, WI, 53573. Tel: 608-739-3510. p. 2463

Meister, Nina, Libr Dir, Jenkintown Library, 460 York Rd, Jenkintown, PA, 19046. Tel: 215-884-0593. p. 1947

Meister, Nina, Dir, Womelsdorf Community Library, 203 W High St, Womelsdorf, PA, 19567-1307. Tel: 610-589-1424. p. 2024

Meitzen, Katelynn, Librn, Cuero Public Library, 207 E Main St, Cuero, TX, 77954. Tel: 361-275-2864. p. 2162

Meizner, Kathie, Br Mgr, Montgomery County Public Libraries, White Oak Library, 11701 New Hampshire Ave, Silver Spring, MD, 20904-2898. Tel: 240-777-9558. p. 975

Mejia, Josua, Coordr, Harvard Library, History Department Library, Robinson Hall, 35 Quincy St, Cambridge, MA, 02138. Tel: 617-495-2556. p. 1007

Mejia, Rebecca, Librn, Stella Ellis Hart Public Library, 103 FM 108 North, Smiley, TX, 78159. Tel: 830-587-6101. p. 2244

Mejia, Yajaira, Libr Mgr, New York Public Library - Astor, Lenox & Tilden Foundations, Bloomingdale Branch, 150 W 100th St, (Between Amsterdam & Columbus Aves), New York, NY, 10025-5196. Tel: 212-222-8030. p. 1594

Mejia-Suarez, Silvia, Ref Librn, Regis College Library, 235 Wellesley St, Weston, MA, 02493. Tel: 781-768-7300. p. 1068

Mejias, Nelba, Actg Dir, Harrison Public Library, 415 Harrison Ave, Harrison, NJ, 07029. Tel: 973-483-2366. p. 1407

Mejstrik, Jeannie, Dir, O'Neill Public Library, 601 E Douglas, O'Neill, NE, 68763. Tel: 402-336-3110. p. 1331

Mekelburg, Mary, Asst Librn, Theresa Public Library, 290 Mayville St, Theresa, WI, 53091-0307. Tel: 920-488-2342. p. 2481

Meko, John, Exec Dir, Union League of Philadelphia Library, 140 S Broad St, Philadelphia, PA, 19102. Tel: 215-587-5583. p. 1987

Melamed, Vladimir, Archivist, Historian, New Center for Psychoanalysis Library, 2014 Sawtelle Blvd, Los Angeles, CA, 90025. Tel: 310-478-6541. p. 167

Melancon, Christopher, Librn, Louisiana House of Representatives, 900 N Third St, Baton Rouge, LA, 70804. Tel: 225-342-2432. p. 883

Meland, Jane, Libr Dir, Michigan State University College of Law Library, Law College Bldg, Rm 115, 648 N Shaw Lane, East Lansing, MI, 48824-1300. Tel: 517-432-6860. p. 1101

Meland, Jane, Asst Dir, Pub Serv, Michigan State University College of Law Library, Law College Bldg, Rm 115, 648 N Shaw Lane, East Lansing, MI, 48824-1300. Tel: 517-432-6867. p. 1102

Melander, Hope, ILL, Baldwin Public Library, 400 Cedar St, Baldwin, WI, 54002. Tel: 715-684-3813. p. 2422

Melberg, Dawn, Librn, Kaiser-Permanente Medical Center, Medical Office One, 1st Flr, 99 Montecillo Rd, San Rafael, CA, 94903. Tel: 707-393-4526. p. 236

Melch, Spencer, Br Supvr, Wellington County Library, Marden Branch, 7368 Wellington Rd 30, RR 5, Guelph, ON, N1H 6J2, CANADA. Tel: 519-763-7445. p. 2641

Melcher, Amanda, Head, Tech Serv, University of Montevallo, Bloch St, Montevallo, AL, 35115. Tel: 205-665-6104. p. 27

Melchi, Jen, Adult Serv, Burlington Public Library, 166 E Jefferson St, Burlington, WI, 53105. Tel: 262-342-1130. p. 2426

Melchor, Lynn, ILL, Reserves, Spec, Elon University, 308 N O'Kelly Ave, Elon, NC, 27244-0187. Tel: 336-278-6600. p. 1688

Melendez, Marie Eleane, Librn, Literacy Serv, Inter-American University of Puerto Rico, 104 Parque Industrial Turpeaux, Rd 1, Mercedita, PR, 00715-1602. Tel: 787-284-1912, Ext 2114. p. 2512

Melendez-Barden, John R, Dir, Maine State Law & Legislative Reference Library, 43 State House Sta, Augusta, ME, 04333-0043. Tel: 207-287-1600. p. 914

Melfi, Susan, Teen Librn, Newburgh Chandler Public Library, 4111 Lakeshore Dr, Newburgh, IN, 47630-2274. Tel: 812-589-5468, Ext 304. p. 709

Melgar, Kathleen, Libr Dir, Asbury Park Public Library, 500 First Ave, Asbury Park, NJ, 07712. Tel: 732-774-4221. p. 1387

Melgoza, Ezequiel, Syst Librn, University of Texas Rio Grande Valley, One W University Blvd, Brownsville, TX, 78520. Tel: 956-882-7591. p. 2150

Melham, Shannon, Br Mgr, Anoka County Library, Rum River, 4201 Sixth Ave, Anoka, MN, 55303. Tel: 763-324-1520. p. 1165

Melia, Marcy, Ch Serv, Goodland Public Library, 812 Broadway, Goodland, KS, 67735. Tel: 785-899-5461. p. 810

Melia, Patricia, Dir, Libr Serv, Baptist Health System, 8400 Datapoint Dr, San Antonio, TX, 78229. Tel: 210-297-7639. p. 2236

Melican, Tori, Ch Serv, Normal Public Library, 206 W College Ave, Normal, IL, 61761. Tel: 309-452-1757. p. 625

Melick, Cindy, Asst Librn, Danvers Township Library, 117 E Exchange St, Danvers, IL, 61732-9347. Tel: 309-963-4269. p. 575

Melilli, Amanda, Head, Libr Develop, University of Nevada, Las Vegas Univ Libraries, Teacher Development & Resources Library, 4505 S Maryland Pkwy, Box 453009, Las Vegas, NV, 89154-3009. Tel: 702-895-1963. p. 1347

Melillo, Mike, Librn, McDonald Hopkins, LLC, 600 Superior Ave E, Ste 2100, Cleveland, OH, 44114. Tel: 216-348-5400. p. 1770

Melillo, Paolo, Br Mgr, Orange County Library System, Southeast Branch, 5575 S Semoran Blvd, Orlando, FL, 32822. p. 431

Melinn, Carmen, Br Mgr, McDowell County Public Library, Marion Davis Memorial Branch / Old Fort Library, 65 Mitchell St, Old Fort, NC, 28762. Tel: 828-668-7111. p. 1702

Melione, Andrea, Asst Head, Science Library, State University of New York at Binghamton, Science Library, Vestal Pkwy E, Binghamton, NY, 13902. Tel: 607-777-6323. p. 1494

Melis, Rachel, Learning Librn, Huron University College, 1349 Western Rd, London, ON, N6G 1H3, CANADA. Tel: 519-438-7224, Ext 235. p. 2653

Melissa, Adler, Libr Found Dir, Springfield-Greene County Library District, 4653 S Campbell Ave, Springfield, MO, 65810-1723. Tel: 417-882-0714. p. 1281

Mellang, Mark, Dir, Osgood Public Library, 136 W Ripley St, Osgood, IN, 47037-1229. Tel: 812-689-4011. p. 712

Melliere, Lori, Client Serv Librn, Outreach Librn, North Carolina Biotechnology Center Life Science Intelligence, 15 T W Alexander Dr, Research Triangle Park, NC, 27709. Tel: 919-541-9366. p. 1712

Mellingen, Andrea, Librn, Montmorency County Public Libraries, 11901 Haymeadow Rd, Atlanta, MI, 49709. Tel: 989-785-3941. p. 1081

Mellinger, Margaret, Head, Emerging Tech & Serv, Oregon State University Libraries, 121 The Valley Library, Corvallis, OR, 97331-4501. Tel: 541-737-9642. p. 1876

Mello, David, Ch Serv, Fall River Public Library, 104 N Main St, Fall River, MA, 02720. Tel: 508-324-2700. p. 1018

Mello, Marjo, Dir, Brawley Public Library, 400 Main St, Brawley, CA, 92227-2491. Tel: 760-344-1891. p. 124

Mello, Peggy, Adult Serv, Coll Develop, The William K Sanford Town Library, 629 Albany Shaker Rd, Loudonville, NY, 12211-1196. Tel: 518-458-9274. p. 1565

Mellon, Joelle, Res & Instruction Librn, Monterey Institute of International Studies, 425 Van Buren St, Monterey, CA, 93940. Tel: 831-647-4136. p. 179

Mellon, Kimberly, Head Librn, Lake Alfred Public Library, 245 N Seminole Ave, Lake Alfred, FL, 33850. Tel: 863-291-5378. p. 415

Mellon, Laura, Br Mgr, Wyoming County Public Library, Oceana Public, 1519 Cook Pkwy, Oceana, WV, 24870. Tel: 304-682-6784. p. 2412

Mellor, Beth Ann, Dir, Oakmont Carnegie Library, 700 Allegheny River Blvd, Oakmont, PA, 15139. Tel: 412-828-9532. p. 1972

Mellor, Karen, Chief, Libr Serv, State of Rhode Island, Department of Administration, One Capitol Hill, 2nd Flr, Providence, RI, 02908. Tel: 401-574-9304. p. 2041

Mellor, Karen, Chief, Libr Serv, Library of Rhode Island Network, One Capitol Hill, Providence, RI, 02908. Tel: 401-574-9300. p. 2774

Mellott, Annie, Acq Librn, Loyola Law School, 919 S Albany St, Los Angeles, CA, 90015-1211. Tel: 213-736-1174. p. 166

Melnick, Todd G E, Dir, Fordham University School of Law, 150 W 62nd St, New York, NY, 10023. Tel: 212-636-7677. p. 1585

Melnyk, Yuli, Circ, River Grove Public Library District, 8638 W Grand Ave, River Grove, IL, 60171. Tel: 708-453-4484. p. 639

Melo, Olivia, Dir, New Bedford Free Public Library, 613 Pleasant St, New Bedford, MA, 02740-6203. Tel: 508-991-6275. p. 1038

Melo, Olivia, Dir, New Bedford Free Public Library, Casa da Saudade Branch, 58 Crapo St, New Bedford, MA, 02740. Tel: 508-991-6218. p. 1038

Melochick, Michael, Exec Dir, Bangor Historical Society Library, 159 Union St, Bangor, ME, 04401. Tel: 207-942-1900. p. 915

Melodie, Hoffman, Asst Br Librn, Emery County Library System, Orangeville Branch, 125 S Main, Orangeville, UT, 84537. Tel: 435-748-2726. p. 2262

Melone, Colleen, Head, Adult Serv, Lincolnwood Public Library District, 4000 W Pratt Ave, Lincolnwood, IL, 60712. Tel: 847-677-5277. p. 609

Melone, Nicole, Libr Serv Coordr, Moretown Memorial Library, 1147 Rte 100-B, Moretown, VT, 05660. Tel: 802-496-9728. p. 2289

Meloy, William, Discovery Serv Librn, Pennsylvania Western University - California, 250 University Ave, California, PA, 15419-1394. Tel: 724-938-4067. p. 1917

Melquist, Maddison, Humanities Librn, North Dakota State University Libraries, 1201 Albrecht Blvd, Fargo, ND, 58108. Tel: 701-231-8394. p. 1733

Melroy, Virginia, Conbtiuning Coll Librn, University of Iowa Libraries, College of Law Library, 200 Boyd Law Bldg, Iowa City, IA, 52242-1166. Tel: 319-335-9077. p. 761

Melsness, Leanne Drury, Mgr, Edmonton Public Library, Whitemud Crossing, 145 Whitemud Crossing Shopping Ctr, 4211 106 St, Edmonton, AB, T6J 6L7, CANADA. Tel: 780-496-8348. p. 2537

Melson, Maggie, Youth Serv Mgr, Saint Charles City-County Library District, 77 Boone Hills Dr, Saint Peters, MO, 63376. Tel: 636-441-2300. p. 1277

Melton, Dana, Dir & Librn, Swayzee Public Library, 301 S Washington St, Swayzee, IN, 46986. Tel: 765-922-7526. p. 720

Melton, Edward, Dir, Harris County Public Library, 5749 S Loop E, Houston, TX, 77033. Tel: 713-274-6600. p. 2192

Melton, Eric, Librn, Northeast Regional Library, Ripley Public Library, 308 N Commerce St, Ripley, MS, 38663-1721. Tel: 662-837-7773. p. 1216

Melton, Janet, Br Mgr, Pamunkey Regional Library, Goochland Branch, 3075 River Rd W, Goochland, VA, 23063. Tel: 804-556-4774. p. 2323

Melton, John, Libr Mgr, Lancaster Veterans Memorial Library, 1600 Veterans Memorial Pkwy, Lancaster, TX, 75134. Tel: 972-275-1419. p. 2209

Melton, Maureen, Dir, Archives, Museum of Fine Arts, Boston, 465 Huntington Ave, Boston, MA, 02115. Tel: 617-369-3385. p. 997

Melton, Pam, Prog Coordr, Griffin Memorial Hospital, Bldg 54 205, 900 E Main St, Norman, OK, 73071. Tel: 405-573-6602. p. 1855

Melton, Sara Olivia, Libr Mgr, New Orleans Public Library, Robert E Smith Library, 6301 Canal Blvd, New Orleans, LA, 70124-3117. Tel: 504-596-2638. p. 903

Meluskey, Andrea, Libr Dir, Shelter Rock Public Library, 165 Searingtown Rd, Albertson, NY, 11507. Tel: 516-248-7343. p. 1484

Melvie, Ann Marie, Librn, Saskatchewan Justice, Court of Appeal Library, Court House, 2425 Victoria Ave, Regina, SK, S4P 4W6, CANADA. Tel: 306-787-7399. p. 2747

Melville, Catherine, Dir, Juneau Public Libraries, 292 Marine Way, Juneau, AK, 99801. Tel: 907-586-5249. p. 47

Melvin, Joann, Libr Asst, Sampson-Clinton Public Library, Roseboro Public Library, 300 W Roseboro St, Roseboro, NC, 28382. Tel: 910-525-5436. p. 1682

Melvin, Mary, Librn, CoxHealth Libraries, Cox Medical Ctr N, 1423 N Jefferson Ave, J-209-210, Springfield, MO, 65802. Tel: 417-269-3460. p. 1280

Menanteaux, Bob, Ref (Info Servs), Seattle University, School of Law Library, Sullivan Hall, 901 12th Ave, Seattle, WA, 98122-4411. Tel: 206-398-4221. p. 2380

Menard, Christine, Head, Res Serv, Williams College, 26 Hopkins Hall Dr, Williamstown, MA, 01267. Tel: 413-597-2515. p. 1069

Menard, Denise M, Cataloger, Scarborough Public Library, 48 Gorham Rd, Scarborough, ME, 04074. Tel: 207-396-6274. p. 939

Menard, Lois, Asst Dir, Rolla Public Library, 14 SE First St, Rolla, ND, 58367. Tel: 701-477-3849. p. 1739

Menard, Margie, Dir, Kingston Library, 55 Franklin St, Kingston, NY, 12401. Tel: 845-339-4260, Ext 14. p. 1560

Menard, Norma, Co-Dir, Mooers Free Library, 25 School St, Mooers, NY, 12958. Tel: 518-236-7744. p. 1574

Mendell, Rebecca, Access Serv Librn, Folsom Lake College Library, Ten College Pkwy, Folsom, CA, 95630. Tel: 916-608-6708. p. 142

Mendell, Sean, Asst Dir, Behringer-Crawford Museum Library, 1600 Montague Rd, Devou Park, Covington, KY, 41011. Tel: 859-491-4003. p. 852

Mendenhall, Mae, Libr Dir, University of Alaska Fairbanks, 604 Third Ave, Kotzebue, AK, 99752. Tel: 907-442-2410. p. 49

Mendenhall, Michael R, Pres & Chief Exec Officer, Nielsen Engineering & Research, Inc, 900 Lafayette St, Ste 600, Santa Clara, CA, 95050. Tel: 408-454-5246. p. 241

Mendes, Stephanie, Access Services & ILL Coord, Holy Family University Library, 9801 Frankford Ave, Philadelphia, PA, 19114. Tel: 267-341-3315. p. 1981

Mendez, Deixter, Library Contact, University of Puerto Rico, Marine Science, PO Box 9022, Mayaguez, PR, 00681-9022. Tel: 787-832-4040, Ext 2513. p. 2511

Mendez, Ignacio, Libr Dir, Red Lake Nation College, 15480 Migizi Dr, Red Lake, MN, 56671. Tel: 218-382-1169. p. 1193

Mendez, Jerry, Computer Lab/Per Supvr, Yuma County Free Library District, 2951 S 21st Dr, Yuma, AZ, 85364. Tel: 928-314-2456. p. 85

Mendez, Lisa J, Dir, Yuma County Free Library District, 2951 S 21st Dr, Yuma, AZ, 85364. Tel: 928-373-6462. p. 85

Mendez, Monica, Acq, California State University, Bakersfield, 9001 Stockdale Hwy, 60 LIB, Bakersfield, CA, 93311. Tel: 661-654-3249. p. 119

Mendez, Samatha, Pub Serv Coordr, Arlington Public Library System, Southwest, 3311 SW Green Oaks Blvd, Arlington, TX, 76017. p. 2136

Mendez-Brady, Marisa, Ref & Instruction Librn, California Institute of the Arts, 24700 McBean Pkwy, Valencia, CA, 91355. Tel: 661-291-3024. p. 255

Mendez-DeMaio, Doris, Br Mgr, Palm Beach County Library System, Acreage Branch, 15801 Orange Blvd, Loxahatchee, FL, 33470. Tel: 561-681-4100. p. 454

Mendieta, Toni, Br Supvr, Yolo County Library, Esparto Branch, 17065 Yolo Ave, Esparto, CA, 95627. Tel: 530-787-3426. p. 260

Mendieta, Toni, Br Supvr, Yolo County Library, Winters Branch, 708 Railroad Ave, Winters, CA, 95694. Tel: 530-795-3177. p. 260

Mendive, Toni, Archivist, Northeastern Nevada Museum Library, 1515 Idaho St, Elko, NV, 89801. Tel: 775-738-3418. p. 1345

Mendoza, Arrial, Circ Mgr, Joe Barnhart Bee County Public Library, 110 W Corpus Christi St, Beeville, TX, 78102-5604. Tel: 361-362-4901. p. 2146

Mendoza, Frank, Circ Mgr, Charlotte Mecklenburg Library, ImaginOn: The Joe & Joan Martin Center, 300 E Seventh St, Charlotte, NC, 28202. Tel: 704-416-4600. p. 1679
Mendoza, Jorge, Sr Librn, The National Academies of Sciences, Engineering & Medicine, 500 Fifth St NW, Keck 304, Washington, DC, 20001-2721. Tel: 202-334-2125. p. 371
Mendoza, Karina, Br Mgr, Stanislaus County Library, David F Bush Library (Oakdale Branch), 151 S First Ave, Oakdale, CA, 95361-3902. Tel: 209-847-4204. p. 178
Mendoza, Rebecca, Libr Asst, Imperial County Free Library, Heber Branch, 1132 Heber Ave, Heber, CA, 92249. Tel: 442-265-7131. p. 140
Mendoza, Tracey, Dean of Libr, University of the Incarnate Word, 4301 Broadway, CPO 297, San Antonio, TX, 78209-6397. p. 2240
Meneades, Rachel, Head, Adult Serv, Abbot Public Library, Three Brook Rd, Marblehead, MA, 01945. Tel: 781-631-1481. p. 1031
Meneely, Becky, Research Librn, Northwest Missouri State University, 800 University Dr, Maryville, MO, 64468-6001. Tel: 660-562-1193. p. 1261
Menefee, Melissa, Dir, Fontanelle Public Library, 303 Washington St, Fontanelle, IA, 50846. Tel: 641-745-4981. p. 753
Menendez, Carolina, Dir, US Customs & Border Protection Information Resources Center, 90 K St NE, Washington, DC, 20229. Tel: 202-325-0130. p. 380
Menendez-Cuesta, Loanis, Asst Dir, Delray Beach Public Library, 100 W Atlantic Ave, Delray Beach, FL, 33444. Tel: 561-819-6406. p. 394
Meneses, Brian, Ref Librn, Sandwich Public Library, 142 Main St, Sandwich, MA, 02563. Tel: 508-888-0625. p. 1052
Mengel, Bea, Youth Serv Librn, Flint River Regional Library System, 800 Memorial Dr, Griffin, GA, 30223. Tel: 770-412-4770. p. 481
Mengel, Elizabeth, Head, Coll Mgt, Johns Hopkins University Libraries, The Sheridan Libraries, 3400 N Charles St, Baltimore, MD, 21218. Tel: 410-516-8325. p. 954
Mengler, Paula, Asst Librn, Belle Plaine Community Library, 904 12th St, Belle Plaine, IA, 52208-1711. Tel: 319-444-2902. p. 734
Menish, Marcia, Ch, O'Neill Public Library, 601 E Douglas, O'Neill, NE, 68763. Tel: 402-336-3110. p. 1331
Menk, Bobb, Info Mgt & Metadata Team Lead, Massachusetts Institute of Technology, 244 Wood St, Lexington, MA, 02420-9176. Tel: 781-981-5354. p. 1028
Menke, Roberta, Librn, Newton Public Library & Museum, 100 S Van Buren St, Newton, IL, 62448. Tel: 618-783-8141. p. 624
Menker, Bill, Patron Serv Mgr, Washington-Centerville Public Library, 111 W Spring Valley Rd, Centerville, OH, 45458. Tel: 937-610-4412. p. 1757
Mennenga, Karen, Dir, Wellsburg Public Library, 411 N Adams St, Wellsburg, IA, 50680. Tel: 641-869-5234. p. 790
Menocal, Elizabeth, Sr Dir, Miami Children's Health System, 3100 SW 62nd Ave, Miami, FL, 33155-3009. Tel: 786-624-4470. p. 422
Menschel, Ronay, Pres & Dir, Museum of the City of New York, 1220 Fifth Ave, New York, NY, 10029. Tel: 212-534-1672. p. 1592
Mensing, Donna, Circ Tech, Wagoner City Public Library, 302 N Main St, Wagoner, OK, 74467-3834. Tel: 918-485-2126. p. 1868
Mensing, Marion, Br Mgr, Jackson County Library Services, Shady Cove Branch, 22477 Hwy 62, Shady Cove, OR, 97539-9718. Tel: 541-878-2270. p. 1886
Mentch, Fran, Librn, Cleveland State University, Michael Schwartz Library, Rhodes Tower, Ste 501, 2121 Euclid Ave, Cleveland, OH, 44115-2214. Tel: 216-687-2365. p. 1769
Menter, Joshua, Br Librn, East Central Regional Library, Hinckley Public Library, 106 First St SE, Hinckley, MN, 55037. Tel: 320-384-6351. p. 1168
Menter, Joshua, Br Librn, East Central Regional Library, Sandstone Public Library, 119 N Fourth St, Sandstone, MN, 55072. Tel: 320-245-2270. p. 1168
Mentink, Joy, Libr Dir, Crawford County Library District, PO Box 1250, Steelville, MO, 65565-1250. Tel: 573-775-5035. p. 1282
Mentkowski, Annie, Head Librn, United States Railroad Retirement Board Library, 844 N Rush St, Chicago, IL, 60611-2031. Tel: 312-751-4926. p. 569
Mentzel, Nina, Automation Serv, Cat, Metadata Librn, South Dakota State Library, 800 Governors Dr, Pierre, SD, 57501-2294. Tel: 605-773-3131. p. 2080
Mentzer, Kristen, Technology Spec, Northern Virginia Community College Libraries, Medical Education Campus, 6699 Springfield Center Dr, Rm 341, Springfield, VA, 22150. Tel: 703-822-9052. p. 2304
Mentzer, Michelle, Librn, Gallitzin Public Library, DeGol Plaza, Ste 30, 411 Convent St, Gallitzin, PA, 16641-1244. Tel: 814-886-4041. p. 1934
Menzel, Jacqueline, Archit Librn, Florida Agricultural & Mechanical University Libraries, 525 Orr Dr, Tallahassee, FL, 32307-4700. Tel: 850-599-8770. p. 446
Menzel, Kelly, Ch Serv, North Tonawanda Public Library, 505 Meadow Dr, North Tonawanda, NY, 14120. Tel: 716-693-4132. p. 1608
Menzies, Xavier, Libr Dir, Harvey Public Library District, 15441 Turlington Ave, Harvey, IL, 60426. Tel: 708-331-0757. p. 597
Menzies, Xavier, Dir, Markham Public Library, 16640 Kedzie Ave, Markham, IL, 60428. Tel: 708-331-0130. p. 614
Meola, Dawn, Coordr, Ch Serv, Woodstock Public Library District, Five Library Lane, Woodstock, NY, 12498. Tel: 845-679-2213. p. 1667
Mera, Kristine, Dir, Smyrna Public Library, 107 S Main St, Smyrna, DE, 19977. Tel: 302-653-4579. p. 356
Merasty, Geraldine, Librn, Ayamicikiwikamik Public Library, PO Box 240, Sandy Bay, SK, S0P 0G0, CANADA. Tel: 306-754-2139. p. 2748
Meraz, Gloria, Dir, State Librn, Texas State Library & Archives Commission, 1201 Brazos St, Austin, TX, 78701. Tel: 512-463-5474. p. 2141
Merboth, Mallorie, Dir of Medical Staff Services, Boulder Community Hospital, 4715 Arapahoe Ave, Boulder, CO, 80303. Tel: 303-415-7496. p. 266
Mercadante, Jolene, Asst Dir, Agawam Public Library, 750 Cooper St, Agawam, MA, 01001. Tel: 413-789-1550. p. 983
Mercado, Alexandra, Head, Library Programs & Newsletter, Sachem Public Library, 150 Holbrook Rd, Holbrook, NY, 11741. Tel: 631-588-5024. p. 1547
Mercado, Fatima, Librn, Toronto International Film Festival Inc, TIFF Bell Lightbox, 350 King St W, Toronto, ON, M5V 3X5, CANADA. Tel: 416-599-8433. p. 2693
Mercado, Peter, Head, Info Syst, Arcadia Public Library, 20 W Duarte Rd, Arcadia, CA, 91006. Tel: 626-821-5567. p. 117
Mercatante, Mike, Commun Relations Coordr, Friends Coordr, Saint Clair County Library System, 210 McMorran Blvd, Port Huron, MI, 48060-4098. Tel: 810-987-7323. p. 1142
Mercer, Crystal, Libr Tech II, College of the North Atlantic Library Services, Seal Cove Campus, 1670 Conception Bay Hwy, Conception Bay South, NL, A1X 5C7, CANADA. Tel: 709-744-2047. p. 2609
Mercer, Holly, Dir, Dodge City Community College Library, 2501 N 14th, Dodge City, KS, 67801. Tel: 620-225-1321, Ext 287, 620-227-9287. p. 804
Mercer, Holly, Assoc Dean, Res, Coll & Scholarly Communication, University of Tennessee, Knoxville, 1015 Volunteer Blvd, Knoxville, TN, 37996-1000. Tel: 865-974-4351. p. 2107
Mercer, Jeff, Dep Chief Librn, South Shore Public Libraries, 135 North Park St, Unit B, Bridgewater, NS, B4V 9B3, CANADA. Tel: 902-543-2548. p. 2616
Mercer, Linda, Dir, Fonda Public Library, 104 W Second St, Fonda, IA, 50540. Tel: 712-288-4467. p. 753
Mercer, Lynn, Mgr, Human Res, Muskingum County Library System, 220 N Fifth St, Zanesville, OH, 43701-3587. Tel: 740-453-0391, Ext 133. p. 1836
Mercer, Megan, Br Mgr, Neuse Regional Library, Trenton Public Library, 204 Lakeview Dr, Trenton, NC, 28585. Tel: 252-448-4261. p. 1699
Mercer, Melissa G, Librn, Washington County Library, 235 E High St, Potosi, MO, 63664. Tel: 573-438-4691. p. 1266
Mercer, Nora, Ref Librn, Notre Dame de Namur University Library, 1500 Ralston Ave, Belmont, CA, 94002-1908. Tel: 650-508-3748. p. 121
Mercer, Patrica, Libr Tech, Michigan Department of Corrections, Ernest C Brooks Correctional Facility Library, 2500 S Sheridan Rd, Muskegon, MI, 49444. Tel: 231-773-9200, Ext 1916. p. 1089
Mercer, Scout, Youth Serv Librn II, Keene Public Library, 60 Winter St, Keene, NH, 03431. Tel: 603-352-0157. p. 1369
Mercer, Shirley, Asst Dir, Union County Public District Library, 126 S Morgan St, Morganfield, KY, 42437. Tel: 270-389-1696. p. 870
Merchant, Arthur, Tech Serv Librn, Clarence Dillon Public Library, 2336 Lamington Rd, Bedminster, NJ, 07921. Tel: 908-234-2325. p. 1389
Mercier, Mellanie, Asst Dir, Automation Syst Coordr, Bridges Library System, 741 N Grand Ave, Ste 210, Waukesha, WI, 53186. Tel: 262-896-8084. p. 2484
Mercier, Pierre, Interim Archivist, Leeds & the Thousand Islands Public Library, Archives, 1365 County Rd 2, Mallorytown, ON, K0E 1R0, CANADA. Tel: 613-659-3800. p. 2652
Mercier, Sandra, Team Leader, Bibliotheques de Trois-Rivieres, Bibliotheque Aline-Piche, 5575 boul Jean-XXIII, Trois-Rivieres, QC, G8Z 4A8, CANADA. Tel: 819-374-6525. p. 2738
Mercure, Mireille, Libr Dir, Fundy Library Region, Bibliothèque Le Cormoran, Centre Samuel de Champlain, 67 Ragged Point Rd, Saint John, NB, E2K 5C3, CANADA. Tel: 506-658-4610. p. 2604
Mercurio, Courtney, Dir, Coffee County Lannom Memorial Public Library, 312 N Collins St, Tullahoma, TN, 37388-3229. Tel: 931-455-2460. p. 2128
Mercurio, Jill, Dir, Newton Free Library, 330 Homer St, Newton Centre, MA, 02459-1429. Tel: 617-796-1360. p. 1039
Meredith, Jessica, Community Engagement & Youth Educ Librn, New Port Richey Public Library, 5939 Main St, New Port Richey, FL, 34652. Tel: 727-853-1264. p. 428
Meredith, Julie, Dir, Clarkston Independence District Library, 6495 Clarkston Rd, Clarkston, MI, 48346. Tel: 248-625-2212. p. 1091
Meredith, Maggie, Librn, Montana Historical Society, 225 N Roberts St, Helena, MT, 59601-4514. Tel: 406-444-9526. p. 1296
Meredith, Mary, Dir, Stephenville Public Library, 174 N Columbia, Stephenville, TX, 76401-3492. Tel: 254-918-1240. p. 2245
Meredith, Tamara, Dr, Dir, Jefferson County Rural Library District, 620 Cedar Ave, Port Hadlock, WA, 98339. Tel: 360-385-6544. p. 2374
Merges, Lucy, Librn, Auglaize County Law Library, County Courthouse, 201 Willipie St, Ste 207, Wapakoneta, OH, 45895. Tel: 419-739-6749. p. 1827

Merguerian, Gayane Karen, Head of Arts, & Social Sciences, Northeastern University Libraries, 360 Huntington Ave, Boston, MA, 02115. Tel: 617-373-2747. p. 998

Merida, Melissa, Dir, New Albany-Floyd County Public Library, 180 W Spring St, New Albany, IN, 47150. Tel: 812-949-3525. p. 709

Meriwether, Taylor, Dir, Hinton Public Library, 123 E Main St, Hinton, OK, 73047. Tel: 405-542-6167. p. 1849

Merkey, Bonnie, Asst Librn, Ulysses Library Association, 401 N Main St, Ulysses, PA, 16948. Tel: 814-848-7226. p. 2014

Merkley, Cari, Librn, Mount Royal University Library, 4825 Mount Royal Gate SW, Calgary, AB, T3E 6K6, CANADA. Tel: 403-440-5068. p. 2528

Merlin, Cate, Dir, Peabody Institute Library, 82 Main St, Peabody, MA, 01960-5553. Tel: 951-531-0100, Ext 16. p. 1045

Merlo, Loretta, Circ Mgr, Cornell University Library, Samuel J Wood Library & C V Starr Biomedical Information Center, 1300 York Ave, C115, Box 67, New York, NY, 10065-4896. Tel: 646-962-2557. p. 1552

Merly, Lisa, Circ Supvr, Louisville Public Library, 951 Spruce St, Louisville, CO, 80027. Tel: 303-335-4849. p. 290

Meroth, Gena, Univ Archivist, Nova Southeastern University Libraries, 3100 Ray Ferrero Jr Blvd, Fort Lauderdale, FL, 33314. Tel: 954-262-4641. p. 402

Merrell, April, Pres, Pittsburgh Toy Lending Library, c/o First United Methodist Church, 5401 Centre Ave, Rear, Pittsburgh, PA, 15232. Tel: 412-682-4430. p. 1995

Merrell, Becky, Acq, Curtis Laws Wilson Library, 400 W 14th St, Rolla, MO, 65409-0060. Tel: 573-341-4013. p. 1268

Merrell, Jessie T, Archival Assoc, Columbus State University Libraries, 4225 University Ave, Columbus, GA, 31907. Tel: 706-507-8673. p. 472

Merriam, Helena, Prof, Algonquin College of Applied Arts & Technology, School of Health & Community Studies, Rm C230, 1385 Woodroffe Ave, Ottawa, ON, K2G 1V8, CANADA. Tel: 613-727-4723. p. 2796

Merrick, Andrea, Br Mgr, Mercer County Library System, Hopewell Branch, 245 Pennington-Titusville Rd, Pennington, NJ, 08534. Tel: 609-737-2610. p. 1411

Merrigan, Roberta, ILL, Enfield Public Library, 104 Middle Rd, Enfield, CT, 06082. Tel: 860-763-7510. p. 311

Merrill, Alex, Head, Systems & Technical Ops, Washington State University Libraries, 100 Dairy Rd, Pullman, WA, 99164. Tel: 509-335-5426. p. 2374

Merrill, Holly, Librn, Morenci Community Library, 346 Plaza Dr, Morenci, AZ, 85540. Tel: 928-865-7042. p. 67

Merrill, Jason, Head, Tech Serv, Longmont Public Library, 409 Fourth Ave, Longmont, CO, 80501-6006. Tel: 303-651-8470. p. 290

Merrill, Paul, Pub Info Officer, Maine Department of Transportation Library, Transportation Headquarters Bldg, 1st Flr, 24 Child St, Augusta, ME, 04330. Tel: 207-624-3000, 207-624-3230. p. 914

Merrill, Sarah, Librn, Brookside Congregational Church Library, 2013 Elm St, Manchester, NH, 03104. Tel: 603-669-2807. p. 1372

Merriman, Gary, Head Librn, Life Pacific College Library, 1100 W Covina Blvd, San Dimas, CA, 91773. Tel: 909-706-3008. p. 223

Merriman, Jennifer, Librn, Supreme Court of Illinois Library, Supreme Court Bldg, 200 E Capital Ave, Springfield, IL, 62701-1791. Tel: 217-782-2424. p. 650

Merriman, Kaitlyn, Pres, Toronto Health Libraries Association, c/o University of Toronto Libraries, 130 Saint George St, Toronto, ON, M5S 1A5, CANADA. Tel: 416-978-2280. p. 2778

Merriman, Selena, Dir, Mott Public Library, 203 Third St E, Mott, ND, 58646-7525. Tel: 701-824-2163. p. 1739

Merritt, Ashlee, Res Sharing Tech, Southwestern Oklahoma State University, 100 Campus Dr, Weatherford, OK, 73096-3002. Tel: 580-774-7023. p. 1868

Merritt, Erica, Youth Serv Librn, Sierra Vista Public Library, 2600 E Tacoma, Sierra Vista, AZ, 85635. Tel: 520-458-4225. p. 78

Merritt, Jackie, Br Mgr, Jackson District Library, Parma Branch, 102 Church St, Parma, MI, 49269. Tel: 517-531-4908. p. 1120

Merritt, Jackie, Br Mgr, Jackson District Library, Springport Branch, 116 Mechanic St, Springport, MI, 49284. Tel: 517-905-1459. p. 1120

Merritt, Jill, Sr Librn, Pierce County Library System, South Hill Branch, 15420 Meridian E, Puyallup, WA, 98375. Tel: 253-548-3303. p. 2386

Merritt, Joey, Assessment & Planning, Librn, Merced College, 3600 M St, Merced, CA, 95348. Tel: 209-384-6283. p. 176

Merritt, John, Dir, Libr Tech, Southern Baptist Theological Seminary, 2825 Lexington Rd, Louisville, KY, 40280-0294. p. 866

Merritt, Julia, Chief Exec Officer, Annapolis Valley Regional Library, 236 Commercial St, Berwick, NS, B0P 1E0, CANADA. Tel: 902-538-2665. p. 2616

Merritt, Karen, Librn, Public Library of Steubenville & Jefferson County, Brilliant Branch, 103 Steuben St, Brilliant, OH, 43913. Tel: 740-598-4028. p. 1822

Merritt, Kelly, Mgr, Libr Media Serv, Ithaca College Library, 953 Danby Rd, Ithaca, NY, 14850-7060. Tel: 607-274-3880. p. 1552

Merritt, Rhonda, Ch, Lincoln County Library System, Thayne Branch, 250 Van Noy Pkwy, Thayne, WY, 83127. Tel: 307-883-7323. p. 2496

Merritt, Zack, Educ Dir, The Clay Center for the Arts & Sciences of West Virginia, One Clay Sq, Charleston, WV, 25301. Tel: 304-561-3570. p. 2400

Merry, Allen, Head Librn, Free Library of Philadelphia, Science & Wellness Center, 1901 Vine St, Rm 202, Philadelphia, PA, 19103. Tel: 215-686-5394. p. 1980

Merry, Barbara, Staff Librn, Hopewell Public Library, 13 E Broad St, Hopewell, NJ, 08525. Tel: 609-466-1625. p. 1409

Merry, Elizabeth, ILL, Antigo Public Library, 617 Clermont St, Antigo, WI, 54409. Tel: 715-623-3724. p. 2420

Merryman, Ann, Coordr, Archives & Spec Coll, Pub Serv Librn, University of South Carolina Upstate Library, 800 University Way, Spartanburg, SC, 29303. Tel: 864-503-5275. p. 2070

Mersand, Shannon, Lecturer, University at Albany, State University of New York, Draper 015, 135 Western Ave, Albany, NY, 12203. Tel: 518-888-6761. p. 2789

Mersch, Toni, Ms, Asst Librn, Monterey-Tippecanoe Township Public Library, 6260 E Main St, Monterey, IN, 46960. Tel: 574-542-2171. p. 707

Merseal, Mary, Librn, Missouri Department of Corrections, Missouri Eastern Correctional Center, 18701 US Hwy 66, Pacific, MO, 63069-3525. Tel: 636-257-3322. p. 1252

Mershon, Mark, Libr Mgr, HealthPartners Libraries, 6600 Excelsior Blvd, Ste 101, Saint Louis Park, MN, 55426. Tel: 953-993-7079. p. 1199

Mershon, Mark, Librn, Park Nicollet Methodist Hospital, 6600 Excelsior Blvd, Ste 101, Saint Louis Park, MN, 55426. Tel: 952-993-5451. p. 1199

Merson, Donna, Librn, Bremer Pond Memorial Library, 12 School St, Pittsburg, NH, 03592. Tel: 603-538-7032. p. 1378

Mertl, Gloria L, Library Contact, Nielsen Engineering & Research, Inc, 900 Lafayette St, Ste 600, Santa Clara, CA, 95050. Tel: 408-454-5246. p. 241

Merucci, Kathy, Head, Youth Serv, Salem-South Lyon District Library, 9800 Pontiac Trail, South Lyon, MI, 48178-7021. Tel: 248-437-6431, Ext 205. p. 1151

Merucci, Kathy, Interim Dir, Salem-South Lyon District Library, 9800 Pontiac Trail, South Lyon, MI, 48178-7021. Tel: 248-437-6431. p. 1151

Mesa, Tina, Dean, Learning Res, Palo Alto College, 1400 W Villaret St, San Antonio, TX, 78224-2499. Tel: 210-486-3901. p. 2237

Mesecher, Susan, Dir, Clinton Public Library, 306 Eighth Ave S, Clinton, IA, 52732. Tel: 563-242-8441. p. 740

Meserve, Deborah, Librn/Br Mgr, Allen County Public Library, Pontiac, 2215 S Hanna St, Fort Wayne, IN, 46803. Tel: 260-421-1350. p. 683

Meserve, Tracy, Librn, The George Washington University Museum & The Textile Museum, 701 21st St NW, Washington, DC, 20052. Tel: 202-994-5918. p. 367

Meservey, Laura, Circ, Tech Serv Librn, Rockport Public Library, 485 Commercial St, Rockport, ME, 04856. Tel: 207-236-3642. p. 939

Mesiti, Martha, Asst Dir, Mount Pleasant Public Library, 350 Bedford Rd, Pleasantville, NY, 10570. Tel: 914-769-0548. p. 1620

Meslener, Jenny, Dir, Garrett College, 687 Mosser Rd, McHenry, MD, 21541. Tel: 301-387-3022. p. 971

Mesmer, Renate, Head, Conserv, Folger Shakespeare Library, 201 E Capitol St SE, Washington, DC, 20003-1094. Tel: 202-675-0332. p. 366

Messana, Valerie, Dir, Berry Memorial Library, 93 Main St, Bar Mills, ME, 04004. Tel: 207-929-5484. p. 916

Messana, Valerie, Dir, Chase Emerson Memorial Library, 17 Main St, Deer Isle, ME, 04627. Tel: 207-348-2899. p. 923

Messely, Maryse, Librn, College Merici - Bibliotheque, 755 Grande Allée Ouest, Quebec, QC, G1S 1C1, CANADA. Tel: 418-683-2104, Ext 2213. p. 2730

Messer, Joanne, Adminr, Alvan Bolster Ricker Memorial Library, 1211 Maine St, Poland, ME, 04274. Tel: 207-998-4390. p. 935

Messer Kimmit, Joanna, Dir, Prog & Serv, Cabrillo College, 6500 Soquel Dr, Aptos, CA, 95003-3198. Tel: 831-479-6473. p. 117

Messerly, Dorajo, Ch, Soda Springs Public Library, 149 S Main, Soda Springs, ID, 83276. Tel: 208-547-2606. p. 531

Messina, Nancy, Mgr, Ref Serv, Lindenwood University Library, 209 S Kingshighway, Saint Charles, MO, 63301. Tel: 636-949-4842. p. 1268

Messinger, Luke, Exec Dir, The Dawes Arboretum Library, 7770 Jacksontown Rd SE, Newark, OH, 43056. Tel: 740-323-2355. p. 1807

Messman-Mandicott, Lea, Dr, Libr Dir, Frostburg State University, One Susan Eisel Dr, Frostburg, MD, 21532. Tel: 301-687-4395. p. 967

Messner, Kevin, Head of Instruction, Miami University Libraries, 151 S Campus Ave, Oxford, OH, 45056. Tel: 513-529-7204. p. 1811

Messner, Mary Ellen, First Dep Commissioner, Chicago Public Library, 400 S State St, Chicago, IL, 60605. Tel: 312-747-4300. p. 555

Messner, Tom, Exec Dean, Florida State College at Jacksonville, South Campus Library & Learning Commons, 11901 Beach Blvd, Jacksonville, FL, 32246-6624. Tel: 904-646-2174. p. 411

Mest, Darlene S, Asst Dir, Exeter Community Library, 4569 Prestwick Dr, Reading, PA, 19606. Tel: 610-406-9431. p. 2000

Metallo, Charmaine, Law Librn, United States Courts Library, US Courthouse, Rm 3625, 101 W Lombard St, Baltimore, MD, 21201. Tel: 410-962-0997. p. 957

Metcalf, Julia, Dir, Oxford Public Library, 129 S Franklin St, Oxford, WI, 53952. Tel: 608-586-4458. p. 2468

Metcalf, Karen, Ch, Weare Public Library, Ten Paige Memorial Lane, Weare, NH, 03281. Tel: 603-529-2044. p. 1383

Metcalf, Pam, Librn, North Central Washington Libraries, Republic Public Library, 794 S Clark Ave, Republic, WA, 99166-8823. Tel: 509-775-3328. p. 2394

Metcalf, Stella, Pub Serv Mgr, Ashland Public Library, 224 Claremont Ave, Ashland, OH, 44805. Tel: 419-289-8188. p. 1746

Metcalfe, William, Tech Serv Asst, Chowan University, One University Pl, Murfreesboro, NC, 27855. Tel: 252-398-6271. p. 1705

Metevier, Molly, Asst Prof of Practice, Simmons University, 300 The Fenway, Boston, MA, 02115. Tel: 617-521-2800. p. 2786

Metgares, Meagan, Br Mgr, Fort Bend County Libraries, Mamie George Branch, 320 Dulles Ave, Stafford, TX, 77477-4704. Tel: 281-238-2880. p. 2232

Metheny, Heather, Dir, Chippewa Branch Library, 2811 Darlington Rd, Beaver Falls, PA, 15010. Tel: 724-847-1450. p. 1909

Metheny, Lisa, Libr Dir, Griswold Public Library, 505 Main, Griswold, IA, 51535. Tel: 712-778-4130. p. 756

Metheny, Lisa, Head Librn, Lewis Public Library & Heritage Center, 412 W Main, Lewis, IA, 51544. Tel: 712-769-2228. p. 765

Methot, Rosalie, Libr Tech, Cegep de Saint-Laurent Bibliotheque, 625 Ave Sainte-Croix, Saint-Laurent, QC, H4L 3X7, CANADA. Tel: 514-747-6521, Ext 7213. p. 2735

Metrick, Kathleen, Tech Serv Librn, Haddonfield Public Library, 60 Haddon Ave, Haddonfield, NJ, 08033-2422. Tel: 856-429-1304. p. 1406

Metro, Julie, Asst Librn, Coll Develop Librn, Southern Arkansas University, 100 E University, Magnolia, AR, 71753-5000. Tel: 870-235-4181. p. 103

Metrock, Emily, Ch Mgr, Salem Public Library, 28 E Main St, Salem, VA, 24153. Tel: 540-375-3089. p. 2347

Metsack, Susan, Adminr, Acworth Silsby Library, Five Lynn Hill Rd, Acworth, NH, 03601. Tel: 603-835-2150. p. 1353

Metscher, Allen, Pres, Central Nevada Museum & Historical Society, 1900 Logan Field Rd, Tonopah, NV, 89049. Tel: 775-482-9676. p. 1351

Metterville, Brenda, Libr Dir, Merrick Public Library, Two Lincoln St, Brookfield, MA, 01506. Tel: 508-867-6339. p. 1003

Metts, Pamela Thomas, Dir, John L Street Library, 244 Main St, Cadiz, KY, 42211-9153. Tel: 270-522-6301. p. 850

Metz, Bob, Dir, Wilkinsburg Public Library, 605 Ross Ave, Pittsburgh, PA, 15221-2195. Tel: 412-244-2940. p. 1997

Metz, Edward J, Head Librn, US Fire Administration, 16825 S Seton Ave, Emmitsburg, MD, 21727. Tel: 301-447-1030. p. 965

Metz, Elizabeth, Librn, Ivy Tech Community College-Northeast, 3800 N Anthony Blvd, Fort Wayne, IN, 46805-1430. Tel: 260-480-4172. p. 684

Metz, John D, Dep Dir, Coll & Prog, The Library of Virginia, 800 E Broad St, Richmond, VA, 23219-8000. Tel: 804-692-3500. p. 2341

Metz-Andrews, Nicole, Libr Mgr, Camp Verde Community Library, 130 N Black Bridge Rd, Camp Verde, AZ, 86322. Tel: 928-554-8389. p. 57

Metzel, Nina, Librn, Collier County Public Library, Estates, 1266 Golden Gate Blvd W, Naples, FL, 34120. Tel: 239-455-8088. p. 427

Metzenbaum, Barbara, Sr Librn, Los Angeles Public Library System, Woodland Hills Branch Library, 22200 Ventura Blvd, Woodland Hills, CA, 91364-1517. Tel: 818-226-0017. p. 166

Metzger, Elizabeth, Dir, Canastota Public Library, 102 W Center St, Canastota, NY, 13032. Tel: 315-697-7030. p. 1513

Metzger, Jodi, Dir, Sullivan County Law Library, Court House, 245 Muncy St, Laporte, PA, 18626. Tel: 570-946-4053. p. 1953

Metzger, Joy, Asst Dir, Whittemore Public Library, 405 Fourth St, Whittemore, IA, 50598. Tel: 515-884-2680. p. 792

Metzger, Kelly, State Data Coordr, State of Rhode Island, Department of Administration, One Capitol Hill, 2nd Flr, Providence, RI, 02908. Tel: 401-574-9305. p. 2041

Metzger, Kristen L, Dir, Libr & Info Serv, CSA Ocean Sciences Inc Library, 8502 SW Kansas Ave, Stuart, FL, 34997. Tel: 772-219-3000. p. 444

Metzger, Melanie, Asst Libr Dir, Albany Public Library, 161 Washington Ave, Albany, NY, 12210. Tel: 518-427-4300. p. 1482

Metzger, Melanie, Asst Dir, Ch, Lone Star College System, CyFair Library, 9191 Barker Cypress Rd, Cypress, TX, 77433. Tel: 281-290-3214, 281-290-3219. p. 2197

Metzger, Michael, Tech & Syst Librn, Northeast Georgia Regional Library System, 204 Ellison St, Ste F, Clarkesville, GA, 30523. Tel: 706-754-0416. p. 471

Metzger, Michael, Tech Serv Librn, Oconee County Public Library, 501 W South Broad St, Walhalla, SC, 29691. Tel: 864-638-4133. p. 2072

Metzger, Michelle, Educ Adminr, Graham Correctional Center Library, 12078 Illinois Rte 185, Hillsboro, IL, 62049. Tel: 217-532-6961. p. 599

Metzke, Kim, Dir, Greenwood Public Library, 102 N Main St, Greenwood, WI, 54437. Tel: 715-267-7103. p. 2440

Metzler, Janet, Sr Librn, Los Angeles Public Library System, Chatsworth Branch Library, 21052 Devonshire St, Chatsworth, CA, 91311. Tel: 818-341-4276. p. 164

Metzler, Jeff, Libr Dir, Hanover Town Library, 130 Etna Rd, Etna, NH, 03750. Tel: 603-643-3116. p. 1363

Metzler, Laura, Br Mgr, Albuquerque-Bernalillo County Library System, South Broadway Library, 1025 Broadway Blvd SE, Albuquerque, NM, 87102. Tel: 505-764-1742. p. 1460

Metzner, Nancy, Div Mgr, Reader Serv, High Point Public Library, 901 N Main St, High Point, NC, 27262. Tel: 336-883-3650. p. 1696

Meulemans, Connie, Acq, Doc Delivery Spec, Saint Norbert College, 400 Third St, De Pere, WI, 54115. p. 2430

Meulemans, Yvonne N, Dir, Learning & Tech Res, California State University, 333 S Twin Oaks Valley Rd, San Marcos, CA, 92096. Tel: 760-750-4348. p. 234

Meunier, Élisabeth, Head of Libr, Cinematheque Quebecoise, 335 boul de Maisonneuve est, Montreal, QC, H2X 1K1, CANADA. Tel: 514-842-9768, Ext 262. p. 2722

Meunier, Suzanne, Metadata Librn, Framingham State University, 100 State St, Framingham, MA, 01701. Tel: 508-626-4783. p. 1019

Meunler, Chad, Librn, Arizona State Parks, HCR63, Box 5, Winslow, AZ, 86047. Tel: 928-289-4106. p. 84

Mevis, Susan Mary, Dir, Beaver Dam Community Library, 311 N Spring St, Beaver Dam, WI, 53916-2043. Tel: 920-887-4631, Ext 101. p. 2423

Mewborn, Shirley, Librn, Grifton Public Library, 568 Queen St, Grifton, NC, 28530. Tel: 252-524-0345. p. 1694

Mewton, Sean, ILL, Grove City Community Library, 125 W Main St, Grove City, PA, 16127-1569. Tel: 724-458-7320. p. 1939

Meyer, Alicia, County Librn, Tehama County Library, 545 Diamond Ave, Red Bluff, CA, 96080. Tel: 530-527-0604. p. 198

Meyer, Amy, Head, Tech Serv, ILL, Warren-Newport Public Library District, 224 N O'Plaine Rd, Gurnee, IL, 60031. Tel: 847-244-5150, Ext 3048. p. 596

Meyer, Andrew, Dir, Archives, North Park University, Covenant Archives & Historical Library, Brandel Library, F M Johnson Archives, 3225 W Foster Ave, Box 38, Chicago, IL, 60625-4823. Tel: 773-244-6224. p. 566

Meyer, Ashley, Dir, Delphi Public Library, 222 E Main St, Delphi, IN, 46923. Tel: 765-564-2929. p. 679

Meyer, Bethany, Asst Libr Dir, South Milwaukee Public Library, 1907 Tenth Ave, South Milwaukee, WI, 53172. Tel: 414-768-8195. p. 2478

Meyer, Betty, Libr Dir, Real County Public Library Leakey, 225 Main St, Leakey, TX, 78873. Tel: 830-232-5199. p. 2210

Meyer, Brady, Asst Librn, Stubbs Memorial Library, 207 E Second St, Holstein, IA, 51025. Tel: 712-368-4563. p. 758

Meyer, Carol, Dir, Charter Oak Public Library, 461 Railroad, Charter Oak, IA, 51439. Tel: 712-678-3425. p. 739

Meyer, Clarice, Dir, Daykin Public Library, 201 Mary Ave, Daykin, NE, 68338. p. 1312

Meyer, Connie, Dir, Crawford County Library, 201 Plum St, Grayling, MI, 49738. Tel: 989-348-9214. p. 1112

Meyer, Cory, Information Specialist III, University of New Mexico, Valencia Campus, 280 La Entrada, Los Lunas, NM, 87031. Tel: 505-925-8992. p. 1463

Meyer, Currie, Mgr, Poudre River Public Library District, Council Tree Library, 2733 Council Tree Ave, Ste 200, Fort Collins, CO, 80525. Tel: 970-221-6740. p. 281

Meyer, Darla, Asst Libr Dir, Benedictine College Library, 1020 N Second St, Atchison, KS, 66002-1499. Tel: 913-360-7516. p. 797

Meyer, Deborah, Ch, Clyde Public Library, 222 W Buckeye St, Clyde, OH, 43410. Tel: 419-547-7174. p. 1771

Meyer, Desiree, Circ, West Hartford Public Library, Bishop's Corner, 15 Starkel Rd, West Hartford, CT, 06117. Tel: 860-561-8210. p. 346

Meyer, Elizabeth, Visual Res Librn, University of Cincinnati Libraries, Design, Architecture Art & Planning, 5480 Aronoff Ctr, Cincinnati, OH, 45221. Tel: 513-556-0279. p. 1765

Meyer, Eric T, Dean, University of Texas at Austin, 1616 Guadalupe St, Ste 5.202, Austin, TX, 78712-0390. Tel: 512-471-3821. p. 2793

Meyer, Gail, Mgr, Indian Temple Mound Museum Library, 139 Miracle Strip Pkwy SE, Fort Walton Beach, FL, 32548. Tel: 850-833-9595. p. 405

Meyer, Hannah, Asst Dir, Kenai Community Library, 163 Main St Loop, Kenai, AK, 99611. Tel: 907-283-4378. p. 48

Meyer, Holly, Br Mgr, Whitman County Rural Library District, Colton Branch, 760 Broadway Ave, Colton, WA, 99113. Tel: 509-229-3887. p. 2362

Meyer, Holly, Br Mgr, Whitman County Rural Library District, Uniontown Branch, 110 S Montgomery, Uniontown, WA, 99179. Tel: 509-229-3880. p. 2362

Meyer, Janet F, Librn, South Carolina Supreme Court Library, 1231 Gervais St, Columbia, SC, 29211. Tel: 803-734-1080. p. 2055

Meyer, Jeff, E-Res/Instrul Librn, Iowa Wesleyan University, 107 W Broad St, Mount Pleasant, IA, 52641. Tel: 319-385-6316. p. 771

Meyer, Jeffrey, Dir, Mount Pleasant Public Library, 307 E Monroe, Ste 101, Mount Pleasant, IA, 52641. Tel: 319-385-1490. p. 771

Meyer, John, Libr Spec II, University of Missouri-Columbia, Math Sciences Library, 206 Math Sciences Bldg, Columbia, MO, 65211. Tel: 573-882-7286. p. 1244

Meyer, Julie, Librn, Southeastern Community College Library, Fred Karre Memorial Library-Keokuk Campus, 335 Messenger Rd, Rm 201, Keokuk, IA, 52632. Tel: 319-524-3221, Ext 1961. p. 791

Meyer, Katie, Librn, Libr Dir, Elizabethtown Community & Technical College Library, 600 College Street Rd, Elizabethtown, KY, 42701. Tel: 270-706-8443. p. 854

Meyer, Lars, Sr Leader, Content Div, Emory University Libraries, Robert W Woodruff Library, 540 Asbury Circle, Atlanta, GA, 30322-2870. Tel: 404-727-2437. p. 463

Meyer, Laura, Ch Serv, Evergreen Park Public Library, 9400 S Troy Ave, Evergreen Park, IL, 60805-2383. Tel: 708-422-8522. p. 587

Meyer, Lawrence R, Dir, Law Library for San Bernardino County, 402 North D St, San Bernardino, CA, 92401. Tel: 909-885-3020. p. 212

Meyer, Margo, Adult Literacy Coordr, Manitowoc Public Library, 707 Quay St, Manitowoc, WI, 54220. Tel: 920-686-3000. p. 2453

Meyer, Margo, Homebound Serv, Manitowoc Public Library, 707 Quay St, Manitowoc, WI, 54220. Tel: 920-686-3000. p. 2453

Meyer, Marian L, Dir, Bellevue Public Library, 106 N Third St, Ste 1, Bellevue, IA, 52031. Tel: 563-872-4991. p. 734

Meyer, Mary Jane, Library Contact, Brunswick Public Library, 115 W Broadway, Brunswick, MO, 65236-1214. Tel: 660-548-1026. p. 1239

Meyer, Matthew, Digital Archivist, Wabash College, 301 W Wabash Ave, Crawfordsville, IN, 47933. Tel: 765-361-6343. p. 677

Meyer, Melinda, Mgr, Miami-Dade Public Library System, Concord Branch, 3882 SW 112th Ave, Miami, FL, 33165. Tel: 305-207-1344. p. 423

Meyer, Mona, Metadata Librn, Spec Coll & Archives Librn, University of Southern Indiana, 8600 University Blvd, Evansville, IN, 47712. Tel: 812-464-1920. p. 682

Meyer, Odessa, Ch, South Sioux City Public Library, 2121 Dakota Ave, South Sioux City, NE, 68776. Tel: 402-494-7545. p. 1336

Meyer, Pat, Ref (Info Servs), Putnam County District Library, The Educational Service Ctr, 136 Putnam Pkwy, Ottawa, OH, 45875-1471. Tel: 419-523-3747. p. 1811

Meyer, Patrick, Libr Dir, University of Detroit Mercy School of Law, 651 E Jefferson, Detroit, MI, 48226. Tel: 313-596-0240. p. 1099

Meyer, Patsy, Dir, Struckman-Baatz Public Library, 104 S West St, Western, NE, 68464. Tel: 402-433-2177. p. 1340

Meyer, Patti, Dir, Larsen Family Public Library, 7401 Main St W, Webster, WI, 54893-0510. Tel: 715-866-7697. p. 2486

Meyer, Rene, Librn, West Rutland Free Library, 595 Main St, West Rutland, VT, 05777. Tel: 802-438-2964. p. 2298

Meyer, Rick, City Librn, Decatur Public Library, 130 N Franklin St, Decatur, IL, 62523. Tel: 217-424-2900. p. 576

Meyer, Sydni, Ref & Instrul Serv Librn, Iona University, 715 North Ave, New Rochelle, NY, 10801-1890. Tel: 914-633-2525. p. 1577

Meyer, Tiffany, Libr Dir, Ellsworth Public Library, 312 W Main St, Ellsworth, WI, 54011. Tel: 715-273-3209. p. 2434

Meyer, Tom, Dir, Lansdale Public Library, 301 Vine St, Lansdale, PA, 19446-3690. Tel: 215-855-3228. p. 1952

Meyer-Ryerson, Sarah, Dir, Waverly Public Library, 1500 W Bremer Ave, Waverly, IA, 50677. Tel: 319-352-1223. p. 789

Meyer-Stearns, Jennifer, Asst Dir, Operations, Milwaukee Public Library, 814 W Wisconsin Ave, Milwaukee, WI, 53233-2309. Tel: 414-286-3000. p. 2459

Meyers, Amanda, Youth Serv Mgr, Freeport Public Library, 100 E Douglas St, Freeport, IL, 61032. Tel: 815-233-3000, Ext 238. p. 590

Meyers, Ashley, Principal Cataloger, Kokomo-Howard County Public Library, 220 N Union St, Kokomo, IN, 46901-4614. Tel: 765-457-3242. p. 700

Meyers, Donna, Br Mgr, Cuyahoga County Public Library, Strongsville Branch, 18700 Westwood Dr, Strongsville, OH, 44136-3431. Tel: 440-238-5530. p. 1813

Meyers, Eric, Assoc Prof, University of British Columbia, The Irving K Barber Learning Ctr, 1961 E Mall, Ste 470, Vancouver, BC, V6T 1Z1, CANADA. Tel: 604-822-2404. p. 2795

Meyers, Karyn, Tech Serv Librn, United States Equal Employment Opportunity Commission Library, 131 M St NE, Rm 4SW16N, Washington, DC, 20507. Tel: 202-921-3119. p. 379

Meyers, Mary, Dir, Savanna Public Library District, 326 Third St, Savanna, IL, 61074. Tel: 815-273-3714. p. 645

Meyers, Sally, Ch, Tom Green County Library System, 33 W Beauregard, San Angelo, TX, 76903. Tel: 325-655-7321. p. 2235

Meyerson, Valerie, Dir, Petoskey District Library, 500 E Mitchell St, Petoskey, MI, 49770. Tel: 231-758-3100. p. 1140

Meyn, Marie, Librn, Westlock Municipal Library, M Alice Frose Library, Fawcett Community Hall, Fawcett, AB, T0G 0Y0, CANADA. Tel: 780-809-2244. p. 2559

Meza, Jody, Libr Dir, Willows Public Library, 201 N Lassen St, Willows, CA, 95988-3010. Tel: 530-934-5156. p. 259

Meza, Jody Halsey, City Librn, Orland Free Library, 333 Mill St, Orland, CA, 95963. Tel: 530-865-1640. p. 189

Meza, Joy, ILL Coordr, The John P Holt Brentwood Library, 8109 Concord Rd, Brentwood, TN, 37027. Tel: 615-371-0090. p. 2089

Meza, Kelsea, Circ Serv Supvr, Helen Hall Library, 100 W Walker, League City, TX, 77573-3899. Tel: 281-554-1123. p. 2210

Mezynski, Andy, Bibliog Instruction/Ref, Los Angeles City College Library, 855 N Vermont Ave, Los Angeles, CA, 90029. Tel: 323-953-4000, Ext 2403. p. 162

Mhiripiri, John, Dir, Anthology Film Archives, 32 Second Ave, New York, NY, 10003. Tel: 212-505-5181. p. 1579

Mi, Jia, Electronic Res, The College of New Jersey, 2000 Pennington Rd, Ewing, NJ, 08628-1104. Tel: 609-771-2311. p. 1402

Mi, Misa, Librn, Children's Hospital of Michigan, Medical Library, 3901 Beaubien Blvd, 1st Flr, Detroit, MI, 48201. Tel: 313-745-0252, 313-745-5322. p. 1097

Miah, Farid, Dr, Mgr, Libr Serv, Sunnybrook Health Sciences Centre - Library Services, Dr R Ian MacDonald Library, 2075 Bayview Ave, Toronto, ON, M4N 3M5, CANADA. Tel: 416-480-6100, Ext 4562. p. 2693

Miah, Md Farid, Mgr, Libr Serv, Sunnybrook Health Sciences Centre - Library Services, Sunnybrook Library Services, 2075 Bayview Ave, Rm EG-29, Toronto, ON, M4N 3M5, CANADA. Tel: 416-480-6100, Ext 2560. p. 2693

Miao, Hong, Res & Instruction Librn, Marywood University Library & Learning Commons, 2300 Adams Ave, Scranton, PA, 18509. Tel: 570-961-4707. p. 2004

Mibbs, Ellen R, Asst Dir, Children's Serv Coordr, Havana Public Library District, 201 W Adams St, Havana, IL, 62644-1321. Tel: 309-543-4701. p. 598

Micalizzi, Paula, Head, Children's Dept, Free Public Library & Cultural Center of Bayonne, 697 Avenue C, Bayonne, NJ, 07002. Tel: 201-858-6970. p. 1388

Miceli, Caren, Head, Circ, Free Public Library & Cultural Center of Bayonne, 697 Avenue C, Bayonne, NJ, 07002. Tel: 201-858-6970. p. 1388

Michael, Cari, Asst Dir, Youth Serv, Paola Free Library, 101 E Peoria, Paola, KS, 66071. Tel: 913-259-3655. p. 830

Michael, Courtney, Ref & Prog Librn, Wayland Free Public Library, Five Concord Rd, Wayland, MA, 01778. Tel: 508-358-2311. p. 1063

Michael, Inbar, Res & Instruction Librn, Texas A&M University-Commerce, 2600 S Neal St, Commerce, TX, 75428. Tel: 903-886-5718. p. 2158

Michael, Joshua B, Dean, Libr Serv, Cedarville University, 251 N Main St, Cedarville, OH, 45314-0601. Tel: 937-766-7840. p. 1757

Michael, Shari, Coordr, Acq, Taylor University, 1846 Main St, Upland, IN, 46989. Tel: 765-998-5264. p. 722

Michaels, Becky, Librn, United States Army, USA MEDDAC, Keller Army Community Hospital, Bldg 900, US Military Academy, West Point, NY, 10996-1197. Tel: 845-938-4883. p. 1662

Michaels, Beverly, Br Mgr, Tredyffrin Public Library, Paoli Branch, 18 Darby Rd, Paoli, PA, 19301-1416. Tel: 610-296-7996. p. 2010

Michaels, Jolene E, Dir, Mackinaw Area Public Library, 528 W Central Ave, Mackinaw City, MI, 49701-9681. Tel: 231-436-5451. p. 1128

Michaels, Stephen, Ref Serv Librn, University of North Georgia, Oconee Campus Library, 1201 Bishop Farms Pkwy, Watkinsville, GA, 30677. Tel: 706-310-6297. p. 493

Michaels, Stephen E, Emerging Tech Librn, Libr Dir, Western Theological Seminary, 101 E 13th St, Holland, MI, 49423. Tel: 616-392-8555, Ext 187. p. 1116

Michaelson, Elaine, Asst Librn, Buffalo Center Public Library, 221 N Main St, Buffalo Center, IA, 50424. Tel: 641-562-2546. p. 736

Michaelson Schmidt, Tessa, Dir, University of Wisconsin-Madison, Cooperative Children's Book Center, Teacher Education Bldg, Rm 401, 225 N Mills St, Madison, WI, 53706. Tel: 608-263-3720. p. 2451

Michalak, Russell, Dir, Goldey-Beacom College, Jones Ctr, 4701 Limestone Rd, Wilmington, DE, 19808. Tel: 302-225-6247. p. 357

Michalik, Carole, Dir, Universite de Saint-Boniface, 0140-200 Ave de la Cathedrale, Winnipeg, MB, R2H 0H7, CANADA. Tel: 204-945-1342. p. 2594

Michalowska, Magdalena, Chef de Div, Bibliotheques de Montreal, Haut-Anjou, 7070 rue Jarry Est, Anjou, QC, H1J 1G4, CANADA. Tel: 514-493-8262. p. 2718

Michalowska, Magdalena, Chef de Div, Bibliotheques de Montreal, Jean-Corbeil, 7500 Ave Goncourt, Anjou, QC, H1K 3X9, CANADA. Tel: 514-493-8262. p. 2719

Michalowskij, Patricia, Circuit Librn, United States Court of Appeals for the District of Columbia, US Court House, 333 Constitution Ave NW, Rm 3205, Washington, DC, 20001. Tel: 202-216-7400. p. 377

Michalski, Corky, Prog Coordr, Ord Township Library, 1718 M St, Ord, NE, 68862. Tel: 308-728-3012. p. 1331

Michalski, Corky, Prog Coordr, Gallatin Public Library, 123 E Main St, Gallatin, TN, 37066-2509. Tel: 615-452-1722. p. 2099

Michaluk, Cheryl, Asst Librn, Pinawa Public Library, Vanier Rd, Pinawa, MB, R0E 1L0, CANADA. Tel: 204-753-2496. p. 2589

Michaud, Bronson, Curator of Coll, Old Colony History Museum, 66 Church Green, Taunton, MA, 02780. Tel: 508-822-1622. p. 1059

Michaud, Carolyn, Dir, Libr Serv, Massachusetts Maritime Academy, ABS IC-123, 101 Academy Dr, Buzzards Bay, MA, 02532. Tel: 508-830-5034. p. 1004

Michaud, Julie, Librn, Bibliotheque Le Tournesol, Centre Communitaire Paul-Emile-Beaulieu, 530 rue Delage, Ste 2, Lac Saint-Charles, QC, G3G 1J2, CANADA. Tel: 418-641-6121. p. 2715

Michaud, Louis, Librn, Universite du Quebec a Rimouski - Service de la bibliotheque, 300 Allee des Ursulines, Rimouski, QC, G5L 3A1, CANADA. Tel: 418-723-1986, Ext 1213. p. 2732

Michaud, Monique, Library Contact, Planetary Association for Clean Energy Inc, 100 Bronson Ave, Ste 1001, Ottawa, ON, K1R 6G8, CANADA. Tel: 613-236-6265. p. 2669

Michaud, Sandy, Ch Serv, Lincoln Memorial Library, 21 W Broadway, Lincoln, ME, 04457. Tel: 207-794-2765. p. 930

Michaud, Sylvie, Chief Librn, Bibliotheque Municipale Francoise-Bedard, 67 rue du Rocher, Riviere-du-Loup, QC, G5R 1J8, CANADA. Tel: 418-867-6669. p. 2732
Michaud, Zoraida, Research Servs Librn, Lowenstein Sandler LLP Library, One Lowenstein Dr, Roseland, NJ, 07068. Tel: 973-597-2500. p. 1440
Michel, Karin, Head, Youth Serv, Chapel Hill Public Library, 100 Library Dr, Chapel Hill, NC, 27514. Tel: 919-968-2777. p. 1678
Michel, Kristin, Asst Dir, Westerville Public Library, 126 S State St, Westerville, OH, 43081. Tel: 614-882-7277. p. 1830
Michel, Megan, Library Contact, Doniphan-Ripley County Library, Annex, 202 Pine St, Doniphan, MO, 63935. p. 1245
Michel, Stephanie, Ref & Instruction Librn, University of Portland, 5000 N Willamette Blvd, Portland, OR, 97203-5743. Tel: 503-943-7111. p. 1894
Michel, Tina, Dir, Centerburg Public Library, 49 E Main St, Centerburg, OH, 43011. Tel: 740-625-6538. p. 1757
Michelman, Norma, Dir, Librn, Nancy Fawcett Memorial Library, 724 Oberfelder St, Lodgepole, NE, 69149-0318. Tel: 308-483-5714. p. 1323
Michelon, Lori, Librn, Mono County Free Library, Crowley Lake, 3627 Crowley Lake Dr, Crowley Lake, CA, 93546. Tel: 760-935-4505. p. 172
Michelson, Alan R, Head of Libr, University of Washington Libraries, Built Environments Library, 334 Gould Hall, Box 355730, Seattle, WA, 98195-5730. Tel: 206-543-7091. p. 2381
Michelson, Craig, Library Contact, American Society of Military History Museum, 1918 Rosemead Blvd, South El Monte, CA, 91733. Tel: 626-442-1776. p. 247
Michie, Barry, Pres, Riley County Kansas Genealogical Society Library, 2005 Claflin Rd, Manhattan, KS, 66502-3415. Tel: 785-565-6495. p. 823
Michie, Jeanne, ILL, Parkersburg & Wood County Public Library, 3100 Emerson Ave, Parkersburg, WV, 26104-2414. Tel: 304-420-4587. p. 2411
Michki, Kevin, Music Librn, Syst Librn, State University of New York at Fredonia, 280 Central Ave, Fredonia, NY, 14063. Tel: 716-673-3117. p. 1535
Michrowski, Andrew, Dr, Pres, Planetary Association for Clean Energy Inc, 100 Bronson Ave, Ste 1001, Ottawa, ON, K1R 6G8, CANADA. Tel: 613-236-6265. p. 2669
Mick, Dawn, Head, Access Serv, Iowa State University Library, 302 Parks Library, 701 Morrill Rd, Ames, IA, 50011-2102. Tel: 515-294-0728. p. 731
Mick, Rita, Br Mgr, Park County Public Libraries, Guffey Branch, 1625B Park County Rd 102, Guffey, CO, 80820. Tel: 719-689-9280. p. 265
Mick, Trisha, Br Supvr, Boise Public Library, Library! at Cole & Ustick, 7557 W Ustick Rd, Boise, ID, 83704. Tel: 208-972-8300. p. 516
Micke, Beth, Asst Dir, Obion County Public Library, 1221 E Reelfoot Ave, Union City, TN, 38261. Tel: 731-885-7000, 731-885-9411. p. 2128
Mickells, Greg, Dir, Madison Public Library, 201 W Mifflin St, Madison, WI, 53703. Tel: 608-266-6300. p. 2449
Mickelson, Dan, Dir, Springville Public Library, 45 S Main St, Springville, UT, 84663. Tel: 801-489-2720. p. 2273
Mickens, Barbara, Librn, Noxubee County Library System, Brooksville Branch, 13758 W Main St, Brooksville, MS, 39739. Tel: 662-738-4559. p. 1225
Mickles, Marsha, Dir, Libr Serv, Bishop State Community College, 351 N Broad St, Mobile, AL, 36603-5898. p. 25
Micks, Daniel, Dir, Mountain Lake Public Library, 1054 Fourth Ave, Mountain Lake, MN, 56159-1455. Tel: 507-427-2506. p. 1190
Micona, Hannah, Tech Serv, Green River College, 12401 SE 320th St, Auburn, WA, 98092-3699. Tel: 253-833-9111, Ext 2098. p. 2357
Micucci, Kathleen, Head, Circ, Bryant Library, Two Paper Mill Rd, Roslyn, NY, 11576. Tel: 516-621-2240. p. 1633
Miculek, Sally, Libr Dir, Georgetown Public Library, 402 W Eighth St, Georgetown, TX, 78626. Tel: 512-930-3551. p. 2184
Middaugh, Nancy, Asst Librn, Hamburg Public Library, 1301 Main St, Hamburg, IA, 51640. Tel: 712-382-1395. p. 757
Middendorf, Julie, Dir, Scotia Public Library, 110 S Main St, Scotia, NE, 68875. Tel: 308-245-3191. p. 1335
Middlemas, Julie, Colls Librn, Dept Chair, Grossmont College Library, 8800 Grossmont College Dr, El Cajon, CA, 92020-1799. Tel: 619-644-7371. p. 139
Middleton, Alex, Chief Operating Officer, Museum of Arts & Sciences, 352 S Nova Rd, Daytona Beach, FL, 32114. Tel: 386-255-0285. p. 392
Middleton, Ann, Mgr, Bossier Parish Libraries, History Center, 2206 Beckett St, Bossier City, LA, 71111. Tel: 318-746-7717. p. 886
Middleton, Charles, Bookmobile Driver, Baldwin County Library Cooperative, Inc, PO Box 399, Robertsdale, AL, 36567-0399. Tel: 251-970-4010. p. 34
Middleton, Cheryl, Librn, Buncombe County Public Libraries, Oakley/South Asheville, 749 Fairview Rd, Asheville, NC, 28803. Tel: 828-250-4754. p. 1672
Middleton, Joseph, Head, Ref, Stonehill College, 320 Washington St, Easton, MA, 02357. Tel: 508-565-1433. p. 1016
Middleton, Katherine, Librn, Palliser Regional Library, Holdfast Branch, 125 Robert St, Holdfast, SK, S0G 2H0, CANADA. Tel: 306-488-2101. p. 2742
Middleton, Kathy, Dep Dir, Pub Serv, Sacramento Public Library, 828 I St, Sacramento, CA, 95814. Tel: 916-264-2700, 916-264-2920. p. 209
Middleton, Kelsey, Br Head, Winnipeg Public Library, Westwood, 66 Allard Ave, Winnipeg, MB, R3K 0T3, CANADA. Tel: 204-805-0109. p. 2597
Middleton, Mike, Circ Supvr, Weber State University, Davis Campus Library, 2750 University Park Blvd, D2 Rm 212, Layton, UT, 84041-9099. Tel: 801-395-3472. p. 2268
Midgette Spence, Juanita, Dr, Dir, Libr Serv, Elizabeth City State University, 1704 Weeksville Rd, Elizabeth City, NC, 27909. Tel: 252-335-3427. p. 1687
Midgley, Katie, Br Mgr, Toledo-Lucas County Public Library, Lagrange, 3422 Lagrange St, Toledo, OH, 43608. Tel: 419-259-5280. p. 1824
Midlik, Gina, Dir, Admin Serv, Case Western Reserve University, 11055 Euclid Ave, Cleveland, OH, 44106. Tel: 216-368-5292. p. 1766
Midthun, Steve, Ref Librn, Milwaukee Area Technical College, 6665 S Howell Ave, Oak Creek, WI, 53154. p. 2465
Midwood, Stan, Asst Mgr, Louisville Free Public Library, Newburg, 4800 Exeter Ave, Louisville, KY, 40218. Tel: 502-479-6160. p. 865
Midyett, Shannon, Asst Dir, Poplar Bluff Municipal Library, 318 N Main St, Poplar Bluff, MO, 63901. Tel: 573-686-8639, Ext 21. p. 1266
Miears, Dawn, Libr Asst, Jay C Byers Memorial Library, 215 E Wichita Ave, Cleveland, OK, 74020. Tel: 918-358-2676. p. 1844
Mielczarek, Mary, Asst Libr Dir, Librn, Oldham County Public Library, 308 Yager Ave, La Grange, KY, 40031. Tel: 502-222-9713. p. 861
Miele, Jennifer, Dir, Libr Serv, Groton Public Library, 52 Newtown Rd, Groton, CT, 06340. Tel: 860-441-6750. p. 314
Mielenhausen, Laura, Libr Dir, Ulysses Philomathic Library, 74 E Main St, Trumansburg, NY, 14886. Tel: 607-387-5623. p. 1653
Mielke, Kristen, Dir, Brownsville Public Library, 379 Main St, Brownsville, WI, 53006. Tel: 920-583-4325. p. 2426
Mielke, Ruth Anne, Teen Serv Mgr, Youth Serv, Bartlett Public Library District, 800 S Bartlett Rd, Bartlett, IL, 60103. Tel: 630-837-2855. p. 540
Mielke, Sally, Acq & Coll, Eastern Oregon University, One University Blvd, La Grande, OR, 97850. Tel: 541-962-3865. p. 1884
Mientka, Katie, Asst Librn, Island Pond Public Library, 49 Mill St Extension, Island Pond, VT, 05846. Tel: 802-723-6134. p. 2286
Mier, Karen, Dir, Plattsmouth Public Library, 401 Ave A, Plattsmouth, NE, 68048. Tel: 402-296-4154. p. 1333
Mierop, Kerrie, Youth Serv Librn, City of Calabasas Library, 200 Civic Center Way, Calabasas, CA, 91302. Tel: 818-225-7616. p. 126
Mierow, Tammy, Asst Libr Dir, Dripping Springs Community Library, 501 Sportsplex Dr, Dripping Springs, TX, 78620. Tel: 512-858-7825. p. 2171
Miessler, Robert, Syst Librn, Gettysburg College, 300 N Washington St, Gettysburg, PA, 17325. Tel: 717-337-7020. p. 1935
Migaldi, Karen K, Asst Dir, Crystal Lake Public Library, 126 Paddock St, Crystal Lake, IL, 60014. Tel: 815-459-1687. p. 574
Migdalski, Alyssa, Ref & Instruction Librn, University of Oklahoma, Schusterman Ctr, 4502 E 41st St, Tulsa, OK, 74135. Tel: 918-660-3224. p. 1867
Migotsky, Jennifer, Youth Librn, Ingalls Memorial Library, 203 Main St, Rindge, NH, 03461. Tel: 603-899-3303. p. 1379
Miguel-Stearns, Teresa, Assoc Dean, Legal Info Innovation, Dir, University of Arizona Libraries, Daniel F Cracchiolo Law Library, James E Rogers College of Law, 1201 E Speedway, Tucson, AZ, 85721. Tel: 520-621-5477. p. 83
Miguez, Darren, Dir, Plainsboro Free Public Library, Nine Van Doren St, Plainsboro, NJ, 08536. Tel: 609-275-2897. p. 1435
Mihaly, Sara, Circ Supvr, University of Cincinnati Libraries, Design, Architecture Art & Planning, 5480 Aronoff Ctr, Cincinnati, OH, 45221. Tel: 513-556-1321. p. 1765
Mihlrad, Leigh, Syst Librn, United States Coast Guard Academy Library, 35 Mohegan Ave, New London, CT, 06320. Tel: 860-444-8519. p. 329
Mika, Stephanie, ILL, Libr Office Mgr, Sidney Public Library, 1112 12th Ave, Sidney, NE, 69162. Tel: 308-254-3110. p. 1336
Mikaberidze, Alexander, Curator, James Smith Noel Coll, Louisiana State University, One University Pl, Shreveport, LA, 71115. Tel: 318-798-4161. p. 907
Mikalson-Andron, Bonnie, Coordr, Youth Serv, Lethbridge Public Library, 810 Fifth Ave S, Lethbridge, AB, T1J 4C4, CANADA. Tel: 403-320-3026. p. 2546
Mike, Julie, Br Mgr, Marion County Public Library, Fairview Public, 500 Main St, Fairview, WV, 26570. Tel: 304-449-1021. p. 2402
Mikel, Amy, Customer Experience Dir, Brooklyn Public Library, Ten Grand Army Plaza, Brooklyn, NY, 11238. Tel: 718-230-2100. p. 1502
Mikesell, Brian, Libr Dir, Bard College at Simon's Rock, 84 Alford Rd, Great Barrington, MA, 01230. Tel: 413-528-7274. p. 1022
Mikesell, Debbie, Adult Serv Mgr, Rodman Public Library, 215 E Broadway St, Alliance, OH, 44601-2694. Tel: 330-821-2665. p. 1745
Mikkelsen, Michele, Dir, Admin Serv, American University Library, 4400 Massachusetts Ave NW, Washington, DC, 20016-8046. Tel: 202-885-3234. p. 361
Mikles, Amber, Br Mgr, Arkansas River Valley Regional Library System, Boyd T & Mollie Gattis-Logan County, 100 E Academy, Paris, AR, 72855-4432. Tel: 479-963-2371. p. 93

Mikolic, Ed, IT Mgr, Mentor Public Library, 8215 Mentor Ave, Mentor, OH, 44060. Tel: 440-255-8811. p. 1802

Mikos, Ilishe, Instruction Coordr, Ref Librn, Louisburg College, 501 N Main St, Louisburg, NC, 27549-7704. Tel: 919-497-3349. p. 1701

Mikruta, Marion, Libr Asst, Venice Public Library, 260 Nokomis Ave S, Venice, FL, 34285. Tel: 941-861-1336. p. 452

Miksa, Shawne, Dr, Assoc Prof, University of North Texas, 3940 N Elm St, Ste E292, Denton, TX, 76207. Tel: 940-565-2445. p. 2793

Miksicek, Barbara, Librn, Saint Louis Metropolitan Police Department, 315 S Tucker Blvd, Saint Louis, MO, 63102. Tel: 314-444-5581. p. 1274

Mikula, Susan, Youth Serv, Ventura County Library, Ray D Prueter Library, 510 Park Ave, Port Hueneme, CA, 93041. Tel: 805-486-5460. p. 256

Mikytyshyn, Susan, Mgr, Edmonton Public Library, Highlands, 6710 118 Ave NW, Edmonton, AB, T5B 0P3, CANADA. Tel: 780-496-4299. p. 2536

Milam, Lindsey, Libr Dir, Autauga Prattville Public Library, 254 Doster St, Prattville, AL, 36067-3933. Tel: 334-365-3396. p. 33

Milan, Jerry, Pres, Czechoslovak Heritage Museum, 2050 Finly Rd, Lombard, IL, 60148. Tel: 630-472-0500. p. 610

Milan, Sheila, Librn, Halifax County Library, W C Jones Jr Memorial, 127 W S Main St, Littleton, NC, 27850. Tel: 252-586-3608. p. 1694

Milani, Rachel, Asst Librn, Minnesota North College - Hibbing, Bldg M, Rm 160, 1515 E 25th St, Hibbing, MN, 55746. Tel: 218-293-6928. p. 1178

Milano, Andrea, Mgr, Tech Serv, Youth Serv Mgr, Lake Oswego Public Library, 706 Fourth St, Lake Oswego, OR, 97034-2399. Tel: 503-675-2539. p. 1884

Milano, Nicole, Head, Archives, Cornell University Library, Samuel J Wood Library & C V Starr Biomedical Information Center, 1300 York Ave, C115, Box 67, New York, NY, 10065-4896. Tel: 646-746-6072. p. 1552

Milas, T Patrick, Dr, Dir, New Brunswick Theological Seminary, 21 Seminary Pl, New Brunswick, NJ, 08901. Tel: 732-247-5241. p. 1424

Milavec, Julie, Libr Dir, Downers Grove Public Library, 1050 Curtiss St, Downers Grove, IL, 60515. Tel: 630-960-1200, Ext 4300. p. 579

Milberg, Craig, Univ Librn, Willamette University, 900 State St, Salem, OR, 97301. Tel: 503-370-6561. p. 1897

Milburn, Gina Gail, Dir, Barry-Lawrence Regional Library, 213 Sixth St, Monett, MO, 65708-2147. Tel: 417-235-6646. p. 1262

Milchman, Lisa, Asst Dir, Norwich Public Library, 368 Main St, Norwich, VT, 05055-9453. Tel: 802-649-1184. p. 2290

Milczarski, Vivian, Dir, Mount Saint Mary College, 330 Powell Ave, Newburgh, NY, 12550-3494. Tel: 845-569-3601. p. 1605

Mildenstein, Lynne, Asst Dir, Operational Serv, Deschutes Public Library District, 507 NW Wall St, Bend, OR, 97703. Tel: 541-312-1028. p. 1874

Mileham, Patricia, Dean of the Library, Valparaiso University, 1410 Chapel Dr, Valparaiso, IN, 46383-6493. Tel: 219-464-5693. p. 723

Miles, Alisha, Exec Dir, University of Tampa, 401 W Kennedy Blvd, Tampa, FL, 33606-1490. Tel: 813-253-6231. p. 450

Miles, Beverly, Br Mgr, Bossier Parish Libraries, East 80 Branch, 1050 Bellevue Rd, Haughton, LA, 71037. Tel: 318-949-2665. p. 886

Miles, David, Library Contact, Multnomah County Library, Kenton, 8226 N Denver Ave, Portland, OR, 97217. p. 1892

Miles, Emily, Libr Dir, Babson College, 11 Babson College Dr, Babson Park, MA, 02457-0310. Tel: 781-239-4596. p. 987

Miles, Evan, Evening Librn, North Carolina School of Science & Mathematics Library, Library, Instructional Technologies & Communications, 1219 Broad St, Durham, NC, 27705. Tel: 919-416-2916. p. 1686

Miles, Kathleen, Dir, Iberia Parish Library, 445 E Main St, New Iberia, LA, 70560-3710. Tel: 337-364-7024, 337-364-7074. p. 900

Miles, Margaret, Br Mgr, Marin County Free Library, Fairfax Library, 2097 Sir Francis Drake Blvd, Fairfax, CA, 94930-1198. Tel: 415-453-8151. p. 237

Miles, Margaret, Supv Librn, New Hanover County Public Library, 201 Chestnut St, Wilmington, NC, 28401. Tel: 910-798-6361. p. 1723

Miles, Marsha, Digital Initiatives Librn, Cleveland State University, Michael Schwartz Library, Rhodes Tower, Ste 501, 2121 Euclid Ave, Cleveland, OH, 44115-2214. Tel: 216-687-2369. p. 1769

Miles, Rhonda, Libr Asst, Coastal Pines Technical College, Hazlehurst Learning Resource Center, 677 Douglas Hwy, Rm 102, Hazlehurst, GA, 31513. Tel: 912-379-0041. p. 503

Miles, Russell, Tech Asst, North Carolina Legislative Library, 500 Legislative Office Bldg, 300 N Salisbury St, Raleigh, NC, 27603-5925. Tel: 919-733-9390. p. 1709

Miles, Susan Ambrose, Tech Serv Librn, Tampa-Hillsborough County Public Library System, Bruton Memorial Library, 302 W McLendon St, Plant City, FL, 33563. Tel: 813-757-9215. p. 448

Mileshosky, Carin, Libr Dir, Fleetwood Area Public Library, 110 W Arch St, Ste 209, Fleetwood, PA, 19522-1301. Tel: 610-944-0146. p. 1933

Milewicz, Liz, PhD, Head, Digital Scholarship Serv, Duke University Libraries, 411 Chapel Dr, Durham, NC, 27708. Tel: 919-660-5911. p. 1684

Miley, Jay, Customer Serv Mgr, Serving Every Ohioan Service Center, 40780 Marietta Rd, Caldwell, OH, 43724. Tel: 740-783-5705. p. 2773

Milfajt, Kathy, Tech Serv, McHenry Public Library District, 809 Front St, McHenry, IL, 60050. Tel: 815-385-0036. p. 616

Milillo, Joe, Asst Librn, National Humanities Center Library, Seven Alexander Dr, Research Triangle Park, NC, 27709. Tel: 919-549-0661. p. 1712

Milite, William, Reserves, Fordham University Libraries, 441 E Fordham Rd, Bronx, NY, 10458-5151. Tel: 718-817-3570. p. 1498

Militello, Teresa, Archivist, National Museum of Transportation, 2933 Barrett Station Rd, Saint Louis, MO, 63122. Tel: 314-821-1190. p. 1272

Millar, Ellen, Corporate & Municipal Records Archivist, Simcoe County Archives, 1149 Hwy 26, Minesing, ON, L9X 0Z7, CANADA. Tel: 705-726-9300, Ext 1288. p. 2658

Millar, Janet, Librn, United States Army, Consumer Health Library, Eisenhower Army Medical Ctr, Rm 3-D-15, Fort Gordon, GA, 30905. Tel: 706-787-6765. p. 479

Millar, Janet, Librn, United States Army, Eisenhower Army Medical Center, Health Sciences Libr, DDEAMC, Fort Gordon, GA, 30905-5650. Tel: 706-787-6765. p. 479

Millar, Major Ron, Dir, The Salvation Army Archives, 26 Howden Rd, Scarborough, ON, M1R 3E4, CANADA. Tel: 416-285-4344. p. 2677

Millard, Jane, Dir, Jefferson Public Library, 200 W Lincoln Way, Jefferson, IA, 50129-2185. Tel: 515-386-2835. p. 761

Millard, John, Asst Dean, Miami University Libraries, 151 S Campus Ave, Oxford, OH, 45056. Tel: 513-529-6789. p. 1811

Millard, Sandra K, Dr, Assoc Univ Librn, Pub Serv, Dep Univ Librn, Outreach Serv, University of Delaware Library, 181 S College Ave, Newark, DE, 19717-5267. Tel: 302-831-2965. p. 355

Millay, Laura, Br Mgr, Enoch Pratt Free Library, Hamilton Branch, 5910 Harford Rd, Baltimore, MD, 21214-1845. Tel: 443-984-4935. p. 953

Millen, Megan, Exec Dir, Joliet Public Library, 150 N Ottawa St, Joliet, IL, 60432. Tel: 815-740-2670. p. 603

Millen, Patricia E, Exec Dir, Hunterdon County Historical Society, 114 Main St, Flemington, NJ, 08822. Tel: 908-782-1091. p. 1403

Miller, Aaron, Dir, Keene Public Library, Main St, Keene, NY, 12942. Tel: 518-576-2200. p. 1559

Miller, Alan, Dir, Sullivan County Library, 206 Center St, Dushore, PA, 18614. Tel: 570-928-9352. p. 1928

Miller, Alison, Libr Dir, Rehoboth Beach Public Library, 226 Rehoboth Ave, Rehoboth Beach, DE, 19971-2134. Tel: 302-227-8044, Ext 108. p. 356

Miller, Amanda, Libr Dir, Bonne Terre Memorial Library, Five SW Main St, Bonne Terre, MO, 63628. Tel: 573-358-2260. p. 1238

Miller, Amanda, Libr Syst Spec, Big Bend Community College Library, 1800 Bldg, 7662 Chanute St NE, Moses Lake, WA, 98837. Tel: 509-793-2350. p. 2371

Miller, Amy, Asst Mgr, Northwest Regional Library System, Harrell Memorial Library of Liberty County, 13016 NW CR 12, Bristol, FL, 32321. Tel: 850-643-2247. p. 435

Miller, Amy, Dir, La Marque Public Library, 1011 Bayou Rd, La Marque, TX, 77568-4195. Tel: 409-938-9270. p. 2207

Miller, Andrew, Adult Serv Mgr, Erie County Public Library, 160 E Front St, Erie, PA, 16507. Tel: 814-451-6932. p. 1931

Miller, Angela, Br Librn, Mingo County Library, Gilbert Branch, City Hall, Gilbert, WV, 25621. Tel: 304-664-8886. p. 2402

Miller, Ann, Dir, Plover Public Library, 301 Main St, Plover, IA, 50573. Tel: 712-857-3532. p. 777

Miller, Ann, Interim Assoc Dean, University of Oregon Libraries, 1501 Kincaid St, Eugene, OR, 97403-1299. Tel: 541-346-3053. p. 1879

Miller, Anne, Prog & Vols Coordr, Jaquith Public Library, Old Schoolhouse Common, 122 School St, Rm 2, Marshfield, VT, 05658. Tel: 802-426-3581. p. 2288

Miller, Annette, Ch, Tomahawk Public Library, 300 W Lincoln Ave, Tomahawk, WI, 54487. Tel: 715-453-2455. p. 2481

Miller, April, Access Serv Librn, Outreach Serv Librn, Southwestern Oklahoma State University, 100 Campus Dr, Weatherford, OK, 73096-3002. Tel: 580-774-7023. p. 1868

Miller, Ashley, Programming, Children's, Covington-Veedersburg Public Library, Veedersburg Public, 408 N Main St, Veedersburg, IN, 47987. Tel: 765-294-2808. p. 677

Miller, Audrey, Dir, Blue Mound Memorial Library District, 213 N St Marie, Blue Mound, IL, 62513. Tel: 217-692-2774. p. 543

Miller, Barb, Asst Dir, Plattsmouth Public Library, 401 Ave A, Plattsmouth, NE, 68048. Tel: 402-296-4154. p. 1333

Miller, Barb, Media Intelligence Analyst, Repsol Oil & Gas Inc, 2000, 888 Third St SW, Calgary, AB, T2P 5C5, CANADA. Tel: 403-237-1429. p. 2528

Miller, Barbara, Res & Instruction Librn, California State University, Fullerton, 800 N State College Blvd, Fullerton, CA, 92831. Tel: 657-278-4460. p. 147

Miller, Barratt, Youth Serv Librn, Oregon City Public Library, 606 John Adams St, Oregon City, OR, 97045. Tel: 503-657-8269. p. 1890

Miller, Benjamin, Dir, Wisconsin Department of Public Instruction, Resources for Libraries & Lifelong Learning, 2109 S Stoughton Rd, Madison, WI, 53716-2899. Tel: 608-224-6168. p. 2452

Miller, Beth, Copyright Librn, Washington & Jefferson College Library, 60 S Lincoln St, Washington, PA, 15301. Tel: 724-223-6069. p. 2018

Miller, Bethany, Ref Librn, Lorain County Community College, 1005 Abbe Rd N, North Elyria, OH, 44035-1691. Tel: 440-366-4026. p. 1810
Miller, Betty Sue, Dir, Hoag Library, 134 S Main St, Albion, NY, 14411. Tel: 585-589-4246. p. 1484
Miller, Beverly, Librn, Nixon Peabody LLP, 799 Ninth St NW, Ste 500, Washington, DC, 20001. Tel: 202-585-8000, Ext 8320. p. 373
Miller, Bonnie, Mgr, United States Marine Corps, Bldg 633, Yuma, AZ, 85369. Tel: 928-269-2785. p. 85
Miller, Brandy M, Assoc Warden of Prog, Northern Regional Jail Correctional Facility, 112 Northern Regional Correctional Dr, Moundsville, WV, 26041. Tel: 304-843-4067, Ext 106. p. 2410
Miller, Brenda, Br Head, Currituck County Public Library, 4261 Caratoke Hwy, Barco, NC, 27917-9707. Tel: 252-453-8345. p. 1673
Miller, Brenda, Dir, New Madison Public Library, 142 S Main St, New Madison, OH, 45346. Tel: 937-996-1741. p. 1806
Miller, Brett T, Archivist, Dir, Libr Serv, West Virginia Wesleyan College, 59 College Ave, Buckhannon, WV, 26201. Tel: 304-473-8013. p. 2399
Miller, Cassidy, Asst Dir, Tech, Community Library of DeWitt & Jamesville, 5110 Jamesville Rd, DeWitt, NY, 13078. Tel: 315-446-3578. p. 1525
Miller, Catherine A, Law Libr Asst, New York State Supreme Court, 163 Arsenal St, Watertown, NY, 13601. Tel: 315-785-3064. p. 1660
Miller, Cathy, Libr Tech, Yakama Nation Library, 100 Spiel-Yi Loop, Toppenish, WA, 98948. Tel: 509-865-2800, Ext 6. p. 2388
Miller, Cheryl, Sr Mgr, Tech Serv, Autry National Center, Autry Library, 4700 Western Heritage Way, Los Angeles, CA, 90027-1462. Tel: 323-667-2000, Ext 349. p. 160
Miller, Christina, Access Serv Supvr, Indiana University Kokomo Library, 2300 S Washington St, Kokomo, IN, 46902. Tel: 765-455-9237. p. 699
Miller, Chuck, Exec Dir, National Railway Historical Society, Atlanta Chapter, 3595 Buford Hwy, Duluth, GA, 30096. Tel: 770-476-2013. p. 477
Miller, Cindy, Br Mgr, Saint Charles City-County Library District, Deer Run Branch, 1300 N Main, O'Fallon, MO, 63366-2013. Tel: 636-978-3251, 636-980-1332. p. 1278
Miller, Claire, Res & Instruction Librn, Seminole State College of Florida, 850 S SR 434, Altamonte Springs, FL, 32714. Tel: 407-404-6025. p. 383
Miller, Clara, Co-Librn, Waubay Public Library, 94 N Main St, Waubay, SD, 57273. Tel: 605-947-4748. p. 2085
Miller, Creighton, Librn, Res & Bibliog Instruction, Washburn University, School of Law Library, 1700 SW College Ave, Topeka, KS, 66621. Tel: 785-670-1041. p. 840
Miller, Crystal, Libr Supvr, Spokane County Library District, Airway Heights Library, 1213 S Lundstrom, Airway Heights, WA, 99001-9000. Tel: 509-893-8250. p. 2384
Miller, Damion, Acq, Coll Develop Librn, Pfeiffer University, 48380 US Hwy 52 N, Misenheimer, NC, 28109. Tel: 704-463-3352. p. 1703
Miller, Danielle, Regional Libr Dir, Washington Talking Book & Braille Library, 2021 Ninth Ave, Seattle, WA, 98121. Tel: 206-615-0400. p. 2382
Miller, Daphne, Head, Coll Mgt, Xavier University, 1535 Musketeer Dr, Cincinnati, OH, 45207. Tel: 513-745-1007. p. 1765
Miller, Dave, Libr Mgr, Bartholomew County Public Library, Hope Branch, 635 Harrison St, Hope, IN, 47246. Tel: 812-546-5310. p. 676
Miller, David, Head, Tech Serv, Curry College, 1071 Blue Hill Ave, Milton, MA, 02186-9984. Tel: 617-333-2101. p. 1036
Miller, Dawn, Dir, Tabor Public Library, 723 Main St, Tabor, IA, 51653. Tel: 712-629-2735. p. 786
Miller, Diane Wilson, Mgr, Palm Beach County Law Library, County Courthouse, Rm 12200, 205 N Dixie Hwy, West Palm Beach, FL, 33401. Tel: 561-355-3149. p. 454
Miller, Dianne, Br Librn, Southeast Regional Library, Alameda Branch, 200-Fifth St, Alameda, SK, S0C 0A0, CANADA. Tel: 306-489-2066. p. 2753
Miller, Don, Dr, Dean, Learning Commons, Piedmont Community College, 1715 College Dr, Roxboro, NC, 27573. Tel: 336-599-1181, Ext 2247. p. 1714
Miller, Donna Lynn, Instruction & Ref Librn, Lebanon Valley College, 101 N College Ave, Annville, PA, 17003-1400. Tel: 717-867-6977. p. 1906
Miller, Doreen, Ch Serv Librn, Rockwall County Library, 1215 E Yellowjacket Lane, Rockwall, TX, 75087. Tel: 972-204-7700. p. 2234
Miller, Doreen, Librn, Chinook Regional Library, Leader Branch, 151 First St W, Leader, SK, S0N 1H0, CANADA. Tel: 306-628-3830. p. 2752
Miller, E Ethelbert, Dir, Howard University Libraries, Afro-American Studies Resource Center, 500 Howard Pl NW, Rm 300, Washington, DC, 20059. Tel: 202-806-7686. p. 369
Miller, Ed, Spec Serv Mgr, Library System of Lancaster County, 1866 Colonial Village Lane, Ste 107, Lancaster, PA, 17601. Tel: 717-207-0500. p. 1952
Miller, Elise, Dir, Acton Public Library, 35 H Rd, Acton, ME, 04001. Tel: 207-636-2781. p. 913
Miller, Elizabeth, Librn, Gallitzin Public Library, DeGol Plaza, Ste 30, 411 Convent St, Gallitzin, PA, 16641-1244. Tel: 814-886-4041. p. 1934
Miller, Elizabeth M, Dir, Goshen College, Mennonite Historical Library, 1700 S Main, Goshen, IN, 46526. Tel: 574-535-7418. p. 687
Miller, Ellen, Head, Ad Ref Serv, Shelter Rock Public Library, 165 Searingtown Rd, Albertson, NY, 11507. Tel: 516-248-7343. p. 1484
Miller, Erica, Periodicals/Documents Manager, Willamette University, 900 State St, Salem, OR, 97301. Tel: 503-370-6739. p. 1897
Miller, Erin E, Dir, Boulder County Corrections Library, 3200 Airport Rd, Boulder, CO, 80301. Tel: 303-441-4686. p. 266
Miller, Eve-Marie, Tech Serv Librn, Santa Rosa Junior College, 1501 Mendocino Ave, Santa Rosa, CA, 95401. Tel: 707-527-4544. p. 245
Miller, Evelyn C, Head Librn, Flatonia Public Library, 208 N Main St, Flatonia, TX, 78941. Tel: 361-772-2088. p. 2176
Miller, Fayrene, Dir, Bean Station Public Library, 895 Broadway Dr, Bean Station, TN, 37708. Tel: 865-993-3068. p. 2088
Miller, Fran, Dir, Berkshire Free Library, 12519 State Rte 38, Berkshire, NY, 13736. Tel: 607-657-4418. p. 1493
Miller, Gail Cross, Dir, Libr Serv, Pub Serv Dir, Missouri Supreme Court Library, Supreme Court Bldg, 207 W High St, 2nd Flr, Jefferson City, MO, 65101. Tel: 573-751-2636. p. 1253
Miller, Garnet, Youth Serv Coordr, Zion-Benton Public Library District, 2400 Gabriel Ave, Zion, IL, 60099. Tel: 847-872-4680. p. 665
Miller, Hanalorraine, Libr Dir, Rockland School Community Library, 321 E Center St, Rockland, ID, 83271. Tel: 208-548-2221. p. 530
Miller, Hannah, Digital Initiatives Librn, Regis University, 3333 Regis Blvd, D20, Denver, CO, 80221-1099. Tel: 303-458-4030, 303-458-4031. p. 276
Miller, Hannah, Head Librn, Cheltenham Township Library System, Glenside Free Library, 215 S Keswick Ave, Glenside, PA, 19038-4420. Tel: 215-885-0455. p. 1937
Miller, Heather, Dir, Dongola Public Library District, 114 NE Front St, Dongola, IL, 62926. Tel: 618-827-3622. p. 579
Miller, Heather, Dir, Ashland Public Library, 224 Claremont Ave, Ashland, OH, 44805. Tel: 419-289-8188. p. 1746
Miller, Helen, Libr Mgr, Indian River Area Library, 3546 S Straits Hwy, Indian River, MI, 49749. Tel: 231-238-8581. p. 1118
Miller, Holly, Dr, Dean of Libr, Florida Institute of Technology, 150 W University Blvd, Melbourne, FL, 32901-6988. Tel: 321-674-8871. p. 420
Miller, Ivy, Dir of Libr, Wyoming Seminary, Stettler Learning Resouces Ctr, 2nd Flr, 201 N Sprague Ave, Kingston, PA, 18704-3593. Tel: 570-270-2168. p. 1949
Miller, Jackie, Br Mgr, South Mississippi Regional Library, Frank L Leggett Public Library, 161 General Robert E Blount Blvd, Bassfield, MS, 39421. Tel: 601-943-5420. p. 1215
Miller, Jackie, Libr Supvr, South Mississippi Regional Library, Prentiss Public, 2229 Pearl St, Prentiss, MS, 39474. Tel: 601-792-5845. p. 1215
Miller, Jaimi, Libr Asst, University of Rochester Medical Center, Basil G Bibby Library, Eastman Dental, Rm 208, 625 Elmwood Ave, Rochester, NY, 14620. Tel: 585-275-5010. p. 1631
Miller, James, Discovery Librn, Hollins University, 7950 E Campus Dr, Roanoke, VA, 24020. Tel: 540-362-6653. p. 2345
Miller, Janelle, Libr Dir, Hildebrand Memorial Library, 1033 Wisconsin Ave, Boscobel, WI, 53805. Tel: 608-375-5723. p. 2425
Miller, Janet, Asst Librn, Kirkland Public Library, 513 W Main St, Kirkland, IL, 60146. Tel: 815-522-6260. p. 605
Miller, Jen, Admin Serv Coordr, Iowa City Public Library, 123 S Linn St, Iowa City, IA, 52240. Tel: 319-887-6003. p. 760
Miller, Jen, Tech Mgr, Dover Public Library, 525 N Walnut St, Dover, OH, 44622. Tel: 330-343-6123. p. 1782
Miller, Jenna, Ref Librn, Santa Fe College, 3000 NW 83rd St, Bldg Y, Gainesville, FL, 32606. Tel: 352-395-5329. p. 407
Miller, Jennifer, Libr Tech, Phillips Community College of the University of Arkansas, 1210 Ricebelt Ave, DeWitt, AR, 72042. Tel: 870-946-3506, Ext 1621. p. 94
Miller, Jennifer, Dir, Heisey Collectors of America, Inc, 169 W Church St, Newark, OH, 43055. Tel: 740-345-2932, Ext 3. p. 1807
Miller, Jessica, Dir, Cleve J Fredricksen Library, 100 N 19th St, Camp Hill, PA, 17011-3900. Tel: 717-761-3900, Ext 227. p. 1918
Miller, Jessica, Exec Dir, Washington County Library System, 55 S College St, Washington, PA, 15301. Tel: 724-222-2400, Ext 231. p. 2018
Miller, Jessica M, Libr Dir, Somers Public Library, Two Vision Blvd, Somers, CT, 06071. Tel: 860-763-3501. p. 337
Miller, John, Tech Librn, Traverse Des Sioux Library Cooperative, 1400 Madison Ave, Ste 622, Mankato, MN, 56001-5488. Tel: 833-837-5422. p. 1181
Miller, John, Dir, Paul Smith Library of Southern York County, 80 Constitution Ave, Shrewsbury, PA, 17361-1710. Tel: 717-235-4313. p. 2007
Miller, John M, Head Librn, Snead State Community College, 102 Elder St, Boaz, AL, 35957. Tel: 256-840-4173. p. 10
Miller, Jolene, Dir, University of Toledo, Mulford Library Bldg, 4th Flr, 3025 Library Circle, Toledo, OH, 43614-8000. Tel: 419-383-4225. p. 1825
Miller, Jolene M, Dir, Health Sci Libr, University of Toledo, 2975 W Centennial Dr, Toledo, OH, 43606-3396. Tel: 419-383-4959. p. 1825
Miller, Jonathan, Dir of Libr, Williams College, 26 Hopkins Hall Dr, Williamstown, MA, 01267. Tel: 413-597-2502. p. 1069
Miller, Joyce Cortright, Med Librn, Luminis Anne Arundel Medical Library, 2001 Medical Pkwy, Annapolis, MD, 21401. Tel: 443-481-4877. p. 950
Miller, Julie, ILL, Warren Library Association, 205 Market St, Warren, PA, 16365. Tel: 814-723-4650. p. 2017

Miller, Julie R, Dean of Libr, Butler University Libraries, 4600 Sunset Ave, Indianapolis, IN, 46208. Tel: 317-940-9227. p. 690
Miller, Kallei, Librn, Mount Pleasant Public Library, 24 E Main St, Mount Pleasant, UT, 84647-1429. Tel: 435-462-3240. p. 2267
Miller, Karen, Br Mgr, Montgomery County Public Libraries, Kensington Park Library, 4201 Knowles Ave, Kensington, MD, 20895-2408. Tel: 240-773-9505. p. 974
Miller, Katharine, Br Mgr, El Dorado County Library, South Lake Tahoe Branch, 1000 Rufus Allen Blvd, South Lake Tahoe, CA, 96150. Tel: 530-573-3185. p. 195
Miller, Katherine, ILL Tech, University of Detroit Mercy Libraries, 4001 W McNichols Rd, Detroit, MI, 48221-3038. Tel: 313-993-1072. p. 1099
Miller, Kathryn, Head of Music, Art & Drama Libraries, University of Washington Libraries, Art, Arts Bldg, Rm 101, Box 353440, Seattle, WA, 98195-3440. Tel: 206-543-0648. p. 2381
Miller, Kathryn, Head of Music, Art & Drama Libraries, University of Washington Libraries, Drama, Hutchinson Hall, Rm 145, Box 353950, Seattle, WA, 98195-3950. Tel: 206-543-5148. p. 2381
Miller, Kathryn, Head of Music, Art & Drama Libraries, University of Washington Libraries, Music, 113 Music Bldg, Box 353450, Seattle, WA, 98195-3450. Tel: 206-543-1159, 206-543-1168. p. 2382
Miller, Katie, Dir, Aiken Technical College Library, 2276 Jefferson Davis Hwy, Graniteville, SC, 29829. Tel: 803-508-7430. p. 2060
Miller, Katilyn, Br Mgr, Fairfax County Public Library, Reston Regional, 11925 Bowman Towne Dr, Reston, VA, 20190-3311. Tel: 703-689-2700. p. 2316
Miller, Katrina, Librn, Tri-County Community College, 21 Campus Circle, Murphy, NC, 28906. Tel: 828-835-4218, 828-837-6810. p. 1705
Miller, Katy, Head, Student Learning & Engagement, University of Central Florida Libraries, 12701 Pegasus Dr, Orlando, FL, 32816-8030. Tel: 407-823-2564. p. 432
Miller, Kayla, Interim Dir, Patagonia Public Library, 346 Duquesne, Patagonia, AZ, 85624. Tel: 520-394-2010. p. 68
Miller, Keisha, Vols Coordr, Youth Serv, South Orange Public Library, 65 Scotland Rd, South Orange, NJ, 07079. Tel: 973-762-0230. p. 1443
Miller, Kelle, Ch, Bridge City Public Library, 101 Parkside Dr, Bridge City, TX, 77611. Tel: 409-735-4242. p. 2150
Miller, Kelli, Asst Dir, Pike-Amite-Walthall Library System, 1022 Virginia Ave, McComb, MS, 39648. Tel: 601-684-7034, Ext 15. p. 1225
Miller, Ken, Ref (Info Servs), Buncombe County Public Libraries, 67 Haywood St, Asheville, NC, 28801. Tel: 828-250-4700. p. 1672
Miller, Ken Enright, Dir, Milton-Union Public Library, 560 S Main St, West Milton, OH, 45383. Tel: 937-698-5515. p. 1830
Miller, Kenneth, Coordr, Tech Serv, Allen Parish Libraries, 320 S Sixth St, Oberlin, LA, 70655. Tel: 318-491-4543. p. 905
Miller, Kenneth S, Libr Dir, Copiague Memorial Public Library, 50 Deauville Blvd, Copiague, NY, 11726. Tel: 631-691-1111. p. 1522
Miller, Kent, Exec Assoc Dean, University of Kansas Libraries, 1425 Jayhawk Blvd, Lawrence, KS, 66045-7544. p. 819
Miller, Kevin, Interim Head, Spec Coll, Univ Archivist, University of California, Davis, 100 NW Quad, Davis, CA, 95616. Tel: 530-752-8792. p. 134
Miller, Kim, Br Mgr, Pines & Plains Libraries, Kiowa Branch, 331 Comanche, Kiowa, CO, 80117. Tel: 303-621-2111. p. 279
Miller, Kimberly, Librn, Palliser Regional Library, Mossbank Branch, 310 Main St, Mossbank, SK, S0H 3G0, CANADA. Tel: 306-354-2474. p. 2743
Miller, Kris, Dir, Dowling Public Library, 1765 E Dowling Rd, Hastings, MI, 49058-9332. Tel: 269-721-3743. p. 1114
Miller, Kristi, Youth & Teen Serv Mgr, Westmont Public Library, 428 N Cass Ave, Westmont, IL, 60559-1502. Tel: 630-869-6150, 630-869-6160. p. 661
Miller, Laniece, Scholarly Communications Librn, Argonne National Laboratory, 9700 S Cass Ave, Bldg 240, Lemont, IL, 60439-4801. Tel: 630-252-0007. p. 608
Miller, Laura, Libr Mgr, Arizona State University Libraries, Fletcher Library, 4701 W Thunderbird Rd, Glendale, AZ, 85306. Tel: 602-543-7781. p. 79
Miller, Laurie B, Dir, Pierce County Law Library, County-City Bldg, 930 Tacoma Ave S, Rm 1A - 105, Tacoma, WA, 98402. Tel: 253-798-2691. p. 2386
Miller, Lee, Librn, Indian Rocks Beach Library, 1507 Bay Palm Blvd, Indian Rocks Beach, FL, 33785. Tel: 727-596-1822. p. 411
Miller, Lee, Tech Serv, Platte County Public Library, 904 Ninth St, Wheatland, WY, 82201. Tel: 307-322-2689. p. 2500
Miller, Lesa, Br Mgr, Shreve Memorial Library, Belcher-Wyche Branch, 409 Charles St, Belcher, LA, 71004. Tel: 318-378-4567. p. 908
Miller, Linda, Librn, Barton Public Library, Huttig Branch, Frost St, Huttig, AR, 71747. Tel: 870-943-3411. p. 94
Miller, Liz, Libr Dir, Colorado Mountain College, 901 S US Hwy 24, Leadville, CO, 80461. Tel: 719-486-4248. p. 289
Miller, Loftan, Dr, Coordr, J Sargeant Reynolds Community College Library, Downtown Campus-Library & Information Services, 700 E Jackson St, 2nd Flr, Rm 231, Richmond, VA, 23219-1543. Tel: 804-523-5776. p. 2341
Miller, Louise Jay, Exec Dir, Aria Health, Health Sciences Libraries, Red Lion & Knights Rds, Philadelphia, PA, 19114-1436. Tel: 206-209-5261. p. 1974
Miller, Lynne, Br Mgr, Shaker Heights Public Library, Bertram Woods Branch, 20600 Fayette Rd, Shaker Heights, OH, 44122. Tel: 216-991-2421. p. 1820
Miller, Marcella, Admin Officer, McNeese State University, , 300 Beauregard Dr, Lake Charles, LA, 70609. Tel: 337-475-5410. p. 894
Miller, Margaret, Research Librn, Fort Lauderdale Historical Society, 219 SW Second Ave, Fort Lauderdale, FL, 33301. Tel: 954-463-4431. p. 401
Miller, Marla, Librn, Carnegie-Schuyler Library, 303 E Second St, Pana, IL, 62557. Tel: 217-562-2326. p. 632
Miller, Martha, Curator, Librn, Salmon Brook Historical Society, 208 Salmon Brook St, Granby, CT, 06035. Tel: 860-653-9713. p. 314
Miller, Martin, Dean, Libr Serv, Butler County Community College, 107 College Dr, Butler, PA, 16002. Tel: 724-284-8511. p. 1917
Miller, Mary, Libr Dir, Mississippi College, 151 E Griffith St, Jackson, MS, 39201-1391. Tel: 601-925-7120. p. 1222
Miller, Mary, Libr Dir, Lakewood Memorial Library, 12 W Summit St, Lakewood, NY, 14750. Tel: 716-763-6234. p. 1561
Miller, Mary Jo, Dir, Western Town Library, 9172 Main St, Westernville, NY, 13486. Tel: 315-827-4118. p. 1663
Miller, Mary Kay, Asst Librn, Fair Haven Free Library, 107 N Main St, Fair Haven, VT, 05743. Tel: 802-265-8011. p. 2284
Miller, Marybeth, Interim Dir, Clinton Public Library, 214 Mill St, Clinton, WI, 53525-9459. Tel: 608-676-5569. p. 2428
Miller, Matt, Chief Tech Officer, Maricopa County Library District, 2700 N Central Ave, Ste 700, Phoenix, AZ, 85004. Tel: 602-652-3000. p. 70
Miller, Melanie, Libr Assoc, Rutgers University Libraries, Mathematical Sciences & Physics Library, Hill Ctr for Mathematical Sciences, 110 Frelinghuysen Rd, Piscataway, NJ, 08854-8019. Tel: 848-445-5919. p. 1425
Miller, Melba, Librn, Missouri Department of Corrections, South Central Correctional Center, 255 W Hwy 32, Licking, MO, 65542-9069. Tel: 573-674-4470. p. 1252
Miller, Melissa, Assoc Univ Librn, University of Southern California Libraries, Hoose Library of Philosophy, Mudd Memorial Hall of Philos, 3709 Trousdale Pkwy, Los Angeles, CA, 90089-0182. Tel: 213-740-7434. p. 170
Miller, Melissa, Ch, Schroeder Public Library, 93 Main St, Keystone, IA, 52249. Tel: 319-442-3329. p. 763
Miller, Michael, Circ, Goshen Public Library, 601 S Fifth St, Goshen, IN, 46526. Tel: 574-533-9531. p. 687
Miller, Michael, Chief Librn, Bronx Community College Library, 2115 University Ave, NL 252A, Bronx, NY, 10453. Tel: 718-289-5431. p. 1497
Miller, Michael, Ref Librn, Sherman Public Library, 421 N Travis St, Sherman, TX, 75090. Tel: 903-892-7240. p. 2243
Miller, Michael M, Bibliographer, Dir, North Dakota State University Libraries, 1201 Albrecht Blvd, Fargo, ND, 58108. Tel: 701-231-8416. p. 1733
Miller, Michael P, Asst Head of MS Processing & Library Registrar, American Philosophical Society Library, 105 S Fifth St, Philadelphia, PA, 19106-3386. Tel: 215-440-3400. p. 1974
Miller, Michelle, Sr Assoc, Tech Serv, Alabama College of Osteopathic Medicine, 445 Health Sciences Blvd, Hwy 84 E, Dothan, AL, 36303. Tel: 334-699-2266. p. 14
Miller, Michelle, Libr Dir, Jay C Byers Memorial Library, 215 E Wichita Ave, Cleveland, OK, 74020. Tel: 918-358-2676. p. 1844
Miller, Mikayla, Youth Serv Coordr, Kuskokwim Consortium Library, Yupiit Picirarait Cultural Ctr, 420 State Hwy, Bethel, AK, 99559. Tel: 907-543-4516. p. 43
Miller, Mina, Librn, New Vineyard Public Library, 20 Lake St, New Vineyard, ME, 04956. Tel: 207-652-2250. p. 933
Miller, Morgan, Exec Dir, Cecil County Public Library, 301 Newark Ave, Elkton, MD, 21921-5441. Tel: 410-996-1055, Ext 122. p. 964
Miller, Nancy, Librn, Stanton Public Library, 600 County 37, Stanton, ND, 58571. Tel: 701-745-3235. p. 1740
Miller, Nancy, Librn, North Central Washington Libraries, Coulee Public Library, 405 W Main St, Coulee City, WA, 99115. Tel: 509-632-8751. p. 2393
Miller, Nancy, Libr Dir, Northwest College, 231 W Sixth St, Powell, WY, 82435. Tel: 307-754-6207. p. 2497
Miller, Nannette D, Dir, Elk Rapids District Library, 300 Isle of Pines, Elk Rapids, MI, 49629. Tel: 231-264-9979. p. 1103
Miller, Nicole, Dir, Cannon Falls Library, 306 W Mill St, Cannon Falls, MN, 55009-2045. Tel: 507-263-2804. p. 1169
Miller, Olivia, Fine Arts Librn, Humanities Librn, University of Massachusetts Dartmouth Library, 285 Old Westport Rd, North Dartmouth, MA, 02747-2300. Tel: 508-999-8526. p. 1041
Miller, Pam, Tech Serv Mgr, Ottawa Library, 105 S Hickory St, Ottawa, KS, 66067. Tel: 785-242-3080. p. 829
Miller, Pamela, Genealogy & Hist Librn, White Cloud Community Library, 1038 Wilcox Ave, White Cloud, MI, 49349. Tel: 231-689-6631. p. 1159
Miller, Pamela, Libr Dir, Burkburnett Library, 215 E Fourth St, Burkburnett, TX, 76354-3446. Tel: 940-569-2991. p. 2151
Miller, Patricia E, Dir, Scottdale Public Library, 106 Spring St, Scottdale, PA, 15683-1711. Tel: 724-887-6140. p. 2004

Miller, Patti, Br Mgr, Colchester-East Hants Public Library, Elmsdale Branch, Lloyd E Matheson Ctr, Ste 100, 15 Commerce Court, Elmsdale, NS, B2S 3K5, CANADA. Tel: 902-883-9838. p. 2623

Miller, Paul, Dir, Libr Serv, American Jewish University, 15600 Mulholland Dr, Los Angeles, CA, 90077. Tel: 310-476-9777, Ext 238. p. 160

Miller, Paul S, Ref Librn, Loyola University New Orleans, Loyola Law Library, School of Law, 7214 St Charles Ave, New Orleans, LA, 70118. p. 902

Miller, Paula, Librn, Oregon County Library District, Thayer Public, 121 N Second St, Thayer, MO, 65791. Tel: 417-264-3091. p. 1237

Miller, Penne, Librn, Scott County Library System, Princeton Branch, 328 River Dr, Princeton, IA, 52768. Tel: 563-289-4282. p. 751

Miller, Pennie E, Chief Librn, Pearl City Public Library District, 221 S Main St, Pearl City, IL, 61062. Tel: 815-443-2832. p. 633

Miller, Peter, Head, Fac & Security, University of Florida Libraries, 1545 W University Ave, Gainesville, FL, 32611-7000. Tel: 352-273-2578. p. 407

Miller, Placedia, Libr Dir, Forsyth Technical Community College Library, 2100 Silas Creek Pkwy, Winston-Salem, NC, 27103. Tel: 336-734-7148. p. 1725

Miller, Placedia, Outreach Librn, Forsyth Technical Community College Library, 2100 Silas Creek Pkwy, Winston-Salem, NC, 27103. Tel: 336-734-7219. p. 1725

Miller, Rachel, Circ Mgr, The Master's University, 21726 W Placerita Canyon Rd, Santa Clarita, CA, 91321-1200. Tel: 661-362-2272. p. 242

Miller, Rachel, Libr Dir, Forsyth Public Library, 268 S Elwood, Forsyth, IL, 62535. Tel: 217-877-8174. p. 589

Miller, Rebecca, Natural Res Librn, University of California, Berkeley, Marian Koshland Bioscience, Natural Resources & Public Health Library, 2101 Valley Life Science Bldg, No 6500, Berkeley, CA, 94720-6500. Tel: 510-643-6475. p. 123

Miller, Rebecca, Mgr, Libr Serv, DLA Piper US LLP, 6225 Smith Ave, Baltimore, MD, 21209-3600. Tel: 410-580-3010. p. 952

Miller, Rebecca, Librn, Aria Health, School of Nursing Library, Three Neshaminy Interflex, Trevose, PA, 19053. Tel: 215-710-3510, Ext 23523. p. 1974

Miller, Regan, Ref & Instruction Librn, Pine Manor College, 400 Heath St, Chestnut Hill, MA, 02467. Tel: 617-731-7081. p. 1011

Miller, Richard, Exec Dir, Osterhout Free Library, 71 S Franklin St, Wilkes-Barre, PA, 18701. Tel: 570-823-0156. p. 2022

Miller, Richard C, Exec Dir, Syst Adminr, Luzerne County Library System, 71 S Franklin St, Wilkes-Barre, PA, 18701. Tel: 570-823-0156, Ext 234. p. 2022

Miller, Rita, Asst Dir, Vermontville Township Library, 120 E First St, Vermontville, MI, 49096. Tel: 517-726-1362. p. 1156

Miller, Robbie, Operations Assoc, Spec, Virginia Baptist Historical Society & the Center for Baptist Heritage & Studies Library, 261 Richmond Way, University of Richmond, Richmond, VA, 23173. Tel: 804-289-8434. p. 2343

Miller, Robert, Chief Exec Officer, LYRASIS, 1438 W Peachtree St NW, Ste 150, Atlanta, GA, 30309. Tel: 800-999-8558, Ext 4898. p. 2764

Miller, Robin, Head, Discovery & Assessment, University of Wisconsin-Eau Claire, 103 Garfield Ave, Eau Claire, WI, 54701-4932. Tel: 715-836-3132. p. 2433

Miller, Robyn, Supv Librn, Monmouth County Library, 125 Symmes Dr, Manalapan, NJ, 07726. Tel: 732-431-7220. p. 1415

Miller, Roxanne J, Dir, Knox Public Library, 305 N Main St, Knox, PA, 16232. Tel: 814-797-1054. p. 1949

Miller, Sally, Asst Librn, Central Manitoulin Public Libraries, Providence Bay Branch, 11 Mutchmor St, Providence Bay, ON, P0P 1T0, CANADA. Tel: 705-377-4503. p. 2658

Miller, Samantha, Libr Dir, Edgemont Public Library, 412 Second Ave, Edgemont, SD, 57735. Tel: 605-662-7712. p. 2076

Miller, Sara, Dep Dir, Burleson Public Library, 248 SW Johnson Ave, Burleson, TX, 76028. Tel: 817-426-9210. p. 2152

Miller, Sarah, Br Serv Supvr, Gaston County Public Library, 1555 E Garrison Blvd, Gastonia, NC, 28054. Tel: 704-868-2164. p. 1690

Miller, Scott, Interim Dir, Smithsonian Libraries, Natural History Bldg, Tenth St & Constitution Ave NW, Washington, DC, 20560. Tel: 647-264-7328. p. 375

Miller, Scott, Circ Serv Mgr, Monticello-Union Township Public Library, 321 W Broadway St, Monticello, IN, 47960. Tel: 574-583-2665. p. 707

Miller, Shakema, Outreach & Partnership Specialist, Nassau Library System, 900 Jerusalem Ave, Uniondale, NY, 11553-3039. Tel: 516-292-8920. p. 1654

Miller, Shantry, Tech Serv Librn, Blessing-Rieman College of Nursing & Health Sciences, 3609 N Marx Dr, Quincy, IL, 62305. Tel: 217-228-5520, Ext 6970. p. 637

Miller, Sharon, Mgr, Ward County Library, Grandfalls Public, 209 Ave D, Grandfalls, TX, 79742. Tel: 432-547-2861. p. 2220

Miller, Sheldon, Mus Dir, Gila County Historical Museum Library, 1330 N Broad St, Globe, AZ, 85501. Tel: 928-425-7385. p. 62

Miller, Sheri, Assoc Dir, Youth Serv Mgr, Whitman County Rural Library District, 102 S Main St, Colfax, WA, 99111-1863. Tel: 509-397-4366. p. 2362

Miller, Sonora, Libr Dir, Youngstown Free Library, 240 Lockport St, Youngstown, NY, 14174. Tel: 716-745-3555. p. 1668

Miller, Stephanie, Tech Serv Librn, Garrett College, 687 Mosser Rd, McHenry, MD, 21541. Tel: 301-387-3009. p. 971

Miller, Susan A, Dir, Bedford Public Library, 1323 K St, Bedford, IN, 47421. Tel: 812-275-4471. p. 669

Miller, Susanna, Assoc Dean, Admin Serv, Florida State University Libraries, Strozier Library Bldg, 116 Honors Way, Tallahassee, FL, 32306. Tel: 850-644-2706. p. 446

Miller, Susi, Libr Mgr, Ohio State University LIBRARIES, Grant Morrow III MD Library at Nationwide Children's Hospital, 700 Children's Dr, Rm ED-244, Columbus, OH, 43205. Tel: 614-722-3200. p. 1776

Miller, Tashia, Librn, Washtenaw Community College, 4800 E Huron River Dr, Ann Arbor, MI, 48105-4800. Tel: 734-973-5464. p. 1081

Miller, Tawnya, Br Mgr, Sublette County Libraries, Big Piney Library, 106 Fish St, Big Piney, WY, 83113. Tel: 307-276-3515. p. 2497

Miller, Terri, Asst Univ Librn, Pub Serv, Michigan State University Libraries, Main Library, 366 W Circle Dr, East Lansing, MI, 48824-1048. Tel: 517-884-0841. p. 1102

Miller, Terry J, Mgr, Illinois Historic Preservation Agency, 307 Decatur St, Galena, IL, 61036. Tel: 815-777-3310. p. 590

Miller, Tierney, Adult Serv Supvr, Cherry Hill Public Library, 1100 Kings Hwy N, Cherry Hill, NJ, 08034. Tel: 856-667-0300. p. 1395

Miller, Tim, Dir, Pines & Plains Libraries, 651 W Beverly St, Elizabeth, CO, 80107-7560. Tel: 303-358-8820. p. 279

Miller, Tim, Dir, Rampart Library District, 218 E Midland Ave, Woodland Park, CO, 80863. Tel: 719-687-9281. p. 298

Miller, Tim, Exec Dir, Western Plains Library System, 501 S 28th St, Clinton, OK, 73601-3996. Tel: 580-323-0974. p. 1844

Miller, Todd, Digital Serv Librn, Niles-Maine District Library, 6960 Oakton St, Niles, IL, 60714. Tel: 847-663-1234. p. 624

Miller, Tracy, Br Mgr, Harford County Public Library, Fallston Branch, 1461 Fallston Rd, Fallston, MD, 21047-1699. Tel: 410-638-3003. p. 959

Miller, Tracy, Br Mgr, Cecil County Public Library, Cecilton Branch, 215 E Main St, Cecilton, MD, 21913-1000. Tel: 410-275-1091. p. 964

Miller, Tristan, Mgr, Miami-Dade Public Library System, Little River Branch, 160 NE 79th St, Miami, FL, 33138. Tel: 305-751-8689. p. 423

Miller, Vicki, Ch Serv, Saint Mary's Public Library, 127 Center St, Saint Marys, PA, 15857. Tel: 814-834-6141. p. 2002

Miller, Viki, Asst Dir, Yutan Public Library, 410 First St, Yutan, NE, 68073. Tel: 402-625-2111. p. 1341

Miller Waltz, Rebecca K, Head, Learning Serv, Pennsylvania State University Libraries, Library Learning Services, 216 Pattee Tower, University Park, PA, 16802-1803. Tel: 814-865-3064. p. 2015

Miller, Wonda, Asst Dir, John Jermain Memorial Library, 201 Main St, Sag Harbor, NY, 11963. Tel: 631-725-0049, Ext 234. p. 1634

Miller-Francisco, Emily, Coll Develop Librn, Southern Oregon University, 1250 Siskiyou Blvd, Ashland, OR, 97520. Tel: 541-552-6819. p. 1872

Miller-Marion, Amanda, Libr Asst, James Township Public Library, 19 First St, Elk Lake, ON, P0J 1G0, CANADA. Tel: 705-678-2340. p. 2640

Miller-McCollum, Keyunda, Dr, Dir, Libr Serv, Shaw University, 118 E South St, Raleigh, NC, 27601. Tel: 919-546-8539. p. 1710

Miller-Ridlon, Ramona, Ref Librn, Santa Fe College, 3000 NW 83rd St, Bldg Y, Gainesville, FL, 32606. Tel: 352-381-3637. p. 407

Millican, Evans, Local Hist Librn, Flint River Regional Library System, 800 Memorial Dr, Griffin, GA, 30223. Tel: 770-412-4770. p. 481

Millican, Lisa, Tech Serv Asst, Gordon State College, 419 College Dr, Barnesville, GA, 30204. Tel: 678-359-5076. p. 468

Millier, Deborah, Dir, Libr Serv, Emmanuel University, 2261 W Main St, Franklin Springs, GA, 30639. Tel: 706-245-2852. p. 480

Milligan, Aleina, Children's & YA Librn, Adair County Public Library, 307 Greensburg St, Columbia, KY, 42728-1488. Tel: 270-384-2472. p. 852

Milligan, Brittany, Libr Tech, Black River Technical College Library, 1410 Hwy 304 E, Pocahontas, AR, 72455. Tel: 870-248-4060. p. 108

Milligan, Debra, Dir, Libr Serv, Carver Bible College Library, 3870 Cascade Rd, Atlanta, GA, 30331. Tel: 404-527-4520. p. 462

Milligan, Javier, Head of Modern Library, Hispanic Society of America Library, 613 W 155th St, New York, NY, 10032. Tel: 212-926-2234, Ext 262. p. 1587

Milligan, Jessica, Computer Lab Librn/Circ, Benton County Public Library, 121 S Forrest Ave, Camden, TN, 38320-2055. Tel: 731-584-4772. p. 2090

Milligan, Lisa, Br Mgr, Brunswick County Library, Leland Branch, 487 Village Rd, Leland, NC, 28451. Tel: 910-371-9442. p. 1716

Milligan, Lora, Dir, Hamilton Parks Public Library, 74 Parks Plaza, Trimble, TN, 38259. Tel: 731-297-3601. p. 2128

Millikan, Karyn, Libr Dir, Danville Public Library, 101 S Indiana St, Danville, IN, 46122-1809. Tel: 317-745-2604. p. 678

Milliken, Jamie, Libr Tech, Phillips Community College of the University of Arkansas, 2807 Hwy 165 S, Box A, Stuttgart, AR, 72160. Tel: 870-673-4201, Ext 1819. p. 111

Milliken, Larry, Ref Librn, Drexel University Libraries, Hagerty Library, 33rd & Market Sts, Philadelphia, PA, 19104-2875. Tel: 215-895-2765. p. 1976

Milliken, Sheena, Br Mgr, Columbus County Public Library, Chadbourn Community, 301 N Wilson St, Chadbourn, NC, 28431. Tel: 910-654-3322. p. 1722

Milliman, Leanne, Dir, Crooked Tree District Library, 2203 Walloon St, Walloon Lake, MI, 49796. Tel: 231-535-2111. p. 1157

Millington, Brittany, Dep Dir, Champaign Public Library, 200 W Green St, Champaign, IL, 61820-5193. Tel: 217-403-2000. p. 551

Mills, Adam, Circ Mgr, University of St Augustine for Health Sciences, One University Blvd, Saint Augustine, FL, 32086. Tel: 904-770-3593. p. 440

Mills, Alexandria, Head Librn, Betty Foster Public Library, 405 Shaffner St, Ponder, TX, 76259. Tel: 940-479-2683. p. 2228

Mills, Candice, Librn, Gulf Correctional Institution Library, 500 Ike Steel Rd, Wewahitchka, FL, 32465. Tel: 850-639-1000. p. 454

Mills, Caroline, Dr, Dir of Libr, Furman University Libraries, 3300 Poinsett Hwy, Greenville, SC, 29613-4100. Tel: 864-294-2190. p. 2061

Mills, Catherine, Curator, Archives & Libr, History San Jose, 1661 Senter Rd, San Jose, CA, 95112. Tel: 408-521-5025. p. 230

Mills, Christine, Br Mgr, Huron County Community Library, Greenwich Public Library, Four New St, Greenwich, OH, 44837. Tel: 419-752-7331. p. 1832

Mills, Christine, Br Mgr, Huron County Community Library, North Fairfield Public Library, Five E Main St, North Fairfield, OH, 44855. Tel: 419-744-2285. p. 1832

Mills, Deana, Dir, Rector Public Library, 121 W Fourth St, Rector, AR, 72461. Tel: 870-595-2410. p. 108

Mills, Deborah, Cataloger, Art Gallery of Ontario, 317 Dundas St W, Toronto, ON, M5T 1G4, CANADA. Tel: 416-979-6642. p. 2686

Mills, Emily, Youth Serv Librn, Cromwell Belden Public Library, 39 West St, Cromwell, CT, 06416. Tel: 860-632-3460. p. 307

Mills, Jackie A, Libr Dir, Mount Angel Public Library, 290 E Charles St, Mount Angel, OR, 97362. Tel: 503-845-6401. p. 1887

Mills, Janet, Dep Dir, Hennepin County Library, 12601 Ridgedale Dr, Minnetonka, MN, 55305-1909. Tel: 612-543-8535. p. 1186

Mills, Judith, Med Librn, Santa Clara Valley Medical Center, 751 S Bascom Ave, Rm 2E063, San Jose, CA, 95128. Tel: 408-885-5651. p. 232

Mills, Kathy, Circ Mgr, George F Johnson Memorial Library, 1001 Park St, Endicott, NY, 13760. Tel: 607-757-5350. p. 1531

Mills, Katie, Librn, Mid-Mississippi Regional Library System, Walnut Grove Public, 146 Main St, Walnut Grove, MS, 39189. Tel: 601-253-2483. p. 1224

Mills, Laura, Univ Archivist, Roosevelt University, 430 S Michigan Ave, Chicago, IL, 60605. Tel: 312-341-2280. p. 567

Mills, Lori, Librn, McLaren Macomb Medical Center, 1000 Harrington Blvd, Mount Clemens, MI, 48043. Tel: 586-493-8047. p. 1134

Mills, Lynnette, Dep Dir, Davis County Library, 133 S Main St, Farmington, UT, 84025. Tel: 801-451-3030. p. 2263

Mills, Maggie, Mgr, Salt Lake County Library Services, Hunter Branch, 4740 W 4100 S, West Valley City, UT, 84120-4948. p. 2274

Mills, Margret, Dept Chair, Pub Serv Librn, Skagit Valley College, 2405 E College Way, Mount Vernon, WA, 98273-5899. Tel: 360-416-7760. p. 2371

Mills, Mari, Br Mgr, Lake Blackshear Regional Library System, Cordele-Crisp Carnegie, 115 E 11th Ave, Cordele, GA, 31010. Tel: 229-276-1300. p. 458

Mills, Maribeth, Librn, Phillips Murrah, Corporate Tower, 13th Flr, 101 N Robinson Ave, Oklahoma City, OK, 73102. Tel: 405-235-4100. p. 1859

Mills, Mary, Dir, Exhibitions & Coll, Museum of American Glass, Wheaton Arts & Cultural Ctr, 1501 Glasstown Rd, Millville, NJ, 08332. Tel: 856-825-6800, Ext 142. p. 1419

Mills, Maryanne, Outreach & Instruction Librn, West Valley Community College Library, 14000 Fruitvale Ave, Saratoga, CA, 95070-5698. Tel: 408-741-4661. p. 245

Mills, Moira, Head, Circ, Dover Town Library, 56 Dedham St, Dover, MA, 02030-2214. Tel: 508-785-8113. p. 1014

Mills, Moira, Circ Supvr, Medfield Public Library, 468 Main St, Medfield, MA, 02052-2008. Tel: 508-359-4544. p. 1033

Mills, Nancy, Librn, English Lutheran Church Library, 1509 King St, La Crosse, WI, 54601. Tel: 608-784-9335. p. 2446

Mills, Paul, Exec Dir, Fountaindale Public Library District, 300 W Briarcliff Rd, Bolingbrook, IL, 60440. Tel: 630-685-4157. p. 543

Mills, Samantha, Br Head, Vancouver Public Library, Dunbar Branch, 4515 Dunbar St, Vancouver, BC, V6S 2G7, CANADA. Tel: 604-665-3968. p. 2581

Mills, Sharde', Librn, Spokane Falls Community College Library, 3410 W Whistalks Way, Spokane, WA, 99224-5204. Tel: 509-533-3224. p. 2385

Mills, Susan, Asst Dir, Warren Public Library, 123 E Third St, Warren, IN, 46792. Tel: 260-375-3450. p. 724

Mills, Thomas, Dir, University of Notre Dame, 2345 Biolchini Hall of Law, Notre Dame, IN, 46556-4640. Tel: 574-631-7024. p. 711

Millsap, Katie, Ad, Bossier Parish Libraries, 2206 Beckett St, Bossier City, LA, 71111. Tel: 318-746-1693. p. 885

Millsap, Matthew, Dir, Libr Serv, Midwestern Baptist Theological Seminary Library, 5001 N Oak Trafficway, Kansas City, MO, 64118-4620. Tel: 816-414-3729. p. 1256

Millsap, Melissa, Dir, Chetwynd Public Library, 5012 46th St, Chetwynd, BC, V0C 1J0, CANADA. Tel: 250-788-2559. p. 2564

Millwood, Kent, Dir, Libr Serv, Anderson University Library, 316 Boulevard, Anderson, SC, 29621. Tel: 864-231-2049. p. 2047

Milne, Debbie, Librn, Cimarron City Library, Ingalls Branch, 220 S Main St, Ingalls, KS, 67853. Tel: 620-335-5580. p. 801

Milne, Deborah, Asst Librn, The Hartford Library, 1587 Maple St, Hartford, VT, 05047. Tel: 802-296-2568. p. 2285

Milner, Alice, Librn, Virginia Department of Corrections, 1900 River Rd W, Crozier, VA, 23039. Tel: 804-784-6800, 804-784-6841. p. 2314

Milner, Kay, Head Librn, Wayne County Historical Society, Hwy 2, 515 E Jefferson St, Corydon, IA, 50060. Tel: 641-872-2211. p. 742

Milner, Megan, Superintendent, Kansas Department of Corrections, 1430 NW 25th St, Topeka, KS, 66618-1499. Tel: 785-354-9800. p. 838

Milnor, Elaine, Circ Supvr, Naugatuck Valley Community College, 750 Chase Pkwy, Rm K512, Waterbury, CT, 06708. Tel: 203-575-8147. p. 344

Milone Hill, Nanci, Libr Dir, Moses Greeley Parker Memorial Library, 28 Arlington St, Dracut, MA, 01826. Tel: 978-454-5474. p. 1015

Milton, Connie, Ref Librn, SOWELA Technical Community College Library, Arts & Humanities Bldg, 2000 Merganser St, Lake Charles, LA, 70616. Tel: 337-421-6928. p. 894

Milton, Danielle, Br Mgr, Spokane County Library District, Spokane Valley Library, 12004 E Main Ave, Spokane Valley, WA, 99206-5114. Tel: 509-893-8400. p. 2385

Milton, Denise, Dir, Jasper Public Library, 175 E Water St, Jasper, TX, 75951. Tel: 409-384-3791. p. 2203

Milton, Joan, Br Mgr, Washington County Library System, Arcola Library, 106 Martin Luther King Dr, Arcola, MS, 38722. Tel: 662-827-5262. p. 1217

Milton, Kristen, Mgr, West Georgia Regional Library, Crossroads Public Library, 909 Harmony Grove Church Rd, Acworth, GA, 30101. Tel: 770-975-0197. p. 470

Milton, LaTrisha, Br Mgr, Enoch Pratt Free Library, Walbrook Branch, 3203 W North Ave, Baltimore, MD, 21216-3015. Tel: 443-984-4934. p. 953

Milton, Terri, Campus Librn, Nova Scotia Community College, Kingstec Campus Library, 236 Belcher St, Kentville, NS, B4N 0A6, CANADA. Tel: 902-679-7380. p. 2620

Milton, Vikki, Dir, Learning Res, Chipola College Library, 3094 Indian Circle, Marianna, FL, 32446. Tel: 850-718-2371. p. 420

Milum, Amber, Dir, Llano County Library System, Kingsland Library, 125 W Polk St, Kingsland, TX, 78639. Tel: 325-388-3170. p. 2212

Milunovich, Kent, Tech Serv, Seattle University, School of Law Library, Sullivan Hall, 901 12th Ave, Seattle, WA, 98122-4411. Tel: 206-398-4221. p. 2380

Mimms, Mike, Media Serv Spec, University of Cincinnati, 2540 Clifton Ave, Cincinnati, OH, 45219. Tel: 513-556-0161. p. 1764

Mimms, Rachel, Head, Circ, Gale Free Library, 23 Highland St, Holden, MA, 01520. Tel: 508-210-5560. p. 1025

Mims, Gloria, Sr Librn, Atlanta-Fulton Public Library System, Auburn Avenue Research Library on African-American Culture & History, 101 Auburn Ave NE, Atlanta, GA, 30303-2503. Tel: 404-730-4001, Ext 108. p. 460

Mims, Lisa M, Br Mgr, Dixie Regional Library System, Houston Carnegie Branch, 105 W Madison St, Houston, MS, 38851. Tel: 662-456-3381. p. 1230

Mims, Sarah, Cataloger, ILL, Elizabeth Jones Library, 1050 Fairfield Ave, Grenada, MS, 38901. Tel: 662-226-2072. p. 1217

Min, Junghee, Librn, New York School of Interior Design Library, 170 E 70th St, New York, NY, 10021. Tel: 212-452-4174. p. 1598

Mina, Laura, Head Librn, Charleston Library Society, 164 King St, Charleston, SC, 29401. Tel: 843-723-9912. p. 2050

Minars, Kelley, Res Sharing Librn, University of Texas Health Science Center at San Antonio Libraries, 7703 Floyd Curl Dr, MSC 7940, San Antonio, TX, 78229-3900. Tel: 210-567-2450. p. 2240

Mincey, Jennifer, Evening Librn, Wake Technical Community College, Scott Northern Wake Library, 6600 Louisburg Rd, NF 241, Raleigh, NC, 27616. Tel: 919-532-5550. p. 1711

Minchillo, Carlo, Learning Commons Coord, Ref Serv, The College of New Rochelle, 29 Castle Pl, New Rochelle, NY, 10805-2308. Tel: 914-654-5345. p. 1577

Mincin, Denise, Ref Librn, Chappaqua Public Library, 195 S Greeley Ave, Chappaqua, NY, 10514. Tel: 914-238-4779. p. 1516

Minder, Irene, Exec Dir, Harvard Library, George David Birkhoff Mathematical Library, Science Ctr 337, One Oxford St, Cambridge, MA, 02138. Tel: 617-495-2171. p. 1005

Mindus, Tracy, Libr Mgr, Blue Ridge Community Library, 117 Second Ave, Blue Ridge, AB, T0E 0B0, CANADA. Tel: 780-648-3991. p. 2524

Minehardt, Jennifer, Head, Youth Serv, Perrot Memorial Library, 90 Sound Beach Ave, Old Greenwich, CT, 06870. Tel: 203-637-8802. p. 332

Miner, Alana, Librn, Mount Pleasant Public Library, 24 E Main St, Mount Pleasant, UT, 84647-1429. Tel: 435-462-3240. p. 2267

Miner, Brenda, Dir, Libr Serv, Rich Mountain Community College, 1100 College Dr, Mena, AR, 71953-2503. Tel: 479-394-7622, Ext 1370. p. 104

Miner, Brenda, Regional Librn, Ouachita Mountains Regional Library, 145 A Whittington St, Mount Ida, AR, 71957. p. 105

Miner, Karen, Bus Mgr, Acorn Public Library District, 15624 S Central Ave, Oak Forest, IL, 60452-3204. Tel: 708-687-3700. p. 627

Miner, Meg, Spec Coll Librn, Univ Archivist, Illinois Wesleyan University, One Ames Plaza, Bloomington, IL, 61701-7188. Tel: 309-556-1538. p. 543

Minervini, Michelle, Head, Children's Servx, Uniondale Public Library, 400 Uniondale Ave, Uniondale, NY, 11553. Tel: 516-489-2220, Ext 215. p. 1654

Mingo, David, Library Contact, Lafayette Public Library, Butler Memorial & Martin Luther King Center, 309 Cora St, Lafayette, LA, 70501. Tel: 337-234-0363. p. 892

Mingo, David, Library Contact, Lafayette Public Library, Chenier Center, 220 W Willow St, Bldg C, Lafayette, LA, 70501. Tel: 337-291-2941. p. 892

Minica, Kelley, Res Sharing Librn, Madison Area Technical College, 3550 Anderson St, Rm A3000, Madison, WI, 53704. Tel: 608-243-4086. p. 2449

Minich, Barb, Libr Dir, Ivy Tech Community College-Northwest, 130 W 35th Ave, Gary, IN, 46408. Tel: 219-981-4410. p. 687

Minix, Amy, Health Sci Librn, Indiana University Bloomington, Optometry Library, Optometry 202, 800 E Atwater Ave, Bloomington, IN, 47405. Tel: 812-855-8629. p. 671

Minkel, Sean, Asst Dir, Circ & Tech Serv Librn, Rapid City Public Library, 610 Quincy St, Rapid City, SD, 57701-3630. Tel: 605-394-6139. p. 2081

Minkiewicz, Carol, Tech Serv Librn, Kellogg-Hubbard Library, 135 Main St, Montpelier, VT, 05602. Tel: 802-223-3338. p. 2289

Minkoff, Meredith, Ch Serv, Mineola Memorial Library, 195 Marcellus Rd, Mineola, NY, 11501. Tel: 516-746-8488. p. 1572

Minnehan, Shari, Dir, Churdan City Library, 414 Sand St, Churdan, IA, 50050. Tel: 515-389-3423. p. 740

Minnella, Rosemary, Chief Exec Officer, West Perth Public Library, 105 Saint Andrew St, Mitchell, ON, N0K 1N0, CANADA. Tel: 519-348-9234. p. 2659

Minner, Ann, Dir, Texas State Library & Archives Commission, 1201 Brazos St, Austin, TX, 78701. Tel: 512-463-5428. p. 2141

Minner, Brook, Libr Dir, Brooksville Free Public Library, Inc, Townhouse Bldg, One Townhouse Rd, Brooksville, ME, 04617-3647. Tel: 207-326-4560. p. 919

Minnick, Cindy, Br Supvr, Montgomery-Floyd Regional Library System, Meadowbrook Public, 267 Alleghany Springs Rd, Shawsville, VA, 24162. Tel: 540-268-1964. p. 2313

Minnick, Gannon, User Services Admin, Washburn University, School of Law Library, 1700 SW College Ave, Topeka, KS, 66621. Tel: 785-670-1776. p. 840

Minnick, Mimi, Coordr, Northwest Regional Library System, Corinne Costin Gibson Memorial Public Library, 110 Library Dr, Port Saint Joe, FL, 32456. Tel: 850-229-8879. p. 435

Minnigh, Joel D, Dir, Wilkinsburg Public Library, Eastridge, 1900 Graham Blvd, Pittsburgh, PA, 15235. Tel: 412-342-0056. p. 1997

Minnis, Mary Lee, Asst Dir, Ch Serv, Meadville Public Library, 848 N Main St, Meadville, PA, 16335. Tel: 814-336-1773. p. 1960

Minock, Adrienne, Libr Mgr, Henrico County Public Library, Libbie Mill Library, 2100 Libbie Lake E St, Henrico, VA, 23230. Tel: 804-501-1940. p. 2326

Minor Harris, DeLisa, Asst Dir, Libr Serv, Fisk University, 1000 17th Ave N, Nashville, TN, 37208-3051. Tel: 615-329-8646. p. 2118

Minor, Laura, Br Mgr, Jacksonville Public Library, Bradham-Brooks Northwest Branch, 1755 Edgewood Ave W, Jacksonville, FL, 32208-7206. Tel: 904-765-5402. p. 412

Minor, Michell, ILL, Saint Mary Parish Library, 206 Iberia St, Franklin, LA, 70538. Tel: 337-828-1624, 337-828-1627. p. 890

Minor, Scott, Head Librn, California Northstate University Library, 9700 W Taron Dr, Elk Grove, CA, 95757. Tel: 916-686-8363. p. 140

Minshall, Kate, Asst Librn, Enfield Free Public Library, 23 Main St, Enfield, NH, 03748. Tel: 603-632-7145. p. 1363

Minshull, Mary-Anne, Dir & Librn, Southwestern Manitoba Regional Library, Pierson Library, 64 Railway Ave, Pierson, MB, R0M 1S0, CANADA. Tel: 204-634-2215. p. 2588

Minson, Ashlee, Br Mgr, Lonoke County Libraries, 204 E Second St, Lonoke, AR, 72086-2858. p. 102

Minson, Val, Assoc Dean, Research, University of Florida Libraries, 1545 W University Ave, Gainesville, FL, 32611-7000. Tel: 352-273-2880. p. 407

Minter, Elizabeth, Librn, East Central Community College, 275 E Broad St, Decatur, MS, 39327. Tel: 601-635-2111, Ext 219, 601-635-6219. p. 1216

Minton, JoNell, Dir, Dunklin County Library, 209 N Main, Kennett, MO, 63857. Tel: 573-888-2261, 573-888-3561. p. 1258

Minton, Kyle, Librn, Durham Technical Community College, Northern Durham Center, 2401 Snow Hill Rd, Durham, NC, 27712. Tel: 919-536-7240. p. 1685

Mintz, Loren, Health Sci Librn, Carroll University, 100 N East Ave, Waukesha, WI, 53186. Tel: 262-524-7674. p. 2484

Minuti, Aurelia, Archivist, Head, Ref, Albert Einstein College of Medicine, Jack & Pearl Resnick Campus, 1300 Morris Park Ave, Bronx, NY, 10461-1924. Tel: 718-430-3108. p. 1497

Minx, Christine, Mkt & Commun Relations Mgr, Upper Arlington Public Library, 2800 Tremont Rd, Columbus, OH, 43221. Tel: 614-486-9621. p. 1778

Mirabal, Margot, Coordr, Pub Relations & Outreach, Mkt, Murrell Library & Commons, Missouri Valley College, 500 E College St, Marshall, MO, 65340. Tel: 660-831-4180, 660-831-4181. p. 1260

Miracle, Maggie, Librn, Pulaski County Public Library, Science Hill Branch, 215 Main St, Science Hill, KY, 42553. Tel: 606-423-4221. p. 875

Miracle, Manuela, Br Mgr, Somerset County Library System of New Jersey, Mary Jacobs Memorial, 64 Washington St, Rocky Hill, NJ, 08553. Tel: 908-458-8430. p. 1392

Miramontes, Mercedes, Fac Librn, Phoenix College, 1202 W Thomas Rd, Phoenix, AZ, 85013. Tel: 602-285-7457. p. 72

Mirams, Doug, Mgr, Br Serv, Pickering Public Library, One The Esplanade, Pickering, ON, L1V 2R6, CANADA. Tel: 905-831-6265, Ext 6003. p. 2672

Mirams, Doug, Mgr, Br Serv, Pickering Public Library, Claremont Branch, 4941 Old Brock Rd, Claremont, ON, L1Y 1A9, CANADA. Tel: 905-649-3341. p. 2673

Mirams, Doug, Mgr, Br Serv, Pickering Public Library, George Ashe Library, 470 Kingston Rd, Pickering, ON, L1V 1A4, CANADA. Tel: 905-420-2254. p. 2673

Miranda, Elisabeth, Dir, Blossburg Memorial Library, 307 Main St, Blossburg, PA, 16912. Tel: 570-638-2197. p. 1913

Miranda, Jack J, ILL Tech, United States Naval War College Library, 686 Cushing Rd, Newport, RI, 02841-1207. Tel: 401-841-2641. p. 2035

Miranda, Joseph, Budget Analyst/Journal Ed, Northeastern University School of Law Library, 416 Huntington Ave, Boston, MA, 02115. Tel: 617-373-3552. p. 999

Miranda, Odalys, Cat, Oakwood University, 7000 Adventist Blvd NW, Huntsville, AL, 35896. Tel: 256-726-7246. p. 22

Miranda, Salvatore, Head, Adult Serv, Tarpon Springs Public Library, 138 E Lemon St, Tarpon Springs, FL, 34689. Tel: 727-943-4922. p. 450

Mirando, Louis, Dir, Torys LLP Library, 79 Wellington St W, Ste 3000, Toronto, ON, M5K 1N2, CANADA. Tel: 416-865-8158. p. 2697

Mire, Heather, Asst Librn, Sharp HealthCare, 7901 Frost St, San Diego, CA, 92123. Tel: 858-939-3242. p. 222

Mire, Jaime, Ref Librn, Trinity Valley Community College Library, 100 Cardinal Dr, Athens, TX, 75751. Tel: 903-675-6260. p. 2137

Mireles, Pura, Dir, Laguna Vista Public Library, 1300 Palm Blvd, Laguna Vista, TX, 78578. Tel: 956-943-7155. p. 2208

Miriello, Susan, Exec Dir, Mifflin County Library, 123 N Wayne St, Lewistown, PA, 17044-1794. Tel: 717-242-2391. p. 1955

Mirkin, Sima, Digital Res/Metadata Librn, American University, 4300 Nebraska Ave NW, Washington, DC, 20016-8182. Tel: 202-274-4344. p. 360

Mirra, Teresa, Youth Serv Librn, Lakeville Public Library, Four Precinct St, Lakeville, MA, 02347. Tel: 508-947-9028. p. 1026

Miser, Lisa, Librn, Proctor Free Library, Four Main St, Proctor, VT, 05765. Tel: 802-459-3539. p. 2292

Misfeldt, Rian, Dir, Libr Serv, SIAST-Saskatchewan Institute of Applied Science & Technology, 600 Saskatchewan St W, Moose Jaw, SK, S6H 4R4, CANADA. Tel: 306-775-7710. p. 2743

Miskewitch, Annie, Exec Dir, Schaumburg Township District Library, 130 S Roselle Rd, Schaumburg, IL, 60193. Tel: 847-923-3200. p. 645

Misko, Nicole, Ch, Licia & Mason Beekley Community Library, Ten Central Ave, New Hartford, CT, 06057. Tel: 860-379-7235. p. 325

Misner, Ann, Dir, Notus Public Library, 387 First St, PO Box 169, Notus, ID, 83656-0169. Tel: 208-459-8247. p. 528

Misner, Doug, Colls Mgr, Libr Mgr, Utah State Historical Society, 7292 S State St, Midvale, UT, 84047. Tel: 801-245-7227. p. 2266

Misquez, Sarah, Br Mgr, San Diego County Library, Jacumba Branch, 44605 Old Hwy 80, Jacumba, CA, 91934. Tel: 619-766-4608. p. 217

Missaghieh Klawitter, Sahra, Circ & Reserves Mgr, University of California, Riverside, 900 University Ave, Riverside, CA, 92521. Tel: 951-827-3220. p. 203

Missaghieh Klawitter, Sahra, Circulation/Reserves Services Mgr, University of California, Riverside, Raymond L Orbach Science Library, 900 University Ave, Riverside, CA, 92521. Tel: 951-827-3701. p. 203

Misselt, Tanya, Libr Dir, River Falls Public Library, 140 Union St, River Falls, WI, 54022. Tel: 715-426-3498. p. 2474

Missner, Emily, Ref Librn, Drexel University Libraries, Hagerty Library, 33rd & Market Sts, Philadelphia, PA, 19104-2875. Tel: 215-895-6164. p. 1976

Missonis, George E, AV, Albright College, 13th & Exeter Sts, Reading, PA, 19604. Tel: 610-921-7203. p. 2000

Mistery, Deepam, Outreach Coordr, Syst, Slippery Rock University of Pennsylvania, 109 Campus Loop, Slippery Rock, PA, 16057. Tel: 724-738-2058. p. 2007

Mistry, Kirti, Acq Assoc, Sheridan College Library, 1430 Trafalgar Rd, Oakville, ON, L6H 2L1, CANADA. Tel: 905-459-7533, Ext 2487. p. 2663

Mitch, Joseph, Librn, Buffalo & Erie County Public Library System, Crane, 633 Elmwood Ave, Buffalo, NY, 14222. Tel: 716-883-6651. p. 1508

Mitchel, Sam, Dir, Libr Serv, Ankeny Kirkendall Public Library, 1250 SW District Dr, Ankeny, IA, 50023. Tel: 515-965-6460. p. 731

Mitchell, Adriana, Managing Librn, Brooklyn Public Library, Brighton Beach, 16 Brighton First Rd, Brooklyn, NY, 11235. Tel: 718-946-2917. p. 1502

Mitchell, Amy, Marketing & Communications Coord, Beloit Public Library, 605 Eclipse Blvd, Beloit, WI, 53511. Tel: 608-364-5743. p. 2423

Mitchell, Ashley, Mgr, District of Columbia Public Library, Dorothy I Height/Benning Neighborhood Library, 3935 Benning Rd NE, Washington, DC, 20019. Tel: 202-281-2583. p. 364
Mitchell, Ashley, Ad, Camden County Library System, 203 Laurel Rd, Voorhees, NJ, 08043. Tel: 856-772-1636. p. 1450
Mitchell, Ashley, Ms, Br Mgr, Enoch Pratt Free Library, Edmondson Avenue Branch, 4330 Edmondson Ave, Baltimore, MD, 21229-1615. Tel: 443-984-4930. p. 953
Mitchell, Barb, Librn, Henry A Malley Memorial Library, 101 S Lincoln, Broadus, MT, 59317. Tel: 406-436-2812. p. 1290
Mitchell, Barb, County Coordr, Cambria County Library System & District Center, 248 Main St, Johnstown, PA, 15901. Tel: 814-536-5131. p. 1947
Mitchell, Becky, Dir, Challis Public Library, 531 W Main St, Challis, ID, 83226. Tel: 208-879-4267. p. 519
Mitchell, Beverly, Art & Dance Librn, Southern Methodist University, Hamon Arts Library, 6101 N Bishop Blvd, Dallas, TX, 75275. Tel: 214-768-1855. p. 2168
Mitchell, Carol, Br Mgr, Dayton Metro Library, Huber Heights, 6160 Chambersburg Rd, Dayton, OH, 45424. Tel: 937-496-8934. p. 1779
Mitchell, Chiquita, Libr Tech, Ser, Elizabeth City State University, 1704 Weeksville Rd, Elizabeth City, NC, 27909. Tel: 252-335-8519. p. 1687
Mitchell, Christie, Exec Dir, Library Association of La Jolla, 1008 Wall St, La Jolla, CA, 92037. Tel: 858-454-5872. p. 154
Mitchell, Christie, Sr Ref Librn, Ridgefield Library Association Inc, 472 Main St, Ridgefield, CT, 06877-4585. Tel: 203-438-2282. p. 335
Mitchell, Constance, Libr Dir, Eureka Public Library, 606 N Main St, Eureka, KS, 67045. Tel: 620-583-6222. p. 807
Mitchell, Cory, Coll Develop Librn, University of Wisconsin-Stout, 315 Tenth Ave, Menomonie, WI, 54751-0790. Tel: 715-232-2363. p. 2456
Mitchell, Dana, Project Leader, United States Forest Service, George W Andrews Forestry Sciences Lab, 521 Devall Dr, Auburn, AL, 36849-5418. Tel: 334-826-8700, Ext 123. p. 6
Mitchell, Danijela, Br Mgr, Carteret County Public Library, Bogue Banks, 320 Salter Path Rd, Ste W, Pine Knoll Shores, NC, 28512. Tel: 252-648-7726. p. 1674
Mitchell, Danijela, Br Mgr, Carteret County Public Library, Newport Public Library, 210 Howard Blvd, Newport, NC, 28570. Tel: 252-648-7727. p. 1674
Mitchell, Debbie, Libr Dir, Lovington Public Library, 115 S Main Ave, Lovington, NM, 88260. Tel: 575-396-3144. p. 1472
Mitchell, Deborah, Archivist, Museum of North Idaho, 115 Northwest Blvd, Coeur d'Alene, ID, 83814. Tel: 208-664-3448. p. 519
Mitchell, Devan, Mgr, Info Tech, Fraser Valley Regional Library, 34589 Delair Rd, Abbotsford, BC, V2S 5Y1, CANADA. Tel: 604-859-7141. p. 2561
Mitchell, Eileen, Principal Libr Asst, Beach Haven Public Library, 219 N Beach Ave, Beach Haven, NJ, 08008. Tel: 609-492-7081. p. 1389
Mitchell, Eleanor, Dir, Libr Serv, Dickinson College, 28 N College St, Carlisle, PA, 17013-2311. Tel: 717-245-1864. p. 1919
Mitchell, Emanuel, Dir, Libr Serv, Georgia Department of Corrections, Office of Library Services, 7175 Manor Rd, Columbus, GA, 31907. Tel: 706-568-2439. p. 472
Mitchell, Emanuel S, Dir, Augusta-Richmond County Public Library, 823 Telfair St, Augusta, GA, 30901. Tel: 706-821-2600. p. 466
Mitchell, Erik, Univ Librn, University of California, San Diego, 9500 Gilman Dr, Mail Code 0175G, La Jolla, CA, 92093-0175. Tel: 858-534-3060. p. 154
Mitchell, Greg, Dir, Denison Public Library, 300 W Gandy St, Denison, TX, 75020-3153. Tel: 903-465-1797. p. 2170
Mitchell, Gretchen, Asst Dir, Support Serv, Jacksonville Public Library, 303 N Laura St, Jacksonville, FL, 32202-3505. Tel: 904-630-1666. p. 411
Mitchell, Heather, Exec Dir, Hopkinton Historical Society, 300 Main St, Hopkinton, NH, 03229. Tel: 603-746-3825. p. 1368
Mitchell, Jana, Ref Mgr, Pine Bluff & Jefferson County Library System, Main Library, 600 S Main St, Pine Bluff, AR, 71601. Tel: 870-534-4802. p. 107
Mitchell, Jarrett, Supvr, Elkhart Public Library, Pierre Moran Branch, 2400 Benham Ave, Elkhart, IN, 46517. Tel: 574-294-6418. p. 680
Mitchell, Jeanette L, Circ, Libr Assoc I, Texas A&M University-Texarkana, 7101 University Ave, Texarkana, TX, 75503. Tel: 903-223-3100. p. 2248
Mitchell, Jennifer, Br Supvr, Licking County Library, Hervey Memorial, 15 N Main, Utica, OH, 43080. Tel: 740-892-2400. p. 1808
Mitchell, Jesse, Tech Serv, Huntington Woods Public Library, 26415 Scotia Rd, Huntington Woods, MI, 48070. Tel: 248-543-9720. p. 1118
Mitchell, John, Dir, Highwood Public Library, 102 Highwood Ave, Highwood, IL, 60040-1597. Tel: 847-432-5404. p. 599
Mitchell, Joshua, Br Mgr, San Diego County Library, Julian Branch, 1850 Hwy 78, Julian, CA, 92036. Tel: 760-765-0370. p. 217
Mitchell, Julie, Librn, Willow Public Library, 23557 W Willow Community Center Circle, Willow, AK, 99688. Tel: 907-861-7655. p. 52
Mitchell, Julie, Asst Dir, University of British Columbia Library, Irving K Barber Learning Centre, 1961 East Mall, Vancouver, BC, V6T 1Z1, CANADA. Tel: 604-827-4307. p. 2580
Mitchell, Kelly, Ref Librn, St Charles Community College, 4601 Mid Rivers Mall Dr, Cottleville, MO, 63376. Tel: 636-922-8798. p. 1244
Mitchell, Kim, Libr Asst, Skagit Valley College, Whidbey Island Campus Library, 1900 SE Pioneer Way, Oak Harbor, WA, 98277-3099. Tel: 360-679-5322. p. 2371
Mitchell, Kimberly, Interim Dir, Libr Serv, Albany College of Pharmacy & Health Sciences, 106 New Scotland Ave, Albany, NY, 12208. Tel: 518-694-7124. p. 1481
Mitchell, Lany, Dir, Wesley Public Library, 206 W Main St, Wesley, IA, 50483. Tel: 515-679-4214. p. 790
Mitchell, Lisa, Research Librn, Alabama Power Co, 600 N 18th St, Birmingham, AL, 35203-2206. Tel: 205-257-4466. p. 6
Mitchell, Lise, Dir, Grand Ledge Area District Library, 131 E Jefferson St, Grand Ledge, MI, 48837-1534. Tel: 517-622-3550. p. 1109
Mitchell, Margaret, Librn, Abington Township Public Library, Roslyn Branch, 2412 Avondale Ave, Roslyn, PA, 19001-4203. Tel: 215-886-9818. p. 1903
Mitchell, Marilyn, Librn, South Haven Township Library, 104 W Baird, South Haven, KS, 67140. Tel: 620-892-5268. p. 836
Mitchell, Mary, Br Mgr, Phoenix Public Library, Ocotillo Library & Workforce Literacy Center, 102 W Southern Ave, Phoenix, AZ, 85041. p. 72
Mitchell, Mary, Librn, Arlington Public Library, City Hall, 500 W First St, Arlington, OR, 97812. Tel: 541-454-2444. p. 1872
Mitchell, Mason, Dir, Dir, University of Saint Thomas, Archbishop Ireland Memorial Library, 2260 Summit Ave, Mail Stop IRL, Saint Paul, MN, 55105. Tel: 651-962-5456. p. 1202
Mitchell, Michael, Head, E-Res & Ser, University of Louisiana at Lafayette, 400 E St Mary Blvd, Lafayette, LA, 70503. Tel: 337-482-6197. p. 893
Mitchell, Michael, Chairperson, Houston Community College - Southeast College, Eastside Campus Library, 6815 Rustic St, Houston, TX, 77087. Tel: 713-718-7050. p. 2194
Mitchell, Michael, Chairperson, Houston Community College - Southeast College, Felix Fraga ERC, 301 N Drennan St, Houston, TX, 77003. Tel: 713-718-6960. p. 2195
Mitchell, Michele, Dir, Birmingham Public Library, 310 Main St, Birmingham, IA, 52535. Tel: 319-498-4423. p. 735
Mitchell, Michele, Head, Circ, Hillside Public Library, John F Kennedy Plaza, 1409 Liberty Ave, Hillside, NJ, 07205. Tel: 973-923-4413. p. 1408
Mitchell, Michelle, Libr Asst, Phillips County Library, Ten S Fourth St E, Malta, MT, 59538. Tel: 406-654-2407. p. 1299
Mitchell, Michelle K, Instrul Serv Librn, State University of New York, PO Box 901, Morrisville, NY, 13408. Tel: 315-684-6055. p. 1574
Mitchell, Nicole Mesich, Exec Dir, Flenniken Public Library, 102 E George St, Carmichaels, PA, 15320-1202. Tel: 724-966-5263. p. 1919
Mitchell, Patsy, Br Mgr, Aiken-Bamberg-Barnwell-Edgefield Regional Library, Johnston Branch, 407 Calhoun St, Johnston, SC, 29832. Tel: 803-275-5157. p. 2045
Mitchell, Paula, Librn, Branchville Correctional Facility, 21390 Old State Rd 37, Branchville, IN, 47514. Tel: 812-843-5921, Ext 4328. p. 672
Mitchell, Paula, Spec Coll Librn, Southern Utah University, 351 W University Blvd, Cedar City, UT, 84720. Tel: 435-586-7976. p. 2262
Mitchell, Perida, Ref (Info Servs), Thomas County Public Library System, 201 N Madison St, Thomasville, GA, 31792-5414. Tel: 229-225-5252. p. 499
Mitchell, Rebecca, Libr Dir, Stewart Public Library, 322 Fifth Ave, Stewart, BC, V0T 1W0, CANADA. Tel: 236-749-2003. p. 2576
Mitchell, Robin Lynn, Exec Dir of Advancement, University of Virginia, 160 McCormick Rd, Charlottesville, VA, 22903. Tel: 434-924-3021. p. 2310
Mitchell, Ronda, Libr Mgr, Boone Daniel Regional Library, Southern Boone County Public Library, 109 N Main St, Ashland, MO, 65010. Tel: 573-657-7378. p. 1243
Mitchell, Sarah, Actg Br Mgr, Asst Dir, Kanawha County Public Library, Marmet Branch, 9303 Oregon Ave, Marmet, WV, 25315. Tel: 304-949-6628. p. 2400
Mitchell, Sarah, Actg Br Mgr, Asst Dir, Kanawha County Public Library, Riverside, One Warrior Way, Belle, WV, 25015. Tel: 304-949-2400. p. 2400
Mitchell, Sarah, Asst Dir, Kanawha County Public Library, 123 Capitol St, Charleston, WV, 25301. Tel: 304-343-4646. p. 2400
Mitchell, Sarah, Asst Dir, Kanawha County Public Library, Saint Albans Branch, 602 Fourth St, Saint Albans, WV, 25177. Tel: 304-722-4244. p. 2400
Mitchell, Sharyn, Res Serv Spec, Berea College, 100 Campus Dr, Berea, KY, 40404. Tel: 859-985-3892. p. 849
Mitchell, Stephanie, Librn, Pima County Juvenile Court Center Library, 2225 E Ajo Way, Tucson, AZ, 85713-6295. Tel: 520-724-2082. p. 82
Mitchell, Sylvia, Head, Circ, Milton Public Library, 476 Canton Ave, Milton, MA, 02186-3299. Tel: 617-698-5757. p. 1036
Mitchell, Tracey, Libr Asst, Vista Grande Public Library, 14 Avenida Torreon, Santa Fe, NM, 87508-9199. Tel: 505-466-7323. p. 1477
Mitchell, Treavan, Tech, Jackson-Madison County Library, North Branch, Eight Stonebridge Blvd, Ste F & G, Jackson, TN, 38305. p. 2102
Mitchell, Valencia, Adjunct Ref Librn, Cerritos College Library, 11110 Alondra Blvd, Norwalk, CA, 90650. Tel: 562-860-2451, Ext 2430. p. 184
Mitchell-Botts, Heather, Instruction Librn, University of Cincinnati, 4200 Clermont College Dr, Batavia, OH, 45103-1785. Tel: 513-732-5271. p. 1749

Mitchem, Crystal, Library Teacher/Resource Specialist, New Mexico School for the Deaf, 1060 Cerrillos Rd, Santa Fe, NM, 87505. Tel: 505-216-2047. p. 1475

Mitchener, Andy, IT Mgr, Central Kansas Library System, 1409 Williams St, Great Bend, KS, 67530-4020. Tel: 620-792-4865. p. 810

Mitchener, Crystal L, Libr Mgr, Wake County Public Library System, Wendell Community Library, 207 S Hollybrook Rd, Wendell, NC, 27591. Tel: 919-365-2600. p. 1711

Mitcheroney, Paul, Pres, Canton Historical Society Library, 1400 Washington St, Canton, MA, 02021. Tel: 781-615-9040. p. 1009

Mitnick, Eva, Dir, Engagement & Learning, Los Angeles Public Library System, 630 W Fifth St, Los Angeles, CA, 90071. Tel: 213-228-7527. p. 163

Mitschelen, Donna, Supvr, Elkhart Public Library, Osolo, 3429 E Bristol St, Elkhart, IN, 46514. Tel: 574-264-7234. p. 680

Mitschke, Julia, Libr Dir, Cedar Park Public Library, 550 Discovery Blvd, Cedar Park, TX, 78613. Tel: 512-401-5630. p. 2154

Mittag, Carol, Access Serv, ILL, Ref Serv, Concordia University Wisconsin, 12800 N Lake Shore Dr, Mequon, WI, 53097-2402. Tel: 262-243-4330. p. 2456

Mittge, Kevin, Ref Serv, Ad, Siuslaw Public Library District, 1460 Ninth St, Florence, OR, 97439. Tel: 541-997-3132. p. 1879

Mittge, Kevin K, Br Mgr, Siuslaw Public Library District, Mapleton Branch, 88148 Riverview Ave, Mapleton, OR, 97453. Tel: 541-268-4033. p. 1880

Mittman, Lisa, Br Mgr, Harford County Public Library, Abingdon Branch, 2510 Tollgate Rd, Abingdon, MD, 21009. Tel: 410-638-3990. p. 959

Mitton, Doris, Librn, Dalton Public Library, Town of Dalton Municipal Bldg, 756 Dalton Rd, Dalton, NH, 03598. Tel: 603-837-2751. p. 1360

Mitton, Lisa, Asst Librn, Attica Public Library, 305 S Perry St, Attica, IN, 47918. Tel: 765-764-4194. p. 668

Mitzenmacher, Joe, Reference & Electronic Services Librn, Loyola University Chicago Libraries, School of Law Library, Philip H Corboy Law Ctr, 25 E Pearson St, Chicago, IL, 60611. Tel: 312-915-6844. p. 564

Mixdorf, David, Libr Dir, South Sioux City Public Library, 2121 Dakota Ave, South Sioux City, NE, 68776. Tel: 402-494-7545. p. 1336

Mixon, JoAnn, Br Mgr, Southern Oklahoma Library System, Atoka County Library, 279 East A St, Atoka, OK, 74525. Tel: 580-889-3555. p. 1841

Mixon, Katherine, Br Mgr, Bienville Parish Library, Gibsland Branch, 1141 First St, Gibsland, LA, 71028. Tel: 318-843-1690. p. 881

Miyamoto, Jeannie, Librn, Kauai Community Correctional Center Library, 3-5351 Kuhio Hwy, Lihue, HI, 96766. Tel: 808-241-3050, Ext 235. p. 514

Miyamoto, Rob, PhD, Library Contact, Shriners Hospitals for Children, 1310 Punahou St, Honolulu, HI, 96826-1099. Tel: 808-951-3693. p. 512

Miyaoka, Mayumi, Archivist, Ref & Instruction Librn, Saint Joseph's College, 222 Clinton Ave, Brooklyn, NY, 11205-3697. Tel: 718-940-5883. p. 1506

Mizak, Megan, Br Mgr, Roanoke Public Libraries, Gainsboro, 15 Patton Ave NW, Roanoke, VA, 24016. Tel: 540-853-2540. p. 2345

Mize, Jennifer, Asst Dir, Graysville Public Library, 136 Harrison Ave, Graysville, TN, 37338. Tel: 423-775-9242, Ext 4. p. 2100

Mize, Marie, Access Serv Mgr, University of Georgia, Alexander Campbell King Law Library, 225 Herty Dr, Athens, GA, 30602-6018. Tel: 706-542-1922. p. 459

Mize, Robin, Cat Librn, Dir, Tech Serv, University of Illinois at Springfield, One University Plaza, MS BRK-140, Springfield, IL, 62703-5407. Tel: 217-206-7113. p. 651

Mizell, Amy, Br Mgr, Catahoula Parish Library, Jonesville Branch, 205 Pond St, Jonesville, LA, 71343. Tel: 318-339-7070. p. 891

Mizikar, Alisa, Ref Librn, Wittenberg University, 801 Woodlawn Ave, Springfield, OH, 45504. Tel: 937-327-7515. p. 1821

Mizla, Susan, Asst Dir, Levi E Coe Library, 414 Main St, Middlefield, CT, 06455-1207. Tel: 860-349-3857. p. 321

Mizzy, Danianne, Assoc Univ Librn, Cornell University Library, 201 Olin Library, Ithaca, NY, 14853. Tel: 607-254-5257. p. 1551

Mlinar, Courtney, Head Librn, Austin Community College, Elgin Campus Library, 1501 W US Hwy 290, 3rd Flr, Rm 1376, Elgin, TX, 78621. Tel: 512-223-9433. p. 2138

Mlsna, Kathryn, Asst Dir, Scholarly Resource Mgmt, Medical College of Wisconsin Libraries, Health Research Ctr, 3rd Flr, 8701 Watertown Plank Rd, Milwaukee, WI, 53226-0509. Tel: 414-955-8305. p. 2459

Moa, Juan, Mgr, Dallas Public Library, Dallas West, 2332 Singleton Blvd, Dallas, TX, 75212-3790. Tel: 214-670-6445. p. 2165

Moa, Juan, Br Mgr, Dallas Public Library, North Oak Cliff, 302 W Tenth St, Dallas, TX, 75208-4617. Tel: 214-670-7555. p. 2166

Moak, Tom, Supvr, Mid-Columbia Libraries, West Richland Branch, 3803 W Van Giesen St, West Richland, WA, 99353. Tel: 509-967-3191. p. 2367

Moan, Jerry, Dr, Dir, Learning Res, Free Lutheran Bible College & Seminary, Heritage Hall, 2nd Flr, 3134 E Medicine Lake Blvd, Plymouth, MN, 55441-3008. Tel: 763-412-2035. p. 1193

Moats, Jean, Dir, Libr Serv, Johnson & Wales University, 801 W Trade St, Charlotte, NC, 28202. Tel: 980-598-1608. p. 1680

Moats, Linda, Circ Supvr, Perry Public Library, 3753 Main St, Perry, OH, 44081-9501. Tel: 440-259-3300. p. 1815

Moberly, Amy, Asst Dir, Tech & Admin Serv, California Western School of Law Library, 290 Cedar St, San Diego, CA, 92101. Tel: 619-525-1421. p. 215

Mobley, Corisa, Libr Asst, Rutgers University Libraries, George F Smith Library of the Health Sciences, 30 12th Ave, Newark, NJ, 07101. Tel: 973-972-6528. p. 1425

Mobley, Darlynn, Dir, Woodruff Community Library, 6414 W First St, Woodruff, AZ, 85942. Tel: 928-524-3885. p. 85

Mobley, LaTrelle, Sr Libr Mgr, Live Oak Public Libraries, Southwest Chatham Branch, 14097 Abercorn St, Savannah, GA, 31419. Tel: 912-927-4079. p. 496

Mobley, Therese, Outreach & Instruction Librn, Fletcher Technical Community College Library, 1407 Hwy 311, Rm 128, Schriever, LA, 70395. Tel: 985-448-7945. p. 907

Moblo, Brandon, Archivist & Spec Coll Librn, Hobart & William Smith Colleges, 334 Pulteney St, Geneva, NY, 14456. Tel: 315-781-3550. p. 1538

Mock, Marci, Coll Develop Librn, Sheridan County Public Library System, 335 W Alger St, Sheridan, WY, 82801. Tel: 307-674-8585. p. 2499

Mockovak, Holly E, Head Librn, Boston University Libraries, Music Library, 771 Commonwealth Ave, Boston, MA, 02215. Tel: 617-353-3705. p. 993

Moczygemba, Keri, Head Librn, Austin Community College, Hays Campus Library, 1200 Kohlers Crossing, 3rd Flr, Rm 1305, Kyle, TX, 78640. Tel: 512-223-1585. p. 2138

Modisette, Tabitha, Circ Assoc, Union University, 1050 Union University Dr, Jackson, TN, 38305-3697. Tel: 731-661-5070. p. 2102

Modrell, Carolyn, Asst Librn, Anita Public Library, 812 Third St, Anita, IA, 50020. Tel: 712-762-3639. p. 731

Modrow, William, Head, Spec Coll & Archives, Miami University Libraries, 151 S Campus Ave, Oxford, OH, 45056. Tel: 513-529-2024. p. 1811

Modys, Rebecca, Principal Librn, Youth Coll Develop Librn, Lee County Library System, Library Processing, 881 Gunnery Rd N, Ste 2, Lehigh Acres, FL, 33971-1246. Tel: 239-533-4170. p. 403

Moe, Rebecca, Dir, Alden-Ewell Free Library, 13280 Broadway, Alden, NY, 14004. Tel: 716-937-7082. p. 1484

Moe, Tammi, Dir, Octavia Fellin Public Library, 115 W Hill Ave, Gallup, NM, 87301. Tel: 505-863-1291, Ext 14017. p. 1468

Moeckel, Lisa, Assoc Dean, Academic Undergrad Success, Syracuse University Libraries, 222 Waverly Ave, Syracuse, NY, 13244-2010. Tel: 315-443-9790. p. 1650

Moeller, Amanda, E-Resources & Systems Librn, University of Wisconsin-River Falls, 410 S Third St, River Falls, WI, 54022. Tel: 715-425-3963. p. 2474

Moeller, Brittany, Libr Dir, Carnegie Public Library, 513 N Orleans Ave, Dell Rapids, SD, 57022-1637. Tel: 605-428-3595. p. 2076

Moeller, Mary Catherine, Fac Res Serv/Ref Serv Librn, University of Michigan, Kresge Library Services, Stephen M Ross School of Business, 701 Tappan St, Ann Arbor, MI, 48109-1234. Tel: 734-647-4936. p. 1079

Moeller, Max, Curator, Hagley Museum & Library, 298 Buck Rd E, Wilmington, DE, 19807. Tel: 302-658-2400. p. 357

Moeller, Paul, Team Lead, Digital Asset Mgmt, Team Lead, Discovery Servs Team, Team Lead, Metadata Ops, University of Colorado Boulder, 1720 Pleasant St, Boulder, CO, 80309. Tel: 303-492-8705. p. 267

Moeller, Robin, Dr, Assoc Prof, Appalachian State University, Reich College of Education, Ste 204, 151 College St, ASU Box 32086, Boone, NC, 28608. Tel: 828-262-2243. p. 2789

Moeller-Peiffer, Kathleen, Dep State Librn, Libr Support Serv, New Jersey State Library, 185 W State St, Trenton, NJ, 08608. Tel: 609-278-2640, Ext 157. p. 1448

Moellering, Katie, Head, Adult Serv, Emmet O'Neal Library, 50 Oak St, Mountain Brook, AL, 35213. Tel: 205-879-0459. p. 31

Moen, Caitlin, Circ Coordr, Charlotte Mecklenburg Library, 310 N Tryon St, Charlotte, NC, 28202-2176. Tel: 704-416-0100. p. 1679

Moen, Lindsay, Pub Serv Librn, University of Iowa Libraries, Special Collections & Archives, 100 Main Library, 125 W Washington St, Iowa City, IA, 52242-1420. Tel: 319-384-3536. p. 761

Moennig, Nancy, Librn, South County Public Library District, 106 Main St, Brussels, IL, 62013. Tel: 618-883-2522. p. 545

Moerschell, Deborah, Co-Dir of Youth Services, Kent Library Association, 32 N Main St, Kent, CT, 06757. Tel: 860-927-3761. p. 319

Moesel, Tanya, Head, Youth Serv, George H & Ella M Rodgers Memorial Library, 194 Derry Rd, Hudson, NH, 03051. Tel: 603-886-6030. p. 1368

Moffat, Kael, Info Literacy Librn, Saint Martin's University, 5000 Abbey Way SE, Lacey, WA, 98503. Tel: 360-688-2257. p. 2368

Moffat, Lorne, IT Mgr, Wapiti Regional Library, 145 12th St E, Prince Albert, SK, S6V 1B7, CANADA. Tel: 306-764-0712. p. 2745

Moffatt, Karyn, Assoc Prof, McGill University, 3661 Peel St, Montreal, QC, H3A 1X1, CANADA. Tel: 514-398-4204. p. 2796

Moffett, Robert, Div Chief of Access Serv, Gail Borden Public Library District, 270 N Grove Ave, Elgin, IL, 60120-5596. Tel: 847-429-5989. p. 583

Moffitt, Amy, Dir, Iowa Central Community College, One Triton Circle, Fort Dodge, IA, 50501. Tel: 515-576-7201, Ext 1156. p. 754

Moffitt, Mallory, Tech Serv, Musser Public Library, 408 E Second St, Muscatine, IA, 52761. Tel: 563-263-3065, Ext 122. p. 772

Moffler-Daykin, Kirsten, Learning Commons Mgr, Western Technical College Library, 400 Seventh St N, La Crosse, WI, 54601. Tel: 608-785-9142. p. 2447

Moga, John, Curator, Berrien County Historical Association Library, 313 N Cass St, Berrien Springs, MI, 49103-1038. Tel: 269-471-1202. p. 1085

Mogren, Diane, Libr Mgr, Federal Reserve Bank of Cleveland, 1455 E Sixth St, Cleveland, OH, 44114. p. 1770

Mohammad, Sandra, Br Mgr, Chicago Public Library, South Shore, 2505 E 73rd St, Chicago, IL, 60649. Tel: 312-747-5281. p. 557

Mohammad, Tamerlane, Br Mgr, Jefferson County Library System, McCollum Public, 405 N Main St, Wrens, GA, 30833-1142. Tel: 706-547-7567. p. 486

Mohammadi, Jane, Syst Librn, United States Army, Casey Memorial Library, 72nd St & 761st Tank Battalion, Bldg 3202, Fort Hood, TX, 76544-5024. Tel: 254-287-0025. p. 2178

Mohammed, G Salim, Librn, San Jose City College Library, LRC Bldg, 2nd & 3rd Flrs, 2100 Moorpark Ave, San Jose, CA, 95128-2799. Tel: 408-288-3775. p. 230

Mohammed, Yatty, Librn, Little Priest Tribal College Library, 601 E College Dr, Winnebago, NE, 68071. Tel: 402-878-2380, Ext 131. p. 1341

Mohanty, Suchi, Head of Libr, University of North Carolina at Chapel Hill, Robert B House Undergraduate, 203 South Rd, CB 3942, Chapel Hill, NC, 27514-3942. Tel: 919-962-1355. p. 1678

Mohd Shah, Zarina, Libr Serv Mgr, Wisconsin Talking Book & Braille Library, 813 W Wells St, Milwaukee, WI, 53233-1436. Tel: 414-286-3045. p. 2461

Mohess, Neera, ILL Librn, Ref & Instruction, Queensborough Community College, City University of New York, 222-05 56th Ave, Bayside, NY, 11364-1497. Tel: 718-281-5067. p. 1491

Mohl, Pam, Ch, Village Library of Morgantown, 207 N Walnut St, Morgantown, PA, 19543. Tel: 610-286-1022. p. 1966

Mohr, Deborah, Database Control Librn, Monroe Community College, LeRoy V Good Library, 1000 E Henrietta Rd, Rochester, NY, 14692. Tel: 585-292-2316. p. 1629

Mohr, Philip, Exec Dir, Des Plaines Historical Society Library, 781 Pearson St, Des Plaines, IL, 60016. Tel: 847-391-5399. p. 578

Mohr-Elzeki, Dahlal, Patient Educ Librn, McGill University Health Centre - Glen Site, 1001 Boul DeCarie, Rm B RC 0078, Montreal, QC, H4A 3J1, CANADA. Tel: 514-934-1934, Ext 22054. p. 2726

Mohundro, Margaret, Dir, Sanibel Public Library District, 770 Dunlop Rd, Sanibel, FL, 33957. Tel: 239-472-2483. p. 442

Moir, Jean, Supvr, Middlesex County Library, Strathroy Branch, 34 Frank St, Strathroy, ON, N7G 2R4, CANADA. Tel: 519-245-1290. p. 2682

Moir, Michael, Univ Archivist, York University Libraries, 4700 Keele St, North York, ON, M3J 1P3, CANADA. Tel: 416-736-2100, Ext 22457. p. 2661

Moisan, Jerome, Dir Gen, Department of Canadian Heritage, 1030 Innes Rd, Ottawa, ON, K1B 4S7, CANADA. Tel: 613-998-3721, Ext 157. p. 2666

Moisan, Patty, Head, Children's Servx, Harborfields Public Library, 31 Broadway, Greenlawn, NY, 11740. Tel: 631-757-4200. p. 1541

Moisio, Rebecca, Mkt/Pub Relations Coordr, Ashtabula County District Library, 4335 Park Ave, Ashtabula, OH, 44004. Tel: 440-997-9343, Ext 333. p. 1747

Moist, Shannon, Head, Ref Serv, Douglas College Library & Learning Centre, 700 Royal Ave, Rm N2100, New Westminster, BC, V3M 5Z5, CANADA. Tel: 604-527-5189. p. 2572

Mokia, Rosemary N, Dr, Head, Acq, Ser Librn, Grambling State University, 403 Main St, Grambling, LA, 71245-2761. Tel: 318-274-6122. p. 890

Mokonyama, John, Med Librn, Penn Medicine, Chester County Hospital Library, 701 E Marshall St, West Chester, PA, 19380. Tel: 610-431-5204. p. 2020

Molander, Shane, State Archivist, State Historical Society of North Dakota, North Dakota Heritage Ctr, 612 E Boulevard Ave, Bismarck, ND, 58505-0830. Tel: 701-328-2091. p. 1730

Molaro, Anthony, PhD, Assoc Prof, Prog Dir, Saint Catherine University, 2004 Randolph Ave, Mailstop No 4125, Saint Paul, MN, 55105. Tel: 651-690-6802. p. 2787

Molde, Angela, Librn, Palliser Regional Library, Mortlach Branch, 118 Rose St, Mortlach, SK, S0H 3E0, CANADA. Tel: 306-355-2202. p. 2743

Moldrem, Kristy, Actg Sr Librn, Los Angeles Public Library System, John Muir Branch Library, 1005 W 64th St, Los Angeles, CA, 90044-3605. Tel: 323-789-4800. p. 165

Moldrup, Wanda, Libr Mgr, Western Plains Library System, Seiling Public Library, 209 N Main St, Seiling, OK, 73663. Tel: 580-922-4259. p. 1845

Mole, Deborah, Ref & Instruction, University of Alaska Anchorage, Consortium Library, 3211 Providence Dr, Anchorage, AK, 99508-8176. Tel: 907-786-1871. p. 43

Mole, Jessica, Chief Exec Officer, New Tecumseth Public Library, 17 Victoria St E, Alliston, ON, L9R 1V6, CANADA. Tel: 705-435-0250. p. 2627

Moles, Sandrah, Head, Children's & Teen Serv, Lower Providence Community Library, 50 Parklane Dr, Eagleville, PA, 19403-1171. Tel: 610-666-6640. p. 1928

Molestina-Kurlat, Maria, Head, Reader Serv, The Morgan Library & Museum, 225 Madison Ave, New York, NY, 10016. Tel: 212-685-0008. p. 1592

Molina, Crissie, Br Mgr, Saint Tammany Parish Library, Covington Branch, 310 W 21st Ave, Covington, LA, 70433. Tel: 985-893-6280. p. 888

Molina, Daniel, Dir, Res Serv, Stearns, Weaver, Miller, Weissler, Alhadeff & Sitterson, 2200 Museum Tower, 150 W Flagler St, Miami, FL, 33130. Tel: 305-789-3225. p. 425

Molina, Hilda, Libr Dir, Elsa Public Library, 711 N Hidalgo St, Elsa, TX, 78543. Tel: 956-262-3061. p. 2175

Molina, Miguelina, Commun Serv, Suffern Free Library, 210 Lafayette Ave, Suffern, NY, 10901. Tel: 845-357-1237. p. 1647

Molinet, Andi, Head, Tech Serv, University of Denver, Westminster Law Library, Sturm College of Law, 2255 E Evans Ave, Denver, CO, 80208. Tel: 303-871-6363. p. 278

Molineux, Mary S, Ref Librn, College of William & Mary in Virginia, Earl Gregg Swem Library, One Landrum Dr, Williamsburg, VA, 23187. Tel: 757-221-3076. p. 2353

Molinski, Jennifer, Libr Dir, William H & Lucy F Rand Memorial Library, 160 Railroad St, Ste 2, North Troy, VT, 05859-9492. Tel: 802-988-4741. p. 2290

Molitor, Jackie, Ch, Germantown Community Library, N112W16957 Mequon Rd, Germantown, WI, 53022. Tel: 262-253-7760. p. 2437

Moll, Kirk, Dr, Electronic Res Librn, Pub Serv Librn, Shippensburg University, 1871 Old Main Dr, Shippensburg, PA, 17257. Tel: 717-477-1473. p. 2007

Mollenkamp, Amy, Mgr, West Georgia Regional Library, Dallas Public Library, 1010 E Memorial Dr, Dallas, GA, 30132. Tel: 770-445-5680. p. 470

Mollenkamp, Amy, Mgr, West Georgia Regional Library, New Georgia Public Library, 94 Ridge Rd, Dallas, GA, 30157. Tel: 770-459-8163. p. 470

Molleston, Missy, Libr Spec, Kirkwood Community College, Iowa City Campus Library, 107 Credit Center Bldg, 1816 Lower Muscatine Rd, Iowa City, IA, 52240. Tel: 319-887-3612, 319-887-3613. p. 738

Mollet, Angela, Adult Serv Mgr, Cedar Mill Community Library, 1080 NW Saltzman Rd, Portland, OR, 97229-5603. Tel: 503-644-0043, Ext 132. p. 1891

Mollette, Sarah, Librn, Research & Instruction Services, Marshall University Libraries, One John Marshall Dr, Huntington, WV, 25755-2060. Tel: 304-696-2335. p. 2405

Molleur, Elaine, Circ Librn, Weeks Public Library, 36 Post Rd, Greenland, NH, 03840-2312. Tel: 603-436-8548. p. 1365

Mollick, Nicole, Head, Ref, Plainedge Public Library, 1060 Hicksville Rd, North Massapequa, NY, 11758. Tel: 516-735-4133. p. 1607

Molloy, Larisa, Admin Librn, Hill Library, 1151 Parker Mountain Rd, Strafford, NH, 03884. Tel: 603-664-2800. p. 1381

Molloy, Patrick, Dir, Chicago Public Library, Government Publications Division, 400 S State St, Chicago, IL, 60605. Tel: 312-747-4051. p. 556

Molly, Lane A, Dir, Rowe Town Library, 318 Zoar Rd, Rowe, MA, 01367. Tel: 413-339-4761. p. 1050

Molnar, Stephanie, Br Mgr, Librn, Hamburg Public Library, Lake Shore, S-4857 Lake Shore Rd, Hamburg, NY, 14075. Tel: 716-627-3017. p. 1543

Moloney, Cathy, Libr Mgr, Florida Department of State, Division of Library & Information Services, R A Gray Bldg, 500 S Bronough St, Tallahassee, FL, 32399-0250. Tel: 850-245-6687. p. 446

Moloney, Cathy, Bur Chief, Florida Library Information Network, State Library & Archives of Florida, R A Gray Bldg, 500 S Bronough St, Tallahassee, FL, 32399-0250. Tel: 850-245-6687. p. 2763

Moloney, Patrick, Sr Librn, California Department of Corrections Library System, California Men's Colony-West, Colony Dr, Hwy 1, San Luis Obispo, CA, 93409. Tel: 805-547-7900, Ext 7185. p. 206

Molseed, Kelsey, Res & Instruction Librn, Randolph College, 2500 Rivermont Ave, Lynchburg, VA, 24503. Tel: 434-947-8133. p. 2330

Molstad, Diane, Libr Asst, Briar Cliff University, 3303 Rebecca St, Sioux City, IA, 51104. Tel: 712-279-5449. p. 782

Molstre, Rachel, Librn, Free Lutheran Bible College & Seminary, Heritage Hall, 2nd Flr, 3134 E Medicine Lake Blvd, Plymouth, MN, 55441-3008. Tel: 763-412-2035. p. 1193

Mombourquette, Mary Pat, Exec Dir, Cape Brenton Miners' Museum Library, 17 Museum St, Glace Bay, NS, B1A 5T8, CANADA. Tel: 902-849-4522. p. 2618

Momeni, Farzaneh, Commun Libr Mgr, Queens Library, Mitchell-Linden Community Library, 31-32 Union St, Flushing, NY, 11354. Tel: 718-539-2330. p. 1555

Mona, Corinne, Asst Librn, American Institute of Physics, One Physics Ellipse, College Park, MD, 20740. Tel: 301-209-3177. p. 962

Monaco, Beth, Libr Supvr, Neiswander Library of Homeopathy, 1006 W 8th Ave, Ste B, King of Prussia, PA, 19406. Tel: 800-456-7818, Ext 2251. p. 1948

Monaghan, Mary Ann, Access & Collection Services Specialist, St John's University Library, Rittenberg Law Library, 8000 Utopia Pkwy, Jamaica, NY, 11439. Tel: 718-990-6829. p. 1556

Monahan, Agatha, Adult Serv, West Hartford Public Library, 20 S Main St, West Hartford, CT, 06107-2432. Tel: 860-561-6950. p. 345

Monbarren, Denise, Spec Coll Librn, The College of Wooster Libraries, 1140 Beall Ave, Wooster, OH, 44691-2364. Tel: 330-263-2527. p. 1833

Moncada, Joseph, Dir, Innovation & Integration, Oakville Public Library, 120 Navy St, Oakville, ON, L6J 2Z4, CANADA. Tel: 905-815-2042. p. 2662

Moncada, Julie D, Assoc Dir, Beauregard Parish Library, 205 S Washington Ave, DeRidder, LA, 70634. Tel: 337-463-6217. p. 888

Monchar, Leslie, Mrs, Librn, Assumption College for Sisters Library, 200 A Morris Ave, Denville, NJ, 07834. Tel: 973-957-0188. p. 1399

Moncrief, Charlotte, Syst Coordr, Library Management Network, Inc, 1405 Plaza St SE, Decatur, AL, 35603. Tel: 256-822-2371. p. 2761

Moncrief, Connie, Br Mgr, Pine Mountain Regional Library, Yatesville Public, 77 Childs Ave, Yatesville, GA, 31097-3661. Tel: 706-472-3048. p. 488

Moncrief, Erica, Libr Serv Mgr, Capital Health Medical Center-Hopewell, One Capital Way, Pennington, NJ, 08534. Tel: 609-303-4125. p. 1434

Moncrief, Erica, Dir, Libr Serv, Capital Health Regional Medical Center, 750 Brunswick Ave, Trenton, NJ, 08638. Tel: 609-303-4125. p. 1447

Moncrief, Lisa, Asst to the Dir, Athens Regional Library System, 2025 Baxter St, Athens, GA, 30606-6331. Tel: 706-613-3650, Ext 351. p. 458

Monday, Joyce, Librn, Butte County Public Law Library, 1675 Montgomery St, Oroville, CA, 95965. Tel: 530-538-7122. p. 190

Monday, Laura, Head, Circ, Worth Public Library District, 6917 W 111th St, Worth, IL, 60482. Tel: 708-448-2855. p. 665

Mondello, Gail, Circ Supvr, Gloucester, Lyceum & Sawyer Free Library, Two Dale Ave, Gloucester, MA, 01930. Tel: 978-325-5500. p. 1021

Mondo, John, Delivery Coordr, ILL Coordr, University at Buffalo Libraries-State University of New York, Charles B Sears Law Library, John Lord O'Brian Hall, 211 Mary Talbert Way, Buffalo, NY, 14260-1110. Tel: 716-645-6765. p. 1511

Mondon, Laurent, Coordr, Youth Serv, Ludington Public Library, Five S Bryn Mawr Ave, Bryn Mawr, PA, 19010-3471. Tel: 610-525-1776. p. 1916

Mondor, Jenny Kobiela, Asst Dir, Eckhart Public Library, 603 S Jackson St, Auburn, IN, 46706-2298. Tel: 206-925-2414, Ext 702. p. 668

Mondoux, Caleb, Head Student Librn, Bibliotheque du College Universitaire Dominicain, 96 Empress Ave, Ottawa, ON, K1R 7G3, CANADA. Tel: 613-233-5696, Ext 216. p. 2665

Mondovich, Rachelle, Dir, Quinerly Olschner Public Library, 451 Second St, Ayden, NC, 28513-7179. Tel: 252-481-5836. p. 1673

Mondowney, Jo Anne G, Exec Dir, Detroit Public Library, 5201 Woodward Ave, Detroit, MI, 48202. Tel: 313-481-1300. p. 1097

Mones, James, Dir, New York Times, Photo Library, 620 Eighth Ave, 5th Flr, New York, NY, 10018. Tel: 212-556-1642. p. 1598

Monette, Sophie, Librn, Bibliotheque Municipale de Mont-Laurier, 385 rue du Pont, Mont-Laurier, QC, J9L 2R5, CANADA. Tel: 819-623-1221, Ext 750. p. 2716

Money, Cindy, Librn, Brumback Library, Convoy Branch, 116 E Tully St, Convoy, OH, 45832. Tel: 419-749-4000. p. 1827

Money, Kim, Student Success Librn, Middlesex Community College, Federal Bldg, E Merrimack St, Lowell, MA, 01852. Tel: 978-656-3005. p. 1029

Money, Leslie, Library Contact, United States Navy, NAS Whidbey Island, 3535 N Princeton St, Bldg 2510, Oak Harbor, WA, 98278. Tel: 360-257-8541. p. 2372

Monge, Robert, Instruction & Outreach, Western Oregon University, 345 N Monmouth Ave, Monmouth, OR, 97361-1396. Tel: 803-838-8887. p. 1887

Mongeau, Deborah, Head Govt Publ, University of Rhode Island, 15 Lippitt Rd, Kingston, RI, 02881-2011. Tel: 401-874-4610. p. 2033

Mongeon, Beth, Librn, Rolette City Library, 208 Main St, Rolette, ND, 58366. p. 1739

Mongeon, Philippe, Dr, Asst Prof, Dalhousie University, Kenneth C Rowe Management Bldg, Ste 4010, 6100 University Ave, Halifax, NS, B3H 4R2, CANADA. Tel: 902-494-3656. p. 2795

Monger, Leah, Asst Dean, Coll & Access, Ferris State University Library, 1010 Campus Dr, Big Rapids, MI, 49307-2279. Tel: 231-591-3500. p. 1085

Mongold, Tonya, Br Mgr, Keyser-Mineral County Public Library, Burlington Public, Patterson Creek Rd S, Burlington, WV, 26710. Tel: 304-289-3690. p. 2406

Mongomery, Heather, Br Mgr, Richmond Public Library, Broad Rock, 4820 Warwick Rd, Richmond, VA, 23224. Tel: 804-646-8488. p. 2341

Monhaut, Jennifer, Br Mgr, La Porte County Public Library, Rolling Prairie Branch, One E Michigan St, Rolling Prairie, IN, 46371. Tel: 219-778-2390. p. 700

Monica, Dawn, Br Supvr, Saint John the Baptist Parish Library, Frazee-Harris Memorial Library, 111 Historic Front St, Garyville, LA, 70051. Tel: 985-535-6868. p. 895

Moninger, Rachel, Bus Mgr, Citizens Library, 55 S College St, Washington, PA, 15301. Tel: 724-222-2400. p. 2018

Moniz, Richard, Dr, Dir, Libr Serv, Horry-Georgetown Technical College, 2050 Hwy 501 E, Conway, SC, 29526-9521. Tel: 843-349-5268. p. 2057

Monk, Lisa, Asst Librn, Jennifer Reinke Public Library, 311 E Pearl St, Deshler, NE, 68340. Tel: 402-365-4107. p. 1312

Monk, Lori, Syst Adminr, Immaculata University, 1145 King Rd, Immaculata, PA, 19345-0705. Tel: 484-323-3839. p. 1945

Monk, Nicole, Head, Children's Servx, Bedford Free Public Library, Seven Mudge Way, Bedford, MA, 01730. Tel: 781-275-9440. p. 987

Monk, Shelby, Access Serv Mgr, Circ Supvr, Tarleton State University Library, 201 Saint Felix, Stephenville, TX, 76401. Tel: 254-968-9246. p. 2246

Monley, Randi, Ch Serv, Minot Public Library, 516 Second Ave SW, Minot, ND, 58701-3792. Tel: 701-838-0606. p. 1738

Monlux, Carrie L, PhD, Dean of Libr & Instrul Serv, Butte College Library, 3536 Butte Campus Dr, Oroville, CA, 95965. Tel: 530-879-4017. p. 189

Monner, Joanne, Libr & Archives Mgr, Milo Municipal Library, 116 Center St, Milo, AB, T0L 1L0, CANADA. Tel: 403-599-3850. p. 2548

Monnier, Ruth, Head, Ref & Instruction, Librn II, Mount Saint Joseph University, 5701 Delhi Rd, Cincinnati, OH, 45233-1671. Tel: 513-244-4880. p. 1761

Monnig, Donna, Dir, Library & Academic Resource Ctr, Moberly Area Community College Library & Academic Resource Center, Main Bldg, 2nd Flr, 101 College Ave, Moberly, MO, 65270-1304. Tel: 660-263-4110, Ext 11244. p. 1262

Monnin, Caroline, Health Sci Librn, University of Manitoba Libraries, Neil John Maclean Health Sciences Library, Brodie Center Atrium, Mezzanine Level, 2nd Flr, 727 McDermot Ave, Winnipeg, MB, R3E 3P5, CANADA. Tel: 204-789-3342. p. 2595

Monobe, DH, Dr, Lecturer, University of Oklahoma, Bizzell Memorial Library, 401 W Brooks, Rm 120, Norman, OK, 73019-6032. Tel: 405-325-3921. p. 2791

Monochello, Ashley, Youth Serv Librn, The Free Public Library of the Borough of Pompton Lakes, 333 Wanaque Ave, Pompton Lakes, NJ, 07442. Tel: 973-835-0482. p. 1435

Monroe, Alexandra, Dir, Delaware City Public Library, 250 Fifth St, Delaware City, DE, 19706. Tel: 302-834-4148. p. 351

Monroe, Haley, Digital Serv Librn, Tech Serv Librn, East Central University, 1100 E 14th St, Ada, OK, 74820. Tel: 580-559-5842. p. 1839

Monroe, Kaliyah, Circ, Dundee Public Library, 202 E Main St, PO Box 1000, Dundee, FL, 33838. Tel: 863-439-9424. p. 394

Monroe, Marcia, Supvr, Access Serv, University of Washington Libraries, Tacoma Library, 1900 Commerce St, Box 358460, Tacoma, WA, 98402-3100. Tel: 253-692-4446. p. 2382

Monroe, Pamela, Dir, Collins LeRoy Leon County Public Library System, Dr B L Perry Jr Branch, 2817 S Adams St, Tallahassee, FL, 32301. Tel: 850-606-2950. p. 445

Monroe, Pamela, Head, Ref, Florida Agricultural & Mechanical University Libraries, 525 Orr Dr, Tallahassee, FL, 32307-4700. Tel: 850-599-8576. p. 446

Monroe, Savannah, Librn, Maud Public Library, 335 Houston St, Maud, TX, 75567-0388. Tel: 903-585-2121. p. 2216

Monroe, Shelly, Libr Dir, Monroe Public Library, 49 N Main St, Monroe, UT, 84754. Tel: 435-527-4019. p. 2266

Monroe, Susan, Youth Serv Librn, Emmaus Public Library, 11 E Main St, Emmaus, PA, 18049. Tel: 610-965-9284. p. 1930

Monroe, Tacey, Dir, Scotland County Memorial Library, 306 W Madison, Memphis, MO, 63555. Tel: 660-465-7042. p. 1261

Monroe, Will, Asst Dir for Instructional Tech, Louisiana State University Libraries, Paul M Hebert Law Center, One E Campus Dr, Baton Rouge, LA, 70803-1000. Tel: 225-578-7838. p. 884

Monroe-Gulick, Amalia, Librn, University of Kansas Life Span Institute, 4089 Dole Ctr, 1000 Sunnyside Dr, Lawrence, KS, 66045-7555. Tel: 785-864-4095. p. 820

Monsalve-Jones, Leslie, Libr Dir, Southwestern College, 3960 San Felipe Rd, Santa Fe, NM, 87507. Tel: 505-467-6825. p. 1477

Monson, Rachel, Libr Spec, Nunez Community College Library, 3710 Paris Rd, Chalmette, LA, 70043. Tel: 504-278-6295, Ext 230. p. 887

Monsour, Kate, Head, Adult Serv, Port Washington Public Library, One Library Dr, Port Washington, NY, 11050. Tel: 516-883-3728, Ext 1302. p. 1622

Montague, Lynn, Head, Youth Serv, Sun Prairie Public Library, 1350 Linnerud Dr, Sun Prairie, WI, 53590. Tel: 608-825-7323. p. 2480

Montague, Rae-Anne, Dr, Prog Coordr, Chicago State University, Education Bldg, Rm 208, 9501 S King Dr, Chicago, IL, 60628-1598. Tel: 773-995-2598. p. 2784

Montague, Sharon, Spec Serv Dir, Rolling Meadows Library, 3110 Martin Lane, Rolling Meadows, IL, 60008. Tel: 847-259-6050. p. 642

Montalbano, JoAnn, Libr Dir, Saint Joseph Seminary College, 75376 River Rd, Saint Benedict, LA, 70457-9900. Tel: 985-867-2237. p. 907

Montalbano, Michelle, Prog Dir, Starr Library, 68 W Market St, Rhinebeck, NY, 12572. Tel: 845-876-4030. p. 1626

Montalvo, Cynthia, Research Librn, Baker & Botts LLP, One Shell Plaza, 910 Louisiana St, Houston, TX, 77002. Tel: 713-229-1643. p. 2191

Montanaro, Mark, Curator, New Year Shooters & Mummers Museum Library, 1100 S Second St, Philadelphia, PA, 19147. Tel: 215-336-3050. p. 1983

Montanaro, Michelle, Library Contact, National Park Service, PO Box 210, Yorktown, VA, 23690-0210. Tel: 757-898-2410. p. 2355

Montaner, Thane, Coll Mgt Librn, Prairie State College Library, 202 S Halsted St, Chicago Heights, IL, 60411-8200. Tel: 708-709-3552. p. 571

Montano, Amber, Access Serv Mgr, University of New Haven, 300 Boston Post Rd, West Haven, CT, 06516. Tel: 203-932-7189. p. 346

Montaño, Estevan, Univ Librn, Dominican University, 7900 W Division St, River Forest, IL, 60305-1066. Tel: 708-524-6873. p. 639

Montano, Estevan, Br Mgr, Albuquerque-Bernalillo County Library System, San Pedro Library, 5600 Trumbull Ave SE, Albuquerque, NM, 87108. Tel: 505-256-2067. p. 1460
Montano, Vita, Libr Mgr, Dona Ana Community College, East Mesa Library, 2800 N Sonoma Ranch Blvd, Las Cruces, NM, 88011. Tel: 575-528-7260. p. 1470
Monte, Bailey, Access Serv Asst, Yale University Library, Center for Science & Social Science Information, Kline Biology Tower, Concourse Level, 219 Prospect St, New Haven, CT, 06520. Tel: 203-432-3300. p. 327
Monte, Catherine M, Chief Innovation Officer, Chief Knowledge Officer, Fox Rothschild LLP, 2000 Market St, 20th Flr, Philadelphia, PA, 19103-3291. Tel: 215-299-2140. p. 1977
Monte, Molly, Br Mgr, Atlantic County Library System, Mays Landing Branch, 40 Farragut Ave, Mays Landing, NJ, 08330. Tel: 609-625-2776. p. 1417
Montefinise, Angela, Dir, Pub Relations, Dir, Mkt, The New York Public Library - Astor, Lenox & Tilden Foundations, 476 Fifth Ave, (@ 42nd St), New York, NY, 10018. Tel: 212-592-7506. p. 1594
Monteith, Robin, Develop, University of Nevada-Reno, 1664 N Virginia St, Mailstop 0322, Reno, NV, 89557-0322. Tel: 775-682-5656. p. 1349
Montejano, Maria, Ch Serv Librn, Cameron Public Library, 304 E Third St, Cameron, TX, 76520. Tel: 254-697-2401. p. 2152
Montella, Fabio, Ref, Suffolk County Community College, Montaukett Learning Center, 121 Speonk Riverhead Rd, Riverhead, NY, 11901-3499. Tel: 631-548-2569. p. 1627
Montelongo, Tracey, Br Mgr, San Luis Obispo County Library, Santa Margarita Library, 9630 Murphy Ave, Santa Margarita, CA, 93453. Tel: 805-438-5622. p. 234
Montelongo, Tracey, Br Mgr, San Luis Obispo County Library, Shandon Library, 240 E Centre St, Shandon, CA, 93461. Tel: 805-237-3009. p. 234
Montenegro, Debbie, Dep Dir, National Network of Libraries of Medicine Region 3, UNT Health Sci Ctr, Gibson D Lewis Health Sci Libr, 3500 Camp Bowie Blvd, Rm 110, Fort Worth, TX, 76107. Tel: 817-735-2469. p. 2775
Montero, Jesse, Libr Dir, Brooklyn Public Library, Ten Grand Army Plaza, Brooklyn, NY, 11238. Tel: 718-230-2100. p. 1502
Montes, Esmeralda, Librn, Los Angeles Mission College Library, 13356 Eldridge Ave, Sylmar, CA, 91342. Tel: 818-639-2221. p. 251
Montes, Rachel, Libr Dir, Elkhart Lake Public Library, 40 Pine St, Elkhart Lake, WI, 53020. Tel: 920-876-2554. p. 2433
Montesano, Vito, Sr Mgr, Human Res, Milton Public Library, 1010 Main St E, Milton, ON, L9T 6H7, CANADA. Tel: 905-875-2665, Ext 3232. p. 2658
Montesclaros, Van, IT Coordr, Chattahoochee Valley Libraries, 3000 Macon Rd, Columbus, GA, 31906-2201. Tel: 706-243-2686. p. 471
Montesinos, Delia, Pres, Northern California Association of Law Libraries, 268 Bush St, No 4006, San Francisco, CA, 94104. p. 2762
Montet, Margaret, Communications Librn, Info Literacy Librn, Bucks County Community College Library, 275 Swamp Rd, Newtown, PA, 18940-0999. Tel: 215-968-8373. p. 1970
Montfort, Jessica, Br Mgr, Norfolk Public Library, Larchmont Branch, 6525 Hampton Blvd, Norfolk, VA, 23508. Tel: 757-441-5335. p. 2335
Montgomery, Adrienne, Dir, San Augustine Public Library, 413 E Columbia St, San Augustine, TX, 75972. Tel: 936-275-5367. p. 2240
Montgomery, Alyson, Dir, Shedd-Porter Memorial Library, Two Main St, Alstead, NH, 03602. Tel: 603-835-6661. p. 1353
Montgomery, Barbara J, Adjunct Prof, North Carolina Central University, 1801 Fayetteville St, Durham, NC, 27707. Tel: 919-530-6485. p. 2790
Montgomery, Becky, Librn, Oregon County Library District, 20 Court Sq, Alton, MO, 65606. Tel: 417-778-6414. p. 1237
Montgomery, Bernard, Brother, Archives, Conception Abbey & Seminary Library, 37174 State Hwy VV, Conception, MO, 64433. Tel: 660-944-2828. p. 1244
Montgomery, Carol, Br Supvr, Birchard Public Library of Sandusky County, Gibsonburg Branch, 100 N Webster St, Gibsonburg, OH, 43431. Tel: 419-637-2173. p. 1786
Montgomery, Chauncey G, Dir/Fiscal Officer, Community Library, 44 Burrer Dr, Sunbury, OH, 43074. Tel: 740-965-3901. p. 1822
Montgomery, Chuck, Dir, Hall of Flame, 6101 E Van Buren St, Phoenix, AZ, 85008. Tel: 602-275-3473. p. 70
Montgomery, Debbie, Assoc Libr Dir, Tech Serv, University of Texas at Dallas, 800 W Campbell Rd, Richardson, TX, 75080. Tel: 972-883-2963. p. 2231
Montgomery, Doug, Network Adminr, Preble County District Library, 450 S Barron St, Eaton, OH, 45320-2402. Tel: 937-456-4250. p. 1784
Montgomery, Erika, Pub Serv Librn, University of South Carolina Upstate Library, 800 University Way, Spartanburg, SC, 29303. Tel: 864-503-5530. p. 2070
Montgomery, Hannah, Libr Supvr, Allegheny Wesleyan College Library, 2161 Woodsdale Rd, Salem, OH, 44460. Tel: 330-337-6403, Ext 302. p. 1819
Montgomery, Jeff, Circ/Ser Mgr, University of Kansas Libraries, Wheat Law Library, Green Hall, Rm 200, 1535 W 15th St, Lawrence, KS, 66045-7608. Tel: 785-864-3025. p. 820
Montgomery, Mary, Dir, Bridge City Public Library, 101 Parkside Dr, Bridge City, TX, 77611. Tel: 409-735-4242. p. 2150
Montgomery, Melissa, Br Mgr, Hawkins County Library System, 407 E Main St, Ste 1, Rogersville, TN, 37857. Tel: 423-272-8710. p. 2125
Montgomery, Nicole, Librn, CoxHealth Libraries, Cox Medical Ctr N, 1423 N Jefferson Ave, J-209-210, Springfield, MO, 65802. Tel: 417-269-8018. p. 1280
Montgomery Reinert, Patti, Exec Dir, Michigan Maritime Museum, 91 Michigan Ave, South Haven, MI, 49090. Tel: 269-637-9156. p. 1150
Montgomery, Sarah, Dir, Bent Northrop Memorial Library, 164 Park St, Fairfield, VT, 05455. Tel: 802-827-3945. p. 2284
Montgomery, Susan, Res & Instruction Librn, Rollins College, 1000 Holt Ave, Campus Box 2744, Winter Park, FL, 32789-2744. Tel: 407-646-2295. p. 456
Monti, Kathleen, Librn, US Environmental Protection Agency, 701 Mapes Rd, Fort George G Meade, MD, 20755-5350. Tel: 410-305-3031. p. 966
Montminy, Eve, Libr Tech, Natural Resources Canada-Forestry, 1055 rue du PEPS, Quebec City, QC, G1V 4C7, CANADA. Tel: 418-648-4428. p. 2732
Montoya, Cathy, Librn, Houston Community College - Southwest College, Alief Continuing Education Center, 13803 Bissonnet, Houston, TX, 77083. Tel: 713-718-5447. p. 2195
Montoya, Dee Dee, Librn, National Scouting Museum, Philmont Scout Ranch, 17 Deer Run Rd, Cimarron, NM, 87714. Tel: 575-376-1136, 575-376-2281, Ext 1256. p. 1465
Montoya, Vanessa, Tech Serv, Pueblo of Pojoaque Public Library, 37 Camino del Rincon, Ste 2, Santa Fe, NM, 87506-9810. Tel: 505-455-7511. p. 1476
Montoya, Vivian, Librn, California Thoroughbred Breeders Association, 201 Colorado Pl, Arcadia, CA, 91007. Tel: 626-445-7800. p. 117
Montroy, Rebecca, Youth Serv Librn, Warren County Public Library District, 62 Public Sq, Monmouth, IL, 61462. Tel: 309-734-3166. p. 619
Monypeny, David, Homebound Serv/Computer Access, Yuma County Free Library District, 2951 S 21st Dr, Yuma, AZ, 85364. Tel: 928-782-1871. p. 85
Monypeny, Derek, Librn, Copper Mountain College, 6162 Rotary Way, Joshua Tree, CA, 92252. Tel: 760-366-5293. p. 154
Moodey, Chris, Dir, Info Tech, Fayetteville Public Library, 401 W Mountain St, Fayetteville, AR, 72701. Tel: 479-856-7000. p. 95
Moody, Bill, Librn, Har Zion Temple, 1500 Hagys Ford Rd, Penn Valley, PA, 19072. Tel: 610-667-5000. p. 1974
Moody, Daniel, Web Serv & Emerging Tech Librn, Auburn University, 7440 East Dr, Montgomery, AL, 36117. Tel: 334-244-3200. p. 28
Moody, David, Circ, Chapman University Fowler School of Law, One University Dr, Orange, CA, 92866. p. 188
Moody, Donna, Dir, Claymont Public Library, 215 E Third St, Uhrichsville, OH, 44683. Tel: 740-922-3626. p. 1826
Moody, Donna J, Dir, Claymont Public Library, Dennison Branch, 15 N Fourth St, Dennison, OH, 44621. Tel: 740-922-3626. p. 1826
Moody, Hortense, Librn, Georgia Department of Corrections, Georgia State Prison, 300 First Ave S, Reidsville, GA, 30453. Tel: 912-557-7301. p. 493
Moody, Karen, Librn, Warrior Public Library, Ten First St, Warrior, AL, 35180. Tel: 205-647-3006. p. 39
Moody, Madeline, Library Contact, Logan Correctional Center Library, 1096 1350th St, Lincoln, IL, 62656. Tel: 217-735-5581. p. 609
Moody, Mieka, Br Mgr, Free Library of Philadelphia, Lillian Marrero Branch, 601 W Lehigh Ave, Philadelphia, PA, 19133-2228. Tel: 215-685-9794. p. 1979
Moody, Natorra, Mgr, Okefenokee Regional Library, Alma-Bacon County Public, 201 N Pierce St, Alma, GA, 31510. Tel: 912-632-4710. p. 503
Moody, Renee, Br Mgr, Jersey City Free Public Library, Miller, 489 Bergen Ave, Jersey City, NJ, 07304. Tel: 201-547-4551. p. 1409
Moody, Sharon, Ch, Paul Pratt Memorial Library, 35 Ripley Rd, Cohasset, MA, 02025. Tel: 781-383-1348. p. 1012
Moody-Goo, Hannah, Dir, Pueblo Community College Library, 900 W Orman Ave, Pueblo, CO, 81004-1430. Tel: 719-549-3305. p. 293
Mooers, Margaret, Circ, Weeks Public Library, 36 Post Rd, Greenland, NH, 03840-2312. Tel: 603-436-8548. p. 1365
Moog, Emily, Res Analyst, New York Law Institute Library, 120 Broadway, Rm 932, New York, NY, 10271-0094. Tel: 212-732-8720. p. 1594
Moolathara, Titus, Br Mgr, Free Library of Philadelphia, Widener Branch, 2808 W Lehigh Ave, Philadelphia, PA, 19132-3296. Tel: 215-685-9799. p. 1980
Moon, Carolann, Ref & Instrul Outreach Librn, Saint Leo University, 33701 State Rd 52, Saint Leo, FL, 33574. Tel: 352-588-8261. p. 441
Moon, Fletcher, Head, Ref (Info Serv), Tennessee State University, 3500 John A Merritt Blvd, Nashville, TN, 37209. Tel: 615-963-5205. p. 2121
Moon, Sarah, Dir, Finger Lakes Community College, 3325 Marvin Sands Dr, Canandaigua, NY, 14424-8405. Tel: 585-785-1371. p. 1512
Moon, Stephen, Br Mgr, Duchesne Library, Roosevelt Branch, 70 W Lagoon 44-4, Roosevelt, UT, 84066-2841. Tel: 435-722-4441. p. 2262
Moon, Tarsha, Admin Officer, Federal Library & Information Network, Library of Congress FEDLINK, Adams Bldg, Rm 217, 101 Independence Ave SE, Washington, DC, 20540-4935. Tel: 202-707-9452. p. 2763
Moon, Tera, Dir, Bloomfield Township Public Library, 1099 Lone Pine Rd, Bloomfield Township, MI, 48302-2410. Tel: 248-642-5800. p. 1086

Moon, Young, Head, Continuing & E-Res, Boston College Libraries, Thomas P O'Neill Jr Library (Main Library), 140 Commonwealth Ave, Chestnut Hill, MA, 02467. Tel: 617-552-3207. p. 1011
Moonan, Jeanne, Tech Serv, Normal Public Library, 206 W College Ave, Normal, IL, 61761. Tel: 309-452-1757. p. 625
Moonan, Lee, Supvr, Springfield City Library, East Springfield Branch, 21 Osborne Terrace, Springfield, MA, 01104. Tel: 413-263-6840. p. 1056
Mooney, Barrie, Res & Instruction Librn, Assumption University, 500 Salisbury St, Worcester, MA, 01609. Tel: 508-767-7035. p. 1071
Mooney, David, Librn, Community College of Allegheny County, Allegheny Campus Library, 808 Ridge Ave, Pittsburgh, PA, 15212-6003. Tel: 412-237-2585. p. 1993
Mooney, Ellen, Libr Tech, Cambrian College Library, 1400 Barrydowne Rd, 3rd Flr, Rm 3021, Sudbury, ON, P3A 3V8, CANADA. Tel: 705-524-7333. p. 2682
Mooney, Joan, Exec Dir, Waseca County Historical Society, 315 Second Ave NE, Waseca, MN, 56093. Tel: 507-835-7700. p. 1207
Mooney, Kris, Mr, Asst Dir, Admin, Saint Louis County Library, 1640 S Lindbergh Blvd, Saint Louis, MO, 63131-3598. Tel: 314-994-3300. p. 1273
Mooney, Laura, ILL, Research Librn, Brookings Institution Library, 1775 Massachusetts Ave NW, Washington, DC, 20036. Tel: 202-797-6240. p. 361
Mooney, Monica, Dir, Clarence Public Library, Three Town Pl, Clarence, NY, 14031. Tel: 716-741-2650. p. 1518
Mooney, Robin, Br Mgr, Tahlequah Public Library, 120 S College Ave, Tahlequah, OK, 74464. Tel: 918-456-2581. p. 1863
Mooney, Tom, Curator of Ms, Nebraska History Library, 1500 R St, Lincoln, NE, 68508. Tel: 402-471-6396. p. 1322
Moonitz, Allison, Dir, Bergenfield Public Library, 50 W Clinton Ave, Bergenfield, NJ, 07621-2799. Tel: 201-387-4040. p. 1390
Moor, Rikki, Online Serv, Syst Librn, Academy of Art University Library, 180 New Montogomery, 6th Flr, San Francisco, CA, 94105. Tel: 415-274-2270. p. 223
Moore, Aleah, Asst Dir, Libr Serv, Oakland City University, 605 W Columbia St, Oakland City, IN, 47660. Tel: 812-749-1269. p. 712
Moore, Alexa, Circ Librn, Reader Serv Librn, Amherst Town Library, 14 Main St, Amherst, NH, 03031. Tel: 603-673-2288. p. 1353
Moore, Alitta, Ch Serv, Ozark County Volunteer Library, 200 Elm St, Gainesville, MO, 65655. Tel: 417-679-4442. p. 1247
Moore, Allison, Mgr, Tech Serv, Fairfield County District Library, Northwest Branch, 2855 Helena Dr NW, Carroll, OH, 43112. Tel: 740-756-4391. p. 1794
Moore, Alyssa, Pub Serv Mgr, Springfield Township Library, 70 Powell Rd, Springfield, PA, 19064-2446. Tel: 610-543-2113. p. 2009
Moore, Amy, Libr Mgr, MaineHealth, 22 Bramhall St, 5th Flr, Portland, ME, 04102. Tel: 207-662-2202. p. 936
Moore, Andrew, Asst Dir, Wayland Free Public Library, Five Concord Rd, Wayland, MA, 01778. Tel: 508-358-2311. p. 1063
Moore, Angie, Dir, Faulkner University, 5345 Atlanta Hwy, Montgomery, AL, 36109-3398. Tel: 334-386-7207. p. 28
Moore, Anita W, Head Librn, Rust College, 150 E Rust Ave, Holly Springs, MS, 38635. Tel: 662-252-8000, Ext 4100. p. 1220
Moore, Beth, Circ, Libr Asst, Kaskaskia College Library, 27210 College Rd, Centralia, IL, 62801. Tel: 618-545-3133. p. 551
Moore, Betty, Coll Mgr, Hampton Historical Society, 40 Park Ave, Hampton, NH, 03842. Tel: 603-929-0781. p. 1366
Moore, Billy, Ref & Instruction Librn, Concordia University, 800 N Columbia Ave, Seward, NE, 68434. Tel: 402-643-7254. p. 1335
Moore, Bobbi, Librn, Woodbury County Library, Hornick Branch, 510 Main St, Hornick, IA, 51026. Tel: 712-874-3616. p. 772
Moore, Bonnie, Libr Coord, Georgia Northwestern Technical College, Gordon County Campus Library, Bldg 4236, 1151 Hwy 53 Spur, Calhoun, GA, 30701. Tel: 706-378-1718. p. 494
Moore, Bonnie, Libr Coord, Georgia Northwestern Technical College, Polk County Campus Library, Bldg 500, Rm D103, 466 Brock Rd, Rockmart, GA, 30153. Tel: 706-378-1781. p. 494
Moore, Brittany, Br Mgr, Eufaula Memorial Library, 301 S First St, Eufaula, OK, 74432-3201. Tel: 918-689-2291. p. 1847
Moore, Bryant, First Year Experience Librn, Texas A&M University-San Antonio, One University Way, San Antonio, TX, 78224. Tel: 210-784-1507. p. 2239
Moore, Cassandra, Librn, Riverside Regional Medical Center, 500 J Clyde Morris Blvd, Newport News, VA, 23601. Tel: 757-240-2403. p. 2334
Moore, Catherine, Librn, Signature Healthcare - Brockton Hospital Library, 680 Centre St, Brockton, MA, 02302. Tel: 508-941-7000. p. 1003
Moore, Christine, Chair, Phoenix College, 1202 W Thomas Rd, Phoenix, AZ, 85013. Tel: 602-285-7457. p. 72
Moore, Christine, Music Librn, Prairie View A&M University, L W Minor St, University Dr, Prairie View, TX, 77446-0519. Tel: 936-261-3322. p. 2229
Moore, Cindy, Br Mgr, Volusia County Public Library, Port Orange Public Library, 1005 City Center Circle, Port Orange, FL, 32119. Tel: 386-322-5152. p. 393
Moore, Cindy, Dir, Converse County Library, 300 E Walnut St, Douglas, WY, 82633. Tel: 307-358-3644. p. 2494
Moore, Cynthia, Br Mgr, Peach Public Libraries, Byron Public, 105 W Church St, Byron, GA, 31008. Tel: 478-956-2200. p. 480
Moore, Dallas, Tech Serv Coordr, Shenandoah County Library, 514 Stoney Creek Blvd, Edinburg, VA, 22824. Tel: 540-984-8200. p. 2315
Moore, Dan, Tech Serv Librn, Edmonds College Library, 20000 68th Ave W, Lynnwood, WA, 98036. Tel: 425-640-1529. p. 2370
Moore, Daniel R, Automation Syst Coordr, Garnet A Wilson Public Library of Pike County, 207 N Market St, Waverly, OH, 45690-1176. Tel: 740-947-4921. p. 1829
Moore, Danielle, Head, Pub Serv, The Citadel, 171 Moultrie St, Charleston, SC, 29409-6140. p. 2050
Moore, David, Dir, University of Alabama in Huntsville, 4700 Holmes Ave, Huntsville, AL, 35805. Tel: 256-824-6530. p. 22
Moore, David, Asst Dir, Flint Public Library, One S Main St, Middleton, MA, 01949. Tel: 978-774-8132. p. 1035
Moore, Deborah, County Libr Dir, Lonoke County Libraries, 204 E Second St, Lonoke, AR, 72086-2858. p. 102
Moore, Deborah, Ref Librn, Highline College Library, 2400 S 240th St, MS 25-4, Des Moines, WA, 98198. Tel: 206-592-3518. p. 2363
Moore, Debra, Syst & Tech Serv Librn, Cerritos College Library, 11110 Alondra Blvd, Norwalk, CA, 90650. Tel: 562-860-2451, Ext 2418. p. 184
Moore, Deirdre, Mgr, Libr Serv, Natural Resources Canada-Forestry, 1055 rue du PEPS, Quebec City, QC, G1V 4C7, CANADA. Tel: 418-648-4850. p. 2732
Moore, Dillon, Head, Digital Initiatives, Wilfrid Laurier University Library, 75 University Ave W, Waterloo, ON, N2L 3C5, CANADA. Tel: 519-884-0701, Ext 4126. p. 2703
Moore, Donna, Asst Dean, Instruction, Pittsburgh Institute of Aeronautics, Five Allegheny County Airport, West Mifflin, PA, 15122-2674. Tel: 412-346-2100, 412-462-9011. p. 2021
Moore, Douglas, Info Spec, Concord University, Vermillion St, Athens, WV, 24712. Tel: 304-384-5372. p. 2397
Moore, Ellen, Tech Serv, Peter White Public Library, 217 N Front St, Marquette, MI, 49855. Tel: 906-226-4316. p. 1130
Moore, Emily, Ch Serv, Camden County Library System, 203 Laurel Rd, Voorhees, NJ, 08043. Tel: 856-772-1636, Ext 7321. p. 1450
Moore, Emma, Librn, Institute for Advanced Study Libraries, One Einstein Dr, Princeton, NJ, 08540. Tel: 609-734-8000. p. 1436
Moore, Erik, Librn, University of New Brunswick Libraries, Five Macaulay Lane, Fredericton, NB, E3B 5H5, CANADA. Tel: 506-452-6202. p. 2601
Moore, Felecia, Archives Specialist, La Grange College, 601 Broad St, LaGrange, GA, 30240-2999. Tel: 706-880-8995. p. 484
Moore, Gerald, Br Mgr, Charleston County Public Library, Dorchester Road Regional, 6325 Dorchester Rd, North Charleston, SC, 29418. Tel: 843-552-6466. p. 2049
Moore, Grace, Teen Librn, Winter Park Public Library, 460 E New England Ave, Winter Park, FL, 32789. Tel: 407-623-3300, Ext 114. p. 456
Moore, Heather, Head, Spec Coll, Mississippi College, 130 W College St, Clinton, MS, 39058. Tel: 601-925-3434. p. 1214
Moore, Hilary, Dir, Gladys J Craig Memorial Library, 57 Exchange St, Ashland, ME, 04732. Tel: 207-435-6532. p. 913
Moore, Jacqueline, Interim Head Librn, Roanoke Rapids Public Library, 319 Roanoke Ave, Roanoke Rapids, NC, 27870. Tel: 252-533-2890. p. 1713
Moore, Jake, Dir, Lawrenceburg Public Library District, 150 Mary St, Lawrenceburg, IN, 47025. Tel: 812-537-2775. p. 702
Moore, Jake, Br Mgr, Boone County Public Library, Florence Branch, 7425 US 42, Florence, KY, 41042. Tel: 859-342-2665. p. 850
Moore, James, City Librn, San Mateo Public Library, 55 W Third Ave, San Mateo, CA, 94402. Tel: 650-522-7802. p. 236
Moore, Janice, Outreach Librn, Northwest Area Health Education Center, Catawba Valley Medical Ctr, 810 Fairgrove Church Rd, Hickory, NC, 28602. Tel: 828-326-3662, Ext 3482. p. 1696
Moore, Janice D, Professional Outreach Librn, Northwest AHEC Library Information Network, One Medical Center Blvd, Winston-Salem, NC, 27157. Tel: 336-618-0310. p. 2772
Moore, Jay, Archivist/Librn, Mariners' Museum & Park Library, 100 Museum Dr, Newport News, VA, 23606-3759. Tel: 757-591-7782. p. 2333
Moore, Jennette, Librn, Mid-Mississippi Regional Library System, Goodman Public, 9792 Main St, Goodman, MS, 39079. Tel: 662-472-0550. p. 1224
Moore, Jennifer, Interim Librn, Washington University Libraries, Kopolow Business Library, One Brookings Dr, Campus Box 1061, Saint Louis, MO, 63130. Tel: 314-935-6739. p. 1277
Moore, Jessica, Dir, Marlette District Library, 3116 Main St, Marlette, MI, 48453. Tel: 989-635-2838. p. 1130
Moore, Jessica, Ref & Instruction Librn, University of Northwestern-St Paul, 3003 Snelling Ave N, Saint Paul, MN, 55113. Tel: 651-631-5241. p. 1202
Moore, Jodie, Libr Dir, Red Lodge Carnegie Library, Three W Eighth St, Red Lodge, MT, 59068. Tel: 406-446-1905. p. 1301
Moore, Johnetta, Ref & Instrul Serv Librn, Edmonds College Library, 20000 68th Ave W, Lynnwood, WA, 98036. Tel: 425-640-1529. p. 2370

Moore, Joi L, Assoc Prof, University of Missouri-Columbia, 303 Townsend Hall, Columbia, MO, 65211. Tel: 573-882-4546. p. 2787
Moore, Jordyn, Dir, Cresco Public Library, 320 N Elm St, Cresco, IA, 52136-1452. Tel: 563-547-2540. p. 743
Moore, Judi, Br Mgr, Free Library of Philadelphia, McPherson Square Branch, 601 E Indiana Ave, Philadelphia, PA, 19134-3042. Tel: 215-685-9995. p. 1979
Moore, Judy, Access Serv Mgr, Columbus State University Libraries, Music Library, 900 Broadway, Columbus, GA, 31901-2735. Tel: 706-641-5044. p. 472
Moore, Judy, Acq, Cat, Bristol Public Library, 701 Goode St, Bristol, VA, 24201. Tel: 276-821-6195. p. 2308
Moore, Judy, Chief Librn, Thompson-Nicola Regional District Library System, 300-465 Victoria St, Kamloops, BC, V2C 2A9, CANADA. Tel: 250-377-8673. p. 2567
Moore, Juli, Dir, Iredell County Public Library, 201 N Tradd St, Statesville, NC, 28677. Tel: 704-878-3092. p. 1717
Moore, Julianne, Mgr, Carnegie Library of Pittsburgh, Beechview, 1910 Broadway Ave, Pittsburgh, PA, 15216-3130. Tel: 412-563-2900. p. 1991
Moore, Karen, Dir, Wright County Library, 160 E Marshfield St, Hartville, MO, 65667-9998. Tel: 417-741-7595. p. 1248
Moore, Karen, Dir, Forest-Jackson Public Library, 102 W Lima St, Forest, OH, 45843-1128. Tel: 419-273-2400. p. 1786
Moore, Katelyn, Mkt, Outreach Coordr, Bourbonnais Public Library District, 250 W John Casey Rd, Bourbonnais, IL, 60914. Tel: 815-933-1727. p. 544
Moore, Katie, Mgr, Township of Springwater Public Library, Minesing Branch, Minesing Community Ctr, 2347 Ronald Rd, Minesing, ON, L0L 1Y0, CANADA. Tel: 705-722-6440. p. 2658
Moore, Kevin, Ref Spec, Mount Hood Community College Libraries, Maywood Campus, Community Skills Ctr, 10100 NE Prescott, Portland, OR, 97220. Tel: 503-491-6122. p. 1881
Moore, Kevin, Br Librn, London Public Library, Pond Mills, 1166 Commissioners Rd E, London, ON, N5Z 4W8, CANADA. Tel: 519-685-1333. p. 2654
Moore, Lauren, State Librn, New York State Library, Cultural Education Ctr, 222 Madison Ave, Albany, NY, 12230. p. 1483
Moore, Lavonnia, Mgr, Okefenokee Regional Library, Pierce County Public, 785 College Ave, Blackshear, GA, 31516. Tel: 912-449-7040. p. 503
Moore, Linda, Dir, Millbrook Public Library, 3650 Grandview Rd, Millbrook, AL, 36054. Tel: 334-285-6688, Ext 101. p. 25
Moore, Linda M, Asst Librn, Illinois Prairie District Public Library, Springbay Branch, 411 Illinois St, Springbay, IL, 61611. Tel: 309-822-0444. p. 617
Moore, Lindsay, ILL, Coeur d'Alene Public Library, 702 E Front Ave, Coeur d'Alene, ID, 83814-2373. Tel: 208-769-2315. p. 519
Moore, Lindsey, Dir, Munford-Tipton Memorial Library, 1476 Munford Ave, Munford, TN, 38058. Tel: 901-837-2665. p. 2117
Moore, Lisa, Head, Res Serv, Amistad Research Center, Tulane University, Tilton Hall, 6823 St Charles Ave, New Orleans, LA, 70118. Tel: 504-862-3233. p. 900
Moore, Lisa, Librn, North Central Washington Libraries, Grand Coulee Public Library, 225 Federal St, Grand Coulee, WA, 99133. Tel: 509-633-0972. p. 2394
Moore, Lynn, Librn, Warren County Historical Society & Genealogy, 313 Mansfield St, Belvidere, NJ, 07823-1828. Tel: 908-475-4246. p. 1389
Moore, Marcy, Dir, Boise Basin Library District, 123 Montgomery St, Idaho City, ID, 83631. Tel: 208-392-4558. p. 522
Moore, Marissa, Librn, Alberta Bible College Library, 635 Northmount Dr NW, Calgary, AB, T2K 3J6, CANADA. Tel: 403-282-2994. p. 2525
Moore, Martha, Cat, Tech Serv, Rhode Island State Law Library, Frank Licht Judicial Complex, 250 Benefit St, Providence, RI, 02903. Tel: 401-222-3275. p. 2040
Moore, Mary, Br Mgr, Davis County Library, Bountiful/South Branch, 725 S Main St, Bountiful, UT, 84010. Tel: 451-451-1760. p. 2263
Moore, Mary Carole, Ch, Bryant Library, Two Paper Mill Rd, Roslyn, NY, 11576. Tel: 516-621-2240. p. 1633
Moore, Mary Wallace, Dir, Smyrna Public Library, 100 Village Green Circle, Smyrna, GA, 30080-3478. Tel: 770-431-2860. p. 497
Moore, Meagan, Br Mgr, Mississippi County Library System, Keiser Public, 112 E Main St, Keiser, AR, 72351. Tel: 870-526-2073. p. 91
Moore, Melissa, Libr Dir, Union University, 1050 Union University Dr, Jackson, TN, 38305-3697. Tel: 731-661-5408. p. 2102
Moore, Meredith, Digital Curation & A-V Archives Specialist, Maryland Institute College of Art, 1401 W Mount Royal Ave, Baltimore, MD, 21217. Tel: 410-225-2304, 410-225-2311. p. 955
Moore, Michelle, Asst Dir, Loutit District Library, 407 Columbus Ave, Grand Haven, MI, 49417. Tel: 616-842-6920. p. 1109
Moore, Mike, ILL/Tech Serv Librn, United States Geological Survey Library, 345 Middlefield Rd, Bldg 15 (MS-955), Menlo Park, CA, 94025-3591. Tel: 650-329-5009. p. 176
Moore, Nancy, Dir, Five Rivers Public Library, 301 Walnut St, Parsons, WV, 26287. Tel: 304-478-3880. p. 2411
Moore, Natalie, Resource Management Specialist, Arnold & Porter Kaye Scholar LLP, 777 S Figueroa St, 44th Flr, Los Angeles, CA, 90017-5844. Tel: 213-243-4000. p. 160
Moore, Nicole, Dep Dir, Mgr, Ch Serv, Ella M Everhard Public Library, 132 Broad St, Wadsworth, OH, 44281-1897. Tel: 330-335-1295. p. 1827
Moore, Pamela, Dr, Coordr, University of South Alabama, UCOM 3800, Mobile, AL, 36688. Tel: 251-380-2153. p. 2781
Moore, Pat, Curriculum Materials, William Paterson University, 300 Pompton Rd, Wayne, NJ, 07470. Tel: 973-720-2174. p. 1452
Moore, Patricia, Ad, Oliver Wolcott Library, 160 South St, Litchfield, CT, 06759-0187. Tel: 860-567-8030. p. 320
Moore, Paul, Govt Doc Librn, Eastern New Mexico University - Portales, 1500 S Ave K, Portales, NM, 88130-7402. Tel: 575-562-2650. p. 1473
Moore, Peter, IT Coordr, Mansfield-Richland County Public Library, 43 W Third St, Mansfield, OH, 44902-1295. Tel: 419-521-3105. p. 1798
Moore, Phyllis, Br Mgr, Jackson Parish Library, Chatham Branch, 1500 Pine St, Chatham, LA, 71226. Tel: 318-249-2980, 318-249-2981. p. 892
Moore, Precious, Dir, Alvarado Public Library, 210 N Baugh St, Alvarado, TX, 76009. Tel: 817-783-7323. p. 2133
Moore, Rachel, Librn, Glasco City Library, 206 E Main St, Glasco, KS, 67445. Tel: 785-568-2313. p. 809
Moore, Rebecca K, Info Literacy, Youngstown State University, One University Plaza, Youngstown, OH, 44555-0001. Tel: 330-941-1720. p. 1836
Moore, Rick, Dir, Perry-Lecompton Community Library, Highland College, Perry Center, 203 W Bridge St, Perry, KS, 66073. Tel: 785-329-3430. p. 831
Moore, Robert, Librn, Miami Correctional Facility, Phase I Library, 3038 W 850 S, Bunker Hill, IN, 46914. Tel: 765-689-8920, Ext 5344. p. 673
Moore, Rosemary, Asst Dir, Rocky J Adkins Public Library, 207 S KY Rte 7, Sandy Hook, KY, 41171. Tel: 606-738-5796. p. 874
Moore, Samantha, Dir, McCord Memorial Library, 32 W Main St, North East, PA, 16428. Tel: 814-725-4057. p. 1971
Moore, Sandy, Assoc Dir, New York Institute of Technology, 1855 Broadway, New York, NY, 10023-7692. Tel: 212-261-1525. p. 1593
Moore, Sarah, Exec Dir, Hussey-Mayfield Memorial Public Library, 250 N Fifth St, Zionsville, IN, 46077-1324. Tel: 317-873-3149. p. 728
Moore, Savannah, County Librn, Petroleum County Community Library, 305 S Broadway, Winnett, MT, 59087. Tel: 406-429-2451. p. 1304
Moore, Shelley, Br Mgr, Memphis Public Library, Frayser Branch, 3712 Argonne St, Memphis, TN, 38127-4414. Tel: 901-415-2768. p. 2113
Moore, Sherri, Librn, Mount San Jacinto College, Menifee Valley, 800/LRC Bldg, 2nd Flr, 28237 La Piedra Rd, Menifee Valley, CA, 92584. Tel: 951-639-5451. p. 230
Moore, Stew, Mgr, Canadian Broadcasting Corp, Reference & Image Research Libraries, 250 Front St W, Toronto, ON, M5V 3G5, CANADA. Tel: 416-205-7153. p. 2687
Moore, Susan, Dep Dir, San Diego County Library, MS 070, 5560 Overland Ave, Ste 110, San Diego, CA, 92123. Tel: 858-694-2448. p. 216
Moore, Susan, Collections Strategist Librn, Coordr, Cat, University of Northern Iowa Library, 1227 W 27th St, Cedar Falls, IA, 50613-3675. Tel: 319-273-3787. p. 737
Moore, Suzanne, Mgr, Thomas County Public Library System, Boston Carnegie Public Library, 250 S Main St, Boston, GA, 31626-3674. Tel: 229-498-5101. p. 499
Moore, Suzanne, County Librn, Wilkes County Public Library, 215 Tenth St, North Wilkesboro, NC, 28659. Tel: 336-838-2818. p. 1706
Moore, Sylvia, ILL, Yuma County Free Library District, 2951 S 21st Dr, Yuma, AZ, 85364. Tel: 928-373-6488. p. 85
Moore, Thomas, Head Librn, Capital Area District Libraries, Haslett Library, 1590 Franklin St, Haslett, MI, 48840. Tel: 517-339-2324. p. 1124
Moore, Thomas, Head Librn, Capital Area District Libraries, Okemos Library, 4321 Okemos Rd, Okemos, MI, 48864. Tel: 517-347-2021. p. 1124
Moore, Tim, Dean, Learning Res, Elgin Community College, 1700 Spartan Dr, Elgin, IL, 60123. Tel: 847-214-7337. p. 584
Moore, Tom, Ad, Delta Township District Library, 5130 Davenport Dr, Lansing, MI, 48917-2040. Tel: 517-321-4014. p. 1124
Moore, Tony, Libr Asst, Community District Library, Bentley Memorial, 135 S Main St, Perry, MI, 48872-0017. Tel: 517-625-3166. p. 1095
Moore, Tonya, ILL Mgr, Virginia Military Institute, 345 Letcher Ave, Lexington, VA, 24450. Tel: 540-464-7570. p. 2329
Moore, Vanja, Circ, Port Isabel Public Library, 213 Yturria St, Port Isabel, TX, 78578. Tel: 956-943-1822. p. 2228
Moore, Vicky, Br Mgr, Camden County Library District, Osage Beach Branch, 1064 Gutridge Lane, Osage Beach, MO, 65065. Tel: 573-348-3282. p. 1239
Moore, Wayne, Asst State Archivist, Tennessee State Library & Archives, 403 Seventh Ave N, Nashville, TN, 37243-0312. Tel: 615-253-3458. p. 2121
Moore, Wendy, Acq Librn, University of Georgia, Alexander Campbell King Law Library, 225 Herty Dr, Athens, GA, 30602-6018. Tel: 706-542-5081. p. 459
Moorefield-Lang, Heather, Dr, Assoc Prof, University of North Carolina at Greensboro, School of Education Bldg, Rm 446, 1300 Spring Garden St, Greensboro, NC, 27412. Tel: 336-334-3477. p. 2790
Moorehead, Cortny, Univ Librn, Midwestern State University, 3410 Taft Blvd, Wichita Falls, TX, 76308-2099. Tel: 940-397-4173. p. 2257
Moorehead, Grayce J, Assoc Dir, Marian J Mohr Memorial Library, One Memorial Ave, Johnston, RI, 02919-3221. Tel: 401-231-4980. p. 2033

Moorer, Laura, Librn, DC Court of Appeals Library, 430 E St NW, Rm 203, Washington, DC, 20001. Tel: 202-879-2767. p. 363
Moores, Beth, Dean, Libr Serv, TriHealth, Inc, 375 Dixmyth Ave, Cincinnati, OH, 45220-2489. Tel: 513-862-2433. p. 1764
Moorhead, Susan, Mgr, New Rochelle Public Library, Huguenot Children's Library, 794 North Ave, New Rochelle, NY, 10801. Tel: 914-632-8954. p. 1577
Moorman, Deborah, Br Mgr, Coastal Plain Regional Library System, Irwin County, 310 S Beech St, Ocilla, GA, 31774. Tel: 229-468-2148. p. 500
Moorman, Jayne, Asst County Librn, Spartanburg County Public Libraries, 151 S Church St, Spartanburg, SC, 29306. Tel: 864-596-3500. p. 2069
Moorman, Josh, Interim Dir, Seaside Public Library, 1131 Broadway, Seaside, OR, 97138. Tel: 503-738-6742. p. 1898
Moorman, Rebecca, Govt Doc Librn, Head, Tech Serv, University of Alaska Anchorage, Consortium Library, 3211 Providence Dr, Anchorage, AK, 99508-8176. Tel: 907-786-1974. p. 43
Moose, Samantha, Libr Mgr, Richmond Hill-Bryan County Library, 9607 Ford Ave, Richmond Hill, GA, 31324. Tel: 912-756-3580. p. 493
Moosmann, Linnea, Ch, Larchmont Public Library, 121 Larchmont Ave, Larchmont, NY, 10538. Tel: 914-834-2281. p. 1562
Moquin, Sherrie, Dir, Hammond Free Library, 17 N Main St, Hammond, NY, 13646. Tel: 315-324-5139. p. 1544
Morais, Yasmin, Cat Librn, University of the District of Columbia, David A Clarke School of Law, Charles N & Hilda H M Mason Law Library, Bldg 39, Rm B-16, 4200 Connecticut Ave NW, Washington, DC, 20008. Tel: 202-274-7310. p. 380
Morales, Ada, Circ Asst, Mitchell Public Library, 221 N Duff St, Mitchell, SD, 57301. Tel: 605-995-8480. p. 2079
Morales, Adrian, Librn, El Paso Community College Library, 919 Hunter St, Rm C200, El Paso, TX, 79915. Tel: 915-831-2442. p. 2173
Morales, Alaina, Libr Dir, Saint Norbert College, 400 Third St, De Pere, WI, 54115. p. 2430
Morales, Cheryl, Exec Dir, Pinellas Public Library Cooperative, 1330 Cleveland St, Clearwater, FL, 33755-5103. Tel: 727-441-8408. p. 389
Morales, Cheryl, Exec Dir, Pinellas Talking Book Library, 1330 Cleveland St, Clearwater, FL, 33755-5103. Tel: 727-441-9958. p. 389
Morales, David, Circ Mgr, College of William & Mary in Virginia, Earl Gregg Swem Library, One Landrum Dr, Williamsburg, VA, 23187. Tel: 757-221-3050. p. 2353
Morales, Fernando, Circ Mgr, Banning Library District, 21 W Nicolet St, Banning, CA, 92220. Tel: 951-849-3192. p. 120
Morales, Hailey, Libr Asst, New Mexico Junior College, One Thunderbird Circle, Hobbs, NM, 88240. Tel: 575-492-2875. p. 1469
Morales, Irma, Regional Mgr, Sr City Librn, Ventura County Library, 5600 Everglades St, Ste A, Ventura, CA, 93003. Tel: 805-677-7150. p. 256
Morales, Jaclyn, Sr Librn, North Shore University Hospital, 300 Community Dr, Manhasset, NY, 11030. Tel: 516-562-4324. p. 1568
Morales, Jonathan, Libr Asst, North Shore Community College Library, One Ferncroft Rd, Danvers Campus Library, Danvers, MA, 01923-4093. Tel: 978-462-5443. p. 1013
Morales, Karen, Circ Supvr, Moreno Valley Public Library, 25480 Alessandro Blvd, Moreno Valley, CA, 92553. Tel: 951-413-3880. p. 180
Morales, Omero, Head, Ref, Dustin Michael Sekula Memorial Library, 1906 S Closner Blvd, Edinburg, TX, 78539. Tel: 956-383-6246. p. 2173
Moralez, Kristine, Sr Librn, Oceanside Public Library, 330 N Coast Hwy, Oceanside, CA, 92054. Tel: 760-435-5571. p. 187
Moran, Alex, ILL, University of San Diego, Helen K & James S Copley Library, 5998 Alcala Park, San Diego, CA, 92110. p. 222
Moran, David, Tech Serv, Southern Oklahoma Library System, 601 Railway Express St, Ardmore, OK, 73401. Tel: 580-223-3164. p. 1840
Moran, Hayley, Principal, Department of Human Services-Youth Corrections, 1427 W Rio Grande St, Colorado Springs, CO, 80905. Tel: 719-385-3370. p. 271
Moran, Kate, Br Mgr, Arlington County Department of Libraries, Westover, 1644 N McKinley Rd, Ste 3, Arlington, VA, 22205. Tel: 703-228-5260. p. 2305
Moran, Kyle, Digital Librn, Free Methodist Church - USA, 5235 Decatur Blvd, Indianapolis, IN, 46241. Tel: 317-244-3660. p. 692
Moran, Mary, Sr Content Strategist, College of the Holy Cross, One College St, Worcester, MA, 01610. Tel: 508-793-2478. p. 1072
Moran, Mary Kay, Dir, Cheltenham Township Library System, 215 S Keswick Ave, Glenside, PA, 19038-4420. Tel: 215-885-0457. p. 1937
Moran, Pat, Archivist, Community College of Allegheny County, Allegheny Campus Library, 808 Ridge Ave, Pittsburgh, PA, 15212-6003. Tel: 412-237-2585. p. 1993
Moran Savakinus, Mary Ann, Exec Dir, Lackawanna Historical Society Library, 232 Monroe Ave, Scranton, PA, 18510. Tel: 570-344-3841. p. 2004
Moran, Shane, Archives & Spec Coll Librn, Juniata College, 1700 Moore St, Huntingdon, PA, 16652-2119. Tel: 814-641-5323. p. 1945
Morant, Wantanisha, Human Res Dir, Alachua County Library District, 401 E University Ave, Gainesville, FL, 32601-5453. Tel: 352-334-0158. p. 406
Morasch, James, Computer Syst Adminr, Whitman County Rural Library District, 102 S Main St, Colfax, WA, 99111-1863. Tel: 509-397-4366. p. 2362
Morash, Meagan, Dir, Libr Serv, Booth University College, 300-290 Vaughan St, Winnipeg, MB, R3B 2L9, CANADA. Tel: 204-924-4857. p. 2592
Morbitzer, Sarah, Children's Mgr, North Manchester Public Library, 405 N Market St, North Manchester, IN, 46962. Tel: 260-982-4773. p. 710
Morcerf, Nancy, Asst Libr Dir, Northport-East Northport Public Library, 151 Laurel Ave, Northport, NY, 11768. Tel: 631-261-6930. p. 1608
Morchower, Gail, Librn, International Game Fish Association, 300 Gulf Stream Way, Dania Beach, FL, 33004. Tel: 954-927-2628. p. 391
More, Katherine, Prof, Seneca College of Applied Arts & Technology, 1750 Finch Ave E, Toronto, ON, M2J 2X5, CANADA. Tel: 416-491-5050, Ext 33701. p. 2796
More, Kathleen, Libr Assoc, Lee Memorial Health System Library, 2776 Cleveland Ave, 1st Flr, Fort Myers, FL, 33901. Tel: 239-343-2410. p. 404
Morea, Michael, Dir, Gold Coast Public Library, 50 Railroad Ave, Glen Head, NY, 11545. Tel: 516-759-8300. p. 1539
Moreau, Carolyn, Team Lead, Comms Team, University of Colorado Boulder, 1720 Pleasant St, Boulder, CO, 80309. Tel: 303-492-8705. p. 267
Moreau, Isabelle, Chef de Section, Bibliotheques de Montreal, Henri-Bourassa, 5400 Blvd Henri-Bourassa Est, Montreal-Nord, QC, H1G 2S9, CANADA. Tel: 514-328-4000, Ext 5620. p. 2718
Moreau, Isabelle, Chef de Section, Bibliotheques de Montreal, Yves-Ryan, 4740 rue de Charleroi, Montreal-Nord, QC, H1H 1V2, CANADA. Tel: 514-328-4000, Ext 5620. p. 2721
Moreau, Julie, Team Leader, Bibliotheques de Trois-Rivieres, 1425 Place de l'Hotel de Ville, Trois-Rivieres, QC, G9A 5L9, CANADA. Tel: 819-372-4615. p. 2737
Moree, Laura, Br Mgr, Walton County Public Library System, Three Circle Dr, De Funiak Springs, FL, 32435-2542. Tel: 850-892-3624. p. 393
Morehart, Lis Ann, Libr Dir, Shelbyville-Bedford County Public Library, 220 S Jefferson St, Shelbyville, TN, 37160. Tel: 931-684-7323. p. 2126
Morehart, Tami, Dir, The Wagnalls Memorial Library, 150 E Columbus St, Lithopolis, OH, 43136. Tel: 614-837-4765. p. 1796
Morehouse, Lorraine, Access Serv, Head, Circ, New Brunswick Public Library Service (NBPLS), 570 Two Nations Crossing, Ste 2, Fredericton, NB, E3A 0X9, CANADA. Tel: 506-453-2354. p. 2601
Morel, Rebecca, Youth Serv Librn, Cresskill Public Library, 53 Union Ave, Cresskill, NJ, 07626. Tel: 201-567-3521. p. 1398
Morel, Rebecca, Youth Serv Librn, River Vale Free Public Library, 412 Rivervale Rd, River Vale, NJ, 07675. Tel: 201-391-2323. p. 1440
Moreland, Lisa, Dir, Caldwell Public Library, 120 S Main St, Caldwell, KS, 67022. Tel: 620-845-6879. p. 800
Moreland, Riley, Ms, Libr Dir, Sidney Public Library, 1002 Illinois St, Sidney, IA, 51652. Tel: 712-374-6203. p. 782
Morell, Brian, Commun Libr Mgr, Queens Library, Queens Village Community Library, 94-11 217th St, Queens Village, NY, 11428. Tel: 718-776-6800. p. 1555
Morency, Martine, Digital Res Librn, SIAST Libraries, 1100 15th St E, Prince Albert, SK, S6V 6G1, CANADA. Tel: 306-765-1547. p. 2745
Moreno, Cynthia, Dir, Engagement & Learning, Mint Museum, 2730 Randolph Rd, Charlotte, NC, 28207. Tel: 704-337-2000, 704-337-2023. p. 1680
Moreno, Deborah, Libr Mgr, Chandler Public Library, Sunset, 4930 W Ray Rd, Chandler, AZ, 85226-6219. p. 58
Moreno, Jeanette, Libr Asst, Township of Georgian Bay Public Library, Port Severn Public, 71 Lone Pine Rd, Port Severn, ON, L0K 1S0, CANADA. Tel: 705-818-7749. p. 2648
Moreno, Jennie, Children & Youth Serv Librn, Hennessey Public Library, 525 S Main, Hennessey, OK, 73742. Tel: 405-853-2073. p. 1849
Moreno, Judith, Dir, Learning Commons, Pub Serv Librn, Central Maine Community College Library, Jalbert Hall, Main Flr, 1250 Turner St, Auburn, ME, 04210. Tel: 207-755-5265. p. 914
Moreno, Maria, Circ, Valencia College, East Campus Library, 701 N Econlockhatchee Trail, Orlando, FL, 32825. Tel: 407-582-2467. p. 432
Moreno, Olivia, Libr Dir, W Walworth Harrison Public Library, One Lou Finney Ln, Greenville, TX, 75401-5988. Tel: 903-457-2992. p. 2186
Moreno, Pat, Br Librn, Sweetwater County Library System, Reliance Branch Library, 1329 Main St, Reliance, WY, 82943. Tel: 307-352-6670. p. 2495
Moreno, Rafael, Librn II, Kern County Library, Beale Memorial, 701 Truxtun Ave, Bakersfield, CA, 93301-4816. Tel: 661-868-0701. p. 119
Moreno, Shilo, Acq Asst, California State University Dominguez Hills, 1000 E Victoria St, Carson, CA, 90747. Tel: 310-243-2850. p. 129
Moreno, Shirley, Cat Librn, University of Health Sciences & Pharmacy in Saint Louis Library, One Pharmacy Pl, Saint Louis, MO, 63110. Tel: 314-446-8364. p. 1276
Morenus, Carlyn, Br Librn, Macon County Public Library, Hudson Library, 554 Main St, Highlands, NC, 28741. Tel: 828-526-3031. p. 1690

Moretz, Connie, Dir, Manly Public Library, 127 S Grant, Manly, IA, 50456. Tel: 641-454-2982. p. 767

Morey, Linda, Library Asst, Acquisitions, East Texas Baptist University, One Tiger Dr, Marshall, TX, 75670-1498. Tel: 903-923-2261. p. 2215

Morey, Ophelia, Outreach Librn, University at Buffalo Libraries-State University of New York, Health Sciences Library, Abbott Hall, 3435 Main St, Bldg 28, Buffalo, NY, 14214-3002. Tel: 716-829-5748. p. 1510

Morey, Sarah, Syst Adminr, Tech Serv Mgr, Wayne Township Library, 80 N Sixth St, Richmond, IN, 47374. Tel: 765-966-8291, Ext 1107. p. 715

Morey, Tammy, Libr Mgr, Rochester Municipal Library, 5202-47 St, Rochester, AB, T0G 1Z0, CANADA. Tel: 780-698-3970. p. 2552

Morfitt, Paige, Digital Assets Librn, Metadata Librn, Whitman College, 345 Boyer Ave, Walla Walla, WA, 99362. Tel: 509-527-5920. p. 2393

Morgan, Alison, Asst Dir, Pub Serv, Xavier University, 1535 Musketeer Dr, Cincinnati, OH, 45207. Tel: 513-745-3931. p. 1765

Morgan, Alyssa, Youth Serv Librn, Morgan County Public Library, 110 S Jefferson St, Martinsville, IN, 46151. Tel: 765-342-3451. p. 705

Morgan, Anna Beth, Exec Dir, Mayo Clinic Libraries, 200 First St SW, Rochester, MN, 55905. Tel: 507-284-2061. p. 1194

Morgan, Anne, Tech Serv Librn, A T Still University, Kirksville Campus, 800 W Jefferson St, Kirksville, MO, 63501. Tel: 660-626-2635. p. 1258

Morgan, Anne, Librn, Institute of Historical Survey Foundation Library, 3035 S Main, Las Cruces, NM, 88005-3756. Tel: 575-525-3035. p. 1470

Morgan, Beth, Tech Serv, Centre College of Kentucky, 600 W Walnut St, Danville, KY, 40422. Tel: 859-238-5272. p. 853

Morgan, Beth, Dir, United States Navy, 1002 Balch Blvd, Stennis Space Center, MS, 39522-5001. Tel: 228-688-4398. p. 1233

Morgan, Bettie, Dir, Wilcox County Library, 100 Broad St, Camden, AL, 36726-1702. Tel: 334-682-4355. p. 11

Morgan, Bill, Head, Syst, Head, Tech Serv, Colchester-East Hants Public Library, 754 Prince St, Truro, NS, B2N 1G9, CANADA. Tel: 902-895-4183. p. 2623

Morgan, Brian, Dir, Finance & Operations, Somerset County Library System of New Jersey, One Vogt Dr, Bridgewater, NJ, 08807-2136. Tel: 908-458-8402. p. 1392

Morgan, Carl, Acq Librn, Orange Coast College Library, 2701 Fairview Rd, Costa Mesa, CA, 92626. Tel: 714-432-5885. p. 132

Morgan, Cheryl, Dir, Somerset County Library, 6022 Glades Pike, Ste 120, Somerset, PA, 15501-4300. Tel: 814-445-5907. p. 2008

Morgan, Cheryl A, Adminr, Somerset County Federated Library System, 6022 Glades Pike, Ste 120, Somerset, PA, 15501-0043. Tel: 814-445-5907. p. 2008

Morgan, Christi, Dir, Orleans Town & Township Public Library, 174 N Maple St, Orleans, IN, 47452. Tel: 812-865-3270. p. 712

Morgan, Cindi, Dir, La Valle Public Library, 101 W Main, La Valle, WI, 53941-9564. Tel: 608-985-7323. p. 2447

Morgan, Coleen, Ch, Tri-Township Public Library District, 209 S Main St, Troy, IL, 62294. Tel: 618-667-2133. p. 654

Morgan, Cynthia, Br Mgr, Jackson-George Regional Library System, Lucedale-George County Public Library, 507 Oak St, Lucedale, MS, 39452. Tel: 601-947-2123. p. 1228

Morgan, Darlene, Dir, Pike-Amite-Walthall Library System, 1022 Virginia Ave, McComb, MS, 39648. Tel: 601-684-7034, Ext 11. p. 1225

Morgan, Deborah, Archivist, US National Park Service, One Bear Valley Rd, Point Reyes Station, CA, 94956. Tel: 415-464-5125. p. 196

Morgan, Dell, Circ Supvr, Doc Delivery Supvr, Converse College, 580 E Main St, Spartanburg, SC, 29302. Tel: 864-596-9020, 864-596-9071. p. 2069

Morgan, Donna, Br Mgr, Pulaski County Library District, Crocker Library, 602 N Commercial St, Crocker, MO, 65452. Tel: 573-736-5592. p. 1285

Morgan, Elizabeth, Doc Delivery, Librn, UPMC Pinnacle - Harrisburg, Brady Bldg, 1st flr, 205 S Front St, Harrisburg, PA, 17101-2099. Tel: 717-782-5511. p. 1941

Morgan, Ellie, Libr Coord, North Florida College Library, 325 NW Turner Davis Dr, Madison, FL, 32340. Tel: 850-973-1624. p. 419

Morgan, Emily, Ad, Leesburg Public Library, 100 E Main St, Leesburg, FL, 34748. Tel: 352-728-9790. p. 418

Morgan, Heather, Librn, Spokane Falls Community College Library, 3410 W Whistalks Way, Spokane, WA, 99224-5204. Tel: 509-533-3807. p. 2385

Morgan, J C, Libr Dir, Campbell County Public Library District, 3920 Alexandria Pike, Cold Spring, KY, 41076. Tel: 859-781-6166. p. 851

Morgan, Jennifer Bryan, Doc Librn, Indiana University, School of Law Library, Maurer School of Law, 211 S Indiana Ave, Bloomington, IN, 47405. Tel: 812-855-4611. p. 670

Morgan, Jo-Ann, Libr Mgr, Taylor County Public Library, 403 N Washington St, Perry, FL, 32347. Tel: 850-838-3512. p. 437

Morgan, Joyce, Ref (Info Servs), Stanly County Public Library, 133 E Main St, Albemarle, NC, 28001. Tel: 704-986-3759. p. 1671

Morgan, Justine, Dir, Venable LLP Library, 600 Massachusetts Ave NW, Washington, DC, 20001. Tel: 202-344-4000. p. 381

Morgan, Katherine, Dir, Haywood Community College, 185 Freedlander Dr, Clyde, NC, 28721. Tel: 828-627-4551. p. 1682

Morgan, Kathleen, Community Partnerships, Dir of Develop, Lawrence Public Library, 707 Vermont St, Lawrence, KS, 66044-2371. Tel: 785-843-3833, Ext 131. p. 819

Morgan, Kathy, Librn, Tok Community Library, Mile 1314 Alaska Hwy, Tok, AK, 99780. Tel: 907-940-0046. p. 52

Morgan, Kimberly, Dir, Heart of America Library, 201 Third St SW, Rugby, ND, 58368-1793. Tel: 701-776-6223. p. 1740

Morgan, Lisa, Div Mgr, Pasco County Library System, Hudson Branch Library, 8012 Library Rd, Hudson, FL, 34667. Tel: 727-861-3040. p. 410

Morgan, Lisa, Br Mgr, Pamunkey Regional Library, Atlee Branch, 9161 Atlee Rd, Mechanicsville, VA, 23116. Tel: 804-559-0654. p. 2323

Morgan, Lori, Youth Serv Mgr, Jeffersonville Township Public Library, 211 E Court Ave, Jeffersonville, IN, 47130. Tel: 812-285-5630. p. 698

Morgan, Louis F, Dr, Dir, Libr Serv, Lee University, 260 11th St NE, Cleveland, TN, 37311. Tel: 423-614-8551. p. 2093

Morgan, Marianne, Librn, C G Jung Institute of San Francisco, 2040 Gough St, San Francisco, CA, 94109. Tel: 415-771-8055, Ext 207. p. 225

Morgan, Marina, Metadata Librn, Florida Southern College, 111 Lake Hollingsworth Dr, Lakeland, FL, 33801-5698. Tel: 863-616-6450. p. 417

Morgan, Marsha, Librn, Stroud Public Library, 301 W Seventh St, Stroud, OK, 74079. Tel: 918-968-2567. p. 1863

Morgan, Melanie, Dir of Libr, Neuse Regional Library, 510 N Queen St, Kinston, NC, 28501. Tel: 252-527-7066. p. 1699

Morgan, Melissa, Br Serv Mgr, Winnetka-Northfield Public Library District, Northfield Branch, 1785 Orchard Ln, Winnetka, IL, 60093. Tel: 847-446-5990. p. 664

Morgan, Mendell D, Jr, Dir of Develop, El Progreso Memorial Library, 301 W Main St, Uvalde, TX, 78801. Tel: 830-278-2017. p. 2251

Morgan, Natalie, Asst Libr Dir, Boerne Public Library, 451 N Main St, Bldg 100, Boerne, TX, 78006. Tel: 830-249-3053. p. 2148

Morgan, Nicole, Dir, Sheldon Public Library, 925 Fourth Ave, Sheldon, IA, 51201. Tel: 712-324-2442. p. 781

Morgan, Pam, Librn, Eva Public Library, 4549 Hwy 55 E, Eva, AL, 35621. Tel: 256-796-8638. p. 16

Morgan, Pamela, Actg Assoc Univ Librn, Memorial University of Newfoundland, Health Sciences Library, Memorial University, 300 Prince Philip Dr, St. John's, NL, A1B 3V6, CANADA. Tel: 709-777-6025. p. 2610

Morgan, Pamela, Programmer, West Perth Public Library, 105 Saint Andrew St, Mitchell, ON, N0K 1N0, CANADA. Tel: 519-348-9234. p. 2659

Morgan, Patrick, Student Success Librn, Savannah State University, 2200 Tompkins Rd, Savannah, GA, 31404. Tel: 912-358-4324. p. 496

Morgan, Rebecca, Sr Librn, The National Academies of Sciences, Engineering & Medicine, 500 Fifth St NW, Keck 304, Washington, DC, 20001-2721. Tel: 202-334-2125. p. 371

Morgan, Rebecca, Spec Coll Archivist, American Museum of Natural History, 200 Central Park W, New York, NY, 10024-5192. Tel: 212-769-5211. p. 1578

Morgan, Samantha, Dir, Adams Free Library, Two N Main St, Adams, NY, 13605. Tel: 315-232-2265. p. 1481

Morgan, Sarah, Librn, Winterton Public Library, Perlwin Elementary School, 102 Main Rd, Winterton, NL, A0B 3M0, CANADA. Tel: 709-583-2119. p. 2611

Morgan, Sarah Kline, Dir, East Hartford Public Library, 840 Main St, East Hartford, CT, 06108. Tel: 860-290-4340. p. 310

Morgan, Saronda, Bus Mgr, Transylvania County Library, 212 S Gaston St, Brevard, NC, 28712. Tel: 828-884-3151. p. 1675

Morgan, Scott, Fiscal Officer, Operations Dir, Cuyahoga County Public Library, 2111 Snow Rd, Parma, OH, 44134-2728. Tel: 216-398-1800. p. 1813

Morgan, Sharon, Asst Dir, Mount Sterling Public Library, 60 W Columbus St, Mount Sterling, OH, 43143. Tel: 740-869-2430. p. 1804

Morgan, Sonja, Libr Dir, Mark & Emily Turner Memorial Library, 39 Second St, Presque Isle, ME, 04769. Tel: 207-764-2571. p. 938

Morgan, Stephanie, Ch Serv, Kingston Library, 55 Franklin St, Kingston, NY, 12401. Tel: 845-331-0507. p. 1560

Morgan, Susan, Libr Dir, Onondaga Free Library, 4840 W Seneca Tpk, Syracuse, NY, 13215. Tel: 315-492-1727. p. 1650

Morgan, Tammie, Br Mgr, Knox County Public Library System, North Knoxville Branch, 2901 Ocoee Trail, Knoxville, TN, 37917. Tel: 865-525-7036. p. 2106

Morgan, Tara, Br Mgr, Harrison County Library System, Margaret Sherry Branch Library, 2141 Popps Ferry Rd, Biloxi, MS, 39532-4251. Tel: 228-388-1633. p. 1218

Morgan, Teresa, Asst Dir, Carter County Library District, 403 Ash St, Van Buren, MO, 63965. Tel: 573-323-4315. p. 1284

Morgan, William, Circ Supvr, Vanguard University of Southern California, 55 Fair Dr, Costa Mesa, CA, 92626. Tel: 714-966-6380. p. 133

Morgan-Benson, Kim, Ad, San Marcos Public Library, 625 E Hopkins, San Marcos, TX, 78666. Tel: 512-393-8200. p. 2241

Morgano, Anthony, Assoc Dir, Access Serv, Art Institute of Chicago, 111 S Michigan Ave, Chicago, IL, 60603. Tel: 312-443-3666. p. 554

Morgano, Anthony, Archivist/Librn, Milwaukee Art Museum Research Center, 1201 N Prospect Ave, Milwaukee, WI, 53202. Tel: 414-224-3270. p. 2459

Morganstein, Nori, Asst Dir, Youth Serv Librn, Brewster Ladies' Library, 1822 Main St, Brewster, MA, 02631. Tel: 508-896-3913. p. 1001

Morganstein, Nori, Dir, Nahant Public Library, 15 Pleasant St, Nahant, MA, 01908. Tel: 781-581-0306. p. 1037

Morgenstern, Karen, Libr Spec, Wilshire Boulevard Temple, 3663 Wilshire Blvd (Mid-Wilshire)), Los Angeles, CA, 90010. Tel: 424-208-8945. p. 170

Morgeson, Amy, Dir, Outreach Librn, Marion County Public Library, 201 E Main St, Lebanon, KY, 40033-1133. Tel: 270-692-4698. p. 861

Morian, Juliane, Libr Dir, Rochester Hills Public Library, 500 Olde Towne Rd, Rochester, MI, 48307-2043. Tel: 248-656-2900. p. 1144

Morihara, Chizu, Art Librn, University of California, Santa Barbara, Arts Library, UCSB Library, Santa Barbara, CA, 93106-9010. Tel: 805-893-2766. p. 241

Morin, Brian, Ref, Mount Angel Abbey Library, One Abbey Dr, Saint Benedict, OR, 97373. Tel: 503-845-3303. p. 1895

Morin, Brian, Dr, Libr Dir, Mount Angel Abbey Library, One Abbey Dr, Saint Benedict, OR, 97373. Tel: 503-845-3303. p. 1895

Morin, Cheryl, Libr Office Mgr, First Baptist Church Library, 304 Main St S, Cambridge, MN, 55008. Tel: 763-689-1173. p. 1168

Morin, Chris, Br Mgr, Nashville Public Library, Donelson Branch, 2315 Lebanon Pike, Nashville, TN, 37214. Tel: 615-862-5859. p. 2119

Morin, Emily, Head Law Librn, Plymouth Law Library, 52 Obery St, Ste 0117, Plymouth, MA, 02360. Tel: 508-747-4796. p. 1047

Morin, Jodie, Libr Dir, Buena Vista University Library, H W Siebens School of Business/Forum, 610 W Fourth St, Storm Lake, IA, 50588. Tel: 712-749-2097. p. 784

Morin, Julie, Sr Prog Officer, Canadian Association of Research Libraries, 309 Cooper St, Ste 203, Ottawa, ON, K2P 0G5, CANADA. Tel: 613-482-9344, Ext 107. p. 2778

Morin, Kayla, Ch, Madbury Public Library, Nine Town Hall Rd, Madbury, NH, 03823. Tel: 603-743-1400. p. 1371

Morin, Lise, Dir, Human Res, Bibliotheque et Archives Nationales du Quebec, 475 de Maisonneuve E, Montreal, QC, H2L 5C4, CANADA. Tel: 514-873-1101, Ext 3241. p. 2717

Morin, Maegan, Asst Mgr, Bibliotheque Dentinger, 27 Central Ave SE, Falher, AB, T0H 1M0, CANADA. Tel: 780-837-2776. p. 2539

Morin, Meghan, YA Librn, New Milford Public Library, 24 Main St, New Milford, CT, 06776. Tel: 860-355-1191, Ext 204. p. 329

Morin, Rebecca, Head Librn, Worcester Art Museum Library, 55 Salisbury St, Worcester, MA, 01609. Tel: 508-793-4382. p. 1072

Morine, Jeanine, Br Supvr, Wellington County Library, Erin Branch, 14 Boland Dr, Erin, ON, N0B 1T0, CANADA. Tel: 519-833-9762. p. 2641

Moring, Jessica, Coordr, Libr Serv, Graham Hospital Association, 210 W Walnut St, Canton, IL, 61520. Tel: 309-647-5240, Ext 2343. p. 548

Moriorty, Audrey, Exec Dir, Given Memorial Library & Tufts Archives, 150 Cherokee Rd, Pinehurst, NC, 28370. Tel: 910-295-6022. p. 1707

Morissette, Brenda, Libr Tech, Northern College, Haileybury Campus Library, 640 Latchford St, Haileybury, ON, P0J 1K0, CANADA. Tel: 705-672-3376, Ext 8806. p. 2679

Morita, Linda, Archivist/Librn, McMichael Canadian Art Collection, 10365 Islington Ave, Kleinburg, ON, L0J 1C0, CANADA. Tel: 905-893-1121, Ext 2255. p. 2652

Mork, Mark, Libr Asst, North Palm Beach Public Library, 303 Anchorage Dr, North Palm Beach, FL, 33408. Tel: 561-841-3383. p. 429

Morlan, Aimee, Dir, Weeping Water Public Library, 101 W Eldora Ave, Ste 2, Weeping Water, NE, 68463. Tel: 402-267-3050. p. 1340

Morlan, Chelsea, Libr Asst, Library Services, Three Rivers Library System, 11929 Elm St, Ste 18, Omaha, NE, 68144. Tel: 402-330-7884. p. 1330

Morlan, Heather, Dir, Poseyville Carnegie Public Library, 55 S Cale St, Poseyville, IN, 47633. Tel: 812-874-3418. p. 714

Morlan, Wendy, Libr Dir, Linn County Library District No 5, 752 Main St, Pleasanton, KS, 66075. Tel: 913-352-8554. p. 832

Morley, Anne, Libr Dir, Swan Lake Public Library, 70900 Hwy 83, Swan Lake, MT, 59911-5115. Tel: 406-886-2086. p. 1303

Morley, Deb, Libr Dir, Widener University, One University Pl, Chester, PA, 19013. Tel: 610-499-4087. p. 1921

Morley, Gabriel, Exec Dir & State Librn, New Orleans Public Library, 219 Loyola Ave, New Orleans, LA, 70112-2044. Tel: 504-529-7323, 504-596-2570. p. 902

Morley, Juliana, Head, Pub Serv, Biola University Library, 13800 Biola Ave, La Mirada, CA, 90639. Tel: 562-944-0351, Ext 5620. p. 155

Morley, Katherine, Admin Coordr, Tufts University, Hirsh Health Sciences Library, 145 Harrison Ave, Boston, MA, 02111. Tel: 617-636-6705. p. 1034

Morningstar-Gray, Andria, Dir, Hiram College Library, 11694 Hayden St, Hiram, OH, 44234. Tel: 330-569-5489. p. 1790

Moroney, Mary J, Exec Dir, Eastern Oklahoma Library System, 14 E Shawnee, Muskogee, OK, 74403-1001. Tel: 918-683-2846, Ext 239. p. 1854

Morong, Michele, Dir, Albert F Totman Public Library, 28 Parker Head Rd, Phippsburg, ME, 04562. Tel: 207-389-2309. p. 935

Morra, Joseph, Asst Dir, Attleboro Public Library, 74 N Main St, Attleboro, MA, 02703. Tel: 508-222-0157. p. 986

Morral, Sally, Dir, United States Air Force, Nine SVS/SVMG, 17849 16th St, Bldg 25219, Beale AFB, CA, 95903-1611. Tel: 530-634-2314. p. 121

Morran, Sherry, Head Librn, Parkland Regional Library-Manitoba, Grandview Branch, 408 Main St, Grandview, MB, R0L 0Y0, CANADA. Tel: 204-546-5257. p. 2586

Morreale, Cheri, Adult Programs, Ref Librn, Hendrick Hudson Free Library, 185 Kings Ferry Rd, Montrose, NY, 10548. Tel: 914-739-5654. p. 1574

Morrell, Julie, Youth Serv, North Palm Beach Public Library, 303 Anchorage Dr, North Palm Beach, FL, 33408. Tel: 561-841-3383. p. 429

Morrell, Susan, Br Supvr, Elgin County Library, Fred Bodsworth Public Library of Port Burwell, 21 Pitt St, Port Burwell, ON, N0J 1T0, CANADA. Tel: 519-874-4754. p. 2681

Morrell, Susan, Br Supvr, Elgin County Library, Straffordville Library, 9366 Plank Rd, Straffordville, ON, N0J 1Y0, CANADA. Tel: 519-866-3584. p. 2681

Morrell, Tina, Librn, Colorado Technical University Library, 4435 N Chestnut, Colorado Springs, CO, 80907. Tel: 719-590-6708. p. 270

Morrill, Allen S, Cat & Ref Librn, Thiel College, 75 College Ave, Greenville, PA, 16125-2183. Tel: 724-589-2205. p. 1939

Morrill, Brooke, Jr, Teen Librn, Somers Public Library, Two Vision Blvd, Somers, CT, 06071. Tel: 860-763-3501. p. 337

Morrill, Linda, Dir, Lincoln Memorial Library, 21 W Broadway, Lincoln, ME, 04457. Tel: 207-794-2765. p. 930

Morrill, Madison, Libr Assoc, Butler Community College Library & Archives, Butler of Andover Library, Library Rm 5012, 715 E 13th St, Andover, KS, 67002. Tel: 316-323-6371. p. 806

Morrill, Mary Beth, Head, Tech Serv, Canton Public Library, 40 Dyer Ave, Canton, CT, 06019. Tel: 860-693-5800. p. 305

Morrill, Richard, Dr, Librn, Clark Maxwell Jr Library, 1405 CR 526A, Sumterville, FL, 33585. Tel: 352-568-3074. p. 445

Morris, Alicia, Asst Dir, Tufts University, 35 Professors Row, Medford, MA, 02155-5816. Tel: 617-627-3345. p. 1034

Morris, Amy, Br Mgr, Kansas City Public Library, Irene H Ruiz Biblioteca de las Americas, 2017 W Pennway St, Kansas City, MO, 64108. Tel: 816-701-3565. p. 1255

Morris, Angela, Dir, Pub Serv, North Central Washington Libraries, 16 N Columbia St, Wenatchee, WA, 98801. Tel: 509-663-1117, Ext 119. p. 2393

Morris, Angela G, Assoc Libr Dir, Louisville Presbyterian Theological Seminary, 1044 Alta Vista Rd, Louisville, KY, 40205-1798. Tel: 502-992-9398. p. 866

Morris, Audreigh, Librn, Bridge Academy Public Library, 44 Middle Rd, Dresden, ME, 04342. Tel: 207-737-8810. p. 923

Morris, Carol, Dir, Auld-Doudna Public Library, 155 W Grant St, Guide Rock, NE, 68942. Tel: 402-257-4015. p. 1317

Morris, Charlotte, Librn, Northeast Regional Library, Burnsville Public Library, Norman Ave, Burnsville, MS, 38833. Tel: 662-427-9258. p. 1215

Morris, Chris, Web Librn, Kennesaw State University Library System, 385 Cobb Ave NW, MD 1701, Kennesaw, GA, 30144. Tel: 470-578-3909. p. 483

Morris, Christine, Dep Dir, OhioNET, 1500 W Lane Ave, Columbus, OH, 43221-3975. Tel: 614-486-2966. p. 2773

Morris, Christopher, Head, Circ, Coronado Public Library, 640 Orange Ave, Coronado, CA, 92118-1526. Tel: 619-522-2472. p. 132

Morris, Coralie Frances, Dir, United States Air Force, 744 Douhet Dr, Bldg 4244, Barksdale AFB, LA, 71110. Tel: 318-456-4101. p. 881

Morris, David, Br Mgr, Tulsa City-County Library, Judy Z Kishner Library, 10150 N Cincinnati Ave E, Tulsa, OK, 74073. p. 1866

Morris, Deborah, Asst Librn, Liberal & Performing Arts Librn, Online Serv Librn, Southern Arkansas University, 100 E University, Magnolia, AR, 71753-5000. Tel: 870-235-4170. p. 103

Morris, Emerson, Coordr of Res Serv, Colorado Mesa University, 1100 North Ave, Grand Junction, CO, 81501. Tel: 970-248-1091. p. 283

Morris, Eric, Govt Doc, Res & Instrul Serv Librn, North Carolina Central University, 1801 Fayetteville St, Durham, NC, 27707-3129. Tel: 919-530-6598. p. 1685

Morris, Gail, Chief Financial Officer, Tulsa City-County Library, 400 Civic Ctr, Tulsa, OK, 74103. Tel: 918-549-7323. p. 1866

Morris, James, Libr Supvr, Columbia University, Social Work Library, School of Social Work, 2nd Flr, 1255 Amsterdam Ave, New York, NY, 10027. Tel: 212-851-2197. p. 1583

Morris, Jeffory, Curator, i.d.e.a. Museum Library, 150 W Pepper Pl, Mesa, AZ, 85201. Tel: 480-644-5769. p. 66

Morris, Jennifer, Dir, Hulbert Public Library of the Town of Concord, 18 Chapel St, Springville, NY, 14141. Tel: 716-592-7742. p. 1644

Morris, Jill, Exec Dir, Partnership for Academic Library Collaborative & Innovation, 1005 Pontiac Rd, Ste 330, Drexel Hill, PA, 19026. Tel: 215-567-1755. p. 2774

Morris, Julie, Tech Serv Librn, Benzie Shores District Library, 630 Main St, Frankfort, MI, 49635. Tel: 231-352-4671. p. 1108

Morris, Kate, Head, Spec Coll, James Madison University Libraries, 880 Madison Dr, MSC 1704, Harrisonburg, VA, 22807. Tel: 540-568-3444. p. 2324

Morris, Katherine, Dir, Phinehas S Newton Library, 19 On the Common, Royalston, MA, 01368. Tel: 978-249-3572. p. 1050

Morris, Katherine, Dir, Wayne County Public Library, 525A Hwy 64 E, Waynesboro, TN, 38485. Tel: 931-722-5537. p. 2129

Morris, Kathleen, Dir, Public Library of Catasauqua, Third & Bridge Sts, Catasauqua, PA, 18032-2510. Tel: 610-264-4151. p. 1919

Morris, Laurel, Dir, Gaston County Public Library, 1555 E Garrison Blvd, Gastonia, NC, 28054. Tel: 704-868-2164. p. 1690

Morris, Lisa, Libr Asst, Hamilton Public Library, 312 N Davis St, Hamilton, MO, 64644. Tel: 816-583-4832. p. 1247

Morris, Madison, Br Mgr, Saint Charles City-County Library District, Corporate Parkway Branch, 1200 Corporate Pkwy, Wentzville, MO, 63385-4828. Tel: 636-327-4010, 636-332-8280. p. 1278

Morris, Pamela, Libr Mgr, Dawson Creek Municipal Public Library, 1001 McKellar Ave, Dawson Creek, BC, V1G 4W7, CANADA. Tel: 250-782-4661. p. 2565

Morris, Pat, Med Librn, Saint Edward Mercy Medical Center Library, 7301 Rogers Ave, Fort Smith, AR, 72917. Tel: 479-314-6520. p. 96

Morris, Patricia, Coordr, Libr Res, Florida Gateway College, 149 SE College Pl, Lake City, FL, 32025-2006. Tel: 386-754-4391. p. 415

Morris, Peter J, Syst Librn, Clarkson University Libraries, Andrew S Schuler Educational Resources Ctr, CU Box 5590, Eight Clarkson Ave, Potsdam, NY, 13699-5590. Tel: 315-268-4459. p. 1622

Morris, Petra, Head, Children's Servx, Arcadia Public Library, 20 W Duarte Rd, Arcadia, CA, 91006. Tel: 626-821-5568. p. 117

Morris, Pru, Exec Dir of Library & Special Colls, Head, Coll Serv, Texas A&M University-San Antonio, One University Way, San Antonio, TX, 78224. Tel: 210-784-1502. p. 2239

Morris, Rachel, Archivist, Middle Tennessee State University, Center for Popular Music, John Bragg Media & Entertainment Bldg, Rm 140, 1301 E Main St, Murfreesboro, TN, 37132. Tel: 615-898-5884. p. 2117

Morris, Rita, Circ Asst, Lordsburg-Hidalgo Library, 208 E Third St, Lordsburg, NM, 88045. Tel: 575-542-9646. p. 1471

Morris, Scott, Br Mgr, Saint Louis Public Library, Divoll, 4234 N Grand Blvd, Saint Louis, MO, 63107. Tel: 314-534-0313. p. 1275

Morris, Sylvia, Head, Circ, Willingboro Public Library, Willingboro Town Ctr, 220 Willingboro Pkwy, Willingboro, NJ, 08046. Tel: 609-877-0476, 609-877-6668. p. 1455

Morris, Tara, Head, Youth Serv, Haverstraw King's Daughters Public Library, 10 W Ramapo Rd, Garnerville, NY, 10923. Tel: 845-786-3800. p. 1537

Morris, Teresa M, Ref & Instruction Librn, College of San Mateo Library, Bldg 9, 1700 W Hillsdale Blvd, San Mateo, CA, 94402-3795. Tel: 650-574-6579. p. 235

Morris, Todd, Dir, Mesalands Community College Library, 911 S Tenth St, Bldg A, Tucumcari, NM, 88401. Tel: 575-461-4413, Ext 121. p. 1479

Morris, Troy, Head, Info Tech, State Library of Louisiana, 701 N Fourth St, Baton Rouge, LA, 70802-5232. Tel: 225-342-4923. p. 885

Morris, Vicki, Cataloger, Govt Doc, Henry Ford College, 5101 Evergreen Rd, Dearborn, MI, 48128-1495. Tel: 313-845-9761. p. 1096

Morris-Holmes, Karla A, Mgr, Res, Husch Blackwell LLP, 190 Carondelet Plaza, Ste 600, Saint Louis, MO, 63105. Tel: 314-480-1500. p. 1271

Morrish, Jeanette F, Libr Dir, Thomas E Fleschner Memorial Library, 11935 Silver Creek Dr, Birch Run, MI, 48415-9767. Tel: 989-624-5171. p. 1086

Morrison, Bill, Tech Serv, Franklin County Library, 906 N Main St, Louisburg, NC, 27549-2199. Tel: 919-496-2111. p. 1701

Morrison, Brian, Access Serv Mgr, Greenville County Library System, 25 Heritage Green Pl, Greenville, SC, 29601-2034. Tel: 864-242-5000, Ext 2257. p. 2061

Morrison, Catherine, Adult Serv Mgr, Asst Dir, Scarborough Public Library, 48 Gorham Rd, Scarborough, ME, 04074. Tel: 207-396-6270. p. 939

Morrison, Christine, Youth Serv Librn, Randall Library, 19 Crescent St, Stow, MA, 01775. Tel: 978-897-8572. p. 1058

Morrison, Corrinne, Libr Mgr, Uxbridge Public Library, Nine Toronto St S, Uxbridge, ON, L9P 1P7, CANADA. Tel: 905-852-9747. p. 2701

Morrison, Drake, Br Supvr, Kern County Library, Southwest Branch, 8301 Ming Ave, Bakersfield, CA, 93311-2020. Tel: 661-664-7716. p. 120

Morrison, Gregory, Head, Ref, Wheaton College, 510 Irving Ave, Wheaton, IL, 60187-4234. Tel: 630-752-5847. p. 662

Morrison, Jenny, Dir, Eau Gallie Public Library, 1521 Pineapple Ave, Melbourne, FL, 32935-6594. Tel: 321-255-4304. p. 420

Morrison, Julia, Chief Financial Officer, Dir, Corporate Serv, Vancouver Public Library, 350 W Georgia St, Vancouver, BC, V6B 6B1, CANADA. Tel: 604-331-3603. p. 2581

Morrison, Kim, Dr, Info Literacy, Libr Coord, Chabot College Library, 25555 Hesperian Blvd, Hayward, CA, 94545. Tel: 510-723-6762. p. 150

Morrison, Kirk, Br Mgr, New Haven Free Public Library, Fair Haven, 182 Grand Ave, New Haven, CT, 06513. Tel: 203-946-8116. p. 326

Morrison, Lauren, Dir, Law Librn, Hamilton County Law Library, Hamilton County Court House, 1000 Main St, Rm 601, Cincinnati, OH, 45202. Tel: 513-946-5300. p. 1760

Morrison, Laurie, Coll Librn, Head of Liaison Services, Brock University, 1812 Sir Isaac Brock Way, St. Catharines, ON, L2S 3A1, CANADA. Tel: 905-688-5550, Ext 5281. p. 2679

Morrison, Marcia, Dir, Libr Develop, California State University, Fresno, Henry Madden Library, 5200 N Barton Ave, Mail Stop ML-34, Fresno, CA, 93740-8014. Tel: 559-278-7177. p. 144

Morrison, Nyia, Br Mgr, Free Library of Philadelphia, Paschalville Branch, 6942 Woodland Ave, Philadelphia, PA, 19142-1823. Tel: 215-685-2662. p. 1979

Morrison, Pat, Br Mgr, Jacksonville Public Library, Highlands Branch, 1826 Dunn Ave, Jacksonville, FL, 32218-4712. Tel: 904-757-7702. p. 412

Morrison Putcher, Julie, Dir, Ahira Hall Memorial Library, 37 W Main St, Brocton, NY, 14716-9747. Tel: 716-792-9418. p. 1497

Morrison, Rob, Assoc Librn, National Louis University Library, 18 S Michigan Ave, 3rd Flr, Chicago, IL, 60603. Tel: 312-261-3372. p. 565

Morrison, Ruth W, Agency Mgr, Memphis Public Library, Business/Sciences, 3030 Poplar Ave, Memphis, TN, 38111. Tel: 901-415-2736. p. 2113

Morrison, Sara B, Dir, Briggs District Library, 108 E Railroad St, Saint Johns, MI, 48879-1526. Tel: 989-224-4702. p. 1148

Morrison, Sara M, Asst Prof, Librn, Erskine College & Theological Seminary, One Depot St, Due West, SC, 29639. Tel: 864-379-8747. p. 2058

Morrison Spinney, Ann, Dir, Northern Maine Community College Library, 33 Edgemont Dr, Presque Isle, ME, 04769. Tel: 207-768-2718. p. 938

Morrison, Sue, Asst Dir, Traer Public Library, 531 Second St, Traer, IA, 50675. Tel: 319-478-2180. p. 787

Morrison, Vanessa, Adult Serv, Franklin Park Public Library District, 10311 Grand Ave, Franklin Park, IL, 60131. Tel: 847-455-6016, Ext 247. p. 590

Morrison-Korajczyk, Lisa, Asst Libr Dir, Head, Adult Serv, Pub Serv Coordr, Matteson Area Public Library District, 801 S School St, Matteson, IL, 60443-1897. Tel: 708-748-4431. p. 615

Morriss, Jessie, Librn, Seymour Community Library, 123 N Fifth St, Seymour, IA, 52590. Tel: 641-898-2966. p. 781

Morrissey, Carla, Circ, Mount Wachusett Community College Library, 444 Green St, Gardner, MA, 01440. Tel: 978-630-9125. p. 1020

Morrissey, Carla, Evening Supvr, Anna Maria College, 50 Sunset Lane, Paxton, MA, 01612-1198. Tel: 508-849-3405. p. 1045

Morrissey, Jake, ILL Coordr, Lindenwood University Library, 209 S Kingshighway, Saint Charles, MO, 63301. Tel: 636-949-4758. p. 1268

Morrissey, Margaret, Libr Dir, Jacob Edwards Library, 236 Main St, Southbridge, MA, 01550-2598. Tel: 508-764-5426, Ext 101. p. 1055

Morrissey, Renee, Librn, Alberta Innovates, 250 Karl Clark Rd, Edmonton, AB, T6N 1E4, CANADA. Tel: 780-450-5229. p. 2535

Morrow, Abby, Youth Serv Librn, Jesup Memorial Library, 34 Mount Desert St, Bar Harbor, ME, 04609-1727. Tel: 207-288-4245. p. 916

Morrow, Abby, Commun Engagement Librn, Ellsworth Public Library, 20 State St, Ellsworth, ME, 04605. Tel: 207-667-6363. p. 924

Morrow, Diana, Dir, Gary Public Library, 220 W Fifth Ave, Gary, IN, 46402-1215. Tel: 219-886-2484. p. 686

Morrow, Erin, District Consultant, Easton Area Public Library & District Center, 515 Church St, Easton, PA, 18042-3587. Tel: 610-258-2917. p. 1928

Morrow, Paula, Libr Tech, Holy Cross College, 54515 State Rd 933 N, Notre Dame, IN, 46556-0308. Tel: 574-239-8391. p. 711

Morrow, Terran, Libr Tech, Mesabi Range Community & Technical College Library, 1001 Chestnut St W, Virginia, MN, 55792. Tel: 218-749-7740. p. 1206

Morry, Lisa, Library Tech, Reserves & Circulation, University of the Fraser Valley, Chilliwack Campus, 45190 Caen Ave, Bldg A, Chilliwack, BC, V2R 0N3, CANADA. Tel: 604-504-7441, Ext 2471. p. 2562

Morse, Barbara, Head, Tech Serv, New Britain Public Library, 20 High St, New Britain, CT, 06051. Tel: 860-224-3155, Ext 126. p. 324

Morse, Betsy, Dir, Riceville Public Library, 307 Woodland Ave, Riceville, IA, 50466. Tel: 641-985-2273. p. 779

Morse, Carey, Interim Dean of Libr, Quinsigamond Community College, 670 W Boylston St, Worcester, MA, 01606-2092. Tel: 508-854-4366. p. 1072

Morse, Kara, Head, Children's Servx, Head, Teen Serv, Rockville Public Library, 52 Union St, Vernon, CT, 06066-3155. Tel: 860-875-5892. p. 342

Morse, Karen Walton, Director, Distinctive Collections, University of Rhode Island, 15 Lippitt Rd, Kingston, RI, 02881-2011. Tel: 401-874-2666. p. 2033

Morse, Lori, Head Librn, Free Library of Philadelphia, General Information Department, 1901 Vine St, Rm 215, Philadelphia, PA, 19103-1116. Tel: 215-686-5322. p. 1978

Morse, Nicole, Dir, Gill Memorial Library, 145 E Broad St, Paulsboro, NJ, 08066. Tel: 856-423-5155. p. 1434

Morse, Sara, Br Mgr, Nashville Public Library, East Branch, 206 Gallatin Ave, Nashville, TN, 37206. Tel: 615-862-5860. p. 2119

Morse, Terry, Chief Exec Officer, National Ground Water Association, 601 Dempsey Rd, Westerville, OH, 43081. Tel: 614-898-7791. p. 1830

Morstatt, Tara, Dir, Haledon Free Public Library, Municipal Bldg, 3rd Flr, 510 Belmont Ave, Haledon, NJ, 07508. Tel: 973-790-3808. p. 1407

Mort, Dori, IT Spec, Milton-Union Public Library, 560 S Main St, West Milton, OH, 45383. Tel: 937-698-5515. p. 1830

Mort, Rhonda, Ch, Willard Library of Evansville, 21 First Ave, Evansville, IN, 47710-1294. Tel: 812-425-4309. p. 682

Mortensen, Annabelle, Dir, Access Serv, Skokie Public Library, 5215 Oakton St, Skokie, IL, 60077-3680. Tel: 847-673-7774. p. 647

Mortensen-Torres, Heidi J, Med Librn, Sutter Roseville Medical Center Library, One Medical Plaza, Roseville, CA, 95661-3037. Tel: 916-781-1580. p. 205
Mortenson, Autumn, Circ, Ref Librn, Ouachita Baptist University, 410 Ouachita St, OBU Box 3742, Arkadelphia, AR, 71998-0001. Tel: 870-245-5123. p. 89
Mortenson, Wina, Youth Serv, Galesville Public Library, 16787 S Main St, Galesville, WI, 54630. Tel: 608-582-2552. p. 2436
Mortimer, Leslie, Adult Serv Mgr, Patten Free Library, 33 Summer St, Bath, ME, 04530. Tel: 207-443-5141, Ext 21. p. 916
Morton, Andy, Librn, Emerging Web Tech, University of Richmond, 261 Richmond Way, Richmond, VA, 23173. Tel: 804-287-6047. p. 2342
Morton, Hope, Coll Develop Librn, Northeast Regional Library, 1023 Fillmore St, Corinth, MS, 38834-4199. Tel: 662-287-7311. p. 1215
Morton, Jeri, Librn, Youth & Family Serv, Chesapeake Public Library, Greenbrier, 1214 Volvo Pkwy, Chesapeake, VA, 23320-7600. Tel: 757-410-7069. p. 2311
Morton, Judy, Asst Br Librn, Pottawatomie Wabaunsee Regional Library, Eskridge Branch, 115 S Main St, Eskridge, KS, 66423. Tel: 785-449-2296. p. 834
Morton, Karen, Coll Mgr, Perot Museum of Nature & Science, 2021 Postal Way, Dallas, TX, 75212. Tel: 214-428-5555. p. 2167
Morton, Mark, Dir, Leland Township Public Library, 203 E Cedar, Leland, MI, 49654. Tel: 231-256-9152. p. 1126
Morton, Michelle, Instruction Librn, Cabrillo College, 6500 Soquel Dr, Aptos, CA, 95003-3198. Tel: 831-479-6473. p. 117
Morton, Pam, Tech Serv, Dixie Regional Library System, 111 N Main St, Pontotoc, MS, 38863. Tel: 662-489-3961. p. 1229
Morton, Rachel, Br Mgr, Heavener Public Library, 203 E Ave C, Heavener, OK, 74937. Tel: 918-653-2870. p. 1849
Morton, Sandra, Br Librn, Roane County Public Library, Geary Library-Health Care Facility, One Library Lane, Ste 1, Left Hand, WV, 25251. Tel: 304-565-4608. p. 2415
Morton, Tim, Asst Librn, Kiowa County Library, 320 S Main, Ste 120, Greensburg, KS, 67054. Tel: 620-723-1118. p. 811
Morton, Velma, Libr Mgr, New York Public Library - Astor, Lenox & Tilden Foundations, 125th Street Branch, 224 E 125th St, (Near Third Ave), New York, NY, 10035-1786. Tel: 212-534-5050. p. 1596
Morton-Owens, Emily, Asst Univ Librn, Digital Libr Developer, University of Pennsylvania Libraries, 3420 Walnut St, Philadelphia, PA, 19104-6206. Tel: 215-898-7556. p. 1987
Mosbo Ballestro, Julie, Asst Provost, Univ Librn, Texas A&M University Libraries, 400 Spence St, College Station, TX, 77843. p. 2157
Moscatello, Sarah, Br Coordr, Marathon County Public Library, Joseph Dessert Branch, 123 Main St, Mosinee, WI, 54455. Tel: 715-693-2144. p. 2485
Moschansky, Sandra, Libr Mgr, Radway Public Library, 4915 50th St, Radway, AB, T0A 2V0, CANADA. Tel: 780-736-3548. p. 2550
Mosele, Marcia, Circ, Carroll County Library, 625 High St, Ste 102, Huntingdon, TN, 38344-3903. Tel: 731-986-1919. p. 2101
Moseley, Caroline, Archivist, Bowdoin College Library, 3000 College Sta, Brunswick, ME, 04011-8421. p. 919
Moseley, Coco, Exec Dir, Henry Sheldon Museum of Vermont History, One Park St, Middlebury, VT, 05753. Tel: 802-388-2117. p. 2288
Moseley, Maggie, Co-Dir, Coldspring Area Public Library, 14221 State Hwy 150 W, Coldspring, TX, 77331. Tel: 936-653-3104. p. 2157
Moser, Anna, Youth Serv Mgr, Lincoln Library, 326 S Seventh St, Springfield, IL, 62701. Tel: 217-753-4900. p. 650
Moser, Anne, Sr Spec Librn, University of Wisconsin-Madison, Wisconsin Water Library, 1975 Willow Dr, 2nd Flr, Madison, WI, 53706-1177. Tel: 608-262-3069. p. 2452
Moser, Janna, Dir, Stayton Public Library, 515 N First Ave, Stayton, OR, 97383-1703. Tel: 503-769-3313. p. 1899
Moser, Joseph, Libr Tech 1, Guerra Joe A Laredo Public Library, Barbara Fasken Branch Library, 15201 Cerralvo Dr, Laredo, TX, 78045. Tel: 956-795-2400, Ext 2600. p. 2209
Moser, Sarah, Dir, Haverhill Public Library, 99 Main St, Haverhill, MA, 01830-5092. Tel: 978-373-1586, Ext 621. p. 1024
Moses, Donald, Univ Librn, University of Prince Edward Island, 550 University Ave, Charlottetown, PE, C1A 4P3, CANADA. Tel: 902-566-0343. p. 2707
Moses, Erica, Libr Dir, Genesee Area Library, 301 Main St, Genesee, PA, 16923-8805. Tel: 814-228-3328. p. 1935
Moses, Ginny, Dir, Bell-Whittington Public Library, 2400 Memorial Pkwy, Portland, TX, 78374. Tel: 361-777-4560. p. 2229
Moses, James, Br Mgr, Saint Louis Public Library, Buder, 4401 Hampton Ave, Saint Louis, MO, 63109-2237. Tel: 314-352-2900. p. 1275
Moses, Roslind, Tech Asst, California State Department of Water Resources, 1416 Ninth St, Rm 1118-13, Sacramento, CA, 95814. Tel: 916-653-0474. p. 208
Moses, Seth, Br Mgr, Mid-Continent Public Library, Colbern Road Branch, 1000 NE Colbern Rd, Lee's Summit, MO, 64086. Tel: 816-525-9924. p. 1250
Moses, Sherod, Libr Syst Coordr, Virginia State University, One Hayden Dr, Petersburg, VA, 23806. Tel: 804-524-5942. p. 2337
Mosey, Sara, Libr Operations Supvr, Carroll University, 100 N East Ave, Waukesha, WI, 53186. Tel: 262-524-7179. p. 2484
Mosher, Jeri, Librn, Reading Community Library, 104 N Main St, Reading, MI, 49274. Tel: 517-283-3916. p. 1143
Mosher, Laura, Engagement Librn, United States Military Academy Library, Jefferson Hall Library & Learning Ctr, 758 Cullum Rd, West Point, NY, 10996. Tel: 845-938-8301. p. 1663
Moshier, Caleb, Head, Outreach Serv, Manchester City Library, 405 Pine St, Manchester, NH, 03104-6199. Tel: 603-624-6550. p. 1372
Moshier, Caleb, Head, Outreach Serv, Manchester City Library, West Manchester Branch Library, 76 N Main St, Manchester, NH, 03102-4084. Tel: 603-624-6560. p. 1372
Moshiri, Farhad L, AV Librn, University of the Incarnate Word, 4301 Broadway, CPO 297, San Antonio, TX, 78209-6397. Tel: 210-829-3842. p. 2240
Mosier, Cindy, Assoc Librn, Scott County Library System, Buffalo Branch, 329 Dodge St, Buffalo, IA, 52728. Tel: 563-381-1797. p. 750
Mosier, Shawna, Storytime Dir, Towanda Public Library, 620 Highland, Towanda, KS, 67144-9042. Tel: 316-536-2464. p. 840
Mosier, Vikijane, Dir, Palacios Library, Inc, 326 Main St, Palacios, TX, 77465. Tel: 361-972-3234. p. 2224
Mosing, Steve, Automation Syst Mgr, Rochester Public Library, 101 Second St SE, Rochester, MN, 55904-3776. Tel: 507-328-2361. p. 1194
Moskala, Suzanne, Librn, United States Army, West Point Post Library, 622 Swift Rd, West Point, NY, 10996-1981. Tel: 845-938-2974. p. 1663
Moskowitz, Paula, Head of Instruction, Manhattanville University Library, 2900 Purchase St, Purchase, NY, 10577. Tel: 914-323-3159. p. 1624
Moskowitz, Sharon, Dir, Youth Librn, Jackson Memorial Library, 71 Main St, Tenants Harbor, ME, 04860. Tel: 207-372-8961. p. 943
Moskwa, Alyssa, Tech Serv Librn, Owens Community College Library, 30335 Oregon Rd, Perrysburg, OH, 43551. Tel: 567-661-7015. p. 1815
Mosley, Erica, Br Mgr, Scenic Regional Library, Owensville Branch, 503 S Olive St, Owensville, MO, 65066. Tel: 573-437-2188. p. 1283
Mosley, Joyce A, Dir, Ellendale Public Library, 75 First Ave S, Ellendale, ND, 58436. Tel: 701-349-3852. p. 1732
Mosley, Nancy, Cataloger, Mint Museum, 2730 Randolph Rd, Charlotte, NC, 28207. Tel: 704-337-2000, 704-337-2023. p. 1680
Mosley, Sherry, Asst Mgr, Ref Spec, First Regional Library, B J Chain Public Library, 6619 Hwy 305 N, Olive Branch, MS, 38654. Tel: 662-895-5900. p. 1219
Mosley, Shonnye, Br Mgr, Richland Parish Library, Mangham Branch, 302 Hixon St, Mangham, LA, 71259. Tel: 318-248-2493. p. 906
Mosorjak, Therese, Head, Tech Serv, Thomas Crane Public Library, 40 Washington St, Quincy, MA, 02269-9164. Tel: 617-376-1300. p. 1048
Mospan, Tara, Assoc Dir, Head, Res Serv, Arizona State University, College of Law, Arizona State University MC 9620, 111 E Taylor St, Ste 350, Phoenix, AZ, 85004. Tel: 480-965-4868. p. 69
Moss, Alesia, Asst Mgr, Portland Public Library of Sumner County, 301 Portland Blvd, Portland, TN, 37148-1229. Tel: 615-325-2279. p. 2124
Moss, Alison, Dir, Parkland Regional Library-Manitoba, 504 Main St N, Dauphin, MB, R7N 1C9, CANADA. Tel: 204-638-6410. p. 2586
Moss, Bess, Librn, Mississippi State University, Bldg 1532, 82 Stoneville Rd, Stoneville, MS, 38776. Tel: 662-686-3260. p. 1233
Moss, Charlene, Dir, Medford Public Library, 123 S Main St, Medford, OK, 73759. Tel: 580-395-2342. p. 1853
Moss, Emily, Instrul Serv Librn, Diablo Valley College Library, 321 Golf Club Rd, Pleasant Hill, CA, 94523-1576. Tel: 925-969-2587. p. 195
Moss, Geneva, Commun Libr Mgr, Contra Costa County Library, Clayton Library, 6125 Clayton Rd, Clayton, CA, 94517. Tel: 925-673-0659. p. 174
Moss, Julie, Librn, Anshe Chesed Fairmount Temple, 23737 Fairmount Blvd, Beachwood, OH, 44122-2296. Tel: 216-464-1330, Ext 123. p. 1749
Moss, Julie, Librn, Park Synagogue, 27500 Shaker Blvd, Pepper Pike, OH, 44124. Tel: 216-371-2244, Ext 223, 216-831-5363, Ext 223. p. 1815
Moss, Katherine, Coll Mgt Librn, Clarkson University Libraries, Andrew S Schuler Educational Resources Ctr, CU Box 5590, Eight Clarkson Ave, Potsdam, NY, 13699-5590. Tel: 315-268-4452. p. 1622
Moss, Maria, Libr Dir, Linwood Public Library, 301 Davis Ave, Linwood, NJ, 08221. Tel: 609-926-7991, Ext 1. p. 1412
Moss, Melba, Coordr, Pub Serv, Saint Clair County Library System, 210 McMorran Blvd, Port Huron, MI, 48060-4098. Tel: 810-987-7323. p. 1142
Moss, Nicole, Law Librn, Preti Flaherty Beliveau & Pachios, One City Ctr, Portland, ME, 04112. Tel: 207-791-3000. p. 937
Moss, Sara, Associate Dir of Education, Howard C Raether Library, 13625 Bishop's Dr, Brookfield, WI, 53005. Tel: 262-789-1880. p. 2425
Moss, Stuart, Dir, Nathan S Kline Institute for Psychiatric Research, 140 Old Orangeburg Rd, Bldg 35, Orangeburg, NY, 10962. p. 1612
Moss, Susan, Circ Spec, Outreach Serv Spec, Prog Spec, Richard Bland College Library, Commons Bldg, 11301 Johnson Rd, Petersburg, VA, 23805. Tel: 804-862-6226. p. 2337
Moss, Thomas, Tech Serv, United States Army, 562 Quarters Rd, Bldg 12420, Fort Lee, VA, 23801-1705. Tel: 804-765-8170. p. 2319
Mossey, Kasey, Communications Coordr, Laramie County Library System, 2200 Pioneer Ave, Cheyenne, WY, 82001-3610. Tel: 307-773-7225. p. 2492

Mosshammer, Greg, Marketing Lead, Wyoming State Library, 2800 Central Ave, Cheyenne, WY, 82002. Tel: 307-777-6338. p. 2493
Mossing, Cary, Br Mgr, San Mateo County Library, Brisbane Library, 250 Visitacion Ave, Brisbane, CA, 94005. Tel: 415-467-2060. p. 235
Most, Carmel, Librn, Ceresco Community Library, 425 S Second St, Ceresco, NE, 68017. Tel: 402-665-2112. p. 1310
Most, Gregory, Image Coll, National Gallery of Art Library, Fourth St & Pennsylvania Ave NW, Washington, DC, 20565. Tel: 202-842-6511. p. 372
Most, Kathi, Dir, Red Oak Public Library, 400 N Second St, Red Oak, IA, 51566. Tel: 712-623-6516. p. 778
Mostad-Jensen, Liv, Dir, Coleraine Public Library, 203 Cole Ave, Coleraine, MN, 55722. Tel: 218-245-2315. p. 1170
Mostyn, Kristine, Dir, Lee-Whedon Memorial Library, 620 West Ave, Medina, NY, 14103. Tel: 585-798-3430. p. 1570
Mota, Vanessa, Admin Librn, Seekonk Public Library, 410 Newman Ave, Seekonk, MA, 02771. Tel: 508-336-8230, Ext 56100. p. 1052
Moten, Kelley, Dir, Libr Serv, Northland Public Library, 300 Cumberland Rd, Pittsburgh, PA, 15237-5455. Tel: 412-366-8100, Ext 146. p. 1994
Mothmiller, Emily, Librn, Miami County Law Library, 201 W Main St, 3rd Flr, Troy, OH, 45373. Tel: 937-440-5994. p. 1826
Motl, Melissa, Assoc Librn, University of Wisconsin Oshkosh, 801 Elmwood Ave, Oshkosh, WI, 54901. Tel: 920-929-1148. p. 2467
Motley, Gwen, Br Mgr, Franklin-Springboro Public Library, Springboro Branch, 125 Park Lane, Springboro, OH, 45066. Tel: 937-748-3200. p. 1786
Motlong, Alice, Librn, Township of Sioux Narrows-Nestor Falls, Sioux Narrows Public Library, 5689 Hwy 71, Sioux Narrows, ON, P0X 1N0, CANADA. Tel: 807-226-5204. p. 2678
Motszko, Jennifer, Head, Archives, University of Wisconsin-Whitewater, 750 W Main St, Whitewater, WI, 53190-1790. Tel: 262-472-5515. p. 2488
Mott, Jaime, Youth Serv Librn, John Jermain Memorial Library, 201 Main St, Sag Harbor, NY, 11963. Tel: 631-725-0049, Ext 230. p. 1634
Mott, Lori, Dir of Collections & Exhibitions, Toledo Museum of Art Reference Library, 2445 Monroe St, Toledo, OH, 43620. Tel: 419-255-8000. p. 1825
Mott, Richard, Mgr, Strategic Initiatives, Jacksonville Public Library, 303 N Laura St, Jacksonville, FL, 32202-3505. Tel: 904-630-2407. p. 411
Motte, Flora, Librn, Emery County Library System, Huntington Branch, 92 S Main, Huntington, UT, 84528. Tel: 435-687-9590. p. 2262
Motter, Laura, Law Librn, Dauphin County Law Library, Dauphin County Courthouse, 4th Flr, 101 Market St, Harrisburg, PA, 17101. Tel: 717-780-6605. p. 1940
Mottinger, Nathaniel, Dir, Burlington Township Library, 135 Elm St, Burlington, MI, 49029. Tel: 517-765-2702. p. 1087
Moul, Rick, Exec Dir, Partnership Among South Carolina Academic Libraries, 1122 Lady St, Ste 400, Columbia, SC, 29201. Tel: 803-734-0900. p. 2775
Moulaison Sandy, Heather, Assoc Prof, University of Missouri-Columbia, 303 Townsend Hall, Columbia, MO, 65211. Tel: 573-882-4546. p. 2787
Mouland, Tracy, Libr Tech II, College of the North Atlantic Library Services, Bonavista Campus, 301 Confederation Dr, Bonavista, NL, A0C 1B0, CANADA. Tel: 709-468-1716. p. 2609
Moulds, Loren, Head, Digital Preservation & Scholarship, University of Virginia, Arthur J Morris Law Library, 580 Massie Rd, Charlottesville, VA, 22903-1738. Tel: 434-924-3877. p. 2310
Moull, Erin, Dir, Croton Township Library, 8260 S Croton-Hardy Dr, Newaygo, MI, 49337. Tel: 231-652-1615, Ext 305. p. 1137
Moulton, Joan, Libr Dir, Blanche R Solomon Memorial Library, 17 Park St, Headland, AL, 36345. Tel: 334-693-2706. p. 20
Moulton, Maria, Dir, Ossipee Public Library, 74 Main St, Center Ossipee, NH, 03814. Tel: 603-539-6390. p. 1357
Moulton, Teresa, Head, Pub Serv, New Albany-Floyd County Public Library, 180 W Spring St, New Albany, IN, 47150. Tel: 812-944-8464. p. 709
Moulton, Wendy, Dir, Abilene Public Library, 209 NW Fourth, Abilene, KS, 67410-2690. Tel: 785-263-3082. p. 795
Mounce, Michael, Ref (Info Servs), Delta State University, Laflore Circle at Fifth Ave, Cleveland, MS, 38733-2599. Tel: 662-846-4430. p. 1214
Mount, Davina, Dir, Brantley Public Library, Ten MLK Dr, Brantley, AL, 36009. Tel: 334-527-8624, Option 2. p. 10
Mount, Lisa, Circ Mgr, University of Nebraska at Kearney, 2508 11th Ave, Kearney, NE, 68849-2240. Tel: 308-865-8850. p. 1319
Mount, Stephen, Syst Librn, Union University, 1050 Union University Dr, Jackson, TN, 38305-3697. Tel: 731-661-5419. p. 2102
Mountain, Mary, Exec Dir, Laramie Plains Museum Association Inc Library, 603 Ivinson Ave, Laramie, WY, 82070-3299. Tel: 307-742-4448. p. 2496
Mountford, Britt, Electronic Res Librn, Instruction Librn, Lipscomb University, One University Park Dr, Nashville, TN, 37204-3951. Tel: 615-966-5803. p. 2119
Mountford, Kelli, Libr Dir, Karl Junginger Memorial Library, 625 N Monroe St, Waterloo, WI, 53594-1183. Tel: 920-478-3344. p. 2483
Mounts, Mark, Bus & Econ Librn, Eng Librn, Dartmouth College Library, Feldberg Business & Engineering Library, 6193 Murdough Ctr, Hanover, NH, 03755-3560. Tel: 603-646-2191. p. 1366
Mouratidis, Roxann, Head, Scholarly Communications, Florida State University Libraries, Charlotte Edwards Maguire Medical Library, 1115 W Call St, Tallahassee, FL, 32306-4300. Tel: 850-645-9398. p. 447
Moussot, Julie, Circ Supvr, Wallkill Public Library, Seven Bona Ventura Ave, Wallkill, NY, 12589-4422. Tel: 845-895-3707. p. 1658
Moutes, Patty, Bus Mgr, Fiscal Officer, Ella M Everhard Public Library, 132 Broad St, Wadsworth, OH, 44281-1897. Tel: 330-335-1297. p. 1827
Mouton, Jessica, Pub Relations Coordr, Terrebonne Parish Library, 151 Library Dr, Houma, LA, 70360. Tel: 985-876-5861. p. 891
Mouton, Jessica, Tech Serv Librn, Fletcher Technical Community College Library, 1407 Hwy 311, Rm 128, Schriever, LA, 70395. Tel: 985-488-7907. p. 907
Mouton, Lenna, Direct Serv Coordr, Rapides Parish Library, 411 Washington St, Alexandria, LA, 71301-8338. Tel: 318-445-6436, Ext 1002. p. 880
Mouton, Osaria, Libr Mgr, Saint Mary Parish Library, 206 Iberia St, Franklin, LA, 70538. Tel: 337-828-1624, 337-828-1627. p. 890
Mouw, Christine, Curator, National Archives & Records Administration, 1200 President Clinton Ave, Little Rock, AR, 72201. Tel: 501-374-4242, 501-748-0419. p. 101
Mouw, James, Assoc Univ Librn, Coll & Access, The University of Chicago Library, 1100 E 57th St, Chicago, IL, 60637-1502. Tel: 773-702-8732. p. 569
Mouyios, Alex, Br Mgr, Brooklyn Public Library, Walt Whitman Branch, 93 Saint Edwards St, Brooklyn, NY, 11205. Tel: 718-935-0244. p. 1504
Mowdy, Brenda S, Dir, John B Curtis Free Public Library, 435 Main Rd, Bradford, ME, 04410. Tel: 207-327-2111. p. 918
Mowen, Mary Beth, Asst Dir, Keyser-Mineral County Public Library, 105 N Main St, Keyser, WV, 26726. Tel: 304-788-3222. p. 2406
Mowery, Rose, Br Mgr, Brumback Library, Willshire Branch, 323 State St, Willshire, OH, 45898. Tel: 419-495-4138. p. 1827
Mowery, Rose, Br Mgr, Brumback Library, Wren Branch, 103 State Rte 49, Wren, OH, 45899. Tel: 419-495-4174. p. 1827
Moxham, Tiffany, Assoc UniveLibrn for Content & Discovery, University of California, Riverside, 900 University Ave, Riverside, CA, 92521. Tel: 951-827-3220. p. 203
Moxley, Clinton J, Regional Dir, Three Rivers Regional Library System, 280 S Mahogany St, Jesup, GA, 31546. Tel: 912-559-2391. p. 483
Moxley, Mallory, Evening Libr Asst, Florida Southern College, 111 Lake Hollingsworth Dr, Lakeland, FL, 33801-5698. Tel: 863-680-4164. p. 417
Moy, Walter, Online Serv, New York State Supreme Court, First Judicial District Criminal Law Library, 100 Centre St, 17th Flr, New York, NY, 10013. Tel: 646-386-3890, 646-386-3891. p. 1598
Moya, Jesus, Acq Mgr, Adult Serv, Galveston County Library System, 2310 Sealy Ave, Galveston, TX, 77550. Tel: 409-763-8854, Ext 137. p. 2183
Moya, Zhaina, Ref Serv, Minot Public Library, 516 Second Ave SW, Minot, ND, 58701-3792. Tel: 701-852-1045. p. 1738
Moye, Allen, Assoc Dean for IT & Library Servs, DePaul University Libraries, Vincent G Rinn Law Library, 25 E Jackson Blvd, 5th Flr, Chicago, IL, 60604-2287. Tel: 312-362-6893. p. 560
Moye, Tanya, Mgr, Elsmere Public Library, 30 Spruce Ave, Wilmington, DE, 19805. Tel: 302-892-2210. p. 357
Moye, Tanya, Mgr, Woodlawn Library, 2020 W Ninth St, Wilmington, DE, 19805. Tel: 302-571-7425. p. 358
Moyer, Debora, Coordr, Jackson Community College, 2111 Emmons Rd, Jackson, MI, 49201-8399. Tel: 517-796-8621. p. 1119
Moyer, Diane, Dir, Dryden Township Library, 5480 Main St, Dryden, MI, 48428-9968. Tel: 810-796-3586. p. 1101
Moyer, Forrest L, Archivist, Mennonite Historians of Eastern Pennsylvania, 565 Yoder Rd, Harleysville, PA, 19438-1020. Tel: 215-256-3020. p. 1939
Moyer, Heidi Abbey, Humanities Librn, Pennsylvania State University-Harrisburg Library, 351 Olmsted Dr, Middletown, PA, 17057-4850. Tel: 717-948-6056. p. 1963
Moyer Hotz, Carla, Head, Access Serv, Calvin University & Calvin Theological Seminary, 1855 Knollcrest Circle SE, Grand Rapids, MI, 49546-4402. Tel: 616-526-5256. p. 1110
Moyer, Katherine, Coordr, User Serv, Spring Arbor University, 106 E Main St, Spring Arbor, MI, 49283. Tel: 517-750-6439. p. 1152
Moyer, Lisa, Circ Supvr, Info Res, Penn State Behrend, 4951 College Dr, Erie, PA, 16563-4115. Tel: 814-898-6106. p. 1932
Moyer, Lynette, Dir, Schuylkill Haven Free Public Library, 104 Saint John St, Schuylkill Haven, PA, 17972. Tel: 570-385-0542. p. 2003
Moyer, Susan, Dir, Dorothy Bramlage Public Library, 230 W Seventh St, Junction City, KS, 66441-3097. Tel: 785-238-4311. p. 816
Moynihan, Brooke, Asst Dir, Coll Mgt, Michigan State University College of Law Library, Law College Bldg, Rm 115, 648 N Shaw Lane, East Lansing, MI, 48824-1300. Tel: 517-432-6864. p. 1102
Moynihan, Gail, Youth Serv Librn, Deerfield Public Library, 12 W Nelson St, Deerfield, WI, 53531-9669. Tel: 608-764-8102. p. 2430

Moyo, Lesley, Assoc Univ Librn, Pub Serv, University of Wisconsin-Madison, 728 State St, Madison, WI, 53706. Tel: 608-262-3193. p. 2450

Moyryla, Jenny, Instrul Serv Librn, University of Massachusetts at Boston, 100 Morrissey Blvd, Boston, MA, 02125-3300. Tel: 617-287-5905. p. 1000

Moyses, Courtnei, Br Mgr, Grand Rapids Public Library, Ottawa Hills, 1150 Giddings Ave SE, Grand Rapids, MI, 49506. Tel: 616-988-5412. p. 1111

Mozee, Pam, Br Mgr, Mexico-Audrain County Library District, Ed French Memorial, 204 E Second St, Laddonia, MO, 63352. Tel: 573-373-2393. p. 1262

Mozer, Sada, Sr Librn, Los Angeles Public Library System, Baldwin Hills Branch Library, 2906 S La Brea Ave, Los Angeles, CA, 90016-3902. Tel: 323-733-1196. p. 163

Mozo, Hope, Circ Supvr, Trinity International University, 2065 Half Day Rd, Deerfield, IL, 60015-1241. Tel: 847-317-4002. p. 577

Mrazik, Michele, Pub Serv, DeSales University, 2755 Station Ave, Center Valley, PA, 18034. Tel: 610-282-1100, Ext 1266. p. 1920

Mrofchak, Mark, Chief Fiscal Officer, Public Library of Youngstown & Mahoning County, 305 Wick Ave, Youngstown, OH, 44503. Tel: 330-744-8636. p. 1835

Mross, Emily, Bus Librn, Pennsylvania State University-Harrisburg Library, 351 Olmsted Dr, Middletown, PA, 17057-4850. Tel: 717-948-6130. p. 1963

Mrozowski, Molly, Interim Deputy Director, Hamilton East Public Library, One Library Plaza, Noblesville, IN, 46060. Tel: 317-773-1384. p. 710

Mslila, Taryn, Libr Mgr, Pikes Peak Library District, Manitou Springs Library, 701 Manitou Ave, Manitou Springs, CO, 80829-1887. Tel: 719-531-6333, Ext 6041. p. 271

Msyo, Jason, Tech Serv, Neshoba County Public Library, 230 Beacon St, Philadelphia, MS, 39350. Tel: 601-656-4911. p. 1229

Mszal, Nicole, Dir, Hustisford Community Library, 609 W Juneau St, Hustisford, WI, 53034. Tel: 920-349-4542. p. 2442

Mubarek, Elizabeth M, Archives Mgr, Lexington Historical Society, 1332 Massachusetts Ave, Lexington, MA, 02420-3809. Tel: 781-862-0928. p. 1028

Muccari, Cesare, Exec Dir, Westmoreland County Federated Library System, 226 Donohoe Rd, Ste 202, Greensburg, PA, 15601. Tel: 724-420-5638. p. 1938

Mucciarone, Lisa, Libr Dir, Chelsea Public Library, 569 Broadway, Chelsea, MA, 02150. Tel: 617-466-4350. p. 1010

Muchin Young, Rachel, Libr Dir, Frank L Weyenberg Library of Mequon-Thiensville, 11345 N Cedarburg Rd, Mequon, WI, 53092-1998. Tel: 262-242-2593, Ext 331. p. 2456

Muchmore, Amy, Adult Serv Mgr, Carnegie-Stout Public Library, 360 W 11th St, Dubuque, IA, 52001. Tel: 563-589-4225. p. 748

Muchow, Michael, Humanities Librn, University of Missouri-Columbia, Elmer Ellis Library, 104 Ellis Library, Columbia, MO, 65201-5149. Tel: 573-882-6824. p. 1243

Muck, Donna, Vols Librn, Gaylord City Library, 504 Main St, Gaylord, KS, 67638. p. 809

Mudd, Laura, Info & Res Mgr, Sutin, Thayer & Browne, 6100 Uptown Blvd NE, Ste 400, Albuquerque, NM, 87110. Tel: 505-883-2500. p. 1462

Muehlberg, Mary, Electronic Res Librn, Minnesota State University Moorhead, 1104 Seventh Ave S, Moorhead, MN, 56563. Tel: 218-477-2922. p. 1189

Mueller, Libby, Tech Serv & Circ Supvr, Kent Library Association, 32 N Main St, Kent, CT, 06757. Tel: 860-927-3761. p. 319

Mueller, Melanie, Dir, American Institute of Physics, One Physics Ellipse, College Park, MD, 20740. Tel: 301-209-3177. p. 962

Mueller, Mitzi, Ch Serv, North Platte Public Library, 120 W Fourth St, North Platte, NE, 69101-3993. Tel: 308-535-8036. p. 1327

Mueller, Nathan, Tech & Instruction Librn, Northern Virginia Community College Libraries, Manassas Campus, Colgan Hall, Rm 129, 10950 Campus Dr, Manassas, VA, 20109. Tel: 703-257-6564. p. 2304

Mueller, Rebecca, Dir, Richmond Free Library, 201 Bridge St, Richmond, VT, 05477. Tel: 802-434-3036. p. 2293

Mueller, Sara, Asst Br Mgr, Chesterfield County Public Library, Clover Hill, 6701 Deer Run Rd, Midlothian, VA, 23112. Tel: 804-751-2275. p. 2312

Mueller, Susan, Spec Projects Librn, University of Nebraska at Kearney, 2508 11th Ave, Kearney, NE, 68849-2240. Tel: 308-865-8143. p. 1319

Mueller, Toby, Libr Dir, Lillooet Area Library Association, 930 Main St, Lillooet, BC, V0K 1V0, CANADA. Tel: 250-256-7944. p. 2569

Mueller, Veronica, Librn, Joseph Patch Library, 320 New Hampshire, Rte 25, Warren, NH, 03279. Tel: 603-764-9072. p. 1383

Mueller-Alexander, Jeanette, Librn, Arizona State University Libraries, Polytechnic Campus, Academic Ctr, Lower Level, 5988 S Backus Mall, Mesa, AZ, 85212. Tel: 480-965-3084. p. 79

Muench, Sarah, Dir, Elm Grove Public Library, 13600 Juneau Blvd, Elm Grove, WI, 53122. Tel: 262-782-6717. p. 2434

Muether, Elizabeth, Dir, Fiscal Officer, Mercer County District Library, 303 N Main St, Celina, OH, 45822. Tel: 419-586-4442. p. 1757

Muether, John R, Dr, Dean of Libr, Reformed Theological Seminary Library, 1231 Reformation Dr, Oviedo, FL, 32765. Tel: 407-278-4483, 407-366-9493, Ext 217. p. 433

Muffley, Laurie, Ref Librn, New Mexico Junior College, One Thunderbird Circle, Hobbs, NM, 88240. Tel: 575-492-2870. p. 1469

Mugdan, Walter, Regional Adminr, Environmental Protection Agency, 290 Broadway, 16th Flr, New York, NY, 10007-1866. Tel: 212-637-3185. p. 1585

Mugford, John, Regional Librn, New Mexico State Library, Library for the Blind and Print Disabled, 1209 Camino Carlos Rey, Santa Fe, NM, 87507. Tel: 505-476-9772. p. 1475

Mugridge, Rebecca L, Dean of Libr, University at Albany, State University of New York, 1400 Washington Ave, Albany, NY, 12222-0001. Tel: 518-442-3570. p. 1483

Muhammad, Tenisha, Exec Dir, Odessa College, 201 W University Blvd, Odessa, TX, 79764. Tel: 432-335-6640. p. 2223

Muhlbach, Cynthia, Libr Dir, East Smithfield Public Library, 50 Esmond St, Smithfield, RI, 02917-3016. Tel: 401-231-5150. p. 2042

Muhlbaier, Brenda, Head, Pub Serv, Gloucester County Library System, 389 Wolfert Station Rd, Mullica Hill, NJ, 08062. Tel: 856-223-6041. p. 1423

Muhlbauer, Linda, Dir, Manning Public Library, 123 Main St, Manning, IA, 51455. Tel: 712-655-2260. p. 767

Muhlenbruch, Pam, Board Pres, Thornton Public Library, 412 Main St, Thornton, IA, 50479. Tel: 641-998-2261, 641-998-2416. p. 786

Muhlenkamp, Shelley, Libr Dir, Rockford Carnegie Library, 162 S Main St, Rockford, OH, 45882-9260. Tel: 419-363-2630. p. 1818

Muhlhauser, Mike, Evening Circ Supvr, Santa Fe College, 3000 NW 83rd St, Bldg Y, Gainesville, FL, 32606. Tel: 352-395-5937. p. 407

Muhm, Kathy, Asst Dir, Westfield Memorial Library, 550 E Broad St, Westfield, NJ, 07090. Tel: 908-789-4090. p. 1454

Muhr, Charlene, Asst Dir, Half Hollow Hills Community Library, Chestnut Hill School, 600 S Service Rd, Dix Hills, NY, 11746. Tel: 631-421-4530. p. 1526

Muhr, Peter, AV, Lindenhurst Memorial Library, One Lee Ave, Lindenhurst, NY, 11757-5399. Tel: 631-957-7755. p. 1563

Muia, Cristina, Librn, Rutland Regional Medical Center, 160 Allen St, Rutland, VT, 05701. Tel: 802-747-3777. p. 2293

Muilenburg, Lisa, Br Librn, Del Mar College, Windward Campus, Barth Learning Resource Center, 4101 Old Brownsville Rd, Corpus Christi, TX, 78405. Tel: 361-698-1754. p. 2160

Muir, Gordon, Coll Develop Librn, State University of New York College at Plattsburgh, Two Draper Ave, Plattsburgh, NY, 12901. Tel: 518-564-5304. p. 1619

Muir, Nancy, Br Chief, National Institutes of Health Library, Ten Center Dr, Rm 1L25A, Bethesda, MD, 20892. Tel: 301-827-3839. p. 959

Muirhead, Leslie, Br Mgr, Hamilton Public Library, Ancaster, 300 Wilson St E, Ancaster, ON, L9G 2B9, CANADA. Tel: 905-546-3200, Ext 3463. p. 2645

Muirhead, Leslie, Br Mgr, Hamilton Public Library, Lynden Branch, 79 Lynden Rd, Lynden, ON, L0R 1T0, CANADA. Tel: 519-647-2571. p. 2646

Mukai, Matt, Actg Libr Mgr, Vancouver Island Regional Library, Campbell River Branch, 1240 Shoppers Row, Campbell River, BC, V9W 2C8, CANADA. Tel: 250-287-3655. p. 2570

Mukooza, Margaret N, Dir & Head Librn, Morris College, 100 W College St, Sumter, SC, 29150-3599. Tel: 803-934-3230. p. 2071

Mulak, Lisa, Regional Librn, Cape Breton Regional Library, 50 Falmouth St, Sydney, NS, B1P 6X9, CANADA. Tel: 902-562-3279. p. 2622

Mulalic, Cheyenne, Br Supvr, Kern County Library, Baker Branch, 1400 Baker St, Bakersfield, CA, 93305-3731. Tel: 661-861-2390. p. 119

Mulalic, Cheyenne, Br Supvr, Kern County Library, Northeast Branch, 2671 Oswell St, Ste B, Bakersfield, CA, 93306. Tel: 661-871-9017. p. 120

Mulberry, Faith, Br Mgr, Kenton County Public Library, William E Durr Branch, 1992 Walton-Nicholson Rd, Independence, KY, 41051. Tel: 859-962-4036. p. 852

Mulcahy, Elyssa, Librn, Pennsylvania College of Optometry at Salus University, 8360 Old York Rd, Elkins Park, PA, 19027. Tel: 215-780-1262. p. 1930

Mulcahy, Julie, Dir, Laughlin Memorial Library, 99 Eleventh St, Ambridge, PA, 15003-2305. Tel: 724-266-3857. p. 1906

Mulcahy, Melissa, Circ Serv, Sadie Pope Dowdell Library of South Amboy, 100 Harold G Hoffman Plaza, South Amboy, NJ, 08879. Tel: 732-721-6060. p. 1443

Mulcahy, Noreen, Lead Librn, Mount Carmel, Center for Learning & Education, 127 S Davis Ave, 3rd-4th Flrs, Columbus, OH, 43222. Tel: 614-234-5337. p. 1774

Mulcahy, Regan, Ref & Tech Librn, Milton Public Library, 476 Canton Ave, Milton, MA, 02186-3299. Tel: 617-698-5757. p. 1036

Mulcaster, Melanie, Librn, Peel District School Board, 5650 Hurontario St, Mississauga, ON, L5R 1C6, CANADA. Tel: 905-890-1099, Ext 2601. p. 2659

Mulcrone, Carina, Circ Mgr, Bettendorf Public Library Information Center, 2950 Learning Campus Dr, Bettendorf, IA, 52722. Tel: 593-344-4195. p. 735

Mulder, Celia, Head, Coll Mgt, Clinton-Macomb Public Library, 40900 Romeo Plank Rd, Clinton Township, MI, 48038-2955. Tel: 586-226-5000. p. 1092

Mulder, Glenda, Dir, Laurens Public Library, 273 N Third St, Laurens, IA, 50554. Tel: 712-841-4612. p. 765

Mulder, Jillian, Curator, Glens Falls-Queensbury Historical Association, 348 Glen St, Glens Falls, NY, 12801. Tel: 518-793-2826. p. 1539
Mulder, Jim, Info Serv Librn, Missouri Western State University, 4525 Downs Dr, Saint Joseph, MO, 64507-2294. Tel: 816-271-4368. p. 1268
Mulder-LeBlanc, Anna, Res Archivist, Amistad Research Center, Tulane University, Tilton Hall, 6823 St Charles Ave, New Orleans, LA, 70118. Tel: 504-862-3224. p. 900
Mule, Joseph J, Dir, Thayer Memorial Library, 717 Main St, Lancaster, MA, 01523-2248. Tel: 978-368-8928. p. 1026
Mulford, Ella, Mgr, Public Library of Cincinnati & Hamilton County, Popular, South Bldg, 1st Flr, 800 Vine St, Cincinnati, OH, 45202-2009. Tel: 513-369-6919. p. 1763
Mulhall, Kevin, Dir, Libr Serv, Mars Hill University, 100 Athletic St, Mars Hill, NC, 28754. Tel: 828-689-1561. p. 1703
Mulhall, Kevin, Dir, Antioch College, One Morgan Pl, Yellow Springs, OH, 45387-1694. Tel: 937-319-0104. p. 1835
Mulholland, Kathy, Libr Dir, Freehold Public Library, 28 1/2 E Main St, Freehold, NJ, 07728. Tel: 732-462-5135. p. 1404
Mull, Linda, ILL, State University of New York at Fredonia, 280 Central Ave, Fredonia, NY, 14063. Tel: 716-673-3180. p. 1535
Mull, Zachary, Br Mgr, Alexander County Library, Stony Point Branch, 431 Ruritan Park Rd, Stony Point, NC, 28678. p. 1719
Mulla, Catherine, Dir, Libr Serv, Miller Canfield Paddock & Stone Library, PLC, 150 W Jefferson, Ste 2500, Detroit, MI, 48226. Tel: 313-963-6420. p. 1099
Mullarkey, Joseph, Coll Mgt Librn, Pub Serv, Moraine Valley Community College Library, 9000 W College Pkwy, Palos Hills, IL, 60465. Tel: 708-974-5293. p. 632
Mullen, Angie, Adminr, Donald W Reynolds Community Center & Library, 1515 W Main St, Durant, OK, 74701. Tel: 580-924-3486, 580-931-0231. p. 1846
Mullen, Deborah, Br Mgr, Willoughby-Eastlake Public Library, Willoughby Branch, 30 Public Sq, Willoughby, OH, 44094. Tel: 440-942-3200. p. 1783
Mullen, Kara, Head, User Services & Tech Support, Georgia State University, 100 Decatur St SE, Atlanta, GA, 30303-3202. Tel: 404-413-2822. p. 464
Mullen, Laura, Access Serv, Behav Sci Librn, Rutgers University Libraries, Library of Science & Medicine, 165 Bevier Rd, Piscataway, NJ, 08854-8009. Tel: 848-445-3663. p. 1425
Mullen, Marilynn, Dir, Cranbury Public Library, 30 Park Place W, Cranbury, NJ, 08512. Tel: 609-799-6992. p. 1397
Mullen, Norma, Dir & Librn, Logan Public Library, 109 W Main St, Logan, KS, 67646. Tel: 785-689-4333. p. 822
Mullen, Sue, Br Mgr, Annapolis Valley Regional Library, Murdoch C Smith Memorial Library - Port Williams, 1045 Main St, Port Williams, NS, B0P 1T0, CANADA. Tel: 902-542-3005. p. 2616
Mullen, Susan, Libr Dir, Herrin City Library, 120 N 13th St, Herrin, IL, 62948-3233. Tel: 618-942-6109. p. 598
Mullen-Neem, Barbara, Librn, Pope John XXIII National Seminary, 558 South Ave, Weston, MA, 02493. Tel: 781-810-1931, Ext 138. p. 1067
Mullenix, Sita, Archives, Tech, National Archives of The Christian & Missionary Alliance, 731 Chapel Hill Dr, Colorado Springs, CO, 80920. Tel: 719-265-2198. p. 271
Muller, Jennifer, District Librn, United States Army Corps of Engineers, US Army Corps of Engineers, Portland District Library, 333 SW First Ave, Portland, OR, 97204. Tel: 503-808-5140. p. 1894
Muller, Joy, Assoc Dir, Libr Serv, Seneca College of Applied Arts & Technology, 13990 Dufferin St N, King City, ON, L7B 1B3, CANADA. Tel: 416-491-5050. p. 2649
Muller, Joy, Dir of Libr, Seneca College of Applied Arts & Technology, 13990 Dufferin St N, King City, ON, L7B 1B3, CANADA. Tel: 416-491-5050. p. 2649
Muller, Joy, Dir, Seneca College of Applied Arts & Technology, Newnham Campus (Main), 1750 Finch Ave E, North York, ON, M2J 2X5, CANADA. Tel: 416-491-5050, Ext 22099. p. 2649
Muller, Karen, Library Mgr, Connect, Hillsboro Public Library, 2850 NE Brookwood Pkwy, Hillsboro, OR, 97124. Tel: 503-615-6500. p. 1881
Muller, Kathy, Br Mgr, Saint Louis County Library, Thornhill Branch, 12863 Willowyck Dr, Saint Louis, MO, 63146-3771. Tel: 314-994-3300, Ext 3900. p. 1274
Muller, Mary, Cat Tech, Tech Serv Technician, Wharton County Junior College, 911 Boling Hwy, Wharton, TX, 77488-3298. Tel: 979-532-6443. p. 2256
Muller, Michelle, Asst Dir, Head, Youth Serv, Goshen Public Library & Historical Society, 366 Main St, Goshen, NY, 10924. Tel: 845-294-6606. p. 1539
Muller, Sheri, Access Serv Librn, Archivist, Grand View University Library, 1350 Morton Ave, Des Moines, IA, 50316. Tel: 515-263-6199. p. 746
Mullican, Melinda, Br Mgr, Indianapolis Public Library, Wayne, 198 S Girls School Rd, Indianapolis, IN, 46231-1120. Tel: 317-275-4537. p. 696
Mulligan, Meredith, Mgr, Resources & Systems Mgmt, Weil, Gotshal & Manges LLP, 767 Fifth Ave, New York, NY, 10153. Tel: 212-310-8444. p. 1603
Mulligan, Mundy, Tech Mgr, Walla Walla County Rural Library District, 37 Jade Ave, Walla Walla, WA, 99362. Tel: 509-527-3284. p. 2392
Mulligan, Nora, Head, Adult Serv, The Field Library, Four Nelson Ave, Peekskill, NY, 10566. Tel: 914-737-1212. p. 1616
Mulliken, Adina, Soc Work Librn, Hunter College Libraries, Schools of Social Work & Public Health Library, 2180 Third Ave, New York, NY, 10035. Tel: 212-396-7665. p. 1588
Mullikin, Elizabeth, Library Contact, Carondelet Health Network Medical Libraries, St Mary's Hospital, 1601 W St Mary's Rd, 2nd Flr Central, Tucson, AZ, 85745. Tel: 925-785-9367. p. 81
Mullin, Casey, Head, Metadata & Cat, Western Washington University, 516 High St, MS 9103, Bellingham, WA, 98225. Tel: 360-650-7458. p. 2358
Mullin, Linda, Technical Servs & Staff Educ, Rice Lake Public Library, Two E Marshall St, Rice Lake, WI, 54868. Tel: 715-234-4861, Ext 1116. p. 2473
Mullin, Susan, Head, Ref, John Jermain Memorial Library, 201 Main St, Sag Harbor, NY, 11963. Tel: 631-725-0049, Ext 232. p. 1634
Mullings, Garcia, Bus Librn, University of Arkansas Libraries, 365 N McIlroy Ave, Fayetteville, AR, 72701-4002. Tel: 479-575-4101. p. 95
Mullins, Cecilia, Mgr, Sharp County Library, 201 Church St, Hardy, AR, 72542. Tel: 870-856-3934. p. 97
Mullins, Cheryl, Ref Mgr, Canal Fulton Public Library, 154 Market St NE, Canal Fulton, OH, 44614-1196. Tel: 330-854-4148. p. 1754
Mullins, Christina, Ref Librn, University of Massachusetts at Boston, 100 Morrissey Blvd, Boston, MA, 02125-3300. Tel: 617-287-5933. p. 1000
Mullins, Dakota, Br Mgr, Lonesome Pine Regional Library, C Bascom Slemp Memorial Library, 11 Proctor St N, Big Stone Gap, VA, 24219. Tel: 276-523-1334. p. 2355
Mullins, Elizabeth, Youth Serv Mgr, Carroll County Public Library, 136 Court St, Carrollton, KY, 41008. Tel: 502-732-7020. p. 851
Mullins, Greg, Dean, Libr & Media Serv, Evergreen State College, Library Bldg, Rm 2300, 2700 Evergreen Pkwy NW, Olympia, WA, 98505-0002. Tel: 360-867-6250. p. 2372
Mullins, Kelly, Learning Commons Specialist, Lincoln Trail College, 11220 State Hwy 1, Robinson, IL, 62454-5707. Tel: 618-544-8657, Ext 1425. p. 640
Mullins, Lauren, Head Librn, Middle Georgia Regional Library System, 1180 Washington Ave, Macon, GA, 31201-1790. Tel: 478-744-0828. p. 486
Mullins, Lindsey, Dir, Moundville Public Library, 279 Market St, Moundville, AL, 35474. Tel: 205-371-2283. p. 30
Mullins, Rachel, Librn, Farmington Public Library, 101 North A St, Farmington, MO, 63640. Tel: 573-756-5779. p. 1245
Mullins, Rob, Pub Serv Mgr, Perry County Public Library, 289 Black Gold Blvd, Hazard, KY, 41701. Tel: 606-436-2475, 606-436-4747. p. 858
Mullins, Stephanie, Circ Mgr, Massanutten Regional Library, Elkton Community Library, 106 N Terrace Ave, Elkton, VA, 22827. Tel: 540-434-4475, Ext 2. p. 2324
Mullins, Terry, Law Librn, Washington County Law Library, 205 Putnam St, Marietta, OH, 45750-3017. Tel: 740-373-6623, Ext 214. p. 1799
Mullins, Tom, Spec Coll Librn, Public Library of Anniston-Calhoun County, 108 E Tenth St, Anniston, AL, 36201. Tel: 256-237-8501, p. 4
Mullins, Wendy, Dir, Ririe City Library, 464 Main St, Ririe, ID, 83443. Tel: 208-538-7974. p. 530
Mullis, Geri Lynn, Dir, Saint Simons Island Public Library, 530A Beachview Dr, Saint Simons Island, GA, 31522. Tel: 912-279-3750. p. 495
Mullis, Gerri, Dir, Marshes of Glynn Libraries, 208 Gloucester St, Brunswick, GA, 31520. Tel: 912-279-3740. p. 468
Mullis, Mark, Libr Mgr, Englewood Public Library, 1000 Englewood Pkwy, Englewood, CO, 80110. Tel: 303-762-2566. p. 279
Mulloy, Katherine, Ch Serv, Lafayette Public Library, 301 W Congress, Lafayette, LA, 70501-6866. Tel: 337-261-5786. p. 892
Mulnik, Barbara, Library Contact, Saint Louis Psychiatric Rehabilitation Center, 5300 Arsenal St, Saint Louis, MO, 63139. Tel: 314-768-5051, 314-877-6500. p. 1274
Mulrenan, Mary, Mkt & Communications Mgr, Fairfax County Public Library, 12000 Government Center Pkwy, Ste 324, Fairfax, VA, 22035-0012. Tel: 703-324-3100. p. 2316
Mulroy, Kevin, PhD, Col Librn, Occidental College Library, 1600 Campus Rd, Los Angeles, CA, 90041. p. 167
Mulvany, Patrick, Library Contact, Missouri Department of Natural Resources - Missouri Geological Survey, 111 Fairgrounds Rd, Rolla, MO, 65401-2909. Tel: 573-368-2139. p. 1267
Mulvenna, Lisa, Head, Youth Serv, Clinton-Macomb Public Library, 40900 Romeo Plank Rd, Clinton Township, MI, 48038-2955. Tel: 586-226-5031. p. 1092
Mulvey, Emily, Teen Librn, New Britain Public Library, 20 High St, New Britain, CT, 06051. Tel: 860-224-3155, Ext 119. p. 324
Mulvey, Theodore, Info Literacy Librn, University of Wisconsin Oshkosh, 801 Elmwood Ave, Oshkosh, WI, 54901. Tel: 920-424-7329. p. 2467
Mulvihill-Jones, Jane, Exec Dir, Mid-America Library Alliance, 15624 E US Hwy 24, Independence, MO, 64050. Tel: 816-521-7257. p. 2769
Mumford, Nancy, Librn, Historical Society of Old Yarmouth Library, 11 Strawberry Lane, Yarmouth Port, MA, 02675. Tel: 508-362-3021. p. 1073

Mumford, Scott, Ad, Ref Serv Librn, Franklin County Library, 906 N Main St, Louisburg, NC, 27549-2199. Tel: 919-496-2111. p. 1701

Mumm, James A, Ref/Copyright Librn, Marquette University, Ray & Kay Eckstein Law Library, 1215 Michigan St, Milwaukee, WI, 53201. Tel: 414-288-7092. p. 2458

Mumma, Polly, Librn, Des Moines Area Community College Library, 1100 Seventh St, Des Moines, IA, 50314. Tel: 515-697-7739. p. 745

Mummert, Kelly, Libr Dir, Wheeling Jesuit University, 316 Washington Ave, Wheeling, WV, 26003-6295. Tel: 304-243-2226. p. 2418

Munch, Janet B, Dr, Spec Coll & Archives Librn, Lehman College, City University of New York, 250 Bedford Park Blvd W, Bronx, NY, 10468. Tel: 718-960-8603. p. 1499

Mundava, Maud, Campus Libr Dir, Distance Support Librn, Liaison Librn, A T Still University, Kirksville Campus, 800 W Jefferson St, Kirksville, MO, 63501. Tel: 660-626-2340. p. 1258

Mundle, Todd, Univ Librn, Kwantlen Polytechnic University Library, 12666 72nd Ave, Surrey, BC, V3W 2M8, CANADA. Tel: 604-599-3400. p. 2576

Mundt, Virginia, Dir, Mesquite Public Library, 300 W Grubb Dr, Mesquite, TX, 75149. Tel: 972-216-6220. p. 2219

Mundy, Jessica, Head, Coll Mgt, Thurgood Marshall State Law Library, Courts of Appeals Bldg, 361 Rowe Blvd, Annapolis, MD, 21401. Tel: 410-260-1430. p. 950

Mune, Christina, Assoc Dean, Innovation & Resource Mgmt, San Jose State University, One Washington Sq, San Jose, CA, 95192-0028. Tel: 408-808-2000. p. 232

Munger, Lucinda, Dir, Orange County Public Library, 137 W Margaret Lane, Hillsborough, NC, 27278. Tel: 919-245-2525. p. 1697

Muniak, Suzie, Asst Dir, Medina County District Library, 210 S Broadway, Medina, OH, 44256. Tel: 330-725-0588. p. 1801

Munias, Mercedes, Mgr, Miami-Dade Public Library System, West Flagler Branch, 5050 W Flagler St, Miami, FL, 33134. Tel: 305-442-8710. p. 424

Municino, Albert, Libr Mgr, Dauphin County Library System, Kline Library, 530 S 29th St, Harrisburg, PA, 17104. Tel: 717-234-3934. p. 1940

Muniz, Cris, Libr Supvr, City of Commerce Public Library, Bandini Library, 2269 S Atlantic Blvd, Commerce, CA, 90040. Tel: 323-887-4494. p. 132

Muñiz, Jennifer, Libr Dir, Pearsall Public Library, 200 E Trinity St, Pearsall, TX, 78061. Tel: 830-334-2496. p. 2225

Muniz, Michelle, Asst Librn, Dr Hector P Garcia Memorial Library, 434 S Ohio St, Mercedes, TX, 78570. Tel: 956-565-2371. p. 2218

Munk, Beth, Youth Serv Mgr, Kendallville Public Library, 221 S Park Ave, Kendallville, IN, 46755-2248. Tel: 260-343-2010. p. 698

Munk, Kindra, Dir, American Falls District Library, 308 Roosevelt St, American Falls, ID, 83211. Tel: 208-226-2335. p. 515

Munns, Kelli, Dr, Professional Practice Asst Professor, Utah State University, 2830 Old Main Hill, Education, Bldg 215, Logan, UT, 84322. Tel: 435-797-1583. p. 2794

Munoz, Cindy, Info Spec, Driscoll Children's Hospital, 3533 S Alameda St, 3rd Flr, Corpus Christi, TX, 78411-1721. Tel: 361-694-5467. p. 2160

Munoz, Jeff, Collection Servs & Digital Initiatives Spec, St John's University Library, Rittenberg Law Library, 8000 Utopia Pkwy, Jamaica, NY, 11439. Tel: 718-990-6660. p. 1556

Munoz, Laura, Adult Serv, Circ, Steger-South Chicago Heights Public Library District, 54 E 31st St, Steger, IL, 60475. Tel: 708-755-5040. p. 651

Munoz, Mary Beth, Libr Supvr, Ed Rachal Memorial Library, 203 S Calixto Mora Ave, Falfurrias, TX, 78355. Tel: 361-325-2144. p. 2176

Munoz, Rebecca, Mgr, Ad Serv, Northland Public Library, 300 Cumberland Rd, Pittsburgh, PA, 15237-5455. Tel: 412-366-8100, Ext 110. p. 1994

Munozospina, Carlos, Head, Tech Serv, Jericho Public Library, One Merry Lane, Jericho, NY, 11753. Tel: 516-935-6790. p. 1558

Munro, Denise, Youth Serv Coordr, Massanutten Regional Library, 174 S Main St, Harrisonburg, VA, 22801. Tel: 540-434-4475, Ext 108. p. 2324

Munro, Karen, Assoc Univ Librn, Learning & Res Serv, Simon Fraser University - Burnaby Campus, 8888 University Dr, Burnaby, BC, V5A 1S6, CANADA. Tel: 778-782-3252. p. 2563

Munroe, Dana Signe, Cabinet Keeper & Library Colls Mgr, Rhode Island Historical Society, 121 Hope St, Providence, RI, 02906. Tel: 401-273-8107, Ext 416. p. 2039

Munsee, Jeanie, Dir, Edmonson County Public Library, 280 Ferguson St, Brownsville, KY, 42210. Tel: 270-597-2146. p. 850

Munson, Deanna, Librn, Anoka Technical College Library, 1355 W Hwy 10, Anoka, MN, 55303. Tel: 763-576-4154. p. 1163

Munson, Doris, Libr Tech, University of Oregon, Institute of Marine Biology, 63466 Boat Basin Dr, Charleston, OR, 97420. Tel: 541-888-2581. p. 1875

Munson, Judith, Ch Serv, South Kingstown Public Library, Kingston Free Branch, 2605 Kingstown Rd, Kingston, RI, 02881. Tel: 401-783-8254. p. 2037

Munson, Kathy, ILL, De Anza College, 21250 Stevens Creek Blvd, Cupertino, CA, 95014-5793. Tel: 408-864-8335. p. 133

Munson, Sally, Ref Librn, Willkie Farr & Gallagher LLP, 787 Seventh Ave, New York, NY, 10019. Tel: 212-728-8700. p. 1604

Munson, Stephanie, Vols Mgr, Hayner Public Library District, 326 Belle St, Alton, IL, 62002. Tel: 618-462-0677. p. 536

Munson, Walter, Asst Librn, Berlin Free Library, 834 Worthington Ridge, Berlin, CT, 06037. Tel: 860-828-3344. p. 302

Muokebe, Theodora, Admin Serv, Div Dir, Br Serv, Harris County Public Library, 5749 S Loop E, Houston, TX, 77033. Tel: 713-274-6600. p. 2192

Mupratt, Beth, Library Contact, Potter Anderson & Corroon LLP, Hercules Plaza, 1313 N Market St, Wilmington, DE, 19801. Tel: 302-984-6000. p. 358

Murad, Hafsa, Info Literacy Librn, North Carolina Central University, 1801 Fayetteville St, Durham, NC, 27707-3129. Tel: 919-530-7315. p. 1685

Muradyan, Inna, Head, Circ, University of San Diego, Katherine M & George M Pardee Jr Legal Research Center, 5998 Alcala Park, San Diego, CA, 92110-2492. Tel: 619-260-7479. p. 222

Murakami, Trisha, Br Mgr, Hawaii State Public Library System, Kalihi-Palama Public Library, 1325 Kalihi St, Honolulu, HI, 96819. Tel: 808-832-3466. p. 508

Muralidharan, Malavika, E-rate Coord for Public Libraries, Arizona State Library, Archives & Public Records, 1901 W Madison St, Phoenix, AZ, 85009. Tel: 602-364-4855. p. 69

Muraski, Terri, Info Syst Librn, University of Wisconsin-Stevens Point, 900 Reserve St, Stevens Point, WI, 54481-1985. Tel: 715-346-3349. p. 2479

Murata, Claire, Assoc Dean, Edmonds College Library, 20000 68th Ave W, Lynnwood, WA, 98036. Tel: 425-640-1529. p. 2370

Murcray, Keri, Circ, California Baptist University, 8432 Magnolia Ave, Riverside, CA, 92504. Tel: 951-343-4228. p. 201

Murdoch, Robert, Assoc Univ Librn for Coll & Tech Serv(s), Brigham Young University, Harold B Lee Library, 2060 HBLL, Provo, UT, 84602. Tel: 801-422-2927. p. 2269

Murdock, Catherine, Asst Librn, YA Librn, Fremont Public Library, Seven Jackie Bernier Dr, Fremont, NH, 03044. Tel: 603-895-9543. p. 1364

Murdock, Cheri, Admin Officer, Bureau of Land Management, 1300 Airport Lane, North Bend, OR, 97459. Tel: 541-756-0100. p. 1889

Murdock, Colleen, Librn, Emery County Library System, Ferron Branch, 55 N 200 West, Ferron, UT, 84523. Tel: 435-384-2637. p. 2262

Murdock, Justin, Res Asst, New York Legislative Service, Inc Library, 120 Broadway, Ste 920, New York, NY, 10271. Tel: 212-962-2826, 212-962-2827, 212-962-2828. p. 1594

Murdock, Kelley, Libr Mgr, Sno-Isle Libraries, Brier Library, 23303 Brier Rd, Brier, WA, 98036-8247. Tel: 425-483-0888. p. 2370

Murdock, Ronda, Dir of Libr/Media Serv, French Institute-Alliance Francaise Library, 22 E 60th St, New York, NY, 10022-1011. Tel: 646-388-6636. p. 1586

Murdock, Tina, Libr Spec, Hendrix College, 1600 Washington Ave, Conway, AR, 72032. Tel: 501-450-1302. p. 92

Murff, Laura, Dir, Tech Serv, Lisle Library District, 777 Front St, Lisle, IL, 60532-3599. Tel: 630-971-1675. p. 610

Murgas, Andy, Head, Computer Serv, Matteson Area Public Library District, 801 S School St, Matteson, IL, 60443-1897. Tel: 708-748-4431. p. 615

Murgu, Cal, Res & Instruction Librn, New College of Florida University of South Florida Sarasota Manatee, 5800 Bay Shore Rd, Sarasota, FL, 34243-2109. Tel: 941-487-4412. p. 443

Murillo, Kimberly, Commun Engagement Librn, Ardmore Public Library, 320 E St NW, Ardmore, OK, 73401. Tel: 580-223-8290. p. 1840

Murillo, Maci, Dir, Wamego Public Library, 431 Lincoln, Wamego, KS, 66547. Tel: 785-456-9181. p. 841

Murillo, Nancy, Archives Librn, Libr Instruction, Orange County Community College Library, 115 South St, Middletown, NY, 10940. Tel: 845-341-4258. p. 1571

Muriuki, Agnes, Asst Dir, Fort Valley State University, 1005 State University Dr, Fort Valley, GA, 31030-4313. Tel: 478-825-6753. p. 479

Murnaghan, Kent, Ref Serv, Canadian Memorial Chiropractic College, 6100 Leslie St, Toronto, ON, M2H 3J1, CANADA. Tel: 416-482-2340, Ext 205. p. 2687

Murnion, Carrie, Libr Dir, Garfield County Free Library, 208 Main St, Jordan, MT, 59337. Tel: 406-557-2297. p. 1297

Murphree, Stephanie, Br Mgr, Fort Bend County Libraries, Albert George Branch, 9230 Gene St, Needville, TX, 77461-8313. Tel: 281-238-2850. p. 2232

Murphree, Yvonne, Dir, Blountsville Public Library, 65 Chestnut St, Blountsville, AL, 35031. Tel: 205-429-3156. p. 10

Murphrey, Mary, Senior Admin Coord, Billings Public Library, 510 N Broadway, Billings, MT, 59101. Tel: 406-657-8258. p. 1288

Murphy, Alexa, ILL Librn, Bard College, One Library Rd, Annandale-on-Hudson, NY, 12504. Tel: 845-758-6822. p. 1487

Murphy, Andrew, Ref Librn, Mill Valley Public Library, 375 Throckmorton Ave, Mill Valley, CA, 94941. Tel: 415-389-4292, Ext 4729. p. 177

Murphy, Anita, Br Mgr, Jasper-Dubois County Public Library, Dubois Branch Library, 5506 E Main St, Dubois, IN, 47527. Tel: 812-678-2548, Ext 112. p. 697

Murphy, Anne M, Dir, Bedford Park Public Library District, 7816 W 65th Pl, Bedford Park, IL, 60501. Tel: 708-458-6826. p. 540

Murphy, Anne Marie, Sister, Dir, IHM Sisters, 610 W Elm Ave, Monroe, MI, 48162. Tel: 734-240-9713. p. 1133

Murphy, Bart, Chief Info Officer, Chief Tech Officer, OCLC Online Computer Library Center, Inc, 6565 Kilgour Pl, Dublin, OH, 43017-3395. Tel: 614-764-6000. p. 2772

Murphy, Beverly, Asst Dir, Communications & Web Content Mgt, Duke University Libraries, Medical Center Library & Archives, DUMC Box 3702, Ten Searle Dr, Durham, NC, 27710-0001. Tel: 919-660-1127. p. 1684

Murphy, Britt Anne, Dir & Librn, Hendrix College, 1600 Washington Ave, Conway, AR, 72032. Tel: 501-450-1288. p. 92

Murphy, Carolyn, Librn, Massachusetts Department of Corrections, 500 Colony Rd, Gardner, MA, 01440. Tel: 978-632-2000, Ext 325. p. 1020

Murphy, Cheryl, Actg Mgr, Coll Develop, Supreme Court of Canada Library, 301 Wellington St, Ottawa, ON, K1A 0J1, CANADA. Tel: 613-996-8120. p. 2670

Murphy, Darin, Head of Libr, Tufts University, W Van Alan Clark Library, School of the Museum of Fine Arts at Tufts, 230 The Fenway, Boston, MA, 02115. p. 1034

Murphy, Donna, Libr Mgr, New York Public Library - Astor, Lenox & Tilden Foundations, 58th Street Branch, 127 E 58th St, (Between Park & Lexington Aves), New York, NY, 10022-1211. Tel: 212-759-7358. p. 1595

Murphy, Doug, Dean, Moody Bible Institute, 820 N LaSalle Blvd, Chicago, IL, 60610-3284. Tel: 312-329-4136. p. 564

Murphy, Ed, Sr Librn, New York State Supreme Court Ninth Judicial District, Ninth Judicial District, 9th Flr, 111 Dr Martin Luther King Blvd, White Plains, NY, 10601. Tel: 914-824-5660. p. 1665

Murphy, Edward, Librn/Br Mgr, Palmer College of Chiropractic, 4777 City Center Pkwy, Port Orange, FL, 32129. Tel: 386-763-2670. p. 439

Murphy, Elizabeth, Asst Dir, Turner Free Library, Two N Main St, Randolph, MA, 02368. Tel: 781-961-0932. p. 1049

Murphy, Ellie, Libr Asst, Waynesville Township Library, 303 E Second St, Waynesville, IL, 61778. Tel: 217-949-5111. p. 660

Murphy, Emily, Hist Coll Librn, Ref Serv, US National Park Service, 160 Derby St, Salem, MA, 01970. Tel: 978-740-1650. p. 1051

Murphy, Eva, ILL, United States Army, Marquat Memorial Library, Bank Hall, Bldg D-3915, 3004 Ardennes St, Fort Bragg, NC, 28310-9610. Tel: 910-432-9222. p. 1689

Murphy, Gerard, Librn, Middlesex County Adult Correction Center Library, Apple Orchard Lane, Rte 130, North Brunswick, NJ, 08902. Tel: 732-297-3636, Ext 6224. p. 1429

Murphy, Gillian, Dir, Elting Memorial Library, 93 Main St, New Paltz, NY, 12561-1593. Tel: 845-255-5030. p. 1576

Murphy, Greg, Head, Research & Circulation Services, Pace University Library, 15 Beekman St, New York, NY, 10038. Tel: 212-346-1332. p. 1600

Murphy, Gretchen, Dir, Head Librn, Casey Township Library, 307 E Main St, Casey, IL, 62420. Tel: 217-932-2105. p. 551

Murphy, Heidi, Dir, Pleasanton Public Library, 400 Old Bernal Ave, Pleasanton, CA, 94566. Tel: 925-931-3400. p. 196

Murphy, Holly, Libr Dir, Waynesville Township Library, 303 E Second St, Waynesville, IL, 61778. Tel: 217-949-5111. p. 660

Murphy, Hunter, Engagement Librn, Learning Librn, Stetson University, 421 N Woodland Blvd, Unit 8418, DeLand, FL, 32723. Tel: 386-822-7176. p. 393

Murphy, Irene, Dir, Unadilla Public Library, 193 Main St, Unadilla, NY, 13849. Tel: 607-369-3131. p. 1654

Murphy, James, Asst Librn, University of Calgary Library, Gallagher Library, 170 Earth Sciences, 2500 University Dr NW, Calgary, AB, T2N 1N4, CANADA. Tel: 403-220-3740. p. 2529

Murphy, Jan, Br Mgr, Lake County Library District, Paisely Branch, 723 Chewaucan St, Paisley, OR, 97636. Tel: 541-943-3911. p. 1884

Murphy, Jane, Youth Serv, Millicent Library, 45 Centre St, Fairhaven, MA, 02719. Tel: 508-992-5342. p. 1017

Murphy, Jane, Libr Asst, CMU Health, CMU College of Medicine, Educ Bldg, 1632 Stone St, Saginaw, MI, 48602. Tel: 989-746-7577. p. 1146

Murphy, Jean, Head, Processing Services, Jericho Public Library, One Merry Lane, Jericho, NY, 11753. Tel: 516-935-6790. p. 1558

Murphy, Jen, Syst Librn, Preble County District Library, 450 S Barron St, Eaton, OH, 45320-2402. Tel: 937-456-4250. p. 1784

Murphy, Jennifer, Cat, Libr Asst, Ser, Cardinal Stafford Library, 1300 S Steele St, Denver, CO, 80210-2526. Tel: 303-715-3234. p. 273

Murphy, Jessica, Librn, North Central Washington Libraries, Wenatchee Public Library, 30 S Wenatchee Ave, Wenatchee, WA, 98801. Tel: 509-662-5021. p. 2394

Murphy, John, Law Libr Dir/Law Librn, Anoka County Law Library, 2100 Third Ave, Ste E130, Anoka, MN, 55303. Tel: 763-324-5560. p. 1163

Murphy, Julie, Dir, Libr Serv, Pacific Institute for Research & Evaluation, 180 Grand Ave, Ste 1200, Oakland, CA, 94612. Tel: 510-486-1111, 510-883-5746. p. 186

Murphy Kao, Regan, Dir, Stanford University Libraries, East Asia Library, Lathrop Library Bldg, 518 Memorial Way, Stanford, CA, 94305. Tel: 650-725-3435. p. 248

Murphy, Karen, Br Mgr, Warren-Trumbull County Public Library, Cortland Branch, 578 Lakeview Dr, Cortland, OH, 44410. Tel: 330-638-6335. p. 1828

Murphy, Katherine, Dr, Libr Coord, Res Spec, Marshall University Libraries, South Charleston Campus Library, 100 Angus E Peyton Dr, South Charleston, WV, 25303-1600. Tel: 304-746-8900. p. 2405

Murphy, Kathy, Br Mgr, Allegany County Library System, Westernport Library, 66 Main St, Westernport, MD, 21562. Tel: 301-359-0455. p. 964

Murphy, Kathy, Tech Serv, Wareham Free Library, 59 Marion Rd, Wareham, MA, 02571. Tel: 508-295-2343, Ext 1015. p. 1062

Murphy, Kelli, Br Serv Mgr, Albuquerque-Bernalillo County Library System, Westgate Library, 1300 Delgado SW, Albuquerque, NM, 87121. Tel: 505-833-6984. p. 1460

Murphy, Kellie, Chief Operating Officer, Museum of the American Railroad Library, 6455 Page St, Frisco, TX, 75034. Tel: 214-428-0101. p. 2182

Murphy, Kelly, Dir, Aspen Historical Society Archives, 620 W Bleeker St, Aspen, CO, 81611. Tel: 970-925-3721, Ext 101. p. 264

Murphy, Kim, Head, Adult Serv, Prospect Heights Public Library District, 12 N Elm St, Prospect Heights, IL, 60070-1450. Tel: 847-259-3500. p. 637

Murphy, Kimberly, Libr Mgr, McPherson Municipal Library, 5113 50 St, Ryley, AB, T0B 4A0, CANADA. Tel: 780-663-3999. p. 2552

Murphy, Kit, Mrs, Library Contact, Christ United Methodist Church Library, 44 Highland Rd, Bethel Park, PA, 15102. Tel: 412-835-6621. p. 1911

Murphy, Kris, Dir, Chariton Free Public Library, 803 Braden Ave, Chariton, IA, 50049. Tel: 641-774-5514. p. 739

Murphy, Lee Ann, Ch Serv, YA Serv, Upton Town Library, Two Main St, Upton, MA, 01568-1608. Tel: 508-529-6272. p. 1060

Murphy, Liam, Librn, Pub Info, United Nations Information Center, 1775 K St NW, Ste 400, Washington, DC, 20006. Tel: 202-331-8670. p. 377

Murphy, Lisa, Archivist, Kalamazoo College Library, 1200 Academy St, Kalamazoo, MI, 49006-3285. Tel: 269-337-7151. p. 1121

Murphy, Liz, Tech Serv, Sampson-Clinton Public Library, 217 Graham St, Clinton, NC, 28328. Tel: 910-592-4153. p. 1681

Murphy, Lynette, Tech Coordr, Graham Hospital Association, 210 W Walnut St, Canton, IL, 61520. Tel: 309-647-5240, Ext 2343. p. 548

Murphy, Maria, Mkt Mgr, Weston Hurd, LLP, The Tower at Erieview, Ste 1900, 1301 E Ninth St, Cleveland, OH, 44114-1862. Tel: 216-241-6602, Ext 3383. p. 1771

Murphy, Mary, Libr Dir, Perry Public Library, 1101 Willis Ave, Perry, IA, 50220. Tel: 515-465-3569. p. 777

Murphy, Mary, Asst Dir, Hackley Public Library, 316 W Webster Ave, Muskegon, MI, 49440. Tel: 231-722-8004. p. 1135

Murphy, Mary Margaret, Exec Dir, Baby's Breath Library, 5 Race St, St. Catharines, ON, L2R 3M1, CANADA. Tel: 905-688-8884. p. 2679

Murphy, Maureen, Libr Asst, Duplin County Library, Phillip Leff Memorial Library, 807 Broad St, Beulaville, NC, 28518. Tel: 910-298-4677. p. 1698

Murphy, Michael, Librn & Archivist, New Canaan Museum & Historical Society Library, 13 Oenoke Ridge, New Canaan, CT, 06840. Tel: 203-966-1776. p. 324

Murphy, Michael, Asst Dir, Cora J Belden Library, 33 Church St, Rocky Hill, CT, 06067-1568. Tel: 860-258-7621. p. 335

Murphy, Miriam A, Assoc Dir, Indiana University, Ruth Lilly Law Library, 530 W New York St, Indianapolis, IN, 46202-3225. Tel: 317-274-3884, 317-274-4028. p. 693

Murphy, Nora, Archivist, Res Serv, Massachusetts Institute of Technology Libraries, Distinctive Collections, Bldg 14N-118, Hayden Library, 160 Memorial Dr, Cambridge, MA, 02139-4307. Tel: 617-253-8066. p. 1008

Murphy, Ondrea, Exec Dir, Libr Serv, Delaware State University, 1200 N Dupont Hwy, Dover, DE, 19901-2277. Tel: 302-857-6192. p. 352

Murphy, Peggy, Colls Serv Mgr, Los Angeles Public Library System, 630 W Fifth St, Los Angeles, CA, 90071. Tel: 213-228-7191. p. 163

Murphy Plankinton, Helen, Tech Serv & Automation, Beck Bookman Library, 420 W Fourth St, Holton, KS, 66436-1572. Tel: 785-364-3532. p. 813

Murphy, Samantha, Libr Dir, Trail & District Public Library, 1505 Bay Ave, Trail, BC, V1R 4B2, CANADA. Tel: 250-364-1731. p. 2577

Murphy, Sarah, Libr Dir, Greenwich Free Library, 148 Main St, Greenwich, NY, 12834. Tel: 518-692-7157. p. 1542

Murphy, Shar, Dir, Lassen Community College Library, 478-200 Hwy 139, Susanville, CA, 96130. Tel: 530-251-8830. p. 251

Murphy, Shari-Lynn, Br Mgr, Hawaii State Public Library System, Ewa Beach Public & School Library, 91-950 North Rd, Ewa Beach, HI, 96706. Tel: 808-689-1204. p. 507

Murphy, Sondra, Dir, Gladys E Kelly Public Library, Two Lake St, Webster, MA, 01570. Tel: 508-949-3880. p. 1063

Murphy, Stephanie, Exec Dir, Saint Joseph County Public Library, 304 S Main St, South Bend, IN, 46601. Tel: 574-282-4604. p. 718

Murphy, Susan, Br Mgr, Summit County Library, Coalville Branch, 82 N 50 E, Coalville, UT, 84017. Tel: 435-336-3070. p. 2269

Murphy, Susan, Br Mgr, Tazewell County Public Library, Bluefield Branch, 108 Huffard Dr, Bluefield, VA, 24605. Tel: 276-326-1577. p. 2348

Murphy, Tina, Head, Circ, Dunlap Public Library District, 302 S First St, Dunlap, IL, 61525. Tel: 309-243-5716. p. 580

Murphy, Tony, Chief Exec Officer, Regional Dir, Wapiti Regional Library, 145 12th St E, Prince Albert, SK, S6V 1B7, CANADA. Tel: 306-764-0712. p. 2745

Murphy, Tracee, Dir, Wellsville Carnegie Public Library, 115 Ninth St, Wellsville, OH, 43968-1431. Tel: 330-532-1526. p. 1829
Murphy, Tracey, Asst Dir, Duval County Law Library, 501 W Adams St, Rm 2291, Jacksonville, FL, 32202. Tel: 904-255-1150. p. 411
Murphy, Yvonne, Br Mgr, Phoenix Public Library, Agave Library, 23550 N 36th Ave, Phoenix, AZ, 85310. p. 72
Murr, Meghan, Dir, Fayetteville-Lincoln County Public Library, 306 Elk Ave N, Fayetteville, TN, 37334. Tel: 931-433-3286. p. 2098
Murr, Olga, Librn, Dallas College, 5001 N MacArthur Blvd, Irving, TX, 75062. Tel: 972-273-3400. p. 2202
Murray, Ann, Br Librn, Menominee County Library, Hermansville Branch, W5480 First St, Hermansville, MI, 49847. Tel: 906-498-2253. p. 1152
Murray, Annie, Archives & Spec Coll Librn, Assoc Univ Librn, University of Calgary Library, 2500 University Dr NW, Calgary, AB, T2N 1N4, CANADA. Tel: 403-210-9521. p. 2529
Murray, Anton, Communications Officer I, Alexandria Library, 5005 Duke St, Alexandria, VA, 22304. Tel: 703-746-1702. p. 2302
Murray, Autumn, Tech Serv, Berkshire Athenaeum, One Wendell Ave, Pittsfield, MA, 01201-6385. Tel: 413-499-9480. p. 1046
Murray, Chelsea, Mgr, Calgary Public Library, Country Hills, 11950 Country Village Link NE, Calgary, AB, T3K 6E3, CANADA. p. 2526
Murray, Chelsea, Mgr, Calgary Public Library, Judith Umbach, 6617 Centre St N, Calgary, AB, T2K 4Y5, CANADA. p. 2527
Murray, Chelsea, Mgr, Calgary Public Library, Sage Hill, 19 Sage Hill Passage NW, Calgary, AB, T3R 0J6, CANADA. p. 2527
Murray, Christine, Soc Sci Librn, Bates College, 48 Campus Ave, Lewiston, ME, 04240. Tel: 207-786-6268. p. 929
Murray, David, Humanities Librn, The College of New Jersey, 2000 Pennington Rd, Ewing, NJ, 08628-1104. Tel: 609-771-2311. p. 1402
Murray, Debi, Chief Curator, Historical Society of Palm Beach County, 300 N Dixie Hwy, West Palm Beach, FL, 33401. Tel: 561-832-4164, Ext 105. p. 453
Murray, Deirdre, Br Mgr, Athens Regional Library System, Winterville Branch, 115 Marigold Lane, Winterville, GA, 30683. Tel: 706-742-7735. p. 459
Murray, Donna, Dir, Purchase Free Library, 3093 Purchase St, Purchase, NY, 10577. Tel: 914-948-0550. p. 1624
Murray, Donna, Dir, Wyandanch Public Library, 14 S 20th St, Wyandanch, NY, 11798. Tel: 631-643-4848. p. 1667
Murray, Donna, Libr Dir, Ridley Township Public Library, 100 E MacDade Blvd, Folsom, PA, 19033-2592. Tel: 610-583-0593. p. 1933
Murray, Elizabeth, Ch Serv Librn, Stillwater Public Library, 1107 S Duck St, Stillwater, OK, 74074. Tel: 405-372-3633, Ext 8116. p. 1862
Murray, Erin, Dir, Lehigh Public Library, 241 Elm St, Lehigh, IA, 50557. Tel: 515-359-2967. p. 765
Murray, Felicia, Dir, Eldorado Memorial Public Library District, 1001 Grant St, Eldorado, IL, 62930-1714. Tel: 618-273-7922. p. 583
Murray, Frederic, Instrul Serv Librn, Southwestern Oklahoma State University, 100 Campus Dr, Weatherford, OK, 73096-3002. Tel: 580-774-7113. p. 1868
Murray, Greg, Pres, Southeastern Pennsylvania Theological Library Association, c/o Biblical Seminary, 200 N Main St, Hatfield, PA, 19440. Tel: 2215-368-5000, Ext 234. p. 2774
Murray, Helena, Education Program Mgr, The Arboretum at Flagstaff Library, 4001 S Woody Mountain Rd, Flagstaff, AZ, 86005. Tel: 928-774-1442. p. 60
Murray, Janice, Dir, Merritt Island Public Library, 1195 N Courtenay Pkwy, Merritt Island, FL, 32953-4596. Tel: 321-455-1369. p. 421
Murray, Jean-Luc, Dir of Educ, Bibliotheque et Archives Nationales du Quebec, 475 de Maisonneuve E, Montreal, QC, H2L 5C4, CANADA. Tel: 514-873-1101, Ext 6714. p. 2717
Murray, Jeanne, Br Mgr, Mercer County Library System, Twin Rivers Branch, 276 Abbington Dr, East Windsor, NJ, 08520. Tel: 609-443-1880. p. 1411
Murray, Jennifer, Asst Dir, Judicial Branch of Arizona, Maricopa County, 101 W Jefferson St, Phoenix, AZ, 85003. Tel: 602-506-7353. p. 70
Murray, Jennifer, Dir, Libr Syst & Tech Serv, University of North Florida, Bldg 12-Library, One UNF Dr, Jacksonville, FL, 32224-2645. Tel: 904-620-5160. p. 413
Murray, Jennifer, Libr Dir, South Burlington Community Library, 180 Market St, South Burlington, VT, 05403. Tel: 802-846-4140. p. 2294
Murray, Jill, Br Mgr, North Madison County Public Library System, Ralph E Hazelbaker Library, 1013 W Church St, Summitville, IN, 46070. Tel: 765-536-2335. p. 681
Murray, Josh, Mgr, County of Los Angeles Public Library, Clifton M Brakensiek Library, 9945 E Flower St, Bellflower, CA, 90706-5486. Tel: 562-925-5543. p. 135
Murray, Juanita, Dir, Archives, Dir, Spec Coll, Vanderbilt University, Special Collections & University Archives, 419 21st Ave S, Nashville, TN, 37203-2427. Tel: 615-322-2807. p. 2122
Murray, Kathy, Head, Alaska Med Libr, University of Alaska Anchorage, Consortium Library, 3211 Providence Dr, Anchorage, AK, 99508-8176. Tel: 907-786-1870. p. 43
Murray, Laura, Ch Serv Librn, Peterborough Public Library, 345 Aylmer St N, Peterborough, ON, K9H 3V7, CANADA. Tel: 705-745-5382, Ext 2362. p. 2672
Murray, LaVonne, Librn, Scio Public Library, Town Hall, 38957 NW First Ave, Scio, OR, 97374. Tel: 503-394-3342. p. 1898
Murray, Lisa, Dir, Cardington-Lincoln Public Library, 128 E Main St, Cardington, OH, 43315. Tel: 419-864-8181. p. 1756
Murray, Lisa, Bus Mgr, Menomonie Public Library, 600 Wolske Bay Rd, Menomonie, WI, 54751. Tel: 715-232-2164. p. 2456
Murray, Mary Jo, Dir, Twentieth Century Club Library, 49 N Main St, Almond, NY, 14804. Tel: 607-276-6311. p. 1485
Murray, Miranda, Libr Mgr, New York Public Library - Astor, Lenox & Tilden Foundations, Hudson Park Branch, 66 Leroy St, (Off Seventh Ave, South), New York, NY, 10014-3929. Tel: 212-243-6876. p. 1595
Murray, Nondus, Br Mgr, Sullivan County Public Libraries, Shelburn Public, 17 W Griffith, Shelburn, IN, 47879. Tel: 812-397-2210. p. 720
Murray, Patricia, Res & Instruction Librn, Fairleigh Dickinson University, 1000 River Rd, Teaneck, NJ, 07666-1914. Tel: 201-692-2285. p. 1445
Murray, Sara, Dir, Algonquin Area Public Library District, 2600 Harnish Dr, Algonquin, IL, 60102-5900. Tel: 847-458-6060. p. 536
Murray, Scott, Assessment Librn, User Experience Librn, Oklahoma State University - Center for Health Sciences, 1111 W 17th St, Tulsa, OK, 74107-1898. Tel: 918-561-8221. p. 1864
Murray, Shannon, Student Success Librn, University Canada West, 1461 Granville St, Vancouver, BC, V6Z 0E5, CANADA. p. 2580
Murray, Tara, Libr Dir, American Philatelic Research Library, 100 Match Factory Pl, Bellefonte, PA, 16823. Tel: 814-933-3803. p. 1909
Murray, Tara, Librn, Pennsylvania State University Libraries, George & Sherry Middlemas Arts & Humanities Library, Pennsylvania State University, W 337 Pattee Library, University Park, PA, 16802-1801. Tel: 814-865-0660. p. 2016
Murray, Telishia, Dir, Libr & Learning Res, Galveston College, 4015 Ave Q, Galveston, TX, 77550. Tel: 409-944-1240. p. 2183
Murray, William G, Head, Syst, United States Naval Academy, 589 McNair Rd, Annapolis, MD, 21402-5029. Tel: 410-293-6945. p. 951
Murray-Donaldson, Colleen, Br Mgr, Erie County Public Library, Lincoln Community Center, 1255 Manchester Rd, Erie, PA, 16505-2614. Tel: 814-451-7085. p. 1931
Murray-McKay, Darice, Br Mgr, San Francisco Public Library, Park Branch Library, 1833 Page St, San Francisco, CA, 94117-1909. Tel: 415-355-5656. p. 228
Murrell, Angela, Assoc Librn, University of Arizona Libraries, Health Sciences Library, 1501 N Campbell Ave, Tucson, AZ, 85724. Tel: (520) 626-2739. p. 83
Murrell, Gayle, Adminr, Circ Asst, Louisiana College, 1140 College Dr, Pineville, LA, 71359. Tel: 318-487-7109. p. 905
Murrell, Rachel, Archivist, California Baptist University, 8432 Magnolia Ave, Riverside, CA, 92504. Tel: 951-343-4250. p. 201
Murrie, Kelli, Sr Libr Asst, Roanoke County Public Library, Bent Mountain Branch, 10148 Tinsley Lane, Bent Mountain, VA, 24059. Tel: 540-929-4700. p. 2345
Murry, Chris, Pub Serv Librn, Northern Wyoming Community College District - Sheridan College, Griffith Memorial Bldg, One Whitney Way, Sheridan, WY, 82801. Tel: 307-675-0220. p. 2498
Murry, Christopher, Dir, Libr Serv, Western Wyoming Community College, 2500 College Dr, Rock Springs, WY, 82902. Tel: 307-382-1701. p. 2498
Murry, Joellyn, Childrens & Family Services, Liverpool Public Library, 310 Tulip St, Liverpool, NY, 13088-4997. Tel: 315-457-0310. p. 1564
Murtha, Helene, Asst Prof, Southern Connecticut State University, 501 Crescent St, New Haven, CT, 06515. Tel: 203-392-8387. p. 2783
Murtha, Leslie, Ref Serv, Atlantic Cape Community College, 5100 Black Horse Pike, Mays Landing, NJ, 08330. Tel: 609-343-4951. p. 1417
Murthy, Uma, Br Librn, Boston Public Library, Brighton Branch, 40 Academy Hill Rd, Brighton, MA, 02135. Tel: 617-782-6032. p. 992
Musacchio, Amanda, Asst Prof, College of Dupage, 425 Fawell Blvd, Glen Ellyn, IL, 60137. Tel: 630-942-3787. p. 2784
Muscarella, Mary, Dir, Town of Tonawanda Public Library, 160 Delaware Rd, Kenmore, NY, 14217. Tel: 716-873-2842. p. 1559
Muscarella, Mary, Dir, Town of Tonawanda Public Library, Kenilworth, 318 Montrose Ave, Buffalo, NY, 14223. Tel: 716-834-7657. p. 1559
Musch, Cheryl, Head, Spec Coll, University Archives, Truman State University, 100 E Normal, Kirksville, MO, 63501-4211. Tel: 660-785-7571. p. 1259
Muse, Clifford L, Jr, Dr, Interim Dir, Univ Archivist, Howard University Libraries, 500 Howard Pl NW, Ste 203, Washington, DC, 20059. Tel: 202-806-7498. p. 368
Muse, Julia, Humanities & Soc Sci Librn, Earlham College, 801 National Rd W, Richmond, IN, 47374-4095. p. 715
Musgrave, Delpha, Microfilm Presv Spec, State Historical Society of Iowa, 600 E Locust, Des Moines, IA, 50319-0290. Tel: 515-281-6200. p. 747
Musgrove, Camilla, Interim Librn, Geological Survey of Alabama Library, Walter Bryan Jones Hall, Rm 200, 420 Hackberry Lane, Tuscaloosa, AL, 35401. Tel: 205-247-3634. p. 37
Musial, Britney, Adult Serv Mgr, North Riverside Public Library District, 2400 S Des Plaines Ave, North Riverside, IL, 60546. Tel: 708-447-0869, Ext 245. p. 626
Musick, Donna, Tech Serv, Concord University, Vermillion St, Athens, WV, 24712. Tel: 304-384-5369. p. 2397

Muska, Deborah, Ch Serv, Stafford Library, Ten Levinthal Run, Stafford Springs, CT, 06075. Tel: 860-684-2852. p. 338

Muske, Erin, Sr Librn, Pierce County Library System, Bonney Lake Branch, 18501 90th St E, Bonney Lake, WA, 98391. Tel: 253-548-3308. p. 2386

Muskiewicz, Marion, Ref Librn, University of Massachusetts Lowell Library, Lydon Library, 84 University Ave, Lowell, MA, 01854-2896. Tel: 978-934-3209. p. 1030

Musko, Amanda, Dir, Frank D Campbell Memorial Library, 209 Hillsville Rd, Bessemer, PA, 16112. Tel: 724-667-7939. p. 1911

Mussehl, Vince, Dir, Chippewa Valley Technical College Library, 620 W Clairemont Ave, Eau Claire, WI, 54701-6162. Tel: 715-833-6285. p. 2432

Musselman, Jon, Head, Syst, University of Wisconsin - Platteville, One University Plaza, Platteville, WI, 53818. Tel: 608-342-1649. p. 2470

Musselman, Pam, Asst Librn, Claysburg Area Public Library, 957 Bedford St, Claysburg, PA, 16625. Tel: 814-239-2782. p. 1922

Musselman-Leister, Angela, Children's & Youth Serv, Librn, Bloomsburg Public Library, 225 Market St, Bloomsburg, PA, 17815-1726. Tel: 570-784-0883. p. 1913

Musser, Linda, Distinguished Librn, Head of Libr, Pennsylvania State University Libraries, Fletcher L Byrom Earth & Mineral Sciences Library, 105 Deike Bldg, University Park, PA, 16802. Tel: 814-863-7073. p. 2015

Musser, Nancy, Adult Serv Coordr, Baldwin Borough Public Library, 5230 Wolfe Dr, Pittsburgh, PA, 15236. Tel: 412-885-2255. p. 1990

Musser, Steven, Acq, Whittier College, Bonnie Bell Wardman Library, 7031 Founders Hill Rd, Whittier, CA, 90608-9984. Tel: 562-907-4247. p. 259

Mussett, Marianne, Sr Legal Ref Librn, University of Toledo, LaValley Law Library, Mail Stop 508, 2801 W Bancroft St, Toledo, OH, 43606-3390. Tel: 419-530-2733. p. 1825

Mussig, Jennifer, Dir, Perry Public Library, 3753 Main St, Perry, OH, 44081-9501. Tel: 440-259-3300. p. 1815

Mussulman, David, Asst Teaching Prof, University of Illinois at Urbana-Champaign, Library & Information Science Bldg, 501 E Daniel St, Champaign, IL, 61820-6211. Tel: 217-333-3280. p. 2784

Mustard, Jessica, Br Mgr, Carbon County Library System, Elk Mountain Branch, 105 Bridge St, Elk Mountain, WY, 82324. Tel: 307-348-7421. p. 2498

Mustic, Sabina, Librn, Staff Develop, Siouxland Libraries, 200 N Dakota Ave, Sioux Falls, SD, 57104. Tel: 605-367-8730. p. 2082

Muszkiewicz, Rachael, Assoc Professor of Library Science, Valparaiso University, 1410 Chapel Dr, Valparaiso, IN, 46383-6493. Tel: 219-464-5464. p. 723

Mutch, Kate, Asst Dir, Natrona County Library, 307 E Second St, Casper, WY, 82601. Tel: 307-577-7323. p. 2492

Mutford, John, Pub Serv Librn, Yellowknife Public Library, Centre Square Mall, 5022 49th St, 2nd Flr, Yellowknife, NT, X1A 2N5, CANADA. Tel: 867-920-5642. p. 2613

Muth, Catherine, Librn, FHN Memorial Hospital, 1045 W Stephenson St, Freeport, IL, 61032. Tel: 219-922-4868, Ext 1009. p. 590

Mutka, Martin E, Exec Dir, Library Consortium of Health Institutions in Buffalo, Abbott Hall, SUNY at Buffalo, 3435 Main St, Buffalo, NY, 14214. Tel: 716-829-3900, Ext 143. p. 2771

Mutum, Alana, Br Head, Great Neck Library, Lakeville, 475 Great Neck Rd, Great Neck, NY, 11021. Tel: 516-466-8055, Ext 231, 516-466-8055, Ext 232. p. 1541

Mutum, Alana, Br Head, Great Neck Library, Station, 26 Great Neck Rd, Great Neck, NY, 11021. Tel: 516-466-8055, Ext 233, 516-466-8055, Ext 234, 516-466-8055, Ext 235. p. 1541

Mutz, Bertha, Tech Serv, National Society of the Daughters of the American Revolution, DAR Library, 1776 D St NW, Washington, DC, 20006-5303. Tel: 202-879-3229. p. 373

Mutz, Janice, User Experience Librn, Lakehead University, 955 Oliver Rd, Thunder Bay, ON, P7B 5E1, CANADA. Tel: 807-343-8147. p. 2685

Muyumba, Valentine, Chair, Tech Serv, Indiana State University, 510 North 6 1/2 St, Terre Haute, IN, 47809. Tel: 812-237-3700. p. 720

Myc, Brenda, Librn, Canizaro Library at Ave Maria University, 5251 Donahue St, Ave Maria, FL, 34142. Tel: 239-280-2426. p. 384

Myers, Ada, Circ Supvr, Licking County Library, 101 W Main St, Newark, OH, 43055-5054. Tel: 740-349-5531. p. 1807

Myers, Adam, Librn, National Intelligence University Library, Defense Intelligence Agency, Attn: NIU-3A, 7400 Pentagon, Washington, DC, 20301-7400. p. 372

Myers, Amanda, Pub Serv Librn, Pearl River Community College, 101 Hwy 11 N, Poplarville, MS, 39470. p. 1230

Myers, Anne, Music Librn, University of Northern Colorado Libraries, 1636 Tenth Ave, Greeley, CO, 80639. Tel: 970-351-2327. p. 285

Myers, Ashton, Dir, Saint Mary Parish Library, 206 Iberia St, Franklin, LA, 70538. Tel: 337-828-1624, 337-828-1627. p. 890

Myers, Carla V, Ser, Washington & Jefferson College Library, 60 S Lincoln St, Washington, PA, 15301. Tel: 724-223-6547. p. 2018

Myers, Carolyn, Br Mgr, Davis County Library, Kaysville Branch, 215 N Fairfield Rd, Kaysville, UT, 84037. Tel: 801-451-1800. p. 2263

Myers, Claire, Fac Res Serv/Ref Serv Librn, University of Michigan, Kresge Library Services, Stephen M Ross School of Business, 701 Tappan St, Ann Arbor, MI, 48109-1234. Tel: 734-647-3380. p. 1079

Myers, Cynthia, Head, Coll Develop, Tech Serv, George Mason University Libraries, Law Library, 3301 N Fairfax Dr, Arlington, VA, 22201-4426. Tel: 703-993-8100. p. 2317

Myers, Gretchen, Head, Tech Serv, Hudson Library & Historical Society, 96 Library St, Hudson, OH, 44236-5122. Tel: 330-653-6658. p. 1790

Myers, Heather, Pub Serv Librn, Anderson University, 1100 E Fifth St, Anderson, IN, 46012-3495. Tel: 765-641-4288. p. 668

Myers, Jerome, Commun Libr Mgr, Queens Library, Ozone Park Community Library, 92-24 Rockaway Blvd, Ozone Park, NY, 11417. Tel: 718-845-3127. p. 1555

Myers, John, Libr Assoc, West Virginia University, 300 Campus Dr, Rm 1332, Parkersburg, WV, 26104-8647. Tel: 304-424-8260. p. 2411

Myers, Jordan, Dir, Keller Public Library, 402 W Grant St, Dexter, MO, 63841. Tel: 573-624-3764. p. 1245

Myers, Kathy, Info Mgr, Carthage College, 2001 Alford Park Dr, Kenosha, WI, 53140-1900. Tel: 262-551-5950. p. 2444

Myers, Kelli, Asst Librn, State Correctional Institution, 11 Fairview Dr, Waymart, PA, 18472. Tel: 570-488-5811, Ext 3459. p. 2018

Myers, Ken, Br Head, Naval Surface Warfare Center, 9500 MacArthur Blvd, West Bethesda, MD, 20817-5700. Tel: 301-227-1319. p. 980

Myers, Kim, Asst Dir, York Public Library, 15 Long Sands Rd, York, ME, 03909. Tel: 207-363-2818. p. 947

Myers, Klarissa, Libr Mgr, Cisco College, 101 College Heights, Cisco, TX, 76437. Tel: 254-442-5011. p. 2155

Myers, Klarissa, Libr Mgr, Cisco College, Abilene Educational Center Library, 717 E Industrial Blvd, Abilene, TX, 79602. Tel: 325-794-4466. p. 2155

Myers, Linda, Dir, Bloomfield Public Library, 200 Seneca St, Bloomfield, MO, 63825. Tel: 573-568-3626. p. 1237

Myers, Marci, Outreach Serv Librn, Tech Serv, Virginia Western Community College, 3095 Colonial Ave SW, Roanoke, VA, 24015. Tel: 540-857-6693. p. 2346

Myers, Marilyn, Assoc Dean, Pub Serv, University of Houston, M D Anderson Library, 114 University Libraries, Houston, TX, 77204-2000. Tel: 713-743-9800. p. 2199

Myers, Mary, Finance Mgr, Palatine Public Library District, 700 N North Ct, Palatine, IL, 60067. Tel: 847-907-3600. p. 631

Myers, Megan, Libr Dir, Coolidge Library, 17 S Main St, Solon, ME, 04979. Tel: 207-643-2562. p. 940

Myers, Melanie, Dir, Organization & Mgmt, The Westport Library, 20 Jesup Rd, Westport, CT, 06880. Tel: 203-291-4820. p. 347

Myers, Michelle, Data Spec, Saint Mark's Hospital, 1200 E 3900 South, Salt Lake City, UT, 84124. Tel: 801-268-7111, 801-268-7676. p. 2271

Myers, Nanci, Librn, Haverhill Library Association, 67 Court St, Haverhill, NH, 03765. Tel: 603-989-5578. p. 1367

Myers, Nancy, Patron Serv Mgr, North Canton Public Library, 185 N Main St, North Canton, OH, 44720-2595. Tel: 330-499-4712. p. 1809

Myers, Randall, Evening Circ, Libr Syst Mgr, Georgetown College, 400 E College St, Georgetown, KY, 40324. Tel: 502-863-8406. p. 856

Myers, Ray, Asst Dir, Madison County Library System, 102 Priestley St, Canton, MS, 39046. p. 1213

Myers, Rene, Mgr, Muskogee Public Library, 801 W Okmulgee, Muskogee, OK, 74401. Tel: 918-682-6657. p. 1854

Myers, Robert, Assoc Dir for Operations, Case Western Reserve University, School of Law Library, 11075 East Blvd, Cleveland, OH, 44106-7148. Tel: 216-368-8656. p. 1766

Myers, Roger, Res & Instruction Librn, Maryville College, 502 E Lamar Alexander Pkwy, Maryville, TN, 37804-5907. Tel: 865-981-8259. p. 2111

Myers, Sally, Asst Dean, Libr Serv, Clinton Community College Library, 1000 Lincoln Blvd, Clinton, IA, 52732. Tel: 563-244-7046. p. 740

Myers, Sarah K, Pub Serv Librn, Messiah University, One University Ave, Ste 3002, Mechanicsburg, PA, 17055. Tel: 717-691-6006, Ext 3590. p. 1960

Myers, Steph, Adult Serv Supvr, Duluth Public Library, 520 W Superior St, Duluth, MN, 55802. Tel: 218-730-4246. p. 1172

Myers, Susan, Dir, Teen Serv, Spartanburg County Public Libraries, 151 S Church St, Spartanburg, SC, 29306. Tel: 864-596-3500. p. 2069

Myers, Tara, Libr Office Mgr, Gavilan College Library, 5055 Santa Teresa Blvd, Gilroy, CA, 95020. p. 148

Myers, Teresa, Circ Mgr, County Br Mgr, Chillicothe & Ross County Public Library, 140 S Paint St, Chillicothe, OH, 45601. Tel: 740-702-4145. p. 1758

Myers, Tim, Sr Mgr, National Endowment for Democracy Library, 1201 Pennsylvania Ave NW, Ste 1100, Washington, DC, 20004. Tel: 202-378-9700. p. 372

Myers, Tommi, Dir, Llano County Library System, 102 E Haynie St, Llano, TX, 78643. Tel: 325-247-5248. p. 2212

Myers, Tori L, Curator, Research Librn, San Juan County Archaeological Research Center & Library at Salmon Ruins, 6131 US Hwy 64, Bloomfield, NM, 87413. Tel: 505-632-2013. p. 1464

Myers, Tracy, Mgr, District of Columbia Public Library, Chevy Chase, 5625 Connecticut Ave NW, Washington, DC, 20015. Tel: 202-282-0021. p. 364

Nance, Anita, Ch Prog, Quitman Public Library, 202 E Goode St, Quitman, TX, 75783-2533. Tel: 903-763-4191. p. 2230

Nance, Heidi, Libr Dir, College of Physicians of Philadelphia, 19 S 22nd St, Philadelphia, PA, 19103. Tel: 215-399-2301. p. 1975

Nance, Karolyn, Dir, Bartlett Public Library District, 800 S Bartlett Rd, Bartlett, IL, 60103. Tel: 630-837-2855. p. 540

Nance, Megan, Access Serv Coordr, Archives Asst, Palm Beach Atlantic University, 300 Pembroke Pl, West Palm Beach, FL, 33401-6503. Tel: 561-803-2231. p. 453

Nance, Nadine F, Head, Access Serv, Williams College, 26 Hopkins Hall Dr, Williamstown, MA, 01267. Tel: 413-597-2920. p. 1069

Nandi, Raka, Dir of Exhibits & Colls, Memphis Museum of Science & History, 3050 Central Ave, Memphis, TN, 38111. Tel: 901-636-2387. p. 2112

Nanes, Roberto, Univ Archivist, University of Houston - Clear Lake, Bayou Bldg 2402, 2700 Bay Area Blvd, Houston, TX, 77058-1002. Tel: 281-283-3933. p. 2199

Nann, John, Assoc Law Librn, Yale University Library, Lillian Goldman Library Yale Law School, 127 Wall St, New Haven, CT, 06511. Tel: 203-432-1259. p. 328

Nantanapibul, Armando, Br Mgr, Riverside County Library System, Romoland Library, 26001 Briggs Rd, Menifee, CA, 92585. Tel: 951-325-2090. p. 202

Napier, Rhonda, Regional Librn, Alabama Public Library Service, 6030 Monticello Dr, Montgomery, AL, 36130. Tel: 334-213-3921. p. 28

Naples, Kim, Adult/YA Serv Librn, Katonah Village Library, 26 Bedford Rd, Katonah, NY, 10536-2121. Tel: 914-232-3508. p. 1559

Naples, Kim, Teen Librn, The Nyack Library, 59 S Broadway, Nyack, NY, 10960. Tel: 845-358-3370, Ext 238. p. 1609

Naples, Pam, Dir, Mount Carroll District Library, 208 N Main St, Mount Carroll, IL, 61053-1022. Tel: 815-244-1751. p. 620

Napoles, Leticia, Mgr, County of Los Angeles Public Library, Graham Library, 1900 E Firestone Blvd, Los Angeles, CA, 90001-4126. Tel: 323-582-2903. p. 136

Naputi, Erlinda C, Libr Dir, Joeten-Kiyu Public Library, 2745 Insatto St, Saipan, MP, 96950. Tel: 670-235-7322, 670-235-7323. p. 2507

Naranjilla, Carina, Library Contact, Alberta Historical Resources Foundation Library, 8820 112th St, Edmonton, AB, T6G 2P8, CANADA. Tel: 780-431-2305. p. 2535

Naranjo, Becky, ILL, Midland County Public Library, 301 W Missouri Ave, Midland, TX, 79701. Tel: 432-688-4320. p. 2219

Naranjo, Teresa, Librn, Santa Clara Pueblo Community Library, 578 Kee St, Espanola, NM, 87532. Tel: 505-692-6295. p. 1467

Narayan, Lakshmi, Librn, Krotona Institute of Theosophy Library, Two Krotona Hill, Ojai, CA, 93023. Tel: 805-646-2653. p. 188

Nardi, Christopher, Chief Operating Officer, USS Massachusetts Memorial Committee, Inc, Battleship Cove, Five Water St, Fall River, MA, 02721-1540. Tel: 508-678-1100. p. 1018

Nardiello, Cheryl, Asst Dir, Wicomico Public Library, 122 S Division St, Salisbury, MD, 21801. Tel: 410-749-3612, Ext 142. p. 976

Nardin, Peter, Librn, United States Air Force, 72nd FSS/FSDL, Bldg 5702, 6120 Arnold St, Tinker AFB, OK, 73145. Tel: 405-734-2626. p. 1864

Narkiewicz, Jacqueline, Br Librn, Huntington Public Library, Huntington Station Branch, 1335 New York Ave, Huntington Station, NY, 11746. Tel: 631-421-5053, Ext 124. p. 1549

Nartker, Gail Ann, Dir, Sandusky District Library, 55 E Sanilac Ave, Sandusky, MI, 48471-1146. Tel: 810-648-2644. p. 1149

Naru, Linda, Asst Univ Librn, Admin Serv, University of Illinois at Chicago, MC 234, 801 S Morgan St, Chicago, IL, 60607. Tel: 312-413-0394. p. 570

Narum, Dianne, Cat Librn, Govt Doc Librn, Bemidji State University, 1500 Birchmont Dr NE, No 28, Bemidji, MN, 56601-2699. Tel: 218-755-3340. p. 1165

Narvaez-Rodriguez, Franisco, Circ Evening Coordr, Saint Leo University, 33701 State Rd 52, Saint Leo, FL, 33574. Tel: 352-588-8273. p. 441

Naseman, Peggy, Pub Relations, Shelby County Libraries, 230 E North St, Sidney, OH, 45365-2785. Tel: 937-492-8354. p. 1820

Nash, Amanda, Asst Dean, Libr, Head Librn - Gainesville Campus, University of North Georgia, 3820 Mundy Mill Rd, Oakwood, GA, 30566. Tel: 678-717-3825. p. 493

Nash, Barbara, Br Librn, Plaquemines Parish Library, Belle Chasse Branch, 8442 Hwy 23, Belle Chasse, LA, 70037. Tel: 504-393-0449, 504-394-3570. p. 885

Nash, Bonnie, Libr Assoc, East Georgia State College Library, 131 College Circle, Swainsboro, GA, 30401-2699. Tel: 478-289-2085. p. 498

Nash, Cassie, Library Systems Admin, Batesville Memorial Public Library, 131 N Walnut St, Batesville, IN, 47006. Tel: 812-934-4706. p. 669

Nash, Crystal, Libr Dir, Lewis County Public Library & Archives, 15 Kyle Ave, Hohenwald, TN, 38462-1434. Tel: 931-796-5365. p. 2101

Nash, Cyndal, Br Mgr, Campbell County Public Library, Patrick Henry Memorial, 204 Lynchburg Ave, Brookneal, VA, 24528. Tel: 434-376-3363. p. 2346

Nash, Jennifer, Asst Dir, Cyrenius H Booth Library, 25 Main St, Newtown, CT, 06470. Tel: 203-426-4533. p. 330

Nash, Lawrence, Sr Librn, Los Angeles Public Library System, Encino-Tarzana Branch Library, 18231 Ventura Blvd, Tarzana, CA, 91356-3620. Tel: 818-343-1983. p. 164

Nash, Maribel, Instrul & Access Serv Librn, Northwestern University Libraries, Pritzker Legal Research Center, 375 E Chicago Ave, Chicago, IL, 60611. Tel: 312-503-0300. p. 587

Nash, Michelle, Curator of Coll, Elkhart County Historical Society Museum, Inc, 304 W Vistula St, Bristol, IN, 46507. Tel: 574-848-4322. p. 672

Nash, Rachel, City Librn, Soldotna Public Library, 235 N Binkley St, Soldotna, AK, 99669. Tel: 907-262-4227. p. 51

Nash, Tiffany, Head, Circ, Arcadia Public Library, 20 W Duarte Rd, Arcadia, CA, 91006. Tel: 626-294-4804. p. 117

Nash-Weninger, Celeste, Exec Secy, American Federation of Astrologers, Inc Library, 6535 S Rural Rd, Tempe, AZ, 85283-3746. Tel: 480-838-1751. p. 79

Nashak, Catherine, Asst Dir, Hewlett-Woodmere Public Library, 1125 Broadway, Hewlett, NY, 11557-0903. Tel: 516-374-1967. p. 1546

Naslund, Donna, Dir, Ransom Memorial Public Library, 110 E Main St, Altona, IL, 61414. Tel: 309-484-6193. p. 536

Nason, Ella, Dir, Client Serv, Operations Dir, New Brunswick Public Library Service (NBPLS), 570 Two Nations Crossing, Ste 2, Fredericton, NB, E3A 0X9, CANADA. Tel: 506-453-2354. p. 2601

Nason, Jennifer L, Mgr, University of Michigan, Sumner & Laura Foster Library, 265 Lorch Hall, Ann Arbor, MI, 48109-1220. Tel: 734-763-6609. p. 1079

Nason, Mike, Librn, University of New Brunswick Libraries, Five Macaulay Lane, Fredericton, NB, E3B 5H5, CANADA. Tel: 506-452-6325. p. 2601

Nasr, Mandy, Libr Dir, Camarillo Public Library, 4101 Las Posas Rd, Camarillo, CA, 93010. Tel: 805-388-5222. p. 126

Nasr, Mandy, Sr Librn, Los Angeles Public Library System, Northridge Branch Library, 9051 Darby Ave, Northridge, CA, 91325-2743. Tel: 818-886-3640. p. 165

Nass, Janice, Mgr, Ser, Martin Luther College Library, 1995 Luther Ct, New Ulm, MN, 56073-3965. Tel: 507-354-8221, Ext 327. p. 1190

Nassar, Anne, Libr Dir, Little Falls Public Library, Ten Waverly Pl, Little Falls, NY, 13365. Tel: 315-823-1542. p. 1563

Nassar, Jennifer, Dir, Chapin Memorial Library, 400 14th Ave N, Myrtle Beach, SC, 29577. Tel: 843-918-1275. p. 2066

Nasta, Jesse, Dir, Middlesex County Historical Society Library, 151 Main St, Middletown, CT, 06457-3423. Tel: 860-346-0746. p. 322

Nasto, Ellen S, Libr Dir, Floyd Memorial Library, 539 First St, Greenport, NY, 11944-1399. Tel: 631-477-0660. p. 1541

Natal, Gerald, Health Sci Librn, University of Toledo, Mulford Library Bldg, 4th Flr, 3025 Library Circle, Toledo, OH, 43614-8000. Tel: 419-383-4225. p. 1825

Natale, Melissa, Ref Librn, Endicott College Library, 376 Hale St, Beverly, MA, 01915. Tel: 978-232-2244. p. 989

Natale, Michael, Br Mgr, Pamunkey Regional Library, Richard S Gillis Jr - Ashland Branch, 201 S Railroad Ave, Ashland, VA, 23005. Tel: 804-798-4072. p. 2323

Natarajan, Vani, Res & Instruction Librn, Barnard College, 3009 Broadway, New York, NY, 10027-6598. Tel: 212-854-8595. p. 1579

Natches, Jane, E-Res & Ser Librn, Tufts University, Hirsh Health Sciences Library, 145 Harrison Ave, Boston, MA, 02111. Tel: 617-636-2452. p. 1034

Natenzon, Galina, Asst Dir, Library of the Chathams, 214 Main St, Chatham, NJ, 07928. Tel: 973-635-0603. p. 1395

Nathan, Carr, Info Tech, Newton Public Library, 720 N Oak, Newton, KS, 67114. Tel: 316-283-2890. p. 826

Nathan, Lisa, Assoc Prof, University of British Columbia, The Irving K Barber Learning Ctr, 1961 E Mall, Ste 470, Vancouver, BC, V6T 1Z1, CANADA. Tel: 604-822-2404. p. 2795

Nathan, Smith, Br Mgr, Jefferson Parish Library, Terrytown Branch, 680 Heritage Ave, Terrytown, LA, 70056. Tel: 504-364-2717. p. 897

Nathanson, Jill, Ref & Instruction Librn, Rutgers University Libraries, Library of Science & Medicine, 165 Bevier Rd, Piscataway, NJ, 08854-8009. p. 1425

Nation, Fred, Exec Dir, Sheldon Swope Art Museum Library, 25 S Seventh St, Terre Haute, IN, 47807. Tel: 812-238-1676. p. 721

Nations, Callie, Pub Serv Librn, South Plains College Library, 1401 S College Ave - Box E, Levelland, TX, 79336. Tel: 806-716-2298. p. 2211

Nations, Maureen, Mgr, Tri-County Regional Library, Ashdown Community Library, 160 E Commerce St, Ashdown, AR, 71822. Tel: 870-898-3233. p. 106

Natriello, Gary J, Dr, Dir, Teachers College, Columbia University, 525 W 120th St, New York, NY, 10027-6696. Tel: 212-678-3087. p. 1602

Natzke, Teresa, Dir, Franklin Public Library, 32455 Franklin Rd, Franklin, MI, 48025. Tel: 248-851-2254. p. 1108

Naughton, Amy, Libr Dir, Minneapolis College of Art & Design Library, 2501 Stevens Ave, Minneapolis, MN, 55404. Tel: 612-874-3752. p. 1184

Naughton, Michael, Head, Tech, Boynton Beach City Library, 115 N Federal Hwy, Boynton Beach, FL, 33435. Tel: 561-742-6390. p. 386

Naughton, Robin, PhD, Digital Projects Mgr, New York Academy of Medicine Library, 1216 Fifth Ave, New York, NY, 10029. Tel: 212-822-7325. p. 1593

Naughton, Sarah, Archivist, Edgewood College Library, 959 Edgewood College Dr, Madison, WI, 53711-1997. Tel: 608-663-3300. p. 2449

Naugle, Mallory, Circ Tech, Wagoner City Public Library, 302 N Main St, Wagoner, OK, 74467-3834. Tel: 918-485-2126. p. 1868

Nault, Andre J, Head Librn, University of Minnesota Libraries-Twin Cities, Veterinary Medical Library, 450 Veterinary Science Bldg, 1971 Commonwealth Ave, Saint Paul, MN, 55108. Tel: 612-624-5376. p. 1186

Nauman, Susan, Libr Dir, Mound City Public Library, 207 E Sixth St, Mound City, MO, 64470. Tel: 660-442-5700. p. 1263

Nauta, Laura R, Head, Cat, United States Naval Academy, 589 McNair Rd, Annapolis, MD, 21402-5029. Tel: 410-293-6945. p. 951

Nauyuq, Lorna, Librn, Nunavut Public Library Services, Qimiruvik Library, PO Box 403, Pangnirtung, NU, X0A 0R0, CANADA. Tel: 867-473-8678. p. 2625

Nava, Penny, Ch, Oakland Public Library, 18 Church St, Oakland, ME, 04963. Tel: 207-465-7533. p. 934

Navare, Anuja, Dir of Coll, Pasadena Museum of History, 470 W Walnut St, Pasadena, CA, 91103. Tel: 626-577-1660, Ext 204. p. 194

Navarrete, Paul, Pub Serv Mgr, California College of the Arts Libraries, Simpson Library, 1111 Eighth St, San Francisco, CA, 94107. p. 185

Navarro, Amalia, Dir, Olga V Figueroa - Zapata County Public Library, 901 Kennedy St, Zapata, TX, 78076. Tel: 956-765-5351. p. 2259

Navarro, Danielle, Libr Coord, Yavapai County Free Library District, Cordes Lakes Public Library, 15989 S Cordes Lake Dr, Cordes Lakes, AZ, 86333. Tel: 928-632-5492. p. 75

Navarro, Diana, Dir, Cocopah Tribal Library, 14250 S Ave 1, Somerton, AZ, 85350. Tel: 928-627-8026. p. 78

Navarro, Nallely, Libr Dir, Elvis Maxine Gilliam Memorial Public Library, 205 E Beltline Rd, Wilmer, TX, 75172. Tel: 972-441-3335. p. 2258

Navarro, Veronica, Circ Librn, Donna Public Library, 301 S Main St, Donna, TX, 78537. Tel: 956-464-2221. p. 2171

Navarro, Yesenia, Asst Dir, Libr Serv, University of Miami, Louis Calder Memorial Library, Miller School of Medicine, 1601 NW Tenth Ave, Miami, FL, 33136. Tel: 305-243-6403. p. 425

Navarro-Rodriguez, Erica, Literacy Service Coord, Braille Institute Library, Anaheim Center, 527 N Dale Ave, Anaheim, CA, 92801. Tel: 714-821-5000. p. 160

Navratil, Heather, Cat/Ref Librn, Carroll College, 1601 N Benton Ave, Helena, MT, 59625. Tel: 406-447-4340. p. 1295

Nawalaniec, Theresa, Librn, Cleveland State University, Michael Schwartz Library, Rhodes Tower, Ste 501, 2121 Euclid Ave, Cleveland, OH, 44115-2214. Tel: 216-687-3504. p. 1769

Nawar, Essraa, Asst Dean, Chapman University, One University Dr, Orange, CA, 92866. Tel: 714-532-7756. p. 188

Nawrocki, Bob, Chief Librn, Saint Augustine Historical Society, Six Artillery Lane, 2nd Flr, Saint Augustine, FL, 32084. Tel: 904-825-2333. p. 440

Nay, Jessica, Librn, State Historical Society of Iowa, 600 E Locust, Des Moines, IA, 50319-0290. Tel: 515-725-3402. p. 747

Naya, Denise, Sr Law Librn, Queens County Supreme Court Library, General Court House, 88-11 Sutphin Blvd, Jamaica, NY, 11435. Tel: 718-298-1206. p. 1553

Naylor, Kim, Librn, Mohave Community College Library, North Mohave Campus, 480 S Central, Colorado City, AZ, 86021. Tel: 928-875-2799, Ext 2224. p. 64

Naylor, Leigh Ann, Dir, Hist & Archives, Fort Worth Museum of Science & History Library, 1600 Gendy St, Fort Worth, TX, 76107. Tel: 817-255-9305. p. 2180

Naylor, Mary, Libr Mgr, San Antonio Public Library, Forest Hills, 5245 Ingram Rd, San Antonio, TX, 78228. Tel: 210-207-9230. p. 2239

Naylor, Nicole, Br Mgr, Toledo-Lucas County Public Library, West Toledo, 1320 Sylvania Ave, Toledo, OH, 43612. Tel: 419-259-5290. p. 1825

Naylor, Tammy, Cat, West Virginia State University, Campus Box L17, Institute, WV, 25112. Tel: 304-766-3116. p. 2406

Nayyer, Kim, Dir, Cornell University Library, Law Library, Myron Taylor Hall, 524 College Ave, Ithaca, NY, 14853-4901. Tel: 607-255-7236. p. 1552

Nazar, Marilyn, Archivist, Art Gallery of Ontario, 317 Dundas St W, Toronto, ON, M5T 1G4, CANADA. Tel: 416-979-6642. p. 2686

Nazarenko, Nadia, Head Librn, Alvin Community College Library, 3110 Mustang Rd, Alvin, TX, 77511. Tel: 281-756-3559. p. 2133

Nazarian, Katie, User Serv Librn, Mitchell College Library, 437 Pequot Ave, New London, CT, 06320. Tel: 860-701-7789. p. 329

Nazario, Carmen, Librn, University of Florida, 2725 S Binion Rd, Apopka, FL, 32703-8504. Tel: 407-410-6929, 407-884-2034, Ext 140. p. 383

Nazarko, Daniel, Supvr, Ad Serv, Madison Public Library, 39 Keep St, Madison, NJ, 07940. Tel: 973-377-0722. p. 1415

Nazionale, Nina, Dir of Libr Operations, New York Historical Society Museum & Library, 170 Central Park W, New York, NY, 10024. Tel: 212-873-3400. p. 1593

Ndulute, Asteria, Govt Doc/Ref Librn, Tuskegee University, 1200 W Old Mongtomery Rd, Ford Motor Company Library, Tuskegee, AL, 36088. Tel: 334-727-8891. p. 38

Neacsu, Dana, Ref Librn, Columbia University, Arthur W Diamond Law Library, 435 W 116th St, New York, NY, 10027. Tel: 212-854-3922. p. 1583

Neacsu, Dana, Dir, Allegheny County Law Library, 921 City-County Bldg, 414 Grant St, Pittsburgh, PA, 15219-2543. Tel: 412-396-6300. p. 1990

Nead, Marge, Dir, Libr Serv, Colgate Rochester Crozer Divinity School, 1100 S Goodman St, Rochester, NY, 14620-2592. Tel: 585-340-9601. p. 1628

Neagle, Eric, Assoc Dir for Operations, Illinois Institute of Technology, Chicago-Kent College of Law Library, 565 W Adams St, 9th Flr, Chicago, IL, 60661. Tel: 312-906-5600. p. 562

Neagle, Eric, Tech Serv Librn, Library of the US Courts of the Seventh Circuit, 219 S Dearborn St, Rm 1637, Chicago, IL, 60604-1769. Tel: 312-435-5660. p. 563

Neal, Alan, Br Librn, Oxnard Public Library, South Oxnard, 4300 Saviers Rd, Oxnard, CA, 93033. Tel: 805-385-8129. p. 190

Neal, Alan, Br Mgr, Oxnard Public Library, Colonia, 1500 Camino del Sol, No 26, Oxnard, CA, 93030. Tel: 805-385-8108. p. 190

Neal, Alan, Branch Services, Sr Librn, Oxnard Public Library, 251 South A St, Oxnard, CA, 93030. Tel: 805-247-8951. p. 190

Neal, Albert, Head, Patron Services, Manhattanville University Library, 2900 Purchase St, Purchase, NY, 10577. Tel: 914-323-3133. p. 1624

Neal, Ben, Libr Dir, Blackwater Regional Library, 22511 Main St, Courtland, VA, 23837. Tel: 757-653-2821. p. 2313

Neal, Ben, Mgr, Portsmouth Public Library, 601 Court St, Portsmouth, VA, 23704. Tel: 757-393-8501, Ext 6509. p. 2338

Neal, Cassaundra, Asst Librn, Fannie Brown Booth Memorial Library, 619 Tenaha St, Center, TX, 75935. Tel: 936-598-5522. p. 2155

Neal, Dan, Interim Libr Dir, Wentworth Institute of Technology, 550 Huntington Ave, Boston, MA, 02115-5998. Tel: 617-989-4790. p. 1000

Neal, Elizabeth, Youth Serv Librn, Dorchester County Library, Summerville Branch, 76 Old Trolley Rd, Summerville, SC, 29485. Tel: 843-871-5075. p. 2069

Neal, Hattie, Br Mgr, Concordia Parish Library, Vidalia Branch, 408 Texas St, Vidalia, LA, 71373. Tel: 318-336-5043. p. 889

Neal, Jessica, Col Archivist, Hampshire College Library, 893 West St, Amherst, MA, 01002. Tel: 413-559-5440. p. 984

Neal, Kailah, Communications Spec, Pub Serv, Wilmington University Library, 320 N DuPont Hwy, New Castle, DE, 19720. Tel: 302-669-6602. p. 355

Neal, Karen, Youth Serv Librn, Drake Community Library, 930 Park St, Grinnell, IA, 50112-2016. Tel: 641-236-2661. p. 756

Neal, Larry, Libr Dir, Clinton-Macomb Public Library, 40900 Romeo Plank Rd, Clinton Township, MI, 48038-2955. Tel: 586-226-5011. p. 1092

Neal, Linda, Asst Librn, Beaman Community Memorial Library, 223 Main St, Beaman, IA, 50609. Tel: 641-366-2912. p. 734

Neal, Lisa, Youth Serv Librn, Hickory Public Library, 375 Third St NE, Hickory, NC, 28601. Tel: 828-304-0500. p. 1696

Neal, Lisa Sue, Librn, Hatch Public Library, 530 E Hall, Hatch, NM, 87937. Tel: 575-267-5132. p. 1469

Neal, Raymond, Continuing Educ Coordr, Northeast Florida Library Information Network, 2233 Park Ave, Ste 402, Orange Park, FL, 32073. Tel: 904-278-5620. p. 2763

Neal, Sally, Assoc Dean, Instruction & User Servs, Butler University Libraries, 4600 Sunset Ave, Indianapolis, IN, 46208. Tel: 317-940-9949. p. 690

Neal, Shari, Libr Tech, Southwest Minnesota State University Library, 1501 State St, Marshall, MN, 56258. Tel: 507-537-7232. p. 1182

Neale, Evelyn, Dir, The William K Sanford Town Library, 629 Albany Shaker Rd, Loudonville, NY, 12211-1196. Tel: 518-458-9274. p. 1565

Nealis, Karen, Br Mgr, Monmouth County Library, Holmdel Branch, 101 Crawfords Corner Rd, Ste 2110, Holmdel, NJ, 07733. Tel: 732-946-4118. p. 1416

Nealon, Robert, Head, Tech, Maplewood Memorial Library, 129 Boyden Ave, Maplewood, NJ, 07040. Tel: 973-762-1688. p. 1416

Neame, Simon, Dean, Univ Libr, University of Washington Libraries, Box 352900, Seattle, WA, 98195-2900. Tel: 206-543-0242. p. 2381

Neary, Corinne, Libr Mgr, New York Public Library - Astor, Lenox & Tilden Foundations, Tompkins Square Branch, 331 E Tenth St, New York, NY, 10009-5099. Tel: 212-228-4747. p. 1597

Neary, Kay, Ref Librn, Massasoit Community College, One Massasoit Blvd, Brockton, MA, 02302. Tel: 508-588-9100, Ext 1941. p. 1003

Neary, Kevin, Supervisory Library Asst, Elmwood Park Public Library, 210 Lee St, Elmwood Park, NJ, 07407. Tel: 201-796-8888. p. 1401

Neate, Janet, Coordr, York University Libraries, Map Library, Scott Library, Main Flr, 4700 Keele St, North York, ON, M3J 1P3, CANADA. Tel: 416-736-2100, Ext 33353. p. 2662

Neath, Jessica, Asst Librn, Nesbitt Memorial Library, 529 Washington St, Columbus, TX, 78934-2326. Tel: 979-732-3392. p. 2158

Neathery, Jennifer, Libr Dir, River Oaks Public Library, 4900 River Oaks Blvd, River Oaks, TX, 76114. Tel: 817-624-7344. p. 2233

Neaton, Allison, Supvr, Lowry Nature Center Library, 7025 Victoria Dr, Victoria, MN, 55386. Tel: 763-694-7650. p. 1206

Neault, Martha, Ch, Berlin Free Library, 834 Worthington Ridge, Berlin, CT, 06037. Tel: 860-828-3344. p. 302

Nechiporenko, Jolene, Access Serv Librn, Minot State University, 500 University Ave W, Minot, ND, 58707. Tel: 701-858-3868. p. 1738

Nederhoff, Laura, Libr Dir, Shaw Public Library, Nine Lily Bay Rd, Greenville, ME, 04441. Tel: 207-695-3579. p. 926

Nee, Julia, Ad, Asst Dir, Hanson Public Library, 132 Maquan St, Hanson, MA, 02341. Tel: 781-293-2151. p. 1023

Needham, Greg, Dir, Sheppard Memorial Library, 530 S Evans St, Greenville, NC, 27858. Tel: 252-329-4585. p. 1694

Needham, Jennifer, Head, Children's Servx, Berlin-Peck Memorial Library, 234 Kensington Rd, Berlin, CT, 06037. Tel: 860-828-7117. p. 302

Needham, Tamara, Chief Exec Officer, Head Librn, Marathon Public Library, 22 Peninsula Rd, Marathon, ON, P0T 2E0, CANADA. Tel: 807-229-1340, Ext 2266. p. 2656

Neel, Becca, Assoc Dir, Res Mgt, Assoc Dir, User Experience, University of Southern Indiana, 8600 University Blvd, Evansville, IN, 47712. Tel: 812-461-5328. p. 682

Neely, Allison, Univ Archivist, Michigan Technological University, 1400 Townsend Dr, Houghton, MI, 49931-1295. Tel: 906-487-2816. p. 1116

Neely, Colton, Ch, Vinton Public Library, 510 Second Ave, Vinton, IA, 52349. Tel: 319-472-4208. p. 788

Neely, Jason, Dir of Libr, Enfield Public Library, 104 Middle Rd, Enfield, CT, 06082. Tel: 860-763-7510. p. 311

Neely, Jennifer, Ch, Dunellen Public Library, 100 New Market Rd, Dunellen, NJ, 08812. Tel: 732-968-4585. p. 1399

Neely, Peter, Digital Serv Librn, Columbia College, 1001 Rogers St, Columbia, MO, 65216. Tel: 573-875-7372. p. 1243

Neely-Sardon, Angie, Ref Librn, Indian River State College, Brackett Library - Mueller Campus, Indian River State College, Mueller Campus, 6155 College Lane, Vero Beach, FL, 32966. Tel: 772-226-2544. p. 404

Neemann, Joanne, Libr Dir, Beatrice Public Library, 100 N 16th St, Beatrice, NE, 68310-4100. Tel: 402-223-3584. p. 1307

Neenan, Thomas, Access Serv Coordr, Salem State University, 352 Lafayette St, Salem, MA, 01970-5353. Tel: 978-542-6368. p. 1051

Nees, Cindy, Ch, The Frances Banta Waggoner Community Library, 505 Tenth St, DeWitt, IA, 52742-1335. Tel: 563-659-5523. p. 747

Neese, Rachael, Tech Serv Mgr, Alexandria-Monroe Public Library, 117 E Church St, Alexandria, IN, 46001-2005. Tel: 765-724-2196. p. 667

Neeves, Dan, Sr Librn, Staff Develop, Siouxland Libraries, 200 N Dakota Ave, Sioux Falls, SD, 57104. Tel: 605-367-8718. p. 2082

Neff, Dee L, Dir, Annville Free Library, 216 E Main St, Annville, PA, 17003-1599. Tel: 717-867-1802. p. 1906

Neff, Linda, Head, Ref Serv, Goshen Public Library, 601 S Fifth St, Goshen, IN, 46526. Tel: 574-533-9531. p. 687

Neff, Victoria, Res & Instruction Librn, University of South Carolina at Beaufort Library, Eight E Campus Dr, Bluffton, SC, 29909. Tel: 843-208-8031. p. 2048

Neff-Rohs, Ann, Dir of Coll, Grand Rapids Public Library, 111 Library St NE, Grand Rapids, MI, 49503-3268. Tel: 616-988-5400. p. 1111

Negley, Jared, Archives, Slippery Rock University of Pennsylvania, 109 Campus Loop, Slippery Rock, PA, 16057. Tel: 724-738-2058. p. 2007

Negrete, Jesse, Libr Coord, Woodbury University Library, San Diego Campus, 2212 Main St, San Diego, CA, 92113. Tel: 619-235-2900. p. 125

Negrimovskaya, Svetlana, Managing Librn, Brooklyn Public Library, Sheepshead Bay, 2636 E 14th St, Brooklyn, NY, 11235. Tel: 718-368-1815. p. 1504

Negron, JoAnna, Asst Librn, Fowler Public Library, 411 Sixth St, Fowler, CO, 81039. Tel: 719-263-4472. p. 282

Neher, Jeff, Mgr, District of Columbia Public Library, Petworth, 4200 Kansas Ave NW, Washington, DC, 20011. Tel: 202-243-1188. p. 364

Neher, Sheryl, Exec Dir, Saskatchewan Choral Federation Library, 1415-B Albert St, Regina, SK, S4K 2R8, CANADA. Tel: 306-780-9230. p. 2747

Nehls, Jennifer, Libr Dir, City of Melissa Public Library, 3411 Barker Ave, Melissa, TX, 75454. Tel: 972-837-4540. p. 2218

Nehrebecky, Diane, Br Librn, Southeast Regional Library, Manor Branch, 23 Main St, Manor, SK, S0C 1R0, CANADA. Tel: 306-448-2266. p. 2754

Nehrkorn, Paula, Human Res Mgr, Mansfield-Richland County Public Library, 43 W Third St, Mansfield, OH, 44902-1295. Tel: 419-521-3147. p. 1798

Neiburger, Eli, Libr Dir, Ann Arbor District Library, Malletts Creek Branch, 3090 E Eisenhower Pkwy, Ann Arbor, MI, 48108. p. 1078

Neiburger, Eli, Libr Dir, Ann Arbor District Library, Pittsfield Branch, 2359 Oak Valley Dr, Ann Arbor, MI, 48103. p. 1078

Neiburger, Eli, Libr Dir, Ann Arbor District Library, Traverwood, 3333 Traverwood Dr, Ann Arbor, MI, 48105. p. 1078

Neiburger, Eli, Libr Dir, Ann Arbor District Library, Washtenaw Library for the Blind & Physically Disabled, 343 S Fifth Ave, Ann Arbor, MI, 48104. Tel: 734-327-4224. p. 1078

Neiburger, Eli, Libr Dir, Ann Arbor District Library, West Branch, 2503 Jackson Rd, Ann Arbor, MI, 48103. p. 1078

Neidermier, Ginny, Libr Dir, Josephine-Louise Public Library, Five Scofield St, Walden, NY, 12586. Tel: 845-778-7621. p. 1658

Neidermyer, Kim, Mkt Mgr, Naperville Public Library, 95th Street, 3015 Cedar Glade Dr, Naperville, IL, 60564. Tel: 630-961-4100, Ext 4913. p. 623

Neidert, Sarah, Head, Coll, Head, Pub Serv, Brighton District Library, 100 Library Dr, Brighton, MI, 48116. Tel: 810-229-6571, Ext 213. p. 1087

Neidhamer, Brenda, Br Mgr, Tangipahoa Parish Library, Ponchatoula Branch, 380 N Fifth St, Ponchatoula, LA, 70454. Tel: 985-386-6554. p. 881

Neigel, Christina, Dr, Univ Librn, Capilano College Library, 2055 Purcell Way, North Vancouver, BC, V7J 3H5, CANADA. Tel: 604-984-4944. p. 2572

Neighbors, Sammie, Asst Dir, Tri-County Library, 132 E Market St, Mabank, TX, 75147. Tel: 903-887-9622. p. 2215

Neihouse, Kristina, Dir, Learning Res Ctr, College of the Florida Keys, Bldg A, 2nd Fl, 5901 College Rd, Key West, FL, 33040. Tel: 305-809-3194. p. 413

Neil, Brooke, Dir, Craigsville Public Library, 63 Library Lane, Craigsville, WV, 26205. Tel: 304-742-3532. p. 2401

Neill, Heather, Asst Mgr, Saint Louis County Library, Weber Road Branch, 4444 Weber Rd, Saint Louis, MO, 63123-6744. Tel: 314-994-3300, Ext 3950. p. 1274

Neill, Margaret M, Libr Adminr, Las Cruces Public Libraries, 200 E Picacho Ave, Las Cruces, NM, 88001-3499. Tel: 575-528-4017. p. 1470

Neils, Donna, Br Librn, Kemper-Newton Regional Library System, Union Public, 101 Peachtree, Union, MS, 39365-2617. Tel: 601-774-5096. p. 1234

Neilson, Christine, Health Sci Librn, University of Manitoba Libraries, Neil John Maclean Health Sciences Library, Brodie Center Atrium, Mezzanine Level, 2nd Flr, 727 McDermot Ave, Winnipeg, MB, R3E 3P5, CANADA. Tel: 204-789-3342. p. 2595

Neiman, Miriam, Access Serv Librn, Bay Path College, 539 Longmeadow St, Longmeadow, MA, 01106. Tel: 413-565-1376. p. 1029

Neinstadt, Karen, Ref/Outreach Librn, Minnesota Department of Transportation Library, 395 John Ireland Blvd, MS 155, Saint Paul, MN, 55155. Tel: 651-366-3796. p. 1200

Neiport, Donna, Adult Serv Coordr, South Park Township Library, 2575 Brownsville Rd, South Park, PA, 15129-8527. Tel: 412-833-5585. p. 2009

Neises, Sarah, Libr Dir, University of Wisconsin-Fond du Lac Library, 400 University Dr, Fond du Lac, WI, 54935-2950. Tel: 920-929-1146. p. 2435

Neises, Sarah, Dir, University of Wisconsin Oshkosh, 801 Elmwood Ave, Oshkosh, WI, 54901. Tel: 920-424-2147. p. 2467

Neithercut, Rachel, Libr Dir, Greeley & Hansen Engineering Library, 100 S Wacker Dr, Ste 1400, Chicago, IL, 60606-4004. Tel: 312-578-2328. p. 561

Nelka, John, Dir, Sinking Spring Public Library, 3940 Penn Ave, Sinking Spring, PA, 19608. Tel: 610-678-4311. p. 2007

Nelke, Barbara, Head of Libr, University of Regina, Dr John Archer Library, 3737 Wascana Pkwy, Regina, SK, S4S 0A2, CANADA. Tel: 306-585-5099. p. 2748

Nellis, Rachel, Research Servs Librn, Society of the Cincinnati Library, 2118 Massachusetts Ave NW, Washington, DC, 20008. Tel: 202 785-2040, Ext 424. p. 376

Nellums, Olivia, Acq Librn, Mercer County Community College Library, 1200 Old Trenton Rd, West Windsor, NJ, 08550. Tel: 609-570-3559. p. 1453

Nelsen, Kim, Dir, Sac City Public Library, 1001 W Main St, Sac City, IA, 50583. Tel: 712-662-7276. p. 780

Nelsen, Kristie, Br Mgr, Anchorage Public Library, Scott & Wesley Gerrish Library, 250 Egloff Dr, Girdwood, AK, 99587. Tel: 907-343-4024. p. 42

Nelsen, Whitney, Librn, Lord Fairfax Community College, 173 Skirmisher Lane, Middletown, VA, 22645. Tel: 540-868-7170. p. 2332

Nelson, Alicisa, Ref Librn, The Edward Waters College Library, 1658 Kings Rd, Jacksonville, FL, 32209-6199. Tel: 904-470-8084. p. 411

Nelson, Amelia, Dir, Libr & Archives, Nelson-Atkins Museum of Art, Bloch Bldg, 2nd Flr, 4525 Oak St, Kansas City, MO, 64111. Tel: 816-751-1215. p. 1257

Nelson, Amy, Libr Mgr, Pueblo City-County Library District, 100 E Abriendo Ave, Pueblo, CO, 81004-4290. Tel: 719-562-5600. p. 293

Nelson, Becky, Cat, Ch, Salida Regional Library, 405 E St, Salida, CO, 81201. Tel: 719-539-4826. p. 295

Nelson, Carol, Dir, Planning & Communication, Vancouver Public Library, 350 W Georgia St, Vancouver, BC, V6B 6B1, CANADA. Tel: 604-331-3603. p. 2581

Nelson, Carrie, Acq, Tech Serv, Flathead Valley Community College Library, 777 Grandview Dr, Kalispell, MT, 59901. Tel: 406-756-3855. p. 1297

Nelson, Christine, Pub Serv Librn, Beloit College, 731 College St, Beloit, WI, 53511. Tel: 608-363-2483. p. 2423

Nelson, Colleen, Libr Mgr, Vancouver Island Regional Library, Comox Branch, 101-1729 Comox Ave, Comox, BC, V9M 1R7, CANADA. Tel: 250-339-2971. p. 2570

Nelson, Colleen, Libr Mgr, Vancouver Island Regional Library, Cumberland Branch, 2746 Dunsmuir Ave, Cumberland, BC, V0R 1S0, CANADA. Tel: 250-336-8121. p. 2570

Nelson, Colleen, Libr Mgr, Vancouver Island Regional Library, Hornby Island Branch, New Horizons Ctr, 1765 Sollans Rd, Hornby Island, BC, V0R 1Z0, CANADA. Tel: 250-335-0044. p. 2571

Nelson, Cynthia, Curator, Kenosha County Historical Society, 220 51st Pl, Kenosha, WI, 53140. Tel: 262-654-5770. p. 2444

Nelson, Debra, Dir, Elk Grove Village Public Library, 1001 Wellington Ave, Elk Grove Village, IL, 60007-3391. Tel: 847-439-0447. p. 584

Nelson, Demetrius, Librn, Nottoway County Public Libraries, Blackstone Library - Louis Spenser Epes Library, 415 S Main St, Blackstone, VA, 23824. Tel: 434-292-3587. p. 2314

Nemmers, John, Interim Chair, Special & Area Studies Colls, University of Florida Libraries, 1545 W University Ave, Gainesville, FL, 32611-7000. Tel: 352-273-2766. p. 407

Nenninger, Danielle, Asst Mgr, Saint Louis County Library, Bridgeton Trails Branch, 3455 McKelvey Rd, Bridgeton, MO, 63044-2500. Tel: 314-994-3300, Ext 3000. p. 1273

Nenstiel, Susan, Br Mgr, York County Library System, Kreutz Creek Valley Library, 66 Walnut Springs Rd, Hellam, PA, 17406. Tel: 717-252-4080. p. 2026

Neppel, Brenda, Librn, Saint Thomas Aquinas Church, 2210 Lincoln Way, Ames, IA, 50014. Tel: 515-292-3810. p. 731

Nepton, Isabel, Library Contact, Bibliotheque Municipale de Jonquiere, 2850 Davis Pl, Jonquiere, QC, G7X 7W7, CANADA. Tel: 418-699-6068, 418-699-6069. p. 2714

Neraasen, Lisa, Libr Mgr, Alliance Public Library, 101 First Ave E, Alliance, AB, T0B 0A0, CANADA. Tel: 780-879-3733. p. 2521

Nerbonne, Elizabeth, Ref Serv, Rochester Public Library, 65 S Main St, Rochester, NH, 03867-2707. Tel: 603-332-1428. p. 1380

Nero, Muriel, Head, Cat, University of South Alabama Libraries, Marx Library, 5901 USA Drive N, Mobile, AL, 36688. Tel: 251-460-2837. p. 27

Neron, Yves, Presv, National Gallery of Canada Library & Archives, 380 Sussex Dr, Ottawa, ON, K1N 9N4, CANADA. Tel: 613-714-6000, Ext 6323. p. 2667

Nerone, Lisa, Asst Librn, Riverton Village Library, 1200 E Riverton Rd, Riverton, IL, 62561-8200. Tel: 217-629-6353. p. 639

Nersesian, Abigail, Admin Librn, Br Mgr, Main Libr, Chandler Public Library, 22 S Delaware, Chandler, AZ, 85225. Tel: 480-782-2804. p. 58

Nesbit, Andrea, Asst Librn, Industry Public Library, 1646 N Main St, Industry, TX, 78944. Tel: 979-357-4434. p. 2202

Nesbit, Angus, Ref Librn, University of Oregon Libraries, John E Jaqua Law Library, William W Knight Law Ctr, 2nd Flr, 1515 Agate St, Eugene, OR, 97403. Tel: 541-346-1673. p. 1879

Nesbitt, Cindy, Dir, Giles County Public Library, 122 S Second St, Pulaski, TN, 38478-3285. Tel: 931-363-2720. p. 2124

Nesbitt, Melissa, Archives Mgr, Southwest Arkansas Regional Archives, 201 Hwy 195, Washington, AR, 71862. Tel: 870-983-2633. p. 112

Nesbitt, Robin, Mgr, Columbus Metropolitan Library, Hilliard Branch, 4500 Hickory Chase Way, Hilliard, OH, 43026. p. 1772

Nesbitt, Sam, Pub Serv Librn, State University of New York Polytechnic Institute, 100 Seymour Rd, Utica, NY, 13502. Tel: 315-792-7245. p. 1655

Nesmith, Stephanie, Head, Youth Serv, Hillside Public Library, John F Kennedy Plaza, 1409 Liberty Ave, Hillside, NJ, 07205. Tel: 973-923-4413. p. 1408

Nesnick, Alyson, Asst Br Mgr, Troup-Harris Regional Library System, Harris County Public Library, 7511 George Hwy 116, Hamilton, GA, 31811. Tel: 706-628-4685. p. 484

Nesselroad, Lara, Mgr, University of Oregon Libraries, Allan Price Science Commons & Research Library, Onyx Bridge, Lower Level, 1344 Franklin Blvd, Eugene, OR, 97403. Tel: 541-346-3075. p. 1879

Nesselroad, Lara, Mgr, University of Oregon Libraries, Design Library, 200 Lawrence Hall, 1190 Franklin Blvd, Eugene, OR, 97403-1299. Tel: 541-346-3637. p. 1879

Nessman, Cheryl, Support Serv Mgr, Mead Public Library, 710 N Eight St, Sheboygan, WI, 53081-4563. Tel: 920-459-3400, Ext 2010. p. 2476

Nestor, Sara, Dir, Glenwood Public Library, 108 First Ave SE, Glenwood, MN, 56334. Tel: 320-634-3375. p. 1176

Nestory, Michele, Librn, Fairleigh Dickinson University, Dickinson Hall, 140 University Plaza Dr, Hackensack, NJ, 07601. Tel: 201-692-2608. p. 1406

Nestory, Michelle, Librn, Outreach Coordr, Fairleigh Dickinson University, 1000 River Rd, Teaneck, NJ, 07666-1914. Tel: 201-692-2279. p. 1445

Neth, Martha, Libr Dir, Rocky Mountain College of Art & Design Library, 1600 Pierce St, Lakewood, CO, 80214. Tel: 303-753-6046, Ext 22405. p. 289

Nethery, Darlene, Mgr, Salt Lake County Library Services, West Jordan Branch, 8030 S 1825 W, West Jordan, UT, 84088. p. 2275

Netscher, Marianne, Libr Dir, Gerald Area Library, 357 S Main St, Gerald, MO, 63037. Tel: 573-764-7323. p. 1247

Nett, Cara, Mgr, Computer Ctr & Cat Serv, Laramie County Library System, 2200 Pioneer Ave, Cheyenne, WY, 82001-3610. Tel: 307-773-7231. p. 2492

Nettles, Judy, Info Processing Librn, State of Mississippi Judiciary, Carroll Gartin Justice Bldg, 450 High St, Jackson, MS, 39201. Tel: 601-359-3672. p. 1223

Nettles, Willie, Br Librn, Ascension Parish Library, 500 Mississippi St, Donaldsonville, LA, 70346. Tel: 225-473-8052. p. 889

Netzer, Mary Jo, Br Coordr, Marathon County Public Library, Stratford Branch, 213201 Scholar St, Stratford, WI, 54484. Tel: 715-687-4420. p. 2486

Neubauer, Michelle, Mgr, Libr Serv, New Berlin Public Library, 15105 Library Lane, New Berlin, WI, 53151. Tel: 262-785-4980. p. 2464

Neubauer, Penny, Dep Fiscal Officer, Dir, Ashtabula County District Library, 4335 Park Ave, Ashtabula, OH, 44004. Tel: 440-997-9341, Ext 322. p. 1747

Neuendorf, Jamie, Br Librn, Ref Librn, Wisconsin State Law Library, Milwaukee County Law Library, Courthouse, Rm G8, 901 N Ninth St, Milwaukee, WI, 53233. Tel: 414-278-4900. p. 2453

Neuenschwander, Robert, Dir, Warren Public Library, 123 E Third St, Warren, IN, 46792. Tel: 260-375-3450. p. 724

Neufeldt, Tim, Actg Head, University of Toronto Libraries, Faculty of Music Library, Edward Johnson Bldg, 80 Queens Park Crescent, Toronto, ON, M5S 2C5, CANADA. Tel: 416-978-3734. p. 2698

Neugebauer, Jenna, Early Childhood Librn, Siouxland Libraries, 200 N Dakota Ave, Sioux Falls, SD, 57104. Tel: 605-367-8708. p. 2082

Neuhaus, Chris, Liaison & Instruction Librn, University of Northern Iowa Library, 1227 W 27th St, Cedar Falls, IA, 50613-3675. Tel: 319-273-3718. p. 737

Neuhaus, Ellen, Digital Scholarship Librn, University of Northern Iowa Library, 1227 W 27th St, Cedar Falls, IA, 50613-3675. Tel: 319-273-3739. p. 737

Neujahr, Denise, YA Librn, Community Library Network, 8385 N Government Way, Hayden, ID, 83835-9280. Tel: 208-772-5612. p. 522

Neujahr, Joyce, Asst Dean, Dir, Patron Serv, University of Nebraska at Omaha, 6001 Dodge St, Omaha, NE, 68182-0237. Tel: 402-554-3607. p. 1330

Neuman, Lisa, Libr Dir, RCS Community Library, 95 Main St, Ravena, NY, 12143. Tel: 518-756-2053. p. 1625

Neuman, Mary, Asst Dir, Youth Serv, Asotin County Library, 417 Sycamore St, Clarkston, WA, 99403-2666. Tel: 509-758-5454, Ext 103. p. 2361

Neuman, Randy, Assoc Dir, Libr Serv, Huntington University, 2303 College Ave, Huntington, IN, 46750. Tel: 260-359-4060. p. 690

Neumann, Amy, Museum Curator, US National Park Service, 8523 W State Hwy 4, Beatrice, NE, 68310. Tel: 402-223-3514. p. 1307

Neumann, Joseph, Digital Legal Res & Syst Librn, University of Maryland, Baltimore, Thurgood Marshall Law Library, 501 W Fayette St, Baltimore, MD, 21201-1768. Tel: 410-706-2736. p. 957

Neumann, Paige, Admin Serv, Texas Historical Commission Library, 1511 Colorado St, Austin, TX, 78701. Tel: 512-463-6100. p. 2140

Neumayer, Alisa, Youth Serv, Roosevelt Public Library, Children's Room, 27 W Fulton Ave, Roosevelt, NY, 11575. Tel: 516-378-0222. p. 1633

Neumeyer, Robert, Mgr, UPMC Mercy Hospital of Pittsburgh, 1400 Locust St, Pittsburgh, PA, 15219. Tel: 412-232-7520. p. 1997

Neunaber, Beth, Adult Serv Mgr, Nampa Public Library, 215 12th Ave S, Nampa, ID, 83651. Tel: 208-468-5807. p. 527

Neurohr, Karen A, Research Librn, Oklahoma State University Libraries, Athletic Ave, 216, Stillwater, OK, 74078. Tel: 405-744-2376. p. 1862

Neusbaum, Erin, Br Mgr, Queen Anne's County Free Library, 121 S Commerce St, Centreville, MD, 21617. Tel: 410-758-0980, Ext 202. p. 961

Nevels, Tiwanna S, Dir, Libr Serv, Saint Augustine's College, 1315 Oakwood Ave, Raleigh, NC, 27610-2298. Tel: 919-516-4150. p. 1710

Nevers, Norma, Asst Dir, Head, Children's Servx, Manchester Public Library, 586 Main St, Manchester, CT, 06040. Tel: 860-643-2471. p. 320

Neves, Kendra, Libr Mgr, Fundy Library Region, Grand Manan Library, 1144, Rte 776, Grand Manan, NB, E5G 4E8, CANADA. Tel: 506-662-7099. p. 2604

Neveu, Sabrina, Ch, Superior District Library, 541 Library Dr, Sault Sainte Marie, MI, 49783. Tel: 906-632-9331. p. 1149

Nevill, Emily, Adult Ref, Palisades Free Library, 19 Closter Rd, Palisades, NY, 10964. Tel: 845-359-0136. p. 1614

Neville, Anne, Shared Automation Syst Coordr, The Library Network, 41365 Vincenti Ct, Novi, MI, 48375. Tel: 248-536-3100. p. 2767

Nevins, Kim, Tech Serv Coordr, Zion-Benton Public Library District, 2400 Gabriel Ave, Zion, IL, 60099. Tel: 847-872-4680. p. 665

Nevins, Tiffanie, Circ Supvr, University of Akron, University Libraries, School of Law Library, 150 University Ave, Akron, OH, 44325. Tel: 330-972-7330. p. 1745

New, Sarah, Web Serv Librn, University of Virginia, Arthur J Morris Law Library, 580 Massie Rd, Charlottesville, VA, 22903-1738. Tel: 434-924-4988. p. 2310

New, Terry, Human Res Mgr, Kalamazoo Public Library, 315 S Rose St, Kalamazoo, MI, 49007-5264. Tel: 269-553-7931. p. 1121

Newbatt, Glenda, Mgr, Libr Serv, Essa Public Library, 8505 County Rd 10, Unit 1, Angus, ON, L0M 1B1, CANADA. Tel: 705-424-6531. p. 2628

Newbegin, Gisela, Asst Dir, DeForest Area Public Library, 203 Library St, DeForest, WI, 53532. Tel: 608-846-5482. p. 2430

Newberry, Julianne, Metadata Librn, Rockhurst University, 1100 Rockhurst Rd, Kansas City, MO, 64110-2561. Tel: 816-501-4131. p. 1257

Newborg, Anna, Dir, Baldwin Borough Public Library, 5230 Wolfe Dr, Pittsburgh, PA, 15236. Tel: 412-885-2255. p. 1990

Newborn, Michele, Br Librn, Plaquemines Parish Library, Buras Branch, 35572 Hwy 11, Buras, LA, 70041. Tel: 504-564-0921, 504-564-0944. p. 885

Newbury, Rachel, Discovery Serv Librn, Pennsylvania Western University - Clarion, 840 Wood St, Clarion, PA, 16214. Tel: 814-393-2746. p. 1922

Newbury, Susan, Head, Cat & Metadata Serv, Brown University, John Carter Brown Library, Brown University, 94 George St, Providence, RI, 02906. Tel: 401-863-2725. p. 2037

Newby, Gayle, Librn, Northeast Regional Library, Walnut Public Library, 650 N Main St, Walnut, MS, 38683. Tel: 662-223-6768. p. 1216

Newby, Katie, Tech Serv Mgr, North Madison County Public Library System, 1600 Main St, Elwood, IN, 46036. Tel: 765-552-5001. p. 680

Newby, Laura, Dir, Union Public Library, 406 Commercial St, Union, IA, 50258. Tel: 641-486-5561. p. 787

Newby, Lilith, Librn, College of New Rochelle, Brooklyn Campus, 1368 Fulton St, Brooklyn, NY, 11216. Tel: 718-638-2500. p. 1577

Newcity, Katherine, Br Mgr, Stark County District Library, DeHoff Memorial Branch, 216 Hartford Ave SE, Canton, OH, 44707. Tel: 330-452-9014. p. 1755

Newcomb, Franky, Ref & Instrul Serv Librn, Marquette University, Ray & Kay Eckstein Law Library, 1215 Michigan St, Milwaukee, WI, 53201. Tel: 414-288-7092. p. 2458

Newcombe, Lisa, Supvr, Pub Serv, Charlottetown Library Learning Centre, 97 Queen St, Charlottetown, PE, C1A 4A9, CANADA. Tel: 902-368-4642. p. 2707

Newcombe, Pat, Assoc Dean, Libr & Info Serv, Western New England University, 1215 Wilbraham Rd, Springfield, MA, 01119-2689. Tel: 413-782-1616. p. 1057

Newcomer, Nara, Head Music Libr, Media Serv, University of Missouri-Kansas City Libraries, 800 E 51st St, Kansas City, MO, 64110. Tel: 816-235-1679. p. 1257

Newell, Amanda, Tech Asst, Galveston College, 4015 Ave Q, Galveston, TX, 77550. Tel: 409-844-1246. p. 2183

Newell, Bonnie, Curator, Burt County Museum, Inc Library, 319 N 13th St, Tekamah, NE, 68061. Tel: 402-374-1505. p. 1338

Newell, Brian, Librn, Logansport State Hospital, 1098 S State Rd 25, Logansport, IN, 46947. Tel: 574-737-3712. p. 703

Newell, Cathy, Asst Librn, United States Army, Medical Library, Bldg 36000, Carl R Darnall Medical Ctr, Fort Hood, TX, 76544-5063. Tel: 254-288-8366. p. 2178

Newell, Crystal, Dir, Libr Serv, Piedmont Virginia Community College, 501 College Dr, Charlottesville, VA, 22902. Tel: 434-961-5339. p. 2309

Newell, Ellie, Head, Youth Serv, Bozeman Public Library, 626 E Main St, Bozeman, MT, 59715. Tel: 406-582-2400. p. 1289

Newell, Natalie, Br Librn, Brazoria County Library System, Freeport Branch, 410 Brazosport Blvd, Freeport, TX, 77541. Tel: 979-233-3622. p. 2135

Newell, Natalie, Ch Serv, Brazoria County Library System, Brazoria Branch, 620 S Brooks, Brazoria, TX, 77422-9022. Tel: 979-798-2372. p. 2135

Newell, Patrick, Res, Instruction & Outreach Librn, California State University, Chico, 400 W First St, Chico, CA, 95929-0295. Tel: 530-898-6501. p. 129

Newell, Patrick, Head, Libr Info Tech, California State University, Fresno, Henry Madden Library, 5200 N Barton Ave, Mail Stop ML-34, Fresno, CA, 93740-8014. Tel: 559-278-6528. p. 144

Newell, Patti, Asst Dir, Sullivan Free Library, 101 Falls Blvd, Chittenango, NY, 13037. Tel: 315-687-6331. p. 1518

Newell, Wendy A, Ref (Info Servs), United States Army, 4300 Camp Hale Rd, Fort Drum, NY, 13602. Tel: 315-772-9099. p. 1534

Newell, Zach, Dean, Libr Serv, Eastern Illinois University, 600 Lincoln Ave, Charleston, IL, 61920. p. 552

Newell, Zach, Dean of Libr, University of Southern Maine Libraries, 314 Forest Ave, Portland, ME, 04103. Tel: 207-780-4276. p. 937

Newgard, Ben, Communications Research Librn, Elon University, 308 N O'Kelly Ave, Elon, NC, 27244-0187. Tel: 336-278-6600. p. 1688

Newgren, Andy, Libr Dir, Rockford University, 5050 E State St, Rockford, IL, 61108-2393. Tel: 815-226-4000, 815-226-4035. p. 642

Newhall, Claudette, Librn, Braintree Historical Society, Inc Library & Resource Center, Gilbert Bean Barn & Mary Bean Cunningham Resource Ctr, 31 Tenney Rd, Braintree, MA, 02184-4416. Tel: 781-848-1640. p. 1001

Newhart, Colleen, Access Serv Mgr, Misericordia University, 301 Lake St, Dallas, PA, 18612-1098. Tel: 570-674-3036. p. 1925

Newhouse, Ria, Head Librn, Atwater Public Library, 322 Atlantic Ave W, Atwater, MN, 56209. Tel: 320-974-3363. p. 1164

Newland, Melissa, Dir, Tri-County Library, 132 E Market St, Mabank, TX, 75147. Tel: 903-887-9622. p. 2215

Newland, Patty, Libr Mgr, Flint River Regional Library System, Tyrone Public Library, 143 Commerce Dr, Tyrone, GA, 30290. Tel: 770-487-1565. p. 481

Newland, Sally, Librn, Amerind Museum Library, 2100 N Amerind Rd, Dragoon, AZ, 85609. Tel: 520-586-3666. p. 59

Newland, Traci, Librn, Mount Carmel Library, 100 Main St, Mount Carmel, TN, 37645-9999. Tel: 423-357-4011. p. 2117

Newlin, Lotte, Dir, Boonton Holmes Public Library, 621 Main St, Boonton, NJ, 07005. Tel: 973-334-2980. p. 1391

Newlin, Nicholas, Br Mgr, Albuquerque-Bernalillo County Library System, Los Griegos Library, 1000 Griegos Rd NW, Albuquerque, NM, 87107. Tel: 505-761-4020. p. 1460

Newman, Anna, Digital Projects Mgr, Connecticut State Library, 231 Capitol Ave, Hartford, CT, 06106. Tel: 860-757-6525. p. 317

Newman, Anne, Librn, Paxton Carnegie Library, 254 S Market St, Paxton, IL, 60957-1452. Tel: 217-379-3431. p. 633

Newman, Arthur, Outreach Coordr, Northumberland Public Library, Inc, 7204 Northumberland Hwy, Heathsville, VA, 22473. Tel: 804-580-5051. p. 2325

Newman, Cheryl, Br Mgr, Tulsa City-County Library, Jenks Branch, 523 West B St, Jenks, OK, 74037. p. 1866

Newman, Dai, Cataloging & Instruction Librn, Columbus College of Art & Design, 60 Cleveland Ave, Columbus, OH, 43215. Tel: 614-222-3273. p. 1772

Newman, Dana, Dir, Talbot County Free Library, 100 W Dover St, Easton, MD, 21601-2620. Tel: 410-822-1626. p. 964

Newman, Donnie, Dir, Media Serv, Carson-Newman University, 1634 Russell Ave, Jefferson City, TN, 37760. Tel: 865-471-3220. p. 2103

Newman, Elizabeth, Br Mgr, Southeast Arkansas Regional Library, Monticello Branch, 114 W Jefferson Ave, Monticello, AR, 71655. Tel: 870-367-8583. p. 105

Newman, Emily, Dep Circuit Librn, United States Court of Appeals for the Ninth Circuit Library, James R Browning Courthouse, 95 Seventh St, San Francisco, CA, 94103. Tel: 415-355-8650. p. 229

Newman, Frances, Chief Exec Officer, Oshawa Public Library, 65 Bagot St, Oshawa, ON, L1H 1N2, CANADA. Tel: 905-579-6111, Ext 5200. p. 2663

Newman, Gary, Head, Ref, Mount Vernon Public Library, 28 S First Ave, Mount Vernon, NY, 10550. Tel: 914-668-1840, Ext 209. p. 1575

Newman, Jeff, Col Librn, University of Toronto Libraries, New College - D G Ivey Library, 20 Willcocks St, Toronto, ON, M5S 1C6, CANADA. Tel: 416-978-2493. p. 2699

Newman, John, Asst Librn, Libr Tech, OhioHealth Grant Medical Center, 340 E Town St, Ste 7-200, 7th flr, Columbus, OH, 43215. Tel: 614-566-9467, 614-566-9468. p. 1777

Newman, Ken, Br Mgr, Chippewa River District Library, Tate Memorial Library, 324 Main St, Blanchard, MI, 49310. Tel: 989-561-2480. p. 1135

Newman, Mary, Librn, Frank Bertetti Benld Public Library, 308 E Central Ave, Benld, IL, 62009. Tel: 217-835-4045. p. 541

Newman, Rebecca, Health Sci Librn, University of Charleston, 2300 MacCorkle Ave SE, Charleston, WV, 25304-1099. Tel: 304-357-4986. p. 2400

Newman, Sara, Br Mgr, Paulding County Carnegie Library, Payne Branch, 101 N Main St, Payne, OH, 45880. Tel: 419-263-3333. p. 1814

Newman, Sara Molitor, Br Mgr, Paulding County Carnegie Library, Antwerp Branch, 205 N Madison St, Antwerp, OH, 45813-8411. Tel: 419-258-2855. p. 1814

Newman, Susan, Dir, New Madrid County Library, 309 E Main St, Portageville, MO, 63873. Tel: 573-379-3583. p. 1266

Newnam, Brenda, Br Mgr, Grove Public Library, 1140 NEO Loop, Grove, OK, 74344-8602. Tel: 918-786-2945. p. 1848

Newnham, Dan, Law Librn, Cox, Castle & Nicholson LLP Library, 2029 Century Park E, 21st Flr, Los Angeles, CA, 90067. Tel: 310-277-4222, Ext 2417. p. 161

Newport, Cindy, Coordr, Circ, Pfeiffer University, 48380 US Hwy 52 N, Misenheimer, NC, 28109. Tel: 704-463-3363. p. 1703

Newsom, Elizabeth, Librn, The Book Club of California, 312 Sutter St, Ste 500, San Francisco, CA, 94108-4320. Tel: 415-781-7532, Ext 4. p. 223

Newsome, Kriston, Ch Serv, Desoto Parish Library, Pelican Branch, 145 Jackson Ave, Pelican, LA, 71063-2803. Tel: 318-755-2353. p. 896

Newson, Gloria, Library Contact, Presbyterian Church of Chatham Township Library, 240 Southern Blvd, Chatham, NJ, 07928. Tel: 973-635-2340. p. 1395

Newsum, Janice, Asst Prof, University of Houston-Clear Lake, 2700 Bay Area Blvd, Bayou Ste 1321, Houston, TX, 77058. Tel: 281-283-3537. p. 2793

Newton, Allison, Libr Asst, Kellogg Community College, 450 North Ave, Battle Creek, MI, 49017-3397. Tel: 269-565-7916. p. 1083

Newton, Alyssa, Adult/YA Serv Librn, Asst Libr Dir, Onondaga Free Library, 4840 W Seneca Tpk, Syracuse, NY, 13215. Tel: 315-492-1727. p. 1650

Newton, Cammie, Br Head, Volusia County Public Library, DeBary Public Library, 200 N Charles R Beall Blvd, DeBary, FL, 32713. Tel: 386-668-3835. p. 393

Newton, Erin, Dir, Libr Serv, Georgia Military College, 201 E Greene St, Milledgeville, GA, 31061. Tel: 478-387-4729. p. 491

Newton, Jonathan, Access Serv Mgr, University of South Carolina Upstate Library, 800 University Way, Spartanburg, SC, 29303. Tel: 864-503-5679. p. 2070

Newton, Laura, Head of Instruction, University of North Florida, Bldg 12-Library, One UNF Dr, Jacksonville, FL, 32224-2645. Tel: 904-620-2615. p. 413

Newton, Lillian, Mgr, Loudoun County Public Library, Lovettsville Branch, 12 N Light St, Lovettsville, VA, 20180. Tel: 703-737-8050. p. 2328

Newton, Marilyn, Mgr, Innisfree Public Library, 5317-48 Ave, Innisfree, AB, T0B 2G0, CANADA. Tel: 780-592-2122. p. 2543

Newton, Matthew, Cat, Bloomberg Industry Group Library, 1801 S Bell St, Arlington, VA, 22202. Tel: 703-341-3308. p. 2305

Newton, Morgan, YA Serv, Public Library of Mount Vernon & Knox County, 201 N Mulberry St, Mount Vernon, OH, 43050-2413. Tel: 740-392-2665. p. 1804

Newton, Patricia, Asst Librn, Richmond Public Library, 19 Winchester Rd, Richmond, NH, 03470. Tel: 603-239-6164. p. 1379

Newton, Renee, Asst Dir, Circ Serv Librn, Dickinson Area Public Library, 139 Third St W, Dickinson, ND, 58601-5147. Tel: 701-456-7023. p. 1732

Newton, Susan, Dir, Spaulding Memorial Library, 282 Sebago Rd, Sebago, ME, 04029. Tel: 207-787-2321. p. 940

Newton, Teresa, Dir, Lawrence County Public Library, 519 E Gaines St, Lawrenceburg, TN, 38464-3599. Tel: 931-762-4627. p. 2108

Newton, Tiffany, Libr Dir, Green Forest Public Library, 206 E Main St, Green Forest, AR, 72638-2627. Tel: 870-438-6700. p. 97

Newville, Natalie, Pub Info, Missouri River Regional Library, 214 Adams St, Jefferson City, MO, 65101. Tel: 573-634-2464. p. 1253

Ney, Diane, Head Archivist, Washington National Cathedral, 3101 Wisconsin Ave NW, Washington, DC, 20016. Tel: 202-537-6200. p. 381

Ney, Jessica, Communications Coordr, Mansfield-Richland County Public Library, 43 W Third St, Mansfield, OH, 44902-1295. Tel: 419-521-3101. p. 1798

Ney, Mamie Anthoine, Dir, Auburn Public Library, 49 Spring St, Auburn, ME, 04210. Tel: 207-333-6640, Ext 2020. p. 913

Ney, Nikki, Br Mgr, Phoenix Public Library, Cesar Chavez Library, 3635 W Baseline Rd, Laveen, AZ, 85339. p. 72

Neylon, Valerie, Assoc Prof, City Colleges of Chicago, Richard J Daley College Library, 7500 S Pulaski Rd, Chicago, IL, 60652-1200. Tel: 773-838-7667. p. 558

Neyman, Barb, Librn, Virginia Department of Transportation (VDOT) Research Library, 530 Edgemont Rd, Charlottesville, VA, 22903. Tel: 434-293-1902. p. 2310

Neymoss, Chantez, Adult Serv Coordr, Charlotte Mecklenburg Library, 310 N Tryon St, Charlotte, NC, 28202-2176. Tel: 704-416-0100. p. 1679

Nez, Ann, Coordr, Tech Serv, University of Washington Libraries, Gallagher Law Library, William H Gates Hall, 4000 15th Ave NE, Seattle, WA, 98195-3020. Tel: 206-221-6114. p. 2382

Nez, Jean, Librn, Elwood Township Carnegie Library, 104 N State St, Ridge Farm, IL, 61870. Tel: 217-247-2820. p. 639

Ng, Judy, Libr Tech, Scarborough Hospital, Health Information Resource Centre, 3050 Lawrence Ave E, Scarborough, ON, M1P 2V5, CANADA. Tel: 416-431-8200, Ext 6593. p. 2677

Ng, Kwong Bor, Dir, Prof, Queens College of the City University of New York, Benjamin Rosenthal Library, Rm 254, 65-30 Kissena Blvd, Flushing, NY, 11367-1597. Tel: 718-997-3790. p. 2789

Ng, Wendy, Automation Syst Coordr, United States Air Force, Air University - Muir S Fairchild Research Information Center, 600 Chennault Circle, Maxwell AFB, AL, 36112-6010. Tel: 334-953-6498. p. 25

Ng-Chin, Eva, Tech Serv Librn, Merritt College Library, 12500 Campus Dr, Oakland, CA, 94619. Tel: 510-436-2461. p. 185

Ng-Wan, Vicki, Dir, Mkt & Communications, Centre d'acces a l'information juridique/Legal Informatin Access Center, 480 Saint-Laurent, Bur 503, Montreal, QC, H2Y 3Y7, CANADA. Tel: 514-844-2245. p. 2721

Ngai, Laura, Coordr, ILL & Doc Delivery Serv, University of Utah, S J Quinney Law Library, 332 S 1400 East, Salt Lake City, UT, 84112-0731. Tel: 801-581-3804. p. 2272

Ngan, Ashley, Cat Librn, Palmer Public Library, 1455 N Main St, Palmer, MA, 01069. Tel: 413-283-3330. p. 1045

Ngo, Lisa, Eng Librn, University of California, Berkeley, Kresge Engineering Library, 110 Bechtel Engineering Ctr, Berkeley, CA, 94720-6000. Tel: 510-643-4299. p. 123

Nguyen, Chieu, Mgr, San Jose Public Library, Seven Trees, 3590 Cas Dr, San Jose, CA, 95111-2499. Tel: 408-808-3056. p. 232

Nguyen, Chieu, Mgr, San Jose Public Library, Tully Community, 880 Tully Rd, San Jose, CA, 95111. Tel: 408-808-3030. p. 232

Nguyen, Hang, Librn, State Historical Society of Iowa, 600 E Locust, Des Moines, IA, 50319-0290. Tel: 515-281-6200. p. 747

Nguyen, Hang, Ref Librn, State Historical Society of Iowa, 402 Iowa Ave, Iowa City, IA, 52240-1806. Tel: 319-335-3926. p. 760

Nguyen, Jen, Dir, Student Ctr for Academic Achievement, California State University, East Bay Library, CSU East Bay Library, 25800 Carlos Bee Blvd, Hayward, CA, 94542-3052. Tel: 510-885-4759. p. 150

Nguyen, Jenny, Dir, Communications, Linda Hall Library of Science, Engineering & Technology, 5109 Cherry St, Kansas City, MO, 64110. Tel: 816-363-4600. p. 1255

Nguyen, John, Law Libr Asst, Middlesex Law Library, Superior Courthouse, 200 Trade Ctr, 3rd Flr, Woburn, MA, 01801. Tel: 781-939-2920. p. 1070

Nguyen, Kathy, Prog Spec, University of Nevada, Las Vegas Univ Libraries, Teacher Development & Resources Library, 4505 S Maryland Pkwy, Box 453009, Las Vegas, NV, 89154-3009. Tel: 702-895-4617. p. 1347

Nguyen, Lynn, Principal Librn, Tech & Support, Santa Ana Public Library, 26 Civic Ctr Plaza, Santa Ana, CA, 92701-4010. Tel: 714-647-5259. p. 239

Nguyen, Minh, Circ Librn, Prescott Public Library, 215 E Goodwin St, Prescott, AZ, 86303. Tel: 928-777-1508. p. 73

Nguyen, Nate, Tech Coordr, Grandview Heights Public Library, 1685 W First Ave, Columbus, OH, 43212. Tel: 614-486-2951. p. 1773

Nguyen, Phu, Digitization & Tech Librarian, Duke University Libraries, Divinity School Library, 407 Chapel Dr, Durham, NC, 27708. Tel: 919-660-3453. p. 1684

Nguyen, Tri, Asst Systems Manager, Circ Supvr, Houston Baptist University, 7502 Fondren Rd, Houston, TX, 77074-3298. Tel: 281-649-3304. p. 2194

Niazov, Irene, Circ, De Anza College, 21250 Stevens Creek Blvd, Cupertino, CA, 95014-5793. Tel: 408-864-8763. p. 133

Nibbe, Kristin, Br Mgr, San Luis Obispo County Library, Morro Bay Library, 625 Harbor St, Morro Bay, CA, 93442. Tel: 805-772-6394. p. 234

Nibblins, Charlene, Libr Spec II, Germanna Community College, Culpeper Campus Library, 18121 Technology Dr, Culpeper, VA, 22701. Tel: 540-937-2923. p. 2320

Niberg, Robin, Ms, Librn, State Correctional Institution, 10745 Rte 18, Albion, PA, 16475-0001. Tel: 814-756-5778. p. 1904

Niblick, William, Chief, US Army Maneuver Center of Excellence, 7533 Holtz St, Bldg 70, Ste 1025, Fort Benning, GA, 31905. Tel: 706-545-8591. p. 479

Nicasio, Sandra, Circ Supvr, Yuma County Free Library District, 2951 S 21st Dr, Yuma, AZ, 85364. Tel: 928-373-6491. p. 85

Nicastro, Kathleen, Libr Asst, University of Rochester, Charlotte Whitney Allen Library, Memorial Art Gallery, 500 University Ave, Rochester, NY, 14607. Tel: 585-276-8901. p. 1631

Nice, Rebecca, Libr Tech, Lamont Public Library, Lamont High School, 4811 50 Ave, Lamont, AB, T0B 2R0, CANADA. Tel: 780-895-2299. p. 2545

Nicely, Beth, Med Librn, Owensboro Medical Health System, 1201 Pleasant Valley Rd, Owensboro, KY, 42303. Tel: 270-417-2000, 270-417-6864. p. 871

Nichol, Amy, Dir, Wichita County Public Library, 208 S Fourth St, Leoti, KS, 67861. Tel: 620-375-4322. p. 821

Nicholas, Patty, Archives Asst, Ellis County Historical Society Archives, 100 W Seventh St, Hays, KS, 67601. Tel: 785-628-2624. p. 812

Nicholas-Kahalley, Rachel, Br Mgr, West Florida Public Library, Molino Branch, 6450-A Hwy 95A, Molino, FL, 32577. Tel: 850-435-1760. p. 437

Nicholl-Lynam, Marie, Br Mgr, Las Vegas-Clark County Library District, Clark County Library, 1401 E Flamingo Rd, Las Vegas, NV, 89119. Tel: 702-507-3400. p. 1346

Nicholls Harrison, Tim, Chief Librn/CEO, Owen Sound & North Grey Union Public Library, 824 First Ave W, Owen Sound, ON, N4K 4K4, CANADA. Tel: 519-376-6623. p. 2671

Nichols, Aaron, Tech Serv, Susquehanna County Historical Society & Free Library Association, 458 High School Rd, Montrose, PA, 18801. Tel: 570-278-1881. p. 1965

Nichols, Andrea, Asst Br Mgr, Yadkin County Public Library, 233 E Main St, Yadkinville, NC, 27055. Tel: 336-679-8792. p. 1727

Nichols, Ann, Dir, East Bonner County Library District, 1407 Cedar St, Sandpoint, ID, 83864-2052. Tel: 208-263-6930. p. 531

Nichols, Anna L, Librn, Charles H Stone Memorial Library, 319 W Main St, Pilot Mountain, NC, 27041. Tel: 336-368-2370. p. 1707

Nichols, Beatrice, Librn, United States Army, Medical Library, Bldg 36000, Carl R Darnall Medical Ctr, Fort Hood, TX, 76544-5063. Tel: 254-288-8366. p. 2178

Nichols, Becky, Dir, Public Library of Selma & Dallas County, 1103 Selma Ave, Selma, AL, 36703-4498. Tel: 334-874-1725. p. 35

Nichols, Brenette, Dir, Human Res, Jackson/Hinds Library System, 300 N State St, Jackson, MS, 39201-1705. Tel: 601-968-5825. p. 1221

Nichols, Carrie, Head, Archives, Head, Tech Serv, Meredith College, 3800 Hillsborough St, Raleigh, NC, 27607-5298. Tel: 919-760-8532. p. 1708

Nichols, Cherise, Librn, Ellen Brooks West Memorial Library, 1800 College Ave, Forney, TX, 75126. Tel: 972-564-7027. p. 2177

Nichols, Danita, Libr Mgr, New York Public Library - Astor, Lenox & Tilden Foundations, Inwood Branch, 4790 Broadway, (Near Dyckman St), New York, NY, 10034-4916. Tel: 212-942-2445. p. 1596

Nichols, Donna, Dir, Arthur Temple Sr Memorial Library, 106 Timberland Hwy, Pineland, TX, 75968-0847. Tel: 409-584-2546. p. 2226

Nichols, Ginni, Ch, Gardiner Public Library, 152 Water St, Gardiner, ME, 04345. Tel: 207-582-3312. p. 926

Nichols, Jane, Head Teaching & Engagement, Oregon State University Libraries, 121 The Valley Library, Corvallis, OR, 97331-4501. Tel: 541-737-7269. p. 1876

Nichols, Jonathan, Dir, Swampscott Public Library, 61 Burrill St, Swampscott, MA, 01907. Tel: 781-596-8867. p. 1059

Nichols, Kate, Libr Mgr, Gibbs Library, 40 Old Union Rd, Washington, ME, 04574. Tel: 207-845-2663. p. 944

Nichols, Kathleen, Librn, United States Army, 705 Washington Blvd, Rm 56, Fort Eustis, VA, 23604. Tel: 757-501-7138. p. 2319

Nichols, Katie, Br Mgr, Pulaski County Public Library, Burnside Branch, 85 E French Ave, Burnside, KY, 42519. Tel: 606-561-5287. p. 875

Nichols, Laura, Librn, Susquehanna County Historical Society & Free Library Association, Susquehanna Branch, 83 Erie Blvd, Ste C, Susquehanna, PA, 18847. Tel: 570-853-4106. p. 1965

Nichols, Lauren, Dir, Amagansett Free Library, 215 Main St, Amagansett, NY, 11930. Tel: 631-267-3810. p. 1486

Nichols, LeaAnn, Asst Librn, Willow Public Library, 23557 W Willow Community Center Circle, Willow, AK, 99688. Tel: 907-861-7655. p. 52

Nichols, Mary A, Sr Lecturer, Kent State University, 314 University Library, 1125 Risman Dr, Kent, OH, 44242-0001. Tel: 330-672-2782. p. 2790

Nichols, Sara, Libr Dir, Seldovia Public Library, 260 Seldovia St, Seldovia, AK, 99663. Tel: 907-234-7662. p. 50
Nichols, Sarah, Dir, Carnegie Public Library, 127 S North St, Washington Court House, OH, 43160. Tel: 740-335-2540. p. 1828
Nichols, Scott, Branch Lead, Saint Clair County Library System, Algonac-Clay Branch Library, 2011 St Clair River Dr, Algonac, MI, 48001. Tel: 810-794-4471. p. 1142
Nichols, Sharon, Library Contact, Palermo Community Library, 2789 Rte 3, Palermo, ME, 04354. Tel: 207-993-6088. p. 935
Nichols, Vicki, Head Librn, Sumiton Public Library, Town Hall, 416 State St, Sumiton, AL, 35148. Tel: 205-648-7451. p. 36
Nichols-Tucker, Carrie, Br Mgr, Shreve Memorial Library, Gilliam Branch, 12797 Main St, Gilliam, LA, 71029. Tel: 318-296-4227. p. 909
Nicholson, Beth, Dir, Clarksburg-Harrison Public Library, 404 W Pike St, Clarksburg, WV, 26301. Tel: 304-627-2236. p. 2401
Nicholson, Christine, Circ Mgr/ILL, Mgr, Vols Serv, Phoenixville Public Library, 183 Second Ave, Phoenixville, PA, 19460-3420. Tel: 610-933-3013, Ext 122. p. 1989
Nicholson, Christy, Librn, Doddridge County Public Library, Center Point Outpost Public Library, 8871 WV Rte 23, Salem, WV, 26426. Tel: 304-782-2461. p. 2417
Nicholson, Cindy, Admin Serv Coordr, Queens University of Charlotte, 1900 Selwyn Ave, Charlotte, NC, 28274. Tel: 704-337-2708. p. 1681
Nicholson, Elizabeth, Dir, Tidioute Public Library, 197 Main St, Tidioute, PA, 16351. Tel: 814-484-3581. p. 2012
Nicholson, Janet, State Law Librn, West Virginia State Law Library, Bldg 1, Rm E-404, 1900 Kanawha Blvd E, Charleston, WV, 25305. Tel: 304-558-2607. p. 2401
Nicholson, Jeffie, Mrs, Adult Serv Mgr, Williamson County Public Library, 1314 Columbia Ave, Franklin, TN, 37064. Tel: 615-595-1269. p. 2098
Nicholson, Joey, Dept Chair, NYU Langone Hospital, 550 First Ave, New York, NY, 10016. p. 1599
Nicholson, Kinsey, Dir, Dallam-Hartley County Library, 420 Denrock Ave, Dalhart, TX, 79022. Tel: 806-244-2761. p. 2162
Nicholson, Lauren, Libr Mgr, Wake County Public Library System, Athens Drive Community Library, 1420 Athens Dr, Raleigh, NC, 27606. Tel: 919-233-4000. p. 1710
Nicholson, Lauren, Libr Mgr, Wake County Public Library System, Duraleigh Road Community Library, 5800 Duraleigh Rd, Raleigh, NC, 27612. Tel: 919-881-1344. p. 1711
Nicholson, Luanne, Pub Info Officer, Guilderland Public Library, 2228 Western Ave, Guilderland, NY, 12084. Tel: 518-456-2400, Ext 112. p. 1542
Nicholson, Marian, Head, Bus Serv, Canton Public Library, 1200 S Canton Center Rd, Canton, MI, 48188-1600. Tel: 734-397-0999. p. 1088
Nicholson, Robin, Libr Tech, Geophysical Institute, International Arctic Research Ctr, 2156 Koyukuk Dr, Fairbanks, AK, 99775. Tel: 907-474-7512. p. 45
Nicholson, Shawn, Asst Dir, Digital Serv, Michigan State University Libraries, Gerald M Kline Digital & Multimedia Center, W432 Main Library, 366 W Circle Dr, East Lansing, MI, 48824. Tel: 517-884-6448. p. 1102
Nicholson, Shawn, Asst Dir, Digital Serv, Michigan State University Libraries, Voice Library, W422 Library, 366 W Circle Dr, East Lansing, MI, 48824. Tel: 517-884-6470. p. 1102
Nicholson, Shawn, Asst Univ Librn, Digital Serv, Michigan State University Libraries, Main Library, 366 W Circle Dr, East Lansing, MI, 48824-1048. Tel: 517-884-6448. p. 1102
Nickel, Evelyn, Librn, Chinook Regional Library, Herbert Branch, 517 Herbert Ave, Herbert, SK, S0H 2A0, CANADA. Tel: 306-784-2484. p. 2752
Nickel, Karen, Libr Mgr, Three Hills Municipal Library, 135 Third Ave S, Three Hills, AB, T0M 2A0, CANADA. Tel: 403-443-2360. p. 2557
Nickel, Kristin, Tech Mgr, L E Phillips Memorial Public Library, 400 Eau Claire St, Eau Claire, WI, 54701. Tel: 715-839-1684. p. 2432
Nickel, Lisa T, Assoc Dean, Res & Pub Serv, College of William & Mary in Virginia, Earl Gregg Swem Library, One Landrum Dr, Williamsburg, VA, 23187. Tel: 757-221-1777. p. 2353
Nickel, Shannon, Librn, Walton Community Library, 122 Main St, Walton, KS, 67151. Tel: 620-837-3252. p. 841
Nickell, Lynette, Ch Serv, Ector County Library, 321 W Fifth St, Odessa, TX, 79761-5066. Tel: 432-332-0633. p. 2223
Nickell, Rene, Br Librn, Fayette County Public Libraries, Ansted Public, 102 Oak St, Ansted, WV, 25812. Tel: 304-658-5472. p. 2411
Nickels, April, Head, Youth Serv, Chester County Library & District Center, 450 Exton Square Pkwy, Exton, PA, 19341-2496. Tel: 610-344-5600. p. 1932
Nickerson, Caroline, Libr Dir, West Buxton Public Library, 34 River Rd, Buxton, ME, 04093-0348. Tel: 207-727-5898. p. 920
Nickerson, Caroline, Libr Dir, Hollis Center Public Library, 14 Little Falls Rd, Hollis Center, ME, 04042. Tel: 207-929-3911. p. 927
Nickerson, Daniel H, Libr Dir, Sugar Grove Free Library, 22 Harmon St, Sugar Grove, PA, 16350. Tel: 814-489-7872. p. 2011
Nickerson, Matthew, Exec Dir, Southern Utah University, 351 W University Blvd, Cedar City, UT, 84720. Tel: 435-586-1955. p. 2262
Nickerson-Harper, Carolyn Jo, Asst Dir, Carlsbad Public Library, 101 S Halagueno St, Carlsbad, NM, 88220. Tel: 575-885-6776. p. 1465
Nickisch Duggan, Heidi, Assoc Dir, Health Sci Libr, Northwestern University Libraries, Galter Health Sciences Library, Montgomery Ward Bldg, 303 E Chicago Ave, Chicago, IL, 60611. Tel: 312-503-8133. p. 586
Nicklas, Dana, Libr Dir, Waterford Township Public Library, 386 White Horse Pike, Atco, NJ, 08004. Tel: 856-767-7727. p. 1387
Nickle, Holly, Br Mgr, United States Geological Survey Library, Mail Stop 150, 12201 Sunrise Valley Dr, Reston, VA, 20192. p. 2340
Nickleberry-Brooks, Pam, Br Mgr, Memphis Public Library, South Branch, 1929 S Third St, Memphis, TN, 38109. Tel: 901-415-2780. p. 2114
Nickles, Tim, Dir, Grand Encampment Museum, Inc Library, 807 Barnett Ave, Encampment, WY, 82325. Tel: 307-327-5308. p. 2494
Nicklom, Judy, Libr Mgr, Delburne Municipal Library, 2210 20th St, Delburne, AB, T0M 0V0, CANADA. Tel: 403-749-3848. p. 2532
Nickolay, Hannah, Library Services Asst, Western Theological Seminary, 101 E 13th St, Holland, MI, 49423. Tel: 616-392-8555, Ext 143. p. 1116
Nickolopoulos, May, Circ, Franklin County Public Library, 355 Franklin St, Rocky Mount, VA, 24151. Tel: 540-483-3098. p. 2346
Nickson, Claudia, Head Librn, Saint Augustine College Library, 1345 W Argyle St, Chicago, IL, 60640. Tel: 773-878-3752. p. 567
Nickum, Lisa, Systems Discovery Librn, Colorado School of Mines, 1400 Illinois St, Golden, CO, 80401-1887. Tel: 303-273-3695. p. 283
Nicol, Erica, Liaison Services, Libr Instruction, Team Leader, Washington State University Libraries, 100 Dairy Rd, Pullman, WA, 99164. Tel: 509-335-8614. p. 2374
Nicolai, Elizabeth, Asst Dir, Anchorage Public Library, 3600 Denali St, Anchorage, AK, 99503. Tel: 907-343-2909. p. 42
Nicolas, Angel, Mgr, County of Los Angeles Public Library, Lynwood Library, 11320 Bullis Rd, Lynwood, CA, 90262-3661. Tel: 310-635-7121. p. 137
Nicolas, Barnaby, Dir, NYU Grossman Long Island School of Medicine, 259 First St, Mineola, NY, 11501. Tel: 516-663-2783. p. 1572
Nicolaus, Melissa, Libr Mgr, Live Oak Public Libraries, Springfield Branch, 810 Hwy 119 S, Springfield, GA, 31329. Tel: 912-754-3003. p. 496
Nicolazzi, Maureen, Librn III, North Babylon Public Library, 815 Deer Park Ave, North Babylon, NY, 11703-3812. Tel: 631-669-4020. p. 1607
Nicolazzo, Lily, Teen Librn, Goodnow Library, 21 Concord Rd, Sudbury, MA, 01776-2383. Tel: 978-443-1035. p. 1058
Nicoletti, Jeanette, Circ, Garden City Public Library, 60 Seventh St, Garden City, NY, 11530. Tel: 516-742-8405. p. 1536
Nicoll, Jonathan, Br Librn, Southeast Regional Library, Carlyle Branch, 119 Souris Ave W, Carlyle, SK, S0C 0R0, CANADA. Tel: 306-453-6120. p. 2753
Nicolosi, David, Br Mgr, Iberville Parish Library, White Castle Branch, 32835 Bowie St, White Castle, LA, 70788. Tel: 225-545-8424. p. 906
Nie, Caroline, Tech Serv Coordr, Concord Free Public Library, 129 Main St, Concord, MA, 01742. Tel: 978-318-3368. p. 1012
Niebuhr, Elizabeth M, Libr Dir, Winthrop Public Library, 305 N Main St, Winthrop, MN, 55396. Tel: 507-647-5308. p. 1209
Niederberger, Erin, Ref Librn, Metropolitan Community College, Maple Woods Library, 2601 NE Barry Rd, Kansas City, MO, 64156. Tel: 816-604-3080. p. 1256
Niederhauser, Julie, Continuing Educ Coordr, Alaska State Library, 395 Whittier St, Juneau, AK, 99801. Tel: 907-465-2920. p. 47
Niedermeier, Bernadette, Youth Serv Librn, Eustis Memorial Library, 120 N Center St, Eustis, FL, 32726. Tel: 352-357-0896. p. 395
Niedringhaus, Kris, Assoc Dean, Libr & Info Serv, Georgia State University, College of Law Library, 140 Decatur St, Atlanta, GA, 30302. Tel: 404-413-9140. p. 464
Nieland, Jayne, Dir, Sisseton Memorial Library, 305 E Maple St, Sisseton, SD, 57262. Tel: 605-698-7391. p. 2083
Nielsen, Bruce, Dr, Archivist, Pub Serv Librn, Herbert D Katz Center for Advanced Judaic Studies Library, 420 Walnut St, Philadelphia, PA, 19106-3703. Tel: 215-746-1290, 215-746-5154. p. 1982
Nielsen, Bryan, Libr Asst, Moffat County Libraries, Dinosaur Branch, 400 W School St, Dinosaur, CO, 81610. Tel: 970-374-2700. p. 272
Nielsen, Christine, Dir, Renwick Public Library, 204 Stoddard St, Renwick, IA, 50577. Tel: 515-824-3209. p. 778
Nielsen, Darth, Regional Mgr, The Seattle Public Library, 1000 Fourth Ave, Seattle, WA, 98104-1109. Tel: 206-386-4636. p. 2379
Nielsen, Elizabeth A, Univ Archivist, Oregon State University Libraries, Special Collections & Archives Research Center, 121 The Valley Library, 5th Flr, Corvallis, OR, 97331. Tel: 541-737-0543. p. 1877
Nielsen, Jerel, Libr Mgr, Chatfield Music Lending Library, 81 Library Lane SW, Chatfield, MN, 55923. Tel: 507-867-3275. p. 1169
Nielsen, Joy, Libr Dir, M-C Community Library, 200 W Grace St, Cleghorn, IA, 51014. Tel: 712-436-2521. p. 740
Nielsen, Juliet, Libr Mgr, SIAST-Saskatchewan Institute of Applied Science & Technology, 600 Saskatchewan St W, Moose Jaw, SK, S6H 4R4, CANADA. Tel: 306-775-7412. p. 2743
Nielsen, Juliet, Libr Mgr, Saskatchewan Polytechnic, 4500 Wascana Pkwy, Regina, SK, S4P 3A3, CANADA. Tel: 306-775-7412. p. 2748
Nielsen, Kjerstine, Asst Dir, Dallas Public Library, 1515 Young St, Dallas, TX, 75201-5415. Tel: 214-670-1400. p. 2165
Nielsen, Maegan, Br Librn, Southeast Regional Library, Moosomin Branch, 701 Main St, Moosomin, SK, S0G 3N0, CANADA. Tel: 306-435-2107. p. 2754

Nielsen, Robin, Br Mgr, Washington County Library System, New Harmony Branch, 34 S 2900 E, New Harmony, UT, 84757. Tel: 435-867-0065. p. 2270
Nielsen, Sara, Adult Serv Mgr, Saint Charles City-County Library District, 77 Boone Hills Dr, Saint Peters, MO, 63376. Tel: 636-441-2300. p. 1277
Nielsen, Tina, Chief Librn, Bowen Island Public Library, 430 Bowen Island Trunk Rd, Bowen Island, BC, V0N 1G0, CANADA. Tel: 604-947-9788. p. 2563
Nielson Corning, Kristie, Dir, Angie Williams Cox Public Library, 119 N Main St, Pardeeville, WI, 53954. Tel: 608-429-2354. p. 2468
Nielson, Joan, Assoc Dir, Access Serv, Kenyon College Library & Information Services, Olin & Chalmers Libraries, 103 College Dr, Gambier, OH, 43022. p. 1787
Nieman, Dan, Asst Dir, South Sioux City Public Library, 2121 Dakota Ave, South Sioux City, NE, 68776. Tel: 402-494-7545. p. 1336
Nieman, Deb, Dir, Benny Gambaiani Public Library, 104 S Cherry St, Shell Rock, IA, 50670. Tel: 319-885-4345. p. 781
Niemeier, Cheryl, Libr Dir, Meridian Public Library, 118 N Main St, Meridian, TX, 76665. Tel: 254-435-9100. p. 2218
Niemeier, Trish, Dir, Galva Public Library, 203 S Main St, Galva, IA, 51020. Tel: 712-282-4400. p. 754
Niemi, Carol, Academy Librn, Interlochen Center for the Arts, Bonisteel Library - Seabury Academic Library, 4000 M-137, Interlochen, MI, 49643. Tel: 231-276-7420. p. 1118
Niemi, Jessica, Assoc Mgr, Edmonton Public Library, Heritage Valley, 2755 119A St SW, Edmonton, AB, T6W 3R3, CANADA. Tel: 780-442-6861. p. 2536
Niemi, Jessica, Assoc Mgr, Edmonton Public Library, Whitemud Crossing, 145 Whitemud Crossing Shopping Ctr, 4211 106 St, Edmonton, AB, T6J 6L7, CANADA. Tel: 780-442-6861. p. 2537
Niemla, Karen, Ref & Tech Librn, Mercyhurst University, 501 E 38th St, Erie, PA, 16546. Tel: 814-824-3871. p. 1932
Niepsuj, Bonnie, ILL, McHenry Public Library District, 809 Front St, McHenry, IL, 60050. Tel: 815-385-0036. p. 616
Nierman, Carla, Exec Dir, Art Center Manatee, 209 Ninth St W, Bradenton, FL, 34205. Tel: 941-746-2862. p. 386
Niese, Joe, Dir, Chippewa Falls Public Library, 105 W Central St, Chippewa Falls, WI, 54729-2397. Tel: 715-723-1146. p. 2427
Nietfeld, Linda, Dir, Fort Recovery Public Library, 113 N Wayne St, Fort Recovery, OH, 45846. Tel: 419-375-2869. p. 1786
Nieto, Suzy, Librn, North Central Washington Libraries, Entiat Public Library, 14138 Kinzel St, Entiat, WA, 98822. Tel: 509-784-1517. p. 2393
Niette, Alan, Deputy Dir, Technology, Natchitoches Parish Library, 450 Second St, Natchitoches, LA, 71457-4649. Tel: 318-238-9226. p. 899
Niette, Alan, Outreach Coordr, Natchitoches Parish Library, 450 Second St, Natchitoches, LA, 71457-4649. Tel: 318-238-9236. p. 899
Nieves, Cassandra, Info Serv Librn, Northampton Community College, Essa Bank & Trust Foundation Library, Keystone Hall, 2411 Rte 715, Tannersville, PA, 18372. Tel: 570-369-1810. p. 1912
Nieves, Jennifer, Archives Mgr, Colls Mgr, Cleveland Health Sciences Library, Allen Memorial Medical Library, 11000 Euclid Ave, Cleveland, OH, 44106-7130. Tel: 216-368-3648. p. 1767
Nieves, Stephanie, Digital Serv Spec, Rollins College, 1000 Holt Ave, Campus Box 2744, Winter Park, FL, 32789-2744. Tel: 407-691-1322. p. 456
Nieves-Goss, Jacqueline, Ch, Circ Desk Mgr, Libr Asst, Groves Public Library, 5600 W Washington St, Groves, TX, 77619. Tel: 409-962-6281. p. 2186
Niewinski, Brian, Head, Res Serv, Pennsylvania Fish & Boat Commission, 1735 Shiloh Rd, State College, PA, 16801-8495. Tel: 814-355-4837. p. 2010
Niewyk, Ellen Buie, Curator, Spec Coll, Southern Methodist University, Hamon Arts Library, 6101 N Bishop Blvd, Dallas, TX, 75275. Tel: 214-768-1855. p. 2168
Niggel, Nancy, Dir, Chester Springs Library, 1709 Art School Rd, Chester Springs, PA, 19425-1402. Tel: 610-827-9212. p. 1921
Nightingale, Eileen, Ch, Sidney Public Library, 1112 12th Ave, Sidney, NE, 69162. Tel: 308-254-3110. p. 1336
Nigoche, Jennifer, Br Supvr, East Travis Gateway Library District, Garfield Library, 5121 Albert Brown Dr, Del Valle, TX, 78617. Tel: 512-247-7371. p. 2169
Nikolis, Sally, Ch Prog, Youth Serv, South Huntington Public Library, 145 Pidgeon Hill Rd, Huntington Station, NY, 11746. Tel: 631-549-4411. p. 1549
Nikolopoulou, Evgenia, Librn, Anderson Kill PC, 1251 Avenue of the Americas, New York, NY, 10020-1182. Tel: 212-278-1069. p. 1579
Niles, Mary Ann, Asst Dean, Libr Serv, Middlesex Community College, Academic Resources Bldg 1A, 591 Springs Rd, Bedford, MA, 01730. Tel: 781-280-3708. p. 988
Niles, Naomi, Assoc Librn, Metropolitan Museum of Art, Library & Teacher Resource Center in the Uris Center for Education, 1000 Fifth Ave, New York, NY, 10028-0198. Tel: 212-570-3788. p. 1591
Niles, Phyllis, Head, Access & Delivery Serv, Borough of Manhattan Community College Library, 199 Chambers St, S410, New York, NY, 10007. Tel: 212-220-1450. p. 1580
Niles, Stephen, Asst Dir, Dorset Village Library, Rte 30 & Church St, Dorset, VT, 05251. Tel: 802-867-5774. p. 2283
Nilova, Olga, Operations Librn, Spec Coll, The Rockefeller University, Welch Hall, 1230 York Ave, RU Box 203, New York, NY, 10065. Tel: 212-327-8868. p. 1601
Nilsen, Heather, Ch Serv, Clifton Public Library, Allwood Branch, 44 Lyall Rd, Clifton, NJ, 07012. Tel: 973-471-0555. p. 1397
Nilson, Wendy, Tech Serv Librn, Edith B Siegrist Vermillion Public Library, 18 Church St, Vermillion, SD, 57069-3093. Tel: 605-677-7060. p. 2084
Nilsson, Frances, Head, Res Mgt, Merrimack College, 315 Turnpike St, North Andover, MA, 01845. Tel: 978-837-5064. p. 1040
Nilsson, Kirsten, Youth Serv Librn, Summit County Library, 1885 W Ute Blvd, Park City, UT, 84098. Tel: 435-615-3903. p. 2268
Nilsson, Monnie, Br Mgr, Boulder Public Library, Meadows Branch, 4800 Baseline Rd, Ste C112, Boulder, CO, 80303-2678. Tel: 303-441-4390. p. 266
Nimersheim, Susan, Dir, Grant County Public Library District, 201 Barnes Rd, Williamstown, KY, 41097-9482. Tel: 859-824-2080. p. 877
Nimmer, David, Asst Dir, Cedarburg Public Library, W63 N589 Hanover Ave, Cedarburg, WI, 53012. Tel: 262-375-7640, Ext 201. p. 2427
Nimmo, Maureen, Dir, Lawrence Public Library, South Lawrence Branch, 135 Parker St, South Lawrence, MA, 01843. Tel: 978-682-1727. p. 1027
Nims, Joyce, Asst Librn, Robertsdale Public Library, 18301 Pennsylvania St, Robertsdale, AL, 36567. Tel: 251-947-8960. p. 34
Nimz, Timothy, Dir, Littleton Museum Research Center, 6028 S Gallup, Littleton, CO, 80120. Tel: 303-795-3950. p. 290
Ninemire, David, Head Librn, Free Library of Philadelphia, Government Publications, 1901 Vine St, Rm 201, Philadelphia, PA, 19103-1116. Tel: 215-686-5330. p. 1978
Ninemire, David, Head Librn, Free Library of Philadelphia, Social Science & History, 1901 Vine St, Rm 201, Philadelphia, PA, 19103-1116. Tel: 215-686-5396. p. 1980
Nino, Ana, Librn, Botanical Research Institute of Texas Library, 1700 University Dr, Fort Worth, TX, 76107. Tel: 817-332-4441, 817-463-4102. p. 2179
Nino, Tylan, Circ, Hudson Valley Community College, 80 Vandenburgh Ave, Troy, NY, 12180. Tel: 518-629-7330. p. 1652
Niotis, Vivy, Br Mgr, Loudoun County Public Library, Gum Spring Library, 24600 Millstream Dr, Aldie, VA, 20105. Tel: 571-258-3838. p. 2328
Nipper, Elena, Ref & Instruction Librn, Vanguard University of Southern California, 55 Fair Dr, Costa Mesa, CA, 92626. Tel: 714-966-6378. p. 133
Nippert, Jennifer, Asst Dir, Mgr, Human Res, Bullitt County Public Library, 127 N Walnut St, Shepherdsville, KY, 40165-6083. Tel: 502-543-7675. p. 874
Niraula, Abha, Acq Librn, Northwest Missouri State University, 800 University Dr, Maryville, MO, 64468-6001. Tel: 660-562-1193. p. 1261
Nishimura, Sunni, Exec Dir, British Columbia Electronic Library Network, WAC Bennett Library, 7th Flr, Simon Fraser University, 8888 University Dr, Burnaby, BC, V5A 1S6, CANADA. Tel: 778-782-7003. p. 2777
Nishimura, Sunni, Exec Dir, Electronic Health Library of British Columbia, c/o Bennett Library, 8888 University Dr, Burnaby, BC, V5A 1S6, CANADA. Tel: 778-782-7003. p. 2777
Nisly, Hope, Acq, Fresno Pacific University, 1717 S Chestnut Ave, Fresno, CA, 93702. Tel: 559-453-2223. p. 146
Niss, John, Interim Dean, Valencia College, 850 W Morse Blvd, Winter Park, FL, 32789. Tel: 407-582-6814. p. 456
Nissen, Jill, Dir, University of Health Sciences & Pharmacy in Saint Louis Library, One Pharmacy Pl, Saint Louis, MO, 63110. Tel: 314-446-8362. p. 1276
Nissen, Theron, Br Mgr, Las Vegas-Clark County Library District, 7060 W Windmill Lane, Las Vegas, NV, 89113. Tel: 702-507-6030, 702-734-7323. p. 1346
Nitcher, Caren, Cat Librn, University of Tennessee at Martin, Ten Wayne Fisher Dr, Martin, TN, 38238. Tel: 731-881-7096. p. 2111
Nitcher, Teresa, Acq Spec, Libr Asst III, Washburn University, 1700 SW College Ave, Topeka, KS, 66621. Tel: 785-670-1985. p. 839
Nitecki, Danuta, Dean, Univ Libr, Drexel University Libraries, Hagerty Library, 33rd & Market Sts, Philadelphia, PA, 19104-2875. Tel: 215-895-2750. p. 1976
Nitschke, Barbara, Librn, Ashley Public Library, 113 First Ave NW, Ashley, ND, 58413-7037. Tel: 701-288-3510. p. 1729
Nittmo, Madeleine, Outreach Serv Librn, Tyler Junior College, 1327 S Baxter St, Tyler, TX, 75701. Tel: 903-510-2759. p. 2250
Nitzel, Heather, Youth Serv Librn, Robert L F Sikes Public Library, 1445 Commerce Dr, Crestview, FL, 32539. Tel: 850-682-4432. p. 391
Niu, Jinfang, Dr, Asst Prof, University of South Florida, 4202 Fowler Ave, CIS 1040, Tampa, FL, 33620-7800. Tel: 813-974-6837. p. 2783
Niver, Tim, Dir, Victor Farmington Library, 15 W Main, Victor, NY, 14564. Tel: 585-924-2637. p. 1657
Nivitanont, Shelby, Scholarly Communications Librn, University of Wyoming, 1820 E Willett Dr, Laramie. Tel: 307-766-5731. p. 2496
Niwinski, Julie, Librn/Mgr, Buncombe County Public Libraries, North Asheville, 1030 Merrimon Ave, Asheville, NC, 28804. Tel: 828-250-4752. p. 1672

Nix, Alexi, Asst Dir, Boylston Public Library, 695 Main St, Boylston, MA, 01505. Tel: 508-869-2371. p. 1001
Nix, Jaime, Dir of Libr, Wichita Public Library, 711 W Second St, Wichita, KS, 67203. Tel: 316-261-8500. p. 843
Nix, Stacey, Dir, Coos County Library Service District, 525 Anderson Ave, Coos Bay, OR, 97420. Tel: 541-269-1101. p. 1876
Nix, Trish, Dir, Eagle Public Library, Second & Amundsen, Eagle, AK, 99738. Tel: 907-547-2334. p. 44
Nix, Tyler, Assoc Dir, University of Michigan, Taubman Health Sciences Library, 1135 E Catherine St, Ann Arbor, MI, 48109-2038. Tel: 734-615-1516. p. 1080
Nix, Vicki, Dir, Tawakoni Area Public Library, 340 W Hwy 276, West Tawakoni, TX, 75474-2644. Tel: 903-447-3445. p. 2256
Nixon, Destynee, Libr Adminr, Royal Oak Township Public Library, 21131 Garden Lane, 2nd Flr, Ferndale, MI, 48220. Tel: 248-542-9205. p. 1105
Nixon, Stephanie, Libr Dir, Hale County Public Library, 1103 Main St, Greensboro, AL, 36744. Tel: 334-624-3409. p. 19
Niziolek, Natalie, Libr Dir, Franklin Township Public Library, 1584 Coles Mill Rd, Franklinville, NJ, 08322. Tel: 856-694-2833. p. 1404
Nizolek, Margaret, Chief Deputy, State Librn, Dir, SLIC, New Jersey State Library, 185 W State St, Trenton, NJ, 08608. Tel: 609-278-2640, Ext 148. p. 1448
Njoroge, Judy, Bibliog Serv, Syst Librn, Library Connection, Inc, 599 Matianuck Ave, Windsor, CT, 06095-3567. Tel: 860-937-8263. p. 2763
Nkwor, Jude, Media Serv Spec, Yeshiva University Libraries, Dr Lillian & Dr Rebecca Chutick Law Library, Benjamin N Cardozo School of Law, 55 Fifth Ave, New York, NY, 10003-4301. Tel: 212-790-0223. p. 1604
No Braid, Avanelle, Dir, Oglala Lakota College, Pahin Sinte College Center, PO Box 220, Porcupine, SD, 57772. Tel: 605-867-5404. p. 2078
Noack, Jaime, Libr Dir, Polk City Community Library, 1500 W Broadway St, Polk City, IA, 50226-2001. Tel: 515-984-6119. p. 777
Noack, Katelyn, Dir, Mondovi Public Library, 146 W Hudson St, Mondovi, WI, 54755. Tel: 715-926-4403. p. 2462
Noah, Kathy, Interim Dir, Carrollton North-Carrollton Public Library, 1102 Lexington St, Carrollton, MS, 38917. Tel: 662-237-6268. p. 1213
Noakes, Amy, Circ Supvr, Mississippi Valley Library District, 408 W Main St, Collinsville, IL, 62234. Tel: 618-344-1112. p. 573
Noark, Erika, Mgr, Geauga County Public Library, Geauga West Branch, 13455 Chillicothe Rd, Chesterland, OH, 44026. Tel: 440-729-4250. p. 1758
Nobbs, Karen, Collection Access Mgt, University of Iowa Libraries, College of Law Library, 200 Boyd Law Bldg, Iowa City, IA, 52242-1166. Tel: 319-335-9029. p. 761
Nobel, Hope, Libr Dir, Tamarack District Library, 832 S Lincoln Ave, Lakeview, MI, 48850. Tel: 989-352-6274. p. 1123
Nobiling, Christina, Dir of Circ, Rock Island Public Library, 401 19th St, Rock Island, IL, 61201. Tel: 309-732-7370. p. 641
Noble, Amy, Ch, Greenville Area Public Library, 330 Main St, Greenville, PA, 16125-2615. Tel: 724-588-5490. p. 1938
Noble, Catherine, Librn, Iowa Veteran's Home Library, 1301 Summit St, Marshalltown, IA, 50158. Tel: 641-753-4412. p. 768
Noble, Jennifer, Sr Librn, Los Angeles Public Library System, Westwood Branch Library, 1246 Glendon Ave, Los Angeles, CA, 90024. Tel: 310-474-1739. p. 166
Noble, Leslie, Asst Dir, Tech Serv Mgr, Urbandale Public Library, 3520 86th St, Urbandale, IA, 50322. Tel: 515-278-3945. p. 787
Noble, Michele, Br Mgr, Arundel Anne County Public Library, Eastport-Annapolis Neck Library, 269 Hillsmere Dr, Annapolis, MD, 21403. Tel: 410-222-1770. p. 950
Noble, Nancy, Librn, Stoel Rives LLP, One Union Sq, 600 University St, Ste 3600, Seattle, WA, 98101. Tel: 206-386-7502. p. 2380
Noble, Stephanie, Dep Circuit Librn, United States Court of Appeals for the District of Columbia, US Court House, 333 Constitution Ave NW, Rm 3205, Washington, DC, 20001. Tel: 202-216-7400. p. 377
Noble, Terri, Libr Tech, Nova Scotia Community College, Burridge Campus Library, 372 Pleasant St, Yarmouth, NS, B5A 2L2, CANADA. Tel: 902-742-3416. p. 2619
Noblick, Martha, Dir & Librn, Goshen Free Public Library, 42 Main St, Goshen, MA, 01032. Tel: 413-268-8236, Ext 111. p. 1021
Noblitt, Scott, Librn, Placer County Library, Granite Bay Branch, 6475 Douglas Blvd, Granite Bay, CA, 95746. Tel: 916-791-5590. p. 118
Nocera, Christian, Mgr, Info Tech & Media Serv, Newport News Public Library System, Main Street, 110 Main St, Newport News, VA, 23601. Tel: 757-591-4858. p. 2334
Nochimson, David, Access Serv Librn, Media Librn, Ser Librn, Molloy College, 1000 Hempstead Ave, Rockville Centre, NY, 11571. Tel: 516-323-3928. p. 1632
Nodes, Jennifer, Dir, Libr Serv, Canizaro Library at Ave Maria University, 5251 Donahue St, Ave Maria, FL, 34142. Tel: 239-348-4710. p. 384
Noe, Christopher, Asst Dir, Head, Pub Serv, University of Mississippi, 481 Chuckie Mullins Dr, University, MS, 38677. Tel: 662-915-6850. p. 1234
Noe, Jennifer, Access Serv, Kingsborough Community College, 2001 Oriental Blvd, Brooklyn, NY, 11235. Tel: 718-368-5438. p. 1504
Noe, Katherine, Coll Mgr, Martin County Library System, 2351 SE Monterey Rd, Stuart, FL, 34996. Tel: 772-219-4968. p. 444
Noe, Lori, Dir, Illinois Eastern Community Colleges, Two Frontier Dr, Fairfield, IL, 62837-2601. Tel: 618-847-9128, Ext 4510. p. 587
Noe, Marie, Customer Serv Mgr, Abilene Public Library, 202 Cedar St, Abilene, TX, 79601-5793. Tel: 325-437-4537. p. 2131
Noe, Reiley, Govt Doc, Hanover College, 121 Scenic Dr, Hanover, IN, 47243. Tel: 812-866-7165. p. 689
Noe, Teresa, Asst Dir, Claiborne County Public Library, 1304 Old Knoxville Rd, Tazewell, TN, 37879. Tel: 423-626-5414. p. 2127
Noel, Audreanne, Libr Coord, De Grandpre Chait Library, 800 Blvd Rene-Levesque, 26th Flr, Montreal, QC, H3B 1X9, CANADA. Tel: 514-878-4311. p. 2724
Noel, Caryn, Libr Dir, Walsh College, 3838 Livernois Rd, Troy, MI, 48083-5066. Tel: 248-823-1254. p. 1155
Noel, Casandra, Circ Librn, State of Mississippi Judiciary, Carroll Gartin Justice Bldg, 450 High St, Jackson, MS, 39201. Tel: 601-359-3672. p. 1223
Noel, Chantel, Library Contact, Robinson, Sheppard & Shapiro, 800 Place Victoria, Ste 4700, Montreal, QC, H4Z 1H6, CANADA. Tel: 514-393-4004. p. 2727
Noel, Fred, Libr Dir, Salish Kootenai College, PO Box 70, Pablo, MT, 59855. Tel: 406-275-4873. p. 1300
Noel, Kim, Mgr, Access Serv, Mgr, Circ Serv, Springfield Technical Community College Library, One Armory Sq, Bldg 27, Ste 1, Springfield, MA, 01105. Tel: 413-755-4564. p. 1057
Noel, Louanne, Libr Mgr, Boyce Ditto Public Library, 2300 Martin Luther King Jr St, Mineral Wells, TX, 76067. Tel: 940-328-7880. p. 2220
Noel, Patrick, Mgr, Miami-Dade Public Library System, Braille & Talking Books Library, c/o North Dade Regional Library, 2455 NW 183rd St, Miami, FL, 33056. Tel: 305-751-8687. p. 423
Noel, Patrick, Mgr, Miami-Dade Public Library System, North Dade Regional, 2455 NW 183rd St, Miami, FL, 33056. Tel: 305-625-6424. p. 424
Noeske, Ben, Asst Librn, University of Maine at Machias, 116 O'Brien Ave, Machias, ME, 04654. Tel: 207-255-1356. p. 931
Noffke, Emily, Circ Supvr, Mount Horeb Public Library, 105 Perimeter Rd, Mount Horeb, WI, 53572. Tel: 608-437-9372. p. 2463
Noffke, Lynne, Dir, Limestone Township Library District, 2701 W Tower Rd, Kankakee, IL, 60901. Tel: 815-939-1696. p. 604
Noffsinger, Martha, Circ Mgr, Carroll County Public Library, 136 Court St, Carrollton, KY, 41008. Tel: 502-732-7020. p. 851
Nofire, David, Br Mgr, Tulsa City-County Library, Kendall-Whittier Branch, 21 S Lewis St, Tulsa, OK, 74104. p. 1866
Nofsinger, Christine, Libr Dir, Marcellus Township-Wood Memorial Library, 205 E Main St, Marcellus, MI, 49067. Tel: 269-646-9654. p. 1129
Noftz, Cassandra, Br Mgr, Park County Public Libraries, Lake George Branch, 37900 Hwy 24, Lake George, CO, 80827. Tel: 719-748-3812. p. 265
Noga, Jennifer, Assoc Dir, Tech Serv, Wake Forest University, Law Library, Worrell Professional Ctr, 1834 Wake Forest Rd, Winston-Salem, NC, 27109. Tel: 336-758-4520. p. 1726
Noganosh, Wanda, Librn, Magnetawan First Nation Public Library, Ten Regional Rd & Hwy 529, Britt, ON, P0G 1A0, CANADA. Tel: 705-383-2477. p. 2633
Nogel, Kim, Education Program Mgr, North Idaho Correctional Institution Library, 236 Radar Rd, Cottonwood, ID, 83522. Tel: 208-962-3276, Ext 174. p. 520
Noggle, Deb, Librn/Br Mgr, Allen County Public Library, Little Turtle, 2201 Sherman Blvd, Fort Wayne, IN, 46808. Tel: 260-421-1335. p. 683
Noggle, Deborah L, Librn/Br Mgr, Allen County Public Library, Tecumseh, 1411 E State Blvd, Fort Wayne, IN, 46805. Tel: 260-421-1361. p. 683
Noguchi, Setsuko, Librn, Princeton University, East Asian Library, 33 Frist Campus Ctr, Rm 317, Princeton, NJ, 08544. Tel: 609-258-6159. p. 1437
Noguera, Ruben, ILS Adminr, Kansas City Library Service Program, Kansas City Public Library, 14 W Tenth St, Kansas City, MO, 64105-1702. Tel: 816-701-3520. p. 2769
Nohrenberg, LaVena, Customer Experience Mgr, Eugene Public Library, 100 W Tenth Ave, Eugene, OR, 97401. Tel: 541-682-5450. p. 1878
Nojonen, Matthew, Libr Dir, Leavenworth Public Library, 417 Spruce St, Leavenworth, KS, 66048. Tel: 913-682-5666. p. 820
Nolan, Brandi, Librn, Kearney & Area Public Library, Eight Main St, Kearney, ON, P0A 1M0, CANADA. Tel: 705-636-5849. p. 2649
Nolan, Connie, Libr Asst, Belmar Public Library, 517 Tenth Ave, Belmar, NJ, 07719. Tel: 732-681-0775. p. 1389
Nolan, Ed, Head, Spec Coll, Washington State History Research Center, 315 N Stadium Way, Tacoma, WA, 98403. Tel: 253-798-5914. p. 2388
Nolan, Kimberly, Info Res Mgr, SUNY Upstate Medical University, 766 Irving Ave, Syracuse, NY, 13210-1602. Tel: 315-464-7113. p. 1650
Nolan, Mary Ellen, Librn, New Hanover County Public Library, Pine Valley, 3802 S College Rd, Wilmington, NC, 28412. Tel: 910-798-6391. p. 1723
Nolan, Maureen D, Librn, University of Washington Libraries, Friday Harbor Library, 620 University Rd, Box 351812, Friday Harbor, WA, 98250-2900. Tel: 206-685-2126. p. 2382

Nolan, Maureen M, Sci Librn, University of Washington Libraries, Fisheries-Oceanography, Suzzallo Library, Research Services, Box 352900, Seattle, WA, 98195-2900. Tel: 206-685-2126. p. 2382

Nolan, Nicole, Assoc Univ Librn, Brock University, 1812 Sir Isaac Brock Way, St. Catharines, ON, L2S 3A1, CANADA. Tel: 905-688-5550, Ext 5868. p. 2679

Nolan, Sarah, Librn, Clackamas Community College Library, 19600 Molalla Ave, Oregon City, OR, 97045. Tel: 503-594-3316. p. 1889

Nolan, Stephen, Librn II, College of the North Atlantic Library Services, Carbonear Campus, Four Pikes Lane, Carbonear, NL, A1Y 1A7, CANADA. Tel: 709-596-8925, 709-596-8940. p. 2609

Nolan, Susan, Head, Children's Servx, Shelter Rock Public Library, 165 Searingtown Rd, Albertson, NY, 11507. Tel: 516-248-7343. p. 1484

Noland-Hughes, Amy, Ch, Estill County Public Library, 246 Main St, Irvine, KY, 40336-1026. Tel: 606-723-3030. p. 860

Nolasco, Kristie, Library Contact, Olympic College, Johnson Library, 937 W Alpine Way, Shelton, WA, 98584-1200. Tel: 360-432-5460. p. 2360

Nolen, Jennifer, Librn, Chaffee Public Library, 202 Wright Ave, Chaffee, MO, 63740. Tel: 573-887-3298. p. 1241

Nolen, Michelle, Dir, Elizabeth Titus Memorial Library, Two W Water St, Sullivan, IL, 61951. Tel: 217-728-7221. p. 652

Nolen, Tina, Librn, Ashland City Library, 113 Second Ave N, Ashland, AL, 36251. Tel: 256-354-3427. p. 5

Nolette, Brenda, Asst Librn, Youth Serv, Rye Public Library, 581 Washington Rd, Rye, NH, 03870. Tel: 603-964-8401. p. 1380

Nolidis, Carla, Circ Serv Supvr, Naperville Public Library, 95th Street, 3015 Cedar Glade Dr, Naperville, IL, 60564. Tel: 630-961-4100, Ext 4920. p. 623

Nolin, Kate-Lee, Libr Dir, Southeast Regional Library, 49 Bison Ave, Weyburn, SK, S4H 0H9, CANADA. Tel: 306-848-3100. p. 2753

Noll, Charlene, Libr Dir, Hillside Public Library, 155 Lakeville Rd, New Hyde Park, NY, 11040. Tel: 516-355-7850. p. 1576

Noll, Claire, Ref & Info Literacy Librn, Texas Chiropractic College, 5912 Spencer Hwy, Pasadena, TX, 77505. Tel: 281-998-6049. p. 2225

Nollette, Patrice, Br Mgr, Mid-Continent Public Library, Riverside Branch, 2700 NW Vivion Rd, Riverside, MO, 64150. Tel: 816-741-6288. p. 1251

Nolte, Jim, Dir, Emeritus, Vermont College of Fine Arts, Vermont College of Fine Arts Library, 36 College St, Montpelier, VT, 05602. Tel: 802-828-8512. p. 2289

Nolting, Dan, Head, Tech Serv, Chatham College, Woodland Rd, Pittsburgh, PA, 15232. Tel: 412-365-1243. p. 1992

Nomeland, Elana, Asst Librn, Minneota Public Library, 200 N Jefferson St, Minneota, MN, 56264. Tel: 507-872-5473. p. 1186

Nones, Irene, Mgr, Libr Admin, Lakeland Library Region, 1302 100 St, North Battleford, SK, S9A 0V8, CANADA. Tel: 306-445-6108. p. 2743

Noon, Kristin Z, Exec Dir, Wenham Museum, 132 Main St, Wenham, MA, 01984. Tel: 978-468-2377. p. 1064

Noonan, Cathy, Br Mgr, Fairfax County Public Library, Martha Washington Branch, 6614 Fort Hunt Rd, Alexandria, VA, 22307-1799. Tel: 703-768-6700. p. 2316

Noonan, Claudia, Ref Librn, Marshfield Clinic, 1000 N Oak Ave, Marshfield, WI, 54449. Tel: 715-389-3532. p. 2454

Noonan, Jennifer, Ch, Prog Coordr, Lewes Public Library, 111 Adams Ave, Lewes, DE, 19958. Tel: 302-645-2733. p. 354

Noonan, Kathryn, Dir, Libr Serv, Lemuel Shattuck Hospital, 170 Morton St, Jamaica Plain, MA, 02130. Tel: 617-971-3225. p. 1026

Noonburg, Tess, Research & Archives Librn, Richmont Graduate University, 1900 The Exchange SE, Bldg 100, Atlanta, GA, 30339. Tel: 404-835-6137. p. 466

Noone, Lynne, Commun Libr Mgr, Contra Costa County Library, San Pablo Library, 13751 San Pablo Ave, San Pablo, CA, 94806. Tel: 510-374-3998. p. 175

Noorhani, Piret, Head Archivist, Tartu Institute, 310 Bloor St W, Toronto, ON, M5S 1W4, CANADA. Tel: 416-925-9405. p. 2693

Noorwood, Sherrie C, Systems & Metadata Librn, University of Arkansas at Little Rock, William H Bowen School of Law / Pulaski County Law Library, 1201 McMath Ave, Little Rock, AR, 72202. Tel: 501-916-5446. p. 102

Norberg, Lisa, Libr Dir, Cooper Union for Advancement of Science & Art Library, Seven E Seventh St, New York, NY, 10003. Tel: 212-353-4187. p. 1584

Norborg, Heather, Asst Dir, Evanston Public Library, 1703 Orrington, Evanston, IL, 60201. Tel: 847-448-8600. p. 586

Norbury, Chris, Mr, Ch, Tumbler Ridge Public Library, 340 Front St, Tumbler Ridge, BC, V0C 2W0, CANADA. Tel: 250-242-4778. p. 2578

Norcross, Mary, AV Tech, Per, Dine College, One Circle Dr, Rte 12, Tsaile, AZ, 86556. Tel: 928-724-6757. p. 80

Norcross-Love, April, Br Supvr, Guelph Public Library, East Side Branch, One Starwood Dr, Guelph, ON, N1E 0H5, CANADA. Tel: 519-829-4405. p. 2643

Norcutt, Hannah, Br Mgr, Hickory Public Library, Ridgeview, 706 First St SW, Hickory, NC, 28602. Tel: 828-345-6037. p. 1696

Nord, Lucinda, Exec Dir, Indiana Library Federation, 941 E 86th St, Ste 260, Indianapolis, IN, 46240. Tel: 317-257-2040, Ext 101. p. 2765

Nordberg, Erik, Dean, University of Tennessee at Martin, Ten Wayne Fisher Dr, Martin, TN, 38238. Tel: 731-881-7070. p. 2111

Norden, Emma Q, Librn, New Haven Museum & Historical Society, 114 Whitney Ave, New Haven, CT, 06510-1025. Tel: 203-562-4183, Ext 115. p. 326

Norden, Laurie, Fiscal Officer, Napoleon Public Library, 310 W Clinton St, Napoleon, OH, 43545. Tel: 419-592-2531. p. 1805

Nordin, Andy, Syst Adminr, East Central Regional Library, 111 Dellwood St, Cambridge, MN, 55008-1588. Tel: 763-689-7390. p. 1167

Nordmann, Stephanie, Adminr, Support Serv, Saint Louis County Library, 1640 S Lindbergh Blvd, Saint Louis, MO, 63131-3598. Tel: 314-994-3300, Ext 2220. p. 1273

Nordmeyer, Marcia, Circ & Ref Asst, Union College Library, 3800 S 48th St, Lincoln, NE, 68506-4386. Tel: 402-486-2600, Ext 2151. p. 1323

Nordon-Parks, Kim, Br Mgr, Pasco County Library System, South Holiday Branch, 4649 Mile Stretch Rd, Holiday, FL, 34690. Tel: 727-834-3331. p. 410

Nordstrom, Gail, Pub Libr Consult, Viking Library System, 1915 Fir Ave W, Fergus Falls, MN, 56537. Tel: 218-739-5286. p. 1175

Nordt, Dustin, Youth Serv, Farmers Branch Manske Library, 13613 Webb Chapel Rd, Farmers Branch, TX, 75234. Tel: 972-919-9813. p. 2176

Norenberg, Bethany, Br Mgr, Cass Lake Community Library, 223 Cedar, Cass Lake, MN, 56633. Tel: 218-335-8865. p. 1169

Norgren, Dianne, Dir, Platteville Public Library, 504 Marion Ave, Platteville, CO, 80651. Tel: 970-785-2231. p. 293

Norheim, Gwen, Sr Knowledge Mgmt Specialist, American Pharmacists Association Library, 2215 Constitution Ave, Washington, DC, 20037. Tel: 202-429-7524. p. 360

Nori, Uma, Head, Youth Serv, Thomas Ford Memorial Library, 800 Chestnut St, Western Springs, IL, 60558. Tel: 708-246-0520. p. 661

Noriega, Ana, Head, Coll, Colby College Libraries, 5100 Mayflower Hill, Waterville, ME, 04901. Tel: 207-859-5142. p. 945

Noriega, Tessa, Circ, Cañada College Library, Bldg 9, 3rd Flr, 4200 Farm Hill Blvd, Redwood City, CA, 94061-1099. p. 200

Norko, Catherine, Librn, Charles W Gibson Public Library, 105 E Main St, Buckhannon, WV, 26201. Tel: 304-472-2339. p. 2399

Norko, Paul, Dir, Upshur County Public Library, 1150 Rte 20 South Rd, Buckhannon, WV, 26201. Tel: 304-473-4219. p. 2399

Norling, Jane, Libr Dir, Beresford Public Library, 115 S Third St, Beresford, SD, 57004. Tel: 605-763-2782. p. 2074

Norman, Amy, Ref & Instruction Librn, Tulsa Community College Libraries, Southeast Campus, 10300 E 81st St, Tulsa, OK, 74133-4513. Tel: 918-595-7702. p. 1867

Norman, Amy, Librn, Calhoun County Public Library, 250 Mill St N, Grantsville, WV, 26147. Tel: 304-354-6300. p. 2403

Norman, Angela, Libr Dir, Grangeville Centennial Library, 215 W North St, Grangeville, ID, 83530. Tel: 208-983-0951. p. 521

Norman, Annie, Dr, Dir, State of Delaware, 121 Martin Luther King Jr Blvd N, Dover, DE, 19901. Tel: 302-257-3001. p. 352

Norman, Carolyn, Dean, Sierra College Library, 5100 Sierra College Blvd, Rocklin, CA, 95677. Tel: 916-660-7230. p. 203

Norman, Cathy, Ad, Fairport Harbor Public Library, 335 Vine St, Fairport Harbor, OH, 44077-5799. Tel: 440-354-8191, Ext 6526. p. 1785

Norman, Dana, Dir, Maxfield Public Library, 8 Rte 129, Loudon, NH, 03307. Tel: 603-798-5153. p. 1371

Norman, Elizabeth, Univ Librn, Hardin-Simmons University, 2200 Hickory St, Abilene, TX, 79698. Tel: 325-670-1236. p. 2132

Norman, Gary, Mgr, Village Library of Morris, 152 Main St, Morris, NY, 13808. Tel: 607-263-2080. p. 1574

Norman, Jeffrey, Music Libr Mgr, Arizona State University Libraries, Music, Music Bldg, 50 E Gammage Pk, Tempe, AZ, 85287. Tel: 480-965-4270. p. 79

Norman, Jenine, Head Librn, Parkland Regional Library-Manitoba, Ochre River Branch, 203 Mann St, Ochre River, MB, R0L 1K0, CANADA. Tel: 204-733-2293. p. 2587

Norman, Julie, Libr Coord, Georgia Northwestern Technical College, Whitfield Murray Campus Library, Bldg B101, 2310 Maddox Chapel Rd, Dalton, GA, 30721. Tel: 706-272-2941. p. 494

Norman, Kristy, Pub Support Serv Coordr, Derby Public Library, 1600 E Walnut Grove, Derby, KS, 67037. Tel: 316-788-0760. p. 804

Norman, Liz, Children's Coordr, Edgecombe County Memorial Library, 909 N Main St, Tarboro, NC, 27886. Tel: 252-823-1141. p. 1718

Norman, Michael, Interim Head of Libr, University of Illinois Library at Urbana-Champaign, Mathematics, 216 Altgeld Hall, 1409 W Green St, Urbana, IL, 61801. Tel: 217-333-8350. p. 656

Norman, Ola K, Br Mgr, Wilkes County Public Library, Traphill Branch, 6938 Traphill Rd, Traphill, NC, 28685. Tel: 336-957-2534. p. 1707

Norman, Robina, Br Mgr, Beaufort, Hyde & Martin County Regional Library, Hazel W Guilford Memorial, 524 E Main St, Aurora, NC, 27806. Tel: 252-322-5046. p. 1720

Norman, Steve, Libr Dir, Belfast Free Library, 106 High St, Belfast, ME, 04915. Tel: 207-338-3884. p. 916

Norman, Trish, Colls Mgr, Arizona Historical Society, 949 E Second St, Tucson, AZ, 85719. Tel: 520-617-1179. p. 81

Normandin, Brittany, Libr Tech, James White Memorial Library, Five Washburn Rd E, East Freetown, MA, 02717-1220. Tel: 508-763-5344. p. 1016

Nosko, Nancy, Tech Asst, West Virginia Northern Community College Library, Weirton Campus, 150 Park Ave, Weirton, WV, 26062-2797. Tel: 304-723-2210, Ext 4609. p. 2418

Nossett, Denise, Sr Librn, Los Angeles Public Library System, Wilmington Branch Library, 1300 N Avalon Blvd, Wilmington, CA, 90744. Tel: 310-834-1082. p. 166

Notarangelo, Maria, Librn, San Bernardino Valley College Library, 701 S Mount Vernon Ave, San Bernardino, CA, 92410. Tel: 909-384-8576. p. 214

Notenboom, Leanne, Mgr, Res Serv, Blake, Cassels & Graydon LLP, Commerce Ct W, 199 Bay St, Ste 4000, Toronto, ON, M5L 1A9, CANADA. Tel: 416-863-2650. p. 2686

Notley, Sunya, Ref & Instruction Librn, Alliance University, Two Washington St, New York, NY, 10004-1008. Tel: 646-378-6100, Ext 7707. p. 1578

Nott, Philip, Dir, Criswell College, 4010 Gaston Ave, Dallas, TX, 75246. Tel: 214-818-1378. p. 2163

Nouri, Sara, Assoc Law Librn, Harris County Robert W Hainsworth Law Library, Congress Plaza, 1019 Congress, 1st Flr, Houston, TX, 77002. Tel: 713-755-5183. p. 2191

Novacescu, Jenny, Chief Librn, Space Telescope Science Institute Library, 3700 San Martin Dr, Baltimore, MD, 21218. Tel: 410-338-4961. p. 956

Novak, Christopher, Head, Info Tech, San Francisco State University, 1630 Holloway Ave, San Francisco, CA, 94132-4030. Tel: 415-338-1854. p. 228

Novak, Frank, Dir, Huntley Area Public Library District, 11000 Ruth Rd, Huntley, IL, 60142-7155. Tel: 847-669-5386. p. 601

Novak, Matt, Ref (Info Servs), University of Nebraska-Lincoln, Marvin & Virginia Schmid Law Library, 1875 N 42nd St, Lincoln, NE, 68583. Tel: 402-472-3547. p. 1323

Novak, Michael, Campus Librn, Front Range Community College, 2190 Miller Dr, Longmont, CO, 80501. Tel: 303-678-3720, 303-678-3721. p. 290

Novak, Stephen, Head, Archives & Spec Coll, Columbia University, Augustus C Long Health Sciences Library, 701 W 168th St, Lobby Level, New York, NY, 10032. Tel: 212-305-3605. p. 1583

Novalis, Jenny, Libr Dir, Bedford Public Library System, 321 N Bridge St, Bedford, VA, 24523-1924. Tel: 540-586-8911, Ext 1140. p. 2306

Novara, Vincent J, Curator, University of Maryland Libraries, Michelle Smith Performing Arts Library, 8270 Alumni Dr, College Park, MD, 20742-1630. Tel: 301-405-9220. p. 963

Novell, Megan E, Head, Circulation & User Servs, University of Detroit Mercy Libraries, 4001 W McNichols Rd, Detroit, MI, 48221-3038. Tel: 313-993-1070. p. 1099

Novelo, Laura, Asst Dir, Lucas County Law Library, Lucas County Family Court Ctr, 905 Jackson St, Toledo, OH, 43604-5512. Tel: 419-213-4747. p. 1824

Novicki, Elizabeth, Dir of Libr, Salem College, 626 S Church St, Winston-Salem, NC, 27101. Tel: 336-917-5417. p. 1725

Novin, Dolores, Circ, McCowan Memorial Library, 15 Pitman Ave, Pitman, NJ, 08071. Tel: 856-589-1656. p. 1435

Novitt, Adam, Dir, Lilly Library, 19 Meadow St, Florence, MA, 01062. Tel: 413-587-1500. p. 1019

Novoa, Vincent, Head, Access Serv, University of California, Riverside, 900 University Ave, Riverside, CA, 92521. Tel: 951-827-3220. p. 203

Novosad, Matt, Adult Serv, Asst Librn II, Ledyard Public Library, Gales Ferry Library, 18 Hurlbutt Rd, Gales Ferry, CT, 06335. Tel: 860-464-9912. p. 320

Novosad, Matthew, Adult Serv, Asst Librn II, Ledyard Public Library, 718 Colonel Ledyard Hwy, Ledyard, CT, 06339. Tel: 860-464-9912. p. 319

Novotny, Allana, Tech & Access Serv Librn, Nebraska Library Commission, The Atrium, 1200 N St, Ste 120, Lincoln, NE, 68508-2023. Tel: 402-471-6681. p. 1322

Novotny, Heidi, Libr Mgr, San Antonio Public Library, Brook Hollow, 530 Heimer Rd, San Antonio, TX, 78232. Tel: 210-207-9030. p. 2238

Novotny, Jessica, Adult Serv, Herrick Memorial Library, 101 Willard Memorial Sq, Wellington, OH, 44090-1342. Tel: 440-647-2120. p. 1829

Novotny, Tom, Library Contact, National Academy of Social Insurance, 1441 L St NW, Ste 530, Washington, DC, 20005. Tel: 202-452-8097. p. 371

Novy, Jim, IT Mgr, Prairie Lakes Library System (PLLS), 29134 Evergreen Dr, Ste 600, Waterford, WI, 53185. Tel: 262-514-4500, Ext 65. p. 2483

Nowak, Barbara, Dir, Mount Hope Public Library, 109 S Ohio St, Mount Hope, KS, 67108. Tel: 316-667-2665. p. 826

Nowak, Bonnie, ILL, Huntington Beach Public Library System, 7111 Talbert Ave, Huntington Beach, CA, 92648. Tel: 714-842-4481. p. 151

Nowak, Christopher, Head, Bus Serv, Mastics-Moriches-Shirley Community Library, 407 William Floyd Pkwy, Shirley, NY, 11967. Tel: 631-399-1511. p. 1640

Nowak, Ingrid, Br Mgr, Cambridge Public Library, O'Connell Branch, 48 Sixth St, Cambridge, MA, 02141. Tel: 617-349-4019. p. 1004

Nowak, Izabela, Dir, Myers Memorial Library, Six Falconer St, Frewsburg, NY, 14738. Tel: 716-569-5515. p. 1535

Nowak, Kathy, Circ Librn, Young Men's Library Association Library, 37 Main St, Ware, MA, 01082-1317. p. 1062

Nowak, Rose, Libr Assoc/Teen Serv, Morris Area Public Library District, 604 Liberty St, Morris, IL, 60450. Tel: 815-942-6880. p. 619

Noward, Karen, Head, Circ & Adult Serv, Evergreen Community Library, 253 Maple St, Metamora, OH, 43540. Tel: 419-644-2771. p. 1802

Nowell, Dea, Tech Serv Mgr, Umatilla County Special Library District, 425 S Main St, Pendleton, OR, 97801. Tel: 541-966-0917. p. 1890

Nowell, Garnet, Tech Serv Librn, Northeastern State University, Broken Arrow Campus Library, 3100 E New Orleans St, Broken Arrow, OK, 74014. Tel: 918-449-6459. p. 1863

Nowell, Michelle C, Evening Supvr, Columbus State University Libraries, Music Library, 900 Broadway, Columbus, GA, 31901-2735. Tel: 706-641-4025. p. 472

Nowell, Rachel, Br Mgr, Saint Louis County Library, Florissant Valley Branch, 195 New Florissant Rd S, Florissant, MO, 63031-6796. Tel: 314-994-3300, Ext 3250. p. 1273

Nowels, Nieca, Dir, Marysville Public Library, 231 S Plum St, Marysville, OH, 43040-1596. Tel: 937-642-1876, Ext 33. p. 1800

Nowels, Nieca, Dir, Marysville Public Library, Raymond Branch, 21698 Main St, Raymond, OH, 43067. Tel: 937-246-4795. p. 1800

Nowesnick, Monica A, Mgr, Franciscan Health Crown Point, 1201 S Main St, Crown Point, IN, 46307. Tel: 219-757-6345. p. 678

Nowicki, Stacy, Dr, Libr Dir, Kalamazoo College Library, 1200 Academy St, Kalamazoo, MI, 49006-3285. Tel: 269-337-5750. p. 1121

Nowlin, Bridget, Dir, Libr Serv, Cornish College of the Arts Library, 1000 Lenora St, Seattle, WA, 98121. Tel: 206-726-5041. p. 2376

Nowling, B Michelle, Exec Dir, Ravalli County Museum, 205 Bedford St, Hamilton, MT, 59840. Tel: 406-363-3338. p. 1295

Nowroozian, Bijan, Sr Librn, Pierce County Library System, Parkland-Spanaway Branch, 13718 Pacific Ave S, Tacoma, WA, 98444. Tel: 253-548-3304. p. 2386

Nowroozian, Dorothy, Librn, California Department of Corrections Library System, Richard J Donovan Correctional Facility at Rock Mountain, 480 Alta Rd, San Diego, CA, 92179. Tel: 619-661-6500. p. 206

Nowviskie, Bethany, Dean of Libr, James Madison University Libraries, 880 Madison Dr, MSC 1704, Harrisonburg, VA, 22807. Tel: 540-568-6150. p. 2324

Noyce, Linda, Division Head, Public Services, Kenosha Public Library, 7979 38th Ave, Kenosha, WI, 53142. Tel: 262-564-6100. p. 2444

Noyd, Pam, Info Res Mgr, Foley & Lardner, 777 E Wisconsin Ave, Milwaukee, WI, 53202-5306. Tel: 414-271-2400. p. 2458

Noyes, Esther, ILL, Anacortes Public Library, 1220 Tenth St, Anacortes, WA, 98221-1988. Tel: 360-293-1910, Ext 25. p. 2357

Noyes, Jonathan, Head, Circ, Berlin-Peck Memorial Library, 234 Kensington Rd, Berlin, CT, 06037. Tel: 860-828-7119. p. 302

Nsilo-Swai, Fyiane, Ref & Instruction Librn, Quinebaug Valley Community College Library, 742 Upper Maple St, Danielson, CT, 06239. Tel: 860-932-4056. p. 308

Nubern, Nancy, Libr Mgr, Pembroke Public Library, 1018 Camelia Dr, Pembroke, GA, 31321. Tel: 912-653-2822. p. 493

Nuckells, Todd, Pub Serv Librn, Wake Technical Community College, Scott Northern Wake Library, 6600 Louisburg Rd, NF 241, Raleigh, NC, 27616. Tel: 919-532-5550. p. 1711

Nuding, Cathy, Youth Serv Librn, East Fishkill Community Library, 348 Rte 376, Hopewell Junction, NY, 12533-6075. Tel: 845-221-9943, Ext 233. p. 1548

Nuelle, Shannon, Dir, Cavalier County Library, 600 Fifth Ave, Langdon, ND, 58249. Tel: 701-256-5353. p. 1737

Nugent, Bryan, Libr Serv Dir, Banner - University Medical Center - Phoenix, 1111 E McDowell Rd, Phoenix, AZ, 85006. Tel: 602-839-4353. p. 69

Nugent, Debbie, Br Mgr, Grant Parish Library, Georgetown Branch, 4570 Hwy 500, Georgetown, LA, 71432. Tel: 318-827-9427. p. 887

Nugent, Jeny, Syst Librn, University of Indianapolis, 1400 E Hanna Ave, Indianapolis, IN, 46227-3697. Tel: 317-788-3268. p. 697

Nugent, Michael, Libr Assoc/Tech Serv, Ref Librn, University of Texas at Austin, 3925 W Braker Lane, Ste 4.909, Austin, TX, 78759. Tel: 512-232-3126. p. 2141

Nugent, Rebecca, Coll Develop, West Hartford Public Library, 20 S Main St, West Hartford, CT, 06107-2432. Tel: 860-561-6950. p. 345

Nugent, Sara, Dir, Tappan Library, 93 Main St, Tappan, NY, 10983. Tel: 845-359-3877. p. 1651

Nugent, Trish, Coordr, Archives & Spec Coll, Loyola University New Orleans, 6363 Saint Charles Ave, New Orleans, LA, 70118. Tel: 504-864-7111. p. 902

Nui, Jeffrey, Res Asst, New York Legislative Service, Inc Library, 120 Broadway, Ste 920, New York, NY, 10271. Tel: 212-962-2826, 212-962-2827, 212-962-2828. p. 1594

Nulph, Christopher, Libr Mgr, New Orleans Public Library, East New Orleans Regional Library, 5641 Read Blvd, New Orleans, LA, 70127-3105. Tel: 504-596-0200. p. 903

Nulph, Christopher, Libr Mgr, Richland Public Library, 955 Northgate Dr, Richland, WA, 99352. Tel: 509-942-7454. p. 2375

Numa, Terry, Head, Children's Servx, Mamaroneck Public Library, 136 Prospect Ave, Mamaroneck, NY, 10543. Tel: 914-698-1250. p. 1568

Nummela-Hanel, Bethany, Digital Initiatives Librn, Olivet Nazarene University, One University Ave, Bourbonnais, IL, 60914-2271. Tel: 815-939-5145. p. 544

Nunes, Charlotte, Interim Dean of Libr, Lafayette College, 710 Sullivan Rd, Easton, PA, 18042-1797. Tel: 610-330-5151. p. 1928

Nunes, Patricia, Tech Serv Librn, Oklahoma Historical Society, Oklahoma History Ctr, 800 Nazih Zuhdi Dr, Oklahoma City, OK, 73105. Tel: 405-522-4025. p. 1859
Nunez, Annabelle, Assoc Dir, University of Arizona Libraries, Health Sciences Library, 1501 N Campbell Ave, Tucson, AZ, 85724. Tel: 520-626-3660. p. 83
Nunez, Deliz, Librn II, Arizona Department of Corrections, 6911 N BDI Blvd, Douglas, AZ, 85608. Tel: 520-364-7521, Ext 34522. p. 59
Nunez, Katia, Assoc Dir, Learning Res, Miami Dade College, Wolfson Campus Library, 300 NE Second Ave, Miami, FL, 33132. Tel: 305-237-7385. p. 422
Nunez, Max, Ch, New Hanover County Public Library, Northeast Regional Library, 1241 Military Cutoff Rd, Wilmington, NC, 28405. Tel: 910-798-6376. p. 1723
Nunez, Robert, Division Head, Support Services, Kenosha Public Library, 7979 38th Ave, Kenosha, WI, 53142. Tel: 262-564-6100. p. 2444
Nunley, Ashley, Literacy Coordr, Prog Dir, Donald W Reynolds Community Center & Library, 1515 W Main St, Durant, OK, 74701. Tel: 580-924-3486, 580-931-0231. p. 1846
Nunley, Ben, Pub Serv Mgr, Boyd County Public Library, 1740 Central Ave, Ashland, KY, 41101. Tel: 606-329-0090. p. 847
Nunley, Ben, Pub Serv Mgr, Boyd County Public Library, Catlettsburg Branch, 2704 Louisa St, Catlettsburg, KY, 41129. Tel: 606-329-0518, Ext 1210. p. 847
Nunley, Ben, Pub Serv Mgr, Boyd County Public Library, Midland Branch, 6686 US Rte 60, Ashland, KY, 41102. Tel: 606-329-0518, Ext 1210. p. 848
Nunley, Erin, Library Contact, St Thomas Health Services Library, 2000 Church St, Nashville, TN, 37236. Tel: 615-222-3051, 615-284-5373. p. 2120
Nunley, Kellie, Tech Serv Supvr, Boyd County Public Library, 1740 Central Ave, Ashland, KY, 41101. Tel: 606-329-0090. p. 847
Nunley, Sandy, Asst Dir, Marion County Public Library, 201 E Main St, Lebanon, KY, 40033-1133. Tel: 270-692-4698. p. 861
Nunn, Dana, Acq & Cat, IU Ball Memorial Hospital, 2401 W University Ave, Muncie, IN, 47303-3499. Tel: 765-747-4470. p. 708
Nunn-Smith, Ashley, Chief Librn, South Shore Public Libraries, 135 North Park St, Unit B, Bridgewater, NS, B4V 9B3, CANADA. Tel: 902-543-2548. p. 2616
Nunnally, Tori, Br Mgr, Richmond Public Library, Westover Hills, 1408 Westover Hills Blvd, Richmond, VA, 23225. Tel: 804-646-8833. p. 2342
Nunziato, Debbie, Pub Relations Mgr, Chillicothe & Ross County Public Library, 140 S Paint St, Chillicothe, OH, 45601. Tel: 740-702-4145. p. 1758
Nurbrum, Karen, Br Coordr, Lennox & Addington County Public Library, Tamworth Branch, One Ottawa St, Tamworth, ON, K0K 3G0, CANADA. Tel: 613-379-3082. p. 2660
Nureddin, Najla, Libr Tech, Waterloo Region Law Association, 85 Frederick St, Kitchener, ON, N2H 0A7, CANADA. Tel: 519-742-0872. p. 2652
Nurse, Carol, Ref Librn, Montclair State University, One Normal Ave, Montclair, NJ, 07043-1699. Tel: 973-655-7667. p. 1420
Nurse, Julie, Libr Dir, Centralia College, 600 Centralia College Blvd, Centralia, WA, 98531. Tel: 360-623-8567. p. 2361
Nusbaum, Lynn, Exec Dir, Temple - Congregation Shomer Emunim Library, 6453 Sylvania Ave, Sylvania, OH, 43560. Tel: 419-885-3341. p. 1823
Nusco, Kimberly, Asst Librn, Res & Ref Serv, Brown University, John Carter Brown Library, Brown University, 94 George St, Providence, RI, 02906. Tel: 401-863-2725. p. 2037
Nuss, Katherine, Mgr, Info & Archive Serv, United States Conference of Catholic Bishops -Catholic News Service, 3211 Fourth St NE, Washington, DC, 20017-1194. Tel: 202-541-3286. p. 377
Nussbaum, Katherine, Libr Spec, University of Pittsburgh at Bradford, 300 Campus Dr, Bradford, PA, 16701. Tel: 814-362-7619. p. 1914
Nussbaumer, Alison, Dir, Libr Serv, British Columbia Institute of Technology Library, 3700 Willingdon Ave, SE14, Burnaby, BC, V5G 3H2, CANADA. Tel: 604-432-8370. p. 2563
Nutefall, Jennifer, Dean of Libr, University of Northern Colorado Libraries, 1400 22nd Ave, Greeley, CO, 80631. Tel: 970-351-2671. p. 285
Nutefall, Jennifer, Dean, Libr & Mus, Saint Louis University, 3650 Lindell Blvd, Saint Louis, MO, 63108-3302. Tel: 314-977-3087. p. 1275
Nuth, Alana, Head, Coll Mgt, State University of New York College, SUNY Geneseo, One College Circle, Geneseo, NY, 14454-1498. Tel: 585-245-5594. p. 1537
Nutley, Becky, Dir, Viborg Public Library, 114 N Main St, Viborg, SD, 57070. Tel: 605-326-5481. p. 2085
Nuttall, Harry, Ref Librn, Jacksonville State University Library, 700 Pelham Rd N, Jacksonville, AL, 36265. Tel: 256-782-5758. p. 23
Nutter, Charlotte, Electronic Res Librn, Reserves Librn, Denver Seminary, 6399 S Santa Fe Dr, Littleton, CO, 80120. Tel: 303-762-6962. p. 290
Nutter, Ed, Circ, Fairmont State University, 1201 Locust Ave, Fairmont, WV, 26554. Tel: 304-367-4733. p. 2402
Nutzman, Erica, Head, Tech Serv, Minnesota State Law Library, Minnesota Judicial Ctr, Rm G25, 25 Rev Dr Martin Luther King Jr Blvd, Saint Paul, MN, 55155. Tel: 651-297-2090. p. 1201
Nuvayestewa, Grace, Libr Spec, Institute of American Indian Arts Library, 83 Avan Nu Po Rd, Santa Fe, NM, 87508. Tel: 505-424-2398. p. 1474
Nwachuku, Ugochi, Ref Librn, Lincoln University, 1570 Baltimore Pike, Lincoln University, PA, 19352. Tel: 484-365-7350. p. 1956
Nyberg, Cheryl, Librn, Digital Initiatives, University of Washington Libraries, Gallagher Law Library, William H Gates Hall, 4000 15th Ave NE, Seattle, WA, 98195-3020. Tel: 206-685-4924. p. 2382
Nyce, Lori, Librn, Train Collectors Association, 300 Paradise Lane, Ronks, PA, 17572. Tel: 717-687-8623, Ext 108. p. 2002
Nyce, Lori A, Head, Coll & Tech Serv, Lebanon Valley College, 101 N College Ave, Annville, PA, 17003-1400. Tel: 717-867-6971. p. 1906
Nycum, James, Librn, Martin Correctional Institution Library, 1150 SW Allapattah Rd, Indiantown, FL, 34956. Tel: 772-597-3705. p. 411
Nycum, Peter S, Dir, Lewis & Clark College, Paul L Boley Law Library, Lewis & Clark Law School, 10015 SW Terwilliger Blvd, Portland, OR, 97219. Tel: 503-768-6776. p. 1891
Nye, Ashly, Co-Dir, Glover Spencer Memorial Library, 100 S Sixth St, Corner SE Sixth & Blakely Ave, Rush Springs, OK, 73082. Tel: 580-476-2108. p. 1861
Nye, August, ILL Librn, Brevard College, One Brevard College Dr, Brevard, NC, 28712-4283. Tel: 828-641-0954. p. 1675
Nye, Beth, Librn, Sheldon Municipal Library, 1640 Main St, Sheldon, VT, 05483. Tel: 802-933-2524, 802-933-2524, Ext 7. p. 2294
Nye, Shelli, Dir, Church of Jesus Christ of Latter-Day Saints-Philadelphia, 721 Paxon Hollow Rd, Broomall, PA, 19008. Tel: 610-356-8507. p. 1915
Nye, Valeria, Libr Dir, Santa Fe Community College Library, 6401 Richards Ave, Santa Fe, NM, 87508-4887. Tel: 505-428-1506. p. 1476
Nye, Valerie, Pres, New Mexico Consortium of Academic Libraries, c/o UNM-Taos Library, 1157 County Rd 110, Ranchos de Taos, NM, 87557. Tel: 505-428-1506. p. 2770
Nyer, Shoshana, Exec Dir, Librn, Suburban Temple - Kol Ami, 22401 Chagrin Blvd, Beachwood, OH, 44122-5345. Tel: 216-991-0700. p. 1749
Nylander, Elisabeth, Librn, Seattle Children's Hospital, 4800 Sand Point Way NE, OB.8.520, Seattle, WA, 98105. Tel: 206-987-2098. p. 2378
Nyman, Mary, Ch, Westbrook Public Library, 61 Goodspeed Dr, Westbrook, CT, 06498. Tel: 860-399-6422. p. 346
Nyquist, Benjamin, Circ Supvr, Regis College Library, 235 Wellesley St, Weston, MA, 02493. Tel: 781-768-7302. p. 1068
Nzediegwu, Blessing, Circ, Libr Tech, Lakeland College Library, 5707 College Dr, Vermilion, AB, T9X 1K5, CANADA. Tel: 780-853-8463. p. 2558
O'Bannon, Randall, Dr, Dir of Educ, Dir, Res Serv, National Right to Life Library, 512 Tenth St NW, Washington, DC, 20004. Tel: 202-626-8800. p. 373
O'Barto, Danielle, Dir, Libr Serv, Ottawa University, 1001 S Cedar St, Ottawa, KS, 66067. p. 829
O'Brian, Katie, School Services Librn, Fremont Public Library District, 1170 N Midlothian Rd, Mundelein, IL, 60060. Tel: 847-566-8702. p. 622
O'Brian, Katie, Head, Youth Serv, Prospect Heights Public Library District, 12 N Elm St, Prospect Heights, IL, 60070-1450. Tel: 847-259-3500. p. 637
O'Brien, Anita, Libr Dir, Little Silver Public Library, 484 Prospect Ave, Little Silver, NJ, 07739. Tel: 732-747-9649. p. 1413
O'Brien, Bill, Head of Libr, Public Libraries of Saginaw, Zauel Memorial Library, 3100 N Center Rd, Saginaw, MI, 48603. Tel: 989-799-2771. p. 1147
O'Brien, Brendan, Sister, Univ Archivist, Holy Family University Library, 9801 Frankford Ave, Philadelphia, PA, 19114. Tel: 267-341-3414. p. 1981
O'Brien, Cortni, Ad, Columbia Heights Public Library, 3939 Central Ave NE, Columbia Heights, MN, 55421. Tel: 763-706-3690. p. 1170
O'Brien, Daniel, Electronic Res Librn, Ashland University Library, 509 College Ave, Ashland, OH, 44805. Tel: 419-289-5146. p. 1747
O'Brien, David, Head, Access Serv, Hope College, Van Wylen Library, 53 Graves Pl, Holland, MI, 49422. Tel: 616-395-7791. p. 1115
O'Brien, DeAnne, Adult Serv, Indian Valley Public Library, 100 E Church Ave, Telford, PA, 18969. Tel: 215-723-9109. p. 2012
O'Brien, Debora, Dir, New Marlborough Town Library, One Mill River Great Barrington Rd, Mill River, MA, 01244-0239. Tel: 413-229-6668. p. 1035
O'Brien Dermott, Maureen, Assoc Dir, Access Serv, Dickinson College, 28 N College St, Carlisle, PA, 17013-2311. Tel: 717-245-1397. p. 1919
O'Brien, Diane, Committee Chair, All Souls Unitarian Church, 5805 E 56th St, Indianapolis, IN, 46226-1526. Tel: 317-545-6005. p. 690
O'Brien, Elizabeth, Public Affairs Mgr, Smithsonian Libraries, Natural History Bldg, Tenth St & Constitution Ave NW, Washington, DC, 20560. Tel: 203-633-1522. p. 375
O'Brien, Ellen, Ch Serv, Warwick Public Library, 600 Sandy Lane, Warwick, RI, 02889-8298. Tel: 401-739-5440, Ext 9748. p. 2043
O'Brien, Eve, Youth Serv Librn, Department of Human Services-Youth Corrections, 13500 E Fremont Pl, Englewood, CO, 80112. Tel: 303-768-7529, 303-768-7597. p. 279
O'Brien, Glenda, Senior Reference Tech, Gowling WLG (Canada) Library, One First Canadian Pl, 100 King St W, Ste 1600, Toronto, ON, M5X 1G5, CANADA. Tel: 416-862-5735. p. 2689
O'Brien, Heather, Prof, University of British Columbia, The Irving K Barber Learning Ctr, 1961 E Mall, Ste 470, Vancouver, BC, V6T 1Z1, CANADA. Tel: 604-822-2404. p. 2795
O'Brien, Jackie, Asst Dir, Rogers Free Library, 525 Hope St, Bristol, RI, 02809. Tel: 401-253-6948. p. 2030

O'Brien Jenks, Kelly, Instruction Coordr, Gonzaga University, 502 E Boone Ave, Spokane, WA, 99258-0095. Tel: 509-313-3829. p. 2383

O'Brien, Jennifer, Ser Librn, Western Connecticut State University, 181 White St, Danbury, CT, 06810. Tel: 203-837-9100. p. 307

O'Brien, Jessica, Coordr, Instrul Tech, Lenoir-Rhyne University Libraries, 625 7th Ave NE, Hickory, NC, 28601. Tel: 828-328-7236. p. 1696

O'Brien, Julie, Dir, Menlo Public Library, Menlo Community Bldg, 504 Fifth St, Menlo, IA, 50164. Tel: 641-524-4201. p. 769

O'Brien, Kaley, Youth Serv Librn, Whistler Public Library, 4329 Main St, Whistler, BC, V8E 1B2, CANADA. Tel: 604-935-8433. p. 2584

O'Brien, Karen L, Libr Dir, Raynham Public Library, 760 S Main St, Raynham, MA, 02767. Tel: 508-823-1344. p. 1049

O'Brien, Kate, Br Supvr, Marion County Public Library System, Dunnellon Public Library, 20351 Robinson Rd, Dunnellon, FL, 34431. Tel: 352-438-2520. p. 430

O'Brien, Leslie, Dir, Commun & Tech Serv, Virginia Polytechnic Institute & State University Libraries, 560 Drillfield Dr, Blacksburg, VA, 24061. Tel: 540-231-4945. p. 2307

O'Brien, Linda, Dir, Bailey Memorial Library, 111 Moulton Ave, North Clarendon, VT, 05759-9327. Tel: 802-747-7743. p. 2290

O'Brien, Lisa, Dir, Communications & Develop, Saint Joseph County Public Library, 304 S Main St, South Bend, IN, 46601. Tel: 574-282-4646. p. 718

O'Brien, Lupita, Head, Youth Serv, Librn, Closter Public Library, 280 High St, Closter, NJ, 07624-1898. Tel: 201-768-4197. p. 1397

O'Brien, Mary Jane, Adult & Tech Serv Mgr, Bartlett Public Library District, 800 S Bartlett Rd, Bartlett, IL, 60103. Tel: 630-837-2855. p. 540

O'Brien, Mary Lee, Dir, Brantingham Greig Reading & Technology Center, 5186 Greig Rd, Greig, NY, 13345. Tel: 315-348-8272, Ext 5. p. 1542

O'Brien, Maryellen, Dir, Robeson Community College, Bldg 4, 5160 Fayetteville Rd, Lumberton, NC, 28360-2158. Tel: 910-272-3324. p. 1701

O'Brien, Maureen, Librn & Archivist, Massachusetts Horticultural Society Library, 900 Washington St, Rte 16, Wellesley, MA, 02482. Tel: 617-933-4900, 617-933-4912. p. 1063

O'Brien, Michael, Syst Coordr, University of San Diego, Helen K & James S Copley Library, 5998 Alcala Park, San Diego, CA, 92110. p. 222

O'Brien, Nancy, Head of Libr, University of Illinois Library at Urbana-Champaign, Social Sciences, Health & Education Library, 101 Main Library, MC-522, 1408 W Gregory Dr, Urbana, IL, 61801. Tel: 217-333-2408. p. 656

O'Brien, Nancy, Dir, Iowa Methodist Medical Center, 1200 Pleasant St, Des Moines, IA, 50309. Tel: 515-241-6490. p. 746

O'Brien, Rory, Coordr, Info Tech, Thomas Crane Public Library, 40 Washington St, Quincy, MA, 02269-9164. Tel: 617-376-1319. p. 1048

O'Brien, Sharon, Mem Serv Librn, Mohawk Valley Library System, 858 Duanesburg Rd, Schenectady, NY, 12306. Tel: 518-355-2010. p. 1638

O'Brien, Shelley, Local Hist Librn, Ref Serv, Melrose Public Library, 263 W Foster St, Melrose, MA, 02176. Tel: 781-665-2313. p. 1034

O'Brien, Sue, Asst Dir, Support Serv, Downers Grove Public Library, 1050 Curtiss St, Downers Grove, IL, 60515. Tel: 630-960-1200. p. 579

O'Brien, Susan, Cat, Quinnipiac University, 275 Mount Carmel Ave, Hamden, CT, 06518. Tel: 203-582-8634. p. 316

O'Brien, Suzanne, Dir, Jewish General Hospital, Hope & Cope Library, 3755 Cote Ste Catherine Rd, Montreal, QC, H3T 1E2, CANADA. Tel: 514-340-8255. p. 2725

O'Brien, Tara, Dir, Presv & Conserv, Historical Society of Pennsylvania, 1300 Locust St, Philadelphia, PA, 19107-5699. Tel: 215-732-6200, Ext 245. p. 1981

O'Brien, Theresa, Youth Serv Supvr, Catherine Schweinsberg Rood Central Library, 308 Forrest Ave, Cocoa, FL, 32922. Tel: 321-633-1792. p. 390

O'Brien, Wendy, Librn, Richmond Public Library, 19 Winchester Rd, Richmond, NH, 03470. Tel: 603-239-6164. p. 1379

O'Bryant, Katie, Libr Assoc, Louisiana State University Health Sciences Center, 1501 Kings Hwy, Shreveport, LA, 71130. Tel: 318-675-5446. p. 908

O'Byrne, Christopher, Research Librn, University of Notre Dame, 2345 Biolchini Hall of Law, Notre Dame, IN, 46556-4640. Tel: 574-631-5664. p. 712

O'Callaghan, Patricia, Librn, Carmelitana Collection, Whitefriars Hall, 1600 Webster St NE, Washington, DC, 20017. Tel: 202-526-1221, Ext 4. p. 362

O'Callaghan, Patricia, Librn, Society of Mount Carmel, Whitefriars Hall, 1600 Webster St NE, Washington, DC, 20017-3145. Tel: 202-526-1221, Ext 4. p. 376

O'Connell, Brendan, Dir, Res, Teaching & Learning, Smith College Libraries, Young Library, Four Tyler Dr, Northampton, MA, 01063. p. 1043

O'Connell, Cecilia, Head, Circ, Bacon Memorial District Library, 45 Vinewood, Wyandotte, MI, 48192-5221. Tel: 734-246-8357. p. 1160

O'Connell, Dan, Ref & Instruction Librn, Wentworth Institute of Technology, 550 Huntington Ave, Boston, MA, 02115-5998. Tel: 617-989-4096. p. 1000

O'Connell, Eileen, Sister, Communications Dir, St Walburg Monastery Archives, 2500 Amsterdam Rd, Covington, KY, 41017. Tel: 859-331-6771. p. 852

O'Connell, Heath, Mgr, Fermi National Accelerator Laboratory, Kirk & Wilson Sts, Batavia, IL, 60510. Tel: 630-840-3401. p. 540

O'Connell, Jane, Assoc Dir, University of Florida Libraries, Holland Law Ctr, 309 Village Dr, Gainesville, FL, 32611. Tel: 352-273-0715. p. 408

O'Connell, John, Archives, Tech, National Archives & Records Administration, 1000 Beal Ave, Ann Arbor, MI, 48109. Tel: 734-205-0559. p. 1079

O'Connell, Kathleen Mary, Assoc Dir, Pub Serv, Washington County Free Library, 100 S Potomac St, Hagerstown, MD, 21740. Tel: 301-739-3250. p. 968

O'Connell, Katie, Head Archivist, Harrison Memorial Library, Ocean Ave & Lincoln St, Carmel, CA, 93921. Tel: 831-624-1615. p. 128

O'Connell, Mary, Libr Dir, Northwest Community Hospital, 800 W Central Rd, Arlington Heights, IL, 60005-2392. Tel: 847-618-5180. p. 537

O'Connell, Mary, Ref & Instruction Librn, College of Lake County, 19351 W Washington St, Grayslake, IL, 60030. Tel: 847-543-2071. p. 595

O'Connell, Nancy, Librn, East Troy Lions Public Library, 3094 Graydon Ave, East Troy, WI, 53120. Tel: 262-642-6262. p. 2432

O'Connell, Peggy, Dir, Minocqua Public Library, 415 Menominee St, Minocqua, WI, 54548. Tel: 715-356-4437. p. 2462

O'Connell, Susan, Dir, Craftsbury Public Library, 12 Church St, Craftsbury Common, VT, 05827. Tel: 802-586-9683. p. 2282

O'Connell, Terence, Cat Librn, Northwestern University Libraries, Pritzker Legal Research Center, 375 E Chicago Ave, Chicago, IL, 60611. Tel: 312-503-7364. p. 587

O'Connor, Brian, Interim Dir, Libr Serv, North Country Community College Libraries, 23 Santanoni Ave, Saranac Lake, NY, 12983-2046. Tel: 518-891-2915, Ext 222. p. 1636

O'Connor, Brian C, Dr, Prof, University of North Texas, 3940 N Elm St, Ste E292, Denton, TX, 76207. Tel: 940-565-2445. p. 2793

O'Connor, Carin, Br Librn, Boston Public Library, Honan-Allston Branch, 300 N Harvard St, Allston, MA, 02134. Tel: 617-787-6313. p. 992

O'Connor, Daragh, Mr, Dir, River Edge Free Public Library, 685 Elm Ave, River Edge, NJ, 07661. Tel: 201-261-1663. p. 1439

O'Connor, Diane, Library Contact, Ticonderoga Historical Society Library, Hancock House, Six Moses Circle, Ticonderoga, NY, 12883. Tel: 518-585-7868. p. 1651

O'Connor, Helene, Coll Develop Librn, Palmer Public Library, 1455 N Main St, Palmer, MA, 01069. Tel: 413-283-3330. p. 1045

O'Connor, Katie, Adult Serv, Libr Supvr, Tempe Public Library, 3500 S Rural Rd, Tempe, AZ, 85282. Tel: 480-350-5557. p. 80

O'Connor, Kelly, Research Librn, Napa County Historical Society, 1219 First St, Napa, CA, 94559. Tel: 707-224-1739. p. 181

O'Connor, Lisa, Dr, Assoc Prof, Dept Chair, University of North Carolina at Greensboro, School of Education Bldg, Rm 446, 1300 Spring Garden St, Greensboro, NC, 27412. Tel: 336-334-3477. p. 2790

O'Connor, Madeline, Ref Librn, Endicott College Library, 376 Hale St, Beverly, MA, 01915. Tel: 978-232-2293. p. 989

O'Connor, Margaret, Prog Coordr, Belmar Public Library, 517 Tenth Ave, Belmar, NJ, 07719. Tel: 732-681-0775. p. 1389

O'Connor, Matthew, Evening Supvr, Maryville College, 502 E Lamar Alexander Pkwy, Maryville, TN, 37804-5907. Tel: 865-981-8258. p. 2111

O'Connor, Michael, Curator, Hofstra University, Special Collections/Long Island Studies Institute, 032 Axinn Library, 123 Hofstra University, Hempstead, NY, 11549-1230. Tel: 516-463-6404, 516-463-6411. p. 1545

O'Connor, Nikki, Asst Librn, Pinawa Public Library, Vanier Rd, Pinawa, MB, R0E 1L0, CANADA. Tel: 204-753-2496. p. 2589

O'Connor, Rhonda R, Libr Assoc II, Missouri State University, Haseltine Library, Greenwood Laboratory School, 1024 E Harrison St, Rm 3, Springfield, MO, 65897. Tel: 417-836-8563. p. 1281

O'Connor, Rory, Cat Librn, Denver Botanic Gardens, 1007 York St, Denver, CO, 80206. Tel: 720-865-3570. p. 275

O'Connor, Samantha, Pub Serv Librn, Central Carolina Community College Libraries, 1105 Kelly Dr, Sanford, NC, 27330. Tel: 919-718-7340. p. 1715

O'Connor, Stephanie, Dir, Alliance Public Library, 1750 Sweetwater Ave, Ste 101, Alliance, NE, 69301-4438. Tel: 308-762-1387. p. 1305

O'Connor, Susie, Circ Librn, Govt Doc Librn, University of South Carolina Aiken, 471 University Pkwy, Aiken, SC, 29801. Tel: 803-641-3261. p. 2046

O'Connor, Zachary, Librn, Dentons Bingham Greenebaum LLP, 300 W Vine St, Ste 1200, Lexington, KY, 40507-1622. Tel: 859-231-8500, 859-288-4717. p. 862

O'Daniel, Heather, Librn, United States Air Force, AFRL/RVIL, 3550 Aberdeen Ave SE Bldg 570, Kirtland AFB, NM, 87117-5776. Tel: 505-846-4767. p. 1470

O'Daniel, Patrick, Exec Dir, Southwest Tennessee Community College, 737 Union Ave, Memphis, TN, 38103. Tel: 901-333-5140. p. 2114

O'Day, Curry, Dir, Media Serv, Loyola University New Orleans, 6363 Saint Charles Ave, New Orleans, LA, 70118. Tel: 504-864-7111. p. 902

O'Dea, Dale, Librn, Whitewood Public Library, 1201 Ash St, Whitewood, SD, 57793. Tel: 605-269-2616. p. 2085

O'Dell, Kathleen, Commun Relations Mgr, Springfield-Greene County Library District, 4653 S Campbell Ave, Springfield, MO, 65810-1723. Tel: 417-882-0714. p. 1281

O'Dell, Katie, Dir, Programming, Multnomah County Library, 919 NE 19th Ave, Ste 250, Portland, OR, 97232. Tel: 503-988-5123. p. 1892
O'Dell, Sue, Sci Librn, Bowdoin College Library, 3000 College Sta, Brunswick, ME, 04011-8421. p. 919
O'Dell, Sue, Sci Librn, Bowdoin College Library, Hatch Science Library, Hatch Science Bldg, 2nd Flr, 3100 College Sta, Brunswick, ME, 04011. Tel: 207-725-3265. p. 919
O'Donnell, Courtney, Asst Librn, American Chemical Society Information Resource Center, 1155 16th St NW, Washington, DC, 20036. Tel: 202-872-4513. p. 359
O'Donnell, Danielle, Dir, Libr Serv, Everglades University, Sarasota Campus, 6001 Lake Osprey Dr, Ste 110, Sarasota, FL, 34240. Tel: 941-907-2262. p. 385
O'Donnell, Debra, Interim Head Librn, Bristol Law Library, Superior Court House, Nine Court St, Taunton, MA, 02780. Tel: 508-824-7632. p. 1059
O'Donnell, James J, Univ Librn, Arizona State University Libraries, Hayden Library, 300 E Orange Mall Dr, Tempe, AZ, 85287. Tel: 480-965-3417. p. 79
O'Donnell, John, Dir, Westcliff University, 16735 Von Karman, Ste 100, Irvine, CA, 92606. Tel: 714-459-1110. p. 153
O'Donnell, John, Ref/Fac Serv Librn, Saint Thomas University Library, Alex A Hanna Law Library, 16401 NW 37th Ave, Miami Gardens, FL, 33054. Tel: 305-623-2339. p. 425
O'Donnell, Kerry, Br Mgr, Wicomico Public Library, Centre Branch, 2300 N Salisbury Blvd, Salisbury, MD, 21801. Tel: 410-546-5397. p. 977
O'Donnell, Kerry, Br Mgr, Wicomico Public Library, Pittsville Branch, 34372 Old Ocean City Rd, Pittsville, MD, 21850-2008. Tel: 410-835-2353. p. 977
O'Donnell, Renee, Mgr, Brandywine Hundred Library, 1300 Foulk Rd, Wilmington, DE, 19803. Tel: 302-477-3150. p. 356
O'Donnell, Tom, Dir, West Warwick Public Library, 1043 Main St, West Warwick, RI, 02893. Tel: 401-828-3750. p. 2043
O'Donnell-Bobadilla, Kellie, Access Serv Librn, Eastern Connecticut State University, 83 Windham St, Willimantic, CT, 06226-2295. Tel: 860-465-5719. p. 347
O'Donnell-Leach, Karen, Outreach Librn, Aldrich Public Library, Six Washington St, Barre, VT, 05641. Tel: 802-476-7550. p. 2278
O'Donoghue, Maura, Asst Librn, Brescia University, 717 Frederica St, Owensboro, KY, 42301. Tel: 270-686-4213. p. 871
O'Dowd, Clare, Electronic Res Librn, Rockland Community College Library, 145 College Rd, Suffern, NY, 10901. Tel: 845-754-4402. p. 1647
O'Driscoll, Sandra, Pres, Maritimes Health Libraries Association, WK Kellogg Health Sciences Library, 5850 College St, Halifax, NS, B3H 1X5, CANADA. Tel: 902-494-2483. p. 2778
O'Flaherty, Dave, Circ Supvr, Rutherford County Library System, 105 W Vine St, Murfreesboro, TN, 37130-3673. Tel: 615-893-4131. p. 2117
O'Gara, Genya, Actg Dir, Dep Dir, Virginia's Academic Library Consortium, George Mason University, 4400 University Dr, Fenwick 5100, Fairfax, VA, 22030. Tel: 703-993-4654. p. 2776
O'Gara, Noreen, Asst Dir, Bedford Free Public Library, Seven Mudge Way, Bedford, MA, 01730. Tel: 781-275-9440. p. 987
O'Gorman, Mary Ann, Teen Serv, Kinnelon Public Library, 132 Kinnelon Rd, Kinnelon, NJ, 07405. Tel: 973-838-1321. p. 1410
O'Grady, Beth, Dir, Carson City Public Library, 102 W Main St, Carson City, MI, 48811-0699. Tel: 989-584-3680. p. 1089
O'Grady, Ryan, Asst Dir, Fac Serv, University of Maryland, Hornbake Library, Ground Flr, Rm 0220, 4130 Campus Dr, College Park, MD, 20742-4345. Tel: 301-405-2039. p. 2786
O'Hanlon, Colin R, Sr, Supvry Librn, United States Army, Bldg 465, Rm 113, White Sands Missile Range, NM, 88002-5039. Tel: 575-678-5820. p. 1479
O'Hanlon, Donna, Ch Serv, Wanaque Public Library, 616 Ringwood Ave, Wanaque, NJ, 07465. Tel: 973-839-4434. p. 1451
O'Hanlon, Laura, Coll Develop Spec, Loyola-Notre Dame Library, Inc, 200 Winston Ave, Baltimore, MD, 21212. Tel: 410-617-6801. p. 954
O'Hanlon, Pat, Dir, Truth or Consequences Public Library, 325 Library Lane, Truth or Consequences, NM, 87901-2375. Tel: 575-894-3027. p. 1479
O'Hanlon, Pat, Dir, Truth or Consequences Public Library, Downtown, 401 N Foch St, Truth or Consequences, NM, 87901. Tel: 575-740-8295. p. 1479
O'Hanlon, Patrick, Asst Mgr, Access Services, Babson College, 11 Babson College Dr, Babson Park, MA, 02457-0310. Tel: 781-239-4484. p. 987
O'Hara, Carolyn, ILL, Chouteau County Library, 1518 Main St, Fort Benton, MT, 59442. Tel: 406-622-5222. p. 1293
O'Hara, Chris, Coordr, Youth Serv, Manatee County Public Library System, 1301 Barcarrota Blvd W, Bradenton, FL, 34205-7522. Tel: 941-748-5555, Ext 6319. p. 386
O'Hara, Helen, Youth Serv Librn, Whitinsville Social Library, 17 Church St, Whitinsville, MA, 01588. Tel: 508-234-2151. p. 1069
O'Hara, Ian, Research & Instruction Librarian for Health Sciences, University of Scranton, 800 Linden St, Scranton, PA, 18510-4634. Tel: 570-941-7802. p. 2005
O'Hara, Kelly, Mr, Libr Spec, Jefferson Community & Technical College, Southwest Campus Library, 1000 Community College Dr, Louisville, KY, 40272. Tel: 502-213-7222. p. 865
O'Hara, Lisa, Univ Librn, University of Manitoba Libraries, Elizabeth Dafoe Library, Rm 156, 25 Chancellors Circle, Winnipeg, MB, R3T 2N2, CANADA. Tel: 204-474-8749. p. 2595
O'Hara, Martha Cordeniz, Head, Adult Serv, Lake Bluff Public Library, 123 E Scranton Ave, Lake Bluff, IL, 60044. Tel: 847-234-2540. p. 606
O'Hara, Steven, Exec Dir, Bucknell University, 220 Bertrand Library, One Dent Dr, Lewisburg, PA, 17837. Tel: 570-577-1557. p. 1955
O'Hare, Heidi, Dir, Tomahawk Public Library, 300 W Lincoln Ave, Tomahawk, WI, 54487. Tel: 715-453-2455. p. 2481
O'Hare, Liam, Syst Librn, Prince Edward Island Public Library Service, 89 Red Head Rd, Morell, PE, C0A 1S0, CANADA. Tel: 902-961-7323. p. 2708
O'Hearn, Will, Exec Dir, Chattanooga Public Library, 1001 Broad St, Chattanooga, TN, 37402-2652. Tel: 423-643-7700. p. 2091
O'Hearn, Will, Exec Dir, Chattanooga Public Library, Eastgate, 5900 Bldg, 5705 Marlin Rd, Ste 1500, Chattanooga, TN, 37411. Tel: 423-643-7770. p. 2091
O'Hearn, Will, Exec Dir, Chattanooga Public Library, Northgate, 278 Northgate Mall Dr, Chattanooga, TN, 37415-6924. Tel: 423-643-7785. p. 2091
O'Hearn, Will, Exec Dir, Chattanooga Public Library, South Chattanooga, 925 W 39th St, Chattanooga, TN, 37410. Tel: 423-643-7780. p. 2091
O'Heren, Samantha, Mgr, Baltimore County Public Library, Hereford Branch, 16940 York Rd, Monkton, MD, 21111. Tel: 410-887-1919. p. 979
O'Hora, Ryan, Dir, Pembroke Town Library, 313 Pembroke St, Pembroke, NH, 03275. Tel: 603-485-7851. p. 1377
O'Keefe, Alex, Instruction Librn, Res, School of the Art Institute of Chicago, 37 S Wabash Ave, Chicago, IL, 60603-3103. Tel: 312-899-5097. p. 568
O'Keefe, Anne, Develop Officer, Rockford Public Library, 214 N Church St, Rockford, IL, 61101-1023. Tel: 815-965-7606. p. 642
O'Keefe, Briana, Tech Serv Librn, Eckerd College, 4200 54th Ave S, Saint Petersburg, FL, 33711. Tel: 727-864-8337. p. 441
O'Keefe, Ellen, Dir, Glen Rock Public Library, 315 Rock Rd, Glen Rock, NJ, 07452. Tel: 201-670-3970. p. 1405
O'Keefe, Kathie, Asst Librn, Antlers Public Library, 104 SE Second St, Antlers, OK, 74523-4000. Tel: 580-298-5649. p. 1840
O'Keefe, Margaret Rose, Cat, ILS LIbrn, Bergen County Cooperative Library System, Inc, 21-00 Route 208 S, Ste 130, Fair Lawn, NJ, 07410. Tel: 201-498-7316. p. 2770
O'Keefe, Megan, Adult & Teen Serv Mgr, Batavia Public Library District, Ten S Batavia Ave, Batavia, IL, 60510-2793. Tel: 630-879-1393. p. 540
O'Keeffe, Rhonda, Libr Mgr, Piedmont Regional Library System, Harold S Swindle Public Library, 5466 US Hwy 441 S, Nicholson, GA, 30565. Tel: 706-757-3577. p. 482
O'Kelly, Kevin, Head, Ref, Somerville Public Library, 79 Highland Ave, Somerville, MA, 02143. Tel: 617-623-5000. p. 1053
O'Kelly, Mary, Assoc Dean for Education & User Services, Western Michigan University, 1903 W Michigan Ave, WMU Mail Stop 5353, Kalamazoo, MI, 49008-5353. Tel: 269-387-5239. p. 1122
O'Leary, Heather, Coll Develop Librn, Stonehill College, 320 Washington St, Easton, MA, 02357. Tel: 508-565-1318. p. 1016
O'Leary, Jody, Dir, Combined Community Library, 1007 Main St, Ordway, CO, 81063-1316. Tel: 719-267-3823. p. 292
O'Leary, Laura, Managing Librn, Brooklyn Public Library, Flatlands, 2065 Flatbush Ave, Brooklyn, NY, 11234. Tel: 718-253-4409. p. 1503
O'Leary, Laura, Managing Librn, Brooklyn Public Library, Ulmer Park, 2602 Bath Ave, Brooklyn, NY, 11214. Tel: 718-265-3443. p. 1504
O'Leary, Patrick, Asst Dir, South Country Library, 22 Station Rd, Bellport, NY, 11713. Tel: 631-286-0818. p. 1492
O'Leary, Robert, Ref Librn, California Western School of Law Library, 290 Cedar St, San Diego, CA, 92101. Tel: 619-515-1584. p. 215
O'Leary, Theresa, Dir, Res Serv, Paul, Weiss, Rifkind, Wharton & Garrison LLP Library, 1285 Avenue of the Americas, New York, NY, 10019-6064. Tel: 212-373-2401. p. 1600
O'Leary-Storer, Bridget, Libr Mgr, Central New Mexico Community College Libraries, Montoya Campus Library, 4700 Morris St NE, RB 101, Albuquerque, NM, 87111. Tel: 505-224-4000, Ext 52548. p. 1461
O'Malley, Caris, Dep Dir, Spokane Public Library, Station Plaza, 2nd Flr, 701 W Riverside Ave, Spokane, WA, 99201. Tel: 509-444-5310. p. 2385
O'Malley, Charlene, Tech Serv Librn, K O Lee Aberdeen Public Library, 215 S E Fourth Ave, Aberdeen, SD, 57401. Tel: 605-626-7097. p. 2073
O'Malley, Cheryl, Librn, Medfield Historical Society Library, Six Pleasant St, Medfield, MA, 02052. Tel: 508-613-6606. p. 1033
O'Malley, Donna, Interim Dir, University of Vermont Libraries, Dana Medical Library, 81 Colchester Ave, Burlington, VT, 05405. Tel: 802-656-4415. p. 2281
O'Malley, Elena, Asst Dir, Collections & Systems, Emerson College, 120 Boylston St, Boston, MA, 02116-4624. Tel: 613-824-8339. p. 995
O'Malley, Karen, Dir, Union Public Library, 1980 Morris Ave, Union, NJ, 07083. Tel: 908-851-5450. p. 1449
O'Malley, Karen, Dir, Union Public Library, Vauxhall Branch, 123 Hilton Ave, Vauxhall, NJ, 07088. Tel: 908-851-5451. p. 1449

O'Malley, Michael, Archivist, Berry College, 2277 Martha Berry Hwy, Mount Berry, GA, 30149. Tel: 706-238-5886. p. 492

O'Malley, Sean, Adult Serv, Prairie Trails Public Library District, 8449 S Moody, Burbank, IL, 60459-2525. Tel: 708-430-3688. p. 546

O'Mara, Timothy, Dir, Brookdale University Hospital & Medical Center, Schulman Institute, 1st Flr, 555 Rockaway Pkwy, Brooklyn, NY, 11212. Tel: 718-240-5312. p. 1501

O'Neal, Amanda, Ch, Winneconne Public Library, 31 S Second St, Winneconne, WI, 54986. Tel: 920-582-7091. p. 2489

O'Neal, Ashley, Head, Circ, Middle Georgia Regional Library System, 1180 Washington Ave, Macon, GA, 31201-1790. Tel: 478-744-0800, 478-744-0841. p. 486

O'Neal, Betty, Br Mgr, Wyoming County Public Library, Mullens Area Public, 102 Fourth St, Mullens, WV, 25882. Tel: 304-294-6687. p. 2412

O'Neal, Emily, Tech Serv Mgr, Deschutes Public Library District, 507 NW Wall St, Bend, OR, 97703. Tel: 541-617-7061. p. 1874

O'Neal, James, Head, Pub Serv, Middle Georgia Regional Library System, 1180 Washington Ave, Macon, GA, 31201-1790. Tel: 478-744-0836. p. 487

O'Neal, Nick, Dir, Tech Serv, Kirkwood Public Library, 140 E Jefferson Ave, Kirkwood, MO, 63122. Tel: 314-821-5770, Ext 1027. p. 1259

O'Neil, Barbara, Librn, East Mississippi Regional Library System, Clarke County-Quitman Public, 116 Water St, Quitman, MS, 39355. Tel: 601-776-2492. p. 1231

O'Neil, Betsy, Adult Serv Mgr, Ref Librn, Natrona County Library, 307 E Second St, Casper, WY, 82601. Tel: 307-577-7323. p. 2492

O'Neil, Betty, Br Mgr, Reading Public Library, Northeast, 1348 N 11th St, Reading, PA, 19604-1509. Tel: 610-655-6361. p. 2001

O'Neil, Cheryl, ILL Librn, Conway Public Library, 15 Main Ave, Conway, NH, 03818. Tel: 603-447-5552. p. 1360

O'Neil, Emily, Librn, Florida State College at Jacksonville, South Campus Library & Learning Commons, 11901 Beach Blvd, Jacksonville, FL, 32246-6624. Tel: 904-646-2174. p. 411

O'Neil, Gail, Dir, Warburg Public Library, 5212 50 Ave, Warburg, AB, T0C 2T0, CANADA. Tel: 780-848-2391. p. 2559

O'Neil, Genevieve, Circ Tech, Librn, Yukon College Library, 500 College Dr, Whitehorse, YT, Y1A 5K4, CANADA. Tel: 867-668-8870. p. 2758

O'Neil, Kelly, Librn, Lennox & Addington County Public Library, Yarker Branch, 4315 County Rd 1, Yarker, ON, K0K 3N0, CANADA. Tel: 613-377-1673. p. 2660

O'Neil, Laura, Outreach Serv Mgr, Athens County Public Libraries, 95 W Washington, Nelsonville, OH, 45764-1177. Tel: 740-753-2118. p. 1805

O'Neil, Margaret, Librn, Penfield Public Library, 1985 Baird Rd, Penfield, NY, 14526. Tel: 585-340-8720. p. 1616

O'Neil, Rhonda, Libr Mgr, Stettler Public Library, 6202 44th Ave, 2nd Flr, Stettler, AB, T0C 2L1, CANADA. Tel: 403-742-2292. p. 2555

O'Neil, Shannon, Curator, New York University, Tamiment Library/Robert F Wagner Labor Archives, Special Collections Ctr, 70 Washington Sq S, 2nd Flr, New York, NY, 10012. Tel: 212-998-2436. p. 1599

O'Neill, Darren, Dir, Morris County Library, 30 E Hanover Ave, Whippany, NJ, 07981. Tel: 973-285-6930. p. 1455

O'Neill, Francis, Sr Ref Librn, Maryland Center for History & Culture Library, 610 Park Ave, Baltimore, MD, 21201. Tel: 410-685-3750. p. 954

O'Neill, Isabella, Head, Spec Coll & Univ Archives, Bucknell University, 220 Bertrand Library, One Dent Dr, Lewisburg, PA, 17837. Tel: 570-577-3230. p. 1955

O'Neill, Jennifer, Exec Dir, Mamaroneck Public Library, 136 Prospect Ave, Mamaroneck, NY, 10543. Tel: 914-698-1250. p. 1568

O'Neill, Jennifer, Tech Serv Mgr, Barberton Public Library, 602 W Park Ave, Barberton, OH, 44203-2458. Tel: 330-745-1194. p. 1749

O'Neill, John, Dr, Curator, Hispanic Society of America Library, 613 W 155th St, New York, NY, 10032. Tel: 212-926-2234, Ext 251. p. 1587

O'Neill, Katy, Dir, Loyola-Notre Dame Library, Inc, 200 Winston Ave, Baltimore, MD, 21212. Tel: 410-617-6801. p. 954

O'Neill, Leslie, Dir, Catholic Historical Research Center of the Archdiocese of Philadelphia, 6740 Roosevelt Blvd, Philadelphia, PA, 19149. Tel: 215-904-8149. p. 1975

O'Neill, Libby, Libr Dir, Boyden Library, Ten Bird St, Foxborough, MA, 02035. Tel: 508-543-1245. p. 1019

O'Neill, Libby, Libr Dir, Norfolk Public Library, Two Liberty Lane, Norfolk, MA, 02056. Tel: 508-528-3380. p. 1040

O'Neill, Mary, Visual Res Curator, University of the South, 178 Georgia Ave, Sewanee, TN, 37383-1000. Tel: 931-598-1660. p. 2126

O'Neill, Michael, Br Supvr, Kern County Library, Holloway-Gonzales Branch, 506 E Brundage Lane, Bakersfield, CA, 93307-3337. Tel: 661-861-2083. p. 119

O'Neill, Michael, Br Supvr, Kern County Library, Bryce C Rathbun Branch, 200 W China Grade Loop, Bakersfield, CA, 93308-1709. Tel: 661-393-6431. p. 120

O'Neill, Philip M, Sr Ref & Instruction Librn, Barry University, 11300 NE Second Ave, Miami Shores, FL, 33161-6695. Tel: 305-899-3762. p. 426

O'Rahilly, Andy, Supvr, Machine Lending, New Jersey State Library, Talking Book & Braille Center, 2300 Stuyvesant Ave, Trenton, NJ, 08618. Tel: 609-406-7179, Ext 819. p. 1448

O'Reilly, Anne, Electronic Res Librn, Fiorello H LaGuardia Community College Library, 31-10 Thomson Ave, Long Island City, NY, 11101. Tel: 718-482-6021. p. 1565

O'Reilly, Kathleen, Cat, National Gallery of Canada Library & Archives, 380 Sussex Dr, Ottawa, ON, K1N 9N4, CANADA. Tel: 613-714-6000, Ext 6323. p. 2667

O'Reilly, Margaret, Exec Dir, New Jersey State Museum-Fine Art Bureau, 205 W State St, Trenton, NJ, 08625. Tel: 609-984-3899. p. 1448

O'Riley, Jane, Libr Dir, Southern University at Shreveport, 3050 Martin Luther King Jr Dr, Shreveport, LA, 71107. Tel: 318-670-9401. p. 910

O'Riordan, Gerry, Libr Serv Coordr, Edmonton Public Library, Mill Woods, 2610 Hewes Way, Edmonton, AB, T6L 0A9, CANADA. Tel: 780-496-1821. p. 2537

O'Rourke, Ashlee, Asst Dir, Burkburnett Library, 215 E Fourth St, Burkburnett, TX, 76354-3446. Tel: 940-569-2991. p. 2151

O'Rourke, Edward, Libr Mgr, Baker Botts LLP, 700 K St NW, Washington, DC, 20001-5692. Tel: 202-639-7967. p. 361

O'Rourke, Joan, Cat Asst, Coordr, Acq, Assumption University, 500 Salisbury St, Worcester, MA, 01609. Tel: 508-767-7076. p. 1071

O'Rourke, Joseph, Adult Serv Mgr, Delaware County District Library, 84 E Winter St, Delaware, OH, 43015. Tel: 740-362-3861. p. 1781

O'Rourke, Sadie, Dir, Sandisfield Free Public Library, 23 Sandisfield Rd, Sandisfield, MA, 01255. Tel: 413-258-4966. p. 1051

O'Shea, Constance, ILL, Olympic College, 1600 Chester Ave, Bremerton, WA, 98337. Tel: 360-475-7250. p. 2360

O'Shea, Denise, Head, Access Serv Dept, Syst Librn, Montclair State University, One Normal Ave, Montclair, NJ, 07043-1699. Tel: 973-655-2098. p. 1420

O'Shea, Sarah, Head, Youth Serv, Tompkins County Public Library, 101 E Green St, Ithaca, NY, 14850-5613. Tel: 607-272-4557, Ext 262. p. 1553

O'Shea, Sarah, Dir, Newfane Public Library, 2761 Maple Ave, Newfane, NY, 14108. Tel: 716-778-9344. p. 1606

O'Steen, Sheila, Br Mgr, Free Library of Philadelphia, Fishtown Community Branch, 1217 E Montgomery Ave, Philadelphia, PA, 19125-3445. Tel: 215-685-9990. p. 1978

O'Sullivan, Catherine, Dir, Pequea Valley Public Library, 31 Center St, Intercourse, PA, 17534. Tel: 717-768-3160. p. 1946

O'Sullivan, Kevin, Curator, Texas A&M University Libraries, Cushing Memorial Library & Archives, 400 Spencer St, College Station, TX, 77843. Tel: 979-845-1951. p. 2157

O'Sullivan, Nancy, Head, Access Serv, Assumption University, 500 Salisbury St, Worcester, MA, 01609. Tel: 508-767-7271. p. 1071

O'Sullivan, Pamela, Assoc Librn, Coll & Scholarly Communications, State University of New York College at Brockport, 350 New Campus Dr, Brockport, NY, 14420-2997. Tel: 585-395-5688. p. 1497

O'Tool, Joyce, Asst Librn, Sac City Public Library, 1001 W Main St, Sac City, IA, 50583. Tel: 712-662-7276. p. 780

O'Toole, Mary Jo, Br Mgr, Chicago Public Library, Lincoln Park, 1150 W Fullerton Ave, Chicago, IL, 60614. Tel: 312-744-1926. p. 557

O'Toole, Susan, Asst Br Supvr, Region of Waterloo Library, Bloomingdale Branch, 860A Sawmill Rd, Bloomingdale, ON, N0B 1K0, CANADA. Tel: 519-745-3151. p. 2629

Oakes, Marcia Lakomsi, Ref Librn, Rhode Island State Law Library, Frank Licht Judicial Complex, 250 Benefit St, Providence, RI, 02903. Tel: 401-222-3275. p. 2040

Oakes, Rita, Chief of Br Serv, Ocean County Library, 101 Washington St, Toms River, NJ, 08753. Tel: 732-914-5409. p. 1446

Oakland, Jane, Circ Mgr, ILL, University of North Dakota, Thormodsgard Law Library, 215 Centennial Dr, Grand Forks, ND, 58202. Tel: 701-777-2204. p. 1734

Oakley, Kim, Circ Supvr, Allen Park Public Library, 8100 Allen Rd, Allen Park, MI, 48101. Tel: 313-381-2425. p. 1077

Oakley, Whitney, Br Mgr, Anythink Libraries, Anythink Bennett, 495 Seventh St, Bennett, CO, 80102. Tel: 303-405-3231. p. 296

Oaks, Chris, Br Mgr, Public Library of Cincinnati & Hamilton County, Oakley, 4033 Gilmore Ave, Cincinnati, OH, 45209. Tel: 513-369-6038. p. 1763

Oaks Gallaway, Teri, Exec Dir, Statewide California Electronic Library Consortium, 617 S Olive St, Ste 1210, Los Angeles, CA, 90014. Tel: 310-775-9807. p. 2762

Oaks, Jodi, Ref Librn, Mohawk Valley Community College Library, Rome Campus, 1101 Floyd Ave, Rome, NY, 13440. Tel: 315-334-7728. p. 1655

Oaksmith, Ashley, Br Mgr, Kitsap Regional Library, Silverdale Branch, 3450 NW Carlton St, Silverdale, WA, 98383-8325. Tel: 360-692-2779. p. 2360

Oanes, Kari, Col Librn, Minnesota State Community & Technical College, 1900 28th Ave S, Moorhead, MN, 56560. Tel: 218-299-6514, 218-299-6552. p. 1188

Oates, Jennifer, Dr, Dir, Carroll College, 1601 N Benton Ave, Helena, MT, 59625. Tel: 406-447-4340. p. 1295

Oates, Jennifer, Dr, Assoc Prof, Head Music Libr, Queens College, Aaron Copland School of Music Library, 65-30 Kissena Blvd, Flushing, NY, 11367. Tel: 718-997-3900. p. 1533

Oathout, Larry, Dir, Portage County Public Library, Charles M White Library Bldg, 1001 Main St, Stevens Point, WI, 54481-2860. Tel: 715-346-1544. p. 2479

Oathout, Lesa, Ch, Marrowbone Public Library District, 216 W Main St, Bethany, IL, 61914. Tel: 217-665-3014. p. 542
Oatis, Victoria, Dir, Ch Serv, Norwalk Public Library, One Belden Ave, Norwalk, CT, 06850. Tel: 203-899-2780, Ext 15127. p. 332
Oatman, Linda, Dir, Hansen Community Library, 120 W Maple Ave, Hansen, ID, 83334-4975. Tel: 208-423-4122. p. 522
Obee, Jenna, Librn, Colorado Technical University Library, 4435 N Chestnut, Colorado Springs, CO, 80907. Tel: 719-590-6708. p. 270
Oberg, Brandon, Head, Res & Instrul Serv, Northeastern State University, 711 N Grand Ave, Tahlequah, OK, 74464-2333. Tel: 918-456-5511, Ext 3200. p. 1863
Oberg, Dave, Exec Dir, Elmhurst Historical Museum, 120 E Park Ave, Elmhurst, IL, 60126. Tel: 630-833-1457. p. 585
Oberg, Judy, Mgr, Libr & Res Serv, Bishop & McKenzie LLP, 10180 101st St NW, Ste 2300, Edmonton, AB, T5J 1V3, CANADA. Tel: 780-426-5550. p. 2535
Oberhansli, Courtney, Dir, Mineral County Library, 110 First St, Hawthorne, NV, 89415. Tel: 775-945-2778. p. 1345
Oberhoffer, Michelle, Circ Mgr, Carnegie-Stout Public Library, 360 W 11th St, Dubuque, IA, 52001. Tel: 563-589-4139. p. 748
Oberlander, Cyril, Dean of Libr, Humboldt State University Library, One Harpst St, Arcata, CA, 95521-8299. p. 117
Oberlin, Jessica, Info Tech, Librn, Pennsylvania College of Technology, 999 Hagan Way, Williamsport, PA, 17701. Tel: 570-327-4523. p. 2023
Obermaier, Jennifer, Asst Dir, Clearwater Public Library System, 100 N Osceola Ave, Clearwater, FL, 33755. Tel: 727-562-4970. p. 388
Oberstar, Cari, Lead Libr Tech, Buhl Public Library, 400 Jones Ave, Buhl, MN, 55713. Tel: 218-258-3391. p. 1167
Oberweiser, Jodi, Dir, Drummond School & Community Library, 124 First St, Drummond, MT, 59832. Tel: 406-288-3700. p. 1292
Obien, Rodney, Head, Archives & Spec Coll, Keene State College, 229 Main St, Keene, NH, 03435-3201. Tel: 603-358-2717. p. 1369
Obregon, Lydia, Digital Ref Librn, Parker University Library, 2540 Walnut Hill Lane, Dallas, TX, 75220. Tel: 972-438-6932, Ext 7517. p. 2167
Obremski, Tracy, Tech Serv, Springfield Town Library, 43 Main St, Springfield, VT, 05156. Tel: 802-885-3108. p. 2295
Obrigewitch, Stacey Noel, Libr Mgr, Hines Creek Municipal Library, 212-10 St, Hines Creek, AB, T0H 2A0, CANADA. Tel: 780-494-3879. p. 2543
Obrist, Krist, Libr Dir, Monmouth Public Library, 168 S Ecols St, Monmouth, OR, 97361. Tel: 503-838-1932. p. 1887
Obrochta, William, Exec Dir, Beth Ahabah Museum & Archives, 1109 W Franklin St, Richmond, VA, 23220. Tel: 804-353-2668. p. 2340
Obydzinski, Beata, Br Mgr, Monterey County Free Libraries, Seaside Branch, 550 Harcourt Ave, Seaside, CA, 93955. Tel: 831-899-2055. p. 173
Obynon, Olivia, Ch Serv, Sheffield Public Library, 316 N Montgomery Ave, Sheffield, AL, 35660. Tel: 256-386-5633. p. 35
Ocadiz, Jose, Br Mgr, San Diego County Library, Lincoln Acres Branch, 2725 Granger Ave, National City, CA, 91950-0168. Tel: 619-475-9880. p. 217
Ocampo, Adolfo R, Br Mgr, San Diego Public Library, San Ysidro, 4235 Beyer Blvd, San Diego, CA, 92173. Tel: 619-424-0475. p. 221
Ocampo, Cheryl, Asst Dir, Coll, Mount Saint Mary's University, 12001 Chalon Rd, Los Angeles, CA, 90049-1599. Tel: 310-954-4372. p. 166
Ocampo, Raleigh, Asst Dir, Head, Guest Serv, Northlake Public Library District, 231 N Wolf Rd, Northlake, IL, 60164. Tel: 708-562-2301. p. 627
Ocampos, Jaime, Ms, Librn, Canadian Lutheran Bible Institute Library, 4837 52A St, Camrose, AB, T4V 1W5, CANADA. Tel: 780-672-4454. p. 2530
Ocana, Angela, Actg Dir, Eugene Public Library, 100 W Tenth Ave, Eugene, OR, 97401. Tel: 541-682-5450. p. 1878
Ocasio, Wilma Gual, Mrs, Librn, Inter-American University of Puerto Rico, Bo Machete, Carr 744, Guayama, PR, 00784. Tel: 787-864-2222. p. 2510
Ocepek, Melissa, Asst Prof, University of Illinois at Urbana-Champaign, Library & Information Science Bldg, 501 E Daniel St, Champaign, IL, 61820-6211. Tel: 217-333-3280. p. 2784
Ochoa, Ana E, Librn, El Paso Community College Library, Library Technical Services, 919 Hunter St, Rm C300M, El Paso, TX, 79915. Tel: 915-831-2484, 915-831-2671. p. 2173
Ochoa, Marilyn, Dir, Middlesex College Library, 2600 Woodbridge Ave, Edison, NJ, 08818. Tel: 732-906-4252. p. 1401
Ochoa, Rose, Acq Asst, City University of New York, 365 Fifth Ave, New York, NY, 10016-4309. Tel: 212-817-7061. p. 1582
Ochsner, James, Dir, Libr Serv, Sutter County Library, 750 Forbes Ave, Yuba City, CA, 95991. Tel: 530-822-7137. p. 261
Ochtera, Tabitha, Digital Commons Curator, Electronic Res Librn, Molloy College, 1000 Hempstead Ave, Rockville Centre, NY, 11571. Tel: 516-323-3917. p. 1632
Octave, Betsy, Br Mgr, Saint James Parish Library, Vacherie Library, 2593 Hwy 20, Vacherie, LA, 70090-5601. Tel: 225-265-9066. p. 895
Octobre, Marie, Librn, College of New Rochelle, Brooklyn Campus, 1368 Fulton St, Brooklyn, NY, 11216. Tel: 718-638-2500. p. 1577
Odahowski, Kris, Ch Serv, Gadsden County Public Library, 732 S Pat Thomas Pkwy, Quincy, FL, 32351. Tel: 850-627-7106. p. 439
Odam, Teresa, Ser, Brigham Young University, Howard W Hunter Law Library, 256 JRCB, Provo, UT, 84602-8000. Tel: 801-422-3593. p. 2269
Odeh, Hussein, Chief Librn, Jersey City Free Public Library, 472 Jersey Ave, Jersey City, NJ, 07302-3499. Tel: 201-547-4304. p. 1409
Odell, Paul, Youth Serv Mgr, Bettendorf Public Library Information Center, 2950 Learning Campus Dr, Bettendorf, IA, 52722. Tel: 563-344-4189. p. 735
Odell, Paula, Adult Serv, Woodward Public Library, 1500 W Main St, Woodward, OK, 73801. Tel: 580-254-8544. p. 1869
Odems, Vanessa, Managing Librn, Milling, Benson, Woodward LLP, 909 Poydras St, Ste 2300, New Orleans, LA, 70112. Tel: 504-569-7000. p. 902
Oden, Fred A, Pres, Fulton County Historical Society, Inc, 37 E 375 N, Rochester, IN, 46975. Tel: 574-223-4436. p. 716
Odess-Harnish, Kerri, Dir, Res & Instruction Serv, Gettysburg College, 300 N Washington St, Gettysburg, PA, 17325. Tel: 717-337-7018. p. 1935
Odgren, Ben, Youth Serv Librn, Rockport Public Library, 485 Commercial St, Rockport, ME, 04856. Tel: 207-236-3642. p. 939
Odlevak, Jane, Librn, Spokane Community College/Community Colleges of Spokane Library, MS 2160, 1810 N Greene St, Spokane, WA, 99217-5399. Tel: 509-533-7046. p. 2384
Odom, Dennis, Head, Tech Serv, Texas Christian University, 2913 Lowden St, TCU Box 298400, Fort Worth, TX, 76129. Tel: 817-257-7106. p. 2181
Odom, Melanie, Ref Serv, Venice Public Library, 260 Nokomis Ave S, Venice, FL, 34285. Tel: 941-861-1336. p. 452
Odom, Rhoda, Mgr, Suwannee River Regional Library, Jo Kennon Public Library, 10655 Dowling Park Dr, Live Oak, FL, 32064. Tel: 386-658-2670. p. 419
Odom, Shi, Br Mgr, Carteret County Public Library, Down East Public, 108 Straits Rd, Beaufort, NC, 28516. Tel: 252-648-7729. p. 1674
Odoski, Diane, Dir, Gilbert Public Library, 628 Second St, Friend, NE, 68359. Tel: 402-947-5081. p. 1315
Odum, Donna, Dir, Libr Serv, Sampson Community College Library, Kitchin Hall, 1801 Sunset Ave, Clinton, NC, 28328. Tel: 910-900-4038. p. 1682
Odum, Mark X, Dir, National Rehabilitation Information Center, 8400 Corporate Dr, Ste 500, Landover, MD, 20785. Tel: 301-459-5900. p. 970
Oedel, Elizabeth, Ref Librn, The Brookfield Library, 182 Whisconier Rd, Brookfield, CT, 06804. Tel: 203-775-6241, Ext 103. p. 304
Oehler, Gail, Exec Dir, Southern Oklahoma Library System, 601 Railway Express St, Ardmore, OK, 73401. Tel: 580-223-3164. p. 1840
Oehlers, Joy, Info Literacy Librn, Kapi'olani Community College Library, 4303 Diamond Head Rd, Honolulu, HI, 96816. Tel: 808-734-9352. p. 512
Oehlke, Vailey, Ms, Dir of Libr, Multnomah County Library, 919 NE 19th Ave, Ste 250, Portland, OR, 97232. Tel: 503-988-5123. p. 1892
Oelrich, Cathy, Adult Serv, Rhinelander District Library, 106 N Stevens St, Rhinelander, WI, 54501-3193. Tel: 715-365-1070. p. 2472
Oels, Phil, Interim Dir, Libr Serv, National University Library, 9393 Lightwave Ave, San Diego, CA, 92123-1447. Tel: 858-541-7942. p. 215
Oelther, Jessica, Head, Ref, Patchogue-Medford Library, 54-60 E Main St, Patchogue, NY, 11772. Tel: 631-654-4700. p. 1615
Oestreich, Melanie, Librn, University of Valley Forge, 1401 Charlestown Rd, Phoenixville, PA, 19460. Tel: 610-917-2003. p. 1989
Oestriecher, Cheryl, Head, Spec Coll & Archives, Boise State University, 1865 Cesar Chavez Lane, Boise, ID, 83725. Tel: 208-426-1204. p. 517
Oeth, Kathy, Circ Mgr, University of Southern Indiana, 8600 University Blvd, Evansville, IN, 47712. Tel: 812-464-1922. p. 682
Offerdahl, John, Ref Librn, Atlanta-Fulton Public Library System, Ocee Branch, 5090 Abbotts Bridge Rd, Johns Creek, GA, 30005-4601. Tel: 404 613-6840, 770-360-8897. p. 461
Offerman, Lauren, Exec Dir, Three Rivers Public Library District, 25207 W Channon Dr, Channahon, IL, 60410-5028. Tel: 815-467-6200, Ext 303. p. 552
Offutt, Edie, Adult Serv, Bolivar-Harpers Ferry Public Library, 151 Polk St, Harpers Ferry, WV, 25425. Tel: 304-535-2301. p. 2403
Ofslager, Ken, Libr Dir, Smithton Public Library, Center & Second St, Smithton, PA, 15479. Tel: 724-872-0701. p. 2008
Ogawa, Rikke S, Dir, University of California Los Angeles Library, Science & Engineering Libraries, 8270 Boelter Hall, Los Angeles, CA, 90095. Tel: 310-825-5781. p. 169
Ogburn, Alyssa, Dir, Corning Public Library, 603 Ninth St, Corning, IA, 50841-1304. Tel: 641-322-3866. p. 742
Ogburn, Christopher, PhD, Dir, Programming, Moravian Music Foundation, 457 S Church St, Winston-Salem, NC, 27101. Tel: 336-725-0651. p. 1725
Ogden, James, III, Historian, National Park Service, 3370 LaFayette Rd, Fort Oglethorpe, GA, 30742. Tel: 706-866-9241. p. 479
Ogden, Sarah, District Libr Mgr, Timberland Regional Library, 415 Tumwater Blvd SW, Tumwater, WA, 98501-5799. Tel: 360-943-5001. p. 2388
Ogea, Angelique, Dr, Dean, McNeese State University, 4205 Ryan St, Lake Charles, LA, 70605. Tel: 337-475-5432, 337-475-5433. p. 2786
Ogea, Stacey, Libr Mgr, Frances T Bourne Jacaranda Public Library, 4143 Woodmere Park Blvd, Venice, FL, 34293. Tel: 941-861-1277. p. 452

Ogg, Harry, Adult Serv Supvr, Per, Midland County Public Library, 301 W Missouri Ave, Midland, TX, 79701. Tel: 432-688-4320. p. 2219
Ogg, Mary Jane, Pub Serv Librn, Pere Marquette District Library, 185 E Fourth St, Clare, MI, 48617. Tel: 989-386-7576. p. 1091
Ogg, Mary-Jane, Pub Serv Librn, Harrison Community Library, 105 E Main St, Harrison, MI, 48625. Tel: 989-539-6711, Ext 2. p. 1113
Ogilvie, Connie, Head Ref Librn, Chemung County Library District, 101 E Church St, Elmira, NY, 14901. Tel: 607-733-9173. p. 1530
Ogle, Angela, Librn, Cutler Memorial Library, 151 High St, Plainfield, VT, 05667. Tel: 802-454-8504. p. 2291
Ogle, Joyce, Coordr, Methodist Hospital of Southern California, 300 W Huntington Dr, Arcadia, CA, 91007. Tel: 626-898-8000, Ext 3681. p. 117
Ogle, Lizzi, Youth Serv Dir, Tremont District Public Library, 215 S Sampson St, Tremont, IL, 61568. Tel: 309-925-5432, 309-925-5597. p. 654
Oglesbee, Audra, Access Serv Coordr, Circ Supvr, Bluffton University, One University Dr, Bluffton, OH, 45817-2104. Tel: 419-358-3271. p. 1751
Oglesby, Shelley, ILL, Ref (Info Servs), High Point Public Library, 901 N Main St, High Point, NC, 27262. Tel: 336-883-8585. p. 1696
Ogletree, Asti, Operations Mgr, East Central Arkansas Regional Library, 410 E Merriman Ave, Wynne, AR, 72396. Tel: 870-238-3850. p. 112
Ogora, Jane, Library Contact, University of Maryland Prince George's Hospital Center, 3001 Hospital Dr, Cheverly, MD, 20785-1193. Tel: 301-618-2000, Ext 82490, 301-618-2490. p. 961
Ogora, Jane, Lead Librn, Adventist HealthCare Shady Grove Medical Center, 9901 Medical Center Dr, Rockville, MD, 20850. Tel: 240-826-6101. p. 973
Ogreenc, Joann, Supvr, United States Army, Fort Wainwright Post Library, Santiago Ave, Bldg 3700, Fort Wainwright, AK, 99703. Tel: 907-353-2642. p. 45
Ogreenc, JoAnn, Asst Dir, McMillan Memorial Library, 490 E Grand Ave, Wisconsin Rapids, WI, 54494-4898. Tel: 715-422-5144. p. 2489
Ogrodowski, Jennifer, Head, Adult Serv, Saratoga Springs Public Library, 49 Henry St, Saratoga Springs, NY, 12866. Tel: 518-584-7860, Ext 205. p. 1636
Oguz, Fatih, PhD, Assoc Prof, University of North Carolina at Greensboro, School of Education Bldg, Rm 446, 1300 Spring Garden St, Greensboro, NC, 27412. Tel: 336-334-3477. p. 2790
Oh, Kyong Eun, Assoc Prof, PhD Prog Dir, Simmons University, 300 The Fenway, Boston, MA, 02115. Tel: 617-521-2800. p. 2786
Oh, Michelle, Educ Librn, Northeastern Illinois University, 5500 N Saint Louis Ave, Chicago, IL, 60625-4699. Tel: 773-442-4400. p. 566
Oh, Michelle, Librarian for Open Access & Equity, Oakton College Library, 1600 E Golf Rd, Rm 1406, Des Plaines, IL, 60016. Tel: 847-635-1642, 847-635-1644. p. 578
Ohigashi Oasay, Lauree H, Continuing Educ Chair, Hawaii-Pacific Chapter of the Medical Library Association, Health Sciences Library, 651 Ilalo St MEB, Honolulu, HI, 96813. Tel: 808-692-0810. p. 2764
Ohlson, Jodi, Br Mgr, Pima County Public Library, Caviglia-Arivaca, 17050 W Arivaca Rd, Arivaca, AZ, 85601. Tel: 520-594-5235. p. 82
Ohlson-Martin, Terry, Co-Dir, New Hampshire Family Voices Library, Dept Health & Human Servs, Spec Med Servs, Thayer Bldg, 129 Pleasant St, Concord, NH, 03301. Tel: 603-271-4525. p. 1359
Ohotnicky, Frank J, Dir, Keystone College, One College Green, La Plume, PA, 18440-0200. Tel: 570-945-8332. p. 1950
Ohr, Donna, Dep Dir, San Diego County Library, MS 070, 5560 Overland Ave, Ste 110, San Diego, CA, 92123. Tel: 858-694-3786. p. 216
Ohrenberg, Laura, Adminr, The Ninety-Nines, Inc, 4300 Amelia Earhart Rd, Oklahoma City, OK, 73159-0040. Tel: 405-685-7969. p. 1858
Ohrt, Julia E, Libr Dir, Albion Municipal Library, 400 N Main St, Albion, IA, 50005. Tel: 641-488-2226. p. 730
Ohrtman, Krista, Access Serv, Augustana University, 2001 S Summit Ave, Sioux Falls, SD, 57197-0001. Tel: 605-274-4921. p. 2081
Ohs, Steve, Adminr, Prairie Lakes Library System (PLLS), 29134 Evergreen Dr, Ste 600, Waterford, WI, 53185. Tel: 262-514-4500, Ext 68. p. 2483
Ohzourk, Jen, Head, Adult Serv, West Des Moines Public Library, 4000 Mills Civic Pkwy, West Des Moines, IA, 50265-2049. Tel: 515-222-3400. p. 791
Oistad, Kay, Br Mgr, Collier County Public Library, Naples Regional Library, 650 Central Ave, Naples, FL, 34102. Tel: 239-262-4130. p. 427
Oiver, Nate, Mgr, Columbus Metropolitan Library, Gahanna Branch, 310 Granville St, Gahanna, OH, 43230. p. 1772
Oja, Lori Anne, Exec Dir, Health Science Information Consortium of Toronto, c/o Gerstein Sci Info Ctr, Univ Toronto, Nine King's College Circle, Toronto, ON, M5S 1A5, CANADA. Tel: 416-978-6359. p. 2778
Ojeda, Santa, Reserves Mgr, Hostos Community College Library, Shirley J Hinds Allied Health & Science Bldg, 475 Grand Concourse, Rm A308, Bronx, NY, 10451. Tel: 718 518-4224. p. 1499
Ojennus, Paul, Head, Coll Mgt, Whitworth University, 300 W Hawthorne Rd, Spokane, WA, 99251-0001. Tel: 509-777-4480. p. 2385
Ojezua, Teresa, Ref & Instruction Librn, Philander Smith College, 900 Daisy Bates Dr, Little Rock, AR, 72202. Tel: 501-370-5366. p. 101
Ojo-Ohikuare, Laurianne, Archivist, University of Maryland, Baltimore County, 1000 Hilltop Circle, Baltimore, MD, 21250. Tel: 410-455-2356. p. 958
Ojuri, Esther, Research Librn, United States Equal Employment Opportunity Commission Library, 131 M St NE, Rm 4SW16N, Washington, DC, 20507. Tel: 202-921-3119. p. 379
Okada, Elinor, Operations Mgr, Indiana University Bloomington, 1320 E Tenth St, Bloomington, IN, 47405. Tel: 812-855-7711. p. 670
Okafor, Tamara, Outreach Serv, Shelton State Community College, Martin Campus, 9500 Old Greensboro Rd, Tuscaloosa, AL, 35405. Tel: 205-391-2248. p. 37
Okamoto, Karen, ILL Librn, John Jay College of Criminal Justice, 899 Tenth Ave, New York, NY, 10019. Tel: 212-237-8246. p. 1589
Okamura, Jill, Instruction Librn, Fullerton College, 321 E Chapman Ave, Fullerton, CA, 92832-2095. Tel: 714-992-7380. p. 147
Okandan, Amanda, Med Librn, Presbyterian Hospital, 1100 Central Ave SE, Albuquerque, NM, 87125. Tel: 505-841-1516. p. 1461
Okano, Sarah, Head, Ref (Info Serv), Jericho Public Library, One Merry Lane, Jericho, NY, 11753. Tel: 516-935-6790. p. 1558
Okazaki, Gail, Head Librn, O'Melveny & Myers LLP, 400 S Hope St, Los Angeles, CA, 90071-2899. Tel: 213-430-6000. p. 167
Okechukwu, Susan, Ch, Englewood Public Library, 31 Engle St, Englewood, NJ, 07631. Tel: 201-568-2215, Ext 241. p. 1402
Okeefe, Sean, Support Serv Mgr, Lake County Library System, 418 W Alfred St, Ste C, Tavares, FL, 32778. Tel: 352-253-6180. p. 450
Okerblom, Melissa, Dir, Rockaway Borough Public Library, 82 E Main St, Rockaway, NJ, 07866. Tel: 973-627-5709. p. 1440
Okin, Avery Eli, Exec Dir, Brooklyn Bar Association Foundation Inc Library, 123 Remsen St, 2nd flr, Brooklyn, NY, 11201. Tel: 718-624-0868. p. 1501
Okrafka, Heather, Interim Libr Dir, Heritage College & Seminary Library, 175 Holiday Inn Dr, Cambridge, ON, N3C 3T2, CANADA. Tel: 519-651-2869. p. 2635
Okuhara, Keiko, Syst Librn, University of Hawaii, 2525 Dole St, Honolulu, HI, 96822-2328. Tel: 808-956-9953. p. 513
Olaka, Musa, Dr, Dir of Libr, Prairie View A&M University, L W Minor St, University Dr, Prairie View, TX, 77446-0519. Tel: 936-261-1533. p. 2229
Olawski, Suzanne, Asst Dir, Solano County Library, 1150 Kentucky St, Fairfield, CA, 94533. p. 142
Olawski, Suzanne A, Dir, Libr Serv, Solano County Library, 1150 Kentucky St, Fairfield, CA, 94533. p. 142
Olberding, Angie, Dir, Stuart Township Library, Second & Main St, Stuart, NE, 68780. Tel: 402-924-3242. p. 1337
Olberding, Suzanne, Dir, Glidden Public Library, 110 Idaho St, Glidden, IA, 51443. Tel: 712-659-3781. p. 755
Olbrys, Cindy D, Sr Exec Dir of Libraries, State University of New York at Binghamton, 4400 Vestal Pkwy E, Binghamton, NY, 13902. Tel: 607-777-4607. p. 1494
Old Chief, Kimberly, Libr Tech, Blackfeet Community College, 504 SE Boundary St, Browning, MT, 59417. Tel: 406-338-5441. p. 1290
Old, Lisa, Dir, Westlock Municipal Library, Heritage Bldg No 1, 10007 100 Ave, Westlock, AB, T7P 2H5, CANADA. Tel: 780-349-3060. p. 2559
Oldal, Maria, Mgr, Coll Serv, Mgr, Libr Syst, The Morgan Library & Museum, 225 Madison Ave, New York, NY, 10016. Tel: 212-685-0008. p. 1592
Oldfield, Jennie, Librn, Atlanta History Center, Cherokee Garden Library, 130 W Paces Ferry Rd, Atlanta, GA, 30305. Tel: 404-814-4124. p. 462
Oldfield, Robert, Sr Librn, California Department of Corrections Library System, Central California Women's Facility, 23370 Rd 22, Chowchilla, CA, 93610. Tel: 559-665-5531, Ext 7210. p. 206
Oldham, Barbara, Ref Librn, Wenatchee Valley College, 1300 Fifth St, Wenatchee, WA, 98801. Tel: 509-682-6714. p. 2395
Oldham, Doug, Librn, Mono County Free Library, 400 Sierra Park Rd, Mammoth Lakes, CA, 93546. Tel: 760-934-4777. p. 172
Oldham, Krista, Col Archivist, Rec Mgr, Haverford College, 370 Lancaster Ave, Haverford, PA, 19041-1392. Tel: 610-896-1284. p. 1942
Oldham Messick, Linda, Head, Children's Servx, Greenwood Public Library, 310 S Meridian St, Greenwood, IN, 46143-3135. Tel: 317-881-1953. p. 688
Oldham, Peggy, Dir, Glen Rose Public Library, 108 Allen Dr, Glen Rose, TX, 76043. Tel: 254-897-4582. p. 2185
Oldham, Peggy, Librn, Somervell County Library, 108 Allen Dr, Glen Rose, TX, 76043. Tel: 254-897-4582. p. 2185
Olds, Barbara, Electronic Res, Libr Assessment Coordr, Stephen F Austin State University, 1936 North St, Nacogdoches, TX, 75962. Tel: 936-468-4636. p. 2221
Olds, Victoria, Asst Dir, Sabina Public Library, 11 E Elm St, Sabina, OH, 45169-1330. Tel: 937-584-2319. p. 1818
Oldt, Carolyn, Br Mgr, Gloucester County Library System, Logan Township Branch, 498 Beckett Rd, Logan Township, NJ, 08085. Tel: 856-241-0202. p. 1423
Olea, Marion, Head, Adult Serv, Northlake Public Library District, 231 N Wolf Rd, Northlake, IL, 60164. Tel: 708-562-2301. p. 627
Oleen, Melissa, Libr Dir, Rowan Public Library, 201 W Fisher St, Salisbury, NC, 28144-4935. Tel: 704-216-8228, 980-432-8670. p. 1715
Oleka, OJ, Dr, Pres, Association of Independent Kentucky Colleges & Universities, 484 Chenault Rd, Frankfort, KY, 40601. Tel: 502-695-5007. p. 2765

Olemida, Sharaya, Librn, California Department of Corrections Library System, California Men's Colony-East, Colony Dr, Hwy 1, San Luis Obispo, CA, 93409. Tel: 805-547-7900, Ext 4721. p. 206

Olendorf, Rob, Dir, North Carolina State University Libraries, Natural Resources Library, Jordan Hall, Rm 1102, 2800 Faucette Dr, Campus Box 7114, Raleigh, NC, 27695-7114. Tel: 919-515-2306. p. 1710

Olesh, Elizabeth, Dir, Baldwin Public Library, 2385 Grand Ave, Baldwin, NY, 11510-3289. Tel: 516-223-6228. p. 1490

Oleskevich, Carmen, Libr Dir, Southern Gulf Islands Community Libraries, 4407 Bedwell Harbour Rd, Pender Island, BC, V0N 2M1, CANADA. Tel: 250-629-3722. p. 2573

Oleston, Jason, Dir, Libr Serv, Department of Veterans Affairs, 1660 S Columbian Way, Bldg 1, Seattle, WA, 98108-1597. Tel: 206-764-2075. p. 2376

Oleston, Jason M, Chief, Libr Serv, VA Puget Sound Health Care System, American Lake Div, 9600 Veterans Dr SW, Bldg 71, Tacoma, WA, 98493-5000. Tel: 253-583-1510. p. 2388

Olewine, Linda, Cat, University of Texas, M D Anderson Cancer Center Research Medical Library, 1400 Pressler St, Houston, TX, 77030-3722. Tel: 713-745-3086. p. 2200

Oling, Rebecca, Dir, Digital Accessibility, State University of New York, 735 Anderson Hill Rd, Purchase, NY, 10577-1400. Tel: 914-251-6417. p. 1625

Olinik, Andrew, Librn, District of Columbia Superior Court Library, 500 Indiana Ave NW, Rm 5400, Washington, DC, 20001. Tel: 202-879-1435. p. 365

Olinkiewicz, Janet, Adult Prog Coordr, Floyd Memorial Library, 539 First St, Greenport, NY, 11944-1399. Tel: 631-477-0660. p. 1541

Oliphant, Tami, PhD, Assoc Prof, Graduate Program Coord, University of Alberta, 7-104 Education N, University of Alberta, Edmonton, AB, T6G 2G5, CANADA. Tel: 780-492-7625. p. 2795

Oliva, Victor, Res & Instruction Librn, Adelphi University, One South Ave, Garden City, NY, 11530. Tel: 516-877-3587. p. 1536

Olivar-Snair, Joyce, Library Contact, Eastern Counties Regional Library, Port Hawkesbury Branch, 304 Pitt St (SAERC), Unit 3, Port Hawkesbury, NS, B9A 2T9, CANADA. Tel: 902-625-2729. p. 2621

Olivares, Cynthia, Librn, Slaton City Library, 200 W Lynn St, Slaton, TX, 79364-4136. Tel: 806-828-2008. p. 2244

Olivares, Karla, Libr Asst, Penitas Public Library, 1111 S Main St, Penitas, TX, 78576. Tel: 956-583-5656. p. 2226

Olivares, Lizbeth, Circ Mgr, Union County Public Library, 316 E Windsor St, Monroe, NC, 28112. Tel: 704-283-8184. p. 1703

Olivares, Veronica, Librn, Cochise County Law Library, 100 Quality Hill Rd, Bisbee, AZ, 85603. Tel: 520-432-8513. p. 56

Olivas, Antonia, Educ Librn, California State University, 333 S Twin Oaks Valley Rd, San Marcos, CA, 92096. Tel: 760-750-4348. p. 234

Olive, Fred J, III, Dr, Head, User Serv/Circ, University of Alabama at Birmingham, Mervyn H Sterne Library, 917 13th St S, Birmingham, AL, 35205. Tel: 205-934-6364. p. 9

Olive, Joel D, Supvr, Pub Serv, Williams Baptist University, 60 W Fulbright, Walnut Ridge, AR, 72476. Tel: 870-759-4139. p. 112

Oliveira, Michael C, Ref & Instruction Librn, ONE National Gay & Lesbian Archives at the USC Libraries, 909 W Adams Blvd, Los Angeles, CA, 90007. Tel: 213-821-2771. p. 167

Oliver, Amanda, Head, Spec Coll & Archives, Wilfrid Laurier University Library, 75 University Ave W, Waterloo, ON, N2L 3C5, CANADA. Tel: 519-884-0710, Ext 3825. p. 2703

Oliver, Astrid, Dir, E-Resources Librn, Fort Lewis College, 1000 Rim Dr, Durango, CO, 81301-3999. Tel: 970-247-7250. p. 278

Oliver, Catherine, Cataloging & Metadata Librn, Northern Michigan University, 1401 Presque Isle Ave, Marquette, MI, 49855-5376. Tel: 906-227-2123. p. 1130

Oliver, Denita, Librn, Central Alabama Community College, 1675 Cherokee Rd, Alexander City, AL, 35010. Tel: 256-215-4293. p. 3

Oliver, Diana, Librn, New Sharon Jim Ditzler Memorial Library, 37 Library Rd, New Sharon, ME, 04955. Tel: 207-779-1128. p. 933

Oliver, Felicia, Br Mgr, Calcasieu Parish Public Library System, Epps Memorial, 1320 N Simmons St, Lake Charles, LA, 70601. Tel: 337-721-7090. p. 893

Oliver, Jackie, Dir, Aurora Public Library, 401 Woodruff St, Aurora, IA, 50607. Tel: 319-634-3960. p. 733

Oliver, Jade, Asst Librn, Bette Winner Public Library, 235 Mattonnabee Ave, Gillam, MB, R0B 0L0, CANADA. Tel: 204-652-2617. p. 2587

Oliver, Jeni, Br Librn, Community District Library, Morrice-Perry Township, 300 Main St, Morrice, MI, 48857. Tel: 517-625-7911. p. 1095

Oliver, Jodi, Dir, Beaver County Library System, 109 Pleasant Dr, Ste 101, Aliquippa, PA, 15001. Tel: 724-378-6227. p. 1904

Oliver, John, Info Literacy Librn, The College of New Jersey, 2000 Pennington Rd, Ewing, NJ, 08628-1104. Tel: 609-771-2311. p. 1402

Oliver, Kimberly, Br Mgr, Clayton County Library System, Jonesboro Branch, 124 Smith St, Jonesboro, GA, 30236. Tel: 770-478-7120. p. 483

Oliver, Kurt, Cataloger, Wentworth Institute of Technology, 550 Huntington Ave, Boston, MA, 02115-5998. Tel: 617-989-4094. p. 1000

Oliver, Phillip, Web Coordr, University of North Alabama, One Harrison Plaza, Box 5028, Florence, AL, 35632-0001. Tel: 256-765-4559. p. 17

Oliver, Rhonda, Br Mgr, Indianapolis Public Library, Brightwood, 2435 N Sherman Dr, Indianapolis, IN, 46218-3852. Tel: 317-275-4315. p. 694

Oliver, Richard E, Libr Dir, Evangel University, 1111 N Glenstone Ave, Springfield, MO, 65802. Tel: 417-865-2815, Ext 7268. p. 1280

Oliver, Rick, Dir, Univ Libr, Assemblies of God Theological Seminary, 1435 N Glenstone Ave, Springfield, MO, 65802-2131. Tel: 417-865-2815, Ext 7267. p. 1280

Oliver, Sarah, Library Contact, Multnomah County Library, Troutdale, 2451 SW Cherry Park Rd, Troutdale, OR, 97060. p. 1893

Oliver, Scott, Asst Dir, Talbot County Free Library, 100 W Dover St, Easton, MD, 21601-2620. Tel: 410-822-1626. p. 964

Olivera, Travis, Dir, Hamilton Public Library, 13 Broad St, Hamilton, NY, 13346. Tel: 315-824-3060. p. 1543

Oliverio, Rob, Head Librn, Arizona Christian University, One W Firestorm Way, Glendale, AZ, 85306. Tel: 602-489-5300, Ext 3031. p. 61

Oliverius, Kilee, Library Contact, Western Nebraska Veterans Home Library, 1102 W 42nd St, Scottsbluff, NE, 69361-4713. Tel: 308-632-0300. p. 1335

Olivier, Ana, Tech Serv, Augustana University, 2001 S Summit Ave, Sioux Falls, SD, 57197-0001. Tel: 605-274-4921. p. 2081

Olivieri, Blynne, Head, Spec Coll, University of West Georgia, 1601 Maple St, Carrollton, GA, 30118. Tel: 678-839-5455. p. 469

Olivieri, Jody, Circ Mgr, Youth Serv Mgr, Homer Township Public Library District, 14320 W 151st St, Homer Glen, IL, 60491. Tel: 708-301-7908. p. 600

Olivigni, Lisa, Ms, Br Mgr, Lincoln City Libraries, Dan A Williams Branch, 5000 Mike Scholl St, Lincoln, NE, 68524. Tel: 402-441-4252. p. 1321

Olivigni, Lisa, Ms, Br Mgr, Lincoln City Libraries, Loren Corey Eiseley Branch, 1530 Superior St, Lincoln, NE, 68521. Tel: 402-441-4252. p. 1321

Olivos, Dori, Adult Serv Mgr, Rocky River Public Library, 1600 Hampton Rd, Rocky River, OH, 44116-2699. Tel: 440-895-3753. p. 1818

Olle-LaJoie, Maureen, Dir, University of Wisconsin-River Falls, 410 S Third St, River Falls, WI, 54022. Tel: 715-425-3799. p. 2474

Ollhoff, Laurie, Libr Dir, T B Scott Library, 106 W First St, Merrill, WI, 54452-2398. Tel: 715-536-7191. p. 2457

Olliff, Martin, Dr, Archivist, Troy University, 502 University Dr, Dothan, AL, 36304. Tel: 334-983-6556, Ext 1327. p. 15

Olliges, Rhonda, Br Mgr, Nelson County Public Library, Bloomfield Branch, 34 Arnold Lane, Bloomfield, KY, 40008. Tel: 502-252-9129. p. 848

Olman, Tiffany, YA Serv, Flat River Community Library, 200 W Judd St, Greenville, MI, 48838. Tel: 616-754-6359. p. 1112

Olmi, Adria P, Dir, United States Army, 562 Quarters Rd, Bldg 12420, Fort Lee, VA, 23801-1705. Tel: 804-765-8170. p. 2319

Olmstadt, Will, Exec Dir, Louisiana State University Health Sciences Center, 1501 Kings Hwy, Shreveport, LA, 71130. Tel: 318-675-6487. p. 908

Olmstead, Barrie, Ad, Lewiston City Library, 411 D St, Lewiston, ID, 83501. Tel: 208-798-2525. p. 524

Olmsted, Jenny, Colls Mgr, Three Rivers Regional Library System, 280 S Mahogany St, Jesup, GA, 31546. Tel: 912-559-2391. p. 483

Olmsted, Linda, Libr Dir, George Gamble Library, 29 Rte 104, Danbury, NH, 03230. Tel: 603-768-3765. p. 1360

Olney, Daniel, Libr Tech, Heritage University, 3240 Fort Rd, Toppenish, WA, 98948. Tel: 509-865-8610. p. 2388

Olney, James, Libr Dir, Northport-East Northport Public Library, 151 Laurel Ave, Northport, NY, 11768. Tel: 631-261-6930. p. 1608

Olney, Kyle, Access Serv Librn, Olivet Nazarene University, One University Ave, Bourbonnais, IL, 60914-2271. Tel: 815-928-5490. p. 544

Olsen, Amy, Libr Dir, Lanpher Memorial Library, 141 Main St, Hyde Park, VT, 05655. Tel: 802-888-4628. p. 2286

Olsen, Anne, Head of Libr, University of British Columbia Library, Humanities & Social Sciences, Koerner Library, 1958 Main Mall, Vancouver, BC, V6T 1Z2, CANADA. Tel: 604-822-3018. p. 2580

Olsen, Bev, Librn, Stavely Municipal Library, 4823 49th St, Stavely, AB, T0L 1Z0, CANADA. Tel: 403-549-2190. p. 2555

Olsen, Chris, Univ Librn, Brigham Young University-Idaho, 525 S Center St, Rexburg, ID, 83460. Tel: 208-496-9510. p. 529

Olsen, Hannah, Tech Serv Librn, Duncanville Public Library, 201 James Collins Blvd, Duncanville, TX, 75116. Tel: 972-780-5050. p. 2172

Olsen, Janet, Archivist/Librn, National Woman's Christian Temperance Union, 1730 Chicago Ave, Evanston, IL, 60201. Tel: 847-864-1397. p. 586

Olsen, Jennifer, Br Mgr, Western Sullivan Public Library, 19 Center St, Jeffersonville, NY, 12748. Tel: 845-482-4350. p. 1558

Olsen, Josh, Dir, Madonna University Library, 36600 Schoolcraft Rd, Livonia, MI, 48150-1173. Tel: 734-432-5703. p. 1127

Olsen, Kathy, Ad, Haywood County Public Library, 678 S Haywood St, Waynesville, NC, 28786. Tel: 828-356-2507. p. 1721

Olsen, Kolleen, Libr Mgr, Twin Cities Biomedical Consortium, c/o Fairview Health Services, 2450 Riverside Ave, Minneapolis, MN, 55455. Tel: 612-273-3000. p. 2768

Olsen, Marilyn, Asst Librn, Emery County Library System, Elmo Branch, 15 S 100 East, Elmo, UT, 84521. Tel: 435-653-2558. p. 2262

Olsen, Matthew, Coordr, Instrul Serv, Millikin University, 1184 W Main St, Decatur, IL, 62522. Tel: 217-424-6214. p. 576

Olsen, Michelle, Dir, Egegik Village Library, 289 Airport Rd, Egegik, AK, 99579. Tel: 907-233-2211. p. 45

Olsen, Michelle, Dir, Richfield Public Library, 83 E Center St, Richfield, UT, 84701. Tel: 435-896-5169. p. 2270

Olsen, Robin, Dir, Blue Hill Public Library, 317 W Gage St, Blue Hill, NE, 68930. Tel: 402-756-2701. p. 1308

Olsen, Serena, Prog Coordr, Lighthouse for the Blind & Visually Impaired, 1155 Market St, 10th Flr, San Francisco, CA, 94103. Tel: 415-431-1481. p. 226

Olsen, Sue, Acq Asst, Tech Serv, Hanson Public Library, 132 Maquan St, Hanson, MA, 02341. Tel: 781-293-2151. p. 1023

Olsen, Tom, Adminr, Las Vegas-Clark County Library District, City of Las Vegas Detention Facility, 3100 E Stewart Ave, Las Vegas, NV, 89101. Tel: 702-384-4887. p. 1346

Olsen, Tom, Librn, Las Vegas-Clark County Library District, Clark County Detention Facility, 330 S Casino Center Blvd, Las Vegas, NV, 89101. Tel: 702-384-4887. p. 1346

Olsen-Lynch, Ellen, Learning Librn, Liaison Librn, Trent University, 1600 West Bank Dr, Peterborough, ON, K9J 7B8, CANADA. Tel: 705-748-1011. p. 2672

Olshin, Josh, Adult Serv, Ref Serv, Stoughton Public Library, 84 Park St, Stoughton, MA, 02072-2974. Tel: 781-344-2711. p. 1058

Olson, Alice, Librn, Dr Shaw Memorial Library, 344 Pond Rd, Mount Vernon, ME, 04352. Tel: 207-293-2565. p. 932

Olson, Ashley, Exec Dir, The Willa Cather Foundation, 413 N Webster St, Red Cloud, NE, 68970-2466. Tel: 402-746-2653. p. 1334

Olson, Carol, Dir, Bullard Community Library, 211 W Main, Bullard, TX, 75757. Tel: 903-894-6125. p. 2151

Olson, Charlotte, Head, ILL, University of Alabama in Huntsville, 4700 Holmes Ave, Huntsville, AL, 35805. Tel: 256-824-6522. p. 22

Olson, David A, Archivist, Columbia University, Rare Book & Manuscript, Butler Library, 6th Flr E, 535 W 114th St, New York, NY, 10027. Tel: 212-854-5590. p. 1583

Olson, Deb, Dir, Dows Community Library, 114 Ellsworth, Dows, IA, 50071. Tel: 515-852-4326. p. 748

Olson, Elena, Dir, Marquette University, Ray & Kay Eckstein Law Library, 1215 Michigan St, Milwaukee, WI, 53201. Tel: 414-288-7092. p. 2458

Olson, Elizabeth, Librn, Archer & Greiner Library, 1025 Laurel Oak Rd, Voorhees, NJ, 08043. Tel: 856-795-2121. p. 1450

Olson, Gail, Br Librn, Wapiti Regional Library, Smeaton Public Library, Village Office, Main St, Smeaton, SK, S0J 2J0, CANADA. Tel: 306-426-2049. p. 2746

Olson, Jennifer, Tech Serv Librn, University of Hartford Harrison Libraries, Mildred P Allen Memorial, 200 Bloomfield Ave, West Hartford, CT, 06117-0395. Tel: 860-768-4491. p. 345

Olson, Josh, Chief Info Officer, Michigan Technological University, 1400 Townsend Dr, Houghton, MI, 49931-1295. Tel: 906-487-1217. p. 1116

Olson, Julie, Librn, Maine Charitable Mechanic Association, 519 Congress St, Portland, ME, 04101. Tel: 207-773-8396. p. 936

Olson, Kathy, Chief Exec Officer, Owensboro Area Museum of Science & History Library, 122 E Second St, Owensboro, KY, 42303-4108. Tel: 270-687-2732. p. 871

Olson, Kelly, Access Serv, Buena Vista University Library, H W Siebens School of Business/Forum, 610 W Fourth St, Storm Lake, IA, 50588. Tel: 712-749-2203. p. 784

Olson, Kim, Assoc Librn, Scott County Library System, Durant Branch, 402 Sixth St, Durant, IA, 52747. Tel: 563-785-4725. p. 751

Olson, Kim, Circ, Ledding Library of Milwaukie, 10660 SE 21st Ave, Milwaukie, OR, 97222. Tel: 503-786-7582. p. 1887

Olson, Marcia, Mgr, Gradient, 20 University Ave, Cambridge, MA, 02138. Tel: 617-395-5562. p. 1005

Olson, Maripat, Head, Tech Serv, Barrington Area Library, 505 N Northwest Hwy, Barrington, IL, 60010. Tel: 847-382-1300. p. 539

Olson, Melissa, Libr Dir, Alice L Pendleton Library, 309 Main Rd, Islesboro, ME, 04848. Tel: 207-734-2218. p. 928

Olson, Melissa, Head, Archives, University of Wisconsin-Parkside Library, 900 Wood Rd, Kenosha, WI, 53141. Tel: 262-595-3432. p. 2445

Olson, Mitzi, Dir, Gladstone Public Library, 135 E Dartmouth St, Gladstone, OR, 97027-2435. Tel: 503-656-2411. p. 1880

Olson, Mitzi, Dir, Clackamas County Library, 16201 SE McLoughlin Blvd, Oak Grove, OR, 97267. Tel: 503-655-8543. p. 1889

Olson, Mitzi, Dir, Clackamas County Library, Gladstone Public Library, 135 E Dartmouth St, Gladstone, OR, 97027. Tel: 503-655-8540. p. 1889

Olson, Robert, Librn, Centre for Suicide Prevention, 105 12 Ave SE, Ste 320, Calgary, AB, T2G 1A1, CANADA. Tel: 403-245-3900, Ext 227. p. 2528

Olson, Roberta, Dir, Church of Jesus Christ of Latter Day Saints, 160 Washington Ave, Plainview, NY, 11803. Tel: 516-433-0122. p. 1618

Olson, Shaye, Academic Specialist, Minnesota State Community & Technical College, 1900 28th Ave S, Moorhead, MN, 56560. Tel: 218-299-6514, 218-299-6552. p. 1188

Olson, Stephanie Mallak, Dir, Iosco-Arenac District Library, 120 W Westover St, East Tawas, MI, 48730. Tel: 989-362-2651. p. 1102

Olson, Susanne, Ref, Webmaster, Groton Public Library, 99 Main St, Groton, MA, 01450. Tel: 978-448-8000, Ext 1316. p. 1022

Olson, Terrie, Circ, Tarpon Springs Public Library, 138 E Lemon St, Tarpon Springs, FL, 34689. Tel: 727-943-4922. p. 450

Olson, Theresa, Libr Operations Mgr, Maryville University Library, 650 Maryville University Dr, Saint Louis, MO, 63141. Tel: 314-529-9493. p. 1271

Olson, Thomas, Br Mgr, Las Vegas-Clark County Library District, East Las Vegas Library, 2851 E Bonanza Rd, Las Vegas, NV, 89101. Tel: 702-507-3500. p. 1346

Olson-Charles, Kim, Head, Pub Serv, University of Western States Library, 8000 NE Tillamook St, Portland, OR, 97213. Tel: 503-251-5752. p. 1894

Olson-Kopp, Kim, Dir, Viterbo University, 900 Viterbo Dr, La Crosse, WI, 54601. Tel: 608-796-3263. p. 2446

Oltivero, Sulema, Asst Dir, Rhoads Memorial Library, 103 SW Second St, Dimmitt, TX, 79027. Tel: 806-647-3532. p. 2171

Oltman, Lenah, Teen Serv Librn, Kling Memorial Library, 708 Seventh St, Grundy Center, IA, 50638-1430. Tel: 319-825-3607. p. 757

Oltmann, Shannon M, Dr, Asst Prof, University of Kentucky, 320 Little Library Bldg, Lexington, KY, 40506-0224. Tel: 859-257-8876. p. 2785

Oltmanns, Judith, Tech Serv, Lied Scottsbluff Public Library, 1809 Third Ave, Scottsbluff, NE, 69361-2493. Tel: 308-630-6207. p. 1335

Oltrop, Monique, Mgr, Point Pelee National Park Library, 1118 Point Pelee Dr, Leamington, ON, N8H 3V4, CANADA. Tel: 519-322-5700, Ext 21. p. 2652

Olund, Ashley, Librn, Eastern Florida State College, Philip F Nohrr Learning Resource Ctr, 3865 N Wickham Rd, Melbourne, FL, 32935-2399. Tel: 321-433-5575, 321-433-5580. p. 420

Olvera, Jane, Lead Librn, Tech Serv, Board of Governors of The Federal Reserve System, Research Library, 20th & C St NW, MS 102, Washington, DC, 20551. Tel: 202-452-3333. p. 361

Olzewski, Lisa, Dir, Cape Canaveral Public Library, 201 Polk Ave, Cape Canaveral, FL, 32920-3067. Tel: 321-868-1101. p. 388

Olzewski, Lisa, Libr Dir, Cocoa Beach Public Library, 550 N Brevard Ave, Cocoa Beach, FL, 32931. Tel: 321-868-1106. p. 390

Omer, Jessica, Circ Librn, Bellevue University, 1028 Bruin Blvd, Bellevue, NE, 68005. Tel: 402-557-7318. p. 1308

Omlor, Lisa, Asst Head Librn, Seymour Public Library, 46 Church St, Seymour, CT, 06483. Tel: 203-888-3903. p. 336

Omodt, Kelly, Ref & Instruction Librn, University of Idaho Library, 850 S Rayburn St, Moscow, ID, 83844. Tel: 208-885-6495. p. 526

Omorogbe-Osagie, Ogie, Libr Mgr, New York Public Library - Astor, Lenox & Tilden Foundations, Mariners Harbor Library, 206 South Ave, (Between Arlington Pl & Brabant St), Staten Island, NY, 10303. Tel: 212-621-0690. p. 1596

Omowale, Yusef, Dir, Southern California Library for Social Studies & Research, 6120 S Vermont Ave, Los Angeles, CA, 90044. Tel: 323-759-6063. p. 168

Omstead, Jenny, Br Mgr, Brampton Library, Mount Pleasant Village Branch, 100 Commuter Dr, Brampton, ON, L7A 0G2, CANADA. Tel: 905-793-4636, Ext 74231. p. 2633

Omstead, Jenny, Br Mgr, Brampton Library, South West Branch, 8405 Financial Dr, Brampton, ON, L6Y 1M1, CANADA. p. 2633

Onate, Missy, Dir, Gibbon Public Library, 116 LaBarre, Gibbon, NE, 68840. Tel: 308-468-5889. p. 1315

Ondricka, Deborah, Pub Serv Librn, American River College Library, 4700 College Oak Dr, Sacramento, CA, 95841. Tel: 916-484-8455. p. 205

Ong, Belinda, Dr, Dir of Research, Info & User Services, University of Alabama in Huntsville, 4700 Holmes Ave, Huntsville, AL, 35805. Tel: 256-824-6432. p. 22

Ong, Jean, Librn I, Orange Public Library & History Center, El Modena Branch, 380 S Hewes Ave, Orange, CA, 92869. Tel: 714-288-2445. p. 189

Onianwa, Chukwuji, Sr Librn, Los Angeles Public Library System, Sylmar Branch Library, 14561 Polk St, Sylmar, CA, 91342-4055. Tel: 818-367-6102. p. 165

Onishi, Yuichiro, Actg Dir, University of Minnesota Libraries-Twin Cities, Immigration History Research Center Archives, Elmer L Andersen Library, 222 21st Ave S, Ste 311, Minneapolis, MN, 55455. Tel: 612-625-4800. p. 1185

Onofrio, Rosalba, Patron Serv Librn, Nichols College, 127 Center Rd, Dudley, MA, 01571. Tel: 508-213-2234. p. 1015

Ontko, Mike, Ref Librn, Coshocton Public Library, 655 Main St, Coshocton, OH, 43812-1697. Tel: 740-622-0956. p. 1778

Onufer, Jaylene, Dir, Redbank Valley Public Library, 720 Broad St, New Bethlehem, PA, 16242-1107. Tel: 814-275-2870. p. 1968

Onyemaechi, Uzoma, Br Mgr, Montgomery County Public Libraries, Silver Spring Library, 900 Wayne Ave, Silver Spring, MD, 20910-4339. Tel: 240-777-9416. p. 975

Onyett, Marie, Head Librn, Beaver Valley Public Library, 1847 First St, Fruitvale, BC, V0G 1L0, CANADA. Tel: 250-367-7114. p. 2566

Oommen, T Anil, Dir, Pacific University Libraries, Eugene Campus, 4000 E 30th Ave, Eugene, OR, 97405. Tel: 541-632-8800. p. 1880

Oonk, Tricia, ILL Librn, Oostburg Public Library, 213 N Eighth St, Oostburg, WI, 53070. Tel: 920-564-2934. p. 2467

Opasik, Scott, Dir, Access Support, Indiana University South Bend, 1700 Mishawaka Ave, South Bend, IN, 46615. Tel: 574-520-4446. p. 718

Opatik, Caitlin, Libr Dir, Lone Rock Community Library, 234 N Broadway, Lone Rock, WI, 53556. Tel: 608-583-2034. p. 2448

Openo, Phuong, Cataloger, Dover Public Library, 73 Locust St, Dover, NH, 03820-3785. Tel: 603-516-6050. p. 1361

Openshaw, Charlotte, Sister, Co-Dir, Las Vegas FamilySearch Genealogy Library, 509 S Ninth St, Las Vegas, NV, 89101. Tel: 702-382-9695. p. 1347

Openshaw, Jeri, Prog Spec, Utah State Library Division, 250 N 1950 West, Ste A, Salt Lake City, UT, 84116-7901. Tel: 801-715-6737. p. 2272

Openshaw, Ken, Co-Dir, Las Vegas FamilySearch Genealogy Library, 509 S Ninth St, Las Vegas, NV, 89101. Tel: 702-382-9695. p. 1347

Opoien, Teresa, Br Mgr, Trails Regional Library, Holden Branch, 207 S Main St, Holden, MO, 64040. Tel: 816-732-4545. p. 1285

Oppenheim, Gabriel, Dir, Adult Serv, La Grange Park Public Library District, 555 N LaGrange Rd, La Grange Park, IL, 60526-5644. Tel: 708-352-0100. p. 606

Oppenheim, Michael, Bus Res Librn, Colls Librn, University of California Los Angeles Library, Eugene & Maxine Rosenfeld Management Library, UCLA Anderson School of Management, 110 Westwood Plaza, E-301, Los Angeles, CA, 90095. Tel: 310-825-0769. p. 169

Oprean, Danielle, Asst Prof, University of Missouri-Columbia, 303 Townsend Hall, Columbia, MO, 65211. Tel: 573-882-4546. p. 2787

Opuszynski, Cheryl, Br Mgr, Cape May County Library, Sea Isle City Branch, 4800 Central Ave., Sea Isle City, NJ, 08243. Tel: 609-263-8485. p. 1395

Orange, Donna, Bus Mgr, Penn Area Library, 2001 Municipal Court, Harrison City, PA, 15636. Tel: 724-744-4414. p. 1941

Orange, Jonathan, Circ Mgr, University of Mississippi, 481 Chuckie Mullins Dr, University, MS, 38677. Tel: 662-915-6824. p. 1234

Oravetz, Alysha, Dir, William Paton Public Library, 105 Main St, Paton, IA, 50217. Tel: 515-968-4559. p. 776

Orbanus, Christen, Br Mgr, Merchantville Public Library, 130 S Centre St, Merchantville, NJ, 08109-2201. Tel: 856-665-3128. p. 1418

Orbanus, Christen, Mgr, Camden County Library System, Merchantville Public Library, 130 S Centre St, Merchantville, NJ, 08109. Tel: 856-665-3128. p. 1450

Orcutt, Rose, Assoc Librn, University at Buffalo Libraries-State University of New York, Architecture & Planning, 303 Abbott Hall, 3435 Main St, Buffalo, NY, 14214-3087. Tel: 716-829-5682. p. 1510

Ordner, Chelsea, Libr Dir, Stonington Historical Society, 40 Palmer St, Stonington, CT, 06378. Tel: 860-535-1131. p. 339

Ordonez-Mercado, Maria E, Chief Librn, University of Puerto Rico Library System, Puerto Rican Collection, Rio Piedras Campus, Jose M Lazaro Bldg, 2nd Flr, San Juan, PR, 00931. Tel: 787-764-0000, Ext 85735, 787-764-0000, Ext 85736. p. 2515

Oreatha, Alex, Br Mgr, Shreve Memorial Library, Atkins Branch, 3704 Greenwood Rd, Shreveport, LA, 71109. Tel: 318-635-6222. p. 908

Orebaugh, Melinda, Dir, Gundersen Lutheran Health System, 1900 South Ave, H01-011, La Crosse, WI, 54601-9980. Tel: 608-775-5410. p. 2446

Oregero, Jacqueline, Librn, Sussex County Library System, Dennis Memorial, 101 Main St, Newton, NJ, 07860. Tel: 973-383-4810. p. 1429

Orenic, Ken, Ref Librn, College of DuPage Library, 425 Fawell Blvd, Glen Ellyn, IL, 60137-6599. Tel: 630-942-2338. p. 593

Orenstein, David I, Dr, Librn, Charles E Stevens American Atheist Library & Archives, Inc, 225 Cristiani St, Cranford, NJ, 07016. Tel: 908-276-7300. p. 1398

Oreste, Jimenez, Evening/Weekend Supvr, Drexel University Libraries, Hagerty Library, 33rd & Market Sts, Philadelphia, PA, 19104-2875. Tel: 215-895-2750. p. 1976

Orgeron, Jean-Paul, Dir, Hudson Valley Community College, 80 Vandenburgh Ave, Troy, NY, 12180. Tel: 518-629-7388. p. 1652

Oria, Chris, Doc Delivery, University of Texas, M D Anderson Cancer Center Research Medical Library, 1400 Pressler St, Houston, TX, 77030-3722. Tel: 713-745-4531. p. 2200

Oringer, Judith, Exec Secy, The Huguenot Society of America Library, General Society of Mechanics & Tradesmen Bldg, Ste 510, 20 W 44th St, New York, NY, 10036. Tel: 212-755-0592. p. 1588

Oriol, Deborah, Br Mgr, Jersey City Free Public Library, West Bergen, 546 West Side Ave, Jersey City, NJ, 07304. Tel: 201-547-4554. p. 1409

Orischak, Emily, Commun Relations Coordr, Berks County Public Libraries, 1040 Berk Rd, Leesport, PA, 19533. Tel: 610-378-5260. p. 1954

Orkiszewski, Paul, Dean, Radford University, 101 Elm Ave SE, 5th Flr, Roanoke, VA, 24013. Tel: 540-831-5471. p. 2345

Orlandini, Rosa, Maps Librn, York University Libraries, Map Library, Scott Library, Main Flr, 4700 Keele St, North York, ON, M3J 1P3, CANADA. Tel: 416-736-2100, Ext 33353. p. 2662

Orlando, Bathsheba, Br Mgr, Catskill Public Library, Palenville Branch, 3303 Rte 23A, Palenville, NY, 12463. Tel: 518-678-3357. p. 1515

Orlando, Katie, Exec Dir, The New England Electric Railway Historical Society, 195 Log Cabin Rd, Kennebunkport, ME, 04046. Tel: 207-967-2800. p. 928

Orlando, Lucia, Research Support Services Librn, University of California, 1156 High St, Santa Cruz, CA, 95064. Tel: 831-459-1279. p. 243

Orlando, Rosemary, Libr Dir, Saint Clair Shores Public Library, 22500 11 Mile Rd, Saint Clair Shores, MI, 48081-1399. Tel: 586-771-9020. p. 1147

Orlik, Mary, Client Serv Librn, Environment Canada Library, 867 Lakeshore Rd, Burlington, ON, L7S 1A1, CANADA. Tel: 905-336-4982. p. 2634

Orlomoski, Amy E, Dir, Librn, Andover Public Library, 355 Rte 6, Andover, CT, 06232. Tel: 860-742-7428. p. 301

Orlomoski, Bobbi Ann, ILL, Canterbury Public Library, One Municipal Dr, Canterbury, CT, 06331-1453. Tel: 860-546-9022. p. 305

Orlomoski, Caitlyn, Adult Serv, Saxton B Little Free Library, Inc, 319 Rte 87, Columbia, CT, 06237-1143. Tel: 860-228-0350. p. 306

Orlov, Ariel, Ms, Mgr, Libr Serv, Adler University, 17 N Dearborn St, 15th Flr, Chicago, IL, 60602. Tel: 312-662-4230. p. 553

Orlov, Stanislav, Syst Librn, Mount Saint Vincent University Library & Archives, 15 Lumpkin Rd, Halifax, NS, B3M 2J6, CANADA. Tel: 902-457-6250. p. 2619

Orlowska, Daria, Data Librn, Western Michigan University, 1903 W Michigan Ave, WMU Mail Stop 5353, Kalamazoo, MI, 49008-5353. Tel: 269-387-5149. p. 1122

Orlowski, Laura, Dir, Jonesville District Library, 310 Church St, Jonesville, MI, 49250-1087. Tel: 517-849-9701. p. 1121

Ornat, Michelle, Dep Dir, Pub Serv, San Jose Public Library, 150 E San Fernando St, San Jose, CA, 95112-3580. Tel: 408-808-2112. p. 231

Ornelas, Cristina, Mgr, Satilla Regional Library, Pearson Public Library, 56 E Bullard Ave, Pearson, GA, 31642. Tel: 912-422-3500. p. 476

Ornelas, Jacquelyn, Circ, Northeast Wisconsin Technical College Library, 2740 W Mason St, Green Bay, WI, 54303-4966. Tel: 920-498-5732. p. 2439

Orner, Sylvia, Coll Res Mgt Librn, University of Scranton, 800 Linden St, Scranton, PA, 18510-4634. Tel: 570-941-7811. p. 2005

Ornstein, Sarah, Dir, Cross' Mills Public Library, 4417 Old Post Rd, Charlestown, RI, 02813. Tel: 401-364-6211. p. 2030

Oro, Robyn R, Access Serv, Spec Coll Coordr, Kansas City University, 1750 Independence Ave, Kansas City, MO, 64106-1453. Tel: 816-654-7267. p. 1256

Orologas, Claire, Chief Curator, Exec Dir, Polk Museum of Art, 800 E Palmetto St, Lakeland, FL, 33801-5529. Tel: 863-688-7743. p. 417

Oropeza, Rachel, ILL Librn, Grand Prairie Public Library System, 901 Conover Dr, Grand Prairie, TX, 75051. Tel: 972-237-5700. p. 2185

Orosco, Melanie, Br Mgr, San Bernardino County Library, Carter Branch, 2630 N Linden Ave, Rialto, CA, 92377. Tel: 909-854-4100, Ext 28148. p. 212

Orosco, Melanie, Libr Adminr, Regional Mgr, San Bernardino County Library, 777 E Rialto Ave, San Bernardino, CA, 92415-0035. Tel: 909-520-2352. p. 212

Orosco, Melanie, Br Mgr, San Bernardino County Library, Kaiser Branch, 11155 Almond Ave, Fontana, CA, 92337. Tel: 909-357-5900, Ext 14174. p. 213

Orosco, Melanie, Br Mgr, San Bernardino County Library, Summit Branch Library, 15551 Summit Ave, Fontana, CA, 92336. Tel: 909-357-5950, Ext 15113. p. 213

Orosco, Michelle, Librn, North Central Washington Libraries, Bridgeport Public Library, 1206 Columbia Ave, Bridgeport, WA, 98813. Tel: 509-686-7281. p. 2393

Orozco, Monica, PhD, Dir, Santa Barbara Mission, 2201 Laguna St, Santa Barbara, CA, 93105. Tel: 805-682-4713. p. 240

Orozco, Rachel, Asst Dir, Pub Serv, Brazoria County Library System, 912 N Velasco, Angleton, TX, 77515. Tel: 979-864-1505. p. 2135

Orozco, Rachel, Dir, Rita & Truett Smith Public Library, 300 Country Club Rd, Bldg 300, Wylie, TX, 75098. Tel: 972-516-6250. p. 2258

Orpia, Karima, Dir, Spring Grove Hospital Center, Tuerk Bldg, 55 Wade Ave, Catonsville, MD, 21228. Tel: 410-402-7040. p. 961

Orr, Alexa, Managing Librn, Brooklyn Public Library, Windsor Terrace, 160 E Fifth St, Brooklyn, NY, 11218. Tel: 718-686-9707. p. 1504

Orr, Blanche, Br Mgr, Huntsville-Madison County Public Library, Triana Public Library, 357 Record Rd, Madison, AL, 35756. Tel: 256-772-9943. p. 22

Orr, Melissa, Interim Dir, Scottsdale Public Library, 3839 N Drinkwater Blvd, Scottsdale, AZ, 85251-4467. Tel: 480-312-7323. p. 77

Orrange, Thomas M, Libr Dir, Medaille College Library, 18 Agassiz Circle, Buffalo, NY, 14214. Tel: 716-880-2283. p. 1509

Orrick, Rita, Br Mgr, Ozark Regional Library, Annapolis Branch, 204 N Allen St, Annapolis, MO, 63620. Tel: 573-598-3706. p. 1251

Orrico, Jeff, Interim Univ Librn, Sacred Heart University, 5151 Park Ave, Fairfield, CT, 06825-1000. Tel: 203-365-4841. p. 312

Orsak, Patricia, Br Mgr, Wharton County Library, East Bernard Branch, 746 Clubside Dr, East Bernard, TX, 77435. Tel: 979-335-6142. p. 2256

Orsini, Andrea, Dir, Cape May County Library, 30 Mechanic St, Cape May Court House, NJ, 08210. Tel: 609-463-6350. p. 1394

Orsini, Anthony, Dir, Belmont County District Library, 20 James Wright Pl, Martins Ferry, OH, 43935. Tel: 740-633-0314. p. 1800

Orsini, Erin, Access Serv Coordr, Roger Williams University, Ten Metacom Ave, Bristol, RI, 02809-5171. Tel: 401-254-4546. p. 2029

Orsini, Sue Ann, Res, Fried, Frank, Harris, Shriver & Jacobson LLP, 801 17th St NW, Ste 600, Washington, DC, 20006. Tel: 202-639-7000. p. 367

Ortale, Monica, Assoc Dir, Pub Serv, South Texas College of Law Houston, 1303 San Jacinto St, Houston, TX, 77002-7006. Tel: 713-646-1721. p. 2198

Ortega, Aizul, Ms, Tech Serv Supvr, Travis County Law Library, Ned Granger, 314 W 11th St, Ste 140, Austin, TX, 78701. Tel: 512-854-9019. p. 2141

Ortega, Alma, Ref Serv, University of San Diego, Helen K & James S Copley Library, 5998 Alcala Park, San Diego, CA, 92110. p. 222

Ortega, Laurie, Exec Dir, Pioneerland Library System, Wilmar Public Library, 410 Fifth St SW, 2nd Flr, Willmar, MN, 56201. Tel: 320-235-6106, Ext 28. p. 1208

Ortega, Lina, Assoc Curator, University of Oklahoma Libraries, Western History Collection, Western History Collection, 452 MH, 630 Parrington Oval, Norman, OK, 73019. Tel: 405-325-3641. p. 1856

Ortega, Marcelina, Supvr, Yakima Valley Libraries, Sunnyside Library, 621 Grant Ave, Sunnyside, WA, 98944. Tel: 509-837-3234. p. 2396

Ortega, Teresa, Circ Mgr, Coastal Carolina Community College, 444 Western Blvd, Jacksonville, NC, 28546. Tel: 910-938-6147. p. 1697

Orten, Zach, Libr Tech, Pulaski Technical College, 13000 Interstate 30, Little Rock, AR, 72210. Tel: 501-812-2878. p. 102

Orth, Pam, Dir, Kismet Public Library, 503 Main St, Kismet, KS, 67859-9615. Tel: 620-563-7357. p. 818

Ortiz, Allison, Mgr, County of Los Angeles Public Library, La Mirada Library, 13800 La Mirada Blvd, La Mirada, CA, 90638. Tel: 562-943-0277. p. 136

Ortiz Del Valle, Pilar, ILL, Inter-American University of Puerto Rico, 100 Calle Francisco Sein, San Juan, PR, 00919. Tel: 787-250-1912, Ext 2160, 787-250-1912, Ext 2514. p. 2513

Ortiz, J J, Libr Dir, Dimmit County Public Library, 200 N Ninth St, Carrizo Springs, TX, 78834. Tel: 830-876-5788. p. 2153

Ortiz, Jhensen, Librn, City College of the City University of New York, Dominican Studies Institute Archives & Library, NAC 2/202, 160 Convent Ave, New York, NY, 10031. Tel: 212-650-7170, 212-650-7496. p. 1582

Ortiz, Jonathan, Libr Operations Mgr, Worcester Polytechnic Institute, 100 Institute Rd, Worcester, MA, 01609-2280. Tel: 508-831-5410. p. 1073

Ortiz, Josefina, Head, Ser, University of Puerto Rico, Law School Library, Avenidas Ponce de Leon & Gandara, San Juan, PR, 00931. Tel: 787-999-9691. p. 2514

Ortiz, Marie-Elena, Dir, Highland Falls Library, 298 Main St, Highland Falls, NY, 10928. Tel: 845-446-3113. p. 1546

Ortiz, Raquel, Asst Dean, Libr & Info Serv, Roger Williams University, Ten Metacom Ave, Bristol, RI, 02809-5171. Tel: 401-254-4530. p. 2029

Ortiz, Veronica, Br Mgr, San Diego County Library, Potrero Branch, 24883 Potrero Valley Rd, Potrero, CA, 91963-0051. Tel: 619-478-5978. p. 217

Ortiz Zapata, Daniel, Chief Librn, Hunter College Libraries, East Bldg, 695 Park Ave, New York, NY, 10065. Tel: 212-772-4161. p. 1588

Ortiz-Hernandez, Evelyn N, Circ, Head, Pub Serv, Supreme Court Library of Puerto Rico, Ave Munoz Rivera Parada 8 1/2 Puerta de Tierra, Parque Munoz Rivera, San Juan, PR, 00902. p. 2514

Ortman, Matt, Community Outreach & Marketing Specialist, New Port Richey Public Library, 5939 Main St, New Port Richey, FL, 34652. Tel: 727-853-1275. p. 428

Ortmeier, Carole, Library Contact, Lincoln Family Medicine Program Library, 4600 Valley Rd, Ste 210, Lincoln, NE, 68510-4892. Tel: 402-483-4591. p. 1321

Orton, Carla, Librn, Chinook Regional Library, Gull Lake Branch, 1377 Conrad Ave, Gull Lake, SK, S0N 1A0, CANADA. Tel: 306-672-3277. p. 2752

Orton, Laurie, Libr Dir, San Juan Island Library, 1010 Guard St, Friday Harbor, WA, 98250-9612. Tel: 360-378-2798. p. 2364

Ortyl, Sheila, Dir, Mary Esther Public Library, 100 Hollywood Blvd W, Mary Esther, FL, 32569-1957. Tel: 850-243-5731. p. 420

Orvis, Julie, ILL, University of Wisconsin-Rock County Library, 2909 Kellogg Ave, Janesville, WI, 53546-5606. Tel: 608-898-5046. p. 2443

Orwig, Angela, Dir, Arthur Hufnagel Public Library of Glen Rock, 32 Main St, Glen Rock, PA, 17327. Tel: 717-235-1127. p. 1937

Orwig, Jordan, Dir, Pub Serv, Vigo County Public Library, 680 Poplar St, Terre Haute, IN, 47807. Tel: 812-232-1113, Ext 1005. p. 721

Orwig, Jordan C, Dir, Sullivan County Public Libraries, 100 S Crowder St, Sullivan, IN, 47882. Tel: 812-268-4957. p. 719

Oryall, Lyn, Libr Dir, Santaquin City Library, 20 W 100 South, Santaquin, UT, 84655. Tel: 801-754-3030, Ext 261. p. 2273

Orzel, Anna, Head, Tech Serv, Acorn Public Library District, 15624 S Central Ave, Oak Forest, IL, 60452-3204. Tel: 708-687-3700. p. 627

Orzel, Linda, Coordr, Spec Serv, Interim Dir, Harris-Stowe State University Library, 3026 Laclede Ave, Saint Louis, MO, 63103. Tel: 314-340-3624. p. 1271

Osborn, Don, Discovery Librn, Pub Serv Librn, Stevenson University Library, 1525 Greenspring Valley Rd, Stevenson, MD, 21153. Tel: 443-334-4233. p. 978

Osborn, Edmond, Mgr, County of Los Angeles Public Library, Maywood Cesar Chavez Library, 4323 E Slauson Ave, Maywood, CA, 90270-2837. Tel: 323-771-8600. p. 137

Osborn, Elizabeth, Librn, Potomac Public Library, 110 E State St, Potomac, IL, 61865. Tel: 217-987-6457. p. 636

Osborn, Jamie, Ms, Br Mgr, Knox County Public Library System, Halls Branch, 4518 E Emory Rd, Knoxville, TN, 37938. Tel: 865-922-2552. p. 2106

Osborn, Melissa, Info Res & Serv Support Spec, Penn State Behrend, 4951 College Dr, Erie, PA, 16563-4115. Tel: 814-898-6106. p. 1932

Osborn, Olivia, Acq & ILL Asst, Dallas Baptist University, 3000 Mountain Creek Pkwy, Dallas, TX, 75211-9299. Tel: 214-333-5260. p. 2163

Osborn, Pam, Asst Dir, White Lake Community Library, 3900 White Lake Dr, Whitehall, MI, 49461-9257. Tel: 231-894-9531. p. 1159

Osborn, Sandra, Dep Dir, Libr Serv, Mooresville Public Library, 220 W Harrison St, Mooresville, IN, 46158-1633. Tel: 317-831-7323. p. 707

Osborn, Susan, Librn, Waterford Public Library, 24 S Park Row, Waterford, PA, 16441. Tel: 814-796-4729. p. 2018

Osborn-Bensaada, Charlotte, Competitive Intelligence Librn, Thompson Coburn LLP Library, 1909 K St NW, Ste 600, Washington, DC, 20006. Tel: 202-585-6900. p. 377

Osborne, Amy, Br Head, Chatham-Kent Public Library, Tilbury Branch, Two Queen St, Tilbury, ON, N0P 2L0, CANADA. Tel: 519-682-0100. p. 2636

Osborne, Amy, Br Head, Chatham-Kent Public Library, Wheatley Branch, 35 Talbot St W, Wheatley, ON, N0P 2P0, CANADA. Tel: 519-825-7131. p. 2636

Osborne, Anne Reever, Asst Dir, Buffalo River Regional Library, 230 E James Campbell Blvd, Ste 108, Columbia, TN, 38401-3359. Tel: 931-388-9282. p. 2094

Osborne, Bridget, Asst Dir, Badger Public Library, 211 First Ave SE, Badger, IA, 50516. Tel: 515-545-4793. p. 733

Osborne, Caroline, Dir, West Virginia University Libraries, George R Farmer Jr College of Law Library, One Law Center Dr, Morgantown, WV, 26506. Tel: 304-293-7641. p. 2409

Osborne, Cindy, Dir, Western Library System, 615 S Beltline Hwy W, Scottsbluff, NE, 69361. Tel: 308-632-1350. p. 1335

Osborne, Crystal M, Dir, Elizabeth Jones Library, 1050 Fairfield Ave, Grenada, MS, 38901. Tel: 662-226-2072. p. 1217

Osborne, Diane, Tech Serv Spec, Bellevue University, 1028 Bruin Blvd, Bellevue, NE, 68005. Tel: 402-557-7312. p. 1308

Osborne, Donna, Chief Fiscal Officer, Chief Operations Officer, Texas State Library & Archives Commission, 1201 Brazos St, Austin, TX, 78701. Tel: 512-463-5440. p. 2141

Osborne, Jennifer, Head, Adult Serv, Brighton District Library, 100 Library Dr, Brighton, MI, 48116. Tel: 810-229-6571, Ext 225. p. 1087

Osborne, Mary Lou, Asst Dir, Winthrop Public Library & Museum, Two Metcalf Sq, Winthrop, MA, 02152-3157. Tel: 617-846-1703. p. 1070

Osborne, Michele, Libr Asst, Buffalo Creek Memorial Library, 511 E McDonald Ave, Man, WV, 25635. Tel: 304-583-7887. p. 2407

Osborne, Michelle, Br Mgr, Gaston County Public Library, Stanley Branch, 205 N Peterson St, Stanley, NC, 28164. Tel: 704-263-4166. p. 1690

Osborne, Zachary, Mgr, Health Inf & Knowledge Mobilization, St Joseph's Health Centre (Unity Health Toronto), 30 The Queensway, Toronto, ON, M6R 1B5, CANADA. Tel: 416-530-6726. p. 2692

Osborne, Zachary, Mgr, St Michael's Hospital, 209 Victoria St, Toronto, ON, M5B 1W8, CANADA. Tel: 416-864-6060, Ext 77694. p. 2692

Osburn, Wade, Libr Dir, Freed-Hardeman University, 158 E Main St, Henderson, TN, 38340-2399. Tel: 731-989-6067. p. 2101

Osepchook, Felicity, Head Librn, New Brunswick Museum Archives & Research Library, 277 Douglas Ave, Saint John, NB, E2K 1E5, CANADA. Tel: 506-643-2324. p. 2605

Oser, Cynthia, Outreach Librn, Ref Librn, Central Texas College, Bldg 102, 6200 W Central Texas Expressway, Killeen, TX, 76549. Tel: 254-526-1475. p. 2206

Oser, Eleanor, Adult Serv Coordr, Kuskokwim Consortium Library, Yupiit Picirarait Cultural Ctr, 420 State Hwy, Bethel, AK, 99559. Tel: 907-543-4516. p. 43

Oshiro, Wayde, Head Librn, Leeward Community College Library, 96-045 Ala Ike St, Pearl City, HI, 96782. Tel: 808-455-0378. p. 514

Oskam, Alison, Digital Collections Supvr, State Library of Pennsylvania, Forum Bldg, 607 South Dr, Harrisburg, PA, 17120. Tel: 717-783-3122. p. 1941

Osland, Sunny, Br Mgr, Jackson County Library, Heron Lake Branch, 401 Ninth St, Heron Lake, MN, 56137-1440. Tel: 507-793-2641. p. 1179

Osmer, Jonathan, Librn, Central Arizona College, 8470 N Overfield Rd, Coolidge, AZ, 85128. Tel: 520-494-5286. p. 58

Osmundson, Sarah, Libr Asst, Phillips County Library, Ten S Fourth St E, Malta, MT, 59538. Tel: 406-654-2407. p. 1299

Osolin, Jessica, Head, Circ, Bloomfield Public Library, 90 Broad St, Bloomfield, NJ, 07003. Tel: 973-566-6200. p. 1391

Ossman, Abir, Chef de Section, Bibliotheques de Montreal, Du Boise, 2727 Blvd Thimens, Saint-Laurent, QC, H4R 1T4, CANADA. Tel: 514-855-6130, Ext 4728. p. 2718

Ost, Kim, Asst Dir, Rock County Public Library, 201 E Bertha St, Bassett, NE, 68714. Tel: 402-684-3800. p. 1306

Ostapchuk, Halyna, Librn, Saint Vladimir Institute Library, 620 Spadina Ave, Toronto, ON, M5S 2H4, CANADA. Tel: 416-923-3318. p. 2692

Ostby, Keri, Head, Tech Serv, Rochester Public Library, 101 Second St SE, Rochester, MN, 55904-3776. Tel: 507-328-2355. p. 1194

Osteen, Jerry, Info Tech, Greenville County Library System, 25 Heritage Green Pl, Greenville, SC, 29601-2034. Tel: 864-242-5000, Ext 4231. p. 2061

Osteen, Timothy, Cat Librn, Bossier Parish Community College Library, 6220 E Texas St, Bldg A, Bossier City, LA, 71111. Tel: 318-678-6543. p. 885

Ostendorf, Molly, Ser & Electronic Res Librn, Cardinal Stritch University Library, 6801 N Yates Rd, Milwaukee, WI, 53217. Tel: 414-410-4265. p. 2458

Ostendorf, Molly, Cat & Metadata, ILL Librn, Milwaukee School of Engineering, 500 E Kilbourn Ave, Milwaukee, WI, 53202. Tel: 414-277-7180. p. 2460

Ostendorp, Emma, Adult Literacy Coordr, Howard County Library System, Central Branch, 10375 Little Patuxent Pkwy, Columbia, MD, 21044-3499. Tel: 410-313-7900. p. 965

Oster, Dianne, Archivist, Govt Doc Librn, ILL & Ser, Seton Hall University School of Law, One Newark Ctr, Newark, NJ, 07102. Tel: 973-642-8195. p. 1428

Ostercamp, Matthew, Dir, North Park University, Brandel Library, 5114 N Christiana Ave, Chicago, IL, 60625. Tel: 773-244-5580, 773-244-6200. p. 566

Osterhoudt, Reesa, Br Mgr, El Dorado County Library, Cameron Park Branch, 2500 Country Club Dr, Cameron Park, CA, 95682. Tel: 530-621-5500. p. 195

Osterhout, Laura, Exec Dir, Rochester Regional Library Council, 3445 Winton Pl, Ste 204, Rochester, NY, 14623. Tel: 585-223-7570. p. 2771

Osterloh, Cassandra, Librn, National Hispanic Cultural Center Library, 1701 Fourth St SW, Albuquerque, NM, 87102. Tel: 505-383-4778. p. 1461

Osterman, Linda, Libr Tech, Montana State University-Northern, 300 13th St W, Havre, MT, 59501. Tel: 406-265-3506. p. 1295

Ostermayer, Fiona, Libr Dir, Hinsdale Public Library, 58 Maple St, Hinsdale, MA, 01235. Tel: 413-655-2303. p. 1024

Ostertag-Holtkamp, Barbara, Libr Dir, Leach Library, 276 Mammoth Rd, Londonderry, NH, 03053. Tel: 603-432-1132. p. 1371

Osterud, Amelia, Br Mgr, Milwaukee Public Library, Mill Road, 6431 N 76th St, Milwaukee, WI, 53223. p. 2460

Osther, Jennifer, Coop Librn, Arcadis Corporate Library, 55 St Clair Ave W, 7th Flr, Toronto, ON, M4V 2Y7, CANADA. Tel: 416-596-1930, Ext 61332. p. 2686

Ostiguy, Karen, Head, Circ, Sandwich Public Library, 142 Main St, Sandwich, MA, 02563. Tel: 508-888-0625. p. 1052

Ostler, Jon, Dir of Libr, Snow College, 141 E Center St, Ephraim, UT, 84627. Tel: 435-283-7363. p. 2263

Ostness, Diana, Adult Serv, Thomas St Angelo Public Library, 1305 Second Ave, Cumberland, WI, 54829. Tel: 715-822-2767. p. 2429

Ostos, Manuel, Librn, Pennsylvania State University Libraries, George & Sherry Middlemas Arts & Humanities Library, Pennsylvania State University, W 337 Pattee Library, University Park, PA, 16802-1801. Tel: 814-865-3693. p. 2016

Ostoyich, Rebecca, Coordr, Archives & Spec Coll, Valparaiso University, 1410 Chapel Dr, Valparaiso, IN, 46383-6493. Tel: 219-464-5808. p. 723

Ostrander, Mary, Ch Serv, Stoughton Public Library, 304 S Fourth St, Stoughton, WI, 53589. Tel: 608-873-6281. p. 2479

Ostrander, Sunday, Dir, Howe Memorial Library, 128 E Saginaw St, Breckenridge, MI, 48615. Tel: 989-842-3202. p. 1087

Ostrofsky, Kathryn, Archivist, Dedham Historical Society, 612 High St, Dedham, MA, 02026. Tel: 781-326-1385. p. 1014

Ostrom, Franki, Instrul Librn, Washburn University, 1700 SW College Ave, Topeka, KS, 66621. Tel: 785-670-1932. p. 839

Ostroski, Sandra, Br Mgr, Jacksonville Public Library, University Park Branch, 3435 University Blvd N, Jacksonville, FL, 32277-2464. Tel: 904-630-1265. p. 412

Osuch, Barbara Byrne, Dir, Park Forest Public Library, 400 Lakewood Blvd, Park Forest, IL, 60466. Tel: 708-748-3731. p. 633

Osuji, Cassandra, Circ Mgr, United States Army, Grant Library, 1637 Flint St, Fort Carson, CO, 80913-4105. Tel: 719-526-2350. p. 280

Osuna, Linda, Library Mgr, Explore, Hillsboro Public Library, 2850 NE Brookwood Pkwy, Hillsboro, OR, 97124. Tel: 503-615-6500. p. 1881

Oswald, Aime, Br Mgr, Coweta Public Library System, A Mitchell Powell Jr Public Library, 25 Hospital Rd, Newnan, GA, 30263. Tel: 770-253-3625. p. 492

Oswald, Dawn, Info Res, Libr Serv Mgr, Penn State University York, 1031 Edgecomb Ave, York, PA, 17403. Tel: 717-777-4021. p. 2026

Oswald, Debra, Dir, Sinclair Community College Library, 444 W Third St, Dayton, OH, 45402-1460. Tel: 937-512-3007. p. 1780

Oswald, Tina, Research Librn, Stephen F Austin State University, 1936 North St, Nacogdoches, TX, 75962. Tel: 936-468-1861. p. 2221

Oswalt, Julie, Bus Mgr, Pendleton Community Library, 595 E Water St, Pendleton, IN, 46064-1070. Tel: 765-778-7527. p. 713

Oszakiewski, Robert, Ref Librn, Porter, Wright, Morris & Arthur, LLP, Huntington Ctr, 41 S High St, Columbus, OH, 43215-6194. p. 1777

Ota, Kelii, Mgr, Clark County Law Library, 309 S Third St, Ste 400, Las Vegas, NV, 89101. Tel: 702-455-4696. p. 1346

Ota, Stella, Head Librn, Stanford University Libraries, Chemistry & Chemical Engineering Library, Robin Li & Melissa Ma Science Library, 376 Lomita Dr, Stanford, CA, 94305. Tel: 650-725-1039. p. 248

Ota, Stella, Head Librn, Stanford University Libraries, Robin Li & Melissa Ma Science Library, Sapp Ctr for Science Teaching & Learning, Rm 315, 376 Lomita Dr, Stanford, CA, 94305. Tel: 650-723-1528. p. 248

Otero, Maria M, Dir, University of Puerto Rico, Law School Library, Avenidas Ponce de Leon & Gandara, San Juan, PR, 00931. Tel: 787-999-9684, 787-999-9702. p. 2514

Oti, Felicia, Dir, Franklin Public Library, 118 Main St, Franklin, MA, 02038. Tel: 508-520-4941. p. 1020

Otieno, Evaline, Circ, Oakwood University, 7000 Adventist Blvd NW, Huntsville, AL, 35896. Tel: 256-726-7246. p. 22

Otsuki, Sachiko, Curator, Oregon Coast History Center, Burrows House, 545 SW Ninth St, Newport, OR, 97365. Tel: 541-265-7509. p. 1888

Ott, Elaine, Libr Dir, Marble Rock Public Library, 122 S Main St, Marble Rock, IA, 50653. Tel: 641-315-4480. p. 767

Ott, Elaine, Libr Asst, Aultman Hospital, Aultman Education Ctr, C2-230, 2600 Seventh St SW, Canton, OH, 44710-1799. Tel: 330-363-5000. p. 1755

Ott, Michelle Nielsen, Dir, Libr Serv, Methodist College Library, 7600 N Academic Dr, Peoria, IL, 61615. Tel: 309-672-5513. p. 634

Ott, Nora, Human Res Coordr, Marigold Library System, 710 Second St, Strathmore, AB, T1P 1K4, CANADA. Tel: 403-934-5334, Ext 222. p. 2555

Ott, Sandra, Dir, Res, Alva Public Library, 504 Seventh St, Alva, OK, 73717. Tel: 580-327-1833. p. 1840

Otte, Bobbi, Libr Dir, Rocky Mountain College, 1511 Poly Dr, Billings, MT, 59102-1796. Tel: 406-657-1086. p. 1288

Otte, Michelle, Dir, Kenyon Public Library, 709 Second St, Kenyon, MN, 55946-1339. Tel: 507-789-6821. p. 1179

Otter, Saralyn, Commun Librn, Santa Clara County Library District, Saratoga Community Library, 13650 Saratoga Ave, Saratoga, CA, 95070. Tel: 408-867-6126. p. 127

Otterson, Linda, Dir, Programming, Kindred Public Library, 330 Elm St, Kindred, ND, 58051. Tel: 701-428-3456. p. 1736

Ottinger, Jeanne M, Dir, Law Librn, Law Library of Montgomery County, Court House, Two E Airy St, Norristown, PA, 19404. Tel: 610-278-3806. p. 1971

Ottman, Claire, Libr Mgr, Cherry Valley Memorial Library, 61 Main St, Cherry Valley, NY, 13320. Tel: 607-264-8214. p. 1517

Otto, Jessica, Ad, Digital Content Librn, Newberg Public Library, 503 E Hancock St, Newberg, OR, 97132. Tel: 503-554-7733. p. 1888

Otto, Jessica, Research & Statistics Consultant, Wyoming State Library, 2800 Central Ave, Cheyenne, WY, 82002. Tel: 307-777-6330. p. 2493

Otto, Justin, Interim Dean of Libr, Eastern Washington University, 320 Media Lane, 100 LIB, Cheney, WA, 99004-2453. Tel: 509-359-7888. p. 2361

Otto, Tonya, Online Learning Librn, Pennsylvania Western University - Clarion, 840 Wood St, Clarion, PA, 16214. Tel: 814-393-2329. p. 1922

Ottolenghi, Carol, Dir, Libr Serv, Ohio Attorney General, 30 E Broad St, 15th Flr, Columbus, OH, 43215. Tel: 614-466-2465. p. 1774

Ottoson, Carolyn, Doc Librn, West Texas A&M University, 110 26th St, Canyon, TX, 79016. Tel: 806-651-2204. p. 2153

Oubre, Marcia, Librn, Fred Heutte Horticultural Library, 6700 Azalea Garden Rd, Norfolk, VA, 23518-5337. Tel: 757-441-5830. p. 2334

Ouellet, Nathalie, Librn, College Edouard-Montpetit Bibliotheque, Ecole Nationale d'Aerotechnique Bibliotheque, 5555, rue de l'ENA, Longueuil, QC, J3Y 0Y3, CANADA. Tel: 450-678-3561, Ext 4599. p. 2716

Ouellette, Amanda, Libr Assoc, Maine State Law & Legislative Reference Library, 43 State House Sta, Augusta, ME, 04333-0043. Tel: 207-287-1600. p. 914

Ouellette, Brigitte, Libr Tech, Bibliothèque du CISSS de l'Outaouais, CISSS de l'Outaouais - Hôpital Pierre-Janet, 20 rue Pharand, Gatineau, QC, J9A 1K7, CANADA. Tel: 819-966-6187. p. 2712

Ouellette, Brigitte, Documentation Tech, Centre Hospitalier des Vallees de l'Outaouais Bibliotheque, 116, Blvd Lionel-Emond, local C-001, Gatineau, QC, J8Y 1W7, CANADA. Tel: 819-966-6050. p. 2713

Ouellette, Cheryl Stern, Ch, Sherborn Library, Four Sanger St, Sherborn, MA, 01770-1499. Tel: 508-653-0770. p. 1053

Ouellette, Erika, Libr Dir, Strong Public Library, 14 S Main St, Strong, ME, 04983. Tel: 207-684-4003. p. 943

Ouellette, Francois, Dir, Teluq University, 455 rue du Parvis, F015-B, Quebec, QC, G1K 9H6, CANADA. Tel: 418-657-2262, Ext 5044. p. 2732

Ouellette, Sue, Dir, Wolcott Public Library, 469 Boundline Rd, Wolcott, CT, 06716. Tel: 203-879-8110. p. 349

Ouimet, Reba, Coordr, Electronic Health Library of British Columbia, c/o Bennett Library, 8888 University Dr, Burnaby, BC, V5A 1S6, CANADA. Tel: 236-333-2955. p. 2777

Ould, Jennifer, Coordr, Association of Chicago Theological Schools, Univ of St Mary of the Lake, 1000 E Maple Ave, Mundelein, IL, 60060. p. 2764

Oumano, Emily, Law Librn, Connecticut Judicial Branch Law Libraries, Rockville Law Library, Rockville Courthouse, 69 Brooklyn St, Rockville, CT, 06066. Tel: 860-896-4955. p. 316

Ourada, Kari, Dir, Westbrook Public Library, 556 First Ave, Westbrook, MN, 56183. Tel: 507-274-6174. p. 1207

Ousley, LaDora, Mgr, Libr Serv, Hocking College Library, Davidson Hall, First Flr, 3301 Hocking Pkwy, Nelsonville, OH, 45764. Tel: 740-753-6338. p. 1805

Outhier, Sara, Performing Arts & Humanities Librn, University of Kansas Libraries, Thomas Gorton Music & Dance Library, 1530 Naismith Dr, Lawrence, KS, 66045-3102. Tel: 785-864-0389. p. 820

Outhouse, Dale, Tech Serv Librn, University of Bridgeport, 126 Park Ave, Bridgeport, CT, 06604-5620. Tel: 203-576-4528. p. 304

Outlaw, Shirley, Libr Serv Coordr, College of the Albemarle Library, 1208 N Road St, Elizabeth City, NC, 27906. Tel: 252-335-0821, Ext 2270. p. 1687

Outler, Jan, Br Mgr, Ohoopee Regional Library System, 610 Jackson St, Vidalia, GA, 30474-2835. Tel: 912-537-9283, Ext 104. p. 501

Ouwinga, Heidi, Admin Serv, Sioux Center Public Library, 102 S Main Ave, Sioux Center, IA, 51250-1801. Tel: 712-722-2138. p. 782

Ouyang, Han, Asst Dir, Tech Serv, University of the District of Columbia, David A Clarke School of Law, Charles N & Hilda H M Mason Law Library, Bldg 39, Rm B-16, 4200 Connecticut Ave NW, Washington, DC, 20008. Tel: 202-274-7358. p. 380

Ouzts, Tracey, Libr Dir, Greenwood County Library, 600 S Main St, Greenwood, SC, 29646. Tel: 864-941-4650. p. 2062

Ovadia, Steven, Dep Chief Librn, Fiorello H LaGuardia Community College Library, 31-10 Thomson Ave, Long Island City, NY, 11101. Tel: 718-482-6022. p. 1565

Ovalle, Norma, Dir, Mathis Public Library, 103 Lamar St, Mathis, TX, 78368. Tel: 361-547-6201. p. 2216

Ovando, Eden, Br Mgr, Riverside County Library System, Nuview Library, 29990 Lakeview Ave, Nuevo, CA, 92567. Tel: 951-928-0769. p. 202

Ovando, Eden, Br Mgr, Riverside County Library System, Paloma Valley Library, 31375 Bradley Rd, Menifee, CA, 92584. Tel: 951-301-3682. p. 202

Overall, Scott, Assoc Dir, University Club Library, One W 54th St, New York, NY, 10019. Tel: 212-572-3418. p. 1603

Overbeck, Nicole, Children's & Teen Serv, Berlin Public Library, 121 W Park Ave, Berlin, WI, 54923. Tel: 920-361-5420. p. 2424

Overbeck, Nicole, Libr Dir, Markesan Public Library, 75 N Bridge St, Markesan, WI, 53946. Tel: 920-398-3434. p. 2454

Overbeck, Rachel, Dir, Stoneham Public Library, 431 Main St, Stoneham, MA, 02180. Tel: 781-438-1324. p. 1058

Overdorf, Ryan, Sr Electronic/Media Serv Librn, University of Toledo, LaValley Law Library, Mail Stop 508, 2801 W Bancroft St, Toledo, OH, 43606-3390. Tel: 419-530-2733. p. 1825

Overfield, Daniel, Asst Prof, Librn, Cuyahoga Community College, Metropolitan Campus Library, 2900 Community College Ave, Cleveland, OH, 44115. Tel: 216-987-4296. p. 1769

Overman, Marcina, Dir, Newkirk Public Library, 116 N Maple Ave, Newkirk, OK, 74647-4011. Tel: 580-362-3934. p. 1855

Overman, Mark, Mgr, Mann-Grandstaff VA Medical Center, 4815 N Assembly St, Spokane, WA, 99205-2697. Tel: 509-434-7575. p. 2383

Overstreet, Leslie K, Curator, Natural Hist Rare Bks, Smithsonian Libraries, Joseph F Cullman III, Library of Natural History, Nat Museum of Natural History, Tenth St & Constitution Ave NW, Washington, DC, 20560. Tel: 202-633-1176. p. 375

Overton, Brittany, Librn, Minot-Sleeper Library, 35 Pleasant St, Bristol, NH, 03222-1407. Tel: 603-744-3352. p. 1356

Overton, Catherine, Libr Dir, Rockville Centre Public Library, 221 N Village Ave, Rockville Centre, NY, 11570. Tel: 516-766-6257. p. 1632

Overton, Jen, Dir, Roseland Free Public Library, 20 Roseland Ave, Roseland, NJ, 07068-1235. Tel: 973-226-8636. p. 1441

Overton, Robert, Jr, Exec Dir, University of West Florida Historic Trust, 117 E Government St, Pensacola, FL, 32502. Tel: 850-595-5985, Ext 106. p. 437

Overton, Tammy, Br Mgr, Desoto Parish Library, Stonewall Branch, 808 Hwy 171, Stonewall, LA, 71078. Tel: 318-925-9191. p. 896

Overton, Tracy, Tech Serv, Pueblo Community College Library, 900 W Orman Ave, Pueblo, CO, 81004-1430. Tel: 719-549-3307. p. 293

Owad, Cynthia, Dir, York Haven Community Library, Two N Front St, York Haven, PA, 17370. Tel: 717-266-4712. p. 2027

Owczarski, Beata, Dir, Cardinal Adam Maida Alumni Library, SS Cyril & Methodius Seminary, 3535 Indian Trail, Orchard Lake, MI, 48324. Tel: 248-392-9963. p. 1139

Owen, Ann, Digital Serv Librn, Sacred Heart Seminary & School of Theology, 7335 Lovers Lane Rd, Franklin, WI, 53132. Tel: 414-858-4659. p. 2436

Owen, Dana, ILL Spec, Longwood University, Redford & Race St, Farmville, VA, 23909. p. 2318

Owen, Dana L, Info Serv, Warsaw Community Public Library, 310 E Main St, Warsaw, IN, 46580-2882. Tel: 574-267-6011. p. 724

Owen, Eric, Dir, Libr Serv, Sam Houston State University, 1830 Bobby K Marks Dr, Huntsville, TX, 77340. Tel: 936-294-1613. p. 2201

Owen, Frosty, Librn, Hunton Andrews Kurth LLP, Riverfront Plaza, E Tower, 951 E Byrd St, Richmond, VA, 23219-4074. Tel: 804-788-8200. p. 2340

Owen Hasting, Emily, Dir, Canton Free Library, Eight Park St, Canton, NY, 13617. Tel: 315-386-3712. p. 1513

Owen, Henry, III, Bus Librn, Northeastern Illinois University, 5500 N Saint Louis Ave, Chicago, IL, 60625-4699. Tel: 773-442-4400. p. 566

Owen, John, Libr Dir, Maryland State Library for the Blind & Print Disabled, 415 Park Ave, Baltimore, MD, 21201-3603. Tel: 410-230-2424. p. 955

Owen, John, Dir, Maryland State Library, 25 S Charles St, Ste 1310, Baltimore, MD, 21201. Tel: 410-230-2452. p. 955

Owen, Karen, Librn, Benewah County District Library, 304 C St, Tensed, ID, 83870. Tel: 208-274-2922. p. 531

Owen, Keitha, Dir, Ocean Shores Public Library, 573 Point Brown Ave NW, Ocean Shores, WA, 98569. Tel: 360-289-3919. p. 2372

Owen, Matt, College Library Director, Syst Librn, San Diego Christian College & Southern California Seminary Library, c/o San Diego Christian College, 200 Riverview Pkwy, Santee, CA, 92071. Tel: 619-201-8680. p. 245

Owen, Melesha, Supv Librn, Hayward Public Library, Weekes Branch, 27300 Patrick Ave, Hayward, CA, 94544. Tel: 510-293-5239. p. 151

Owen, Rebecca, Head, Access Serv, University of Virginia, Arthur J Morris Law Library, 580 Massie Rd, Charlottesville, VA, 22903-1738. Tel: 434-924-3384. p. 2310

Owen, Sarah, Libr Dir, Independence Community College Library, 1057 W College Ave, Independence, KS, 67301. Tel: 620-331-4100, 620-332-5468. p. 815

Owen, Sheila, Assoc Librn, Harding School of Theology, 1000 Cherry Rd, Memphis, TN, 38117. Tel: 901-761-1354. p. 2112

Owens, Becky, Mgr, South Texas College Library, 3201 W Pecan Blvd, McAllen, TX, 78501-6661. Tel: 956-872-6487. p. 2217

Owens, Bethia, Dir, Muldrow Public Library, 711 W Shanntel Smith Blvd, Muldrow, OK, 74948. Tel: 918-427-6703. p. 1854

Owens, Bethia, Mgr, Stanley Tubbs Memorial Library, 101 E Cherokee St, Sallisaw, OK, 74955. Tel: 918-775-4481. p. 1861

Owens, Brandon A, PhD, Dean of the Library, Fisk University, 1000 17th Ave N, Nashville, TN, 37208-3051. Tel: 615-668-8731. p. 2118

Owens, Carla, Mgr, Libr Serv, Chicago Zoological Society, 3300 Golf Rd, Brookfield, IL, 60513. p. 545

Owens, Carla, Librn II, National Opinion Research Center Library, 1155 E 60th St, Rm 369, Chicago, IL, 60637-2667. Tel: 773-256-6206. p. 565

Owens, Chris, Dir, Blanchester Public Library, 110 N Broadway, Blanchester, OH, 45107-1250. Tel: 937-783-3585. p. 1751

Owens, Dan, Dir, Neill Public Library, 210 N Grand Ave, Pullman, WA, 99163-2693. Tel: 509-334-3595. p. 2374

Owens, David, Head, Tech Serv, University of Missouri-Saint Louis Libraries, Thomas Jefferson Library, One University Blvd, Saint Louis, MO, 63121-4400. Tel: 314-516-5060. p. 1276

Owens, David, Asst Dir, Adult Serv, Cabell County Public Library, 455 Ninth Street Plaza, Huntington, WV, 25701. Tel: 304-528-5700. p. 2404

Owens, Debbie, Ch, West Plains Public Library, 750 W Broadway St, West Plains, MO, 65775. Tel: 417-256-4775. p. 1286

Owens, Ellen, Libr Mgr, Crouse Health Library, 736 Irving Ave, Syracuse, NY, 13210. Tel: 315-470-7380. p. 1648

Owens, Fonda, Dir, La Porte County Public Library, 904 Indiana Ave, La Porte, IN, 46350. Tel: 219-362-6156. p. 700

Owens, Geoff, Librn, Mount Royal University Library, 4825 Mount Royal Gate SW, Calgary, AB, T3E 6K6, CANADA. Tel: 403-440-7737. p. 2528

Owens, Glenda, Circ, Nelson County Public Library, Bloomfield Branch, 34 Arnold Lane, Bloomfield, KY, 40008. Tel: 502-252-9129. p. 848

Owens, Jacqulyn, Libr Dir, Memphis Public Library, 303 S Eighth St, Memphis, TX, 79245. Tel: 806-259-2062. p. 2218

Owens, Jessica, Syst Librn, Grossmont College Library, 8800 Grossmont College Dr, El Cajon, CA, 92020-1799. Tel: 619-644-7356. p. 139

Owens, Jonah, Exec Dir, Caroline County Public Library, 100 Market St, Denton, MD, 21629. Tel: 410-479-1343. p. 964

Owens, Katherine, Spec Coll Librn, Flagler College, 44 Sevilla St, Saint Augustine, FL, 32084-4302. Tel: 904-819-6206. p. 439

Owens, Kristine, Cataloger, Electronic Serv, Instruction & Ref Librn, Malone University, 2600 Cleveland Ave NW, Canton, OH, 44709-3308. Tel: 330-471-8557. p. 1755

Owens, Krystal, Br Mgr, El Dorado County Library, Pollock Pines Branch, 6210 Pony Express Trail, Pollock Pines, CA, 95726. Tel: 530-644-2498. p. 195

Owens, L, Dir, Viola Public Library, 137 S Main St, Viola, WI, 54664-7037. Tel: 608-627-1850. p. 2482

Owens, Michelle, Coll Develop Librn, Rogers State University Library, 1701 W Will Rogers Blvd, Claremore, OK, 74017-3252. Tel: 918-343-7720. p. 1844

Owens, Paige, Dir, New Hanover County Public Library, 201 Chestnut St, Wilmington, NC, 28401. Tel: 910-798-6321. p. 1723

Owens, Rachel, Coll Develop, Fac Serv Librn, Daytona State College Library, Bldg 115, Rm 314, 1200 W International Speedway Blvd, Daytona Beach, FL, 32114. Tel: 386-506-3842. p. 392

Owens, Rita, Outreach Coordr, Polk County Public Library, 1289 W Mills St, Columbus, NC, 28722. Tel: 828-894-8721. p. 1682

Owens, Rodney, Librn, Green Bay Correctional Institution Library, PO Box 19033, Green Bay, WI, 54307-9033. Tel: 920-432-4877, Ext 3457. p. 2438

Owens, Ronna, ILL, Mkt Librn, North Central Missouri College Library, Geyer Hall, 1st & 2nd Flr, 1301 Main St, Trenton, MO, 64683. Tel: 660-359-3948, Ext 1322, 660-359-3948, Ext 1325, 660-359-3948, Ext 1335. p. 1282

Owens, Ruth, ILL, State University of New York, College of Environmental Science & Forestry, One Forestry Dr, Syracuse, NY, 13210. Tel: 315-470-4780. p. 1650
Owens, Sharon, Br Mgr, Newark Public Library, Springfield, 50 Hayes St, Newark, NJ, 07103. Tel: 973-733-7736. p. 1427
Owens, Sheldon, Interim Asst Dir, Chattanooga Public Library, 1001 Broad St, Chattanooga, TN, 37402-2652. Tel: 423-643-7700. p. 2091
Owens, Stephanie, Dir, Libr Serv, God's Bible School & College Library, 507 Ringgold St, Cincinnati, OH, 45202. Tel: 513-721-7944, Ext 5112. p. 1760
Owens, Tammie, Head Librn, Knott County Public Library, 238 Hwy 160 S, Hindman, KY, 41822. Tel: 606-785-5412. p. 859
Owens, Wendy, Fac Librn, City College of San Francisco, 50 Frida Kahlo Way, 4th Flr, San Francisco, CA, 94112. Tel: 415-452-5433. p. 224
Owens, Whitney, Learning Technologies & Systems Spec, Catawba College, 2300 W Innes St, Salisbury, NC, 28144-2488. Tel: 704-637-4239. p. 1714
Owings, Connie, Circ, Tech Serv, Scott County Library System, 200 N Sixth Ave, Eldridge, IA, 52748. Tel: 563-285-4794. p. 750
Owings, David, Head, Archives & Spec Coll, Columbus State University Libraries, 4225 University Ave, Columbus, GA, 31907. Tel: 706-507-8674. p. 472
Owings, Heather, Br Mgr, Carroll County Public Library, Finksburg Branch, 2265 Old Westminster Pike, Finksburg, MD, 21048. p. 971
Owings, Kathy, Dir, Demopolis Public Library, 211 E Washington, Demopolis, AL, 36732. Tel: 334-289-1595. p. 14
Owiny, Sylvia A, PhD, Soc Sci Librn, Pennsylvania State University Libraries, Social Sciences & Education, 208 Paterno Library, 2nd & 5th Flrs, University Park, PA, 16802-1809. Tel: 814-865-8864. p. 2016
Ownby, David, Tech Serv Mgr, Johnson City Public Library, 100 W Millard St, Johnson City, TN, 37604. Tel: 423-434-4343. p. 2104
Owusu, Jaclyn, Pub Awareness Coordr, Texas State Library & Archives Commission, 1201 Brazos St, Austin, TX, 78701. Tel: 512-463-5452. p. 2141
Owusu-Ansah, Edward, Dr, Dean of Libr, William Paterson University, 300 Pompton Rd, Wayne, NJ, 07470. Tel: 973-720-3179. p. 1451
Owusu-Nkwantabisa, Nana, Dir, Libr & Learning Commons, Howard Community College Library, 10901 Little Patuxent Pkwy, 2nd Flr, Columbia, MD, 21044. Tel: 443-518-4634. p. 963
Oxendine, Kara, Asst Dir, Tech Serv, Syst Librn, University of North Carolina at Pembroke, One University Dr, Pembroke, NC, 28372. Tel: 910-521-6516. p. 1707
Oxford, Mary-Catherine, Dean, Learning Res, Santa Rosa Junior College, 1501 Mendocino Ave, Santa Rosa, CA, 95401. Tel: 707-527-4392. p. 245
Oxford, Mary-Catherine, Dir, Learning Res, College of the Sequoias Library, 915 S Mooney Blvd, Visalia, CA, 93277. Tel: 559-730-3824. p. 257
Oxford, Ron, Librn, West Hills College Lemoore Library, 555 College Ave, Lemoore, CA, 93245. Tel: 559-925-3403. p. 156
Oxild, Ryan, Ch, Verona Public Library, 17 Gould St, Verona, NJ, 07044-1928. Tel: 973-857-4848. p. 1449
Oxley, Peter, Assoc Dir, Res Serv, Cornell University Library, Samuel J Wood Library & C V Starr Biomedical Information Center, 1300 York Ave, C115, Box 67, New York, NY, 10065-4896. Tel: 646-962-2576. p. 1552
Oxley, Rebecca, Mgr, District of Columbia Public Library, Rosedale, 1701 Gales St NE, Washington, DC, 20002. Tel: 202-727-5012. p. 364
Oyerly, Anne, Mgr, Spec Coll, Andrews University, 4190 Administration Dr, Berrien Springs, MI, 49104-1400. Tel: 269-471-3976. p. 1085
Ozanich, Nicole E, Youth Serv Librn, Portage County Public Library, Charles M White Library Bldg, 1001 Main St, Stevens Point, WI, 54481-2860. Tel: 715-346-1544. p. 2479
Ozburn, Britt, Asst Dir, Conyers-Rockdale Library System, 864 Green St SW, Conyers, GA, 30012. Tel: 770-388-5040. p. 472
Ozier, Crystal, Dir, Everett Horn Public Library, 702 W Church St, Lexington, TN, 38351-1713. Tel: 731-968-3239. p. 2109
Ozimek, Jo, Circ Supvr, Saint Paris Public Library, 127 E Main St, Saint Paris, OH, 43072. Tel: 937-663-4349. p. 1819
Ozmore, Brittany, Libr Assoc, Georgia Highlands College Libraries, 5441 Hwy 20 NE, Cartersville, GA, 30121. Tel: 678-872-8400. p. 470
Ozoh, Ruthina, Br Mgr, Henry County Public Library System, 1001 Florence McGarity Blvd, McDonough, GA, 30252. Tel: 678-432-5353. p. 490
Paap-Young, Melissa, Youth Serv Librn, Butler Public Library, 12808 W Hampton Ave, Butler, WI, 53007. Tel: 262-783-2535. p. 2426
Paarsmith, Allie, Dir, West Liberty Free Public Library, 400 N Spencer St, West Liberty, IA, 52776. Tel: 319-627-2084. p. 791
Paavola, Morgan, Univ Archivist & Rec Mgr, University of Wisconsin-River Falls, 410 S Third St, River Falls, WI, 54022. Tel: 715-425-3567. p. 2474
Pabarja, Julie, Libr Mgr, Mgr, Res, Latham & Watkins, 330 N Wabash Ave, Ste 2800, Chicago, IL, 60611. Tel: 312-876-7700. p. 563
Pabian, Linda R, Info Serv Librn, Oradell Free Public Library, 375 Kinderkamack Rd, Oradell, NJ, 07649-2122. Tel: 201-262-2613. p. 1431
Pablo, Carmella, Libr Asst, Tohono O'odham Community College Library, Hwy 86 Milepost 111 W, Sells, AZ, 85634. Tel: 520-383-0032. p. 78
Pac, Rebecca, Ref & Instruction Librn, Anna Maria College, 50 Sunset Lane, Paxton, MA, 01612-1198. Tel: 508-849-3405. p. 1045
Pacciotti, Jessica, Libr Dir, Perry Public Library, 70 N Main St, Perry, NY, 14530-1299. Tel: 585-237-2243. p. 1617
Pacciotti, Jessica, Dir, Warner Library, 121 N Broadway, Tarrytown, NY, 10591. Tel: 914-631-7734. p. 1651
Pace, Andrew, Exec Dir, Association of Research Libraries, 21 Dupont Circle NW, Ste 800, Washington, DC, 20036. Tel: 202-296-2296. p. 2763
Pace, Charles, Exec Dir, Gwinnett County Public Library, 1001 Lawrenceville Hwy NW, Lawrenceville, GA, 30046-4707. Tel: 770-978-5154. p. 485
Pace Dickenson, Jen, Youth Serv Librn, Polk County Public Library, 1289 W Mills St, Columbus, NC, 28722. Tel: 828-894-8721. p. 1682
Pace, Michael, Ref, Neumann University Library, One Neumann Dr, Aston, PA, 19014-1298. Tel: 610-558-5543. p. 1907
Pace, Rebecca, Dir, Peru Free Library, 3024 Rte 22, Peru, NY, 12972. Tel: 518-643-8618. p. 1617
Pace-McGowan, Sarah, Adult Serv Mgr, McCracken County Public Library, 555 Washington St, Paducah, KY, 42003. Tel: 270-442-2510. p. 872
Pacella, Veronica, Dir, Ellwood City Area Public Library, 415 Lawrence Ave, Ellwood City, PA, 16117-1944. Tel: 724-758-6458. p. 1930
Pacenza, Joyce M, Exec Dir, Tulsa County Law Library, Courthouse, 2nd Flr, 500 S Denver Ave, Tulsa, OK, 74103. Tel: 918-596-5404. p. 1867
Pacheco, Ana, Asst Librn, University of New Mexico, Taos Campus, 115 Civic Plaza Dr, Taos, NM, 87571. Tel: 575-737-6242. p. 1463
Pacheco, Christine, Pres, Dighton Historical Society Museum Library, 1217 Williams St, Dighton, MA, 02715-1013. Tel: 508-669-5514. p. 1014
Pacheco, Patricia, Mgr, Loudoun County Public Library, Outreach Services, 380 Old Waterford Rd NW, Leesburg, VA, 20176. Tel: 703-771-3107. p. 2328
Pachman, Frederic C, Libr Dir, Monmouth Medical Center, 300 Second Ave, Long Branch, NJ, 07740. Tel: 732-923-6645. p. 1414
Pachnanda, Swadesh, Dir, Tuckahoe Public Library, 71 Columbus Ave, Tuckahoe, NY, 10707. Tel: 914-961-2121. p. 1653
Pacion, Kelee, Librn, Princeton University, Lewis Science Library, Washington Rd, Princeton, NJ, 08544-0001. Tel: 609-258-8601. p. 1437
Pack, Mary, Br Mgr, Sumter County Library, Wesmark Branch Library, 180 W Wesmark Blvd, Sumter, SC, 29150. Tel: 803-469-8110. p. 2071
Pack, Nancy, Dir, Alabama Public Library Service, 6030 Monticello Dr, Montgomery, AL, 36130. Tel: 334-213-3902., Dir, Alabama Public Library Service, 6030 Monticello Dr, Montgomery, AL, 36130. Tel: 334-213-3902. p. 27, 28
Pack, Suzy, Libr Dir, Merkel Public Library, 100 Kent St, Merkel, TX, 79536. Tel: 325-928-5054. p. 2218
Packard, Anne, Dir, United Methodist Church - South Georgia Conference, Epworth-by-the-Sea, 100 Arthur Moore Dr, Saint Simons Island, GA, 31522. Tel: 912-638-4050. p. 495
Packard, Marko, Ref & Coll Develop Librn, Springfield Technical Community College Library, One Armory Sq, Bldg 27, Ste 1, Springfield, MA, 01105. Tel: 413-755-4565. p. 1057
Packard, Sarah, Br Librn, Wilson County Public Library, Black Creek Branch, 103 Central Ave, Black Creek, NC, 27813. Tel: 252-237-3715. p. 1724
Packer, Cheri, Librn, Emery County Library System, Green River Branch, 85 S Long St, Green River, UT, 84525. Tel: 435-564-3349. p. 2262
Paddick, Courtney, Research Librn, Education, Bloomsburg University of Pennsylvania, 400 E Second St, Bloomsburg, PA, 17815-1301. Tel: 570-389-4656. p. 1913
Paddock, Denise, Librn II, Ohio Department of Rehabilitation & Correction, 1580 State Rte 56 SW, London, OH, 43140. Tel: 740-490-6700. p. 1797
Paddock, Sue, Mgr, Carbon County Library System, Saratoga Branch, 503 W Elm St, Saratoga, WY, 82331. Tel: 307-326-8209. p. 2498
Paddock, Susan, Libr Mgr, Virginia Beach Public Library, Bayside Area & Special Services Library, 936 Independence Blvd, Virginia Beach, VA, 23455. Tel: 757-385-2680. p. 2350
Paden, Hardy, Br Mgr, Stanislaus County Library, Hughson Branch, 2412 Third St, Ste A, Hughson, CA, 95326. Tel: 209-883-2293. p. 178
Paden, Treva, Ch, ILL Librn, Ellinwood School & Community Library, 210 N Schiller Ave, Ellinwood, KS, 67526. Tel: 620-564-2306. p. 806
Padgett, Juliet, Br Mgr, Atlanta-Fulton Public Library System, Roswell Branch, 115 Norcross St, Roswell, GA, 30075. Tel: 770-640-3075. p. 461
Padgett, Kenan, Interlibrary Loan/Info Servs Librn, Rhodes College, 2000 North Pkwy, Memphis, TN, 38112-1694. Tel: 901-843-3890. p. 2114
Padilla Bowen, Jessica, Commun Relations Mgr, Carlsbad City Library, 1775 Dove Lane, Carlsbad, CA, 92011. Tel: 760-602-2024. p. 127
Padilla, Dora, Res Tech, Southwest Texas Junior College, 207 Wildcat Dr, Del Rio, TX, 78840. Tel: 830-703-1563. p. 2169
Padilla, Gregory, Access Serv Mgr, Massachusetts Institute of Technology Libraries, Dewey Library for Management & Social Sciences, MIT Bldg, Rm E53-100, 30 Wadsworth St, Cambridge, MA, 02139. Tel: 617-253-2722. p. 1008
Padilla, Irene, State Librn, Maryland State Library, 25 S Charles St, Ste 1310, Baltimore, MD, 21201. Tel: 667-219-4801. p. 955

Padilla, Virginia, Head Librn, Truchas Community Library, 60 County Rd 75, Truchas, NM, 87578. Tel: 505-689-2683. p. 1479
Padua, Noelia, Dir, Pontifical Catholic University, Monsignor Fremiot Torres Oliver Law Library, 2250 Blvd Luis A Ferre Aguayo, Ste 544, Ponce, PR, 00717-9997. Tel: 787-841-2000, Ext 1852. p. 2512
Pagan, Alberto, Br Mgr, Free Library of Philadelphia, Charles L Durham Branch, 3320 Haverford Ave, Philadelphia, PA, 19104-2021. Tel: 215-685-7436. p. 1978
Pagán, Evelyn, Libr Tech, USDA Forest Service, Jardin Botanico Sur, 1201 Calle Ceiba, San Juan, PR, 00926-1119. Tel: 787-764-2250. p. 2515
Pagan, Maria G, Dir, Holyoke Public Library, 250 Chestnut St, Holyoke, MA, 01040-4858. Tel: 413-420-8101. p. 1025
Pagan, Maribel, Librn, Klamath Community College, 7390 S Sixth St, Klamath Falls, OR, 97603. Tel: 541-880-2206. p. 1882
Pagan Martinez, Jose, Chief Librn, University of Puerto Rico Library System, Library Services for Persons with Disabilities, Rio Piedras Campus, Jose M Lazaro Bldg, San Juan, PR, 00931. Tel: 787-764-0000, Ext 85840, 787-764-0000, Ext 85849. p. 2515
Pagan, Natha, Br Supvr, Greater Victoria Public Library, Juan de Fuca Branch, 1759 Island Hwy, Victoria, BC, V9B 1J1, CANADA. Tel: 250-940-4875, Ext 804. p. 2583
Paganelli, Andrea, Dr, Assoc Prof, Graduate Program Coord, Western Kentucky University, School of Teacher Education, Gary A Ransdell Hall, Office 1005, 1906 College Heights Blvd, No 61030, Bowling Green, KY, 42101-1030. Tel: 270-745-5414. p. 2785
Pagani, Regina, Experiential Learning Librn, Northeastern University Libraries, 360 Huntington Ave, Boston, MA, 02115. Tel: 617-373-3197. p. 998
Pagano, James, Asst Dir, Franklin Square Public Library, 19 Lincoln Rd, Franklin Square, NY, 11010. Tel: 516-488-3444. p. 1535
Pagdon, Briana, Libr Dir, Etowah Carnegie Public Library, 723 Ohio Ave, Etowah, TN, 37331. Tel: 423-263-9475. p. 2098
Page, Brian, IT Dir, Putnam County Library System, 50 E Broad St, Cookeville, TN, 38501. Tel: 931-526-2416. p. 2095
Page, Deborah, Librn, Cleveland County Library System, Spangler Branch Library, 112 Piedmont Dr, Lawndale, NC, 28090. Tel: 704-538-7005. p. 1716
Page, Elaine Fetyko, Head, Tech Serv, Elmhurst University, 190 Prospect St, Elmhurst, IL, 60126. Tel: 630-617-3166. p. 585
Page, Indya, ILL, Bedford Public Library System, 321 N Bridge St, Bedford, VA, 24523-1924. Tel: 540-586-8911, Ext 1112. p. 2306
Page, Isolda, Youth Serv, West Branch Public Library, 300 N Downey, West Branch, IA, 52358. Tel: 319-643-2633. p. 790
Page, Jennifer, Mgr, Angola Public Library, 34 N Main St, Angola, NY, 14006. Tel: 716-549-1271. p. 1487
Page, Jessica, Veterinary Med Librn, Ohio State University LIBRARIES, Veterinary Medicine, 225 Veterinary Medicine Academic Bldg, 1900 Coffey Rd, Columbus, OH, 43210. Tel: 614-292-6107. p. 1777
Page, Kayla, Sr Ref Librn, Cape Fear Community College, 415 N Second St, Wilmington, NC, 28401-3905. Tel: 910-362-7530. p. 1722
Page, Leslie, Dir, Woonsocket Harris Public Library, 303 Clinton St, Woonsocket, RI, 02895. Tel: 401-769-9044. p. 2044
Page, Michelle, Ch Serv, Bristol Public Library, 701 Goode St, Bristol, VA, 24201. Tel: 276-821-6193. p. 2308
Page, Paul, Librn, Delaware Technical & Community College, 400 Stanton-Christiana Rd, Rm D 201, Newark, DE, 19713-2197. Tel: 302-453-3716. p. 355
Page, Rachael, Asst Dir, Deerfield Public Library, 12 W Nelson St, Deerfield, WI, 53531-9669. Tel: 608-764-8102. p. 2430
Page, Scott, PhD, Dept Chair, Minnesota State University, Mankato, College of Education, Armstrong Hall AH 313, Mankato, MN, 56001-8400. Tel: 507-389-1788. p. 2787
Page, Tammy, Head, Circ, Holliston Public Library, 752 Washington St, Holliston, MA, 01746. Tel: 508-429-0617. p. 1025
Page, Yvette, Head Librn, Ref & Instruction, Mercy College Libraries, Manhattan Campus, 47 W 34th St, New York, NY, 10001. Tel: 212-615-3364. p. 1526
Page, Yvette, Coordr, Libr Serv, The College of New Rochelle, 29 Castle Pl, New Rochelle, NY, 10805-2308. Tel: 914-654-5345. p. 1577
Page, Yvette, Librn, College of New Rochelle, Cardinal John O'Connor Campus, 332 E 149 St, Bronx, NY, 10451. Tel: 718-665-1310. p. 1577
Pagel, Scott B, Dir, George Washington University, Jacob Burns Law Library, 716 20th St NW, Washington, DC, 20052. Tel: 202-994-7337. p. 367
Paggi, Paula, Dept Chair, Pierce College Library, 6201 Winnetka Ave, Woodland Hills, CA, 91371. Tel: 818-710-2843. p. 260
Paglia, Tanya, YA Librn, Barrington Public Library, 281 County Rd, Barrington, RI, 02806. Tel: 401-247-1920. p. 2029
Pagos, Hollin Elizabeth, Libr Dir, West Dennis Free Public Library, 260 Main St, Rte 28, West Dennis, MA, 02670. Tel: 508-398-2050. p. 1065
Pahl, Jeanine, Librn, Oakes Public Library, 804 Main Ave, Oakes, ND, 58474. Tel: 701-742-3234, Ext 155. p. 1739
Pahr, Marilyn, Bus Librn, Emory University Libraries, Goizueta Business Library, 540 Asbury Circle, Atlanta, GA, 30322. Tel: 404-727-1641. p. 463
Pahvitse, Lori, Dir, Shoshone-Bannock Library, Pima & Bannock Dr, Fort Hall, ID, 83203. Tel: 208-478-3882. p. 521
Pai, Sunny, Digital Initiatives Librn, Kapi'olani Community College Library, 4303 Diamond Head Rd, Honolulu, HI, 96816. Tel: 808-734-9755. p. 512
Paicely, Jamie L, Mrs, Libr Dir, Flossmoor Public Library, 1000 Sterling Ave, Flossmoor, IL, 60422-1295. Tel: 708-798-3600. p. 588
Paige, LaVerne, Tech Serv Mgr, Sweet Briar College, 134 Chapel Rd, Sweet Briar, VA, 24595. Tel: 434-381-6135. p. 2348
Paige, Sarah, Instr Librn, Eastern Florida State College, 250 Community College Pkwy, Palm Bay, FL, 32909. Tel: 321-433-5270. p. 434
Paige, Thomas, Mgr, Circ Serv, University of Massachusetts Amherst Libraries, 154 Hicks Way, University of Massachusetts, Amherst, MA, 01003-9275. Tel: 413-577-2103. p. 985
Paille, Jamie, Libr Dir, Houghton Lake Public Library, 4431 W Houghton Lake Dr, Houghton Lake, MI, 48629-8713. Tel: 989-366-9230. p. 1116
Paille, Mario, Librn, College de Maisonneuve Centre des Medias, 3800 Est rue Sherbrooke E, 4th Flr, Rm D-4690, Montreal, QC, H1X 2A2, CANADA. Tel: 514-254-7131, Ext 4770. p. 2723
Paine, Beth, Libr Dir, Richmond Memorial Library, 19 Ross St, Batavia, NY, 14020. Tel: 585-343-9550. p. 1491
Paine, Beth, Dir, Sidney Memorial Public Library, Eight River St, Sidney, NY, 13838. Tel: 607-563-1200, 607-563-8021. p. 1641
Paine, Laura, Supvr, Ventura County Library, Avenue Library, 606 N Ventura Ave, Ventura, CA, 93001. Tel: 805-643-6393. p. 256
Paino, Frank, Admin Supvr, Baldwin Wallace University, 57 E Bagley Rd, Berea, OH, 44017. Tel: 440-826-2204. p. 1750
Painter, Christine, Dir, Bud Werner Memorial Library, 1289 Lincoln Ave, Steamboat Springs, CO, 80487. Tel: 970-879-0240, Ext 304. p. 295
Painter, Joy, Librn, California Institute of Technology, Astrophysics, 1201 E California Blvd, M/C 11-17, Pasadena, CA, 91125. Tel: 626-395-2290. p. 193
Painter, Marsia, Govt Doc Librn, Ref Librn, Saint Bonaventure University, 3261 W State Rd, Saint Bonaventure, NY, 14778. Tel: 716-375-2153. p. 1635
Painter, Tina, Br Librn, Carson County Public Library, Groom Branch, 201 Broadway St, Groom, TX, 79039. Tel: 806-248-7353. p. 2225
Paisley, Danielle, Dir, Patchogue-Medford Library, 54-60 E Main St, Patchogue, NY, 11772. Tel: 631-654-4700. p. 1615
Paisley, Tiffany, Libr Mgr, Pikes Peak Library District, Penrose Library, 20 N Cascade Ave, Colorado Springs, CO, 80903. Tel: 719-531-6333, Ext 6350. p. 271
Paitl, Sandy, Librn, Ashland County Law Library, Courthouse, Rm 304, 201 W Main St, Ashland, WI, 54806. Tel: 715-682-7016. p. 2421
Pajor, Sue, Adult Serv Mgr, Alsip-Merrionette Park Public Library District, 11960 S Pulaski Rd, Alsip, IL, 60803. Tel: 708-371-5666. p. 536
Pakhtigian, Alice, Ref Librn, Harcum College, 750 Montgomery Ave, Bryn Mawr, PA, 19010-3476. Tel: 610-526-6085. p. 1916
Pakulski, Dana, Asst Librn, Finlandia University, 601 Quincy St, Hancock, MI, 49930. Tel: 906-487-7502. p. 1113
Pal, Pam, Chief Exec Officer, Chief Librn, Wasaga Beach Public Library, 120 Glenwood Dr, Wasaga Beach, ON, L9Z 2K5, CANADA. Tel: 705-429-5481, Ext 2404. p. 2702
Palacio, Maria, Dir, Acton Memorial Library, 486 Main St, Acton, MA, 01720. Tel: 978-929-6655. p. 983
Palacio, Maria, Asst Libr Dir, Chelmsford Public Library, 25 Boston Rd, Chelmsford, MA, 01824. Tel: 978-256-5521. p. 1010
Palacios, Kristine, Dir, Dennis P McHugh Piermont Public Library, 25 Flywheel Park W, Piermont, NY, 10968. Tel: 845-359-4595. p. 1618
Paladino, Emily, Acq, Robert Morris University Library, 6001 University Blvd, Moon Township, PA, 15108-1189. Tel: 412-397-6880. p. 1965
Paladino, Mary, Head, Cataloging, Ordering, Receiving & Processing Servs, Montrose Regional Library District, 320 S Second St, Montrose, CO, 81401. Tel: 970-249-9656. p. 291
Paladino, Paul H, Dir, Montrose Regional Library District, 320 S Second St, Montrose, CO, 81401. Tel: 970-249-9656, Ext 2550. p. 291
Palani, Selva, Access & Circ Serv Librn, Hamline University, School of Law Library, 1536 Hewitt Ave, Saint Paul, MN, 55104. Tel: 651-523-2379. p. 1199
Palay, Jaime, Librn, Howard Hughes Medical Institute, 19700 Helix Dr, Ashburn, VA, 20147. Tel: 571-209-4124. p. 2306
Palazzo, Meghan, Asst Dir, Georgetown Public Library, 123 W Pine St, Georgetown, DE, 19947. Tel: 302-856-7958. p. 353
Palazzola, Robert, Librn, American Aviation Historical Society, Flabob Airport, 4130 Mennes Ave, Bldg 56, Riverside, CA, 92509. Tel: 951-777-1332. p. 201
Palencia, Katherine, Ch, Chelsea Public Library, 569 Broadway, Chelsea, MA, 02150. Tel: 617-466-4350. p. 1010
Palermo, Jill C, Dir, Lewiston Public Library, 305 S Eighth St, Lewiston, NY, 14092. Tel: 716-754-4720. p. 1563
Palermo, Natalie, Asst Dir for Resource Mgmt, Louisiana State University Libraries, Paul M Hebert Law Center, One E Campus Dr, Baton Rouge, LA, 70803-1000. Tel: 225-578-6530. p. 884
Palermo, Renée, Syst Dir, Ocean State Libraries, 300 Centerville Rd, Ste 103S, Warwick, RI, 02886. Tel: 401-593-2162. p. 2774
Paley, Valerie, Dir, Sr VPres, New York Historical Society Museum & Library, 170 Central Park W, New York, NY, 10024. Tel: 212-873-3400. p. 1593

Panella, Heather, Dir, Moon Township Public Library, 1700 Beaver Grade Rd, Ste 100, Moon Township, PA, 15108. Tel: 412-269-0334. p. 1965
Panella, Jessica, Head, Access & Admin Services, University of Connecticut, Thomas J Meskill Law Library, 39 Elizabeth St, Hartford, CT, 06105. Tel: 860-570-5106. p. 340
Pang, Lily, Head, Access Serv, Head, Resource Sharing, University of Florida Libraries, 1545 W University Ave, Gainesville, FL, 32611-7000. Tel: 352-273-2910. p. 407
Paniccia, Christina, Youth Serv Librn, Dunham Public Library, 76 Main St, Whitesboro, NY, 13492. Tel: 315-736-9734. p. 1665
Panik, Tina, Ref & Adult Serv Mgr, Avon Free Public Library, 281 Country Club Rd, Avon, CT, 06001. Tel: 860-673-9712. p. 301
Panitz, Zimra, Head, Tech Serv, School of Visual Arts Library, 380 Second Ave, 2nd Flr, New York, NY, 10010. Tel: 212-592-2662. p. 1601
Pankey, Amanda, Librn, Memorial Hospital Library, 4500 Memorial Dr, Belleville, IL, 62226-5360. Tel: 618-233-7750. p. 541
Pankey, William, Coordr, Tech, William Rainey Harper College Library, 1200 W Algonguin Rd, Palatine, IL, 60067. Tel: 847-925-6498. p. 631
Pankiw, Suzanne, Librn, Rainbow Lake Municipal Library, One Atco Rd, Rainbow Lake, AB, T0H 2Y0, CANADA. Tel: 780-956-3656. p. 2551
Panko, Sergiy, Bibliographer, Librn, Shevchenko Scientific Society Inc, 63 Fourth Ave, New York, NY, 10003. Tel: 212-254-5130. p. 1602
Pankowsky, Susan, Librn, West End Synagogue, 3810 W End Ave, Nashville, TN, 37205. Tel: 615-269-4592. p. 2122
Pankratz, Harley, Library Contact, Wood, 5681-70 St, Edmonton, AB, T6B 3P6, CANADA. Tel: 204-488-2997. p. 2538
Pankratz, Karen, Curator, Boot Hill Museum, 500 W Wyatt Earp Blvd, Dodge City, KS, 67801. Tel: 620-227-8188. p. 804
Pannabecker, Ginny, Asst Dean, Dir, Research Collaboration & Engagement, Virginia Polytechnic Institute & State University Libraries, 560 Drillfield Dr, Blacksburg, VA, 24061. Tel: 540-231-7980. p. 2307
Pannier, Karin, Libr Dir, Vienna Correctional Center Library, 6695 State Rte 146 E, Vienna, IL, 62995. Tel: 618-658-8371. p. 657
Pannkuk, Jill, Libr Dir, Clear Lake Public Library, 200 N Fourth St, Clear Lake, IA, 50428-1698. Tel: 641-357-6133. p. 740
Pannkuk, Matt, Dir, Watonwan County Library, 125 Fifth St S, Saint James, MN, 56081. Tel: 507-375-1278. p. 1198
Panta, Manju, Assoc Librn, West Virginia University Institute of Technology, 405 Fayette Pike, Montgomery, WV, 25136-2436. Tel: 304-442-3230. p. 2409
Panté, Jane, Head Librn, Mattawamkeag Public Library, 327 Main St, Mattawamkeag, ME, 04459. Tel: 207-736-7013. p. 931
Pantel, Marilynne, Chairperson, Rural Municipality of Argyle Public Library, 627 Elizabeth Ave, Hwy 23, Baldur, MB, R0K 0B0, CANADA. Tel: 204-535-2314. p. 2585
Panter, Laura, Head, Teen Serv, Sachem Public Library, 150 Holbrook Rd, Holbrook, NY, 11741. Tel: 631-588-5024. p. 1547
Pao, Florence, Emerging Tech Librn, Teen Librn, Tenafly Public Library, 100 Riveredge Rd, Tenafly, NJ, 07670-1962. Tel: 201-568-8680. p. 1445
Paoli, Tessa, Mkt Coordr, Prog Coordr, Sausalito Public Library, 420 Litho St, Sausalito, CA, 94965. Tel: 415-289-4100, Ext 501. p. 246
Paon, Michelle, Head Librn, Dalhousie University, Sexton Design & Technology Library, Bldg B, 3rd Flr, 5260 DaCosta Row, Halifax, NS, B3H 4R2, CANADA. Tel: 902-476-8437. p. 2618
Paone, Kimberly, Dir, Matawan-Aberdeen Public Library, 165 Main St, Matawan, NJ, 07747. Tel: 732-583-9100. p. 1417
Papa, Carrie, Dir, Libr Serv, Wheaton Franciscan Healthcare - All Saints, Library & Community Center, 3801 Spring St, Racine, WI, 53405. Tel: 262-687-4300. p. 2472
Papadopoulos, John, Nicholls Librn & Dir Graham Libr, University of Toronto Libraries, Trinity College, John W Graham Library, Munk School of Global Affairs Bldg, 3 Devonshire Pl, East House, Toronto, ON, M5S 3K7, CANADA. p. 2700
Papadourakis, Laurie, Asst Dir, Des Plaines Public Library, 1501 Ellinwood St, Des Plaines, IL, 60016. Tel: 847-827-5551. p. 578
Papandrea, Jamie, Dir, Brookhaven Free Library, 273 Beaver Dam Rd, Brookhaven, NY, 11719. Tel: 631-286-1923. p. 1500
Papandrea, Jamie, Dir, West Islip Public Library, Three Higbie Lane, West Islip, NY, 11795-3999. Tel: 631-661-7080, Ext 211. p. 1662
Papas, Katie, Supvr, University of Rochester, Rossell Hope Robbins Library, Rush Rhees Library, Rm 416, Rochester, NY, 14627. Tel: 585-275-0110. p. 1631
Papas, Philip R, Archivist, Touro College Libraries, 320 W 31st St, New York, NY, 10001. Tel: 212-463-0400, Ext 55321. p. 1603
Papazian, Jodi, Asst Dir, Burlington Public Library, 34 Library Lane, Burlington, CT, 06013. Tel: 860-673-3331. p. 305
Pape, Whitney, Dir, Blanding Free Public Library, 124 Bay State Rd, Rehoboth, MA, 02769. Tel: 508-252-4236. p. 1049
Papenfuss, Larry, IT Dir, South Central Kansas Library System, 321 N Main St, South Hutchinson, KS, 67505. Tel: 620-663-3211. p. 837
Papillo, Jo, Dir, Saint Clairsville Public Library, 108 W Main St, Saint Clairsville, OH, 43950-1225. Tel: 740-695-2062. p. 1819
Papineau-Archambault, Véronic, Chef de Section, Bibliotheques de Montreal, Haut-Anjou, 7070 rue Jarry Est, Anjou, QC, H1J 1G4, CANADA. Tel: 514-493-8270. p. 2718
Papineau-Archambault, Véronic, Chef de Section, Bibliotheques de Montreal, Jean-Corbeil, 7500 Ave Goncourt, Anjou, QC, H1K 3X9, CANADA. Tel: 514-493-8270. p. 2719
Papini, Allison, Asst Dir, Instruction & Research Mgr, Bryant University, 1150 Douglas Pike, Smithfield, RI, 02917-1284. Tel: 401-232-6125. p. 2042
Pappani, Laura, Br Mgr, Nevada County Community Library, Doris Foley Library for Historical Research, 211 N Pine St, Nevada City, CA, 95959. Tel: 530-265-4606. p. 182
Pappas, Dan, Head, Ref, NASA Ames Research Center, Technical Library, Bldg 202, Mail Stop 202-3, Moffett Field, CA, 94035-1000. Tel: 650-604-6325. p. 178
Pappas, Daniel, Tech Serv, Schulte Roth & Zabel LLP, 919 Third Ave, New York, NY, 10022. Tel: 212-756-2237. p. 1601
Pappas, John, Head Librn, Ardmore Free Library, 108 Ardmore Ave, Ardmore, PA, 19003-1399. Tel: 610-642-5187. p. 1907
Pappas, Lisa, Libr Dir, Plainfield Public Library District, 15025 S Illinois St, Plainfield, IL, 60544. Tel: 815-439-2874. p. 635
Pappas, Lydia, Asst Dir, University of South Carolina, Moving Image Research Collections, 707 Catawba St, Columbia, SC, 29201. Tel: 803-777-6841. p. 2055
Pappert, John, Librn, Gateway Seminary, 7393 S Alton Way, Centennial, CO, 80112-2302. Tel: 303-779-6431, Ext 204. p. 270
Papple, Sarah, Chief Librn/CEO, Township of Georgian Bay Public Library, 2586 Honey Harbour Rd, Honey Harbour, ON, P0E 1E0, CANADA. Tel: 705-756-8851. p. 2648
Paprocki, Laura, Librn, St Mary's General Hospital, 911 Queen's Blvd, Kitchener, ON, N2M 1B2, CANADA. Tel: 519-749-6549. p. 2652
Paquet, Anna, Weekend Librn, Endicott College Library, 376 Hale St, Beverly, MA, 01915. Tel: 978-232-2279. p. 989
Paquet, Simone, Team Leader, Bibliotheques de Trois-Rivieres, Bibliotheque de Pointe-du-Lac (Simone-L-Roy), 500 rue de la Grande-Allee, Trois-Rivieres, QC, G0X 1Z0, CANADA. Tel: 819-377-4289. p. 2738
Paquette, Dan, Libr Dir, Willimantic Public Library, 905 Main St, Willimantic, CT, 06226. Tel: 860-465-3079. p. 347
Paquette, Dan, Syst Librn, Springfield Technical Community College Library, One Armory Sq, Bldg 27, Ste 1, Springfield, MA, 01105. Tel: 413-755-4550. p. 1057
Paquette, Jennifer, Adult & Teen Serv, Midland Public Library, 320 King St, Midland, ON, L4R 3M6, CANADA. Tel: 705-526-4216. p. 2658
Paquette, Lynn, ILL, Libr Asst, Nation Municipality Public Library, 4531 Ste-Catherine St, St. Isidore, ON, K0C 2B0, CANADA. Tel: 613-524-2252. p. 2680
Paquette, Meghan, Ch, Tiverton Public Library, 34 Roosevelt Ave, Tiverton, RI, 02878. Tel: 401-625-6796, Ext 3. p. 2042
Paquette, Michele, Libr Dir, Sherman Free Library, 20 Church St, Port Henry, NY, 12974. Tel: 518-546-7461. p. 1621
Paquette, Racheal, Asst Librn, Poultney Public Library, 205 Main St, Ste 1, Poultney, VT, 05764. Tel: 802-287-5556. p. 2291
Paquette-Lalonde, Lise, Lead Librn, Greater Sudbury Public Library, Azilda Gilles Pelland Library, 120 Ste-Agnus St, Azilda, ON, P0M 1B0, CANADA. Tel: 705-983-3955. p. 2683
Paquette-Lalonde, Lise, Lead Librn, Greater Sudbury Public Library, Chelmsford Public Library-Norman Huneault Branch, Citizen Service Centre, 3502 Errington St, Chelmsford, ON, P0M 1L0, CANADA. Tel: 705-688-3963. p. 2683
Paquette-Lalonde, Lise, Lead Librn, Greater Sudbury Public Library, Dowling Public Library-Lionel Rheaume Branch, Citizen Service Centre, 79 Main St W, Dowling, ON, P0M 1R0, CANADA. Tel: 705-688-3956. p. 2683
Paquette-Lalonde, Lise, Lead Librn, Greater Sudbury Public Library, Levack/Onaping Public Library-Earle Jarvis Branch, One Hillside Ave, Onaping, ON, P0M 2R0, CANADA. Tel: 705-688-3951. p. 2683
Paquin, Émilie, Chef de Section, Bibliotheques de Montreal, La Petite-Patrie, 6707 Ave de Lorimier, Montreal, QC, H2G 2P8, CANADA. Tel: 514-872-3910. p. 2719
Paquin, Émilie, Chef de Section, Bibliotheques de Montreal, Rosemont, 3131 Blvd Rosemont, Montreal, QC, H1Y 1M4, CANADA. Tel: 514-872-1734. p. 2720
Paquin, Johanne, Head of Libr, Centre d'acces a l'Information Juridique-Bibliotheque de Quebec, 300 boul Jean-Lesage, 3.5 Local, Quebec, QC, G1K 8K6, CANADA. Tel: 418-525-0057. p. 2730
Paradis, Claire, Libr Dir, Nakusp Public Library Association, 92 Sixth Ave NW, Nakusp, BC, V0G 1R0, CANADA. Tel: 250-265-3363. p. 2570
Paradise, Laurin, Res & Instruction Librn, Manhattan College, 4513 Manhattan College Pkwy, Riverdale, NY, 10471. Tel: 718-862-7743. p. 1627
Paraham, Greg, Electronic Res Librn, Rhodes College, 2000 North Pkwy, Memphis, TN, 38112-1694. Tel: 901-843-3890. p. 2114
Parang, Elizabeth, Res & Instruction Librn, Pepperdine University Libraries, 24255 Pacific Coast Hwy, Malibu, CA, 90263. Tel: 310-506-4252. p. 171
Paraskevas, Marie-Chantal, Syst Librn, Bibliothèque Municipale de Gatineau, Ville de Gatineau, CP 1970 Succ. Hull, Gatineau, QC, J8X 3Y9, CANADA. Tel: 819-243-2345. p. 2712
Parcell-Greene, Joyce, Br Supvr, Mecklenburg County Public Library, Butler Memorial, 515 Marshall St, Chase City, VA, 23924. Tel: 434-372-4286. p. 2308

Pardee, Jamie, Head, Fiscal Serv, State Library of Ohio, 274 E First Ave, Ste 100, Columbus, OH, 43201. Tel: 614-644-6879. p. 1777
Pardi, Sarah, Admin Librn, Head, Youth Serv, Fort Lee Public Library, 320 Main St, Fort Lee, NJ, 07024. Tel: 201-592-3615. p. 1403
Pardi, Sarah, Head, Pub Serv, Millburn Free Public Library, 200 Glen Ave, Millburn, NJ, 07041. Tel: 973-376-1006, Ext 117. p. 1419
Pardo, Leslie A., Digital Serv Librn, Arizona State University, College of Law, Arizona State University MC 9620, 111 E Taylor St, Ste 350, Phoenix, AZ, 85004. Tel: 480-965-3579. p. 69
Pardo, Patricia, Librn, University of Miami, 1311 Miller Dr, Coral Gables, FL, 33146. Tel: 305-284-2251. p. 390
Pardo, Travis, Ref & Instruction Librn, Northwest University, 5520 108th Ave NE, Kirkland, WA, 98083. Tel: 425-889-5301. p. 2368
Pardue, Diana, Chief Curator, Heard Museum, 2301 N Central Ave, Phoenix, AZ, 85004-1323. Tel: 602-252-8840. p. 70
Pardue, Laura, Asst Librn, Tallassee Community Library, 99 Freeman Ave, Tallassee, AL, 36078. Tel: 334-283-2732. p. 36
Paredes, Susan, Commun Libr Mgr, Queens Library, Kew Gardens Hills Community Library, 72-33 Vleigh Pl, Flushing, NY, 11367. Tel: 718-261-6654. p. 1555
Pareja, Jose Ignacio, Sci Tech Learning Spec, Earlham College, 801 National Rd W, Richmond, IN, 47374-4095. Tel: 765-983-1612. p. 715
Parent, Laura, Br Mgr, Trails Regional Library, Knob Noster Branch, 202 N Adams, Knob Noster, MO, 65336. Tel: 660-563-2997. p. 1285
Parent, Suzanne, Coll Develop, University of Maine School of Law, 246 Deering Ave, Portland, ME, 04102. Tel: 207-780-4353. p. 937
Parent-Touchette, Arianne, Head, Youth Serv, Tech Serv, Kirkland Public Library, 17100 Hymus Blvd, Kirkland, QC, H9J 2W2, CANADA. Tel: 514-630-2726. p. 2714
Parente, Christy, Libr Office Mgr, Midlothian Public Library, 14701 S Kenton Ave, Midlothian, IL, 60445-4122. Tel: 708-535-2027. p. 617
Parente, Dianna, Br Librn, Tiverton Public Library, Union Public Library, 3832 Main Rd, Tiverton, RI, 02878. Tel: 401-625-6796, Ext 2. p. 2042
Parente, Sharon, Distance Learning Serv, Middle Tennessee State University, 1611 Alumni Dr, Murfreesboro, TN, 37132. Tel: 615-898-2549. p. 2117
Parenteau, Anna, Libr Mgr, Manitoba Indigenous Culture-Educational Center, 119 Sutherland Ave, Winnipeg, MB, R2W 3C9, CANADA. Tel: 204-942-0228. p. 2594
Parenteau, Susan, Asst Librn, Gill Memorial Library, 145 E Broad St, Paulsboro, NJ, 08066. Tel: 856-423-5155. p. 1434
Parham, Carl, Cat Librn, South College, 3904 Lonas Dr, Knoxville, TN, 37909. Tel: 865-251-1832. p. 2107
Parham, Karen, Libr Asst, Sampson-Clinton Public Library, 217 Graham St, Clinton, NC, 28328. Tel: 910-592-4153. p. 1681
Parham, Loretta, Chief Exec Officer, Libr Dir, Atlanta University Center, 111 James P Brawley Dr SW, Atlanta, GA, 30314. Tel: 404-978-2000. p. 462
Parham, Marita, Libr Assoc, Roselle Free Public Library, 104 W Fourth Ave, Roselle, NJ, 07203. Tel: 908-245-5809. p. 1441
Parham, Rita, Info Serv Librn, Louisiana State University Libraries, Paul M Hebert Law Center, One E Campus Dr, Baton Rouge, LA, 70803-1000. Tel: 225-578-4043. p. 884
Parham, Sandra, Exec Dir, Meharry Medical College Library, 2001 Albion St, Nashville, TN, 37208. Tel: 615-327-5770. p. 2119
Parham, Scott, Asst Dir, Develop, Project Mgr, Clayton County Library System, 865 Battlecreek Rd, Jonesboro, GA, 30236. Tel: 770-473-3850. p. 483
Parham, Vivian, Managing Librn, Brooklyn Public Library, Kings Highway, 2115 Ocean Ave, Brooklyn, NY, 11229. Tel: 718-375-3037. p. 1503
Paridis, Marie-Eve, Director, Research Support, Universite Laval Bibliotheque, Pavillon Jean-Charles-Bonenfant, 2345, allée des Bibliothèques, Quebec, QC, G1V 0A6, CANADA. Tel: 418-656-3344. p. 2732
Parilac, Rory, Children's & Teen Serv, Youth Serv Supvr, Bourbonnais Public Library District, 250 W John Casey Rd, Bourbonnais, IL, 60914. Tel: 815-295-1366. p. 544
Parillo, Michael, Dir, Walter Elwood Museum Library, 100 Church St, Amsterdam, NY, 12010. Tel: 518-843-5151. p. 1486
Paris, Andrew, Sr Librn, Edgewater Free Public Library, 49 Hudson Ave, Edgewater, NJ, 07020. Tel: 201-224-6144. p. 1400
Paris, Cheyenne, Asst Librn, Albion Area Public Library, 111 E Pearl St, Albion, PA, 16401-1202. Tel: 814-756-5400. p. 1903
Paris, Dona, Asst Admin, Martin County Historical Society, Inc, 304 E Blue Earth Ave, Fairmont, MN, 56031. Tel: 507-235-5178. p. 1174
Paris, Jennifer, Electronic Res Librn, MiraCosta College Library, One Barnard Dr, Bldg 1200, Oceanside, CA, 92056-3899. Tel: 760-634-7814. p. 187
Paris, Liz, Colls Mgr, McNay Art Museum Library, 6000 N New Braunfels Ave, San Antonio, TX, 78209. Tel: 210-805-1737. p. 2237
Paris, Melissa, Library Asst, Children's, Manor Public Library, 44 Main St, Manor, PA, 15665. Tel: 724-864-6850. p. 1957
Parise, Kelly, Ref, Allentown Public Library, 1210 Hamilton St, Allentown, PA, 18102. Tel: 610-820-2400. p. 1904
Pariseau, Joanne, Dir, Goodrich Memorial Library, 202 Main St, Newport, VT, 05855. Tel: 802-334-7902. p. 2290
Parish, Daniela, Librn, Warsaw Public Library, 1025 Webster St, Warsaw, IL, 62379. Tel: 217-256-3417. p. 659
Parish, Elizabeth K, Asst Librn, University of Arkansas-Monticello Library, 514 University Dr, Monticello, AR, 71656. Tel: 870-460-1280. p. 105
Parish, Melissa, Librn, Flagler Beach Library, 315 S Seventh St, Flagler Beach, FL, 32136-3640. Tel: 386-517-2030. p. 396
Parish, Shar, Acq, Spooner Memorial Library, 421 High St, Spooner, WI, 54801. Tel: 715-635-2792. p. 2478
Parisher, Deborah B, Dir, Libr Serv, Edgecombe Community College, 2009 W Wilson St, Tarboro, NC, 27886. Tel: 252-618-6570. p. 1718
Parisher, Deborah B, Dir, Libr Serv, Edgecombe Community College, Rocky Mount Campus, 225 Tarboro St, Rocky Mount, NC, 27801. Tel: 252-618-6694. p. 1718
Parisi, Bianca, Tech Coordr, Niagara College of Applied Arts & Technology, 100 Niagara College Blvd, Welland, ON, L3C 7L3, CANADA. Tel: 905-735-2211, Ext 7767. p. 2703
Parisi, Mark, Tech Serv Librn, Everett Public Libraries, 410 Broadway, Everett, MA, 02149. Tel: 617-394-2305. p. 1017
Park, Candice, Libr Tech, Regis College Library, 100 Wellesley St W, Toronto, ON, M5S 2Z5, CANADA. Tel: 416-922-5474, Ext 236. p. 2692
Park, Christina, Bus Mgr, Bergen County Cooperative Library System, Inc, 21-00 Route 208 S, Ste 130, Fair Lawn, NJ, 07410. Tel: 201-498-7311. p. 2770
Park, Cyndi, Libr Dir, Mary Gilkey City Library, 416 Ferry St, Dayton, OR, 97114-9774. Tel: 503-864-2221. p. 1877
Park Dahlen, Sarah, Assoc Prof, University of Illinois at Urbana-Champaign, Library & Information Science Bldg, 501 E Daniel St, Champaign, IL, 61820-6211. Tel: 217-333-3280. p. 2784
Park, Janet, Exec Dir, Onondaga County Public Libraries, The Galleries of Syracuse, 447 S Salina St, Syracuse, NY, 13202-2494. Tel: 315-435-1900. p. 1649
Park, Jessie, Youth Serv, Saint Charles City-County Library District, Deer Run Branch, 1300 N Main, O'Fallon, MO, 63366-2013. Tel: 636-978-3251, 636-980-1332. p. 1278
Park, Kathryn, Libr Dir, College of the Mainland Library, 1200 Amburn Rd, Texas City, TX, 77591-2499. Tel: 409-938-8471. p. 2248
Park, Kylie, Library Contact, Multnomah County Library, Fairview-Columbia Branch, 1520 NE Village St, Fairview, OR, 97024. p. 1892
Park, Linda, Dir, Keuka College, 141 Central Ave, Keuka Park, NY, 14478. Tel: 315-279-5208. p. 1559
Park, Margo, Dir, Bloomfield Public Library, Nine Church St, Bloomfield, NY, 14469. Tel: 585-657-6264. p. 1495
Park, Nicky, Br Head, Mariposa County Library, Bassett Memorial, 7971 Chilnualna Falls Rd, Wawona, CA, 95389. Tel: 209-375-6510. p. 173
Park, Pamala, Human Res Mgr, Salt Lake County Library Services, 8030 S 1825 W, West Jordan, UT, 84088. Tel: 801-943-4636. p. 2274
Park, Sang, Dir, United States Navy, One Administration Circle, Stop 6203, China Lake, CA, 93555-6100. Tel: 760-939-3389. p. 129
Park, Steven, Principal Librn, Huntington Beach Public Library System, 7111 Talbert Ave, Huntington Beach, CA, 92648. Tel: 714-842-4481. p. 151
Park, Sunyoung, Metadata Librn, Museum of Fine Arts, Houston, 1001 Bissonnet St, Houston, TX, 77005. Tel: 713-639-7325. p. 2197
Park, Taeyeol, Dr, Dir, Instrul Tech, Georgetown University, Dahlgren Memorial Library, Preclinical Science Bldg GM-7, 3900 Reservoir Rd NW, Washington, DC, 20007. Tel: 202-687-5089. p. 368
Park, Young, Dr, Cat Supvr, Naval History & Heritage Command, 805 Kidder-Breese St SE, Washington Navy Yard, DC, 20374-5060. Tel: 202-433-2060. p. 382
Parke, Julie, Mgr, Elkhart County Historical Society Museum, Inc, 304 W Vistula St, Bristol, IN, 46507. Tel: 574-848-4322. p. 672
Parke, Kiyoshi, Br Mgr, Glendale Public Library, Heroes Regional Park, 6075 N 83rd Ave, Glendale, AZ, 85303. Tel: 623-930-4466. p. 62
Parke, Lyndy, Ser Librn, Missoula Public Library, 301 E Main, Missoula, MT, 59802-4799. Tel: 406-721-2665. p. 1300
Parker, Ann, Dir, King Memorial Library, 9538 Rte 16, Machias, NY, 14101. Tel: 716-353-9915. p. 1567
Parker, Barbara, Libr Mgr, Charlton Public Library, Inc, 1291 Indian Trail, Folkston, GA, 31537. Tel: 912-496-2041. p. 479
Parker, Barry, Dr, Ser, California Baptist University, 8432 Magnolia Ave, Riverside, CA, 92504. Tel: 951-343-4228. p. 201
Parker, Beth, Assoc Dir, Operations & Colls, Nova Southeastern University Libraries, Panza Maurer Law Library, Shepard Broad College of Law, Leo Goodwin Sr Bldg, 3305 College Ave, Davie, FL, 33314. Tel: 954-262-6204. p. 402
Parker, Betty, Ad, Conway Public Library, 15 Main Ave, Conway, NH, 03818. Tel: 603-447-5552. p. 1360
Parker, Beverly, Librn, Northeast Regional Library, Margaret Rae Memorial, Margaret Rae Memorial Bldg, Hwy 25 & Main St, Tishomingo, MS, 38873. Tel: 662-438-7640. p. 1216
Parker, Carmen, Tech Serv, Hillside Public Library, 405 N Hillside Ave, Hillside, IL, 60162-1295. Tel: 708-449-7510. p. 599
Parker, Carol, Tech Serv, Gulfport Public Library, 5501 28th Ave S, Gulfport, FL, 33707. Tel: 727-893-1076. p. 408
Parker, Charlene, Br Mgr, High Plains Library District, Farr Regional Library, 1939 61st Ave, Greeley, CO, 80634. p. 285

Parker, Dana, Br Mgr, Hawkins County Library System, Church Hill Public Library, 412 E Main Blvd, Church Hill, TN, 37642. Tel: 423-357-4591. p. 2125

Parker, Dawn, Librn, Southern Technical College, Brandon Campus, 608 E Bloomingdale Ave, Brandon, FL, 33511. Tel: 813-820-0200. p. 404

Parker, Don, Dir, Wanatah Public Library, 114 S Main St, Wanatah, IN, 46390. Tel: 219-733-9303. p. 724

Parker, Elaine, Acq, Tech, Oakwood University, 7000 Adventist Blvd NW, Huntsville, AL, 35896. Tel: 256-726-7251. p. 22

Parker, Englisa, Libr Tech, Nevada Legislative Counsel Bureau, 401 S Carson St, Carson City, NV, 89701-4747. Tel: 775-684-6827. p. 1344

Parker, Eric C, Acq Librn, Northwestern University Libraries, Pritzker Legal Research Center, 375 E Chicago Ave, Chicago, IL, 60611. Tel: 312-503-7920. p. 587

Parker, Gretchen, Librn, King Public Library, 101 Pilot View Dr, King, NC, 27021. Tel: 336-983-3868. p. 1699

Parker, Hannah, Br Mgr, Ohoopee Regional Library System, Nelle Brown Memorial Library, 166 W Liberty St, Lyons, GA, 30436-1432. Tel: 912-526-6511. p. 502

Parker, Jaime, Asst Dir, Beene-Pearson Public Library, 208 Elm Ave, South Pittsburg, TN, 37380-1312. Tel: 423-837-6513. p. 2127

Parker, Jean, Asst Dean for Coll Mgt, Head, Coll Mgt, Saint Louis University, 3650 Lindell Blvd, Saint Louis, MO, 63108-3302. Tel: 314-977-3093. p. 1275

Parker, Jeanette, Ref & Instruction Librn, Newman University, 3100 McCormick Ave, Wichita, KS, 67213. Tel: 316-942-4291, Ext 2104. p. 843

Parker, Jennifer, Br Mgr, Clay County Public Library System, Green Cove Springs Branch, 403 Ferris St, Green Cove Springs, FL, 32043. Tel: 904-269-6315, 904-284-6315. p. 396

Parker, Jennifer, Archit Librn, Hesburgh Libraries, Architecture, 150 Walsh Family Hall of Architecture, Notre Dame, IN, 46556-5652. Tel: 574-631-9401. p. 711

Parker, Joan Elliott, Tech Serv, Newburgh Chandler Public Library, 4111 Lakeshore Dr, Newburgh, IN, 47630-2274. Tel: 812-853-5468. p. 709

Parker, Julie, Libr Dir, Clayton Public Library District, 211 E Main St, Clayton, IL, 62324. Tel: 217-894-6519. p. 572

Parker, Karen, Ref & Acq Librn, Lone Star College System, North Harris College Library, 2700 W W Thorne Dr, Houston, TX, 77073. Tel: 281-618-5491. p. 2197

Parker, Katherine, Br Head, Vancouver Public Library, Fraserview Branch, 1950 Argyle Dr, Vancouver, BC, V5P 2A8, CANADA. Tel: 604-665-3957. p. 2581

Parker, Kathy, Dir, Libr Serv, United States Navy, Naval Medical Center, Library Bldg 5-2, Naval Medical Ctr, San Diego, CA, 92134-5200. Tel: 619-532-7950. p. 222

Parker, Kayla, Br Mgr, Bladen County Public Library, Bridger Memorial, 313 S Main St, Bladenboro, NC, 28320. Tel: 910-863-4586. p. 1687

Parker, Kim, Adult Serv, D A Hurd Library, 41 High St, North Berwick, ME, 03906. Tel: 207-676-2215. p. 933

Parker, Lee, Libr Dir, Norton Public Library, 68 E Main St, Norton, MA, 02766. Tel: 508-285-0265. p. 1043

Parker, Lettice, Librn, Snohomish County Law Library, M/S 703 Basement/Courthouse, 3000 Rockefeller Ave, Everett, WA, 98201. Tel: 425-388-3010. p. 2364

Parker, Lindsay, Mgr, Okefenokee Regional Library, Appling County Public, 242 Parker Ave, Baxley, GA, 31513. Tel: 912-367-8103. p. 503

Parker, Lois, Dir, Community Library of Western Perry County, 104 E Main St, Blain, PA, 17006. Tel: 717-536-3761. p. 1913

Parker, Lynn Stewart, Libr Asst, Starksboro Public Library, 2827 VT Rte 116, Starksboro, VT, 05487. Tel: 802-453-3732. p. 2295

Parker, Marie, Libr Tech, Gadsden County Public Library, Cowen Public Library, 300 Maple St, Chattahoochee, FL, 32324. Tel: 850-663-2707. p. 439

Parker, Mary Ellen D, Librn, Queen of the Holy Rosary Center Library, 43326 Mission Circle, Fremont, CA, 94539. Tel: 510-657-2468. p. 144

Parker, Mary Jo, Head Librn, Lake Andes Carnegie Public Library, 500 Main St, Lake Andes, SD, 57356. Tel: 605-487-7524. p. 2078

Parker, Michelle, Br Supvr, Auglaize County Libraries, New Knoxville Community Library, 304 S Main St, New Knoxville, OH, 45871. Tel: 419-753-2724. p. 1828

Parker, Onie, Libr Dir, Franklin Parish Library, 705 Prairie St, Winnsboro, LA, 71295. Tel: 318-435-4336. p. 912

Parker, Pam, Circ Coordr, The Community Library, 415 Spruce Ave N, Ketchum, ID, 83340. Tel: 208-726-3493. p. 523

Parker, Pamela, ILL, IWK Health, 5850/5980 University Ave, Halifax, NS, B3K 6R8, CANADA. Tel: 902-470-8646. p. 2619

Parker, Ron, Chief of Interpretation, National Park Service, Chickasaw National Recreation Area, 901 W First St, Sulphur, OK, 73086. Tel: 580-622-7231. p. 1863

Parker, Rosa, Actg Dir, Aquinnah Public Library, One Church St, Aquinnah, MA, 02535. Tel: 508-645-2314. p. 985

Parker, Rosalind, Deputy Dir, Personnel, Natchitoches Parish Library, 450 Second St, Natchitoches, LA, 71457-4649. Tel: 318-238-9226. p. 899

Parker, Sally, Br Mgr, Pine Forest Regional Library System - Headquarters, Stone County Public, 242 S Second St, Wiggins, MS, 39577. Tel: 601-928-4993. p. 1232

Parker, Shawn, Bus Mgr, University of Maryland, Baltimore County, 1000 Hilltop Circle, Baltimore, MD, 21250. Tel: 410-455-2356. p. 958

Parker, Shelli, Br Supvr, Auglaize County Libraries, New Bremen Public Library, 45 S Washington St, New Bremen, OH, 45869. Tel: 419-629-2158. p. 1828

Parker, Sheri, Library Services & Assessment Mgr, Texas Wesleyan University, 1201 Wesleyan St, Fort Worth, TX, 76105. Tel: 817-531-4800. p. 2181

Parker Smith, Jessica, Univ Archivist, Mississippi State University, 395 Hardy Rd, Mississippi State, MS, 39762. Tel: 662-325-7668. p. 1227

Parker, Susan, Cataloger, Ch, Dennis Memorial Library Association, 1020 Old Bass River Rd, Dennis, MA, 02638. Tel: 508-385-2255. p. 1014

Parker, Susan, Univ Librn, University of British Columbia Library, 1961 East Mall, Vancouver, BC, V6T 1Z1, CANADA. Tel: 604-827-3434. p. 2580

Parker, Susy, Librn, Stella Ellis Hart Public Library, 103 FM 108 North, Smiley, TX, 78159. Tel: 830-587-6101. p. 2244

Parker, Suzan, Head, Coll, Head, Support Serv, University of Washington Libraries, Bothell Campus/Cascadia College Library, University of Washington Bothell, 18225 Campus Way NE, Box 358550, Bothell, WA, 98011-8245. Tel: 425-352-5340. p. 2381

Parker, Tammy, Br Mgr, Kanawha County Public Library, Clendenin, 107 Koontz Ave, Ste 100, Clendenin, WV, 25045. Tel: 304-548-6370. p. 2400

Parker, Tara G, Libr Dir, Eunice Public Library, 1003 Ave N, Eunice, NM, 88231. Tel: 575-394-2336. p. 1467

Parker, Vincent, Librn II, Arizona State Prison Complex Florence Libraries, 1305 E Butte Ave, Florence, AZ, 85132. Tel: 520-868-4011, Ext 6010. p. 61

Parker, Visnja, Libr Tech, Nova Scotia Department of Education & Early Childhood Dev, 2021 Brunswick St, Halifax, NS, B3J 2S9, CANADA. Tel: 902-424-5168. p. 2620

Parker Wonderly, Lisa, Libr Dir, Newell Public Library, 208 Girard Ave, Newell, SD, 57760. Tel: 605-456-2179. p. 2080

Parker-Gibson, Necia, Agr Librn, University of Arkansas Libraries, 365 N McIlroy Ave, Fayetteville, AR, 72701-4002. Tel: 479-575-8421. p. 95

Parkins, Susan, Outreach Specialist, Sr Serv, Laramie County Library System, 2200 Pioneer Ave, Cheyenne, WY, 82001-3610. Tel: 307-773-7228. p. 2492

Parkinson, Carol, Libr Dir, Ivy Tech Community College of Indiana, 200 Daniels Way, Bloomington, IN, 47404. Tel: 812-330-6080. p. 671

Parkinson, Scott, Tech Serv Librn, DeSales University, 2755 Station Ave, Center Valley, PA, 18034. Tel: 610-282-1100, Ext 1266. p. 1920

Parkinson, Stephanie, Head Librn, Parkland Regional Library-Manitoba, Foxwarren Branch, 312 Webster Ave, Foxwarren, MB, R0J 0R0, CANADA. Tel: 204-847-2080. p. 2586

Parkinson, Susan, Libr Dir, Calmar Public Library, 4705 50th Ave, Calmar, AB, T0C 0V0, CANADA. Tel: 780-985-3472. p. 2529

Parkison, Samantha, Communications Coordr, Mkt, Addison Public Library, Four Friendship Plaza, Addison, IL, 60101. Tel: 630-458-3303. p. 535

Parkoff, Cara, Assoc Col Librn, Fisher College Library, 118 Beacon St, Boston, MA, 02116. Tel: 617-236-8875. p. 995

Parkomaki, Shara H, Dir & Librn, Ashtabula County Law Library, County Courthouse, 25 W Jefferson St, Jefferson, OH, 44047. Tel: 440-576-3690. p. 1792

Parks, Bonnie, Coll Tech Librn, University of Portland, 5000 N Willamette Blvd, Portland, OR, 97203-5743. Tel: 503-943-7111. p. 1894

Parks, Elysa, Outreach Librn, Hopkinsville-Christian County Public Library, 1101 Bethel St, Hopkinsville, KY, 42240. Tel: 270-887-4262, Ext 124. p. 860

Parks, Elysa, Dir, Libr Serv, Hopkinsville Community College Library, 720 North Dr, Hopkinsville, KY, 42240. Tel: 270-707-3764. p. 860

Parks, Harriette, Dir, Br, Cleveland Public Library, 325 Superior Ave, Cleveland, OH, 44114-1271. Tel: 216-623-7652. p. 1767

Parks, Karin, Head Librn, Robertson Memorial Library, 849 Greenfield Rd, Leyden, MA, 01301-9419. Tel: 413-773-9334. p. 1028

Parks, Sheila, Dir, Lanesborough Public Library, Town Hall, 83 N Main St, Lanesborough, MA, 01237. Tel: 413-442-0222. p. 1027

Parks, Stephen, State Librn, State of Mississippi Judiciary, Carroll Gartin Justice Bldg, 450 High St, Jackson, MS, 39201. Tel: 601-359-3672. p. 1223

Parks, Stephen, Chairperson, Central Mississippi Library Council, c/o Millsaps College Library, 1701 N State St, Jackson, MS, 39210. Tel: 601-974-1070. p. 2768

Parks, Stuart, Archivist, North Carolina Office of Archives & History, One Festival Park Blvd, Manteo, NC, 27954. Tel: 252-473-2655. p. 1702

Parks, Sue, Assoc Dean for Special Libraries, University of North Texas Libraries, 1155 Union Circle, No 305190, Denton, TX, 76203-5017. Tel: 940-369-7249. p. 2170

Parlier, Rachael, Adult Prog Coordr, Children's Prog Coordr, Autauga Prattville Public Library, 254 Doster St, Prattville, AL, 36067-3933. Tel: 334-365-3396. p. 33

Parliman, Lynn, Head, Ser & Electronic Res, Fordham University Libraries, 441 E Fordham Rd, Bronx, NY, 10458-5151. Tel: 718-817-3570. p. 1498

Parmele, Alicia, Youth Serv Mgr, Algonquin Area Public Library District, 2600 Harnish Dr, Algonquin, IL, 60102-5900. Tel: 847-458-6060. p. 536
Parmenter, Robert, Head Librn, Mendocino College Library, 1000 Hensley Creek Rd, Ukiah, CA, 95482. Tel: 707-468-3245. p. 254
Parno, Travis, Director, Collections & Research, Historic Saint Mary's City, 18751 Hogaboom Ln, Saint Mary's City, MD, 20686. Tel: 240-895-4974. p. 976
Parnprome, Tetima, Librn, Cochise College Library, Andrea Cracchiolo Library, Bldg 900, 901 N Colombo Ave, Sierra Vista, AZ, 85635. Tel: 520-515-5320. p. 59
Paronto, Linda, Librn, United States Air Force, Bldg 1152, 7356 Fourth Ave N, Malmstrom AFB, MT, 59402-7506. Tel: 406-731-4638. p. 1299
Parpart, Paulette, Cat Librn, Missoula Public Library, 301 E Main, Missoula, MT, 59802-4799. Tel: 406-721-2665. p. 1300
Parr, Marilyn, Asst Librn, Crystal City Public Library, 736 Mississippi Ave, Crystal City, MO, 63019-1646. Tel: 636-937-7166. p. 1244
Parra, Joanne, Adult Serv, Ref Librn, Moorestown Public Library, 111 W Second St, Moorestown, NJ, 08057. Tel: 856-234-0333. p. 1421
Parrick, Ann, Res & Instrul Serv Librn, Keystone College, One College Green, La Plume, PA, 18440-0200. Tel: 570-945-8332. p. 1950
Parrigin, James, Info Literacy/Instruction Coordr, Salisbury University, 1101 Camden Ave, Salisbury, MD, 21801-6863. Tel: 410-543-6130. p. 976
Parrilla, Nilca, Dir, Tech Serv, University of Puerto Rico, Conrado F Asenjo Library, Medical Sciences Campus, Main Bldg, Unit C, San Juan, PR, 00935. Tel: 787-758-2525, Ext 1346. p. 2514
Parrillo, Whitney, Dir, Hutchinson Memorial Library, 228 N High St, Randolph, WI, 53956. Tel: 920-326-4640. p. 2472
Parrington-Wright, Sharon, Head, Adult Serv, Turner Free Library, Two N Main St, Randolph, MA, 02368. Tel: 781-961-0932. p. 1049
Parris, Brenda P, Ref Librn, Tech Serv, Calhoun Community College, Hwy 31 N, Decatur, AL, 35609. Tel: 256-306-2778. p. 14
Parris, Eileen, Sr Archivist, Virginia Historical Society Library, 428 North Blvd, Richmond, VA, 23220. Tel: 804-340-1800. p. 2344
Parris, Keisha, Educ Tech Librn, Johnson C Smith University, 100 Beatties Ford Rd, Charlotte, NC, 28216. Tel: 704-371-6731, 704-371-6740. p. 1680
Parrish, Alex, Methodist Curator, Drew University Library, 36 Madison Ave, Madison, NJ, 07940. Tel: 973-408-3910. p. 1414
Parrish, Andi, Dir, Kansas State University Libraries, Veterinary Medical Library, Veterinary Medical Complex, 408 Trotter Hall, Manhattan, KS, 66506-5614. Tel: 785-532-6006. p. 823
Parrish, Dana, Ref & Instruction Librn, Southeastern University, 1000 Longfellow Blvd, Lakeland, FL, 33801. Tel: 863-667-5225. p. 417
Parrish, Evie, Br Librn, Jasper County Public Library, Wheatfield Branch, 350 S Bierma St, Wheatfield, IN, 46392. Tel: 219-956-3774. p. 715
Parrish, Lila, Pub Serv Librn, Austin Presbyterian Theological Seminary, 100 E 27th St, Austin, TX, 78705-5797. Tel: 512-404-4878. p. 2138
Parrish, Michelle, Curator, Henry Whitfield State Museum, 248 Old Whitfield St, Guilford, CT, 06437. Tel: 203-453-2457. p. 315
Parrish, Michelle, Dir, Livingston Parish Library, 13986 Florida Blvd, Livingston, LA, 70754. Tel: 225-686-4100. p. 895
Parrish, Peggy, Dir, Leander Public Library, 1011 S Bagdad Rd, Leander, TX, 78641. Tel: 512-259-5259, Ext 5. p. 2210
Parrish, Sandra, Exec Dir, Campbell River Museum & Archives, 470 Island Hwy, Campbell River, BC, V9W 2B7, CANADA. Tel: 250-287-3103. p. 2564
Parrott, Jaclyn, Coll Develop, Eastern Washington University, 320 Media Lane, 100 LIB, Cheney, WA, 99004-2453. Tel: 509-359-7895. p. 2361
Parrott, James, Coll Develop Librn, Lewis & Clark Library, 120 S Last Chance Gulch, Helena, MT, 59601. Tel: 406-447-1690. p. 1296
Parrott, Kiera, Dir, Darien Library, 1441 Post Rd, Darien, CT, 06820-5419. Tel: 203-655-1234. p. 308
Parrott, Neva, Asst Librn, Missouri State University-West Plains, 304 W Trish Knight St, West Plains, MO, 65775. Tel: 417-255-7947. p. 1286
Parry, Daria A, Chief Operations Officer, Harford County Public Library, 1221-A Brass Mill Rd, Belcamp, MD, 21017-1209. Tel: 410-273-5702. p. 958
Parry, Karen, Info Serv Mgr, East Brunswick Public Library, Two Jean Walling Civic Ctr, East Brunswick, NJ, 08816-3599. Tel: 732-390-6950. p. 1399
Parry, Kim, Br Head, Winnipeg Public Library, St John's, 500 Salter St, Winnipeg, MB, R2W 4M5, CANADA. Tel: 204-226-1047. p. 2596
Parry, Norm, Dir, New Woodstock Free Library, 2106 Main St, New Woodstock, NY, 13122-8718. Tel: 315-662-3134. p. 1577
Parshall, Shelly, Br Mgr, La Crosse County Library, F J Robers Library, Campbell Town Hall, 2548 Lakeshore Dr, La Crosse, WI, 54603. Tel: 608-783-0052. p. 2441
Parsons, Aaron P, Dir, West Virginia Archives & History Library, Culture Ctr, 1900 Kanawha Blvd E, Charleston, WV, 25305-0300. Tel: 304-558-0230, Ext 165. p. 2400
Parsons, Ann Marie, Libr Dir, United States Patent & Trademark Office, 600 Dulany St, MDE OA50, Alexandria, VA, 22314-5791. Tel: 571-272-9694. p. 2303
Parsons, Cassie, Dir, Logan Area Public Library, 16 Wildcat Way, Logan, WV, 25601. Tel: 304-752-6652. p. 2407
Parsons, Dianna, Mgr, Richard T Liddicoat Gemological Library & Information Center, 5345 Armada Dr, Carlsbad, CA, 92008. Tel: 760-603-4046, 760-603-4068. p. 128
Parsons, Jeff, Dir, Hueytown Public Library, 1372 Hueytown Rd, Hueytown, AL, 35023-2443. Tel: 205-491-1443. p. 21
Parsons, Jillian, Sr Librn, Peabody Institute Library, South, 78 Lynn St, Peabody, MA, 01960. Tel: 978-535-3380, Ext 11. p. 1045
Parsons, Karen, Librn, Oxford Public Library, 115 S Sumner St, Oxford, KS, 67119. Tel: 620-455-2221. p. 830
Parsons, Karen, Ref Librn, Spring Arbor University, 106 E Main St, Spring Arbor, MI, 49283. Tel: 517-750-6436. p. 1152
Parsons, Katherine, Interim Head, Access Serv, Bronx Community College Library, 2115 University Ave, NL 252A, Bronx, NY, 10453. Tel: 718-289-5431. p. 1497
Parsons, Lewis, Head, Tech Serv, Hamilton-Wenham Public Library, 14 Union St, South Hamilton, MA, 01982. Tel: 978-468-5577, Ext 23. p. 1055
Parsons, Matthew, Librn, University of Washington Libraries, Map Collection & Cartographic Information Services, Suzzallo Library, Ground Flr, Universtiy of Washington, Box 352900, Seattle, WA, 98195-2900. Tel: 206-543-2725. p. 2382
Parsons, Maura, YA Serv, North Shore Public Library, 250 Rte 25A, Shoreham, NY, 11786-9677. Tel: 631-929-4488. p. 1641
Parsons, Melody, Interim Dir, Atchison Public Library, 401 Kansas Ave, Atchison, KS, 66002. Tel: 913-367-1902. p. 797
Parsons, Robert, Dir, Laurel Community Learning Center & Public Library, 502 Wakefield St, Laurel, NE, 68745-0248. Tel: 402-256-3133, Ext 4144. p. 1320
Parsons, Ruth, Circ Librn, Wyalusing Public Library, 115 Church St, Wyalusing, PA, 18853. Tel: 570-746-1711. p. 2024
Parsons, Stephen Copel, Ch, Porter Memorial Library, 92 Court St, Machias, ME, 04654-2102. Tel: 207-255-3933. p. 931
Parsons, Stu, Ch, Sandwich Public Library, 142 Main St, Sandwich, MA, 02563. Tel: 508-888-0625. p. 1052
Parsons, Tamika, Br Mgr, Memphis Public Library, North Branch, 1192 Vollintine Ave, Memphis, TN, 38107-2899. Tel: 901-415-2775. p. 2113
Parsons, Vicki L, Dir, Siena College, 515 Loudon Rd, Loudonville, NY, 12211. Tel: 518-783-2545. p. 1566
Partanen, Kimberly, Dir, Castlegar & District Public Library, 1005 Third St, Castlegar, BC, V1N 2A2, CANADA. Tel: 250-365-7751. p. 2564
Partelow, Donald, Adult Prog Coordr, Pawling Free Library, 11 Broad St, Pawling, NY, 12564. Tel: 845-855-3444. p. 1616
Partenheimer, Meta, Digital Projects Archivist, Cambridge Historical Commission Archive, 831 Massachusetts Ave, 2nd Flr, Cambridge, MA, 02139. Tel: 617-349-4683. p. 1004
Partida, Stephanie, Libr Dir, Athena Public Library, 418 E Main St, Athena, OR, 97813. Tel: 541-566-2470. p. 1872
Partington, Elizabeth, Libr Asst, Florida Southern College, 111 Lake Hollingsworth Dr, Lakeland, FL, 33801-5698. Tel: 863-680-4164. p. 417
Partington, Linda, Sr Librn, Canadian Broadcasting Corp, Radio Archives, 205 Wellington St W, Toronto, ON, M5G 3G7, CANADA. Tel: 416-205-5880. p. 2687
Partlow, Lacey, Asst Dir, Sump Memorial Library, 222 N Jefferson St, Papillion, NE, 68046. Tel: 402-597-2040. p. 1332
Partney, Sam, Ad, Cragin Memorial Library, Eight Linwood Ave, Colchester, CT, 06415. Tel: 860-537-5752. p. 306
Parton, Kerri, Br Mgr, Greater Clarks Hill Regional Library System, Lincoln County Library, 181 N Peachtree St, Lincolnton, GA, 30817. Tel: 706-359-4014. p. 478
Parton, Pam, Outreach Librn, Daviess County Library, Jamesport Branch, 101 E Main, Jamesport, MO, 64648. Tel: 660-684-6120. p. 1247
Parton, Yvonne, Br Mgr, Jackson-George Regional Library System, Ocean Springs Municipal Library, 525 Dewey Ave, Ocean Springs, MS, 39564. Tel: 228-875-1193. p. 1228
Partrick, Cindy, Dir, Central Square Library, 637 S Main St, Central Square, NY, 13036. Tel: 315-668-6104. p. 1516
Partridge, Elizabeth, Libr Dir, Kennedale Public Library, 316 W Third St, Kennedale, TX, 76060-2202. Tel: 817-985-2136. p. 2205
Partridge, Leslie, Asst Dir, Kinchafoonee Regional Library System, 913 Forrester Dr SE, Dawson, GA, 39842-2106. Tel: 229-995-6331. p. 474
Partridge, Leslie, Librn, Kinchafoonee Regional Library System, Webster County Library, 40 Cemetey Rd, Preston, GA, 31824. Tel: 229-828-5740. p. 475
Partridge, Norm, Evening Supvr, Saint Mary's College Library, 1928 Saint Mary's Rd, Moraga, CA, 94575. Tel: 925-631-4229. p. 180
Partridge, Tracie, Br Mgr, Wichita Public Library, Westlink Branch, 8515 Bekemeyer St, Wichita, KS, 67212. Tel: 316-337-9456. p. 844
Parus, Dale, Dir, Ionia Community Library, 126 E Main St, Ionia, MI, 48846. Tel: 616-527-3680, Ext 104. p. 1118
Parveen, Nasim, Head Librn, Boston University Libraries, Stone Science Library, 771 Commonwealth Ave, Boston, MA, 02215. Tel: 617-353-5679. p. 994
Pasackow, Lee, Bus Librn, Emory University Libraries, Goizueta Business Library, 540 Asbury Circle, Atlanta, GA, 30322. Tel: 404-727-1641. p. 463
Pasanda, Lois, Circ, Belleville Public Library & Information Center, 221 Washington Ave, Belleville, NJ, 07109-3189. Tel: 973-450-3434. p. 1389

Pascale, Christee, Head, Acq, University of South Carolina, 1322 Greene St, Columbia, SC, 29208-0103. Tel: 803-777-3142. p. 2055

Pascale, Claudine, Dir, Caldwell Public Library, 268 Bloomfield Ave, Caldwell, NJ, 07006-5198. Tel: 973-226-2837. p. 1393

Pascale, Claudine, Libr Dir, Verona Public Library, 17 Gould St, Verona, NJ, 07044-1928. Tel: 973-857-4848. p. 1449

Pasch, Teresa, Br Mgr, Crawford County Library District, Bourbon Branch, 575 Elm St, Bourbon, MO, 65441. Tel: 573-732-3277. p. 1282

Paschal, Dawn, Sr Assoc Dean for Collections & Discovery, Colorado State University Libraries, Morgan Library, 1201 Center Ave Mall, Fort Collins, CO, 80523. Tel: 970-491-1838. p. 280

Pasche, Stacy, Asst Libr Dir, Benzie Shores District Library, 630 Main St, Frankfort, MI, 49635. Tel: 231-352-4671. p. 1108

Paschel, Shannon, Librn, Ruthven Public Library, 1301 Gowrie St, Ruthven, IA, 51358. Tel: 712-837-4820. p. 780

Paschen, Ken, Head, Circ, Ellensburg Public Library, 209 N Ruby St, Ellensburg, WA, 98926-3397. Tel: 509-962-7250. p. 2363

Paschild, Cristine, Head, Spec Coll, Univ Archivist, Portland State University Library, 1875 SW Park Ave, Portland, OR, 97201-3220. Tel: 503-725-5874. p. 1893

Pascoe, Rachel, Dir, Oconto Falls Community Library, 251 N Main St, Oconto Falls, WI, 54154. Tel: 920-846-2673. p. 2466

Pascucci, Sandy, Dir, Woodgate Free Library, 11051 Woodgate Dr, Woodgate, NY, 13494. Tel: 315-392-4814. p. 1667

Pascuzzi, Kathleen, Asst Help Desk Mgr/Circ Supvr, Iona University, 715 North Ave, New Rochelle, NY, 10801-1890. Tel: 914-633-2351. p. 1577

Pashaie, Billy, Coordr, Instruction & Outreach, Cypress College Library, 9200 Valley View St, Cypress, CA, 90630-5897. Tel: 714-484-7418. p. 133

Pashia, Angela, Head, Learning Serv, Head, Res Support Serv, University of West Georgia, 1601 Maple St, Carrollton, GA, 30118. Tel: 678-839-6495. p. 469

Pasi, Gino, Archivist, Curator, University of Cincinnati Libraries, Henry R Winkler Center for the History of the Health Professions, 231 Albert Sabin Way, Cincinnati, OH, 45267. Tel: 513-558-5123. p. 1765

Pasicznyuk, Bob, Exec Dir, Douglas County Libraries, 100 S Wilcox, Castle Rock, CO, 80104. Tel: 303-688-7654. p. 269

Pasillas, Manuel, Jr, Libr Dir, Gilbreath Memorial Library, 916 N Main St, Winnsboro, TX, 75494. Tel: 903-342-6866. p. 2258

Pasini, Nicole, Dep Dir, Libr Serv, San Mateo County Library, Library Administration, 125 Lessingia Ct, San Mateo, CA, 94402-4000. Tel: 650-312-5251. p. 235

Pasley, Anthony, Dir & Curator, Dodge County Historical Society, 1643 N Nye Ave, Fremont, NE, 68025. Tel: 402-721-4515. p. 1314

Pasley, Kristina, Ref Librn, Clearwater Public Library System, East, 2465 Drew St, Clearwater, FL, 33765. Tel: 727-562-4970. p. 389

Pasos, Manuel, ILL/Doc Delivery Serv, Libr Mgr, University of Miami, Louis Calder Memorial Library, Miller School of Medicine, 1601 NW Tenth Ave, Miami, FL, 33136. Tel: 305-243-6749. p. 425

Pasquale, Jessica, Asst Dir, Scholarly Publishing Servs Librn, University of Michigan, Law Library, 801 Monroe St, Ann Arbor, MI, 48109-1210. Tel: 734-647-8713. p. 1080

Pass, Amy, Student Success Librn, Russell Sage College Libraries, 109 Second St, Troy, NY, 12180. Tel: 518-244-2431. p. 1653

Pass, Gregory, PhD, Asst Dean, Spec Coll, Saint Louis University, 3650 Lindell Blvd, Saint Louis, MO, 63108-3302. Tel: 314-977-3096. p. 1275

Passalacqua, Julie, Asst City Librn, Santa Clara City Library, 2635 Homestead Rd, Santa Clara, CA, 95051. Tel: 408-615-2900. p. 241

Passannant, Rachel, Colls Mgr, American Independence Museum Library, One Governors Lane, Exeter, NH, 03833. Tel: 603-772-2622. p. 1363

Passaretti, Cathy, Supvr, Haliburton County Public Library, Cardiff Branch, 2778 Monck Rd, Cardiff, ON, K0L 1M0, CANADA. Tel: 613-339-2712. p. 2644

Passaro, Patricia L, Library Contact, United States Army, Kimbrough Ambulatory Care Center Medical Library, 2480 Llewellyn Ave, Ste 5800, Fort George G Meade, MD, 20755-5800. Tel: 301-677-8228. p. 965

Passeri, Brian, Circ Librn, Converse Free Library, 38 Union St, Lyme, NH, 03768-9702. Tel: 603-795-4622. p. 1371

Passey, Samuel J, Libr Dir, Uintah County Library, 204 E 100 North, Vernal, UT, 84078. Tel: 435-789-0091. p. 2274

Passi McCue, Paula, Libr Asst, Bacon Free Library, 58 Eliot St, Natick, MA, 01760. Tel: 508-653-6730. p. 1037

Passiglia, Francesca, Teen Librn, Greenfield Public Library, 412 Main St, Greenfield, MA, 01301. Tel: 413-772-1544. p. 1022

Paster, Amy, Head Librn, Pennsylvania State University Libraries, Life Sciences, 408 Paterno Library, University Park, PA, 16802-1811. Tel: 814-865-3708. p. 2015

Pastuch, Carisa, Outreach Librn, Ref Librn, US Customs & Border Protection Information Resources Center, 90 K St NE, Washington, DC, 20229. Tel: 202-325-0130. p. 380

Pastula, Matthew, Dir, Northern Marianas College, Fina Sisu Lane, Bldg O, Saipan, MP, 96950. Tel: 670-237-6799. p. 2507

Paszek, Alicea, Library Services, Mgr, Redwater Public Library, 4915 48th St, Redwater, AB, T0A 2W0, CANADA. Tel: 780-942-3464. p. 2552

Paszko, Laurie, Head Law Librn, Lawrence Law Library, Two Appleton St, Lawrence, MA, 01840-1525. Tel: 978-687-7608. p. 1027

Paszkowski, Diane, Mgr, Libr Serv, Crowley Fleck PLLP Library, 490 N 31st St, Ste 500, Billings, MT, 59101-1267. Tel: 406-252-3441. p. 1288

Patalita, Sara, Head, Ref Serv, Rochester Public Library, 101 Second St SE, Rochester, MN, 55904-3776. Tel: 507-328-2369. p. 1194

Pate, Brandi, Circ Coordr, Southeastern Oklahoma State University, 425 W University, Durant, OK, 74701-0609. Tel: 580-745-2107. p. 1846

Pate, Davin, Asst Dir, Scholarly Communications & Coll, University of Texas at Dallas, 800 W Campbell Rd, Richardson, TX, 75080. Tel: 972-883-2908. p. 2231

Pate, Lisa, Br Mgr, Albuquerque-Bernalillo County Library System, Tony Hillerman Library, 8205 Apache Ave NE, Albuquerque, NM, 87110. Tel: 505-291-6264. p. 1460

Pate, Margetta, Asst Librn, Latimer County Public Library, 301 W Ada Ave, Wilburton, OK, 74578. Tel: 918-465-3751. p. 1869

Pate, Michael, Librn, South Florida State College Library, 600 W College Dr, Avon Park, FL, 33825-9356. Tel: 863-784-7305. p. 384

Pate, Tim, Libr Mgr, Vaughan Public Libraries, Ansley Grove Library, 350 Ansley Grove Rd, Woodbridge, ON, L4L 5C9, CANADA. Tel: 905-653-7323. p. 2701

Patel, Anita, Br Mgr, Fort Bend County Libraries, Missouri City Branch, 1530 Texas Pkwy, Missouri City, TX, 77489-2170. Tel: 281-238-2100. p. 2232

Patel, Samir, Dept Chair, Murray State University, College of Education & Human Services, 3201 Alexander Hall, Murray, KY, 42071-3309. Tel: 270-809-2500. p. 2785

Pateman, John, Chief Librn/CEO, Thunder Bay Public Library, 285 Red River Rd, Thunder Bay, ON, P7B 1A9, CANADA. Tel: 807-684-6802. p. 2685

Paterick, Rick, Coordr, Ref (Info Servs), Lehigh Carbon Community College Library, 4750 Orchard Rd, Schnecksville, PA, 18078. Tel: 610-799-1150. p. 2003

Paterra, Alice, Br Mgr, Worcester County Library, Berlin Branch, 13 Harrison Ave, Berlin, MD, 21811. Tel: 410-641-0650. p. 978

Paterson, Bill, Libr Dir, Lansdowne Public Library, 55 S Lansdowne Ave, Lansdowne, PA, 19050-2804. Tel: 610-623-0239, Ext 307. p. 1953

Paterson, Kurt, Pres, Alberta Genealogical Society Library & Research Centre, No 162-14315-118 Ave, Edmonton, AB, T5L 4S6, CANADA. Tel: 780-424-4429. p. 2534

Paterson, Raeanna, Digital Serv Librn, Instrul Serv Librn, Westmoreland County Community College Library, Student Achievement Ctr, Youngwood Campus, 145 Pavilion Lane, Youngwood, PA, 15697-1814. Tel: 724-925-4100. p. 2027

Paterson, Seale, Libr Mgr, New Orleans Public Library, Cita Dennis Hubbell Library, 725 Pelican Ave, New Orleans, LA, 70114. Tel: 504-596-3113. p. 903

Patillo, David, Info Tech, Springfield-Greene County Library District, 4653 S Campbell Ave, Springfield, MO, 65810-1723. Tel: 417-882-0714. p. 1281

Patillo, Ericka, Assoc Dean of Libr, Appalachian State University, 218 College St, Boone, NC, 28608. p. 1674

Patillo, Ericka, Dir, University of Houston, Music Library, 220 Moores School of Music Bldg, Houston, TX, 77204-4017. Tel: 713-743-3770. p. 2199

Patkus, Ronald, Head, Spec Coll, Vassar College Library, 124 Raymond Ave, Box 20, Poughkeepsie, NY, 12604. Tel: 845-437-5798. p. 1624

Paton, Jennie, Librn, United States Air Force, Air Force Flight Test Center Technical Research Library, 812 TSS/ENTL, 307 E Popson Ave, Bldg 1400, Rm 106, Edwards AFB, CA, 93524-6630. Tel: 661-275-5516. p. 139

Patricia Castaneda-Rocha, Patricia, Dep Dir, Finance, East Chicago Public Library, Robert A Pastrick Branch, 1008 W Chicago Ave, East Chicago, IN, 46312. Tel: 219-397-5505. p. 680

Patricia, Ford, Dir, Truro Public Library, Seven Standish Way, North Truro, MA, 02652. Tel: 508-487-1125. p. 1042

Patrick, James, Spec Serv Librn, Yuma County Free Library District, 2951 S 21st Dr, Yuma, AZ, 85364. Tel: 928-373-6484. p. 85

Patrick, Jean, Ch Serv Librn, Mitchell Public Library, 221 N Duff St, Mitchell, SD, 57301. Tel: 605-995-8480. p. 2079

Patrick, Kari, Librn, Maryland Correctional Training Center Library, 18800 Roxbury Rd, Hagerstown, MD, 21746. Tel: 240-420-1607. p. 968

Patrick, Lindsey, Br Mgr, Nashville Public Library, Southeast Branch, 5260 Hickory Hollow Pkwy, # 201, Antioch, TN, 37013. Tel: 615-862-5871. p. 2120

Patrick, Lorraine, Ref & Instruction Librn, Bellevue University, 1028 Bruin Blvd, Bellevue, NE, 68005. Tel: 402-557-7316. p. 1308

Patrick, Mary, Dean, Allan Hancock College, 800 S College Dr, Santa Maria, CA, 93455. Tel: 805-922-6966, Ext 3475. p. 243

Patrick, Mathis, Database Mgr, Syst Coordr, Parkland Regional Library-Saskatchewan, Hwy 52 W, Yorkton, SK, S3N 3Z4, CANADA. Tel: 306-783-7022. p. 2755

Patrick, Michele, Dir, Indianola Public Library, 207 North B St, Indianola, IA, 50125. Tel: 515-961-9418. p. 759

Patrick, Peggi, Libr Mgr, Florida State College at Jacksonville, Deerwood Center Library, 9911 Old Baymeadows Rd, Jacksonville, FL, 32256. Tel: 904-997-2562. p. 411

Patrick, Skye, County Librn, County of Los Angeles Public Library, 7400 E Imperial Hwy, Downey, CA, 90242-3375. Tel: 562-940-8400. p. 134

Patrick, Vrena, Asst Dir, Richardson Public Library, 2360 Campbell Creek Blvd, Ste 500, Richardson, TX, 75082. Tel: 972-744-4352. p. 2231

Patridge, Emily, Asst Dir, University of Washington Libraries, Health Sciences Library, T-334 Health Sciences Bldg, 1959 NE Pacific St, Box 357155, Seattle, WA, 98195-7155. Tel: 206-221-3489. p. 2382

Patry, Catherine, Dir, Bibliotheque de la ville de Shawinigan, 205 6e rue de la Pointe, Shawinigan, QC, G9N 6V3, CANADA. Tel: 819-537-4989, Ext 227. p. 2736

Patry, Claudine, Pub Serv Librn, Bibliothèque Municipale de Gatineau, Ville de Gatineau, CP 1970 Succ. Hull, Gatineau, QC, J8X 3Y9, CANADA. Tel: 819-243-2345. p. 2712

Patry, Janice, Dir, Libr Serv, Windham Free Library Association, Seven Windham Green Rd, Windham, CT, 06280. Tel: 860-423-0636. p. 348

Patt, Dorothy, Libr Mgr, Wolcott Public Library, 5890 New Hartford St, Wolcott, NY, 14590. Tel: 315-594-2265. p. 1667

Pattee, Amy, Prof, Simmons University, 300 The Fenway, Boston, MA, 02115. Tel: 617-521-2800. p. 2786

Patten, Christine, Mgr, Libr Serv, Seminole County Public Library System, 215 N Oxford Rd, Casselberry, FL, 32707. Tel: 407-665-1500. p. 388

Patten, Hannah, Colls Mgr, Wisconsin Maritime Museum, 75 Maritime Dr, Manitowoc, WI, 54220. Tel: 920-684-0218, Ext 112. p. 2453

Patten, Heather, Asst Dir, Brown County Public Library, 613 S High St, Mount Orab, OH, 45154. Tel: 937-444-0181. p. 1804

Patten, Heather, Mgr, Brown County Public Library, Mt Orab Branch, 613 S High St, Mount Orab, OH, 45154. Tel: 937-444-1414. p. 1804

Patten, Marlene, Libr Asst, Gardiner Public Library, 152 Water St, Gardiner, ME, 04345. Tel: 207-582-3312. p. 926

Patterson, Ann, Librn, Mono County Free Library, Benton, 25553 Hwy 6, Benton, CA, 93512. Tel: 760-933-2542. p. 172

Patterson, Bettie, Libr Asst, Alexander Memorial Library, 201 S Center St, Cotulla, TX, 78014-2255. Tel: 830-879-2601. p. 2161

Patterson, Bettie, Libr Asst, Alexander Memorial Library, La Salle County Library - Encinal Branch, 201 Center St, Cotulla, TX, 78014. p. 2161

Patterson, Cadene, Circ Mgr, Long Branch Free Public Library, 328 Broadway, Long Branch, NJ, 07740. Tel: 732-222-3900. p. 1413

Patterson, Carol, Tech Serv, Public Library of Mount Vernon & Knox County, 201 N Mulberry St, Mount Vernon, OH, 43050-2413. Tel: 740-392-2665. p. 1804

Patterson, Carolyn Sue, Acq Librn, Mercer County Public Library, 109 W Lexington St, Harrodsburg, KY, 40330-1542. Tel: 859-734-3680. p. 858

Patterson, Cassie, Asst Dir, Greenville Public Library, 573 Putnam Pike, Greenville, RI, 02828-2195. Tel: 401-949-3630. p. 2032

Patterson, Cynthia, Supvr, Circ, Lawrence University, 113 S Lawe St, Appleton, WI, 54911-5683. p. 2420

Patterson, Darla, Dir, Kittanning Public Library, 280 N Jefferson, Kittanning, PA, 16201. Tel: 724-543-1383. p. 1949

Patterson, Deborah, Dir, Volusia County Law Library, Courthouse Annex, Rm 208, 125 E Orange Ave, Daytona Beach, FL, 32114. Tel: 386-257-6041. p. 392

Patterson, Elizabeth, Librn, Washburn Public Library, 705 Main Ave, Washburn, ND, 58577. Tel: 701-462-8180. p. 1741

Patterson, Emily, Librn, North Central Washington Libraries, Curlew Public Library, 11 River St, Curlew, WA, 99118. Tel: 509-779-0321. p. 2393

Patterson, Eva, Br Mgr, Marin County Free Library, Civic Center Library, 3501 Civic Center Dr, Rm 427, San Rafael, CA, 94903-4177. Tel: 415-473-6057, 415-499-6056. p. 237

Patterson, Gail, Children & Teen Librn, South Haven Memorial Library, 314 Broadway St, South Haven, MI, 49090. Tel: 269-637-2403. p. 1150

Patterson, Greg, Head, Knowledge Mgt, United States Navy, Naval Hospital Library, HP01 One Boone Rd, Bremerton, WA, 98312-1898. Tel: 360-475-4316. p. 2360

Patterson, Greg, Br Mgr, Richmond Hill Public Library, Oak Ridges Moraine Library, 13085 Yonge St, Unit 12, Richmond Hill, ON, L4E 3L2, CANADA. Tel: 905-773-5533. p. 2675

Patterson Harris, Emily, Dr, Interim Dean of Libr, Langston University, 701 Sammy Davis Jr Dr, Langston, OK, 73050. Tel: 405-466-3292. p. 1851

Patterson, James, Dir, Northwestern Connecticut Community College Library, Park Pl E, Winsted, CT, 06098. Tel: 860-738-6480. p. 348

Patterson, Jenna, Law Librn, Federal Communications Commission Library, 45 L St NE, Washington, DC, 20554. Tel: 202-418-0450. p. 366

Patterson, Jennie P, Dir, Pleasant Grove Public Library, 501 Park Rd, Pleasant Grove, AL, 35127. Tel: 205-744-1742. p. 33

Patterson, Jennifer, Libr Serv Dir, Thousand Oaks Library, Newbury Park Branch, 2331 Borchard Rd, Newbury Park, CA, 91320-3206. Tel: 805-449-2660 x7316. p. 252

Patterson, Jennifer, State Librn, State Library of Oregon, 250 Winter St NE, Salem, OR, 97301-3950. Tel: 503-378-4367. p. 1897

Patterson, Jennifer R, Libr Serv Dir, Thousand Oaks Library, 1401 E Janss Rd, Thousand Oaks, CA, 91362-2199. Tel: 805-449-2660, Ext 7316. p. 252

Patterson, Jordan, Assoc Librn, Saint Peter's Seminary, 1040 Waterloo St N, London, ON, N6A 3Y1, CANADA. Tel: 519-646-7125. p. 2655

Patterson, Kelly, Dir, Crew Public Library, 107 E Cherry St, Salem, IA, 52649. Tel: 319-258-9007. p. 780

Patterson, Kenneth J, Exec Dir, Harvard Library, Baker Library & Special Collections, Harvard Business School, Bloomberg Ctr, Ten Soldiers Field Rd, Boston, MA, 02163. Tel: 617-495-6040. p. 1005

Patterson, Lauren, Admin Officer, Riverside County Law Library, 3989 Lemon St, Riverside, CA, 92501-4203. Tel: 951-368-0361. p. 201

Patterson, MariBeth, Libr Asst, Ahira Hall Memorial Library, 37 W Main St, Brocton, NY, 14716-9747. Tel: 716-792-9418. p. 1497

Patterson, Maribeth, Tech Serv, State University of New York at Fredonia, 280 Central Ave, Fredonia, NY, 14063. Tel: 716-673-3192. p. 1535

Patterson, Mary, Br Mgr, Monmouth County Library, Hazlet Branch, 251 Middle Rd, Hazlet, NJ, 07730. Tel: 732-264-7164. p. 1416

Patterson, Michele, Ad, Indianapolis Public Library, Beech Grove Branch, 1102 Main St, Beech Grove, IN, 46107. Tel: 317-275-4560. p. 694

Patterson, Mindy, Libr Dir, Kendallville Public Library, 221 S Park Ave, Kendallville, IN, 46755-2248. Tel: 260-343-2010. p. 698

Patterson, Nancy, Outreach Librn, National Network of Libraries of Medicine Region 1, Univ Md Health Scis & Human Servs Libr, 601 W Lombard St, Baltimore, MD, 21201-1512. Tel: 410-706-2858. p. 2766

Patterson, Nick, Head Music Libr, Columbia University, The Gabe M Wiener Music & Arts Library, 701 Dodge Hall, 2960 Broadway, New York, NY, 10027. Tel: 212-854-8523. p. 1584

Patterson, Renee, Tech Serv Adminr, Alachua County Library District, 401 E University Ave, Gainesville, FL, 32601-5453. Tel: 352-334-3960. p. 406

Patterson, Robyn, Librn, Idaho State Correctional Institution Library, South Idaho Correctional Institution Library, 13900 S Pleasant Valley Rd, Kuna, ID, 83634. Tel: 208-336-1260. p. 517

Patterson, Rory, Assoc Dean, Planning, Administration & Ops, Liberty University, 1971 University Blvd, Lynchburg, VA, 24515. Tel: 434-582-2230. p. 2330

Patterson, Savannah, Pub Serv Librn, Union University, 1050 Union University Dr, Jackson, TN, 38305-3697. Tel: 731-661-6544. p. 2102

Patterson, Stephanie, Dir, Maryville Public Library, 509 N Main St, Maryville, MO, 64468. Tel: 660-582-5281. p. 1261

Patterson, Tabitha, Cataloging & Metadata Librn, Baylor University Libraries, Sheridan & John Eddie Williams Legal Research & Technology Center, 1114 S University Parks Dr, Waco, TX, 76706. Tel: 254-710-2168. p. 2253

Patterson, Tara, Libr Mgr, George Washington University, Virginia Science & Technology Campus Library, 44983 Knoll Sq, Ste 179, Ashburn, DC, 20147-2604. Tel: 571-553-8230. p. 367

Patterson-Day, Cassaundra, Dir, Ivy Tech Community College, 815 E 60th St, Anderson, IN, 46013. Tel: 765-643-7133, Ext 2079. p. 668

Patteson, Jason, Br Mgr, Tulsa City-County Library, Herman & Kate Kaiser Library, 5202 S Hudson Ave, Ste B, Tulsa, OK, 74135. p. 1866

Patti, Angela, Librn, New York Supreme Court, 77 W Eagle St, Buffalo, NY, 14202. Tel: 716-845-9391. p. 1509

Patti, Kupka, Dir, Clutier Public Library, 404 Main St, Clutier, IA, 52217. Tel: 319-479-2171. p. 741

Pattison, Katy, Br Mgr, Springfield-Greene County Library District, Schweitzer Brentwood Branch, 2214 Brentwood Blvd, Springfield, MO, 65804. Tel: 417-883-1974. p. 1281

Pattison, Toni, Project Mgr, Charleston County Public Library, 68 Calhoun St, Charleston, SC, 29401. Tel: 843-805-6801. p. 2048

Patton, Amy, Circ, Tech Serv, Lake County Library, 1425 N High St, Lakeport, CA, 95453-3800. Tel: 707-263-8817. p. 156

Patton, Julia, Libr Dir, University of Valley Forge, 1401 Charlestown Rd, Phoenixville, PA, 19460. Tel: 610-917-2004. p. 1989

Patton, Katie, Ch, Dir, Towanda Public Library, 104 Main St, Towanda, PA, 18848. Tel: 570-265-2470. p. 2013

Patton, Sherrie, Dir, Lexington Public Library District, 207 S Cedar St, Lexington, IL, 61753. Tel: 309-365-7801. p. 608

Patton, Stephen, Chair, Systems, Indiana State University, 510 North 6 1/2 St, Terre Haute, IN, 47809. Tel: 812-237-3700. p. 720

Patzner, Joseph, Interim Librn, Chancellor Robert R Livingston Masonic Library of Grand Lodge, 71 W 23rd St, 14th Flr, New York, NY, 10010-4171. Tel: 212-337-6623. p. 1581

Patzold, Karen, Librn II, College of the North Atlantic Library Services, Gander Campus, One Magee Rd, Gander, NL, A1V 1W8, CANADA. Tel: 709-651-4815. p. 2609

Pau, Tiffany, Coordr, MFL Occupational Health Centre, 167 Sherbrook St, Winnipeg, MB, R3C 2B7, CANADA. Tel: 204-926-7909. p. 2594

Paul, Angela, Instruction & Outreach Librn, Wichita State University Libraries, 1845 Fairmount, Wichita, KS, 67260-0068. Tel: 316-978-5084. p. 844

Paul, Angie, Develop Dir, Evansville State Hospital, 3400 Lincoln Ave, Evansville, IN, 47714. Tel: 812-469-6800, Ext 4979. p. 681

Paul, Beth, Cat, Tech Serv Spec, Federal Reserve Bank of Philadelphia, 100 N Sixth St, 4th Flr, Philadelphia, PA, 19106. Tel: 215-574-6540. p. 1977

Paul, Cassandra, Library & Archives Assoc, Wildlife Conservation Society Library, 2300 Southern Blvd, Bronx, NY, 10460. Tel: 718-220-5100. p. 1500

Paul, Eddie, Head Biblio & Info Serv, Bibliotheque Publique Juive, 5151 Cote Ste Catherine, Montreal, QC, H3W 1M6, CANADA. Tel: 514-345-2627. p. 2717
Paul, Elizabeth, Ch, Andover Public Library, 142 W Main St, Andover, OH, 44003-9318. Tel: 440-293-6792. p. 1746
Paul, Ellen, Libr Dir, East Hampton Public Library, 105 Main St, East Hampton, CT, 06424. Tel: 860-267-6621. p. 309
Paul, Ellen, Exec Dir, Connecticut Library Consortium, 234 Court St, Middletown, CT, 06457-3304. Tel: 860-344-8777. p. 2762
Paul, Laura, Circ Supvr, Agawam Public Library, 750 Cooper St, Agawam, MA, 01001. Tel: 413-789-1550. p. 984
Paul, Morgan, Ms, Dir, St Marys Community Public Library, 140 S Chestnut St, Saint Marys, OH, 45885. Tel: 419-394-7471. p. 1819
Paul, Nichole, Discovery Librn, Western Nevada Community College, Dini Bldg, 2201 W College Pkwy, Carson City, NV, 89703. Tel: 775-445-3229. p. 1344
Paul, Paula, Dir, Steep Falls Public Library, 1128 Pequawket Trail, Steep Falls, ME, 04085. Tel: 207-675-3132. p. 942
Paulene, Rebecca, Librn, West Blocton Public Library, 109 Florida St, West Blocton, AL, 35184. Tel: 205-938-3570. p. 39
Paulette, Meg, Dir, Buchanan District Library, 128 E Front St, Buchanan, MI, 49107. Tel: 269-695-3681. p. 1087
Pauley, Nathan, Tech Serv Mgr, Daniel Boone Regional Library, 100 W Broadway, Columbia, MO, 65203. Tel: 573-443-3161. p. 1242
Pauley, Shannon, Head, Youth Serv, Peters Township Public Library, 616 E McMurray Rd, McMurray, PA, 15317-3495. Tel: 724-941-9430. p. 1959
Pauli, Ron, Dep Dir, Support Serv, Poplar Creek Public Library District, 1405 S Park Ave, Streamwood, IL, 60107-2997. Tel: 630-837-6800. p. 652
Paulic, Mary Ann, Libr Coord, Yavapai County Free Library District, Congress Public Library, 26750 Santa Fe Rd, Congress, AZ, 85332. Tel: 928-427-3945. p. 74
Pauline, Tami, Ch, South Park Township Library, 2575 Brownsville Rd, South Park, PA, 15129-8527. Tel: 412-833-5585. p. 2009
Pauling, Laura, Dir, Libbie A Cass Memorial Library, 2748 Main St, Springfield, NH, 03284. Tel: 603-763-4381. p. 1381
Paulios, Jason, Adult Serv Coordr, Iowa City Public Library, 123 S Linn St, Iowa City, IA, 52240. Tel: 319-887-6075. p. 760
Paulk, J Sara, Dir, Houston County Public Library System, 1201 Washington Ave, Perry, GA, 31069. Tel: 478-987-3050. p. 493
Paulk, Lesley, Br Mgr, Coastal Plain Regional Library System, Fitzgerald-Ben Hill County Library, 123 N Main St, Fitzgerald, GA, 31750. Tel: 229-426-5080. p. 500
Paulls, Linda, Med Librn, Mount Sinai Phillips School of Nursing, Beth Israel, 148 E 126th St, 2nd Flr, New York, NY, 10035. p. 1592
Paulraj, Rebecca, Ref & Instruction Librn, University of Wisconsin-Whitewater, 750 W Main St, Whitewater, WI, 53190-1790. Tel: 262-472-5519. p. 2488
Pauls, Anna, Head, Youth Serv, Round Lake Area Public Library District, 906 Hart Rd, Round Lake, IL, 60073. Tel: 847-546-7060, Ext 120. p. 643
Pauls, Becky, Br Mgr, Pioneer Library System, Blanchard Public, 205 NE Tenth St, Blanchard, OK, 73010. Tel: 405-485-2275. p. 1855
Pauls, Katie, Libr Dir, Maquoketa Public Library, 126 S Second St, Maquoketa, IA, 52060. Tel: 563-652-3874. p. 767
Pauls, Stuart, Libr Mgr, Vermilion Public Library, 5001 49th Ave, Vermilion, AB, T9X 1B8, CANADA. Tel: 780-853-4288. p. 2558
Paulsen, Carolyn, Library Contact, Finley Public Library, 302 Broadway, Finley, ND, 58230. p. 1733
Paulsen, Cathy, Head, Teen Serv, Chappaqua Public Library, 195 S Greeley Ave, Chappaqua, NY, 10514. Tel: 914-238-4779. p. 1516
Paulsen, Cathy, Ref Librn, Chappaqua Public Library, 195 S Greeley Ave, Chappaqua, NY, 10514. Tel: 914-238-4779. p. 1516
Paulsen, Jessica, Mgr, Jefferson County Public Library, Evergreen Branch, 5000 Country Rd 73, Evergreen, CO, 80439. p. 288
Paulsen, Julia, Librn, Seattle Children's Hospital, 4800 Sand Point Way NE, OB.8.520, Seattle, WA, 98105. Tel: 206-987-2098. p. 2378
Paulson, Anne, Dir, Rouses Point Dodge Memorial Library, 144 Lake St, Rouses Point, NY, 12979. Tel: 518-297-6242. p. 1633
Paulson, Justine, Dir, Withee Public Library, 511 Division St, Withee, WI, 54498. Tel: 715-229-2010. p. 2489
Paulson, Keri-Lynn, Electronic Serv Librn, King University, 1350 King College Rd, Bristol, TN, 37620. Tel: 423-652-4897. p. 2090
Paulus, Kory, Coll Mgt Librn, Wingate University, 110 Church ST, Wingate, NC, 28174. Tel: 704-233-8089. p. 1724
Pauly, Regina, Head, Instrul Mat Lab, University of Wisconsin - Platteville, One University Plaza, Platteville, WI, 53818. Tel: 608-342-1099. p. 2470
Pause, Tracey, Asst Dir, Voorheesville Public Library, 51 School Rd, Voorheesville, NY, 12186. Tel: 518-765-2791. p. 1657
Paustian, Lauren, Coll Mgr, Registrar, Center for Jewish History, 15 W 16 St, New York, NY, 10011. Tel: 212-294-8340, 212-744-6400. p. 1580
Pava, Joseph, Coll Develop, South Windsor Public Library, 1550 Sullivan Ave, South Windsor, CT, 06074. Tel: 860-644-1541. p. 337
Pavlica, Carol, Br Librn, Community District Library, Bentley Memorial, 135 S Main St, Perry, MI, 48872-0017. Tel: 517-625-3166. p. 1095
Pavlina, Amber, Ref & Instruction Librn, University of Saint Francis, Pope John Paul II Ctr, 2701 Spring St, Rm 102 & 202, Fort Wayne, IN, 46808. Tel: 260-399-7700, Ext 6067. p. 685
Pavloff, Matt, Dir, Kinderhook Memorial Library, 18 Hudson St, Kinderhook, NY, 12106-2003. Tel: 518-758-6192. p. 1560
Pavlov, Deanna, Circ Mgr, Boulder City Library, 701 Adams Blvd, Boulder City, NV, 89005-2207. Tel: 702-293-1281. p. 1343
Pavlov, Nadine, Circ Supvr, Green River College, 12401 SE 320th St, Auburn, WA, 98092-3699. Tel: 253-833-9111, Ext 2088. p. 2357
Pavlovsky, Taras, Dean of Libr, The College of New Jersey, 2000 Pennington Rd, Ewing, NJ, 08628-1104. Tel: 609-771-2332. p. 1402
Pavluk, Linda, Circ, Wilmington Memorial Library, 175 Middlesex Ave, Wilmington, MA, 01887-2779. Tel: 978-658-2967. p. 1070
Pavoldi, Teresa, Libr Dir, Middleburgh Library, 323 Main St, Middleburgh, NY, 12122. Tel: 518-827-5142. p. 1571
Pavy, Jeanne, Dept Chair, Resource Management, Scholarly Communications Officer, University of New Orleans, 2000 Lakeshore Dr, New Orleans, LA, 70148. Tel: 504-280-6547. p. 904
Pawlak, James, Libr Dir, Eastern New Mexico University - Ruidoso, 709 Mechem Dr, Ruidoso, NM, 88345. Tel: 575-315-1135. p. 1474
Pawlak, Jenna, Ch Serv Librn, Lebanon Public Library, 101 S Broadway, Lebanon, OH, 45036. Tel: 513-932-2665. p. 1795
Pawlak, Mark, Lending Servs, William Paterson University, 300 Pompton Rd, Wayne, NJ, 07470. Tel: 973-720-2542. p. 1452
Pawlak, Nicole, Libr Dir, Invermere Public Library, 646 Fourth St, Invermere, BC, V0A 1K0, CANADA. Tel: 250-342-6416. p. 2567
Pawlarczyk, Bonnie, Head, Youth Serv, Worth Public Library District, 6917 W 111th St, Worth, IL, 60482. Tel: 708-448-2855. p. 665
Pawloski, Lynn, Ch, Southington Public Library & Museum, 255 Main St, Southington, CT, 06489. Tel: 860-628-0947. p. 337
Pawlowski, Amy, Exec Dir, Ohio Library & Information Network, 1224 Kinnear Rd, Columbus, OH, 43215. Tel: 614-485-6722. p. 2773
Pawlowski, Cindy, Br Mgr, Nevada County Community Library, Bear River Station, 11130 Magnolia Rd, Grass Valley, CA, 95949. p. 182
Pawlowski, Cindy, Br Mgr, Nevada County Community Library, Madelyn Helling Library, 980 Helling Way, Nevada City, CA, 95959. Tel: 530-265-7078. p. 183
Pawlowski, Cindy, Br Mgr, Nevada County Community Library, Penn Valley Station, 11336 Pleasant Valley Rd, Penn Valley, CA, 95946. Tel: 530-432-5764. p. 183
Pawlowski, Jack, Circ & Info Serv Librn, Colleyville Public Library, 110 Main St, Colleyville, TX, 76034. Tel: 817-503-1150, 817-503-1154 (Youth Serv), 817-503-1155 (Adult Serv). p. 2158
Pawluk, Alanna, Librn, Chinook Regional Library, Cabri Branch, Town Hall, 202 Centre St, Cabri, SK, S0N 0J0, CANADA. Tel: 306-587-2911. p. 2752
Pawlus, Erin, Adminr, Arizona Talking Book Library, 1030 N 32nd St, Phoenix, AZ, 85008. Tel: 602-255-5578. p. 69
Paxson, Holly, Libr Mgr, Timberland Regional Library, Lacey Branch, 500 College St SE, Lacey, WA, 98503-1240. Tel: 360-491-3860. p. 2389
Paxton, Michelle, Head, Youth Serv, York County Public Library, 100 Long Green Blvd, Yorktown, VA, 23693. Tel: 757-890-5100. p. 2355
Paxton, Sharlene, Librn, Cerro Coso Community College Library, 3000 College Heights Blvd, Ridgecrest, CA, 93555-9571. Tel: 760-384-6216. p. 200
Payer, Angela, Br Mgr, Kenton County Public Library, Erlanger Branch, 401 Kenton Lands Rd, Erlanger, KY, 41018. Tel: 859-962-4001. p. 852
Payette, Suzanne, Dir, Bibliotheque de Brossard, 7855 ave San Francisco, Brossard, QC, J4X 2A4, CANADA. Tel: 450-923-6304. p. 2710
Payne, Ben, Reader Serv, Alabama Institute for the Deaf & Blind, 705 South St E, Talladega, AL, 35160. Tel: 256-761-3237. p. 36
Payne, Christine, Tech Serv Librn, Katten Muchin Rosenman LLP, 50 Rockefeller Plaza, New York, NY, 10020-1605. Tel: 212-940-7029. p. 1590
Payne, Chuck, Exec Dir, Medicine Hat College Library, 299 College Dr SE, Medicine Hat, AB, T1A 3Y6, CANADA. Tel: 403-529-3870. p. 2548
Payne, Cindy, Circ Supvr, Centralia Regional Library District, 515 E Broadway, Centralia, IL, 62801. Tel: 618-532-5222. p. 551
Payne, David, Br Mgr, Montgomery County Public Libraries, Aspen Hill Library, 4407 Aspen Hill Rd, Rockville, MD, 20853-2899. Tel: 240-773-9401. p. 974
Payne, David, Actg Br Mgr, Montgomery County Public Libraries, Potomac Library, 10101 Glenolden Dr, Potomac, MD, 20854-5052. Tel: 240-777-0696. p. 975
Payne, David, Dir, Avon Grove Library, 117 Rosehill Ave, West Grove, PA, 19390. Tel: 610-869-2004. p. 2021
Payne, Dianna, Dir, Lincoln Public Library, 107 W Bean St, Lincoln, AR, 72744. Tel: 479-824-3294. p. 99
Payne, Elizabeth, Adult Serv, Ashe County Public Library, 148 Library Dr, West Jefferson, NC, 28694. Tel: 336-846-2041. p. 1722
Payne, John, Dir of Libr, St Lawrence University, 23 Romoda Dr, Canton, NY, 13617. Tel: 315-229-5424. p. 1513
Payne, Kayla, Ch Serv, Alexandria Library, James M Duncan Jr Branch, 2501 Commonwealth Ave, Alexandria, VA, 22301. Tel: 703-746-1705. p. 2302

Payne, Lee, Br Mgr, Phoenix Public Library, Saguaro Library, 2808 N 46th St, Phoenix, AZ, 85008. p. 72
Payne, Nina, Dir, Winthrop Public Library, 354 W Madison St, Winthrop, IA, 50682. Tel: 319-935-3374. p. 792
Payne, Ophelia, Br Mgr, Jefferson-Madison Regional Library, Louisa County, 881 Davis Hwy, Mineral, VA, 23117. Tel: 540-894-5853. p. 2309
Payne, Rebecca, Dir, Stone County Library, 322 West State Hwy 248, Galena, MO, 65656. Tel: 417-357-6410. p. 1247
Payne, Steven, Dr, Dir, Bronx County Historical Society, 3309 Bainbridge Ave, Bronx, NY, 10467. Tel: 718-881-8900, Ext 105. p. 1498
Payne, Suzanne, Sr Librn, Placer County Library, Auburn Branch, 350 Nevada St, Auburn, CA, 95603-3789. Tel: 530-886-4500. p. 118
Payonk, Karen, Asst Dir, Ch, Lititz Public Library, 651 Kissel Hill Rd, Lititz, PA, 17543. Tel: 717-626-2255. p. 1956
Payovich, Tracy Gierada, Curator, The Heritage Museum & Cultural Center, 601 Main St, Saint Joseph, MI, 49085. Tel: 269-983-1191. p. 1148
Payton, Stephanie, Dir, Karlen Memorial Library, 215 Blaine St, Beemer, NE, 68716. Tel: 402-528-3476. p. 1307
Payton, Wendy, Interim Libr Dir, Pub Serv Librn, Dallas International University Library, 7500 W Camp Wisdom Rd, Dallas, TX, 75236-5699. Tel: 972-708-7416. p. 2164
Payton-Johnson, Lori, Lecturer, North Carolina Central University, 1801 Fayetteville St, Durham, NC, 27707. Tel: 919-530-6485. p. 2790
Paz, Daniel, IT Mgr, Yuma County Free Library District, 2951 S 21st Dr, Yuma, AZ, 85364. Tel: 928-373-6467. p. 85
Paz Vera, Mari, Head, Pub Serv, Vancouver Community College, 250 W Pender St, Vancouver, BC, V6B 1S9, CANADA. Tel: 604-871-7000, Ext 7319. p. 2581
Peacemaker, Bettina, Head, Acad Outreach, Virginia Commonwealth University Libraries, 901 Park Ave, Richmond, VA, 23284. Tel: 804-828-8960. p. 2343
Peach, Amanda, Asst Dir, Libr Serv, Berea College, 100 Campus Dr, Berea, KY, 40404. Tel: 859-985-3279. p. 849
Peach, Brenda, Libr Tech II, College of the North Atlantic Library Services, Carbonear Campus, Four Pikes Lane, Carbonear, NL, A1Y 1A7, CANADA. Tel: 709-596-8925, 709-596-8940. p. 2609
Peach, Paula, Circ, Wabash Valley College, 2200 College Dr, Mount Carmel, IL, 62863. Tel: 618-263-5096. p. 620
Peachin, Lorna, Librn, Kristine Mann Library, C G Jung Ctr of New York, 28 E 39th St, 4th Flr, New York, NY, 10016. Tel: 212-697-7877. p. 1590
Peacock, Beth, Asst Dir, Gloucester, Lyceum & Sawyer Free Library, Two Dale Ave, Gloucester, MA, 01930. Tel: 978-325-5555. p. 1021
Peacock, Elayna, Asst to the Dir, The Baptist College of Florida, 5400 College Dr, Graceville, FL, 32440-1833. Tel: 850-263-3261, Ext 424. p. 408
Peacock, Hannah, Asst Dir, Burnham Memorial Library, 898 Main St, Colchester, VT, 05446. Tel: 802-264-5660. p. 2282
Peacock, Jennifer, Dir, Admin Serv Bur, Mississippi Library Commission, 3881 Eastwood Dr, Jackson, MS, 39211. Tel: 601-432-4042. p. 1222
Peacock, Joyce, Ref, Cypress College Library, 9200 Valley View St, Cypress, CA, 90630-5897. Tel: 714-484-7068. p. 133
Peacock, Lizzie, Site Supvr, Albuquerque-Bernalillo County Library System, Ernie Pyle Library, 900 Girard Blvd SE, Albuquerque, NM, 87106. Tel: 505-256-2065. p. 1460
Peacock, Lynn S, Library Contact, Florida State University Libraries, Center for Demography & Population Health, 601 Bellamy Bldg, 113 Collegiate Loop, Tallahassee, FL, 32306-2240. Tel: 850-644-1762. p. 447
Peacock, Roberta, Dir, Martin Public Library, 100 Main St, Martin, TN, 38237-2445. Tel: 731-587-3148. p. 2110
Peak, Caroline, Br Mgr, Cleveland Public Library, Collinwood, 856 E 152nd St, Cleveland, OH, 44110. Tel: 216-623-6934. p. 1768
Peak, Natalie, Libr Tech, Mount Hope-Funks Grove Townships Library District, 111 S Hamilton St, McLean, IL, 61754-7624. Tel: 309-874-2291. p. 616
Peak, Tina M, Dir, Lake Wales Public Library, 290 Cypress Garden Lane, Lake Wales, FL, 33853. Tel: 863-678-4004. p. 416
Peake, Beryle, Br Librn, Wapiti Regional Library, Leask Public Library, 231 First Ave, Leask, SK, S0J 1M0, CANADA. Tel: 306-466-4577. p. 2745
Peake, Connie, Br Librn, Wapiti Regional Library, Leask Public Library, 231 First Ave, Leask, SK, S0J 1M0, CANADA. Tel: 306-466-4577. p. 2745
Peaks, Nicole, Librn, United States Court of Appeals, King Courthouse, Rm 5007, 50 Walnut St, Newark, NJ, 07102. Tel: 973-645-3034. p. 1428
Pealer, Lindsay, Supv Librn, Office of Legislative Counsel, State of California, 925 L St, Lower Level, Sacramento, CA, 95814-3772. Tel: 916-341-8036. p. 209
Pealer, Meghan, Ch, Malvern Public Library, One E First Ave, Ste 2, Malvern, PA, 19355-2743. Tel: 610-644-7259. p. 1957
Pearce, Alexa L, Assoc Univ Librn, Res & Learning, University of Michigan, 818 Hatcher Graduate Library South, 913 S University Ave, Ann Arbor, MI, 48109-1190. Tel: 734-764-0400. p. 1080
Pearce, Amy, Librn, Brookes Bible College Library, 10257 St Charles Rock Rd, Saint Ann, MO, 63074. Tel: 314-773-0083. p. 1268
Pearce, Ann, Mgr, McMaster University Library, H G Thode Library of Science & Engineering, 1280 Main St W, Hamilton, ON, L8S 4P5, CANADA. Tel: 905-525-9140, Ext 28691. p. 2647
Pearce, Beverley, Br Mgr, Whitman County Rural Library District, Palouse Branch, E 120 Main, Palouse, WA, 99149. Tel: 508-878-1513. p. 2362
Pearce, Eileen, Ad, Windsor Locks Public Library, 28 Main St, Windsor Locks, CT, 06096. Tel: 860-627-1495. p. 348
Pearcy, Gloria, Supvr, Yakima Valley Libraries, Southeast Yakima Library, 1211 S Seventh St, Yakima, WA, 98901. Tel: 509-576-0723. p. 2396
Pearcy, Kevin, Dir, Greenville-Butler County Public Library, 309 Ft Dale St, Greenville, AL, 36037. Tel: 334-382-3216. p. 19
Pearish, Rebecca, Youth Serv Librn, Brown Public Library, 93 S Main St, Northfield, VT, 05663. Tel: 802-485-4621. p. 2290
Pearl, Glenn, Asst Dir, Ref, Ser Librn, Southeastern University, 1000 Longfellow Blvd, Lakeland, FL, 33801. Tel: 863-667-5089. p. 417
Pearlman, Nancy, Dir, The Educational Communications Corp, PO Box 351419, Los Angeles, CA, 90035-9119. Tel: 213-705-4992. p. 161
Pearlman, Stefanie, Ref (Info Servs), University of Nebraska-Lincoln, Marvin & Virginia Schmid Law Library, 1875 N 42nd St, Lincoln, NE, 68583. Tel: 402-472-3547. p. 1323
Pearman, Carlos, Head, Circ, Manchester City Library, 405 Pine St, Manchester, NH, 03104-6199. Tel: 603-624-6550. p. 1372
Pearman, Connie, Librn, Potter County Library, 205 W Commercial Ave, Gettysburg, SD, 57442. Tel: 605-765-9518. p. 2076
Pearson, Alicia, Head, Cat & Metadata Serv, Siena College, 515 Loudon Rd, Loudonville, NY, 12211. Tel: 518-783-2591. p. 1566
Pearson, Andrew, Dir, Bridgewater College, 402 E College St, Bridgewater, VA, 22812. Tel: 540-828-5410. p. 2308
Pearson, Anna, Libr Mgr, Yukon Energy Mines & Resources Library, 335-300 Main St, Whitehorse, YT, Y1A 2B5, CANADA. Tel: 867-667-3111. p. 2758
Pearson, Brittany, Ref (Info Servs), North Haven Memorial Library, 17 Elm St, North Haven, CT, 06473. Tel: 203-239-5803. p. 331
Pearson, Brittany, Asst Librn, Westbrook Public Library, 61 Goodspeed Dr, Westbrook, CT, 06498. Tel: 860-399-6422. p. 346
Pearson, Demetra W, Mrs, Head, Tech Serv, Librn, Francis Marion University, 4822 E Palmetto St, Florence, SC, 29506. Tel: 843-661-1308. p. 2059
Pearson, Dottie, Librn, Atlantic Cape Community College, 341 Court House S Dennis Rd, Cape May Court House, NJ, 08210. Tel: 609-463-3713. p. 1394
Pearson, Drew D, Outreach Serv Mgr, Public Library of Cincinnati & Hamilton County, Outreach Services, 800 Vine St, Cincinnati, OH, 45202-2009. Tel: 513-665-3352. p. 1763
Pearson, Jeffrey, Assoc Librn, University of Michigan, Askwith Media Library, Shapiro Library, 919 S University Ave, Ann Arbor, MI, 48109-1185. Tel: 734-763-3758. p. 1080
Pearson, Jennifer, Dir, Marshall County Memorial Library, 310 Old Farmington Rd, Lewisburg, TN, 37091. Tel: 931-359-3335. p. 2109
Pearson, Jennifer Gladden, Exec Dir, Tuscaloosa Public Library, 1801 Jack Warner Pkwy, Tuscaloosa, AL, 35401-1027. Tel: 205-345-5820, Ext 1102. p. 38
Pearson, Jesse, Dir, Admin Serv, Lehigh University, Eight A E Packer Ave, Bethlehem, PA, 18015. Tel: 610-758-3825. p. 1912
Pearson, Jimmy, Dir, Astoria Public Library, 450 Tenth St, Astoria, OR, 97103. Tel: 503-325-7323. p. 1872
Pearson, Katie, Libr Dir, Danbury Public Library, 170 Main St, Danbury, CT, 06810. Tel: 203-797-4505. p. 307
Pearson, Katy, Coordr, Navajo County Library District, 121 W Buffalo, Holbrook, AZ, 86025. Tel: 928-524-4745. p. 63
Pearson, Kristen, Exec Adminir, Grand Forks Public Library, 2110 Library Circle, Grand Forks, ND, 58201-6324. Tel: 701-772-8116, Ext 14. p. 1734
Pearson, Lisa, Dir, Ketchikan Public Library, 1110 Copper Ridge Lane, Ketchikan, AK, 99901. Tel: 907-225-3331. p. 48
Pearson, Lisa E, Head of Libr & Archives, Harvard Library, Arnold Arboretum Horticultural Library, 125 Arborway, Jamaica Plain, MA, 02130. Tel: 617-384-5330. p. 1005
Pearson, M Emily, Instruction Coordr, Outreach Librn, Whitman College, 345 Boyer Ave, Walla Walla, WA, 99362. Tel: 509-527-5918. p. 2393
Pearson, Peggy, Librn, Northwest Regional Library, Hallock Public Library, 163 Third St S, Hallock, MN, 56728. Tel: 218-843-2401. p. 1205
Pearson, Peggy, Librn, Northwest Regional Library, Karlstad Public Library, 104 First St S, Karlstad, MN, 56732. Tel: 218-436-7323. p. 1205
Pearson, Sarah, Librn, Florida State University Libraries, The Career Center Library, Dunlap Success Ctr 1200, 100 S Woodward Ave, Tallahassee, FL, 32304. Tel: 850-644-9779. p. 447
Pearson, Shamika, Libr Assoc/Teen Serv, Coweta Public Library System, 85 Literary Lane, Newnan, GA, 30265. Tel: 770-683-2052. p. 492
Pearson, Sherry, Ch, Spanish Peaks Library District, 415 Walsen Ave, Walsenburg, CO, 81089. Tel: 719-738-2774. p. 297
Pearson, Wendy, Libr Dir, Stockbridge Library Association, 46 Main St, Stockbridge, MA, 01262. Tel: 413-298-5501. p. 1058
Pease, Josie, Asst Dir, Tech Librn, Skowhegan Free Public Library, Nine Elm St, Skowhegan, ME, 04976. Tel: 207-474-9072. p. 940
Pease, Renee, Ch Serv Librn, Welles-Turner Memorial Library, 2407 Main St, Glastonbury, CT, 06033. Tel: 860-652-7718. p. 313

Peasley, Tammy, Libr Dir, Black River Falls Public Library, 222 Fillmore St, Black River Falls, WI, 54615. Tel: 715-284-4112. p. 2424

Peaster, Max C, Librn, Erie County Law Library, Court House, Rm 01, 140 W Sixth St, Erie, PA, 16501. Tel: 814-451-6319. p. 1931

Peavy, Kristina C, Libr Dir, Wesleyan College, 4760 Forsyth Rd, Macon, GA, 31210. Tel: 478-757-5201. p. 487

Peay, Jana Lee, Libr Dir, Kanab City Library, 374 N Main St, Kanab, UT, 84741-3259. Tel: 435-644-2394. p. 2265

Pecina, Carmelita, Access Serv Librn, University of Texas Rio Grande Valley, One W University Blvd, Brownsville, TX, 78520. Tel: 956-882-7428. p. 2150

Pecina, Kayla, Prog Mgr, Hewitt Public Library, 200 Patriot Ct, Hewitt, TX, 76643. Tel: 254-666-2442. p. 2189

Peck, Barbara, Asst Dir, Westport Historical Society Library, 25 Avery Pl, Westport, CT, 06880-3215. Tel: 203-222-1424, Ext 106. p. 346

Peck, Betsy, Libr Mgr, Pinetop-Lakeside Public Library, 1595 Johnson Dr, Lakeside, AZ, 85929. Tel: 928-368-6688, Ext 4. p. 65

Peck, Bob, Archivist, Historic Mobile Preservation Society, 300 Oakleigh Pl, Mobile, AL, 36604. Tel: 251-432-1281. p. 26

Peck, Brian M, Tech Librn & Indexer, North Carolina Legislative Library, 500 Legislative Office Bldg, 300 N Salisbury St, Raleigh, NC, 27603-5925. Tel: 919-733-9390. p. 1709

Peck, Celeste, Circ Mgr, Johnson City Public Library, 100 W Millard St, Johnson City, TN, 37604. Tel: 423-434-4472. p. 2104

Peck, Darcie, Librn, Newman Regional Library District, 207 S Coffin St, North Entrance, Newman, IL, 61942. Tel: 217-837-2412. p. 624

Peck, Jane, Br Mgr, Framingham Public Library, Christa Corrigan McAuliffe Branch, Ten Nicholas Rd, Framingham, MA, 01701-3469. Tel: 508-532-5636. p. 1019

Peck, Jane, Libr Dir, Regis College Library, 235 Wellesley St, Weston, MA, 02493. Tel: 781-768-7307. p. 1068

Peck, Kate, Head, Tech Serv, Butte-Silver Bow Public Library, 226 W Broadway St, Butte, MT, 59701. Tel: 406-792-1080. p. 1290

Peck, Mona, Asst Librn, Lane County Library, 144 South Lane, Dighton, KS, 67839. Tel: 620-397-2808. p. 804

Peck, Monica, Libr Dir, Boyne District Library, 201 E Main St, Boyne City, MI, 49712. Tel: 231-582-7861. p. 1087

Peckar, Rissa, Libr Dir, Cadwalader, Wickersham & Taft, 700 Sixth St NW, Ste 300, Washington, DC, 20001. Tel: 202-862-2289. p. 362

Pecora, Emily, Dir, Allens Hill Free Library, 3818 County Rd 40, Bloomfield, NY, 14469. Tel: 585-229-5636. p. 1495

Pecotte, Rachel, Bus Librn, Texas A&M University-San Antonio, One University Way, San Antonio, TX, 78224. Tel: 210-784-1510. p. 2239

Peden, Brenda, ILL, Normal Public Library, 206 W College Ave, Normal, IL, 61761. Tel: 309-452-1757. p. 625

Peden, Sarah, Children's & Youth Serv, Humboldt Public Library, 115 S 16th Ave, Humboldt, TN, 38343-3403. Tel: 731-784-2383. p. 2101

Pedersen, Chris, Head, Info Tech, Ela Area Public Library District, 275 Mohawk Trail, Lake Zurich, IL, 60047. Tel: 847-438-3433. p. 607

Pedersen, Emily, Br Librn, Grand County Library District, Kremmling Branch, 300 S Eighth St, Kremmling, CO, 80459. Tel: 970-724-9228. p. 283

Pedersen, Melodee, Customer Services, Columbus Public Library, 2500 14th St, Ste 2, Columbus, NE, 68601. Tel: 402-562-4214. p. 1311

Pedersen, Nate, Ref/Archives Librn, Georgia Historical Society, 501 Whitaker St, Savannah, GA, 31401. Tel: 912-651-2128. p. 495

Pedersen-Faria, Sarah, Children's Prog Dir, Cumston Public Library, 796 Main St, Monmouth, ME, 04259. Tel: 207-933-4788. p. 932

Pederson, Brooke, Br Mgr, Whatcom County Library System, Island Branch, 2144 S Nugent Rd, Lummi Island, WA, 98262. Tel: 360-758-7145. p. 2359

Pederson, Randy, Head, Syst, University of North Dakota, 3051 University Ave, Stop 9000, Grand Forks, ND, 58202-9000. Tel: 701-777-4643. p. 1735

Pedley, Elayne, Mgr, Contra Costa County Library, Dougherty Station Library, 17017 Bollinger Canyon Rd, San Ramon, CA, 94582. Tel: 925-973-3380. p. 174

Pedley, Genevieve, Events Coord, Rehoboth Beach Public Library, 226 Rehoboth Ave, Rehoboth Beach, DE, 19971-2134. Tel: 302-227-8044, Ext 107. p. 356

Pedraza, Mary, Archivist, Fine Arts Museums of San Francisco Library & Archives, Golden Gate Park, 50 Hagiwara Tea Garden Dr, San Francisco, CA, 94118. Tel: 415-750-7603. p. 225

Pedri, Lynne, Dir, Hurley Public Library, 405 Fifth Ave N, Hurley, WI, 54534-1170. Tel: 715-561-5707. p. 2442

Pedrick, Afton, Youth Serv Librn, Fairfield Public Library, 104 W Adams Ave, Fairfield, IA, 52556. Tel: 641-472-6551, Ext 114. p. 752

Pedroza, Edward, Br Supvr, Colton Public Library, Luque Branch, 294 East O St, Colton, CA, 92324. Tel: 909-370-5182. p. 131

Pedroza, Edward, Libr Supvr, Colton Public Library, 656 N Ninth St, Colton, CA, 92324. Tel: 909-370-5189. p. 131

Pedu, Bambi, Dir, Lake Placid Public Library, 2471 Main St, Lake Placid, NY, 12946. Tel: 518-523-3200. p. 1561

Peebles, Kyle, Communications Mgr, Illinois Library & Information Network, c/o Illinois State Library, Gwendolyn Brooks Bldg, 300 S Second St, Springfield, IL, 62701-1796. Tel: 217-558-4029. p. 2764

Peebles, Margaret, Div Chief of Public Serv, Gail Borden Public Library District, 270 N Grove Ave, Elgin, IL, 60120-5596. Tel: 847-429-5983. p. 583

Peel, Glenice, Br Supvr, Chemung County Library District, Big Flats Library, 78 Canal St, Big Flats, NY, 14814. Tel: 607-562-3300. p. 1530

Peele, Holly, Libr Dir, Editorial Projects in Education Library, 6935 Arlington Rd, Bethesda, MD, 20814. Tel: 301-280-3100. p. 959

Peeler, Dana, Syst Adminr, Cherokee County Public Library, 300 E Rutledge Ave, Gaffney, SC, 29340-2227. Tel: 864-487-2711. p. 2059

Peeler, Stacey, Dir, Tipton County Public Library, Bldg C, 3149 Hwy 51 S, Covington, TN, 38019. Tel: 901-476-8289. p. 2095

Peeling, Mary Alice, Head, Outreach Serv, Widener University, School of Law Library, 4601 Concord Pike, Wilmington, DE, 19803. Tel: 302-477-2244. p. 358

Peeples, Jacqueline, Dir, Wheaton Community Library, 901 First Ave N, Wheaton, MN, 56296. Tel: 320-563-8487. p. 1207

Peeples, Martin, Libr Supvr, University of Miami Libraries, Marta & Austin Weeks Music Library, 5469 San Amaro Dr, Coral Gables, FL, 33146. Tel: 305-284-9885. p. 391

Peeples, Stacey, Archivist, Curator, Pennsylvania Hospital, Medical Library, Three Pine Ctr, 800 Spruce St, Philadelphia, PA, 19107-6192. Tel: 215-829-3370. p. 1984

Peeples, Stacey, Curator, Lea Archivist, Pennsylvania Hospital, 800 Spruce St, Philadelphia, PA, 19107. Tel: 215-829-3370. p. 1984

Peeples, Stacey C, Archivist, Pennsylvania Hospital, Historic Library, Three Pine Ctr, 800 Spruce St, Philadelphia, PA, 19107-6192. Tel: 215-829-5434. p. 1984

Peercy, Lisa, Dir, Human Res, Akron-Summit County Public Library, 60 S High St, Akron, OH, 44326. Tel: 330-643-9104. p. 1744

Peerenboom, Tina, Youth Serv, Reedsburg Public Library, 370 Vine St, Reedsburg, WI, 53959. Tel: 608-768-7323. p. 2472

Peerenboom, Tina, Ch, Watertown Public Library, 100 S Water St, Watertown, WI, 53094-4320. Tel: 920-262-2330. p. 2484

Peery, Ian, Asst Libr Dir, Glenside Public Library District, 25 E Fullerton Ave, Glendale Heights, IL, 60139-2697. Tel: 630-260-1550. p. 593

Peery, Katie Musick, Assoc Univ Librn, University of Texas at Arlington Library, 702 Planetarium Pl, Arlington, TX, 76019. Tel: 817-272-1714. p. 2136

Peevyhouse, Janice, Libr Mgr, Newbern City Library, 220 E Main St, Newbern, TN, 38059-1528. Tel: 731-627-3153. p. 2122

Pegg-Wheat, Amanda, Br Librn, Crane Thomas Public Library, Wollaston Branch, 41 Beale St, Quincy, MA, 02170. Tel: 617-376-1330. p. 1048

Pegnataro, Rachel, Dir, Mkt & Communications, The Westport Library, 20 Jesup Rd, Westport, CT, 06880. Tel: 203-291-4820. p. 347

Pegues, Bronwyn, Head, Circ, Longview Public Library, 222 W Cotton St, Longview, TX, 75601. Tel: 903-237-1350. p. 2213

Pegues, Jutta Catharine, Pres, Worthington Historical Society Library, 50 W New England Ave, Worthington, OH, 43085. Tel: 614-885-1247. p. 1833

Pei, Jingru, Commun Libr Mgr, Queens Library, Woodside Community Library, 54-22 Skillman Ave, Woodside, NY, 11377. Tel: 718-429-4700. p. 1556

Peiffer, Joan, Dir, Grove Family Library, 101 Ragged Edge Rd S, Chambersburg, PA, 17202. Tel: 717-264-9663. p. 1920

Peil, Carolyn, Colls Mgr, Mat Mgr, Waukesha Public Library, 321 Wisconsin Ave, Waukesha, WI, 53186-4713. Tel: 262-522-3690. p. 2484

Peine, Kim, Info Tech, ILL, Ref & Instrul Serv Librn, Dorothy Alling Memorial Library, 21 Library Lane, Williston, VT, 05495. Tel: 802-878-4918. p. 2299

Peirce, Leah, Circ Supvr, Cornerstone University, 1001 E Beltline Ave NE, Grand Rapids, MI, 49525. Tel: 616-254-1650, Ext 1976. p. 1110

Peischel Mull, Valerie, Br Mgr, Saint Johns County Public Library System, Main Branch, 1960 N Ponce de Leon Blvd, Saint Augustine, FL, 32084. Tel: 904-827-6941. p. 440

Pek, Alice, Libr Dir, Mackenzie Public Library, 400 Skeena Dr, Mackenzie, BC, V0J 2C0, CANADA. Tel: 250-997-6343. p. 2569

Pekar, Paula Sue, Dir, Shiner Public Library, 115 E Wolters/Second St, Shiner, TX, 77984. Tel: 361-594-3044. p. 2243

Pekel, Sue Ann, Ch, Bentonville Public Library, 405 S Main St, Bentonville, AR, 72712. Tel: 479-271-6816. p. 91

Peladeau, Ginette, Br Head, Alfred & Plantagenet Public Library System, Alfred Branch, 555 Saint-Philippe St, Alfred, ON, K0B 1A0, CANADA. Tel: 613-679-2663. p. 2652

Pelaia, Jennifer Korpacz, Dir, Libr Serv, Covington & Burling LLP, One City Ctr, 850 Tenth St, NW, Washington, DC, 20001. Tel: 202-662-6158. p. 363

Pelanne, Joel, Tech Serv Librn, Museum of Fine Arts, Houston, 1001 Bissonnet St, Houston, TX, 77005. Tel: 713-639-7325. p. 2197

Pelchat, Chris, Dean, Spokane Falls Community College Library, 3410 W Whistalks Way, Spokane, WA, 99224-5204. Tel: 509-533-3800. p. 2385

Pelchat, Pat, Br Librn, Wapiti Regional Library, Shell Lake Public Library, Main St, Village Office, Shell Lake, SK, S0J 2G0, CANADA. Tel: 306-427-2272. p. 2746

Pelczynski, Tony, Instrul Serv Librn, University of California, 200 McAllister St, San Francisco, CA, 94102-4978. Tel: 415-565-4757. p. 229

Pelekis, Nikolaos, Libr Mgr, Sonoma County Public Law Library, 2604 Ventura Ave, Santa Rosa, CA, 95403. Tel: 707-565-2668. p. 245

Pelepchuk, Anna, Head, Circ, Bloomfield Township Public Library, 1099 Lone Pine Rd, Bloomfield Township, MI, 48302-2410. Tel: 248-642-5800. p. 1086

Peletich, Darcy, Librn, Kino Institute Diocesan Library, 400 E Monroe St, Phoenix, AZ, 85004-2336. Tel: 602-354-2311. p. 70

Pelfrey, Carlie, Dir, Lawrence County Public Library, 102 W Main St, Louisa, KY, 41230. Tel: 606-638-4497. p. 864

Pelfrey, Debbie, Dir, Graysville Public Library, 136 Harrison Ave, Graysville, TN, 37338. Tel: 423-775-9242, Ext 4. p. 2100

Pelger, Jada, Tech Coordr, University of Puget Sound, 1604 N Warner St, Upper Loading Dock, Tacoma, WA, 98416. Tel: 253-879-3287. p. 2387

Pelish, Nora, Mgr, Pub Serv, Irondequoit Public Library, 1290 Titus Ave, Rochester, NY, 14617. Tel: 585-210-2390 ((Text)), 585-336-6060. p. 1628

Pelkey, Eva, Br Mgr, Springfield-Greene County Library District, Midtown Carnegie Branch, 397 E Central St, Springfield, MO, 65802-3834. Tel: 417-862-0135. p. 1281

Pelkey, Lori, Br Mgr, Corvallis-Benton County Public Library, Monroe Community Library, 668 Commercial St, Monroe, OR, 97456. Tel: 541-847-5174. p. 1876

Pell, John, Instrul & Ref Librn, Hunter College Libraries, Health Professions Library, Hunter College Brookdale Campus, 425 E 25th St, New York, NY, 10010. Tel: 212-481-5117. p. 1588

Pell, Susan, Dr, Exec Dir, United States Botanic Garden Library, 245 First St SW, Washington, DC, 20024. Tel: 202-225-8333. p. 377

Pellack, Lorraine, Head, Research & Outreach, Iowa State University Library, 302 Parks Library, 701 Morrill Rd, Ames, IA, 50011-2102. Tel: 515-294-5569. p. 731

Pelland, Kelli, Dir, Baudette Public Library, 110 First Ave SW, Baudette, MN, 56623. Tel: 218-634-2329. p. 1164

Pellegrene, Tom, Mgr, News Tech, Journal Gazette Library, 600 W Main St, Fort Wayne, IN, 46802. Tel: 260-461-8377. p. 685

Pellegrino, Catherine, Ref & Instruction Librn, Saint Mary's College, Notre Dame, IN, 46556-5001. Tel: 574-284-5286. p. 711

Pellegrino, Roberto, ILL, Alberta Innovates, 250 Karl Clark Rd, Edmonton, AB, T6N 1E4, CANADA. Tel: 780-450-5057. p. 2535

Pellerite, Kathryn, Circ Supvr, Leominster Public Library, 30 West St, Leominster, MA, 01453. Tel: 978-534-7522, Ext 3603. p. 1028

Pellersels, Michelle, Br Mgr, Spruce Pine Public Library, 142 Walnut Ave, Spruce Pine, NC, 28777. Tel: 828-765-4673. p. 1717

Pelletier, Brenda, Acq, Ser, University of Maine at Fort Kent, 23 University Dr, Fort Kent, ME, 04743. Tel: 207-834-7523. p. 925

Pelletier, Josee, Info Access Coordr, Universite du Quebec a Rimouski - Service de la bibliotheque, 300 Allee des Ursulines, Rimouski, QC, G5L 3A1, CANADA. Tel: 418-723-1986, Ext 1479. p. 2732

Pelletier, Marie, Archivist, Centre d'Archives Regionales Seminaire de Nicolet Library, 645, boul Louis-Frechette, Nicolet, QC, J3T 1L6, CANADA. Tel: 819-293-4838. p. 2728

Pelletier, MaryAnne, Dir, Merriam-Gilbert Public Library, Three W Main St, West Brookfield, MA, 01585. Tel: 508-867-1410. p. 1065

Pelletier, Michaela, Head, Circ, Amesbury Public Library, 149 Main St, Amesbury, MA, 01913. Tel: 978-388-8148. p. 984

Pelletier, Odette, Tech Serv, Bibliotheques de Trois-Rivieres, 1425 Place de l'Hotel de Ville, Trois-Rivieres, QC, G9A 5L9, CANADA. Tel: 819-372-4641, Ext 4251. p. 2737

Pelletier, Rick, Br Mgr, Charleston County Public Library, Cooper River Memorial, 3503 Rivers Ave, Charleston, SC, 29405. Tel: 843-744-2489. p. 2049

Pelletier, Saxanee-Rae Hynes, Asst Admin, Flin Flon Public Library, 58 Main St, Flin Flon, MB, R8A 1J8, CANADA. p. 2587

Pelletier, Sheryl, Libr Dir, Shannon Municipal Library, Sexsmith Civic Centre, 9917 99th Ave, Sexsmith, AB, T0H 3C0, CANADA. Tel: 780-568-4333. p. 2553

Pelletier, Suzie, Coordr, Tech Serv & Syst, Universite du Quebec a Rimouski - Service de la bibliotheque, 300 Allee des Ursulines, Rimouski, QC, G5L 3A1, CANADA. Tel: 418-723-1986, Ext 1502. p. 2732

Pelletier, Trish, Libr Supvr, Apache Junction Public Library, 1177 N Idaho Rd, Apache Junction, AZ, 85119. Tel: 480-474-8558. p. 55

Pelletier, Wendy L, Libr Dir, Moosilauke Public Library, 165 Lost River Rd, North Woodstock, NH, 03262. Tel: 603-745-9971. p. 1377

Pelley, Nate, Mgr, Public Library of Cincinnati & Hamilton County, MakerSpace, North Bldg, 2nd Flr, 800 Vine St, Cincinnati, OH, 45202-2009. Tel: 513-369-6900. p. 1763

Pellis, Mark, Head Librn, DLA Piper US LLP, 1251 Avenue of Americas, 27th Flr, New York, NY, 10020-1104. Tel: 212-776-3732. p. 1585

Pellissier, Viola, Libr Tech, Truckee Meadows Community College, William N Pennington Applied Technology Learning Resource Center, Technical Institute, 475 Edison Way, Reno, NV, 89502-4103. Tel: 775-857-4990. p. 1349

Pellman, Adam, Cat & Acq, Seton Hill University, One Seton Hill Dr, Greensburg, PA, 15601. Tel: 724-838-2438. p. 1938

Peloquin, Jeanne, Regional Mgr, Greater Clarks Hill Regional Library System, 7022 Evans Town Center Blvd, Evans, GA, 30809. Tel: 706-863-1946. p. 478

Peloquin, Jeanne, Communications Coordr, Outreach Coordr, Tigard Public Library, 13500 SW Hall Blvd, Tigard, OR, 97223-8111. Tel: 503-684-6537, Ext 2508. p. 1900

Peloquin, Margaret, Head Librn, Austin Community College, Eastview Campus Library, 3401 Webberville Rd, 2nd Flr, Rm 2200, Austin, TX, 78702. Tel: 512-223-5117. p. 2138

Peltier, Janet, Asst Librn, Lincoln Public Library, 22 Church St, Lincoln, NH, 03251. Tel: 603-745-8159. p. 1370

Peltier, Matt, Univ Librn, King University, 1350 King College Rd, Bristol, TN, 37620. Tel: 423-652-4750. p. 2090

Peltz-Steele, Misty, Asst Dean of Libr, University of Massachusetts School of Law Library, 333 Faunce Corner Rd, North Dartmouth, MA, 02747. Tel: 508-985-1121. p. 1041

Pelyhes, Marlene, Head, Tech Serv, Geauga County Public Library, 12701 Ravenwood Dr, Chardon, OH, 44024-1336. Tel: 440-286-6811, Ext 2519. p. 1758

Pelzek, Geoff, Head Librn, Supreme Court of Illinois Library, Supreme Court Bldg, 200 E Capital Ave, Springfield, IL, 62701-1791. Tel: 217-782-2424. p. 650

Pembelton, Chris, Supvry Archivist, National Archives & Records Administration, 1000 George Bush Dr W, College Station, TX, 77845. Tel: 979-691-4000. p. 2157

Pemberton, David, Instruction/Periodicals Librn, School of Visual Arts Library, 380 Second Ave, 2nd Flr, New York, NY, 10010. Tel: 212-592-2664. p. 1601

Pemberton, Patrick, Access Serv Supvr, National University Library, 9393 Lightwave Ave, San Diego, CA, 92123-1447. Tel: 858-541-7909. p. 215

Pemstein, Ira, Actg Dep Dir, National Archives & Records Administration, 40 Presidential Dr, Simi Valley, CA, 93065. Tel: 805-577-4073. p. 246

Pena, Amanda, Libr Dir, Hollis & Helen Baright Public Library, 5555 S 77th St, Ralston, NE, 68127-2899. Tel: 402-331-7636. p. 1333

Pena, David, Dir, Palm Beach State College, 3160 PGA Blvd, Palm Beach Gardens, FL, 33410-2893. Tel: 561-207-5810. p. 434

Pena, Marie, Br Mgr, Starr County Public Library, 4192 W Hwy 83, Larosita, TX, 78582. Tel: 956-849-2606. p. 2210

Peña Nicolau, Juanita, Dir, Pontifical Catholic University, Encarnacion Valdes Library, 2250 Avenida Las Americas, Ste 509, Ponce, PR, 00717-0777. Tel: 787-841-2000, Ext 1801, 787-841-2000, Ext 1802. p. 2512

Pena, Patricia, Acq Mgr, Northern Virginia Community College Libraries, Media Processing Services, 8333 Little River Tpk, Annandale, VA, 22003-3796. Tel: 703-323-3095. p. 2304

Pena, Ricardo, Libr Supvr, University of Southern California Libraries, Science & Engineering, Seaver Science Ctr, 920 W 37th Pl, Los Angeles, CA, 90089-0481. Tel: 213-740-4419, 213-740-8507. p. 170

Pena, Sylvia, Dir, Kenedy Public Library, 303 W Main St, Kenedy, TX, 78119. Tel: 830-583-3313. p. 2205

Pender, Constance, Libr Mgr, University of South Carolina Sumter, 200 Miller Rd, Sumter, SC, 29150-2498. Tel: 803-938-3797. p. 2071

Pendergraph, Cindy, Libr Experience Mgr, Wayne County Public Library, 1001 E Ash St, Goldsboro, NC, 27530. Tel: 919-735-1824. p. 1691

Pendergrass, Andrew, Br Mgr, Fairfax County Public Library, Pohick Regional, 6450 Sydenstricker Rd, Burke, VA, 22015-4274. Tel: 703-644-7333. p. 2316

Pendergrass, Darrell, Dir, Washburn Public Library, 307 Washington Ave, Washburn, WI, 54891-1165. Tel: 715-373-6172. p. 2483

Pendergrass, Linda, Head, Ref, Bloomfield Public Library, 90 Broad St, Bloomfield, NJ, 07003. Tel: 973-566-6200. p. 1391

Pendleton, Ann, Libr Dir, Isabelle Hunt Memorial Public Library, 6124 N Randall Pl, Pine, AZ, 85544. Tel: 928-476-3678. p. 73

Pendleton, Gretchen, Director, Curatorial Operations, George Washington Foundation, 1201 Washington Ave, Fredericksburg, VA, 22401. Tel: 540-373-3381. p. 2320

Pendley, Margaret, Br Mgr, Fulton County Public Library, Fulton Branch, 514 State Rd 25, Fulton, IN, 46931. Tel: 574-857-3895. p. 716

Pendroff, Petra, Head of Br Serv, Jones Library, Inc, Munson Memorial, 1046 S East St, South Amherst, MA, 01002. Tel: 413-259-3095. p. 984

Penegar, Kaye, Br Mgr, Chesterfield County Library System, Fannie D Lowry Memorial Library, 500 N Main St, Jefferson, SC, 29718. Tel: 843-658-3966. p. 2052

Penick, Marguerite W, PhD, Graduate Program Coord, Prof, University of Wisconsin Oshkosh College of Education & Human Services, 800 Algoma Blvd, Oshkosh, WI, 54901. Tel: 920-424-0881. p. 2794

Penick, Patti, Asst Dir, Head, Youth Serv, Goffstown Public Library, Two High St, Goffstown, NH, 03045-1910. Tel: 603-497-2102. p. 1364

Penick, Steve, Head Archivist, Ref (Info Servs), Stearns History Museum, 235 33rd Ave S, Saint Cloud, MN, 56301-3752. Tel: 320-253-8424. p. 1198

Penke, Ann, Dir, Libr Serv, Lakeland University, W3718 South Dr, Plymouth, WI, 53073. Tel: 920-565-1038, Ext 2416. p. 2470

Penkova, Emilia, Br Supvr, Greater Victoria Public Library, Esquimalt, 1231 Esquimalt Rd, Victoria, BC, V9A 3P1, CANADA. Tel: 250-940-4875, Ext 764. p. 2583

Penland, Tammy, Support Serv Mgr, Wichita Public Library, 711 W Second St, Wichita, KS, 67203. Tel: 316-261-8534. p. 843

Penley, Nicole, Outreach Serv Spec, South Central Kansas Library System, 321 N Main St, South Hutchinson, KS, 67505. Tel: 620-663-3211. p. 837

Penn, Kim, Br Mgr, Toledo-Lucas County Public Library, Mott, 1010 Dorr St, Toledo, OH, 43607. Tel: 419-259-5230. p. 1824

Penn, Margaret, Dir, Br Serv, Gwinnett County Public Library, 1001 Lawrenceville Hwy NW, Lawrenceville, GA, 30046-4707. Tel: 770-978-5154. p. 485

Penn, Maureen, Libr Dir, Lac La Biche County Libraries, 8702 91st Ave, Lac La Biche, AB, T0A 2C0, CANADA. Tel: 780-623-7467. p. 2544

Penn, Maureen, Libr Dir, Lac La Biche County Libraries, Plamondon Municipal Library, Ecole Plamondon, 9814 100 St, Plamondon, AB, T0A 2T0, CANADA. Tel: 780-623-7467. p. 2545

Penn, Michele, Law Librn II, Connecticut Judicial Branch Law Libraries, New Haven Law Library, New Haven Courthouse, 235 Church St, New Haven, CT, 06510. Tel: 203-503-6828. p. 316

Penn, Michele, Research Librn, Williams & Connolly Library, 680 Maine Ave SW, Washington, DC, 20024. Tel: 202-434-5000. p. 381

Penn, Michelle, Fac Serv Librn, University of Denver, Westminster Law Library, Sturm College of Law, 2255 E Evans Ave, Denver, CO, 80208. Tel: 303-871-6827. p. 278

Penna, Mary Lena, Dir, Port St John Public Library, 6500 Carole Ave, Cocoa, FL, 32927. Tel: 321-633-1867. p. 390

Penna, Mary Lena, Libr Dir, Catherine Schweinsberg Rood Central Library, 308 Forrest Ave, Cocoa, FL, 32922. Tel: 321-633-1792. p. 390

Pennala, Lisa, Dir, Babbitt Public Library, 71 South Dr, Babbitt, MN, 55706. Tel: 218-827-3345. p. 1164

Pennell, Janeen Bradley, Student Success Librn, Milligan College, 200 Blowers Blvd, Milligan College, TN, 37682. Tel: 423-461-8900. p. 2116

Penner, Bradley, Libr Divisional Mgr, Oceanside Public Library, 330 N Coast Hwy, Oceanside, CA, 92054. Tel: 760-435-5575. p. 187

Penner, Frances, Tech Serv Librn, Horsham Township Library, 435 Babylon Rd, Horsham, PA, 19044-1224. Tel: 215-443-2609, Ext 211. p. 1944

Penner, Katherine, Music Librn, University of Manitoba Libraries, Eckhardt-Gramatté Music Library, T257 Taché Arts Complex, 136 Dafoe Rd, Winnipeg, MB, R3T 2N2, CANADA. Tel: 204-474-9567. p. 2595

Penner, Les, Library Technologist, Summit Pacific College, 35235 Straiton Rd, Abbotsford, BC, V2S 7Z1, CANADA. Tel: 604-851-7230. p. 2562

Penner, Wanda, Libr Mgr, La Glace Community Library, 9924 97 Ave, La Glace, AB, T0H 2J0, CANADA. Tel: 780-568-4696. p. 2544

Penney, Jamie, Head, Tech Serv, Reading Public Library, 64 Middlesex Ave, Reading, MA, 01867-2550. Tel: 781-944-0840. p. 1049

Penney, Jeanne, Dir & Librn, Campbell Public Library, 721 Broad St, Campbell, NE, 68932. Tel: 402-756-8121. p. 1309

Penney, Kaitlyn, Librn, Clarenville Public Library, 98 Manitoba Dr, Clarenville, NL, A5A 1K7, CANADA. Tel: 709-466-7634. p. 2607

Penniman, Sarah, Libr Dir, Elizabethtown College, One Alpha Dr, Elizabethtown, PA, 17022-2227. Tel: 717-361-1428. p. 1929

Pennington, Annie, Librn, Copper Mountain College, 6162 Rotary Way, Joshua Tree, CA, 92252. Tel: 760-366-3791, Ext 5904. p. 154

Pennington, Eric, Br Mgr, Public Library of Cincinnati & Hamilton County, Cheviot, 3711 Robb Ave, Cincinnati, OH, 45211. Tel: 513-369-6015. p. 1762

Pennington, Teresa, Dir, Paris Carnegie Public Library, 207 S Main St, Paris, IL, 61944. Tel: 217-463-3950. p. 632

Pennington, Theresa, Dir, Martelle Public Library, 202 South St, Martelle, IA, 52305. Tel: 319-482-4121. p. 768

Pennisi, Roseann, ILL, Caldwell University, 120 Bloomfield Ave, Caldwell, NJ, 07006. Tel: 973-618-3337. p. 1393

Penny, Keely, Tech Serv, Plainville Public Library, 198 South St, Plainville, MA, 02762-1512. Tel: 508-695-1784. p. 1047

Penny, Victoria, Instrul Librn, Northwest Mississippi Community College, Senatobia Learning Resource Ctr, 4975 Hwy 51 N, Senatobia, MS, 38668-1701. Tel: 662-562-3278. p. 1232

Pennycuff, Tim, Archivist, University of Alabama at Birmingham, Lister Hill Library of the Health Sciences, 1700 University Blvd, Birmingham, AL, 35294-0013. Tel: 205-934-5460. p. 9

Pennywell, Darryl, Dir, Mount Vernon Public Library, 19180 Shepard Lake Rd, Mount Vernon, AL, 36560. Tel: 251-829-9497. p. 31

Penon, Leticia, Libr Asst, Kansas Department of Corrections, 500 Reformatory St, Hutchinson, KS, 67501. Tel: 620-625-7377. p. 814

Penoyer, Jenny, Libr Mgr, Timberland Regional Library, South Bend Branch, First & Pacific, South Bend, WA, 98586. Tel: 360-875-5532. p. 2389

Penrod, Michael, Dir, Wood County District Public Library, 251 N Main St, Bowling Green, OH, 43402. Tel: 419-352-5104. p. 1752

Penrod, Pamela, Librn, Norborne Public Library, 109 E Second St, Norborne, MO, 64668. Tel: 660-593-3514. p. 1264

Pensa, Shannon, Head, Spec Coll & Archives, University of Texas Rio Grande Valley, 1201 W University Blvd, Edinburg, TX, 78541-2999. Tel: 956-665-5288. p. 2173

Pensgard, Sara, Libr Dir, Patrick Henry College Library, Ten Patrick Henry Circle, Purcellville, VA, 20132. Tel: 540-441-8400. p. 2339

Pentecost, Carol, Ch, Centerville-Center Township Public Library, 126 E Main St, Centerville, IN, 47330-1206. Tel: 765-855-5223. p. 674

Penteliuk, David, Libr Mgr, Mississauga Library System, Erin Meadows, 2800 Erin Centre Blvd, Mississauga, ON, L5M 6R5, CANADA. Tel: 905-615-4750. p. 2659

Penteliuk, David, Libr Mgr, Mississauga Library System, Streetsville, 112 Queen St S, Mississauga, ON, L5M 1K8, CANADA. Tel: 905-615-4785. p. 2659

Pentz, Alice, Dir, Willoughby Wallace Memorial Library, 146 Thimble Islands Rd, Stony Creek, CT, 06405-5739. Tel: 203-488-8702. p. 339

Penwell, Jason, Syst Librn, Kennesaw State University Library System, 385 Cobb Ave NW, MD 1701, Kennesaw, GA, 30144. Tel: 470-578-6189. p. 483

Penz, Niki, Dir, Coll & Tech, Surrey Libraries, 10350 University Dr, Surrey, BC, V3T 4B8, CANADA. Tel: 604-598-7300. p. 2577

Penza, Pam, Sr Librn, New Hanover County Public Library, Northeast Regional Library, 1241 Military Cutoff Rd, Wilmington, NC, 28405. Tel: 910-798-6366. p. 1723

Penziwol, Shelley, Head Librn, Bibliothèque Allard Regional Library, 104086 PTH 11, Saint Georges, MB, R0E 1V0, CANADA. Tel: 204-367-8443. p. 2590

People, Janice, Head, Children's Dept, Plainfield Public Library, 800 Park Ave, Plainfield, NJ, 07060-2594. Tel: 908-757-1111, Ext 129. p. 1435

Peoples, Brock, Exec Dir, Southeast Florida Library Information Network, Inc, Florida Atlantic University, Wimberly Library, Office 452, 777 Glades Rd, Boca Raton, FL, 33431. Tel: 561-208-0984. p. 2763

Peoples, Lee, Dir, Oklahoma City University, School of Law Library, 2501 N Blackwelder, Oklahoma City, OK, 73106. Tel: 405-208-6030. p. 1858

Pepich, Bruce W, Curator of Coll, Exec Dir, Racine Art Museum Library, 441 Main St, Racine, WI, 53403. Tel: 262-638-8300, Ext 106. p. 2471

Pepin, Jessie, Asst Dir, Cochrane Public Library, 405 Railway St W, Cochrane, AB, T4C 2E2, CANADA. Tel: 403-932-4353. p. 2531

Pepin, Pascal, Librn, Ministere de la Culture, 587 rue Radisson, Trois-Rivieres, QC, G9A 2C8, CANADA. Tel: 819-371-6748, Ext 228. p. 2738

Pepmiller, Catherine, Librn, United States Department of Energy, PO Box 62, Oak Ridge, TN, 37831-0062. Tel: 865-576-1188. p. 2123

Peppers, Marla, Assoc Dean, California State University, Los Angeles, 5151 State University Dr, Los Angeles, CA, 90032-8300. Tel: 323-343-3950. p. 161

Perales, Carol, Youth Serv Coordr, Fayette Public Library, 855 S Jefferson St, La Grange, TX, 78945. Tel: 979-968-3765. p. 2207

Perales, Evelyn, Circ, Marshall Memorial Library, 110 S Diamond St, Deming, NM, 88030. Tel: 575-546-9202. p. 1467

Perales, Rebecca, Pub Serv Librn, El Paso Community College Library, Rio Grande Campus Library, 100 W Rio Grande Ave, Rm E100, El Paso, TX, 79902. Tel: 915-831-4019. p. 2173

Perault, Maureen, Librn, Washtenaw Community College, 4800 E Huron River Dr, Ann Arbor, MI, 48105-4800. Tel: 734-973-3407. p. 1081

Peraza, Zayne, Tech Asst II, Crafton Hills College Library, 11711 Sand Canyon Rd, Yucaipa, CA, 92399. Tel: 909-389-3321. p. 262

Percic, Melissa A W, Dir, Carnegie Public Library, 219 E Fourth St, East Liverpool, OH, 43920-3143. Tel: 330-385-2048. p. 1783

Percival, Katherine, Libr Supvr, North Island College, 1685 S Dogwood St, Campbell River, BC, V9W 8C1, CANADA. Tel: 250-923-9787. p. 2564

Percy, Janet, Br Librn, Southeast Regional Library, Maryfield Branch, 201 Barrows St, Maryfield, SK, S0G 3K0, CANADA. Tel: 306-646-2148. p. 2754

Percy, Joanne, Teen & Adult Librn, Liberty Lake Municipal Library, 23123 E Mission Ave, Liberty Lake, WA, 99019-7613. Tel: 509-232-2510. p. 2369

Percy, Kiley, Coordr, Commun Engagement, Clarington Public Library, Courtice Branch, 2950 Courtice Rd, Courtice, ON, L1E 2H8, CANADA. Tel: 905-404-0707. p. 2632

Perdew, Lori Jane, Br Mgr, Scenic Regional Library, Pacific Branch, 111 Lamar Pkwy, Pacific, MO, 63069. Tel: 636-257-2712. p. 1283

Perdue, Derek, Pub Serv Coordr, Arlington Public Library System, Lake Arlington, 4000 W Green Oaks Blvd, Arlington, TX, 76016. p. 2136

Perea, Lee, Librn, Miller Stratvert PA, 500 Marquette Ave NW, Ste 1100, Albuquerque, NM, 87102. Tel: 505-842-1950. p. 1461

Pereira, Beth, Youth Serv, South Huntington Public Library, 145 Pidgeon Hill Rd, Huntington Station, NY, 11746. Tel: 631-549-4411. p. 1549

Pereira, Cornelius, Head, Tech Serv, University of South Carolina, Law Library, 1525 Senate St, Columbia, SC, 29208. Tel: 803-777-5942. p. 2055

Pereira, Diana, Ms, Libr Assoc, American Samoa Community College Library, Malaeimi Village, Malaeimi Rd, Mapusaga, AS, 96799. p. 2503

Pereira, Heather, Br Mgr, Santa Cruz City-County Library System, Aptos Branch, 7695 Soquel Dr, Aptos, CA, 95003-3899. Tel: 831-427-7702. p. 242

Pereira, K L, Youth Serv Librn, Rockport Public Library, 17 School St, Rockport, MA, 01966. Tel: 978-546-6934. p. 1050

Pereira, Kathy, Asst Librn, Waverly Public Library, 291 N Pearl St, Waverly, IL, 62692. Tel: 217-435-2051. p. 660

Perekrestov, Michael, Curator, Dir & Librn, Holy Trinity Orthodox Seminary, 1407 Robinson Rd, Jordanville, NY, 13361-0036. Tel: 315-858-0945. p. 1558

Perelman, Rimma, Med Librn, Nassau University Medical Center, 2201 Hempstead Tpk, East Meadow, NY, 11554. Tel: 516-572-8742. p. 1528

Perelyubskiy, Hillary, Actg Sr Librn, Los Angeles Public Library System, Playa Vista Branch Library, 6400 Playa Vista Dr, Los Angeles, CA, 90094. Tel: 310-437-6680. p. 165

Perera, Michelle, Dir, Sunnyvale Public Library, 665 W Olive Ave, Sunnyvale, CA, 94086-7622. Tel: 408-730-7300. p. 251

Peres, Marcela, Libr Dir, Lewiston Public Library, 200 Lisbon St, Lewiston, ME, 04240. Tel: 207-513-3004. p. 929

Perev, Kristen, Librn, Nelson, Mullins, Riley & Scarborough, 104 S Main St, Ste 900, Greenville, SC, 29601. Tel: 864-250-2300. p. 2062

Perez, Alex, Br Mgr, City of Palo Alto Library, 270 Forest Ave, Palo Alto, CA, 94301. Tel: 650-838-2981. p. 191

Perez, Alex, Br Mgr, City of Palo Alto Library, Children's, 1276 Harriet St, Palo Alto, CA, 94301. Tel: 650-838-2981. p. 191

Perez, Alex, Mgr, Libr Serv, City of Palo Alto Library, College Terrace, 2300 Wellesley St, Palo Alto, CA, 94306. Tel: 650-838-2981. p. 192

Perez, Alex, Mgr, Libr Serv, City of Palo Alto Library, Downtown, 270 Forest Ave, Palo Alto, CA, 94301. Tel: 650-838-2981. p. 192

Perez, Alex, Mgr, Libr Serv, City of Palo Alto Library, Rinconda Library, 1213 Newell Rd, Palo Alto, CA, 94303. Tel: 650-383-2981. p. 192

Perez, Celia, Instr, City Colleges of Chicago, Harold Washington College Library, 30 E Lake St, Chicago, IL, 60601-9996. Tel: 312-553-5635. p. 559

Perez, Christa, Research Coordr, C D Howe Institute Library, 67 Yonge St, Ste 300, Toronto, ON, M5E 1J8, CANADA. Tel: 416-865-1904, Ext 2606. p. 2689

Perez Gomez, Analiza, Librn IV, Guerra Joe A Laredo Public Library, Santa Rita Express Branch Library, 301 Castro Urdiales Loop, Laredo, TX, 78046. Tel: 956-568-5952. p. 2209

Perez Gomez, Analiza, Librn IV, Guerra Joe A Laredo Public Library, Sophie Christen McKendrick, Francisco Ochoa & Fernando A Salinas Branch, 1920 Palo Blanco St, Laredo, TX, 78046. Tel: 956-795-2400, Ext 2403. p. 2209

Perez Gonzalez, Carmen T, Dir, Universidad Ana G Mendez, Calle 190, Esquina 220 Bo Sabana Abajo, Carolina, PR, 00983. Tel: 787-257-7373, Ext 2550. p. 2510

Perez, Jessy, Archivist, City College of the City University of New York, Dominican Studies Institute Archives & Library, NAC 2/202, 160 Convent Ave, New York, NY, 10031. Tel: 212-650-7170, 212-650-7496. p. 1582

Perez, Jorge, Head Librn, Saint Petersburg College, Tarpon Springs Campus Library, 600 Klosterman Rd, Tarpon Springs, FL, 34689. Tel: 727-712-5728. p. 438

Perez, Jorge, Dir, River Grove Public Library District, 8638 W Grand Ave, River Grove, IL, 60171. Tel: 708-453-4484. p. 639

Perez, Jose Eddie, Automated Syst Coordr, Laredo College, West End Washington St, Laredo, TX, 78040. Tel: 956-721-5282. p. 2209

Perez, Joshua, Syst Coordr, Indian River County Library System, 1600 21st St, Vero Beach, FL, 32960. Tel: 772-770-5060. p. 452

Perez, Julian, Ref & Instruction Librn, Carlos Albizu University Library, 2173 NW 99 Ave, Miami, FL, 33172. Tel: 305-593-1223, Ext 3131. p. 421

Perez, Luis, Librn, Southern Technical College, Auburndale Campus, 450 Havendale Blvd, Auburndale, FL, 33823. Tel: 863-551-1112. p. 404

Perez Martinez, Margarita, Cataloging & Metadata Librn, University of Miami, 1311 Miller Dr, Coral Gables, FL, 33146. Tel: 305-284-2251. p. 390

Perez Rios, Osvaldo, Br Mgr, Grand Rapids Public Library, West Side, 713 Bridge St NW, Grand Rapids, MI, 49504. Tel: 616-988-5414. p. 1111

Perez, Rochelle, Dr, Instruction & Outreach, Pub Serv, Cosumnes River College Library, 8401 Center Pkwy, Sacramento, CA, 95823. Tel: 916-691-7629. p. 208

Perez, Sheena, Digital Serv Librn, Oklahoma State University - Tulsa Library, 700 N Greenwood Ave, Tulsa, OK, 74106-0702. Tel: 918-594-8134. p. 1865

Perez Shelton, Andrea, Health Educ Asst, Sutter Health Memorial Medical Center, 1800 Coffee Rd, Ste 43, Modesto, CA, 95355-2700. p. 178

Perez, Victoria, Libr Supvr, City of Commerce Public Library, Veterans Library, 6134 Greenwood Ave, Commerce, CA, 90040. Tel: 562-887-4493. p. 132

Perez, Wendi, Exec Adminr, American Rhinologic Society Library, PO Box 269, Oak Ridge, NJ, 07438. Tel: 973-545-2735. p. 1430

Perez-Balesky, Liz, Libr Asst, Cragin Memorial Library, Eight Linwood Ave, Colchester, CT, 06415. Tel: 860-537-5752. p. 306

Perez-Cavazos, Lizbeth, Bilingual Library Asst, Adrian District Library, 143 E Maumee St, Adrian, MI, 49221-2773. Tel: 517-265-2265. p. 1075

Perez-Gilbe, Hector, Head Librn/Prog Dir, Saint Petersburg College, Health Education Center, 7200 66th St N, Pinellas Park, FL, 33781. Tel: 727-341-3657. p. 437

Perfenova, Darina, Br Supvr, Greater Victoria Public Library, Emily Carr Branch, 101-3521 Blanshard St, Victoria, BC, V8Z 0B9, CANADA. Tel: 250-940-4875, Ext 744. p. 2583

Perger, Vanessa, Programming Librn, Camas Public Library, 625 NE Fourth Ave, Camas, WA, 98607. Tel: 360-834-4692. p. 2360

Peri, Janet, Asst Libr Dir, University of Texas, Health Science Center at Houston, Dental Branch Library, 7500 Cambridge St, Houston, TX, 77054. Tel: 713-486-4204. p. 2200

Perillo, Alexa, Membership & Development Assoc, The Athenaeum of Philadelphia, East Washington Sq, 219 S Sixth St, Philadelphia, PA, 19106-3794. Tel: 215-925-2688. p. 1975

Perin, Debra, Br Mgr, Watertown Library Association, Oakville Branch, 55 Davis St, Oakville, CT, 06779. Tel: 860-945-5368. p. 345

Perini, Michael, Head, Ref, Cocoa Beach Public Library, 550 N Brevard Ave, Cocoa Beach, FL, 32931. Tel: 321-868-1104. p. 390

Perish, Cathy, Libr Serv Coordr, Great River Regional Library, Eagle Bend Library, 127 E Main, Eagle Bend, MN, 56446. Tel: 218-738-4590. p. 1196

Perish, Cathy, Libr Serv Coordr, Great River Regional Library, Staples Public Library, 122 Sixth St NE, Staples, MN, 56479. Tel: 218-894-1401. p. 1197

Perisho, Stephen, Info Spec, Seattle Pacific University Library, 3307 Third Ave W, Seattle, WA, 98119. Tel: 206-281-2417. p. 2379

Peritz, Loreen, Head of Legal Research Instruction, Brooklyn Law School Library, 250 Joralemon St, Brooklyn, NY, 11201. Tel: 718-780-7538. p. 1501

Perkins, Candace, Librn, Norwich Community Library, 209 South Pkwy, Norwich, KS, 67188-0397. Tel: 620-478-2235. p. 828

Perkins, Catherine, Tech Serv & Syst Librn, Wagner College, One Campus Rd, Staten Island, NY, 10301. Tel: 718-390-3377. p. 1645

Perkins, Cathy, Cat, Tech Serv, Waterville Public Library, 73 Elm St, Waterville, ME, 04901-6078. Tel: 207-872-5433. p. 945

Perkins, Christine, Exec Dir, Whatcom County Library System, 5205 Northwest Dr, Bellingham, WA, 98226. Tel: 360-305-3600. p. 2359

Perkins, Cindy, Librn, Ascension Via Christi, 929 N Saint Francis Ave, Wichita, KS, 67214. Tel: 316-268-6799. p. 842

Perkins, Cindy, Librn, CHI Health Creighton University Medical Center-Bergan Mercy, 7500 Mercy Rd, Omaha, NE, 68124-9832. Tel: 402-398-6092. p. 1327

Perkins, Dan, Dir, Wallkill Public Library, Seven Bona Ventura Ave, Wallkill, NY, 12589-4422. Tel: 845-895-3707. p. 1658

Perkins, Daniel, Ref & Instruction Librn, Wagner College, One Campus Rd, Staten Island, NY, 10301. Tel: 718-390-3379. p. 1645

Perkins, Debra, Br Mgr, Jackson/Hinds Library System, Beverley J Brown Library, 7395 South Siwell Rd, Byram, MS, 39272-8741. Tel: 601-372-0954. p. 1221

Perkins, Gail, Libr Assoc, Stanly Community College Library, Snyder Bldg, 141 College Dr, 1st Flr, Albemarle, NC, 28001. Tel: 704-991-0259. p. 1671

Perkins, George, Archivist, McLean County Museum of History, 200 N Main, Bloomington, IL, 61701. Tel: 309-827-0428. p. 543

Perkins, Iris, Librn, Glades County Public Library, 201 Riverside Dr SW, Moore Haven, FL, 33471. Tel: 863-946-0744. p. 427

Perkins, Jeanne, Libr Asst, Holderness Library, 866 US Rte 3, Holderness, NH, 03245. Tel: 603-968-7066. p. 1368

Perkins, John M, Ref (Info Servs), Mercer University, Walter F George School of Law, Furman Smith Law Library, 1021 Georgia Ave, Macon, GA, 31201-1001. Tel: 478-301-2667. p. 486

Perkins, Laura, Libr Dir, Brown Memorial Library, 53 Railroad St, Clinton, ME, 04927. Tel: 207-426-8686. p. 922

Perkins, Lauren, Dir, Big Rapids Community Library, 426 S Michigan Ave, Big Rapids, MI, 49307. Tel: 231-796-5234. p. 1085

Perkins, Lee, Dir, Rice Public Library, Eight Wentworth St, Kittery, ME, 03904. Tel: 207-439-1553. p. 929

Perkins, Margaret Y, Dir, Medway Public Library, 26 High St, Medway, MA, 02053. Tel: 508-533-3217. p. 1034

Perkins, Mark, Learning Librn, Madison Area Technical College, 3550 Anderson St, Rm A3000, Madison, WI, 53704. Tel: 608-246-6923. p. 2449

Perkins, Megan, Br Mgr, Sebastopol Public Library, 17403 Hwy 21 N, Sebastopol, MS, 39359. Tel: 601-625-8826. p. 1232

Perkins, Nicole, Dir, San Juan County Public Library, Monument Valley Branch, 100 Cougar Lane, Monument Valley, UT, 84536. Tel: 435-727-3204. p. 2267

Perkins, Priscilla L, Dir, Western New England University, 1215 Wilbraham Rd, Springfield, MA, 01119. Tel: 413-782-1535. p. 1057

Perkins, Rebecca, Dir, United States Air Force, 21 FSS/FSDL, 201 W Stewart Ave, Bldg 1171, Peterson AFB, CO, 80914-1600. Tel: 719-556-7643. p. 292

Perkins, Roseanne, Asst Prof, Kutztown University, 12 Rohrbach Library, Kutztown, PA, 19530. Tel: 610-683-4902. p. 2791

Perkins, Ruth, Ref (Info Servs), Kutztown University, 15200 Kutztown Rd, Bldg 5, Kutztown, PA, 19530. Tel: 610-683-4480. p. 1949

Perkins, Samantha, Libr Dir, Prof, Murrell Library & Commons, Missouri Valley College, 500 E College St, Marshall, MO, 65340. Tel: 660-831-4180, 660-831-4181. p. 1260

Perkins, Seth, Fac Librn, Laramie County Community College, Laramie Campus Library, 1125 Boulder Dr, Rm 105, Laramie, WY, 82070. Tel: 307-772-4285. p. 2492

Perkins, Susan R, Dir, Herkimer County Historical Society Library, Eckler Bldg, 406 N Main St, Herkimer, NY, 13350. Tel: 315-866-6413. p. 1546

Perkins, Sylvia, Ch, Audubon Public Library, 401 N Park Pl, Audubon, IA, 50025-1258. Tel: 712-563-3301. p. 733

Perles, Patricia, Br Mgr, Dougherty County Public Library, Northwest, 2507 Dawson Rd, Albany, GA, 31707. Tel: 229-420-3270. p. 457

Perlin, Daniel, Ref Librn, York University Libraries, Osgoode Hall Law School Library, 92 Scholar's Walk, Keele Campus, Toronto, ON, M3J 1P3, CANADA. Tel: 416-736-5380. p. 2662

Perlin, Marjorie, Head, Circ, Chappaqua Public Library, 195 S Greeley Ave, Chappaqua, NY, 10514. Tel: 914-238-4779, Ext 201. p. 1516

Perlman, James, Tech Serv, Morrill Memorial Library, 33 Walpole St, Norwood, MA, 02062-1206. Tel: 781-769-0200. p. 1044

Perlmupper, Shira, Dir, U.S. Copyright Office, Register of Copyrights, Library of Congress, James Madison Memorial Bldg, 101 Independence Ave SE, Washington, DC, 20540. Tel: 202-707-5000. p. 370

Permenter, Cindi, Br Mgr, Palm Beach County Library System, West Boynton Branch, 9451 Jog Rd, Boynton Beach, FL, 33437. Tel: 561-734-5556. p. 454

Pernell, Rebecca Ione, Head, Access Serv, Librn, Stanford University Libraries, Stanford Auxiliary Library, 691 Pampas Lane, Stanford, CA, 94305. Tel: 650-725-1277. p. 249

Perolli, Donna, Dir, Dover Plains Library, 1797 Rte 22, Wingdale, NY, 12594-1444. Tel: 845-832-6605. p. 1666

Perone, Karen, Head, Tech Serv, Head, Tech, Rodman Public Library, 215 E Broadway St, Alliance, OH, 44601-2694. Tel: 330-821-2665, p. 1745

Perone, Robert, Dir, Bradford County Public Library, 456 W Pratt St, Starke, FL, 32091. Tel: 904-368-3911. p. 444

Perpich, Jaime, Mgr, Mem Serv, Warrenville Public Library District, 28 W 751 Stafford Pl, Warrenville, IL, 60555. Tel: 630-393-1171. p. 659

Perras, Connie, Br Librn, Southeast Regional Library, Sedley Branch, 224 Broadway St, Sedley, SK, S0G 4K0, CANADA. Tel: 306-885-4505. p. 2754

Perrault, Claudine, Dir, Estes Valley Library, 335 E Elkhorn Ave, Estes Park, CO, 80517. Tel: 970-586-8116. p. 280

Perrault, Conor, Syst Librn, Gateway Community College Library & Learning Commons, 20 Church St, New Haven, CT, 06510. Tel: 203-285-2089. p. 325

Perrault, Nicole, YA Serv, Medford Public Library, 200 Boston Ave, Ste G-350, Medford, MA, 02155. Tel: 781-395-7950. p. 1033

Perreault, Tina, Libr Serv Coordr, Edmonton Public Library, Lois Hole Library, 17650 69 Ave NW, Edmonton, AB, T5T 3X9, CANADA. Tel: 780-442-0882. p. 2536

Perrie, Vicki, Dir, Superior Public Library, 449 N Kansas, Superior, NE, 68978-1852. Tel: 402-879-4200. p. 1337

Perrien, Shane, Chief Info Officer, Midland University, 900 N Clarkson, Fremont, NE, 68025. Tel: 402-941-6250. p. 1315

Perrigo, Janet, Library Contact, Christ Central Institute, 110 Park St NW, Wagener, SC, 29164. Tel: 803-564-5902, Ext 5000. p. 2071

Perrin, Diane, Br Librn, Wapiti Regional Library, Duck Lake Public Library, 410 Victoria Ave, Duck Lake, SK, S0K 1J0, CANADA. Tel: 306-467-2016. p. 2745

Perrin, Julie M, Libr Dir, Jaffrey Public Library, 38 Main St, Jaffrey, NH, 03452-1196. Tel: 603-532-7301. p. 1369

Perrin, Sara, Prog Asst, Cragin Memorial Library, Eight Linwood Ave, Colchester, CT, 06415. Tel: 860-537-5752. p. 306

Perrin-Mohr, Maryalice, Archivist, New England Conservatory of Music, 255 St Butolph St, Boston, MA, 02115. Tel: 617-585-1252. p. 998

Perrin-Ramos, Dawn, Libr Dir, Hebron Public Library, 811 Main Ave, Hebron, ND, 58638. Tel: 701-878-4110. p. 1736

Perritt, Patsy, Dr, Librn, University Baptist Church Library, 5775 Highland Rd, Baton Rouge, LA, 70808. Tel: 225-766-9474. p. 885

Perrizo, Gail, Dir, Minneota Public Library, 200 N Jefferson St, Minneota, MN, 56264. Tel: 507-872-5473. p. 1186

Perron, Sandra, Asst Dir, Silsby Free Public Library, 226 Main St, Charlestown, NH, 03603. Tel: 603-826-7793. p. 1357

Perrone, Fernanda H, Head, Exhibitions Prog Curator/William E Griffis Coll, Univ Archivist, Rutgers University Libraries, Special Collections & University Archives, Alexander Library, 169 College Ave, New Brunswick, NJ, 08901-1163. Tel: 848-932-6154. p. 1425

Perrone, Peggy, Librn, Baiting Hollow Free Library, Four Warner Dr, Calverton, NY, 11933. Tel: 631-727-8765. p. 1511

Perry, Allison, Librn, Hawley Troxell Ennis & Hawley, 877 Main St, Ste 200, Boise, ID, 83702. Tel: 208-344-6000. p. 517

Perry, Allison, Law Librn, Bond, Schoeneck & King, PLLC, One Lincoln Ctr, 110 W Fayette St, Syracuse, NY, 13202-1355. Tel: 315-218-8000. p. 1648

Perry, Amy, Commun Engagement Librn, Middleton Public Library, 7425 Hubbard Ave, Middleton, WI, 53562-3117. Tel: 608-827-7417. p. 2457

Perry, Angela, Librn, United States Army, United States Disciplinary Barracks Library, 1301 N Warehouse Rd, Fort Leavenworth, KS, 66027-2304. Tel: 913-758-3864. p. 808

Perry, Annette, Asst Librn, Albemarle Regional Library, Ahoskie Public Library, 210 E Church St, Ahoskie, NC, 27910. Tel: 252-332-5500. p. 1727

Perry, Beth, Research Servs Librn, Mercer University Atlanta, 3001 Mercer University Dr, Atlanta, GA, 30341. Tel: 678-547-6435. p. 465

Perry, Betsy, Asst Dir, Head, Adult Serv, Charlton Public Library, 40 Main St, Charlton, MA, 01507. Tel: 508-248-0452. p. 1010

Perry, Bob, Exec Dir, Charles River Museum of Industry Library, 154 Moody St, Waltham, MA, 02453. Tel: 781-893-5410. p. 1062

Perry, Bonnie, Br Mgr, Hawaii State Public Library System, Mountain View Public & School Library, 18-1235 Volcano Hwy, Mountain View, HI, 96771. Tel: 808-968-2322. p. 510

Perry, Candace, Curator, Schwenkfelder Library & Heritage Center, 105 Seminary St, Pennsburg, PA, 18073. Tel: 215-679-3103, Ext 12. p. 1974

Perry, Cara, Head, Ref, Sachem Public Library, 150 Holbrook Rd, Holbrook, NY, 11741. Tel: 631-588-5024. p. 1547

Perry, Charmette, Interim Br Mgr, Chattahoochee Valley Libraries, South Columbus Branch, 2034 S Lumpkin Rd, Columbus, GA, 31903-2728. Tel: 706-683-8805. p. 472

Perry, Danica, Br Mgr, Mansfield-Richland County Public Library, Lexington Branch, 25 Lutz Ave, Lexington, OH, 44904. Tel: 419-884-2500. p. 1798

Perry, Debra, Librn, Atlanta-Fulton Public Library System, Dogwood Branch, 1838 Donald L Hollowell Pkwy NW, Atlanta, GA, 30318. Tel: 404-612-3900. p. 461

Perry, Donte', Ref Librn, Johnson & Wales University, 801 W Trade St, Charlotte, NC, 28202. Tel: 980-598-1604. p. 1680

Perry, Erica, Ch, Clarksburg-Harrison Public Library, 404 W Pike St, Clarksburg, WV, 26301. Tel: 304-627-2236. p. 2401

Perry, Gail, Libr Mgr, Valhalla Community Library, PO Box 68, Valhalla Centre, AB, T0H 3M0, CANADA. Tel: 780-356-3834. p. 2557

Perry, Gerald, Assoc Dean, University of Arizona Libraries, 1510 E University Blvd, Tucson, AZ, 85721. Tel: 520-621-8132. p. 83

Perry, Heather, ILL, Ref Serv, Stonehill College, 320 Washington St, Easton, MA, 02357. Tel: 508-565-1538. p. 1016

Perry, Heather Brodie, Dir, Ashby Free Public Library, 812 Main St, Ashby, MA, 01431. Tel: 978-386-5377. p. 986

Perry, Joseph, Librn, Pres, Grand Army of the Republic Civil War Museum & Archive, 8110 Frankford Ave, Philadelphia, PA, 19136. Tel: 215-613-0350. p. 1981

Perry, Karen, Ch, Raymond Village Library, Three Meadow Rd, Raymond, ME, 04071-6461. Tel: 207-655-4283. p. 938

Perry, Karin, Dr, Asst Chair, Library Services, Assoc Prof, Prog Coordr, Sam Houston State University, 1905 Bobby K Marks Dr, Huntsville, TX, 77340. Tel: 936-294-4641. p. 2793

Perry, Kendra, Coord, Libr & Learning Support Services, Hagerstown Community College Library, Learning Resource Ctr, No 200B, 11400 Robinwood Dr, Hagerstown, MD, 21742-6590. Tel: 240-500-2237. p. 967

Perry, Kim, Head Librn, Camden County Library, 104 Investors Way, Units CDEF, Camden, NC, 27921. Tel: 252-331-2543. p. 1677

Perry, Kristy, Dir, Theresa Free Library, 301 Main St, Theresa, NY, 13691. Tel: 315-628-5972. p. 1651

Perry, Lewis, Network Adminr, University of the District of Columbia, David A Clarke School of Law, Charles N & Hilda H M Mason Law Library, Bldg 39, Rm B-16, 4200 Connecticut Ave NW, Washington, DC, 20008. Tel: 202-274-7310. p. 380

Perry, Linda, Dir, Deaf Smith County Library, 211 E Fourth St, Hereford, TX, 79045. Tel: 806-364-1206. p. 2189

Perry, Lora R, Dir, Walter J Hanna Memorial Library, 4615 Gary Ave, Fairfield, AL, 35064. Tel: 205-783-6007. p. 16

Perry Lundgren, Martha, Asst Dir, Ref & Instruction Librn, Bellarmine University, 2001 Newburg Rd, Louisville, KY, 40205-0671. Tel: 502-272-8139. p. 864

Perry, Maureen, Research Librn, University of Southern Maine Libraries, Lewiston-Auburn College Library, 51 Westminster St, Lewiston, ME, 04240. Tel: 207-753-6546. p. 938

Perry, Michael, County Librn, Siskiyou County Library, Technical Services, 719 Fourth St, Yreka, CA, 96097. Tel: 530-842-8805. p. 261

Perry, Michele, Tech Serv, Vermont State University - Castleton, 178 Alumni Dr, Castleton, VT, 05735. Tel: 802-468-1256. p. 2281

Perry, Nichelle, Interim Dir, North Carolina Central University, School of Law Library, 640 Nelson St, Durham, NC, 27707. Tel: 919-530-5188. p. 1685

Perry, Pamela, Campus Librn, Online Serv Librn, MiraCosta College Library, San Elijo Campus, 3333 Manchester Ave, Bldg 100, Cardiff, CA, 92007-1516. Tel: 760-634-7824. p. 187

Perry, Pamela, Online Serv Librn, MiraCosta College Library, One Barnard Dr, Bldg 1200, Oceanside, CA, 92056-3899. Tel: 760-795-6719. p. 187

Perry, Patricia, Libr Dir, Bancroft Memorial Library, 50 Hopedale St, Hopedale, MA, 01747-1799. Tel: 508-634-2209. p. 1025

Perry, Rhiannon, Br Mgr, Harris County Public Library, La Porte Community Library, 600 S Broadway, La Porte, TX, 77571. Tel: 281-471-4022. p. 2193

Perry, Robin, Asst Librn, Massachusetts Trial Court Law Libraries, Superior Courthouse, 186 S Main St, Fall River, MA, 02721. Tel: 508-491-3475. p. 1018

Perry, Sara, Asst Dir, Operations, Westfield Washington Public Library, 17400 Westfield Blvd, Unit A, Westfield, IN, 46074-9283. Tel: 317-896-9391. p. 726

Perry, Scott, Libr Tech II, Clark Maxwell Jr Library, 1405 CR 526A, Sumterville, FL, 33585. Tel: 352-568-3074. p. 445

Perry, Spence, Children's Prog Coordr, Sevier County Public Library System, Seymour Branch, 137 W Macon Lane, Seymour, TN, 37865. Tel: 865-573-0728. p. 2126

Perry, Sue Chesley, Head, Digital Initiatives, University of California, 1156 High St, Santa Cruz, CA, 95064. Tel: 831-459-5590. p. 243

Perry, Suzanne, Fac Mgr, Indiana University of Pennsylvania, Punxsutawney Campus Library, 1012 Winslow St, Punxsutawney, PA, 15767. Tel: 814-938-4870. p. 1946

Perry, Teresa, Librn, Mason County Library System, Hannan, 6760 Ashton-Upland Rd, Ashton, WV, 25503. Tel: 304-743-6200. p. 2413

Perry, Tessa, Dean of Libr, Virginia State University, One Hayden Dr, Petersburg, VA, 23806. Tel: 804-524-5040. p. 2337

Perry, Valerie, Head of Libr, University of Kentucky Libraries, Agricultural Information Center, N24 Agricultural Science Bldg N, 1100 Nicholasville Rd, Lexington, KY, 40546-0091. Tel: 859-257-8360. p. 863

Perry, Valerie, Dir, University of Kentucky Libraries, Science & Engineering Library, 211 King Bldg, 179 Funkhouser Dr, Lexington, KY, 40506-0039. Tel: 859-257-0121. p. 864

Perry, Vanessa, Dep Dir, West Virginia State Law Library, Bldg 1, Rm E-404, 1900 Kanawha Blvd E, Charleston, WV, 25305. Tel: 304-558-2607. p. 2401

Perry-Davis, Amanda, Coll Mgt Librn, Shelby County Public Library, 309 Eighth St, Shelbyville, KY, 40065. Tel: 502-633-3803. p. 874

Perryman, Bobbi, Ms, Exec Dir, Vespasian Warner Public Library District, 310 N Quincy, Clinton, IL, 61727. Tel: 217-935-5174. p. 572

Persic, Peter, Dir, Pub Relations, Los Angeles Public Library System, 630 W Fifth St, Los Angeles, CA, 90071. Tel: 213-228-7556. p. 163

Persick, Jenna, Tech Serv Mgr, Chester County Library & District Center, 450 Exton Square Pkwy, Exton, PA, 19341-2496. Tel: 610-344-5600. p. 1932

Persick, Mike, Head, Acq & Ser, Haverford College, 370 Lancaster Ave, Haverford, PA, 19041-1392. Tel: 610-896-2971. p. 1942

Persinger, Austin, Dir, Summers County Public Library, 201 Temple St, Hinton, WV, 25951. Tel: 304-466-4490. p. 2404

Persohn, Gretchen, Adult Serv Coordr, Licking County Library, 101 W Main St, Newark, OH, 43055-5054. Tel: 740-349-5524. p. 1807

Personeus, Jackie, Libr Mgr, Sno-Isle Libraries, Sultan Library, 319 Main St, Ste 100, Sultan, WA, 98294. Tel: 360-793-1695. p. 2371

Persons, Nancy, Librn, Santa Rosa Junior College, 1501 Mendocino Ave, Santa Rosa, CA, 95401. Tel: 707-521-6902. p. 245

Persons, Seth, Syst Librn, Tech Serv Librn, Bard Graduate Center Library, 38 W 86th St, New York, NY, 10024. Tel: 212-501-3037. p. 1579

Persons, Sharon, Libr Dir, Northeastern University School of Law Library, 416 Huntington Ave, Boston, MA, 02115. Tel: 617-373-3332. p. 999

Persson, Brittany, Assoc Prof, Head, Pub Serv, Seton Hall University School of Law, One Newark Ctr, Newark, NJ, 07102. Tel: 973-642-8767. p. 1428

Persson, Brittany, Libr Dir, Brooklyn Law School Library, 250 Joralemon St, Brooklyn, NY, 11201. Tel: 718-780-7975. p. 1501

Peruchi, Andrew, Legal Serv Adminr, James T Vaughn Correctional Center Law Library, 1181 Paddock Rd, Smyrna, DE, 19977. Tel: 302-653-9261. p. 356

Perugino, Patricia, Libr Dir, Bloomingdale Free Public Library, Municipal Bldg, 101 Hamburg Tpk, Bloomingdale, NJ, 07403. Tel: 973-838-0077. p. 1391

Perveen, Rowshon A, Managing Librn, Brooklyn Public Library, Cypress Hills, 1197 Sutter Ave, Brooklyn, NY, 11208. Tel: 718-277-6004. p. 1502

Perzeski, Donna, Dir, Libr Serv, Kent State University College of Podiatric Medicine, 6000 Rockside Woods Blvd, Independence, OH, 44131. Tel: 216-916-7506. p. 1791

Pesale, Robert, IT Coordr, West Bloomfield Township Public Library, 4600 Walnut Lake Rd, West Bloomfield, MI, 48323. Tel: 248-232-2315. p. 1158

Pescador, Katrina, Libr Dir, San Diego Air & Space Museum, Inc, 2001 Pan American Plaza, Balboa Park, San Diego, CA, 92101-1636. Tel: 619-234-8291, Ext 123. p. 216

Pesce, Donna, Libr Dir, Briarcliff Manor Public Library, One Library Rd, Briarcliff Manor, NY, 10510. Tel: 914-941-7072. p. 1496

Pesch, Wendy, Librn, Baton Rouge General Medical Center, 3600 Florida Blvd, Baton Rouge, LA, 70806. Tel: 225-387-7000, 225-387-7012. p. 882

Peschang, Kathy, Dir, River Valley District Library, 214 S Main St, Port Byron, IL, 61275. Tel: 309-523-3440. p. 636

Peschel, Shelley, Campus Librn, Milwaukee Area Technical College, 1200 S 71st St, Rm 213, West Allis, WI, 53214-3110. Tel: 414-456-5392. p. 2486

Pesik, Lori, Cat Librn, Saint Mary's University of Minnesota, 700 Terrace Heights, No 26, Winona, MN, 55987-1399. Tel: 507-457-6665. p. 1209

Pesko, Robin, Librn, Orangeburg-Calhoun Technical College Library, 3250 Saint Matthews Rd NE, Orangeburg, SC, 29118. Tel: 803-535-1262. p. 2066

Petcavage, Stephanie, Colls Mgr, Akron Art Museum, One S High St, Akron, OH, 44308-1801. Tel: 330-376-9186, Ext 228. p. 1743

Pete, Donovan, Supvr, Navajo Nation Library, Hwy 264, Post Office Loop Rd, Window Rock, AZ, 86515. Tel: 928-871-7303. p. 84

Peter, Phylis, Youth Serv Librn, Newton Public Library, 100 N Third Ave W, Newton, IA, 50208. Tel: 641-792-4108. p. 773

Peter, Samantha, Instrul Design Librn, University of Wyoming Libraries, 13th & Ivinson Ave, 1000 E University Ave, Laramie, WY, 82071. Tel: 307-766-3190. p. 2496

Peterman, Aaron, Assoc Dir, Providence Public Library, 150 Empire St, Providence, RI, 02903-3283. Tel: 401-455-8000. p. 2039

Peterman, Michala, Asst Librn, Culver-Stockton College, One College Hill, Canton, MO, 63435. Tel: 573-288-6711. p. 1240

Petermann, Marta, Adult Programming, Vols Coordr, Hiawatha Public Library, 150 W Willman St, Hiawatha, IA, 52233. Tel: 319-393-1414. p. 758

Petermeier, Preston, Genealogy Librn, Research Historian, Polk County Historical & Genealogical Library, Historic Courthouse, 100 E Main St, Bartow, FL, 33830. Tel: 863-534-4380. p. 384

Petermon, Jonathan, Libr Asst, Wisconsin School for the Deaf, 309 W Walworth Ave, Delavan, WI, 53115. Tel: 262-728-7127, Ext 7133. p. 2431

Peters, Alison, Commun Libr Mgr, Contra Costa County Library, Crockett Library, 991 Loring Ave, Crockett, CA, 94525. Tel: 510-787-2345. p. 174

Peters, Alison, Sr Commun Libr Mgr, Contra Costa County Library, Hercules Library, 109 Civic Dr, Hercules, CA, 94547. Tel: 510-245-2420. p. 174

Peters, Andy, Assoc Dir, Tech, Pioneer Library System, 300 Norman Ctr Ct, Norman, OK, 73072. Tel: 405-801-4560. p. 1855

Peters, Anne, Libr Asst, Oblate School of Theology, 285 Oblate Dr, San Antonio, TX, 78216. Tel: 210-341-1366, Ext 311. p. 2237

Peters, Carolyn, Adminr, Bud Werner Memorial Library, 1289 Lincoln Ave, Steamboat Springs, CO, 80487. Tel: 970-879-0240, Ext 316. p. 295

Peters, Cassandra, Asst Dir, Public Library of Mount Vernon & Knox County, 201 N Mulberry St, Mount Vernon, OH, 43050-2413. Tel: 740-392-2665. p. 1804

Peters, Chad, Pub Serv Coordr, Raritan Valley Community College, Theater Bldg Branchburg, 118 Lamington Rd, Somerville, NJ, 08876. Tel: 908-218-8865. p. 1442

Peters, Daniel T, Fac Mgr, Res, Manchester Historic Association Library, 129 Amherst St, Manchester, NH, 03101. Tel: 603-622-7531. p. 1372

Peters, Ellen, Dir, Fowlerville District Library, 130 S Grand Ave, Fowlerville, MI, 48836. Tel: 517-223-9089. p. 1107

Peters, Ellen, Br Mgr, Spokane Public Library, East Side, 524 S Stone Ave, Spokane, WA, 99202. p. 2385

Peters, Ellen, Br Mgr, Spokane Public Library, South Hill, 3324 S Perry St, Spokane, WA, 99203. p. 2385

Peters, Graeme, Br Mgr, New Tecumseth Public Library, Memorial Branch, 17 Victoria St E, Alliston, ON, L9R 1V6, CANADA. Tel: 705-435-5651. p. 2628

Peters, Jamie, Library Contact, National Park Service, 725 Ruins Rd, Aztec, NM, 87410. Tel: 505-334-6174, Ext 232. p. 1463

Peters, Jay, Mgr, Mkt, Communications & Develop, Coquitlam Public Library, 575 Poirier St, Coquitlam, BC, V3J 6A9, CANADA. Tel: 604-937-4147. p. 2565

Peters, Jennifer, Digital Serv Librn, E-Learning Librn, Seneca College of Applied Arts & Technology, Newnham Campus (Main), 1750 Finch Ave E, North York, ON, M2J 2X5, CANADA. Tel: 416-491-5050, Ext 22070. p. 2649

Peters, Julie A, Libr Dir, Rutgers University Libraries, James B Carey Library, School of Management & Labor Relations, 50 Labor Center Way, New Brunswick, NJ, 08901-8553. Tel: 848-932-9608. p. 1424

Peters, Kristen, Ref Librn, Wittenberg University, 801 Woodlawn Ave, Springfield, OH, 45504. Tel: 937-327-7533. p. 1821

Peters, Lisa, Circ Supvr, Norfolk Public Library, 308 W Prospect Ave, Norfolk, NE, 68701-4138. Tel: 402-844-2100. p. 1326

Peters, Lisa, Access Serv, Case Western Reserve University, School of Law Library, 11075 East Blvd, Cleveland, OH, 44106-7148. Tel: 216-368-2793. p. 1766

Peters, Lynne, Librn, MedStar Franklin Square Medical Center, 9000 Franklin Square Dr, Baltimore, MD, 21237. Tel: 443-777-7363. p. 955

Peters, Magnolia, Br Mgr, Cleveland Public Library, Memorial-Nottingham, 17109 Lake Shore Blvd, Cleveland, OH, 44110. Tel: 216-623-7039. p. 1768

Peters, Margie, Exec Dir, Upper Moreland Free Public Library, 109 Park Ave, Willow Grove, PA, 19090-3277. Tel: 215-659-0741. p. 2024

Peters, Michael, Div Chief, Subject Area Services, Chicago Public Library, 400 S State St, Chicago, IL, 60605. Tel: 312-747-4485. p. 555

Peters, Mindy L, Librn, Carpenter Technology Corp, 1600 Centre Ave, Reading, PA, 19601. Tel: 610-208-2807. p. 2000

Peters, Roger A, Asst Dir, Concordia Theological Seminary, 6600 N Clinton St, Fort Wayne, IN, 46825. Tel: 260-452-2145. p. 684

Peters, Sharon, Supvr, The Mohawk Council of Akwesasne, PO Box 90, Akwesasne, QC, H0M 1A0, CANADA. Tel: 613-575-2250. p. 2709

Peters, Tess, Libr Dir, Millersville Public Library of Sumner County, 1174 Louisville Hwy, Millersville, TN, 37072. Tel: 615-448-6959. p. 2116

Peters, Thomas, Dean, Missouri State University, 850 S John Q Hammons Pkwy, Springfield, MO, 65807. p. 1281

Peters, Timothy, Assoc Dean, Univ Libr Serv, Central Michigan University, 250 E Preston St, Mount Pleasant, MI, 48859. Tel: 989-774-6420. p. 1134

Peters, Victoria M, Cat, DePauw University, 405 S Indiana St, Greencastle, IN, 46135. Tel: 765-658-4420. p. 687

Petersen, Chris, Sr Res Asst, Oregon State University Libraries, Special Collections & Archives Research Center, 121 The Valley Library, 5th Flr, Corvallis, OR, 97331. Tel: 541-737-2810. p. 1877

Petersen, Jeffrey, Assoc Univ Librn, Cornell University Library, 201 Olin Library, Ithaca, NY, 14853. Tel: 607-255-4144. p. 1551
Petersen, Jeffrey, Assoc Univ Librn, Cornell University Library, Division of Asia Collections (Carl A Kroch Library), Kroch Library, Level 1, Ithaca, NY, 14853. Tel: 607-255-8199. p. 1551
Petersen, Julie, Ref Librn, Kirkwood Community College, Benton Hall, 6301 Kirkwood Blvd SW, Cedar Rapids, IA, 52404-5260. Tel: 319-398-5553. p. 738
Petersen, Kris, Libr Dir, Springmier Community Library, 311 W Marengo Rd, Tiffin, IA, 52340-9308. Tel: 319-545-2960. p. 786
Petersen, Kristi, Libr Tech, Southwest Minnesota State University Library, 1501 State St, Marshall, MN, 56258. Tel: 507-537-6162. p. 1182
Petersen, Lisa, Libr Dir, J Turner Moore Memorial Library, 1330 Lands End Rd, Manalapan, FL, 33462. Tel: 561-383-2541, 561-588-7577. p. 419
Petersen, Loralee, Dir, Owen Public Library, 414 Central Ave, Owen, WI, 54460-9777. Tel: 715-229-2939. p. 2468
Petersen, Lori, Youth Serv Librn, Waterloo Public Library, 415 Commercial St, Waterloo, IA, 50701-1385. Tel: 319-291-4521. p. 789
Petersen, Meghan, Librn & Archivist, Currier Museum of Art, 150 Ash St, Manchester, NH, 03104. Tel: 603-518-4927, 603-669-6144. p. 1372
Petersen, Sheila, Dir, Battle Creek Public Library, 115 Main St, Battle Creek, IA, 51006. Tel: 712-365-4912. p. 734
Petersilie, Laurie, Dir, Ness City Public Library, 113 S Iowa Ave, Ness City, KS, 67560-1992. Tel: 785-798-3415. p. 826
Peterson, Adrianne, Br Mgr, San Diego Public Library, Rancho Peñasquitos, 13330 Salmon River Rd, San Diego, CA, 92129-2640. Tel: 858-538-8159. p. 220
Peterson, Amy, Dir, Lena Public Library, 200 E Main St, Lena, WI, 54139. Tel: 920-829-5335. p. 2448
Peterson, Amy, Libr Dir, Farnsworth Public Library, 715 Main St, Oconto, WI, 54153. Tel: 920-834-7730. p. 2466
Peterson, Andrea, Librn, Western Washington University, 516 High St, MS 9103, Bellingham, WA, 98225. Tel: 360-650-3894. p. 2358
Peterson, Anecia, Br Mgr, Ohoopee Regional Library System, Tattnall County Library, 129 Tattnall St, Reidsville, GA, 30453-0338. Tel: 912-557-6247. p. 502
Peterson, Anndee, Asst Dir, Pittsburg Public Library, 308 N Walnut, Pittsburg, KS, 66762-4732. Tel: 620-230-5567. p. 831
Peterson, Anne, Curator, Southern Methodist University, DeGolyer Library of Special Collections, 6404 Robert S Hyer Lane, Dallas, TX, 75275. Tel: 214-768-2661. p. 2168
Peterson, Beth, Libr Spec, Spartanburg Community College Library, Peeler Academic Bldg, 1st Flr, 523 Chesnee Hwy, Gaffney, SC, 29341. Tel: 864-206-2656. p. 2060
Peterson, Brice, Exec Dir, Libr Serv, Rosemont College Library, 1400 Montgomery Ave, Rosemont, PA, 19010-1631. Tel: 610-527-0200, Ext 2271. p. 2002
Peterson, Coral, Librn, Canada Department of National Defence, Royal Artillery Park, Bldg No 3, 5460 Royal Artillery Court, Halifax, NS, B3J 0A8, CANADA. Tel: 902-427-4494. p. 2618
Peterson, Cynthia Lynn, Librn, Unger Memorial Library, 825 Austin St, Plainview, TX, 79072-7235. Tel: 806-296-1148. p. 2227
Peterson, David, Dir, Rowan College at Burlington County Library, 900 College Circle, Mount Laurel, NJ, 08054-5308. Tel: 856-222-9311, Ext 2021. p. 1422
Peterson, Debra, Archivist, San Mateo County Historical Association, 2200 Broadway St, Redwood City, CA, 94063. Tel: 650-299-0104. p. 200
Peterson, Dee, Dir of Libr, Ohio Wesleyan University, 43 Rowland Ave, Delaware, OH, 43015-2370. Tel: 740-368-3240. p. 1782
Peterson, Doris, Librn, University of South Dakota, I D Weeks Library, 414 E Clark St, Vermillion, SD, 57069. Tel: 605-658-3380. p. 2084
Peterson, Ellen, Head Librn, University of Hawaii, 310 Kaahumanu Ave, Kahului, HI, 96732. Tel: 808-984-3233, 808-984-3715. p. 513
Peterson, Ellen, Br Mgr, Davis County Library, Layton/Central Branch, 155 N Wasatch Dr, Layton, UT, 84041. Tel: 801-451-1820. p. 2263
Peterson, Emily, Pub Serv Dir, Columbia Theological Seminary, 701 S Columbia Dr, Decatur, GA, 30030. Tel: 404-687-4661. p. 475
Peterson, Eric, Access Serv Mgr, University of California San Francisco, Mission Bay FAMRI Library, William J Rutter Conference Ctr, Rm 150, 1675 Owens St, San Francisco, CA, 94143-2119. Tel: 415-514-4060. p. 229
Peterson, Gabriel, Assoc Prof, North Carolina Central University, 1801 Fayetteville St, Durham, NC, 27707. Tel: 919-530-6485. p. 2790
Peterson, Gretchen, Research Librn, American Society for Quality, 600 N Plankinton Ave, Milwaukee, WI, 53203. Tel: 414-272-8575. p. 2457
Peterson, Harriet, Dir, Granger Public Library, 2216 Broadway, Granger, IA, 50109. Tel: 515-999-2088. p. 756
Peterson, Heather, Ad, Asst Dir, Sanbornton Public Library, 27 Meetinghouse Hill Rd, Sanbornton, NH, 03269. Tel: 603-286-8288. p. 1380
Peterson, Herman, Col Librn, Dine College, One Circle Dr, Rte 12, Tsaile, AZ, 86556. Tel: 928-724-6764. p. 80
Peterson, Herman, Col Librn, Dine College, State Hwy 371 & Navajo Service Rte 9, Crownpoint, NM, 87313. Tel: 505-786-7391, Ext 7205. p. 1466
Peterson, Jeanne, Tech Serv Coordr, Chippewa Falls Public Library, 105 W Central St, Chippewa Falls, WI, 54729-2397. Tel: 715-723-1146. p. 2427
Peterson, Jennifer, Evening Librn, Milwaukee Area Technical College, 1200 S 71st St, Rm 213, West Allis, WI, 53214-3110. Tel: 414-456-5393. p. 2486
Peterson, Jessi, Children's Serv Coordr, Chippewa Falls Public Library, 105 W Central St, Chippewa Falls, WI, 54729-2397. Tel: 715-723-1146. p. 2427
Peterson, Jim, Media/IT Mgr, Goodnight Memorial Public Library, 203 S Main St, Franklin, KY, 42134. Tel: 270-586-8397. p. 856
Peterson, John, Archivist, Lutheran Theological Seminary, United Lutheran Seminary, 7301 Germantown Ave, Philadelphia, PA, 19119-1794. Tel: 215-248-6383. p. 1982
Peterson, Jonna, Interim Dir, Loyola University Chicago Libraries, Health Sciences Library, Bldg 125, Rm 1526, 2160 S First Ave, Maywood, IL, 60153. Tel: 708-216-6328. p. 563
Peterson, Julie, Coordr, Yavapai County Free Library District, Bagdad Public Library, 700 Palo Verde, Bldg C, Bagdad, AZ, 86321. Tel: 928-633-2325. p. 74
Peterson, Justine, Dir, Seville Township Public Library, 6734 N Lumberjack Rd, Riverdale, MI, 48877. Tel: 989-833-7776. p. 1144
Peterson, Kathi Bower, Librn, Library Association of La Jolla, 1008 Wall St, La Jolla, CA, 92037. Tel: 858-454-5872. p. 154
Peterson, Kathy, Dir, Red River County Public Library, 307 N Walnut St, Clarksville, TX, 75426. Tel: 903-427-3991. p. 2156
Peterson, Kenneth, Assoc Librn, Access Serv, Dartmouth College Library, 6025 Baker Berry Library, Rm 115, Hanover, NH, 03755-3527. Tel: 603-646-2236. p. 1366
Peterson, Marika, Campus Librn, Southside Virginia Community College Libraries, 109 Campus Dr, Alberta, VA, 23821. Tel: 434-949-1065. p. 2302
Peterson, Marika, Librn, Southside Virginia Community College, 200 Daniel Rd, Keysville, VA, 23947. Tel: 434-949-1064. p. 2327
Peterson, Mark, Fac Librn, Mt Hood Community College Libraries, 26000 SE Stark St, Gresham, OR, 97030. Tel: 503-491-7693. p. 1881
Peterson, Melissa, Dir, Daemen University Library, Research & Information Commons, 4380 Main St, Amherst, NY, 14226-3592. Tel: 716-839-8243. p. 1486
Peterson, Merlin, Dir, Pope County Historical Society, 809 S Lakeshore Dr, Glenwood, MN, 56334. Tel: 320-634-3293. p. 1176
Peterson, Myrene, Librn, Enderlin Municipal Library, 303 Railway St, Enderlin, ND, 58027. Tel: 701-437-2953. p. 1732
Peterson, Nan, Br Mgr, Manville Public Library, 100 S Tenth Ave, Manville, NJ, 08835. Tel: 908-458-8425. p. 1416
Peterson, Patricia I, Dir, Riley City Library, 115 S Broadway St, Riley, KS, 66531. Tel: 785-485-2978. p. 833
Peterson, Rick, Mgr, Access Serv, Lewis & Clark College, Aubrey R Watzek Library, 0615 SW Palatine Hill Rd, Portland, OR, 97219-7899. Tel: 503-768-7274. p. 1892
Peterson, Rose, Mgr, Coll Mgt, Mgr, Info Tech, Rockford Public Library, 214 N Church St, Rockford, IL, 61101-1023. Tel: 815-965-7606. p. 642
Peterson, Shauna, Libr Dir, Chocorua Public Library, 25 Deer Hill Rd, Chocorua, NH, 03817. Tel: 603-323-8610. p. 1358
Peterson, Sherri, Libr Dir, Newell Public Library, 205 E Second St, Newell, IA, 50568. Tel: 712-272-4334. p. 773
Peterson, Sue, Youth Serv Librn, Atlantic Public Library, 507 Poplar St, Atlantic, IA, 50022. Tel: 712-243-5466. p. 733
Peterson, Susan, Asst Librn, Griswold Public Library, 505 Main, Griswold, IA, 51535. Tel: 712-778-4130. p. 756
Peterson, Sylvia, Library Contact, Wilkin County Museum Library, 704 Nebraska Ave, Breckenridge, MN, 56520. Tel: 218-643-1303. p. 1166
Peterson, Terry, Library Contact, Minnesota West Community & Technical College, Pipestone Campus, 1314 N Hiawatha Ave, Pipestone, MN, 56164. Tel: 507-825-6832. p. 1210
Peterson, Toby, Dir, Hood College, 401 Rosemont Ave, Frederick, MD, 21701. Tel: 301-696-3924. p. 966
Peterson-Fairchild, Kelly, Dean of Library & Open Learning Services, Dixie State University Library, 225 S 700 E, Saint George, UT, 84770. Tel: 435-652-7711. p. 2270
Petersons, Nancy, Dir, Mechanic Falls Public Library, 108 Lewiston St, Third Flr, Mechanic Falls, ME, 04256. Tel: 207-345-9450. p. 931
Petipas-Haggerty, Casey, Youth Serv Librn, Maynard Public Library, 77 Nason St, Maynard, MA, 01754-2316. Tel: 978-897-1010. p. 1033
Petkova, Veneta, Br Supvr, Greater Victoria Public Library, Bruce Hutchison Branch, 4636 Elk Lake Dr, Victoria, BC, V8Z 7K2, CANADA. Tel: 250-940-4875, Ext 704. p. 2583
Petraits, Ellen, Res & Instruction Librn, Rhode Island School of Design Library, 15 Westminster St, Providence, RI, 02903. Tel: 401-709-5905. p. 2040
Petrakis, Sophia, Br Mgr, Stanislaus County Library, Newman Branch, 1305 Kern St, Newman, CA, 95360-1603. Tel: 209-862-2010. p. 178
Petranovich, Katie, Dir, Western Taylor County Public Library, 380 E Main St, Gilman, WI, 54433. Tel: 715-447-5486. p. 2437
Petrarca, Jackie, Br Mgr, Warwick Public Library, Conimicut, 55 Beach Ave, Warwick, RI, 02889. Tel: 401-737-6546. p. 2043
Petretti, Dawn, Principal Libr Asst/Tech Serv & Circ, Glen Ridge Free Public Library, 240 Ridgewood Ave, Glen Ridge, NJ, 07028. Tel: 973-748-5482. p. 1405

Pfannenstiel, Mendy, Dir, Arkansas City Public Library, 120 E Fifth Ave, Arkansas City, KS, 67005-2695. Tel: 620-442-1280. p. 796
Pfarr, Jason, Dean, Acad Support, Pittsburgh Institute of Aeronautics, Five Allegheny County Airport, West Mifflin, PA, 15122-2674. Tel: 412-346-2100, 412-462-9011. p. 2021
Pfarr, Tracey, Mgr, Masonic Grand Lodge Library, 201 14th Ave N, Fargo, ND, 58102. Tel: 701-235-8321. p. 1733
Pfeifer, Brian, Library Contact, Newton Correctional Facility, NCF Library, 307 S 60th Ave W, Newton, IA, 50208. Tel: 641-792-7552, Ext 568. p. 773
Pfeifer, Karen, Coll Spec, Resource Dev Specialist, Fort Hays State University, 502 S Campus Dr, Hays, KS, 67601. Tel: 785-628-4343. p. 812
Pfeifer, Thomas, Libr Dir, Avila University, 11901 Wornall Rd, Kansas City, MO, 64145. Tel: 816-501-2912. p. 1254
Pfeifer, Veronica Ann, Asst Librn, Cedar Rapids Public Library, 423 W Main St, Cedar Rapids, NE, 68627. Tel: 308-358-0603. p. 1309
Pfeiffer, Julie, Librn, Hooker County Library, 102 N Cleveland Ave, Mullen, NE, 69152. Tel: 308-546-2240. p. 1325
Pfeiffer, Lisa, Cat Librn, Rawlins Municipal Library, 1000 E Church St, Pierre, SD, 57501. Tel: 605-773-7421. p. 2080
Pfister, Jude, Curator, National Park Service, 30 Washington Pl, Morristown, NJ, 07960-4299. Tel: 973-539-2016, Ext 204. p. 1422
Pfisterer, Matthew, Dir, Middletown Thrall Library, 11-19 Depot St, Middletown, NY, 10940. Tel: 845-341-5454. p. 1571
Pfitzinger, Scott, Circ, University of Wisconsin-La Crosse, 1631 Pine St, La Crosse, WI, 54601-3748. Tel: 608-785-8943. p. 2446
Pfledderer, Cynthia, City Librn, Southlake Public Library, 1400 Main St, Ste 130, Southlake, TX, 76092-7640. Tel: 817-748-8243. p. 2245
Pflum, Sara, Mgr, Northeast Missouri Library Service, Knox County Public, 118 S Main St, Edina, MO, 63537-1427. Tel: 660-397-2460. p. 1254
Pfohl, Tina, Dir, Brickl Memorial Library, 500 East Ave, Dickeyville, WI, 53808. Tel: 608-568-3142. p. 2431
Pham, John, Sr Librn, Los Angeles Public Library System, Harbor City-Harbor Gateway Branch Library, 24000 S Western Ave, Los Angeles, CA, 90710. Tel: 310-534-9520. p. 164
Pham, Sylvia, Outreach & Student Engagement, Kutztown University, 15200 Kutztown Rd, Bldg 5, Kutztown, PA, 19530. Tel: 610-683-4480. p. 1949
Pham, Vannie, Libr Asst II, Saddleback College, 28000 Marguerite Pkwy, Mission Viejo, CA, 92692. Tel: 949-582-4285. p. 177
Phan, Hao, Curator, Northern Illinois University Libraries, 217 Normal Rd, DeKalb, IL, 60115-2828. Tel: 815-753-1809. p. 577
Phares, Carol, Syst Dir, Pearl River County Library System, 900 Goodyear Blvd, Picayune, MS, 39466. Tel: 601-798-5081. p. 1229
Phares, Jennifer, Dep Libr Dir, Boulder Public Library, 1001 Arapahoe Rd, Boulder, CO, 80302. Tel: 303-441-3100. p. 266
Phares, Karen, Ch Serv Librn, Orange Public Library, 220 N Fifth St, Orange, TX, 77630. Tel: 409-883-1086. p. 2224
Pharo, Sam, Dir, Free Library of New Hope & Solebury, 93 W Ferry St, New Hope, PA, 18938-1332. Tel: 215-862-2330. p. 1969
Phelan, Paul, Dir, Libr Serv, Kyle Public Library, 550 Scott St, Kyle, TX, 78640. Tel: 512-268-7411. p. 2207
Phelps, Ann, Br Mgr, Beaufort, Hyde & Martin County Regional Library, Martin Memorial, 200 N Smithwick St, Williamston, NC, 27892. Tel: 252-792-7476. p. 1720
Phelps, Dana, Br Mgr, Martinsburg-Berkeley County Public Library, Hedgesville Public Library, 207 N Mary St, Hedgesville, WV, 25427. Tel: 304-754-3949. p. 2408
Phelps, Dana, Br Mgr, Martinsburg-Berkeley County Public Library, North Berkeley Public Library, 125 T J Jackson Dr, Falling Waters, WV, 25419. Tel: 304-274-3443. p. 2408
Phelps, Jessica, Libr Dir, Custer County Library, 447 Crook St, Ste 4, Custer, SD, 57730. Tel: 605-673-4803. p. 2075
Phelps, Lena, Chair, Libr Serv, Lead Librn, South Florida State College Library, 600 W College Dr, Avon Park, FL, 33825-9356. Tel: 863-784-7303. p. 384
Phelps, Luellen Kay, Dir, Sioux Rapids Memorial Library, 215 Second St, Sioux Rapids, IA, 50585. Tel: 712-283-2064. p. 783
Phelps, Priscilla, Libr Coord, Yavapai County Free Library District, Yarnell Public Library, 22278 N Hwy 89, Yarnell, AZ, 85362. Tel: 928-427-3191. p. 75
Phemester, Erin, Dir, Youth Serv, Programming, Public Library of Youngstown & Mahoning County, 305 Wick Ave, Youngstown, OH, 44503. Tel: 330-744-8636. p. 1835
Phenessa, Gray, Br Mgr, Jacksonville Public Library, Raiford A Brown Eastside Branch, 1390 Harrison St, Jacksonville, FL, 32206-5324. Tel: 904-630-5466. p. 412
Phetterplace, Peggy, Circ Serv Coordr, Florida SouthWestern State College, 8099 College Pkwy SW, Bldg J-212, Fort Myers, FL, 33919. Tel: 239-489-9299. p. 403
Philbert, Medaline, Asst Univ Librn, Pace University, 861 Bedford Rd, Pleasantville, NY, 10570-2799. Tel: 914-773-3945. p. 1620
Philbin, Paul, Dir, Media Serv, Tech & Access Serv Dir, University of Vermont Libraries, 538 Main St, Burlington, VT, 05405-0036. Tel: 802-656-1369. p. 2281
Philbin, Timothy, ILL, William Rainey Harper College Library, 1200 W Algonguin Rd, Palatine, IL, 60067. Tel: 847-925-6584. p. 631
Philbrick, Virginia, Dir, Buhler Public Library, 121 N Main St, Buhler, KS, 67522. Tel: 620-543-2241. p. 799
Philbrook, Wayne, Br Mgr, Stanislaus County Library, Salida Branch, 4835 Sisk Rd, Salida, CA, 95368-9445. Tel: 209-543-7353. p. 178
Philipot, Julie, Br Coordr, Shelby County Libraries, Russia Branch, 200 Raider St, Russia, OH, 45363. Tel: 937-526-4300. p. 1820
Philippe-Gagnon, Mylène, Cataloger & Acq, Officer, Canadian Museum of Nature Library & Archives, 1740 Pink Rd, Gatineau, QC, J9J 3N7, CANADA. Tel: 613-566-4734. p. 2712
Philippon, Patricia, Exec Dir, American Clock & Watch Museum, Inc, 100 Maple St, Bristol, CT, 06010-5092. Tel: 860-583-6070. p. 304
Philips, Warren, Library Contact, Validata Computer & Research Corp Library, 600 S Court St, Montgomery, AL, 36104. Tel: 334-834-2324. p. 30
Phillabaum, Winona, Mgr, County of Los Angeles Public Library, Lloyd Taber-Marina del Rey Library, 4533 Admiralty Way, Marina del Rey, CA, 90292-5416. Tel: 310-821-3415. p. 138
Phillibert, Margaret, Br Librn, Boston Public Library, Lower Mills, 27 Richmond St, Dorchester, MA, 02124-5610. Tel: 617-298-7841. p. 992
Phillip, Roberta, Br Dir, Custer County Library, Hermosa Branch, 234 Main St, Hermosa, SD, 57744. Tel: 605-255-5597. p. 2075
Phillipo, Zeta, Ch, County of Brant Public Library, Burford Branch, 24 Park Ave, Burford, ON, N0E 1A0, CANADA. Tel: 519-449-5371. p. 2671
Phillipps, Bobby, AV Coordr, Laramie County Library System, 2200 Pioneer Ave, Cheyenne, WY, 82001-3610. Tel: 307-773-7212. p. 2492
Phillips, Abigail L, Dr, Asst Prof, University of Wisconsin-Milwaukee, NWQD, Rm 3860, 2025 E Newport, Milwaukee, WI, 53211. Tel: 414-229-4707. p. 2794
Phillips, Amy, Dir, Loveland Public Library, 300 N Adams Ave, Loveland, CO, 80537. Tel: 970-962-2404. p. 290
Phillips, Amy, Spec Coll Cataloger, Woodstock Theological Center Library, Georgetown University, Lauinger Library, PO Box 571170, Washington, DC, 20057-1170. Tel: 202-687-2902. p. 382
Phillips, Andrew, Br Mgr, Mid-Continent Public Library, North Independence Branch, 317 W US Hwy 24, Independence, MO, 64050. Tel: 816-252-0950. p. 1251
Phillips, Anne Marie, Rec Mgr, Princeton University, Seeley G Mudd Manuscript Library, 65 Olden St, Princeton, NJ, 08544. Tel: 609-258-3213. p. 1438
Phillips, Annie, Br Mgr, Huntsville-Madison County Public Library, Eleanor E Murphy Library, 7910 Charlotte Dr SW, Huntsville, AL, 35802. Tel: 256-881-5620. p. 22
Phillips, Audrey, Dir, Goodnight Memorial Public Library, 203 S Main St, Franklin, KY, 42134. Tel: 270-586-8397. p. 856
Phillips, Becky, Libr Mgr, Brown County Library, Weyers-Hilliard Branch, 2680 Riverview Dr, Green Bay, WI, 54313. Tel: 920-448-4405. p. 2438
Phillips, Becky J, Libr Mgr, Brown County Library, Pulaski Branch, 222 W Pulaski St, Pulaski, WI, 54162. Tel: 920-822-3220. p. 2438
Phillips, Bob, Dir, Libr Serv, Gateway Seminary, 3200 NE 109th Ave, Vancouver, WA, 98682-7749. Tel: 360-882-2200. p. 2391
Phillips, Brian, IT Mgr, Chillicothe & Ross County Public Library, 140 S Paint St, Chillicothe, OH, 45601. Tel: 740-702-4145. p. 1758
Phillips, Carrie, Archives & Spec Coll Librn, Bluffton University, One University Dr, Bluffton, OH, 45817-2104. Tel: 419-358-3275. p. 1751
Phillips, Cathy, Head, Tech Serv, Lawrence Technological University Library, 21000 W Ten Mile Rd, Southfield, MI, 48075-1058. Tel: 248-204-3000. p. 1151
Phillips, Christie, Ch, Dartmouth Public Libraries, 732 Dartmouth St, Dartmouth, MA, 02748. Tel: 508-999-0726. p. 1013
Phillips, Crystal, Librn, Cook Public Library, 103 S River St, Cook, MN, 55723. Tel: 218-666-2210. p. 1171
Phillips, David, Dir, Jefferson City Public Library, 108 City Center Dr, Jefferson City, TN, 37760. Tel: 865-475-9094. p. 2103
Phillips, David, Br Mgr, Sevier County Public Library System, Seymour Branch, 137 W Macon Lane, Seymour, TN, 37865. Tel: 865-573-0728. p. 2126
Phillips, Deborah, Br Mgr, Mountain Regional Library System, Towns County Public Library, 99 S Berrong St, Hiawassee, GA, 30546. Tel: 706-896-6169. p. 504
Phillips, Denise, ILL, Hershey Public Library, 701 Cocoa Ave, Hershey, PA, 17033. Tel: 717-533-6555. p. 1943
Phillips, Donna, Dir, Wayne County Public Library, 1001 E Ash St, Goldsboro, NC, 27530. Tel: 919-735-1880. p. 1690
Phillips, Donna, Dir, Parrott-Wood Memorial Library, 3133 W Old Andrew Johnson Hwy, Strawberry Plains, TN, 37871. Tel: 865-933-1311. p. 2127
Phillips, Elizabeth, Dir, Libr Serv, Washington County Community College Library, One College Dr, Calais, ME, 04619. Tel: 207-454-1050. p. 920
Phillips, Ellen, Ch, West Hartford Public Library, Faxon Branch, 1073 New Britain Ave, West Hartford, CT, 06110. Tel: 860-561-8200. p. 346
Phillips, Emily, Bus Mgr, Willard Library of Evansville, 21 First Ave, Evansville, IN, 47710-1294. Tel: 812-425-4309. p. 682
Phillips, Erin, Librn, Cape Breton Regional Library, Baddeck Public, 520 Chebucto St, Baddeck, NS, B0E 1B0, CANADA. Tel: 902-562-3279. p. 2622
Phillips, Erin, Librn, Cape Breton Regional Library, Victoria North Regional, 36243 Cabot Trail, Ingonish, NS, B0C 1K0, CANADA. Tel: 902-285-2544. p. 2622

Phillips, Faith, Dir, Cumberland County Public Library & Information Center, 300 Maiden Lane, Fayetteville, NC, 28301-5032. Tel: 910-483-7727. p. 1688
Phillips, Grace, Libr Asst II, Shippensburg University, 1871 Old Main Dr, Shippensburg, PA, 17257. Tel: 717-477-1461. p. 2007
Phillips, Heather, Asst Dir, Delanco Public Library, M Joan Pearson School, 1303 Burlington Ave, Delanco, NJ, 08075. Tel: 856-461-6850. p. 1398
Phillips, Holly, Dir, Moultrie-Colquitt County Library, 204 Fifth St SE, Moultrie, GA, 31768. Tel: 229-985-6540. p. 492
Phillips, Janet, Dir, Jemez Springs Public Library, 30 Jemez Plaza, Jemez Springs, NM, 87025. Tel: 575-829-9155. p. 1470
Phillips, Jed T, Exec Dir, Bridgewater Public Library, 15 South St, Bridgewater, MA, 02324. Tel: 508-697-3331. p. 1002
Phillips, Jennifer, Dir, National Center for Atmospheric Research Library, Mesa Lab Campus, 1850 Table Mesa Dr, Boulder, CO, 80305. Tel: 303-497-1173. p. 267
Phillips, Jessica, Head, Children's Servx, Duxbury Free Library, 77 Alden St, Duxbury, MA, 02332. Tel: 781-934-2721. p. 1015
Phillips, Jessica, Dir, Bolivar-Hardeman County Library, 213 N Washington St, Bolivar, TN, 38008-2020. Tel: 731-658-3436. p. 2089
Phillips, John, Chief of Staff, American Indian Higher Education Consortium, 121 Oronoco St, Alexandria, VA, 22314. Tel: 703-838-0400. p. 2776
Phillips, Joi, Asst Dir, Delta State University, Laflore Circle at Fifth Ave, Cleveland, MS, 38733-2599. Tel: 662-846-4430. p. 1214
Phillips, Julie, Libr Dir, Botetourt County Libraries, 28 Avery Row, Roanoke, VA, 24012. Tel: 540-928-2900. p. 2344
Phillips, Kara, Coll Develop, Seattle University, School of Law Library, Sullivan Hall, 901 12th Ave, Seattle, WA, 98122-4411. Tel: 206-398-4221. p. 2380
Phillips, Kat, Nursing Librn, Pennsylvania State University Libraries, Life Sciences, 408 Paterno Library, University Park, PA, 16802-1811. Tel: 814-865-7313. p. 2015
Phillips, Kathy, Circ Supvr, Boyle County Public Library, 307 W Broadway, Danville, KY, 40422. Tel: 859-236-8466, 859-238-7323. p. 853
Phillips, Kathy, Asst Librn, Five Rivers Public Library, 301 Walnut St, Parsons, WV, 26287. Tel: 304-478-3880. p. 2411
Phillips, Kerry, Br Mgr, Richmond Public Library, Ginter Park, 1200 Westbrook Ave, Richmond, VA, 23227. Tel: 804-646-1236. p. 2342
Phillips, Lauren, Colls Mgr, New Canaan Library, 151 Main St, New Canaan, CT, 06840. Tel: 203-594-5070. p. 324
Phillips, Lauri, Libr Asst, Patrick Henry School District Public Library, 208 N East Ave, Deshler, OH, 43516. Tel: 419-278-3616. p. 1782
Phillips, Laurie, Dean of Libr, Loyola University New Orleans, 6363 Saint Charles Ave, New Orleans, LA, 70118. Tel: 504-864-7111. p. 902
Phillips, Lois, Libr Dir, Essential Club Free Library, 11 Pratt St, Canaseraga, NY, 14822. Tel: 607-545-6443. p. 1513
Phillips, Lori, Head, Tech Serv, Croton Free Library, 171 Cleveland Dr, Croton-on-Hudson, NY, 10520. Tel: 914-271-6612. p. 1523
Phillips, Marissa, Pub Serv Librn, Maitland Public Library, 501 S Maitland Ave, Maitland, FL, 32751-5672. Tel: 407-647-7700. p. 419
Phillips, Mark, Assoc Dean for Digital Libraries, University of North Texas Libraries, 1155 Union Circle, No 305190, Denton, TX, 76203-5017. Tel: 940-565-2415. p. 2170
Phillips, Marlena, Br Supvr, Wythe-Grayson Regional Library, Whitetop Public, 16309 Highlands Pkwy, Whitetop, VA, 24292. Tel: 276-388-2873. p. 2326
Phillips, Mary Lynn, Libr Asst, Sangudo Public Library, 5028 50 Ave, Sangudo, AB, T0E 2A0, CANADA. Tel: 780-785-2955. p. 2553
Phillips, Maryam, Exec Dir, Health Sciences Libraries Consortium, 3600 Market St, Ste 550, Philadelphia, PA, 19104-2646. Tel: 215-222-1532. p. 2774
Phillips, Matthew, Mobile Library Services, Henrico County Public Library, 1700 N Parham Rd, Henrico, VA, 23229. Tel: 804-501-1900. p. 2325
Phillips, Melissa, Ch Serv, Sr Mgr, Cook Memorial Public Library District, 413 N Milwaukee Ave, Libertyville, IL, 60048-2280. Tel: 847-362-2330. p. 608
Phillips, Merrilyn, Librn, Rupert J Smith Law Library of Saint Lucie County, 221 S Indian River Dr, Fort Pierce, FL, 34950. Tel: 772-462-2370. p. 405
Phillips, Nancy Kim, Dir, Commun Engagement, Skokie Public Library, 5215 Oakton St, Skokie, IL, 60077-3680. Tel: 847-673-7774. p. 647
Phillips, Rachael, Br Mgr, Augusta County Library, Churchville Branch, 3714 Churchville Ave, Churchville, VA, 24421. Tel: 540-245-5287. p. 2318
Phillips, Roberta, Chief Exec Officer, Prince George's County Memorial Library System, 9601 Capital Lane, Largo, MD, 20774. Tel: 301-699-3500. p. 970
Phillips, Sara, Br Mgr, Cleveland Heights-University Heights Public Library, University Heights Branch, 13866 Cedar Rd, University Heights, OH, 44118-3201. Tel: 216-321-4700. p. 1771
Phillips, Sharon, Head Librn, Montgomery City-County Public Library System, Coliseum Boulevard Branch Library, 840 Coliseum Blvd, Montgomery, AL, 36109. Tel: 334-271-7005. p. 29
Phillips, Sue, Librn, Elk City Community Library, 100 School Rd, Elk City, ID, 83525. Tel: 208-926-2270. p. 520
Phillips, Susan J, Libr Dir, Hall Memorial Library, 93 Main St, Ellington, CT, 06029. Tel: 860-870-3160. p. 310
Phillips, Tenecia, Br Coordr, Mesa Public Library, Red Mountain Branch, 635 N Power Rd, Mesa, AZ, 85205. Tel: 480-644-3183. p. 67
Phillips, Tenecia, Br Mgr, Pima County Public Library, Sahuarita, 725 W Via Rancho Sahuarita, Sahuarita, AZ, 85629. Tel: 520-594-5490. p. 82
Phillips, Terrance, Libr Assoc, Gateway Community College Library & Learning Commons, 20 Church St, New Haven, CT, 06510. Tel: 203-285-2058. p. 325
Phillips, Thomas, Dr, Dean of Libr, Info Res, Claremont School of Theology Library, Center for Process Studies, 1325 N College Ave, Claremont, CA, 91711-3154. Tel: 909-447-2512. p. 130
Phillips, Tom, Dr, Dean, Libr & Info Tech, Claremont School of Theology Library, 1325 N College Ave, Claremont, CA, 91711. Tel: 909-447-2512. p. 130
Phillips, Yvonne, Librn, Red Deer College Library, 100 College Blvd, Red Deer, AB, T4N 5H5, CANADA. Tel: 403-342-4855. p. 2551
Phillips-Bell, Allen, Dir, Pender County Public Library, 103 S Cowan St, Burgaw, NC, 28425. Tel: 910-259-0306. p. 1676
Philo, Thomas, Archivist, Cataloger, California State University Dominguez Hills, 1000 E Victoria St, Carson, CA, 90747. Tel: 310-243-3361. p. 129
Philp, Sandra, Coordr, Cabell County Public Library, Services for the Blind & Physically Handicapped, 455 Ninth St, 1st Flr, Huntington, WV, 25701. Tel: 304-528-5700, Ext 118. p. 2405
Philpot, Carlee, Libr Spec, Central New Mexico Community College Libraries, Rio Rancho Campus Library, 2601 Campus Blvd NE, Rm 112, Rio Rancho, NM, 87144. Tel: 505-224-4953. p. 1461
Philpot, Kecia, Br Mgr, Scenic Regional Library, Sullivan Branch, 525 Cumberland Way, Sullivan, MO, 63080. Tel: 573-468-4372. p. 1283
Philpotts, Joanna, Supvr, Center for Naval Analyses Library, 3003 Washington Blvd, Arlington, VA, 22201. Tel: 703-824-2111. p. 2305
Phinney, Alicia, Circ Serv Dir, Williamsburg Regional Library, 7770 Croaker Rd, Williamsburg, VA, 23188-7064. Tel: 757-741-3353. p. 2353
Phinney, Jason, Ref Librn, Jefferson County Library, Windsor, 7479 Metropolitian Blvd, Barnhart, MO, 63012. Tel: 636-461-1914. p. 1249
Phinney, John, Librn, Southern Methodist University, Institute for Study of Earth & Man Reading Room, N L Heroy Science Hall, Rm 129, 3225 Daniels Ave, Dallas, TX, 75275. Tel: 214-768-2430. p. 2168
Phinney, Scott, Head, Cat, University of South Carolina, 1322 Greene St, Columbia, SC, 29208-0103. Tel: 803-777-3142. p. 2055
Phipps, Desarae, Librn, Caprock Public Library, 106 N First, Quitaque, TX, 79255. Tel: 806-455-1225. p. 2230
Phipps, Heather, Human Res Coordr, Saline County Public Library, 1800 Smithers Dr, Benton, AR, 72015. Tel: 501-778-4766. p. 90
Pho, Annie, Head, Instruction & Outreach, University of San Francisco, 2130 Fulton St, San Francisco, CA, 94117-1080. Tel: 415-422-2759. p. 229
Phoenix, Colene, Asst Dir, Nassau Free Library, 18 Church St, Nassau, NY, 12123. Tel: 518-766-2715. p. 1575
Piacenti, Sue, Librn, Hazleton Area Public Library, McAdoo, Southside Branch, 15 Kelayres Rd, McAdoo, PA, 18237. Tel: 570-929-1120. p. 1943
Piacentini, Lynne, Instruction Librn, Ref Serv, University of Saint Joseph, 1678 Asylum Ave, West Hartford, CT, 06117-2791. Tel: 860-231-5751. p. 345
Piacun, Maria, Br Mgr, Jefferson Parish Library, Harahan Branch, 219 Soniat Ave, Harahan, LA, 70123. Tel: 504-736-8745. p. 897
Piantigini, Cathy, Dir, Somerville Public Library, 79 Highland Ave, Somerville, MA, 02143. Tel: 617-623-5000, Ext 2910. p. 1053
Piasecki, Sara, Archivist, Anchorage Museum, 625 C St, Anchorage, AK, 99501. Tel: 907-929-9235. p. 42
Piatt, Audrey, Br Librn, Wapiti Regional Library, St Brieux Public Library, 50 Third Ave, St. Brieux, SK, S0K 3V0, CANADA. Tel: 306-275-2133. p. 2746
Pic, Sara, Head, Pub Serv, Law Library of Louisiana, Louisiana Supreme Court, 2nd Flr, 400 Royal St, New Orleans, LA, 70130-2104. Tel: 504-310-2412. p. 901
Picard, Patrick, IT Tech, University of Sudbury Library, 935 Ramsey Lake Rd, Sudbury, ON, P3E 2C6, CANADA. Tel: 705-673-5661. p. 2683
Picato, Laura, Head, Circ & Adult Serv, O'Fallon Public Library, 120 Civic Plaza, O'Fallon, IL, 62269-2692. Tel: 618-632-3783. p. 629
Picazio, Steve, Head, Circ, Librn, Kellogg-Hubbard Library, 135 Main St, Montpelier, VT, 05602. Tel: 802-223-3338. p. 2289
Picazio, Steven, Librn, Vermont Historical Society, Vermont History Ctr, 60 Washington St, Barre, VT, 05641-4209. Tel: 802-479-8508. p. 2278
Picca, David, Librn, Miami Dade College, Kendall Campus Library, 11011 SW 104th St, Miami, FL, 33176-3393. Tel: 305-237-0996, 305-237-2015, 305-237-2291. p. 422
Piccini, Sarah, Asst Dir, Lackawanna Historical Society Library, 232 Monroe Ave, Scranton, PA, 18510. Tel: 570-344-3841. p. 2004
Piccininni, James, Dean of Libr, University of Saint Thomas, 3800 Montrose Blvd, Houston, TX, 77006. Tel: 713-525-2192. p. 2200
Pichardo, Dorothy, Mgr, Washington County Library, Sam Mitchell Public Library, 3731 Roche Ave, Vernon, FL, 32462. Tel: 850-535-1208. p. 388
Pichette, Julia, Metadata Serv, Palm Beach Atlantic University, 300 Pembroke Pl, West Palm Beach, FL, 33401-6503. Tel: 561-803-2225. p. 454
Pichette, Melissa, ILL Supvr, Pepperdine University Libraries, 24255 Pacific Coast Hwy, Malibu, CA, 90263. Tel: 310-506-4252. p. 171

Pichler, Susanne, Libr Dir, Andrew W Mellon Foundation, 140 E 62nd St, New York, NY, 10065. Tel: 212-838-8400. p. 1591
Pick, Peggy, Libr Dir, Maryville Community Library, Eight Schiber Ct, Maryville, IL, 62062. Tel: 618-288-3801. p. 614
Pickell, Barbara, Dir, Clearwater Public Library System, 100 N Osceola Ave, Clearwater, FL, 33755. Tel: 727-562-4970. p. 388
Pickens, Kathleen, Coll Develop, Instrul Serv Librn, Ref (Info Servs), Cincinnati State Technical & Community College, 3520 Central Pkwy, Rm 170, Cincinnati, OH, 45223-2690. Tel: 513-569-1611. p. 1760
Pickens, Sindee, Librn II/Youth Serv, Sch Serv, El Segundo Public Library, 111 W Mariposa Ave, El Segundo, CA, 90245. Tel: 310-524-2771. p. 140
Pickering, Bob, Interim Dean of Libr, University of Tulsa Libraries, 2933 E Sixth St, Tulsa, OK, 74104-3123. Tel: 918-631-2871. p. 1867
Pickering, Kathleen, Dir, Belen Public Library, 333 Becker Ave, Belen, NM, 87002. Tel: 505-966-2604. p. 1464
Pickering, Kelly, Librn, Frenchtown Free Public Library, 29 Second St, Frenchtown, NJ, 08825. Tel: 908-996-4788. p. 1404
Pickering, Richard, Dep Dir, Plimoth Plantation, 137 Warren Ave, Plymouth, MA, 02360. Tel: 508-746-1622, Ext 8379. p. 1047
Pickett, Ashley, Ref Librn, Roswell P Flower Memorial Library, 229 Washington St, Watertown, NY, 13601-3388. Tel: 315-785-7714. p. 1659
Pickett, Jennifer, Ref Librn, Brooks Free Library, 739 Main St, Harwich, MA, 02645. Tel: 508-430-7562. p. 1023
Pickett, Keith, Coordr, Res Serv, Tulane University, Rudolph Matas Library of the Health Sciences, Tulane Health Sciences Campus, 1430 Tulane Ave, SL-86, New Orleans, LA, 70112-2699. Tel: 504-988-2406. p. 904
Pickett, Kelly, Asst Librn, Ohio Legislative Service Commission Library, 77 S High St, 9th Flr, Columbus, OH, 43215-6136. Tel: 614-466-2242. p. 1774
Pickett, Kenny, Assoc Dir, Classroom Tech & Media Services, Yeshiva University Libraries, Dr Lillian & Dr Rebecca Chutick Law Library, Benjamin N Cardozo School of Law, 55 Fifth Ave, New York, NY, 10003-4301. Tel: 212-790-0223. p. 1604
Pickett, Lisa, Mgr, Ouachita County Libraries, 405 Cash Rd SW, Camden, AR, 71701-3735. Tel: 870-836-5083. p. 92
Pickett, Lorri, Cataloging & Processing Supvr, McDaniel College, 2 College Hill, Westminster, MD, 21157-4390. Tel: 410-857-2789. p. 981
Picklesimer, Olivia, Mgr, Cabell County Public Library, West Huntington, 901 W 14th St, Huntington, WV, 25704. Tel: 304-528-5697. p. 2405
Pickthon, Barbara, Interim Asst Dir, Cameron University Library, 2800 W Gore Blvd, Lawton, OK, 73505-6377. Tel: 580-581-2855. p. 1851
Pickup McMullin, Kate, Asst Dir, Southwest Harbor Public Library, 338 Main St, Southwest Harbor, ME, 04679. Tel: 207-244-7065. p. 942
Picollo, Rio, Electronic Resources & Assessment Librn, University Canada West, 1461 Granville St, Vancouver, BC, V6Z 0E5, CANADA. p. 2580
Picone, Allison, Circ Asst, Grafton Public Library, 35 Grafton Common, Grafton, MA, 01519. Tel: 508-839-4649. p. 1021
Picone, Deborah, Librn, American Academy of Dramatic Arts, 120 Madison Ave, New York, NY, 10016. Tel: 212-686-9244, Ext 337. p. 1578
Piech, Allison, Head, Youth Serv, Hammond Public Library, 564 State St, Hammond, IN, 46320-1532. Tel: 219-931-5100, Ext 330. p. 689
Piechowski, Bernice, Libr Dir, Browns Valley Public Library, 15 S Third St, Browns Valley, MN, 56219. Tel: 320-695-2318. p. 1167
Piehler, Heide, Ch Serv, Shorewood Public Library, 3920 N Murray Ave, Shorewood, WI, 53211-2385. Tel: 414-847-2670. p. 2477
Piekarski, Cory, Dir, Westport Library Association, Six Harris Lane, Westport, NY, 12993. Tel: 518-962-8219. p. 1664
Piekielek, Nathan, Librn, Pennsylvania State University Libraries, Donald W Hamer Center for Maps & Geospatial Information, One Central Pattee Library, Lower Level, University Park, PA, 16802-1807. Tel: 814-865-3703. p. 2015
Piel, Sue, Libr Dir, Woodbury Public Library, 269 Main St S, Woodbury, CT, 06798. Tel: 203-263-3502. p. 349
Pienkowski, Kathy, Operations Mgr, Citizens Library, 55 S College St, Washington, PA, 15301. Tel: 724-222-2400. p. 2018
Pieper, Scott, Assoc Dept Head, Georgia State University, Decatur Campus, 3251 Panthersville Rd, Decatur, GA, 30034. Tel: 678-891-2587. p. 464
Piepho, Kristin, Libr Mgr, Sno-Isle Libraries, Mountlake Terrace Library, 23300 58th Ave W, Mountlake Terrace, WA, 98043-4630. Tel: 425-776-8722. p. 2371
Pierce, Alison, Circ Librn, Brownell Library, Six Lincoln St, Essex Junction, VT, 05452-3154. Tel: 802-878-6955. p. 2284
Pierce, Amy, Vols Serv Coordr, Nashville Public Library, 615 Church St, Nashville, TN, 37219-2314. Tel: 615-862-5769. p. 2119
Pierce, Andrew, Supvr, Circ, Gaston County Public Library, 1555 E Garrison Blvd, Gastonia, NC, 28054. Tel: 704-868-2164. p. 1690
Pierce, Bryan, Dr, Archivist, Digital Serv Librn, Philander Smith College, 900 Daisy Bates Dr, Little Rock, AR, 72202. Tel: 501-370-5263. p. 101
Pierce, Diane, Head, Circ Serv, Brighton District Library, 100 Library Dr, Brighton, MI, 48116. Tel: 810-229-6571, Ext 216. p. 1087
Pierce, Donna, Libr Dir, Krum Public Library, 815 E McCart St, Krum, TX, 76249-6823. Tel: 940-482-3455. p. 2207
Pierce, Erin, Libr Dir, C C Mellor Memorial Library, One Pennwood Ave, Edgewood, PA, 15218-1627. Tel: 412-731-0909. p. 1929
Pierce, Glen, Archivist, Messiah University, One University Ave, Ste 3002, Mechanicsburg, PA, 17055. Tel: 717-691-6006, Ext 6048. p. 1960
Pierce, Glen A, Dir, Messiah University, Brethren in Christ Historical Library & Archives, One College Ave, Mechanicsburg, PA, 17055. Tel: 717-691-6048. p. 1960
Pierce, Jeannette, Assoc Dir, Res & Info Serv, University of Missouri-Columbia, Elmer Ellis Library, 104 Ellis Library, Columbia, MO, 65201-5149. Tel: 573-882-4701. p. 1243
Pierce, Jennifer, Dir, Libr & Acad Info Serv, Salem Community College Library, Donaghay Hall, Rm DON 111, 460 Hollywood Ave, Carneys Point, NJ, 08069. Tel: 856-351-2681. p. 1395
Pierce, Jennifer Burek, Dr, Interim Dir, University of Iowa, 3087 Main Library, 125 W Washington St, Iowa City, IA, 52242-1420. Tel: 319-335-5707. p. 2785
Pierce, Karen, Dir, Henderson Memorial Public Library Association, 54 E Jefferson St, Jefferson, OH, 44047-1198. Tel: 440-576-3761. p. 1792
Pierce, Karen, Dir, Erie County Public Library, 160 E Front St, Erie, PA, 16507. Tel: 814-451-6900. p. 1931
Pierce, Karen, Dir & Librn, Slippery Rock Community Library, 465 N Main St, Slippery Rock, PA, 16057. Tel: 724-738-9179. p. 2007
Pierce, Kellie, Mgr, McGrath Community Library, 12 Chinana Ave, McGrath, AK, 99627. Tel: 907-524-3843. p. 49
Pierce, Kirsten, Dir, Swaney Memorial Library, 210 S Court St, New Cumberland, WV, 26047. Tel: 304-564-3471. p. 2410
Pierce, LeeAnn, Br Mgr, Jackson County Library Services, Butte Falls Branch, 626 Fir Ave, Butte Falls, OR, 97522. Tel: 541-865-3511. p. 1886
Pierce, LeeAnn, Br Mgr, Jackson County Library Services, Prospect Branch, 150 Mill Creek Dr, Prospect, OR, 97536. Tel: 541-560-3668. p. 1886
Pierce, Lora, Dir, Akron Public Library, 350 Reed St, Akron, IA, 51001. Tel: 712-568-2601. p. 729
Pierce, Lori, Children's Serv Coordr, Youth Serv Coordr, Meaford Public Library, 11 Sykes St N, Meaford, ON, N4L 1V6, CANADA. Tel: 519-538-3500. p. 2657
Pierce, Melissa, Circ Supvr, Libr Tech, Pennsylvania Western University - Clarion, 840 Wood St, Clarion, PA, 16214. Tel: 814-393-2304. p. 1922
Pierce, Michael, Principal Librn, Pasadena Public Library, 285 E Walnut St, Pasadena, CA, 91101. Tel: 626-744-4066. p. 194
Pierce, Pat, Head, Children's Servx, Lucy Robbins Welles Library, 95 Cedar St, Newington, CT, 06111. Tel: 860-665-8783. p. 330
Pierce, Patricia, Dr, Librn, Georgia Department of Corrections, Office of Library Services, 27823 Main St, Morgan, GA, 39866. Tel: 229-849-5000, Ext 5058. p. 491
Pierce, Shawn, Pub Serv Coordr, Arkansas Supreme Court Library, 625 Marshall St, Ste 1500, Little Rock, AR, 72201. Tel: 501-682-2147. p. 101
Pierce, Susan, ILL Librn, Brownell Library, Six Lincoln St, Essex Junction, VT, 05452-3154. Tel: 802-878-6955. p. 2284
Pierce, Valerie, Libr Mgr, Wake County Public Library System, Wake Forest Community Library, 400 E Holding Ave, Wake Forest, NC, 27587. Tel: 919-554-8498. p. 1711
Pierce, Virginia, Ref & Instruction Librn, Francis Marion University, 4822 E Palmetto St, Florence, SC, 29506. Tel: 843-661-1302. p. 2059
Pierce, Yvette, Media Spec, Florence-Darlington Technical College Libraries, Segars Library, Health Sciences Campus, 320 W Cheves St, Florence, SC, 29501. Tel: 843-676-8575. p. 2059
Pierceall, Tracy, Librn II, Illinois State Museum Library, 1011 East Ash, Springfield, IL, 62703. Tel: 217-524-0496. p. 650
Pierceall, Tracy, Librn II, Illinois State Museum Library, Research & Collections Ctr, 1011 E Ash St, Springfield, IL, 62703. Tel: 217-524-0496. p. 650
Piermarini, Nicole, Asst Dir, Leominster Public Library, 30 West St, Leominster, MA, 01453. Tel: 978-534-7522, Ext 3507. p. 1028
Piermarini, Nicole, YA Librn, Lunenburg Public Library, 1023 Massachusetts Ave, Lunenburg, MA, 01462. Tel: 978-582-4140. p. 1030
Pierpoint, Christine, Br Mgr, Tuscarawas County Public Library, Sugarcreek Branch, 120 S Broadway, Sugarcreek, OH, 44681. Tel: 330-852-2813. p. 1807
Pierpont, Lucy C, Marketing & Special Events Dir, Kent Library Association, 32 N Main St, Kent, CT, 06757. Tel: 860-927-3761. p. 319
Pierre, Jodi, Res & Instruction Librn, University of Wisconsin-Green Bay, 2420 Nicolet Dr, Green Bay, WI, 54311-7001. p. 2439
Pierre, Vivica Smith, PhD, Dir, Libr & Learning Commons, Bunker Hill Community College, E Bldg, 3rd Flr, Rm E300, 250 New Rutherford Ave, Boston, MA, 02129-2925. Tel: 617-228-3240. p. 994
Pierre-Louis, Jemmy, Mgr, Miami-Dade Public Library System, Model City Branch, 2211 NW 54th St, Miami, FL, 33142. Tel: 305-636-2233. p. 423
Pierrot, Lennora, Archit Librn, Tuskegee University, 1200 W Old Mongtomery Rd, Ford Motor Company Library, Tuskegee, AL, 36088. Tel: 334-727-4572. p. 38
Piers-Gamble, Dawne, Libr Dir, Russell Public Library, 162 Main St, Russell, MA, 01071. Tel: 413-862-6221. p. 1050
Pierschalla, Linda, Dir, Cedarburg Public Library, W63 N589 Hanover Ave, Cedarburg, WI, 53012. Tel: 262-375-7640, Ext 202. p. 2427

Pierson, Alice, Asst Br Mgr, Johnson County Library, Cedar Roe, 5120 Cedar St, Roeland Park, KS, 66205. p. 830
Pierson, Alice, Asst Br Mgr, Johnson County Library, Shawnee Branch, 13811 Johnson Dr, Shawnee, KS, 66216. p. 830
Pierson, Bonnie, Libr Dir, Bastrop Public Library, 1100 Church St, Bastrop, TX, 78602. Tel: 512-332-8880. p. 2144
Pierson, Ivy, Dir, Nigel Sprouse Memorial Library, 102 E Kimball, Callaway, NE, 68825. Tel: 308-836-2610. p. 1309
Pierson, Jessica, Managing Dir, Linden Municipal Library, 215 First St SE, Linden, AB, T0M 1J0, CANADA. Tel: 403-546-3757. p. 2546
Pierson, Leif, Re/Ser Librn, Tyler Junior College, 1327 S Baxter St, Tyler, TX, 75701. Tel: 903-510-2502, 903-510-2503. p. 2250
Pierson, Margo, Asst Libr Dir, Sci/Eng Librn, Tech Serv & Syst Librn, Southern Arkansas University, 100 E University, Magnolia, AR, 71753-5000. Tel: 870-235-4177. p. 103
Pierson, Mike, Br Mgr, Pioneer Library System, Norman Public Library West, 300 Norman Ctr Court, Norman, OK, 73069. Tel: 405-701-2645, Ext 588. p. 1855
Pierson, Patricia, Librn, University of Montana Helena, 1115 N Roberts St, Helena, MT, 59601. Tel: 406-447-6370. p. 1297
Pierson, Sami, Dir, Coos Bay Public Library, 525 Anderson Ave, Coos Bay, OR, 97420-1678. Tel: 541-269-1101. p. 1876
Pierson, Terri, Librn, Arcadia Township Library, 100 S Reynolds, Arcadia, NE, 68815. Tel: 308-789-6346. p. 1305
Piertsma, Eleanor, Libr Support Serv Asst, Stormont, Dundas & Glengarry County Library, Iroquois Branch, One Dundas St & Elizabeth St, Iroquois, ON, K0E 1K0, CANADA. Tel: 613-652-4377. p. 2638
Pieterss, Rachel, Admin Librn, Rowan College at Burlington County Library, 900 College Circle, Mount Laurel, NJ, 08054-5308. Tel: 856-894-9311, Ext 2100. p. 1422
Pietila, Lyn, Asst Dir, Edward U Demmer Memorial Library, 6961 W School St, Three Lakes, WI, 54562. Tel: 715-546-3391. p. 2481
Pietras, Angela, Dir, Barbara S Ponce Public Library, 7770 52nd St, Pinellas Park, FL, 33781. Tel: 727-369-0590. p. 437
Pietraszewski, Pete, Bus Librn, Hesburgh Libraries, Thomas Mahaffey Jr Business Library, L001 Mendoza College of Business, Notre Dame, IN, 46556. Tel: 574-631-9099. p. 711
Pietrobono, Judy, Asst Dir, South Brunswick Public Library, 110 Kingston Lane, Monmouth Junction, NJ, 08852. Tel: 732-329-4000, Ext 7351. p. 1419
Pietsch, Karen, Mgr, Omaha Public Library, Benson Branch, 6015 Binney St, Omaha, NE, 68104-3498. Tel: 402-444-4846. p. 1329
Pifer, Elizabeth, Br Tech, Monroe County Library System, Blue Bush Branch Library, 2210 Blue Bush Rd, Monroe, MI, 48162-9643. Tel: 734-242-4085. p. 1133
Pifer, Jill, Dir, Fairview Heights Public Library, 10017 Bunkum Rd, Fairview Heights, IL, 62208-1703. Tel: 618-489-2070. p. 588
Pifher, Karen, Br Mgr, Somerset County Library System of New Jersey, Hillsborough Public, Hillsborough Municipal Complex, 379 S Branch Rd, Hillsborough, NJ, 08844. Tel: 908-458-8420. p. 1392
Pigeon, Darla, Dir, Aldrich Free Public Library, 299 Main St, Moosup, CT, 06354. Tel: 860-564-8760. p. 323
Pike, Angela, Dir, Sebewaing Township Library, 41 N Center St, Sebewaing, MI, 48759-1406. Tel: 989-883-3520. p. 1150
Pike, Ashley, Patron Serv Mgr, Frank L Weyenberg Library of Mequon-Thiensville, 11345 N Cedarburg Rd, Mequon, WI, 53092-1998. Tel: 262-242-2593. p. 2456
Pike, George H, Dir, Northwestern University Libraries, Pritzker Legal Research Center, 375 E Chicago Ave, Chicago, IL, 60611. Tel: 312-503-0295. p. 587
Pike, Jeffrey, Ref, Syst Tech, Groton Public Library, 99 Main St, Groton, MA, 01450. Tel: 978-448-8000, Ext 1316. p. 1022
Pike, Jordan, Librn, Eastern Health, St Claire's Mercy Hospital Library, 154 Le Marchant Rd, St. John's, NL, A1C 5B8, CANADA. Tel: 709-777-5414. p. 2610
Pike, June, Br Mgr, Galax-Carroll Regional Library, Carroll County Public, 101 Beaver Dam Rd, Hillsville, VA, 24343. Tel: 276-728-2228, 276-728-3334. p. 2321
Pike, Katy, Mgr, Libraries of Stevens County, Hunters Branch, 5014 Columbia River Rd, Bldg No 11, Hunters, WA, 99157. Tel: 509-722-3877. p. 2369
Pike, Katy, Mgr, Libraries of Stevens County, Kettle Falls Branch, 605 Meyers St, Kettle Falls, WA, 99141. Tel: 509-738-6817. p. 2369
Pike, Katy, Mgr, Libraries of Stevens County, Northport Community Library, 521 Center Ave, Northport, WA, 99157. Tel: 509-732-8928. p. 2369
Pike, Katy, Mgr, Libraries of Stevens County, Onion Creek Library Station, 2191 Clugston-Onion Creek Rd, Colville, WA, 99114. Tel: 509-738-6817. p. 2370
Pike, Lisa, Librn, Mat, Manitowoc Public Library, 707 Quay St, Manitowoc, WI, 54220. Tel: 920-686-3000. p. 2453
Pike, Nancy, Asst Librn, Canaan Town Library, 1173 US Rte 4, Canaan, NH, 03741. Tel: 603-523-9650. p. 1356
Pike, Roberta A, Cat, Kingsborough Community College, 2001 Oriental Blvd, Brooklyn, NY, 11235. Tel: 718-368-5639. p. 1504
Pikora, Joel, Mgr, Digital Assets, Tri-Township Public Library District, 209 S Main St, Troy, IL, 62294. Tel: 618-667-2133. p. 654
Pikramenos, Tony, Librn, Reading Public Library, 717 Vermont Rte 106, Reading, VT, 05062. Tel: 802-484-5588. p. 2293
Pilatich, Barbara, Libr Serv Librn, Media Serv Librn, Columbia-Greene Community College Library, 4400 Rte 23, Hudson, NY, 12534. Tel: 518-828-4181, Ext 3286. p. 1549
Pilcher, David, Dir, Mississippi Department of Archives & History, William F Winter Archives & History Bldg, 200 North St, Jackson, MS, 39201. Tel: 601-576-6991. p. 1222
Pilcher, Heather, Spec Coll Coordr, University of Louisiana at Monroe Library, 700 University Ave, Monroe, LA, 71209-0720. Tel: 318-342-1054. p. 899
Pilger, Barbara, Br Mgr, Starke County Public Library System, Hamlet Branch, Six N Starke St, Hamlet, IN, 46532. Tel: 574-867-6033. p. 699
Pilkington, Angela, Children's Serv Coordr, Iowa City Public Library, 123 S Linn St, Iowa City, IA, 52240. Tel: 319-887-6019. p. 760
Pilla, Amie, Dir, Berthoud Public Library, 236 Welch Ave, Berthoud, CO, 80513. Tel: 970-532-2757. p. 266
Pilla, Linda, Dir, George H & Ella M Rodgers Memorial Library, 194 Derry Rd, Hudson, NH, 03051. Tel: 603-886-6030. p. 1368
Pillard, Mallory, Br Mgr, High Plains Library District, Centennial Park Library, 2227 23rd Ave, Greeley, CO, 80634-6632. p. 285
Pillatzki, Kathy, Dir, Henry County Public Library System, 1001 Florence McGarity Blvd, McDonough, GA, 30252. Tel: 678-432-5353. p. 490
Piller, Michael, Dir, Acad Tech, American University Library, 4400 Massachusetts Ave NW, Washington, DC, 20016-8046. Tel: 202-885-3228. p. 361
Pillon, Karen, Assoc Univ Librn, University of Windsor, 401 Sunset Ave, Windsor, ON, N9B 3P4, CANADA. Tel: 519-253-3000, Ext 3201. p. 2704
Pillow, Lisa, Head, Loan Services, Carleton College, One N College St, Northfield, MN, 55057-4097. Tel: 507-222-5447. p. 1191
Pilmanis, Aldona, Head, Youth Serv, The Nyack Library, 59 S Broadway, Nyack, NY, 10960. Tel: 845-358-3370, Ext 231. p. 1609
Piloiu, Rares, Info Literacy Librn, Otterbein University, 138 W Main St, Westerville, OH, 43081. Tel: 614-823-1314. p. 1830
Pilon, Isabelle, Chef de Div, Bibliotheques de Montreal, Ahuntsic, 10300 rue Lajeunesse, Montreal, QC, H3L 2E5, CANADA. Tel: 514 872-0850. p. 2718
Pilon, Isabelle, Chef de Div, Bibliotheques de Montreal, Cartierville, 5900 rue De Salaberry, Montreal, QC, H4J 1J8, CANADA. Tel: 514-872-0850. p. 2718
Pilon, Isabelle, Chef de Div, Bibliotheques de Montreal, De Salaberry, 4170 rue De Salaberry, Montreal, QC, H4J 1H1, CANADA. Tel: 514-872-0850. p. 2718
Pilon, Isabelle, Dir, Libr Network, Centre d'acces a l'information juridique/Legal Informatin Access Center, 480 Saint-Laurent, Bur 503, Montreal, QC, H2Y 3Y7, CANADA. Tel: 514-844-2245. p. 2721
Pilon, Steven, Assoc Librn, Christendom College, 263 St Johns Way, Front Royal, VA, 22630. Tel: 540-551-9194. p. 2320
Pilsing, Margaret, Librn, Dunklin County Library, Clarkton Branch, 113 S Main St, Clarkton, MO, 63837. Tel: 573-448-3803. p. 1258
Pilston, Anna, Librn, Spartanburg County Public Libraries, Landrum Library, 111 E Asbury Dr, Landrum, SC, 29356. Tel: 864-457-2218. p. 2070
Pinc, Amy, Dir, Libr Syst & Tech Serv, Triton College Library, Bldg A, Rm 200, 2000 Fifth Ave, River Grove, IL, 60171. Tel: 708-456-0300, Ext 3215. p. 639
Pinder, Garrett, Libr Dir, Kent Memorial Library, 50 N Main St, Suffield, CT, 06078-2117. Tel: 860-668-3896. p. 341
Pinder, Liz, Br Mgr, Free Library of Philadelphia, David Cohen Ogontz Library, 6017 Ogontz Ave, Philadelphia, PA, 19141. Tel: 215-685-3566. p. 1979
Pineau, Jill, Librn, Vancouver Holocaust Education Centre, 50-950 W 41st Ave, Vancouver, BC, V5Z 2N7, CANADA. Tel: 604-264-0499. p. 2581
Pineau, Priscilla, Ch, Jay-Niles Memorial Library, 983 Main St, North Jay, ME, 04262. Tel: 207-645-4062. p. 933
Pineda, Shalyn, Regional Librn, Kern County Library, 701 Truxtun Ave, Bakersfield, CA, 93301. Tel: 661-868-0700. p. 119
Pineda, Shalyn, Regional Supvr, Kern County Library, McFarland Branch, 500 W Kern Ave, McFarland, CA, 93250-1355. Tel: 661-792-2318. p. 120
Pineda, Tracey, Librn, South Plains College Library, 1401 S College Ave - Box E, Levelland, TX, 79336. Tel: 806-716-4694. p. 2211
Ping, Jin, Acq/Ser Librn, Indiana University of Pennsylvania, 431 S 11th St, Rm 203, Indiana, PA, 15705-1096. Tel: 724-357-2330. p. 1946
Pinger, Judith, Asst Libr Dir, Info Tech, Milwaukee Public Library, 814 W Wisconsin Ave, Milwaukee, WI, 53233-2309. Tel: 414-286-3000. p. 2459
Pingle, Peggy, Br Mgr, Perry County District Library, Corning Branch, 113 11th Hill St, Corning, OH, 43730. Tel: 740-347-4763. p. 1806
Pingolt, Darlene, Asst Dir, East Alton Public Library District, 250 Washington Ave, East Alton, IL, 62024-1547. Tel: 618-259-0787. p. 580
Pini, Paula, Ref Serv, Manchester Community College Library, Great Path, Manchester, CT, 06040. Tel: 860-512-2877. p. 320
Pinilla, Lynn, Dep Dir, Libr Serv, Clay County Public Library System, 1895 Town Center Blvd, Fleming Island, FL, 32003. Tel: 904-278-3720. p. 396

Pinkard, Courtney, Head, Res Serv, Alabama Department of Archives & History Research Room, 624 Washington Ave, Montgomery, AL, 36130. Tel: 334-353-9272. p. 27
Pinkard, James, Dir, Covington County Library System, 403 S Fir Ave, Collins, MS, 39428. Tel: 601-765-4612. p. 1214
Pinkerton, Kristen, Ref Librn, College of Physicians of Philadelphia, 19 S 22nd St, Philadelphia, PA, 19103. Tel: 215-399-2301. p. 1975
Pinkerton, Lois, Asst Librn, Quimby Public Library, 120 N Main, Quimby, IA, 51049. Tel: 712-445-2413. p. 778
Pinkner, Kerry, Commun Engagement Mgr, Waukesha Public Library, 321 Wisconsin Ave, Waukesha, WI, 53186-4713. Tel: 262-524-3692. p. 2484
Pinkston, Jerry, IT Dir, New Orleans Public Library, 219 Loyola Ave, New Orleans, LA, 70112-2044. Tel: 504-529-7323, 504-596-2570. p. 902
Pinnell, Julie, Univ Librn, Nebraska Wesleyan University, 5000 St Paul Ave, Lincoln, NE, 68504. Tel: 402-465-2405. p. 1322
Pinney, Tom, Jr, Pres, Northeast Wisconsin Masonic Library & Museum, 1950 Bond St, Green Bay, WI, 54303. Tel: 920-493-3727. p. 2439
Pinney-Benjamin, Arlene, Actg Dir, Elaine Ione Sprauve Library, Enighed Estate, Cruz Bay, Saint John, VI, 00831. Tel: 340-776-6359. p. 2517
Pinnick, Denise J, Dr, Dir, Libr Serv, Oakland City University, 605 W Columbia St, Oakland City, IN, 47660. Tel: 812-749-1267. p. 712
Pinnick, Maggie, Tech Serv Mgr, Frankfort Community Public Library, 208 W Clinton St, Frankfort, IN, 46041. Tel: 765-654-8746. p. 685
Pinnix, Laura, Tech Proc Mgr, Chillicothe & Ross County Public Library, 140 S Paint St, Chillicothe, OH, 45601. Tel: 740-702-4145. p. 1758
Pino, Janine, Cat Librn, Pellissippi State Community College, Hardin Valley Library, 10915 Harding Valley Rd, Knoxville, TN, 37933. Tel: 865-694-6621. p. 2106
Pino, Ricardo, Dir, Wayne Public Library, 461 Valley Rd, Wayne, NJ, 07470. Tel: 973-694-4272, Ext 5101. p. 1451
Pinshower, Jason, Exec Dir, Barrington Area Library, 505 N Northwest Hwy, Barrington, IL, 60010. Tel: 847-382-1300. p. 539
Pinshower, Jason, Head, Adult Serv, Barrington Area Library, 505 N Northwest Hwy, Barrington, IL, 60010. Tel: 847-382-1300. p. 539
Pinskey, Nicole, Coll Coordr, Tech Innovation Librn, Saint Clair County Library System, 210 McMorran Blvd, Port Huron, MI, 48060-4098. Tel: 810-987-7323. p. 1142
Pinsonat, Rhonda, Bus Mgr, East Baton Rouge Parish Library, 7711 Goodwood Blvd, Baton Rouge, LA, 70806-7625. Tel: 225-231-3705. p. 882
Pintado, Vanessa, Asst Curator, Hispanic Society of America Library, 613 W 155th St, New York, NY, 10032. Tel: 212-926-2234, Ext 229. p. 1587
Pintar, Judith, Teaching Prof, University of Illinois at Urbana-Champaign, Library & Information Science Bldg, 501 E Daniel St, Champaign, IL, 61820-6211. Tel: 217-333-3280. p. 2784
Pintcke, Kathleen, Librn, Mancelona Township Library, 202 W State St, Mancelona, MI, 49659. Tel: 231-587-9451. p. 1128
Pinto, Holly, Dir, Knowledge & Res Serv, Holland & Hart, 555 17th St, Ste 3200, Denver, CO, 80201-3950. Tel: 303-295-8485. p. 276
Pinto, Mark, Dir, Adult Serv, Ref Librn, Phoenixville Public Library, 183 Second Ave, Phoenixville, PA, 19460-3420. Tel: 610-933-3013, Ext 132. p. 1989
Pinto, Usha, Commun Libr Mgr, Queens Library, Maspeth Community Library, 69-70 Grand Ave, Maspeth, NY, 11378. Tel: 718-639-5228. p. 1555
Piorun, Mary, Dir, University of Massachusetts Medical School, 55 Lake Ave N, Worcester, MA, 01655-0002. p. 1072
Piorun, Mary, Dir, National Network of Libraries of Medicine Region 7, Univ of Massachusetts Chan Med Sch, Lamar Soutter Libr, 55 Lake Ave N, Rm S4-241, Worcester, MA, 01655. Tel: 508-856-2206. p. 2767
Piorunski, Michael, Librn, Friedenwald-Romano Library, Johns Hopkins Hospital, Woods Res Bldg, 600 N Wolfe St, Rm 3B-50, Baltimore, MD, 21287-9105. Tel: 410-955-3127. p. 953
Piotrow, Meredith, Ch, Jackson Public Library, 125 Main St, Jackson, NH, 03846. Tel: 603-383-9731. p. 1369
Piotrowicz, Lynn, Dir, Tucker Free Library, 31 Western Ave, Henniker, NH, 03242. Tel: 603-428-3471. p. 1367
Piotrowski, Pattie, Dean, Libr Instrul Serv, Univ Librn, University of Illinois at Springfield, One University Plaza, MS BRK-140, Springfield, IL, 62703-5407. Tel: 217-206-6597. p. 651
Piper, Claudia, Br Mgr, Orange County Library System, Washington Park Branch, 5151 Raleigh St, Ste A, Orlando, FL, 32811. p. 431
Piper, Jessica, Br Mgr, Nashville Public Library, Madison Branch, 610 Gallatin Pike S, Madison, TN, 37115. Tel: 615-862-5868. p. 2120
Piperno-Jones, Carla, Librn, Springport Free Library, 171 Cayuga St, Union Springs, NY, 13160. Tel: 315-889-7766. p. 1654
Pipes, Robert, Tech Serv Coordr, Mount San Jacinto College, 300 Bldg, 1499 N State St, San Jacinto, CA, 92583-2399. Tel: 951-487-3453. p. 230
Pipins, Charles, Research Librn, University of Maryland, Baltimore, Thurgood Marshall Law Library, 501 W Fayette St, Baltimore, MD, 21201-1768. Tel: 410-706-9784. p. 957
Pipins, Charles, Pres, Southeastern Chapter of the American Association of Law Libraries, c/o University of Baltimore School of Law, 1420 N Charles St, Baltimore, MD, 21201. Tel: 410-837-4373. p. 2766
Pipins, Charles A, II, Dir, Law Libr, University of Baltimore, Law Library, Angelos Law Center, 7th thru 12th Flrs, 1401 N Charles St, Baltimore, MD, 21201. Tel: 410-837-4373. p. 957
Pippin, Donald, Dir, Philo Public Library District, 115 E Washington St, Philo, IL, 61864. Tel: 217-684-2896. p. 635
Pippin, Johnnie, Libr Dir, Sampson-Clinton Public Library, 217 Graham St, Clinton, NC, 28328. Tel: 910-592-4153. p. 1681
Pippitt, Amanda, Libr Dir, Millikin University, 1184 W Main St, Decatur, IL, 62522. Tel: 217-424-3957. p. 576
Piquet, Jeanette, Libr Dir, Richmond Heights Memorial Library, 8001 Dale Ave, Richmond Heights, MO, 63117. Tel: 314-645-6202. p. 1267
Piraneo, Carl, Mem Serv Coordr, Partnership for Academic Library Collaborative & Innovation, 1005 Pontiac Rd, Ste 330, Drexel Hill, PA, 19026. Tel: 215-567-1755. p. 2774
Pirillo, Joe, Distance Learning Librn, Info Literacy, University of Wisconsin Oshkosh, 801 Elmwood Ave, Oshkosh, WI, 54901. Tel: 920-424-7332. p. 2467
Piroli, Vivienne, Libr Dir, Simmons University, 300 The Fenway, Boston, MA, 02115-5898. Tel: 617-521-2752. p. 999
Pirtle, Jeff, Dir, Baylor University Libraries, Texas Collection & University Archives, 1429 S Fifth St, Waco, TX, 76706. Tel: 254-710-1268. p. 2253
Pisano, Concetta, Coll Develop, Carroll County Public Library, 1100 Green Valley Rd, New Windsor, MD, 21776. Tel: 410-386-4500. p. 971
Pisarski, Alyssa, Asst Dir, North Shore Library, 6800 N Port Washington Rd, Glendale, WI, 53217. Tel: 414-351-3461. p. 2437
Pisciotta, Henry, Archit/Art Librn, Pennsylvania State University Libraries, George & Sherry Middlemas Arts & Humanities Library, Pennsylvania State University, W 337 Pattee Library, University Park, PA, 16802-1801. Tel: 814-865-6778. p. 2016
Piscitelli, Felicia, Rare Bk Cataloger, Texas A&M University Libraries, Cushing Memorial Library & Archives, 400 Spencer St, College Station, TX, 77843. Tel: 979-845-1951. p. 2157
Pisha, Louis, ILL Librn, Long Island University Post, 720 Northern Blvd, Brookville, NY, 11548. Tel: 516-299-4143. p. 1507
Pisklak, Georgia, Electronic Serv, Midland College, 3600 N Garfield, Midland, TX, 79705. Tel: 432-685-4703. p. 2219
Pitcher, Ellen, Head, Ref, Starke County Public Library System, 152 W Culver Rd, Knox, IN, 46534-2220. Tel: 574-772-7323. p. 699
Pitcher, Karen, Health Sci Ref Librn, SUNY Broome Community College, 907 Front St, Binghamton, NY, 13905-1328. Tel: 607-778-5468. p. 1494
Pitchford, Veronda, Asst Dir, Califa, 330 Townsend St, Ste 133, San Francisco, CA, 94107. Tel: 888-239-2289. p. 2761
Pitchon, Cindy A, Dir, Libr Serv, Health Sciences Libraries Consortium, 3600 Market St, Ste 550, Philadelphia, PA, 19104-2646. Tel: 215-222-1532. p. 2774
Piticco, Stacey, Libr Support Serv Asst, Stormont, Dundas & Glengarry County Library, Morrisburg Branch, 34 Ottawa St, Morrisburg, ON, K0C 1X0, CANADA. Tel: 613-543-3384. p. 2638
Pitkin, Lisa, Head, Cat & Coll, Guilderland Public Library, 2228 Western Ave, Guilderland, NY, 12084. Tel: 518-456-2400, Ext 118. p. 1542
Pitko, Mike, Pres, Greenwood County Historical Society Library, 120 W Fourth St, Eureka, KS, 67045-1445. Tel: 316-583-6682. p. 807
Pitsch, Madeleine, Librn, Blackhawk Technical College Library, 6004 S County Rd G, Janesville, WI, 53547. Tel: 608-757-7705. p. 2443
Pitt, Jaime, Cat Librn, Tech Serv, Indiana Wesleyan University, 4201 S Washington St, Marion, IN, 46953. Tel: 765-677-2445. p. 704
Pittam, Joyce, Librn, Woolworth Community Library, 100 E Utah Ave, Jal, NM, 88252. Tel: 505-395-3268. p. 1470
Pittenger, Hilary, Curator of Coll, White River Valley Museum Research Library, 918 H St SE, Auburn, WA, 98002. Tel: 253-288-7438. p. 2358
Pitterman, Michael, Br Mgr, El Paso Public Library, Jose Cisneros Cielo Vista, 1300 Hawkins Blvd, El Paso, TX, 79907-6803. Tel: 915-212-0450. p. 2174
Pittman, Betsy, Univ Archivist, University of Connecticut, 369 Fairfield Rd, Storrs, CT, 06269-1005. p. 339
Pittman, Betsy, Univ Archivist, University of Connecticut, Archives & Special Collections, 405 Babbidge Rd, Unit 1205, Storrs, CT, 06269-1205. Tel: 860-486-4507. p. 340
Pittman, Donna, Dir, Champaign Public Library, 200 W Green St, Champaign, IL, 61820-5193. Tel: 217-403-2000. p. 551
Pittman, Kristyn, Fac Librn, Austin Community College, Round Rock Campus Library, 4400 College Park Dr, Round Rock, TX, 78665. Tel: 512-223-0119. p. 2138
Pittman, Mary Jane, Campus Librn, Nova Scotia Community College, Lunenburg Campus Library, 75 High St, Bridgewater, NS, B4V 1V8, CANADA. Tel: 902-543-0690. p. 2620
Pittman, Vanessa, Cat Supvr, ILL, Mountain Regional Library System, 698 Miller St, Young Harris, GA, 30582. Tel: 706-379-3732. p. 503
Pittman-Hassett, Amy, Librn Supvr, William T Cozby Public Library, 177 N Heartz Rd, Coppell, TX, 75019. Tel: 972-304-3656. p. 2159
Pitts, Amy, Library Contact, East Moline Correctional Center Library, 100 Hillcrest Rd, East Moline, IL, 61244. Tel: 309-755-4511, Ext 2326. p. 580
Pitts, Ashley, Public & Collection Dev Librarian, University of Saint Thomas, Cardinal Beran Library at Saint Mary's Seminary, 9845 Memorial Dr, Houston, TX, 77024-3498. Tel: 713-654-5773. p. 2200

Pitts, Chrisler, Librn, Kean University, 1000 Morris Ave, Union, NJ, 07083. Tel: 908-737-4629. p. 1449

Pitts, Diane, Ch Serv, Desoto Parish Library, Logansport Branch, 203 Hwy 5, Logansport, LA, 71049. Tel: 318-697-2311. p. 896

Pitts, Diane, Libr Asst, Desoto Parish Library, Logansport Branch, 203 Hwy 5, Logansport, LA, 71049. Tel: 318-697-2311. p. 896

Pitts Diedrichs, Carol, Dir, Ohio State University LIBRARIES, Jerome Lawrence & Robert E Lee Theatre Research Institute, 1430 Lincoln Tower, 1800 Cannon Dr, Columbus, OH, 43210-1230. Tel: 614-292-6614. p. 1775

Pitts, Laura, Dir, Scottsboro Public Library, 1002 S Broad St, Scottsboro, AL, 35768. Tel: 256-574-4335. p. 35

Pitts, Mary Margaret, Br Librn, Boston Public Library, Hyde Park Branch, 35 Harvard Ave, Hyde Park, MA, 02136. Tel: 617-361-2524. p. 992

Pitts, Nina, Libr Supvr, Peninsula College Library, 1502 E Lauridsen Blvd, Port Angeles, WA, 98362-6698. Tel: 360-417-6280. p. 2374

Pitts, Rob, Syst Adminr, Starke County Public Library System, 152 W Culver Rd, Knox, IN, 46534-2220. Tel: 574-772-7323. p. 699

Pitts, Ted, Digital Strategies Librarian, Libr Tech, Case Western Reserve University, 11055 Euclid Ave, Cleveland, OH, 44106. Tel: 216-368-3654. p. 1766

Pitz, Lauren, Asst Dir, Saint Charles Parish Library, 160 W Campus Dr, Destrehan, LA, 70047. Tel: 985-764-2366. p. 888

Piush, Evelyn, Br Head, Winnipeg Public Library, West Kildonan, 365 Jefferson Ave, Winnipeg, MB, R2V 0N3, CANADA. Tel: 204-986-4387. p. 2597

Pixley, Bill, Libr Dir, C E Brehm Memorial Public Library District, 101 S Seventh St, Mount Vernon, IL, 62864. Tel: 618-242-6322. p. 621

Pizarro, Luz D, Librn III, Inter-American University of Puerto Rico, PO Box 70351, Hato Rey, PR, 00936. Tel: 787-751-1912. p. 2511

Pizzi, Tracy, Metadata & Discovery Librn, Winthrop University, 824 Oakland Ave, Rock Hill, SC, 29733. Tel: 803-323-2179. p. 2068

Pizzuta, Holly, Dir, Weehawken Free Public Library, 49 Hauxhurst Ave, Ste 1, Weehawken, NJ, 07086. Tel: 201-863-7823. p. 1452

Pizzuto, Katherine, Libr Assoc, Hilbert College, 5200 S Park Ave, Hamburg, NY, 14075. Tel: 716-926-8913. p. 1543

Place, Lindsay, Asst Libr Dir, Athens County Public Libraries, 95 W Washington, Nelsonville, OH, 45764-1177. Tel: 740-753-2118. p. 1805

Place, Lynn, Dir, Germantown Library, 31 Palatine Park Rd, Germantown, NY, 12526-5309. Tel: 518-537-5800. p. 1538

Placer, Chandra, Dir, Learning Res, Sherman College of Chiropractic, 2020 Springfield Rd, Boiling Springs, SC, 29316-7251. Tel: 864-578-8770, Ext 258. p. 2048

Placer, Jordan, Teen Librn, Citizens Library, 55 S College St, Washington, PA, 15301. Tel: 724-222-2400. p. 2018

Placher, Andrea, Libr Dir, Williston Community Library, 1302 Davidson Dr, Williston, ND, 58801. Tel: 701-774-8805. p. 1741

Placke, Margaret, State Librn, State Library of Louisiana, 701 N Fourth St, Baton Rouge, LA, 70802-5232. Tel: 225-342-4923. p. 884

Placzek, Sandy, Assoc Dir, University of Nebraska-Lincoln, Marvin & Virginia Schmid Law Library, 1875 N 42nd St, Lincoln, NE, 68583. Tel: 402-472-3547. p. 1323

Plageman, Kathryn, Supvr, Circ, South Burlington Community Library, 180 Market St, South Burlington, VT, 05403. Tel: 802-846-4140. p. 2294

Plagman, Karen, Dir, Lied Irwin Public Library, 509 Ann St, Irwin, IA, 51446. Tel: 712-782-3335. p. 761

Plaisance, Aimee, Cat Librn, University of Maryland, Baltimore County, 1000 Hilltop Circle, Baltimore, MD, 21250. Tel: 410-455-2356. p. 958

Plaisance, Heather, Head, Ref & Res Serv, University of Louisiana at Lafayette, 400 E St Mary Blvd, Lafayette, LA, 70503. Tel: 337-482-1172. p. 893

Plank, Elissa, Head, Circ, Louisiana State University Libraries, 295 Middleton Library, Baton Rouge, LA, 70803. Tel: 225-578-3216. p. 884

Plankinton, Nikki, Librn, Lyon County, Library District One, 421 Main St, Allen, KS, 66833. Tel: 620-528-3451. p. 795

Plant, Randy, Br Head, Winnipeg Public Library, Munroe, 489 London St, Winnipeg, MB, R2K 2Z4, CANADA. Tel: 204-986-3738. p. 2596

Plantak, Zorislav, Head, Libr Syst, Andrews University, 4190 Administration Dr, Berrien Springs, MI, 49104-1400. Tel: 269-471-6242. p. 1085

Plante, Pierre, Librn, Bibliotheque Municipale de Sorel-Tracy, 145 rue George, Sorel-Tracy, QC, J3P 7K1, CANADA. Tel: 450-780-5600. p. 2737

Plaskon, Denise, Br Mgr, New Bedford Free Public Library, Francis J Lawler Branch, 745 Rockdale Ave, New Bedford, MA, 02740. Tel: 508-991-6216. p. 1038

Plasterer, Rick, Library Contact, Presbyterian Church of the Atonement Library, 10613 Georgia Ave, Silver Spring, MD, 20902. Tel: 301-649-4131. p. 978

Plastow, Kristine, Dir, Libr Serv, Red Deer College Library, 100 College Blvd, Red Deer, AB, T4N 5H5, CANADA. Tel: 403-342-3578. p. 2551

Platfoot, Joyce, Exec Dir, Radnor Memorial Library, 114 W Wayne Ave, Wayne, PA, 19087. Tel: 610-687-1124. p. 2018

Plath, Lisa, Libr Dir, Lucius E & Elsie C Burch Jr Library, 501 Poplar View Pkwy, Collierville, TN, 38017. Tel: 901-457-2600. p. 2094

Platkowski, Melissa, Syst Librn, University of Wisconsin-Green Bay, 2420 Nicolet Dr, Green Bay, WI, 54311-7001. Tel: 920-465-2764. p. 2439

Plato, Terra, Chief Exec Officer, Lethbridge Public Library, 810 Fifth Ave S, Lethbridge, AB, T1J 4C4, CANADA. Tel: 403-380-7341. p. 2546

Platt, Carolyn, Head, Tech Serv, Jones Library, Inc, 43 Amity St, Amherst, MA, 01002-2285. Tel: 413-259-3214. p. 984

Platt, Christopher, County Libr Dir, Mono County Free Library, 400 Sierra Park Rd, Mammoth Lakes, CA, 93546. Tel: 760-934-4777. p. 172

Platt, Elizabeth, Librn, Eastford Public Library, Ivy Glenn Memorial Bldg, 179 Eastford Rd, Eastford, CT, 06242. Tel: 860-974-0125. p. 310

Platt, Ellen, Fac Serv Librn, Research Librn, Santa Clara University Library, Edwin A Heafey Law Library, School of Law, 500 El Camino Real, Santa Clara, CA, 95053-0430. Tel: 408-554-5139. p. 242

Platt, Kathie, Dir, Bern Community Library, 405 Main St, Bern, KS, 66408. Tel: 785-336-3000. p. 798

Platt, Mary, Mountain View Campus Librn, Chattahoochee Technical College Library, 980 S Cobb Dr, Marietta, GA, 30060. Tel: 770-528-4536. p. 488

Platt, Mary, Librn, Library Services, Chattahoochee Technical College Library, Woodstock Campus Library, 8371 Main St, Woodstock, GA, 30188. Tel: 770-720-6687. p. 489

Platt, Stephen, Librn/Br Mgr, Allen County Public Library, Georgetown, 6600 E State Blvd, Fort Wayne, IN, 46815. Tel: 260-421-1320. p. 683

Platte, Amy, Libr Tech, Michigan Department of Corrections, Carson City Correctional Facility Library, PO Box 5000, Carson City, MI, 48811-5000. Tel: 989-548-3941, Ext 6331. p. 1089

Platte, Kelly, Dir, Denver Public Library, 100 Washington St, Denver, IA, 50622. Tel: 319-984-5140. p. 745

Platte, Michael, Libr Tech III, University of Nevada, Las Vegas Univ Libraries, Music Library, 4505 S Maryland Pkwy, Box 457002, Las Vegas, NV, 89154-7002. Tel: 702-895-2547. p. 1347

Platts, Barbara, Mgr, Libr Serv, Munson Healthcare, Department of Library Services, 1105 Sixth St, Traverse City, MI, 49684. Tel: 231-935-6544. p. 1154

Platts, Lorna, District Supervisor, Stormont, Dundas & Glengarry County Library, Lancaster Branch, 195 S Rd Military, Lancaster, ON, K0C 1N0, CANADA. Tel: 613-347-2311. p. 2638

Platts, Lorna, Libr Serv Tech, Stormont, Dundas & Glengarry County Library, Avonmore Branch, 16299 Fairview Dr, Avonmore, ON, K0C 1C0, CANADA. Tel: 613-346-2137. p. 2638

Plaut, Suzanne, Librn, Lubec Memorial Library, 55 Water St, Lubec, ME, 04652-1122. Tel: 207-733-2491. p. 930

Player, Nathanael, Dir, Utah State Law Library, 450 S State St, W-13, Salt Lake City, UT, 84111-3101. Tel: 801-238-7990. p. 2272

Plazyk, Judy, Br Librn, Platte County Public Library, Glendo Branch, 204 S Yellowstone, Glendo, WY, 82213. Tel: 307-735-4480. p. 2500

Pleasants, Nina, Librn, Norridgewock Public Library, 40 Mercer Rd, Norridgewock, ME, 04957. Tel: 207-634-2828. p. 933

Pleil, Otto, E-Br Mgr, Alachua County Library District, 401 E University Ave, Gainesville, FL, 32601-5453. Tel: 352-334-3936. p. 406

Plesman, Joanne, Libr Asst, Sparwood Public Library, 110 Pine Ave, Sparwood, BC, V0B 2G0, CANADA. Tel: 250-425-2299. p. 2576

Plessel, Sam, YA Librn, Willmar Public Library, 410 Fifth St SW, Willmar, MN, 56201-3298. Tel: 320-235-3162. p. 1208

Pletcher, Sandra, Corrections Librn, State Correctional Institution, Laurel Highlands Library, 5706 Glades Pike, Somerset, PA, 15501. Tel: 814-445-6501. p. 2008

Pletka, Scott, Asst Dir, Logansport-Cass County Public Library, 616 E Broadway, Logansport, IN, 46947. Tel: 574-753-6383. p. 703

Plett, Katherine, Dir, College of New Caledonia Library, 3330 22nd Ave, Prince George, BC, V2N 1P8, CANADA. Tel: 250-561-5811, 250-562-2131, Ext 5298. p. 2574

Plett, Rachel, Br Librn, Evergreen Regional Library, Arborg Branch, 292 Main St, Arborg, MB, R0C 0A0, CANADA. Tel: 204-376-5388. p. 2587

Plett, Vanessa, Libr Mgr, Rosemary Community Library, Rosemary School, 622 Dahlia St, Rosemary, AB, T0J 2W0, CANADA. Tel: 403-378-4493, Ext 150. p. 2552

Pliakas, Kristin, Liaison Librn, Grafton Public Library, 35 Grafton Common, Grafton, MA, 01519. Tel: 508-839-4649. p. 1021

Plimpton, Becky, Dir, Joshua Hyde Public Library, 306 Main St, Sturbridge, MA, 01566-1242. Tel: 508-347-2512. p. 1058

Plimpton, Nancy, ILL, University of New Hampshire Library, 18 Library Way, Durham, NH, 03824. Tel: 603-862-1173. p. 1362

Plocharczyk, Leah, Dir, Florida Atlantic University, 5353 Parkside Dr, Jupiter, FL, 33458. Tel: 561-799-8685. p. 413

Plodowski, Katherin, Bus Operations Mgr, Indiana University South Bend, 1700 Mishawaka Ave, South Bend, IN, 46615. Tel: 574-520-4380. p. 718

Plohr, Jennifer, Adult Serv, Sr Mgr, Cook Memorial Public Library District, 413 N Milwaukee Ave, Libertyville, IL, 60048-2280. Tel: 847-362-2330. p. 608

Plomske, Maureen, Librn, Kitchener Public Library, Pioneer Park, 150 Pioneer Dr, Kitchener, ON, N2H 2H1, CANADA. Tel: 519-748-2740. p. 2651

Plonkey, Deborah, Youth Serv Prog Coordr, John C Fremont Library District, 130 Church Ave, Florence, CO, 81226. Tel: 719-784-4649, Ext 2. p. 280

Ploof, Charmaine, Librn, Iosco-Arenac District Library, Omer Little Eagles Nest Library, 205 E Center St, Omer, MI, 48749. Tel: 989-653-2230. p. 1102

Plotke, Kassia, Head, Adult Serv, East Islip Public Library, 381 E Main St, East Islip, NY, 11730-2896. Tel: 631-581-9200. p. 1528

Plotner, Elizabeth, Libr Dir, Daviess County Library, 306 W Grand, Gallatin, MO, 64640-1132. Tel: 660-663-3222. p. 1247

Plotner, Elizabeth S, Dir, Daviess County Library, Jamesport Branch, 101 E Main, Jamesport, MO, 64648. Tel: 660-684-6120. p. 1247

Plouffe, Martine, Ref Serv Mgr, Bibliothèque Municipale de Gatineau, Ville de Gatineau, CP 1970 Succ. Hull, Gatineau, QC, J8X 3Y9, CANADA. Tel: 819-243-2345. p. 2712

Plourde, Vickie, Librn, Milan Public Library, 20 Bridge St, Milan, NH, 03588. Tel: 603-449-7307. p. 1373

Plowman, Stephanie, Spec Coll Librn, Gonzaga University, 502 E Boone Ave, Spokane, WA, 99258-0095. Tel: 509-323-3847. p. 2383

Plowman, Tammy, Ch, Lincoln County Library System, Cokeville Branch, 240 E Main St, Cokeville, WY, 83114. Tel: 307-279-3213. p. 2496

Plude, Victoria, Dir, Fort Edward Free Library, 23 East St, Fort Edward, NY, 12828. Tel: 518-747-6743. p. 1534

Plum, Kristi, Dir, Glenn A Jones, MD Memorial Library, 400 S Parish Ave, Johnstown, CO, 80534. Tel: 970-587-2459. p. 287

Plumb, Erick, Libr Dir, Waunakee Public Library, 210 N Madison St, Waunakee, WI, 53597. Tel: 608-849-4217. p. 2485

Plumb, Jo, Dir, Wellington Public Library, 121 W Seventh St, Wellington, KS, 67152. Tel: 620-326-2011. p. 842

Plumb, Tawnya, Libr Dir, University of Wyoming, 1820 E Willett Dr, Laramie. Tel: 307-766-5733. p. 2496

Plumb-Larrick, C Andrew, Dir, Law Libr, Case Western Reserve University, School of Law Library, 11075 East Blvd, Cleveland, OH, 44106-7148. Tel: 216-368-2792. p. 1766

Plumer, Mary, Ch, Mansfield Public Library, 255 Hope St, Mansfield, MA, 02048-2353. Tel: 508-261-7380. p. 1031

Plumley, Jeff, Circ Mgr, Librn, Crowell Public Library, 1890 Huntington Dr, San Marino, CA, 91108-2595. Tel: 626-300-0777. p. 234

Plummer, Ashley, Dir, Marion Military Institute, 1101 Washington St, Marion, AL, 36756. Tel: 334-683-2371. p. 25

Plummer, Jennifer, Libr Coord, North Gorham Public Library, Two Standish Neck Rd, Gorham, ME, 04038-2469. Tel: 207-892-2575. p. 926

Plummer, Pamela, Dir, Judge George W Armstrong Library, 220 S Commerce St, Natchez, MS, 39120. Tel: 601-445-8862. p. 1227

Plunket, Linda, Assoc Univ Librn, Grad & Res Serv, Boston University Libraries, Mugar Memorial Library, 771 Commonwealth Ave, Boston, MA, 02215. Tel: 617-353-3710. p. 993

Plunket, Linda, Librn, Boston University Libraries, Pickering Educational Resources Library, Two Sherborn St, Boston, MA, 02215. Tel: 617-353-3735. p. 993

Plunkett, Becki, Spec Coll & Archives Librn, State Historical Society of Iowa, 600 E Locust, Des Moines, IA, 50319-0290. Tel: 515-281-6200. p. 747

Plunkett, David, Dir, Jefferson-Madison Regional Library, 201 E Market St, Charlottesville, VA, 22902-5287. Tel: 434-979-7151, Ext 6671. p. 2309

Plunkett, Judy, Br Mgr, Robinson Public Library District, Oblong Branch, 110 E Main St, Oblong, IL, 62449. Tel: 618-592-3001. p. 640

Plunkett, Stephanie, Chief Curator, Dep Dir, Norman Rockwell Museum, Nine Rte 183, Stockbridge, MA, 01262. Tel: 413-298-4100, Ext 208. p. 1057

Pluss, Deborah, Head, Bibliog Serv, William Paterson University, 300 Pompton Rd, Wayne, NJ, 07470. Tel: 973-720-3143. p. 1452

Plutchak, T Scott, Dir, University of Alabama at Birmingham, Lister Hill Library of the Health Sciences, 1700 University Blvd, Birmingham, AL, 35294-0013. Tel: 205-934-5460. p. 9

Poage, Alison, Dir, Episcopal Theological Seminary of the Southwest, 501 E 32nd St, Austin, TX, 78705. Tel: 512-472-4133, 512-478-5212. p. 2139

Pochan, Jan, Library Representative, Newark United Methodist Church, 69 E Main St, Newark, DE, 19711-4645. Tel: 302-368-8774. p. 355

Pochatko, Andy, Head, Ref & Adult Serv, Harbor-Topky Memorial Library, 1633 Walnut Blvd, Ashtabula, OH, 44004. Tel: 440-964-9645. p. 1748

Podell, Roger, Dr, Exec Dir, Cold Spring Harbor Library, 95 Harbor Rd, Cold Spring Harbor, NY, 11724. Tel: 631-692-6820. p. 1520

Podhradsky, Anne, Librn, Wagner Public Library, 106 Sheridan Ave SE, Wagner, SD, 57380. Tel: 605-384-5248. p. 2085

Podlaski, Paula, Libr Assoc, Norwalk Community College, 188 Richards Ave, Norwalk, CT, 06854-1655. Tel: 203-857-7201. p. 331

Podlowski, Rachel, Libr Assoc, Trent University, Durham Greater Toronto Area Campus Library & Learning Centre, 55 Thornton Rd S, Ste 102, Oshawa, ON, L1J 5Y1, CANADA. Tel: 905-435-5102, Ext 5062. p. 2672

Podollan, Christine, Mgr, Russell & District Regional Library, 339 Main St, Russell, MB, R0J 1W0, CANADA. Tel: 204-773-3127. p. 2589

Podolsky, Jennifer, Exec Dir, Princeton Public Library, 65 Witherspoon St, Princeton, NJ, 08542. Tel: 609-924-9529. p. 1436

Podzemny, Todd, Mgr, Libr Operations, Metropolitan Library System in Oklahoma County, Southern Oaks Library, 6900 S Walker Ave, Oklahoma City, OK, 73139-7203. p. 1857

Poe, Jodi, Head, Tech Serv, Jacksonville State University Library, 700 Pelham Rd N, Jacksonville, AL, 36265. Tel: 256-782-5758. p. 23

Poe, Judy, Dir, Community Library Sedona, 3250 White Bear Rd, Sedona, AZ, 86336. Tel: 928-282-7714. p. 77

Poe, Laura, Actg Dir, Athens-Limestone Public Library, 603 S Jefferson St, Athens, AL, 35611. Tel: 256-232-1233. p. 5

Poe, Sherry, Dir, Cheaha Regional Library, 935 Coleman St, Heflin, AL, 36264. Tel: 256-463-7125. p. 20

Poet, Patricia, Instrul Media, York College of Pennsylvania, 441 Country Club Rd, York, PA, 17403-3651. Tel: 717-815-1458. p. 2026

Poffenberger, Robin, Support Serv Mgr, Washington-Centerville Public Library, 111 W Spring Valley Rd, Centerville, OH, 45458. Tel: 937-610-4444. p. 1757

Pogosyan, Nina, Br Mgr, San Francisco Public Library, Ingleside Branch Library, 1298 Ocean Ave, San Francisco, CA, 94112-1717. Tel: 415-355-2898. p. 228

Pogue, Andi Adkins, Pub Serv Librn, Cosumnes River College Library, 8401 Center Pkwy, Sacramento, CA, 95823. Tel: 916-691-7904. p. 208

Pohl, Denise, Dir, Rockwell City Public Library, 424 Main St, Rockwell City, IA, 50579-1415. Tel: 712-297-8422. p. 779

Pohrte, Shannon, Assoc Dean of Libr, Elgin Community College, 1700 Spartan Dr, Elgin, IL, 60123. Tel: 847-214-7337. p. 584

Poignant, Nicholas, Youth Serv Librn, Bradford Public Library District, 111 S Peoria St, Bradford, IL, 61421. Tel: 309-897-8400. p. 544

Pointon, Scott, Dir, White Oak Library District, 201 W Normantown Rd, Romeoville, IL, 60446. Tel: 815-886-2030. p. 643

Pointon, Scott, Dir, White Oak Library District, Crest Hill Branch, 20670 Len Kubinski Dr, Crest Hill, IL, 60403. Tel: 815-725-0234. p. 643

Poirier, Eve, Head Librn, NorQuest College, 10215-108th St, 5th Flr, Edmonton, AB, T5J 1L6, CANADA. Tel: 708-644-6070. p. 2537

Poirier, Isabelle, Exec Dir, Centre Regional de Services aux Bibliotheques Publiques de la Capitale-Nationale et de la Chaudiere-Appalaches Inc, 3189 rue Albert-Demers, Charny, QC, G6X 3A1, CANADA. Tel: 418-832-6166. p. 2710

Poirier, Isabelle, Dir, Bibliotheque Henri-Brassard, 505A rue Saint-Laurent, Saint-Simeon, QC, G0T 1X0, CANADA. Tel: 418-471-0550. p. 2736

Poirier, Noel, Exec Dir, Ohio Genealogical Society, 611 State Rte 97 W, Bellville, OH, 44813-8813. Tel: 419-886-1903. p. 1750

Poirier, Sarah-Kim, Librn, Reseau Bibliotheques du Bas-Saint-Laurent, 465 St Pierre, Riviere-du-Loup, QC, G5R 4T6, CANADA. Tel: 418-714-6007. p. 2733

Poissant, Roxanne, Town Librn, College de Valleyfield, 80 rue Saint Thomas, Salaberry-de-Valleyfield, QC, J6T 4J7, CANADA. Tel: 450-373-9441, Ext 200. p. 2736

Poitras, Anne-Marie, Chef de Div, Bibliotheques de Montreal, Robert-Bourassa, 41 Ave Saint-Just, Outremont, QC, H2V 4T7, CANADA. Tel: 514-495-6270. p. 2720

Poitras, Melanie, Chef de Div, Bibliotheques de Montreal, L'Octogone, 1080 Ave Dollard, LaSalle, QC, H8N 2T9, CANADA. Tel: 514-367-6376. p. 2719

Pojman, Paul, Librn, Bedford Historical Society Library, 30 S Park St, Bedford, OH, 44146-3635. Tel: 440-232-0796. p. 1749

Pokorny, Renee, Br Mgr, Free Library of Philadelphia, South Philadelphia Branch, 1700 S Broad St, Philadelphia, PA, 19145-2392. Tel: 215-685-1866. p. 1980

Poku, Brenda, Dir, Conyers-Rockdale Library System, 864 Green St SW, Conyers, GA, 30012. Tel: 770-388-5040. p. 472

Pol, Cindy, Mgr, Human Res, Baltimore County Public Library, 320 York Rd, Towson, MD, 21204-5179. Tel: 410-887-6100. p. 979

Poladian, B, Librn, Musick, Peeler & Garrett Library, 333 S Hope St, Ste 2900, Los Angeles, CA, 90071. Tel: 213-629-7600. p. 167

Polak, Gail, Librn, Faulkner-Van Buren Regional Library System, Greenbrier Branch, 13 Wilson Farm Rd, Greenbrier, AR, 72058. Tel: 501-679-6344. p. 92

Poland, Anna, Dir, Hampshire County Public Library, 153 W Main St, Romney, WV, 26757. Tel: 304-822-3185. p. 2413

Poland, Kandace, Co-Librn, Archer Public Library, 203 Sanford St, Archer, IA, 51231. Tel: 712-723-5629. p. 732

Poland, Robin, Ref Librn, Vermont State University - Williston, 401 Lawrence Pl, Rm 409, Williston, VT, 05495. Tel: 802-879-8249. p. 2299

Polard, Sharna, Mgr, Libr Serv, Covenant Health Grey Nuns Community Hospital, 1100 Youville Dr W, Rm 0634, Edmonton, AB, T6L 5X8, CANADA. Tel: 780-306-7618. p. 2536

Polard, Sharna, Mgr, Libr Serv, Covenant Health Misericordia Community Hospital, 16940 87 Ave NW, Edmonton, AB, T5R 4H5, CANADA. Tel: 780-735-9329. p. 2536

Polardino, Linda S, Chief Librn, Department of Veterans Affairs, Bldg 9, Rm 104, 5500 Armstrong Rd, Battle Creek, MI, 49015. Tel: 269-223-6491. p. 1083

Polashek, Roseann, Youth Serv Mgr, Scott County Public Library, 104 S Bradford Lane, Georgetown, KY, 40324-2335. Tel: 502-863-3566. p. 856

Polasko, Julie Ann, Ch, Chappaqua Public Library, 195 S Greeley Ave, Chappaqua, NY, 10514. Tel: 914-238-4779. p. 1516

Ponville, Myra, Br Mgr, Fort Bend County Libraries, Cinco Ranch, 2620 Commercial Center Blvd, Katy, TX, 77494. Tel: 281-395-1311. p. 2232

Ponzio, Renee, Ref Serv, South Dakota School of Mines & Technology, 501 E Saint Joseph St, Rapid City, SD, 57701-3995. p. 2081

Pool, Cassandra, Libr Dir, Old Town Public Library, 46 Middle St, Old Town, ME, 04468. Tel: 207-827-3972. p. 934

Pool, Clancy, Br Mgr, Whitman County Rural Library District, St John Branch, One E Front St, Saint John, WA, 99171. Tel: 509-648-3319. p. 2362

Pool, Jenny, Cat, Libr Spec II, Texas A&M University-Texarkana, 7101 University Ave, Texarkana, TX, 75503. Tel: 903-334-6696. p. 2248

Pool, Jesse, Br Librn, First Regional Library, Jessie J Edwards Public Library, 610 E Central Ave, Coldwater, MS, 38618. Tel: 662-622-5573. p. 1220

Pool, Jesse, Br Librn, First Regional Library, Senatobia Public Library, 222 Ward St, Senatobia, MS, 38668. Tel: 662-562-6791. p. 1220

Pool, Jesse, Head Librn, First Regional Library, Hernando Public Library, 370 W Commerce St, Hernando, MS, 38632. Tel: 662-429-4439. p. 1220

Pool, Jesse, Head Librn, First Regional Library, Walls Public Library, 7181 Delta Bluff Pkwy, Walls, MS, 38680. Tel: 662-781-3664. p. 1220

Pool, Kristen, Adult Serv Mgr, Kent Free Library, 312 W Main St, Kent, OH, 44240-2493. Tel: 330-673-4414. p. 1792

Pool, Rebecca, Libr Serv Dir, Deer Park Public Library, 3009 Center St, Deer Park, TX, 77536. Tel: 281-478-7208. p. 2169

Poole, Chelsea, Asst Dir, Meigs County District Public Library, 216 W Main St, Pomeroy, OH, 45769. Tel: 740-992-5813. p. 1816

Poole, Eva, Dir, Virginia Beach Public Library, Municipal Ctr, Bldg 19, Rm 210, 2416 Courthouse Dr, Virginia Beach, VA, 23452. Tel: 757-385-8709. p. 2350

Poole, Jason, Ch Serv Librn, Webster Public Library, Webster Plaza, 980 Ridge Rd, Webster, NY, 14580. Tel: 585-872-7075. p. 1661

Poole, Kelly, Dir, Lexington County Public Library System, 5440 Augusta Rd, Lexington, SC, 29072. Tel: 803-785-2643. p. 2064

Poole, Laura, Librn, Hickman County Memorial Library, 110 Craig Lane, Clinton, KY, 42031-1427. Tel: 270-653-2225. p. 851

Pooler, Jacqueline, Dir, Evelyn Goldberg Briggs Memorial Library, 68235 S Main St, Iron River, WI, 54847. Tel: 715-372-5451. p. 2442

Pooloa, Elizabeth, Dir of Coll, Dir, Operations, Hawaiian Mission Children's Society Library, 553 S King St, Honolulu, HI, 96813. Tel: 808-531-0481. p. 512

Poon, Cindy, Colls Mgr, Commun Engagement Mgr, Ajax Public Library, 55 Harwood Ave S, Ajax, ON, L1S 2H8, CANADA. Tel: 905-683-4000, Ext 8801. p. 2627

Poorbaugh, Susan, Br Mgr, Knox County Public Library System, Bearden Branch, 100 Golfclub Rd, Knoxville, TN, 37919. Tel: 865-588-8813. p. 2105

Poore, Erin, Asst Dir, Bethlehem Area Public Library, 11 W Church St, Bethlehem, PA, 18018. Tel: 610-867-3761, Ext 256. p. 1911

Poore, Jolene, Dir, Ada Public Library, 124 S Rennie, Ada, OK, 74820. Tel: 580-436-8125. p. 1839

Poore, Sami, Supvr, Leath Thomas H Memorial Library, Kemp-Sugg Memorial, 279 Second St, Ellerbe, NC, 28338-9001. Tel: 910-652-6130. p. 1713

Poorman, Jamie, Head Librn, Marshall Public Library, 612 Archer Ave, Marshall, IL, 62441. Tel: 217-826-2535. p. 614

Poorman, Kathy, Asst Dir, Tech Serv, University of Texas at El Paso Library, 500 W University Ave, El Paso, TX, 79968-0582. Tel: 915-747-5394. p. 2175

Poorte, Judi, Ch Assoc, North Logan City Library, 475 E 2500 N, North Logan, UT, 84341. Tel: 435-755-7169. p. 2267

Poortenga, Linda, HQ Librn, Jasper County Public Library, 208 W Susan St, Rensselaer, IN, 47978. Tel: 219-866-5881. p. 714

Popadak, John, Acq Librn, Youngstown State University, One University Plaza, Youngstown, OH, 44555-0001. Tel: 330-941-3679. p. 1836

Popadick, Caroline, Head Librn, Lakeland Library Region, North Battleford Public Library, 1392-101 St, North Battleford, SK, S9A 1A2, CANADA. Tel: 306-445-3206. p. 2744

Pope, Aaron, Head, Access Serv, Northeastern State University, 711 N Grand Ave, Tahlequah, OK, 74464-2333. Tel: 918-456-5511, Ext 3200. p. 1863

Pope, Alyson, Head, Pub Serv, Pittsburgh Theological Seminary, 616 N Highland Ave, Pittsburgh, PA, 15206. Tel: 412-924-1356. p. 1995

Pope, Barbara, Per Librn, Pittsburg State University, 1605 S Joplin St, Pittsburg, KS, 66762-5889. Tel: 620-235-4884. p. 831

Pope, Brittainy, Asst Br Mgr, Bossier Parish Libraries, East 80 Branch, 1050 Bellevue Rd, Haughton, LA, 71037. Tel: 318-949-2665. p. 886

Pope, Cristina, Dir, SUNY Upstate Medical University, 766 Irving Ave, Syracuse, NY, 13210-1602. Tel: 315-464-7091. p. 1650

Pope, Donna, Br Mgr, Blackwater Regional Library, 22511 Main St, Courtland, VA, 23837. Tel: 757-653-2821. p. 2313

Pope, Jessica, Library Contact, US National Park Service, 151 Hwy 76, Harpers Ferry, IA, 52146. Tel: 563-873-3491. p. 757

Pope, Kitty, Chief Exec Officer, Windsor Public Library, 850 Ouellette Ave, Windsor, ON, N9A 4M9, CANADA. Tel: 519-255-6770. p. 2704

Pope, Michele, Ser/Govt Doc Librn, Loyola University New Orleans, Loyola Law Library, School of Law, 7214 St Charles Ave, New Orleans, LA, 70118. p. 902

Pope Robbins, Laura, Assoc Dir, Access Serv, Embry-Riddle Aeronautical University, 3700 Willow Creek Rd, Prescott, AZ, 86301-3720. Tel: 928-777-6686. p. 73

Pope, Sanya, Br Mgr, Whitman County Rural Library District, Oakesdale Branch, 101 E Steptoe, Oakesdale, WA, 99158. Tel: 509-285-4310. p. 2362

Popescu, Adriana, Dean, Libr Serv, California Polytechnic State University, One Grand Ave, San Luis Obispo, CA, 93407. Tel: 805-756-2345. p. 233

Popinchalk, Kara, Librn I, Pub Relations/Mkt Librn, Groton Public Library, 52 Newtown Rd, Groton, CT, 06340. Tel: 860-441-6750. p. 314

Popken, Rachel, Access Serv Coordr, Northwestern College, 101 Seventh St SW, Orange City, IA, 51041. Tel: 712-707-7237. p. 774

Popko, John, Univ Librn, Seattle University, A A Lemieux Library, 901 12th Ave, Seattle, WA, 98122-4411. Tel: 206-296-6201. p. 2380

Poplau, Jim, Br Mgr, Kansas City Public Library, Waldo Community, 201 E 75th St, Kansas City, MO, 64114. Tel: 816-701-3586. p. 1255

Poplawska, Paulina, Libr Dir, New Ulm Public Library, 17 N Broadway, New Ulm, MN, 56073-1786. Tel: 507-359-8331. p. 1190

Poplees, Julie A, Head, Children's Servx, Pleasant Valley Free Library, Three Maggiacomo Lane, Pleasant Valley, NY, 12569. Tel: 845-635-8460. p. 1620

Popma, Paula, Head, Pub Serv, California State University, Fresno, Henry Madden Library, 5200 N Barton Ave, Mail Stop ML-34, Fresno, CA, 93740-8014. Tel: 559-278-5794. p. 144

Popoff, Jordan, Cat Librn, Curry Public Library, 94341 Third St, Gold Beach, OR, 97444. Tel: 541-247-7246. p. 1880

Popovich, Emily, Libr Mgr, Timberland Regional Library, Raymond Branch, 507 Duryea St, Raymond, WA, 98577-1829. Tel: 360-942-2408. p. 2389

Popovich, Mary, Dir, Thousand Island Park Library, 42743 Saint Lawrence Ave, Thousand Island Park, NY, 13692. Tel: 315-482-9098, 315-559-7460. p. 1651

Popowich, Emma, Languages Librarian, University of Manitoba Libraries, Elizabeth Dafoe Library, 25 Chancellor's Circle, Winnipeg, MB, R3T 2N2, CANADA. Tel: 204-474-6211. p. 2595

Poppen, Rachel, Coll Archivist, University of Iowa Libraries, Special Collections & Archives, 100 Main Library, 125 W Washington St, Iowa City, IA, 52242-1420. Tel: 319-335-5921. p. 761

Poppendeck, Caroline, Ref Librn, Chemung County Library District, 101 E Church St, Elmira, NY, 14901. Tel: 607-733-9173. p. 1530

Poppens, Lex, Exec Dir, Bureau County Historical Society Museum & Library, 109 Park Ave W, Princeton, IL, 61356-1927. Tel: 815-875-2184. p. 636

Poppino, Stephen, Ref (Info Servs), College of Southern Idaho Library, 315 Falls Ave, Twin Falls, ID, 83301-3367. Tel: 208-732-6500. p. 531

Poquet, Ginette, Librn, Bibliotheque Fleur de Lin, 260 Pettigrew St, Saint-Leonard de Portneuf, QC, G0A 4A0, CANADA. Tel: 418-337-3961. p. 2736

Poray, Reann, Ind Rm Librn, Plainfield-Guilford Township Public Library, 1120 Stafford Rd, Plainfield, IN, 46168. Tel: 317-839-6602, Ext 2114. p. 713

Porben, Eduardo, Ref & Instruction Librn, Barry University, 11300 NE Second Ave, Miami Shores, FL, 33161-6695. Tel: 305-981-1195. p. 426

Porcaro, J P, Dir, East Orange Public Library, 21 S Arlington Ave, East Orange, NJ, 07018. Tel: 973-266-5600. p. 1400

Poremba, David, Orlando Campus Libr Dir, Keiser University Library System, 1500 NW 49th St, Fort Lauderdale, FL, 33309. Tel: 954-351-4035. p. 401

Poretta, Jill M, Dir, Research & Business Intelligence, Cozen O'Connor, 1650 Market St, Ste 2800, Philadelphia, PA, 19103. Tel: 215-665-4709. p. 1976

Porfiri, Amy, Dep Dir, American Psychiatric Association Foundation, 800 Maine Ave SW, Ste 900, Washington, DC, 20024. Tel: 202-683-8312. p. 360

Porfirio-Milton, Dawn, Br Mgr, Phoenix Public Library, Acacia Library, 750 E Townley Ave, Phoenix, AZ, 85020. p. 72

Porn, Whitney, Youth Serv Supvr, Norfolk Public Library, 308 W Prospect Ave, Norfolk, NE, 68701-4138. Tel: 402-844-2108. p. 1326

Porpiglia, Johanna, Dir, Miami-Dade County Law Library, County Courthouse, Rm 321A, 73 W Flagler St, Miami, FL, 33130. Tel: 305-349-7548. p. 422

Porpora, Pasquale, Library Contact, New York State Supreme Court Ninth Judicial District, Supreme Court Law Library, 2nd Flr, Rm 2002, 285 Main St, Goshen, NY, 10924. Tel: 845-476-3473. p. 1540

Portelance, Julie, Dir, Libr Serv, Hearst Public Library, 801 George St, Hearst, ON, P0L 1N0, CANADA. Tel: 705-372-2843. p. 2648

Portelli, Justin, Circ, Maurice M Pine Free Public Library, 10-01 Fair Lawn Ave, Fair Lawn, NJ, 07410. Tel: 201-796-3400. p. 1402

Portelli, Kathryn, Librn, Alaska State Court Law Library, Juneau Branch, Dimond Court Bldg, 123 Fourth St, Juneau, AK, 99811. Tel: 907-463-4761. p. 42

Porter, Abigail, Asst Dir, Head, Adult Serv, Lynnfield Public Library, 18 Summer St, Lynnfield, MA, 01940-1837. Tel: 781-334-5411, 781-334-6404. p. 1031

Porter, Amanda, Br Mgr, Huntsville-Madison County Public Library, Elizabeth Carpenter Public Library of New Hope, 5498 Main St, New Hope, AL, 35760. Tel: 256-723-2995. p. 22

Porter, Barbara, Dir, Kinney Memorial Library, 3140 County Hwy 11, Hartwick, NY, 13348-3007. Tel: 607-293-6600. p. 1544

Porter, Brandi, Dr, Dir, Libr Serv, American National University, 1813 E Main St, Salem, VA, 24153-4598. Tel: 540-444-4189, 540-986-1800, Ext 189. p. 2346

Porter, Christa, Dir, Libr Develop, Nebraska Library Commission, The Atrium, 1200 N St, Ste 120, Lincoln, NE, 68508-2023. Tel: 402-471-2045. p. 1322

Porter, Deanna, Br Head, Thompson-Nicola Regional District Library System, Ashcroft Branch, 201 Brink St, Ashcroft, BC, V0K 1A0, CANADA. Tel: 250-453-9042. p. 2567

Porter, Donna, Asst Dir, Dorothy Bramlage Public Library, 230 W Seventh St, Junction City, KS, 66441-3097. Tel: 785-238-4311. p. 816

Porter, Elizabeth, Libr Spec, Inyo County Free Library, Big Pine Branch, 500 S Main St, Big Pine, CA, 93513. Tel: 760-938-2420. p. 152

Porter, Emily, Dir, Byron Public Library District, 100 S Washington St, Byron, IL, 61010. Tel: 815-234-5107. p. 547

Porter, Gayle, Cat Librn, Chicago State University, 9501 S Martin Luther King Jr Dr, LIB 440, Chicago, IL, 60628-1598. Tel: 773-995-2551. p. 558

Porter, George, Eng Librn, California Institute of Technology, Sherman Fairchild Library of Engineering & Applied Science, Fairchild Library I-43, Pasadena, CA, 91125. Tel: 626-395-3409. p. 193

Porter, George, Librn, California Institute of Technology, Earthquake Engineering Research, Sherman Fairchild Library, 200 E California Blvd, M/C 1-43, Pasadena, CA, 91125. Tel: 626-395-3409. p. 193

Porter, Jean, Circ Serv, Spring Green Community Library, 230 E Monroe St, Spring Green, WI, 53588-8035. Tel: 608-588-2276. p. 2478

Porter, Jill, Libr Dir, Everett Roehl Marshfield Public Library, 105 S Maple Ave, Marshfield, WI, 54449. Tel: 715-387-8494. p. 2454

Porter, Kate, Asst Dir, Upper Arlington Public Library, 2800 Tremont Rd, Columbus, OH, 43221. Tel: 614-486-9621. p. 1778

Porter, Kayla, Br Librn, Southeast Regional Library, Wawota Branch, 308 Railway Ave, Wawota, SK, S0G 5A0, CANADA. Tel: 306-739-2375. p. 2755

Porter, Kim, Dir, Batesville Memorial Public Library, 131 N Walnut St, Batesville, IN, 47006. Tel: 812-934-4706. p. 669

Porter, Lawrence, PhD, Rev, Dir, Seton Hall University, 400 S Orange Ave, South Orange, NJ, 07079. Tel: 973-761-9198, 973-761-9336. p. 1443

Porter, Linda, Circ, Beck Bookman Library, 420 W Fourth St, Holton, KS, 66436-1572. Tel: 785-364-3532. p. 813

Porter, Lori, Dir, Madison Public Library, 208 W Third St, Madison, NE, 68748. Tel: 402-454-3500. p. 1324

Porter, Mary, Archivist, Scituate Historical Society Library, 43 Cudworth Rd, Scituate, MA, 02066-3802. Tel: 781-545-1083. p. 1052

Porter, Mary, Tech Serv, Indian Valley Public Library, 100 E Church Ave, Telford, PA, 18969. Tel: 215-723-9109. p. 2012

Porter, Michael, Electronic Res Mgr, Maricopa County Library District, 2700 N Central Ave, Ste 700, Phoenix, AZ, 85004. Tel: 602-652-3000. p. 70

Porter, Samantha H, Research, Instruction & Web Services Librn, Babson College, 11 Babson College Dr, Babson Park, MA, 02457-0310. Tel: 781-239-4471. p. 987

Porter, Toccara, ILL, Tennessee State University, 3500 John A Merritt Blvd, Nashville, TN, 37209. Tel: 615-963-5211. p. 2121

Porter, Will, Libr Dir, Sussex County Library System, 125 Morris Tpk, Newton, NJ, 07860. Tel: 973-948-3660. p. 1429

Porter-Reynolds, Daisy, Chief Public Services Officer, Saint Louis Public Library, 1301 Olive St, Saint Louis, MO, 63103. Tel: 314-539-0300. p. 1274

Porterfield, Amy, Br Mgr, Rockbridge Regional Library System, Bath Public, 96 Courthouse Hill Rd, Warm Springs, VA, 24484. Tel: 540-839-7286. p. 2329

Porterfield, Angela, Libr Dir, Madison Public Library, 827 N College Ave, Huntsville, AR, 72740. Tel: 479-738-2754. p. 99

Porterfield, David, Asst Dir, Martinsburg-Berkeley County Public Library, 101 W King St, Martinsburg, WV, 25401. Tel: 304-267-8933, Ext 4012. p. 2408

Porterfield, David, Br Mgr, Martinsburg-Berkeley County Public Library, Musselman-South Berkeley Community Library, 126 Excellence Way, Inwood, WV, 25428. Tel: 304-229-2220. p. 2408

Porterfield, Diane, Libr Dir, Central Penn College, 600 Valley Rd, Summerdale, PA, 17093. Tel: 717-728-2500. p. 2011

Porterfield, Lori, Asst Librn, Pearisburg Public Library, 209 Fort Branch Rd, Pearisburg, VA, 24134. Tel: 540-921-2556. p. 2337

Porterfield, Margaret, Br Mgr, Moore County Library, Page Memorial, 100 N Poplar St, Aberdeen, NC, 28315. Tel: 910-944-1200. p. 1677

Portillo, Elizabeth, Head, Youth Serv, Finkelstein Memorial Library, 24 Chestnut St, Spring Valley, NY, 10977. Tel: 845-352-5700, Ext 235. p. 1644

Portley, Mary Beth, Adult Reference Servs & Collection Dev, Jervis Public Library Association, Inc, 613 N Washington St, Rome, NY, 13440-4296. Tel: 315-336-4570. p. 1632

Portman, Sally, Librn, North Central Washington Libraries, Winthrop Public Library, 49 State Rte 20, Winthrop, WA, 98862. Tel: 509-996-2685. p. 2394

Portugal, Rhoda, Ref Librn, Rutherford Public Library, 150 Park Ave, Rutherford, NJ, 07070. Tel: 201-939-8600. p. 1441

Portwood, Alyssa, Med Librn, Mary Hower Medical Library, One Perkins Sq, Akron, OH, 44308-1062. Tel: 330-543-8250. p. 1745

Posa, Dylan, Acq, Lebanon Public Library, 101 S Broadway, Lebanon, OH, 45036. Tel: 513-932-2665. p. 1795

Poser, Cletus, Dir, Fort Myers Beach Public Library, 2755 Estero Blvd, Fort Myers Beach, FL, 33931. Tel: 239-463-9691. p. 404

Posey, Betty, Librn, American Donkey & Mule Society Library, 1346 Morningside Ave, Lewisville, TX, 75057. Tel: 972-219-0781. p. 2211

Posey, Donna, Br Mgr, Harrison County Library System, Woolmarket Library, 13034 Kayleigh Cove, Biloxi, MS, 39532. Tel: 228-354-9464. p. 1218

Posey, Jake, Access Serv Librn, John Brown University Library, 2000 W University, Siloam Springs, AR, 72761. Tel: 479-524-7202. p. 110

Posey, Jamie, Dean of Libr, Walters State Community College, 500 S Davy Crockett Pkwy, Morristown, TN, 37813-6899. Tel: 423-585-6903. p. 2116

Posinger, Barbara, Dir, Sandwich Public Library District, 925 S Main St, Sandwich, IL, 60548-2304. Tel: 815-786-8308, Ext 212. p. 644

Position Open, Br Mgr, Pine Forest Regional Library System - Headquarters, State Line Public, 229 Main St, State Line, MS, 39362. Tel: 601-848-7011. p. 1232

Posmantur, Craig, Librn, Temple Beth Tzedek, 1641 N Forest Rd, Williamsville, NY, 14221. Tel: 716-838-3232. p. 1666

Posner, Beth, Head, Resource Sharing, City University of New York, 365 Fifth Ave, New York, NY, 10016-4309. Tel: 212-817-7051. p. 1582

Post, Amanda T, Br Mgr, Fairfax County Public Library, Herndon Fortnightly Branch, 768 Center St, Herndon, VA, 20170-4640. Tel: 703-437-8855. p. 2316

Post, Bradley, Acq Mgr, SUNY Delhi, Bush Hall, 454 Delhi Dr, Delhi, NY, 13753. Tel: 607-746-4640. p. 1524

Post, Chelsea, Syst Librn, Eastern University, 1300 Eagle Rd, Saint Davids, PA, 19087-3696. Tel: 610-225-5003. p. 2002

Post, Colin, Dr, Asst Prof, University of North Carolina at Greensboro, School of Education Bldg, Rm 446, 1300 Spring Garden St, Greensboro, NC, 27412. Tel: 336-334-3477. p. 2790

Post, Corrie, Dir, Jane I & Annetta M Herr Memorial Library, 500 Market St, Mifflinburg, PA, 17844. Tel: 570-966-0831. p. 1963

Post, Diana, Dr, Pres, Rachel Carson Landmark Alliance, 11701 Berwick Rd, Silver Spring, MD, 20904-2767. Tel: 301-593-4900. p. 977

Post, Jacob, Head Librn, Oak Brook Public Library, 600 Oak Brook Rd, Oak Brook, IL, 60523. Tel: 630-368-7712. p. 627

Post, Joy, Dir, Springboro Public Library, 110 S Main St, Springboro, PA, 16435-1108. Tel: 814-587-3901. p. 2009

Post, Julie, Librn, A H Meadows Library, 921 S Ninth St, Midlothian, TX, 76065-3636. Tel: 972-775-3417. p. 2220

Post, Penny, Librn, Webb Public Library, 124 Main St, Webb, IA, 51366. Tel: 712-838-7719. p. 790

Post, Phyllis, Head, Tech Serv, Capital University, Law School Library, 303 E Broad St, Columbus, OH, 43215. Tel: 614-236-6483. p. 1772

Post, Rita, Youth Serv Librn, South River Public Library, 55 Appleby Ave, South River, NJ, 08882-2499. Tel: 732-254-2488. p. 1444

Post-Petkus, Cindy, Br Mgr, Roscommon Area District Library, Lyon Branch, 7851 W Higgins Lake Dr, Higgins Lake, MI, 48627. Tel: 989-281-9111. p. 1146

Postar, Adeen, Dir, Law Libr, American University, 4300 Nebraska Ave NW, Washington, DC, 20016-8182. Tel: 202-274-4374. p. 360

Postel, Kersten, Ch, Carroll Public Library, 118 E Fifth St, Carroll, IA, 51401. Tel: 712-792-3432. p. 737

Postelle, Yvette, Adult Programming, Rogers Memorial Library, 91 Coopers Farm Rd, Southampton, NY, 11968. Tel: 631-283-0774. p. 1643

Postema, Beth E, Dep Dir, Fargo Public Library, 102 N Third St, Fargo, ND, 58102. Tel: 701-241-1472. p. 1733

Posthumus, Michaela, Br Supvr, Bruce County Public Library, Kincardine Branch, 727 Queen St, Kincardine, ON, N2Z 1Z9, CANADA. Tel: 519-396-3289. p. 2673

Posthumus, Michaela, Br Supvr, Bruce County Public Library, Tiverton Branch, 56 King St, Tiverton, ON, N0G 2T0, CANADA. Tel: 519-368-5655. p. 2674

Postlethwaite, Bonnie, Dean, Univ Libr, University of Missouri-Kansas City Libraries, 800 E 51st St, Kansas City, MO, 64110. Tel: 816-235-1531. p. 1257

Postma, Jill, Librn, Homewood Public Library, 17917 Dixie Hwy, Homewood, IL, 60430-1703. Tel: 708-798-0121. p. 601

Poston, Ed, Instrul Serv Librn, Berea College, 100 Campus Dr, Berea, KY, 40404. Tel: 859-985-3172. p. 849

Poston, Linda, Dir, Messiah University, One University Ave, Ste 3002, Mechanicsburg, PA, 17055. Tel: 717-691-6006, Ext 3820. p. 1960

Postyn, Anita, Law Librn, Supreme Court Library, Richmond Supreme Court Law Library, 25 Hyatt St, Rm 515, Staten Island, NY, 10301-1968. Tel: 718-675-8711. p. 1645

Poswencyk, Doug, Br Mgr, Somerset County Library System of New Jersey, Somerville Public Library, 35 West End Ave, Somerville, NJ, 08876. Tel: 908-458-8445. p. 1392

Potance, Rebecca, Librn, Museum of New Mexico, Museum of Fine Arts Library, 107 W Palace Ave, Santa Fe, NM, 87501. Tel: 505-476-5061. p. 1475

Potap, Olga, Acq Librn, Boston University Libraries, School of Theology Library, 745 Commonwealth Ave, 2nd Flr, Boston, MA, 02215. Tel: 617-353-3034. p. 993

Potdevin, Nicole, University Librn for User Services, Fairleigh Dickinson University, 285 Madison Ave, M-LAO-03, Madison, NJ, 07940. Tel: 973-443-8627. p. 1415

Potemkin, Alexis (Alex), Dir, Libr Serv, Tarrant County College, Northwest Campus Walsh Library, 4801 Marine Creek Pkwy, Fort Worth, TX, 76179. Tel: 817-515-7725. p. 2180

Potje, Linda, Mgr, Township of Springwater Public Library, Minesing Branch, Minesing Community Ctr, 2347 Ronald Rd, Minesing, ON, L0L 1Y0, CANADA. Tel: 705-722-6440. p. 2658

Potter, Cara, Dir, Defiance Public Library, 320 Fort St, Defiance, OH, 43512-2186. Tel: 419-782-1456. p. 1781

Potter, Geoffrey, Webmaster, University of Texas at Austin, 3925 W Braker Lane, Ste 4.909, Austin, TX, 78759. Tel: 512-232-3126. p. 2141

Potter, Heidi, Libr Dir, Princeton Public Library, 40 Main St, Princeton, ME, 04668. Tel: 207-796-5333. p. 938

Potter, Jeffrey, Interim Libr Dir, Prince George's Community College Library, 301 Largo Rd, Largo, MD, 20774-2199. Tel: 301-546-0468. p. 970

Potter, Jo-Ann, Libr Tech, Nova Scotia Community College, Cumberland Campus Library, One Main St, Springhill, NS, B0M 1X0, CANADA. Tel: 902-597-4109. p. 2619

Potter, Jonathan, Asst Dir, Eastern Washington University, 600 N Riverpoint Blvd, Rm 230, Spokane, WA, 99202. Tel: 509-358-7930. p. 2383

Potter, Kelley, Mgr, Pub Serv, Caledon Public Library, 150 Queen St S, Bolton, ON, L7E 1E3, CANADA. Tel: 905-857-1400, Ext 238. p. 2631

Potter, Liz, Dir, Phoenicia Library, 48 Main St, Phoenicia, NY, 12464. Tel: 845-688-7811. p. 1618

Potter, Melissa, Asst Libr Serv Dir, Burbank Public Library, 110 N Glenoaks Blvd, Burbank, CA, 91502-1203. Tel: 818-238-5600. p. 125

Potter, Michelle, Librn, Holyrood Public Library, Holyrood Access Rd, Exit 36, Holyrood, NL, A0A 2R0, CANADA. Tel: 709-229-7852. p. 2608

Potter, Nick, Dir, Commun Relations, Pueblo City-County Library District, 100 E Abriendo Ave, Pueblo, CO, 81004-4290. Tel: 719-562-5605. p. 293

Potter, Nicole, Curator of Coll, Margaret Chase Smith Library, 56 Norridgewock Ave, Skowhegan, ME, 04976. Tel: 207-474-7133. p. 940

Potter, Patricia, Ref Spec, University of Southern Maine Libraries, 314 Forest Ave, Portland, ME, 04103. Tel: 207-780-5451. p. 937

Potter, Steven, Exec Dir, Missouri Evergreen, 1190 Meramec Station Rd, Ste 207, Ballwin, MO, 63021-6902. p. 2769

Potter, Steven V, Dir of Libr, Mid-Continent Public Library, 15616 E US Hwy 24, Independence, MO, 64050. Tel: 816-836-5200. p. 1250

Potter, Ted, Head, Pub Serv, University of Iowa Libraries, College of Law Library, 200 Boyd Law Bldg, Iowa City, IA, 52242-1166. Tel: 319-335-9017. p. 761

Potter, Teresa, City Librn, Helen Hall Library, 100 W Walker, League City, TX, 77573-3899. Tel: 281-554-1111. p. 2210

Potters, Bonnie, Tech Serv Mgr, Clearwater Public Library System, 100 N Osceola Ave, Clearwater, FL, 33755. Tel: 727-562-4970. p. 388

Potthoff, Renita, Dir, Monterey-Tippecanoe Township Public Library, 6260 E Main St, Monterey, IN, 46960. Tel: 574-542-2171. p. 707

Pottinger, J, Librn, Dixon Correctional Center Library, 2600 N Brinton Ave, Dixon, IL, 61021. Tel: 815-288-5561. p. 579

Potts, Amy, Circ Mgr, Salida Regional Library, 405 E St, Salida, CO, 81201. Tel: 719-539-4826. p. 295

Potts, Brian, Libr Operations Coordr, Wright Memorial Public Library, 1776 Far Hills Ave, Oakwood, OH, 45419-2598. Tel: 937-294-7171. p. 1810

Potts, Jennifer, Curator of Objects & Textiles, Delaware Historical Society Research Library, 505 N Market St, Wilmington, DE, 19801. Tel: 302-655-7161. p. 357

Potts, Linda, Br Mgr, Idabel Public Library, 103 E Main St, Idabel, OK, 74745. Tel: 580-286-6406. p. 1850

Potts, Renee, Libr Spec, Saint Louis Community College, Forest Park Campus Library, 5600 Oakland Ave, Saint Louis, MO, 63110-1316. Tel: 314-644-9681. p. 1273

Potvin, Gail, Librn, Grantsburg Public Library, 415 S Robert St, Grantsburg, WI, 54840-7423. Tel: 715-463-2244. p. 2438

Potwin, Sarah, Executive Library Dir, Niagara Falls Public Library, Earl W Brydges Bldg, 1425 Main St, Niagara Falls, NY, 14305. Tel: 716-286-4914. p. 1606

Potwin, Sarah, Executive Library Dir, Niagara Falls Public Library, LaSalle Branch, 8728 Buffalo Ave, Niagara Falls, NY, 14304. Tel: 716-283-8309. p. 1606

Poulin, Eric, Asst Prof of Practice, Simmons University, 300 The Fenway, Boston, MA, 02115. Tel: 617-521-2800. p. 2786

Poulin, Lisa, Libr Mgr, Maricopa County Sheriff's Office Inmate Library, 3150 W Lower Buckeye Rd, Ste C, Phoenix, AZ, 85009. Tel: 602-876-5633, 602-876-5638. p. 71

Poulin, Mike, Head, Coll Mgt, Colgate University, 13 Oak Dr, Hamilton, NY, 13346-1398. Tel: 315-228-7025. p. 1543

Poulin, Priscilla, Librn, Andover Public Library, 11 School St, Andover, NH, 03216. Tel: 603-735-5333. p. 1353

Poulin, Sonia, Dir, Alberta Law Libraries, LRTC Calgary, Calgary Court Ctr, Ste 501-N, 601 Fifth St SW, Calgary, AB, T2P 5P7, CANADA. Tel: 780-422-1011. p. 2525

Pouliot, Amber, Dir, Margaret Shontz Memorial Library, 145 Second St, Conneaut Lake, PA, 16316. Tel: 814-382-6666. p. 1924

Pouliot, Jeremie, Head of Libr, Cegep Riviere du-Loup-Bibliotheque, 80 rue Frontenac, Riviere-du-Loup, QC, G5R 1R1, CANADA. Tel: 418-862-6903, Ext 2579. p. 2732

Pound, Danean, Libr Coord, Enterprise State Community College, 600 Plaza Dr, Enterprise, AL, 36330. Tel: 334-347-2623, Ext 2308. p. 15

Povero, Kelly, Asst Libr Dir, Montour Falls Memorial Library, 406 W Main St, Montour Falls, NY, 14865. Tel: 607-535-7489. p. 1573

Povilaitis, Bonnie, Dir, Pathfinder Community Library, 812 Michigan Ave, Baldwin, MI, 49304. Tel: 231-745-4010. p. 1082

Pow, Virginia, Librn, University of Alberta, William C Wonders Map Collection, 1-55 Cameron Library, Edmonton, AB, T6G 2J8, CANADA. Tel: 780-492-7919. p. 2538

Powe, Kymberlee, Ch Serv, YA Serv, Connecticut State Library, 231 Capitol Ave, Hartford, CT, 06106. Tel: 860-704-2207. p. 317

Powel, Jessie, Libr Asst, Dora Bee Woodyard Memorial Library, 411 Mulberry St, Elizabeth, WV, 26143. Tel: 304-275-4295. p. 2402

Powell Allen, Shannon, Outreach Serv Librn, Gadsden County Public Library, 732 S Pat Thomas Pkwy, Quincy, FL, 32351. Tel: 850-627-7106. p. 439

Powell, Angela, Br Mgr, Defiance Public Library, Johnson Memorial, 116 W High St, Hicksville, OH, 43526. Tel: 419-542-6200. p. 1781

Powell, Anne, Cat Librn, Campbell University, Norman Adrian Wiggins School of Law Library, 225 Hillsborough St, Ste 203H, Raleigh, NC, 27603. Tel: 919-865-5869. p. 1676

Powell, Anne-Elizabeth, Head, Tech Serv & Syst, Point Loma Nazarene University, 3900 Lomaland Dr, San Diego, CA, 92106-2899. Tel: 619-849-2312. p. 216

Powell, Antoinette, Music Librn, Ref Librn, Lawrence University, 113 S Lawe St, Appleton, WI, 54911-5683. Tel: 920-832-6995. p. 2420

Powell, Barb, Librn, Thomas St Angelo Public Library, 1305 Second Ave, Cumberland, WI, 54829. Tel: 715-822-2767. p. 2429

Powell, Benson, Support Serv Coordr, Woods Rogers, PLC, Wells Fargo Tower, 10 S Jefferson St, Ste 1800, Roanoke, VA, 24011. Tel: 540-983-7600. p. 2346

Powell, Brad, Br Mgr, Saint Johns County Public Library System, Hastings Branch, 6195 S Main St, Hastings, FL, 32145. Tel: 904-827-6971. p. 440

Powell, Brenda, Asst Librn, Wallace Community College, 3000 Earl Goodwin Pkwy, Selma, AL, 36701. Tel: 334-876-9344, 334-876-9345. p. 35

Powell, Charles, Dir, Dalton Public Library, 306 Main St, Dalton, NE, 69131. Tel: 308-377-2413. p. 1312

Powell, Charles A, Dir, University of Florida, 2199 S Rock Rd, Fort Pierce, FL, 34945-3138. Tel: 772-468-3922. p. 405

Powell, Claire, Dir, Libr Serv, Ringling College of Art & Design, 2700 N Tamiami Trail, Sarasota, FL, 34234-5895. Tel: 941-359-7587. p. 443

Powell, David, Asst Librn, Ref (Info Servs), Methodist Theological School, 3081 Columbus Pike, Delaware, OH, 43015. Tel: 740-362-3438. p. 1782

Powell, Devon, Dean of Libr, South Suburban College Library, 15800 S State St, Rm 1249, South Holland, IL, 60473-1200. Tel: 708-210-5751. p. 648

Powell, Erica, Metadata & Spec Coll Librn, University of Miami, Louis Calder Memorial Library, Miller School of Medicine, 1601 NW Tenth Ave, Miami, FL, 33136. Tel: 305-243-6931. p. 425

Powell, Gina, Outreach & Vols Serv Librn, North Carolina Regional Library for the Blind & Physically Handicapped, 1841 Capital Blvd, Raleigh, NC, 27635. Tel: 919-733-4376. p. 1709

Powell, Jeanette, Dir, Jones Memorial Library, One Water St, Orleans, VT, 05860. Tel: 802-754-6660. p. 2291

Powell, Jennifer, Dir, Tyrone-Snyder Public Library, 1000 Pennsylvania Ave, Tyrone, PA, 16686. Tel: 814-684-1133. p. 2014

Powell, Jessica, Dir, Oldham County Public Library, 308 Yager Ave, La Grange, KY, 40031. Tel: 502-222-9713. p. 861

Powell, Joyce, Br Mgr, Ouachita Parish Public Library, Carver McDonald Branch, 2941 Renwick St, Monroe, LA, 71201. Tel: 318-327-1477. p. 898

Powell, Judy, Libr Mgr, Columbus County Public Library, Tabor City Public, 101 E Fifth St, Tabor City, NC, 28463. Tel: 910-653-3774. p. 1722

Powell, Karen, Dir, Eric M Taylor Center, 10-10 Hazen St, East Elmhurst, NY, 11370. Tel: 718-546-7359. p. 1527

Powell, Kathleen, Curator, St Catharines Museum, 1932 Welland Canals Pkwy, St. Catharines, ON, L2R 7K6, CANADA. Tel: 905-984-8880. p. 2680

Powell, Kathryn, Ch, Chester County Library, 100 Center St, Chester, SC, 29706. Tel: 803-377-8145. p. 2052
Powell, Kristie, Cat Librn, University of Dallas, 1845 E Northgate Dr, Irving, TX, 75062-4736. Tel: 972-721-4031. p. 2203
Powell, Laura, Ch & Youth Librn, Talbot County Free Library, 100 W Dover St, Easton, MD, 21601-2620. Tel: 410-822-1626. p. 964
Powell, Marilyn, Materials Handling Coord, New Albany-Floyd County Public Library, 180 W Spring St, New Albany, IN, 47150. Tel: 812-944-8464. p. 709
Powell, Mary Jo, ILL/Doc Delivery Serv, Mohave Community College Library, Lake Havasu City Campus, 1977 W Acoma Blvd, Lake Havasu City, AZ, 86403-2999. Tel: 928-453-5809. p. 64
Powell, Melanie, Br Mgr, Wayne County Public Library, Steele Memorial, 119 W Main St, Mount Olive, NC, 28365. Tel: 919-299-8105. p. 1691
Powell, Niki, Br Mgr, Southern Oklahoma Library System, Love County Library, 500 S Hwy 77, Marietta, OK, 73448. Tel: 580-276-3783. p. 1841
Powell, Reese, Dir of Libr, William Carey University Libraries, 710 William Carey Pkwy, Hattiesburg, MS, 39401. Tel: 601-318-6169. p. 1219
Powell, Steve, Chief Operating Officer, Orange County Library System, 101 E Central Blvd, Orlando, FL, 32801. Tel: 407-835-7323. p. 431
Powell, Steve, Regional Mgr, Cobb County Public Library System, West Cobb Regional Library, 1750 Dennis Kemp Lane, Kennesaw, GA, 30152. Tel: 770-528-4699. p. 489
Powell, Steve, Libr Dir, Orange Public Library, 348 Main St, Orange, NJ, 07050. Tel: 973-786-3988. p. 1431
Powell, Susan, Maps Librn, University of California, Berkeley, Earth Sciences & Maps, 50 McCone Hall, Berkeley, CA, 94720-6000. Tel: 510-642-2997. p. 122
Powell, Tracy, Per, Emory University Libraries, Pitts Theology Library, Candler School of Theology, 1531 Dickey Dr, Ste 560, Atlanta, GA, 30322-2810. Tel: 404-727-4166. p. 463
Powell, Vicky, Br Mgr, Ouachita Parish Public Library, Cpl J R Searcy Memorial Library, 5775 Jonesboro Rd, West Monroe, LA, 71292. Tel: 318-327-1240. p. 898
Powelson, Susan, Assoc Univ Librn, Digital & Discovery Serv, Tech, University of Calgary Library, 2500 University Dr NW, Calgary, AB, T2N 1N4, CANADA. Tel: 403-220-5930. p. 2529
Power, Amy, Youth Serv Librn, Burlington Public Library, 210 Court St, Burlington, IA, 52601. Tel: 319-753-1647. p. 736
Power, Marlene, Libr Dir, Redeemer University, 777 Garner Rd E, Ancaster, ON, L9K 1J4, CANADA. Tel: 905-648-2131. p. 2628
Power, Mary Alice, Ref Librn, Lawrence Technological University Library, 21000 W Ten Mile Rd, Southfield, MI, 48075-1058. Tel: 248-204-3000. p. 1151
Power, Rebecca, Youth Serv Librn, Smyrna Public Library, 100 Village Green Circle, Smyrna, GA, 30080-3478. Tel: 770-431-2860. p. 497
Power, Rose, Libr Assoc, College of the North Atlantic Library Services, Placentia Campus, One Roosevelt Ave, Placentia, NL, A0B 2Y0, CANADA. Tel: 709-227-6264. p. 2609
Powers, Alla, Instrul Serv Librn, Oregon Institute of Technology Library, 3201 Campus Dr, Klamath Falls, OR, 97601-8801. Tel: 541-885-1774. p. 1883
Powers, Allison, Dir, Roy Downs Memorial Calera Library, 9700 Hwy 25, Calera, AL, 35040. Tel: 205-668-7200. p. 11
Powers, Annie, Mgr, Info Tech, Volusia County Public Library, 1290 Indian Lake Rd, Daytona Beach, FL, 32124. Tel: 386-248-1745. p. 392
Powers, Anthony, Br Mgr, Chicago Public Library, Austin-Irving, 6100 W Irving Park Rd, Chicago, IL, 60634. Tel: 312-744-6222. p. 556
Powers, Carla, Libr Mgr, Duluth Public Library, 520 W Superior St, Duluth, MN, 55802. Tel: 218-730-4225. p. 1172
Powers, Dan, Dir, Crestwood Public Library District, 4955 W 135th St, Crestwood, IL, 60418. Tel: 708-371-4090. p. 574
Powers, Donna, Dir, Fair Haven Public Library, 748 River Rd, Fair Haven, NJ, 07704. Tel: 732-747-0241, Ext 220. p. 1402
Powers, Heidi, Supvr, Deschutes Public Library District, Sunriver Area Branch, 56855 Venture Lane, Sunriver, OR, 97707. Tel: 541-312-1085. p. 1874
Powers, Jackie, Asst Dir, Lucius Beebe Memorial Library, 345 Main St, Wakefield, MA, 01880-5093. Tel: 781-246-6334. p. 1061
Powers, Jeanne, Adult Serv, Bristol Public Library, 701 Goode St, Bristol, VA, 24201. Tel: 276-645-8780. p. 2308
Powers, Jo, Info Serv Librn, Talbot County Free Library, 100 W Dover St, Easton, MD, 21601-2620. Tel: 410-822-1626. p. 964
Powers, Joan, Ch, Moses Greeley Parker Memorial Library, 28 Arlington St, Dracut, MA, 01826. Tel: 978-454-5474. p. 1015
Powers, Luke, Ad, Plain City Public Library, 305 W Main St, Plain City, OH, 43064-1148. Tel: 614-873-4912, Ext 130. p. 1816
Powers, Mary, Ch Serv, Midland County Public Library, 301 W Missouri Ave, Midland, TX, 79701. Tel: 432-688-4320. p. 2219
Powers, Matthew, Exec Dir, Woodstock History Center, 26 Elm St, Woodstock, VT, 05091. Tel: 802-457-1822. p. 2300
Powers, Meredith, Head, Electronic Res, York College Library, 94-20 Guy R Brewer Blvd, Jamaica, NY, 11451. Tel: 718-262-2018. p. 1556
Powers, Monica, Libr Dir, Amityville Public Library, 19 John St, Amityville, NY, 11701. Tel: 631-264-0567. p. 1486
Powers, Robert, Access & Learning Serv Librn, Rockhurst University, 1100 Rockhurst Rd, Kansas City, MO, 64110-2561. Tel: 816-501-4121. p. 1257
Powers, Shannon, Head, Info Serv, Chelsea District Library, 221 S Main St, Chelsea, MI, 48118-1267. Tel: 734-475-8732. p. 1090
Powers, Susan, Mgr, Access Serv, Central Michigan University, 250 E Preston St, Mount Pleasant, MI, 48859. Tel: 989-774-1212. p. 1134
Powers, Tammy, Libr Dir, Dona Ana Community College, 3400 S Espina, Rm 260, Las Cruces, NM, 88003. Tel: 575-527-7555. p. 1470
Powers, Tina, Br Librn, Riverside Regional Library, Benton Branch, 54 N Winchester, Hwy 61, Benton, MO, 63736. Tel: 573-545-3581. p. 1252
Powers, Vicki L, Librn, Eula & David Wintermann Library, 101 N Walnut Ave, Eagle Lake, TX, 77434. Tel: 979-234-5411. p. 2172
Powers-Jones, Martha, Dir, Okefenokee Regional Library, 401 Lee Ave, Waycross, GA, 31501. Tel: 912-287-4978. p. 503
Powes, Shyla, Libr Tech, Placentia Public Library, 14 Atlantic Ave, Placentia, NL, A0B 2Y0, CANADA. Tel: 709-227-3621. p. 2608
Powhida, Elizabeth, Dir, Valatie Free Library, 1036 Kinderhook St, Valatie, NY, 12184. Tel: 518-758-9321. p. 1656
Poworoznek, Emily L, Librn, University of New Hampshire Library, Engineering, Mathematics & Computer Science, Kingsbury Hall, 33 Academic Way, Durham, NH, 03824. Tel: 603-862-4168. p. 1362
Poworoznek, Emily LeViness, Librn, University of New Hampshire Library, Chemistry, Parsons Hall, 23 College Rd, Durham, NH, 03824-3598. Tel: 603-862-4168. p. 1362
Poworoznek, Emily LeViness, Librn, University of New Hampshire Library, David G Clark Memorial Physics Library, DeMeritt Hall, Nine Library Way, Durham, NH, 03824-3568. Tel: 603-862-2348. p. 1362
Poyer, Helen, Dir, Cobb County Public Library System, 266 Roswell St, Marietta, GA, 30060-2004. Tel: 770-528-2320. p. 489
Poyer, Judy, Head, Mat Mgt, Anne Arundel County Public Library, Five Harry Truman Pkwy, Annapolis, MD, 21401. Tel: 410-222-2503. p. 950
Poynor, Dee Ann, Campus Librn, Amarillo College, West Campus, 6100 W Ninth Ave, Amarillo, TX, 79106. Tel: 806-356-3627. p. 2134
Pozzi, Ellen, Dr, Prog Dir, William Paterson University, College of Education, 1600 Valley Rd, Wayne, NJ, 07470. Tel: 973-720-3784. p. 2788
Pradhan, Pramod, Commun Outreach Liaison, West Hartford Public Library, 20 S Main St, West Hartford, CT, 06107-2432. Tel: 860-561-6950. p. 345
Praest, Jenny, Libr Dir, John Rogers Memorial Public Library, 703 Second St, Dodge, NE, 68633. Tel: 402-693-2512. p. 1312
Prager, Stephen, Br Mgr, Mobile Public Library, Moorer/Spring Hill Branch, Four McGregor Ave, Mobile, AL, 36608. Tel: 251-470-7770. p. 26
Prak, Margo, Libr Dir, Dansville Public Library, 200 Main St, Dansville, NY, 14437. Tel: 585-335-6720. p. 1524
Prasad, Neelam, Ms, Br Mgr, Enoch Pratt Free Library, Clifton Branch, 2001 N Wolfe St, Baltimore, MD, 21213-1477. Tel: 443-984-4973. p. 952
Prater, Angela, Mgr, Confluence Health - Central Washington Hospital, 1201 S Miller St, Wenatchee, WA, 98801. Tel: 509-664-3476. p. 2393
Pratesi, Angela L, Head Librn, Bowling Green State University Libraries, Music Library & Bill Schurk Sound Archives, Jerome Library, 3rd Flr, Bowling Green, OH, 43403. Tel: 419-372-9929. p. 1752
Prather, Cindy, Asst Dir, Conneaut Public Library, 304 Buffalo St, Conneaut, OH, 44030-2658. Tel: 440-593-1608. p. 1778
Prather, David, Ref Librn, Lee-Itawamba Library System, 219 N Madison St, Tupelo, MS, 38804-3899. Tel: 662-841-9027. p. 1233
Prato, Stephanie C, Head, Children's Servx, Simsbury Public Library, 725 Hopmeadow St, Simsbury, CT, 06070. Tel: 860-658-7663. p. 337
Pratt, Alexandra, Libr Dir, West Tisbury Free Public Library, 1042 State Rd, Vineyard Haven, MA, 02568. Tel: 508-693-3366. p. 1061
Pratt, Caitlin, Dir, Critical Path Learning Center, 1233 Locust St, 2nd Flr, Philadelphia, PA, 19107. Tel: 215-985-4851. p. 1976
Pratt, Carolyn A, Librn, Mitchell Silberberg & Knupp LLP, 11377 W Olympic Blvd, Los Angeles, CA, 90064-1683. Tel: 310-312-2000. p. 166
Pratt, Charles, Libr Mgr, Sno-Isle Libraries, Stanwood Library, 9701 271st St NW, Stanwood, WA, 98292-8097. Tel: 360-629-3132. p. 2371
Pratt, Christine, Coll Develop Librn, Framingham Public Library, 49 Lexington St, Framingham, MA, 01702-8278. Tel: 508-879-5570, Ext 4359. p. 1019
Pratt, Diane, Libr Dir, Modale Public Library, 210 N Main St, Modale, IA, 51556. Tel: 712-645-2826. p. 770
Pratt, Ellen, Ref & Instruction Librn, Mount Wachusett Community College Library, 444 Green St, Gardner, MA, 01440. Tel: 978-630-9285. p. 1020
Pratt, Estina, Adjunct Librn, Compton College Library, 1111 E Artesia Blvd, Compton, CA, 90221. Tel: 310-900-1600, Ext 2179. p. 132
Pratt, Greg, Sr Info Spec, University of Texas, M D Anderson Cancer Center Research Medical Library, 1400 Pressler St, Houston, TX, 77030-3722. Tel: 713-745-5156. p. 2200
Pratt, Jane, Dir, Richmond Public Library, 325 Civic Center Plaza, Richmond, CA, 94804-9991. Tel: 510-620-6561. p. 200

Pratt, Jill, Ch, Greensburg-Decatur County Public Library, 1110 E Main St, Greensburg, IN, 47240. Tel: 812-663-2826. p. 688

Pratt, JoEllen, Libr Dir, Cameron Public Library, 312 N Chestnut St, Cameron, MO, 64429. Tel: 816-632-2311. p. 1239

Pratt, Kathleen, Cat, Cotuit Library, 871 Main St, Cotuit, MA, 02635. Tel: 508-428-8141. p. 1013

Pratt, Mark, Learning Res Spec, Trinity Valley Community College Library, Terrell HSC Campus, 1551 SH 34 S, Terrell, TX, 75160. Tel: 469-416-3805. p. 2137

Pratt, Michele, Dir, Delta College Library, 1961 Delta Rd, University Center, MI, 48710. Tel: 989-686-9006. p. 1155

Pratt, Tricia, Librn, Burnet County Library System, Oakalla Public Library, 29011 FM 963, Oakalla, TX, 78608. Tel: 512-556-9085. p. 2152

Pratt, Vallarie, Exec Dir, Whitfield-Murray Historical Society, 715 Chattanooga Ave, Dalton, GA, 30720. Tel: 706-278-0217. p. 474

Pratt-McHugh, Sheli, Learning Commons Coord, Research & Instruction Librarian for Technology & Outreach, University of Scranton, 800 Linden St, Scranton, PA, 18510-4634. Tel: 570-941-4006. p. 2005

Praught, Melissa, Dir, Rising City Community Library, 675 Main St, Rising City, NE, 68658. Tel: 402-954-0270. p. 1334

Prazak, Catherine, Libr Mgr, San Antonio Public Library, Great Northwest, 9050 Wellwood, San Antonio, TX, 78251. Tel: 210-207-9210. p. 2239

Prchal, Alyson, Head, Youth Serv, Barrington Area Library, 505 N Northwest Hwy, Barrington, IL, 60010. Tel: 847-382-1300. p. 539

Prchal, Laurel, Br Mgr, Jackson County Library Services, Jacksonville Branch, 340 West C St, Jacksonville, OR, 97530. Tel: 541-899-1665. p. 1886

Prchal, Robb, Head, Property Mgmt & Security, Russell Library, 123 Broad St, Middletown, CT, 06457. Tel: 860-347-2528. p. 322

Preas, Chelsea, Br Mgr, Green Tom County Library System, North Branch, 3001 N Chadbourne St, San Angelo, TX, 76903. Tel: 325-653-8412. p. 2236

Prechel, Amelia, Asst Librn, Prairie Trails Public Library District, 8449 S Moody, Burbank, IL, 60459-2525. Tel: 708-430-3688. p. 546

Prechtel, Karyn, Dep Dir, Pub Serv, Pima County Public Library, 101 N Stone Ave, Tucson, AZ, 85701. Tel: 520-594-5600. p. 82

Preece, Diana, Ref Serv, Milford Public Library, 57 New Haven Ave, Milford, CT, 06460. Tel: 203-783-3290. p. 323

Preece, Kerry, Youth Serv Mgr, McMillan Memorial Library, 490 E Grand Ave, Wisconsin Rapids, WI, 54494-4898. Tel: 715-422-5136. p. 2489

Prefontaine, Gabrielle, Dean, Univ Libr, University of Winnipeg Library, 515 Portage Ave, Winnipeg, MB, R3B 2E9, CANADA. Tel: 204-786-9488. p. 2596

Pregler, Maria, Asst Dir, Antigo Public Library, 617 Clermont St, Antigo, WI, 54409. Tel: 715-623-3724. p. 2420

Preilis, Wendy, Adult Learning Ctr Spec, Johnson County Public Library, 49 E Monroe St, Franklin, IN, 46131. p. 686

Preisler, Dennis, PhD, Dir, Archives & Rec Mgt, State Archivist, Arizona State Library, Archives & Public Records, 1901 W Madison St, Phoenix, AZ, 85009. Tel: 602-926-4035. p. 69

Prellwitz, Andrew R, Libr Dir, User Serv Librn, Ripon College, 300 Seward St, Ripon, WI, 54971. Tel: 920-748-8175. p. 2474

Premuto, J, Ch Serv, Bellmore Memorial Library, 2288 Bedford Ave, Bellmore, NY, 11710. Tel: 516-785-2990. p. 1492

Prendergast, Kevin, ILL, Ref Librn, Montclair State University, One Normal Ave, Montclair, NJ, 07043-1699. Tel: 973-655-4301. p. 1420

Prendergast, Neville, Dir, Tulane University, Rudolph Matas Library of the Health Sciences, Tulane Health Sciences Campus, 1430 Tulane Ave, SL-86, New Orleans, LA, 70112-2699. Tel: 504-988-2060. p. 904

Prendergast, Tess, Lecturer, University of British Columbia, The Irving K Barber Learning Ctr, 1961 E Mall, Ste 470, Vancouver, BC, V6T 1Z1, CANADA. Tel: 604-822-2404. p. 2795

Prendergast, Tim, Dir, Hodgkins Public Library District, 6500 Wenz Ave, Hodgkins, IL, 60525. Tel: 708-579-1844. p. 600

Prendergust, Sue, Ref Mgr, Jackson/Hinds Library System, Eudora Welty Library (Main Library), 300 North State St, Jackson, MS, 39201-1705. Tel: 601-968-5811. p. 1221

Preneta, Julie, Dir, Leelanau Township Public Library, 119 E Nagonaba St, Northport, MI, 49670. Tel: 231-386-5131. p. 1138

Prenger, Becky, Br Supvr, Auglaize County Libraries, Francis J Stallo Memorial Library, 196 E Fourth St, Minster, OH, 45865. Tel: 419-628-2925. p. 1828

Preniczky, Danielle, Head, Program Dev, Marine Corps Recruit Depot Library, 3800 Chosin Ave, Bldg 7 W, San Diego, CA, 92140-5196. Tel: 619-524-1849. p. 215

Prentice, Julian, Fac Librn, City College of San Francisco, 50 Frida Kahlo Way, 4th Flr, San Francisco, CA, 94112. Tel: 415-452-5433. p. 224

Prentice, Katie, Assoc Dir, University of Oklahoma, Schusterman Ctr, 4502 E 41st St, Tulsa, OK, 74135. Tel: 918-660-3216. p. 1867

Prentice, Katie, Exec Dir, Houston Academy of Medicine, 1133 John Freeman Blvd, No 100, Houston, TX, 77030. Tel: 713-795-4200. p. 2193

Prentice, Melissa, Dep Dir, Mead Public Library, 710 N Eight St, Sheboygan, WI, 53081-4563. Tel: 920-459-3400, Ext 2033. p. 2476

Prentiss, Erin, Outreach Librn, Augusta-Richmond County Public Library, 823 Telfair St, Augusta, GA, 30901. Tel: 706-821-2600. p. 466

Prescott, Carolyn, Supvr, Access Serv, Oral Roberts University Library, 7777 S Lewis Ave, Tulsa, OK, 74171. Tel: 918-495-6723. p. 1865

Prescott, Joan C, Dir, Rogers Free Library, 525 Hope St, Bristol, RI, 02809. Tel: 401-253-6948. p. 2030

Prescott, Martha, Libr Dir, Berkshire Medical Center, 725 North St, Pittsfield, MA, 01201. Tel: 413-447-2734. p. 1047

Prescott, Patricia M, Libr Dir, Webb Institute, 298 Crescent Beach Rd, Glen Cove, NY, 11542. Tel: 516-671-0439. p. 1539

Presedo, Vivian, Bus Mgr, Yonkers Public Library, One Larkin Ctr, Yonkers, NY, 10701. Tel: 914-337-1500. p. 1668

Preskitt, Sarah, Adult Serv Coordr, Anchorage Public Library, 3600 Denali St, Anchorage, AK, 99503. Tel: 907-343-2856. p. 42

Presler, Melanie, Adult Serv Mgr, Amherst Public Library, 221 Spring St, Amherst, OH, 44001. Tel: 440-988-4230. p. 1746

Presley, Beverly, Librn, Clark University, Guy H Burnham Map & Aerial Photography Library, 950 Main St, Worcester, MA, 01610-1477. Tel: 508-793-7706. p. 1071

Presley, Chrystal, Librn, Ragland Public Library, 26 Providence Rd, Ragland, AL, 35131. Tel: 205-472-2007. p. 33

Presley, Melisa, Br Mgr, Buncombe County Public Libraries, Black Mountain Branch, 105 Dougherty St, Black Mountain, NC, 28711. Tel: 828-250-4756. p. 1672

Presley, Sondra, Br Mgr, Public Library of Cincinnati & Hamilton County, West End, 805 Ezzard Charles Dr, Cincinnati, OH, 45203. Tel: 513-369-6026. p. 1763

Pressey, Jenna, Libr Assoc, Sadie Pope Dowdell Library of South Amboy, 100 Harold G Hoffman Plaza, South Amboy, NJ, 08879. Tel: 732-721-6060. p. 1442

Prestamo, Anne M, Dean, Univ Libr, Florida International University, 11200 SW Eighth St, Miami, FL, 33199. Tel: 305-348-2461. p. 421

Presti, Cathy, Ch Serv, Kinnelon Public Library, 132 Kinnelon Rd, Kinnelon, NJ, 07405. Tel: 973-838-1321. p. 1410

Preston, Deborah, Fiscal Officer, MidPointe Library System, 125 S Broad St, Middletown, OH, 45044. Tel: 513-424-1251. p. 1802

Preston, Janine, Dir, Belfast Public Library, 75 S Main St, Belfast, NY, 14711-8605. Tel: 585-365-2072. p. 1492

Preston, Karen, Dir, Life University, 1269 Barclay Circle, Marietta, GA, 30060. Tel: 770-426-2692. p. 489

Preston, Kathleen, Head, Tech Serv & Cat, Finkelstein Memorial Library, 24 Chestnut St, Spring Valley, NY, 10977. Tel: 845-352-5700, Ext 218. p. 1644

Preston, Leslie, Head, Acquisitions & Metadata Servs, Fashion Institute of Technology-SUNY, Seventh Ave at 27th St, 227 W 27th St, New York, NY, 10001-5992. Tel: 212-217-4346. p. 1585

Preston, Margaret, Ref Librn, New Hartford Public Library, Two Library Lane, New Hartford, NY, 13413-2815. Tel: 315-733-1535. p. 1576

Preston, Marie, Libr Tech, North Carolina Central University, School of Library & Information Sciences, James E Shepard Memorial Library, 3rd Flr, 1801 Fayetteville St, Durham, NC, 27707. Tel: 919-530-6400. p. 1686

Preston, Michelle, Libr Dir, Canmore Public Library, 101-700 Railway Ave, Canmore, AB, T1W 1P4, CANADA. Tel: 403-678-2468. p. 2530

Preston, Rosalind, Asst Commissioner, New Jersey State Prison, PO Box 861, Trenton, NJ, 08625. Tel: 609-292-9700, Ext 4285. p. 1448

Preston, Sherry, Pub Serv Librn, Gering Public Library, 1055 P St, Gering, NE, 69341. Tel: 308-436-7433. p. 1315

Preston, Steve, Dir, Amherst County Public Library, 382 S Main St, Amherst, VA, 24521. Tel: 434-946-9488. p. 2304

Preston, Steve, Dir, Amherst County Public Library, Madison Heights Branch, 200 River James Shopping Ctr, Madison Heights, VA, 24572. Tel: 434-846-8171. p. 2304

Preston-Schreck, Catherine, Coordr, Libr Asst, College of the Atlantic, 105 Eden St, Bar Harbor, ME, 04609-1198. Tel: 207-801-5664. p. 916

Presutti, Robert, Archivist, Emory University Libraries, Pitts Theology Library, Candler School of Theology, 1531 Dickey Dr, Ste 560, Atlanta, GA, 30322-2810. Tel: 404-727-4166. p. 463

Pretzer, Nannette, Dir, Saint Charles District Library, 132 S Saginaw St, Saint Charles, MI, 48655. Tel: 989-865-9451. p. 1147

Preudhomme, Gene, Dir, Supreme Court, Appellate Division, 27 Madison Ave, New York, NY, 10010. Tel: 212-340-0478. p. 1602

Preuit, Theresa, Assoc Dir, Coll Mgt, Assoc Dir, Pub Serv, Mercer University, Jack Tarver Library, 1300 Edgewood Ave, Macon, GA, 31207. Tel: 478-301-2960. p. 486

Preuss, Karen, Asst Libr Dir, Montgomery City-County Public Library System, 245 High St, Montgomery, AL, 36104. Tel: 334-240-4922. p. 29

Preuss, Nathan, Head, Pub Serv, University of Tennessee, Taylor Law Ctr, 1505 W Cumberland Ave, Knoxville, TN, 37996-1800. Tel: 865-974-6736. p. 2107

Prevatte, Crystal, Acq, Libr Asst, Central Carolina Community College Libraries, 1105 Kelly Dr, Sanford, NC, 27330. Tel: 919-718-7207. p. 1715

Prevette, Sunnie, Cataloger, Northwestern Regional Library, 111 N Front St, 2nd Flr, Elkin, NC, 28621. Tel: 336-835-4894, Ext 1005. p. 1688

Prevey-Levin, Kathy, Tech Serv, Wadleigh Memorial Library, 49 Nashua St, Milford, NH, 03055. Tel: 603-249-0645. p. 1374

Priest, Michael, Dir, Prairie-River Library District, 103 N Main St, Lapwai, ID, 83540. Tel: 208-843-7254. p. 524
Priest, Michael, Pres, Cooperative Information Network, Community Library Network, Post Falls Branch, 821 N Spokane St, Post Falls, ID, 83854. Tel: 208-769-2315, Ext 436. p. 2764
Priester, Amber, Youth Serv, Clearwater Public Library System, North Greenwood, 905 N Martin Luther King Jr Ave, Clearwater, FL, 33755. Tel: 727-562-4970. p. 389
Priester, Wanda L, Ref & Info Serv, South Carolina State University, 300 College St NE, Orangeburg, SC, 29115. Tel: 803-536-8647, p. 2067
Priestley, Holly, Br Mgr, Main Libr, Ouachita Parish Public Library, 1800 Stubbs Ave, Monroe, LA, 71201. Tel: 318-327-1490. p. 898
Prieth, Geraldine, Asst Dir, Melbourne Public Library, 540 E Fee Ave, Melbourne, FL, 32901. Tel: 321-952-4514. p. 421
Prieth, Jeri, Asst Libr Serv Dir, Brevard County Public Libraries, 308 Forrest Ave, 2nd Flr, Cocoa, FL, 32922. Tel: 321-633-1801. p. 389
Prieto, Adolfo, Ref & Instruction Librn, California State University, Fullerton, 800 N State College Blvd, Fullerton, CA, 92831. Tel: 657-278-5238. p. 147
Prieto, John, Archivist, Canal Society of New Jersey, 35 Waterview Blvd, Ste 103, Parsippany, NJ, 07054. Tel: 551-579-2791. p. 1432
Prieto-Seijas, Marta, Sr Librn, Youth Serv, Kalkaska County Library, 247 S Cedar St, Kalkaska, MI, 49646. Tel: 231-258-9411. p. 1122
Prieur, Linda, Br Support, Stormont, Dundas & Glengarry County Library, Ingleside Branch, Ten Memorial Sq, Ingleside, ON, K0C 1M0, CANADA. Tel: 613-537-2592. p. 2638
Prifogle, Sue, Dir, Rushville Public Library, 130 W Third St, Rushville, IN, 46173-1899. Tel: 765-932-3496. p. 717
Prilliman, Jennifer, Assoc Law Libr Dir, Oklahoma City University, School of Law Library, 2501 N Blackwelder, Oklahoma City, OK, 73106. Tel: 405-208-5271. p. 1858
Prime, Jacqueline, Dir, Phillipston Free Public Library, 25 Templeton Rd, Phillipston, MA, 01331-9704. Tel: 978-249-1734. p. 1046
Prime, Jacqueline, Dir, Boynton Public Library, 27 Boynton Rd, Templeton, MA, 01468-1412. Tel: 978-939-5582. p. 1059
Prime, Kaylea, Br Head, Thompson-Nicola Regional District Library System, Clearwater Branch, 422 Murtle Crescent, Clearwater, BC, V0E 1N1, CANADA. Tel: 250-674-2543. p. 2567
Primeau, Emma, Br Mgr, Oakville Public Library, White Oaks, 1070 McCraney St E, Oakville, ON, L6H 2R6, CANADA. Tel: 905-815-2038. p. 2662
Primeau, Emma, Br Mgr, Oakville Public Library, Woodside, 1274 Rebecca St, Oakville, ON, L6L 1Z2, CANADA. Tel: 905-815-2036, Ext 5141. p. 2662
Primeau, Melanie, Supvr, Pub Serv, Vancouver Community College, 250 W Pender St, Vancouver, BC, V6B 1S9, CANADA. Tel: 604-871-7000, Ext 8342. p. 2581
Primeaux, Beckie, Br Mgr, Cameron Parish Library, Grand Chenier Branch, 2863 Grand Chenier Hwy, Grand Chenier, LA, 70643. Tel: 337-538-2214. p. 886
Primiano, Amanda, Exec Dir, Monroe Free Library, 44 Millpond Pkwy, Monroe, NY, 10950. Tel: 845-783-4411. p. 1573
Prince, DeAnn, Acq & Coll Develop Librn, Asst Dir, Southeastern Oklahoma State University, 425 W University, Durant, OK, 74701-0609. Tel: 580-745-2702. p. 1846
Prince, Heather, Dir, Parrottsville Community Library, 2060 Canary Dr, Parrottsville, TN, 37843. Tel: 423-625-8990. p. 2123
Prince, J Dale, Dir of Libr, Louisiana State University Health Sciences Center, 433 Bolivar St, Box B3-1, New Orleans, LA, 70112-2223. Tel: 504-568-6100. p. 901
Prince, Tanya, Access Serv Mgr, York University Libraries, Leslie Frost Library, Glendon Campus, 2275 Bayview Ave, North York, ON, M4N 3M6, CANADA. Tel: 416-487-6726. p. 2662
Prince, William, ILL, Ref, Niceville Public Library, 206 Partin Dr N, Niceville, FL, 32578. p. 428
Prince-Richard, Celia P, Libr Mgr, University of the Virgin Islands, RR 2, Box 10000, Kingshill, VI, 00850-9781. Tel: 340-692-4134. p. 2517
Princz, Marina, Libr Coord, Yosef Wosk Library & Resource Centre, 5151 Oak St, Vancouver, BC, V6M 4H1, CANADA. Tel: 604-257-8668. p. 2582
Prindle, Wynne, Br Mgr, Lyon County Library System, Silver-Stage Branch, 3905 Hwy 50 W, Silver Springs, NV, 89429. Tel: 775-577-5015. p. 1352
Prine, Elaine, Br Librn, Community District Library, New Lothrop-Hazelton Township, 9387 Genesee St, New Lothrop, MI, 48460. Tel: 810-638-7575. p. 1095
Pring, Johnathan, Mgr, User Serv, Sheridan College Library, Davis Campus, 7899 McLaughlin Rd, Brampton, ON, L6V 1G6, CANADA. Tel: 905-459-7533, Ext 4338. p. 2663
Pringle, LaJuan, Branch Lead, Charlotte Mecklenburg Library, West Boulevard Branch, 2157 West Blvd, Charlotte, NC, 28208. Tel: 704-416-7400. p. 1680
Prinn, Charles, Circ & Tech Serv Coordr, Saint Joseph's College, 278 Whites Bridge Rd, Standish, ME, 04084-5263. Tel: 207-893-7725, p. 942
Prinos, Matt, Br Mgr, Oswego Public Library District, , Montgomery Campus, 1111 Reading Dr, Montgomery, IL, 60538. Tel: 630-978-1207. p. 631
Prinsen, Charlene, Br Mgr, Jackson County Library Services, Eagle Point Branch, 239 W Main St, Eagle Point, OR, 97524. Tel: 541-826-3313. p. 1886
Priola, Michelle, Dir, New Berlin Library, 15 S Main St, New Berlin, NY, 13411. Tel: 607-847-8564. p. 1575
Prioletti, Laurie, Human Res Mgr, Northbrook Public Library, 1201 Cedar Lane, Northbrook, IL, 60062-4581. Tel: 847-272-6224. p. 627
Prior, Alix, Br Mgr, Whatcom County Library System, Ferndale Branch, 2125 Main St, Ferndale, WA, 98248. Tel: 360-384-3647. p. 2359
Prior, Elizabeth, Branch Services, Palm Beach County Library System, 3650 Summit Blvd, West Palm Beach, FL, 33406-4198. Tel: 561-233-2600. p. 454
Prior, Susan, Div Mgr, Provincial Information & Library Resources Board, Arts & Culture Ctr, 125 Allandale Rd, St. John's, NL, A1B 3A3, CANADA. Tel: 709-737-3418. p. 2611
Priore, Charles, Sci Librn, Saint Olaf College, Rolvaag Memorial Library, Hustad Science Library, Halvorson Music Library, 1510 Saint Olaf Ave, Northfield, MN, 55057-1097. Tel: 507-786-3099. p. 1191
Prisbrey, Mary, Br Mgr, Fairfax County Public Library, Dolley Madison Branch, 1244 Oak Ridge Ave, McLean, VA, 22101-2818. Tel: 703-356-0770. p. 2316
Priscilla, Coatney, Dir, William Leonard Public Library District, 13820 Central Park Ave, Robbins, IL, 60472-1999. Tel: 708-597-2760. p. 640
Pritchard, Alicia, Managing Librn, Brooklyn Public Library, Bedford, 496 Franklin Ave, Brooklyn, NY, 11238. Tel: 718-623-0012. p. 1502
Pritchard, Colleen, Div Dir, Tech Serv, United States Department of Health & Human Services, FDA Library, WO2, Rm 3302, 10903 New Hampshire Ave, Silver Spring, MD, 20993. Tel: 301-796-2373. p. 975
Pritchard, Dan, Assoc Dir, Curricular Engagement, United States Military Academy Library, Jefferson Hall Library & Learning Ctr, 758 Cullum Rd, West Point, NY, 10996. Tel: 845-938-8301. p. 1663
Pritchard, Debra, Dir, Spalding Public Library, 159 W St Joseph St, Spalding, NE, 68665. Tel: 308-497-2705. p. 1336
Pritchard, Lisa, Dir, Libr Serv, Jefferson College Library, 1000 Viking Dr, Hillsboro, MO, 63050. Tel: 636-481-3160. p. 1249
Pritchard, Skip, Pres & Chief Exec Officer, OCLC Online Computer Library Center, Inc, 6565 Kilgour Pl, Dublin, OH, 43017-3395. Tel: 614-764-6000. p. 2772
Pritchard, Tamar, Librn III, New Jersey Department of Law & Public Safety, 25 Market St, West Wing, 6th Flr, Trenton, NJ, 08625. Tel: 973-648-4849. p. 1447
Pritchard, Trisha, Mgr, County of Los Angeles Public Library, Littlerock Library, 35119 80th St E, Littlerock, CA, 93543. Tel: 661-944-4138. p. 137
Pritchard, Vanessa, Pub Serv Librn, Quinte West Public Library, Seven Creswell Dr, Trenton, ON, K8V 6X5, CANADA. Tel: 613-394-3381, Ext 3311. p. 2700
Pritchett, Carla, Govt Doc/Micro Ref Librn, Tulane University, Law Library, Weinmann Hall, 3rd Flr, 6329 Freret St, New Orleans, LA, 70118-6231. Tel: 504-865-5994. p. 904
Pritchett, Erin, Supvry Librn, United States Army, Bldg 38, Screaming Eagle Blvd, Fort Campbell, KY, 42223. Tel: 270-798-5729. p. 855
Pritchett, Hallie, Interim Dean of Libr, North Dakota State University Libraries, 1201 Albrecht Blvd, Fargo, ND, 58108. Tel: 701-231-8897. p. 1733
Pritsky, Richard, Asst Dir, Carpenter-Carse Library, 69 Ballards Corner Rd, Hinesburg, VT, 05461. Tel: 802-482-2878. p. 2286
Pritt, Andrea, STEM Librarian, Pennsylvania State University-Harrisburg Library, 351 Olmsted Dr, Middletown, PA, 17057-4850. Tel: 717-948-6071. p. 1963
Pritt, Rachelle, Libr Asst, Burnsville Public Library, 235 Kanawha Ave, Burnsville, WV, 26335. Tel: 304-853-2338. p. 2399
Prive, Monique, Coordr, Acq, Per, Vermont State University - Lyndon, 1001 College Rd, Lyndonville, VT, 05851. p. 2288
Privitera, Allison, Children's & Teen Serv, Newburyport Public Library, 94 State St, Newburyport, MA, 01950-6619. Tel: 978-465-4428, Ext 227. p. 1039
Probst, Laura, Dir, Concordia College, 901 S Eighth St, Moorhead, MN, 56562. Tel: 218-299-4642. p. 1187
Procell, James, Dir, University of Louisville Libraries, Dwight Anderson Music Library, 105 W Brandeis Ave, Louisville, KY, 40208. Tel: 502-852-0528. p. 867
Prochnik, Bernie, Ms, Libr Dir, Bath Public Library, Four W Bath Rd, Bath, NH, 03740. Tel: 603-747-3372. p. 1354
Procious, Jean Marie, Exec Dir, Salem Athenaeum, 337 Essex St, Salem, MA, 01970. Tel: 978-744-2540. p. 1051
Procious, Kate, Asst Dir, Pittsford Community Library, 24 State St, Pittsford, NY, 14534. Tel: 585-248-6275. p. 1618
Prock, Krista, Info Literacy, Kutztown University, 15200 Kutztown Rd, Bldg 5, Kutztown, PA, 19530. Tel: 610-683-4480. p. 1949
Procko, Claudia, Support Serv Mgr, Leesburg Public Library, 100 E Main St, Leesburg, FL, 34748. Tel: 352-728-9790. p. 418
Proctor, JoAnn, Br Supvr, Saint John the Baptist Parish Library, Roland Borne Sr Memorial Library, 2979 Hwy 18, Edgard, LA, 70049. Tel: 985-497-3453. p. 895
Proctor, Julia, Coll & Instruction Librn, Dodge City Community College Library, 2501 N 14th, Dodge City, KS, 67801. Tel: 620-225-1321, Ext 287, 620-227-9287. p. 804
Proctor, Julia, Exec Dir, ConnectNY, Inc, 6721 US Hwy 11, Potsdam, NY, 13676. p. 2771
Proctor, Nancy, Librn, Tennessee Valley Authority, , WT CC - K, 400 W Summit Hill Dr, Knoxville, TN, 37902. Tel: 865-632-3464. p. 2107

Puccio, Andrea, Dir, Sterling & Francine Clark Art Institute Library, 225 South St, Williamstown, MA, 01267. Tel: 413-458-0532. p. 1069

Puccio, Anya, Adult Ref, North Tonawanda Public Library, 505 Meadow Dr, North Tonawanda, NY, 14120. Tel: 716-693-4132. p. 1608

Puccio, Todd, Exec Dir, Nova Southeastern University, 3200 S University Dr, Fort Lauderdale, FL, 33328. Tel: 954-262-3114. p. 401

Puchalski, Irene, Librn, University of Toronto Libraries, Architecture, Landscape & Design, Eberhard Zeidler Library, One Spadina Crescent, Toronto, ON, M5S 2J5, CANADA. Tel: 416-978-6787. p. 2698

Puchalski, Leigh-Ann, Youth Serv Librn, Carbondale Public Library, Five N Main St, Carbondale, PA, 18407. Tel: 570-282-4281. p. 1918

Puchalski, Leigh-Ann, Asst Dir, Youth Serv Coordr, Abington Community Library, 1200 W Grove St, Clarks Summit, PA, 18411-9501. Tel: 570-587-3440. p. 1922

Puckett, Elina, Syst Librn, Indiana Tech, Academic Ctr, West Wing, 1600 E Washington Blvd, Fort Wayne, IN, 46803. Tel: 260-422-5561, Ext 2223. p. 684

Puckett, Ellie, Librn, Ivy Tech Community College-Northeast, 3800 N Anthony Blvd, Fort Wayne, IN, 46805-1430. Tel: 260-480-4172. p. 684

Puckett, Jonathan, Lead Libr Asst, Ivy Tech Community College-Northeast, 3800 N Anthony Blvd, Fort Wayne, IN, 46805-1430. Tel: 260-480-4172. p. 684

Puckett, Michele Morante, Dir, Consumers Energy, Corporate Library, One Energy Plaza, EP1-244, Jackson, MI, 49201. Tel: 517-788-0541. p. 1119

Puckitt, Sarah, Photo Archivist, Mariners' Museum & Park Library, 100 Museum Dr, Newport News, VA, 23606-3759. Tel: 757-591-7782. p. 2333

Pudas, Matt, Ch Serv, Magee Public Library, 120 First St NW, Magee, MS, 39111. Tel: 601-849-3747. p. 1225

Puddephatt, Lee, Libr Asst Supvr, Region of Waterloo Library, Ayr Branch, 137 Stanley St, Ayr, ON, N0B 1E0, CANADA. Tel: 519-632-7298. p. 2629

Puddephatt, Lee, Mgr, Pub Serv, Milton Public Library, 1010 Main St E, Milton, ON, L9T 6H7, CANADA. Tel: 905-875-2665, Ext 3260. p. 2658

Puderak, Danylo, Exec Dir, Ukrainian Canadian Congress - Saskatchewan Provincial Council Inc, 4-2345 Avenue C North, Saskatoon, SK, S7L 5Z5, CANADA. Tel: 306-652-5850. p. 2750

Puderbaugh, Dena, Br Mgr, Prairie-River Library District, Kooskia Community, 26 S Main St, Kooskia, ID, 83539. Tel: 208-926-4539. p. 524

Puentes, Margaret, Coord, Coll Develop, Chapman University, One University Dr, Orange, CA, 92866. Tel: 714-532-7756. p. 188

Puestow, Allison, Asst Dir, Tomahawk Public Library, 300 W Lincoln Ave, Tomahawk, WI, 54487. Tel: 715-453-2455. p. 2481

Pufahl, Penny, Dir, Charles Ralph Holland Memorial Library, 205 W Hull Ave, Gainesboro, TN, 38562. Tel: 931-268-9190. p. 2099

Pugh, Daniela, Asst Librn, ILL, Weil, Gotshal & Manges LLP, 767 Fifth Ave, New York, NY, 10153. Tel: 212-310-8444. p. 1603

Pugh, Nancy, Libr Supvr, University of South Alabama Libraries, Health Information Resource Center, USA Medical Center, 2451 Fillingim St, Mobile, AL, 36617. Tel: 251-471-7855. p. 27

Pugh, Rosanne, Libr Dir, Slatington Public Library, 650 Main St, Slatington, PA, 18080. Tel: 610-767-6461. p. 2007

Pugh, Susan, Extended Serv, Breathitt County Public Library, 1024 College Ave, Jackson, KY, 41339. Tel: 606-666-5541. p. 860

Puglisi, Andrea, Adult Serv, Richard Salter Storrs Library, 693 Longmeadow St, Longmeadow, MA, 01106. Tel: 413-565-4181. p. 1029

Puhl, Rebecca, Dir, Phillips Public Library, 286 Cherry St, Phillips, WI, 54555. Tel: 715-339-2868. p. 2469

Pujals, Michael, Scholarly Communications Librn, Dominican University of California, 50 Acacia Ave, San Rafael, CA, 94901-2298. Tel: 415-485-3254. p. 236

Pukansky, Ann, Br Mgr, Stark County District Library, East Canton Branch, 224 N Wood St, East Canton, OH, 44730. Tel: 330-488-1501. p. 1755

Pukherjee, Poonam, Br Mgr, Enoch Pratt Free Library, Govans Branch, 5714 Bellona Ave, Baltimore, MD, 21212-3508. Tel: 443-984-4941. p. 953

Pukkila, Marilyn R, Humanities & Soc Sci Librn, Colby College Libraries, 5100 Mayflower Hill, Waterville, ME, 04901. Tel: 207-859-5145. p. 945

Pukteris, Marek, Chairperson, Librn, John Abbott College, 21275 Lakeshore Dr, Sainte-Anne-de-Bellevue, QC, H9X 3L9, CANADA. Tel: 514-457-6610, Ext 5337. p. 2734

Puleio, Erin, Youth Serv Librn, Rockland Memorial Library, 20 Belmont St, Rockland, MA, 02370-2232. Tel: 781-878-1236. p. 1049

Puley, Ken, Sr Librn, Canadian Broadcasting Corp, Radio Archives, 205 Wellington St W, Toronto, ON, M5G 3G7, CANADA. Tel: 416-205-5880. p. 2687

Pulfer, Richard, Ad, Oregon Public Library District, 300 Jefferson St, Oregon, IL, 61061. Tel: 815-732-2724. p. 630

Pulgino Stout, Denise, Dir, Boyertown Community Library, 24 N Reading Ave, Boyertown, PA, 19512. Tel: 610-369-0496. p. 1914

Pulice, Daniela L, Dir, Pleasant Valley Free Library, Three Maggiacomo Lane, Pleasant Valley, NY, 12569. Tel: 845-635-8460. p. 1620

Pulido, Daisy, Sr Librn, Los Angeles Public Library System, Leon H Washington Jr Memorial-Vernon Branch Library, 4504 S Central Ave, Los Angeles, CA, 90011-3632. Tel: 213-234-9106. p. 165

Pulido, Luis B, Libr Asst, Belmar Public Library, 517 Tenth Ave, Belmar, NJ, 07719. Tel: 732-681-0775. p. 1389

Pulkkinen, Tyler, Dir, Hibbing Public Library, 2020 E Fifth Ave, Hibbing, MN, 55746. Tel: 218-362-5959. p. 1178

Pullen, Craig, Computer Serv Librn, Lindenhurst Memorial Library, One Lee Ave, Lindenhurst, NY, 11757-5399. Tel: 631-957-7755. p. 1563

Pullen, Melanie, Youth Serv Supvr, Sequoyah Regional Library System, 116 Brown Industrial Pkwy, Canton, GA, 30114. Tel: 770-479-3090. p. 469

Pullen, Steve, Mgr, Columbus Metropolitan Library, Franklinton Branch, 1061 W Town St, Columbus, OH, 43222. p. 1772

Pulley, Natalie, Ch, Greater Clarks Hill Regional Library System, 7022 Evans Town Center Blvd, Evans, GA, 30809. Tel: 706-447-7664. p. 478

Pulliam, Cheryl, Operations Mgr, Three Rivers Regional Library System, 176 SW Community Circle, Ste B, Mayo, FL, 32066. Tel: 386-294-3858. p. 420

Pullman, Beatrice, Dir, Info Serv, Dir, Tech Serv, Providence Public Library, 150 Empire St, Providence, RI, 02903-3283. Tel: 401-455-8000. p. 2039

Pullman, ShienDee, Libr Dir, Gibbs Memorial Library, 305 E Rusk St, Mexia, TX, 76667. Tel: 254-562-3231. p. 2219

Puls, Grace, Librn, Grace Lutheran Church Library, 200 N Catherine Ave, La Grange, IL, 60525-1826. Tel: 708-352-0730. p. 605

Pulsford, Cindy, Head Librn, Johnston City Public Library, 506 Washington Ave, Johnston City, IL, 62951. Tel: 618-983-6359. p. 603

Pulver, A Issac, Libr Dir, Saratoga Springs Public Library, 49 Henry St, Saratoga Springs, NY, 12866. Tel: 518-584-7860, Ext 201. p. 1636

Pulver, Brianna, Cataloging & Continuing Resources Specialist, Albany Law School, 80 New Scotland Ave, Albany, NY, 12208. p. 1482

Pulver, Brianna, ILL, Sr Libr Spec, The Sage Colleges, 140 New Scotland Ave, Albany, NY, 12208. Tel: 518-292-1721. p. 1483

Pulver, Emilie, Metadata Librn, Lutheran School of Theology At Chicago & McCormick Theological Seminary, 5416 S Cornell Ave, Chicago, IL, 60615. Tel: 773-256-0730. p. 564

Pummill, Cathy, Librn II, Chillicothe Correctional Institution, 15802 State Rte 104 N, Chillicothe, OH, 45601. Tel: 740-774-0103. p. 1758

Pumroy, Eric, Dir, Spec Coll, Bryn Mawr College, 101 N Merion Ave, Bryn Mawr, PA, 19010-2899. Tel: 610-526-5272. p. 1916

Pundlik, Rohan, Libr Asst, Tech, Metuchen Public Library, 480 Middlesex Ave, Metuchen, NJ, 08840. Tel: 732-632-8526. p. 1418

Pundsack, Karen, Exec Dir, Great River Regional Library, 1300 W St Germain St, Saint Cloud, MN, 56301. Tel: 320-650-2512. p. 1196

Pundzak, Robin, Libr Dir, Community Library of the Shenango Valley, Stey-Nevant Branch Library, 1000 Roemer Blvd, Farrell, PA, 16121-1899. Tel: 724-983-2714. p. 2006

Pundzak, Robin, Mrs, Dir, Community Library of the Shenango Valley, 11 N Sharpsville Ave, Sharon, PA, 16146. Tel: 724-981-4360. p. 2006

Pupino, Kaaren, Acq, Head, Tech Serv, Ser, University of North Dakota, Thormodsgard Law Library, 215 Centennial Dr, Grand Forks, ND, 58202. Tel: 701-777-2204. p. 1734

Purcell, Aaron, Dir, Spec Coll, Virginia Polytechnic Institute & State University Libraries, 560 Drillfield Dr, Blacksburg, VA, 24061. Tel: 540-231-9672. p. 2307

Purcell, Camille, Libr Dir, Sea Cliff Village Library, 300 Sea Cliff Ave, Sea Cliff, NY, 11579. Tel: 516-671-4290. p. 1639

Purcell, Elsie, Libr Dir, Hondo Public Library, 2003 Ave K, Hondo, TX, 78861-2431. Tel: 830-426-5333. p. 2190

Purcell, Megan, Colls Mgr, Campbell River Museum & Archives, 470 Island Hwy, Campbell River, BC, V9W 2B7, CANADA. Tel: 250-287-3103. p. 2564

Purcell, Michael, Syst Librn, Thompson Rivers University, 900 McGill Rd, Kamloops, BC, V2C 5N3, CANADA. Tel: 250-828-5000. p. 2568

Purcell, Sandi, Librn, North Central Washington Libraries, East Wenatchee Public Library, 271 Ninth St NE, East Wenatchee, WA, 98802-4438. Tel: 509-886-7404. p. 2393

Purdie, Leslie, Librn, California Department of Corrections Library System, Folsom State Prison, 300 Prison Rd, Represa, CA, 95671. Tel: 916-985-2561, Ext 4236. p. 206

Purdue, Jeff, Teaching, Learning & Media Librn, Western Washington University, 516 High St, MS 9103, Bellingham, WA, 98225. Tel: 360-650-7750. p. 2358

Purdy, Char, Br Mgr, Volusia County Public Library, Deltona Regional, 2150 Eustace Ave, Deltona, FL, 32725. Tel: 386-789-7207, 407-328-4912 (osteen). p. 393

Purdy, David, Head Librn, Crandall University, 333 Gorge Rd, Moncton, NB, E1C 3H9, CANADA. Tel: 506-858-8970, Ext 171. p. 2603

Purdy, Dorothy, Ref Librn, Amesbury Public Library, 149 Main St, Amesbury, MA, 01913. Tel: 978-388-8148. p. 984

Purdy, Erin, Dep Exec Dir, University of Texas Libraries, Briscoe Center for American History, Sid Richard Hall, Unit 2, Rm 2106, 2300 Red River St, Austin, TX, 78712-1426. Tel: 512-947-7774. p. 2142

Purdy, Kristen, Mgr, Tech Serv, Ohio State University LIBRARIES, Agricultural Technical Institute Library, Halterman Hall, 1328 Dover Rd, Wooster, OH, 44691-4000. Tel: 330-287-1225. p. 1774

Purdy, Lillian, Dir, Libr Serv, Louisiana State University at Alexandria, 8100 Hwy 71 S, Alexandria, LA, 71302. Tel: 318-473-6437. p. 879

Purdy, Rebecca, Dep Dir, Central Rappahannock Regional Library, 125 Olde Greenwich Dr, Ste 160, Fredericksburg, VA, 22408. Tel: 540-372-1144, Ext 7004. p. 2319

Purgiel, Alison, Librn, Muskegon Area District Library, Norton Shores Branch, 705 Seminole Rd, Muskegon, MI, 49441-4797. Tel: 231-780-8844. p. 1136

Purifoy, Marian, ILL, Putnam County Library System, 601 College Rd, Palatka, FL, 32177-3873. Tel: 386-329-0126. p. 433

Purifoy, Sara, Head, Ref, Easton Area Public Library & District Center, 515 Church St, Easton, PA, 18042-3587. Tel: 610-258-2917. p. 1928

Purintun, Mary, Dir, Hazel L Meyer Memorial Library, 114 First St, De Smet, SD, 57231. Tel: 605-854-3842. p. 2075

Purrenhage, Ingrid, Assoc Dir of Libr, Pasco-Hernando State College-East Campus, 36727 Blanton Rd, Rm C124, Dade City, FL, 33523-7599. Tel: 352-518-1211. p. 391

Purrenhage, Ingrid, Dir of Libr, Pasco-Hernando State College-West Campus, 10230 Ridge Rd, Rm C124, New Port Richey, FL, 34654-5122. Tel: 727-816-3229. p. 428

Purrenhage, Ingrid, Sr Dir, Libr, Pasco-Hernando State College-Porter Campus, 2727 Mansfield Blvd, Rm C428, Wesley Chapel, FL, 33543-7168. Tel: 727-816-3418. p. 453

Purser, Cynthia, Assoc Dir, Scott County Library System, 1615 Weston Ct, Shakopee, MN, 55379. Tel: 952-496-8010. p. 1203

Purser, Lori, Dean & Dir, Libr Serv, Central Texas College, Bldg 102, 6200 W Central Texas Expressway, Killeen, TX, 76549. Tel: 254-526-1486. p. 2206

Purses, Jeanna, Dir, Lake Erie College, 391 W Washington St, Painesville, OH, 44077-3309. Tel: 440-375-7400. p. 1812

Purtee, Beth, Coll Serv Librn, Trevecca Nazarene University, 333 Murfreesboro Rd, Nashville, TN, 37210. Tel: 615-248-1455. p. 2121

Purtee, Beth, Coll Serv Librn, Christian Library Consortium, c/o ACL, PO Box 4, Cedarville, OH, 45314. Tel: 937-766-2255. p. 2772

Purtee, Sharon Ann, Tech Serv Librn, University of Cincinnati Libraries, Donald C Harrison Health Sciences Library, 231 Albert Sabin Way, Cincinnati, OH, 45267. Tel: 513-558-1019. p. 1765

Purviance, Janice, Library Contact, Lynch Public Library, 423 W Hoffman St, Lynch, NE, 68746. Tel: 402-569-3491. p. 1324

Purvis, Alyssa, Ch Mgr, Jackson County Public Library System, 2929 Green St, Marianna, FL, 32446. Tel: 850-482-9631. p. 420

Pusateri, Judy, Fiscal Officer, Tiffin-Seneca Public Library, 77 Jefferson St, Tiffin, OH, 44883. Tel: 419-447-3751. p. 1823

Pusateri, Julia, Dir, Mercer Public Library, 2648 W Margaret St, Mercer, WI, 54547. Tel: 715-476-2366. p. 2456

Pusey, Anne, Br Mgr, Arundel Anne County Public Library, Edgewater Library, 25 Stepneys Lane, Edgewater, MD, 21037. Tel: 410-222-1538. p. 950

Pushkina, Natalya, Librn, Massachusetts Department of Corrections, Institutional Library at Massachusetts Treatment Center, One Administration Rd, Bridgewater, MA, 02324. Tel: 508-279-8100, Ext 8443. p. 1002

Pushman, Stephanie, Libr Mgr, Hunter Public Library, 7965 Main St, Hunter, NY, 12442. Tel: 518-263-4655. p. 1549

Puskas, Amy, Dir, Whippanong Library, 1000 Rte 10, Whippany, NJ, 07981. Tel: 973-428-2460. p. 1455

Pustejovsky, Cynthia, Librn, Butte County Library, Biggs Branch, 464A B St, Biggs, CA, 95917-9796. Tel: 530-868-5724. p. 190

Pustejovsky, Cynthia, Librn, Butte County Library, Durham Branch, 2545 Durham-Dayton Hwy, Durham, CA, 95938-9615. Tel: 530-879-3835. p. 190

Pustejovsky, Cynthia, Librn, Butte County Library, Gridley Branch, 299 Spruce St, Gridley, CA, 95948-0397. Tel: 530-846-3323. p. 190

Pustejovsky, Cynthia, Librn, Butte County Library, Paradise Branch, 5922 Clark Rd, Paradise, CA, 95969-4896. Tel: 530-872-6320. p. 190

Pustz, Jennifer, Mus Historian, Historic New England, 141 Cambridge St, Boston, MA, 02114-2702. Tel: 617-227-3956. p. 996

Puterbaugh, Colleen, Research Librn, Maryland National Capital Park & Planning Commission, 9118 Brandywine Rd, Clinton, MD, 20735. Tel: 301-868-1121. p. 962

Puterbaugh, Savanna, Asst Dir, United Methodist Church - South Georgia Conference, Epworth-by-the-Sea, 100 Arthur Moore Dr, Saint Simons Island, GA, 31522. Tel: 912-638-4050. p. 495

Putnam, Candice, Librn, Red Deer Public Library, Timberlands Branch, 300 Timothy Dr, Red Deer, AB, T4P 0L1, CANADA. p. 2551

Putnam, Jenny, Instrul Res Coordr, Wayne State College, 1111 Main St, Wayne, NE, 68787. Tel: 402-375-7732. p. 1340

Putnam, Lucy, Archivist, Home Missioners of America, 4119 Glenmary Trace, Fairfield, OH, 45014. Tel: 513-881-7439. p. 1785

Putnam, Patricia, Librn, Truchas Community Library, 60 County Rd 75, Truchas, NM, 87578. Tel: 505-689-2683. p. 1479

Putnam, Samuel, Dir, The NYU Tandon School of Engineering, Five MetroTech Ctr, Brooklyn, NY, 11201-3840. Tel: 718-260-3530. p. 1505

Putnam-Bailey, Gwen, Ad, Rye Public Library, 581 Washington Rd, Rye, NH, 03870. Tel: 603-964-8401. p. 1380

Putt, Janice, Academic Services Librn, Davenport University, 6191 Kraft Ave SE, Grand Rapids, MI, 49512. Tel: 616-554-5664. p. 1110

Putt, Steven, Syst Librn, Web Librn, Grand Rapids Community College, 140 Ransom NE Ave, Grand Rapids, MI, 49503. Tel: 616-234-3868. p. 1110

Putt, Twyla R, Communications Spec, SEARCH Group, Inc Library, 1900 Point West Way, Ste 161, Sacramento, CA, 95815. Tel: 916-392-2550. p. 210

Putz, Denise, Cataloger, Tri-Township Public Library District, 209 S Main St, Troy, IL, 62294. Tel: 618-667-2133. p. 654

Pyati, Ajit, Assoc Prof, Western University, FIMS & Nursing Bldg, Rm 2020, London, ON, N6A 5B9, CANADA. Tel: 519-661-2111, Ext 85616. p. 2796

Pyatt, Katharine, Circ Librn, Mineral County Library, 110 First St, Hawthorne, NV, 89415. Tel: 775-945-2778. p. 1345

Pyatt, Tim, Dean, Wake Forest University, 1834 Wake Forest Rd, Winston-Salem, NC, 27109. Tel: 335-758-5090. p. 1726

Pye, Beth, Ref & Instrul Serv Librn, Gordon State College, 419 College Dr, Barnesville, GA, 30204. Tel: 678-359-5076. p. 468

Pyko, Marie, Chief Exec Officer, Topeka & Shawnee County Public Library, 1515 SW Tenth Ave, Topeka, KS, 66604-1374. Tel: 785-580-4400. p. 839

Pyle, Carol, Br Mgr, Barton County Library, Hylton Library - Golden City Branch, 607 Main St, Golden City, MO, 64748-8211. Tel: 417-537-4991. p. 1259

Pyle, Erica, Dir, New Athens District Library, 201 N Van Buren St, New Athens, IL, 62264. Tel: 618-475-3255. p. 623

Pyle, Perri, Archivist, Librn, Arizona Historical Society, 949 E Second St, Tucson, AZ, 85719. Tel: 520-617-1147. p. 81

Pyles, Kathy, ILL, Andover Public Library, 1511 E Central Ave, Andover, KS, 67002. Tel: 316-558-3500. p. 796

Pyles, Keshia, Dir, R Iris Brammer Public Library, 109 Mary St, Narrows, VA, 24124. Tel: 540-726-2884. p. 2333

Pylman, Cricket, Ch Serv, Libr Assoc II, Vail Public Library, 292 W Meadow Dr, Vail, CO, 81657. Tel: 970-479-2179. p. 297

Pynes, Caroline, Libr Dir, Chichester Town Library, 161 Main St, Chichester, NH, 03258. Tel: 603-798-5613. p. 1358

Pype, Paul, Digital Serv Librn, Alberta Government Library, Capital Blvd, 11th Flr, 10044 - 108 St, Edmonton, AB, T5J 5E6, CANADA. Tel: 780-427-2985. p. 2534

Pyrzynski, Mary Ann, Mgr, Patron Serv, Tinley Park Public Library, 7851 Timber Dr, Tinley Park, IL, 60477-3398. Tel: 708-532-0160, Ext 3. p. 653

Pysarchyk, Marianne, Libr Dir, Royalton Memorial Library, 23 Alexander Pl, South Royalton, VT, 05068. Tel: 802-763-7094. p. 2295

Pysarenko, Jackie, Dir, Hillsboro Public Library, 819 High Ave, Hillsboro, WI, 54634. Tel: 608-489-2192. p. 2441

Pyzinski, Susan, Assoc Librn, Tech Serv, Harvard Library, Houghton Library-Rare Books & Manuscripts, Houghton Library, Harvard Yard, Cambridge, MA, 02138. Tel: 617-495-2440. p. 1007

Qi, Lianglei, Info Syst Librn, Cheyney University, 1837 University Circle, Cheyney, PA, 19319. Tel: 610-399-2715. p. 1921

Qin, Dijia, Br Mgr, Hamilton Public Library, Terryberry, 100 Mohawk Rd W, Hamilton, ON, L9C 1W1, CANADA. Tel: 905-546-3200, Ext 7065. p. 2646

Qin, Liping, Head, Cat, The John Marshall Law School, 300 S State St, 6th Flr, Chicago, IL, 60604. Tel: 312-427-2737. p. 564

Qiu, Sandy, Lead Research & Knowledge Analyst, Skadden, Arps, Slate, Meagher & Flom LLP Library, 155 N Wacker Dr, Suite 2700, Chicago, IL, 60606. Tel: 312-407-0700, 312-407-0925. p. 568

Qiu, Shu, Dir, Dalton Community Library, 113 E Main St, Dalton, PA, 18414. Tel: 570-563-2014. p. 1925

Quackenbush, Pam, Tech Serv, Lyon Township Public Library, 27005 S Milford Rd, South Lyon, MI, 48178. Tel: 248-437-8800. p. 1150

Quada, Erin, Libr Tech II, Youth Serv, Ledyard Public Library, 718 Colonel Ledyard Hwy, Ledyard, CT, 06339. Tel: 860-464-9912. p. 319

Quaile, Deb, ILL, Guelph Public Library, 100 Norfolk St, Guelph, ON, N1H 4J6, CANADA. Tel: 519-824-6220, Ext 261. p. 2643

Quain, Katarina, Youth Librn, Hamtramck Public Library, 2360 Caniff St, Hamtramck, MI, 48212. Tel: 313-733-6822. p. 1113

Qualls, Elizabeth, Coll Develop Mgr, Blackwater Regional Library, 22511 Main St, Courtland, VA, 23837. Tel: 757-653-2821. p. 2313

Qualls, Melissa, Libr Asst, Young Public Library, 124 S Midway Ave, Young, AZ, 85554. Tel: 928-462-3588. p. 85

Quam, Allison, Archives & Spec Coll Librn, Winona State University, 175 W Mark St, Winona, MN, 55987. Tel: 507-457-2644. p. 1209

Quam, Sonya, Actg Librn, Zuni Public Library, 27 E Chavez Circle, Zuni, NM, 87327. Tel: 505-782-4575. p. 1479

Quan, Vanessa, Libr Tech, Department of Veterans Affairs, Medical Library 142D, 4150 Clement St, San Francisco, CA, 94121. Tel: 415-221-4810, Ext 23302. p. 224

Quan-Haase, Anabel, Assoc Dean, Prof, Western University, FIMS & Nursing Bldg, Rm 2020, London, ON, N6A 5B9, CANADA. Tel: 519-661-2111, Ext 81405. p. 2796

Quance, Marilyn, Tech Serv Librn, Wayne State College, 1111 Main St, Wayne, NE, 68787. Tel: 402-375-7474. p. 1340

Quarella, Gary, Dir, Moore Memorial Library, 59 Genesee St, Greene, NY, 13778-1298. Tel: 607-656-9349. p. 1541

Quarles, Brandon, Dir, Baylor University Libraries, Sheridan & John Eddie Williams Legal Research & Technology Center, 1114 S University Parks Dr, Waco, TX, 76706. Tel: 254-710-2168. p. 2253

Quarles, Jessica, Res & Instruction Librn, Embry-Riddle Aeronautical University, 3700 Willow Creek Rd, Prescott, AZ, 86301-3720. Tel: 928-777-6658. p. 73

Quarles, Melissa, Head, Children's Servx, Monroe Free Library, 44 Millpond Pkwy, Monroe, NY, 10950. Tel: 845-783-4411. p. 1573

Quarles, Robert, Libr Dir, Atlanta Metropolitan State College Library, 1630 Metropolitan Pkwy SW, Atlanta, GA, 30310. Tel: 404-756-4010. p. 462

Quashnick, Amanda, Librn, United States Navy, Command Library, Puget Sound Naval Shipyard & Intermediate Maintenance Facility, 1400 Farragut Ave, Bremerton, WA, 98314-5001. Tel: 360-476-2767. p. 2360

Quatraro, Harry, Registrar, Saint Lucie County Regional History Center, 414 Seaway Dr, Fort Pierce, FL, 34949. Tel: 772-462-1795. p. 405

Queisar, Susan, Dir, Barron Public Library, Ten N Third St, Barron, WI, 54812-1119. Tel: 715-537-3881. p. 2422

Queler, Reva, ILL, Ref Librn, John C Hart Memorial Library, 1130 Main St, Shrub Oak, NY, 10588. Tel: 914-245-5262. p. 1641

Quesada, Darryl, Librn, Whiteriver Public Library, 100 E Walnut St, Whiteriver, AZ, 85941. Tel: 928-594-3164. p. 84

Quesenberry, Amy, Tech Serv Mgr, Charleston County Public Library, 68 Calhoun St, Charleston, SC, 29401. Tel: 843-805-6801. p. 2048

Quesnel, Helene, Br Head, Township of Russell Public Library, 1053 Concession St, Box 280, Russell, ON, K4R 1E1, CANADA. Tel: 613-445-5331. p. 2676

Quiballo, Kari, Librn, Venito Garcia Public Library, PO Box 837, Sells, AZ, 85634-0837. Tel: 520-383-5756. p. 78

Quick, Angela Myatt, Dir, Maryville College, 502 E Lamar Alexander Pkwy, Maryville, TN, 37804-5907. Tel: 865-981-8038. p. 2111

Quick, Brenda, Circ Supvr, Sandhills Community College, 3395 Airport Rd, Pinehurst, NC, 28374. Tel: 910-695-3969. p. 1707

Quick, Janet, Library Contact, Schenectady County Public Library, Glenville Branch, 20 Glenridge Rd, Scotia, NY, 12302. Tel: 518-386-2243. p. 1638

Quick, Sarah, Archivist, Trinity Church Archives, 120 Broadway, 38th Flr, New York, NY, 10271. Tel: 212-602-9652, 212-602-9687. p. 1603

Quick, Shuana, Librn, Brandon Township Public Library, 304 South St, Ortonville, MI, 48462. Tel: 248-627-1472. p. 1139

Quick, Spring, Ad, Silver Falls Library District, 410 S Water St, Silverton, OR, 97381. Tel: 503-873-5173. p. 1899

Quick, Suzy, Curator, Vigo County Historical Museum Library, 929 Wabash Ave, Terre Haute, IN, 47803. Tel: 812-235-9717. p. 721

Quidachay-Swan, Seth, Asst Dir, Colls & Access Services, University of Michigan, Law Library, 801 Monroe St, Ann Arbor, MI, 48109-1210. Tel: 734-764-6150. p. 1080

Quigel, James, Head, Hist Coll & Labor Archives, Pennsylvania State University Libraries, Eberly Family Special Collections Library, 104 Paterno Library, University Park, PA, 16802-1808. Tel: 814-863-3181. p. 2015

Quigley, Anne, Dir, Valentine Public Library, 324 N Main St, Valentine, NE, 69201. Tel: 402-376-3160. p. 1339

Quigley, Brian, Math Librn, Statistics Librn, University of California, Berkeley, Mathematics-Statistics, 100 Evans Hall, No 6000, Berkeley, CA, 94720-6000. Tel: 510-642-3381. p. 123

Quigley, Brian, Research & Technical Servs Librn, Nova Southeastern University Libraries, Panza Maurer Law Library, Shepard Broad College of Law, Leo Goodwin Sr Bldg, 3305 College Ave, Davie, FL, 33314. Tel: 954-262-6213. p. 402

Quigley, Brian, Legal Info Librn & Lecturer in Law, Boston College, 885 Centre St, Newton Centre, MA, 02459. Tel: 617-552-1525. p. 1039

Quigley, D Samuel, Dir, Lyman Allyn Art Museum Library, 625 Williams St, New London, CT, 06320-4130. Tel: 860-443-2545, Ext 113. p. 328

Quigley, Jane, Dept Head, Smithsonian Libraries, National Museum of Natural History Library, Tenth St & Constitution Ave NW, 1st Flr, Washington, DC, 20013-0712. Tel: 202-633-1680. p. 375

Quigley, Lindsey, Tech Serv Supvr, Bushnell University, 1188 Kincade, Eugene, OR, 97401. Tel: 541-684-7246. p. 1878

Quigley, Megan, Ch, Saxton B Little Free Library, Inc, 319 Rte 87, Columbia, CT, 06237-1143. Tel: 860-228-0350. p. 306

Quigley, Sarah, Archives, Dir, Spec Coll, University of Nevada, Las Vegas University Libraries, 4505 S Maryland Pkwy, Box 457001, Las Vegas, NV, 89154-7001. Tel: 702-895-2293. p. 1347

Quigley, Shelagh, Dir, Human Res, Kingston Frontenac Public Library, 130 Johnson St, Kingston, ON, K7L 1X8, CANADA. Tel: 613-549-8888. p. 2650

Quiles, David, Circ Supvr, Mercy College Libraries, Bronx Campus, 1200 Waters Pl, Bronx, NY, 10461. Tel: 718-678-8390. p. 1526

Quiles Martinez, Yariliz R, Libr Dir, USDA Forest Service, Jardin Botanico Sur, 1201 Calle Ceiba, San Juan, PR, 00926-1119. Tel: 787-764-7257. p. 2515

Quillen, Amy-Celeste, Dir, Hawkins County Library System, 407 E Main St, Ste 1, Rogersville, TN, 37857. Tel: 423-272-8710. p. 2125

Quillen, C L, Dir, Churchill County Library, 553 S Maine St, Fallon, NV, 89406-3387. Tel: 775-423-7581. p. 1345

Quillen, Ev, Librn Supvr, White & Williams, LLP, One Liberty Pl, Ste 1800, 1650 Market St, Philadelphia, PA, 19103. Tel: 215-864-7000. p. 1989

Quillen, Steven, Acq Librn, National Oceanic & Atmospheric Administration, 1315 East West Hwy, SSMC 3, 2nd Flr, Silver Spring, MD, 20910. Tel: 301-713-2607, Ext 157. p. 977

Quilty, Morgann, Dean, Parkland College Library, 2400 W Bradley Ave, Champaign, IL, 61821-1899. p. 552

Quimby, Sara, Dir, Institute of American Indian Arts Library, 83 Avan Nu Po Rd, Santa Fe, NM, 87508. Tel: 505-424-2397. p. 1474

Quimby, Sean, Dir, University of Pennsylvania Libraries, Kislak Center for Special Collections, Rare Books & Manuscripts, 3420 Walnut St, Philadelphia, PA, 19104. Tel: 215-898-7088. p. 1988

Quin, Sarah, Digital Serv Librn, Ref & Instruction Librn, Hawkeye Community College Library, 1501 E Orange Rd, Waterloo, IA, 50701-9014. Tel: 319-296-4006, Ext 1227. p. 788

Quiner, Theresa, Libr Dir, Kuskokwim Consortium Library, Yupiit Picirarait Cultural Ctr, 420 State Hwy, Bethel, AK, 99559. Tel: 907-543-4516. p. 43

Quinlan, Elizabeth, Found Librn, John D & Catherine T MacArthur Foundation Library, 140 S Dearborn St, Ste 1200, Chicago, IL, 60603-5285. Tel: 312-726-8000. p. 564

Quinlan, Maureen P, Govt Doc Law Librn, Ref Serv, University of Maine School of Law, 246 Deering Ave, Portland, ME, 04102. Tel: 207-780-4835. p. 937

Quinlan, Nora, Dir, Ref Serv, Dir, Instrul Serv, Nova Southeastern University Libraries, 3100 Ray Ferrero Jr Blvd, Fort Lauderdale, FL, 33314. Tel: 954-262-4637. p. 402

Quinn, Anne, Head, Children's Servx, Carnegie Public Library, 127 S North St, Washington Court House, OH, 43160. Tel: 740-335-2540. p. 1828

Quinn, Arthur G, Libr Dir, St Vincent de Paul Regional Seminary Library, 10701 S Military Trail, Boynton Beach, FL, 33436-4811. Tel: 561-732-4424, Ext 8578. p. 386

Quinn, Bridget, Pres & Chief Exec Officer, Hartford Public Library, 500 Main St, Hartford, CT, 06103. Tel: 860-695-6285. p. 317

Quinn, Colleen, Ref & Instruction Librn, University of Maryland, 3501 University Blvd E, Adelphi, MD, 20783. Tel: 240-684-2020. p. 949

Quinn, Cynthia, Ch, Berkley Public Library, Two N Main St, Berkley, MA, 02779. Tel: 508-822-3329. p. 989

Quinn, Debbie, Libr Dir, Hastings-on-Hudson Public Library, Seven Maple Ave, Hastings-on-Hudson, NY, 10706. Tel: 914-478-3307. p. 1544

Quinn, Dennis, Asst Dir, William T Cozby Public Library, 177 N Heartz Rd, Coppell, TX, 75019. Tel: 972-304-3660. p. 2159

Quinn, Doreen, Librn, Harbour Grace Public Library, 106 Harvey St, Harbour Grace, NL, A0A 2M0, CANADA. Tel: 709-596-3894. p. 2608

Quinn, Frank, Dr, Dean, Univ Libr Serv, Lenoir-Rhyne University Libraries, 625 7th Ave NE, Hickory, NC, 28601. Tel: 828-328-7236. p. 1696

Quinn, Gretchen, Ref Serv Mgr, Barberton Public Library, 602 W Park Ave, Barberton, OH, 44203-2458. Tel: 330-745-1194. p. 1748

Quinn, Jacqueline, Dr, Dir of Libr, Copiah-Lincoln Community College, 1028 J C Redd Dr, Wesson, MS, 39191. Tel: 601-643-8364. p. 1235

Quinn, Jamie, Dir, Libr Serv, Amberton University, 1700 Eastgate Dr, Garland, TX, 75041. Tel: 972-279-6511, Ext 136. p. 2183

Quinn, Jamie, Chair, Health Libraries Information Network, 3500 Camp Bowie Blvd, LIB-222, Fort Worth, TX, 76107-2699. Tel: 817-735-2590. p. 2775

Quinn, Jamie Furrh, Outreach Serv Librn, Texas Health Harris Methodist Fort Worth Hospital, 1301 Pennsylvania Ave, Fort Worth, TX, 76104. Tel: 817-250-3191. p. 2181

Quinn, Jamie, Ms, Dir, Baylor University Libraries, Nursing Learning Resource Center, Louise Herrington School of Nursing, 333 N Washington Ave, Dallas, TX, 75246-9100. Tel: 972-576-9200. p. 2253

Quinn, Karen, Dir, Corbit-Calloway Memorial Library, 115 High St, Odessa, DE, 19730. Tel: 302-378-8838. p. 356

Quinn, Karen, Tech Serv Mgr, North Riverside Public Library District, 2400 S Des Plaines Ave, North Riverside, IL, 60546. Tel: 708-447-0869, Ext 236. p. 626

Quinn, Kathryn, Librn, North Haven Library, 33 Main St, North Haven, ME, 04853. Tel: 207-867-9797. p. 933

Quinn, Linda, Asst Dir, Weedsport Library, 2795 E Brutus St, Weedsport, NY, 13166. Tel: 315-834-6222. p. 1661

Quinn, Lisa, Sr Librn, Canton Public Library, 786 Washington St, Canton, MA, 02021. Tel: 781-821-5027. p. 1009

Quinn, Lisa, Adult Ref Librn, Massapequa Public Library, Bar Harbour Bldg, 40 Harbor Lane, Massapequa Park, NY, 11762. Tel: 516-799-0770. p. 1569

Quinn, Lori-Ann, Dir, Waldwick Public Library, 19 E Prospect St, Waldwick, NJ, 07463-2099. Tel: 201-652-5104. p. 1451

Quinn, Mary, Br Mgr, Jersey City Free Public Library, The Heights, 14 Zabriskie St, Jersey City, NJ, 07307. Tel: 201-547-4556. p. 1409

Quinn, Mary Anne, Adult Serv, Warwick Public Library, 600 Sandy Lane, Warwick, RI, 02889-8298. Tel: 401-739-5440, Ext 9766. p. 2043

Quinn, Mary Rose, Head, State Programs & Gov Liaison, Massachusetts Board of Library Commissioners, 90 Canal St, Ste 500, Boston, MA, 02114. Tel: 617-725-1860. p. 996

Quinn, Maryse, Youth Serv Librn, Your Home Public Library, 107 Main St, Johnson City, NY, 13790. Tel: 607-797-4816. p. 1558

Quinn, Robin, Dir, Hastings Memorial Library, 505 Central Ave, Grant, NE, 69140-3017. Tel: 308-352-4894. p. 1316

Quinn, Sue, Interim Dir, Forest Park Public Library, 7555 Jackson Blvd, Forest Park, IL, 60130. Tel: 708-366-7171. p. 588

Quinn, Susan, Dir, Ocean County Library, 101 Washington St, Toms River, NJ, 08753. Tel: 732-914-5400. p. 1446

Quinn, Tim, Dir, Mkt & Communications, Princeton Public Library, 65 Witherspoon St, Princeton, NJ, 08542. Tel: 609-924-9529. p. 1436

Quinnell, Katherine, Dr, Dean, Univ Libr, Tarleton State University Library, 201 Saint Felix, Stephenville, TX, 76401. Tel: 254-968-9246. p. 2246

Quinones, Aida, Br Mgr, Athens Regional Library System, Biblioteca Centro Educativo de la Communidad de Pinewoods (Pinewoods Library & Learning Center), North Lot F-12, 1465 US Hwy 29 N, Athens, GA, 30601-1103. Tel: 706-613-3708. p. 458

Quinones, Philip, Chief Librn, United States Army, John L Throckmorton Library, IMSE-BRG-MWR-L Bldg 1-3346, Randolph St, Fort Bragg, NC, 28310-5000. Tel: 910-396-2665. p. 1689

Quinones-Mauras, Irma, Dr, Dir, University of Puerto Rico, Conrado F Asenjo Library, Medical Sciences Campus, Main Bldg, Unit C, San Juan, PR, 00935. Tel: 787-751-8199, 787-758-2525, Ext 1200. p. 2514

Quint, Amanda, Ad, Outreach Librn, Metropolis Public Library, 317 Metropolis St, Metropolis, IL, 62960. Tel: 618-524-4312. p. 617

Quint, Emily, Librn, Stewart Public Library, 37 Elm St, North Anson, ME, 04958. Tel: 207-635-3212. p. 933

Quintanilla, Carmen F, Libr Tech II, University of Guam, Guam & Micronesia Collection, UOG Sta, Mangilao, GU, 96923. Tel: 671-735-2161. p. 2505

Quintanilla, Caroline, Br Mgr, Seminole County Public Library System, Jean Rhein Central Library, 215 N Oxford Rd, Casselberry, FL, 32707. p. 388

Quintanilla, Kristen, Librn, National Park College Library, 101 College Dr, Hot Springs, AR, 71913. Tel: 501-760-4101, 501-760-4110. p. 99

Quintero, Ivonne, Dr, Librn III, Inter-American University of Puerto Rico, PO Box 70351, Hato Rey, PR, 00936. Tel: 787-751-1912, Ext 2160. p. 2511

Quintero, Lisa, YA Serv, Shorewood Public Library, 3920 N Murray Ave, Shorewood, WI, 53211-2385. Tel: 414-847-2670. p. 2477

Quintero, Minnie, Librn, Iraan Public Library, 120 W Fifth St, Iraan, TX, 79744. Tel: 432-639-2235. p. 2202

Quintero, Patricia, Librn, Tech Serv Coordr, Odessa College, 201 W University Blvd, Odessa, TX, 79764. Tel: 432-335-6640. p. 2223

Quinton, Jennifer, Br Librn, London Public Library, Landon, 167 Wortley Rd, London, ON, N6C 3P6, CANADA. Tel: 519-439-6240. p. 2654

Quinton, Laura, Libr Mgr, Stirling Theodore Brandley Municipal Library, 409 Second St, Stirling, AB, T0K 2E0, CANADA. Tel: 403-756-3665. p. 2555

Quintrell, Kim, Colls Mgr, Mgr, Info Tech, Allen County Public Library, 900 Library Plaza, Fort Wayne, IN, 46802. Tel: 260-421-1284. p. 683

Quintus, Rebecca, Col Librn for Health Professions, Pharm & Sci, The University of Findlay, 1000 N Main St, Findlay, OH, 45840-3695. Tel: 419-434-4549. p. 1785

Quirin, Chiquita, Sr Mgr, Alachua County Library District, Millhopper Branch, 3145 NW 43rd St, Gainesville, FL, 32606-6107. Tel: 352-334-1272. p. 406

Quiring, Anne Marie, Librn, Morneau Shepell, 1060 Boul Robert-Bourassa, Ste 900, Montreal, QC, H3B 4V3, CANADA. Tel: 514-878-9090. p. 2727

Quiros-Laso, Miriam, Mgr, Miami-Dade Public Library System, Coral Reef Branch, 9211 SW 152nd St, Miami, FL, 33157. Tel: 305-233-8324. p. 423

Quiroz, Eloisa, Br Librn, Moore County Library System, Cactus Branch Library, 407 Sherri, Cactus, TX, 79013. Tel: 806-966-3706. p. 2172

Quiroz, Sally, Dir, Wayland Baptist University, 1900 W Seventh St, Plainview, TX, 79072-6957. Tel: 806-291-3702. p. 2227

Quist, Valerie, Librn, Tracy Public Library, 189 Third St, Tracy, MN, 56175. Tel: 507-629-5548. p. 1205

Qurashi, Zoma, Libr Asst, Manor College, 700 Fox Chase Rd, Jenkintown, PA, 19046-3399. Tel: 215-885-5752. p. 1947

Raab, Barbara, Ch Serv, Wilmington Memorial Library, 175 Middlesex Ave, Wilmington, MA, 01887-2779. Tel: 978-658-2967. p. 1070

Raab, Christopher, Assoc Librn, Archives & Spec Coll, Franklin & Marshall College, Martin Library of the Sciences, Bldg 22, 681 Williamson Way, Lancaster, PA, 17604. Tel: 717-358-4225. p. 1951

Raab, Gretchen, Dir, Neenah Public Library, 240 E Wisconsin Ave, Neenah, WI, 54956. Tel: 920-886-6300. p. 2463

Raatz, Tari, Asst Dir, Wisconsin Department of Public Instruction, Instructional Media & Technology Team, 125 S Webster St, Madison, WI, 53707. Tel: 608-267 2920. p. 2452

Rabalais, Annette, Br Mgr, Avoyelles Parish Library, Mansura Branch, 2111 Cleco Rd, Mansura, LA, 71350. Tel: 318-964-2118. p. 897

Rabasca, Nancy, Librn, Nathan & Henry B Cleaves Law Library, 142 Federal St, Portland, ME, 04101. Tel: 207-773-9712. p. 936

Rabbito, Seana, Head, Children's Dept, Waltham Public Library, 735 Main St, Waltham, MA, 02451. Tel: 781-314-3425. p. 1062

Raber, Ericka, Dir, Wartburg Theological Seminary, 333 Wartburg Pl, Dubuque, IA, 52003. Tel: 563-589-0278. p. 749

Raber, Steven, Mgr, Gibson, Dunn & Crutcher, 200 Park Ave, 48th Flr, New York, NY, 10166-0193. Tel: 212-351-4005. p. 1587

Rabideau, Tammy, Bus & Career Ctr Coordr, Dir, Waterville Public Library, 73 Elm St, Waterville, ME, 04901-6078. Tel: 207-872-5433. p. 945

Rabie, Ryan, Digital Scholarship Librn, Huron University College, 1349 Western Rd, London, ON, N6G 1H3, CANADA. Tel: 519-438-7224, Ext 195. p. 2653

Rabine, Julie, Ref & Instruction Librn, Bowling Green State University Libraries, 1001 E Wooster St, Bowling Green, OH, 43403-0170. p. 1752

Rabinowitz, Celia, Dean, Keene State College, 229 Main St, Keene, NH, 03435-3201. Tel: 603-358-2711. p. 1369

Rabiola, Keith W, Pub Serv Librn, Wisconsin Historical Society Library, 816 State St, 2nd Flr, Madison, WI, 53706. Tel: 608-264-6535. p. 2452

Raboin, Diane, Librn, Rainy River Community College Library, 1501 Hwy 71, International Falls, MN, 56649. Tel: 218-285-2250. p. 1178

Raboin, Regina, Assoc Dir, University of Massachusetts Medical School, 55 Lake Ave N, Worcester, MA, 01655-0002. Tel: 508-856-2099. p. 1072

Rabold, Catherine, Circ & ILL, Green River College, 12401 SE 320th St, Auburn, WA, 98092-3699. Tel: 253-833-9111, Ext 2093. p. 2357

Rabson, Emily, Cataloger, Lower Providence Community Library, 50 Parklane Dr, Eagleville, PA, 19403-1171. Tel: 610-666-6640. p. 1928

Race, Stephanie, Head, Outreach Serv, Head, Res Serv, University of North Florida, Bldg 12-Library, One UNF Dr, Jacksonville, FL, 32224-2645. Tel: 904-620-2615. p. 413

Race, Tammera, Dean of Libr, New College of Florida University of South Florida Sarasota Manatee, 5800 Bay Shore Rd, Sarasota, FL, 34243-2109. Tel: 941-487-4405. p. 443

Rachal, Michelle, Ref Librn, University of Nevada-Reno, Pennington Medical Education Bldg, 1664 N Virginia St, Reno, NV, 89557. Tel: 775-784-4625. p. 1349

Rachar, Kurt, Supvr, Oakland County Jail Library, 1201 N Telegraph Rd, Pontiac, MI, 48341-1044. Tel: 248-858-2925. p. 1141

Rachels, Ryan, Supervisory Library Branch Tech, Marine Corps Logistics Bases, Base Library, Bldg 7122, 814 Radford Blvd, Ste 20311, Albany, GA, 31704-1130. Tel: 229-639-5242. p. 457

Rachetta, Laurie, Dir, East Syracuse Free Library, 4990 James St, East Syracuse, NY, 13057. Tel: 315-437-4841. p. 1528

Rachwal, Jacob, Mgr, Town of North Collins Public Library, 2095 School St, North Collins, NY, 14111. Tel: 716-337-3211. p. 1607

Rackley, Nora, Open Educational Resources Librn, Ref, Lake-Sumter State College Library, 9501 US Hwy 441, Leesburg, FL, 34788. Tel: 352-365-3586. p. 418

Rackover, Suzanne, Dir, Libr Serv, Langara College Library, 100 W 49th Ave, Vancouver, BC, V5Y 2Z6, CANADA. Tel: 604-323-5243. p. 2579

Raczkowski, Betsy, Head, Youth Serv, Rochester Hills Public Library, 500 Olde Towne Rd, Rochester, MI, 48307-2043. Tel: 248-650-7142. p. 1144

Rad, Fatoma, Tech Serv, Farmingdale State College of New York, 2350 Broadhollow Rd, Farmingdale, NY, 11735-1021. Tel: 934-420-2040. p. 1532

Rada, Kristal, Head, Libr Operations, Crown Point Community Library, 122 N Main St, Crown Point, IN, 46307. Tel: 219-663-0270. p. 678

Radandt, Gina, Mgr of Collections & Exhibitions, Kenosha Public Museum Library, 5500 First Ave, Kenosha, WI, 53140. Tel: 262-653-4140, 262-653-4426. p. 2445

Radcliff, Christine, Libr Dir, Texas A&M University-Kingsville, 1050 University Blvd, MSC 197, Kingsville, TX, 78363. Tel: 361-593-3319. p. 2206

Radcliff, Joyce, Ser Librn, Tennessee State University, Avon Williams Library, 330 Tenth Ave N, Nashville, TN, 37203. Tel: 615-963-7383. p. 2121

Radcliff, Sharon, Assoc Librn, California State University, East Bay Library, CSU East Bay Library, 25800 Carlos Bee Blvd, Hayward, CA, 94542-3052. Tel: 510-885-7452. p. 150

Radcliffe, Katharina, Dir, Delanco Public Library, M Joan Pearson School, 1303 Burlington Ave, Delanco, NJ, 08075. Tel: 856-461-6850. p. 1398

Radcliffe, Tim, Libr Dir, Mount Vernon Nazarene University, 800 Martinsburg Rd, Mount Vernon, OH, 43050-9500. Tel: 740-397-9000, Ext 4240. p. 1804

Rademacher, Cyndi, Exec Dir, Niles-Maine District Library, 6960 Oakton St, Niles, IL, 60714. Tel: 847-663-1234. p. 624

Rader, Conrad, Asst Mgr, Saint Louis County Library, Grand Glaize Branch, 1010 Meramec Station Rd, Manchester, MO, 63021-6943. Tel: 314-994-3300, Ext 3300. p. 1273

Rader, Mary, Humanities Liaison Librn, University of Texas Libraries, Fine Arts Library, Doty Fine Arts Bldg 3-200, 2306 Trinity St, Austin, TX, 78712. Tel: 512-495-4119. p. 2142

Rader, Mary, Librn, University of Texas Libraries, South Asian Library Program, 120 Inner Campus Dr, SG 9300, Austin, TX, 78712. Tel: 512-495-4119. p. 2143

Radford, Kate, Br Librn, Lewis & Clark Library, Lincoln Branch, 102 Ninth Ave S, Lincoln, MT, 59639. Tel: 406-362-4300. p. 1296

Radford, Trent, Access Serv, University of Mount Olive, 646 James B Hunt Dr, Mount Olive, NC, 28365-1699. Tel: 919-658-7869. p. 1705

Radick, Caryn, Digital Archivist, Rutgers University Libraries, Special Collections & University Archives, Alexander Library, 169 College Ave, New Brunswick, NJ, 08901-1163. Tel: 848-932-6152. p. 1425

Radigan, Barbara, Dir, Pulteney Free Library, 9226 County Rte 74, Pulteney, NY, 14874. Tel: 607-868-3652. p. 1624

Radisauskas, Christina, Libr Dir, Aquinas College, 1700 Fulton St E, Grand Rapids, MI, 49506. Tel: 616-632-2124. p. 1109

Radke, Kate, Outreach & Programming Librn, Walker Memorial Library, 800 Main St, Westbrook, ME, 04092. Tel: 207-854-0630. p. 946

Radke, Ruth, Dir, Lewellen Public Library, 208 Main St, Lewellen, NE, 69147. Tel: 308-778-5421. p. 1320

Radman, Carrie, Youth Serv Mgr, Columbiana Public Library, 332 N Middle St, Columbiana, OH, 44408. Tel: 330-482-5509. p. 1771

Radovsky, Jennie, Br Mgr, Norfolk Public Library, Janaf Branch, 124 Janaf Shopping Ctr, 5900 E Virginia Beach Blvd, Norfolk, VA, 23502. Tel: 757-441-5660. p. 2335

Radthorne, Daniel, Research Librn, University of Virginia, Arthur J Morris Law Library, 580 Massie Rd, Charlottesville, VA, 22903-1738. Tel: 434-982-5090. p. 2310

Radwan, Randa, Dir, University of North Carolina at Chapel Hill, Highway Safety Research Center, Boiling Creek Ctr, Ste 300, 730 Martin Luther King Jr Blvd, Chapel Hill, NC, 27514. Tel: 919-962-2202. p. 1678

Radzvickas, Adrienne, Tech Serv Librn, Lincoln College, 300 Keokuk St, Lincoln, IL, 62656. Tel: 217-735-7291. p. 609

Rae, Abby, Dir, Libr Serv, Fielding Graduate University, 2020 De La Vina St, Santa Barbara, CA, 93105. Tel: 805-690-4373. p. 239

Rae, Cailin, Librn, Union Free Public Library, 979 Buckley Hwy, Union, CT, 06076. Tel: 860-684-4913. p. 342

Rae, Gina, Dir, Wilton Public Library, 400 East St, Wilton, WI, 54670. Tel: 608-435-6710. p. 2489

Rae, Rosemary, Chief Librn/CEO, Espanola Public Library, 245 Avery Dr, Espanola, ON, P5E 1S4, CANADA. Tel: 705-869-2940. p. 2640

Rael, Sylvia, Libr Dir, Colorado Mesa University, 1100 North Ave, Grand Junction, CO, 81501. Tel: 970-248-1029. p. 283

Raezer-Stursa, Trista, Archivist, Minnesota State University Moorhead, 1104 Seventh Ave S, Moorhead, MN, 56563. Tel: 218-477-2922. p. 1189

Rafael, Robin, Literacy Supvr, Napa County Library, 580 Coombs St, Napa, CA, 94559-3396. Tel: 707-253-4283. p. 182

Rafal, Andy, Exec Dir, CEO, OLI Systems, Inc Library, Two Gatehall Dr, Ste 1D, Parsippany, NJ, 07054. Tel: 973-539-4996, Ext 21. p. 1432

Raff, Amy, Libr Dir, Provincetown Public Library, 356 Commercial St, Provincetown, MA, 02657-2209. Tel: 508-487-7094, Ext 216. p. 1048

Rafferty, Emily Connell, Mgr, Tech Serv, St John's College Library, 60 College Ave, Annapolis, MD, 21401. Tel: 410-626-2548. p. 951

Rafferty, John, Pres & Chief Exec Officer, Canadian National Institute for the Blind, 1929 Bayview Ave, Toronto, ON, M4G 3E8, CANADA. p. 2688

Rafferty, Rusty P, Chief Doc Librn, United States Army, Combined Arms Research Library, US Army Command & General Staff College, Eisenhower Hall, 250 Gibbon Ave, Fort Leavenworth, KS, 66027-2314. Tel: 913-758-3128. p. 808

Rafferty, Sharon, Tech Serv, Seabrook Library, 25 Liberty Lane, Seabrook, NH, 03874-4506. Tel: 603-474-2044. p. 1381

Raffo, Cecilia, Adult Serv, Circ Supvr, Saint Helena Public Library, 1492 Library Lane, Saint Helena, CA, 94574-1143. Tel: 707-963-5244. p. 210

Rafter, William, Head, Libr Syst, West Virginia University Libraries, 1549 University Ave, Morgantown, WV, 26506. Tel: 304-293-4040. p. 2409

Raftery, Patrick, Librn, Westchester County Historical Society Library, 2199 Saw Mill River Rd, Elmsford, NY, 10523. Tel: 914-231-1401. p. 1531

Ragan, McKenzie, Dir, Libr Serv, Andrew College, 501 College St, Cuthbert, GA, 39840. Tel: 229-732-5956. p. 473

Ragas, Diana, Med Librn, Southcoast Health Medical Library, 101 Page St, New Bedford, MA, 02740. Tel: 508-973-5267. p. 1038

Rager, Janie, Assoc Dean, Saint Francis University, 106 Franciscan Way, Loretto, PA, 15940. Tel: 814-472-3160. p. 1956

Raglin, Mary Grace, Head Librn, Letcher County Public Library District, Blackey Branch, 295 Main St Loop, Blackey, KY, 41804. Tel: 606-633-4013. p. 877

Ragnow, Marguerite, Dr, Curator, University of Minnesota Libraries-Twin Cities, James Ford Bell Library, Elmer L Andersen Library, 222 21st Ave S, Ste 15, Minneapolis, MN, 55455. Tel: 612-624-1528. p. 1185

Ragsdale, Lesley, Syst Librn, Moore Memorial Public Library, 1701 Ninth Ave N, Texas City, TX, 77590. Tel: 409-643-5964. p. 2248

Rahming, Jamar, Dir, Wilmington Public Library, Ten E Tenth St, Wilmington, DE, 19801. Tel: 302-571-7400. p. 358

Rahmoeller, Brenda, Ref Librn, Jefferson County Library, Northwest, 5680 State Rd PP, High Ridge, MO, 63049. Tel: 636-677-8186. p. 1249

Rahn, Katrina, Fac Librn, City College of San Francisco, 50 Frida Kahlo Way, 4th Flr, San Francisco, CA, 94112. Tel: 415-452-5433. p. 224

Rai, Balwinder, Dir, Human Res, Vancouver Public Library, 350 W Georgia St, Vancouver, BC, V6B 6B1, CANADA. Tel: 604-331-3603. p. 2581

Raia, Ann, Dir, Libr Serv, Oklahoma City Community College, 7777 S May Ave, Oklahoma City, OK, 73159. Tel: 405-682-1611, Ext 7468. p. 1858

Raia, Deborah, Librn II, Santa Fe Springs City Library, 11700 E Telegraph Rd, Santa Fe Springs, CA, 90670-3600. Tel: 562-868-7738. p. 243

Raiche, Amanda, Coordr, Ch & Youth Serv, South Dakota State Library, 800 Governors Dr, Pierre, SD, 57501-2294. Tel: 605-773-3131. p. 2080

Raiche, Amanda, Youth Serv Librn, Edith B Siegrist Vermillion Public Library, 18 Church St, Vermillion, SD, 57069-3093. Tel: 605-677-7060. p. 2084

Raiche, Kristin, Head, Children's & Teen Serv, Enfield Public Library, 104 Middle Rd, Enfield, CT, 06082. Tel: 860-763-7510. p. 311

Raidy-Klein, Susan, Coll Develop, Tech Serv, University of Massachusetts Dartmouth Library, 285 Old Westport Rd, North Dartmouth, MA, 02747-2300. Tel: 508-999-8666. p. 1041

Railey, Cecilia, Med Librn, Norton Healthcare, 200 E Chestnut St, Louisville, KY, 40202. Tel: 502-629-8125. p. 866

Railey, Valerie A, Br Mgr, United States Courts Library, Edward J Schwartz US Courthouse, 221 W Broadway, Rm 3185, San Diego, CA, 92101. Tel: 619-557-5066. p. 222

Railsback, Beth, Dir, Carnegie City-County Library, 2810 Wilbarger St, Vernon, TX, 76384. Tel: 940-552-2462. p. 2251

Rainbolt, Darryl, ILL, Southeastern Oklahoma State University, 425 W University, Durant, OK, 74701-0609. Tel: 580-745-2931. p. 1846

Raine, Kristy, Dir, Mount Mercy University, 1330 Elmhurst Dr NE, Cedar Rapids, IA, 52402-4797. Tel: 319-368-6465. p. 738

Raine, Michele, Dep Dir, Wood County District Public Library, 251 N Main St, Bowling Green, OH, 43402. Tel: 419-352-5104. p. 1752

Raines, Karen, Special Collections Public Services Coord, University of California, Riverside, Special Collections & University Archives, 900 University Ave, Riverside, CA, 92521. Tel: 951-827-3233. p. 203

Rainey, Betty, Br Mgr, Middle Georgia Regional Library System, Ideal Public Library, 605 Tom Watson Ave, Ideal, GA, 31041. Tel: 478-949-2720. p. 487

Rainey, Cassie, Asst Dir, Lincoln Public Library, 145 Old River Rd, Lincoln, RI, 02865. Tel: 401-333-2422, Ext 17. p. 2034

Rainey, David, Readers' Advisory, Supvr, State Library of Louisiana, 701 N Fourth St, Baton Rouge, LA, 70802. Tel: 225-342-5148. p. 885

Rainey, Lynn, Br Mgr, Jackson-George Regional Library System, Ina Thompson Moss Point Library, 4119 Bellview St, Moss Point, MS, 39563. Tel: 228-475-7462. p. 1228

Rainford, Denise, Youth Serv Dir, Rochester Public Library District, One Community Dr, Rochester, IL, 62563. Tel: 217-498-8454. p. 640

Rainier, Heather, Dir, Hooksett Public Library, 31 Mount Saint Mary's Way, Hooksett, NH, 03106-1852. Tel: 603-485-6092. p. 1368

Rainville, Ellen, Dir, J V Fletcher Library, 50 Main St, Westford, MA, 01886-2599. Tel: 978-399-2312. p. 1067

Rainwater, Pat, Dir, Reynolds County Library District, 2306 Pine St, Centerville, MO, 63633. Tel: 573-648-2471. p. 1241

Rais, Shirley, Per, Loma Linda University, 11072 Anderson St, Loma Linda, CA, 92350-0001. Tel: 909-558-4581. p. 157

Raish, Victoria, Online Learning Librn, Pennsylvania State University Libraries, Library Learning Services, 216 Pattee Tower, University Park, PA, 16802-1803. Tel: 814-863-9750. p. 2015

Raith, Jenny, Librn, Oregon County Library District, Thomasville Public Library, 132 Old St, Birch Tree, MO, 65438. Tel: 417-764-3603. p. 1237

Raitz, Brian E, Dir, Parkersburg & Wood County Public Library, 3100 Emerson Ave, Parkersburg, WV, 26104-2414. Tel: 304-420-4587. p. 2411

Rajamani, Karthi, Chief Exec Officer, Pembroke Public Library, 237 Victoria St, Pembroke, ON, K8A 4K5, CANADA. Tel: 613-732-8844. p. 2671

Rajcevic, Peter, Chief Tech Officer, Plainfield Public Library, 800 Park Ave, Plainfield, NJ, 07060-2594. Tel: 908-757-1111, Ext 130. p. 1435

Rajguru, Nalini, Mgr, Libr Serv, Caplin & Drysdale Library, One Thomas Circle, NW, Ste 1100, Washington, DC, 20005-5802. Tel: 202-862-5073. p. 362

Rajotte, Anne, Head, Ref Serv, University of Connecticut, Thomas J Meskill Law Library, 39 Elizabeth St, Hartford, CT, 06105. Tel: 860-510-5081. p. 340

Raju, Pearl, Sr Manager, Library Services, George Brown College Library Learning Commons, PO Box 1015, Sta B, Toronto, ON, M5T 2T9, CANADA. Tel: 416-415-5000, Ext 8255. p. 2689

Rakas, Laurel, Ch Serv, Pemberville Public Library, 375 E Front St, Pemberville, OH, 43450. Tel: 419-287-4012. p. 1814

Rake, John, Libr Assoc, Media Serv, Rutgers University Libraries, Blanche & Irving Laurie Performing Arts Library, Mabel Smith Douglass Library, Eight Chapel Dr, New Brunswick, NJ, 08901-8527. Tel: 848-932-5038. p. 1425

Rakes, Howard, Info Serv Coordr, Chippewa Falls Public Library, 105 W Central St, Chippewa Falls, WI, 54729-2397. Tel: 715-723-1146. p. 2427

Rakestraw, Lacy, Dir, Saint Louis County Law Library, Courts Bldg, 105 S Central Ave, 6th Flr, Clayton, MO, 63105. Tel: 314-615-4726. p. 1242

Rakestraw, Renee, Asst Dir, Cultural & Community Services, Oxnard Public Library, 251 South A St, Oxnard, CA, 93030. Tel: 805-385-8022. p. 190

Rakestraw, Scott, Head, Tech, Chelsea District Library, 221 S Main St, Chelsea, MI, 48118-1267. Tel: 734-475-8732. p. 1090

Rakhminova, Basanda, Commun Libr Mgr, Queens Library, Poppenhusen Community Library, 121-23 14th Ave, College Point, NY, 11356. Tel: 718-359-1102. p. 1555

Rakhshani, Diane, Mgr, Pine Mountain Regional Library, Manchester Public, 218 W Perry St, Manchester, GA, 31816-0709. Tel: 706-846-3851. p. 488

Raleigh, Denise, Div Chief of Public Relations & Develop, Gail Borden Public Library District, 270 N Grove Ave, Elgin, IL, 60120-5596. Tel: 847-429-5981. p. 583

Raleigh, Rebekah, Head, Youth Serv, Warren-Newport Public Library District, 224 N O'Plaine Rd, Gurnee, IL, 60031. Tel: 847-244-5150, Ext 3040. p. 596

Raley, Kelly, Assoc Dir, University of Texas Libraries, Population Research Center Library, 305 E 23rd St, Stop G1800, Austin, TX, 78712-1699. Tel: 512-471-5514. p. 2143

Ralph, Stephanie, Libr Dir, Summit County Libraries, County Commons Bldg, 0037 Peak One Dr, Frisco, CO, 80443. Tel: 970-668-4138. p. 282

Ralph, Stephanie, Dir, Grand County Library District, 225 E Jasper Ave, Granby, CO, 80446. Tel: 970-887-9411. p. 283

Ralston, Andrea, Outreach Serv Mgr, Washington County Public Library, 615 Fifth St, Marietta, OH, 45750-1973. Tel: 740-373-1057. p. 1799

Ralston, Carrie, Libr Dir, Walled Lake City Library, 1499 E West Maple Rd, Walled Lake, MI, 48390. Tel: 248-624-3772. p. 1156

Ralston, Carson, Adult Serv, Camp Verde Community Library, 130 N Black Bridge Rd, Camp Verde, AZ, 86322. Tel: 928-554-8391. p. 57

Ralston, Jennifer, Mat Mgt Adminr, Harford County Public Library, 1221-A Brass Mill Rd, Belcamp, MD, 21017-1209. Tel: 410-273-5600, Ext 6539. p. 958

Ralston, Rick, Asst Dir, Libr Operations, Indiana University, Ruth Lilly Medical Library, 975 W Walnut St, IB 100, Indianapolis, IN, 46202. Tel: 317-274-1409. p. 693

Ralston, Tracy, Dir, Post University, 800 Country Club Rd, Waterbury, CT, 06723-2540. Tel: 203-596-4564. p. 344

Ram, Elizabeth, Br Mgr, Riverside County Library System, El Cerrito Library, 7581 Rudell Rd, Corona, CA, 92881. Tel: 951-270-5012. p. 202

Ramage, Gregory, Dir, Support Serv, Upper Arlington Public Library, 2800 Tremont Rd, Columbus, OH, 43221. Tel: 614-486-9621. p. 1778

Ramage, Janet, Chief Exec Officer, White River Public Library, 123 Superior St, White River, ON, P0M 3G0, CANADA. Tel: 807-822-1113. p. 2704

Ramarge, Sue, ILL, Librn, Cameron County Public Library, 27 W Fourth St, Emporium, PA, 15834. Tel: 814-486-8011. p. 1930

Ramaswamy, Mohan, Dean, US Department of Defense, Fort McNair, Marshall Hall, Washington, DC, 20319-5066. Tel: 202-685-3511. p. 378

Rambo, Arielle, Chief Cataloger, Digital Initiatives Librn, Library Company of Philadelphia, 1314 Locust St, Philadelphia, PA, 19107. Tel: 215-546-3181. p. 1982

Rambo, Bob, ILL Mgr, Martin Memorial Library, 159 E Market St, York, PA, 17401-1269. Tel: 717-846-5300. p. 2026

Rambow, Judi, Lead Librn, Kalamazoo Public Library, Alma Powell Branch, 1000 W Paterson St, Kalamazoo, MI, 49007. Tel: 269-553-7961. p. 1121

Rambow, Judi, Lead Librn, Kalamazoo Public Library, Eastwood, 1112 Gayle St, Kalamazoo, MI, 49048. Tel: 269-553-7810. p. 1121

Ramdial, Opal, Treas, Lakeview Public Library, 1120 Woodfield Rd, Rockville Centre, NY, 11570. Tel: 516-536-3071. p. 1632

Ramer, Allie, Asst Librn, Dixonville Community Library, PO Box 206, Dixonville, AB, T0H 1E0, CANADA. Tel: 780-971-2593. p. 2533

Ramer, Donna, Asst Dir, Tech Serv Librn, University of Mobile, 5735 College Pkwy, Mobile, AL, 36613-2842. Tel: 251-442-2478. p. 26

Ramer, Sheryl, Dir, NYC Health & Hospital - Elmhurst, 79-01 Broadway, D3-52A, Elmhurst, NY, 11373. Tel: 718-334-2040. p. 1530

Ramey, Cindy, Librn, Northeast Regional Library, Marietta Public Library, Park Rd, Marietta, MS, 38856. Tel: 662-728-9320. p. 1216

Ramey, Robyn, Adult Serv, Fleming County Public Library, 202 Bypass Blvd, Flemingsburg, KY, 41041-1298. Tel: 606-845-7851. p. 854

Ramezani, Sara, Asst Dir, Cabell County Public Library, 455 Ninth Street Plaza, Huntington, WV, 25701. Tel: 304-528-5700. p. 2404

Ramirez, Al, IT Mgr, Bartlett Public Library District, 800 S Bartlett Rd, Bartlett, IL, 60103. Tel: 630-837-2855. p. 540

Ramirez, Alyssa, County Librn, Amador County Law Library, Amador County Library, 530 Sutter St, Jackson, CA, 95642. p. 153

Ramirez, Alyssa, Dir, Lincoln County Public Libraries, 220 W Sixth St, Libby, MT, 59923-1898. Tel: 406-293-2778. p. 1298

Ramirez, Ana, Libr Asst, Saint Elizabeth School of Nursing Division of Franciscan Health, 1501 Hartford St, St Elizabeth School of Nursing, Lafayette, IN, 47904-2198. Tel: 765-423-6125. p. 701

Ramirez, Anneka, Patron Serv Supvr, Norfolk Public Library, 308 W Prospect Ave, Norfolk, NE, 68701-4138. Tel: 402-844-2104. p. 1326

Ramirez, Dan, Br Mgr, Arundel Anne County Public Library, Riviera Beach Library, 8485A Fort Smallwood Rd, Pasadena, MD, 21122. Tel: 410-222-6285. p. 950

Ramirez, Danae, Dep Dir, Libr Serv, San Mateo County Library, Library Administration, 125 Lessingia Ct, San Mateo, CA, 94402-4000. Tel: 650-312-5236. p. 235

Ramirez, Diane, Br Mgr, Stanislaus County Library, Empire Branch, 18 S Abbie St, Empire, CA, 95319. Tel: 209-524-5505. p. 178

Ramirez, Isaac, Tech Serv Mgr, University of La Verne, 320 E D St, Ontario, CA, 91764. Tel: 909-460-2070. p. 188

Ramirez, Itzel, Ch Serv, Seagoville Public Library, 702 N Hwy 175, Seagoville, TX, 75159-1774. Tel: 972-287-7720. p. 2242

Ramirez, Laura, Interim Dir of Reference, Nova Southeastern University Libraries, 3100 Ray Ferrero Jr Blvd, Fort Lauderdale, FL, 33314. Tel: 954-262-8423. p. 402

Ramirez, Lourdes, Chief Librn, University of Puerto Rico Library System, Planning Library, Rio Piedras Campus, Plaza Universitaria, 6th Flr, San Juan, PR, 00931. Tel: 787-764-0000, Ext 85524. p. 2515

Ramirez, Marianne, Head, Teen Serv, Sayville Library, 88 Greene Ave, Sayville, NY, 11782. Tel: 631-589-4440. p. 1637

Ramirez, Marvin, Spec, Air Line Pilots Association International, 7950 Jones Branch Dr, Ste 400-S, McLean, VA, 22102. Tel: 703-689-4204. p. 2332

Ramirez, Penny, Head, Automation & Tech Serv, Crystal Lake Public Library, 126 Paddock St, Crystal Lake, IL, 60014. Tel: 815-459-1687. p. 574

Ramirez, Perla Tineda, Library Contact, Colusa County Free Library, Williams Branch, 901 E St, Williams, CA, 95987. Tel: 530-473-5955. p. 131

Ramirez, Rachel, Dir, Wilmette Historical Museum, 609 Ridge Rd, Wilmette, IL, 60091-2721. Tel: 847-853-7666. p. 663

Ramirez, Rolando, Br Mgr, McAllen Public Library, Palm View Branch, 3401 Jordan Rd W, McAllen, TX, 78503. Tel: 956-681-3113. p. 2217

Ramirez, Selena, Dir, Lamb County Library, 110 E Sixth St, Littlefield, TX, 79339. Tel: 806-385-5223. p. 2212

Ramirez, Stephanie, Libr Dir, Delafield Public Library, 500 Genesee St, Delafield, WI, 53018-1895. Tel: 262-646-6230. p. 2431

Ramirez, Yanira, Tech Serv Assoc, Drew University Library, 36 Madison Ave, Madison, NJ, 07940. Tel: 973-408-3672. p. 1414

Ramirez, Yesianne, Actg Br Supvr, Madison Public Library, Meadowridge, 5726 Raymond Rd, Madison, WI, 53711. Tel: 608-288-6160. p. 2449

Ramirez-Luhrs, Ana, Librn, Lafayette College, Kirby Library of Government & Law, Kirby Hall of Civil Rights, 716 Sullivan Rd, Easton, PA, 18042-1797. Tel: 610-330-5398. p. 1928

Ramler, Joe, Sr Res Economist, Montana Department of Commerce, 301 S Park Ave, Helena, MT, 59620. Tel: 406-841-2719. p. 1296

Ramlow, Edith, Librn/Mgr, College of Central Florida Learning Resources Center, 3800 S Lecanto Hwy, C2-202, Lecanto, FL, 34461. Tel: 352-249-1205. p. 418

Rammer, Jacqueline, Libr Dir, Menomonee Falls Public Library, W156 N8436 Pilgrim Rd, Menomonee Falls, WI, 53051. Tel: 262-532-8900. p. 2455

Ramon, Dinorah, Cat Spec, Laredo College, West End Washington St, Laredo, TX, 78040. Tel: 956-721-5272. p. 2209

Ramos Caban, Edwin, Libr Dir, Pontifical Catholic University of Puerto Rico, Ramon Emeterio Betances St 482, Mayaguez, PR, 00680. Tel: 787-834-5151, Ext 5008, 787-834-5151, Ext 5051. p. 2511

Ramos, Carolina, Fiscal Officer, Atlantic County Library System, 40 Farragut Ave, Mays Landing, NJ, 08330-1750. Tel: 609-625-2776. p. 1417

Ramos, Jane, Libr Dir, Sherburne Memorial Library, 2998 River Rd, Killington, VT, 05751. Tel: 802-422-4251, 802-422-9765. p. 2287

Ramos, Mario, Supvr, Computer Serv & Ref (Info Serv), High Point Public Library, 901 N Main St, High Point, NC, 27262. Tel: 336-883-3633. p. 1696

Ramos, Mary, Asst Dir, Maryland State Library for the Blind & Print Disabled, 415 Park Ave, Baltimore, MD, 21201-3603. Tel: 410-230-2424. p. 955

Ramos, Nitza, Br Mgr, Osceola Library System, Kenansville Branch, 1154 S Canoe Creek Rd, Kenansville, FL, 34739. Tel: 407-742-8888. p. 414

Ramos, Nitza, Br Mgr, Osceola Library System, Veterans Memorial Library, 810 13th St, Saint Cloud, FL, 34769. Tel: 407-742-8888. p. 414

Ramos, Rebecca, Outreach Librn, Ref Librn, Aiso Library, 543 Lawton Rd, Ste 617A, Monterey, CA, 93944-3214. p. 179

Ramos, Stacey, Br Mgr, San Bernardino County Library, Rialto Branch, 251 W First St, Rialto, CA, 92376. Tel: 909-875-0144. p. 213

Ramos-Ankrum, Angeles, Tech Serv Librn, Louisville Presbyterian Theological Seminary, 1044 Alta Vista Rd, Louisville, KY, 40205-1798. Tel: 502-895-3411, Ext 397. p. 866

Ramos-Cruz, Karen, Br Supvr, Kern County Library, Arvin Branch, 201 Campus Dr, Arvin, CA, 93203. Tel: 661-854-5934. p. 119

Ramos-Cruz, Karen, Br Supvr, Kern County Library, Lamont Branch, 8304 Segrue Rd, Lamont, CA, 93241-2123. Tel: 661-845-3471. p. 120

Ramos-Goyette, Sharon, Learning Commons Coord, Bristol Community College, Taunton Campus, Two Hamilton St, 3rd Flr, Taunton, MA, 02780. Tel: 774-357-2569. p. 1017

Ramos-Wing, Isabel, Librn, Paul D Camp Community College Library, 100 N College Dr, Franklin, VA, 23851. Tel: 757-569-6741. p. 2319

Rampa, Justyn, Customer Experience Mgr, Public Library of Cincinnati & Hamilton County, 800 Vine St, Cincinnati, OH, 45202-2009. Tel: 513-369-6926. p. 1761

Ramsay, Amy, Libr Mgr, Innisfail Public Library, 5300A 55th St Close, Innisfail, AB, T4G 1R6, CANADA. Tel: 403-227-4407. p. 2543

Ramsay, Lisa, Circ Supvr, Rutherford County Library System, 105 W Vine St, Murfreesboro, TN, 37130-3673. Tel: 615-893-4131, Ext 123. p. 2117

Ramsden, Ann, Exec Dir, Musee Heritage Museum, Five Saint Anne St, St. Albert, AB, T8N 3Z9, CANADA. Tel: 780-459-1528. p. 2554

Ramsden, Karen, Res Spec, Montclair State University, One Normal Ave, Montclair, NJ, 07043-1699. Tel: 973-655-5276. p. 1420

Ramsell, Michelle, Dir, Tuscarawas County Public Library, 121 Fair Ave NW, New Philadelphia, OH, 44663-2600. Tel: 330-364-4474. p. 1807

Ramsey, Beccy, Dir, Ridgemont Public Library, 124 E Taylor St, Mount Victory, OH, 43340. Tel: 937-354-4445. p. 1805

Ramsey, Carolyn, Librn, Alaska Housing Finance Corp, 4300 Boniface Pkwy, Anchorage, AK, 99504. Tel: 907-330-8166. p. 41

Ramsey, Cassidy, Digital Res Librn, Cleveland Community College, 137 S Post Rd, Shelby, NC, 28152. Tel: 704-669-4125. p. 1716

Ramsey, Donna, Librn, United States Army, Van Noy Library, 5966 12th St, Bldg 1024, Fort Belvoir, VA, 22060-5554. Tel: 703-806-3238. p. 2319

Ramsey, Jacinda, Admin Librn, Pryor Public Library, 505 E Graham, Pryor, OK, 74361. Tel: 918-825-0777. p. 1861

Ramsey, James, Libr Dir, Stoughton Public Library, 304 S Fourth St, Stoughton, WI, 53589. Tel: 608-873-6281. p. 2479

Ramsey, Kathy, Dir, Aubrey Area Library, 226 Countryside Dr, Aubrey, TX, 76227. Tel: 940-365-9162. p. 2137

Ramsey, Kendall, Br Mgr, Gaston County Public Library, TECH@Lowell, 203 McAdenville Rd, Lowell, NC, 28098. Tel: 704-824-1266. p. 1690

Ramsey, Kristi, Supvry Librn, Joint Base Lewis-McChord Library System, Grandstaff Library, 2109 N Tenth St & Pendleton Ave, Joint Base Lewis McChord, WA, 98433. Tel: 253-967-5889. p. 2366

Ramsey, Ryan, Chief of Staff, Library of Congress, James Madison Memorial Bldg, 101 Independence Ave SE, Washington, DC, 20540. Tel: 202-707-5000. p. 370

Ramsour, Mariah, Communications Coordr, Events Coord, San Jose State University, One Washington Sq, San Jose, CA, 95192-0028. Tel: 408-808-2050. p. 232

Ranadive, Mary, Assoc Univ Librn, Admin Serv, Towson University, 8000 York Rd, Towson, MD, 21252. Tel: 410-704-2618. p. 980

Ranburger, Carol, Cat, ILL, Brescia University, 717 Frederica St, Owensboro, KY, 42301. Tel: 270-686-4214. p. 871

Rance, Darla, Asst City Librn, Pub Serv, Helen Hall Library, 100 W Walker, League City, TX, 77573-3899. Tel: 281-554-1102. p. 2210

Rance, Donald, Ref Librn, Art Gallery of Ontario, 317 Dundas St W, Toronto, ON, M5T 1G4, CANADA. Tel: 416-979-6642. p. 2686

Ranck, Jennifer, Dir, Worcester County Library, 307 N Washington St, Snow Hill, MD, 21863. Tel: 410-632-2600. p. 978

Rancourt, Lichen J, Libr Dir, Jackson Public Library, 125 Main St, Jackson, NH, 03846. Tel: 603-383-9731. p. 1369

Rand, Angela, Dr, Libr Dir, University of South Alabama Libraries, Marx Library, 5901 USA Drive N, Mobile, AL, 36688. Tel: 251-460-7028. p. 27

Rand, Denise, Ch, Evansdale Public Library, 123 N Evans Rd, Evansdale, IA, 50707. Tel: 319-232-5367. p. 752

Rand, Kathy, Dir, Parker Public Library, 290 N Main, Parker, SD, 57053. Tel: 605-297-5552. p. 2080

Randall, Chase, Libr Dir, Tooele City Public Library, 128 W Vine St, Tooele, UT, 84074-2059. Tel: chaser@tooelecity.org. p. 2274

Randall, Rebecca, Ref, Southbury Public Library, 100 Poverty Rd, Southbury, CT, 06488. Tel: 203-262-0626. p. 337

Randall, Todd, Librn, Penfield Public Library, 1985 Baird Rd, Penfield, NY, 14526. Tel: 585-340-8720. p. 1616

Randazzo, Jennifer, Library Contact, Ascension Macomb-Oakland Hospital Warren Campus Library, 11800 E 12 Mile Rd, Warren, MI, 48093. Tel: 586-573-5117. p. 1157

Randeiro, Charlene, Dir, Fallsington Library, 139 Yardley Ave, Fallsington, PA, 19054-1118. Tel: 215-295-4449. p. 1933

Randell, Kent, Col Archivist, Ref Librn, Saint Mary's College of Maryland Library, 47645 College Dr, Saint Mary's City, MD, 20686-3001. Tel: 240-895-4196. p. 976

Randeree, Ebrahim, Asst Dean, Florida State University, College of Communication & Information, 142 Collegiate Loop, Tallahassee, FL, 32306-2100. Tel: 850-645-5674. p. 2783

Randhawa, Sarwan, Libr Mgr, Fraser Valley Regional Library, Terry Fox Library, 2470 Mary Hill Rd, Port Coquitlam, BC, V3C 3B1, CANADA. Tel: 604-927-7999. p. 2561

Randle, Deanne, Asst Dir, Burnet County Library System, 100 E Washington St, Burnet, TX, 78611. Tel: 512-715-5228. p. 2152

Randlett, Betsy, Dir, Allenstown Public Library, 59 Main St, Allenstown, NH, 03275-1716. Tel: 603-485-7651. p. 1353

Rando, Julie, Dir, Learning Commons, Allegany College of Maryland Library, 12401 Willowbrook Rd SE, Cumberland, MD, 21502. Tel: 301-784-5269. p. 963

Rando, Julie, Dir, Learning Commons, Allegany College of Maryland Library, 18 N River Lane, Everett, PA, 15537. Tel: 814-652-9528. p. 1932

Rando, Ruth, Dir & Librn, Closter Public Library, 280 High St, Closter, NJ, 07624-1898. Tel: 201-768-4197. p. 1397

Randolph, Ann, Ch Serv, Saint Charles City-County Library District, McClay, 2760 McClay Rd, Saint Charles, MO, 63303-5427. Tel: 636-441-7577. p. 1278

Randolph, Bailey, Head, Children's Servx, Grande Prairie Public Library, 101-9839 103 Ave, Grande Prairie, AB, T8V 6M7, CANADA. Tel: 780-357-7477. p. 2541

Randolph, Mari, Br Mgr, Public Library of Cincinnati & Hamilton County, Corryville, 2802 Vine St, Cincinnati, OH, 45219. Tel: 513-369-6034. p. 1762

Randolph, Michelle, Assoc Dir, Benny Gambaiani Public Library, 104 S Cherry St, Shell Rock, IA, 50670. Tel: 319-885-4345. p. 781

Randolph, Morgan, Libr Dir, Minor Hill Public Library, 108 Pickett Dr, Minor Hill, TN, 38473. Tel: 931-565-3699. p. 2116

Randolph, Susan, Circ Mgr, Gallia County District Library, Seven Spruce St, Gallipolis, OH, 45631. Tel: 740-446-7323. p. 1787

Randolph, Terri, Libr Dir, Riegelsville Public Library, 615 Easton Rd, Riegelsville, PA, 18077. Tel: 610-749-2357. p. 2001

Randolph, Tracie, Br Mgr, Riverside County Library System, Glen Avon Library, 9244 Galena St, Jurupa Valley, CA, 92509. Tel: 951-685-8121. p. 202

Randolphe, Nadine, Library Contact, Clara Maass Medical Center, One Clara Maass Dr, Belleville, NJ, 07109. Tel: 973-450-2294. p. 1389

Rands, Tammy, Dir, Libr Serv, Coastal Bend College, 3800 Charco Rd, Beeville, TX, 78102. Tel: 361-354-2741. p. 2146

Rands, Tammy, Dir, Coastal Bend College, 1814 S Brahma Blvd, Rm 135A, Kingsville, TX, 78363. Tel: 361-354-2741. p. 2206

Randsdell, Eden, Head, Youth Serv, Harrison County Public Library, 105 N Capitol Ave, Corydon, IN, 47112. Tel: 812-738-4110. p. 677

Randtke, Wilhelmina, Head, Libr Syst & Tech, Georgia Southern University, 11935 Abercorn St, Savannah, GA, 31419. Tel: 912-344-3027. p. 495

Randtke, Wilhelmina, Head, Libr Syst & Tech, Georgia Southern University, 1400 Southern Dr, Statesboro, GA, 30458. Tel: 912-478-5115. p. 497

Rane, Joel J, Sr Librn, Metropolitan State Hospital Library, Enhancement Services, 11401 Bloomfield Ave, Norwalk, CA, 90650. Tel: 562-474-2873. p. 184

Ranelli, Julie, Br Mgr, Queen Anne's County Free Library, Kent Island Branch, 200 Library Circle, Stevensville, MD, 21666. Tel: 410-643-8161, Ext 102. p. 961

Rangarajan, Latha, Head, Tech Serv, University of Detroit Mercy School of Law, 651 E Jefferson, Detroit, MI, 48226. Tel: 313-596-9824. p. 1099

Rangel, Angela, Executive Admin Mgr, Rob & Bessie Welder Wildlife Foundation Library, 10429 Welder Wildlife, Hwy 77 N, Sinton, TX, 78387. Tel: 361-364-2643. p. 2244

Ranger, Joshua, Archivist & Communications Librn, Head, Pub Serv, University of Wisconsin Oshkosh, 801 Elmwood Ave, Oshkosh, WI, 54901. Tel: 920-424-0828. p. 2467

Ranisate, Allison, ILL, University of North Dakota, Harley E French Library of the Health Sciences, School of Medicine & Health Sciences, 501 N Columbia Rd, Stop 9002, Grand Forks, ND, 58202-9002. Tel: 701-777-3993. p. 1734

Rank, Robin, Ref & Instruction Librn, Kalamazoo College Library, 1200 Academy St, Kalamazoo, MI, 49006-3285. Tel: 269-337-7153. p. 1121

Rankin, Aimee, Electronic Serv Librn, Christian Brothers University, 650 East Pkwy S, Memphis, TN, 38104. Tel: 901-321-3432. p. 2112

Rankin, Amy, Mgr, Royal Canadian Mounted Police Resource Centre, Depot Division Library, 5600 11th Ave W, Regina, SK, S4P 3J7, CANADA. Tel: 639-625-3537, 639-625-3552. p. 2747

Rankin, Billy, Interim Pres & Chief Exec Officer, Shaker Village of Pleasant Hill Museum Library, 3501 Lexington Rd, Harrodsburg, KY, 40330. Tel: 859-734-1549, 859-734-5411. p. 858

Rankin, Bonnie, Ch Serv, Chelmsford Public Library, MacKay, 43 Newfield St, North Chelmsford, MA, 01863-1799. Tel: 978-251-3212. p. 1010

Rankin, Gina, Br Coordr, Lake County Library, Upper Lake Branch, 310 Second St, Upper Lake, CA, 95485. Tel: 707-275-2049. p. 156

Rankin, Julie, Dir, Libr Serv, Oklahoma Baptist University, 500 W University, OBU Box 61309, Shawnee, OK, 74804-2504. Tel: 405-585-4500. p. 1861

Rankin, Matthew, Br Librn, Southeast Regional Library, Weyburn Branch, 45 Bison Ave NE, Weyburn, SK, S4H 0H9, CANADA. Tel: 306-842-4352. p. 2755

Rankin, Shannon, Libr Tech, Georgian College, Main Bldg, 1st Flr, Rm 206, 1450 Eighth St E, Owen Sound, ON, N4K 5R4, CANADA. Tel: 519-372-3211. p. 2671

Rankin, Teri, Head, Youth Serv, O'Fallon Public Library, 120 Civic Plaza, O'Fallon, IL, 62269-2692. Tel: 618-632-3783. p. 629

Rankin, Zephyr, Marketing & Communication Librn, Texas A&M University-Commerce, 2600 S Neal St, Commerce, TX, 75428. Tel: 903-468-8661. p. 2158

Ransom, Barbara, Dir Customer Experience, Main, Richmond Hill Public Library, One Atkinson St, Richmond Hill, ON, L4C 0H5, CANADA. Tel: 905-884-9288. p. 2675

Ransom, Emily, Librn, Texarkana College, 1024 Tucker St, Texarkana, TX, 75501. Tel: 903-832-3215. p. 2248

Ransom, Joan, Br Librn, South Interlake Regional Library, 419 Main St, Stonewall, MB, R0C 2Z0, CANADA. Tel: 204-467-8415. p. 2591

Ransom, John, Head Librn, Rutherford B Hayes Presidential Library & Museums, Spiegel Grove, Fremont, OH, 43420-2796. Tel: 419-332-2081. p. 1786
Ransom, Kathy, Br Mgr, Azalea Regional Library System, Hancock County Library, 8984 E Broad St, Sparta, GA, 31087. Tel: 706-444-5389. p. 488
Ransom, Marcia, Dir, Springdale Public Library, 405 S Pleasant St, Springdale, AR, 72764. Tel: 479-750-8180. p. 110
Ransone, Jennifer, Ch Serv, Marion County Public Library System, 2720 E Silver Springs Blvd, Ocala, FL, 34470. Tel: 352-671-8551. p. 430
Ranzan, David, Head, Archives & Spec Coll, Adelphi University, One South Ave, Garden City, NY, 11530. Tel: 516-877-3543. p. 1536
Rao, Dittakavi, Assoc Dir, Duquesne University, Center for Legal Information, 900 Locust St, Pittsburgh, PA, 15282. Tel: 412-396-5014. p. 1993
Rao, Sai, Mrs, Dir, North Bergen Free Public Library, 8411 Bergenline Ave, North Bergen, NJ, 07047. Tel: 201-869-4715. p. 1429
Rapalee, Elizabeth, Librn, Wadhams Free Library, 763 NYS Rte 22, Wadhams, NY, 12993. Tel: 518-962-8717. p. 1658
Raphael, Brian, Asst Dir, Pub Serv, University of Southern California Libraries, Asa V Call Law Library, 699 Exposition Blvd, LAW 202, MC 0072, Los Angeles, CA, 90089-0072. Tel: 213-740-6482. p. 170
Raphael, Honora, Music Librn, Brooklyn College Library, Walter W Gerboth Music Library, 2900 Bedford Ave, 2nd Flr, Brooklyn, NY, 11210. Tel: 718-951-5845. p. 1501
Raphael-Lubin, Camina, Dir, Lakeview Public Library, 1120 Woodfield Rd, Rockville Centre, NY, 11570. Tel: 516-536-3071. p. 1631
Rapier, Jennifer, Mgr, Cobb County Public Library System, Powder Springs Library, 4181 Atlanta St, Bldg 1, Powder Springs, GA, 30127. Tel: 770-439-3600. p. 489
Rapp, Andrea, Librn, Isaac M Wise Temple, 8329 Ridge Rd, Cincinnati, OH, 45236. Tel: 513-793-2556. p. 1765
Rapp, Anne, Dir, McKay Library, 105 S Webster St, Augusta, MI, 49012-9601. Tel: 269-731-4000. p. 1082
Rapp, Megan, Dir, Mark Twain Home Foundation, 120 N Main St, Hannibal, MO, 63401-3537. Tel: 573-221-9010. p. 1248
Rapp, Melissa, Content & Collection Librn, Huron University College, 1349 Western Rd, London, ON, N6G 1H3, CANADA. Tel: 519-438-7224, Ext 283. p. 2653
Rapp-Weiss, Melanie, Br Mgr, Cuyahoga County Public Library, Brecksville Branch, 9089 Brecksville Rd, Brecksville, OH, 44141-2313. Tel: 440-526-1102. p. 1813
Rapp-Weiss, Melanie, Br Mgr, Cuyahoga County Public Library, Independence Branch, 6361 Selig Dr, Independence, OH, 44131-4926. Tel: 216-447-0160. p. 1813
Rappaport, Karen, Libr Dir, Wells Memorial Library, 12230 NYS Rte 9N, Upper Jay, NY, 12987. Tel: 518-946-2644. p. 1654
Rappaport, Sharon, Adult Serv Supvr, Manhasset Public Library, 30 Onderdonk Ave, Manhasset, NY, 11030. Tel: 516 627-2300, Ext 209. p. 1568
Rappoport, Robin, Ref Librn, Lincoln Public Library, Three Bedford Rd, Lincoln, MA, 01773. Tel: 781-259-8465. p. 1028
Rapuano, Jennifer, YA Librn, Vineyard Haven Public Library, 200 Main St, Vineyard Haven, MA, 02568. Tel: 508-696-4211, Ext 118. p. 1061
Rapue, Danielle, Adjunct Librn, West Hills College Lemoore Library, 555 College Ave, Lemoore, CA, 93245. Tel: 559-925-3403. p. 156
Rasberry, Kayla, Asst Librn, Bus Librn, Pub Serv Librn, Southern Arkansas University, 100 E University, Magnolia, AR, 71753-5000. Tel: 870-235-4175. p. 103
Rasberry, Margaret, Libr Asst, Shaw University, 118 E South St, Raleigh, NC, 27601. Tel: 919-546-8324. p. 1710
Rasby, Ruth M, Head, Access Serv, Howard University Libraries, 500 Howard Pl NW, Ste 203, Washington, DC, 20059. Tel: 202-806-7213. p. 369
Raschke, Aaron, Dir, Westfield Public Library, 117 E Third St, Westfield, WI, 53964-9107. Tel: 608-296-2544. p. 2487
Raschke, Greg, Dir, Vice Provost, North Carolina State University Libraries, James B Hunt Jr Library, 1070 Partners Way, Campus Box 7132, Raleigh, NC, 27606. p. 1709
Raschke, Gregory, Dir, Senior Vice Provost, North Carolina State University Libraries, D H Hill Jr Library, Two Broughton Dr, Raleigh, NC, 27695. Tel: 919-515-7188. p. 1709
Raschke-Janchenko, Alissa, Youth Serv Mgr, New Lenox Public Library District, 120 Veterans Pkwy, New Lenox, IL, 60451. Tel: 815-485-2605. p. 624
Rasczyk, Kristen, Teen/Tech Librnb, Glen Rock Public Library, 315 Rock Rd, Glen Rock, NJ, 07452. Tel: 201-670-3970. p. 1405
Rasel, John, Librn, Cuyahoga Community College, Eastern Campus Library, 4250 Richmond Rd, Highland Hills, OH, 44122-6195. Tel: 216-987-2321. p. 1769
Rash, Elaine, Head, Youth Serv, Osterhout Free Library, 71 S Franklin St, Wilkes-Barre, PA, 18701. Tel: 570-823-0156. p. 2022
Rash, Kathleen, Dir, Hart Area Public Library, 415 S State St, Hart, MI, 49420-1228. Tel: 231-873-4476. p. 1113
Rash, Katrina, Br Mgr, Pasco County Library System, Hudson Branch Library, 8012 Library Rd, Hudson, FL, 34667. Tel: 727-861-3040. p. 410
Raska-Engelson, Marilyn, Dir, Radcliffe Public Library, 210 Isabella St, Radcliffe, IA, 50230. Tel: 515-899-7914. p. 778
Rasmussen, Anne, Exec Dir, Vernon Area Public Library District, 300 Olde Half Day Rd, Lincolnshire, IL, 60069. Tel: 847-634-3650. p. 609
Rasmussen, Anne, Mgr, Br, Pub Serv Mgr, Milwaukee Public Library, 814 W Wisconsin Ave, Milwaukee, WI, 53233-2309. Tel: 414-286-3000. p. 2459
Rasmussen, Julie, Dir, Cravath Memorial Library, 243 N Main, Hay Springs, NE, 69347. Tel: 308-638-4541. p. 1318
Rasmussen, Kasey, Public Services Assoc, San Juan Island Library, 1010 Guard St, Friday Harbor, WA, 98250-9612. Tel: 360-378-2798. p. 2364
Rasmussen, Nathaniel, Head, Info Tech, Schlow Centre Region Library, 211 S Allen St, State College, PA, 16801-4806. Tel: 814-237-6236. p. 2010
Rasmussen, Pam, Mgr, Washoe County Library System, Incline Village Library, 845 Alder Ave, Incline Village, NV, 89451. Tel: 775-832-4130. p. 1350
Rasmussen, Paul, Pres, Great Lakes Bible College Library, 470 Glenelm Crescent, Waterloo, ON, N2L 5C8, CANADA. Tel: 519-342-3040. p. 2702
Rasmussen-Schramm, Carol, Head Librn, Siletz Public Library, 255 S Gaither St, Siletz, OR, 97380. Tel: 541-444-2855. p. 1898
Rasnick, Rebecca, Br Mgr, MidPointe Library System, Trenton Branch, 200 Edgewood Dr, Trenton, OH, 45067. Tel: 513-988-9930. p. 1802
Rasnick, Rebecca, Br Mgr, MidPointe Library System, West Chester Branch, 9363 Centre Pointe Dr, West Chester, OH, 45069. Tel: 513-777-3131. p. 1802
Raso, Christopher, Br Supvr, Guelph Public Library, West End Branch, 21 Imperial Rd S, Guelph, ON, N1K 1X3, CANADA. Tel: 519-829-4403. p. 2643
Raspuzzi, Callie, Colls Mgr, Bennington Museum, 75 Main St, Bennington, VT, 05201. Tel: 802-447-1571. p. 2279
Rassaei, Virginia, Head, Cat, University of Texas at El Paso Library, 500 W University Ave, El Paso, TX, 79968-0582. Tel: 915-747-5683. p. 2175
Rastogi, Sonal, Dir of Libr, Norfolk Public Library, Administrative Offices & Service Ctr, 1155 Pineridge Rd, Norfolk, VA, 23502. p. 2335
Raszewski, Thomas, Libr Dir, Saint Mary's Seminary & University, 5400 Roland Ave, Baltimore, MD, 21210-1994. Tel: 410-864-3621. p. 956
Rataic-Lang, Joan, Exec Dir, Libr Dir, Toronto Lawyers Association Library, Courthouse, 3rd Flr, 361 University Ave, Toronto, ON, M5G 1T3, CANADA. Tel: 416-327-6012. p. 2693
Ratch, Noel, Dir, Reynolds-Alberta Museum Reference Centre, 6426 40th Ave, Wetaskiwin, AB, T9A 2G1, CANADA. Tel: 780-312-2080. p. 2559
Ratchenski, Rebecca, Dir, Cavalier Public Library, 200 Bjornson Dr, Cavalier, ND, 58220. Tel: 701-265-4746. p. 1731
Ratcliffe, Jill, Br Mgr, Green Tom County Library System, West Branch, 3013 Vista del Arroyo, San Angelo, TX, 76904. Tel: 325-659-6436. p. 2236
Ratcliffe, Sam, Head, Spec Coll, Southern Methodist University, Hamon Arts Library, 6101 N Bishop Blvd, Dallas, TX, 75275. Tel: 214-768-1855. p. 2168
Ratclliffe, Zane, Instruction & Res Serv Librn, Oklahoma State University - Tulsa Library, 700 N Greenwood Ave, Tulsa, OK, 74106-0702. Tel: 918-594-8146. p. 1865
Ratelle, Sallie, Circ Mgr, Pauline Haass Public Library, N64 W23820 Main St, Sussex, WI, 53089-3120. Tel: 262-246-5180. p. 2481
Rath, Linda, Grad Serv Librn, Baruch College-CUNY, 151 E 25th St, Box H-0520, New York, NY, 10010-2313. Tel: 646-312-1622. p. 1580
Rath, Logan, Assoc Librn, Instrul Serv, State University of New York College at Brockport, 350 New Campus Dr, Brockport, NY, 14420-2997. Tel: 585-395-2568. p. 1497
Rath, Nancy, Asst Dir, Mooresville Public Library, 304 S Main St, Mooresville, NC, 28115. Tel: 704-664-2927. p. 1704
Rath, Zoe, Ad, Norwell Public Library, 64 South St, Norwell, MA, 02061-2433. Tel: 781-659-2015. p. 1043
Rath-Tickle, Stephanie, Ad, Phillipsburg Free Public Library, 200 Broubalow Way, Phillipsburg, NJ, 08865. Tel: 908-454-3712. p. 1434
Rathbone, Cathy, Librn, Yakima Valley Libraries, Richard E Ostrander West Valley Community Library, 223 S 72nd Ave, Yakima, WA, 98908. Tel: 509-966-7070. p. 2395
Rathbun, James, Dir, Baxter Memorial Library, 71 South St, Gorham, ME, 04038. Tel: 207-222-1190. p. 926
Rathbun, Maria, Br Mgr, Branch District Library, Lucille E Dearth Union Township Branch, 195 N Broadway, Union City, MI, 49094-1153. Tel: 517-741-5061, Ext 602. p. 1092
Rathbun-Grubb, Susan R, PhD, Assoc Prof, University of South Carolina, 1501 Greene St, Columbia, SC, 29208. Tel: 803-777-3858. p. 2792
Rathemacher, Andree J, Head, Acq, University of Rhode Island, 15 Lippitt Rd, Kingston, RI, 02881-2011. Tel: 401-874-5096. p. 2033
Rathi, Dinesh, PhD, Prof, University of Alberta, 7-104 Education N, University of Alberta, Edmonton, AB, T6G 2G5, CANADA. Tel: 780-492-7625. p. 2795
Rathke, Bekah, ILL Coordr, University of Saint Thomas, 2115 Summit Ave, Mail Box 5004, Saint Paul, MN, 55105. Tel: 651-962-5494. p. 1202
Rathnam, Priya, Libr Dir, Shrewsbury Public Library, 609 Main St, Shrewsbury, MA, 01545. Tel: 508-841-8609. p. 1053

Ratke, Joanne, Tech Librn, Oak Creek Public Library, Drexel Town Sq, 8040 S Sixth St, Oak Creek, WI, 53154. Tel: 414-766-7900. p. 2465

Ratliff, Debi, Adult Serv Mgr, Rockbridge Regional Library System, 138 S Main St, Lexington, VA, 24450-2316. Tel: 540-463-4324. p. 2329

Ratliff, Diana, Circ, Mendocino College Library, 1000 Hensley Creek Rd, Ukiah, CA, 95482. Tel: 707-468-3245. p. 254

Ratliff, Jim, Instruction Librn, Librn, Arcadia Commons Campus, Kalamazoo Valley Community College Libraries, 6767 West O Ave, Rm 3210, Kalamazoo, MI, 49003. Tel: 269-488-4328, 269-488-4380. p. 1122

Ratliff, Lori, Br Mgr, Southern Oklahoma Library System, Healdton Community Library, 554 S Fourth St, Healdton, OK, 73438. Tel: 580-229-0590. p. 1841

Ratliff, Ramona, Info Spec, York College, 1125 E Eighth St, York, NE, 68467-2699. Tel: 402-363-5703. p. 1341

Ratliff, Rosanna, Dir, Baylor Health Sciences Library, 3302 Gaston Ave, Dallas, TX, 75246. Tel: 214-820-2377, 214-828-8151. p. 2163

Ratliff, Sarah, Tech Serv, Plumas County Library, 445 Jackson St, Quincy, CA, 95971. Tel: 530-283-6310. p. 197

Ratliff Warren, Dena, Dir, Trimble County Public Library, 35 Equity Dr, Bedford, KY, 40006. Tel: 502-255-7362. p. 848

Ratt, Chad, Librn, Peayamechikee Public Library, Pinehouse Ave, Pinehouse Lake, SK, S0J 2B0, CANADA. Tel: 306-884-4888. p. 2744

Rattermann, Carrie, Br Supvr, Campbell County Public Library District, Alexandria Branch, 8333 Alexandria Pike, Alexandria, KY, 41001. Tel: 859-572-7463. p. 851

Rattray, Russ, Assoc Dir, New England College, 196 Bridge St, Henniker, NH, 03242-3298. Tel: 603-428-2344. p. 1367

Ratz, Heather, Chief Exec Officer, Brighton Public Library, 35 Alice St, Brighton, ON, K0K 1H0, CANADA. Tel: 613-475-2511. p. 2633

Ratzlaff, Jon, Fac Mgr, Lawrence Public Library, 707 Vermont St, Lawrence, KS, 66044-2371. Tel: 785-843-3833, Ext 135. p. 819

Rau, Erik, Dir, Libr Serv, Hagley Museum & Library, 298 Buck Rd E, Wilmington, DE, 19807. Tel: 302-658-2400. p. 357

Rau, JoElle, Librn, Nyssa Public Library, 319 Main St, Nyssa, OR, 97913-3845. Tel: 541-372-2978. p. 1889

Rau, Rebecca, Libr Asst, Lincoln Heritage Public Library, 105 Wallace St, Dale, IN, 47523-9267. Tel: 812-937-7170. p. 678

Rauch, Barbara, Br Mgr, Ross Annie Halenbake Library, Renovo Area Library, 317 Seventh St, Renovo, PA, 17764. Tel: 570-923-0390. p. 1956

Rauch, Steve, Med Librn, Community Hospital, 2351 G Rd, Grand Junction, CO, 81505. Tel: 970-242-0920, 970-256-6209. p. 284

Rauchwerger, Diane, Librn, Congregation Beth Am Library, 26790 Arastradero Rd, Los Altos Hills, CA, 94022. Tel: 650-493-4661. p. 159

Rauh, Jill, Doc, Ref (Info Servs), Benton Harbor Public Library, 213 E Wall St, Benton Harbor, MI, 49022-4499. Tel: 269-926-6139. p. 1084

Raum, Tamar, Sr Librn, New York City Law Department, 100 Church St, Rm 6-310, New York, NY, 10007. Tel: 212-356-2005. p. 1593

Rausch, Mary, Head, Cat, West Texas A&M University, 110 26th St, Canyon, TX, 79016. Tel: 806-651-2219. p. 2153

Rausch, Stacy, Dir, Br Serv, Borden Gail Public Library District, Rakow Library, 2751 W Bowes Rd, Elgin, IL, 60124. Tel: 847-531-7271. p. 583

Rausch, Stacy, Dir, Br Serv, Borden Gail Public Library District, South Elgin Library, 127 S McLean Blvd, South Elgin, IL, 60177. Tel: 847-931-2090. p. 583

Rausch, Stephanie, Dir, Farmer City Public Library, 109 E Green St, Farmer City, IL, 61842-1508. Tel: 309-928-9532. p. 588

Rautenstrauch, Denine, City Librn, Enterprise Public Library, 101 NE First St, Enterprise, OR, 97828-1173. Tel: 541-426-3906. p. 1878

Ravanbakhsh, Heather, Br Mgr, Arundel Anne County Public Library, Broadneck Library, 1275 Green Holly Dr, Annapolis, MD, 21401. Tel: 410-222-1905. p. 950

Rave, Melissa, Librn, Salt River Tribal Library, 11725 E Indian School Rd, Scottsdale, AZ, 85256. Tel: 480-362-2557. p. 77

Raven, Janna, Br Mgr, Fort Bend County Libraries, Mission Bend, 8421 Addicks Clodine Rd, Houston, TX, 77083. Tel: 832-471-5900. p. 2232

Raven, Meg, Colls Librn, Mount Saint Vincent University Library & Archives, 15 Lumpkin Rd, Halifax, NS, B3M 2J6, CANADA. Tel: 902-457-6403. p. 2619

Ravenell, Alma, Librn, Panola College, 1109 W Panola St, Carthage, TX, 75633. Tel: 903-693-1162. p. 2154

Ravenholt, Amy, Mgr, Borrower Serv, Outreach Serv, Washington Talking Book & Braille Library, 2021 Ninth Ave, Seattle, WA, 98121. Tel: 206-615-0400. p. 2382

Ravera, Laura, Dir, Minoa Library, 242 N Main St, Minoa, NY, 13116. Tel: 315-656-7401. p. 1572

Ravichandran, Radha, Info Serv, William Paterson University, 300 Pompton Rd, Wayne, NJ, 07470. Tel: 973-720-2769. p. 1452

Ravishanker, Ravi, Assoc Provost, Chief Info Officer, Wellesley College, 106 Central St, Wellesley, MA, 02481. Tel: 781-283-2166. p. 1064

Rawlings, Shari, Dir, Hope Welty Public Library District, 100 S Madison St, Cerro Gordo, IL, 61818. Tel: 217-763-5001. p. 551

Rawlins, Sharon, Youth Serv Spec, Lifelong Learning, New Jersey State Library, 185 W State St, Trenton, NJ, 08608. Tel: 609-278-2640, Ext 116. p. 1448

Rawlins, Stephanie, Dir, Pike County Public Library, 1008 E Maple St, Petersburg, IN, 47567-1736. Tel: 812-354-6257. p. 713

Rawlins, Stephanie, Dir, Pike County Public Library, Winslow Branch, 105 E Center St, Winslow, IN, 47598. Tel: 812-789-5423. p. 713

Rawls, Alexandria, Tech Serv Librn, Smyrna Public Library, 100 Village Green Circle, Smyrna, GA, 30080-3478. Tel: 770-431-2860. p. 497

Rawls, Mallory, Library Contact, Florida State University Libraries, Department of Religion Library, 301-B Dodd Hall, 641 University Way, Tallahassee, FL, 32306-1520. Tel: 850-644-1020. p. 447

Rawls, Maria, Br Mgr, Harris County Public Library, North Channel Branch, 15741 Wallisvillle Rd, Houston, TX, 77049. Tel: 832-927-5550. p. 2193

Rawls, Ronnie, Head, Circ, Pearl River County Library System, Poplarville Public Library, 202 W Beers St, Poplarville, MS, 39470. Tel: 601-795-8411. p. 1229

Rawls, Tess, Librn II, Guerra Joe A Laredo Public Library, Barbara Fasken Branch Library, 15201 Cerralvo Dr, Laredo, TX, 78045. Tel: 956-795-2400, Ext 2600. p. 2209

Rawn, Rachel, Dir, Havre Hill County Library, 402 Third St, Havre, MT, 59501. Tel: 406-265-2123. p. 1295

Rawson, Katie, Dir of Libr Operations, University of Pennsylvania Libraries, Annenberg School of Communication, 3620 Walnut St, Philadelphia, PA, 19104-6220. Tel: 215-898-7027. p. 1988

Rawson, Wendy, Libr Dir, Fitchburg Public Library, 5530 Lacy Rd, Fitchburg, WI, 53711. Tel: 608-729-1764. p. 2435

Ray, Allie, Asst Ch, Osceola Public Library, 131 N Main, Osceola, NE, 68651. Tel: 402-747-4301. p. 1331

Ray, Camille, Mgr, County of Los Angeles Public Library, View Park Bebe Moore Campbell Library, 3854 W 54th St, Los Angeles, CA, 90043-2297. Tel: 323-293-5371. p. 138

Ray, Daniel, Commun Librn, Bitterroot Public Library, 306 State St, Hamilton, MT, 59840. Tel: 406-363-1670. p. 1294

Ray, Elaine, Librn, Zelle LLP, 500 Washington Ave S, Ste 4000, Minneapolis, MN, 55415. Tel: 612-339-2020. p. 1186

Ray, Jacquelyn, Dir, Libr Serv, Walla Walla Community College Library, 500 Tausick Way, Walla Walla, WA, 99362-9267. Tel: 509-527-4277. p. 2392

Ray, Jeffrey, Head, Circ, Morton Grove Public Library, 6140 Lincoln Ave, Morton Grove, IL, 60053-2989. Tel: 847-965-4220. p. 620

Ray, June, Dir, Henry A Malley Memorial Library, 101 S Lincoln, Broadus, MT, 59317. Tel: 406-436-2812. p. 1290

Ray, Kathlin L, Dean, Libr & Teaching & Learning Tech, University of Nevada-Reno, 1664 N Virginia St, Mailstop 0322, Reno, NV, 89557-0322. Tel: 775-682-5684. p. 1349

Ray, Kelly, Ref Librn, Bacon Memorial District Library, 45 Vinewood, Wyandotte, MI, 48192-5221. Tel: 734-246-8357. p. 1160

Ray, Laura, Educ Prog Librn, Cleveland State University, Cleveland-Marshall Law Library, Cleveland-Marshall College of Law, 1801 Euclid Ave, Cleveland, OH, 44115-2223. Tel: 216-687-6880. p. 1769

Ray, Linda, User Serv Librn, Milligan College, 200 Blowers Blvd, Milligan College, TN, 37682. Tel: 423-461-8495. p. 2116

Ray, Michelle, Adult, Tech & Media Serv Coordr, LeRoy Collins Leon County Public Library System, 200 W Park Ave, Tallahassee, FL, 32301-7720. Tel: 850-606-2665. p. 445

Ray, Michelle, Br Coordr, Collins LeRoy Leon County Public Library System, Lake Jackson, Huntington Oaks Plaza, 3840-302 N Monroe, Tallahassee, FL, 32303. Tel: 850-606-2850. p. 445

Ray, Morgan E, Dir, Libr Serv, Flathead Valley Community College Library, 777 Grandview Dr, Kalispell, MT, 59901. Tel: 406-756-3856. p. 1297

Ray, Patsy, Br Mgr, Choctaw County Public Library, Silas Branch, 130 Indian Way, Silas, AL, 36919. Tel: 251-542-9379. p. 11

Ray, Phyllis, Br Mgr, Norfolk Public Library, Horace C Downing Branch, 555 E Liberty St, Norfolk, VA, 23523. Tel: 757-441-1968. p. 2335

Ray, Rebekah, Admin Librn, Free Library of Philadelphia, Business Resource & Innovaton Center, 1901 Vine St, Ground Flr, Philadelphia, PA, 19103. Tel: 215-686-8663. p. 1977

Ray, Rob, Head, Spec Coll & Univ Archives, San Diego State University, 5500 Campanile Dr, San Diego, CA, 92182-8050. Tel: 619-594-4303. p. 221

Ray, Shelley, Head Librn, Parkland Regional Library-Manitoba, Gladstone Branch, 42 Morris Ave N, Gladstone, MB, R0J 0T0, CANADA. Tel: 204-385-2641. p. 2586

Ray, Susan, Head, Adult Serv, Simsbury Public Library, 725 Hopmeadow St, Simsbury, CT, 06070. Tel: 860-658-7663. p. 336

Ray, Susan, Dir, Catskill Public Library, One Franklin St, Catskill, NY, 12414-1496. Tel: 518-943-4230. p. 1515

Ray, Theri, Ms, Dep Dir, Public Library of Enid & Garfield County, 120 W Maine, Enid, OK, 73701-5606. Tel: 580-234-6313. p. 1847

Rayburn, Barbara, Youth Serv Librn, Monon Town & Township Public Library, 427 N Market St, Monon, IN, 47959. Tel: 219-253-6517. p. 707

Rayford, Christyn, Libr Dir, South Holland Public Library, 16250 Wausau Ave, South Holland, IL, 60473. Tel: 708-527-3104. p. 648

Rayhill, Gladys, Libr Dir, Belt Public Library, 404 Millard St, Belt, MT, 59412. Tel: 406-277-3136. p. 1287

Rayl, Heather, Dir, Tech & Special Services, Vigo County Public Library, 680 Poplar St, Terre Haute, IN, 47807. Tel: 812-232-1113, Ext 1004. p. 721

Rayment, Rianne, Mgr, Crossfield Municipal Library, 1210 Railway St, Crossfield, AB, T0M 0S0, CANADA. Tel: 403-946-4232. p. 2532
Raymond, Brooke, Sr Res Analyst, New York Law Institute Library, 120 Broadway, Rm 932, New York, NY, 10271-0094. Tel: 212-732-8720. p. 1594
Raymond, Donna, Libr Asst, Boscawen Public Library, 116 N Main St, Boscawen, NH, 03303-1123. Tel: 603-753-8576. p. 1355
Raymond, John, Access Serv, Siena College, 515 Loudon Rd, Loudonville, NY, 12211. Tel: 518-783-2522. p. 1566
Raymond, Kirk, Dir, Publications & Communications, American Correctional Association, 206 N Washington St, Alexandria, VA, 22314. Tel: 703-224-0194. p. 2303
Raymond, Laura, Br Mgr, Fairfax County Public Library, City of Fairfax Regional Library, 10360 North St, Fairfax, VA, 22030-2514. Tel: 703-293-6227. p. 2316
Raymond, Mark, Br Mgr, Fort Smith Public Library, Dallas Street, 8100 Dallas St, Fort Smith, AR, 72903. Tel: 479-484-5650. p. 96
Raymond, Melanie, Area Mgr, Vaughan Public Libraries, Bathurst Clark Resource Library, 900 Clark Ave W, Thornhill, ON, L4J 8C1, CANADA. Tel: 905-653-7323. p. 2701
Raymond, Nancy, Chef de Div, Bibliotheques de Montreal, Ile-des-Soeurs, 260 rue Elgar, Verdun, QC, H3E 1C9, CANADA. Tel: 514-765-7154. p. 2719
Raymond, Nancy, Chef de Div, Bibliotheques de Montreal, Jacqueline-De Repentigny, 5955 rue Bannantyne, Verdun, QC, H4H 1H6, CANADA. Tel: 514-765-7154. p. 2719
Raymond, Sandy, Ms, Libr Dir, Wayland Free Public Library, Five Concord Rd, Wayland, MA, 01778. Tel: 508-358-2311. p. 1063
Rayner, Ashley, Br Mgr, Chicago Public Library, Greater Grand Crossing, 1000 E 73rd St, Chicago, IL, 60619. Tel: 312-745-1608. p. 556
Rayner, Ashley, Librn II, National Opinion Research Center Library, 1155 E 60th St, Rm 369, Chicago, IL, 60637-2667. Tel: 773-256-6206. p. 565
Raynor, Andrea, Digital Serv Librn, Berlin-Peck Memorial Library, 234 Kensington Rd, Berlin, CT, 06037. Tel: 860-828-7118. p. 302
Raynor, Jennifer, Assoc Dean of Libr, University of Rochester Medical Center, 601 Elmwood Ave, Rochester, NY, 14642. Tel: 716-275-4869. p. 1631
Raynor, John, Ref (Info Servs), High Point Public Library, 901 N Main St, High Point, NC, 27262. Tel: 336-883-3216. p. 1696
Raynor, Julie, Supvr, AV & Media Serv, High Point Public Library, 901 N Main St, High Point, NC, 27262. Tel: 336-883-3093. p. 1696
Razee, Jennifer, Asst Librn, Pettee Memorial Library, 16 S Main St, Wilmington, VT, 05363. Tel: 802-464-8557. p. 2299
Razer, Jennifer, Digital Serv Mgr, Arkansas State Library, 900 W Capitol, Ste 100, Little Rock, AR, 72201-3108. Tel: 501-682-2550. p. 100
Razer, Lee, ILL, Central Arkansas Library System, 100 Rock St, Little Rock, AR, 72201-4698. Tel: 501-918-3000. p. 101
Razor, Mary, Br Mgr, Mississippi County Library System, Blytheville Public, 200 N Fifth St, Blytheville, AR, 72315. Tel: 870-762-2431. p. 91
Razzo, Marilyn, Asst Librn, Fernie Heritage Library, 492 Third Ave, Fernie, BC, V0B 1M0, CANADA. Tel: 250-423-4458. p. 2566
Re, Tina, Special Collections & Arts Librn, Southern Connecticut State University, 501 Crescent St, New Haven, CT, 06515. Tel: 203-392-5597. p. 326
Rea, Colin, Dir, Fern Ridge Public Library, 88026 Territorial Rd, Veneta, OR, 97487. Tel: 541-935-7512. p. 1901
Rea, Jackie, Br Librn, Stockton-San Joaquin County Public Library, Weston Ranch Branch, 1453 W French Camp Rd, Stockton, CA, 95206. p. 250
Rea, Michael, Asst Dir, Schuyler Public Library, 108 E 18th St, Schuyler, NE, 68661-1929. Tel: 402-352-2221. p. 1335
Read, Allison, Campus Librn, Greenville Technical College Libraries, Northwest Campus, Bldg 402, Rm 122, 8109 White Horse Rd, Greenville, SC, 29617. Tel: 864-250-8018. p. 2062
Read, Allison, Pub Serv Librn, University of South Carolina Upstate Library, 800 University Way, Spartanburg, SC, 29303. Tel: 864-503-5613. p. 2070
Read, April, Dir, Cherryvale Public Library, 329 E Main St, Cherryvale, KS, 67335. Tel: 620-336-3460. p. 801
Read, Steve, Dir, McPherson Public Library, 214 W Marlin, McPherson, KS, 67460-4299. Tel: 620-245-2570. p. 825
Read, Vicki, Head, Patron Serv, Utah State University, 3000 Old Main Hill, Logan, UT, 84322-3000. Tel: 435-797-2914. p. 2265
Reade Law, Elisabeth K, Dir, Mkt, Reade International Corp, PO Drawer 15039, East Providence, RI, 02915-0039. Tel: 401-433-7000. p. 2032
Reader-Jones, Melodie, Asst Librn, Bartlett-Carnegie Sapulpa Public Library, 27 W Dewey Ave, Sapulpa, OK, 74066. Tel: 918-224-5624. p. 1861
Reading, Alexandra, Ad, Saint Clair Shores Public Library, 22500 11 Mile Rd, Saint Clair Shores, MI, 48081-1399. Tel: 586-771-9020. p. 1147
Readman, Samuel, ILL, Ref Librn, Ser, University of Holy Cross, 4123 Woodland Dr, New Orleans, LA, 70131. Tel: 504-398-2101. p. 904
Ready, Belinda, Librn, Bennett County Library, 101 Main St, Martin, SD, 57551. Tel: 605-685-6556. p. 2078
Reagan, Barbara, Libr Asst, Helper City Library, 19 S Main St, Helper, UT, 84526. Tel: 435-472-5601. p. 2264
Reagan, Katherine, Asst Dir, Curator, Cornell University Library, Division of Rare & Manuscript Collections (Carl A Kroch Library), 2B Carl A Kroch Library, Ithaca, NY, 14853. Tel: 607-255-3530. p. 1551
Reagan-Kershner, Suzan, Sr Prog Mgr, University of New Mexico, Bureau of Business & Economic Research Data Bank, 1919 Las Lomas NE, Albuquerque, NM, 87106. Tel: 505-277-3038. p. 1462
Reakes, Patrick J, Sr Assoc Dean, Scholarly Resources & Servs, University of Florida Libraries, 1545 W University Ave, Gainesville, FL, 32611-7000. Tel: 352-273-2505. p. 407
Real, A J, Head, Acq, Dominican University of California, 50 Acacia Ave, San Rafael, CA, 94901-2298. Tel: 415-257-0104. p. 236
Real, Brian, Dr, Asst Prof, University of Kentucky, 320 Little Library Bldg, Lexington, KY, 40506-0224. Tel: 859-257-8876. p. 2785
Real, Travis, Asst Dir, Texas Tech University Health Sciences, Odessa Campus, 800 W Fourth St, Odessa, TX, 79763. Tel: 432-703-5035. p. 2214
Reale, Michelle, Dr, Access Serv Mgr, Outreach Librn, Arcadia University, 450 S Easton Rd, Glenside, PA, 19038. Tel: 215-572-2139. p. 1937
Reale, Sue Ann, Head, Children's Servx, Syosset Public Library, 225 S Oyster Bay Rd, Syosset, NY, 11791-5897. Tel: 516-921-7161. p. 1648
Ream, Dan, Coordr, Rappahannock Community College, 52 Campus Dr, Warsaw, VA, 22572. Tel: 804-333-6716. p. 2352
Reaman, Kim, Asst Librn, Brighton Public Library, 35 Alice St, Brighton, ON, K0K 1H0, CANADA. Tel: 613-475-2511. p. 2633
Reams, Don, Correctional Education & Reference Librn, Ashland University Library, 509 College Ave, Ashland, OH, 44805. Tel: 419-289-5410. p. 1747
Reardon, Craig, Electronic Serv Librn, Nashotah House, 2777 Mission Rd, Nashotah, WI, 53058-9793. Tel: 262-646-6537. p. 2463
Reash, Aimee, Dir, Pub Serv, Allegheny College, 520 N Main St, Meadville, PA, 16335. Tel: 814-332-3768. p. 1959
Reason, Judy, Librn, Fulton County Public Library, Hickman Public, 902 Moscow Ave, Hickman, KY, 42050. Tel: 270-236-2464. p. 856
Reason, Shunde, Bus Off Adminr, Hinds Community College, 505 E Main St, Raymond, MS, 39154. Tel: 601-857-3355. p. 1231
Reasoner, Brenda, Dir, Murray Public Library, 416 Maple St, Murray, IA, 50174. Tel: 641-447-2711. p. 772
Reasoner, Mary Beth, Ch Serv Librn, Tecumseh District Library, 215 N Ottawa St, Tecumseh, MI, 49286-1564. Tel: 517-423-2238. p. 1153
Reaux, Angela, Coll Serv Librn, Law Library of Louisiana, Louisiana Supreme Court, 2nd Flr, 400 Royal St, New Orleans, LA, 70130-2104. Tel: 504-310-2432. p. 901
Reaveley, Melanie, Exec Dir, Kootenay Library Federation, PO Box 3125, Castlegar, BC, V1N 3H4, CANADA. Tel: 250-608-4490. p. 2564
Reaves, Damon, Head of Education, National Gallery of Art Library, Learning Resources, Fourth St & Pennsylvania Ave NW, Washington, DC, 20565. Tel: 202-842-6280. p. 372
Reaves, Jennifer, Tech Serv Mgr, Denton Public Library, 502 Oakland St, Denton, TX, 76201. Tel: 940-349-8752. p. 2170
Reavie, Keir, Mr, Dir, Libr Serv, City of Hope, 1500 E Duarte Rd, Duarte, CA, 91010. Tel: 626-301-8497. p. 139
Reavis, Paul, Librn, Hopkins & Carley Library, 70 S First St, San Jose, CA, 95113. Tel: 408-286-9800. p. 230
Reay, Danielle, Digital Scholarship Tech Mgr, Drew University Library, 36 Madison Ave, Madison, NJ, 07940. Tel: 973-408-3855. p. 1414
Reazer, John, Instrul & Ref Librn, University of Miami, Louis Calder Memorial Library, Miller School of Medicine, 1601 NW Tenth Ave, Miami, FL, 33136. Tel: 305-243-3999. p. 425
Rebertus, Diane, Dir, Libr Serv, Gloucester County Library, 6920 Main St, Gloucester, VA, 23061. Tel: 804-693-2998. p. 2321
Rebertus, Diane, Dir, Libr Serv, Gloucester County Library, Point Branch, 2354 York Crossing Dr, Gloucester, VA, 23072. Tel: 804-642-9790. p. 2321
Rebori, Lisa, VPres, Coll, Houston Museum of Natural Science, 5555 Hermann Park Dr, Houston, TX, 77030-1799. Tel: 713-639-4670. p. 2195
Rechnitz, Andrew, Dir, Systems & Tech Strategies, Texas State University, 601 University Dr, San Marcos, TX, 78666-4684. Tel: 512-408-4006. p. 2241
Rechsteiner, Kelly, YA Librn, North Merrick Public Library, 1691 Meadowbrook Rd, North Merrick, NY, 11566. Tel: 516-378-7474. p. 1607
Recio, Frances, Libr Dir, Muleshoe Area Public Library, 322 W Second St, Muleshoe, TX, 79347. Tel: 806-272-4707. p. 2221
Reck, Jhanna, Coordr, Prog, Anderson County Library, 300 N McDuffie St, Anderson, SC, 29621-5643. Tel: 864-260-4500. p. 2046
Recka, Lindsey, Head, Children's & Young Adult Serv, Topsfield Town Library, One S Common St, Topsfield, MA, 01983. Tel: 978-887-1528. p. 1060
Reckamp, Julie, Head, Youth Serv, Byron Public Library District, 100 S Washington St, Byron, IL, 61010. Tel: 815-234-5107. p. 547
Reckemeier, Nils, Evening Libr Asst, Queens University of Charlotte, 1900 Selwyn Ave, Charlotte, NC, 28274. Tel: 704-337-7585. p. 1681
Reckhow, Susan, Interim Dir, Liverpool Public Library, 310 Tulip St, Liverpool, NY, 13088-4997. Tel: 315-457-0310. p. 1564
Reckner, Alessandra, Librn, Portage County Law Library, 241 S Chestnut St, 1st Flr, Ravenna, OH, 44266. Tel: 330-297-3661. p. 1817
Reckson, Ivy, Ch, Lakeview Public Library, 1120 Woodfield Rd, Rockville Centre, NY, 11570. Tel: 516-536-3071. p. 1631

Record, Rachelle, Mgr, Miami-Dade Public Library System, Fairlawn Branch, 6376 SW Eighth St, Miami, FL, 33144. Tel: 305-261-1571. p. 423

Rector, Aubrey, Acq Librn, Tulane University, Law Library, Weinmann Hall, 3rd Flr, 6329 Freret St, New Orleans, LA, 70118-6231. Tel: 504-862-8866. p. 904

Rector, Eric, Libr Dir, Arkansas Tech University, 305 West Q St, Russellville, AR, 72801. Tel: 479-968-0417. p. 108

Rector, Joe, Dir, James River Valley Library System, Stutsman County Library, 910 Fifth St SE, Jamestown, ND, 58401. Tel: 701-252-1531. p. 1736

Rector, Joseph, Libr Dir, James River Valley Library System, 105 Third St SE, Jamestown, ND, 58401. Tel: 701-252-2990. p. 1736

Reczkowski, Alex, Libr Dir, Berkshire Athenaeum, One Wendell Ave, Pittsfield, MA, 01201-6385. Tel: 413-499-9480, Ext 102. p. 1046

Redburn, Maria, Dir, Bedford Public Library, 2424 Forest Ridge Dr, Bedford, TX, 76021. Tel: 817-952-2350. p. 2146

Redcay, Sheila, Libr Dir, Matthews Public Library, 102 W Main St, Fredericksburg, PA, 17026. Tel: 717-865-5523. p. 1934

Redd, Kay, Br Mgr, Saint Tammany Parish Library, Abita Springs Branch, 71683 Leveson St, Abita Springs, LA, 70420. Tel: 985-893-6285. p. 887

Redd, Rea Andrew, Libr Dir, Waynesburg College, 51 W College St, Waynesburg, PA, 15370. Tel: 724-852-3419. p. 2019

Reddell, Becky, ILL, Metropolitan Community College, Longview Campus Library, 500 SW Longview Rd, Lee's Summit, MO, 64081-2105. Tel: 816-604-2267. p. 1256

Redden, Carla, Librn III, Maysville Community & Technical College, 1755 US Hwy 68, Maysville, KY, 41056. Tel: 606-759-7141, Ext 66206. p. 869

Redden, Melanie, Dir, Robertson County Carnegie Library, 315 E Decherd St, Franklin, TX, 77856. Tel: 979-828-4331. p. 2181

Redden, Teresa, Interim Head, Coll Develop, Frye Art Museum Curatorial Library, 704 Terry Ave, Seattle, WA, 98104. Tel: 206-432-8228. p. 2376

Redding, Carmen, Head, Libr Serv, North Dakota State Library, Liberty Memorial Bldg, Dept 250, 604 East Blvd Ave, Bismarck, ND, 58505-0800. Tel: 701-328-4676. p. 1730

Redding, Lorna I, Acq, Normandale Community College Library, 9700 France Ave S, Bloomington, MN, 55431. Tel: 952-487-8292. p. 1166

Redding, Yvonne, Dir, Rosebud County Library, 201 N Ninth Ave, Forsyth, MT, 59327. Tel: 406-346-7561. p. 1293

Redepenning, Barb, Curator, Lac Qui Parle County Historical Society, 250 Eighth Ave S, Madison, MN, 56256. Tel: 320-598-7678. p. 1181

Redfield, Lauren, Interim Dir, Durham Public Library, Seven Maple Ave, Durham, CT, 06422. Tel: 860-349-9544. p. 309

Redford, John, Music, Spec Projects Librn, Biola University Library, 13800 Biola Ave, La Mirada, CA, 90639. Tel: 562-944-0351, Ext 5613. p. 155

Redigan, Mary, Coordr, Saint Clair County Library System, Blind & Physically Handicapped Library, 210 McMorran Blvd, Port Huron, MI, 48060. Tel: 810-982-3600. p. 1142

Rediker, Adam, Educ Mgr, Bartholomew County Historical Society, 524 Third St, 2nd Flr, Columbus, IN, 47201. Tel: 812-372-3541. p. 676

Reding, Diana, Libr Dir, Corfu Free Library, Seven Maple Ave, Corfu, NY, 14036. Tel: 585-599-3321. p. 1522

Reding, Sue, Dir, Arcade Free Library, 365 W Main St, Arcade, NY, 14009. Tel: 585-492-1297. p. 1487

Redinger, Gloria, Operations Mgr, Tech Serv Mgr, Illinois Wesleyan University, One Ames Plaza, Bloomington, IL, 61701-7188. Tel: 309-556-3526. p. 543

Redington, Daniel L, Dir, Mary Meuser Memorial Library, 1803 Northampton St, Easton, PA, 18042-3183. Tel: 610-258-3040. p. 1928

Redington, Deirdre, Tech Serv Librn, Bradley University, 1501 W Bradley Ave, Peoria, IL, 61625. Tel: 309-677-2850. p. 634

Redker, Amanda, Children's Mgr, Thomas County Public Library System, 201 N Madison St, Thomasville, GA, 31792-5414. Tel: 229-225-5252. p. 499

Redlecki, Darlene, Dir, Clymer-French Creek Free Library, 564 Clymer-Sherman Rd, Clymer, NY, 14724. Tel: 716-355-8823. p. 1519

Redman, Tony, Ad, Abilene Public Library, Mockingbird Branch, 1326 N Mockingbird, Abilene, TX, 79603. Tel: 325-437-7323. p. 2132

Redmer, Jill, Acq, ILL Spec, Yavapai County Free Library District, 1971 Commerce Ctr Circle, Ste D, Prescott, AZ, 86301. Tel: 928-771-3191. p. 74

Redmer, Michelle, Librn, Ward County Public Library, Kenmare Branch, Memorial Hall, Five NE Third St, Kenmare, ND, 58746. Tel: 701-385-4090. p. 1738

Redmond, Charles, Librn, New York State Supreme Court Third Judicial District, Hon John L Larkin Memorial Law Library, Ulster County Courthouse, 285 Wall St, Kingston, NY, 12401. Tel: 845-481-9391. p. 1560

Redmond, David, Tech Coordr, Massapequa Public Library, Bar Harbour Bldg, 40 Harbor Lane, Massapequa Park, NY, 11762. Tel: 516-799-0770. p. 1569

Redmond, Jana, Instrul Serv/Ref Librn, Carson-Newman University, 1634 Russell Ave, Jefferson City, TN, 37760. Tel: 865-471-3338. p. 2103

Redmond, Malissa, Admin Serv Coordr, Wentworth Institute of Technology, 550 Huntington Ave, Boston, MA, 02115-5998. Tel: 617-989-4299. p. 1000

Redpath, Hayley, Libr Serv Coordr, Edmonton Public Library, Capilano, 9915 67 St NW, Edmonton, AB, T6A 0H2, CANADA. Tel: 780-496-8426. p. 2536

Reece, Courtenay, Dir, Millville Public Library, 210 Buck St, Millville, NJ, 08332. Tel: 856-825-7087. p. 1419

Reece, Elizabeth, Pres, Tama County Historical Society & Genealogy Library, 200 N Broadway, Toledo, IA, 52342. Tel: 641-484-6767. p. 786

Reece, Gwendolyn, Dir, Res, Teaching & Learning, American University Library, 4400 Massachusetts Ave NW, Washington, DC, 20016-8046. Tel: 202-885-3281. p. 361

Reece, Jessica Dixon, Res Analyst, North Carolina Biotechnology Center Life Science Intelligence, 15 T W Alexander Dr, Research Triangle Park, NC, 27709. Tel: 919-541-9366. p. 1712

Reece, Sheila, Area Mgr, Albuquerque-Bernalillo County Library System, Cherry Hills Library, 6901 Barstow NE, Albuquerque, NM, 87111. Tel: 505-857-8321. p. 1460

Reece, Stephenie, Libr Mgr, Timberland Regional Library, Aberdeen Branch, 121 E Market St, Aberdeen, WA, 98520-5292. Tel: 360-533-2360. p. 2388

Reecer, Crystal, Br Mgr, Albuquerque-Bernalillo County Library System, Lomas-Tramway Library, 908 Eastridge Dr NE, Albuquerque, NM, 87123. Tel: 505-291-6295. p. 1460

Reecy, Agnes, Asst Librn, Edgemont Public Library, 412 Second Ave, Edgemont, SD, 57735. Tel: 605-662-7712. p. 2076

Reed, Amber, Commun Librn, Monroe County Library System, Dorsch Memorial Branch Library, 18 E First St, Monroe, MI, 48161-2227. Tel: 734-241-7878. p. 1133

Reed, Amber, Commun Librn, Monroe County Library System, L S Navarre Branch, 1135 E Second St, Monroe, MI, 48161-1920. Tel: 734-241-5577. p. 1134

Reed, Anne, Asst Dir, Admin, Public Library of Brookline, 361 Washington St, Brookline, MA, 02445. Tel: 617-730-2370. p. 1003

Reed, Ashley, Head, Circ, Starke County Public Library System, 152 W Culver Rd, Knox, IN, 46534-2220. Tel: 574-772-7323. p. 699

Reed, Brenda, Head, Educ Libr, Queen's University, Education Library, Duncan McArthur Hall, 511 Union St at Sir John A Macdonald Blvd, Kingston, ON, K7M 5R7, CANADA. Tel: 613-533-6000, Ext 77644. p. 2651

Reed, Brennan, Children's Coordr, Kokomo-Howard County Public Library, 220 N Union St, Kokomo, IN, 46901-4614. Tel: 765-457-3242. p. 700

Reed, Brittany, Br Operations Mgr, University of Colorado Boulder, Jerry Crail Johnson Earth Sciences & Map Library, Benson Earth Sciences, 2200 Colorado Ave, Boulder, CO, 80309. Tel: 303-492-4488. p. 268

Reed, Carol, Ref (Info Servs), United States Air Force, Air Force Research Laboratory, Wright Research Site, Det 1 AFRL/WSC, Bldg 642, Rm 1300, 2950 Hobson Way, Wright-Patterson AFB, OH, 45433-7765. Tel: 937-255-5511, Ext 4271. p. 1834

Reed, Carolyn, Mgr, County of Los Angeles Public Library, Hawaiian Gardens Library, 11940 Carson St, Hawaiian Gardens, CA, 90716-1137. Tel: 562-496-1212. p. 136

Reed, Chay, Access Serv Coordr, University of Connecticut, Avery Point Campus Library, 1084 Shennecossett Rd, Groton, CT, 06340. Tel: 860-486-9147. p. 340

Reed, Cindy, Head, Cat, Harrison Regional Library System, 50 Lester St, Columbiana, AL, 35051. Tel: 205-669-3910. p. 13

Reed, Danielle Renee, Dr, Assoc Dir, Monell Chemical Senses Center, 3500 Market St, Philadelphia, PA, 19104. Tel: 267-280-3248. p. 1983

Reed, David, Dean, Cañada College Library, Bldg 9, 3rd Flr, 4200 Farm Hill Blvd, Redwood City, CA, 94061-1099. p. 200

Reed, Donna, Dr, Dean, Learning & Libr Serv, City College of San Francisco, 50 Frida Kahlo Way, 4th Flr, San Francisco, CA, 94112. Tel: 415-452-5455. p. 224

Reed, Emily, Ref & Instruction Librn, Pennsylvania State University-Harrisburg Library, 351 Olmsted Dr, Middletown, PA, 17057-4850. Tel: 717-948-6373. p. 1963

Reed, Erich, Dir, Southwest Harbor Public Library, 338 Main St, Southwest Harbor, ME, 04679. Tel: 207-244-7065. p. 942

Reed, Erika, Dir, Marion County Public Library, 321 Monroe St, Fairmont, WV, 26554-2952. Tel: 304-366-1210. p. 2402

Reed, Gabrielle, Access Serv Librn, Massachusetts College of Art & Design, 621 Huntington Ave, Boston, MA, 02115-5882. Tel: 617-879-7102. p. 996

Reed, Heidi, Libr Dir, Young Men's Library Association Library, 37 Main St, Ware, MA, 01082-1317. Tel: 413-967-5491. p. 1062

Reed, Jason, Dir, Acad Res, Greenville Technical College Libraries, Bldg 102, 506 S Pleasantburg Dr, Greenville, SC, 29607. Tel: 864-236-6500. p. 2062

Reed, Jason, Head Librn, Orangeburg-Calhoun Technical College Library, 3250 Saint Matthews Rd NE, Orangeburg, SC, 29118. Tel: 803-535-1262. p. 2066

Reed, Jenna, Branch Lead, Saint Clair County Library System, G Lynn Campbell Branch Library, 1955 N Allen Rd, Kimball, MI, 48074. Tel: 810-982-9171. p. 1142

Reed, Jessica, Ref Coordr, Springdale Public Library, 405 S Pleasant St, Springdale, AR, 72764. Tel: 479-750-8180. p. 110

Reed, Jodi, Interim Dean of Info Tech & Learning Resources, Cuyamaca College Library, 900 Rancho San Diego Pkwy, El Cajon, CA, 92019. Tel: 619-660-4400. p. 139

Reed, Joyce, Adult Serv, Barry-Lawrence Regional Library, Monett Branch, 2200 Park St, Monett, MO, 65708. Tel: 417-235-7350. p. 1263

Reed, Kathryn, Ch, Russell Adelia M Library, Mamie's Place Children's Library & Learning Center, 284 Church St, Alexander City, AL, 35010. Tel: 256-234-4644. p. 4

Reed, Kayla, Discovery, Systems & Digital Strategy Librarian, Grinnell College Libraries, 1111 Sixth Ave, Grinnell, IA, 50112-1770. Tel: 641-269-4775. p. 756

Reed, Kelsey, Circ Supvr, United States Army, Combined Arms Research Library, US Army Command & General Staff College, Eisenhower Hall, 250 Gibbon Ave, Fort Leavenworth, KS, 66027-2314. Tel: 913-758-3005. p. 808

Reed, Kerry, Ch Serv, Tinley Park Public Library, 7851 Timber Dr, Tinley Park, IL, 60477-3398. Tel: 708-532-0160, Ext 2. p. 653

Reed, Kerry, Dir, Newton Falls Public Library, 204 S Canal St, Newton Falls, OH, 44444-1694. Tel: 330-872-1282. p. 1808

Reed, Kim, Ms, Dir, Libr Serv, College of Western Idaho, Nampa Campus Multipurpose Bldg, 1st Flr, Rm 105/103, 6042 Birch Lane, Nampa, ID, 83687. Tel: 208-562-3114. p. 527

Reed, Krissy, Dir, Gretna Public Library, 736 South St, Gretna, NE, 68028. Tel: 402-332-4480. p. 1316

Reed, Laura, Mgr, Mississauga Library System, 301 Burnhamthorpe Rd W, Mississauga, ON, L5B 3Y3, CANADA. Tel: 905-615-3500, p. 2659

Reed, Leeanne, Coll Serv Mgr, Charleston Carnegie Public Library, 712 Sixth St, Charleston, IL, 61920. Tel: 217-345-4913. p. 552

Reed, Linda, Librn, Township Library of Silver Creek, 309 Vine St, Silver Creek, NE, 68663. Tel: 308-773-2594. p. 1336

Reed, Liz, Adult Serv, Morrill Memorial Library, 33 Walpole St, Norwood, MA, 02062-1206. Tel: 781-769-0200. p. 1044

Reed, Marci, Br Mgr, Louisville Free Public Library, Fairdale Branch, 10620 W Manslick Rd, Fairdale, KY, 40118. Tel: 502-375-2051. p. 865

Reed, Marcia, Assoc Dir, Getty Research Institute, 1200 Getty Center Dr, Ste 1100, Los Angeles, CA, 90049-1688. Tel: 310-440-7390. p. 161

Reed, Margaret, Per Librn, Ouachita Baptist University, 410 Ouachita St, OBU Box 3742, Arkadelphia, AR, 71998-0001. Tel: 870-245-5125. p. 89

Reed, Marie, Br Assoc, Las Vegas-Clark County Library District, Indian Springs Library, 715 Gretta Lane, Indian Springs, NV, 89018. Tel: 702-879-3845. p. 1346

Reed, Maryruth, Libr Dir, Mitchell Public Library, 1449 Center Ave, Mitchell, NE, 69357. Tel: 308-623-2222. p. 1325

Reed, Melanie, Spec Coll & Univ Archives, Shippensburg University, 1871 Old Main Dr, Shippensburg, PA, 17257. Tel: 717-477-1325. p. 2007

Reed, Mignon G, Dir, Calloway County Public Library, 710 Main St, Murray, KY, 42071. Tel: 270-753-2288, Ext 101. p. 870

Reed, Neil, Archivist, US Court of Appeals for the Sixth Circuit Library, 540 Potter Stewart US Courthouse, 100 E Fifth St, Cincinnati, OH, 45202-3911. Tel: 513-564-7321. p. 1764

Reed, Nyama, Libr Dir, Whitefish Bay Public Library, 5420 N Marlborough Dr, Whitefish Bay, WI, 53217. Tel: 414-755-6551. p. 2488

Reed, Olivia, Archives, Coordr, Spec Coll, Taylor University, 1846 Main St, Upland, IN, 46989. Tel: 765-998-5520. p. 722

Reed, Pamela, Librn, Morris, Nichols, Arsht & Tunnell, LLP, 1201 N Market St, Wilmington, DE, 19801. Tel: 302-658-9200. p. 357

Reed, Pamela, Dir, Clarendon College, 1122 College Dr, Clarendon, TX, 79226. Tel: 806-874-4815. p. 2156

Reed, Patricia, Librn, North Central Washington Libraries, Peshastin Public Library, 8396 Main St, Peshastin, WA, 98847-9734. Tel: 509-548-7821. p. 2394

Reed, Regina, Libr Dir, Leon Valley Public Library, 6425 Evers Rd, Leon Valley, TX, 78238-1453. Tel: 210-684-0720. p. 2211

Reed, Robyn, Head, Access Serv, Union College, 807 Union St, Schenectady, NY, 12308. Tel: 518-388-6277. p. 1638

Reed, Robyn, Biomedical Info & Emerging Technologies, Pennsylvania State University, College of Medicine, Penn State Hershey, 500 University Dr, Hershey, PA, 17033. Tel: 717-531-6137. p. 1943

Reed, Shelly A, Asst Librn, Sutton Memorial Library, 201 S Saunders, Sutton, NE, 68979. Tel: 402-773-5259. p. 1337

Reed, Stefanie, Dir, Flat River Community Library, 200 W Judd St, Greenville, MI, 48838. Tel: 616-754-6359. p. 1112

Reed, Stephanie, Asst Libr Mgr, Siloam Springs Public Library, 205 E Jefferson, Siloam Springs, AR, 72761. Tel: 479-524-4236. p. 110

Reed, Sujaniah, Libr Assoc, American Samoa Community College Library, Malaeimi Village, Malaeimi Rd, Mapusaga, AS, 96799. p. 2503

Reed, Susan L, Dir, Pawtucket Public Library, 13 Summer St, Pawtucket, RI, 02860. Tel: 401-725-3714. p. 2036

Reed, Todd, Dir, Sturgis District Library, 255 North St, Sturgis, MI, 49091. Tel: 269-659-7225. p. 1153

Reed, Tracey, Dir, Warminster Township Free Library, 1076 Emma Lane, Warminster, PA, 18974. Tel: 215-672-4362. p. 2017

Reed, Trina, Dir, Levittown Public Library, One Bluegrass Lane, Levittown, NY, 11756-1292. Tel: 516-731-5728. p. 1562

Reed, Trish, Chief Exec Officer, Head Librn, Asphodel-Norwood Public Library, 2363 County Rd 45, Norwood, ON, K0L 2V0, CANADA. Tel: 705-639-2228. p. 2662

Reed, Trish, Chief Exec Officer, Head Librn, Asphodel-Norwood Public Library, Westwood Branch, 312 Centre Line, Westwood, ON, K0L 3B0, CANADA. Tel: 705-768-2548. p. 2662

Reed, William, Mgr, Cleveland Public Library, Ohio Library for the Blind & Physically Disabled, 17121 Lake Shore Blvd, Cleveland, OH, 44110-4006. Tel: 216-623-2911. p. 1768

Reed, Yvonne, Syst Librn, Victor Valley College Library, 18422 Bear Valley Rd, Victorville, CA, 92395-5850. Tel: 760-245-4271, Ext 2262. p. 256

Reed-Armbrister, Tracey, Supvr, Youth Serv, Smyth County Public Library, 118 S Sheffey St, Marion, VA, 24354. Tel: 276-783-2323, Ext 223. p. 2331

Reed-Benge, Catherine, Librn, United States Air Force, 71 FTW/ASRCC-CSSL, 446 McAffrey Ave, Bldg 314, Ste 24, Vance AFB, OK, 73705-5710. Tel: 580-213-7368. p. 1867

Reeder, Candace, Br Librn, Northport-East Northport Public Library, East Northport Public, 185 Larkfield Rd, East Northport, NY, 11731. Tel: 631-261-2313. p. 1608

Reeder, Jeremy, Dir, Maricopa County Library District, 2700 N Central Ave, Ste 700, Phoenix, AZ, 85004. Tel: 602-652-3000. p. 70

Reeder, Kathy, Admin Support Coordr, Lycoming College, One College Pl, Williamsport, PA, 17701. Tel: 570-321-4106. p. 2023

Reedy, Lisa, Br Mgr, Putnam County Library, Eleanor Branch, 401 Roosevelt Blvd, Eleanor, WV, 25070. Tel: 304-586-4295. p. 2406

Reedy, Melanie, Bus Mgr, Wyoming State Library, 2800 Central Ave, Cheyenne, WY, 82002. Tel: 307-777-5917. p. 2493

Reel, Ellyn, Asst Librn, Earlham Public Library, 120 S Chestnut Ave, Earlham, IA, 50072. Tel: 515-758-2121. p. 750

Reel, Teresa, Head, Tech Serv, Paulding County Carnegie Library, 205 S Main St, Paulding, OH, 45879-1492. Tel: 419-399-2032. p. 1814

Reems, Carmen, Mgr, Libr Serv, Northern Alberta Institute of Technology, 11762 106 St NW, Edmonton, AB, T5G 2R1, CANADA. Tel: 780-471-8777. p. 2537

Rees, Jamie, Historical Colls Mgr, Kansas University Medical Center, 1020-1030 Robinson Bldg, 3901 Rainbow Blvd, Kansas City, KS, 66160-7311. Tel: 913-588-7244. p. 817

Rees, Joshua, Librn, Daly City Public Library, John D Daly Branch, 134 Hillside Blvd, Daly City, CA, 94014. Tel: 650-991-8073. p. 134

Rees, Lisa, Chief Librn, Granisle Public Library, Two Village Sq, McDonald Ave, Granisle, BC, V0J 1W0, CANADA. Tel: 250-697-2713. p. 2567

Rees, Marilyn, Head, Circ, Louis Bay 2nd Library, 345 Lafayette Ave, Hawthorne, NJ, 07506-2546. Tel: 973-427-5745, Ext 10. p. 1407

Rees, Pam, Dir, Grand View University Library, 1350 Morton Ave, Des Moines, IA, 50316. Tel: 515-263-6098. p. 746

Reese, Amy, Head, Systems & Digital Strategies, North Dakota State University Libraries, 1201 Albrecht Blvd, Fargo, ND, 58108. Tel: 701-231-7288. p. 1733

Reese, Diana, Tech Serv, Colorado Department of Corrections, Centennial Correctional Facility Library, PO Box 600, Canon City, CO, 81215-0600. Tel: 719-269-5546. p. 269

Reese, Ginny, Br Mgr, Jefferson-Madison Regional Library, Greene County, 222 Main St, Ste 101, Standardsville, VA, 22973. Tel: 434-985-5227. p. 2309

Reese, Joel, Local Hist Librn, Iredell County Public Library, 201 N Tradd St, Statesville, NC, 28677. Tel: 704-878-3093. p. 1717

Reese, Noreen, Dep Dir, Warren-Newport Public Library District, 224 N O'Plaine Rd, Gurnee, IL, 60031. Tel: 847-244-5150, Ext 3026. p. 596

Reese, Sue, Librn, US National Park Service, 99 Marconi Site Rd, Wellfleet, MA, 02667. Tel: 508-771-2144. p. 1064

Reese-Hornsby, Twyla, Pub Serv Librn, Tarrant County College, 828 W Harwood Rd, Hurst, TX, 76054. Tel: 817-515-6365. p. 2201

Reeser, Ann, Librn, Albert W Thompson Memorial Library, 17 Chestnut St, Clayton, NM, 88415. Tel: 575-374-9423. p. 1465

Reesman, Nancy, Education Analyst, Department of Veterans Affairs, 353 N Duffy Rd, Butler, PA, 16001. Tel: 878-271-6924. p. 1917

Reetz, Vicky, Dir, Onarga Community Public Library District, 209 W Seminary Ave, Onarga, IL, 60955-1131. Tel: 815-268-7626. p. 630

Reeve, Carole, Br Head, Winnipeg Public Library, Osborne, 625 Osborne St, Winnipeg, MB, R3L 2B3, CANADA. Tel: 204-986-4776. p. 2596

Reeves, Ann, Dir, Eureka Public Library District, 202 S Main St, Eureka, IL, 61530. Tel: 309-467-2922. p. 586

Reeves, Betty, Ref Librn, Carnegie Evans Public Library Albia Public, 203 Benton Ave E, Albia, IA, 52531-2036. Tel: 641-932-2469. p. 729

Reeves, Bobby, Tech Serv, Virginia's Academic Library Consortium, George Mason University, 4400 University Dr, Fenwick 5100, Fairfax, VA, 22030. Tel: 703-993-4654. p. 2776

Reeves, David, Access Serv Asst, Rockhurst University, 1100 Rockhurst Rd, Kansas City, MO, 64110-2561. Tel: 816-501-4142. p. 1257

Reeves, Deidrah, Br Mgr, Harford County Public Library, Norrisville Branch, 5310 Norrisville Rd, White Hall, MD, 21161-8924. Tel: 410-692-7850. p. 959

Reeves, Deidrah, Br Mgr, Harford County Public Library, Whiteford Branch, 2407 Whiteford Rd, Whiteford, MD, 21160-1218. Tel: 410-452-8831, 410-638-3608. p. 959

Reeves, Donna, Bus Mgr, Haverford Township Free Library, 1601 Darby Rd, Havertown, PA, 19083-3798. Tel: 610-446-3082, Ext 512. p. 1942

Reeves, Florence, Dir, Burnet County Library System, 100 E Washington St, Burnet, TX, 78611. Tel: 512-715-5228. p. 2152

Reeves, Greg, Libr Mgr, Boone Daniel Regional Library, Callaway County Public Library, 710 Court St, Fulton, MO, 65251. Tel: 573-642-7261. p. 1242

Reeves, Jessica, Librn, Mid-Arkansas Regional Library, Grant County Library, 210 N Oak St, Sheridan, AR, 72150-2495. Tel: 870-942-4436. p. 103
Reeves, Kelly, Mr, ILL Spec, Troy University Library, 309 Wallace Hall, Troy, AL, 36082. Tel: 334-670-3257. p. 37
Reeves, Kimberly, Br Mgr, East Baton Rouge Parish Library, Fairwood Branch, 12910 Old Hammond Hwy, Baton Rouge, LA, 70816. Tel: 225-924-9380. p. 883
Reeves, Larry, Assoc Dean, Dir, Law Libr, Vanderbilt University, Alyne Queener Massey Law Library, 131 21st Ave S, Nashville, TN, 37203. Tel: 615-322-0020. p. 2122
Reeves, Linda, Ref Librn, Northwest Vista College, Redbud Learning Ctr, 3535 N Ellison Dr, San Antonio, TX, 78251. Tel: 210-486-4569. p. 2237
Reeves, Lynn, Dep Law Librn, Third Judicial Circuit Court, Wayne County, Office of the General Counsel, Coleman A Young Municipal Ctr, Two Woodward Ave, Ste 780, Detroit, MI, 48226-3461. Tel: 313-224-5265. p. 1099
Reeves, Rochelle, Curric Librn, University of Nebraska at Kearney, 2508 11th Ave, Kearney, NE, 68849-2240. Tel: 308-865-8276. p. 1319
Reeves, Tolley, Asst Dir, Rochester Public Library, 115 South Ave, Rochester, NY, 14604-1896. Tel: 585-428-8345. p. 1630
Reeves, Tolley, Librn, Houston Community College - Northeast College, Pinemont Campus Library, 1265 Pinemont, Houston, TX, 77018-1303. Tel: 713-718-8443. p. 2194
Reff, Yvonne, Libr Dir, Roswell P Flower Memorial Library, 229 Washington St, Watertown, NY, 13601-3388. Tel: 315-785-7701. p. 1659
Regalado, Mariana, Assoc Librn, Info Serv, Brooklyn College Library, 2900 Bedford Ave, Brooklyn, NY, 11210. Tel: 718-758-8215. p. 1501
Regan, Alison, Assoc Univ Librn, Pub Serv, University of California Irvine Libraries, PO Box 19557, Irvine, CA, 92623-9557. Tel: 949-824-9753. p. 153
Regan, Laurie, Librn, South Shore Hospital, 55 Fogg Rd, South Weymouth, MA, 02190. Tel: 781-340-8000, 781-624-8528. p. 1055
Regan, Leila, City Librn, Sierra Madre Public Library, 440 W Sierra Madre Blvd, Sierra Madre, CA, 91024-2399. Tel: 626-355-7186. p. 246
Regeimbal, Katherine, Br Mgr, Arlington County Department of Libraries, Cherrydale, 2190 N Military Rd, Arlington, VA, 22207. Tel: 703-228-6330. p. 2305
Regenberg, Pat, Libr Mgr, Basic Health Sciences Library Network, Overlook Medical Center, 99 Beauvoir Ave, Summit, NJ, 07902. Tel: 908-522-2886. p. 2769
Regenberg, Patricia, Libr Mgr, Overlook Medical Center, 99 Beauvoir Ave, Summit, NJ, 07901. Tel: 908-522-2119. p. 1445
Regenberg, Patricia, Libr Mgr, New Jersey Health Sciences Library Network, Overlook Hospital Library, 99 Beauvoir Ave, Summit, NJ, 07902. Tel: 908-522-2886. p. 2770
Regensburg, Brooke, Access Serv Tech-ILL, Washtenaw Community College, 4800 E Huron River Dr, Ann Arbor, MI, 48105-4800. Tel: 734-973-3429. p. 1081
Regester, Charlotte, Dir, Red Waller Community Library, 109 Melton St, Malakoff, TX, 75148. Tel: 903-489-1818. p. 2215
Regier, Elaine, Librn, Federal Aviation Administration, Mike Monroney Aeronautical Center Library, Academy Bldg 14, Rm 114, 6500 S MacArthur Blvd, Oklahoma City, OK, 73169. Tel: 405-954-2665. p. 1856
Regier, Jenny, Dir, Cherokee-City-County Public Library, 123 S Grand Ave, Cherokee, OK, 73728. Tel: 580-596-2366. p. 1843
Regina, Bernadette, Ch Serv, North Shore Public Library, 250 Rte 25A, Shoreham, NY, 11786-9677. Tel: 631-929-4488. p. 1641
Regina, Kristen, Dir, Libr & Archive Serv, Philadelphia Museum of Art Library, Ruth & Raymond G Perelman Bldg, 2525 Pennsylvania Ave, Philadelphia, PA, 19130. Tel: 215-684-7650. p. 1984
Regis, Paul, IT Mgr, Downers Grove Public Library, 1050 Curtiss St, Downers Grove, IL, 60515. Tel: 630-960-1200, Ext 4291. p. 579
Register, Renee, Libr Dir, Tech Serv, Tennessee State Library & Archives, 403 Seventh Ave N, Nashville, TN, 37243-0312. Tel: 615-741-2764. p. 2121
Regler, Lori, Dir, Human Res, San Francisco Public Library, 100 Larkin St, San Francisco, CA, 94102. Tel: 415-557-4585. p. 227
Regula, Kristen, Cat, William Paterson University, 300 Pompton Rd, Wayne, NJ, 07470. Tel: 973-720-2295. p. 1452
Reha, Jodie, Cat Librn, Chesapeake Public Library, 298 Cedar Rd, Chesapeake, VA, 23322-5512. Tel: 757-926-5740. p. 2311
Rehborg, Sarah, Ch Serv, Peter White Public Library, 217 N Front St, Marquette, MI, 49855. Tel: 906-226-4319. p. 1130
Rehder, Jim, Dir, Idaho State Correctional Institution Library, Idaho Correctional Institution-Orofino Library, 23 Hospital Dr N, Orofino, ID, 83544. Tel: 208-476-3655. p. 517
Rehkopf, Sue, Archivist, Registrar, The Episcopal Diocese of Missouri Archives, 1210 Locust St, Saint Louis, MO, 63103-2322. Tel: 314-231-1220, Ext 1375. p. 1270
Rehm, Sadie, Coordr, Youth Serv, Lake County Public Library, 1115 Harrison Ave, Leadville, CO, 80461-3398. Tel: 719-486-0569. p. 289
Rehmeyer, Barb, Libr Dir, Liberty Library, 59 Main St, Liberty, ME, 04949. Tel: 207-589-3161. p. 929
Reibach, Lois, Access Serv Librn, Resource Description Mgr, The Athenaeum of Philadelphia, East Washington Sq, 219 S Sixth St, Philadelphia, PA, 19106-3794. Tel: 215-925-2688. p. 1975
Reich, Barbara S, Dir, Hackensack University Medical Center, 30 Prospect Ave, Hackensack, NJ, 07601. Tel: 551-996-2326. p. 1406
Reich, Steve, Managing Librn, Austin Public Library, Pleasant Hill, 211 E William Cannon Dr, Austin, TX, 78745. Tel: 512-974-3940. p. 2139
Reichardt, Beth, Head, Ref, Lake County Library System, Cooper Memorial Library, 2525 Oakley Seaver Dr, Clermont, FL, 34711. Tel: 352-536-2275. p. 451
Reichardt, Kayla, Acq, Libr Asst, Giles County Public Library, 122 S Second St, Pulaski, TN, 38478-3285. Tel: 931-363-2720. p. 2124
Reichert, Allen, Electronic Access Librn, Otterbein University, 138 W Main St, Westerville, OH, 43081. Tel: 614-823-1164. p. 1830
Reichert, Andrea, Curator, Manitoba Crafts Museum & Library, 1-329 Cumberland Ave, Winnipeg, MB, R3B 1T2, CANADA. Tel: 204-615-3951. p. 2593
Reichert, Marisa, Pub Serv Librn, Tri-County Technical College Library, 7900 Hwy 76, Pendleton, SC, 29670. Tel: 864-646-1750. p. 2067
Reichert, Tom, PhD, Dean, University of South Carolina, 1501 Greene St, Columbia, SC, 29208. Tel: 803-777-4105. p. 2792
Reichert-Simpson, Jennifer, Dep Dir, Dakota County Library System, 1340 Wescott Rd, Eagan, MN, 55123-1099. Tel: 651-450-2900. p. 1173
Reichl, Patricia, Libr Dir, Mifflin Community Library, Six Philadelphia Ave, Shillington, PA, 19607. Tel: 610-777-3911. p. 2006
Reichler, Deborah, Mgr, Med Librn, Department of Veterans Affairs, 3200 Vine St, Cincinnati, OH, 45220-2213. Tel: 513-861-3100, Ext 204342. p. 1760
Reichling, Sue, Supvr, Missouri State University, Music Library, Ellis Hall, Rm 209, 901 S National, Springfield, MO, 65804-0095. Tel: 417-836-5105. p. 1281
Reichmann, Doug, Media Tech, Syst Tech, Southwestern Oklahoma State University, 100 Campus Dr, Weatherford, OK, 73096-3002. Tel: 580-774-7069. p. 1868
Reichwein, Chuck, Libr Dir, Hebron Secrest Library, 146 N Fourth St, Hebron, NE, 68370. Tel: 402-768-6701. p. 1318
Reicks, Elaine, Libr Asst, West Union Community Library, 210 N Vine St, West Union, IA, 52175. Tel: 563-422-3103. p. 791
Reid, Adele, Actg Chief Exec Officer, King Township Public Library, 1970 King Rd, King City, ON, L7B 1A6, CANADA. Tel: 905-833-5101. p. 2649
Reid, Annie, Univ Archivist, University of San Francisco, 2130 Fulton St, San Francisco, CA, 94117-1080. Tel: 415-422-5352. p. 229
Reid, Benjamin, Mgr, Columbus Metropolitan Library, New Albany Branch, 200 Market St, New Albany, OH, 43054. p. 1773
Reid, Courtney, Asst Dir, Ch, El Paso Public Library, 149 W First St, El Paso, IL, 61738. Tel: 309-527-4360. p. 583
Reid, Danielle, Dir, Reese Unity District Library, 2065 Gates St, Reese, MI, 48757. Tel: 989-868-4120. p. 1144
Reid, Diana, Librn, Vermontville Township Library, 120 E First St, Vermontville, MI, 49096. Tel: 517-726-1362. p. 1156
Reid, Jeff, Coll Develop Librn, Dayton Metro Library, 215 E Third St, Dayton, OH, 45402. Tel: 937-463-2665. p. 1779
Reid, Julie, Br Mgr, Morgan County Public Library, Waverly Branch, 9410 State Rd 144, Martinsville, IN, 46151. Tel: 317-422-9915. p. 705
Reid, Julie, Archivist, La Societe Historique de Saint-Boniface Bibliotheque, Centre du patrimoine, 340 Provencher Blvd, Saint Boniface, MB, R2H 0G7, CANADA. Tel: 204-233-4888. p. 2589
Reid, Kevin, Ref Librn, Henderson Community College, 2660 S Green St, Henderson, KY, 42420. Tel: 270-831-9766. p. 859
Reid, Lynda, Mgr, Coll & Fac Serv, Collingwood Public Library, 55 Ste. Marie St, Collingwood, ON, L9Y 0W6, CANADA. Tel: 705-445-1571, Ext 6223. p. 2637
Reid, Marg, Asst Head Librn, Carstairs Public Library, 1402 Scarlett Ranch Blvd, Carstairs, AB, T0M 0N0, CANADA. Tel: 403-337-3943. p. 2530
Reid, Melissa, Br Mgr, Western Sullivan Public Library, Delaware Free Branch, 45 Lower Main St, Callicoon, NY, 12723. Tel: 845-887-4040. p. 1558
Reid, Ruth, Br Mgr, Massanutten Regional Library, Shenandoah Community, 418 S Third St, Shenandoah, VA, 22849. Tel: 540-434-4475, Ext 6, 540-652-2665. p. 2325
Reid, Samantha, Librn, Runnells Community Library, 6575 SE 116th St, Runnells, IA, 50237-1193. Tel: 515-957-5662. p. 780
Reid, Sarah, Outreach Coordr, Youth Serv Coordr, Four County Library System, 304 Clubhouse Rd, Vestal, NY, 13850-3713. Tel: 607-723-8236, Ext 350. p. 1657
Reid, Sarah, Libr Assoc, Langston University, 701 Sammy Davis Jr Dr, Langston, OK, 73050. Tel: 405-466-3292. p. 1851
Reid, Shannon, Dir, Lillie Russell Memorial Library, 200 E Hubbard St, Lindale, TX, 75771-3397. Tel: 903-882-1900. p. 2212
Reid, Sharon, Circ Mgr, Fairfield Public Library, Fairfield Woods, 1147 Fairfield Woods Rd, Fairfield, CT, 06825. Tel: 203-255-7310. p. 312
Reid, Shawn, Ms, Library Contact, Virginia Aquarium & Marine Science Center, 717 General Booth Blvd, Virginia Beach, VA, 23451. Tel: 757-385-3474. p. 2350
Reid, Stacey, Mgr, Greensboro Public Library, 219 N Church St, Greensboro, NC, 27402. Tel: 336-373-2471. p. 1692

Reid, Sue, Asst Dir, Columbus Junction Public Library, 232 Second St, Columbus Junction, IA, 52738-1028. Tel: 319-728-7972. p. 741

Reid, Susan, Circ Supvr, Vols Coordr, Cedar Mill Community Library, Bethany Branch, 15325 NW Central Dr, Ste J-8, Portland, OR, 97229-0986. Tel: 503-617-7323, Ext 203. p. 1891

Reid, Teresa, Exec Dir, Northport Historical Society, 215 Main St, Northport, NY, 11768. Tel: 631-757-9859. p. 1608

Reid, Tina, Br Mgr, Loudoun County Public Library, Middleburg Branch, 101 Reed St, Middleburg, VA, 20117. Tel: 540-687-5730. p. 2328

Reid, Trish, Dir, Cambridge Hospital-Cambridge Health Alliance, 1493 Cambridge St, Cambridge, MA, 02139. Tel: 617-665-1439. p. 1004

Reid-Goldberg, Samantha, Dir, Hesperia Community Library, 80 S Division St, Hesperia, MI, 49421-9004. Tel: 231-854-5125. p. 1114

Reid-Wheat, Shannon, Libr Dir, Council Grove Public Library, 829 W Main St, Council Grove, KS, 66846. Tel: 620-767-5716. p. 803

Reidhead, Doris, Dir, Clay Springs Public Library, 2106 Granite Rd, Clay Springs, AZ, 85923. Tel: 928-535-7142. p. 58

Reidler, Danette, ILL, Pottsville Free Public Library, 215 W Market St, Pottsville, PA, 17901. Tel: 570-622-8105, 570-622-8880. p. 1999

Reidy, Brent, Andrew W Mellon Dir of the New York Pub Libr, The New York Public Library - Astor, Lenox & Tilden Foundations, 476 Fifth Ave, (@ 42nd St), New York, NY, 10018. Tel: 212-930-0710. p. 1594

Reidy, Karen, Asst Librn, Sacred Heart Academy, c/o Sacred Heart Academy, 265 Benham St, Hamden, CT, 06514. Tel: 203-288-2309. p. 316

Reif, Eric, Music Librn, Hampton University, Music, Armstrong Hall, Dewitt Wing, 129 William R Harvey Way, Hampton, VA, 23668. Tel: 757-727-5411. p. 2323

Reifenrath, LaVaille, Library Contact, Emerson Public Library, 205 W Third St, Emerson, NE, 68733. Tel: 402-695-2449. p. 1313

Reigle, Alexandra, Ref Librn, Smithsonian Libraries, Smithsonian American Art Museum/National Portrait Gallery Library, Victor Bldg, Rm 2100, 750 Ninth St NW, Washington, DC, 20560. Tel: 202-633-8235. p. 376

Reihman, Gregory, Vice Provost for Libr & Tech Serv, Lehigh University, Eight A E Packer Ave, Bethlehem, PA, 18015. Tel: 610-758-6840. p. 1912

Reiling, Lexie, Asst Dir, Davenport Public Library, 321 Main St, Davenport, IA, 52801-1490. Tel: 563-326-7832. p. 743

Reilly, Anne, Tech Serv Mgr, Worthington Libraries, 820 High St, Worthington, OH, 43085. Tel: 614-807-2631. p. 1834

Reilly, Brandon, Br Mgr, East Baton Rouge Parish Library, Greenwell Springs Road Regional, 11300 Greenwell Springs Rd, Baton Rouge, LA, 70814. Tel: 225-274-4480. p. 883

Reilly, Candace, Mgr, Spec Coll, Drew University Library, 36 Madison Ave, Madison, NJ, 07940. Tel: 973-408-3590. p. 1414

Reilly, Candace, Mgr, Spec Coll, United Methodist Church, 36 Madison Ave, Madison, NJ, 07940. Tel: 973-408-3590. p. 1415

Reilly, Heather, Children's Prog Mgr, Pomfret Public Library, 449 Pomfret St, Pomfret, CT, 06258. Tel: 860-928-3475. p. 334

Reilly, Jamie, Br Mgr, Harford County Public Library, Havre de Grace Branch, 120 N Union Ave, Havre de Grace, MD, 21078-3000. Tel: 410-939-6700. p. 959

Reilly, Joseph, Interim Dir, Libr Serv, Tunxis Community College Library, 271 Scott Swamp Rd, Farmington, CT, 06032. Tel: 860-773-1371. p. 312

Reilly, Karen, Br Mgr, San Diego Public Library, Mission Valley, 2123 Fenton Pkwy, San Diego, CA, 92108. Tel: 858-573-5007. p. 220

Reilly, Karen, Assoc Dir, College of the Holy Cross, One College St, Worcester, MA, 01610. Tel: 508-793-2520. p. 1072

Reilly, Katie, Library Contact, Sheboygan County Historical Research Center Library, 518 Water St, Sheboygan Falls, WI, 53085. Tel: 920-467-4667. p. 2477

Reilly, Leila, Br Mgr, East Baton Rouge Parish Library, Jones Creek Regional, 6222 Jones Creek Rd, Baton Rouge, LA, 70817. Tel: 225-756-1180. p. 883

Reilly, Patrick, Mgr, Dallas Public Library, Pleasant Grove, 7310 Lake June Rd, Dallas, TX, 75217. Tel: 214-670-0965. p. 2166

Reilly, Richard, Dep Dir, Martin County Library System, 2351 SE Monterey Rd, Stuart, FL, 34996. Tel: 772-219-4964. p. 444

Reilly, Susan, Dir, Moundsville-Marshall County Public Library, 700 Fifth St, Moundsville, WV, 26041. Tel: 304-845-6911. p. 2410

Reilly, Susan, Dir, Moundsville-Marshall County Public Library, Benwood-McMechen Public, 201 Marshall St, McMechen, WV, 26040. Tel: 304-232-9720. p. 2410

Reily, Gaye, Dir, Rhoads Memorial Library, 103 SW Second St, Dimmitt, TX, 79027. Tel: 806-647-3532. p. 2171

Reiman, Karel, Librn, Haakon County Public Library, Midland Community Library, 401 Russel Ave, Midland, SD, 57552. Tel: 605-843-2158. p. 2080

Reiman, Lorraine, Libr Dir, McLeod Health, 144 N Ravenel St, Florence, SC, 29506. Tel: 843-777-2275. p. 2059

Reimer, Lucille, Dir, Limon Memorial Library, 205 E Ave, Limon, CO, 80828. Tel: 719-775-2163. p. 289

Reimer, Torsten L, Dean & Univ Librn, The University of Chicago Library, 1100 E 57th St, Chicago, IL, 60637-1502. Tel: 773-702-8740. p. 569

Reimers, Dawn, Asst Librn, Gardner Public Library, 114 W Third St, Wakefield, NE, 68784. Tel: 402-287-2334. p. 1339

Reimert, JoLynne, Dir, Hamann Memorial Library, 311 E Main, Anthon, IA, 51004. Tel: 712-373-5275. p. 732

Rein, Allison, Asst Dir, American Institute of Physics, One Physics Ellipse, College Park, MD, 20740. Tel: 301-209-3177. p. 962

Rein, Danielle, Dir, Greenwood Public Library, 619 Main St, Greenwood, NE, 68366. Tel: 402-789-2301. p. 1316

Rein, Diane, Dr, Assoc Librn, University at Buffalo Libraries-State University of New York, Health Sciences Library, Abbott Hall, 3435 Main St, Bldg 28, Buffalo, NY, 14214-3002. Tel: 716-829-5749. p. 1510

Rein, Jack, Exec Dir, Oscar Getz Museum of Bourbon History Library, Spalding Hall, 114 N Fifth St, Bardstown, KY, 40004. Tel: 502-348-2999. p. 848

Reinbold, Marissa, Prog Dir, Kansas Department of Corrections, 1430 NW 25th St, Topeka, KS, 66618-1499. Tel: 785-354-9800. p. 838

Reinboldt, Valerie, Librn, Chinook Regional Library, Fox Valley Branch, 85 Centre St E, Fox Valley, SK, S0N 0V0, CANADA. Tel: 306-666-2045. p. 2752

Reinecke, Ann, Director of Library & Academic Support, Chesapeake College, 1000 College Circle, Wye Mills, MD, 21679. Tel: 410-827-5860. p. 981

Reineke, Beth, Asst Dir, Estherville Public Library, 613 Central Ave, Estherville, IA, 51334-2294. Tel: 712-362-7731. p. 751

Reiner, Casie, Head, Cat, Tech Serv Librn, Traverse Des Sioux Library Cooperative, 1400 Madison Ave, Ste 622, Mankato, MN, 56001-5488. Tel: 833-837-5422. p. 1181

Reiner, MaryAnn, Head, Circ, Monroe Township Public Library, Four Municipal Plaza, Monroe Township, NJ, 08831-1900. Tel: 732-521-5000, Ext 101. p. 1419

Reinert, Ann, Asst Librn, Smith Center Public Library, 117 W Court St, Smith Center, KS, 66967. Tel: 785-282-3361. p. 836

Reinert, Claire, Res & Instruction Librn, McKendree University, 701 College Rd, Lebanon, IL, 62254-1299. Tel: 618-537-6950. p. 607

Reinhardt, Ann, Archivist, American Philosophical Society Library, 105 S Fifth St, Philadelphia, PA, 19106-3386. Tel: 215-440-3400. p. 1974

Reinhardt, Matthew, ILL, University of Wisconsin Oshkosh, 801 Elmwood Ave, Oshkosh, WI, 54901. Tel: 920-424-3348. p. 2467

Reinhardt, Michelle, Librn, South New Berlin Free Library, 3320 State Hwy 8, South New Berlin, NY, 13843. Tel: 607-859-2420. p. 1642

Reinhardt, Stephanie, Br Head, Public Libraries of Saginaw, Butman-Fish, 1716 Hancock St, Saginaw, MI, 48602. Tel: 989-799-9160. p. 1147

Reinhart, Ermal, Access Serv Mgr, Carson City Library, 900 N Roop St, Carson City, NV, 89701. Tel: 775-283-7595. p. 1343

Reinhart, Julia, Chief Librn/CEO, Gravenhurst Public Library, 180 Sharpe St W, Gravenhurst, ON, P1P 1J1, CANADA. Tel: 705-687-3382. p. 2643

Reinhart, Lore, Dir, Randolph Township Free Public Library, 28 Calais Rd, Randolph, NJ, 07869. Tel: 973-895-3556. p. 1438

Reinhart, Sean, Libr Serv Dir, Menlo Park Public Library, 800 Alma St, Alma & Ravenswood, Menlo Park, CA, 94025-3455. Tel: 650-330-2500. p. 175

Reinhart, Sean, Libr Serv Dir, Menlo Park Public Library, Belle Haven, 413 Ivy Dr, Menlo Park, CA, 94025. Tel: 650-330-2540. p. 175

Reinhart, Tricia, Dir, Info Serv, Regis College Library, 235 Wellesley St, Weston, MA, 02493. Tel: 781-768-7378. p. 1068

Reinke, Fern, Libr Mgr, Bawlf Public Library, 203 Hanson St, Box 116, Bawlf, AB, T0B 0J0, CANADA. Tel: 780-373-3882. p. 2523

Reinke, Kristin, Managing Librn, Washoe County Library System, Northwest Reno Library, 2325 Robb Dr, Reno, NV, 89523. Tel: 775-787-4100. p. 1350

Reinke, Kristin, Managing Librn, Washoe County Library System, Verdi Community Library, 270 Bridge St, Verdi, NV, 89439. Tel: 775-345-8104. p. 1351

Reinl, Cynthia, Librn, Bellin College, 3201 Eaton Rd, Green Bay, WI, 54311. Tel: 920-433-6660. p. 2438

Reinman, Suzanne, Head Librn, Oklahoma State University Libraries, Government Documents Department, Edmon Low Library, 5th Flr, Stillwater, OK, 74078. Tel: 405-744-9788. p. 1862

Reinmann, Kris, Libr Tech, Department of Veterans Affairs, Lyons Campus Patient's Library, 151 Knollcroft Rd, Lyons, NJ, 07939. Tel: 908-647-0180, Ext 6421, 973-676-1000. p. 1414

Reinoehl, Ayla, Asst Dir, Northern Cambria Public Library, 4200 Crawford Ave, Northern Cambria, PA, 15714-1399. Tel: 814-948-8222. p. 1972

Reinold, Healther, Archivist, Arkansas State Archives, One Capitol Mall, Ste 215, Little Rock, AR, 72201. Tel: 501-682-6900. p. 100

Reinsfelder, Tom, Head Librn, Pennsylvania State University, 320 Campus Dr, Mont Alto, PA, 17237. Tel: 717-749-6040. p. 1965

Reinwald, Donovan, Librn, Middlesex Community College, 100 Training Hill Rd, Middletown, CT, 06457. Tel: 860-343-5835. p. 322

Reisdorf, JoLyn, Br Mgr, Tacoma Public Library, Swasey Branch, 7001 Sixth Ave, Tacoma, WA, 98406. Tel: 253-280-2970. p. 2387

Reiser, Bill, Libr Mgr, Monroe County Library System, Ellis Library & Reference Center, 3700 S Custer Rd, Monroe, MI, 48161-9716. Tel: 734-241-5277. p. 1133

Reish, Gregory, Dr, Dir, Middle Tennessee State University, Center for Popular Music, John Bragg Media & Entertainment Bldg, Rm 140, 1301 E Main St, Murfreesboro, TN, 37132. Tel: 615-898-2449. p. 2117

Reisig, Allison, Librn, Libr Tech II, Western Nebraska Community College Library, 1601 E 27th NE, Scottsbluff, NE, 69361-1899. Tel: 308-635-6040. p. 1335
Reisig, Allison, Librn, Western Nebraska Community College Library, Sidney Learning Resource Center, Sidney Campus, 371 College Dr, Sidney, NE, 69162. Tel: 308-254-7452. p. 1335
Reiskind, Alix, Digital Initiatives Librn, Harvard Library, Frances Loeb Library, Harvard Graduate School of Design, 48 Quincy St, Gund Hall, Cambridge, MA, 02138. Tel: 617-495-9163. p. 1007
Reisler, Reina, Dir, Community Medical Center, 99 Hwy 37 W, Toms River, NJ, 08755. Tel: 732-557-8117. p. 1446
Reisman, Victoria, Curator, National Museum of Racing & Hall of Fame, 191 Union Ave, 2nd Flr, Saratoga Springs, NY, 12866. Tel: 518-584-0400, Ext 113. p. 1636
Reiss, Laurel M, Dir, Erie Public Library District, 802 Eighth Ave, Erie, IL, 61250. Tel: 309-659-2707. p. 585
Reissaus, Lexie, Librn, Indiana Hand to Shoulder Center Library, 8501 Harcourt Rd, Indianapolis, IN, 46260-2046. Tel: 317-471-4340. p. 692
Reist, Marie, Acq Librn, Circ, Pryor Public Library, 505 E Graham, Pryor, OK, 74361. Tel: 918-825-0777. p. 1861
Reiste, Carolyn, Dir, Adamstown Area Library, 110 W Main St, Adamstown, PA, 19501. Tel: 717-484-4200. p. 1903
Reister, Brenda, Researcher, Carver County Historical Society Library, 555 W First St, Waconia, MN, 55387. Tel: 952-442-4234. p. 1206
Reitan, Beth, Dir, Bottineau County Public Library, 314 W Fifth St, Bottineau, ND, 58318-9600. Tel: 701-228-2967. p. 1730
Reiten, Julie, Dir, United States Air Force, 156 Missile Ave, Ste 1, Minot AFB, ND, 58705-5026. Tel: 701-723-3344, 701-723-4418. p. 1738
Reiter, Lauren, Bus Liaison Librn, Pennsylvania State University Libraries, William & Joan Schreyer Business Library, 309 Paterno Library, 3rd Flr, University Park, PA, 16802-1810. Tel: 814-865-4414. p. 2016
Reiter, Nancy, Br Mgr, Riverside County Library System, Home Gardens Library, 3785 Neece St, Corona, CA, 92879. Tel: 951-279-2148. p. 202
Reiter, Sue, Coll Mgt, ILL, University of Dubuque Library, 2000 University Ave, Dubuque, IA, 52001. Tel: 563-589-3100. p. 749
Reiterman, Sue, Br Mgr, Burlingame Public Library, Easton Drive Branch, 1800 Easton Dr, Burlingame, CA, 94010. Tel: 650-340-6180. p. 126
Reith, David, Ref Librn, Kelley Drye & Warren LLP, 101 Park Ave, New York, NY, 10178. Tel: 212-808-7800. p. 1590
Reitmire, Georgia, Ms, Managing Librn, Yakima Valley Libraries, 102 N Third St, Yakima, WA, 98901. Tel: 509-452-8541. p. 2395
Reitsma, Denise, Youth Serv Mgr, Howe Library, 13 South St, Hanover, NH, 03755. Tel: 603-640-3254. p. 1367
Reitz, Dawn, Circ Serv, Pueblo Community College Library, 900 W Orman Ave, Pueblo, CO, 81004-1430. Tel: 719-549-3113. p. 293
Reitz, Joan, Instruction Librn, Western Connecticut State University, 181 White St, Danbury, CT, 06810. Tel: 203-837-8308. p. 307
Rekowski, Michelle, Librn, Wisconsin Lutheran College Library, 8800 W Bluemound Rd, Milwaukee, WI, 53226. Tel: 414-443-8864. p. 2461
Rekowski, Richard G, Dir, Mary H Weir Public Library, 3442 Main St, Weirton, WV, 26062. Tel: 304-797-8510. p. 2416
Rekuc, Robert, Libr Operations Mgr, Rancho Mirage Library & Observatory, 71-100 Hwy 111, Rancho Mirage, CA, 92270. Tel: 760-341-7323. p. 198
Relyveld-Osnato, Charisse, Bus Mgr, Nassau Library System, 900 Jerusalem Ave, Uniondale, NY, 11553-3039. Tel: 516-292-8920. p. 1654
Remak-Honnef, Elizabeth, Distinguished Librn, Librn Emeritus, University of California, 1156 High St, Santa Cruz, CA, 95064. Tel: 831-239-3567. p. 243
Remaklus, David, Dir, Operations, University of Toledo, 2975 W Centennial Dr, Toledo, OH, 43606-3396. Tel: 419-530-4030. p. 1825
Remavich, Patricia, Tech Serv, Cumberland Public Library, 1464 Diamond Hill Rd, Cumberland, RI, 02864-5510. Tel: 401-333-2552, Ext 131. p. 2031
Remer, Patrick, Commun Libr Mgr, Contra Costa County Library, Pleasant Hill Library, 1750 Oak Park Blvd, Pleasant Hill, CA, 94523. Tel: 925-646-6434. p. 174
Remhof, Tamara, Coordr, Libr Serv, Germanna Community College, Science & Engineering Bldg, 10000 Germanna Point Dr, Fredericksburg, VA, 22408-9543. Tel: 540-891-3013. p. 2320
Remhof, Tamara, Libr Serv Coordr, Germanna Community College, Locust Grove Campus Library, 2130 Germanna Hwy, Locust Grove, VA, 22508-2102. Tel: 540-423-9163. p. 2320
Remillard, Kerry Ann, Head, Tech Serv, Amesbury Public Library, 149 Main St, Amesbury, MA, 01913. Tel: 978-388-8148. p. 984
Remillard, Lyne, Libr Asst Supvr, Bibliotheque Louis-Ange-Santerre, 500, ave Jolliet, Sept Iles, QC, G4R 2B4, CANADA. Tel: 418-964-3355. p. 2736
Remillard, Stephanie, Dir, Campbellsport Public Library, 220 N Helena St, Campbellsport, WI, 53010-0405. Tel: 920-533-8534. p. 2427
Remington, Cheri, Br Mgr, Saint Louis County Library, Samuel C Sachs Branch, 16400 Burkhardt Pl, Chesterfield, MO, 63017-4660. Tel: 314-994-3300, Ext 3800. p. 1274
Remington, Diana, Dir, Free Library of Northampton Township, 25 Upper Holland Rd, Richboro, PA, 18954-1514. Tel: 215-357-3050. p. 2001
Remington, Kerry J, Dir, Rutland Free Public Library, 280 Main St, Rutland, MA, 01543. Tel: 508-886-4108, Option 5. p. 1050
Remington, Lori, Div Dir, Human Res, Harris County Public Library, 5749 S Loop E, Houston, TX, 77033. Tel: 713-274-6600. p. 2192
Rempel, Clark, Br Head, Winnipeg Public Library, Windsor Park, 1195 Archibald St, Winnipeg, MB, R2J 0Y9, CANADA. Tel: 204-619-4152. p. 2597
Rempel, Heidi, Circ, East Orange Public Library, 21 S Arlington Ave, East Orange, NJ, 07018. Tel: 973-266-5600. p. 1400
Remple, Bonny, Ch, Burns Lake Public Library, 585 Government St, Burns Lake, BC, V0J 1E0, CANADA. Tel: 250-692-3192. p. 2564
Remsen, Ben, Br Mgr, Free Library of Philadelphia, Kingsessing Branch, 1201 S 51st, Philadelphia, PA, 19143-4353. Tel: 215-685-2690. p. 1979
Remson, Regina, ILL, Benedictine University Library, 5700 College Rd, Lisle, IL, 60532-0900. Tel: 630-829-6061. p. 610
Remus, Ed, Soc Sci Librn, Northeastern Illinois University, 5500 N Saint Louis Ave, Chicago, IL, 60625-4699. Tel: 773-442-4400. p. 566
Remy, Alex, Head, Children's Servx, Windsor Public Library, 323 Broad St, Windsor, CT, 06095. Tel: 860-285-1917. p. 348
Remy, Alexandra, Ch Serv Librn, Windsor Public Library, Wilson, 365 Windsor Ave, Windsor, CT, 06095-4550. Tel: 860-247-8960. p. 348
Remy, Charles, Electronic Res, University of Tennessee at Chattanooga Library, 400 Douglas Ave, Dept 6456, Chattanooga, TN, 37403-2598. Tel: 423-425-4501. p. 2092
Ren, Xiaoai, Dr, Assoc Prof, Valdosta State University, Odum Library, 1500 N Patterson St, Valdosta, GA, 31698. Tel: 229-249-2726. p. 2784
Renaud, John, Assoc University Librn, Resources, Res, University of California Irvine Libraries, PO Box 19557, Irvine, CA, 92623-9557. Tel: 949-824-5216. p. 153
Renaud, Matthew, Liaison Librn, University of Manitoba Libraries, E K Williams Law Library, 401 Robson Hall, 224 Dysart Rd, Winnipeg, MB, R3T 2N2, CANADA. Tel: 204-474-6371. p. 2596
Rencher, Natalie, Dir, Kings County Library, 401 N Douty St, Hanford, CA, 93230. Tel: 559-582-0261. p. 150
Renda, Sarah, Law Librn, Wood County Law Library, One Courthouse Sq, Bowling Green, OH, 43402. Tel: 419-353-3921. p. 1752
Render, Felicia, Ms Curator, Amistad Research Center, Tulane University, Tilton Hall, 6823 St Charles Ave, New Orleans, LA, 70118. Tel: 504-314-2137. p. 900
Rendle, Hugh, Dir, Tyndale University College & Seminary, 3377 Bayview Ave, Toronto, ON, M2M 3S4, CANADA. Tel: 416-226-6620, Ext 6716. p. 2697
Rendler, Cheri, Mgr, Mat Serv, Meridian Library District, 1326 W Cherry Lane, Meridian, ID, 83642. Tel: 208-888-4451. p. 525
Rene, France, Exec Dir, Centre Regional de Services aux Bibliotheques Publiques, 3125 rue Girard, Trois-Rivieres, QC, G8Z 2M4, CANADA. Tel: 819-375-9623. p. 2738
Renear, Allen, Prof, University of Illinois at Urbana-Champaign, Library & Information Science Bldg, 501 E Daniel St, Champaign, IL, 61820-6211. Tel: 217-333-3280. p. 2784
Renehan, Kelly, Res Mgr, Three Crowns LLP, 3000 K St NW, Ste 101, Washington, DC, 20007. Tel: 202-540-9460. p. 377
Renell, Allyson, Mgr, Ch Serv, Downers Grove Public Library, 1050 Curtiss St, Downers Grove, IL, 60515. Tel: 630-960-1200, Ext 4260. p. 579
Renevier, Amanda, Chair, University of Saint Thomas, Cardinal Beran Library at Saint Mary's Seminary, 9845 Memorial Dr, Houston, TX, 77024-3498. Tel: 713-654-5771. p. 2200
Renfro, Crystal, Graduate Engineering Librn, Kennesaw State University Library System, 385 Cobb Ave NW, MD 1701, Kennesaw, GA, 30144. Tel: 470-578-4530. p. 483
Renfro, Pam, Librn, Cimarron City Library, Ensign Branch, 108 Aubrey, Ensign, KS, 67841. Tel: 620-865-2199. p. 801
Renfro, Susan, Develop Officer, Fresno County Public Library, 2420 Mariposa St, Fresno, CA, 93721. Tel: 559-600-7323. p. 145
Renfro, Terrie, Head, Circ, Head, Per, Duncan Public Library, 2211 N Hwy 81, Duncan, OK, 73533. Tel: 580-255-0636. p. 1845
Renfroe, Tasha, Ms, Admin Coordr, Medical University of South Carolina Libraries, 171 Ashley Ave, Ste 419, Charleston, SC, 29425-0001. Tel: 843-792-9211. p. 2051
Renfrow, Debbie, Pub Serv Librn, Riverside Community College District, 16130 Lasselle St, Moreno Valley, CA, 92551. Tel: 951-571-6356. p. 181
Renga, Alan, Archivist, San Diego Air & Space Museum, Inc, 2001 Pan American Plaza, Balboa Park, San Diego, CA, 92101-1636. Tel: 619-234-8291, Ext 125. p. 216
Renick, Debbie, Circ, Fairmont State University, 1201 Locust Ave, Fairmont, WV, 26554. Tel: 304-367-4733. p. 2402
Renick, Martha, Dir, Multnomah Law Library, County Courthouse, 4th Flr, 1021 SW Fourth Ave, Portland, OR, 97204. Tel: 503-988-3394. p. 1893
Renick, Martha, Librn, Marion County Law Library, Marion County Courthouse, 100 High St NE, Basement B181, Salem, OR, 97301. Tel: 503-588-5090. p. 1896
Renick, Mary, Librn, Polk County Library, 410 Eighth St, Mena, AR, 71953. Tel: 479-394-2314. p. 104

Renkema, Megan, Mgr, Info Serv, Caledon Public Library, 150 Queen St S, Bolton, ON, L7E 1E3, CANADA. Tel: 905-857-1400, Ext 232. p. 2631
Renken, Kathy, Instruction Librn, Weatherford College Library, 225 College Park Dr, Weatherford, TX, 76086. Tel: 817-598-6251. p. 2255
Renker, Laura, Asst Dir, Outreach Librn, Crete Public Library, 1515 Forest Ave, Crete, NE, 68333. Tel: 402-826-3809. p. 1311
Renkosiak, Chris, Dep Dir, Lincolnwood Public Library District, 4000 W Pratt Ave, Lincolnwood, IL, 60712. Tel: 847-677-5277. p. 609
Rennaker, Stacie, Libr Dir, Darby Community Public Library, 101 1/2 Marshall St, Darby, MT, 59829. Tel: 406-821-4771. p. 1291
Renne, Stephanie, Head, Ref Serv, Free Library of Springfield Township, 8900 Hawthorne Lane, Wyndmoor, PA, 19038. Tel: 215-836-5300. p. 2024
Renner, Kathy, Coordr, Ser & Electronic Res, Westminster College, Reeves Memorial Library, 501 Westminster Ave, Fulton, MO, 65251-1299. Tel: 573-592-5248. p. 1246
Renners, Tim, Libr Dir, Ivy Tech Community College, 590 Ivy Tech Dr, Madison, IN, 47250. Tel: 812-265-2580, Ext 4106. p. 704
Rennick, Brian, Assoc Univ Librn, Interim Univ Librn, Brigham Young University, Harold B Lee Library, 2060 HBLL, Provo, UT, 84602. Tel: 801-422-2927. p. 2269
Rennie, Elizabeth, Instruction Librn, Outreach Librn, Thompson Rivers University, 900 McGill Rd, Kamloops, BC, V2C 5N3, CANADA. Tel: 250-828-5000. p. 2568
Rennix, Joanna, Dir, Russell Memorial Public Library, 10038 Seneca Trail, Mill Creek, WV, 26280. Tel: 304-335-6277. p. 2408
Reno, Carolyn, Asst Dir, Colls Mgr, Shiloh Museum of Ozark History Library, 118 W Johnson Ave, Springdale, AR, 72764. Tel: 479-750-8165. p. 110
Reno, Trista, Youth & Teen Serv Mgr, Commerce Township Community Library, 180 E Commerce, Commerce Township, MI, 48382. Tel: 248-669-8101, Ext 106. p. 1093
Reno, Trista, Youth Serv Librn, Commerce Township Community Library, 180 E Commerce, Commerce Township, MI, 48382. Tel: 248-669-8108. p. 1093
Renshaw, Laura, Mgr, Salt Lake County Library Services, Calvin S Smith Branch, 810 E 3300 S, Salt Lake City, UT, 84106. p. 2275
Rensler, Jenny, Research Librn, University of Maryland, Baltimore, Thurgood Marshall Law Library, 501 W Fayette St, Baltimore, MD, 21201-1768. Tel: 410-706-2466. p. 957
Renteria, Roxanne, Commun Librn, Deschutes Public Library District, Sunriver Area Branch, 56855 Venture Lane, Sunriver, OR, 97707. Tel: 541-312-1080. p. 1874
Rentz, Palvi, Lead Systems Admin, Texas State University, 601 University Dr, San Marcos, TX, 78666-4684. Tel: 512-908-4423. p. 2241
Renz, Jes, Asst Dir, Converse County Library, 300 E Walnut St, Douglas, WY, 82633. Tel: 307-358-3644. p. 2494
Renz, Lisa, Ch, Utica Public Library, 303 Genesee St, Utica, NY, 13501. Tel: 315-735-2279. p. 1656
Renzi-Falge, Suzie, Ch, Roswell P Flower Memorial Library, 229 Washington St, Watertown, NY, 13601-3388. Tel: 315-785-7709. p. 1659
Repolesk, Gloria, Head, Children's Servx, Emmet O'Neal Library, 50 Oak St, Mountain Brook, AL, 35213. Tel: 205-879-0459. p. 31
Repp, Ann, Dir, Moravia Public Library, 100 E Chariton, Moravia, IA, 52571. Tel: 641-724-3440. p. 771
Reppe, Liz, State Law Librn, Minnesota State Law Library, Minnesota Judicial Ctr, Rm G25, 25 Rev Dr Martin Luther King Jr Blvd, Saint Paul, MN, 55155. Tel: 651-297-7651. p. 1201
Repplinger, John, Sci Librn, Willamette University, 900 State St, Salem, OR, 97301. Tel: 503-370-6525. p. 1897
Repzynski, Allison, Director of Library & Academic Support, Central Georgia Technical College Library, I Bldg, 2nd Flr, 3300 Macon Tech Dr, Macon, GA, 31206-3628. Tel: 478-757-3547. p. 486
Rerat, Cari, Libr Dir, Pryor Public Library, 505 E Graham, Pryor, OK, 74361. Tel: 918-825-0777. p. 1861
Reseigh, Melanie, Br Mgr, Knox County Public Library System, Carter Branch, 9036 Asheville Hwy, Knoxville, TN, 37924. Tel: 865-933-5438. p. 2105
Reser, Mary, Libr Dir, Gilliam County Public Library, 134 S Main St, Condon, OR, 97823. p. 1875
Reside, Marilyn, Libr Dir, Monroe College, King Hall, 2501 Jerome Ave, Bronx, NY, 10468. Tel: 718-933-6700, Ext 8342. p. 1499
Resner, Samantha, Library Systems Admin, Bellevue University, 1028 Bruin Blvd, Bellevue, NE, 68005. Tel: 402-557-7307. p. 1308
Resnik, Rachel, Chair, Tech Serv Librn, Massachusetts College of Art & Design, 621 Huntington Ave, Boston, MA, 02115-5882. Tel: 617-879-7115. p. 996
Resor-Whicker, Jennifer, Univ Librn, Radford University, 925 E Main St, Radford, VA, 24142. Tel: 540-831-6624. p. 2339
Ressel, Maggie, Access Serv, Outreach Serv, Spec Coll & Basque Libr, University of Nevada-Reno, 1664 N Virginia St, Mailstop 0322, Reno, NV, 89557-0322. Tel: 775-682-5653. p. 1349
Resto Ortiz, Maria de Lourdes, Dir, Inter-American University of Puerto Rico, 100 Calle Francisco Sein, San Juan, PR, 00919. Tel: 787-250-1912, Ext 2160, 787-250-1912, Ext 2514. p. 2513
Retherford, Julie, Access Serv, Team Leader, Chillicothe & Ross County Public Library, 140 S Paint St, Chillicothe, OH, 45601. Tel: 740-702-4145. p. 1758
Rethlefsen, Melissa, Dir, University of New Mexico, Health Sciences Library & Informatics Center, MSC09-5100, One University of New Mexico, Albuquerque, NM, 87131-0001. Tel: 505-272-0635. p. 1463
Rettig, Chris, Br Head, Lake County Public Library, 1919 W 81st Ave, Merrillville, IN, 46410-5488. Tel: 219-769-3541. p. 705
Rettinger, Karin, Archives Mgr, Marshall County Historical Society Library, 123 N Michigan St, Plymouth, IN, 46563. Tel: 574-936-2306. p. 714
Retzlaff, Karen, Librn, Carnegie Regional Library, Aneta Public Library, 309 Main Ave, Aneta, ND, 58212. Tel: 701-326-4107. p. 1734
Reuter, Bradley, Head, Tech Serv, Clarkston Independence District Library, 6495 Clarkston Rd, Clarkston, MI, 48346. Tel: 248-625-2212. p. 1091
Reuter, Kristin, Cat Spec, Hartwick College, One Hartwick Dr, Oneonta, NY, 13820. Tel: 607-431-4478. p. 1611
Reuter, Nicole, Access Serv Mgr, College of Saint Benedict, 37 S College Ave, Saint Joseph, MN, 56374. Tel: 320-363-5159. p. 1199
Reuter, Pat, Curator, Canadian County Historical Museum Library, 300 S Grand Ave, El Reno, OK, 73036. Tel: 405-262-5121. p. 1846
Reutter, Lori, Dir, Leonard A Good Community Library, 208 W Mulberry St, Ogden, IA, 50212. Tel: 515-275-4550. p. 774
Revas, Bob, Librn, US Courts Library - Tenth Circuit Court of Appeals, US Court House, Ste 5.200, 351 S West Temple St, Salt Lake City, UT, 84101. Tel: 801-535-4220. p. 2272
Revels, Mary Beth, Dir, St Joseph Public Library, 927 Felix St, Saint Joseph, MO, 64501-2799. Tel: 816-232-7729. p. 1269
Reverdy, Sophie, Distance Educ, Anne Arundel Community College, 101 College Pkwy, Arnold, MD, 21012-1895. Tel: 410-777-2211. p. 951
Revesz, Richard L, Dir, American Law Institute Library, 4025 Chestnut St, Philadelphia, PA, 19104. Tel: 215-243-1627. p. 1974
Revie, Gretchen, Ref Librn, Lawrence University, 113 S Lawe St, Appleton, WI, 54911-5683. p. 2420
Revilla, Dana, Dep Dir, Arlington Heights Memorial Library, 500 N Dunton Ave, Arlington Heights, IL, 60004-5966. Tel: 847-392-0100. p. 537
Revilla, Dana, Dir, Chicago Public Library, Conrad Sulzer Regional, 4455 N Lincoln Ave, Chicago, IL, 60625. Tel: 312-744-7616. p. 557
Revis, Polly, Tech Serv Mgr, Bryan College Library, 585 Bryan Dr, Dayton, TN, 37321. Tel: 423-775-7307. p. 2096
Revitt, Eva, Interim Dean, MacEwan University Library, 10700 104th Ave, Edmonton, AB, T5J 4S2, CANADA. Tel: 780-497-5850. p. 2537
Rexford, Victoria, Libr Mgr, Timberland Regional Library, North Mason, 23081 NE State Rte 3, Belfair, WA, 98528-9334. Tel: 360-275-3232. p. 2389
Rexhepi, Teuta, Secy Gen, Rehabilitation International, 866 United Nations Plaza, Off 422, New York, NY, 10017. Tel: 212-420-1500. p. 1600
Rey, Jorge R, Dir, University of Florida, 200 Ninth St SE, Vero Beach, FL, 32962. Tel: 772-226-6644. p. 453
Reycraft, Kim, Asst Librn, Florida Gulf Coast University Library, 10501 FGCU Blvd S, Fort Myers, FL, 33965. Tel: 239-590-1339. p. 403
Reyes Ayala, Brenda, PhD, Asst Prof, University of Alberta, 7-104 Education N, University of Alberta, Edmonton, AB, T6G 2G5, CANADA. Tel: 780-492-7625. p. 2795
Reyes, Deyanira, Circ Mgr, Lewis University Library, One University Pkwy, Romeoville, IL, 60446. Tel: 815-836-5307. p. 642
Reyes, Dolores, Br Mgr, Jersey City Free Public Library, Marion, 1017 West Side Ave, Jersey City, NJ, 07306. Tel: 201-547-4552. p. 1409
Reyes, Estella, ILL, Alhambra Civic Center Library, 101 S First St, Alhambra, CA, 91801-3432. Tel: 626-570-5008. p. 115
Reyes, Juan, Media Serv Mgr, Highland Park Public Library, 494 Laurel Ave, Highland Park, IL, 60035-2690. Tel: 847-432-0216. p. 599
Reyes, Lara, Br Mgr, Riverside County Library System, Thousand Palms Library, 31189 Robert Rd, Thousand Palms, CA, 92276. Tel: 760-343-1556. p. 202
Reyes, Michelle C, Librn, Wilmington University Library, 320 N DuPont Hwy, New Castle, DE, 19720. Tel: 302-356-6857. p. 354
Reyes, Misty, Bus & Human Res Mgr, Cherokee Regional Library System, 305 S Duke St, LaFayette, GA, 30728. Tel: 706-638-2992. p. 484
Reyes, Roger, Asst Dir, Bus Operations, Suffolk Cooperative Library System, 627 N Sunrise Service Rd, Bellport, NY, 11713. Tel: 631-286-1600. p. 1492
Reyes-Gavilan, Richard, Exec Dir, District of Columbia Public Library, 1990 K St NW, Washington, DC, 20006. Tel: 202-727-1101. p. 363
Reykdal, Sandra, Head Librn, Evergreen Regional Library, 65 First Ave, Gimli, MB, R0C 1B0, CANADA. Tel: 204-642-7912. p. 2587
Reyna, Kayli, Dir, Person County Public Library, 319 S Main St, Roxboro, NC, 27573. Tel: 336-597-7881. p. 1714
Reyna, Peter, Circulation/Course Reserves Asst, University of California, Riverside, Raymond L Orbach Science Library, 900 University Ave, Riverside, CA, 92521. Tel: 951-827-3701. p. 203
Reynard, Colleen, Br Librn, Southeast Regional Library, Indian Head Branch, 419 Grand Ave, Indian Head, SK, S0G 2K0, CANADA. Tel: 306-695-3922. p. 2753
Reynders, Su, Exec Dir, Mount Prospect Public Library, Ten S Emerson St, Mount Prospect, IL, 60056. Tel: 847-253-5675. p. 621

Reynolds, Arlene, Librn, Henry Henley Public Library, 102 N Main St, Carthage, IN, 46115. Tel: 765-565-8022. p. 674

Reynolds, Carol, Libr Dir, Congregation Beth Israel, 10460 N 56th St, Scottsdale, AZ, 85253. Tel: 480-951-0323, Ext 121. p. 77

Reynolds, Carol, Librn, Rush Center Library, 220 Washington, 2396 W Hwy 96, Rush Center, KS, 67575. Tel: 785-372-4222. p. 833

Reynolds, Cathy, Dir, Rutledge Public Library, 8030 Rutledge Pk, Rutledge, TN, 37861. Tel: 865-828-4784. p. 2125

Reynolds, Celia, Ref & ILL Serv Coordr, University of North Alabama, One Harrison Plaza, Box 5028, Florence, AL, 35632-0001. Tel: 256-765-4625. p. 17

Reynolds, Christine Gale, Br Head, Mariposa County Library, Yosemite National Park Branch, Girls Club Bldg, 58 Cedar Ct, Yosemite National Park, CA, 95389. Tel: 209-372-4552. p. 173

Reynolds Cooper, Amanda, Dir, Lane Memorial Library, Two Academy Ave, Hampton, NH, 03842. Tel: 603-926-3368. p. 1366

Reynolds, Danielle, Asst Librn, Grangeville Centennial Library, 215 W North St, Grangeville, ID, 83530. Tel: 208-983-0951. p. 521

Reynolds, Danielle, Ref Librn, Neligh Public Library, 710 Main St, Neligh, NE, 68756-1246. Tel: 402-887-5140. p. 1326

Reynolds, Danielle, Colls Mgr, Tech Mgr, Camas Public Library, 625 NE Fourth Ave, Camas, WA, 98607. Tel: 360-834-4692. p. 2360

Reynolds, Denitra, Branch Lead, Live Oak Public Libraries, West Broad Branch, YMCA Bldg, 1110 May St, Savannah, GA, 31415. Tel: 912-201-9246. p. 496

Reynolds, Genea, Libr Dir, Lyndon Carnegie Library, 127 E Sixth, Lyndon, KS, 66451. Tel: 785-828-4520. p. 822

Reynolds, Holly, Head, Circ, ILL, College of Our Lady of the Elms, 291 Springfield St, Chicopee, MA, 01013-2839. Tel: 413-265-2280. p. 1011

Reynolds, Jane, Br Mgr, Monmouth County Library, Atlantic Highlands Branch, 100 First Ave, Atlantic Highlands, NJ, 07716. Tel: 732-291-1956. p. 1415

Reynolds, Janet, Asst Librn, Ch Serv, Tech Serv, Linn County Library District No 2, 209 N Broadway, La Cygne, KS, 66040. Tel: 913-757-2151. p. 818

Reynolds, Jennifer, Br Mgr, Chicago Public Library, Edgebrook, 5331 W Devon Ave, Chicago, IL, 60646. Tel: 312-744-8313. p. 556

Reynolds, John, Ref & Educ Librn, University of Miami, Louis Calder Memorial Library, Miller School of Medicine, 1601 NW Tenth Ave, Miami, FL, 33136. Tel: 305-243-5439. p. 425

Reynolds, Judith K, Dir, Meigs County - Decatur Public Library, 120 E Memorial Dr, Decatur, TN, 37322. Tel: 423-334-3332. p. 2096

Reynolds, Karen, Adult Ref Librn, Atlanta-Fulton Public Library System, Sandy Springs Branch, 395 Mount Vernon Hwy NE, Sandy Springs, GA, 30328. Tel: 404-612-7000. p. 461

Reynolds, Kelly, Ref Librn, University of Oregon Libraries, John E Jaqua Law Library, William W Knight Law Ctr, 2nd Flr, 1515 Agate St, Eugene, OR, 97403. Tel: 541-346-1567. p. 1879

Reynolds, Kristie, Youth Librn, Portland District Library, 334 Kent St, Portland, MI, 48875-1735. Tel: 517-647-6981. p. 1143

Reynolds, Kristina, Dir, Bath Township Public Library, 14033 Webster Rd, Bath, MI, 48808. Tel: 517-641-7111. p. 1082

Reynolds, Kristy, Doc Serv Coordr, Mgr, Libr Admin, University of Texas Southwestern Medical Center, 5323 Harry Hines Blvd, Dallas, TX, 75390-9049. Tel: 214-648-9070. p. 2169

Reynolds, Leslie, Sr Assoc Dean, University of Colorado Boulder, 1720 Pleasant St, Boulder, CO, 80309. Tel: 303-492-8705. p. 267

Reynolds, Linda, Dir, E Tex Res Ctr, Stephen F Austin State University, 1936 North St, Nacogdoches, TX, 75962. Tel: 936-468-1562. p. 2221

Reynolds, Lindsey, Art Librn, University of Georgia Libraries, Art, Main Art Bldg, Rm N201, Lamar Dodd School of Art, Athens, GA, 30602. Tel: 706-542-2712. p. 459

Reynolds, Marianne, Exec Dir, Nebraska State Historical Society, 306 W Elm, Bancroft, NE, 68004. Tel: 402-648-3388. p. 1306

Reynolds, Melissa, Regional Librn, Volusia County Public Library, 1290 Indian Lake Rd, Daytona Beach, FL, 32124. Tel: 386-257-6036. p. 392

Reynolds, Nicole, Spec Coll Librn, University of Kentucky Libraries, Law Library, J David Rosenberg College of Law, 620 S Limestone St, Lexington, KY, 40506-0048. Tel: 859-257-2437. p. 863

Reynolds, Phil, Scholarly Communications Librn, Stephen F Austin State University, 1936 North St, Nacogdoches, TX, 75962. Tel: 936-468-1453. p. 2221

Reynolds, Polly, Head, Adult Serv, Hudson Library & Historical Society, 96 Library St, Hudson, OH, 44236-5122. Tel: 330-653-6658. p. 1790

Reynolds, Ron, Head, Tech Serv, Western Michigan University-Cooley Law School Libraries, 300 S Capitol Ave, Lansing, MI, 48933. Tel: 517-371-5140, Ext 3405. p. 1126

Reynolds, Sarah, Research Servs Librn, Longwood University, Redford & Race St, Farmville, VA, 23909. Tel: 434-395-2437. p. 2318

Reynolds, Susan, ILL, Tech Serv, Marion County Public Library System, 2720 E Silver Springs Blvd, Ocala, FL, 34470. Tel: 352-671-8551. p. 430

Reynolds, Trent, Dir, Thomas County Public Library System, 201 N Madison St, Thomasville, GA, 31792-5414. Tel: 229-225-5252. p. 499

Reynolds, Valerie, Libr Supvr, Copperas Cove Public Library, 501 S Main St, Copperas Cove, TX, 76522. Tel: 254-547-3826. p. 2160

Reynolds, Veronica, Head, Commun Relations, New City Library, 198 S Main St, New City, NY, 10956. Tel: 845-634-4997. p. 1575

Reynoso, Jennifer, Sr Librn, Lee County Library System, North Fort Myers Public Library, 2001 N Tamiami Trail, North Fort Myers, FL, 33903-2802. Tel: 239-533-4320. p. 403

Reynoso, Pedro, Instruction & Outreach, Chabot College Library, 25555 Hesperian Blvd, Hayward, CA, 94545. Tel: 510-723-6767. p. 150

Rezabek, Charlene, Database Mgt Librn, Monroe Community College, LeRoy V Good Library, 1000 E Henrietta Rd, Rochester, NY, 14692. Tel: 585-292-2330. p. 1629

Rezac, June, Br Supvr, Waseca-Le Sueur Regional Library, Elysian Branch, 132 Main St E, Elysian, MN, 56028. Tel: 507-267-4411. p. 1207

Rezac, June, Br Supvr, Waseca-Le Sueur Regional Library, Waterville Public, 210 E Paquin St, Waterville, MN, 56096. Tel: 507-362-8462. p. 1207

Rezaei, Fatemeh, Archivist, University of Baltimore, 1420 Maryland Ave, Baltimore, MD, 21201. Tel: 410-837-5047. p. 957

Rezai-Atrie, Maryam, Chief Admin, Saint Augustine's Seminary Library, 2661 Kingston Rd, Scarborough, ON, M1M 1M3, CANADA. Tel: 416-261-7207, Ext 271. p. 2677

Rezak, Sheila A, Educ Librn, Purdue University, 2200 169th St, Hammond, IN, 46323. Tel: 219-989-2677. p. 689

Rezeau, Michelle, Acq & Ser Librn, Eastern Florida State College, 1519 Clearlake Rd, Cocoa, FL, 32922. Tel: 321-433-7189. p. 389

Rezek, Rachael, Commun Serv Librn, Fremont Public Library District, 1170 N Midlothian Rd, Mundelein, IL, 60060. Tel: 847-566-8702. p. 622

Rezendes, Cathy, Ch, Young Men's Library Association Library, 37 Main St, Ware, MA, 01082-1317. Tel: 413-967-9691. p. 1062

Rezendes, Karin, Youth Serv Mgr, Manheim Township Public Library, 595 Granite Run Dr, Lancaster, PA, 17601. Tel: 717-560-6441. p. 1952

Reznicek, Amy, Dir, North Bend Public Library, 110 E 13th St, North Bend, NE, 68649. Tel: 402-652-8356. p. 1326

Reznick, Carolyn, Dir, Ruth Keeler Memorial Library, 276 Titicus Rd, North Salem, NY, 10560-1708. Tel: 914-669-5161. p. 1608

Reznik, Alex, Librn, Legal Aid Society, 199 Water St, New York, NY, 10038. Tel: 212-577-3300. p. 1590

Reznik-Zellen, Rebecca, Head, Sci & Eng, University of Massachusetts Amherst Libraries, 154 Hicks Way, University of Massachusetts, Amherst, MA, 01003-9275. Tel: 413-545-6739. p. 985

Rhan, Cathy, Talking Bks Consult, Central Kansas Library System, Subregional Library for the Blind & Physically Handicapped, 1409 Williams St, Great Bend, KS, 67530-4020. p. 810

Rhea, Caitlin, Curator of Education & Programming, Pensacola Museum of Art, 407 S Jefferson St, Pensacola, FL, 32502. Tel: 850-432-6247. p. 436

Rhea, Pam, Bus Mgr, Columbus-Lowndes Public Library, 314 Seventh St N, Columbus, MS, 39701. Tel: 662-329-5300. p. 1215

Rheaume, Marty, Dir, Aitkin Memorial District Library, 111 N Howard Ave, Croswell, MI, 48422. Tel: 810-679-3627. p. 1095

Rheaume, Sylvie A, Tech Coordr, Bibliotheque Gabrielle Roy, Bibliotheque Etienne-Parent, 3515 rue Clemenceau, Quebec, QC, G1C 7R5, CANADA. Tel: 418-641-6110. p. 2729

Rheinecker, Rachel, Dir, Steeleville Area Public Library District, 625 S Sparta St, Steeleville, IL, 62288-2147. Tel: 618-965-9732. p. 651

Rheingrover, Daniel, Br Mgr, Charles County Public Library, Two Garrett Ave, La Plata, MD, 20646. Tel: 301-934-9001. p. 969

Rhilinger, Amy, Dir, Attleboro Public Library, 74 N Main St, Attleboro, MA, 02703. Tel: 508-222-0157. p. 986

Rhim, Choonhee, AV/Periodicals Librn, Chairperson, East Los Angeles College, Bldg F3, 1301 Avenida Cesar Chaves, Monterey Park, CA, 91754. Tel: 323-265-8758. p. 180

Rhine, Zoe, Spec Coll Librn, Buncombe County Public Libraries, 67 Haywood St, Asheville, NC, 28801. Tel: 828-250-4700. p. 1672

Rhinehart, Judy, Br Mgr, Aiken-Bamberg-Barnwell-Edgefield Regional Library, Jackson Branch, 106 Main St, Jackson, SC, 29831-2616. Tel: 803-471-3811. p. 2045

Rhoades-Swartz, Linda, Admin Mgr, Union County Historical Society Library, Union County Courthouse, 103 S Second St, Lewisburg, PA, 17837. Tel: 570-524-8666. p. 1955

Rhoads, Bertha, Librn, Udall Public Library, 109 E First St, Udall, KS, 67146. Tel: 620-782-3435. p. 840

Rhoads, Howardean, Librn, Fairfax Public Library, 158 E Elm, Fairfax, OK, 74637. Tel: 918-642-5535. p. 1847

Rhoads, Kirstin, Commun Relations Coordr, Milanof-Schock Library, 1184 Anderson Ferry Rd, Mount Joy, PA, 17552. Tel: 717-653-1510. p. 1966

Rhoads, Mary, Asst Dir, Ch Serv, Johnson County Library, 171 N Adams Ave, Buffalo, WY, 82834. Tel: 307-684-5546. p. 2491

Rhoda, Alan R, Dr, Sysy & Acad Tech Librn, Christian Theological Seminary, 1000 W 42nd St, Indianapolis, IN, 46208. Tel: 317-931-2362. p. 691

Rhoda, Martha, Librn, The Seattle Metaphysical Library (As-You-Like-It Library), 3450 40th Ave W, Seattle, WA, 98199. Tel: 206-551-8277. p. 2379

Richard, Beth, Libr Dir, Copiah-Lincoln Community College, 11 Co-Lin Circle, Natchez, MS, 39120. Tel: 601-446-1101. p. 1227

Richard, Bonnie, Br Supvr, Vermilion Parish Library, Delcambre Branch, 206 W Main St, Delcambre, LA, 70528-2918. Tel: 337-685-2388. p. 879

Richard, Bonnie, Br Mgr, Iberia Parish Library, Delcambre Branch, 206 W Main St, Delcambre, LA, 70528-2918. Tel: 337-685-2388. p. 900

Richard, Gwendolyn, Dir, Libr Serv, Houston Community College - Northeast College, Northline Library, 8001 Fulton St, Houston, TX, 77022. Tel: 713-718-8045. p. 2194

Richard, Gwendolyn, NE Dir of Libr Serv, Houston Community College - Northeast College, Pinemont Campus Library, 1265 Pinemont, Houston, TX, 77018-1303. Tel: 713-718-8443. p. 2194

Richard, Jenn, Head, Adult Serv, Town of Ballston Community Library, Two Lawmar Lane, Burnt Hills, NY, 12027. Tel: 518-399-8174. p. 1511

Richard, Jennifer, Acting Dean, Library & Archives, Acadia University, 50 Acadia St, Wolfville, NS, B4P 2R6, CANADA. Tel: 902-670-0294. p. 2623

Richard, Krystal, Libr Assoc, Cloud County Community College Library, 2221 Campus Dr, Concordia, KS, 66901-5305. Tel: 785-243-1435, Ext 227. p. 803

Richard, Léa, Br Adminr, Government of Quebec - Agriculture Fisheries & Foods, 96 Montee de Sandy-Beach, Rez-de-chaussee, Gaspe, QC, G4X 2V6, CANADA. Tel: 418-368-6371. p. 2712

Richard, Michel, Librn, Canadian Radio-Television & Telecommunications Commission Information Resource Centre, One Promenade du Portage, Ottawa, ON, K1A 0N2, CANADA. Tel: 819-997-4484. p. 2666

Richard, Nathalie, Ref Librn, Universite de Moncton, 18, ave Antonine-Maillet, Moncton, NB, E1A 3E9, CANADA. Tel: 506-858-4012. p. 2604

Richard, Susan, Assoc Dean, University of Louisiana at Lafayette, 400 E St Mary Blvd, Lafayette, LA, 70503. Tel: 337-482-6396. p. 893

Richards, Amanda, Br Mgr, Montrose Regional Library District, Naturita Branch, 107 W First Ave, Naturita, CO, 81422. Tel: 970-787-2270. p. 291

Richards, Anne, Circ Serv Mgr, Grandview Heights Public Library, 1685 W First Ave, Columbus, OH, 43212. Tel: 614-486-2951. p. 1773

Richards, Carol, IT Dir, Wellesley Free Library, 530 Washington St, Wellesley, MA, 02482. Tel: 781-235-1610, Ext 1130. p. 1064

Richards, David, Dean, Libr Serv, University of Nebraska at Omaha, 6001 Dodge St, Omaha, NE, 68182-0237. Tel: 402-554-3208. p. 1330

Richards, David L, PhD, Dr, Dir, Margaret Chase Smith Library, 56 Norridgewock Ave, Skowhegan, ME, 04976. Tel: 207-474-7133. p. 940

Richards, Deborah, Head, Archives & Spec Coll, Mount Holyoke College Library, 50 College St, South Hadley, MA, 01075. Tel: 413-538-2013. p. 1054

Richards, Holly, Dir, Tech Serv, Dayton Metro Library, 215 E Third St, Dayton, OH, 45402. Tel: 937-463-2665. p. 1779

Richards, Janette, Youth Serv, Hagerstown Jefferson Township Library, Ten W College St, Hagerstown, IN, 47346. Tel: 765-489-5632. p. 689

Richards, Jennifer Tys, Mgr of Archives & Research, Natick Historical Society, 58 Eliot St, Natick, MA, 01760. Tel: 508-647-4841. p. 1037

Richards, Jules, Youth Serv Librn, Metuchen Public Library, 480 Middlesex Ave, Metuchen, NJ, 08840. Tel: 732-632-8526. p. 1418

Richards, Katie, Dir, Shapleigh Community Library, 607 Shapleigh Corner Rd, Shapleigh, ME, 04076. Tel: 207-636-3630. p. 940

Richards, Kayla, Tech Serv Asst, Monroe County Community College, 1555 S Raisinville Rd, Monroe, MI, 48161-9047. Tel: 734-384-4182. p. 1133

Richards, Kelly, Pres & Dir, Free Library of Philadelphia, 1901 Vine St, Philadelphia, PA, 19103. Tel: 215-567-7710, 215-686-5322. p. 1977

Richards, Kelsey, Br Mgr, Lincoln County Library System, Thayne Branch, 250 Van Noy Pkwy, Thayne, WY, 83127. Tel: 307-883-7323. p. 2496

Richards, Lanelle, Acad Librn, Northern Wyoming Community College District - Sheridan College, Griffith Memorial Bldg, One Whitney Way, Sheridan, WY, 82801. Tel: 307-675-0220. p. 2498

Richards, Maegan, Learning Commons Coord, Kent State University, 2491 State Rte 45-S, Salem, OH, 44460-9412. Tel: 330-337-4211. p. 1819

Richards, Meredith, Ad, Ref Librn, George Hail Free Library, 530 Main St, Warren, RI, 02885. Tel: 401-245-7686. p. 2042

Richards, Rob, Archives Dir, National Archives & Records Administration, 5780 Jonesboro Rd, Morrow, GA, 30260. Tel: 770-968-2485. p. 491

Richards, Samuel, Assoc Dir for Finance & Personnel, United States Military Academy Library, Jefferson Hall Library & Learning Ctr, 758 Cullum Rd, West Point, NY, 10996. Tel: 845-938-8301. p. 1663

Richards, Serenity, Br Librn, Albert Carlton-Cashiers Community Library, 249 Frank Allen Rd, Cashiers, NC, 28717. Tel: 828-743-0215. p. 1678

Richards, Sonia, Asst to the Dir, New York Public Library - Astor, Lenox & Tilden Foundations, Schomburg Center for Research in Black Culture, 515 Malcolm X Blvd, (135th & Malcolm X Blvd), New York, NY, 10037-1801. p. 1597

Richards, Stacy, Head Librn, Westside Public Library, 5151 Walnut Grove Rd, Walnut Grove, AL, 35990. Tel: 205-589-6699. p. 39

Richards, Tiffany, Br Mgr, Scenic Regional Library, Hermann Branch, 123-A Bavarian Hills Blvd, Hermann, MO, 65041. Tel: 573-486-2024. p. 1283

Richards-Jones, Jane, Asst Librn, Frost Free Library, 28 Jaffrey Rd, Marlborough, NH, 03455. Tel: 603-876-4479. p. 1373

Richardson, Aaron, Ref & Instruction Librn, Dominican University of California, 50 Acacia Ave, San Rafael, CA, 94901-2298. Tel: 415-485-3251. p. 236

Richardson, Alison, Assoc Dir of Finance & Admin, Harvard Library, Francis A Countway Library of Medicine, Ten Shattuck St, Boston, MA, 02115. Tel: 617-432-2136. p. 1005

Richardson, Allison, Electronic Res Librn, Kwantlen Polytechnic University Library, 12666 72nd Ave, Surrey, BC, V3W 2M8, CANADA. Tel: 604-598-6026. p. 2576

Richardson, Angela, Circ & ILL, Dir, Illinois Mathematics & Science Academy, 1500 Sullivan Rd, Aurora, IL, 60506-1000. Tel: 630-907-5920. p. 539

Richardson, Athena, Coordr, Prog, Goodnight Memorial Public Library, 203 S Main St, Franklin, KY, 42134. Tel: 270-586-8397. p. 856

Richardson, Barbara, Asst Dir, Phinehas S Newton Library, 19 On the Common, Royalston, MA, 01368. Tel: 978-249-3572. p. 1050

Richardson, Beatrice, Dir, Info Tech, North Carolina State University Libraries, D H Hill Jr Library, Two Broughton Dr, Raleigh, NC, 27695. Tel: 919-513-8031. p. 1709

Richardson, Brittany, Web Serv Librn, University of Tennessee at Chattanooga Library, 400 Douglas Ave, Dept 6456, Chattanooga, TN, 37403-2598. Tel: 423-425-4501. p. 2092

Richardson, Caitlin, Campus Libr Dir, Miami Dade College, 500 College Terrace, Bldg D, Rm D-101, Homestead, FL, 33030-6009. Tel: 305-237-5245. p. 409

Richardson, Christopher K, Dr, Seminary Librarian, Union Presbyterian Seminary Library, 3401 Brook Rd, Richmond, VA, 23227. Tel: 804-278-4310. p. 2342

Richardson, Connie, Board Pres, O'Brien Memorial Library, 51771 Blue River Dr, Blue River, OR, 97413. p. 1874

Richardson, Dana, Dir, Macon County Public Library, 311 Church St, Lafayette, TN, 37083. Tel: 615-666-4340. p. 2108

Richardson, Dana, Dir, Macon County Public Library, Red Boiling Springs Branch, 335 E Main St, Red Boiling Springs, TN, 37150. Tel: 615-699-3701. p. 2108

Richardson, Daneen, Librn, Illinois Department of Corrections, 1300 W Locust St, Canton, IL, 61520-8791. Tel: 309-647-7030. p. 548

Richardson, David, Librn, Mgr, Libr Serv, Whitehead Institute for Biomedical Research, 455 Main St, Cambridge, MA, 02142. Tel: 617-258-5132. p. 1009

Richardson, Debra J, Exec Dir, Fillmore County History Center, 202 County Rd 8, Fountain, MN, 55935. Tel: 507-268-4449. p. 1175

Richardson, Diana, Librn, Texas County Library, Summersville Branch, 480 First St, Summersville, MO, 65571. Tel: 417-932-5261. p. 1249

Richardson, Evallou, Tech Serv, Sheffield Public Library, 316 N Montgomery Ave, Sheffield, AL, 35660. Tel: 256-386-5633. p. 35

Richardson, Gail P, Dir, Audubon Public Library, 401 N Park Pl, Audubon, IA, 50025-1258. Tel: 712-563-3301. p. 733

Richardson, Ian, Head, Distance Learning Servs, University of Louisiana at Lafayette, 400 E St Mary Blvd, Lafayette, LA, 70503. Tel: 337-482-6452. p. 893

Richardson, Janice, Coordr, Oregon County Library District, 20 Court Sq, Alton, MO, 65606. Tel: 417-778-6414. p. 1237

Richardson, Janie, Research Librn, Stephen F Austin State University, 1936 North St, Nacogdoches, TX, 75962. Tel: 936-468-1896. p. 2221

Richardson, Jeanne, Chief Officer, Coll Serv, Scholarly Communications Officer, Arizona State University Libraries, Collections & Scholarly Communication, PO Box 871006, Tempe, AZ, 85287-1006. Tel: 480-965-5345. p. 79

Richardson, Juanita, Librn, Michener Institute of Education at UHN, 222 Saint Patrick St, 2nd Flr, Toronto, ON, M5T 1V4, CANADA. Tel: 416-596-3123. p. 2690

Richardson, Katherine, Dir, Camden Archives & Museum Library, 1314 Broad St, Camden, SC, 29020-3535. Tel: 803-425-6050. p. 2048

Richardson, Kathleen, Tech Serv Librn, Bluegrass Community & Technical College, 221 Oswald Bldg, 470 Cooper Dr, Lexington, KY, 40506-0235. Tel: 859-246-6386. p. 862

Richardson, Kelley, Br Mgr, Hancock County Public Library, Lewisport Branch, 400 Second St, Lewisport, KY, 42351. Tel: 270-295-3765. p. 858

Richardson, Krista, Pub Serv Librn, Quinte West Public Library, Seven Creswell Dr, Trenton, ON, K8V 6X5, CANADA. Tel: 613-394-3381, Ext 3325. p. 2700

Richardson, Laura, Br Librn, Washington State Library, Washington Corrections Center, 2321 W Dayton Airport Rd, Shelton, WA, 98584. Tel: 360-432-1509. p. 2390

Richardson, Laurie, Tech Serv Librn, United States Army, Center Library, Bldg 212, Corner of Ruf Ave & Novosel, Fort Rucker, AL, 36362-5000. Tel: 334-255-3885. p. 18

Richardson, Maria, Ch, Head, Youth Serv, Kennebunk Free Library, 112 Main St, Kennebunk, ME, 04043. Tel: 207-985-2173. p. 928

Richardson, Marisa, Curator, Bossier Parish Libraries, History Center, 2206 Beckett St, Bossier City, LA, 71111. Tel: 318-746-7717. p. 886

Ridgeway, Bernice, ILL Coordr, University of California, Riverside, 900 University Ave, Riverside, CA, 92521. Tel: 951-827-3220. p. 203
Ridgeway, Beth, Dir, Sheffield Public Library, 316 N Montgomery Ave, Sheffield, AL, 35660. Tel: 256-386-5633. p. 35
Ridgeway, Jeff, Head, Children's Servx, Washington County Free Library, 100 S Potomac St, Hagerstown, MD, 21740. Tel: 301-739-3250, p. 968
Ridgway, Laurie, Ch, Wiscasset Public Library, 21 High St, Wiscasset, ME, 04578-4119. Tel: 207-882-7161. p. 947
Ridinger, Robert, Res & Ref Librn, Northern Illinois University Libraries, 217 Normal Rd, DeKalb, IL, 60115-2828. Tel: 815-753-1367. p. 577
Ridley, Astoria, Law Librn II, Connecticut Judicial Branch Law Libraries, New Haven Law Library, New Haven Courthouse, 235 Church St, New Haven, CT, 06510. Tel: 203-503-6828. p. 316
Ridley, Connie, Circ Serv, Belen Public Library, 333 Becker Ave, Belen, NM, 87002. Tel: 505-966-2607. p. 1464
Ridley, Jennifer, Dir, Human Res, Mid-Continent Public Library, 15616 E US Hwy 24, Independence, MO, 64050. Tel: 816-836-5200. p. 1250
Ridnour, Sue, Libr Dir, Flower Mound Public Library, 3030 Broadmoor Lane, Flower Mound, TX, 75022. Tel: 972-874-6200. p. 2177
Rieck, Wendy, Librn, Montmorency County Public Libraries, Lewiston Public, 2851 Kneeland St, Lewiston, MI, 49756. Tel: 989-786-2985. p. 1081
Rieckenberg, Tammy, Librn, Coulterville Public Library, 103 S Fourth St, Coulterville, IL, 62237. Tel: 618-758-3013. p. 574
Riedel, Christina, Asst Dir, Clarksville-Montgomery County Public Library, 350 Pageant Lane, Ste 501, Clarksville, TN, 37040. Tel: 931-648-8826. p. 2092
Riedel, Gayle, Asst Dir, Student Serv Librn, Mount Vernon Nazarene University, 800 Martinsburg Rd, Mount Vernon, OH, 43050-9500. Tel: 740-397-9000, Ext 4240. p. 1804
Rieder, Mary, Acq Librn, Outreach Librn, Viterbo University, 900 Viterbo Dr, La Crosse, WI, 54601. Tel: 608-796-3266. p. 2446
Riederer, Diana, Br Mgr, Tangipahoa Parish Library, Hammond Branch, 314 E Thomas, Hammond, LA, 70401. Tel: 985-345-0937, 985-345-3909. p. 881
Riedlinger, Jean E, Ref Serv, American College of Obstetricians & Gynecologists, 409 12th St SW, Washington, DC, 20024-2188. Tel: 202-863-2518. p. 360
Rief, Allison, Circ Asst, ILL, Somers Public Library, Two Vision Blvd, Somers, CT, 06071. Tel: 860-763-3501. p. 337
Rieger, Jamie, Fiscal Officer, Dover Public Library, 525 N Walnut St, Dover, OH, 44622. Tel: 330-343-6123. p. 1782
Riegler, Sue, Dir, Alden District Library, 8751 Helena Rd, Alden, MI, 49612. Tel: 231-331-4318. p. 1076
Riegner, Amy, Dir, Murrysville Community Library, 4130 Sardis Rd, Murrysville, PA, 15668. Tel: 724-327-1102. p. 1967
Riehl, Christian, Assistive Tech Coordr, New Jersey State Library, Talking Book & Braille Center, 2300 Stuyvesant Ave, Trenton, NJ, 08618. Tel: 609-406-7179, Ext 821. p. 1448
Riehl, Jennifer, Library Contact, Nogales-Santa Cruz County Public Library, Sonoita Community Library, County Complex Bldg, 3147 State Rte 83, Sonoita, AZ, 85637. Tel: 520-455-5517. p. 67
Riehl, Sue, Archivist, Pub Serv Librn, Tech Serv, Carroll University, 100 N East Ave, Waukesha, WI, 53186. Tel: 262-650-4832. p. 2484
Riehle, Caitlyn, Curator of Coll, Monroe County Historical Museum, 126 S Monroe St, Monroe, MI, 48161. Tel: 734-240-7787, 734-240-7794. p. 1133
Riehle, Tina, Br Mgr, Public Library of Cincinnati & Hamilton County, Sharonville, 10980 Thornview Dr, Cincinnati, OH, 45241. Tel: 513-369-6049. p. 1763
Riehman-Murphy, Christina E, Ref & Instruction Librn, Pennsylvania State University, 1600 Woodland Rd, Abington, PA, 19001. Tel: 215-881-7911. p. 1903
Riek, Lisa, Library Contact, Nelson, Mullins, Riley & Scarborough, Pinnacle Corporate Ctr, Ste 300, 3751 Robert M Grissom Pkwy, Myrtle Beach, SC, 29577. Tel: 843-448-3500. p. 2066
Riel, Kathryn, Acq, Ser Librn, Massachusetts College of Art & Design, 621 Huntington Ave, Boston, MA, 02115-5882. Tel: 617-879-7112. p. 996
Riener, Alexandra, Librn, Austrian Cultural Forum Library, 11 E 52nd St, New York, NY, 10022. Tel: 212-319-5300. p. 1579
Rienti, Beth, Head, Youth Serv, Guilderland Public Library, 2228 Western Ave, Guilderland, NY, 12084. Tel: 518-456-2400, Ext 152. p. 1542
Rienzo, Theresa, Assoc Librn, Health Sci Librn, Molloy College, 1000 Hempstead Ave, Rockville Centre, NY, 11571. Tel: 516-323-3930. p. 1632
Rienzo, Theresa, Treas, Medical & Scientific Libraries of Long Island, Molloy College, 1000 Hempstead Ave, Rockville Centre, NY, 11571. p. 2771
Ries, Rachael, Br Mgr, Fort Vancouver Regional Library District, Cascade Park Community Library, 600 NE 136th Ave, Vancouver, WA, 98684. p. 2391
Ries, Rachael, Br Mgr, Fort Vancouver Regional Library District, Washougal Community Library, 1661 C St, Washougal, WA, 98671. p. 2391
Ries-Taggart, Jennifer, Exec Dir, Brighton Memorial Library, 2300 Elmwood Ave, Rochester, NY, 14618. Tel: 585-784-5300. p. 1628
Riesenberg, Lisa, Dir, West Bend Public Library, 316 S Broadway, West Bend, IA, 50597. Tel: 515-887-6411. p. 790
Riess, Rosemary, Head, Spec Coll & Archives, Palmer College of Chiropractic-Davenport Campus, 1000 Brady St, Davenport, IA, 52803-5287. Tel: 563-884-5641. p. 744
Rieur, Elizabeth, Head, Info Serv, Head, Ref, Haverhill Public Library, 99 Main St, Haverhill, MA, 01830-5092. Tel: 978-373-1586. p. 1024
Riewerts, Emily, Circ Asst, River Valley District Library, 214 S Main St, Port Byron, IL, 61275. Tel: 309-523-3440. p. 636
Rife, Jennifer, Head, Exhibitions, Supvr, Laramie County Library System, 2200 Pioneer Ave, Cheyenne, WY, 82001-3610. Tel: 307-773-7218. p. 2492
Rifenburg, Leigh, Chief Curator, Delaware Historical Society Research Library, 505 N Market St, Wilmington, DE, 19801. Tel: 302-295-2386. p. 357
Riffle, Vera, Br Mgr, Warren-Trumbull County Public Library, Lordstown Branch, 1471 Salt Springs Rd, Warren, OH, 44481. Tel: 330-824-2094. p. 1828
Rifkin, Laura, Dir, Township of Washington Public Library, 144 Woodfield Rd, Washington Township, NJ, 07676. Tel: 201-664-4586. p. 1451
Rigaux, Ryan, Actg Br Mgr, Toledo-Lucas County Public Library, Toledo Heights, 423 Shasta Dr, Toledo, OH, 43609. Tel: 419-259-5220. p. 1825
Rigby, Mary, Libr Coord, Yavapai County Free Library District, Ash Fork Public Library, 450 W Lewis Ave, Ash Fork, AZ, 86320. Tel: 928-637-2442. p. 74
Rigby, Sarah, Libr Dir, Newton Town Library, 51 S Center St, Newton, UT, 84327. Tel: 435-563-9283. p. 2267
Rigby, Virginia, Doc, Ref Librn, Lone Star College System, North Harris College Library, 2700 W W Thorne Dr, Houston, TX, 77073. Tel: 281-618-5490. p. 2197
Rigdon, Helen, Dir, Sioux City Public Library, 529 Pierce St, Sioux City, IA, 51101-1203. Tel: 712-255-2933. p. 783
Rigg, Pamela, Libr Dir, Perry Carnegie Library, 302 N Seventh St, Perry, OK, 73077. Tel: 580-336-4721. p. 1860
Riggi, Christine, Circ Coordr, University at Buffalo Libraries-State University of New York, Charles B Sears Law Library, John Lord O'Brian Hall, 211 Mary Talbert Way, Buffalo, NY, 14260-1110. Tel: 716-645-5631. p. 1511
Riggi, Wendy, Cataloger, Technology Spec, Grove City Community Library, 125 W Main St, Grove City, PA, 16127-1569. Tel: 724-458-7320. p. 1939
Riggie, Joseph W, Head, Info Mgt, Buffalo State University of New York, 1300 Elmwood Ave, Buffalo, NY, 14222. Tel: 716-878-6320. p. 1508
Riggins, Adina, Univ Archivist, University of North Carolina Wilmington Library, 601 S College Rd, Wilmington, NC, 28403. Tel: 910-962-4233. p. 1723
Riggs, Alexia, Libr Dir, Southwestern University, 1100 E University Ave, Georgetown, TX, 78626. p. 2184
Riggs, Krista, Libr Dir, Madera County Library, 121 North G St, Madera, CA, 93637-3592. Tel: 559-675-7871. p. 171
Riggs, Laura, Health Sci Librn, Liaison Librn, Mohawk College Library, 135 Fennell Ave W, Hamilton, ON, L9C 0E5, CANADA. Tel: 905-575-1212, Ext 6720. p. 2647
Riggs, Laura, Liaison Librn, Mohawk College Library, IAHS (Institute for Applied Health Sciences) Library, 1400 Main St W, Hamilton, ON, L8S 1C7, CANADA. Tel: 905-575-1212 x6720. p. 2647
Riggs, LaVeda, Ch Serv, Linn County Library District No 2, 209 N Broadway, La Cygne, KS, 66040. Tel: 913-757-2151. p. 818
Riggs, Lisa, Dir, Moore County Public Library, 17 Majors Blvd, Lynchburg, TN, 37352. Tel: 931-759-7285. p. 2110
Riggs, Lisa, Libr Mgr, Hutto Public Library, 500 W Live Oak St, Hutto, TX, 78634. Tel: 512-459-4008. p. 2201
Riggs, Shannon, Head, Circ, Neuse Regional Library, 510 N Queen St, Kinston, NC, 28501. Tel: 252-527-7066. p. 1699
Riggs, Timothy, Libr Tech, College of Central Florida Learning Resources Center, 3800 S Lecanto Hwy, C2-202, Lecanto, FL, 34461. Tel: 352-746-6721, Ext 6119. p. 418
Riggs, Vincent, Library Contact, Fayette County Law Library, 120 N Limestone St, Ste C-357, 3rd Flr, Lexington, KY, 40507. Tel: 859-246-2141. p. 862
Righter, Loretta, Head, Ref, Montgomery County-Norristown Public Library, 1001 Powell St, Norristown, PA, 19401-3817. Tel: 610-278-5100, Ext 116. p. 1971
Rightnowar, Hayley, Asst Head, Circ Serv, Eisenhower Public Library District, 4613 N Oketo Ave, Harwood Heights, IL, 60706. Tel: 708-867-7828. p. 597
Rigsby, Lisa, Dir, De Soto Trail Regional Library System, 145 E Broad St, Camilla, GA, 31730. Tel: 229-336-8372. p. 468
Rigsby, Lisa, Tech Serv Mgr, Eckhart Public Library, 603 S Jackson St, Auburn, IN, 46706-2298. Tel: 206-925-2414, Ext 503. p. 669
Rigsby, Olivia, Circ, Reserves, Lamar University, 4400 Martin Luther King Jr Pkwy, Beaumont, TX, 77705. Tel: 409-880-8980. p. 2146
Rigual, Michelle, Dir, University of New Mexico, Law Library, 1117 Stanford Dr NE, Albuquerque, NM, 87131-1441. Tel: 505-277-6236. p. 1463
Riker, Pat, Br Mgr, Martin County Library System, Hobe Sound Branch, 10595 SE Federal Hwy, Hobe Sound, FL, 33455. Tel: 772-546-2257. p. 445
Riker, Ross, Automation Mgr, Goshen Public Library, 601 S Fifth St, Goshen, IN, 46526. Tel: 574-533-9531. p. 687
Rilee, Savannah, Ch Serv, Perry Carnegie Library, 302 N Seventh St, Perry, OK, 73077. Tel: 580-336-4721. p. 1860

Rinz, Beth Maher, Librn, Sherwin-Williams Automotive Finishes Corp Library, 4440 Warrensville Center Rd, Cleveland, OH, 44128. Tel: 216-332-8427. p. 1770

Rio, Julie, Asst Dir, Wallingford Public Library, 200 N Main St, Wallingford, CT, 06492. Tel: 203-284-6422. p. 342

Riopel, Dianne, Exec Dir, Ojibway & Cree Cultural Centre, 150 Brousseau Ave, Unit B, Timmins, ON, P4N 5Y4, CANADA. Tel: 705-267-7911. p. 2685

Riordan, Elizabeth, Lead Outreach & Instruction Librn, University of Iowa Libraries, Special Collections & Archives, 100 Main Library, 125 W Washington St, Iowa City, IA, 52242-1420. Tel: 319-384-2802. p. 761

Riordan, Johanna, Electronic Res Librn, Haverford College, 370 Lancaster Ave, Haverford, PA, 19041-1392. Tel: 610-896-1168. p. 1942

Rios, David, Ref Supvr, McAllen Public Library, 4001 N 23rd St, McAllen, TX, 78504. Tel: 956-681-3000. p. 2217

Rios, Gabe, Dir, Indiana University, Ruth Lilly Medical Library, 975 W Walnut St, IB 100, Indianapolis, IN, 46202. Tel: 317-274-1408. p. 693

Rios, Joanna, Rec Mgr, Columbia University, Archives, Butler Library, 6th Flr, 535 W 114th St, MC 1127, New York, NY, 10027. Tel: 212-854-1331. p. 1582

Rios, Julie, Ch, ILL Librn, Walpole Town Library, Bridge Memorial Library, 48 Main St, Walpole, NH, 03608. Tel: 603-756-9806. p. 1383

Rios, Laura, Head, Ref, Free Public Library of Hasbrouck Heights, 320 Boulevard, Hasbrouck Heights, NJ, 07604. Tel: 201-288-0484, 201-288-0488. p. 1407

Rios, Leslie, Librn, Lincoln Land Community College Library, Sangamon Hall, 5250 Shepherd Rd, Springfield, IL, 62794. Tel: 217-786-4617. p. 650

Rios, Lizeth, Libr Tech, Ridgewater College Library, 2101 15th Ave NW, Willmar, MN, 56201. Tel: 320-222-7536. p. 1208

Rios, Michael, Ref Librn, Fordham University Libraries, Quinn Library at Lincoln Center, 140 W 62nd St, New York, NY, 10023. Tel: 212-636-6050. p. 1498

Rios, Molly, Youth Serv Mgr, Herrick District Library, 300 S River Ave, Holland, MI, 49423. Tel: 616-355-3731. p. 1115

Rios, Rosa, Circ Supvr, Laredo College, West End Washington St, Laredo, TX, 78040. Tel: 956-721-5275. p. 2209

Rios, Senele, Sr Librn, Los Angeles Public Library System, Mark Twain Branch Library, 9621 S Figueroa St, Los Angeles, CA, 90003. Tel: 323-755-4088. p. 165

Rioux, Jean-Francois, Librn, Universite du Quebec a Rimouski - Service de la bibliotheque, 300 Allee des Ursulines, Rimouski, QC, G5L 3A1, CANADA. Tel: 418-723-1986, Ext 1669. p. 2732

Rioux, Kevin, PhD, Assoc Prof, St John's University, Saint Augustine Hall, Rm 408A, 8000 Utopia Pkwy, Jamaica, NY, 11439. Tel: 718-990-1458. p. 2789

Rioux, Nicole, Pub Serv Librn, Chesapeake College, 1000 College Circle, Wye Mills, MD, 21679. Tel: 410-827-5860. p. 981

Ripka, Beverly, Dir, Williamstown Library, 2877 County Rte 17N, Williamstown, NY, 13493. Tel: 315-964-2802. p. 1666

Ripley, George, Br Mgr, New Bedford Free Public Library, Howland-Green Branch, Three Rodney French Blvd, New Bedford, MA, 02744. Tel: 508-991-6212. p. 1038

Ripley, George, Dir, Westport Free Public Library, 408 Old County Rd, Westport, MA, 02790. Tel: 508-636-1100. p. 1068

Ripoll-Leal, Otto, Libr Tech II, First Nations University of Canada, Northern Campus Library, 1301 Central Ave, Prince Albert, SK, S6V 4W1, CANADA. Tel: 306-765-3333. p. 2746

Riportella, Molly, Asst Dir, Walpole Public Library, 143 School St, Walpole, MA, 02081. Tel: 508-660-6358. p. 1061

Riportella, Molly, Head, Adult Serv, Westwood Public Library, 660 High St, Westwood, MA, 02090. Tel: 718-320-1004. p. 1068

Ripp, Chantal, Research Librn, University of Ottawa Libraries, Geographic, Statistical & Government Information Centre, Morisset Hall, 3rd Flr, 65 University, Ottawa, ON, K1N 9A5, CANADA. Tel: 613-562-5211. p. 2670

Rippel, Kali, Librn, Las Positas College Library, 3000 Campus Hill Dr, Livermore, CA, 94551. Tel: 925-424-1150. p. 156

Rippel, Kathleen, Dir & Librn, Bison Community Library, 202 Main St, Bison, KS, 67520. Tel: 785-356-4803. p. 798

Rippins, Gina, ILL Spec, Eastern Florida State College, 1519 Clearlake Rd, Cocoa, FL, 32922. Tel: 321-433-7262. p. 389

Ripplinger, Anna, Cataloger, Columbia Public Library, 106 N Metter Ave, Columbia, IL, 62236-2299. Tel: 618-281-4237. p. 573

Ripplinger, Lillian, Br Librn, Southeast Regional Library, Montmartre Branch, 136 Central Ave, Montmartre, SK, S0G 3M0, CANADA. Tel: 306-424-2029. p. 2754

Rippstein, Kathy, Circ Supvr, Concordia University, 800 N Columbia Ave, Seward, NE, 68434. Tel: 402-643-7254. p. 1335

Rippy, Linda, Exec Dir, Marshall County Historical Society Library, 123 N Michigan St, Plymouth, IN, 46563. Tel: 574-936-2306. p. 714

Risa, Terry, Br Librn, Opheim Community Library, 100 Rock St, Opheim, MT, 59250. Tel: 406-762-3213. p. 1300

Risch, Laurie, Exec Dir, Behringer-Crawford Museum Library, 1600 Montague Rd, Devou Park, Covington, KY, 41011. Tel: 859-491-4003. p. 852

Riseley, David, Librn, Arbor Road Church, 5336 E Arbor Rd, Long Beach, CA, 90808. Tel: 562-420-1471. p. 158

Risen, Deb, Asst Librn, Stratford Public Library, 816 Shakespeare, Stratford, IA, 50249. Tel: 515-838-2131. p. 785

Rish, Jane, Librn, VA Pittsburgh Healthcare System, Medical Library University Drive Division, University Dr, Pittsburgh, PA, 15240. Tel: 412-360-3054. p. 1997

Rish, Jane, Librn, VA Pittsburgh Healthcare System, University Dr C, Pittsburgh, PA, 15240. Tel: 412-360-3054, 412-822-1748. p. 1997

Risher, Amanda, YA Librn, Alexandrian Public Library, 115 W Fifth St, Mount Vernon, IN, 47620. Tel: 812-838-3286. p. 708

Risinger, Michele, Dir, Hartford City Public Library, 314 N High St, Hartford City, IN, 47348-2143. Tel: 765-348-1720. p. 689

Riskedahl, Laura, Dir, Libr Serv, Univ Archivist, Coe College, 1220 First Ave NE, Cedar Rapids, IA, 52402. p. 738

Risley, Carine, Dep Dir, Libr Serv, San Mateo County Library, Library Administration, 125 Lessingia Ct, San Mateo, CA, 94402-4000. Tel: 650-312-5312. p. 235

Risolo, Glenn, Principal Librn, Coronado Public Library, 640 Orange Ave, Coronado, CA, 92118-1526. Tel: 619-522-2470. p. 132

Risolo, Glenn, Br Mgr, San Diego Public Library, Skyline Hills, 7900 Paradise Valley Rd, San Diego, CA, 92139. Tel: 619-527-3485. p. 221

Risse, Sherri, Dir, Spencer County Public Library, 210 Walnut St, Rockport, IN, 47635-1398. Tel: 812-649-4866. p. 716

Rist, Julianne, Dir, Pub Serv, Jefferson County Public Library, 10200 W 20th Ave, Lakewood, CO, 80215. Tel: 303-275-2236. p. 288

Rist, Kelly, Dir, Delphos Public Library, 309 W Second St, Delphos, OH, 45833-1695. Tel: 419-695-4015. p. 1782

Ristau, April, Br Mgr, Collier County Public Library, 2385 Orange Blossom Dr, Naples, FL, 34109. Tel: 239-593-0334. p. 427

Rister, Kathleen, Dir, Groffe Memorial Library, 118 South Middle St, Grayville, IL, 62844. Tel: 618-375-7121. p. 595

Rita, Agnes, Supv Librn, Adult Serv, Murrieta Public Library, 8 Town Sq, Murrieta, CA, 92562. Tel: 951-461-6130. p. 181

Ritcher-Sanchez, Carolina, Evening Supvr, Berry College, 2277 Martha Berry Hwy, Mount Berry, GA, 30149. Tel: 706-238-5887. p. 492

Ritchey, Sandi, ILL, Mount Angel Abbey Library, One Abbey Dr, Saint Benedict, OR, 97373. Tel: 503-845-3303. p. 1895

Ritchhart, Tandy, Bus Mgr, Southwest Kansas Library System, 100 Military Ave, Ste 210, Dodge City, KS, 67801. Tel: 620-225-1231, Ext 200. p. 805

Ritchie, Ellen, Dir, Saginaw Public Library, 355 W McLeroy Blvd, Saginaw, TX, 76179. Tel: 817-232-0300. p. 2235

Ritchie, James, Br Mgr, Arkansas River Valley Regional Library System, Johnson County, Two Taylor Circle, Clarksville, AR, 72830-3653. Tel: 479-754-3135. p. 93

Ritchie, Jessica, Head, Spec Coll & Univ Archives, Old Dominion University Libraries, 4427 Hampton Blvd, Norfolk, VA, 23529-0256. Tel: 757-683-4483. p. 2336

Ritchie, Vanessa, Asst Dean, Mississippi Gulf Coast Community College, Hwy 49 S, Perkinston, MS, 39573. Tel: 601-928-6242. p. 1229

Ritchot, Dominique, Coordr, Societe Genealogique Canadienne-Francaise Bibliotheque, 3440 rue Davidson, Montreal, QC, H1W 2Z5, CANADA. Tel: 514-527-1010. p. 2728

Riter, Robert B, Dr, Asst Prof, University of Alabama, 7035 Gorgas Library, Campus Box 870252, Tuscaloosa, AL, 35487-0252. Tel: 205-348-4610. p. 2781

Ritter, Anne, Br Mgr, Acadia Parish Library, Iota Branch, 119 Duson Ave, Iota, LA, 70543. Tel: 337-779-2770. p. 888

Ritter, Clay, Dir, Payette Public Library, 24 S Tenth St, Payette, ID, 83661-2861. Tel: 208-642-6029. p. 528

Ritter, Dawn, Adult Serv, Joliet Public Library, 150 N Ottawa St, Joliet, IL, 60432. Tel: 815-740-2660. p. 603

Ritter, Heather, Libr Mgr, Northwestern State University Libraries, 3329 University Pkwy, Leesville, LA, 71446. Tel: 337-392-3126. p. 895

Ritter, James, Archivist, State Librn, Tennessee State Library & Archives, 403 Seventh Ave N, Nashville, TN, 37243-0312. Tel: 615-741-2764. p. 2121

Ritter, Katy, Circ Mgr, Illinois Wesleyan University, One Ames Plaza, Bloomington, IL, 61701-7188. Tel: 309-556-3172. p. 543

Ritter, Marian, Head Music Libr, Western Washington University, 516 High St, MS 9103, Bellingham, WA, 98225. Tel: 630-650-3696. p. 2358

Ritter, Vern, Chief Financial Officer, LYRASIS, 1438 W Peachtree St NW, Ste 150, Atlanta, GA, 30309. Tel: 800-999-8558, Ext 4828. p. 2764

Ritter, William, Dir, Greensboro College, 815 W Market St, Greensboro, NC, 27401. Tel: 336-272-7102, Ext 5734. p. 1692

Rittgers, Melinda, Univ Archivist, Baker University, 518 Eighth St, Baldwin City, KS, 66006. Tel: 785-594-8380. p. 797

Rittner, Stephen, Librn, Rittners School of Floral Design Library, 345 Marlborough St, Boston, MA, 02115. Tel: 617-267-3824. p. 999

Ritzert, Lindsey A, Head, Circ Serv, University of Central Florida Libraries, 12701 Pegasus Dr, Orlando, FL, 32816-8030. Tel: 407-823-2527. p. 432

Riva, Pat, Assoc Univ Librn, Coll & Serv, Concordia University Libraries, 1400 de Maisonneuve Blvd W, LB 2, Montreal, QC, H3G 1M8, CANADA. Tel: 514-848-2424, Ext 5255. p. 2723

Rivard, Bernadette D, Dir, Bellingham Public Library, 100 Blackstone St, Bellingham, MA, 02019. Tel: 508-966-1660. p. 988

Rivard, Timothy, Dir, Learning Serv, MassBay Community College, 50 Oakland St, Wellesley, MA, 02481. Tel: 781-239-2631. p. 1063

Rivas, Claudia, Librn, Rio Hondo College Library, 3600 Workman Mill Rd, 2nd Flr, Whittier, CA, 90601. Tel: 562-908-3378. p. 259

Rivas, Vianela, Libr Mgr, New York Public Library - Astor, Lenox & Tilden Foundations, Washington Heights Branch, 1000 St Nicholas Ave, (@ W 160th St), New York, NY, 10032-5202. Tel: 212-923-6054. p. 1598

Rivera, Amanda, ILL Spec, Midwestern State University, 3410 Taft Blvd, Wichita Falls, TX, 76308-2099. Tel: 940-397-4757. p. 2257

Rivera, Andrew, Dir, Libr Serv, St Philip's College, 1801 Martin Luther King Dr, San Antonio, TX, 78203-2098. Tel: 210-486-2330. p. 2238

Rivera, Angel, Coordr, Info Literacy, Berea College, 100 Campus Dr, Berea, KY, 40404. Tel: 859-985-3372. p. 849

Rivera Caraballos, Melva L, Interim Libr Dir, Universidad del Turabo, Rd 189 Km 3.3, Gurabo, PR, 00778. Tel: 787-743-7979, Ext 4501. p. 2511

Rivera, Daniel, Textbook Services Mgr, University of Wisconsin-River Falls, 410 S Third St, River Falls, WI, 54022. Tel: 715-425-4721. p. 2474

Rivera, Deanna, Dir, Human Res, Somerset County Library System of New Jersey, One Vogt Dr, Bridgewater, NJ, 08807-2136. Tel: 908-458-8407. p. 1392

Rivera, Destiny, Access & Info Serv Librn, Menlo College, 1000 El Camino Real, Atherton, CA, 94027. Tel: 650-543-3826. p. 118

Rivera, Dorothy, Mgr, Res, The Mary Baker Eddy Library, Research & Reference Services, 210 Massachusetts Ave, P04-10, Boston, MA, 02115-3017. Tel: 617-450-7002. p. 994

Rivera, Elizabeth, Archives, Spec Coll Librn, Lipscomb University, One University Park Dr, Nashville, TN, 37204-3951. Tel: 615-966-6033. p. 2119

Rivera, Felix A, Ref & Flm Librn, Hunter College Libraries, Centro - Center for Puerto Rican Studies Library, 2180 Third Ave, Rm 121, New York, NY, 10035. Tel: 212-396-7880. p. 1588

Rivera González, Juliemar, Auxiliary Librarian, Evangelical Seminary of Puerto Rico, 776 Ponce de Leon Ave, San Juan, PR, 00925-9907. Tel: 787-763-6700. p. 2513

Rivera, Graciela, Br Mgr, Hartford Public Library, Park, 744 Park St, Hartford, CT, 06106. Tel: 860-695-7500. p. 318

Rivera, Harold, Library Contact, Almena City Library, 415 Main, Almena, KS, 67622. Tel: 785-669-2336. p. 795

Rivera, Jose, Mgr, County of Los Angeles Public Library, Cudahy Library, 5218 Santa Ana St, Cudahy, CA, 90201-6098. Tel: 323-771-1345. p. 135

Rivera, Katja, Curator, Colorado Springs Fine Arts Center Library, 30 W Dale St, Colorado Springs, CO, 80903. Tel: 719-477-4323. p. 270

Rivera, Kim, Chair, Dermott O'Toole Memorial Library, 707 W Tenakee Ave, Tenakee Springs, AK, 99841. Tel: 907-736-2248. p. 52

Rivera, Liza, Ref Serv, Los Alamos County Library System, 2400 Central Ave, Los Alamos, NM, 87544. Tel: 505-662-8240. p. 1472

Rivera, Liza, Dir, Boricua College, 3755 Broadway, New York, NY, 10032. Tel: 212-694-1000, Ext 335. p. 1580

Rivera, Melissa, Per, Manchester Community College Library, Great Path, Manchester, CT, 06040. Tel: 860-512-2884. p. 320

Rivera, Mildred I, Dir, Med Libr, Universidad Central Del Caribe, Avenida Laurel, Santa Juanita, Bayamon, PR, 00956. Tel: 787-798-3001, Ext 2305. p. 2510

Rivera, Nicole, Pub Serv Librn, Cedar Crest College, 100 College Dr, Allentown, PA, 18104-6196. Tel: 610-606-4666, Ext 3387. p. 1904

Rivera, Raven, Children's Serv Coordr, McBride Memorial Library, 500 N Market St, Berwick, PA, 18603. Tel: 570-752-2241, Ext 206. p. 1910

Rivera-Negron, Veronica, Mgr, Ch & Youth Serv, Takoma Park Maryland Library, 7505 New Hampshire Ave, Ste 205, Takoma Park, MD, 20912. Tel: 301-891-7259. p. 979

Rivera-Sierra, Ismael, Dir, St John's University Library, Kathryn & Shelby Cullom Davis Library, 101 Astor Pl, 2nd Flr, New York, NY, 10003. Tel: 212-277-5135. p. 1556

Rivers, Claudia, Head, Spec Coll, University of Texas at El Paso Library, 500 W University Ave, El Paso, TX, 79968-0582. Tel: 915-747-6725. p. 2175

Rivers, David, Dir, Pub Info & Commun Outreach, Medical University of South Carolina Libraries, 171 Ashley Ave, Ste 419, Charleston, SC, 29425-0001. Tel: 843-792-5546. p. 2051

Rivers, Jan, Dir, Dorsey & Whitney, 50 S Sixth St, Minneapolis, MN, 55402. Tel: 612-340-2600. p. 1183

Rivers-Moore, Agnes, Chief Exec Officer, Chief Librn, Hanover Public Library, 451 Tenth Ave, Hanover, ON, N4N 2P1, CANADA. Tel: 519-364-1420. p. 2647

Riviere, Sharon, Librn, Rideau Lakes Public Library, Portland Branch, 2792 Hwy 15, Portland, ON, K0G 1V0, CANADA. Tel: 613-272-2832. p. 2640

Rixon, Jennifer, Supvr, Circ, Wellesley Free Library, 530 Washington St, Wellesley, MA, 02482. Tel: 781-235-1610, Ext 1131. p. 1064

Rizvi, Ahtasham, Coll Develop Librn, Sheridan College Library, 1430 Trafalgar Rd, Oakville, ON, L6H 2L1, CANADA. Tel: 905-845-9430, Ext 2495. p. 2663

Rizzo, Carl, Cat, Rider University, 2083 Lawrenceville Rd, Lawrenceville, NJ, 08648, p. 1411

Rizzo, Gaye, Dir, Windsor Public Library, 323 Broad St, Windsor, CT, 06095. Tel: 860-285-1912. p. 348

Rizzo, Leda, Libr Tech, Central New Mexico Community College Libraries, 525 Buena Vista SE, Albuquerque, NM, 87106-4023. Tel: 505-224-4000, Ext 52538. p. 1460

Rizzo, Linda, Librn, Buffalo & Erie County Public Library System, Frank E Merriweather Jr Library, 1324 Jefferson Ave, Buffalo, NY, 14208. Tel: 716-883-4418. p. 1508

Rizzo, Linda, Librn, Buffalo & Erie County Public Library System, Isaias Gonzalez-Soto Branch Library, 280 Porter Ave, Buffalo, NY, 14201-1030. Tel: 716-882-1537. p. 1508

Roach, Brenda, Libr Supvr, Lindenwold Public Library, 310 E Linden Ave, Lindenwold, NJ, 08021. Tel: 856-784-5602. p. 1412

Roach, Deneen, Librn, Mather Memorial Library, 23866 Rte 220, Ulster, PA, 18850. Tel: 570-358-3595. p. 2014

Roach, Julie, Mgr, Youth Serv, Cambridge Public Library, 449 Broadway, Cambridge, MA, 02138. Tel: 617-349-4041. p. 1004

Roach, Mary, Exec Assoc Dean, University of Kansas Libraries, 1425 Jayhawk Blvd, Lawrence, KS, 66045-7544. p. 819

Roach, Melissa, Library Contact, Colusa County Free Library, Princeton Branch, 232 Prince St, Princeton, CA, 95970. Tel: 530-439-2235. p. 131

Roache, Andrew, Assoc Law Librn, Maine State Law & Legislative Reference Library, 43 State House Sta, Augusta, ME, 04333-0043. Tel: 207-287-1600. p. 914

Roache, James, Curator, Canton Historical Society Library, 1400 Washington St, Canton, MA, 02021. Tel: 781-615-9040. p. 1009

Roadpouch, Marlene, Dir, Mineral City Nicole Donant Library, 8503 N High St, Mineral City, OH, 44656. Tel: 330-859-9100. p. 1803

Roane, Mandy, Dir, Marfa Public Library, 115 E Oak St, Marfa, TX, 79843. Tel: 432-729-4631. p. 2215

Roane, Sherry, Librn, Buncombe County Public Libraries, West Asheville, 942 Haywood Rd, Asheville, NC, 28806. Tel: 828-250-4750. p. 1672

Roane, Teresa, Archivist, United Daughters of the Confederacy, 328 N Arthur Ashe Blvd, Richmond, VA, 23220-4009. Tel: 804-355-1636. p. 2342

Roark, Barbara, Asst Dir, Hancock County Public Library, 900 W McKenzie Rd, Greenfield, IN, 46140-1741. Tel: 317-462-5141. p. 688

Roark, Christy, Dir, Waveland-Brown Township Public Library, 115 E Green, Waveland, IN, 47989. Tel: 765-435-2700. p. 725

Roark, Joan, Cat, Rainbow City Public Library, 3702 Rainbow Dr, Rainbow City, AL, 35906. Tel: 256-442-8477. p. 33

Roark, Nancy, Regional Libr Dir, Tennessee State Library & Archives, 403 Seventh Ave N, Nashville, TN, 37243-0312. Tel: 615-741-2764. p. 2121

Rob, MacKenzie, Libr Tech, Capital Health/Nova Scotia Hospital, Hugh Bell Bldg, Rm 200, 300 Pleasant St, Dartmouth, NS, B2Y 3Z9, CANADA. Tel: 902-464-3255. p. 2617

Roba, Kaiden, Libr Support Serv Asst, Blue Mountain Community College Library, 2411 NW Carden Ave, Pendleton, OR, 97801. Tel: 541-278-5915. p. 1890

Robarts, Barbara R, Dir, William D Weeks Memorial Library, 128 Main St, Lancaster, NH, 03584-3031. Tel: 603-788-3352. p. 1370

Robayo, Jessica, Ch Serv, Flagler County Public Library, 2500 Palm Coast Pkwy NW, Palm Coast, FL, 32137. Tel: 386-446-6763. p. 434

Robb, Carol Ann, Head, Adult Serv, Pittsburg Public Library, 308 N Walnut, Pittsburg, KS, 66762-4732. Tel: 620-230-5568. p. 831

Robb, Carrie, Head, Coll Serv, Head, Syst Admin, Alexandrian Public Library, 115 W Fifth St, Mount Vernon, IN, 47620. Tel: 812-838-3286. p. 708

Robb, Jen, ILL, Brooks Memorial Library, 224 Main St, Brattleboro, VT, 05301. Tel: 802-254-5290. p. 2280

Robb, Jenny E, Curator, Ohio State University LIBRARIES, Billy Ireland Cartoon Library & Museum, 27 W 17th Ave Mall, Columbus, OH, 43210-1393. Tel: 614-292-0538. p. 1775

Robb, Joan, Asst Dir, Coll Develop & Mgt Librn, University of Wisconsin-Green Bay, 2420 Nicolet Dr, Green Bay, WI, 54311-7001. Tel: 920-465-2384. p. 2439

Robb, Laurie, Librn, Rowan-Cabarrus Community College, South Campus, 1531 Trinity Church Rd, Concord, NC, 28027. Tel: 704-216-3681. p. 1715

Robb, Marilynn, Br Mgr, Georgetown County Library, Carvers Bay, 13048 Choppee Rd, Hemingway, SC, 29554-3318. Tel: 843-545-3515. p. 2060

Robbeloth, Hilary, Discovery Librn, Syst, University of Puget Sound, 1604 N Warner St, Upper Loading Dock, Tacoma, WA, 98416. Tel: 253-879-3677. p. 2387

Robben, Krista, Libr Dir, Maria College Library, 700 New Scotland Ave, Albany, NY, 12208. Tel: 518-861-2515. p. 1482

Robbins, Angie, Dir, Waucoma Public Library, 103 First Ave SW, Waucoma, IA, 52171. Tel: 563-776-4042. p. 789

Robbins, Ann, Circ, Northwest Regional Library System, 898 W 11th St, Panama City, FL, 32401. Tel: 850-522-2100. p. 435

Robbins, Anna, Electronic Serv Librn, Essentia Institute of Rural Health, Essentia Health St Mary's Medical Center, 407 E Third St, Duluth, MN, 55805-1984. Tel: 218-786-5488. p. 1172

Robbins, Annette, Libr Dir, Bovina Public Library, 33 Maple Ave, Bovina Center, NY, 13740. Tel: 607-832-4884. p. 1496

Robbins, Diane, Exec Dir, Bartholomew County Historical Society, 524 Third St, 2nd Flr, Columbus, IN, 47201. Tel: 812-372-3541. p. 676

Robbins, Jan, Br Mgr, El Dorado County Library, El Dorado Hills Branch, 7455 Silva Valley Pkwy, El Dorado Hills, CA, 95762. Tel: 916-358-3500. p. 195

Robbins, Joan, Circ Supvr, New Bern-Craven County Public Library, 400 Johnson St, New Bern, NC, 28560-4098. Tel: 252-638-7800. p. 1706

Robbins, Kathy, Librn, Quatrefoil Library, 1220 E Lake St, Minneapolis, MN, 55407. Tel: 612-729-2543. p. 1184

Robbins, Kim, Circ Librn, Middlesex Community College, Academic Resources Bldg 1A, 591 Springs Rd, Bedford, MA, 01730. Tel: 781-280-3708. p. 988

Robbins, Kim, Circ Librn, Middlesex Community College, Federal Bldg, E Merrimack St, Lowell, MA, 01852. Tel: 978-656-3005. p. 1029

Robbins, Lee, Head Librn, University of Toronto Libraries, Astronomy & Astrophysics Library, 60 St George St, Rm 1306, Toronto, ON, M5S 3H8, CANADA. Tel: 416-978-4268. p. 2698

Robbins, Lucy, Asst Dir, Access & Technical Servs, Loyola University Chicago Libraries, School of Law Library, Philip H Corboy Law Ctr, 25 E Pearson St, Chicago, IL, 60611. Tel: 312-915-7198. p. 564

Robbins, Miranda, Access Serv Librn, Alamo Colleges District, 1201 Kitty Hawk Rd, Universal City, TX, 78148. Tel: 210-486-5466. p. 2250

Robbins, Molly, Asst Dir, Ossining Public Library, 53 Croton Ave, Ossining, NY, 10562. Tel: 914-941-2416. p. 1613

Robbins, Patrick Randall, Dir, Libr Serv, Bob Jones University, 1700 Wade Hampton Blvd, Greenville, SC, 29614. Tel: 864-370-1800, Ext 6015. p. 2060

Robbins, Sarah, Mgr Strategic Research, Sr Dir, University of Oklahoma Libraries, 401 W Brooks St, Norman, OK, 73019. Tel: 405-325-3341. p. 1856

Robbins-Gigee, Tiffany, Dir, Spalding Memorial Library, 724 S Main St, Athens, PA, 18810-1010. Tel: 570-888-7117. p. 1908

Roberge, Kelly, Libr Spec, Yavapai County Free Library District, 1971 Commerce Ctr Circle, Ste D, Prescott, AZ, 86301. Tel: 928-771-3191. p. 74

Roberson, Baronica, Deputy Commissioner for Admin & Finance, Chicago Public Library, 400 S State St, Chicago, IL, 60605. Tel: 312-747-4030. p. 555

Roberson, Caprice, Dir, College of Southern Nevada, Bldg L, 1st Flr, 6375 W Charleston Blvd, Las Vegas, NV, 89146. Tel: 702-651-7693. p. 1346

Roberson, Casey, Res & Instruction Librn, St Lawrence University, 23 Romoda Dr, Canton, NY, 13617. Tel: 315-229-5479. p. 1513

Roberson, Colleen, Library Contact, Hendrick Medical Center, 1900 Pine St, Abilene, TX, 79601. Tel: 325-670-2375. p. 2132

Roberson, Gina, Br Mgr, Santa Clarita Public Library, Old Town Newhall Library, 24500 Main St, Santa Clarita, CA, 91321. p. 242

Roberson, Grace, Librn, Roberts County Library, 122 E Water St, Miami, TX, 79059. Tel: 806-278-8147. p. 2219

Roberson, Jerome, PhD, Fac Mgr, Howard University Libraries, Law Library, 2929 Van Ness St NW, Washington, DC, 20008. Tel: 202-806-8224. p. 369

Roberson, Kip, Libr Dir, Teton County Library, 125 Virginian Lane, Jackson, WY, 83001. Tel: 307-733-2164, Ext 1300. p. 2495

Roberson, Lynette, Dir, Irving Public Library, 801 W Irving Blvd, Irving, TX, 75015. p. 2202

Roberson, Lynette, Libr Mgr, Little Elm Public Library, 100 W Eldorado Pkwy, Little Elm, TX, 75068. Tel: 214-975-0430. p. 2212

Roberson, Pamela, Communications Spec, Department of Veterans Affairs-Memphis, 1030 Jefferson Ave, Memphis, TN, 38104-2193. Tel: 901-523-8990, Ext 5883. p. 2112

Roberson, Sara, Asst Dir, Clay County Public Library, 116 Guffey St, Celina, TN, 38551-9802. Tel: 931-243-3442. p. 2090

Roberson, Todd, Tech Serv, Coastal Plain Regional Library System, 2014 Chestnut Ave, Tifton, GA, 31794. Tel: 229-386-3400. p. 500

Robert, Lindsey, Adult Serv, Lynn Public Library, Five N Common St, Lynn, MA, 01902. Tel: 781-595-0567. p. 1030

Robert, Philip, Br Mgr, Ottawa Public Library/Bibliothèque publique d'Ottawa, Rideau, 377 Rideau St, Ottawa, ON, K1N 5Y6, CANADA. p. 2669

Robert, Philip, Br Mgr, Ottawa Public Library/Bibliothèque publique d'Ottawa, Rockcliffe Park, 380 Springfield Rd, Ottawa, ON, K1M 0K7, CANADA. p. 2669

Robert, Philip, Br Mgr, Ottawa Public Library/Bibliothèque publique d'Ottawa, St-Laurent, 515 Cote St, Ottawa, ON, K1K 0Z0, CANADA. p. 2669

Robert, Philip, Br Mgr, Ottawa Public Library/Bibliothèque publique d'Ottawa, Vanier Branch, 310 Pères Blancs Ave, Ottawa, ON, K1L 7L5, CANADA. p. 2669

Robert, Susan, Head, Circ, Blanding Free Public Library, 124 Bay State Rd, Rehoboth, MA, 02769. Tel: 508-252-4236. p. 1049

Robertelli, Darlene, Dir, Med Libr, Jersey Shore University Medical Center, 1945 Route 33, Neptune, NJ, 07753. Tel: 732-776-4266. p. 1423

Roberto, Bianca, Head, Circ, Baldwin Public Library, 2385 Grand Ave, Baldwin, NY, 11510-3289. Tel: 516-223-6228. p. 1490

Roberts, Aimee, ILL, Council Grove Public Library, 829 W Main St, Council Grove, KS, 66846. Tel: 620-767-5716. p. 803

Roberts, Angie, Dir, Clayton-Liberty Township Public Library, 5199 Iowa St, Clayton, IN, 46118-9174. Tel: 317-539-2991. p. 675

Roberts, Bethany, Teen Prog Coordr, South Hadley Public Library, Two Canal St, South Hadley, MA, 01075. Tel: 413-538-5045. p. 1054

Roberts, Bianca, Asst Dir, Tangipahoa Parish Library, 204 NE Central Ave, Amite, LA, 70422. Tel: 985-748-7559. p. 880

Roberts, Bonnie, Circ Librn, Gallatin County Public Library, 209 W Market St, Warsaw, KY, 41095. Tel: 859-567-7323. p. 876

Roberts, Brandi, Tech Proc Mgr, Cass District Library, 319 M-62 N, Cassopolis, MI, 49031. Tel: 269-533-4793, Ext 104. p. 1089

Roberts, Brent, Dean of Libr, Longwood University, Redford & Race St, Farmville, VA, 23909. p. 2318

Roberts, Bridget, Circ Serv, Spring Green Community Library, 230 E Monroe St, Spring Green, WI, 53588-8035. Tel: 608-588-2276. p. 2478

Roberts, Carly, Archivist, National Gallery of Canada Library & Archives, 380 Sussex Dr, Ottawa, ON, K1N 9N4, CANADA. Tel: 613-714-6000, Ext 6323. p. 2667

Roberts, Carol, Libr Mgr, Apache County Library District, Concho Public, 18 County Rd 5101, Concho, AZ, 85924. Tel: 928-337-2167. p. 76

Roberts, Carol, Head, Youth Serv, Troy Public Library, 100 Second St, Troy, NY, 12180. Tel: 518-274-7071. p. 1653

Roberts, Christine A, Youth Serv Librn, Springfield Township Library, 70 Powell Rd, Springfield, PA, 19064-2446. Tel: 610-543-2113. p. 2009

Roberts, Cynthia, Dir, Libr Serv, Community College of Baltimore County, Y Bldg, 800 S Rolling Rd, Catonsville, MD, 21228. Tel: 443-840-2711. p. 960

Roberts, Dawn, Dir of Coll, Chicago Academy of Sciences/Peggy Notebaert Nature Museum, CAS/PNNM Collections Facility, 4001 N Ravenswood Ave, Ste 201, Chicago, IL, 60613. Tel: 773-755-5100. p. 555

Roberts, Deanna, Ref/Outreach Librn, Emory University Libraries, Pitts Theology Library, Candler School of Theology, 1531 Dickey Dr, Ste 560, Atlanta, GA, 30322-2810. Tel: 404-727-4166. p. 463

Roberts, Donna, Assoc Dean, Humphreys University Library, 6650 Inglewood Ave, Stockton, CA, 95207. Tel: 209-235-2933. p. 249

Roberts, Ellen, Br Mgr, Robinson Public Library District, Susie Wesley Memorial, 105 S Main, Flat Rock, IL, 62427. Tel: 618-584-3636. p. 640

Roberts, Evyan, Coordr, Holy Cross Hospital of Silver Spring, 1500 Forest Glen Rd, Silver Spring, MD, 20910. Tel: 301-754-7987. p. 977

Roberts, Geri, Asst Admin, Beaumont Public Library System, 801 Pearl St, Beaumont, TX, 77701. Tel: 409-981-5911. p. 2145

Roberts, Geri, Asst Admin, Br Mgr, Beaumont Public Library System, Elmo Willard Branch, 3590 E Lucas Dr, Beaumont, TX, 77708. Tel: 409-892-4988. p. 2146

Roberts, Jakob, Libr Asst, Mount Allison University Libraries & Archives, Alfred Whitehead Music Library, 134 Main St, Sackville, NB, E4L 1A6, CANADA. Tel: 506-364-2561. p. 2604

Roberts, Jan, Br Mgr, Franklin Parish Library, Wisner Branch, 129 Fort Scott St, Wisner, LA, 71378. Tel: 318-724-7399. p. 912

Roberts, Janice, Libr Asst, Washington County Public Library, McIntosh Branch, Melva Jean Daughtery Bldg, 83 Olin Rd, McIntosh, AL, 36553. Tel: 251-944-2047. p. 11

Roberts, Jennifer, Head, Children's Servx, Upper Dublin Public Library, 520 Virginia Ave, Fort Washington, PA, 19034. Tel: 215-628-8744. p. 1933

Roberts, Jo Amy, Br Mgr, Mineral County Public Library, St Regis Branch, St Regis Public School Bldg, Six Tiger St, Saint Regis, MT, 59866. Tel: 406-649-2427, Ext 215. p. 1303

Roberts, Joanna, Br Mgr, Nashville Public Library, Z Alexander Looby Branch, 2301 Rosa L Parks Blvd, Nashville, TN, 37228. Tel: 615-862-5867. p. 2120

Roberts, JoDee, Br Mgr, Cameron Parish Library, Grand Lake, 10200 Gulf Hwy, Lake Charles, LA, 70607. Tel: 337-598-5950. p. 886

Roberts, Joel, Dr, Head, Br Libr, Music Librn, University Libraries, University of Memphis, Music Library, Rudi E Scheidt Music Bldg, Rm 115, 3775 Central Ave, Memphis, TN, 38152-3250. Tel: 901-678-4412. p. 2115

Roberts, John, Dir, Kalkaska County Library, 247 S Cedar St, Kalkaska, MI, 49646. Tel: 231-258-9411. p. 1122

Roberts, John, Libr Dir, Wyoming Free Library, 358 Wyoming Ave, Wyoming, PA, 18644-1822. Tel: 570-693-1364. p. 2025

Roberts, Joni R, Assoc Univ Librarian for Collections, Teaching & Research, Willamette University, 900 State St, Salem, OR, 97301. Tel: 503-370-6741. p. 1897

Roberts, Josh, Dir, Univ Libr, University of the Arts University Libraries, Anderson Hall, 1st Flr, 333 S Broad St, Philadelphia, PA, 19102. Tel: 215-717-6244. p. 1988

Roberts, Juanita M, Dir, Libr Serv - Univ Archives & Mus, Tuskegee University, 1200 W Old Mongtomery Rd, Ford Motor Company Library, Tuskegee, AL, 36088. Tel: 334-727-8892. p. 38

Roberts, Kathy, Children's & Youth Serv, Coordr, Central Mississippi Regional Library System, 100 Tamberline St, Brandon, MS, 39042. Tel: 601-825-0100. p. 1212

Roberts, Kelly, Coordr, Ch Serv, New Woodstock Free Library, 2106 Main St, New Woodstock, NY, 13122-8718. Tel: 315-662-3134. p. 1577

Roberts, Kim, Head Librn, Albert L Scott Library, 100 Ninth St NW, Alabaster, AL, 35007-9172. Tel: 205-664-6822. p. 3

Roberts, Kim, Circ Librn, Hamburg Township Library, 10411 Merrill Rd, Hamburg, MI, 48139. Tel: 810-231-1771. p. 1112

Roberts, Kyle, Exec Dir, American Congregational Association, 14 Beacon St, 2nd Flr, Boston, MA, 02108-9999. Tel: 617-523-0470. p. 990

Roberts, Lauren, Libr Dir, Oxford Public Library, 112 Augusta Ave, Oxford, IA, 52322. Tel: 319-828-4087. p. 775

Roberts, Lauren, Mgr, User Serv, Limestone University Library, 1115 College Dr, Gaffney, SC, 29340. Tel: 864-488-4612. p. 2060

Roberts, Lisa, Dean of Libr, Wofford College, 429 N Church St, Spartanburg, SC, 29303-3663. Tel: 864-597-4300. p. 2070

Roberts, Mandie, Dir, Spencer Public Library, 21 E Third St, Spencer, IA, 51301-4131. Tel: 712-580-7290. p. 783

Roberts, Marie, Libr Asst, Gadsden State Community College, Cherokee Center Library, 801 Cedar Bluff Rd, Centre, AL, 35960. Tel: 256-927-1808. p. 18

Roberts, Mark E, PhD, Dean, Learning Res, Oral Roberts University Library, 7777 S Lewis Ave, Tulsa, OK, 74171. Tel: 918-495-6723. p. 1865

Roberts, Meghin, Ch Serv Librn, Baldwinsville Public Library, 33 E Genesee St, Baldwinsville, NY, 13027-2575. Tel: 315-635-5631. p. 1490

Roberts, Morgan, Ref & Instruction Librn, Butler Community College Library & Archives, Library 600 Bldg, 901 S Haverhill Rd, El Dorado, KS, 67042-3280. Tel: 316-323-6843. p. 805

Roberts, Roberta, Head Librn, FPInnovations, 570 Blvd St-Jean, Pointe-Claire, QC, H9R 3J9, CANADA. Tel: 514-630-4100, Option 9. p. 2729

Roberts, Ron, Actg Br Mgr, Cleveland Public Library, Brooklyn, 3706 Pearl Rd, Cleveland, OH, 44109. Tel: 216-623-6920. p. 1768

Roberts, Ryan, Librn, Lincoln Land Community College Library, Sangamon Hall, 5250 Shepherd Rd, Springfield, IL, 62794. Tel: 217-786-2771. p. 650

Roberts, Sally, Tech Serv, United States Geological Survey Library, Mail Stop 150, 12201 Sunrise Valley Dr, Reston, VA, 20192. Tel: 703-648-7182. p. 2340

Roberts, Sara Kate, Ref Librn, United States Army, Redstone Arsenal Family & MWR Library, 3323 Redeye Rd, Redstone Arsenal, AL, 35898. Tel: 256-876-4741. p. 34

Roberts, Sarah, Ref Librn, Abington Public Library, 600 Gliniewicz Way, Abington, MA, 02351. Tel: 781-982-2139. p. 983

Roberts, Sharon A, Asst Dean, Coll Res Mgt, Ball State University Libraries, 2000 W University Ave, Muncie, IN, 47306-1099. Tel: 765-285-1305. p. 708

Roberts, Steve, Circ Mgr, Nova Southeastern University, 3200 S University Dr, Fort Lauderdale, FL, 33328. Tel: 954-262-3110. p. 401

Roberts, Susan, Asst Dir, Wayne County Public Library, 220 W Liberty St, Wooster, OH, 44691. Tel: 330-262-4087. p. 1833

Roberts, Suzanne, Dir, Highland County District Library, Ten Willettsville Pike, Hillsboro, OH, 45133. Tel: 937-393-3114. p. 1789

Roberts, Sylvia, Liaison Librn, Simon Fraser University - Vancouver Campus, 515 W Hastings St, Vancouver, BC, V6B 5K3, CANADA. Tel: 778-782-5050. p. 2579

Roberts, Virginia, Exec Dir, Rhinelander District Library, 106 N Stevens St, Rhinelander, WI, 54501-3193. Tel: 715-365-1070. p. 2472

Roberts, Vivalda, Asst Dir, La Harpe Carnegie Public Library District, 209 E Main St, La Harpe, IL, 61450. Tel: 217-659-7729. p. 606

Roberts, Wendy, Dir, Cushing Public Library, 39 Cross Rd, Cushing, ME, 04563. Tel: 207-354-8860. p. 922

Roberts-Reilley, Jennifer, Resources & Scholarly Comms Librn, Susquehanna University, 514 University Ave, Selinsgrove, PA, 17870-1050. Tel: 570-372-4301. p. 2005

Robertson, Brenda, Librn, University of North Texas Libraries, Dallas Campus Library, 7350 University Hills Blvd, 3rd Flr, Dallas, TX, 75241. Tel: 972-338-1617. p. 2170

Robertson, Brianna, Libr Asst, Mooneyham Public Library, 240 E Main St, Forest City, NC, 28043. Tel: 828-248-5224. p. 1689

Robertson, Catherine, Libr Dir, Montserrat College of Art, 23 Essex St, Beverly, MA, 01915. p. 989

Robertson, Darrell, Br Mgr, Carroll County Public Library, North Carroll, 2255 Hanover Pike, Greenmount, MD, 21074. Tel: 410-386-4480. p. 972

Robertson, Deb, Dir, Kilgore Memorial Library, 520 N Nebraska Ave, York, NE, 68467-3035. Tel: 402-363-2620. p. 1341

Robertson, Debbie, Librn, Chinook Regional Library, Kincaid Branch, Village Office, Dominion Ave, Kincaid, SK, S0H 2J0, CANADA. Tel: 306-264-3910. p. 2752

Robertson, Gina, Adult Serv, Gardendale - Martha Moore Public Library, 995 Mt Olive Rd, Gardendale, AL, 35071. Tel: 205-631-6639. p. 19

Robertson, Ginni, Librn, Independent Presbyterian Church, 3100 Highland Ave S, Birmingham, AL, 35205. Tel: 205-933-1830. p. 8

Robertson, Grant, Br Supvr, Bruce County Public Library, Chesley Branch, 72 Second Ave SE, Chesley, ON, N0G 1L0, CANADA. Tel: 519-363-2239. p. 2673

Robertson, Grant, Br Supvr, Bruce County Public Library, Paisley Branch, 274 Queen St, Paisley, ON, N0G 2N0, CANADA. Tel: 519-353-7225. p. 2674

Robertson, Grant, Br Supvr, Bruce County Public Library, Tara Branch, 67 Yonge St, Tara, ON, N0H 2N0, CANADA. Tel: 519-934-2626. p. 2674

Robertson, Gretchen, Dean of Instruction, Skagit Valley College, 2405 E College Way, Mount Vernon, WA, 98273-5899. Tel: 360-416-7850. p. 2371

Robertson, Holly, Curator, University of Virginia, Albert & Shirley Small Special Collections Library, 170 McCormick Rd, Charlottesville, VA, 22904. Tel: 434-243-1776. p. 2310

Robertson, Jacob, Supvr, Pub Serv, Arizona State University Libraries, Design & Fine Arts, 810 S Forest Mall, CDN 153, Tempe, AZ, 85287. Tel: 480-965-6400. p. 79

Robertson, Jamie, Ch/Children's Serv, Hobbs Public Library, 509 N Shipp St, Hobbs, NM, 88240. Tel: 575-397-9328. p. 1469

Robertson, Jennifer, Dir, Carbondale Public Library, 405 W Main St, Carbondale, IL, 62901-2995. Tel: 618-457-0354. p. 548

Robertson, Jennifer, Librn, University of Toronto Libraries, Noranda Earth Sciences Library, Five Bancroft Ave, 2nd Flr, Room 2091, Toronto, ON, M5S 1A5, CANADA. Tel: 416-978-6673. p. 2699

Robertson, John, Br Supvr, Warren Public Library, Arthur J Miller Branch, 5460 Arden St, Ste 303, Warren, MI, 48092. Tel: 586-751-5377. p. 1157

Robertson, Katherine, Librn, Olmsted Public Library, 160 N Front St, Olmsted, IL, 62970. Tel: 618-742-8296. p. 629

Robertson, Kristin, Br Librn, Bedford Public Library System, Montvale Library, 11575 W Lynchburg-Salem Tpk, Montvale, VA, 24122. Tel: 540-425-7006. p. 2306

Robertson, Kym, Mgr, Alexandria Library, Talking Books, 5005 Duke St, Alexandria, VA, 22304-2903. Tel: 703-746-1760. p. 2302

Robertson, Lorrie, Dir, Cambridge Community Library, 120 S Superior St, Cambridge, ID, 83610. Tel: 208-257-3434. p. 519

Robertson, Lynn, Mr, Libr Spec, University of Kentucky Libraries, Lexmark Library, 740 New Circle Rd NW, Lexington, KY, 40511. Tel: 859-232-3783. p. 863

Robertson, Mark, Univ Librn, Brock University, 1812 Sir Isaac Brock Way, St. Catharines, ON, L2S 3A1, CANADA. Tel: 905-688-5550, Ext 5980. p. 2679

Robertson, Meg, Br Mgr, Ramsey County Library, New Brighton Branch, 400 Tenth St NW, New Brighton, MN, 55112-6806. Tel: 651-724-6050. p. 1204

Robertson, Melinda, Asst Dir, Med Librn, University of Pikeville, 147 Sycamore St, Pikeville, KY, 41501-9118. Tel: 606-218-5157. p. 872

Robertson, Melinda, Asst Library Dir for Health Sciences, Med Librn, University of Pikeville, 147 Sycamore St, Pikeville, KY, 41501. Tel: 606-218-5157. p. 872

Robertson, Michele, Youth Serv Spec, Carlsbad Public Library, 101 S Halagueno St, Carlsbad, NM, 88220. Tel: 575-885-6776. p. 1465

Robertson, Michelle, Systems & Resource Mgmt, Anne Arundel Community College, 101 College Pkwy, Arnold, MD, 21012-1895. Tel: 410-777-2211. p. 951

Robertson, Nathan, Dir, Info Policy & Mgt, University of Maryland, Baltimore, Thurgood Marshall Law Library, 501 W Fayette St, Baltimore, MD, 21201-1768. Tel: 410-706-1213. p. 957

Robertson, R John, Dean of Libr, Seattle Pacific University Library, 3307 Third Ave W, Seattle, WA, 98119. Tel: 206-281-2228. p. 2379

Robertson, Raechael, Br Mgr, Louisville Free Public Library, South Central Regional, 7300 Jefferson Blvd, Louisville, KY, 40219. Tel: 502-964-3515. p. 866

Robertson, Sally, Cat, Ser, Nashville State Technical Community College, 120 White Bridge Rd, Nashville, TN, 37209-4515. Tel: 615-353-3270. p. 2120

Robertson, Sandra, ILL, Chickasha Public Library, 527 W Iowa Ave, Chickasha, OK, 73018. Tel: 405-222-6075. p. 1844

Robertson, Sigrid A, Dir, Leroy Community Library, 104 W Gilbert St, LeRoy, MI, 49655. Tel: 231-768-4493. p. 1127

Robertson, Susan, Librn, Dolores County Public Library, Rico Public, Two N Commercial St, Rico, CO, 81332. Tel: 970-967-2103. p. 278

Robertson, Susie, Br Mgr, Mesa County Public Library District, Orchard Mesa, 230 Lynwood St, Grand Junction, CO, 81503. Tel: 970-243-0181. p. 284

Robertson, Terry, Assoc Dean, Seminary Librarian, Andrews University, 4190 Administration Dr, Berrien Springs, MI, 49104-1400. Tel: 269-471-3269. p. 1085

Robeson, Mary Ann, Libr Mgr, Hudson Yablonski Community Library, 205 Illinois St, Hudson, WY, 82515. Tel: 307-332-5770. p. 2495

Robichaud, Jeremy, Asst Dir, Ref, Maynard Public Library, 77 Nason St, Maynard, MA, 01754-2316. Tel: 978-897-1010. p. 1033

Robichaud, Marie-Josée, Pub Serv, Universite de Moncton, Centre de Ressources Pédagogiques, Pavillon Jeanne-de-Valois, local B-010, 68, rue Notre-Dame-du-Sacré-Coeur, Moncton, NB, E1A 3E9, CANADA. Tel: 506-858-4356. p. 2604

Robichaud, Nadine, Libr Mgr, Chaleur Library Region, Laval-Goupil Public Library, 128 Mgr Chiasson St, Shippagan, NB, E8S 1X7, CANADA. Tel: 506-336-3920. p. 2599

Robichaud, Pierre, Libr Coord, Libr Tech, Administrative Tribunals Support Services of Canada, CD Howe Bldg West Tower, 6th Flr, 240 rue Sparks St 645F, Ottawa, ON, K1A 0E1, CANADA. Tel: 613-990-1809. p. 2664

Robichaud, Stephen, Dir, Pollard Memorial Library, 401 Merrimack St, Lowell, MA, 01852. Tel: 978-674-4120. p. 1029

Robicheau, Rosalie, Libr Asst II, Universite Sainte-Anne, 1695 Hwy 1, Church Point, NS, B0W 1M0, CANADA. Tel: 902-769-2114, Ext 7170. p. 2617

Robicheau, Wendy, Archivist, Acadia University, 50 Acadia St, Wolfville, NS, B4P 2R6, CANADA. Tel: 902-585-1249. p. 2623

Robidoux, Danielle, Br Head, Winnipeg Public Library, St Boniface, 100-131 Provencher Blvd, Winnipeg, MB, R2H 0G2, CANADA. Tel: 204-986-4272. p. 2596

Robillard, Diane, Syst Librn, Chicopee Public Library, 449 Front St, Chicopee, MA, 01013. Tel: 413-594-1800. p. 1011

Robillard, Gail, Libr Spec, Wilshire Boulevard Temple, 3663 Wilshire Blvd (Mid-Wilshire)), Los Angeles, CA, 90010. p. 170
Robins, David, Dr, Assoc Prof, Kent State University, 314 University Library, 1125 Risman Dr, Kent, OH, 44242-0001. Tel: 330-672-2782. p. 2790
Robins, Judith, Registrar, Wood Library-Museum of Anesthesiology, 1061 American Lane, Schaumburg, IL, 60173. Tel: 847-268-9168. p. 645
Robins, Kathy, Syst Adminr, Billings Public Library, 510 N Broadway, Billings, MT, 59101. Tel: 406-657-8258. p. 1288
Robins, Sharani, Ref Librn, Dartmouth Public Libraries, 732 Dartmouth St, Dartmouth, MA, 02748. Tel: 508-999-0726. p. 1013
Robins, Simon, Ref Librn, Northeast Ohio Medical University, 4209 State Rte 44, Rootstown, OH, 44272. Tel: 330-325-6378. p. 1818
Robinson, Alan, Dir, Jamaica Public Library, 316 Main St, Jamaica, IA, 50128. Tel: 641-429-3362. p. 761
Robinson, Alan M, Historian, James E Whalley Museum & Library, 351 Middle St, Portsmouth, NH, 03801. Tel: 603-436-3712. p. 1379
Robinson, Alexis, ILL Spec, Midwestern State University, 3410 Taft Blvd, Wichita Falls, TX, 76308-2099. Tel: 940-397-4171. p. 2257
Robinson, Alfenette, Br Mgr, Jackson/Hinds Library System, Annie Thompson Jeffers Library, 111 Madison St, Bolton, MS, 39041. Tel: 601-866-4247. p. 1221
Robinson, Allison, Br Mgr, Hightower Sara Regional Library, Cedartown Branch, 245 East Ave, City Complex, Cedartown, GA, 30125-3001. Tel: 770-748-5644. p. 494
Robinson, Alvin R, Libr Assoc, Atlanta-Fulton Public Library System, Auburn Avenue Research Library on African-American Culture & History, 101 Auburn Ave NE, Atlanta, GA, 30303-2503. Tel: 404-613-4001. p. 461
Robinson, Alyce, Youth Serv, North Scituate Public Library, 606 W Greenville Rd, North Scituate, RI, 02857. Tel: 401-647-5133. p. 2036
Robinson, Andrea, Ch, Atlanta-Fulton Public Library System, Hapeville Branch, 525 King Arnold St, Hapeville, GA, 30354. Tel: 404-762-4065. p. 461
Robinson, Annette, Supvr, Circ, Elko-Lander-Eureka County Library System, 720 Court St, Elko, NV, 89801. Tel: 775-738-3066. p. 1344
Robinson, Ashley, Library Contact, Chillicothe & Ross County Public Library, 841 E Main St, Chillicothe, OH, 45601. Tel: 740-702-4145. p. 1758
Robinson, Barbara, Br Mgr, Nicholson Memorial Library System, North Garland Branch, 3845 N Garland Ave, Garland, TX, 75040. Tel: 972-205-2803. p. 2184
Robinson, Ben, Children & Teen Librn, Guelph Public Library, 100 Norfolk St, Guelph, ON, N1H 4J6, CANADA. Tel: 519-824-6220, Ext 277. p. 2643
Robinson, Beth, Youth Serv Librn, Exeter Public Library, 773 Ten Rod Rd, Exeter, RI, 02822. Tel: 401-294-4109. p. 2032
Robinson, Bill, Presv Librn, Delaware Historical Society Research Library, 505 N Market St, Wilmington, DE, 19801. Tel: 302-655-7161. p. 357
Robinson, Camille, Asst Dir, Rosebud County Library, Bicentennial Library of Colstrip, 419 Willow Ave, Colstrip, MT, 59323. Tel: 406-748-3040. p. 1293
Robinson, Chad, Ad, Matheson Memorial Library, 101 N Wisconsin, Elkhorn, WI, 53121. Tel: 262-723-2678. p. 2433
Robinson, Chad, Dir, Matheson Memorial Library, 101 N Wisconsin, Elkhorn, WI, 53121. Tel: 262-723-2678. p. 2433
Robinson, Cherie, Dir, Jackson County Memorial Library, 411 N Wells St, Rm 121, Edna, TX, 77957-2734. Tel: 361-782-2162. p. 2173
Robinson, Courtney, Libr Mgr, Fraser Valley Regional Library, Ladner Pioneer Library, 4683 - 51st St, Delta, BC, V4K 2V8, CANADA. Tel: 604-946-6215. p. 2561
Robinson, Courtney, Libr Mgr, Fraser Valley Regional Library, George Mackie Library, 8440 112th St, Delta, BC, V4C 4W9, CANADA. Tel: 604-594-8155. p. 2562
Robinson, Courtney, Libr Mgr, Fraser Valley Regional Library, Tsawwassen Library, 1321A 56th St, Delta, BC, V4L 2A6, CANADA. Tel: 604-943-2271. p. 2562
Robinson, Cyndee, Tech Serv Librn, San Joaquin College of Law Library, 901 Fifth St, Clovis, CA, 93612. Tel: 559-323-2100, Ext 121. p. 131
Robinson, David, Ad, Shenandoah County Library, 514 Stoney Creek Blvd, Edinburg, VA, 22824. Tel: 540-984-8200. p. 2315
Robinson, Deborah, Librn, Coastal Alabama Community College, Kathryn Tucker Windham Library & Museum, 30755 Hwy 43, Thomasville, AL, 36784-2519. Tel: 334-637-3146. p. 6
Robinson, Dee, Mgr, Richland Library, North Main, 5306 N Main St, Columbia, SC, 29203-6114. Tel: 803-754-7734. p. 2054
Robinson, Denise, Dir, Brownsburg Public Library, 450 S Jefferson St, Brownsburg, IN, 46112-1310. Tel: 317-852-3167. p. 673
Robinson, Denise K, Head Librn, Central Carolina Technical College Library, 506 N Guignard Dr, Sumter, SC, 29150. Tel: 803-778-7851. p. 2071
Robinson, Eric, Dir, Fairfield County Library, 300 W Washington St, Winnsboro, SC, 29180. Tel: 803-635-4971. p. 2072
Robinson, Eric, Dir, Dwight Foster Public Library, 209 Merchants Ave, Fort Atkinson, WI, 53538-2049. Tel: 920-563-7790. p. 2435
Robinson, Erik, Archivist, Florida Supreme Court Library, 500 S Duval St, Tallahassee, FL, 32399-1926. Tel: 850-488-8919. p. 447
Robinson, Erin, Dir, Cordelia A Greene Library, 11 S Main St, Castile, NY, 14427. Tel: 585-493-5466. p. 1514
Robinson, Guffie, Operations Supvr, Texas State Library & Archives Commission, 1201 Brazos St, Austin, TX, 78701. Tel: 512-463-5458. p. 2141
Robinson, Heather, Chief Exec Officer, St Thomas Public Library, 153 Curtis St, St. Thomas, ON, N5P 3Z7, CANADA. Tel: 519-631-6050, Ext 8027. p. 2681
Robinson, Heidi, Dir, Wimodaughsian Free Library, 19 W Main St, Canisteo, NY, 14823-1005. Tel: 607-698-4445. p. 1513
Robinson, Jennifer, Tech Serv Librn, Averett University Library, 344 W Main St, Danville, VA, 24541-2849. Tel: 434-791-5693. p. 2314
Robinson, Jennifer, Dep Chief Librn, Western University Libraries, 1151 Richmond St, Ste 200, London, ON, N6A 3K7, CANADA. Tel: 519-661-2111, Ext 86897. p. 2655
Robinson, Jontyule, Dr, Curator, Tuskegee University, 1200 W Old Mongtomery Rd, Ford Motor Company Library, Tuskegee, AL, 36088. Tel: 334-727-8888. p. 38
Robinson, Joy, Ad, Piscataway Township Free Public Library, 500 Hoes Lane, Piscataway, NJ, 08854. Tel: 732-463-1633. p. 1435
Robinson, Julia, Ref Librn, Ohio University-Lancaster Library, 1570 Granville Pike, Lancaster, OH, 43130-1097. Tel: 740-681-3348. p. 1794
Robinson, Kara L, Assoc Dean, Kent State University Libraries, Risman Plaza, 1125 Risman Dr, Kent, OH, 44242. Tel: 330-672-1664. p. 1792
Robinson, Kathy, Youth Librn, Pittsfield Public Library, 205 N Memorial St, Pittsfield, IL, 62363-1406. Tel: 217-285-2200. p. 635
Robinson, Keitha, Librn, Houston Community College - Southeast College, Eastside Campus Library, 6815 Rustic St, Houston, TX, 77087. Tel: 713-718-7050. p. 2194
Robinson, Ken, Br Mgr, Athens County Public Libraries, The Plains Public, 14 S Plains Rd, The Plains, OH, 45780. Tel: 740-797-4579. p. 1805
Robinson, Kishier, Br Mgr, Morehouse Parish Library, Dunbar, 1102 Perry St, Bastrop, LA, 71220. Tel: 318-281-1137. p. 882
Robinson, Krista, Actg Chief Exec Officer, Syst Librn, Stratford Public Library, 19 Saint Andrew St, Stratford, ON, N5A 1A2, CANADA. Tel: 519-271-0220, Ext 112. p. 2682
Robinson, Kristine, Admin Librn, Instrul Librn, Belmont Abbey College, 100 Belmont-Mt Holly Rd, Belmont, NC, 28012. Tel: 704-461-6748. p. 1674
Robinson, Lauren, Ref Librn, Sandwich Public Library, 142 Main St, Sandwich, MA, 02563. Tel: 508-888-0625. p. 1052
Robinson, Lauren, Dir, Preble County District Library, 450 S Barron St, Eaton, OH, 45320-2402. Tel: 937-456-4250. p. 1784
Robinson, Lauren, Dir, Preble County District Library, Library Administration & Resource Center, 450 S Barron St, Eaton, OH, 45320-2402. Tel: 937-456-4520. p. 1784
Robinson, Leigh, Supvr, Middlesex County Library, Lucan Branch, 270 Main St, Lucan, ON, N0M 2J0, CANADA. Tel: 519-227-4682. p. 2682
Robinson, Lyndsey, Asst Librarian I, Adult Services, Ledyard Public Library, Gales Ferry Library, 18 Hurlbutt Rd, Gales Ferry, CT, 06335. Tel: 860-464-9912. p. 320
Robinson, Lyndsie, Info Literacy & Instructional Librn, Hartwick College, One Hartwick Dr, Oneonta, NY, 13820. Tel: 607-431-4475. p. 1611
Robinson, Margaret (Bess), Head, Res & Instrul Serv, University Libraries, University of Memphis, 3785 Norriswood Ave, Memphis, TN, 38152. Tel: 901-678-8214. p. 2115
Robinson, Mark, Libr Operations Asst, Riverside Community College District, 16130 Lasselle St, Moreno Valley, CA, 92551. Tel: 951-571-6356. p. 181
Robinson, Marline C, Coordr, Josey Health Sciences Library, Prisma Health Richland, Five Richland Medical Park, Columbia, SC, 29203. Tel: 803-434-6312. p. 2053
Robinson, Mary M, Dir, Buffalo Bill Historical Center, 720 Sheridan Ave, Cody, WY, 82414. Tel: 307-578-4063. p. 2493
Robinson, Melissa, Ch Serv, Bloomington Public Library, 205 E Olive St, Bloomington, IL, 61701. Tel: 309-828-6091. p. 543
Robinson, Mike, Head, Libr Syst, University of Alaska Anchorage, Consortium Library, 3211 Providence Dr, Anchorage, AK, 99508-8176. Tel: 907-786-1001. p. 43
Robinson, Mike, Ref & ILL Librn, US Department of Commerce, 325 Broadway, R/ESRL5, Boulder, CO, 80305-3328. Tel: 303-497-3271. p. 267
Robinson, Nicole, Dep Dir, Houston Public Library, 500 McKinney Ave, Houston, TX, 77002-2534. Tel: 832-393-1313. p. 2195
Robinson, Nydia, Head, Patron Serv, Morris Area Public Library District, 604 Liberty St, Morris, IL, 60450. Tel: 815-942-6880. p. 619
Robinson, Pamela J, Librn, Hunterdon County Historical Society, 114 Main St, Flemington, NJ, 08822. Tel: 908-782-1091. p. 1403
Robinson, Pasha Moncrief, Br Mgr, Cleveland Public Library, Fleet, 7224 Broadway Ave, Cleveland, OH, 44105. Tel: 216-623-6962, p. 1768
Robinson, Paula, Ref & Document Delivery Librn, Duke University Libraries, Ford Library, 100 Fuqua Dr, Durham, NC, 27708. Tel: 919-660-7942. p. 1684
Robinson, Robbie, Br Mgr, Middle Georgia Regional Library System, Marshallville Public Library, 106 Camellia Blvd, Marshallville, GA, 31057. Tel: 478-967-2413. p. 487

Robinson, Shannon, Head of Libr, University of Southern California Libraries, Helen Topping Architecture & Fine Arts Library, Watt Hall Rm 4, Los Angeles, CA, 90089-0182. Tel: 213-740-1956. p. 170
Robinson, Shirley, Exec Dir, Texas Council of Academic Libraries, VC/UHV Library, 2602 N Ben Jordan, Victoria, TX, 77901. Tel: 361-570-4150. p. 2775
Robinson, Sue, Dir, Galien Township Public Library, 302 N Main St, Galien, MI, 49113. Tel: 269-545-8281. p. 1108
Robinson, Sue, Dir, Communications, Pub Relations, Virginia Commonwealth University Libraries, 901 Park Ave, Richmond, VA, 23284. Tel: 804-828-0129. p. 2343
Robinson, Susan, Br Mgr, Upper Darby Township & Sellers Memorial Free Public Library, Primos Branch, 409 Ashland Ave, Secane, PA, 19018. Tel: 610-622-8091. p. 2016
Robinson, Suzanne, Dir, Lynn-Washington Township Public Library, 107 N Main St, Lynn, IN, 47355. Tel: 765-874-1488. p. 704
Robinson, Suzanne, Br Mgr, Nashville Public Library, Inglewood Branch, 4312 Gallatin Pike, Nashville, TN, 37216. Tel: 615-862-5866. p. 2119
Robinson, Tammy, Chief Exec Officer, Cobourg Public Library, 200 Ontario St, Cobourg, ON, K9A 5P4, CANADA. Tel: 905-372-9271, Ext 6200. p. 2636
Robinson, Tayce, Dir, Burley Public Library, 1300 Miller Ave, Burley, ID, 83318-1729. Tel: 208-878-7708. p. 518
Robinson, Taylor, Libr Dir, NIH, National Institute of Allergy & Infectious Diseases, 903 S Fourth St, Hamilton, MT, 59840-2932. p. 1295
Robinson, Terri, Exec Dir, Northeast Ohio Medical University, 4209 State Rte 44, Rootstown, OH, 44272. Tel: 330-325-6600. p. 1818
Robinson, Tracey D, Asst Libr Dir, Tarrant County College, Bldg ESED 1200, 2100 Southeast Pkwy, Arlington, TX, 76018. Tel: 817-515-3082. p. 2136
Robinson, Tracy, Pub Relations Coordr, Salem-South Lyon District Library, 9800 Pontiac Trail, South Lyon, MI, 48178-7021. Tel: 248-437-6431. p. 1151
Robinson, Trina, Asst Dir, Info Resources Mgmt Services, George Washington University, Jacob Burns Law Library, 716 20th St NW, Washington, DC, 20052. Tel: 202-994-8550. p. 367
Robinson, Will, Dir, Granville County Library System, 210 Main St, Oxford, NC, 27565-3321. Tel: 919-693-1121. p. 1707
Robison, Kim, Youth Serv, Barry-Lawrence Regional Library, Miller Branch, 112 E Main St, Miller, MO, 65707. Tel: 417-452-3466. p. 1263
Robison, Louisa, Chief Exec Officer, Peace Library System, 8301 110 St, Grande Prairie, AB, T8W 6T2, CANADA. Tel: 780-538-4656. p. 2541
Robison, Richard, Dean of Libr, Diablo Valley College Library, 321 Golf Club Rd, Pleasant Hill, CA, 94523-1576. Tel: 925-969-2610. p. 195
Robison, Sharon, Libr Dir, Thelma Dingus Bryant Library, 409 W Main St, Wallace, NC, 28466-2909. Tel: 910-285-3796. p. 1720
Robitaille, Anne, Tech Serv, Institut National de la Recherche Scientifique, 490 de la Couronne, Quebec, QC, G1K 9A9, CANADA. Tel: 418-654-2588. p. 2731
Robitaille, Patricia, Dir, Bibliothèque Raymond-Laberge, 25 Maple Blvd, Chateauguay, QC, J6J 3P7, CANADA. Tel: 450-698-3080. p. 2710
Robitaille, Suzanne, Vols Coordr, Paso Robles City Library, 1000 Spring St, Paso Robles, CA, 93446-2207. Tel: 805-237-3870. p. 194
Robling, Cathy, Dir, Free Methodist Church - USA, 5235 Decatur Blvd, Indianapolis, IN, 46241. Tel: 317-244-3660. p. 692
Roblyer, Cheryl Sue, Dir, Taylor Public Library, PO Box 207, Taylor, NE, 68879-0207. Tel: 308-346-4395. p. 1338
Robson, Ian, Head, Coll Develop, University of Waterloo Library, 200 University Ave W, Waterloo, ON, N2L 3G1, CANADA. Tel: 519-888-4567, Ext 41586. p. 2702
Roby, Megan, Develop Dir, Cleve J Fredricksen Library, 100 N 19th St, Camp Hill, PA, 17011-3900. Tel: 717-761-3900, Ext 244. p. 1918
Roby, Tameka, Outreach Serv, East Baton Rouge Parish Library, 7711 Goodwood Blvd, Baton Rouge, LA, 70806-7625. Tel: 225-231-3710. p. 882
Roccanti, Kim, Youth Serv Librn, Lake County Library System, Cagan Crossings Community Library, 16729 Cagan Oaks, Clermont, FL, 34714. Tel: 352-243-1840. p. 450
Rocchio, Avelina, Libr Mgr, Community Libraries of Providence, Washington Park Library, 1316 Broad St, Providence, RI, 02905. Tel: 401-781-3136. p. 2038
Rocchio, Mary, Library Contact, East West Gateway Council of Governments Library, One Memorial Dr, Ste 1600, Saint Louis, MO, 63102. Tel: 314-421-4220, Ext 201. p. 1270
Rocco, Brian, Libr Dir, Marymount Manhattan College, 221 E 71st St, New York, NY, 10021. Tel: 212-774-4802. p. 1591
Rocha, Maria, Archives, Fayette Public Library, 855 S Jefferson St, La Grange, TX, 78945. Tel: 979-968-3765. p. 2207
Rocha, Mayra, Libr Dir, Speer Memorial Library, 801 E 12th St, Mission, TX, 78572. Tel: 956-580-8750. p. 2220
Rochat, Julie, Dir, Hamline University, Bush Memorial Library, 1536 Hewitt, Saint Paul, MN, 55104. Tel: 651-523-2375. p. 1199
Rochat, Laura, Librn, Brookfield Free Public Library, 40 Ralph Rd, Brookfield, VT, 05036. Tel: 802-276-3358. p. 2280
Roche, Bernadette, Dir, United States Air Force, Maxwell Gunter Community Library System, MSD/MSEL, 481 Williamson St, Bldg 1110 Gunter Annex, Maxwell AFB, AL, 36114. Tel: 334-416-3179. p. 25
Roché, Carly, Librn, Attorney General's Office, 200 Saint Paul Pl, 18th Flr, Baltimore, MD, 21202. Tel: 410-576-6400. p. 951
Roche, Catherine, Dir, Libr Serv, Braswell Memorial Public Library, 727 N Grace St, Rocky Mount, NC, 27804-4842. Tel: 252-442-1951. p. 1713
Roche, Jill, Mgr, Community Library Network, Athol Branch, 30399 Third St, Athol, ID, 83801. Tel: 208-683-2979. p. 522
Roche, Katie, Dir of Develop, Iowa City Public Library, 123 S Linn St, Iowa City, IA, 52240. Tel: 319-356-5249. p. 760
Roche, Mary Beth, Libr Dir, Lackawanna College, 406 N Washington Ave, Scranton, PA, 18503. Tel: 570-504-1589. p. 2004
Roche, Michael, Libr Dir, Rockingham County Public Library, 527 Boone Rd, Eden, NC, 27288. Tel: 336-627-1106. p. 1686
Roche, Phil, Dir, Libr Serv, Brazosport College Library, 500 College Dr, Lake Jackson, TX, 77566. Tel: 979-230-3259. p. 2208
Roche, Philip, Head Librn, Austin Community College, San Gabriel Campus, 449 San Gabriel Campus Dr, 2nd Flr, Rm 1200, Leander, TX, 78641. Tel: 512-223-2564. p. 2138
Rochford-Volk, Jake, Libr Dir, Hawkins Memorial Library, 308 Main St, La Porte City, IA, 50651. Tel: 319-342-3025. p. 763
Rock, Erik, Mgr, Libr Tech, Loveland Public Library, 300 N Adams Ave, Loveland, CO, 80537. Tel: 970-962-2665. p. 290
Rock, Jessica, Libr Dir, Palos Park Public Library, 12330 S Forest Glen Blvd, Palos Park, IL, 60464. Tel: 708-448-1530. p. 632
Rock, Laura, E-Learning Librn, Info Literacy, Misericordia University, 301 Lake St, Dallas, PA, 18612-1098. Tel: 570-674-6351. p. 1925
Rock, Marie-Hélène, Ad, Bibliothèque Municipale de Gatineau, Ville de Gatineau, CP 1970 Succ. Hull, Gatineau, QC, J8X 3Y9, CANADA. Tel: 819-243-2345. p. 2712
Rockafellow, Patty, Dir, White Pine Library, 106 E Walnut, Stanton, MI, 48888-9294. Tel: 989-831-4327. p. 1152
Rockey, Jennifer, Tech Serv Coordr, Eureka College, 301 E College Ave, Eureka, IL, 61530-1563. Tel: 309-467-6380. p. 585
Rockstead, Angela, Libr Asst, Arizona Christian University, One W Firestorm Way, Glendale, AZ, 85306. Tel: 602-386-4117. p. 61
Rockwell, Jenny, Commun Libr Mgr, Contra Costa County Library, Kensington Library, 61 Arlington Ave, Kensington, CA, 94707. Tel: 510-524-3043. p. 174
Rockwell, Maegan, Librn, Dolores County Public Library, 525 N Main St, Dove Creek, CO, 81324. Tel: 970-677-2389. p. 278
Rockwell, Mary Ann, Campus Librn, North Country Community College Libraries, Ticonderoga Campus Library, 11 Hawkeye Trail, Ticonderoga, NY, 12883. Tel: 518-585-4454, Ext 2208. p. 1636
Rockwell-Kincannon, Janeanne, Pub Serv, Western Oregon University, 345 N Monmouth Ave, Monmouth, OR, 97361-1396. Tel: 503-838-9493. p. 1887
Rodarte, Antonio, Pub Serv Librn, El Paso Community College Library, Rio Grande Campus Library, 100 W Rio Grande Ave, Rm E100, El Paso, TX, 79902. Tel: 915-831-4019. p. 2173
Rodarte, Janie, Treas, Westerners International Library, c/o Panhandle-Plains Historical Museum, 2503 Fourth Ave, Canyon, TX, 79015. Tel: 806-654-6920. p. 2153
Rodda, Amy, Mgr, Libr Serv, Westminster Public Library, 3705 W 112th Ave, Westminster, CO, 80031. p. 298
Roddam, Barbara, Ser Tech, Southwestern Oklahoma State University, 100 Campus Dr, Weatherford, OK, 73096-3002. Tel: 580-774-7022. p. 1868
Roddrick, Michael, Head, Circ, Paul Pratt Memorial Library, 35 Ripley Rd, Cohasset, MA, 02025. Tel: 781-383-1348. p. 1012
Roddy, Shannon, Student Serv Librn, American University, 4300 Nebraska Ave NW, Washington, DC, 20016-8182. Tel: 202-274-4332. p. 360
Rode, Sheila S, Court Adminr, Greene County Courthouse, 10 E High St, Waynesburg, PA, 15370. Tel: 724-852-5237. p. 2019
Rodeffer, Tef, Prog Mgr, National Park Service, 255 N Commerce Park Loop, Tucson, AZ, 85745. Tel: 520-791-6416. p. 81
Rodegerdts, Alexis, Support Serv Librn, Walla Walla Public Library, 238 E Alder St, Walla Walla, WA, 99362. Tel: 509-524-4609. p. 2392
Rodela, Rudy, Chief Tech Officer, Anne Arundel County Public Library, Five Harry Truman Pkwy, Annapolis, MD, 21401. Tel: 410-222-2830. p. 950
Roden, Netanya, Access Serv Coordr, Concordia University, 1282 Concordia Ave, Saint Paul, MN, 55104. Tel: 651-641-8240. p. 1199
Rodenbeck, Erica, Curator, Grand County Historical Association Library, 110 E Byers Ave, Hot Sulphur Springs, CO, 80451. Tel: 970-725-3939. p. 286
Rodenberg, Denise, Asst Librn, Evansville Public Library, 602 Public St, Evansville, IL, 62242. Tel: 618-853-4649. p. 587
Rodenberg, Trisha, Circ Mgr, Pine Bluff & Jefferson County Library System, Main Library, 600 S Main St, Pine Bluff, AR, 71601. Tel: 870-534-4802. p. 107
Roderer, Debbie, Asst Dir, Dorothy Alling Memorial Library, 21 Library Lane, Williston, VT, 05495. Tel: 802-878-4918. p. 2299
Roderick, Amy, Ad, Asst Dir, Rowley Public Library, 141 Main St, Rowley, MA, 01969. Tel: 978-948-2850. p. 1050

Rodger, Julie, Mgr, Info Serv, Government of the Northwest Territories, Scotia Centre, Basement, 5102 50th Ave, Ste 600, Yellowknife, NT, X1A 3S8, CANADA. Tel: 867-767-9170, Ext 15505. p. 2613

Rodgers, Brenda, ILL Tech, Saint Mary's College of Maryland Library, 47645 College Dr, Saint Mary's City, MD, 20686-3001. Tel: 240-895-4264. p. 976

Rodgers, Crystal, Librn, South Routt Library District, 227 Dodge Ave, Oak Creek, CO, 80467. Tel: 970-736-8371. p. 292

Rodgers, Crystal, Librn, South Routt Library District, Yampa Public Library, 116 Main St, Yampa, CO, 80483. Tel: 970-638-4654. p. 292

Rodgers, Haley, Tech Serv, University of Mobile, 5735 College Pkwy, Mobile, AL, 36613-2842. Tel: 251-442-2479. p. 26

Rodgers, Jessica, Computer Spec, Teen Librn, Belen Public Library, 333 Becker Ave, Belen, NM, 87002. Tel: 505 966 2602. p. 1464

Rodgers, Linda, Dir, Skene Memorial Library, 1017 Main St, Fleischmanns, NY, 12430. Tel: 845-254-4581. p. 1533

Rodgers, Samantha, Dir, Doniphan-Ripley County Library, 207 Locust St, Doniphan, MO, 63935. Tel: 573-996-2616. p. 1245

Rodgers, Sara, Adult Ref Librn, Head, Ad Ref Serv, Dobbs Ferry Public Library, 55 Main St, Dobbs Ferry, NY, 10522. Tel: 914-231-3057. p. 1526

Rodio, Joseph, Dir, South Hadley Public Library, Two Canal St, South Hadley, MA, 01075. Tel: 413-538-5045. p. 1054

Rodio, Joseph, Libr Dir, South Hadley Public Library, Gaylord Memorial Library, 47 College St, South Hadley, MA, 01075. Tel: 413-538-5047. p. 1054

Rodiquez, MaryBeth, Circ, Swansea Free Public Library, 69 Main St, Swansea, MA, 02777. Tel: 508-674-9609. p. 1059

Rodkey, Ashley, Libr Asst, Patron Serv, Pelham Library, Two S Valley Rd, Pelham, MA, 01002. Tel: 413-253-0657. p. 1045

Rodne, Mary, Libr Dir, Colleyville Public Library, 110 Main St, Colleyville, TX, 76034. Tel: 817-503-1150, 817-503-1154 (Youth Serv), 817-503-1155 (Adult Serv). p. 2158

Rodney-Hill, Cyanna, Libr Spec, Norfolk State University Library, 700 Park Ave, Norfolk, VA, 23504-8010. Tel: 757-823-2224. p. 2335

Rodricks, Karen, Sr Libr Supvr, Washington County Library, Lake Elmo Branch, 3537 Lake Elmo Ave N, Lake Elmo, MN, 55042. Tel: 651-275-8515. p. 1210

Rodrigues, Denyse, Research & E-Learning Librn, Mount Saint Vincent University Library & Archives, 15 Lumpkin Rd, Halifax, NS, B3M 2J6, CANADA. Tel: 902-457-6200. p. 2619

Rodrigues, Elizabeth, Humanities & Digital Scholarship Librn, Grinnell College Libraries, 1111 Sixth Ave, Grinnell, IA, 50112-1770. Tel: 641-269-3362. p. 756

Rodrigues, Isa, Asst Librn II, Mariposa County Law Library, 4978 Tenth St, Mariposa, CA, 95338. Tel: 209-966-2140. p. 173

Rodrigues, Jessica, Ref, Youth Serv, Steger-South Chicago Heights Public Library District, 54 E 31st St, Steger, IL, 60475. Tel: 708-755-5040. p. 651

Rodrigues, Kimberly A, Dir, Hopland Research & Extension Center Library, 4070 University Rd, Hopland, CA, 95449. Tel: 707-744-1424, Ext 115. p. 151

Rodrigues, Ronald, Ref Librn, United States Geological Survey Library, 345 Middlefield Rd, Bldg 15 (MS-955), Menlo Park, CA, 94025-3591. Tel: 650-329-5427. p. 176

Rodrigues, Tyler, Student Engagement Librn, University of Idaho Library, 850 S Rayburn St, Moscow, ID, 83844. Tel: 208-885-9807. p. 526

Rodriguez, Amanda, Libr Dir, Lumberton Public Library, 130 E Chance Rd, Lumberton, TX, 77657-7763. Tel: 409-755-7400. p. 2214

Rodriguez, Carlos, Dean, California State University, Los Angeles, 5151 State University Dr, Los Angeles, CA, 90032-8300. Tel: 323-343-3950. p. 161

Rodriguez, Carmen, General Services Mgr, Oblate School of Theology, 285 Oblate Dr, San Antonio, TX, 78216. Tel: 210-341-1366, Ext 311. p. 2237

Rodriguez, Catalina, Dir, Human Res, Stanford University Libraries, 557 Escondido Mall, Stanford, CA, 94305-6063. Tel: 650-725-1064. p. 248

Rodriguez, Corey, Libr Mgr, New York Public Library - Astor, Lenox & Tilden Foundations, Woodstock Branch, 761 E 160th St, (West of Prospect Ave), Bronx, NY, 10456. Tel: 718-665-6255. p. 1598

Rodriguez, Cynthia Y, Libr Dir, Laredo College, West End Washington St, Laredo, TX, 78040. Tel: 956-721-5845. p. 2209

Rodriguez, Dawn, Circ, Passaic Public Library, 195 Gregory Ave, Passaic, NJ, 07055. Tel: 973-779-0474. p. 1433

Rodriguez, Diane M, Asst Dir, San Francisco Law Library, 1145 Market St, 4th Flr, San Francisco, CA, 94103. Tel: 415-554-1772. p. 227

Rodriguez, Elisabeth, Librn, Estrella Mountain Community College Library, 3000 N Dysart Rd, Avondale, AZ, 85392. Tel: 623-935-8191. p. 55

Rodriguez, Hector, Br Supvr, University of Texas Libraries, Life Science (Biology, Pharmacy), Main Bldg, 2400 Inner Campus Dr, Austin, TX, 78712. Tel: 512-495-4630. p. 2142

Rodriguez, Jenny, Youth Serv, New Braunfels Public Library, 700 E Common St, New Braunfels, TX, 78130-5689. Tel: 830-221-4314. p. 2222

Rodriguez, Jessica, Dir, Steger-South Chicago Heights Public Library District, 54 E 31st St, Steger, IL, 60475. Tel: 708-755-5040. p. 651

Rodriguez, Juana, Library Contact, Colusa County Free Library, Grimes Branch, 240 Main St, Grimes, CA, 95950. Tel: 530-437-2428. p. 131

Rodriguez, Judith, Br Mgr, Prince William Public Libraries, Dumfries Library, 18115 Triangle Shopping Plaza, Dumfries, VA, 22026. Tel: 703-792-5678. p. 2338

Rodriguez, Julia, Health Sci, Nursing & Fac Res Support Librn, Oakland University Library, 100 Library Dr, Rochester, MI, 48309-4479. Tel: 248-370-2490. p. 1144

Rodriguez, Julio, Mgr, Miami-Dade Public Library System, West Dade Regional, 9445 Coral Way, Miami, FL, 33165. Tel: 305-553-1134. p. 424

Rodriguez, Kathryn G, Res Asst, Stearns, Weaver, Miller, Weissler, Alhadeff & Sitterson, 2200 Museum Tower, 150 W Flagler St, Miami, FL, 33130. Tel: 813-222-5020. p. 425

Rodriguez, Ketty, Chief Librn, University of Puerto Rico Library System, Library & Information Sciences, Rio Piedras Campus, Jose M Lazaro Bldg, 3rd Flr, San Juan, PR, 00931. Tel: 787-764-0000, Ext 85980. p. 2515

Rodriguez, Luis, Br Mgr, Bridgeport Public Library, East Side Branch, 1174 E Main St, Bridgeport, CT, 06608. Tel: 203-576-7634. p. 303

Rodriguez, Luis, Dir, Butler Public Library, One Ace Rd, Butler, NJ, 07405. Tel: 973-838-3262. p. 1393

Rodriguez, Mark, Br Librn, Stockton-San Joaquin County Public Library, Thornton Branch, 26341 N Thornton Rd, Thornton, CA, 95686. p. 250

Rodriguez, Martha, Librn, Florida National University Library, South Campus Resource Room, 11865 SW 26th St, Unit H-3, Miami, FL, 33175. Tel: 305-226-9999, Ext 1320. p. 408

Rodriguez, Matthew, Sr Librn, Los Angeles Public Library System, Angeles Mesa Branch Library, 2700 W 52nd St, Los Angeles, CA, 90043-1953. Tel: 323-292-4328. p. 163

Rodriguez, Mayra, Libr Dir, Inter-American University of Puerto Rico, San German Campus, Ave Inter-American University, Rd 102, K 30.6, San German, PR, 00683-9801. Tel: 787-264-1912, Ext 7521. p. 2512

Rodriguez, Nicolas, Br Adminr, Atlanta-Fulton Public Library System, Auburn Avenue Research Library on African-American Culture & History, 101 Auburn Ave NE, Atlanta, GA, 30303-2503. Tel: 404-613-4001. p. 460

Rodriguez, Rafael, Member & Visitor Services Mgr, The New York Society Library, 53 E 79th St, New York, NY, 10075. Tel: 212-288-6900, Ext 232. p. 1598

Rodriguez, Rebecca, Librn, Ft Lauderdale Campus, Keiser University Library System, 1500 NW 49th St, Fort Lauderdale, FL, 33309. Tel: 954-351-4035. p. 401

Rodriguez, Richard, Libr Supvr, San Juan Memorial Library, 1010 S Standard Ave, San Juan, TX, 78589. Tel: 956-702-0926. p. 2241

Rodriguez, Robert, Dir, Robert J Kleberg Public Library, 220 N Fourth St, Kingsville, TX, 78363. Tel: 361-592-6381. p. 2206

Rodriguez, Ronald, Dean, Libr Serv, California State University, Stanislaus, One University Circle, Turlock, CA, 95382. Tel: 209-667-3607. p. 253

Rodriguez, Shalyn, Asst Dir, Ch Mgr, Shorewood-Troy Public Library District, 650 Deerwood Dr, Shorewood, IL, 60404. Tel: 815-725-1715. p. 647

Rodriguez, Sharesly, User Experience Librn, San Jose State University, One Washington Sq, San Jose, CA, 95192-0028. Tel: 408-808-2000. p. 232

Rodriguez, Susan Ayala, Br Mgr, Pamunkey Regional Library, King & Queen Branch, 396 Newtown Rd, Saint Stephens Church, VA, 23148. Tel: 804-769-1623. p. 2324

Rodriguez, Susan Ayala, Br Mgr, Pamunkey Regional Library, Upper King William Branch, Sharon Office Park, 694-J Sharon Rd, King William, VA, 23086. Tel: 804-769-3731. p. 2324

Rodriguez, Tomasa, Tech Serv, Port Chester-Rye Brook Public Library, One Haseco Ave, Port Chester, NY, 10573. Tel: 914-939-6710, Ext 107. p. 1620

Rodriguez, Walberto, Webmaster, Inter-American University of Puerto Rico, 104 Parque Industrial Turpeaux, Rd 1, Mercedita, PR, 00715-1602. Tel: 787-284-1912, Ext 2128. p. 2512

Rodriguez-Parrilla, Iris D, Dr, Chief Librn, University of Puerto Rico Library System, Arts Collection, Rio Piedras Campus, Jose M Lazaro Bldg, 2nd Flr, San Juan, PR, 00931. Tel: 787-764-0000, Ext 85535, 787-764-0000, Ext 85539. p. 2514

Rodriquez, Marcy, Asst Dir, Elmhurst Public Library, 125 S Prospect Ave, Elmhurst, IL, 60126-3298. Tel: 630-279-8696. p. 585

Rodriquez, Safia, Librn, Wales Public Library, 77 Main St, Wales, MA, 01081. Tel: 413-245-9072. p. 1061

Roduin, Cheyenne, Libr Mgr, Seattle Children's Hospital, 4800 Sand Point Way NE, OB.8.520, Seattle, WA, 98105. Tel: 206-987-2098. p. 2378

Roe, Andrea, Libr Dir, Fulton County Public Library, 320 W Seventh St, Rochester, IN, 46975-1332. Tel: 574-223-2713. p. 716

Roe, Brent, Univ Librn, Laurentian University Library & Archives, 935 Ramsey Lake Rd, Sudbury, ON, P3E 2C6, CANADA. Tel: 705-675-1151, Ext 4841. p. 2683

Roe, Joyce, Librn, Gypsum Community Library, 521 Maple St, Gypsum, KS, 67448. Tel: 785-536-4319. p. 811

Roe, Kit, Librn, West Georgia Technical College, Douglas Campus, 4600 Timber Ridge Dr, Douglasville, GA, 30135. Tel: 770-947-7240. p. 502

Roe, Lisa, Br Mgr, Chicago Public Library, Bucktown-Wicker Park, 1701 N Milwaukee Ave, Chicago, IL, 60647. Tel: 312-744-6022. p. 556

Roe, Merry, Librn, Beaver Island District Library, 26400 Donegal Bay Rd, Beaver Island, MI, 49782. Tel: 231-448-2701. p. 1083

Roedel, Deb, Asst Librn, Loyal Public Library, 214 N Main St, Loyal, WI, 54446. Tel: 715-255-8189. p. 2448

Roeder, Renee, Br Mgr, Cherokee Regional Library System, Chickamauga Public, 306 Cove Rd, Chickamauga, GA, 30707. Tel: 706-375-3004. p. 484

Roeder, Tracie, Asst Librn, Fairfield/Teton Public Library, 14 N Fourth St, Fairfield, MT, 59436. Tel: 406-467-2477. p. 1292

Roen, Elisabeth, Asst Dir, Palm Harbor Library, 2330 Nebraska Ave, Palm Harbor, FL, 34683. Tel: 727-784-3332, Ext 3007. p. 435

Roepke, Rebecca, Libr Dir, Cudahy Family Library, 3500 Library Dr, Cudahy, WI, 53110. Tel: 414-769-2244. p. 2429

Roes, Paulette, Dir, North Country Library System, 22072 County Rte 190, Watertown, NY, 13601-1066. Tel: 315-782-5540. p. 1660

Roese, Sonja, Youth Serv, Westhampton Free Library, Seven Library Ave, Westhampton Beach, NY, 11978-2697. Tel: 631-288-3335, Ext 166. p. 1664

Roeth, Cherie, Dir, Bradford Public Library, 138 E Main St, Bradford, OH, 45308-1108. Tel: 937-448-2612. p. 1752

Roeth, Cherie, Dir, J R Clarke Public Library, 102 E Spring St, Covington, OH, 45318. Tel: 937-473-2226. p. 1778

Roethemeyer, Robert V, Dir, Libr Serv, Concordia Theological Seminary, 6600 N Clinton St, Fort Wayne, IN, 46825. Tel: 260-452-2145. p. 684

Roether, Diane, Dean of Libr, North Central Texas College Library, 1525 W California St, Gainesville, TX, 76240-0815. Tel: 940-668-4283, Ext 4338. p. 2182

Roewe, Patrick, Exec Dir, Spokane County Library District, 4322 N Argonne Rd, Spokane, WA, 99212. Tel: 509-893-8200. p. 2384

Roffer, Michael, Assoc Librn, New York Law School, 185 W Broadway, New York, NY, 10013. Tel: 212-431-2332. p. 1594

Rofini, Laurie A, Dir, Chester County Archives & Records Services Library, 601 Westtown Rd, Ste 080, West Chester, PA, 19382-4958. Tel: 610-344-6760. p. 2020

Rogalla, Mike, Ch Mgr, Champaign Public Library, 200 W Green St, Champaign, IL, 61820-5193. Tel: 217-403-2000. p. 551

Rogan, Mary Ellen, Dir, Plainfield Public Library, 800 Park Ave, Plainfield, NJ, 07060-2594. Tel: 908-757-1111. p. 1435

Rogan, Rebecca, Ref Librn, Chappaqua Public Library, 195 S Greeley Ave, Chappaqua, NY, 10514. Tel: 914-238-4779. p. 1516

Rogers, Alexander, Curator, Maturango Museum, 100 E Las Flores Ave, Ridgecrest, CA, 93555. Tel: 760-375-6900. p. 200

Rogers, Ashley, Br Mgr, Arundel Anne County Public Library, Severn Library, 2624 Annapolis Rd, Rte 175, Severn, MD, 21144. Tel: 410-222-6280. p. 950

Rogers Beal, Mary, Dir, Mississippi Library Commission, 3881 Eastwood Dr, Jackson, MS, 39211-6473. Tel: 601-432-4116. p. 1223

Rogers, Beth, Librn, Western Canadian Universities Marine Sciences Society, 100 Pachena Rd, Bamfield, BC, V0R 1B0, CANADA. Tel: 250-728-3301, Ext 213. p. 2562

Rogers, Brandie, Dir, William H Bush Memorial Library, 5605 Whitaker Rd, Martinsburg, NY, 13404. Tel: 315-376-7490. p. 1569

Rogers, Brian, Assoc Librn, New London Maritime Society-Custom House Maritime Museum, 150 Bank St, New London, CT, 06320. Tel: 860-447-2501. p. 329

Rogers, Brian, Dir, Info Tech, University of Tennessee at Chattanooga Library, 400 Douglas Ave, Dept 6456, Chattanooga, TN, 37403-2598. Tel: 423-425-4501. p. 2092

Rogers, Christopher, Libr Dir, University of Saint Mary of the Lake - Mundelein Seminary, 1000 E Maple Ave, Mundelein, IL, 60060. Tel: 847-970-4833. p. 622

Rogers, Darrah, Circ, ILL, Flathead Valley Community College Library, 777 Grandview Dr, Kalispell, MT, 59901. Tel: 406-756-3856. p. 1297

Rogers, Doris, Asst Dir, North Kansas City Public Library, 2251 Howell St, North Kansas City, MO, 64116. Tel: 816-221-3360. p. 1264

Rogers, Elizabeth, Sr Librn, Long Beach Public Library, Brewitt, 4036 E Anaheim St, Long Beach, CA, 90804. Tel: 562-570-1040. p. 159

Rogers, Elizabeth, Archivist, Keene Valley Library Association, 1796 Rte 73, Keene Valley, NY, 12943. Tel: 518-576-4335. p. 1559

Rogers, Emily, Dep Dir, Brown County Library, 515 Pine St, Green Bay, WI, 54301. Tel: 920-448-5808. p. 2438

Rogers, Evelyn, Br Librn, Newport Beach Public Library, Balboa Branch, 100 E Balboa Blvd, Balboa, CA, 92661. Tel: 949-644-3076. p. 183

Rogers, Evelyn, Libr Dir, Port Jervis Free Library, 138 Pike St, Port Jervis, NY, 12771. Tel: 845-856-7313, Ext 6. p. 1621

Rogers, Georgette, Circ Supvr, Liberty Lake Municipal Library, 23123 E Mission Ave, Liberty Lake, WA, 99019-7613. Tel: 509-435-0778. p. 2369

Rogers, Ginger, Dir, Owen County Public Library, Ten S Montgomery St, Spencer, IN, 47460-1738. Tel: 812-829-3392. p. 719

Rogers, James, Asst to the Dir, Salem University, 223 W Main St, Salem, WV, 26426. Tel: 304-326-1390. p. 2414

Rogers, Jenica, Dir, Libr Serv, State University of New York College at Potsdam, Lougheed Learning Commons, 44 Pierrepont Ave, Potsdam, NY, 13676-2294. Tel: 315-267-3328. p. 1622

Rogers, Jennifer, Asst Librn, John Mosser Public Library District, 106 W Meek St, Abingdon, IL, 61410-1451. Tel: 309-462-3129. p. 535

Rogers, Jennifer, Br Mgr, Jonesville Public Library, 112 N Swain St, Jonesville, NC, 28642. Tel: 336-526-4226. p. 1698

Rogers, Jesse, Dir, Oostburg Public Library, 213 N Eighth St, Oostburg, WI, 53070. Tel: 920-564-2934. p. 2467

Rogers, Jim, Br Librn, Phillips-Lee-Monroe Regional Library, Jacobs Memorial Library, 270 Madison St, Clarendon, AR, 72029-2792. Tel: 870-747-5593. p. 98

Rogers, Joan M, Libr Dir, Waterford Township Public Library, 5168 Civic Center Dr, Waterford, MI, 48329. Tel: 248-618-7691. p. 1158

Rogers, Joanne, Librn, Orr's Island Library, 1699 Harpswell Islands Rd, Orr's Island, ME, 04066. Tel: 207-833-7811. p. 934

Rogers, Joy, Outreach Serv, Kokomo-Howard County Public Library, 220 N Union St, Kokomo, IN, 46901-4614. Tel: 765-457-3242. p. 700

Rogers, Julie, Curator, Mgr, Lake County Historical Society Library, 317 W Main St, Tavares, FL, 32778. Tel: 352-343-9890. p. 450

Rogers, Justin, Port St Lucie Campus Libr Dir, Keiser University Library System, 1500 NW 49th St, Fort Lauderdale, FL, 33309. Tel: 954-351-4035. p. 401

Rogers, Kalah, Evening Librn, Northeast Mississippi Community College, 101 Cunningham Blvd, Booneville, MS, 38829. Tel: 662-720-7237, 662-728-7751. p. 1212

Rogers, Kandace, Libr Dir, Sullivan University Library, Lexington Campus, 2355 Harrodsburg Rd, Lexington, KY, 40504. Tel: 859-514-3309. p. 867

Rogers, Keith, Tech Serv Librn, Friendswood Public Library, 416 S Friendswood Dr, Friendswood, TX, 77546-3897. Tel: 281-482-7135. p. 2182

Rogers, Lacy, Mgr, Charlestown-Clark County Public Library, Henryville Branch, 214 E Main St, Henryville, IN, 47126. Tel: 812-294-4246. p. 674

Rogers, Lala, Br Mgr, Chicago Public Library, Sherman Park, 5440 S Racine Ave, Chicago, IL, 60609. Tel: 312-747-0477. p. 557

Rogers, Leslie, Asst Dir, Will Rogers Library, 1515 N Florence Ave, Claremore, OK, 74017. Tel: 918-341-1564. p. 1844

Rogers, Lisa, Instruction Coordr, Ref Librn, Utica University, 1600 Burrstone Rd, Utica, NY, 13502-4892. Tel: 315-792-3342. p. 1656

Rogers, Marsha, Librn, Selden Public Library, 109 S Kansas Ave, Selden, KS, 67757. Tel: 785-386-4321. p. 836

Rogers, Mary, Assoc Dir, Info Syst, Trumbull Library System, 33 Quality St, Trumbull, CT, 06611. Tel: 203-452-5197. p. 342

Rogers, Mary, Mgr, West Georgia Regional Library, Warren P Sewell Memorial Library of Bowdon, 450 West Ave, Bowdon, GA, 30108. Tel: 770-258-8991. p. 470

Rogers, Mary, Libr Mgr, Live Oak Public Libraries, Garden City Branch, 104 Sunshine Ave, Garden City, GA, 31405. Tel: 912-644-5932. p. 496

Rogers, Mary, Libr Mgr, Live Oak Public Libraries, Islands Branch, 50 Johnny Mercer Blvd, Savannah, GA, 31410. Tel: 912-897-4061. p. 496

Rogers, Mike, County Librn, Regional Dir, Greene County Public Library, 120 N 12th St, Paragould, AR, 72450. Tel: 870-236-8711. p. 107

Rogers, Mike E, Dir, Northeast Arkansas Regional Library System, 120 N 12th St, Paragould, AR, 72450. Tel: 870-236-8711. p. 107

Rogers, Paula, Asst Librn, David M Hunt Library, 63 Main St, Falls Village, CT, 06031. Tel: 860-824-7424. p. 312

Rogers, Ruth, Spec Coll Librn, Wellesley College, 106 Central St, Wellesley, MA, 02481. Tel: 781-283-3592. p. 1064

Rogers, Samantha, Ref Librn, Southwestern Illinois College, 2500 Carlyle Ave, Belleville, IL, 62221. Tel: 618-235-2700, Ext 5204. p. 541

Rogers, Sara, Libr Dir, Berlin Free Town Library, 47 S Main St, Berlin, NY, 12022. Tel: 518-658-2231. p. 1493

Rogers, Scarlett, Catalog & Archives Librn, Brevard College, One Brevard College Dr, Brevard, NC, 28712-4283. Tel: 828-641-0114. p. 1675

Rogers, Shelley, Sr Cataloger, University of West Georgia, 1601 Maple St, Carrollton, GA, 30118. Tel: 678-839-6495. p. 469

Rogers, Sonya, Libr Dir, Altamont Public Library, 1433 Main St, Altamont, TN, 37301. Tel: 931-692-2457. p. 2087

Rogers, Stephen, Head, Guest Serv, Westminster College, America's National Churchill Museum, 501 Westminster Ave, Fulton, MO, 65251-1299. Tel: 573-592-5610. p. 1246

Rogers, Susan, Asst Librn, Nakusp Public Library Association, 92 Sixth Ave NW, Nakusp, BC, V0G 1R0, CANADA. Tel: 250-265-3363. p. 2570

Rogers, Tim, Libr Dir, Jacksonville Public Library, 303 N Laura St, Jacksonville, FL, 32202-3505. Tel: 904-630-2665. p. 411

Rogers, Tim, Br Mgr, Pittsylvania County Public Library, Brosville/Cascade, 11948 Martinsville Hwy, Danville, VA, 24541. Tel: 434-685-1285. p. 2311

Rogers, Tina, Acq Asst, Circ Asst, Harding School of Theology, 1000 Cherry Rd, Memphis, TN, 38117. Tel: 901-761-1354. p. 2112

Rogers-Snyr, Andrea, Librn, Beaumont Hospital, 3601 W 13 Mile Rd, Royal Oak, MI, 48073-6769. Tel: 248-898-1750. p. 1146

Roggenstein, Carol, Br Mgr, Palm Beach County Library System, Gardens Branch, 11303 Campus Dr, Palm Beach Gardens, FL, 33410. Tel: 561-626-6133. p. 454

Roghair, Nicholas, Archivist, Tech Serv Librn, Tuzzy Consortium Library, 5421 North Star St, Barrow, AK, 99723. Tel: 907-852-4050. p. 43

Rogler, Hilary, Circ, ILL, Per, Hellenic College-Holy Cross Greek Orthodox School of Theology, 50 Goddard Ave, Brookline, MA, 02445-7496. Tel: 617-850-1244. p. 1003

Rognlie, Lori, Administrative Specialist, Washburn University, 1700 SW College Ave, Topeka, KS, 66621. Tel: 785-670-1179. p. 839

Rohan, Jennifer, Fac Librn, Green River College, 12401 SE 320th St, Auburn, WA, 98092-3699. Tel: 253-833-9111, Ext 2102. p. 2357
Rohde, Annie, ILL, Perry Public Library, 3753 Main St, Perry, OH, 44081-9501. Tel: 440-259-3300. p. 1815
Rohe, Tiffany, Youth Serv Librn, Winterset Public Library, 123 N Second St, Winterset, IA, 50273-1508. Tel: 515-462-1731. p. 792
Rohen, Melissa, Libr Dir, Reed City Area District Library, 829 S Chestnut St, Reed City, MI, 49677-1152. Tel: 231-832-2131. p. 1143
Rohlfing, Alexis, Col Librn, Thomas More College of Liberal Arts, Six Manchester St, Merrimack, NH, 03054-4805. Tel: 603-880-0425. p. 1373
Rohlwing, Brett, Br Mgr, Milwaukee Public Library, Martin Luther King Branch, 310 W Locust St, Milwaukee, WI, 53212. p. 2460
Rohmiller, Thomas, Chief, Acq & Res Flight, United States Air Force, National Air & Space Intelligence Center Research Center, 4180 Watson Way, Wright-Patterson AFB, OH, 45433-5648. Tel: 937-257-3531. p. 1834
Rohner, Susan, Librn, Johns Hopkins University Libraries, William H Welch Medical Library, 1900 E Monument St, Baltimore, MD, 21205. Tel: 410-955-3028. p. 954
Rohrer, Lorie, Head, Youth Serv, Lake Forest Library, 360 E Deerpath Rd, Lake Forest, IL, 60045. Tel: 847-810-4632. p. 606
Roi, Charlotte, Librn, California Department of Corrections Library System, Pelican Bay State Prison, 5905 Lake Earl Dr, Crescent City, CA, 95532. Tel: 707-465-1000, Ext 7995. p. 207
Roiger, Linda, Dir, Springfield Public Library, 120 N Cass Ave, Springfield, MN, 56087-1506. Tel: 507-723-3510. p. 1204
Roirdan, Jim, Head, Ref (Info Serv), Peabody Institute Library, 15 Sylvan St, Danvers, MA, 01923. Tel: 978-774-0554. p. 1013
Rojas, Alexandra, Head, Ref & Pub Serv, Fiorello H LaGuardia Community College Library, 31-10 Thomson Ave, Long Island City, NY, 11101. Tel: 718-482-6020. p. 1565
Rojas, Irene, ILL Coordr, Ingleside Public Library, 2775 Waco St, Ingleside, TX, 78362. Tel: 361-776-5355. p. 2202
Rojas, Lilia, Libr Asst, Sunland Park Community Library, 984 McNutt Rd, Sunland Park, NM, 88063-9039. Tel: 575-874-0873. p. 1478
Rojas, Lupi, Circ Mgr, Arizona Western College, 2020 S Ave 8E, Yuma, AZ, 85366. Tel: 928-344-7768. p. 85
Rokicki, Russell, Library Contact, Dechert LLP, Cira Ctr, 2929 Arch St, Philadelphia, PA, 19104. Tel: 215-994-4000. p. 1976
Rokicki, Ryan, Dir, Working Men's Institute Museum & Library, 407 W Tavern St, New Harmony, IN, 47631. Tel: 812-682-4806. p. 709
Rokolj, Tea, Art Librn, University of Ottawa Libraries, Morisset Library (Arts & Sciences), 65 University Private, Ottawa, ON, K1N 9A5, CANADA. Tel: 613-562-5213. p. 2671
Rokos, Sue Z, Asst Dir, Ch Serv, Mohawk Valley Library System, 858 Duanesburg Rd, Schenectady, NY, 12306. Tel: 518-355-2010. p. 1638
Roksandic, Stevo, Regional Dir, Library Services, Mercy Medical Center - North Iowa, 1000 Fourth St SW, Mason City, IA, 50401. Tel: 641-428-7699. p. 768
Roksandic, Stevo, Regional Libr Serv Dir, Mount Carmel, Center for Learning & Education, 127 S Davis Ave, 3rd-4th Flrs, Columbus, OH, 43222. Tel: 614-234-1644. p. 1774
Rokusek, Steve, Asst Librn, Florida Gulf Coast University Library, 10501 FGCU Blvd S, Fort Myers, FL, 33965. Tel: 239-590-7632. p. 403
Rol, Brigette, Dir, Lake City Public Library, 201 S High St, Lake City, MN, 55041. Tel: 651-345-4013. p. 1180
Roland, Bridget, Asst Dir, Markham Public Library, 16640 Kedzie Ave, Markham, IL, 60428. Tel: 708-331-0130. p. 614
Roland, Debbie, Dir, Calhoun County Museum & Cultural Center, 313 Butler St, Saint Matthews, SC, 29135. Tel: 803-874-3964. p. 2069
Roles, Eryn, Res & Instruction Librn, Marshall University Libraries, One John Marshall Dr, Huntington, WV, 25755-2060. Tel: 304-696-2336. p. 2405
Rolfe, Alexander, Head, Tech Serv, Univ Librn, George Fox University, 416 N Meridian St, Newberg, OR, 97132. Tel: 503-554-2410. p. 1888
Rolfe, Kate, Librn, Lake Superior College, 2101 Trinity Rd, Duluth, MN, 55811. Tel: 218-733-5980. p. 1172
Rolfe, Susan, Head, Circ, Plainville Public Library, 198 South St, Plainville, MA, 02762-1512. Tel: 508-695-1784. p. 1047
Rolfsmeyer, Deana, Youth Serv, Irvin L Young Memorial Library, 431 W Center St, Whitewater, WI, 53190. Tel: 262-473-0530. p. 2488
Rolison, Edith, Mgr, L C Anderson Memorial Library, 50 S Kennedy St, Metter, GA, 30439-4442. Tel: 912-685-2455. p. 490
Roll, Jarrod, Dir, Monroe County Local History Room, 200 W Main St, Sparta, WI, 54656. Tel: 608-269-8680. p. 2478
Roll, Samantha, Librn, Highlands County Library, Lake Placid Memorial Library, 205 W Interlake Blvd, Lake Placid, FL, 33852. Tel: 863-699-3705. p. 444
Roll, Todd, Head Librn, University of Wisconsin - Platteville, One University Plaza, Platteville, WI, 53818. Tel: 608-342-1229. p. 2470
Roller, Elizabeth, Teen Serv Librn, Giles County Public Library, 122 S Second St, Pulaski, TN, 38478-3285. Tel: 931-363-2720. p. 2124
Roller, Sarah, Libr Dir, Happy Valley Library, 13793 SE Sieben Park Way, Happy Valley, OR, 97015. Tel: 503-783-3456. p. 1881
Rollings, Susan, Dir, Indian Lake Public Library, 113 Pelon Rd, Indian Lake, NY, 12842. Tel: 518-648-5444. p. 1550
Rollins, Alison, Dir, Uniformed Services University of the Health Sciences, 4301 Jones Bridge Rd, Bethesda, MD, 20814-4799. Tel: 301-295-3350. p. 960
Rollins, Deborah, Head, Coll Serv, University of Maine, 5729 Fogler Library, Orono, ME, 04469-5729. Tel: 207-581-1659. p. 934
Rollins, Kristin, Archives Dir, National Archives of The Christian & Missionary Alliance, 731 Chapel Hill Dr, Colorado Springs, CO, 80920. Tel: 719-265-2172. p. 271
Rollins, Shannon, Dir, Kingman-Millcreek Public Library, 123 W State St, Kingman, IN, 47952. Tel: 765-397-3138. p. 699
Rollins, Stephanie, Dr, Electronic Serv, United States Air Force, Air University - Muir S Fairchild Research Information Center, 600 Chennault Circle, Maxwell AFB, AL, 36112-6010. Tel: 334-953-8301. p. 25
Rollins, Stephen, Dean of Libr, University of Alaska Anchorage, Consortium Library, 3211 Providence Dr, Anchorage, AK, 99508-8176. Tel: 907-786-1825. p. 43
Rollins, Steve, Exec Dir, Alaska Library Network, PO Box 230051, Anchorage, AK, 99523-0051. Tel: 907-786-0618. p. 2761
Rollins, Tina, Dir, Hampton University, 129 William R Harvey Way, Hampton, VA, 23668. Tel: 757-727-5388. p. 2323
Rollins, Valerie, Coll Develop Coordr, Rutherford County Library System, 105 W Vine St, Murfreesboro, TN, 37130-3673. Tel: 615-962-7424, p. 2117
Rollison, Jeff, Dir, Immaculata University, 1145 King Rd, Immaculata, PA, 19345-0705. Tel: 484-323-3839. p. 1945
Rollison, Kaylee, Dir, George P & Susan Platt Cady Library, 42 E River St, Nichols, NY, 13812. Tel: 607-699-3835. p. 1606
Roloff, Raina, Dir, North Freedom Public Library, 105 N Maple St, North Freedom, WI, 53951. Tel: 608-522-4571. p. 2465
Roma, Mark, Br Mgr, Dayton Metro Library, Belmont, 1041 Watervliet Ave, Dayton, OH, 45420. Tel: 937-496-8920. p. 1779
Roman, Ann, Campus Librn, Nova Scotia Community College, Ivany Campus Library, 80 Mawiomi Pl, Dartmouth, NS, B2Y 0A5, CANADA. Tel: 902-491-1035. p. 2620
Roman, Cynthia, Curator, Yale University Library, Lewis Walpole Library, 154 Main St, Farmington, CT, 06032. Tel: 860-677-2140. p. 328
Roman, Dedra, Br Mgr, Volusia County Public Library, Daytona Beach Regional, 105 E Magnolia Ave, Daytona Beach, FL, 32114. Tel: 386-257-6036. p. 393
Roman, Kenny, YA Librn, George F Johnson Memorial Library, 1001 Park St, Endicott, NY, 13760. Tel: 607-757-5350. p. 1531
Roman, Marcia, Librn, State Correctional Institution, Somerset Library, 1590 Walters Mill Rd, Somerset, PA, 15510-0001. Tel: 814-443-8100. p. 2008
Roman, Monica, Ch, Covina Public Library, 234 N Second Ave, Covina, CA, 91723-2198. Tel: 626-384-5312. p. 133
Roman, Sharon, Head, Circ, Patchogue-Medford Library, 54-60 E Main St, Patchogue, NY, 11772. Tel: 631-654-4700. p. 1615
Romaniuk, Elena, Coordr, Ser, University of Victoria Libraries, McPherson Library, PO Box 1800, Victoria, BC, V8W 3H5, CANADA. Tel: 250-721-8211. p. 2583
Romaniuk, Mary-Jo, Vice Provost & Univ Librn, University of Calgary Library, 2500 University Dr NW, Calgary, AB, T2N 1N4, CANADA. Tel: 403-220-3765. p. 2529
Romano, Anne, Dir, Libr Serv, Silver Hill Hospital, 208 Valley Rd, New Canaan, CT, 06840. Tel: 203-966-3561, Ext 2270. p. 325
Romano, Eileen, Coordr, Circ, Gwynedd Mercy University, 1325 Sumneytown Pike, Gwynedd Valley, PA, 19437. Tel: 215-646-7300, Ext 21492. p. 1939
Romano, Joanne, Head, Res Mgt, Houston Academy of Medicine, 1133 John Freeman Blvd, No 100, Houston, TX, 77030. Tel: 713-799-7144. p. 2193
Romano, Leigh, Librn, Seymour Public Library District, 176-178 Genesee St, Auburn, NY, 13021. Tel: 315-252-2571. p. 1489
Romano, Nicoletta, Manager, Library & Learning Commons, University Canada West, 1461 Granville St, Vancouver, BC, V6Z 0E5, CANADA. p. 2580
Romano, Pia, Ref & Instruction Librn, Wentworth Institute of Technology, 550 Huntington Ave, Boston, MA, 02115-5998. Tel: 617-989-4043. p. 1000
Romano, Stephanie, Libr Dir, Chester Public Library, 21 W Main St, Chester, CT, 06412. Tel: 860-526-0018. p. 306
Romano, Tony, ILL, Eastern Monroe Public Library, 1002 N Ninth St, Stroudsburg, PA, 18360. Tel: 570-421-0800. p. 2010
Romanosky, Neil, Librn, Michigan State University Libraries, Area Studies, Main Library, 366 W Circle Dr, East Lansing, MI, 48824. Tel: 517-884-6392. p. 1102
Romanowski, Cynthia Morrow, Tech Serv Librn, Governors State University Library, One University Pkwy, University Park, IL, 60466-0975. Tel: 708-534-4116. p. 655
Romansky, Moira, Mgr, NASA, 12600 NASA Rd, Las Cruces, NM, 88012. Tel: 575-524-5683. p. 1471
Rombouts, Stephen, Archivist, Saint Francis University, 106 Franciscan Way, Loretto, PA, 15940. Tel: 814-472-2761. p. 1957
Rome, Alan K, Dr, Librn, Saint Mary Seminary, 28700 Euclid Ave, Wickliffe, OH, 44092. Tel: 440-943-7665. p. 1831
Romeo, Cara, Asst Dir, Commun Serv, K O Lee Aberdeen Public Library, 215 S E Fourth Ave, Aberdeen, SD, 57401. Tel: 605-626-7097. p. 2073

Rosburg, Thomas, Library Contact, Saint Peter Regional Treatment Center Libraries, MSH Education Dept Library, 2100 Sheppard Dr, Saint Peter, MN, 56082. Tel: 507-985-2320. p. 1203
Roscello, Annemarie, Ref (Info Servs), Bergen Community College, 400 Paramus Rd, Paramus, NJ, 07652-1595. Tel: 301-447-5569. p. 1432
Rosch, Angie, Ref, Jefferson Public Library, 321 S Main St, Jefferson, WI, 53549-1772. Tel: 920-674-7733. p. 2443
Roschen, Jessica, Outreach Coordr, Traverse Des Sioux Library Cooperative, 1400 Madison Ave, Ste 622, Mankato, MN, 56001-5488. Tel: 833-837-5422. p. 1181
Rosco, Dina, Head, Circ, West Nyack Free Library, 65 Strawtown Rd, West Nyack, NY, 10994. Tel: 845-358-6081. p. 1662
Roscup, Roxanne, Libr Dir, Sodus Community Library, 17 Maple Ave, Sodus, NY, 14551. Tel: 315-483-9292. p. 1642
Rose, Ahniwake, Pres & Chief Exec Officer, American Indian Higher Education Consortium, 121 Oronoco St, Alexandria, VA, 22314. Tel: 703-838-0400, Ext 111. p. 2776
Rose, Alisa, Asst Dir, Morgan County Library, 50 N 100 West, Morgan, UT, 84050. Tel: 801-829-3481. p. 2267
Rose, Amanda, Dir, Burnet County Library System, Marble Falls Public Library, 101 Main St, Marble Falls, TX, 78654. Tel: 830-693-3023. p. 2152
Rose, Amy, Sr Mgr, Library, Archives & Research Fellowship Program, National Gallery of Canada Library & Archives, 380 Sussex Dr, Ottawa, ON, K1N 9N4, CANADA. Tel: 613-714-6000, Ext 6146. p. 2667
Rose, Camille, Asst Dir, Library Engagement, Kankakee Public Library, 201 E Merchant St, Kankakee, IL, 60901. Tel: 815-939-4564. p. 604
Rose, Carrie, Co-Librn, Connecticut Legislative Library, Legislative Office Bldg, Rm 5400, 300 Capitol Ave, Hartford, CT, 06106-1591. Tel: 860-240-8888. p. 317
Rose, Cedric, Librn, Mercantile Library Association, 414 Walnut St, Cincinnati, OH, 45202. Tel: 513-621-0717. p. 1761
Rose, Coleen, Tech Serv Librn, Southwest Baptist University Libraries, 1600 University Ave, Bolivar, MO, 65613. Tel: 417-328-1631. p. 1238
Rose, Donna, Metadata Lead Librn, University of Arkansas at Little Rock, 2801 S University Ave, Little Rock, AR, 72204. Tel: 501-916-6182. p. 102
Rose, Elizabeth, Head, Tech Serv, University of Alabama in Huntsville, 4700 Holmes Ave, Huntsville, AL, 35805. Tel: 256-824-6537. p. 22
Rose, Elizabeth, Dr, Libr Dir, Fairfield Museum & History Center, 370 Beach Rd, Fairfield, CT, 06824. Tel: 203-259-1598, Ext 106. p. 311
Rose, Ellen, Librn I, Kansas Department of Corrections, 1607 State St, Ellsworth, KS, 67439. Tel: 785-472-5501, Ext 250, 785-472-6250. p. 806
Rose, Erica, Prog Coordr, University of Nebraska at Omaha, College of Education, Roskens Hall, Omaha, NE, 68182. Tel: 402-554-2119. p. 2788
Rose, Jacqueline, Dir, Ref/Tech Proc, Fort Meade Public Library, 75 E Broadway, Fort Meade, FL, 33841-2998. Tel: 863-285-8287. p. 402
Rose, Jesse, Dir, Ford-MacNichol Home, Wyandotte Museum, Archives, 2624 Biddle Ave, Wyandotte, MI, 48192. Tel: 734-324-7297. p. 1160
Rose, Kari, Dir, Eckels Memorial Library, 207 S Hwy 6, Oakland, IA, 51560. Tel: 712-482-6668. p. 774
Rose, Ken, Dir, Prog & Project Develop, Carnegie Mellon University, Hunt Library, 4909 Frew St, Pittsburgh, PA, 15213. Tel: 412-268-2444. p. 1992
Rose, Kimberley, Br Mgr, Lonesome Pine Regional Library, Jonnie B Deel Memorial, 198 Chase St, Clintwood, VA, 24228. Tel: 276-926-6617. p. 2354
Rose, Kimberley, Br Mgr, Lonesome Pine Regional Library, Haysi Public, 157 O'Quinn St, Haysi, VA, 24256. Tel: 276-865-4851. p. 2355
Rose, Kirsten, Ch, David & Joyce Milne Public Library, 1095 Main St, Williamstown, MA, 01267-2627. Tel: 413-458-5369. p. 1069
Rose, Laura, Asst Dir, Marshall Community Library, 605 Waterloo Rd, Marshall, WI, 53559. Tel: 608-655-3123. p. 2454
Rose, Lin, Librn, American Geological Institute Library, 4220 King St, Alexandria, VA, 22302-1502. Tel: 703-379-2480, Ext 239. p. 2303
Rose, Lourdes, Adul Prog Coordr/LAII, Yuma County Free Library District, 2951 S 21st Dr, Yuma, AZ, 85364. Tel: 928-782-1871. p. 85
Rose, Mark, Dir, Hermiston Public Library, 235 E Gladys Ave, Hermiston, OR, 97838. Tel: 541-567-2882. p. 1881
Rose, Mary, Archival Library Research Mgr, Madison County Historical Museum & Archival Library, 801 N Main St, Edwardsville, IL, 62025. Tel: 618-656-7569. p. 582
Rose, Matthew, Br Mgr, Sonoma County Library, Sebastopol Regional Library, 7140 Bodega Ave, Sebastopol, CA, 95472. Tel: 707-823-7691. p. 204
Rose, Ruthe, Asst Libr Dir, New York University School of Law, Vanderbilt Hall, 40 Washington Sq S, New York, NY, 10012-1099. Tel: 212-998-6306. p. 1599
Rose, Yvonne, Dir, Pawhuska Public Library, 1801 Lynn Ave, Pawhuska, OK, 74056. Tel: 918-287-3989. p. 1860
Roseberry, Jackilyn, Dir, Fremont Area District Library, 104 E Main St, Fremont, MI, 49412. Tel: 231-924-3480. p. 1108
Roseblatt, Hal, Adminr, United Lodge of Theosophists, 347 E 72nd St, New York, NY, 10021. Tel: 212-535-2230. p. 1603
Roseburg, Chad, Asst Dir, Info Tech, North Central Washington Libraries, 16 N Columbia St, Wenatchee, WA, 98801. Tel: 509-663-1117, Ext 134. p. 2393
Rosedale, Jeff, Dir, Manhattanville University Library, 2900 Purchase St, Purchase, NY, 10577. Tel: 914-323-5277. p. 1624
Rosekrans, Rick, Controller, The Library Network, 41365 Vincenti Ct, Novi, MI, 48375. Tel: 248-536-3100. p. 2767
Roseland, Mary, Librn, Marshall-Lyon County Library, Cottonwood Community, 86 W Main St, Cottonwood, MN, 56229. Tel: 507-423-6488. p. 1182
Rosell, Lea, Dir, Milford Public Library, 11 SE Front St, Milford, DE, 19963. Tel: 302-422-8996. p. 354
Roselle, Ann, Fac Librn, Phoenix College, 1202 W Thomas Rd, Phoenix, AZ, 85013. Tel: 602-285-7457. p. 72
Rosen, C Martin, Dir, Libr Serv, Kentuckiana Metroversity, Inc, 200 W Broadway, Ste 800, Louisville, KY, 40202. Tel: 812-941-2262. p. 2765
Rosen, Eric, Libr Tech, Alcohol Research Group Library, 6001 Shellmound St, Ste 450, Emeryville, CA, 94608. Tel: 510-898-5800. p. 140
Rosen, Fran, Colls Librn, Ferris State University Library, 1010 Campus Dr, Big Rapids, MI, 49307-2279. Tel: 231-591-3500. p. 1085
Rosen, Jack, Programmer, YA Serv, Patterson Library, 40 S Portage St, Westfield, NY, 14787. Tel: 716-326-2154. p. 1664
Rosen, Janice, Librn for Deaf, District of Columbia Talking Book & Braille Library, Center for Accessibility, Rm 215, 901 G St NW, Washington, DC, 20001. Tel: 202-727-2142. p. 365
Rosen, Lisa, Mgr, Shirley Ryan AbilityLab, 355 E Erie St, 10th Flr, Chicago, IL, 60611. Tel: 312-238-5433. p. 568
Rosen, Meeghan, Asst Dir, Head, Tech Serv, Chapel Hill Public Library, 100 Library Dr, Chapel Hill, NC, 27514. Tel: 919-969-2046. p. 1678
Rosen, Sam, Multimedia Support Librn, Deerfield Public Library, 920 Waukegan Rd, Deerfield, IL, 60015. Tel: 847-945-3311. p. 577
Rosen, Wendy L, Ref Librn, New Bern-Craven County Public Library, 400 Johnson St, New Bern, NC, 28560-4098. Tel: 252-638-7800. p. 1706
Rosenbalm, Sandy, Dir, Claiborne County Public Library, 1304 Old Knoxville Rd, Tazewell, TN, 37879. Tel: 423-626-5414. p. 2127
Rosenbaum, David, Dir, Plymouth Public Library, 103 N Jefferson Ave, Plymouth, NE, 68424. Tel: 402-656-4335. p. 1333
Rosenbaum, Lois, Dir, Hancock County Public Library, 138 Willow St, Sneedville, TN, 37869. Tel: 423-733-2020. p. 2126
Rosenberg, Judy, Commun Relations Mgr, Brighton Memorial Library, 2300 Elmwood Ave, Rochester, NY, 14618. Tel: 585-784-5300. p. 1628
Rosenberg, Rachel A, Dir, Communications, The University of Chicago Library, 1100 E 57th St, Chicago, IL, 60637-1502. Tel: 773-834-1519. p. 569
Rosenberg-Justman, Gayle, Tech Serv, Wilmette Public Library District, 1242 Wilmette Ave, Wilmette, IL, 60091-2558. Tel: 847-256-6920. p. 663
Rosenbloom, Megan, Assoc Dir, Coll Serv, University of Southern California Libraries, Norris Medical Library, 2003 Zonal Ave, Los Angeles, CA, 90089-9130. Tel: 323-442-1116. p. 170
Rosenblum, Lisa G, Exec Dir, King County Library System, 960 Newport Way NW, Issaquah, WA, 98027. Tel: 425-462-9600. p. 2365
Rosenblum, Sarah, Dir, Marshalltown Public Library, 105 W Boone St, Marshalltown, IA, 50158-4911. Tel: 641-754-5738. p. 768
Rosenbrook, Margaret B, Dir, Falmouth Area Library, 219 E Prosper Rd, Falmouth, MI, 49632-0602. Tel: 231-826-3738. p. 1104
Rosendahl, Matt, Libr Dir, University of Minnesota Duluth, 416 Library Dr, Duluth, MN, 55812. Tel: 218-726-6562. p. 1173
Rosendale, Nadine, Br Mgr, Carroll County Public Library, Eldersburg Branch, 6400 W Hemlock Dr, Eldersburg, MD, 21784-6538. Tel: 410-386-4460. p. 971
Rosenkrans, Korin, Br Mgr, Parsippany-Troy Hills Free Public Library, Lake Hiawatha Branch, 68 Nokomis Ave, Lake Hiawatha, NJ, 07034. Tel: 973-335-0952. p. 1433
Rosenkrans, Korin, Br Mgr, Parsippany-Troy Hills Free Public Library, Mount Tabor Branch, 31 Trinity Park, Mount Tabor, NJ, 07878. Tel: 973-627-9508. p. 1433
Rosenmiller, Leah, Ref/Outreach Librn, Lindenwood University Library, 209 S Kingshighway, Saint Charles, MO, 63301. Tel: 636-949-4820. p. 1268
Rosenstein, Jennifer, Libr Dir, Pace University Library, 15 Beekman St, New York, NY, 10038. Tel: 212-346-1778. p. 1600
Rosenthal, Adam, Dir of Libr, Hebrew Union College-Jewish Institute of Religion, Brookdale Ctr, HUC-JIR, One W Fourth St, New York, NY, 10012. Tel: 212-824-2258. p. 1587
Rosenthal, Adam, Dir of Libr, Hebrew Union College-Jewish Institute of Religion, 3101 Clifton Ave, Cincinnati, OH, 45220-2488. Tel: 513-221-1875. p. 1760
Rosenthal, Danielle Zino, Head, Tech, Univ Librn, Florida Gulf Coast University Library, 10501 FGCU Blvd S, Fort Myers, FL, 33965. Tel: 239-590-7633. p. 403
Rosenthal, Laurie, Dir, Commack Public Library, 18 Hauppauge Rd, Commack, NY, 11725-4498. Tel: 631-499-0888. p. 1521
Rosenthal, Robert, Dir, Mecklenburg County Public Library, 1294 Jefferson St, Boydton, VA, 23917. Tel: 434-738-6580. p. 2308
Rosenthal, Roger C, Exec Dir, Migrant Legal Action Program Library, 1001 Connecticut Ave NW, Ste 915, Washington, DC, 20036. Tel: 202-775-7780. p. 371

Rosenzweig, Sheri L, Digital Initiatives, Ref Librn, Boston Architectural College, 320 Newbury St, Boston, MA, 02115. Tel: 617-585-0257. p. 991
Roser, Missy, Head, Res & Instruction, Amherst College, 61 Quadrangle Dr, Amherst, MA, 01002. p. 984
Rosetto, Ashley, Youth Serv Librn, Commerce Township Community Library, 180 E Commerce, Commerce Township, MI, 48382. Tel: 248-669-8108. p. 1093
Rosewicz, Lee Ann, Computer Tech, Barry-Lawrence Regional Library, 213 Sixth St, Monett, MO, 65708-2147. Tel: 417-235-6646. p. 1262
Rosfeld, Amy, Librn, Goessel Public Library, 101 S Cedar, Goessel, KS, 67053. Tel: 620-367-8440. p. 810
Roshia, Jackie, Assoc Curator, New York State Division for Historic Preservation, 17 Rippleton Rd, Cazenovia, NY, 13035. Tel: 315-655-3200. p. 1515
Rosier, Deanna, Dir, New Lisbon Memorial Library, 115 W Park St, New Lisbon, WI, 53950-1250. Tel: 608-562-3213. p. 2464
Rosillo, Sylvia, Student Engagement Librn, Oakton College Library, 1600 E Golf Rd, Rm 1406, Des Plaines, IL, 60016. Tel: 847-635-1642, 847-635-1644. p. 578
Rosinski-Kauz, Donna, Dir, Libr Serv, Ocean County College Library, College Dr, Toms River, NJ, 08754. Tel: 732-255-0392. p. 1446
Roske, Peggy, Archivist, Saint John's University, 2835 Abbey Plaza, Collegeville, MN, 56321. Tel: 320-363-2129. p. 1170
Roske, Peggy, Archivist, College of Saint Benedict, 37 S College Ave, Saint Joseph, MN, 56374. Tel: 320-363-5019. p. 1199
Rosko, Tom, Univ Librn, Naval Postgraduate School, 411 Dyer Rd, Monterey, CA, 93943. Tel: 831-656-2947. p. 179
Roslund, Matthew, Med Librn, Bassett Mary Imogene Hospital, Bassett Medical Ctr, One Atwell Rd, Cooperstown, NY, 13326. Tel: 607-547-3115. p. 1521
Roslund, Matthew, Research Librn, New York Center for Agricultural Medicine & Health Library, 6160 State Hwy 28, Fly Creek, NY, 13337. Tel: 607-547-3116. p. 1534
Rosman, Phillipa, Archives & Spec Coll Librn, Phillips Theological Seminary Library, 901 N Mingo Rd, Tulsa, OK, 74116. Tel: 918-270-6488. p. 1865
Rosolowski, Karen, Dir, Stevens Memorial Community Library, 146 Main St, Attica, NY, 14011-1243. Tel: 585-591-2733. p. 1488
Ross, Alexander, Asst Prof, University of British Columbia, The Irving K Barber Learning Ctr, 1961 E Mall, Ste 470, Vancouver, BC, V6T 1Z1, CANADA. Tel: 604-822-2404. p. 2795
Ross, Alexandra, Assoc Dir, Humber College, Lakeshore Campus Library, 3199 Lakeshore Blvd W, Toronto, ON, M8V 1K8, CANADA. Tel: 416-675-6622, Ext 3250. p. 2690
Ross, Andrea, Br Mgr, Washington County Library System, Torrey Wood Memorial, 302 East Ave N, Hollandale, MS, 38748-3714. Tel: 662-827-2335. p. 1217
Ross, Ann Marie, Circ, Hanson Public Library, 132 Maquan St, Hanson, MA, 02341. Tel: 781-293-2151. p. 1023
Ross, Bernadette, Ref Librn, United States Army, John L Throckmorton Library, IMSE-BRG-MWR-L Bldg 1-3346, Randolph St, Fort Bragg, NC, 28310-5000. Tel: 910-396-2665. p. 1689
Ross, Bonnie, Br Mgr, Johnson County Library, Kaycee Branch, 231 Ritter Ave, Kaycee, WY, 82639. Tel: 307-738-2473. p. 2491
Ross, Carla, Librn, Holmes Community College, 1180 W Monroe St, Grenada, MS, 38901. Tel: 662-227-2363. p. 1217
Ross, Carr, Web Technologies Librn, Bowdoin College Library, 3000 College Sta, Brunswick, ME, 04011-8421. p. 919
Ross, Celia, Fac Res Serv/Ref Serv Librn, University of Michigan, Kresge Library Services, Stephen M Ross School of Business, 701 Tappan St, Ann Arbor, MI, 48109-1234. Tel: 734-763-5452. p. 1079
Ross, Charles, Human Res Dir, Harford County Public Library, 1221-A Brass Mill Rd, Belcamp, MD, 21017-1209. Tel: 410-273-5704. p. 958
Ross, Christina, Dir, Brandon Public Library, 117 E Main St, Brandon, WI, 53919. Tel: 920-346-2350. p. 2425
Ross, Christopher, Libr Dir, Stonington Public Library, 64 Main St, Stonington, ME, 04681. Tel: 207-367-5926. p. 943
Ross, Collette, Dir, Leon-Saxeville Township Library, N4715 County Rd E, Pine River, WI, 54965. Tel: 920-987-5110. p. 2469
Ross, Cooper, Libr Tech, Paul Smiths College of Arts & Sciences, 7833 New York 30, Paul Smiths, NY, 12970. Tel: 518-327-6312. p. 1615
Ross, Dan, Head, Access Serv, State University of New York College, SUNY Geneseo, One College Circle, Geneseo, NY, 14454-1498. Tel: 585-245-5594. p. 1537
Ross, David, Commun Librn, Monroe County Library System, Carleton Branch Library, 1444 Kent St, Carleton, MI, 48117. Tel: 734-654-2180. p. 1133
Ross, David, Commun Librn, Monroe County Library System, South Rockwood Branch, 5676 Carleton Rockwood Rd, Ste C, South Rockwood, MI, 48179. Tel: 734-379-3333. p. 1134
Ross, David, Head Librn, Head, Res Serv, University of New Brunswick, Saint John Campus, 100 Tucker Park Rd, Saint John, NB, E2L 4L5, CANADA. Tel: 506-648-5832. p. 2605
Ross, David E, Commun Librn, Monroe County Library System, Newport Branch, 8120 N Dixie Hwy, Newport, MI, 48166. Tel: 734-586-2117. p. 1134
Ross, Debbie, Librn, Illinois Department of Corrections, 2268 E Morton Ave, Jacksonville, IL, 62650. Tel: 217-245-1481, Ext 334. p. 602
Ross, Deborah, Doc Librn, Thiel College, 75 College Ave, Greenville, PA, 16125-2183. Tel: 724-589-2127. p. 1939
Ross, Doris, Chief Cataloger, Mgr, Desoto Parish Library, 109 Crosby St, Mansfield, LA, 71052. Tel: 318-872-6100. p. 895
Ross, Gail, Libr Mgr, York Library Region, Upper Miramichi Community Library, Central New Brunswick Academy Bldg, 7263 Rte 8, Unit 1, New Bandon, NB, E9C 2A7, CANADA. Tel: 506-365-2096. p. 2603
Ross, Heather, Br Mgr, Pima County Public Library, Himmel Park, 1035 N Treat Ave, Tucson, AZ, 85716. Tel: 520-594-5305. p. 82
Ross, Ishmael, Collections Cataloger, Historic New Orleans Collection, 410 Chartres St, New Orleans, LA, 70130. Tel: 504-556-7131. p. 901
Ross, Janet, Librn, Stanly Community College Library, Snyder Bldg, 141 College Dr, 1st Flr, Albemarle, NC, 28001. Tel: 704-991-0337. p. 1671
Ross, Jeannie, Libr Dir, Barclay College, 100 E Cherry St, Haviland, KS, 67059. Tel: 620-862-5274. p. 812
Ross, Jeffrey, Indexer, Columbia University, Avery Architectural & Fine Arts Library, 300 Avery Hall, 1172 Amsterdam Ave, MC 0301, New York, NY, 10027. Tel: 212-854-6199. p. 1583
Ross, Jennifer, Dir, Lacon Public Library District, 205 Sixth St, Lacon, IL, 61540. Tel: 309-246-2855. p. 606
Ross, Jennifer, Br Mgr, Washington County Free Library, Boonsboro Free Library, 401 Potomac St, Boonsboro, MD, 21713. Tel: 301-432-5723. p. 968
Ross, Jennifer, Br Mgr, Washington County Free Library, Keedysville Branch, 22 Taylor Dr, Keedysville, MD, 21756. Tel: 301-432-6641. p. 968
Ross, Jessica, Dir, Washington County Public Library, 14102 Saint Stephens Ave, Chatom, AL, 36518. Tel: 251-847-2097. p. 11
Ross, Jessica, Dir, Adult Serv, Durham Public Library, 49 Madbury Rd, Durham, NH, 03824. Tel: 603-868-6699. p. 1361
Ross, Jody, Tech Serv Librn, Indianola Public Library, 207 North B St, Indianola, IA, 50125. Tel: 515-961-9418. p. 759
Ross, Joleen, Dir, Halstead Public Library, 264 Main St, Halstead, KS, 67056-0285. Tel: 316-835-2170. p. 811
Ross, Kate, Acq Librn, Head, Tech Serv, Saint John Fisher University, 3690 East Ave, Rochester, NY, 14618-3599. Tel: 585-385-8136. p. 1630
Ross, Kathryn, Sr Librn, Los Angeles Public Library System, West Los Angeles Regional Library, 11360 Santa Monica Blvd, Los Angeles, CA, 90025-3152. Tel: 310-575-8323. p. 165
Ross Kelliher, Sarah, Spec Coll Librn, Midland County Public Library, 301 W Missouri Ave, Midland, TX, 79701. Tel: 432-688-4320. p. 2219
Ross, Kevin, Dean, Leatherby Libr, Chapman University, One University Dr, Orange, CA, 92866. Tel: 714-532-7756. p. 188
Ross, Krista, Exec Dir, Southeast Library System (SELS), 2600 19th St, Rochester, MN, 55901. Tel: 507-288-5513. p. 1195
Ross, Krista, Exec Dir, Southeastern Libraries Cooperating, 2600 19th St NW, Rochester, MN, 55901-0767. Tel: 507-288-5513. p. 2768
Ross, Laura, Head, Pub Serv, Touro University, 225 Eastview Dr, Central Islip, NY, 11722-4539. Tel: 631-761-7150. p. 1516
Ross, Laurence, Head, ILL, Head, Ref Serv, Morris County Library, 30 E Hanover Ave, Whippany, NJ, 07981. Tel: 973-285-6930. p. 1455
Ross, Leanne, Programming Coord, Children & Adults, Elmwood Park Public Library, 210 Lee St, Elmwood Park, NJ, 07407. Tel: 201-796-8888. p. 1401
Ross, Marc, Head Librn, University of Pittsburgh at Bradford, 300 Campus Dr, Bradford, PA, 16701. Tel: 814-362-4452. p. 1914
Ross, Marc, Head of Libr, University of Pittsburgh at Titusville, 504 E Main St, Titusville, PA, 16354. Tel: 814-827-4452. p. 2013
Ross, Matthew, Libr Dir, Tiffin-Seneca Public Library, 77 Jefferson St, Tiffin, OH, 44883. Tel: 419-447-3751. p. 1823
Ross, Michelle, Libr Dir, Samuels Public Library, 330 E Criser Rd, Front Royal, VA, 22630. Tel: 540-635-3153, Ext 110. p. 2321
Ross, Pam, Exec Dir, Snyder County Libraries, One North High St, Selinsgrove, PA, 17870-1548. Tel: 570-374-7163. p. 2005
Ross, Philip, Sr Librn, Torrance Public Library, Walteria, 3815 W 242nd St, Torrance, CA, 90505-6410. Tel: 310-375-8418. p. 253
Ross, Sandie, Info Res Spec, Fishbeck, Thompson, Carr & Huber, 1515 Arboretum Dr SE, Grand Rapids, MI, 49546. Tel: 616-575-3824. p. 1110
Ross, Sarah, Libr Mgr, New York Public Library - Astor, Lenox & Tilden Foundations, Dongan Hills Branch, 1617 Richmond Rd, (Between Seaview & Liberty Aves), Staten Island, NY, 10304. Tel: 718-351-1444. p. 1595
Ross, Sarah, Libr Dir, Norris Public Library, 132 N Main, Rutherfordton, NC, 28139. Tel: 828-287-4981, Ext 3. p. 1714
Ross, Saundra, Librn, Birmingham Public Library, North Avondale, 501 43rd St N, Birmingham, AL, 35222-1417. Tel: 205-592-2082. p. 7
Ross, Seamus, Dr, Prof, University of Toronto, 140 St George St, Toronto, ON, M5S 3G6, CANADA. Tel: 416-978-5763. p. 2796
Ross, Shelley, Chief Exec Officer, Red Deer Public Library, 4818 49th St, Red Deer, AB, T4N 1T9, CANADA. Tel: 403-346-4576. p. 2551
Ross, Sheri, PhD, Assoc Prof, Saint Catherine University, 2004 Randolph Ave, Mailstop No 4125, Saint Paul, MN, 55105. Tel: 651-690-6802. p. 2787

Ross, Steve, Chief Exec Officer, World Research Foundation Library, 41 Bell Rock Plaza, Sedona, AZ, 86351. Tel: 928-284-3300. p. 78

Ross, Susan, Libr Mgr, Office of the Auditor General of Canada, West Tower, 240 Sparks St, 11th Flr, Ottawa, ON, K1A 0G6, CANADA. Tel: 613-952-0213. p. 2668

Ross, Taylor, Govt Doc, Libr Assoc, University of Georgia Libraries, Map & Government Information, 320 S Jackson St, Athens, GA, 30602. Tel: 706-542-0489. p. 459

Ross, Tesa, Head, Pub Serv, Reed Memorial Library, 167 E Main St, Ravenna, OH, 44266-3197. Tel: 330-296-2827, Ext 401. p. 1817

Ross, Trent, Dep Dir, Rocky River Public Library, 1600 Hampton Rd, Rocky River, OH, 44116-2699. Tel: 440-895-3727. p. 1818

Ross, William E, Dr, Spec Coll Librn, University of New Hampshire Library, 18 Library Way, Durham, NH, 03824. Tel: 603-862-0346. p. 1362

Rosseel, Trish, Dir, Learning Resources & Records Mgmt, Douglas College Library & Learning Centre, 700 Royal Ave, Rm N2100, New Westminster, BC, V3M 5Z5, CANADA. Tel: 604-527-5182. p. 2572

Rosser, Chris, Instrul Librn, Theological Librn, Oklahoma Christian University, 2501 E Memorial Rd, Edmond, OK, 73013. Tel: 405-425-5323. p. 1846

Rosset, Marie, Chief Exec Officer, Powassan & District Union Public Library, 324 Clark St, Powassan, ON, P0H 1Z0, CANADA. Tel: 705-724-3618. p. 2674

Rossetto, Gail, Librn, Northumberland Public Library, 31 State St, Groveton, NH, 03582. Tel: 603-636-2066. p. 1366

Rossi, Jessica, Tech Serv, Community College of Philadelphia Library, Mint Bldg, Level 1, 1700 Spring Garden St, Philadelphia, PA, 19130. Tel: 215-751-8394. p. 1975

Rossi, Maureen, Dir, Libr Serv, Pepper, Hamilton LLP, 4000 Town Ctr, Ste 1800, Southfield, MI, 48075. Tel: 248-359-7300. p. 1151

Rossini, Adriana, Registrar & Dir, Student Serv, University of Toronto, 140 St George St, Toronto, ON, M5S 3G6, CANADA. Tel: 416-978-8589. p. 2796

Rossiter, Debra, Dir, Camp Point Public Library, 206 E State St, Camp Point, IL, 62320. Tel: 217-593-7021. p. 548

Rossiter, Shannon, Dir, Mohave County Historical Society, 400 W Beale St, Kingman, AZ, 86401. Tel: 928-753-3195. p. 64

Rossman, Doralyn, Head, Digital Libr Initiatives, Montana State University Library, One Centennial Mall, Bozeman, MT, 59717. Tel: 406-994-3153. p. 1289

Rossman, Janet N, Youth Serv Librn, Perry Public Library, 70 N Main St, Perry, NY, 14530-1299. Tel: 585-237-2243. p. 1617

Rossman, Michelle, Chairperson, Ref (Info Servs), Lakeland Community College Library, Bldg C, Rm 3051, 7700 Clocktower Dr, Kirtland, OH, 44094-5198. Tel: 440-525-7069. p. 1793

Rossman, Nick, Libr Dir, Carnegie-Stout Public Library, 360 W 11th St, Dubuque, IA, 52001. Tel: 563-589-4126. p. 748

Rossman, Rhonda, Dir, West Nyack Free Library, 65 Strawtown Rd, West Nyack, NY, 10994. Tel: 845-358-6081. p. 1662

Rossmann, Brian, Assoc Dean of Libr, Montana State University Library, One Centennial Mall, Bozeman, MT, 59717. Tel: 406-994-5298. p. 1289

Rossner, Marilyn, Dr, Library Contact, International Institute of Integral Human Sciences Library, 1974 de Maisonneuve W, Montreal, QC, H3H 1K5, CANADA. Tel: 514-937-8359. p. 2725

Rosso, Christy, Ch, Gloucester, Lyceum & Sawyer Free Library, Two Dale Ave, Gloucester, MA, 01930. Tel: 978-325-5506. p. 1021

Rosson, Jennifer, Dir, Caney City Library, 211 W Fifth Ave, Caney, KS, 67333. Tel: 620-879-5341. p. 800

Rosson, Loren, Circ Supvr, Nashua Public Library, Two Court St, Nashua, NH, 03060. Tel: 603-589-4617. p. 1374

Rosson, Michael, Libr Instruction, Kingsborough Community College, 2001 Oriental Blvd, Brooklyn, NY, 11235. Tel: 718-368-5146. p. 1504

Rostami, Amanda, Dir, Sigourney Public Library, 720 E Jackson, Sigourney, IA, 52591-1505. Tel: 641-622-2890. p. 782

Rostomian, Patricia, Sr Librn, Los Angeles Public Library System, Valley Plaza Branch Library, 12311 Vanowen St, North Hollywood, CA, 91605. Tel: 818-765-9251. p. 165

Rostron, Stephanie, Dir, Piqua Public Library, 116 W High St, Piqua, OH, 45356. Tel: 937-773-6753. p. 1815

Rostron, Stephenie, Dir, Wilberforce University, 1055 N Bickett Rd, Wilberforce, OH, 45384-5801. Tel: 937-502-3955. p. 1831

Rote, Wendy, Dir, West End Library, 45 Ball Park Rd, Laurelton, PA, 17835. Tel: 570-922-4773. p. 1953

Roten, Caroline, Asst Dir, Haywood County Public Library, 678 S Haywood St, Waynesville, NC, 28786. Tel: 828-356-2518. p. 1721

Rotenfeld, Michoel, Assoc Dir of Libr, Touro College Libraries, 320 W 31st St, New York, NY, 10001. Tel: 212-463-0400, Ext 55224. p. 1603

Roth, Andrew, Customer Experience Supervisor, Douglas County Libraries, Castle Pines Branch, 360 Village Square Lane, Castle Pines, CO, 80108. Tel: 303-791-7323. p. 270

Roth, Arla, Head Librn, Elgin Public Library, 121 Main St N, Elgin, ND, 58533. Tel: 701-584-2181. p. 1732

Roth, Ashley, Librn, Kirwin City Library, First & Main, Kirwin, KS, 67644. Tel: 785-543-6652. p. 817

Roth, James, Dep Dir, National Archives & Records Administration, Columbia Point, Boston, MA, 02125. Tel: 617-514-1600. p. 997

Roth, Jennifer, Libr Dir, Westland Public Library, 6123 Central City Pkwy, Westland, MI, 48185. Tel: 734-326-6123. p. 1159

Roth, Linda, Dir, Libr Serv, Reform Congregation Keneseth Israel, 8339 Old York Rd, Elkins Park, PA, 19027. Tel: 215-887-8700, Ext 417. p. 1930

Roth, Noah, Electronic Res Librn, SUNY Broome Community College, 907 Front St, Binghamton, NY, 13905-1328. Tel: 607-778-5528. p. 1494

Rothauge, Fred A, Dir, National Ground Water Association, 601 Dempsey Rd, Westerville, OH, 43081. Tel: 614-898-7791. p. 1830

Rothausen, Brittany, Br Mgr, Kanawha County Public Library, Cross Lanes, 5449 Big Tyler Rd, Charleston, WV, 25313. Tel: 304-776-5999. p. 2400

Rothbauer, Paulette, Assoc Prof, Western University, FIMS & Nursing Bldg, Rm 2020, London, ON, N6A 5B9, CANADA. Tel: 519-661-2111, Ext 88512. p. 2796

Rothbaum, Ellen, Librn, Saint Francis Hospital & Heart Center, 100 Port Washington Blvd, Roslyn, NY, 11576. Tel: 516-562-6673. p. 1633

Rothchild, Jessica, Librn, Burr Oak Community Library, 231 Pennsylvania St, Burr Oak, KS, 66936. Tel: 785-647-5597. p. 800

Rothenberg, Sandra, Instruction Coordr, Ref Librn, Framingham State University, 100 State St, Framingham, MA, 01701. Tel: 508-626-4083. p. 1019

Rothenberger, Maria, Res Serv, Fashion Institute of Technology-SUNY, Seventh Ave at 27th St, 227 W 27th St, New York, NY, 10001-5992. Tel: 212-217-4340. p. 1585

Rothenbuehler, Erin Denis, Dir, Bellaire Public Library, 330 32nd St, Bellaire, OH, 43906. Tel: 740-676-9421. p. 1750

Rotherman, Chantal, Digital Serv Librn, Tech Librn, Onondaga Free Library, 4840 W Seneca Tpk, Syracuse, NY, 13215. Tel: 315-492-1727. p. 1650

Rothfuss, Matthew, Head, Adult Serv, Bethlehem Area Public Library, 11 W Church St, Bethlehem, PA, 18018. Tel: 610-867-3761, Ext 212. p. 1911

Rothhaar, Jan, Tech Serv, Broward College, Bldg 17, 3501 SW Davie Rd, Davie, FL, 33314. Tel: 954-201-6655. p. 391

Rothman, Lorraine, Dir, Staatsburg Library, 70 Old Post Rd, Staatsburg, NY, 12580-0397. Tel: 845-889-4683. p. 1644

Rothrock, Donna, Assoc Librn, Salem College, Lorraine F Rudolph Fine Arts Center Library, 500 Salem Rd, Winston-Salem, NC, 27101. Tel: 336-917-5475. p. 1726

Rothstein, Cara, Ch Serv, Thelma Dingus Bryant Library, 409 W Main St, Wallace, NC, 28466-2909. Tel: 910-285-3796. p. 1720

Rothstein, Jane, Archivist/Librn, Congregation Mishkan Or, Jack & Lilyan Mandel Bldg, 26000 Shaker Blvd, Beachwood, OH, 44122. Tel: 216-455-1724. p. 1749

Rothstein, Jill, Head Librn, JBI Library, 110 E 30th St, New York, NY, 10016. Tel: 212-889-2525. p. 1589

Rothstein, Jill, Chief Librn, New York Public Library - Astor, Lenox & Tilden Foundations, Andrew Heiskell Braille & Talking Book Library, 40 W 20th St, (Between Fifth & Sixth Aves), New York, NY, 10011-4211. Tel: 212-206-5400. p. 1595

Rothstein, Kathleen, Regional Br Mgr, Pasco County Library System, Land O' Lakes Branch, 2818 Collier Pkwy, Land O'Lakes, FL, 34639. Tel: 813-929-1214. p. 410

Rothstein, Linda, Asst Dir, Clearwater Public Library System, 100 N Osceola Ave, Clearwater, FL, 33755. Tel: 727-562-4970. p. 388

Rothweiler, Jeffrey, Dir/Fiscal Officer, Pataskala Public Library, 101 S Vine St, Pataskala, OH, 43062. Tel: 740-927-9986. p. 1814

Rothwell, Barbara, Managing Librn, Foster Garvey PC, 1111 Third Ave, Ste 3000, Seattle, WA, 98101. Tel: 206-447-2811. p. 2376

Rotman, Chloe, Mgr, Libr Serv, Boston Children's Hospital Medical Library, 300 Longwood Ave, Boston, MA, 02115. Tel: 617-355-7232. p. 991

Rotroff, Kristi, Libr Dir, Northwest State Community College Library, 22600 State Rte 34, Archbold, OH, 43502-9517. Tel: 419-267-1271. p. 1746

Rotvik, Cordelle, Libr Mgr, Big Valley Municipal Library, 29 First Ave S, Big Valley, AB, T0J 0G0, CANADA. Tel: 403-876-2642. p. 2523

Rouan, Judith, Dir Gen, Centre de documentation sur l'education des adultes et la condition feminine, 469 rue Jean Talon Ouest, bureau 229, Montreal, QC, H3N 1R4, CANADA. Tel: 514-876-1180. p. 2722

Roubal, Michelle Y, Librn, Technical Assistant Program Coord, Joliet Junior College Library, Campus Ctr (A-Bldg), 2nd Flr, 1215 Houbolt Rd, Joliet, IL, 60431. Tel: 815-280-2350. p. 603

Roubal, Rylie, Dir, Hinckley Public Library District, 100 N Maple St, Hinckley, IL, 60520. Tel: 815-286-3220. p. 600

Roughen, Patrick, Asst Prof, North Carolina Central University, 1801 Fayetteville St, Durham, NC, 27707. Tel: 919-530-6485. p. 2790

Rouhana, Lauren, Coll Mgr, Hernando County Public Library System, 238 Howell Ave, Brooksville, FL, 34601. Tel: 352-754-4043. p. 387

Roulett, Margaret, Mgr, Archives & Spec Coll, Western Reserve Historical Society Research Library, 10825 East Blvd, Cleveland, OH, 44106. Tel: 216-721-5722, Ext 1519. p. 1770

Roulhac, Tomeka, Br Mgr, Albemarle Regional Library, Hertford County Library, 303 W Tryon St, Winton, NC, 27986. Tel: 252-358-7855. p. 1727

Roulston, Linda, Librn, University of New Brunswick Libraries, Five Macaulay Lane, Fredericton, NB, E3B 5H5, CANADA. Tel: 506-451-6879. p. 2601

Round, Nancy, Dir Educ & Outreach, Joslyn Art Museum, 2200 Dodge St, Omaha, NE, 68102-1292. Tel: 402-661-3859. p. 1328

Rounds, Chris, Automation/Pub Serv Librn, Dyer Library, 371 Main St, Saco, ME, 04072. Tel: 207-283-3861. p. 939

Rounds, Laura, Acq Librn, Cat Librn, University of Tampa, 401 W Kennedy Blvd, Tampa, FL, 33606-1490. Tel: 813-257-3649. p. 450

Rounds, Leslie L, Exec Dir, Dyer Library, 371 Main St, Saco, ME, 04072. Tel: 207-283-3861. p. 939

Rounds, Mary, Librn, Corvallis-Benton County Public Library, Alsea Community Library, 19192 Alsea Hwy, Alsea, OR, 97324. Tel: 541-487-5061. p. 1876

Rounds, Michelle, Libr Mgr, Morrisville Public Library, 83 E Main St, Morrisville, NY, 13408. Tel: 315-684-9130. p. 1574

Roundtree, Koven, Chief, Human Resources, Anne Arundel County Public Library, Five Harry Truman Pkwy, Annapolis, MD, 21401. Tel: 410-222-1892. p. 950

Roundtree, Whitney, Libr Dir, Franklin County Public Library, 160 Hickory Dip, Eastpoint, FL, 32328. Tel: 850-670-8151. p. 394

Rounsville, Lorine, Dir, Hamlin Memorial Library, 123 S Mechanic St, Smethport, PA, 16749. Tel: 814-887-9262. p. 2008

Rountree, Brian, Brother, Librn, Grand Lodge of Manitoba, 420 Corydon Ave, Winnipeg, MB, R3L 0N8, CANADA. Tel: 204-453-7410. p. 2593

Rountree, Christi, Info Spec, Air Force Research Laboratory, Technical Library, 203 W Eglin Blvd, Ste 300, Eglin AFB, FL, 32542-6843. Tel: 850-882-3212, 850-882-5586. p. 395

Rountree, Renae, Dir, Washington County Library, 1444 Jackson Ave, Chipley, FL, 32428. Tel: 850-638-1314. p. 388

Roupe, Cindy, Dir, Ref, State Library of Kansas, State Capitol Bldg, Rm 312-N, 300 SW Tenth Ave, Topeka, KS, 66612. Tel: 785-296-3296. p. 839

Rourke, Lorna, Univ Librn, Saint Jerome's University Library, 290 Westmount Rd N, Waterloo, ON, N2L 3G3, CANADA. Tel: 519-884-8111, Ext 28271. p. 2702

Rouse, Catherina, Chief Exec Officer, Clarence-Rockland Public Library, 1525 du Parc Ave, Unit 2, Rockland, ON, K4K 1C3, CANADA. Tel: 613-446-5680. p. 2676

Rouse, Deborah, Campus Librn, Greenville Technical College Libraries, Brashier Campus, Bldg 202, Rm 103, 1830 W Georgia Rd, Simpsonville, SC, 29680. Tel: 864-250-4162. p. 2062

Rouse, Zachary, Access Serv Supvr, Columbia University, Avery Architectural & Fine Arts Library, 300 Avery Hall, 1172 Amsterdam Ave, MC 0301, New York, NY, 10027. Tel: 212-854-6199. p. 1583

Roush, Adrienne, Fac Librn, Grays Harbor College, 1620 Edward P Smith Dr, Aberdeen, WA, 98520. Tel: 360-538-4053. p. 2357

Rousiouk, Anjela, Libr Tech, Conservatoire de Musique de Montreal Bibliotheque, 4750 Ave Henri-Julien, 3rd Flr, Montreal, QC, H2T 2C8, CANADA. Tel: 514-873-4031, Ext 250. p. 2724

Rousseau, Randi, Head, Cat, Clark University, 950 Main St, Worcester, MA, 01610-1477. Tel: 508-793-7156. p. 1071

Rousseau, Susan, Dir, Brownell Library, 44 Commons, Little Compton, RI, 02837. Tel: 401-635-8562. p. 2034

Rousseau, Thais, Assoc Dir, Coll Serv, Capital Area District Libraries, 401 S Capitol Ave, Lansing, MI, 48933. Tel: 517-367-6325. p. 1124

Rousseau, Tyler, Ref (Info Servs), Monroe Township Public Library, Four Municipal Plaza, Monroe Township, NJ, 08831-1900. Tel: 732-521-5000, Ext 123. p. 1419

Roussel, Denis, Br Mgr, Government of Canada, Federal Courts & Tax Court of Canada, Courts Administration Service-Library Services, 90 Sparks St, Ottawa, ON, K1A 0H9, CANADA. Tel: 613-992-1704. p. 2667

Roussel, Denis, Librn, Government of Canada, Courts Administration Service, Tax Library, 200 Kent St, Ottawa, ON, K1A 0M1, CANADA. Tel: 613-992-1704. p. 2667

Roussel, Mark, Circ Mgr, School of Visual Arts Library, 380 Second Ave, 2nd Flr, New York, NY, 10010. Tel: 212-592-2689. p. 1601

Roussin, Jackie, Children's Prog Librn, Flint Public Library, One S Main St, Middleton, MA, 01949. Tel: 978-774-8132. p. 1035

Rout, Les, Br Librn, Genesee District Library, Vera B Rison-Beecher Library, 1386 W Coldwater Rd, Flint, MI, 48505. Tel: 810-789-2800. p. 1106

Routhier, Edith, Asst Regional Dir, Haut-Saint-Jean Regional Library, 15 rue de l'Eglise St, Ste 102, Edmundston, NB, E3V 1J3, CANADA. Tel: 506-735-2074. p. 2600

Routsong, Scott, Dir, Brooks County Public Library, 404 Barwick Rd, Quitman, GA, 31643. Tel: 229-263-4412. p. 493

Roux, Johanne, Archives, Tech, Libr Tech, Ministry of Northern Development & Mines, 933 Ramsey Lake Rd, Level A-3, Sudbury, ON, P3E 6B5, CANADA. Tel: 705-670-5614. p. 2683

Rovatti-Leonard, Angela, Ch, Montague Public Libraries, 201 Ave A, Turners Falls, MA, 01376-1989. Tel: 413-863-3214, Ext 2. p. 1060

Rovi, Laura, Asst Librn, Bayfield Carnegie Library, 37 N Broad St, Bayfield, WI, 54814. Tel: 715-779-3953. p. 2422

Row, Christine, Chief Exec Officer, Mississippi Mills Libraries, 155 High St, Almonte, ON, K0A 1A0, CANADA. Tel: 613-256-1037. p. 2628

Row, Christine, Chief Exec Officer, Mississippi Mills Libraries, Pakenham Library, 128 MacFarlane St, Pakenham, ON, K0A 2X0, CANADA. Tel: 613-624-5306. p. 2628

Rowan, Carey, Dir, Contra Costa County Public Law Library, 1020 Ward St, 1st Flr, Martinez, CA, 94553-1360. Tel: 925-646-2783. p. 175

Rowe, Alina, Br Mgr, Pima County Public Library, Woods Memorial Branch, 3455 N First Ave, Tucson, AZ, 85719. Tel: 520-594-5445. p. 83

Rowe, Andy, Circ Supvr, Belleville Public Library, 121 E Washington St, Belleville, IL, 62220. Tel: 618-234-0441. p. 541

Rowe, Dora, Instrul Res, Instrul Serv Librn, Union Presbyterian Seminary Library, 3401 Brook Rd, Richmond, VA, 23227. Tel: 804-278-4324. p. 2342

Rowe, Helen, Fiscal Serv Mgr, Baltimore County Public Library, 320 York Rd, Towson, MD, 21204-5179. Tel: 410-887-6100. p. 979

Rowe, Kathryn, Head, Acq & Ser, University of North Carolina School of the Arts Library, 1533 S Main St, Winston-Salem, NC, 27127. Tel: 336-770-3270. p. 1726

Rowe, Kathy, Librn, Powell Memorial Library, 951 W College St, Troy, MO, 63379. Tel: 636-462-4874. p. 1283

Rowe, Max, Pub Serv Spec, Library Connection, Inc, 599 Matianuck Ave, Windsor, CT, 06095-3567. Tel: 860-937-8263. p. 2763

Rowe, Monk, Dir, Jazz Archives, Hamilton College, 198 College Hill Rd, Clinton, NY, 13323. Tel: 315-859-4071. p. 1519

Rowe, Pam, Br Mgr, Bullitt County Public Library, Mount Washington Branch, 214 N Bardstown Rd, Mount Washington, KY, 40047. Tel: 502-538-7560. p. 875

Rowe, Robert, Head, Info Tech, Finkelstein Memorial Library, 24 Chestnut St, Spring Valley, NY, 10977. Tel: 845-352-5700, Ext 294. p. 1644

Rowe, Ronda, Communications Librn, Syst Librn, University of Texas Libraries, 101 E 21st St, Austin, TX, 78705. Tel: 512-495-4110. p. 2142

Rowe, Ruth, Libr Mgr, West Winfield Library, Bisby Hall, 179 South St, West Winfield, NY, 13491-2826. Tel: 315-822-6394. p. 1663

Rowe, Shannon, Library Contact, US National Park Service, 41 Cockspur Island Rd, Savannah, GA, 31410. Tel: 912-219-4233. p. 497

Rowe, Sylvia, Cat/Ref Librn, Jackson State Community College Library, 2046 North Pkwy, Jackson, TN, 38301. Tel: 731-425-2609. p. 2102

Rowe, Terri, Coordr, Tech Serv, North Tonawanda Public Library, 505 Meadow Dr, North Tonawanda, NY, 14120. Tel: 716-693-4132. p. 1608

Rowe, Wendy, Ch, Barrington Public Library, 105 Ramsdell Lane, Barrington, NH, 03825-7469. Tel: 603-664-9715. p. 1354

Rowell, Barbara, Dir, Jacksonville Public Library, 200 Pelham Rd S, Jacksonville, AL, 36265. Tel: 256-435-6332. p. 23

Rowell, Charlotte, Ref Librn, Seymour Public Library, 46 Church St, Seymour, CT, 06483. Tel: 203-888-3903. p. 336

Rowell, Cheryl, Ch, Fremont Public Library, Seven Jackie Bernier Dr, Fremont, NH, 03044. Tel: 603-895-9543. p. 1364

Rowell, Regina Ann, Info Spec, United States Air Force, David Grant USAF Medical Center Learning Resource Center, 101 Bodin Circle, Travis AFB, CA, 94535-1800. Tel: 707-423-5344. p. 253

Rowell, Ruth, Libr Asst, Glover Public Library, 51 Bean Hill Rd, Glover, VT, 05839. Tel: 802-525-4365. p. 2284

Rowland, Alexandra, Librn, Arizona Department of Corrections, Arizona State Prison Phoenix-West, 3402 W Cocopah St, Phoenix, AZ, 85009. Tel: 602-352-0350, Ext 109. p. 68

Rowland, Carra, Circ Mgr, Saint Tammany Parish Library, Mandeville Branch, 844 Girod St, Mandeville, LA, 70448. Tel: 985-626-4293. p. 888

Rowland, Jane, Dir, Calumet City Public Library, 660 Manistee Ave, Calumet City, IL, 60409. Tel: 708-862-6220, Ext 244. p. 548

Rowland, Lori F, Head, Access Serv, University of Pennsylvania Libraries, Biddle Law Library, 3501 Sansom St, Philadelphia, PA, 19104. Tel: 215-746-1755. p. 1988

Rowland, Mark, Distance Serv Librn, Instruction Librn, New England College, 196 Bridge St, Henniker, NH, 03242-3298. Tel: 603-428-2344. p. 1367

Rowland, Sara, Head, Tech Serv, Eastern Oregon University, One University Blvd, La Grande, OR, 97850. Tel: 541-962-3546. p. 1884

Rowlands, Brian, Libr Mgr, Solvay Public Library, 615 Woods Rd, Solvay, NY, 13209-1681. Tel: 315-468-2441. p. 1642

Rowlands, Jeffrey, Dir, Admin & Finance, Princeton University, One Washington Rd, Princeton, NJ, 08544-2098. Tel: 609-258-4158. p. 1437

Rowlands, Rebecca, Circ Mgr, Cambridge Public Library, 449 Broadway, Cambridge, MA, 02138. Tel: 617-349-4041. p. 1004

Rowlands, Wendy, Librn, Colorado Department of Corrections, Colorado State Penitentiary Library, PO Box 777, Canon City, CO, 81215-0777. Tel: 719-269-5268. p. 269

Rowlandson, David, Circ Serv Supvr, Redeemer University, 777 Garner Rd E, Ancaster, ON, L9K 1J4, CANADA. Tel: 905-648-2131. p. 2628

Rowler, Joan, Asst Librn, Stonington Historical Society, 40 Palmer St, Stonington, CT, 06378. Tel: 860-535-1131. p. 339

Rowley, Mary, Educ Coordr, Wildwood Correctional Complex Library, Ten Chugach Ave, Kenai, AK, 99611. Tel: 907-260-7200. p. 48

Rowley, Mary, Educ Coordr, Wildwood Pre-Trial Facility Library, Five Chugach Ave, Kenai, AK, 99611. Tel: 907-260-7265. p. 48

Rowley, Tina, Dir, Price City Library, 159 E Main St, Price, UT, 84501-3046. Tel: 435-636-3188. p. 2269

Rowlison, Nikki, Librn, Jennings City Library, 133 S Kansas Ave, Jennings, KS, 67643. Tel: 785-678-2666. p. 816

Rowse, Melissa A, Libr Dir, Degenstein Community Library, 40 S Fifth St, Sunbury, PA, 17801. Tel: 570-286-2461. p. 2011
Rowzee, B, Sr Librn, Coxsackie Correctional Facility Library, 11260 Rte 9W, Coxsackie, NY, 12051. Tel: 518-731-2781. p. 1523
Roxburgh, Teresa, Dir, Minor Memorial Library, 23 South St, Roxbury, CT, 06783. Tel: 860-350-2181. p. 335
Roxbury, Carol, Facilities Dir, Akron-Summit County Public Library, 60 S High St, Akron, OH, 44326. Tel: 330-643-9175. p. 1744
Roy, Anjana, Mgr, Good Samaritan Medical Center, 1309 N Flagler Dr, West Palm Beach, FL, 33401. Tel: 561-650-6315. p. 453
Roy, April, Br Dir, Kansas City Public Library, Plaza, 4801 Main St, Kansas City, MO, 64112. Tel: 816-701-3690. p. 1255
Roy, Christopher, Law Librn II, Connecticut Judicial Branch Law Libraries, New Britain Law Library, New Britain Courthouse, 20 Franklin Sq, New Britain, CT, 06051. Tel: 860-515-5110. p. 316
Roy, David A, Info Res Spec, Workplace Safety & Insurance Board, 200 Front St W, 17th Flr, Toronto, ON, M5V 3J1, CANADA. Tel: 416-344-4585. p. 2700
Roy, Debra J, Dir, Hazen Memorial Library, Three Keady Way, Shirley, MA, 01464. Tel: 978-425-2620. p. 1053
Roy, Harriet, Asst Dir, Pahkisimon Nuye?ah Library System, 118 Avro Pl, Air Ronge, SK, S0J 3G0, CANADA. Tel: 306-425-4525. p. 2741
Roy, Jo-Ann, Head, Libr Serv, Moultonborough Public Library, Four Holland St, Moultonborough, NH, 03254. Tel: 603-476-8895. p. 1374
Roy, Leila, Head Librn, Community Library, Ten John St, Lyman, ME, 04002-7312. Tel: 207-499-7114. p. 930
Roy, Michael D, Dean, Middlebury College, 110 Storrs Ave, Middlebury, VT, 05753. Tel: 802-443-5490. p. 2288
Roy, Rachel, Dir, Libr Serv, North Carolina Wesleyan University, 3400 N Wesleyan Blvd, Rocky Mount, NC, 27804. Tel: 252-985-5343. p. 1713
Roy, Suzie, Coordr, Cegep St Jean Sur Richelieu Bibliotheque, 30 boul du Seminaire Nord, Saint-Jean-Sur-Richelieu, QC, J3B 5J4, CANADA. Tel: 450-347-5301, Ext 2283, 450-347-5301, Ext 2333. p. 2735
Roy, Terry, Libr Adminr, Lafayette Public Library, 301 W Congress, Lafayette, LA, 70501-6866. Tel: 337-261-5781. p. 892
Roy, Theresa, Regional Libr Mgr, Lafayette Public Library, South Regional Library, 6101 Johnston St, Lafayette, LA, 70503. Tel: 337-981-1028. p. 892
Royal, Elias, Tech Serv Librn, Saint Thomas University Library, Alex A Hanna Law Library, 16401 NW 37th Ave, Miami Gardens, FL, 33054. Tel: 305-623-2336. p. 425
Royal, Marian, Dir, Ruidoso Public Library, 107 Kansas City Rd, Ruidoso, NM, 88345. Tel: 575-258-3704. p. 1474
Royan, Nancy, Dir, Wedsworth Memorial Library, 13 Front St N, Cascade, MT, 59421. Tel: 406-468-2848. p. 1290
Royce, Joni, Librn, Coldwater-Wilmore Regional Library, Wilmore Branch, 100 S Taft St, Wilmore, KS, 67155. Tel: 620-738-4464. p. 803
Royer, Jennifer, Curator, Landis Valley Village & Farm Museum, 2451 Kissel Hill Rd, Lancaster, PA, 17601. Tel: 717-569-0401, Ext 227. p. 1951
Royer, Michelle, Head, Commun Serv, Lucy Robbins Welles Library, 95 Cedar St, Newington, CT, 06111. Tel: 860-665-8707. p. 330
Royster, Melody, Chair, Marston Sci Libr, University of Florida Libraries, 1545 W University Ave, Gainesville, FL, 32611-7000. Tel: 352-273-2661. p. 407
Rozario, Shamol, Librn, York Correctional Institution Library, 201 W Main St, Niantic, CT, 06357. Tel: 860-451-3001. p. 330
Rozas, Nicole, Bus Mgr, Louisiana State University, 267 Coates Hall, Baton Rouge, LA, 70803. Tel: 225-578-3158, 225-578-3159. p. 2785
Rozek, William J, Chief Financial Officer, OCLC Online Computer Library Center, Inc, 6565 Kilgour Pl, Dublin, OH, 43017-3395. Tel: 614-764-6000. p. 2772
Rozelle, Brandi, Libr Mgr, Waterloo Library & Historical Society, 31 E Williams St, Waterloo, NY, 13165. Tel: 315-539-3313. p. 1659
Rozelle, Liz, Dir, Yorktown Public Library, 8920 W Adaline St, Yorktown, IN, 47396. Tel: 765-759-9723. p. 727
Rozen, Celia, Coll Develop Coordr, Alaska Resources Library & Information Services ARLIS, Library Bldg, 3211 Providence Dr, Ste 111, Anchorage, AK, 99508-4614. Tel: 907-786-7676. p. 41
Rozmarynowski, Mark, Dir, Sheboygan Falls Memorial Library, 330 Buffalo St, Sheboygan Falls, WI, 53085-1399. Tel: 920-467-7908. p. 2477
Roznoy, Cynthia, Curator, Mattatuck Museum of the Mattatuck Historical Society, 144 W Main St, Waterbury, CT, 06702. Tel: 203-753-0381, Ext 115. p. 343
Rozycki, Jennie, Libr Dir, John G McCullough Free Library, Two Main St N, North Bennington, VT, 05257. Tel: 802-447-7121. p. 2290
Rozycki, Jennie, Pres, Catamount Library Network, 43 Main St, Springfield, VT, 05156. Tel: 802-885-3108. p. 2776
Rozzell, Ronald, Archivist, Bus Mgr, Butler Community College Library & Archives, Library 600 Bldg, 901 S Haverhill Rd, El Dorado, KS, 67042-3280. Tel: 316-322-3234. p. 805
Rua-Bashir, Patricia, Mgr, Ch Serv, Nashville Public Library, 615 Church St, Nashville, TN, 37219-2314. Tel: 615-862-5800. p. 2119
Rua-Larsen, Marybeth, Ref Librn, Somerset Public Library, 1464 County St, Somerset, MA, 02726. Tel: 508-646-2829. p. 1053
Ruane Rogers, Monica, Assessment & Research Services Librn, Pennsylvania Western University - California, 250 University Ave, California, PA, 15419-1394. Tel: 724-938-4048. p. 1917
Ruback, Jane, Adult Serv, La Grange Public Library, Ten W Cossitt Ave, La Grange, IL, 60525. Tel: 708-215-3200. p. 605
Ruban, John, IT Serv, Ocean City Free Public Library, 1735 Simpson Ave, Ste 4, Ocean City, NJ, 08226. Tel: 609-399-2434. p. 1430
Rubel, Dejah, Electronic Res Mgt Librn, Metadata Librn, Ferris State University Library, 1010 Campus Dr, Big Rapids, MI, 49307-2279. Tel: 231-591-3500. p. 1085
Rubendall, Gary, Dir, Dublin Public Library, 2249 E Cumberland, Dublin, IN, 47335. Tel: 765-478-6206. p. 679
Rubenstein, Ellen, PhD, Dr, Assoc Prof, University of Oklahoma, Bizzell Memorial Library, 401 W Brooks, Rm 120, Norman, OK, 73019-6032. Tel: 405-325-3921. p. 2791
Rubenstein, Kristin, Libr Assoc/Ch, Coweta Public Library System, 85 Literary Lane, Newnan, GA, 30265. Tel: 770-683-2052. p. 492
Rubero, Robert, Archivist, Florida State University Libraries, Claude Pepper Library & Archives, 636 W Call St, Tallahassee, FL, 32304. Tel: 850-644-3271, 850-644-9217. p. 447
Rubin, Catherine, Asst Regional Librn, North Carolina Regional Library for the Blind & Physically Handicapped, 1841 Capital Blvd, Raleigh, NC, 27635. Tel: 919-733-4376. p. 1709
Rubin Irish, Erica, Youth Serv Librn, Belfast Free Library, 106 High St, Belfast, ME, 04915. Tel: 207-338-3884. p. 916
Rubin, J Adam, Dir, Libr Serv, John A Logan College Library, 700 Logan College Dr, Carterville, IL, 62918. Tel: 618-985-3741, Ext 8338. p. 550
Rubin, Katharine, Acq, Cat, University of Holy Cross, 4123 Woodland Dr, New Orleans, LA, 70131. Tel: 504-398-2119. p. 904
Rubin, Melissa, Dir, Pub Relations, Bryant Library, Two Paper Mill Rd, Roslyn, NY, 11576. Tel: 516-621-2240. p. 1633
Rubin, Rachel, Dean of Libraries & Archives, Mount Allison University Libraries & Archives, 49 York St, Sackville, NB, E4L 1C6, CANADA. Tel: 506-364-2567. p. 2604
Rubin, Victoria, Prof, Western University, FIMS & Nursing Bldg, Rm 2020, London, ON, N6A 5B9, CANADA. Tel: 519-661-2111, Ext 88479. p. 2796
Rubin, William, Br Mgr, Cuyahoga County Public Library, Mayfield Branch, 500 SOM Ctr Rd, Mayfield Village, OH, 44143-2103. Tel: 440-473-0350. p. 1813
Rubin, William, Br Mgr, Cuyahoga County Public Library, Richmond Heights Branch, 5235 Wilson Mills Rd, Richmond Heights, OH, 44143-3016. Tel: 440-449-2666. p. 1813
Rubino, Cynthia, Dir, Tufts University, Edwin Ginn Library, Mugar Bldg, 1st Flr, 160 Packard St, Medford, MA, 02155-7082. Tel: 617-627-2175. p. 1034
Rubino, Cynthia, Dir, Lewisboro Library, 15 Main St, South Salem, NY, 10590. Tel: 914-763-3857, 914-875-9004. p. 1643
Rubino, Johanna, Librn, Donora Public Library, 510 Meldon Ave, Donora, PA, 15033-1333. Tel: 724-379-7940. p. 1926
Rubino, Kit, Tech Serv, Roselle Park Veterans Memorial Library, 404 Chestnut St, Roselle Park, NJ, 07204. Tel: 908-245-2456. p. 1441
Rubino, Michelle, Info Literacy Librn, Outreach Librn, Greenville Technical College Libraries, Bldg 102, 506 S Pleasantburg Dr, Greenville, SC, 29607. Tel: 864-236-6439. p. 2062
Rubinstein, Sally, Tech Serv, Newburyport Public Library, 94 State St, Newburyport, MA, 01950-6619. Tel: 978-465-4428, Ext 230. p. 1039
Ruby, Christy, Pub Relations Librn, Eastern New Mexico University - Portales, 1500 S Ave K, Portales, NM, 88130-7402. Tel: 575-562-2640. p. 1473
Ruby, Christy, Dr, Dir, Libr Serv, Tech Serv, Wharton County Junior College, 911 Boling Hwy, Wharton, TX, 77488-3298. Tel: 979-532-6953. p. 2256
Ruby, Patti, Libr Dir, Clear Lake City Library, 125 Third Ave S, Clear Lake, SD, 57226. Tel: 605-874-2013. p. 2075
Ruby, Penny, Libr Asst, Clallam County Law Library, County Courthouse Basement, 223 E Fourth St, Rm 175, Port Angeles, WA, 98362. Tel: 360-417-2287. p. 2373
Ruby, Shelia, Librn, Lapeer District Library, Metamora Branch, 4018 Oak St, Metamora, MI, 48455. Tel: 810-678-2991. p. 1126
Ruby, Veneda, Youth Spec, First Regional Library, Emily Jones Pointer Public Library, 104 Main St, Como, MS, 38619. Tel: 662-526-5283. p. 1220
Rucchetto, Leah, Br Mgr, Markham Public Library, Markham Village Branch, 6031 Hwy 7, Markham, ON, L3P 3A7, CANADA. Tel: 905-513-7977, Ext 4277. p. 2656
Rucinski, Paula Jean, Mgr, Richard T Liddicoat Gemological Library & Information Center, 5345 Armada Dr, Carlsbad, CA, 92008. Tel: 760-603-4046, 760-603-4068. p. 128
Rucinski, Taryn, Dep Dir, United States Court of International Trade, One Federal Plaza, New York, NY, 10278. Tel: 212-264-2816. p. 1603
Rucker, John, Libr Dir, Branch District Library, Ten E Chicago St, Coldwater, MI, 49036-1615. Tel: 517-278-2341, Ext 115. p. 1092
Rucker, Melissa, Cat Librn, University of the Incarnate Word, 4301 Broadway, CPO 297, San Antonio, TX, 78209-6397. Tel: 210-829-6097. p. 2240
Rucker, Rob, Chief Strategist, Student Success, North Carolina State University Libraries, D H Hill Jr Library, Two Broughton Dr, Raleigh, NC, 27695. Tel: 919-513-3657. p. 1709

Rucker, Ryan, Dr, Lecturer, Valdosta State University, Odum Library, 1500 N Patterson St, Valdosta, GA, 31698. Tel: 229-333-5966. p. 2784
Rudd, Lynda, Br Mgr, Alexandria Library, Technical Services, 5005 Duke St, Alexandria, VA, 22304-2903. Tel: 703-746-1764. p. 2302
Rudd, Lynda, Tech Serv, Alexandria Library, 5005 Duke St, Alexandria, VA, 22304. Tel: 703-746-1764. p. 2302
Rudd, Pam, Br Head, Thompson-Nicola Regional District Library System, Barriere Branch, 4511 Barriere Town Rd, Barriere, BC, V0E 1E0, CANADA. Tel: 250-672-5811. p. 2567
Rudd, Patrick, Coordr, Instruction & Outreach, Elon University, 308 N O'Kelly Ave, Elon, NC, 27244-0187. Tel: 336-278-6600. p. 1688
Rudd, Patrick, Interim Dean of Libr, Elon University, 308 N O'Kelly Ave, Elon, NC, 27244-0187. Tel: 336-278-6600. p. 1688
Ruddell, Teresa C, Librn, Baptist Health Madisonville, 900 Hospital Dr, Madisonville, KY, 42431-1694. Tel: 270-825-5252. p. 868
Rudder, Leah, Dir, Laurel County Public Library District, 120 College Park Dr, London, KY, 40741. Tel: 606-864-5759. p. 864
Ruddick, Deja, Dir, Horseshoe Bend Regional Library, 207 N West St, Dadeville, AL, 36853. Tel: 256-825-9232. p. 13
Ruddy, Mary, Ref (Info Servs), Jenner & Block Library, 353 N Clark St, Ste 4300, Chicago, IL, 60654. Tel: 312-222-9350. p. 562
Rude, Charles, Dir, Kewanna Union Township Public Library, 210 E Main St, Kewanna, IN, 46939-9529. Tel: 574-653-2011. p. 698
Rudecoff, Christine, Dir of Libr, State University of New York, PO Box 901, Morrisville, NY, 13408. Tel: 315-684-6055. p. 1574
Ruder, Susan, Dir, Pittsford Public Library, 9268 E Hudson Rd, Pittsford, MI, 49271. Tel: 517-523-2565. p. 1141
Rudikoff, Leigh, Ref Librn, MassBay Community College, 50 Oakland St, Wellesley, MA, 02481. Tel: 781-239-2622. p. 1063
Rudisill, Mark, Interim Dean of Libr, College of DuPage Library, 425 Fawell Blvd, Glen Ellyn, IL, 60137-6599. Tel: 630-942-3334. p. 593
Rudloff, Liz, Cataloger, Missouri Evergreen, 1190 Meramec Station Rd, Ste 207, Ballwin, MO, 63021-6902. p. 2769
Rudner, Andrea, Libr Dir, Richmond University Medical Center, 355 Bard Ave, Staten Island, NY, 10310-1664. Tel: 718-818-3117. p. 1645
Rudnick, Tracey, Head Librn, University of Hartford Harrison Libraries, Mildred P Allen Memorial, 200 Bloomfield Ave, West Hartford, CT, 06117-0395. Tel: 860-768-4491. p. 345
Rudolf, Kenneth, Dir, University of La Verne, 320 E D St, Ontario, CA, 91764. Tel: 909-460-2065. p. 188
Rudolfo, Lynette, Pub Serv Mgr, University of Hawaii, 2525 Dole St, Honolulu, HI, 96822-2328. Tel: 808-956-5581, 808-956-7583. p. 513
Rudolph, Arwen, Asst Dir, Rural Br Supvr, Palliser Regional Library, 366 Coteau St W, Moose Jaw, SK, S6H 5C9, CANADA. Tel: 306-693-3669. p. 2742
Rudshteyn, Alex, Dir, Libr Tech Serv, Director, Systems & Network Support, Brooklyn College Library, 2900 Bedford Ave, Brooklyn, NY, 11210. Tel: 718-951-5335. p. 1501
Rudy, Clint, Dir, Suffolk Public Library System, 443 W Washington St, Suffolk, VA, 23434. Tel: 757-514-7323. p. 2348
Rudy, Joel, Libr Serv Coordr, Virginia Highlands Community College Library, 100 VHCC Dr, Abingdon, VA, 24210. Tel: 276-739-2542. p. 2301
Rudzinski, Monica, Br Mgr, Cleveland Public Library, Sterling, 2200 E 30th St, Cleveland, OH, 44115. Tel: 216-623-7074. p. 1769
Rue, Trista, Dir, Melton Public Library, 8496 W College St, French Lick, IN, 47432-1026. Tel: 812-936-2177. p. 686
Rueckert, Michelle, Library Contact, Wisconsin Center for the Blind & Visually Impaired, 1700 W State St, Janesville, WI, 53546-5344. Tel: 608-758-6118. p. 2443
Rueda, Eric, Br Mgr, Phoenix Public Library, Century Library, 1750 E Highland Ave, Phoenix, AZ, 85016-4648. p. 72
Rueff, Mary, Asst Dir, Hussey-Mayfield Memorial Public Library, 250 N Fifth St, Zionsville, IN, 46077-1324. Tel: 317-873-3149. p. 728
Ruegg, Lillie, Pub Serv Librn, Greenville Technical College Libraries, Bldg 102, 506 S Pleasantburg Dr, Greenville, SC, 29607. Tel: 864-250-8321. p. 2062
Ruelle, Maggie, Dir, Learning Commons, Tyler Junior College, 1327 S Baxter St, Tyler, TX, 75701. Tel: 903-510-2502, 903-510-2503. p. 2249
Ruetzel, Jessica, Mgr, Corteva Agriscience Library, 9330 Zionsville Rd, Indianapolis, IN, 46268. Tel: 833-267-8382. p. 691
Rufai, Fumilayo, Archives, Cat, Tech Serv, City Colleges of Chicago, Malcolm X College - Carter G Woodson Library, 1900 W Jackson St, 2nd Flr, Chicago, IL, 60612. Tel: 312-850-7244. p. 558
Ruff, David C, Libr Dir, Rolling Meadows Library, 3110 Martin Lane, Rolling Meadows, IL, 60008. Tel: 847-259-6050. p. 642
Ruffcorn, Katie, Supvr, Yakima Valley Libraries, Terrace Heights Library, 4011 Commonwealth Dr, Yakima, WA, 98901. Tel: 509-457-5319. p. 2396
Ruffin, Ingrid, Assoc Dean, University of Nevada, Las Vegas University Libraries, 4505 S Maryland Pkwy, Box 457001, Las Vegas, NV, 89154-7001. Tel: 702-895-4127. p. 1347
Ruffin, Rhonda, Info Serv Mgr, Glenwood-Lynwood Public Library District, 19901 Stony Island Ave, Lynwood, IL, 60411. Tel: 708-758-0090. p. 611
Rufty, Beverly, Libr Coord, Mitchell Community College, 500 W Broad St, Statesville, NC, 28677. Tel: 704-878-3249. p. 1717
Rufty, Sandra, Admin Assoc, Northwestern State University College of Nursing & Allied Health - Library, 1800 Line Ave, Rm 101, Shreveport, LA, 71101. p. 908
Ruggiero, Madeline, Acquisitions & Instruction Librn, Queensborough Community College, City University of New York, 222-05 56th Ave, Bayside, NY, 11364-1497. Tel: 718-281-5072. p. 1491
Ruggles, Aaron, Asst Dir, Clear Lake Public Library, 200 N Fourth St, Clear Lake, IA, 50428-1698. Tel: 641-357-6133. p. 740
Ruhe, Amy, Planning & Resource Mgmt, US Department of Interior, National Park Service, Two Mark Bird Lane, Elverson, PA, 19520. Tel: 610-582-8773, Ext 240. p. 1930
Ruhl, Meredith, Asst Dir, Children's Librn, Bacon Free Library, 58 Eliot St, Natick, MA, 01760. Tel: 508-653-6730. p. 1037
Ruiz Alvarez, Jose, Libr Mgr, San Antonio Public Library, Las Palmas, 515 Castroville Rd, San Antonio, TX, 78237. Tel: 210-207-9200. p. 2239
Ruiz, Anjelica, Dir, Libr & Archives, Temple Emanu-El, 8500 Hillcrest Rd, Dallas, TX, 75225. Tel: 214-706-0000, Ext 185. p. 2168
Ruiz, Anjelica, Dir, Libr & Archives, Temple Emanu-El, William P Budner Youth Library, 8500 Hillcrest Rd, Dallas, TX, 75225. Tel: 214-706-0000, Ext 114. p. 2168
Ruiz, Cristina, Br Supvr, Yolo County Library, Clarksburg Branch, 52915 Netherlands Ave, Clarksburg, CA, 95612-5007. Tel: 916-744-1755. p. 260
Ruiz, Deborah, Instruction & Ref Librn, Monterey Peninsula College Library, 980 Fremont St, Monterey, CA, 93940. Tel: 831-646-1309. p. 179
Ruiz, Faithe, Libr Dir, College of Central Florida, 3001 SW College Rd, Ocala, FL, 34474-4415. Tel: 352-873-5805. p. 429
Ruiz, John Martin, Fr, Librn, Dominican Theological Library, 487 Michigan Ave NE, Washington, DC, 20017-1585. Tel: 202-655-4651. p. 365
Ruiz, Jose, Circ Mgr, Manhattan School of Music, 130 Claremont Ave, New York, NY, 10027. Tel: 917-493-4511. p. 1590
Ruiz, Leticia, Circ, El Progreso Memorial Library, 301 W Main St, Uvalde, TX, 78801. Tel: 830-278-2017. p. 2251
Ruiz, Lissette, Campus Libr Dir, San Marcos, Nicaragua, Keiser University Library System, 1500 NW 49th St, Fort Lauderdale, FL, 33309. Tel: 954-351-4035. p. 401
Ruiz, Lorraine, Libr Dir, Kenilworth Public Library, 548 Boulevard, Kenilworth, NJ, 07033. Tel: 908-276-2451. p. 1410
Ruiz, Lynn, Circ Supvr, North Palm Beach Public Library, 303 Anchorage Dr, North Palm Beach, FL, 33408. Tel: 561-841-3383. p. 429
Ruiz McCall, Linda, Info Geologist & Res Ctr Mgr, University of Texas Libraries, Bureau of Economic Geology & Resource Center, 10100 Burnet Rd, Bldg 131, Austin, TX, 78758-4445. Tel: 512-471-1534, 512-471-7144. p. 2142
Ruiz, Michelle, Br Mgr, San Diego Public Library, North University Community, 8820 Judicial Dr, San Diego, CA, 92122. Tel: 858-581-9637. p. 220
Ruiz, Raul, Libr Serv Mgr, Metropolitan State University, 645 E Seventh St, Saint Paul, MN, 55106. Tel: 651-793-1632. p. 1200
Ruiz, Ricardo, Regional Librn, Florida Technical College Library, 12900 Challenger Pkwy, Ste 130, Orlando, FL, 32826. Tel: 407-447-7300, Ext 8339. p. 431
Ruiz-Hearne, Norma Jean, Libr Dir, Edwards Public Library, 210 W Gilbert St, Henrietta, TX, 76365-2816. Tel: 940-538-4791. p. 2189
Rukhelman, Svetlana K, Librn, Harvard Library, Davis Center for Russian & Eurasian Studies Fung Library, Knafel Bldg, Concourse Level, 1737 Cambridge St, Cambridge, MA, 02138. Tel: 617-496-8421. p. 1006
Rumbaugh, Christopher, Adult Serv Mgr, Salem Public Library, 585 Liberty St SE, Salem, OR, 97301. Tel: 503-588-6449. p. 1897
Rumble, Beth, County Librn, Huron County Library, Administration Office, 77722B London Rd, RR 5 Hwy 4, Clinton, ON, N0M 1L0, CANADA. Tel: 519-482-5457. p. 2636
Rumery, Elizabeth, Res & Instruction Librn, University of Connecticut, Avery Point Campus Library, 1084 Shennecossett Rd, Groton, CT, 06340. Tel: 860-405-9148. p. 340
Rumery, Joyce, Dean of Libr, University of Maine, 5729 Fogler Library, Orono, ME, 04469-5729. Tel: 207-581-1661. p. 934
Rumig, Joanne, Head, Access Serv, Carleton University Library, 1125 Colonel By Dr, Ottawa, ON, K1S 5B6, CANADA. Tel: 613-520-2600, Ext 1018. p. 2666
Ruminson, Kevin, Admin Serv, Assoc Univ Librn, University of California Irvine Libraries, PO Box 19557, Irvine, CA, 92623-9557. Tel: 949-824-4440. p. 153
Rummel, Jennifer, Ch, YA Librn, Cragin Memorial Library, Eight Linwood Ave, Colchester, CT, 06415. Tel: 860-537-5752. p. 306
Rumpca-Shafer, Hope, Libr Dir, Caribou Public Library, 30 High St, Caribou, ME, 04736. Tel: 207-493-4214. p. 920
Rumple, Jayanne, Dir, Montezuma Public Library, 270 Crawford St, Montezuma, IN, 47862. Tel: 765-245-2772. p. 707
Rumrill, Alan, Dir, Historical Society of Cheshire County, 246 Main St, Keene, NH, 03431. Tel: 603-352-1895. p. 1369
Rumschlag, Denise, Librn, Department of Veterans Affairs, 1481 W Tenth St, Indianapolis, IN, 46202. Tel: 317-988-4084. p. 691
Rumsey, Carla, Dir, Vermontville Township Library, 120 E First St, Vermontville, MI, 49096. Tel: 517-726-1362. p. 1156
Rumsey, LeighAnn, Dir, Dormann Library, 101 W Morris St, Bath, NY, 14810. Tel: 607-776-4613. p. 1491

Rundle, Emily, Children's Servs & Local History Librn, Jervis Public Library Association, Inc, 613 N Washington St, Rome, NY, 13440-4296. Tel: 315-336-4570. p. 1632

Rundquist, Christy, Dir, Pepin Public Library, 510 Second St, Pepin, WI, 54759. Tel: 715-442-4932. p. 2468

Rundquist Corbett, Kirsten, Dir, Dudley-Tucker Library, Six Epping St, Raymond, NH, 03077. Tel: 603-895-7057. p. 1379

Rundquist, Robert, Interim Dean, Support Serv, Chaffey College Library, 5885 Haven Ave, Rancho Cucamonga, CA, 91737-3002. Tel: 909-652-6800. p. 197

Rung, Michelle, Head, Adult/Teen Serv, Northport-East Northport Public Library, 151 Laurel Ave, Northport, NY, 11768. Tel: 631-261-6930. p. 1608

Runge, Donna, Dir, Wessington Public Library, 240 Wessington St, Wessington, SD, 57381. Tel: 605-458-2596. p. 2085

Runion, Susan, Dir, Mohawk Community Library, 200 S Sycamore Ave, Sycamore, OH, 44882. Tel: 419-927-2407. p. 1822

Runkle, Amy, Dir, Winifred Knox Memorial Library, 112 S Elm St, Franklin Grove, IL, 61031. Tel: 815-456-2823. p. 589

Runksmeiier, Nancy, Head Librn, Ledyard Public Library, 220 Edmunds St, Ledyard, IA, 50556. Tel: 515-646-3111. p. 765

Runnels, Jason, Dr, Music Librn, Southwestern Baptist Theological Seminary Libraries, 2001 W Seminary Dr, Fort Worth, TX, 76115-2157. Tel: 817-923-1921, Ext 4000. p. 2180

Runnels, Marquenez, Circ Supvr, DeSoto Public Library, 211 E Pleasant Run Rd, Ste C, DeSoto, TX, 75115. Tel: 972-230-9656. p. 2170

Runser, Kathleen E, Dep Dir, Elyria Public Library System, 211 2nd St, Elyria, OH, 44035. Tel: 440-322-0174. p. 1784

Runstadler, Angelica, Circ Supvr, Northwest University, 5520 108th Ave NE, Kirkland, WA, 98083. Tel: 425-889-4205. p. 2368

Runyon, Amanda, Assoc Dean & Dir, University of Pennsylvania Libraries, Biddle Law Library, 3501 Sansom St, Philadelphia, PA, 19104. Tel: 215-898-7488. p. 1988

Runyon, Ashley, Ch Serv, Saint Charles City-County Library District, Kisker Road Branch, 1000 Kisker Rd, Saint Charles, MO, 63304-8726. Tel: 636-447-7323, 636-926-7323. p. 1278

Runyon, Carolyn, Dir, Spec Coll, University of Tennessee at Chattanooga Library, 400 Douglas Ave, Dept 6456, Chattanooga, TN, 37403-2598. Tel: 423-425-4501. p. 2092

Runyon, David, Univ Librn, Harrisburg University of Science & Technology, 326 Market St, Harrisburg, PA, 17101. Tel: 717-901-5188. p. 1940

Runyon, Joanna, Libr Dir, Smith Center Public Library, 117 W Court St, Smith Center, KS, 66967. Tel: 785-282-3361. p. 836

Rupe, Kathrine, Dir, Lyman Public Library, 313 Jeffers St, Lyman, NE, 69352. Tel: 308-787-1366. p. 1324

Rupkalvis, Cari, Dir, Tarpon Springs Public Library, 138 E Lemon St, Tarpon Springs, FL, 34689. Tel: 727-943-4922. p. 450

Rupp, Amanda, Exec Dir, Ellis County Historical Society Archives, 100 W Seventh St, Hays, KS, 67601. Tel: 785-628-2624. p. 812

Ruppert, Dean, Digital Librn, Society of Actuaries Library, 475 N Martingale Rd, Ste 600, Schaumburg, IL, 60173. Tel: 847-706-3575. p. 645

Ruppert, Jamie, Teen Librn, Council Bluffs Public Library, 400 Willow Ave, Council Bluffs, IA, 51503-9042. Tel: 712-323-7553, Ext 5422. p. 742

Ruppert, Valerie, Libr Asst, Brevard College, One Brevard College Dr, Brevard, NC, 28712-4283. Tel: 828-641-0114. p. 1675

Rurode, Brett, Cat Librn, ILL Librn, State Library of Kansas, State Capitol Bldg, Rm 312-N, 300 SW Tenth Ave, Topeka, KS, 66612. Tel: 785-296-3296. p. 839

Rusch, Adam, Asst Teaching Prof, University of Illinois at Urbana-Champaign, Library & Information Science Bldg, 501 E Daniel St, Champaign, IL, 61820-6211. Tel: 217-333-3280. p. 2784

Rusch, Cortnye, Ref Librn, Arapahoe Community College, 5900 S Santa Fe Dr, Littleton, CO, 80160. Tel: 303-797-5210. p. 289

Rusch, Evan, Govt Doc, Ref & Instruction Librn, Minnesota State University, Mankato, 601 Maywood Ave, Mankato, MN, 56001. Tel: 507-389-5952. p. 1181

Rusch, Maggie, Head, Circ, Plainedge Public Library, 1060 Hicksville Rd, North Massapequa, NY, 11758. Tel: 516-735-4133. p. 1607

Ruschak, Iren, Tech Serv, New Brunswick Free Public Library, 60 Livingston Ave, New Brunswick, NJ, 08901-2597. Tel: 732-745-5108, Ext 27. p. 1424

Rusche, Jennifer, Adult Serv, Ref Librn, William Jeanes Memorial Library, 4051 Joshua Rd, Lafayette Hill, PA, 19444-1400. Tel: 610-828-0441, Ext 107. p. 1950

Rusek, Stacey, Librn, Northwest Regional Library, Roseau Public Library, 121 Center St E, Ste 100, Roseau, MN, 56751. Tel: 218-463-2825. p. 1205

Rusell, Katie, Cataloger, Circ Mgr, Wood River Public Library, 326 E Ferguson Ave, Wood River, IL, 62095-2098. Tel: 618-254-4832. p. 664

Rush, Abigail, Coordr, Electronic Serv & Syst, Presbyterian College, 211 E Maple St, Clinton, SC, 29325. Tel: 864-833-7026. p. 2052

Rush, Brianna, Libr Dir, Treat Memorial Library, 56 Main St, Livermore Falls, ME, 04254. Tel: 207-897-3631. p. 930

Rush, Erin, Dir, Anamosa Public Library & Learning Center, 600 E First St, Anamosa, IA, 52205. Tel: 319-462-2183. p. 731

Rush, John, Librn, Emmaus Bible College Library, 2570 Asbury Rd, Dubuque, IA, 52001-3096. Tel: 563-588-8000, Ext 1003. p. 748

Rush, Katherine, Circ, Tech Serv Mgr, Northfield Public Library, 210 Washington St, Northfield, MN, 55057. Tel: 507-645-1800. p. 1191

Rush, Martha, Access Serv, College of William & Mary in Virginia, The Wolf Law Library, 613 S Henry St, Williamsburg, VA, 23187. Tel: 757-221-3255. p. 2353

Rush, Nicole, Dir, Saint Paris Public Library, 127 E Main St, Saint Paris, OH, 43072. Tel: 937-663-4349. p. 1819

Rushay, Samuel W, Supvry Archivist, National Archives & Records Administration, 500 W US Hwy 24, Independence, MO, 64050-1798. Tel: 816-268-8200. p. 1251

Rushing, Ann, Br Mgr, Jackson-George Regional Library System, East Central Public Library, 21801 Slider Rd, Moss Point, MS, 39562. Tel: 228-588-6263. p. 1228

Rushing, Ann, Br Mgr, Jackson-George Regional Library System, Kathleen McIlwain-Gautier Public Library, 2100 Library Lane, Gautier, MS, 39553. Tel: 228-497-4531. p. 1228

Rushing, Beth, Pres, Appalachian College Association, 7216 Jewel Bell Lane, Bristol, TN, 37620. Tel: 859-986-4584. p. 2775

Rushing, Dale, Br Mgr, Madera County Library, Oakhurst Branch, 49044 Civic Circle, Oakhurst, CA, 93644-0484. Tel: 559-683-4838. p. 171

Rushing, Mary, Dir, Fleming County Public Library, 202 Bypass Blvd, Flemingsburg, KY, 41041-1298. Tel: 606-845-7851. p. 854

Rushing, Robin, Asst Librn, Riverton Village Library, 1200 E Riverton Rd, Riverton, IL, 62561-8200. Tel: 217-629-6353. p. 639

Rushing, Trina, Dir, Henderson County Public Library, 301 N Washington St, Hendersonville, NC, 28739. Tel: 828-697-4725, Ext 2334. p. 1695

Rushton, Christine, Dir, Springfield Township Library, 70 Powell Rd, Springfield, PA, 19064-2446. Tel: 610-543-2113. p. 2009

Rushton, Margot, Asst Librn, Madison Public Library, 12 Old Point Ave, Madison, ME, 04950. Tel: 207-696-5626. p. 931

Rusin, Andrew, Access Serv Coordr, University of Chicago Library, Eckhart Library, 1118 E 58th St, Chicago, IL, 60637. Tel: 773-702-8778. p. 570

Rusk, Denise, Sr Librn, California Department of Corrections Library System, Pelican Bay State Prison, 5905 Lake Earl Dr, Crescent City, CA, 95532. Tel: 707-465-1000, Ext 7995. p. 207

Rusk, Samantha, Bus Mgr, Vespasian Warner Public Library District, 310 N Quincy, Clinton, IL, 61727. Tel: 217-935-5174. p. 572

Ruskamp, Lori, Librn, Pilger Public Library, 120 Main St, Pilger, NE, 68768. Tel: 402-396-3550. p. 1333

Ruskin, Suzy, Dir, Community Library of Allegheny Valley, 1522 Broadview Blvd, Natrona Heights, PA, 15065. Tel: 724-226-3491. p. 1968

Russ, Bridget, Circ Mgr, Rocky River Public Library, 1600 Hampton Rd, Rocky River, OH, 44116-2699. Tel: 440-895-3739. p. 1818

Russ, Cathy, Libr Dir, Troy Public Library, 510 W Big Beaver Rd, Troy, MI, 48084-5289. Tel: 248-524-3538. p. 1155

Russ, Jodi, Commun Librn, Monroe County Library System, Bedford Branch Library, 8575 Jackman Rd, Temperance, MI, 48182. Tel: 734-847-6747. p. 1133

Russelburg, Erin, Dir, Webster County Public Library, 101 State Rte 132 E, Dixon, KY, 42409. Tel: 270-639-9171. p. 853

Russell, Alissa, Spec Coll Librn, Midwestern State University, 3410 Taft Blvd, Wichita Falls, TX, 76308-2099. Tel: 940-397-4755. p. 2257

Russell, Allison, Librn, Oregon Public Library, 103 S Washington St, Oregon, MO, 64473. Tel: 660-446-3586. p. 1264

Russell, Amy, Head, Genealogy & Local Hist, Kokomo-Howard County Public Library, 220 N Union St, Kokomo, IN, 46901-4614. Tel: 765-457-3242. p. 699

Russell, Anita, Librn, Mason County Library System, New Haven Public, 106 Main St, New Haven, WV, 25265. Tel: 304-882-3252. p. 2413

Russell, Ann, Tech Librn, Gardiner Public Library, 152 Water St, Gardiner, ME, 04345. Tel: 207-582-3312. p. 926

Russell, Ann, Asst Librn, Garland Smith Public Library, 702 W. Main, Marlow, OK, 73055. Tel: 580-658-5354. p. 1852

Russell, Ann, Sr Dir, Michener Institute of Education at UHN, 222 Saint Patrick St, 2nd Flr, Toronto, ON, M5T 1V4, CANADA. Tel: 416-596-3123. p. 2690

Russell, Anna, Librn, United States Courts Library, 222 W Seventh Ave, Rm 181, Anchorage, AK, 99513-7586. Tel: 907-271-5655. p. 43

Russell, Anna, Electronic Serv Librn, University of San Diego, Katherine M & George M Pardee Jr Legal Research Center, 5998 Alcala Park, San Diego, CA, 92110-2492. Tel: 619-260-4542. p. 223

Russell, Arthur James, III, Libr Tech, VA Puget Sound Health Care System, American Lake Div, 9600 Veterans Dr SW, Bldg 71, Tacoma, WA, 98493-5000. Tel: 253-583-1513. p. 2388

Russell, Brandi, Circ Supvr, Saint Ambrose University Library, 518 W Locust St, Davenport, IA, 52803. Tel: 563-333-5813. p. 744

Russell, Carolyn, Asst Dir, Laurel-Jones County Library System, Inc, 530 Commerce St, Laurel, MS, 39440. Tel: 601-428-4313, Ext 103. p. 1224

Russell, Cayley, Libr Mgr, Dixonville Community Library, PO Box 206, Dixonville, AB, T0H 1E0, CANADA. Tel: 780-971-2593. p. 2533

Russell, Celisa, Br Mgr, Dixie Regional Library System, Sherman Public, 20 W Lamar St, Sherman, MS, 38869. Tel: 662-840-2513. p. 1230

Rutherford, Linda, Archives Librn, Tech Serv Librn, Mott Community College, 1401 E Court St, Flint, MI, 48503. Tel: 810-762-0400, 810-762-0401. p. 1107

Rutherford, Matthew, Curator, Genealogy, Newberry Library, 60 W Walton St, Chicago, IL, 60610-3305. Tel: 312-255-3671. p. 565

Rutherford, Noel, Coll Develop Mgr, Nashville Public Library, 615 Church St, Nashville, TN, 37219-2314. Tel: 615-862-5800. p. 2119

Rutherford, Patti, Libr Coord, Yavapai County Free Library District, Yarnell Public Library, 22278 N Hwy 89, Yarnell, AZ, 85362. Tel: 928-427-3191. p. 75

Rutigliano, Eugene, Curator, Digital Initiatives Librn, Ohio Wesleyan University, 43 Rowland Ave, Delaware, OH, 43015-2370. Tel: 740-368-3233. p. 1782

Rutkowski, Andrzej, Actg Head, Libr, University of Southern California Libraries, Von KleinSmid Center Library, Von KleinSmid Ctr, 3518 Trousdale Pkwy, Los Angeles, CA, 90089-0182. Tel: 213-740-1768. p. 170

Rutkowski, Barb, Head, Info Tech, Novi Public Library, 45255 W Ten Mile Rd, Novi, MI, 48375. Tel: 248-349-0720. p. 1138

Rutkowski, Ed, Asst Dir, Brighton District Library, 100 Library Dr, Brighton, MI, 48116. Tel: 810-229-6571, Ext 222. p. 1087

Rutkowski, Kelsey, Libr Dir, Indian River Area Library, 3546 S Straits Hwy, Indian River, MI, 49749. Tel: 231-238-8581. p. 1118

Rutkowski, Melissa, Br Mgr, Ocean County Library, Bay Head Reading Center, 136 Meadow Ave, Bay Head, NJ, 08742-5080. Tel: 732-892-0662. p. 1446

Rutkowski, Melissa, Br Mgr, Ocean County Library, Upper Shores Branch, 112 Jersey City Ave, Lavallette, NJ, 08735. Tel: 732-793-3996. p. 1447

Rutkowski, Patricia, Dir, New Britain Public Library, 20 High St, New Britain, CT, 06051. Tel: 860-224-3155, Ext 113. p. 324

Rutkowski, Sandra, Sister, Dir, Libr Serv, Lourdes University, 6832 Convent Blvd, Sylvania, OH, 43560. Tel: 419-824-3762. p. 1822

Rutland, David, Coll Serv Mgr, University of Georgia, Alexander Campbell King Law Library, 225 Herty Dr, Athens, GA, 30602-6018. Tel: 706-542-1922. p. 459

Rutland, Jessie, Coll Develop Librn, Flagler College, 44 Sevilla St, Saint Augustine, FL, 32084-4302. Tel: 904-819-6206. p. 439

Rutledge, Hannah, Dir, Libr & Info Serv, Longwood Gardens Library & Archives, 1001 Longwood Rd, Kennett Square, PA, 19348. Tel: 610-388-1000, Ext 5241. p. 1948

Rutledge, Jillian, Interim Dir, Pub Serv, Waterloo Public Library, 415 Commercial St, Waterloo, IA, 50701-1385. Tel: 319-291-4521. p. 789

Rutledge, John, Deputy Chief Info Officer, Library of Congress, James Madison Memorial Bldg, 101 Independence Ave SE, Washington, DC, 20540. Tel: 202-707-5000. p. 370

Rutter, Deb, Interim Dir, Brainerd Memorial Library, 920 Saybrook Rd, Haddam, CT, 06438. Tel: 860-345-2204. p. 315

Rutz, Linda, Head, Tech Serv, Way Public Library, 101 E Indiana Ave, Perrysburg, OH, 43551. Tel: 419-874-3135, Ext 114. p. 1815

Ruzicka, Joyce, Librn, North Bend Public Library, 110 E 13th St, North Bend, NE, 68649. Tel: 402-652-8356. p. 1326

Ruzicka, Lori, Human Res Mgr, Springfield-Greene County Library District, 4653 S Campbell Ave, Springfield, MO, 65810-1723. Tel: 417-882-0714. p. 1281

Ruzicka, Nancy, Ch, Guttenberg Public Library, 603 S Second St, Guttenberg, IA, 52052. Tel: 563-252-3108. p. 757

Ryan, Amy, Dir, Vineyard Haven Public Library, 200 Main St, Vineyard Haven, MA, 02568. Tel: 508-696-4211, Ext 111. p. 1060

Ryan, Amy E, Interim Dir, Boston Athenaeum, Ten 1/2 Beacon St, Boston, MA, 02108-3777. Tel: 617-227-0270. p. 991

Ryan, Angela, Trades, Tech & Physical Sciences Librn, Kwantlen Polytechnic University Library, 12666 72nd Ave, Surrey, BC, V3W 2M8, CANADA. Tel: 604-598-6040. p. 2576

Ryan, Beth, Dir, Johnsburg Public Library District, 3000 N Johnsburg Rd, Johnsburg, IL, 60051. Tel: 815-344-0077. p. 603

Ryan, Beth Ann, Head Librn, Delaware Technical & Community College, Wilmington Campus, West Bldg, First Flr, 300 N Orange St, Wilmington, DE, 19801. Tel: 302-573-5431. p. 357

Ryan, Brendan, Tech Serv Librn, Providence Athenaeum, 251 Benefit St, Providence, RI, 02903. Tel: 401-421-6970. p. 2039

Ryan, Christine, Librn, Vermont Law School, 164 Chelsea St, South Royalton, VT, 05068. Tel: 802-831-1448. p. 2295

Ryan, Dan, Head Librn, Free Library of Philadelphia, Interlibrary Loan, 1901 Vine St, Philadelphia, PA, 19103-1116. Tel: 215-686-5360. p. 1978

Ryan, Dan, Head, ILL, Free Library of Philadelphia, Fiction & Popular Culture Library & Central Circulation Department, Philbrick Hall, 1901 Vine St, Rm 103, Philadelphia, PA, 19103-1116. Tel: 215-686-5320. p. 1978

Ryan, Ellen, Supv Librn, Ch, Bernards Township Library, 32 S Maple Ave, Basking Ridge, NJ, 07920-1216. Tel: 908-204-3031. p. 1388

Ryan, Ellen M, Head, Spec Coll, Idaho State University, 850 S Ninth Ave, Pocatello, ID, 83209. Tel: 208-282-3608. p. 528

Ryan, Janet, Head, Prog & Outreach, Jones Library, Inc, 43 Amity St, Amherst, MA, 01002-2285. Tel: 413-259-3223. p. 984

Ryan, Jeanne Marie, Libr Dir, Roselle Free Public Library, 104 W Fourth Ave, Roselle, NJ, 07203. Tel: 908-245-5809. p. 1441

Ryan, Jessica, Head, Youth Serv, Rye Public Library, 581 Washington Rd, Rye, NH, 03870. Tel: 603-964-8401. p. 1380

Ryan, Joyce, City Librn, National City Public Library, 1401 National City Blvd, National City, CA, 91950-4401. Tel: 619-470-5800. p. 182

Ryan, Joyce, Dir, Libr Serv, Santa Fe Springs City Library, 11700 E Telegraph Rd, Santa Fe Springs, CA, 90670-3600. Tel: 562-868-7738. p. 243

Ryan, Karen, Circ & ILL, Wiggin Memorial Library, Ten Bunker Hill Ave, Stratham, NH, 03885. Tel: 603-772-4346. p. 1381

Ryan, Kimberly, Head Librn, Atwater Library & Computer Centre, 1200 Atwater Ave, Westmount, QC, H3Z 1X4, CANADA. Tel: 514-935-7344. p. 2739

Ryan, Laura, Library Contact, Community College of Rhode Island, One Hilton St, Providence, RI, 02905-2304. Tel: 401-455-6078. p. 2038

Ryan, Lauren, Mgr, Br Serv, Somerset County Library System of New Jersey, One Vogt Dr, Bridgewater, NJ, 08807-2136. Tel: 908-458-8451. p. 1392

Ryan, Lauren, Br Mgr, Somerset County Library System of New Jersey, Warren Township Branch, 42 Mountain Blvd, Warren, NJ, 07059. Tel: 908-458-8450. p. 1393

Ryan, Lisa, Head, Ref, Beverly Public Library, 32 Essex St, Beverly, MA, 01915-4561. Tel: 978-921-6062. p. 989

Ryan, Lisa, Head, Adult Serv, Dexter District Library, 3255 Alpine St, Dexter, MI, 48130. Tel: 734-426-4477. p. 1100

Ryan, Marianne, Dean of Libr, Loyola University Chicago Libraries, 1032 W Sheridan Rd, Chicago, IL, 60660. Tel: 773-508-2657. p. 563

Ryan, Mary, Head, Coll Serv, Curry College, 1071 Blue Hill Ave, Milton, MA, 02186-9984. Tel: 617-333-2937. p. 1036

Ryan, Mary, Youth Serv, Crook County Library, 175 NW Meadow Lakes Dr, Prineville, OR, 97754. Tel: 541-447-7978. p. 1895

Ryan, Meghan, Spec Coll Cat Librn, National Louis University Library, 18 S Michigan Ave, 3rd Flr, Chicago, IL, 60603. Tel: 312-261-3122. p. 565

Ryan, Michele, Dir, Oneida Public Library, 220 Broad St, Oneida, NY, 13421. Tel: 315-363-3050. p. 1611

Ryan, Michelle, Mgr, Elyria Public Library System, South Branch, 340 15th St, Elyria, OH, 44035. Tel: 440-323-7519. p. 1784

Ryan, Nancy, Librn, Arkansas Methodist Hospital, 900 W Kingshighway, Paragould, AR, 72450. Tel: 870-239-7165. p. 106

Ryan, Nancy, Br Coordr, Fairfax County Public Library, 12000 Government Center Pkwy, Ste 324, Fairfax, VA, 22035-0012. Tel: 703-324-3100. p. 2316

Ryan, Nanette, Head, Children's Servx, West Bridgewater Public Library, 80 Howard St, West Bridgewater, MA, 02379-1710. Tel: 508-894-1255. p. 1065

Ryan, Pam, Dir, Serv Develop, Toronto Public Library, 789 Yonge St, Toronto, ON, M4W 2G8, CANADA. Tel: 416-393-7131. p. 2693

Ryan, Samantha, Circ Librn, ILL, Old Town Public Library, 46 Middle St, Old Town, ME, 04468. Tel: 207-827-3972. p. 934

Ryan, Sue, Br Mgr, Saint Tammany Parish Library, Slidell Branch, 555 Robert Blvd, Slidell, LA, 70458. Tel: 985-646-6470. p. 888

Ryan, Susan, Librn, Seyfarth Shaw, 975 F St NW, Washington, DC, 20004. Tel: 202-828-5345. p. 374

Ryan, Susan, Asst Librn, Filger Public Library, 261 E Fifth St, Minonk, IL, 61760. Tel: 309-432-2929. p. 618

Ryan, Susan M, Dean of the Library & Learning Technologies, Stetson University, 421 N Woodland Blvd, Unit 8418, DeLand, FL, 32723. Tel: 386-822-7181. p. 393

Ryan, Tarri, Ch Serv Librn, Saint Clair County Library System, 210 McMorran Blvd, Port Huron, MI, 48060-4098. Tel: 810-987-7323. p. 1142

Ryan, Tim, Librn, East Rochester Public Library, 317 Main St, East Rochester, NY, 14445. Tel: 585-586-8302. p. 1528

Ryan, Tom, Automation & Networking Mgr, Council Bluffs Public Library, 400 Willow Ave, Council Bluffs, IA, 51503-9042. Tel: 712-323-7553. p. 742

Ryan, Victoria, Libr Dir, Shamokin & Coal Township Public Library, Inc, 210 E Independence St, Shamokin, PA, 17872-6888. Tel: 570-648-3202. p. 2006

Ryan, William, Fgn, Intl & Rare Books Librarian, American University, 4300 Nebraska Ave NW, Washington, DC, 20016-8182. Tel: 202-274-4331. p. 360

Rybarczyk, Nathan, Ad, Asst Dir, Carnegie-Schadde Memorial Public Library, 230 Fourth Ave, Baraboo, WI, 53913. Tel: 608-356-6166. p. 2422

Rybin Koob, Amanda, Dir, Naropa University Library, 2130 Arapahoe Ave, Boulder, CO, 80302. Tel: 303-546-3507. p. 267

Rychlik, Marjorie, Dir, Sheridan Memorial Library, 5805 S Logan Park Dr, Sheridan, TX, 77475. Tel: 979-234-5154. p. 2243

Ryczek, Marianne, Head, Youth Serv, Northlake Public Library District, 231 N Wolf Rd, Northlake, IL, 60164. Tel: 708-562-2301. p. 627

Ryden, Tricia, Adult Serv Coordr, Wiggin Memorial Library, Ten Bunker Hill Ave, Stratham, NH, 03885. Tel: 603-772-4346. p. 1381

Ryder, Becky, Libr Dir, Keeneland Association, Keeneland Race Course, 4201 Versailles Rd, Lexington, KY, 40510. Tel: 859-280-4761. p. 862

Ryder, Jen, Br Mgr, Sonoma County Library, Rohnert Park Cotati Regional Library, 6250 Lynne Conde Way, Rohnert Park, CA, 94928. Tel: 707-584-9121. p. 204

Ryder, Jill, Coll Develop, Southern Adirondack Library System, 22 Whitney Pl, Saratoga Springs, NY, 12866-4596. Tel: 518-584-7300, Ext 216. p. 1636

Ryder, Suzanne, Chief Librn, Naval Research Laboratory, 4555 Overlook Ave SW, Code 5500, Washington, DC, 20375-5337. Tel: 202-767-2357. p. 373
Ryder, Vanessa, Circ, Sunderland Public Library, 20 School St, Sunderland, MA, 01375. Tel: 413-665-2642. p. 1058
Rydgren, Erin, Dir, Washta Public Library, 100 S Fifth Ave, Washta, IA, 51061. Tel: 712-447-6546. p. 788
Rydin, Roger, Archives, Rec Mgr, Oral Roberts University Library, 7777 S Lewis Ave, Tulsa, OK, 74171. Tel: 918-495-6750. p. 1865
Rydin, Roger, Archivist, Oral Roberts University Library, Holy Spirit Research Center, 7777 S Lewis Ave, Tulsa, OK, 74171. Tel: 918-495-6750. p. 1865
Ryer, Sharon Galbraith, Br Mgr, Mercer County Library System, Hickory Corner Branch, 138 Hickory Corner Rd, East Windsor, NJ, 08520. Tel: 609-448-1330. p. 1411
Ryjewski, Jen, Asst Dir, Downers Grove Public Library, 1050 Curtiss St, Downers Grove, IL, 60515. Tel: 630-960-1200, Ext 4299. p. 579
Ryker, Amy, Dir, Duncan Public Library, 2211 N Hwy 81, Duncan, OK, 73533. Tel: 580-255-0636. p. 1845
Rylander, Deidre, Pres, Yonkers Historical Society, Grinton I Will Library, 1500 Central Park Ave, Yonkers, NY, 10710. Tel: 914-961-8940. p. 1668
Rymsza-Pawlowska, Elzbieta, Dir, Res Mgt & Digital Serv, Catholic University of America, 315 Mullen Library, 620 Michigan Ave NE, Washington, DC, 20064. Tel: 202-319-5554. p. 362
Ryner, Katherine H, Head, Coll Support Serv, Saint Mary's College of Maryland Library, 47645 College Dr, Saint Mary's City, MD, 20686-3001. Tel: 240-895-4260. p. 976
Rynkiewicz, Robert P, Dir, Atlantic City Free Public Library, William K Cheatham Bldg, One N Tennessee Ave, Atlantic City, NJ, 08401. Tel: 609-345-2269. p. 1388
Rynning, Connie, Br Mgr, Riverside County Library System, Woodcrest Library, 16625 Krameria, Riverside, CA, 92504. Tel: 951-789-7324. p. 203
Ryu, Christine, Br Mgr, Stanislaus County Library, Keyes Branch, 4420 Maud Ave, Keyes, CA, 95328-0367. Tel: 209-664-8006. p. 178
Ryzner, Vanessa, Circ Coordr, Upper St Clair Township Library, 1820 McLaughlin Run Rd, Upper St Clair, PA, 15241-2397. Tel: 412-835-5540. p. 2016
Rzasa, Steve, Dir, Johnson County Library, 171 N Adams Ave, Buffalo, WY, 82834. Tel: 307-684-5546. p. 2491
Rzepczynski, Mary, Dir, Delta Township District Library, 5130 Davenport Dr, Lansing, MI, 48917-2040. Tel: 517-321-4014. p. 1124
Saab, Lila, Br Mgr, Oakville Public Library, Glen Abbey, 1415 Third Line, Oakville, ON, L6M 3G2, CANADA. Tel: 905-815-2039, Ext 3596. p. 2662
Saadaoui, Leila, Librn, Laurentian University Library & Archives, 935 Ramsey Lake Rd, Sudbury, ON, P3E 2C6, CANADA. Tel: 705-675-1151, Ext 3319. p. 2683
Saalfeld, Kim, Br Mgr, Eagle Valley Library District, Avon Public Library, 200 Benchmark Rd, Avon, CO, 81620. Tel: 970-949-6797. p. 279
Saar, Michael, Head, Instructional Service & Assessment, Interim Dean of Libr, Lamar University, 4400 Martin Luther King Jr Pkwy, Beaumont, TX, 77705. Tel: 409-880-7264. p. 2146
Saathoff, Colette, Tech Serv, Cordova District Library, 402 Main Ave, Cordova, IL, 61242. Tel: 309-654-2330. p. 573
Saavedra, Adriana, Dir, Central Arizona College, Aravaipa Campus Learning Resource Center, 80440 E Aravaipa Rd, Winkelman, AZ, 85192. Tel: 520-357-2821. p. 58
Saba, Bea, Dir, Libr Syst, Bryan College Station Public Library System, 201 E 26th St, Bryan, TX, 77803-5356. Tel: 979-209-5600. p. 2151
Saba, Beatrice, Dir, Cent Libr Serv, Live Oak Public Libraries, 2002 Bull St, Savannah, GA, 31401. Tel: 912-652-3600. p. 496
Saba, Meredith, Head, Access, Research & Instructional Servs, Western Carolina University, 176 Central Dr, Cullowhee, NC, 28723. Tel: 828-227-3746. p. 1683
Sabados, Laura, Br Librn, Southeast Regional Library, Stoughton Branch, 232 Main St, Stoughton, SK, S0G 4T0, CANADA. Tel: 306-457-2484. p. 2755
Sabala, John, IT Mgr, Fox River Valley Public Library District, 555 Barrington Ave, East Dundee, IL, 60118-1496. Tel: 847-428-3661. p. 580
Sabanos, Jacqueline, Head, Acq, University of San Diego, Helen K & James S Copley Library, 5998 Alcala Park, San Diego, CA, 92110. p. 222
Sabatier, Sophie, Sr Assoc, National Economic Research Associates, Inc, 360 Hamilton Ave, 10th Flr, White Plains, NY, 10601. Tel: 914-448-4000. p. 1664
Sabbagh, Lia, Coordr, Englewood Health, 350 Engle St, Englewood, NJ, 07631. Tel: 201-894-3069. p. 1401
Sabbar, Carol, Dir, Libr Serv & Instrul Tech, Carthage College, 2001 Alford Park Dr, Kenosha, WI, 53140-1900. Tel: 262-551-5950. p. 2444
Sabbe, Nancy, Libr Dir, Madison Public Library, 209 E Center St, Madison, SD, 57042. Tel: 605-256-7525. p. 2078
Sabel, Myra, Tech Serv Librn, Alabama Supreme Court & State Law Library, Heflin-Torbert Judicial Bldg, 300 Dexter Ave, Montgomery, AL, 36104. Tel: 334-229-0580. p. 28
Sabin, Marion, Libr Tech, South Piedmont Community College, Carpenter Library, Technical Education Bldg, 4209 Old Charlotte Hwy, Monroe, NC, 28110. Tel: 704-290-5851. p. 1708
Sabine, Virnna, Dir, Libr Serv, Kingswood University, 248 Main St, Sussex, NB, E4E 1R3, CANADA. Tel: 506-432-4417. p. 2605
Sable, Courtney, Dir, Cresson Public Library, 231 Laurel Ave, Cresson, PA, 16630-1118. Tel: 814-886-2619. p. 1925
Sabo, Joshua, Dep Libr Dir, Huntsville Public Library, 1219 13th St, Huntsville, TX, 77340. Tel: 936-291-5485. p. 2201
Sabo, Sara, Chief Op Officer, Library Servs, Gail Borden Public Library District, 270 N Grove Ave, Elgin, IL, 60120-5596. Tel: 847-429-5984. p. 583
Sabolcik, Cara, Assoc Libr Dir, St John's College Library, 60 College Ave, Annapolis, MD, 21401. Tel: 410-295-6927. p. 951
Sabonya, Jamie, Head, Youth Serv, Library of the Chathams, 214 Main St, Chatham, NJ, 07928. Tel: 973-635-0603. p. 1395
Sabourin, Francoise, Librn, Bibliotheque Montcalm Library, 113, 2e Ave, Saint-Jean-Baptiste, MB, R0G 2B0, CANADA. Tel: 204-758-3137. p. 2590
Sabourin, Helene, Chief Exec Officer, Canadian Association of Occupational Therapists, 103-2685 Queensview Dr, Ottawa, ON, K2B 8K2, CANADA. Tel: 613-523-2268. p. 2665
Sabourin, Julie, Libr Mgr, Community Libraries of Providence, Fox Point Library, 90 Ives St, Providence, RI, 02906. Tel: 401-331-0390. p. 2038
Sacco, Barbara, Libr Mgr, Eatontown Library, 33 Broad St, Eatontown, NJ, 07724. Tel: 732-389-2665. p. 1400
Sacco, Christina, Pub Relations Coordr, Chattanooga Public Library, 1001 Broad St, Chattanooga, TN, 37402-2652. Tel: 423-643-7700. p. 2091
Sacco, Karen, ILL, Ridley Township Public Library, 100 E MacDade Blvd, Folsom, PA, 19033-2592. Tel: 610-583-0593. p. 1933
Sacco, Kathleen, Dean of Library & Learning Services, Lake-Sumter State College Library, 9501 US Hwy 441, Leesburg, FL, 34788. Tel: 352-365-3541. p. 418
Sacher, Laurie, Supvr, Deschutes Public Library District, Bend Branch, 601 NW Wall St, Bend, OR, 97703. Tel: 541-312-7052. p. 1874
Sachez, Rashell, Ms, Library Contact, Colusa County Free Library, Stonyford Branch, 5080 Stonyford-Lodoga Rd, Stonyford, CA, 95979. Tel: 530-963-3722. p. 131
Sachs, Aimee, Head Librn, Connell Foley Law Library, 56 Livingston Ave, Roseland, NJ, 07068. Tel: 973-535-0500. p. 1440
Sachs, Dianna, Health & Human Services Librn, Western Michigan University, 1903 W Michigan Ave, WMU Mail Stop 5353, Kalamazoo, MI, 49008-5353. Tel: 269-387-5182. p. 1122
Sackett, Jennifer, Dir, Lincoln County Public Library, 306 W Main St, Lincolnton, NC, 28092. Tel: 704-735-8044. p. 1701
Sackett, Nancy, Outreach Serv Librn, Lewistown Public Library, 701 W Main St, Lewistown, MT, 59457. Tel: 406-538-5212. p. 1298
Sackmann, Anna, Sci/Eng Librn, University of California, Berkeley, Kresge Engineering Library, 110 Bechtel Engineering Ctr, Berkeley, CA, 94720-6000. Tel: 510-642-9478. p. 123
Sacolic, Brian, Head, Pub Serv, Wilkes University, 84 W South St, Wilkes-Barre, PA, 18766. Tel: 570-408-3206. p. 2023
Saddler, Nancy, Adult Serv, ILL, Pioneer Memorial Library, 375 W Fourth St, Colby, KS, 67701-2197. Tel: 785-460-4470. p. 802
Sadeghi Pari, Akram, Bibliog Serv Librn, Spec Coll Librn, University of Cincinnati, 2540 Clifton Ave, Cincinnati, OH, 45219. Tel: 513-556-0154. p. 1764
Sadkin, Amy, Commun Serv, Outreach Serv, Framingham Public Library, 49 Lexington St, Framingham, MA, 01702-8278. Tel: 508-879-5570, Ext 4347. p. 1019
Sadkin, Amy, Dir, Bacon Free Library, 58 Eliot St, Natick, MA, 01760. Tel: 508-653-6730. p. 1037
Sadkin, Amy, Asst Dir, Morse Institute Library, 14 E Central St, Natick, MA, 01760. Tel: 508-647-6526. p. 1037
Sadowitz, Daniel, Libr Dir, United States Army, Van Noy Library, 5966 12th St, Bldg 1024, Fort Belvoir, VA, 22060-5554. Tel: 703-806-3323. p. 2319
Sadowski, Kristi, Exec Dir, Southington Public Library & Museum, 255 Main St, Southington, CT, 06489. Tel: 860-628-0947. p. 337
Sadowski, Serena, Asst Law Librn, Wood County Law Library, One Courthouse Sq, Bowling Green, OH, 43402. Tel: 419-353-3921. p. 1752
Sadusky, Lynda, ILL Coordr, Drexel University Libraries, Hahnemann Library, 245 N 15th St MS 449, Philadelphia, PA, 19102-1192. p. 1976
Saecker, Tasha, Asst Dir, Appleton Public Library, 225 N Oneida St, Appleton, WI, 54911-4780. Tel: 920-832-6173. p. 2420
Saeger, Lynnette, Libr Dir, Southern Lehigh Public Library, 3200 Preston Lane, Center Valley, PA, 18034. Tel: 610-282-8825. p. 1920
Saeli, Marie, Exec Dir, Franklin Park Public Library District, 10311 Grand Ave, Franklin Park, IL, 60131. Tel: 847-455-6016, Ext 226. p. 590
Saenz, Janie, Br Mgr, Duval County-San Diego Public Library, Benavides Branch, 131 Mesquite St, Benavides, TX, 78341. Tel: 361-256-4646. p. 2241
Saenz, Patricia, Acq Librn, Coll Mgt Librn, Librn III, South Texas College Library, 3201 W Pecan Blvd, McAllen, TX, 78501-6661. Tel: 956-872-2323. p. 2217
Saffell, Kathleen, Br Mgr, San Luis Obispo County Library, Creston Library, 6290 Adams, Creston, CA, 93432. Tel: 805-237-3010. p. 234
Saffell, Mary, Sr Archivist, Texas Christian University, 2913 Lowden St, TCU Box 298400, Fort Worth, TX, 76129. Tel: 817-257-7106. p. 2181

Saffer, Sam, Database Librn, The National Academies, Keck 439, 500 Fifth St NW, Washington, DC, 20001. Tel: 202-334-2989. p. 371
Safford, Beth, Head, Ref, Boxford Town Library, Seven-A Spofford Rd, Boxford, MA, 01921. Tel: 978-887-7323. p. 1001
Safier, Neil, Dir & Librn, Brown University, John Carter Brown Library, Brown University, 94 George St, Providence, RI, 02906. Tel: 401-863-2725. p. 2037
Safin, Kelly, Ref & Pub Serv Librn, University of Pittsburgh at Greensburg, Greensburg Campus, 150 Finoli Dr, Greensburg, PA, 15601-5804. Tel: 724-836-7961. p. 1938
Safley, Ellen Derey, Dean of Libr, University of Texas at Dallas, 800 W Campbell Rd, Richardson, TX, 75080. Tel: 972-883-2916. p. 2231
Safratowich, Michael, Cat, University of North Dakota, Harley E French Library of the Health Sciences, School of Medicine & Health Sciences, 501 N Columbia Rd, Stop 9002, Grand Forks, ND, 58202-9002. Tel: 701-777-2602. p. 1734
Saft, Roger, Dir, Prescott Public Library, 215 E Goodwin St, Prescott, AZ, 86303. Tel: 928-777-1523. p. 73
Sagaas, Christopher, Dir, Utica Public Library, 303 Genesee St, Utica, NY, 13501. Tel: 315-735-2279. p. 1656
Sagan, Kim, Circ Supvr, Brookfield Public Library, 1900 N Calhoun Rd, Brookfield, WI, 53005. Tel: 262-782-4140. p. 2425
Sagar, Mary, Asst Libr Mgr, Chandler Public Library, 22 S Delaware, Chandler, AZ, 85225. Tel: 480-782-2820. p. 58
Sage, Audrey L, Preservation Services Mgr, University of North Carolina at Greensboro, 320 College Ave, Greensboro, NC, 27412-0001. Tel: 336-334-3591. p. 1693
Sage, Hess, Asst Dir, Galva Public Library District, 120 NW Third Ave, Galva, IL, 61434. Tel: 309-932-2180. p. 591
Sage, Joy, Ref Librn, California State University, Fullerton, 800 N State College Blvd, Fullerton, CA, 92831. Tel: 657-278-2151. p. 147
Sagevick, Cathy, Ref Serv, Mineola Memorial Library, 195 Marcellus Rd, Mineola, NY, 11501. Tel: 516-746-8488. p. 1572
Sahm, Tatiana, Librn, Onondaga County Public Libraries, Syracuse Northeast Community Center, 716 Hawley Ave, Syracuse, NY, 13203. Tel: 315-472-6343. p. 1649
Said, Mildred, Commun Libr Mgr, Queens Library, South Ozone Park Community Library, 128-16 Rockaway Blvd, South Ozone Park, NY, 11420. Tel: 718-529-1660. p. 1555
Sailing, Sharilyn, Dir, Barneveld Public Library, 107 W Orbison St, Barneveld, WI, 53507. Tel: 608-924-3711. p. 2422
Sain, Annette, Mus Dir, College of the Ozarks, Brownell Research Center Library, Ralph Foster Museum, One Cultural Ct, Point Lookout, MO, 65726. Tel: 417-690-3407. p. 1266
Saini, Sanjeev, Mr, Librn, Independent Institute Library, 100 Swan Way, Oakland, CA, 94621-1428. Tel: 510-632-1366, Ext 143. p. 185
Saint-Paen, Robyn, Asst Dir, Br Serv, Clayton County Library System, 865 Battlecreek Rd, Jonesboro, GA, 30236. Tel: 770-473-3850. p. 483
Saito Lincoln, Emma, Spec Coll Librn, Augustana College Library, 3435 9 1/2 Ave, Rock Island, IL, 61201-2296. Tel: 309-794-7317. p. 641
Sajja, Prasada, Dir, Luther Rice University & Seminary, 3038 Evans Mill Rd, Lithonia, GA, 30038. Tel: 770-484-1204, Ext 5756. p. 485
Saka, Tim, Librn, Onondaga Community College, 4585 W Seneca Tpk, Syracuse, NY, 13215-4585. Tel: 315-498-2340. p. 1649
Sakai, Chiaki, Librn, Columbia University, C V Starr East Asian Library, 300 Kent Hall, MC 3901, 1140 Amsterdam Ave, New York, NY, 10027. Tel: 212-854-4318. p. 1584
Sakarya, Mustafa, Libr Dir, Sarah Lawrence College, One Mead Way, Bronxville, NY, 10708. Tel: 914-395-2471. p. 1500
Sakarya, Mustafa, Libr Dir, Sarah Lawrence College, William Schuman Music Library, One Mead Way, Bronxville, NY, 10708. Tel: 914-395-2375. p. 1500
Sakiestewa, Noreen E, Dr, Dir, Hopi Public Library, c/o Hopi Educ Dept, One Main St, Kykotsmovi Village, AZ, 86039. Tel: 928-734-3501. p. 65
Sakmann, Lindsay, ILL, Albright College, 13th & Exeter Sts, Reading, PA, 19604. Tel: 610-921-7517. p. 2000
Sakovich, Sherry, Dir, Decatur Public Library, 504 Cherry St NE, Decatur, AL, 35601. Tel: 256-353-2993, Ext 102. p. 14
Sala, Christine, Archit Librn, Columbia University, Avery Architectural & Fine Arts Library, 300 Avery Hall, 1172 Amsterdam Ave, MC 0301, New York, NY, 10027. Tel: 212-854-6199. p. 1583
Salaam, Karen, Br Mgr, Norfolk Public Library, Blyden Branch, 879 E Princess Anne Rd, Norfolk, VA, 23504. Tel: 757-441-2852. p. 2335
Salaba, Athena, Dr, Prof, Kent State University, 314 University Library, 1125 Risman Dr, Kent, OH, 44242-0001. Tel: 330-672-2782. p. 2790
Saladino, Richard, Archit/Art Librn, University of Nevada, Las Vegas Univ Libraries, Architecture Studies Library, Paul B Sogg Architecture Bldg, 4505 S Maryland Pkwy, Box 454049, Las Vegas, NV, 89154-4049. Tel: 702-895-2148. p. 1348
Salami, Lola, Law Librn, Alberta Law Libraries, Judicial, Calgary Courts Ctr, 601-Five St SW, Ste 501N, Calgary, AB, T2P 5P7, CANADA. Tel: 403-297-3231. p. 2525
Salamon, Anaïs, Head Librn, McGill University Libraries, Islamic Studies, Morrice Hall, 3485 McTavish St, Montreal, QC, H3A 1Y1, CANADA. Tel: 514-398-4688. p. 2726
Salamone, Sue, Ch Serv Librn, Johnson County Public Library, Clark Pleasant Library, 530 Tracy Rd, Ste 250, New Whiteland, IN, 46184-9699. Tel: 317-535-6206. p. 686
Salantrie, Theresa, Head, Circ, Head, Tech Serv, Mandel Public Library of West Palm Beach, 411 Clematis St, West Palm Beach, FL, 33401. Tel: 561-868-7700. p. 453
Salas, Jennifer, Libr Dir, Martin County Library System, 2351 SE Monterey Rd, Stuart, FL, 34996. Tel: 772-221-1410. p. 444
Salas, Victor, Evening Ref Librn, The John Marshall Law School, 300 S State St, 6th Flr, Chicago, IL, 60604. Tel: 312-427-2737. p. 564
Salathe, Kate, Syst Librn, St Lawrence University, 23 Romoda Dr, Canton, NY, 13617. Tel: 315-229-1823. p. 1514
Salaz, Alicia, Vice Provost & Univ Librn, University of Oregon Libraries, 1501 Kincaid St, Eugene, OR, 97403-1299. Tel: 541-346-3053. p. 1879
Salazar, Gerardo, Libr Dir, San Benito Public Library, 101 W Rose St, San Benito, TX, 78586-5169. Tel: 956-361-3860. p. 2240
Salazar, Janet, Dir, Queen Anne's County Free Library, 121 S Commerce St, Centreville, MD, 21617. Tel: 410-758-0980, Ext 203. p. 961
Salazar, Linda, Mgr, Luna Community College, 366 Luna Dr, Las Vegas, NM, 87701. Tel: 505-454-5333. p. 1471
Salazar, Ramiro S, Dir, San Antonio Public Library, 600 Soledad, San Antonio, TX, 78205-2786. Tel: 210-207-2500. p. 2238
Salazar-Mallorquin, Jenny, Ser Librn, Inter-American University of Puerto Rico, San German Campus, Ave Inter-American University, Rd 102, K 30 6, San German, PR, 00683-9801. Tel: 787-264-1912, Ext 7537. p. 2512
Saldaña, David, Per Librn, Ser Librn, Universidad Central Del Caribe, Avenida Laurel, Santa Juanita, Bayamon, PR, 00956. Tel: 787-798-3001, Ext 2344. p. 2510
Saldana, Samantha, Librn, Shafter Library & Learning Center, 236 James St, Shafter, CA, 93263. Tel: 661-746-5055. p. 246
Saldanha, Guy, ILL Supvr, Bowdoin College Library, 3000 College Sta, Brunswick, ME, 04011-8421. p. 919
Saldarriaga, Juliana, Collection Strategies Specialist, Adelphi University, One South Ave, Garden City, NY, 11530. Tel: 516-877-3533. p. 1536
Saldarriaga-Osorio, Maria Luisa, Ref Librn, Surry Community College, R Bldg, 630 S Main St, Dobson, NC, 27017. Tel: 336-386-3501. p. 1683
Saldivar, Hope, Libr Assoc, Yolo County Library, Knights Landing Branch, 42351 Third St, Knights Landing, CA, 95645. Tel: 530-735-6593. p. 260
Saldivar, Krystal, Circ Spec, Coastal Bend College, 3800 Charco Rd, Beeville, TX, 78102. Tel: 361-354-2737. p. 2146
Saldivar, Tanya, Librn, Collier County Public Library, Immokalee Branch, 417 N First St, Immokalee, FL, 34142. Tel: 239-657-2882. p. 427
Saldutte, Catherine (Katie), Outreach Librn, Wisconsin Talking Book & Braille Library, 813 W Wells St, Milwaukee, WI, 53233-1436. Tel: 414-286-6918. p. 2461
Saleh, Ahlam, Dr, Assoc Librn, University of Arizona Libraries, Health Sciences Library, 1501 N Campbell Ave, Tucson, AZ, 85724. Tel: 520-626-5450. p. 83
Salehudres, Dejare, Financial Dir, Prince George's County Memorial Library System, 9601 Capital Lane, Largo, MD, 20774. Tel: 301-699-3500. p. 970
Salem, Joe, Univ Librn, Michigan State University Libraries, Main Library, 366 W Circle Dr, East Lansing, MI, 48824-1048. Tel: 517-432-6123. p. 1102
Salem, Lea, Managing Librn, Brooklyn Public Library, New Lots, 665 New Lots Ave, Brooklyn, NY, 11207. Tel: 718-649-0311. p. 1503
Salem, Linda, Head, Ref Serv, San Diego State University, 5500 Campanile Dr, San Diego, CA, 92182-8050. Tel: 619-594-5148. p. 221
Salem, Sara, Dir, Buckland Public Library, 30 Upper St, Buckland, MA, 01338. Tel: 413-625-9412. p. 1003
Salemme, Kevin, Dir, Media Instrul Serv, Merrimack College, 315 Turnpike St, North Andover, MA, 01845. Tel: 978-837-5377. p. 1040
Salerno, Ann Marie, Circ, West Hartford Public Library, 20 S Main St, West Hartford, CT, 06107-2432. Tel: 860-561-6950. p. 345
Salerno, Cheryl, Tech Serv Librn, Oklahoma Wesleyan University Library, 2201 Silver Lake Rd, Bartlesville, OK, 74006. Tel: 918-335-6298. p. 1842
Salgado, Eliamar, Libr Asst, Penitas Public Library, 1111 S Main St, Penitas, TX, 78576. Tel: 956-583-5656. p. 2226
Salgado, Gaby, Head, Circ, Head, Tech Serv, Elmwood Park Public Library, One Conti Pkwy, Elmwood Park, IL, 60707. Tel: 708-395-1205. p. 585
Salgado, Kathy, Ref Librn, Kettering College, 3737 Southern Blvd, Kettering, OH, 45429-1299. Tel: 937-395-8053, Ext 6. p. 1793
Salgat, Jennifer, Dir, Lake Odessa Community Library, 1007 Fourth Ave, Lake Odessa, MI, 48849-1023. Tel: 616-374-4591. p. 1123
Salhany, Stephen R, Cat Librn, Ser, University of Maine School of Law, 246 Deering Ave, Portland, ME, 04102. Tel: 207-780-4832. p. 937
Saliba, Elizabeth, Dept Chair, Glendale Community College - Main, 6000 W Olive Ave, Glendale, AZ, 85302. Tel: 623-845-3109. p. 61
Salie, Paul, Assessment Specialist, Tarleton State University Library, 201 Saint Felix, Stephenville, TX, 76401. Tel: 254-968-9246. p. 2246
Salierno, Kristen, Dir, Howland Public Library, 313 Main St, Beacon, NY, 12508. Tel: 845-831-1134. p. 1491

Salieron, Kristen, Dir, East Fishkill Community Library, 348 Rte 376, Hopewell Junction, NY, 12533-6075. Tel: 845-221-9943, Ext 227. p. 1548

Salinas, Erica, Dep Dir, Pilot Point Community Library, 324 S Washington St, Pilot Point, TX, 76258. Tel: 940-686-5004. p. 2226

Salinas, Karla, ILL Coordr, California State University Dominguez Hills, 1000 E Victoria St, Carson, CA, 90747. Tel: 310-243-3758. p. 129

Salinas, Roberto, Br Mgr, Irving Public Library, Valley Ranch Library, 401 Cimmaron Trail, Irving, TX, 75063-4680. Tel: 972-721-4669. p. 2202

Salinas, Roberto, Br Mgr, Irving Public Library, West Irving Library, 4444 W Rochelle Rd, Irving, TX, 75062. Tel: 972-721-2691. p. 2203

Salinero, David, Doc, Ref (Info Servs), Delta State University, Laflore Circle at Fifth Ave, Cleveland, MS, 38733-2599. Tel: 662-846-4430. p. 1214

Salino, Stephen, Dir, Watkins Glen Public Library, 610 S Decatur St, Watkins Glen, NY, 14891. Tel: 607-535-2346. p. 1660

Salisbury, Adam, Access Serv Mgr, Salve Regina University, 100 Ochre Point Ave, Newport, RI, 02840-4192. Tel: 401-341-2330. p. 2035

Salisbury, Kim, Dir, Maple Rapids Public Library, 130 S Maple Ave, Maple Rapids, MI, 48853. Tel: 989-682-4464. p. 1129

Salisbury, Lisa, Asst Librn, Jackson Memorial Library, 71 Main St, Tenants Harbor, ME, 04860. Tel: 207-372-8961. p. 943

Salisbury, Lutishoor, Dir, Chemistry & Biochemistry Library, University of Arkansas Libraries, 365 N McIlroy Ave, Fayetteville, AR, 72701-4002. Tel: 479-575-8418. p. 95

Salisbury, Lutishoor, Head of Libr, University of Arkansas Libraries, Chemistry & Biochemistry, University of Arkansas, 225 CHEM, Fayetteville, AR, 72701-4002. Tel: 479-575-2557. p. 95

Salisbury, Mackenzie, Info Literacy Librn, School of the Art Institute of Chicago, 37 S Wabash Ave, Chicago, IL, 60603-3103. Tel: 312-899-5097. p. 568

Salisbury, Meghan, Youth Serv Librn, Belgrade Community Library, 106 N Broadway, Belgrade, MT, 59714. Tel: 406-388-4346. p. 1287

Salkowitz, Lauren, Br Co-Mgr, Iberia Parish Library, Lydia Branch, 4800 Freyou Rd, New Iberia, LA, 70560. Tel: 337-364-7808. p. 900

Sallberg, Steven, Librn, California Department of Corrections Library System, California Men's Colony-East, Colony Dr, Hwy 1, San Luis Obispo, CA, 93409. Tel: 805-547-7185. p. 206

Sallee, Donna, Dir, Inman Public Library, 100 N Main, Inman, KS, 67546. Tel: 620-585-2474. p. 815

Sallee, Lisa, Asst Dir, Ocean State Libraries, 300 Centerville Rd, Ste 103S, Warwick, RI, 02886. Tel: 401-593-2167. p. 2774

Salmen, Katelyn, Tech Coordr, Columbiana Public Library, 332 N Middle St, Columbiana, OH, 44408. Tel: 330-482-5509. p. 1771

Salmers, Greg, Dir, Support Serv, Saskatchewan Legislative Library, 234-2405 Legislative Dr, Regina, SK, S4S 0B3, CANADA. Tel: 306-787-2278. p. 2748

Salminen, Amy, Circ, Peter White Public Library, 217 N Front St, Marquette, MI, 49855. Tel: 906-226-4310. p. 1130

Salmon, Elizabeth, Research Servs Librn, University of California, Merced Library, 5200 N Lake Rd, Merced, CA, 95343. Tel: 209-631-6954. p. 176

Salmon, Helen, Librn, Colls & Content, University of Guelph, 50 Stone Rd E, Guelph, ON, N1G 2W1, CANADA. Tel: 519-824-4120, Ext 52121. p. 2644

Salmon, Lori, Head Librn, New York University, Stephen Chan Library of Fine Arts & Conservation Center Library, One E 78th St, New York, NY, 10075. Tel: 212-992-5908. p. 1599

Salmon, Michael W, AV Coordr, Librn, Ref (Info Servs), LA84 Foundation, 2141 W Adams Blvd, Los Angeles, CA, 90018. Tel: 323-730-4646. p. 162

Salmon, Robin, Curator, Brookgreen Gardens Library, 1931 Brookgreen Dr, Murrells Inlet, SC, 29576. Tel: 843-235-6000. p. 2066

Salmon, Virginia, Librn, Northeast State Community College, 2425 Hwy 75, Blountville, TN, 37617. Tel: 423-354-2429. p. 2088

Salmons, Laura, Librn, Currituck County Public Library, 4261 Caratoke Hwy, Barco, NC, 27917-9707. Tel: 252-453-8345. p. 1673

Salmons, Nadine, Tech Serv Mgr, United States Army, Grant Library, 1637 Flint St, Fort Carson, CO, 80913-4105. Tel: 719-526-8140. p. 280

Salo, Pam, Asst Dir, Buchanan District Library, 128 E Front St, Buchanan, MI, 49107. Tel: 269-695-3681. p. 1087

Salomon, Danielle, Dir of Libr, Mount Saint Mary's University, 12001 Chalon Rd, Los Angeles, CA, 90049-1599. Tel: 310-954-4371. p. 166

Salomon, Kathleen, Assoc Dir, Getty Research Institute, 1200 Getty Center Dr, Ste 1100, Los Angeles, CA, 90049-1688. Tel: 310-440-7390. p. 161

Salomon, Yvette, Br Mgr, Van Buren District Library, Bangor Branch, 420 Division St, Bangor, MI, 49013. Tel: 269-427-8810. p. 1096

Salomone, Pam, Mkt & Communications Mgr, St Charles Public Library District, One S Sixth Ave, Saint Charles, IL, 60174-2105. Tel: 630-584-0076, Ext 246. p. 644

Saloom, Joe, Asst Dir, Flagler County Public Library, 2500 Palm Coast Pkwy NW, Palm Coast, FL, 32137. Tel: 386-446-6763. p. 434

Salopek, Alexander, Coll Develop Librn, Trinity University, 125 Michigan Ave NE, Washington, DC, 20017. Tel: 202-884-9359. p. 377

Salotto, Lori, Asst Dir, Head, Adult Serv, Haverstraw King's Daughters Public Library, 10 W Ramapo Rd, Garnerville, NY, 10923. Tel: 845-786-3800. p. 1537

Salpeter, Michael, Asst Br Mgr, Atlanta-Fulton Public Library System, Alpharetta Branch, Ten Park Plaza, Alpharetta, GA, 30009. Tel: 404-613-6735. p. 460

Salrin, Melissa, Spec Coll Librn, Simon Fraser University - Burnaby Campus, 8888 University Dr, Burnaby, BC, V5A 1S6, CANADA. Tel: 778-782-4626. p. 2564

Salsbury, Kathleen, Libr Serv Dir, Munson-Williams-Proctor Arts Institute Library, 310 Genesee St, Utica, NY, 13502. Tel: 315-797-0000, Ext 2228. p. 1655

Salsedo, Elizabeth, Dir, Robinson & Cole LLP, 280 Trumbull St, Hartford, CT, 06103. Tel: 860-275-8200. p. 318

Salsman, Joseph, Tech Serv Librn, Churchill County Library, 553 S Maine St, Fallon, NV, 89406-3387. Tel: 775-423-7581. p. 1345

Salter, Elaine, Cat, Wellington County Library, 190 Saint Andrews St W, Fergus, ON, N1M 1N5, CANADA. Tel: 519-846-0918, Ext 6229. p. 2641

Salter, Krewasky, Dr, Pres, Pritzker Military Museum & Library, 104 S Michigan Ave, 2nd Flr, Chicago, IL, 60603. Tel: 312-374-9333. p. 567

Salting, Julia B, Asst Libr Dir, Saint Ambrose University Library, 518 W Locust St, Davenport, IA, 52803. Tel: 563-333-6244. p. 744

Saltman, David, Dir, Institute for Defense Analyses, 805 Bunn Dr, Princeton, NJ, 08540. Tel: 609-924-4600. p. 1436

Saltman, Jennifer, Children's Coordr, Hopewell Public Library, 13 E Broad St, Hopewell, NJ, 08525. Tel: 609-466-1625. p. 1409

Saltzman, Maureen, Ref Librn, Stoneham Public Library, 431 Main St, Stoneham, MA, 02180. Tel: 781-438-1324. p. 1058

Salubi, Oghenere (Gabriel), Asst Prof, Southern Connecticut State University, 501 Crescent St, New Haven, CT, 06515. Tel: 203-392-5708. p. 2783

Salvado, Lucy, Mgr, Ch Serv, Yorba Linda Public Library, 4852 Lakeview Ave, Yorba Linda, CA, 92886. Tel: 714-777-2873. p. 261

Salvarrey Iranzo, Gustavo, Spec Coll Librn, University of Puerto Rico Library, Cayey Campus, 205 Ave Antonio R Barcelo, Ste 205, Cayey, PR, 00736. Tel: 787-738-2161, Ext 2026. p. 2510

Salvato, Bridget, Libr Mgr, New York Public Library - Astor, Lenox & Tilden Foundations, Richmondtown Branch, 200 Clarke Ave, (@ Amber St), Staten Island, NY, 10306. Tel: 718-668-0413. p. 1597

Salvesen, Linda, Syst Librn, William Paterson University, 300 Pompton Rd, Wayne, NJ, 07470. Tel: 973-720-3127. p. 1452

Salvo, Angelo, Librn, Tech Proc, Bethune-Cookman University, 640 Mary McLeod Bethune Blvd, Daytona Beach, FL, 32114. Tel: 386-481-2186. p. 392

Salvo-Eaton, Jen, Head, Resource Sharing, University of Missouri-Kansas City Libraries, 800 E 51st St, Kansas City, MO, 64110. Tel: 816-235-2225. p. 1257

Salyards, Jackie, Dir, Randolph County Library, 111 W Everett St, Pocahontas, AR, 72455. Tel: 870-892-5617. p. 108

Salyer, Anna, Head, Commun Outreach, University of Washington Libraries, Tacoma Library, 1900 Commerce St, Box 358460, Tacoma, WA, 98402-3100. Tel: 253-692-4448. p. 2382

Salzer, Adele, Br Mgr, Saint Tammany Parish Library, Pearl River Branch, 64580 Hwy 41, Pearl River, LA, 70452. Tel: 985-863-5518. p. 888

Salzman, Scott, Web Discovery Librn, Furman University Libraries, 3300 Poinsett Hwy, Greenville, SC, 29613-4100. Tel: 864-294-2190. p. 2061

Samaie, Parisa, Dept Chair, Librn, Los Angeles Southwest College, Cox Bldg, 1600 W Imperial Hwy, Los Angeles, CA, 90047-4899. Tel: 323-241-5235. p. 166

Samaras, Julie, Librn, Waverly Public Library, 291 N Pearl St, Waverly, IL, 62692. Tel: 217-435-2051. p. 660

Samargia, Ashlyn, Children's Programmer, New Hartford Public Library, Two Library Lane, New Hartford, NY, 13413-2815. Tel: 315-733-1535. p. 1576

Sambets, Nancy, Dir, Archives, Museum of York County, 210 E Jefferson St, York, SC, 29745. Tel: 803-329-2121. p. 2072

Samblanet, Thomas, Dir, Fort Lupton Public & School Library, 370 S Rollie Ave, Fort Lupton, CO, 80621. Tel: 303-339-4089. p. 281

Samek, Toni, PhD, Prof, University of Alberta, 7-104 Education N, University of Alberta, Edmonton, AB, T6G 2G5, CANADA. Tel: 780-492-7625. p. 2795

Samet, Oneka, District Dean, LRC Serv, Wayne County Community College District, Arthur Cartwright LRC Library, Downtown Campus, 1001 W Fort St, Detroit, MI, 48226-3096. Tel: 313-496-2858. p. 1099

Samhammer, Taran, Innovations Mgr, Sr Res Libr Mgr, New Jersey State League of Municipalities, 222 W State St, Trenton, NJ, 08608. Tel: 609-695-3481. p. 1447

Sammis, Marc, Curator, US Army Transportation Museum Library, Besson Hall, 300 Washington Blvd, Fort Eustis, VA, 23604. Tel: 757-878-1115. p. 2319

Sammon, Lisa, Libr Dir, Sofia University Library, 1069 E Meadow Circle, Palo Alto, CA, 94303. Tel: 888-820-1484, Ext 10391. p. 192

Sammon, Tiffany, Librn, Navasota Public Library, 1411 E Washington Ave, Navasota, TX, 77868. Tel: 936-825-6744. p. 2221

Samoil, Tom, Libr Serv Mgr, Inuvik Centennial Library, 100 Mackenzie Rd, Inuvik, NT, X0E 0T0, CANADA. Tel: 867-777-8620. p. 2613

Samokishyn, Marta, Coll Develop Librn, Saint Paul University Library, Guides Hall, 1st Flr, 223 Main St, Ottawa, ON, K1S 1C4, CANADA. Tel: 613-236-1393, Ext 2313. p. 2670
Samora, Tara-jean, Archives Coordr, Cataloger, Vermont State University - Lyndon, 1001 College Rd, Lyndonville, VT, 05851. p. 2288
Samoussev, Amber, Librn I, Dyersburg State Community College, 1510 Lake Rd, Dyersburg, TN, 38024. Tel: 901-475-3121. p. 2097
Sampaio, Gina, Exec Dir, Red Mill Museum Library, 56 Main St, Clinton, NJ, 08809. Tel: 908-735-4101, Ext 101. p. 1397
Sample, Angela, Dr, Head, Access Serv, Webmaster, Oral Roberts University Library, 7777 S Lewis Ave, Tulsa, OK, 74171. Tel: 918-495-6895. p. 1865
Sample, George, Human Res Dir, Cuyahoga County Public Library, 2111 Snow Rd, Parma, OH, 44134-2728. Tel: 216-398-1800. p. 1813
Sample, Holbrook, Chief Tech Officer, Public Library of Cincinnati & Hamilton County, 800 Vine St, Cincinnati, OH, 45202-2009. Tel: 513-369-4408. p. 1761
Samples, Courtney, Asst Dir, Russell Memorial Public Library, 10038 Seneca Trail, Mill Creek, WV, 26280. Tel: 304-335-6277. p. 2408
Sampley, Lisa, Coll Serv, Springfield-Greene County Library District, 4653 S Campbell Ave, Springfield, MO, 65810-1723. Tel: 417-882-0714. p. 1281
Sampson, April, Campus Librn, Nova Scotia Community College, Strait Area Campus Library, 226 Reeves St, Port Hawkesbury, NS, B9A 2W2, CANADA. Tel: 902-625-4075. p. 2620
Sampson, Debra, Libr Dir, Academy of Art University Library, 180 New Montogomery, 6th Flr, San Francisco, CA, 94105. Tel: 415-274-2270. p. 223
Sampson, Jo Ann, Acq Mgr, Orange County Library System, 101 E Central Blvd, Orlando, FL, 32801. Tel: 407-835-7323. p. 431
Sampson, Linda, Asst Librn, Abington Public Library, 600 Gliniewicz Way, Abington, MA, 02351. Tel: 781-982-2139. p. 983
Sampson, Lydia, Asst Dir, Head, Tech Serv, Morrill Memorial Library, 33 Walpole St, Norwood, MA, 02062-1206. Tel: 781-769-0200. p. 1044
Sampson, Lynda, Adjunct Ref Librn, Cerritos College Library, 11110 Alondra Blvd, Norwalk, CA, 90650. Tel: 562-860-2451, Ext 2430. p. 184
Sampson, Margaret, Mgr, Libr Serv, Children's Hospital of Eastern Ontario, 401 Smyth Rd, Ottawa, ON, K1H 8L1, CANADA. Tel: 613-737-7600, Ext 2206. p. 2666
Sampson, Michelle, Dir, York Public Library, 15 Long Sands Rd, York, ME, 03909. Tel: 207-363-2818. p. 947
Sampson, Sara, Dir, Law Libr, Ohio State University LIBRARIES, Michael E Moritz Law Library, 55 W 12th Ave, Columbus, OH, 43210-1391. Tel: 614-292-2964. p. 1776
Samra, Gurpreet, Libr Dir, River Rouge Public Library, 221 Burke St, River Rouge, MI, 48218. Tel: 313-843-2040. p. 1144
Sams, Geoff, Libr Mgr, Roanoke Public Library, 308 S Walnut St, Roanoke, TX, 76262. Tel: 817-491-2691. p. 2233
Sams, Jenn, Instruction & Learning Librn, Michigan Technological University, 1400 Townsend Dr, Houghton, MI, 49931-1295. Tel: 906-487-2698. p. 1116
Sams, Tonya, Librn, Ashmont Public Library, Box 330 Main St, Ashmont, AB, T0A 0C0, CANADA. Tel: 780-726-3777. p. 2522
Samson, Kathy, Asst Dir, Bruce County Public Library, 1243 MacKenzie Rd, Port Elgin, ON, N0H 2C6, CANADA. Tel: 519-832-6935. p. 2673
Samson, Kathy, Br Supvr, Bruee County Public Library, Port Elgin Branch, 708 Goderich St, Port Elgin, ON, N0H 2C0, CANADA. Tel: 519-832-2201. p. 2674
Samson, Kathy, Br Supvr, Bruce County Public Library, Southampton Branch, 215 High St, Southampton, ON, N0H 2L0, CANADA. Tel: 519-797-3586. p. 2674
Samsundar, Devica, Dir, Doctor's Hospital, Baptist Health, 5000 University Dr, Coral Gables, FL, 33146. Tel: 305-669-2360. p. 390
Samsundar, Devica, Dir, Baptist Hospital of Miami, 8900 N Kendall Dr, Miami, FL, 33176. Tel: 786-596-6506. p. 421
Samsundar, Devica, Dir, South Miami Hospital, 6200 SW 73rd St, Miami, FL, 33143. Tel: 786-662-8219. p. 424
Samudio, Kyle, Adult Serv Mgr, Fullerton Public Library, 353 W Commonwealth Ave, Fullerton, CA, 92832. Tel: 714-738-6333. p. 147
Samuel, Eunice G, Head, Ref Serv, Tuskegee University, 1200 W Old Mongtomery Rd, Ford Motor Company Library, Tuskegee, AL, 36088. Tel: 334-727-8892. p. 38
Samuel, Libby, Med Librn, Inova Fairfax Hospital, 3300 Gallows Rd, Falls Church, VA, 22042. Tel: 703-776-3234. p. 2317
Samuel, Mariann, Head, Scholarly Communications, University of Georgia Libraries, Science, Boyd Graduate Studies Bldg, 210 D W Brooks Dr, Athens, GA, 30602. Tel: 706-542-0698. p. 460
Samuel, Sandra, Libr Dir, Media-Upper Providence Free Library, One E Front St, Media, PA, 19063. Tel: 610-566-1918. p. 1961
Samuel, Tabitha, Digital Archivist, Medical University of South Carolina Libraries, 171 Ashley Ave, Ste 419, Charleston, SC, 29425-0001. Tel: 843-792-6749. p. 2051
Samuel, Tabitha, Digital Archivist, Medical University of South Carolina Libraries, Waring Historical Library, 175 Ashley Ave, Charleston, SC, 29425-0001. Tel: 843-792-6749. p. 2051
Samuel, Tom, Br Mgr, Middlesex County Public Library, Deltaville Branch, 35 Lovers Lane, Deltaville, VA, 23043. Tel: 804-776-7362. p. 2349
Samuel-Wade, Sharon, Br Mgr, Shreve Memorial Library, David Raines Branch, 2855 Martin Luther King Jr Dr, Shreveport, LA, 71107. Tel: 318-222-0824. p. 910
Samuels, Merrily, Asst Dir/Ref Librn, Hampstead Public Library, Nine Mary E Clark Dr, Hampstead, NH, 03841. Tel: 603-329-6411. p. 1366
Samuelson, Georgeanne, Librn, Oakridge Public Library, 48326 E First St, Oakridge, OR, 97463. Tel: 541-782-2258, Option 9. p. 1889
Samuelson, Jacob, Ref Librn, Loyola Law School, 919 S Albany St, Los Angeles, CA, 90015-1211. Tel: 213-736-1413. p. 166
Samuelson, Jacob, Legal Info Librn & Lecturer in Law, Boston College, 885 Centre St, Newton Centre, MA, 02459. Tel: 617-552-2897. p. 1039
Samuelson, Rick, Youth Serv Coordr, Henrico County Public Library, 1700 N Parham Rd, Henrico, VA, 23229. Tel: 804-501-1900. p. 2325
Samuelson, Ryan, Assoc Univ Librn, Midwestern State University, 3410 Taft Blvd, Wichita Falls, TX, 76308-2099. Tel: 940-397-4177. p. 2257
Samulak, Kendra, Mgr, Human Res, Allen County Public Library, 900 Library Plaza, Fort Wayne, IN, 46802. Tel: 260-421-1234. p. 683
San Miguel, Ana, Librn, Alberta Law Libraries, Departmental Library, 400A Bowker Bldg, North, 9833 - 109 St, Edmonton, AB, T5K 2E8, CANADA. Tel: 780-422-6264. p. 2535
Sanabria, Diane, Local Hist & Genealogy Librn, Leominster Public Library, 30 West St, Leominster, MA, 01453. Tel: 978-534-7522, Ext 3605. p. 1028
Sanborn, Cerese, Tech Serv Librn, Aldrich Public Library, Six Washington St, Barre, VT, 05641. Tel: 802-476-7550. p. 2278
Sanborn, Colin, Circ Librn, Fiske Free Library, 108 Broad St, Claremont, NH, 03743-2673. Tel: 603-542-7017. p. 1358
Sanborn, Deborah, Tech Serv Spec, Golden Gate University - Otto & Velia Butz Libraries, 536 Mission St, San Francisco, CA, 94105-2967. Tel: 415-442-5215. p. 225
Sanborn, Lorrie, Libr Dir, Hartland Public Library, 16 Mill St, Hartland, ME, 04943. Tel: 207-938-4702. p. 927
Sanchez, Alice, Libr Dir, Costilla County Library, 418 Gasper St, San Luis, CO, 81152. Tel: 719-672-3309. p. 295
Sanchez, Alice, Libr Dir, Costilla County Library, Blanca-Ft Garland Branch, Garland Community Ctr, 2nd Flr, 17591 E Hwy 160, Blanca, CO, 81123. Tel: 719-379-3945. p. 295
Sanchez, Ana, Libr Dir, Palestine Public Library, 2000 S Loop 256, Ste 42, Palestine, TX, 75801-5932. Tel: 903-729-4121. p. 2224
Sanchez, Anna, Br Mgr, Pima County Public Library, El Pueblo, 101 W Irvington Rd, Tucson, AZ, 85714. Tel: 520-594-5250. p. 82
Sanchez, Aurelia, Head Librn, Rivkin Radler LLP, West Tower, 926 RXR Plaza, Uniondale, NY, 11556-0926. Tel: 516-357-3453, 516-357-3454, 516-357-3455. p. 1654
Sanchez, Cynthia, Lead Res & Instruction Librn, Palo Alto College, 1400 W Villaret St, San Antonio, TX, 78224-2499. Tel: 210-486-3579. p. 2237
Sanchez, Edward, Head, Libr Info Tech, Marquette University, 1355 W Wisconsin Ave, Milwaukee, WI, 53233. Tel: 414-288-6043. p. 2458
Sanchez, Gale, Head Librn, El Paso Community College Library, Rio Grande Campus Library, 100 W Rio Grande Ave, Rm E100, El Paso, TX, 79902. Tel: 915-831-4019. p. 2173
Sanchez, Gladis, Dean, Cosumnes River College Library, 8401 Center Pkwy, Sacramento, CA, 95823. Tel: 916-691-7266. p. 208
Sanchez, Hector Ruben, Asst Prof, Libr Dir, Inter-American University of Puerto Rico, PO Box 70351, Hato Rey, PR, 00936. Tel: 787-751-1912. p. 2511
Sanchez, Ignacio, Electronic Res Librn, John Jay College of Criminal Justice, 899 Tenth Ave, New York, NY, 10019. Tel: 212-237-8234. p. 1589
Sanchez, Iris, Dir, Aransas County Public Library, 701 E Mimosa St, Rockport, TX, 78382-4150. Tel: 361-790-0153. p. 2233
Sanchez, Jose, Asst Prof, Queens College of the City University of New York, Benjamin Rosenthal Library, Rm 254, 65-30 Kissena Blvd, Flushing, NY, 11367-1597. Tel: 718-997-3790. p. 2789
Sanchez, Joseph, Dir, University of Hawaii at Hilo Library, 200 W Kawili St, Hilo, HI, 96720. Tel: 808-932-7315. p. 505
Sanchez, Karen, Librn, Los Angeles County Counsel Law Library, Kenneth Hahn Hall of Administration, 500 W Temple St, Los Angeles, CA, 90012. Tel: 213-974-1982. p. 162
Sanchez, Lauren, Ch Serv, Groton Public Library, 99 Main St, Groton, MA, 01450. Tel: 978-448-1168, Ext 1319. p. 1022
Sanchez, Leovigildo, Librn, California Department of Corrections Library System, California Medical Facility, 1600 California Dr, Vacaville, CA, 95696. Tel: 707-448-6841, Ext 2585. p. 206
Sanchez, Leticia, Librn, Central Oklahoma Juvenile Center Library, 700 S Ninth St, Tecumseh, OK, 74873. Tel: 405-598-2135. p. 1864
Sanchez, Lorena, Head, Ser, Southwestern Law School, Bullock Wilshire Bldg, 1st Flr, 3050 Wilshire Blvd, Los Angeles, CA, 90010. Tel: 213-738-5771. p. 168
Sanchez, Lynn E, Dir, Librn, El Paso County Law Library, Court House, 12th Flr, 500 E San Antonio St, Rm 1202, El Paso, TX, 79901. Tel: 915-273-3699. p. 2174
Sanchez, Magali, Dir, Western Oklahoma State College, 2801 N Main St, Altus, OK, 73521. Tel: 580-477-7770. p. 1840
Sanchez, Margaret, Circ Serv, Liverpool Public Library, 310 Tulip St, Liverpool, NY, 13088-4997. Tel: 315-457-0310. p. 1564

Sanchez, Mary, Br Mgr, Pima County Public Library, Eckstrom-Columbus, 4350 E 22nd St, Tucson, AZ, 85711. Tel: 520-594-5285. p. 82
Sanchez, Monica, Sr Librn, Englewood Public Library, 31 Engle St, Englewood, NJ, 07631. Tel: 201-568-2215. p. 1402
Sanchez, Nilda, Librn, City College of the City University of New York, Architecture Library, Spitzer Bldg, Rm 101, 160 Convent Ave, New York, NY, 10031. Tel: 212-650-8768. p. 1581
Sanchez, Rafael, Sr Res Serv Librn, Cooley LLP, 55 Hudson Yards, New York, NY, 10001-2157. Tel: 212-479-6000. p. 1584
Sanchez, Rosa, Interim Dir, Reber Memorial Library, 193 N Fourth St, Raymondville, TX, 78580-1994. Tel: 956-689-2930. p. 2230
Sanchez, Titiana, Library & Archives Coord, Freeborn County Historical Museum Library, 1031 N Bridge Ave, Albert Lea, MN, 56007. Tel: 507-373-8003 (museum), 507-552-2053. p. 1163
Sanchez, Toshia, ILL, Amarillo Public Library, 413 E Fourth Ave, Amarillo, TX, 79101. Tel: 806-378-3054. p. 2134
Sanchez-Herman, Jillyann, Br Coordr, Collins LeRoy Leon County Public Library System, Fort Braden, 16327 Blountstown Hwy, Tallahassee, FL, 32310. Tel: 850-606-2900. p. 445
Sanchez-Himes, Aileen, Libr Dir, Hudson Public Library, Three Washington St, Hudson, MA, 01749-2499. Tel: 978-568-9644. p. 1025
Sanchez-Lugo, Jose, Prof, University of Puerto Rico, Rio Piedras Campus, PO Box 21906, San Juan, PR, 00931-1906. Tel: 787-764-0000, Ext 85272. p. 2795
Sanchez-Tucker, Maria, Libr Dir, Santa Fe Public Library, 145 Washington Ave, Santa Fe, NM, 87501. Tel: 505-955-6780. p. 1476
Sand, Amy, Regional Mgr, Braille Institute Library, Coachella Valley Center, 74-245 Hwy 111, E101, Palm Desert, CA, 92260. Tel: 760-321-1111. p. 160
Sand, Jeff, Automation Serv Coordr, Villa Park Public Library, 305 S Ardmore Ave, Villa Park, IL, 60181-2698. Tel: 630-834-1164. p. 658
Sandak, Cathy, Asst Dir, Tuxedo Park Library, 227 Rte 17, Tuxedo Park, NY, 10987. Tel: 845-351-2207. p. 1654
Sandarin, Barbara, Librn, Anoka-Ramsey Community College, 11200 Mississippi Blvd NW, Coon Rapids, MN, 55433-3470. Tel: 763-433-1466. p. 1171
Sandberg, Louise, Spec Coll Librn, Lawrence Public Library, 51 Lawrence St, Lawrence, MA, 01841. Tel: 978-620-3600. p. 1027
Sandberg, Tami, Mgr, Libr Serv, National Renewable Energy Laboratory Library, 15013 Denver West Pkwy, Golden, CO, 80401-3305. Tel: 303-275-4024. p. 283
Sandblade, Mark, IT Mgr, Library System of Lancaster County, 1866 Colonial Village Lane, Ste 107, Lancaster, PA, 17601. Tel: 717-207-0500. p. 1952
Sandefur, Shannon, Dir, Henderson County Public Library, 101 S Main St, Henderson, KY, 42420. Tel: 270-826-3712. p. 859
Sandell, Ami, Dir, Mary Wood Weldon Memorial Library, 1530 S Green St, Glasgow, KY, 42141. Tel: 270-651-2824. p. 857
Sandell, Denise, Coll & Electronic Res Librn, Libr Dir, Wilson College, 1015 Philadelphia Ave, Chambersburg, PA, 17201-1285. Tel: 717-262-2724. p. 1921
Sander, Christine, Dir, Stockton Public Library, 124 N Cedar, Stockton, KS, 67669-1636. Tel: 785-425-6372. p. 837
Sander, Sandra, Dir, Libr Serv, Northampton Community College, College Ctr, 3835 Green Pond Rd, Bethlehem, PA, 18020-7599. Tel: 610-861-3360. p. 1912
Sander, Sandra L, Dir, Libr Serv, Northampton Community College, 3835 Green Pond Rd, Bethlehem, PA, 18020. Tel: 610-861-4150. p. 2791
Sanders, A Carolyn, Media Spec, Central State University, 1400 Brush Row Rd, Wilberforce, OH, 45384. Tel: 937-376-6213. p. 1831
Sanders, Anne, Br Librn, Jackson/Hinds Library System, Medgar Evers Library, 4215 Medgar Evers Blvd, Jackson, MS, 39213-5210. Tel: 601-982-2867. p. 1221
Sanders, Audrey, Children & Youth Serv Librn, Kingfisher Memorial Library, 505 W Will Rogers Dr, Kingfisher, OK, 73750. Tel: 405-375-3384. p. 1851
Sanders, Blanche, Dr, Dean, Univ Libr, Alcorn State University, 1000 ASU Dr, Alcorn State, MS, 39096-7500. Tel: 601-877-6350. p. 1211
Sanders, Cherette J, Libr Tech 1, Howard University Libraries, Social Work, 601 Howard Pl NW, Rm 200, Washington, DC, 20059. Tel: 202-806-4737. p. 369
Sanders, Dara, Dir, West Point Public Library, 317 Fifth St, West Point, IA, 52656. Tel: 319-837-6315. p. 791
Sanders, Emily, Coordr, Ch Serv, Meigs County District Public Library, 216 W Main St, Pomeroy, OH, 45769. Tel: 740-992-5813. p. 1816
Sanders, Emma, Circ, Waupun Public Library, 123 S Forest St, Waupun, WI, 53963. Tel: 920-324-7925. p. 2485
Sanders, Hannah, Technology Spec, Hubbard Public Library, 436 W Liberty St, Hubbard, OH, 44425. Tel: 330-534-3512. p. 1790
Sanders, Jacque, County Librn, Gila County Library District, 1400 E Ash St, Globe, AZ, 85501-1414. Tel: 928-402-8768, 928-402-8770. p. 62
Sanders, Jean, Head, Ref, Glenview Public Library, 1930 Glenview Rd, Glenview, IL, 60025. Tel: 847-729-7500. p. 594
Sanders, Jesse, Br Mgr, Cuyahoga County Public Library, Fairview Park Branch, 21255 Lorain Rd, Fairview Park, OH, 44126-2120. Tel: 440-333-4700. p. 1813
Sanders, Jesse, Br Mgr, Cuyahoga County Public Library, Metrohealth Medical Center Branch, 2500 MetroHealth Dr, Cleveland, OH, 44109. Tel: 216-778-7670. p. 1813
Sanders, Jill, Libr Dir, Bondurant Community Library, 104 Second St NE, Bondurant, IA, 50035. Tel: 515-967-4790. p. 735
Sanders, Joey, Ref Librn, Piedmont Community College, 1715 College Dr, Roxboro, NC, 27573. Tel: 336-599-1181, Ext 2247. p. 1714
Sanders, Joey, Ref Librn, Piedmont Community College, Caswell Learning Commons, 331 Piedmont Dr, Yanceyville, NC, 27379. Tel: 336-694-5707, Ext 8072. p. 1714
Sanders, John, Admin Librn, Hinds Community College, Rankin Library, 3805 Hwy 80 E, Pearl, MS, 39208-4295. Tel: 601-936-5538. p. 1231
Sanders, Kathy, Actg Libr Dir, Three Rivers College Library, 2080 Three Rivers Blvd, Poplar Bluff, MO, 63901. Tel: 573-840-9654. p. 1266
Sanders, Krishanda, Libr Dir, East Carroll Parish Library, 109 Sparrow St, Lake Providence, LA, 71254-2645. Tel: 318-559-2615. p. 894
Sanders, Laura, Dir, Lafourche Parish Public Library, 314 Saint Mary St, Thibodaux, LA, 70301. Tel: 985-446-1163. p. 911
Sanders, Laura, Head Librn, Lower Canada College Library, 4090 Royal Ave, Montreal, QC, H4A 2M5, CANADA. Tel: 514-482-9797, Ext 473. p. 2725
Sanders, Laurie, Co-Executive Dir, Historic Northampton, 46 Bridge St, Northampton, MA, 01060. Tel: 413-584-6011. p. 1042
Sanders, Mark, Asst Dir, Pub Serv, East Carolina University, J Y Joyner Library, E Fifth St, Greenville, NC, 27858-4353. Tel: 242-328-2900. p. 1693
Sanders, Martha, Asst Dir, Ch, Buda Public Library, 405 Loop St, Bldg 100, Buda, TX, 78610. Tel: 512-295-5899. p. 2151
Sanders, Mary, Br Mgr, Bossier Parish Libraries, Anna P Tooke Memorial Branch, 451 Fairview Point Rd, Elm Grove, LA, 71051. Tel: 318-987-3915. p. 886
Sanders, Mary, Chief Librn, Head, Children's Servx, Head, Reader Serv, Morris County Library, 30 E Hanover Ave, Whippany, NJ, 07981. Tel: 973-285-6930. p. 1455
Sanders, Melissa, Br Mgr, Pope County Library System, Dover Branch, 80 Library Rd, Dover, AR, 72837. Tel: 479-331-2173. p. 109
Sanders, Patricia, Media Ctr Mgr, University of Tennessee at Martin, Ten Wayne Fisher Dr, Martin, TN, 38238. Tel: 731-881-7069. p. 2111
Sanders, Patrick, Cat Librn, Pike-Amite-Walthall Library System, 1022 Virginia Ave, McComb, MS, 39648. Tel: 601-684-2661, Ext 14. p. 1225
Sanders, Rebekah, Br Mgr, San Diego County Library, Fletcher Hills Branch, 576 Garfield Ave, El Cajon, CA, 92020-2792. Tel: 619-466-1132. p. 217
Sanders, Richard, Dir, Hart County Library, 150 Benson St, Hartwell, GA, 30643. Tel: 706-376-4655. p. 482
Sanders, Rob, Interim Dean of Libr, Rollins College, 1000 Holt Ave, Campus Box 2744, Winter Park, FL, 32789-2744. Tel: 407-646-2521. p. 455
Sanders, Scott, Col Archivist, Antioch College, One Morgan Pl, Yellow Springs, OH, 45387-1694. Tel: 973-319-0111. p. 1835
Sanders, Sharon K, Librn, Southeast Missourian Newspaper Library, 301 Broadway, Cape Girardeau, MO, 63701. Tel: 573-388-3653. p. 1240
Sanders, Stuart, Dir, Research & Publications, Kentucky Historical Society, 100 W Broadway St, Frankfort, KY, 40601. Tel: 502-782-8080. p. 855
Sanders, Suzanne, Mgr, Prog & Outreach, San Marcos Public Library, 625 E Hopkins, San Marcos, TX, 78666. Tel: 512-393-8200. p. 2241
Sanders, Tammy, Librn, Bevill State Community College, Hamilton Campus, 1481 Military St S, Hamilton, AL, 35570. Tel: 205-921-3177, Ext 5356. p. 17
Sanders, Tara, Youth Serv Librn, Kutztown Community Library, 70 Bieber Alley, Kutztown, PA, 19530-1113. Tel: 610-683-5820. p. 1949
Sanders-Kroft, Farris, Med Librn, St Luke's Hospital, 915 E First St, Duluth, MN, 55805. Tel: 218-249-5320. p. 1172
Sandersfeld, Emily, Teen Prog, North Valley Public Library, 208 Main St, Stevensville, MT, 59870. Tel: 406-777-5061. p. 1302
Sanderson, Cherie, Libr Dir, Boulder Junction Public Library, 5392 Park St, Boulder Junction, WI, 54512-9605. Tel: 715-385-2050. p. 2425
Sanderson, Cortney, Br Mgr, Kemper-Newton Regional Library System, DeKalb Branch, 141 Bell St, DeKalb, MS, 39328. Tel: 601-743-5981. p. 1234
Sanderson, Denise, Br Mgr, San Francisco Public Library, Noe Valley/Sally Brunn Branch Library, 451 Jersey St, San Francisco, CA, 94114-3632. Tel: 415-355-5707. p. 228
Sanderson, Kim, Cat/Metadata Librn, Davidson College, 209 Ridge Rd, Davidson, NC, 28035-0001. Tel: 704-894-2331. p. 1683
Sanderson, Sarah, Dir, Sioux County Public Library, 182 W Third St, Harrison, NE, 69346. Tel: 308-668-9431. p. 1317
Sanderson, Suzanne, Librn, Plymouth Church, 1217 Sixth Ave, Seattle, WA, 98101-3199. Tel: 206-622-4865. p. 2378
Sandford, Betsy, Tech Serv Librn, West Valley Community College Library, 14000 Fruitvale Ave, Saratoga, CA, 95070-5698. Tel: 408-741-2478. p. 245
Sandford, Mark, Syst Librn, Colgate University, 13 Oak Dr, Hamilton, NY, 13346-1398. Tel: 315-228-7363. p. 1543
Sandford, Wendy, Dir, Ringwood Public Library, 30 Cannici Dr, Ringwood, NJ, 07456. Tel: 973-962-6256, Ext 114. p. 1439

Sandgathe, Trevor, Coordr, Pub Serv, Oregon State University Libraries, Special Collections & Archives Research Center, 121 The Valley Library, 5th Flr, Corvallis, OR, 97331. Tel: 541-737-2075. p. 1877
Sandifer, Kevin, Library Contact, First Baptist Church of Blanchard, 201 Attaway St, Blanchard, LA, 71009. Tel: 318-929-2346. p. 885
Sandin, Vicky, Asst Dir, Head, Info Tech, Head, Tech Serv, George H & Ella M Rodgers Memorial Library, 194 Derry Rd, Hudson, NH, 03051. Tel: 603-886-6030. p. 1368
Sandino, Margarita, Dir of Educ, Dixon Gallery & Gardens Library, 4339 Park Ave, Memphis, TN, 38117. Tel: 901-761-5250. p. 2112
Sandlin, Linda, Dir, Clay County Public Library, 211 Bridge St, Manchester, KY, 40962. Tel: 606-598-2617. p. 868
Sandlin, Miyo, Res & Instrul Serv Librn, Fashion Institute of Technology-SUNY, Seventh Ave at 27th St, 227 W 27th St, New York, NY, 10001-5992. Tel: 212-217-4340. p. 1585
Sandor, Jill, Librn, American Bar Association Library, 1050 Connecticut Ave NW, Ste 400, Washington, DC, 20036. Tel: 202-662-1015. p. 359
Sandoro, Mary Ann, Librn, Collector Car Appraisers Association Library, 24 Myrtle Ave, Buffalo, NY, 14204. Tel: 716-855-1931. p. 1509
Sandoval, Aaron, Coll Develop & Acq Librn, Wesleyan University, 252 Church St, Middletown, CT, 06459. Tel: 860-685-3834. p. 322
Sandoval, Bertha, Librn, Montgomery & Andrews, 325 Paseo de Peralta, Santa Fe, NM, 87501. Tel: 505-982-3873. p. 1475
Sandoval, Carlos, Tech, George Mason University Libraries, Law Library, 3301 N Fairfax Dr, Arlington, VA, 22201-4426. Tel: 703-993-8100. p. 2317
Sandoval, Lucy, Cat, El Progreso Memorial Library, 301 W Main St, Uvalde, TX, 78801. Tel: 830-278-2017. p. 2251
Sandoval, Maribel, Ch, Grant County Library, 215 E Grant Ave, Ulysses, KS, 67880. Tel: 620-356-1433. p. 840
Sandoval, Martha, Libr Asst, International Center of Photography, 79 Essex St, New York, NY, 10002. Tel: 212-857-0004. p. 1589
Sandoval, Rachel, Syst Librn, West Valley Community College Library, 14000 Fruitvale Ave, Saratoga, CA, 95070-5698. Tel: 408-741-2479. p. 245
Sandridge, Suzanne, Br Mgr, Dayton Metro Library, Vandalia Branch, 330 S Dixie Dr, Vandalia, OH, 45377. Tel: 937-496-8960. p. 1779
Sands, Joyce, Exec Dir, Manheim Township Public Library, 595 Granite Run Dr, Lancaster, PA, 17601. Tel: 717-560-6441. p. 1952
Sands, Tonya, Br Mgr, Athens Regional Library System, East Athens Resource Center, East Athens Community Ctr, 3rd Flr, 400 McKinley Dr, Athens, GA, 30601. Tel: 706-613-3657. p. 458
Sandusky, Robert, Assoc Univ Librn, Info Tech, University of Illinois at Chicago, MC 234, 801 S Morgan St, Chicago, IL, 60607. Tel: 312-996-2716. p. 570
Sandusky, Timothy, Electronic Resources & Affordable Learning Librn, Ohio Dominican University Library, 1216 Sunbury Rd, Columbus, OH, 43219. Tel: 614-251-4752. p. 1774
Sandvick, Erin, Br Mgr, Rupp Ida Public Library, Marblehead Peninsula Branch, 710 W Main St, Marblehead, OH, 43440. Tel: 419-798-0477. p. 1816
Sandy, Julie, Archivist, Librn, New York School of Interior Design Library, 170 E 70th St, New York, NY, 10021. Tel: 212-452-4196. p. 1598
Sanfilippo, Madelyn Rose, Asst Prof, University of Illinois at Urbana-Champaign, Library & Information Science Bldg, 501 E Daniel St, Champaign, IL, 61820-6211. Tel: 217-333-3280. p. 2784
Sanfilippo, Sarah, Asst Dir, Access Serv, Rhode Island College, 600 Mt Pleasant Ave, Providence, RI, 02908-1924. p. 2039
Sanford, Amanda, Ch Serv, Weston County Library System, 23 W Main St, Newcastle, WY, 82701. Tel: 307-746-2206. p. 2497
Sanford, Cheryl, Asst Librn, Asphodel-Norwood Public Library, 2363 County Rd 45, Norwood, ON, K0L 2V0, CANADA. Tel: 705-639-2228. p. 2662
Sanford, Chris, Ms, Libr Dir, Davis County Library, 133 S Main St, Farmington, UT, 84025. Tel: 801-451-3051. p. 2263
Sanford, Heather, Librn, Central Georgia Technical College Library, 80 Cohen Walker Dr, Warner Robins, GA, 31088. Tel: 478-988-6863. p. 502
Sanford, Robin, Cat, University of New England Libraries, Josephine S Abplanalp Library, Portland Campus, 716 Stevens Ave, Portland, ME, 04103. Tel: 207-221-4328. p. 918
Sanford, Travis, Librn, Spartanburg County Public Libraries, Boiling Springs Library, 871 Double Bridge Rd, Boiling Springs, SC, 29316. Tel: 864-578-3665. p. 2070
Sangston, Tari, Dir, Richard A Mautino Memorial Library, 215 E Cleveland St, Spring Valley, IL, 61362. Tel: 815-663-4741. p. 649
Sanidas, Oli, Exec Dir, Arapahoe Library District, 12855 E Adam Aircraft Circle, Englewood, CO, 80112. Tel: 303-542-7279. p. 279
Saniga, Liz, Br Mgr, Arundel Anne County Public Library, Deale Library, 5940 Deale-Churchton Rd, Deale, MD, 20751. Tel: 410-222-1925. p. 950
Sankam, Melinda, Br Mgr, Juneau Public Libraries, Douglas Public, 1016 Third St, Douglas, AK, 99824. Tel: 907-364-2378. p. 47
Sankam, Melinda, Electronic Serv, Juneau Public Libraries, 292 Marine Way, Juneau, AK, 99801. Tel: 907-586-5249. p. 47
Sanks, Megan, Youth Serv Librn, Deerfield Public Library, 920 Waukegan Rd, Deerfield, IL, 60015. Tel: 847-945-3311. p. 577
Sanoubane, Dara, Dr, Educ Spec, Pennsylvania State University, N Atherton St, State College, PA, 16801. Tel: 814-865-0451. p. 2010
Sanow, Caitlyn, Circ Supvr, Southwest Minnesota State University Library, 1501 State St, Marshall, MN, 56258. Tel: 507-537-6688. p. 1182
Sansing, Jocelyne, Dir, Middleton Public Library, 7425 Hubbard Ave, Middleton, WI, 53562-3117. Tel: 608-831-5564. p. 2457
Sansing, Tori, Br Mgr, Columbus-Lowndes Public Library, Caledonia Public, 754 Main St, Caledonia, MS, 39740. Tel: 662-356-6384. p. 1215
Sansom, Jean, Libr Office Mgr, Walla Walla County Rural Library District, 37 Jade Ave, Walla Walla, WA, 99362. Tel: 509-527-3284. p. 2392
Sansone, Marguerite, Circ Supvr, Englewood Public Library, 31 Engle St, Englewood, NJ, 07631. Tel: 201-568-2215, Ext 226. p. 1402
Santa Cruz, Norma, Libr Tech, California Department of Justice Library, 600 W Broadway, Ste 1800, San Diego, CA, 92101. Tel: 619-738-9000. p. 215
Santa Cruz, Theresa, Libr Spec, Chandler-Gilbert Community College Library, 2626 E Pecos Rd, Chandler, AZ, 85225-2499. Tel: 480-857-5104. p. 58
Santa, Susan, Libr Dir, North Merrick Public Library, 1691 Meadowbrook Rd, North Merrick, NY, 11566. Tel: 516-378-7474, Ext 10. p. 1607
Santa, Susan, Dir, Plainedge Public Library, 1060 Hicksville Rd, North Massapequa, NY, 11758. Tel: 516-735-4133. p. 1607
Santa, Susan A, Asst Libr Dir, Shelter Rock Public Library, 165 Searingtown Rd, Albertson, NY, 11507. Tel: 516-248-7343. p. 1484
Santagata, Dana, Head, Circ Serv, Cranston Public Library, 140 Sockanosset Cross Rd, Cranston, RI, 02920-5539. Tel: 401-943-9080. p. 2031
Santaliz, Lorraine, Youth Serv, Whitehall Township Public Library, 3700 Mechanicsville Rd, Whitehall, PA, 18052. Tel: 610-432-4339. p. 2021
Santamaria, Daniel, Univ Archivist, Tufts University, 35 Professors Row, Medford, MA, 02155-5816. Tel: 617-627-2696. p. 1034
Santana Gabriell, Silvana, Library Contact, Multnomah County Library, Holgate, 7905 SE Holgate Blvd, Portland, OR, 97206. p. 1892
Santana, Gilda, Head, Archit Libr, University of Miami Libraries, Architecture Research Center (ARC), 1223 Dickison Dr, Bldg 48, Coral Gables, FL, 33146. Tel: 305-284-5282. p. 391
Santana, John, Ref & Circ Librn, Columbia-Greene Community College Library, 4400 Rte 23, Hudson, NY, 12534. Tel: 518-828-4181, Ext 3287. p. 1549
Santana, Tanisha, Librn, California Highway Patrol, 601 N Seventh St, Sacramento, CA, 95811. Tel: 916-843-3370. p. 207
Santangelo, Chloe, Libr Dir, Hilbert College, 5200 S Park Ave, Hamburg, NY, 14075. Tel: 716-649-7900, Ext 365. p. 1543
Santangelo, Michael, Librn, Lesbian, Bisexual, Gay & Transgender Community Center, 208 W 13th St, New York, NY, 10011. Tel: 212-620-7310. p. 1590
Santeford, Jim, Tech Serv Librn, Phoenix Seminary Library, 7901 E Shea Blvd, Scottsdale, AZ, 85260. Tel: 602-429-4974. p. 77
Santiago, Edny, Dir, Inter-American University of Puerto Rico, Bo Machete, Carr 744, Guayama, PR, 00784. Tel: 787-864-2222. p. 2510
Santiago, Hilarie, Youth Serv Dir, Swanton Public Library, One First St, Swanton, VT, 05488. Tel: 802-868-7656. p. 2296
Santiago, Kristina, Librn, Mesa Community College Library, Red Mountain, 7110 E McKellips Rd, Mesa, AZ, 85207. Tel: 480-654-7741. p. 66
Santiago, Lillian E, Spec Coll Librn, Inter-American University of Puerto Rico, PO Box 70351, Hato Rey, PR, 00936. Tel: 787-751-1912, Ext 2300. p. 2511
Santiago, Roshni, Researcher, White & Case LLP, 701 13th St NW, Washington, DC, 20005-3807. Tel: 202-626-3600, 202-626-6475. p. 381
Santiago, Tina, Sr Libr Asst, Columbia-Greene Community College Library, 4400 Rte 23, Hudson, NY, 12534. Tel: 518-828-4181, Ext 3284. p. 1549
Santiago-Canchani, Carmen I, Admin Serv, Libr Tech, Department of Veterans Affairs, Library Service 142D, Ten Calle Casia, San Juan, PR, 00921-3201. Tel: 787-641-7582, Ext 12276, 787-641-7582, Ext 31905. p. 2513
Santiago-Vazquez, Nivea, Actg Dir, University of Puerto Rico RP College of Natural Sciences Library, 17 Ave Universidad, Ste 1701, San Juan, PR, 00925-2537. Tel: 787-764-0000, Ext 88399. p. 2515
Santiapillai, Terry, Brother, Evening Librn, Ref, Quincy University, 1800 College Ave, Quincy, IL, 62301-2699. Tel: 217-228-5432, Ext 3801. p. 638
Santillan, Brooke, Libr Mgr, Des Moines Public Library, South Side, 1111 Porter Ave, Des Moines, IA, 50315. Tel: 515-283-4152. p. 746
Santino, Joanne, Libr Mgr, Nixon Peabody LLP, 100 Summer St, Boston, MA, 02110-2131. Tel: 617-345-1000. p. 998
Santo, Jennifer, Ref (Info Servs), Locust Valley Library, 170 Buckram Rd, Locust Valley, NY, 11560-1999. Tel: 516-671-1837. p. 1564
Santora, Deirdre, Assoc Librn, Access Serv, James Blackstone Memorial Library, 758 Main St, Branford, CT, 06405-3697. Tel: 203-488-1441, Ext 311. p. 303
Santoro, Anita, Head, Tech Serv, Lake Villa District Library, 140 N Munn Rd, Lindenhurst, IL, 60046. Tel: 847-245-5111. p. 609
Santoro, Kathy, Dir, Harvard Library, Faculty of Arts & Sciences Office of Career Services Library, 54 Dunster St, Cambridge, MA, 02138. Tel: 617-495-2595. p. 1006

Santoro, Mary Catherine, Outreach & Instruction Librn, Radford University, 101 Elm Ave SE, 5th Flr, Roanoke, VA, 24013. Tel: 540-831-1823. p. 2345

Santos, Carmen, Spec Coll Librn, University of Puerto Rico, Conrado F Asenjo Library, Medical Sciences Campus, Main Bldg, Unit C, San Juan, PR, 00935. Tel: 787-758-2525, Ext 1224. p. 2514

Santos, Daisy, Supervisor, Client Services, University of Manitoba Libraries, Neil John Maclean Health Sciences Library, Brodie Center Atrium, Mezzanine Level, 2nd Flr, 727 McDermot Ave, Winnipeg, MB, R3E 3P5, CANADA. Tel: 204-789-3462. p. 2595

Santos, David, Br Supvr, Kern County Library, Rosamond Branch, 3611 Rosamond Blvd, Rosamond, CA, 93560-7653. Tel: 661-256-3236. p. 120

Santos, Dawn, Librn, Winhall Memorial Library, Two Lower Tayler Hill Rd, Bondville, VT, 05340. Tel: 802-297-9741. p. 2279

Santos, Eileen, Assoc Dir, Interim Dir, Howard University Libraries, Law Library, 2929 Van Ness St NW, Washington, DC, 20008. Tel: 202-806-8301. p. 369

Santos, Eliane, Advisor, Knowledge Mgmt & Networks, Pan American Health Organization Headquarters Library, 525 23rd St NW, Washington, DC, 20037. Tel: 202-974-3160, 202-974-3734. p. 374

Santos, Eunice E, Prof & Dean, University of Illinois at Urbana-Champaign, Library & Information Science Bldg, 501 E Daniel St, Champaign, IL, 61820-6211. Tel: 217-333-3280. p. 2784

Santos, Jill, Circ Supvr, W T Bland Public Library, 1995 N Donnelly St, Mount Dora, FL, 32757. Tel: 352-735-7180. p. 427

Santos, Jovemay, Dept Head, NYC Health & Hospitals - Coler, 900 Main St, Roosevelt Island, New York, NY, 10044. Tel: 212-848-5849. p. 1599

Santos, Julian, Head Law Librn, Massachusetts Trial Court, Lowell Justice Ctr, 370 Jackson St, Lowell, MA, 01852. Tel: 978-452-9301. p. 1029

Santos, Kathryn, Archivist, California State Railroad Museum Library, Big Four Bldg, 111 I St, 2nd Flr, Sacramento, CA, 95814. Tel: 916-322-0375. p. 208

Santos, Leon, Coll Develop, University of Puerto Rico, Sector Las Dunas, Carr 653 Km 0.8, Arecibo, PR, 00612. Tel: 787-815-0000, Ext 3161. p. 2509

Santos, Mercedes, Mgr, County of Los Angeles Public Library, Dr Martin Luther King, Jr Library, 17906 S Avalon Blvd, Carson, CA, 90746-1598. Tel: 310-327-4830. p. 136

Santos, Rafael, Libr Asst, Universidad Central Del Caribe, Avenida Laurel, Santa Juanita, Bayamon, PR, 00956. Tel: 787-785-6039, 787-798-3001, Ext 2304. p. 2510

Santos, Rodner, AV Tech Equip Mgr, Dona Ana Community College, 3400 S Espina, Rm 260, Las Cruces, NM, 88003. Tel: 575-527-7555. p. 1470

Santos, Sarah, Dir of Develop, Brown University, John Carter Brown Library, Brown University, 94 George St, Providence, RI, 02906. Tel: 401-863-2725. p. 2037

Santoso, Dee, Dep Libr Dir, Manchester City Library, 405 Pine St, Manchester, NH, 03104-6199. Tel: 603-624-6550. p. 1372

Santoviz, Jennifer, Dep Dir, Bullard Sanford Memorial Library, 520 W Huron Ave, Vassar, MI, 48768. Tel: 989-823-2171. p. 1156

Santoyo, Laura, Archivist, American Academy of Pediatrics, 345 Park Blvd, Itasca, IL, 60143. Tel: 630-626-6421. p. 602

Santucci, Kendall, Dir, Schiller Park Public Library, 4200 Old River Rd, Schiller Park, IL, 60176. Tel: 847-678-0433. p. 645

Santucci, Lisa, Dir, Tipp City Public Library, 11 E Main St, Tipp City, OH, 45371. Tel: 937-667-3826. p. 1823

Santulli, Joan, Admin Serv, Chemung County Library District, 101 E Church St, Elmira, NY, 14901. Tel: 607-733-9173. p. 1530

Santy, Gail, Dir, Great Bend Public Library, 1409 Williams St, Great Bend, KS, 67530. Tel: 620-792-2409. p. 811

Sanudo, Manuel, Ref (Info Servs), Queens College, Benjamin S Rosenthal Library, 65-30 Kissena Blvd, Flushing, NY, 11367-0904. Tel: 718-997-3700. p. 1534

Saperstein, Michael, Br Mgr, Harris County Public Library, Parker Williams Branch, 10851 Scarsdale Blvd, Ste 510, Houston, TX, 77089. Tel: 832-927-7870. p. 2193

Saporito-Emler, Gwendolyn, Music Cataloger, Florida State University Libraries, Warren D Allen Music Library, Housewright Music Bldg, 122 N Copeland St, Tallahassee, FL, 32306. Tel: 850-644-5028. p. 447

Saposnik, Susan, Circ Asst, Yarmouth Port Library, 297 Main St, Rte 6A, Yarmouth Port, MA, 02675. Tel: 508-362-3717. p. 1073

Sapp-Nelson, Megan, Head of Libr, University of Illinois Library at Urbana-Champaign, Grainger Engineering Library Information Center, 1301 W Springfield Ave, MC-274, Urbana, IL, 61801. Tel: 217-333-3576. p. 656

Sappington, Jayne, Assoc Librn, Texas Tech University Libraries, 2802 18th St, Lubbock, TX, 79409. Tel: 806-834-4734. p. 2214

Sappington, Kay, Dir, Union County Library, 219 King St, New Albany, MS, 38652. Tel: 662-534-1991. p. 1228

Sapse, Paula, Coordr, Ch Serv, Minor Memorial Library, 23 South St, Roxbury, CT, 06783. Tel: 860-350-2181. p. 335

Saragossi, Jamie, Head of Libr, Stony Brook University, Science & Engineering Library, Frank Melville Jr Memorial Library N-1001, Stony Brook, NY, 11794-3301. Tel: 631-632-7148. p. 1647

Saragossi, Jamie, Head, Health Sci Libr, Stony Brook University, Health Sciences Library, HST Level 3, Rm 136, 8034 SUNY Stony Brook, Stony Brook, NY, 11794-8034. Tel: 631-444-2512. p. 1647

Sarajean, Petite, Govt Doc, Case Western Reserve University, School of Law Library, 11075 East Blvd, Cleveland, OH, 44106-7148. Tel: 216-368-6356. p. 1766

Saranteas, Edie, Libr Asst, North Shore Community College Library, McGee Bldg, LE127, 300 Broad St, Lynn, MA, 01901. Tel: 978-762-4000, Ext 6251. p. 1030

Sarazin, Stephen, Dir, Aston Public Library, 3270 Concord Rd, Aston, PA, 19014. Tel: 610-494-5877. p. 1907

Sarff, Michelle, Dir, Library Servs, Res & Outreach, Ohio Dominican University Library, 1216 Sunbury Rd, Columbus, OH, 43219. Tel: 614-251-4752. p. 1774

Sarg, Tamara, Libr Mgr, Virginia Beach Public Library, Windsor Woods Area, 3612 S Plaza Trail, Virginia Beach, VA, 23452. Tel: 757-385-2630. p. 2351

Sarge Miller, Laura, Youth Serv Librn, Centre County Library & Historical Museum, 200 N Allegheny St, Bellefonte, PA, 16823-1601. Tel: 814-355-1516. p. 1910

Sargeant, Jeff, Sr Librn, Los Angeles Public Library System, Frances Howard Goldwyn-Hollywood Regional Library, 1623 Ivar Ave, Los Angeles, CA, 90028-6304. Tel: 323-856-8260. p. 164

Sargent, Aloha, Tech Serv Librn, Cabrillo College, 6500 Soquel Dr, Aptos, CA, 95003-3198. Tel: 831-479-6473. p. 117

Sargent, Bill, Coordr, Access Serv, University of Southern Maine Libraries, 314 Forest Ave, Portland, ME, 04103. Tel: 207-780-8154. p. 937

Sargent, Elizabeth, Tech Serv Mgr, Montgomery County Memorial Library System, 104 I-45 N, Conroe, TX, 77301-2720. Tel: 936-788-8377, Ext 2118. p. 2159

Sargent, Elizabeth A, Vols Librn, Brainerd Memorial Library, 4215 Bruce Badger Memorial Hwy, Danville, VT, 05828. Tel: 802-424-1403. p. 2282

Sargent, Judith, Br Assoc, Las Vegas-Clark County Library District, Mesquite Library, 121 W First North St, Mesquite, NV, 89027-4759. Tel: 702-507-4312. p. 1347

Sargent, Robert, Dir, Franklin Public Library, 310 Central St, Franklin, NH, 03235. Tel: 603-934-2911. p. 1364

Sargente, Michael, Asst Dir, Atlantic Cape Community College, 1535 Bacharach Blvd, Atlantic City, NJ, 08401. Tel: 609-343-4800, Ext 4726. p. 1387

Sargente, Michael, Asst Director, Academic Support Services, Atlantic Cape Community College, 5100 Black Horse Pike, Mays Landing, NJ, 08330. Tel: 609-343-5631. p. 1417

Sarjeant, Bruce, Govt Doc, Maps Librn, Northern Michigan University, 1401 Presque Isle Ave, Marquette, MI, 49855-5376. Tel: 906-227-1580. p. 1130

Sarjeant-Jenkins, Rachel, Assoc Dean, University of Saskatchewan Libraries, Three Campus Dr, Saskatoon, SK, S7N 5A4, CANADA. Tel: 306-966-5958. p. 2750

Sark, Stephanie, Librn, Wabash Valley Correctional Facility, Level Three Library, 6908 S Old US Hwy 41, Carlisle, IN, 47838. Tel: 812-398-5050, Ext 3271. p. 674

Sarmiento, Beatriz, Dir, Libr Serv, City of Commerce Public Library, 5655 Jillson St, Commerce, CA, 90040. Tel: 323-722-6660. p. 131

Sarna, Susan, Chief of Cultural Resources, Sagamore Hill National Historic Site Library, 20 Sagamore Hill Rd, Oyster Bay, NY, 11771-1899. Tel: 516-922-4788. p. 1614

Sarneso, Anna, Dir, Lasell College, 80 A Maple Ave, Newton, MA, 02466. Tel: 617-243-2243. p. 1039

Sarno, Deborah, Circ, John C Hart Memorial Library, 1130 Main St, Shrub Oak, NY, 10588. Tel: 914-245-5262. p. 1641

Sarnoff, Tamar, Dir, Maryland State Library, 25 S Charles St, Ste 1310, Baltimore, MD, 21201. Tel: 667-219-4802. p. 955

Saroff, Kristyn, Sr Librn, New Hanover County Public Library, 201 Chestnut St, Wilmington, NC, 28401. Tel: 910-798-6252. p. 1723

Saroff, Kristyn, Libr Mgr, Henrico County Public Library, Fairfield Area Library, 1401 N Laburnum Ave, Henrico, VA, 23223. Tel: 804-501-1930. p. 2325

Sarr, Debra, Asst Dir, Edison Township Free Public Library, 340 Plainfield Ave, Edison, NJ, 08817. Tel: 732-287-2298. p. 1400

Sarracino, Theresa, Head, Circ & Adult Serv, Glen Rock Public Library, 315 Rock Rd, Glen Rock, NJ, 07452. Tel: 201-670-3970. p. 1405

Sarratt, Carla, Dir of Libr, University of Mount Union Library, Kolenbrander-Harter Information Ctr, 1972 Clark Ave, Alliance, OH, 44601-3993. Tel: 330-823-3847. p. 1746

Sarto, Janine, Head, Circ, Mount Prospect Public Library, Ten S Emerson St, Mount Prospect, IL, 60056. Tel: 847-253-5675. p. 621

Sartwell, Allison, Head, Adult Serv, Rochester Hills Public Library, 500 Olde Towne Rd, Rochester, MI, 48307-2043. Tel: 248-650-7132. p. 1144

Sarty, Tim, Libr Mgr, York Library Region, Stanley Community Library, 28 Bridge St, Unit 2, Stanley, NB, E6B 1B2, CANADA. Tel: 506-367-2492. p. 2602

Sarver, Alston, Ms, Educ Mgr, Libr Mgr, Princeton Community Hospital Library, 122 12th St, Princeton, WV, 24740-2352. Tel: 304-487-7000, 304-487-7714. p. 2413

Sarver, Jennifer, Dir of Educ, Cedarhurst Center for the Arts, 2600 Richview Rd, Mount Vernon, IL, 62864. Tel: 618-242-1236, Ext 224. p. 621

Sas, Heather, Acq & Ser Coordr, Northwestern College, 101 Seventh St SW, Orange City, IA, 51041. Tel: 712-707-7235. p. 774

Saslow, Lauren, Syst Librn, Pierce College Library, 6201 Winnetka Ave, Woodland Hills, CA, 91371. Tel: 818-710-4442. p. 260

Sass, Rivkah K, Ms, Libr Dir, Sacramento Public Library, 828 I St, Sacramento, CA, 95814. Tel: 916-264-2700, 916-264-2920. p. 209

Sasselli, Jennifer, Dir, Skagway Public Library, 769 State St, Skagway, AK, 99840. Tel: 907-983-2665. p. 51

Sasser, Patricia, Music & Outreach Librn, Furman University Libraries, 3300 Poinsett Hwy, Greenville, SC, 29613-4100. Tel: 864-294-2192. p. 2061

Sasser, Patricia, Music Librn, Furman University Libraries, Maxwell Music Library, Herring Music Pavilion, 3300 Poinsett Hwy, Greenville, SC, 29613. Tel: 864-294-3795. p. 2061

Sasser, Shasta, Dir, Wilsonville Public Library, 8200 SW Wilsonville Rd, Wilsonville, OR, 97070. Tel: 503-682-2744. p. 1902

Sasseville, Rebecca, Dir, Whitinsville Social Library, 17 Church St, Whitinsville, MA, 01588. Tel: 508-234-2151. p. 1069

Sassi, Lisa, Head, Circ, La Grange Association Library, 1110 Route 55, 2nd Flr, LaGrangeville, NY, 12540. Tel: 845-452-3141. p. 1561

Sassian, Maria, Dir, Res, Insurance Information Institute Library, 110 William St, New York, NY, 10038. Tel: 212-346-5500. p. 1589

Sassman, Cheryl, Head, Circ, Texas Christian University, 2913 Lowden St, TCU Box 298400, Fort Worth, TX, 76129. Tel: 817-257-7106. p. 2181

Sasso, Carol, Mgr, Off of the Dean of Libr & Info Serv, Hofstra University, 123 Hofstra University, Hempstead, NY, 11549. Tel: 516-463-5943. p. 1545

Sasso, Maureen Diana, Asst Univ Librn, Res Serv & User Engagement Librn, Duquesne University, 600 Forbes Ave, Pittsburgh, PA, 15282. Tel: 412-396-5680. p. 1993

Satersmoen, Carol, Librn, Aims Community College, College Ctr, 5401 W 20th St, 7501, Greeley, CO, 80634-3002. Tel: 970-339-6589. p. 284

Sathler, Julia, Br Librn, United States Courts for the Ninth Circuit Library, 1000 SW Third Ave, 7A40, Portland, OR, 97204. Tel: 503-326-8140. p. 1894

Sathler, Julia, Br Librn, United States Courts for the Ninth Circuit Library, Mark O Hatfield US Courthouse, 1000 SW Third Ave, 7A40, Portland, OR, 97204. Tel: 503-326-8140. p. 1894

Satrang, Peggy, Libr Mgr, Britton Public Library, 759 Seventh St, Britton, SD, 57430. Tel: 605-448-2800. p. 2074

Satterfield, Jay, Head, Spec Coll, Dartmouth College Library, Rauner Special Collections Library, 6065 Webster Hall, Hanover, NH, 03755-3519. Tel: 603-646-0538. p. 1366

Satterfield, Kristen, Dir, Claud H Gilmer Memorial Library, 201 N Hwy 377, Rocksprings, TX, 78880. Tel: 830-683-8130. p. 2234

Satterthwaite, Mimi, Ref (Info Servs), Abington Township Public Library, 1030 Old York Rd, Abington, PA, 19001-4594. Tel: 215-885-5180. p. 1903

Satterwhite, Melissa, Dir, Teague Public Library, 400 Main St, Teague, TX, 75860. Tel: 254-739-3311. p. 2247

Satyavolu, Sreedevi, Access Serv Librn, Adler University, 17 N Dearborn St, 15th Flr, Chicago, IL, 60602. Tel: 312-662-4230. p. 553

Sauceda, Eduardo, Chair, Access Serv, Chapman University, One University Dr, Orange, CA, 92866. Tel: 714-532-7756. p. 188

Sauceda, Jon, Assoc Dean, University of Rochester, Sibley Music Library, 27 Gibbs St, Rochester, NY, 14604-2596. Tel: 585-274-1350. p. 1631

Sauceda, Jonathan, Music & Performing Arts Librn, Rutgers University Libraries, Mabel Smith Douglass Library, Eight Chapel Dr, New Brunswick, NJ, 08901-8527. Tel: 848-932-9023. p. 1425

Saucedo, Ed, Social Servs Coord, City of Commerce Public Library, 5655 Jillson St, Commerce, CA, 90040. Tel: 323-722-6660. p. 131

Saucier, Denise, Dir, Long Beach Public Library, 209 Jeff Davis Ave, Long Beach, MS, 39560. Tel: 228-863-0711. p. 1225

Sauder, Molly, Archivist/Librn, The Old Jail Art Center, 201 S Second St, Albany, TX, 76430. Tel: 325-762-2269. p. 2132

Sauer, Abby, Outreach & Programming Supvr, East Moline Public Library, 745 16th Ave, East Moline, IL, 61244-2122. Tel: 309-755-9614, Ext 105. p. 580

Sauer, Brita, Libr Mgr, Public Programs, Las Cruces Public Libraries, 200 E Picacho Ave, Las Cruces, NM, 88001-3499. Tel: 575-528-4085. p. 1470

Sauer, Jeff, Interim Dir, Anderson County Public Library, 114 N Main St, Lawrenceburg, KY, 40342. Tel: 502-839-6420. p. 861

Sauer, Laurie, IT Librn, Knox College, 371 S West St, Galesburg, IL, 61401. Tel: 309-341-7788. p. 591

Sauers, Mary, Govt Info Librn, Nebraska Library Commission, The Atrium, 1200 N St, Ste 120, Lincoln, NE, 68508-2023. Tel: 402-471-4017. p. 1322

Sauers, Richard A, Dr, Curator, Western Museum of Mining & Industry Library, 225 N Gate Blvd, Colorado Springs, CO, 80921. Tel: 719-488-0880. p. 272

Saul, Jackie, Dir, Admin & Finance, Whatcom County Library System, 5205 Northwest Dr, Bellingham, WA, 98226. Tel: 360-305-3600. p. 2359

Saul, Nancy, Ref (Info Servs), Simon Wiesenthal Center & Museum of Tolerance, 1399 S Roxbury Dr, 3rd Flr, Los Angeles, CA, 90035-4709. Tel: 310-772-7605. p. 168

Saulat, Zohra, Student Success Librn, Lake Forest College, 555 N Sheridan Rd, Lake Forest, IL, 60045. Tel: 847-735-5056. p. 606

Saulnier, Jason, Libr Asst I, Universite Sainte-Anne, 1695 Hwy 1, Church Point, NS, B0W 1M0, CANADA. Tel: 902-769-2114, Ext 7158. p. 2617

Saulter, Sarah, Librn, Cuyamaca College Library, 900 Rancho San Diego Pkwy, El Cajon, CA, 92019. Tel: 619-660-4416. p. 139

Saunders, Barbara, Librn, Dolores County Public Library, Pioneer Reading Center, Pioneer Reading Ctr, 8540 Rd 7 2, Dove Creek, CO, 81324. Tel: 970-677-2787. p. 278

Saunders, Beth, Head, Spec Coll, University of Maryland, Baltimore County, 1000 Hilltop Circle, Baltimore, MD, 21250. Tel: 410-455-2356. p. 958

Saunders, Beth, Quaker Collections Associate, Guilford College, Quaker Archives, Hege Library, 5800 W Friendly Ave, Greensboro, NC, 27410. Tel: 336-316-2264. p. 1692

Saunders, Cindy, Library Contact, Department of Natural Resources, Government of Newfoundland & Labrador, Natural Resources Bldg, 50 Elizabeth Ave, St. John's, NL, A1B 4J6, CANADA. Tel: 709-729-6280. p. 2610

Saunders, Deborah, Dir, Gallia County District Library, Seven Spruce St, Gallipolis, OH, 45631. Tel: 740-446-7323. p. 1787

Saunders, Desiree, Prog Mgr, WYLD Network, c/o Wyoming State Library, 2800 Central Ave, Cheyenne, WY, 82002-0060. Tel: 307-777-6258. p. 2777

Saunders, Heather, Dir, Cleveland Museum of Art, 11150 East Blvd, Cleveland, OH, 44106-1797. Tel: 216-707-2530. p. 1767

Saunders, Jeffrey, Adminr, Anthroposophical Society In Canada Library, 130A-1 Hesperus Rd, Thornhill, ON, L4J 0G9, CANADA. Tel: 416-892-3656. p. 2684

Saunders, Jesse, Asst Head Librn, Austin Community College, Round Rock Campus Library, 4400 College Park Dr, Round Rock, TX, 78665. Tel: 512-223-0118. p. 2138

Saunders, Laura, Assoc Dean, Prof, Simmons University, 300 The Fenway, Boston, MA, 02115. Tel: 617-521-2800. p. 2786

Saunders, Marc, Dir, Libr Serv, Port Moody Public Library, 100 Newport Dr, Port Moody, BC, V3H 5C3, CANADA. Tel: 604-469-4575. p. 2574

Saunders, Mark, Facilities Dir, Stark County District Library, 715 Market Ave N, Canton, OH, 44702. Tel: 330-458-2685. p. 1755

Saunders, Mike, Ser, National Gallery of Canada Library & Archives, 380 Sussex Dr, Ottawa, ON, K1N 9N4, CANADA. Tel: 613-714-6000, Ext 6323. p. 2667

Saunders, Nicholas, Br Mgr, Chicago Public Library, Altgeld, 13281 S Corliss Ave, Chicago, IL, 60827. Tel: 312-747-3270. p. 555

Saunders, Pat, Br Mgr, Beaufort, Hyde & Martin County Regional Library, Belhaven Public, 333 E Main St, Belhaven, NC, 27810. Tel: 252-943-2993. p. 1720

Saunders, Perri, Dir, White Pigeon Township Library, 102 N Kalamazoo St, White Pigeon, MI, 49099-9726. Tel: 269-483-7409. p. 1159

Saunders, Phyllis, Admin Librn, Chandler Public Library, Hamilton, 3700 S Arizona Ave, Chandler, AZ, 85248-4500. p. 58

Saunders, Richard L, Dr, Coll Develop, Dean, Libr Serv, Southern Utah University, 351 W University Blvd, Cedar City, UT, 84720. Tel: 435-586-7933, 435-865-8240. p. 2262

Saunders, Steve, Head, Info Tech, Orion Township Public Library, 825 Joslyn Rd, Lake Orion, MI, 48362. Tel: 248-693-3000, Ext 440. p. 1123

Saunders, Teresa, Libr Tech, Western Connecticut State University, Robert S Young Business Library, 181 White St, Danbury, CT, 06810-6885. Tel: 203-837-9139. p. 308

Saunders, Wesley, Asst Dir, Support Serv, Rapides Parish Library, 411 Washington St, Alexandria, LA, 71301-8338. Tel: 318-445-2412, Ext 1044. p. 880

Sauter, Katie, Libr Dir, American Alpine Club Library, 710 Tenth St, Ste 15, Golden, CO, 80401. Tel: 303-384-0112. p. 282

Sauter, Rodney, Library Contact, National Park Service, 800 S San Marcial St, El Paso, TX, 79905-4123. Tel: 915-532-7273, Ext 127. p. 2174

Sautter, Betty, Tech Serv, Southwest Wisconsin Library System, 1300 Industrial Dr, Ste 2, Fennimore, WI, 53809. Tel: 608-822-3393. p. 2435

Sautter, Carolyn, Dir, Spec Coll & Archives, Gettysburg College, 300 N Washington St, Gettysburg, PA, 17325. Tel: 717-337-7002. p. 1935

Sauvé, Jean-Sébastien, Asst Prof, Universite de Montreal, 3150, rue Jean-Brillant, bur C-2004, Montreal, QC, H3T 1N8, CANADA. Tel: 514-343-6044. p. 2797

Sauve, Jennifer, Pub Serv, College of New Caledonia Library, 3330 22nd Ave, Prince George, BC, V2N 1P8, CANADA. Tel: 250-561-5811, 250-562-2131, Ext 5298. p. 2574

Sauzer, Jennifer, Head, Access Servs & Assessment, Columbia College Chicago Library, 624 S Michigan Ave, Chicago, IL, 60605-1996. Tel: 312-369-8540. p. 559

Savage, Adam, Head, Libr Tech & Fac Serv, University of Waterloo Library, 200 University Ave W, Waterloo, ON, N2L 3G1, CANADA. Tel: 519-888-4567, Ext 44141. p. 2702

Savage, Carolyn, Asst Dir, Ref Librn, Mashpee Public Library, 64 Steeple St, Mashpee, MA, 02649. Tel: 508-539-1435, Ext 3005. p. 1033

Savage, Cassandra, Ch, Wilton Free Public Library, Six Goodspeed St, Wilton, ME, 04294. Tel: 207-645-4831. p. 946

Savage, Catherine, Head, Integrated Comms, Vernon Area Public Library District, 300 Olde Half Day Rd, Lincolnshire, IL, 60069. Tel: 847-634-3650. p. 609

Savage, Devin, Dean of Libr, Illinois Institute of Technology, 35 W 33rd St, Chicago, IL, 60616. Tel: 312-567-3615. p. 562

Savage, Hilary, Asst Dir, Belleville Area District Library, 167 Fourth St, Belleville, MI, 48111. Tel: 734-699-3291. p. 1084
Savage, Laura, Librn, Mississippi Gulf Coast Community College, Hwy 49 S, Perkinston, MS, 39573. Tel: 601-928-6380. p. 1229
Savage, Meghan, Br Mgr, Surrey Libraries, Guildford, 15105 105th Ave, Surrey, BC, V3R 7G8, CANADA. Tel: 604-598-7374. p. 2577
Savage, Meghan, Br Mgr, Surrey Libraries, Port Kells, 18885 88th Ave, Surrey, BC, V4N 5T1, CANADA. Tel: 604-598-7374. p. 2577
Savage, Sharon, YA Spec, New Castle Public Library, 207 E North St, New Castle, PA, 16101-3691. Tel: 724-658-6659, Ext 111. p. 1969
Savage, Tiffany, Ch, Sampson-Clinton Public Library, 217 Graham St, Clinton, NC, 28328. Tel: 910-592-4153. p. 1681
Savage, Will, Dir, Youth Serv, Lisle Library District, 777 Front St, Lisle, IL, 60532-3599. Tel: 630-971-1675. p. 610
Savard, Tracy, Libr Dir, Apalachin Library, 719 Main St, Apalachin, NY, 13732. Tel: 607-625-3333. p. 1487
Savaria, Kristen, Tech Serv, East Longmeadow Public Library, 60 Center Sq, East Longmeadow, MA, 01028-2459. Tel: 413-525-5400. p. 1016
Savarino, Michael, IT Coordr, Boone County Public Library, 1786 Burlington Pike, Burlington, KY, 41005. Tel: 859-342-2665. p. 850
Savary, Karine, Archivist, La Societe d'Histoire de Sherbrooke, 275, rue Dufferin, Sherbrooke, QC, J1H 4M5, CANADA. Tel: 819-821-5406. p. 2737
Savedchuk, Lesia, Librn, St Volodymyr's Cultural Centre, 404 Meredith Rd NE, Calgary, AB, T2E 5A6, CANADA. Tel: 403-264-3437. p. 2529
Savelesky, Mike, Rev, Archivist, Catholic Diocesan Archives, 525 E Mission Ave, Spokane, WA, 99202. Tel: 509-358-7336. p. 2383
Savery, Wendy, Librn, Gilbert Hart Library, 14 S Main St, Wallingford, VT, 05773. Tel: 802-446-2685. p. 2297
Savitsky, Tanya, Librn, Ringtown Area Library, 132 W Main St, Ringtown, PA, 17967-9538. Tel: 570-889-5503. p. 2002
Savitts, Patricia A, Circ Serv Coordr, University of Scranton, 800 Linden St, Scranton, PA, 18510-4634. Tel: 570-941-6139. p. 2005
Savoie, Denise M, Head, ILL, Universite de Moncton, 18, ave Antonine-Maillet, Moncton, NB, E1A 3E9, CANADA. Tel: 506-858-4012. p. 2603
Savoie, Marina, ILL Coordr, Bradley University, 1501 W Bradley Ave, Peoria, IL, 61625. Tel: 309-677-2850. p. 634
Savolainen, Jaclyn, Libr Dir, Starr Library, 68 W Market St, Rhinebeck, NY, 12572. Tel: 845-876-4030. p. 1626
Savonius-Wroth, Celestina, Head of Libr, University of Illinois Library at Urbana-Champaign, History, Philosophy & Newspaper, 246 Main Library, MC-522, 1408 W Gregory Dr, Urbana, IL, 61801. Tel: 217-300-3520. p. 656
Savopol, Florin, Mgr, Natural Resources Canada, National Air Photo Library, 615 Booth St, Rm 180, Ottawa, ON, K1A 0E9, CANADA. Tel: 613-943-0234. p. 2668
Savoy, Patrice, Instrul Media, Alcorn State University, 1000 ASU Dr, Alcorn State, MS, 39096-7500. Tel: 601-877-6359. p. 1211
Saw, Kevin, Learning Res Coordr, State University of New York, 111 Livingston St, Ste 306, Brooklyn, NY, 11201. Tel: 718-802-3300, 718-802-3314. p. 1506
Sawa, Maureen, Chief Exec Officer, Greater Victoria Public Library, 735 Broughton St, Victoria, BC, V8W 3H2, CANADA. Tel: 250-940-1193. p. 2582
Sawatsky, Melissa, ILL, Pub Relations, Smithers Public Library, 3817 Alfred Ave, Smithers, BC, V0J 2N0, CANADA. Tel: 250-847-3043. p. 2576
Sawatzky, Jay, Libr Mgr, Claresholm Public Library, 211 49th Ave W, Claresholm, AB, T0L 0T0, CANADA. Tel: 403-625-4168. p. 2531
Sawchuk, Natalka, Asst Dir, Lib, Iona University, 715 North Ave, New Rochelle, NY, 10801-1890. Tel: 914-633-2220. p. 1577
Sawh, Michelle, Dir, Admin Serv, Markham Public Library, 6031 Hwy 7, Markham, ON, L3P 3A7, CANADA. Tel: 905-513-7977, Ext 4233. p. 2656
Sawhney, Delia, Libr Dir, Federal Reserve Bank of Boston, 600 Atlantic Ave, Boston, MA, 02210-2204. Tel: 617-973-3397. p. 995
Sawicki, Michelle, Dir, Barclay Public Library District, 220 S Main St, Warrensburg, IL, 62573-9657. Tel: 217-672-3621. p. 658
Sawisch, Kate, Head, Knowledge & Community Servs, Morse Institute Library, 14 E Central St, Natick, MA, 01760. Tel: 508-647-6400, Ext 1527. p. 1037
Sawtelle, Julie, Librn, Cumston Public Library, 796 Main St, Monmouth, ME, 04259. Tel: 207-933-4788. p. 932
Sawyer, Barbara, Libr Mgr, Ida Hilton Public Library, 1105 North Way, Darien, GA, 31305. Tel: 912-437-2124. p. 474
Sawyer, Cara Elizabeth, Dir, Cherryfield Free Public Library, 35 Main St, Cherryfield, ME, 04622. Tel: 207-546-4228. p. 922
Sawyer, Ginger, Ch Serv, York County Library, 138 E Black St, Rock Hill, SC, 29730. Tel: 803-981-5882. p. 2068
Sawyer, Jack, Instruction & Ref Librn, College of Southern Nevada, Cheyenne Campus, 3200 E Cheyenne Ave, Rm 201, North Las Vegas, NV, 89030. Tel: 702-651-4444. p. 1346
Sawyer, Rachel, Librn, Farmington Public Library, 175 W Cimarron Pl, Farmington, AR, 72730. Tel: 479-267-2674. p. 95
Sawyer, Stephanie, Libr Dir, Kennedy Library of Konawa, 701 W South St, Konawa, OK, 74849. Tel: 580-925-3662. p. 1851
Sawyer, Sueann, Libr Dir, Protection Township Library, 404 N Broadway, Protection, KS, 67127. Tel: 620-622-4886. p. 833
Sawyer, Suzanne, Librn, Utah Geological Survey Library, 1594 W North Temple, Salt Lake City, UT, 84114. Tel: 801-537-3333, 801-538-4846. p. 2272
Sawyer, Sylvia, Acq, Carson-Newman University, 1634 Russell Ave, Jefferson City, TN, 37760. Tel: 865-471-4847. p. 2103
Sawyer, Tamara, Knowledge Mgr, CMU Health, St Mary's Branch, 800 S Washington, 2nd Flr, Saginaw, MI, 48601-2551. Tel: 989-746-7577. p. 1146
Sawyer, Tamara, Libr Mgr, CMU Health, CMU College of Medicine, Educ Bldg, 1632 Stone St, Saginaw, MI, 48602. Tel: 989-746-7577. p. 1146
Sax, Anthony, Digital Initiatives Coordr, South Dakota State University, 1300 N Campus Dr, Box 2115, Brookings, SD, 57007. Tel: 605-688-5576. p. 2074
Saxe, Coleen, Librn, SSM Health - Good Samaritan Hospital, One Good Samaritan Way, Mount Vernon, IL, 62864. Tel: 618-899-3095. p. 622
Saxe-Eyler, Amy, Develop Dir, San Juan Island Library, 1010 Guard St, Friday Harbor, WA, 98250-9612. Tel: 360-378-2798. p. 2364
Saxon, Jared, Librn, Dallas College, 3030 N Dallas Ave, Lancaster, TX, 75134-3799. Tel: 972-860-8140. p. 2209
Saxton, Amy, Distance Learning Librn, University of Hawaii at Hilo Library, 200 W Kawili St, Hilo, HI, 96720. Tel: 808-932-7331. p. 505
Saxton, Jennifer, Librn, Miami Dade College, Kendall Campus Library, 11011 SW 104th St, Miami, FL, 33176-3393. Tel: 305-237-0996, 305-237-2015, 305-237-2291. p. 422
Saxton, Sara, Youth Serv Librn, Wasilla Public Library, 500 N Crusey St, Wasilla, AK, 99654. Tel: 907-864-9173. p. 52
Saxton, Stephanie, Libr Tech, Nashua Community College, 505 Amherst St, Nashua, NH, 03063-1026. Tel: 603-578-8905. p. 1374
Sayed, Ellen, Dir, Medical College of Wisconsin Libraries, Health Research Ctr, 3rd Flr, 8701 Watertown Plank Rd, Milwaukee, WI, 53226-0509. Tel: 414-955-4852. p. 2459
Sayer, Lauren, Law Librn, Administrative Office of the United States Courts Library, One Columbus Circle NE, Ste 4-400, Washington, DC, 20544. Tel: 202-502-2418. p. 359
Sayers, John, Dir, Cambridge Public Library District, 212 W Center St, Cambridge, IL, 61238-1239. Tel: 309-937-2233. p. 548
Sayles, Tammy, Actg Chief, Pub Serv, Pikes Peak Library District, 20 N Cascade Ave, Colorado Springs, CO, 80903. Tel: 719-531-6333. p. 271
Saylor, Elke, Head, Pub Serv, Muskego Public Library, S73 W16663 Janesville Rd, Muskego, WI, 53150. Tel: 262-971-2100. p. 2463
Saylor, Gerard, Dir, L D Fargo Public Library, 120 E Madison St, Lake Mills, WI, 53551-1644. Tel: 920-648-2166. p. 2447
Saylor, Helen, Dir, Gallitzin Public Library, DeGol Plaza, Ste 30, 411 Convent St, Gallitzin, PA, 16641-1244. Tel: 814-886-4041. p. 1934
Saylor, Trina, Mrs, Asst Ch, Stewart County Public Library, 102 Natcor Dr, Dover, TN, 37058. Tel: 931-232-3127. p. 2097
Sayre Batton, Susan, Exec Dir, San Jose Museum of Art Library, 110 S Market St, San Jose, CA, 95113. Tel: 408-271-6840. p. 231
Sayre, Brad, IT Dir, Stark County District Library, 715 Market Ave N, Canton, OH, 44702. Tel: 330-458-3140. p. 1755
Sayre, Janet, Cat, Tech Serv, Houston County Public Library System, 1201 Washington Ave, Perry, GA, 31069. Tel: 478-987-3050. p. 493
Sayre, Tessa, Pub Serv Mgr, Mercyhurst University, 501 E 38th St, Erie, PA, 16546. Tel: 814-824-2236. p. 1932
Saywell, Lisa, Director, Public Servs & Ref, Wisconsin Historical Society Library, 816 State St, 2nd Flr, Madison, WI, 53706. Tel: 608-264-6535. p. 2452
Sbar, Shelley, Librn, Jack Balaban Memorial Library of Temple Sinai, 2101 New Albany Rd, Cinnaminson, NJ, 08077-3536. Tel: 856-829-0658. p. 1396
Sbaschnik, Werner, Syst Librn, State University of New York, 223 Store Hill Rd, Old Westbury, NY, 11568. Tel: 516-876-3154. p. 1610
Scace, Kim, Dir, Libr Serv, Stockton Township Public Library, 140 W Benton Ave, Stockton, IL, 61085. Tel: 815-947-2030. p. 651
Scaggs, Andy, Coordr, Outreach Serv, London Public Library, 20 E First St, London, OH, 43140. Tel: 740-852-9543. p. 1796
Scaggs, Deirdre, Assoc Dean, Spec Coll, Interim Dean of Libr, University of Kentucky Libraries, 401 Hilltop Ave, Lexington, KY, 40506. Tel: 859-257-3653. p. 863
Scaggs, Deirdre, Libr Dir, University of Kentucky Libraries, Special Collections Research Center, Margaret I King Library, 179 Funkhouser Dr, Lexington, KY, 40506-0039. Tel: 859-257-3653. p. 864
Scagnelli-Townley, Melody, Libr Dir, Free Public Library & Cultural Center of Bayonne, 697 Avenue C, Bayonne, NJ, 07002. Tel: 201-858-6970. p. 1388
Scales, Angela, Dir, Ida Grove Public Library, 100 E Second St, Ida Grove, IA, 51445. Tel: 712-364-2306. p. 759
Scales, Jane, Instrul Librn, Cleary University Library, 3750 Cleary Dr, Howell, MI, 48843. p. 1117
Scalese, Gisella, Educ Librn, Lakehead University, 955 Oliver Rd, Thunder Bay, ON, P7B 5E1, CANADA. Tel: 807-343-8719. p. 2685
Scalese, Gisella, Educ Librn, Lakehead University, Education Library, Bora Laskin Bldg, 1st Flr, 955 Oliver Rd, Thunder Bay, ON, P7B 5E1, CANADA. Tel: 807-343-8719. p. 2685
Scalia, Liz, Librn, American Institutes for Research Library, 10720 Columbia Pike, Ste 500, Silver Spring, MD, 20901. Tel: 301-592-3347. p. 977

Scalise, Rachel Yost, Br Serv Librn, Monmouth County Library, 125 Symmes Dr, Manalapan, NJ, 07726. Tel: 732-431-7220. p. 1415
Scalzi, Mell, Registrar, Florence Griswold Museum, 96 Lyme St, Old Lyme, CT, 06371. Tel: 860-434-5542. p. 332
Scambler, Sarah, Libr Asst, Irene Ingle Public Library, 124 Second Ave, Wrangell, AK, 99929. Tel: 907-874-3535. p. 53
Scammell, Rochelle, Libr Mgr, Cadogan Public Library, 112 Second St, Cadogan, AB, T0B 0T0, CANADA. Tel: 780-753-6933. p. 2525
Scandling, Christopher, Dir, Bremen Public Library, 304 N Jackson St, Bremen, IN, 46506. Tel: 574-546-2849. p. 672
Scanlan, Allison, Dir, Pinson Public Library, 4509 Pinson Blvd, Pinson, AL, 35126. Tel: 205-680-9298. p. 33
Scanlan, Molly, Dir, O'Fallon Public Library, 120 Civic Plaza, O'Fallon, IL, 62269-2692. Tel: 618-632-3783. p. 629
Scanlon, Bridget, Coordr, Staten Island University Hospital/Northwell Health, 475 Seaview Ave, Staten Island, NY, 10305. Tel: 718-226-9545. p. 1645
Scanlon, Seamus, Librn, City College of the City University of New York, Center for Worker Education Library, 25 Broadway, 7-28, New York, NY, 10004. Tel: 212-925-6625, Ext 228. p. 1581
Scannell, Fiona, Dir, Libr Serv, Global Affairs Canada, Lester B Pearson Bldg, 125 Sussex Dr, Ottawa, ON, K1A 0G2, CANADA. Tel: 343-203-2644. p. 2667
Scannell, Kathryn Geoffrion, Dir, Merrimack College, 315 Turnpike St, North Andover, MA, 01845. Tel: 978-837-5211. p. 1040
Scannell, Kim, Librn, The Center - Resources for Teaching & Learning Library, 2626 S Clearbrook Dr, Arlington Heights, IL, 60005-4626. Tel: 224-366-8590. p. 537
Scapple, Karren, Asst Archivist, Unity Archives, 1901 NW Blue Pkwy, Unity Village, MO, 64065-0001. Tel: 816-347-5539, 816-524-3550, Ext 2020. p. 1284
Scarbeck, Denise, Patron Serv, Sachem Public Library, 150 Holbrook Rd, Holbrook, NY, 11741. Tel: 631-588-5024. p. 1547
Scarberry, Laura, Ch, Pataskala Public Library, 101 S Vine St, Pataskala, OH, 43062. Tel: 740-927-9986. p. 1814
Scarborough, James, Media Spec, Orem Public Library, 58 N State St, Orem, UT, 84057. Tel: 801-229-7050. p. 2268
Scarbrough, Jill, Dir, Brazil Public Library, 204 N Walnut St, Brazil, IN, 47834. Tel: 812-446-1331, 812-448-1981. p. 672
Scarbrough, Karly, Dir, Libr Serv, Cochise College Library, Andrea Cracchiolo Library, Bldg 900, 901 N Colombo Ave, Sierra Vista, AZ, 85635. Tel: 520-515-5320. p. 59
Scarbrough, Karly, Dir, Libr Serv, Cochise College Library, Bldg 300, 4190 W Hwy 80, Douglas, AZ, 85607. Tel: 520-417-4082. p. 59
Scarfo, Michael, User Experience Supvr, Richland Public Library, 955 Northgate Dr, Richland, WA, 99352. Tel: 50-942-7446. p. 2375
Scarlet, Jeremy, Ad, Simi Valley Library, 2969 Tapo Canyon Rd, Simi Valley, CA, 93063. Tel: 805-526-1735. p. 246
Scarlet, Rose, Ref/Cat Librn, Missouri State University-West Plains, 304 W Trish Knight St, West Plains, MO, 65775. Tel: 417-255-7945. p. 1286
Scarnati, Brandi, Dir, Libr Serv, Truckee Meadows Community College, 7000 Dandini Blvd, Reno, NV, 89512-3999. Tel: 775-674-7600. p. 1349
Scarpa, Sunnie, Dir, E C Scranton Memorial Library, 1250 Durham Rd, Ste F, Madison, CT, 06443. Tel: 203-245-7365. p. 320
Scarpa, Sunnie, Dir, Wallingford Public Library, 200 N Main St, Wallingford, CT, 06492. Tel: 203-284-6411. p. 342
Scarpelli, Rosalie, Mgr, Mem Serv, Palatine Public Library District, 700 N North Ct, Palatine, IL, 60067. Tel: 847-907-3600. p. 631
Scarpitti, Michelle, Fiscal Officer, Akron-Summit County Public Library, 60 S High St, Akron, OH, 44326. Tel: 330-643-9000. p. 1744
Scarpola, Cindy, Br Mgr, Harford County Public Library, Darlington Branch, 1134 Main St, Darlington, MD, 21034-1418. Tel: 410-638-3750. p. 959
Scates, Trisha M, Libr Dir, Shawneetown Public Library, 320 N Lincoln Blvd E, Shawneetown, IL, 62984. Tel: 618-269-3761. p. 646
Schaad, Gerrianne, Col Archivist, Florida Southern College, 111 Lake Hollingsworth Dr, Lakeland, FL, 33801-5698. Tel: 863-680-4994. p. 417
Schaade, Becky, Libr Dir, Fairfield County District Library, 219 N Broad St, Lancaster, OH, 43130-3098. Tel: 740-653-2745. p. 1794
Schaaf, Libby, Library Contact, US National Park Service, 13063 E Bonita Canyon Rd, Willcox, AZ, 85643-9737. Tel: 520-824-3560, Ext 9307. p. 84
Schaafsma, Roberta, Dir & J S Bridwell Endowed Librn, Southern Methodist University, Bridwell Library-Perkins School of Theology, 6005 Bishop Blvd, Dallas, TX, 75205. Tel: 214-768-3483. p. 2167
Schaal, Donna, Dir, Argenta-Oreana Public Library District, 100 E Water St, Argenta, IL, 62501. Tel: 217-468-2340, 217-795-2144. p. 537
Schaal, Donna, Dir, Argenta-Oreana Public Library District, 211 S Rte 48, Oreana, IL, 62554. Tel: 217-468-2340. p. 630
Schaal, Kate, Libr Dir, Quechee Public Library, 1957 Quechee Main St, Quechee, VT, 05059. Tel: 802-295-1232. p. 2292
Schaal, Kate, Dir, Wilder Library, 78 Norwich Ave, Wilder, VT, 05088. Tel: 802-295-6341. p. 2299
Schaarschmidt, Erin, YA Serv, Port Jefferson Free Library, 100 Thompson St, Port Jefferson, NY, 11777. Tel: 631-473-0022. p. 1621
Schabel, Christine, Br Mgr, Milwaukee Public Library, Capitol, 3969 N 74th St, Milwaukee, WI, 53216. p. 2460
Schaben, Carmen, Ms, Supvr, Mid-Columbia Libraries, West Pasco Branch, 7525 Wrigley Dr, Pasco, WA, 99301. Tel: 509-546-8055. p. 2367
Schable, Kathy, Dir, Dakota City Public Library, 1710 Broadway, Dakota City, NE, 68731. Tel: 402-987-3778. p. 1312
Schacht, Katherine, Head, Tech Serv, Mansfield Public Library, 255 Hope St, Mansfield, MA, 02048-2353. Tel: 508-261-7380. p. 1031
Schachte, Margaret, Libr Dir, Ashland Public Library, 1229 Centre St, Ashland, PA, 17921-1207. Tel: 570-875-3175. p. 1907
Schachter, Debbie, Dr, Dir, Centre for Accessible Post-Secondary Education Resources, Langara College Library, 100 W 49th Ave, Vancouver, BC, V5Y 2Z6, CANADA. Tel: 604-323-5639. p. 2777
Schack, Amy, Head, Circ, American International College, 1000 State St, Springfield, MA, 01109. Tel: 413-205-3225. p. 1056
Schack, Bridget, Librn, Bare Hill Correctional Facility Library, Caller Box 20, 181 Brand Rd, Malone, NY, 12953-0020. Tel: 518-483-8411. p. 1567
Schack Jensen, Sue, Libr Dir, Seattle Genealogical Society Library, 6200 Sand Point Way NE, Seattle, WA, 98115. Tel: 206-522-8658. p. 2378
Schad, Marian, Cataloger, Delaware Valley University, 700 E Butler Ave, Doylestown, PA, 18901-2699. Tel: 215-489-2385. p. 1927
Schade, Cynthia, Libr Asst, Linn County Library District No 5, 752 Main St, Pleasanton, KS, 66075. Tel: 913-352-8554. p. 832
Schadrie, Rebecca, Dir, Manitowoc-Calumet Library System, 707 Quay St, Manitowoc, WI, 54220. Tel: 920-686-3051. p. 2453
Schaebler, Alice, Sister, ILL, Ref Librn, Immaculata University, 1145 King Rd, Immaculata, PA, 19345-0705. Tel: 484-323-3839. p. 1945
Schaefer, Judy, Libr Asst II, Schreiner Memorial Library, Potosi Branch, 103 N Main St, Potosi, WI, 53820. Tel: 608-763-2115. p. 2448
Schaefer, Julie, Dep Dir, Dearborn Public Library, 16301 Michigan Ave, Dearborn, MI, 48126. Tel: 313-943-2338. p. 1095
Schaefer, Patricia M, Researcher, New London County Historical Society Library, 11 Blinman St, New London, CT, 06320. Tel: 860-443-1209. p. 329
Schaefer, Sharon, Ref Librn, Hayner Public Library District, 326 Belle St, Alton, IL, 62002. Tel: 618-462-0677. p. 536
Schaefer, Tanya, Br Mgr, Broken Bow Public Library, 404 N Broadway St, Broken Bow, OK, 74728. p. 1843
Schaeffer, Amy, Dir, Arlington Baptist University, 3001 W Division, Arlington, TX, 76012. Tel: 817-461-8741, Ext 127. p. 2136
Schaeffer, Elissa, Ch Serv Librn, Brighton Memorial Library, 2300 Elmwood Ave, Rochester, NY, 14618. Tel: 585-784-5300. p. 1628
Schaeffer, John, Chief Info Security Officer, Dir Network, Servers and Security, Connecticut College, 270 Mohegan Ave, New London, CT, 06320-4196. Tel: 860-439-2655. p. 328
Schaeffer, Kelly, Coordr, Cornell University Library, Adelson Library, Laboratory of Ornithology, 159 Sapsucker Woods Rd, Ithaca, NY, 14850-1999. Tel: 607-254-2165. p. 1551
Schaeffer, Laurie, Assoc Chief Info Officer, Connecticut College, 270 Mohegan Ave, New London, CT, 06320-4196. Tel: 860-439-2655. p. 328
Schaeffer, Lyndsey, Librn, OhioHealth Grant Medical Center, 340 E Town St, Ste 7-200, 7th flr, Columbus, OH, 43215. Tel: 614-566-9467, 614-566-9468. p. 1777
Schaeffer, Stuart, Head, Ref, Farmingdale Public Library, 116 Merritts Rd, Farmingdale, NY, 11735. Tel: 516-249-9090, Ext 203. p. 1532
Schaefferkoetter, Robin, Br Mgr, Scenic Regional Library, Warrenton Branch, 912 S Hwy 47, Warrenton, MO, 63383. Tel: 636-456-3321. p. 1283
Schaefgen, Susan M, Dir, Libr Serv, Porter, Wright, Morris & Arthur, LLP, Huntington Ctr, 41 S High St, Columbus, OH, 43215-6194. p. 1777
Schaepperkoetter, Kelsey, Libr Dir, Nashville Public Library, 219 E Elm St, Nashville, IL, 62263. Tel: 618-327-3827. p. 623
Schafer, Allison, Resource Sharing Circulation Specialist, Bellevue University, 1028 Bruin Blvd, Bellevue, NE, 68005. Tel: 402-557-7314. p. 1308
Schafer, Andrew, Digital Coll Librn, State Library of Kansas, 300 SW Tenth Ave, Rm 312-N, Topeka, KS, 66612-1593. Tel: 785-296-8152. p. 2765
Schafer, Andy, Dir, Statewide Libr Serv, State Library of Kansas, State Capitol Bldg, Rm 312-N, 300 SW Tenth Ave, Topeka, KS, 66612. Tel: 785-296-3296. p. 839
Schafer, Bethany, Librn, Lidgerwood City Library, 15 Wiley Ave N, Lidgerwood, ND, 58053. Tel: 701-538-4669. p. 1737
Schafer, Crystal, Dir, Prescott Public Library, 607 Second St, Prescott, IA, 50859-0177. Tel: 641-335-2238. p. 777
Schafer, Curtis, Dir, Arcanum Public Library, 101 W North St, Arcanum, OH, 45304-1185. Tel: 937-692-8484. p. 1746
Schafer, Curtis, Chair, Consortium of Ohio Libraries, 1500 W Lane Ave, Columbus, OH, 43221. Tel: 614-484-1061. p. 2772
Schafer, Elyshia, Dir, Hopkins Public Library, 118 E Main St, Hopkins, MI, 49328-0366. Tel: 269-793-7516. p. 1116
Schafer, Jason, Ser & Electronic Res Librn, Cleveland Museum of Art, 11150 East Blvd, Cleveland, OH, 44106-1797. Tel: 216-707-2530. p. 1767
Schafer, Jessica, Adult Serv, Asst Dir, West Branch Public Library, 300 N Downey, West Branch, IA, 52358. Tel: 319-643-2633. p. 790

Schafer, Johnny, Ref (Info Servs), Howard County Library, 500 Main St, Big Spring, TX, 79720. Tel: 432-264-2260. p. 2148

Schafer, Juliane, Ch, Morton Township Library, 110 S James, Mecosta, MI, 49332-9334. Tel: 231-972-8315, Ext 209. p. 1131

Schafer, Kristin, Libr Mgr, Lidgerwood City Library, 15 Wiley Ave N, Lidgerwood, ND, 58053. Tel: 701-538-4669. p. 1737

Schafer, Laura, Librn, Northwest Regional Library, Red Lake Falls Public Library, 105 Champagne Ave SW, Red Lake Falls, MN, 56750. Tel: 218-253-2992. p. 1205

Schafer, Mindy, Circ Serv, Libr Asst III, DeWitt District Library, 13101 Schavey Rd, DeWitt, MI, 48820-9008. Tel: 517-669-3156. p. 1100

Schafer, Ron, Library Contact, Nevada Department of Corrections, Ely State Prison Library, 4569 N State Rte 490, Ely, NV, 89301. Tel: 775-289-8800, Ext 2244. p. 1345

Schafer, Ruth, Commun Librn, Fort Vancouver Regional Library District, White Salmon Valley Community Library, 77 NE Wauna Ave, White Salmon, WA, 98672. Tel: 509-493-1132. p. 2391

Schaff, Kimberly, Dir, Oak Park Public Library, 14200 Oak Park Blvd, Oak Park, MI, 48237-2089. Tel: 248-691-7480. p. 1138

Schaffer, Gary, Dir, Libr, Arts & Culture, Glendale Library, Arts & Culture, 222 E Harvard St, Glendale, CA, 91205. Tel: 818-548-2021. p. 148

Schaffer, Janette, Asst State Librn, State of Vermont Department of Libraries, 60 Washington St, Ste 2, Barre, VT, 05641. Tel: 802-636-0040. p. 2278

Schaffer, Marysue, Assoc Dir, Coll Mgt, Washington University Libraries, Bernard Becker Medical Library, 660 S Euclid Ave, Campus Box 8132, Saint Louis, MO, 63110. Tel: 314-362-0997. p. 1277

Schaffer, Steve, Asst Archivist, Milwaukee County Historical Society, 910 N Old World Third St, Milwaukee, WI, 53203. Tel: 414-273-7487, 414-273-8288. p. 2459

Schaffner, Brad, Librn, Carleton College, One N College St, Northfield, MN, 55057-4097. Tel: 507-222-4267. p. 1191

Schaffner, Jane, Dir, McComb Public Library, 113 S Todd St, McComb, OH, 45858. Tel: 419-293-2425. p. 1801

Schaffrick, Rebecca, Head Librn, Plymouth Library Association, 692 Main St, Plymouth, CT, 06782. Tel: 860-283-5977. p. 334

Schaffter, David A., Assoc Dir, Tech Serv, United States Air Force Academy Libraries, 2354 Fairchild Dr, Ste 3A15, USAF Academy, CO, 80840-6214. Tel: 719-333-4406. p. 297

Schaible, Fran, Tech Serv Mgr, Cherry Valley Public Library District, 755 E State St, Cherry Valley, IL, 61016-9699. Tel: 815-332-5161, Ext 32. p. 553

Schalk Bjornson, Bonita, Mgr, The King's University, 9125 50th St, Edmonton, AB, T6B 2H3, CANADA. Tel: 780-465-8304. p. 2537

Schallenberger, Melissa, Asst Librn, Centuria Public Library, 409 Fourth St, Centuria, WI, 54824-7468. Tel: 715-646-2630. p. 2427

Schaller, Kati, Educ Librn, Res & Instruction Librn, University of Wisconsin-Eau Claire, 103 Garfield Ave, Eau Claire, WI, 54701-4932. Tel: 715-836-4522. p. 2433

Schaller, Phil, Ref Serv Librn, Berry College, 2277 Martha Berry Hwy, Mount Berry, GA, 30149. Tel: 706-233-4093. p. 492

Schalm, Colleen, Mgr, Parkland Regional Library-Alberta, 5404 56th Ave, Lacombe, AB, T4L 1G1, CANADA. Tel: 403-782-3850. p. 2545

Schambow, Betty, Dir, Allen Dietzman Library, 220 W Barber Ave, Livingston, WI, 53554. Tel: 608-943-6801. p. 2448

Schander, Deborah, State Librn, Connecticut State Library, 231 Capitol Ave, Hartford, CT, 06106. Tel: 860-757-6500. p. 317

Schander, Deborah, Assoc Prof of Law, Dir, Law Libr, Seton Hall University School of Law, One Newark Ctr, Newark, NJ, 07102. Tel: 973-642-8773. p. 1428

Schanely, Carissa, Dir, Collingswood Public Library, 771 Haddon Ave, Collingswood, NJ, 08108. Tel: 856-858-0649. p. 1397

Schanock, Carly, Clinical Serv Librn, Medical College of Wisconsin Libraries, Froedtert Hospital Library, Froedtert Specialty Clinics Bldg, 2nd Flr, 9200 W Wisconsin Ave, Milwaukee, WI, 53226. Tel: 414-805-4311. p. 2459

Schapiro, Katya, Dir, Emily Williston Memorial Library, Nine Park St, Easthampton, MA, 01027. Tel: 413-527-1031. p. 1016

Schapiro, Moshe, Ref Librn, Yeshiva University Libraries, Mendel Gottesman Library of Hebraica-Judaica, 2520 Amsterdam Ave, New York, NY, 10033. Tel: 646-592-4190. p. 1604

Schappert, David, Libr Dir, King's College, 14 W Jackson St, Wilkes-Barre, PA, 18711. Tel: 570-208-5944. p. 2022

Scharcklet, Lakreasha, Libr Assoc, Union University, 1050 Union University Dr, Jackson, TN, 38305-3697. Tel: 731-661-5070. p. 2102

Schard, Robin, Dir, University of Miami, 1311 Miller Dr, Coral Gables, FL, 33146. Tel: 305-284-2251. p. 390

Schardt, Jan, Disability Serv Librn, Napa Valley College, 1700 Bldg, 2277 Napa-Vallejo Hwy, Napa, CA, 94558. Tel: 707-256-7412. p. 182

Schardt, Jill, Dir, Edwardsville Public Library, 112 S Kansas St, Edwardsville, IL, 62025. Tel: 618-692-7556. p. 581

Scharf, Davida, Dir, Ref, New Jersey Institute of Technology, 186 Central Ave, Newark, NJ, 07103. Tel: 973-596-4397. p. 1426

Scharf, Emily, Head, Ref & Instruction, Carleton College, One N College St, Northfield, MN, 55057-4097. Tel: 507-222-5304. p. 1191

Schattle, Ann, Libr Tech, Mattapoisett Free Public Library, Seven Barstow St, Mattapoisett, MA, 02739-0475. Tel: 508-758-4171. p. 1033

Schatvet, Susan, Dir, Seabrook Library, 25 Liberty Lane, Seabrook, NH, 03874-4506. Tel: 603-474-2044. p. 1381

Schatzke, Bethany, Libr Assoc, Rocky Mountain College, 1511 Poly Dr, Billings, MT, 59102-1796. Tel: 406-657-1087. p. 1288

Schaub, Denis, Libr Dir, Wagner College, One Campus Rd, Staten Island, NY, 10301. Tel: 718-390-3378. p. 1645

Schaub, Emily, Co-Dir, Peru Public Library, 1409 11th St, Peru, IL, 61354. Tel: 815-223-0229. p. 635

Schaub, Mary-Elizabeth, Head Librn, Dominican College Library, 480 Western Hwy, Blauvelt, NY, 10913-2000. Tel: 845-848-7500. p. 1494

Schaubhut, Diana, Libr Dir, University of Holy Cross, 4123 Woodland Dr, New Orleans, LA, 70131. Tel: 504-398-2103. p. 904

Schaubhut, Diana, Chair, Health Sciences Library Association of Louisiana, c/o National World War II Museum Library, 945 New Orleans, Shreveport, LA, 70130. Tel: 318-675-5679. p. 2766

Schauntz, Brittany, Br Supvr, Wellington County Library, Puslinch Branch, 29 Brock Rd S, Puslinch, ON, N0B 2J0, CANADA. Tel: 519-763-8026. p. 2641

Schauppeet, Sallie, Br Mgr, Beaufort, Hyde & Martin County Regional Library, Robersonville Public, 119 S Main St, Robersonville, NC, 27871. Tel: 252-508-0342. p. 1720

Schaus, Margaret, Lead Res & Instruction Librn, Haverford College, 370 Lancaster Ave, Haverford, PA, 19041-1392. Tel: 610-896-1166. p. 1942

Schautteet, Sallie, Libr Mgr, Robersonville Public Library, 119 S Main St, Robersonville, NC, 27871. Tel: 252-508-0342. p. 1713

Schawang, Hope, Dir, The Falls City Library & Arts Center, 1400 Stone St, Falls City, NE, 68355. Tel: 402-245-2913. p. 1314

Schechinger, Elizabeth, Ad, Harlan Community Library, 718 Court St, Harlan, IA, 51537. Tel: 712-755-5934. p. 757

Schechter, Carol, Med Librn, St Jude Medical Center, 101 E Valencia Mesa Dr, Fullerton, CA, 92835. Tel: 714-992-3000, Ext 3708. p. 148

Schechter, Steven, Dir, Govt & Commun Affairs, Brooklyn Public Library, Ten Grand Army Plaza, Brooklyn, NY, 11238. Tel: 718-230-2100. p. 1502

Schecter, Karen, Chief Librn, Smiths Falls Public Library, 81 Beckwith St N, Smiths Falls, ON, K7A 2B9, CANADA. Tel: 613-283-2911. p. 2678

Scheer, Frank R, Dr, Curator, Pres, Railway Mail Service Library, Inc, 117 E Main St, Boyce, VA, 22620-9639. Tel: 540-837-9090. p. 2308

Scheer, John, Tech Serv Librn, Willard Library of Evansville, 21 First Ave, Evansville, IN, 47710-1294. Tel: 812-425-4309. p. 682

Scheeren, Jyna, Prog Coordr, Manatee County Public Library System, 1301 Barcarrota Blvd W, Bradenton, FL, 34205-7522. Tel: 941-748-5555, Ext 6308. p. 386

Scheeren, Melissa, Research Librn, University of Virginia, Arthur J Morris Law Library, 580 Massie Rd, Charlottesville, VA, 22903-1738. Tel: 434-924-3495. p. 2310

Scheetz, Anita A, Dir, Fort Peck Community College Library, 604 Assiniboine Ave, Poplar, MT, 59255. Tel: 406-768-6340. p. 1301

Scheffler, Bridget, Libr Dir, El Reno Carnegie Library, 215 E Wade St, El Reno, OK, 73036-2753. Tel: 405-262-2409. p. 1846

Scheg, Mary Clare, Supvr, Rochester Public Library, Monroe, 809 Monroe Ave, Rochester, NY, 14607. Tel: 585-428-8202. p. 1630

Scheiberg, Susan, Assoc Dir, RAND Corporation Library, 1776 Main St, M1LIB, Santa Monica, CA, 90407. Tel: 310-393-0411, Ext 7788. p. 244

Scheibler, Molly, Youth Serv Mgr, Indian Trails Public Library District, 355 S Schoenbeck Rd, Wheeling, IL, 60090. Tel: 847-459-4100. p. 662

Scheid, Kate, Youth Serv Mgr, Brandon Township Public Library, 304 South St, Ortonville, MI, 48462. Tel: 248-627-1473. p. 1139

Scheid, Kristofer, Ref (Info Servs), Hamline University, Bush Memorial Library, 1536 Hewitt, Saint Paul, MN, 55104. Tel: 651-523-2375. p. 1199

Scheidler, Ann, VPres, Pro-Life Action League Library, 6160 N Cicero Ave, Ste 600, Chicago, IL, 60646. Tel: 773-777-2900. p. 567

Scheidler, Joe, Dir, Pro-Life Action League Library, 6160 N Cicero Ave, Ste 600, Chicago, IL, 60646. Tel: 773-777-2900. p. 567

Scheielberg, Nicole, Librn, Prog Mgr, United States Department of Justice, National Institute of Corrections Information Ctr, 11900 E Cornell Ave, Unit C, Aurora, CO, 80014. Tel: 303-338-6648. p. 265

Scheier, Robert, Syst, College of the Holy Cross, One College St, Worcester, MA, 01610. Tel: 508-793-3495. p. 1072

Schein, Cindi, Asst Librn, Galesville Public Library, 16787 S Main St, Galesville, WI, 54630. Tel: 608-582-2552. p. 2436

Scheiner, Meredith, Head, Circ, Head, YA, Supv Libr Asst, Fanwood Memorial Library, Five Forest Rd, Fanwood, NJ, 07023. Tel: 908-322-6400. p. 1402

Schell, Jennifer, Assoc Mgr, Edmonton Public Library, Mill Woods, 2610 Hewes Way, Edmonton, AB, T6L 0A9, CANADA. Tel: 780-496-7842. p. 2537

Schell, Michael, Syst Adminr, Fort Erie Public Library, 136 Gilmore Rd, Fort Erie, ON, L2A 2M1, CANADA. Tel: 905-871-2546, Ext 301. p. 2642

Schellenberg, Tammy, Head Librn, La Crete Community Library, 10102 100 Ave, La Crete, AB, T0H 2H0, CANADA. Tel: 780-928-3166. p. 2544

Schelleng, Jessica, Ref Librn, Pamunkey Regional Library, 7527 Library Dr, Hanover, VA, 23069. Tel: 804-537-6211. p. 2323
Schellenger, Sarah, Br Mgr, Public Library of Cincinnati & Hamilton County, Northside, 4219 Hamilton Ave, Cincinnati, OH, 45223. Tel: 513-369-4449. p. 1763
Schellinger, Jana, Health Sci Librn, Emory & Henry College, 30480 Armbrister Dr, Emory, VA, 24327. Tel: 276-944-6208. p. 2315
Schembri, Elizabeth, Ref & Instruction, Sheridan College Library, Hazel McCallion Campus, 4180 Duke of York Blvd, Mississauga, ON, L5B 0G5, CANADA. Tel: 905-845-9430, Ext 2467. p. 2663
Schemm, Karyn, Asst Dir, Andover Public Library, 1511 E Central Ave, Andover, KS, 67002. Tel: 316-558-3500. p. 796
Schemrich, Pam, Br Mgr, Wayne County Public Library, Rittman Branch, 49 W Ohio Ave, Rittman, OH, 44270. Tel: 330-925-2761. p. 1833
Schena, Judith, Libr Asst, North Shore Community College Library, One Ferncroft Rd, Danvers Campus Library, Danvers, MA, 01923-4093. Tel: 978-739-5412. p. 1013
Schenk, Joseph, Dir, Texas A&M University-Corpus Christi, Art Museum of South Texas Library, 1902 N Shoreline, Corpus Christi, TX, 78401-1164. Tel: 361-825-3500. p. 2161
Schenkel, Hunt, Archivist, Schwenkfelder Library & Heritage Center, 105 Seminary St, Pennsburg, PA, 18073. Tel: 215-679-3103, Ext 13. p. 1974
Schenkel, Nick, Dir, West Lafayette Public Library, 208 W Columbia St, West Lafayette, IN, 47906. Tel: 765-743-2261. p. 726
Scheppke, Jane, Asst Dir, Crook County Library, 175 NW Meadow Lakes Dr, Prineville, OR, 97754. Tel: 541-447-7978, Ext 303. p. 1895
Scher, Adam, VPres, Coll, Virginia Historical Society Library, 428 North Blvd, Richmond, VA, 23220. Tel: 804-340-1800. p. 2344
Scherb, Meredith, Knowledge Mgmt & Operations Specialist, Drake University, 2725 University Ave, Des Moines, IA, 50311. Tel: 515-271-2119. p. 746
Scherber, Marla, Libr Serv Coordr, Great River Regional Library, Monticello Library, 200 W Sixth St, Monticello, MN, 55362-8832. Tel: 763-295-2322. p. 1197
Scherer, Helga, Head, Tech Serv, Morton Grove Public Library, 6140 Lincoln Ave, Morton Grove, IL, 60053-2989. Tel: 847-965-4220. p. 620
Scherer, Irene, Head, Pub Serv, Community Library, 24615 89th St, Salem, WI, 53168. Tel: 262-843-3348. p. 2475
Scherer, Janet, Dir, South Huntington Public Library, 145 Pidgeon Hill Rd, Huntington Station, NY, 11746. Tel: 631-549-4411. p. 1549
Scherer, Kristi, Dir, Creston-Dement Public Library District, 107 S Main St, Creston, IL, 60113-0056. Tel: 815-384-3111. p. 574
Scherer, Nicole, Asst Dir, Nassau Library System, 900 Jerusalem Ave, Uniondale, NY, 11553-3039. Tel: 516-292-8920. p. 1654
Scherf, Scott, Dir, Kaubisch Memorial Public Library, 205 Perry St, Fostoria, OH, 44830-2265. Tel: 419-435-2813. p. 1786
Scherger, Jonathan, User Serv Librn, Western Michigan University, 1903 W Michigan Ave, WMU Mail Stop 5353, Kalamazoo, MI, 49008-5353. Tel: 269-387-5881. p. 1122
Schermeister-Simons, Christal, Dir, Presque Isle Community Library, 8306 School Loop Rd, Presque Isle, WI, 54557. Tel: 715-686-7613. p. 2471
Schermerhorn, Steve, Syst Librn, Tech Serv Coordr, San Joaquin Delta College, 5151 Pacific Ave, Stockton, CA, 95207. Tel: 209-954-5152. p. 249
Scherrer, John, Fac Serv Librn, Ref, George Mason University Libraries, Law Library, 3301 N Fairfax Dr, Arlington, VA, 22201-4426. Tel: 703-993-8100. p. 2317
Scherry, Rejoice, Spec Coll Librn, Univ Archivist, Delaware State University, 1200 N Dupont Hwy, Dover, DE, 19901-2277. Tel: 302-857-6130. p. 352
Scherzinger, Christine, Dir, Libr & Res Serv, Duane Morris LLP Library, 30 S 17th St, Philadelphia, PA, 19103-4196. Tel: 215-979-1000, 215-979-1720. p. 1977
Schettler, Holly, Ref & Instruction Librn, Morningside University, 1501 Morningside Ave, Sioux City, IA, 51106. Tel: 712-274-5246. p. 782
Schettler, Holly, Library Liaison, Research Librn, Buena Vista University Library, H W Siebens School of Business/Forum, 610 W Fourth St, Storm Lake, IA, 50588. Tel: 712-749-2089. p. 784
Scheu, Allison, Br Mgr, Waco-McLennan County Library System, West Waco Library & Genealogy Center, 5301 Bosque Blvd, Ste 275, Waco, TX, 76710. Tel: 254-750-5975. p. 2254
Scheu, Jonathan, Dir, Carrollton Public Library, 1700 N Keller Springs Rd, Carrollton, TX, 75006. Tel: 972-466-3362. p. 2153
Scheuerman, Jeff, Finance Mgr, Naperville Public Library, Naper Boulevard, 2035 S Naper Blvd, Naperville, IL, 60565-3353. Tel: 630-961-4100, Ext 2228. p. 623
Scheuher, Joel, Fac Res Serv/Ref Serv Librn, University of Michigan, Kresge Library Services, Stephen M Ross School of Business, 701 Tappan St, Ann Arbor, MI, 48109-1234. Tel: 734-647-0469. p. 1079
Scheuler, Steven, Circ, Lending Serv Coordr, Valdosta State University, 1500 N Patterson St, Valdosta, GA, 31698-0150. Tel: 229-259-5363. p. 501
Scheuring, Lynnette, Librn, Hankinson Public Library, 319 Main Ave S, Hankinson, ND, 58041. Tel: 701-242-7929. p. 1735
Schewe, Judy, Libr Dir, Naples Library, 118 S Main, Naples, NY, 14512. Tel: 585-374-2757. p. 1575
Schiappacasse, Angie, Pub Serv Librn, University of Wisconsin-Madison, MERIT Library (Media, Education Resources & Information Technology), 368 Teacher Education Bldg, 225 N Mills St, Madison, WI, 53706. Tel: 608-262-9950. p. 2451
Schiavo, Julie, Asst Dir, Louisiana State University Health Sciences Center, 433 Bolivar St, Box B3-1, New Orleans, LA, 70112-2223. Tel: 504-941-8162. p. 901
Schiavo, Julie, Assoc Librn, Louisiana State University Health Sciences Center, School of Dentistry Library, 1100 Florida Ave, New Orleans, LA, 70119. Tel: 504-941-8162. p. 902
Schiavone, Joseph, Commun Libr Mgr, Queens Library, Sunnyside Community Library, 43-06 Greenpoint Ave, Long Island City, NY, 11104. Tel: 718-784-3033. p. 1556
Schick, Brittany, Librn, Dallas College, 5001 N MacArthur Blvd, Irving, TX, 75062. Tel: 972-273-3400. p. 2202
Schieman, Sara, Librn, Mabel C Fry Public Library, 1200 Lakeshore Dr, Yukon, OK, 73099. Tel: 405-354-8232. p. 1870
Schienle, David, Archives Coordr, Catholic Diocese of Fairbanks, Chancery Bldg, 1316 Peger Rd, Fairbanks, AK, 99709-5199. Tel: 907-374-9555. p. 45
Schierhorst, Gisele Ira, Head Librn, Stony Brook University, Music, Melville Library, Rm W1530, Stony Brook, NY, 11794-3333. Tel: 631-632-7097. p. 1647
Schierschmidt, Erin, Librn, Michigan Department of Corrections, N6141 Industrial Park Dr, Munising, MI, 49862. Tel: 906-628-7100. p. 1135
Schieuer, Jane, Librn, Woodbury County Library, Pierson Branch, 201 Main St, Pierson, IA, 51048. Tel: 712-375-7535. p. 772
Schiff, Christopher, Art Librn, Music Librn, Bates College, 48 Campus Ave, Lewiston, ME, 04240. Tel: 207-786-6274. p. 929
Schiffer, Michael, Director, IT & Digital Resources, DePaul University Libraries, Vincent G Rinn Law Library, 25 E Jackson Blvd, 5th Flr, Chicago, IL, 60604-2287. Tel: 312-362-6311. p. 560
Schill, Vicki, Commun Librn, Cariboo Regional District Library, Likely Branch, 6163 Keithly Creek Rd, Likely, BC, V0L 1N0, CANADA. Tel: 250-790-2234. p. 2584
Schillace, Michael, Syst/Tech Serv, Cayuga County Community College, 197 Franklin St, Auburn, NY, 13021. Tel: 315-294-8596. p. 1488
Schiller, Margo, Br Head, Thompson-Nicola Regional District Library System, Kamloops Branch, 100-465 Victoria St, Kamloops, BC, V2C 2A9, CANADA. Tel: 250-372-5145. p. 2567
Schiller, Margo, Br Head, Thompson-Nicola Regional District Library System, North Kamloops Branch, 693 Tranquille Rd, Kamloops, BC, V2B 3H7, CANADA. Tel: 250-554-1124. p. 2567
Schillig, Jennifer E, Ad, Free Public Library of Monroe Township, 713 Marsha Ave, Williamstown, NJ, 08094. Tel: 856-629-1212, Ext 204. p. 1455
Schilling, Amanda, Librn, National Weather Center Library, 120 David L Boren Blvd, Ste 4300, Norman, OK, 73072-7303. Tel: 405-325-1171. p. 1855
Schilling, Dora, Principal Librn, Lee County Library System, Cape Coral-Lee County Public Library, 921 SW 39th Terrace, Cape Coral, FL, 33914-5721. Tel: 239-533-4500. p. 403
Schilling, Evan, Archit Librn, University of Waterloo Library, Musagetes Architecture Library, Seven Melville St S, Cambridge, ON, N1S 2H4, CANADA. Tel: 519-888-4567, Ext 27620. p. 2702
Schilling, Lisa K, Acq Librn, Ref Librn, Neumann University Library, One Neumann Dr, Aston, PA, 19014-1298. Tel: 610-558-5557. p. 1907
Schillinger, Michele, Library Contact, First Congregational Church Library, 128 Central St, Auburn, MA, 01501. Tel: 508-832-2845. p. 987
Schilperoort, Hannah, Head of Libr, University of Southern California Libraries, Jennifer Ann Wilson Dental Library & Learning Center, 925 W 34th St, DEN 21, University Park - MC 0641, Los Angeles, CA, 90089-0641. Tel: 213-740-6476. p. 170
Schiltz, Judy, Adult Serv Spec, Algona Public Library, 210 N Phillips St, Algona, IA, 50511. Tel: 515-295-5476. p. 730
Schimanski-Gross, Suzanne, Ref & Ser Librn, Lawrence Technological University Library, 21000 W Ten Mile Rd, Southfield, MI, 48075-1058. Tel: 248-204-3000. p. 1151
Schimanski-Gross, Suzanne, Treas, Southeastern Michigan League of Libraries, UM-Dearborn Mardigian Library, 4901 Evergreen Rd, Dearborn, MI, 48128. Tel: 313-593-5617. p. 2767
Schimdt, Bart, Digital Projects Librn, Drake University, 2725 University Ave, Des Moines, IA, 50311. Tel: 515-271-2940. p. 746
Schimelman, Ashley, Ch, San Marcos Public Library, 625 E Hopkins, San Marcos, TX, 78666. Tel: 512-393-8200. p. 2241
Schimelpfenig, Robert, Archivist, Washington State University Libraries, 14204 NE Salmon Creek Ave, Vancouver, WA, 98686. Tel: 360-546-9249. p. 2391
Schimizzi, Tony, Cataloger, University of Alabama at Birmingham, Mervyn H Sterne Library, 917 13th St S, Birmingham, AL, 35205. Tel: 205-934-3512. p. 9
Schimpf, Crystal, Dir, Tracy Memorial Library, 304 Main St, New London, NH, 03257-7813. Tel: 603-526-4656. p. 1376
Schindele-Cupples, Carrie, Libr Mgr, Springfield Public Library, 225 Fifth St, Springfield, OR, 97477-4697. Tel: 541-726-3766. p. 1899

Schindler, Amy, Dir, Archives & Spec Coll, University of Nebraska at Omaha, 6001 Dodge St, Omaha, NE, 68182-0237. Tel: 402-554-6046. p. 1330

Schindler, Michelle, Librn, Presho Public Library, 108 N Main Ave, Presho, SD, 57568. Tel: 605-895-2443. p. 2081

Schink, Christy, Assoc Dir of Youth & Outreach Services, Scenic Regional Library, 251 Union Plaza Dr, Union, MO, 63084. Tel: 636-583-0652, Ext 105. p. 1283

Schink, Raechel, Teen Prog Coordr, DeForest Area Public Library, 203 Library St, DeForest, WI, 53532. Tel: 608-846-5482. p. 2430

Schinkai, Adrianne, Head, Circ & Ref, Vicksburg District Library, 215 S Michigan Ave, Vicksburg, MI, 49097. Tel: 269-649-1648. p. 1156

Schipper, Christopher, Dir, Libr Serv, San Juan College Library, 4601 College Blvd, Farmington, NM, 87402. Tel: 505-566-3449. p. 1468

Schipper, Rachel, Dr, Libr Dir, The Society of the Four Arts, 101 Four Arts Plaza, Palm Beach, FL, 33480. Tel: 561-655-2766. p. 434

Schippers, Betsy, Liaison Librn, Outreach Coordr, User Experience Coord, Colorado State University - Pueblo, 2200 Bonforte Blvd, Pueblo, CO, 81001-4901. Tel: 719-549-2826. p. 293

Schira, Rainer, Interim Univ Librn, Brandon University, 270 18th St, Brandon, MB, R7A 6A9, CANADA. p. 2585

Schiraldi, Hilary, Bus Librn, University of California, Berkeley, Thomas J Long Business Library, Haas School of Business, Rm S350, 2220 Piedmont Ave, Berkeley, CA, 94720-6000. Tel: 510-642-0370. p. 123

Schirer-Suter, Myron, Dr, Dir, Libr Serv, Gordon College, 255 Grapevine Rd, Wenham, MA, 01984-1899. Tel: 978-867-4083. p. 1064

Schirmer, Deirdré, Pub Serv Mgr, Wayne Township Library, 80 N Sixth St, Richmond, IN, 47374. Tel: 765-966-8291, Ext 1116. p. 715

Schirmer, Susan, Circ, Beck Bookman Library, 420 W Fourth St, Holton, KS, 66436-1572. Tel: 785-364-3532. p. 813

Schisler, Cheri, Dir, Mulberry Public Library, 905 NE Fifth St, Mulberry, FL, 33860. Tel: 863-425-3246. p. 427

Schissel, Heather, Librn, Farmersburg Public Library, 208 S Main St, Farmersburg, IA, 52047. Tel: 563-536-2229. p. 753

Schkade, Heather, Dir, Breckenridge Library, 209 N Breckenridge Ave, Breckenridge, TX, 76424. Tel: 254-559-5505. p. 2149

Schlaack, Emily, Curric Librn, University of Michigan, Kresge Library Services, Stephen M Ross School of Business, 701 Tappan St, Ann Arbor, MI, 48109-1234. Tel: 734-763-7765. p. 1079

Schlachter, Virginia, ILL Coordr, Mount Prospect Public Library, Ten S Emerson St, Mount Prospect, IL, 60056. Tel: 847-253-5675. p. 621

Schlagel, Nicole, Asst Br Mgr, Mid-Continent Public Library, Midwest Genealogy Center, 3440 S Lee's Summit Rd, Independence, MO, 64055. Tel: 816-252-7228. p. 1251

Schlak, Tim, Dean, Univ Libr, Robert Morris University Library, 6001 University Blvd, Moon Township, PA, 15108-1189. Tel: 412-397-6868. p. 1965

Schlechte, Todd, Asst Dir, Southeast Library System (SLS), 5730 R St, Ste C1, Lincoln, NE, 68505. Tel: 531-530-3010. p. 1323

Schlegel, Carolyn, Librn, Virgil Biegert Public Library, 214 N Market, Shickley, NE, 68436. Tel: 402-627-3365. p. 1336

Schlekau, Linda, Br Mgr, Fairfax County Public Library, Sherwood Regional, 2501 Sherwood Hall Lane, Alexandria, VA, 22306-2799. Tel: 703-765-3645. p. 2316

Schlembach, Mary, Head Librn, University of Illinois Library at Urbana-Champaign, Chemistry, 170 Noyes Lab, MC-712, 505 S Mathews Ave, Urbana, IL, 61801. Tel: 213-333-3158. p. 655

Schlembach, Mary, Chem Librn, Phys Sci Librn, University of Illinois Library at Urbana-Champaign, Geology Virtual Library, 1301 W Springfield Ave, Urbana, IL, 61801. Tel: 217-333-3158. p. 656

Schlembach, Mary, Librn, University of Illinois Library at Urbana-Champaign, Physics-Astronomy Virtual Library, 1301 W Springfield Ave, Urbana, IL, 61801. Tel: 217-333-3158. p. 656

Schleper, Susan, Librn, CentraCare - Saint Cloud Hospital, 1406 Sixth Ave N, Saint Cloud, MN, 56303. Tel: 320-251-2700, Ext 54686. p. 1196

Schleppy, Francesca, Circ Librn, Hampton Falls Free Public Library, Seven Drinkwater Rd, Hampton Falls, NH, 03844. Tel: 603-926-3682. p. 1366

Schlernitzauer, Anna, Dir, Smyrna Public Library, Seven E Main St, Smyrna, NY, 13464. Tel: 607-627-6271. p. 1642

Schlernitzauer, Lori, Tech Serv, Northbrook Public Library, 1201 Cedar Lane, Northbrook, IL, 60062-4581. Tel: 847-272-6224. p. 627

Schlesinger, Kenneth, Chief Librn, Lehman College, City University of New York, 250 Bedford Park Blvd W, Bronx, NY, 10468. Tel: 718-960-8577. p. 1499

Schley, Mackenzie, Asst Dir, Jackson County Library, 311 Third St, Jackson, MN, 56143-1600. Tel: 507-847-4748. p. 1179

Schlicht, Erin, Assoc Circuit Librarian, Library of the US Courts of the Seventh Circuit, 219 S Dearborn St, Rm 1637, Chicago, IL, 60604-1769. Tel: 312-435-5660. p. 563

Schlichte, Kayla, YA Librn, Spencer Public Library, 21 E Third St, Spencer, IA, 51301-4131. Tel: 712-580-7290. p. 783

Schlichter, Marcus, Acq Librn, Archivist, Wayne State College, 1111 Main St, Wayne, NE, 68787. Tel: 402-375-7266. p. 1340

Schlichting, Eunice, Br Librn, Riverside Regional Library, Altenburg Branch, 66 Poplar St, Altenburg, MO, 63732. Tel: 573-824-5267. p. 1252

Schlinck, Olivia Smith, Head of Research Instruction, Yeshiva University Libraries, Dr Lillian & Dr Rebecca Chutick Law Library, Benjamin N Cardozo School of Law, 55 Fifth Ave, New York, NY, 10003-4301. Tel: 212-790-0223. p. 1604

Schlinke, John, Archit/Art Librn, Roger Williams University Library, Architecture, One Old Ferry Rd, Bristol, RI, 02809-2921. Tel: 401-254-3833. p. 2030

Schlinke, John, Archit/Art Librn, Roger Williams University Library, One Old Ferry Rd, Bristol, RI, 02809. Tel: 401-254-3833. p. 2030

Schlipp, John, Intellectual Property Librn, Northern Kentucky University, University Dr, Highland Heights, KY, 41099. Tel: 859-572-5723. p. 859

Schlossberg, Jennifer, Access Serv Librn, Hobart & William Smith Colleges, 334 Pulteney St, Geneva, NY, 14456. Tel: 315-781-3550. p. 1538

Schlotterbeck, Brooke, Dir, Hamilton City Library, 21 E Main St, Hamilton, KS, 66853. Tel: 620-678-3646. p. 811

Schlotzhauer, Nonny, Interim Head of Libr, Pennsylvania State University Libraries, Social Sciences & Education, 208 Paterno Library, 2nd & 5th Flrs, University Park, PA, 16802-1809. Tel: 814-863-4644. p. 2016

Schmalenberg, Mojgan, Mgr, Info Tech, Caledon Public Library, 150 Queen St S, Bolton, ON, L7E 1E3, CANADA. Tel: 905-857-1400, Ext 237. p. 2631

Schmall, Anna, Instruction Librn, Res, Mount Mercy University, 1330 Elmhurst Dr NE, Cedar Rapids, IA, 52402-4797. Tel: 319-368-6465. p. 738

Schmand, Kathleen L, Dean, Middle Tennessee State University, 1611 Alumni Dr, Murfreesboro, TN, 37132. Tel: 615-898-2773. p. 2117

Schmandt, Erin, Dir, Caro Area District Library, 840 W Frank St, Caro, MI, 48723. Tel: 989-673-4329, Ext 102. p. 1088

Schmaus, Meg, Head, Circ, Warren-Newport Public Library District, 224 N O'Plaine Rd, Gurnee, IL, 60031. Tel: 847-244-5150, Ext 3024. p. 596

Schmehl, Charlie, Librn, Urban Research & Development Corp Library, 81 Highland Ave, Ste 120, Bethlehem, PA, 18017. Tel: 610-865-0701. p. 1912

Schmeisser, Kayla, Acq, University of Montana Western, 710 S Atlantic St, Dillon, MT, 59725. Tel: 406-683-7542. p. 1292

Schmenk, Mike, Fiscal Officer, Marysville Public Library, 231 S Plum St, Marysville, OH, 43040-1596. Tel: 937-642-1876, Ext 30. p. 1800

Schmersal, David, Ref & Digital Librn, Southern Methodist University, Bridwell Library-Perkins School of Theology, 6005 Bishop Blvd, Dallas, TX, 75205. Tel: 214-768-3483. p. 2167

Schmid, Allison, Tech Serv Mgr, Bloomington Public Library, 205 E Olive St, Bloomington, IL, 61701. Tel: 309-828-6091. p. 543

Schmid, Ellen, Law Librn, Kane County Law Library & Self Help Legal Center, Kane County Judicial Ctr, 2nd Flr, 37W777W IL Rte 38, Saint Charles, IL, 60175. Tel: 630-406-7126. p. 644

Schmid, Jena, Asst Dir, Main Libr, Nashville Public Library, 615 Church St, Nashville, TN, 37219-2314. Tel: 615-862-5806. p. 2119

Schmid, Kay, Exec Dir, Roman L & Victoria E Hruska Memorial Public Library, 399 N Fifth St, David City, NE, 68632. Tel: 402-367-3100. p. 1312

Schmid, Kim, Co-Dir, Cedar County Library District, 717 East St, Stockton, MO, 65785. Tel: 417-276-3413. p. 1282

Schmid, Patti, Head Librn, Rowan College of South Jersey, 3322 College Dr, Vineland, NJ, 08360. Tel: 856-200-4624. p. 1450

Schmid, Peter F, Visual Res Archivist, Providence Archives, 4800 37th Ave SW, Seattle, WA, 98126. Tel: 206-923-4012. p. 2378

Schmid, Taryn, Campus Librn, Okanagan College Library, Salmon Arm Campus, 2552 Tenth Ave NE (THC), Salmon Arm, BC, V1E 2S4, CANADA. Tel: 250-804-8851, Ext 8253. p. 2568

Schmidkunz, Linnett, Libr Assoc, North Dakota State University Libraries, 1201 Albrecht Blvd, Fargo, ND, 58108. Tel: 701-231-8888. p. 1733

Schmidkunz, Linnette, Libr Assoc, North Dakota State University Libraries, Sanford Health Library, Sudro Hall 136, 512 N Seventh St, Bismarck, ND, 58501. Tel: 791-224-3835. p. 1733

Schmidlen, Roberta, Ad, Saint Albans Free Library, 11 Maiden Lane, Saint Albans, VT, 05478. Tel: 802-524-1507. p. 2293

Schmidt, Amy, Br Mgr, Walla Walla County Rural Library District, Burbank Library, 875 Lake Rd, Burbank, WA, 99323. Tel: 509-545-6549. p. 2392

Schmidt, Angela, Film Archivist, University of Alaska Fairbanks, 1732 Tanana Dr, Fairbanks, AK, 99775. Tel: 907-474-5357. p. 45

Schmidt, Carol, Educ Serv, Bryn Mawr Presbyterian Church, 625 Montgomery Ave, Bryn Mawr, PA, 19010-3599. Tel: 610-525-2821. p. 1916

Schmidt, Catherine, Asst Dir, Shelby Township Library, 51680 Van Dyke, Shelby Township, MI, 48316-4448. Tel: 586-739-7414. p. 1150

Schmidt, Dana, Libr Dir, Yankton Community Library, 515 Walnut St, Yankton, SD, 57078. Tel: 605-668-5275. p. 2086

Schmidt, Dara, Libr Dir, Cedar Rapids Public Library, 3750 Williams Blvd SW, Cedar Rapids, IA, 52404. Tel: 319-398-5123. p. 738

Schmidt, Denise, Bus Mgr, Kinchafoonee Regional Library System, 913 Forrester Dr SE, Dawson, GA, 39842-2106. Tel: 229-995-6331. p. 474

Schmidt, Doreen, Br Mgr, Prairie-River Library District, Craigmont Community, 113 W Main St, Craigmont, ID, 83523-9700. Tel: 208-924-5510. p. 524

Schmidt, Doreen, Br Mgr, Prairie-River Library District, Peck Community, 217 N Main St, Peck, ID, 83545. Tel: 208-486-6161. p. 524

Schmidt, Elizabeth, Ref Serv, Wright Memorial Public Library, 1776 Far Hills Ave, Oakwood, OH, 45419-2598. Tel: 937-294-7171. p. 1810

Schmidt, Evelyn, Cat, Orem Public Library, 58 N State St, Orem, UT, 84057. Tel: 801-229-7050. p. 2268

Schmidt, Hannah, Circ Coordr, Milwaukee Institute of Art & Design Library & Learning Commons, 273 E Erie St, Milwaukee, WI, 53202-6003. Tel: 414-847-3342. p. 2459

Schmidt, Janice, Dir, Stanislaus County Law Library, 1101 13th St, Modesto, CA, 95354. Tel: 209-558-7759. p. 178

Schmidt, Jen, Communications Mgr, Develop Mgr, Indian Trails Public Library District, 355 S Schoenbeck Rd, Wheeling, IL, 60090. Tel: 847-459-4100. p. 662

Schmidt, Jennifer Gauthier, Access Serv Librn, South Louisiana Community College-Lafayette Campus, Devalcourt Bldg, 1st Flr, 1101 Bertrand Dr, Lafayette, LA, 70506. Tel: 337-521-8935. p. 893

Schmidt, Jim, Assoc Dir, Springfield-Greene County Library District, 4653 S Campbell Ave, Springfield, MO, 65810-1723. Tel: 417-882-0714. p. 1281

Schmidt, Kari, Assoc Dir, Coll, Assoc Dir, Resources, Montgomery College Library, 51 Mannakee St, Macklin Tower, Rockville, MD, 20850. Tel: 240-567-4135. p. 973

Schmidt, Kristen, Actg Br Mgr, Cleveland Public Library, Harvard-Lee, 16918 Harvard Ave, Cleveland, OH, 44128. Tel: 216-623-6990. p. 1768

Schmidt, Larry, Chair, Res & Instrul Serv, Support Librn, University of Wyoming Libraries, Brinkerhoff Geology Library (Brinkerhoff Earth Resources Information Center), Geology Bldg, Rm 121, 121 SH Knight, Laramie, WY, 82071. Tel: 307-766-2844. p. 2497

Schmidt, Larry, Research & Instruction Services, University of Wyoming Libraries, Rocky Mountain Herbarium Reference Collection, Aven Nelson Bldg, 3rd Flr, 1000 E University Ave, Laramie, WY, 82071. Tel: 307-766-2844. p. 2497

Schmidt, Lili, Libr Dir, Milton-Freewater Public Library, Eight SW Eighth Ave, Milton-Freewater, OR, 97862. Tel: 541-938-8247. p. 1887

Schmidt, Lydia, Youth Serv Librn, Hackley Public Library, 316 W Webster Ave, Muskegon, MI, 49440. Tel: 231-722-8013. p. 1135

Schmidt, Mark, Exec Dir, Falmouth Historical Society & Museums on the Green, 65 Palmer Ave, Falmouth, MA, 02540. Tel: 508-548-4857. p. 1018

Schmidt, Martin, Ref Librn, Maharishi International University Library, 1000 N Fourth St, Fairfield, IA, 52557. Tel: 641-472-1148. p. 752

Schmidt, Myra, Librn, Nipawin Bible College Library, Hwy 35 S, Nipawin, SK, S0E 1E0, CANADA. Tel: 306-862-5095. p. 2743

Schmidt, Nancy, Coordr, South Central Federation, 720 W Third St, Laurel, MT, 59044. Tel: 406-628-4961. p. 1298

Schmidt, Nancy L, Libr Dir, Laurel Public Library, 720 W Third St, Laurel, MT, 59044. Tel: 406-628-4961. p. 1298

Schmidt, Renee, Syst/Tech Serv, Cayuga County Community College, 197 Franklin St, Auburn, NY, 13021. Tel: 315-294-8596. p. 1488

Schmidt, Rhonda, Libr Mgr, Western Plains Library System, Cordell Public Library, 208 S College, Cordell, OK, 73632-5210. Tel: 580-832-3530. p. 1845

Schmidt, Rich, Dir, Archives & Info Resources, Linfield University, 900 SE Baker St, McMinnville, OR, 97128. Tel: 508-883-2734. p. 1885

Schmidt, Rita, Dir, Fort Dodge Public Library, 424 Central Ave, Fort Dodge, IA, 50501. Tel: 515-573-8167, Ext 6229. p. 754

Schmidt, Ronna, Libr Dir, Greeley County Library, 517 Broadway, Tribune, KS, 67879. Tel: 620-376-4801. p. 840

Schmidt, Rosa, Dir, Oakland Public Library, 110 E Third St, Oakland, NE, 68045-1356. Tel: 402-685-5113. p. 1327

Schmidt, Sabine, Libr Dir, St Paul Public Library, 145 Fifth St, Saint Paul, AR, 72760. Tel: 479-677-2907. p. 109

Schmidt, Sarah, Chair, Libr Serv, Res & Instruction Librn, Keyano College Library, 8115 Franklin Ave, Fort McMurray, AB, T9H 2H7, CANADA. Tel: 780-791-8911. p. 2540

Schmidt, Shannon, Head, Support Serv, Orion Township Public Library, 825 Joslyn Rd, Lake Orion, MI, 48362. Tel: 248-693-3000, Ext 402. p. 1123

Schmidt, Stacie, Ref & Instruction Librn, Biola University Library, 13800 Biola Ave, La Mirada, CA, 90639. Tel: 562-944-0351, Ext 5154. p. 155

Schmidt, Stephanie, Dir, Crandon Public Library, 110 W Polk St, Crandon, WI, 54520-1458. Tel: 715-478-3784. p. 2429

Schmidtgall, Kathleen, Librn, Weston Public Library, 108 E Main St, Weston, OR, 97886. Tel: 541-566-2378. p. 1902

Schmidtke, David, Dep Dir, Minnesota Legislative Reference Library, 645 State Office Bldg, 100 Rev Dr Martin Luther King Jr Blvd, Saint Paul, MN, 55155-1050. Tel: 651-215-9058. p. 1201

Schmidtke, Emma, Research & Education Librn, Western Colorado University, One Western Way, Gunnison, CO, 81231. Tel: 970-943-2898. p. 285

Schmiedel, Tom, Educ Librn, Pub Serv, Western Connecticut State University, 181 White St, Danbury, CT, 06810. Tel: 203-837-9100. p. 307

Schmiedicke, Laura, Adult Serv, Monroe Public Library, 925 16th Ave, Monroe, WI, 53566-1497. Tel: 608-328-7010. p. 2462

Schmitt, Carol J, Info Res Mgr, Reinhart Boerner Van Deuren SC, 1000 N Water St, Ste 1700, Milwaukee, WI, 53202. Tel: 608-229-2232. p. 2461

Schmitt, Rebecca, Library Contact, Osterhout Free Library, South, Two Airy St, Wilkes-Barre, PA, 18702. Tel: 570-823-5544. p. 2022

Schmitt, Stephanie, Head, Tech Serv, University of California, 200 McAllister St, San Francisco, CA, 94102-4978. Tel: 415-565-4757. p. 229

Schmittle, Lisa, Mgr, York County Library System, Dover Area Community Library, 3700-3 Davidsburg Rd, Dover, PA, 17315. Tel: 717-292-6814. p. 2026

Schmitz, Gail, Circ, Beck Bookman Library, 420 W Fourth St, Holton, KS, 66436-1572. Tel: 785-364-3532. p. 813

Schmitz, Julie, Assoc Dir, Human Res, Great River Regional Library, 1300 W St Germain St, Saint Cloud, MN, 56301. Tel: 320-650-2511. p. 1196

Schmitz, Kris, Central Servs Mgr, Montana State Library, 1515 E Sixth Ave, Helena, MT, 59620. Tel: 406-444-3117. p. 1296

Schmitz-Garrett, Susan, Libr Dir, Security Public Library, 715 Aspen Dr, Security, CO, 80911-1807. Tel: 719-390-2814. p. 295

Schmitzer, Debra, Br Mgr, Cabarrus County Public Library, Kannapolis Branch, 850 Mountain St, Kannapolis, NC, 28081. Tel: 704-920-2303. p. 1682

Schmoyer, Katie, Dir, Winnebago Public Library District, 210 N Elida St, Winnebago, IL, 61088. Tel: 815-335-7050. p. 664

Schmukal, Marie, Dir, Warren Public Library, 413 Main St, Warren, VT, 05674. Tel: 802-496-3913. p. 2297

Schmuland, Arlene, Head, Archives & Spec Coll, University of Alaska Anchorage, Consortium Library, 3211 Providence Dr, Anchorage, AK, 99508-8176. Tel: 907-786-1849. p. 43

Schnack, Allison, Librn, Claud H Gilmer Memorial Library, 201 N Hwy 377, Rocksprings, TX, 78880. Tel: 830-683-8130. p. 2234

Schnackenberg, Janell, Cat Librn, Museum of Flight, 9404 E Marginal Way S, Seattle, WA, 98108-4097. Tel: 206-764-5700. p. 2377

Schnackenberg, Laura, Hed, Bkmobile Dept, Washington County Free Library, 100 S Potomac St, Hagerstown, MD, 21740. Tel: 301-739-3250. p. 968

Schnacky, Kati, Coordr, ILL, Rice Lake Public Library, Two E Marshall St, Rice Lake, WI, 54868. Tel: 715-234-4861, Ext 1112. p. 2473

Schnaible, Lydia, Librn, Bowdle Public Library, 3043 Main St, Bowdle, SD, 57428. Tel: 605-285-6464. p. 2074

Schnarr, Chris, Librn, Kitchener Public Library, Forest Heights, 251 Fischer-Hallman Rd, Kitchener, ON, N2H 2H1, CANADA. Tel: 519-743-0644. p. 2651

Schnarre, Virginia, Research Librn, Warner University, 13895 Hwy 27, Lake Wales, FL, 33859. Tel: 863-638-7620. p. 416

Schneeflock, Melanie, Librn, Central Arizona College, 805 S Idaho Rd, Apache Junction, AZ, 85119. Tel: 480-677-7747. p. 55

Schneider, Alexandra L, Dir, Brooke County Public Library, Follansbee Branch, 844 Main St, Follansbee, WV, 26037. Tel: 304-527-0860. p. 2417

Schneider, Cary, Dir, Los Angeles Times, 2300 E Imperial Hwy, El Segundo, CA, 90245. Tel: 213-237-5000. p. 140

Schneider, Edward, Dr, Asst Prof, University of South Florida, 4202 Fowler Ave, CIS 1040, Tampa, FL, 33620-7800. Tel: 813-974-7540. p. 2783

Schneider, Elizabeth, Dir, Massachusetts General Hospital, Treadwell Library, Bartlett Hall Ext-I, 55 Fruit St, Boston, MA, 02114-2696. Tel: 617-726-8600. p. 997

Schneider, Gretchen, Coordr, Access Serv, Oakton College Library, 1600 E Golf Rd, Rm 1406, Des Plaines, IL, 60016. Tel: 847-635-1642, 847-635-1644. p. 578

Schneider, Janet, Prog Coordr, Peninsula Public Library, 280 Central Ave, Lawrence, NY, 11559. Tel: 516-239-3262, Ext 216. p. 1562

Schneider, Jodi, Assoc Prof, University of Illinois at Urbana-Champaign, Library & Information Science Bldg, 501 E Daniel St, Champaign, IL, 61820-6211. Tel: 217-333-3280. p. 2784

Schneider, Jordan, Libr Dir, Red Jacket Community Library, 89 S Main St, Manchester, NY, 14504. Tel: 585-289-3559. p. 1568

Schneider, Julia, Assessment Librn, Scholarly Resources Librn, Hesburgh Libraries, Medieval Institute Library, 715 Hesburgh Library, Notre Dame, IN, 46556-5629. Tel: 574-631-5724, 574-631-6603. p. 711

Schneider, Karen, Dean, Sonoma State University Library, 1801 E Cotati Ave, Rohnert Park, CA, 94928. Tel: 707-664-2375. p. 204

Schneider, Karen, Head Librn, The Phillips Collection Library, 1600 21st St NW, Washington, DC, 20009. Tel: 202-387-2151, Ext 212. p. 374

Schneider, Karin, Asst Dir, Licia & Mason Beekley Community Library, Ten Central Ave, New Hartford, CT, 06057. Tel: 860-379-7235. p. 325

Schneider, Katie, Libr Dir, Spring Valley Public Library, E 121 S Second St, Spring Valley, WI, 54767. Tel: 715-778-4590. p. 2478

Schneider, Lynne, Head, Adult Serv, Sewickley Public Library, 500 Thorn St, Sewickley, PA, 15143. Tel: 412-741-6920. p. 2006

Schneider, Melissa, Head, Circ, Winter Park Public Library, 460 E New England Ave, Winter Park, FL, 32789. Tel: 407-623-3300, Ext 107. p. 456

Schneider, Michael, Librn, Minnesota Department of Corrections, 7525 Fourth Ave, Lino Lakes, MN, 55014. Tel: 651-717-6100, Ext 684. p. 1180
Schneider, Rob, Mgr, District of Columbia Public Library, West End, 2301 L St NW, Washington, DC, 20037. Tel: 202-724-8707. p. 365
Schneider, Sabine, Cat, Kent Memorial Library, 50 N Main St, Suffield, CT, 06078-2117. Tel: 860-668-3896. p. 341
Schneider, Sheri, Electronic Res, Info & Instrul Serv Librn, Cedar Crest College, 100 College Dr, Allentown, PA, 18104-6196. Tel: 610-606-4666, Ext 3387. p. 1904
Schneider, Tina, Dir, Libr Serv, Ohio State University LIBRARIES, Lima Campus Library, 4240 Campus Dr, Lima, OH, 45804. Tel: 419-995-8401. p. 1776
Schneider, Wendy, Br Mgr, Alachua County Library District, Micanopy Branch, Micanopy Town Hall, 706 NE Cholokka Blvd, Micanopy, FL, 32667-4113. Tel: 352-466-3122. p. 406
Schneiderman, Victoria, Ref (Info Servs), Medford Public Library, 200 Boston Ave, Ste G-350, Medford, MA, 02155. Tel: 781-395-7950. p. 1033
Schneidermann, Lynn, ILL Spec, Creighton University, 2500 California Plaza, Omaha, NE, 68178-0209. Tel: 402-280-2260. p. 1328
Schnell, Eric H, Info Tech, Ohio State University LIBRARIES, John A Prior Health Sciences Library, 376 W Tenth Ave, Columbus, OH, 43210-1240. Tel: 614-292-4870. p. 1776
Schneller, Lenora, Music Librn, Cornell University Library, Sidney Cox Library of Music & Dance, 220 Lincoln Hall, Ithaca, NY, 14853. Tel: 607-255-7126. p. 1551
Schnepp, Sarah, Head, Tech Serv, Harborfields Public Library, 31 Broadway, Greenlawn, NY, 11740. Tel: 631-757-4200. p. 1541
Schnitzer, Sue, Asst Dir, Outreach & Spec Projects, Memphis Public Library & Information Center, 3030 Poplar Ave, Memphis, TN, 38111. Tel: 901-415-2871. p. 2113
Schnupp, Joy, Dir, Barrett Memorial Library, 65 W Geneva St, Williams Bay, WI, 53191. Tel: 262-245-2709. p. 2488
Schnur, Lesia, Br Mgr, Alachua County Library District, Archer Branch, 13266 SW State Rd 45, Archer, FL, 32618-5524. Tel: 352-495-3367. p. 406
Schnurer, Daphne, Libr Mgr, Elk Point Municipal Library, PO Box 750, Elk Point, AB, T0A 1A0, CANADA. Tel: 780-724-3737. p. 2539
Schober, Amber, Libr Tech, Ser, University of Arkansas-Monticello Library, 514 University Dr, Monticello, AR, 71656. Tel: 870-460-1080. p. 105
Schock, Molly, Dir, Washington County Public Library, 205 Oak Hill St, Abingdon, VA, 24210. Tel: 276-676-6222, 276-676-6233. p. 2301
Schoedel, Mary, Dir, John Graham Public Library, Nine Parsonage St, Newville, PA, 17241-1399. Tel: 717-776-5900. p. 1970
Schoen, David, Dir of Libr, Niagara University Library, Four Varsity Dr, Niagara University, NY, 14109. Tel: 716-286-8001. p. 1606
Schoenenberger, Ginger, Dir, Boone County Library, 221 W Stephenson, Harrison, AR, 72601-4225. Tel: 870-741-5913. p. 97
Schoenfelder, Jonathan, Coord of Reference & Digital Experience, Instrul Serv Librn, Lycoming College, One College Pl, Williamsport, PA, 17701. Tel: 570-321-4053. p. 2023
Schoenhals, Mandi, Ad, Alva Public Library, 504 Seventh St, Alva, OK, 73717. Tel: 580-327-1833. p. 1840
Schoening, Paul, Assoc Dean & Dir, Washington University Libraries, Bernard Becker Medical Library, 660 S Euclid Ave, Campus Box 8132, Saint Louis, MO, 63110. Tel: 314-362-3119. p. 1277
Schoenknecht, John, Volunteer Archivist, Waukesha County Historical Society & Museum, 101 W Main St, Waukesha, WI, 53186. Tel: 262-521-2859, Ext 225. p. 2484
Schoep, Thea, Libr Dir, Claverack Free Library, Nine Rte 9H, Claverack, NY, 12513. Tel: 518-851-7120. p. 1518
Schoepe, Kathy, Tech Serv Mgr, Tempe Public Library, 3500 S Rural Rd, Tempe, AZ, 85282. Tel: 480-350-5540. p. 80
Schoerner, Jeff, Librn, Morrison & Foerster LLP Library, 707 Wilshire Blvd, Los Angeles, CA, 90017-3543. Tel: 213-892-5359. p. 166
Schoess, Tori, Dir, Hazel Mackin Community Library, 311 W Warren St, Roberts, WI, 54023. Tel: 715-749-3849. p. 2474
Schoettgen, Thea, Libr Asst III, Alpine County Library, Bear Valley Branch, 367 Creekside Dr, Bear Valley, CA, 95223. Tel: 209-753-6219. p. 173
Schofer, Sheila, Dir, Neighborhood Libr, Brooklyn Public Library, Ten Grand Army Plaza, Brooklyn, NY, 11238. Tel: 718-230-2100. p. 1502
Schofield, Amy, Dir, Kershaw County Library, 1304 Broad St, Camden, SC, 29020. Tel: 803-425-1508, Ext 3210. p. 2048
Schofield, Cindy, Prof, Southern Connecticut State University, 501 Crescent St, New Haven, CT, 06515. Tel: 203-392-5778. p. 2783
Schofield, Elise, Chief Exec Officer, Ramara Township Public Library, 5482 Hwy 12 S, Ramara, ON, L3V 0S2, CANADA. Tel: 705-325-5776. p. 2675
Schofield, Elise, Commun Engagement Mgr, Sault Ste Marie Public Library, 50 East St, Sault Ste. Marie, ON, P6A 3C3, CANADA. Tel: 705-759-5243. p. 2677
Schoknecht, Patricia A, Col Librn, VPres, Libr & Info Tech, Bates College, 48 Campus Ave, Lewiston, ME, 04240. Tel: 207-786-6260. p. 929
Scholl, Miki, Manager, Systems & Collections, Walden University Library, 100 Washington Ave S, Ste 900, Minneapolis, MN, 55401. p. 1186
Scholl, Shauna, Dir, Mattituck-Laurel Library, 13900 Main Rd, Mattituck, NY, 11952. Tel: 631-298-4134. p. 1569
Scholten, Sarah, Br Mgr, Saint Johns County Public Library System, Anastasia Island Branch, 124 Seagrove Main St, Saint Augustine Beach, FL, 32080. Tel: 904-209-3730. p. 440
Scholtz, James C, Exec Dir, McHenry Public Library District, 809 Front St, McHenry, IL, 60050. Tel: 815-385-0036. p. 616
Scholz, James, Instruction & Assessment Librn, Cameron University Library, 2800 W Gore Blvd, Lawton, OK, 73505-6377. Tel: 580-581-5916. p. 1851
Scholz, James, Coordr, Tennessee State University, 3500 John A Merritt Blvd, Nashville, TN, 37209. Tel: 615-963-5211. p. 2121
Scholz, James, Libr Coord, Tennessee State University, Avon Williams Library, 330 Tenth Ave N, Nashville, TN, 37203. Tel: 615-963-7188. p. 2121
Schomber, Jeni, Head, Libr Serv, Beloit Public Library, 605 Eclipse Blvd, Beloit, WI, 53511. Tel: 608-364-5754. p. 2423
Schomberg, Jessica, Librn, Minnesota State University, Mankato, 601 Maywood Ave, Mankato, MN, 56001. Tel: 507-389-5952. p. 1181
Schoner-Saunders, Lisl, Acad Librn, Algoma University, 1520 Queen St E, Sault Ste. Marie, ON, P6A 2G4, CANADA. Tel: 705-949-2101, Ext 4614. p. 2676
Schoolcraft, Cindy, Res Sharing Librn, Westminster College, Reeves Memorial Library, 501 Westminster Ave, Fulton, MO, 65251-1299. Tel: 573-592-5245. p. 1246
Schoon, Sarah, Libr Dir, Central Citizens' Library District, 1134 E 3100 North Rd, Ste C, Clifton, IL, 60927-7088. Tel: 815-694-2800. p. 572
Schoonover, Erin, Sr Librn, Redondo Beach Public Library, 303 N Pacific Coast Hwy, Redondo Beach, CA, 90277. Tel: 310-318-0675. p. 199
Schoonover, Jessica, Dir, Shirley M Wright Memorial Library, 11455 Fremont St, Trempealeau, WI, 54661. Tel: 608-534-6197. p. 2481
Schoop, Lynda, Dir, Chicago Public Library, Carter G Woodson Regional, 9525 S Halsted St, Chicago, IL, 60628. Tel: 312-747-6900. p. 557
Schopp, Mary Lynn, ILL, Pontiac Public Library, 211 E Madison St, Pontiac, IL, 61764. Tel: 815-844-7229. p. 636
Schoppert, John, Univ Librn, Oregon Institute of Technology Library, 3201 Campus Dr, Klamath Falls, OR, 97601-8801. Tel: 541-885-1783. p. 1883
Schorr, Andrea, Assoc Dir, Res Mgt, University of Texas Health Science Center at San Antonio Libraries, 7703 Floyd Curl Dr, MSC 7940, San Antonio, TX, 78229-3900. Tel: 210-567-2450. p. 2240
Schorr, Jill, Asst Librn, Montgomery County Circuit Court, Judicial Ctr, 50 Maryland Ave, Ste 3420, Rockville, MD, 20850. Tel: 240-777-9120. p. 974
Schott, Jane, Librn, Pocahontas Public Library, 14 Second Ave NW, Pocahontas, IA, 50574. Tel: 712-335-4471. p. 777
Schott, Kai, Librn, Copper Mountain College, 6162 Rotary Way, Joshua Tree, CA, 92252. Tel: 760-366-3791. p. 154
Schott, Lynn, Ref (Info Servs), Bergen Community College, 400 Paramus Rd, Paramus, NJ, 07652-1595. Tel: 201-447-8889. p. 1432
Schouwstra, DeAnna, Programmer, West Perth Public Library, 105 Saint Andrew St, Mitchell, ON, N0K 1N0, CANADA. Tel: 519-348-9234. p. 2659
Schow, Elizabeth, Circ/Adult Serv, Brigham City Library, 26 E Forest St, Brigham City, UT, 84302. Tel: 435-723-5850. p. 2261
Schow, Leslie, Mgr, Salt Lake County Library Services, Herriman Branch, 5380 W Herriman Main St, Herriman, UT, 84096. p. 2274
Schrade, Scott, Br Mgr, Akron-Summit County Public Library, Fairlawn-Bath Branch, 3101 Smith Rd, Akron, OH, 44333. Tel: 330-666-4888. p. 1744
Schrader, Beth, Commun Relations Mgr, Cromaine District Library, 3688 N Hartland Rd, Hartland, MI, 48353. Tel: 810-632-5200, Ext 118. p. 1114
Schrader, Greta, Libr Mgr, Reading Room Association of Gouverneur, 60 Church St, Gouverneur, NY, 13642. Tel: 315-287-0191, p. 1540
Schrader, Richard, Dir, Louis B Goodall Memorial Library, 952 Main St, Sanford, ME, 04073. Tel: 207-324-4714. p. 939
Schram, Jennifer, Supvr, Mayo Clinic Health System, 1221 Whipple St, Eau Claire, WI, 54703. Tel: 715-838-3248. p. 2432
Schram, Kathleen, Asst Dir, Bonner Springs City Library, 201 N Nettleton Ave, Bonner Springs, KS, 66012. Tel: 913-441-2665. p. 799
Schram, Nancy, Dir, Ventura County Library, 5600 Everglades St, Ste A, Ventura, CA, 93003. Tel: 805-677-7150. p. 256
Schramek, Sarah, Librn, Stewartville Public Library, 110 Second St SE, Stewartville, MN, 55976-1306. Tel: 507-533-4902. p. 1205
Schramm, Liz, Libr Assoc II, Tech Serv, Vail Public Library, 292 W Meadow Dr, Vail, CO, 81657. Tel: 970-479-2193. p. 297
Schrandt, Dawn, Asst Libr Dir, James Kennedy Public Library, 320 First Ave E, Dyersville, IA, 52040. Tel: 563-875-8912. p. 749
Schranz, Stefanie, Libr Mgr, Graham Community Library, Ralston Community Ctr, R35 Dugway Dr, Ralston, AB, T0J 2N0, CANADA. Tel: 403-544-3670. p. 2551
Schraut, Debbie, Cat Librn, Missouri Historical Society, 225 S Skinker Blvd, Saint Louis, MO, 63105. Tel: 314-746-4500. p. 1272
Schrauth, Mark, Dir, Saint Francis Seminary, 3257 S Lake Dr, Saint Francis, WI, 53235-0905. Tel: 414-747-6479. p. 2475

Schrecengost, Judy, Librn, Walnut Public Library, 224 Antique City Dr, Walnut, IA, 51577. Tel: 712-784-3533. p. 788

Schreck, Liz, Dir, Ocoee River Regional Library, 718 George St NW, Athens, TN, 37303-2214. Tel: 423-745-5194. p. 2088

Schreck, Liz, Regional Libr Dir, Tennessee State Library & Archives, 403 Seventh Ave N, Nashville, TN, 37243-0312. Tel: 423-745-8086. p. 2121

Schrecker, Diane, Head, Instruction Serv, Ashland University Library, 509 College Ave, Ashland, OH, 44805. Tel: 419-289-5406. p. 1747

Schreiber, Andrea, Pub Serv Librn, North Las Vegas Library District, Alexander Library, 1755 W Alexander Rd, North Las Vegas, NV, 89032. Tel: 702-633-2880. p. 1348

Schreiber, Kathleen, Libr Dir, Harlowton Public Library, 13 S Central Ave, Harlowton, MT, 59036. Tel: 406-632-5584. p. 1295

Schreiber, Kelly, Ch, Marion Public Library, 120 N Main St, Marion, WI, 54950. Tel: 715-754-5368. p. 2454

Schreiber, Linda M, Libr Dir, Bertolet Memorial Library District, 705 S Main St, Leaf River, IL, 61047. Tel: 815-738-2742. p. 607

Schreibstein, Florence, Assoc Dir, Albert Einstein College of Medicine, Jack & Pearl Resnick Campus, 1300 Morris Park Ave, Bronx, NY, 10461-1924. Tel: 718-430-3110. p. 1497

Schreiner, Sally, Adminr, Nebraska Center for the Education of Children Who Are Blind or Visually Impaired, 824 Tenth Ave, Nebraska City, NE, 68410. Tel: 402-873-5513. p. 1325

Schretzenmaire, Ja'Nelle, Circ & ILL Mgr, Yeadon Public Library, 809 Longacre Blvd, Yeadon, PA, 19050. Tel: 610-623-4090. p. 2025

Schrey, Carol, Coll Serv Mgr, Saint Charles City-County Library District, 77 Boone Hills Dr, Saint Peters, MO, 63376. Tel: 636-441-2300. p. 1277

Schreyer, Alice, VPres, Coll, VPres, Libr Serv, Newberry Library, 60 W Walton St, Chicago, IL, 60610-3305. Tel: 312-255-3590. p. 565

Schriar, Suzanne, Assoc Dir, Libr Automation & Tech, Illinois State Library, Gwendolyn Brooks Bldg, 300 S Second St, Springfield, IL, 62701-1796. Tel: 217-785-1533. p. 649

Schriber, Cynthia, Law Librn, Thomson Reuters Westlaw, 610 Opperman Dr, MS DLL N750, Eagan, MN, 55123. Tel: 651-687-7000. p. 1173

Schriefer-McClean, Carol, Br Supvr, Frankfort Community Public Library, Mulberry Community Library, 615 E Jackson St, Mulberry, IN, 46058. Tel: 765-296-2604. p. 685

Schriek, Robert, Head, Ref, Library of the Chathams, 214 Main St, Chatham, NJ, 07928. Tel: 973-635-0603. p. 1395

Schriftman, Lindsay, Executive Dir of Libr, Community College of Allegheny County, North Campus Library & Learning Services, 8701 Perry Hwy, Pittsburgh, PA, 15237-5372. Tel: 412-369-3681. p. 1993

Schriner, Stephanie, Tech Processing Supervisor, Kankakee Public Library, 201 E Merchant St, Kankakee, IL, 60901. Tel: 815-939-4564. p. 604

Schrock, Amy, Asst Dir, New Carlisle & Olive Township Public Library, 408 S Bray St, New Carlisle, IN, 46552. Tel: 574-654-3046. p. 709

Schrock, Lee Ann, Dir, Mary S Biesecker Public Library, 230 S Rosina Ave, Somerset, PA, 15501. Tel: 814-445-4011. p. 2008

Schrodt, Dee, Dir, Alexander Public Library, 409 Harriman St, Alexander, IA, 50420. Tel: 641-692-3238. p. 730

Schroeder, Alison, Br Mgr, Kitchener Public Library, Country Hills Community, 1500 Block Line Rd, Kitchener, ON, N2C 2S2, CANADA. Tel: 519-743-3558. p. 2651

Schroeder, Annette, Ch, McComb Public Library, 113 S Todd St, McComb, OH, 45858. Tel: 419-293-2425. p. 1801

Schroeder, Courtney, Head, Youth Serv, Morton Grove Public Library, 6140 Lincoln Ave, Morton Grove, IL, 60053-2989. Tel: 847-965-4220. p. 620

Schroeder, Dave, Dir, Kenton County Public Library, 502 Scott Blvd, Covington, KY, 41011. Tel: 859-962-4060. p. 852

Schroeder, David E, Dir, Kenton County Public Library, Administration Center, 3095 Hulbert Ave, Erlanger, KY, 41018. Tel: 859-578-3600. p. 852

Schroeder, Diane, Librn, Ulysses Township Library, 410 C St, Ulysses, NE, 68669. Tel: 402-641-3652. p. 1338

Schroeder, Edwin, Dir, Yale University Library, Beinecke Rare Book & Manuscript Library, 121 Wall St, New Haven, CT, 06511. Tel: 203-432-2959. p. 327

Schroeder, Greta, Dir, Thompson Free Library, 186 E Main St, Dover-Foxcroft, ME, 04426. Tel: 207-564-3350. p. 923

Schroeder, Jennifer, Dir, Libr Serv, Cloud County Community College Library, 2221 Campus Dr, Concordia, KS, 66901-5305. Tel: 785-243-1435, Ext 226. p. 803

Schroeder, Kimberly A, Lecturer, Wayne State University, 106 Kresge Library, Detroit, MI, 48202. Tel: 313-577-1825. p. 2787

Schroeder, Lauren, Ref Serv, University of Houston, The O'Quinn Law Library, 12 Law Library, Houston, TX, 77204-6054. Tel: 713-743-2300. p. 2199

Schroeder, Mark, Librn, University of South Dakota, Wegner Health Sciences Library, Sanford School of Medicine, 1400 W 22nd St, Ste 100, Sioux Falls, SD, 57105. Tel: 605-357-1400. p. 2084

Schroeder, Patrick A, Historian, Library Contact, National Park Service, PO Box 218, Appomattox, VA, 24522. Tel: 434-352-8987, Ext 232. p. 2304

Schroeder, Randall, Dir, Williamsburg Public Library, 300 W State St, Williamsburg, IA, 52361. Tel: 319-668-1195. p. 792

Schroeder, Sarah, Dir, Libr Serv, South Carolina State Library, 1500 Senate St, Columbia, SC, 29201. Tel: 803-734-6061. p. 2054

Schroeder-Green, Suzanna, Dir, Ursuline College, 2550 Lander Rd, Pepper Pike, OH, 44124-4398. Tel: 440-449-4202. p. 1815

Schroer, Alyssa, Sr Mgr, Ropes & Gray LLP Library, 1211 Avenue of the Americas, New York, NY, 10036. Tel: 212-596-9000. p. 1601

Schroer, Ronda, Dir, Oberlin City Library, 104 E Oak, Oberlin, KS, 67749-1997. Tel: 785-475-2412. p. 828

Schroer, Tara, Dir, Colby Community College, 1255 S Range Ave, Colby, KS, 67701. Tel: 785-460-4689. p. 802

Schroth, Kristin, Br Librn, United States Court of Appeals, One J F Gerry Plaza, Fourth & Cooper, Camden, NJ, 08101. Tel: 856-968-4859. p. 1394

Schroth, Kristin, Librn, US Courts Library, Clarkson S Fisher Judicial Complex, Rm 300, 402 E State St, Trenton, NJ, 08608. Tel: 609-989-2345. p. 1448

Schrott, Judy, Dir, Flewellin Memorial Library, 108 W Comanche Ave, Shabbona, IL, 60550. Tel: 815-824-2079. p. 646

Schrum, Jamie, Ch, New Hanover County Public Library, 201 Chestnut St, Wilmington, NC, 28401. Tel: 910-798-6362. p. 1723

Schu, Joshu, Mgr, Ad Serv, Cromaine District Library, 3688 N Hartland Rd, Hartland, MI, 48353. Tel: 810-632-5200, Ext 113. p. 1114

Schubart, Mary, Dir, Islip Public Library, 71 Monell Ave, Islip, NY, 11751. Tel: 631-581-5933. p. 1551

Schubert, Carolyn, Dir, Research & Education Services, James Madison University Libraries, 880 Madison Dr, MSC 1704, Harrisonburg, VA, 22807. Tel: 540-568-4264. p. 2324

Schubert, Jason, Curator, J M Davis Arms & Historical Museum, 330 N JM Davis Blvd, Claremore, OK, 74017. Tel: 918-341-5707. p. 1844

Schuele, Jane, ILL Coordr, Benedictine College Library, 1020 N Second St, Atchison, KS, 66002-1499. Tel: 913-360-7609. p. 797

Schuele, Marilyn Jo, Dir, Cedar Rapids Public Library, 423 W Main St, Cedar Rapids, NE, 68627. Tel: 308-358-0603. p. 1309

Schuermann, Keith, Dir, Troup-Harris Regional Library System, Harris County Public Library, 7511 George Hwy 116, Hamilton, GA, 31811. Tel: 706-628-4685. p. 484

Schuermann, Keith, Libr Mgr, Regional Libr Dir, Troup-Harris Regional Library System, 115 Alford St, LaGrange, GA, 30240. Tel: 706-882-7784. p. 484

Schuette, Kay, Ch, Louis Latzer Memorial Public Library, 1001 Ninth St, Highland, IL, 62249. Tel: 618-654-5066. p. 599

Schuetter, Jordan, Libr Experience Mgr, Jasper-Dubois County Public Library, 1116 Main St, Jasper, IN, 47546-2899. Tel: 812-482-2712, Ext 6108. p. 697

Schuffert, Sandra, Children's & Youth Serv, Smithers Public Library, 3817 Alfred Ave, Smithers, BC, V0J 2N0, CANADA. Tel: 250-847-3043. p. 2576

Schuh, Laurie, Circ, Oostburg Public Library, 213 N Eighth St, Oostburg, WI, 53070. Tel: 920-564-2934. p. 2467

Schukat, Rachel, Youth Serv Coordr, Berkeley Public Library, 1637 N Taft Ave, Berkeley, IL, 60163-1499. Tel: 708-544-6017. p. 542

Schuld, Sue, Tech Serv Mgr, Medina County District Library, 210 S Broadway, Medina, OH, 44256. Tel: 330-725-0588. p. 1801

Schuldt, Anna, Curator, Medical University of South Carolina Libraries, Waring Historical Library, 175 Ashley Ave, Charleston, SC, 29425-0001. Tel: 843-792-2288. p. 2051

Schuler, Amy C, Dir, Libr & Info Serv, Cary Institute of Ecosystem Studies Library, Ecosystem Science Bldg, 2801 Sharon Tpk, Millbrook, NY, 12545. Tel: 845-677-7600, Ext 164. p. 1572

Schuler, Belinda, Dir, E J Cottrell Memorial Library, 30 W Main St, Atlanta, NY, 14808-0192. Tel: 585-534-5030. p. 1488

Schuler, Deanna, Br Mgr, Trails Regional Library, Leeton Express Branch, 500 N Main St, Leeton, MO, 64761. Tel: 660-653-2301, Ext 125, 660-653-4731. p. 1285

Schuler, Genelle, Br Mgr, Alexandria Library, Ellen Coolidge Burke Branch, 4701 Seminary Rd, Alexandria, VA, 22304. Tel: 703-746-1704. p. 2302

Schuler, Genelle, Br Mgr, Arlington County Department of Libraries, Shirlington, 4200 Campbell Ave, Arlington, VA, 22206. Tel: 703-228-6546. p. 2305

Schuler, Nancy, E-Resources Librn, Eckerd College, 4200 54th Ave S, Saint Petersburg, FL, 33711. Tel: 727-864-8337. p. 441

Schuller, Annemarie, Dir, John A H Murphree Law Library, Alachua County Courthouse, Family/ Civil Justice Ctr, 201 E University Ave, Rm 413, Gainesville, FL, 32601. Tel: 352-548-3781. p. 407

Schulman, Ronnie, Res Analyst, Sidley Austin LLP, 1501 K St NW, Washington, DC, 20005. Tel: 202-736-8525. p. 374

Schult, Julia, Experiential Learning Librn, Baldwinsville Public Library, 33 E Genesee St, Baldwinsville, NY, 13027-2575. Tel: 315-635-5631. p. 1490

Schulte, Jeff, Interlibrary Loan, Cataloging & Serials Mgr, Coe College, 1220 First Ave NE, Cedar Rapids, IA, 52402. Tel: 319-399-8028. p. 738

Schulte, Jessi, Sr Libr Mgr, Washington County Library, Park Grove Branch, 7900 Hemingway Ave S, Cottage Grove, MN, 55016-1833. Tel: 651-459-2040. p. 1210

Schulte, Mary, Pub Serv Librn, Bellevue University, 1028 Bruin Blvd, Bellevue, NE, 68005. Tel: 402-557-7315. p. 1308

Schulte, Stephanie S, Interim Dir, Ohio State University LIBRARIES, John A Prior Health Sciences Library, 376 W Tenth Ave, Columbus, OH, 43210-1240. Tel: 614-292-4893. p. 1776
Schulteis, Ramie, Librn, Sylvan Grove Public Library, 122 S Main St, Sylvan Grove, KS, 67481. Tel: 785-526-7188. p. 837
Schultis, Cathy, Br Mgr, Cuyahoga County Public Library, Berea Branch, Seven Berea Commons, Berea, OH, 44017-2524. Tel: 440-234-5475. p. 1813
Schultz, Allison Mead, Librn, Shawano County Library, Bonduel Branch, 125 N Washington St, Bonduel, WI, 54107. Tel: 715-758-2267. p. 2476
Schultz, Amie, Dir, Tom Burnett Memorial Library, 400 W Alameda St, Iowa Park, TX, 76367. Tel: 940-592-4981. p. 2202
Schultz, Beth, Libr Mgr, Hay Lakes Municipal Library, 110 Main St, Hay Lakes, AB, T0B 1W0, CANADA. Tel: 780-878-2665. p. 2542
Schultz, Bill, Cat Librn, Eastern Illinois University, 600 Lincoln Ave, Charleston, IL, 61920. Tel: 217-581-8457. p. 552
Schultz, Brenda, Dir, San Joaquin County Law Library, Kress Legal Ctr, 20 N Sutter St, Stockton, CA, 95202. Tel: 209-468-3920. p. 249
Schultz, George, Tech Info Spec, United States Army, Aviation Applied Technology Directorate, Technical Library, Bldg 401, Rm 100C, Fort Eustis, VA, 23604-5577. Tel: 757-878-0083. p. 2319
Schultz, Jamie, Circ, Fairmont State University, 1201 Locust Ave, Fairmont, WV, 26554. Tel: 304-367-4733. p. 2402
Schultz, Jennifer, Youth Serv Librn, Fauquier County Public Library, 11 Winchester St, Warrenton, VA, 20186. Tel: 540-422-8500, Ext 1. p. 2351
Schultz, Jodi, Br Mgr, Park Rapids Area Library, 210 W First St, Park Rapids, MN, 56470-8925. Tel: 218-732-4966. p. 1192
Schultz, Karen, Librn, Dodge Memorial Public Library, 22440 Railroad St, Olive Branch, IL, 62969. Tel: 618-776-5115. p. 629
Schultz, Karen, Br Mgr, Saint Joseph Public Library, Washington Park, 1821 N Third St, Saint Joseph, MO, 64505-2533. Tel: 816-232-2052. p. 1269
Schultz, Leslie, Libr Dir, Slinger Community Library, 220 Slinger Rd, Slinger, WI, 53086. Tel: 262-644-6171. p. 2477
Schultz, Lisa, Ref Librn, Loyola Law School, 919 S Albany St, Los Angeles, CA, 90015-1211. Tel: 213-736-1132. p. 166
Schultz, Lisa, Syst Mgr, John Michael Kohler Arts Center, 608 New York Ave, Sheboygan, WI, 53081-4507. Tel: 920-458-6144. p. 2476
Schultz, Lois, Assoc Dean Coll Mgt, Northern Kentucky University, University Dr, Highland Heights, KY, 41099. Tel: 859-572-5275. p. 859
Schultz, Marci, Br Mgr, Atlantic County Library System, Egg Harbor City Branch, 134 Philadelphia Ave, Egg Harbor City, NJ, 08215. Tel: 609-804-1063. p. 1417
Schultz, Melissa, Libr Asst, Indian Hills Community College, 721 N First St, Bldg CV06, Centerville, IA, 52544. Tel: 641-856-2143, Ext 2237. p. 739
Schultz, Rachael, Archives, Ref Librn, Spec Coll Librn, Saint Bonaventure University, 3261 W State Rd, Saint Bonaventure, NY, 14778. Tel: 716-375-2322. p. 1635
Schultz, Rob, Circ, Everett Roehl Marshfield Public Library, 105 S Maple Ave, Marshfield, WI, 54449. Tel: 715-387-8494, Ext 2755. p. 2454
Schultz, Skyler, Cat, Staff Librn, Marshall University Libraries, One John Marshall Dr, Huntington, WV, 25755-2060. Tel: 304-696-2320. p. 2405
Schultz-Jones, Barbara, Assoc Chair, Assoc Prof, University of North Texas, 3940 N Elm St, Ste E292, Denton, TX, 76207. Tel: 940-565-2445. p. 2793
Schultz-Nielsen, Sarah, Dir, Lithgow Public Library, 45 Winthrop St, Augusta, ME, 04330-5599. Tel: 207-626-2415. p. 914
Schultze, Phyllis, Librn, Rutgers University Libraries, Don M Gottfredson Library of Criminal Justice, 123 Washington St, Ste 350, Newark, NJ, 07102-3094. Tel: 973-353-3118. p. 1428
Schulz, Christine, Libr Dir, Janet Carlson Calvert Library, One Tyler Dr, Franklin, CT, 06254. Tel: 860-642-6207. p. 313
Schulz, Judy, Circ Mgr, Mentor Public Library, 8215 Mentor Ave, Mentor, OH, 44060. Tel: 440-255-8811. p. 1802
Schulz, Kristin, Library Contact, Immanuel Evangelical Lutheran Church Library, 645 Poplar St, Terre Haute, IN, 47807. Tel: 812-232-4972. p. 720
Schulz, Kristina, Univ Archivist & Coordr of Spec Coll, University of Dayton Libraries, 300 College Park Dr, Dayton, OH, 45469. Tel: 937-229-4256. p. 1780
Schulz, Lindsey, Cat/Acq Tech, Stormont, Dundas & Glengarry County Library, 26 Pitt St, Ste 106, Cornwall, ON, K6J 3P2, CANADA. Tel: 613-936-8777, Ext 225. p. 2637
Schulz, Nora, Librn, White Earth Tribal & Community College Library, 2250 College Rd, Rm 202, Mahnomen, MN, 56557. Tel: 218-935-0417, Ext 8332. p. 1181
Schulz, Suzanne, Librn, Reardan Memorial Library, 120 S Oak, Reardan, WA, 99029. Tel: 509-994-9997. p. 2375
Schulze, Amber, Br Mgr, Jackson-George Regional Library System, St Martin Public Library, 15004 LeMoyne Blvd, Biloxi, MS, 39532. Tel: 228-392-3250. p. 1228
Schumacher, Beth, Dir, Moore Public Library, 7239 Huron Ave, Lexington, MI, 48450. Tel: 810-359-8267. p. 1127
Schumacher, Claudia, Ref Librn, Fiske Public Library, 110 Randall Rd, Wrentham, MA, 02093. Tel: 508-384-5440. p. 1073
Schumacher, Fred, Team Lead, Core Tech & Apps Team, University of Colorado Boulder, 1720 Pleasant St, Boulder, CO, 80309. Tel: 303-492-8705. p. 267
Schumacher, Julia, Br Mgr, Riverside County Library System, Palm Desert Library, 73-300 Fred Waring Dr, Palm Desert, CA, 92260. Tel: 760-346-6552. p. 202
Schumacher, Zoe, Supvr, Deschutes Public Library District, Sisters Branch, 110 N Cedar St, Sisters, OR, 97759. Tel: 541-617-1076. p. 1874
Schumann, Amy, Head, Ref, Cyrenius H Booth Library, 25 Main St, Newtown, CT, 06470. Tel: 203-426-4533. p. 330
Schumann, Amy, Libr Dir, Thomaston Public Library, 248 Main St, Thomaston, CT, 06787. Tel: 860-283-4339. p. 341
Schumann, Michele, Ch Serv, Brigham City Library, 26 E Forest St, Brigham City, UT, 84302. Tel: 435-723-5850. p. 2261
Schumm, Aimee, Mgr, E-Serv, Boulder Public Library, 1001 Arapahoe Rd, Boulder, CO, 80302. Tel: 303-441-3100. p. 266
Schuppe, Lauren, Dir, Madeline Island Public Library, One Library St, La Pointe, WI, 54850. Tel: 715-747-3662. p. 2447
Schur, Brandi, Asst Dir, Pub Serv Librn, East Central University, 1100 E 14th St, Ada, OK, 74820. Tel: 580-559-5308. p. 1839
Schureman, Jennifer, Head, Youth Serv, Gloucester County Library System, 389 Wolfert Station Rd, Mullica Hill, NJ, 08062. Tel: 856-223-6027. p. 1423
Schurk, Anna, Br Mgr, Saint Louis County Library, Eureka Hills Branch, 156 Eureka Towne Center Dr, Eureka, MO, 63025-1032. Tel: 314-994-3300, Ext 3200. p. 1273
Schurr, Andrea, Digital Development Librn, University of Tennessee at Chattanooga Library, 400 Douglas Ave, Dept 6456, Chattanooga, TN, 37403-2598. Tel: 423-425-4501. p. 2092
Schuster, Janice, Ser & Electronic Res Librn, Providence College, One Cunningham Sq, Providence, RI, 02918. Tel: 401-865-2631. p. 2039
Schuster, Mark, Mgr, Libr Operations, Metropolitan Library System in Oklahoma County, Northwest Library, 5600 NW 122nd St, Oklahoma City, OK, 73142-4204. p. 1857
Schuster, Rudy, Br Chief, US Geological Survey, 2150 Centre Ave, Bldg C, Fort Collins, CO, 80526. Tel: 970-226-9165. p. 281
Schuster, Tess, Cataloger, Wells Public Library, 1434 Post Rd, Wells, ME, 04090-4508. Tel: 207-646-8181. p. 945
Schuttler, Stacy, Dir, Townsend Public Library, 12 Dudley Rd, Townsend, MA, 01469. Tel: 978-597-1714. p. 1060
Schutz, Alexandra, Univ Archivist, Stephen F Austin State University, 1936 North St, Nacogdoches, TX, 75962. Tel: 936-468-1536. p. 2221
Schutz, Christine, Libr Dir, The College of Idaho, 2112 Cleveland Blvd, Caldwell, ID, 83605. p. 518
Schutz, Melody, Head, Adult Serv, North Shore Library, 6800 N Port Washington Rd, Glendale, WI, 53217. Tel: 414-351-3461. p. 2437
Schwab-Kjelland, Susan, Librn, North Dakota School for the Deaf Library, 1401 College Dr N, Devils Lake, ND, 58301. Tel: 701-665-4433. p. 1732
Schwake, Theresa, Libr Asst, Riverside County Law Library, 82-995 Hwy 111, Ste 102, Indio, CA, 92201. Tel: 760-848-7151. p. 152
Schwarting, Paulette, Dir, Tech Serv, Virginia Historical Society Library, 428 North Blvd, Richmond, VA, 23220. Tel: 804-340-1800. p. 2344
Schwartz, Andrew, Dir, Claremont School of Theology Library, Center for Process Studies, 1325 N College Ave, Claremont, CA, 91711-3154. Tel: 909-447-2559. p. 130
Schwartz, Cristine, Pub Info Officer, Nebraska Department of Correctional Services, 2309 N Hwy 83, McCook, NE, 69001. Tel: 308-345-8405. p. 1324
Schwartz, Daniel, Br Mgr, Corpus Christi Public Libraries, Owen R Hopkins Public Library, 3202 McKinzie Rd, Corpus Christi, TX, 78410. Tel: 361-826-2350. p. 2160
Schwartz, Eleanor, Circ Coordr, Syst Adminr, T B Scott Library, 106 W First St, Merrill, WI, 54452-2398. Tel: 715-536-7191. p. 2457
Schwartz, Eric, Librn, New Jersey Department of Transportation, 1035 Parkway Ave, Trenton, NJ, 08618-2309. Tel: 609-530-5289. p. 1447
Schwartz, Judith, Interim Chief Librn, Medgar Evers College, 1650 Bedford Ave, Brooklyn, NY, 11225. Tel: 718-270-4873. p. 1505
Schwartz, Kathryn, Dir, Libr Serv, Flint Public Library, 1026 E Kearsley St, Flint, MI, 48503. Tel: 810-249-3038. p. 1105
Schwartz, Larry, Info Serv Librn, Minnesota State University Moorhead, 1104 Seventh Ave S, Moorhead, MN, 56563. Tel: 218-477-2922. p. 1189
Schwartz, Laura, Br Mgr, Adams Public Library System, Geneva Branch, 305 E Line St, Geneva, IN, 46740-1026. Tel: 260-368-7270. p. 679
Schwartz, Lee, Br Supvr, Marion County Public Library System, Belleview Public Library, 13145 SE Hwy 484, Belleview, FL, 34420. Tel: 352-438-2500. p. 430
Schwartz, Linda, Dir, Lehigh Valley Hospital, 1200 Cedar Crest Blvd, Allentown, PA, 18105. Tel: 610-402-8410. p. 1905
Schwartz, Mary, Librn, H F Brigham Free Public Library, 104 Main St, Bakersfield, VT, 05441. Tel: 802-827-4414. p. 2277
Schwartz, Pat, Circ Asst, Harrison County Public Library, Lanesville Branch, 7340 E Pennington St NE, Lanesville, IN, 47136. Tel: 812-952-3759. p. 677
Schwartz, Ray, Head, Libr Info Serv, William Paterson University, 300 Pompton Rd, Wayne, NJ, 07470. Tel: 973-720-3192. p. 1452
Schwartz, Roberta, Archivist, Res Serv, Bowdoin College Library, 3000 College Sta, Brunswick, ME, 04011-8421. Tel: 207-725-3134. p. 919

Schwartz, Stephanie, Res, Historical Society of Princeton, Updike Farmstead, 345 Quaker Road, Princeton, NJ, 08540. Tel: 609-921-6748, Ext 103. p. 1436
Schwartz, Tami, Br Mgr, Whitman County Rural Library District, LaCrosse Branch, 201 S Main, LaCrosse, WA, 99143. Tel: 509-549-3770. p. 2362
Schwartz, Thomas, Dr, Dir, National Archives & Records Administration, 210 Parkside Dr, West Branch, IA, 52358-9685. Tel: 319-259-8331. p. 790
Schwarz, Brenda, Youth Serv Librn, Lexington Public Library, 907 N Washington St, Lexington, NE, 68850. Tel: 308-324-2151, p. 1320
Schwarz, Tracy, Ms, Dir, Wayne County Public Library, 1406 Main St, Honesdale, PA, 18431. Tel: 570-253-1220, p. 1944
Schwarzenbach, Alicia, Youth Serv Librn, Ascension Parish Library, 500 Mississippi St, Donaldsonville, LA, 70346. Tel: 225-473-8052. p. 889
Schwarzwalder, Robert, Assoc Univ Librn, Eng & Sci, Stanford University Libraries, 557 Escondido Mall, Stanford, CA, 94305-6063. Tel: 650-725-1064. p. 248
Schwass, Cheryl, Br Supvr, Whitby Public Library, Rossland Branch, 701 Rossland Rd E, Whitby, ON, L1N 8Y9, CANADA. Tel: 905-668-1886. p. 2704
Schwebel, Sara L, Dir, Ctr for Children's Books, Prof, University of Illinois at Urbana-Champaign, Library & Information Science Bldg, 501 E Daniel St, Champaign, IL, 61820-6211. Tel: 217-333-3280. p. 2784
Schween, Tom, Mgr, Contra Costa County Library, El Sobrante Library, 4191 Appian Way, El Sobrante, CA, 94803. Tel: 510-374-3991. p. 174
Schwegel, Richard, Head, Access Serv, North Park University, Brandel Library, 5114 N Christiana Ave, Chicago, IL, 60625. Tel: 773-244-5580, 773-244-6200. p. 566
Schweigert, Gretchen, Libr Dir, Royalton Hartland Community Library, 9 South Vernon St, Middleport, NY, 14105. Tel: 716-735-3281. p. 1571
Schweigert, Robbi, Librn, Five Towns College Library, 305 N Service Rd, Dix Hills, NY, 11746. Tel: 631-656-3187. p. 1525
Schweikhard, April, Math Librn, Scholarly Communications Librn, Sci Librn, Kennesaw State University Library System, 385 Cobb Ave NW, MD 1701, Kennesaw, GA, 30144. Tel: 470-578-7639. p. 483
Schweinfest, Cindy, Br Mgr, Montgomery County Public Libraries, Gaithersburg Library, 18330 Montgomery Village Ave, Gaithersburg, MD, 20879. Tel: 240-773-9494. p. 974
Schweiss, Joe, Dir, Bullitt County Public Library, 127 N Walnut St, Shepherdsville, KY, 40165-6083. Tel: 502-543-7675. p. 874
Schweisthal, Katie, Libr Serv Coordr, Palmer Public Library, 655 S Valley Way, Palmer, AK, 99645. Tel: 907-745-4690, p. 50
Schweitzer, Andrea, Br Mgr, Coshocton Public Library, West Lafayette Branch, 601 E Main St, West Lafayette, OH, 43845. Tel: 740-545-6672. p. 1778
Schweitzer Smith, Andrea, Br Mgr, Coshocton Public Library, 655 Main St, Coshocton, OH, 43812-1697. Tel: 740-622-0956. p. 1778
Schweizer, Brenna, Ser, Kent State University, 6000 Frank Ave NW, North Canton, OH, 44720-7548. Tel: 330-244-3248. p. 1809
Schwelm, Meaghan, Dir, Westhampton Public Library, One North Rd, Westhampton, MA, 01027. Tel: 413-527-5386. p. 1067
Schwenk, Cindy, Cataloger, Circ, Pub Serv, Andover Public Library, 142 W Main St, Andover, OH, 44003-9318. Tel: 440-293-6792. p. 1746
Schwenk, Larissa, Head Librn, Clara City Public Library, 126 N Main St, Clara City, MN, 56222. Tel: 320-847-3535. p. 1170
Schwenk, Larissa, Head Librn, Granite Falls Public Library, 155 Seventh Ave, Granite Falls, MN, 56241. Tel: 320-564-3738. p. 1177
Schwenk, Larissa, Head Librn, Maynard Public Library, 331 Mason Ave, Maynard, MN, 56260. Tel: 320-367-2143. p. 1182
Schwenk, Larissa, Head Librn, Milan Public Library, 235 Main St, Milan, MN, 56262. Tel: 320-734-4792. p. 1182
Schwenk, Larissa, Head Librn, Montevideo Public Library, 224 S First St, Montevideo, MN, 56265. Tel: 320-269-6501. p. 1187
Schweppe, Janet, Libr Mgr, Hayner Public Library District, Alton Square, 132 Alton Sq, Alton, IL, 62002-6115. p. 536
Schwerzler, Shelly, Develop Mgr, Gwinnett County Public Library, 1001 Lawrenceville Hwy NW, Lawrenceville, GA, 30046-4707. Tel: 770-978-5154. p. 485
Schwichtenberg, Suzanne, Adult Serv, Lewis & Clark Library, 120 S Last Chance Gulch, Helena, MT, 59601. Tel: 406-447-1690. p. 1296
Schwieger, Pamela, Youth Serv Coordr, East Providence Public Library, 41 Grove Ave, East Providence, RI, 02914. Tel: 401-434-2453. p. 2032
Schwien, Lacy, Dir, Willow Springs Public Library, 214 N Harris St, Willow Springs, MO, 65793. Tel: 417-469-3482. p. 1286
Schwimmer, Deena, Archivist, Yeshiva University Libraries, 2520 Amsterdam Ave, New York, NY, 10033. Tel: 646-592-4107. p. 1604
Schwing, Laurie J, Library Services, Syst Mgr, UPMC Pinnacle - Harrisburg, Brady Bldg, 1st flr, 205 S Front St, Harrisburg, PA, 17101-2099. Tel: 717-782-5533. p. 1941
Sciacotta, Tony, Head, Fac & Security, Eisenhower Public Library District, 4613 N Oketo Ave, Harwood Heights, IL, 60706. Tel: 708-867-7828. p. 597
Sciaky, Jenifer, Head, Tech Serv, Mokena Community Public Library District, 11327 W 195th St, Mokena, IL, 60448. Tel: 708-479-9663. p. 618
Sciboz, Joelle, Coordr, United Nations System Electronic Information Acquisitions Consortium, c/o United Nations Library, 450 E 42nd St, Rm L-0204, New York, NY, 10017. Tel: 212-963-1344. p. 2771
Scinta, Diane, Asst Dir, Cold Spring Harbor Library, 95 Harbor Rd, Cold Spring Harbor, NY, 11724. Tel: 631-692-6820. p. 1520
Sciochetti, Melanie, Sr Mgr, Archives & Library, Pew Charitable Trusts Library, 901 E St NW, 5th Flr, Washington, DC, 20004. Tel: 215-575-9050. p. 374
Sciranka, Kim, Libr Assoc, Lima Public Library, Cairo Branch, 108 Everrett Dr, Cairo, OH, 45820. Tel: 419-641-7744. p. 1796
Scircle, Kathy, Br Operations Mgr, Frankfort Community Public Library, Rossville Community Library, 400 W Main St, Rossville, IN, 46065. Tel: 765-379-2246. p. 685
Scire, Debby, Dr, Pres, New Hampshire College & University Council, Three Barrell Ct, Ste 100, Concord, NH, 03301-8543. Tel: 603-225-4199. p. 2769
Sciurba, Frances, Tech Serv Librn, Barry University, 11300 NE Second Ave, Miami Shores, FL, 33161-6695. Tel: 305-899-4029. p. 426
Sclafani, Maria, Coordr, Instrul Serv, Wichita State University Libraries, 1845 Fairmount, Wichita, KS, 67260-0068. Tel: 316-978-6331. p. 844
Scobedo, Ramses, Libr Mgr, San Mateo County Library, East Palo Alto Library, 2415 University Ave, East Palo Alto, CA, 94303. Tel: 650-321-7712, Ext 227. p. 235
Scoggins, Adrianna, Asst Librn, Charles Ralph Holland Memorial Library, 205 W Hull Ave, Gainesboro, TN, 38562. Tel: 931-268-9190. p. 2099
Scoggins, Rebekah, Pub Serv & Instruction Librn, Museum of Fine Arts, Houston, 1001 Bissonnet St, Houston, TX, 77005. Tel: 713-639-7325. p. 2197
Scoggins, Slade, ILL & Circ, Cleveland State Community College Library, 3535 Adkisson Dr, Cleveland, TN, 37312-2813. Tel: 423-473-2277, 423-478-6209. p. 2093
Scoles, Bridget, Student Success & Instruction Librn, Whitman College, 345 Boyer Ave, Walla Walla, WA, 99362. Tel: 509-527-5917. p. 2393
Scondras, Susan, Asst Dir, Dalton Community Library, 113 E Main St, Dalton, PA, 18414. Tel: 570-563-2014. p. 1925
Scot, Diane, Daytona Beach Campus Libr Dir, Keiser University Library System, 1500 NW 49th St, Fort Lauderdale, FL, 33309. Tel: 954-351-4035. p. 401
Scotese, Ariel, Assoc Dir, User Serv, University of Chicago Library, D'Angelo Law Library, 1121 E 60th St, Chicago, IL, 60637-2786. Tel: 773-702-9616. p. 570
Scotka, Rebecca, Ch, YA Librn, East Lyme Public Library, 39 Society Rd, Niantic, CT, 06357. Tel: 860-739-6926. p. 330
Scott, Amanda, Dir, Cambridge Springs Public Library, 158 McClellan St, Cambridge Springs, PA, 16403-1018. Tel: 814-398-2123. p. 1917
Scott, Amie, Asst Dir, Brownsburg Public Library, 450 S Jefferson St, Brownsburg, IN, 46112-1310. Tel: 317-852-3167. p. 673
Scott, Andy, Ref Serv, Franklin Public Library, 9151 W Loomis Rd, Franklin, WI, 53132. Tel: 414-425-8214. p. 2436
Scott, Angela, Dir, Ligonier Public Library, 300 S Main St, Ligonier, IN, 46767-1812. Tel: 260-894-4511. p. 703
Scott, Angie, Librn, Breckinridge County Public Library, Irvington Branch, 1109 West US 60, Irvington, KY, 40146. Tel: 270-547-7404. p. 857
Scott, Ann, Exec Dir, Nantucket Atheneum, One India St, Nantucket, MA, 02554-3519. Tel: 508-228-1974. p. 1037
Scott, Anne, Libr Dir, Columbia State Community College, 1665 Hampshire Pike, Columbia, TN, 38401. Tel: 931-540-2560. p. 2094
Scott, Antoinette, Librn, Mercer County Community College Library, James Kerney Campus, 102 N Broad St, Trenton, NJ, 08690. Tel: 609-570-3179. p. 1453
Scott, April, Librn, Mason County Library System, Mason City Public, 502 Brown St, Mason, WV, 25260. Tel: 304-773-5580. p. 2413
Scott, Barbara, Ch, Bucyrus Public Library, 200 E Mansfield St, Bucyrus, OH, 44820-2381. Tel: 419-562-7327, Ext 104. p. 1753
Scott, Brooke, Mgr, Libr Serv, Royal Columbian Hospital, 330 E Columbia St, New Westminster, BC, V3L 3W7, CANADA. Tel: 604-520-4755. p. 2572
Scott, Carol, Librn, Fair Haven Free Library, 107 N Main St, Fair Haven, VT, 05743. Tel: 802-265-8011. p. 2284
Scott, Carrie, Commun Outreach Supvr-Literacy, Carlsbad City Library, Library Learning Center, 3368 Eureka Pl, Carlsbad, CA, 92008. Tel: 760-931-4515. p. 128
Scott, Charles, Libr Tech, State Historical Society of Iowa, 402 Iowa Ave, Iowa City, IA, 52240-1806. Tel: 319-335-3911. p. 760
Scott, Christy, Educ Serv Librn, Walla Walla University Libraries, 104 S College Ave, College Place, WA, 99324-1159. Tel: 509-527-2134. p. 2362
Scott, Connie, Br Mgr, Indianapolis Public Library, Warren, 9701 E 21st St, Indianapolis, IN, 46229-1707. Tel: 317-275-4550. p. 696
Scott, Craig, Libr Dir, Gadsden Public Library, 254 S College St, Gadsden, AL, 35901. Tel: 256-549-4699. p. 18
Scott, Craig, Dir, Presv Serv, Royal Tyrrell Museum of Palaeontology Library, Midland Provincial Park, Hwy 838 N Dinosaur Trail, Box 7500, Drumheller, AB, T0J 0Y0, CANADA. Tel: 403-823-7707. p. 2534
Scott, Cynthia, Tech Serv Coordr, North Central College, 320 E School St, Naperville, IL, 60540. Tel: 630-637-5712. p. 623

Scott, Cynthia, Dir, Middleton Community Library, 110 Bolton Ave, Middleton, TN, 38052. Tel: 731-376-0680. p. 2115
Scott, Cynthia L, Dir, Wolfeboro Public Library, 259 S Main St, Wolfeboro, NH, 03894. Tel: 603-569-2428. p. 1384
Scott, Dana E, Dir of Libr Operations, Marion County Library, 308 Old Main, Yellville, AR, 72687. Tel: 870-449-6015. p. 113
Scott, Daniel, Librn, Laurentian University Library & Archives, 935 Ramsey Lake Rd, Sudbury, ON, P3E 2C6, CANADA. Tel: 705-675-1151, Ext 3315. p. 2683
Scott, Darwin, Music Librn, Princeton University, Mendel Music Library, Woolworth Ctr for Musical Studies, Princeton, NJ, 08544. Tel: 609-258-4251. p. 1438
Scott, David, Br Mgr, Palm Beach County Library System, Greenacres Branch, 3750 Jog Rd, Greenacres, FL, 33467. Tel: 561-641-9100. p. 454
Scott, Dorrie, Ref Librn, Lone Star College System, CyFair Library, 9191 Barker Cypress Rd, Cypress, TX, 77433. Tel: 281-290-3214, 281-290-3219. p. 2197
Scott, Elijah, Exec Dir, Florida Virtual Campus, Library Services, 1753 W Paul Dirac Dr, Tallahassee, FL, 32310. Tel: 850-922-6044. p. 2763
Scott, Elizabeth, Archivist & Spec Coll Librn, East Stroudsburg University, 200 Prospect Ave, East Stroudsburg, PA, 18301-2999. Tel: 570-422-3584. p. 1928
Scott, Emily, Libr Coord, Jane Norman College, 60 Lorne St, Ste 1, Truro, NS, B2N 3K3, CANADA. Tel: 902-893-3342. p. 2623
Scott, Eric, Assoc Univ Librn, Libr Operations, University of California, Merced Library, 5200 N Lake Rd, Merced, CA, 95343. Tel: 209-675-8040. p. 176
Scott, Glenda, Librn, Dunklin County Library, Hornersville Branch, 502 School St, Hornersville, MO, 63855. Tel: 573-737-2728. p. 1258
Scott, Jacque, Dir, Carnegie Public Library, 314 McLeod St, Big Timber, MT, 59011. Tel: 406-932-5608. p. 1288
Scott, Jamie, Dir, North Madison County Public Library System, 1600 Main St, Elwood, IN, 46036. Tel: 765-552-5001. p. 680
Scott, Jamie, Librn, Walnut Public Library, 511 W Robbins, Walnut, KS, 66780. Tel: 620-354-6794. p. 841
Scott, Janet L, Librn, Sweet Springs Public Library, 217 Turner St, Sweet Springs, MO, 65351. Tel: 660-335-4314. p. 1282
Scott, Jeannine, Br Mgr, Chattahoochee Valley Libraries, North Columbus Branch, 5689 Armour Rd, Columbus, GA, 31909-4513. Tel: 706-748-2855. p. 472
Scott, Jeff, Dir, Washoe County Library System, 301 S Center St, Reno, NV, 89501-2102. p. 1350
Scott, Jennifer, Dir, Wilton Free Public Library, Six Goodspeed St, Wilton, ME, 04294. Tel: 207-645-4831. p. 946
Scott, Juanita, Bookmobile Librn, Adair County Public Library, 307 Greensburg St, Columbia, KY, 42728-1488. Tel: 270-384-2472. p. 852
Scott, Judy, Dir, J H Wootters Crockett Public Library, 709 E Houston Ave, Crockett, TX, 75835-2124. Tel: 936-544-3089. p. 2161
Scott, Julie, Exec Dir, Rosicrucian Order, AMORC, Rosicrucian Park, 1660 Park Ave, San Jose, CA, 95191. Tel: 408-947-3600. p. 230
Scott, Karen, Br Coordr, Lennox & Addington County Public Library, Bath Branch, 197 Davey St, Bath, ON, K0H 1G0, CANADA. Tel: 613-352-5600. p. 2660
Scott, Kerry, Assoc Univ Librn, Coll & Serv, University of California, 1156 High St, Santa Cruz, CA, 95064. Tel: 831-459-2802. p. 243
Scott, Kim, Br Mgr, Chattahoochee Valley Libraries, Marion County Public Library, 123 E Fifth Ave, Buena Vista, GA, 31803-2113. Tel: 229-649-6385. p. 472
Scott, Kim, Ch, Cambridge City Public Library, 600 W Main St, Cambridge City, IN, 47327. Tel: 765-478-3335. p. 673
Scott, Kristy, Libr Tech II, Colorado Department of Corrections, LaVista Correctional Facility Library, 1401 W 17th St, Pueblo, CO, 81003. Tel: 719-544-4800, Ext 3721. p. 293
Scott, Laura, Ref Serv Mgr, Park Ridge Public Library, 20 S Prospect, Park Ridge, IL, 60068. Tel: 847-825-3123. p. 633
Scott, Laura M, Asst Dir, Reference, Clinics, & Outreach, Duke University Libraries, J Michael Goodson Law Library, 210 Science Dr, Durham, NC, 27708. Tel: 919-613-7164. p. 1684
Scott, Leslie, Libr Dir, The Amargosa Valley Library, 1660 E Amargosa Farm Rd, Amargosa Valley, NV, 89020. Tel: 775-372-5340. p. 1343
Scott, Leslie, Dir, Libr Serv, Prosper Community Library, 200 S Main St, Prosper, TX, 75078. Tel: 972-569-1185. p. 2229
Scott, Linda, Librn, Lebanon-Community Library, 404½ Main St, Lebanon, KS, 66952. Tel: 785-389-5711. p. 820
Scott, Lynn, Ms, Br Mgr, Enoch Pratt Free Library, Cherry Hill Branch, 606 Cherry Hill Rd, Baltimore, MD, 21225. Tel: 443-984-4932. p. 952
Scott, Margaret, Chief Exec Officer, Chief Librn, Port Hope Public Library, 31 Queen St, Port Hope, ON, L1A 2Y8, CANADA. Tel: 905-885-4712. p. 2674
Scott, Margaret, Chief Librn, Port Hope Public Library, Hub at Canton, 5325 County Rd 10, Canton, ON, L1A 3V5, CANADA. Tel: 905-753-0031. p. 2674
Scott, Marleena, Dir, Harrington Public Library, 110 E Center St, Harrington, DE, 19952. Tel: 302-398-4647. p. 353
Scott, Mary, Circ & Reserves Supvr, University of Maryland Libraries, Michelle Smith Performing Arts Library, 8270 Alumni Dr, College Park, MD, 20742-1630. Tel: 301-405-9223. p. 963
Scott, Mary Jo, Dir, Div Archives, Alabama Department of Archives & History Research Room, 624 Washington Ave, Montgomery, AL, 36130. Tel: 334-353-4694. p. 27
Scott, Megan, Mgr, Northeast Missouri Library Service, Lewis County Branch-LaGrange, 114 S Main St, LaGrange, MO, 63448. Tel: 573-655-2288. p. 1254
Scott, Melissa, Asst Dir, Youth Serv Librn, Fayette County Public Library, 828 N Grand Ave, Connersville, IN, 47331. Tel: 765-827-0883. p. 676
Scott, Michael, State Librn, State of Iowa Libraries Online, State Library of Iowa, 1112 E Grand, Des Moines, IA, 50319. Tel: 515-281-4105. p. 2765
Scott, Michelle, Head Librn, Boissevain-Morton Library & Archives, 409 S Railway, Boissevain, MB, R0K 0E0, CANADA. Tel: 204-534-6478. p. 2585
Scott, Mitchell, Coll Mgt Librn, Saint Norbert College, 400 Third St, De Pere, WI, 54115. Tel: 920-403-3422. p. 2430
Scott, Mona, Bus Mgr, Metropolitan Library Service Agency, 1619 Dayton Ave, Ste 314, Saint Paul, MN, 55104. Tel: 651-645-5731. p. 2768
Scott, Morgan, Operations Mgr, University of Kansas Libraries, Anschutz Library, 1301 Hoch Auditoria Dr, Lawrence, KS, 66045-7537. Tel: 785-864-1080. p. 819
Scott Moxon, Kaitlyn, Exec Dir, Napa County Historical Society, 1219 First St, Napa, CA, 94559. Tel: 707-224-1739. p. 181
Scott, Patricia, Dir, Loyola University Chicago Libraries, School of Law Library, Philip H Corboy Law Ctr, 25 E Pearson St, Chicago, IL, 60611. Tel: 312-915-8515. p. 564
Scott, Paula, Dr, Libr Dir, Driscoll Children's Hospital, 3533 S Alameda St, 3rd Flr, Corpus Christi, TX, 78411-1721. Tel: 361-694-5467. p. 2160
Scott, Penny, Ref Librn, University of San Francisco, 2130 Fulton St, San Francisco, CA, 94117-1080. Tel: 415-422-5389. p. 229
Scott, Rachel, Assoc Dean for Information Assets, Illinois State University, Campus Box 8900, 201 N School St, Normal, IL, 61790. Tel: 309-438-3451. p. 625
Scott, Rebecca, Dean, Libr & Learning Res, Napa Valley College, 1700 Bldg, 2277 Napa-Vallejo Hwy, Napa, CA, 94558. Tel: 707-256-7438. p. 182
Scott, Rebekah, Pub Serv Librn, Alamance Community College Library, 1247 Jimmie Kerr Rd, Graham, NC, 27253. Tel: 336-506-4198. p. 1691
Scott, Sandy, Librn, Public Library of Steubenville & Jefferson County, Dillonvale-Mt Pleasant Branch, 192 Cole St, Dillonvale, OH, 43917. Tel: 740-769-2090. p. 1822
Scott, Sarah, Local Hist Librn, The Field Library, Four Nelson Ave, Peekskill, NY, 10566. Tel: 914-737-1212. p. 1616
Scott, Sheila, Br Librn, Boston Public Library, West Roxbury Branch, 1961 Centre St, West Roxbury, MA, 02132. Tel: 617-325-3147. p. 993
Scott, Shelley Ann, Dir, M Alice Chapin Memorial Library, 120 E Main St, Marion, MI, 49665. Tel: 231-743-2421. p. 1129
Scott, Susan, Dir, Gale Free Library, 23 Highland St, Holden, MA, 01520. Tel: 508-210-5566. p. 1025
Scott, Teresa, Libr Mgr, Delia Municipal Library, 205 Third Ave N, Delia, AB, T0J 0W0, CANADA. Tel: 403-364-3777. p. 2533
Scott, Timothy, Adminr, Saint Joseph's Abbey, 167 N Spencer Rd, Spencer, MA, 01562-1233. Tel: 508-885-8700, Ext 521. p. 1056
Scott, Tracie, Dir, Holland Public Library, 27 Sturbridge Rd, Unit 9, Holland, MA, 01521. Tel: 413-245-3607. p. 1025
Scott, Tracy, Mgr, Tulsa City-County Library, Outreach Services, 2901 S Harvard, Ste A, Tulsa, OK, 74114. Tel: 918-549-7481. p. 1866
Scott, Una, Interlibrary Loan Services Mgr, University of Texas at Dallas, 800 W Campbell Rd, Richardson, TX, 75080. Tel: 972-883-2955. p. 2231
Scott, Wilbertine, Ref Librn, Cleveland Bradley County Public Library, 795 Church St NE, Cleveland, TN, 37311-5295. Tel: 423-472-2163. p. 2092
Scott-Branch, Jamillah, Asst Dir, Libr Serv, North Carolina Central University, 1801 Fayetteville St, Durham, NC, 27707-3129. Tel: 919-530-7312. p. 1685
Scott-Childress, Katie, Libr Dir, Rosendale Library, 264 Main St, Rosendale, NY, 12472. Tel: 845-658-9013. p. 1633
Scottaline, Lauren, Head, Children's Servx, East Islip Public Library, 381 E Main St, East Islip, NY, 11730-2896. Tel: 631-581-9200. p. 1528
Scoufopolous, Fifi, Libr Assoc, Petersham Memorial Library, 23 Common St, Petersham, MA, 01366. Tel: 978-724-3405. p. 1046
Scoular, Heather, Customer Experience Dir, Fraser Valley Regional Library, 34589 Delair Rd, Abbotsford, BC, V2S 5Y1, CANADA. Tel: 604-859-7141. p. 2561
Scoular, Heather, Interim Libr Mgr, Fraser Valley Regional Library, Maple Ridge Public Library, 130 - 22470 Dewdney Trunk Rd, Maple Ridge, BC, V2X 5Z6, CANADA. Tel: 604-467-7417. p. 2562
Scoular, Heather, Interim Libr Mgr, Fraser Valley Regional Library, Pitt Meadows Public Library, 200-12099 Harris Rd, Pitt Meadows, BC, V3Y 0E5, CANADA. Tel: 604-465-4113. p. 2562
Scovil, Sheri, Br Mgr, Bartow County Public Library System, Cartersville Main Street, 429 W Main St, Cartersville, GA, 30120. Tel: 770-382-4203. p. 470
Scovil, Sheri, Br Mgr, Bartow County Public Library System, Emmie Nelson Branch, 116 Covered Bridge Rd, Cartersville, GA, 30120. Tel: 770-382-2057. p. 470

Scoville, Karen, Coll Serv Mgr, Arizona State University, College of Law, Arizona State University MC 9620, 111 E Taylor St, Ste 350, Phoenix, AZ, 85004. Tel: 480-965-4869. p. 69

Scoville, Nikki, Asst Dir, Person County Public Library, 319 S Main St, Roxboro, NC, 27573. Tel: 336-597-7881. p. 1714

Scoville, Tabitha, Dir, Cortland County Historical Society, 25 Homer Ave, Cortland, NY, 13045. Tel: 607-756-6071. p. 1522

Scramuzza, Lynn A, Dir, Hamlin Community Library, 518 Easton Tpk, Lake Ariel, PA, 18436-4797. Tel: 570-689-0903. p. 1950

Scretchen, Denise, Br Mgr, Public Library of Cincinnati & Hamilton County, Anderson, 7450 State Rd, Cincinnati, OH, 45230. Tel: 513-369-6030. p. 1762

Scrimshire, Natalie, Assoc Librn, Henderson State University, 1100 Henderson St, Arkadelphia, AR, 71999-0001. Tel: 870-230-5958. p. 89

Scripa, Allison, Interim Campus Librarian, Ref & Instruction Librn, Pellissippi State Community College, Magnolia Avenue Library, 1610 E Magnolia Ave, Knoxville, TN, 37917. Tel: 865-539-7237. p. 2107

Scritchfield, Larry, Syst Adminr, Cochise County Library District, 100 Clawson Ave, Bisbee, AZ, 85603. Tel: 520-432-8930. p. 56

Scritchfield, Teresa, Br Mgr, White County Regional Library System, Searcy Public, 113 E Pleasure Ave, Searcy, AR, 72143. p. 110

Scrivener, Chris, Br Coordr, County of Brant Public Library, Burford Branch, 24 Park Ave, Burford, ON, N0E 1A0, CANADA. Tel: 519-449-5371. p. 2671

Scrivner, Kristie, Asst Librn, Winchester Public Library, 203 Fourth St, Winchester, KS, 66097. Tel: 913-774-4967. p. 844

Scroggins, Alexis, Dir, Youth Serv, Outreach Coordr, Conway County Library Headquarters, 101 W Church St, Morrilton, AR, 72110. Tel: 501-354-5204. p. 105

Scroggins, Lisa, Exec Dir, Natrona County Library, 307 E Second St, Casper, WY, 82601. Tel: 307-577-7323. p. 2492

Scruggs, Jennifer, Tech Serv, South Carolina School for the Deaf & the Blind, 355 Cedar Springs Rd, Spartanburg, SC, 29302-4699. Tel: 864-577-7642, 864-585-7711. p. 2069

Scruggs, Melissa, Dir, Beersheba Springs Public Library, Hwy 56, Beersheba Springs, TN, 37305. Tel: 931-692-3029. p. 2088

Scruggs, Rose, Libr Syst Coordr, University of Southern Indiana, 8600 University Blvd, Evansville, IN, 47712. Tel: 812-464-1828. p. 682

Scuccimarri, Erin, Chief Librn/CEO, Innisfil Public Library, 20 Church St, Cookstown, ON, L0L 1L0, CANADA. Tel: 705-431-7410. p. 2637

Scudder, Mary Jean, Dir, Roxbury Library Association, 53742 State Hwy 30, Roxbury, NY, 12474. Tel: 607-326-7901. p. 1634

Scudo, Sally, Head, Tech Serv, Chappaqua Public Library, 195 S Greeley Ave, Chappaqua, NY, 10514. Tel: 914-238-4779. p. 1516

Scull, Barbara, Librn, Middletown Public Library, 20 N Catherine St, Middletown, PA, 17057-1401. Tel: 717-944-6412. p. 1962

Scullin, Katy, Spec Coll Librn, Marietta College, 215 Fifth St, Marietta, OH, 45750. Tel: 740-376-4464. p. 1798

Scully, Mike, Med Librn, Swedish Medical Center Library, First Hill Campus, 747 Broadway, Seattle, WA, 98122-4307. Tel: 206-386-2484. p. 2380

Scurka, Lori, Br Mgr, Cleveland Public Library, Mount Pleasant, 14000 Kinsman Rd, Cleveland, OH, 44120. Tel: 216-623-7032. p. 1768

Scurry, Paulette, Br Mgr, Augusta-Richmond County Public Library, Friedman Branch, 1447 Jackson Rd, Augusta, GA, 30909. Tel: 706-736-6758. p. 466

Seaborn, Rebecca, Dir, Farmington Area Public Library District, 411 N Lightfoot Rd, Farmington, IL, 61531-1276. Tel: 309-245-2175. p. 588

Seadler, Amanda, Colls Mgr, Exhibitions Mgr, Orange County Museum of Art Library, 3333 Avenue of the Arts, Costa Mesa, CA, 92626. Tel: 714-780-2130. p. 132

Seager, Tiffany, Librn, Nebraska Department of Correctional Services, 3216 W Van Dorn St, Lincoln, NE, 68522. Tel: 402-471-2861. p. 1321

Seagren, Lana, Librn, Montana Department of Corrections, Four N Haynes Ave, Miles City, MT, 59301. Tel: 406-232-1377, 406-233-2230. p. 1299

Seaholm, Jill, Head, Genealogical Serv, Swenson Swedish Immigration Research Center, Augustana College, 3520 Seventh Ave, Rock Island, IL, 61201. Tel: 309-794-7204. p. 641

Seal, Debbie, Br Mgr, Moore County Library, Vass Branch, 128 Seaboard St, Vass, NC, 28394. Tel: 910-245-2200. p. 1677

Seal, Marnie, Libr Mgr, Cambrian College Library, 1400 Barrydowne Rd, 3rd Flr, Rm 3021, Sudbury, ON, P3A 3V8, CANADA. Tel: 705-524-7651. p. 2682

Seale, Kathleen, Coordr, State Historical Society of Missouri - Rolla, University of Missouri, G-3 Curtis Laws Wilson Library, 400 W 14th St, Rolla, MO, 65409-0060. Tel: 573-341-4440. p. 1267

Seale, Rachel, Br Mgr, Yuma County Free Library District, San Luis Branch, 1075 N Sixth Ave, San Luis, AZ, 85349. Tel: 928-627-8344. p. 86

Sealine, Holly, Libr Dir, Johnston Public Library, 6700 Merle Hay Rd, Johnston, IA, 50131-0327. Tel: 515-278-5233. p. 762

Sealine, Holly, Libr Dir, Norwalk Easter Public Library, 1051 North Ave, Norwalk, IA, 50211. Tel: 515-981-0217. p. 774

Seally, Janet, Info Serv Mgr, Waterloo Public Library, 35 Albert St, Waterloo, ON, N2L 5E2, CANADA. Tel: 519-886-1310, Ext 126. p. 2702

Seals, Tiffany, Adminr, Pesticide Action Network North American, 2029 University Ave, Ste 200, Berkeley, CA, 94704. Tel: 510-788-9020, Ext 332. p. 122

Seaman, David, Dean of Libr, Univ Librn, Syracuse University Libraries, 222 Waverly Ave, Syracuse, NY, 13244-2010. Tel: 315-443-5533. p. 1650

Seaman, David, Interim Dean, Syracuse University, 114 Hinds Hall, Syracuse, NY, 13244-1190. Tel: 315-443-2736. p. 2789

Seaman, Mary, Dir, Burnet County Library System, Joanne Cole-Mitte Memorial Library, 170 N Gabriel St, Bertram, TX, 78605. Tel: 512-355-2113. p. 2152

Seaman, Scott, Dean of Libr, Ohio University Libraries, 30 Park Pl, Athens, OH, 45701. Tel: 740-593-2705. p. 1748

Seaman, Terri, Librn, Project Mgr, United States Army, Fort Riley Post Library, Bldg 5306, Hood Dr, Fort Riley, KS, 66442-6416. Tel: 785-239-5305. p. 808

Seamans, Sue, Outreach Coordr, Falconer Public Library, 101 W Main St, Falconer, NY, 14733. Tel: 716-665-3504. p. 1532

Seamon, George, Dir, Northwest Kansas Library System, Two Washington Sq, Norton, KS, 67654-1615. Tel: 785-877-5148. p. 827

Seamon, George, State Librn, South Dakota State Library, 800 Governors Dr, Pierre, SD, 57501-2294. Tel: 605-773-3131. p. 2080

Searcy, Ashley, Libr Tech, United States District Court, Page Belcher Federal Bldg, 4th Flr, 333 W Fourth St, Tulsa, OK, 74103. Tel: 918-699-4744. p. 1867

Searle, Emily, Dir, Chester Library, 250 W Main St, Chester, NJ, 07930. Tel: 908-879-7612. p. 1396

Searle, Melissa, Ref/Tech Serv, Coeur d'Alene Public Library, 702 E Front Ave, Coeur d'Alene, ID, 83814-2373. Tel: 208-769-2315. p. 519

Searles, Mary S, Dir, The John W King New Hampshire Law Library, Supreme Court Bldg, One Charles Doe Dr, Concord, NH, 03301-6160. Tel: 603-271-3777. p. 1358

Searles, Melissa, Asst Dir, GEP Dodge Library, Two Main St, Bennington, NH, 03442. Tel: 603-588-6585. p. 1355

Sears, Amy, Ch Serv, Teaneck Public Library, 840 Teaneck Rd, Teaneck, NJ, 07666. Tel: 201-837-4171. p. 1445

Sears, Carolyn, Asst Dir, Chesterfield County Public Library, 9501 Lori Rd, Chesterfield, VA, 23832. Tel: 804-748-1761. p. 2312

Sears, Deborah, Ref Serv Coordr, Jackson District Library, 244 W Michigan Ave, Jackson, MI, 49201. Tel: 517-788-4087. p. 1120

Sears, Debra, Extn Serv Mgr, LeRoy Collins Leon County Public Library System, 200 W Park Ave, Tallahassee, FL, 32301-7720. Tel: 850-606-2665. p. 445

Sears, Dennis, Ref (Info Servs), Brigham Young University, Howard W Hunter Law Library, 256 JRCB, Provo, UT, 84602-8000. Tel: 801-422-3593. p. 2269

Sears Ilnicki, Wendy, Asst Dir, Mgr, Bibliog Serv, Yellowhead Regional Library, 433 King St, Spruce Grove, AB, T7X 3B4, CANADA. Tel: 780-962-2003, Ext 225. p. 2554

Sears, Jan, Dir, Kimball Public Library, 208 S Walnut St, Kimball, NE, 69145. Tel: 308-235-4523. p. 1320

Sears, Jean, Library Contact, Auburn Correctional Facility Library, 135 State St, Auburn, NY, 13024-9000. Tel: 315-253-8401, Ext 4650. p. 1488

Sears, JoAnn, Librn, Ivy Tech Community College, 3101 S Creasy Lane, Lafayette, IN, 47905. Tel: 765-269-5395. p. 701

Sears, Jon, Br Mgr, Davis County Library, Clearfield/North Branch, 562 S 1000 East, Clearfield, UT, 84015. Tel: 801-451-1840. p. 2263

Sears, Sandra, Dir, Perry Memorial Library, 22 SE Fifth Ave, Perryton, TX, 79070. Tel: 806-435-5801. p. 2226

Sears, Stephen A, Assoc Dir, Johns Hopkins University School of Advanced International, 1740 Massachusetts Ave NW, 6th Flr, Washington, DC, 20036. Tel: 202-663-5907. p. 370

Seary, Cathy, Head, Adult Serv, George F Johnson Memorial Library, 1001 Park St, Endicott, NY, 13760. Tel: 607-757-5350. p. 1531

Seaton, Christine, Dir, Shell Lake Public Library, 501 First St, Shell Lake, WI, 54871. Tel: 715-468-2074. p. 2477

Seaton, Linda, Br Mgr, Park County Library System, Meeteetse Branch, 2107 Idaho St, Meeteetse, WY, 82433. Tel: 307-868-2248. p. 2494

Seaton-Martin, Marcia, Tech Serv, Patrick Henry Community College, 645 Patriot Ave, Martinsville, VA, 24115. Tel: 276-656-0276. p. 2332

Seaver, Carolyn, Dir, Albertson Memorial Library, 200 N Water St, Albany, WI, 53502. Tel: 608-862-3491. p. 2419

Seay, Cynthia, Br Mgr, Norfolk Public Library, Mary D Pretlow Anchor Branch Library, 111 W Ocean View Ave, Norfolk, VA, 23503-1608. Tel: 757-441-1750. p. 2335

Seay, Scott, Dr, Dir, Libr & Info Serv, Christian Theological Seminary, 1000 W 42nd St, Indianapolis, IN, 46208. Tel: 317-931-2347. p. 691

Sebanc, Denise, Br Mgr, Chicago Public Library, North Pulaski, 4300 W North Ave, Chicago, IL, 60639. Tel: 312-744-9573. p. 557

Sebastian, Diane, Dir, Dover Free Public Library, 32 E Clinton St, Dover, NJ, 07801. Tel: 973-366-0172. p. 1399

Sebastian, Joanie, Head, Adult Serv, Des Plaines Public Library, 1501 Ellinwood St, Des Plaines, IL, 60016. Tel: 847-827-5551. p. 578

Sebela, Mary, Dir of Circ, Rolling Meadows Library, 3110 Martin Lane, Rolling Meadows, IL, 60008. Tel: 847-259-6050. p. 642

Sebert, Patricia, Dir, City of Bayou La Batre Public Library, 12747 Padgett Switch Rd, Irvington, AL, 36544. Tel: 251-824-4213. p. 23

Sebrasky, Josh, Br Mgr, Mentor Public Library, Headlands, 4669 Corduroy Rd, Mentor, OH, 44060. Tel: 440-257-2000. p. 1802

Sebrowski, Ben, Dir, Technology, Commerce Township Community Library, 180 E Commerce, Commerce Township, MI, 48382. Tel: 248-669-8101, Ext 107. p. 1093

Sebuck, Chris, Dir, Bridgeview Public Library, 7840 W 79th St, Bridgeview, IL, 60455. Tel: 708-458-2880, Ext 100. p. 545

Sechler, Michael W, Archivist, Cat Librn, Randolph College, 2500 Rivermont Ave, Lynchburg, VA, 24503. Tel: 434-947-8133. p. 2330

Secil, Breanna, Circ Mgr, Mustang Public Library, 1201 N Mustang Rd, Mustang, OK, 73064. Tel: 405-376-2226. p. 1854

Seckelson, Linda, Reader Serv, Metropolitan Museum of Art, Thomas J Watson Library, 1000 Fifth Ave, New York, NY, 10028-0198. Tel: 212-570-3759. p. 1592

Seckman, David, Dir, Jeffersonville Township Public Library, 211 E Court Ave, Jeffersonville, IN, 47130. Tel: 812-285-5630. p. 698

Secor, Dane, Electronic Res Librn, Blue Ridge Community College Library, 180 W Campus Dr, Flat Rock, NC, 28731. Tel: 828-694-1824. p. 1689

Seda, Felichia, Asst Librn, Gladbrook Public Library, 301 Second St, Gladbrook, IA, 50635. Tel: 641-473-3236. p. 755

Sedberry, Ashlee, Librn, Stonewall County Library, 516 S Washington Ave, Aspermont, TX, 79502. Tel: 940-989-2730. p. 2137

Seddon, Joan, Librn, Leaf Rapids Public Library, 20 Town Ctr Complex, Leaf Rapids, MB, R0B 1W0, CANADA. Tel: 204-473-2742. p. 2588

Sederlund, Olivia, Head, Tech Serv, Goodnow Library, 21 Concord Rd, Sudbury, MA, 01776-2383. Tel: 978-440-5555. p. 1058

Sederstrom, Kyle, Libr Dir, Overbrook Public Library, 317 Maple St, Overbrook, KS, 66524. Tel: 785-862-9840. p. 829

Sedestrom, Dave, Financial Mgr, Allen County Public Library, 900 Library Plaza, Fort Wayne, IN, 46802. Tel: 260-421-1270. p. 683

Sedey, Joe, Br Mgr, Saint Louis Public Library, Kingshighway, 2260 S Vandeventer Ave, Saint Louis, MO, 63110. Tel: 314-771-5450. p. 1275

Sedig, Kamran, Prof, Western University, FIMS & Nursing Bldg, Rm 2020, London, ON, N6A 5B9, CANADA. Tel: 519-661-2111, Ext 86612. p. 2796

Sedlacek, Gretchen, Actg Libr Mgr, Murrieta Public Library, 8 Town Sq, Murrieta, CA, 92562. Tel: 951-304-2665. p. 181

Sedlak, Belinda, Tech Serv Librn, Westmoreland County Community College Library, Student Achievement Ctr, Youngwood Campus, 145 Pavilion Lane, Youngwood, PA, 15697-1814. Tel: 724-925-4100. p. 2027

Sedlock, Barbara, Archives Coordr, Lead Librn, Metadata Coordr, Defiance College, 201 College Pl, Defiance, OH, 43512-1667. Tel: 419-783-2487. p. 1781

Sednek, Sam, Youth Serv, Medford Public Library, 200 Boston Ave, Ste G-350, Medford, MA, 02155. Tel: 781-395-7950. p. 1033

Sedy, Josh, Librn, Grays Harbor County Law Library, 100 W Broadway Ave, Montesano, WA, 98563. Tel: 360-249-5311, Ext 3. p. 2371

Seeber, Kevin, Head Librn, Pennsylvania State University, 1600 Woodland Rd, Abington, PA, 19001. Tel: 215-881-7462. p. 1903

Seedorff, Sherri, Dir, Arlington Public Library, 711 Main St, Arlington, IA, 50606. Tel: 563-633-3475. p. 732

Seeds, Jeanne, Librn, Hodgson Russ LLP, 140 Pearl St, Ste 100, Buffalo, NY, 14202-4040. Tel: 716-848-1282, 716-856-4000. p. 1509

Seeger, Erin, Circ Mgr, Northbrook Public Library, 1201 Cedar Lane, Northbrook, IL, 60062-4581. Tel: 847-272-2011. p. 626

Seegert, Lynda, Mgr, Mat Serv, Six Mile Regional Library District, Niedringhaus Bldg, 2001 Delmar Ave, Granite City, IL, 62040-4590. Tel: 618-452-6238. p. 594

Seegraber, Lori, Br Librn, Ch, Crane Thomas Public Library, Adams Shore Branch, 519 Sea St, Quincy, MA, 02169. Tel: 617-376-1325, 617-376-1326. p. 1048

Seeland, Megan, Youth Serv, Red Wing Public Library, 225 East Ave, Red Wing, MN, 55066-2298. Tel: 651-385-3673. p. 1194

Seelbach, Diane, Dir, Girard Township Library, 201 W Madison St, Girard, IL, 62640-1551. Tel: 217-627-2414. p. 592

Seeley, Lois, Asst Librn, Palliser Regional Library, Assiniboia & District Public Library, 201 Third Ave W, Assiniboia, SK, S0H 0B0, CANADA. Tel: 306-642-3631. p. 2742

Seeley, Nathan, Colls Mgr, Frankenmuth Historical Association, 613 S Main St, Frankenmuth, MI, 48734. Tel: 989-652-9701, Ext 103. p. 1107

Seeley, Susan, Youth Serv, Holderness Library, 866 US Rte 3, Holderness, NH, 03245. Tel: 603-968-7066. p. 1368

Seely, Amber, Coll, Div Dir, Tech Serv, Harris County Public Library, 5749 S Loop E, Houston, TX, 77033. Tel: 713-274-6600. p. 2192

Seely, Julie, Br Mgr, Prairie-River Library District, 103 N Main St, Lapwai, ID, 83540. Tel: 208-843-7254. p. 524

Seely, Kristi, Dir, Lehi City Library, 120 N Center St, Lehi, UT, 84043. Tel: 385-201-1050. p. 2265

Seeman, Corey, Dir, University of Michigan, Kresge Library Services, Stephen M Ross School of Business, 701 Tappan St, Ann Arbor, MI, 48109-1234. Tel: 734-764-9969. p. 1079

Seeman, Kay, Asst Librn, Smith Center Public Library, 117 W Court St, Smith Center, KS, 66967. Tel: 785-282-3361. p. 836

Seeman, Samantha, Dir, Cambridge Community Library, 101 Spring Water Alley, Cambridge, WI, 53523. Tel: 608-423-3900. p. 2426

Seerengan, Krishnan, Mr, Dir, Guam Public Library System, 254 Martyr St, Hagatna, GU, 96910. Tel: 671-475-4753, 671-475-4754. p. 2505

Seese, Joshua, Libr Dir, Windber Public Library, 1909 Graham Ave, Windber, PA, 15963-2011. Tel: 814-467-4950. p. 2024

Seewald, Joel, Sci, Tech, Eng & Math Librn, University of Michigan-Dearborn, 4901 Evergreen Rd, Dearborn, MI, 48128-2406. Tel: 313-583-6326. p. 1096

Sefton, Cindy C, Dir, Cincinnati State Technical & Community College, 3520 Central Pkwy, Rm 170, Cincinnati, OH, 45223-2690. Tel: 513-569-1699. p. 1760

Segal, Barbara, Dir Learning Ctr, Temple Beth El, 1351 S 14th Ave, Hollywood, FL, 33020-6499. Tel: 954-920-8225. p. 409

Segal, Jody, Fac Librn, Green River College, 12401 SE 320th St, Auburn, WA, 98092-3699. Tel: 253-833-9111, Ext 2103. p. 2357

Segal, Julia, Patient Educ Librn, Department of Veterans Affairs, New York Harbor Healthcare, 423 E 23rd St, New York, NY, 10010. Tel: 212-686-7500, Ext 7681. p. 1585

Seger, Cindy, Ch, Old Town Public Library, 46 Middle St, Old Town, ME, 04468. Tel: 207-827-3972. p. 934

Seger, Dana, Br Mgr, Azalea Regional Library System, Monroe - Walton County Library, 217 W Spring St, Monroe, GA, 30655. Tel: 770-267-4630. p. 488

Seger, Kristen, Head, Circ, Montrose Regional Library District, 320 S Second St, Montrose, CO, 81401. Tel: 970-249-9656. p. 291

Seger, Peg, Assoc Dir of Outreach & Community Engagement, University of Texas Health Science Center at San Antonio Libraries, 7703 Floyd Curl Dr, MSC 7940, San Antonio, TX, 78229-3900. Tel: 210-567-2450. p. 2240

Segota, Courtney, Head, Instrul Serv, University of South Dakota, McKusick Law Library, Knudson School of Law, 414 E Clark St, Vermillion, SD, 57069-2390. Tel: 605-658-3523. p. 2084

Segroves, Doris, Coll Develop, Shelbyville-Bedford County Public Library, 220 S Jefferson St, Shelbyville, TN, 37160. Tel: 931-684-7323. p. 2126

Seguin, Brian, Coll Develop Librn, Pub Serv, North Idaho College Library, 1000 W Garden Ave, Coeur d'Alene, ID, 83814-2199. Tel: 208-769-3255. p. 520

Séguin-Couture, France, Chief Exec Officer, Township of Russell Public Library, 1053 Concession St, Box 280, Russell, ON, K4R 1E1, CANADA. Tel: 613-445-5331. p. 2676

Segura, Jean, Br Mgr, Iberia Parish Library, Coteau Branch, 6308 Coteau Rd, New Iberia, LA, 70560. Tel: 337-364-7430. p. 900

Segura, Stella, ESL Coordr, Plainfield Public Library, 800 Park Ave, Plainfield, NJ, 07060-2594. Tel: 908-757-1111, Ext 121. p. 1435

Seguro, Leo, Br Mgr, Las Vegas-Clark County Library District, West Las Vegas Library, 951 W Lake Mead Blvd, Las Vegas, NV, 89106. Tel: 702-507-3980. p. 1347

Sehgal, Gurmeet, Ref (Info Servs), Loma Linda University, 11072 Anderson St, Loma Linda, CA, 92350-0001. Tel: 909-558-4581. p. 157

Sehgal, Vandana, Head, Bus Serv, Lincolnwood Public Library District, 4000 W Pratt Ave, Lincolnwood, IL, 60712. Tel: 847-677-5277. p. 609

Sehring, Hope, Dir, Jeannette Public Library, 500 Magee Ave, Jeannette, PA, 15644-3416. Tel: 724-523-5702. p. 1946

Seibach-Larsen, Anna, Dir, University of Rochester, Rossell Hope Robbins Library, Rush Rhees Library, Rm 416, Rochester, NY, 14627. Tel: 585-275-9197. p. 1631

Seiber, Kellie, Asst Dir, Springfield Memorial Library, 665 Main St, Springfield, NE, 68059. Tel: 402-253-2797. p. 1337

Seiberling, Tom, Dir, Mahanoy City Public Library, 17-19 W Mahanoy St, Mahanoy City, PA, 17948-2615. Tel: 570-773-1610. p. 1957

Seibert, Michael, Cultural Res Spec, Fort Frederica National Monument Library, 6515 Frederica Rd, Saint Simons Island, GA, 31522. Tel: 912-638-3639, Ext 114. p. 495

Seidel, Aaron, Asst Mgr, Saint Louis County Library, Jamestown Bluffs Branch, 4153 N Hwy 67, Florissant, MO, 63034-2825. Tel: 314-994-3300, Ext 3400. p. 1274

Seidel, Shelma, Cat, Havre Hill County Library, 402 Third St, Havre, MT, 59501. Tel: 406-265-2123. p. 1295

Seidl, Nicolette, Dir, Evergreen Park Public Library, 9400 S Troy Ave, Evergreen Park, IL, 60805-2383. Tel: 708-422-8522. p. 587

Seifer, Marc, Librn, Metascience Foundation Library, PO Box 32, Kingston, RI, 02881-0032. Tel: 401-294-2414. p. 2033

Seifert, Cindy, Asst Librn, Franklin Public Library, 1502 P St, Franklin, NE, 68939. Tel: 308-425-3162. p. 1314

Seigel, Caroline, Librn, Santa Fe Institute Library, 1399 Hyde Park Rd, Santa Fe, NM, 87501. Tel: 505-946-2707. p. 1476

Seil, Michelle, Dir, Carrington City Library, 87 Eighth Ave N, Carrington, ND, 58421. Tel: 701-652-3921. p. 1731

Seiler, Dimitra A, Fiscal Mgr, Abington Township Public Library, 1030 Old York Rd, Abington, PA, 19001-4594. Tel: 215-885-5180, Ext 117. p. 1903

Seiler, River, Ref & Instruction Librn, College of Lake County, 19351 W Washington St, Grayslake, IL, 60030. Tel: 847-543-2071. p. 595

Seiler, Sherry, YA Librn, Bucyrus Public Library, 200 E Mansfield St, Bucyrus, OH, 44820-2381. Tel: 419-562-7327, Ext 110. p. 1753

Seim, Cindy, Circ, The William K Sanford Town Library, 629 Albany Shaker Rd, Loudonville, NY, 12211-1196. Tel: 518-458-9274. p. 1565

Seimer, Jacqueline, Head, Support Serv, Oxford Public Library, 530 Pontiac St, Oxford, MI, 48371-4844. Tel: 248-628-3034. p. 1140

Seipke, Amy, Chair, Southeastern Michigan League of Libraries, UM-Dearborn Mardigian Library, 4901 Evergreen Rd, Dearborn, MI, 48128. Tel: 313-593-5617. p. 2767

Seipp, Rebecca, Asst Univ Librn, Hollins University, 7950 E Campus Dr, Roanoke, VA, 24020. Tel: 540-362-6328. p. 2345

Seisser, Colleen, Asst Dir, Westmont Public Library, 428 N Cass Ave, Westmont, IL, 60559-1502. Tel: 630-869-6150, 630-869-6160. p. 661

Seita, Valarie, Media Coordr, Tulare County Office of Education, 7000 Doe Ave, Ste A, Visalia, CA, 93291. Tel: 559-651-3031. p. 257

Seitter, Barbara, Br Mgr, Trails Regional Library, Lexington Branch, 1008 Main St, Lexington, MO, 64067. Tel: 660-259-3071. p. 1285

Seitz, Lola, Dir, Pawnee City Public Library, 735 Eighth St, Pawnee City, NE, 68420. Tel: 402-852-2118. p. 1332

Sekula, Jennifer, Ref Serv, College of William & Mary in Virginia, The Wolf Law Library, 613 S Henry St, Williamsburg, VA, 23187. Tel: 757-221-3255. p. 2353

Selakovich, Tabitha, Dir, John C Fremont Library District, 130 Church Ave, Florence, CO, 81226. Tel: 719-784-4649, Ext 4. p. 280

Selander, Vicki, Dir, Castle Rock Public Library, 137 Cowlitz St W, Castle Rock, WA, 98611. Tel: 360-274-6961. p. 2361

Selbee, Aileen, Libr Tech 1, North Island College, 3699 Roger St, Port Alberni, BC, V9Y 8E3, CANADA. Tel: 250-724-8760. p. 2573

Selby, Cheryl, Dir, Grand Valley Public Library, One N School St, Orwell, OH, 44076. Tel: 440-437-6545. p. 1811

Selby, Courtney, Assoc Dean, Libr Serv, St John's University Library, Rittenberg Law Library, 8000 Utopia Pkwy, Jamaica, NY, 11439. p. 1556

Selby, Gay Kozak, Chief Librn, County of Brant Public Library, Burford Branch, 24 Park Ave, Burford, ON, N0E 1A0, CANADA. Tel: 519-449-5371. p. 2671

Selden, Karen, Metadata Librn, University of Colorado Boulder, William A Wise Law Library, Wolf Law Bldg, 2nd Flr, 2450 Kittredge Loop Dr, Boulder, CO, 80309-0402. Tel: 303-492-7535. p. 268

Selden, Kellee, Mgr, Ascension Columbia-Saint Mary's Hospital, Women's Hospital, 2nd Flr, 2323 N Lake Dr, Milwaukee, WI, 53211. Tel: 414-585-1626. p. 2458

Selden, Laura, Business Office Coord, Duluth Public Library, 520 W Superior St, Duluth, MN, 55802. Tel: 218-730-4223. p. 1172

Selden, Laura, Pub Relations, Webmaster, Duluth Public Library, 520 W Superior St, Duluth, MN, 55802. Tel: 218-730-4236. p. 1172

Selders, Shana, Br Mgr, Audubon Regional Library, 12220 Woodville St, Clinton, LA, 70722. Tel: 225-683-8753. p. 887

Seldin, Sian, Sr Res Librn, Board of Governors of The Federal Reserve System, Research Library, 20th & C St NW, MS 102, Washington, DC, 20551. Tel: 202-452-3333. p. 361

Self, Amber, Ch, Librn, Carnegie Library of Ballinger, 204 N Eighth St, Ballinger, TX, 76821. Tel: 325-365-9315. p. 2144

Self, Deb, Exec Dir, Farallones Marine Sanctuary Association, Bldg 991, Old Coast Guard Sta, Marine Dr, San Francisco, CA, 94129. Tel: 415-561-6625. p. 224

Self, Leigh Ann, Youth Serv, Barry-Lawrence Regional Library, Aurora Branch, 202 Jefferson, Aurora, MO, 65605. Tel: 417-678-2036. p. 1263

Self, Melanie, Asst Dir, Hampshire County Public Library, 153 W Main St, Romney, WV, 26757. Tel: 304-822-3185. p. 2413

Self, Steve, Fac Librn, Austin Community College, Eastview Campus Library, 3401 Webberville Rd, 2nd Flr, Rm 2200, Austin, TX, 78702. Tel: 512-223-5134. p. 2138

Selfridge, Anna B, Curator of Archives, Curator of Ms, Librn, Allen County Historical Society, 620 W Market St, Lima, OH, 45801. Tel: 419-222-9426. p. 1795

Selima, Ashley, State Archivist, Rhode Island State Archives, 337 Westminster St, Providence, RI, 02903. Tel: 401-222-2353. p. 2040

Selin-Love, Greta, Commun Serv Librn, Victor Farmington Library, 15 W Main, Victor, NY, 14564. Tel: 585-924-2637. p. 1657

Selinder, Sven, Archivist, Westport Historical Society Library, 25 Avery Pl, Westport, CT, 06880-3215. Tel: 203-222-1424. p. 346

Selk, Nanci, Br Mgr, Whitman County Rural Library District, Endicott Branch, 324 E St, Endicott, WA, 99125. Tel: 509-657-3429. p. 2362

Sell, Elizabeth, Br Mgr, Allegany County Library System, LaVale Branch, 815 National Hwy, LaVale, MD, 21502. Tel: 301-729-0855. p. 964

Sell, Marcia, Dir, Elmendaro Township Library, 224 Commercial St, Hartford, KS, 66854. Tel: 620-392-5518. p. 812

Sell, Paula, Asst Dir, Youth Serv Coordr, Roaring Spring Community Library, 320 E Main St, Roaring Spring, PA, 16673-1009. Tel: 814-224-2994. p. 2002

Sellal, Walid, Librn, Embassy of Oman, 1100 16th St NW, Washington, DC, 20036. Tel: 202-677-3967, Ext 104. p. 365

Sellal, Walid, Cat, Coll Develop Librn, Middle East Institute, 1761 N St NW, Washington, DC, 20036. Tel: 202-785-1141, Ext 222. p. 371

Sellen, Mary, Univ Librn, Christopher Newport University, One Avenue of the Arts, Newport News, VA, 23606. Tel: 757-594-7130. p. 2333

Seller, S, Archivist, Vancouver Holocaust Education Centre, 50-950 W 41st Ave, Vancouver, BC, V5Z 2N7, CANADA. Tel: 604-264-0499. p. 2581

Sellers, Connie, ILL, New England Law, 154 Stuart St, Boston, MA, 02116-5687. Tel: 617-422-7288. p. 998

Sellers, Dawson, Mgr, Pike County Library, 210 Second Ave, Murfreesboro, AR, 71958. Tel: 870-285-2575. p. 106

Sellers, Gregory, Admin Librn, Hinds Community College, Vicksburg Campus, 755 Hwy 27, Vicksburg, MS, 39180-8699. Tel: 601-629-6846. p. 1231

Sellers, Laura, Youth Spec, First Regional Library, Senatobia Public Library, 222 Ward St, Senatobia, MS, 38668. Tel: 662-562-6791. p. 1220

Sellers, Rhonda, Operations Mgr, VPres, Fly Fishers International, 5237 US Hwy 89 S, Ste 11, Livingston, MT, 59047. Tel: 406-222-9369, Ext 4. p. 1299

Sellers, Sherri, Br Mgr, Snyder County Libraries, Beavertown Community Library, 111 W Walnut St, Beavertown, PA, 17813. Tel: 570-658-3437. p. 2005

Sellie, Alycia, Coll Develop Librn, City University of New York, 365 Fifth Ave, New York, NY, 10016-4309. Tel: 212-817-7078. p. 1582

Sellmer, Alvin, Libr Mgr, National Park Service Library, 12795 W Alameda Pkwy, Lakewood, CO, 80228. Tel: 303-969-2133. p. 288

Sello, Charmaine, Mgr, County of Los Angeles Public Library, Sorensen Library, 6934 Broadway Ave, Whittier, CA, 90606-1994. Tel: 562-695-3979. p. 138

Sellon, Sarah L, Dir, Ely Public Library, 1595 Dows St, Ely, IA, 52227. Tel: 319-848-7616. p. 751

Sells, Julie, Libr Coord, Mildred Stevens Williams Memorial Library, 2916 Sennebec Rd, Appleton, ME, 04862. Tel: 207-785-5656. p. 913

Sells, Rebecca, Archives, E-Publications, Federal Reserve Bank of Philadelphia, 100 N Sixth St, 4th Flr, Philadelphia, PA, 19106. Tel: 215-574-6540. p. 1977

Sells, Vicki, Assoc Provost, Info & Tech Serv, University of the South, 178 Georgia Ave, Sewanee, TN, 37383-1000. Tel: 931-598-3220. p. 2126

Selly, Lynn, Br Supvr, Waseca-Le Sueur Regional Library, Le Center Public, Ten W Tyrone St, Le Center, MN, 56057. Tel: 507-357-6792. p. 1207

Selmeister, Annette, Head Librn, Hometown Public Library, 4331 Southwest Hwy, Hometown, IL, 60456-1161. Tel: 708-636-0997. p. 601

Selter, Angela, Cataloger, Marion County Public Library, 201 E Main St, Lebanon, KY, 40033-1133. Tel: 270-692-4698. p. 861

Seltzer, Barb, Mgr, Dauphin County Library System, Elizabethville Area Library, 80 N Market St, Elizabethville, PA, 17023. Tel: 717-362-9825. p. 1940

Selvaggio, Donna, Dr, Libr Dir, United States Merchant Marine Academy, 300 Steamboat Rd, Kings Point, NY, 11024. Tel: 516-726-5751. p. 1560

Selwitschka, Holly, Dir, Kimberly Public Library, 515 W Kimberly Ave, Kimberly, WI, 54136. Tel: 920-788-7515. p. 2445

Selwitschka, Holly, Dir, Winneconne Public Library, 31 S Second St, Winneconne, WI, 54986. Tel: 920-582-7091. p. 2489

Sembler, Kristina, Libr Dir, South Country Library, 22 Station Rd, Bellport, NY, 11713. Tel: 631-286-0818. p. 1492

Semenchuk, Nicole, Archive Spec, Digital Spec, Culinary Institute of America, 1946 Campus Dr, Hyde Park, NY, 12538-1430. Tel: 845-451-1270. p. 1550

Semenza, Jenny, Assoc Univ Librn, Res Serv, Idaho State University, 850 S Ninth Ave, Pocatello, ID, 83209. Tel: 208-282-2581. p. 528

Semenza, Lisa, Dir, Hazard Library Association, 2487 Rte 34 B, Poplar Ridge, NY, 13139. Tel: 315-364-7975. p. 1620

Semifero, Angela, Dir, Marshall District Library, 124 W Green St, Marshall, MI, 49068. Tel: 269-781-7821, Ext 11. p. 1130

Seminara, Michael, Archives & Spec Coll Librn, University of South Dakota, I D Weeks Library, 414 E Clark St, Vermillion, SD, 57069. Tel: 605-658-3379. p. 2084

Semling, Agnes, Circ Supvr, University of Nevada, Las Vegas Univ Libraries, Wiener-Rogers Law Library, William S Boyd School of Law, 4505 S Maryland Pkwy, Las Vegas, NV, 89154. Tel: 702-895-2400. p. 1348

Semmerling, Lee, Distance Educ, Moraine Valley Community College Library, 9000 W College Pkwy, Palos Hills, IL, 60465. Tel: 708-608-4009. p. 632

Semrinec, Vickie, Circ & Ref Asst, Lake Michigan College, 2755 E Napier Ave, Benton Harbor, MI, 49022. Tel: 269-927-8605. p. 1084

Sena, Josephine, Head, Govt Doc & Per Div/Librn, New Mexico Highlands University, 802 National Ave, Las Vegas, NM, 87701. Tel: 505-454-3411. p. 1471

Sendelbach, Judy, Libr Tech, ProMedica Toledo Hospital, 2142 N Cove Blvd, Toledo, OH, 43606. Tel: 419-291-4404. p. 1824

Sender, Pablo, Co-Librn, Krotona Institute of Theosophy Library, Two Krotona Hill, Ojai, CA, 93023. Tel: 805-646-2653. p. 188

Seneca, Jennifer, Asst Dir, Livingston Parish Library, 13986 Florida Blvd, Livingston, LA, 70754. Tel: 225-686-4100. p. 895

Senecal, Melody J, Med Librn, AdventHealth Shawnee Mission Medical Library, 9100 W 74th St, Shawnee Mission, KS, 66204. Tel: 913-676-2101. p. 836

Senechal, Molly, Libr Mgr, Brown County Library, Wrightstown Branch, 615 Main St, Wrightstown, WI, 54180. Tel: 920-532-4011. p. 2438

Senechal, Molly A, Br Mgr, Brown County Library, Kress Family Branch, 333 N Broadway, De Pere, WI, 54115. Tel: 920-448-4407. p. 2438

Senechal, Rachael, Coordr of Develop, Kellogg-Hubbard Library, 135 Main St, Montpelier, VT, 05602. Tel: 802-223-3338. p. 2289
Senesac, Katie, Librn, Illinois Veteran's Home Library, One Veterans Dr, Manteno, IL, 60950. Tel: 815-468-6581. p. 613
Senger, Jennifer, Asst Dir, James River Valley Library System, Stutsman County Library, 910 Fifth St SE, Jamestown, ND, 58401. Tel: 701-252-1531. p. 1736
Sengupta, Mimi, Head, Circ Serv, Scotch Plains Public Library, 1927 Bartle Ave, Scotch Plains, NJ, 07076-1212. Tel: 908-322-5007. p. 1441
Senior, David, Head of Libr & Archives, San Francisco Museum of Modern Art, 151 Third St, San Francisco, CA, 94103-3107. Tel: 415-357-4121. p. 227
Senior, Heidi, Ref & Instruction Librn, University of Portland, 5000 N Willamette Blvd, Portland, OR, 97203-5743. Tel: 503-943-7111. p. 1894
Senn, Holly, Virtual Ref, Pacific Lutheran University, 12180 Park Ave S, Tacoma, WA, 98447-0001. Tel: 253-535-7500. p. 2386
Senn, Roy, Info Tech, New Hartford Public Library, Two Library Lane, New Hartford, NY, 13413-2815. Tel: 315-733-1535. p. 1576
Senning, Amy, Adult Info Serv Mgr, Mentor Public Library, 8215 Mentor Ave, Mentor, OH, 44060. Tel: 440-255-8811. p. 1802
Sennott, Emily, Head, Children's Servx, Bedford Public Library, Three Meetinghouse Rd, Bedford, NH, 03110. Tel: 603-472-2300. p. 1354
Sensabaugh, Elizabeth, Libr Dir, Radford Public Library, 30 W Main St, Radford, VA, 24141. Tel: 540-731-3621. p. 2339
Sensabaugh, Zach, Libr Asst, James Madison University Libraries, Music Library, MSC 7301, Harrisonburg, VA, 22807. Tel: 540-568-8035. p. 2324
Sensale-Guerin, Marianne, Dir of Finance, Portland Public Library, Five Monument Sq, Portland, ME, 04101. Tel: 207-871-1700, Ext 760. p. 937
Sentes, Shelley, Br Librn, Southeast Regional Library, Milestone Branch, 112 Main St, Milestone, SK, S0G 3L0, CANADA. Tel: 306-436-2112. p. 2754
Sentman-Paz, Joy, Librn, Fresno County Genealogical Society Library, Fresno Public Library, 2420 Mariposa St, Fresno, CA, 93721. Tel: 559-600-6230. p. 145
Sentman-Paz, Joy, Branch Cluster Supvr, Fresno County Public Library, 2420 Mariposa St, Fresno, CA, 93721. Tel: 559-600-7323. p. 145
Seo, Hilary, Dean, Iowa State University Library, 302 Parks Library, 701 Morrill Rd, Ames, IA, 50011-2102. Tel: 515-294-1443. p. 731
Seo, JooYoung, Asst Prof, University of Illinois at Urbana-Champaign, Library & Information Science Bldg, 501 E Daniel St, Champaign, IL, 61820-6211. Tel: 217-333-3280. p. 2784
Seper, Jennifer, Libr Mgr, Vancouver Island Regional Library, Nanaimo North, 6250 Hammond Bay Rd, Nanaimo, BC, V9T 5M4, CANADA. Tel: 250-933-2665. p. 2571
Seper, Jennifer, Libr Mgr, Vancouver Island Regional Library, Nanaimo Wellington, 3200 N Island Hwy, Nanaimo, BC, V9T 1W1, CANADA. Tel: 250-758-5544. p. 2571
Sepnafski, Marla Rae, Dir, Wisconsin Valley Library Service, 300 N First St, Wausau, WI, 54403. Tel: 715-261-7250. p. 2777
Sepulveda, Efrem, Acq Librn, Wichita Falls Public Library, 600 11th St, Wichita Falls, TX, 76301-4604. Tel: 940-767-0868, Ext 4241. p. 2258
Sequeira, Andrea, Libr Mgr, Ontario Ministry of Education, College Park, 777 Bay St, Ste 3201, Toronto, ON, M7A 1L2, CANADA. Tel: 416-215-0855. p. 2691
Serafin, Stacia, Head, Youth & Teen Serv, Clarkston Independence District Library, 6495 Clarkston Rd, Clarkston, MI, 48346. Tel: 248-625-2212. p. 1091
Seraphine, Marcus, Head Librn, Dunwoody College of Technology, 818 Dunwoody Blvd, Minneapolis, MN, 55403. Tel: 612-381-3306. p. 1183
Serban, Raluca, Libr Tech, Toronto Rehab, 550 University Ave, Rm 2-055, Toronto, ON, M5G 2A2, CANADA. Tel: 416-597-3422, Ext 3050. p. 2697
Serdjenian, Tina, Librn, Waterville Historical Society Library, 62 Silver St, Unit B, Waterville, ME, 04901. Tel: 207-872-9439. p. 945
Serdyuk, Yana, Dir, Concordia University, 7400 Augusta St, River Forest, IL, 60305-1499. Tel: 708-209-3053. p. 639
Serdyuk, Yana, Libr Dir, Seneca Public Library District, 210 N Main St, Seneca, IL, 61360. Tel: 815-357-6566. p. 646
Seredey, Bridget, Dir, Prospect Community Library, 357 Main St, Prospect, PA, 16052. Tel: 724-865-9718. p. 1999
Serfass, Melissa, Electronic Res & Ref Librn, University of Arkansas at Little Rock, William H Bowen School of Law / Pulaski County Law Library, 1201 McMath Ave, Little Rock, AR, 72202. Tel: 501-916-5459. p. 102
Sergel, Tori, Head, Circ, Lake Forest Library, 360 E Deerpath Rd, Lake Forest, IL, 60045. Tel: 847-810-4616. p. 606
Serico, Susan, Dir, North Haledon Free Public Library, 129 Overlook Ave, North Haledon, NJ, 07508-2533. Tel: 973-427-6213. p. 1429
Serkownek, Edith, Head Librn, Kent State University Libraries, Fashion, Rockwell Hall, Rm 131, 515 Hilltop Dr, Kent, OH, 44242. Tel: 330-672-9502. p. 1792
Serlis-McPhillips, Sophia, Dir, Middle Country Public Library, 101 Eastwood Blvd, Centereach, NY, 11720. Tel: 631-585-9393, Ext 219. p. 1515
Serlis-McPhillips, Sophia, Dir, Middle Country Public Library, Selden Branch, 575 Middle Country Rd, Selden, NY, 11784. p. 1516
Serna, Kimberly, Assoc Dir, Research Servs, Jones Day, 717 Texas St, Ste 3300, Houston, TX, 77002. Tel: 832-239-3939, p. 2196
Serna, Nellie, Br Mgr, Madera County Library, Chowchilla Branch, 300 Kings Ave, Chowchilla, CA, 93610-2059. Tel: 559-665-2630. p. 171
Serpico, Joan, Dir, Moorestown Public Library, 111 W Second St, Moorestown, NJ, 08057. Tel: 856-234-0333. p. 1421
Serran, Stacey, Dir, Rice Avenue Community Public Library, 705 Rice Ave, Girard, PA, 16417. Tel: 814-774-8286. p. 1936
Serrano, Samuel, Head, Circ, University of Puerto Rico, Law School Library, Avenidas Ponce de Leon & Gandara, San Juan, PR, 00931. Tel: 787-999-9898. p. 2514
Serrata, Amy, Youth Serv Spec, Nueces County Public Libraries, 100 Terry Shamsie Blvd, Robstown, TX, 78380. Tel: 361-387-3431. p. 2233
Servaes, Brita, Undergrad Serv Librn, New School, Raymond Fogelman Library, 55 W 13th St, New York, NY, 10011. Tel: 212-229-5307, Ext 3163. p. 1592
Servais, Arlene, Tech Serv Assoc, Arcadia Free Public Library, 730 Raider Dr, Ste 3140, Arcadia, WI, 54612. Tel: 608-323-7505. p. 2421
Servais, Cheryl, Info Serv Coordr, Stormont, Dundas & Glengarry County Library, 26 Pitt St, Ste 106, Cornwall, ON, K6J 3P2, CANADA. Tel: 613-936-8777. p. 2637
Servais, Cheryl, District Supervisor, Stormont, Dundas & Glengarry County Library, Ingleside Branch, Ten Memorial Sq, Ingleside, ON, K0C 1M0, CANADA. Tel: 613-537-2592. p. 2638
Servant, Allison, Archivist, Societe d'histoire de la Haute-Gaspesie, 5B First Ave W, Sainte-Anne-des-Monts, QC, G4V 1B4, CANADA. Tel: 418-763-7871. p. 2734
Servatius-Brown, Sheryl, ILL, Ottawa Library, 105 S Hickory St, Ottawa, KS, 66067. Tel: 785-242-3080. p. 829
Servey, Patsy, Ad, Waupaca Area Public Library, 107 S Main St, Waupaca, WI, 54981-1521. Tel: 715-258-4414. p. 2485
Sesin, Armandina, Libr Dir, San Juan Memorial Library, 1010 S Standard Ave, San Juan, TX, 78589. Tel: 956-702-0926. p. 2241
Sessions, Denise, Librn, Shaw Memorial Library, 312 Main St, Plainfield, MA, 01070-9709. Tel: 413-634-5406. p. 1047
Sestokas, Frank, Br Supvr, Worcester Public Library, Frances Perkins Branch, 470 W Boylston St, Worcester, MA, 01606-3226. Tel: 508-799-1687. p. 1073
Sestrick, Tim, Music Librn, West Chester University, 25 W Rosedale Ave, West Chester, PA, 19383. Tel: 610-436-2379. p. 2020
Sestrick, Tim, Music Librn, West Chester University, Presser Music Library, Wells School of Music & Performing Arts Ctr, West Chester, PA, 19383. Tel: 610-436-2379, 610-436-2430. p. 2020
Setchell, Lori, Tech Info Spec, Carus LLC, 1500 Eighth St, LaSalle, IL, 61301-3500. Tel: 815-223-1500. p. 607
Setser, Laurel, Libr Dir, Avon-Washington Township Public Library, 498 N Avon Ave, Avon, IN, 46123. Tel: 317-272-4818. p. 669
Settle, Nicole, Branch Cluster Supvr, Fresno County Public Library, 2420 Mariposa St, Fresno, CA, 93721. Tel: 559-600-7323. p. 145
Settoon, Paula, Dean, Tulsa Community College Libraries, Metro Campus, 909 S Boston Ave, Tulsa, OK, 74119-2011. Tel: 918-595-7461. p. 1866
Settoon, Paula, Dir, Tulsa Community College Libraries, Northeast Campus, 3727 E Apache St, Tulsa, OK, 74115-3151. Tel: 918-595-7501. p. 1866
Setty, Linda, Librn, Belle Center Free Public Library, 103 S Elizabeth St, Belle Center, OH, 43310. Tel: 937-464-3611. p. 1750
Setzer, Jason, Dir, Libr Serv, Davidson-Davie Community College Library, 297 DCC Rd, Thomasville, NC, 27360-7385. Tel: 336-249-8186, Ext 6207. p. 1719
Setzkorn, Kirsten, Humanities Librn, Cedarville University, 251 N Main St, Cedarville, OH, 45314-0601. Tel: 937-766-7840. p. 1757
Seuell, Ashley, Campus Librn, Gateway Seminary, 3200 NE 109th Ave, Vancouver, WA, 98682-7749. Tel: 360-882-2179. p. 2391
Seufert, Joshua, Librn, Princeton University, East Asian Library, 33 Frist Campus Ctr, Rm 317, Princeton, NJ, 08544. Tel: 609-258-5336. p. 1437
Seuling, Robbin, Circ Supvr, South River Public Library, 55 Appleby Ave, South River, NJ, 08882-2499. Tel: 732-254-2488. p. 1444
Sevenski, Pam, Dir, West Frankfort Public Library, 402 E Poplar St, West Frankfort, IL, 62896. Tel: 618-932-3313. p. 660
Sever, Sarah, Asst Dir, Neuse Regional Library, 510 N Queen St, Kinston, NC, 28501. Tel: 252-527-7066. p. 1699
Severson, Matthew, Libr Dir, Academy of Motion Picture Arts & Sciences, 333 S La Cienega Blvd, Beverly Hills, CA, 90211. Tel: 310-247-3036, Ext 2200. p. 124
Severson, Robin, Cat Supvr, Northwest University, 5520 108th Ave NE, Kirkland, WA, 98083. Tel: 425-889-5264. p. 2368
Severy, Robin, Asst Librn, Platt Memorial Library, 279 Main St, Shoreham, VT, 05770. Tel: 802-897-2647. p. 2294
Sevett, Annice, Asst Dir, Albert Lea Public Library, 211 E Clark St, Albert Lea, MN, 56007. Tel: 507-377-4350. p. 1163
Sevigny-Killen, Brenda, Asst Dir, Libr Serv, Coll Develop, University of Maine at Augusta Libraries, 46 University Dr, Augusta, ME, 04330-9410. Tel: 207-621-3351. p. 915
Seville, Andy, Asst Dir, Tech Serv, St John's University Library, Kathryn & Shelby Cullom Davis Library, 101 Astor Pl, 2nd Flr, New York, NY, 10003. Tel: 212-277-5135. p. 1556

Seward, Katherine, Library Contact, The Aspen Institute, 1000 N Third St, Aspen, CO, 81611-1361. Tel: 970-925-7010. p. 264

Sewell, Bethany, Access Serv Librn, The College of New Jersey, 2000 Pennington Rd, Ewing, NJ, 08628-1104. Tel: 609-771-2311. p. 1402

Sewell, Carly, Cat, Ref Serv, Neiswander Library of Homeopathy, 1006 W 8th Ave, Ste B, King of Prussia, PA, 19406. Tel: 610-283-7567. p. 1948

Sewell, Jeff, Dir, Shook, Hardy & Bacon, 2555 Grand Blvd, 3rd Flr, Kansas City, MO, 64108-2613. Tel: 816-474-6550. p. 1257

Sewell, Justin, Syst Librn, Holy Family University Library, 9801 Frankford Ave, Philadelphia, PA, 19114. Tel: 267-341-3573. p. 1981

Sewell, Kaylee, Programming Librn, Rosebud County Library, 201 N Ninth Ave, Forsyth, MT, 59327. Tel: 406-346-7561. p. 1293

Sewell, Lisa, Librn, NASA Ames Research Center, Life Sciences Library, Mail Stop 239-13, Moffett Field, CA, 94035-1000. Tel: 650-604-5387. p. 178

Sewell, Peter, Libr Coord, Nebraska Department of Corrections, 4201 S 14th St, Lincoln, NE, 68502. Tel: 402-479-3267. p. 1321

Sexton, Amy, Collection Mgmt Assoc, The College of Wooster Libraries, 1140 Beall Ave, Wooster, OH, 44691-2364. Tel: 330-263-2107. p. 1833

Sexton, Barbara, Asst Librn, Wayne County Public Library, 157 Rolling Hills Blvd, Monticello, KY, 42633. Tel: 606-348-8565. p. 869

Sexton, Chris, Ref Serv Mgr, Research Librn, Taft, Stettinius & Hollister LLP, 2200 IDS Ctr, 80 S Eighth St, Minneapolis, MN, 55402. Tel: 612-977-8400. p. 1185

Sexton, Ellen, Chief Librn, John Jay College of Criminal Justice, 899 Tenth Ave, New York, NY, 10019. Tel: 212-237-8246. p. 1589

Sexton, Jill, Assoc Dir, Digital Initiatives & Org Strategy, North Carolina State University Libraries, D H Hill Jr Library, Two Broughton Dr, Raleigh, NC, 27695. Tel: 919-515-7188. p. 1709

Sexton, John, Exec Dir, Greenburgh Public Library, 300 Tarrytown Rd, Elmsford, NY, 10523. Tel: 914-721-8200. p. 1531

Sexton, Lexi, Dir, Liberty Center Public Library, 124 East St, Liberty Center, OH, 43532. Tel: 419-533-5721. p. 1795

Sexton, Manda, Assessment Librn, Kennesaw State University Library System, 385 Cobb Ave NW, MD 1701, Kennesaw, GA, 30144. Tel: 470-578-6511. p. 483

Sexton, Marcia, Tech Serv Librn, Ramapo College of New Jersey, 505 Ramapo Valley Rd, Mahwah, NJ, 07430-1623. Tel: 201-684-7362. p. 1415

Sexton, Nancy D, Head, Tech Serv, Emmet O'Neal Library, 50 Oak St, Mountain Brook, AL, 35213. Tel: 205-879-0459. p. 31

Sexton, Will, Head, Digital Projects, Duke University Libraries, 411 Chapel Dr, Durham, NC, 27708. Tel: 919-660-6931. p. 1684

Sexton-Mayes, Robin, Acting Collections Mgmt Librn, Fundy Library Region, One Market Sq, Saint John, NB, E2L 4Z6, CANADA. Tel: 506-643-7222. p. 2604

Seybold, Linda S, Librn, Grove United Methodist Church Library, 490 W Boot Rd, West Chester, PA, 19380. Tel: 610-696-2663. p. 2020

Seyl, Sara, Tech Serv Librn, San Marcos Public Library, 625 E Hopkins, San Marcos, TX, 78666. Tel: 512-393-8200. p. 2241

Seymour, Anne, Assoc Dir, Johns Hopkins University Libraries, Carol J Gray Nursing Information Resource Center, 525 N Wolfe St, Rm 313, Baltimore, MD, 21202. Tel: 410-955-7559. p. 954

Seymour, Denise, Libr Assoc, Massasoit Community College, Canton Campus Library, 900 Randolph St, Canton, MA, 02021. Tel: 508-588-9100, Ext 2942. p. 1003

Seymour, Felicia, Br Librn, Southeast Regional Library, Gainsborough Branch, 401 Railway Ave, Gainsborough, SK, S0C 0Z0, CANADA. Tel: 306-685-2229. p. 2753

Seymour, Jason, Asst Libr Dir, Carolina University, 420 S Broad St, Winston-Salem, NC, 27101-5025. Tel: 336-714-7952. p. 1724

Seymour, Nancy S, Libr Operations Mgr, Jones Day, 325 John H McConnell Blvd, Ste 600, Columbus, OH, 43215-2673. Tel: 614-469-3939. p. 1773

Seymour, Olivia, Ch, Portsmouth Free Public Library, 2658 E Main Rd, Portsmouth, RI, 02871. Tel: 401-683-9457. p. 2037

Sezzi, Peter H, Chair, Librn, Ventura College, 4667 Telegraph Rd, Ventura, CA, 93003. Tel: 805-289-6189. p. 255

Sfanos, Ben H, Data Mgt, Dir, IT, Howard County Library System, 9411 Frederick Rd, Ellicott City, MD, 21042. Tel: 410-313-7750. p. 965

Sferra, Maria, Regional Br Operations Mgr, Public Library of Cincinnati & Hamilton County, 800 Vine St, Cincinnati, OH, 45202-2009. Tel: 513-369-4419. p. 1761

Sgammato, Judith, Asst Dir, Head, Adult Serv, Perrot Memorial Library, 90 Sound Beach Ave, Old Greenwich, CT, 06870. Tel: 203-637-1066. p. 332

Sgombick, Meg, Dir, Florida Public Library, Four Cohen Circle, Florida, NY, 10921-1514. Tel: 845-651-7659. p. 1533

Sgro, Holly, Ch, Highland Public Library, 14 Elting Pl, Highland, NY, 12528. Tel: 845-691-2275. p. 1546

Shackelford, Philip, Dir, South Arkansas Community College, 300 S West Ave, El Dorado, AR, 71730. Tel: 870-864-7115. p. 94

Shackle, Ashley, Br Head, Henderson County Public Library, Green River, 50 Green River Rd, Zirconia, NC, 28790. Tel: 828-697-4969. p. 1695

Shackles, Maria, Br Mgr, Tacoma Public Library, Wheelock Branch, 3722 N 26th St, Tacoma, WA, 98407. Tel: 253-280-2980. p. 2387

Shacklett, Rita, Dir of Libr, Rutherford County Library System, 105 W Vine St, Murfreesboro, TN, 37130-3673. Tel: 615-962-7424. p. 2117

Shaddy, Robert, Chief Librn, Queens College, Benjamin S Rosenthal Library, 65-30 Kissena Blvd, Flushing, NY, 11367-0904. Tel: 718-997-3700. p. 1533

Shade, Leslie, Dr, Prof, University of Toronto, 140 St George St, Toronto, ON, M5S 3G6, CANADA. Tel: 416-978-3234. p. 2796

Shade, Stephanie, Br Mgr, Mid-Continent Public Library, Claycomo Branch, 309 NE US Hwy 69, Claycomo, MO, 64119. Tel: 816-455-5030. p. 1250

Shader, Robin, Libr Dir, Northwest Regional Library System, 898 W 11th St, Panama City, FL, 32401. Tel: 850-522-2100. p. 435

Shadid, Jennifer M, Library Contact, Peoria County Law Library, Peoria County Court House, Rm 211, 324 Main St, Peoria, IL, 61602. Tel: 309-672-6084. p. 634

Shadowens, Melissa, Libr Mgr, Plano Public Library System, Gladys Harrington Library, 1501 18th St, Plano, TX, 75074. Tel: 972-941-7175. p. 2227

Shadowens, Paulina, Community Experience Librn, Lane Memorial Library, Two Academy Ave, Hampton, NH, 03842. Tel: 603-926-3368. p. 1366

Shadrix, Pam, Ref & Instruction, Life University, 1269 Barclay Circle, Marietta, GA, 30060. Tel: 770-426-2688. p. 489

Shafer, Connie, Dir, Shubert Public Library & Museum, 313 Main St, Shubert, NE, 68437. Tel: 402-883-2059. p. 1336

Shafer, John, Research Librn, University of San Francisco, Zief Law Library, 2101 Fulton St, San Francisco, CA, 94117-1004. Tel: 415-422-6679. p. 230

Shafer, Leesa, Dir, Spearville Township Library, 414 N Main St, Spearville, KS, 67876. Tel: 620-385-2501. p. 837

Shafer, Lori, Adult Serv, Briggs Lawrence County Public Library, 321 S Fourth St, Ironton, OH, 45638. Tel: 740-532-1124. p. 1791

Shafer, Maribeth, Asst Dir, Central Kansas Library System, 1409 Williams St, Great Bend, KS, 67530-4020. Tel: 620-792-4865. p. 810

Shafer, Pam, Dir, Lone Star College System, Tomball College Library, 30555 Tomball Pkwy, Tomball, TX, 77375-4036. Tel: 832-559-4217. p. 2197

Shafer, Typhanie, Archivist, Becker County Historical Society, 714 Summit Ave, Detroit Lakes, MN, 56501. Tel: 218-847-2938. p. 1171

Shaffer, Brandi, Dir, Burlingame Community Library, 122 W Santa Fe Ave, Burlingame, KS, 66413. Tel: 785-654-3400. p. 799

Shaffer, Chris, Asst Vice Chancellor, Univ Librn, University of California San Francisco, 530 Parnassus Ave, San Francisco, CA, 94143. Tel: 415-476-5557. p. 229

Shaffer, Chris, Dr, Dean, Univ Libr, Troy University Library, 309 Wallace Hall, Troy, AL, 36082. Tel: 334-670-3694. p. 37

Shaffer, David, Dir, Rappahannock County Library, Four Library Rd, Washington, VA, 22747. Tel: 540-675-3780. p. 2352

Shaffer, Duane, Coll Develop, Sanibel Public Library District, 770 Dunlop Rd, Sanibel, FL, 33957. Tel: 239-472-2483. p. 442

Shaffer, Eleonore, Br Head, Vancouver Public Library, South Hill Branch, 6076 Fraser St, Vancouver, BC, V5W 2Z7, CANADA. Tel: 604-665-3965. p. 2582

Shaffer, Elizabeth, Asst Prof, University of British Columbia, The Irving K Barber Learning Ctr, 1961 E Mall, Ste 470, Vancouver, BC, V6T 1Z1, CANADA. Tel: 604-822-2404. p. 2795

Shaffer, Jaimie, Circ Supvr, University of Dubuque Library, 2000 University Ave, Dubuque, IA, 52001. Tel: 563-589-3100. p. 749

Shaffer, Larina, Ch, Logansport-Cass County Public Library, 616 E Broadway, Logansport, IN, 46947. Tel: 574-753-6383. p. 703

Shaffer, Leigh Ann, Br Mgr, Mercer County District Library, Mendon Branch, 105 W Market St, Mendon, OH, 45862. Tel: 419-795-6472. p. 1757

Shaffer, Lisa, Head Librn, Albany College of Pharmacy & Health Sciences, 106 New Scotland Ave, Albany, NY, 12208. Tel: 518-694-7270. p. 1481

Shaffer, Michael, Librn, Maryland Correctional Institution-Hagerstown Library, 18601 Roxbury Rd, Hagerstown, MD, 21746. Tel: 240-420-1000, Ext 2347, 240-420-1340, 301-733-2800, Ext 2347. p. 968

Shaffer, Ryan, Pres, Japan-American Society of Washington DC Library, 1819 L St NW, Level 410, Washington, DC, 20036. Tel: 202-833-2210. p. 370

Shaffer, Seth, Per, Ref Librn, Southern Adventist University, 4851 Industrial Dr, Collegedale, TN, 37315. Tel: 423-236-2792. p. 2094

Shaffer, Stephanie, Dep Fiscal Officer, North Canton Public Library, 185 N Main St, North Canton, OH, 44720-2595. Tel: 330-499-4712. p. 1809

Shaffer, Virginia, Libr Dir, Allen Community College Library, 1801 N Cottonwood, Iola, KS, 66749-1648. Tel: 620-365-5116, Ext 6235. p. 815

Shaffer-Duong, Amy, Ch Serv, Palmyra Public Library, 50 Landings Dr, Ste B, Annville, PA, 17003. Tel: 717-838-1347. p. 1906

Shaffett, John, Dir, Libr & Info Serv, Brewton-Parker College, 201 David-Eliza Fountain Circle, Mount Vernon, GA, 30445. Tel: 912-583-3235. p. 492

Shafiroff, Jodi, Dir, Becket Athenaeum, Inc, 3367 Main St, Becket, MA, 01223. Tel: 413-623-5483. p. 987

Shah, Alpesh, IT Mgr, East Brunswick Public Library, Two Jean Walling Civic Ctr, East Brunswick, NJ, 08816-3599. Tel: 732-390-6950. p. 1399
Shah, Bijal, Electronic Res, ILL, Ref, University of Baltimore, Law Library, Angelos Law Center, 7th thru 12th Flrs, 1401 N Charles St, Baltimore, MD, 21201. Tel: 410-837-4554. p. 957
Shah, Sharad J, Coll Mgt Librn, Smithsonian Libraries, Museum Support Center Library, Smithsonian Museum Support Center, Rm C-2000, 4210 Silver Hill Rd, Suitland, DC, 20746-2863. Tel: 301-238-1030. p. 375
Shah, Stacey, Distance Learning Librn, Elgin Community College, 1700 Spartan Dr, Elgin, IL, 60123. Tel: 847-214-7337. p. 584
Shah, Zahid, Managing Librn, Brooklyn Public Library, Gerritsen Beach, 2808 Gerritsen Ave, Brooklyn, NY, 11229. Tel: 718-368-1435. p. 1503
Shah, Zahid, Managing Librn, Brooklyn Public Library, Jamaica Bay, 9727 Seaview Ave, Brooklyn, NY, 11236. Tel: 718-241-3571. p. 1503
Shahlaei, Faraz, Supvr, Pub Serv, Pepperdine University Libraries, School of Law-Jerene Appleby Harnish Law Library, 24255 Pacific Coast Hwy, Malibu, CA, 90263. Tel: 310-506-4643. p. 171
Shain, Zar, Br Mgr, San Diego Public Library, North Park, 3795 31st St, San Diego, CA, 92104. Tel: 619-533-3972. p. 220
Shainidze-Krebs, Teona, Chief Exec Officer, Interim Chief Librn, Pikes Peak Library District, 20 N Cascade Ave, Colorado Springs, CO, 80903. Tel: 719-531-6333. p. 271
Shake, Miranda, Libr Dir, Lakeview College of Nursing, 903 N Logan Ave, Danville, IL, 61832. Tel: 217-709-0927. p. 575
Shaker, Jennifer, Dir, Willett Free Library, 45 Ferry Rd, Saunderstown, RI, 02874. Tel: 401-294-2081. p. 2041
Shaknovich, Rebecca, Head Librn, Free Library of Philadelphia, Children's Department, 1901 Vine St, Rm 22, Philadelphia, PA, 19103-1116. Tel: 215-686-5369. p. 1977
Shalley, Doris, Bibliog Instr, Librn, Online Serv, GlaxoSmithKline Pharmaceuticals, Marketing Library, One Franklin Plaza, Philadelphia, PA, 19101. Tel: 215-751-5576. p. 1981
Shalongo, Joette, Head, Cat, Thomas Beaver Free Library, 317 Ferry St, Danville, PA, 17821-1939. Tel: 570-275-4180. p. 1925
Shaltry, Huda, Br Supvr, Boise Public Library, Library! at Hillcrest, 5246 W Overland Rd, Boise, ID, 83705. Tel: 208-972-8340. p. 517
Shamchuk, Lisa, Asst Prof, MacEwan University, 10700-104 Ave NW 5-306W, Edmonton, AB, T5J 4S2, CANADA. Tel: 780-633-3574. p. 2795
Shams, Chabha, Br Mgr, Volusia County Public Library, DeLand Regional Library, 130 E Howry Ave, DeLand, FL, 32724. Tel: 386-822-6430. p. 393
Shamy, Selwa, Asst Dir, Montclair Public Library, 50 S Fullerton Ave, Montclair, NJ, 07042. Tel: 973-744-0500. p. 1420
Shan, Yi, Librn, University of Texas Libraries, East Asian Library Program, Perry-Castaneda Library, 2.302, Mail Code S5431, 101 E 21st St, Austin, TX, 78712-1474. Tel: 512-495-4325. p. 2142
Shanda, Subia, Dir, Lampasas Public Library, 201 S Main St, Lampasas, TX, 76550. Tel: 512-556-3251. p. 2209
Shaner, Arlene, Hist Coll Librn, New York Academy of Medicine Library, 1216 Fifth Ave, New York, NY, 10029. Tel: 212-822-7313. p. 1593
Shank, Amy J, Dir, Luther Area Public Library, 115 State St, Luther, MI, 49656. Tel: 231-797-8006. p. 1128
Shank, John, Head Librn, Pennsylvania State University, Berks Campus, Tulpehocken Rd, Reading, PA, 19610. Tel: 610-396-6339. p. 2000
Shank, Karin, Sr Res Analyst, North Carolina Biotechnology Center Life Science Intelligence, 15 T W Alexander Dr, Research Triangle Park, NC, 27709. Tel: 919-541-9366. p. 1712
Shank, Matthew, Mgr, Dallas Public Library, Mountain Creek, 6102 Mountain Creek Pkwy, Dallas, TX, 75249. Tel: 214-670-6704. p. 2166
Shank, Patrick, Asst Archivist, Catholic Historical Research Center of the Archdiocese of Philadelphia, 6740 Roosevelt Blvd, Philadelphia, PA, 19149. Tel: 215-904-8149. p. 1975
Shank, Sarah, ILL, Ithaca College Library, 953 Danby Rd, Ithaca, NY, 14850-7060. Tel: 607-274-3206. p. 1553
Shank-Chapman, Karen, Exec Dir, Wayne County, Indiana, Historical Museum Library, 1150 North A St, Richmond, IN, 47374. Tel: 765-962-5756. p. 715
Shanks, Jean, Librn, Birmingham Public Library, Wylam Branch, 4300 Seventh Ave, Birmingham, AL, 35224-2624. Tel: 205-785-0349. p. 8
Shankweiler, Joseph, Spec Coll Cat Librn, Western Kentucky University Libraries, Helm-Cravens Library Complex, 1906 College Heights Blvd, No 11067, Bowling Green, KY, 42101-1067. Tel: 270-745-6306. p. 849
Shannahan, Annette, Dir, North English Public Library, 123 S Main, North English, IA, 52316. Tel: 319-664-3725. p. 773
Shannon, Callie, ILL Librn, Indiana Free Library, Inc, 845 Philadelphia St, Indiana, PA, 15701-3907. Tel: 724-465-8841. p. 1945
Shannon, Carol, Dir, East Rochester Public Library, 935 Portland St, East Rochester, NH, 03868. Tel: 603-923-0126. p. 1362
Shannon, Crystal, Interim Dean of Libr, Indiana University Northwest, 3400 Broadway, Gary, IN, 46408. Tel: 219-980-6547. p. 686
Shannon, Judy, Colls Mgr, Lee County Library System, Library Processing, 881 Gunnery Rd N, Ste 2, Lehigh Acres, FL, 33971-1246. Tel: 239-533-4170. p. 403
Shannon, Kate, Communications Mgr, Libr Assoc, Roeliff Jansen Community Library, 9091 Rte 22, Hillsdale, NY, 12529. Tel: 518-325-4101. p. 1547
Shannon, Kathy, Exec Dir, Petroleum Museum Library & Hall of Fame, 1500 Interstate 20 W, Midland, TX, 79701. Tel: 432-683-4403. p. 2219
Shannon, Kit, Interim Dean of Libr, University of Alaska Fairbanks, 1732 Tanana Dr, Fairbanks, AK, 99775. Tel: 907-474-6194. p. 45
Shannon, Mandy, Assoc Univ Librn, Pub Serv, Wright State University Libraries, 126 Dunbar Library, 3640 Colonel Glenn Hwy, Dayton, OH, 45435-0001. Tel: 937-775-3594. p. 1781
Shanton, Kristina, Music Librn, Ithaca College Library, 953 Danby Rd, Ithaca, NY, 14850-7060. Tel: 607-274-3206. p. 1552
Shapiola, Annemarie, Ch Serv, Borough of Totowa Public Library, 537 Totowa Rd, Totowa, NJ, 07512-1699. Tel: 973-790-3265, Ext 10. p. 1447
Shapiro, Carey, Libr Dir, Palmyra Memorial Library, 525 Illinois Pl, Palmyra, NE, 68418. Tel: 402-780-5344. p. 1332
Shapiro, Danielle, Managing Librn, Brooklyn Public Library, Highlawn, 1664 W 13th St, Brooklyn, NY, 11223. Tel: 718-234-7208. p. 1503
Shapiro, Fred, Assoc Librn, Coll, Yale University Library, Lillian Goldman Library Yale Law School, 127 Wall St, New Haven, CT, 06511. Tel: 203-432-4840. p. 328
Shapiro, Jocelyn, Mgr, Federal Library & Information Network, Library of Congress FEDLINK, Adams Bldg, Rm 217, 101 Independence Ave SE, Washington, DC, 20540-4935. Tel: 202-707-4168. p. 2763
Shapiro, Martin, Coll Develop, American University Library, 4400 Massachusetts Ave NW, Washington, DC, 20016-8046. Tel: 202-885-3854. p. 361
Shapiro, Robert, Dir, South East Area Health Education Center Medical Library, 2131 S 17th St, Wilmington, NC, 28401. Tel: 910-343-2180. p. 1723
Shapiro, Robert M, II, Dir, Libr Serv, Novant Health Library Services, 3333 Silas Creek Pkwy, Winston-Salem, NC, 27103-3090. Tel: 336-718-5995. p. 1725
Shapiro, Stacey, Programming Librn, YA Librn, Cranford Free Public Library, 224 Walnut Ave, Cranford, NJ, 07016-2931. Tel: 908-709-7272. p. 1398
Shapiro, Steven, Electronic Res Librn, Multimedia, Montclair State University, One Normal Ave, Montclair, NJ, 07043-1699. Tel: 973-655-4428. p. 1420
Shapka, Jalisa, Libr Asst, Grassland Public Library, Hwy 63, Box 150, Grassland, AB, T0A 1V0, CANADA. Tel: 780-525-3733. p. 2541
Shapoval, Sandy, Dean of the Library & Research Servs, Phillips Theological Seminary Library, 901 N Mingo Rd, Tulsa, OK, 74116. Tel: 918-270-6437. p. 1865
Shappee, Lisa, Dir, Kansas State University at Salina, Technology Ctr Bldg, Rm 111, 2310 Centennial Rd, Salina, KS, 67401. Tel: 785-826-2636. p. 835
Sharbaugh, Lisa, Tech Coordr, South Central Kansas Library System, 321 N Main St, South Hutchinson, KS, 67505. Tel: 620-663-3211. p. 837
Share, Ellen, Librn, Washington Hebrew Congregation Libraries, 3935 Macomb St NW, Washington, DC, 20016-3741. Tel: 301-354-3212. p. 381
Shari, Ferda, Br Mgr, Belmont County District Library, Victoria Read Flushing Branch, 300 High St, Flushing, OH, 43977. Tel: 740-968-3891. p. 1800
Sharkey, Kathleen, Head, Circ, Lower Providence Community Library, 50 Parklane Dr, Eagleville, PA, 19403-1171. Tel: 610-666-6640. p. 1928
Sharkey, Leslie Ann, Libr Mgr, Fox Creek Municipal Library, 501 Eighth St, Fox Creek, AB, T0H 1P0, CANADA. Tel: 780-622-2343. p. 2540
Sharkey, Lisa, Asst Mgr, Adult Serv, Teen Serv, La Grange Public Library, Ten W Cossitt Ave, La Grange, IL, 60525. Tel: 708-215-3228. p. 605
Sharkey, Stephanie, Libr Spec, Northern Virginia Community College Libraries, Woodbridge Library, Bldg WAS, Rm 230, 15200 Neabsco Mills Rd, Woodbridge, VA, 22191. Tel: 703-878-5733. p. 2304
Sharkey, Wendy, Cat Librn, Circ Librn, Bennington Free Library, 101 Silver St, Bennington, VT, 05201. Tel: 802-442-9051. p. 2279
Sharma, Minakshi, Librn, Toronto Public Health Library, 277 Victoria St, 6th Flr, Toronto, ON, M5B 1W2, CANADA. Tel: 416-338-0049. p. 2693
Sharon, Stephanie, Multimedia, Chester County Library & District Center, 450 Exton Square Pkwy, Exton, PA, 19341-2496. Tel: 610-344-5600. p. 1932
Sharp, Alex, Info Serv Librn, Tennessee Wesleyan College, 23 Coach Farmer Dr, Athens, TN, 37303. Tel: 423-746-5249. p. 2088
Sharp, Alexis Fetzer, State Law Librn, Virginia State Law Library, Supreme Court Bldg, 2nd Flr, 100 N Ninth St, Richmond, VA, 23219-2335. Tel: 804-786-2075. p. 2344
Sharp, Andrew, Dir, Jones County Junior College, 900 S Court St, Ellisville, MS, 39437. Tel: 601-477-4055. p. 1216
Sharp, Carla, Head, Youth Serv, Brighton District Library, 100 Library Dr, Brighton, MI, 48116. Tel: 810-229-6571, Ext 209. p. 1087
Sharp, Chris, Access Serv, Interim Dir, Kennesaw State University Library System, 385 Cobb Ave NW, MD 1701, Kennesaw, GA, 30144. Tel: 470-578-6190. p. 483
Sharp, Chris, Syst Adminr, Public Information Network for Electronic Services, Georgia Public Library Service, 2872 Woodcock Blvd, Ste 250, Atlanta, GA, 30341. Tel: 404-235-7147. p. 2764

Sharp, David, Circ Supvr, Ohio State University LIBRARIES, Veterinary Medicine, 225 Veterinary Medicine Academic Bldg, 1900 Coffey Rd, Columbus, OH, 43210. Tel: 614-292-6107. p. 1777
Sharp, David, Head, Acq, Carleton University Library, 1125 Colonel By Dr, Ottawa, ON, K1S 5B6, CANADA. Tel: 613-520-2600, Ext 8372. p. 2666
Sharp, Debra, Branch Lead, Charlotte Mecklenburg Library, Hickory Grove Branch, 5935 Hickory Grove Rd, Charlotte, NC, 28215. Tel: 704-416-4400. p. 1679
Sharp, Debra, Br Mgr, Charlotte Mecklenburg Library, University City Regional, 301 East W T Harris Blvd, Charlotte, NC, 28262. Tel: 704-416-7200. p. 1680
Sharp, Janice, Dir, Valley Center Public Library, 314 E Clay St, Valley Center, KS, 67147. Tel: 316-755-7350. p. 840
Sharp, Jody, Coordr, Tech Serv, Baltimore County Public Library, 320 York Rd, Towson, MD, 21204-5179. Tel: 410-887-6100. p. 979
Sharp, Katherine, Br Coordr, South Shore Public Libraries, Margaret Hennigar Public Library, 135 North Park St, Unit B, Bridgewater, NS, B4V 9B3, CANADA. Tel: 902-543-9222. p. 2616
Sharp, Leslie, Dean of Libr, Georgia Institute of Technology Library, 260 Fourth St NW, Atlanta, GA, 30332. Tel: 404-385-7590. p. 464
Sharp, Lynsey, Supv Librn, Pierce County Library System, Buckley Branch, 123 S River Ave, Buckley, WA, 98321. Tel: 253-548-3310, 360-829-0300. p. 2386
Sharp, Marshana, Br Mgr, Cherokee Regional Library System, Dade County Public Library, 102 Court St, Trenton, GA, 30752. Tel: 706-657-7857. p. 484
Sharp, Melanie, Circ Mgr, Saint Tammany Parish Library, Covington Branch, 310 W 21st Ave, Covington, LA, 70433. Tel: 985-893-6280. p. 888
Sharp, Michelle, Br Mgr, Indianapolis Public Library, Garfield Park, 2502 Shelby St, Indianapolis, IN, 46203-4236. Tel: 317-275-4495. p. 695
Sharp, Shannon, Asst Treasurer, Chief Financial Officer, The New York Public Library - Astor, Lenox & Tilden Foundations, 476 Fifth Ave, (@ 42nd St), New York, NY, 10018. Tel: 212-621-0241. p. 1594
Sharp, Susie, Librn, Eddy-New Rockford Library, Ten Eight St N, New Rockford, ND, 58356. Tel: 701-947-5540. p. 1739
Sharp, Tammie, Human Res Mgr, Kansas City, Kansas Public Library, 625 Minnesota Ave, Kansas City, KS, 66101. Tel: 913-295-8250, Ext 6400. p. 816
Sharpe, Amy, Asst Librn, Sharp HealthCare, 7901 Frost St, San Diego, CA, 92123. Tel: 858-939-3242. p. 222
Sharpe, Delanie, Youth Serv Librn, Clintonville Public Library, 75 Hemlock St, Clintonville, WI, 54929-1461. Tel: 715-823-7133. p. 2428
Sharpe, Elizabeth, Co-Executive Dir, Historic Northampton, 46 Bridge St, Northampton, MA, 01060. Tel: 413-584-6011. p. 1042
Sharpe, Heather, Exec Dir, Lancaster Public Library, 125 N Duke St, Lancaster, PA, 17602. Tel: 717-394-2651, Ext 108. p. 1951
Sharpe, Lori, Health Res Ctr Coordr, Prince County Hospital, 65 Roy Boates Ave, Summerside, PE, C1N 2A9, CANADA. Tel: 902-438-4520. p. 2708
Sharpe, Maddie, Dir, Lake Region Public Library, 423 Seventh St NE, Devils Lake, ND, 58301-2529. Tel: 701-662-2220. p. 1731
Sharpe, Patti, Librn, Patterson Palmer Library, PO Box 1068, Truro, NS, B2N 5B9, CANADA. Tel: 902-897-2000. p. 2623
Sharpe, Paul, Univ Librn, University of Texas Rio Grande Valley, 1201 W University Blvd, Edinburg, TX, 78541-2999. Tel: 956-665-2344. p. 2173
Sharpe, Sally, Dir, Francesville-Salem Township Public Library, 201 W Montgomery St, Francesville, IN, 47946. Tel: 219-567-9433. p. 685
Sharpe, Susan, Mgr, Libr Serv, H Lee Moffitt Cancer Center & Research Institute, 12902 USF Magnolia Dr, Tampa, FL, 33612. Tel: 813-745-4673. p. 448
Sharpe, Tania, Chief Librn/CEO, Chatham-Kent Public Library, 120 Queen St, Chatham, ON, N7M 2G6, CANADA. Tel: 519-354-2940. p. 2635
Sharpensteen, Isabella, Interim Dir, ILL Tech, Cortez Public Library, 202 N Park, Cortez, CO, 81321-3300. Tel: 970-565-8117. p. 272
Sharples, Sarah, Libr Mgr, Pikes Peak Library District, Sand Creek Library, 1821 S Academy Blvd, Colorado Springs, CO, 80916. Tel: 719-531-6333, Ext 6374. p. 271
Sharps, Andrea, Dir, Coll Serv, Spokane County Library District, 4322 N Argonne Rd, Spokane, WA, 99212. Tel: 509-893-8200. p. 2384
Sharron, David, Head, Spec Coll, Univ Archivist, Brock University, 1812 Sir Isaac Brock Way, St. Catharines, ON, L2S 3A1, CANADA. Tel: 905-688-5550, Ext 3264. p. 2679
Sharrow, Zachary, Head, Digital Initiatives, The College of Wooster Libraries, 1140 Beall Ave, Wooster, OH, 44691-2364. Tel: 330-263-2442. p. 1832
Sharry, Sharon A, Dir, Jones Library, Inc, 43 Amity St, Amherst, MA, 01002-2285. Tel: 413-259-3090. p. 984
Sharum, Monica, Assoc Dir, Libr Admin, University of the Pacific - McGeorge School of Law, 3282 Fifth Ave, Sacramento, CA, 95817. Tel: 916-739-7131. p. 210
Sharwell, Erin, Ms, Head, Libr Operations, State University of New York College at Brockport, 350 New Campus Dr, Brockport, NY, 14420-2997. Tel: 585-395-2142. p. 1497
Shary, Patricia, Librn, Broad Brook Public Library, 78 Main St, Broad Brook, CT, 06016. Tel: 860-627-0493. p. 304
Shasteen, Ruth, Libr Consult, Moultrie County Historical & Genealogical Society Library, 1303 S Hamilton St, Sullivan, IL, 61951. Tel: 217-728-4085. p. 652
Shatara, Halimeh, Libr Tech II, Palm Beach State College, 1977 College Dr, Mail Sta 43, Belle Glade, FL, 33430. Tel: 561-993-1155. p. 384
Shatarevyan, Suzie, Head, Access & Collection Mgmt Services, Loyola Law School, 919 S Albany St, Los Angeles, CA, 90015-1211. Tel: 213-736-1147. p. 166
Shatat, Mara, Archivist, Ref & Instruction Librn, Ursuline College, 2550 Lander Rd, Pepper Pike, OH, 44124-4398. Tel: 440-449-4202. p. 1815
Shatzer, Jennifer, Dir, Wayne County Public Library, 220 W Liberty St, Wooster, OH, 44691. Tel: 330-262-0986. p. 1833
Shaub, Kyle, Digital Serv Mgr, IT Mgr, Waukegan Public Library, 128 N County St, Waukegan, IL, 60085. Tel: 847-623-2041. p. 660
Shaughnessy, Amy, Syst Librn, Suburban Library Cooperative, 44750 Delco Blvd, Sterling Heights, MI, 48313. Tel: 586-685-5750. p. 2767
Shaughnessy, Jean, Dir, Athol Public Library, 568 Main St, Athol, MA, 01331. Tel: 978-249-9515. p. 986
Shaughnessy, Kathryn, Assoc Univ Librn, St John's University Library, St Augustine Hall, 8000 Utopia Pkwy, Jamaica, NY, 11439. Tel: 718-990-1454. p. 1556
Shave, Diane, Libr Dir, Breton Municipal Library, 4916-50 Ave, Breton, AB, T0C 0P0, CANADA. Tel: 780-696-3740. p. 2524
Shaver, Paul, Dir, Tampa-Hillsborough County Public Library System, Bruton Memorial Library, 302 W McLendon St, Plant City, FL, 33563. Tel: 813-757-9215. p. 448
Shaw, Amy, Head, Archives & Spec Coll, Saint Catherine University, 2004 Randolph Ave, Saint Paul, MN, 55105. Tel: 651-690-6423. p. 1201
Shaw, Anna, Dir, Beaman Memorial Public Library, Eight Newton St, West Boylston, MA, 01583. Tel: 508-835-3711. p. 1065
Shaw, April, Govt Doc/Ref Librn, State of Vermont Department of Libraries, 60 Washington St, Ste 2, Barre, VT, 05641. Tel: 802-636-0040. p. 2278
Shaw, Benjamin, Mgr, Libr Operations, Newmarket Public Library, 438 Park Ave, Newmarket, ON, L3Y 1W1, CANADA. Tel: 905-953-5110. p. 2660
Shaw, Cathy, Dir, Edgewood Public Library, 203 W Union St, Edgewood, IA, 52042. Tel: 563-928-6242. p. 750
Shaw, Chandra, Circ Tech, Montana State University-Billings Library, 1500 University Dr, Billings, MT, 59101. Tel: 406-657-1671. p. 1288
Shaw, Collen, Circulation & Outreach Services, Bloomington Public Library, 205 E Olive St, Bloomington, IL, 61701. Tel: 309-828-6091. p. 543
Shaw, Courtney, Commun Outreach Librn, Memphis Public Library, Hollywood Branch, 1530 N Hollywood St, Memphis, TN, 38108. Tel: 901-415-2772. p. 2113
Shaw, Dawn, Asst Librn, Nelson Public Library, Ten W Third St, Nelson, NE, 68961. Tel: 402-225-7111. p. 1326
Shaw, Debbie, Br Librn, Community District Library, Lennon-Venice Township, 11904 Lennon Rd, Lennon, MI, 48449. Tel: 810-621-3202. p. 1095
Shaw, Diane, Dir, Archives & Spec Coll, Lafayette College, 710 Sullivan Rd, Easton, PA, 18042-1797. Tel: 610-330-5401. p. 1928
Shaw, Dianne, Circ Spec, Gallaudet University Library, 800 Florida Ave NE, Washington, DC, 20002. Tel: 202-651-2349. p. 367
Shaw, Erin, Asst Prof, University of Central Arkansas, College of Education, PO Box 4918, Conway, AR, 72032-5001. Tel: 501-450-3177, 501-450-5497. p. 2782
Shaw, Heather, Librn, Northeast Texas Community College, 2886 Farm-to-Market Rd 1735, Mount Pleasant, TX, 75456. Tel: 903-434-8100. p. 2221
Shaw, James, Coll Coordr, Govt Doc Librn, University of Nebraska at Omaha, 6001 Dodge St, Omaha, NE, 68182-0237. Tel: 402-554-2225. p. 1330
Shaw, Jane, Asst Librn, Madison Public Library, 12 Old Point Ave, Madison, ME, 04950. Tel: 207-696-5626. p. 931
Shaw, Janet, Librn, Missouri Department of Corrections, Women's Eastern Reception & Diagnostic Correctional Center, 1101 E Hwy 54, Vandalia, MO, 63382-2905. Tel: 573-594-6686. p. 1252
Shaw, Jean, AV, Mercer County District Library, 303 N Main St, Celina, OH, 45822. Tel: 419-586-4442. p. 1757
Shaw, Jean, Librn, Lillooet Area Library Association, Gold Bridge Branch, 40 Hurley St, Gold Bridge, BC, V0K 1P0, CANADA. Tel: 250-238-2521. p. 2569
Shaw, Jocelyn, Ref Serv, Ad, Website Mgr, Hackley Public Library, 316 W Webster Ave, Muskegon, MI, 49440. Tel: 231-722-8005. p. 1135
Shaw, Jon, Assoc Vice-Provost, Dep Univ Librn, University of Pennsylvania Libraries, 3420 Walnut St, Philadelphia, PA, 19104-6206. Tel: 215-898-7556. p. 1987
Shaw, Jordana, Interim Dir, Libr & Info Serv, Middlesex Community College, Academic Resources Bldg 1A, 591 Springs Rd, Bedford, MA, 01730. Tel: 781-280-3708. p. 988
Shaw, Joyce M, Head of Libr, University of Southern Mississippi-Gulf Coast Research Laboratory, 703 E Beach Dr, Ocean Springs, MS, 39564. Tel: 228-872-4213, 228-872-4253. p. 1228
Shaw, Kasidy, Br Mgr, Giles County Public Library, Elkton Public Library, 168 Main St, Elkton, TN, 38455. Tel: 931-468-2506. p. 2124
Shaw, Lee, Mr, Libr Dir, New Gloucester Public Library, 379 Intervale Rd, New Gloucester, ME, 04260. Tel: 207-926-4840. p. 932

Shaw, Lindsay, Ch, Providence Athenaeum, 251 Benefit St, Providence, RI, 02903. Tel: 401-421-6970. p. 2039
Shaw, Lucy, Br Assoc, Yuma County Free Library District, Dateland Branch, Ave 64E & Interstate 8, Dateland, AZ, 85333. Tel: 928-454-2242. p. 86
Shaw, Lucy, Br Assoc, Yuma County Free Library District, Roll Branch, 5151 S Ave 39E, Roll, AZ, 85347. Tel: 928-785-9575. p. 86
Shaw, Mark M, Dir, Southwest Public Libraries, SPL Admin, 3359 Broadway, Grove City, OH, 43123. Tel: 614-875-6716. p. 1789
Shaw, Matthew, Dean, Univ Libr, Ball State University Libraries, 2000 W University Ave, Muncie, IN, 47306-1099. Tel: 765-285-5277. p. 708
Shaw, Mike, Curator, Johnson County Historical Society, 302 N Main St, Warrensburg, MO, 64093. Tel: 660-747-6480. p. 1285
Shaw, Rebekah, Libr Mgr, Walla Walla County Rural Library District, Touchet Community Library, 161 Hanson Rd, Touchet, WA, 99360. Tel: 509-394-2329. p. 2392
Shaw, Roberta, Library Contact, Holy Trinity Lutheran Church Library, 2730 E 31st St, Minneapolis, MN, 55406. Tel: 612-729-8358. p. 1184
Shaw, Ronald, Dir, Chemung County Library District, 101 E Church St, Elmira, NY, 14901. Tel: 607-733-8611. p. 1530
Shaw, Sam, Planning & Data Serv Coordr, Nebraska Library Commission, The Atrium, 1200 N St, Ste 120, Lincoln, NE, 68508-2023. Tel: 402-471-3216. p. 1322
Shaw, Sandra, Dir, Community Free Library, 86 Public Sq, Holley, NY, 14470. Tel: 585-638-6987. p. 1547
Shaw, Scout, ILL/Doc Delivery Serv, Mountain Area Health Education Center, 121 Hendersonville Rd, Asheville, NC, 28803. Tel: 828-257-4444. p. 1672
Shaw, Sherill, Archive Spec, Cat Librn, Utah State University Eastern Library, 451 E & 400 N, Price, UT, 84501. Tel: 435-613-5208. p. 2269
Shaw, Shileen, Br Mgr, Newark Public Library, Weequahic, 355 Osborne Terrace, Newark, NJ, 07112. Tel: 973-733-7751. p. 1428
Shaw, Steve, Librn, Antioch University Library, 900 Dayton St, Yellow Springs, OH, 45387. Tel: 281-639-3158. p. 1835
Shaw, Susan, Acq, Moundsville-Marshall County Public Library, 700 Fifth St, Moundsville, WV, 26041. Tel: 304-845-6911. p. 2410
Shaw, Suzanne, Exec Dir, Temple Israel, 130 Riverside Dr, Dayton, OH, 45405. Tel: 937-496-0050. p. 1780
Shaw, Tamara, Ref Serv, University of San Diego, Helen K & James S Copley Library, 5998 Alcala Park, San Diego, CA, 92110. p. 222
Shaw, Tommy, Asst Dir, Springfield Free Public Library, 66 Mountain Ave, Springfield, NJ, 07081-1786. Tel: 973-376-4930, Ext 235. p. 1444
Shaw-Brunson, Patrice, Asst Br Mgr, Memphis Public Library, Whitehaven Branch, 4120 Mill Branch Rd, Memphis, TN, 38116. Tel: 901-415-2781. p. 2114
Shaw-Spence, Jennifer, Archivist, Asst Librn, Dunwoody College of Technology, 818 Dunwoody Blvd, Minneapolis, MN, 55403. Tel: 612-381-3345. p. 1183
Shawa, Wangyal Tsering, Librn, Princeton University, Lewis Science Library, Washington Rd, Princeton, NJ, 08544-0001. Tel: 609-258-6804. p. 1437
Shawaga, Kathy, Librn, Wapiti Regional Library, Cudworth Public Library, 426 Second Ave, Cudworth, SK, S0K 1B0, CANADA. Tel: 306-256-3530. p. 2745
Shay, Katie, ILL, University of Wisconsin-Stout, 315 Tenth Ave, Menomonie, WI, 54751-0790. Tel: 715-232-1112. p. 2456
Shay, Tysha, Br Mgr, Springfield-Greene County Library District, Republic Branch, 921 N Lindsey Ave, Republic, MO, 65738-1248. Tel: 417-732-7284. p. 1281
Shea, Brenda, Dir, Fairmount Community Library, 406 Chapel Dr, Syracuse, NY, 13219. Tel: 315-487-8933. p. 1648
Shea, Catherine, Br Mgr, Buffalo & Erie County Public Library System, East Clinton, 1929 Clinton St, Buffalo, NY, 14206-3214. Tel: 716-823-5626. p. 1508
Shea, Ellen, Head, Res Serv, Harvard Library, Arthur & Elizabeth Schlesinger Library on the History of Women in America, Three James St, Cambridge, MA, 02138-3766. Tel: 617-495-8647. p. 1007
Shea, Erin, Supvr, Ferguson Library, Weed Memorial & Hollander, 1143 Hope St, Stamford, CT, 06907. Tel: 203-351-8284. p. 338
Shea, Janet, Youth Serv Coordr, South Hadley Public Library, Gaylord Memorial Library, 47 College St, South Hadley, MA, 01075. Tel: 413-538-5047. p. 1054
Shea, Jonathan D, Archivist, Pres, Polish Genealogical Society of Connecticut & The Northeast, Inc, Eight Lyle Rd, New Britain, CT, 06053-2104. Tel: 860-229-8873. p. 324
Shea, Joseph, Day Circ Supvr, American International College, 1000 State St, Springfield, MA, 01109. Tel: 413-205-3225. p. 1056
Shea, Karen, Plebe Experience Librn, United States Military Academy Library, Jefferson Hall Library & Learning Ctr, 758 Cullum Rd, West Point, NY, 10996. Tel: 845-938-8301. p. 1663
Shea, Lisa, Circ, Edwards Public Library, 30 East St, Southampton, MA, 01073. Tel: 413-527-9480. p. 1055
Shea, Maire, Circ, Swansea Free Public Library, 69 Main St, Swansea, MA, 02777. Tel: 508-674-9609. p. 1059
Shea, Mary Ann, Head, Circ, Wadleigh Memorial Library, 49 Nashua St, Milford, NH, 03055. Tel: 603-249-0645. p. 1374
Shea, Patrick, Chief Curator, Archives & Ms, Science History Institute Museum & Library, 315 Chestnut St, Philadelphia, PA, 19106. Tel: 215-873-8205. p. 1985
Shea, Shana, Br Mgr, Mkt & Communications Spec, Farmington Library, Barney Branch, 71 Main St, Farmington, CT, 06032. Tel: 860-673-6791 x5303. p. 312
Shear, Haley, Dir of Coll, Fenimore Art Museum, 5798 State Hwy 80, Cooperstown, NY, 13326. Tel: 607-547-1470. p. 1521
Shear, Joan A, Legal Info Librn & Lecturer in Law, Boston College, 885 Centre St, Newton Centre, MA, 02459. Tel: 617-552-2895. p. 1039
Sheard, Latina, Libr Mgr, Central Arkansas Library System, Sue Cowan Williams Branch, 1800 Chester St, Little Rock, AR, 72206-1010. Tel: 501-376-4282. p. 101
Shearer, Tim, Assoc Univ Librn, Digital Strat, Assoc Univ Librn, Info Tech, University of North Carolina at Chapel Hill, 208 Raleigh St, CB 3916, Chapel Hill, NC, 27515. Tel: 919-962-1053. p. 1678
Shearman, Christine, Archives Asst, Tech Serv Librn, Rivier University, 420 S Main St, Nashua, NH, 03060-5086. Tel: 603-897-8671. p. 1375
Shearrer, Cindy, Assoc Law Librn, University of Missouri-Columbia, Law Library, 203 Hulston Hall, Columbia, MO, 65211-4190. Tel: 573-882-1125. p. 1244
Shearwood, Debbie, Asst Librn, Palliser Regional Library, Davidson Branch, 314 Washington Ave, Davidson, SK, S0G 1A0, CANADA. Tel: 306-567-2022. p. 2742
Sheble, Laura, Dr, Asst Prof, Wayne State University, 106 Kresge Library, Detroit, MI, 48202. Tel: 313-577-3762. p. 2787
Sheck, Alexia, Librn, University of St Augustine for Health Sciences, One University Blvd, Saint Augustine, FL, 32086. Tel: 904-770-3593. p. 440
Sheckells, Diane, Asst Librn, East Kingston Public Library, 47 Maplevale Rd, East Kingston, NH, 03827. Tel: 603-642-8333. p. 1362
Shedd, Shirley, Archivist, Evangel University, 1111 N Glenstone Ave, Springfield, MO, 65802. Tel: 417-865-2815, Ext 7268. p. 1280
Shedd, Stephanie, Tech Serv, Midland College, 3600 N Garfield, Midland, TX, 79705. Tel: 432-685-4583. p. 2219
Sheddan, Ian, Coordr, Tech Serv, Sr Cataloger, Easton Area Public Library & District Center, 515 Church St, Easton, PA, 18042-3587. Tel: 610-258-2917. p. 1928
Shedlofsky, Joel, Tech Serv Librn, Concordia Seminary Library, 801 Seminary Pl, Saint Louis, MO, 63105-3199. Tel: 314-505-7038. p. 1270
Shedloski, Denise, Dir, Support Serv, Grandview Heights Public Library, 1685 W First Ave, Columbus, OH, 43212. Tel: 614-486-2951. p. 1773
Shedrick, Laurie, Asst Dir, Mid-Hudson Library System, 103 Market St, Poughkeepsie, NY, 12601-4098. Tel: 845-471-6060, Ext 220. p. 1623
Sheedy, Linda K, Librn, Kitchell Memorial Library, 300 SE Fifth St, Morrisonville, IL, 62546. Tel: 217-526-4553. p. 619
Sheedy, Lynn, Youth Serv Mgr, Peru Public Library, 1409 11th St, Peru, IL, 61354. Tel: 815-223-0229. p. 635
Sheedy, Sally, Fac Librn, Syst Librn, Whatcom Community College Library, Heiner Bldg, 231 W Kellogg Rd, Bellingham, WA, 98226. Tel: 360-383-3300. p. 2359
Sheedy, Tammy, Dir, Berwyn Public Library, 2701 S Harlem Ave, Berwyn, IL, 60402. Tel: 708-795-8000. p. 542
Sheedy, Tammy, Libr Dir, Stickney-Forest View Public Library District, 6800 W 43rd St, Stickney, IL, 60402. Tel: 708-749-1050. p. 651
Sheehan, Amy, Ref (Info Servs), Hamline University, Bush Memorial Library, 1536 Hewitt, Saint Paul, MN, 55104. Tel: 651-523-2375. p. 1199
Sheehan, Cheryl, Adminr, Pub Serv, San Antonio Public Library, 600 Soledad, San Antonio, TX, 78205-2786. Tel: 210-207-2587. p. 2238
Sheehan, Deborah, Circ, Indian Prairie Public Library District, 401 Plainfield Rd, Darien, IL, 60561-4207. Tel: 630-887-8760. p. 575
Sheehan, Emily, Asst Dir, Libr Serv, Groton Public Library, 52 Newtown Rd, Groton, CT, 06340. Tel: 860-441-6750. p. 314
Sheehan, Kate, Head, Info Tech Serv, Stratford Library Association, 2203 Main St, Stratford, CT, 06615. Tel: 203-385-4163. p. 340
Sheehan, Kevin, Dir, Everett Public Libraries, 410 Broadway, Everett, MA, 02149. Tel: 617-394-2300. p. 1017
Sheehan, Kevin, Dr, Colls Mgr, Maritime Museum of San Diego, 1492 N Harbor Dr, San Diego, CA, 92101. Tel: 619-234-9153, Ext 118. p. 215
Sheehan, Laura, Mgr, Sequoyah Regional Library System, Ball Ground Public, 435 Old Canton Rd, Ball Ground, GA, 30107. Tel: 770-735-2025. p. 469
Sheehan, Michael, Tech Serv Mgr, La Porte County Public Library, 904 Indiana Ave, La Porte, IN, 46350. Tel: 219-362-6156. p. 700
Sheehan, Michelle, Circ Supvr, West Bridgewater Public Library, 80 Howard St, West Bridgewater, MA, 02379-1710. Tel: 508-894-1255. p. 1065
Sheehan, Nancy, Head, Youth Serv, Lucius Beebe Memorial Library, 345 Main St, Wakefield, MA, 01880-5093. Tel: 781-246-6334. p. 1061
Sheehan, Sarah E, Dir, Res & Instruction Serv, Manhattan College, 4513 Manhattan College Pkwy, Riverdale, NY, 10471. Tel: 718-862-7743. p. 1627
Sheehan, Xina, Asst Dir, Franklin Free Library, 334 Main St, Franklin, NY, 13775. Tel: 607-829-2941. p. 1534
Sheehy, Dale, Librn, United States Environmental Protection Agency, 27 Tarzwell Dr, Narragansett, RI, 02882. Tel: 401-782-3025. p. 2034

Sheehy, Louis, Asst Dir, Trumbull Library System, 33 Quality St, Trumbull, CT, 06611. Tel: 203-452-5197. p. 342

Sheehy, Matthew, Univ Librn, Brandeis University, 415 South St, Mailstop 045, Waltham, MA, 02454-9110. Tel: 781-736-5626. p. 1061

Sheely, Amber, Tech Serv Mgr, Westchester Public Library, 200 W Indiana Ave, Chesterton, IN, 46304. Tel: 219-926-7696. p. 675

Sheet, Erica, Instruction & Ser Librn, Gordon College, 255 Grapevine Rd, Wenham, MA, 01984-1899. Tel: 978-867-4345. p. 1064

Sheets, Audrey, Br Mgr, Saint Joseph Public Library, Carnegie Public, 316 Massachusetts St, Saint Joseph, MO, 64504-1449. Tel: 816-238-0526. p. 1269

Sheets, Kris, Br Supvr, Smyth County Public Library, Saltville Public, 111 Palmer Ave, Saltville, VA, 24370. Tel: 276-496-5514. p. 2331

Sheets, Sarah, Electronic Res Coordr, University of California, Merced Library, 5200 N Lake Rd, Merced, CA, 95343. Tel: 209-228-4422. p. 176

Sheets, Shawni, Board Pres, Talmage Public Library, 2994 Main St, Talmage, KS, 67842. Tel: 785-643-9126. p. 838

Sheetz, Christine, Instrul Serv/Ref Librn, Lorain County Community College, 1005 Abbe Rd N, North Elyria, OH, 44035-1691. Tel: 440-366-7288. p. 1810

Sheffer, Polly, Librn, Ossipee Public Library, 74 Main St, Center Ossipee, NH, 03814. Tel: 603-539-6390. p. 1357

Sheffield, Carolyn, Assoc Dir, Library Tech & Digital Strategies, University of Maryland, Baltimore County, 1000 Hilltop Circle, Baltimore, MD, 21250. Tel: 410-455-2356. p. 958

Sheffield, Josh, Librn, Ocmulgee Regional Library System, 531 Second Ave, Eastman, GA, 31023. Tel: 478-374-4711. p. 477

Sheffield, Joshua, Br Mgr, Augusta-Richmond County Public Library, Jeff Maxwell Branch, 1927 Lumpkin Rd, Augusta, GA, 30906. Tel: 706-793-2020. p. 466

Sheffield, Lisa, Adult Serv Coordr, Transylvania County Library, 212 S Gaston St, Brevard, NC, 28712. Tel: 828-884-3151. p. 1675

Sheffield, Mandy, Br Mgr, Harris County Public Library, Stratford Library Highlands, 509 Stratford, Highlands, TX, 77562. Tel: 832-927-5400. p. 2193

Sheffield, Rebecca Susanne, Head of Acq Serv, Ball State University Libraries, 2000 W University Ave, Muncie, IN, 47306-1099. Tel: 765-285-8031. p. 708

Shehan, Kevin, Coord, Content Management Services, University of South Carolina Upstate Library, 800 University Way, Spartanburg, SC, 29303. Tel: 864-503-5639. p. 2070

Sheidlower, Scott, Head, Archives, Head, Circ & Reserves, York College Library, 94-20 Guy R Brewer Blvd, Jamaica, NY, 11451. Tel: 718-262-2017. p. 1556

Sheikh, Abby, Tech Supvr, Billerica Public Library, 15 Concord Rd, Billerica, MA, 01821. Tel: 978-671-0948, 978-671-0949. p. 989

Sheinfeld, Ely, Archivist for Electronic Records & Digital Colls, Ball State University Libraries, Archives & Special Collections, Bracken Library, Rm 210, Muncie, IN, 47306-0161. Tel: 765-285-8723. p. 708

Shelburne, Brian, Head, Digital Scholarship Serv, University of Massachusetts Amherst Libraries, 154 Hicks Way, University of Massachusetts, Amherst, MA, 01003-9275. Tel: 413-545-4061. p. 985

Shelburne, Stephanie, Music Libr Supvr, Bob Jones University, Music Library, 1700 Wade Hampton Blvd, Greenville, SC, 29614. Tel: 864-370-1800, Ext 2706. p. 2060

Shelden, Louise, Dir, Union Carnegie Public Library, 1825 N Main St, Union, OR, 97883. Tel: 541-562-5811. p. 1901

Sheldon, Karen, Instrul Serv Librn, Delaware Valley University, 700 E Butler Ave, Doylestown, PA, 18901-2699. Tel: 215-489-4968. p. 1927

Sheldon, Laci, Youth Serv Dir, McIntosh Memorial Library, 205 S Rock Ave, Viroqua, WI, 54665. Tel: 608-637-7151. p. 2483

Sheldon, Michelle, Tech Serv Asst, Oklahoma Christian University, 2501 E Memorial Rd, Edmond, OK, 73013. Tel: 405-425-5311. p. 1846

Sheldon-Hess, Coral, Web Librn, University of Alaska Anchorage, Consortium Library, 3211 Providence Dr, Anchorage, AK, 99508-8176. Tel: 907-786-1871. p. 43

Sheley, Lisa, Dir, Jamestown Philomenian Library, 26 North Rd, Jamestown, RI, 02835. Tel: 401-423-7280. p. 2033

Shelford, Holly A, Youth Serv Librn, Knoxville Public Library, 213 E Montgomery St, Knoxville, IA, 50138-2296. Tel: 641-828-0585. p. 763

Sheliga, Jeanette, Head Librn, Niagara County Genealogical Society Library, 215 Niagara St, Lockport, NY, 14094. Tel: 716-433-1033. p. 1564

Shell, Lambert, Dr, Dir, Roosevelt Public Library, 27 W Fulton Ave, Roosevelt, NY, 11575. Tel: 516-378-0222. p. 1633

Shellehamer, Denise, Cat, New Cumberland Public Library, One Benjamin Plaza, New Cumberland, PA, 17070-1597. Tel: 717-774-7820. p. 1969

Shelleman, Jessica, Br Mgr, Adams County Library System, Littlestown Library, 232 N Queen St, Littlestown, PA, 17340. Tel: 717-359-0446. p. 1935

Shelley, Alison, Head, Youth Serv, Reed Memorial Library, 167 E Main St, Ravenna, OH, 44266-3197. Tel: 330-296-2827, Ext 301. p. 1817

Shelley, Joseph, VPres, Libr & Info Tech, Hamilton College, 198 College Hill Rd, Clinton, NY, 13323. Tel: 315-859-4181. p. 1519

Shelley, Kim, Br Supvr, Lincoln City Libraries, Bethany Branch, 1810 N Cotner Blvd, Lincoln, NE, 68505. Tel: 402-441-8550. p. 1321

Shelley, Kim, Br Supvr, Lincoln City Libraries, Victor E Anderson Branch, 3635 Touzalin Ave, Lincoln, NE, 68507-1698. Tel: 402-441-8542. p. 1321

Shelley, Lanny, Librn, Colorado Department of Corrections, Limon Correctional Facility-Law Library, 49030 State Hwy 71, Limon, CO, 80826. Tel: 719-775-9221, Ext 3238. p. 289

Shelley, Matt, Head of Instruction, Christopher Newport University, One Avenue of the Arts, Newport News, VA, 23606. Tel: 757-594-7245. p. 2333

Shelley, Sandoval, Dir, Attorney Recruitment & Prof Dev, City of Chicago, 121 N La Salle St, Chicago, IL, 60602. Tel: 312-742-0335. p. 559

Shelley, Zhang, Assoc Dir, Tech Serv, Cobb County Public Library System, 266 Roswell St, Marietta, GA, 30060-2004. Tel: 770-528-2320. p. 489

Shellhouse, Emily, Dir, Granville Public Library, 217 E Broadway, Granville, OH, 43023-1398. Tel: 740-587-0196. p. 1788

Shelly, Jodi, Dir, Libr Serv, Felician University, 262 S Main St, Lodi, NJ, 07644. Tel: 201-559-6070. p. 1413

Shelsy, Sue, Librn, Hinsdale Public Library, 58 Maple St, Hinsdale, MA, 01235. Tel: 413-655-2303. p. 1024

Shelton, Amanda, Libr Dir, Franklin Public Library, 1502 P St, Franklin, NE, 68939. Tel: 308-425-3162. p. 1314

Shelton, Iris, Br Librn, McDowell Public Library, Bradshaw Branch, City Hall Bldg, Main St, Bradshaw, WV, 24817. Tel: 304-967-5140. p. 2416

Shelton, Jennifer, Br Asst, Elko-Lander-Eureka County Library System, Crescent Valley Branch Library, Cresent Valley Town Ctr, 5045 Tenabo Ave, Ste 103, Cresent Valley, NV, 89821. Tel: 775-468-0249. p. 1344

Shelton, John, Asst to the Dir, West Florida Public Library, 239 N Spring St, Pensacola, FL, 32502. Tel: 850-436-5060. p. 437

Shelton, Kelly, Librn, Virginia Department of Corrections, 256 Bland Farm Rd, Bland, VA, 24315. Tel: 276-688-3341, Ext 88721. p. 2307

Shelton, Mark, Dir, College of the Holy Cross, One College St, Worcester, MA, 01610. Tel: 508-793-3371. p. 1072

Shelton, Pamela, Dir, United States Army, Casey Memorial Library, 72nd St & 761st Tank Battalion, Bldg 3202, Fort Hood, TX, 76544-5024. Tel: 254-287-0025. p. 2178

Shelton, Steven D, Digital Development Librn, University of Tennessee at Chattanooga Library, 400 Douglas Ave, Dept 6456, Chattanooga, TN, 37403-2598. Tel: 423-425-4501. p. 2092

Shelton, Tania, Research Librn, Monroe County Historical Association, 900 Main St, Stroudsburg, PA, 18360-1604. Tel: 570-421-7703. p. 2011

Shelton-Council, Lola, Exec Dir, Live Oak Public Libraries, 2002 Bull St, Savannah, GA, 31401. Tel: 912-652-3600. p. 496

Sheltraw, Susie, Librn, Department of Veterans Affairs, 1500 Weiss St, Saginaw, MI, 48602. Tel: 989-497-2500, Ext 11870. p. 1146

Shelvy, Jason, IT Mgr, Missouri River Regional Library, 214 Adams St, Jefferson City, MO, 65101. Tel: 573-634-2464. p. 1252

Shelwood, Bernice, Electronic Res Librn, Jackson State University, 1325 J R Lynch St, Jackson, MS, 39217. Tel: 601-979-2123, 601-979-4270. p. 1222

Shemanski, Lori, Ref Librn, Luzerne County Community College Library, 1333 S Prospect St, Nanticoke, PA, 18634-3899. Tel: 570-740-0415. p. 1967

Shemwell, Daniel, Acq & Cat Librn, Mississippi College, 151 E Griffith St, Jackson, MS, 39201-1391. Tel: 601-925-7120. p. 1222

Shen, Lisa, Head, Ref, Sam Houston State University, 1830 Bobby K Marks Dr, Huntsville, TX, 77340. Tel: 936-294-3587. p. 2201

Shen, Vivian, Conserv Librn, Presv Librn, Fordham University Libraries, 441 E Fordham Rd, Bronx, NY, 10458-5151. Tel: 718-817-3570. p. 1498

Shenk, Melissa, Br Mgr, Horry County Memorial Library, Green Sea-Floyds Branch, 5331 Hwy 9, Green Sea, SC, 29545. Tel: 843-392-0994. p. 2056

Shenoy, Priya, Graduate Health Professions Librn, Drake University, 2725 University Ave, Des Moines, IA, 50311. Tel: 515-271-2879. p. 746

Shenoy, Sandhya, Circ Asst, Grafton Public Library, 35 Grafton Common, Grafton, MA, 01519. Tel: 508-839-4649. p. 1021

Shepard, Brian, Exec Dir, Indian Trails Public Library District, 355 S Schoenbeck Rd, Wheeling, IL, 60090. Tel: 847-459-4100. p. 662

Shepard, Dennis, Dir, Support Serv, Vigo County Public Library, 680 Poplar St, Terre Haute, IN, 47807. Tel: 812-232-1113, Ext 1010. p. 721

Shepard, Elizabeth, Archivist, Cornell University Library, Samuel J Wood Library & C V Starr Biomedical Information Center, 1300 York Ave, C115, Box 67, New York, NY, 10065-4896. Tel: 646-962-6072. p. 1552

Shepard, Jamie, ILL, Salish Kootenai College, PO Box 70, Pablo, MT, 59855. Tel: 406-275-4876. p. 1300

Shepard, John, Curator of Coll, University of California, Berkeley, Jean Gray Hargrove Music Library, Berkeley, CA, 94720-6000. Tel: 510-642-2428. p. 123

Shepard, Patricia, Libraries Mgr, Park County Public Libraries, Fairplay Branch, 400 Front St, Fairplay, CO, 80440. Tel: 719-836-4297. p. 265

Shepard, Sharon, Libr Dir, Cornell Public Library, 117 N Third St, Cornell, WI, 54732. Tel: 715-239-3709. p. 2429

Shepard, Stephanie, Law Librn, First Judicial District of Pennsylvania, City Hall, Rm 600, Broad & Market Sts, Philadelphia, PA, 19107. Tel: 215-686-3799. p. 1977

Sheperdson, Amy, Asst Dir, Carver Public Library, Two Meadowbrook Way, Carver, MA, 02330. Tel: 508-866-3415. p. 1009

Shepherd, Anne B, Ref Librn, Cincinnati Museum Center At Union Terminal, 1301 Western Ave, Ste 2133, Cincinnati, OH, 45203. Tel: 513-287-7069. p. 1760

Shepherd, Christina, Asst Dir, Dougherty County Public Library, 300 Pine Ave, Albany, GA, 31701-2533. Tel: 229-420-3200. p. 457

Shepherd, Jodi, Interim Dean, California State University, Chico, 400 W First St, Chico, CA, 95929-0295. Tel: 530-898-5499. p. 129

Shepherd, Renae, Br Mgr, Harlan County Public Libraries, 107 N Third St, Harlan, KY, 40831. Tel: 606-573-5220. p. 858

Shepherd, Sara, Librn, Dunklin County Library, Campbell Branch, 404 W Grand, Campbell, MO, 63933. Tel: 573-246-2112. p. 1258

Shepherd, Sarah, Head, Circ, Woodbridge Town Library, Ten Newton Rd, Woodbridge, CT, 06525. Tel: 203-389-3498. p. 349

Shepherd, Sonja, Ch Serv, Tully Free Library, 12 State St, Tully, NY, 13159. Tel: 315-696-8606. p. 1653

Shepherd, W John, Univ Archivist & Head, Spec Coll, Catholic University of America, Rare Books Special Collections, 214 Mullen Library, 620 Michigan Ave NE, Washington, DC, 20064. Tel: 202-319-5065. p. 362

Shepley, Tom, Libr Dir, Pamunkey Regional Library, 7527 Library Dr, Hanover, VA, 23069. Tel: 804-537-6211. p. 2323

Sheppard, Annette, Dir, United States Air Force, Air Force Research Laboratory, Wright Research Site, Det 1 AFRL/WSC, Bldg 642, Rm 1300, 2950 Hobson Way, Wright-Patterson AFB, OH, 45433-7765. Tel: 937-255-5511, Ext 4205. p. 1834

Sheppard, April, Assoc Dean, Arkansas State University, 322 University Loop Circle, State University, AR, 72401. Tel: 870-972-3077. p. 111

Sheppard, Denise, Br Mgr, Colchester-East Hants Public Library, Stewiacke Branch, 295 George St, Stewiacke, NS, B0N 2J0, CANADA. Tel: 902-639-2481. p. 2623

Sheppard, Gail, Head, Youth Serv, Pittsburg Public Library, 308 N Walnut, Pittsburg, KS, 66762-4732. Tel: 620-230-5564. p. 831

Sheppard, Maureen, Coordr, Librn, Algonquin College Library, 1385 Woodroffe Ave, Rm C350, Ottawa, ON, K2G 1V8, CANADA. Tel: 613-727-4723, Ext 5944. p. 2664

Sheppard, Michel-Adrien, Mgr, Res, Ref Mgr, Supreme Court of Canada Library, 301 Wellington St, Ottawa, ON, K1A 0J1, CANADA. Tel: 613-944-7723. p. 2670

Sheppard, Nicole, Br Librn, Bedford Public Library System, Stewartsville Library, 45 Cascade Dr, Vinton, VA, 24179. Tel: 540-425-7008. p. 2306

Sheppard, Ronald, Dir, Parkland Regional Library-Alberta, 5404 56th Ave, Lacombe, AB, T4L 1G1, CANADA. Tel: 403-782-3850. p. 2545

Sheppler, Nancy, Bibliog Serv, Cat Spec, Per, Andrews University, 4190 Administration Dr, Berrien Springs, MI, 49104-1400. Tel: 269-471-3033. p. 1085

Shepstone, Carol, Chief Librn, Ryerson University Library, 350 Victoria St, 2nd Flr, Toronto, ON, M5B 2K3, CANADA. Tel: 416-979-5000, Ext 5142. p. 2692

Sher, Meg, Dir, David M Hunt Library, 63 Main St, Falls Village, CT, 06031. Tel: 860-824-7424. p. 312

Sher, Rachel, Libr Mgr, Alameda County Library, Albany Library, 1247 Marin Ave, Albany, CA, 94706-2043. Tel: 510-526-3720. p. 143

Shere, Angie, Ch, Manchester Public Library, 304 N Franklin St, Manchester, IA, 52057. Tel: 563-927-3719. p. 767

Sheret, Larry, Open Education Librn, Scholarly Communications, Marshall University Libraries, One John Marshall Dr, Huntington, WV, 25755-2060. Tel: 304-696-6577. p. 2405

Sherfield, Jeanette, Br Mgr, Hancock County Public Library, Sugar Creek Branch, 5087 W US 52, New Palestine, IN, 46163. Tel: 317-861-6618, Ext 20. p. 688

Sherfield, Megan, Library & Academic Services Support Tech, Maine Maritime Academy, Pleasant St, Box C-1, Castine, ME, 04420. Tel: 207-326-2265. p. 921

Sheridan, April, Colls Mgr, School of the Art Institute of Chicago, 37 S Wabash Ave, Chicago, IL, 60603-3103. Tel: 312-899-5097. p. 568

Sheridan, Cathi, Br Mgr, Ocean County Library, Lakewood Branch, 301 Lexington Ave, Lakewood, NJ, 08701. Tel: 732-363-1435. p. 1446

Sheridan, Christin, Libr Dir, York Library Region, Fay Tidd Public Library, 54 Miramichi Rd, Oromocto, NB, E2V 1S2, CANADA. Tel: 506-357-3329. p. 2602

Sheridan, Gina, Br Mgr, Saint Louis County Library, Lewis & Clark Branch, 9909 Lewis-Clark Blvd, Saint Louis, MO, 63136-5322. Tel: 314-994-3300, Ext 3450. p. 1274

Sheridan, Holly, Head, Circ, J V Fletcher Library, 50 Main St, Westford, MA, 01886-2599. Tel: 978-399-2313. p. 1067

Sheridan, John, Dir, West Branch District Library, 119 N Fourth St, West Branch, MI, 48661. Tel: 989-345-2235. p. 1159

Sheridan, Kelly, Head, YA, Bayport-Blue Point Public Library, 203 Blue Point Ave, Blue Point, NY, 11715-1217. Tel: 631-363-6133. p. 1495

Sheridan, Natalie, Pub Serv Mgr, Cornell University Library, Mathematics, 420 Malott Hall, Ithaca, NY, 14853-4201. Tel: 607-254-3568. p. 1552

Sheridan, Shannon, Ch, Webster County Public Library, 101 State Rte 132 E, Dixon, KY, 42409. Tel: 270-639-9171. p. 853

Sheridan, Terence, Libr Dir, Amridge University Library, 1200 Taylor Rd, Montgomery, AL, 36117. Tel: 334-387-7541. p. 28

Sheridan, Terri, Mus Librn, Santa Barbara Museum of Natural History Library, 2559 Puesta del Sol Rd, Santa Barbara, CA, 93105. Tel: 805-682-4711, Ext 134. p. 240

Sherif, Joan, Dir of Libr, Northwestern Regional Library, 111 N Front St, 2nd Flr, Elkin, NC, 28621. Tel: 336-835-4894, Ext 1001. p. 1688

Sherk, Warren, Assoc Dir, Spec Coll & Archives, Academy of Motion Picture Arts & Sciences, 333 S La Cienega Blvd, Beverly Hills, CA, 90211. Tel: 310-247-2265, Ext 2265. p. 124

Sherlock, Lisa J, Chief Librn, University of Toronto Libraries, Victoria University, E J Pratt Library, 71 Queens Park Crescent E, Toronto, ON, M5S 1K7, CANADA. Tel: 416-585-4472. p. 2700

Sherman, Brian, Dean, Head, Access Serv & Syst, Louisiana State University, One University Pl, Shreveport, LA, 71115. Tel: 318-798-4117. p. 907

Sherman, Carrie, Head, Ref Serv, Attleboro Public Library, 74 N Main St, Attleboro, MA, 02703. Tel: 508-222-0157. p. 986

Sherman, Cynthia, Br Mgr, Iberia Parish Library, Loreauville Branch, 510 N Main St, Loreauville, LA, 70552. Tel: 337-229-6348. p. 900

Sherman, Jacquelynn, Asst Libr Dir, Fairmont State University, 1201 Locust Ave, Fairmont, WV, 26554. Tel: 304-368-3643. p. 2402

Sherman, Jessica, Dir, Monroe Public Library, 19 Plains Rd, Monroe, NH, 03771. Tel: 603-638-4736. p. 1374

Sherman, Jill, Interim Dir, Louisville Presbyterian Theological Seminary, 1044 Alta Vista Rd, Louisville, KY, 40205-1798. Tel: 502-992-9398. p. 866

Sherman, Kris, Asst Libr Mgr, Pub Serv, Chandler Public Library, 22 S Delaware, Chandler, AZ, 85225. Tel: 480-782-2818. p. 58

Sherman, Lisa, Dir, Stuart Public Library, 111 E Front St, Stuart, IA, 50250. Tel: 515-523-2152. p. 785

Sherman, Lorna, Libr Asst, Youth Serv Coordr, Knoxville Public Library, 112 E Main St, Knoxville, PA, 16928. Tel: 814-326-4448. p. 1949

Sherman, Matthew, Digital Content Librn, University of Bridgeport, 126 Park Ave, Bridgeport, CT, 06604-5620. Tel: 203-576-4539. p. 304

Sherman, Natania, Mgr, Coll Serv, Toronto International Film Festival Inc, TIFF Bell Lightbox, 350 King St W, Toronto, ON, M5V 3X5, CANADA. Tel: 416-599-8433. p. 2693

Sherman, Paul, Dr, Assoc Prof, Kent State University, 314 University Library, 1125 Risman Dr, Kent, OH, 44242-0001. Tel: 330-672-2782. p. 2790

Sherman, Rebecca, Asst Librn, United States Courts for the Ninth Circuit Library, 1000 SW Third Ave, 7A40, Portland, OR, 97204. Tel: 503-326-8140. p. 1894

Sherman, Summer, Mgr, Columbus Metropolitan Library, South High Branch, 3540 S High St, Columbus, OH, 43207. p. 1773

Sherman, Susan, Ch, Derby Public Library, 313 Elizabeth St, Derby, CT, 06418. Tel: 203-736-1482. p. 309

Sherman, Ted, Digital Serv Librn, D'Youville College, 320 Porter Ave, Buffalo, NY, 14201-1084. Tel: 716-829-7618. p. 1509

Sherman, Zakariya, Libr Dir, North Palm Beach Public Library, 303 Anchorage Dr, North Palm Beach, FL, 33408. Tel: 561-841-3383. p. 429

Shermer, Jeanmarie, Asst Librn, Ch, Raymond A Whitwer Tilden Public Library, 202 S Center St, Tilden, NE, 68781. Tel: 402-368-5306. p. 1338

Sherock, Gina, Human Res Dir, Public Library of Youngstown & Mahoning County, 305 Wick Ave, Youngstown, OH, 44503. Tel: 330-744-8636. p. 1835

Sherod, James, Sr Librn, Los Angeles Public Library System, Little Tokyo Branch Library, 203 S Los Angeles St, Los Angeles, CA, 90012. Tel: 213-612-0525. p. 164

Sherod, Martha, Sr Librn, Los Angeles Public Library System, Vermont Square Branch Library, 1201 W 48th St, Los Angeles, CA, 90037-2838. Tel: 323-290-7405. p. 165

Sherping, Trevor, Dir, Kalona Public Library, 510 C Ave, Kalona, IA, 52247. Tel: 319-656-3501. p. 762

Sherren, Joseph, Prog Coordr, University of Maryland, Hornbake Library, Ground Flr, Rm 0220, 4130 Campus Dr, College Park, MD, 20742-4345. Tel: 301-405-2039. p. 2786

Sherretts, Kim, Archivist, Crawford County Historical Society, 869 Diamond Park, Meadville, PA, 16335. Tel: 814-724-6080. p. 1960

Sherri, Randall, Br Mgr, Weston County Library System, Upton Branch Library, 722 Fourth St, Upton, WY, 82730. Tel: 307-468-2324. p. 2497

Sherrick, Deb, Dir, Greenup Township Public Library, 101 N Franklin St, Greenup, IL, 62428. Tel: 217-923-3616. p. 595

Sherrill, Butch, Libr Dir, Westminister Presbyterian Church Library, 3906 W Friendly Ave, Greensboro, NC, 27410. Tel: 336-299-3785. p. 1693

Sherrill, Denise, Access Serv, Asst Dir, Operations, Davidson College, 209 Ridge Rd, Davidson, NC, 28035-0001. Tel: 704-894-2331. p. 1683

Sherrill, Jacque, Exec Dir, Jetmore Public Library, 310 Main St, Jetmore, KS, 67854. Tel: 620-357-8336. p. 816

Sherrill, Kate, Research Servs Librn, University of Southern Indiana, 8600 University Blvd, Evansville, IN, 47712. Tel: 812-465-1277. p. 682

Sherrod, Tracey, Dir, Libr Serv, Methodist University, 5400 Ramsey St, Fayetteville, NC, 28311. Tel: 910-630-7123. p. 1689

Sherron, Kelsey, Ch Serv, Muscle Shoals Public Library, 1918 E Avalon, Muscle Shoals, AL, 35661. Tel: 256-386-9212. p. 31

Sherry, Elisabeth, Dir, Elizabeth Taber Library, Eight Spring St, Marion, MA, 02738. Tel: 508-748-1252. p. 1031

Sherry, Suzanne, Dir, Libr Serv, Brightpoint Community College Library, Midlothian Campus, Hamel Hall, Rm H202, 800 Charter Colony Pkwy, Midlothian, VA, 23114-4383. Tel: 804-594-1523. p. 2312

Sherry, Suzanne, Dir, Libr Serv, Brightpoint Community College Library, Moyar Hall, M216, 13101 Rte One, Chester, VA, 23831-5316. Tel: 804-706-5201. p. 2312

Sherwood, David, Libr Dir, Nashotah House, 2777 Mission Rd, Nashotah, WI, 53058-9793. Tel: 262-646-6534. p. 2463

Sherwood, Emily, Univ Librn, RIT Libraries, 90 Lomb Memorial Dr, Rochester, NY, 14623-5604. p. 1629

Sherwood, Julie, Commun Engagement Mgr, Partnerships, Wichita Public Library, 711 W Second St, Wichita, KS, 67203. Tel: 316-261-8590. p. 843

Sherwood, Lena, Libr Asst, Berkshire Free Library, 12519 State Rte 38, Berkshire, NY, 13736. Tel: 607-657-4418. p. 1493

Sherwood, Louis, Jr, Univ Archivist, Texas Wesleyan University, 1201 Wesleyan St, Fort Worth, TX, 76105. Tel: 817-531-4822. p. 2181

Sherwood, Mitzi, Libr Dir, Honey Grove Library & Learning Center, 500 N Sixth St, Honey Grove, TX, 75446. Tel: 903-378-2206. p. 2191

Sherwood, Nancy, Tech Serv, Garden City Public Library, 60 Seventh St, Garden City, NY, 11530. Tel: 516-742-8405. p. 1536

Sherwood, Sherrill, Coll Develop Coordr, Haliburton County Public Library, Administrative Ctr, 78 Maple Ave, Haliburton, ON, K0M 1S0, CANADA. Tel: 705-457-2241. p. 2644

Sherwood, William, Sr Librn, San Leandro Public Library, Manor, 1241 Manor Blvd, San Leandro, CA, 94579. Tel: 510-577-7970. p. 233

Sheterom, Amanda, Human Res Mgr, Delaware County District Library, 84 E Winter St, Delaware, OH, 43015. Tel: 740-362-3861. p. 1781

Shetler, Brian, Head, Spec Coll & Archives, Princeton Theological Seminary Library, 25 Library Pl, Princeton, NJ, 08540. Tel: 609-497-7940. p. 1437

Shetter, Cynthia J, Libr Dir, Los Lunas Public Library, 460 Main St NE, Los Lunas, NM, 87031. Tel: 505-839-3850. p. 1472

Shetty, Minni, Head, Support Serv, Auburn Hills Public Library, 3400 E Seyburn Dr, Auburn Hills, MI, 48326-2759. Tel: 248-370-9466. p. 1081

Shevokas, Jill, Dir, Oglesby Public Library, 111 S Woodland St, Oglesby, IL, 61348. Tel: 815-883-3619. p. 629

Shew, Anne, Dir, California Pacific Medical Center, 1375 Sutter St, Ste 100, San Francisco, CA, 94109. Tel: 415-600-0540. p. 224

Shewdeen, Marie, Acq Librn, Universite de Saint-Boniface, 0140-200 Ave de la Cathedrale, Winnipeg, MB, R2H 0H7, CANADA. Tel: 204-945-8594. p. 2594

Shi, Ruilan, Chief Librn, McGill University Libraries, Geographic Information Centre, Burnside Hall Bldg, 5th Flr, 805 Sherbrooke St W, Montreal, QC, H3A 2K6, CANADA. Tel: 514-398-7438. p. 2726

Shibuyama, Loni, Archives Librn, ONE National Gay & Lesbian Archives at the USC Libraries, 909 W Adams Blvd, Los Angeles, CA, 90007. Tel: 213-821-2771. p. 167

Shideler, Cherri, Acq Spec, Longwood University, Redford & Race St, Farmville, VA, 23909. Tel: 434-395-2742. p. 2318

Shieh, Linnea, Eng Librn, Stanford University Libraries, Terman Engineering Library, Jen-Hsun Huang Engineering Ctr, Rm 201, 475 Via Ortega, Stanford, CA, 94305-4121. Tel: 650-723-0001. p. 249

Shiel, Teri, Head, User Serv, UConn Health Sciences Library, 263 Farmington Ave, Farmington, CT, 06034-4003. Tel: 860-679-4108. p. 313

Shields, Andrew, Head, Tech Serv, Ser & Syst, Goshen College, Harold & Wilma Good Library, 1700 S Main, Goshen, IN, 46526-4794. Tel: 574-535-7427. p. 687

Shields, Catherine, Ref & ILL Librn, East Lyme Public Library, 39 Society Rd, Niantic, CT, 06357. Tel: 860-739-6926. p. 330

Shields, Christopher, Dir, Libr & Archives, Greenwich Historical Society, 47 Strickland Rd, Cos Cob, CT, 06807. Tel: 203-869-6899, Ext 23. p. 306

Shields, Deborah, Librn, Melanee Smith Memorial Library, 2103 Main St, Waller, TX, 77484. Tel: 936-372-3961. p. 2254

Shields, Jeannette, Chief Exec Officer, Chief Librn, Bonfield Public Library, 365 Hwy 531, Bonfield, ON, P0H 1E0, CANADA. Tel: 705-776-2396. p. 2632

Shields, Jerri, Librn, G B Burton Memorial Library, 217 S Kearney, Clarendon, TX, 79226. Tel: 806-874-3685. p. 2156

Shields, Mary, Librn, Northwest Missouri State University, Horace Mann Library, Brown Hall 121, 800 University Dr, Maryville, MO, 64468. Tel: 660-562-1271. p. 1261

Shields, Nicole, Br Serv Supvr, Napa County Library, Calistoga Branch, 1108 Myrtle, Calistoga, CA, 94515-1730. Tel: 707-259-8391. p. 182

Shields, Nicole, Supvr, Extn Serv, Napa County Library, 580 Coombs St, Napa, CA, 94559-3396. Tel: 707-259-8391. p. 182

Shields, Theodosia, Dir of Libr, North Carolina Central University, School of Library & Information Sciences, James E Shepard Memorial Library, 3rd Flr, 1801 Fayetteville St, Durham, NC, 27707. Tel: 919-530-5233. p. 1686

Shields, Theodosia, Dr, Dir, Libr Serv, North Carolina Central University, 1801 Fayetteville St, Durham, NC, 27707-3129. Tel: 919-530-6475. p. 1685

Shier, Andrea, Librn, University of Toronto Libraries, Centre of Criminology & Sociolegal Studies, 14 Queens Park Crescent W, Toronto, ON, M5S 3K9, CANADA. Tel: 416-946-5745. p. 2698

Shier, Konni, Instruction & Ref Librn, Lenoir-Rhyne University, 4201 N Main St, Columbia, SC, 29203. Tel: 803-461-3220, 803-461-3269. p. 2053

Shiff, Debra, Archives, The College of New Jersey, 2000 Pennington Rd, Ewing, NJ, 08628-1104. Tel: 609-771-2311. p. 1402

Shifflett, Selena, Ch Serv, Library of Graham, 910 Cherry St, Graham, TX, 76450-3547. Tel: 940-549-0600. p. 2185

Shifton, Anna, Ch, North Brunswick Free Public Library, 880 Hermann Rd, North Brunswick, NJ, 08902. Tel: 732-246-3545. p. 1429

Shih, Virginia, Curator, University of California, Berkeley, South-Southeast Asia Library, 120 Doe Library, Berkeley, CA, 94720-6000. Tel: 510-643-0850. p. 123

Shije, Jennifer, Library Contact, Zia Enrichment Library, 162B Zia Blvd, Zia Pueblo, NM, 87053-6002. Tel: 505-337-2108. p. 1479

Shilling, Jordin, Youth Serv Librn, Van Zandt County Sarah Norman Library, 317 First Monday Lane, Canton, TX, 75103. Tel: 903-567-4276. p. 2152

Shilton, Savannah, Dir, Putnam District Library, 327 N Main St, Nashville, MI, 49073-9578. Tel: 517-852-9723. p. 1136

Shimabukuro, Kelli, Chief of Programs & Outreach, Enoch Pratt Free Library, 400 Cathedral St, Baltimore, MD, 21201. Tel: 410-396-5430. p. 952

Shimbashi, Kim, Libr Mgr, Barnwell Public Library, 320 Heritage Rd, Barnwell, AB, T0K 0B0, CANADA. Tel: 403-223-2902. p. 2522

Shimmin, Nick, Ad, North Liberty Library, 520 W Cherry St, North Liberty, IA, 52317-9797. Tel: 319-626-5781. p. 773

Shimmin, Nick, Dir, West Branch Public Library, 300 N Downey, West Branch, IA, 52358. Tel: 319-643-2633. p. 790

Shimonishi, Melissa, Libr Asst, Hawaii State Archives, Iolani Palace Grounds, 364 S King St, Honolulu, HI, 96813. Tel: 808-586-0329. p. 506

Shimp, Robert, Dr, Dir, Lakewood Historical Society Library, 13314 Detroit Ave, Lakewood, OH, 44107. Tel: 216-221-7343. p. 1793

Shin, Hee-sook, Librn, Columbia University, C V Starr East Asian Library, 300 Kent Hall, MC 3901, 1140 Amsterdam Ave, New York, NY, 10027. Tel: 212-854-4318. p. 1584

Shin, Helen, Librn, New Orleans Baptist Theological Seminary, 1800 Satellite Blvd NW, Duluth, GA, 30097. Tel: 770-321-1606. p. 477

Shin, Helen, Extn Serv Librn, New Orleans Baptist Theological Seminary, 4110 Seminary Pl, New Orleans, LA, 70126. Tel: 470-655-6717, ext. 7605. p. 902

Shin, Yumi, Access Serv, Ref Coordr, Lamar State College, 317 Stilwell Blvd, Port Arthur, TX, 77640. Tel: 409-984-6221. p. 2228

Shincovich, Ann, Dir, Pocono Mountain Public Library, Coolbaugh Township Municipal Ctr, 5500 Municipal Dr, Tobyhanna, PA, 18466. Tel: 570-894-8860. p. 2013

Shine, Monica, IT Librn, North Brunswick Free Public Library, 880 Hermann Rd, North Brunswick, NJ, 08902. Tel: 732-246-3545. p. 1429

Shinholser, Michele, Supvr, Circ, Southeastern Baptist Theological Seminary Library, 114 N Wingate St, Wake Forest, NC, 27587. Tel: 919-863-2256. p. 1720

Shinn, Tatyana N, Asst Dir, Ref Serv, State Historical Society of Missouri Library, 605 Elm St, Columbia, MO, 65201. Tel: 573-882-1187. p. 1243

Shipala, Kim, Asst Dir, Franklin Public Library, 118 Main St, Franklin, MA, 02038. Tel: 508-520-4941. p. 1020

Shipes, Sherry, Br Mgr, Colleton County Memorial Library, Edisto Beach Branch, 71 Station Ct, Edisto Beach, SC, 29438. Tel: 843-869-2499. p. 2072

Shiplett, Darrell, Asst Librn, United States Air Force, Air Force Flight Test Center Technical Research Library, 812 TSS/ENTL, 307 E Popson Ave, Bldg 1400, Rm 106, Edwards AFB, CA, 93524-6630. Tel: 661-277-3606. p. 139

Shipley, Amy, Libr Dir, Basalt Regional Library District, 14 Midland Ave, Basalt, CO, 81621-8305. Tel: 970-927-4311. p. 265

Shipley, Brenda, Dir, Greenfield Public Library, 515 Chestnut, Greenfield, IL, 62044-1304. Tel: 217-368-2613. p. 595

Shipley, Marcy, Head, Circ, Hudson Library & Historical Society, 96 Library St, Hudson, OH, 44236-5122. Tel: 330-653-6658. p. 1790

Shipley, Virginia, Asst Dir, Rector Public Library, 121 W Fourth St, Rector, AR, 72461. Tel: 870-595-2410. p. 108

Shipman, Charles, Ref/Info Serv Supvr, New Hampshire State Library, 20 Park St, Concord, NH, 03301. Tel: 603-271-3302. p. 1359

Shipman, Peter, Librn, Central Georgia Technical College Library, 80 Cohen Walker Dr, Warner Robins, GA, 31088. Tel: 478-988-6863. p. 502

Shipman, Suzanne, Head, Children's Servx, Redford Township District Library, 25320 W Six Mile, Redford, MI, 48240. Tel: 313-531-5960. p. 1143

Shippey, Stephanie, Assoc Dir, Pub Serv, Texas Tech University Health Sciences Center, 3601 Fourth St, Lubbock, TX, 79430. Tel: 806-743-2200. p. 2214

Shipps, Bradley, Dir, Outagamie Waupaca Library System (OWLS), 225 N Oneida, Appleton, WI, 54911. Tel: 920-832-6368. p. 2420

Shotick, Kimberly, Student Success Librn, Northern Illinois University Libraries, 217 Normal Rd, DeKalb, IL, 60115-2828. Tel: 815-753-5290. p. 577

Shott, Erica, Libr Dir, Dorset Village Library, Rte 30 & Church St, Dorset, VT, 05251. Tel: 802-867-4085. p. 2283

Shott, Shannen, Libr Mgr, Hinton Municipal Library, 803 Switzer Dr, Hinton, AB, T7V 1V1, CANADA. Tel: 780-865-2363. p. 2543

Shoudel, Eric, Librn, Joseph Public Library, 201 N Main, Joseph, OR, 97846. Tel: 541-432-0141. p. 1882

Shoumaker, Brandon, Br Mgr, Calcasieu Parish Public Library System, Carnegie Memorial, 411 Pujo St, Lake Charles, LA, 70601-4254. Tel: 337-721-7084. p. 893

Shoumaker, Brandon, Br Mgr, Calcasieu Parish Public Library System, Southwest Louisiana Genealogical & Historical Library, 411 Pujo St, Lake Charles, LA, 70601-4254. Tel: 337-721-7110. p. 894

Shoup, Jason, Dir, Rio Rancho Public Library, 755 Loma Colorado Blvd NE, Rio Rancho, NM, 87124. Tel: 505-891-5013. p. 1473

Show, Ellen, Archivist, Mint Museum, 2730 Randolph Rd, Charlotte, NC, 28207. Tel: 704-337-2092. p. 1680

Showalter, Janet, AV Coordr, Goshen Public Library, 601 S Fifth St, Goshen, IN, 46526. Tel: 574-533-9531. p. 687

Shrader, Marcia, Circ, Jefferson County Library, Arnold Branch, 1701 Missouri State Rd, Arnold, MO, 63010. Tel: 636-296-2204. p. 1249

Shrake, Peter, Archivist, Circus World Museum, 415 Lynn St, Baraboo, WI, 53913. Tel: 608-356-8341. p. 2422

Shrauger, Kristine, Head, ILL & Doc Delivery, University of Central Florida Libraries, 12701 Pegasus Dr, Orlando, FL, 32816-8030. Tel: 407-823-5422. p. 432

Shreeves, Sarah, Vice Dean, University of Arizona Libraries, 1510 E University Blvd, Tucson, AZ, 85721. Tel: 520-621-6442. p. 83

Shreve, Debbie, Libr Mgr, Wake County Public Library System, West Regional Library, 4000 Louis Stephens Dr, Cary, NC, 27519. Tel: 919-463-8500. p. 1711

Shreves, Thomas E, Mgr, Libr Serv, Kaiser-Permanente Medical Center, 4733 Sunset Blvd, 1st Flr, Los Angeles, CA, 90027. Tel: 323-783-8568. p. 162

Shrewsberry, Debbie, Head, Circ, Tri-Township Public Library District, 209 S Main St, Troy, IL, 62294. Tel: 618-667-2133. p. 654

Shrimplin, Aaron, Assoc Dean, Miami University Libraries, 151 S Campus Ave, Oxford, OH, 45056. Tel: 513-529-6823. p. 1811

Shriver, Emery, Ref, Web Develop Librn, Williams College, 26 Hopkins Hall Dr, Williamstown, MA, 01267. Tel: 413-597-4716. p. 1069

Shroll, Christian, Dir, Bracken County Public Library, 310 W Miami St, Brooksville, KY, 41004. Tel: 606-735-3620. p. 849

Shropshire, Laurie, Dir, Winkler County Library, 307 S Poplar St, Kermit, TX, 79745-4300. Tel: 432-586-3841. p. 2205

Shropshire, Sandra, Interim Dean, Idaho State University, 850 S Ninth Ave, Pocatello, ID, 83209. Tel: 208-282-2958. p. 528

Shropshire, Sandra, Interim Dean, Idaho State University, Idaho Health Sciences Library, 850 S Ninth Ave, Pocatello, ID, 83201-5314. Tel: 208-282-4685. p. 528

Shropshire, Shelly, Libr Dir, Morristown-Hamblen Library, 417 W Main St, Morristown, TN, 37814-4686. Tel: 423-586-6410. p. 2116

Shroyer, Carol, Br Head, Saint Lucie County Library System, Lakewood Park Branch, 7605 Santa Barbara Dr, Fort Pierce, FL, 34951. Tel: 772-462-6870. p. 405

Shtern, Laura, Info Serv, Wellington County Library, 190 Saint Andrews St W, Fergus, ON, N1M 1N5, CANADA. Tel: 519-787-7805. p. 2641

Shtulman, Robin, Asst Dir, Athol Public Library, 568 Main St, Athol, MA, 01331. Tel: 978-249-9515. p. 986

Shu, Evena, Mgr, Tech Serv, Sr Librn, Monterey Park Bruggemeyer Library, 318 S Ramona Ave, Monterey Park, CA, 91754-3399. Tel: 626-307-1368. p. 180

Shu, Yue, Librn, Smithsonian Libraries, National Museum of Asian Art Library - Freer Gallery of Art, Arthur M Sackler Gallery Library, Rm 2058, 1050 Independence Ave SW, MRC 707, Washington, DC, 20560. Tel: 202-633-0479. p. 375

Shubick, Karen, Librn, Hatboro Baptist Church Library, 32 N York Rd, Hatboro, PA, 19040. Tel: 215-675-8400. p. 1942

Shucha, Bonnie, Assoc Dean, Dir, Law Libr, University of Wisconsin-Madison, Law Library, 975 Bascom Mall, Madison, WI, 53706. Tel: 608-262-1128. p. 2451

Shuck, Jessica, Electronic Res Librn, Cornerstone University, 1001 E Beltline Ave NE, Grand Rapids, MI, 49525. Tel: 616-254-1650, Ext 2002. p. 1110

Shuck, John, Libr Dir, Dawson Community College Library, 300 College Dr, Glendive, MT, 59330. Tel: 406-377-9413. p. 1293

Shue, Frannie, Asst Dir, Br Coordr, Centre County Library & Historical Museum, 200 N Allegheny St, Bellefonte, PA, 16823-1601. Tel: 814-355-1516. p. 1910

Shufelt, Craig, Chief Exec Officer, Fort Erie Public Library, 136 Gilmore Rd, Fort Erie, ON, L2A 2M1, CANADA. Tel: 905-871-2546, Ext 303. p. 2642

Shuford, David, Cataloger, School of Visual Arts Library, 380 Second Ave, 2nd Flr, New York, NY, 10010. Tel: 212-592-2630. p. 1601

Shuford, Lindsey, Asst Libr Dir, Union County Public Library, 316 E Windsor St, Monroe, NC, 28112. Tel: 704-283-8184. p. 1703

Shukitt, Pamela A, Librn, Wilmington University Library, 320 N DuPont Hwy, New Castle, DE, 19720. Tel: 302-356-6877. p. 354

Shull, Diana, User Serv Librn, University of Wisconsin-Whitewater, 750 W Main St, Whitewater, WI, 53190-1790. Tel: 262-472-5011. p. 2488

Shull, Kelly, Br Mgr, Darlington County Library System, Lamar Branch, 103 E Main St, Lamar, SC, 29069. Tel: 843-326-5524. p. 2057

Shull, Mindy, Archives Records Analyst, Ball State University Libraries, Archives & Special Collections, Bracken Library, Rm 210, Muncie, IN, 47306-0161. Tel: 765-285-8853. p. 708

Shull, Wanda, Coordr, Piedmont Technical College Library, Library Resource Center - Saluda County Campus, 701 Batesburg Hwy, Rm 111SS, Saluda, SC, 29138. Tel: 864-445-3144, Ext 3102. p. 2063

Shulman, Anne, Librn, Riker, Danzig, Scherer, Hyland & Perretti, Headquarters Plaza, One Speedwell Ave, Morristown, NJ, 07962-1981. Tel: 973-538-0800. p. 1422

Shulman, Rachel, Head, Youth & School Services, Vernon Area Public Library District, 300 Olde Half Day Rd, Lincolnshire, IL, 60069. Tel: 847-634-3650. p. 609

Shultes, Stephanie, Dir, Iroquois Indian Museum Library, 324 Caverns Rd, Howes Cave, NY, 12092. Tel: 518-296-8949. p. 1548

Shults, Natalie, Virtual Serv Librn, Schertz Public Library, 798 Schertz Pkwy, Schertz, TX, 78154. Tel: 210-619-1700. p. 2242

Shultz, Harriet, Dir, Jennings Carnegie Public Library, 303 Cary Ave, Jennings, LA, 70546. Tel: 337-821-5517. p. 892

Shuluk, William, Head Librn, Florida SouthWestern State College, 8099 College Pkwy SW, Bldg J-212, Fort Myers, FL, 33919. Tel: 239-489-9356. p. 403

Shumaker, Deb, Dir, Kirtland Community College Library, 10775 N St Helen Rd, Roscommon, MI, 48653. Tel: 989-275-5000, Ext 235. p. 1145

Shumaker, Jasmine, Ref & Instruction Librn, University of Maryland, Baltimore County, 1000 Hilltop Circle, Baltimore, MD, 21250. Tel: 410-455-2356. p. 958

Shuman, Jay, Interim Libr Dir, New York University School of Law, Vanderbilt Hall, 40 Washington Sq S, New York, NY, 10012-1099. Tel: 212-998-6310. p. 1599

Shumar, Alesha, Univ Archivist, University of Tennessee, Knoxville, Special Collections, 121 Hodges Library, 1015 Volunteer Blvd, Knoxville, TN, 37996. Tel: 865-974-4480. p. 2108

Shumate, Connie, Dir, Concord University, Vermillion St, Athens, WV, 24712. Tel: 304-384-5371. p. 2397

Shumicky, Lisa, Asst Dir, Deer Park Public Library, 44 Lake Ave, Deer Park, NY, 11729. Tel: 631-586-3000. p. 1524

Shumway, Jean, Ref & Instruction Librn, Butler County Community College, 107 College Dr, Butler, PA, 16002. Tel: 724-284-8511. p. 1917

Shupala, Christine, Dir, Texas A&M University-Corpus Christi, Mary & Jeff Bell Library, 6300 Ocean Dr, Corpus Christi, TX, 78412-5501. Tel: 361-825-2643. p. 2161

Shupe, Robert, Dir, Palmdale City Library, 700 E Palmdale Blvd, Palmdale, CA, 93550. Tel: 661-267-5600. p. 191

Shuping, Andrew, ILL/Circ Supvr, Ref Librn, Mercer University, Jack Tarver Library, 1300 Edgewood Ave, Macon, GA, 31207. Tel: 478-301-2251. p. 486

Shuppe, Valetta, Ch Serv, Indiana Free Library, Inc, 845 Philadelphia St, Indiana, PA, 15701-3907. Tel: 724-465-8841. p. 1945

Shurly, Victoria, Dir, Peninsula Community Library, 2699 Island View Rd, Traverse City, MI, 49686. Tel: 231-223-7700. p. 1154

Shurtleff, Jennie, Educ Coordr, Woodstock History Center, 26 Elm St, Woodstock, VT, 05091. Tel: 802-457-1822. p. 2300

Shurtleff, William, Head Librn, Soyinfo Center Library, 1021 Dolores Dr, Lafayette, CA, 94549-2907. Tel: 925-283-2991. p. 155

Shuster, Laurie, Ref & Instruction Librn, Pierce College Library, Fort Steilacoom Campus/Cascade Bldg 4, 9401 Farwest Dr SW, Lakewood, WA, 98498. Tel: 253-964-6305. p. 2368

Shuster, Marjorie, Coordinator, Literary Events, Congregation Emanu-El of the City of New York, One E 65th St, New York, NY, 10065. Tel: 212-507-9560, 212-744-1400. p. 1584

Shute, Daniel J, Dr, Librn, Presbyterian College Library, 3495 University St, Montreal, QC, H3A 2A8, CANADA. Tel: 514-288-5256. p. 2727

Shutkin, Sara, Col Archivist/Rec Mgr, Ref Librn, Alverno College Library, 3401 S 39th St, Milwaukee, WI, 53215. Tel: 414-382-6202. p. 2457

Shutter, Claudia, Librn, Braintree Historical Society, Inc Library & Resource Center, Gilbert Bean Barn & Mary Bean Cunningham Resource Ctr, 31 Tenney Rd, Braintree, MA, 02184-4416. Tel: 781-848-1640. p. 1001

Shutter, Gloria, Dir of Library Technical Services, Harrisburg Area Community College, 735 Cumberland St, Lebanon, PA, 17042. Tel: 717-780-2543. p. 1953

Shuyler, Kristen, Dir, Communications & Outreach, James Madison University Libraries, 880 Madison Dr, MSC 1704, Harrisonburg, VA, 22807. Tel: 540-568-7012. p. 2324

Shymwell, Lynn, Youth Serv Librn, River Rouge Public Library, 221 Burke St, River Rouge, MI, 48218. Tel: 313-843-2040. p. 1144

Siasoco, Hope, Dir, Pinckney Community Public Library, 125 Putnam St, Pinckney, MI, 48169. Tel: 734-878-3888. p. 1141

Sibley, David, Univ Librn, Chicago School of Professional Psychology Library, 325 N Wells St, 6th Flr, Chicago, IL, 60654. Tel: 312-329-6630. p. 558

Sibley, Donna M, Dir of Libr Operations, Becker College, 13 Washburn Sq, Leicester, MA, 01524. Tel: 508-373-9712. p. 1027

Sibley, Jean, Head, Ser, College of William & Mary in Virginia, Earl Gregg Swem Library, One Landrum Dr, Williamsburg, VA, 23187. Tel: 757-221-3103. p. 2353

Sica, Deb, Dep County Librn, Alameda County Library, 2450 Stevenson Blvd, Fremont, CA, 94538-2326. Tel: 510-745-1500. p. 143

Sichaleune, Jeffrey, Mgr, County of Los Angeles Public Library, A C Bilbrew Library, 150 E El Segundo Blvd, Los Angeles, CA, 90061. Tel: 310-538-3350. p. 135

Sichler, Donia, Youth Serv, Redondo Beach Public Library, 303 N Pacific Coast Hwy, Redondo Beach, CA, 90277. Tel: 310-318-0675. p. 199

Sicignano, Charlie, Head, Acq, Head, Electronic Res, University of West Georgia, 1601 Maple St, Carrollton, GA, 30118. Tel: 678-839-6495. p. 469

Sicurella, Tim, Head, Adult Serv, Sayville Library, 88 Greene Ave, Sayville, NY, 11782. Tel: 631-589-4440. p. 1637

Siddell, Kayla, Interim Asst Dir, Xavier University of Louisiana, One Drexel Dr, New Orleans, LA, 70125-1098. Tel: 504-520-7311. p. 904

Sidders, Debbie, Br Mgr, Ouachita Parish Public Library, West Monroe Branch, 315 Cypress St, West Monroe, LA, 71291. Tel: 318-327-1365. p. 898

Siddiqui, Rashid, Syst Mgr, Carnegie Mellon University, Hunt Library, 4909 Frew St, Pittsburgh, PA, 15213. Tel: 412-268-2444. p. 1992

Sideris, Amy, Br Mgr, East Baton Rouge Parish Library, Scotlandville, 7373 Scenic Hwy, Baton Rouge, LA, 70807. Tel: 225-354-7580. p. 883

Siders, Kari, Dir, Pub Serv, Cedarville University, 251 N Main St, Cedarville, OH, 45314-0601. Tel: 937-766-7840. p. 1757

Sides, Patricia, Archivist, Willard Library of Evansville, 21 First Ave, Evansville, IN, 47710-1294. Tel: 812-425-4309. p. 682

Sidie, Jennifer, Br Mgr, Warren County Library, Two Shotwell Dr, Belvidere, NJ, 07823. Tel: 908-818-1280. p. 1389

Sidie, Jennifer, Br Mgr, Warren County Library, Southwest Branch, 404 Rte 519, Phillipsburg, NJ, 08885. Tel: 908-818-1280. p. 1390

Sidon, Yanira, Br Mgr, Santa Clarita Public Library, 18601 Soledad Canyon Rd, Santa Clarita, CA, 91351. Tel: 661-259-0750. p. 242

Sidorick, Kim, Mgr, Ch Serv, Mentor Public Library, 8215 Mentor Ave, Mentor, OH, 44060. Tel: 440-255-8811. p. 1802

Sidwell, Tara, Dir, Kate Love Simpson Morgan County Library, 358 E Main St, McConnelsville, OH, 43756. Tel: 740-962-2533. p. 1801

Siebenaler, Jessica, Instrul Librn, Washburn University, 1700 SW College Ave, Topeka, KS, 66621. Tel: 785-670-1935. p. 839

Siebenberg, Tammy, Dir, Yakima Valley College, S 16th Ave at Nob Hill Blvd, Yakima, WA, 98902. Tel: 509-574-4984. p. 2395

Siebers, Bruce, Br Mgr, Free Library of Philadelphia, Walnut Street West Branch, 201 S 40th St, Philadelphia, PA, 19104. Tel: 215-685-7671. p. 1980

Siebert, M J, YA Serv, Grant County Library, 215 E Grant Ave, Ulysses, KS, 67880. Tel: 620-356-1433. p. 840

Siebert, Sheryl, Dir, Chenoa Public Library, 211 S Division St, Chenoa, IL, 61726. Tel: 815-945-4253. p. 553

Siebol, Mike, Chief Curator of Collections & Archives, Yakima Valley Museum, 2105 Tieton Dr, Yakima, WA, 98902. Tel: 509-248-0747. p. 2396

Siebold, Patrick, Libr Mgr, Vancouver Island Regional Library, Masset Branch, 2123 Collison Ave, Masset, BC, V0T 1M0, CANADA. Tel: 250-626-3663. p. 2571

Siebold, Patrick, Libr Mgr, Vancouver Island Regional Library, Port Clements Branch, 35 Cedar Ave W, Port Clements, BC, V0T 1R0, CANADA. Tel: 250-557-4402. p. 2571

Siebold, Patrick, Libr Mgr, Vancouver Island Regional Library, Queen Charlotte City Branch, Community Hall, 138 Bay, Queen Charlotte, BC, V0T 1S0, CANADA. Tel: 250-559-4518. p. 2571

Siebold, Patrick, Libr Mgr, Vancouver Island Regional Library, Sandspit Branch, Seabreeze Plaza, Beach Rd, Sandspit, BC, V0T 1T0, CANADA. Tel: 250-637-2247. p. 2571

Siecke, Elizabeth J, Col Librn, Ramapo College of New Jersey, 505 Ramapo Valley Rd, Mahwah, NJ, 07430-1623. Tel: 201-684-7575. p. 1415

Sieczka, Ann Marie, Head, Circ, Berkeley Heights Public Library, 29 Park Ave, Berkeley Heights, NJ, 07922. Tel: 908-464-9333. p. 1390

Sieczkiewicz, Rob, Libr Dir, Susquehanna University, 514 University Ave, Selinsgrove, PA, 17870-1050. Tel: 570-372-4329. p. 2005

Sieczkiewicz, Robert, Univ Archivist, Drexel University Libraries, Hagerty Library, 33rd & Market Sts, Philadelphia, PA, 19104-2875. Tel: 215-895-1757. p. 1976

Siedlecki, Armin, Cat, Emory University Libraries, Pitts Theology Library, Candler School of Theology, 1531 Dickey Dr, Ste 560, Atlanta, GA, 30322-2810. Tel: 404-727-4166. p. 463

Sieg, Julie, Dir, Marion County Public Library System, Ocala Public Library (Headquarters), 2720 E Silver Springs Blvd, Ocala, FL, 34470. Tel: 352-671-8551. p. 430

Sieg, Julie H, Dir, Marion County Public Library System, 2720 E Silver Springs Blvd, Ocala, FL, 34470. Tel: 352-671-8551. p. 430

Siegal, Marni, Libr Asst, Nederland Community Library, 200 Hwy 72 N, Nederland, CO, 80466. Tel: 303-258-1101. p. 292

Siegel, Beth, Ad, Bryant Library, Two Paper Mill Rd, Roslyn, NY, 11576. Tel: 516-621-2240. p. 1633

Siegel, Jane Rogers, Bibliog Serv, Rare Bk Librn, Columbia University, Rare Book & Manuscript, Butler Library, 6th Flr E, 535 W 114th St, New York, NY, 10027. Tel: 212-854-8482. p. 1583

Siegel, John, Coordr, Info Literacy, Pub Serv Librn, University of South Carolina Upstate Library, 800 University Way, Spartanburg, SC, 29303. Tel: 864-503-5620. p. 2070

Siegel, Lenny, Dir, Pacific Studies Center, 2423B Old Middlefield Way, Mountain View, CA, 94043. Tel: 650-961-8918. p. 181

Siegel, Leora, Dir, Libr Serv, Lenhardt Library of the Chicago Botanic Garden, 1000 Lake Cook Rd, Glencoe, IL, 60022. Tel: 847-835-8202. p. 593

Siegel, Lori, Ref Librn, Washington University Libraries, George Warren Brown School of Social Work, One Brookings Dr, Campus Box 1196, Saint Louis, MO, 63130-4899. Tel: 314-935-4064. p. 1277

Siegel, Minna, Librn, Temple Beth Sholom, 1901 Kresson Rd, Cherry Hill, NJ, 08003. Tel: 856-751-6663. p. 1396

Siegel, Nancy, Libr Dir, Agawam Public Library, 750 Cooper St, Agawam, MA, 01001. Tel: 413-789-1550. p. 983

Siegele, Hannah, Ad, Asst Dir, West Chester Public Library, 415 N Church St, West Chester, PA, 19380-2401. Tel: 610-696-1721. p. 2020

Siegfried, Cary Ann, Dir, Washington Public Library, 115 W Washington St, Washington, IA, 52353. Tel: 319-653-2726. p. 788

Siegfried, Glennis, Ref Librn, Barberton Public Library, 602 W Park Ave, Barberton, OH, 44203-2458. Tel: 330-745-1194. p. 1748

Siegler, Sara, Asst Dir, Ocean County Library, 101 Washington St, Toms River, NJ, 08753. Tel: 732-914-5412. p. 1446

Siekman, Jill, Tech Serv Supvr, Saint Lucie County Library System, 101 Melody Lane, Fort Pierce, FL, 34950-4402. Tel: 772-462-2198. p. 405

Siemer, Barbara, Mgr, United States Navy, Naval Base Coronado Library, MWR Base Library, 2478 Munda Rd, San Diego, CA, 92155-5396. Tel: 619-437-3026. p. 222

Siemon, Jeff, Electronic Res Librn, Anderson University, 1100 E Fifth St, Anderson, IN, 46012-3495. Tel: 765-641-4280. p. 668

Siemons, Cynthia, Dir, Greene Public Library, 231 W Traer St, Greene, IA, 50636-9406. Tel: 641-816-5642. p. 756

Sienczenko, Nina, Librn, New Kuban Education & Welfare Association, 228 Don Rd, Buena, NJ, 08310. Tel: 856-697-2255. p. 1393

Sieracki, Rita, Ref Librn, Medical College of Wisconsin Libraries, Health Research Ctr, 3rd Flr, 8701 Watertown Plank Rd, Milwaukee, WI, 53226-0509. Tel: 414-955-8327. p. 2459

Sierpe, Eino, Dr, Assoc Prof, Southern Connecticut State University, 501 Crescent St, New Haven, CT, 06515. Tel: 203-392-6883. p. 2783

Sierra, Bianca, Dir, East Moline Public Library, 745 16th Ave, East Moline, IL, 61244-2122. Tel: 309-755-9614. p. 580

Sierra, Carmen J, Chief Librn, Department of Veterans Affairs, Library Service 142D, Ten Calle Casia, San Juan, PR, 00921-3201. Tel: 787-641-7582, Ext 12276, 787-641-7582, Ext 31905. p. 2513

Sierra, Melissa, Dir, Alpha Park Public Library District, 3527 S Airport Rd, Bartonville, IL, 61607-1799. Tel: 309-697-3822. p. 540

Siesing, Gina, Chief Info Officer, Dir of Libr, Bryn Mawr College, 101 N Merion Ave, Bryn Mawr, PA, 19010-2899. Tel: 610-526-7440. p. 1916

Sieve, Leasa, Ref Librn, New Ulm Public Library, 17 N Broadway, New Ulm, MN, 56073-1786. Tel: 507-359-8331. p. 1190

Sievers, Brooke, Asst Dir, Head, Mat Mgt, Addison Public Library, Four Friendship Plaza, Addison, IL, 60101. Tel: 630-458-3329. p. 535

Sievert, Charlotte, Ref (Info Servs), Summa Health System, 55 Arch St, Ste G-3, Akron, OH, 44304. Tel: 330-375-3260. p. 1745

Sieving, Amy, Tech Serv Mgr, Wilkinson Public Library, 100 W Pacific Ave, Telluride, CO, 81435. Tel: 970-728-4519. p. 296

Siewert, Karl, Instruction Librn, Northeastern State University, Broken Arrow Campus Library, 3100 E New Orleans St, Broken Arrow, OK, 74014. Tel: 918-449-6449. p. 1863

Siftar, Tim, Ref Librn, Drexel University Libraries, Hagerty Library, 33rd & Market Sts, Philadelphia, PA, 19104-2875. Tel: 215-895-2762. p. 1976

Siga, Sharon, Chief Exec Officer, Strathcona County Library, 401 Festival Lane, Sherwood Park, AB, T8A 5P7, CANADA. Tel: 780-410-8600. p. 2553

Sigal, Ari, Ref & Instruction Librn, Catawba Valley Community College Library, Cuyler A Dunbar Bldg, 2550 Hwy 70 SE, Hickory, NC, 28602. Tel: 828-327-7000, Ext 4355. p. 1696

Sigal, Myrna, Head, Pub Serv, West Nyack Free Library, 65 Strawtown Rd, West Nyack, NY, 10994. Tel: 845-358-6081. p. 1662

Sigal, Stella, Med Librn, New York Presbyterian Hospital-Weill Cornell, 21 Bloomingdale Rd, White Plains, NY, 10605. Tel: 914-997-5897. p. 1664

Sigety, Stephen, Electronic Res Librn, Indiana University South Bend, 1700 Mishawaka Ave, South Bend, IN, 46615. Tel: 574-520-4416. p. 718

Sigismondi, Anthony, Assoc Librn, University of Wisconsin-Green Bay, Manitowoc Campus Library, 705 Viebahn St, Manitowoc, WI, 54220. Tel: 920-683-4715. p. 2439

Sigismondi, Anthony, Adult Serv, Plymouth Public Library, 130 Division St, Plymouth, WI, 53073. Tel: 920-892-4416. p. 2470

Signater, Jordan, Head, Ref, Southern University, 167 Roosevelt Steptoe Ave, Baton Rouge, LA, 70813-0001. Tel: 225-771-4990. p. 884

Sigua, David, Libr Assoc, City of Palo Alto Library, Downtown, 270 Forest Ave, Palo Alto, CA, 94301. Tel: 650-838-2964. p. 192

Siker, Nancy, Dir, Libr Serv, Milwaukee Institute of Art & Design Library & Learning Commons, 273 E Erie St, Milwaukee, WI, 53202-6003. Tel: 414-847-3342. p. 2459

Sikes, Sherry, Dir, Jones Public Library, 801 South Cleveland, Ste A, Dayton, TX, 77535. Tel: 936-258-7060. p. 2169

Sikma Wallin, Renee, Sr Acad Librn, University of Wisconsin Stevens Point Library, 518 S Seventh Ave, Wausau, WI, 54401-5396. Tel: 715-261-6220. p. 2486

Sikora, David, Br Mgr, Milwaukee Public Library, Tippecanoe, 3912 S Howell Ave, Milwaukee, WI, 53207. p. 2460

Sikora, David, Br Mgr, Milwaukee Public Library, Zablocki, 3501 W Oklahoma Ave, Milwaukee, WI, 53215. p. 2460

Sikora, Sara, Learning Res Spec, Mid-State Technical College, 2600 W Fifth St, Marshfield, WI, 54449. Tel: 715-389-7020. p. 2454

Sikora, Victoria, Sr Librn, Los Angeles Public Library System, Echo Park Branch Library, 1410 W Temple St, Los Angeles, CA, 90026-5605. Tel: 213-250-7808. p. 164

Sikorsky, Donna, Liaison Librn, University of Manitoba Libraries, E K Williams Law Library, 401 Robson Hall, 224 Dysart Rd, Winnipeg, MB, R3T 2N2, CANADA. Tel: 204-474-6372. p. 2596

Silberger, Kathryn, Digital Serv, Sr Librn, Marist College, 3399 North Rd, Poughkeepsie, NY, 12601-1387. Tel: 845-575-3419. p. 1623

Silberman, David, Head, Adult Serv, Clarkston Independence District Library, 6495 Clarkston Rd, Clarkston, MI, 48346. Tel: 248-625-2212. p. 1091

Silbernagel, Tony, Chairperson, Elnora Public Library, 210 Main St, Elnora, AB, T0M 0Y0, CANADA. Tel: 403-773-3966. p. 2539

Silbersack, Barbara, Assoc Dir, Libr Operations, Thompson Hine LLP, 1400 Scripps Ctr, 312 Walnut St, Cincinnati, OH, 45202. Tel: 513-352-6528. p. 1764

Silbiger, Jenny, State Law Librn, Supreme Court Law Library, 417 S King St, Rm 119, Honolulu, HI, 96813. Tel: 808-539-4964. p. 512

Silchuk-Ashcraft, Daphne, Dir, Orrville Public Library, 230 N Main St, Orrville, OH, 44667. Tel: 330-683-1065. p. 1810

Siler, Elizabeth, Assoc Dean, Coll Serv, University of North Carolina at Charlotte, 9201 University City Blvd, Charlotte, NC, 28223-0001. Tel: 704-687-1372. p. 1681

Silfee, Jayne, Supvr, User Serv, Washington & Jefferson College Library, 60 S Lincoln St, Washington, PA, 15301. Tel: 724-223-6070. p. 2018

Silgals, Mary, Head Librn, Ballard-Carlisle-Livingston County Public Library, 257 N Fourth St, Wickliffe, KY, 42087. Tel: 270-335-5059. p. 877

Silka, Marylu, Libr Office Mgr, Adams County Library, 569 N Cedar St, Ste 1, Adams, WI, 53910-9800. Tel: 608-339-4250. p. 2419

Sillars, Jennifer, Libr Asst, Patrick Henry College Library, Ten Patrick Henry Circle, Purcellville, VA, 20132. Tel: 540-441-8400. p. 2339

Silliman, Molly, Sr Archivist, South Carolina Historical Society Library, Addlestone Library, 3rd Flr, 205 Calhoun St, Charleston, SC, 29401. Tel: 843-723-3225, Ext 112. p. 2051

Sillito, Savannah, Info Spec, University of Calgary Library, Doucette Library of Teaching Resources, 370 Education Block, 2500 University Dr NW, Calgary, AB, T2N 1N4, CANADA. Tel: 403-220-3984. p. 2529

Sillius, Irene, Cat, Syst Tech, Sheridan College Library, Davis Campus, 7899 McLaughlin Rd, Brampton, ON, L6V 1G6, CANADA. Tel: 905-459-7533, Ext 4338. p. 2663

Sills, Allison, Librn, Lee County Library, 107 Hawkins Ave, Sanford, NC, 27330. Tel: 919-718-4665. p. 1715

Sills, Frederick, Circ Mgr, Doc Delivery, Saint Augustine's College, 1315 Oakwood Ave, Raleigh, NC, 27610-2298. Tel: 919-516-4148. p. 1710

Sills, Scott, Access Serv Mgr, Pacific Lutheran University, 12180 Park Ave S, Tacoma, WA, 98447-0001. Tel: 253-535-7500. p. 2386

Silmser, Jennifer, Librn, Horry County Memorial Library, Carolina Forest Branch, 2250 Carolina Forest Blvd, Myrtle Beach, SC, 29579. Tel: 843-915-5282. p. 2056

Silsbe, Gail, Ch Serv, Bayport-Blue Point Public Library, 203 Blue Point Ave, Blue Point, NY, 11715-1217. Tel: 631-363-6133. p. 1495

Silva, Elizabeth, Librn, Ohlone College, 43600 Mission Blvd, Fremont, CA, 94539. Tel: 510-659-6000, Ext 7484. p. 144

Silva, Ivan, Tech & Learning Initiatives Librn, Belvedere Tiburon Library, 1501 Tiburon Blvd, Tiburon, CA, 94920. Tel: 415-789-2665. p. 252

Silva, Judy, Archivist, Performing Arts Librn, Slippery Rock University of Pennsylvania, 109 Campus Loop, Slippery Rock, PA, 16057. Tel: 724-738-2058. p. 2007

Silva, Leticia, Educ Supvr, Central Florida Reception Center, 7000 H C Kelley Rd, Orlando, FL, 32831. Tel: 407-208-8283. p. 431

Silva, Mary, Circ Supvr, Ames Free Library, 53 Main St, North Easton, MA, 02356. Tel: 508-238-2000. p. 1041

Silva, Robin, Librn, Portsmouth Athenaeum, Six-Nine Market Sq, Portsmouth, NH, 03801. Tel: 603-431-2538. p. 1379

Silva, Sandra, Supvr, Pub Serv, Mesquite Public Library, 300 W Grubb Dr, Mesquite, TX, 75149. Tel: 972-216-6220. p. 2219

Silva, Taylor, YA Librn, Fall River Public Library, 104 N Main St, Fall River, MA, 02720. Tel: 508-324-2700. p. 1018

Silva, Victoria, Libr Dir, Safford City-Graham County Library, 808 S Seventh Ave, Safford, AZ, 85546. Tel: 928-432-4151. p. 76

Silvas, Georgina, Librn, Taft Public Library, 501 Green Ave, Taft, TX, 78390. Tel: 361-528-3512. p. 2246

Silver, Ilana, Head, Youth Serv, West Babylon Public Library, 211 Rte 109, West Babylon, NY, 11704. Tel: 631-669-5445. p. 1661

Silver, Joel, Dir, Indiana University Bloomington, Lilly Library Rare Books & Manuscripts, 1200 E Seventh St, Bloomington, IN, 47405-5500. Tel: 812-855-2452. p. 671

Silver, Lynda, Librn, Nova Scotia Department of Education & Early Childhood Dev, 2021 Brunswick St, Halifax, NS, B3J 2S9, CANADA. Tel: 902-424-5168. p. 2620

Silver, Rachel, Circ/Ser, Vineyard Haven Public Library, 200 Main St, Vineyard Haven, MA, 02568. Tel: 508-696-4210. p. 1061

Silver, Samantha, Electronic Res Librn, Mount Saint Mary's University, J Thomas McCarthy Library, Doheny Campus, Ten Chester Pl, Los Angeles, CA, 90007. Tel: 213-477-2754. p. 166

Silver, Steve, Dir, Bushnell University, 1188 Kincade, Eugene, OR, 97401. Tel: 541-684-7237. p. 1878

Silver-Morillo, Jackie, Archivist, Head, Ref, Atlantic City Free Public Library, William K Cheatham Bldg, One N Tennessee Ave, Atlantic City, NJ, 08401. Tel: 609-345-2269, Ext 3063. p. 1388

Silvera, Vicki, Head, Spec Coll, Univ Archivist, Florida International University, 11200 SW Eighth St, Miami, FL, 33199. Tel: 305-348-3136. p. 421

Silverman, Alan, Dir, Easttown Library & Information Center, 720 First Ave, Berwyn, PA, 19312-1769. Tel: 610-644-0138. p. 1910

Silverman, Daniel, Dir of Educ, Dir, Programming, Beth Tzedec Congregation, 1700 Bathurst St, Toronto, ON, M5P 3K3, CANADA. Tel: 416-781-3514, Ext 225. p. 2686

Silverman, Eleanor, Librn, Chilton Memorial Hospital, 97 West Pkwy, Pompton Plains, NJ, 07444. Tel: 973-831-5058. p. 1436

Silverman, Evelyn, Access Serv, ILL, Queens College, Benjamin S Rosenthal Library, 65-30 Kissena Blvd, Flushing, NY, 11367-0904. Tel: 718-997-3700. p. 1534

Silverman, Mark, Actg Dir, University of Pittsburgh Library System, Law Bldg, 3900 Forbes Ave, 4th Flr, Pittsburgh, PA, 15260. Tel: 412-648-1376. p. 1996

Silverman, Rachel, Youth Serv Librn, Millis Public Library, 961 Main St, Millis, MA, 02054. Tel: 508-376-8282. p. 1036

Silverman, Sue, Ref Librn, Brooklyn Law School Library, 250 Joralemon St, Brooklyn, NY, 11201. Tel: 718-780-0678. p. 1501

Silvernail, Sean, Head, Info Tech, Guilderland Public Library, 2228 Western Ave, Guilderland, NY, 12084. Tel: 518-456-2400, Ext 199. p. 1542

Silvers, Stephanie, Libr Dir, Harmony Public Library, 225 Third Ave SW, Harmony, MN, 55939-6635. Tel: 507-886-8133. p. 1177

Silversides, Brock, Dept Head, University of Toronto Libraries, Media Commons, Robarts Library, 130 St George St, 3rd flr, Toronto, ON, M5S 1A5, CANADA. Tel: 416-978-7119. p. 2699

Silverstein, Bruce, Head, Automation & Tech Serv, Patchogue-Medford Library, 54-60 E Main St, Patchogue, NY, 11772. Tel: 631-654-4700. p. 1615

Silverstein, Isabel, Librn, St John's Hospital, 800 E Carpenter, Springfield, IL, 62769. Tel: 217-544-6464, Ext 44563. p. 650

Silverstein, Marcia, Dir, Mkt & Outreach, Nova Southeastern University Libraries, 3100 Ray Ferrero Jr Blvd, Fort Lauderdale, FL, 33314. Tel: 954-262-4562. p. 402

Silverstein, Russell, Dir, Info Tech, Syracuse University Libraries, 222 Waverly Ave, Syracuse, NY, 13244-2010. Tel: 315-443-4300. p. 1650

Silvestrini, Maria, Info Access Ctr Dir, Inter-American University of Puerto Rico, 104 Parque Industrial Turpeaux, Rd 1, Mercedita, PR, 00715-1602. Tel: 787-284-1912. p. 2512

Silvey, Layce, Legislative Librn, Idaho Legislative Research Library, State Capitol, 700 W Jefferson St, Boise, ID, 83702. Tel: 208-334-4822. p. 517

Silvey, Sandra, Dir, George H & Laura E Brown Library, 122 Van Norden St, Washington, NC, 27889. Tel: 252-946-4300. p. 1721

Silvey, Sharon, Mgr, Eastern Shore Public Library, Cape Charles Memorial Library, 201 Mason Ave, Cape Charles, VA, 23310. Tel: 757-331-1300. p. 2301

Silvia, Jessica L, Faculty & Digital Services Asst, Roger Williams University, Ten Metacom Ave, Bristol, RI, 02809-5171. Tel: 401-254-4546. p. 2029

Sim, Lisa, Admin Officer, Learning Resources, Douglas College Library & Learning Centre, 700 Royal Ave, Rm N2100, New Westminster, BC, V3M 5Z5, CANADA. Tel: 604-527-5180. p. 2572

Simard, Aliela, Treas, Kapuskasing Public Library, 24 Mundy Ave, Kapuskasing, ON, P5N 1P9, CANADA. Tel: 705-335-3363. p. 2648

Simard, Fabienne, Ref (Info Servs), Cegep de Jonquiere, 2505 rue St Hubert, Jonquiere, QC, G7X 7W2, CANADA. Tel: 418-547-2191, Ext 6268. p. 2714

Simard, Guylaine, Libr Serv Mgr, Bibliotheque, Institut de Tourisme et d'Hotellerie du Quebec, 3535, rue Saint-Denis, Local 1.97, Montreal, QC, H2X 3P1, CANADA. Tel: 514-282-5111, Ext 4525. p. 2717

Simard, Marie-Eve, Head of Libr, Conservatoire de Musique de Quebec Bibliotheque, 270 rue Jacques-Parizeau, Quebec, QC, G1R 5G1, CANADA. Tel: 418-643-2190, Ext 224. p. 2730

Simard, Pauline, Asst Chief Librn, Universite de Moncton, 18, ave Antonine-Maillet, Moncton, NB, E1A 3E9, CANADA. Tel: 506-858-4012. p. 2603

Simco, Kristie, Tech Serv Supvr, East Fishkill Community Library, 348 Rte 376, Hopewell Junction, NY, 12533-6075. Tel: 845-221-9943, Ext 222. p. 1548

Sime, Tanya, Admin Serv Mgr, Capital Area Regional Planning Commission Library, 100 State St, Ste 400, Madison, WI, 53703. Tel: 608-474-6017. p. 2449

Simek, Elizabeth, Outreach Serv, Antigo Public Library, 617 Clermont St, Antigo, WI, 54409. Tel: 715-623-3724. p. 2420

Simensen, Kristen, Dir, Calhoun County Library, 900 FR Huff Dr, Saint Matthews, SC, 29135. Tel: 803-874-3389. p. 2069

Simeon, Cindy Lee, Libr Dir, Raymond A Whitwer Tilden Public Library, 202 S Center St, Tilden, NE, 68781. Tel: 402-368-5306. p. 1338

Simerlink, Cindy, Br Mgr, Ocean County Library, Tuckerton Branch, 380 Bay Ave, Tuckerton, NJ, 08087-2557. Tel: 609-296-1470. p. 1447

Simic, Robert, Head, Children's Servx, New Rochelle Public Library, Huguenot Children's Library, 794 North Ave, New Rochelle, NY, 10801. Tel: 914-632-8954. p. 1577

Simmons, Andrea, Dir & Librn, Ballston Spa Public Library, 21 Milton Ave, Ballston Spa, NY, 12020. Tel: 518-885-5022. p. 1490

Simmons, Angie, Coll Develop, Dir, Pretty Prairie Public Library, 119 W Main St, Pretty Prairie, KS, 67570. Tel: 620-459-6392. p. 833

Simmons, Anne, Research & Programs Librn, National Gallery of Art Library, Fourth St & Pennsylvania Ave NW, Washington, DC, 20565. Tel: 202-842-6511. p. 372

Simmons, Arthur, Exec Dir, Rome Historical Society, 200 Church St, Rome, NY, 13440. Tel: 315-336-5870. p. 1632

Simmons, Christopher, Dir, Leetonia Community Public Library, 181 Walnut St, Leetonia, OH, 44431. Tel: 330-427-6635. p. 1795

Simmons, Cindy, Librn, North Central Washington Libraries, Manson Public Library, 80 Wapato Way, Manson, WA, 98831-9210. Tel: 509-687-3420. p. 2394

Simmons, Don, Asst Prof, Simmons University, 300 The Fenway, Boston, MA, 02115. Tel: 617-521-2800. p. 2786

Simmons, Elizabeth, Research Librn, Thurgood Marshall State Law Library, Courts of Appeals Bldg, 361 Rowe Blvd, Annapolis, MD, 21401. Tel: 410-260-1430. p. 950

Simmons, Gwen, Dir, College of the Ozarks, Lyons Memorial Library, One Opportunity Ave, Point Lookout, MO, 65726. Tel: 417-690-3411. p. 1266

Simmons, Laquodra, Supvr, Cuyahoga Community College, Library Technical Services, 2900 Community College Ave, MRC507, Cleveland, OH, 44115-3123. Tel: 216-987-3383. p. 1769

Simmons, Liz, Syst/Electronic Serv Librn, Genesee Community College, One College Rd, Batavia, NY, 14020-9704. Tel: 585-343-0055, Ext 6458. p. 1490

Simmons, Mark, Librn, Phoenix VA Health Care System, 650 E Indian School Rd, Phoenix, AZ, 85012. Tel: 602-222-6411. p. 72

Simmons, Martha, Tech Serv Librn, Hooksett Public Library, 31 Mount Saint Mary's Way, Hooksett, NH, 03106-1852. Tel: 603-485-6092. p. 1368

Simmons, Meriam D, Tech Serv, United States Army, Fort Stewart Main Post Library, 316 Lindquist Rd, Fort Stewart, GA, 31314-5126. Tel: 912-767-2260, 912-767-2828. p. 479

Simmons, Michael, Libr Mgr, Med Librn, Sparrow Health System, Two South, Sparrow Hospital, 1215 E Michigan Ave, Lansing, MI, 48912. Tel: 517-364-2200. p. 1125

Simmons, Nathan, Ref Serv, Rock Island Public Library, 401 19th St, Rock Island, IL, 61201. Tel: 309-732-7302. p. 641

Simmons, Rachel, Archivist, Winter Park Public Library, 460 E New England Ave, Winter Park, FL, 32789. Tel: 407-623-3300, Ext 106. p. 456

Simmons, Rachel, Br Mgr, Sampson-Clinton Public Library, Bryan Memorial, 302 W Weeksdale St, Newton Grove, NC, 28366. Tel: 910-594-1260. p. 1681

Simmons, Sabrina, ILL Coordr, University of California, Riverside, 900 University Ave, Riverside, CA, 92521. Tel: 951-827-3220. p. 203

Simmons, Stephanie, Br Mgr, Bullitt County Public Library, Nichols Branch, 10729 Hwy 44 W, West Point, KY, 40177. Tel: 502-324-7699. p. 875

Simmons, Valerie, Libr Dir, Four Star Public Library District, 132 W South St, Mendon, IL, 62351. Tel: 217-936-2131. p. 616

Simmons, Valerie, Br Mgr, Lane Public Libraries, Fairfield Lane Library, 1485 Corydale Dr, Fairfield, OH, 45014. Tel: 513-858-3238. p. 1789

Simmons, Vicki, Fiscal Officer, Willoughby-Eastlake Public Library, 35150 Lakeshore Blvd, Eastlake, OH, 44095. Tel: 440-943-2203. p. 1783

Simmons-Henry, Linda, Dir, Libr Serv, Texas College, 2404 N Grand Ave, Tyler, TX, 75702-4500. Tel: 903-593-8311, Ext 2349. p. 2249

Simms, Eileen, Interim Dir, Boone Area Library, 129 N Mill St, Birdsboro, PA, 19508-2340. Tel: 610-582-5666. p. 1912

Simms, Eileen, Asst Dir, Muhlenberg Community Library, 3612 Kutztown Rd, Laureldale, PA, 19605-1842. Tel: 610-929-0589. p. 1953

Simms, Gail, Libr Tech, Atlantic Provinces Special Education Authority Library, 102-7071 Bayers Rd, Halifax, NS, B3L 2C2, CANADA. Tel: 902-423-8094. p. 2618

Simms, Grace, Tech Librn, Samford University Library, Lucille Stewart Beeson Law Library, 800 Lakeshore Dr, Birmingham, AL, 35229. Tel: 205-726-2714. p. 9

Simms, Jennifer, Head of Libr, Indiana University Bloomington, Sciences Library, Chemistry C002, 800 E Kirkwood Ave, Bloomington, IN, 47405-7102. Tel: 812-855-5609. p. 671

Simms, Jonathan, Tech Coordr, University of North Alabama, One Harrison Plaza, Box 5028, Florence, AL, 35632-0001. Tel: 256-765-4470. p. 17

Simms, Mary, Librn, Pleasant Grove Christian Church Library, 1324 Pleasant Dr, Dallas, TX, 75217. Tel: 214-391-3159. p. 2167

Simms, Sheree, Br Mgr, Putnam County Library System, Melrose Public Library, 312 Wynnwood Ave, Melrose, FL, 32666. Tel: 352-475-3382. p. 433

Simoes, Brian, IT Tech, Bergen County Cooperative Library System, Inc, 21-00 Route 208 S, Ste 130, Fair Lawn, NJ, 07410. Tel: 201-498-7315. p. 2770

Simon, Adam, Exec Dir, Kehillat Israel Reconstructionist Congregation of Pacific Palisades Library, 16019 W Sunset Blvd, Pacific Palisades, CA, 90272. Tel: 310-459-2328. p. 191

Simon, Alan C, Dir, Network Serv, Health Sciences Libraries Consortium, 3600 Market St, Ste 550, Philadelphia, PA, 19104-2646. Tel: 215-222-1532. p. 2774

Simon, Anna, Head of Libr, University of Wisconsin-Madison, Kohler Art Library, 160 Conrad A Elvehjem Bldg, 800 University Ave, Madison, WI, 53706. Tel: 608-263-2258. p. 2451

Simon, Bashe, Dir of Libr, Touro College Libraries, 320 W 31st St, New York, NY, 10001. Tel: 212-463-0400, Ext 55523. p. 1603

Simon, Jenny, Dir, Spring Valley Public Library, 121 W Jefferson St, Spring Valley, MN, 55975. Tel: 507-346-2100. p. 1204

Simon, Karen, Bus Mgr, Saint John the Baptist Parish Library, 2920 New Hwy 51, LaPlace, LA, 70068. Tel: 985-652-6857. p. 894

Simon, Leanna R, Mgr, Honigman Miller Schwartz & Cohn LLP, 2290 First National Bldg, 660 Woodward Ave, Detroit, MI, 48226-3583. Tel: 313-465-7169. p. 1099

Simon, Leslie, Archives Dir, National Archives & Records Administration, Mid Atlantic Region (Center City Philadelphia), 14700 Townsend Rd, Philadelphia, PA, 19154. Tel: 215-305-9347. p. 1983

Simon, Leslie, Dir, National Archives & Records Administration, Mid Atlantic Region (Northeast Philadelphia), 14700 Townsend Rd, Philadelphia, PA, 19154-1096. Tel: 215-305-9347. p. 1983

Simon, Lorita, Librn I, Hurley Medical Center, One Hurley Plaza, Flint, MI, 48503. Tel: 810-262-9055. p. 1106

Simon, Melissa, Circ, Stetson University, 421 N Woodland Blvd, Unit 8418, DeLand, FL, 32723. Tel: 386-822-7187. p. 393

Simon, Michelle, Dep Dir, Support Serv, Pima County Public Library, 101 N Stone Ave, Tucson, AZ, 85701. Tel: 520-594-5600. p. 82

Simon, Mindi, Dir, Lee County Library System, 2201 Second St, Ste 400, Fort Myers, FL, 33901. Tel: 239-533-4800. p. 403

Simon, R Raphael, Dr, Librn, Temple on the Heights, 27501 Fairmount Blvd, Pepper Pike, OH, 44124. Tel: 216-831-6555. p. 1815

Simon, Robert, Librn, College of the Holy Cross, Fenwick Music Library, Fenwick Bldg, Worcester, MA, 01610-2394. Tel: 508-793-2295. p. 1072

Simon, Rubi, Libr Dir, Howe Library, 13 South St, Hanover, NH, 03755. Tel: 603-643-4120. p. 1367

Simon, Stephen E, Archivist, Simsbury Historical Society Archives, 800 Hopmeadow St, Simsbury, CT, 06070. Tel: 860-658-2500. p. 336

Simon, Vesna, Commun Libr Mgr, Queens Library, Middle Village Community Library, 72-31 Metropolitan Ave, Middle Village, NY, 11379. Tel: 718-326-1390. p. 1555

Simone, Joann, Asst Dir, J Lewis Crozer Library, 620 Engle St, Chester, PA, 19013-2199. Tel: 610-494-3454. p. 1921

Simoneau, Lorraine, Libr Dir, Kurth Memorial Library, 706 S Raguet St, Lufkin, TX, 75904. Tel: 936-630-0560. p. 2214

Simoneaux, Julie, Ser, Iberville Parish Library, 24605 J Gerald Berret Blvd, Plaquemine, LA, 70764. Tel: 225-687-2520, 225-687-4397. p. 906

Simons, Brian, Dir, San Leandro Public Library, Mulford-Marina, 13699 Aurora Dr, San Leandro, CA, 94577-4036. Tel: 510-577-7976. p. 233

Simons, Brian, Libr Dir, San Leandro Public Library, 300 Estudillo Ave, San Leandro, CA, 94577. Tel: 510-577-3942. p. 233

Simons, Kirk, Adminr, Meserve, Mumper & Hughes, 800 Wilshire Blvd, Ste 500, Los Angeles, CA, 90017-2611. Tel: 213-620-0300. p. 166

Simons, Marilyn, Tech Serv Librn, Brookline Public Library, 16 Main St, Brookline, NH, 03033. Tel: 603-673-3330. p. 1356

Simons, Renee, Ch, Eagle Grove Memorial Library, 101 S Cadwell Ave, Eagle Grove, IA, 50533. Tel: 515-448-4115. p. 750

Simons, Spencer, Dir, University of Houston, The O'Quinn Law Library, 12 Law Library, Houston, TX, 77204-6054. Tel: 713-743-2300. p. 2199

Simonsen, Doreen, Humanities & Fine Arts Librarian, Willamette University, 900 State St, Salem, OR, 97301. Tel: 503-375-5343. p. 1897

Simonson, Anna, Health Sci Librn, Research Servs Librn, University of South Dakota, 1400 W 22nd St, Ste 100, Sioux Falls, SD, 57105. Tel: 605-658-3388. p. 2083

Simonson, Anna, Health Science & Research Servs Librn, University of South Dakota, I D Weeks Library, 414 E Clark St, Vermillion, SD, 57069. Tel: 605-658-3388. p. 2084

Simonson, Lizeth, Commun Outreach Supvr-Bilingual, Carlsbad City Library, Library Learning Center, 3368 Eureka Pl, Carlsbad, CA, 92008. Tel: 760-931-4509. p. 128

Simonson, Scott, Libr Tech, The Learning Center, 500 W Broadway, Missoula, MT, 59802. Tel: 406-329-5712. p. 1300

Simonton, Lilia, Br Mgr, Jacksonville Public Library, San Marco Branch, 1513 LaSalle St, Jacksonville, FL, 32207-8653. Tel: 904-858-2907. p. 412

Simopoulos, Jennie, Ch, Marlborough Public Library, 35 W Main St, Marlborough, MA, 01752-5510. Tel: 508-624-6900. p. 1032

Simpkin, Sarah, Head, Res Support Serv, Head, Spec Coll, University of Ottawa Libraries, 65 University Private, Ottawa, ON, K1N 6N5, CANADA. Tel: 613-562-5213. p. 2670

Simpkins, Charlie, Br Mgr, Northwest Point Reservoir Library, 2230 Spillway Rd, Brandon, MS, 39047. Tel: 601-992-2539. p. 1212

Simpkins, Jennifer, Circ Serv, Donald W Reynolds Community Center & Library, 1515 W Main St, Durant, OK, 74701. Tel: 580-924-3486, 580-931-0231. p. 1846

Simpkins, Karen, Dir, Darcy Library of Beulah, 7238 Commercial Ave, Beulah, MI, 49617. Tel: 231-882-4037. p. 1085

Simpkins, Terry, Dir, Discovery & Access, Middlebury College, 110 Storrs Ave, Middlebury, VT, 05753. Tel: 802-443-5045. p. 2288

Simpson, Alison, Pub Serv Mgr, Wingate University, 110 Church ST, Wingate, NC, 28174. Tel: 704-233-8089. p. 1724

Simpson, Anita, Libr Operations Supvr, Tuolumne County Public Library, 480 Greenley Rd, Sonora, CA, 95370-5956. Tel: 209-533-5507. p. 247

Simpson, Anita, Libr Operations Supvr, Tuolumne County Public Library, Tuolumne City Branch, 18636 Main St, Tuolumne, CA, 95379. Tel: 209-928-3612. p. 247

Simpson, Carrie, Librn, Benton County Library System, 247 Court St, Ashland, MS, 38603. Tel: 662-224-6400. p. 1211

Simpson, Cathy, Chief Librn, Niagara-on-the-Lake Public Library, Ten Anderson Lane, Niagara-on-the-Lake, ON, L0S 1J0, CANADA. Tel: 905-468-2023. p. 2661

Simpson, Cynthia, Coordr, Access Serv, Lawrence Technological University Library, 21000 W Ten Mile Rd, Southfield, MI, 48075-1058. Tel: 248-204-3000. p. 1151

Simpson, Cynthia, Librn, Middlesex Law Association, Ground Flr, Unit N, 80 Dundas St, London, ON, N6A 6A1, CANADA. Tel: 519-679-7046. p. 2654

Simpson, Diana, Cataloger, Tech Serv, Alma Public Library, 500 E Superior St, Alma, MI, 48801-1999. Tel: 989-463-3966, Ext 9582. p. 1077

Simpson, Evan, Assoc Dean, Res & Learning Serv, Northeastern University Libraries, 360 Huntington Ave, Boston, MA, 02115. Tel: 617-373-4920. p. 998

Simpson, Haley R, Libr Supvr, Ohio State University LIBRARIES, Food, Agricultural & Environmental Sciences, 045 Agriculture Administration Bldg, 2120 Fyffe Rd, Columbus, OH, 43210-1066. Tel: 614-292-6125. p. 1775

Simpson, Heather, Family & Youth Serv Coordr, Chesapeake Public Library, 298 Cedar Rd, Chesapeake, VA, 23322-5512. Tel: 757-410-7127. p. 2311

Simpson, Jean, Dir, Elmont Memorial Library, 700 Hempstead Tpk, Elmont, NY, 11003-1896. Tel: 516-354-5280. p. 1531

Simpson, Jenny, Asst Librn, Cat, Nyssa Public Library, 319 Main St, Nyssa, OR, 97913-3845. Tel: 541-372-2978. p. 1889

Simpson, Julia, Libr Mgr, Piedmont Regional Library System, Winder Public Library, 189 Bellview St, Winder, GA, 30680-1706. Tel: 770-867-2762. p. 483

Simpson, Katie, Asst Librn, Orangeville Public Library, 301 Mill St, Orangeville, PA, 17859-0177. Tel: 570-683-5354. p. 1973

Simpson, Kay, Pres, Lyman & Merrie Wood Museum of Springfield History, 21 Edwards St, Springfield, MA, 01103. Tel: 413-263-6800, Ext 230. p. 1057

Simpson, Keri, Dir, Libr Serv, Phillips Community College of the University of Arkansas, 2807 Hwy 165 S, Box A, Stuttgart, AR, 72160. Tel: 870-338-6474, Ext 1145. p. 111

Simpson, King, Dir, Logan County Public Library, 225 Armory Dr, Russellville, KY, 42276. Tel: 270-726-6129. p. 874

Simpson, Laura, Cataloger, University of Alabama at Birmingham, Mervyn H Sterne Library, 917 13th St S, Birmingham, AL, 35205. Tel: 205-934-6364. p. 9

Simpson, Livy I, Librn, Volunteer State Community College Library, 1480 Nashville Pike, Gallatin, TN, 37066-3188. Tel: 615-230-3414. p. 2099

Simpson, Lynne, Dr, Mgr, Info Serv, Morehouse School of Medicine, Medical Education Bldg, 1st Flr, Ste 100, 720 Westview Dr SW, Atlanta, GA, 30310-1495. Tel: 404-752-1533. p. 465

Simpson, Melissa, Dir, Adult Serv, Williamsburg Regional Library, 7770 Croaker Rd, Williamsburg, VA, 23188-7064. Tel: 757-741-3355. p. 2353

Simpson, Pamela, Librn, Orangeville Public Library, 301 Mill St, Orangeville, PA, 17859-0177. Tel: 570-683-5354. p. 1973

Simpson, Robert, Dir, Atchison County Library, 200 S Main St, Rock Port, MO, 64482. Tel: 660-744-5404. p. 1267

Simpson, Sam, Circ Mgr, Valparaiso University, 1410 Chapel Dr, Valparaiso, IN, 46383-6493. Tel: 219-464-5500. p. 723

Simpson, Samanatha, Prog Mgr, Partners Library Action Network, 5806 Mesa Dr, Ste 375, Austin, TX, 78731. Tel: 512-583-0704. p. 2775

Simpson, Sherry, Dir, Florala Public Library, 1214 Fourth St, Florala, AL, 36442. Tel: 334-858-3525. p. 17

Simpson, Sherry, Syst Dir, Pope County Library System, 116 E Third St, Russellville, AR, 72801. Tel: 479-968-4368. p. 109

Simpson, Sonja, Librn, United States Courts Library, Birch Bayh Federal Bldg, 46 E Ohio St, Rm 445, Indianapolis, IN, 46204. Tel: 317-229-3928. p. 697

Simpson, Susan N, Spec Projects Librn, East Carolina University, William E Laupus Health Sciences Library, 500 Health Sciences Dr, Greenville, NC, 27834. Tel: 252-744-2904. p. 1693

Simpson, Susanne, Dir, Licking County Library, 101 W Main St, Newark, OH, 43055-5054. Tel: 740-349-5500. p. 1807

Simpson, Terri, Library Contact, Eastern Counties Regional Library, Cyril Ward Memorial, 27 Pleasant St, Guysborough, NS, B0H 1N0, CANADA. Tel: 902-533-3586. p. 2621

Simpson, Todd, Head, Ref, York College Library, 94-20 Guy R Brewer Blvd, Jamaica, NY, 11451. Tel: 718-262-2022. p. 1556

Simpson, Valerie, Regional Mgr, Broward County Libraries Division, 100 S Andrews Ave, Fort Lauderdale, FL, 33301. Tel: 954-765-1596. p. 396

Simpson, William, ILL, Pasadena Public Library, 1201 Jeff Ginn Memorial Dr, Pasadena, TX, 77506. Tel: 713-477-0276. p. 2225

Sims, Adam, Tech Serv Asst, Blue Mountain Community College Library, 2411 NW Carden Ave, Pendleton, OR, 97801. Tel: 541-278-5912. p. 1890

Sims, Arlie, Head, Ref & Instruction, Columbia College Chicago Library, 624 S Michigan Ave, Chicago, IL, 60605-1996. Tel: 312-369-7059. p. 559

Sims, Carmen Melinda, Dir, Bartow County Public Library System, 429 W Main St, Cartersville, GA, 30120. Tel: 770-382-4203. p. 470

Sims, Emily, Children's Dir, Programming Dir, Chelsea Public Library, 16623 US 280, Chelsea, AL, 35043. Tel: 205-847-5750. p. 12

Sims, Iyanna, Head, Bibliog & Metadata Serv, Head, Discovery Serv, North Carolina Agricultural & Technical State University, 1601 E Market St, Greensboro, NC, 27411-0002. Tel: 336-285-4164. p. 1693

Sims, Jay, Computer Serv Mgr, Galveston County Library System, 2310 Sealy Ave, Galveston, TX, 77550. Tel: 409-763-8854, Ext 131. p. 2183

Sims, Jonathan, Asst Law Librn, Curt B Henderson Law Library, Russell A Steindam Courts Bldg, 2100 Bloomdale Rd, McKinney, TX, 75071. Tel: 972-424-1460, Ext 4255, 972-424-1460, Ext 4260. p. 2217

Sims, Kim, Assoc Univ Librn, Spec Coll & Archives Librn, Washington & Lee University, University Library, 204 W Washington St, Lexington, VA, 24450-2116. Tel: 540-458-8643. p. 2329

Sims, Lee, Head, User Serv, Rutgers University Library for the Center for Law & Justice, 123 Washington St, Newark, NJ, 07102-3094. Tel: 973-353-3121. p. 1428

Sims, Melanie, Head, Access Services & Govt Info, Louisiana State University Libraries, Paul M Hebert Law Center, One E Campus Dr, Baton Rouge, LA, 70803-1000. Tel: 225-578-8815. p. 884

Sims, Pat, Librn, Bunker Hill Public Library District, 220 E Warren St, Bunker Hill, IL, 62014. Tel: 618-585-4736. p. 545

Sims, Richard, Librn, Centennial College of Applied Arts & Technology, Progress Campus, 941 Progress Ave, L3-06, Scarborough, ON, M1G 3T8, CANADA. Tel: 416-289-5000, Ext 5400. p. 2677

Sims, Sandra, Libr Dir, Leonard Public Library, 102 S Main St, Leonard, TX, 75452. Tel: 903-587-2391. p. 2211

Sims, Steven C, Head, Access Serv, ILL Librn, Francis Marion University, 4822 E Palmetto St, Florence, SC, 29506. Tel: 843-661-1299. p. 2059

Sims, Suzette S, Prog Serv Coordr, Craft Memorial Library, 600 Commerce St, Bluefield, WV, 24701. Tel: 304-325-3943. p. 2398

Sinclair, Bryan, Assoc Dean, Pub Serv, Georgia State University, 100 Decatur St SE, Atlanta, GA, 30303-3202. Tel: 404-413-2721. p. 464

Sinclair, Charlie, Librn, Spartanburg County Public Libraries, Cowpens Library, 181 School St, Cowpens, SC, 29330. Tel: 864-463-0430. p. 2070

Sinclair, Dylan, Libr Tech II, Maine State Law & Legislative Reference Library, 43 State House Sta, Augusta, ME, 04333-0043. Tel: 207-287-1600. p. 914

Sinclair, Emily, Ref Librn, Ontario Workplace Tribunals Library, 505 University Ave, 7th Flr, Toronto, ON, M5G 2P2, CANADA. Tel: 416-314-3700. p. 2691

Sinclair, Jac, Diversity, Equity & Inclusion Librn, Alverno College Library, 3401 S 39th St, Milwaukee, WI, 53215. Tel: 414-392-6184. p. 2457

Sinclair, Mary Beth, Ch, Marshall-Lyon County Library, 201 C St, Marshall, MN, 56258. Tel: 507-537-6188. p. 1182

Sinclair, Patricia, Electronic Res Mgr, South Carolina State Library, 1500 Senate St, Columbia, SC, 29201. Tel: 803-734-8851. p. 2054

Sinclair, Tammie L, Dir, El Progreso Memorial Library, 301 W Main St, Uvalde, TX, 78801. Tel: 830-278-2017. p. 2251

Sinclair, Tracey, Chief Exec Officer, Librn, Atikokan Public Library, Civic Centre, Atikokan, ON, P0T 1C0, CANADA. Tel: 807-597-4406. p. 2629

Sindelar, Rachel, Medical Educ Librn, Broadlawns Medical Center, 1801 Hickman Rd, Des Moines, IA, 50314. Tel: 515-282-2200, 515-282-2394. p. 745

Sindelar, Rachel, Medical Educ Librn, Polk County Biomedical Consortium, c/o Unity Point Health Sciences Library, 1200 Pleasant St, Des Moines, IA, 50309. Tel: 515-241-6490. p. 2765

Sines, Dottie, ILL Assoc, The College of Wooster Libraries, 1140 Beall Ave, Wooster, OH, 44691-2364. Tel: 330-263-2442. p. 1833

Singarella, Irma, Dr, Health Sci Librn, University Libraries, University of Memphis, Baptist Memorial Health Care Library, Community Health Bldg, 4055 North Park Loop, Memphis, TN, 38152-3250. Tel: 901-678-3829. p. 2115

Singer, Dev, Tech Serv, Lasell College, 80 A Maple Ave, Newton, MA, 02466. Tel: 617-243-2207. p. 1039

Singer, Jeffrey, Dir, Bradford County Library System, 16093 Rte 6, Troy, PA, 16947. Tel: 570-297-2436. p. 2013

Singer, Joel, Cat Asst, City University of New York, 365 Fifth Ave, New York, NY, 10016-4309. Tel: 212-817-7064. p. 1582

Singh, Carolyn, Info & Instruction Librn, Shasta College Library, 11555 Old Oregon Trail, Redding, CA, 96003-7692. Tel: 530-242-2347. p. 198

Singh, Devi, ILL, Miami Dade College, North Campus Learning Resources, 11380 NW 27th Ave, Miami, FL, 33167. Tel: 305-237-1142. p. 422

Singh, Genevieve, Cataloger, Washington Adventist University, 7600 Flower Ave, Takoma Park, MD, 20912-7796. Tel: 301-891-4221. p. 979

Singh, Indrajeet, Dir, Helene Fuld College of Nursing, 24 E 120th St, New York, NY, 10035. Tel: 212-616-7200, 212-616-7269. p. 1586

Singh, Judy, Librn, Canadian Tax Foundation, 145 Wellington St W, Ste 1400, Toronto, ON, M5J 1H8, CANADA. Tel: 416-599-0283. p. 2688

Singh, Lynnette, IT Mgr, Geneva Public Library District, 127 James St, Geneva, IL, 60134. Tel: 630-232-0780, Ext 310. p. 592

Singh, Monica, Bus Librn, Evening Librn, University of California, Berkeley, Thomas J Long Business Library, Haas School of Business, Rm S350, 2220 Piedmont Ave, Berkeley, CA, 94720-6000. Tel: 510-642-0370. p. 123

Singh, Nanne, Librn, California Christian College, 5364 E Belmont Ave, Fresno, CA, 93727. Tel: 559-302-9653, Ext 1008. p. 144

Singh, Rajesh, PhD, Assoc Prof, St John's University, Saint Augustine Hall, Rm 408A, 8000 Utopia Pkwy, Jamaica, NY, 11439. Tel: 718-990-6200. p. 2789

Singh, Vandana, Assoc Prof, University of Tennessee, Knoxville, 451 Communications Bldg, 1345 Circle Park Dr, Knoxville, TN, 37996-0332. Tel: 865-974-2785. p. 2792

Singletary, Adam, Assoc Dir, The Library of Hattiesburg, Petal, Forrest County, 329 Hardy St, Hattiesburg, MS, 39401-3496. Tel: 601-582-4461. p. 1218

Singletary, Adam, Dir, Library of Hattiesburg, Petal, Forrest County, Petal Branch, 714 S Main St, Petal, MS, 39465. Tel: 601-584-7610. p. 1218

Singletary, Jon, Libr Syst Spec, Carnegie Mellon University, Hunt Library, 4909 Frew St, Pittsburgh, PA, 15213. Tel: 412-268-2444. p. 1992

Singletary, Virginia, Dir, Stella Hill Memorial Library, 158 W San Antonio St, Alto, TX, 75925. Tel: 936-858-4343. p. 2133

Singleton, Brent, Coordr of Ref Serv, California State University, San Bernardino, 5500 University Pkwy, San Bernardino, CA, 92407-2318. Tel: 909-537-5083. p. 212

Singleton, Charnette, Dean of Libr, Trident Technical College, Berkeley Campus Learning Resources, LR-B, PO Box 118067, Charleston, SC, 29423-8067. Tel: 843-574-6088. p. 2051

Singleton, Charnette, Dean of Libr, Trident Technical College, Main Campus Learning Resources Center, LR-M, PO Box 118067, Charleston, SC, 29423-8067. Tel: 843-574-6087. p. 2051

Singleton, Erin, Youth Serv Librn, George F Johnson Memorial Library, 1001 Park St, Endicott, NY, 13760. Tel: 607-757-5350. p. 1531

Singleton, Jeanetta, Libr Dir, Irvington Public Library, Civic Sq, Irvington, NJ, 07111-2498. Tel: 973-372-6400. p. 1409

Singleton, Latoya, Evening Librn, Georgetown University, Dahlgren Memorial Library, Preclinical Science Bldg GM-7, 3900 Reservoir Rd NW, Washington, DC, 20007. Tel: 202-687-3791. p. 368

Singleton, Margie, Chief Exec Officer, Vaughan Public Libraries, 2191 Major MacKenzie Dr, Vaughan, ON, L6A 4W2, CANADA. Tel: 905-653-7323. p. 2701

Singleton, Maureen, Chief Operating Officer, San Francisco Public Library, 100 Larkin St, San Francisco, CA, 94102. Tel: 415-557-4400. p. 227

Singleton, Suzanne, Archivist, Head, Ref, Librn, Francis Marion University, 4822 E Palmetto St, Florence, SC, 29506. Tel: 843-661-1319. p. 2059

Singleton, Veronica, Br Mgr, Horry County Memorial Library, Bucksport, 7657 Hwy 701 S, Conway, SC, 29527. Tel: 843-397-1950. p. 2056

Singley, Emily, Assoc Univ Librn, Systems & Technology, Boston College Libraries, 140 Commonwealth Ave, Chestnut Hill, MA, 02467. Tel: 617-552-2918. p. 1010

Sinha, Luzviminda, Med Librn, Research Librn, Dayton Children's Hospital, One Children's Plaza, Dayton, OH, 45404-1815. Tel: 937-641-3307. p. 1779

Sinhart, Angela, Cat Librn, Fordham University School of Law, 150 W 62nd St, New York, NY, 10023. Tel: 212-636-7041. p. 1585

Sink, Martha, Assoc Dir, Tech Serv, Alamance County Public Libraries, 342 S Spring St, Burlington, NC, 27215. Tel: 336-513-4754. p. 1676

Sinkinson, Caroline, Team Lead, Learning & Engagement Team, University of Colorado Boulder, 1720 Pleasant St, Boulder, CO, 80309. Tel: 303-492-8705. p. 267

Sinn, Donghee, Dr, Assoc Prof, University at Albany, State University of New York, Draper 015, 135 Western Ave, Albany, NY, 12203. Tel: 518-442-5117. p. 2789

Sinn, Stefanie, Managing Librn, Brooklyn Public Library, Rugby, 1000 Utica Ave, Brooklyn, NY, 11203. Tel: 718-566-0053. p. 1504

Sinnamon, Luanne, Dr, Assoc Prof, Dir, University of British Columbia, The Irving K Barber Learning Ctr, 1961 E Mall, Ste 470, Vancouver, BC, V6T 1Z1, CANADA. Tel: 604-822-2404. p. 2795

Sinnett, Heidi, Asst Librn, Ch Serv, Carleton Place Public Library, 101 Beckwith St, Carleton Place, ON, K7C 2T3, CANADA. Tel: 613-257-2702. p. 2635

Sinnett, Scott, Br Mgr, Saint Joseph County Public Library, Roger B Francis Branch, 52655 N Ironwood Rd, South Bend, IN, 46635. Tel: 574-282-4641. p. 719

Sinniger, Sherri, Br Mgr, La Crosse County Library, Onalaska Public, 741 Oak Ave S, Onalaska, WI, 54650. Tel: 608-781-9568. p. 2441

Sinnott, Susan, Dir, Madbury Public Library, Nine Town Hall Rd, Madbury, NH, 03823. Tel: 603-743-1400. p. 1371

Sinon, Stephen, Archives, Curator, Spec Coll, Res, The LuEsther T Mertz Library, The New York Botanical Garden, 2900 Southern Blvd, Bronx, NY, 10458-5126. Tel: 718-817-8728. p. 1499

Sinotte, Jillian, Learning Services, Librn, Okanagan College Library, 1000 KLO Rd, Kelowna, BC, V1Y 4X8, CANADA. Tel: 250-762-5445, Ext 4257. p. 2568

Sinovic, Dianne, Librn, Pipersville Free Library, 7114 Durham Rd, Pipersville, PA, 18947-9998. Tel: 215-766-7880. p. 1990

Sinsuan, Elaine, Br Mgr, San Diego Public Library, University Heights, 4193 Park Blvd, San Diego, CA, 92103. Tel: 619-692-4912. p. 221

Siong, Chamong, Br Mgr, Tulsa City-County Library, Maxwell Park, 1313 N Canton Ave, Tulsa, OK, 74115. p. 1866

Sipeki, Julianna, Mgr, Jefferson County Public Library, Golden Library, 1019 Tenth St, Golden, CO, 80401. Tel: 303-403-5120. p. 288

Sipman, Glorian, Tech Serv Librn, MiraCosta College Library, One Barnard Dr, Bldg 1200, Oceanside, CA, 92056-3899. Tel: 760-795-6722. p. 187

Sipocz, Joseph, Br Mgr, Saint Joseph County Public Library, River Park Branch, 2022 Mishawaka Ave, South Bend, IN, 46615. Tel: 574-282-4635. p. 719

Sippel, Colleen, Dir, J H Robbins Memorial Library, 219 N Lincoln Ave, Ellsworth, KS, 67439-3313. Tel: 785-472-3969. p. 806

Sippel, Jennifer, Libr Operations Coordr, Minneapolis Community & Technical College Library, Wheelock Whitney Hall, 1501 Hennepin Ave, Minneapolis, MN, 55403. Tel: 612-659-6434. p. 1184

Siragusa, Debbie, Asst Dir, Kansas City Public Library, Lucile H Bluford Branch, 3050 Prospect Ave, Kansas City, MO, 64128. Tel: 816-701-3482. p. 1255

Siragusa, Debbie, Asst Dir, The Kansas City Public Library, 14 W Tenth St, Kansas City, MO, 64105. Tel: 816-701-3515. p. 1255

Sirak, Jennifer, Dir, Lambertville Free Public Library, Six Lilly St, Lambertville, NJ, 08530. Tel: 609-397-0275. p. 1411

Sirianni, Christina, Br Mgr, Camden County Library System, William G Rohrer Memorial Library - Haddon Township, 15 MacArthur Blvd, Westmont, NJ, 08108. Tel: 856-854-2752. p. 1450

Sirigos, Cecilia, Ref Librn, University of Massachusetts at Boston, 100 Morrissey Blvd, Boston, MA, 02125-3300. Tel: 617-287-4071. p. 1000

Sirois, Christina, Exec Dir, Harvard Library, John F Kennedy School of Government Library, 79 John F Kennedy St, Cambridge, MA, 02138. Tel: 617-495-1300. p. 1007

Sirois, Kim, Tech Serv Librn, Harnett County Public Library, 601 S Main St, Lillington, NC, 27546-6107. Tel: 910-893-3446. p. 1700

Sirois, Ricky, Asst Libr Dir, Concord Free Public Library, 129 Main St, Concord, MA, 01742. Tel: 978-318-3383. p. 1012

Sirois, Ricky, Asst Dir, Haverhill Public Library, 99 Main St, Haverhill, MA, 01830-5092. Tel: 978-373-1586, Ext 641. p. 1024

Sisco, Chantel, Asst Librn, Danvers Township Library, 117 E Exchange St, Danvers, IL, 61732-9347. Tel: 309-963-4269. p. 575

Sise, Heidi, Circ, Johnson University, 7902 Eubanks Dr, Knoxville, TN, 37998. Tel: 865-251-2277. p. 2105

Sise, Marjorie, Pub Serv Librn, Rust College, 150 E Rust Ave, Holly Springs, MS, 38635. Tel: 662-252-8000, Ext 4100. p. 1220

Sisk, Emily, Head, Circ, King's College, 14 W Jackson St, Wilkes-Barre, PA, 18711. Tel: 570-208-5840. p. 2022

Sisk, Lisa, Dir, Park Hills Public Library, 16 S Coffman St, Park Hills, MO, 63601. Tel: 573-431-4842. p. 1265

Sisler, Beth, Interim Dir, Stinson Memorial Public Library District, 409 S Main St, Anna, IL, 62906. Tel: 618-833-2521. p. 536

Sisler, Thomas, Asst Dir, Stinson Memorial Public Library District, 409 S Main St, Anna, IL, 62906. Tel: 618-833-2521. p. 536

Sisneros, Caroline, Dir, Libr Serv, Phillips Graduate University Library, 19900 Plummer St, Chatsworth, CA, 91311. Tel: 818-386-5642. p. 129

Sissel, Delana, Dir, Sara Hightower Regional Library, 205 Riverside Pkwy NE, Rome, GA, 30161-2922. Tel: 706-236-4609. p. 494

Sissen, Melissa M, Pub Serv Librn, Siena Heights University Library, 1247 E Siena Heights Dr, Adrian, MI, 49221-1796. Tel: 517-264-7150. p. 1076

Sisti, Elena, Archives Librn, Ref, Rosemont College Library, 1400 Montgomery Ave, Rosemont, PA, 19010-1631. Tel: 610-527-0200, Ext 2204. p. 2002

Sistrunk, Allen, Exec Dir, Historic Westville Library, 3557 S Lumpkin Rd, Columbus, GA, 31903. Tel: 706-940-0057. p. 472

Sistrunk, Wendy, Head, Metadata Serv, Presv, University of Missouri-Kansas City Libraries, 800 E 51st St, Kansas City, MO, 64110. Tel: 816-235-5291. p. 1257

Sites, Sara-Jo, Head, Youth Serv, George F Johnson Memorial Library, 1001 Park St, Endicott, NY, 13760. Tel: 607-757-5350. p. 1531

Sitkus, Hance M, Exec Dir, Allaire Village Inc, 4263 Atlantic Ave, Farmingdale, NJ, 07727. Tel: 732-919-3500. p. 1402

Sittler, Ryan, Dr, Instrul Tech Librn, User Experience Librn, Pennsylvania Western University - California, 250 University Ave, California, PA, 15419-1394. Tel: 724-938-4923. p. 1917

Sitton, Cara, Dir, The Dell Dehay Law Library of Tarrant County, Tarrant County Historical Courthouse, 100 W Weatherford St, Rm 420, Fort Worth, TX, 76196-0800. Tel: 817-884-1481. p. 2179

Sitton, Nancy, Librn, Pike-Amite-Walthall Library System, Osyka Branch, 112 W Railroad Ave, Osyka, MS, 39657. Tel: 601-542-5147. p. 1226

Sitzman, Kelly, Br Mgr, Pioneer Library System, Norman Public Library East, 3051 Alameda St, Norman, OK, 73071. Tel: 405-217-0770. p. 1855

Sitzman, Kelly, Dir, Communications, Pioneer Library System, 300 Norman Ctr Ct, Norman, OK, 73072. Tel: 405-801-4500. p. 1855

Siudut, Joanna, ILL Coordr, National Louis University Library, 18 S Michigan Ave, 3rd Flr, Chicago, IL, 60603. Tel: 312-261-5502. p. 565

Siufanua, Maia, Admin Coordr, Oregon Health & Science University Library, 3181 SW Sam Jackson Park Rd, MC LIB, Portland, OR, 97239-3098. Tel: 503-494-8601. p. 1893

Siverson, Julie, Dir, Lineville City Library, 60119 Hwy 9, Lineville, AL, 36266. Tel: 256-396-5162. p. 24

Sivigny, Robert, Ref Librn, Dallas International University Library, 7500 W Camp Wisdom Rd, Dallas, TX, 75236-5699. Tel: 972-708-7416. p. 2164

Six, Amanda, Dir, The Libraries of Stevens County, 4008 Cedar St, Loon Lake, WA, 99148-9676. Tel: 509-675-5102. p. 2369

Six-Means, Amy, Consumer Health Ref Librn, SCLHS Saint Joseph Hospital, Gervasini Health Library, 1375 E 19th Ave, 1st Flr, Denver, CO, 80218. Tel: 303 812-3622. p. 277

Sixt, Tina, Coll Develop, Ref Serv, Sierra College Library, 5100 Sierra College Blvd, Rocklin, CA, 95677. Tel: 916-660-7230. p. 203

Sizemore, C Jason, Br Mgr, Wyoming County Public Library, Hanover Public, 5556 Interstate Hwy, Hanover, WV, 24839. Tel: 304-664-5580. p. 2412

Sizemore, Daardi, Archivist, Spec Coll Librn, Minnesota State University, Mankato, 601 Maywood Ave, Mankato, MN, 56001. Tel: 507-389-5952. p. 1181

Sizemore, Mary M, Libr Dir, High Point Public Library, 901 N Main St, High Point, NC, 27262. Tel: 336-883-3694. p. 1696

Sizemore, Stacy, Mgr, Br, Denton Public Library, 502 Oakland St, Denton, TX, 76201. Tel: 940-349-8761. p. 2170

Sizemore, Stacy, Mgr, Denton Public Library, South Branch, 3228 Teasley Lane, Denton, TX, 76210. p. 2170

Sizemore, Vicki, Mgr, West Georgia Regional Library, Mount Zion Public Library, 4455 Mount Zion Rd, Mount Zion, GA, 30150. Tel: 770-832-0056, Ext 104. p. 470

Skaar, Michelle, Ad, Ref, Mattapoisett Free Public Library, Seven Barstow St, Mattapoisett, MA, 02739-0475. Tel: 508-758-4171. p. 1033

Skaggs, Angela L, Asst Dir, Access Serv, Angelo State University Library, 2025 S Johnson, San Angelo, TX, 76904-5079. Tel: 325-486-6524. p. 2235

Skakum, Janet, Head, Circ Serv, Library of the Chathams, 214 Main St, Chatham, NJ, 07928. Tel: 973-635-0603. p. 1395

Skalbeck, Roger V, Assoc Dean, Info Tech, University of Richmond, William T Muse Law Library, 203 Richmond Way, Richmond, VA, 23173. Tel: 804-289-8218. p. 2343

Skantz, Amber, Circ Supvr, Athens State University, 407 E Pryor St, Athens, AL, 35611. Tel: 256-216-6664. p. 5

Skare, Carla, Dir, El Paso Public Library, 149 W First St, El Paso, IL, 61738. Tel: 309-527-4360. p. 583

Skarphol, Molly, Access Serv Coordr, Western Seminary, 5511 SE Hawthorne Blvd, Portland, OR, 97215-3367. Tel: 503-517-1843. p. 1895

Skarzenski, Aaron, Exec Dir, Windham Textile & History Museum, 411 Main St, Willimantic, CT, 06226. Tel: 860-456-2178. p. 347

Skaugset, Chris, Libr Dir, Longview Public Library, 1600 Louisiana St, Longview, WA, 98632-2993. Tel: 360-442-5309. p. 2369

Skawinski, Sarah, Dir, Adult Serv, Portland Public Library, Five Monument Sq, Portland, ME, 04101. Tel: 207-871-1700, Ext 726. p. 937

Skeggs, Jamie, Dir, Library Administrative Operations, California State University, Northridge, 18111 Nordhoff St, Northridge, CA, 91330. Tel: 818-677-2205. p. 184

Skelloway, Stephanie, Librn, Hare Bay-Dover Public Library, Jane Collins Academy, 22 Anstey's Rd, Hare Bay, NL, A0G 2P0, CANADA. Tel: 709-537-2391. p. 2608

Skelly, Julie, Outreach Librn, Fletcher Free Library, 235 College St, Burlington, VT, 05401. Tel: 802-865-7224. p. 2281

Skelly, Linda, Coordr, Spec Serv, Lititz Public Library, 651 Kissel Hill Rd, Lititz, PA, 17543. Tel: 717-626-2255. p. 1956

Skelly, Lois H, Dir, Sarah Hull Hallock Free Library, 56-58 Main St, Milton, NY, 12547. Tel: 845-795-2200. p. 1572

Skelton, Victoria, Head Librn, University of Toronto Libraries, Jean & Dorothy Newman Industrial Relations Library, 121 St George St, Toronto, ON, M5S 2E8, CANADA. Tel: 416-946-7003. p. 2699

Skenandore, Eliza, Libr Mgr, Oneida Community Library, 201 Elm St, Oneida, WI, 54155. Tel: 920-869-2210. p. 2466

Skerrett, Paulette, Dr, Asst Prof, Dalhousie University, Kenneth C Rowe Management Bldg, Ste 4010, 6100 University Ave, Halifax, NS, B3H 4R2, CANADA. Tel: 902-494-6119. p. 2795

Skevington, Wendy, Dir, Holbrook Public Library, 403 Park St, Holbrook, AZ, 86025. Tel: 928-524-3732. p. 63

Skib, Bryan, Assoc Univ Librn, Coll Develop, University of Michigan, 818 Hatcher Graduate Library South, 913 S University Ave, Ann Arbor, MI, 48109-1190. Tel: 734-764-0400. p. 1080

Skiba, Bob, Archives, Curator, John J Wilcox Jr Archives & Library, William Way LGBT Community Ctr, 1315 Spruce St, Philadelphia, PA, 19107. Tel: 215-732-2220. p. 1989

Skidmore, Phyllis, Dir, Martha Canfield Memorial Free Library, 528 E Arlington Rd, Arlington, VT, 05250. Tel: 802-375-6153. p. 2277

Skiles, Kayla, Circ, Kokomo-Howard County Public Library, 220 N Union St, Kokomo, IN, 46901-4614. Tel: 765-457-3242. p. 700

Skillen, Amy, Archives, Tech, Florida Southern College, 111 Lake Hollingsworth Dr, Lakeland, FL, 33801-5698. Tel: 863-616-6487. p. 417

Skillern, Gary D, Librn, Grand Lodge of Ancient Free & Accepted Masons of Wyoming Library, Masonic Temple, 1820 Capitol Ave, Cheyenne, WY, 82001. Tel: 307-630-5933. p. 2492

Skilton, Sarah, Dir, Oswego Public Library District, Oswego Campus, 32 W Jefferson St, Oswego, IL, 60543. Tel: 630-978-1506. p. 630

Skinner, Brittany, Genealogy Librn, Tech Librn, Gallatin County Public Library, 209 W Market St, Warsaw, KY, 41095. Tel: 859-567-7323. p. 876

Skinner, Deborah, Libr Dir, Moore County Library System, 124 S Bliss Ave, Dumas, TX, 79029-3889. Tel: 806-935-4941. p. 2172

Skinner, Debra, Head, Coll Serv, Georgia Southern University, 1400 Southern Dr, Statesboro, GA, 30458. Tel: 912-478-5114. p. 497

Skinner, Jackie, Asst Dir, Otsego County Library, 700 S Otsego Ave, Gaylord, MI, 49735-1723. Tel: 989-732-5841. p. 1109

Skinner, Jane, Librn, Omaha Correctional Center Library, 2323 E Ave J, Omaha, NE, 68110-0099. Tel: 402-595-3964. p. 1329

Skinner, Jeremy, Libr Dir, Curry Public Library, 94341 Third St, Gold Beach, OR, 97444. Tel: 541-247-7246. p. 1880

Skinner, Kathy, Dir, White & Case Law Library, 1221 Avenue of the Americas, New York, NY, 10020-1095. Tel: 212-819-8200. p. 1604

Skinner, Lakesha, Admin Librn, Tidewater Community College, 1428 Cedar Rd, Chesapeake, VA, 23322. p. 2312

Skinner, Michelle, Libr Asst, Chickasha Public Library, 527 W Iowa Ave, Chickasha, OK, 73018. Tel: 405-222-6075. p. 1844

Skinner, Patti, Libr Dir, Mason County District Library, Scottville Branch, 204 E State St, Scottville, MI, 49454. Tel: 231-757-2588. p. 1128

Skinner, Sophia, Circ/Shelving Supvr, Missouri State University-West Plains, 304 W Trish Knight St, West Plains, MO, 65775. Tel: 417-255-7945. p. 1286

Skinner, Susan, Interim Dir, Campton Public Library, 1110 New Hampshire Rte 175, Ste B, Campton, NH, 03223. Tel: 603-726-4877. p. 1356

Skirvin, Rebecca, Coordr, Archives & Spec Coll, North Central College, 320 E School St, Naperville, IL, 60540. Tel: 630-637-5714. p. 623

Skitowski, Susan, Br Mgr, Toledo-Lucas County Public Library, Kent, 3101 Collingwood Blvd, Toledo, OH, 43610. Tel: 419-259-5340. p. 1824

Sklow, David, Libr Dir, American Numismatic Association Library, 818 N Cascade Ave, Colorado Springs, CO, 80903-3279. Tel: 719-482-9821. p. 270

Skobrak, Cassie, Ad, Memorial & Library Association, 44 Broad St, Westerly, RI, 02891. Tel: 401-596-2877, Ext 312. p. 2044

Skocdopole, Patti, Libr Mgr, Eckville Municipal Library, 4855 51 Ave, Eckville, AB, T0M 0X0, CANADA. Tel: 403-746-3240. p. 2534

Skodack, Adam, Technology Spec, Hackley Public Library, 316 W Webster Ave, Muskegon, MI, 49440. Tel: 231-722-8006. p. 1135

Skog, Aaron, Exec Dir, System Wide Automated Network, c/o Metropolitan Library System, 800 Quail Ridge Dr, Westmont, IL, 60559. Tel: 630-734-5153. p. 2765

Skoog, Jason, Archives, Syst Librn, Viterbo University, 900 Viterbo Dr, La Crosse, WI, 54601. Tel: 608-796-3262. p. 2446

Skoog, Marija, Libr Dir, Lower Providence Community Library, 50 Parklane Dr, Eagleville, PA, 19403-1171. Tel: 610-666-6640. p. 1928

Skopelja, Elaine, Knowledge Mgr, Outreach Coordr, Indiana University, Ruth Lilly Medical Library, 975 W Walnut St, IB 100, Indianapolis, IN, 46202. Tel: 317-274-8358. p. 693

Skopp, Sharon, Ref & ILL Librn, Saint Thomas Aquinas College, 125 Rte 340, Sparkill, NY, 10976. Tel: 845-398-4215. p. 1643

Skora, Adrienne, Youth Serv Librn, Sandown Public Library, 305 Main St, Sandown, NH, 03873. Tel: 603-887-3428. p. 1380

Skorina, Diane, Dir of Research, Teaching & Learning Servs, Ursinus College Library, 601 E Main St, Collegeville, PA, 19426. Tel: 610-409-3022. p. 1923

Sleister, Patricia, Dir, Mary J Barnett Memorial Library, 400 Grand St, Guthrie Center, IA, 50115-1439. Tel: 641-747-8110. p. 757

Slepecki, Kristen, Youth Serv Librn, Durham Public Library, Seven Maple Ave, Durham, CT, 06422. Tel: 860-349-9544. p. 309

Slessor, Janet, Dir, Reinbeck Public Library, 501 Clark St, Reinbeck, IA, 50669. Tel: 319-788-2652. p. 778

Slick, Suzanne, Info Assoc, Fort Wayne Museum of Art, 311 E Main St, Fort Wayne, IN, 46802. Tel: 260-422-6467. p. 684

Slider, Nelda, Youth Serv Librn, Kingman Carnegie Public Library, 455 N Main St, Kingman, KS, 67068-1395. Tel: 620-532-3061. p. 817

Slife, Daniel, Dir, Ella M Everhard Public Library, 132 Broad St, Wadsworth, OH, 44281-1897. Tel: 330-334-5761. p. 1827

Slimman, Katherine, Coordr, Ontario Library Consortium, c/o Georgina Public Library, 90 Wexford Dr, Keswick, ON, L4P 3P7, CANADA. Tel: 905-627-8662. p. 2778

Slinchum, Nathan, Br Mgr, Roanoke Public Libraries, Jackson Park, 1101 Morningside St SE, Roanoke, VA, 24013-2515. Tel: 540-853-2640. p. 2345

Slingluff, Deborah, Assoc Dir, Johns Hopkins University Libraries, The Sheridan Libraries, 3400 N Charles St, Baltimore, MD, 21218. Tel: 410-516-8254. p. 954

Slingluff, Lola, Dir, Garwin Public Library, 308 Fourth St, Garwin, IA, 50632. Tel: 641-499-2024. p. 755

Slingsby, Jacque, Br Mgr, Mid-Continent Public Library, South Independence Branch, 13700 E 35th St S, Independence, MO, 64055. Tel: 816-461-2050. p. 1251

Slipp, Kathleen, Ad, Everett Public Libraries, 410 Broadway, Everett, MA, 02149. Tel: 617-394-2300. p. 1017

Sliter, Justina, Librn, Harrington Public Library, 11 S Third St, Harrington, WA, 99134. Tel: 509-253-4345, Option 5. p. 2365

Slive, Daniel, Head, Spec Coll, Southern Methodist University, Bridwell Library-Perkins School of Theology, 6005 Bishop Blvd, Dallas, TX, 75205. Tel: 214-768-3483. p. 2167

Slivka, Krystal K, Chief Med Librn, Aultman Hospital, Aultman Education Ctr, C2-230, 2600 Seventh St SW, Canton, OH, 44710-1799. Tel: 330-363-5000. p. 1755

Sliwka, Agnieszka, History/Special Colls Librn, University of New Brunswick Libraries, Five Macaulay Lane, Fredericton, NB, E3B 5H5, CANADA. Tel: 506-453-5017. p. 2601

Sloan, Catherine, Librn, United States Navy, Naval Undersea Warfare Center Division, Newport Technical Library, 1176 Howell St, Bldg 101, Newport, RI, 02841. Tel: 401-832-4338. p. 2036

Sloan, Chris, Libr Dir, Bensenville Community Public Library, 200 S Church Rd, Bensenville, IL, 60106. Tel: 630-766-4642. p. 541

Sloan, Corey, Head, Adult Programming & Outreach, Bozeman Public Library, 626 E Main St, Bozeman, MT, 59715. Tel: 406-582-2400. p. 1289

Sloan, Nancy, Cat/Metadata Librn, Furman University Libraries, 3300 Poinsett Hwy, Greenville, SC, 29613-4100. Tel: 864-294-2197. p. 2061

Sloan, Steve, Superintendent of Libraries, Sunnyvale Public Library, 665 W Olive Ave, Sunnyvale, CA, 94086-7622. Tel: 408-730-7300. p. 251

Sloat, Ian, Dir, Rahway Public Library, Two City Hall Plaza, Rahway, NJ, 07065. Tel: 732-340-1551. p. 1438

Sloat, Timi, Libr Dir, Nottawa Township Library, 685 E Main St, Centreville, MI, 49032-9603. Tel: 269-467-6289. p. 1090

Slobodian, Terry, Curator, Pres & Chief Exec Officer, Royal Aviation Museum of Western Canada Library-Archives, 2088 Wellington Ave, Winnipeg, MB, R3H 1C5, CANADA. Tel: 204-786-5503. p. 2594

Slobuski, Teresa, Head Librn, Pennsylvania State University Libraries, Vairo Library, Brandywine Campus, 25 Yearsley Mill Rd, Media, PA, 19063-5596. Tel: 610-892-1380. p. 2016

Slocum, Christine, Librn, Union City Public Library, S Main & Stranahan Sts, Union City, PA, 16438. Tel: 814-438-3209. p. 2014

Slocum, Cristi, Dir, Librn, Mason County M Beven Eckert Memorial Library, 410 Post Hill, Mason, TX, 76856. Tel: 325-347-5446. p. 2216

Slocum, Melonee, Fac Librn, Florida State College at Jacksonville, Nassau Center Library & Learning Commons, 76346 William Burgess Blvd, Yulee, FL, 32097. Tel: 904-548-4467. p. 411

Slocum, Sam, Digital Serv & Emerging Tech Librn, Rapid City Public Library, 610 Quincy St, Rapid City, SD, 57701-3630. Tel: 605-394-6139. p. 2081

Slomsky, Jodi, Ch Serv, Libr Tech, Georgetown Peabody Library, Two Maple St, Georgetown, MA, 01833. Tel: 978-352-5728. p. 1020

Slonaker, Michelle, Dir, Chico Public Library Inc, 106 W Jacksboro St, Chico, TX, 76431. Tel: 940-644-2330. p. 2155

Slone, Nicholas, Exec Dir, Adams County Public Library, 157 High St, Peebles, OH, 45660. Tel: 937-587-2085. p. 1814

Slone, Terry, Dir, Waskom Public Library, 103 Waskom Ave, Waskom, TX, 75692-9281. Tel: 903-687-3041. p. 2254

Slone, William, Pub Serv Librn, Alice Lloyd College, 100 Purpose Rd, Pippa Passes, KY, 41844. Tel: 606-368-6117. p. 873

Sloniker, Benthe, Bus Mgr, Cherry Valley Public Library District, 755 E State St, Cherry Valley, IL, 61016-9699. Tel: 815-332-5161. p. 553

Slopek, Linda, Dir, Carnegie Free Library, 61 Ninth St, Midland, PA, 15059. Tel: 724-643-8980. p. 1963

Slossar, Bobbi Lee, Tech Res Librn, New Hampshire State Library, 20 Park St, Concord, NH, 03301. Tel: 603-271-2143. p. 1359

Slough, Barbara, Br Mgr, Rockbridge Regional Library System, Glasgow Public, 1108 Blue Ridge Rd, Glasgow, VA, 24555. Tel: 540-258-2509. p. 2329

Slough, Eileen, Ch, Atlanta-Fulton Public Library System, Evelyn G Lowery Library at Southwest, 3665 Cascade Rd SW, Atlanta, GA, 30331. Tel: 404-699-6363. p. 461

Slovasky, Stephen, Cat Mgr, Connecticut State Library, 231 Capitol Ave, Hartford, CT, 06106. Tel: 860-757-6546. p. 317

Slowik, Amy, Head, Borrowing & Discovery, Russell Library, 123 Broad St, Middletown, CT, 06457. Tel: 860-347-2528. p. 322

Slowik, Rae, Education & Collections Mgr, Lombard Historical Society Library, 23 W Maple St, Lombard, IL, 60148. Tel: 630-629-1885. p. 611

Slozat, Dan, Exec Dir, Meadville Public Library, 848 N Main St, Meadville, PA, 16335. Tel: 814-336-1773. p. 1960

Sluck, Jeanie, Dir, Taylor Community Library, 710 S Main St, Taylor, PA, 18517-1774. Tel: 570-562-1234. p. 2012

Slugoski, Lisa, Libr Adminr, Flin Flon Public Library, 58 Main St, Flin Flon, MB, R8A 1J8, CANADA. p. 2587

Slupe, Julie, Dir, Mustang Public Library, 1201 N Mustang Rd, Mustang, OK, 73064. Tel: 405-376-2226. p. 1854

Slusher, Robyn, Librn, Anoka-Ramsey Community College, 300 Spirit River Dr S, Cambridge, MN, 55008. Tel: 763-433-1819. p. 1167

Slutsky, Carol, Ref Serv, Norton Rose Fulbright Canada LLP Library, One Place Ville Marie, Ste 2500, Montreal, QC, H3B 1R1, CANADA. Tel: 514-847-4701. p. 2727

Slutzky, Amy, Ref Librn, SUNY Upstate Medical University, 766 Irving Ave, Syracuse, NY, 13210-1602. Tel: 315-464-7104. p. 1650

Sluzenski, Karen, Bus & Econ Librn, Eng Librn, Dartmouth College Library, Feldberg Business & Engineering Library, 6193 Murdough Ctr, Hanover, NH, 03755-3560. Tel: 603-646-2191. p. 1366

Sly, Dana, Assoc Libr Dir, Boston Architectural College, 320 Newbury St, Boston, MA, 02115. Tel: 617-585-7337. p. 991

Sly, Emily, Br Mgr, North Olympic Library System, Sequim Branch, 630 N Sequim Ave, Sequim, WA, 98382. Tel: 360-683-1161. p. 2374

Sly, Margery, Dir, Spec Coll Res Ctr, Temple University Libraries, 1210 W Berks St, Philadelphia, PA, 19122-6088. Tel: 215-204-8231. p. 1986

Slye, Greg D, Asst Dir of Library & Archives, Historical Society of York County, York County Heritage Trust, 121 N Pershing Ave, York, PA, 17401. Tel: 717-848-1587, Ext 223. p. 2026

Slymon, Sara F, Dir, Public Library of Brookline, 361 Washington St, Brookline, MA, 02445. Tel: 617-730-2360. p. 1003

Slyter, Frederick, Dir, JBER Library, Bldg 7, Fourth St, JBER, AK, 99505. Tel: 907-384-1640. p. 47

Smaby, Alisha, Head, Circ, Round Lake Area Public Library District, 906 Hart Rd, Round Lake, IL, 60073. Tel: 847-546-7060, Ext 115. p. 643

Smailes, Suzanne, Head, Tech Serv, Wittenberg University, 801 Woodlawn Ave, Springfield, OH, 45504. Tel: 937-327-7020. p. 1821

Smale, Jody, Librn, Pennsylvania Department of Conservation & Natural Resources, 3240 Schoolhouse Rd, Middletown, PA, 17057-3534. Tel: 717-702-2020. p. 1963

Smale, Maura, Chief Librn, City University of New York, 365 Fifth Ave, New York, NY, 10016-4309. Tel: 212-817-7058. p. 1582

Small, Amy, Dir, Texas State Law Library, Tom C Clark Bldg, 205 W 14th St, Rm G01, Austin, TX, 78701-1614. Tel: 512-463-1722. p. 2141

Small, Ann, Libr Coord, St Lawrence College Library, Two Saint Lawrence Dr, Cornwall, ON, K6H 4Z1, CANADA. Tel: 613-544-5400, Ext 2171. p. 2637

Small, Anne, Dir, Bethlehem Public Library, 32 Main St S, Bethlehem, CT, 06751. Tel: 203-266-7510. p. 302

Small, Erin, Cat Librn, William Carey University Libraries, 710 William Carey Pkwy, Hattiesburg, MS, 39401. Tel: 601-318-6169. p. 1219

Small, Isa, Mgr, Communications, Mgr, Programming, L E Phillips Memorial Public Library, 400 Eau Claire St, Eau Claire, WI, 54701. Tel: 715-839-5094. p. 2432

Small, Kevin, ILL, Grayson County Public Library, 163 Carroll Gibson Blvd, Leitchfield, KY, 42754-1488. Tel: 270-259-5455. p. 861

Small, Lillian, Libr Asst, Hutchinson Community College, 1300 N Plum St, Hutchinson, KS, 67501. Tel: 620-665-3547. p. 814

Small, Melissa, Librn, Readfield Community Library, 1151 Main St, Readfield, ME, 04355. Tel: 207-685-4089. p. 938

Smallery, Kimberly, Interim Dir, Northern Michigan University, 1401 Presque Isle Ave, Marquette, MI, 49855-5376. Tel: 906-227-2261. p. 1130

Smalley, Ann Walker, Exec Dir, Metronet, 1619 Dayton Ave, Ste 314, Saint Paul, MN, 55104. Tel: 651-646-0475. p. 2768

Smalley, Krystal, Soc Media Coordr, Upper Sandusky Community Library, 301 N Sandusky Ave, Upper Sandusky, OH, 43351-1139. Tel: 419-294-1345. p. 1826

Smalley, Pam, Asst Librn, McGregor Public Library, 334 Main St, McGregor, IA, 52157. Tel: 563-873-3318. p. 769

Smalley-King, Samantha, Librn, New Hampshire Department of Corrections, 138 E Milan Rd, Berlin, NH, 03570. Tel: 603-752-0460. p. 1355

Smalling, Pat, Br Mgr, Calaveras County Library, Angels Camp Branch, 426 N Main St, Angels Camp, CA, 95222. Tel: 209-736-2198. p. 211

Smalling, Sheigla, Dir, Montefiore Medical Center, Moses Research Tower, 2nd Flr, 111 E 210th St, Bronx, NY, 10467. Tel: 718-920-4666. p. 1499

Smith, Bradley, Archivist, Berks History Center, 160 Spring St, Reading, PA, 19601. Tel: 610-375-4375. p. 2000
Smith, Brandi, Circ Serv Coordr, Chippewa Falls Public Library, 105 W Central St, Chippewa Falls, WI, 54729-2397. Tel: 715-723-1146. p. 2427
Smith, Brandie, Librn, Texas County Library, Licking Branch, 126 S Main St, Licking, MO, 65542. Tel: 573-674-2038. p. 1249
Smith, Brandon, Librn, Birmingham Public Library, Eastwood, 4500 Montevallo Rd, Birmingham, AL, 35210. Tel: 205-591-4944. p. 7
Smith, Breanne, Assoc Dep Dir, South Carolina State Library, 1500 Senate St, Columbia, SC, 29201. Tel: 803-734-8626. p. 2054
Smith, Brena, Dir, Lake County Public Library, 1115 Harrison Ave, Leadville, CO, 80461-3398. Tel: 719-486-0569. p. 289
Smith, Brenda, Distance Learning Librn, Doc Delivery, Thompson Rivers University, 900 McGill Rd, Kamloops, BC, V2C 5N3, CANADA. Tel: 250-828-5000. p. 2568
Smith, Brittany, Circ Coordr, La Grange Park Public Library District, 555 N LaGrange Rd, La Grange Park, IL, 60526-5644. Tel: 708-352-0100. p. 606
Smith, Brooke, Br Mgr, Jackson-Madison County Library, North Branch, Eight Stonebridge Blvd, Ste F & G, Jackson, TN, 38305. p. 2102
Smith, Brooke, Br Librn, Marinette County Library System, Coleman-Pound Library, 123 W Main St, Coleman, WI, 54112. Tel: 920-897-2400. p. 2453
Smith, Calvert, Extn Serv, Pub Serv, Rockingham County Public Library, 527 Boone Rd, Eden, NC, 27288. Tel: 336-349-8476. p. 1686
Smith, Calvin, Libr Coord, Trinidad State Junior College, 600 Prospect St, Trinidad, CO, 81082. Tel: 719-846-5593. p. 297
Smith, Cameron, Dir, Libr Serv, Guthrie Public Library, 201 N Division St, Guthrie, OK, 73044-3201. Tel: 405-282-0050. p. 1849
Smith, Carl, Interim Mgr, Delta County Libraries, Crawford Public, 545 Hwy 92, Crawford, CO, 81415. Tel: 970-399-7783. p. 286
Smith, Carl, Mgr, Delta County Libraries, Hotchkiss Public, 149 E Main St, Hotchkiss, CO, 81419. Tel: 970-399-7781. p. 286
Smith, Carl, Br Mgr, Harris County Public Library, Aldine Branch, 11331 Airline Dr, Houston, TX, 77037. Tel: 832-927-5410. p. 2192
Smith, Carla, Ch, Colo Public Library, 309 Main St, Colo, IA, 50056. Tel: 641-377-2900. p. 741
Smith, Carly, Library Contact, Finney County Public Library, 605 E Walnut St, Garden City, KS, 67846. Tel: 620-272-3680. p. 809
Smith, Carol, Genealogy Serv, Cherokee Regional Library System, 305 S Duke St, LaFayette, GA, 30728. Tel: 706-638-4912. p. 484
Smith, Carol, Tech Coordr, Pulaski County Public Library System, 60 W Third St, Pulaski, VA, 24301. Tel: 540-980-7770. p. 2339
Smith, Carol V, Univ Librn, Colorado School of Mines, 1400 Illinois St, Golden, CO, 80401-1887. Tel: 303-273-3698. p. 282
Smith, Caroline, Knowledge Mgr, Aerospace Corp, 2360 E El Segundo Blvd, El Segundo, CA, 90245. Tel: 310-336-5000. p. 140
Smith, Carolyn, Br Mgr, Martin County Library System, Peter & Julie Cummings Library, 2551 SW Matheson Ave, Palm City, FL, 34990. Tel: 772-288-2551. p. 445
Smith, Carolyn, Br Librn, Dearborn Heights City Libraries, John F Kennedy Jr Library, 24602 Van Born Rd, Dearborn Heights, MI, 48125. Tel: 313-791-6055. p. 1096
Smith, Carrie, Dir, US Department of Commerce, 325 Broadway, R/ESRL5, Boulder, CO, 80305-3328. Tel: 303-497-3271. p. 267
Smith, Catherine, Librn, Sevier County Library, Horatio Branch, 108 Main St, Horatio, AR, 71842. Tel: 870-832-6882. p. 93
Smith, Catherine, Dr, Assoc Prof, Kent State University, 314 University Library, 1125 Risman Dr, Kent, OH, 44242-0001. Tel: 330-672-2782. p. 2790
Smith, Cathy, Dir, Dwight T Parker Public Library, 925 Lincoln Ave, Fennimore, WI, 53809-1743. Tel: 608-822-6294. p. 2434
Smith, Celena, Circ Supvr, Learning Commons Supvr, Northwest Nazarene University, 804 E Dewey St, Nampa, ID, 83686. Tel: 208-467-8614. p. 527
Smith, Charlotte, Libr Mgr, Mid Arkansas Regional Library, 202 E Third St, Malvern, AR, 72104. Tel: 501-332-5441. p. 103
Smith, Chas, Educ Tech Spec, SouthWest Ohio & Neighboring Libraries, 10250 Alliance Rd, Ste 112, Cincinnati, OH, 45242. Tel: 513-751-4423. p. 2773
Smith, Cheryl, Dir, O'Melveny & Myers LLP, 400 S Hope St, Los Angeles, CA, 90071-2899. Tel: 213-430-6000. p. 167
Smith, Cheryl, Dir, Timothy C Hauenstein Reynolds Township Library, 117 W Williams St, Howard City, MI, 49329. Tel: 231-937-5575. p. 1117
Smith, Cheryl, Libr Tech, St Clair College, 1001 Grand Ave W, Chatham, ON, N7M 5W4, CANADA. Tel: 519-354-9100, Ext 3232, 519-354-9100, Ext 3273. p. 2636
Smith, Chris-Tina, Libr Supvr, Corona Public Library, 650 S Main St, Corona, CA, 92882. Tel: 951-739-4860. p. 132
Smith, Christa, Br Mgr, Librn, Clearwater Public Library System, 100 N Osceola Ave, Clearwater, FL, 33755. Tel: 727-562-4970. p. 388
Smith, Claudia, Librn, Northwest-Shoals Community College, 800 George Wallace Blvd, Muscle Shoals, AL, 35661-3206. Tel: 256-331-5283. p. 31
Smith, Colleen, Sr Librn, Lee County Library System, Pine Island Public Library, 10701 Russell Rd, Bokeelia, FL, 33922. Tel: 239-533-4350. p. 403
Smith, Connie, Dir, Gardendale - Martha Moore Public Library, 995 Mt Olive Rd, Gardendale, AL, 35071. Tel: 205-631-6639. p. 19
Smith, Connie, Asst Dir, Lake City Public Library, 110 E Washington St, Lake City, IA, 51449. Tel: 712-464-3413. p. 763
Smith, Corbin, Circ Supvr, Goucher College Library, 1021 Dulaney Valley Rd, Baltimore, MD, 21204. Tel: 410-337-6360. p. 953
Smith, Cory, Libr Dir, Abbott Memorial Library, 15 Library St, South Pomfret, VT, 05067. Tel: 802-457-2236. p. 2295
Smith, Craig, Head, Info & Tech, Winchester Public Library, 80 Washington St, Winchester, MA, 01890. Tel: 781-721-7171. p. 1070
Smith Curtis, Karen, Libr Bus Adminr, St Catharines Public Library, 54 Church St, St. Catharines, ON, L2R 7K2, CANADA. Tel: 905-688-6103. p. 2680
Smith, Cynthia, Br Mgr, Peoria Public Library, Lincoln, 1312 W Lincoln Ave, Peoria, IL, 61605-1976. Tel: 309-497-2601. p. 634
Smith, Cynthia, Dir, Limerick Public Library, 55 Washington St, Limerick, ME, 04048-3500. Tel: 207-793-8975. p. 929
Smith, Cynthia, Libr Tech, Rhode Island Hospital, Aldrich Bldg, 593 Eddy St, Providence, RI, 02902. Tel: 401-444-5450. p. 2040
Smith, Dale, Ch Serv, Morse Institute Library, 14 E Central St, Natick, MA, 01760. Tel: 508-647-6520. p. 1037
Smith, Dan, Librn, Onondaga County Public Libraries, Southwest Community Center, 401 South Ave, Syracuse, NY, 13204. Tel: 315-671-5814. p. 1649
Smith, Dan A, Dir, University of Wisconsin-Green Bay, Sheboygan Campus Library, One University Dr, Sheboygan, WI, 53081-4789. Tel: 920-459-6625. p. 2439
Smith, Daniel, Ref Librn, Newburgh Chandler Public Library, 4111 Lakeshore Dr, Newburgh, IN, 47630-2274. Tel: 812-589-5468, Ext 303. p. 709
Smith, Daniella, Dr, Assoc Prof, University of North Texas, 3940 N Elm St, Ste E292, Denton, TX, 76207. Tel: 940-565-2445. p. 2793
Smith, Danielle, Town Librn, Stamford Community Library, 986 Main Rd, Stamford, VT, 05352. Tel: 802-694-1379. p. 2295
Smith, Danny, Libr Dir, Canby Public Library, 220 NE Second Ave, Canby, OR, 97013-3732. Tel: 503-266-3394. p. 1875
Smith, Darlene, Dir, Libr Serv, Winchester Public Library, 215 N Main St, Winchester, IL, 62694. Tel: 217-742-3150. p. 663
Smith, Darlene, Libr Dir, Winchester Public Library, 2117 Lake St, Winchester, WI, 54557-9104. Tel: 715-686-2926. p. 2489
Smith, David, Assoc Dir, Libr Serv, Thomas College Library, 180 W River Rd, Waterville, ME, 04901. Tel: 207-859-1235. p. 945
Smith, David C, Cat, United States Forest Service, One Gifford Pinchot Dr, Madison, WI, 53726-2398. Tel: 608-231-9200. p. 2450
Smith, Dawn, Asst Dean, Pub Serv, Florida Atlantic University, 777 Glades Rd, Boca Raton, FL, 33431. Tel: 561-297-1029. p. 385
Smith, Dawn, Asst Dir, Illinois Prairie District Public Library, 208 E Partridge St, Metamora, IL, 61548. Tel: 309-921-5074. p. 617
Smith, Dean P, Dir, Albuquerque-Bernalillo County Library System, 501 Copper Ave NW, Albuquerque, NM, 87102. p. 1459
Smith, Deanna, Youth Serv, Pender County Public Library, 103 S Cowan St, Burgaw, NC, 28425. Tel: 910-259-1234. p. 1676
Smith, Deb, Librn, Greensburg-Decatur County Public Library, Westport Branch, 205 W Main St, Westport, IN, 47283-9601. Tel: 812-591-2330. p. 688
Smith, Debara, Libr Dir, Brownsdale Grace Gillette Public Library, 103 E Main St, Brownsdale, MN, 55918-8817. Tel: 507-567-9951. p. 1167
Smith, Deborah, Exec Dir, Essex Library Association, Inc, 33 West Ave, Essex, CT, 06426-1196. Tel: 860-767-1560. p. 311
Smith, Deborah, Dir, Jones Memorial Library, Lynchburg Public Library Bldg, 2nd Flr, 2311 Memorial Ave, Lynchburg, VA, 24501. Tel: 434-846-0501. p. 2330
Smith, Debra, Ref Librn, College of DuPage Library, 425 Fawell Blvd, Glen Ellyn, IL, 60137-6599. Tel: 630-942-4305. p. 593
Smith, Deena, Librn, Federal Judicial Center, One Columbus Circle NE, Washington, DC, 20002-8003. Tel: 202-502-4153. p. 366
Smith, Deena, Libr Dir, Sharon Public Library, 133 E Main St, Sharon, TN, 38255. Tel: 731-456-2707. p. 2126
Smith, Denise, Dir, Tipton Public Library, 206 Cedar St, Tipton, IA, 52772-1753. Tel: 563-886-6266. p. 786
Smith, Dennis, Assoc Dean, West Virginia University Libraries, 1549 University Ave, Morgantown, WV, 26506. Tel: 304-293-4040. p. 2409
Smith, Diana, Dir, New Salem Public Library, 23 S Main St, New Salem, MA, 01355. Tel: 978-544-6334. p. 1038
Smith, Diana, ILL, Saint Mary's Public Library, 127 Center St, Saint Marys, PA, 15857. Tel: 814-834-6141. p. 2002
Smith, Diane, Co-Dir, National Society of Sons of Utah Pioneers, 3301 E 2920 South, Salt Lake City, UT, 84109. Tel: 801-484-4441. p. 2271
Smith, Donald R, Dir, Morehouse Parish Library, 524 E Madison Ave, Bastrop, LA, 71220. Tel: 318-281-3696. p. 881
Smith, Donna, Discovery Serv, E-Resources Librn, Interim Head, Coll Develop, Northern Kentucky University, University Dr, Highland Heights, KY, 41099. Tel: 859-572-6140. p. 859
Smith, Donna, Librn, Clarendon College, 1122 College Dr, Clarendon, TX, 79226. Tel: 806-874-4815. p. 2156
Smith, Dorothy, Dir, Libr Serv, Shorter University, 315 Shorter Ave NW, Rome, GA, 30165. Tel: 706-233-7296, 770-748-0231, Ext 7296. p. 495

Smith, Dorothy, Acq, Southwestern Baptist Theological Seminary Libraries, 2001 W Seminary Dr, Fort Worth, TX, 76115-2157. Tel: 817-923-1921, Ext 4000. p. 2180
Smith, Dreda, Libr Dir, Centralia Community Library, 520 Fourth St, Centralia, KS, 66415. Tel: 785-857-3331. p. 801
Smith, Dylan, Health Sci Librn, Mount Saint Mary's University, J Thomas McCarthy Library, Doheny Campus, Ten Chester Pl, Los Angeles, CA, 90007. Tel: 213-234-9834. p. 166
Smith, Edward J, Exec Dir, Abilene Library Consortium, 3305 N Third St, Abilene, TX, 79603. Tel: 325-672-7081. p. 2775
Smith, Elizabeth, Res Ctr Mgr, North Carolina Synod of the ELCA, 1988 Lutheran Synod Dr, Salisbury, NC, 28144. Tel: 704-633-4861, Ext 9573. p. 1715
Smith, Ellen, Mat Mgt Mgr, Hinsdale Public Library, 20 E Maple St, Hinsdale, IL, 60521. Tel: 630-986-1976. p. 600
Smith, Ellesha, Libr Supvr, Weekend Cir Mgr, Valparaiso University, 1410 Chapel Dr, Valparaiso, IN, 46383-6493. Tel: 219-464-5500. p. 723
Smith, Ellie, Br Asst, Pictou - Antigonish Regional Library, Stellarton Library, 248 Foord St, Stellarton, NS, B0K 1S0, CANADA. Tel: 902-755-1638. p. 2622
Smith, Elliott, Emerging Tech Librn, University of California, Berkeley, Marian Koshland Bioscience, Natural Resources & Public Health Library, 2101 Valley Life Science Bldg, No 6500, Berkeley, CA, 94720-6500. Tel: 510-643-6482. p. 123
Smith, Emily, Libr Dir, Concord Free Public Library, 129 Main St, Concord, MA, 01742. Tel: 978-318-3377. p. 1012
Smith, Emily, Dep Dir, Head, Tech, Cary Memorial Library, 1874 Massachusetts Ave, Lexington, MA, 02420. Tel: 781-862-6288, Ext 84402. p. 1028
Smith, Emily, Dir, Montour Falls Memorial Library, 406 W Main St, Montour Falls, NY, 14865. Tel: 607-535-7489. p. 1573
Smith, Emily, Res & Instruction Librn, University of South Carolina at Beaufort Library, Eight E Campus Dr, Bluffton, SC, 29909. Tel: 843-208-8028. p. 2048
Smith, Eric, Libr Dir, Mason County District Library, 217 E Ludington Ave, Ludington, MI, 49431. Tel: 231-843-8465. p. 1127
Smith, Erin, Asst Librn, Dr Grace O Doane Alden Public Library, 1012 Water St, Alden, IA, 50006. Tel: 515-859-3820. p. 730
Smith, Erin, Tech Serv Librn, Albion College, 602 E Cass St, Albion, MI, 49224-1879. p. 1076
Smith, Erin, Ch Assoc, Liberty Lake Municipal Library, 23123 E Mission Ave, Liberty Lake, WA, 99019-7613. Tel: 509-232-2510. p. 2369
Smith, Erin T, Assoc Dean, Libr & Info Serv, Westminster College, S Market St, New Wilmington, PA, 16172-0001. Tel: 724-946-6000. p. 1970
Smith, Frederick, Dir, New Jersey City University, 2039 Kennedy Blvd, Jersey City, NJ, 07305-1597. Tel: 201-200-3474. p. 1409
Smith, Gabrielle, Sr Librn, California Department of Corrections Library System, California Correctional Center, 711-045 Center Rd, Susanville, CA, 96127. Tel: 530-257-2181, Ext 4370. p. 206
Smith, Garrette, Br Mgr, Charlotte Mecklenburg Library, ImaginOn: The Joe & Joan Martin Center, 300 E Seventh St, Charlotte, NC, 28202. Tel: 704-416-4600. p. 1679
Smith, Gary, Head Law Librn, Massachusetts Trial Court, Court House, 76 East St, Pittsfield, MA, 01201. Tel: 413-442-5059. p. 1047
Smith, Genevieve, Libr Dir, Pitkin County Library, 120 N Mill St, Aspen, CO, 81611. Tel: 970-429-1900. p. 264
Smith, Giselle, Br Mgr, Mesa County Public Library District, Fruita Branch, 324 N Coulson, Fruita, CO, 81521. Tel: 970-858-7703. p. 284
Smith, Greg, Assoc Dean, Library Technologies & Collection Servs, Liberty University, 1971 University Blvd, Lynchburg, VA, 24515. Tel: 434-592-4892. p. 2330
Smith Hale, Fiona, Dir, Libr & Archive Serv, Canada Science & Technology Museum, 1865 St Laurent, Ottawa, ON, K1G 5A3, CANADA. Tel: 613-993-2303. p. 2665
Smith, Heather, Br Mgr, Bossier Parish Libraries, Benton Branch, 115 Courthouse Dr, Benton, LA, 71006. Tel: 318-965-2751. p. 886
Smith, Heather, Info Fluency Librn, Learning Tech Librn, Belmont Abbey College, 100 Belmont-Mt Holly Rd, Belmont, NC, 28012. Tel: 704-461-6748. p. 1674
Smith, Heather, Libr Tech, Department of Veterans Affairs, 215 N Main St, White River Junction, VT, 05009. Tel: 802-295-9363. p. 2298
Smith, Heather, Librn/Coll Develop/Info Literacy, University College of the North Libraries, 436 Seventh St E, The Pas, MB, R9A 1M7, CANADA. Tel: 204-627-8561. p. 2591
Smith, Heidi, Exec Dir, Highland Park Public Library, 494 Laurel Ave, Highland Park, IL, 60035-2690. Tel: 847-432-0216, Ext 121. p. 599
Smith, Helen, Agr Sci Librn, Pennsylvania State University Libraries, Life Sciences, 408 Paterno Library, University Park, PA, 16802-1811. Tel: 814-865-3706. p. 2015
Smith Hoogasian, Lori, Head, Mat Serv, Bloomfield Township Public Library, 1099 Lone Pine Rd, Bloomfield Township, MI, 48302-2410. Tel: 248-642-5800. p. 1086
Smith, Ina, Dir, Bonnyville Municipal Library, 4804 49th Ave, Bonnyville, AB, T9N 2J3, CANADA. Tel: 780-826-3071. p. 2524
Smith, Ivan, Br Librn, Genesee District Library, Swartz Creek-Perkins Library, 8095 Civic Dr, Swartz Creek, MI, 48473. Tel: 810-635-3900. p. 1106
Smith, Jacqueline, Libr Assoc, Tech Serv, Marshall University Libraries, One John Marshall Dr, Huntington, WV, 25755-2060. Tel: 304-696-2320. p. 2405
Smith, James, Librn, Houston Community College - Northeast College, Codwell Campus Library, 555 Community College Dr, Houston, TX, 77013-6127. Tel: 713-718-8354. p. 2194
Smith, Jane E, Assoc Dir for Library Writing Support, Bard College, One Library Rd, Annandale-on-Hudson, NY, 12504. Tel: 845-758-7892. p. 1487
Smith, Janet, Dir, Palliser Regional Library, 366 Coteau St W, Moose Jaw, SK, S6H 5C9, CANADA. Tel: 306-693-3669. p. 2742
Smith, Jason, Metadata Librn, Medical University of South Carolina Libraries, 171 Ashley Ave, Ste 419, Charleston, SC, 29425-0001. Tel: 843-792-8727. p. 2051
Smith, Jean, Librn, Faulkner-Van Buren Regional Library System, Mayflower Branch, Six Ashmore Dr, Mayflower, AR, 72106. Tel: 501-470-9678. p. 92
Smith, Jean, Br Coordr, Phillips-Lee-Monroe Regional Library, West Helena Library, 721 Plaza St, West Helena, AR, 72390-2698. Tel: 870-572-2861. p. 98
Smith, Jean, Ch Serv, Clarion Free Library, 644 Main St, Clarion, PA, 16214. Tel: 814-226-7172. p. 1922
Smith, Jeffrey, Curator, Columbia River Maritime Museum, 1792 Marine Dr, Astoria, OR, 97103. Tel: 503-325-2323. p. 1872
Smith, Jen, Libr Mgr, Bighorn Library, Two Heart Mountain Dr, Exshaw, AB, T0L 2C0, CANADA. Tel: 403-673-3571. p. 2539
Smith, Jennie, Br Mgr, Camden County Library District, Macks Creek Branch, 90 State Rd N, Macks Creek, MO, 65786. Tel: 573-363-5530. p. 1239
Smith, Jennifer, Head, Children's Servx, Suffern Free Library, 210 Lafayette Ave, Suffern, NY, 10901. Tel: 845-357-1237. p. 1647
Smith, Jennifer L, Libr Dir, Ledyard Public Library, 718 Colonel Ledyard Hwy, Ledyard, CT, 06339. Tel: 860-464-9912. p. 319
Smith, Jennifer L, Libr Dir, Ledyard Public Library, Gales Ferry Library, 18 Hurlbutt Rd, Gales Ferry, CT, 06335. Tel: 860-464-9917. p. 320
Smith, Jennifer, PhD, Res & Instruction Librn, Northern Kentucky University, University Dr, Highland Heights, KY, 41099. Tel: 859-572-6620. p. 859
Smith, Jessica, Head, Children's Servx, Woodridge Public Library, Three Plaza Dr, Woodridge, IL, 60517-5014. Tel: 630-487-2567. p. 664
Smith, Jill, Dir, Bayport Public Library, 582 N Fourth St, Bayport, MN, 55003-1111. Tel: 651-275-4416. p. 1164
Smith, Jim, Chief Financial Officer, Daniel Boone Regional Library, 100 W Broadway, Columbia, MO, 65203. Tel: 573-443-3161. p. 1242
Smith, Joan, ILL Spec, Northwest Nazarene University, 804 E Dewey St, Nampa, ID, 83686. Tel: 208-467-8605. p. 527
Smith, John, Co-Dir, National Society of Sons of Utah Pioneers, 3301 E 2920 South, Salt Lake City, UT, 84109. Tel: 801-484-4441. p. 2271
Smith, John A, Dir of Collection Operations, American University, 4300 Nebraska Ave NW, Washington, DC, 20016-8182. Tel: 202-274-4354. p. 360
Smith, Jonathan, Access Serv, Interim Asst Dean, Tech Serv, Sonoma State University Library, 1801 E Cotati Ave, Rohnert Park, CA, 94928. Tel: 707-664-2375. p. 204
Smith, Jordyn, Teen Librn, Tiverton Public Library, 34 Roosevelt Ave, Tiverton, RI, 02878. Tel: 401-625-6796, Ext 4. p. 2042
Smith, Josefine, Instruction & Assessment Librn, Shippensburg University, 1871 Old Main Dr, Shippensburg, PA, 17257. Tel: 717-477-1634. p. 2007
Smith, Josh, Libr Mgr, Cornelia-Habersham County Library, 301 Main St N, Cornelia, GA, 30531. Tel: 706-778-2635. p. 473
Smith, Josh, Digital Preservation Specialist, Pacific Lutheran University, 12180 Park Ave S, Tacoma, WA, 98447-0001. Tel: 253-535-7500. p. 2386
Smith, Joyce, Librn, Saint Johns River State College, 5001 St Johns Ave, Palatka, FL, 32177-3897. Tel: 386-312-4153. p. 433
Smith, Joyce, Ch, Charleston Library Society, 164 King St, Charleston, SC, 29401. Tel: 843-723-9912. p. 2050
Smith, Jude, Pub Relations, Great Falls Public Library, 301 Second Ave N, Great Falls, MT, 59401-2593. Tel: 406-453-0181, Ext 220. p. 1294
Smith, Judy, Br Mgr, Southwest Georgia Regional Library, Seminole County Public Library, 103 W Fourth St, Donalsonville, GA, 39845. Tel: 229-524-2665. p. 467
Smith, Judy, Librn, Travis Avenue Baptist Church Library, 800 W Berry St, Fort Worth, TX, 76110. Tel: 817-924-4266. p. 2181
Smith, Julia, Br Mgr, Forsyth County Public Library, Southside, 3185 Buchanan St, Winston-Salem, NC, 27127. Tel: 336-703-2980. p. 1725
Smith, Julianne, Asst Dir, Ypsilanti District Library, 5577 Whittaker Rd, Ypsilanti, MI, 48197. Tel: 734-879-1301. p. 1160
Smith, Julie, Exec Dir, Prince Edward Island Association for Community Living, 40 Enman Crescent, Rm 273, Charlottetown, PE, C1E 1E6, CANADA. Tel: 902-439-4607. p. 2707
Smith, Juliet, Pres, American-Canadian Genealogical Society Library, One Sundial Ave, Ste 317N, Manchester, NH, 03103-7242. Tel: 603-622-1554. p. 1371
Smith, Justin, Mgr, Nestle Purina Pet Care Co, One Checkerboard Sq, Saint Louis, MO, 63164. Tel: 314-982-5913. p. 1272
Smith, Karen, Head, Youth Serv, Livonia Public Library, Civic Center, 32777 Five Mile Rd, Livonia, MI, 48154-3045. Tel: 734-466-2450. p. 1127

Smith, Karen M, Dir, Whitesville Public Library, 500 Main St, Whitesville, NY, 14897-9703. Tel: 607-356-3645. p. 1665
Smith, Karla, ILL Mgr, Winnefox Library System, 106 Washington Ave, Oshkosh, WI, 54901-4985. Tel: 920-236-5220. p. 2468
Smith, Kate, Bus Mgr, Mahomet Public Library District, 1702 E Oak St, Mahomet, IL, 61853-7427. Tel: 217-586-2611. p. 612
Smith, Katelyn, Circ, Calmar Public Library, 4705 50th Ave, Calmar, AB, T0C 0V0, CANADA. Tel: 780-985-3472. p. 2529
Smith, Kathelene McCarty, Head, Spec Coll & Univ Archives, University of North Carolina at Greensboro, 320 College Ave, Greensboro, NC, 27412-0001. Tel: 336-334-5648. p. 1693
Smith, Kathleen, Exec Dir, Southern California University of Health Sciences, 16200 E Amber Valley Dr, Whittier, CA, 90604-4098. Tel: 562-902-3368. p. 259
Smith, Kathleen, Dir, Waynoka Public Library, 1659 Cecil St, Waynoka, OK, 73860. Tel: 580-824-6181. p. 1868
Smith, Kathy, Dir, San Manuel Public Library, 108 Fifth Ave, San Manuel, AZ, 85631. Tel: 520-385-4470. p. 76
Smith, Kathy, Br Mgr, Scottsville Free Library, Mumford Branch, 883 George St, Mumford, NY, 14511. Tel: 718-538-6124. p. 1639
Smith, Kathy, Br Mgr, Jim Lucas Checotah Public Library, 626 W Gentry, Checotah, OK, 74426-2218. Tel: 918-473-6715. p. 1843
Smith, Katie, Br Mgr, Mid-Continent Public Library, Midwest Genealogy Center, 3440 S Lee's Summit Rd, Independence, MO, 64055. Tel: 816-252-7228. p. 1251
Smith, Katie, Teen Serv Librn, Wood Library Association, 134 N Main St, Canandaigua, NY, 14424-1295. Tel: 585-394-1381, Ext 302. p. 1512
Smith, Katie, Libr Dir, Hazeltine Public Library, 891 Busti-Sugar Grove Rd, Jamestown, NY, 14701. Tel: 716-487-1281. p. 1557
Smith, Katy, Dr, Pres, Saint Louis Regional Library Network, c/o Amigos Library Services, 1190 Meramec Station Rd, Ste 207, Ballwin, MO, 63021-6902. p. 2769
Smith, Kawana, Dir, Horicon Free Public Library, 6604 State Rte 8, Brant Lake, NY, 12815. Tel: 518-494-4189. p. 1496
Smith, Kelli, Circ Supvr, Topeka & Shawnee County Public Library, 1515 SW Tenth Ave, Topeka, KS, 66604-1374. Tel: 785-580-4400. p. 839
Smith, Kelly, Readers' Advisory, Arkansas State Library for the Blind & Print Disabled, 900 W Capitol Ave, Ste 100, Little Rock, AR, 72201-3108. Tel: 501-682-2871. p. 100
Smith, Ken, Dir, Coll Serv, Dir, Res Serv, Valdosta State University, 1500 N Patterson St, Valdosta, GA, 31698-0150. Tel: 229-259-3734. p. 501
Smith, Kendra, Librn, Lincoln-Lawrence-Franklin Regional Library, Lawrence County Public Library, 142 Courthouse Sq, Monticello, MS, 39654. Tel: 601-587-2471. p. 1213
Smith, Kendra, Tech Serv, South Mississippi Regional Library, 900 Broad St, Columbia, MS, 39429. Tel: 601-736-5516. p. 1215
Smith, Kevin L, Dean of Libr, University of Kansas Libraries, 1425 Jayhawk Blvd, Lawrence, KS, 66045-7544. Tel: 785-864-4711. p. 819
Smith, Kevin W, Libr Dir, York County Public Library, 100 Long Green Blvd, Yorktown, VA, 23693. Tel: 757-890-5134. p. 2355
Smith, Kim, Librn, Monterey Public Library, 625 Pacific St, Monterey, CA, 93940. Tel: 831-646-3933. p. 179
Smith, Kim Ann, Circ Mgr, Northland Public Library, 300 Cumberland Rd, Pittsburgh, PA, 15237-5455. Tel: 412-366-8100, Ext 115. p. 1994
Smith, Kimberley, Asst Univ Librn, Coll Develop, California State University, Fresno, Henry Madden Library, 5200 N Barton Ave, Mail Stop ML-34, Fresno, CA, 93740-8014. Tel: 559-278-4578. p. 144
Smith, Kimberly, Librn, Hinds Community College, 505 E Main St, Raymond, MS, 39154. Tel: 601-857-3355. p. 1231
Smith, Kimberly, Librn, South Dakota State Historical Society, 900 Governors Dr, Pierre, SD, 57501. Tel: 605-773-4233. p. 2080
Smith, Kirk, Head, Circ, Lamar University, 4400 Martin Luther King Jr Pkwy, Beaumont, TX, 77705. Tel: 409-880-8133. p. 2146
Smith, Kristen, E-Res & Research Serv Librn, Loras College Library, 1450 Alta Vista St, Dubuque, IA, 52004-4327. Tel: 563-588-7042. p. 748
Smith, Kristi, Circ, Head, Ref, Ouachita Baptist University, 410 Ouachita St, OBU Box 3742, Arkadelphia, AR, 71998-0001. Tel: 870-245-5119. p. 89
Smith, Kristin, Dir, Richmond Free Public Library, 2821 State Rd, Richmond, MA, 01254-9472. Tel: 413-563-7795. p. 1049
Smith, Krystle, Mgr, Miami-Dade Public Library System, Coconut Grove Branch, 2875 McFarlane Rd, Coconut Grove, FL, 33133. Tel: 305-442-8695. p. 423
Smith, Lakesha, Admin Librn, Hinds Community College, Jackson Academic & Technical Center, 3925 Sunset Dr, Jackson, MS, 39213-5899. Tel: 601-987-8123. p. 1231
Smith, Lana, Br Mgr, Wayne County Public Library, Wayne Public, 325 Keyser St, Wayne, WV, 25570. Tel: 304-272-3756. p. 2406
Smith, Laura, Coll & Instruction Librn, Santa Fe Community College Library, 6401 Richards Ave, Santa Fe, NM, 87508-4887. Tel: 505-428-1368. p. 1476
Smith, Laurie, Librn, New Creation Family Church, 100 Pasadena Ave N, Saint Petersburg, FL, 33710-8315. Tel: 727-345-0148. p. 441
Smith, Lavada, Cat Librn, University of Michigan-Dearborn, 4901 Evergreen Rd, Dearborn, MI, 48128-2406. Tel: 313-593-3284. p. 1096
Smith, Lawrence, Coll Mgt Serv Dir, Mississippi Library Commission, 3881 Eastwood Dr, Jackson, MS, 39211. Tel: 601-432-4120. p. 1222
Smith, Leah, Asst Dir, Prospect Public Library, 17 Center St, Prospect, CT, 06712. Tel: 203-758-0813. p. 334
Smith, Lee, Dir, Adams Memorial Library, 205 Central St, Central Falls, RI, 02863. Tel: 401-727-7440. p. 2030
Smith, Lee Roy, Exec Dir, National Wrestling Hall of Fame Library & Museum, 405 W Hall of Fame Ave, Stillwater, OK, 74075. Tel: 405-377-5243. p. 1862
Smith, Lela, Outreach Mgr, The Indiana Youth Institute, 603 E Washington St, Ste 800, Indianapolis, IN, 46204. Tel: 317-396-2700. p. 693
Smith, Leslie, Admin Serv Mgr, Sumter County Library System, 7375 Powell Rd, Ste 150, Wildwood, FL, 34785. Tel: 352-689-4400. p. 455
Smith, Leslie, Br Mgr, Brazoria County Library System, Sweeny Branch, 205 W Ashley-Wilson Rd, Sweeny, TX, 77480. Tel: 979-548-2567. p. 2135
Smith, Leslie, Asst Librn, Greenwood Public Library, 346 S Copper Ave, Greenwood, BC, V0H 1J0, CANADA. Tel: 250-445-6111. p. 2567
Smith, Lesly M, Dir, Libr Serv, Haltom City Public Library, 4809 Haltom Rd, Haltom City, TX, 76117-3622. Tel: 817-222-7791. p. 2187
Smith, Lilly, Coll Develop Librn, Tyler Junior College, 1327 S Baxter St, Tyler, TX, 75701. Tel: 903-510-2645. p. 2249
Smith, Lily, Youth Serv Librn, Solon Public Library, 320 W Main St, Solon, IA, 52333-9504. Tel: 319-624-2678. p. 783
Smith, Linda, Br Mgr, Huntington City-Township Public Library, Markle Public Library, 155 W Sparks St, Markle, IN, 46770. Tel: 260-758-3332. p. 690
Smith, Linda, Br Mgr, Cape May County Library, Cape May City Branch, 110 Ocean St, Cape May, NJ, 08204. Tel: 609-884-9568. p. 1395
Smith, Lindsey, ILL, Teen Prog, Oscar Foss Memorial Library, 111 S Barnstead Rd, Center Barnstead, NH, 03225. Tel: 603-269-3900. p. 1357
Smith, Lisa, Cat, Ada Public Library, 124 S Rennie, Ada, OK, 74820. Tel: 580-436-8125. p. 1839
Smith, Lissie, Circ Supvr, Willoughby Wallace Memorial Library, 146 Thimble Islands Rd, Stony Creek, CT, 06405-5739. Tel: 203-488-8702. p. 339
Smith, Liz, Library Contact, Twin Valley Behavioral Healthcare, Forensic Patients' Library, 2200 W Broad St, Columbus, OH, 43223. Tel: 614-752-0333, Ext 5451. p. 1778
Smith, Lora, Libr Dir, Richmond Public Library, 38 W Main St, Richmond, UT, 84333-1409. Tel: 435-258-5525. p. 2270
Smith, Loretta, Dir, Texas County Library, 117 W Walnut St, Houston, MO, 65483. Tel: 417-967-2258. p. 1249
Smith, Lorraine, Librn, Camden County College Library, 200 College Dr, Blackwood, NJ, 08012. Tel: 856-227-7200, Ext 4407. p. 1390
Smith, Lorraine, Library Contact, Somerset County Law Library, Court House, 111 E Union St, Ste 50, Somerset, PA, 15501. Tel: 814-445-1510. p. 2008
Smith, Lorrie, Dir, Beaverdale Public Library, 506 Jefferson Ave, Beaverdale, PA, 15921. Tel: 814-487-7742. p. 1909
Smith, Lydia, Ad, Harwinton Public Library, 80 Bentley Dr, Harwinton, CT, 06791. Tel: 860-485-9113. p. 319
Smith, Lynn, Historian, Registrar, Episcopal Diocese of Massachusetts, 138 Tremont St, Boston, MA, 02111. Tel: 617-482-4826, Ext 488. p. 995
Smith, MacKenzie, Univ Librn, University of California, Davis, 100 NW Quad, Davis, CA, 95616. Tel: 530-752-8792. p. 134
Smith, Maddie, Library Asst, Periodicals & Archives, Christian Brothers University, 650 East Pkwy S, Memphis, TN, 38104. Tel: 901-321-3432. p. 2112
Smith, Margaret, Dir, Armada Free Public Library, 73930 Church St, Armada, MI, 48005. Tel: 586-784-5921. p. 1081
Smith, Margit, Head, Cat, University of San Diego, Helen K & James S Copley Library, 5998 Alcala Park, San Diego, CA, 92110. p. 222
Smith, Maria, Br Librn, Greenstone Public Library, 405 Second St W, Geraldton, ON, P0T 1M0, CANADA. Tel: 807-854-1490. p. 2642
Smith, Mark, Pub Serv Librn, University of South Carolina Upstate Library, 800 University Way, Spartanburg, SC, 29303. Tel: 864-503-5672. p. 2070
Smith, Mark, Dir & Librn, TexSHARE - Texas State Library & Archives Commission, 1201 Brazos St, Austin, TX, 78701. Tel: 512-463-5460. p. 2776
Smith, Mark A, Dir, Libr Serv, Alfred University, Scholes Library of Ceramics, New York State College of Ceramics at Alfred University, Two Pine St, Alfred, NY, 14802-1297. p. 1485
Smith, Marta, Asst Dir, Fiske Free Library, 108 Broad St, Claremont, NH, 03743-2673. Tel: 603-542-7017. p. 1358
Smith, Martha, Acq/Coll Develop Librn, Winthrop University, 824 Oakland Ave, Rock Hill, SC, 29733. Tel: 803-323-2274. p. 2068
Smith, Martin, Head, Automation, Redford Township District Library, 25320 W Six Mile, Redford, MI, 48240. Tel: 313-531-5960. p. 1143
Smith, Mary, Head, Kids' Libr, Elmhurst Public Library, 125 S Prospect Ave, Elmhurst, IL, 60126-3298. Tel: 630-279-8696. p. 585
Smith, Mary, Head, Youth Serv, Mount Prospect Public Library, Ten S Emerson St, Mount Prospect, IL, 60056. Tel: 847-253-5675. p. 621
Smith, Mary Ann, Sr Libr Tech, Imperial Valley College, 380 E Ira Aten Rd, Imperial, CA, 92251. Tel: 760-355-6380. p. 152

Smith, Mary Jo, Ch, Gates Public Library, 902 Elmgrove Rd, Rochester, NY, 14624. Tel: 585-247-6446. p. 1628
Smith, Mary Lee, Dep Dir, Farmington Public Library, 2101 Farmington Ave, Farmington, NM, 87401. Tel: 505-566-2205. p. 1468
Smith, Matthew R, Dir of Libr, State University of New York, College of Environmental Science & Forestry, One Forestry Dr, Syracuse, NY, 13210. Tel: 315-470-6724. p. 1650
Smith, Megan, Asst Dir, Ch Serv, YA Serv, Thomas Memorial Library, Six Scott Dyer Rd, Cape Elizabeth, ME, 04107. Tel: 207-799-1720. p. 920
Smith, Meghan Wanucha, Head of Liaison Librarian Servs, University of North Carolina Wilmington Library, 601 S College Rd, Wilmington, NC, 28403. Tel: 910-962-3272, 910-962-3760. p. 1723
Smith, Melissa, Archivist, McPherson Public Library, 214 W Marlin, McPherson, KS, 67460-4299. Tel: 620-245-2570. p. 825
Smith, Melissa, Br Mgr, Tulsa City-County Library, Bixby Branch, 20 E Breckinridge, Bixby, OK, 74008. p. 1866
Smith, Melissa, Educ Librn, Simon Fraser University - Fraser Campus, Central City, Podium 3, 250-13450 102 Ave, Surrey, BC, V3T 0A3, CANADA. Tel: 778-782-7419. p. 2577
Smith, Michael, Ref & Instruction Librn, Butte College Library, 3536 Butte Campus Dr, Oroville, CA, 95965. Tel: 530-879-4066. p. 189
Smith, Michael, Head, Ref, College of Our Lady of the Elms, 291 Springfield St, Chicopee, MA, 01013-2839. Tel: 413-265-2280. p. 1011
Smith, Micky, Libr Dir, United States Air Force, 75 MSG/SVMG, Bldg 440, 7415 Weiner St, Hill AFB, UT, 84056-5006. Tel: 801-777-2533, 801-777-3833. p. 2264
Smith, Mike, Librn, Smithsonian Libraries, National Museum of Asian Art Library - Freer Gallery of Art, Arthur M Sackler Gallery Library, Rm 2058, 1050 Independence Ave SW, MRC 707, Washington, DC, 20560. Tel: 202-633-0480. p. 375
Smith, Misti, Head, Tech Serv, Saint Francis University, 106 Franciscan Way, Loretto, PA, 15940. Tel: 814-472-3160. p. 1957
Smith, Mitchell, Br Mgr, Chicago Public Library, Whitney M Young Jr Branch, 415 E 79th St, Chicago, IL, 60619. Tel: 312-747-0039. p. 558
Smith, Monica, Ch, Sandy Public Library, 38980 Proctor Blvd, Sandy, OR, 97055-8040. Tel: 503-668-5537. p. 1898
Smith, Monica A, Dir, Louis Bay 2nd Library, 345 Lafayette Ave, Hawthorne, NJ, 07506-2546. Tel: 973-427-5745. p. 1407
Smith, Monica L, Librn, Cairo Public Library, 1609 Washington Ave, Cairo, IL, 62914. Tel: 618-734-1840. p. 547
Smith, Moria, Librn, American Chemical Society Information Resource Center, 1155 16th St NW, Washington, DC, 20036. Tel: 202-872-4513. p. 359
Smith, Nancy, Lead Librn, Kalamazoo Public Library, Oshtemo, 7265 W Main St, Kalamazoo, MI, 49009. Tel: 269-553-7980. p. 1121
Smith, Nathan M, Librn, Utah State University, Young Educational Technology Center, UMC 2845 - 170 EDUC, Utah State University, Logan, UT, 84322-2845. Tel: 435-797-3377. p. 2266
Smith, Ngaire, Librn, Technology Spec, Haywood Community College, 185 Freedlander Dr, Clyde, NC, 28721. Tel: 828-565-4172. p. 1682
Smith, Olga, Coordr, Cape Cod Hospital, 27 Park St, Hyannis, MA, 02601-5230. Tel: 508-862-5443. p. 1026
Smith, Owen G, Circuit Librn, US Court of Appeals for the Sixth Circuit Library, 540 Potter Stewart US Courthouse, 100 E Fifth St, Cincinnati, OH, 45202-3911. Tel: 513-564-7324. p. 1764
Smith, Pam, Archives, Tech, Montana Historical Society, 225 N Roberts St, Helena, MT, 59601-4514. Tel: 406-444-4739. p. 1296
Smith, Pam, Asst Dir, Howe Library, 13 South St, Hanover, NH, 03755. Tel: 603-640-3257. p. 1367
Smith, Pamela, Br Mgr, Central Rappahannock Regional Library, Salem Church, 2607 Salem Church Rd, Fredericksburg, VA, 22407-6451. Tel: 540-785-9267. p. 2320
Smith, Pamela, Br Mgr, Central Rappahannock Regional Library, Spotsylvania Towne Centre Branch, 390 Spotsylvania Mall, Fredericksburg, VA, 22407. p. 2320
Smith, Parker, Librn, Walter T A Hansen Memorial Library, Ten Hansen St, Mars Hill, ME, 04758. Tel: 207-429-9625. p. 931
Smith, Pat, Libr Dir, San Juan County Public Library, 80 N Main St, Monticello, UT, 84535. Tel: 435-587-2281. p. 2266
Smith, Patricia, Dir, Monaca Public Library, 998 Indiana Ave, 2nd Flr, Monaca, PA, 15061. Tel: 724-775-9608. p. 1964
Smith, Paul, Ref Librn, Pennsylvania State University, 1600 Woodland Rd, Abington, PA, 19001. Tel: 215-881-7424. p. 1903
Smith, Paula, Circ Supvr, Knox County Public Library, 502 N Seventh St, Vincennes, IN, 47591-2119. Tel: 812-886-4380. p. 723
Smith, Paula, Libr Spec, Clemson University Libraries, Gunnin Architecture Library, 2-112 Lee Hall, Clemson University, Clemson, SC, 29634. Tel: 864-656-3933. p. 2052
Smith, Paulette, Ref (Info Servs), Valencia College, Raymer Maguire Jr Learning Resources Center, West Campus, 1800 S Kirkman Rd, Orlando, FL, 32811. Tel: 407-582-1210. p. 433
Smith, Peggy, Librn, Putnam County Public Library District, Magnolia Branch, 112 N Chicago St, Magnolia, IL, 61336. Tel: 815-869-6038. p. 598
Smith, Peggy, Ref & Data Librn, University of Wisconsin-Madison, Business Library, Grainger Hall, Rm 1320, 975 University Ave, Madison, WI, 53706. Tel: 608-890-1901. p. 2451
Smith, Philip Alan, Dir, Florence County Library System, 509 S Dargan St, Florence, SC, 29506. Tel: 843-662-8424. p. 2058
Smith, Rachel, Br Mgr, Fort Smith Public Library, Windsor Drive, 4701 Windsor Dr, Fort Smith, AR, 72904. Tel: 479-785-0405. p. 96
Smith, Rachel, Br Mgr, Louisville Free Public Library, Northeast Regional, 15 Bellevoir Circle, Louisville, KY, 40223. Tel: 502-394-0379. p. 866
Smith, Rachel, Dir, Discovery & Access, Mount Holyoke College Library, 50 College St, South Hadley, MA, 01075. Tel: 413-538-2061. p. 1054
Smith, Raeanne, Libr Dir, Genesee Library, 8351 State Rte 417, Little Genesee, NY, 14754. Tel: 585-928-1915. p. 1563
Smith, Raeanne, Libr Dir, Scio Memorial Library, 3980 NY-19, Scio, NY, 14880. Tel: 585-593-4816. p. 1639
Smith, Rana, Libr Mgr, New York Public Library - Astor, Lenox & Tilden Foundations, Woodlawn Heights Branch, 4355 Katonah Ave, (@ E 239th St), Bronx, NY, 10470. Tel: 718-519-9627. p. 1598
Smith, Randy, Presv Mgr, Hampton University, 129 William R Harvey Way, Hampton, VA, 23668. Tel: 757-727-5553. p. 2323
Smith, Rashond, Ref (Info Servs), East Orange Public Library, 21 S Arlington Ave, East Orange, NJ, 07018. Tel: 973-266-5600. p. 1400
Smith, Rebecca, Dir, Historic New Orleans Collection, 410 Chartres St, New Orleans, LA, 70130. Tel: 504-598-7167. p. 901
Smith, Rebecca, Br Mgr, Rockingham County Public Library, Eden Branch, 598 S Pierce St, Eden, NC, 27288. Tel: 336-623-3168. p. 1686
Smith, Rebecca, Ref (Info Servs), Rockingham County Public Library, 527 Boone Rd, Eden, NC, 27288. Tel: 336-623-3168. p. 1686
Smith, Rebekah, Admin Librn, Ad, Balsam Lake Public Library, 404 Main St, Balsam Lake, WI, 54810. Tel: 715-485-3215. p. 2422
Smith, Renee, Media/Instruction Librn, Glendale Community College - Main, 6000 W Olive Ave, Glendale, AZ, 85302. Tel: 623-845-3110. p. 61
Smith, Rhonda B, Circ Mgr, Waynesboro Public Library, 600 S Wayne Ave, Waynesboro, VA, 22980. Tel: 540-942-6746. p. 2352
Smith, Rita Hunt, Children & Teen Librn, Hershey Public Library, 701 Cocoa Ave, Hershey, PA, 17033. Tel: 717-533-6555. p. 1943
Smith, Robin, Membership Serv(s) Mgr, Highland Park Public Library, 494 Laurel Ave, Highland Park, IL, 60035-2690. Tel: 847-432-0216. p. 599
Smith, Rochelle, Humanities Librn, University of Idaho Library, 850 S Rayburn St, Moscow, ID, 83844. Tel: 208-885-7850. p. 526
Smith, Roger, Assoc Univ Librn, Scholarly Resources & Serv, University of California, San Diego, 9500 Gilman Dr, Mail Code 0175G, La Jolla, CA, 92093-0175. Tel: 858-534-1235. p. 154
Smith, Ronnie, Dir, Eufaula Carnegie Library, 217 N Eufaula Ave, Eufaula, AL, 36027. Tel: 334-687-2337. p. 15
Smith, Samantha, Dir, Libr Serv, Lamar State College Orange Library, 410 Front St, Orange, TX, 77630-5796. Tel: 409-882-3083. p. 2224
Smith, Sandra, Br Mgr, Ouachita Parish Public Library, Sterlington Memorial Branch, 305 Keystone Rd, Monroe, LA, 71203. Tel: 318-327-1382. p. 898
Smith, Sandra, Archives, Wilson County Public Libraries, Wilson County Historical Commission Archives, 1144 C St, Floresville, TX, 78114. p. 2177
Smith, Sandra, Dir, Libr Serv, New River Community College, 226 Martin Hall, 5255 College Dr, Dublin, VA, 24084. Tel: 540-674-3600, Ext 4345. p. 2315
Smith, Sara, Br Mgr, Pine Forest Regional Library System - Headquarters, Leakesville Public Library, 301 Lafayette Ave, Leakesville, MS, 39451. Tel: 601-394-2897. p. 1232
Smith, Sarah, Sr Ref & Instruction Librn, Suffolk University, 73 Tremont St, 2nd Flr, Boston, MA, 02108. Tel: 617-573-8535. p. 1000
Smith, Sarah, Asst Dir, Camargo Township District Library, 14 N Main St, Villa Grove, IL, 61956. Tel: 217-832-5211. p. 658
Smith, Sarah, Mgr, Baltimore County Public Library, Randallstown Branch, 8604 Liberty Rd, Randallstown, MD, 21133-4797. Tel: 410-887-0770. p. 980
Smith, Sarah, District Dean of Libraries, Saint Louis Community College, Instructional Resources, 11333 Big Bend Rd, Saint Louis, MO, 63122. Tel: 314-984-7615. p. 1273
Smith, Scott, Mgr, Western Michigan University, Zhang Legacy Collections Center, 1650 Oakland Dr, Kalamazoo, MI, 49008. Tel: 269-387-8496. p. 1122
Smith, Scott, Head, Acq & Coll Develop, Stevens Institute of Technology, One Castle Point Terrace, Hoboken, NJ, 07030. Tel: 201-216-5419. p. 1408
Smith, Sean, Head, Borrower Serv, Chelmsford Public Library, 25 Boston Rd, Chelmsford, MA, 01824. Tel: 978-256-5521. p. 1010
Smith, Shanna, Libr Dir, Mulvane Public Library, 408 N Second Ave, Mulvane, KS, 67110. Tel: 316-777-1211. p. 826
Smith, Shannon, Br Mgr, Fairfield County District Library, Northwest Branch, 2855 Helena Dr NW, Carroll, OH, 43112. Tel: 740-756-4391. p. 1794
Smith, Sharaya, Circ Mgr, Sacred Heart University, 5151 Park Ave, Fairfield, CT, 06825-1000. Tel: 203-371-7703. p. 312
Smith, Sharon, Dir, Facilities, Indianapolis Public Library, 2450 N Meridian St, Indianapolis, IN, 46208. Tel: 317-275-4301. p. 694
Smith, Shawn, Educ Mgr, Wyoming Department of Corrections, 40 Honor Farm Rd, Riverton, WY, 82501-8400. Tel: 307-856-9578. p. 2498

Smith, Sheila, Bus Mgr, Liverpool Public Library, 310 Tulip St, Liverpool, NY, 13088-4997. Tel: 315-457-0310. p. 1564
Smith, Sherri, Webmaster, La Grange Association Library, 1110 Route 55, 2nd Flr, LaGrangeville, NY, 12540. Tel: 845-452-3141. p. 1561
Smith, Shirley, Mat Mgr, Supvr, Licking County Library, 101 W Main St, Newark, OH, 43055-5054. Tel: 740-349-5530. p. 1807
Smith, Sisi, Library Contact, Federal Correctional Institution Library, 501 Capital Circle NE, Tallahassee, FL, 32301. Tel: 850-878-2173. p. 445
Smith, Sorcha, Youth Serv Coordr, Boyertown Community Library, 24 N Reading Ave, Boyertown, PA, 19512. Tel: 610-369-0496. p. 1914
Smith, Spencer, Dir of Libr, McKinney Memorial Public Library, 101 E Hunt St, McKinney, TX, 75069. Tel: 972-547-7323. p. 2217
Smith, Stacey J, Dir, Libr & Info Serv, LeMoyne-Owen College, 807 Walker Ave, Memphis, TN, 38126. Tel: 901-435-1351. p. 2112
Smith, Stephanie, Law Librn, Mercer County Law Library, Mercer County Courthouse, 125 S Diamond St, Ste 305, Mercer, PA, 16137. Tel: 724-662-3800, Ext 2302. p. 1962
Smith, Stephanie, Archives, Exec Dir, Nova Scotia Museum Library, 1747 Summer St, 3rd Flr, Halifax, NS, B3H 3A6, CANADA. Tel: 902-424-7344. p. 2621
Smith, Stephanny, Commun Engagement Mgr, Allen County Public Library, 900 Library Plaza, Fort Wayne, IN, 46802. Tel: 260-421-1265. p. 683
Smith, Stephen, Reserves, University of Tennessee Southern, 433 W Madison St, Pulaski, TN, 38478-2799. Tel: 931-363-9844. p. 2124
Smith, Steve, Admin Librn, Dearborn Public Library, 16301 Michigan Ave, Dearborn, MI, 48126. Tel: 313-943-2812. p. 1095
Smith, Steve, Dir, Res Serv, Historical Society of Pennsylvania, 1300 Locust St, Philadelphia, PA, 19107-5699. Tel: 215-732-6200, Ext 238. p. 1981
Smith, Steven, Dean of Libr, University of Tennessee, Knoxville, 1015 Volunteer Blvd, Knoxville, TN, 37996-1000. Tel: 865-974-4351. p. 2107
Smith, Steven A, Tech Serv Librn, Limestone University Library, 1115 College Dr, Gaffney, SC, 29340. Tel: 864-488-4611. p. 2060
Smith Stewart, Donetta, Dir, Auburn Public Library, 209 Pine St, Auburn, IA, 51433. Tel: 712-688-2264. p. 733
Smith, Sue, Academic Liaison, University of Kentucky Libraries, Science & Engineering Library, 211 King Bldg, 179 Funkhouser Dr, Lexington, KY, 40506-0039. Tel: 859-257-0121. p. 864
Smith, Susan, Ch, Beaman Memorial Public Library, Eight Newton St, West Boylston, MA, 01583. Tel: 508-835-3711. p. 1065
Smith, Susan, Ref/ILL, Sumter County Library, 111 N Harvin St, Sumter, SC, 29150. Tel: 803-773-7273. p. 2071
Smith, Susan, Br Mgr, Lunenburg County Public Library System Inc, Victoria Public, 1417 Seventh St, Victoria, VA, 23974. Tel: 434-696-3416. p. 2327
Smith, Susanna, Instrul Designer, Library & Information Science, Georgia Highlands College Libraries, 3175 Cedartown Hwy SE, Rome, GA, 30161. Tel: 706-295-6318. p. 494
Smith, Tamela M, Dir, Belington Public Library, 88 Elliott Ave, Belington, WV, 26250. Tel: 304-823-1026. p. 2398
Smith, Tammy, Br Mgr, Jackson/Hinds Library System, Richard Wright Library, 515 W McDowell Rd, Jackson, MS, 39204-5547. Tel: 601-372-1621. p. 1222
Smith, Tammy, Principal Library Clerk, North Tonawanda Public Library, 505 Meadow Dr, North Tonawanda, NY, 14120. Tel: 716-693-4132. p. 1608
Smith, Tanja, Dir, Marble Public Library, 302 Alice Ave, Marble, MN, 55764. Tel: 218-247-7676. p. 1182
Smith, Tariana, Ref Librn, Southern University in New Orleans, 6400 Press Dr, New Orleans, LA, 70126. Tel: 504-286-5225. p. 903
Smith, Ted J, Libr Dir, Newport Public Library, 35 NW Nye St, Newport, OR, 97365-3714. Tel: 541-265-2153. p. 1888
Smith, Teri, Dir, Libr Serv, Redwood Falls Public Library, 509 S Lincoln St, Redwood Falls, MN, 56283. Tel: 507-616-7420. p. 1194
Smith, Terri, Res & Instruction Librn, Taft College Library, 29 Cougar Ct, Taft, CA, 93268. Tel: 661-763-7707. p. 251
Smith, Theresa, Access Serv Librn, Dir, Shepherd University, 301 N King St, Shepherdstown, WV, 25443. p. 2414
Smith, Thomas W, PhD, Dean, Catholic University of America, 620 Michigan Ave NE, Washington, DC, 20064. Tel: 202-319-5085. p. 2783
Smith, Tienya, Commun Libr Mgr, Queens Library, Long Island City Community Library, 37-44 21 St, Long Island City, NY, 11101. Tel: 718-752-3700. p. 1555
Smith, Tienya, Dir of Engagement, Outreach & Partnerships, The New York Society Library, 53 E 79th St, New York, NY, 10075. Tel: 212-288-6900, Ext 243. p. 1598
Smith, Tiffany, Librn, Calvary University, 15800 Calvary Rd, Kansas City, MO, 67417. Tel: 816-425-6210. p. 1254
Smith, Traci, Asst Dir, Carbondale City Library, 302 Main St, Carbondale, KS, 66414-9635. Tel: 785-836-7638. p. 800
Smith, Tracy D, Libr Dir, Arkansas State University, 1000 W Iowa St, Beebe, AR, 72012. Tel: 501-882-8806. p. 90
Smith, Tracy H, Dir of Libr, Pearl River Community College, 101 Hwy 11 N, Poplarville, MS, 39470. p. 1230
Smith, Travis, Head, General Services, University of Richmond, 261 Richmond Way, Richmond, VA, 23173. Tel: 804-289-8672. p. 2342
Smith, Trent, Libr Dir, Garden City Community College, 801 Campus Dr, Garden City, KS, 67846. Tel: 620-276-9510. p. 809
Smith, Trevor, Chair, Mesa Community College Library, 1833 W Southern Ave, Mesa, AZ, 85202. Tel: 480-461-7631. p. 66
Smith, Trevor, Syst Adminr, Harrison County Public Library, 105 N Capitol Ave, Corydon, IN, 47112. Tel: 812-738-4110. p. 677
Smith, Tricia, Librn III, Saint Petersburg Public Library, James Weldon Johnson Branch, 1059 18th Ave S, Saint Petersburg, FL, 33705. Tel: 727-893-7113. p. 441
Smith, Tricia, Librn III, Saint Petersburg Public Library, South, 2300 Roy Hanna Dr S, Saint Petersburg, FL, 33712. Tel: 727-893-7244. p. 442
Smith, Trina, Ch, Saint John the Baptist Parish Library, 2920 New Hwy 51, LaPlace, LA, 70068. Tel: 985-652-6857. p. 894
Smith, Trisha, Univ Librn, Trinity University, 125 Michigan Ave NE, Washington, DC, 20017. Tel: 202-884-9351. p. 377
Smith, Trisha, Dir, Germantown Community Library, N112W16957 Mequon Rd, Germantown, WI, 53022. Tel: 262-253-7760. p. 2437
Smith, Trista, Dir, Newburgh Chandler Public Library, 4111 Lakeshore Dr, Newburgh, IN, 47630-2274. Tel: 812-942-9997. p. 709
Smith, Trudy, Librn, Faulkner-Van Buren Regional Library System, Twin Groves Branch, Ten Twin Groves Lane, Twin Groves, AR, 72039. Tel: 501-335-8088. p. 92
Smith, Vanessa, Health Info Coordr, Meharry Medical College Library, 2001 Albion St, Nashville, TN, 37208. Tel: 615-327-6463. p. 2119
Smith, Veronica, Tech Coordr, Westminster Public Library, 3705 W 112th Ave, Westminster, CO, 80031. Tel: 303-658-2645. p. 298
Smith, Ward, Syst Librn, Orange Coast College Library, 2701 Fairview Rd, Costa Mesa, CA, 92626. Tel: 714-432-5885. p. 132
Smith, Warren, Ref Librn, Walpole Public Library, 143 School St, Walpole, MA, 02081. Tel: 508-660-7341. p. 1061
Smith, William, Asst Dir, Syst Adminr, Desoto Parish Library, 109 Crosby St, Mansfield, LA, 71052. Tel: 318-872-6100. p. 895
Smith, William L, Librn, Wilmington University Library, 320 N DuPont Hwy, New Castle, DE, 19720. Tel: 302-356-6878. p. 355
Smith-Borne, Holling, Dir, Vanderbilt University, Anne Potter Wilson Music Library, Blair School of Music, 2400 Blakemore Ave, Nashville, TN, 37212. Tel: 615-322-5227. p. 2122
Smith-Brown, Stacey, Librn, Roosevelt Public Library, 27 W Fulton Ave, Roosevelt, NY, 11575. Tel: 516-378-0222. p. 1633
Smith-Duhaney, Tricia, Circ Serv, Uniondale Public Library, 400 Uniondale Ave, Uniondale, NY, 11553. Tel: 516-489-2220, Ext 235. p. 1654
Smith-Ennis, Theresa, Libr Supvr, State College of Florida Manatee-Sarasota Library, Venice Campus Dr Bill Jervey Jr Library, 8000 S Tamiami Trail, Venice, FL, 34293. Tel: 941-408-1434. p. 387
Smith-Farrell, Melanie F, Asst Dean, Public Services & Facilities, University of Akron, University Libraries, 315 Buchtel Mall, Akron, OH, 44325-1701. Tel: 330-972-7047. p. 1745
Smith-Roselle, Donna, Libr Tech, Royal Victoria Regional Health Centre, 201 Georgian Dr, Barrie, ON, L4M 6M2, CANADA. Tel: 705-728-9090, Ext 42630. p. 2630
Smith-Vaughan, Brigitte, Br Mgr, Wharton County Library, El Campo Branch, 200 W Church St, El Campo, TX, 77437. Tel: 979-543-2362. p. 2256
Smither, Doriene, Br Mgr, Indianapolis Public Library, East Washington, 2822 E Washington St, Indianapolis, IN, 46201-4215. Tel: 317-275-4365. p. 695
Smithers, Karen, Librn, Knoedler Memorial Library, 315 Main St, Augusta, KY, 41002. Tel: 606-756-3911. p. 848
Smithey, Richard, Circ, Warren County Memorial Library, 119 South Front St, Warrenton, NC, 27589. Tel: 252-257-4990, Ext 201. p. 1720
Smithglass, Margaret, Digital Content Librn, Registrar, Columbia University, Avery Architectural & Fine Arts Library, 300 Avery Hall, 1172 Amsterdam Ave, MC 0301, New York, NY, 10027. Tel: 212-854-6199. p. 1583
Smithson, Suzanne, Dir, Libr & Cultural Serv, Carlsbad City Library, 1775 Dove Lane, Carlsbad, CA, 92011. Tel: 760-602-2049. p. 127
Smithson, Suzanne, Dep Libr Dir, Carlsbad City Library, Georgina Cole Library, 1250 Carlsbad Village Dr, Carlsbad, CA, 92008. Tel: 760-434-2876. p. 128
Smits, Brandi, Youth Serv Mgr, Orland Park Public Library, 14921 Ravinia Ave, Orland Park, IL, 60462. Tel: 708-428-5135. p. 630
Smits, Christine, Asst Librn, Bellin College, 3201 Eaton Rd, Green Bay, WI, 54311. Tel: 920-433-6659. p. 2438
Smitz, Danijela, Support Serv Mgr, Community Library, 24615 89th St, Salem, WI, 53168. Tel: 262-843-3348. p. 2475
Smitz, Danijela, Support Serv Mgr, Community Library, Twin Lakes Branch, 110 S Lake Ave, Twin Lakes, WI, 53181. Tel: 262-877-4281. p. 2475
Smock, Jason, Law Librn, Minnesota Attorney General Library, Bremer Tower, Ste 1050, 445 Minnesota St, Saint Paul, MN, 55101-2109. Tel: 651-757-1055. p. 1200
Smock, Jason, Consortium Contact, Capital Area Library Consortium, c/o Attorney General Library, Bremer Tower, Ste 1050, 445 Minnesota St, Saint Paul, MN, 55101-2109. Tel: 651-757-1055. p. 2768

Smodic, Monica, Dir, Delmont Public Library, 75 School St, Delmont, PA, 15626. Tel: 724-468-5329. p. 1926
Smolarek, Dennis, Ref Librn, Lake County Library System, Cooper Memorial Library, 2525 Oakley Seaver Dr, Clermont, FL, 34711. Tel: 352-536-2275. p. 451
Smolinsky, Susan, Libr Dir, Peacham Library, 656 Bayley Hazen Rd, Peacham, VT, 05862. Tel: 802-592-3216. p. 2291
Smolzer, Jo, Head, Collections Mgmt, Huntley Area Public Library District, 11000 Ruth Rd, Huntley, IL, 60142-7155. Tel: 847-669-5386. p. 601
Smook, Dana, Dir, Essex Public Library, 117 N Church Lane, Tappahannock, VA, 22560. Tel: 804-443-4945. p. 2348
Smoot, Carmin I, Mgr, Digital Production Ctr, University of Utah, Spencer S Eccles Health Sciences Library, Bldg 589, 10 N 1900 E, Salt Lake City, UT, 84112-5890. Tel: 801-581-8771. p. 2272
Smothers, Diann, Dir, Marion County Library System, 101 East Court St, Marion, SC, 29571. Tel: 843-423-8300. p. 2065
Smothers, Stephanie, Adult Programming, Librn, Marion County Public Library, 201 E Main St, Lebanon, KY, 40033-1133. Tel: 270-692-4698. p. 861
Smoyak, Rachael, Br Supvr, Lake County Library System, Cagan Crossings Community Library, 16729 Cagan Oaks, Clermont, FL, 34714. Tel: 352-243-1840. p. 450
Smyk, Laura, Coll Serv, Canadian Museum of Nature Library & Archives, 1740 Pink Rd, Gatineau, QC, J9J 3N7, CANADA. Tel: 613-364-4046. p. 2712
Smyrl, Rebecca, Conservator, Spec Coll, University of North Carolina at Chapel Hill, 208 Raleigh St, CB 3916, Chapel Hill, NC, 27515. Tel: 919-962-1053. p. 1678
Smyth, Charla, Br Librn, Southeast Regional Library, Kipling Branch, 207 Sixth Ave, Kipling, SK, S0G 2S0, CANADA. Tel: 306-736-2911. p. 2754
Snaith, Helen, Dir of Libr, West Virginia Junior College Library, 5514 Big Tyler Rd, Ste 200, Charleston, WV, 25313. Tel: 304-769-0011. p. 2400
Snapp, Dale, Mgr of Computing, University of California, Davis, 100 NW Quad, Davis, CA, 95616. Tel: 530-752-8792. p. 134
Snapp, Heather, First Year Experience & Outreach Librn, Florida Gulf Coast University Library, 10501 FGCU Blvd S, Fort Myers, FL, 33965. Tel: 239-745-4224. p. 403
Snarr, Alicia, Br Operations Adminr, Maricopa County Library District, 2700 N Central Ave, Ste 700, Phoenix, AZ, 85004. Tel: 602-652-3000. p. 70
Snavely, Sarah, Dir, Bowman Regional Public Library, 18 E Divide St, Bowman, ND, 58623. Tel: 701-523-3797. p. 1731
Snawder, Kristin, User Experience Librn, Northern Virginia Community College Libraries, Medical Education Campus, 6699 Springfield Center Dr, Rm 341, Springfield, VA, 22150. Tel: 703-822-6682. p. 2304
Snead, Fran, Dir, Bassett Historical Center, 3964 Fairystone Park Hwy, Bassett, VA, 24055. Tel: 276-629-9191. p. 2306
Snead, Ragan, Continuing Educ Coordr, Northeast Ohio Regional Library System, 1737 Georgetown Rd, Ste B, Hudson, OH, 44236. Tel: 330-655-0531, Ext 105. p. 2772
Sneathen, Pete, IT Mgr, Herrick District Library, 300 S River Ave, Holland, MI, 49423. Tel: 616-355-4948. p. 1115
Snedden Yates, Emily, Exhibitions Mgr, Folger Shakespeare Library, 201 E Capitol St SE, Washington, DC, 20003-1094. Tel: 202-675-8776. p. 366
Snee, Toni, Asst Dir, Scituate Town Library, 85 Branch St, Scituate, MA, 02066. Tel: 781-545-8727. p. 1052
Sneed, Thomas, Dir, Washburn University, School of Law Library, 1700 SW College Ave, Topeka, KS, 66621. Tel: 785-670-1658. p. 839
Sneig, Anne, Librn, Department of Veterans Affairs, VA Medical Ctr, 5000 W National Ave, Milwaukee, WI, 53295. Tel: 414-384-2000, Ext 42341. p. 2458
Snell, Cynthia, Libr Dir, Columbia International University, 7435 Monticello Rd, Columbia, SC, 29203-1599. Tel: 803-807-5107. p. 2053
Snell, Gina, Br Asst, Pictou - Antigonish Regional Library, Westville Library, 2042 Queen St, Unit 3, Westville, NS, B0K 2A0, CANADA. Tel: 902-396-5022. p. 2622
Snelling, Brad, Asst Prof, Coll Develop, Per Librn, The College of Saint Scholastica Library, 1200 Kenwood Ave, Duluth, MN, 55811-4199. Tel: 218-723-6644. p. 1171
Snelling, Charlene, Chair, Libr & Instruction Serv, Chicago State University, 9501 S Martin Luther King Jr Dr, LIB 440, Chicago, IL, 60628-1598. Tel: 773-995-2557. p. 558
Snelling, Lindsey, Generalist Librn, Rockwall County Library, 1215 E Yellowjacket Lane, Rockwall, TX, 75087. Tel: 972-204-7700. p. 2234
Snellman, Scott, Librn, Central Arizona College, Maricopa Campus Learning Resource Center, 17945 N Regent Dr, Maricopa, AZ, 85138. Tel: 520-494-6407. p. 59
Snider, Allen, Librn, Rainier City Library, 106 B St W, Rainier, OR, 97048. Tel: 503-556-7301, Ext 207. p. 1895
Snider, Chloe, Br Mgr, Collier County Public Library, Vanderbilt Beach, 788 Vanderbilt Beach Rd, Naples, FL, 34108. Tel: 239-597-8444. p. 427
Snider, Christina, Libr Supvr, University of Southern California Libraries, Hoose Library of Philosophy, Mudd Memorial Hall of Philos, 3709 Trousdale Pkwy, Los Angeles, CA, 90089-0182. Tel: 213-821-4443. p. 170
Snider, Karen, Br Mgr, Riverside County Library System, Mead Valley, 21580 Oakwood St, Mead Valley, CA, 92570. Tel: 951-943-4727. p. 202
Snider, Linda L, Libr Asst, University of Wisconsin-Eau Claire, 1800 College Dr, Rice Lake, WI, 54868-2497. Tel: 715-788-6250. p. 2473
Snider, Nancy, Librn, Patoka Public Library, 210 W Bond St, Patoka, IL, 62875. Tel: 618-432-5019. p. 633
Snider, Sarah, Librn, Dunklin County Library, Malden Branch, 1203 Stokelan, Malden, MO, 63863. Tel: 573-276-3674. p. 1258
Sniderman, Erin, Outreach Librn, Hampton Falls Free Public Library, Seven Drinkwater Rd, Hampton Falls, NH, 03844. Tel: 603-926-3682. p. 1366
Snively, Karen, Libr Serv Mgr, James Madison University Libraries, Music Library, MSC 7301, Harrisonburg, VA, 22807. Tel: 540-568-3542. p. 2324
Snively, Sharon, Dir, Delphos Public Library, 114 W Second, Delphos, KS, 67436. Tel: 785-523-4668. p. 804
Snoblen, Patricia, Br Mgr, Jackson District Library, Meijer Branch, 2699 Airport Rd, Jackson, MI, 49202. Tel: 517-788-4480. p. 1120
Snodgrass, Renee, Dir, West Shore Community College, 3000 N Stiles Rd, Scottville, MI, 49454. Tel: 231-843-5529, 231-845-6211. p. 1150
Snoeberger, Mark, Dr, Dir, Libr Serv, Detroit Baptist Theological Seminary Library, 4801 Allen Rd, Allen Park, MI, 48101. Tel: 313-381-0111, Ext 412. p. 1077
Snoek-Brown, Jennifer, Librn, Tacoma Community College Library, Bldg 7, 6501 S 19th St, Tacoma, WA, 98466-6100. Tel: 253-460-3936. p. 2387
Snook, Carol, Br Mgr, Lawrence County Public Library, Loretto Branch, 102 S Main St, Loretto, TN, 38469-2110. Tel: 931-853-7323. p. 2108
Snook, Justin, Dir, Simon Fairfield Public Library, 290 Main St, East Douglas, MA, 01516. Tel: 508-476-2695. p. 1016
Snook, Myra, Library Contact, Sussex County Historical Society Library, 82 Main St, Newton, NJ, 07860-2046. Tel: 973-383-6010. p. 1429
Snow, Karen, Dir, PhD Prog, Dominican University, Crown Library 300, 7900 W Division St, River Forest, IL, 60305. Tel: 708-524-6845. p. 2784
Snow, Maggie, Dir, Minitex, University of Minnesota, Wilson Library, Rm 60, 309 19th Ave S, Minneapolis, MN, 55455. Tel: 612-624-4002. p. 2768
Snow, Randy, Pres, New England Wireless & Steam Museum Inc Library, 1300 Frenchtown Rd, East Greenwich, RI, 02818. Tel: 401-885-0545. p. 2032
Snow, Renae, Librn, Maine Department of Corrections, 17 Mallison Falls Rd, Windham, ME, 04062. Tel: 207-893-7000. p. 946
Snow, Sarah, Dir, Ainsworth Public Library, 2338 VT Rte 14, Williamstown, VT, 05679. Tel: 802-433-5887. p. 2299
Snow, Shannon, Dr, Co-Dir, Cedar County Library District, 717 East St, Stockton, MO, 65785. Tel: 417-276-3413. p. 1282
Snow, Timothy M, Ref Librn, University of Rio Grande, 218 N College Ave, Rio Grande, OH, 45674. Tel: 740-245-7005. p. 1817
Snow-Croft, Sheila, Dir, Network of Alabama Academic Libraries, c/o Alabama Commission on Higher Education, 100 N Union St, Montgomery, AL, 36104. Tel: 334-242-2211. p. 2761
Snowden, Audrey, Children's & YA Librn, Medway Public Library, 26 High St, Medway, MA, 02053. Tel: 508-533-3217. p. 1034
Snowman, Ann, Head, Access Serv, Head, User Serv, Pennsylvania State University Libraries, 510 Paterno Library, University Park, PA, 16802. Tel: 814-863-1362. p. 2015
Snyder, Amber, Dir, Everett Free Library, 137 E Main St, Everett, PA, 15537-1259. Tel: 814-652-5922. p. 1932
Snyder, Amy, Educ Librn, Pennsylvania College of Health Sciences, 850 Greenfield Rd, Lancaster, PA, 17601. Tel: 717-947-6215. p. 1952
Snyder, Angie, Dir, Monroe County Public Library, 121 Pineville Rd, Monroeville, AL, 36460. Tel: 251-743-3818. p. 27
Snyder, Anna, Head, Ref Serv, Wayne County Public Library, 1001 E Ash St, Goldsboro, NC, 27530. Tel: 919-735-1824, Ext 5106. p. 1691
Snyder, Betty, Librn, Library District Number One, Doniphan County, Highland Branch, 306 W Main, Highland, KS, 66035. Tel: 785-442-3078. p. 840
Snyder, Chris, Librn, Snyder County Libraries, Middleburg Community Library, 13 N Main St, Middleburg, PA, 17842. Tel: 570-837-5931. p. 2005
Snyder, Christine, Br Mgr, Pamunkey Regional Library, Cochrane Rockville Branch, 16600 Pouncey Tract Rd, Rockville, VA, 23146. Tel: 804-749-3146. p. 2323
Snyder, Colleen, Fiscal Officer, Mentor Public Library, 8215 Mentor Ave, Mentor, OH, 44060. Tel: 440-255-8811. p. 1802
Snyder, Connie, Youth Serv Mgr, Bellevue Public Library, 224 E Main St, Bellevue, OH, 44811-1467. Tel: 419-483-4769. p. 1750
Snyder, Crystal, Asst Dir, Commun Engagement Librn, Columbia Public Library, 106 N Metter Ave, Columbia, IL, 62236-2299. Tel: 618-281-4237. p. 573
Snyder, Gretchen, Dir, Rye Historical Society, 265 Rye Beach Ave, Rye, NY, 10580. Tel: 914-967-7588. p. 1634
Snyder, Ian, Libr Dir, Clarion Free Library, 644 Main St, Clarion, PA, 16214. Tel: 814-226-7172. p. 1922
Snyder, Jane, Librn, Underberg & Kessler Law Library, 300 Bausch & Lomb Pl, Rochester, NY, 14604. Tel: 585-258-2800. p. 1631

Snyder, Jennifer, Dir, Pleasant Mount Public Library, 375 Great Bend Tpk, Pleasant Mount, PA, 18453-4580. Tel: 570-448-2573. p. 1998

Snyder, Jill, Asst Librn, Arapahoe Public Library, 306 Nebraska Ave, Arapahoe, NE, 68922. Tel: 308-962-7806. p. 1305

Snyder, Julee, Law Librn, Charles County Circuit Court, 200 Charles St, La Plata, MD, 20646-9602. Tel: 301-932-3322. p. 969

Snyder, Laine, Dir, Zanesville Museum of Art, 620 Military Rd, Zanesville, OH, 43701. Tel: 740-452-0741. p. 1837

Snyder, Natalie, Dir, Neuschafer Community Library, 317 Wolf River Dr, Fremont, WI, 54940. Tel: 920-446-2474. p. 2436

Snyder, Patti, Libr Asst, Highgate Library & Community Center, 17 Mill Hill Rd, Highgate Center, VT, 05459. Tel: 802-868-3970. p. 2286

Snyder, Rebecca, Dir, Res, Dakota County Historical Society, 130 Third Ave N, South Saint Paul, MN, 55075. Tel: 651-552-7548. p. 1204

Snyder, Robert, Chair, Libr Teaching & Learning, Bowling Green State University Libraries, 1001 E Wooster St, Bowling Green, OH, 43403-0170. p. 1752

Snyder, Sally, Children's Coordr, Young Adult Serv Coordr, Nebraska Library Commission, The Atrium, 1200 N St, Ste 120, Lincoln, NE, 68508-2023. Tel: 402-471-4003. p. 1322

Snyder, Samantha, Libr Dir, Free Public Library of Monroe Township, 713 Marsha Ave, Williamstown, NJ, 08094. Tel: 856-629-1212, Ext 200. p. 1455

Snyder, Sandra, Br Mgr, Campbell County Public Library System, Wright Branch, 305 Wright Blvd, Wright, WY, 82732. Tel: 307-464-0500. p. 2494

Snyder, Sarah, Ad, Jacksonville Public Library, 201 W College Ave, Jacksonville, IL, 62650-2497. Tel: 217-243-5435. p. 602

Snyder, Stori, Dir, Brown County Public Library, 205 Locust Lane, Nashville, IN, 47448. Tel: 812-988-2850. p. 709

Snyder, Terry, Librn of the Col, Haverford College, 370 Lancaster Ave, Haverford, PA, 19041-1392. Tel: 610-896-1272. p. 1942

Snyder, Tina, Dir, Hancock County Public Library, 1210 Madison St, Hawesville, KY, 42348. Tel: 270-927-6760. p. 858

Snyder, Tony, Copyright & Interlibrary Loan Associate, Kent State University Libraries, Risman Plaza, 1125 Risman Dr, Kent, OH, 44242. Tel: 330-672-1634. p. 1792

Snyder, Tracey, Instruction Librn, Music Cat Librn, Cornell University Library, Sidney Cox Library of Music & Dance, 220 Lincoln Hall, Ithaca, NY, 14853. Tel: 607-255-6160. p. 1551

Snyder, Tressa A, Libr Dir, Thiel College, 75 College Ave, Greenville, PA, 16125-2183. Tel: 724-589-2119. p. 1939

Snyder-Morse, Stacy, Dir, Orleans Public Library, 36263 SR 180, La Fargeville, NY, 13656. Tel: 315-658-2271. p. 1560

Snyders, Christy, Circ Mgr, Roselle Public Library District, 40 S Park St, Roselle, IL, 60172-2020. Tel: 630-529-1641, Ext 241. p. 643

Soares, Danny, Head of Doc Delivery, San Jose State University, One Washington Sq, San Jose, CA, 95192-0028. Tel: 408-808-2078. p. 232

Soares, Zach, AV Tech Spec, College of the Atlantic, 105 Eden St, Bar Harbor, ME, 04609-1198. Tel: 207-801-5663. p. 916

Sobba, Andrea, Dir, Garnett Public Library, 125 W Fourth St, Garnett, KS, 66032-1350. Tel: 785-448-3388. p. 809

Sobczak, Elizabeth, Libr Supvr, Essentia Institute of Rural Health, Essentia Health St Mary's Medical Center, 407 E Third St, Duluth, MN, 55805-1984. Tel: 218-786-4145. p. 1172

Sobczyk, Connie, Br Mgr, Latah County Library District, Genesee Branch, 140 E Walnut St, Genesee, ID, 83832. Tel: 208-285-1398. p. 526

Sobocinski, Scott, Dir, Wabasso Public Library, 1248 Oak St, Wabasso, MN, 56293. Tel: 507-342-5279. p. 1206

Soborowski, Sheryl, Head, Circ, Outreach Serv, Olean Public Library, 134 N Second St, Olean, NY, 14760. Tel: 716-372-0200. p. 1611

Sobotka, Clare, Dir, Libr & Learning Res, Tillamook Bay Community College Library, 4301 Third St, Tillamook, OR, 97141. Tel: 503-842-8222, Ext 1710. p. 1900

Socha, Kelsey, Youth Serv, Ventress Memorial Library, 15 Library Plaza, Marshfield, MA, 02050. Tel: 781-834-5535. p. 1032

Socha, Lisa, Ch Serv Librn, Helen Hall Library, 100 W Walker, League City, TX, 77573-3899. Tel: 281-554-1112. p. 2210

Sochacka, E Tamara, Dir, Hamtramck Public Library, 2360 Caniff St, Hamtramck, MI, 48212. Tel: 313-733-6822. p. 1113

Soden, Martina, Head, Ref Serv, Scranton Public Library, 500 Vine St, Scranton, PA, 18509-3298. Tel: 570-348-3000, Ext 3051. p. 2004

Soder, Jessie, Admin Dir, Gustavus Public Library, PO Box 279, Gustavus, AK, 99826-0279. Tel: 907-697-2350. p. 46

Soderlund, Tyler, Dir, Cattaraugus Free Library, 21 Main St, Cattaraugus, NY, 14719. Tel: 716-257-9500. p. 1515

Sodha, Komal, Ref Asst, Belmont Abbey College, 100 Belmont-Mt Holly Rd, Belmont, NC, 28012. Tel: 704-461-6748. p. 1674

Sodoski, Marianne, Instruction & Ref Librn, King's College, 14 W Jackson St, Wilkes-Barre, PA, 18711. Tel: 570-208-5840. p. 2022

Sodt, Jill, Dir, Libr Serv, Mott Community College, 1401 E Court St, Flint, MI, 48503. Tel: 810-762-0400, 810-762-0401. p. 1107

Soehl, Kathy, Asst Dir, Ch, Dickinson Public Library, 4411 Hwy 3, Dickinson, TX, 77539. Tel: 281-534-3812. p. 2171

Soehner, Catherine, Assoc Dean, Res & Learning Serv, University of Utah, J Willard Marriott Library, 295 S 1500 East, Salt Lake City, UT, 84112-0860. Tel: 801-581-8558. p. 2272

Soehner, Catherine, Dir, University of Utah, Spencer S Eccles Health Sciences Library, Bldg 589, 10 N 1900 E, Salt Lake City, UT, 84112-5890. Tel: 801-581-8771. p. 2272

Soehner, Catherine, Exec Dir, National Network of Libraries of Medicine Region 4, Univ Utah, Spencer S Eccles Health Sci Libr, Bldg 589, 10 North 1900 East, Salt Lake City, UT, 84112-5890. Tel: 801-587-3412. p. 2776

Soehner, Kenneth, Chief Librn, Metropolitan Museum of Art, Thomas J Watson Library, 1000 Fifth Ave, New York, NY, 10028-0198. Tel: 212-570-3934. p. 1592

Soelberg, Debbie, Adult Programming, Outreach Coordr, Bulverde-Spring Branch Library, 131 Bulverde Crossing, Bulverde, TX, 78163. Tel: 830-438-4864. p. 2151

Soencer, Mary Ellen, Dean, Libr Serv, Pellissippi State Community College, Hardin Valley Library, 10915 Harding Valley Rd, Knoxville, TN, 37933. Tel: 865-694-6517. p. 2106

Soergel, Dagobert, Dr, Prof, University at Buffalo, The State University of New York, 534 Baldy Hall, Buffalo, NY, 14260. Tel: 716-645-2412. p. 2789

Sofge, Robin, Br Mgr, Prince William Public Libraries, Potomac Library, 2201 Opitz Blvd, Woodbridge, VA, 22191. Tel: 703-792-8330. p. 2339

Softa, Amy, Libr Dir, Curtis Memorial Library, 116 S Main, Wheatland, IA, 52777. Tel: 563-374-1534. p. 791

Sogigian, Sara, Exec Dir, Massachusetts Library System, 225 Cedar Hill St, Ste 229, Marlborough, MA, 01752. Tel: 508-357-2121. p. 1032

Sogoian, Mariam, Acq Librn, Pittsburgh Theological Seminary, 616 N Highland Ave, Pittsburgh, PA, 15206. Tel: 412-924-1361. p. 1995

Sohigian, Jason, Exec Dir, Armenian Museum of America, Inc, Mugar Bldg, 4th Flr, 65 Main St, Watertown, MA, 02472. Tel: 617-926-2562, Ext 111. p. 1062

Sohl, Morgan, Libr Mgr, Timberland Regional Library, Olympia Branch, 313 Eighth Ave SE, Olympia, WA, 98501-1307. Tel: 360-352-0595. p. 2389

Soileau, Debra, Br Mgr, Pointe Coupee Parish Library, Julian Poydras Branch, 4985 Poydras Lane, Rougon, LA, 70773. Tel: 225-627-5846. p. 905

Sojka, Kristina, Circ Mgr, Friends University, 2100 W University Ave, Wichita, KS, 67213-3397. Tel: 316-295-5880. p. 842

Sokol, Chris, Dir, Latah County Library District, 110 S Jefferson St, Moscow, ID, 83843-2833. Tel: 208-882-3925. p. 526

Sokol, Veronika, Asst Librn, Fitzwilliam Town Library, 11 Templeton Tpk, Fitzwilliam, NH, 03447. Tel: 603-585-6503. p. 1363

Sokoll, Susan, Law Librn, Department of Veterans Affairs, Office of the General Counsel Law Library, 810 Vermont Ave NW, Washington, DC, 20420. Tel: 202-273-6558. p. 363

Sokolnicki, Marcia, Asst Dir, E C Scranton Memorial Library, 1250 Durham Rd, Ste F, Madison, CT, 06443. Tel: 203-245-7365. p. 320

Sola-Fernandez, Sylvia, Chief Librn, University of Puerto Rico Library System, Reference Collection, Rio Piedras Campus, Jose M Lazaro Bldg, 1st Flr, San Juan, PR, 00931. Tel: 787-764-0000, Ext 85750, 787-764-0000, Ext 85757, 787-764-0000, Ext 85764. p. 2515

Solaita-Malele, Emma, Territorial Librn, Feleti Barstow Public Library, PO Box 997687, Pago Pago, AS, 96799. Tel: 684-633-5816. p. 2503

Solar, Vivian, Cat Librn, Ascension Parish Library, 500 Mississippi St, Donaldsonville, LA, 70346. Tel: 225-473-8052. p. 889

Solares, Gina, Digital Coll Librn, University of San Francisco, 2130 Fulton St, San Francisco, CA, 94117-1080. Tel: 415-422-5361. p. 229

Solberg, Bonnie, Coordr, Br Serv, Hartford Public Library, Ropkins Branch, 1750 Main St, Hartford, CT, 06120. Tel: 860-695-7520. p. 318

Solberg, Judy, Dir, Instrul & Pub Serv, Seattle University, A A Lemieux Library, 901 12th Ave, Seattle, WA, 98122-4411. Tel: 206-296-6274. p. 2380

Soldat, Nicole, Coordr, Silver Cross Hospital Medical Library, 1900 Silver Cross Blvd, New Lenox, IL, 60451-9509. Tel: 815-300-7491. p. 624

Solecki, Amy, Commun Outreach Coordr, Meaford Public Library, 11 Sykes St N, Meaford, ON, N4L 1V6, CANADA. Tel: 519-538-3500. p. 2657

Solek, VivianLea, Archivist, Knights of Columbus Supreme Council Archives, One State St, New Haven, CT, 06511-6702. Tel: 203-752-4578. p. 325

Solensky, Jeanne, Librn, Historic Deerfield Inc & Pocumtuck Valley Memorial, Six Memorial St, Deerfield, MA, 01342-9736. Tel: 413-775-7126. p. 1014

Soler-Lopez, Lillian D, Librn, Southern Technical College, Orlando Campus, 1485 Florida Mall Ave, Orlando, FL, 32809. Tel: 407-438-6000. p. 404

Soles, Amanda, Librn, Horry County Memorial Library, North Myrtle Beach Branch, 910 First Ave S, North Myrtle Beach, SC, 29582. Tel: 843-915-5281. p. 2056

Soles, Lovella, Libr Asst, La Glace Community Library, 9924 97 Ave, La Glace, AB, T0H 2J0, CANADA. Tel: 780-568-4696. p. 2544

Soles, Tammy, Libr Mgr, Columbus County Public Library, Fair Bluff Community, 315 Railroad St, Fair Bluff, NC, 28439. Tel: 910-649-7098. p. 1722

Soliday, Jennifer E, Libr Dir, Punxsutawney Memorial Library, 301 E Mahoning St, Punxsutawney, PA, 15767-2198. Tel: 814-938-5020. p. 1999

Solis, Amy, Dir, Nueta Hidatsa Sahnish College, 301 College Dr, New Town, ND, 58763. Tel: 701-627-8055. p. 1739

Solis, Jacqueline, Dir, Res, Instrul Serv, University of North Carolina at Chapel Hill, 208 Raleigh St, CB 3916, Chapel Hill, NC, 27515. Tel: 919-962-1053. p. 1678

Solis, Laura, Libr Dir, Sargeant Fernando de la Rosa Memorial Library, 416 N Tower Rd, Alamo, TX, 78516-2795. Tel: 956-787-6160. p. 2132

Solis Ortiz, Francisco, Librn II, University of the Sacred Heart, Rosales St, PO Box 12383, Santurce, PR, 00914-0383. Tel: 787-728-1515, Ext 4357. p. 2515

Solis, Tony, Dir, Superior Public Library, 99 N Kellner Ave, Superior, AZ, 85173. Tel: 520-689-2327. p. 79

Soliven, Andrew, Dir, Libr Serv, Rose State College, 6420 SE 15th St, Midwest City, OK, 73110. Tel: 405-733-7914. p. 1853

Soliz, Maria G, Dir, Joe A Guerra Laredo Public Library, 1120 E Calton Rd, Laredo, TX, 78041. Tel: 956-795-2400. p. 2209

Sollars, Sheryl A, Exec Dir, Westfield Washington Public Library, 17400 Westfield Blvd, Unit A, Westfield, IN, 46074-9283. Tel: 317-896-9391. p. 726

Sollenberger, Lori, Head, Circ, Ela Area Public Library District, 275 Mohawk Trail, Lake Zurich, IL, 60047. Tel: 847-438-3433. p. 607

Sollitt, Marie, Br Mgr, Charleston County Public Library, Edgar Allan Poe Branch, 1921 I'On Ave, Sullivan's Island, SC, 29482. Tel: 843-883-3914. p. 2049

Solomon, Adam, Dir, Libr Res, Point University, 507 W Tenth St, West Point, GA, 31833-1200. Tel: 706-385-1000. p. 503

Solomon, Autumn, Assoc Dir, Westbank Community Library District, 1309 Westbank Dr, Austin, TX, 78746. Tel: 512-327-3045. p. 2143

Solomon, Darren, Chief Exec Officer, Richmond Hill Public Library, One Atkinson St, Richmond Hill, ON, L4C 0H5, CANADA. Tel: 905-884-9288. p. 2675

Solomon, Geri, Asst Dean, Hofstra University, Special Collections/Long Island Studies Institute, 032 Axinn Library, 123 Hofstra University, Hempstead, NY, 11549-1230. Tel: 516-463-6404, 516-463-6411. p. 1545

Solomon, Jon, Dir, Longmont Public Library, 409 Fourth Ave, Longmont, CO, 80501-6006. Tel: 303-651-8470. p. 290

Solomon, Laura, Libr Serv Mgr, Ohio Public Library Information Network, 2323 W Fifth Ave, Ste 130, Columbus, OH, 43204. Tel: 614-728-5252. p. 2773

Solomon, Meredith I, Libr Tech, Tuality Healthcare, Health Sciences Library, 335 SE Eighth Ave, Hillsboro, OR, 97123. Tel: 503-681-1121. p. 1881

Solomon, Rachel, Br Mgr, Free Library of Philadelphia, Whitman Branch, 200 Snyder Ave, Philadelphia, PA, 19148-2620. Tel: 215-685-1754. p. 1980

Solomonson, Sheryl, Dir, Gridley Public Library District, 320 Center St, Gridley, IL, 61744. Tel: 309-747-2284. p. 596

Solon, Betsy, Libr Dir, Wadleigh Memorial Library, 49 Nashua St, Milford, NH, 03055. Tel: 603-249-0645. p. 1374

Solorzano, Jeannie, Dir, Bagley Public Library, 117 Main, Bagley, IA, 50026. Tel: 641-427-5214. p. 734

Solorzano, Ron, City Librn, Regional Mgr, West Region, Ventura County Library, 5600 Everglades St, Ste A, Ventura, CA, 93003. Tel: 805-677-7150. p. 256

Solove, Dan, Head, Acq, Syst & Tech, Bethlehem Area Public Library, 11 W Church St, Bethlehem, PA, 18018. Tel: 610-867-3761, Ext 216. p. 1911

Soltau, Elena, Res & Instruction Librn, Seminole State College of Florida, 850 S SR 434, Altamonte Springs, FL, 32714. Tel: 407-404-6025. p. 383

Soltis, John, Asst City Librn, Bridgeport Public Library, 925 Broad St, Bridgeport, CT, 06604. Tel: 203-576-7400. p. 303

Solz, Julie, Librn & Archivist, Historic New England, 141 Cambridge St, Boston, MA, 02114-2702. Tel: 617-227-3956. p. 996

Somathilake, Sheryl, Br Mgr, Mobile Public Library, Saraland Public Library, 111 Saraland Loop, Saraland, AL, 36571-2418. Tel: 251-675-2879. p. 26

Somerhalder, Holly, Br Mgr, Door County Library, Fish Creek Branch, 4097 Hwy 42, Fish Creek, WI, 54212. Tel: 920-868-3471. p. 2480

Somers, Ana, Res Spec, Douglas County Historical Society, 5730 N 30th St, No 11A, Omaha, NE, 68111. Tel: 402-455-9990. p. 1328

Somers, Emma, Libr Operations Coordr, Emily Carr University of Art & Design, 520 E First Ave, Vancouver, BC, V5T 0H2, CANADA. Tel: 604-844-3840. p. 2578

Somers, Jennifer, Digital Media Spec, Washburn University, 1700 SW College Ave, Topeka, KS, 66621. Tel: 785-670-1275. p. 839

Somers, Lynn, Dir, Nova Scotia Provincial Library, 6016 University Ave, 5th Flr, Halifax, NS, B3H 1W4, CANADA. Tel: 902-424-2457. p. 2621

Somerton, Gloria, Librn, Whitbourne Public Library, 494 Main St, Whitbourne, NL, A0B 3K0, CANADA. Tel: 709-759-2461. p. 2611

Somerville, Alex, Exec Dir, Dawson City Museum, 595 Fifth Ave, Dawson City, YT, Y0B 1G0, CANADA. Tel: 867-993-5291, Ext 21. p. 2757

Somerville, Jane, Libr Dir, Stanley Community Public Library, 240 Niece Ave, Stanley, ID, 83278. Tel: 208-774-2470. p. 531

Sommer, Jamie, Res & Instrul Serv Librn, Northwestern University Libraries, Pritzker Legal Research Center, 375 E Chicago Ave, Chicago, IL, 60611. Tel: 312-503-0314. p. 587

Sommer, MaryAnne, Access Serv Librn, Concordia Theological Seminary, 6600 N Clinton St, Fort Wayne, IN, 46825. Tel: 260-452-2145. p. 684

Sommer, MaryAnne, Br Mgr, Cumberland County Public Library & Information Center, Hope Mills Branch, 3411 Golfview Rd, Hope Mills, NC, 28348-2266. p. 1688

Sommer, Rachael, Mgr, Kershaw County Library, Elgin Branch, 2652 Main St, Elgin, SC, 29045. Tel: 803-438-7881, Ext 3302. p. 2048

Sommer, Shelly, Dir, Info Outreach, University of Colorado Boulder, Institute of Arctic & Alpine Research Information Center, 4001 Discovery Dr, Boulder, CO, 80303. Tel: 303-492-1867, 303-492-6387. p. 268

Sommer, Valerie, Dir, South San Francisco Public Library, 840 W Orange Ave, South San Francisco, CA, 94080-3125. Tel: 650-829-3872. p. 247

Sommers, Hannah, Dep Univ Librn, Sr Assoc Dean, The George Washington University, 2130 H St NW, Washington, DC, 20052. Tel: 202-994-6558. p. 367

Sommers, Meredith, Head, Ref, Superior District Library, 541 Library Dr, Sault Sainte Marie, MI, 49783. Tel: 906-632-9331. p. 1149

Sommersmith, Clairellyn, Dir, Princeton Public Library, 424 W Water St, Princeton, WI, 54968-9147. Tel: 920-295-6777. p. 2471

Somodi, Szilvia, Access Serv, Libr Assoc, University of Georgia, Alexander Campbell King Law Library, 225 Herty Dr, Athens, GA, 30602-6018. Tel: 706-542-1922. p. 459

Somsen, Chelle, State Archivist, South Dakota State Historical Society, 900 Governors Dr, Pierre, SD, 57501. Tel: 605-773-3804. p. 2080

Soncrant, Roy, Br Librn, Genesee District Library, Clio Area Library, 2080 W Vienna Rd, Clio, MI, 48420. Tel: 810-686-7130. p. 1106

Soncrant, Roy, Br Librn, Genesee District Library, Davison Area Library, 203 E Fourth St, Davison, MI, 48423. Tel: 810-653-2022. p. 1106

Sones, Linda, Dir, Quimby Public Library, 120 N Main, Quimby, IA, 51049. Tel: 712-445-2413. p. 778

Song, Connie, Libr Dir, Athenaeum of Ohio, 6616 Beechmont Ave, Cincinnati, OH, 45230-2091. Tel: 513-233-6136. p. 1759

Song, Sophie, IT Serv Mgr, Alberta Law Libraries, Edmonton, Law Courts Bldg, 2nd Flr S, 1A Sir Winston Churchill Sq, Edmonton, AB, T5J 0R2, CANADA. Tel: 780-415-8580. p. 2535

Song, Sophie, IT Serv Mgr, Alberta Law Libraries, North Library, Law Courts North, 5th Flr, 1A Sir Winston Churchill Sq, Edmonton, AB, T5J 0R2, CANADA. Tel: 780-427-3327. p. 2535

Song, Yiluo, Syst Librn, Rock Valley College, 3301 N Mulford Rd, Rockford, IL, 61114. Tel: 815-921-4602. p. 641

Song, Yoo-Seong, Assoc Prof, University of Illinois at Urbana-Champaign, Library & Information Science Bldg, 501 E Daniel St, Champaign, IL, 61820-6211. Tel: 217-333-3280. p. 2784

Songster, Jennifer, Sr Librn, Long Beach Public Library, Mark Twain Branch, 1401 E Anaheim St, Long Beach, CA, 90813. Tel: 562-570-1046. p. 159

Sonnek, Therese, Br Mgr, Ramsey County Library, White Bear Lake Branch, 2150 Second St, White Bear Lake, MN, 55110. Tel: 651-724-6130. p. 1204

Sonnenberg, Edmund, Govt Doc, Ref Serv, Widener University, Harrisburg Campus Law Library, 3800 Vartan Way, Harrisburg, DE, 17110. Tel: 717-541-3932. p. 358

Sonnenfelt, Karen, Dir, Michael Nivison Public Library, 90 Swallow Pl, Cloudcroft, NM, 88317. Tel: 575-682-1111. p. 1465

Sonnichsen, Amy, Asst Dir of User Experience & Digital Initiatives, Mount Saint Mary's University, 12001 Chalon Rd, Los Angeles, CA, 90049-1599. Tel: 310-954-4389. p. 166

Sonnie, Amy, Br Mgr, Marin County Free Library, South Novato Library, 931 C St, Novato, CA, 94949. Tel: 415-506-3165. p. 237

Sonnier, Denice, Mgr, Davis Jefferson Parish Library, McBurney Memorial, 301 S Sarah St, Welsh, LA, 70591. Tel: 337-734-3262. p. 892

Sonsteby, Alec, Fac Chair, Libr Serv, Metropolitan State University, 645 E Seventh St, Saint Paul, MN, 55106. Tel: 651-793-1636. p. 1200

Sonstegaard, Elizabeth, Adult Serv, Albany Public Library, 2450 14th Ave SE, Albany, OR, 97322. Tel: 541-917-0014. p. 1871

Sontag, Bryan, Br Operations Mgr, Stanislaus County Library, 1500 I St, Modesto, CA, 95354-1166. Tel: 209-558-7800. p. 178

Soohoo, Jason, Res & Instruction Librn, Salem State University, 352 Lafayette St, Salem, MA, 01970-5353. Tel: 978-542-6967. p. 1051

Sookralli, Pamela, Libr Assoc, Vaughn College Library, 8601 23rd Ave, Flushing, NY, 11369. Tel: 718-429-6600, Ext 184. p. 1534

Soontornsaratool, Arthur, Digital Projects, Spec, Maryland Institute College of Art, 1401 W Mount Royal Ave, Baltimore, MD, 21217. Tel: 410-225-2304, 410-225-2311. p. 955

Soper, Kristin, Outreach & Events Coord, Lawrence Public Library, 707 Vermont St, Lawrence, KS, 66044-2371. Tel: 785-843-3833, Ext 122. p. 819

Sorbel, Stephanie, Dir, Oglala Lakota College, Pejuta Haka College Center, PO Box 370, Kyle, SD, 57752-0370. Tel: 605-455-2450. p. 2078

Sorci, Joanna, Librn, Monterey Institute for Research & Astronomy, 200 Eighth St, Marina, CA, 93933. Tel: 831-883-1000. p. 173

Sordan, Janet, Librn, Southern Technical College, Port Charlotte Campus, 950 Tamiami Trail, No 109, Port Charlotte, FL, 33953. Tel: 941-391-8888. p. 404

Sorell, Katrina, Dir, Belleville Public Library, 1327 19th St, Belleville, KS, 66935. Tel: 785-527-5305. p. 798

Sorensen, Charlene, Assoc Dean of Libr, University of Saskatchewan Libraries, Three Campus Dr, Saskatoon, SK, S7N 5A4, CANADA. Tel: 306-966-5958. p. 2750

Sorensen, Emma, Acq & Coll Develop Librn, Fresno Pacific University, 1717 S Chestnut Ave, Fresno, CA, 93702. Tel: 559-453-8018. p. 146

Sorensen, Janet, Libr Dir, Elmwood Public Library, 124 West D St, Elmwood, NE, 68349. Tel: 402-994-4125. p. 1313

Sorensen, Julie, Mgr, County of Los Angeles Public Library, San Gabriel Library, 500 S Del Mar Ave, San Gabriel, CA, 91776-2408. Tel: 626-287-0761. p. 138

Sorensen, Kristi, Dir, Belle Plaine Community Library, 904 12th St, Belle Plaine, IA, 52208-1711. Tel: 319-444-2902. p. 734

Sorensen, Kristy, Assoc Dir, Head, Archives & Rec Libr, Austin Presbyterian Theological Seminary, 100 E 27th St, Austin, TX, 78705-5797. Tel: 512-404-4875. p. 2138

Sorensen, Lee, Visual Studies Librarian, Duke University Libraries, William R Perkins Lilly Library, 1348 Campus Dr, Campus Box 90725, Durham, NC, 27708-0725. Tel: 919-660-5995. p. 1684

Sorensen, Luke, Sr Librn, Walker Memorial Library, 800 Main St, Westbrook, ME, 04092. Tel: 207-854-0630. p. 946

Sorensen, Marianna, Youth Serv Librn, Southborough Library, 25 Main St, Southborough, MA, 01772. Tel: 508-485-5031. p. 1055

Sorensen, Mirissa, Libr Spec II, Eastern Shore Community College, 29300 Lankford Hwy, Melfa, VA, 23410. Tel: 757-789-1721. p. 2332

Sorenson, Beth, Libr Dir, Cloquet Public Library, 320 14th St, Cloquet, MN, 55720. Tel: 218-879-1531. p. 1170

Sorenson, Beth K, Dir, Milford Memorial Library, 1009 Ninth St, Ste 5, Milford, IA, 51351. Tel: 712-338-4643. p. 770

Sorenson, Brandi, Librn, Chinook Regional Library, Abbey Branch, 336 Cathedral Ave, Abbey, SK, S0N 0A0, CANADA. Tel: 306-689-2202. p. 2752

Sorenson, Karolee, Admin/Personnel Mgr, Twin Falls Public Library, 201 Fourth Ave E, Twin Falls, ID, 83301-6397. Tel: 208-733-2964. p. 532

Sorenson, Melanie, Educ Dir, Oregon Zoo Animal Management Library, 4001 SW Canyon Rd, Portland, OR, 97221. Tel: 503-226-1561. p. 1893

Sorenson, Susan, Libr Dir, LDS Business College Library, 95 N 300 West, Salt Lake City, UT, 84101. Tel: 801-524-8150. p. 2271

Soria, Lucila, Libr Asst II, Saddleback College, 28000 Marguerite Pkwy, Mission Viejo, CA, 92692. Tel: 949-582-4314. p. 177

Soriano, Jo Ann, Syst Librn, United States Air Force Academy Libraries, 2354 Fairchild Dr, Ste 3A15, USAF Academy, CO, 80840-6214. Tel: 719-333-4406. p. 297

Sorlie, Kathy, Asst Dir, Larchwood Public Library, 1020 Broadway, Larchwood, IA, 51241. Tel: 712-477-2583. p. 764

Soroya, Saira, Assoc Prof, Southern Connecticut State University, 501 Crescent St, New Haven, CT, 06515. Tel: 203-392-6655. p. 2783

Sorrell, Eva, Coordr, Cat, California State University, San Bernardino, 5500 University Pkwy, San Bernardino, CA, 92407-2318. Tel: 909-537-7392. p. 212

Sorrell, Iva, Libr Dir, Prairie Grove Public Library, 123 S Neal St, Prairie Grove, AR, 72753. Tel: 479-846-3782. p. 108

Sorrell, Paul, Creative Projects Coordr, Union University, 1050 Union University Dr, Jackson, TN, 38305-3697. Tel: 731-661-5417. p. 2102

Sorrells, Mitzi, Cat, Spec Coll Librn, Philadelphia College of Osteopathic Medicine, 4170 City Ave, Philadelphia, PA, 19131-1694. Tel: 215-871-6470. p. 1984

Sorrells, Wanda, Library Contact, Phillips State Prison, 2989 W Rock Quarry Rd NE, Buford, GA, 30519. Tel: 770-932-4500, 770-932-4732. p. 468

Sorrentino, Bobbi, Dir, Walworth Memorial Library, 525 Kenosha St, Walworth, WI, 53184. Tel: 262-275-6322. p. 2483

Sorscher, Holly, Assoc Dir, Head, User Serv, University of Michigan-Dearborn, 4901 Evergreen Rd, Dearborn, MI, 48128-2406. Tel: 313-593-5695. p. 1096

Sorth, Kristen L, Libr Dir, Saint Louis County Library, 1640 S Lindbergh Blvd, Saint Louis, MO, 63131-3598. Tel: 314-994-3300. p. 1273

Sosnowski, Maria, Law Librn, Clark County Law Library, 1200 Franklin St, Vancouver, WA, 98660. Tel: 564-397-2268. p. 2390

Sossi, Catherine, Ad, Chelsea District Library, 221 S Main St, Chelsea, MI, 48118-1267. Tel: 734-475-8732. p. 1090

Sota, Hai-Thom, Libr Dir, Samuel Merritt University, Health Education Center, 400 Hawthorne Ave, Oakland, CA, 94609. Tel: 510-879-9264. p. 187

Sotak, Diane, Ref & Instruction Librn, University of Portland, 5000 N Willamette Blvd, Portland, OR, 97203-5743. Tel: 503-943-7111. p. 1894

Sotelo, Susie, Libr Dir, Umatilla Public Library, 700 Sixth St, Umatilla, OR, 97882-9507. Tel: 541-922-5704. p. 1901

Sotilleo, Sophia, Dean of the Library, Bowie State University, 14000 Jericho Park Rd, Bowie, MD, 20715. Tel: 301-860-3870. p. 960

Soto, Evelyn, Sr Libr Asst, Freehold Public Library, 28 1/2 E Main St, Freehold, NJ, 07728. Tel: 732-462-5135. p. 1404

Soto, Jammilah, Tech Serv Librn, Universidad Central Del Caribe, Avenida Laurel, Santa Juanita, Bayamon, PR, 00956. Tel: 787-798-3001, Ext 2306. p. 2510

Soto, Sharon, Br Coordr, Indiana University, Indiana Institute on Disability & Community, 2853 E Tenth St, Bloomington, IN, 47408-2601. Tel: 812-855-9396. p. 670

Soto, Tricia, Info Serv Librn, Menlo College, 1000 El Camino Real, Atherton, CA, 94027. Tel: 650-543-3826. p. 118

Soto-Barra, Laura, Chief, NPR RAD-Research Archive & Data Strategy, 1111 N Capitol St NE, Washington, DC, 20002. p. 373

Soto-Rodriguez, Omar, Div Head, Kirkland Public Library, 17100 Hymus Blvd, Kirkland, QC, H9J 2W2, CANADA. Tel: 514-630-2726. p. 2714

Sotolotto, Rebecca, Head, Children's Servx, Seymour Public Library, 46 Church St, Seymour, CT, 06483. Tel: 203-888-3903. p. 336

Sottong, Renee, Br Mgr, Pamunkey Regional Library, Lois Wickham Jones - Montpelier Branch, 17205 Sycamore Tavern Lane, Montpelier, VA, 23192. Tel: 804-883-7116. p. 2324

Souannavong, Anna, Libr Dir, Gates Public Library, 902 Elmgrove Rd, Rochester, NY, 14624. Tel: 585-247-6446. p. 1628

Soucie, Mary, State Librn, North Dakota State Library, Liberty Memorial Bldg, Dept 250, 604 East Blvd Ave, Bismarck, ND, 58505-0800. Tel: 701-328-2492. p. 1730

Soucy, Jennifer, ILL, The William K Sanford Town Library, 629 Albany Shaker Rd, Loudonville, NY, 12211-1196. Tel: 518-458-9274. p. 1565

Souid, Dania, YA Librn, Baldwinsville Public Library, 33 E Genesee St, Baldwinsville, NY, 13027-2575. Tel: 315-635-5631. p. 1490

Soukup, Hannah, Archivist, Govt Doc, Montana Historical Society, 225 N Roberts St, Helena, MT, 59601-4514. Tel: 406-444-7427. p. 1296

Soukup, Lynne, Asst Dir, Westborough Public Library, 55 W Main St, Westborough, MA, 01581. Tel: 508-366-3050. p. 1066

Soule, Rebecca, Ch Serv, Pasquotank County Library, 100 E Colonial Ave, Elizabeth City, NC, 27909. Tel: 252-335-2473. p. 1687

Soulek, Rachel, Circ Asst, Mitchell Public Library, 221 N Duff St, Mitchell, SD, 57301. Tel: 605-995-8480. p. 2079

Soulen, Rita, Dr, Asst Prof, East Carolina University, 104B Ragsdale Hall, Greenville, NC, 27858. Tel: 252-737-4352. p. 2790

Soules, Aline, Librn, California State University, East Bay Library, CSU East Bay Library, 25800 Carlos Bee Blvd, Hayward, CA, 94542-3052. Tel: 510-885-4596. p. 150

Soules, Rebecca, Collections & Education Dir, Shaker Village of Pleasant Hill Museum Library, 3501 Lexington Rd, Harrodsburg, KY, 40330. Tel: 859-734-1549, 859-734-5411. p. 858

Soulier, Ashley, Adult Serv, Manville Public Library, 100 S Tenth Ave, Manville, NJ, 08835. Tel: 908-458-8425. p. 1416

Soulliere, Robert, Digital Syst Librn, Mohawk College Library, 135 Fennell Ave W, Hamilton, ON, L9C 0E5, CANADA. Tel: 905-575-1212, Ext 3936. p. 2647

Soultoukis, Donna, Librn, Our Lady of Lourdes, School of Nursing Library, 1600 Haddon Ave, Camden, NJ, 08103. Tel: 856-757-3722. p. 1394

Soussana, Kevin, Libr Mgr, Chaleur Library Region, Raymond Lagace Public Library, 275 rue Notre-Dame, Atholville, NB, E3N 4T1, CANADA. Tel: 506-789-2914. p. 2599

South, Cheryl, Br Coordr, Shelby County Libraries, Jackson Center Memorial, 205 S Linden St, Jackson Center, OH, 45334. Tel: 937-596-5300. p. 1820

South, Elizabeth, Asst Librn, Access & Tech Services, Interim Dir, Indiana University East Campus Library, Hayes Hall, 2325 Chester Blvd, Richmond, IN, 47374. Tel: 765-973-8204. p. 715

South, Kathy, Dir, Monroe County District Library, 96 Home Ave, Woodsfield, OH, 43793. Tel: 740-472-1954. p. 1832

Southard, Christy, Tech Serv Mgr, Sequoyah Regional Library System, 116 Brown Industrial Pkwy, Canton, GA, 30114. Tel: 770-479-3090. p. 469

Southard, Sophia, Archivist, State Historical Society of Missouri, 306 Miller Nichols Library UMKC, 800 E 51st St, Kansas City, MO, 64110. Tel: 816-235-1544. p. 1257

Souther, Randy, Head, Reference & Access Servs, University of San Francisco, 2130 Fulton St, San Francisco, CA, 94117-1080. Tel: 412-422-5388. p. 229

Souther, Travis, Local Hist Librn, New Hanover County Public Library, 201 Chestnut St, Wilmington, NC, 28401. Tel: 910-798-6356. p. 1723

Southern, Melanie, Chief Librn, Halton Hills Public Library, Nine Church St, Georgetown, ON, L7G 2A3, CANADA. Tel: 905-873-2681, Ext 2513. p. 2642

Southern, Melanie, Libr Mgr, Mississauga Library System, Burnhamthorpe, 3650 Dixie Rd, Mississauga, ON, L4Y 3V9, CANADA. Tel: 905-615-4635. p. 2659

Southern, Melanie, Libr Mgr, Mississauga Library System, Lakeview, 1110 Atwater Ave, Mississauga, ON, L5E 1M9, CANADA. Tel: 905-615-4805. p. 2659

Southern, Rana, Librn, Mount Airy Public Library, 145 Rockford St, Mount Airy, NC, 27030-4759. Tel: 336-789-5108. p. 1705

Southwood, Karen, Journalism & Graphic Communication Res, Florida Agricultural & Mechanical University Libraries, 525 Orr Dr, Tallahassee, FL, 32307-4700. Tel: 850-599-3704. p. 446

Southwood, Roxanne, Regional Mgr, North Central Washington Libraries, Moses Lake Public Library, 418 E Fifth Ave, Moses Lake, WA, 98837-1797. Tel: 509-765-3489. p. 2394

Southworth, Denise, Circ Serv Librn, Southwest Public Libraries, Westland Area Library, 4740 W Broad St, Columbus, OH, 43228. Tel: 614-878-1301. p. 1789

Soutter, Jennifer, Head, Syst, University of Windsor, 401 Sunset Ave, Windsor, ON, N9B 3P4, CANADA. Tel: 519-253-3000, Ext 3402. p. 2704

Souza, Carol Jean, Br Mgr, Mineral County Library, Mina-Luning Library, 908 B St, Mina, NV, 89422. Tel: 775-573-2505. p. 1345

Souza, Laurie, Asst Dir, Endicott College Library, 376 Hale St, Beverly, MA, 01915. Tel: 978-232-2276. p. 989
Souza-Mort, Susan, Res & Instruction Librn, Bristol Community College, New Bedford Campus, 800 Purchase St, LL06, New Bedford, MA, 02740. Tel: 774-357-2183. p. 1017
Sova, DeeAnna, Dir, Hopkinsville-Christian County Public Library, 1101 Bethel St, Hopkinsville, KY, 42240. Tel: 270-887-4262, Ext 106. p. 860
Sowards, Jason, Librn, Nevada Supreme Court Law Library, Supreme Court Bldg, 201 S Carson St, Ste 100, Carson City, NV, 89701-4702. Tel: 775-684-1671. p. 1344
Sowards, Steven, Assoc Univ Librn, Coll, Michigan State University Libraries, Main Library, 366 W Circle Dr, East Lansing, MI, 48824-1048. Tel: 517-884-6391. p. 1102
Sowchek, Ellen, Univ Archivist, Pace University Library, 15 Beekman St, New York, NY, 10038. Tel: 212-346-1787. p. 1600
Sowell, Cary, Fac Librn, Austin Community College, Eastview Campus Library, 3401 Webberville Rd, 2nd Flr, Rm 2200, Austin, TX, 78702. Tel: 512-223-5232. p. 2138
Sowell, Diane, Archives Asst, Troy University, 502 University Dr, Dothan, AL, 36304. Tel: 334-983-6556, Ext 1320. p. 15
Sowell, Lacee, Mkt Coordr, Outreach Coordr, Bulverde-Spring Branch Library, 131 Bulverde Crossing, Bulverde, TX, 78163. Tel: 830-438-4864. p. 2151
Sowell, Stevie, Asst Dir, Autauga Prattville Public Library, 254 Doster St, Prattville, AL, 36067-3933. Tel: 334-365-3396. p. 33
Sowell, Tom, Head Fac Mgt, Kalamazoo Public Library, 315 S Rose St, Kalamazoo, MI, 49007-5264. Tel: 269-553-7883. p. 1121
Sowers, Barb, Dir, Readlyn Community Library, 309 Main St, Readlyn, IA, 50668. Tel: 319-279-3432. p. 778
Sowers, Bill, State Doc Cataloger, State Library of Kansas, State Capitol Bldg, Rm 312-N, 300 SW Tenth Ave, Topeka, KS, 66612. Tel: 785-296-3296. p. 839
Sowers, Dawn, Pub Serv Mgr, Fauquier County Public Library, 11 Winchester St, Warrenton, VA, 20186. Tel: 540-422-8500, Ext 1. p. 2351
Sowers, Susan, Libr Dir, Hoyt Lakes Public Library, 206 Kennedy Memorial Dr, Hoyt Lakes, MN, 55750. Tel: 218-225-2412. p. 1178
Sowinski, Brad, Youth Serv Mgr, Alexandria-Monroe Public Library, 117 E Church St, Alexandria, IN, 46001-2005. Tel: 765-724-2196. p. 667
Sowles, Glen, Ad, Romeo District Library, 65821 Van Dyke, Washington, MI, 48095. Tel: 586-752-0603. p. 1157
Sowles, Julie A, Libr Dir, Rancho Cucamonga Public Library, 12505 Cultural Center Dr, Rancho Cucamonga, CA, 91739. Tel: 909-477-2720. p. 197
Soyka, Heather, Asst Prof, Kent State University, 314 University Library, 1125 Risman Dr, Kent, OH, 44242-0001. Tel: 330-672-2782. p. 2790
Space, Cheryl, Libr Dir, Community Libraries of Providence, PO Box 9267, Providence, RI, 02940. Tel: 401-467-2700, Ext 1616. p. 2038
Spachkan, Kimberly, Head, Info Servs & Adult Learning, Russell Library, 123 Broad St, Middletown, CT, 06457. Tel: 860-347-2528. p. 322
Spadaro, Joanne, Sr Asst Librn, Ref, State University of New York, 223 Store Hill Rd, Old Westbury, NY, 11568. Tel: 516-876-2896. p. 1610
Spade, Jennifer, Dir, Honey Brook Community Library, 687 Compass Rd, Honey Brook, PA, 19344. Tel: 610-273-3303. p. 1944
Spade, Kendra, Asst Dir, Operations, Emporia Public Library, 110 E Sixth Ave, Emporia, KS, 66801-3960. Tel: 620-340-6462. p. 806
Spadoni, Ambi, Library Contact, Hunterdon Developmental Center Library, 40 Pittstown Rd, Clinton, NJ, 08809. Tel: 908-735-4031, Ext 1038. p. 1397
Spadoni, Cindy, Head, Ref, O'Melveny & Myers LLP, 400 S Hope St, Los Angeles, CA, 90071-2899. Tel: 213-430-6000. p. 167
Spadoni, Cindy, Dir, Bibliog Serv, Dir, Coll Mgt, University of California Los Angeles Library, Hugh & Hazel Darling Law Library, 1112 Law Bldg, 385 Charles E Young Dr E, Los Angeles, CA, 90095-1458. Tel: 310-825-7826. p. 169
Spaeth, Paul J, Spec Coll Librn, Saint Bonaventure University, 3261 W State Rd, Saint Bonaventure, NY, 14778. Tel: 716-375-2327. p. 1635
Spague, James, Libr Mgr, American Watchmakers-Clockmakers Institute, 701 Enterprise Dr, Harrison, OH, 45030-1696. Tel: 513-367-9800. p. 1789
Spahn, Kathleen, Dir, Access Serv, Portland Public Library, Five Monument Sq, Portland, ME, 04101. Tel: 207-871-1700, Ext 709. p. 937
Spaine, Jamie Lee, Adminr, Coordr, Spec Projects, University of Puget Sound, 1604 N Warner St, Upper Loading Dock, Tacoma, WA, 98416. Tel: 253-879-3243. p. 2387
Spak, Judy, Asst Dir, Res & Educ, Yale University Library, Harvey Cushing/John Hay Whitney Medical Library, Sterling Hall of Medicine, 333 Cedar St, New Haven, CT, 06510. Tel: 203-737-2961. p. 327
Spalding, Jeff, Cat Librn, Florida Supreme Court Library, 500 S Duval St, Tallahassee, FL, 32399-1926. Tel: 850-488-8919. p. 447
Spalding, Kate, Head, Tech Serv, Waltham Public Library, 735 Main St, Waltham, MA, 02451. Tel: 781-314-3425. p. 1062
Spalsbury, Jeff, Dir, Porterville College Library, 100 E College Ave, Porterville, CA, 93257. Tel: 559-791-2271, 559-791-2318. p. 197
Spalti, Michael, Assoc Univ Librn, Syst, Willamette University, 900 State St, Salem, OR, 97301. Tel: 503-370-6356. p. 1897
Spanbock, Addie, Mgr, Contra Costa County Library, Walnut Creek Library, 1644 N Broadway, Walnut Creek, CA, 94596. Tel: 925-977-3340. p. 175
Spanburgh, Sarah, Librn II, Plattsburgh Public Library, 19 Oak St, Plattsburgh, NY, 12901. Tel: 518-563-0921. p. 1619
Spaner, Megan, Asst Librn, Rotary Club of Slave Lake Public Library, 50 Main St SW, Slave Lake, AB, T0G 2A0, CANADA. Tel: 780-849-5250. p. 2554
Spangenberg, Lisa, Librn, Susquehanna County Historical Society & Free Library Association, Forest City Branch, 531 Main St, Forest City, PA, 18421-1421. Tel: 570-785-5590. p. 1965
Spangler, Alison, Ch, Lewis County Public Library, 27 Third St, Vanceburg, KY, 41179. Tel: 606-796-2532. p. 876
Spangler, Cheryl, Librn, Harrisburg Public Library, 354 Smith St, Harrisburg, OR, 97446. Tel: 541-995-6949. p. 1881
Spangler, Loretta, Coordr, Info Literacy, McDaniel College, 2 College Hill, Westminster, MD, 21157-4390. Tel: 410-386-4679. p. 981
Spangler, Michelle, Asst Dir, Peru Public Library, 102 E Main St, Peru, IN, 46970-2338. Tel: 765-473-3069. p. 713
Spanier, Jennifer, Libr Dir, Blake Memorial Library, 676 Village Rd, East Corinth, VT, 05040. Tel: 802-439-5338. p. 2283
Spann, Julie, Dir, Libr Serv, Blodgett Memorial Library, 37 Broad St, Fishkill, NY, 12524-1836. Tel: 845-896-9215. p. 1533
Spann, Marla K, Dir, East Chicago Public Library, 2401 E Columbus Dr, East Chicago, IN, 46312-2998. Tel: 219-397-2453. p. 680
Spano, Desiree, Outreach Serv Librn, Safety Harbor Public Library, 101 Second St N, Safety Harbor, FL, 34695. Tel: 727-724-1525. p. 439
Spano, Nadine, Ch, Elmont Memorial Library, 700 Hempstead Tpk, Elmont, NY, 11003-1896. Tel: 516-354-5280. p. 1531
Spar, Lisa, Interim Dir, Hofstra University Law Library, 122 Hofstra University, Hempstead, NY, 11549-1220. Tel: 516-463-5898. p. 1545
Sparagna, Betty, Asst Libr Dir, Tuolumne County Genealogical Society Library, 158 Bradford St, Sonora, CA, 95370. Tel: 209-532-1317. p. 247
Spare, Amy, Assoc Dir, Res & Info Serv, Villanova University, Law Library, Villanova University Charles Widger School of Law, 299 N Spring Mill Rd, Villanova, PA, 19085. Tel: 610-519-7188. p. 2017
Sparenberg, Jessica, Dir, Parlin Ingersoll Public Library, 205 W Chestnut St, Canton, IL, 61520. Tel: 309-647-0328. p. 548
Sparkman, Olivia, Libr Coord, Forrest College Library, 601 E River St, Anderson, SC, 29624. Tel: 864-225-7653. p. 2047
Sparks, Barbara, Circ Serv Supvr, Bedford Public Library, 2424 Forest Ridge Dr, Bedford, TX, 76021. Tel: 817-952-2350. p. 2146
Sparks, Courtney, Dir, Freeport Community Library, Ten Library Dr, Freeport, ME, 04032. Tel: 207-865-3307. p. 925
Sparks, Jamie, Ms, Dir, Sedalia Public Library, 311 W Third St, Sedalia, MO, 65301-4399. Tel: 660-826-1314. p. 1279
Sparks, Mary Ann, Libr Mgr, Edgerton Public Library, 5037-50 Ave, Edgerton, AB, T0B 1K0, CANADA. Tel: 780-755-3933, Ext 7. p. 2534
Sparks, Rhonda, Ch, Pendleton Community Library, 595 E Water St, Pendleton, IN, 46064-1070. Tel: 765-778-7527. p. 713
Sparks-Jamal, Ashley, Librn, Los Angeles Mission College Library, 13356 Eldridge Ave, Sylmar, CA, 91342. Tel: 818-364-7750. p. 251
Sparling, Kathy, Tech Serv, Ohlone College, 43600 Mission Blvd, Fremont, CA, 94539. Tel: 510-659-6160. p. 144
Sparrow, Cathleen, Exec Dir, Found, Anne Arundel County Public Library, Five Harry Truman Pkwy, Annapolis, MD, 21401. Tel: 410-222-2509. p. 950
Spasojevich, Helen, Tech Serv Asst, University of Wisconsin-River Falls, 410 S Third St, River Falls, WI, 54022. Tel: 715-425-4628. p. 2474
Spaulding, Caitlyn, Children's Serv Coordr, Springdale Public Library, 405 S Pleasant St, Springdale, AR, 72764. Tel: 479-750-8180. p. 110
Spaulding, Cheryl, Circ Coordr, Dyer Library, 371 Main St, Saco, ME, 04072. Tel: 207-283-3861. p. 939
Spaulding, Diana, Interim Br Mgr, Sonoma County Library, Sonoma Valley Regional Library, 755 W Napa St, Sonoma, CA, 95476. Tel: 707-996-5217. p. 204
Spaulding, Donna, Br Mgr, Saint Louis County Library, Bridgeton Trails Branch, 3455 McKelvey Rd, Bridgeton, MO, 63044-2500. Tel: 314-994-3300, Ext 3000. p. 1273
Spaulding, Jim, Library Contact, Saint Peter's University Hospital Medical Library, 254 Easton Ave, New Brunswick, NJ, 08903. Tel: 732-745-8600, Ext 5185. p. 1425
Spaulding, JoAnn, Coll Develop Librn, Lenox Library Association, 18 Main St, Lenox, MA, 01240. Tel: 413-637-0197. p. 1028
Spaw, Shawn, Teen Librn, Pulaski County Public Library, 304 S Main St, Somerset, KY, 42501. Tel: 606-679-8401. p. 875
Speare, April, Libr Serv Tech, Mohawk College Library, STARRT (Skilled Trades & Apprenticeship Research, Resources & Training) Library, 481 Barton St E, Stoney Creek, ON, L8E 2L7, CANADA. Tel: 905-575-2504, Ext 5028. p. 2647
Speare, Marie, Assoc Librn, University of Manitoba Libraries, Donald W Craik Engineering Library, E3-361 Engineering Information & Technology Ctr, 75B Chancellors Circle, Winnipeg, MB, R3T 5V6, CANADA. Tel: 204-474-9445. p. 2595
Speare, Marie, Actg Head, Libr, University of Manitoba Libraries, Sciences & Technology Library, 211 Machray Hall, 186 Dysart Rd, Winnipeg, MB, R3T 2N2, CANADA. Tel: 204-789-7063. p. 2596

Spearman, Leander, Dir, Belleville Public Library, 121 E Washington St, Belleville, IL, 62220. Tel: 618-234-0441. p. 541

Spearman, Sallee, Dir, Budget & Fiscal Operations, San Diego State University, 5500 Campanile Dr, San Diego, CA, 92182-8050. Tel: 619-594-4921. p. 221

Spearmon, Senatra, Ad, Onslow County Public Library, 58 Doris Ave E, Jacksonville, NC, 28540. Tel: 910-455-7350, Ext 1417. p. 1697

Spears, David, Library Contact, Virginia Division of Geology & Mineral Resources Library, 900 Natural Resources Dr, Ste 500, Charlottesville, VA, 22903-2982. Tel: 434-951-6341. p. 2311

Spears, Jessica, Research Servs Librn, Southern Adventist University, 4851 Industrial Dr, Collegedale, TN, 37315. Tel: 423-236-2009. p. 2094

Spears, John, Dir, Buffalo & Erie County Public Library System, One Lafayette Sq, Buffalo, NY, 14203-1887. Tel: 716-858-8900. p. 1507

Spears, R, Supvr of Educ, Federal Correctional Institution, 1100 River Rd, Hopewell, VA, 23860. Tel: 804-733-7881. p. 2326

Speas, Bonnie, Acq Librn, Ser Librn, Lake Superior State University, 906 Ryan Ave, Sault Sainte Marie, MI, 49783. Tel: 906-635-2861. p. 1149

Speca, Janelle, Dir, Honeoye Public Library, 8708 Main St, Honeoye, NY, 14471. Tel: 585-229-5020. p. 1548

Spece, Lacey, Dir, Gowrie Public Library, 1204 Market St, Gowrie, IA, 50543. Tel: 515-352-3315. p. 755

Specht, Leota, Library Contact, Village of Verdon Library, 312 1/2 Main St, Verdon, NE, 68457. Tel: 402-883-2044. p. 1339

Special, Cathy, Asst Dir, Otis Library, 261 Main St, Norwich, CT, 06360. Tel: 860-889-2365. p. 332

Special, Lori, Dir, Libr Develop, Colorado State Library, 201 E Colfax Ave, Rm 309, Denver, CO, 80203-1799. Tel: 303-866-6730. p. 274

Speck, Jason, Head, Archives & Spec Coll, Hillwood Estate, Museum & Gardens Library, 4155 Linnean Ave NW, Washington, DC, 20008. Tel: 202-243-3953. p. 368

Speck, Karen A, Dir, Ozark Dale County Library, Inc, 416 James St, Ozark, AL, 36360. Tel: 334-774-2399, 334-774-5480. p. 32

Speck, Michele, Electronic Res Librn, Mission College Library, 3000 Mission College Blvd, Santa Clara, CA, 95054-1897. Tel: 408-855-5169. p. 241

Spector, Carol, Reference & Government Info Librn, University of San Francisco, 2130 Fulton St, San Francisco, CA, 94117-1080. Tel: 415-422-2040. p. 229

Spector, Jennifer, Computer Serv, Thompson Coburn LLP, One US Bank Plaza, Saint Louis, MO, 63101-1693. Tel: 314-552-6000. p. 1276

Spedowski, Jeff, Tech Serv, Morton Township Library, 110 S James, Mecosta, MI, 49332-9334. Tel: 231-972-8315. p. 1131

Speed, Beth, Librn, Woolworth Community Library, 100 E Utah Ave, Jal, NM, 88252. Tel: 505-395-3268. p. 1470

Speed, Lancia, Libr Tech, Pierce County Law Library, County-City Bldg, 930 Tacoma Ave S, Rm 1A - 105, Tacoma, WA, 98402. Tel: 253-798-2691. p. 2386

Speer, Jacob, State Librn, Indiana State Library, 315 W Ohio St, Indianapolis, IN, 46202. Tel: 317-232-3675. p. 692

Speer, Lisa, Archivist, Ouachita Baptist University, 410 Ouachita St, OBU Box 3742, Arkadelphia, AR, 71998-0001. Tel: 870-245-5332. p. 89

Speer, Margaret, Asst Br Librn, East Bend Public Library, 420 Flint Hill Rd, East Bend, NC, 27018. Tel: 336-699-3890. p. 1686

Speer, Priscilla, Ref Serv Librn, Trevecca Nazarene University, 333 Murfreesboro Rd, Nashville, TN, 37210. Tel: 615-248-1347. p. 2121

Speer, Priscilla, Assoc Prof, Trevecca Nazarene University, School of Education, 333 Murfreesboro Rd, Nashville, TN, 37210-2877. Tel: 615-248-1201, 615-248-1206. p. 2792

Speers, Beth, Libr Dir, Altamont Public Library, 121 W Washington Ave, Altamont, IL, 62411. Tel: 618-483-5457. p. 536

Speetzen, Alexander, Fac Librn, Austin Community College, Highland Campus Library, 6101 Airport Blvd, 1st Flr, Rm 1325, Austin, TX, 78752. Tel: 512-223-7387. p. 2138

Speich, Robert, Br Mgr, Pasco County Library System, Land O' Lakes Branch, 2818 Collier Pkwy, Land O'Lakes, FL, 34639. Tel: 813-929-1214. p. 410

Speidel, Dan, Libr Dir, Rivier University, 420 S Main St, Nashua, NH, 03060-5086. Tel: 603-897-8576. p. 1375

Spellman, Rekesha, Pub Serv Librn, Chesapeake Public Library, Russell Memorial, 2808 Taylor Rd, Chesapeake, VA, 23321-2210. Tel: 757-410-7020. p. 2311

Spelock, DeAnnia, Res Mgr, West Virginia Legislative Reference Library, Capitol Bldg, Rm MB 27, 1900 Kanawha Blvd E, Charleston, WV, 25305-0591. Tel: 304-347-4830. p. 2400

Spence, Anna, Circ, Lasalle Parish Library, 3165 N First St, Jena, LA, 71342. Tel: 318-992-5675. p. 891

Spence, Camilla, Asst Librn, Madison Library, 1895 Village Rd, Madison, NH, 03849. Tel: 603-367-8545. p. 1371

Spence, David, Circ, Ref, Warren County Memorial Library, 119 South Front St, Warrenton, NC, 27589. Tel: 252-257-4990, Ext 202. p. 1720

Spence, Hannah, Co-Dir, New England Conservatory of Music, 255 St Butolph St, Boston, MA, 02115. Tel: 617-585-1250. p. 998

Spence, Melissa, Asst Dir, Elko-Lander-Eureka County Library System, 720 Court St, Elko, NV, 89801. Tel: 775-738-3066. p. 1344

Spence, Sarah, Librn, Daly City Public Library, Westlake, 275 Southgate Ave, Daly City, CA, 94015-3471. Tel: 650-991-8071. p. 134

Spence, Travis, Head, Library Tech & Admin Services, University of Arizona Libraries, Daniel F Cracchiolo Law Library, James E Rogers College of Law, 1201 E Speedway, Tucson, AZ, 85721. p. 83

Spence, Wayne, Dir, Catahoula Parish Library, 300 Bushley St, Harrisonburg, LA, 71340. Tel: 318-744-5271. p. 891

Spence-Wilcox, Sharon, Ref Librn, Seattle Central College, 1701 Broadway, BE Rm 2101, Seattle, WA, 98122. Tel: 206-934-4069. p. 2378

Spencer, Alia, Ref (Info Servs), Palm Beach State College, 3160 PGA Blvd, Palm Beach Gardens, FL, 33410-2893. Tel: 561-207-5800. p. 434

Spencer, Carol, Med Librn, Lahey Hospital & Medical Center, 41 Mall Rd, Burlington, MA, 01805. Tel: 781-744-2409. p. 1004

Spencer, Darron, Ch, Desoto Parish Library, 109 Crosby St, Mansfield, LA, 71052. Tel: 318-872-6100. p. 895

Spencer, Deirdre, Librn, University of Michigan, Fine Arts Library, 260 Tappan Hall, 2nd Flr, 855 S University Ave, Ann Arbor, MI, 48109-1357. Tel: 734-763-8963. p. 1080

Spencer, Eric, Libr Mgr, Sno-Isle Libraries, Marysville Library, 6120 Grove St, Marysville, WA, 98270-4127. Tel: 360-658-5000. p. 2370

Spencer, Estelle, Dir, Libr Serv, American International College, 1000 State St, Springfield, MA, 01109. Tel: 413-205-3461. p. 1056

Spencer, Gene, Chief Info Officer, Ursinus College Library, 601 E Main St, Collegeville, PA, 19426. Tel: 610-409-3064. p. 1923

Spencer, Jane, Libr Asst, Rappahannock Community College Library, 12745 College Dr, Glenns, VA, 23149. Tel: 804-758-6710. p. 2321

Spencer, Jesse, ILL Librn, Christopher Newport University, One Avenue of the Arts, Newport News, VA, 23606. Tel: 757-594-7130. p. 2333

Spencer, Jo, Ms, Dep Dir, Bus Operations, Central Arkansas Library System, 100 Rock St, Little Rock, AR, 72201-4698. Tel: 501-918-3000. p. 101

Spencer, John, Ref Coordr, Gonzaga University, 502 E Boone Ave, Spokane, WA, 99258-0095. Tel: 509-313-6110. p. 2383

Spencer, Judy, Head, Pub Serv, Amherst County Public Library, 382 S Main St, Amherst, VA, 24521. Tel: 434-946-9488. p. 2304

Spencer, Kevin, Br Librn, Waseca-Le Sueur Regional Library, Montgomery Public, 104 Oak Ave SE, Montgomery, MN, 56069. Tel: 507-364-7615. p. 1207

Spencer, Korin, Dir, Fenton Free Library, 1062 Chenango St, Binghamton, NY, 13901-1736. Tel: 607-724-8649. p. 1494

Spencer, Laura, Tech Serv, James V Brown Library of Williamsport & Lycoming County, 19 E Fourth St, Williamsport, PA, 17701. Tel: 570-326-0536. p. 2023

Spencer, Lindsay, Mkt Dir, Sheridan Public Library, 103 W First St, Sheridan, IN, 46069. Tel: 317-758-5201. p. 718

Spencer, Meg C, Libr Dir, Siuslaw Public Library District, 1460 Ninth St, Florence, OR, 97439. Tel: 541-997-3132. p. 1879

Spencer, Nancy, Dir, Pinhole Resource Library, 224 Royal John Mine Rd, San Lorenzo, NM, 88041. Tel: 505-536-9942. p. 1474

Spencer, Nicole, Dir, Harrisville Free Library, 8209 Main St, Harrisville, NY, 13648. Tel: 315-543-2577. p. 1544

Spencer, Patricia, Pub Info Officer, Lewis & Clark Library, 120 S Last Chance Gulch, Helena, MT, 59601. Tel: 406-447-1690. p. 1296

Spencer, Richard, Ref Librn, NASA Headquarters Library, 300 E St SW, Rm 1W53, Washington, DC, 20546. Tel: 202-358-0172. p. 371

Spencer, Rose, Dir, Alderson Public Library, 115 Walnut Ave, Alderson, WV, 24910. Tel: 304-445-7221. p. 2397

Spencer, Shannon, Per, Ref Librn, University of Tampa, 401 W Kennedy Blvd, Tampa, FL, 33606-1490. Tel: 813-257-3847. p. 450

Spencer, Shayna, Dir, Zearing Public Library, 101 E Main, Zearing, IA, 50278. Tel: 641-487-7888. p. 793

Spencer, Shelia, Dir, Ruth Holliman Public Library, 287 Main St, Gordo, AL, 35466. Tel: 205-364-7148. p. 19

Spencer, Suzette, Dir, Libr & Info Serv, Montgomery College Library, 51 Mannakee St, Macklin Tower, Rockville, MD, 20850. Tel: 240-567-7915. p. 973

Spencer, Verlaine, Ch, Garfield County-Panguitch City Library, 25 S 200 East, Panguitch, UT, 84759. Tel: 435-676-2431. p. 2268

Spencer, Vickie V, Head, Access Serv, North Carolina Central University, 1801 Fayetteville St, Durham, NC, 27707-3129. Tel: 919-530-7305. p. 1685

Spera, Joanna, Circ Mgr, St Catharines Public Library, 54 Church St, St. Catharines, ON, L2R 7K2, CANADA. Tel: 905-688-6103. p. 2680

Speranza, Ginger, Librn, Washington School for the Deaf, 611 Grand Blvd, Vancouver, WA, 98661-4498. Tel: 360-696-6525, Ext 4352. p. 2391

Spero, Patrick, Dr, Dir & Librn, American Philosophical Society Library, 105 S Fifth St, Philadelphia, PA, 19106-3386. Tel: 215-440-3403. p. 1974

Spero, Rebecca, Adult Serv, William E Dermody Free Public Library, 420 Hackensack St, Carlstadt, NJ, 07072. Tel: 201-438-8866. p. 1395

Sperry, Jamee, Libr Dir, Osburn Public Library, 921 E Mullan, Osburn, ID, 83849. Tel: 208-752-9711. p. 528

Sperry, Kim, Br Mgr, Blackwater Regional Library, Claremont Public, 91 Mancha Ave, Claremont, VA, 23899. Tel: 757-866-8627. p. 2313

Sperry, Kim, Br Mgr, Blackwater Regional Library, Surry Public, 270 Colonial Trail E, Surry, VA, 23883. Tel: 757-294-3949. p. 2313

Sperry, Regina, Dir & Librn, Northwest Regional Library, Winfield Public Library, 185 Ashwood Dr, Winfield, AL, 35594. Tel: 205-487-2484. p. 40

Sperry, Regina, Dir, Northwest Regional Library, 185 Ashwood Dr, Winfield, AL, 35594-5436. Tel: 205-487-2330. p. 40

Spetter, Stephanie, Head, Youth Serv, Des Plaines Public Library, 1501 Ellinwood St, Des Plaines, IL, 60016. Tel: 847-827-5551. p. 578

Sphar, Laurie, Libr Mgr, St Mary's Library, 100 Herb Bauer Dr, Saint Marys, GA, 31558-3300. Tel: 912-882-4800. p. 495

Spicer, Larry, Pres, Great Falls Genealogy Society Library, 301 Second Ave N, 3rd Flr, Great Falls, MT, 59404. Tel: 406-727-3922. p. 1294

Spicer, Tom, Dep Dir, Aurora Public Library District, 101 S River St, Aurora, IL, 60506. Tel: 630-264-4100. p. 539

Spicher, Carl, Asst Dir, Chadron Public Library, 507 Bordeaux, Chadron, NE, 69337. Tel: 308-432-0531. p. 1310

Spickett, Donna, Supvr, Essex County Library, LaSalle - Bill Varga Branch, 5950 Malden Rd, LaSalle, ON, N9H 1S4, CANADA. Tel: 226-946-1529, Ext 210. p. 2641

Spicola, Lisa, Dir, Univ Libr, Johnson & Wales University Library, Yena Ctr, 2nd Flr, 111 Dorrance St, Providence, RI, 02903. Tel: 401-598-1282. p. 2038

Spiegelberg, Shirley, Br Librn, Albany County Public Library, Rock River Branch, 386 Ave D, Rock River, WY, 82083. p. 2496

Spiegelglass, Howard, Adult Serv, South Huntington Public Library, 145 Pidgeon Hill Rd, Huntington Station, NY, 11746. Tel: 631-549-4411. p. 1549

Spiel, Karen, Regional Mgr, The Seattle Public Library, 1000 Fourth Ave, Seattle, WA, 98104-1109. Tel: 206-386-4636. p. 2379

Spieldenner, Sharon, Archivist, Newburyport Public Library, 94 State St, Newburyport, MA, 01950-6619. Tel: 978-465-4428, Ext 231. p. 1038

Spiering, Rosanne, AV, Br Mgr, Outreach Serv, Park County Library System, Powell Branch, 217 E Third St, Powell, WY, 82435-1903. Tel: 307-754-8828. p. 2494

Spiers, Teresa, Youth Serv Spec, First Regional Library, B J Chain Public Library, 6619 Hwy 305 N, Olive Branch, MS, 38654. Tel: 662-895-5900. p. 1219

Spiese, Kelly, Ref & Instruction Librn, Wilson College, 1015 Philadelphia Ave, Chambersburg, PA, 17201-1285. Tel: 717-262-2008. p. 1921

Spiess, Rhonda, Br Mgr, Saint Tammany Parish Library, Lacombe Branch, 28027 Hwy 190, Lacombe, LA, 70445. Tel: 985-882-7858. p. 888

Spieth, Bethany, Instruction & Access Services Librn, Ohio Northern University, 525 S Main St, Ada, OH, 45810. Tel: 419-772-2473. p. 1743

Spiker, Regina, Br Mgr, Allegany County Library System, George's Creek, 76 Main St, Lonaconing, MD, 21539. Tel: 301-463-2629. p. 963

Spikes, Janet, Librn, Wilson Woodrow International Center for Scholars Library, Kennan Institute for Advanced Russian Studies Library, 1300 Pennsylvania Ave NW, Washington, DC, 20004-3027. p. 381

Spikes, Janet, Librn, Woodrow Wilson International Center for Scholars Library, 1300 Pennsylvania Ave NW, Washington, DC, 20004-3027. Tel: 202-691-4150. p. 381

Spikes, TiKeecha, Coord, Tutoring Services, Southeast Arkansas College, 1900 Hazel St, Pine Bluff, AR, 71603. Tel: 870-850-4840. p. 107

Spilinek, Elizabeth, Library Contact, Adams County Historical Society Archives, Hastings Museum of Natural & Cultural History, 1330 N Burlington Ave, Hastings, NE, 68902. Tel: 402-463-5838. p. 1317

Spilker, Chris, Dir, Sacred Heart Major Seminary, 2701 Chicago Blvd, Detroit, MI, 48206. Tel: 313-883-8651. p. 1099

Spill, Sally, Dir, Libr Serv, Winters Public Library, 120 N Main St, Winters, TX, 79567. Tel: 325-754-4251. p. 2258

Spiller, Janet, Ref Librn, Lincoln Public Library, Three Bedford Rd, Lincoln, MA, 01773. Tel: 781-259-8465. p. 1028

Spillum, Kirsten, Access Serv, Head, Circ Serv, Interim Co-Dir, University of Washington Libraries, Box 352900, Seattle, WA, 98195-2900. Tel: 206-685-3987. p. 2381

Spilman, Karen, Ref Librn, National Cowboy & Western Heritage Museum, 1700 NE 63rd St, Oklahoma City, OK, 73111. Tel: 405-839-7782. p. 1858

Spilver, Rebecca, Customer Experience Supervisor, Douglas County Libraries, Roxborough Branch, 8357 N Rampart Range Rd, Ste 200, Littleton, CO, 80125. Tel: 303-791-7323. p. 270

Spilver, Rebecca, Supvr, Youth & Family Serv, Douglas County Libraries, Louviers Branch, 7885 Louviers Blvd, Louviers, CO, 80131. Tel: 303-791-7323. p. 270

Spina, Carli, Head, Res & Instrul Serv, Fashion Institute of Technology-SUNY, Seventh Ave at 27th St, 227 W 27th St, New York, NY, 10001-5992. Tel: 212-217-4396. p. 1585

Spina, Kerstin, Bus Mgr, Manlius Library, One Arkie Albanese Ave, Manlius, NY, 13104. Tel: 315-682-6400. p. 1568

Spinato, Diane, Interim Dir, University of New Haven, 300 Boston Post Rd, West Haven, CT, 06516. Tel: 203-479-4554. p. 346

Spindel, Dale T, Libr Dir, Springfield Free Public Library, 66 Mountain Ave, Springfield, NJ, 07081-1786. Tel: 973-376-4930, Ext 227. p. 1444

Spindler, Holly, Resource Librn, Cincinnati Children's Hospital, Edward L Pratt Library, S9.125 ML 3012, 3333 Burnet Ave, Cincinnati, OH, 45229-3039. Tel: 513-636-4230. p. 1759

Spindler, Tim, Exec Dir, Long Island Library Resources Council, 627 N Sunrise Service Rd, Bellport, NY, 11713. Tel: 631-675-1570. p. 2771

Spinelli, Catherine, Librn, Union Congregational Church, 176 Cooper Ave, Montclair, NJ, 07043. Tel: 973-744-7424. p. 1420

Spink, Chris, Tech Serv Librn, Chautauqua-Cattaraugus Library System, 106 W Fifth St, Jamestown, NY, 14701. Tel: 716-484-7135, Ext 248. p. 1557

Spinner, Emily, Librn, Ellis Medicine, 1101 Nott St, Schenectady, NY, 12308. Tel: 518-243-4000, 518-243-4381. p. 1637

Spinney, Ann, Librn, Ivy Tech Community College-Northeast, 3800 N Anthony Blvd, Fort Wayne, IN, 46805-1430. Tel: 260-480-4172. p. 684

Spinney, John, Electronic Res, Ref Serv, Norfolk Public Library, Two Liberty Lane, Norfolk, MA, 02056. Tel: 508-528-3380. p. 1040

Spira, Andrea, Br Mgr, Fairfax County Public Library, Great Falls Branch, 9830 Georgetown Pike, Great Falls, VA, 22066-2634. Tel: 703-757-8560. p. 2316

Spires, Katie, Online & Distance Learning Librn, Ref Librn, Utica University, 1600 Burrstone Rd, Utica, NY, 13502-4892. Tel: 315-792-3761. p. 1656

Spires, Todd, Coll Develop Librn, Bradley University, 1501 W Bradley Ave, Peoria, IL, 61625. Tel: 309-677-2850. p. 634

Spiritas, Jackie, Br Mgr, Jacksonville Public Library, Pablo Creek Regional, 13295 Beach Blvd, Jacksonville, FL, 32246-7259. Tel: 904-992-7101. p. 412

Spirito, Philip, Libr Mgr, Sno-Isle Libraries, Monroe Library, 1070 Village Way, Monroe, WA, 98272-2035. Tel: 360-794-7851. p. 2371

Spiro, Lisa, Exec Dir, Digital Scholarship Serv, Rice University, 6100 Main, MS-44, Houston, TX, 77005. Tel: 713-348-2480. p. 2197

Spisak, April, Youth Serv, Albany Public Library, 2450 14th Ave SE, Albany, OR, 97322. Tel: 541-917-0015. p. 1871

Spiteri, Louise, Dr, Prof, Dalhousie University, Kenneth C Rowe Management Bldg, Ste 4010, 6100 University Ave, Halifax, NS, B3H 4R2, CANADA. Tel: 902-494-2473. p. 2795

Spitler, Cynthia, Mgr, Patron Serv, Blount County Public Library, 508 N Cusick St, Maryville, TN, 37804. Tel: 865-982-0981. p. 2111

Spitzmiller, Susie, Ch, Ozark Regional Library, 402 N Main St, Ironton, MO, 63650. Tel: 573-546-2615. p. 1251

Spitzzeri, Paul R, Dir, Workman & Temple Family Homestead Museum Library, 15415 E Don Julian Rd, City of Industry, CA, 91745-1029. Tel: 626-968-8492. p. 130

Spivak, Howard, Dr, IT Dir, Brooklyn College Library, 2900 Bedford Ave, Brooklyn, NY, 11210. Tel: 718-951-5335. p. 1501

Spivey, Debbie, North Area Libr Coord, Kawartha Lakes Public Library, 190 Kent St W, Lower Level, Lindsay, ON, K9V 2Y6, CANADA. Tel: 705-887-6300. p. 2652

Spizziri, Kara, Head, Adult Serv, Head, Ref, Bellwood Public Library, 600 Bohland Ave, Bellwood, IL, 60104-1896. Tel: 708-547-7393. p. 541

Splane, Justine, Digital Serv Librn, Info Serv Librn, Bracebridge Public Library, 94 Manitoba St, Bracebridge, ON, P1L 2B5, CANADA. Tel: 705-645-4171. p. 2632

Spoerl, Michael, Tech Serv Assoc, Drake University, Drake Law Library, Opperman Hall, 2604 Forest Ave, Des Moines, IA, 50311. Tel: 515-271-2051. p. 746

Spofford, Jennifer, Librn, Fryeburg Public Library, 515 Main St, Fryeburg, ME, 04037. Tel: 207-935-2731. p. 926

Spofford, Katie, YA Serv, Wadleigh Memorial Library, 49 Nashua St, Milford, NH, 03055. Tel: 603-249-0645. p. 1374

Spofford, Michael, Finance Mgr, Clinton-Essex-Franklin Library System, 33 Oak St, Plattsburgh, NY, 12901-2810. Tel: 518-563-5190, Ext 112. p. 1619

Spohalotz, Theresa, Librn, Sandisfield Free Public Library, 23 Sandisfield Rd, Sandisfield, MA, 01255. Tel: 413-258-4966. p. 1051

Spohn, Melissa, Head, Project Mgmt, Kent State University Libraries, Risman Plaza, 1125 Risman Dr, Kent, OH, 44242. Tel: 330-672-1682. p. 1792

Spohn, Rachel, Br Mgr, Summit County Library, Kamas Branch, 110 N Main St, Kamas, UT, 84036. Tel: 435-783-3190. p. 2269

Spohn, Stephen, Exec Dir, Ocean State Libraries, 300 Centerville Rd, Ste 103S, Warwick, RI, 02886. Tel: 401-593-2160. p. 2774

Spomer, Kay, Cat Supvr, Presque Isle District Library, 181 E Erie St, Rogers City, MI, 49779-1709. Tel: 989-734-2477. p. 1145

Spomer, Michelle, Libr Dir, Pittsburgh Theological Seminary, 616 N Highland Ave, Pittsburgh, PA, 15206. Tel: 412-924-1408. p. 1995

Sponaugle, Lisa, Libr Dir, Allegany Highlands Regional Library, 406 W Riverside St, Covington, VA, 24426. Tel: 540-962-3321. p. 2314

Spong, Stephen, Dir, Western University Libraries, John & Dotsa Bitove Family Law Library, Josephine Spencer Niblett Law Bldg, 2nd Flr, 1151 Richmond St, London, ON, N6A 3K7, CANADA. Tel: 519-661-3171. p. 2655

Spongberg, Janet, Circ Coordr, Smith College Libraries, Werner Josten Performing Arts Library, Mendenhall Ctr for the Performing Arts, 122 Green St, Northampton, MA, 01063. Tel: 413-585-2932. p. 1043

Spoo, Melanie, Curator, Library Contact, US National Park Service, 74485 National Park Dr, Twentynine Palms, CA, 92277-3597. Tel: 760-367-5571. p. 254

Spoon, Henrik, Dir, Cornell University Library, Mathematics, 420 Malott Hall, Ithaca, NY, 14853-4201. Tel: 607-255-5268. p. 1552

Spooner, Jessica, Electronic Res Librn, Tech Serv, SUNY Canton, 34 Cornell Dr, Canton, NY, 13617. Tel: 315-386-7054. p. 1514

Spooner, Leiana, Libr Mgr, New York Public Library - Astor, Lenox & Tilden Foundations, Columbus Branch, 742 Tenth Ave, (Between E 50th & 51st Sts), New York, NY, 10019-7019. Tel: 212-586-5098. p. 1595
Spooner, Valerie, Youth Serv, Rusk County Community Library, 418 Corbett Ave W, Ladysmith, WI, 54848-1396. Tel: 715-532-2604. p. 2447
Sporleder, Christine, Circ, Bloomingdale Public Library, 101 Fairfield Way, Bloomingdale, IL, 60108. Tel: 630-529-3120. p. 542
Sporlein, Barb, Interim Dir, Saint Paul Public Library, 90 W Fourth St, Saint Paul, MN, 55102-1668. Tel: 651-266-7000. p. 1202
Spoto, Elizabeth, Head, Ch, Head, Circ, Island Trees Public Library, 38 Farmedge Rd, Levittown, NY, 11756. Tel: 516-731-2211. p. 1562
Spotted Bear, Leishawn, Asst Curator, Fort Worth Museum of Science & History Library, 1600 Gendy St, Fort Worth, TX, 76107. Tel: 817-255-9323. p. 2180
Spottek, Samantha, Ch Serv, Plymouth Public Library, 130 Division St, Plymouth, WI, 53073. Tel: 920-892-4416. p. 2470
Spotts, Lydia, Assoc Archivist, Librn, Indianapolis Museum of Art at Newfields, 4000 Michigan Rd, Indianapolis, IN, 46208-3326. Tel: 317-923-1331, Ext 547. p. 693
Spracklen, Lisa Marie, Co-Dir, Marrowbone Public Library District, 216 W Main St, Bethany, IL, 61914. Tel: 217-665-3014. p. 542
Spradley, Patsy, Libr Dir, Doris Stanley Memorial Library, 300 Bookmark Circle, Moody, AL, 35004. Tel: 205-640-2517. p. 30
Spradlin, Gary, Librn, Monterey History & Art Association, 155 Van Buren St, Monterey, CA, 93940. Tel: 831-747-1027. p. 179
Spradlin, Jenci, Ad, Jackson-Madison County Library, 433 E Lafayette St, Jackson, TN, 38301. Tel: 731-425-8600. p. 2102
Sprague, Arlene, Ch Serv, The Morristown & Morris Township Library, One Miller Rd, Morristown, NJ, 07960. Tel: 973-538-6161. p. 1421
Sprague, Jennifer, Dir, Saint John's College, 1160 Camino Cruz Blanca, Santa Fe, NM, 87505. Tel: 505-984-6041. p. 1476
Sprague, Kayleigh, Head, Teen Serv, Wallingford Public Library, 200 N Main St, Wallingford, CT, 06492. Tel: 203-284-6423. p. 343
Sprague, Kelly, Circ, Framingham Public Library, 49 Lexington St, Framingham, MA, 01702-8278. Tel: 508-879-5570, Ext 4345. p. 1019
Sprague, Lisa, Pub Serv Librn, Enfield Public Library, 104 Middle Rd, Enfield, CT, 06082. Tel: 860-763-7510. p. 311
Sprague, Suzanne, Assoc Dir, Electronic/Tech Libr Serv, Embry-Riddle Aeronautical University, One Aerospace Blvd, Daytona Beach, FL, 32114. Tel: 386-226-6932. p. 392
Sprankle, Ashley, Ref & Circ Librn, Cleveland Law Library, One W Lakeside Ave, 4th Flr, Cleveland, OH, 44113-1078. Tel: 216-861-5070. p. 1767
Spratlin, Amber, Library Research & Instruction Specialist for Online Programs, Maryville University Library, 650 Maryville University Dr, Saint Louis, MO, 63141. Tel: 314-529-6528. p. 1271
Spratlin Hasskarl, Marie, Libr Dir, Burlington Public Library, 34 Library Lane, Burlington, CT, 06013. Tel: 860-673-3331. p. 305
Spratling, Cynthia, Bus Mgr, Houston County Public Library System, 1201 Washington Ave, Perry, GA, 31069. Tel: 478-987-3050. p. 493
Spratt, Debra, Dir, Lawrence Library, 15 Main St, Pepperell, MA, 01463. Tel: 978-433-0330. p. 1046
Spratt, Stephanie, Asst Dir, Tech Serv, Missouri Western State University, 4525 Downs Dr, Saint Joseph, MO, 64507-2294. Tel: 816-271-4368. p. 1268
Spring, Kathy, Youth Serv Librn, Socorro Public Library, 401 Park St, Socorro, NM, 87801. Tel: 575-835-1114. p. 1478
Springer, Carol, Asst Dir, House Memorial Public Library, 220 Thurston Ave, Pender, NE, 68047. Tel: 402-385-2521. p. 1332
Springer, Carrie, Mgr, Somerset County Park Commission, 190 Lord Stirling Rd, Basking Ridge, NJ, 07920. Tel: 908-722-1200, Ext 5002. p. 1388
Springer, Chris, Librn, Grays Harbor College, 1620 Edward P Smith Dr, Aberdeen, WA, 98520. Tel: 360-538-4050. p. 2357
Springer, Christopher, Libr Mgr, Timberland Regional Library, Montesano Branch, 125 Main St S, Montesano, WA, 98563-3794. Tel: 360-249-4211. p. 2389
Springer, Elizabeth, Ch Serv, Alexandria Library, Kate Waller Barrett Branch, 717 Queen St, Alexandria, VA, 22314. Tel: 703-746-1703. p. 2302
Springer, Joe A, Curator, Goshen College, Mennonite Historical Library, 1700 S Main, Goshen, IN, 46526. Tel: 574-535-7418. p. 687
Springer, John, Libr Dir, Lorain County Law Library, 226 Middle Ave, Elyria, OH, 44035. Tel: 440-329-5567. p. 1784
Springer, Josh, Libr Serv Mgr, Muskingum University, Ten College Dr, New Concord, OH, 43762. Tel: 740-826-8156. p. 1806
Springer, Kelley, Br Mgr, Marion County Library System, Mullins Branch, 210 N Main St, Mullins, SC, 29574. Tel: 843-464-9621. p. 2065
Springer, Kortni, Head, Adult Serv, Acorn Public Library District, 15624 S Central Ave, Oak Forest, IL, 60452-3204. Tel: 708-687-3700. p. 627
Springer, Lori, Dir, Valparaiso Public Library, 300 W Second St, Valparaiso, NE, 68065. Tel: 402-784-6141. p. 1339
Springer, Paul, Jr, Libr Asst, Tech Serv, Fisk University, 1000 17th Ave N, Nashville, TN, 37208-3051. Tel: 615-329-8733. p. 2118
Springer-Ali, Nadja, Librn, Ref (Info Servs), Oakland Community College, Bldg K, 27055 Orchard Lake Rd, Farmington Hills, MI, 48334-4579. Tel: 248-522-3531. p. 1104
Springfield, Cristina, Open Education Librn, California State University Dominguez Hills, 1000 E Victoria St, Carson, CA, 90747. Tel: 310-243-2062. p. 129
Springfield, Cristina, Bus Librn, Career Dev, Outreach Librn, Madison Area Technical College, 3550 Anderson St, Rm A3000, Madison, WI, 53704. Tel: 608-246-6637. p. 2449
Springfield, Edwin, Asst Librn, Little Big Horn College Library, 8645 S Weaver Dr, Crow Agency, MT, 59022. Tel: 406-638-3160. p. 1291
Springston, Lorna, Dir, Libr Serv, IU Ball Memorial Hospital, 2401 W University Ave, Muncie, IN, 47303-3499. Tel: 765-747-4229. p. 708
Sprinkles, Amy, Dir, Grand Prairie Public Library System, 901 Conover Dr, Grand Prairie, TX, 75051. Tel: 972-237-5700. p. 2185
Sproul, Laurel, Br Mgr, Manistee County Library System, Onekama Branch, 5283 Main St, Onekama, MI, 49675-9701. Tel: 231-889-4041. p. 1129
Sproul, Stephanie, Br Mgr, Blackwater Regional Library, Ruth Camp Campbell Memorial, 280 N College Dr, Franklin, VA, 23851. Tel: 757-562-4801. p. 2313
Sprowls, Charles, Ref Librn/Circ Syst, Duquesne University, Center for Legal Information, 900 Locust St, Pittsburgh, PA, 15282. Tel: 412-396-5533. p. 1993
Spruill, Octavious, Head, Access Serv, Head Bldg Serv, North Carolina Agricultural & Technical State University, 1601 E Market St, Greensboro, NC, 27411-0002. Tel: 336-285-4164. p. 1693
Spruill, Tom, Libr Asst, Grand County Public Library, Castle Valley, Castle Valley Community Ctr, Two Castle Valley Dr, Moab, UT, 84532. Tel: 435-259-9998. p. 2266
Sprung, David, Dir, Ohio Public Library District, 112 N Main St, Ohio, IL, 61349. Tel: 815-376-5422. p. 629
Spunaugle, Emily, Humanities Librn, Rare Bk Librn, Oakland University Library, 100 Library Dr, Rochester, MI, 48309-4479. Tel: 248-370-2498. p. 1144
Spurlock, Brad, Mgr, Smith Library of Regional History, 441 S Locust St, Oxford, OH, 45056. Tel: 513-523-3035. p. 1812
Spurlock, Patrick, Libr Dir, SIT Graduate Institute/SIT Study Abroad, One Kipling Rd, Brattleboro, VT, 05302. Tel: 802-258-3354. p. 2280
Spurrier, Jennifer, Assoc Dean of Libr, Texas Tech University Libraries, 2802 18th St, Lubbock, TX, 79409. Tel: 806-834-2252. p. 2214
Spurway, Tracy, Univ Librn, Algoma University, 1520 Queen St E, Sault Ste. Marie, ON, P6A 2G4, CANADA. Tel: 705-949-2101, Ext 4612. p. 2676
Spybuck, Crystal, Libr Dir, Blanco County South Library District, 1118 Main St, Blanco, TX, 78606. Tel: 830-833-4280. p. 2148
Spyker, Kristine, Libr Serv Mgr, Auglaize County Libraries, 203 S Perry St, Wapakoneta, OH, 45895-1999. Tel: 419-738-2921. p. 1827
Squier, Carol, Asst Librn, Brenizer Public Library, 430 W Center Ave, Merna, NE, 68856. Tel: 308-643-2268. p. 1325
Squier, Cynthia, Librn, Chesterfield Public Library, 408 Main Rd, Chesterfield, MA, 01012-9708. Tel: 413-296-4735. p. 1010
Squier, Jackie, Dir, Lacona Public Library, 107 E Main St, Lacona, IA, 50139. Tel: 641-534-4400. p. 763
Squillante, Michael, Dir, Bay Shore-Brightwaters Public Library, One S Country Rd, Brightwaters, NY, 11718-1517. Tel: 631-665-4350. p. 1497
Squire, Brittney, Outreach Specialist, Fort Hays State University, 502 S Campus Dr, Hays, KS, 67601. Tel: 785-628-5566. p. 812
Squires, David, Asst Librn, Kern County Library, Buttonwillow Branch, 101 Main St, Buttonwillow, CA, 93206. Tel: 661-764-5337. p. 119
Squires, David, Br Supvr, Kern County Library, Taft Branch, 27 Cougar Ct, Taft, CA, 93268-2327. Tel: 661-763-3294. p. 120
Squires, Doug, Fac Mgr, Anythink Libraries, 5877 E 120th Ave, Thornton, CO, 80602. Tel: 303-288-2001. p. 296
Squires, Lorraine, Head, Tech Serv, Mastics-Moriches-Shirley Community Library, 407 William Floyd Pkwy, Shirley, NY, 11967. Tel: 631-399-1511. p. 1640
Squires, Richard, Coll Develop Librn, Monroe Community College, LeRoy V Good Library, 1000 E Henrietta Rd, Rochester, NY, 14692. Tel: 585-292-2314. p. 1629
Squires, Tracey, Circ Mgr, East Brunswick Public Library, Two Jean Walling Civic Ctr, East Brunswick, NJ, 08816-3599. Tel: 732-390-6950. p. 1399
Sridaran, Geetha, Asst Dir, Life University, 1269 Barclay Circle, Marietta, GA, 30060. Tel: 770-426-2691. p. 489
Srinath, Lavanya, Libr Assoc/Circ, Mercer County Community College Library, 1200 Old Trenton Rd, West Windsor, NJ, 08550. Tel: 609-570-3558. p. 1453
Sriram, Rashmita, Librn, San Francisco Center for Psychoanalysis Library, 444 Natoma St, San Francisco, CA, 94103. Tel: 415-563-4477, 415-563-5815, Ext 105. p. 227
Sroka, Marek, Librn, University of Illinois Library at Urbana-Champaign, Literatures & Languages, 225 Main Library, MC-522, 1408 W Gregory Dr, Urbana, IL, 61801. Tel: 217-265-8025. p. 656
St Amant, Alisa, Asst Dir, Coll Mgt, Jackson-George Regional Library System, 3214 Pascagoula St, Pascagoula, MS, 39567. Tel: 228-769-3227. p. 1228
St Amant, Kyara, Dir, Tech Serv, New Orleans Baptist Theological Seminary, 4110 Seminary Pl, New Orleans, LA, 70126. Tel: 504-816-8475. p. 902

St Amour, Cindy, Libr Dir, Brewster Ladies' Library, 1822 Main St, Brewster, MA, 02631. Tel: 508-896-3913. p. 1001

St Clair, Cate, Dir, Robey Memorial Library, 401 First Ave NW, Waukon, IA, 52172. Tel: 563-568-4424. p. 789

St Clair, Heather, Dir, Libr Serv, Bryan College of Health Sciences, 1535 S 52nd St, Lincoln, NE, 68506. Tel: 402-481-3908. p. 1320

St Clair, Jason, Cat, Pacific Union College, One Angwin Ave, Angwin, CA, 94508-9705. Tel: 707-965-6640. p. 116

St George, Beth, Libr Assoc, Lopez Island Library, 2225 Fisherman Bay Rd, Lopez Island, WA, 98261. Tel: 360-468-2265. p. 2370

St George, Hillary, Sr Librn, Los Angeles Public Library System, Cahuenga Branch Library, 4591 Santa Monica Blvd, Los Angeles, CA, 90029-1937. Tel: 323-664-6418. p. 163

St George, Jayne, Libr Dir, Lodi Memorial Library, One Memorial Dr, Lodi, NJ, 07644. Tel: 973-365-4044. p. 1413

St Germain, Jan, Dir, Richmond Township Library, 304 Snyder St, Palmer, MI, 49871. Tel: 906-401-0316. p. 1140

St Germain, Joe, Libr Dir, Billerica Public Library, 15 Concord Rd, Billerica, MA, 01821. Tel: 978-671-0948, 978-671-0949. p. 989

St John, Amanda, Libr Dir, Grand Marais Public Library, 104 Second Ave W, Grand Marais, MN, 55604. Tel: 218-387-1140. p. 1176

St John, Faith, Dir, Argyle Free Library, 21 Sheridan St, Argyle, NY, 12809. Tel: 518-638-8911. p. 1488

St John, Nicole, Electronic Res Librn, University of Mary Washington, 1801 College Ave, Fredericksburg, VA, 22401-5300. Tel: 540-654-1772. p. 2320

St Laurent, Laurie, Dep Dir, Saint Charles City-County Library District, 77 Boone Hills Dr, Saint Peters, MO, 63376. Tel: 636-441-2300. p. 1277

St Martin, Dora, Dir, Malden Public Library, 36 Salem St, Malden, MA, 02148-5291. Tel: 781-324-0218. p. 1031

St Martin, Sarah, Head, Tech Serv, Manchester City Library, 405 Pine St, Manchester, NH, 03104-6199. Tel: 603-624-6550. p. 1372

St Martin, Sarah, Syst Librn, GMILCS, Inc, 31 Mount Saint Mary's Way, Hooksett, NH, 03106. p. 2769

St Onge, Anne L, Librn, Mackinac Island Public Library, 903 Main St, Mackinac Island, MI, 49757. Tel: 906-847-3421. p. 1128

St Pierre, Anne, Circ Supvr, Saint Charles Parish Library, Paradis Branch, 307 Audubon St, Paradis, LA, 70080. Tel: 985-758-1868. p. 888

St Pierre, Dominic, Asst Librn, Pouce Coupe Public Library, 5010-52 Ave, Pouce Coupe, BC, V0C 2C0, CANADA. Tel: 250-786-5765. p. 2574

St-Aubin, Diane, Mgr, Centre Hospitalier de l'Universite de Montreal, 3840, rue Saint-Urbain, Montreal, QC, H2W 1T8, CANADA. Tel: 514-890-8000, Ext 14355. p. 2722

St-Aubin, Diane, Dir, Hopital Hotel-Dieu du CHUM, 3840 rue St-Urbain, Montreal, QC, H2W 1T8, CANADA. Tel: 514-890-8000, Ext 35867. p. 2724

St-Martin, Ginette, Documentation Tech, Cegep de Granby, 235 Saint Jacques St, Granby, QC, J2G 3N1, CANADA. Tel: 450-372-6614, Ext 1204. p. 2713

St-Martin, Helene, Pub Serv, Ref Serv, Bibliotheque Charles-Edouard-Mailhot, Bibliotheque Alcide-Fleury, 841, blvd des Bois-Francs Sud, Victoriaville, QC, G6P 5W3, CANADA. Tel: 819-357-8240. p. 2738

St-Onge, Christiane, Chef de Section, Bibliotheques de Montreal, Robert-Bourassa, 41 Ave Saint-Just, Outremont, QC, H2V 4T7, CANADA. Tel: 514-495-6209. p. 2720

St-Onge, Tania, Libr Mgr, Haut-Saint-Jean Regional Library, Monseigneur Plourde Public, 15 Bellevue St, Saint Francois, NB, E7A 1A4, CANADA. Tel: 506-992-6052. p. 2600

St-Pierre, Anne, Br Head, Alfred & Plantagenet Public Library System, Wendover Branch, 5000 rue du Centre, Wendover, ON, K0A 3K0, CANADA. Tel: 613-673-2923. p. 2652

St-Pierre, Karyne, Chef de Div, Bibliotheques de Montreal, Saint-Leonard, 8420 Blvd Lacordaire, Saint-Leonard, QC, H1R 3G5, CANADA. Tel: 514-328-8500, Ext 8517. p. 2720

St-Pierre, Therese, Library Contact, Bibliotheque Municipale, 25A rue Saint Pierre, Saint-Clement, QC, G0L 2N0, CANADA. Tel: 418-963-2258. p. 2734

St-Vincent, Jade, Libr Tech, Centre Jeunesse de Montreal - Institut universitaire, 1001 boul de Maisonneuve est, 5ieme etage, Montreal, QC, H2L 4P9, CANADA. Tel: 514-896-3396. p. 2722

St. Peter, Nora, Mgr, Northwestern Memorial Hospital, Galter Pavilion, Ste 3-304, 251 E Huron St, Chicago, IL, 60611. Tel: 312-926-5465. p. 566

St. Pierre, Dina, Dir of Libr, Dartmouth Public Libraries, 732 Dartmouth St, Dartmouth, MA, 02748. Tel: 508-999-0726. p. 1013

St. Pierre, Dina, Dir of Libr, Dartmouth Public Libraries, North Dartmouth, 1383 Tucker Rd, Dartmouth, MA, 02747. Tel: 508-999-0728. p. 1013

Staab, Katherine, Libr Serv Mgr, Kaiser-Permanente Medical Center, 10800 Magnolia Ave, Riverside, CA, 92505. Tel: 951-353-3658. p. 201

Stabler, Sydney, Teen Librn, Redford Township District Library, 25320 W Six Mile, Redford, MI, 48240. Tel: 313-531-5960. p. 1143

Stabryla, Kathleen, Librn, CDC National Institute for Occupational Safety & Health, 626 Cochrans Mill Rd, Pittsburgh, PA, 15236. Tel: 412-386-4431. p. 1992

Stacchini, Pauline, Exec Dir, Emporia Public Library, 110 E Sixth Ave, Emporia, KS, 66801-3960. Tel: 620-340-6462. p. 806

Stacey, Carolyn, Dir, Escanaba Public Library, 400 Ludington St, Escanaba, MI, 49829. Tel: 906-789-7332. p. 1103

Stacey, Kathleen, Coll Serv Librn, University of Hawaii at Hilo Library, 200 W Kawili St, Hilo, HI, 96720. Tel: 808-932-7285. p. 505

Stacey, Sean, Head, Ref & Instruction, Washburn University, 1700 SW College Ave, Topeka, KS, 66621. Tel: 785-670-1484. p. 839

Stachacz, John, Dean, Wilkes University, 84 W South St, Wilkes-Barre, PA, 18766. Tel: 570-408-4254. p. 2023

Stachnick, Charlene M, Supvr, University of Michigan, Shapiro Science Library, Shapiro Library Bldg, 3rd & 4th Flrs, 919 S University Ave, Ann Arbor, MI, 48109-1185. p. 1080

Stachnik, Lu Ann, Dir, Potterville Benton Township District Library, 150 Library Lane, Potterville, MI, 48876. Tel: 517-645-2989. p. 1143

Stachnik-Hollis, Charlene M, Coll & Access Serv Librn, University of Michigan, Museums Library, Research Museums Ctr, 3600 Varsity Dr, Ann Arbor, MI, 48108. Tel: 734-764-0467. p. 1080

Stacie, Cohen B, Librn, CDM Smith InfoCenter, 75 State St, Boston, MA, 02109. Tel: 617-452-6824. p. 994

Stack, Bryan, Ser, Creighton University, Health Sciences Library-Learning Resource Center, 2770 Webster St, Omaha, NE, 68178-0210. Tel: 402-280-5137. p. 1328

Stack, Elizabeth, Mgr, Baltimore County Public Library, Sollers Point Branch, 323 Sollers Point Rd, Baltimore, MD, 21222-6169. Tel: 410-887-2485. p. 980

Stackhouse, Emily, Access Serv Asst, Mkt Coordr, Outreach Coordr, DeSales University, 2755 Station Ave, Center Valley, PA, 18034. Tel: 610-282-1100, Ext 1361. p. 1920

Stackhouse, Eric, Chief Librn, Pictou - Antigonish Regional Library, 182 Dalhousie St, New Glasgow, NS, B2H 5E3, CANADA. Tel: 902-755-6031. p. 2622

Stackpole, Mark, Library Technologist, The California Maritime Academy Library, 200 Maritime Academy Dr, Vallejo, CA, 94590. Tel: 707-654-1090. p. 255

Stacy, Julie, Youth Serv Mgr, Washington County Public Library, 615 Fifth St, Marietta, OH, 45750-1973. Tel: 740-373-1057. p. 1799

Stacy-Ann, Brown, Libr Tech, Conestoga College, Library Services-Brantford Campus, 274 Colborne St, Rm 138, Brantford, ON, N3T 2L6, CANADA. Tel: 519-748-5220, Ext 7343. p. 2651

Stade, Kelly, Libr Serv Mgr, Hennepin County Library, 12601 Ridgedale Dr, Minnetonka, MN, 55305-1909. Tel: 612-543-8749. p. 1186

Stadick, Anna, Dir, University of Wisconsin-Parkside Library, 900 Wood Rd, Kenosha, WI, 53141. Tel: 262-595-2167. p. 2445

Stadler, Derek, Web Serv Librn, Fiorello H LaGuardia Community College Library, 31-10 Thomson Ave, Long Island City, NY, 11101. Tel: 718-482-5031. p. 1565

Staedter, Jessica, Youth Serv Librn, Hales Corners Library, 5885 S 116th St, Hales Corners, WI, 53130-1707. Tel: 414-529-6150, Ext 17. p. 2440

Staerker, John, Tech Asst, Hudson Valley Community College, 80 Vandenburgh Ave, Troy, NY, 12180. Tel: 518-629-7323. p. 1652

Staff, Rhoda, Dir, Unity Free Public Library, 13 Center Rd, Unity, NH, 03603. Tel: 603-543-3253. p. 1382

Stafford, Ameerah, Assoc Dir, University of Delaware Library Museums & Press, Willard Hall Education Bldg, 16 W Main St, Rm 012, Newark, DE, 19716. Tel: 302-831-8148. p. 355

Stafford, Bill, Adminr, Louisiana Office of the Secretary of State, 3851 Essen Lane, Baton Rouge, LA, 70809-2137. Tel: 225-922-1208. p. 884

Stafford, Cynthia, Knowledge Serv Analyst, Taft, Stettinius & Hollister LLP, 425 Walnut St, Ste 1800, Cincinnati, OH, 45202-3957. Tel: 513-381-2838. p. 1764

Stafford, Daniel, Emerging Tech Librn, Open Educational Resources Librn, Kutztown University, 15200 Kutztown Rd, Bldg 5, Kutztown, PA, 19530. Tel: 610-683-4480. p. 1949

Stafford, Jeffrey, Dir, Robert R Jones Public Library, 900 First St, Coal Valley, IL, 61240. Tel: 309-799-3047. p. 573

Stafford, Jill, Head, Adult Serv, Matawan-Aberdeen Public Library, 165 Main St, Matawan, NJ, 07747. Tel: 732-583-9100. p. 1417

Stafford, Leslie, Tech Support, Eastern Health, Addictions Services Library, Mount Pearl Sq, 760 Topsail Rd, St. John's, NL, A1B 4A4, CANADA. Tel: 709-752-4120, 709-752-4121. p. 2610

Stafford, Ron, Head Librn, Northeastern Technical College Library, Harris Hall, Cheraw Campus, 1201 Chesterfield Hwy, Rm 506, Cheraw, SC, 29520-7015. Tel: 843-921-6953, 843-921-6954. p. 2051

Stafford, Stephen, Librn, Vernon College, 4400 College Dr, Vernon, TX, 76384. Tel: 940-552-6291, Ext 2222. p. 2252

Stage, Teresa, Libr Tech, Tech Serv, Pennsylvania Western University - Clarion, 840 Wood St, Clarion, PA, 16214. Tel: 814-393-2343. p. 1922

Staggs, Geneva, Dir, University of South Alabama Libraries, Biomedical Library, Biomedical Library Bldg, 5791 USA Dr N, Mobile, AL, 36688-0002. Tel: 251-460-7043. p. 27

Staheli, Kory, Coll Develop, Brigham Young University, Howard W Hunter Law Library, 256 JRCB, Provo, UT, 84602-8000. Tel: 801-422-3593. p. 2269

Staheli, Kory, Dir, Brigham Young University, Howard W Hunter Law Library, 256 JRCB, Provo, UT, 84602-8000. Tel: 801-422-3593. p. 2269
Stahl, Frank, Dir, Learning Res, Pratt Community College, 348 NE State Rd 61, Pratt, KS, 67124. Tel: 620-450-2238. p. 832
Stahl, Hannah, Dir, Cohoes Public Library, 169 Mohawk St, Cohoes, NY, 12047. Tel: 518-235-2570. p. 1520
Stahl, Joan, Dir, Res & Instruction Serv, Catholic University of America, 315 Mullen Library, 620 Michigan Ave NE, Washington, DC, 20064. Tel: 202-319-6473. p. 362
Stahl, Michelle M, Exec Dir, Monadnock Center for History & Culture at Peterborough Historical Society, 19 Grove St, Peterborough, NH, 03458. Tel: 603-924-3235. p. 1378
Stahler, Kim R, Instrul Serv Librn, Ref Serv, Reading Area Community College, 30 S Front St, Reading, PA, 19602. Tel: 610-607-6237. p. 2000
Stahr, Shelah, Coord, Coll Develop, Tech Serv, Pickaway County District Public Library, 1160 N Court St, Circleville, OH, 43113-1725. Tel: 740-477-1644, Ext 222. p. 1765
Stainbrook, Bernadette, Dir, Plainfield Public Library, 126 S Main St, Plainfield, WI, 54966-0305. Tel: 715-335-4523. p. 2469
Stainbrook, Laura, Libr Dir, Denton Public Library, 515 Broadway, Denton, MT, 59430. Tel: 406-567-2571. p. 1292
Stainbrook, Lynn, Exec Dir, Rockford Public Library, 214 N Church St, Rockford, IL, 61101-1023. Tel: 815-965-7606. p. 642
Stainer, Lori, Dir, Slayton Public Library, 2451 Broadway Ave, Slayton, MN, 56172. Tel: 507-836-8778. p. 1204
Stainforth, Cheri, Early Literacy Specialist, Frankenmuth James E Wickson District Library, 359 S Franklin St, Frankenmuth, MI, 48734. Tel: 989-652-8323. p. 1107
Stakes, Robert, Libr Dir, Assoc VPres for Univ Advan, University of Texas at El Paso Library, 500 W University Ave, El Paso, TX, 79968-0582. Tel: 915-747-6710. p. 2175
Stakley, Paula, Interim Libr Dir, Maud Preston Palenske Memorial Library, 500 Market St, Saint Joseph, MI, 49085. Tel: 269-983-7167, Ext 10. p. 1148
Stakutis, Lisa, Br Supvr, Dedham Public Library, Endicott Branch, 257 Mount Vernon St, Dedham, MA, 02026. Tel: 781-751-9178. p. 1014
Stalcup, Carrissa, Librn, Stockport Public Library, 113 E Beswick St, Stockport, IA, 52651. Tel: 319-796-4681. p. 784
Stalcup, Derek, Coll, Tech Serv Mgr, Ventura County Library, 5600 Everglades St, Ste A, Ventura, CA, 93003. Tel: 805-677-7150. p. 256
Staley, Vickie, Circ Librn, Cumberland County Public Library, 114 W Hill St, Burkesville, KY, 42717. Tel: 270-864-2207. p. 850
Staley, Walter, Resource Specialist, Moberly Area Community College Library & Academic Resource Center, Mexico Campus, 2900 Doreli Lane, Mexico, MO, 65265. Tel: 573-582-0817, 660-263-4100, Ext 13629. p. 1262
Stalker, Amy, Assoc Dept Head, Georgia State University, Dunwoody Campus, 2101 Womack Rd, Dunwoody, GA, 30338. Tel: 770-274-5088. p. 464
Stalker, Laura, Dep Dir, Henry E Huntington Library & Art Gallery, 1151 Oxford Rd, San Marino, CA, 91108. Tel: 626-405-2100. p. 235
Stall, Lisa, Librn, Preble County District Library, New Paris Branch, 115 N Washington St, New Paris, OH, 45347. Tel: 937-437-7242. p. 1784
Stallings, Jennifer, Circ Mgr, Augusta-Richmond County Public Library, 823 Telfair St, Augusta, GA, 30901. Tel: 706-821-2600. p. 466
Stallings, Melissa, Mgr, County of Los Angeles Public Library, Malibu Library, 23519 W Civic Center Way, Malibu, CA, 90265-4804. Tel: 310-456-6438. p. 137
Stallworth, Rebecca, Asst Prof, Simmons University, 300 The Fenway, Boston, MA, 02115. Tel: 617-521-2800. p. 2786
Stam, Julie, Commun Outreach Liaison, Eisenhower Public Library District, 4613 N Oketo Ave, Harwood Heights, IL, 60706. Tel: 708-867-7828. p. 597
Staman, Johanna, Head, Access Serv, Seattle Pacific University Library, 3307 Third Ave W, Seattle, WA, 98119. Tel: 206-281-2789. p. 2379
Stamas, Stacy, Mgr, Art, Music & Media, Allen County Public Library, 900 Library Plaza, Fort Wayne, IN, 46802. Tel: 260-421-1211. p. 683
Stamatopoulos, Gus, Dir, Libr & Learning Commons, Stockton University, 101 Vera King Farris Dr, Galloway, NJ, 08205-9441. Tel: 609-652-4289. p. 1404
Stambach, Abigail, Head, Archives & Spec Coll, College of the Holy Cross, One College St, Worcester, MA, 01610. Tel: 508-793-2506. p. 1072
Stambaugh, Bradley, Bus Mgr, Central Michigan University, 250 E Preston St, Mount Pleasant, MI, 48859. Tel: 989-774-6415. p. 1134
Stamberg, Michael, YA Serv, Bellmore Memorial Library, 2288 Bedford Ave, Bellmore, NY, 11710. Tel: 516-785-2990. p. 1492
Stamey, Leisa, Librn, Buncombe County Public Libraries, Enka-Candler Branch, 1404 Sand Hill Rd, Enka, NC, 28715. Tel: 828-250-4758. p. 1672
Stamm, Colleen, Dir, Wyomissing Public Library, Nine Reading Blvd, Wyomissing, PA, 19610-2084. Tel: 610-374-2385. p. 2025
Stamm, Timothy, Dean, Libr Serv, Delgado Community College, City Park Campus, Marvin E Thames Sr Learning Resource Ctr, 615 City Park Ave, Bldg 7, New Orleans, LA, 70119. Tel: 504-671-5482. p. 900
Stampahar, Margie, Tech Serv Coordr, Point Park University Library, 414 Wood St, Pittsburgh, PA, 15222. Tel: 412-392-3167. p. 1995
Stamper, Harry Loren, Head, Tech Serv, University of San Diego, Katherine M & George M Pardee Jr Legal Research Center, 5998 Alcala Park, San Diego, CA, 92110-2492. Tel: 619-260-4543. p. 223
Stampler, Carol, Libr Dir, Mason-Dixon Public Library, 250 Bailey Dr, Stewartstown, PA, 17363. Tel: 717-993-2404. p. 2010
Stanbery, Renee, Librn, Jennings, Strouss & Salmon, One E Washington St, Ste 1900, Phoenix, AZ, 85004-2554. Tel: 602-262-5911. p. 70
Stancampiano, Robert, Ref & Instruction Librn, Point Park University Library, 414 Wood St, Pittsburgh, PA, 15222. Tel: 412-392-3166. p. 1995
Stancher, Amber, Dean, Learning Res, Mid-State Technical College, 2600 W Fifth St, Marshfield, WI, 54449. Tel: 715-389-7020. p. 2454
Stancher, Amber, Librn, Mid-State Technical College, 1001 Centerpoint Dr, Stevens Point, WI, 54481. Tel: 715-342-3129. p. 2479
Stancil, Nathan, Instruction & Outreach Librn, Johnston Community College Library, Learning Resource Ctr, Bldg E, 245 College Rd, Smithfield, NC, 27577. Tel: 919-464-2277. p. 1716
Stancliff, Eric, Asst Dir, Libr Serv, Concordia Seminary Library, 801 Seminary Pl, Saint Louis, MO, 63105-3199. Tel: 314-505-7038. p. 1270
Stanczak, Cynthia, Dir, Albion District Library, 501 S Superior St, Albion, MI, 49224. Tel: 517-629-3993. p. 1076
Stanczak, Daniel, Chief Info Officer, Sigma Alpha Epsilon Fraternity & Foundation, 1856 Sheridan Rd, Evanston, IL, 60201-3837. Tel: 847-475-1856. p. 587
Standal, Becky, Youth Serv Librn, Longview Public Library, 1600 Louisiana St, Longview, WA, 98632-2993. Tel: 360-442-5323. p. 2369
Standard, Michael, Studio Librarian, University of Tennessee at Chattanooga Library, 400 Douglas Ave, Dept 6456, Chattanooga, TN, 37403-2598. Tel: 423-425-4501. p. 2092
Standifird, Beth, Librn, San Antonio Conservation Society Foundation Library, 1146 S Alamo St, San Antonio, TX, 78210. Tel: 210-224-6163. p. 2238
Standling, Elizabeth, Libr Asst, Gale Library, 16 S Main St, Newton, NH, 03858. Tel: 603-382-4691. p. 1376
Standridge, Paula, Tech Serv Coordr, Motlow State Community College Libraries, 6015 Ledford Mill Rd, Tullahoma, TN, 37388. Tel: 931-393-1669. p. 2128
Stanek, Tori, Digital Access & Public Servs Librn, Columbia Gorge Community College Library, 400 E Scenic Dr, The Dalles, OR, 97058. Tel: 541-506-6081. p. 1899
Stanfanski, Megan, Libr Mgr, Superior District Library, DeTour Public Library, 202 S Division St, DeTour Village, MI, 49725. Tel: 906-297-2011. p. 1149
Stanfield, Andrea, Interim Dean of Libr, University of West Georgia, 1601 Maple St, Carrollton, GA, 30118. Tel: 678-839-6495. p. 469
Stanfield, Andrea, Libr Dir, Queens University of Charlotte, 1900 Selwyn Ave, Charlotte, NC, 28274. Tel: 704-337-2400. p. 1681
Stanfield, Danielle, Library Contact, ScottHulse, PC, One San Jacinto Plaza, 201 E Main Dr, Ste 1100, El Paso, TX, 79901. Tel: 915-533-2493, Ext 307. p. 2174
Stanfield, Heath, Br Mgr, McAlester Public Library, 401 N Second St, McAlester, OK, 74501. Tel: 918-426-0930. p. 1853
Stanford, Charlie, Circ Asst, McMurry University, Bldg 1601 War Hawk Way, One McMurry University # 218, Abilene, TX, 79697. Tel: 325-793-4688. p. 2132
Stangel, Vickie, Dir, Dodgeville Public Library, 139 S Iowa St, Dodgeville, WI, 53533. Tel: 608-935-3728. p. 2431
Stanger, Rasheil, Prog Dir, Valley of the Tetons Library, 56 N Main St, Victor, ID, 83455. Tel: 208-787-2201. p. 532
Stangle, Rita, Tech Serv, Carroll County Public Library, 136 Court St, Carrollton, KY, 41008. Tel: 502-732-7020. p. 851
Stanhope, Sarah, Cat, Managing Librn, Museum of Fine Arts, Houston, 1001 Bissonnet St, Houston, TX, 77005. Tel: 713-639-7325. p. 2197
Staniec, Jillian, Archivist, Red Deer & District Archives, 4525 47 A Ave, Red Deer, AB, T4N 3T4, CANADA. Tel: 403-309-8403. p. 2551
Stanifer, Laura, Archivist, Wheaton College, Marion E Wade Center, 351 E Lincoln, Wheaton, IL, 60187-4213. Tel: 630-752-5908. p. 662
Staninger, Steve, Assoc Univ Librn, University of San Diego, Helen K & James S Copley Library, 5998 Alcala Park, San Diego, CA, 92110. p. 222
Stanis, Suzanne, VP of Education, Indiana Landmarks, 1201 Central Ave, Indianapolis, IN, 46202-2660. Tel: 317-639-4534. p. 692
Stanishevskaya, Irina, Cataloger, University of Alabama at Birmingham, Mervyn H Sterne Library, 917 13th St S, Birmingham, AL, 35205. Tel: 205-934-6364. p. 10
Stanley, Ben, Ref Librn, Syst Adminr, Cranford Free Public Library, 224 Walnut Ave, Cranford, NJ, 07016-2931. Tel: 908-709-7272. p. 1398
Stanley, Brenda, Libr Dir, Enosburgh Public Library, 241 Main St, Enosburg Falls, VT, 05450. Tel: 802-933-2328. p. 2283
Stanley, Brian, Asst Librn, Vassalboro Public Library, 930 Bog Rd, East Vassalboro, ME, 04935. Tel: 207-923-3233. p. 924
Stanley, Carol, Dir, Libr Serv, Athens Technical College Library, 800 US Hwy 29 N, Athens, GA, 30601-1500. Tel: 706-355-5020. p. 459
Stanley, Cynthia, Libr Adminr, Frenchman's Bay Library, 1776 US Hwy, No 1, Sullivan, ME, 04664. Tel: 207-422-2307. p. 943
Stanley, David H, Dr, Dir, Seton Hill University, One Seton Hill Dr, Greensburg, PA, 15601. Tel: 724-838-4291. p. 1938
Stanley, Jamie, Librn, Minnesota Department of Corrections, 1101 Linden Lane, Faribault, MN, 55021-0730. Tel: 507-334-0727. p. 1175

Stanley, Jamie, Ref Librn, Northfield Public Library, 210 Washington St, Northfield, MN, 55057. Tel: 507-645-6606. p. 1191

Stanley, Janet L, Librn, Smithsonian Libraries, Warren M Robbins Library, National Museum of African Art, National Museum of African Art, 950 Independence Ave SW, Rm 2138, Washington, DC, 20560. Tel: 202-633-4681. p. 376

Stanley, Jennifer, Br Mgr, York County Library, York Public, 21 E Liberty St, York, SC, 29745. Tel: 803-684-3751. p. 2068

Stanley, Karen, Head, Children's Servx, Galveston County Library System, 2310 Sealy Ave, Galveston, TX, 77550. Tel: 409-763-8854, Ext 119. p. 2183

Stanley, Melissa, Library Contact, Queen Elizabeth Hospital, 60 Riverside Dr, Charlottetown, PE, C1A 8T5, CANADA. Tel: 902-894-2371. p. 2707

Stanley, Ruth, Asst Br Mgr, Evangeline Parish Library, Turkey Creek, 13951 Veterans Memorial Hwy, Turkey Creek, LA, 70586. Tel: 337-461-2304. p. 912

Stanley, Sara, Librn, Law Society of Saskatchewan Libraries, Court House, 2425 Victoria Ave, 2nd Flr, Regina, SK, S4P 3M3, CANADA. Tel: 306-569-8020. p. 2746

Stannard, Teresa L, Dir, Parchment Community Library, 401 S Riverview Dr, Parchment, MI, 49004. Tel: 269-343-7747, Ext 203. p. 1140

Stano, Terri, Dir, Thayer Public Library, 798 Washington St, Braintree, MA, 02184. Tel: 781-848-0405. p. 1001

Stanoeva, Milena, Public Affairs Mgr, Canadian Federation of Independent Business, 401-4141 Yonge St, Toronto, ON, M2P 2A6, CANADA. Tel: 416-222-8022. p. 2687

Stansbery, Jill, Coordr, Youth Serv, Upper Sandusky Community Library, 301 N Sandusky Ave, Upper Sandusky, OH, 43351-1139. Tel: 419-294-1345. p. 1826

Stansbury, Mary C, PhD, Assoc Prof, Dept Chair, University of Denver, Morgridge College of Education, Katherine A Ruffatto Hall, 1999 E Evans Ave, Denver, CO, 80208. Tel: 303-871-3217. p. 2783

Stansell, Lewis, Libr Dir, Nellie Pederson Civic Library, 406 Live Oak St, Clifton, TX, 76634. Tel: 254-675-6495. p. 2156

Stansell, Morgan, Access Serv Coordr, Berry College, 2277 Martha Berry Hwy, Mount Berry, GA, 30149. Tel: 706-233-2938. p. 492

Stanton, Chris, Supvry Librn, Museum of Flight, 9404 E Marginal Way S, Seattle, WA, 98108-4097. Tel: 206-764-5700. p. 2377

Stanton, Claire, Pub Serv Librn, The John P Holt Brentwood Library, 8109 Concord Rd, Brentwood, TN, 37027. Tel: 615-371-0090. p. 2089

Stanton, Debbie, Pub Serv Mgr, Topeka & Shawnee County Public Library, 1515 SW Tenth Ave, Topeka, KS, 66604-1374. Tel: 785-580-4400. p. 839

Stanton, Kelsey, Human Res Mgr, Trudeau Institute Library, 154 Algonquin Ave, Saranac Lake, NY, 12983. Tel: 518-891-3080. p. 1636

Stanton, Kenetha, Coll Develop Librn, Christian Theological Seminary, 1000 W 42nd St, Indianapolis, IN, 46208. Tel: 317-931-2367. p. 691

Stanton, Maggie, Dir, Malvern Public Library, One E First Ave, Ste 2, Malvern, PA, 19355-2743. Tel: 610-644-7259. p. 1957

Stanton, Maggie, Libr Dir, West Chester Public Library, 415 N Church St, West Chester, PA, 19380-2401. Tel: 610-696-1721. p. 2020

Stanton, Mary, Coordr, Circ, Pickaway County District Public Library, 1160 N Court St, Circleville, OH, 43113-1725. Tel: 740-477-1644, Ext 225. p. 1765

Stanton, Morgan, Ms, Mgr, Enoch Pratt Free Library, Canton Branch, 1030 S Ellwood Ave, Baltimore, MD, 21224-4930. Tel: 443-984-4959. p. 952

Stanton, Natasha, Ch Serv, Mary Meuser Memorial Library, 1803 Northampton St, Easton, PA, 18042-3183. Tel: 610-258-3040. p. 1928

Stanton, Paula, Circ Serv Mgr, L E Phillips Memorial Public Library, 400 Eau Claire St, Eau Claire, WI, 54701. Tel: 715-839-5098. p. 2432

Stanton, Shelly, Dir, Hannibal Free Library, 162 Oswego St, Hannibal, NY, 13074. Tel: 315-564-5471. p. 1544

Stanton, Staci, Mgr, Prog & Outreach, Urbandale Public Library, 3520 86th St, Urbandale, IA, 50322. Tel: 515-278-3945. p. 787

Stanton, Stephen, Librn, University of Missouri-Columbia, Geological Sciences Library, 201 Geological Sciences, Columbia, MO, 65211. Tel: 573-882-4860. p. 1244

Stanton, Susan, Dir, Access Serv, Dir, Conserv Serv, Provincial Archives of Alberta, Reference Library, 8555 Roper Rd, Edmonton, AB, T6E 5W1, CANADA. Tel: 780-427-1750. p. 2537

Stanton-Roark, Nic Don, Archivist, Anderson University, 1100 E Fifth St, Anderson, IN, 46012-3495. Tel: 765-641-4285. p. 668

Stanwicks, Kabel, Head, Access Serv, University at Albany, State University of New York, Science Library, 1400 Washington Ave, Albany, NY, 12222. Tel: 518-442-3578. p. 1484

Stanwicks, Kabel Nathan, Head, Access Serv, University at Albany, State University of New York, 1400 Washington Ave, Albany, NY, 12222-0001. Tel: 518-442-3578. p. 1484

Stap, Madolene, Doc Delivery Spec, Kalamazoo College Library, 1200 Academy St, Kalamazoo, MI, 49006-3285. Tel: 269-337-7153. p. 1121

Staples, Alyssa, Head, Tech Serv, Lucius Beebe Memorial Library, 345 Main St, Wakefield, MA, 01880-5093. Tel: 781-246-6334. p. 1061

Staples, Caitlin, Tech & Technical Serv Librn, Westborough Public Library, 55 W Main St, Westborough, MA, 01581. Tel: 508-366-3050. p. 1066

Stapleton, Belinda, Cat, Coll Develop, Lasalle Parish Library, 3165 N First St, Jena, LA, 71342. Tel: 318-992-5675. p. 891

Stapleton, Blair, Asst Dean, Pub Serv, University of Louisiana at Lafayette, 400 E St Mary Blvd, Lafayette, LA, 70503. Tel: 337-482-1173. p. 893

Stapleton, Elliot, Art Coll Coordr, Outreach Librn, Camas Public Library, 625 NE Fourth Ave, Camas, WA, 98607. Tel: 360-834-4692. p. 2360

Stapleton, Leslie, Head, Archives & Spec Coll, Texas A&M University-San Antonio, One University Way, San Antonio, TX, 78224. Tel: 210-784-1516. p. 2239

Stapleton, Mary, Dir, Rochester Public Library, 208 W Spring St, Rochester, WI, 53167. Tel: 262-534-3533. p. 2474

Stapleton, Melody, Ref Librn, Mississippi Delta Community College, 414 Hwy 3 S, Moorhead, MS, 38761. Tel: 662-246-6376. p. 1227

Stapp, Jennie, State Librn, Montana State Library, 1515 E Sixth Ave, Helena, MT, 59620. Tel: 406-444-3115. p. 1296

Starasta, Leslie, Dir, Libr Serv, Lincoln Christian University, 100 Campus View Dr, Lincoln, IL, 62656. Tel: 217-732-7788, Ext 2203. p. 608

Starasta, Leslie, Assoc Dir, Libr Operations, Illinois State Library, Gwendolyn Brooks Bldg, 300 S Second St, Springfield, IL, 62701-1796. Tel: 217-785-0052. p. 649

Starasta, Mike, Libr Dir, Lincoln Public Library District, 725 Pekin, Lincoln, IL, 62656. Tel: 217-732-5732, 217-732-8878. p. 609

Starbird, Lauren, Director of Library & Academic Support, Maine Maritime Academy, Pleasant St, Box C-1, Castine, ME, 04420. Tel: 207-326-2260. p. 921

Starbuck, Edith, Info Serv Librn, University of Cincinnati Libraries, Donald C Harrison Health Sciences Library, 231 Albert Sabin Way, Cincinnati, OH, 45267. Tel: 513-558-1433. p. 1765

Starcher, Debbie, Br Supvr, Wayne County Public Library, West Salem Branch, 99 E Buckeye St, West Salem, OH, 44287. Tel: 330-804-4712. p. 1833

Starchuck, Rhonda, Dept Adminr, SIAST-Saskatchewan Institute of Applied Science & Technology, 600 Saskatchewan St W, Moose Jaw, SK, S6H 4R4, CANADA. Tel: 306-775-7709. p. 2743

Starek, Retha, Co-Dir, Ackley Public Library, 401 State St, Ackley, IA, 50601. Tel: 641-847-2233. p. 729

Stares, Sean, Libr Adminr, Alex Robertson Public Library, 1212 Hildebrand Dr, La Ronge, SK, S0J 1L0, CANADA. Tel: 306-425-2160. p. 2742

Stargard, William, Interim Dean, Community College of Rhode Island, 400 East Ave, Warwick, RI, 02886-1807. Tel: 401-825-1189. p. 2043

Stark, Andrea, Dir, Monroe Community Library, Eight Swan Lake Ave, Monroe, ME, 04951. Tel: 207-525-3515. p. 932

Stark, LeAnn, Asst Librn, Green Forest Public Library, 206 E Main St, Green Forest, AR, 72638-2627. Tel: 870-438-6700. p. 97

Stark, Marissa, Dir, Niobrara Public Library, 25414 Park Ave, Ste 3, Niobrara, NE, 68760. Tel: 402-857-3565. p. 1326

Stark, Robin, Archivist, The Morton Arboretum, 4100 Illinois Rte 53, Lisle, IL, 60532-1293. Tel: 630-719-2429. p. 610

Stark, Thomas, Br Mgr, Chicago Public Library, Budlong Woods, 5630 N Lincoln Ave, Chicago, IL, 60659. Tel: 312-742-9590. p. 556

Stark, Tom, Dir, Federal Reserve Bank of Philadelphia, 100 N Sixth St, 4th Flr, Philadelphia, PA, 19106. Tel: 215-574-6540. p. 1977

Stark-Farrow, Marie, Archivist, Shaw University, 118 E South St, Raleigh, NC, 27601. Tel: 919-546-8202. p. 1710

Starkey, Brendan E, Dir, Orange County Public Law Library, 515 N Flower St, Santa Ana, CA, 92703-2354. Tel: 714-338-6790. p. 239

Starkey, Deborah, Librn, Lowe Public Library, 40 Bridge St, Shinnston, WV, 26431. Tel: 304-592-1700. p. 2415

Starkey, Edward D, Univ Librn, University of San Diego, Helen K & James S Copley Library, 5998 Alcala Park, San Diego, CA, 92110. p. 222

Starkey, Jennifer, Dir, Elyria Public Library System, 211 2nd St, Elyria, OH, 44035. Tel: 440-323-5747. p. 1784

Starkey, Monique Delatte, Acq Librn, Fullerton College, 321 E Chapman Ave, Fullerton, CA, 92832-2095. Tel: 714-992-7379. p. 147

Starks, Cindy, Communications Coordr, Coal City Public Library District, 85 N Garfield St, Coal City, IL, 60416. Tel: 815-634-4552. p. 572

Starks, Jacob, Dir, Univ Libr, Graceland University, One University Pl, Lamoni, IA, 50140. p. 764

Starling, Rayel, Libr Mgr, Globe Public Library, 339 S Broad St, Globe, AZ, 85501. Tel: 928-425-6111. p. 62

Starnes, Christie, Br Mgr, Union County Public Library, Union West Regional, 123 Unionville-Indian Trail Rd, Indian Trail, NC, 28079. Tel: 704-821-7475. p. 1704

Starnes, Leda, Br Mgr, Middle Georgia Regional Library System, Crawford County Public Library, 340 McCrary Ave, Roberta, GA, 31078-0580. Tel: 478-836-4478. p. 487

Starosta, Natalie, Dir, North Riverside Public Library District, 2400 S Des Plaines Ave, North Riverside, IL, 60546. Tel: 708-447-0869, Ext 225. p. 626

Starr, Daniel, Dir, Tech Serv, Metropolitan Museum of Art, Thomas J Watson Library, 1000 Fifth Ave, New York, NY, 10028-0198. Tel: 212-650-2582. p. 1592

Starr, Jesse, Circ Supvr, Amarillo College, 2201 S Washington, Amarillo, TX, 79109. Tel: 806-371-5386. p. 2134

Starr, Juniper, Cat Spec, Johnson City Public Library, 100 W Millard St, Johnson City, TN, 37604. Tel: 423-434-4462. p. 2104

Starr, Lea, Assoc Univ Librn, Res Serv, University of British Columbia Library, 1961 East Mall, Vancouver, BC, V6T 1Z1, CANADA. Tel: 604-822-2826. p. 2580

Starr, Valorie, Dir, Weatherford College Library, 225 College Park Dr, Weatherford, TX, 76086. Tel: 817-598-6251. p. 2255

Starr-Ashton, Penny, Libr Mgr, Pennsylvania School for the Deaf Library, 100 W School House Lane, Philadelphia, PA, 19144. Tel: 215-951-4700. p. 1984

Starratt, Jay, Dean of Libr, Washington State University Libraries, 100 Dairy Rd, Pullman, WA, 99164. Tel: 509-335-9671. p. 2374

Start, Amanda, Coll Mgt, University at Buffalo Libraries-State University of New York, Health Sciences Library, Abbott Hall, 3435 Main St, Bldg 28, Buffalo, NY, 14214-3002. Tel: 716-829-5736. p. 1510

Stascak, Rachel, Libr Asst, Lester Public Library of Rome, 1157 Rome Center Dr, Nekoosa, WI, 54457. Tel: 715-325-8990. p. 2464

Stasiak, Denise, Cataloger, Andover Public Library, 142 W Main St, Andover, OH, 44003-9318. Tel: 440-293-6792. p. 1746

Stasinopoulos, Jennifer, Dir, Mayville Public Library, 111 N Main St, Mayville, WI, 53050. Tel: 920-387-7910. p. 2455

Staskowski, Jim, Mgr, Richland Library, Sandhills, 763 Fashion Dr, Columbia, SC, 29229. Tel: 803-699-9230. p. 2054

Statham, Ricky, Dir, Oneonta Public Library, 221 Second St S, Oneonta, AL, 35121. Tel: 205-274-7641. p. 31

Staton, Michael, Dir, Jefferson Davis Parish Library, 118 W Plaquemine St, Jennings, LA, 70546. Tel: 337-824-1210. p. 892

Staton, Michael, Dir, Iberville Parish Library, 24605 J Gerald Berret Blvd, Plaquemine, LA, 70764. Tel: 225-687-2520, 225-687-4397. p. 906

Staton, Vicky, Br Mgr, Calcasieu Parish Public Library System, Central Library, 301 W Claude St, Lake Charles, LA, 70605. Tel: 337-721-7116. p. 893

Statton, Maddy, Tech Serv Mgr, Wicomico Public Library, 122 S Division St, Salisbury, MD, 21801. Tel: 410-749-3612, Ext 164. p. 976

Statz, Mary, Dir, Nelson Public Library, Ten W Third St, Nelson, NE, 68961. Tel: 402-225-7111. p. 1326

Statz, Meagan, Asst Dir, Teen & Adult Librn, Ruth Culver Community Library, 540 Water St, Prairie du Sac, WI, 53578. Tel: 608-643-8318. p. 2471

Staub, Will, Dir, Mount Gilead Public Library, 41 E High St, Mount Gilead, OH, 43338-1429. Tel: 419-947-5866. p. 1804

Stauber, Abbigail, Libr Tech, Geneva College, 3200 College Ave, Beaver Falls, PA, 15010-3599. Tel: 724-847-6563. p. 1909

Stauffer, Julie, Assoc Dir for Collection Servs, University of Chicago Library, D'Angelo Law Library, 1121 E 60th St, Chicago, IL, 60637-2786. Tel: 773-702-0692. p. 570

Stauffer, Suzanne, Dr, Prof, Louisiana State University, 267 Coates Hall, Baton Rouge, LA, 70803. Tel: 225-578-3158, 225-578-3159. p. 2785

Staugler, Brandy, Br Mgr, Mercer County District Library, Saint Henry Granville Township, 200 E Main St, Saint Henry, OH, 45883. Tel: 419-678-3128. p. 1757

Stavenga, Mink, Dean, Southwestern College Library, 900 Otay Lakes Rd, Bldg 64, Chula Vista, CA, 91910-7299. Tel: 619-482-6569. p. 130

Stavros, Crista, Br Head, Lowell Public Library, Schneider Branch, 24002 Parrish Ave, Schneider, IN, 46376. Tel: 219-552-1000. p. 704

Stay, Elisabeth, Coordr, Patron Serv, Bethany Lutheran College Memorial Library, 700 Luther Dr, Mankato, MN, 56001-4490. Tel: 507-344-7000. p. 1181

Staysniak, Geoffrey, Dir, Health Sci Libr, Sacred Heart University, 5151 Park Ave, Fairfield, CT, 06825-1000. Tel: 203-396-6051. p. 312

Stayton, Gonda, Head, Acq, West Texas A&M University, 110 26th St, Canyon, TX, 79016. Tel: 806-651-2218. p. 2153

Stayton, Kevin, Chief Curator, Brooklyn Museum, Wilbour Library of Egyptology, 200 Eastern Pkwy, Brooklyn, NY, 11238. Tel: 718-501-6219. p. 1502

Steadham, Christopher, Dir, University of Kansas Libraries, Wheat Law Library, Green Hall, Rm 200, 1535 W 15th St, Lawrence, KS, 66045-7608. Tel: 785-864-9242. p. 820

Steadman, Diane, Prog Dir, Franklin County Library District, 109 S First E, Preston, ID, 83263. Tel: 208-852-0175. p. 529

Steagall, Jason, Libr Instruction & Ref Spec, Gateway Technical College, North Bldg, Rm N226, 400 County Rd H, Elkhorn, WI, 53121. Tel: 262-741-8438. p. 2433

Steans, Elizabeth, Ref Serv Mgr, L E Phillips Memorial Public Library, 400 Eau Claire St, Eau Claire, WI, 54701. Tel: 715-839-1683. p. 2432

Stearns, Barry, Sr Ref Librn, New England Law, 154 Stuart St, Boston, MA, 02116-5687. Tel: 617-422-7332. p. 998

Stebbins, James, Bus Mgr, Finger Lakes Library System, 1300 Dryden Rd, Ithaca, NY, 14850. Tel: 607-273-4074, Ext 225. p. 1552

Stebbins, Jenna, Instruction Librn, Ref Librn, Naugatuck Valley Community College, 750 Chase Pkwy, Rm K512, Waterbury, CT, 06708. Tel: 203-596-8712. p. 344

Steben, Frederic, Chef de Div, Bibliotheques de Montreal, Hochelaga, 1870 rue Davidson, Montreal, QC, H1W 2Y6, CANADA. Tel: 514-872-3666. p. 2719

Steben, Frederic, Chef de Div, Bibliotheques de Montreal, Langelier, 6473 rue Sherbrooke Est, Montreal, QC, H1N 1C5, CANADA. Tel: 514-872-2640 (Adult Serv), 514-872-4227 (Children's Serv). p. 2719

Steben, Frederic, Chef de Div, Bibliotheques de Montreal, Maisonneuve, 4120 rue Ontario Est, Montreal, QC, H1V 1J9, CANADA. Tel: 514-872-4213 (Adult Serv), 514-872-4214 (Children's Serv). p. 2719

Steben, Frederic, Chef de Div, Bibliotheques de Montreal, Mercier, 8105 rue Hochelaga, Montreal, QC, H1L 2K9, CANADA. Tel: 514-872-8738 (Adult serv). p. 2719

Steckelberg, Helen, Automation Librn, Osmond Public Library, 412 N State St, Osmond, NE, 68765. Tel: 402-748-3382. p. 1331

Stecklein, Heather, Area Research Director, Univ Archivist, University of Wisconsin-Stout, 315 Tenth Ave, Menomonie, WI, 54751-0790. Tel: 715-232-5418. p. 2456

Steding, Jessica, Ref & Tech Librn, Old Lyme, Two Library Lane, Old Lyme, CT, 06371. Tel: 860-434-1684. p. 333

Stedke, Kathy, Circ Supvr, Ohio State University LIBRARIES, Lima Campus Library, 4240 Campus Dr, Lima, OH, 45804. Tel: 419-995-8361. p. 1776

Steed, Jane, Commun Librn, Monroe County Library System, Blue Bush Branch Library, 2210 Blue Bush Rd, Monroe, MI, 48162-9643. Tel: 734-242-4085. p. 1133

Steed, Jane, Commun Librn, Monroe County Library System, Frenchtown-Dixie, 2881 Nadeau Rd, Monroe, MI, 48162-9355. Tel: 734-289-1035. p. 1133

Steed, Jane, Commun Librn, Monroe County Library System, Robert A Vivian Branch, 2664 Vivian Rd, Monroe, MI, 48162-9212. Tel: 734-241-1430. p. 1134

Steel, Kilie, Ch, Oskaloosa Public Library, 301 S Market St, Oskaloosa, IA, 52577. Tel: 641-673-0441. p. 775

Steel, Virginia, Univ Librn, University of California Los Angeles Library, PO Box 951575, Los Angeles, CA, 90095-1575. Tel: 310-825-1201. p. 168

Steele, Amy M, Exec Dir, Northland Public Library, 300 Cumberland Rd, Pittsburgh, PA, 15237-5455. Tel: 412-366-8100, Ext 101. p. 1994

Steele, Andra, Br Mgr, Oakville Public Library, Central, 120 Navy St, Oakville, ON, L6J 2Z4, CANADA. Tel: 905-815-2042, Ext 5063. p. 2662

Steele, Cheryl, Circ, The Parrott Centre, 376 Wallbridge-Loyalist Rd, Belleville, ON, K8N 5B9, CANADA. Tel: 613-969-1913, Ext 2249. p. 2631

Steele, Chrissy, Asst Librn, Alberta School for the Deaf Library, 6240 113 St NW, Edmonton, AB, T6H 3L2, CANADA. Tel: 780-436-0465. p. 2535

Steele, Diane, Asst Dir, Chamberlin Free Public Library, 46 Main St, Greenville, NH, 03048. Tel: 603-878-1105. p. 1365

Steele, Elizabeth, ILL Coordr, Calvin University & Calvin Theological Seminary, 1855 Knollcrest Circle SE, Grand Rapids, MI, 49546-4402. Tel: 616-526-8573. p. 1110

Steele, Emily, Dir, Kingston Public Library, 1004 Bradford Way, Kingston, TN, 37763. Tel: 865-376-9905. p. 2105

Steele, Faith, Exec Dir, National Network of Libraries of Medicine Region 1, Univ Md Health Scis & Human Servs Libr, 601 W Lombard St, Baltimore, MD, 21201-1512. Tel: 410-706-2855. p. 2766

Steele, Jadrien, VPres, Develop, The New York Public Library - Astor, Lenox & Tilden Foundations, 476 Fifth Ave, (@ 42nd St), New York, NY, 10018. Tel: 212-930-0852. p. 1594

Steele, Jan, Dir, Lago Vista Public Library, 5803 Thunderbird, Ste 40, Lago Vista, TX, 78645. Tel: 512-267-3868. p. 2208

Steele, Kathi, Ch, Herbert Wescoat Memorial Library, 120 N Market St, McArthur, OH, 45651-1218. Tel: 740-596-5691. p. 1801

Steele, Linda, Registrar, History Museum of Western Virginia, One Market Sq, 3rd Flr, Roanoke, VA, 24011. Tel: 540-224-1207. p. 2344

Steele, Patty, ILL, Everett Roehl Marshfield Public Library, 105 S Maple Ave, Marshfield, WI, 54449. Tel: 715-387-8494, Ext 2750. p. 2454

Steele, Ruth, Dir, Rawson Memorial District Library, 6495 Pine St, Cass City, MI, 48726-1462. Tel: 989-872-2856. p. 1089

Steele, Ruth, Archivist, Ctr for Pac NW Studies, Western Washington University, 516 High St, MS 9103, Bellingham, WA, 98225. Tel: 360-650-7747. p. 2358

Steele, Sarah, Dean of Libr, Campbell University, 113 Main St, Buies Creek, NC, 27506. Tel: 910-893-1466. p. 1676

Steele, Tracey, Librn, Woonsocket City Library, 101 N Second Ave, Woonsocket, SD, 57385. Tel: 605-796-1412. p. 2086

Steele, Tracie, Youth Serv Mgr, Upper Arlington Public Library, 2800 Tremont Rd, Columbus, OH, 43221. Tel: 614-486-9621. p. 1778

Steele-Jeffers, Betty, Ref Librn, Snow Library, 67 Main St, Orleans, MA, 02653-2413. Tel: 508-240-3760. p. 1044

Steelman, Daniel, Digitization Librn, Bureau of Land Management Library, Denver Federal Ctr, Bldg 85, W-5, Denver, CO, 80225. Tel: 303-236-6650. p. 273

Steelman, Dorothy, Libr Dir, Pleasanton Library & Information Center, 115 N Main, Pleasanton, TX, 78064. Tel: 830-569-5901. p. 2227

Steelman, Stephanie, Early Childhood Librn, Center for Early Education Library, 563 N Alfred St, West Hollywood, CA, 90048-2512. Tel: 323-651-0707. p. 258

Steelman Wilson, Jodie, Asst Dir, Crawfordsville District Public Library, 205 S Washington St, Crawfordsville, IN, 47933. Tel: 765-362-2242. p. 677

Steely, Jeff, Dean of Libr, Georgia State University, 100 Decatur St SE, Atlanta, GA, 30303-3202. Tel: 404-413-2700. p. 464
Steely, Jeff, Pres, Association of Southeastern Research Libraries, c/o Robert W Woodruff Library, 540 Asbury Circle, Ste 316, Atlanta, GA, 30322-1006. Tel: 404-727-0137. p. 2763
Steen Boyer, Ingrid, Dir, Saugatuck-Douglas District Library, 137 Center St, Douglas, MI, 49406. Tel: 269-857-8241. p. 1101
Steen, Patty, Libr Mgr, Rumsey Community Library, 229 Main St, Rumsey, AB, T0J 2Y0, CANADA. Tel: 403-368-3939. p. 2552
Steenbarger, Sharon, Librn, Harvard Public Library, 309 N Clay Ave, Harvard, NE, 68944. Tel: 402-772-7201. p. 1317
Steenken, Beau, Instrul Serv Librn, University of Kentucky Libraries, Law Library, J David Rosenberg College of Law, 620 S Limestone St, Lexington, KY, 40506-0048. Tel: 859-257-1578. p. 863
Steets, Theresa, Librn, High Bridge Public Library, 71 Main St, High Bridge, NJ, 08829. Tel: 908-638-8231. p. 1408
Steever, Judy, Chief Librn, Department of Veterans Affairs, 130 W Kingsbridge Rd, Bronx, NY, 10468. Tel: 718-741-4229. p. 1498
Steeves, Catherine, Vice Provost & Chief Librn, Western University Libraries, 1151 Richmond St, Ste 200, London, ON, N6A 3K7, CANADA. Tel: 519-661-2111, Ext 83165. p. 2655
Steeves, Merle, Head, Tech Serv, Librn, University of New Brunswick Libraries, Five Macaulay Lane, Fredericton, NB, E3B 5H5, CANADA. Tel: 506-453-5043. p. 2601
Stefanelli, Justine, Dir of Publ(s), Dir, Res, American Society of International Law Library, 2223 Massachusetts Ave NW, Washington, DC, 20008. Tel: 202-939-6017. p. 360
Stefani, Christine, Head, Youth Serv, Bridgewater Public Library, 15 South St, Bridgewater, MA, 02324. Tel: 508-697-3331. p. 1002
Stefanik, Karen, Br Mgr, New Bedford Free Public Library, Wilks Branch, 1911 Acushnet Ave, New Bedford, MA, 02746. Tel: 508-991-6214. p. 1038
Stefano, Debbie, Br Mgr, Camden County Library System, Anthony P Infanti Bellmawr Branch Library, 35 E Browning Rd, Bellmawr, NJ, 08031. Tel: 856-931-1400. p. 1450
Stefano, Jessica, Br Mgr, Erie County Public Library, Iroquois Avenue, 4212 Iroquois Ave, Erie, PA, 16511-2198. Tel: 814-451-7082. p. 1931
Stefanow, Meagan, Educ Coordr, Ref Librn, Insurance Library Association of Boston, 156 State St, 2nd Flr, Boston, MA, 02109. Tel: 617-227-2087, Ext 203. p. 996
Steffan, Sandra, Librn, Illinois Prairie District Public Library, Roanoke Branch, 123 E Broad St, Roanoke, IL, 61561. Tel: 309-923-7686. p. 617
Steffen, Elizabeth, Dir, Festus Public Library, 400 W Main, Festus, MO, 63028. Tel: 636-937-2017. p. 1246
Steffen, Josh, Exec Dir, Kingwood Center Gardens Library, 50 N Trimble Rd, Mansfield, OH, 44906. Tel: 419-522-0211. p. 1798
Steffen, Kayla, Business Office & Facilities Dir, Rock Island Public Library, 401 19th St, Rock Island, IL, 61201. Tel: 309-732-7305. p. 641
Steffen, Nicolle, Dir, State Publ & Talking Bk Libr, Colorado State Library, 201 E Colfax Ave, Rm 309, Denver, CO, 80203-1799. Tel: 303-866-6900. p. 274
Steffen, Nicolle, Dir, State Publ & Talking Bk Libr, Colorado Talking Book Library, 180 Sheridan Blvd, Denver, CO, 80226-8101. Tel: 303-727-9277. p. 274
Steffensen, Elizabeth, Head, Pub Serv, Huntley Area Public Library District, 11000 Ruth Rd, Huntley, IL, 60142-7155. Tel: 847-669-5386. p. 601
Steffes, Dale, Mgr, Planning & Forecasting Consultants Library, PO Box 820228, Houston, TX, 77282-0228. Tel: 281-497-2179. p. 2197
Steffey, Jennifer, Interim Branch Admin, Noble County Public Library, West, 120 Jefferson St, Cromwell, IN, 46732-0555. Tel: 260-856-2119. p. 667
Steffey, Shannon, Dir, Lonesome Pine Regional Library, 124 Library Rd SW, Wise, VA, 24293-5907. Tel: 276-328-8325, Ext 103. p. 2354
Steffey, Shannon, Ref Librn, University of Virginia's College at Wise, One College Ave, Wise, VA, 24293. Tel: 276-328-0157. p. 2355
Steffman, Michael, Asst Libr Dir, Godfrey Memorial Library, 134 Newfield St, Middletown, CT, 06457-2534. Tel: 860-346-4375. p. 322
Steffy, Christina, Dir, Libr Serv, Pennsylvania College of Health Sciences, 850 Greenfield Rd, Lancaster, PA, 17601. Tel: 717-947-6142. p. 1952
Stefko, Kat, Dir, Archives & Spec Coll, Bowdoin College Library, 3000 College Sta, Brunswick, ME, 04011-8421. p. 919
Stefl-Mabry, Joette, Dr, Prof, University at Albany, State University of New York, Draper 015, 135 Western Ave, Albany, NY, 12203. Tel: 518-442-5120. p. 2789
Stegall, Lee, Dir, Mound Valley Public Library, 411 Hickory, Mound Valley, KS, 67354. Tel: 620-328-4158. p. 826
Steger, Sheila, Ch Serv, ILL, Mayville Public Library, 111 N Main St, Mayville, WI, 53050. Tel: 920-387-7910. p. 2455
Stegner, Gina, Pub Relations Coordr, Kenton County Public Library, Administration Center, 3095 Hulbert Ave, Erlanger, KY, 41018. Tel: 859-578-3609. p. 852
Stehle, Douglas, Head Librn, University of Colorado Denver/ Anschutz Medical Campus, Anschutz Medical Campus, 12950 E Montview Blvd, Aurora, CO, 80045. Tel: 303-724-2152. p. 265
Stehr, Andy, Circ Serv Mgr, Rochester Public Library, 101 Second St SE, Rochester, MN, 55904-3776. Tel: 507-328-2322. p. 1195
Steidinger, Shawn, Asst Med Librn, Primary Children's Hospital Medical Library, 81 N Mario Capecchi Dr, Salt Lake City, UT, 84113. Tel: 801-662-1390. p. 2271
Steiger, Alexandra, Librn, North Bergen Free Public Library, Kennedy Branch, 2123 Kennedy Blvd, North Bergen, NJ, 07047. Tel: 201-869-4715, Ext 5. p. 1429
Steiger, Jon Miller, Regional Dir, Federal Trade Commission, 1111 Superior Ave, Ste 200, Cleveland, OH, 44114. Tel: 216-263-3442. p. 1770
Steiger, Judi, Dir, Fort Hunter Free Library, 167 Fort Hunter Rd, Amsterdam, NY, 12010. Tel: 518-829-7248. p. 1487
Steiger, Lucy, Teen Serv Librn, Siouxland Libraries, 200 N Dakota Ave, Sioux Falls, SD, 57104. Tel: 605-367-8712. p. 2082
Steigerwalt, Kristy, Sr Med Librn, University of Missouri-Kansas City Libraries, Health Sciences Library, 2411 Holmes St, Kansas City, MO, 64108. Tel: 816-235-1876. p. 1258
Stein, Ardis J, Law Librn, Jefferson County Law Library, 301 Market St, 3rd Flr, Steubenville, OH, 43952. Tel: 740-283-8553. p. 1821
Stein, Margaret, Cat, Nioga Library System, 6575 Wheeler Rd, Lockport, NY, 14094. Tel: 716-434-6167, Ext 18. p. 1564
Stein, Marsha, Chief Info Officer, Ropes & Gray LLP Library, Prudential Tower, 800 Boylston St, Boston, MA, 02199. Tel: 617-951-7000. p. 999
Stein, Mary, Asst Dir, Admin Serv, East Baton Rouge Parish Library, 7711 Goodwood Blvd, Baton Rouge, LA, 70806-7625. Tel: 225-231-3710. p. 882
Stein, Phoebe, Digital Serv Librn, School of Visual Arts Library, 380 Second Ave, 2nd Flr, New York, NY, 10010. Tel: 212-592-2672. p. 1601
Stein, Rachael, Asst Dir, Worcester County Library, 307 N Washington St, Snow Hill, MD, 21863. Tel: 410-632-2600. p. 978
Stein, Stacia, HQ Librn, Library of the US Courts of the Seventh Circuit, 219 S Dearborn St, Rm 1637, Chicago, IL, 60604-1769. Tel: 312-435-5660. p. 563
Stein, Terri, Librn, Iosco-Arenac District Library, Tawas City Branch, 208 North St, Tawas City, MI, 48763. Tel: 989-362-6557. p. 1102
Stein, Zachary, Head, Spec Coll, University of Louisiana at Lafayette, 400 E St Mary Blvd, Lafayette, LA, 70503. Tel: 337-482-6427. p. 893
Stein-Ham, Roberta, Adminr, Support Serv, Scarsdale Public Library, 54 Olmsted Rd, Scarsdale, NY, 10583. Tel: 914-722-1300. p. 1637
Steinbacher, Lorri, Asst Dir, Ridgewood Public Library, 125 N Maple Ave, Ridgewood, NJ, 07450-3288. Tel: 201-670-5600. p. 1439
Steinberg, Desiree, Librn, Larsen Family Public Library, 7401 Main St W, Webster, WI, 54893-0510. Tel: 715-866-7697. p. 2486
Steinberg Gurganus, Alison, Chair, Instrul Serv Librn, Online Serv, San Diego Mesa College Library, 7250 Mesa College Dr, San Diego, CA, 92111-4998. Tel: 619-388-2695. p. 218
Steinbrecker, Jenn, ILL, Hanna Municipal Library, 202 First St W, Hanna, AB, T0J 1P0, CANADA. Tel: 403-854-3865. p. 2542
Steinbrick, Jaye, Chief Tech Officer, Sr Dir, Los Angeles County Law Library, Mildred L Lillie Bldg, 301 W First St, Los Angeles, CA, 90012-3100. Tel: 213-785-2529. p. 162
Steiner, Beth, Dir, Auglaize County Libraries, 203 S Perry St, Wapakoneta, OH, 45895-1999. Tel: 419-738-2921. p. 1827
Steiner, Cyndi, Dir, S White Dickinson Memorial Library, 202 Chestnut Plain Rd, Whately, MA, 01093. Tel: 413-665-2170. p. 1068
Steiner, Danni, Circ Serv, Mamie Doud Eisenhower Public Library, Three Community Park Rd, Broomfield, CO, 80020. Tel: 720-887-2306. p. 268
Steiner, Kimberly, ILL Supvr, Messiah University, One University Ave, Ste 3002, Mechanicsburg, PA, 17055. Tel: 717-691-6006, Ext 7242. p. 1960
Steiner, Rachel, Asst Dir, Omaha Public Library, 215 S 15th St, Omaha, NE, 68102-1629. Tel: 402-444-4800. p. 1329
Steingrubey, Elaine, Dir, Morrison-Talbott Library, 215 Park St, Waterloo, IL, 62298-1305. Tel: 618-939-6232. p. 659
Steinhart, Darlene, Head, Youth Serv, Rockaway Township Free Public Library, 61 Mount Hope Rd, Rockaway, NJ, 07866. Tel: 973-627-2344. p. 1440
Steinhiser, Leah, Br Mgr, Saint Joseph County Public Library, Western Branch, 611 S Lombardy Dr, South Bend, IN, 46619. Tel: 574-282-4639. p. 719
Steinhoff, Cynthia, Libr Dir, Anne Arundel Community College, 101 College Pkwy, Arnold, MD, 21012-1895. Tel: 410-777-2483. p. 951
Steinkuhler, Jae, Br Mgr, Trails Regional Library, 432 N Holden St, Warrensburg, MO, 64093. Tel: 660-747-1699. p. 1285
Steinkuhler, Jae, Br Mgr, Trails Regional Library, Warrensburg Branch, 432 N Holden, Warrensburg, MO, 64093. Tel: 660-747-9177. p. 1285
Steinle, Mary Ann, Dir, Lucas Public Library, 135 S Main, Lucas, KS, 67648-9574. Tel: 785-525-6305. p. 822
Steinmacher, Michael, Dir, Ivy Tech Community College, 8204 Hwy 311, Sellersburg, IN, 47172-1897. Tel: 812-246-3301, Ext 4225. p. 718
Steinmayer, Lynn Barker, Libr Dir, Goshen Public Library, 42 North St, Goshen, CT, 06756. Tel: 860-491-3234. p. 313
Steinmehl, Carrie, Asst Libr Dir, Hoover Public Library, 200 Municipal Dr, Hoover, AL, 35216. Tel: 205-444-7810. p. 21
Steinmetz, Kristin, Ch, Richards Memorial Library, 44 Richards Ave, Paxton, MA, 01612. Tel: 508-754-0793. p. 1045

Steinmeyer, Richard, Circ Supvr, Saint Johns County Public Library System, Main Branch, 1960 N Ponce de Leon Blvd, Saint Augustine, FL, 32084. Tel: 904-827-6946. p. 440

Steinsultz, Erin, Dir, Crab Orchard Public Library District, 20012 Crab Orchard Rd, Marion, IL, 62959. Tel: 618-982-2141. p. 613

Stekel, Susan, Lead Librn, Info Literacy & Instruction, Walden University Library, 100 Washington Ave S, Ste 900, Minneapolis, MN, 55401. p. 1186

Stello, Noelle, Univ Librn, National University of Natural Medicine Library, 49 S Porter St, Portland, OR, 97201. Tel: 503-552-1542. p. 1893

Stellrecht, Elizabeth M, Clinical Librn, University at Buffalo Libraries-State University of New York, Health Sciences Library, Abbott Hall, 3435 Main St, Bldg 28, Buffalo, NY, 14214-3002. Tel: 716-829-5734. p. 1510

Stelly, Amy, Bus Mgr, Vermilion Parish Library, 405 E Saint Victor St, Abbeville, LA, 70510-5101. Tel: 337-893-2655. p. 879

Stelly, John, Dir, Ascension Parish Library, 500 Mississippi St, Donaldsonville, LA, 70346. Tel: 225-473-8052. p. 889

Stelly, Susan, Br Mgr, Vermilion Parish Library, 405 E Saint Victor St, Abbeville, LA, 70510-5101. Tel: 337-893-2655. p. 879

Stelzer, Stuart P, Dir, University of the Ozarks, 415 N College Ave, Clarksville, AR, 72830. Tel: 479-979-1382. p. 92

Stem, Elaine, Dir, Vance-Granville Community College, 200 Community College Rd, Henderson, NC, 27536. Tel: 252-738-3279. p. 1695

Stemberg, Patricia, Bus Mgr, Lewis & Clark Library, 120 S Last Chance Gulch, Helena, MT, 59601. Tel: 406-447-1690. p. 1296

Stembridge, Koren, Libr Dir, Cary Memorial Library, 1874 Massachusetts Ave, Lexington, MA, 02420. Tel: 781-862-6288, Ext 84401. p. 1028

Stemlar, Anne, Managing Dir, Goodwin Procter, 100 Northern Ave, Boston, MA, 02210. Tel: 617-570-1000, 617-570-1994. p. 995

Stemmer, John, PhD, Dir, Bellarmine University, 2001 Newburg Rd, Louisville, KY, 40205-0671. Tel: 502-272-8140. p. 864

Stempel, Kathy, Dir, Berne Public Library, 1763 Helderberg Trail, Berne, NY, 12023. Tel: 518-872-1246. p. 1493

Stempf, Kathryn, Dir, Bruce Area Library, 102 W River St, Bruce, WI, 54819. Tel: 715-868-2005. p. 2426

Stempien, Judy, Br Librn, Wapiti Regional Library, Canwood Public Library, 660 Main St, Canwood, SK, S0J 0K0, CANADA. Tel: 306-468-2501. p. 2745

Stenbak, Judy, Youth Serv, Crook County Library, Moorcroft Branch, 105 E Converse, Moorcroft, WY, 82721. Tel: 307-756-3232. p. 2499

Stenberg Brown, Emily, Dir, North Dakota Vision Services-School for the Blind, 500 Stanford Rd, Grand Forks, ND, 58203. Tel: 701-795-2709. p. 1734

Stencel, Jennifer, Br Mgr, Akron-Summit County Public Library, Richfield Branch, 3761 S Grant St, Richfield, OH, 44286-9603. Tel: 330-659-4343. p. 1744

Stender, Kathy, Dir, Leigh Public Library, 153 N Main St, Leigh, NE, 68643. Tel: 402-487-2507. p. 1320

Stender, Martha, Br Mgr, Free Library of Philadelphia, Lovett Memorial Branch, 6945 Germantown Ave, Philadelphia, PA, 19119-2189. Tel: 215-685-2095. p. 1979

Stengel, Jacque, Asst Librn, Heyworth Public Library District, 119 E Main St, Heyworth, IL, 61745. Tel: 309-473-2313. p. 599

Stengel, Katherine A, Mgr, Human Res, MidPointe Library System, 125 S Broad St, Middletown, OH, 45044. Tel: 513-424-1251. p. 1802

Stenger, Elizabeth, Libr Serv Dir, Indian River County Library System, 1600 21st St, Vero Beach, FL, 32960. Tel: 772-770-5060. p. 452

Stenhouse, Channing, Dir, Peace River Municipal Library, 9807 97th Ave, Peace River, AB, T8S 1H6, CANADA. Tel: 780-624-4076. p. 2550

Stepak, Nishan, Head, Coll, Head, Electronic Res, Mount Vernon Public Library, 28 S First Ave, Mount Vernon, NY, 10550. Tel: 914-668-1840, Ext 228. p. 1575

Stepanek, Darcia, Activity Spec, Iowa Correctional Institution for Women Library, 420 Mill St SW, Mitchellville, IA, 50169. Tel: 515-725-5114. p. 770

Stepaniuk, Sandra, Libr Mgr, Darwell Public Library, 54-225B Hwy 765, Darwell, AB, T0E 0L0, CANADA. Tel: 780-892-3746. p. 2532

Stepaniuk, Sandra, Libr Mgr, Sangudo Public Library, 5028 50 Ave, Sangudo, AB, T0E 2A0, CANADA. Tel: 780-785-2955. p. 2553

Stepanyan, Liana, Mgr, County of Los Angeles Public Library, San Fernando Library, 217 N Maclay Ave, San Fernando, CA, 91340-2433. Tel: 818-365-6928. p. 137

Steph, Crowell, Evening Librn, Outreach Librn, McDaniel College, 2 College Hill, Westminster, MD, 21157-4390. Tel: 410-857-2287. p. 981

Stephan, Elizabeth, Student Success Librn, Western Washington University, 516 High St, MS 9103, Bellingham, WA, 98225. Tel: 360-650-2061. p. 2358

Stephan, Nicholas, Exec Dir, Garrett Public Library, 107 W Houston St, Garrett, IN, 46738. Tel: 260-357-5485. p. 686

Stephan-Strombom, Sandy, Asst Librn, ILL Librn, Dunbar Free Library, 401 Rte 10 S, Grantham, NH, 03753. Tel: 603-863-2172. p. 1365

Stephens, Amy, Acq, Bus Mgr, Ripon College, 300 Seward St, Ripon, WI, 54971. Tel: 920-748-8175. p. 2474

Stephens, Antonia, Dir, Cotuit Library, 871 Main St, Cotuit, MA, 02635. Tel: 508-428-8141. p. 1013

Stephens, Antonio, Dir, Hyannis Public Library, 401 Main St, Hyannis, MA, 02601. Tel: 508-775-2280. p. 1026

Stephens, Austin, Cat Librn, Montgomery County Public Library, 328 N Maysville Rd, Mount Sterling, KY, 40353. Tel: 859-498-2404. p. 870

Stephens, Bradley K, Dir, Salem Public Library, 821 E State St, Salem, OH, 44460-2298. Tel: 330-332-0042. p. 1819

Stephens, Brianna, Acq Librn, Giles County Public Library, 122 S Second St, Pulaski, TN, 38478-3285. Tel: 931-363-2720. p. 2124

Stephens, Daylan, Circ Librn, Belhaven University, 1500 Peachtree St, Jackson, MS, 39202. Tel: 601-968-5948. p. 1221

Stephens, Debbie, Dir, Jasper Free Library, 3807 Preacher St, Jasper, NY, 14855. Tel: 607-792-3494. p. 1557

Stephens, Debra, Head Librn, Hartnell College Library, 411 Central Ave, Salinas, CA, 93901. p. 211

Stephens, Denise, Dean, Univ Libr, University of Oklahoma Libraries, 401 W Brooks St, Norman, OK, 73019. Tel: 405-325-3341. p. 1856

Stephens, Jane, Coordr, Circ, Chipola College Library, 3094 Indian Circle, Marianna, FL, 32446. Tel: 850-718-2279. p. 420

Stephens, Jay, Dir, Halifax County-South Boston Regional Library, 177 S Main St, Halifax, VA, 24558. Tel: 434-476-3357. p. 2322

Stephens, Jennifer S, Tech Serv Librn, Haynes & Boone LLP, 2323 Victory Ave, Ste 700, Dallas, TX, 75219. Tel: 214-651-5711. p. 2167

Stephens, Julia, Dir, Coweta Public Library, 120 E Sycamore St, Coweta, OK, 74429. Tel: 918-486-6532. p. 1845

Stephens, Juliet, YA Serv, Aldrich Public Library, Six Washington St, Barre, VT, 05641. Tel: 802-476-7550. p. 2278

Stephens, Kiyana, Libr Mgr, San Antonio Public Library, Landa, 233 Bushnell Ave, San Antonio, TX, 78212. Tel: 210-207-9090. p. 2239

Stephens, Mark, Dr, Dean, Tennessee Technological University, Graduate Studies, Dewberry Hall 306, One William L Jones Dr, Cookeville, TN, 38505. Tel: 931-372-3224. p. 2792

Stephens, Melody, Librn, Emerson Public Library, 701 Morton Ave, Emerson, IA, 51533. Tel: 712-824-7867. p. 751

Stephens, Nancy, Libr Mgr, Levy County Public Library System, Cedar Key Public, 460 Second St, Cedar Key, FL, 32625. Tel: 352-543-5777. p. 387

Stephens, Priscilla, Chief Librn, United States Department of Veterans Affairs, Library Service (142D), 13000 Bruce B Downs Blvd, Tampa, FL, 33612. Tel: 813-972-2000, Ext 6570. p. 449

Stephens, Raylene, Asst Librn, Cordelia B Preston Memorial Library, 510 Orleans Ave, Orleans, NE, 68966. Tel: 308-473-3425. p. 1331

Stephens, Rebecca, Exec Secy, Enterprise State Community College, 600 Plaza Dr, Enterprise, AL, 36330. Tel: 334-347-2623, Ext 2271. p. 15

Stephens, Ruth, Br Mgr, Kansas City Public Library, Sugar Creek Branch, 102 S Sterling Ave, Sugar Creek, MO, 64054. Tel: 816-701-3583. p. 1255

Stephens, Ruth, Mgr, Kansas City Public Library, Trails West, 11401 E 23rd St, Independence, MO, 64052. Tel: 816-701-3483. p. 1255

Stephens, Seth, Libr Dir, Jefferson Township Public Library, 1031 Weldon Rd, Oak Ridge, NJ, 07438. Tel: 973-208-6244, Ext 207. p. 1430

Stephens, Taylor, Access Serv Librn, Shaw University, 118 E South St, Raleigh, NC, 27601. Tel: 919-546-8337. p. 1710

Stephens, Todd, County Librn, Spartanburg County Public Libraries, 151 S Church St, Spartanburg, SC, 29306. Tel: 864-596-3500. p. 2069

Stephens, Wendy, Dr, Prog Chair, Jacksonville State University, 700 Pelham Rd N, Jacksonville, AL, 36265. Tel: 256-782-5011, 256-782-5096. p. 2781

Stephenson, Amanda, Head, ILL, Head, Ref, Hutchinson Public Library, 901 N Main, Hutchinson, KS, 67501-4492. Tel: 620-663-5441. p. 814

Stephenson, Amy, Children's Programmer, Programmer, Patterson Library, 40 S Portage St, Westfield, NY, 14787. Tel: 716-326-2154. p. 1664

Stephenson, Carol, Licensing Coord, Council of Prairie & Pacific University Libraries, 150B -1711 85th St NW, Calgary, AB, T3R 1J3, CANADA. Tel: 604-827-0578. p. 2777

Stephenson, Christina A, Br Mgr, Santa Fe Public Library, Oliver La Farge Branch Library, 1730 Llano St, Santa Fe, NM, 87505-5460. Tel: 505-955-4868. p. 1476

Stephenson, Corey, Libr Dir, Moretown Memorial Library, 1147 Rte 100-B, Moretown, VT, 05660. Tel: 802-496-9728. p. 2289

Stephenson, Deb, Commun Relations, Supvr, Carnegie-Stout Public Library, 360 W 11th St, Dubuque, IA, 52001. Tel: 563-589-4243. p. 748

Stephenson, Graham, Electronic Serv Librn, Illinois College of Optometry Library, 3241 S Michigan Ave, Chicago, IL, 60616-3878. Tel: 312-949-7160. p. 562

Stephenson, Kit, Asst Dir, Bozeman Public Library, 626 E Main St, Bozeman, MT, 59715. Tel: 406-582-2400. p. 1289

Stephenson, Linda, Head, Info Serv, University of Utah, S J Quinney Law Library, 332 S 1400 East, Salt Lake City, UT, 84112-0731. Tel: 801-581-5800. p. 2272

Stephenson, Marla, Libr Tech, Moffat County Libraries, Maybell Branch, 202 Collom St, Maybell, CO, 81640. Tel: 970-272-9919. p. 272

Stephenson, Martha, Ref & Instruction Librn, University of Wisconsin-Whitewater, 750 W Main St, Whitewater, WI, 53190-1790. Tel: 262-472-4366. p. 2488

Stephenson, Nancy, Mgr, Support Serv & Vols Res, Indianapolis Public Library, 2450 N Meridian St, Indianapolis, IN, 46208. Tel: 317-275-4840. p. 694

Stephenson, Patsy, Govt Doc Librn, Marshall University Libraries, One John Marshall Dr, Huntington, WV, 25755-2060. Tel: 304-696-6573. p. 2405

Stephenson, Suzanne, Law Librn II, Washington County Library, Washington County Law Library, Washington County Courthouse, 14949 62nd St N, Rm 1005, Stillwater, MN, 55082. Tel: 651-430-6330. p. 1210

Stephenson, Valerie D, Libr Dir, Wasco County Library District, Southern Wasco County Public Library, 410 Deschutes Ave, Maupin, OR, 97037. Tel: 541-395-2208. p. 1900

Stepp, Julie, Dr, Assoc Prof, Tennessee Technological University, Graduate Studies, Dewberry Hall 306, One William L Jones Dr, Cookeville, TN, 38505. Tel: 931-372-3103. p. 2792

Stepro, Diane, Local Hist & Genealogy Librn, Jeffersonville Township Public Library, 211 E Court Ave, Jeffersonville, IN, 47130. Tel: 812-285-5630. p. 698

Steranko, Jane, Libr Dir, Minersville Public Library Association Inc, 220 S Fourth St, Minersville, PA, 17954. Tel: 570-544-5196. p. 1964

Sterbenz, John E, Jr, Exec Dir, Detroit Area Library Network, 5150 Anthony Wayne Dr, Detroit, MI, 48202. Tel: 313-577-6789. p. 2767

Stere, Robert, Ref Librn, Mount Aloysius College Library, 7373 Admiral Peary Hwy, Cresson, PA, 16630-1999. Tel: 814-886-6445. p. 1925

Sterk, Joleen, Dir, Menomonie Public Library, 600 Wolske Bay Rd, Menomonie, WI, 54751. Tel: 715-232-2164. p. 2456

Sterle, Christine, Dir, Thorntown Public Library, 124 N Market St, Thorntown, IN, 46071-1144. Tel: 765-436-7348. p. 721

Sterling, Bailey, Tech Coordr, National Network of Libraries of Medicine Region 3, UNT Health Sci Ctr, Gibson D Lewis Health Sci Libr, 3500 Camp Bowie Blvd, Rm 110, Fort Worth, TX, 76107. Tel: 817-735-2370. p. 2775

Sterling, Bonnie, Dir, Milltown Public Library, 20 W Church St, Milltown, NJ, 08850. Tel: 732-247-2270. p. 1419

Sterling, Marcy, Dir, Fairfax Public Library, 158 E Elm, Fairfax, OK, 74637. Tel: 918-642-5535. p. 1847

Sterling, Rayette, Br Mgr, Anchorage Public Library, Mountain View Branch, 120 Bragaw St, Anchorage, AK, 99508. Tel: 907-343-2818. p. 42

Sterling, Rick, Dir, Richard C Sullivan Public Library of Wilton Manors, 500 NE 26th St, Wilton Manors, FL, 33305. Tel: 954-390-2195. p. 455

Sterling, Ruth, Coordr, Teen Serv, Clapp Memorial Library, 19 S Main St, Belchertown, MA, 01007. Tel: 413-323-0417. p. 988

Sterma, Kathy, Head Librn, North-West Regional Library, 610 First St N, Swan River, MB, R0L 1Z0, CANADA. Tel: 204-734-3880. p. 2591

Stern, Eric, Libr Dir, Derry Public Library, 64 E Broadway, Derry, NH, 03038-2412. Tel: 603-432-6140. p. 1361

Stern, Kelly, Dir, Cedar Falls Public Library, 524 Main St, Cedar Falls, IA, 50613. Tel: 319-268-5541. p. 737

Stern, Margie, Dir, Indian Valley Public Library, 100 E Church Ave, Telford, PA, 18969. Tel: 215-723-9109. p. 2012

Stern, Nancy, Lead Librn, Kalamazoo Public Library, Washington Square, 1244 Portage Rd, Kalamazoo, MI, 49001. Tel: 269-553-7970. p. 1121

Sternberg, Brian, Exec Dir, Libr Serv, Santa Ana Public Library, 26 Civic Ctr Plaza, Santa Ana, CA, 92701-4010. Tel: 714-647-5250. p. 239

Sternberg, Guy, Dir, Starhill Forest Arboretum Library, 12000 Boy Scout Trail, Petersburg, IL, 62675. Tel: 217-632-3685. p. 635

Sternberg, Susan, Dir, Rachel Kohl Community Library, 687 Smithbridge Rd, Glen Mills, PA, 19342. Tel: 610-358-3445. p. 1936

Sternburg, Annie, Dir, Libr Serv, University of Sioux Falls, 1101 W 22nd St, Sioux Falls, SD, 57105. Tel: 605-331-6661. p. 2083

Sternemann, Emily, Engagement Librn, Hartland Public Library, 110 E Park Ave, Hartland, WI, 53029. Tel: 262-367-3350. p. 2441

Sternklar, Debbie, Teen Serv Librn, Voorheesville Public Library, 51 School Rd, Voorheesville, NY, 12186. Tel: 518-765-2791. p. 1657

Sterthaus, Elizabeth, ILL Librn, Embry-Riddle Aeronautical University, One Aerospace Blvd, Daytona Beach, FL, 32114. Tel: 386-323-8774. p. 392

Stessman, Hailey, Acq Spec, Bellevue University, 1028 Bruin Blvd, Bellevue, NE, 68005. Tel: 402-557-7306. p. 1308

Stetkus, Sonia, Tech Serv Coordr, Berkeley Public Library, 1637 N Taft Ave, Berkeley, IL, 60163-1499. Tel: 708-544-6017. p. 542

Stetson, Natalie, Exec Dir, Erie Canal Museum Research Library, 318 Erie Blvd E, Syracuse, NY, 13202. Tel: 315-471-0593. p. 1648

Stetson, Ruth, Dir, Tarkington Community Library, 3032 FM 163, Cleveland, TX, 77327. Tel: 281-592-5136. p. 2156

Steuer, Marisa, Head, Youth Serv, Palm Harbor Library, 2330 Nebraska Ave, Palm Harbor, FL, 34683. Tel: 727-784-3332, Ext 3018. p. 435

Steuer, Susan, Spec Coll Librn, Western Michigan University, 1903 W Michigan Ave, WMU Mail Stop 5353, Kalamazoo, MI, 49008-5353. Tel: 269-387-5250. p. 1122

Steuer, Susan, Spec Coll Librn, Western Michigan University, Zhang Legacy Collections Center, 1650 Oakland Dr, Kalamazoo, MI, 49008. Tel: 269-387-5250. p. 1122

Steuernagel, Ann, Dir, Abbie Greenleaf Library, 439 Main St, Franconia, NH, 03580. Tel: 603-823-8424. p. 1364

Steuhm, Abbie, Research & Scholarship Librn, Dakota State University, 820 N Washington Ave, Madison, SD, 57042. Tel: 605-256-5203. p. 2078

Stevens, Allie, Dir, Calhoun County Library, 115 S 2nd St, Hampton, AR, 71744. Tel: 870-798-4492. p. 97

Stevens, Anne, Br Librn, Stockton-San Joaquin County Public Library, Manteca Branch, 320 W Center St, Manteca, CA, 95336. p. 250

Stevens, April, Dir, Osceola Public Library, 131 N Main, Osceola, NE, 68651. Tel: 402-747-4301. p. 1331

Stevens, Brian, Archives & Spec Coll Librn, Western Connecticut State University, 181 White St, Danbury, CT, 06810. Tel: 203-837-9100. p. 307

Stevens, Brooke, Asst Dir, Ch, Starr Library, 68 W Market St, Rhinebeck, NY, 12572. Tel: 845-876-4030. p. 1626

Stevens, Courtney R, Dir, Warren County Public Library, 1225 State St, Bowling Green, KY, 42101. Tel: 270-781-4882, Ext 207. p. 849

Stevens, Daniel, Electronic Res & Cat Librn, Columbia College, 1301 Columbia College Dr, Columbia, SC, 29203-9987. Tel: 803-786-3570. p. 2053

Stevens, Daniel, Ref Serv, Lone Star College System, Montgomery College Library, 3200 College Park Dr, Conroe, TX, 77384. Tel: 936-273-7487. p. 2197

Stevens, David, AV/Multimedia Spec, University of Florida, 3200 E Palm Beach Rd, Belle Glade, FL, 33430. Tel: 561-993-1517. p. 384

Stevens, Deborah, Br Mgr, Memphis Public Library, Cherokee Branch, 3300 Sharpe, Memphis, TN, 38111. Tel: 901-415-2762. p. 2113

Stevens, Deborah, Br Mgr, Memphis Public Library, Parkway Village Branch, 4655 Knight Arnold Rd, Memphis, TN, 38118-3234. Tel: 901-415-2776. p. 2113

Stevens, Elizabeth, Programming & Comms Mgr, Johnston Public Library, 6700 Merle Hay Rd, Johnston, IA, 50131-0327. Tel: 515-278-5233. p. 762

Stevens, Hannah, Archivist/Librn, College of the Atlantic, 105 Eden St, Bar Harbor, ME, 04609-1198. Tel: 207-801-5662. p. 916

Stevens, Jennifer, Evening Librn, Isothermal Community College Library, 286 ICC Loop Rd, Spindale, NC, 28160. Tel: 828-395-1525. p. 1717

Stevens, Jenny, Children's & Youth Serv, Hopkinton Town Library, 61 Houston Dr, Contoocook, NH, 03229. Tel: 603-746-3663. p. 1360

Stevens, Jenny, Admin Serv, Chief, Chesterfield County Public Library, 9501 Lori Rd, Chesterfield, VA, 23832. Tel: 804-751-4998. p. 2312

Stevens, Juliet, Libr Operations Mgr, Vermont College of Fine Arts, Vermont College of Fine Arts Library, 36 College St, Montpelier, VT, 05602. Tel: 802-828-8512. p. 2289

Stevens, Kathryn, Asst Librn, Macsherry Library, 112 Walton St, Alexandria Bay, NY, 13607. Tel: 315-482-2241. p. 1485

Stevens, Kim, Sr Cat Librn, Jacksonville State University Library, 700 Pelham Rd N, Jacksonville, AL, 36265. Tel: 256-782-5758. p. 23

Stevens, Kristen, Regional Mgr, San Bernardino County Library, 777 E Rialto Ave, San Bernardino, CA, 92415-0035. Tel: 909-771-9265. p. 212

Stevens, Kristen, Br Mgr, San Bernardino County Library, Janice Horst Branch, 33103 Old Woman Springs Rd, Lucerne Valley, CA, 92356. Tel: 760-248-7521. p. 213

Stevens, Laura, Youth Serv, Kelley Library, 234 Main St, Salem, NH, 03079-3190. Tel: 603-898-7064. p. 1380

Stevens, Leon, Law Librn, Walter & Haverfield LLP, The Tower at Erieview, Ste 3500, 1301 E Ninth St, Cleveland, OH, 44114-1821. Tel: 216-781-1212. p. 1770

Stevens, Linda, Dir, Prog & Partnerships, Div Head, Harris County Public Library, 5749 S Loop E, Houston, TX, 77033. Tel: 713-274-6600. p. 2192

Stevens, Lisa, Asst Librn, Oakland Public Library, 18 Church St, Oakland, ME, 04963. Tel: 207-465-7533. p. 934

Stevens, Lisa, Mgr, Wayne County Public Library, Pikeville Public, 107 W Main St, Pikeville, NC, 27863. Tel: 919-705-1892. p. 1691

Stevens, Marina, Asst Dir, Head, Adult Serv, Round Lake Area Public Library District, 906 Hart Rd, Round Lake, IL, 60073. Tel: 847-546-7060, Ext 127. p. 643

Stevens, Michelle, Ad, ILL Librn, Lee Public Library, Nine Mast Rd, Lee, NH, 03861. Tel: 603-659-2626. p. 1370

Stevens, Molly, Youth Services & Children's Programming, Grinnell Library, 2642 E Main St, Wappingers Falls, NY, 12590. Tel: 845-297-3428. p. 1658

Stevens, Pam, Br Mgr, Newark Free Library, 750 Library Ave, Newark, DE, 19711. Tel: 302-731-7550. p. 355

Stevens, Russell, Supvr, Ventura County Library, Saticoy Library, 11426 Violeta St, Saticoy, CA, 93004. Tel: 805-647-5736. p. 256

Stevens, Scott, Libr Dir, Baltimore County Circuit Court Library, 401 Bosley Ave, Towson, MD, 21204. Tel: 410-887-3086. p. 979

Stevens, Shelen A, Dir, Weston Public Library, 13153 Main St, Weston, OH, 43569. Tel: 419-669-3415. p. 1831

Stevens, Sheryl, Dir, Coll Serv, University of Toledo, 2975 W Centennial Dr, Toledo, OH, 43606-3396. Tel: 419-530-7981. p. 1825

Stevens, Shirley, Librn, Oscar Johnson Memorial Library, 21967 Sixth St, Silverhill, AL, 36576. Tel: 251-945-5201. p. 35

Stevens, Tina L, Dir, Franklin County Library, 105 S Porter St, Winchester, TN, 37398-1546. Tel: 931-967-3706. p. 2130

Stevens, Valerie, Libr Dir & Chief Exec Officer, Georgina Public Library, 90 Wexford Dr, Keswick, ON, L4P 3P7, CANADA. Tel: 905-476-7233. p. 2649

Stevens-Garmon, Morgan, Assoc Curator, Museum of the City of New York, 1220 Fifth Ave, New York, NY, 10029. Tel: 212-534-1672. p. 1592

Stevenson, April, Head, Info Serv, Novi Public Library, 45255 W Ten Mile Rd, Novi, MI, 48375. Tel: 248-349-0720. p. 1138

Stevenson, April, Libr Dir, White Lake Township Library, 11005 Elizabeth Lake Rd, White Lake, MI, 48386. Tel: 248-698-4942. p. 1159

Stevenson, Arthur, Circ, Pitt Community College, Clifton W Everett Bldg, 1986 Pitt Tech Rd, Winterville, NC, 28590. Tel: 252-493-7350. p. 1727

Stevenson, Ben, Research Services Asst, Rockhurst University, 1100 Rockhurst Rd, Kansas City, MO, 64110-2561. Tel: 816-501-4142. p. 1257

Stevenson, Bryan, Colls Mgr, Prog Mgr, Santa Barbara Mission, 2201 Laguna St, Santa Barbara, CA, 93105. Tel: 805-682-4713. p. 240

Stevenson, Jana, Dep Dir, Warwick Public Library, 600 Sandy Lane, Warwick, RI, 02889-8298. Tel: 401-739-5440, Ext 9759. p. 2043

Stevenson, Joanne, Chief Exec Officer, Grand Valley Public Library, Four Amaranth St E, Grand Valley, ON, L9W 5L2, CANADA. Tel: 519-928-5622. p. 2643

Stevenson, Joy, Libr Dir, Crete Public Library, 1515 Forest Ave, Crete, NE, 68333. Tel: 402-826-3809. p. 1311

Stevenson, Justin, Digital Res Librn, Siouxland Libraries, 200 N Dakota Ave, Sioux Falls, SD, 57104. Tel: 605-367-8734. p. 2082

Stevenson, Lacy, Br Mgr, Portsmouth Public Library, South Webster Branch, 496 Webster St, South Webster, OH, 45682. Tel: 740-778-2122. p. 1816

Stevenson, Lindsey, Libr Tech II, Lamar State College Orange Library, 410 Front St, Orange, TX, 77630-5796. Tel: 409-882-3065. p. 2224

Stevenson, Marilyn, Librn III, Supvr, New Hampshire State Library, Gallen State Office Park, Dolloff Bldg, 117 Pleasant St, Concord, NH, 03301-3852. Tel: 603-271-2417, 603-271-3429. p. 1359

Stevenson, Mark, Tech Coordr, Beaver County Library System, 109 Pleasant Dr, Ste 101, Aliquippa, PA, 15001. Tel: 724-378-6227. p. 1904

Stevenson, Martha, Dir, Libr Serv, Kutztown University, 15200 Kutztown Rd, Bldg 5, Kutztown, PA, 19530. Tel: 610-683-4480. p. 1949

Stevenson, Mathew, Library Contact, Christ Church Cathedral, 125 Monument Circle, Indianapolis, IN, 46204-2921. Tel: 317-636-4577. p. 691

Stevenson, Michael, Coll Develop Librn, Quinsigamond Community College, 670 W Boylston St, Worcester, MA, 01606-2092. Tel: 508-854-2793. p. 1072

Stevenson, Sarah, Head of Libr, Dalhousie University, 6225 University Ave, Halifax, NS, B3H 4H8, CANADA. Tel: 902-494-1325. p. 2618

Stevenson, Sherri, Dir, Aurelia Public Library, 232 Main St, Aurelia, IA, 51005. Tel: 712-434-5330. p. 733

Stevenson, Vicki, Chief Exec Officer, Rideau Lakes Public Library, 26 Halladay St, Elgin, ON, K0G 1E0, CANADA. Tel: 613-359-5334. p. 2640

Stevenson, Wilma, Asst Libr Dir, Garrett Memorial Library, 123 S Main, Moulton, IA, 52572. Tel: 641-642-3664. p. 771

Stever, Deborah, Dir, Deposit Free Library, 159 Front St, Deposit, NY, 13754. Tel: 607-467-2577. p. 1525

Stevick, David, Libr Dir, Houghton University, One Willard Ave, Houghton, NY, 14744. Tel: 585-567-9242. p. 1548

Steward, Barbara, Librn, Kansas State University Libraries, Mathematics & Physics Library, 105 Cardwell Hall, Manhattan, KS, 66506. Tel: 785-532-6827. p. 823

Steward, Bonnie, Asst Librn, Georgia O'Keeffe Museum, 217 Johnson St, Santa Fe, NM, 87501. p. 1476

Steward, Celeste, Libr Supvr, Mechanics' Institute Library, 57 Post St, Ste 504, San Francisco, CA, 94104-5003. Tel: 415-393-0118. p. 226

Steward, Darla, Br Supvr, Hernando County Public Library System, West Hernando, 6335 Blackbird Ave, Brooksville, FL, 34613. Tel: 352-754-4043. p. 388

Steward, Jenna, Librn, Louisiana House of Representatives, 900 N Third St, Baton Rouge, LA, 70804. Tel: 225-342-2433. p. 883

Steward, Karilyn, Principal Librn, City of Calabasas Library, 200 Civic Center Way, Calabasas, CA, 91302. Tel: 818-225-7616. p. 126

Steward, Noreen, Librn, Saranac Public Library, Clarksville Branch, 130 S Main St, Clarksville, MI, 48815. Tel: 616-693-1001. p. 1149

Stewart, Amanda, Dir, Richland Parish Library, 1410 Louisa St, Rayville, LA, 71269. Tel: 318-728-4806. p. 906

Stewart, Amanda, Youth Serv Dir, Utica Public Library, 303 Genesee St, Utica, NY, 13501. Tel: 315-735-2279. p. 1656

Stewart, Andrea, Dir, Libr & Educ, Nova Scotia Community College, Burridge Campus Library, 372 Pleasant St, Yarmouth, NS, B5A 2L2, CANADA. Tel: 902-742-3416. p. 2619

Stewart, Andrea, Dir of Libr, Nova Scotia Community College, Pictou Campus Library, 39 Acadia Ave, Stellarton, NS, B0K 1S0, CANADA. Tel: 902-755-7201. p. 2620

Stewart, Angela, Librn, Palliser Regional Library, Rockglen Branch, 1018 Centre St, Rockglen, SK, S0H 3R0, CANADA. Tel: 306-476-2350. p. 2743

Stewart, Ann-Marie, Supvry Librn, Environmental Protection Agency, West Bldg, Rm 3340, 1301 Constitution Ave NW, Washington, DC, 20004. Tel: 202-566-0578. p. 365

Stewart, Ariel, Br Mgr, Shreve Memorial Library, Broadmoor Branch, 1212 Captain Shreve Dr, Shreveport, LA, 71105. Tel: 318-869-0120. p. 908

Stewart, Ashley, Pub Serv Librn, Alaska State Court Law Library, 303 K St, Anchorage, AK, 99501. Tel: 907-264-0585. p. 41

Stewart, Audrey, Subject Liaison Librn, Coastal Carolina Community College, 444 Western Blvd, Jacksonville, NC, 28546. Tel: 910-938-6278. p. 1697

Stewart, Barbara, Cataloger, Capitan Public Library, 101 E Second St, Capitan, NM, 88316. Tel: 575-354-3035. p. 1464

Stewart, Brandi, Asst Dir, Ch, Monroe County Public Library, 500 W Fourth St, Tompkinsville, KY, 42167. Tel: 270-487-5301. p. 876

Stewart, Carolyn, Dir, Jasper Public Library, 14 W Second St, Jasper, TN, 37347-3409. Tel: 423-942-3369. p. 2103

Stewart, Cassandra, Librn, Sumpter Township Library, 148 Courthouse Sq, Toledo, IL, 62468. Tel: 217-849-2072. p. 654

Stewart, Catherine, Asst Dir, Head, Children's Servx, Memorial Library of Nazareth & Vicinity, 295 E Center St, Nazareth, PA, 18064. Tel: 610-759-4932. p. 1968

Stewart, Charles, Librn, Sheehan Phinney Library, 1000 Elm St, 17th Flr, Manchester, NH, 03101. Tel: 603-627-8175. p. 1372

Stewart, Christina, Br Mgr, Florence County Library System, Dozier M Munn Pamplico Public Library, 100 E Main St, Pamplico, SC, 29583. Tel: 843-493-5441. p. 2058

Stewart, Christina A, Dir, Wilmington Memorial Library, 175 Middlesex Ave, Wilmington, MA, 01887-2779. Tel: 978-658-2967. p. 1070

Stewart, Christopher, Web Coordr, State University of New York Downstate Health Sciences University, 395 Lenox Rd, Brooklyn, NY, 11203. Tel: 718-270-7400. p. 1506

Stewart, Claire, Dean, Libr & Univ Librn, University of Illinois Library at Urbana-Champaign, 1408 W Gregory Dr, Urbana, IL, 61801. Tel: 217-333-2291. p. 655

Stewart, Claire, Dean, Libr & Univ Librn, University of Illinois Library at Urbana-Champaign, Information Sciences Virtual Library, 100 Main Library, 1408 W Gregory Dr, Urbana, IL, 61801. Tel: 217-333-07900. p. 656

Stewart, Claire, Dean of Libr, University of Nebraska-Lincoln, 318 Love Library, 13th & R Strs, Lincoln, NE, 68588. Tel: 402-472-2526. p. 1323

Stewart, Cortiz, Library Contact, United States Navy, Medical Library, Code 185, 6000 W Hwy 98, Code 185, Pensacola, FL, 32512-0003. Tel: 850-505-6635. p. 436

Stewart, Danny, Dir, Pell City Library, 1000 Bruce Etheredge Pkwy, Ste 100, Pell City, AL, 35128. Tel: 205-884-1015. p. 32

Stewart, Darren, Br Mgr, Indianapolis Public Library, West Indianapolis, 1216 S Kappes St, Indianapolis, IN, 46221-1540. Tel: 317-275-4540. p. 696

Stewart, David, Dir, Bethel University Library, 3900 Bethel Dr, Saint Paul, MN, 55112. Tel: 651-638-6540. p. 1199

Stewart, Deborah, Br Mgr, Milwaukee Public Library, Villard Square, 5190 N 35th St, Milwaukee, WI, 53209. p. 2460

Stewart, Deborah Brown, Head of Libr, University of Pennsylvania Libraries, Museum Library, 3260 South St, Philadelphia, PA, 19104-6324. Tel: 215-898-4021. p. 1988

Stewart, Elizabeth, Sr Librn, City of Palo Alto Library, Children's, 1276 Harriet St, Palo Alto, CA, 94301. Tel: 650-838-2975. p. 191

Stewart, Erin, Br Librn, The Cavan Monaghan Libraries, One Dufferin St, Millbrook, ON, L0A 1G0, CANADA. Tel: 705-932-2919. p. 2658

Stewart, Hazel, Tech Serv, Parkersburg & Wood County Public Library, 3100 Emerson Ave, Parkersburg, WV, 26104-2414. Tel: 304-420-4587, Ext 513. p. 2411

Stewart, Jacquline, Mrs, Asst Librn, Mary Berry Brown Memorial Library, 1318 Hinton Waters Ave, Midland City, AL, 36350. Tel: 334-983-1191. p. 25

Stewart, James, Br Mgr, Montgomery County Public Libraries, Quince Orchard Library, 15831 Quince Orchard Rd, Gaithersburg, MD, 20878. Tel: 240-777-0212. p. 975

Stewart, Jamie, Asst Librn, Chapman & Cutler, 320 S Canal St, 27th Flr, Chicago, IL, 60606. Tel: 312-845-3435. p. 555

Stewart, Jennifer, Librn, Arley Public Library, 6788 Hwy 41, Arley, AL, 35541. Tel: 205-387-0129. p. 4

Stewart, John, Director, Operations & Tech, Serving Every Ohioan Service Center, 40780 Marietta Rd, Caldwell, OH, 43724. Tel: 740-783-5705. p. 2773

Stewart, Julia, Libr Dir, York Library Region, Fredericton Public Library, 12 Carleton St, Fredericton, NB, E3B 5P4, CANADA. Tel: 506-460-2800. p. 2602

Stewart, Karen, Consulting Research Librn, Desert Research Institute, 755 E Flamingo Rd, Las Vegas, NV, 89119-7363. Tel: 702-862-5405. p. 1346

Stewart, Kathleen, Acq Mgr, George Mason University Libraries, Law Library, 3301 N Fairfax Dr, Arlington, VA, 22201-4426. Tel: 703-993-8100. p. 2317

Stewart, Kelly, Cat, Paola Free Library, 101 E Peoria, Paola, KS, 66071. Tel: 913-259-3655. p. 830

Stewart, Kim, Dir, Marion-Perry County Library, 202 Washington St, Marion, AL, 36756. Tel: 334-683-6411. p. 25

Stewart, Kristen, Asst Br Librn/Ref, Brazoria County Library System, Pearland Branch, 3522 Liberty Dr, Pearland, TX, 77581. Tel: 281-485-4876. p. 2135

Stewart, Kristin, Tech Serv, Balch Springs Library-Learning Center, 12450 Elam Rd, Balch Springs, TX, 75180. Tel: 972-913-3000. p. 2144

Stinson, Jeffrey, Br Mgr, Atlanta-Fulton Public Library System, Alpharetta Branch, Ten Park Plaza, Alpharetta, GA, 30009. Tel: 404-613-6735. p. 460

Stinson, Judy, Doc/Ref Serv, Washington & Lee University, Wilbur C Hall Law Library, Lewis Hall, E Denny Circle, Lexington, VA, 24450. Tel: 540-458-8544. p. 2329

Stinson, Kaitlynn, Ref Librn, MGH Institute of Health Professions Library, Charlestown Navy Yard, 38 Third Ave, 4th Flr, Charlestown, MA, 02129. p. 1009

Stinson, Michelle, Youth Serv Librn, Springfield Town Library, 43 Main St, Springfield, VT, 05156. Tel: 802-885-3108. p. 2295

Stinson, Nichole, Dir, Thomasville Public Library, 1401 Mosley Dr, Thomasville, AL, 36784. Tel: 334-636-5343. p. 37

Stinson, Willette F, PhD, Dr, Dir, West Virginia State University, Campus Box L17, Institute, WV, 25112. Tel: 304-766-3116. p. 2406

Stipek, Elizabeth, Coll Mgt Librn, Chestatee Regional Library System, 56 Mechanicsville Rd, Dahlonega, GA, 30533. Tel: 706-864-3668. p. 474

Stipek-Long, Paula, Librn, Grace Hall Memorial Library, 161 Main Rd, Montgomery, MA, 01085-9525. Tel: 413-862-3894. p. 1036

Stirek, Valerie, Libr Tech, Arizona Christian University, One W Firestorm Way, Glendale, AZ, 85306. Tel: 602-386-4117. p. 61

Stirling, Casey, Libr Asst, Bacon Free Library, 58 Eliot St, Natick, MA, 01760. Tel: 508-653-6730. p. 1037

Stirm, David, Libr Tech II, Great Basin College Library, 1500 College Pkwy, Elko, NV, 89801. Tel: 775-327-2122. p. 1345

Stith, Ed, Librn, Dallas College, 3030 N Dallas Ave, Lancaster, TX, 75134-3799. Tel: 972-860-8140. p. 2209

Stiver, David, Spec Coll Librn, Graduate Theological Union Library, 2400 Ridge Rd, Berkeley, CA, 94709-1212. Tel: 510-649-2523. p. 122

Stivers, Rachelle, Dir, Libr & Info Serv, Heartland Community College Library, 1500 W Raab Rd, Normal, IL, 61761. Tel: 309-268-8274. p. 625

Stivers, Tracey, Archives, Database Coordr, Tech Serv, Cincinnati State Technical & Community College, 3520 Central Pkwy, Rm 170, Cincinnati, OH, 45223-2690. Tel: 513-569-1608. p. 1760

Stiverson, Cynthia, Acq Mgr, Maryland Department of Legislative Services Library, B-00 Legislative Services Bldg, 90 State Circle, Annapolis, MD, 21401. Tel: 410-946-5400. p. 951

Stiwinter, Katherine, Dir, Spartanburg Community College Library, Giles Campus, 107 Community College Dr, Spartanburg, SC, 29303. Tel: 864-592-4764. p. 2069

Stock, Jennifer, Dir, Upper Darby Township & Sellers Memorial Free Public Library, 76 S State Rd, Upper Darby, PA, 19082. Tel: 610-789-4440. p. 2016

Stock, Kara, Dir, Lancaster Public Library, 5466 Broadway, Lancaster, NY, 14086. Tel: 716-683-1120. p. 1562

Stock, Matt, Librn, University of Oklahoma Libraries, Architecture Library, LLG8, 830 Van Vleet Oval, Norman, OK, 73019. Tel: 405-325-5521. p. 1856

Stock, Matt, Librn, University of Oklahoma Libraries, Fine Arts, 500 W Boyd St, Norman, OK, 73019. Tel: 405-325-4243. p. 1856

Stockall, Janice, Cat, Reserves, University of New Brunswick Libraries, Gerard V La Forest Law Library, Law School, 2nd Flr, 41 Dineen Dr, Fredericton, NB, E3B 5A3, CANADA. Tel: 506-458-7979. p. 2602

Stocker, Corrine, Dir, Hazel Park Memorial District Library, 123 E Nine Mile Rd, Hazel Park, MI, 48030. Tel: 248-542-0940, 248-546-4095. p. 1114

Stockman, Cyndi, Chief Exec Officer, James Township Public Library, 19 First St, Elk Lake, ON, P0J 1G0, CANADA. Tel: 705-678-2340. p. 2640

Stockment, Jennifer, Mgr, Miami-Dade Public Library System, Palmetto Bay Branch, 17641 Old Cutler Rd, Miami, FL, 33157. Tel: 305-232-1771. p. 424

Stockton, David, Assoc Dir, Coll Serv, United States Military Academy Library, Jefferson Hall Library & Learning Ctr, 758 Cullum Rd, West Point, NY, 10996. Tel: 845-938-8301. p. 1663

Stockwell, Claudette, Dir, Killingly Public Library, 25 Westcott Rd, Danielson, CT, 06239. Tel: 860-779-5383. p. 308

Stoddard, Ashley, Coll Spec, Northeastern State University, 711 N Grand Ave, Tahlequah, OK, 74464-2333. Tel: 918-456-5511, Ext 3200. p. 1863

Stoddard, Lauren, Br Mgr, Washington County Library System, Hurricane Branch, 36 S 300 W, Hurricane, UT, 84737. Tel: 435-635-4621. p. 2270

Stoddard, Laurie, Librn, Renfrew County Law Association, 297 Pembroke St E, Ste 1211, Pembroke, ON, K8A 3K2, CANADA. Tel: 613-732-4880. p. 2671

Stoddart, Joan, Dep Dir, University of Utah, Spencer S Eccles Health Sciences Library, Bldg 589, 10 N 1900 E, Salt Lake City, UT, 84112-5890. Tel: 801-581-8771. p. 2272

Stoeger, Kristin, Libr Dir, Manitowoc Public Library, 707 Quay St, Manitowoc, WI, 54220. Tel: 920-686-3000. p. 2453

Stoelb, Barbara, ILL, Edwin A Bemis Public Library, 6014 S Datura St, Littleton, CO, 80120-2636. Tel: 303-795-3961. p. 290

Stoesz, Rachel, Libr Mgr, DeBolt Public Library, PO Box 480, DeBolt, AB, T0H 1B0, CANADA. Tel: 780-957-3770. p. 2532

Stofel, Christopher, Mgr, Libr Operations, Metropolitan Library System in Oklahoma County, Choctaw Library, 2525 Muzzy St, Choctaw, OK, 73020-8717. p. 1857

Stofel, Christopher, Mgr, Libr Operations, Metropolitan Library System in Oklahoma County, Harrah Library, 1930 N Church Ave, Harrah, OK, 73045. p. 1857

Stofer, Kelly, Chief Admin Officer, British Columbia Land Surveyors Foundation, No 301-2400 Bevan Ave, Sidney, BC, V8L 1W1, CANADA. Tel: 250-655-7222. p. 2576

Stoffle, Carla, Prof, University of Arizona, Harvill Bldg, 4th Flr, 1103 E Second St, Tucson, AZ, 85721. Tel: 520-621-3565. p. 2782

Stofocik, Jai, Ref Serv, Tidewater Community College Learning Resources Center, 300 Granby St, Norfolk, VA, 23510. Tel: 757-822-1775. p. 2336

Stohr, Nicki, Dir & Librn, Wilson County Public Libraries, 1103 Fourth St, Floresville, TX, 78114. Tel: 830-393-7361. p. 2177

Stohr, S, Asst Dir, Nissen Public Library, 217 W Fifth St, Saint Ansgar, IA, 50472. Tel: 641-713-2218. p. 780

Stohr, Sarah, Instruction Librn, Rio Salado College, 2323 W 14th St, Tempe, AZ, 85281. Tel: 480-517-8281. p. 79

Stohs, Cindy, Dir, Coffey County Library, LeRoy Branch, 725 Main St, LeRoy, KS, 66857. Tel: 620-964-2321. p. 800

Stoiber, Rosaleen, Sister, Libr Asst, Queen of the Holy Rosary Center Library, 43326 Mission Circle, Fremont, CA, 94539. Tel: 510-657-2468. p. 144

Stokanovich, Bree, Adult Serv, Hamburg Township Library, 10411 Merrill Rd, Hamburg, MI, 48139. Tel: 810-231-1771. p. 1112

Stokem, Lori, Dir, Bancroft Public Library, 181 Main St, Salem, NY, 12865. Tel: 518-854-7463. p. 1635

Stoker, Storm, Tech Serv, University of Hawaii, 2525 Dole St, Honolulu, HI, 96822-2328. Tel: 808-956-5582. p. 513

Stokes, Brian, Dir, Falmouth Public Library, 300 Main St, Falmouth, MA, 02540. Tel: 508-457-2555. p. 1018

Stokes, Brian, Libr Mgr, New York Public Library - Astor, Lenox & Tilden Foundations, New Amsterdam Branch, Nine Murray St, (Between Broadway and Church St), New York, NY, 10007-2223. Tel: 212-732-8186. p. 1596

Stokes, Joan, Dir, Libr Syst, Plumb Memorial Library, 65 Wooster St, Shelton, CT, 06484. Tel: 203-924-1580. p. 336

Stokes, Katrina, Dir, Warren County-Vicksburg Public Library, 700 Veto St, Vicksburg, MS, 39180-3595. Tel: 601-636-6411. p. 1235

Stokes, Laura, Children's Activities Dir, Pike-Amite-Walthall Library System, 1022 Virginia Ave, McComb, MS, 39648. Tel: 601-684-2661, Ext 12. p. 1225

Stokes, Laura, Librn, Brown University, Orwig Music Library, Orwig Music Bldg, One Young Orchard Ave, Providence, RI, 02912. Tel: 401-863-3759. p. 2037

Stokes, Leslie, Mgr, West Georgia Regional Library, Heard County Public Library, 564 Main St, Franklin, GA, 30217. Tel: 706-675-6501. p. 470

Stokes, Perry, Libr Dir, Baker County Public Library, 2400 Resort St, Baker City, OR, 97814-2798. Tel: 541-523-6419. p. 1872

Stolarz, Erika, Br Serv Coordr, Lake County Public Library, 1919 W 81st Ave, Merrillville, IN, 46410-5488. Tel: 219-769-3541. p. 705

Stolfer, Karen, Libr Dir, Hanson Public Library, 132 Maquan St, Hanson, MA, 02341. Tel: 781-293-2151. p. 1023

Stolfi, Maria, Tech Serv, John C Hart Memorial Library, 1130 Main St, Shrub Oak, NY, 10588. Tel: 914-245-5262. p. 1641

Stolins, Leslie, Sr Librn, New York Supreme Court, 235 Elizabeth St, Utica, NY, 13501. Tel: 315-266-4570. p. 1655

Stoll, Carla, Br Mgr, Starke County Public Library System, San Pierre Branch, 103 S Broadway, San Pierre, IN, 46374. Tel: 219-828-4352. p. 699

Stoll, Christina, Adult Serv Mgr, Indian Trails Public Library District, 355 S Schoenbeck Rd, Wheeling, IL, 60090. Tel: 847-459-4100. p. 662

Stoll, Laura, Asst Dir, Kirkland Town Library, 55 1/2 College St, Clinton, NY, 13323. Tel: 315-853-2038. p. 1519

Stoll, Lisa, Libr Coord, Warren County Community College, 475 Rte 57 W, Washington, NJ, 07882-4343. Tel: 908-835-2336. p. 1451

Stoll, Sandra J, Chief Admin, Law Librn, Hancock County Law Library Association, 300 S Main St, 4th Flr, Findlay, OH, 45840. Tel: 419-424-7077. p. 1785

Stoller, Elyse, Head, Circ, Finkelstein Memorial Library, 24 Chestnut St, Spring Valley, NY, 10977. Tel: 845-352-5700, Ext 227. p. 1644

Stoltenburg, Jeanne M, Libr Dir, Supvry Librn, United States Air Force, 28 FSS/FSDL, 2650 Doolittle Dr, Bldg 3910, Ellsworth AFB, SD, 57706-4820. Tel: 605-385-1686, 605-385-1688. p. 2076

Stoltz, Carol, Head, Pub Serv, Saint Francis University, 106 Franciscan Way, Loretto, PA, 15940. Tel: 814-472-3165. p. 1957

Stoltz, Dorothy, Outreach Serv Librn, Prog Serv, Carroll County Public Library, 1100 Green Valley Rd, New Windsor, MD, 21776. Tel: 410-386-4500. p. 971

Stoltz, Zoe Ann, Ref Historian, Montana Historical Society, 225 N Roberts St, Helena, MT, 59601-4514. Tel: 406-444-1988. p. 1296

Stolz, Jacqueline, Outreach Specialist, Youth Programmer, Urbandale Public Library, 3520 86th St, Urbandale, IA, 50322. Tel: 515-278-3945. p. 787

Stonbraker, Jayme, Dir, Joseph & Elizabeth Shaw Public Library, One S Front St, Clearfield, PA, 16830. Tel: 814-765-3271. p. 1922

Stone, Aleya, Ref Librn, Tyler Public Library, 201 S College Ave, Tyler, TX, 75702-7381. Tel: 903-593-7323. p. 2250

Stone, Amy, Dir, Bridgton Public Library, One Church St, Bridgton, ME, 04009. Tel: 207-647-2472. p. 918
Stone, Bethany, Br Chief, Orange County Library System, 101 E Central Blvd, Orlando, FL, 32801. Tel: 407-835-7323. p. 431
Stone, Bridget, Dir, Georgia Public Library, 1697 Ethan Allen Hwy, Georgia, VT, 05454. Tel: 802-524-4643. p. 2284
Stone, Bridgette, Dir of Educ, Berkshire Botanical Garden Library, PO Box 826, Stockbridge, MA, 01262-0826. Tel: 413-298-3926. p. 1057
Stone, Carla, Mgr, Fulton County Library, 325 Main St, Mammoth Spring, AR, 72554. Tel: 870-625-3205. p. 103
Stone, Danae, Dir, Barnard Library, 521 Elm, La Crosse, KS, 67548. Tel: 785-222-2826. p. 818
Stone, Europonda, Dir, United States Air Force, 37 Harris St, Columbus AFB, MS, 39710-5102. Tel: 662-434-2934. p. 1215
Stone, Glenice, Dir, Northeast Mississippi Community College, 101 Cunningham Blvd, Booneville, MS, 38829. Tel: 662-720-7237, 662-728-7751. p. 1212
Stone, Jan, Head, Fac Serv, University of North Dakota, Thormodsgard Law Library, 215 Centennial Dr, Grand Forks, ND, 58202. Tel: 701-777-2204. p. 1734
Stone, Janet, Libr Dir, Glendora Public Library & Cultural Center, 140 S Glendora Ave, Glendora, CA, 91741. Tel: 626-852-4896. p. 149
Stone, Jeannie, Dir, Bayard Public Library, 315 Main St, Bayard, IA, 50029. Tel: 712-651-2238. p. 734
Stone, Jennifer, Librn I, Plattsburgh Public Library, 19 Oak St, Plattsburgh, NY, 12901. Tel: 518-563-0921. p. 1619
Stone, Jenny, Librn, Dallas Museum of Art, 1717 N Harwood, Dallas, TX, 75201. Tel: 214-922-1277. p. 2164
Stone, Joan, Dir, Crosby County Library, Lorenzo Branch, 409 Van Buren, Lorenzo, TX, 79343-2553. Tel: 806-634-5639. p. 2162
Stone, John, Libr Dir, The Master's Seminary Library, 13248 Roscoe Blvd, Sun Valley, CA, 91352. Tel: 818-909-5545. p. 251
Stone, John W, Libr Dir, The Master's University, 21726 W Placerita Canyon Rd, Santa Clarita, CA, 91321-1200. Tel: 661-362-2271. p. 242
Stone, Karen E, Adminr, Semmes, Bowen & Semmes Library, 25 S Charles St, Ste 1400, Baltimore, MD, 21201. Tel: 410-385-3936. p. 956
Stone, Kathleen, Librn, Jefferson Public Library, 48 Washington Rd, Jefferson, ME, 04348. Tel: 207-549-7491. p. 928
Stone, Kenneth H, Dep Dir-Chief Financial Officer, Buffalo & Erie County Public Library System, One Lafayette Sq, Buffalo, NY, 14203-1887. Tel: 716-858-8900. p. 1507
Stone, Libby, ILL, Pub Serv, Gaston College, 201 Hwy 321 S, Dallas, NC, 28034-1499. Tel: 704-922-6359. p. 1683
Stone, Linda, Curator, Woolaroc Museum Library, 1925 Woolaroc Ranch Rd, Bartlesville, OK, 74003. Tel: 918-336-0307, Ext 32. p. 1842
Stone, Margaret, Dir, Dakota County Library System, 1340 Wescott Rd, Eagan, MN, 55123-1099. Tel: 651-450-2900. p. 1173
Stone, Martha, Ref (Info Servs), Massachusetts General Hospital, Treadwell Library, Bartlett Hall Ext-I, 55 Fruit St, Boston, MA, 02114-2696. Tel: 617-726-8600. p. 997
Stone, Phillip, Archivist, Wofford College, 429 N Church St, Spartanburg, SC, 29303-3663. Tel: 864-597-4300. p. 2070
Stone, Roberta, Mgr, Collier County Public Library, Everglades Branch, City Hall, Everglades City, FL, 34139. Tel: 239-695-2511. p. 427
Stone, Steve, Pub Serv Librn, Bluegrass Community & Technical College, 221 Oswald Bldg, 470 Cooper Dr, Lexington, KY, 40506-0235. Tel: 859-246-6387. p. 862
Stone, Sue, Librn, Missoula Public Library, Seeley Lake Community, 456 Airport Rd, Seeley Lake, MT, 59868. Tel: 406-677-8995. p. 1300
Stone, Susan, Adminr, Librn, Susquehanna County Historical Society & Free Library Association, 458 High School Rd, Montrose, PA, 18801. Tel: 570-278-1881. p. 1965
Stone, Tina, Dir, Julesburg Public Library, 320 Cedar St, Julesburg, CO, 80737-1545. Tel: 970-474-2608. p. 287
Stoneback, Sharon, Libr Spec, Mercer County Community College Library, 1200 Old Trenton Rd, West Windsor, NJ, 08550. Tel: 609-5586-4800 x3560. p. 1453
Stonebraker, Jeanette, Mgr, Mercy Medical Center, 1111 Sixth Ave, Des Moines, IA, 50314-2611. Tel: 515-247-4189. p. 747
Stonebraker, Llana, Dept Head, Indiana University Bloomington, Business/SPEA Information Commons, SPEA 150, 1315 E Tenth St, Bloomington, IN, 47405. Tel: 812-855-2448. p. 670
Stonehocker, Lori, Libr Dir, Redfield Public Library, 1112 Thomas St, Redfield, IA, 50233. Tel: 515-833-2200. p. 778
Stonehouse, Jordan, Libr Mgr, Coronation Memorial Library, 5001 Royal St, Coronation, AB, T0C 1C0, CANADA. Tel: 403-578-3445. p. 2532
Stoneking, Shannon, Dir, Ramsey County Law Library, 1815 Court House, Saint Paul, MN, 55102. Tel: 651-266-8391. p. 1201
Stoner, Angela, Librn, Patton State Hospital, Staff Library, 3102 E Highland Ave, Patton, CA, 92369. Tel: 909-425-7484. p. 195
Stoner, Joe, Libr Mgr, Alameda County Library, Newark Library, 6300 Civic Terrace Ave, Newark, CA, 94560-3766. Tel: 510-284-0675. p. 143
Stoner, Mary, Dir, Anne West Lindsey District Library, 600 N Division St, Carterville, IL, 62918. Tel: 618-985-3298. p. 550
Stoner, Ruth, Librn, Niagara Parks Botanical Gardens & School of Horticulture, 2565 Niagara Pkwy N, Niagara Falls, ON, L2E 6S4, CANADA. Tel: 905-356-8554, Ext 6207. p. 2660
Stoner, Shannon Nichola, Libr Dir, Gillett Public Library, 200 E Main St, Gillett, WI, 54124. Tel: 920-855-6224. p. 2437
Stonesifer, Susan, Br Mgr, Howard County Library System, Miller Branch & Historical Center, 9421 Frederick Rd, Ellicott City, MD, 21042-2119. Tel: 410-313-1978. p. 965
Stonewall, Hannah, Youth Serv Librn, Pineville-Bell County Public Library, 214 Walnut St, Pineville, KY, 40977. Tel: 606-337-3422. p. 873
Stonewell, Steve, ILL Mgr, Saint Mary's College Library, 1928 Saint Mary's Rd, Moraga, CA, 94575. Tel: 925-631-4229. p. 180
Stoops, Jaime, Supv Librn, Pamunkey Regional Library, 7527 Library Dr, Hanover, VA, 23069. Tel: 804-537-6211. p. 2323
Stopsky, Korine, Youth Serv Librn, Dixon Homestead Library, 180 Washington Ave, Dumont, NJ, 07628. Tel: 201-384-2030. p. 1399
Storey, Kim, ILL Spec, Laramie County Library System, 2200 Pioneer Ave, Cheyenne, WY, 82001-3610. Tel: 307-773-7233. p. 2492
Storey, Nicholas, Libr Mgr, Kinchafoonee Regional Library System, Webster County Library, 40 Cemetey Rd, Preston, GA, 31824. Tel: 229-828-5740. p. 475
Stork, Jackie, Youth Serv Librn, Itasca Community Library, 500 W Irving Park Rd, Itasca, IL, 60143. Tel: 630-773-1699. p. 602
Stork, Veronica, Dir, Pine Plains Free Library, 7775 S Main St, Pine Plains, NY, 12567-5653. Tel: 518-398-1927. p. 1618
Storlien, Jessica, Archivist, Ref (Info Servs), Stearns History Museum, 235 33rd Ave S, Saint Cloud, MN, 56301-3752. Tel: 320-253-8424. p. 1198
Storm, Abigail, Dir, Conant Public Library, 111 Main St, Winchester, NH, 03470. Tel: 603-239-4331. p. 1384
Storm, Jill, Youth Serv Supvr, Seminole Community Library at St Petersburg College, 9200 113th St N, Seminole, FL, 33772. Tel: 727-394-6915. p. 444
Storm, Misha, Libr Dir, Leverett Library, 75 Montague Rd, Leverett, MA, 01054. Tel: 413-548-9220. p. 1028
Storm, Misha, Dir, Dickinson Memorial Library, 115 Main St, Northfield, MA, 01360. Tel: 413-498-2455. p. 1043
Storm, Waneta, Libr Dir, Klyte Burt Memorial Public Library, 316 Center Ave, Curtis, NE, 69025. Tel: 308-367-4148. p. 1312
Stormberg, Amy, Dir, Amery Area Public Library, 255 Scholl Ct, Amery, WI, 54001. Tel: 715-268-9340. p. 2420
Stormo, Kaylinn, Doc Delivery, ILL, Essentia Institute of Rural Health, Essentia Health St Mary's Medical Center, 407 E Third St, Duluth, MN, 55805-1984. Tel: 218-786-4396. p. 1172
Storms, Elizabeth, Mgr, Baltimore County Public Library, North Point Branch, 1716 Merritt Blvd, Baltimore, MD, 21222. Tel: 410-887-7255. p. 980
Stortdedt, Joy, Tech Coordr, Shenandoah Public Library, 201 S Elm St, Shenandoah, IA, 51601. Tel: 712-246-2315. p. 781
Story, Betty, Ref Librn, Bethune-Cookman University, 640 Mary McLeod Bethune Blvd, Daytona Beach, FL, 32114. Tel: 386-481-2186. p. 392
Story, Christopher, Librn, Oklahoma State Reformatory Library, 1700 E First St, Granite, OK, 73547. Tel: 580-480-3700. p. 1848
Story, Daniel, Digital Scholarship Librn, University of California, 1156 High St, Santa Cruz, CA, 95064. Tel: 831-459-3187. p. 243
Story, Edwynne, Librn, Phillips-Lee-Monroe Regional Library, Marvell Library, 806 Carruth St, Marvell, AR, 72366. Tel: 870-829-3183. p. 98
Story, Moriah, Br Mgr, Blue Ridge Summit Free Library, 13676 Monterey Lane, Blue Ridge Summit, PA, 17214. Tel: 717-794-2240. p. 1914
Story-Huffman, Ru, Dean, Libr Serv, Georgia Southwestern State University, 800 Georgia Southwestern State University Dr, Americus, GA, 31709. Tel: 229-931-2259. p. 457
Storz, Kim, Chief Librn/CEO, West Grey Public Library, 453 Garafraxa St S, Durham, ON, N0G 1R0, CANADA. Tel: 519-369-2107. p. 2639
Stotelmyer, Christopher, Head, Electronic Res & Serv, Clayton State University Library, 2000 Clayton State Blvd, Morrow, GA, 30260. Tel: 678-466-4347. p. 491
Stothert-Maurer, Molly, Head Librn, Arizona State Museum Library, University of Arizona, 1013 E University Blvd, Tucson, AZ, 85721-0026. Tel: 520-621-4695. p. 81
Stouffer, Christine, Librn, Thompson, Hine LLP, 3900 Key Ctr, 127 Public Sq, Cleveland, OH, 44114-1291. Tel: 216-566-5651. p. 1770
Stouffer, Joe, Access Services Assoc, Drake University, Drake Law Library, Opperman Hall, 2604 Forest Ave, Des Moines, IA, 50311. Tel: 515-271-4960. p. 746
Stough, Tom, Librn, Oxnard College Library, 4000 S Rose Ave, Oxnard, CA, 93033-6699. Tel: 805-986-5819. p. 190
Stoughton, Judy, Ch, Mansfield Public Library, 54 Warrenville Rd, Mansfield Center, CT, 06250. Tel: 860-423-2501. p. 321
Stout, Aleisha, Ch Serv, Idaho Falls Public Library, 457 W Broadway, Idaho Falls, ID, 83402. Tel: 208-612-8460. p. 523
Stout, Andrew, Assoc Librn, Pub Serv, Covenant Theological Seminary, 478 Covenant Ln, Saint Louis, MO, 63141. Tel: 314-392-4100, 314-434-4044. p. 1270
Stout, Ashley, Pub Serv Librn, Pendleton Community Library, 595 E Water St, Pendleton, IN, 46064-1070. Tel: 765-778-7527. p. 713
Stout, Carlton, Mgr, Carnegie Library of Pittsburgh, Allegheny, 1230 Federal St, Pittsburgh, PA, 15212. Tel: 412-237-1890. p. 1991

Stout, David, Mgr, Research & Digital Scholarship, Christian Theological Seminary, 1000 W 42nd St, Indianapolis, IN, 46208. Tel: 317-931-2364. p. 691

Stout, Jenna, Archivist, Saint Louis Art Museum, One Fine Arts Dr, Forest Park, Saint Louis, MO, 63110. Tel: 314-655-5452. p. 1272

Stout, Julie, Circ, Charles A Ransom District Library, 180 S Sherwood Ave, Plainwell, MI, 49080-1896. Tel: 269-685-8024. p. 1141

Stout, Justin, Head, Ref, Neuse Regional Library, 510 N Queen St, Kinston, NC, 28501. Tel: 252-527-7066. p. 1699

Stout, Nancy, Asst Librn, New York Psychoanalytic Society & Institute, 247 E 82nd St, New York, NY, 10028-2701. Tel: 212-879-6900. p. 1594

Stoutenburgh, Delaine, Asst Br Mgr, First Regional Library, Jessie J Edwards Public Library, 610 E Central Ave, Coldwater, MS, 38618. Tel: 662-622-5573. p. 1220

Stovall, Ann, Tech Serv, Tech Serv, Indian Prairie Public Library District, 401 Plainfield Rd, Darien, IL, 60561-4207. Tel: 630-887-8760. p. 575

Stovall, Barbara, Dr, Archivist, Oakwood University, 7000 Adventist Blvd NW, Huntsville, AL, 35896. Tel: 256-726-7249. p. 22

Stovall, Brack, Br Mgr, Alexandria Library, James M Duncan Jr Branch, 2501 Commonwealth Ave, Alexandria, VA, 22301. Tel: 703-746-1705. p. 2302

Stovall, Jerry, Dir, South Georgia Technical College, Hicks Hall, Rm 115, 900 S Georgia Tech Pkwy, Americus, GA, 31709. Tel: 229-931-2562. p. 458

Stovall, Jerry, Dir, South Georgia Technical College, Crisp County Ctr, Rm A37, 402 N Midway Rd, Cordele, GA, 31015. Tel: 229-271-4071. p. 473

Stovall, Melanee, Br Mgr, San Bernardino County Library, Cal Aero Preserve Academy Branch, 15850 Main St, Chino, CA, 91708. Tel: 909-606-2173. p. 212

Stovall, Melanee, Regional Mgr, San Bernardino County Library, 777 E Rialto Ave, San Bernardino, CA, 92415-0035. Tel: 909-665-0296. p. 212

Stovall, Melanee, Br Mgr, San Bernardino County Library, Chino Branch, 13180 Central Ave, Chino, CA, 91710. Tel: 909-465-5280. p. 213

Stovall, Rebecca, Adminr, Memphis Public Library & Information Center, 3030 Poplar Ave, Memphis, TN, 38111. Tel: 901-415-2700. p. 2113

Stovall, Sheila, Dir, Allen County Public Library, 106 W Public Sq, Scottsville, KY, 42164. Tel: 270-237-3861. p. 874

Stover, Amy, Dir, Raleigh County Public Library, 221 N Kanawha St, Beckley, WV, 25801-4716. Tel: 304-255-0511. p. 2397

Stover, Ivy, Dir, Magdalena Public Library, 108 N Main St, Magdalena, NM, 87825. Tel: 575-854-2361. p. 1472

Stover, Jennifer, Head, Tech Serv, Merrimack Public Library, 470 Daniel Webster Hwy, Merrimack, NH, 03054-3694. Tel: 603-424-5021. p. 1373

Stover, Mark, PhD, Dean, California State University, Northridge, 18111 Nordhoff St, Northridge, CA, 91330. Tel: 818-677-2285. p. 183

Stover, Robin, Ms, Br Mgr, Bland County Library, 697 Main St, Bland, VA, 24315. Tel: 276-688-3737. p. 2307

Stover, Sheila, Librn, Esmeralda County Public Libraries, Fish Lake Library, Hwy 264 Bluebird Lane, Dyer, NV, 89010. Tel: 775-572-3311. p. 1351

Stover, Teri, Dir, Texas A&M University-Texarkana, 7101 University Ave, Texarkana, TX, 75503. Tel: 903-223-3100. p. 2248

Stovin, Lorraine, Librn, Bren Del Win Centennial Library, 211 N Railway W, Deloraine, MB, R0M 0M0, CANADA. Tel: 204-747-2415. p. 2587

Stow, Elizabeth, Asst Dir, Pub Serv, Columbia Theological Seminary, 701 S Columbia Dr, Decatur, GA, 30030. Tel: 404-687-4617. p. 475

Stowell, Genoveve, Managing Librn, New York Public Library - Astor, Lenox & Tilden Foundations, 53rd Street Branch, 18 W 53rd St, New York, NY, 10019. Tel: 212-714-8400. p. 1594

Stoyanova, Penka, Sr Librn, Trillium Health Partners - Credit Valley Hospital, 2200 Eglinton Ave W, Mississauga, ON, L5M 2N1, CANADA. Tel: 905-813-2111, Ext 6479. p. 2659

Strachan, Elisabeth, Ch, Thayer Public Library, 798 Washington St, Braintree, MA, 02184. Tel: 781-848-0405, Ext 4426. p. 1001

Strackeljahn, Anna, Head, Coll Mgt, Saint Louis Public Library, 1301 Olive St, Saint Louis, MO, 63103. Tel: 314-539-0300. p. 1274

Strader, Linda, Dir, Belleville Philomathean Free Library, 8086 County Rte 75, Belleville, NY, 13611. Tel: 315-846-5103. p. 1492

Stradiotto, Nicole, Scholarly Communications Librn, Lakehead University, 955 Oliver Rd, Thunder Bay, ON, P7B 5E1, CANADA. Tel: 807-343-8315. p. 2685

Stradling-Collins, SueAn, Dir, Apache County Library District, 30 S Second W, Saint Johns, AZ, 85936. Tel: 928-337-4923. p. 76

Straffolino, Laura, Curator, Free Library of Philadelphia, Print & Picture, 1901 Vine St, 2nd Flr, Philadelphia, PA, 19103-1116. Tel: 215-686-5405. p. 1979

Strahan, Michael, Distance Educ, Ref, Northern Michigan University, 1401 Presque Isle Ave, Marquette, MI, 49855-5376. Tel: 906-227-2463. p. 1130

Strahl, Sarah, City Librn, Salem Public Library, 585 Liberty St SE, Salem, OR, 97301. Tel: 503-588-6315. p. 1897

Strahm, Rachel, Youth Serv Librn, Delphos Public Library, 309 W Second St, Delphos, OH, 45833-1695. Tel: 419-695-4015. p. 1782

Strain, Amy, Br Mgr, Saint Tammany Parish Library, Folsom Branch, 82393 Railroad Ave, Folsom, LA, 70437. Tel: 985-796-9728. p. 888

Strain, Jennifer, Instruction & Scholarly Communications Librn, Elizabethtown College, One Alpha Dr, Elizabethtown, PA, 17022-2227. Tel: 717-361-1480. p. 1929

Strain, Judson, Ref Librn, Olivet Nazarene University, One University Ave, Bourbonnais, IL, 60914-2271. Tel: 815-928-5438. p. 544

Strain, Pam, Adult Serv, McHenry Public Library District, 809 Front St, McHenry, IL, 60050. Tel: 815-385-0036. p. 616

Strain Swint, Darlene, Coordr, Cincinnati Children's Hospital, Edward L Pratt Library, S9.125 ML 3012, 3333 Burnet Ave, Cincinnati, OH, 45229-3039. Tel: 513-636-4230. p. 1759

Strait, Angela, Coll Res Mgt Librn, Marshall University Libraries, One John Marshall Dr, Huntington, WV, 25755-2060. Tel: 304-696-4356. p. 2405

Straitiff, Donna, Dir, Ingalls Memorial Library, 203 Main St, Rindge, NH, 03461. Tel: 603-899-3303. p. 1379

Straka, Brett, Tech Serv, Whatcom Community College Library, Heiner Bldg, 231 W Kellogg Rd, Bellingham, WA, 98226. Tel: 360-383-3300. p. 2359

Straka, Carrie, Ad, Itasca Community Library, 500 W Irving Park Rd, Itasca, IL, 60143. Tel: 630-773-1699. p. 602

Straka, Mary, Libr Res Serv Mgr, Argonne National Laboratory, 9700 S Cass Ave, Bldg 240, Lemont, IL, 60439-4801. Tel: 630-252-7770. p. 608

Stranack, Kevin, Univ Librn, University of Northern British Columbia Library, 333 University Way, Prince George, BC, V2N 4Z9, CANADA. Tel: 250-960-6612. p. 2574

Strand, Jennifer, Librn, Osceola Township Public & School Library, 48475 Maple Dr, Dollar Bay, MI, 49922. Tel: 906-482-5800. p. 1101

Strand, Kyle, Head of Libr, Inter-American Development Bank, 1300 New York Ave NW, Stop W-0102, Washington, DC, 20577. Tel: 202-623-3210. p. 369

Strand, Rose, Cat Tech, Alamosa Public Library, 300 Hunt Ave, Alamosa, CO, 81101. Tel: 719-587-2539. p. 263

Strandquist, Wanda, Libr Mgr, Elnora Public Library, 210 Main St, Elnora, AB, T0M 0Y0, CANADA. Tel: 403-773-3966. p. 2539

Strandt, Laura, Youth Serv, Hamburg Township Library, 10411 Merrill Rd, Hamburg, MI, 48139. Tel: 810-231-1771. p. 1112

Strang, Anne, Ch Serv Librn, Ogden Farmers' Library, 269 Ogden Center Rd, Spencerport, NY, 14559. Tel: 585-617-6181. p. 1643

Strang, Jane, Libr Asst, Cascade Public Library, 310 First Ave W, Cascade, IA, 52033. Tel: 563-852-3222. p. 737

Strang, Mark, Mgr, Libr Info Tech, Bowling Green State University Libraries, 1001 E Wooster St, Bowling Green, OH, 43403-0170. p. 1752

Strang, Su Ying, Exec Dir, Southern Alberta Art Gallery Library, 601 Third Ave S, Lethbridge, AB, T1J 0H4, CANADA. Tel: 403-327-8770, Ext 26. p. 2546

Strange, Jennifer, Sr Pub Serv Librn, Plano Public Library System, Christopher A Parr Library, 6200 Windhaven Pkwy, Plano, TX, 75093. Tel: 972-769-4300. p. 2227

Strange, Kathleen, Adult Ref Librn, Clarendon Hills Public Library, Seven N Prospect Ave, Clarendon Hills, IL, 60514. Tel: 630-323-8188. p. 572

Strange, Michael, Library Contact, Lafayette County Public Library, 219 E Third St, Lewisville, AR, 71845. Tel: 870-921-4757. p. 99

Stranger, Jennifer, Dir, Roachdale-Franklin Township Public Library, 100 E Washington St, Roachdale, IN, 46172. Tel: 765-522-1491. p. 716

Stransky, Barbara, Ref Librn, Kansas City Kansas Community College Library, 7250 State Ave, Kansas City, KS, 66112. Tel: 913-288-7650. p. 816

Stranz, Dennis, Libr Dir, Township Library of Lower Southampton, 1983 Bridgetown Pike, Feasterville, PA, 19053-4493. Tel: 215-355-1183. p. 1933

Strass, David, Ref Librn, Kirkwood Community College, Iowa City Campus Library, 107 Credit Center Bldg, 1816 Lower Muscatine Rd, Iowa City, IA, 52240. Tel: 319-887-3612, 319-887-3613. p. 738

Stratman, Jason D, Ref & Info Serv, Web Coordr, Missouri Historical Society, 225 S Skinker Blvd, Saint Louis, MO, 63105. Tel: 314-746-4500. p. 1272

Stratton, Jane, Br Mgr, Belmont County District Library, Powhatan Point Branch, 297 N State Rte 7, Powhatan Point, OH, 43942. Tel: 740-795-4624. p. 1800

Stratton, Judy, Dir, Pomona Community Library, 115 E Franklin St, Pomona, KS, 66076. Tel: 785-566-3300. p. 832

Stratton, Karin, Operations Supvr, University of Michigan, Music Library, Earl V Moore Bldg, 3rd Flr, 1100 Baits Dr, Ann Arbor, MI, 48109-2085. Tel: 734-764-2512. p. 1080

Stratton, Michael, Libr Coord, Bryant & Stratton College Library, 1259 Central Ave, Albany, NY, 12205. Tel: 518-437-1802. p. 1482

Stratton, Monica, Br Mgr, Ramsey County Library, Maplewood Branch, 3025 Southlawn Dr, Maplewood, MN, 55109. Tel: 651-724-6063. p. 1203

Stratton-Thompson, Cynthia, Dir, Amelia S Givin Free Library, 114 N Baltimore Ave, Mount Holly Springs, PA, 17065-1201. Tel: 717-486-3688. p. 1966

Straube, Karen, Cat Librn, Yavapai County Free Library District, 1971 Commerce Ctr Circle, Ste D, Prescott, AZ, 86301. Tel: 928-771-3191. p. 74

Strauch, Susan, Circ, Pontiac Public Library, 211 E Madison St, Pontiac, IL, 61764. Tel: 815-844-7229. p. 636

Straughn, Chris, Dr, Continuing Resources Librn, Metadata Librn, Northeastern Illinois University, 5500 N Saint Louis Ave, Chicago, IL, 60625-4699. Tel: 773-442-4477. p. 566

Strausman, Jeanne, Chief Librn, New York Institute of Technology, Northern Blvd, Old Westbury, NY, 11568-8000. Tel: 516-686-3779. p. 1610

Strauss, Barbara, Asst Dir, Discovery Support Services, Cleveland State University, Michael Schwartz Library, Rhodes Tower, Ste 501, 2121 Euclid Ave, Cleveland, OH, 44115-2214. Tel: 216-687-2362. p. 1769

Strauss, Catina, Head, Ref & Adult Prog, Monroe Free Library, 44 Millpond Pkwy, Monroe, NY, 10950. Tel: 845-783-4411. p. 1573

Strauss, Douglas, Dir, Learning Commons, Aims Community College, College Ctr, 5401 W 20th St, 7501, Greeley, CO, 80634-3002. Tel: 970-339-6458. p. 284

Strauss, Jason, Libr Dir, Wright Institute Library, 2728 Durant Ave, Berkeley, CA, 94704. Tel: 510-841-9230, Ext 140. p. 124

Strauss, Jason, Pres, Northern & Central California Psychology Libraries, c/o Wright Institute Library, 2728 Durant Ave, Berkeley, CA, 94704. Tel: 510-841-9230. p. 2762

Strauss, Leah, Reader Serv Librn, Jewish Community Library, 1835 Ellis St, San Francisco, CA, 94115. Tel: 415-567-3327, Ext 706. p. 225

Strauss, Liz, Outreach Serv Mgr, Teen Serv Mgr, Dover Public Library, 525 N Walnut St, Dover, OH, 44622. Tel: 330-343-6123. p. 1782

Strauss, Matthew, Dir, Libr & Archives, Historical Society of Western Pennsylvania, 1212 Smallman St, Pittsburgh, PA, 15222. Tel: 412-454-6364. p. 1994

Strauss, Todd, Head, Tech, Waltham Public Library, 735 Main St, Waltham, MA, 02451. Tel: 781-314-3425. p. 1062

Strauss-De Groote, Jeanne, Br Mgr, Public Library of Cincinnati & Hamilton County, Clifton, 3400 Brookline Ave, Cincinnati, OH, 45220. Tel: 513-369-4447. p. 1762

Straw, Joseph, Ref & Instruction Librn, Marietta College, 215 Fifth St, Marietta, OH, 45750. Tel: 740-376-4541. p. 1798

Straw, Melissa, Dir, Presv & Conserv, Goucher College Library, 1021 Dulaney Valley Rd, Baltimore, MD, 21204. Tel: 410-337-6360. p. 953

Strawbridge, Laurie, Libr Asst, Asphodel-Norwood Public Library, 2363 County Rd 45, Norwood, ON, K0L 2V0, CANADA. Tel: 705-639-2228. p. 2662

Strawbridge, Laurie, Libr Asst, Asphodel-Norwood Public Library, Westwood Branch, 312 Centre Line, Westwood, ON, K0L 3B0, CANADA. Tel: 705-768-2548. p. 2662

Strawn, Scott, Dir, Allendale-Hampton-Jasper Regional Library, 297 Main St, Allendale, SC, 29810. Tel: 803-584-2371, 803-584-3513. p. 2046

Strawn, Tim, Coll, Dir, California Polytechnic State University, One Grand Ave, San Luis Obispo, CA, 93407. Tel: 805-756-1485. p. 233

Strayer, Susan, Communications Librn, Valley of the Tetons Library, Driggs Branch, 79 N Main St, Driggs, ID, 83422. Tel: 208-354-5522. p. 532

Strayhorn, Jennifer, Dir, Texarkana Public Library, 600 W Third St, Texarkana, TX, 75501-5054. Tel: 903-794-2149. p. 2248

Strayton, Melissa, Dir, Morrill Memorial & Harris Library, 220 Justin Morrill Memorial Hwy, Strafford, VT, 05072-9730. Tel: 802-765-4037. p. 2296

Strbo, Ellie, Mgr, Children's Dept, Middletown Township Public Library, 55 New Monmouth Rd, Middletown, NJ, 07748. Tel: 732-671-3700. p. 1418

Streb, Emma, Libr Asst, Historical Society of York County, York County Heritage Trust, 121 N Pershing Ave, York, PA, 17401. Tel: 717-848-1587, Ext 223. p. 2026

Streb, Theresa, Libr Dir, Lyons Public Library, 122 Broad St, Lyons, NY, 14489. Tel: 315-946-9262. p. 1566

Streby, Paul, Coll Develop Librn, University of Michigan-Flint, 303 E Kearsley St, Flint, MI, 48502. Tel: 810-762-3405. p. 1107

Streckert, Toni, Info Serv Coordr, Monona Public Library, 1000 Nichols Rd, Monona, WI, 53716. Tel: 608-216-7457. p. 2462

Streckmann, Jennifer, Coordr, Vancouver Public Library, Accessible Services, 350 W Georgia St, Level 3, Vancouver, BC, V6B 6B1, CANADA. Tel: 604-331-4100. p. 2581

Streeby, Suzanne, Dir, Eldon Carnegie Public Library, 608 W Elm St, Eldon, IA, 52554. Tel: 641-652-7517. p. 750

Streese, Germano, First Year Experience Librn, Luther College, 700 College Dr, Decorah, IA, 52101. Tel: 563-387-2223. p. 745

Street, Kathy, Dir, Oregon Trail Library District, 200 Main St, Boardman, OR, 97818. Tel: 541-481-3365. p. 1874

Streeter, Becky, Libr Dir, Stratton Free Library, Nine Main St, West Swanzey, NH, 03446. Tel: 603-352-9391. p. 1384

Streeter, Erin, Ch Serv, Warsaw Community Public Library, 310 E Main St, Warsaw, IN, 46580-2882. Tel: 574-267-6011. p. 724

Streeter, Gillian, Youth Serv Librn, Muskegon Area District Library, Norton Shores Branch, 705 Seminole Rd, Muskegon, MI, 49441-4797. Tel: 231-780-8844. p. 1136

Streett, Laura, Access Serv Librn, Digital Archivist, Vassar College Library, 124 Raymond Ave, Box 20, Poughkeepsie, NY, 12604. Tel: 845-437-5716. p. 1624

Stregger, Elizabeth, Data & Digital Services Librn, Mount Allison University Libraries & Archives, 49 York St, Sackville, NB, E4L 1C6, CANADA. Tel: 506-364-2610. p. 2604

Streif, Kim F, Cat, Southwest Wisconsin Library System, 1300 Industrial Dr, Ste 2, Fennimore, WI, 53809. Tel: 608-822-3393. p. 2435

Streiff, Marian, Mgr, Carnegie Library of Pittsburgh, Mount Washington, 315 Grandview Ave, Pittsburgh, PA, 15211-1549. Tel: 412-381-3380. p. 1991

Strelka, Debra, Coordr, Cat, University of Wisconsin-Green Bay, 2420 Nicolet Dr, Green Bay, WI, 54311-7001. Tel: 920-465-2960. p. 2439

Stremming, Stacey, Libr Dir, Windsor Storm Memorial Public Library District, 102 S Maple, Windsor, IL, 61957. Tel: 217-459-2498. p. 663

Strempke-Durgin, Ryan, Mr, Digital Serv Librn, Kirkwood Community College, Benton Hall, 6301 Kirkwood Blvd SW, Cedar Rapids, IA, 52404-5260. Tel: 319-398-5553. p. 738

Stretshberry, Sonya, Circ Supvr, Bartholomew County Public Library, 536 Fifth St, Columbus, IN, 47201-6225. Tel: 812-379-1257. p. 676

Stretton, Larissa, Ch, Boylston Public Library, 695 Main St, Boylston, MA, 01505. Tel: 508-869-2371. p. 1001

Streyle, Linda, Head, Circ, Door County Library, 107 S Fourth Ave, Sturgeon Bay, WI, 54235. Tel: 920-746-5599. p. 2479

Streyle, Linda, Circ, Door County Library, Sturgeon Bay Branch, 107 S Fourth Ave, Sturgeon Bay, WI, 54235. p. 2480

Stricker, Michele, Dep State Librn, Lifelong Learning, New Jersey State Library, 185 W State St, Trenton, NJ, 08608. Tel: 609-278-2640, Ext 164. p. 1448

Stricker, Warren, Dir, Panhandle-Plains Historical Museum, 2503 Fourth Ave, Canyon, TX, 79015. Tel: 806-651-2254. p. 2153

Strickland, Denise, Libr Coord, Mooneyham Public Library, 240 E Main St, Forest City, NC, 28043. Tel: 828-248-5224. p. 1689

Strickland, Jay, Dir, University of Arkansas Community College Batesville, 2005 White Dr, Batesville, AR, 72501. Tel: 870-612-2020. p. 90

Strickland, Laura, Assoc Librn, Southern Baptist Theological Seminary, 2825 Lexington Rd, Louisville, KY, 40280-0294. p. 866

Strickland, Michele, Asst Mgr, Elsie Quirk Public Library of Englewood, 100 W Dearborn St, Englewood, FL, 34223. Tel: 941-861-1216. p. 395

Strickland, Regina, Asst Dir, Horseshoe Bend Regional Library, 207 N West St, Dadeville, AL, 36853. Tel: 256-825-9232. p. 13

Strickland, Renae, Br Mgr, Horry County Memorial Library, Loris Branch, 4316 Main St, Loris, SC, 29569. Tel: 843-756-8101. p. 2056

Strickland, Stacey L, Dir, Youth Serv, Stevens County Library, 500 S Monroe, Hugoton, KS, 67951-2639. Tel: 620-544-2301. p. 814

Strickland, Vicki, Library Contact, Saskatchewan Justice, Civil Law Library, 900 - 1874 Scarth St, Regina, SK, S4P 4B3, CANADA. Tel: 306-787-8382. p. 2747

Strickler, Mara, Libr Dir, Pella Public Library, 603 Main St, Pella, IA, 50219. Tel: 641-628-4268. p. 776

Stricklin, David, Dr, Dir, Spec Coll, Central Arkansas Library System, 100 Rock St, Little Rock, AR, 72201-4698. Tel: 501-918-3000. p. 101

Stricklin, Torrey, Dir, Libr Serv, Howe Community Library, 315 S Collins Freeway, Howe, TX, 75459. Tel: 903-745-4050. p. 2201

Strieb, Karla, Assoc Dir, Coll & Tech Serv, Ohio State University LIBRARIES, William Oxley Thompson Library, 1858 Neil Ave Mall, Columbus, OH, 43210-1286. Tel: 614-292-6785. p. 1776

Striebel, Heather, Librn, Curtis, Mallet-Prevost, Colt & Mosle Library, 101 Park Ave, New York, NY, 10178-0061. Tel: 212-696-6138. p. 1584

Striepe, Thomas J, Fac Serv Librn, University of Georgia, Alexander Campbell King Law Library, 225 Herty Dr, Athens, GA, 30602-6018. Tel: 706-542-5077. p. 459

Strife, Mary L, Univ Librn, West Virginia University Institute of Technology, 405 Fayette Pike, Montgomery, WV, 25136-2436. Tel: 304-442-3230. p. 2409

Striker, Bridgit, Genealogy Mgr, Local Hist Mgr, Boone County Public Library, 1786 Burlington Pike, Burlington, KY, 41005. Tel: 859-342-2665. p. 850

Strillacci, Claire, Ref Supvr, Bristol Public Library, Five High St, Bristol, CT, 06010. Tel: 860-584-7787. p. 304

Strine, Scott, Dir, Effingham Community Library, 414 Main St, Effingham, KS, 66023. Tel: 913-833-5881. p. 805

Stringer, Alison, Mgr, Covington County Library System, Conner-Graham Memorial, 101 Willow St, Seminary, MS, 39479. Tel: 601-722-9041. p. 1214

Stringer, Elaine, Circ Serv, Somerset County Library System of New Jersey, Watchung Public, 12 Stirling Rd, Watchung, NJ, 07069. Tel: 908-458-8455. p. 1393

Stringer, Ellen, YA Serv, Lexington County Public Library System, 5440 Augusta Rd, Lexington, SC, 29072. Tel: 803-785-2632. p. 2064

Stringer, Kayla, Libr Dir, Dixon Township Library, 120 W Walnut, Argonia, KS, 67004. Tel: 620-435-6979. p. 796

Stringer, Sybyl, Admin Librn, Hinds Community College, 505 E Main St, Raymond, MS, 39154. Tel: 601-857-3355. p. 1231

Stringfellow, Julia, Archivist, Central Washington University, 400 E University Way, Ellensburg, WA, 98926-7548. Tel: 509-963-1901. p. 2363

Stringfellow, Patty, Dir, Jasper County Public Library, 208 W Susan St, Rensselaer, IN, 47978. Tel: 219-866-5881. p. 714

Strittmatter, Conni L, Coordr, Youth Serv, Baltimore County Public Library, 320 York Rd, Towson, MD, 21204-5179. Tel: 410-887-6100. p. 979

Strniste, Bryan, Ref & Instrul Serv Librn, Southern Maine Community College Library, Two Fort Rd, South Portland, ME, 04106. Tel: 207-741-5521. p. 941
Strobel, Michele, Librn, Trinity Presbyterian Church Library, 499 Rte 70E, Cherry Hill, NJ, 08034. Tel: 856-428-2050. p. 1396
Strobel, Tracy, Exec Dir, Cuyahoga County Public Library, 2111 Snow Rd, Parma, OH, 44134-2728. Tel: 216-749-9419. p. 1813
Strode, Cindy, Pub Serv Librn, Monroe County Public Library, 500 W Fourth St, Tompkinsville, KY, 42167. Tel: 270-487-5301. p. 876
Strodtman, Erin, Dir, Dulany Memorial Library, 501 S Broadway, Salisbury, MO, 65281. Tel: 660-388-5712. p. 1278
Strodtman, Leasa, Tech Serv, Central Methodist University, 411 Central Methodist Sq, Fayette, MO, 65248. Tel: 660-248-6271. p. 1245
Stroh, Kristen, Asst Dir, Sachem Public Library, 150 Holbrook Rd, Holbrook, NY, 11741. Tel: 631-588-5024. p. 1547
Stroh, Scott, Dir, Gunston Hall Plantation Library & Archives, 10709 Gunston Rd, Mason Neck, VA, 22079-3901. Tel: 703-550-9220. p. 2332
Strohm, Ben, Youth Serv Dir, Williamsburg Regional Library, 7770 Croaker Rd, Williamsburg, VA, 23188-7064. Tel: 757-741-3368. p. 2353
Strohm, Janine, Dir, Rebecca M Arthurs Memorial Library, 223 Valley St, Brookville, PA, 15825-0223. Tel: 814-849-5512. p. 1915
Strohmeyer, Kristin, Engagement Librn, Hamilton College, 198 College Hill Rd, Clinton, NY, 13323. Tel: 315-859-4481. p. 1519
Strohschein, Alex, Mr, Circ Coordr, Regent College, 5800 University Blvd, Vancouver, BC, V6T 2E4, CANADA. Tel: 604-221-3340. p. 2579
Strojny, Brittany, Mgr, Libr & Res Serv, Adler Pollock & Sheehan PC Library, One Citizens Plaza, 8th Flr, Providence, RI, 02903. Tel: 401-427-6103. p. 2037
Strojny, Duane, Assoc Dean & Dir, Western Michigan University-Cooley Law School Libraries, 300 S Capitol Ave, Lansing, MI, 48933. Tel: 517-371-5140, Ext 3401. p. 1126
Stroker, Frank, Hist Coll Dir, Pittsburgh History & Landmarks Foundation, 100 W Station Square Dr, Ste 450, Pittsburgh, PA, 15219. Tel: 412-471-5808. p. 1995
Strokis, Jennifer, Bkmobile/Outreach Serv Mgr, York County Library, 138 E Black St, Rock Hill, SC, 29730. Tel: 803-981-5841. p. 2068
Strom, Mike, State Archivist, The Library of Virginia, 800 E Broad St, Richmond, VA, 23219-8000. Tel: 804-692-3500. p. 2341
Stromberger, Eileen, Librn, United States Air Force, Two W Castle St, Fairchild AFB, WA, 99011-8532. Tel: 509-247-5228, 509-247-5556. p. 2364
Stromgren, Jeanette, Libr Dir, Osage City Public Library, 515 Main St, Osage City, KS, 66523. Tel: 785-528-2620, 785-528-3727. p. 828
Stromgren, Rena, Head, Circ, South Hadley Public Library, Two Canal St, South Hadley, MA, 01075. Tel: 413-538-5045. p. 1054
Stromquist, John, Chief Exec Officer, ProConsort, 118 N Bedford Rd, Ste 100, Mount Kisco, NY, 10549. p. 2771
Stromwall, Marie, Ch, Somers Public Library, Two Vision Blvd, Somers, CT, 06071. Tel: 860-763-3501. p. 337
Strong, Angela Z, Dir, The Nyack Library, 59 S Broadway, Nyack, NY, 10960. Tel: 845-358-3370, Ext 221. p. 1609
Strong, Angie, Libr Dir, Madrid Public Library, 100 W Third St, Madrid, IA, 50156. Tel: 515-795-3846. p. 766
Strong, Bess, Br Mgr, Allendale-Hampton-Jasper Regional Library, Allendale County Library, 297 N Main St, Allendale, SC, 29810. Tel: 803-584-2371. p. 2046
Strong, Carrie, Dir, Alexandria Public Library, Ten Maple Dr, Alexandria, OH, 43001. Tel: 740-924-3561. p. 1745
Strong, Cindy, Info Spec, Seattle Pacific University Library, 3307 Third Ave W, Seattle, WA, 98119. Tel: 206-281-2074. p. 2379
Strong, Kathy, Dir, Newman Grove Public Library, 615 Hale Ave, Newman Grove, NE, 68758. Tel: 402-447-2331. p. 1326
Strong, Lauren, Family & Youth Serv Coordr, Riverhead Free Library, 330 Court St, Riverhead, NY, 11901-2885. Tel: 631-727-3228. p. 1627
Strong, Marjorie, Asst Librn, Vermont Historical Society, Vermont History Ctr, 60 Washington St, Barre, VT, 05641-4209. Tel: 802-479-8509. p. 2278
Strope, Susan, Asst Libr Dir, Tuolumne County Genealogical Society Library, 158 Bradford St, Sonora, CA, 95370. Tel: 209-532-1317. p. 247
Strother, Lara, Dir, Libr & Commun Serv, Mary Lou Reddick Public Library, 7005 Charbonneau Rd, Lake Worth, TX, 76135. Tel: 817-237-9681. p. 2208
Stroud, Austin, Dir, Monon Town & Township Public Library, 427 N Market St, Monon, IN, 47959. Tel: 219-253-6517. p. 707
Stroud, Ellen, Dir, Serv Delivery, Oshawa Public Library, 65 Bagot St, Oshawa, ON, L1H 1N2, CANADA. Tel: 905-579-6111, Ext 5200. p. 2664
Stroud, Victoria, Libr Mgr, Albert-Westmorland-Kent Regional Library, Hillsborough Public, 2849 Main St, Unit 2, Hillsborough, NB, E4H 2X7, CANADA. Tel: 506-734-3722. p. 2603
Strougal, Pat, Dir, United States Environmental Protection, Region 4 OEA Information-Research Center, 61 Forsyth St SW, Atlanta, GA, 30303-3104. Tel: 404-562-9654. p. 466
Stroup, Debbie, Head, Circ, Southampton Free Library, 947 Street Rd, Southampton, PA, 18966. Tel: 215-322-1415. p. 2009
Stroup, Richard, Asst Dir, Public Law Library of King County, King County Courthouse, 516 Third Ave, Ste W621, Seattle, WA, 98104. Tel: 206-477-1305. p. 2378
Strouse, Lisa, Asst Librn, Boone Area Library, 129 N Mill St, Birdsboro, PA, 19508-2340. Tel: 610-582-5666. p. 1912
Strube, Kim, Chief Financial Officer, Topeka & Shawnee County Public Library, 1515 SW Tenth Ave, Topeka, KS, 66604-1374. Tel: 785-580-4400. p. 839
Struble, Evan, Assoc State Librn, Libr Develop, State Library of Ohio, 274 E First Ave, Ste 100, Columbus, OH, 43201. Tel: 614-644-6914. p. 1777
Struck, Monica, Univ Librn, Dickinson State University, 291 Campus Dr, Dickinson, ND, 58601. Tel: 701-483-2136. p. 1732
Strudwick, Tracy, Chief Exec Officer, Chief Librn, Greater Madawaska Public Library, 12629 Lanark Rd, Calabogie, ON, K0J 1H0, CANADA. Tel: 613-752-2317. p. 2634
Strunk, Emily, Library Contact, Flagler Community Library, 311 Main Ave, Flagler, CO, 80815. Tel: 719-765-4310. p. 280
Strunk, Sheila, Br Coordr, Shelby County Libraries, Anna Community, 304 N Second St, Anna, OH, 45302. Tel: 937-394-2761. p. 1820
Strunz, Sarah, Dir, Orfordville Public Library, 519 E Beloit St, Orfordville, WI, 53576. Tel: 608-879-9229. p. 2467
Strusienski, Julia, Mgr, District of Columbia Public Library, Southeast, 403 Seventh St SE, Washington, DC, 20003. Tel: 202-698-3377. p. 364
Struthers, Lisa A, Libr Dir, San Jacinto Museum & Battlefield Association, One Monument Circle, La Porte, TX, 77571-9585. Tel: 281-479-2421. p. 2208
Struthers, Randy, Circ Serv, Plano Community Library District, 15 W North St, Plano, IL, 60545. Tel: 630-552-2009. p. 635
Struve, Molly, Dir, Academic Support Services, Iowa Lakes Community College Libraries, Emmetsburg Campus, 3200 College Dr, Emmetsburg, IA, 50536. Tel: 712-362-7935. p. 752
Struve, Molly, Dir, Iowa Lakes Community College Libraries, 300 S 18th St, Estherville, IA, 51334. Tel: 712-362-7985. p. 752
Struve, Molly, Libr Dir, Iowa Lakes Community College Libraries, Spirit Lake Campus, 800 21st St, Spirit Lake, IA, 51360. Tel: 712-336-3439, 712-336-6564. p. 752
Struzynski, Melinda, Admin Operations Specialist, Mercer County Community College Library, 1200 Old Trenton Rd, West Windsor, NJ, 08550. Tel: 609-570-3554, 609-570-3560. p. 1453
Struzziero, Peter, Dir, Belmont Public Library, 336 Concord Ave, Belmont, MA, 02478-0904. Tel: 617-489-2000, Ext 2852. p. 988
Stryker, Samantha, Asst Dir, Community & Adult Services Librn, Richmond Memorial Library, 19 Ross St, Batavia, NY, 14020. Tel: 585-343-9550. p. 1491
Strynadka, Melissa, Head Librn, Parkland Regional Library-Manitoba, McCreary Branch, 615 Burrows Rd, McCreary, MB, R0J 1B0, CANADA. Tel: 204-835-2629. p. 2587
Stuart, Beverly, Librn, Antioch University Library, 900 Dayton St, Yellow Springs, OH, 45387. Tel: 206-268-4507. p. 1835
Stuart, Beverly, Dir, Libr Serv, Antioch University Library, 2400 Third Ave, Ste 200, Seattle, WA, 98121. Tel: 206-268-4109, 206-268-4210. p. 2376
Stuart, Jennifer, Br Mgr, Haywood County Public Library, Canton Branch, 11 Pennsylvania Ave, Canton, NC, 28716. Tel: 828-648-2561. p. 1721
Stuart, Nancy, Coordr, ILL, University of Victoria Libraries, McPherson Library, PO Box 1800, Victoria, BC, V8W 3H5, CANADA. Tel: 250-721-8211. p. 2583
Stuart, Patricia, Library Contact, US Department of the Interior, Bureau of Reclamation, 2800 Cottage Way, Rm W-1825, Sacramento, CA, 95825-1898. Tel: 916-978-5594. p. 210
Stubblefield, Laura, Coll Develop, Head of Libr, Sharp HealthCare, 7901 Frost St, San Diego, CA, 92123. Tel: 858-939-3242. p. 222
Stubbs, Alyssa, Info Spec, University of New Mexico, 4000 University Dr, Los Alamos, NM, 87544. Tel: 505-662-0343. p. 1472
Stubbs, Brian, Libr Supvr, Rutgers University Libraries, Archibald Stevens Alexander Library, 169 College Ave, New Brunswick, NJ, 08901-1163. Tel: 848-932-6054. p. 1424
Stubbs-Trevino, Alex, Head Librn, Dentons US, 1221 Avenue of the Americas, 24th Flr, New York, NY, 10020-1089. Tel: 212-768-6700. p. 1585
Stuck, Christina, Youth Serv Librn, Charlotte Community Library, 226 S Bostwick St, Charlotte, MI, 48813-1801. Tel: 517-543-8859. p. 1090
Stuckel, Jon, IT Dir, Mid-Columbia Libraries, 405 S Dayton St, Kennewick, WA, 99336. p. 2367
Stuckey, Sheila A, Dir, Libr Serv, Kentucky State University, 400 E Main St, Frankfort, KY, 40601-2355. Tel: 502-597-6852. p. 855
Stuckey-Weber, Emily, Head, Adult/Teen Serv, Goshen Public Library, 601 S Fifth St, Goshen, IN, 46526. Tel: 574-533-9531. p. 687
Stucky, Renae, Access Serv Librn, Bethel College Library, 300 E 27th St, North Newton, KS, 67117-0531. Tel: 316-284-5361. p. 827
Stucky, Stephanie, Br Librn, Fairbanks North Star Borough Libraries, North Pole Branch, 656 NPHS Blvd, North Pole, AK, 99705. Tel: 907-488-6101. p. 45
Studebaker, Nancy, Libr Dir, Van Meter Public Library, 505 Grant St, Van Meter, IA, 50261. Tel: 515-996-2435. p. 787
Studer, Jan, Dir, Beattie Public Library, 715 Main St, Beattie, KS, 66406. Tel: 785-353-2348. p. 798

Studholme, Claire, Head, Children's & Teen Serv, Longmont Public Library, 409 Fourth Ave, Longmont, CO, 80501-6006. Tel: 303-651-8470. p. 290

Studnicka, Nicholas, Dir, Kraemer Library & Community Center, 910 Main St, Plain, WI, 53577. Tel: 608-546-4201. p. 2469

Stueve, Sarah, Librn, Minnesota Department of Corrections, 2305 Minnesota Blvd SE, Saint Cloud, MN, 56304. Tel: 320-240-3071. p. 1198

Stuffel, Karen, Cat, Coll Develop, Hagerstown Jefferson Township Library, Ten W College St, Hagerstown, IN, 47346. Tel: 765-489-5632. p. 689

Stuffles, Pamela, Librn, Westport Public Library, Three Spring St, Westport, ON, K0G 1X0, CANADA. Tel: 613-273-3223. p. 2703

Stuhlmann, Jason, Actg Dir, Elmwood Park Public Library, One Conti Pkwy, Elmwood Park, IL, 60707. Tel: 708-395-1241. p. 585

Stukes, Margo, Br Supvr, Sumter County Library, South Sumter Branch, 337 Manning Ave, Sumter, SC, 29150. Tel: 803-775-7132. p. 2071

Stulgate, Kelly, Youth Serv Mgr, St Charles Public Library District, One S Sixth Ave, Saint Charles, IL, 60174-2105. Tel: 630-584-0076, Ext 263. p. 644

Stull, April, Dir, Newhall Public Library, 109 Railroad St E, Newhall, IA, 52315. Tel: 319-223-5510. p. 773

Stull, Rachel, Dir, Blackburn College, 700 College Ave, Carlinville, IL, 62626. Tel: 217-854-5665. p. 549

Stultz, Amy, Head, Youth Serv, Lake County Library System, Cooper Memorial Library, 2525 Oakley Seaver Dr, Clermont, FL, 34711. Tel: 352-536-2275. p. 451

Stultz, Amy, Libr Dir, Umatilla Public Library, 412 Hatfield Dr, Umatilla, FL, 32784-8913. Tel: 352-669-3284. p. 452

Stultz, Kris, Libr Tech, Brunswick Community College Library, 50 College Rd, Supply, NC, 28462. Tel: 910-755-8514. p. 1718

Stumbough, Doug, Operations Dir, Spokane County Library District, 4322 N Argonne Rd, Spokane, WA, 99212. Tel: 509-893-8200. p. 2384

Stumme, Mark, Ref Librn, Drake University, 2725 University Ave, Des Moines, IA, 50311. Tel: 515-271-3192. p. 746

Stump, Christina, Br Mgr, Tuscarawas County Public Library, Bolivar Branch, 455 W Water St, Bolivar, OH, 44612-9224. Tel: 330-874-2720. p. 1807

Stump, Sandra L, Assoc Prof, Coll Mgt Librn, Interim Dir, Albright College, 13th & Exeter Sts, Reading, PA, 19604. Tel: 610-921-7205. p. 2000

Stumpf, Susan, Info Res & Serv Support Spec, Pennsylvania State Lehigh Valley Library, 2809 E Saucon Valley Rd, Center Valley, PA, 18034-8447. Tel: 610-285-5027. p. 1920

Stupegia, Cristy, Dir, LaSalle Public Library, 305 Marquette St, LaSalle, IL, 61301. Tel: 815-223-2341. p. 607

Stuppi, Karen, Ch Serv, New Brunswick Free Public Library, 60 Livingston Ave, New Brunswick, NJ, 08901-2597. Tel: 732-745-5108, Ext 15. p. 1424

Stupski, Betsy L, Dir, Libr Serv, Florida Attorney General's Law Library, Collins Bldg, 107 W Gaines St, Rm 437, Tallahassee, FL, 32399-1050. Tel: 850-414-3300. p. 446

Sturdevant, Meg, Br Mgr, Davidson County Public Library System, North Davidson Public, 559 Critcher Dr, Welcome, NC, 27374. Tel: 336-242-2050. p. 1700

Sturdivant, Dewey P, Asst Librn, Charles H Stone Memorial Library, 319 W Main St, Pilot Mountain, NC, 27041. Tel: 336-368-2370. p. 1707

Sturdy, Michelle, Br Supvr, Latah County Library District, Troy Branch, 402 S Main St, Troy, ID, 83871. Tel: 208-835-4311. p. 526

Sturgeon, Holly, Circ Mgr, Seattle University, A A Lemieux Library, 901 12th Ave, Seattle, WA, 98122-4411. Tel: 206-296-6234. p. 2380

Sturgeon, Kendall, Libr Asst, University of Western Ontario, FNB 3020, London, ON, N6A 5B9, CANADA. Tel: 519-661-2111, Ext 88488. p. 2655

Sturgeon, Roy, Foreign, Comparative & Intl Law/Ref Librn, Tulane University, Law Library, Weinmann Hall, 3rd Flr, 6329 Freret St, New Orleans, LA, 70118-6231. Tel: 504-865-5953. p. 904

Sturgeon, Stephen, Head, Coll, Boston College Libraries, Thomas P O'Neill Jr Library (Main Library), 140 Commonwealth Ave, Chestnut Hill, MA, 02467. Tel: 617-552-4470. p. 1011

Sturgeon, Tammy, Cataloger, Hancock County Public Library, 1210 Madison St, Hawesville, KY, 42348. Tel: 270-927-6760. p. 858

Sturgeon, Walter, Librn, International Wild Waterfowl Association, 1633 Bowden Rd, Spring Hope, NC, 27882. Tel: 252-478-5610. p. 1717

Sturges, Amber, Libr Asst, North Georgia Technical College Library, 121 Meeks Ave, Blairsville, GA, 30512. Tel: 706-439-6326. p. 468

Sturges, Debra, Sr Librn, Creighton University, 2500 California Plaza, Omaha, NE, 68178-0209. Tel: 402-280-4756. p. 1328

Sturges, Michelle, Tech Serv Librn, Kapi'olani Community College Library, 4303 Diamond Head Rd, Honolulu, HI, 96816. Tel: 808-734-9163. p. 512

Sturgill, Carrie, Head, Children's Servx, Radnor Memorial Library, 114 W Wayne Ave, Wayne, PA, 19087. Tel: 610-687-1124. p. 2018

Sturm, Brian, Assoc Dean, Acad Affairs, Prof, University of North Carolina at Chapel Hill, Manning Hall, 216 Lenoir Dr, Campus Box 3360, Chapel Hill, NC, 27599-3360. Tel: 919-962-8366. p. 2790

Sturm, Heather, Dir, Neighborhood Servs, Aurora Public Library District, 101 S River St, Aurora, IL, 60506. Tel: 630-264-3410. p. 539

Sturm, Heather, Dir, Neighborhood Servs, Aurora Public Library District, Eola Road Branch, 555 S Eola Rd, Aurora, IL, 60504-8992. Tel: 630-264-3400. p. 539

Sturm, Shannon L, Head, Special Colls & Programs, Angelo State University Library, 2025 S Johnson, San Angelo, TX, 76904-5079. Tel: 325-486-6555. p. 2235

Sturman, Debbie, Dir, Niobrara County Library, 425 S Main St, Lusk, WY, 82225. Tel: 307-334-3490. p. 2497

Sturtz, Carmaline, Br Mgr, Muskingum County Library System, New Concord Branch, 77 W Main St, New Concord, OH, 43762. Tel: 740-826-4184. p. 1837

Stutes, Angela, Dir, Human Res, Calcasieu Parish Public Library System, 301 W Claude St, Lake Charles, LA, 70605-3457. Tel: 337-721-7147. p. 893

Stutzman, Karl, Dir, Anabaptist Mennonite Biblical Seminary Library, 3003 Benham Ave, Elkhart, IN, 46517. Tel: 574-296-6280. p. 680

Stutzman-Fry, Jhanna, Dir, Agness Community Library, 3905 Cougar Lane, Agness, OR, 97406. Tel: 541-247-6323. p. 1871

Stylianopoulos, Lucie, Research Librn, University of Virginia, Fiske Kimball Fine Arts Library, Bayly Dr, Charlottesville, VA, 22903. Tel: 434-924-6604. p. 2310

Stymiest, Carl W, Archivist, United Empire Loyalists' Association of Canada Library, Cornwall Community Museum, 160 Water St W, Cornwall, ON, K6H 5T5, CANADA. Tel: 778-822-4290. p. 2638

Styons, Jessica, Dir, Jefferson Parish Library, 4747 W Napoleon Ave, Metairie, LA, 70001. Tel: 504-838-1190. p. 897

Su, Di, Head, ILL, Head, Info Literacy, York College Library, 94-20 Guy R Brewer Blvd, Jamaica, NY, 11451. Tel: 718-262-2031. p. 1556

Su, Julie, Head, Ser, San Diego State University, 5500 Campanile Dr, San Diego, CA, 92182-8050. Tel: 619-594-0904. p. 221

Su, Ken, Chief Exec Officer, St Catharines Public Library, 54 Church St, St. Catharines, ON, L2R 7K2, CANADA. Tel: 905-688-6103. p. 2680

Su, Min, Librn, Lanier Technical College, 3410 Ronald Reagan Blvd, Cumming, GA, 30041. Tel: 678-341-6636. p. 473

Suarez, Dora, Sr Librn, Los Angeles Public Library System, Arroyo Seco Regional Library, 6145 N Figueroa St, Los Angeles, CA, 90042-3565. Tel: 323-255-0537. p. 163

Suarez, Jillian, Head, Libr Serv, The Museum of Modern Art, 11 W 53th St, New York, NY, 10019. Tel: 212-708-9433. p. 1592

Suarez, Kristen, Youth Serv, Mount Olive Public Library, 202 Flanders-Drakestown Rd, Flanders, NJ, 07836. Tel: 973-691-8686. p. 1403

Suarez, Rocio, Libr Spec, Organization of American States, 19th & Constitution Ave NW, Washington, DC, 20006-4499. Tel: 202-370-0628. p. 373

Suarez, Shari, Br Librn, Genesee District Library, Genesee-Johnson Library, 7397 N Genesee Rd, Genesee, MI, 48437. Tel: 810-640-1410. p. 1106

Suarez, Steven, AV, Valencia College, East Campus Library, 701 N Econlockhatchee Trail, Orlando, FL, 32825. Tel: 407-582-2467. p. 432

Suarez, Yamil, Assoc Dir, Libr Serv, Berklee College of Music Library, 150 Massachusetts Ave, Boston, MA, 02115. Tel: 617-747-2617. p. 990

Suarez-Balseiro, Carlos, Prof, University of Puerto Rico, Rio Piedras Campus, PO Box 21906, San Juan, PR, 00931-1906. Tel: 787-764-0000, Ext 85284. p. 2795

Suazo, Ron, IT Tech, Santa Clara Pueblo Community Library, 578 Kee St, Espanola, NM, 87532. Tel: 505-692-6295. p. 1467

Sucec, Sharon, Librn, Kosciusko County Historical Society, 121 N Indiana St, Warsaw, IN, 46581. Tel: 574-269-1078. p. 724

Suchaski, Alysha, Br Mgr, Waco-McLennan County Library System, East Waco, 901 Elm Ave, Waco, TX, 76704-2659. Tel: 254-750-8418. p. 2254

Suchy, Mary Jo, Dir, Belleville Area District Library, 167 Fourth St, Belleville, MI, 48111. Tel: 734-699-3291. p. 1084

Sucre, Natalia, Digital Serv Librn, Instruction Librn, Metropolitan College of New York Library, 60 West St, 7th Flr, New York, NY, 10006. Tel: 212-343-1234, Ext 2001. p. 1591

Suda, Jane, Head, Ref & Info Serv, Fordham University Libraries, 441 E Fordham Rd, Bronx, NY, 10458-5151. Tel: 718-817-3570. p. 1498

Suda, Kristin, Tech Serv, Delaware County Libraries, Bldg 19, 340 N Middletown Rd, Media, PA, 19063-5597. Tel: 610-891-8622. p. 1961

Suddarth, Matthew, Dir, Winfield Public Library, 0S291 Winfield Rd, Winfield, IL, 60190. Tel: 630-653-7599. p. 663

Sudduth, Elizabeth, Assoc Dean, Spec Coll, Dir, University of South Carolina, Ernest F Hollings Special Collections Library, 1322 Greene St, Columbia, SC, 29208. Tel: 807-777-5487. p. 2055

Sudduth, Elizabeth, Assoc Dean, Spec Coll, Dir, University of South Carolina, Irvin Department of Rare Books & Special Collections, Ernest F Hollings Special Collections Library, 1322 Greene St, Columbia, SC, 29208. Tel: 803-777-3847. p. 2055

Suellentrop, Tricia, County Librn, Johnson County Library, 9875 W 87th St, Overland Park, KS, 66212. Tel: 913-826-4600. p. 830

Sueme, Zana, Dir, Libr Serv, Missouri Baptist University, One College Park Dr, Saint Louis, MO, 63141-8698. Tel: 314-434-1115. p. 1271

Suero, Priscilla M, Dep Dir, Free Library of Philadelphia, 1901 Vine St, Philadelphia, PA, 19103. Tel: 215-567-7710, 215-686-5322. p. 1977

Suess, Eric, Dir, Marshall Public Library, 113 S Garfield Ave, Pocatello, ID, 83204. Tel: 208-232-1263. p. 529

Suffoletta, Kathryn, Supvr, Middlesex County Library, Dorchester Branch, 2123 Dorchester Rd, Dorchester, ON, N0L 1G0, CANADA. Tel: 519-268-3451. p. 2682

Sufi, Narinder, County Librn, Butte County Library, 1820 Mitchell Ave, Oroville, CA, 95966-5387. Tel: 530-552-5652, Ext 4. p. 189

Sugarman, Tammy, Assoc Dean for Colls, Discovery & Budget, Virginia Commonwealth University Libraries, 901 Park Ave, Richmond, VA, 23284. Tel: 804-827-3624. p. 2343

Sugawara, Sumiye, Librn, Corporation of the Township of Nipigon Public Library Board, 52 Front St, Nipigon, ON, P0T 2J0, CANADA. Tel: 807-887-3142. p. 2661

Sugden, Sarah, Exec Dir, Brown County Library, 515 Pine St, Green Bay, WI, 54301. Tel: 920-448-5810. p. 2438

Suggs, Pamela, Dir, Claiborne Parish Library, 909 Edgewood Dr, Homer, LA, 71040. Tel: 318-927-3845. p. 891

Sugihara, Takeo, Teen Serv, Belleville Public Library & Information Center, 221 Washington Ave, Belleville, NJ, 07109-3189. Tel: 973-450-3434. p. 1389

Sugiyama, Justin, Sr Librn, Los Angeles Public Library System, Hyde Park Miriam Matthews Branch Library, 2205 W Florence Ave, Los Angeles, CA, 90043. Tel: 323-750-7241. p. 164

Suholutsky, Inna, Librn, JBI Library, 110 E 30th St, New York, NY, 10016. Tel: 212-889-2525. p. 1589

Suhrstedt, Angel, Mgr, Libr Operations, Metropolitan Library System in Oklahoma County, Del City Library, 4509 SE 15th St, Del City, OK, 73115-3098. p. 1857

Suico, Richard, Mgr, Sno-Isle Libraries, Edmonds Library, 650 Main St, Edmonds, WA, 98020-3056. Tel: 425-771-1933. p. 2370

Suiter, Jody, Libr Dir, Macksville City Library, 333 N Main St, Macksville, KS, 67557. Tel: 620-348-3555. p. 822

Sukenic, Harvey, Libr Dir, Hebrew College, 1860 Washington St, Newton, MA, 02466. Tel: 617-559-8757. p. 1039

Sulavik, Andrew, Dr, Head, Metadata & Res Description Serv, Howard University Libraries, 500 Howard Pl NW, Ste 203, Washington, DC, 20059. Tel: 202-806-4224. p. 369

Sulima, Kelly, Head, Community Engagement, Sachem Public Library, 150 Holbrook Rd, Holbrook, NY, 11741. Tel: 631-588-5024. p. 1547

Sullenger, Paula, Head, Acq, Auburn University, Ralph Brown Draughon Library, 231 Mell St, Auburn, AL, 36849. Tel: 334-844-1725. p. 5

Sullivan, Amy, Dir, Libr Serv, West Kentucky Community & Technical College, 4810 Alben Barkley Dr, Paducah, KY, 42001. Tel: 270-534-3171. p. 872

Sullivan, Andie, Dir of Libr, Kern County Library, 701 Truxtun Ave, Bakersfield, CA, 93301. Tel: 661-868-0700. p. 119

Sullivan, Andrea, Head, Ref & Instruction, Daemen University Library, Research & Information Commons, 4380 Main St, Amherst, NY, 14226-3592. Tel: 716-839-8243. p. 1486

Sullivan, Bessie, Chief Exec Officer, Orillia Public Library, 36 Mississaga St W, Orillia, ON, L3V 3A6, CANADA. Tel: 705-325-2338. p. 2663

Sullivan, Brian, Instrul Librn, Alfred University, Herrick Memorial Library, One Saxon Dr, Alfred, NY, 14802. Tel: 607-871-2268. p. 1485

Sullivan, Brian, Ref Librn, Grinnell Library, 2642 E Main St, Wappingers Falls, NY, 12590. Tel: 845-297-3428. p. 1658

Sullivan, Brice, Operations Mgr, University of California, Berkeley, Marian Koshland Bioscience, Natural Resources & Public Health Library, 2101 Valley Life Science Bldg, No 6500, Berkeley, CA, 94720-6500. Tel: 510-642-2531. p. 123

Sullivan, Bridget, Cat Librn, Bureau of Land Management Library, Denver Federal Ctr, Bldg 85, W-5, Denver, CO, 80225. Tel: 303-236-6650. p. 273

Sullivan, Bruce, Network Analyst, Poughkeepsie Public Library District, 93 Market St, Poughkeepsie, NY, 12601. Tel: 845-485-3445, Ext 3322. p. 1623

Sullivan, Camrin, Dir, Lomira QuadGraphics Community Library, 427 S Water St, Lomira, WI, 53048-9581. Tel: 920-269-4115, Ext 3. p. 2448

Sullivan, Camrin, Dir, Lakeview Community Library, 112 Butler St, Random Lake, WI, 53075. Tel: 920-994-4825. p. 2472

Sullivan, Charles M, Exec Dir, Cambridge Historical Commission Archive, 831 Massachusetts Ave, 2nd Flr, Cambridge, MA, 02139. Tel: 617-349-4683. p. 1004

Sullivan, Christine, Dir, Franklin T Degroodt Library, 6475 Minton Rd SE, Palm Bay, FL, 32909. Tel: 321-952-6317. p. 434

Sullivan, Christine, Dir, Palm Bay Public Library, 1520 Port Malabar Blvd NE, Palm Bay, FL, 32905. Tel: 321-952-4519. p. 434

Sullivan, Colleen, ILL, University of Alaska Fairbanks, 1732 Tanana Dr, Fairbanks, AK, 99775. Tel: 907-474-5348. p. 45

Sullivan, Connie, Prog Asst, Braille & Talking Bks, South Dakota State Library, Braille & Talking Book Program, McKay Bldg, 800 Governors Dr, Pierre, SD, 57501-2294. Tel: 605-773-3131. p. 2080

Sullivan, Debbie, Dir, Colchester District Library, 203 Macomb St, Colchester, IL, 62326. Tel: 309-776-4861. p. 573

Sullivan, Deirdre, Coll Develop Librn, Thomas Crane Public Library, 40 Washington St, Quincy, MA, 02269-9164. Tel: 617-376-1306. p. 1048

Sullivan, Denis, Tech Serv Asst, Massachusetts College of Art & Design, 621 Huntington Ave, Boston, MA, 02115-5882. Tel: 617-879-7111. p. 996

Sullivan, Elizabeth, Head, Children's Servx, West Islip Public Library, Three Higbie Lane, West Islip, NY, 11795-3999. Tel: 631-661-7080. p. 1662

Sullivan, Erin, Adminr, Pub Relations, Orange County Library System, 101 E Central Blvd, Orlando, FL, 32801. Tel: 407-835-7323. p. 431

Sullivan, Gerald, Head, Circ, Bayport-Blue Point Public Library, 203 Blue Point Ave, Blue Point, NY, 11715-1217. Tel: 631-363-6133. p. 1495

Sullivan, Jason, Chief Admin Officer, Chattanooga Public Library, 1001 Broad St, Chattanooga, TN, 37402-2652. Tel: 423-643-7700. p. 2091

Sullivan, Jennifer, Head, Adult Serv, Woodbridge Town Library, Ten Newton Rd, Woodbridge, CT, 06525. Tel: 203-389-3487. p. 349

Sullivan, Jennifer, Mgr, Youth & Family Serv, Anderson County Public Library, 114 N Main St, Lawrenceburg, KY, 40342. Tel: 502-839-6420. p. 861

Sullivan, Jennifer, Ref Librn, SUNY Upstate Medical University, 766 Irving Ave, Syracuse, NY, 13210-1602. Tel: 315-464-7084. p. 1650

Sullivan, Jeremy, VPres, Northern California Association of Law Libraries, 268 Bush St, No 4006, San Francisco, CA, 94104. p. 2762

Sullivan, Jill, Exec Dir, Winfred L & Elizabeth C Post Foundation, 1901 E 20th St, Joplin, MO, 64804. Tel: 417-623-7953, Ext 1041. p. 1254

Sullivan, Joan, Cataloger, Marstons Mills Public Library, 2160 Main St, Marstons Mills, MA, 02648. Tel: 508-428-5175. p. 1033

Sullivan, John, Dr, Instr, University of South Florida, 4202 Fowler Ave, CIS 1040, Tampa, FL, 33620-7800. Tel: 813-974-2370. p. 2783

Sullivan, John M, Jr, Dir, Frothingham Free Library, 28 W Main St, Fonda, NY, 12068. Tel: 518-853-3016. p. 1534

Sullivan, Kathleen, Br Mgr, Cuyahoga County Public Library, Parma Branch, 6996 Powers Blvd, Parma, OH, 44129-6602. Tel: 440-885-5362. p. 1813

Sullivan, Kathryn, Head, Ref Serv, University of Maryland, Baltimore County, 1000 Hilltop Circle, Baltimore, MD, 21250. Tel: 410-455-2356. p. 958

Sullivan, Laura, Interim Head, Access Serv, Northern Kentucky University, University Dr, Highland Heights, KY, 41099. Tel: 859-572-5724. p. 859

Sullivan, Libby, Librn, Skagit Valley College, Whidbey Island Campus Library, 1900 SE Pioneer Way, Oak Harbor, WA, 98277-3099. Tel: 360-679-5322. p. 2371

Sullivan, Lisa, Collections & Instructional Services Librn, Canisius College, 2001 Main St, Buffalo, NY, 14208-1098. Tel: 716-888-8403. p. 1509

Sullivan, Madison, Fine & Performing Arts Librn, University of Washington Libraries, Art, Arts Bldg, Rm 101, Box 353440, Seattle, WA, 98195-3440. Tel: 206-543-0648. p. 2381

Sullivan, Madison, Fine & Performing Arts Librn, University of Washington Libraries, Drama, Hutchinson Hall, Rm 145, Box 353950, Seattle, WA, 98195-3950. Tel: 206-543-5148. p. 2381

Sullivan, Margaret, Dr, Scholarly Comms Specialist, Marshall University Libraries, One John Marshall Dr, Huntington, WV, 25755-2060. Tel: 304-696-6780. p. 2405

Sullivan, Marisha, Head Librn, Cleveland Botanical Garden, 11030 East Blvd, Cleveland, OH, 44106. Tel: 216-721-1600, Ext 195. p. 1766

Sullivan, Marisha, Head Librn, Holden Arboretum, 9550 Sperry Rd, Kirtland, OH, 44094. Tel: 440-946-4400, Ext 225. p. 1793

Sullivan, Mark, Dir, Info & Delivery Services, State University of New York College, SUNY Geneseo, One College Circle, Geneseo, NY, 14454-1498. Tel: 585-245-5594. p. 1537

Sullivan, Michael, Dir, Richards Library, 36 Elm St, Warrensburg, NY, 12885. Tel: 518-623-3011. p. 1658

Sullivan, Michayla, Res Serv Spec, Bose McKinney & Evans LLP, 111 Monument Circle, Ste 2700, Indianapolis, IN, 46204. Tel: 317-684-5166. p. 690

Sullivan, Nancy, Mgr Fac, Charleston County Public Library, 68 Calhoun St, Charleston, SC, 29401. Tel: 843-805-6801. p. 2048

Sullivan, Pat, Librn, McCormick Barstow, LLP, 7647 N Freso St, Fresno, CA, 93720. Tel: 559-433-1300. p. 147

Sullivan, Patrick, Law Librn, Jones Day, 555 S Flower St, 50th Flr, Los Angeles, CA, 90071. Tel: 213-489-3939. p. 162

Sullivan, Patrick, Asst Dir, Hearst Free Library, 401 Main St, Anaconda, MT, 59711. Tel: 406-563-6932. p. 1287

Sullivan, Paulette, Mgr, Monroe County Public Library, Key Largo Branch, Tradewinds Shopping Ctr, 101485 Overseas Hwy, Key Largo, FL, 33037. Tel: 305-451-2396. p. 414

Sullivan, Salena, Br Supvr, Montgomery-Floyd Regional Library System, 125 Sheltman St, Christiansburg, VA, 24073. Tel: 540-382-6965. p. 2312

Sullivan, Sarah, Asst Dir, Nevins Memorial Library, 305 Broadway, Methuen, MA, 01844-6898. Tel: 978-686-4080. p. 1035

Sullivan, Sarah, Chief Financial Officer, Richland Library, 1431 Assembly St, Columbia, SC, 29201-3101. Tel: 803-799-9084. p. 2054

Sullivan, Sheila, Ch Serv, Georgetown County Library, 405 Cleland St, Georgetown, SC, 29440-3200. Tel: 843-545-3300. p. 2060

Sullivan, Stephanie, Librn, East Mississippi Regional Library System, Pachuta Public, Hwy 11 N, Pachuta, MS, 39347. Tel: 601-776-7209. p. 1231

Sullivan, Steve, Chief Operations Officer, Richland Library, 1431 Assembly St, Columbia, SC, 29201-3101. Tel: 803-799-9084. p. 2054

Sullivan, Suzanne, Asst Dir, Head, Coll Serv, Auburn Public Library, 49 Spring St, Auburn, ME, 04210. Tel: 207-333-6640. p. 913

Sullivan, Tara, Br Mgr, Long Branch Free Public Library, Elberon Branch, 168 Lincoln Ave, Elberon, NJ, 07740. Tel: 732-870-1776. p. 1414

Sullivan, Teri, Interim Mgr, Rapides Parish Library, Georgie G Johnson Branch, 1610 Veterans Dr, Lecompte, LA, 71346. Tel: 318-776-5153. p. 880
Sullivan, Thomas, Brother, Spec Coll, Conception Abbey & Seminary Library, 37174 State Hwy VV, Conception, MO, 64433. Tel: 660-944-2860. p. 1244
Sumbulla, Helena, Student Engagement Librn, University of Wisconsin-Eau Claire, 103 Garfield Ave, Eau Claire, WI, 54701-4932. Tel: 715-836-6032. p. 2433
Sumic, Caryn, Circ, Libr Spec, Mat, Lenoir-Rhyne University Libraries, 625 7th Ave NE, Hickory, NC, 28601. Tel: 828-328-7236. p. 1696
Sumida, Jerilyn, Libr Spec, East-West Center, John A Burns Hall, Rm 4063 & 4066, 1601 East-West Rd, Honolulu, HI, 96848-1601. Tel: 808-944-7379. p. 506
Sumlin, Thyra, Librn, East Mississippi Regional Library System, Mary Weems Parker Memorial, 1016 N Pine Ave, Heidelberg, MS, 39439. Tel: 601-787-3857. p. 1231
Summars, Kathy, Dir, Buffalo Public Library, 11 E Turner, Buffalo, OK, 73834. Tel: 580-735-2995. p. 1843
Summerall, Elizabeth, Law Librn, Manatee County Law Library, Manatee County Judicial Ctr, Rm 1101, 1051 Manatee Ave W, Bradenton, FL, 34205. Tel: 941-741-4090. p. 386
Summerfield, Terri, Dir, Clearwater County Free Library District, 204 Wood St, Weippe, ID, 83553. Tel: 208-435-4058. p. 532
Summers, Anita, Exec Dir, Sequoyah Regional Library System, 116 Brown Industrial Pkwy, Canton, GA, 30114. Tel: 770-479-3090, Ext 221. p. 469
Summers, Cheryl, Mgr, University of Virginia, Mathematics, Deparment of Mathematics, Kerchof Hall. Rm 107, Charlottesville, VA, 22903. Tel: 434-924-7806. p. 2310
Summers, Cheryl L, Mgr, University of Virginia, Chemistry, Brown Science & Engineering Library, 291 McCormick Rd, Charlottesville, VA, 22903. Tel: 434-924-3159. p. 2310
Summers, Holly, Teen Serv, Charlotte Mecklenburg Library, ImaginOn: The Joe & Joan Martin Center, 300 E Seventh St, Charlotte, NC, 28202. Tel: 704-416-4600. p. 1679
Summers, Scott, Asst Dir, North Carolina State University Libraries, College of Education Media Center, DH Hill Jr Library, B404, 2 W Broughton Dr, Raleigh, NC, 27695. Tel: 919-515-3191. p. 1709
Summers-Ables, Joy, Dir, University of Oklahoma Health Sciences Center, 1105 N Stonewall Ave, Oklahoma City, OK, 73117-1220. Tel: 405-271-2285. p. 1859
Summers-Ables, Joy, Dir, Oklahoma Health Sciences Library Association, University of Oklahoma - HSC Bird Health Science Library, 1101 N Stonewall, Oklahoma City, OK, 73190. Tel: 405-271-2285, Ext 48755. p. 2773
Summers-Gil, Holly, Teen Serv Coordr, Charlotte Mecklenburg Library, 310 N Tryon St, Charlotte, NC, 28202-2176. Tel: 704-416-0100. p. 1679
Summerscales, Deb, Head Librn, Parkland Regional Library-Manitoba, Strathclair Branch, 50 Main St, Strathclair, MB, R0J 2C0, CANADA. Tel: 204-365-2539. p. 2587
Summey, Terri, Res & Ref Serv, Emporia State University, 1200 Commercial St, Box 4051, Emporia, KS, 66801. Tel: 620-341-5207. p. 807
Sumner, Kaytlin, Dir, Portage Public Library, 704 Main St, Portage, PA, 15946-1715. Tel: 814-736-4340. p. 1998
Sumner, Patty, Ch Serv Librn, Piscataway Township Free Public Library, 500 Hoes Lane, Piscataway, NJ, 08854. Tel: 732-463-1633. p. 1435
Sumner, Robyn, Exec Dir, Washington County Historical Society, 135 W Washington St, Hagerstown, MD, 21740. Tel: 301-797-8782. p. 968
Sump-Crethar, Nicole, Data Mgt, Dir, Libr Tech, University of Central Oklahoma, Chambers Library, 100 N University Dr, Edmond, OK, 73034. Tel: 405-974-2883. p. 1846
Sumpter, Jill, Tech Coordr, Fort Bend County Libraries, 1001 Golfview Dr, Richmond, TX, 77469-5199. Tel: 281-633-4760. p. 2232
Sun, Jinong, Acq Librn, Fayetteville State University, 1200 Murchison Rd, Fayetteville, NC, 28301-4298. Tel: 910-672-1642. p. 1689
Sun, Meicen, Asst Prof, University of Illinois at Urbana-Champaign, Library & Information Science Bldg, 501 E Daniel St, Champaign, IL, 61820-6211. Tel: 217-333-3280. p. 2784
Sun, Pam, Collection Strategies Services Coord, University of California, Riverside, 900 University Ave, Riverside, CA, 92521. Tel: 951-827-3220. p. 203
Sun, Ying, Dr, Assoc Prof, University at Buffalo, The State University of New York, 534 Baldy Hall, Buffalo, NY, 14260. Tel: 716-645-2412. p. 2789
Sundberg, Patty, Br Mgr, Carroll County Public Library, Mount Airy Branch, 705 Ridge Ave, Mount Airy, MD, 21771-3911. Tel: 410-386-4470. p. 971
Sunde, Esther, Ref (Info Servs), South Seattle Community College, 6000 16th Ave SW, Seattle, WA, 98106-1499. Tel: 206-768-6663. p. 2380
Sunde, Tena, Dir, Estherville Public Library, 613 Central Ave, Estherville, IA, 51334-2294. Tel: 712-362-7731. p. 751
Sundell-Thomas, Lilly, Asst Dir, Ipswich Public Library, 25 N Main St, Ipswich, MA, 01938. Tel: 978-356-6648. p. 1026
Sunderhaus, Jennifer, Ch Serv, Shelby Township Library, 51680 Van Dyke, Shelby Township, MI, 48316-4448. Tel: 586-739-7414. p. 1150
Sunderland, Debbie, Pres, Portage County Historical Society Museum & Library, 6549 N Chestnut St, Ravenna, OH, 44266. Tel: 330-296-3523. p. 1817
Sundin, Ashley, Head, Pub Serv, Gonzaga University School of Law, 721 N Cincinnati St, Spokane, WA, 99220. Tel: 509-313-3753. p. 2383
Sundin, Kelly, Dean of Libr, California Institute of Integral Studies, 1453 Mission St, 2nd Flr, San Francisco, CA, 94103. Tel: 415-575-6180. p. 223
Sundquist, Jeffery, Libr Dir, Monterey Peninsula College Library, 980 Fremont St, Monterey, CA, 93940. Tel: 831-646-4036. p. 179
Sundt, Chayse, Br Mgr, Anoka County Library, St Francis Branch, 3519 Bridge St NW, Saint Francis, MN, 55070. Tel: 763-324-1580. p. 1165
Sung, Sanga A, Govt Info Librn, University of Illinois Library at Urbana-Champaign, Government Information Services, 450-F Main Library, 1408 W Gregory Dr, Urbana, IL, 61801. Tel: 217-333-2290. p. 656
Sung, Yunah, Tech Serv, University of Michigan, Asia Library, Harlen Hatcher Graduate Library, 913 S University Ave, Ann Arbor, MI, 48109-1190. Tel: 734-936-2408. p. 1080
Suni, Karin, Curator, Free Library of Philadelphia, Rare Book, 1901 Vine St, 3rd Flr, Philadelphia, PA, 19103-1116. Tel: 215-686-5416. p. 1979
Sunio, Maria, Libr Dir, Moreno Valley Public Library, 25480 Alessandro Blvd, Moreno Valley, CA, 92553. Tel: 951-413-3880. p. 180
Sunio, Maria V, Libr Dir, Moreno Valley Public Library, Iris Plaza, 16170 Perris Blvd, Ste C3, Moreno Valley, CA, 92551. Tel: 951-413-3670. p. 181
Sunio, Maria V, Libr Dir, Moreno Valley Public Library, Moreno Valley Mall, 22500 Town Circle, Ste 2078, Moreno Valley, CA, 92553. Tel: 951-413-3761. p. 181
Sunny, Sophie, Colls Mgr, Asbury University, One Macklem Dr, Wilmore, KY, 40390-1198. Tel: 859-858-3511, Ext 2425. p. 878
Sunrich, Matt, Librn, West Georgia Technical College, 176 Murphy Campus Blvd, Waco, GA, 30182. Tel: 770-537-6066. p. 502
Supnick, Patricia, Librn, Children's Hospital of Michigan, Phyllis Ann Colburn Memorial Family Library, 3901 Beaubien Blvd, 5th Flr, Detroit, MI, 48201. Tel: 313-745-5437. p. 1097
Supnick, Patricia, Dir, Michigan Department of Health and Human Services, 8303 Platt Rd, Saline, MI, 48176. Tel: 734-429-2531, Ext 4296. p. 1148
Supp, Melinda, Libr Mgr, Jordanville Public Library, 189 Main St, Jordanville, NY, 13361. Tel: 315-858-2874. p. 1558
Suprunova, Yelena, Digital Res Librn, Howard University Libraries, Louis Stokes Health Sciences Library, 501 W St NW, Washington, DC, 20059. Tel: 202-884-1730. p. 369
Surak, Amy, Dir, Archives & Spec Coll, Manhattan College, 4513 Manhattan College Pkwy, Riverdale, NY, 10471. Tel: 718-862-7743. p. 1627
Surbaugh, Holly, Ref Librn, Georgetown University, Blommer Science Library, 302 Reiss Science Bldg, Washington, DC, 20057. Tel: 202-662-5685. p. 368
Surbaugh, Kris, Dir, Frederic Public Library, 127 Oak St W, Frederic, WI, 54837. Tel: 715-327-4979. p. 2436
Sureck, Connie, Mgr, Medina County District Library, Brunswick Community, 3649 Center Rd, Brunswick, OH, 44212-0430. Tel: 330-273-4150. p. 1801
Surerus, Lorrie, Dir, Snake River School Community Library, 924 W Hwy 39, Blackfoot, ID, 83221. Tel: 208-684-3063. p. 516
Surgenor, Trevor, Dir, Manitoba Culture, Heritage & Tourism, B10 - 340 9th St, Brandon, MB, R7A 6C2, CANADA. Tel: 204-726-6590. p. 2586
Surjan, Ed, Libr Dir, The Frederick Gunn School, 99 Green Hill Rd, Washington, CT, 06793. Tel: 860-868-7334, Ext 224. p. 343
Surles, Alma, Pub Serv Librn, Alabama Supreme Court & State Law Library, Heflin-Torbert Judicial Bldg, 300 Dexter Ave, Montgomery, AL, 36104. Tel: 334-229-0569. p. 28
Surovich, Linda, Head, Youth Serv, Mount Kisco Public Library, 100 E Main St, Mount Kisco, NY, 10549. Tel: 914-864-0039. p. 1574
Surprise-Tolj, Christie, Br Mgr, Annapolis Valley Regional Library, Annapolis Royal Branch, 143 Ritchie St, Annapolis Royal, NS, B0S 1A0, CANADA. Tel: 902-532-2226. p. 2616
Surratt, Greg, Tech Serv, US Courts Library - Tenth Circuit Court of Appeals, 333 Lomas Blvd NW, Ste 230, Albuquerque, NM, 87102. Tel: 505-348-2135. p. 1462
Susag, Peter, Assoc Dir, Luther Seminary Library, 2375 Como Ave, Saint Paul, MN, 55108. Tel: 651-641-3447. p. 1200
Susie, Bloom, Assoc Librn, Head, Instrul Serv, Molloy College, 1000 Hempstead Ave, Rockville Centre, NY, 11571. Tel: 516-323-3927. p. 1632
Susin, Nancy, Br Mgr, Newton County Public Library, Roselawn Library, 4421 East State Rd 10, Roselawn, IN, 46372. Tel: 219-345-2010. p. 702
Suson, Gina, Librn, Walters Public Library, 202 N Broadway St, Walters, OK, 73572-1226. Tel: 580-875-2006. p. 1868
Sussenbach, Michelle, Dean of Academic Services, Greenville University, 301 N Elm, Greenville, IL, 62246. Tel: 618-664-6603. p. 596
Sussman, Benjamin, Fac Mgr, Georgetown University, Dahlgren Memorial Library, Preclinical Science Bldg GM-7, 3900 Reservoir Rd NW, Washington, DC, 20007. Tel: 202-687-1665. p. 368
Sussmier, Stephanie, Bibliog Control Librn, Rider University, Katharine Houk Talbott Library, Franklin F Moore Library Bldg, 3rd & 4th Flrs, 2083 Lawrenceville Rd, Lawrenceville, NJ, 08648. Tel: 609-921-7100, Ext 8305. p. 1411
Sustache, Rafael, Electronic Res Librn, Info Syst Librn, Amaury Veray Music Library, 951 Ave Ponce de Leon, San Juan, PR, 00907-3373. Tel: 787-751-0160, Ext 238. p. 2513

Suszek, Ron, Dir, Muskegon Area District Library, 4845 Airline Rd, Unit 5, Muskegon, MI, 49444-4503. Tel: 231-737-6248. p. 1136

Suter, Gwen, Br Mgr, Portsmouth Public Library, W Gordon Ryan Branch, 103 Lucasville-Minford Rd, Lucasville, OH, 45648-0744. Tel: 740-259-6119. p. 1816

Sutera, Karen, Dir, Harvard Diggins Public Library, 900 E McKinley St, Harvard, IL, 60033. Tel: 815-943-4671. p. 597

Sutherland, Amy, Pub Serv Librn, Haut-Saint-Jean Regional Library, 15 rue de l'Eglise St, Ste 102, Edmundston, NB, E3V 1J3, CANADA. Tel: 506-735-2074. p. 2600

Sutherland, Janet, Mgr, Warren County Historical Society, 102 W Walton St, Warrenton, MO, 63383. Tel: 636-456-3820. p. 1285

Sutherland, Judy, Pres, West Hennepin County Pioneers Association Library, 1953 W Wayzata Blvd, Long Lake, MN, 55356. Tel: 952-473-6557. p. 1180

Sutherland, Leslie, Dir, Carroll County Public Library, 136 Court St, Carrollton, KY, 41008. Tel: 502-732-7020. p. 851

Sutherland, Linda, Fiscal Officer, Stow-Munroe Falls Public Library, 3512 Darrow Rd, Stow, OH, 44224. Tel: 330-688-3295. p. 1822

Sutherland Mills, Kimberly, Mgr, Prog & Outreach, Kingston Frontenac Public Library, 130 Johnson St, Kingston, ON, K7L 1X8, CANADA. Tel: 613-549-8888. p. 2650

Sutherland, Norma, Br Mgr, Lincoln County Libraries, Guyan River Public Library, 5320 McClellan Hwy, Branchland, WV, 25506. Tel: 304-824-4640. p. 2403

Sutherland, Peggy, Br Mgr, Sullivan County Public Library, Sullivan Gardens Branch, 104 Bluegrass Dr, Kingsport, TN, 37660. Tel: 423-349-5990. p. 2089

Sutherland, Shelley, Youth Serv Mgr, Skokie Public Library, 5215 Oakton St, Skokie, IL, 60077-3680. Tel: 847-673-7774. p. 647

Sutherland, Tonia, Dr, Asst Prof, University of Hawaii, 2550 McCarthy Mall, Hamilton Library, Rm 002, Honolulu, HI, 96822. Tel: 808-956-7321. p. 2784

Sutherlin, Leslie, Dir, Aurora Public Library District, 414 Second St, Aurora, IN, 47001-1384. Tel: 812-926-0646. p. 669

Sutherlin, Leslie, Dir, Aurora Public Library District, Dillsboro Public, 10151 Library Lane, Dillsboro, IN, 47018. Tel: 812-954-4151. p. 669

Suto, Lisa, Circ Mgr, Albany Law School, 80 New Scotland Ave, Albany, NY, 12208. p. 1482

Sutrina-Haney, Katie, Dir, Spec Coll, Univ Archivist, Indiana State University, 510 North 6 1/2 St, Terre Haute, IN, 47809. Tel: 812-237-3700. p. 720

Sutro, Douglas, Libr Tech, Sonoma County Public Law Library, 2604 Ventura Ave, Santa Rosa, CA, 95403. Tel: 707-565-2668. p. 245

Suttee, Valerie, Br Mgr, Fairfax County Public Library, Richard Byrd Branch, 7250 Commerce St, Springfield, VA, 22150-3499. Tel: 703-451-8055. p. 2316

Sutter, Amy, Digital Initiatives, Illinois Wesleyan University, One Ames Plaza, Bloomington, IL, 61701-7188. Tel: 309-556-3728. p. 543

Sutterfield, Debra, Dir, Izard County Library, 301 Second St, Calico Rock, AR, 72519. Tel: 870-297-3785. p. 92

Sutterfield, Debra, Regional Librn, White River Regional Library, PO Box 1107, Mountain View, AR, 72560. Tel: 870-269-4682. p. 105

Sutton, Angela, Coordr, National Park Service, One Indian Well Headquarters, Tulelake, CA, 96134. Tel: 530-667-8113, 530-667-8119. p. 253

Sutton, Ann, Tech Serv, Pike County Public Library, 1008 E Maple St, Petersburg, IN, 47567-1736. Tel: 812-354-6257. p. 713

Sutton, Annie, Head, Access Serv, Anderson County Library, 300 N McDuffie St, Anderson, SC, 29621-5643. Tel: 864-260-4500. p. 2046

Sutton, Carolyn, Br Mgr, Hightower Sara Regional Library, Cave Spring Branch, 17 Cedartown St SW, Cave Spring, GA, 30124-2702. Tel: 706-777-3346. p. 494

Sutton, Donna, Dir, Carter County Library District, 403 Ash St, Van Buren, MO, 63965. Tel: 573-323-4315. p. 1284

Sutton, Erica, Cat/Acq Tech, Stormont, Dundas & Glengarry County Library, 26 Pitt St, Ste 106, Cornwall, ON, K6J 3P2, CANADA. Tel: 613-936-8777, Ext 213. p. 2637

Sutton, Gloria, Adult Serv Mgr, Asst Dir, Braswell Memorial Public Library, 727 N Grace St, Rocky Mount, NC, 27804-4842. Tel: 252-442-1951. p. 1713

Sutton, Kameron, Librn, New Waverly Public Library, 9372 State Hwy 75 S, New Waverly, TX, 77358. Tel: 936-344-2198. p. 2222

Sutton, Karen, Br Head, Mariposa County Library, El Portal Branch, 9670 Rancheria Flat Rd, 1st Flr, El Portal, CA, 95318. Tel: 209-379-2401. p. 173

Sutton, Kay, Librn, Galeton Public Library, Five Park Ln, Galeton, PA, 16922. Tel: 814-435-2321. p. 1934

Sutton, Kristine, Dir, Newstead Public Library, 33 Main St, Akron, NY, 14001-1020. Tel: 716-542-2327. p. 1481

Sutton, Lea, Ch, Davis Memorial Library, 928 Cape Rd, Limington, ME, 04049. Tel: 207-637-2422. p. 930

Sutton, Melanie, Asst Librn, Kirbyville Public Library, 210 S Elizabeth St, Kirbyville, TX, 75956. Tel: 409-423-4653. p. 2207

Sutton, Norma, Ref Serv, North Park University, Brandel Library, 5114 N Christiana Ave, Chicago, IL, 60625. Tel: 773-244-6239. p. 566

Sutton, Quentin, Br Mgr, Edgecombe County Memorial Library, Pinetops Branch, 201 S First St, Pinetops, NC, 27864. Tel: 252-827-4621. p. 1718

Sutton, Roxanne, Tech Serv Librn, Harcum College, 750 Montgomery Ave, Bryn Mawr, PA, 19010-3476. Tel: 610-526-6022. p. 1916

Sutton, Shan C, Dean, Univ Libr, University of Arizona Libraries, 1510 E University Blvd, Tucson, AZ, 85721. Tel: 520-621-0717. p. 83

Sutton, Shannon, Br Supvr, Duplin County Library, 107 Bowden Dr, Kenansville, NC, 28349. Tel: 910-296-2117. p. 1698

Sutton, Tonya, Asst Dir, Ref & Circ Librn, Carl Albert State College, 1507 S McKenna, Poteau, OK, 74953. Tel: 918-647-1311. p. 1860

Suurtramm, Karen, Archivist, Trent University, 1600 West Bank Dr, Peterborough, ON, K9J 7B8, CANADA. Tel: 705-748-1011, Ext 7410. p. 2672

Suzuki, Mari, Head of Libr, University of Michigan, Asia Library, Harlen Hatcher Graduate Library, 913 S University Ave, Ann Arbor, MI, 48109-1190. Tel: 734-764-0406. p. 1080

Suzuki, Naoe, Admin Coordr, Harvard Library, Fine Arts Library, Littauer Ctr, 1805 Cambridge St, Cambridge, MA, 02138. Tel: 617-495-3374. p. 1006

Svansson, Pat, Cat Asst, Circ Asst, Glocester Libraries, Harmony Library, 195 Putnam Pike, Harmony, RI, 02829. Tel: 401-949-2850. p. 2030

Svedin, Tam, Co-Dir, Kuna Library District, 457 N Locust, Kuna, ID, 83634-1926. Tel: 208-922-1025. p. 523

Svehla, Louise, Ad, Three Rivers Public Library District, 25207 W Channon Dr, Channahon, IL, 60410-5028. Tel: 815-467-6200, Ext 306. p. 552

Svendsen, Melissa, Librn, Thompson Rivers University, 1250 Western Ave, Williams Lake, BC, V2G 1H7, CANADA. Tel: 250-392-8030. p. 2584

Svenningsen, Julie, Libr Assoc, Scott County Library System, 1615 Weston Ct, Shakopee, MN, 55379. Tel: 952-496-8010. p. 1203

Svenpladsen, Alexandra, Br Mgr, Williamson County Public Library, Nolensville Branch, 915 Oldham Dr, Nolensville, TN, 37135. Tel: 615-776-5490. p. 2099

Svitavsky, Bill, Access Serv Librn, Rollins College, 1000 Holt Ave, Campus Box 2744, Winter Park, FL, 32789-2744. Tel: 407-464-2679. p. 456

Svitavsky, Bonnie, Sr Librn, Pierce County Library System, University Place Branch, 3609 Market Pl W, Ste 100, University Place, WA, 98466. Tel: 253-548-3307. p. 2387

Svoboda, Cynthia, Head, Access Serv, Bridgewater State University, Ten Shaw Rd, Bridgewater, MA, 02325. Tel: 508-531-1740. p. 1002

Svoboda, Megan, Dir, Broken Bow Public Library, 626 South D St, Broken Bow, NE, 68822. Tel: 308-872-2927. p. 1309

Svoboda, Rachael, Bus Serv Coordr, Laramie County Library System, 2200 Pioneer Ave, Cheyenne, WY, 82001-3610. Tel: 307-773-7200. p. 2492

Swadley, Thresa, Interim Br Mgr, Pioneer Library System, Shawnee Public, 101 N Philadelphia, Shawnee, OK, 74801. Tel: 405-275-6353. p. 1855

Swafford, James, Head, Info Tech, Pittsburg Public Library, 308 N Walnut, Pittsburg, KS, 66762-4732. Tel: 620-230-5511. p. 831

Swafford, William, Sr Librn, California Department of Corrections, Fifth St & Western, Norco, CA, 92860. Tel: 951-737-2683, Ext 4202. p. 183

Swaggart, Keri, Clinical Serv Librn, Children's Mercy Hospital, 2401 Gillham Rd, Kansas City, MO, 64108. Tel: 816-234-3800, 816-234-3900. p. 1254

Swails, Mark, Copyright Librn, Johnson County Community College, 12345 College Blvd, Overland Park, KS, 66210. Tel: 913-469-8500, Ext 3773. p. 829

Swain, Deborah E, Asst Prof, North Carolina Central University, 1801 Fayetteville St, Durham, NC, 27707. Tel: 919-530-6485. p. 2790

Swain, Dorothy J, Dir, Greenville Public Library, 573 Putnam Pike, Greenville, RI, 02828-2195. Tel: 401-949-3630. p. 2032

Swale, Hannah, Adult Serv Supvr, Kankakee Public Library, 201 E Merchant St, Kankakee, IL, 60901. Tel: 815-939-4564. p. 604

Swallow, Kendra, Libr Tech, Algonquin College Library, Perth Campus, Seven Craig St, Rm 117, Perth, ON, K7H 1X7, CANADA. Tel: 613-267-2859, Ext 6225. p. 2664

Swan, Celine, Libr Dir, Grand Island Public Library, 1124 W Second St, Grand Island, NE, 68801. Tel: 308-385-5333. p. 1316

Swan, Evan, Circ, Syst Librn, Wayne State College, 1111 Main St, Wayne, NE, 68787. Tel: 402-375-7161. p. 1340

Swan, Morgan, Outreach & Spec Coll Librn, Dartmouth College Library, Rauner Special Collections Library, 6065 Webster Hall, Hanover, NH, 03755-3519. Tel: 603-646-0538. p. 1367

Swan, Philip, Head, Res & Instruction, Hunter College Libraries, East Bldg, 695 Park Ave, New York, NY, 10065. Tel: 212-396-6733. p. 1588

Swan, Ruth, Dr, Dir, Oakwood University, 7000 Adventist Blvd NW, Huntsville, AL, 35896. Tel: 256-726-7250. p. 22

Swan, Tiger, Ref & Instruction Librn, Quinsigamond Community College, 670 W Boylston St, Worcester, MA, 01606-2092. Tel: 508-854-4210. p. 1072

Swanay, Bob, Dir, Carmel Clay Public Library, 425 E Main St, Carmel, IN, 46032-2278. Tel: 317-814-3901. p. 674

Swanberg, Carl, Head, Info Tech, Canton Public Library, 1200 S Canton Center Rd, Canton, MI, 48188-1600. Tel: 734-397-0999. p. 1088

Swanburg, Karen, Librn, Lenawee District Library, Addison Branch, 102 S Talbot St, Addison, MI, 49220. Tel: 517-547-3414. p. 1075

Swane, Michelle, Libr Dir, Ozark Regional Library, 402 N Main St, Ironton, MO, 63650. Tel: 573-546-2615. p. 1251

Swane, Michelle, Librn, Ozark Regional Library, Ironton Branch, 402 N Main St, Ironton, MO, 63650. Tel: 573-546-2615. p. 1251

Swanger, Maggie, Electronic Res Librn, Laramie County Community College, 1400 E College Dr, Cheyenne, WY, 82007-3204. Tel: 307-778-1283. p. 2492
Swann, Donica, Director, Champaign County Historical Archives, The Urbana Free Library, 210 W Green St, Urbana, IL, 61801. Tel: 217-367-4025. p. 657
Swann, Linda, Mgr, Suwannee River Regional Library, Lee Public Library, 7883 E US Hwy 90, Lee, FL, 32059-0040. Tel: 850-971-5665. p. 419
Swann, Oliver, Tech Serv Spec, Parkland College Library, 2400 W Bradley Ave, Champaign, IL, 61821-1899. p. 552
Swanner, Alex, Access Serv Librn, De Anza College, 21250 Stevens Creek Blvd, Cupertino, CA, 95014-5793. Tel: 408-864-8486. p. 133
Swanson, Brent, Bus Mgr, Head, Bus Serv, Iowa State University Library, 302 Parks Library, 701 Morrill Rd, Ames, IA, 50011-2102. Tel: 515-294-4954. p. 731
Swanson, Dawn, Dir, Kennedy Free Library, 649 Second St, Kennedy, NY, 14747. Tel: 716-267-4265. p. 1559
Swanson, Douglas, Librn, Arizona Department of Corrections - Adult Institutions, 7125 E Juan Sanchez Blvd, San Luis, AZ, 85349. Tel: 928-627-8871. p. 76
Swanson, Ellie, Tech Serv Librn, Elgin Community College, 1700 Spartan Dr, Elgin, IL, 60123. Tel: 847-214-7337. p. 584
Swanson, Emily, Libr Dir, Westminster College, 1840 S 1300 East, Salt Lake City, UT, 84105-3697. Tel: 801-832-2250. p. 2273
Swanson, Heather, Youth Serv Mgr, Ella Johnson Memorial Public Library District, 109 S State St, Hampshire, IL, 60140. Tel: 847-683-4490. p. 597
Swanson, Hillary, Adminr, Exec Dir, Crow Wing County Historical Society Archives Library, 320 Laurel St, Brainerd, MN, 56401-3523. Tel: 218-829-3268. p. 1166
Swanson, Jessica, Libr Dir, New Port Richey Campus, Keiser University Library System, 1500 NW 49th St, Fort Lauderdale, FL, 33309. Tel: 954-351-4035. p. 401
Swanson, Joe, Jr, Dir, Morehouse School of Medicine, Medical Education Bldg, 1st Flr, Ste 100, 720 Westview Dr SW, Atlanta, GA, 30310-1495. Tel: 404-752-1542. p. 465
Swanson, Julie, Ref Librn, Locke Lord Bissell & Liddell LLP, 111 S Wacker Dr, Chicago, IL, 60606. Tel: 312-443-0646. p. 563
Swanson, Karen, Supvry Librn, United States Environmental Protection Agency, 77 W Jackson Blvd (ML-16J), Chicago, IL, 60604. Tel: 312-886-6822. p. 569
Swanson, Kari, Acq & Coll Develop Librn, Southern Connecticut State University, 501 Crescent St, New Haven, CT, 06515. Tel: 203-392-5774. p. 326
Swanson, Laura, Libr Mgr, Chartiers-Houston Community Library, 730 W Grant St, Houston, PA, 15342. Tel: 724-745-4300. p. 1944
Swanson, Linda, Coll Mgr, Ohio Genealogical Society, 611 State Rte 97 W, Bellville, OH, 44813-8813. Tel: 419-886-1903. p. 1750
Swanson, Robin, Supvry Librn, Environmental Protection Agency, 2000 Traverwood Dr, Ann Arbor, MI, 48105. Tel: 734-214-4311. p. 1079
Swanson, Sara, Asst Dir, Research, Learning & Scholarly Comms, Davidson College, 209 Ridge Rd, Davidson, NC, 28035-0001. Tel: 704-894-2331. p. 1683
Swanson, Troy, Dept Chair, Pub Serv, Teaching & Learning Librn, Moraine Valley Community College Library, 9000 W College Pkwy, Palos Hills, IL, 60465. Tel: 708-974-5439. p. 632
Swanson, Victoria, Libr Dir, Caldwell University, 120 Bloomfield Ave, Caldwell, NJ, 07006. Tel: 973-618-3311. p. 1393
Swanson-Farmarco, Cindy, Mgr, Baltimore County Public Library, Lansdowne Branch, 500 Third Ave, Baltimore, MD, 21227. Tel: 410-887-5602. p. 979
Swantek, Shuana, Head, Pub Serv, Marshall District Library, 124 W Green St, Marshall, MI, 49068. Tel: 269-781-7821, Ext 18. p. 1130
Swanton, Abby, Wis Doc Dep Prog/Wis Digital Archives, Wisconsin Department of Public Instruction, Resources for Libraries & Lifelong Learning, 2109 S Stoughton Rd, Madison, WI, 53716-2899. Tel: 608-224-6174. p. 2452
Swanzy, Geri, Ch Serv, Brazoria County Library System, Angleton Branch, 401 E Cedar St, Angleton, TX, 77515-4652. Tel: 979-864-1519. p. 2135
Swaren, Chantelle, Outreach & Assessment Librn, University of Tennessee at Chattanooga Library, 400 Douglas Ave, Dept 6456, Chattanooga, TN, 37403-2598. Tel: 423-425-4501. p. 2092
Swarm, Darryl, Assessment Librn, Asst Prof, University of La Verne, 2040 Third St, La Verne, CA, 91750. Tel: 909-593-3511, Ext 4305. p. 155
Swarm, Darryl, Libr Dir, Feather River College Library, 570 Golden Eagle Ave, Quincy, CA, 95971-9124. Tel: 530-283-0202, Ext 236. p. 197
Swarr, Lisa, Acq Asst, Lancaster Bible College, Teague Learning Commons, 901 Eden Rd, Lancaster, PA, 17601-5036. Tel: 717-569-7071, Ext 5385. p. 1951
Swart, Colleen, Cat Librn, Oostburg Public Library, 213 N Eighth St, Oostburg, WI, 53070. Tel: 920-564-2934. p. 2467
Swart, Katherine, Coll Develop, Calvin University & Calvin Theological Seminary, 1855 Knollcrest Circle SE, Grand Rapids, MI, 49546-4402. Tel: 616-526-6311. p. 1110
Swart, Kathy, Ref & Instruction Librn, Pierce College Library, Puyallup Campus, 1601 39th Ave SE, Puyallup, WA, 98374. Tel: 253-840-8305. p. 2368
Swartz, Donna, Dir, Shrewsbury Public Library, 98 Town Hill Rd, Cuttingsville, VT, 05738. Tel: 802-492-3410. p. 2282
Swartz, Jane, Librn, Missouri Department of Corrections, Fulton Reception & Diagnostic Center, PO Box 190, Fulton, MO, 65251-0190. Tel: 573-592-4040. p. 1252
Swartz, Pat, Archivist/Librn, Fairbanks Museum & Planetarium, 1302 Main St, Saint Johnsbury, VT, 05819. Tel: 802-748-2372. p. 2294
Swartz, Pauline, Dept Chair, Librn, Mt San Antonio College Library, 1100 N Grand Ave, Walnut, CA, 91789. Tel: 909-274-4260. p. 258
Swartzendruber, Brent, Library Contact, Bethesda Mennonite Church Library, 930 16th St, Henderson, NE, 68371. Tel: 402-723-4562. p. 1318
Swartzlander, Barbara, Research & Teaching Librn, University of New England Libraries, 11 Hills Beach Rd, Biddeford, ME, 04005. Tel: 207-602-2315. p. 917
Swary, Lynn, Dir, Holgate Community Library, 204 Railway Ave, Holgate, OH, 43527. Tel: 419-264-7965. p. 1790
Swatos, Elizabeth, Dir, Henry C Adams Memorial Library, 209 W Third St, Prophetstown, IL, 61277. Tel: 815-537-5462. p. 637
Swatski, Joseph, Ref Librn, State University of New York, 735 Anderson Hill Rd, Purchase, NY, 10577-1400. Tel: 914-251-6411. p. 1625
Swayney, Robin, Genealogist, Museum of the Cherokee People, 589 Tsali Blvd, Cherokee, NC, 28719. Tel: 828-497-3481, 828-554-0479. p. 1681
Sweany, Brent, Head, Libr Operations, University of Missouri-Kansas City Libraries, Health Sciences Library, 2411 Holmes St, Kansas City, MO, 64108. Tel: 816-235-2062. p. 1258
Swearingen, Christina, Libr Dir, Schreiner Memorial Library, 113 W Elm St, Lancaster, WI, 53813-1202. Tel: 608-723-7304. p. 2447
Swearingen, Christinna, Dir, Rusk County Community Library, 418 Corbett Ave W, Ladysmith, WI, 54848-1396. Tel: 715-532-2604. p. 2447
Sweatlock, Diane, Libr Dir, River Vale Free Public Library, 412 Rivervale Rd, River Vale, NJ, 07675. Tel: 201-391-2323. p. 1440
Sweatlock, Donna Z, Circ Mgr, Oradell Free Public Library, 375 Kinderkamack Rd, Oradell, NJ, 07649-2122. Tel: 201-262-2613. p. 1431
Swed, Kevin, Mgr, Appoquinimink Community Library, 651 N Broad St, Middletown, DE, 19709. Tel: 302-378-5588. p. 354
Sweeney, Abigail, Reserves Mgr, Massachusetts College of Art & Design, 621 Huntington Ave, Boston, MA, 02115-5882. Tel: 617-879-7104. p. 996
Sweeney, Charlotte, Campus Librn, Pensacola State College, Milton Campus, Bldg 4100, 5988 Hwy 90, Milton, FL, 32583-1798. Tel: 850-484-4465. p. 436
Sweeney, Chris, Cat, George H & Ella M Rodgers Memorial Library, 194 Derry Rd, Hudson, NH, 03051. Tel: 603-886-6030. p. 1368
Sweeney, Debbie, Asst Dir, Augusta County Library, 1759 Jefferson Hwy, Fishersville, VA, 22939. Tel: 540-885-3961, 540-949-6354. p. 2318
Sweeney, Felesha, Asst Br Mgr, Bossier Parish Libraries, Haughton Branch, 116 E McKinley Ave, Haughton, LA, 71037. Tel: 318-949-0196. p. 886
Sweeney, J Mark, Deputy Librarian of Congress, Principal, Library of Congress, James Madison Memorial Bldg, 101 Independence Ave SE, Washington, DC, 20540. Tel: 202-707-5000. p. 370
Sweeney, Jacqui, Research Librn, Texas Ranger Hall of Fame & Museum, 100 Texas Ranger Trail, Waco, TX, 76706. Tel: 254-750-8639. p. 2254
Sweeney, Julie, Instrul Serv Librn, Point Loma Nazarene University, 3900 Lomaland Dr, San Diego, CA, 92106-2899. Tel: 619-849-2312. p. 216
Sweeney Marsh, Joan, Assoc Vice Provost, Academic & Career Learning Resources, Sheridan College Library, 1430 Trafalgar Rd, Oakville, ON, L6H 2L1, CANADA. Tel: 905-845-9430, Ext 2480. p. 2663
Sweeney, Michael, Libr Mgr, Texas A&M University at Galveston, Bldg 3010, 200 Seawolf Pkwy, Galveston, TX, 77554. Tel: 409-740-4560. p. 2183
Sweeney, Miriam, Dr, Assoc Prof, University of Alabama, 7035 Gorgas Library, Campus Box 870252, Tuscaloosa, AL, 35487-0252. Tel: 205-348-4610. p. 2781
Sweeney, Nancy, Br Mgr, Fairfield Public Library, Fairfield Woods, 1147 Fairfield Woods Rd, Fairfield, CT, 06825. Tel: 203-255-7310. p. 312
Sweeney, Sarah, Digital Repository Librn, Northeastern University Libraries, 360 Huntington Ave, Boston, MA, 02115. Tel: 617-373-5062. p. 998
Sweeney, Stephen, Libr Dir, Cardinal Stafford Library, 1300 S Steele St, Denver, CO, 80210-2526. Tel: 303-715-3192. p. 273
Sweeney, Teresa Curran, Cat, Ser, Big Bend Community College Library, 1800 Bldg, 7662 Chanute St NE, Moses Lake, WA, 98837. Tel: 509-793-2350. p. 2371
Sweeney, Vicky, Asst Dir, Franklin-Springboro Public Library, 44 E Fourth St, Franklin, OH, 45005. Tel: 937-746-2665. p. 1786
Sweeper, Darren L, Govt Doc & Data Librn, Montclair State University, One Normal Ave, Montclair, NJ, 07043-1699. Tel: 973-655-7145. p. 1420
Sweet, Amanda, Tech Innovation Librn, Nebraska Library Commission, The Atrium, 1200 N St, Ste 120, Lincoln, NE, 68508-2023. Tel: 402-471-3106. p. 1322
Sweet, Arlene, Asst Librn, Aldrich Free Public Library, 299 Main St, Moosup, CT, 06354. Tel: 860-564-8760. p. 323
Sweet, Barbara, Dir/Chief Exec Officer, Prince Edward County Public Library, 208 Main St, Picton, ON, K0K 2T0, CANADA. Tel: 613-476-5962. p. 2673

Sweet, Barbee, Dir, Clarks Public Library, 101 W Amity, Clarks, NE, 68628. Tel: 308-548-2864. p. 1310
Sweet, Beth, Dir, D A Hurd Library, 41 High St, North Berwick, ME, 03906. Tel: 207-676-2215. p. 933
Sweet, Bob, Mgr, University of Michigan, Transportation Research Institute Library, 2901 Baxter Rd, Ann Arbor, MI, 48109-2150. Tel: 734-936-1073. p. 1080
Sweet, Christopher, Info Literacy Librn, Scholarly Communications Librn, Illinois Wesleyan University, One Ames Plaza, Bloomington, IL, 61701-7188. Tel: 309-556-3984. p. 543
Sweet, Dorene, Circ Mgr, Amherst Public Library, 221 Spring St, Amherst, OH, 44001. Tel: 440-988-4230. p. 1746
Sweet, Kimberly, Sr Res Librn, Ropes & Gray LLP Library, Prudential Tower, 800 Boylston St, Boston, MA, 02199. Tel: 617-951-7000. p. 999
Sweet, Russell, Assoc Dir, Boston University Libraries, Pappas Law Library, 765 Commonwealth Ave, Boston, MA, 02215. Tel: 617-353-8877. p. 993
Sweeter, Kristine, Librn, Whitingham Free Public Library, 2948 Vt Rte 100, Jacksonville, VT, 05342. Tel: 802-368-7506. p. 2286
Sweetland, Jessica, Head, Cat & Circ, Manchester Public Library, 586 Main St, Manchester, CT, 06040. Tel: 860-643-2471, p. 320
Sweetman, Kimberly, Assoc Dean of Libr, University of New Hampshire Library, 18 Library Way, Durham, NH, 03824. Tel: 603-862-1974. p. 1361
Sweetser, Michlle, Head Univ Archivist, Bowling Green State University Libraries, Center for Archival Collections, Jerome Library, 5th Flr, Bowling Green, OH, 43403. Tel: 419-372-2411. p. 1752
Swendsrud, Christina, History & Archives, Research Servs Librn, Le Moyne College, 1419 Salt Springs Rd, Syracuse, NY, 13214. Tel: 315-445-4153. p. 1648
Swensen, Rolf, Web Coordr, Queens College, Benjamin S Rosenthal Library, 65-30 Kissena Blvd, Flushing, NY, 11367-0904. Tel: 718-997-3700. p. 1534
Swenson, Beth, Adult Serv, Idaho Falls Public Library, 457 W Broadway, Idaho Falls, ID, 83402. Tel: 208-612-8460. p. 523
Swenson, Mark, Head, Info Tech, Winnetka-Northfield Public Library District, 768 Oak St, Winnetka, IL, 60093-2515. Tel: 847-446-7220. p. 664
Swenson, Suzanna, Dir, Lindsborg Community Library, 111 S Main St, Lindsborg, KS, 67456. Tel: 785-227-2710. p. 821
Swetel, Jeremiah, Chief Operating Officer, Cleveland Public Library, 325 Superior Ave, Cleveland, OH, 44114-1271. Tel: 216-623-2800. p. 1767
Swetman, Barbara, Acq/Ser Librn, Hamilton College, 198 College Hill Rd, Clinton, NY, 13323. Tel: 315-859-4470. p. 1519
Swets, Heidi, Libr Asst, Decorah Public Library, 202 Winnebago St, Decorah, IA, 52101. Tel: 563-382-3717. p. 744
Sweyko-Kuhlman, Dylan, Sr Archivist, Kansas Historical Society, 6425 SW Sixth Ave, Topeka, KS, 66615-1099. Tel: 785-272-8681. p. 838
Swiatek, Emma, Head, Res & Info Serv, King's University College at the University of Western Ontario, 266 Epworth Ave, London, ON, N6A 2M3, CANADA. Tel: 519-433-3491, Ext 4390. p. 2653
Swiatosz, Susan, Head, Spec Coll & Archives, University of North Florida, Bldg 12-Library, One UNF Dr, Jacksonville, FL, 32224-2645. Tel: 904-620-2615. p. 413
Swick, Jeremy, Curator, Historian, National Football Foundation's College, 250 Marietta St, Atlanta, GA, 30313-1591. Tel: 404-880-4800. p. 465
Swierat, Catherine, Circ Supvr, East Fishkill Community Library, 348 Rte 376, Hopewell Junction, NY, 12533-6075. Tel: 845-221-9943, Ext 228. p. 1548
Swierenga, Marianne, Cataloging & Metadata Librn, Western Michigan University, 1903 W Michigan Ave, WMU Mail Stop 5353, Kalamazoo, MI, 49008-5353. Tel: 269-387-4112. p. 1122
Swift, Caitlin, Assoc Dir, Head, Res Serv, Campbell University, Norman Adrian Wiggins School of Law Library, 225 Hillsborough St, Ste 203H, Raleigh, NC, 27603. Tel: 919-865-5869. p. 1676
Swift, Elizabeth, Syst Librn, Web Serv Mgr, Jefferson County Library Cooperative Inc, 2100 Park Place, Birmingham, AL, 35203-2794. Tel: 205-226-3615. p. 2761
Swift, Jim, IT Librn, Fairfield Public Library, 1080 Old Post Rd, Fairfield, CT, 06824. Tel: 203-256-3155. p. 312
Swift, L G, Library Contact, Fort Worth Library, COOL (Cavile Outreach Opportunity Library), 5060 Ave G, Fort Worth, TX, 76105-1906. Tel: 817-392-5512. p. 2179
Swift, L G, Ms, Librn, Fort Worth Library, BOLD (Butler Outreach Library Division), 1801 N South Frwy, Fort Worth, TX, 76102-5742. Tel: 817-392-5514. p. 2179
Swift, L G, Ms, Supvr, Fort Worth Library, eSkills Library & Job Center, 2800 Stark St, Fort Worth, TX, 76112. Tel: 817-392-6621. p. 2179
Swift, L G, Ms, Librn, Fort Worth Library, Ella Mae Shamblee, 1062 Evans Ave, Fort Worth, TX, 76104-5135. Tel: 817-392-5580. p. 2180
Swift, Leah, Library Contact, R V Anderson Associates Ltd Library, 2001 Sheppard Ave E, Ste 400, Toronto, ON, M2J 4Z8, CANADA. Tel: 416-497-8600, Ext 1230. p. 2686
Swift, Matt, State Law Librn, Wyoming Supreme Court, Supreme Court Bldg, 2301 Capitol Ave, Cheyenne, WY, 82002. Tel: 307-777-7509. p. 2493
Swift, Rebecca, Librn, Central Arizona College, Aravaipa Campus Learning Resource Center, 80440 E Aravaipa Rd, Winkelman, AZ, 85192. Tel: 520-357-2821. p. 58
Swihart, Cheryl, Librn, Crestline Public Library, 324 N Thoman St, Crestline, OH, 44827-1410. Tel: 419-683-3909. p. 1779
Swihart, Mona, Librn, Bainum Library, 128 E Broadway, Glenwood, AR, 71943. Tel: 870-356-5193. p. 96
Swilley, Polly, Dir, Libr Serv, Southern Regional Technical College Library Services, 15689 US Hwy 19 N, Thomasville, GA, 31792. Tel: 229-225-3958. p. 498
Swilley, Polly, Dir, Libr Serv, Southern Regional Technical College Library Services, Veterans Parkway Campus, 800 Veterans Pkwy N, Moultrie, GA, 31788. Tel: 229-227-2576. p. 499
Swincicki, Holly, Asst Libr Dir, Morton Township Library, 110 S James, Mecosta, MI, 49332-9334. Tel: 231-972-8315, Ext 204. p. 1131
Swindle, Ginann, Libr Mgr, Central Arkansas Library System, Amy Sanders Branch, 10200 Johnson Dr, Sherwood, AR, 72120. Tel: 501-835-7756. p. 101
Swindle, Janet, Br Mgr, Dixie Regional Library System, Edmondson Memorial, 109 Stovall St, Vardaman, MS, 38878. Tel: 662-682-7333. p. 1230
Swindon, Kara, Libr Spec, Dean College, 99 Main St, Franklin, MA, 02038-1994. Tel: 508-541-1771. p. 1020
Swingen, Lisa, Dir, Crystal Lake Public Library, 225 State Ave S, Crystal Lake, IA, 50432. Tel: 641-565-3325. p. 743
Swingen, Lisa, Dir, Woden Public Library, 304 Main St, Woden, IA, 50484. Tel: 641-926-5716. p. 792
Swingruber, Jurinda, Br Mgr, Fort Vancouver Regional Library District, La Center Community Library, 1411 NE Lockwood Creek Rd, La Center, WA, 98629. Tel: 360-906-4760. p. 2391
Swink, Selena, Br Mgr, Lake Public Library, City Hall, 100 Front St, Lake, MS, 39092. Tel: 601-775-3560. p. 1224
Swinney, Victoria, PhD, Dir, Oklahoma City University, 2501 N Blackwelder, Oklahoma City, OK, 73106. Tel: 405-208-5068. p. 1858
Swiscz, Doug, Asst Libr Dir, Barrington Public Library, 281 County Rd, Barrington, RI, 02806. Tel: 401-247-1920. p. 2029
Swisher, Cody, Pub Serv Asst, United Lutheran Seminary, 66 Seminary Ridge, Gettysburg, PA, 17325. Tel: 717-338-3014. p. 1936
Swisher, Sherry, Br Mgr, Akron-Summit County Public Library, Green Branch, 4046 Massillon Rd, Uniontown, OH, 44685-4046. Tel: 330-896-9074. p. 1744
Swistock, Darlene, Mem Serv Coordr, Bergen County Cooperative Library System, Inc, 21-00 Route 208 S, Ste 130, Fair Lawn, NJ, 07410. Tel: 201-498-7301. p. 2770
Swiszcz, Jane, Ref Serv, Stonehill College, 320 Washington St, Easton, MA, 02357. Tel: 508-565-1452. p. 1016
Switzer, Amy, Dir, Shaker Heights Public Library, 16500 Van Aken Blvd, Shaker Heights, OH, 44120. Tel: 216-991-2030. p. 1820
Switzer, Elizabeth, Libr Dir, Worthington West Franklin Community Library, 214 E Main St, Ste 1, Worthington, PA, 16262. Tel: 724-297-3762. p. 2024
Switzer, Jenny, Libr Asst, Iberia Parish Library, Jeanerette Branch, 411 Kentucky St, Jeanerette, LA, 70544. Tel: 337-276-4014. p. 900
Switzer, Justin, Br Mgr, Enoch Pratt Free Library, Orleans Street Branch, 1303 Orleans St, Baltimore, MD, 21231. Tel: 443-984-3914. p. 953
Switzer, Linda, Librn, Greater West Central Public Library District, Plymouth Branch, 129 W Side Sq, Plymouth, IL, 62367. Tel: 309-458-6616. p. 538
Swonger, Stephanie, Dir, Minneola City Library, 112 Main St, Minneola, KS, 67865. Tel: 620-885-4749. p. 825
Swope, Jeff, Exec Dir, Cumberland County Law Library, Bosler Library, 158 W High St, Carlisle, PA, 17013. Tel: 717-243-4642. p. 1919
Swope, Jeffrey D, Exec Dir, Bosler Memorial Library, 158 W High St, Carlisle, PA, 17013-2988. Tel: 717-243-4642. p. 1918
Swope, Leslie, Dir, Saint Mary's Public Library, 127 Center St, Saint Marys, PA, 15857. Tel: 814-834-6141. p. 2002
Sword, Amee, Dir, Wornstaff Memorial Public Library, 302 E High St, Ashley, OH, 43003. Tel: 740-747-2085. p. 1747
Sword, Shannan, Libr Mgr, Mississauga Library System, Courtneypark, 730 Courtneypark Dr W, Mississauga, ON, L5W 1L9, CANADA. Tel: 905-615-4745. p. 2659
Sword, Shannan, Libr Mgr, Mississauga Library System, Malton Branch, 3540 Morningstar Dr, Malton, ON, L4T 1Y2, CANADA. Tel: 905-615-4640. p. 2659
Swords, Kasey, Br Mgr, Pickens County Library System, Sarlin Branch, 15 S Palmetto St, Liberty, SC, 29658. Tel: 864-843-5805. p. 2058
Swygart-Hobaugh, Mandy, Dr, Head, Res Serv, Georgia State University, 100 Decatur St SE, Atlanta, GA, 30303-3202. Tel: 404-413-2864. p. 464
Sydorenko, Wasyl, Ref Spec, University of Toronto Libraries, Petro Jacyk Central & East European Resource Centre, Robarts Library, 130 St George St,3rd Flr, Rm 3008, Toronto, ON, M5S 1A5, CANADA. Tel: 416-978-0588. p. 2699
Sydow, Caleb, Dir, Bicknell-Vigo Township Public Library, 201 W Second St, Bicknell, IN, 47512. Tel: 812-735-2317. p. 669
Syed, Marvieluz, Asst Librn, Joeten-Kiyu Public Library, Tinian Public, PO Box 520704, Tinian, MP, 96952. Tel: 670-433-0504. p. 2507
Sykes, Diana, Access Serv Librn, Erikson Institute, 451 N LaSalle St, Ste 210, Chicago, IL, 60654. Tel: 312-893-7210. p. 561
Sykes, Frank, Dir, Livonia Public Library, Two Washington St, Livonia, NY, 14487. Tel: 585-346-3450. p. 1564

Syler, Heidi, Dir, Info Literacy, Dir, Instrul Tech, University of the South, 178 Georgia Ave, Sewanee, TN, 37383-1000. Tel: 931-598-1709. p. 2126
Sylka, Christina, Head Librn, University of British Columbia Library, David Lam Management Research Library, UBC Sauder School of Business, 2033 Main Mall, Vancouver, BC, V6T 1Z2, CANADA. Tel: 604-822-9390. p. 2580
Sylvain, Matt, Chair, Libr Serv, University of Massachusetts Dartmouth Library, 285 Old Westport Rd, North Dartmouth, MA, 02747-2300. Tel: 508-999-8682. p. 1041
Sylvester, Brian, Libr Dir, Dover Public Library, 35 Loockerman Plaza, Dover, DE, 19901. Tel: 302-736-7030. p. 352
Sylvester, Cheryl, Libr Dir, Oskaloosa Public Library, 315 Jefferson St, Oskaloosa, KS, 66066. Tel: 785-863-2475. p. 829
Sylvia, Margaret, Asst Dir, Tech Serv, Saint Mary's University, Louis J Blume Library, One Camino Santa Maria, San Antonio, TX, 78228-8608. Tel: 210-436-3441. p. 2238
Symes, Christine, Library Contact, Schenectady County Public Library, Mont Pleasant, 1036 Crane St, Schenectady, NY, 12303. Tel: 518-386-2245. p. 1638
Symington, Nancy, Libr Dir, Dennis Memorial Library Association, 1020 Old Bass River Rd, Dennis, MA, 02638. Tel: 508-385-2255. p. 1014
Symons, Diana, Assoc Dir, Learning & Research, College of Saint Benedict, 37 S College Ave, Saint Joseph, MN, 56374. Tel: 320-363-5296. p. 1199
Symons, John, Mgr, Miami-Dade Public Library System, International Mall Branch, 10315 NW 12 St, Miami, FL, 33172. Tel: 305-594-2514. p. 423
Symons, Ken, Services Administrator, Brantford Public Library, 173 Colborne St, Brantford, ON, N3T 2G8, CANADA. Tel: 519-756-2220, Ext 3320. p. 2633
Sympson, Penny, Librn, Wiss, Janney, Elstner Associates, Inc, 330 Pfingsten Rd, Northbrook, IL, 60062. Tel: 847-272-7400, 847-753-7202. p. 627
Syms, Laura, Librn, Cape Breton University Library, 1250 Grand Lake Rd, Sydney, NS, B1P 6L2, CANADA. Tel: 902-563-1320. p. 2623
Synnestvedt, Betty, Coord, Ad Serv, Minor Memorial Library, 23 South St, Roxbury, CT, 06783. Tel: 860-350-2181. p. 335
Synnett, Veronique, Librn, Bibliotheque de l'Hopital Montfort, 713 Chemin Montreal, 2D-113, Ottawa, ON, K1K 0T2, CANADA. Tel: 613-746-4621, Ext 6045. p. 2664
Synowka, Natasha, Libr Dir, Ivy Tech Community College, 50 W Fall Creek Pkwy N Dr, Indianapolis, IN, 46208. Tel: 317-921-4782. p. 697
Sypert, Juanita, Coll, Govt Doc Coordr, Howard Payne University, 1000 Fisk St, Brownwood, TX, 76801. Tel: 325-649-8096. p. 2150
Szabo, John F, City Librn, Los Angeles Public Library System, 630 W Fifth St, Los Angeles, CA, 90071. Tel: 213-228-7515. p. 163
Szajewski, Michael, Asst Dean, Special Colls & Digital Scholarships, Ball State University Libraries, 2000 W University Ave, Muncie, IN, 47306-1099. Tel: 765-285-5078. p. 708
Szajewski, Michael, Asst Dean, Special Colls & Digital Scholarships, Ball State University Libraries, Archives & Special Collections, Bracken Library, Rm 210, Muncie, IN, 47306-0161. Tel: 765-285-5078. p. 708
Szajewski, Michael, Assoc Dean, Spec Coll, University of Oklahoma Libraries, 401 W Brooks St, Norman, OK, 73019. Tel: 405-325-3341. p. 1856
Szalkowski, Barbara, Core Operations Librn, South Texas College of Law Houston, 1303 San Jacinto St, Houston, TX, 77002-7006. Tel: 713-646-1724. p. 2198
Szarejko, Celia, Dir, Tech/Content Serv, East Tennessee State University, Sherrod Library, Seehorn Dr & Lake St, Johnson City, TN, 37614-0204. Tel: 423-439-4337. p. 2103
Szarek, April, Genealogy Serv, C E Brehm Memorial Public Library District, 101 S Seventh St, Mount Vernon, IL, 62864. Tel: 618-242-6322. p. 621
Szczepaniak, Adam, Jr, Dep State Librn, NJSL Talking Bk & Braille Ctr, Dir, New Jersey State Library, Talking Book & Braille Center, 2300 Stuyvesant Ave, Trenton, NJ, 08618. Tel: 604-406-7179, Ext 801. p. 1448
Szczesny, Gregg, Fac Mgr, Palatine Public Library District, 700 N North Ct, Palatine, IL, 60067. Tel: 847-907-3600. p. 631
Szeles, Lisa, Br Mgr, Stark County District Library, Perry Sippo Branch, 5710 12th St NW, Canton, OH, 44708. Tel: 330-477-8482. p. 1756
Szichak, Ryan, Librn, California Department of Corrections Library System, Mule Creek State Prison, 4001 Hwy 104, Ione, CA, 95640. Tel: 209-274-4911, Ext 6409. p. 207
Szidik, Mark, Chief Info Officer, Midwest Collaborative for Library Services, 1407 Rensen St, Ste 1, Lansing, MI, 48910. p. 2767
Szilagyi, John, Libr Dir, Lansing Community College Library, Technology & Learning Ctr, 400 N Capitol Ave, Lansing, MI, 48933. Tel: 517-483-1650. p. 1125
Szitas, Emily, Coll Develop/E-Res Librn, Indiana University of Pennsylvania, 431 S 11th St, Rm 203, Indiana, PA, 15705-1096. Tel: 724-357-2330. p. 1946
Szitas, Emily M, Pub Serv Librn, Carlow University, 3333 Fifth Ave, Pittsburgh, PA, 15213. Tel: 412-578-2049. p. 1990
Szostak, Sue Crites, Dir, Poplar Bluff Municipal Library, 318 N Main St, Poplar Bluff, MO, 63901. Tel: 573-686-8639, Ext 25. p. 1266
Szosz, Eva, Spec Coll, Libraries of Foster, Tyler Free Library, 81A Moosup Valley Rd, Foster, RI, 02825. Tel: 401-397-7930. p. 2032
Szponar, Pawel, Tech & Syst Librn, Foothill College, 12345 El Monte Rd, Los Altos Hills, CA, 94022-4599. p. 159
Szurek, Jaro, Chair, Cat, Samford University Library, 800 Lakeshore Dr, Birmingham, AL, 35229. Tel: 205-726-4136. p. 8
Szuszkiewicz, Patty, Br Supvr, Clermont County Public Library, Bethel Branch, 611 W Plane St, Bethel, OH, 45106-1302. Tel: 513-734-2619. p. 1803
Szwagiel, Will, Head, Tech Serv, Wayne County Public Library, 1001 E Ash St, Goldsboro, NC, 27530. Tel: 919-299-8105, Ext 8010. p. 1691
Szwed, Michael, Tech Mgr, Palatine Public Library District, 700 N North Ct, Palatine, IL, 60067. Tel: 847-907-3600. p. 631
Szymanik, Susan, Br Mgr, Burlington County Library System, Evesham Library, Evesham Municipal Complex, 984 Tuckerton Rd, Marlton, NJ, 08053. Tel: 856-983-1444. p. 1454
Szymanski, Cynthia, Assoc Librn, Head, Tech Serv, Indiana University Northwest, 3400 Broadway, Gary, IN, 46408. Tel: 219-980-6521. p. 686
Szymanski, Sheri, Libr Dir, Stratford Library Association, 2203 Main St, Stratford, CT, 06615. Tel: 203-385-4160. p. 340
Szymanski, Tina, Librn, Immaculate Heart of Mary Parish Library, 3700 Canyon Rd, Los Alamos, NM, 87544. Tel: 505-662-6193. p. 1472
Szymczak, Victoria, Dir, Law Libr & Assoc Prof of Law, University of Hawaii, 2525 Dole St, Honolulu, HI, 96822-2328. Tel: 808-956-5581, 808-956-7583. p. 513
Tabaei, Sara, Info Literacy Librn, Touro College Libraries, 320 W 31st St, New York, NY, 10001. Tel: 212-463-0400, Ext 55321. p. 1603
Tabah-Percival, Rebekah, VPres, Archives & Libr, Arizona Historical Society Museum Library & Archives, 1300 N College Ave, Tempe, AZ, 85281. Tel: 480-387-5355. p. 79
Tabah-Percival, Rebekah, Coll, VPres, Archives & Libr, Arizona Historical Society, 949 E Second St, Tucson, AZ, 85719. Tel: 520-617-1157. p. 81
Tabatabai, Habib, Exec Dir, University of Central Oklahoma, Chambers Library, 100 N University Dr, Edmond, OK, 73034. Tel: 405-974-2865. p. 1846
Tabb, Winston, Dean, Johns Hopkins University Libraries, The Sheridan Libraries, 3400 N Charles St, Baltimore, MD, 21218. Tel: 410-516-8328. p. 954
Taber, Brenda, Treas, Coles County Historical Society, Mattoon Depot, 1718 Broadway Ave, Mattoon, IL, 61938. Tel: 217-235-6744. p. 615
Taber, Kolette, Sr Mgr, Canadian Life & Health Insurance Association, Inc, 79 Wellington St W, Ste 2300, Toronto, ON, M5K 1G8, CANADA. Tel: 416-777-2221, Ext 3070. p. 2687
Taber, Philip, Librn, University of New Brunswick, Saint John Campus, 100 Tucker Park Rd, Saint John, NB, E2L 4L5, CANADA. Tel: 506-648-5710. p. 2605
Taber, Tory, Dir, Dodge Library, Nine Fisk Rd, West Chazy, NY, 12992. Tel: 518-493-6131. p. 1661
Tabish, Colleen, Librn, Kitscoty Public Library, 4910 51 St, Kitscoty, AB, T0B 2P0, CANADA. Tel: 780-846-2822. p. 2544
Taboada, Monica, Br Mgr, Indianapolis Public Library, Haughville, 2121 W Michigan St, Indianapolis, IN, 46222-3862. Tel: 317-275-4420. p. 695
Tabor, Allison, Youth Serv Coordr, Harrison Village Library, Four Front St, Harrison, ME, 04040. Tel: 207-583-2970. p. 927
Tabor, Emily, Family Serv Librn, North Liberty Library, 520 W Cherry St, North Liberty, IA, 52317-9797. Tel: 319-626-5701. p. 773
Tabor, Kristen, Dep Dir, Art Circle Public Library, Three East St, Crossville, TN, 38555. Tel: 931-484-6790. p. 2095
Tabor, Leslie, Dir, Tompkins County Public Library, 101 E Green St, Ithaca, NY, 14850-5613. Tel: 607-272-4557. p. 1553
Tabusa, Phyllis, Info Spec, East-West Center, John A Burns Hall, Rm 4063 & 4066, 1601 East-West Rd, Honolulu, HI, 96848-1601. Tel: 808-944-7450. p. 506
Taccone, Corrina, Research Librn, Ontario Ministry of Education, College Park, 777 Bay St, Ste 3201, Toronto, ON, M7A 1L2, CANADA. Tel: 416-215-0855. p. 2691
Tacey, Amber, Libr Operations Spec, Mohave Community College Library, 1971 Jagerson Ave, Kingman, AZ, 86409-1238. Tel: 928-692-3008. p. 64
Tacey, Sheila, Libr Tech, United States Navy, Naval Hospital Library, HP01 One Boone Rd, Bremerton, WA, 98312-1898. Tel: 360-475-4316. p. 2360
Tacke, Melissa, Libr Dir, Castleton Public Library, 85 S Main St, Castleton-on-Hudson, NY, 12033. Tel: 518-732-0879. p. 1514
Tackett, Ben, Librn, Fruitland Baptist Bible College, 1455 Gillaim Rd, Hendersonville, NC, 28792. Tel: 828-685-8886, Ext 3. p. 1695
Tackett, Eddie, II, Dir, Buffalo Creek Memorial Library, 511 E McDonald Ave, Man, WV, 25635. Tel: 304-583-7887. p. 2407
Tackett, Sara, Dir, Jackson District Library, 244 W Michigan Ave, Jackson, MI, 49201. Tel: 517-788-4087. p. 1120
Tackett, Sara, Dir, Jackson District Library, Carnegie Library, 244 W Michigan Ave, Jackson, MI, 49201. Tel: 517-788-4087. p. 1120
Tackitt, Suzanne, Coordr, Flagstaff Medical Center, 1200 N Beaver St, Flagstaff, AZ, 86001. Tel: 928-773-2418. p. 60
Tacoma, Laurel, Br Mgr, Fairfax County Public Library, Thomas Jefferson Branch, 7415 Arlington Blvd, Falls Church, VA, 22042-7499. Tel: 703-573-1060. p. 2316

Taddonio, Courtney, Mgr, Libr Operations, Metropolitan Library System in Oklahoma County, Ronald J Norick Downtown Library, 300 Park Ave, Oklahoma City, OK, 73102-3600. p. 1857

Taddonio, Courtney, Mgr, Libr Operations, Metropolitan Library System in Oklahoma County, Wright Extension Library, 2101 Exchange Ave, Oklahoma City, OK, 73108-2625. p. 1858

Tadman, Andrew, Ref Coordr, East Baton Rouge Parish Library, 7711 Goodwood Blvd, Baton Rouge, LA, 70806-7625. Tel: 225-231-3735. p. 882

Taffe, Michael, Brother, Librn, Assumption Abbey Library, 418 Third Ave W, Richardton, ND, 58652-7100. Tel: 701-974-3315. p. 1739

Tafolla, Gabriela, Head, Community Engagement, Addison Public Library, Four Friendship Plaza, Addison, IL, 60101. Tel: 630-543-3617. p. 535

Taft, Alyssa, Teen Librn, Cranston Public Library, 140 Sockanosset Cross Rd, Cranston, RI, 02920-5539. Tel: 401-943-9080. p. 2031

Tag, Sylvia, Children's & YA Literature Librn, Western Washington University, 516 High St, MS 9103, Bellingham, WA, 98225. Tel: 360-650-7992. p. 2358

Tagak, Katharine, Mgr, Libr Serv, Nunavut Arctic College, Bag 002, Rankin Inlet, NU, X0C 0G0, CANADA. Tel: 867-979-7219. p. 2625

Taggar, Harsh, Coordr, Info Serv, Pratt Institute Libraries, Pratt Manhattan Library, 144 W 14th St, Rm 410, New York, NY, 10011-7301. Tel: 212-647-7546. p. 1506

Taggart, Eric, Dir, Rodman Public Library, 215 E Broadway St, Alliance, OH, 44601-2694. Tel: 330-821-2665. p. 1745

Taggart, Jen, Head, Youth Serv, Bloomfield Township Public Library, 1099 Lone Pine Rd, Bloomfield Township, MI, 48302-2410. Tel: 248-642-5800. p. 1086

Taggart, Katherine, Mgr, Res Serv, Lowenstein Sandler LLP Library, One Lowenstein Dr, Roseland, NJ, 07068. Tel: 973-422-6442. p. 1440

Taggart, Susan, Br Mgr, Saint Tammany Parish Library, Bush Branch, 81597 Hwy 41, Bush, LA, 70431. Tel: 985-886-3588. p. 888

Tagge, Natalie, Head Librn, Temple University School of Podiatric Medicine, 148 N Eighth St, Philadelphia, PA, 19107. Tel: 215-777-5775. p. 1986

Tagliaferro, Jessica, Chair, Electronic Res Librn, SUNY Westchester Community College, 75 Grasslands Rd, Valhalla, NY, 10595. Tel: 914-606-6808. p. 1656

Tagtmeyer, Peter, Sci Librn, Colgate University, George R Cooley Science Library, 13 Oak Dr, Hamilton, NY, 13346-1338. Tel: 315-228-7402. p. 1543

Tahaney, Erin, Librn, Princeton Library in New York, 15 W 43rd St, New York, NY, 10036. Tel: 212-596-1250. p. 1600

Tahir, Peggy, Copyright Librn, Research Librn, University of California San Francisco, 530 Parnassus Ave, San Francisco, CA, 94143. Tel: 415-476-5765. p. 229

Tahirkheli, Sharon, Dir, Info Serv, American Geological Institute Library, 4220 King St, Alexandria, VA, 22302-1502. Tel: 703-379-2480, Ext 239. p. 2303

Tai, Andrew, Children & Youth Serv Librn, Gladys E Kelly Public Library, Two Lake St, Webster, MA, 01570. Tel: 508-949-3880. p. 1063

Tai, I-Chene, Tech Serv Librn, Le Moyne College, 1419 Salt Springs Rd, Syracuse, NY, 13214. Tel: 315-445-4331. p. 1648

Tai, Marie, Dir, Harvard Library, Houghton Library-Rare Books & Manuscripts, Houghton Library, Harvard Yard, Cambridge, MA, 02138. Tel: 617-495-2440. p. 1007

Taillieu, Cheryl, Libr Mgr, Seba Beach Public Library, 140 Third St, Seba Beach, AB, T0E 2B0, CANADA. Tel: 780-797-3940. p. 2553

Taillon, Francois, Dir, Societe Historique de la Cote-du-Sud, 100 4e Ave Painchaud, La Pocatiere, QC, G0R 1Z0, CANADA. Tel: 418-856-2104. p. 2714

Taillon, Marie-Claude, Ref Serv, Bibliotheques de Trois-Rivieres, 1425 Place de l'Hotel de Ville, Trois-Rivieres, QC, G9A 5L9, CANADA. Tel: 819-372-4641, Ext 4317. p. 2737

Tairov, Giovanni, Dep State Librn, State Library of Louisiana, 701 N Fourth St, Baton Rouge, LA, 70802-5232. Tel: 225-342-4923. p. 884

Tait, Joe, Librn, Cleveland Museum of Natural History, One Wade Oval Dr, University Circle, Cleveland, OH, 44106-1767. Tel: 216-231-4600, Ext 3222. p. 1767

Tait, Laura, Libr Mgr, Niagara-on-the-Lake Public Library, Ten Anderson Lane, Niagara-on-the-Lake, ON, L0S 1J0, CANADA. Tel: 905-468-2023. p. 2661

Tait, Lori, Librn, Coventry Public Library, Greene Public, 179 Hopkins Hollow Rd, Greene, RI, 02827. Tel: 401-397-3873. p. 2031

Tait, Lori, Youth Serv Coordr, Libraries of Foster, Tyler Free Library, 81A Moosup Valley Rd, Foster, RI, 02825. Tel: 401-397-7930. p. 2032

Tait, Sue, Dir, The Episcopal Diocese of Olympia, 1551 Tenth Ave E, Seattle, WA, 98102. Tel: 206-325-4200, Ext 2043. p. 2376

Tait-Ripperdan, Rachel, Asst Librn, Florida Gulf Coast University Library, 10501 FGCU Blvd S, Fort Myers, FL, 33965. Tel: 239-590-7661. p. 403

Tajerian, Ardem, Sr Librn, Los Angeles Public Library System, Sunland-Tujunga Branch Library, 7771 Foothill Blvd, Tujunga, CA, 91042-2137. Tel: 818-352-4481. p. 165

Takagi, Melissa, Libr Mgr, Grossmont College Library, 8800 Grossmont College Dr, El Cajon, CA, 92020-1799. Tel: 619-644-7359. p. 139

Takahashi, Nina, Libr Tech, Natural Resources Canada Library, 605 Robson St, Ste 1500, Vancouver, BC, V6B 5J3, CANADA. Tel: 604-666-1147. p. 2579

Takala, Paul, Chief Librn/CEO, Hamilton Public Library, 55 York Blvd, Hamilton, ON, L8R 3K1, CANADA. Tel: 905-546-3200, Ext 3215. p. 2645

Takamoto, Tina, Br Mgr, Hawaii State Public Library System, Aiea Public Library, 99-374 Pohai Pl, Aiea, HI, 96701. Tel: 808-483-7333. p. 507

Takasugi, Ross, Librn, Cuyamaca College Library, 900 Rancho San Diego Pkwy, El Cajon, CA, 92019. Tel: 619-660-4416. p. 139

Takorian, Holly, Adult Serv, Asst Librn, Merriam-Gilbert Public Library, Three W Main St, West Brookfield, MA, 01585. Tel: 508-867-1410. p. 1065

Talaroc, Monika, Distance Learning Librn, Baptist Health System, 8400 Datapoint Dr, San Antonio, TX, 78229. Tel: 210-297-7639. p. 2236

Talbert, Carol, Libr Tech, Big Sandy Community & Technical College, Mayo-Paintsville Campus, Bldg C, 513 Third St, Paintsville, KY, 41240. Tel: 606-886-7343. p. 873

Talbert, Cheryl, Dir, Blakesburg Public Library, 407 S Wilson St, Blakesburg, IA, 52536. Tel: 641-938-2834. p. 735

Talbert, Cheryl, Dir, Libr Serv, Indian Hills Community College, 721 N First St, Bldg CV06, Centerville, IA, 52544. Tel: 641-856-2143, Ext 2237. p. 739

Talbert, Penny, Dir, Ephrata Public Library, 550 S Reading Rd, Ephrata, PA, 17522. Tel: 717-738-9291. p. 1930

Talbert, Rachel, YA Librn, Bernards Township Library, 32 S Maple Ave, Basking Ridge, NJ, 07920-1216. Tel: 908-204-3031. p. 1388

Talbot, David, Libr Tech, Centre Jeunesse de Montreal - Institut universitaire, 1001 boul de Maisonneuve est, 5ieme etage, Montreal, QC, H2L 4P9, CANADA. Tel: 514-896-3396. p. 2722

Talbot, Emily, Br Mgr, Nashville Public Library, Hermitage Branch, 3700 James Kay Lane, Hermitage, TN, 37076. Tel: 615-880-3951. p. 2119

Talbot, Faye, Librn, Louisiana State Penitentiary Library, Main Prison Library, A Bldg, 17544 Tunica Trace, Angola, LA, 70712. Tel: 225-655-2031. p. 881

Talbot, Hélène, Libr Tech, Institut de Technologie Agroalimentaire, Campus La Pocatière, 401 rue Poire, local 202, La Pocatiere, QC, G0R 1Z0, CANADA. Tel: 418-856-1110, Ext 1257. p. 2714

Talbot, Kathleen, Br Mgr, Cochise County Library District, Myrtle Kraft Library, 2393 S Rock House Rd, Portal, AZ, 85632. Tel: 520-558-2468. p. 56

Talbott, Lauren, Mgr, County of Los Angeles Public Library, Pico Rivera Library, 9001 Mines Ave, Pico Rivera, CA, 90660-3098. Tel: 562-942-7394. p. 137

Talbott, Lauren, Mgr, County of Los Angeles Public Library, Rivera Library, 7828 S Serapis Ave, Pico Rivera, CA, 90660-4600. Tel: 562-949-5485. p. 137

Talbott, Sherry, Dir, Blandinsville-Hire District Library, 130 S Main St, Blandinsville, IL, 61420. Tel: 309-652-3166. p. 542

Talbott, William, Libr Dir, Sheridan Public Library, 109 E Hamilton St, Sheridan, MT, 59749. Tel: 406-842-5770. p. 1302

Talcott, Becky, Colls Mgr, Woodstock History Center, 26 Elm St, Woodstock, VT, 05091. Tel: 802-457-1822. p. 2300

Tales, Matt, Head, Cat & Metadata Serv, Wilfrid Laurier University Library, 75 University Ave W, Waterloo, ON, N2L 3C5, CANADA. Tel: 519-884-0710, Ext 3839. p. 2703

Talhelm, Katie, Mgr, Programming, Victoria Public Library, 302 N Main St, Victoria, TX, 77901. Tel: 361-485-3302. p. 2252

Talio, Christine, Tech Serv, East Meadow Public Library, 1886 Front St, East Meadow, NY, 11554-1705. Tel: 516-794-2570. p. 1528

Talkington, Lauren, Circ, Shelby County Public Library, 309 Eighth St, Shelbyville, KY, 40065. Tel: 502-633-3803. p. 874

Tallant, Matt, Proc Archivist, North Dakota State University Libraries, 1201 Albrecht Blvd, Fargo, ND, 58108. Tel: 701-231-8877. p. 1733

Tallant, Matt, Proc Archivist, North Dakota State University Libraries, NDSU Archives/Institute For Regional Studies, NDSU West Bldg, Rm 123, 3551 7th Ave N, Fargo, ND, 58102. Tel: 701-231-8877. p. 1733

Tallent, Tony, Chief Innovation Officer, Chief Programs Officer, Richland Library, 1431 Assembly St, Columbia, SC, 29201-3101. Tel: 803-799-9084. p. 2054

Talley, Helen, Br Mgr, McKinney Memorial Public Library, John & Judy Gay Library, 6861 W Eldorado Pkwy, McKinney, TX, 75070. p. 2218

Talley, Lesley, Asst Libr Dir, Safford City-Graham County Library, 808 S Seventh Ave, Safford, AZ, 85546. Tel: 928-432-4169. p. 76

Tallis, Melissa, Youth Serv Coordr, Way Public Library, 101 E Indiana Ave, Perrysburg, OH, 43551. Tel: 419-874-3135, Ext 109. p. 1815

Tallman, Jonathan, Librn, Kingsport Public Library & Archives, 400 Broad St, Kingsport, TN, 37660-4292. Tel: 423-224-2539. p. 2104

Talpey, Carolyn, Dir, Jackman Public Library, 604 Main St, Jackman, ME, 04945. Tel: 207-668-2110. p. 928

Talpos, Paul, Asst Curator, Chief, Dearborn Historical Museum Library, Dearborn Historical Museum, 915 Brady St, Dearborn, MI, 48126. Tel: 313-565-3000. p. 1095

Talucci, Mary, Librn, Dorathea Zeoli Public Library, Two Rd C, Audubon Park, NJ, 08106. Tel: 856-323-8771. p. 1388

Tarala, Carol M, Libr Asst, Ref Librn, Dennis Memorial Library Association, 1020 Old Bass River Rd, Dennis, MA, 02638. Tel: 508-385-2255. p. 1014
Tarango, Adolfo, Actg Head, University of British Columbia Library, Xwi7xwa Library-First Nations House of Learning, 1985 West Mall, Vancouver, BC, V6T 1Z2, CANADA. Tel: 604-822-9615. p. 2580
Tarantino, Jane, Ch, Rutherford Public Library, 150 Park Ave, Rutherford, NJ, 07070. Tel: 201-939-8600. p. 1441
Taranto, Lisa, Head, Tech Serv, Abbot Public Library, Three Brook Rd, Marblehead, MA, 01945. Tel: 781-631-1481. p. 1031
Taranto, Michael, Br Mgr, West Florida Public Library, West Florida Genealogy, 5740 N Ninth Ave, Pensacola, FL, 32504. Tel: 850-494-7373. p. 437
Tarantowicz, Thomas A, Dir, Brentwood Public Library, 34 Second Ave, Brentwood, NY, 11717. Tel: 631-273-7883. p. 1496
Taras, Yolanda, Librn, Balzekas Museum of Lithuanian Culture, 6500 S Pulaski Rd, Chicago, IL, 60629. Tel: 773-582-6500. p. 554
Tarbett, Megan, Dir, Putnam County Library, 4219 State Rte 34, Hurricane, WV, 25526. Tel: 304-757-9680. p. 2405
Tarbox, Anita, Br Mgr, Henrico County Public Library, Sandston Branch Library, 23 E Williamsburg Rd, Sandston, VA, 23150. Tel: 804-501-1990. p. 2326
Tarbox, Scott, Ref Librn, Santa Fe College, 3000 NW 83rd St, Bldg Y, Gainesville, FL, 32606. Tel: 352-395-5233. p. 407
Tarbuck, Barbara, Dir, H A Peine District Library, 202 N Main St, Minier, IL, 61759. Tel: 309-392-3220. p. 618
Tardiff, Anthony, Engagement Librn, Instruction Librn, Gonzaga University, 502 E Boone Ave, Spokane, WA, 99258-0095. Tel: 509-313-3844. p. 2383
Tardy, Joanne, Asst Librn, Monson Free Public Library, 35 Greenville Rd, Monson, ME, 04464-6432. Tel: 207-997-3476. p. 932
Tarmann, Anastasia, Digital Projects Librn, Alaska State Library, 395 Whittier St, Juneau, AK, 99801. Tel: 907-465-2920. p. 47
Tarnowski, Kristin, Libr Spec, Humboldt County Library, Denio Branch, 190 Pueblo Dr, Denio, NV, 89404. Tel: 775-941-0330. p. 1351
Tarpey, Anne, Sr Librn, Texas Department of State Health Services, 1100 W 49th St, Austin, TX, 78756-3199. Tel: 512-776-2882. p. 2140
Tarpley, Kelly, Dir, Ruby Pickens Tartt Public Library, 201 Monroe St, Livingston, AL, 35470. Tel: 205-652-2349. p. 24
Tarply, Kelly, Dir, Sumter County Library System, 201 Monroe St, Livingston, AL, 35470. Tel: 205-652-2349. p. 24
Tarr, Emily, Exec Dir, Texarkana Museums System, 219 N State Line Ave, Texarkana, TX, 75501. Tel: 903-793-4831. p. 2248
Tarr, Sarah, Tech Serv Asst, Endicott College Library, 376 Hale St, Beverly, MA, 01915. Tel: 978-232-2277. p. 989
Tarsetti, Lynda, Libr Tech, Pilot Point Community Library, 324 S Washington St, Pilot Point, TX, 76258. Tel: 940-686-5004. p. 2226
Tarter, Patty, Acq, ILL, Berea College, 100 Campus Dr, Berea, KY, 40404. Tel: 859-985-3364. p. 849
Tarullo, Danielle, Asst Br Mgr, Chesterfield County Public Library, LaPrade, 9000 Hull St Rd, Richmond, VA, 23236. Tel: 804-751-2275. p. 2312
Tarves, Theresa K, Assoc Dir, Law Librn, Pennsylvania State University - Dickinson School of Law, 214 Lewis Katz Bldg, University Park, PA, 16802. Tel: 814-863-6861. p. 2015
Tasch, Rachel, Exec Dir, Congregation Beth Am Library, 26790 Arastradero Rd, Los Altos Hills, CA, 94022. Tel: 650-493-4661. p. 159
Tash, Liz, Library Contact, Peachtree Presbyterian Church, 3434 Roswell Rd NW, Atlanta, GA, 30305. Tel: 404-842-5810. p. 466
Taskey, Robert, Evening Circ Supvr, American International College, 1000 State St, Springfield, MA, 01109. Tel: 413-205-3225. p. 1056
Tassa, Lisa, Br Mgr, Calvert Library, Fairview, 8120 Southern Maryland Blvd, Owings, MD, 20736. Tel: 410-257-2101. p. 973
Tassell, Regina, Admin Assoc, University of Cincinnati Libraries, PO Box 210033, Cincinnati, OH, 45221-0033. Tel: 513-556-1515. p. 1764
Tassone, Alyssa, Dir, Manlius Library, One Arkie Albanese Ave, Manlius, NY, 13104. Tel: 315-682-6400. p. 1568
Taste, Sharon, Br Mgr, Dayton Metro Library, Northwest Branch, 2410 Philadelphia Dr, Dayton, OH, 45406. p. 1779
Tatar, Colleen, Librn, Hazleton Area Public Library, Freeland Branch, 515 Front St, Freeland, PA, 18224. Tel: 570-636-2125. p. 1943
Tatarka, Karen, Dir, University of Connecticut, Hartford Campus, Uconn Library at Hartford Public Library, 500 Main St, Hartford, CT, 06103. Tel: 959-200-3466. p. 340
Tate, Allen, Mgr, Info Tech, Newburgh Chandler Public Library, 4111 Lakeshore Dr, Newburgh, IN, 47630-2274. Tel: 812-942-9991. p. 709
Tate, David, Libr Asst III, Dyersburg State Community College, 1510 Lake Rd, Dyersburg, TN, 38024. Tel: 731-286-3272. p. 2097
Tate, Debbra, Acq, Cataloger, Resource Dev Librn, Kentucky State University, 400 E Main St, Frankfort, KY, 40601-2355. Tel: 502-597-6862. p. 855
Tate, Dorie, Libr Tech, Phillips Community College of the University of Arkansas, 1000 Campus Dr, Helena, AR, 72342. Tel: 870-338-6474, Ext 1167. p. 98
Tate, Erin, Dir, Albion Area Public Library, 111 E Pearl St, Albion, PA, 16401-1202. Tel: 814-756-5400. p. 1903
Tate George, Leanne, Br Mgr, Union County Library, Nance McNeely Public, 1080 Megginson Lane, Myrtle, MS, 38650. Tel: 662-988-2895. p. 1228
Tate, Jack, Curator, Dearborn Historical Museum Library, Dearborn Historical Museum, 915 Brady St, Dearborn, MI, 48126. Tel: 313-565-3000. p. 1095
Tate, Jeff, Digital Serv Mgr, Wichita Public Library, 711 W Second St, Wichita, KS, 67203. Tel: 316-261-8522. p. 843
Tate, Karen, Dir, National Library of Education, 400 Maryland Ave SW, BE-101, Washington, DC, 20202-5523. Tel: 202-453-5620. p. 372
Tate, Lamar, Librn, Kings Mountain National Military Park Library, 2625 Park Rd, Blacksburg, SC, 29702. Tel: 864-936-7921, Ext 3. p. 2047
Tate, Mary Lue, Dir, Sidell District Library, 101 E Market St, Sidell, IL, 61876. Tel: 217-288-9031. p. 647
Tate, Vicki, Head, Govt Doc & Ser, University of South Alabama Libraries, Marx Library, 5901 USA Drive N, Mobile, AL, 36688. Tel: 251-460-2822. p. 27
Tate, Virginia, Circ, Greene County Public Library, 120 N 12th St, Paragould, AR, 72450. Tel: 870-236-8711. p. 107
Tatnall, Amber, Assoc Dean, Acad, York County Community College Library, 112 College Dr, Wells, ME, 04090. Tel: 207-646-9282. p. 946
Tatnall, Kathryn, Youth Serv Librn, New Ulm Public Library, 17 N Broadway, New Ulm, MN, 56073-1786. Tel: 507-359-8331. p. 1190
Tatro, Fred, Dir, Boston Baptist College, 950 Metropolitan Ave, Boston, MA, 02136. Tel: 617-364-3510, Ext 216. p. 991
Tatro, Mary, Tech Serv Librn, Augustana College Library, 3435 9 1/2 Ave, Rock Island, IL, 61201-2296. Tel: 309-794-7824. p. 641
Tatta, Antonietta, Librn, Condon & Forsyth LLP Library, Seven Times Sq, 18th Flr, New York, NY, 10036. Tel: 212-490-9100. p. 1584
Tattersall, Lisa, Mgr, Washington County Cooperative Library Services, 2350 NE Griffin Oaks St, Hillsboro, OR, 97124. Tel: 503-846-3222. p. 2773
Tattonetti, Michael, Govt Doc Librn, Touro University, 225 Eastview Dr, Central Islip, NY, 11722-4539. Tel: 631-761-7150. p. 1516
Tatum, Christina, Instruction & Outreach Librn, Agnes Scott College, 141 E College Ave, Decatur, GA, 30030-3770. Tel: 404-471-6141. p. 475
Taube, John, Exec Dir, Allegany County Library System, 31 Washington St, Cumberland, MD, 21502. Tel: 301-777-1200. p. 963
Taupier, Andrea S, Dir, Springfield College, 263 Alden St, Springfield, MA, 01109-3797. Tel: 413-748-3315. p. 1057
Taurone, Riley, Ms, Br Mgr, Pope County Library System, Atkins Centennial Branch, 216 NE First St, Atkins, AR, 72823. Tel: 479-641-7904. p. 109
Tautkus, Mike, Dir, Kingfisher Memorial Library, 505 W Will Rogers Dr, Kingfisher, OK, 73750. Tel: 405-375-3384. p. 1851
Tavares, Cecelia, Asst Librn, Old Dartmouth Historical Society, 18 Johnny Cake Hill, New Bedford, MA, 02740. Tel: 508-997-0046, Ext 134. p. 1038
Tavares, David, Br Mgr, Monterey County Free Libraries, Castroville Branch, 11160 Speegle St, Castroville, CA, 95012. Tel: 831-769-8724. p. 172
Tavares, Jocelyn, Dir, Dighton Public Library, 979 Somerset Ave, Dighton, MA, 02715. Tel: 508-669-6421. p. 1014
Tavares, Jocelyn, Libr Dir, Swansea Free Public Library, 69 Main St, Swansea, MA, 02777. Tel: 508-674-9609. p. 1059
Tavenner, Debbie, Adminr, Ohio Legislative Service Commission Library, 77 S High St, 9th Flr, Columbus, OH, 43215-6136. Tel: 614-466-2241. p. 1774
Taverna, Linda, Ch, Durand Public Library, 604 Seventh Ave E, Durand, WI, 54736. Tel: 715-672-8730. p. 2431
Tavernier, Joan, Libr Mgr, Wide Awake Club Library, 22 Genesee St, Fillmore, NY, 14735. Tel: 585-567-8301. p. 1533
Taves, Spencer, Libr Tech, Northwood Technical College, 2100 Beaser Ave, Ashland, WI, 54806. Tel: 715-682-4591, Ext 3108. p. 2421
Tawa, Danielle, Archivist, Tech, Needham Free Public Library, 1139 Highland Ave, Needham, MA, 02494-3298. Tel: 781-455-7559, Ext 215. p. 1038
Tawzer, Tiffany, Access Services & Emerging Technologies Librn, Loyola University Chicago Libraries, Health Sciences Library, Bldg 125, Rm 1526, 2160 S First Ave, Maywood, IL, 60153. Tel: 708-216-5308. p. 563
Taxakis, Brooke, Ref & Instruction Librn, Campbell University, 113 Main St, Buies Creek, NC, 27506. Tel: 910-814-5579. p. 1676
Tayag, Elnora Kelly, Dir, Learning Commons, College of San Mateo Library, Bldg 9, 1700 W Hillsdale Blvd, San Mateo, CA, 94402-3795. Tel: 650-574-6569. p. 235
Taychert, Alice Marie, Dir, Hornell Public Library, 64 Genesee St, Hornell, NY, 14843-1651. Tel: 607-324-1210. p. 1548
Taylor, Amanda, Libr Dir, Concordia Parish Library, 1609 Third St, Ferriday, LA, 71334. Tel: 318-757-3550. p. 889
Taylor, Amber Ruth, Cat, Decatur County Library, 20 W Market St, Decaturville, TN, 38329. Tel: 731-852-3325. p. 2096
Taylor, Amy, County Librn, Merced County Library, 2100 O St, Merced, CA, 95340-3637. p. 176
Taylor, Amy, Community Engagement & Instruction Librn, University of Pikeville, 147 Sycamore St, Pikeville, KY, 41501-9118. Tel: 606-218-5504. p. 872

Taylor, Amy, Librn, Spindale Public Library, 131 Tanner St, Spindale, NC, 28160. Tel: 828-286-3879. p. 1717
Taylor, Amy, Pub Serv, University of Texas, School of Public Health Library, 1200 Herman Pressler Blvd, Houston, TX, 77030-3900. Tel: 713-500-9121. p. 2200
Taylor, Angela, Br Mgr, Sullivan County Public Library, Bloomingdale Branch, 3230 Van Horn St, Kingsport, TN, 37660. Tel: 423-288-1310. p. 2089
Taylor, Angela, Br Mgr, Sullivan County Public Library, Thomas Memorial Branch, 481 Cedar St, Bluff City, TN, 37618. Tel: 423-538-1980. p. 2089
Taylor, Anne Cleester, Ref (Info Servs), Washington University Libraries, Law Library, Washington Univ Sch Law, Anheuser-Busch Hall, One Brookings Dr, Campus Box 1171, Saint Louis, MO, 63130. Tel: 314-935-4829. p. 1277
Taylor, Anneliese, Head, Scholarly Communications, University of California San Francisco, 530 Parnassus Ave, San Francisco, CA, 94143. Tel: 415-476-8415. p. 229
Taylor, Ara, Reserves, Whatcom Community College Library, Heiner Bldg, 231 W Kellogg Rd, Bellingham, WA, 98226. Tel: 360-383-3300. p. 2359
Taylor, Athalia Boroughs, Dir, Decatur County Library, 20 W Market St, Decaturville, TN, 38329. Tel: 731-852-3325. p. 2096
Taylor, Audrey, Libr Mgr, Central Arkansas Library System, Oley E Rooker Library, 11 Otter Creek Ct, Little Rock, AR, 72210. Tel: 501-907-5991. p. 101
Taylor, Barbara, Mrs, Asst Dir, Stewart County Public Library, 102 Natcor Dr, Dover, TN, 37058. Tel: 931-232-3127. p. 2097
Taylor, Beth, Head, Tech Serv, University of Michigan-Dearborn, 4901 Evergreen Rd, Dearborn, MI, 48128-2406. Tel: 313-593-5402. p. 1096
Taylor, Brenda, Archivist, Librn, Sharlot Hall Museum Library & Archives, Granite Creek Ctr, 115 S McCormick St, Prescott, AZ, 86301. Tel: 928-277-2003, 928-445-3122. p. 74
Taylor, Brooke, Interim Branch Supervisor, Rowan Public Library, East Branch, 110 Broad St, Rockwell, NC, 28138. p. 1715
Taylor, Carol, Dir, Jefferson County Library System, 306 E Broad St, Louisville, GA, 30434. Tel: 478-625-7079. p. 486
Taylor, Carrie, Exec Dir, Windsor Historical Society Library, 96 Palisado Ave, Windsor, CT, 06095. Tel: 860-688-3813. p. 348
Taylor, Casey, Libr Dir, Cascade Public Library, 105 Front St, Cascade, ID, 83611. Tel: 208-382-4757. p. 519
Taylor, Celeste Felix, Br Mgr, Toledo-Lucas County Public Library, South, 1736 Broadway St, Toledo, OH, 43609. Tel: 419-259-5395. p. 1825
Taylor, Chandler, Br Mgr, Ascension Parish Library, Dutchtown Branch, 13278 Hwy 73, Geismar, LA, 70734. Tel: 225-673-8699. p. 889
Taylor, Chantelle, Dep Chief Librn, Cumberland Public Libraries, 21 Acadia St, 2nd Flr, Amherst, NS, B4H 4W3, CANADA. Tel: 902-667-2135. p. 2615
Taylor, Charlene, Librn, Dry Point Township Library, S Rte 128, Cowden, IL, 62422. Tel: 217-783-2616. p. 574
Taylor, Charlene, Head, Ref & Adult Serv, Englewood Public Library, 31 Engle St, Englewood, NJ, 07631. Tel: 201-568-2215, Ext 229. p. 1401
Taylor, Cindy, Ch Serv, Unicoi County Public Library, 201 Nolichucky Ave, Erwin, TN, 37650. Tel: 423-743-6533. p. 2098
Taylor, Corlis, Librn, Fairbanks Memorial Hospital Library, 1650 Cowles St, Fairbanks, AK, 99701-5998. Tel: 907-458-5580. p. 45
Taylor, Cory, Dir, Walton Erickson Public Library, 4808 Northland Dr, Morley, MI, 49336-9522. Tel: 231-856-4298. p. 1134
Taylor, Curtice, Mr, Br Librn, Genesee District Library, Headquarters, 4195 W Pasadena Ave, Flint, MI, 48504. Tel: 810-732-0110. p. 1106
Taylor, Dan, Libr Tech Spec, Ithaca College Library, 953 Danby Rd, Ithaca, NY, 14850-7060. Tel: 607-274-3206. p. 1553
Taylor, Danielle, Head, Youth Serv, Richton Park Public Library District, 22310 Latonia Lane, Richton Park, IL, 60471. Tel: 708-481-5333. p. 638
Taylor, Danielle, Head, Youth Serv, Stickney-Forest View Public Library District, 6800 W 43rd St, Stickney, IL, 60402. Tel: 708-749-1050. p. 651
Taylor, Diann, Interim Dir, Akron Public Library, 207 First Ave S, Akron, AL, 35441. Tel: 205-372-3148. p. 3
Taylor, Dominique, Ref Serv, National Gallery of Canada Library & Archives, 380 Sussex Dr, Ottawa, ON, K1N 9N4, CANADA. Tel: 613-714-6000, Ext 6323. p. 2667
Taylor, Dorthea, Head, Access Serv, East Carolina University, Music Library, A J Fletcher Music Ctr, Rm A110, Greenville, NC, 27858. Tel: 252-328-1242. p. 1694
Taylor, Elaine, Br Mgr, Montgomery County Memorial Library System, Malcolm Purvis Library, 510 Melton St, Magnolia, TX, 77354. Tel: 936-788-8324. p. 2159
Taylor, Elisha, Ref Librn, Univ Archivist, University of Pikeville, 147 Sycamore St, Pikeville, KY, 41501-9118. Tel: 606-218-5625. p. 872
Taylor, Erika, Statewide Servs Asst, State Library of Kansas, 300 SW Tenth Ave, Rm 312-N, Topeka, KS, 66612-1593. Tel: 785-296-2146. p. 2765
Taylor, Erna, Br Mgr, Park County Public Libraries, 350 Bulldogger Rd, Bailey, CO, 80421. Tel: 303-838-5539. p. 265
Taylor, Evelyn, Asst Dir, Deaf Smith County Library, 211 E Fourth St, Hereford, TX, 79045. Tel: 806-364-1206. p. 2189
Taylor, Gabrielle, Br Mgr, Atlanta-Fulton Public Library System, Adamsville-Collier Heights Branch, 3424 Martin Luther King Jr Dr, Atlanta, GA, 30331. Tel: 404-699-4206. p. 460
Taylor, George, Dir, Libr Serv, Lake County Library System, 418 W Alfred St, Ste C, Tavares, FL, 32778. Tel: 352-253-6180. p. 450
Taylor, Gloria, Br Supvr, Mecklenburg County Public Library, R T Arnold Public, 110 E Danville St, South Hill, VA, 23970. Tel: 434-447-8162. p. 2308
Taylor, Hali, Dir, Shepherdstown Public Library, 100 E German St, Shepherdstown, WV, 25443. Tel: 304-876-2783. p. 2414
Taylor, Heidi, Libr Dir, Mendon Library, 15 N Main St, Mendon, UT, 84325. Tel: 435-774-2200. p. 2266
Taylor, Jacqui, Youth Serv Coordr, Wright Memorial Public Library, 1776 Far Hills Ave, Oakwood, OH, 45419-2598. Tel: 937-294-7171. p. 1810
Taylor, Jane, Br Mgr, Atlanta-Fulton Public Library System, Buckhead Branch, 269 Buckhead Ave NE, Atlanta, GA, 30305. Tel: 404-814-3500. p. 461
Taylor, Jane, Br Librn, Siouxland Libraries, Ronning Branch, 3100 E 49th St, Sioux Falls, SD, 57103-5877. Tel: 605-367-8140. p. 2082
Taylor, Janet L, Bus & Finance Mgr, Coordr, Outreach Serv, Coordr, Pub Serv, South Dakota School of Mines & Technology, 501 E Saint Joseph St, Rapid City, SD, 57701-3995. p. 2081
Taylor, Jeannie, Asst Dir, Boynton Beach City Library, 115 N Federal Hwy, Boynton Beach, FL, 33435. Tel: 561-742-6390. p. 386
Taylor, Jeff, Br Mgr, Fort Bend County Libraries, Sienna Branch, 8411 Sienna Springs Blvd, Missouri City, TX, 77459. Tel: 281-238-2900. p. 2232
Taylor, Jennifer, Chair, Spec Coll, Samford University Library, 800 Lakeshore Dr, Birmingham, AL, 35229. Tel: 205-726-4103. p. 9
Taylor, Jennifer, Circ Serv Coordr, LeRoy Collins Leon County Public Library System, 200 W Park Ave, Tallahassee, FL, 32301-7720. Tel: 850-606-2665. p. 445
Taylor, Jennifer, Adult & Teen Serv, Tech Serv, Hagerstown Jefferson Township Library, Ten W College St, Hagerstown, IN, 47346. Tel: 765-489-5632. p. 688
Taylor, Jennifer, ILL, Walla Walla Community College Library, 500 Tausick Way, Walla Walla, WA, 99362-9267. Tel: 509-527-4277. p. 2392
Taylor, Jenny, Asst Dir, Electronic Resources, Consortium of Academic & Research Libraries in Illinois, 1704 Interstate Dr, Champaign, IL, 61822. Tel: 217-265-8437. p. 2764
Taylor, Jerri, Mgt Analyst, University of Arkansas-Pine Bluff, Music Lab, 1200 N University Dr, Mail Stop 4956, Pine Bluff, AR, 71601. Tel: 870-575-7036. p. 108
Taylor, Jill, Br Librn, Southeast Regional Library, Windthorst Branch, 202 Angus St, Windthorst, SK, S0G 5G0, CANADA. Tel: 306-224-2159. p. 2755
Taylor, John, Dean, Libr & Learning Support, Orange Coast College Library, 2701 Fairview Rd, Costa Mesa, CA, 92626. Tel: 714-432-5885. p. 132
Taylor, Julie, Cat Librn, Vermont State University - Randolph, Main St, Randolph Center, VT, 05061. Tel: 802-728-1237. p. 2292
Taylor, Julie, Br Mgr, Antigo Public Library, Elcho Branch, Elcho High School, Hwy 45 N, Elcho, WI, 54428. Tel: 715-275-3225, Ext 1815. p. 2420
Taylor, Karen A, Dir, East Greenwich Free Library, 82 Peirce St, East Greenwich, RI, 02818. Tel: 401-884-9510. p. 2031
Taylor, Karin, Dir, Andalusia Public Library, 212 S Three Notch St, Andalusia, AL, 36420. Tel: 334-222-6612. p. 4
Taylor, Karin, Dir, Beardsley & Memorial Library, 40 Munro Pl, Winsted, CT, 06098. Tel: 860-379-6043. p. 348
Taylor, Kathy, Pres, Canton Historical Society Library, 11 Front St, Collinsville, CT, 06019. Tel: 860-693-2793. p. 306
Taylor, Kevin, Librn, First District Court of Appeal Library, 2000 Drayton Dr, Tallahassee, FL, 32399. Tel: 850-487-1000. p. 446
Taylor, Kolleen, Dir, Bertha Bartlett Public Library, 503 Broad St, Story City, IA, 50248-1133. Tel: 515-733-2685. p. 785
Taylor, Laura, Coll & Res Librn, Macomb Community College Libraries, Center Campus, 44575 Garfield Rd, C-Bldg, Clinton Township, MI, 48038-1139. Tel: 586-445-7419. p. 1157
Taylor, Laura, Dep Chief Exec Officer, Marigold Library System, 710 Second St, Strathmore, AB, T1P 1K4, CANADA. Tel: 403-934-5334, Ext 242. p. 2555
Taylor, Linda, Circ Mgr, Richmond County Public Library, Rappahannock Community College Library Ctr, 52 Campus Dr, Warsaw, VA, 22572. Tel: 804-333-6710. p. 2352
Taylor, Lisa, Libr Dir, Sumter County Library System, 7375 Powell Rd, Ste 150, Wildwood, FL, 34785. Tel: 352-689-4560. p. 455
Taylor, Liza, Asst Dir, Hamilton Public Library, 13 Broad St, Hamilton, NY, 13346. Tel: 315-824-3060. p. 1543
Taylor, Lorrie, Tech Serv, Allerton Public Library District, 4000 Green Apple Lane, Monticello, IL, 61856. Tel: 217-762-4676. p. 619
Taylor, Lorrie, Dir & Librn, Alma Public Library, 500 E Superior St, Alma, MI, 48801-1999. Tel: 989-463-3966. p. 1077
Taylor, Lynn, Dir, Richfield Township Public Library, 1410 Saint Helen Rd, Saint Helen, MI, 48656. Tel: 989-389-7630. p. 1147
Taylor, Maria, Interim Libr Dir, Georgetown College, 400 E College St, Georgetown, KY, 40324. Tel: 502-863-8403. p. 856

Taylor, Mark, Libr Asst, Gadsden State Community College, Valley Street Campus Library, 600 Valley St, Gadsden, AL, 35901. Tel: 256-439-6887. p. 18

Taylor, Marsha, Head Librn, Montgomery City-County Public Library System, Pike Road Branch Library, 9585 Vaughn Rd, Pike Road, AL, 36064-2292. Tel: 334-244-8679. p. 30

Taylor, Marsha, Head Librn, Montgomery City-County Public Library System, Pintlala Branch Library, 255 Federal Rd, Pintlala, AL, 36043-9781. Tel: 334-281-8069. p. 30

Taylor, Megan, Dir, Bloomer Public Library, 1519 17th Ave, Bloomer, WI, 54724. Tel: 715-568-2384. p. 2424

Taylor, Melanie, Librn, Pulaski County Public Library, Shopville Branch, 144 Shopville Rd, Somerset, KY, 42503. Tel: 606-274-1671. p. 875

Taylor, Nancy, Dir, Prog & Serv, Presbyterian Historical Society, 425 Lombard St, Philadelphia, PA, 19147-1516. Tel: 215-627-1852. p. 1985

Taylor, Nathan L, Dr, Exec Dir, Virginia Baptist Historical Society & the Center for Baptist Heritage & Studies Library, 261 Richmond Way, University of Richmond, Richmond, VA, 23173. Tel: 804-289-8434. p. 2343

Taylor, Nick, Mgr, Jefferson County Public Library, Edgewater Branch, 1800 Harlan St, Edgewater, CO, 80214. Tel: 303-403-5140. p. 288

Taylor, Nick, Mgr, Jefferson County Public Library, Wheat Ridge Library, 5475 W 32nd Ave, Wheat Ridge, CO, 80212. p. 288

Taylor, Pam, Br Mgr, Harford County Public Library, Joppa Branch, 655 Towne Center Dr, Joppa, MD, 21085-4497. Tel: 410-612-1660. p. 959

Taylor, Pam, Circ Supvr, Delaware County District Library, 84 E Winter St, Delaware, OH, 43015. Tel: 740-362-3861. p. 1781

Taylor, Pat, Libr Office Mgr, Hopkinsville-Christian County Public Library, 1101 Bethel St, Hopkinsville, KY, 42240. Tel: 270-887-4262, Ext 107. p. 860

Taylor, Patrick, Dir of Finance, Capital Area District Libraries, 401 S Capitol Ave, Lansing, MI, 48933. Tel: 517-367-6337. p. 1124

Taylor, Rachel, Law Librn, Walla Walla County Law Library, County Courthouse, 315 W Main St, Walla Walla, WA, 99362. Tel: 509-524-2795. p. 2392

Taylor, Raquel, Coms & Multimedia Engagement Mgr, Norfolk Public Library, Slover Library, 235 E Plume St, Norfolk, VA, 23510. Tel: 757-431-7491. p. 2335

Taylor, Rebbecca, Dir, Ector County Library, 321 W Fifth St, Odessa, TX, 79761-5066. Tel: 432-332-0633. p. 2223

Taylor, Rita, Librn, Missouri Department of Corrections, Western Missouri Correctional Center, 609 E Pence Rd, Cameron, MO, 64429-8823. Tel: 816-632-1390. p. 1252

Taylor, Robbie, Automation Coordr, Info Tech, Manatee County Public Library System, 1301 Barcarrota Blvd W, Bradenton, FL, 34205-7522. Tel: 941-748-5555, Ext 6330. p. 386

Taylor, Robert, Librn, University of North Texas Libraries, Dallas Campus Library, 7350 University Hills Blvd, 3rd Flr, Dallas, TX, 75241. Tel: 972-338-1616. p. 2170

Taylor, Rosemarie Kazda, Mgr, Wilkes-Barre General Hospital, 575 N River St, Wilkes-Barre, PA, 18764. Tel: 570-552-1175. p. 2023

Taylor, Russ, Assoc Univ Librn, Spec Coll, Brigham Young University, Harold B Lee Library, 2060 HBLL, Provo, UT, 84602. Tel: 801-422-2927. p. 2269

Taylor, Russell, Dir, Asheville-Buncombe Technical Community College, 340 Victoria Rd, Asheville, NC, 28801. Tel: 828-398-7307. p. 1672

Taylor, Sarah, Asst Dir, Johnson County Public Library, 49 E Monroe St, Franklin, IN, 46131. p. 686

Taylor, Shari, Dir, Earlville Free Library, Four N Main St, Earlville, NY, 13332. Tel: 315-691-5931. p. 1527

Taylor, Shelia, Librn, United States Department of Transportation, Federal Highway Administration-Chief Counsel's Law Library, 1200 New Jersry Ave SE, Rm E84-464, Washington, DC, 20590. Tel: 202-366-1387. p. 379

Taylor, Sherita, Librn, Northeast Mississippi Community College, 101 Cunningham Blvd, Booneville, MS, 38829. Tel: 662-720-7583. p. 1212

Taylor, Shirley, Dir, Le Mars Public Library, 46 First St SW, Le Mars, IA, 51031. Tel: 712-546-5004. p. 765

Taylor, Stephanie, Interim Dir, Tougaloo College, 500 W County Line Rd, Tougaloo, MS, 39174-9799. Tel: 601-977-7703. p. 1233

Taylor, Sue, Res Analyst, Katten Muchin Rosenman LLP, 50 Rockefeller Plaza, New York, NY, 10020-1605. Tel: 310-788-4675. p. 1590

Taylor, Tammy, Circ Supvr, University of Baltimore, 1420 Maryland Ave, Baltimore, MD, 21201. Tel: 410-837-4263. p. 957

Taylor, Tanna, Dir, Tombigbee Regional Library System, 436 Commerce St, West Point, MS, 39773-2923. Tel: 662-494-4872. p. 1235

Taylor, Tanya, Asst Dir, Geneva Public Library, 244 Main St, Geneva, NY, 14456. Tel: 315-789-5303. p. 1538

Taylor, Terry, Pres & Dir, Shakespeare Society of America, 7981 Moss Landing Rd, Moss Landing, CA, 95039. Tel: 831-633-2989. p. 181

Taylor, Tiffany, Asst Dir, Polk County Library, 1690 W Broadway St, Bolivar, MO, 65613. Tel: 417-326-4531. p. 1238

Taylor, Tobee, Br Mgr, Bullitt County Public Library, Lebanon Junction Branch, 11382 S Preston Hwy, Lebanon Junction, KY, 40150. Tel: 502-833-4648. p. 875

Taylor, Tom, Dir, Andover Public Library, 1511 E Central Ave, Andover, KS, 67002. Tel: 316-558-3500. p. 796

Taylor, Traci, Lead Librn, Bellingham Technical College Library, 3028 Lindbergh Ave, Bellingham, WA, 98225-1599. Tel: 360-752-8488. p. 2358

Taylor, Tucky, Head, Circ, University of South Carolina, 1322 Greene St, Columbia, SC, 29208-0103. Tel: 803-777-3142. p. 2055

Taylor, Valerie, Librn, Chester County Library, Lewisville Community Library, 3771 Lancaster Hwy, Richburg, SC, 29729. Tel: 803-789-7800. p. 2052

Taylor, Wendy, Ch Serv, Kent Memorial Library, 50 N Main St, Suffield, CT, 06078-2117. Tel: 860-668-3896. p. 341

Taylor, Whitney, Tech Serv Librn, University of the Cumberlands, 821 Walnut St, Williamsburg, KY, 40769. Tel: 606-539-4464. p. 877

Taylor, Will, Curator, Kenilworth Historical Society, 415 Kenilworth Ave, Kenilworth, IL, 60043. Tel: 847-251-2565. p. 604

Taylor, William, Head, Tech Proc, Washington County Free Library, 100 S Potomac St, Hagerstown, MD, 21740. Tel: 301-739-3250. p. 968

Taylor, Zoie, Library Applications Developer, Drake University, 2725 University Ave, Des Moines, IA, 50311. Tel: 515-271-2975. p. 746

Taylor-Bader, Tamia, Tech Consult, South Central Kansas Library System, 321 N Main St, South Hutchinson, KS, 67505. Tel: 620-663-3211. p. 837

Taylor-Bandele, Leola, Librn, Essex County College Library, 303 University Ave, Newark, NJ, 07102. Tel: 973-877-3238. p. 1426

Taylor-Pack, Jennifer, Libr Mgr, Live Oak Public Libraries, Pooler Branch, 216 S Rogers St, Pooler, GA, 31322. Tel: 912-748-6979. p. 496

Taylor-Smith, Cheryl, Asst Dir, High River Library, 909 First St SW, High River, AB, T1V 1A5, CANADA. Tel: 403-652-2917. p. 2543

Tchepelev, Gaelle, Cat, Circ, Centre de documentation collegiale, 1111 rue Lapierre, LaSalle, QC, H8N 2J4, CANADA. Tel: 514-364-3327. p. 2715

Te Tan, Robert, ILL, Bloomberg Industry Group Library, 1801 S Bell St, Arlington, VA, 22202. Tel: 703-341-3315. p. 2305

Teachey, Philip, Libr Asst, Sampson-Clinton Public Library, Miriam B Lamb Memorial, 144 S Church St, Garland, NC, 28441. Tel: 910-529-2441. p. 1681

Teaff, Elizabeth Anne, Assoc Univ Librarian, Access & Discovery, Washington & Lee University, University Library, 204 W Washington St, Lexington, VA, 24450-2116. Tel: 540-458-8643. p. 2329

Teaford, Ellie, Br Mgr, Kanawha County Public Library, Elk Valley, 313 The Crossing Mall, Elkview, WV, 25071. Tel: 304-965-3636. p. 2400

Teagle, Ashley, Chief Exec Officer, Southern Maryland Regional Library Association, Inc, 37600 New Market Rd, Charlotte Hall, MD, 20622. Tel: 301-884-0436. p. 961

Teague, Adrienne, Br Head, Thompson-Nicola Regional District Library System, Cache Creek Branch, 1025 Trans-Canada Hwy, Cache Creek, BC, V0K 1H0, CANADA. Tel: 250-457-9953. p. 2567

Teague, Adrienne, Br Head, Thompson-Nicola Regional District Library System, Savona Branch, 60 Savona St, Savona, BC, V0K 2J0, CANADA. Tel: 250-373-2666. p. 2568

Teague, Janie, Librn, Trumann Public Library, 1200 W Main St, Trumann, AR, 72472. Tel: 870-483-7744. p. 111

Teague, Karen, Dir, Nocona Public Library, Ten Cooke St, Nocona, TX, 76255. Tel: 940-825-6373. p. 2222

Teague, Kathy, Mgr, County of Los Angeles Public Library, El Camino Real Library, 4264 E Whittier Blvd, Los Angeles, CA, 90023-2036. Tel: 323-269-8102. p. 136

Teague, Teresa, Asst Librn, Tech Serv, Campbell University, Norman Adrian Wiggins School of Law Library, 225 Hillsborough St, Ste 203H, Raleigh, NC, 27603. Tel: 919-865-5869. p. 1676

Teahen, James, Dep Dir, Marion Public Library, 1101 Sixth Ave, Marion, IA, 52302. Tel: 319-377-3412. p. 768

Teal Lovely, Victoria, Tech Serv Coordr, South Central Library System, 4610 S Biltmore Lane, Ste 101, Madison, WI, 53718-2153. Tel: 608-242-4713. p. 2450

Teasdle, Holly, Dir, Lyon Township Public Library, 27005 S Milford Rd, South Lyon, MI, 48178. Tel: 248-437-8800. p. 1150

Teasley, Tammy, Libr Res Coordr, Lincoln City Libraries, 136 S 14th St, Lincoln, NE, 68508-1899. Tel: 402-441-8575. p. 1321

Tebbe, Michael, Dir, Info & Res, Duff & Phelps, 311 S Wacker Dr, Ste 4200, Chicago, IL, 60606. Tel: 312-697-4535. p. 560

Tebow, Linda, Dir, Scandia City Library, 318 Fourth St, Scandia, KS, 66966. Tel: 785-335-2271. p. 835

Techau, Donna, Dir, Bement Public Library District, 349 S Macon St, Bement, IL, 61813. Tel: 217-678-7101. p. 541

Tecumseh, Ramona, Head Librn, Ira H Hayes Memorial Library, 94 N Church St, Sacaton, AZ, 85147. Tel: 520-562-3225. p. 75

Tedford, Rosalind, Dir, Res & Instruction Serv, Wake Forest University, 1834 Wake Forest Rd, Winston-Salem, NC, 27109. Tel: 336-758-5910. p. 1726

Tedjeske Crane, Julie, Educ Tech Librn, Illinois Institute of Technology, Chicago-Kent College of Law Library, 565 W Adams St, 9th Flr, Chicago, IL, 60661. Tel: 312-906-5600. p. 562

Tedone-Goldstone, Diana, Librn, Cañada College Library, Bldg 9, 3rd Flr, 4200 Farm Hill Blvd, Redwood City, CA, 94061-1099. p. 200

Tedrick, Courtney, Head, Community Engagement, Wheaton Public Library, 225 N Cross St, Wheaton, IL, 60187-5376. Tel: 630-868-7526. p. 662

Teel, April, Dir, Emily Taber Public Library, 14 McIver Ave W, Macclenny, FL, 32063. Tel: 904-259-6464. p. 419

Teel, Dawn, Dir, Whiting Public Library, 407 Whittier St, Whiting, IA, 51063. Tel: 712-455-2612. p. 791

Teel, Linda, Circ Supvr, Oxford Public Library, 48 S Second St, Oxford, PA, 19363-1377. Tel: 610-932-9625. p. 1973

Teeple, Bruce, Pres, Union County Historical Society Library, Union County Courthouse, 103 S Second St, Lewisburg, PA, 17837. Tel: 570-524-8666. p. 1955

Teeter, Enid, Br Mgr, University of Wyoming Libraries, Brinkerhoff Geology Library (Brinkerhoff Earth Resources Information Center), Geology Bldg, Rm 121, 121 SH Knight, Laramie, WY, 82071. Tel: 307-766-2633. p. 2497

Teeter, Kara, Ad, Colleyville Public Library, 110 Main St, Colleyville, TX, 76034. Tel: 817-503-1150, 817-503-1154 (Youth Serv), 817-503-1155 (Adult Serv). p. 2158

Teeter, Keith, Assoc Dir, Educ Serv/Pub Serv, Auraria Library, 1100 Lawrence St, Denver, CO, 80204-2095. Tel: 303-315-7732. p. 273

Teeter, Robert J, Librn, Santa Clara Valley Water District Library, 1020 Blossom Hill Rd, San Jose, CA, 95123. Tel: 408-630-2360, 408-630-3748. p. 232

Tefft, Jessica, Teen Serv Librn, Branch District Library, Ten E Chicago St, Coldwater, MI, 49036-1615. Tel: 517-278-2341, Ext 122. p. 1092

Tegeler, Nancy, Head, Children's Servx, Dover Town Library, 56 Dedham St, Dover, MA, 02030-2214. Tel: 508-785-8113. p. 1014

Tegethoff, Vicki, Librn, Missouri Baptist Medical Center, 3015 N Ballas Rd, Saint Louis, MO, 63131. Tel: 314-996-5531. p. 1271

Teglas, Rebecca, Head, Youth Serv, Larchmont Public Library, 121 Larchmont Ave, Larchmont, NY, 10538. Tel: 914-834-2281. p. 1562

Teh-Frenette, Lillian, Tech Coordr, Red Deer College Library, 100 College Blvd, Red Deer, AB, T4N 5H5, CANADA. Tel: 403-342-3353. p. 2551

Tehan, Bruce, Br Mgr, Rochester Public Library, Arnett, 310 Arnett Blvd, Rochester, NY, 14619. Tel: 585-428-8214. p. 1630

Tehonica, Amanda, Ref, Roswell P Flower Memorial Library, 229 Washington St, Watertown, NY, 13601-3388. Tel: 315-785-7715. p. 1659

Tehrani, Mahnaz, Med Librn, New York Institute of Technology, Northern Blvd, Old Westbury, NY, 11568-8000. Tel: 516-686-3743. p. 1610

Tehrani, Melody, Sr Librn, City of Palo Alto Library, Rinconda Library, 1213 Newell Rd, Palo Alto, CA, 94303. Tel: 650-329-2426. p. 192

Teichmann, Jeffrey, Libr Supvr, Rutgers University Libraries, Archibald Stevens Alexander Library, 169 College Ave, New Brunswick, NJ, 08901-1163. Tel: 848-932-6057. p. 1424

Teifer, Hermann, Head Archivist, Center for Jewish History, 15 W 16 St, New York, NY, 10011. Tel: 212-294-8340, 212-744-6400. p. 1580

Teixeira, Ann, Govt Doc, Rhode Island State Library, State House, Rm 208, 82 Smith St, Providence, RI, 02903. Tel: 401-222-2473. p. 2041

Teixeira, Monica, Ref (Info Servs), Monroe Township Public Library, Four Municipal Plaza, Monroe Township, NJ, 08831-1900. Tel: 732-521-5000. p. 1419

Teixeria, Roy, Dir, Western Philatelic Library, 3004 Spring St, Redwood City, CA, 94063. Tel: 650-306-9150. p. 200

Tejada, Christina, Sr Librn, California Department of Corrections Library System, California Institution for Men, 14901 Central Ave, Chino, CA, 91710. Tel: 909-597-1821, Ext 4368. p. 206

Teketele, Tsigereda, Br Mgr, Dallas Public Library, Paul Laurence Dunbar Lancaster-Kiest Branch, 2008 E Kiest Blvd, Dallas, TX, 75216-4448. Tel: 214-670-1952. p. 2165

Tekin, Kathy, Br Mgr, Jacksonville Public Library, Charles Webb Wesconnett Regional, 6887 103rd St, Jacksonville, FL, 32210-6897. Tel: 904-778-7305. p. 412

Teleha, John, Eng Librn, Spec Projects Librn, North Carolina Agricultural & Technical State University, 1601 E Market St, Greensboro, NC, 27411-0002. Tel: 336-285-4164. p. 1693

Teleha, Sheri, Cat, Ser, High Point University, One University Pkwy, High Point, NC, 27268. Tel: 336-841-4549. p. 1697

Teliha, James K, Dean, Library & Learning Commons, Utica University, 1600 Burrstone Rd, Utica, NY, 13502-4892. Tel: 315-792-3041. p. 1656

Telles, James, Instruction Librn, Folsom Lake College Library, Ten College Pkwy, Folsom, CA, 95630. Tel: 916-608-6528. p. 142

Tellez, Ida, Asst Dir, Port Isabel Public Library, 213 Yturria St, Port Isabel, TX, 78578. Tel: 956-943-1822. p. 2228

Tellman, Patricia, Libr Dir, Navy General Library Program, 1802 Doolittle Ave, NAS Fort Worth JRB, Fort Worth, TX, 76127. Tel: 817-782-7735. p. 2180

Tello, Humberto, Supvr, Ventura County Library, Albert H Soliz Library, 2820 Jourdan St, Oxnard, CA, 93036. Tel: 805-485-4515. p. 256

Temnyk, Mark, Mgr, Libr Student & Instrul Computing, Wayne State University, 106 Kresge Library, Detroit, MI, 48202. Tel: 313-577-5328. p. 2787

Temple, Joan, Librn, Minor Memorial Library, 23 South St, Roxbury, CT, 06783. Tel: 860-350-2181. p. 335

Temple, Kaila, Curator of Coll, Germantown Historical Society, 5501 Germantown Ave, Philadelphia, PA, 19144-2225. Tel: 215-844-1683, Ext 104. p. 1981

Temple-Rhodes, Gina, Govt Doc, Duluth Public Library, 520 W Superior St, Duluth, MN, 55802. Tel: 218-730-4249. p. 1172

Templeton, Teresa, Librn, Northeast Regional Library, Iuka Public Library, 204 N Main St, Iuka, MS, 38852. Tel: 662-423-6300. p. 1216

Templin, Barbara, Library Contact, Leon Public Library, 711 N West St, Leon, KS, 67074. Tel: 316-742-3438. p. 820

Ten Have, Beth, Dir of Libr Operations, Thomas Jefferson University, 1020 Walnut St, Philadelphia, PA, 19107. Tel: 215-503-2827. p. 1986

Ten Have, Elizabeth, Dir, Libr Acad Partnerships, Drexel University Libraries, Hagerty Library, 33rd & Market Sts, Philadelphia, PA, 19104-2875. Tel: 215-895-2751. p. 1976

Tenerife, Wilmer, Libr Tech, Burman University Library, 5410 Ramona Ave, Lacombe, AB, T4L 2B7, CANADA. Tel: 403-782-3381, Ext 4104. p. 2545

Tenewitz, Christie, Br Mgr, Union City Public Library, Summit Branch, 1800 Summit Ave, Union City, NJ, 07087-4320. Tel: 201-866-7503. p. 1449

Tenglund, Ann M, Dir, Library & Faculty Resource Ctr, Saint Bonaventure University, 3261 W State Rd, Saint Bonaventure, NY, 14778. Tel: 716-375-2378. p. 1635

Tenhage, Joyce, Br Supvr, Wellington County Library, Aboyne, 552 Wellington Rd 18, Fergus, ON, N1M 2W3, CANADA. Tel: 519-846-0918. p. 2641

Tennant, Bruce, Evening/Weekend Supvr, University of Maryland Libraries, Michelle Smith Performing Arts Library, 8270 Alumni Dr, College Park, MD, 20742-1630. Tel: 301-405-9218. p. 963

Tennant, Shannon, Coord, Libr Coll, Elon University, 308 N O'Kelly Ave, Elon, NC, 27244-0187. Tel: 336-278-6600. p. 1688

Tennant, Susan, Dir, Lititz Public Library, 651 Kissel Hill Rd, Lititz, PA, 17543. Tel: 717-626-2255. p. 1956

Tennell, Mariah, Syst Librn, Aurora University, 315 S Gladstone Ave, Aurora, IL, 60506-4892. Tel: 630-844-7533. p. 539

Tenney, Martha, Dir, Archives & Spec Coll, Barnard College, 3009 Broadway, New York, NY, 10027-6598. Tel: 212-854-4079. p. 1579

Tenney, Robin, Libr Dir, Lewis Egerton Smoot Memorial Library, 9533 Kings Hwy, King George, VA, 22485. Tel: 540-775-2147. p. 2327

Tennis, Joseph, Dr, Assoc Dean, Assoc Prof, Faculty Servs, University of Washington, Mary Gates Hall, Ste 370, Campus Box 352840, Seattle, WA, 98195-2840. Tel: 206-543-1794. p. 2794

Tennison, Katherine, Coll Mgt, Tech Serv Librn, Southwestern Oklahoma State University, 100 Campus Dr, Weatherford, OK, 73096-3002. Tel: 580-774-7021. p. 1868

Tenopir, Carol, Interim Dir, University of Tennessee, Knoxville, 451 Communications Bldg, 1345 Circle Park Dr, Knoxville, TN, 37996-0332. Tel: 865-974-2148. p. 2792

Tentico, Amanda, Dir, Kinney Memorial Library, 214 Main St, Hanlontown, IA, 50444. Tel: 641-896-2888. p. 757

Teoli, Liz, Ref Serv, Northern Essex Community College, 100 Elliott St, Haverhill, MA, 01830. Tel: 978-556-3426. p. 1024

Teoli, Liz, Ref & Instruction Librn, Umpqua Community College Library, 1140 Umpqua College Rd, Roseburg, OR, 97470. Tel: 541-440-7681. p. 1895

Teolis, Marilyn, Admin Librn, Bay Pines Veterans Affairs Healthcare System, 10000 Bay Pines Blvd, Bay Pines, FL, 33744. Tel: 727-398-9366. p. 384

Teolis, Marilyn, Clinical Med Librn, United States Department of Veterans Affairs, Library Service (142D), 13000 Bruce B Downs Blvd, Tampa, FL, 33612. Tel: 813-972-2000, Ext 6570. p. 449

Tepe, Leslie, Br Mgr, San Bernardino County Library, James S Thalman Branch, 14020 City Center Dr, Chino Hills, CA, 91709-5442. Tel: 909-590-5380. p. 213

Tepe, Nicholas, Dir, Athens County Public Libraries, 95 W Washington, Nelsonville, OH, 45764-1177. Tel: 740-753-2118. p. 1805

Teplitzky, Samantha, Sci Librn, University of California, Berkeley, Earth Sciences & Maps, 50 McCone Hall, Berkeley, CA, 94720-6000. Tel: 510-642-2997. p. 122

Tepper, Andrei, Fr, Dean, Saint Herman Orthodox Theological Seminary Library, 414 Mission Rd, Kodiak, AK, 99615. Tel: 907-486-3524. p. 49

Terbeek, Wendy L, Dir, Hammond Library of Crown Point NY, 2732 Main St, Crown Point, NY, 12928. Tel: 518-597-3616. p. 1523

Terhorst, John, Syst Analyst, Weil, Gotshal & Manges LLP, 767 Fifth Ave, New York, NY, 10153. Tel: 212-310-8444. p. 1603

Terhune, Janet, Dir, Harness Racing Museum & Hall of Fame, 240 Main St, Goshen, NY, 10924-2157. Tel: 845-294-6330. p. 1540

Terifay, Lora, Head, Children's Servx, Southampton Free Library, 947 Street Rd, Southampton, PA, 18966. Tel: 215-322-1415. p. 2009

Terlaga, Amy, Dir, User Serv, Bibliomation Inc, 24 Wooster Ave, Waterbury, CT, 06708. Tel: 203-577-4070, Ext 101. p. 2762

Terlecky, John, Librn, Ukrainian Museum & Library of Stamford, 39 Clovelly Rd, Stamford, CT, 06902-3004. Tel: 203-323-8866, 203-324-0488. p. 339

Terminella, Sue E, Med Librn, J Stephen Lindsey Medical Library, 1602 Skipwith Rd, Richmond, VA, 23229-5205. Tel: 804-289-4728. p. 2341

Ternes, Lexi, Librn, Viola Township Library, 100 N Grice, Viola, KS, 67149. Tel: 620-584-6679. p. 841

Terpening, Judi, Dir, Madison-Jefferson County Public Library, 420 W Main St, Madison, IN, 47250. Tel: 812-265-2744. p. 704

Terpening, Nancy, Head, Tech Serv, Galesburg Public Library, 40 E Simmons St, Galesburg, IL, 61401-4591. Tel: 309-343-6118. p. 591

Terpis, Katherine, Assoc Dean, Interim Dean, New Mexico State University Library, 2911 McFie Circle, Las Cruces, NM, 88003. Tel: 575-646-1508. p. 1471

Terpstra, Charles, Archivist, Librn, Theological School of Protestant Reformed Churches Library, 4949 Ivanrest Ave SW, Wyoming, MI, 49418. Tel: 616-531-1490. p. 1160

Terracino, Haley, Young Adult Coordinator, Ringwood Public Library, 30 Cannici Dr, Ringwood, NJ, 07456. Tel: 973-962-6256, Ext 115. p. 1439

Terrado, Maura, Ad, Hillside Public Library, 405 N Hillside Ave, Hillside, IL, 60162-1295. Tel: 708-449-7510. p. 599

Terrafranca, Deya, Dir, Research Library & Archives, Museum of Ventura County, 100 E Main St, Ventura, CA, 93001. Tel: 805-653-0323, Ext 320. p. 255

Terranova, Terri, Librn, Southwestern Illinois College, 4950 Maryville Rd, Rm 455, Granite City, IL, 62040. Tel: 618-931-0600, ext. 7353. p. 595

Terrazas, Estella, Pub Serv Dir, Altadena Library District, 600 E Mariposa St, Altadena, CA, 91001. Tel: 626-798-0833. p. 116

Terrazas, Estella, Admin Serv, Teton County Library, 125 Virginian Lane, Jackson, WY, 83001. Tel: 307-733-2164, Ext 3101. p. 2495

Terrazas, Julie, Acq, Cat, Golden West College, 15744 Golden West St, Huntington Beach, CA, 92647. Tel: 714-895-8741, Ext 55207. p. 151

Terrazas, Sara, Dir, Kinney County Public Library, 510 S Ellen St, Brackettville, TX, 78832. Tel: 830-563-2884. p. 2149

Terrell, Danielle, Govt Doc Librn, Alcorn State University, 1000 ASU Dr, Alcorn State, MS, 39096-7500. Tel: 601-877-6358. p. 1211

Terrell, Gloria, Dir, Kirchner-French Memorial Library, 101 Main St, Peterson, IA, 51047. Tel: 712-295-6705. p. 777

Terrell, Ian, Technical Spec, Kaiser Permanente, 3800 N Interstate Ave, Portland, OR, 97227-1098. Tel: 503-335-2400. p. 1891

Terrell, Lori Beth, Br Librn, Pottawatomie Wabaunsee Regional Library, Alma Branch, 115 W Third St, Alma, KS, 66401. Tel: 785-765-3647. p. 834

Terrell, Staci, Br Mgr, Indianapolis Public Library, Infozone, The Children's Museum, 3000 N Meridian St, Indianapolis, IN, 46208. Tel: 317-275-4430. p. 695

Terrile, Vikki C, Public Services & Assessment Librn, Queensborough Community College, City University of New York, 222-05 56th Ave, Bayside, NY, 11364-1497. Tel: 718-281-5711. p. 1491

Terrill, Lori, Spec Coll Librn, Black Hills State University, 1200 University St, Unit 9676, Spearfish, SD, 57799-9676. Tel: 605-642-6361. p. 2083

Terrill, Melanie, Libr Dir, West Bridgewater Public Library, 80 Howard St, West Bridgewater, MA, 02379-1710. Tel: 508-894-1255. p. 1065

Terrio, Robert, Chair, Librn, Rider University, Katharine Houk Talbott Library, Franklin F Moore Library Bldg, 3rd & 4th Flrs, 2083 Lawrenceville Rd, Lawrenceville, NJ, 08648. Tel: 609-921-7100, Ext 8237. p. 1411

Territo, Stephen, Head, Libr Operations, Vernon Area Public Library District, 300 Olde Half Day Rd, Lincolnshire, IL, 60069. Tel: 847-634-3650. p. 609

Terro, Jolie, Libr Dir, Cameron Parish Library, 512 Marshall St, Cameron, LA, 70631. Tel: 337-775-5421. p. 886

Terron-Elder, Miriam, Knowledge Servs, Spec, Educational Testing Service, Turnbull Hall, Mail Stop 01-R, 660 Rosedale Rd, Princeton, NJ, 08541. Tel: 609-734-5049. p. 1436

Terrones, Mary, Libr Dir, Hot Springs Public Library, 2005 Library Dr, Hot Springs, SD, 57747-2767. Tel: 605-745-3151. p. 2077

Terry, Beverly, Ref Serv, Logan County Public Library, 225 Armory Dr, Russellville, KY, 42276. Tel: 270-726-6129. p. 874

Terry, Briana, Admin Serv Mgr, Appomattox Regional Library System, 209 E Cawson St, Hopewell, VA, 23860. Tel: 804-458-6329, Ext 2004. p. 2326

Terry, Carol S, Dir, Libr Serv, Rhode Island School of Design Library, 15 Westminster St, Providence, RI, 02903. Tel: 401-709-5900. p. 2040

Terry, Cindy, Coll Mgt Spec, Thurgood Marshall State Law Library, Courts of Appeals Bldg, 361 Rowe Blvd, Annapolis, MD, 21401. Tel: 410-260-1430. p. 950

Terry, Connie, Dir, Woodward Public Library, 1500 W Main St, Woodward, OK, 73801. Tel: 580-254-8544. p. 1869

Terry, Courtney, Ms, Librn III/Ref, McMinnville Public Library, 225 NW Adams St, McMinnville, OR, 97128. Tel: 503-435-5562. p. 1886

Terry, Delbert, Libr Dir, Desoto Parish Library, 109 Crosby St, Mansfield, LA, 71052. Tel: 318-872-6100. p. 895

Terry, Eric, Sr Librn, Adult & YA Serv, Mary Lib Saleh Euless Public Library, 201 N Ector Dr, Euless, TX, 76039-3595. Tel: 817-685-1480. p. 2176

Terry, Gynene, Asst Dir, Troy Public Library, 500 E Walnut St, Troy, AL, 36081. Tel: 334-566-1314. p. 37

Terry, Hilda, Librn, Mid-Arkansas Regional Library, Roy & Christine Sturgis Library of Cleveland County, 203 W Magnolia St, Rison, AR, 71665. Tel: 870-325-7270. p. 103

Terry, Kansas, Ch Serv, Sr Librn, Haltom City Public Library, 4809 Haltom Rd, Haltom City, TX, 76117-3622. Tel: 817-222-7788. p. 2187

Terry, Nicole, Libr Dir, Newton Public Library, 100 N Third Ave W, Newton, IA, 50208. Tel: 641-792-4108. p. 773

Terry, Shannon, Libr Dir, Minersville Public Library, 40 W Main St, Minersville, UT, 84752. Tel: 435-386-2267. p. 2266

Terry, Sondra, Libr Dir, Marengo-Union Library District, 19714 E Grant Hwy, Marengo, IL, 60152. Tel: 815-568-8236. p. 613

Terry, Susan, E-Resources Librn, University of North Carolina at Asheville, One University Heights, Ramsey Library, CPO 1500, Asheville, NC, 28804. Tel: 828-251-6625. p. 1673

Terry, Tammie, Br Mgr, Madison County Library System, Rebecca Baine Rigby Library, 994 Madison Ave, Madison, MS, 39110. Tel: 601-856-2749. p. 1213

Terry, Tessa, Communications Coordr, Nebraska Library Commission, The Atrium, 1200 N St, Ste 120, Lincoln, NE, 68508-2023. Tel: 402-471-3434. p. 1322

Terry, Tracie, Circ Supvr, Davis County Library, Kaysville Branch, 215 N Fairfield Rd, Kaysville, UT, 84037. Tel: 801-451-1800. p. 2263

Teruya, Lynette, Librn, Chaminade University of Honolulu, 3140 Waialae Ave, Honolulu, HI, 96816-1578. Tel: 808-739-4860. p. 506

Tesch, Jennie, Br Mgr, Rampart Library District, Florissant Public Library, 334 Circle Dr, Florissant, CO, 80816. Tel: 719-748-3939. p. 299

Tesch, Rosella, Dir, Chadron Public Library, 507 Bordeaux, Chadron, NE, 69337. Tel: 308-432-0531. p. 1310

Tescher, Joanne, County Librn, Golden Valley County Library, 54 Central Ave S, Beach, ND, 58621. Tel: 701-872-4627. p. 1729

Tesdesco-Blair, Graham, Dir, Darwin R Barker Library Association, Seven Day St, Fredonia, NY, 14063-1891. Tel: 716-672-8051. p. 1535

Teske, Amy, Mgr, Youth Serv, Carol Stream Public Library, 616 Hiawatha Dr, Carol Stream, IL, 60188. Tel: 630-653-0755. p. 549

Teske, Mary Ann, Cat Librn, Luther Seminary Library, 2375 Como Ave, Saint Paul, MN, 55108. Tel: 651-641-3446. p. 1200

Teske, Matt, Mgr, Mat Serv, Indian Trails Public Library District, 355 S Schoenbeck Rd, Wheeling, IL, 60090. Tel: 847-459-4100. p. 662

Tessmer, Wanda, Dir, Carp Lake Township Library, 36349 Mall Circle Dr, White Pine, MI, 49971. Tel: 906-885-5888. p. 1159

Test, Janis, Head, Info Serv, Abilene Public Library, 202 Cedar St, Abilene, TX, 79601-5793. Tel: 325-676-6017. p. 2131

Testa Cinquino, Joy, Asst Deputy Dir-Development & Communications, Buffalo & Erie County Public Library System, One Lafayette Sq, Buffalo, NY, 14203-1887. Tel: 716-858-8900. p. 1507

Testani, Erica, Youth Serv Librn, Lewis Egerton Smoot Memorial Library, 9533 Kings Hwy, King George, VA, 22485. Tel: 540-775-2147. p. 2327

Testerman, Meghan, Behav Sci Librn, Princeton University, Lewis Science Library, Washington Rd, Princeton, NJ, 08544-0001. Tel: 609-258-5481. p. 1437

Testori, Peter, Asst Dean, Exec Dir, Bay Path College, 539 Longmeadow St, Longmeadow, MA, 01106. Tel: 413-565-1058. p. 1029

Teter, Darla, Br Librn, Platte County Public Library, Chugwater Branch, 301 Second St, Chugwater, WY, 82210. Tel: 307-422-3275. p. 2500

Teterenko, Halia, Librn, University of Manitoba, St Andrew's College Library, 29 Dysart Rd, Winnipeg, MB, R3T 2M7, CANADA. Tel: 204-474-8901. p. 2594

Tethong, Zayden, Instruction & Assessment Librn, Westminster College, 1840 S 1300 East, Salt Lake City, UT, 84105-3697. Tel: 801-832-2250. p. 2273

Tetrault, Paul, Exec Dir, Insurance Library Association of Boston, 156 State St, 2nd Flr, Boston, MA, 02109. Tel: 617-227-2087, Ext 201. p. 996

Tetreault, Annie, Head, Ref Serv, Pub Serv, Kirkland Public Library, 17100 Hymus Blvd, Kirkland, QC, H9J 2W2, CANADA. Tel: 514-630-2726. p. 2714

Tetzloff, John, Mgr, Columbus Metropolitan Library, Hilltop Branch, 511 S Hague Ave, Columbus, OH, 43204. p. 1772

Teutsch, Sue, Asst Dir, Ch Serv, Gibson Memorial Library, 200 W Howard St, Creston, IA, 50801-2339. Tel: 641-782-2277. p. 743

Teval, Charles, Asst Dir, Hedberg Public Library, 316 S Main St, Janesville, WI, 53545. Tel: 608-758-6605. p. 2443

Tewell McCord, Eamon C, Head, Res, Outreach & Instruction, Columbia University, Thomas J Watson Library of Business & Economics, 130 Uris Hall, 3022 Broadway, New York, NY, 10027. Tel: 212-854-7803. p. 1584

Tews, Annette, Dir, Bloomfield Public Library, 107 N Columbia St, Bloomfield, IA, 52537-1431. Tel: 641-664-2209. p. 735

Tezak, Katie, Librn, Logan County Libraries, West Liberty Branch, 117 N Detroit St, West Liberty, OH, 43357. Tel: 937-465-3656. p. 1750

Thach, Anh, Ser, University of Michigan-Flint, 303 E Kearsley St, Flint, MI, 48502. Tel: 810-762-3414. p. 1107

Thacker, Avie, Instruction & Collection Mgmt Librn, Blue Ridge Community College, One College Lane, Weyers Cave, VA, 24486. Tel: 540-453-2247. p. 2352

Thacker, Elizabeth, Br Mgr, San Francisco Public Library, Merced Branch Library, 155 Winston Dr, San Francisco, CA, 94132-2032. Tel: 415-355-2825. p. 228

Thacker, Lynn, Cat, Duncan Public Library, 2211 N Hwy 81, Duncan, OK, 73533. Tel: 580-255-0636. p. 1845

Thacker, Tim, Head, Tech Serv, Sussex County Library System, 125 Morris Tpk, Newton, NJ, 07860. Tel: 973-948-3660. p. 1429

Thackson, Sharon, Ch Serv Librn, Gallatin Public Library, 123 E Main St, Gallatin, TN, 37066-2509. Tel: 615-452-1722. p. 2099

Thai, Trung, Syst Coordr, De Anza College, 21250 Stevens Creek Blvd, Cupertino, CA, 95014-5793. Tel: 408-846-8438. p. 133

Thalacker, Reagen, Regional Librn, Southeastern Libraries Cooperating, 2600 19th St NW, Rochester, MN, 55901-0767. Tel: 507-288-5513. p. 2768

Thaler, Lynda, Acq, Metadata Serv, Bucknell University, 220 Bertrand Library, One Dent Dr, Lewisburg, PA, 17837. Tel: 570-577-1557. p. 1955

Thaler, Susan, Dep Dir, Yonkers Public Library, One Larkin Ctr, Yonkers, NY, 10701. Tel: 914-337-1500. p. 1668

Thalhimer, Sheila, Libr Dir, Johns Hopkins University School of Advanced International, 1740 Massachusetts Ave NW, 6th Flr, Washington, DC, 20036. Tel: 202-663-5905. p. 370

Thalman, Jennifer, ILL, Virginia Beach Public Library, Interlibrary Loan Division, 4100 Virginia Beach Blvd, Virginia Beach, VA, 23452. p. 2351

Thalmann, David, Dir, Admin & Finance, Redwood Library & Athenaeum, 50 Bellevue Ave, Newport, RI, 02840. Tel: 401-847-0292. p. 2035

Thampi-Lukose, Usha, Dir, Washington Public Library, 20 W Carlton Ave, Washington, NJ, 07882. Tel: 908-689-0201. p. 1451

Thanh, Quang, Syst Coordr, De Anza College, 21250 Stevens Creek Blvd, Cupertino, CA, 95014-5793. Tel: 408-864-8494. p. 133

Thao, Xia, Br Mgr, Stanislaus County Library, Patterson Branch, 46 N Salado, Patterson, CA, 95363-2587. Tel: 209-892-6473. p. 178

Tharman, Laura, Libr Dir, Hesston College, 301 S Main St, Hesston, KS, 67062. Tel: 620-327-8245. p. 813

Thatcher, Amy, Br Mgr, Free Library of Philadelphia, Richmond Branch, 2987 Almond St, Philadelphia, PA, 19134-4955. Tel: 215-685-9992. p. 1980

Thatcher, Celeste, Supvr of Educ, Correctional Institution for Women, PO Box 4004, Clinton, NJ, 08809-4004. Tel: 908-735-7111, Ext 3641. p. 1397

Thatcher, Wendy, Asst Dir, Head, Ref & ILL Serv, Topsfield Town Library, One S Common St, Topsfield, MA, 01983. Tel: 978-887-1528. p. 1060

Thayer, J Peter, Ref & Access Serv Librn, Marietta College, 215 Fifth St, Marietta, OH, 45750. Tel: 740-376-4361. p. 1798

Thayer, Johnathan, Asst Prof, Queens College of the City University of New York, Benjamin Rosenthal Library, Rm 254, 65-30 Kissena Blvd, Flushing, NY, 11367-1597. Tel: 718-997-3790. p. 2789

Thayer, Marilyn, Libr Tech, Middleborough Public Library, 102 N Main St, Middleborough, MA, 02346. Tel: 508-946-2470. p. 1035

Thebarge, Nathan, Dir, Libr Serv, Trinity International University, 2065 Half Day Rd, Deerfield, IL, 60015-1241. Tel: 847-317-4013. p. 577

Theerman, Paul, PhD, Libr Dir, New York Academy of Medicine Library, 1216 Fifth Ave, New York, NY, 10029. Tel: 212-822-7350. p. 1593

Theimer, Sarah, Cat & Metadata, University of New Hampshire Library, 18 Library Way, Durham, NH, 03824. Tel: 603-862-5603. p. 1362

Theis, Jacob, Libr Asst, Denver Academy Library, 4400 E Iliff Ave, Denver, CO, 80222. Tel: 303-777-5870. p. 275

Theisen, Colleen, Lecturer, University of Iowa, 3087 Main Library, 125 W Washington St, Iowa City, IA, 52242-1420. Tel: 319-335-5707. p. 2785

Theiss, Danielle, Libr Dir, Park University Library, Norrington Ctr, 8700 NW River Park Dr, CMB 61, Parkville, MO, 64152. Tel: 816-584-6285. p. 1265

Theissen, Inga, Colls Mgr, American Swedish Institute, 2600 Park Ave, Minneapolis, MN, 55407. Tel: 612-871-4907. p. 1182

Thelen, Pat, Libr Asst, Lied Randolph Public Library, 111 N Douglas St, Randolph, NE, 68771-5510. Tel: 402-337-0046. p. 1334

Theobald, Maureen, Admin Dir, Gold Coast Library Network, 3437 Empresa Dr, Ste C, San Luis Obispo, CA, 93401-7355. Tel: 805-543-6082. p. 2761

Theobald, Walter, Ref Librn, North Chicago Public Library, 2100 Argonne Dr, North Chicago, IL, 60064. Tel: 847-689-0125. p. 626

Theodore, Kelly, Libr Tech, Connors State College, 700 College Rd, Warner, OK, 74469-9700. Tel: 918-463-6210. p. 1868

Theodore-McIntosh, Roslyn, Dir, Gowling WLG (Canada) Library, One First Canadian Pl, 100 King St W, Ste 1600, Toronto, ON, M5X 1G5, CANADA. Tel: 416-862-5735. p. 2689

Theodori, Judith, Mgr, Exponent, 149 Commonwealth Dr, Menlo Park, CA, 94025. Tel: 650-688-7184. p. 175

Theriault, Bonnie, Asst Dir, ILL Librn, Aldrich Free Public Library, 299 Main St, Moosup, CT, 06354. Tel: 860-564-8760. p. 323

Theriault, Ken, Dir, Madawaska Public Library, 393 Main St, Madawaska, ME, 04756-1126. Tel: 207-728-3606. p. 931

Thériault McGraw, Geneviève, Libr Dir, York Library Region, Bibliothèque Carrefour Beausoleil Library, 300 Chemin Beaverbrook, Miramichi, NB, E1V 1A1, CANADA. Tel: 506-627-4084. p. 2602

Theriot, Clifton, Archivist, Co-Dir, Nicholls State University, 906 E First St, Thibodaux, LA, 70310. Tel: 985-448-4621. p. 911

Thero, Stephanie, Client Serv Mgr, Yellowhead Regional Library, 433 King St, Spruce Grove, AB, T7X 3B4, CANADA. Tel: 780-962-2003, Ext 224. p. 2554

Theroux, Shari, Discovery Librn, Syst Librn, South Dakota State University, 1300 N Campus Dr, Box 2115, Brookings, SD, 57007. Tel: 605-688-5560. p. 2074

Therrien, Eric, Dir, Bibliotheque Gabrielle Roy, 350 rue Saint-Joseph Est, Quebec, QC, G1K 3B2, CANADA. Tel: 418-641-6789. p. 2729

Therrien, Manon, Documentation Tech, Centre de Santé et de Services Sociaux du Nord de Lanaudière, Bibliothèque de l'Hôpital Pierre-Le Gardeur, 911, montée des Pionniers, Terrebonne, QC, J6V 2H2, CANADA. Tel: 450-654-7525, Ext 22207. p. 2733

Therrien, Susan, Dir, Libr Serv, Port Colborne Public Library, 310 King St, Port Colborne, ON, L3K 4H1, CANADA. Tel: 905-834-6512. p. 2673

Therrien, Tracey, Chief Librn, Nelson Public Library, 602 Stanley St, Nelson, BC, V1L 1N4, CANADA. Tel: 250-352-6333. p. 2572

Thevenote, Theresa, Dir, Avoyelles Parish Library, 606 N Main St, Marksville, LA, 71351. Tel: 318-253-7559. p. 896

Thewis, Jennie, Dir, Legion Memorial Library, 106 Iron St, Mellen, WI, 54546. Tel: 715-274-8331. p. 2455

Thexton, Helen, Serv Area Mgr, Halifax Public Libraries, 60 Alderney Dr, Dartmouth, NS, B2Y 4P8, CANADA. Tel: 902-490-5744. p. 2617

Theyer, Hillary, County Librn, Monterey County Free Libraries, 188 Seaside Ctr, Marina, CA, 93933-2500. Tel: 831-883-7573. p. 172

Thibault, Erika, Libr Dir, Sonoma County Library, 6135 State Farm Dr, Rohnert Park, CA, 94928. Tel: 707-545-0831. p. 204

Thibault, Sylvie, Dir Gen, Reseau BIBLIO de l'Outaouais, 2295 Saint-Louis St, Gatineau, QC, J8T 5L8, CANADA. Tel: 819-561-6008. p. 2779

Thibeault, Emelia, Libr Office Mgr, Goodnow Library, 21 Concord Rd, Sudbury, MA, 01776-2383. Tel: 978-440-5511. p. 1058

Thibert, Lori, Tech Librn, Tampa-Hillsborough County Public Library System, Bruton Memorial Library, 302 W McLendon St, Plant City, FL, 33563. Tel: 813-757-9215. p. 448

Thibodaux, Julia, Circ Supvr, Saint Charles Parish Library, Norco Branch, 590 Apple St, Norco, LA, 70079. Tel: 985-764-6581. p. 888

Thibodeau, Marianne, Dir, University of Maine at Machias, 116 O'Brien Ave, Machias, ME, 04654. Tel: 207-255-1234. p. 931

Thibodeau, Nicole, Asst Dir, Taos Public Library, 402 Camino de La Placita, Taos, NM, 87571. Tel: 575-758-3063. p. 1478

Thibodeau, Patricia, Libr & Archives Asst, The California Maritime Academy Library, 200 Maritime Academy Dr, Vallejo, CA, 94590. Tel: 707-654-1089. p. 255

Thibodeau, Sarah, Cat Librn, Ref Archivist, Marian University, 45 S National Ave, Fond du Lac, WI, 54935-4699. Tel: 920-923-8926. p. 2435

Thibodeau, Sean, Commun Planning Coordr, Pollard Memorial Library, 401 Merrimack St, Lowell, MA, 01852. Tel: 978-674-4120. p. 1029

Thibodeaux, Carolyn, Ch, Port Arthur Public Library, 4615 Ninth Ave, Port Arthur, TX, 77642. Tel: 409-985-8838. p. 2228

Thibodeaux, Shandi, Instr, Pub Serv Librn, McNeese State University, 300 S Beauregard Dr, Lake Charles, LA, 70609. Tel: 337-475-5739. p. 894

Thiede, Malina, Assoc Librn, Dept Chair, State University of New York College at Plattsburgh, Two Draper Ave, Plattsburgh, NY, 12901. Tel: 518-564-5329. p. 1619

Thiel, Beth, Circ, University of Wisconsin-Rock County Library, 2909 Kellogg Ave, Janesville, WI, 53546-5606. Tel: 608-898-6533. p. 2443

Thiel, Breanne, Adult Serv, ILL, Park County Library System, Powell Branch, 217 E Third St, Powell, WY, 82435-1903. Tel: 307-754-8828. p. 2494

Thiele, Ronald L, Asst Dean, Advan, Syracuse University Libraries, 222 Waverly Ave, Syracuse, NY, 13244-2010. Tel: 315-443-2537. p. 1650

Thiele-Martin, Dollie, Advanced Cataloger, Cedar County Library District, 717 East St, Stockton, MO, 65785. Tel: 417-276-3413. p. 1282

Thielker, Jennifer, Libr Dir, Taylor Library, 49 E Derry Rd, East Derry, NH, 03041. Tel: 603-432-7186. p. 1362

Thiem, Kimberly, Children's Activities Dir, Genoa Public Library, 421 Willard Ave, Genoa, NE, 68640. Tel: 402-993-2943. p. 1315

Thiem, Tammi, Libr Dir, Genoa Public Library, 421 Willard Ave, Genoa, NE, 68640. Tel: 402-993-2943. p. 1315

Thiem, Tammi, Dir, Three Rivers Library System, 11929 Elm St, Ste 18, Omaha, NE, 68144. Tel: 402-330-7884. p. 1330

Thiem-Menning, Ashley, Dir, Kaukauna Public Library, 207 Thilmany Rd, Ste 200, Kaukauna, WI, 54130-2436. Tel: 920-766-6340. p. 2444

Thier, Karen, Dir, Health Info Mgt, Northwestern Medicine Palos Hospital, 12251 S 80th Ave, Palos Heights, IL, 60463. Tel: 708-923-4000. p. 631

Thiesen, Barbara, Co-Dir, Bethel College, 1001 Bethel Circle, Mishawaka, IN, 46545. Tel: 574-807-7180. p. 706

Thiesen, Barbara, Cat, Bethel College Library, Mennonite Library & Archives, 300 E 27th St, North Newton, KS, 67117-0531. Tel: 316-284-5304. p. 827

Thiesen, Barbara, Co-Dir, Libr & Dir Tech Serv, Bethel College Library, 300 E 27th St, North Newton, KS, 67117-0531. Tel: 316-284-5361. p. 827
Thiesen, John, Archivist, Co-Dir, Bethel College, 1001 Bethel Circle, Mishawaka, IN, 46545. Tel: 574-807-7180. p. 706
Thiesen, John, Archives, Co-Dir, Bethel College Library, 300 E 27th St, North Newton, KS, 67117-0531. Tel: 316-284-5361. p. 827
Thiesen, John, Archivist, Dir, Bethel College Library, Mennonite Library & Archives, 300 E 27th St, North Newton, KS, 67117-0531. Tel: 316-284-5304. p. 827
Thiesen, Matthew, Dir, Libr & Info Serv, Western Seminary, 5511 SE Hawthorne Blvd, Portland, OR, 97215-3367. Tel: 503-517-1841. p. 1895
Thiessen, David, Libr Mgr, Fraser Valley Regional Library, Aldergrove Library, 26770 29th Ave, Aldergrove, BC, V4W 3B8, CANADA. Tel: 604-856-6415. p. 2561
Thiessen, David, Libr Mgr, Fraser Valley Regional Library, Brookswood Library, 20045 40th Ave, Langley, BC, V3A 2W2, CANADA. Tel: 604-534-7055. p. 2561
Thiessen, David, Libr Mgr, Fraser Valley Regional Library, Fort Langley Library, 9167 Glover Rd, Fort Langley, BC, V1M 2R6, CANADA. Tel: 604-888-0722. p. 2561
Thiessen, David, Libr Mgr, Fraser Valley Regional Library, Muriel Arnason Library, Township of Langley Civic Ctr, 130 - 20338 65th Ave, Langley, BC, V2Y 2X3, CANADA. Tel: 604-532-3590. p. 2561
Thiessen, David, Libr Mgr, Fraser Valley Regional Library, Murrayville Library, Unit 100 - 22071 48th Ave, Langley, BC, V3A 3N1, CANADA. Tel: 604-533-0339. p. 2562
Thiessen, David, Libr Mgr, Fraser Valley Regional Library, Walnut Grove Library, Walnut Grove Community Ctr, 8889 Walnut Grove Dr, Langley, BC, V1M 2N7, CANADA. Tel: 604-882-0410. p. 2562
Thiessen, David, Libr Mgr, Fraser Valley Regional Library, White Rock Library, 15342 Buena Vista Ave, White Rock, BC, V4B 1Y6, CANADA. Tel: 604-541-2201. p. 2562
Thiessen, Jean, Libr Dir, Whitewater Memorial Library, 118 E Topeka, Whitewater, KS, 67154. Tel: 316-799-2471. p. 842
Thiessen, Jonquil, Mgr, Acme Municipal Library, 610 Walsh Ave, Acme, AB, T0M 0A0, CANADA. Tel: 403-546-3879. p. 2521
Thiessen, Tanya, Mgr, Strategic Initiatives, Surrey Libraries, City Centre, 10350 University Dr, Surrey, BC, V3T 4B8, CANADA. Tel: 604-598-7430. p. 2577
Thieszen, Ashley, Ch, Lake City Public Library, 110 E Washington St, Lake City, IA, 51449. Tel: 712-464-3413. p. 763
Thigpen, Sandy, Circ Serv Mgr, Victoria Public Library, 302 N Main St, Victoria, TX, 77901. Tel: 361-485-3302. p. 2252
Thill, John, Assoc Dir, Ada Community Library, Hidden Springs Branch, 5868 W Hidden Springs Dr, Boise, ID, 83714. Tel: 208-229-2665. p. 516
Thill, John, Asst Dir, Meridian Library District, 1326 W Cherry Lane, Meridian, ID, 83642. Tel: 208-888-4451. p. 525
Thill, Mary, Humanities Librn, Ref Coordr, Northeastern Illinois University, 5500 N Saint Louis Ave, Chicago, IL, 60625-4699. Tel: 773-442-4400. p. 566
Thimons, Dana, Health Sci Librn, Xavier University of Louisiana, One Drexel Dr, New Orleans, LA, 70125-1098. Tel: 504-520-7311. p. 904
Thind, Harjinder, Br Mgr, Surrey Libraries, Newton, 13795 70th Ave, Surrey, BC, V3W 0E1, CANADA. Tel: 604-598-7410. p. 2577
Thind, Harjinder, Br Mgr, Surrey Libraries, Strawberry Hill, 7399-122nd St, Surrey, BC, V3W 5J2, CANADA. Tel: 604-598-7410. p. 2577
Thirmodson, Kelly, Asst Dir, University of North Dakota, Harley E French Library of the Health Sciences, School of Medicine & Health Sciences, 501 N Columbia Rd, Stop 9002, Grand Forks, ND, 58202-9002. Tel: 701-777-4129. p. 1734
Thiry, Christopher J J, Assoc Librn, Maps Librn, Colorado School of Mines, 1400 Illinois St, Golden, CO, 80401-1887. Tel: 303-273-3697. p. 282
Thiry, Steve, Libr Dir, West Bend Community Memorial Library, 630 Poplar St, West Bend, WI, 53095-3380. Tel: 262-335-5151. p. 2487
Thissault, Sandra, Team Leader, Bibliotheques de Trois-Rivieres, Bibliotheque de La Franciade, 100 rue de la Mairie, Trois-Rivieres, QC, G8W 1S1, CANADA. Tel: 819-374-6419. p. 2738
Thistle, Carol, Mkt & Pub Relations Dir, Concord Museum Library, 53 Cambridge Tpk, Concord, MA, 01742. Tel: 978-369-9763. p. 1012
Thistle, Dawn, Libr Dir, Gardiner Public Library, 152 Water St, Gardiner, ME, 04345. Tel: 207-582-3312. p. 926
Thistle, Dawn R, Libr Dir, Haston Free Public Library, 161 N Main St, North Brookfield, MA, 01535. Tel: 508-867-0208. p. 1041
Thode, Nicole, Libr Mgr, Timberland Regional Library, Tumwater Branch, 7023 New Market St, Tumwater, WA, 98501-6563. Tel: 360-943-7790. p. 2389
Thom, Angie, Dir, Jasper Municipal Library, 500 Robson St, Jasper, AB, T0E 1E0, CANADA. Tel: 780-852-3652. p. 2544
Thomann, Maggie, Mgr, Northbrook Public Library, 1201 Cedar Lane, Northbrook, IL, 60062-4581. Tel: 847-272-6224. p. 627
Thomas, Adrian, Asst Librn, New York Psychoanalytic Society & Institute, 247 E 82nd St, New York, NY, 10028-2701. Tel: 212-879-6900. p. 1594
Thomas, Alice, Dir, Moore County Library, 101 Saunders St, Carthage, NC, 28327. Tel: 910-947-5335. p. 1677
Thomas, Allie, Librn, Byrd Polar Research Center, 176 Scott Hall, 1090 Carmack Rd, Columbus, OH, 43210-1002. Tel: 614-292-6715. p. 1771
Thomas, Amy, Educ Coordr, Alaska State Department of Corrections, 9101 Hesterberg Rd, Eagle River, AK, 99577. Tel: 907-694-9511. p. 45
Thomas, Amy, Dir, Kent State University, 3300 Lake Rd, Ashtabula, OH, 44004-2316. Tel: 440-964-4237. p. 1748
Thomas, Ann Margaret, Dir, Friend Memorial Public Library, One Reach Rd, Brooklin, ME, 04616. Tel: 207-359-2276. p. 918
Thomas, Ann Marie, Head, Circ, Prospect Heights Public Library District, 12 N Elm St, Prospect Heights, IL, 60070-1450. Tel: 847-259-3500. p. 637
Thomas, Anne, Law Libr Asst, Oswego County Supreme Court, 25 E Oneida St, Oswego, NY, 13126. Tel: 315-207-7565. p. 1613
Thomas, Annie, Hawaiian Res Spec, Kapi'olani Community College Library, 4303 Diamond Head Rd, Honolulu, HI, 96816. Tel: 808-734-9599. p. 512
Thomas, Barbara, Pub Serv Librn, Dallas International University Library, 7500 W Camp Wisdom Rd, Dallas, TX, 75236-5699. Tel: 972-708-7416. p. 2164
Thomas, Brad, Br Mgr, Tulsa City-County Library, Schusterman-Benson Library, 3333 E 32nd Pl, Tulsa, OK, 74135. p. 1866
Thomas, Bud, Libr Supvr, Operations Mgr, ONE National Gay & Lesbian Archives at the USC Libraries, 909 W Adams Blvd, Los Angeles, CA, 90007. Tel: 213-821-2771. p. 167
Thomas, Cam, Med Staff Spec, Saint Luke's Hospital, 5901 Monclova Rd, Maumee, OH, 43537-1855. Tel: 419-893-5917. p. 1800
Thomas, Camille, Asst Br Librn, Emery County Library System, 115 N 100 E, Castle Dale, UT, 84513. Tel: 435-381-2554. p. 2261
Thomas, Cecelia, Br Mgr, Charles County Public Library, P D Brown Memorial, 50 Village St, Waldorf, MD, 20602. Tel: 301-645-2864. p. 969
Thomas, Celene, Br Mgr, Pend Oreille County Library District, Newport Public Library, 116 S Washington Ave, Newport, WA, 99156. p. 2372
Thomas, Christina, Head, Circ, Scranton Public Library, 500 Vine St, Scranton, PA, 18509-3298. Tel: 570-348-3000, Ext 3001. p. 2004
Thomas, Chuck, Dean, Libr Serv, Western Carolina University, 176 Central Dr, Cullowhee, NC, 28723. Tel: 828-227-7307. p. 1683
Thomas, Claire, Ad, Cherry Hill Public Library, 1100 Kings Hwy N, Cherry Hill, NJ, 08034. Tel: 856-667-0300. p. 1395
Thomas, Courtlann, Dir, Learning Res, Lakeland, Polk State College, Lakeland Campus Library, 3425 Winter Lake Rd, Sta 62, Lakeland, FL, 33803. Tel: 863-297-1042. p. 455
Thomas, Dallas, Libr Mgr, Levy County Public Library System, Bronson Public, 600 Gilbert St, Bronson, FL, 32621. Tel: 352-486-2015. p. 387
Thomas, Dan, Dir, Technology, Cleveland State University, Cleveland-Marshall Law Library, Cleveland-Marshall College of Law, 1801 Euclid Ave, Cleveland, OH, 44115-2223. Tel: 216-523-7372. p. 1769
Thomas, Debbie, Asst Dir, Derby Public Library, 1600 E Walnut Grove, Derby, KS, 67037. Tel: 316-788-0760. p. 804
Thomas, Deborah, Dir, Greater Baltimore Medical Center, 6701 N Charles St, Baltimore, MD, 21204. Tel: 443-849-2530. p. 953
Thomas, Deborah, Assoc Dir, Health Info Res, Washington University Libraries, Bernard Becker Medical Library, 660 S Euclid Ave, Campus Box 8132, Saint Louis, MO, 63110. Tel: 314-362-9729. p. 1277
Thomas, Deborah, Sr Libr Tech, United States Air Force, Wright-Patterson Air Force Base Library FL2300, 88 MSG/SVMG, Bldg 1226, 5435 Hemlock St, Wright-Patterson AFB, OH, 45433-5420. Tel: 937-257-4340, 937-257-4815. p. 1834
Thomas, Dia, AV Librn, Barberton Public Library, 602 W Park Ave, Barberton, OH, 44203-2458. Tel: 330-745-1194. p. 1748
Thomas, Diane, Br Mgr, Warren-Trumbull County Public Library, Howland Branch, 9095 E Market St, Warren, OH, 44484. Tel: 330-856-2011. p. 1828
Thomas, Erica, Ref Librn, Mohawk Valley Community College Library, Rome Campus, 1101 Floyd Ave, Rome, NY, 13440. Tel: 315-334-7728. p. 1655
Thomas, Felton, Jr, Exec Dir, CEO, Cleveland Public Library, 325 Superior Ave, Cleveland, OH, 44114-1271. Tel: 216-623-2800. p. 1767
Thomas, Floyce, Ser Librn, Alcorn State University, 1000 ASU Dr, Alcorn State, MS, 39096-7500. Tel: 601-877-6362. p. 1211
Thomas, Helen, Libr Dir, Sharon Springs Free Library, 129 Main St, Sharon Springs, NY, 13459. Tel: 518-284-3126. p. 1640
Thomas, Holly, Libr Dir, W H Walters Free Public Library, 1001 East Blvd, Alpha, NJ, 08865. Tel: 908-454-1445. p. 1387
Thomas, Ian, Instruction Coordr, Sci Res & Instruction Librn, University of Georgia Libraries, Science, Boyd Graduate Studies Bldg, 210 D W Brooks Dr, Athens, GA, 30602. Tel: 706-542-0698. p. 460
Thomas, Jamie, Br Mgr, Southeast Arkansas Regional Library, Hermitage Branch, First State Bank Bldg, 122 S Main, Hermitage, AR, 71647. Tel: 870-463-8962. p. 104
Thomas, Jan, Librn, National Oceanic & Atmospheric Administration, Betty Petersen Memorial Library, NOAA Center for Weather & Climate Control Prediction, 5830 University Research Court, Rm 1650 E/0C4, College Park, MD, 20740. Tel: 301-683-1307. p. 977

Thomas, Jane, Libr Operations Coordr, Gunnison Public Library, Crested Butte Library, 504 Maroon Ave, Crested Butte, CO, 81224. Tel: 970-349-6535. p. 285
Thomas, Janelle, Exec Dir, NORWELD, 181 1/2 S Main St, Bowling Green, OH, 43402. Tel: 419-352-2903. p. 2772
Thomas, Janet K, Tech Serv Librn, Ringling College of Art & Design, 2700 N Tamiami Trail, Sarasota, FL, 34234-5895. Tel: 941-359-7586. p. 443
Thomas, Jason, Head, Circ & Tech Serv, Newburgh Free Library, 124 Grand St, Newburgh, NY, 12550. Tel: 845-563-3610. p. 1606
Thomas, Jean, Coordr, Libr Serv, Saint Louis Community College, Forest Park Campus Library, 5600 Oakland Ave, Saint Louis, MO, 63110-1316. Tel: 314-644-9206. p. 1273
Thomas, Jennifer, Br Mgr, Jackson County Public Library System, Graceville Branch, 5314 Brown St, Graceville, FL, 32440. Tel: 850-263-3659. p. 420
Thomas, Jenny, Dir, Libr Serv, Electronic Serv Librn, Randolph Community College Library, 629 Industrial Park Ave, Asheboro, NC, 27205-7333. Tel: 336-633-0204. p. 1671
Thomas, Jessica, Evening Libr Asst, Central Carolina Community College Libraries, 1105 Kelly Dr, Sanford, NC, 27330. Tel: 919-718-7244. p. 1715
Thomas, Jill, Dir, Tech Serv, Lawrence University, 113 S Lawe St, Appleton, WI, 54911-5683. p. 2420
Thomas, Jithin, Library Contact, Meyer, Suozzi, English & Klein, 990 Stewart Ave, Ste 300, Garden City, NY, 11530. Tel: 516-741-6565. p. 1537
Thomas, Jody, City Librn, Carpinteria Community Library, 5141 Carpinteria Ave, Carpinteria, CA, 93013. Tel: 805-684-4314. p. 128
Thomas, Jody, Dir, Bettie M Luke Muenster Public Library, 418 N Elm St, Muenster, TX, 76252. Tel: 940-759-4291. p. 2221
Thomas, JoEllen, Law Librn, Lawrence County Law Library, 430 Court St, New Castle, PA, 16101. Tel: 724-656-2136. p. 1969
Thomas, John, Libr Dir, State University of New York - Jefferson Community College, 1220 Coffeen St, Watertown, NY, 13601-1897. Tel: 315-786-2225. p. 1660
Thomas, Joseph, Dir, Saint Mary's College, Notre Dame, IN, 46556-5001. Tel: 574-284-5280. p. 711
Thomas, Joseph, Asst Dir, Scholarly Communications & Coll, East Carolina University, J Y Joyner Library, E Fifth St, Greenville, NC, 27858-4353. Tel: 252-737-2728. p. 1693
Thomas, Josy, Coordr, Access Serv, Dallas College, 801 Main St, Dallas, TX, 75202-3605. Tel: 214-860-2174. p. 2164
Thomas, Judith, Head of Libr, University of Virginia, Clemons Library, 164 McCormick Rd, Charlottesville, VA, 22904-4710. Tel: 434-924-8814. p. 2310
Thomas, Judy, Library Contact, Donora Public Library, 510 Meldon Ave, Donora, PA, 15033-1333. Tel: 724-379-7940. p. 1926
Thomas, Karen, Librn, Central Alabama Community College, Childersburg Library, 34091 US Hwy 280, Childersburg, AL, 35044. Tel: 256-378-2041. p. 4
Thomas, Karin, Dir, Dutton S Peterson Memorial Library, 106 First St, Odessa, NY, 14869. Tel: 607-594-2791. p. 1609
Thomas, Katherine, Asst Dir, Grand Junction Public Library, 106 E Main St, Grand Junction, IA, 50107. Tel: 515-738-2506. p. 755
Thomas, Kathy, Chief Librn, US Army Institute for Religious Leadership Library, 10100 Lee Rd, Fort Jackson, SC, 29207. Tel: 803-751-8828. p. 2059
Thomas, Kay, Dir, Cooper Landing Community Library, 18511 Bean Creek Rd, Cooper Landing, AK, 99572. Tel: 907-599-1643. p. 44
Thomas, Kayleigh, Asst Dir, Gilford Public Library, 31 Potter Hill Rd, Gilford, NH, 03249-6803. Tel: 603-524-6042. p. 1364
Thomas, Kim, Librn, California Department of Corrections Library System, California Correctional Institution, 24900 Hwy 202, Tehachapi, CA, 93561. Tel: 681-822-4402, Ext 4447. p. 206
Thomas, Kirstin, Instrul Coordr, Libr Serv, Rio Salado College, 2323 W 14th St, Tempe, AZ, 85281. Tel: 480-517-8423. p. 79
Thomas, LaTarsha, Librn, Halifax County Library, Weldon Memorial, Six W First St, Weldon, NC, 27890. Tel: 252-536-3837. p. 1694
Thomas, Laura, Dir, Fort Atkinson Public Library, 302 Third St NW, Fort Atkinson, IA, 52144. Tel: 563-534-2222. p. 754
Thomas, Leigh, Supv Librn, New Hanover County Public Library, Northeast Regional Library, 1241 Military Cutoff Rd, Wilmington, NC, 28405. Tel: 910-798-6327. p. 1723
Thomas, Linda, Libr Mgr, Ascension Resurrection Medical Center Chicago, 7435 W Talcott Ave, Chicago, IL, 60631-3746. Tel: 773-990-7638. p. 554
Thomas, Lisa, Circ Serv, Weston County Library System, 23 W Main St, Newcastle, WY, 82701. Tel: 307-746-2206. p. 2497
Thomas, Lynn M, Head of Libr, University of Illinois Library at Urbana-Champaign, Rare Book & Manuscript Library, 346 Main Library, MC-522, 1408 W Gregory Dr, Urbana, IL, 61801. Tel: 217-333-3777. p. 656
Thomas, Margaret, Ref & Instruction Librn, South Puget Sound Community College Library, 2011 Mottman Rd SW, Olympia, WA, 98512. Tel: 360-596-5271. p. 2373
Thomas, Mark, Teen Librn, Gilford Public Library, 31 Potter Hill Rd, Gilford, NH, 03249-6803. Tel: 603-524-6042. p. 1364
Thomas, Martha, Interim Libr Dir, Marshall County Library System, 109 E Gholson Ave, Holly Springs, MS, 38635. Tel: 662-252-3823. p. 1220
Thomas, Mary, Coll Develop Librn, Foothill College, 12345 El Monte Rd, Los Altos Hills, CA, 94022-4599. p. 159
Thomas, Mary, Regional Dir, Wythe-Grayson Regional Library, 147 S Independence Ave, Independence, VA, 24348. Tel: 276-773-3018. p. 2326
Thomas, Maurice, Jr, Br Mgr, Chicago Public Library, West Englewood, 1745 W 63rd St, Chicago, IL, 60636. Tel: 312-747-3481. p. 557
Thomas, Megan, Assessment Librn, Montana State University-Billings Library, 1500 University Dr, Billings, MT, 59101. Tel: 406-657-1663. p. 1288
Thomas, Melanie, Librn, Mississippi State University, Meridian Campus, 1000 Hwy 19 N, Meridian, MS, 39307. Tel: 601-484-0236. p. 1227
Thomas, Michael, Adult Serv, Neenah Public Library, 240 E Wisconsin Ave, Neenah, WI, 54956. Tel: 920-886-6311. p. 2463
Thomas, Nicole, Access & Delivery Librn, Access & Info Serv Librn, Northeastern University Libraries, 360 Huntington Ave, Boston, MA, 02115. Tel: 617-373-4970. p. 998
Thomas, Nina, Mgr, Westerville Public Library, Anti Saloon League Museum & Local History Resource Center, 126 S State St, Westerville, OH, 43081. Tel: 614-882-7277, Ext 5010. p. 1830
Thomas, Patricia, Dir, Erwin Library & Institute, 104 Schuyler St, Boonville, NY, 13309-1005. Tel: 315-942-4834. p. 1496
Thomas, Patricia, Asst Libr Dir, Smithtown Library, One N Country Rd, Smithtown, NY, 11754. Tel: 631-360-2480. p. 1641
Thomas, Phyllis, Librn, United States Army Corps of Engineers, Ray Bldg, Rm No 4202, 1222 Spruce St, Saint Louis, MO, 63033. Tel: 314-331-8883. p. 1276
Thomas, Rachel, Patron Serv Supvr, Great River Regional Library, 1300 W St Germain St, Saint Cloud, MN, 56301. Tel: 320-650-2525. p. 1196
Thomas, Ray, Librn, Compass Lexecon Library, 332 S Michigan Ave, Ste 1300, Chicago, IL, 60604. Tel: 312-322-0200. p. 559
Thomas, Roger, Libr Serv Supvr, Saint Louis Community College, Florissant Valley Campus Library, 3400 Pershall Rd, Ferguson, MO, 63135-1408. Tel: 314-513-4529. p. 1272
Thomas, Roger, Mgr, Saint Louis Community College, Meramec Campus Library, 11333 Big Bend Rd, Saint Louis, MO, 63122-5720. Tel: 314-984-7616. p. 1273
Thomas, Roxanne, Libr Tech, Gowling WLG (Canada) Library, One First Canadian Pl, 100 King St W, Ste 1600, Toronto, ON, M5X 1G5, CANADA. Tel: 416-862-5735. p. 2689
Thomas, Ruth, Ref Librn, Pulaski County Public Library, 304 S Main St, Somerset, KY, 42501. Tel: 606-679-8401. p. 875
Thomas, Sabrina, Head, Res & Instruction, Marshall University Libraries, One John Marshall Dr, Huntington, WV, 25755-2060. Tel: 304-696-3627. p. 2405
Thomas, Sally, Supv Librn, Hayward Public Library, 835 C St, Hayward, CA, 94541. Tel: 510-293-8685. p. 150
Thomas, Sandra, Electronic Ser Librn, Libr Dir, Southeastern Oklahoma State University, 425 W University, Durant, OK, 74701-0609. Tel: 580-745-2702. p. 1846
Thomas, Sarah, Libr Mgr, Theological Librn, Ashland Theological Seminary, 910 Center St, Ashland, OH, 44805. Tel: 419-289-5169. p. 1747
Thomas, Sarah, Acq Librn, Ashland University Library, 509 College Ave, Ashland, OH, 44805. Tel: 419-289-5168. p. 1747
Thomas, Sarah K, Libr Dir, Embry-Riddle Aeronautical University, 3700 Willow Creek Rd, Prescott, AZ, 86301-3720. Tel: 928-777-3812. p. 73
Thomas, Scott, Chief Exec Officer, Scranton Public Library, 500 Vine St, Scranton, PA, 18509-3298. Tel: 570-348-3000, Ext 3011. p. 2004
Thomas, Shan, Curator, Mineral Point Public Library, 137 High St, Ste 2, Mineral Point, WI, 53565. Tel: 608-987-2447. p. 2462
Thomas, Sherri, Law Librn, University of New Mexico, Law Library, 1117 Stanford Dr NE, Albuquerque, NM, 87131-1441. Tel: 505-277-6236. p. 1463
Thomas, Sheryl, Asst Dir, Erie County Public Library, 160 E Front St, Erie, PA, 16507. Tel: 814-451-6911. p. 1931
Thomas, Shiloa, Dir, Libr Serv, Northern Lakes College Library, 1201 Main St SE, Slave Lake, AB, T0G 2A3, CANADA. Tel: 780-849-8670. p. 2554
Thomas, SinDee, Ad, Tomah Public Library, 716 Superior Ave, Tomah, WI, 54660. Tel: 608-374-7470. p. 2481
Thomas, Stevie, Youth Serv Coordr, West Florida Public Library, 239 N Spring St, Pensacola, FL, 32502. Tel: 850-436-5060. p. 437
Thomas, Susan, Dean, Libr Serv, Indiana University South Bend, 1700 Mishawaka Ave, South Bend, IN, 46615. Tel: 574-520-5500. p. 718
Thomas, Tanya, Ref Librn, Thurgood Marshall State Law Library, Courts of Appeals Bldg, 361 Rowe Blvd, Annapolis, MD, 21401. Tel: 410-260-1430. p. 950
Thomas, Tina, Exec Direc, Strategy & Innovation, Edmonton Public Library, Seven Sir Winston Churchill Sq, Edmonton, AB, T5J 2V4, CANADA. Tel: 780-496-7046. p. 2536
Thomas, Tracey, Dir, B B Comer Memorial Library, 314 N Broadway, Sylacauga, AL, 35150-2528. Tel: 256-249-0961. p. 36
Thomas, Vance M, Libr Dir, Central Baptist Theological Seminary Library, 6601 Monticello Rd, Shawnee, KS, 66226-3513. Tel: 913-667-5700, 913-667-5725. p. 836

Thomas, Vickie, Circ Mgr, Otis College of Art & Design Library, 9045 Lincoln Blvd, Westchester, CA, 90045. Tel: 310-665-6930. p. 259

Thomas, Virginia C, Dir, Wayne State University Libraries, Arthur Neef Law Library, 474 Gilmour Mall, Detroit, MI, 48202. Tel: 313-577-3925. p. 1100

Thomas-Burroughs, Darlene, Br Mgr, Allendale-Hampton-Jasper Regional Library, Hardeeville Community Library, 30 Main St, Hardeeville, SC, 29927. Tel: 843-784-3426. p. 2046

Thomas-Hardy, Rhonda, Library Contact, Chain of Lakes Correctional Facility Library, 3516 E 75th S, Albion, IN, 46701. Tel: 260-636-3114. p. 667

Thomason, Anne, Dir, Knox College, 371 S West St, Galesburg, IL, 61401. Tel: 309-341-7491. p. 591

Thomason, Beth, Librn, Carrier Mills-Stonefort Public Library District, 109 W Oak St, Carrier Mills, IL, 62917. Tel: 618-994-2011. p. 550

Thomason, Christia, Asst Dir, Head, Cat & Metadata Serv, University of North Carolina School of the Arts Library, 1533 S Main St, Winston-Salem, NC, 27127. Tel: 336-770-3270. p. 1726

Thomason, Mary, Dir, Libr Serv, Messenger College Library, 2701 Brown Trail, Ste 401, Bedford, TX, 76039. Tel: 817-554-5950. p. 2146

Thomassie, Jordan, Mgr, Saint Mary Parish Library, Bayou Vista Branch, 1325 Bellview Dr, Bayou Vista, LA, 70380. Tel: 985-399-9866. p. 890

Thomasson, Carol, Mgr, Gloucester County Library System, Newfield Public, 115 Catawba Ave, Newfield, NJ, 08344. Tel: 856-697-0415. p. 1423

Thomaswick, Tracey, Br Mgr, Chestatee Regional Library System, Lumpkin County Library, 56 Mechanicsville Rd, Dahlonega, GA, 30533. p. 474

Thome, Debbie, Interim Dir, Endeavor Public Library, 400 Church St, Endeavor, WI, 53930. Tel: 608-587-2902. p. 2434

Thomerson, Alex, Mgr, Sequoyah Regional Library System, Gilmer County Public, 268 Calvin Jackson Dr, Ellijay, GA, 30540. Tel: 706-635-4528. p. 469

Thomet, Jennifer, Dir, Interlochen Public Library, 9411 Tenth St, Interlochen, MI, 49643. Tel: 231-276-6767. p. 1118

Thomkins, Harriet, Librn, Saint Petersburg College, Clearwater Campus Library, 2465 Drew St, Clearwater, FL, 33765. Tel: 727-791-2614. p. 437

Thompkins, Harriet, Operations Librn, Saint Petersburg College, Processing Center, 6021 142nd Ave N, Clearwater, FL, 33760. Tel: 727-341-3693. p. 437

Thompkins, Marcy, Dir, Fairgrove District Library, 1959 Main St, Fairgrove, MI, 48733. Tel: 989-693-6050. p. 1104

Thompson, Abbey, Asst Dir, Access Services & Spaces, Mount Saint Mary's University, J Thomas McCarthy Library, Doheny Campus, Ten Chester Pl, Los Angeles, CA, 90007. Tel: 213-477-2720. p. 166

Thompson, Agnes, Br Mgr, La Porte County Public Library, Fish Lake, 7981 E State Rd 4, Walkerton, IN, 46574. Tel: 219-369-1337. p. 700

Thompson, Agnes, Br Mgr, La Porte County Public Library, Kingsford Heights Branch, 436 Evanston Rd, Kingsford Heights, IN, 46346. Tel: 219-393-3280. p. 700

Thompson, Alanna, Cataloger, Montgomery House Library, 20 Church St, McEwensville, PA, 17749. Tel: 570-538-1381. p. 1959

Thompson, Alyson, Dir, Marshall Public Library, 612 Archer Ave, Marshall, IL, 62441. Tel: 217-826-2535. p. 614

Thompson, Amanda, Libr Tech, College of the North Atlantic Library Services, Corner Brook Campus, 141 O'Connell Dr, Corner Brook, NL, A2H 6H6, CANADA. Tel: 709-637-8528. p. 2609

Thompson, Amy, Ch, East Granby Public Library, 24 Center St, East Granby, CT, 06026. Tel: 860-653-3002. p. 309

Thompson, Angelica, Mgr, Edmonton Public Library, Mill Woods, 2610 Hewes Way, Edmonton, AB, T6L 0A9, CANADA. Tel: 780-496-7077. p. 2537

Thompson, Angie, Libr Dir, Fertile Public Library, 204 W Main St, Fertile, IA, 50434-1020. Tel: 641-797-2787. p. 753

Thompson, Ann, Head, Adult Serv, Essex Library Association, Inc, 33 West Ave, Essex, CT, 06426-1196. Tel: 860-767-1560. p. 311

Thompson, Anna Cathernine, Acq, Muscle Shoals Public Library, 1918 E Avalon, Muscle Shoals, AL, 35661. Tel: 256-386-9212. p. 31

Thompson, Annie, Head of Libr, University of Southern California Libraries, Norris Medical Library, 2003 Zonal Ave, Los Angeles, CA, 90089-9130. Tel: 323-442-1116. p. 170

Thompson, Barbara, Dept Head, Librn, Community College of Allegheny County, North Campus Library & Learning Services, 8701 Perry Hwy, Pittsburgh, PA, 15237-5372. Tel: 412-369-3671. p. 1993

Thompson, Barbara, Dir, Haslet Public Library, 100 Gammill, Haslet, TX, 76052. Tel: 817-439-4278. p. 2188

Thompson, Beth, Head, Content Org, Metadata, E-Resources & Tech, Western Carolina University, 176 Central Dr, Cullowhee, NC, 28723. Tel: 828-227-3728. p. 1683

Thompson, Betsy, Br Supvr, Sioux City Public Library, Perry Creek Branch Library, Plaza Professional Center, Lower B, 2912 Hamilton Blvd, Sioux City, IA, 51104-2410. Tel: 712-255-2926. p. 783

Thompson, Betty, Ch, Hull Public Library, Nine Main St, Hull, MA, 02045. Tel: 781-925-2295. p. 1026

Thompson, Beverly, Tech Serv, Woburn Public Library, 36 Cummings Park, Woburn, MA, 01801. Tel: 781-933-0148. p. 1070

Thompson, BJ, Lead Libr Asst, Central Carolina Community College Libraries, 1105 Kelly Dr, Sanford, NC, 27330. Tel: 919-718-7375. p. 1715

Thompson, Brian, Curator, Libr Mgr, University of Washington Botanic Gardens, 3501 NE 41st St, Seattle, WA, 98105. Tel: 206-543-0415. p. 2381

Thompson, Bruce, Br Mgr, Cobb County Public Library System, Sewell Mill Library & Cultural Center, 2051 Lower Roswell Rd, Marietta, GA, 30068. Tel: 770-509-2711. p. 489

Thompson, Camille, Br Mgr, Jefferson-Madison Regional Library, Gordon Ave, 1500 Gordon Ave, Charlottesville, VA, 22903-1997. Tel: 434-296-5544. p. 2309

Thompson, Carly, Coll Serv Mgr, Palatine Public Library District, 700 N North Ct, Palatine, IL, 60067. Tel: 847-907-3600. p. 631

Thompson, Carmel, Acq, Electronic Res Mgr, University of Puget Sound, 1604 N Warner St, Upper Loading Dock, Tacoma, WA, 98416. Tel: 253-879-3240. p. 2387

Thompson, Carolyn, Literacy Prog Dir, Pollard Memorial Library, 401 Merrimack St, Lowell, MA, 01852. Tel: 978-674-4120. p. 1029

Thompson, Charlene, Libr Dir, Judson University, 1151 N State St, Elgin, IL, 60123. Tel: 847-628-2030. p. 584

Thompson, Cheral, Br Mgr, Horry County Memorial Library, Aynor Branch, 500 Ninth Ave, Aynor, SC, 29511. Tel: 843-358-3324. p. 2056

Thompson, Christina, Br Mgr, Harris County Public Library, Clear Lake City-County Freeman Branch, 16616 Diana Lane, Houston, TX, 77062. Tel: 832-927-5420. p. 2192

Thompson, Christina, Libr Support Serv Asst, Stormont, Dundas & Glengarry County Library, Williamsburg Branch, 12333 County Rd 18, Williamsburg, ON, K0C 2H0, CANADA. Tel: 613-535-2185. p. 2638

Thompson, Christine, Br Mgr, Loudoun County Public Library, Brambleton Branch, 22850 Brambleton Plaza, Brambleton, VA, 20148. Tel: 571-258-3998. p. 2328

Thompson, Contina, Courier Driver, Baldwin County Library Cooperative, Inc, PO Box 399, Robertsdale, AL, 36567-0399. Tel: 251-970-4010. p. 34

Thompson, Craig, Research Systems Coord, Greenberg Traurig LLP, One Vanderbilt Ave, New York, NY, 10017. Tel: 212-801-9200. p. 1587

Thompson, Cynthia, Br Mgr, San Diego County Library, Borrego Springs Branch, 2580 Country Club Rd, Borrego Springs, CA, 92004. Tel: 760-767-5761. p. 216

Thompson, Cynthia, Assoc Dean, Pub Serv, University of Missouri-Kansas City Libraries, 800 E 51st St, Kansas City, MO, 64110. Tel: 816-235-1511. p. 1257

Thompson, D Leigh, Instrul Serv Librn, University of North Alabama, One Harrison Plaza, Box 5028, Florence, AL, 35632-0001. Tel: 256-765-4466. p. 17

Thompson, Daryl, Ref Librn, Michigan State University College of Law Library, Law College Bldg, Rm 115, 648 N Shaw Lane, East Lansing, MI, 48824-1300. Tel: 517-432-6957. p. 1102

Thompson, Debbie, Libr Mgr, William C Beck Health Science Library & Resource Center, One Guthrie Sq, Sayre, PA, 18840. Tel: 570-887-4700, 570-887-4704. p. 2003

Thompson, Deborah, Access Services Assoc, University of Rio Grande, 218 N College Ave, Rio Grande, OH, 45674. Tel: 740-245-7005. p. 1817

Thompson, Debra, Ch, Hancock Town Library, 25 Main St, Hancock, NH, 03449. Tel: 603-525-4411. p. 1366

Thompson, Deidre, Coll Serv Librn, Maryland Institute College of Art, 1401 W Mount Royal Ave, Baltimore, MD, 21217. Tel: 410-225-2304, 410-225-2311. p. 955

Thompson, Desnee, Circ Supvr, Kankakee Public Library, 201 E Merchant St, Kankakee, IL, 60901. Tel: 815-939-4564. p. 604

Thompson, Elizabeth, Asst Admin, Arizona Talking Book Library, 1030 N 32nd St, Phoenix, AZ, 85008. Tel: 602-255-5578. p. 69

Thompson, Elizabeth, YA Serv, Birchard Public Library of Sandusky County, 423 Croghan St, Fremont, OH, 43420. Tel: 419-334-7101. p. 1786

Thompson, Ellen, Asst Librn, Ch, Warren Public Library, 15 Sackett Hill Rd, Warren, CT, 06754. Tel: 860-868-2195. p. 343

Thompson, Erin, Health Science & Research Servs Librn, Sacred Heart University, 5151 Park Ave, Fairfield, CT, 06825-1000. Tel: 203-520-8196. p. 312

Thompson, Erin, Asst Librn, Wells Village Library, Five E Wells Rd, Wells, VT, 05774-9791. Tel: 802-645-0611. p. 2297

Thompson, Gen, Outreach Serv Librn, Harrison County Library System, 12135 Old Hwy 49, Gulfport, MS, 39501. Tel: 228-539-0110. p. 1217

Thompson, George, Spec Coll Librn, California State University, Chico, 400 W First St, Chico, CA, 95929-0295. Tel: 530-898-6603. p. 129

Thompson, Germaine, Libr Tech, Hinds Community College, Jackson Academic & Technical Center, 3925 Sunset Dr, Jackson, MS, 39213-5899. Tel: 601-987-8123. p. 1231

Thompson, Grant, Br Mgr, San Luis Obispo County Library, San Miguel Library, 254 13th St, San Miguel, CA, 93451. Tel: 805-467-3224. p. 234

Thompson, Gregory C, Assoc Dean, Spec Coll, University of Utah, J Willard Marriott Library, 295 S 1500 East, Salt Lake City, UT, 84112-0860. Tel: 801-581-8863. p. 2272

Thompson, Heather, Head, Youth & Family Services, Kenosha Public Library, 7979 38th Ave, Kenosha, WI, 53142. Tel: 262-564-6100. p. 2444

Thompson, Helen, Head Librn, Mount Pleasant Public Library, 601 N Madison, Mount Pleasant, TX, 75455. Tel: 903-575-4180. p. 2220
Thompson, Holly, Dir, Rantoul Public Library, 106 W Flessner, Rantoul, IL, 61866. Tel: 217-893-3955. p. 638
Thompson, James, Sci Librn, Argonne National Laboratory, 9700 S Cass Ave, Bldg 240, Lemont, IL, 60439-4801. Tel: 630-252-0007. p. 608
Thompson, James, Dir, Libr Serv, Holmes Community College, Goodman Campus, One Hill St, Goodman, MS, 39079. Tel: 662-472-9021. p. 1216
Thompson, James, Dir, Libr Serv, Holmes Community College, 1180 W Monroe St, Grenada, MS, 38901. Tel: 662-227-2363. p. 1217
Thompson, James, Libr Dir, Holmes Community College, Ridgeland Campus, 412 W Ridgeland Ave, Ridgeland, MS, 39158-1410. Tel: 601-605-3303. p. 1232
Thompson, Jane, Assoc Dir, Faculty Servs, University of Colorado Boulder, William A Wise Law Library, Wolf Law Bldg, 2nd Flr, 2450 Kittredge Loop Dr, Boulder, CO, 80309-0402. Tel: 303-492-2705. p. 268
Thompson, Jason, Library Contact, VPres, National Concrete Masonry Association Library, 13750 Sunrise Valley Dr, Herndon, VA, 20171. Tel: 703-713-1900. p. 2326
Thompson, Jay, Curator, Shasta Historical Society, 1449 Market St, Redding, CA, 96001. Tel: 530-243-3720. p. 198
Thompson, Jeffrey, Dir, Libr Serv, Brevard County Public Libraries, 308 Forrest Ave, 2nd Flr, Cocoa, FL, 32922. Tel: 321-633-1801. p. 389
Thompson, Jennifer, Asst Dir, Mercy College of Health Sciences Library, 928 Sixth Ave, Des Moines, IA, 50309-1239. Tel: 515-643-6613. p. 747
Thompson, Jerianne, Libr Dir, Tualatin Public Library, 18878 SW Martinazzi Ave, Tualatin, OR, 97062. Tel: 503-691-3063. p. 1901
Thompson, Jim, Br Mgr, Jackson-George Regional Library System, Pascagoula Public Library, 3214 Pascagoula St, Pascagoula, MS, 39567. p. 1228
Thompson, Jo, Cat, Coll, Enterprise Public Library, 101 E Grubbs St, Enterprise, AL, 36330. Tel: 334-347-2636. p. 15
Thompson, Jody, Archivist, Georgia Institute of Technology, Architecture Core Collection, 260 Fourth St NW, 1st Flr, Atlanta, GA, 30332. Tel: 404-894-4586. p. 464
Thompson, Jody, Head, Archives, Records Mgmt & Digital Curation, Georgia Institute of Technology Library, 260 Fourth St NW, Atlanta, GA, 30332. Tel: 404-894-9626. p. 464
Thompson, Joe, Chief Operations Officer, Bucks County Free Library, Library Center at Doylestown, 150 S Pine St, Doylestown, PA, 18901-4932. Tel: 215-348-9081. p. 1927
Thompson, John, Dir, Inspiring & Facilitating Library Success (IFLS), 1538 Truax Blvd, Eau Claire, WI, 54703. Tel: 715-839-5082. p. 2432
Thompson, John Walters, Syst Librn, Waynesburg College, 51 W College St, Waynesburg, PA, 15370. Tel: 724-852-7668. p. 2019
Thompson, Judy, Librn, Maritime Museum of British Columbia Library, 634 Humboldt St, Unit 100, Victoria, BC, V8W 1A4, CANADA. Tel: 250-385-4222, Ext 116. p. 2583
Thompson, Kara, Campus Librn, Nova Scotia Community College, Marconi Campus Library, 1240 Grand Lake Rd, Sydney, NS, B1P 6J7, CANADA. Tel: 902-563-2102. p. 2620
Thompson, Kate, Develop, Head, Pub Serv, New Brunswick Public Library Service (NBPLS), 570 Two Nations Crossing, Ste 2, Fredericton, NB, E3A 0X9, CANADA. Tel: 506-453-2354. p. 2601
Thompson, Kathryn, Dir, Libr Serv, Lanier Technical College, 3410 Ronald Reagan Blvd, Cumming, GA, 30041. Tel: 770-533-6968. p. 473
Thompson, Kathryn, Dir, Libr Serv, Lanier Technical College, Breeden-Giles Bldg, Rm 1210, 2535 Lanier Tech Dr, Gainesville, GA, 30507-4500. Tel: 770-533-6968. p. 480
Thompson, Katie, Libr Dir, Sac & Fox National Public Library & Archives, 920883 S Hwy 99, Stroud, OK, 74079-5178. Tel: 918-968-3526, Ext 2021. p. 1863
Thompson, Kelly, Digital Initiatives, Augustana University, 2001 S Summit Ave, Sioux Falls, SD, 57197-0001. Tel: 605-274-4921. p. 2081
Thompson, Kelly, Chief Librn, Renfrew Public Library, 13 Railway Ave, Renfrew, ON, K7V 3A9, CANADA. Tel: 613-432-8151. p. 2675
Thompson, Kenneth Wayne, Exec Dir, Charles County Public Library, Two Garrett Ave, La Plata, MD, 20646. Tel: 301-934-9001. p. 969
Thompson, Kira, Head, Ref & Adult Serv, Poughkeepsie Public Library District, 93 Market St, Poughkeepsie, NY, 12601. Tel: 845-485-3445, Ext 3350. p. 1623
Thompson, Kristi, Tech Info Spec, United States Department of the Interior, Denver Fed Ctr, Sixth Ave & Kipling St, Bldg 67, Denver, CO, 80225. Tel: 303-445-2039. p. 277
Thompson, Krystal Ann, Dir, Geauga County Law Library Resources Board, 100 Short Court St, Ste BA, Chardon, OH, 44024. Tel: 440-279-2085, 440-285-2222, Ext 2085. p. 1758
Thompson, L, Interim Dir, Lubbock Public Library, 1306 Ninth St, Lubbock, TX, 79401. Tel: 806-775-2834, 806-775-2835. p. 2213
Thompson, Laura, Head Music Librn, Michigan State University Libraries, Fine Arts-Music, W403 Main Library, 366 W Circle Dr, East Lansing, MI, 48824. Tel: 517-884-6469. p. 1102
Thompson, Laura Anne, Dir, Keeseville Free Library, 1721 Front St, Keeseville, NY, 12944. Tel: 518-834-9054. p. 1559
Thompson, Leann, Libr Mgr, Wandering River Public Library, Main St, Wandering River, AB, T0A 3M0, CANADA. Tel: 780-771-3939. p. 2559
Thompson, Leanne, Res & Presv Librn, Alberta Legislature Library, 216 Legislature Bldg, 10800-97 Ave NW, Edmonton, AB, T5K 2B6, CANADA. Tel: 780-422-9316. p. 2535
Thompson, LeoNard, Br Mgr, Arlington County Department of Libraries, Central Library, 1015 N Quincy St, Arlington, VA, 22201. Tel: 703-228-5990. p. 2305
Thompson, LeoNard, Br Mgr, Div Chief, Cent Serv, Arlington County Department of Libraries, 1015 N Quincy St, Arlington, VA, 22201. Tel: 703-228-5952. p. 2305
Thompson, Linda, Br Mgr, Walton County Public Library System, Coastal, 437 Greenway Trail, Santa Rosa Beach, FL, 32459-5589. Tel: 850-267-2809. p. 393
Thompson, Linda, Assoc Dean of Libr, University of Houston, M D Anderson Library, 114 University Libraries, Houston, TX, 77204-2000. Tel: 713-743-9800. p. 2199
Thompson, Linda, Librn, Springlake-Earth Community Library, 472 Farm Rd 302, Springlake, TX, 79082. Tel: 806-257-3357. p. 2245
Thompson, Lisa, Libr Dir, Barker Public Library, 8673 Church St, Barker, NY, 14012. Tel: 716-795-3344. p. 1490
Thompson, Lolana, Pub Serv, Spec Coll, Dallas Theological Seminary, 3909 Swiss Ave, Dallas, TX, 75204. Tel: 214-887-5290. p. 2166
Thompson, Lori, Head, Archives, Spec Coll, Marshall University Libraries, One John Marshall Dr, Huntington, WV, 25755-2060. Tel: 304-696-3525. p. 2405
Thompson, Lou Ann, Electronic Res Librn, Oklahoma State University - Center for Health Sciences, 1111 W 17th St, Tulsa, OK, 74107-1898. Tel: 918-561-8457. p. 1864
Thompson, Lynn, Dir, Clark Memorial Library, Seven Pinehurst Dr, Carolina, RI, 02812. Tel: 401-364-6100. p. 2030
Thompson, Lynn, Asst Dir, New Braunfels Public Library, 700 E Common St, New Braunfels, TX, 78130-5689. Tel: 830-221-4315. p. 2222
Thompson, Madeleine, Exec Dir, Library & Archives, Wildlife Conservation Society Library, 2300 Southern Blvd, Bronx, NY, 10460. Tel: 718-220-5100. p. 1500
Thompson, Marcella, Head Librn, Crawford Public Library, 601 Second St, Crawford, NE, 69339. Tel: 308-665-1780. p. 1311
Thompson, Marcy, Local Hist Librn, Transylvania County Library, 212 S Gaston St, Brevard, NC, 28712. Tel: 828-884-3151. p. 1675
Thompson, Mari, Br Librn, McDowell Public Library, Northfork Branch, Rte 52, Northfork, WV, 24868. Tel: 304-862-4541. p. 2416
Thompson, Mary, Circ Mgr, Saint Tammany Parish Library, Madisonville Branch, 1123 Main St, Madisonville, LA, 70447. Tel: 985-845-4819. p. 888
Thompson Mayer, Ann, Asst Librn, Southport Memorial Library, 1032 Hendricks Hill Rd, Southport, ME, 04576-3309. Tel: 207-633-2741. p. 942
Thompson, Meaghan, Libr Dir, Turner Free Library, Two N Main St, Randolph, MA, 02368. Tel: 781-961-0932. p. 1049
Thompson, Michel, Bus Mgr, New Orleans Public Library, 219 Loyola Ave, New Orleans, LA, 70112-2044. Tel: 504-529-7323, 504-596-2570. p. 902
Thompson, Molly, Sr Librn, Front Range Community College, Larimer Campus, 4616 S Shields St, Fort Collins, CO, 80526. Tel: 970-221-6740. p. 281
Thompson, Nellie L, Chair, Archives, Chair, Libr Serv, Curator, New York Psychoanalytic Society & Institute, 247 E 82nd St, New York, NY, 10028-2701. Tel: 212-879-6900. p. 1594
Thompson, Noelle, Dir, Galesburg Public Library, 40 E Simmons St, Galesburg, IL, 61401-4591. Tel: 309-343-6118. p. 591
Thompson, Pamela, Dir, Mason County Library System, 508 Viand St, Point Pleasant, WV, 25550. Tel: 304-675-0894. p. 2413
Thompson, Paul, Dir, R K Kittay Public Library, 2827 Hwy 153, Rupert, VT, 05768. Tel: 802-394-2444. p. 2293
Thompson, Rachel, Dir, Hubbard Public Library, 218 E Maple St, Hubbard, IA, 50122. Tel: 641-864-2771. p. 758
Thompson, Rebecca, Instruction & Ref Librn, King's College, 14 W Jackson St, Wilkes-Barre, PA, 18711. Tel: 570-208-5840. p. 2022
Thompson, Rhonda, Dir, Ripley Public Library, 64 W Main St, Ripley, NY, 14775. Tel: 716-736-3913. p. 1627
Thompson, Ronelle, Dir, Libr Serv, Augustana University, 2001 S Summit Ave, Sioux Falls, SD, 57197-0001. Tel: 605-274-4921. p. 2081
Thompson, Ronelle, Libr Dir, Augustana University, Center for Western Studies, 2201 S Summit Ave, Sioux Falls, SD, 57197. Tel: 605-274-4007. p. 2082
Thompson, Rose M, Libr Dir, Leepertown Township Public Library, 201 E Nebraska, Bureau, IL, 61315. Tel: 815-659-3283. p. 546
Thompson, Roslin I, Dir, Knoxville Public Library, 213 E Montgomery St, Knoxville, IA, 50138-2296. Tel: 641-828-0585. p. 763
Thompson, Samantha, Law Librn, Merced County Law Library, 670 W 22nd St, Merced, CA, 95340-3780. Tel: 209-385-7332. p. 176
Thompson, Sandi, Dir, Puskarich Public Library, 200 E Market St, Cadiz, OH, 43907-1185. Tel: 740-942-2623. p. 1754
Thompson, Sandra, Head of Libr, Temple University Libraries, Ambler Campus Library, 580 Meetinghouse Rd, Ambler, PA, 19002. Tel: 267-468-8642. p. 1986
Thompson, Sara, Adult Serv Mgr, Deschutes Public Library District, 507 NW Wall St, Bend, OR, 97703. Tel: 541-312-1038. p. 1874

Thompson, Sarah, Libr Asst, Lake City Public Library, 110 E Washington St, Lake City, IA, 51449. Tel: 712-464-3413. p. 763

Thompson, Shane, Supvr, Mid-Columbia Libraries, Kahlotus Branch, 225 E Weston St, Kahlotus, WA, 99335. Tel: 509-282-3493. p. 2367

Thompson, Shannon, Dir, Marilla Free Library, 11637 Bullis Rd, Marilla, NY, 14102-9727. Tel: 716-652-7449. p. 1569

Thompson, Shirley, Dir, Goodwater Public Library, 36 Coosa County Rd, 66, Goodwater, AL, 35072. Tel: 256-839-5741. p. 19

Thompson Smith, Deanna, Dir, Trinity Valley Community College Library, Terrell Campus, 1200 E I-20, Terrell, TX, 75161. Tel: 972-563-4929. p. 2137

Thompson, Susan M, Assoc Librn, Coordr, California State University, 333 S Twin Oaks Valley Rd, San Marcos, CA, 92096. Tel: 760-750-4373. p. 234

Thompson, Sydney, Dean of Libr, Central Washington University, 400 E University Way, Ellensburg, WA, 98926-7548. Tel: 509-963-1901. p. 2363

Thompson, Tammy, Dir, Kimballton Public Library, 118 Main St, Kimballton, IA, 51543. Tel: 712-773-3002. p. 763

Thompson, Teresa, Mgr, Haldimand County Public Library, Caledonia Branch, 100 Haddington St, Unit 2, Caledonia, ON, N3W 2N4, CANADA. p. 2639

Thompson, Teresa, Sr Librn, Pub, Haldimand County Public Library, Hagersville Branch, 13 Alma St N, Hagersville, ON, N0A 1H0, CANADA. p. 2639

Thompson, Tim, Librn, Holley A G State Hospital, Patients Library, 1199 W Lantana Rd, Lantana, FL, 33465. Tel: 561-582-5666, Ext 3799. p. 417

Thompson-Franklin, Samantha, Collections & Govt Info Librarian, University of Idaho Library, 850 S Rayburn St, Moscow, ID, 83844. Tel: 208-885-2531. p. 526

Thoms, Becky, Head, Digital Libr Serv, Utah State University, 3000 Old Main Hill, Logan, UT, 84322-3000. Tel: 435-797-0816. p. 2265

Thoms, Beth, Ref & Instruction Librn, Pierce College Library, Puyallup Campus, 1601 39th Ave SE, Puyallup, WA, 98374. Tel: 253-840-8303. p. 2368

Thomsen, Cristina, Libr Dir, Southwestern Adventist University, 101 W Magnolia St, Keene, TX, 76059. Tel: 817-202-6242. p. 2204

Thomsen, Elizabeth B, Mgr, Libr Serv, North of Boston Library Exchange, Inc, 42A Cherry Hill Dr, Danvers, MA, 01923. Tel: 978-777-8844. p. 2767

Thomsen, Janette, Dir, Alice M Farr Library, 1603 L St, Aurora, NE, 68818-2132. Tel: 402-694-2272. p. 1306

Thomsen, Jill, Libr Serv Coordr, Peoria Public Library, 8463 W Monroe St, Peoria, AZ, 85345. Tel: 623-773-7566. p. 68

Thomson, Allison, Cent Libr Mgr, Calgary Public Library, W R Castell Central Library, 800 Third St SE, Calgary, AB, T2G 2E7, CANADA. p. 2526

Thomson, Allison, Mgr, Calgary Public Library, Nicholls Family Library, 1421 33rd St SW, Calgary, AB, T3C 1P2, CANADA. p. 2527

Thomson, Cindy, Outreach & Programming Supvr, Dodge City Public Library, 1001 N Second Ave, Dodge City, KS, 67801. Tel: 620-225-0248. p. 804

Thomson, Karen, Circ, West Hartford Public Library, Faxon Branch, 1073 New Britain Ave, West Hartford, CT, 06110. Tel: 860-561-8200. p. 346

Thomson, Mary Beth, Sr Assoc Dean for Coll, Digital Scholarship & Tech Serv, University of Kentucky Libraries, 401 Hilltop Ave, Lexington, KY, 40506. Tel: 859-218-1227. p. 863

Thomson-Mohr, Linda, Adminr, Acworth Silsby Library, Five Lynn Hill Rd, Acworth, NH, 03601. Tel: 603-835-2150. p. 1353

Thomssen, Heidi, Asst Librn, Lake Benton Public Library, 110 E Benton St, Lake Benton, MN, 56149. Tel: 507-368-4641, Ext 3. p. 1179

Thor, Dianna, Br Mgr, Pima County Public Library, Dusenberry-River Branch, 5605 E River Rd, Ste 105, Tucson, AZ, 85750. Tel: 520-594-5345. p. 82

Thorbjornsen, Barbara, Ch Serv, Kingston Public Library, 1004 Bradford Way, Kingston, TN, 37763. Tel: 865-376-9905. p. 2105

Thorenz, Matt, Head, Ref & Adult Serv, Moffat Library of Washingtonville, Six W Main St, Washingtonville, NY, 10992. Tel: 845-496-5483. p. 1659

Thorleifson, Harvey, Dir, Minnesota Geological Survey Library, 2609 W Territorial Rd, Saint Paul, MN, 55114-1009. Tel: 612-626-2969. p. 1201

Thormodson, Kelly, Libr Dir, Pennsylvania State University, College of Medicine, Penn State Hershey, 500 University Dr, Hershey, PA, 17033. Tel: 717-531-8631. p. 1943

Thormoto, Collin, Librn, Las Positas College Library, 3000 Campus Hill Dr, Livermore, CA, 94551. Tel: 925-424-1150. p. 156

Thornburg, Brian, Head, Media Serv, Meredith College, 3800 Hillsborough St, Raleigh, NC, 27607-5298. Tel: 919-760-8457. p. 1708

Thorne, Nancy, Evening/Weekend Ref Librn, Drexel University Libraries, Hagerty Library, 33rd & Market Sts, Philadelphia, PA, 19104-2875. Tel: 215-895-2750. p. 1976

Thorne Rogers, Sheila, Libr Dir, Oakland Public Library, 18 Church St, Oakland, ME, 04963. Tel: 207-465-7533. p. 934

Thorne, Sheila, Libr Dir, Clay County Public Library, 614 Main St, Clay, WV, 25043. Tel: 304-587-4254. p. 2401

Thornhill, Cheryl, Exec Dir, Museum of the Mississippi Delta, 1608 Hwy 82 W, Greenwood, MS, 38930. Tel: 662-453-0925. p. 1217

Thornhill, Jenny, Law Librn, Law Society of Newfoundland Law Library, 196-198 Water St, St. John's, NL, A1C 5M3, CANADA. Tel: 709-753-7770. p. 2610

Thornhill, Vickie, Pub Serv Librn, Patrick Henry College Library, Ten Patrick Henry Circle, Purcellville, VA, 20132. Tel: 540-441-8400. p. 2339

Thornley, Cynthia, Dir, Horry County Memorial Library, 1008 Fifth Ave, Conway, SC, 29526. Tel: 843-915-5285. p. 2056

Thornsbury, Christa, Librn, Welch College, 1045 Bison Trail, Gallatin, TN, 37066. Tel: 615-675-5290. p. 2099

Thornton, Amy J, Law Librn, Wisconsin Department of Justice, 17 W Main St, Madison, WI, 53703. Tel: 608-266-0325. p. 2452

Thornton, Ann T, Vice Provost & Univ Librn, Columbia University, Butler Library, 535 W 114th St, New York, NY, 10027. Tel: 212-854-7309. p. 1582

Thornton, Beth, Distance Educ & Outreach Librn, Athens Technical College Library, Elbert County Campus, Yeargin Blgd, Rm 121, 1317 Athens Hwy, Elberton, GA, 30635. Tel: 706-213-2116. p. 459

Thornton, Caroline, Mgr, Regional Medical Center of Orangeburg & Calhoun Counties, Medical Staff Services, 3000 St Matthews Rd, Orangeburg, SC, 29118. Tel: 803-395-3002. p. 2067

Thornton, Danielle, Br Mgr, Greenville County Library System, Fountain Inn Branch, 311 N Main St, Fountain Inn, SC, 29644. Tel: 864-527-9210. p. 2061

Thornton, Elizabeth, Dir, Bentley Memorial Library, 206 Bolton Center Rd, Bolton, CT, 06043. Tel: 860-646-7349. p. 303

Thornton, Glenda A, Dr, Dir, Cleveland State University, Michael Schwartz Library, Rhodes Tower, Ste 501, 2121 Euclid Ave, Cleveland, OH, 44115-2214. Tel: 216-687-2475. p. 1769

Thornton, Jennifer, Children/Youth Librn, Benton County Public Library, 121 S Forrest Ave, Camden, TN, 38320-2055. Tel: 731-584-4772. p. 2090

Thornton, Joseph, Mgr, Automation Serv, Upper Hudson Library System, 28 Essex St, Albany, NY, 12206. Tel: 518-437-9880, Ext 230. p. 1484

Thornton, Julie, Head, Tech Serv, Mississippi College, 130 W College St, Clinton, MS, 39058. Tel: 601-925-3436. p. 1214

Thornton, Julie, Librn I, East Mississippi Community College, 1512 Kemper St, Scooba, MS, 39358. Tel: 662-476-5054. p. 1232

Thornton, Libby, Librn, East Mississippi Regional Library System, Bay Springs Municipal, 2747 Hwy 15, Bay Springs, MS, 39422. Tel: 601-764-2291. p. 1231

Thornton, Linda, Outreach Serv Librn, Auburn University, Ralph Brown Draughon Library, 231 Mell St, Auburn, AL, 36849. Tel: 334-844-4500. p. 5

Thornton, Lori, Tech Serv Librn, Carson-Newman University, 1634 Russell Ave, Jefferson City, TN, 37760. Tel: 865-471-3339. p. 2103

Thornton, Mary, Libr Mgr, Timberland Regional Library, Hoquiam Branch, 420 Seventh St, Hoquiam, WA, 98550-3616. Tel: 360-532-1710. p. 2389

Thornton, Ruth Anne, Libr Mgr, Emmanuel Bible College, 100 Fergus Ave, Kitchener, ON, N2A 2H2, CANADA. Tel: 519-894-8900, Ext 234, 519-894-8900, Ext 269. p. 2651

Thornton, Tammy, Mgr, Algonquin College Library, 1385 Woodroffe Ave, Rm C350, Ottawa, ON, K2G 1V8, CANADA. Tel: 613-727-4723, Ext 5834. p. 2664

Thorp, David, Br Mgr, Hawaii State Public Library System, Koloa Public & School Library, 3451 Poipu Rd, Koloa, HI, 96756. Tel: 808-742-8455. p. 509

Thorp, Kathryn, Br Mgr, Orange County Library System, Winter Garden Branch, 805 E Plant St, Winter Garden, FL, 34787. Tel: 407-835-7323. p. 432

Thorp, Kristen, Youth Serv Mgr, Eugene Public Library, 100 W Tenth Ave, Eugene, OR, 97401. Tel: 541-682-5450. p. 1878

Thorpe, Gillian, Libr Dir, Julia L Butterfield Memorial Library, Ten Morris Ave, Cold Spring, NY, 10516. Tel: 845-265-3040. p. 1520

Thorpe, Mary, Dir, East Rockaway Public Library, 477 Atlantic Ave, East Rockaway, NY, 11518. Tel: 516-599-1664. p. 1528

Thorsen, Don, Dir, Western District Library, 1111 Fourth St, Orion, IL, 61273. p. 630

Thorsen, Mary, Head, Access Serv, Warner University, 13895 Hwy 27, Lake Wales, FL, 33859. Tel: 863-638-7586. p. 416

Thorson, Elizabeth Cuckow, Mgr, Ad Serv, Laramie County Library System, 2200 Pioneer Ave, Cheyenne, WY, 82001-3610. Tel: 307-773-7230. p. 2492

Thorson, Jennifer, Asst Dir, Reed City Area District Library, 829 S Chestnut St, Reed City, MI, 49677-1152. Tel: 231-832-2131. p. 1143

Thorson, Kip, Dir, Minnesota West Community & Technical College Libraries, 1450 College Way, Worthington, MN, 56187. Tel: 507-372-3462. p. 1210

Thorson, Nancy, Vols Librn, First Lutheran Church, 615 W Fifth St, Red Wing, MN, 55066. Tel: 651-388-9311. p. 1193

Thorson, Shirley, Head Librn, Southbury Public Library, 100 Poverty Rd, Southbury, CT, 06488. Tel: 203-262-0626, Ext 140. p. 337

Thorup, Shawna, Libr Dir, Northwest Arkansas Community College, One College Dr, Bentonville, AR, 72712. Tel: 479-619-4246. p. 91

Thrane, Jannette, Dir, Juneau Public Library, 250 N Fairfield Ave, Juneau, WI, 53039. Tel: 920-386-4805. p. 2444

Thrash, David, Actg Br Mgr, Atlanta-Fulton Public Library System, Gladys S Dennard Library at South Fulton, 4055 Flat Shoals Rd, Union City, GA, 30291-1590. Tel: 770-306-3092. p. 461
Thrash, David, Br Mgr, Atlanta-Fulton Public Library System, Mechanicsville Branch, 400 Formwalt St SW, Atlanta, GA, 30312. Tel: 404-730-4779. p. 461
Thrash, David, Asst Dir, Access Serv, Clayton County Library System, 865 Battlecreek Rd, Jonesboro, GA, 30236. Tel: 770-473-3850. p. 483
Thrasher, Jill, Libr Dir, Sherman Library & Gardens, 614 Dahlia Ave, Corona del Mar, CA, 92625. Tel: 949-673-1880. p. 132
Thrasher, Peggy, Tech & Syst Librn, Dover Public Library, 73 Locust St, Dover, NH, 03820-3785. Tel: 603-516-6050. p. 1361
Thrasher, Shawn, Libr Dir, Ontario City Library, 215 East C St, Ontario, CA, 91764. Tel: 909-395-2004. p. 188
Threatt, Pati, Asst Prof, Head, Archives & Spec Coll, McNeese State University, 300 S Beauregard Dr, Lake Charles, LA, 70609. Tel: 337-475-5731. p. 894
Thresher, John, Ref Librn, North Kingstown Free Library, 100 Boone St, North Kingstown, RI, 02852-5150. Tel: 401-294-3306. p. 2036
Thronson, Linda, Br Mgr, Iberia Parish Library, Parkview Branch, 500 Grand Pre Blvd, New Iberia, LA, 70563. Tel: 337-364-7480. p. 900
Thuma, Jessie, Head, Circ, Reader Serv, Thomas Crane Public Library, 40 Washington St, Quincy, MA, 02269-9164. Tel: 617-376-1300. p. 1048
Thumin, Ling, Ref Librn, Missouri Baptist University, One College Park Dr, Saint Louis, MO, 63141-8698. Tel: 314-434-1115. p. 1271
Thunder Hawk, Jodi, Dir, Sitting Bull College Library, 9299 Hwy 24, Fort Yates, ND, 58538. Tel: 701-854-8008. p. 1734
Thur, Victoria, Head, Spec Coll, Florida Atlantic University, 777 Glades Rd, Boca Raton, FL, 33431. Tel: 561-297-3787. p. 385
Thurber, Amy, Libr Dir, Canaan Town Library, 1173 US Rte 4, Canaan, NH, 03741. Tel: 603-523-9650. p. 1356
Thurman, Britt, Exec Dir, Museum of North Idaho, 115 Northwest Blvd, Coeur d'Alene, ID, 83814. Tel: 208-664-3448. p. 519
Thurman, Kelli, Dir, Crane County Library, 701 S Alford St, Crane, TX, 79731-2521. Tel: 432-558-1142. p. 2161
Thurman, Stacy, Br Mgr, Woodford County Library, Midway Branch, 400 Northside Dr, Midway, KY, 40347. Tel: 859-846-4014. p. 876
Thurston, Michele, Head Librn, Annawan-Alba Township Library, 200 N Meadow Lane, Ste 2, Annawan, IL, 61234-7607. Tel: 309-935-6483. p. 537
Thurston, Robin, Librn, Robert A Frost Memorial Library, 42 Main St, Limestone, ME, 04750. Tel: 207-325-4706. p. 929
Thurston, Sally, Adult Prog Coordr, Maynard Public Library, 77 Nason St, Maynard, MA, 01754-2316. Tel: 978-897-1010. p. 1033
Thynne, Sara, Dir, Learning Res Ctr, Alamance Community College Library, 1247 Jimmie Kerr Rd, Graham, NC, 27253. Tel: 336-506-4116. p. 1691
Tibay, Eunice, Librn, Fort Concho National Historic Landmark, 630 S Oakes St, San Angelo, TX, 76903. Tel: 325-657-4442. p. 2235
Tibben, Ginette, Libr Support Serv Asst, Stormont, Dundas & Glengarry County Library, South Mountain Branch, 10543 Main St, South Mountain, ON, K0E 1W0, CANADA. Tel: 613-989-2199. p. 2638
Tibbits, Victoria, Asst Dir, Essex Free Library, One Browns River Rd, Essex, VT, 05451. Tel: 802-879-0313. p. 2283
Tibbs, Emily, Libr Spec, New Mexico State University at Alamogordo, 2400 N Scenic Dr, Alamogordo, NM, 88310. Tel: 575-439-3851. p. 1459
Tichenor, Jerie, Dir, Meriden-Ozawkie Public Library, 7272 K4 Hwy, Ste D, Meriden, KS, 66512. Tel: 785-484-3393. p. 825
Tichy, Brenda, Br Mgr, Allen Parish Libraries, Oakdale Branch, 405 E Sixth Ave, Oakdale, LA, 71463. Tel: 318-335-2690. p. 905
Tickel, Mary, Dir, Calhoun Public Library, 746 Hwy 163, Calhoun, TN, 37309. Tel: 423-336-2348. p. 2090
Tiddes, Heather, Asst Dir, Pembroke Town Library, 313 Pembroke St, Pembroke, NH, 03275. Tel: 603-485-7851. p. 1377
Tidwell, Bryan, Br Mgr, Libraries of Stevens County, Chewelah Branch, 311 E Clay Ave, Chewelah, WA, 99109. Tel: 509-935-6805. p. 2369
Tidwell, Jessica, Dir, Carmen Public Library, 112 N Sixth St, Carmen, OK, 73726. Tel: 580-987-2301. p. 1843
Tidwell, Judy, Dir, Grandview Public Library, 112 S Third St, Grandview, TX, 76050. Tel: 817-866-3965. p. 2186
Tidwell, Mark J, Dir, Jellico Public Library, 104 N Main St, Jellico, TN, 37762-2004. Tel: 423-784-7488. p. 2103
Tidwell, Teresa, Dir, Caruthersville Public Library, 707 W 13th St, Caruthersville, MO, 63830. Tel: 573-333-2480. p. 1241
Tidyman, Monica, Dir, Stromsburg Public Library, 320 Central St, Stromsburg, NE, 68666. Tel: 402-764-7681. p. 1337
Tieden, Brandy, Asst Librn, Elkader Public Library, 130 N Main St, Elkader, IA, 52043. Tel: 563-245-1446. p. 751
Tieger, Helene, Archivist, Bard College, One Library Rd, Annandale-on-Hudson, NY, 12504. Tel: 845-758-7396. p. 1487
Tiegs, Tracie, Libr Mgr, Frost Brown Todd LLC, 3300 Great American Tower, 301 E Fourth St, Cincinnati, OH, 45202. Tel: 513-651-6982. p. 1760
Tieman, Dana, Head, Adult Serv, Wheaton Public Library, 225 N Cross St, Wheaton, IL, 60187-5376. Tel: 630-868-7527. p. 662
Tiemersma, Anna, Librn, Dale & Lessmann Library, 181 University Ave, Ste 2100, Toronto, ON, M5H 3M7, CANADA. Tel: 416-863-1010. p. 2688
Tiemeyer, Jamie, Head, Tech Serv, Cornerstone University, 1001 E Beltline Ave NE, Grand Rapids, MI, 49525. Tel: 616-254-1650, Ext 1628. p. 1110
Tierney, Barbara, Head, Res & Info Serv, University of Central Florida Libraries, 12701 Pegasus Dr, Orlando, FL, 32816-8030. Tel: 407-823-5464. p. 432
Tierney, Catie, Libr Mgr, Pikes Peak Library District, Library 21c, 1175 Chapel Hills Dr, Colorado Springs, CO, 80920. Tel: 719-531-6333, Ext 6201. p. 271
Tierney, Sarah, Librn, Wasco County Library District, Dufur School-Community Library, 802 NE Fifth St, Dufur, OR, 97021-3034. Tel: 541-467-2509, 541-467-2588. p. 1900
Tietje, Lori, Dir, Patrick Henry School District Public Library, 208 N East Ave, Deshler, OH, 43516. Tel: 419-278-3616. p. 1782
Tietjen, Joan, Dir, Burkley Library & Resource Center, 208 E Fillmore Ave, Dewitt, NE, 68341. Tel: 402-683-2145. p. 1312
Tietjen, Liza, Archivist & Spec Coll Librn, Salve Regina University, 100 Ochre Point Ave, Newport, RI, 02840-4192. Tel: 401-341-2330. p. 2035
Tietze, Larry, Syst Librn, United States Military Academy Library, Jefferson Hall Library & Learning Ctr, 758 Cullum Rd, West Point, NY, 10996. Tel: 845-938-8301. p. 1663
Tiffany, Courtney, Librn, North Central Washington Libraries, Mattawa Public Library, 101 Manson Lane, Mattawa, WA, 99349. Tel: 509-932-5507. p. 2394
Tiffany, Courtney, Librn, North Central Washington Libraries, Wenatchee Public Library, 30 S Wenatchee Ave, Wenatchee, WA, 98801. Tel: 509-662-5021. p. 2394
Tiffany, Joshua, Dir, Gray Public Library, Five Hancock St, Gray, ME, 04039. Tel: 207-657-4110. p. 926
Tiffin, John, Asst Dean of Libr, Electronic Res Librn, Biola University Library, 13800 Biola Ave, La Mirada, CA, 90639. Tel: 562-944-0351, Ext 4837. p. 155
Tiffney, Scott, Librn, American Philatelic Research Library, 100 Match Factory Pl, Bellefonte, PA, 16823. Tel: 814-933-3803, Ext 246. p. 1909
Tig Wartluft, Andrew J, Head, Instrul Serv, Pennsylvania State University - Dickinson School of Law, 214 Lewis Katz Bldg, University Park, PA, 16802. Tel: 814-865-8875. p. 2015
Tighe, Chris, Librn, United States Courts Library, Melvin Price Courthouse, 750 Missouri Ave, East Saint Louis, IL, 62201. Tel: 618-482-9371. p. 581
Tignor, Mia, Emerging Tech Librn, Indian River State College, 3209 Virginia Ave, Fort Pierce, FL, 34981-5599. Tel: 772-462-7124. p. 404
Tignor, Mia, Emerging Tech Librn, Indian River State College, Dixon Hendry Campus Library, 2229 NW Ninth Ave, Okeechobee, FL, 34972. Tel: 863-462-7124. p. 404
Tigue, Kate, Ch, Morrill Memorial Library, 33 Walpole St, Norwood, MA, 02062-1206. Tel: 781-769-0200. p. 1044
Tilbe, Janet, Dir, Bridgewater Free Library, 408 State Rte 8, Bridgewater, NY, 13313. Tel: 315-822-6475. p. 1497
Tileston, Nancy, Tech Serv Librn, Alaska State Court Law Library, 303 K St, Anchorage, AK, 99501. Tel: 907-264-0585. p. 41
Till-Rogers, Margo, Mgr, Edmonton Public Library, Woodcroft, 13420 114 Ave NW, Edmonton, AB, T5M 2Y5, CANADA. Tel: 780-496-6894. p. 2537
Tillequots, Jolena, Libr Tech III, Yakama Nation Library, 100 Spiel-Yi Loop, Toppenish, WA, 98948. Tel: 509-865-2800, Ext 6. p. 2388
Tiller, Cynthia, Librn, Cape Breton Regional Library, Glace Bay Public, 143 Commercial St, Glace Bay, NS, B1A 3B9, CANADA. Tel: 902-849-8657. p. 2622
Tiller, Stacy, Adult Serv, Spencer County Public Library, 168 Taylorsville Rd, Taylorsville, KY, 40071. Tel: 502-477-8137. p. 875
Tillett, Aubree, Humanities Librn, University of Minnesota Libraries-Twin Cities, Architecture & Landscape Architecture Library, 210 Rapson Hall, 89 Church St SE, Minneapolis, MN, 55455. Tel: 612-624-6383. p. 1185
Tilley, Carol, Assoc Prof, University of Illinois at Urbana-Champaign, Library & Information Science Bldg, 501 E Daniel St, Champaign, IL, 61820-6211. Tel: 217-333-3280. p. 2784
Tilley, Marilyn, Youth Serv Dir, Churdan City Library, 414 Sand St, Churdan, IA, 50050. Tel: 515-389-3423. p. 740
Tilley, Sheryl, Mgr, Libr Serv, Region of Waterloo Library, 2017 Nafziger Rd, Baden, ON, N3A 3H4, CANADA. Tel: 519-575-4590. p. 2629
Tillie, Yoder, Libr Asst, Goshen College, Harold & Wilma Good Library, 1700 S Main, Goshen, IN, 46526-4794. Tel: 574-535-7637. p. 687
Tillinghast, Andrea, Dir, Edith B Ford Memorial Library, 7169 N Main St, Ovid, NY, 14521. Tel: 607-869-3031. p. 1613
Tillinghast, Shelby, Head, Customer Serv, Head, Tech Serv, Huron Public Library, 333 Williams St, Huron, OH, 44839. Tel: 419-433-5009. p. 1791
Tillman, Janet, Database Adminr, The Master's Seminary Library, 13248 Roscoe Blvd, Sun Valley, CA, 91352. Tel: 818-909-5545. p. 251
Tillman, Janet L, Ref Librn, Ser Librn, The Master's University, 21726 W Placerita Canyon Rd, Santa Clarita, CA, 91321-1200. Tel: 661-259-3540. p. 242

Tillman, Marvin, Mgr, Library Service Ctr, Duke University Libraries, 411 Chapel Dr, Durham, NC, 27708. Tel: 919-596-3962. p. 1684

Tillman, Mike, Teacher Res Ctr Librn, California State University, Fresno, Henry Madden Library, 5200 N Barton Ave, Mail Stop ML-34, Fresno, CA, 93740-8014. Tel: 559-278-2054. p. 144

Tillmon, Renee C, Dir, Burr Oak Township Library, 220 S Second St, Burr Oak, MI, 49030-5133. Tel: 269-489-2906. p. 1088

Tills, Brenda, Br Mgr, Allen Parish Libraries, Kinder Branch, 833 Fourth Ave, Kinder, LA, 70648. Tel: 318-491-4545. p. 905

Tillson, Linda, Dir, Flagstaff City-Coconino County Public Library System, 300 W Aspen Ave, Flagstaff, AZ, 86001. Tel: 928-213-2331. p. 60

Tilly, Lauren, Prog & Res Coordr, Orangeville Public Library, One Mill St, Orangeville, ON, L9W 2M2, CANADA. Tel: 519-941-0610, Ext 5230. p. 2663

Tilly, Tatyana, Librn, Red Deer Public Library, Dawe Branch, 56 Holt St, Red Deer, AB, T4N 6A6, CANADA. Tel: 403-341-3822. p. 2551

Tillyer, Brenda, Commun Librn, Cariboo Regional District Library, Interlakes Branch, 7170 Levick Circle, Lone Butte, BC, V0K 1X1, CANADA. Tel: 250-593-4545. p. 2584

Tilsy, Emily, Evening/Weekend Supvr, Judson University, 1151 N State St, Elgin, IL, 60123. Tel: 847-628-2030. p. 584

Tilt, Stephanie, Mgr, Salt Lake County Library Services, Riverton Branch, 12877 S 1830 W, Riverton, UT, 84065-3204. p. 2275

Timberlake, Mona, Br Mgr, Bullitt County Public Library, Hillview Branch, 155 Terry Blvd, Hillview, Louisville, KY, 40229. Tel: 502-957-5759. p. 875

Timbs, Jeff, Dir, Allen Public Library, 300 N Allen Dr, Allen, TX, 75013. Tel: 214-509-4902. p. 2133

Timko, Matthew, Academic Technologies & Outreach Servs Librn, Northern Illinois University Libraries, David C Shapiro Memorial Law Library, Swen Parson Hall, 2nd Flr, Normal Rd, DeKalb, IL, 60115-2890. Tel: 815-753-9492. p. 578

Timm, Chris, Chief Curator, Maine Maritime Museum, 243 Washington St, Bath, ME, 04530. Tel: 207-443-1316, Ext 328. p. 916

Timm, Cindy, Vols Librn, Bailey-Matthews National Shell Museum & Aquarium, 3075 Sanibel Captiva Rd, Sanibel, FL, 33957. Tel: 239-395-2233. p. 442

Timm, Jann, Librn, North Central Washington Libraries, Okanogan Public Library, 228 Pine St, Okanogan, WA, 98840. Tel: 509-422-2609. p. 2394

Timm, Sarah, Head, Pub Serv, Texas A&M University-San Antonio, One University Way, San Antonio, TX, 78224. Tel: 210-784-1504. p. 2239

Timme, Kay, Dir, Allan Shivers Library & Museum, 302 N Charlton St, Woodville, TX, 75979. Tel: 409-283-3709. p. 2258

Timmerman, Clara, Dir, Stuttgart Public Library, 2002 S Buerkle St, Stuttgart, AR, 72160-6508. Tel: 870-673-1966. p. 111

Timmerman, Jennifer, Outreach Coordr, Youth Serv Coordr, Boone County Public Library, 1786 Burlington Pike, Burlington, KY, 41005. Tel: 859-342-2665. p. 850

Timmins, Elizabeth M, Libr Dir, Programmer, Muehl Public Library, 436 N Main, Seymour, WI, 54165-1021. Tel: 920-833-2725. p. 2475

Timmins, Leila, Sr Curator, Robert McLaughlin Gallery Library, Civic Centre, 72 Queen St, Oshawa, ON, L1H 3Z3, CANADA. Tel: 905-576-3000. p. 2663

Timmons, Cassidy, Libr Assoc, Hill Correctional Center Library, 600 S Linwood Rd, Galesburg, IL, 61401. Tel: 309-343-4212, Ext 360. p. 591

Timmons, Mary, Managing Librn, Monroe Community College, Damon City Campus Library, 228 E Main St, 4th Flr 4-101, Rochester, NY, 14604. Tel: 585-262-1413. p. 1628

Timmons, Michele, Libr Dir, Elgin Public Library, 1699 Division St, Elgin, OR, 97827. Tel: 541-437-2860. p. 1878

Timmons, Traci, Librn, Mgr, Libr Serv, Seattle Art Museum, Dorothy Stimson Bullitt Library, 1300 First Ave, Seattle, WA, 98101. Tel: 206-654-3220. p. 2378

Timms, Dorothy, Dir, Sun River Terrace Public Library District, 7219 E Chicago St, Sun River Terrace, IL, 60964. Tel: 815-370-5244. p. 653

Timms, Geoffrey A, Librn, Center for Coastal Environmental Health & Biomolecular Research, c/o College of Charleston, Marine Resources Library, 217 Ft Johnson Rd, Bldg 8, Charleston, SC, 29412. Tel: 843-953-9370. p. 2048

Timms, Geoffrey P, Librn, College of Charleston, Marine Resources Library, Bldg 8, 217 Fort Johnson Rd, Charleston, SC, 29412. Tel: 843-953-9370. p. 2050

Timms, Gwendolyn, Libr Asst, Media Serv, Voorhees University, 213 Wiggins Dr, Denmark, SC, 29042. Tel: 803-780-1220. p. 2058

Timony, Patrick, Adaptive Tech Librn, District of Columbia Talking Book & Braille Library, Center for Accessibility, Rm 215, 901 G St NW, Washington, DC, 20001. Tel: 202-727-2142. p. 365

Timothy, Lisa, Exec Dir, East Lyme Public Library, 39 Society Rd, Niantic, CT, 06357. Tel: 860-739-6926. p. 330

Tims, Barbara, Librn, Texas Medical Association, 401 W 15th St, Austin, TX, 78701-1680. Tel: 512-370-1548. p. 2141

Tincher, Tina M, Librn, Michigan Department of Natural Resources, Institute for Fisheries, NIB G250, 400 N Ingalls St, Ann Arbor, MI, 48109-5480. Tel: 734-356-1934. p. 1079

Tindall, Lisa, Libr Dir, Cutler Public Library, Civic Ctr, 409 S Main, Cutler, IL, 62238. Tel: 618-497-2961. p. 575

Tinder, Emi, Asst Librn, Marquette Regional History Center, 145 W Spring St, Marquette, MI, 49855. Tel: 906-226-3571. p. 1130

Tinerella, Sherry, Pub Serv Librn, Arkansas Tech University, 305 West Q St, Russellville, AR, 72801. Tel: 479-964-0571. p. 108

Tingle, Natalia, Bus Ref & Instruction Librn, University of Colorado Boulder, William M White Business Library, Koelbel Bldg, 995 Regent Dr, Boulder, CO, 80309. Tel: 303-492-3034. p. 268

Tingley, Charles, Sr Res Librn, Saint Augustine Historical Society, Six Artillery Lane, 2nd Flr, Saint Augustine, FL, 32084. Tel: 904-825-2333. p. 440

Tinius, Dara, Electronic Res & Ref Librn, Oklahoma Christian University, 2501 E Memorial Rd, Edmond, OK, 73013. Tel: 405-425-5315. p. 1846

Tinker, Scott, Dir, University of Texas Libraries, Bureau of Economic Geology & Resource Center, 10100 Burnet Rd, Bldg 131, Austin, TX, 78758-4445. Tel: 512-471-1534, 512-471-7144. p. 2142

Tinkham, Kelly, Libr Dir, Newaygo Area District Library, 44 N State Rd, Newaygo, MI, 49337-8969. Tel: 231-652-6723. p. 1137

Tinnel, Emily, YA Librn, Mansfield Public Library, 54 Warrenville Rd, Mansfield Center, CT, 06250. Tel: 860-423-2501. p. 321

Tinney, Nancy, Ch Serv, East Orange Public Library, 21 S Arlington Ave, East Orange, NJ, 07018. Tel: 973-266-5600. p. 1400

Tipler, Stephen, Digital Serv Librn, Marshall University Libraries, One John Marshall Dr, Huntington, WV, 25755-2060. Tel: 304-696-2907. p. 2405

Tippey, Paul, Dean, Libr & Info Tech, Asbury Theological Seminary, 204 N Lexington Ave, Wilmore, KY, 40390-1199. Tel: 859-858-2100. p. 877

Tippins, Carol, Principal Asst Librn, Ned R McWherter Weakley County Library, 341 Linden St, Dresden, TN, 38225-1400. Tel: 731-364-2678. p. 2097

Tippitt, Rhonda, Dir, Sevier County Public Library System, 408 High St, Sevierville, TN, 37862. Tel: 865-365-1416. p. 2125

Tipton, Ashley, Assoc Univ Librn, Midwestern State University, 3410 Taft Blvd, Wichita Falls, TX, 76308-2099. Tel: 940-397-4175. p. 2257

Tipton, Jessica, Instruction Librn, Online Librn, Johnson County Community College, 12345 College Blvd, Overland Park, KS, 66210. Tel: 913-469-8500, Ext 3286. p. 829

Tipton, Margie, Asst Ch, Eunice Public Library, 1003 Ave N, Eunice, NM, 88231. Tel: 575-394-2336. p. 1467

Tipton, Martha, Asst Admin, Central Texas College, Bldg 102, 6200 W Central Texas Expressway, Killeen, TX, 76549. Tel: 254-526-1474. p. 2206

Tipton, Roberta, Bus Librn, Information Literacy Coord, Rutgers University Libraries, John Cotton Dana Library, 185 University Ave, Newark, NJ, 07102. Tel: 973-353-5222. p. 1428

Tipton-Llamas, Regina, Hist Coll Librn, Ref Serv, Ellensburg Public Library, 209 N Ruby St, Ellensburg, WA, 98926-3397. Tel: 509-962-7250. p. 2363

Tirona, Pat, Br Mgr, San Diego County Library, Solana Beach Branch, Earl Warren Middle School, 157 Stevens Ave, Solana Beach, CA, 92075-1873. Tel: 858-755-1404. p. 217

Tirschman, Kelly, Br Supvr, Western Manitoba Regional Library, Glenboro/South Cypress Library Branch, 105 Broadway St, Glenboro, MB, R0K 0X0, CANADA. Tel: 204-827-2874. p. 2586

Tisdale, Jessi, Circ Mgr, Worthington Libraries, Northwest Library, 2280 Hard Rd, Columbus, OH, 43235. Tel: 614-807-2655. p. 1834

Tish, Emily, Dir, Trussville Public Library, 201 Parkway Dr, Trussville, AL, 35173. Tel: 205-655-2022. p. 37

Tisi, Madel, Circ Librn, Instruction Librn, Ref Librn, Ramapo College of New Jersey, 505 Ramapo Valley Rd, Mahwah, NJ, 07430-1623. Tel: 201-684-7510. p. 1415

Tissel, Jenni, Youth Serv, Clearwater County Free Library District, 204 Wood St, Weippe, ID, 83553. Tel: 208-435-4058. p. 532

Titkemeier, Susan, Dir, Pemberville Public Library, 375 E Front St, Pemberville, OH, 43450. Tel: 419-287-4012. p. 1814

Titkemeier, Susan, Dir, Pemberville Public Library, Luckey Branch, 335 Park Dr, Luckey, OH, 43443. Tel: 419-287-4012. p. 1814

Titone, Angela, Sr Libr Mgr, Consumer Technology Association (CTA), 1919 S Eads St, Arlington, VA, 22202. Tel: 703-907-7600. p. 2305

Titonis, Georgia, Br Librn, Boston Public Library, Uphams Corner, 500 Columbia Rd, Dorchester, MA, 02125. Tel: 617-265-0139. p. 993

Titschinger, Casey, Br Mgr, Public Library of Cincinnati & Hamilton County, Delhi Township, 5095 Foley Rd, Cincinnati, OH, 45238. Tel: 513-369-6019. p. 1762

Titsworth, Myra, Librn, Oregon County Library District, Koshkonong Public, 302 Diggins St, Koshkonong, MO, 65692. Tel: 417-867-5472. p. 1237

Tittemore, Cecilia, Head, Cat & Metadata Serv, Dartmouth College Library, Baker-Berry Library, 6025 Baker-Berry Library, Hanover, NH, 03755-3527. Tel: 603-646-3236. p. 1366

Tittle, Beth, Circ Serv, ILL, Jerseyville Public Library, 105 N Liberty St, Jerseyville, IL, 62052-1512. Tel: 618-498-9514. p. 603

Tittle, Karen, Dir, May Justus Memorial Library, 24 Dixie Lee Ave, Monteagle, TN, 37356. Tel: 931-924-2638. p. 2116

Titus, Jessica, Dir, Moyer District Library, 618 S Sangamon, Gibson City, IL, 60936. Tel: 217-784-5343. p. 592

Titus, Judy, Media Serv, Cedar Crest College, 100 College Dr, Allentown, PA, 18104-6196. Tel: 610-606-4666, Ext 3387. p. 1904

Titus, Mollie, Librn, Self Regional Healthcare, 1226 Spring St, Greenwood, SC, 29646. Tel: 864-725-4797, 864-725-4851. p. 2063

Titus, Ron, Electronic Serv Librn, Marshall University Libraries, One John Marshall Dr, Huntington, WV, 25755-2060. Tel: 304-696-6575. p. 2405

Titus, Sarah, Archives & Spec Coll Librn, Saint Norbert College, 400 Third St, De Pere, WI, 54115. Tel: 920-403-3282. p. 2430

Titus, Susanne, Head, Libr Serv, Swenson Swedish Immigration Research Center, Augustana College, 3520 Seventh Ave, Rock Island, IL, 61201. Tel: 309-794-7807. p. 641

Tkacs, Becky, Youth Librn, Upper Moreland Free Public Library, 109 Park Ave, Willow Grove, PA, 19090-3277. Tel: 215-659-0741. p. 2024

Tkaczyk, Holly, Circ Librn, E-Resources Librn, Eastern Florida State College, 1519 Clearlake Rd, Cocoa, FL, 32922. Tel: 321-433-7252. p. 389

Tkaczyk, Holly, Instr Librn, Eastern Florida State College, 250 Community College Pkwy, Palm Bay, FL, 32909. Tel: 321-433-5270. p. 434

To, Trisha, Br Librn, Everett Public Libraries, Shute Memorial, 781 Broadway, Everett, MA, 02149. Tel: 617-394-2308. p. 1017

Tobar, Cynthia, Head, Archives, Bronx Community College Library, 2115 University Ave, NL 252A, Bronx, NY, 10453. Tel: 718-289-5436. p. 1497

Tobe, Tamie, Librn, Nixon Peabody LLP, 799 Ninth St NW, Ste 500, Washington, DC, 20001. Tel: 202-585-8000, Ext 8320. p. 373

Tobey, Darren, Dir, Libr Syst, Northeastern State University, 711 N Grand Ave, Tahlequah, OK, 74464-2333. Tel: 918-456-5511, Ext 3200. p. 1863

Tobias, Deb, Cat, Coll Develop, Hiawatha Public Library, 150 W Willman St, Hiawatha, IA, 52233. Tel: 319-393-1414. p. 758

Tobias, Sarah, Ch, Franklin Lakes Public Library, 470 DeKorte Dr, Franklin Lakes, NJ, 07417. Tel: 201-891-2224. p. 1404

Tobichuk, Mary, Dir, Fiske Public Library, 110 Randall Rd, Wrentham, MA, 02093. Tel: 508-384-5440. p. 1073

Tobin, Frances, Commun Libr Mgr, Queens Library, North Forest Park Community Library, 98-27 Metropolitan Ave, Forest Hills, NY, 11375. Tel: 718-261-5512. p. 1555

Tobin, Gail, Br Coordr, Schaumburg Township District Library, Hanover Park Branch, 1266 Irving Park Rd, Hanover Park, IL, 60133. Tel: 847-923-3470. p. 645

Tobin, Helen, Supvr, Mid-Columbia Libraries, Connell Branch, 118 N Columbia Ave, Connell, WA, 99326. Tel: 509-234-4971. p. 2367

Tobin, Joy, Mgr, El Camino Hospital Library & Information Center, 2500 Grant Rd, Mountain View, CA, 94039. Tel: 650-940-7210. p. 181

Tobin, Karen, Asst Dir, Goodnow Library, 21 Concord Rd, Sudbury, MA, 01776-2383. Tel: 978-440-5525. p. 1058

Tobin, Mary, Asst Dir, Head, Info Serv, Ridley Township Public Library, 100 E MacDade Blvd, Folsom, PA, 19033-2592. Tel: 610-583-0593. p. 1933

Toby, Benjamin, Libr Serv Mgr, Seward & Kissel LLP, One Battery Park Plaza, New York, NY, 10004. Tel: 212-574-1200. p. 1601

Toce, Jackie, Head, Tech Serv, Southern Connecticut State University, 501 Crescent St, New Haven, CT, 06515. Tel: 203-392-5777. p. 326

Tock, Emily, Info Serv & Instrul Librn, Indiana University-Purdue University Fort Wayne, 2101 E Coliseum Blvd, Fort Wayne, IN, 46805-1499. Tel: 260-481-6515. p. 684

Tockey, Linda, Exec Dir, Scientists Center for Animal Welfare Library, 2660 NE Hwy 20, Ste 610-115, Bend, OR, 97701. Tel: 301-345-3500. p. 1874

Toczko, Susan, Asst Dir, Shedd Free Library, 46 N Main, Washington, NH, 03280. Tel: 603-495-3592. p. 1383

Todaro, Don, Manager, Access & Tech Serv, Library of Michigan, 702 W Kalamazoo St, Lansing, MI, 48915. Tel: 517-373-2583. p. 1125

Todaro, Julie, Dean, Libr Serv, Austin Community College, 5930 Middle Fiskville Rd, Austin, TX, 78752. Tel: 512-223-7792. p. 2137

Todd, Adam, Br Mgr, Indianapolis Public Library, Irvington, 5625 E Washington St, Indianapolis, IN, 46219-6411. Tel: 317-275-4450. p. 695

Todd, Adam, Br Mgr, Indianapolis Public Library, Nora, 8625 Guilford Ave, Indianapolis, IN, 46240-1835. Tel: 317-275-4473. p. 696

Todd, Alexander C, Exec Dir, Prospect Heights Public Library District, 12 N Elm St, Prospect Heights, IL, 60070-1450. Tel: 847-259-3500. p. 637

Todd, Amanda, Head Librn, Dominy Memorial Library, 201 S Third St, Fairbury, IL, 61739. Tel: 815-692-3231. p. 587

Todd, Andrew, Librn, Eastern Florida State College, 1519 Clearlake Rd, Cocoa, FL, 32922. p. 389

Todd, Carl, Libr Serv Coordr, Holyoke Community College Library, Donahue Bldg, 2nd Flr, 303 Homestead Ave, Holyoke, MA, 01040-1099. Tel: 413-552-2374. p. 1025

Todd, Carrie, Cat, Tech Serv, Fairport Harbor Public Library, 335 Vine St, Fairport Harbor, OH, 44077-5799. Tel: 440-354-8191, Ext 6523. p. 1785

Todd, Chris, Syst & Cat Librn, University of Pittsburgh Library System, Law Bldg, 3900 Forbes Ave, 4th Flr, Pittsburgh, PA, 15260. Tel: 412-648-1326. p. 1996

Todd, Christine, Evening Librn, Nunez Community College Library, 3710 Paris Rd, Chalmette, LA, 70043. Tel: 504-278-6295, Ext 232. p. 887

Todd, Emily, Dir, Stubbs Memorial Library, 207 E Second St, Holstein, IA, 51025. Tel: 712-368-4563. p. 758

Todd, Emily, Br Librn, Boston Public Library, Connolly, 433 Centre St, Jamaica Plain, MA, 02130. Tel: 617-522-1960. p. 992

Todd, Janette, Asst Librn, Judith Basin County Free Library, 93 Third St N, Stanford, MT, 59479. Tel: 406-566-2277, Ext 123. p. 1302

Todd, Jocelyn, Librn, Palliser Regional Library, Wood Mountain Branch, Two Second Ave, Wood Mountain, SK, S0H 4L0, CANADA. Tel: 306-266-2110. p. 2743

Todd, Julia, Circ Serv Team Leader, Clarksburg-Harrison Public Library, 404 W Pike St, Clarksburg, WV, 26301. Tel: 304-627-2236. p. 2401

Todd, Julie, Sr Librn, Ad Serv, El Segundo Public Library, 111 W Mariposa Ave, El Segundo, CA, 90245. Tel: 310-524-2729. p. 140

Todd, Kathleen, Head, Children's Servx, Kenora Public Library, 24 Main St S, Kenora, ON, P9N 1S7, CANADA. Tel: 807-467-2081. p. 2649

Todd, Kathy, Dir, Hudson Carnegie District Library, 205 S Market, Hudson, MI, 49247. Tel: 517-448-3801. p. 1117

Todd, Kimberly, Libr Dir, Luttrell Public Library, 115 Park Rd, Luttrell, TN, 37779. Tel: 865-992-0208. p. 2110

Todd, Kimberly, Libr Dir, Maynardville Public Library, 296 Main St, Maynardville, TN, 37807-3400. Tel: 865-992-7106. p. 2111

Todd, Leslie, Information Literacy Coord, University of the Incarnate Word, 4301 Broadway, CPO 297, San Antonio, TX, 78209-6397. Tel: 210-829-3841. p. 2240

Todd, Matt, Assoc Dean, Tech & Learning Res, Libr Dir, Northern Virginia Community College Libraries, Alexandria Campus, Bisdorf Bldg, Rm 232, 5000 Dawes Ave, Alexandria, VA, 22311. Tel: 703-845-6033. p. 2304

Todd, Melanie, Librn, Lucy Hill Patterson Memorial Library, 201 Ackerman St, Rockdale, TX, 76567. Tel: 512-446-3410. p. 2233

Todd, Patricia, Ref (Info Servs), Alhambra Civic Center Library, 101 S First St, Alhambra, CA, 91801-3432. Tel: 626-570-5008. p. 115

Todd, Star, Youth Serv Spec, Jefferson County Library District, 241 SE Seventh St, Madras, OR, 97741. Tel: 541-475-3351. p. 1885

Todd, Sue, Dir, Eastpointe Memorial Library, 15875 Oak St, Eastpointe, MI, 48021-2390. Tel: 586-445-5096. p. 1102

Todd, Vonda K, Head Librn, Texas Commission on Environment Quality, Bldg A, Rm 102, 12100 Park 35 Circle, Austin, TX, 78753. Tel: 512-239-0024. p. 2140

Todd-Roberts, Vera, Br Head, Chatham-Kent Public Library, Bothwell Branch, 320 Main St, Bothwell, ON, N0P 1C0, CANADA. Tel: 519-695-2844. p. 2635

Todd-Roberts, Vera, Br Head, Chatham-Kent Public Library, Highgate Branch, 291 King St, Highgate, ON, N0P 1T0, CANADA. Tel: 519-678-3313. p. 2635

Todd-Roberts, Vera, Br Head, Chatham-Kent Public Library, Ridgetown Branch, 54 Main St, Ridgetown, ON, N0P 2C0, CANADA. Tel: 519-674-3121. p. 2636

Todman, Judith, Mgr, Queens Library, The Archives at Queens Library, 89-11 Merrick Blvd, Jamaica, NY, 11432. Tel: 718-990-0770. p. 1553

Todorinova, Lilyana, Undergraduate Ed Librn, Rutgers University Libraries, Mabel Smith Douglass Library, Eight Chapel Dr, New Brunswick, NJ, 08901-8527. Tel: 848-932-1696. p. 1425

Todtman, Rhonda, Asst Dir, Peninsula Public Library, 280 Central Ave, Lawrence, NY, 11559. Tel: 516-239-3262. p. 1562

Todwong, Janet, Digital Projects, Spec Coll Librn, Washburn University, School of Law Library, 1700 SW College Ave, Topeka, KS, 66621. Tel: 785-670-3191. p. 840

Toelle, Mae, Asst Dir, Lied Battle Creek Public Library, 100 S Fourth St, Battle Creek, NE, 68715. Tel: 402-675-6934. p. 1307

Toews, Robin, Br Librn, Wapiti Regional Library, Archerwill Public Library, First Ave, Archerwill, SK, S0E 0B0, CANADA. Tel: 306-323-2128. p. 2745

Toews-Neufeldt, Lynette, Asst Libr Dir, Concordia University of Edmonton, 7128 Ada Blvd, Edmonton, AB, T5B 4E4, CANADA. Tel: 780-479-9339. p. 2536

Tofferi, Jill, Dir, Fletcher Memorial Library, 88 Main St, Ludlow, VT, 05149. Tel: 802-228-3517, 802-228-8921. p. 2287

Tointigh, Brandy, Dir, Hobart Public Library, 200 S Main St, Hobart, OK, 73651. Tel: 580-726-2535. p. 1849

Tokar, Liudmyla, Br Librn, Wapiti Regional Library, Prairie River Public Library, Two Arras St, Prairie River, SK, S0E 1J0, CANADA. Tel: 306-889-4521. p. 2746

Tokar, Victoria, Ref Librn, Loyola Law School, 919 S Albany St, Los Angeles, CA, 90015-1211. Tel: 213-736-8132. p. 166

Tokert, Amanda, Libr Dir, Benton County Public Library, 102 N Van Buren Ave, Fowler, IN, 47944. Tel: 765-884-1720. p. 685

Tokheim, Ivon, Dir, Swea City Public Library, 208 Third St N, Swea City, IA, 50590. Tel: 515-272-4216. p. 786

Tokuda, Joyce, Learning Res Librn, Kapi'olani Community College Library, 4303 Diamond Head Rd, Honolulu, HI, 96816. Tel: 808-734-9357. p. 512

Tolan, Michael, Cat, Govt Doc, Black Hills State University, 1200 University St, Unit 9676, Spearfish, SD, 57799-9676. Tel: 605-642-6356. p. 2083

Tolan, Michael, Instructor, Library Media, Black Hills State University, E Y Berry Library Learning Ctr, 1200 University St, Unit 9676, Spearfish, SD, 57799-9676. Tel: 605-642-6356. p. 2792

Toland, Dwight, Fac Mgr, Calcasieu Parish Public Library System, 301 W Claude St, Lake Charles, LA, 70605-3457. Tel: 337-721-7147. p. 893

Toland, Laura, Dir, Dorcas Carey Public Library, 236 E Findlay St, Carey, OH, 43316-1250. Tel: 419-396-7921. p. 1756

Toland, Matthew, Dir, Wood Library-Museum of Anesthesiology, 1061 American Lane, Schaumburg, IL, 60173. Tel: 847-268-9165. p. 645

Tolbert, James, Dir, Milan-Berlin Library District, 19 E Church St, Milan, OH, 44846. Tel: 419-499-4117. p. 1802

Tolbert, Randa, Libr Spec, Gadsden State Community College, Pierce C Cain Learning Resource Center, Ayers Campus, 1801 Coleman Rd, Anniston, AL, 36207. Tel: 256-835-5436. p. 18

Tolchin, Judith, Libr Dir, Monmouth County Library, 125 Symmes Dr, Manalapan, NJ, 07726. Tel: 732-431-7220. p. 1415

Toledo, Ivan, Asst Dir, Miami Dade College, Medical Center Campus Library & Information Resource Center, 950 NW 20th St, Miami, FL, 33127. Tel: 305-237-4325. p. 422

Toles, Dana, Admin Coordr, Texas A&M University-Commerce, Mesquite Metroplex Center Library, 3819 Towne Crossing Blvd, Mesquite, TX, 75150. Tel: 972-613-7591. p. 2159

Tolf, Tracy, Libr Syst & Applications Librn, Whitman College, 345 Boyer Ave, Walla Walla, WA, 99362. Tel: 509-527-5916. p. 2393

Tolias, Kiki, Asst Librn, Keyser-Mineral County Public Library, Burlington Public, Patterson Creek Rd S, Burlington, WV, 26710. Tel: 304-289-3690. p. 2406

Toll, Cathy, PhD, Assoc Prof, Graduate Program Coord, University of Wisconsin Oshkosh College of Education & Human Services, 800 Algoma Blvd, Oshkosh, WI, 54901. Tel: 920-424-0881. p. 2794

Tolle, Audry, Libr Dir, Sanger Public Library, 501 Bolivar St, Sanger, TX, 76266. Tel: 940-458-3257. p. 2241

Tollensdorf, Denise, Dir, Hanover Township Library, 204 Jefferson St, Hanover, IL, 61041. Tel: 815-591-3517. p. 597

Tolleson, Mark, Assoc Dir, County College of Morris, 214 Center Grove Rd, Randolph, NJ, 07869-2086. Tel: 973-328-5311. p. 1438

Tollett, Brenda, Librn, Sevier County Library, Gillham Branch, 202 N Second St, Gillham, AR, 71841-9511. Tel: 870-386-5665. p. 93

Tolley-Stokes, Rebecca, Pub Relations/Mkt Librn, East Tennessee State University, Sherrod Library, Seehorn Dr & Lake St, Johnson City, TN, 37614-0204. Tel: 423-439-4365. p. 2103

Tollison, Sharon, Dir, Vaiden Public Library, 507 Lee St, Vaiden, MS, 39176-0108. Tel: 662-464-7736. p. 1234

Tolliver, Bob, Sci Librn, North Dakota State University Libraries, 1201 Albrecht Blvd, Fargo, ND, 58108. Tel: 701-231-7351. p. 1733

Tolliver, Carol, Libr Assoc, Desoto Parish Library, Stonewall Branch, 808 Hwy 171, Stonewall, LA, 71078. Tel: 318-925-9191. p. 896

Tolly, Lynda, Librn, University of California Los Angeles Library, Grace M Hunt Memorial English Reading Room, 235 Humanities Bldg, 415 Portola Plaza, Los Angeles, CA, 90095. Tel: 310-825-4511. p. 169

Tolmam, Michelle, Libr Dir, Bonneville County Library District, Iona Branch, 3548 N Main St, Iona, ID, 83427. Tel: 208-523-2358. p. 515

Tolman, Michelle, Dir, Bonneville County Library District, 3015 S 25th E, Ammon, ID, 83406. Tel: 208-757-6393. p. 515

Tolppanen, Bradley, Univ Archivist, Eastern Illinois University, 600 Lincoln Ave, Charleston, IL, 61920. Tel: 217-581-7552. p. 552

Tolson, Kim, Libr Dir, Millis Public Library, 961 Main St, Millis, MA, 02054. Tel: 508-376-8282. p. 1036

Tolson, Ruth, Br Mgr, Rockbridge Regional Library System, Goshen Public, 140 Main St, Goshen, VA, 24439. Tel: 540-997-0351. p. 2329

Tom, Martha, Asst Librn, Real County Public Library Leakey, 225 Main St, Leakey, TX, 78873. Tel: 830-232-5199. p. 2210

Tom, May Lee, Head, Tech Serv, Leominster Public Library, 30 West St, Leominster, MA, 01453. Tel: 978-534-7522, Ext 3599. p. 1028

Tom, Michelle, Archivist, Librn, Windsor Historical Society Library, 96 Palisado Ave, Windsor, CT, 06095. Tel: 860-688-3813. p. 348

Tom, Tracy, Br Mgr, Muskingum County Library System, Dresden Branch, 816 Main St, Dresden, OH, 43821. Tel: 740-754-1003. p. 1837

Toman, April, Youth Serv Librn, Schertz Public Library, 798 Schertz Pkwy, Schertz, TX, 78154. Tel: 210-619-1700. p. 2242

Tomasiewicz, Megan, Dir, Tekamah Public Library, 204 S 13th St, Tekamah, NE, 68061. Tel: 402-374-2453. p. 1338

Tomasini, Chris, Librn, Lakehead University, Orillia, 500 University Ave, Orillia, ON, L3Z 0B9, CANADA. Tel: 705-330-2260. p. 2685

Tomaszewski, Carol, Dir, Ashley Public Library District, 70 N Second St, Ashley, IL, 62808. Tel: 618-485-2295. p. 537

Tombarge, John, Res & Instruction Librn, Washington & Lee University, University Library, 204 W Washington St, Lexington, VA, 24450-2116. Tel: 540-458-8643. p. 2329

Tomberlin, Cetoria, Coll Spec, ILL Spec, Berry College, 2277 Martha Berry Hwy, Mount Berry, GA, 30149. Tel: 706-368-6706. p. 492

Tomchak, Tiffany, Libr Spec, Central New Mexico Community College Libraries, South Valley Campus Library, 525 Buena Vista Dr, Albuquerque, NM, 87105. Tel: 505-224-4000, Ext 53275. p. 1461

Tomcik, Laura, Libr Dir, Fall Creek Public Library, 122 E Lincoln Ave, Fall Creek, WI, 54742-9425. Tel: 715-877-3334. p. 2434

Tomczak, Justine, Libr Dir, Clifton Public Library, 292 Piaget Ave, Clifton, NJ, 07011. Tel: 973-772-5500. p. 1397

Tomczak, Patricia, Dean of Libr, Quincy University, 1800 College Ave, Quincy, IL, 62301-2699. Tel: 217-228-5432, Ext 3801. p. 638

Tomek, Nancy, Youth Serv Mgr, Amherst Public Library, 221 Spring St, Amherst, OH, 44001. Tel: 440-988-4230. p. 1746

Tomeo, Bill, Tech Serv Librn, Hamilton County Law Library, Hamilton County Court House, 1000 Main St, Rm 601, Cincinnati, OH, 45202. Tel: 513-946-5300. p. 1760

Tomes, Ann M, Librn, Beverly Hospital Medical Library, 85 Herrick St, Beverly, MA, 01915. Tel: 978-922-3000, Ext 2920. p. 989

Tomilson, Shelley, Sr Librn, California Department of Corrections Library System, Salinas Valley State Prison, 31625 Hwy 101, Soledad, CA, 93960. Tel: 831-678-5500, Ext 6232. p. 207

Tominaga, Mana, Libr Mgr, Oakland Public Library, 125 14th St, Oakland, CA, 94612. Tel: 510-238-6611. p. 186

Tominaga, Mana, Supv Librn, Oakland Public Library, Main Library, 125 14th St, Oakland, CA, 94612. Tel: 510-238-3134. p. 186

Tomita, Kellie, Mkt & Communications Mgr, Cumberland County Public Library & Information Center, 300 Maiden Lane, Fayetteville, NC, 28301-5032. Tel: 910-483-7727. p. 1688

Tomlin, Bryce, Computer Coordr, Tech Serv Coordr, East Baton Rouge Parish Library, 7711 Goodwood Blvd, Baton Rouge, LA, 70806-7625. Tel: 225-231-3700. p. 882

Tomlin, Kathryn, Dir, Luverne Public Library, 148 E Third St, Luverne, AL, 36049. Tel: 334-335-5326. p. 24

Tomlin, Patrick, Dir, Learning Environment, Virginia Polytechnic Institute & State University Libraries, 560 Drillfield Dr, Blacksburg, VA, 24061. Tel: 540-231-9272. p. 2307

Tomlinson, Andie, Librn, Spec Coll Coordr, Vancouver Island University Library, 900 Fifth St, Nanaimo, BC, V9R 5S5, CANADA. Tel: 250-753-3245. p. 2572

Tomlinson, Andrea, Sr Librn, Talbot Research Library & Media Services, 333 Cottman Ave, 3rd Flr, Philadelphia, PA, 19111-2497. Tel: 215-728-2710. p. 1986

Tomlinson, Clint, Circ, Ohio State University LIBRARIES, Fine Arts, Wexner Ctr for the Arts, 1871 N High St, Columbus, OH, 43210. Tel: 614-292-6184. p. 1775

Tomlinson, Elise, Dean of Libr, University of Alaska Southeast, 11066 Auke Lake Way, BE1, Juneau, AK, 99801. Tel: 907-796-6467. p. 47

Tomlinson, Janis A, Dr, Dir of Mus, Dir, Spec Coll, University of Delaware Library, 181 S College Ave, Newark, DE, 19717-5267. Tel: 302-831-2965. p. 355

Tomlinson, Jeff, Dir, Lee-Itawamba Library System, 219 N Madison St, Tupelo, MS, 38804-3899. Tel: 662-841-9027. p. 1233

Tomlinson, Kathryn, Dir, Libr Serv, Wiregrass Georgia Technical College Library, 1676 Elm St, Rm 204, Sparks, GA, 31647. Tel: 229-549-7368, Ext 7941. p. 497

Tomlinson, Kimberly, Ref Librn, Wisconsin Talking Book & Braille Library, 813 W Wells St, Milwaukee, WI, 53233-1436. Tel: 414-286-3045. p. 2461

Tomlinson, Martin, Sr Mgr, Osler, Hoskin & Harcourt Library, One First Canadian Pl, Ste 6200, 100 King St W, Toronto, ON, M5X 1B8, CANADA. Tel: 416-862-4239. p. 2692

Tomlinson, Trish, Dir, Plainville Public Library, 56 East Main St, Plainville, CT, 06062. Tel: 860-793-1446. p. 333

Tommila, Kiki, Coll Develop Librn, Fac Librn, Whatcom Community College Library, Heiner Bldg, 231 W Kellogg Rd, Bellingham, WA, 98226. Tel: 360-383-3300. p. 2359

Tompeck, Kristen, Interim Dir, Wallowa Public Library, 201 N Main, Wallowa, OR, 97885. Tel: 541-886-4265. p. 1901

Tompkins, Alison, Libr Spec, Geisinger Wyoming Valley Medical Center, 1000 E Mountain Dr, Wilkes-Barre, PA, 18711. Tel: 570-808-7809. p. 2022

Tompkins, Allen R, Libr Dir, Fair Haven Public Library, 14426 Richmond Ave, Fair Haven, NY, 13064. Tel: 315-947-5851. p. 1532

Tompkins, Cheri, Libr Asst, Public Library at Tellico Village, 300 Irene Lane, Loudon, TN, 37774. Tel: 865-458-5199. p. 2110

Tompkins, Hayley, Br Mgr, Jefferson-Madison Regional Library, Crozet Branch, 2020 Library Ave, Crozet, VA, 22932. Tel: 434-823-4050. p. 2309

Tompkins, Heather, Dir of Libr Prog, Appalachian College Association, 7216 Jewel Bell Lane, Bristol, TN, 37620. Tel: 859-986-4584. p. 2775

Tomren, Jessie, Ms, Br Mgr, Mid-Columbia Libraries, Kennewick Branch, 1620 S Union St, Kennewick, WA, 99338. Tel: 509-783-7878. p. 2367

Tomschin, Sandra, Dir, Cicero Public Library, 5225 W Cermak Rd, Cicero, IL, 60804. Tel: 708-652-8084. p. 571

Tomzik, Peggy, Head, Circ Serv, Eisenhower Public Library District, 4613 N Oketo Ave, Harwood Heights, IL, 60706. Tel: 708-867-7828. p. 597

Tone, Lyn, Dir, Lawton Public Library, 125 S Main St, Lawton, MI, 49065. Tel: 269-624-5481. p. 1126

Tonelli, Maria, Br Mgr, West Haven Public Library, Ora Mason Branch, 260 Benham Hill Rd, West Haven, CT, 06516-6541. Tel: 203-933-9381. p. 346

Toner, Janelle, Mem Serv Coordr, ConnectNY, Inc, 6721 US Hwy 11, Potsdam, NY, 13676. p. 2771
Toner, Valerie, Supvr, Ch Serv, Bristol Public Library, Five High St, Bristol, CT, 06010. Tel: 860-584-7787. p. 304
Toney, Angela, Libr Asst, Desoto Parish Library, Logansport Branch, 203 Hwy 5, Logansport, LA, 71049. Tel: 318-697-2311. p. 896
Toney, Keaton, Libr Mgr, Davidson County Public Library System, Thomasville Public, 14 Randolph St, Thomasville, NC, 27360-4638. Tel: 336-474-2690. p. 1700
Tong, Jenny, Tech Serv, East Orange Public Library, 21 S Arlington Ave, East Orange, NJ, 07018. Tel: 973-266-5600. p. 1400
Tonner, Paulette, Libr Mgr, Haut-Saint-Jean Regional Library, Nackawic Public-School Library, 30 Landegger Dr, Nackawic, NB, E6G 1E9, CANADA. Tel: 506-575-2136. p. 2600
Tonowski, Sarah, Libr Mgr, Edson & District Public Library, 4726-8 Ave, Edson, AB, T7E 1E3, CANADA. Tel: 780-723-6691. p. 2539
Tonowski, Sarah, Libr Mgr, Forestburg Public Library, 4905 50th St, Forestburg, AB, T0B 1N0, CANADA. Tel: 780-582-4110. p. 2540
Tonubbee, Robbee, Libr Dir, Donald W Reynolds Community Center & Library, 1515 W Main St, Durant, OK, 74701. Tel: 580-924-3486, 580-931-0231. p. 1846
Tooey, M J, Exec Dir, University of Maryland, Baltimore, Health Sciences & Human Services Library, 601 W Lombard St, Baltimore, MD, 21201. Tel: 410-706-7545. p. 957
Tooker, Sue, Asst Librn, O'Neill Public Library, 601 E Douglas, O'Neill, NE, 68763. Tel: 402-336-3110. p. 1331
Toole, Gerri, Librn, Bowerston Public Library, 200 Main St, Bowerston, OH, 44695. Tel: 740-269-8531. p. 1752
Toole, Mary, Ref Librn, Middlesex Public Library, 1300 Mountain Ave, Middlesex, NJ, 08846. Tel: 732-356-6602. p. 1418
Toole, Susan, Br Mgr, Aiken-Bamberg-Barnwell-Edgefield Regional Library, New Ellenton Branch, 113 Pine Hill Ave, New Ellenton, SC, 29809. Tel: 803-652-7845. p. 2045
Toolen, Sandra, Library Contact, Wyoming Women's Center Library, 1000 W Griffith Blvd, Lusk, WY, 82225. Tel: 307-334-3693. p. 2497
Toolsidass, Rebecca, Ref & Instruction Librn, Saint Joseph's College, 222 Clinton Ave, Brooklyn, NY, 11205-3697. Tel: 718-940-5877. p. 1506
Tooman, Joseph P, Chmn, Gardenview Horticultural Park Library, 16711 Pearl Rd, Strongsville, OH, 44136-6048. Tel: 440-238-6653. p. 1822
Toombs, Yvonne, Asst Librn, DeKalb County Public Library, 504 Grand Ave NW, Fort Payne, AL, 35967. Tel: 256-845-2671. p. 18
Toomer, Patrice, Libr Serv Dir, Wiregrass Georgia Technical College, 706 W Baker Hwy, Rm 2125, Douglas, GA, 31533. Tel: 229-468-2226. p. 477
Toomer, Patrice, Dir, Libr Serv, Wiregrass Georgia Technical College, Lowndes Hall, 4089 Val Tech Rd, Rm 7147A, Valdosta, GA, 31602. Tel: 229-259-5177. p. 501
Toon, Ben, Sr Libr Mgr, Irving Public Library, East Library & Learning Center, 440 S Nursery Rd, Irving, TX, 75060. Tel: 972-721-3722. p. 2202
Toon, Ben, Sr Library Services Mgr; Operations & Customer Service, Irving Public Library, 801 W Irving Blvd, Irving, TX, 75015. p. 2202
Toon, Lydia, Librn, Delta County Public Library, 300 W Dallas Ave, Cooper, TX, 75432-1632. Tel: 903-395-4575. p. 2159
Topcik, Heather, Libr Dir, Bard Graduate Center Library, 38 W 86th St, New York, NY, 10024. Tel: 212-501-3036. p. 1579
Topel, Adriana, Ref Supvr, Clearwater Public Library System, 100 N Osceola Ave, Clearwater, FL, 33755. Tel: 727-562-4970. p. 388
Topel, Dennis, Libr Tech, Glendale Community College - North, Bldg GCN B (Beshbito), 5727 W Happy Valley Rd, Glendale, AZ, 85310. p. 62
Topete, Connie, Sr Librn, Los Angeles Public Library System, Benjamin Franklin Branch Library, 2200 E First St, Los Angeles, CA, 90033. Tel: 323-263-6901. p. 163
Topliffe, Jacob, Youth Serv, Colebrook Public Library, 126 Main St, Colebrook, NH, 03576. Tel: 603-237-4808. p. 1358
Topolski, Judy, Asst Librn, Weathersfield Proctor Library, 5181 Rte 5, Ascutney, VT, 05030. Tel: 802-674-2863. p. 2277
Topp-Schefers, Hannah, ILL, St Cloud State University Library, James W Miller Learning Resource Center, 400 Sixth St S, Saint Cloud, MN, 56301. Tel: 320-308-2085. p. 1198
Topper, Joby, Dir, Libr & Info Serv, Lock Haven University of Pennsylvania, 401 N Fairview Ave, Lock Haven, PA, 17745-2390. Tel: 570-484-2309. p. 1956
Topping, Irina, Head, Tech Serv, Union Presbyterian Seminary Library, 3401 Brook Rd, Richmond, VA, 23227. Tel: 804-278-4314. p. 2342
Torabi, Naz, VPres, Canadian Health Libraries Association, 468 Queen St E, Ste LL-02, Toronto, ON, M5A 1T7, CANADA. Tel: 416-646-1600. p. 2778
Torchio, Alex, Archivist, The Evangelical & Reformed Historical Society, 555 W James St, Lancaster, PA, 17603. Tel: 717-290-8734. p. 1950
Torchynowycz, Alexa, Cat Librn, Syst Librn, Davidson College, 209 Ridge Rd, Davidson, NC, 28035-0001. Tel: 704-894-2331. p. 1683
Tordo, Judi, Libr Dir, Brownfield Public Library, 216 Main St, Brownfield, ME, 04010. Tel: 207-935-3003. p. 919
Toren-Jones, Katheryn, Br Mgr, Public Library of Cincinnati & Hamilton County, Norwood, 4325 Montgomery Rd, Cincinnati, OH, 45212. Tel: 513-369-6037. p. 1763
Torgerson Lundin, Jessica, Cat/Acq Tech, Montana State University-Billings Library, 1500 University Dr, Billings, MT, 59101. Tel: 406-657-1664. p. 1288
Torgerson, Rick, Tech Serv, Delta State University, Laflore Circle at Fifth Ave, Cleveland, MS, 38733-2599. Tel: 662-846-4438. p. 1214
Torian, Regina, Sr Librn, New York State Department of Correctional Services, Harriman State Campus, 1220 Washington Ave, Albany, NY, 12226-2050. Tel: 518-485-7109. p. 1482
Torkelson, Kathy, Ch Serv, Willmar Public Library, 410 Fifth St SW, Willmar, MN, 56201-3298. Tel: 320-235-3162, Ext 14. p. 1208
Tormey, Jennifer, Supv Librn, Tech Serv, Des Moines Public Library, 1000 Grand Ave, Des Moines, IA, 50309. Tel: 515-283-4155. p. 745
Tornquist, Kristi, Dean of Libr, South Dakota State University, 1300 N Campus Dr, Box 2115, Brookings, SD, 57007. Tel: 605-688-5106. p. 2074
Toro, Orlando, Acq, Asst Librn, Amaury Veray Music Library, 951 Ave Ponce de Leon, San Juan, PR, 00907-3373. Tel: 787-751-0160, Ext 225. p. 2513
Torok-Oberholtzer, Donna, Assoc Librn, Menil Foundation, 1533 Sul Ross St, Houston, TX, 77006. Tel: 713-535-3102. p. 2197
Torralbas, Grisel, Dir, Hialeah Public Libraries, 190 W 49th St, Hialeah, FL, 33012-3712. Tel: 305-821-2700. p. 408
Torrence, Joshua Campbell, Exec Dir, Florence Griswold Museum, 96 Lyme St, Old Lyme, CT, 06371. Tel: 860-434-5542. p. 332
Torrens, Carol, Adult Serv, Bloomington Public Library, 205 E Olive St, Bloomington, IL, 61701. Tel: 309-828-6091. p. 543
Torres, Ana, Co-Dir, Head, Library Services & Ops, Youngstown State University, One University Plaza, Youngstown, OH, 44555-0001. Tel: 330-941-1717. p. 1836
Torres, Daisy, Div Head, Financial Serv, Harris County Public Library, 5749 S Loop E, Houston, TX, 77033. Tel: 713-274-6600. p. 2192
Torres, Dima, Mr, Librn, KMD Architects Library, 222 Vallejo St, San Francisco, CA, 94111. Tel: 415-398-5191. p. 225
Torres, Elizabeth, Head, Pub Serv, Hawaii Pacific University Libraries, Atherton Library, Cook Academic Ctr, 45-045 Kamehameha Hwy, Kaneohe, HI, 96744. Tel: 808-236-3505. p. 506
Torres, Evelyn, Dir, Puerto Rico Regional Library for the Blind & Physically Handicapped, 705 Hoare Calle, San Juan, PR, 00907. Tel: 787-721-7170, 787-723-2519. p. 2513
Torres, Gabriela, Mgr, County of Los Angeles Public Library, City Terrace Library, 4025 E City Terrace Dr, Los Angeles, CA, 90063-1297. Tel: 323-261-0295. p. 135
Torres, John, Head, Youth & Teen Serv, Poughkeepsie Public Library District, 93 Market St, Poughkeepsie, NY, 12601. Tel: 845-485-3445, Ext 3368. p. 1623
Torres, Juanita, Supvr, Yakima Valley Libraries, Buena Library, 801 Buena Rd, Buena, WA, 98921. Tel: 509-865-2298. p. 2395
Torres, Mark, Interim Dir, Pacifica Foundation, 3729 Cahuenga Blvd W, North Hollywood, CA, 91604. Tel: 818-506-1077, Ext 266. p. 183
Torres, Tracy, Librn II, Youth Serv Coordr, Groton Public Library, 52 Newtown Rd, Groton, CT, 06340. Tel: 860-441-6750. p. 314
Torres-Alvarez, Ivette, Dir, Supreme Court Library of Puerto Rico, Ave Munoz Rivera Parada 8 1/2 Puerta de Tierra, Parque Munoz Rivera, San Juan, PR, 00902. p. 2514
Torres-Aveillez, Magdalena, Ref Librn, Inter-American University of Puerto Rico, San German Campus, Ave Inter-American University, Rd 102, K 30 6, San German, PR, 00683-9801. Tel: 787-264-1912, Ext 7521. p. 2512
Torres-Retana, Raquel, Dean of Libr, Pasadena City College Library, 1570 E Colorado Blvd, Pasadena, CA, 91106. Tel: 626-585-7221. p. 193
Torresdal, Kristin, Dir, Decorah Public Library, 202 Winnebago St, Decorah, IA, 52101. Tel: 563-382-3717. p. 744
Torrey, Charles, Historian, History Museum of Mobile, 111 S Royal St, Mobile, AL, 36602-3101. Tel: 251-208-7569. p. 26
Torrie, Susan, Ch, Glenolden Library, 211 S Llanwellyn Ave, Glenolden, PA, 19036. Tel: 610-583-1010. p. 1937
Torsney, Janet, Libr Dir, Brielle Public Library, 610 South St, Brielle, NJ, 08730. Tel: 732-528-9381. p. 1393
Tortorelli, Amber, Youth Serv Coordr, Easton Area Public Library & District Center, 515 Church St, Easton, PA, 18042-3587. Tel: 610-258-2917. p. 1928
Torvik, Vetle, Assoc Prof, University of Illinois at Urbana-Champaign, Library & Information Science Bldg, 501 E Daniel St, Champaign, IL, 61820-6211. Tel: 217-333-3280. p. 2784
Tosaka, Yuji, Cataloging & Metadata Librn, The College of New Jersey, 2000 Pennington Rd, Ewing, NJ, 08628-1104. Tel: 609-771-2311. p. 1402
Tosh, Christopher, Hospital Libr Serv Coordr, Capital District Library Council, 28 Essex St, Albany, NY, 12206. Tel: 518-438-2500. p. 2770
Tosh, Deidre, Br Mgr, Marshall County Public Library System, Hardin, 4640 Murray Hwy, Hardin, KY, 42048. Tel: 270-527-9969, Ext 324. p. 849
Tosi, Brooke, Dir, Federal Reserve Bank of Minneapolis, 90 Hennepin Ave, Minneapolis, MN, 55401. Tel: 612-204-5000. p. 1183
Tosko, Mike, Br Mgr, Stark County District Library, Madge Youtz Branch, 2921 Mahoning Rd NE, Canton, OH, 44705. Tel: 330-452-2618. p. 1756
Toth, Carolyn, Exec Dir, Sewickley Public Library, 500 Thorn St, Sewickley, PA, 15143. Tel: 412-741-6920. p. 2006
Toth, Dana, Exec Dir, North Central Nevada Historical Society, 175 Museum Ln, Winnemucca, NV, 89445. Tel: 775-623-2912. p. 1352

Toth, Frieda, Teen Librn, Crandall Public Library, 251 Glen St, Glens Falls, NY, 12801-3546. Tel: 518-792-6508. p. 1539

Toth, Gabriela Rae, Pub Programming Librn, Sr Librn, Ad Serv, Peabody Institute Library, 82 Main St, Peabody, MA, 01960-5553. Tel: 951-531-0100, Ext 17. p. 1045

Toth, Gabrielle, Coordr, Instruction & Ref, Chicago State University, 9501 S Martin Luther King Jr Dr, LIB 440, Chicago, IL, 60628-1598. Tel: 773-995-2562. p. 558

Toth, Michelle, Access Serv Tech-Operation, Washtenaw Community College, 4800 E Huron River Dr, Ann Arbor, MI, 48105-4800. Tel: 734-477-8710. p. 1081

Toth, Michelle, Instruction & Ref Librn, State University of New York College at Plattsburgh, Two Draper Ave, Plattsburgh, NY, 12901. Tel: 518-564-5225. p. 1619

Toth, Paulette, Assoc Dir, Research Servs, Kirkland & Ellis LLP, 601 Lexington Ave, New York, NY, 10022. Tel: 212-446-4800. p. 1590

Totman, Jill, Librn, Buncombe County Public Libraries, Weaverville Branch, 41 N Main St, Weaverville, NC, 28787. Tel: 828-250-6482. p. 1672

Toto, Patrick, Children's Mgr, Waukegan Public Library, 128 N County St, Waukegan, IL, 60085. Tel: 847-623-2041. p. 660

Totten, Mark, Mgr, County of Los Angeles Public Library, La Cañada Flintridge Library, 4545 N Oakwood Ave, La Canada Flintridge, CA, 91011-3358. Tel: 818-790-3330. p. 136

Totten, Mark, Pres, Chesapeake & Ohio Historical Society Archives, 312 E Ridgeway St, Clifton Forge, VA, 24422. Tel: 540-862-2210. p. 2313

Totter, Susan, Pub Serv Adminr, Youth Serv, New Haven Free Public Library, 133 Elm St, New Haven, CT, 06510. Tel: 203-946-8139. p. 326

Toub, Austin, Res & Ref Serv, Sr Librn, Los Angeles County Law Library, Mildred L Lillie Bldg, 301 W First St, Los Angeles, CA, 90012-3100. Tel: 213-785-2529. p. 162

Touchet LeBlanc, Angela, Br Supvr, Vermilion Parish Library, Gueydan Branch, 704 Tenth St, Gueydan, LA, 70542-3806. Tel: 337-536-6781. p. 879

Touhey, Laura, Prog Coordr, Leland Township Public Library, 203 E Cedar, Leland, MI, 49654. Tel: 231-256-9152. p. 1126

Toupin, Claude, Chef de Div, Bibliotheques de Montreal, Pointe-aux-Trembles, 14001 rue Notre-Dame Est, Montreal, QC, H1A 1T9, CANADA. Tel: 514-872-2102. p. 2720

Toupin, Claude, Chef de Div, Bibliotheques de Montreal, Riviere-des-Prairies, 9001 Blvd Perras, Montreal, QC, H1E 3J7, CANADA. Tel: 514-872-2102. p. 2720

Toupin-Lefebvre, Camee, Documentation Tech, Cegep de L'Abitibi - Temiscamingue Bibliotheque, 425 Boul du College, Rouyn-Noranda, QC, J9X 5M5, CANADA. Tel: 819-762-0931, Ext 1234. p. 2733

Toups, Danelle, Asst Dir, Tarrant County College, Trinity River Campus Library, 300 Trinity Campus Circle, Fort Worth, TX, 76102. Tel: 817-515-1222. p. 2181

Tour, Debbie, Chief of Lifelong Learning, Orange County Library System, 101 E Central Blvd, Orlando, FL, 32801. Tel: 407-835-7323. p. 431

Tourigny, Manon, Dir, Artexte Information Centre, Two Saint-Catherine St Est, Rm 301, Montreal, QC, H2X 1K4, CANADA. Tel: 514-874-0049. p. 2716

Tourville, Elaine, Libr Dir, Holy Apostles Catholic Church Library, 4925 N Carefree Circle, Colorado Springs, CO, 80917. Tel: 719-597-7571. p. 271

Tousey, Janis, Asst Dir, Ref (Info Servs), North Shore Public Library, 250 Rte 25A, Shoreham, NY, 11786-9677. Tel: 631-929-4488. p. 1641

Toussaint, Arlene, Head, Circ, Mount Laurel Library, 100 Walt Whitman Ave, Mount Laurel, NJ, 08054. Tel: 856-234-7319. p. 1422

Touzin, Francis, Dir, Bibliotheque Municipale de Notre-Dame-du-Lac, 2448 rue Commerciale Sud, Temiscouata-sur-Le-Lac, QC, G0L 1X0, CANADA. Tel: 418-899-2528, Ext 301. p. 2737

Tovar, Bea, Cataloger, Oblate School of Theology, 285 Oblate Dr, San Antonio, TX, 78216. Tel: 210-341-1366, Ext 311. p. 2237

Tovar, Cecilia, Asst City Librn, Santa Monica Public Library, Fairview, 2101 Ocean Park Blvd, Santa Monica, CA, 90405-5013. Tel: 310-458-8681. p. 244

Tovar, Cecilia, Asst City Librn, Santa Monica Public Library, Montana Avenue, 1704 Montana Ave, Santa Monica, CA, 90403. Tel: 310-458-8682. p. 244

Tovar, Cecilia, Asst City Librn, Santa Monica Public Library, Pico Branch Library, 2201 Pico Blvd, Santa Monica, CA, 90404. Tel: 310-458-8684. p. 244

Tovar, Cecilia, Principal Librn, Pub & Br Serv, Santa Monica Public Library, 601 Santa Monica Blvd, Santa Monica, CA, 90401. Tel: 310-458-8600. p. 244

Tow, Hildy, Educ Curator, Woodmere Art Museum Library, 9201 Germantown Ave, Philadelphia, PA, 19118. Tel: 215-247-0948. p. 1989

Towanda, Mathurin, Circ, ILL, Per, SUNY Westchester Community College, 75 Grasslands Rd, Valhalla, NY, 10595. Tel: 914-606-8086. p. 1656

Towell, Fay, Dir, Prisma Health System, 601 Grove Rd, Greenville, SC, 29605. Tel: 864-455-3099. p. 2062

Tower, Karen, Librn, Huntington Woods Public Library, 26415 Scotia Rd, Huntington Woods, MI, 48070. Tel: 248-543-9720. p. 1118

Tower, Susan, Co-Dir, West Warren Library, 2370 Main St, West Warren, MA, 01092. Tel: 413-436-9892. p. 1066

Towers, Sandra, Asst Dir, Williamsburg Regional Library, 7770 Croaker Rd, Williamsburg, VA, 23188-7064. Tel: 757-741-3385. p. 2353

Towers, Sandy, Dir, Williamsburg Regional Library, 7770 Croaker Rd, Williamsburg, VA, 23188-7064. Tel: 757-741-3300. p. 2353

Towle, Jean, Exec Dir, Pottsville Free Public Library, 215 W Market St, Pottsville, PA, 17901. Tel: 570-622-8105, 570-622-8880. p. 1999

Towles, Latasha, Practice Technologist, University at Buffalo Libraries-State University of New York, Charles B Sears Law Library, John Lord O'Brian Hall, 211 Mary Talbert Way, Buffalo, NY, 14260-1110. Tel: 716-645-2050. p. 1511

Towlson, Diane, Communications Coordr, Liverpool Public Library, 310 Tulip St, Liverpool, NY, 13088-4997. Tel: 315-457-0310. p. 1564

Town, Maria, Br Mgr, Pend Oreille County Library District, Calispel Valley Library, 107 First Ave, Cusick, WA, 99119. p. 2372

Town, Marie, Libr Divisional Mgr, Oceanside Public Library, 330 N Coast Hwy, Oceanside, CA, 92054. Tel: 760-435-5597. p. 187

Towne, Daniel, Librn, Fulton-Montgomery Community College, 2805 State Hwy 67, Johnstown, NY, 12095-3790. Tel: 518-736-3622, Ext 8058. p. 1558

Towne, Linda, Librn, United States Army Corps of Engineers, 803 Front St, Norfolk, VA, 23510-1096. Tel: 757-201-7219. p. 2336

Townes, Adam, Dr, Asst Dir, Pub Serv, Henry County Public Library System, 1001 Florence McGarity Blvd, McDonough, GA, 30252. Tel: 678-432-5353. p. 490

Towns, Bobby, Libr Serv Mgr, Mayer Brown LLP, 71 S Wacker Dr, Chicago, IL, 60606. Tel: 312-782-0600. p. 564

Towns-Campbell, Julia, Librn, Columbia Environmental Research Center Library, US Geological Survey, 4200 New Haven Rd, Columbia, MO, 65201-8709. Tel: 573-876-1853. p. 1243

Townsend, Betty, Librn, G V Montgomery VA Medical Center Library, 1500 E Woodrow Wilson Dr, Jackson, MS, 39216. Tel: 601-364-1273. p. 1223

Townsend, Carol, Br Mgr, Alpine Public Library, Marathon Public, 106 N Third St E, Marathon, TX, 79842. Tel: 432-386-4136. p. 2133

Townsend, Darlene, Head, Cat, University of North Alabama, One Harrison Plaza, Box 5028, Florence, AL, 35632-0001. Tel: 256-765-4473. p. 17

Townsend, David, Communications Coordr, Coeur d'Alene Public Library, 702 E Front Ave, Coeur d'Alene, ID, 83814-2373. Tel: 208-769-2315. p. 519

Townsend, David, Mgr, Info Tech, Pickaway County District Public Library, 1160 N Court St, Circleville, OH, 43113-1725. Tel: 740-477-1644, Ext 232. p. 1765

Townsend, Gregory, Br Mgr, US Courts Library - Tenth Circuit Court of Appeals, Byron Rogers Courthouse, 1929 Stout St, Rm 430, Denver, CO, 80294. Tel: 303-844-3591. p. 277

Townsend, Gregory L, Librn, US Courts Library - Tenth Circuit Court of Appeals, 333 Lomas Blvd NW, Ste 230, Albuquerque, NM, 87102. Tel: 505-348-2135. p. 1462

Townsend, Jean, Bkmobile/Outreach Serv, Youth Serv, Marion County Library System, 101 East Court St, Marion, SC, 29571. Tel: 843-423-8300. p. 2065

Townsend, Karen, Law Librn II, Connecticut Judicial Branch Law Libraries, Middletown Law Library, Middletown Courthouse, One Court St, Middletown, CT, 06457. Tel: 860-343-6560. p. 316

Townsend, Karen, Librn, Saint Marys Correctional Center Library, 2880 N Pleasants Hwy, Saint Marys, WV, 26170. Tel: 304-684-5500. p. 2414

Townsend, Kat, Adult Serv, Weston County Library System, 23 W Main St, Newcastle, WY, 82701. Tel: 307-746-2206. p. 2497

Townsend, Kay, Dir, Parsons Public Library, 105 Kentucky Ave S, Parsons, TN, 38363. Tel: 731-847-6988. p. 2124

Townsend, Montoya, Br Mgr, Nashville Public Library, Watkins Park Branch, 612 17th Ave N, Nashville, TN, 37203. Tel: 615-862-5872. p. 2120

Townsend, Ronald, Acq, ILL Librn, Lutheran Theological Seminary, United Lutheran Seminary, 7301 Germantown Ave, Philadelphia, PA, 19119-1794. Tel: 215-248-6329. p. 1982

Townsend, Shannon, Library Contact, Pueblo of San Felipe Community Library, 18 Cougar Rd, San Felipe Pueblo, NM, 87001. Tel: 505-771-9970. p. 1474

Townsend, Wilma, Curator, Ontario County Historical Society Library, 55 N Main St, Canandaigua, NY, 14424. Tel: 585-394-4975. p. 1512

Townsend-Diggs, Melanie, Area Mgr, Prince George's County Memorial, Accokeek Branch, 15773 Livingston Rd, Accokeek, MD, 20607-2249. Tel: 301-292-2880. p. 970

Townsend-Diggs, Melanie, Area Mgr, Prince George's County Memorial, Baden Branch, 13603 Baden-Westwood Rd, Brandywine, MD, 20613-8167. Tel: 301-888-1152. p. 970

Townsend-Diggs, Melanie, Area Mgr, Prince George's County Memorial, Oxon Hill Branch, 6200 Oxon Hill Rd, Oxon Hill, MD, 20745-3091. Tel: 301-839-2400. p. 971

Townsend-Diggs, Melanie, Area Mgr, Prince George's County Memorial, Surratts-Clinton Branch, 9400 Piscataway Rd, Clinton, MD, 20735-3632. Tel: 301-868-9200. p. 971

Townson, Abbie, YA Serv, York County Library, 138 E Black St, Rock Hill, SC, 29730. Tel: 803-981-5830. p. 2068

Townson, Samantha, Br Mgr, Mississippi County Library System, Osceola Public, 320 West Hale Ave, Osceola, AR, 72370-2530. Tel: 870-563-2721. p. 91

Townson, Sharon, Dir, Cullman County Public Library System, 200 Clark St NE, Cullman, AL, 35055. Tel: 256-734-1068. p. 13

Toy, Michael, Liaison & Instruction Librn, Salt Lake Community College Libraries, Jordan Campus, Health & Science Bldg, JHS 235, 3500 W Wights Fort Rd, West Jordan, UT, 84088. Tel: 801-957-6208. p. 2274
Toy, Renee, Librn, Texas School for the Blind, 1100 W 45th St, Austin, TX, 78756. Tel: 512-454-8631. p. 2141
Toyama, Ralph, Syst Librn, Leeward Community College Library, 96-045 Ala Ike St, Pearl City, HI, 96782. Tel: 808-455-0682. p. 514
Toyne, Tonica, Coordr, Acq, Bradley University, 1501 W Bradley Ave, Peoria, IL, 61625. Tel: 309-677-2850. p. 634
Toze, Sandra, Dr, Asst Prof, Dir, Dalhousie University, Kenneth C Rowe Management Bldg, Ste 4010, 6100 University Ave, Halifax, NS, B3H 4R2, CANADA. Tel: 902-494-2488. p. 2795
Tozer, Jennifer, Br Mgr, Pueblo City-County Library District, Frank I Lamb Branch, 2525 S Pueblo Blvd, Pueblo, CO, 81005. p. 293
Tozer, Julie, Br Mgr, Camden County Library System, Nilsa I Cruz-Perez Downtown Branch-Rutgers, Rutgers Campus, 301 N 5th St, Camden, NJ, 08102. Tel: 856-225-6807. p. 1450
Tozer, Rosemary, Sr Librn, Richard T Liddicoat Gemological Library & Information Center, 5345 Armada Dr, Carlsbad, CA, 92008. Tel: 760-603-4046, 760-603-4068. p. 128
Tozier, Sarah, Ch Serv, Preble County District Library, 450 S Barron St, Eaton, OH, 45320-2402. Tel: 937-456-4331. p. 1784
Traas, Wendy, Head of Libr, University of British Columbia Library, Education, 2125 Main Mall, Vancouver, BC, V6T 1Z4, CANADA. Tel: 604-822-5381. p. 2580
Trace, Howard, Dir, Libr & Mus Serv, American Legion National Headquarters Library, 700 N Pennsylvania St, 4th Flr, Indianapolis, IN, 46204. Tel: 317-630-1366. p. 690
Tracey, Jillian, Adult Serv Coordr, River Edge Free Public Library, 685 Elm Ave, River Edge, NJ, 07661. Tel: 201-261-1663. p. 1439
Tracey, Scott, Asst Dir, West Lafayette Public Library, 208 W Columbia St, West Lafayette, IN, 47906. Tel: 765-743-2261. p. 726
Tracey, Stephen, Mgr, Ref Serv, Bentley University, 175 Forest St, Waltham, MA, 02452-4705. Tel: 781-891-2168. p. 1061
Trachim, Caitlin, Access Serv Librn, Flagler College, 44 Sevilla St, Saint Augustine, FL, 32084-4302. Tel: 904-819-6206. p. 439
Tracht, Frances, Head, Tech Serv, Libr Mgr, Inglewood Public Library, 101 W Manchester Blvd, Inglewood, CA, 90301-1771. Tel: 310-412-5397. p. 152
Tracy, Carol, Asst Dir, Ref Serv, Mokena Community Public Library District, 11327 W 195th St, Mokena, IL, 60448. Tel: 708-479-9663. p. 618
Tracy, Elizabeth, Dir, Whistler Public Library, 4329 Main St, Whistler, BC, V8E 1B2, CANADA. Tel: 604-935-8433. p. 2584
Tracy, Hannah, Asst Dir, Brownell Library, Six Lincoln St, Essex Junction, VT, 05452-3154. Tel: 802-878-6955. p. 2284
Tracy, Jami Frazier, Curator, Wichita-Sedgwick County Historical Museum Library, 204 S Main St, Wichita, KS, 67202. Tel: 316-265-9314. p. 844
Tracy, Morgan, Dir, College Libraries, Seminole State College of Florida, 100 Weldon Blvd, Sanford, FL, 32773-6199. Tel: 407-708-2136. p. 442
Traczek, Rozanne, Dir, Fairchild Public Library, 208 Huron St, Fairchild, WI, 54741. Tel: 715-334-4007. p. 2434
Traditi, Lisa, Dep Dir, University of Colorado Denver/ Anschutz Medical Campus, Anschutz Medical Campus, 12950 E Montview Blvd, Aurora, CO, 80045. Tel: 303-724-2152. p. 265
Trafford, Mabel, Librn, Tripler Army Medical Center, One Jarrett White Rd, Honolulu, HI, 96859-5000. Tel: 808-433-4534. p. 512
Trager, Sonya, Dir, Talbot Belmond Public Library, 440 E Main St, Belmond, IA, 50421-1224. Tel: 641-444-4160. p. 734
Trahan, Angel, Br Mgr, Calcasieu Parish Public Library System, Hayes Branch, 7709 Perier St, Hayes, LA, 70646. Tel: 337-721-7098. p. 893
Trahan, Eric, Dir, Mohawk Valley Library System, 858 Duanesburg Rd, Schenectady, NY, 12306. Tel: 518-355-2010. p. 1638
Trahan, Sue, Adult Serv Mgr, YA Mgr, Vermilion Parish Library, 405 E Saint Victor St, Abbeville, LA, 70510-5101. Tel: 337-893-2655. p. 879
Trail, Jennifer, Libr Dir, Glenns Ferry Public Library, 298 S Lincoln St, Glenns Ferry, ID, 83623. Tel: 208-366-2045. p. 521
Trail, Susan, Curator, National Park Service, 302 E Main St, Sharpsburg, MD, 21782. Tel: 301-432-5124, 301-432-8767. p. 977
Trainor, Chris, Head, Archives & Spec Coll, Carleton University Library, 1125 Colonel By Dr, Ottawa, ON, K1S 5B6, CANADA. Tel: 613-520-2600, Ext 6030. p. 2666
Trainor, Kaitlin, Proc Archivist, Moravian Archives, 41 W Locust St, Bethlehem, PA, 18018-2757. Tel: 610-866-3255. p. 1912
Trainor, Kevin, Sr Lecturer, University of Illinois at Urbana-Champaign, Library & Information Science Bldg, 501 E Daniel St, Champaign, IL, 61820-6211. Tel: 217-333-3280. p. 2784
Trame, Anieta, Librn, Sarah Bush Lincoln Health Center, 1000 Health Center Dr, Mattoon, IL, 61938. Tel: 217-258-2262. p. 615
Trammel, Kena, Libr Mgr, Mid-Arkansas Regional Library, Dallas County Library, 501 E Fourth St, Fordyce, AR, 71742. Tel: 870-352-3592. p. 103
Tran, Alice Y, Archivist, Head, Coll Mgt, Hawaii State Archives, Iolani Palace Grounds, 364 S King St, Honolulu, HI, 96813. Tel: 808-586-0329. p. 506
Tran, Alyson, Adult Programming Mgr, Hershey Public Library, 701 Cocoa Ave, Hershey, PA, 17033. Tel: 717-533-6555. p. 1943
Tran, Brandon, Assistant Student Librn, Bibliotheque du College Universitaire Dominicain, 96 Empress Ave, Ottawa, ON, K1R 7G3, CANADA. Tel: 613-233-5696, Ext 216. p. 2665
Tran, Candice, Mgr, San Jose Public Library, Berryessa, 3355 Noble Ave, San Jose, CA, 95132-3198. Tel: 408-808-3050. p. 231
Tran, Clara Y, Sci Librn, Stony Brook University, Chemistry, Chemistry Bldg, C-299, Stony Brook, NY, 11794-3425. Tel: 631-632-7145. p. 1647
Tran, Janet, Dir, National Archives & Records Administration, 40 Presidential Dr, Simi Valley, CA, 93065. Tel: 805-577-4000. p. 246
Tran, Samantha, Academic Success Librarian, Parker University Library, 2540 Walnut Hill Lane, Dallas, TX, 75220. Tel: 214-902-2408. p. 2167
Tran, Tien, Libr Dir, Exeter Public Library, 773 Ten Rod Rd, Exeter, RI, 02822. Tel: 401-294-4109. p. 2032
Tranfaglia, Twyla, Legal Info Librn, Wright & Greenhill PC, 4700 Mueller Blvd, Ste 200, Austin, TX, 78723. Tel: 512-866-6681. p. 2144
Tranquada, Kate, Ref Librn, Lincoln Public Library, Three Bedford Rd, Lincoln, MA, 01773. Tel: 781-259-8465. p. 1028
Transue, Beth, Info Literacy Librn, Messiah University, One University Ave, Ste 3002, Mechanicsburg, PA, 17055. Tel: 717-691-6006, Ext 3810. p. 1960
Trapp Davis, Naomi, Librn, Southwestern College Library, 900 Otay Lakes Rd, Bldg 64, Chula Vista, CA, 91910-7299. p. 130
Trapp, Rachel, Dir, Northwest-Shoals Community College, 800 George Wallace Blvd, Muscle Shoals, AL, 35661-3206. Tel: 256-331-5283. p. 31
Trapp, Rachel, Chair, Northwest-Shoals Community College, 2080 College Rd, Phil Campbell, AL, 35581. Tel: 256-331-6271. p. 33
Trappe, Susan, Asst Dir, Murphy Helwig Library, 111 N Page, Monona, IA, 52159. Tel: 563-539-2356. p. 770
Trask, Greg, Br Mgr, Akron-Summit County Public Library, Northwest Akron Branch, 1720 Shatto Ave, Akron, OH, 44313. Tel: 330-836-1081. p. 1744
Trask, Jay, Head, Archives & Spec Coll, University of Northern Colorado Libraries, 1400 22nd Ave, Greeley, CO, 80631. Tel: 970-351-2322. p. 285
Trask, Richard, Archivist, Peabody Institute Library, 15 Sylvan St, Danvers, MA, 01923. Tel: 978-774-0554. p. 1013
Traub, Adam, Assoc Libr Dir, Monroe County Library System, 115 South Ave, Rochester, NY, 14604. Tel: 585-428-8180. p. 1629
Traub, Adam, Libr Dir, Webster Public Library, Webster Plaza, 980 Ridge Rd, Webster, NY, 14580. Tel: 585-872-7075. p. 1661
Trause, John J, Libr Dir, Oradell Free Public Library, 375 Kinderkamack Rd, Oradell, NJ, 07649-2122. Tel: 201-262-2613. p. 1431
Trauth, Rich, Mgr, Info Tech, Vernon Area Public Library District, 300 Olde Half Day Rd, Lincolnshire, IL, 60069. Tel: 847-634-3650. p. 609
Trautman, Phil, Libr Dir, Clifton Springs Library, Four Railroad Ave, Clifton Springs, NY, 14432. Tel: 315-462-7371. p. 1519
Trautweiler, Courtney, Libr Dir, Cottey College, 1000 W Austin, Nevada, MO, 64772-2763. Tel: 417-667-8181, Ext 2153. p. 1264
Traveny, Carol, Dir, Bryn Athyn College, 2925 College Drive, Bryn Athyn, PA, 19009. Tel: 267-502-2531. p. 1916
Traver, Lorry, Librn, Lapeer District Library, Metamora Branch, 4018 Oak St, Metamora, MI, 48455. Tel: 810-678-2991. p. 1126
Travers, Kimberley, Libr Asst, Memphis Theological Seminary Library, 168 E Parkway S, Memphis, TN, 38104. Tel: 901-334-5858. p. 2114
Travers, Shevonne, Prog Coordr, Joslin Memorial Library, 4391 Main St, Waitsfield, VT, 05673-6155. Tel: 802-496-4205. p. 2297
Traverse, Stephanie, Circ, Vermont State University - Castleton, 178 Alumni Dr, Castleton, VT, 05735. Tel: 802-468-1256. p. 2281
Travi, Lorie, Br Mgr, Hamilton Public Library, Turner Park, 352 Rymal Rd E, Hamilton, ON, L9B 1C2, CANADA. Tel: 905-546-3200, Ext 4224. p. 2646
Travis, Amanda, Dir, Northern Onondaga Public Library, 8686 Knowledge Lane, Cicero, NY, 13039. Tel: 315-699-2032. p. 1518
Travis, Joella, Youth Serv Librn, Rantoul Public Library, 106 W Flessner, Rantoul, IL, 61866. Tel: 217-893-3955. p. 638
Travis, Joella, Youth Serv Librn, Brookline Public Library, 16 Main St, Brookline, NH, 03033. Tel: 603-673-3330. p. 1356
Travis, Linda, Chef de Section, Bibliotheque Municipale Eva-Senecal, 450 Marquette St, Sherbrooke, QC, J1H 1M4, CANADA. Tel: 819-821-5596. p. 2736
Travis, Lindsey, Asst Dir, Pub Relations, Sweetwater County Library System, 300 N First East, Green River, WY, 82935. Tel: 307-352-6669. p. 2495
Travis, Lindsey, Libr Mgr, Sweetwater County Library System, Rock Springs Library, 400 C St, Rock Springs, WY, 82901. Tel: 307-352-6667. p. 2495
Travis, Pam, Dir, West Salem Public Library, 112 W South St, West Salem, IL, 62476-1206. Tel: 618-456-8970. p. 660
Travis, Phyllis, Libr Asst, New Virginia Public Library, 504 Book Alley, New Virginia, IA, 50210. Tel: 641-449-3614. p. 773
Travis, Tina, Br Supvr, Warwick Public Library, Norwood, 328 Pawtuxet Ave, Warwick, RI, 02888. Tel: 401-941-7545. p. 2043
Trawick, Amanda, Librn, Huntsville-Madison County Public Library, Subregional Library for the Blind & Physically Handicapped, 915 Monroe St, Huntsville, AL, 35801-5007. Tel: 256-532-5980. p. 22
Trawick, Theresa, Libr Dir, Tupper Lightfoot Memorial Library, 164 S Main St, Brundidge, AL, 36010. Tel: 334-735-2145. p. 10

Traxel, Sheila, Coordr, Town of Lewis Library, 5213 Osceola Rd, West Leyden, NY, 13489. Tel: 315-225-0450. p. 1662
Tray, Adaena, Dir, Green Tree Public Library, Ten W Manilla Ave, 1st Flr, Pittsburgh, PA, 15220-3310. Tel: 412-921-9292. p. 1994
Traylor, Andrea, Librn, Pike-Amite-Walthall Library System, Progress, 5071 Mt Herman Rd, McComb, MS, 39648-9767. Tel: 601-542-5501. p. 1226
Traylor, Garrett, Cat & Ref Librn, Illinois College, 1101 W College Ave, Jacksonville, IL, 62650-2299. Tel: 217-245-3020. p. 602
Treadway, Sandra G, State Librn, The Library of Virginia, 800 E Broad St, Richmond, VA, 23219-8000. Tel: 804-692-3500. p. 2341
Treadwell, Maria, Instr, University of South Florida, 4202 Fowler Ave, CIS 1040, Tampa, FL, 33620-7800. Tel: 813-974-3520. p. 2783
Treaster, Beth, Dir, Centerville-Center Township Public Library, 126 E Main St, Centerville, IN, 47330-1206. Tel: 765-855-5223. p. 674
Treat, Ben, Libr Dir, Bangor Public Library, 145 Harlow St, Bangor, ME, 04401-1802. Tel: 207-947-8336. p. 915
Treber, Nick, Dir, Bourbon Public Library, 307 N Main St, Bourbon, IN, 46504. Tel: 574-342-5655. p. 672
Trebisky, Ingrid, Br Mgr, Pima County Public Library, Flowing Wells Branch, 1730 W Wetmore Rd, Tucson, AZ, 85705. Tel: 520-594-5225. p. 82
Trebon Boyd, Amanda, Membership Coord, Iowa League of Cities Library, 500 SW Seventh St, Ste 101, Des Moines, IA, 50309-4111. Tel: 515-244-7282. p. 746
Trede, Gail, Libr Dir, Bradford Public Library, 21 S Main St, Bradford, VT, 05033. Tel: 802-222-4536. p. 2280
Tredwell, Susannah, Mgr, Libr Serv, DLA Piper (Canada) LLP, 666 Burrard St, Ste 2800, Vancouver, BC, V6C 2Z7, CANADA. Tel: 604-643-6432. p. 2578
Treece, Staci, Tech Serv, Youth Serv Librn, Swanton Local School District Public Library, 305 Chestnut St, Swanton, OH, 43558. Tel: 419-826-2760. p. 1822
Treese, Kevin, Libr Dir, Oklahoma Library for the Blind & Physically Handicapped, 300 NE 18th St, Oklahoma City, OK, 73105. Tel: 405-521-3514. p. 1859
Treesh, Nicole, Dir, Ivy Tech Community College-Northeast, 3800 N Anthony Blvd, Fort Wayne, IN, 46805-1430. Tel: 260-480-4172. p. 684
Treesh, Zane, Librn, Ref Spec, Anchorage Museum, 625 C St, Anchorage, AK, 99501. Tel: 907-929-9235. p. 42
Treesh, Zane, Dir, Wasilla Public Library, 500 N Crusey St, Wasilla, AK, 99654. Tel: 907-864-9170. p. 52
Trehaeven, Robin, Tech Serv, Edwin A Bemis Public Library, 6014 S Datura St, Littleton, CO, 80120-2636. Tel: 303-795-3961. p. 290
Trehub, Aaron, Head, Syst, Auburn University, Ralph Brown Draughon Library, 231 Mell St, Auburn, AL, 36849. Tel: 334-844-1716. p. 5
Treischmann, Lagan, Circ & ILL, Vineyard Haven Public Library, 200 Main St, Vineyard Haven, MA, 02568. Tel: 508-696-4211, Ext 112. p. 1061
Trejo, Armando, Archivist, ILL Librn, Elgin Community College, 1700 Spartan Dr, Elgin, IL, 60123. Tel: 847-214-7337. p. 584
Trejo, Jeanna, Asst to the Dir, Dr Eugene Clark Library, 217 S Main St, Lockhart, TX, 78644-2742. Tel: 512-398-3223. p. 2212
Trela, Dori, Library Contact, Schenectady County Public Library, Niskayuna Branch, 2400 Nott St E, Niskayuna, NY, 12309. Tel: 518-386-2249. p. 1638
Trembach, Vera, Br Librn, Wapiti Regional Library, Wakaw Public Library, 121 Main St, Wakaw, SK, S0K 4P0, CANADA. Tel: 306-233-5552. p. 2746
Tremblay, Andree, Chef de Div, Bibliotheques de Montreal, Du Boise, 2727 Blvd Thimens, Saint-Laurent, QC, H4R 1T4, CANADA. Tel: 514-855-6130, Ext 4722. p. 2718
Tremblay, Andree, Chef de Div, Bibliotheques de Montreal, Vieux-Saint-Laurent, 1380 rue de l'Eglise, Saint-Laurent, QC, H4L 2H2, CANADA. Tel: 514-855-6130, Ext 4722. p. 2721
Tremblay, Carrie, Ref Librn, Dover Public Library, 73 Locust St, Dover, NH, 03820-3785. Tel: 603-516-6050. p. 1361
Tremblay, Cindy, Sr Libr Mgr, University of New Hampshire at Manchester Library, 88 Commercial St, Manchester, NH, 03101. Tel: 603-641-4173. p. 1373
Tremblay, Claire, Cat, Conservatoire de Musique de Quebec Bibliotheque, 270 rue Jacques-Parizeau, Quebec, QC, G1R 5G1, CANADA. Tel: 418-643-2190, Ext 232. p. 2730
Tremblay, Claudia, Head Librn, Bibliotheque Jean-Marc-Belzile, 378, rue Principale, Lachute, QC, J8H 1Y2, CANADA. Tel: 450-562-3781, Ext 255. p. 2715
Tremblay, David, Chief Exec Officer, Chief Librn, Huntsville Public Library, Seven Minerva St E, Huntsville, ON, P1H 1W4, CANADA. Tel: 705-789-5232. p. 2648
Tremblay, Gina, Chef de Div, Bibliotheques de Montreal, Frontenac, 2550 rue Ontario Est, Montreal, QC, H2K 1W7, CANADA. Tel: 514-872-0831. p. 2718
Tremblay, Gina, Chef de Div, Bibliotheques de Montreal, Pere-Ambroise, 2093 rue de la Visitation, Montreal, QC, H2L 3C9, CANADA. Tel: 514-872-0831. p. 2720
Tremblay, Joanie, Actg Head Librn, College Militaire Royal de Saint-Jean Library, Lahie Bldg, Rm 210, 15 rue Jaques-Cartier Nord, Saint-Jean-Sur-Richelieu, QC, J3B 8R8, CANADA. Tel: 450-358-6777, Ext 5866. p. 2735
Tremblay, Paul, Chief Med Librn, New York College of Podiatric Medicine, 53 E 124th St, New York, NY, 10035. Tel: 212-410-8020, 212-410-8142. p. 1593
Tremblay, Paul, Pres, Brooklyn-Queens-Staten Island-Manhattan-Bronx Health Sciences Librarians, 150 55th St, Brooklyn, NY, 11220. Tel: 718-630-7200. p. 2770
Tremblay, Regina, Libr Asst, Naples Public Library, 940 Roosevelt Trail, Naples, ME, 04055. Tel: 207-693-6841. p. 932
Tremblay, Rene, Dir, Bibliotheque Albert Rousseau, 711 ave Albert Rousseau, Levis, QC, G6J 1Z7, CANADA. Tel: 418-839-2002. p. 2715
Tremblay, Sarah, Ref & Instruction Librn, North Shore Community College Library, One Ferncroft Rd, Danvers Campus Library, Danvers, MA, 01923-4093. Tel: 978-739-5540. p. 1013
Trembley, Cyndi, Mgr, Res Serv, Harris, Beach PLLC, 99 Garnsey Rd, Pittsford, NY, 14534. Tel: 585-419-8800. p. 1618
Trenam, Jami, Assoc Dir, Coll Develop, Great River Regional Library, 1300 W St Germain St, Saint Cloud, MN, 56301. Tel: 320-650-2531. p. 1196
Trendler, Amy E, Archit Librn, Ball State University Libraries, Architecture, Architecture Bldg, Rm 116, Muncie, IN, 47306. Tel: 765-285-5858. p. 708
Trendowski, Edward, Dir, Diocesan of Providence Office of Faith Formation, 34 Fenner St, Providence, RI, 02903. Tel: 401-278-4571. p. 2038
Trenholm, Jerry, Dir, Res, McDermott, Will & Emery Law Library, 444 West Lake St, Chicago, IL, 60606. Tel: 312-984-3289. p. 564
Trent, Emma, Res Assoc, Sam Rayburn Library & Museum, 800 W Sam Rayburn Dr, Bonham, TX, 75418. Tel: 903-583-2455. p. 2148
Trent, Renolds, Dir, United States Army, MWR Library, Bldg 93, Wold Ave, Fort Benning, GA, 31905. Tel: 706-545-8932. p. 479
Tresback, Jo Ann, Circ Librn, New Salem Public Library, 23 S Main St, New Salem, MA, 01355. Tel: 978-544-6334. p. 1038
Tresnan, Joseph, Asst Dir, Libr Serv, Rosemont College Library, 1400 Montgomery Ave, Rosemont, PA, 19010-1631. Tel: 610-527-0200, Ext 2206. p. 2002
Tresp, Teresa, Assoc Dir, Br Serv, Cobb County Public Library System, 266 Roswell St, Marietta, GA, 30060-2004. Tel: 770-528-2320. p. 489
Tressler, Donna, Ref & Instruction Librn, Ivy Tech Community College, 50 W Fall Creek Pkwy N Dr, Indianapolis, IN, 46208. Tel: 317-921-4782. p. 697
Tretiak, Alex, Managing Librn, Brooklyn Public Library, Canarsie, 1580 Rockaway Pkwy, Brooklyn, NY, 11236. Tel: 718-257-6547. p. 1502
Tretiak, Alexander, Managing Librn, Brooklyn Public Library, Brooklyn Heights, 109 Remsen St, Brooklyn, NY, 11201. Tel: 718-623-7100. p. 1502
Tretter, Laura, Libr Mgr, Montana Historical Society, 225 N Roberts St, Helena, MT, 59601-4514. Tel: 406-444-7415. p. 1296
Treves, Richelle, Br Mgr, Louisville Free Public Library, Shawnee, 3912 W Broadway, Louisville, KY, 40211. Tel: 502-574-1722. p. 866
Trevino, Brenda, Head Librn, Brownsville Public Library System, 2600 Central Blvd, Brownsville, TX, 78520-8824. Tel: 956-548-1055, Ext 2121. p. 2150
Trevino, Lisa, Head, Circ, Calumet City Public Library, 660 Manistee Ave, Calumet City, IL, 60409. Tel: 708-862-6220, Ext 240. p. 548
Trevorrow, Alyssa, Asst Librn, Montfort Public Library, 102 E Park St, Montfort, WI, 53569. Tel: 608-943-6265. p. 2462
Trexler, JaNelle, Dir, J R Huffman Public Library, 375 Sabine St, Hemphill, TX, 75948. Tel: 409-787-4829. p. 2188
Trexler, Lisa, Dir, Libr Serv, Cleveland Community College, 137 S Post Rd, Shelby, NC, 28152. Tel: 704-669-4042. p. 1716
Tri, Ben, Librn, Saint Paul College Library, 235 Marshall Ave, Saint Paul, MN, 55102. Tel: 651-846-1489. p. 1202
Trice, Stephanie, Circ, ILL, San Jacinto College North, 5800 Uvalde Rd, Houston, TX, 77049-4599. Tel: 281-998-6150, Ext 7352. p. 2198
Triebel, Sharon, Librn, Edna Public Library, 105 N Delaware, Edna, KS, 67342. Tel: 620-922-3470. p. 805
Trierweiler, Ann, Dir, Elsie Public Library, 145 W Main St, Elsie, MI, 48831. Tel: 989-862-4633. p. 1103
Trigg, Elizabeth, Libr Dir, Osawatomie Public Library, 527 Brown Ave, Osawatomie, KS, 66064. Tel: 913-755-2136. p. 828
Trigg, Morgan, Ch, Marion County Public Library, 201 E Main St, Lebanon, KY, 40033-1133. Tel: 270-692-4698. p. 861
Triggs, Nick, Pub Serv Spec, University of Puget Sound, 1604 N Warner St, Upper Loading Dock, Tacoma, WA, 98416. Tel: 253-879-3618. p. 2387
Triller-Doran, Malinda, Spec Coll Librn, Dickinson College, 28 N College St, Carlisle, PA, 17013-2311. Tel: 717-245-1397. p. 1919
Trimble, Ashtin, Dir, Libr Serv, Black Hawk College, 26230 Black Hawk Rd, Galva, IL, 61434. Tel: 309-796-5143. p. 591
Trimble, Ashtin, Dir, Libr Serv, Black Hawk College, 6600 34th Ave, Moline, IL, 61265. Tel: 309-796-5700. p. 618
Trimble, Carolyn, Librn, Wewoka Public Library, 118 W Fifth St, Wewoka, OK, 74884. Tel: 405-257-3225. p. 1869
Trimble, Donna, Librn, Bowman & Brooke, 150 S Fifth St, Ste 3000, Minneapolis, MN, 55402. Tel: 612-339-8682. p. 1183

Trimble, Dorothy, Asst Librn, Blanco County South Library District, 1118 Main St, Blanco, TX, 78606. Tel: 830-833-4280. p. 2148
Trimble, Frances, Br Mgr, Carnegie Library of McKeesport, White Oak Branch, McAllister Lodge, 169 Victoria Dr, White Oak, PA, 15131. Tel: 412-678-2002. p. 1959
Trimble, Galen, Evening Circ, Libr Tech, Pennsylvania Western University - Clarion, 840 Wood St, Clarion, PA, 16214. Tel: 814-393-2176. p. 1922
Trimble, Julie, Assoc Dir, University of Texas Medical Branch, 914 Market St, Galveston, TX, 77555. Tel: 409-772-3642. p. 2183
Trimble, Kathryn, Libr Dir, Logan County Public Library, 317 Main St, Stapleton, NE, 69163. Tel: 308-636-2343. p. 1337
Trimble, Leanne, Actg Head, Data Librn, University of Toronto Libraries, Map & Data Library, John P Robarts Library, 130 St George St, 5th Flr, Toronto, ON, M5S 1A5, CANADA. Tel: 416-978-5365. p. 2699
Trimboli, Teresa, Librn, North American Center for Marianist Studies Library, Chaminade Ctr, 4435 E Patterson Rd, Dayton, OH, 45430-1083. Tel: 937-429-2521. p. 1780
Trimm, Nancy, Libr Dir, Edwin A Bemis Public Library, 6014 S Datura St, Littleton, CO, 80120-2636. Tel: 303-795-3961. p. 290
Trimmer, Scott, Dir, Global Issues Resource Center Library, Bldg ESS-3100, Cuyahoga Community College, East Student Services, 4250 Richmond Rd, Highland Hills, OH, 44122. Tel: 216-987-0595. p. 1789
Trimper, Wendy, Commun Serv Coordr, Annapolis Valley Regional Library, 236 Commercial St, Berwick, NS, B0P 1E0, CANADA. Tel: 902-538-2665. p. 2616
Trinchitella, Carol, Head, Coll Serv, Connecticut State Library, 231 Capitol Ave, Hartford, CT, 06106. Tel: 860-757-6561. p. 317
Trindle, Joan, Br Librn, Chouteau County Library, Geraldine Branch, 254 Main St, Geraldine, MT, 59446. Tel: 406-737-4331. p. 1293
Trinidad, Stephanie, Access Serv Asst, University of Wisconsin-River Falls, 410 S Third St, River Falls, WI, 54022. Tel: 715-425-4155. p. 2474
Trinidad-Christensen, Jeremiah, Head, Data Serv, Res, Columbia University, Lehman Social Sciences Library, 300 International Affairs Bldg, 420 W 118th St, New York, NY, 10027. Tel: 212-854-3794. p. 1583
Trinkle, Jeff, Dir, Riverside Regional Library, 1997 E Jackson Blvd, Jackson, MO, 63755-1949. Tel: 573-243-8141. p. 1251
Trinoskey, Jessica, Dir of the Univ Libr, Marian University, 3200 Cold Spring Rd, Indianapolis, IN, 46222-1997. Tel: 317-955-6090. p. 697
Triolo, Jennifer, Br Coordr, Marathon County Public Library, Athens Branch, 221 Caroline St, Athens, WI, 54411-0910. Tel: 715-257-7292. p. 2485
Triplett, Jeanne, Dir, Yuma Public Library, 910 S Main St, Yuma, CO, 80759-2402. Tel: 970-848-2368. p. 299
Triplett, John, Cataloger/Ref Librn, United States Army, Fort Riley Post Library, Bldg 5306, Hood Dr, Fort Riley, KS, 66442-6416. Tel: 785-239-9582. p. 808
Triplett, Mary Beth, Br Mgr, Free Library of Philadelphia, Eastwick Branch, 2851 Island Ave, Philadelphia, PA, 19153-2314. Tel: 215-685-4170. p. 1978
Triplett, Robert K, Ref Librn, Palm Beach Atlantic University, 300 Pembroke Pl, West Palm Beach, FL, 33401-6503. Tel: 561-803-2234. p. 453
Triplett, Tonya, ILL, Northwestern Regional Library, 111 N Front St, 2nd Flr, Elkin, NC, 28621. Tel: 336-835-4894, Ext 1004. p. 1688
Tripp, Ann, Dir, Salem Public Library, 28 E Main St, Salem, VA, 24153. Tel: 540-375-3089. p. 2347
Tripp, Billy, Libr Dir, Peach Public Libraries, 315 Martin Luther King Jr Dr, Fort Valley, GA, 31030. Tel: 478-825-1640. p. 480
Tripp, Maureen, Media Res Coordr, Emerson College, 120 Boylston St, Boston, MA, 02116-4624. Tel: 617-824-8407. p. 995
Tripp, Teresa D, Asst Dir, Admin, East Carolina University, William E Laupus Health Sciences Library, 500 Health Sciences Dr, Greenville, NC, 27834. Tel: 252-744-3495. p. 1693
Tripp-Lanser, Brenda, Dir, Monroe Public Library, 416 S Buchanan St, Monroe, IA, 50170. Tel: 641-259-3065. p. 770
Trippodo, Brian, Electronic Res & Syst Librn, Queens University of Charlotte, 1900 Selwyn Ave, Charlotte, NC, 28274. Tel: 704-688-2766. p. 1681
Tripuraneni, Vinaya, Prof, Univ Librn, University of La Verne, 2040 Third St, La Verne, CA, 91750. Tel: 909-593-3511, Ext 4305. p. 155
Triska, Kyle, Spec, Minnesota Library Information Network, University of Minnesota-Minitex, Wilson Library, Rm 60, 309 19th Ave S, Minneapolis, MN, 55455. Tel: 612-624-8096, 612-625-0886. p. 2768
Trisler, Susan, Tech Serv, Morningside University, 1501 Morningside Ave, Sioux City, IA, 51106. Tel: 712-274-5195. p. 782
Tritt, Deborah, Archives, Instruction & Ref Librn, University of South Carolina Aiken, 471 University Pkwy, Aiken, SC, 29801. Tel: 803-641-3589. p. 2046
Triumph, Therese, Actg Head, Info Serv, University of North Carolina at Chapel Hill, Kenan Science Library, G301 Venable Hall, CB 3290, Chapel Hill, NC, 27599-3290. Tel: 919-962-1188. p. 1678
Trivedi, Himanshu, Ref Librn, Elgin Community College, 1700 Spartan Dr, Elgin, IL, 60123. Tel: 847-214-7337. p. 584
Trivette, Karen J, Head, Spec Coll & Archives, Fashion Institute of Technology-SUNY, Seventh Ave at 27th St, 227 W 27th St, New York, NY, 10001-5992. Tel: 212-217-4386. p. 1585
Trizna, Louis, Info & Tech Librn, Hillside Public Library, 405 N Hillside Ave, Hillside, IL, 60162-1295. Tel: 708-449-7510. p. 599
Trkay, Gretchen, Dir of Libr, Saint John's University, 2835 Abbey Plaza, Collegeville, MN, 56321. Tel: 320-363-2121. p. 1170
Trkay, Gretchen, Dir of Libraries & Archives, College of Saint Benedict, 37 S College Ave, Saint Joseph, MN, 56374. Tel: 320-363-5611. p. 1199
Trochta, Jill, Libr Dir, Suring Area Public Library, 604 E Main St, Suring, WI, 54174. Tel: 920-842-4451. p. 2480
Troeger, Nancy, Dir, Abel J Morneault Memorial Library, 153 Main St, Van Buren, ME, 04785. Tel: 207-868-5076. p. 944
Troendle, Mark, Dir, Stillwater Public Library, 224 N Third St, Stillwater, MN, 55082. Tel: 651-275-4338. p. 1205
Trofatter, Deborah, Assoc Librn, Ref, Tech, James Blackstone Memorial Library, 758 Main St, Branford, CT, 06405-3697. Tel: 203-488-1441, Ext 318. p. 303
Trogdon-Livingston, Debra, Br Mgr, Gaston County Public Library, Mount Holly Branch, 245 W Catawba Ave, Mount Holly, NC, 28120. Tel: 704-827-3581. p. 1690
Troha, Amanda, Asst Br Supvr, Public Library of Brookline, Coolidge Corner, 31 Pleasant St, Brookline, MA, 02446. Tel: 617-730-2380. p. 1003
Troianos, Rachel, Br Mgr, Arundel Anne County Public Library, Crofton Library, 1681 Riedel Rd, Crofton, MD, 21114. Tel: 410-222-7915. p. 950
Troini, Cassandra, Ref Librn, Warner Library, 121 N Broadway, Tarrytown, NY, 10591. Tel: 914-631-7734. p. 1651
Trojan, Bogusia, Dir, University Health Network, Health Sciences Library, 610 University Ave, 5th Flr, Toronto, ON, M5G 2M9, CANADA. Tel: 416-946-4482. p. 2698
Trojanowski, James, Regional Dir, Northwest Regional Library, 210 LaBree Ave N, Thief River Falls, MN, 56701. Tel: 218-681-1066. p. 1205
Trojanowski, Jim, Dir, Plum Creek Library System, 290 S Lake St, Worthington, MN, 56187. Tel: 507-376-5803. p. 1210
Trokey, Travis, Dir, Farmington Public Library, 101 North A St, Farmington, MO, 63640. Tel: 573-756-5779. p. 1245
Trombetta, Amy, Br Mgr, Old Bridge Public Library, Laurence Harbor Branch, 302 Laurence Pkwy, Laurence Harbor, NJ, 08879. Tel: 732-696-2011. p. 1431
Trombetta, Amy, ILL, Old Bridge Public Library, One Old Bridge Plaza, Old Bridge, NJ, 08857-2498. Tel: 732-721-5600, Ext 5033. p. 1431
Tromblee, Stacey, Dir, Livingston Manor Free Library, 92 Main St, Livingston Manor, NY, 12758-5113. Tel: 845-439-5440. p. 1564
Trombley, Alexandria, Librn, Galveston College, 4015 Ave Q, Galveston, TX, 77550. Tel: 409-944-1240. p. 2183
Trombley, Michael, Tech Asst, Field Museum of Natural History, 1400 S DuSable Lake Shore Dr, Chicago, IL, 60605-2496. Tel: 312-665-7892. p. 561
Trombly, Christopher, Interim Dean, Southern Connecticut State University, 501 Crescent St, New Haven, CT, 06515. Tel: 203-392-5781. p. 2783
Tromp, Kathleen, Cat, Resource Management, Nicolet Area Technical College, Lakeside Center, 3rd Flr, 5364 College Dr, Rhinelander, WI, 54501. Tel: 715-365-4479. p. 2472
Tronier, Suzanne, Mgr, Salt Lake County Library Services, Millcreek Community Library, 2266 E Evergreen Ave, Salt Lake City, UT, 84109-2927. p. 2275
Tronkowski, Sarah, Librn, SUNY Corning Community College, One Academic Dr, Corning, NY, 14830. Tel: 607-962-9251. p. 1522
Tronley, Robert, Asst Dir, Wauwatosa Public Library, 7635 W North Ave, Wauwatosa, WI, 53213-1718. Tel: 414-471-8484. p. 2486
Troppmann, Kathleen, Mgr, Customer Serv, St Albert Public Library, Five Saint Anne St, St. Albert, AB, T8N 3Z9, CANADA. Tel: 780-459-1530. p. 2555
Trosclair, Charlotte, Dir, Vermilion Parish Library, 405 E Saint Victor St, Abbeville, LA, 70510-5101. Tel: 337-893-2655. p. 879
Trosclair, Mona, Br Mgr, Saint Martin Parish Library, Breaux Bridge Branch, 205 N Main St, Breaux Bridge, LA, 70517. Tel: 337-332-2733. p. 907
Trosper, Summer, Dir, Childress Public Library, 117 Ave B NE, Childress, TX, 79201-4509. Tel: 940-937-8421. p. 2155
Trost, Christine, Exec Dir, University of California, Berkeley, Institute of Governmental Studies, 109 Philosophy Hall, Ground Flr, Berkeley, CA, 94720-2370. Tel: 510-642-1472. p. 123
Trott, Barry, Dir, Tech Serv, Spec Project Dir, Williamsburg Regional Library, 7770 Croaker Rd, Williamsburg, VA, 23188-7064. Tel: 757-741-3330. p. 2353
Trott, Garrett, Univ Librn, Corban University Library, 5000 Deer Park Dr SE, Salem, OR, 97317-9392. Tel: 503-375-7016. p. 1896
Trott, Holly, Coll Mgt, La Porte County Public Library, 904 Indiana Ave, La Porte, IN, 46350. Tel: 219-362-6156. p. 700
Trotta, Marcia, Librn, Berlin Free Library, 834 Worthington Ridge, Berlin, CT, 06037. Tel: 860-828-3344. p. 302
Trotter, Ashley, Mgr, Currituck County Public Library, Moyock Public Library, 126 Campus Dr, Moyock, NC, 27958. Tel: 252-435-6419. p. 1673
Trotter, Terri, Asst Librn, Loogootee Public Library, 106 N Line St, Loogootee, IN, 47553. Tel: 812-295-3713. p. 704

Trotter, Tracy, Dir, Adams Memorial Library, 1112 Ligonier St, Latrobe, PA, 15650. Tel: 724-539-1972. p. 1953
Trottier, Guillaume, Librn, Hopital Maisonneuve-Rosemont, 5415 boul de l'Assomption, Montreal, QC, H1T 2M4, CANADA. Tel: 514-252-3463. p. 2724
Troup, Karen S, Dir, Monroeton Public Library, 149 Dalpiaz Dr, Monroeton, PA, 18832. Tel: 570-265-2871. p. 1964
Troup, Tam, Cat & Metadata, Mgr, Bucknell University, 220 Bertrand Library, One Dent Dr, Lewisburg, PA, 17837. Tel: 570-577-1557. p. 1955
Trout, Amy, Curator, Connecticut River Museum, 67 Main St, Essex, CT, 06426. Tel: 860-767-8269, Ext 115. p. 311
Trout, Daniel, Mgr, Acq & Ser, RIT Libraries, 90 Lomb Memorial Dr, Rochester, NY, 14623-5604. Tel: 585-475-7283. p. 1629
Trout, Karla, Exec Dir, Library System of Lancaster County, 1866 Colonial Village Lane, Ste 107, Lancaster, PA, 17601. Tel: 717-207-0500. p. 1952
Trout, Peggy, Circ Serv, Rochester Public Library, 65 S Main St, Rochester, NH, 03867-2707. Tel: 603-332-1428. p. 1380
Trout, Sami Jo, Asst Dir, Boyertown Community Library, 24 N Reading Ave, Boyertown, PA, 19512. Tel: 610-369-0496. p. 1914
Troutman, Brooke, Research Servs Librn, United States Air Force Academy Libraries, 2354 Fairchild Dr, Ste 3A15, USAF Academy, CO, 80840-6214. Tel: 719-333-4406. p. 297
Troutman, Karen S, Dir, Ref Librn, Walton & Tipton Township Public Library, 110 N Main St, Walton, IN, 46994. Tel: 574-626-2234. p. 724
Trovillo, Michelle, Dir, Info Res, Baker & Hostetler LLP Library, Key Tower, 127 Public Sq, Ste 200, Cleveland, OH, 44114-1214. Tel: 216-621-0200. p. 1766
Trow, Virginia, Prog Mgr, Samaritan Medical Center, 728 Washington St, Watertown, NY, 13601. Tel: 315-785-4191. p. 1660
Troy, Sarah, Head User Serv & Resource Sharing, University of California, 1156 High St, Santa Cruz, CA, 95064. Tel: 831-459-3878. p. 243
Troyan, David, Tech Serv Coordr, Riverhead Free Library, 330 Court St, Riverhead, NY, 11901-2885. Tel: 631-727-3228. p. 1627
Truax, Morgan, Dir, Alberta Health Services, 3942 50A Ave, Red Deer, AB, T4N 4E7, CANADA. Tel: 403-343-4557. p. 2551
Trudeau, Emma, Ad, Ref Serv Librn, Southwest Public Libraries, SPL Admin, 3359 Broadway, Grove City, OH, 43123. Tel: 614-875-6716. p. 1789
Trudeau, Mike, Librn, Legislative Reference Bureau Law Library, 112 State House, Springfield, IL, 62706. Tel: 217-782-6625. p. 650
Trudel, Nancy J, Exec Dir, Centre d'acces a l'information juridique/Legal Informatin Access Center, 480 Saint-Laurent, Bur 503, Montreal, QC, H2Y 3Y7, CANADA. Tel: 514-844-2245. p. 2721
Trueblood, Dianne, Dir, Info Tech, South Georgia Technical College, Crisp County Ctr, Rm A37, 402 N Midway Rd, Cordele, GA, 31015. Tel: 229-271-4071. p. 473
Truesdale, Beverly, Per, Southern California Genealogical Society, 417 Irving Dr, Burbank, CA, 91504-2408. Tel: 818-843-7247. p. 125
Truesdell, Thalia, Br Mgr, Jackson County Library Services, Ruch Branch, 7919 Hwy 238, Ruch, OR, 97530-9728. Tel: 541-899-7438. p. 1886
Truex, Eleanor, Med Librn, Ascension Saint Joseph Hospital-Chicago, 2900 N Lake Shore Dr, 12th Flr, Chicago, IL, 60657. Tel: 773-665-3038. p. 554
Truex, Eleanor, Med Librn, Ascension Saint Francis Hospital-Evanston, 355 Ridge Ave, Evanston, IL, 60202. Tel: 847-316-2460. p. 586
Truex, Eleanor, Librn, AMITA Health Saint Mary's Hospital, 500 W Court St, Kankakee, IL, 60901. Tel: 815-937-2400, 815-937-2477. p. 604
Truhe, Brenna, Head, Tech Serv, University of Kansas Libraries, Wheat Law Library, Green Hall, Rm 200, 1535 W 15th St, Lawrence, KS, 66045-7608. Tel: 785-864-3025. p. 820
Truick, Lyda, Mgr, County of Los Angeles Public Library, Woodcrest Library, 1340 W 106th St, Los Angeles, CA, 90044-1626. Tel: 323-757-9373. p. 138
Truitt, Tabitha, Asst Dir, H Grady Bradshaw Chambers County Library, 3419 20th Ave, Valley, AL, 36854. Tel: 334-768-2161. p. 39
Trujillo, Alice, Br Mgr, Conejos County Library, Antonito Branch, 220 Main St, Antonito, CO, 81120. Tel: 719-376-5904. p. 287
Trujillo, Barbara, Libr Dir, Cuba Public Library, 13 E Cordova Ave, Cuba, NM, 87013. Tel: 575-289-3100. p. 1466
Trujillo, Colin, Dir, College of the Redwoods Library, 7351 Tompkins Hill Rd, Eureka, CA, 95501. Tel: 707-476-4260. p. 141
Trujillo, Enrico, Info Spec I, University of New Mexico, Taos Campus, 115 Civic Plaza Dr, Taos, NM, 87571. Tel: 575-737-6242. p. 1463
Trujillo, Flo, Youth Serv Coordr, Farmington Public Library, 2101 Farmington Ave, Farmington, NM, 87401. Tel: 505-599-1261. p. 1468
Trujillo, Isabel W, Dir, Pueblo de Abiquiu Library & Cultural Center, Bldg 29, County Rd 187, Abiquiu, NM, 87510. Tel: 505-685-4884. p. 1459
Trujillo, Jaclyn, Dir, Walnut Public Library District, 101 Heaton St, Walnut, IL, 61376. Tel: 815-379-2159. p. 658
Trujillo, Julie C, Libr Dir, Truchas Community Library, 60 County Rd 75, Truchas, NM, 87578. Tel: 505-689-2683. p. 1479
Trujillo, Susan, Librn, West Los Angeles College Library, 9000 Overland Ave, Culver City, CA, 90230. Tel: 310-287-4406. p. 133
Trull, Chris, Tech Coordr, Thomasville Public Library, 1401 Mosley Dr, Thomasville, AL, 36784. Tel: 334-636-5343. p. 37
Trulson, Shelly, Librn, United States Army Corps of Engineers, 4735 E Marginal Way S, Seattle, WA, 98134. Tel: 206-316-3728. p. 2381
Truman, Rob, Electronic Res, Lewis & Clark College, Paul L Boley Law Library, Lewis & Clark Law School, 10015 SW Terwilliger Blvd, Portland, OR, 97219. Tel: 503-768-6776. p. 1891
Trumble, Amy, Dir, New Glarus Public Library, 319 Second St, New Glarus, WI, 53574. Tel: 608-527-2003. p. 2464
Trumble, Stephen, Mgr, County of Los Angeles Public Library, Norwood Library, 4550 N Peck Rd, El Monte, CA, 91732-1998. Tel: 626-443-3147. p. 137
Trumbo, Gerri, Libr Mgr, United States Army, Institute of Surgical Research Library, 3698 Chambers Pass, Bldg 3611, Fort Sam Houston, TX, 78234-6315. Tel: 210-539-4559. p. 2178
Trummell, Angelica, Head of Children's & Family Services, Rancho Cucamonga Public Library, 12505 Cultural Center Dr, Rancho Cucamonga, CA, 91739. Tel: 909-477-2720. p. 197
Trump, Betty, Ch Serv Librn, Montgomery County Public Library, 328 N Maysville Rd, Mount Sterling, KY, 40353. Tel: 859-498-2404. p. 870
Trumpy, Julia, Youth Serv Librn, Lucius E & Elsie C Burch Jr Library, 501 Poplar View Pkwy, Collierville, TN, 38017. Tel: 901-457-2600. p. 2094
Truog, Sara, Asst Dir, Head, Children's Servx, Milton Public Library, 476 Canton Ave, Milton, MA, 02186-3299. Tel: 617-698-5757. p. 1036
Truong, Irene, Librn, Rio Hondo College Library, 3600 Workman Mill Rd, 2nd Flr, Whittier, CA, 90601. Tel: 562-908-3377. p. 259
Truscott, Pam, Nebraska Health Care Association Library, 1200 Libra Dr, Ste 100, Lincoln, NE, 68512. Tel: 402-435-3551. p. 1322
Trushenski, Jenny, Dir, Martin County Library, 110 N Park St, Fairmont, MN, 56031-2822. Tel: 507-238-4207. p. 1174
Truslow, Hugh, Head of Libr, Harvard Library, Fung Library, Knafel Bldg, Concourse Level, 1737 Cambridge St, Cambridge, MA, 02138. Tel: 617-495-0485. p. 1006
Truslow, Robyn, Pub Relations Coordr, Calvert Library, 850 Costley Way, Prince Frederick, MD, 20678. Tel: 301-855-1862, 410-535-0291. p. 972
Trussell, Mike, Libr Mgr, Kodiak College, 117 Benny Benson Dr, Kodiak, AK, 99615. Tel: 907-486-1238. p. 48
Trusty, Deborah, Dir, Toledo Public Library, 173 NW Seventh St, Toledo, OR, 97391. Tel: 541-336-3132. p. 1900
Trusty, Jennifer, Br Head, Brazoria County Library System, Alvin Branch, 105 S Gordon, Alvin, TX, 77511. Tel: 281-388-4301. p. 2135
Truszkowski, Christopher, Web & Digital Spec, Roger Williams University Library, One Old Ferry Rd, Bristol, RI, 02809. Tel: 401-254-5548. p. 2030
Trutna, Carrie, Children's Serv Coordr, Wahoo Public Library, 637 N Maple St, Wahoo, NE, 68066-1673. Tel: 402-443-3871. p. 1339
Tryggestad, Michelle, Dir, Sparta Free Library, 124 W Main St, Sparta, WI, 54656. Tel: 608-269-2010, Ext 4. p. 2478
Tryggestad, Michelle, Dir, Bekkum Memorial Library, 206 N Main St, Westby, WI, 54667-1108. Tel: 608-634-4419. p. 2487
Tryon, Rusty, Libr Dir, Saint Mary-of-the-Woods College, One Saint Mary of the Woods College, Saint Mary-of-the-Woods, IN, 47876. Tel: 812-535-5255. p. 717
Tryon, Rusty, Dr, Libr Dir, Louisiana College, 1140 College Dr, Pineville, LA, 71359. Tel: 318-487-7110. p. 905
Trzeciak, Jeffrey, Libr Dir, Jersey City Free Public Library, 472 Jersey Ave, Jersey City, NJ, 07302-3499. Tel: 201-547-4788. p. 1409
Tsahalis, Cate, Executive Asst, Russell Library, 123 Broad St, Middletown, CT, 06457. Tel: 860-347-2528. p. 322
Tsahalis, Courtney, Dir, Millbrook Library, Three Friendly Lane, Millbrook, NY, 12545. Tel: 845-677-3611. p. 1572
Tsang, Kamling, ILL, Carlsbad City Library, 1775 Dove Lane, Carlsbad, CA, 92011. Tel: 760-602-2031. p. 128
Tschanen-Feasel, Kayleigh, Commun Relations Mgr, Tiffin-Seneca Public Library, 77 Jefferson St, Tiffin, OH, 44883. Tel: 419-447-3751. p. 1823
Tschauner, Monica, Exec Dir, Libr Mgr, Shepperd Leadership Institute, 4919 E University Blvd, Odessa, TX, 79762. Tel: 432-552-2850. p. 2223
Tschoerner, Laura, Interim Libr Dir, Rowlett Public Library, 3900 Main St, Ste 200, Rowlett, TX, 75088-5075. Tel: 972-412-6161. p. 2234
Tse, Angela, Br Mgr, Markham Public Library, Aaniin Branch, 5665 14th Ave, Markham, ON, L3S 3K5, CANADA. Tel: 905-513-7977, Ext 4477. p. 2656
Tse, Ronny, Library Contact, Dentons Canada LLP, 77 King St W, Ste 400, Toronto, ON, M5K 0A1, CANADA. Tel: 416-863-4511. p. 2688
Tsekenis, Gus, Br Mgr, Jersey City Free Public Library, Five Corners, 678 Newark Ave, Jersey City, NJ, 07306. Tel: 201-547-4543. p. 1409
Tseng, Peggy, Libr Dir, Frank Sarris Public Library, 36 N Jefferson Ave, Canonsburg, PA, 15317. Tel: 724-745-1308. p. 1918
Tsiakos, George, Actg Head, Libr, University of British Columbia Library, Law, Allard Hall, 1822 Main Mall, Vancouver, BC, V6T 1Z1, CANADA. Tel: 604-822-0093. p. 2580
Tsiouris, Susan, Res & Instruction Librn, Widener University, One University Pl, Chester, PA, 19013. Tel: 610-499-4069. p. 1921
Tsistinas, Olivia, Clinical Libr Coordr, Outreach Coordr, SUNY Upstate Medical University, 766 Irving Ave, Syracuse, NY, 13210-1602. Tel: 315-464-7200. p. 1650
Tsitso, Matthew, Archivist, Fenton History Center, 73 Forest Ave, Jamestown, NY, 14701. Tel: 716-664-6256. p. 1557

Tsomaeva, Elena, Dir, Union City Public Library, 324 43rd St, Union City, NJ, 07087-5008. Tel: 201-866-7500. p. 1449

Tsoumpelis, Chryso, Coordr, Patron Serv, Riverhead Free Library, 330 Court St, Riverhead, NY, 11901-2885. Tel: 631-727-3228. p. 1627

Tsubira, Helene, Dir, Somers Public Library, 502 Sixth St, Somers, IA, 50586. Tel: 515-467-5522. p. 783

Tsui, Tracy, Syst Librn, Southwestern Law School, Bullock Wilshire Bldg, 1st Flr, 3050 Wilshire Blvd, Los Angeles, CA, 90010. Tel: 213-738-5771. p. 168

Tsung, Shu-Chen, Assoc Univ Librn, Digital Serv & Tech Planning, Georgetown University, 37th & O St NW, Washington, DC, 20057-1174. Tel: 202-687-7429. p. 368

Tsutsui, Ilona, Ref Librn, University of Oregon Libraries, John E Jaqua Law Library, William W Knight Law Ctr, 2nd Flr, 1515 Agate St, Eugene, OR, 97403. Tel: 541-346-1657. p. 1879

Tsvetkova, Denitsa, Mrs, Chief Editor, Canadian Centre for Ecumenism Library, 2715, Chemin de la Cote Sainte-Catherine, Montreal, QC, H3T 1B6, CANADA. Tel: 514-937-9176. p. 2721

Tu, Vy, Sr Librn, Tech Serv, Coronado Public Library, 640 Orange Ave, Coronado, CA, 92118-1526. Tel: 619-522-2473. p. 132

Tu-Keefner, Feili, PhD, Assoc Prof, University of South Carolina, 1501 Greene St, Columbia, SC, 29208. Tel: 803-777-3858. p. 2792

Tuai, Cameron, Data & Business Librarian, Drake University, 2725 University Ave, Des Moines, IA, 50311. Tel: 515-271-2924. p. 746

Tubb, Karen, Syst Programmer, Sundre Municipal Library, 96-2 Ave NW, No 2, Sundre, AB, T0M 1X0, CANADA. Tel: 403-638-4000. p. 2556

Tubbs, Camilla, Assoc Dean for Libr & Tech Serv, University of California, 200 McAllister St, San Francisco, CA, 94102-4978. Tel: 415-565-4757. p. 229

Tubbs, Camilla, Actg Dir, University of Maryland, Baltimore, Thurgood Marshall Law Library, 501 W Fayette St, Baltimore, MD, 21201-1768. Tel: 410-706-0792. p. 957

Tubbs, Cecily, Electronic Res & Syst Librn, Rogers State University Library, 1701 W Will Rogers Blvd, Claremore, OK, 74017-3252. Tel: 918-343-7719. p. 1844

Tubbs, Peter, Technology Spec, Library of Rush University Medical Center, Armour Academic Ctr, 600 S Paulina St, Ste 571, Chicago, IL, 60612. Tel: 312-942-8558. p. 563

Tubinis, Jason, IT Librn, University of Georgia, Alexander Campbell King Law Library, 225 Herty Dr, Athens, GA, 30602-6018. Tel: 706-542-7365. p. 459

Tubinis, Martha, Dir, Programs, Dir, Social Media, Andover Center for History & Culture Library, 97 Main St, Andover, MA, 01810. Tel: 978-475-2236. p. 985

Tucci, Gail, Head, Circ, Lucius E & Elsie C Burch Jr Library, 501 Poplar View Pkwy, Collierville, TN, 38017. Tel: 901-457-2600. p. 2094

Tucci, Josephine, Exec Dir, Batavia Public Library District, Ten S Batavia Ave, Batavia, IL, 60510-2793. Tel: 630-879-1393. p. 540

Tucci, Josephine, Dir, Lincolnwood Public Library District, 4000 W Pratt Ave, Lincolnwood, IL, 60712. Tel: 847-677-5277. p. 609

Tucci, Valerie, Librn, The College of New Jersey, 2000 Pennington Rd, Ewing, NJ, 08628-1104. Tel: 609-771-2311. p. 1402

Tuck, Joyce, Librn, Isle La Motte Library, 2238 Main St, Isle La Motte, VT, 05463. Tel: 802-928-4113. p. 2286

Tuck, Nikki, Librn, United States Army, Military Occupational Specialty Library, Bldg 2110, Montgomery Rd, Fort Wainwright, AK, 99703. Tel: 907-353-7297. p. 46

Tuck, Sue, Supvr, Essex County Library, Leamington Branch, One John St, Leamington, ON, N8H 1H1, CANADA. Tel: 226-946-1529, Ext 220. p. 2641

Tucker, Adam, Br Mgr, Jefferson County Library, Windsor, 7479 Metropolitian Blvd, Barnhart, MO, 63012. Tel: 636-461-1914. p. 1249

Tucker, Angel, Youth Serv Mgr, Johnson County Library, 9875 W 87th St, Overland Park, KS, 66212. Tel: 913-826-4600. p. 830

Tucker, Ben, Digital Projects Librn, Scholarly Communications, University of Puget Sound, 1604 N Warner St, Upper Loading Dock, Tacoma, WA, 98416. Tel: 253-879-3667. p. 2387

Tucker, Catherine, Librn, Brooklyn Town Library Association, Ten Canterbury Rd, Brooklyn, CT, 06234. Tel: 860-774-0649. p. 305

Tucker, Dawnn, Dir, Lied Pierce Public Library, 207 W Court St, Pierce, NE, 68767. Tel: 402-329-6324. p. 1332

Tucker, Dayna, Ch Serv, River Grove Public Library District, 8638 W Grand Ave, River Grove, IL, 60171. Tel: 708-453-4484. p. 639

Tucker, Diana, Br Mgr, Saint Charles City-County Library District, Kisker Road Branch, 1000 Kisker Rd, Saint Charles, MO, 63304-8726. Tel: 636-447-7323, 636-926-7323. p. 1278

Tucker, Elissa, Dir, Sharkey-Issaquena County Library, 116 R Morganfield Way, Rolling Fork, MS, 39159. Tel: 662-873-4076. p. 1232

Tucker, Gail, Br Mgr, White County Regional Library System, Bradford Branch, 302 W Walnut St, Bradford, AR, 72020. Tel: 501-344-2558. p. 110

Tucker, Gayle, Human Res Mgr, Bloomington Public Library, 205 E Olive St, Bloomington, IL, 61701. Tel: 309-828-6091. p. 543

Tucker, James, Librn, Johns Hopkins University Libraries, Adolf Meyer Library, 600 N Wolfe St, Baltimore, MD, 21205. Tel: 410-955-5819. p. 954

Tucker, Jennifer, Operations Librn, Southlake Public Library, 1400 Main St, Ste 130, Southlake, TX, 76092-7640. Tel: 817-748-8243. p. 2245

Tucker, Jill, Archives Asst, Huntingdon College, 1500 E Fairview Ave, Montgomery, AL, 36106. Tel: 334-833-4418. p. 29

Tucker, Joe, Dir, Library Access & Research, Bennington College, One College Dr, Bennington, VT, 05201-6001. Tel: 802-440-4610. p. 2279

Tucker, Joel, Dir, Washington County Library System, 88 West 100 S, Saint George, UT, 84770. Tel: 435-634-5737. p. 2270

Tucker, Kari, Asst Dir, Jervis Public Library Association, Inc, 613 N Washington St, Rome, NY, 13440-4296. Tel: 315-336-4570. p. 1632

Tucker, Kristine, Br Mgr, Parkersburg & Wood County Public Library, Waverly, 450 Virginia St, Waverly, WV, 26184. Tel: 304-464-5668. p. 2411

Tucker, Laura, Head, Children's Servx, Homewood Public Library, 1721 Oxmoor Rd, Homewood, AL, 35209-4085. Tel: 205-332-6616. p. 21

Tucker, Laura Ayling, Cat Librn, Lewis & Clark College, Aubrey R Watzek Library, 0615 SW Palatine Hill Rd, Portland, OR, 97219-7899. Tel: 503-768-7274. p. 1892

Tucker, Lawrence, Access Services Tech, Howard University Libraries, Louis Stokes Health Sciences Library, 501 W St NW, Washington, DC, 20059. Tel: 202-884-1500. p. 369

Tucker, Marcia, Librn, Institute for Advanced Study Libraries, One Einstein Dr, Princeton, NJ, 08540. Tel: 609-734-8000. p. 1436

Tucker, Michelle, Human Res Mgr, Kenosha Public Library, 7979 38th Ave, Kenosha, WI, 53142. Tel: 262-564-6100. p. 2444

Tucker, Nancy, Ref & Instruction Librn, Jacksonville University, 2800 University Blvd N, Jacksonville, FL, 32211-3394. Tel: 904-256-7266. p. 413

Tucker, Rachel, Br Mgr, Nevada County Community Library, Grass Valley Library - Royce Branch, 207 Mill St, Grass Valley, CA, 95945. Tel: 530-273-4117. p. 182

Tucker, Sharon, Archives Mgr, Huntingdon College, 1500 E Fairview Ave, Montgomery, AL, 36106. Tel: 334-833-4413. p. 29

Tucker, Sharon, Doc, Jersey City Free Public Library, 472 Jersey Ave, Jersey City, NJ, 07302-3499. Tel: 201-547-4517. p. 1409

Tucker, Shawn, Tech Serv Coordr, North Kawartha Library, 175 Burleigh St, Apsley, ON, K0L 1A0, CANADA. Tel: 705-656-4333. p. 2628

Tucker, Sherri, Lending Servs, William Paterson University, 300 Pompton Rd, Wayne, NJ, 07470. Tel: 973-720-3182. p. 1452

Tucker, Taneisha K, Dir, Vestavia Hills Library in the Forest, 1221 Montgomery Hwy, Vestavia Hills, AL, 35216. Tel: 205-978-0155. p. 39

Tucker, Tina, Dir of Communities, Thunder Bay Public Library, 285 Red River Rd, Thunder Bay, ON, P7B 1A9, CANADA. Tel: 807-684-6813. p. 2685

Tucker, Tracy, Archivist, Educ Dir, The Willa Cather Foundation, 413 N Webster St, Red Cloud, NE, 68970-2466. Tel: 402-746-2653. p. 1334

Tuckman, Joel, Research Coordr, The Beasley Firm, LLC, 1125 Walnut St, Philadelphia, PA, 19107. Tel: 215 592-1000. p. 1975

Tucman, Elizabeth, Dir, Simpson, Thacher & Bartlett, 425 Lexington Ave, New York, NY, 10017. Tel: 212-455-2800. p. 1602

Tudisco, Gayle, Librn, Exeter Hospital Inc, Five Alumni Dr, Exeter, NH, 03833-2160. Tel: 603-580-6226. p. 1363

Tudor, Andrew, Dir of Libr, Wenatchee Valley College, 1300 Fifth St, Wenatchee, WA, 98801. Tel: 509-682-6715. p. 2395

Tudor, Renee, Dir, New Florence Community Library, 122 Ligonier St, New Florence, PA, 15944. Tel: 724-235-2249. p. 1969

Tueller, Korine, Research Admin for Library Collections, Arizona State Library, Archives & Public Records, Polly Rosenbaum Archives & History Bldg, 1901 W Madison St, Phoenix, AZ, 85009. Tel: 602-926-3720. p. 69

Tuffin, Sherry, Digital Projects, Libr Asst, Lawrence Technological University Library, 21000 W Ten Mile Rd, Southfield, MI, 48075-1058. Tel: 248-204-2800. p. 1151

Tuffs, Diane, Librn, Yakima Valley Libraries, Wapato Library, 119 E Third St, Wapato, WA, 98951. Tel: 509-877-2882. p. 2396

Tufts, Sarah, Youth Librn, Windsor Public Library, 43 State St, Windsor, VT, 05089. Tel: 802-674-2556. p. 2299

Tuggle, Donna, Ch, Wayne County Public Library, 157 Rolling Hills Blvd, Monticello, KY, 42633. Tel: 606-348-8565. p. 869

Tuggle, Ellen, Libr Asst, Lantana Public Library, 205 W Ocean Ave, Lantana, FL, 33462. Tel: 561-540-5740. p. 417

Tuggle, John, Exec Dir, Shreve Memorial Library, 424 Texas St, Shreveport, LA, 71101. Tel: 318-226-5897. p. 908

Tugman, Mary Lynn, Adult Serv Mgr, Wilkes County Public Library, 215 Tenth St, North Wilkesboro, NC, 28659. Tel: 336-838-2818. p. 1706

Tugwell, Cindy, Exec Dir, Heritage Winnipeg Corp Library, 63 Albert St, Ste 509, Winnipeg, MB, R3B 1G4, CANADA. Tel: 204-942-2663. p. 2593

Tuinstra, Merri-Jo, Libr Dir, Sparta Township Library, 80 N Union St, Sparta, MI, 49345. Tel: 616-887-9937. p. 1152

Tuite, Brenna, Librn, Carle BroMenn Medical Center, 1304 Franklin Ave, Ste 180, Normal, IL, 61761. Tel: 309-268-5281, 309-454-1400. p. 625

Tukhareli, Natalia, Dir, Canadian Memorial Chiropractic College, 6100 Leslie St, Toronto, ON, M2H 3J1, CANADA. Tel: 416-482-2340, Ext 159. p. 2687

Tule, Abigail, Asst Dir, Bethlehem Public Library, 2245 Main St, Bethlehem, NH, 03574. Tel: 603-869-2409. p. 1355

Tuley-Williams, Dana, Syst Librn, Oklahoma City Community College, 7777 S May Ave, Oklahoma City, OK, 73159. Tel: 405-682-1611, Ext 7390. p. 1858

Tulikangas, June, Head, Tech Serv, Westwood Public Library, 660 High St, Westwood, MA, 02090. Tel: 781-320-1047. p. 1068

Tulis, Susan, Assoc Dean, Southern Illinois University Carbondale, 605 Agriculture Dr, Mailcode 6632, Carbondale, IL, 62901. Tel: 618-453-2522. p. 549

Tulloch, Meg, Dir, Libr Serv, United States Government Accountability Office, 441 G St NW, Rm 6H19, Washington, DC, 20548. p. 379

Tullos, Andrea, Dir, Saint John the Baptist Parish Library, 2920 New Hwy 51, LaPlace, LA, 70068. Tel: 985-652-6857. p. 894

Tullos, Andrea, Asst Dir, Orange County Public Library, 137 W Margaret Lane, Hillsborough, NC, 27278. Tel: 919-245-2525. p. 1697

Tully, Megan, Ref & Ad Serv Librn, Ames Free Library, 53 Main St, North Easton, MA, 02356. Tel: 508-238-2000. p. 1041

Tulp, Anita, Libr Dir, Valley City Barnes County Public Library, 410 N Central Ave, Valley City, ND, 58072-2949. Tel: 701-845-3821. p. 1740

Tuluao, Pauline, Cat Supvr, Libr Assoc, American Samoa Community College Library, Malaeimi Village, Malaeimi Rd, Mapusaga, AS, 96799. p. 2503

Tummeti, Meredith, Fac Librn, Centralia College, 600 Centralia College Blvd, Centralia, WA, 98531. Tel: 360-623-8722. p. 2361

Tuncer-Bayramli, Nurhak, Music Librn, Elizabeth City State University, 1704 Weeksville Rd, Elizabeth City, NC, 27909. Tel: 252-335-3632. p. 1687

Tunnell, Beth, Br Mgr, Latah County Library District, Potlatch Branch, 1010 Onaway Rd, Potlatch, ID, 83855. Tel: 208-875-1036. p. 526

Tunnell, Julie, Head Librn, Metropolitan Transportation Commission, 375 Beale St, Ste 800, San Francisco, CA, 94105. Tel: 415-778-5236. p. 226

Tunnicliff, Melita, Libr Dir, LeClaire Community Library, 323 Wisconsin St, LeClaire, IA, 52753. Tel: 563-289-6007. p. 765

Tuohig, Paul, Res Analyst, United States Army, The Institute of Heraldry Library, 9325 Gunston Rd, Ste S113, Fort Belvoir, VA, 22060-5579. Tel: 703-806-4967, 703-806-4975. p. 2319

Tuohy, Catherine, Assoc Librn, Electronic Res, Emmanuel College, 400 The Fenway, Boston, MA, 02115. Tel: 617-264-7658. p. 995

Tuominen, Liisa, Researcher, Ottawa Citizen Library Collection, 1101 Baxter Rd, Ottawa, ON, K2C 3M4, CANADA. Tel: 613-596-3744. p. 2668

Turbak, Jamie, Dir, Libr Serv, Oakland Public Library, 125 14th St, Oakland, CA, 94612. Tel: 510-238-6610. p. 186

Turbak, Michelle, Ch Serv, Edith Wheeler Memorial Library, 733 Monroe Tpk, Monroe, CT, 06468. Tel: 203-452-2850. p. 323

Turbyne, Susan, Dir, Byron G Merrill Library, Ten Buffalo Rd, Rumney, NH, 03266. Tel: 603-786-9520. p. 1380

Turcotte, Dawna, Regional Librn, Northern Lights College Library, 11401 Eighth St, Dawson Creek, BC, V1G 4G2, CANADA. Tel: 250-784-7533. p. 2565

Turcotte, Dawna, Regional Librn, Northern Lights College, 9820 120 Ave, Fort Saint John, BC, V1J 8C3, CANADA. Tel: 250-787-6213. p. 2566

Turcotte, Vickie, Asst Dir, Support Serv, Chelmsford Public Library, 25 Boston Rd, Chelmsford, MA, 01824. Tel: 978-256-5521. p. 1010

Tureen, Amy, Library Liaison, University of Nevada, Las Vegas Univ Libraries, Music Library, 4505 S Maryland Pkwy, Box 457002, Las Vegas, NV, 89154-7002. Tel: 702-895-2134. p. 1347

Tureski, Tim, Libr Mgr, New York Public Library - Astor, Lenox & Tilden Foundations, Spuyten Duyvil Branch, 650 W 235th St, (@ Independence Ave), Bronx, NY, 10463. Tel: 718-796-1202. p. 1597

Turgasen, Amy, Asst Dir, Altoona Public Library, 700 Eighth St SW, Altoona, IA, 50009. Tel: 515-967-3881. p. 730

Turgeon, David, Chairperson, Hornepayne Public Library, 68 Front St, Hornepayne, ON, P0M 1Z0, CANADA. Tel: 807-868-2332. p. 2648

Turgeon, Tammy, Dir, Sterling Heights Public Library, 40255 Dodge Park Rd, Sterling Heights, MI, 48313-4140. Tel: 586-446-2665. p. 1152

Turgeon, Tammy, Dir, Suburban Library Cooperative, 44750 Delco Blvd, Sterling Heights, MI, 48313. Tel: 586-685-5764. p. 2767

Turhan, Merve, Libr Asst, Waterloo Region Law Association, 85 Frederick St, Kitchener, ON, N2H 0A7, CANADA. Tel: 519-742-0872. p. 2652

Turk, Isabel, Libr Dir, Parsons Memorial Library, 27 Saco Rd, Alfred, ME, 04002. Tel: 207-324-2001. p. 913

Turk, Matthew, Asst Prof, University of Illinois at Urbana-Champaign, Library & Information Science Bldg, 501 E Daniel St, Champaign, IL, 61820-6211. Tel: 217-333-3280. p. 2784

Turk, Zachary, Electronic Services Specialist, University of Detroit Mercy School of Law, 651 E Jefferson, Detroit, MI, 48226. Tel: 313-596-0239. p. 1099

Turkalo, Laury, Head, Libr Syst, University of Rhode Island, 15 Lippitt Rd, Kingston, RI, 02881-2011. Tel: 401-874-2820. p. 2033

Turkington, Barbara, Asst Dir, Advan, Saint Louis County Library, 1640 S Lindbergh Blvd, Saint Louis, MO, 63131-3598. Tel: 314-994-3300, Ext 2152. p. 1273

Turkovic, Dana, Curator, Laumeier Sculpture Park Library & Archive, 12580 Rott Rd, Saint Louis, MO, 63127. Tel: 314-615-5280. p. 1271

Turley, Patty, Regional Mgr, San Bernardino County Library, 777 E Rialto Ave, San Bernardino, CA, 92415-0035. Tel: 909-855-5486. p. 212

Turnage, Karen, Br Mgr, Lincoln-Lawrence-Franklin Regional Library, New Hebron Public Library, 209 Jones St, New Hebron, MS, 39140. Tel: 601-694-2623. p. 1213

Turnbull, Benjamin, Tech Serv Librn, Dominican Theological Library, 487 Michigan Ave NE, Washington, DC, 20017-1585. Tel: 202-655-4652. p. 365

Turnbull, Nancy, Tech Serv Librn, Fitchburg State University, 160 Pearl St, Fitchburg, MA, 01420. Tel: 978-665-4338. p. 1019

Turner, Adrienna, Librn, California Department of Corrections Library System, California State Prison, Sacramento, 100 Prison Rd, Represa, CA, 95671. Tel: 916-985-8610, Ext 7781. p. 206

Turner, Alexis, Circ Supvr, Cragin Memorial Library, Eight Linwood Ave, Colchester, CT, 06415. Tel: 860-537-5752. p. 306

Turner, Ali, Div Mgr, Syst Serv, Hennepin County Library, 12601 Ridgedale Dr, Minnetonka, MN, 55305-1909. Tel: 612-543-8516. p. 1186

Turner, Amber, Mgr, Human Res, Johnson County Public Library, 49 E Monroe St, Franklin, IN, 46131. p. 686

Turner, Amy, Film, Theatre & Communications Librn, Head, Jones Film & Video Coll, Southern Methodist University, Hamon Arts Library, 6101 N Bishop Blvd, Dallas, TX, 75275. Tel: 214-768-1855. p. 2168

Turner, Andrea, Mgr, Spec Coll, Baylor University Libraries, Arts & Special Collections Research Center, Moody Memorial Library, 1312 S Third St, Waco, TX, 76798. Tel: 254-710-4278. p. 2252

Turner, Angela, Adult Serv, Clark County Public Library, 370 S Burns Ave, Winchester, KY, 40391-1876. Tel: 859-744-5661. p. 878

Turner, Angela, Dir, Clark County Public Library, 370 S Burns Ave, Winchester, KY, 40391-1876. Tel: 859-744-5661. p. 878

Turner, Ariel, Interim Dept Chair, Resource Management, Kennesaw State University Library System, 385 Cobb Ave NW, MD 1701, Kennesaw, GA, 30144. Tel: 470-578-6273. p. 483

Turner, Augusta, Dir, Town of Pelham Public Library, 530 Colonial Ave, Pelham, NY, 10803. Tel: 914-738-1234. p. 1616

Turner, Autumn, Librn, Georgia Department of Corrections, Office of Library Services, 650 Alston Rd, Mount Vernon, GA, 30445. Tel: 912-583-3600. p. 492

Turner, Bob, Librn, Harding School of Theology, 1000 Cherry Rd, Memphis, TN, 38117. Tel: 901-761-1354. p. 2112

Turner, Bonnie, Libr Mgr, Kansas City University, Dawson Library, 2901 St John's Blvd, Joplin, MO, 64804. Tel: 417-288-0642. p. 1256

Turner, Brad, Asst Dir, Southeast Steuben County Library, 300 Nasser Civic Center Plaza, Ste 101, Corning, NY, 14830. Tel: 607-936-3713, Ext 208. p. 1522

Turner, Breann, Librn, La Plata Public Library, 103 E Moore St, La Plata, MO, 63549. Tel: 660-332-4945. p. 1259

Turner, Carmanita, Colls Librn, Wofford College, 429 N Church St, Spartanburg, SC, 29303-3663. Tel: 864-597-4300. p. 2070

Turner, Carrie, Acq, Harrison County Library System, 12135 Old Hwy 49, Gulfport, MS, 39501. Tel: 228-539-0110. p. 1217

Turner, Colette, Dir, Vidor Public Library, 440 E Bolivar St, Vidor, TX, 77662. Tel: 409-769-7148. p. 2252

Turner, Geraly, Ch Serv, Jacksonville Public Library, 526 E Commerce St, Jacksonville, TX, 75766. Tel: 903-586-7664. p. 2203

Turner, Hannah, Asst Prof, University of British Columbia, The Irving K Barber Learning Ctr, 1961 E Mall, Ste 470, Vancouver, BC, V6T 1Z1, CANADA. Tel: 604-822-2404. p. 2795

Turner, Heidi, Libr Dir, Kirklin Public Library, 115 N Main St, Kirklin, IN, 46050. Tel: 765-279-8308. p. 699

Turner, Jamie, Br Librn, Stockton-San Joaquin County Public Library, Tracy Branch, 20 E Eaton Ave, Tracy, CA, 95376. p. 250

Turner, Jane, Univ Archivist, University of Victoria Libraries, McPherson Library, PO Box 1800, Victoria, BC, V8W 3H5, CANADA. Tel: 250-721-8211. p. 2583

Turner, Joanne, Ad, Helen Hall Library, 100 W Walker, League City, TX, 77573-3899. Tel: 281-554-1103. p. 2210

Turner, June, Librn, Palo Verde College Library, One College Dr, Blythe, CA, 92225. Tel: 760-921-5518. p. 124

Turner, Kathleen, Evening Supvr, Outreach Librn, Drexel University Libraries, Hahnemann Library, 245 N 15th St MS 449, Philadelphia, PA, 19102-1192. p. 1976

Turner, Kim, Dir, Sammy Brown Library, 319 S Market St, Carthage, TX, 75633. Tel: 903-693-6741. p. 2154

Turner, Kris, Tech Serv, Centerville-Center Township Public Library, 126 E Main St, Centerville, IN, 47330-1206. Tel: 765-855-5223. p. 674

Turner, Lauren, Libr Asst II, Nashville State Technical Community College, 120 White Bridge Rd, Nashville, TN, 37209-4515. Tel: 615-353-3552. p. 2120

Turner, Leah, Adult Serv, Franklin County Public Library District, 919 Main St, Brookville, IN, 47012. Tel: 765-647-4031. p. 673

Turner, Lynne, Librn, Blue Rapids Public Library, 14 Public Sq, Blue Rapids, KS, 66411. Tel: 785-363-7709. p. 799

Turner, Marcellus, City Librn, Exec Dir, The Seattle Public Library, 1000 Fourth Ave, Seattle, WA, 98104-1109. Tel: 206-386-4636. p. 2379

Turner, Marilynn, Libr Operations Mgr, Confederated Tribes of the Colville Reservation, 12 Lakes Ave, Nespelem, WA, 99155. Tel: 509-634-2791. p. 2371

Turner, Marilynn, Libr Operations Mgr, Confederated Tribes of the Colville Reservation, Inchelium Library, 12 Community Loop Rd, Inchelium, WA, 99138. Tel: 509-634-2791. p. 2372

Turner, Marilynn, Libr Operations Mgr, Confederated Tribes of the Colville Reservation, Keller Library, 11673 S Hwy 21, Keller, WA, 99140. Tel: 509-634-2791. p. 2372

Tyndall, Susan, Librn, Nebraska Indian Community College, 1111 Hwy 75, Macy, NE, 68039. Tel: 402-241-5964. p. 1324
Tyner, James, Ad, Fresno County Public Library, 2420 Mariposa St, Fresno, CA, 93721. Tel: 559-600-7323. p. 145
Tyner, Ross, Dir, Libr Serv, Okanagan College Library, 1000 KLO Rd, Kelowna, BC, V1Y 4X8, CANADA. Tel: 250-762-5445, Ext 4665. p. 2568
Tyner, Theresa, Libr Dir, Crawfordsville District Public Library, 205 S Washington St, Crawfordsville, IN, 47933. Tel: 765-362-2242. p. 677
Tyree, Janet, Dir, Springdale Free Public Library, 331 School St, Springdale, PA, 15144. Tel: 724-274-9729. p. 2009
TyRee, Jenks, Instruction Coordr, Ref Librn, Montana State University-Billings Library, 1500 University Dr, Billings, MT, 59101. Tel: 406-657-1654. p. 1288
Tyree, Kathleen, Br Mgr, Rutherford County Library System, Technology Engagement Center, 306 Minerva Dr, Murfreesboro, TN, 37130. Tel: 615-225-8312. p. 2118
Tyree, Theresa, Librn, Prescott/Nevada County Library & Educational Facility, 121 W Main St, Prescott, AR, 71857. Tel: 870-887-5846. p. 108
Tyrell, Meg, Colls Librn, Liaison Librn, Mohawk College Library, 135 Fennell Ave W, Hamilton, ON, L9C 0E5, CANADA. Tel: 905-575-1212, Ext 3129. p. 2647
Tysdal, Bobbie Jo, Dir, Anna Miller Museum Library, 401 Delaware Ave, Newcastle, WY, 82701. Tel: 307-746-4188. p. 2497
Tyson, Bryan, Head, Tech Serv, Bob Jones University, 1700 Wade Hampton Blvd, Greenville, SC, 29614. Tel: 864-370-1800, Ext 6030. p. 2060
Tyson, Christy, Librn, St Thomas Health Services Library, 2000 Church St, Nashville, TN, 37236. Tel: 615-222-3051, 615-284-5373. p. 2120
Tyson, Roberta, Coordr, Tech Serv, Resource Sharing Coord, Horry-Georgetown Technical College, 2050 Hwy 501 E, Conway, SC, 29526-9521. Tel: 843-349-5396. p. 2057
Tyson, Sharon, Asst Br Mgr, Bossier Parish Libraries, Henry L Aulds Memorial Branch, 3950 Wayne Ave, Bossier City, LA, 71112. Tel: 318-742-2337. p. 886
Tyszka, Carrie, Head, Ref & Adult Serv, Berlin-Peck Memorial Library, 234 Kensington Rd, Berlin, CT, 06037. Tel: 860-828-7120. p. 302
Tyus, Emma, Br Mgr, Autauga Prattville Public Library, Marbury Community, 205 County Rd 20 E, Marbury, AL, 36051. Tel: 205-755-8575. p. 33
Tzambazakis, Mary T, Chief Admin Officer, Hartford Public Library, 500 Main St, Hartford, CT, 06103. Tel: 860-695-6312. p. 317
Tzanova, Stefka, Sci Librn, York College Library, 94-20 Guy R Brewer Blvd, Jamaica, NY, 11451. Tel: 718-262-2037. p. 1556
Uccellani, Claudia, Ch, Katonah Village Library, 26 Bedford Rd, Katonah, NY, 10536-2121. Tel: 914-232-3508. p. 1559
Uchida, Tammy, Circ Supvr, Bellarmine University, 2001 Newburg Rd, Louisville, KY, 40205-0671. Tel: 502-272-8308. p. 864
Uchimura, Elizabeth, Music & Digital Serv Librn, Spec Coll Librn, Florida State University Libraries, Warren D Allen Music Library, Housewright Music Bldg, 122 N Copeland St, Tallahassee, FL, 32306. Tel: 850-644-7064. p. 447
Uden, Ryann, Dep Dir, Indian Trails Public Library District, 355 S Schoenbeck Rd, Wheeling, IL, 60090. Tel: 847-459-4100. p. 662
Udstad, Kimberly, Asst Librn, Oswayo Valley Memorial Library, 103 N Pleasant St, Shinglehouse, PA, 16748. Tel: 814-697-6691. p. 2007
Udstrand, Kimberly, Dir, Lostant Community Library, 102 W Third St, Lostant, IL, 61334. Tel: 815-368-3530. p. 611
Uehlein, Sara, Librn, King & Spalding, 1700 Pennsylvania Ave NW, Ste 200, Washington, DC, 20006-4706. Tel: 202-737-0500. p. 370
Uffelman, Molly, Children's Mgr, Security Public Library, 715 Aspen Dr, Security, CO, 80911-1807. Tel: 719-391-3197. p. 295
Ugaldea, Ben, Librn, Spokane Falls Community College Library, 3410 W Whistalks Way, Spokane, WA, 99224-5204. Tel: 509-533-3806. p. 2385
Ugboma, Anayo, Mr, Dir, Libr Serv, Strathmore Municipal Library, 85 Lakeside Blvd, Strathmore, AB, T1P 1A1, CANADA. Tel: 403-934-5440. p. 2556
Uhing, Austin, Libr Tech, Department of Veteran Affairs, 500 E Veterans St, Tomah, WI, 54660. Tel: 608-372-3971, Ext 66267. p. 2481
Uhl, Heather, Acq, Cat, Circ, Everett Community College, 2000 Tower St, Everett, WA, 98201-1352. Tel: 425-388-9139. p. 2363
Uhler, Linda, Mgr, Ch Serv, Tuscarawas County Public Library, 121 Fair Ave NW, New Philadelphia, OH, 44663-2600. Tel: 330-364-4474. p. 1807
Uhlhorn, Melissa, Libr Dir, Schertz Public Library, 798 Schertz Pkwy, Schertz, TX, 78154. Tel: 210-619-1700. p. 2242
Uko, Kenneth, Br Mgr, Jersey City Free Public Library, Earl A Morgan Branch, 1841 Kennedy Blvd, Jersey City, NJ, 07305. Tel: 201-547-4553. p. 1409
Ulaszek, Lisel, Youth Serv Mgr, Batavia Public Library District, Ten S Batavia Ave, Batavia, IL, 60510-2793. Tel: 630-879-1393. p. 540
Ulch, Rosemary, Br Asst, Cumberland Public Libraries, River Hebert Library, 2730 Barronsfield Rd, River Hebert, NS, B0L 1G0, CANADA. Tel: 902-251-2324. p. 2615
Ulland, Haley, City Librn, Park River Public Library, 605 Sixth St W, Park River, ND, 58270. Tel: 701-284-6116. p. 1739
Ullman, Christopher, Head Librn, Pub Serv, Moody Bible Institute, 820 N LaSalle Blvd, Chicago, IL, 60610-3284. Tel: 312-329-4136. p. 564
Ullman, Julie, Mgr, Washoe County Library System, South Valleys Library, 15650A Wedge Pkwy, Reno, NV, 89511. Tel: 775-851-5190. p. 1350
Ulloa, Charlotte, Coll Archivist, Hope College, Archives & Special Collections, Van Wylen Library, 53 Graves Pl, Holland, MI, 49423-3513. Tel: 616-395-7798. p. 1115
Ulloha, Hannah, Librn, Suzette Penton Polk City Community Library, 215 S Bougainvillea Ave, Polk City, FL, 33868. Tel: 863-984-4340. p. 438
Ullrich, Dieter, Head, Spec Coll & Archives, Morehead State University, 150 University Blvd, Morehead, KY, 40351. Tel: 606-783-2200. p. 869
Ullrich, Jennifer, Principal Librn, Santa Monica Public Library, Ocean Park, 2601 Main St, Santa Monica, CA, 90405. Tel: 310-458-8683. p. 244
Ullrich, Melanie, Circ, Johnsburg Public Library District, 3000 N Johnsburg Rd, Johnsburg, IL, 60051. Tel: 815-344-0077. p. 603
Ullucci, Beth, Libr Dir, Jesse M Smith Memorial Library, 100 Tinkham Lane, Harrisville, RI, 02830. Tel: 401-710-7800. p. 2032
Ulmer, Katherine, Supvr, Yakima Valley Libraries, Naches Library, 303 Naches Ave, Naches, WA, 98937. Tel: 509-653-2005. p. 2395
Ulmer, Mary Jane, Asst Librn, Beaver Area Memorial Library, 100 College Ave, Beaver, PA, 15009-2794. Tel: 724-775-1132. p. 1908
Ulmer, Patricia, Dir, Geisinger Health System, 100 N Academy Ave, Danville, PA, 17822-2101. Tel: 570-214-7343. p. 1926
Umansky, Olga, Librn & Archivist, Boston Psychoanalytic Society & Institute, Inc, 141 Herrick Rd, 1st Flr, Newton, MA, 02459. Tel: 617-266-0953, Ext 104. p. 1039
Umba, Marc Mambuku, Librn, Bibliothèque de la Compagnie de Jésus, Collège Jean-de-Brebeuf, Local B4-25, 3200 Chemin Côte-Sainte-Catherine, Montreal, QC, H3T 1C1, CANADA. Tel: 514-342-9342, Ext 5466. p. 2717
Umberger, Sheila, Dir, Roanoke Public Libraries, 706 S Jefferson St, Roanoke, VA, 24016-5191. Tel: 540-853-2473. p. 2345
Umberson, Debra, Dir, University of Texas Libraries, Population Research Center Library, 305 E 23rd St, Stop G1800, Austin, TX, 78712-1699. Tel: 512-471-5514. p. 2143
Umbreit, Hilary, Info Serv Librn, Sharon Public Library, 11 N Main St, Sharon, MA, 02067-1299. Tel: 781-784-1578. p. 1052
Umland, Karla, Asst Dir, Stonington Free Library, 20 High St, Stonington, CT, 06378. Tel: 860-535-0658. p. 339
Umpleby, Elisabeth, Head, Tech Serv, University of Connecticut, Thomas J Meskill Law Library, 39 Elizabeth St, Hartford, CT, 06105. Tel: 860-570-5007. p. 340
Umstead, Wes, Br Mgr, Chippewa River District Library, Fremont Township Community Library, 7959 South Winn Rd, Winn, MI, 48896. Tel: 989-866-2550. p. 1135
Unaeze, Felix, Univ Librn, Savannah State University, 2200 Tompkins Rd, Savannah, GA, 31404. Tel: 912-358-4324. p. 496
Underhill, Christina, Libr Dir, Englewood Public Library, 1000 Englewood Pkwy, Englewood, CO, 80110. Tel: 303-762-2550. p. 279
Underhill, Lisa, Asst Dir, Tech Serv, Rhode Island College, 600 Mt Pleasant Ave, Providence, RI, 02908-1924. p. 2039
Underhill, Michelle, State Librn, State Library of North Carolina, 109 E Jones St, Raleigh, NC, 27601. Tel: 919-814-6780. p. 1710
Underhill, Tracy, Dir, Crawford County Public Library, 203 Indiana Ave, English, IN, 47118. Tel: 812-338-2606. p. 681
Underly, Jill K, State Superintendent, Wisconsin Department of Public Instruction, 125 S Webster St, Madison, WI, 53707. Tel: 608-266-2205. p. 2452
Underwood, Alicia, Librn, East Mississippi Regional Library System, Enterprise Public, 500 River Rd, Enterprise, MS, 39330. Tel: 601-659-3564. p. 1231
Underwood, Anna, Libr Mgr, Wembley Public Library, 9719-99 Ave, Wembley, AB, T0H 3S0, CANADA. Tel: 780-766-3553. p. 2559
Underwood, Beth, Ref Serv, United States Army, Casey Memorial Library, 72nd St & 761st Tank Battalion, Bldg 3202, Fort Hood, TX, 76544-5024. Tel: 254-287-0025. p. 2178
Underwood, Breanna, Commun Libr Rep, Mohave County Library District, South Mohave Valley Community Library, 5744 S Hwy 95, Ste 102, Fort Mohave, AZ, 86426. Tel: 928-768-1151. p. 65
Underwood, Ellen, Dir, Mitchell Community Public Library, 804 Main St, Mitchell, IN, 47446. Tel: 812-849-2412. p. 707
Underwood, Grahm, ILL Supvr, Mississippi Valley Library District, 408 W Main St, Collinsville, IL, 62234. Tel: 618-344-1112. p. 573
Underwood, Jack, Librn, Spartanburg County Public Libraries, Chesnee Library, 100 Pickens Ave, Chesnee, SC, 29323. Tel: 864-461-2423. p. 2070
Underwood, Jane, Columbus Satellite Librn, US Court of Appeals for the Sixth Circuit Library, 540 Potter Stewart US Courthouse, 100 E Fifth St, Cincinnati, OH, 45202-3911. Tel: 614-719-3180. p. 1764
Underwood, Jonna, Coordr, Golden Plains Library Federation, 100 W Laurel Ave, Plentywood, MT, 59254. Tel: 406-765-3463. p. 1301
Underwood, Jonna, Dir, Sheridan County Library, 100 W Laurel Ave, Plentywood, MT, 59254. Tel: 406-765-3510. p. 1301
Underwood, Kim, Libr Mgr, Alamogordo Public Library, 920 Oregon Ave, Alamogordo, NM, 88310. Tel: 575-439-4140. p. 1459
Underwood, Leann, Adult Serv, Lynchburg Public Library, 2315 Memorial Ave, Lynchburg, VA, 24501. Tel: 434-455-6311. p. 2330

Underwood, Patty, Br Mgr, Moore County Library, Pinebluff Branch, 305 E Baltimore Ave, Pinebluff, NC, 28373-8903. Tel: 910-281-3004. p. 1677
Underwood, Sandra, Dir, Carl Elliott Regional Library System, 98 E 18th St, Jasper, AL, 35501. Tel: 205-221-2584. p. 23
Underwood, Sandra, Dir, Jasper Public Library, 98 18th St E, Jasper, AL, 35501. Tel: 205-221-2584, 205-221-8512. p. 23
Underwood, Sandy, Libr Dir, Converse Public Library, 601 S Seguin Rd, Converse, TX, 78109. Tel: 210-659-4160. p. 2159
Underwood, Stephen, Adminr, Info Tech, Carl Elliott Regional Library System, 98 E 18th St, Jasper, AL, 35501. Tel: 205-221-2584. p. 23
Underwood, Ted, Prof, University of Illinois at Urbana-Champaign, Library & Information Science Bldg, 501 E Daniel St, Champaign, IL, 61820-6211. Tel: 217-333-3280. p. 2784
Unger, Debra, Br Supvr, Western Manitoba Regional Library, Neepawa Branch, 280 Davidson St, Neepawa, MB, R0J 1H0, CANADA. Tel: 204-476-5648. p. 2586
Unger, Lesley, Libr Dir, Springvale Public Library, 443 Main St, Springvale, ME, 04083. Tel: 207-324-4624. p. 942
Unger Skinner, Laurie, Info & Reader Serv Mgr, Highland Park Public Library, 494 Laurel Ave, Highland Park, IL, 60035-2690. Tel: 847-432-0216. p. 599
Ungs, Kim, Dir, Hopkinton Public Library, 110 First St SE, Hopkinton, IA, 52237. Tel: 563-926-2514. p. 758
Unker, Christi, Sch Librn, Kentucky School for the Blind Library, 1867 Frankfort Ave, Louisville, KY, 40206. Tel: 502-897-1583, Ext 6301. p. 865
Unruh, Alicia, Circ Supvr, Pioneer Memorial Library, 375 W Fourth St, Colby, KS, 67701-2197. Tel: 785-460-4470. p. 802
Unsold, Doug, Asst Librn, Washington State Community College, 710 Colegate Dr, Marietta, OH, 45750. Tel: 740-568-1914. p. 1799
Unsworth, Alan, Dir, Academic Support, Dir, Res, Surry Community College, R Bldg, 630 S Main St, Dobson, NC, 27017. Tel: 336-386-3317. p. 1683
Unsworth, John M, Dean of Libr, Univ Librn, University of Virginia, 160 McCormick Rd, Charlottesville, VA, 22903. Tel: 434-924-3021. p. 2310
Unsworth, Kelly, Dir, Merrimac Public Library, 86 W Main St, Merrimac, MA, 01860. Tel: 978-346-9441. p. 1034
Unterborn, Lee, Cat, Saint Mary's University, Sarita Kennedy East Law Library, One Camino Santa Maria, San Antonio, TX, 78228-8605. Tel: 210-436-3435. p. 2238
Unterbrink, Rikki, Youth Serv, Shelby County Libraries, 230 E North St, Sidney, OH, 45365-2785. Tel: 937-492-8354. p. 1820
Unterholzner, Dennis, Head, Pub Serv, Carthage College, 2001 Alford Park Dr, Kenosha, WI, 53140-1900. Tel: 262-551-5950. p. 2444
Unthank, Katie, Digital Design & Editorial Content Mgr, PAI Library, 1300 19th St NW, Ste 200, Washington, DC, 20036. Tel: 202-557-3400. p. 374
Upchurch, Inger, Br Mgr, Memphis Public Library, Cornelia Crenshaw Memorial Library, 531 Vance Ave, Memphis, TN, 38126-2116. Tel: 901-415-2765. p. 2113
Upchurch, Inger, Br Mgr, Memphis Public Library, Gaston Park Branch, 1040 S Third St, Memphis, TN, 38106-2002. Tel: 901-415-2769. p. 2113
Upchurch, Rebecca, ILL, Wilson County Public Libraries, 1103 Fourth St, Floresville, TX, 78114. Tel: 830-393-7361. p. 2177
Upole, Susan, Dir, Delmar Public Library, 101 N Bi-State Blvd, Delmar, DE, 19940. Tel: 302-846-9894. p. 352
Upshaw, Megan, Dir, Caroline Library, Inc, 17202 Richmond Tpk, Milford, VA, 22514. Tel: 804-633-5455. p. 2333
Upshaw, Suzanne, Br Mgr, Jefferson Parish Library, Old Metairie, 2350 Metairie Rd, Metairie, LA, 70001. Tel: 504-838-4353. p. 897
Uptigrove, Donna, Dep Dir, Historic Arkansas Museum Library, 200 E Third St, Little Rock, AR, 72201-1608. Tel: 501-324-9701. p. 101
Upton, Becky, Asst Dir, Friona Public Library, 109 W Seventh St, Friona, TX, 79035-2548. Tel: 806-250-3200. p. 2182
Upton, Cody, Exec Dir, American Academy of Arts & Letters Library, 633 W 155th St, New York, NY, 10032. Tel: 212-368-5900. p. 1578
Upton, Connie, Supvr, Olin Corp, 1186 Old Lower River Rd, Charleston, TN, 37310. Tel: 423-336-4347. p. 2091
Urbain, Carole, Dir, Academic Affairs, McGill University Libraries, McLennan Library Bldg, 3459 McTavish St, Montreal, QC, H3A 0C9, CANADA. Tel: 514-398-5725. p. 2726
Urban, Brodie, Mr, Librn, State Correctional Institution, 209 Institution Dr, Houtzdale, PA, 16698. Tel: 814-378-1000, Ext 1556. p. 1944
Urban, Catherine, Acq & Cat, Amarillo Public Library, 413 E Fourth Ave, Amarillo, TX, 79101. Tel: 806-378-3054. p. 2134
Urban, Lori, Dir, Heyworth Public Library District, 119 E Main St, Heyworth, IL, 61745. Tel: 309-473-2313. p. 599
Urban, Oksana, Libr Dir, Warren Public Library, One City Sq, Ste 100, Warren, MI, 48093-2396. Tel: 586-751-0770. p. 1157
Urban, Rhonda, Library Contact, Monroe Clinic, 515 22nd Ave, Monroe, WI, 53566. Tel: 608-324-1090. p. 2462
Urban, Shannon, Br Mgr, Kenosha Public Library, 7979 38th Ave, Kenosha, WI, 53142. Tel: 262-564-6100. p. 2444
Urban, Susan, Exec Dir, Mid-America Law Library Consortium, 800 N Harvey Ave, Oklahoma City, OK, 73102. Tel: 405-208-5393. p. 2773
Urban, Tracey, Dir, Moravian College & Moravian Theological Seminary, 1200 Main St, Bethlehem, PA, 18018. Tel: 610-625-7894. p. 1912
Urbanczyk, Peggy, Librn, City County Library of Munday, 131 S Munday Ave, Munday, TX, 76371. Tel: 940-422-4877. p. 2221
Urbanek, Laura, Dir, Roland Public Library, 221 N Main St, Roland, IA, 50236. Tel: 515-388-4086. p. 779
Urbaniak, Brooke, ILL/Circ Supvr, North Idaho College Library, 1000 W Garden Ave, Coeur d'Alene, ID, 83814-2199. Tel: 208-769-3269. p. 520
Urbano, Christiana, Makerspace Coord, Concord Free Public Library, 129 Main St, Concord, MA, 01742. Tel: 978-318-3384. p. 1012
Urbanski, Denise, Research Librn, Oregon National Primate Research Center, 505 NW 185th Ave, Beaverton, OR, 97006. Tel: 503-346-5044. p. 1873
Urbashich, Mary Ann, Sr Assoc Dir, Alzheimer's Association, 225 N Michigan Ave, 17th Flr, Chicago, IL, 60601. Tel: 312-335-5199. p. 554
Urbick, Tracey, Ref & Instruction Librn, Colorado Mountain College, 1275 Crawford Ave, Steamboat Springs, CO, 80487. Tel: 970-870-4451. p. 295
Urbiel, Martha, Dir, Westwood Public Library, 49 Park Ave, Westwood, NJ, 07675. Tel: 201-664-0583. p. 1454
Urbizagastegui, Shelley, Asst Prof, Info Literacy Librn, University of La Verne, 2040 Third St, La Verne, CA, 91750. Tel: 909-593-3511, Ext 4305. p. 155
Urcinas, Amanda, Children's Programmer, Harwinton Public Library, 80 Bentley Dr, Harwinton, CT, 06791. Tel: 860-485-9113. p. 319
Urena, Silvia, IT Mgr, San Mateo County Library, Library Administration, 125 Lessingia Ct, San Mateo, CA, 94402-4000. Tel: 650-312-5524. p. 235
Urie, Kristin, Librn, Albany Town Library, 530 Main St, Albany, VT, 05820. Tel: 802-755-6107. p. 2277
Urie, Kristin, Librn, John Woodruff Simpson Memorial Library, 1972 E Craftsbury Rd, East Craftsbury, VT, 05826. Tel: 802-586-9692. p. 2283
Urquhart, Connie, Libr Dir, Camas Public Library, 625 NE Fourth Ave, Camas, WA, 98607. Tel: 360-834-4692. p. 2360
Urquiaga, Laurie, Assoc Dir, Access Serv, Brigham Young University, Howard W Hunter Law Library, 256 JRCB, Provo, UT, 84602-8000. Tel: 801-422-3593. p. 2269
Ursery, Sheila, Outreach Coordr, Three Rivers College Library, 2080 Three Rivers Blvd, Poplar Bluff, MO, 63901. Tel: 573-840-9654. p. 1266
Ursprung, Amber, Libr Dir, Liberty Municipal Library, 1710 Sam Houston Ave, Liberty, TX, 77575-4741. Tel: 936-336-8901. p. 2211
Urton, Ellen, Dir, Res & Instruction Serv, University of Arkansas Libraries, 365 N McIlroy Ave, Fayetteville, AR, 72701-4002. Tel: 479-575-4101. p. 95
Urtz, Heather, Libr Dir, Village Library of Cooperstown, 22 Main St, Cooperstown, NY, 13326. Tel: 607-547-8344. p. 1522
Uscio, Joseph, Head, Ref, North Providence Union Free Library, 1810 Mineral Spring Ave, North Providence, RI, 02904. Tel: 401-353-5600. p. 2036
Usher, Brian, Info Syst Coordr, Auburn Public Library, 49 Spring St, Auburn, ME, 04210. Tel: 207-333-6640. p. 913
Usina, Phyllis, Librn, Santa Rosa Junior College, 1501 Mendocino Ave, Santa Rosa, CA, 95401. Tel: 707-527-4547. p. 245
Uskokovich, Sharon, Librn, Florida State College at Jacksonville, 3939 Roosevelt Blvd, C-100, Jacksonville, FL, 32205. Tel: 904-381-3522. p. 411
Ussach, Ivan, Librn, Warwick Free Public Library, Four Hotel Rd, Warwick, MA, 01378-9311. Tel: 978-544-7866. p. 1062
Ussery, Christine, Libr Dir, Providence Presbyterian Church Library, 5497 Providence Rd, Virginia Beach, VA, 23464. Tel: 757-420-6159. p. 2349
Ussery, Regina, Librn, Hardee County Public Library, 315 N Sixth Ave, Wauchula, FL, 33873. Tel: 863-773-6438. p. 453
Utchel, Christine, Head, Ref Serv, Bronxville Public Library, 201 Pondfield Rd, Bronxville, NY, 10708. Tel: 914-337-7680. p. 1500
Utley, Lance, Database Adminr, Librn, National Radio Astronomy Observatory Library, 520 Edgemont Rd, Charlottesville, VA, 22903-2475. Tel: 434-296-0215. p. 2309
Utrecht, Rachel, Tech Serv Librn, William Woods University, One University Ave, Fulton, MO, 65251. p. 1246
Utschig, Katie, Coordr, Southeastern Wisconsin Information Technology Exchange, Inc, 6801 N Yates Rd, Milwaukee, WI, 53217-3985. Tel: 414-351-2423. p. 2777
Uttangi-Matsos, Meg, Br Mgr, Hamilton Public Library, Dundas Branch, 18 Ogilvie St, Dundas, ON, L9H 2S2, CANADA. Tel: 905-627-3507, Ext 1404. p. 2645
Uttangi-Matsos, Meg, Br Mgr, Hamilton Public Library, Greensville, 59 Kirby Ave, Unit 5, Greensville, ON, L9H 4H6, CANADA. Tel: 905-627-4951. p. 2645
Uttaro, Patricia, Regional Dir, Penfield Public Library, 1985 Baird Rd, Penfield, NY, 14526. Tel: 585-340-8720. p. 1616
Uttaro, Patricia, Dir, Monroe County Library System, 115 South Ave, Rochester, NY, 14604. Tel: 585-428-8180. p. 1629
Uttaro, Patricia, Dir, Rochester Public Library, 115 South Ave, Rochester, NY, 14604-1896. Tel: 585-428-8045. p. 1630
Utter, Susan, Br Mgr, Cadillac-Wexford Public Library, Buckley Branch, 305 S First St, Buckley, MI, 49620-9526. Tel: 231-269-3325, Ext 3020. p. 1088

Utz, Bonnie, Dir, Madison County Library, Inc, 402 N Main St, Madison, VA, 22727. Tel: 540-948-4720. p. 2331

Utz, Joy, Asst Dir, Acq, Free Library of Springfield Township, 8900 Hawthorne Lane, Wyndmoor, PA, 19038. Tel: 215-836-5300. p. 2024

Utz, Vinnie, Head, Circ, Grand Valley Public Library, One N School St, Orwell, OH, 44076. Tel: 440-437-6545. p. 1811

Uyengco-Harooch, Myrna Y, Med Librn, White Memorial Medical Center, North Bldg, Basement, 1720 Cesar E Chavez Ave, Los Angeles, CA, 90033. Tel: 323-260-5715. p. 170

Vaala-Olsen, Laurie, Dir, Marin County Law Library, 20 N San Pedro Rd, Ste 2007, San Rafael, CA, 94903. Tel: 415-472-3733. p. 237

Vaca, Arielle, Librn, Halton County Law Association, 491 Steeles Ave E, Milton, ON, L9T 1Y7, CANADA. Tel: 905-878-1272. p. 2658

Vaca, Betsy, Outreach Librn, Cabrillo College, 6500 Soquel Dr, Aptos, CA, 95003-3198. Tel: 831-479-6473. p. 117

Vacca, Maurice, Evening Supvr, William Paterson University, 300 Pompton Rd, Wayne, NJ, 07470. Tel: 973-720-3181. p. 1452

Vaccarelli, Michele, Libr Dir, Oyster Bay-East Norwich Public Library, 89 E Main St, Oyster Bay, NY, 11771. Tel: 516-922-1212. p. 1614

Vaccaro, Rachel, Br Mgr, Tangipahoa Parish Library, Kentwood Branch, 101 Ave F, Kentwood, LA, 70444. Tel: 985-229-3596. p. 881

Vacek, Shelie, Assoc Librn, University of South Dakota, Wegner Health Sciences Library, Sanford School of Medicine, 1400 W 22nd St, Ste 100, Sioux Falls, SD, 57105. Tel: 605-357-1319. p. 2084

Vacha, Victoria, Dir, Howells Public Library, 128 N Third St, Howells, NE, 68641. Tel: 402-986-1210. p. 1319

Vachon Hanlon, Nicole, Libr Dir, Chittenden Public Library, 223 Chittenden Rd, Chittenden, VT, 05737. Tel: 802-773-3531. p. 2282

Vachon, Sandrine, Librn, Universite du Quebec a Rimouski - Service de la bibliotheque, 300 Allee des Ursulines, Rimouski, QC, G5L 3A1, CANADA. Tel: 418-723-1986, Ext 1481. p. 2732

Vachon, Tyler, Asst Dir, Whitman Public Library, 100 Webster St, Whitman, MA, 02382. Tel: 781-447-7613. p. 1069

Vadakin, Teresa, Head, Adult Serv, Tompkins County Public Library, 101 E Green St, Ithaca, NY, 14850-5613. Tel: 607-272-4557, Ext 272. p. 1553

Vadney, Kelly, Dir, Watervliet Public Library, 1501 Broadway, Watervliet, NY, 12189-2895. Tel: 518-274-4471. p. 1660

Vagani, Elizabeth, Br Mgr, San Diego County Library, El Cajon Branch, 201 E Douglas, El Cajon, CA, 92020. Tel: 619-588-3708. p. 217

Vagenas, Vicky, Library Budget & Planning Analyst, St John's University Library, St Augustine Hall, 8000 Utopia Pkwy, Jamaica, NY, 11439. Tel: 718-990-6714. p. 1556

Vagt, Brian, Libr Dir, Glenwood-Lynwood Public Library District, 19901 Stony Island Ave, Lynwood, IL, 60411. Tel: 708-758-0090. p. 611

Vaias, Karen, Supv Librn, Ref, Bernards Township Library, 32 S Maple Ave, Basking Ridge, NJ, 07920-1216. Tel: 908-204-3031. p. 1388

Vail, Deana, Library Contact, First Congregational Church Library, 640 Millsboro Rd, Mansfield, OH, 44903. Tel: 419-756-3046. p. 1798

Vaillancourt, Chris, Med Librn & Coordr Med Educ, McLean Hospital, 115 Mill St, Mail Stop 203, Belmont, MA, 02478. Tel: 617-855-2460. p. 988

Vaillancourt, Chris, Librn, New England Baptist Hospital, 125 Parker Hill Ave, 3rd Flr, Boston, MA, 02120. Tel: 617-754-5155. p. 997

Vaillancourt, Nancy, Br Mgr, Owatonna Public Library, Blooming Prairie Branch, 138 Highway Ave S, Blooming Prairie, MN, 55917. Tel: 507-583-7750. p. 1192

Vajnar, Amy, Br Mgr, Mid-Continent Public Library, Oak Grove Branch, 2320 S Broadway St, Oak Grove, MO, 64075. Tel: 816-690-3213. p. 1251

Vajs, Kristin, Chief Librn, Board of Governors of The Federal Reserve System, Research Library, 20th & C St NW, MS 102, Washington, DC, 20551. Tel: 202-452-3333. p. 361

Valadez, Elva, Dir, Fort Stockton Public Library, 500 N Water St, Fort Stockton, TX, 79735. Tel: 432-336-3374. p. 2178

Valasek, Jana Marie, Exec Dir, Bibliotheque Commemorative Pettes, 276 chemin Knowlton, Lac-Brome, QC, J0E 1V0, CANADA. Tel: 450-243-6128. p. 2715

Valasek, Martha, Asst Librn, Kirkland Public Library, 513 W Main St, Kirkland, IL, 60146. Tel: 815-522-6260. p. 605

Valbuena, Andrew, Head, Ser, Chapman University, One University Dr, Orange, CA, 92866. Tel: 714-532-7756. p. 188

Valdes, Carrie, Libr Dir, Grand County Public Library, 257 E Center St, Moab, UT, 84532. Tel: 435-355-0930. p. 2266

Valdez, Arlene, Librn, Vallejo Naval & Historical Museum, 734 Marin St, Vallejo, CA, 94590. Tel: 707-643-0077. p. 255

Valdez, Jason, Collections Strategy Librn, Museum of Fine Arts, Houston, 1001 Bissonnet St, Houston, TX, 77005. Tel: 713-639-7325. p. 2197

Valdez, Karla, Sr Librn, Los Angeles Public Library System, Jefferson-Vassie D Wright Memorial Branch Library, 2211 W Jefferson Blvd, Los Angeles, CA, 90018-3741. Tel: 323-734-8573. p. 164

Valdez, Mark, Librn, Department of Human Services-Youth Corrections, 1406 W 17th St, Pueblo, CO, 81003. Tel: 719-546-4928. p. 293

Valdez, Raul, Asst Dir, Info Tech, Morgan State University, 1700 E Cold Spring Lane, Baltimore, MD, 21251. Tel: 443-885-3930. p. 956

Valdez, Ruth, Asst Admin, Robert J Kleberg Public Library, 220 N Fourth St, Kingsville, TX, 78363. Tel: 361-592-6381. p. 2206

Valdivia, Alex, Evening/Weekend Librn, University of La Verne, 2040 Third St, La Verne, CA, 91750. Tel: 909-593-3511, Ext 4305. p. 155

Valdivia, Marie, Libr Asst, Kansas Supreme Court, Kansas Judicial Ctr, 301 SW Tenth Ave, 1st Flr, Topeka, KS, 66612-1502. Tel: 785-368-7372. p. 839

Valdmanis, Karin, Libr Tech, Arcadis Corporate Library, 55 St Clair Ave W, 7th Flr, Toronto, ON, M4V 2Y7, CANADA. Tel: 416-596-1930, Ext 61332. p. 2686

Valdovinos, Louise, Ch, DeForest Area Public Library, 203 Library St, DeForest, WI, 53532. Tel: 608-846-5482. p. 2430

Valdry, Andree, Acq Librn, Compton College Library, 1111 E Artesia Blvd, Compton, CA, 90221. Tel: 310-900-1600, Ext 2179. p. 132

Vale, Gina, Dir, Philipsburg Public Library, 106 W Broadway St, Philipsburg, MT, 59858. Tel: 406-859-5030. p. 1301

Valencia, Ernesto, Head, Libr Tech, Northeastern University Libraries, 360 Huntington Ave, Boston, MA, 02115. Tel: 617-373-3398. p. 998

Valencia, Thomas, Library Contact, Lake Mead National Recreation Area Library, Alan Bible Visitor Ctr, Intersection of Hwys 93 & 166, Boulder City, NV, 89005. Tel: 702-293-8990. p. 1343

Valensisi, Josephine, Tech Serv Supvr, Glen Cove Public Library, Four Glen Cove Ave, Glen Cove, NY, 11542-2885. Tel: 516-676-2130. p. 1538

Valenta, Susan, Circ Supvr, Wyckoff Public Library, 200 Woodland Ave, Wyckoff, NJ, 07481. Tel: 201-891-4866. p. 1456

Valente, Elissa, YA Serv, The William K Sanford Town Library, 629 Albany Shaker Rd, Loudonville, NY, 12211-1196. Tel: 518-458-9274. p. 1565

Valente, Tara, Librn, United States Golf Association Museum & Archives, 77 Liberty Corner Rd, Liberty Corner, NJ, 07938. Tel: 908-326-1207. p. 1412

Valenti, Anthony, Board Pres, Southwest Florida Library Network, 13120 Westlinks Tr, Unit 3, Fort Myers, FL, 33913. Tel: 239-313-6338. p. 2763

Valenti, Anthony P, Fac Librn, Florida SouthWestern State College, 7505 Grand Lely Dr, Bldg G, Naples, FL, 34113. Tel: 239-732-3774. p. 427

Valenti Kroski, Ellyssa, Dir, Public Innovation & Engagement, New York Law Institute Library, 120 Broadway, Rm 932, New York, NY, 10271-0094. Tel: 212-732-8720. p. 1594

Valentin, Anidza, Dr, Dir, University of Puerto Rico, Alfonso Valdes Ave, 259 Blvd, Mayaguez, PR, 00681. Tel: 787-265-3810, 787-832-4040, Ext 2151, 787-832-4040, Ext 2155. p. 2511

Valentin, Christal, Head Librn, Greenville Public Library, 414 W Main St, Greenville, IL, 62246-1615. Tel: 618-664-3115. p. 596

Valentin, Ryan, Fac Serv Librn, University of Kentucky Libraries, Law Library, J David Rosenberg College of Law, 620 S Limestone St, Lexington, KY, 40506-0048. Tel: 859-257-8346. p. 863

Valentine, Allyson, Ref & Instruction Librn, Harrisburg Area Community College, 2010 Pennsylvania Ave, York, PA, 17404. Tel: 717-718-3256. p. 2026

Valentine, Hélène, Adminr, Societe de Genealogie de l'Outaouais Bibliotheque, 855, blvd de la Gappe, Gatineau, QC, J8T 8H9, CANADA. Tel: 819-243-0888. p. 2713

Valentine, Jeanne, Adult Serv, Plano Community Library District, 15 W North St, Plano, IL, 60545. Tel: 630-552-2009. p. 635

Valentine, Jennifer, Law Librn, Rackemann, Sawyer & Brewster Library, 160 Federal St, Boston, MA, 02110-1700. Tel: 617-542-2300. p. 999

Valentine, Kat, Chmn of Libr Board, Fairmount Community Library, 1310 W Allen Ave, Fort Worth, TX, 76110. Tel: 682-710-3223. p. 2179

Valentine, Laura, Ref Librn, Wilentz, Goldman & Spitzer, 90 Woodbridge Center Dr, Ste 900, Woodbridge, NJ, 07095. Tel: 732-855-6140. p. 1456

Valentine, Renee, Asst Librn, Madison Public Library, 827 N College Ave, Huntsville, AR, 72740. Tel: 479-738-2754. p. 99

Valentini-Ghosh, Lisa, Dir, Admin Serv, Dir, Info & Res, Financial Accounting Foundation Library, 401 Merritt 7, Norwalk, CT, 06856. Tel: 203-847-0700. p. 331

Valentino, Camille, Dir, Emerson Public Library, 20 Palisade Ave, Emerson, NJ, 07630. Tel: 201-261-5604. p. 1401

Valentino, Erin, Assoc Librn, Research, Instruction & Outreach, Bowdoin College Library, 3000 College Sta, Brunswick, ME, 04011-8421. Tel: 207-725-3749. p. 919

Valenzano, Danielle, YA Librn, Milford Public Library, 57 New Haven Ave, Milford, CT, 06460. Tel: 203-701-4554. p. 323

Valenzuela, Ross, Assoc Librn, Mount San Jacinto College, 300 Bldg, 1499 N State St, San Jacinto, CA, 92583-2399. Tel: 951-487-3455. p. 230

Valera, Janelle, Supvr, Ch Serv, Supvr, Youth Serv, DeSoto Public Library, 211 E Pleasant Run Rd, Ste C, DeSoto, TX, 75115. Tel: 972-230-9656. p. 2170

Valero, Lucinda, Asst Dir, Tech Serv, The University of Memphis, One N Front St, Memphis, TN, 38103. Tel: 901-678-2749. p. 2115

Valeska, Gary, Campus Library Coord, Seminole State College of Florida, 850 S SR 434, Altamonte Springs, FL, 32714. Tel: 407-404-6180. p. 383

Valetutti, Lynn, Dir, National Park College Library, 101 College Dr, Hot Springs, AR, 71913. Tel: 501-760-4101, 501-760-4110. p. 99

Valiente, Evelio, Res Tech, Southwest Texas Junior College, 207 Wildcat Dr, Del Rio, TX, 78840. Tel: 830-703-1563. p. 2169

Valine, Debbie, Assoc Dir, Rhinelander District Library, 106 N Stevens St, Rhinelander, WI, 54501-3193. Tel: 715-365-1070. p. 2472

Valinsky, Lisa, Librn, State Correctional Institution, 1111 Altamont Blvd, Frackville, PA, 17931. Tel: 570-874-4516. p. 1934

Valladares, Kerby, Br Mgr, Arlington County Department of Libraries, Plaza Library, 2100 Clarendon Blvd, Lobby, Arlington, VA, 22201. Tel: 703-228-3352. p. 2305

Vallario, Yahira, YA Librn, Derry Public Library, 64 E Broadway, Derry, NH, 03038-2412. Tel: 603-432-6140. p. 1361

Vallejo, Christina, Acq, ILL, Arcadia Public Library, 20 W Duarte Rd, Arcadia, CA, 91006. Tel: 626-821-5567. p. 117

Vallejos, James, Br Cluster Mgr, Denver Public Library, Ten W 14th Ave Pkwy, Denver, CO, 80204-2731. Tel: 720-865-1111. p. 275

Vallejos, Victoria, Mgr, County of Los Angeles Public Library, Castaic Library, 27971 Sloan Canyon Rd, Castaic, CA, 91384. Tel: 661-257-7410. p. 135

Valles, Jaye, Cat, Libr Spec I, Camp Verde Community Library, 130 N Black Bridge Rd, Camp Verde, AZ, 86322. Tel: 928-554-8388. p. 57

Valliant, Merrie, Tech Serv Librn, Johnson & Wales University, College of Business, 7150 Montview Blvd, Denver, CO, 80220. Tel: 303-256-9445. p. 276

Vallier, John, Head, Media Serv, University of Washington Libraries, Music, 113 Music Bldg, Box 353450, Seattle, WA, 98195-3450. Tel: 206-543-1159, 206-543-1168. p. 2382

Vallone, Richard, Co-Dir, New England Conservatory of Music, 255 St Butolph St, Boston, MA, 02115. Tel: 617-585-1247. p. 998

Valmestad, Liv, Art Librn, University of Manitoba Libraries, Architecture & Fine Arts Library, 206 Russell Bldg, 84 Curry Pl, Winnipeg, MB, R3T 2N2, CANADA. Tel: 204-474-9217. p. 2595

Valor, Candyce, Asst Libr Dir, Red Bank Public Library, 84 W Front St, Red Bank, NJ, 07701. Tel: 732-842-0690. p. 1439

Valosin, Christine, Curator, National Park Service, 648 Rte 32, Stillwater, NY, 12170. Tel: 518-670-2985. p. 1646

Valterza, Loren, Bibliog Instr, San Joaquin Delta College, 5151 Pacific Ave, Stockton, CA, 95207. Tel: 209-954-5154. p. 249

Valverde, Mary Ellen, Head, ILL & Doc Delivery, Stevens Institute of Technology, One Castle Point Terrace, Hoboken, NJ, 07030. Tel: 201-216-5408. p. 1408

Valyi-Hax, Kristen, Dir, Harper Woods Public Library, 19601 Harper, Harper Woods, MI, 48225. Tel: 313-343-2575. p. 1113

Vamanu, Iulian, Asst Prof, University of Iowa, 3087 Main Library, 125 W Washington St, Iowa City, IA, 52242-1420. Tel: 319-335-5714. p. 2785

Van Ackeren, Laurie, Dir, Mead Public Library, 316 S Vine St, Mead, NE, 68041. Tel: 402-624-6605. p. 1324

Van Ackeren, Laurie, Dir, Yutan Public Library, 410 First St, Yutan, NE, 68073. Tel: 402-625-2111. p. 1341

Van Allen, Sharon, Head Librn, Sharon Springs Public Library, 414 N Main St, Sharon Springs, KS, 67758. Tel: 785-852-4685. p. 836

Van Alstyne, Susan, Dir, Univ Librn, Centenary University, 400 Jefferson St, Hackettstown, NJ, 07840. Tel: 908-852-1400, Ext 2345. p. 1406

Van Arsdale, Katharine, Spec Coll Librn, Pacific Union College, One Angwin Ave, Angwin, CA, 94508-9705. Tel: 707-965-6244. p. 116

Van Auken, Kate, Dir, White Pine Library Cooperative, 429 N State St, Ste 207, Caro, MI, 48723. Tel: 989-793-7126. p. 2768

Van Bebber, Greg, Dir, Germantown Public Library, 51 N Plum St, Germantown, OH, 45327. Tel: 937-855-4001. p. 1788

Van Beek, Marie, Dir, Baxter Public Library, 202 E State St, Baxter, IA, 50028. Tel: 641-227-3934. p. 734

Van Berkom, Lindsay, Coordr, Access Serv, Scholars Archive Admin, University at Albany, State University of New York, Thomas E Dewey Graduate Library, 135 Western Ave, Albany, NY, 12222. Tel: 518-442-3517. p. 1484

van Beynen, Kaya, Head, Res & Instruction, University of South Florida Saint Petersburg, 140 Seventh Ave S, POY118, Saint Petersburg, FL, 33701-5016. Tel: 727-873-4626. p. 442

Van Buren, Heather, Dir, University of Kansas School of Medicine-Wichita, 1010 N Kansas, Wichita, KS, 67214-3199. Tel: 316-293-2629. p. 843

Van Buren, Jessica, Dep Dir, Maine State Law & Legislative Reference Library, 43 State House Sta, Augusta, ME, 04333-0043. Tel: 207-287-1600. p. 914

Van Camp, Amanda, Br Mgr, Saint Lucie County Library System, Port Saint Lucie Branch, 180 SW Prima Vista Blvd, Port Saint Lucie, FL, 34983. Tel: 772-871-5450. p. 405

Van Campen, Mike, Dep Dir, Loudoun County Public Library, Admin Offices, 102 North St NW, Ste A, Leesburg, VA, 20176. Tel: 703-777-0368. p. 2328

Van Cleave, Benita, Customer Serv Mgr, Salem Public Library, 28 E Main St, Salem, VA, 24153. Tel: 540-375-3089. p. 2347

Van Cleave, Keith, Br Mgr, United States Geological Survey Library, 345 Middlefield Rd, Bldg 15 (MS-955), Menlo Park, CA, 94025-3591. Tel: 303-236-1004. p. 176

Van Cleave, Keith, Supvr, Tech Info Spec, United States Geological Survey Library, Bldg 41, Rm 145, Denver Federal Ctr, Denver, CO, 80225. Tel: 303-236-1000. p. 277

Van Cleave, Kendra, Dept Chair, San Francisco State University, 1630 Holloway Ave, San Francisco, CA, 94132-4030. Tel: 415-405-0997. p. 228

Van Cleve, Laura, Libr Dir, Richton Park Public Library District, 22310 Latonia Lane, Richton Park, IL, 60471. Tel: 708-481-5333. p. 638

Van Cleve, Stewart, Assoc Dir, Augsburg University, 630 22nd Ave S, Minneapolis, MN, 55454. Tel: 612-330-1604. p. 1182

Van Dam, Dayna, Libr Mgr, Empress Municipal Library, Six Third Ave, Empress, AB, T0J 1E0, CANADA. Tel: 403-565-3936. p. 2539

Van Dam, Edwina, Ref (Info Servs), Floral Park Public Library, 17 Caroline Pl, Floral Park, NY, 11001. Tel: 516-326-6330. p. 1533

Van Dan, Rebecca, Asst Dir, Head, Youth Serv, Eager Free Public Library, 39 W Main St, Evansville, WI, 53536. Tel: 608-882-2260, 608-882-2275. p. 2434

Van Deman, Lori, Coll Serv Mgr, Cedar Mill Community Library, 1080 NW Saltzman Rd, Portland, OR, 97229-5603. Tel: 503-644-0043, Ext 127. p. 1891

Van Den Berg, Becky, Teen Serv Mgr, Pine River Public Library District, 395 Bayfield Center Dr, Bayfield, CO, 81122. Tel: 970-884-2222. p. 266

Van Den Bussche, Denise, Libr Asst, Pinawa Public Library, Vanier Rd, Pinawa, MB, R0E 1L0, CANADA. Tel: 204-753-2496. p. 2589

van den Hoogen, Suzanne, Univ Librn, Saint Mary's University, 923 Robie St, Halifax, NS, B3H 3C3, CANADA. Tel: 902-420-5532. p. 2621

van den Hoogen, Suzanne, Committee Chair, Council of Atlantic Academic Libraries (CAAL), 120 Western Pkwy, Ste 202, Bedford, NS, B4B 0V2, CANADA. Tel: 902-830-6467. p. 2778

Van der Heuvel, Heidi, Acq, Coordr, Cat, Ottawa Library, 105 S Hickory St, Ottawa, KS, 66067. Tel: 785-242-3080. p. 829

van der Heyden, Sarah, Creative Services Coord, Addison Public Library, Four Friendship Plaza, Addison, IL, 60101. Tel: 630-458-3354. p. 535

Van Der Linden, Heather, Librn, Faith Public & School Library, 204 W Fifth St, Faith, SD, 57626. Tel: 605-967-2262. p. 2076

van der Vaart, Lise, Libr Mgr, Smoky Lake Municipal Library, 5010-50 St, Smoky Lake, AB, T0A 3C0, CANADA. Tel: 780-656-4212. p. 2554

van der Valk, Andre, Co-Pres, Chatsworth Historical Society, 10385 Shadow Oak Dr, Chatsworth, CA, 91311. Tel: 818-882-5614. p. 129

van der Valk, Linda, Co-Pres, Chatsworth Historical Society, 10385 Shadow Oak Dr, Chatsworth, CA, 91311. Tel: 818-882-5614. p. 129

Van Deursen, Kathy, Libr Dir, Bartlett Public Library, 1313 US Rte 302, Bartlett, NH, 03812. Tel: 603-374-2755. p. 1354

Van Deusen, Anne, Children's Coordr, Huntington Memorial Library, 62 Chestnut St, Oneonta, NY, 13820-2498. Tel: 607-432-1980. p. 1611

Van Dine, Chelbi, Asst Dir, Salem Township Library, 3007 142nd Ave, Burnips, MI, 49314. Tel: 616-896-8170. p. 1088

Van Doren, Ali, Acad Librn, Lake Superior State University, 906 Ryan Ave, Sault Sainte Marie, MI, 49783. Tel: 906-635-2124. p. 1149

Van Dorp, Kathryn, Libr Mgr, Bow Island Municipal Library, 510 Centre St, Bow Island, AB, T0K 0G0, CANADA. Tel: 403-545-2828. p. 2524

Van Duinen, Rita, Br Mgr, Chatham County Public Libraries, Chatham Community Library, 197 NC Hwy 87 N, Pittsboro, NC, 27312. Tel: 919-545-8084. p. 1707

Van Duzer, Lee, Law Librn, Washington County Law Library, 111 NE Lincoln St, Hillsboro, OR, 97124. Tel: 503-846-8880. p. 1882

Van Duzer, Mary, Tech Serv Librn, Emmaus Public Library, 11 E Main St, Emmaus, PA, 18049. Tel: 610-965-9284. p. 1930

van Dyk, Jacqueline, Dir, Libr Serv, North Vancouver District Public Library, 1277 Lynn Valley Rd, North Vancouver, BC, V7J 0A2, CANADA. Tel: 604-984-0286, 604-990-5800. p. 2573

Van Dyk, Stephen H, Colls Librn, Smithsonian Libraries, Cooper-Hewitt, National Design Library, Two E 91st St, New York, DC, 10128. Tel: 212-849-8335. p. 375

Van Dyne, Heather, Ch, Coffeyville Public Library, 311 W Tenth St, Coffeyville, KS, 67337. Tel: 620-251-1370. p. 802

Van Dyne, Tracy, Actg Dir, Great Neck Library, 159 Bayview Ave, Great Neck, NY, 11023. Tel: 516-466-8055, Ext 212. p. 1540

Van Epps, Amy S, Dir of Science & Engineering Services, Harvard Library, Godfrey Lowell Cabot Science Library, Science Ctr, One Oxford St, Cambridge, MA, 02138. Tel: 617-495-5355. p. 1005

Van Erem, Rochelle, Metadata Specialist, Saint Norbert College, 400 Third St, De Pere, WI, 54115. Tel: 920-403-3270. p. 2430

Van Eyk, Krystal, Br Mgr, Riverside County Library System, Lake Elsinore Library, 600 W Graham, Lake Elsinore, CA, 92530. Tel: 951-674-4517. p. 202

Van Fleet, Heather, Br Librn, Genesee District Library, Mount Morris Library, 685 Van Buren Ave, Mount Morris, MI, 48458. Tel: 810-686-6120. p. 1106

Van Fleet, Tim, Br Mgr, Arundel Anne County Public Library, Odenton Library, 1325 Annapolis Rd, Odenton, MD, 21113. Tel: 410-222-6277. p. 950

Van Gieson, Kathy, Libr Dir, Frackville Free Public Library, 56 N Lehigh Ave, Frackville, PA, 17931-1424. Tel: 570-874-3382. p. 1934

Van Gorp, Lisa, Dir, Colfax Public Library, 25 W Division St, Colfax, IA, 50054. Tel: 515-674-3625. p. 741

Van Hannak, Jen, Libr Dir, Burrell Township Library, 321 Park Dr, Black Lick, PA, 15716. Tel: 724-248-7122. p. 1912

Van Haren, Barbara, Asst State Superintendent, Wisconsin Department of Public Instruction, 125 S Webster St, Madison, WI, 53707. Tel: 608-266-2205. p. 2452

Van Haren, Casey, Libr Dir, Prescott Valley Public Library, 7401 E Skoog Blvd, Prescott Valley, AZ, 86314. Tel: 928-759-3040. p. 75

Van Herreweghe, Christa, Dir, Kirkwood Public Library, 140 E Jefferson Ave, Kirkwood, MO, 63122. Tel: 314-821-5770, Ext 1016. p. 1259

Van Hoeck, Michele, Dean of Libr, Librn, The California Maritime Academy Library, 200 Maritime Academy Dr, Vallejo, CA, 94590. Tel: 707-654-1097. p. 255

Van Hook, Lorie, Youth Serv Librn, Dighton Public Library, 979 Somerset Ave, Dighton, MA, 02715. Tel: 508-669-6421. p. 1014

Van Horn, Ben, Ref & Instruction Librn, Mississippi College, 130 W College St, Clinton, MS, 39058. Tel: 601-925-7390. p. 1214

Van Horsen, Jackie, Ch Serv, Nobles County Library, 407 12th St, Worthington, MN, 56187. Tel: 507-295-5340. p. 1210

Van Houten, Mike, Co-Dir, Albion College, 602 E Cass St, Albion, MI, 49224-1879. Tel: 517-629-0293. p. 1076

Van Houtte, Philippe, Syst Librn, Arkansas Tech University, 305 West Q St, Russellville, AR, 72801. Tel: 479-498-6042. p. 108

Van Hoy, Holly, Ch, Alamosa Public Library, 300 Hunt Ave, Alamosa, CO, 81101. Tel: 719-587-2550. p. 263

Van Iderstine, Anne, Mgr, Info Serv, Nova Scotia Legislative Library, Province House, 2nd Flr, Halifax, NS, B3J 2P8, CANADA. Tel: 902-424-5932. p. 2620

Van Ingen, Rosary, Access Serv Mgr, Hoboken Public Library, 500 Park Ave, Hoboken, NJ, 07030. Tel: 201-420-2346, Ext 5101. p. 1408

Van Ingen, Rosary, Dir, Access Serv, Hoboken Public Library, Grand Street, 124 Grand St, 2nd Flr, Hoboken, NJ, 07030. Tel: 201-420-2346, Ext 5301. p. 1408

van Kalmthout, Frank, Librn, Archives of Ontario Library, 134 Ian Macdonald Blvd, Toronto, ON, M7A 2C5, CANADA. Tel: 416-327-1600. p. 2686

Van Kampen, Doris, Interim Dir, Libr Serv, Saint Leo University, 33701 State Rd 52, Saint Leo, FL, 33574. Tel: 352-588-8485. p. 441

Van Kempen, Peter, Interim Dir, La Grange Public Library, Ten W Cossitt Ave, La Grange, IL, 60525. Tel: 708-215-3273. p. 605

Van Keuren, Linda, Access Serv, Asst Dean, Resource Management, Georgetown University, Dahlgren Memorial Library, Preclinical Science Bldg GM-7, 3900 Reservoir Rd NW, Washington, DC, 20007. Tel: 202-687-1168. p. 368

Van Klooster, Brian, Libr Dir, Greendale Public Library, 5647 Broad St, Greendale, WI, 53129. Tel: 414-423-2136, Ext 225. p. 2439

van Kniest, Rebecca, Archives Librn, Outreach Librn, Univ Librn, Fontbonne University, 6800 Wydown Blvd, Saint Louis, MO, 63105. Tel: 314-719-8046. p. 1270

Van Koevering, Annette, Libr Mgr, Vancouver Island Regional Library, Cowichan Lake, 69 Renfrew Ave, Lake Cowichan, BC, V0R 2G0, CANADA. Tel: 250-749-3431. p. 2570

Van Koevering, Annette, Libr Mgr, Vancouver Island Regional Library, Cowichan, 2687 James St, Duncan, BC, V9L 2X5, CANADA. Tel: 250-746-7661. p. 2570

Van Lare, Rosemary, Sr Librn, Alameda Free Library, Bay Farm Island, 3221 Mecartney Rd, Alameda, CA, 94502. Tel: 510-747-7787. p. 115

Van Leeuwen, Katherine, Adult Serv, Asst Dir, The Brookfield Library, 182 Whisconier Rd, Brookfield, CT, 06804. Tel: 203-775-6241, Ext 108. p. 304

Van Liere, Lori, Librn, Res Serv Spec, Stautzenberger College Library, 1796 Indian Wood Circle, Maumee, OH, 43537. Tel: 419-866-0261. p. 1800

van Lith, Yvonne, Br Mgr, Ottawa Public Library/Bibliothèque publique d'Ottawa, Carlingwood, 281 Woodroffe Ave, Ottawa, ON, K2A 3W4, CANADA. p. 2668

van Lith, Yvonne, Br Mgr, Ottawa Public Library/Bibliothèque publique d'Ottawa, Centennial, 3870 Old Richmond Rd, Ottawa, ON, K2H 5C4, CANADA. p. 2668

van Lith, Yvonne, Br Mgr, Ottawa Public Library/Bibliothèque publique d'Ottawa, Emerald Plaza, 1547 Merivale Rd, Ottawa, ON, K2G 4V3, CANADA. p. 2669

van Lith, Yvonne, Br Mgr, Ottawa Public Library/Bibliothèque publique d'Ottawa, Nepean Centrepointe Branch, 101 Centrepointe Dr, Ottawa, ON, K2G 5K7, CANADA. p. 2669

Van Loon, Jim, Reserves & Res Data Librn, Oakland University Library, 100 Library Dr, Rochester, MI, 48309-4479. Tel: 248-370-2477. p. 1144

Van Maanen, Cathy, Dir, Libr Serv, Huxley Public Library, 515 N Main Ave, Huxley, IA, 50124. Tel: 515-597-2552. p. 759

Van Meter, Dana, Tech Serv Librn, Institute for Advanced Study Libraries, One Einstein Dr, Princeton, NJ, 08540. Tel: 609-734-8000. p. 1436

Van Minnen, Ania, Br Mgr, Hamilton Public Library, Sherwood, 467 Upper Ottawa St, Hamilton, ON, L8T 3T3, CANADA. Tel: 905-546-3200, Ext 3436. p. 2646

Van Minnen, Ania, Br Mgr, Hamilton Public Library, Valley Park, 970 Paramount Dr, Hamilton, ON, L8J 1Y2, CANADA. Tel: 905-573-3141. p. 2646

Van Moorsel, Guillaume, Dir, Stamford Hospital, One Hospital Plaza, Stamford, CT, 06904. Tel: 203-325-7523. p. 339

Van Ness, Cynthia M, Dir, Libr & Archives, Buffalo History Museum Research Library, One Museum Ct, Buffalo, NY, 14216-3199. Tel: 716-873-9644. p. 1508

Van Ness, Elizabeth, Ref Serv, Canton Public Library, 40 Dyer Ave, Canton, CT, 06019. Tel: 860-693-5800. p. 305

Van Niel, Sharon, Circ Librn, Sherburne Memorial Library, 2998 River Rd, Killington, VT, 05751. Tel: 802-422-4251, 802-422-9765. p. 2287

Van Norman, Alison, Outreach & Marketing Librn, Elon University, 308 N O'Kelly Ave, Elon, NC, 27244-0187. Tel: 336-278-6600. p. 1688

Van Nort, Sydney, Archivist, City College of the City University of New York, College Archives & Special Collections, North Academic Ctr-Cohen Library, 160 Convent Ave, New York, NY, 10031. Tel: 212-650-7609. p. 1581

Van Nort, Sydney, Archivist, City College of the City University of New York, North Academic Ctr, 160 Convent Ave, New York, NY, 10031. Tel: 212-650-7609. p. 1581

Van Ostran, Sue, Librn, Witt Township Memorial Library, 18 N Second St, Witt, IL, 62094. Tel: 217-594-7333. p. 664

Van Patten, Margaret A, Libr Dir, Baldwinsville Public Library, 33 E Genesee St, Baldwinsville, NY, 13027-2575. Tel: 315-635-5631. p. 1490

Van Pelt, Martha, Dir, South Central Library System, 4610 S Biltmore Lane, Ste 101, Madison, WI, 53718-2153. Tel: 608-246-7975. p. 2450

Van Rij, Karen, Mgr, Knox County Public Library System, Karns Branch, 7516 Oak Ridge Hwy, Knoxville, TN, 37931. Tel: 865-470-8663. p. 2106

Van Riper, A Bowdoin, Research Librn, Martha's Vineyard Museum Library, 151 Lagoon Pond Rd, Vineyard Haven, MA, 02568. Tel: 508-627-4441, Ext 115. p. 1060

Van Rootselaar, Anna, Asst Br Supvr, Region of Waterloo Library, St Jacobs Branch, 29 Queensway Dr, St. Jacobs, ON, N0B 2N0, CANADA. Tel: 519-664-3443. p. 2629

Van Rybroek, Gregory, Dir, Mendota Mental Health Institute, 301 Troy Dr, Madison, WI, 53704-1599. Tel: 608-301-1196. p. 2449

Van Sant, Debra, Librn, Rock Island County Illinois Genealogical Society Library, 822 11th Ave, Moline, IL, 61265. Tel: 309-764-8590. p. 618

Van Setten, Della, Libr Dir, Choteau/Teton Public Library, 17 N Main Ave, Choteau, MT, 59422. Tel: 406-466-2052. p. 1291

Van Setten, Della, Libr Tech, Lewis & Clark Trail Heritage Foundation, Inc, 4201 Giant Spring Rd, Ste 2, Great Falls, MT, 59405. Tel: 406-454-1234. p. 1294

Van Skaik, Patricia, Exec Dir, Lloyd Library & Museum, 917 Plum St, Cincinnati, OH, 45202. Tel: 513-721-3707. p. 1761

Van Stanley, Zach, Asst Dir, Hudson Public Library, 401 Fifth St, Hudson, IA, 50643. Tel: 319-988-4217. p. 759

Van Thiel, Nikki, Br Cluster Mgr, Denver Public Library, Ten W 14th Ave Pkwy, Denver, CO, 80204-2731. Tel: 720-865-1111. p. 275

Van Tussel, Nicole, Libr Asst, Turner Public Library, 98 Matthews Way, Turner, ME, 04282-3930. Tel: 207-225-2030. p. 943

Van Valkenburg, Kelly, Asst Dir, Beaumont Library District, 125 E Eighth St, Beaumont, CA, 92223-2194. Tel: 951-845-1357. p. 121

Van Valkenburg, Trevor, Dir, Lenawee District Library, 4459 W US Hwy 223, Adrian, MI, 49221-1294. Tel: 517-263-1011. p. 1075

Van Vark, Sue, Libr Office Mgr, Central College, Campus Box 6500, 812 University St, Pella, IA, 50219-1999. Tel: 641-628-5219. p. 776

Van Vleet, Mindy, Libr Dir, Wibaux Public Library, 115 S Wibaux, Wibaux, MT, 59353. Tel: 406-796-2452. p. 1304

Van Vliet, Kim, Br Librn, South Central Regional Library, Morden Branch, 514 Stephen St, Morden, MB, R6M 1T7, CANADA. Tel: 204-822-4092. p. 2592

Van Wagenberg, Anke, PhD, Chief Curator, Academy Art Museum, 106 South St, Easton, MD, 21601. Tel: 410-822-2787. p. 964

van Well, Michelle, Ch, Wayne Public Library, 3737 S Wayne Rd, Wayne, MI, 48184. Tel: 734-721-7832. p. 1158

Van Winkle, Donna, Library Contact, Federal Correctional Institution - Englewood Library, 9595 W Quincy Ave, Littleton, CO, 80123. Tel: 303-763-4300. p. 290

Van Winkle, Joan, Library Contact, First United Methodist Church, Laura Knight Children's Library, 419 NE First St, Gainesville, FL, 32601. Tel: 352-372-8523. p. 407

van Zanten, Denise, Dir, Manchester City Library, 405 Pine St, Manchester, NH, 03104-6199. Tel: 603-624-6550. p. 1372

Van Zyl, Dalene, Br Supvr, Elgin County Library, Aylmer Old Town Hall Library, 38 John St S, Aylmer, ON, N5H 2C2, CANADA. Tel: 519-773-2439. p. 2680

Van't Hul, Sylvia, Dir, Larchwood Public Library, 1020 Broadway, Larchwood, IA, 51241. Tel: 712-477-2583. p. 764

Van-Gils, Hayley, Dir, Lee Public Library, Nine Mast Rd, Lee, NH, 03861. Tel: 603-659-2626. p. 1370

VanBeck, Kimberly, Librn, Harnett County Public Library, Erwin Public, 110 West F St, Erwin, NC, 28339. Tel: 910-897-5780. p. 1701

VanBibber, Dawn, Adult Coll Develop Librn, Kokomo-Howard County Public Library, 220 N Union St, Kokomo, IN, 46901-4614. Tel: 765-457-3242. p. 699

VanCalcar, Ann, Libr Asst, Thorp Public Library, 401 S Conway Dr, Thorp, WI, 54771. Tel: 715-669-5953. p. 2481

Vance, Amanda, Librn/Br Mgr, Allen County Public Library, Waynedale, 2200 Lower Huntington Rd, Fort Wayne, IN, 46819. Tel: 260-421-1365. p. 684

Vance, Ashley, Libr Dir, Vermont Public Library, 101 N Main St, Vermont, IL, 61484. Tel: 309-784-6291. p. 657

Vance, Carey, Libr Mgr, Monrovia Public Library, 321 S Myrtle Ave, Monrovia, CA, 91016-2848. Tel: 626-256-8229. p. 179

Vance, Dara, Exec Dir, Greenbrier Historical Society Archives & Library, 814 Washington St W, Lewisburg, WV, 24901. Tel: 304 645 3398. p. 2407

Vance, Dorothy, Pub Relations Coordr, Central Mississippi Regional Library System, 100 Tamberline St, Brandon, MS, 39042. Tel: 601-825-0100. p. 1212

Vance, Jackson, Clarkston Ctr Libr Coordr, Walla Walla Community College Library, 500 Tausick Way, Walla Walla, WA, 99362-9267. Tel: 509-758-1714. p. 2392

Vance, Kendall, ILL, Waubonsee Community College, Collins Hall, 2nd Flr, State Rte 47 at Waubonsee Dr, Sugar Grove, IL, 60554. Tel: 630-466-2333. p. 652

Vance, Mona, Archivist, Columbus-Lowndes Public Library, 314 Seventh St N, Columbus, MS, 39701. Tel: 662-329-5300. p. 1215

VanCise, Jim, Facilities Servs, Superintendent, Laramie County Library System, 2200 Pioneer Ave, Cheyenne, WY, 82001-3610. Tel: 307-773-7213. p. 2492

Vande Bunte, Lisa, Dir, Salem Township Library, 3007 142nd Ave, Burnips, MI, 49314. Tel: 616-896-8170. p. 1088

VanDeale, Stacey, Br Head, Chatham-Kent Public Library, Wallaceburg Branch, 209 James St, Wallaceburg, ON, N8A 2N4, CANADA. Tel: 519-627-5292. p. 2636

VandeBurgt, Melissa, Head, Archives & Spec Coll, Head, Digital Initiatives, Florida Gulf Coast University Library, 10501 FGCU Blvd S, Fort Myers, FL, 33965. Tel: 239-590-7658. p. 402

VandeCreek, Leanne, Assoc Dean, Pub Serv, Northern Illinois University Libraries, 217 Normal Rd, DeKalb, IL, 60115-2828. Tel: 815-753-9804. p. 577

Vanden Elzen, Angela, Learning Tech Librn, Ref Librn, Lawrence University, 113 S Lawe St, Appleton, WI, 54911-5683. p. 2420

Vanden Heuvel, Kathleen, Dir, University of California, Berkeley, Law, Berkley Law South Addition, 2nd Flr, 2778 Bancroff Way, Berkeley, CA, 94720. Tel: 510-642-0621. p. 123

Vandenbark, Todd, Dir, Libr Serv, Columbia County Rural Library District, 111 S Third St, Dayton, WA, 99328. Tel: 509-382-4131. p. 2363

Vandenberg, Susan, Br Mgr, Akron-Summit County Public Library, Firestone Park Branch, 1486 Aster Ave, Akron, OH, 44301-2104. Tel: 330-724-2126. p. 1744

Vandenberg, Vicki, Asst Dir, Oshkosh Public Library, 106 Washington Ave, Oshkosh, WI, 54901-4985. Tel: 920-236-5201, 920-236-5205. p. 2467

Vandenberghe, Terri, Librn, Reston & District Library, 220 Fourth St, Reston, MB, R0M 1X0, CANADA. Tel: 204-877-3673. p. 2589

Vandenbosch, Trish, Libr Dir, Moores Memorial Library, Nine W Slokom Ave, Christiana, PA, 17509-1202. Tel: 610-593-6683. p. 1921

Vandenburg, Michael, Assoc Univ Librn, Queen's University, 101 Union St, Kingston, ON, K7L 2N9, CANADA. Tel: 613-533-6000, Ext 78844. p. 2650

Vandenburg, Michael, Interim Exec Dir, Ontario Council of University Libraries, 130 Saint George St, 7th Flr, Toronto, ON, M5S 1A5, CANADA. Tel: 613-893-2665. p. 2778

Vandenhengel, Kerry, Youth Serv Mgr, Strathcona County Library, 401 Festival Lane, Sherwood Park, AB, T8A 5P7, CANADA. Tel: 780-410-8600. p. 2553

Vander Esch, Marge, Ch, Hull Public Library, 1408 Main St, Hull, IA, 51239. Tel: 712-439-1321. p. 759

Vander Sluis, Lisa, Ch, Le Mars Public Library, 46 First St SW, Le Mars, IA, 51031. Tel: 712-546-5004. p. 765

Vander Veen, Brian, Managing Librn, Spokane County Library District, North Spokane Library, 44 E Hawthorne Rd, Spokane, WA, 99218-1597. Tel: 509-893-8350. p. 2384

Vander Vorst, Barbara, Dir, Potter County Library, 205 W Commercial Ave, Gettysburg, SD, 57442. Tel: 605-765-9518. p. 2076

Vanderbeck, Norma, Librn, Davies Memorial Library, 612 Thayer St, Butte, NE, 68722. Tel: 402-775-2325, 402-775-2426. p. 1309

Vanderbie, Maria, Commun Librn, Wheatland Regional Library, Young Branch, 114 Main St, Young, SK, S0K 4Y0, CANADA. Tel: 306-259-2227. p. 2751

Vanderhaak, Rosie, Br Mgr, Riverside County Library System, Temecula Public Library, 30600 Pauba Rd, Temecula, CA, 92592. Tel: 951-693-8900. p. 202

VanderHeijden, Michael, Ref Librn, Yale University Library, Lillian Goldman Library Yale Law School, 127 Wall St, New Haven, CT, 06511. Tel: 203-432-4367. p. 328

Vanderhorst, Sheila, Asst Dir, Ingalls Memorial Library, 203 Main St, Rindge, NH, 03461. Tel: 603-899-3303. p. 1379

Vanderhulst, Kyla, Br Librn, Southeast Regional Library, Arcola Branch, 127 Main St, Arcola, SK, S0C 0G0, CANADA. Tel: 306-455-2321. p. 2753

Vanderkruys, Christopher, Dir, Corporate Serv, Barrie Public Library, 60 Worsley St, Barrie, ON, L4M 1L6, CANADA. Tel: 705-728-1010, Ext 2200. p. 2630

Vanderloo, Tom, Digital Serv Librn, US Court of Appeals for the Sixth Circuit Library, 540 Potter Stewart US Courthouse, 100 E Fifth St, Cincinnati, OH, 45202-3911. Tel: 513-564-7305. p. 1764

Vandermeer, Philip, Head of Libr, University of North Carolina at Chapel Hill, Music, 201 South Rd, CB 3906, Chapel Hill, NC, 27514-3906. Tel: 919-966-1113. p. 1678

VanderPloeg, Jennifer, Head, Libr Operations, Bellingham Public Library, 210 Central Ave, Bellingham, WA, 98225. Tel: 360-778-7233. p. 2358

VanderPloeg, Sondra, Circ Mgr, Howe Library, 13 South St, Hanover, NH, 03755. Tel: 603-640-3262. p. 1367

VanderPol, Diane, College Library Director, Pima Community College, 6680 S Country Club Dr, Tucson, AZ, 85709-1790. Tel: 520-206-2782. p. 81

Vanderree, Cara, Libr Dir, Ashland City Library, 604 Main St, Ashland, KS, 67831. Tel: 620-635-2589. p. 797

VanDerslice, Laura, Br Mgr, Libr Asst III, Santa Cruz City-County Library System, Live Oak, 2380 Portola Dr, Santa Cruz, CA, 95062. Tel: 831-427-7711. p. 243

Vandervoort, Charlotte, Access Serv, Syst Librn, University of Dallas, 1845 E Northgate Dr, Irving, TX, 75062-4736. Tel: 972-721-5282. p. 2203

Vandestreek, Joanne, Sr Legis Librn, Legislative Council Service Library, 411 State Capitol, Santa Fe, NM, 87501. Tel: 505-986-4656. p. 1475

VanDetta, Deborah, Youth Serv Librn, Estacada Public Library, 825 NW Wade St, Estacada, OR, 97023. Tel: 503-630-8273. p. 1878

Vandewalker, Amy, Librn, Eastern Oklahoma VA HealthCare System, 1011 Honor Heights Dr, Muskogee, OK, 74401. Tel: 918-577-4082. p. 1854

VanDoran, Chris, Acq Mgr, ILL, Ser, University of Tennessee Southern, 433 W Madison St, Pulaski, TN, 38478-2799. Tel: 931-363-9844. p. 2124

VanDoren, Mary, Br Mgr, Athens County Public Libraries, Wells Public Library, 5200 Washington Rd, Albany, OH, 45710. Tel: 740-698-3059. p. 1805

Vandriel, Caroline, Dir, Sylvan Lake Municipal Library, 4715-50 Ave, Sylvan Lake, AB, T4S 1A2, CANADA. Tel: 403-887-2130. p. 2556

VanDrunen, Katherine, Ref Librn, Westminster Seminary California Library, 1725 Bear Valley Pkwy, Escondido, CA, 92027. Tel: 760-480-8474. p. 141

VanDusen, Sandy, Librn, Superintendent, Sterling Public Library, 420 N Fifth St, Sterling, CO, 80751-3363. Tel: 970-522-2023. p. 296

vanEijnsbergen, Chandra, Commun Librn, Deschutes Public Library District, East Bend Branch, 62080 Dean Swift Rd, Bend, OR, 97701. Tel: 841-330-6764. p. 1874

Vangundy, Amelia C, Cat Librn, University of Virginia's College at Wise, One College Ave, Wise, VA, 24293. Tel: 276-328-0154. p. 2355

Vani, Anna, Cat Librn, Washington University Libraries, Bernard Becker Medical Library, 660 S Euclid Ave, Campus Box 8132, Saint Louis, MO, 63110. Tel: 314-362-3481. p. 1277

Vanis, Michelle, IT Mgr, Midlothian Public Library, 14701 S Kenton Ave, Midlothian, IL, 60445-4122. Tel: 708-535-2027. p. 617

VanKoughnett, Alex, Libr Asst, William Bradford Huie Library of Hartselle, 152 NW Sparkman St, Hartselle, AL, 35640. Tel: 256-773-9880. p. 20

Vanlandingham, Allison, Dir, Powell County Public Library, 725 Breckenridge St, Stanton, KY, 40380. Tel: 606-663-4511. p. 875

Vanlandingham, Taylor, Ms, Libr Dir, John Brown University Library, 2000 W University, Siloam Springs, AR, 72761. Tel: 479-524-7202. p. 110

Vanlaningham, David, Tech Mgr, Crawford County Public Library, 203 Indiana Ave, English, IN, 47118. Tel: 812-338-2606. p. 681

VanMeter, Jeremy, Fiscal Officer, Mount Sterling Public Library, 60 W Columbus St, Mount Sterling, OH, 43143. Tel: 740-869-2430. p. 1804

Vannier, Clarrisa, Interim Librn, Intermountain Health, 400 S Clark St, Butte, MT, 59701. Tel: 406-723-2523. p. 1290

Vannuchi, Anne, Interim Br Mgr, San Francisco Public Library, Eureka Valley-Harvey Milk Memorial Branch Library, One Jose Sarria Ct, San Francisco, CA, 94114-1621. Tel: 415-355-5616. p. 228

Vano, Leslie, Mgr, Ad Serv, Rockford Public Library, 214 N Church St, Rockford, IL, 61101-1023. Tel: 815-965-7606. p. 642

VanOrsdale, Ginny, Br Mgr, Newton County Library System, Porter Memorial Branch Library, 6191 Hwy 212, Covington, GA, 30016. p. 473

VanRaden, Sarah, Mgr, Br, Omaha Public Library, 215 S 15th St, Omaha, NE, 68102-1629. Tel: 402-444-4800. p. 1329

VanScoy, Amy, Dr, Assoc Prof, University at Buffalo, The State University of New York, 534 Baldy Hall, Buffalo, NY, 14260. Tel: 716-645-2412. p. 2789

VanScoyoc, Lilas, Librn, Evart Public Library, 105 N Main St, Evart, MI, 49631. Tel: 231-734-5542. p. 1104

Vansteen, John, Libr Dir, Five Towns College Library, 305 N Service Rd, Dix Hills, NY, 11746. Tel: 631-656-3187. p. 1525

Vanstone, Catherine, Asst Dir, Southwest Georgia Regional Library, 301 S Monroe St, Bainbridge, GA, 39819. Tel: 229-248-2665. p. 467

Vant Sant, Susanna, Acq Librn, Tompkins Cortland Community College Library, Baker Commons, 2nd Flr, 170 North St, Dryden, NY, 13053-8504. Tel: 607-844-8222, Ext 4360. p. 1526

Vantassell, Heather, Dir, Libr Serv, Walla Walla Public Library, 238 E Alder St, Walla Walla, WA, 99362. Tel: 509-524-4433. p. 2392

Vanterpool, Karen, Librn, SUNY Westchester Community College, 75 Grasslands Rd, Valhalla, NY, 10595. Tel: 914-785-6960. p. 1656

Vantran, Anne, Head, Youth Serv, East Bridgewater Public Library, 32 Union St, East Bridgewater, MA, 02333. Tel: 508-378-1616. p. 1015

Vanuytven, Jessica, Librn, Ramsey Public Library, 401 S Superior St, Ramsey, IL, 62080. Tel: 618-423-2019. p. 638

Vanvelzen, Lina, Libr Mgr, Mississauga Library System, Cooksville, 3024 Hurontario St, Ste 212, Mississauga, ON, L5B 4M4, CANADA. Tel: 905-615-4855. p. 2659

VanWingen, Mindy, Asst Dir, Head, Adult Serv, Everett Public Library, 2702 Hoyt Ave, Everett, WA, 98201-3556. Tel: 425-257-8021. p. 2364

Vanya, Dana, Asst Dir, Mickey Reily Public Library, 604 S Matthews St, Corrigan, TX, 75939. Tel: 936-398-4156. p. 2161

VanZant, Ivory, User Serv Librn, Wasilla Public Library, 500 N Crusey St, Wasilla, AK, 99654. Tel: 907-864-9177. p. 52

Vanzant-Salyer, Michelle, Librn, Highland County Law Library, Courthouse, 105 N High St, Hillsboro, OH, 45133. Tel: 937-393-4863. p. 1790

Vanzelzen, Lina, Libr Mgr, Mississauga Library System, Port Credit, 20 Lakeshore Rd E, Mississauga, ON, L5G 1C8, CANADA. Tel: 905-615-4835. p. 2659

Varady, Kathy, Libr Asst, Lyme Public Library, 482 Hamburg Rd, Lyme, CT, 06371-3110. Tel: 860-434-2272. p. 320

Varcoe, Jennifer, Librn, Georgian College, One Georgian Dr, Barrie, ON, L4M 3X9, CANADA. Tel: 705-728-1968. p. 2630

Vardaman, Lisa, Educ Librn, Instrul Media Serv Librn, Troy University Library, 309 Wallace Hall, Troy, AL, 36082. Tel: 334-670-3262. p. 37

Vardanyan, Rouzanna, Dir, Maharishi International University Library, 1000 N Fourth St, Fairfield, IA, 52557. Tel: 641-472-1148. p. 752

Varela, Harry, Mgr, Miami-Dade Public Library System, Allapattah Branch, 1799 NW 35th St, Miami, FL, 33142-5421. Tel: 305-638-6086. p. 423

Varga, Paulette, Br Mgr, Starke County Public Library System, Koontz Lake Branch, 7954 N State Rd 23, Walkerton, IN, 46574. Tel: 574-586-3353. p. 699

Varga, Vicky, Mgr, Edmonton Public Library, Castle Downs, 106 Lakeside Landing, 15379 Castle Downs Rd, Edmonton, AB, T5X 3Y7, CANADA. Tel: 780-496-2708. p. 2536

Vargas, Mandi, Dir, Hansford County Library, 122 Main St, Spearman, TX, 79081. Tel: 806-659-2231. p. 2245

Vargas, Maritza, Head, Circ, New London Public Library, 63 Huntington St, New London, CT, 06320. Tel: 860-447-1411, Ext 102. p. 329

Vargas, Samantha, Librn, San Saba County Library, 103 S Live Oak, San Saba, TX, 76877. Tel: 325-372-3079. p. 2241

Vargas-Minor, Alexandra, Spec Coll & Univ Archives, University of South Florida Saint Petersburg, 140 Seventh Ave S, POY118, Saint Petersburg, FL, 33701-5016. Tel: 727-873-4094. p. 442

Vargas-Minor, Alexandra, Spec Coll & Univ Archives, University of South Florida Saint Petersburg, 140 Seventh Ave S, POY118, Saint Petersburg, FL, 33701-5016. Tel: 727-873-7094. p. 442

Vargas-Pile, Kinshasa, Ms, Mgr, Enoch Pratt Free Library, Brooklyn Branch, 300 E Patapsco Ave, Baltimore, MD, 21225-1828. Tel: 443-984-4947. p. 952

Vargha, Rebecca, Librn, University of North Carolina at Chapel Hill, Information & Library Science, 115B Manning Hall, CB 3360, Chapel Hill, NC, 27599. Tel: 919-962-8361. p. 1678

Vargo, Vicki, Exec Dir, Braddock Carnegie Library, 419 Library St, Braddock, PA, 15104-1609. Tel: 412-351-5356. p. 1914

Varick, Vicki, Libr Dir, Aaron Cutler Memorial Library, 269 Charles Bancroft Hwy, Litchfield, NH, 03052. Tel: 603-424-4044. p. 1371

Varley, Craig, Dir, Alice M Ward Memorial Library, 27 Park St, Canaan, VT, 05903. Tel: 802-266-7135. p. 2281

Varman, Beatriz, Head, Res & Instruction, Houston Academy of Medicine, 1133 John Freeman Blvd, No 100, Houston, TX, 77030. Tel: 713-799-7169. p. 2193

Varner, Douglas, Asst Dean, Georgetown University, Dahlgren Memorial Library, Preclinical Science Bldg GM-7, 3900 Reservoir Rd NW, Washington, DC, 20007. Tel: 202-431-9503. p. 368

Varner, Elizabeth, Asst Dir, Boswell & Grant Township Public Library, 101 N Clinton St, Boswell, IN, 47921. Tel: 765-869-5428. p. 672

Varnes, Kerri, Librn, Mid-Mississippi Regional Library System, Kilmichael Public, 102 First St, Kilmichael, MS, 39747. Tel: 662-262-7615. p. 1224

Varns, Tia, Dir, Clifton Public Library, 150 E Fourth Ave, Clifton, IL, 60927. Tel: 815-694-2069. p. 572

Varnum, Lindsay, Youth Serv Librn, Orono Public Library, 39 Pine St, Orono, ME, 04473. Tel: 207-866-5060. p. 934

Varrett Davis, Stacie Lynn, Libr Dir, West Feliciana Parish Library, 5114 Burnett Rd, Saint Francisville, LA, 70775-4341. Tel: 225-635-3364. p. 907

Varry, Sandra, Dept Head, Special Colls, North Carolina State University Libraries, D H Hill Jr Library, Two Broughton Dr, Raleigh, NC, 27695. Tel: 919-515-8119. p. 1709

Vartabedian, Stefanie, Satellite Librn, United States Courts Library, Sandra Day O'Connor United States Courthouse, Ste 410, 401 W Washington St, SPC16, Phoenix, AZ, 85003-2135. Tel: 602-322-7295. p. 73

Vasconi, Linda, Pub Relations, North Merrick Public Library, 1691 Meadowbrook Rd, North Merrick, NY, 11566. Tel: 516-378-7474. p. 1608

Vashaw, Courtney, Librn, Whitefield Public Library, Eight Lancaster Rd, Whitefield, NH, 03598. Tel: 603-837-2030. p. 1384

Vasica, Christine, Access Serv, Anne Arundel Community College, 101 College Pkwy, Arnold, MD, 21012-1895. Tel: 410-777-2211. p. 951

Vasilic, Sasha, Dir, Mkt & Communications, Arlington Heights Memorial Library, 500 N Dunton Ave, Arlington Heights, IL, 60004-5966. Tel: 847-392-0100. p. 537

Vasinda, Kathleen A, Libr Dir, Runnemede Free Public Library, Two Broadway & Black Horse Pike, Runnemede, NJ, 08078. Tel: 856-939-4688. p. 1441

Vasquez, Aldo, Br Mgr, Chicago Public Library, Little Village, 2311 S Kedzie Ave, Chicago, IL, 60623. Tel: 312-745-1862. p. 557

Vasquez, Alison, Dir, United States Air Force, Edwards Air Force Base Library, Five W Yeager Blvd, Edwards AFB, CA, 93524-1295. Tel: 661-275-2665. p. 139

Vasquez, Barbara J, Chair, Los Angeles City College Library, 855 N Vermont Ave, Los Angeles, CA, 90029. Tel: 323-953-4000, Ext 2407. p. 162

Vasquez, Candace, Managing Librn, Brooklyn Public Library, Pacific, 25 Fourth Ave, Brooklyn, NY, 11217. Tel: 718-638-1531. p. 1503

Vasquez, Ivonne, Tech Serv Librn, North Miami Public Library, 835 NE 132nd St, North Miami, FL, 33161. Tel: 305-891-5535. p. 429

Vasquez, Karln, Asst Dir, Grant Parish Library, 300 Main St, Colfax, LA, 71417-1830. Tel: 318-627-9920. p. 887

Vasquez, Manuel, Dir of Circ, Grande Prairie Public Library District, 3479 W 183rd St, Hazel Crest, IL, 60429. Tel: 708 798-5563. p. 598

Vasquez, Maridza, Youth Librn, Crete Public Library, 1515 Forest Ave, Crete, NE, 68333. Tel: 402-826-3809. p. 1311

Vasquez, Melissa, Children & Youth Serv Librn, Teen Librn, Crittenden County Public Library, 204 W Carlisle St, Marion, KY, 42064-1727. Tel: 270-965-3354. p. 868

Vass, Annie, Asst County Librn, Chambers County Library System, 202 Cummings St, Anahuac, TX, 77514. Tel: 409-267-2554. p. 2134

Vass, Mary, Libr Mgr, Youngtown Public Library, 12035 Clubhouse Sq, Youngtown, AZ, 85363. Tel: 623-974-3401. p. 85

Vassallo, Anita, Interim Dir, Montgomery County Public Libraries, 21 Maryland Ave, Ste 310, Rockville, MD, 20850. Tel: 240-777-0002. p. 974

Vassallo, John Anthony, Chief Librn, United States Army, Fort Jackson Main Post Library, Thomas Lee Hall Main Post Library, Bldg 4679, Fort Jackson, SC, 29207. Tel: 803-751-4816, 803-751-5589. p. 2059

Vassar, David, Ref Librn, Fordham University Libraries, Quinn Library at Lincoln Center, 140 W 62nd St, New York, NY, 10023. Tel: 212-636-6050. p. 1498

Vassilakos-Long, Jill, Coordr, Spec Coll, Govt Doc, California State University, San Bernardino, 5500 University Pkwy, San Bernardino, CA, 92407-2318. Tel: 909-537-7541. p. 212

Vasudev, Shaunda, Student Success Librn, Capital University, One College & Main, Columbus, OH, 43209. Tel: 614-236-6614. p. 1772

Vataha, Cara, Dir, Cibecue Community Library, Six W Third St, Cibecue, AZ, 85911. Tel: 928-532-6240. p. 58

Vatani, Sandra, Dir, Adamsville Public Library, 4825 Main St, Adamsville, AL, 35005-1947. Tel: 205-674-3399. p. 3

Vater-Olsen, Susan, Dir, Scandinavia Public Library, 349 N Main St, Scandinavia, WI, 54977. Tel: 715-467-4636. p. 2475

Vauble, Beth, Dir, Lytton Public Library, 118 Main St, Lytton, IA, 50561. Tel: 712-466-2522. p. 766

Vaughan, Daniel, Reference & User Services Librn, East Texas Baptist University, One Tiger Dr, Marshall, TX, 75670-1498. Tel: 903-923-2260. p. 2215

Vaughan, Emily, Sr Librn, National Endowment for Democracy Library, 1201 Pennsylvania Ave NW, Ste 1100, Washington, DC, 20004. Tel: 202-378-9700. p. 372

Vaughan, Jason, Dir, Technology, University of Nevada, Las Vegas University Libraries, 4505 S Maryland Pkwy, Box 457001, Las Vegas, NV, 89154-7001. Tel: 702-895-2179. p. 1347

Vaughan, K T, Dr, Univ Librn, Washington & Lee University, University Library, 204 W Washington St, Lexington, VA, 24450-2116. Tel: 540-458-8643. p. 2329

Vaughan, Kirsten, Br Mgr, Anoka County Library, Johnsville, 12461 Oak Park Blvd, Blaine, MN, 55434. Tel: 763-324-1550. p. 1165

Vaughan, Kirsten, Br Librn, East Central Regional Library, 111 Dellwood St, Cambridge, MN, 55008-1588. Tel: 763-689-7390. p. 1167

Vaughan, Richard, Acq Librn, Indiana University, School of Law Library, Maurer School of Law, 211 S Indiana Ave, Bloomington, IN, 47405. Tel: 812-855-4199. p. 670

Vaughan, Sarah, Mgr, Okefenokee Regional Library, Clinch County Public, 478 W Dame St, Homerville, GA, 31634. Tel: 912-483-0475. p. 503

Vaughan, Susan, Ser, University of Dallas, 1845 E Northgate Dr, Irving, TX, 75062-4736. Tel: 972-721-4130. p. 2203

Vaughan, Tammy, Libr Assoc, Mississippi State University, Jackson Architecture, 509 E Capitol St, Jackson, MS, 39201. Tel: 601-354-6184. p. 1227

Vaughan-Evans, Tracey, Librn, Carbonear Public Library, 256 Water St, Carbonear, NL, A1Y 1C4, CANADA. Tel: 709-596-3382. p. 2607

Vaughan-Lloyd, Kathy, Asst Dir, Scott County Public Library, 104 S Bradford Lane, Georgetown, KY, 40324-2335. Tel: 502-863-3566. p. 856

Vaughn, April, Br Librn, Fayette County Public Libraries, Meadow Bridge Branch, 53 Montrado St, Meadow Bridge, WV, 25976. Tel: 304-484-7942. p. 2411

Vaughn, Betty H, Dir, Dora Public Library, 56125 Goldbrick Rd, Myrtle Point, OR, 97458. Tel: 541-572-6009. p. 1888

Vaughn, Chris, Digital Serv Librn, Head, Circ, Midwestern Baptist Theological Seminary Library, 5001 N Oak Trafficway, Kansas City, MO, 64118-4620. Tel: 816-414-3729. p. 1256

Vaughn, Chris, Libr Support Spec, William Jewell College, 500 William Jewell College Dr, Liberty, MO, 64068. Tel: 816-415-5062. p. 1260

Vaughn, Connie, Br Asst, Elko-Lander-Eureka County Library System, Austin Branch Library, 88 Main St, Austin, NV, 89310. Tel: 775-964-2428. p. 1344

Vaughn, Faye, Tech Serv, Nashville State Technical Community College, 120 White Bridge Rd, Nashville, TN, 37209-4515. Tel: 615-353-3560. p. 2120

Vaughn, Jan, Asst Dir, Warren-Trumbull County Public Library, 444 Mahoning Ave NW, Warren, OH, 44483. Tel: 330-399-8807. p. 1828

Vaughn, Janaice, Br Mgr, Dixie Regional Library System, Jesse Yancy Memorial Library, 314 N Newberger Ave, Bruce, MS, 38915. Tel: 662-983-2220. p. 1230

Vaughn, Laura, Interim Libr Dir, Roane State Community College Library, 276 Patton Lane, Harriman, TN, 37748-5011. Tel: 865-882-4551. p. 2100

Vaughn, Natalie, ILL Librn, Oklahoma City University, School of Law Library, 2501 N Blackwelder, Oklahoma City, OK, 73106. Tel: 405-208-5271. p. 1858

Vaughn, Patsy, Librn, Scott-Sebastian Regional Library, Scott County Library, 149 Second St, Waldron, AR, 72958. Tel: 479-637-3516. p. 97

Vaughn, Pauline R, Dir, Coffee County-Manchester Library, 1005 Hillsboro Hwy, Manchester, TN, 37355-2099. Tel: 931-723-5143. p. 2110

Vaughn, RaNae, Librn, Knox County Historical Society & Museum Library, 408 E Lafayette St, Edina, MO, 63537. Tel: 660-216-9085. p. 1245

Vaughn, Sandy, Asst Librn, Cataloger, Yalobusha County Public Library System, 14432 Main St, Coffeeville, MS, 38922-2590. Tel: 662-675-8822. p. 1214

Vaughn, Sarah, Head, Access Serv, University of Northern Colorado Libraries, 1400 22nd Ave, Greeley, CO, 80631. Tel: 970-351-1539. p. 285

Vaughn, Sarah, Acad Librn, University of Kentucky Libraries, Education, 227 Dickey Hall, 251 Scott St, Lexington, KY, 40506-0017. Tel: 859-218-4882. p. 863

Vaughn, Vida, Dir, University of Louisville Libraries, Kornhauser Health Sciences Library, Health Sciences Ctr, 500 S Preston St, Louisville, KY, 40202. Tel: 502-852-8540. p. 868

Vaughn-Carr, Wanda, Libr Asst, Casco Public Library, Five Leach Hill Rd, Casco, ME, 04015. Tel: 207-627-4541. p. 921

Vaughn-Tucker, Daenel, Ms, Dir, Libr Serv, Central Louisiana Technical Community College Library, Alexandria Main Campus, 516 Murray St, Alexandria, LA, 71301. Tel: 318-487-5443, Ext 1137, 318-487-5443, Ext 1931. p. 879

Vaught, Dwight, Dir, University of South Dakota, National Music Museum Library, Corner of Clark & Yale St, 414 E Clark St, Vermillion, SD, 57069-2390. Tel: 605-658-3454. p. 2084

Vauthier, Carly, Asst Librn, Harlem Public Library, 37 First Ave SE, Harlem, MT, 59526. Tel: 406-353-2712. p. 1295

Vauthn, Robert, Dir, Libr Serv, Red Rocks Community College, 13300 W Sixth Ave, Lakewood, CO, 80228-1255. Tel: 303-914-6740. p. 288

Vavala, Jane, Assoc Librn, State University of New York, College of Technology, Upper College Dr, Alfred, NY, 14802. Tel: 607-587-4313. p. 1485

Vaver, Anthony, Local Hist Librn, Westborough Public Library, 55 W Main St, Westborough, MA, 01581. Tel: 508-366-3050. p. 1066

Vaverka, Arielle, Youth Serv Librn, Colleyville Public Library, 110 Main St, Colleyville, TX, 76034. Tel: 817-503-1150, 817-503-1154 (Youth Serv), 817-503-1155 (Adult Serv). p. 2158

Vavra, Ashley N, Archivist/Librn, Virginia State Law Library, Supreme Court Bldg, 2nd Flr, 100 N Ninth St, Richmond, VA, 23219-2335. Tel: 804-786-2075. p. 2344

Vay, Peter, Research Servs Librn, George Mason University Libraries, Law Library, 3301 N Fairfax Dr, Arlington, VA, 22201-4426. Tel: 703-993-8100. p. 2317

Vazquez, Alicia, Youth Serv Librn, Newark Public Library, 121 High St, Newark, NY, 14513-1492. Tel: 315-331-4370. p. 1605

Vazquez, Donna, Assoc Dir, Florida Gulf Coast University Library, 10501 FGCU Blvd S, Fort Myers, FL, 33965. Tel: 239-590-7603. p. 402

Vazquez Figueroa, Norma E, Librn I, Inter-American University of Puerto Rico, 500 Carretera Dr, John Will Harris, Bayamon, PR, 00957-6257. Tel: 787-279-7312, Ext 2176. p. 2510

Vazquez, Hector, Mgr, Miami-Dade Public Library System, Bay Harbor Islands Branch, 1175 95 St, Bay Harbor Islands, Miami Beach, FL, 33154. Tel: 786-646-9961. p. 423

Vazquez, Hector, Mgr, Miami-Dade Public Library System, Sunny Isles Beach Branch, 18070 Collins Ave, Sunny Isles Beach, FL, 33160. Tel: 305-682-0726. p. 424

Vazquez, Maria, Coll Develop Librn, Inter-American University of Puerto Rico, Carretera 459, Int 463 Barrio Corrales, Sector Calero, Aguadilla, PR, 00605. Tel: 787-891-0925. p. 2509

Vazquez, Nikki, Libr Tech, Mesalands Community College Library, 911 S Tenth St, Bldg A, Tucumcari, NM, 88401. Tel: 575-461-4413, Ext 121. p. 1479

Vazquez-Duran, Sofia, Cat Librn, Loyola Law School, 919 S Albany St, Los Angeles, CA, 90015-1211. Tel: 213-736-1419. p. 166

Veach, Christopher, Dir, Lake County Library, 1425 N High St, Lakeport, CA, 95453-3800. Tel: 707-263-8817. p. 156

Veale, Miriam, Libr Assoc/Tech Serv, Coweta Public Library System, 85 Literary Lane, Newnan, GA, 30265. Tel: 770-683-2052. p. 492

Vecchi, Betsy, Head, Children's Servx, Pelham Public Library, 24 Village Green, Pelham, NH, 03076. Tel: 603-635-7581. p. 1377

Vecchio, Kaitlyn, Dir, Northwest Library Federation, 1162 McGowan Dr, Prince George, BC, V2M 6R1, CANADA. Tel: 250-981-3507. p. 2777

Vecchiola, Rina, Interim Librn, Washington University Libraries, Chemistry, 549 Louderman Hall, Rm 549, Campus Box 1061, Saint Louis, MO, 63130. Tel: 314-935-4818. p. 1277

Vecchiola, Rina, Librn, Washington University Libraries, Kranzberg Art & Architecture Library, One Brookings Dr, Campus Box 1061, Saint Louis, MO, 63130-4862. Tel: 314-935-7658. p. 1277

Vedas, Mary Ellen, Coll Serv Librn, Texas A&M University at Galveston, Bldg 3010, 200 Seawolf Pkwy, Galveston, TX, 77554. Tel: 409-740-7179. p. 2183

Veeraraghavan, Kalyani, Br Mgr, York County Library, 138 E Black St, Rock Hill, SC, 29730. Tel: 803-981-5853. p. 2068

Vega, Aixa, Dir, Universidad Adventista de las Antillas, Carr 106 Km 2.2, Bo La Quinta, Mayaguez, PR, 00680. Tel: 787-834-9595, Ext 2216. p. 2511

Vega Garcia, Susan, Asst Dean, Inclusion & Equity, Iowa State University Library, 302 Parks Library, 701 Morrill Rd, Ames, IA, 50011-2102. Tel: 515-294-4052. p. 731

Vega, Holiday, Librn, University of Chicago Library, Social Work Library, 969 E 60th St, Chicago, IL, 60637-2627. Tel: 773-702-1199. p. 570

Vega, Natalie, Interim Br Mgr, Chula Vista Public Library, Otay Ranch, 2015 Birch Rd, Ste 1103, Chula Vista, CA, 91915. Tel: 619-397-0124. p. 130

Vega, Patricia, Br Mgr, Biblioteca Criolla, Jersey City Free Public Library, 472 Jersey Ave, Jersey City, NJ, 07302-3499. Tel: 201-547-4541. p. 1409

Vegh-Gaynor, Shoshana, Instruction & Ref Librn, Institute of American Indian Arts Library, 83 Avan Nu Po Rd, Santa Fe, NM, 87508. Tel: 505-424-5715. p. 1474

Vegh-Gaynor, Shoshana Ruth, Libr Spec, University of Illinois Library at Urbana-Champaign, Architecture & Art Library, 208 Architecture Bldg, 608 E Lorado Taft Dr, Urbana, IL, 61801. Tel: 217-300-6422. p. 655

Veghts, Darlene, Head, Tech Serv, Pittsburgh Theological Seminary, 616 N Highland Ave, Pittsburgh, PA, 15206. Tel: 412-924-1352. p. 1995

Veglia, Emily, Circ Spec, Flagler College, 44 Sevilla St, Saint Augustine, FL, 32084-4302. Tel: 904-819-6206. p. 439

Vegors, Rachael, Library Contact, US National Park Service, 46 Volcano Hwy, Capulin, NM, 88414. Tel: 575-278-2201, Ext 232. p. 1465

Vehorn, Jane, Br Coordr, Shelby County Libraries, Philip Sheets Family Botkins Branch, 109 E Lynn St, Botkins, OH, 45306. Tel: 937-693-6671. p. 1820

Veitch, Mike, Historian, National Museum of Racing & Hall of Fame, 191 Union Ave, 2nd Flr, Saratoga Springs, NY, 12866. Tel: 518-584-0400, Ext 122. p. 1636

Vela, Hector, Acq, Robert J Kleberg Public Library, 220 N Fourth St, Kingsville, TX, 78363. Tel: 361-592-6381. p. 2206

Vela, Kathryn, Exec Dir, National Network of Libraries of Medicine Region 5, Univ of Washington, Health Sciences Bldg, Rm T230, 1959 NE Pacific St, Seattle, WA, 98195. Tel: 206-543-8262. p. 2776

Velasquez, Ana, Acq, Supvr, Laredo College, West End Washington St, Laredo, TX, 78040. Tel: 956-721-5271. p. 2209

Velasquez, Angelica, Asst to the Dean of Libraries, University of the Incarnate Word, 4301 Broadway, CPO 297, San Antonio, TX, 78209-6397. p. 2240

Velasquez, Grisel, Br Mgr, Jersey City Free Public Library, Pavonia, 326 Eighth St, Jersey City, NJ, 07302. Tel: 201-547-4808. p. 1409

Velasquez, Jennifer, Coordr, Teen Serv, San Antonio Public Library, 600 Soledad, San Antonio, TX, 78205-2786. Tel: 210-207-2567. p. 2238

Velasquez, Jennifer, Teen Serv Coordr, San Antonio Public Library, Teen Services, 600 Soledad, San Antonio, TX, 78205-2786. Tel: 210-207-2678. p. 2239

Velasquez, Julio, Libr Dir, Duncanville Public Library, 201 James Collins Blvd, Duncanville, TX, 75116. Tel: 972-780-5053. p. 2172

Velasquez, Maggie, Library Contact, Transamerica Occidental Life Insurance, 1150 S Olive St, Ste T-2700, Los Angeles, CA, 90015-2211. Tel: 213-742-3129. p. 168

Velasquez, Terry, Br Mgr, Johnson County Library, Cedar Roe, 5120 Cedar St, Roeland Park, KS, 66205. p. 830

Velasquez, Terry, Br Mgr, Johnson County Library, Shawnee Branch, 13811 Johnson Dr, Shawnee, KS, 66216. p. 830

Velazquez, Flor, Library Contact, Buchalter, 805 SW Broadway, Ste 1500, Portland, OR, 97205. Tel: 503-226-1191. p. 1891

Velazquez, Leida, Libr Mgr, New York Public Library - Astor, Lenox & Tilden Foundations, Throg's Neck Branch, 3025 Cross Bronx Expressway Extension, (@ East Tremont Ave), Bronx, NY, 10465. Tel: 718-792-2612. p. 1597

Veldheer, Kris, Libr Dir, Catholic Theological Union, 5416 S Cornell Ave, Chicago, IL, 60615-5698. Tel: 773-371-5464. p. 555

Veldkamp, Jody, Mkt & Communications Mgr, Johnson County Public Library, 49 E Monroe St, Franklin, IN, 46131. p. 686

Velez, Angelica, Sister, Library Contact, St Thomas More Catholic Newman Center, 1615 E Second St, Tucson, AZ, 85719. Tel: 520-327-4665. p. 83

Velez, LaTesha, Dr, Asst Prof, University of North Carolina at Greensboro, School of Education Bldg, Rm 446, 1300 Spring Garden St, Greensboro, NC, 27412. Tel: 336-334-3477. p. 2790

Velez, Lucy, Bus Mgr, New Jersey Institute of Technology, 186 Central Ave, Newark, NJ, 07103. Tel: 973-596-3207. p. 1426

Velez-Natal, Betsaida, Assoc Prof, University of Puerto Rico, Rio Piedras Campus, PO Box 21906, San Juan, PR, 00931-1906. Tel: 787-764-0000, Ext 8521, 787-764-6199. p. 2795

Velez-Rubio, Daniel, Br Supvr, Lake County Library System, Marion Baysinger Memorial County Library, 756 W Broad St, Groveland, FL, 34736. Tel: 352-429-5840. p. 450

Velez-Vendrell, Norma, Dir, Libr Serv, Northwest Vista College, Redbud Learning Ctr, 3535 N Ellison Dr, San Antonio, TX, 78251. Tel: 210-486-4500. p. 2237

Veli, Ravil, Chief Exec Officer, North Bay Public Library, 271 Worthington St E, North Bay, ON, P1B 1H1, CANADA. Tel: 705-474-4830. p. 2661

Veliz, Kim, Lead Res & Instruction Librn, Butler Community College Library & Archives, Library 600 Bldg, 901 S Haverhill Rd, El Dorado, KS, 67042-3280. Tel: 316-323-6845. p. 805

Velk, Sarah, Libr Dir, Montana State University-Northern, 300 13th St W, Havre, MT, 59501. Tel: 406-265-4140. p. 1295

Vella, Gisi, Dir, Morton Memorial Library, 22 Elm St, Pine Hill, NY, 12465. Tel: 845-254-4222. p. 1618

Vella-Garrido, Rachael, Outreach Librn, Villa Maria College Library, 240 Pine Ridge Rd, Buffalo, NY, 14225. Tel: 716-961-1863. p. 1511

Velo, Jana, Librn, Sons of Norway, 1455 W Lake St, Minneapolis, MN, 55408. Tel: 612-827-3611. p. 1185

Vempala, John, Dir of Library Computing Servs, Nova Southeastern University Libraries, 3100 Ray Ferrero Jr Blvd, Fort Lauderdale, FL, 33314. Tel: 954-262-4695. p. 402

Venard, Paul D, Ref Librn, University of Dayton School of Law, 300 College Park, Dayton, OH, 45469-2772. Tel: 937-229-2314. p. 1780

Venditelli, Michelle, Head, Preservation, Conservation & Library Annex, Brown University, Library Collections Annex, 10 Park Lane, Providence, RI, 02907-3124. Tel: 401-863-3905. p. 2037

Venegas, Cassie, Libr Asst I, Parker Public Library, 1001 S Navajo Ave, Parker, AZ, 85344. Tel: 928-669-2622. p. 68

Venegas, E Frances, Librn, Garcia Venito Public Library, San Lucy District, 1125 C St, Gila Bend, AZ, 85337. Tel: 928-683-2012, 928-683-2796. p. 78

Venegas, Rosina, Br Mgr, Neuse Regional Library, Pollocksville Public Library, 415 Green Hill St, Pollocksville, NC, 28573. Tel: 252-224-5011. p. 1699

Venie, Todd, Asst Dean, Dir, Libr & Info Tech, Louisiana State University Libraries, Paul M Hebert Law Center, One E Campus Dr, Baton Rouge, LA, 70803-1000. Tel: 225-578-4952. p. 884

Venier, Kelli, Br Tech, Monroe County Library System, South Rockwood Branch, 5676 Carleton Rockwood Rd, Ste C, South Rockwood, MI, 48179. Tel: 734-379-3333. p. 1134

Venieri, Joanna, Chief Exec Officer, ILL Coordr, Scientific & Biomedical Information & Documentation Center, 200 S Andrews Ave, Ste 504, Fort Lauderdale, FL, 33301. Tel: 754-333-4565. p. 402

Venne, Carolyn, Exec Dir, Wood Memorial Library, 783 Main St, South Windsor, CT, 06074. Tel: 860-289-1783. p. 337

Venner, Mary Ann, Assoc Dean, Pub Serv, University of North Texas Libraries, 1155 Union Circle, No 305190, Denton, TX, 76203-5017. Tel: 940-565-2868. p. 2170

Ventiere, Dena, Asst Librn, Weare Public Library, Ten Paige Memorial Lane, Weare, NH, 03281. Tel: 603-529-2044. p. 1383

Ventola, Rebecca, Dir, Franklin County Public Library, 355 Franklin St, Rocky Mount, VA, 24151. Tel: 540-483-3098. p. 2346

Ventura, Gerie, Libr Dir, Highline College Library, 2400 S 240th St, MS 25-4, Des Moines, WA, 98198. Tel: 206-592-3230. p. 2363

Ventura, Julie, Br Mgr, Orange County Library System, South Creek Branch, 1702 Deerfield Blvd, Orlando, FL, 32837. p. 431

Venzor, Cynthia, Br Mgr, Hutchinson County Library, Stinnett Branch, Courthouse Basement, 500 S Main St, Borger, TX, 79083. Tel: 806-878-4013. p. 2149

Venzor, Fawn, Libr Dir, Three Forks Community Library, 607 S Main St, Three Forks, MT, 59752. Tel: 406-285-3747. p. 1303

Ver Ploeg, Brad, Dir, Narberth Community Library, 80 Windsor Ave, Narberth, PA, 19072-2296. Tel: 610-664-2878. p. 1967

Ver Steeg, Jennie, Dir, Libr & Media Serv, Mercy College of Health Sciences Library, 928 Sixth Ave, Des Moines, IA, 50309-1239. Tel: 515-643-6613. p. 747

Vera, Cara, Libr Serv Mgr, Rancho Cucamonga Public Library, 12505 Cultural Center Dr, Rancho Cucamonga, CA, 91739. Tel: 909-477-2720. p. 197

Vera, Linda, Libr Mgr, Crowell Public Library, 1890 Huntington Dr, San Marino, CA, 91108-2595. Tel: 626-300-0775. p. 234

Vera, Salvador, Br Supvr, Yuma County Free Library District, Somerton Branch, 240 Canal St, Somerton, AZ, 85350. Tel: 928-627-2149. p. 86

Verba, Sharon, Head, Res & Instruction, University of South Carolina, 1322 Greene St, Columbia, SC, 29208-0103. Tel: 803-777-3142. p. 2055

Verbesey, Kevin, Dir, Suffolk Cooperative Library System, 627 N Sunrise Service Rd, Bellport, NY, 11713. Tel: 631-286-1600. p. 1492

Verbick, Erin, Dir, Morrill Public Library, 431 Oregon, Hiawatha, KS, 66434-2290. Tel: 785-742-3831. p. 813

Verbit, Daniel, Syst Librn, Thomas Jefferson University-East Falls, 4201 Henry Ave, Philadelphia, PA, 19144-5497. Tel: 215-951-5365. p. 1987

Verble, Melissa, ILL & Evening Circ Coordr, Christian Brothers University, 650 East Pkwy S, Memphis, TN, 38104. Tel: 901-321-3432. p. 2112

Verderame, Michael, Dr, Head Librn, Hebrew Theological College, 7135 N Carpenter Rd, Skokie, IL, 60077-3263. Tel: 847-982-2500. p. 647

Verdesca, Anthony, Ref Librn, Palm Beach Atlantic University, 300 Pembroke Pl, West Palm Beach, FL, 33401-6503. Tel: 561-803-2238. p. 453

Verdier, Marie-Claude, Libr Asst, National Theatre School of Canada Library, 5030 rue Saint-Denis, Montreal, QC, H2J 2L8, CANADA. Tel: 514-842-7954, Ext 136. p. 2727

Verdine, Delores, Br Mgr, Calcasieu Parish Public Library System, Westlake Branch, 937 Mulberry St, Westlake, LA, 70669. Tel: 337-721-7113. p. 894

Verdini, Jim, Access Serv, Ref Serv, Averett University Library, 344 W Main St, Danville, VA, 24541-2849. Tel: 434-791-5694. p. 2314

Verdone, Joyce, Ser, NHTI, Concord's Community College, 31 College Dr, Concord, NH, 03301-7425. Tel: 603-230-4028. p. 1359

Verdun, Lynne, Board Pres, Odell Public Library District, 301 E Richard St, Odell, IL, 60460. Tel: 815-998-2012. p. 628

Verdun-Morris, Vanessa, Dir, Taylor Community Library, 12303 Pardee Rd, Taylor, MI, 48180-4219. Tel: 734-287-4840. p. 1153

Veres, Lisa, Circ Supvr, Palm Springs Public Library, 217 Cypress Lane, Palm Springs, FL, 33461-1698. Tel: 561-584-8350. p. 435

Vergara-Bautista, Gina S, Supvr, Hawaii State Archives, Iolani Palace Grounds, 364 S King St, Honolulu, HI, 96813. Tel: 808-586-0329. p. 506

Verge, Lynn, Exec Dir, Atwater Library & Computer Centre, 1200 Atwater Ave, Westmount, QC, H3Z 1X4, CANADA. Tel: 514-935-7344. p. 2739

Verhayden, Rebecca, Dir, Town of Ballston Community Library, Two Lawmar Lane, Burnt Hills, NY, 12027. Tel: 518-399-8174. p. 1511

Verhey, Barb, Asst Librn, Rock County Community Library, 201 W Main, Luverne, MN, 56156. Tel: 507-449-5040. p. 1180

Verillo, Molly, Ch, Southington Public Library & Museum, 255 Main St, Southington, CT, 06489. Tel: 860-628-0947. p. 337

Verkerk, Anne, Library Contact, Selkirk College Library, Silver Campus, 2001 Silver King Rd, Nelson, BC, V1L 1C8, CANADA. Tel: 250-354-3249. p. 2564

Verma, Asha, Head, Circ, Montgomery County-Norristown Public Library, 1001 Powell St, Norristown, PA, 19401-3817. Tel: 610-278-5100, Ext 112. p. 1971

Verma, Louisa, Ref Serv, Huntington Hospital, 100 W California Blvd, Pasadena, CA, 91105-3010. Tel: 626-397-5161. p. 193

Verma, Louisa, Librn, Portland Cement Association, 5420 Old Orchard Rd, Skokie, IL, 60077-1083. Tel: 847-972-9174. p. 647

Vermette, Stephen, Info Tech, Taunton Public Library, 12 Pleasant St, Taunton, MA, 02780. Tel: 508-821-1410. p. 1059

VerMeulen, Amanda, Dir, Libr & Archives, Saint Mary's College of Maryland Library, 47645 College Dr, Saint Mary's City, MD, 20686-3001. Tel: 240-895-4267. p. 976

Vermillion, Jeani, Asst Librn, Ranger College, 1100 College Circle, Ranger, TX, 76470-3298. Tel: 254-647-1414. p. 2230

Vermillion, Kaylie, Circ Mgr, Ohio State University LIBRARIES, Michael E Moritz Law Library, 55 W 12th Ave, Columbus, OH, 43210-1391. Tel: 614-292-6691. p. 1776

Vermillion, Mary, Commun Relations Mgr, Whatcom County Library System, 5205 Northwest Dr, Bellingham, WA, 98226. Tel: 360-305-3600. p. 2359

Vernau, Mary, City Librn, Tyler Public Library, 201 S College Ave, Tyler, TX, 75702-7381. Tel: 903-593-7323. p. 2250

Vernell, Erin, Librn, First Presbyterian Church, 5300 Main St, Houston, TX, 77004. Tel: 713-620-6500. p. 2191

Vernet, Renaud, Head Librn, Bibliotheque de Sorel Tracy, 3015 Place des Loisirs, De Sorel Tracy, QC, J3R 5S5, CANADA. Tel: 450-780-5600, Ext 4442. p. 2711

Verniest, Jo-Ann, Head Librn, Victoria Municipal Library, 102 Stewart Ave, Holland, MB, R0G 0X0, CANADA. Tel: 204-526-2011. p. 2587

Vernon, Angie, Br Mgr, Avoyelles Parish Library, Bunkie Branch, 200 Walnut St, Bunkie, LA, 71322. Tel: 318-346-6122. p. 897

Veronique, Marcotte, Librn, Bibliothèque Raymond-Laberge, 25 Maple Blvd, Chateauguay, QC, J6J 3P7, CANADA. Tel: 450-698-3080. p. 2710

Veronneau, Kevin, Libr Mgr, Community Libraries of Providence, Olneyville Library, One Olneyville Sq, Providence, RI, 02909. Tel: 401-421-4084. p. 2038

Verostek, Jane, Archives, State University of New York, College of Environmental Science & Forestry, One Forestry Dr, Syracuse, NY, 13210. Tel: 315-470-6718. p. 1650

Verostko, Joann, Br Mgr, Montgomery-Floyd Regional Library System, Jessie Peterman Memorial, 321 W Main St, Floyd, VA, 24091. Tel: 540-745-2947. p. 2313

Verquin, Amy, Libr Mgr, Rycroft Municipal Library, 4732-50 St, Rycroft, AB, T0H 3A0, CANADA. Tel: 780-765-3973. p. 2552

Verrilli, Gina, Asst Dir, Phinehas S Newton Library, 19 On the Common, Royalston, MA, 01368. Tel: 978-249-3572. p. 1050

Verrillo, Debra, Ch, North Branford Library Department, Edward Smith Branch, Three Old Post Rd, Northford, CT, 06472. Tel: 203-484-0469. p. 331

Vigliotta, Brooke, Weekend Supvr, Colby-Sawyer College, 541 Main St, New London, NH, 03257-4648. Tel: 603-526-3685. p. 1375

Vigneault, Marie-Soleil, Dir, Reseau BIBLIO de la Cote-Nord, 59 ave Napoleon, Sept Iles, QC, G4R 5C5, CANADA. Tel: 418-962-1020, Ext 222. p. 2736

Vigo-Verestin, Milka, Libr Dir, Evangelical Seminary of Puerto Rico, 776 Ponce de Leon Ave, San Juan, PR, 00925-9907. Tel: 787-763-6700, Ext 233. p. 2513

Vigorito, Angelo, Archivist, The General Society of Mechanics & Tradesmen Library, 20 W 44th St, New York, NY, 10036. Tel: 212-840-1840, Ext 2. p. 1586

Vigue, Jaimie, Br Mgr, Atlantic County Library System, Ventnor Branch, 6500 Atlantic Ave, Ventnor, NJ, 08406. Tel: 609-823-4614. p. 1417

Vigue Picard, Larissa, Exec Dir, Pejepscot History Center, 159 Park Row, Brunswick, ME, 04011. Tel: 207-729-6606. p. 919

Vik, Jean, Assoc Libr Dir, Syst, University of Texas at Dallas, 800 W Campbell Rd, Richardson, TX, 75080. Tel: 972-883-2623. p. 2231

Vikor, Marlene, Sr Librn, Tech Serv, Board of Governors of The Federal Reserve System, Research Library, 20th & C St NW, MS 102, Washington, DC, 20551. Tel: 202-452-3333, p. 361

Vilander, Debi, Sr Librn, Long Beach Public Library, Bay Shore, 195 Bay Shore Ave, Long Beach, CA, 90803. Tel: 562-570-1039. p. 159

Vilas Novas, Jessica V, Dir, Lawrence Public Library, 51 Lawrence St, Lawrence, MA, 01841. Tel: 978-620-3600. p. 1027

Vilaxa, Paola, Mgr, Jefferson County Public Library, Arvada Library, 7525 W 57th Ave, Arvada, CO, 80002. Tel: 303-403-5060. p. 288

Vilelle, Luke, Univ Librn, Hollins University, 7950 E Campus Dr, Roanoke, VA, 24020. Tel: 540-362-7465. p. 2345

Viles, Deborah, Acq Mgr, Mgr, Ser, Maryland Institute College of Art, 1401 W Mount Royal Ave, Baltimore, MD, 21217. Tel: 410-225-2304, 410-225-2311. p. 955

Villa, Cesar, Dir, Eagle Pass Public Library, 589 Main St, Eagle Pass, TX, 78852. Tel: 830-773-7323. p. 2172

Villa, Keilah, Campus Librn, Nelson University, American Indian College, 10020 N 15th Ave, Phoenix, AZ, 85021-2199. Tel: 602-944-3335, Ext 217, 602-944-3335, Ext 252. p. 71

Villa, Lisa, Digital Scholarship Librn, College of the Holy Cross, One College St, Worcester, MA, 01610. Tel: 508-793-2767. p. 1072

Villa, Samantha, Libr Dir, Southeast New Mexico College, 1500 University Dr, Carlsbad, NM, 88220. Tel: 575-234-9330. p. 1465

Villagomez, Oscar, Mgr, County of Los Angeles Public Library, South Whittier Library, 11543 Colima Rd, Whittier, CA, 90604-2966. Tel: 562-946-4415. p. 138

Villalobos, Jennifer, Br Supvr, Boise Public Library, Library! at Collister, 4724 W State St, Boise, ID, 83703. Tel: 208-972-8320. p. 516

Villalobos, Samantha, Head, Tech Serv, Texas A&M University-Kingsville, 1050 University Blvd, MSC 197, Kingsville, TX, 78363. Tel: 361-593-3319. p. 2206

Villalobos, Yoland, Libr Asst, Ward County Library, Barstow Branch, Community Bldg, Barstow, TX, 79719. Tel: 432-445-5205. p. 2220

Villanueva, Andrea, Mgr, Columbus Metropolitan Library, Northern Lights Branch, 4093 Cleveland Ave, Columbus, OH, 43224. p. 1773

Villanueva, Julie, Circ Supvr, Monterey Park Bruggemeyer Library, 318 S Ramona Ave, Monterey Park, CA, 91754-3399. Tel: 626-307-1368. p. 180

Villanueva, Natalie, Mkt Coordr, Greenspoon Marder, 200 E Broward Blvd, Ste 1800, Fort Lauderdale, FL, 33301. Tel: 954-491-1120. p. 401

Villanueva, Sarah, Librn, Northwest Regional Library, Thief River Falls Public Library, 102 First St E, Thief River Falls, MN, 56701. Tel: 218-681-4325. p. 1205

Villar, Ana, Librarian, Math & Sciences, North Seattle Community College, 9600 College Way N, Seattle, WA, 98103. Tel: 206-527-3607. p. 2377

Villarino, Esther, Head, Cat, University of Puerto Rico, Law School Library, Avenidas Ponce de Leon & Gandara, San Juan, PR, 00931. Tel: 787-999-9709. p. 2514

Villarma, Margaret, Libr Dir, Irene Ingle Public Library, 124 Second Ave, Wrangell, AK, 99929. Tel: 907-874-3535. p. 53

Villarreal, Janie, Dir, Port Isabel Public Library, 213 Yturria St, Port Isabel, TX, 78578. Tel: 956-943-1822. p. 2228

Villarreal, Lillian, Librn, Ed & Hazel Richmond Public Library, 110 N Lamont St, Aransas Pass, TX, 78336. Tel: 361-758-2350. p. 2136

Villarreal, Melina, Cat Tech, Laredo College, West End Washington St, Laredo, TX, 78040. Tel: 956-721-5269. p. 2210

Villarreal, Melissa, Dir, Fox Lake Public District Library, 255 E Grand Ave, Fox Lake, IL, 60020. Tel: 847-587-0198. p. 589

Villarreal, Michael, Circ & Reserves Supvr, University of California, Berkeley, Chemistry & Chemical Engineering, 100 Hildebrand Hall, Berkeley, CA, 94720-6000. Tel: 510-643-4477. p. 122

Villarreal, Michael, Circ & Reserves Supvr, University of California, Berkeley, Physics-Astronomy Library, 351 LeConte Hall, Berkeley, CA, 94720-6000. Tel: 510-642-3122. p. 123

Villarreal, Patricia, Librn, United States Navy, 601 Nimitz Ave, Bldg 3766, Kingsville, TX, 78363. Tel: 361-516-6449. p. 2207

Villarreal, Rebecca, Research Librn, Harvard Library, Andover-Harvard Theological Library, Divinity School, 45 Francis Ave, Cambridge, MA, 02138. Tel: 617-495-5788. p. 1005

Villegas, Darlene, Library Contact, Doheny Eye Institute Library, 1355 San Pablo St, Los Angeles, CA, 90033. Tel: 323-342-6600. p. 161

Villegas, Susana, Libr Dir, La Joya Municipal Library, 201 Palm Shores Blvd, La Joya, TX, 78560. Tel: 956-581-4533. p. 2207

Villegas, Victoria, Libr Asst, City of Melissa Public Library, 3411 Barker Ave, Melissa, TX, 75454. Tel: 972-837-4540. p. 2218

Villela, Katrine, Tech Serv Mgr, Victoria Public Library, 302 N Main St, Victoria, TX, 77901. Tel: 361-485-3302. p. 2252

Villeneuve, Nathalie, Dir, Universite du Quebec a Chicoutimi, 555 Blvd de l'Universite E, Chicoutimi, QC, G7H 2B1, CANADA. Tel: 418-545-5011, Ext 5630. p. 2711

Villet, Aimee, Youth Serv Dir, Glen Carbon Centennial Library District, 198 S Main St, Glen Carbon, IL, 62034. Tel: 618-288-1212. p. 593

Villigrana, Rosa, Libr Asst, Lake County Library District, Silver Lake Branch, Hwy 31, Silver Lake, OR, 97638. Tel: 541-576-2146. p. 1884

Villy, Melissa, Prog Spec, Carroll Public Library, 118 E Fifth St, Carroll, IA, 51401. Tel: 712-792-3432. p. 737

Vilshanetskaya, Rimma, Coll Develop Spec, Mount Saint Mary College, 330 Powell Ave, Newburgh, NY, 12550-3494. Tel: 845-569-3243. p. 1605

Vinal, Adra, Operations Supvr, University of Nebraska-Lincoln, Architecture Library, Architecture Hall, Rm 308, City Campus 0108, Lincoln, NE, 68588-0108. p. 1323

Vince, Jeanne, Coll Develop, Ref Librn, University of Tampa, 401 W Kennedy Blvd, Tampa, FL, 33606-1490. Tel: 813-257-3744. p. 450

Vincelli, Deborah, Electronic Res, Metropolitan Museum of Art, Thomas J Watson Library, 1000 Fifth Ave, New York, NY, 10028-0198. Tel: 212-650-2912. p. 1592

Vincelli, Nick J, Head Librn, North Carolina Department of Labor, 111 Hillsborough St, Rm C510, Raleigh, NC, 27603-1762. Tel: 919-707-7880. p. 1709

Vincent, Alyssa, Digital Scholarship Librn, First-Year Experience Coord, Northeastern Illinois University, 5500 N Saint Louis Ave, Chicago, IL, 60625-4699. Tel: 773-442-4400. p. 566

Vincent, Annette, Circ Mgr, Coordr, University of Arkansas-Monticello Library, 514 University Dr, Monticello, AR, 71656. Tel: 870-460-1080. p. 105

Vincent, Anthony, Br Mgr, Chippewa River District Library, Faith Johnston Memorial, 4035 N Mission, Rosebush, MI, 48878. Tel: 989-433-0006. p. 1135

Vincent, Bonnie, Borrower Serv Librn, Barbara S Ponce Public Library, 7770 52nd St, Pinellas Park, FL, 33781. Tel: 727-369-0592. p. 437

Vincent, Dena, Librn, Edward A Block Family Library, 705 Riley Hospital Dr, Rm 1719, Indianapolis, IN, 46202-5109. Tel: 317-944-1149. p. 690

Vincent, John, Pres, Downey Historical Society, 12540 Rives Ave, Downey, CA, 90242-3444. Tel: 562-862-2777. p. 139

Vincent, Lynda, Libr Serv Coordr, Volunteer State Community College Library, 1480 Nashville Pike, Gallatin, TN, 37066-3188. Tel: 615-230-3415. p. 2099

Vincent, Michelle, Libr Engagement Facilitator, St Dominic Hospital, 969 Lakeland Dr, Jackson, MS, 39216. Tel: 601-200-6944. p. 1223

Vincent, Patti, Library Contact, Multnomah County Library, Capitol Hill, 10723 SW Capitol Hwy, Portland, OR, 97219. p. 1892

Vincent, Rachel, Librn, Sterling Public Library, 1183 Plainfield Pike, Oneco, CT, 06373. Tel: 860-564-2692. p. 333

Vincent, Sharla A, Dir, Tekonsha Public Library, 230 S Church St, Tekonsha, MI, 49092. Tel: 517-767-4769. p. 1153

Vincent, Sue, ILL Librn, Dover Public Library, 73 Locust St, Dover, NH, 03820-3785. Tel: 603-516-6050. p. 1361

Vincent, Tammy, Br Mgr, Robeson County Public Library, Pembroke Public, 413 S Blaine St, Pembroke, NC, 28372. Tel: 910-521-1554. p. 1702

Vincent-Ekunwe, Vincent, Tech & Web Support Specialist, Clayton State University Library, 2000 Clayton State Blvd, Morrow, GA, 30260. Tel: 678-466-4325. p. 491

Vincett, Matthew, Librn, James Sprunt Community College, Boyette Bldg, 133 James Sprunt Dr, Kenansville, NC, 28349. Tel: 910-275-6330. p. 1699

Vinciguerra, Antoinette, Librn, Roanoke Public Libraries, Williamson Road, 3837 Williamson Rd NW, Roanoke, VA, 24012. Tel: 540-853-2340. p. 2345

Vincz, Sharon, Dir, Library Company of Burlington, 23 W Union St, Burlington, NJ, 08016. Tel: 609-386-1273. p. 1393

Vine, Scott, Col Librn, Franklin & Marshall College, 450 College Ave, Lancaster, PA, 17604. Tel: 717-358-3840. p. 1950

Vining, Marcia, Libr Dir, Ignacio Community Library, 470 Goddard Ave, Ignacio, CO, 81137. Tel: 970-563-9287. p. 286

Vining, Melissa, Br Mgr, Assumption Parish Library, Labadieville Branch, 105 Cherry St, Labadieville, LA, 70372. Tel: 985-526-7055. p. 899

Vinke, Dana, Principal Librn, Torrance Public Library, 3301 Torrance Blvd, Torrance, CA, 90503. Tel: 310-618-5974. p. 253

Vinke, Dana, Dep Libr Dir, Ventura County Library, 5600 Everglades St, Ste A, Ventura, CA, 93003. Tel: 805-677-7150. p. 256

Vinson, Brenda, Librn, Tombigbee Regional Library System, Dorothy J Lowe Memorial Public Library, 165 Young Ave, Nettleton, MS, 38858. Tel: 662-963-2011. p. 1235

Vinson, Chris, Assoc Librn, Libr Tech, Clemson University Libraries, 116 Sigma Dr, Clemson, SC, 29631. Tel: 864-656-3622. p. 2052
Vinson, Corey, Ref Librn, First Regional Library, Lafayette County-Oxford Public Library, 401 Bramlett Blvd, Oxford, MS, 38655. Tel: 662-234-5751. p. 1220
Vinson, Daniel, Libr Dir, Mount Mary University, 2900 N Menomonee River Pkwy, Milwaukee, WI, 53222-4597. p. 2460
Vinson, Debra, Librn, Louisville Public Library, 1951 Main St, Louisville, AL, 36048. Tel: 334-266-5210. p. 24
Vinton, Cab, Dir, Plaistow Public Library, 85 Main St, Plaistow, NH, 03865. Tel: 603-382-6011. p. 1378
Vinyard, Marc, Assoc University Librn for Graduate Campus Libraries, Pepperdine University Libraries, 24255 Pacific Coast Hwy, Malibu, CA, 90263. Tel: 310-506-4252. p. 171
Viola, Vanessa, Assoc Dir, Librn II, New York Institute of Technology, Art & Architecture Library, Education Hall, New York Institute of Technology, Northern Blvd, Old Westbury, NY, 11568-8000. Tel: 516-686-7422, 516-686-7579. p. 1610
Violette, James, Jr, Pres, Waterville Historical Society Library, 62 Silver St, Unit B, Waterville, ME, 04901. Tel: 207-872-6286. p. 945
Vipperman, Betsy, Libr Dir, New York State Judicial Department, M Dolores Denman Courthouse, 50 East Ave, Ste 100, Rochester, NY, 14604. Tel: 585-530-3250. p. 1629
Virbia, Krizia, Libr Serv Supvr, Covina Public Library, 234 N Second Ave, Covina, CA, 91723-2198. Tel: 626-384-5303. p. 133
Virden, Christine, Archivist, Manchester Historical Museum, Ten Union St, Manchester-by-the-Sea, MA, 01944. Tel: 978-526-7230. p. 1031
Virgil, Barbara, Libr Office Mgr, Marlborough Public Library, 35 W Main St, Marlborough, MA, 01752-5510. Tel: 508-624-6996. p. 1032
Visnak, Kelly, Dr, Univ Librn, Vice Provost, Texas State University, 601 University Dr, San Marcos, TX, 78666-4684. Tel: 512-408-0576. p. 2241
Visser, Dagmar, Ms, Librn, Neerlandia Public Library, 4918 50th St, Neerlandia, AB, T0G 1R0, CANADA. Tel: 780-674-5384. p. 2549
Visser, Marijke, Dir, Libr Develop, Maine State Library, 242 State St, Augusta, ME, 04333. Tel: 207-287-5600. p. 914
Visser, Meghan, Operations Mgr, Southern Alberta Art Gallery Library, 601 Third Ave S, Lethbridge, AB, T1J 0H4, CANADA. Tel: 403-327-8770, Ext 27. p. 2546
Vital, Sarah, Bus Librn, Saint Mary's College Library, 1928 Saint Mary's Rd, Moraga, CA, 94575. Tel: 925-631-4229. p. 180
Vitale, Jeanne, Dir, Three Bridges Public Library, 449 Main St, Three Bridges, NJ, 08887. Tel: 908-782-2908. p. 1445
Vitale, Thomas S, Libr Dir, Patterson Library, 40 S Portage St, Westfield, NY, 14787. Tel: 716-326-2154. p. 1664
Vitas, Gaile, Libr Dir, Lithuanian Research & Studies Center, Inc, 5620 S Claremont Ave, Chicago, IL, 60636-1039. Tel: 773-434-4545. p. 563
Vitella, Franco, Mobile Serv Mgr, Toledo-Lucas County Public Library, 325 Michigan St, Toledo, OH, 43604. Tel: 419-259-5200. p. 1824
Vitez, Gordana, Libr Mgr, Niagara College of Applied Arts & Technology, Daniel J Patterson Campus Library, 135 Taylor Rd, SS 4, Niagara-on-the-Lake, ON, L0S 1J0, CANADA. Tel: 905-641-2252, Ext 4223. p. 2703
Vitiello, Regina, Librn, North Shore University Hospital, 300 Community Dr, Manhasset, NY, 11030. Tel: 516-562-4324. p. 1568
Vitkauskas, Rebecca, Coll Develop Librn, Programming, Richard Salter Storrs Library, 693 Longmeadow St, Longmeadow, MA, 01106. Tel: 413-565-4181. p. 1029
Vitoratos, Stavroula, Pub Serv Librn, Dawson College Library, 3040 Sherbrooke St W, Westmount, QC, H3Z 1A4, CANADA. Tel: 514-931-8731, Ext 1798. p. 2739
Vittek, Robyn E, Dir, Mt Lebanon Public Library, 16 Castle Shannon Blvd, Pittsburgh, PA, 15228-2252. Tel: 412-531-1912. p. 1994
Vitzelio, Tom, Dean of Student Success, Dean, Acad Support, Riverside Community College District, 16130 Lasselle St, Moreno Valley, CA, 92551. Tel: 951-571-6356. p. 181
Viveiros, Jayme, Dir, Lakeville Public Library, Four Precinct St, Lakeville, MA, 02347. Tel: 508-947-9028. p. 1026
Viveros, Juan, Dir, Hidalgo Public Library, 710 Ramon Ayala Dr, Hidalgo, TX, 78557. Tel: 956-843-2093. p. 2190
Vivian, Alexis, Librn, Alamance County Public Libraries, North Park, North Park Community Ctr, 849 Sharpe Rd, Burlington, NC, 27217. Tel: 336-226-7185. p. 1676
Vivian, Jean-Paul, Principal Law Librn, Nassau County Supreme Court, 100 Supreme Court Dr, 2nd Flr, Mineola, NY, 11501. Tel: 516-442-8580. p. 1572
Viviani, Deena, Circ, Prog Coordr, Brighton Memorial Library, 2300 Elmwood Ave, Rochester, NY, 14618. Tel: 585-784-5300. p. 1628
Viviano-Broderick, Tammi, Dr, Dean, College of Central Florida, 3001 SW College Rd, Ocala, FL, 34474-4415. Tel: 352-873-5805. p. 429
Vizecky, Susan, Dir, Ivanhoe Public Library, 401 N Harold, Ivanhoe, MN, 56142. Tel: 507-694-1555. p. 1179
Vizzini, Beth, Head, Circ, West Texas A&M University, 110 26th St, Canyon, TX, 79016. Tel: 806-651-2230. p. 2153
Vlach, Jennine, Access Serv, Team Leader, Case Western Reserve University, 11055 Euclid Ave, Cleveland, OH, 44106. Tel: 216-368-0555. p. 1766
Vloeberghs, Sonja, Dept Head, Lending Serv, Princeton Public Library, 65 Witherspoon St, Princeton, NJ, 08542. Tel: 609-924-9529. p. 1436
Vocino, Michael, Tech Serv Librn, University of Rhode Island, 15 Lippitt Rd, Kingston, RI, 02881-2011. Tel: 401-874-4605. p. 2033
Voebel, Sherri Lynn, Head of Libr, Northwestern State University College of Nursing & Allied Health - Library, 1800 Line Ave, Rm 101, Shreveport, LA, 71101. p. 908
Voekel, Matt, Curator, Klamath County Museum & Baldwin Hotel Museum, 1451 Main St, Klamath Falls, OR, 97601. Tel: 541-883-4208. p. 1883
Voelcker, Aaron, Dr, Dean, Libr & Learning Support Serv, Santiago Canyon College Library, 8045 E Chapman Ave, Orange, CA, 92869. Tel: 714-628-5001. p. 189
Voelkel, James, Curator, Rare Bks, Science History Institute Museum & Library, 315 Chestnut St, Philadelphia, PA, 19106. Tel: 215-873-8205. p. 1985
Voelker, Charley, Ref Serv Mgr, Morley Library, 184 Phelps St, Painesville, OH, 44077-3926. Tel: 440-352-3383. p. 1812
Voelker, Diane, Mgr, UPMC Hamot, 201 State St, Erie, PA, 16550. Tel: 814-877-3628. p. 1932
Voelkers, Emily, Pub Serv Librn, Oklahoma Wesleyan University Library, 2201 Silver Lake Rd, Bartlesville, OK, 74006. Tel: 918-335-6298. p. 1842
Voell, Mary Patricia, Exec Dir, Fond du Lac County Historical Society, 336 Old Pioneer Rd, Fond du Lac, WI, 54935-6126. Tel: 920-922-1166. p. 2435
Voeller, Stacy, Pub Serv Librn, Minnesota State University Moorhead, 1104 Seventh Ave S, Moorhead, MN, 56563. Tel: 218-477-2922. p. 1189
Voels, Sarah, Col Librn, Dir, Wartburg College Library, 100 Wartburg Blvd, Waverly, IA, 50677-0903. Tel: 319-352-8500. p. 789
Vogel, Alicia, Dir, Lamberton Public Library, 101 E Second Ave, Lamberton, MN, 56152. Tel: 507-752-7220. p. 1180
Vogel, Alita, Dir, Letcher County Public Library District, 220 Main St, Whitesburg, KY, 41858. Tel: 606-633-7547. p. 877
Vogel, Gerald, Asst Dir, Avon Lake Public Library, 32649 Electric Blvd, Avon Lake, OH, 44012. Tel: 440-933-8128. p. 1748
Vogel, Jeff, Ad, Anacortes Public Library, 1220 Tenth St, Anacortes, WA, 98221-1988. Tel: 360-293-8128. p. 2357
Vogel, Jeff, Tech Serv Librn, Anacortes Public Library, 1220 Tenth St, Anacortes, WA, 98221-1988. Tel: 360-293-1910, Ext 33. p. 2357
Vogel, Karen, Adjunct Librn, Compton College Library, 1111 E Artesia Blvd, Compton, CA, 90221. Tel: 310-900-1600, Ext 2179. p. 132
Vogel, Pamela J, Ch Serv Librn, Rushville Public Library, 130 W Third St, Rushville, IN, 46173-1899. Tel: 765-932-3496. p. 717
Vogel, Petra, Librn, Sterling College, 1205 N Craftsbury Rd, Craftsbury Common, VT, 05827. Tel: 802-586-7711, Ext 129. p. 2282
Vogel, Samantha Public, Circ Supvr, Waterford Public Library, 101 N River St, Waterford, WI, 53185-4149. Tel: 262-534-3988, Ext 12. p. 2483
Vogel, Victoria, Br Mgr, Huron County Community Library, Wakeman Community Library, 33 Pleasant St, Wakeman, OH, 44889. Tel: 440-839-2976. p. 1832
Vogel-Teeter, Lindsey, Curator, Pueblo Grande Museum & Archaeological Park, 4619 E Washington St, Phoenix, AZ, 85034-1909. Tel: 602-495-0901. p. 72
Vogh, Bryan, Tech Coordr, University of Wisconsin-Stout, 315 Tenth Ave, Menomonie, WI, 54751-0790. Tel: 715-232-1892. p. 2456
Vogl, Ann, Syst Librn, University of Wisconsin-Stout, 315 Tenth Ave, Menomonie, WI, 54751-0790. Tel: 715-232-1553. p. 2456
Vogl, Tom, Chief Exec Officer, Mountaineers Library, 7700 Sand Point Way NE, Seattle, WA, 98115. Tel: 206-521-6000. p. 2377
Vogler, Laura, Assoc Dir, Wabash College, 301 W Wabash Ave, Crawfordsville, IN, 47933. Tel: 765-361-6215. p. 677
Vogt, Lori, Dir, Bailey H Dunlap Memorial Public Library, 400 S Main St, La Feria, TX, 78559. Tel: 956-797-1242. p. 2207
Vogt, Valerie, Ref (Info Servs), Shook, Hardy & Bacon, 2555 Grand Blvd, 3rd Flr, Kansas City, MO, 64108-2613. Tel: 816-474-6550. p. 1257
Voisey, Sarah, Librn, Nunavut Public Library Services, Donald Suluk Library, PO Box 4000, Arviat, NU, X0C 0E0, CANADA. Tel: 867-857-2579. p. 2625
Voitko, Nancy, Br Mgr, Ocean County Library, Brick Branch, 301 Chambers Bridge Rd, Brick, NJ, 08723-2803. Tel: 732-477-4513. p. 1446
Volf, Diane, Asst Librn, White River Public Library, 123 Superior St, White River, ON, P0M 3G0, CANADA. Tel: 807-822-1113. p. 2704
Volin, Eva, Supvr, Ch Serv, Alameda Free Library, 1550 Oak St, Alameda, CA, 94501. Tel: 510-747-7707. p. 115
Volk, Rachel, Acq Spec, Valparaiso University, 1410 Chapel Dr, Valparaiso, IN, 46383-6493. Tel: 219-464-5500. p. 723
Volkanova, Victoria, Ref Librn, Universite de Moncton, 18, ave Antonine-Maillet, Moncton, NB, E1A 3E9, CANADA. Tel: 506-858-4012. p. 2604
Volkert, Jennifer, Libr District Dir, Navajo County Library District, 121 W Buffalo, Holbrook, AZ, 86025. Tel: 928-524-4749. p. 63
Volkman, Karen, Instruction & Ref Librn, State University of New York College at Plattsburgh, Two Draper Ave, Plattsburgh, NY, 12901. Tel: 518-564-5305. p. 1619
Volland, Mark, Communications Mgr, Southern Maryland Regional Library Association, Inc, 37600 New Market Rd, Charlotte Hall, MD, 20622. Tel: 301-884-0436. p. 961

Vollebekk, Marc, Libr Tech, Nova Scotia Community College, Lunenburg Campus Library, 75 High St, Bridgewater, NS, B4V 1V8, CANADA. Tel: 902-543-0684. p. 2620

Vollmer, Timothy, Copyright Librn, Scholarly Communications Librn, University of California, Berkeley, South Hall Rd, Berkeley, CA, 94704. Tel: 510-642-6657. p. 122

Vollum, Nicole, Univ Librn, University of Western States Library, 8000 NE Tillamook St, Portland, OR, 97213. Tel: 503-251-5752. p. 1894

Volpe, Paul, Br Mgr, Newark Public Library, Clinton, 739 Bergen St, Newark, NJ, 07108. Tel: 973-733-7757. p. 1427

Von Behren, Misty, Dep Libr Dir, Perry Public Library, 1101 Willis Ave, Perry, IA, 50220. Tel: 515-465-3569. p. 777

Von Drasek, Lisa, Curator, University of Minnesota Libraries-Twin Cities, Children's Literature Research Collections, Elmer L Andersen Library, 222 21st Ave S, Ste 113, Minneapolis, MN, 55455. Tel: 612-624-4576. p. 1185

Von Dulm, Timothy C, Assoc Dir, Res Serv, University of Pennsylvania Libraries, Biddle Law Library, 3501 Sansom St, Philadelphia, PA, 19104. Tel: 215-898-0844. p. 1988

Von Hassell, Elizabeth, Exec Dir, National Sporting Library & Museum, 102 The Plains Rd, Middleburg, VA, 20117. Tel: 540-687-6542, Ext 30. p. 2332

Von Isenburg, Megan, Assoc Dean, Library Services & Archives, Duke University Libraries, Medical Center Library & Archives, DUMC Box 3702, Ten Searle Dr, Durham, NC, 27710-0001. Tel: 919-660-1148. p. 1684

von Letkemann, Lucia, Teen Librn, Wiggin Memorial Library, Ten Bunker Hill Ave, Stratham, NH, 03885. Tel: 603-772-4346. p. 1381

von Mayrhauser, Kathy, Br Mgr, Burlingame Public Library, 480 Primrose Rd, Burlingame, CA, 94010. Tel: 650-558-7400. p. 125

von Ranson, Julia, Youth Serv Librn, Putney Public Library, 55 Main St, Putney, VT, 05346. Tel: 802-387-4407. p. 2292

von Seldeneck, Robin, Pres & Chief Exec Officer, Woodrow Wilson Presidential Library & Museum, 20 N Coalter St, Staunton, VA, 24401-4332. Tel: 540-885-0897. p. 2347

Von Tungeln, Brittney, Librn, North Texas State Hospital, 4730 College Dr, Vernon, TX, 76384. Tel: 940-552-4117. p. 2251

von Unwerth, Matthew, Libr Dir, New York Psychoanalytic Society & Institute, 247 E 82nd St, New York, NY, 10028-2701. Tel: 212-879-6900. p. 1594

von Wittgenstein, Karin, Dir, Kimberley Public Library, 115 Spokane St, Kimberley, BC, V1A 2E5, CANADA. Tel: 250-427-3112. p. 2569

VonButtgereit, Jason, Head, Info Tech, Baldwin Public Library, 2385 Grand Ave, Baldwin, NY, 11510-3289. Tel: 516-223-6228. p. 1490

Vonderhaar, Shirley J, Dir, James Kennedy Public Library, 320 First Ave E, Dyersville, IA, 52040. Tel: 563-875-8912. p. 749

VonEwegen, Anna, Children & Teen Librn, Butler Public Library, 340 S Broadway St, Butler, IN, 46721. Tel: 260-868-2351. p. 673

Vong, Ronny Phengsouvanna, Circ Supvr, Fort Smith Public Library, 3201 Rogers Ave, Fort Smith, AR, 72903. Tel: 479-783-0229. p. 96

Vonnegut, Shannon, City Librn, Santa Clarita Public Library, 18601 Soledad Canyon Rd, Santa Clarita, CA, 91351. Tel: 661-259-0750. p. 242

VonTauffkirchen, Elizabeth, Ch Mgr, Pine River Public Library District, 395 Bayfield Center Dr, Bayfield, CO, 81122. Tel: 970-884-2222. p. 266

VonVille, Helena M, Dir, Ref (Info Servs), University of Texas, School of Public Health Library, 1200 Herman Pressler Blvd, Houston, TX, 77030-3900. Tel: 713-500-9121. p. 2200

Voorhees, Brittany, Circ Mgr, Fulton County Public Library, 320 W Seventh St, Rochester, IN, 46975-1332. Tel: 574-223-2713. p. 716

Voorhies, Marguerite, Libr Assoc, Volunteer State Community College Library, 1480 Nashville Pike, Gallatin, TN, 37066-3188. Tel: 615-452-8600, Ext 3404. p. 2099

Voorhies, Mary, Br Mgr, Delphi Public Library, Northwest Carroll Branch, 164 W Forest St, Yeoman, IN, 47997. Tel: 574-965-2382. p. 679

Voorhies, Pamela, Coordr, CHRISTUS Santa Rosa Health Care, 333 N Santa Rosa St, Ste F5626, San Antonio, TX, 78207. Tel: 210-704-2701. p. 2236

Voors, Mary, Mgr, Ch Serv, Allen County Public Library, 900 Library Plaza, Fort Wayne, IN, 46802. Tel: 260-421-1221. p. 683

Vopelak, Mark, Univ Archivist, University of Indianapolis, 1400 E Hanna Ave, Indianapolis, IN, 46227-3697. Tel: 317-788-3268. p. 697

Vorbach, James, PhD, Assoc Prof, Dir, Library & Info Science, St John's University, Saint Augustine Hall, Rm 408A, 8000 Utopia Pkwy, Jamaica, NY, 11439. Tel: 718-990-1834. p. 2789

Vorce, Amanda, Youth Serv Librn, Commerce Township Community Library, 180 E Commerce, Commerce Township, MI, 48382. Tel: 248-669-8101, Ext 112. p. 1093

Vorce, Amanda, Head Librn, Capital Area District Libraries, Webberville Library, 115 S Main St, Webberville, MI, 48892. Tel: 517-521-3643. p. 1124

Vorderstrasse, Ellen, Librn, American Historical Society of Germans from Russia, 631 D St, Lincoln, NE, 68502. Tel: 402-474-3363. p. 1320

Vork, Gretchen, Libr Serv Coordr, Great River Regional Library, Paynesville Library, 119 Washburne Ave, Paynesville, MN, 56362. Tel: 320-243-7343. p. 1197

Vos, Jaycie, Spec Coll Coordr, Univ Archivist, University of Northern Iowa Library, 1227 W 27th St, Cedar Falls, IA, 50613-3675. Tel: 319-273-6307. p. 737

Vos, Larry, Div Mgr, Mgr, Learning Serv, Wichita Public Library, 711 W Second St, Wichita, KS, 67203. Tel: 316-261-8540. p. 843

Vosberg, Emily, Access Serv Mgr, Frank L Weyenberg Library of Mequon-Thiensville, 11345 N Cedarburg Rd, Mequon, WI, 53092-1998. Tel: 262-242-2593. p. 2456

Vosberg, Michelle, Br Mgr, Rockford Public Library, East, 6685 E State St, Rockford, IL, 61108. Tel: 815-965-7606. p. 642

Vose, David, Head, Br Libr, State University of New York at Binghamton, Science Library, Vestal Pkwy E, Binghamton, NY, 13902. Tel: 607-777-4903. p. 1494

Vose, David, Head, Br Libr, State University of New York at Binghamton, University Downtown Center Library Information Commons & Services, 67 Washington St, Binghamton, NY, 13902-6000. Tel: 607-777-9275. p. 1494

Vose, Jeanne, Libr Asst, University of Maine at Machias, 116 O'Brien Ave, Machias, ME, 04654. Tel: 207-255-1234. p. 931

Voshall, Lori, Dir, Ephraim Public Library, 30 S Main St, Ephraim, UT, 84627. Tel: 435-283-4544. p. 2263

Voskuil, Bart, Theological Librn, Mid-America Reformed Seminary Library, 229 Seminary Dr, Dyer, IN, 46311. Tel: 219-864-2400, Ext 412. p. 679

Voss, Anke, Curator, Spec Coll, Concord Free Public Library, 129 Main St, Concord, MA, 01742. Tel: 978-318-3342. p. 1012

Voss, Brian, Libr Dir, NOAA Seattle Regional Library, Bldg 3, 7600 Sand Point Way NE, Seattle, WA, 98115. Tel: 206-526-6241. p. 2377

Voss, Carey, Curator, Historic Arkansas Museum Library, 200 E Third St, Little Rock, AR, 72201-1608. Tel: 501-324-9351. p. 101

Voss, Erica, Youth Serv Librn, The Frances Banta Waggoner Community Library, 505 Tenth St, DeWitt, IA, 52742-1335. Tel: 563-659-5523. p. 747

Voss, Julie, Dir, Forreston Public Library, 204 First Ave, Forreston, IL, 61030. Tel: 815-938-2624. p. 589

Vossberg, Susan, Tech Serv, Northwestern Health Sciences University, 2501 W 84th St, Bloomington, MN, 55431-1599. Tel: 952-204-5361. p. 1166

Vossberg, Susan J, Cat Librn, Hamline University, School of Law Library, 1536 Hewitt Ave, Saint Paul, MN, 55104. Tel: 651-523-2379. p. 1199

Vossler, Kathy, Dir, Haywood County Public Library, 678 S Haywood St, Waynesville, NC, 28786. Tel: 828-356-2504. p. 1721

Vote, Thomas, Dir, Ruth Enlow Library of Garrett County, Six N Second St, Oakland, MD, 21550. Tel: 301-334-3996. p. 972

Voth, Kelly, Librn, Turtle Lake Public Library, 107 Eggert St, Turtle Lake, ND, 58575. Tel: 701-448-9170. p. 1740

Voth, Nancy, Libr Tech, Manitoba Hydro Library, 360 Portage Ave, 2nd Flr, Winnipeg, MB, R3C 0G8, CANADA. Tel: 204-360-4708. p. 2593

Votipka, Jessica, Dir, Exeter Public Library, 202 S Exeter Ave, Exeter, NE, 68351. Tel: 402-266-3031. p. 1313

Votruba, Elaine, Pub Serv Librn, Gila County Library District, 1400 E Ash St, Globe, AZ, 85501-1414. Tel: 928-402-8768, 928-402-8770. p. 62

Votruba, Elaine Helen, Libr Mgr, Hayden Public Library, 520 Velasco Ave, Hayden, AZ, 85135. Tel: 520-356-7801, Ext 501. p. 63

Voves, Ed, Head Librn, Free Library of Philadelphia, Education, Philosophy & Religion, 1901 Vine St, Rm 205, Philadelphia, PA, 19103-1116. Tel: 215-686-5392. p. 1978

Vowles, Chris, Ms, Libr Mgr, Taber Public Library, 5415 50 Ave, Taber, AB, T1G 1V2, CANADA. Tel: 403-223-4343. p. 2556

Voyles, Robbie, Librn, Southern Regional Technical College Library Services, Industrial Drive Campus, 361 Industrial Dr, Moultrie, GA, 31788. Tel: 229-217-4208. p. 499

Voyt, Nick, Youth Librn, Muskegon Area District Library, North Muskegon Walker Branch, 1522 Ruddiman Dr, North Muskegon, MI, 49445-3038. Tel: 231-744-6080. p. 1136

Vrattos, Constance, Interim Dean of Libr, Lesley University, South Campus, 89 Brattle St, Cambridge, MA, 02138-2790. Tel: 617-349-8850. p. 1008

Vredenburg, Beth, Head of Br Serv, Poughkeepsie Public Library District, Boardman Road Branch, 141 Boardman Rd, Poughkeepsie, NY, 12603. Tel: 845-485-3445, Ext 3410. p. 1623

Vredevoogdi, Gwen, Librn, Marymount University, 2807 N Glebe Rd, Arlington, VA, 22207-4299. Tel: 703-284-1533. p. 2305

Vreeke, Tracy, Dir, Nicolet Federated Library System, 1595 Allouez Ave, Ste 4, Green Bay, WI, 54311. Tel: 920-448-4410. p. 2438

Vreeland, Kate, Ad, Ogden Farmers' Library, 269 Ogden Center Rd, Spencerport, NY, 14559. Tel: 585-617-6181. p. 1643

Vriesman, Kirk, Library Contact, Missoula Public Library, Potomac Branch, Potomac School District II, 29750 Potomac Rd, Potomac, MT, 59823. Tel: 406-244-5581, Ext 227. p. 1300

Vrieze, Scott, Exec Dir, Metropolitan Library Service Agency, 1619 Dayton Ave, Ste 314, Saint Paul, MN, 55104. Tel: 651-645-5731. p. 2768

Vroegh, Vicki, Dir, Eddyville Public Library, 202 S Second St, Eddyville, IA, 52553. Tel: 641-969-4815. p. 750

Vrooman, David, Info Literacy Librn, Eastern Connecticut State University, 83 Windham St, Willimantic, CT, 06226-2295. Tel: 860-465-4470. p. 347

Vulgares, Sue, Circ Mgr, San Juan Island Library, 1010 Guard St, Friday Harbor, WA, 98250-9612. Tel: 360-378-2798. p. 2364

Vuori, Teneil, Librn, Red Deer College Library, 100 College Blvd, Red Deer, AB, T4N 5H5, CANADA. Tel: 403-342-3478. p. 2551

Vyas, Hetal, Head, Tech Serv, Middle Georgia Regional Library System, 1180 Washington Ave, Macon, GA, 31201-1790. Tel: 478-744-0813. p. 487

Vyas, Isha, Div Head, Middlesex County Cultural & Heritage Commission, 75 Bayard St, New Brunswick, NJ, 08901. Tel: 732-745-4489. p. 1424

Vyortkina, Dina, Dir, Florida State University Libraries, Learning Resource Center, College of Education, 1301 Stone Bldg, Tallahassee, FL, 32306-4450. Tel: 850-644-4553. p. 447

Waage, Thomas, Libr Res Coordr, St Andrews University, 1700 Dogwood Mile, Laurinburg, NC, 28352. Tel: 910-277-5025. p. 1700

Waak, Paul, Asst Exec Dir, Partners Library Action Network, 5806 Mesa Dr, Ste 375, Austin, TX, 78731. Tel: 512-583-0704. p. 2775

Waarala, Karrie, Libr Dir, Saline District Library, 555 N Maple Rd, Saline, MI, 48176. Tel: 734-429-5450. p. 1148

Wac, Christina, Libr Serv Coordr, Portage College Library, 9531 94th Ave, Lac La Biche, AB, T0A 2C0, CANADA. Tel: 780 623-5755. p. 2545

Wacek, Dawn, Youth Serv Mgr, La Crosse Public Library, 800 Main St, La Crosse, WI, 54601. Tel: 608-789-8190. p. 2446

Wachel, Linda, Librn, Park Cities Baptist Church, 3933 Northwest Pkwy, Dallas, TX, 75225. Tel: 214-860-1593. p. 2167

Wachholz, Jacqueline, Dir, Duke University Libraries, David M Rubenstein Rare Book & Manuscript Library, 316 Perkins Library, 411 Chapel Dt, Durham, NC, 27708. Tel: 919-660-5836. p. 1685

Wachowiak, Amanda, Registrar, Chesapeake Bay Maritime Museum Library, 109A Mill St, Saint Michaels, MD, 21663. Tel: 410-745-4996. p. 976

Wachsmann, Melanie, Br Mgr, Harris County Public Library, Lone Star College-CyFair Library, 9191 Barker Cypress Rd, Cypress, TX, 77429. Tel: 281-290-3210. p. 2193

Wachsmann, Melanie S, Libr Dir, Lone Star College System, CyFair Library, 9191 Barker Cypress Rd, Cypress, TX, 77433. Tel: 281-290-3214, 281-290-3219. p. 2196

Wachula-Breckel, Rita, Dir, Lawton Memorial Library, 118 N Bird St, La Farge, WI, 54639. Tel: 608-625-2015. p. 2447

Wacker, Jody, Libr Dir, Meinders Community Library, 1401 Seventh St SW, Pipestone, MN, 56164. Tel: 507-825-6714. p. 1193

Wacondo, Maureen, Librn, Jemez Pueblo Community Library & Archives, 20 Mission Rd, Jemez Pueblo, NM, 87024. Tel: 575-834-9171. p. 1470

Wadas, Linda, Acq Librn, Borough of Manhattan Community College Library, 199 Chambers St, S410, New York, NY, 10007. Tel: 212-220-1443. p. 1580

Waddell, Carla, Chair, Ref & Res Serv, Samford University Library, 800 Lakeshore Dr, Birmingham, AL, 35229. Tel: 205-726-2755. p. 9

Waddell, Christine, Dir, Linn County Library District No 2, 209 N Broadway, La Cygne, KS, 66040. Tel: 913-757-2151. p. 818

Waddell, Phillip, Dir, Baptist Missionary Association Theological Seminary, 1530 E Pine St, Jacksonville, TX, 75766-5407. Tel: 903-586-2501, Ext 215, 903-586-2501, Ext 216. p. 2203

Waddick, Julie, Librn, North York General Hospital, 4001 Leslie St, Toronto, ON, M2K 1E1, CANADA. Tel: 416-756-6142. p. 2690

Waddle, Keith, PhD, ILL Librn, Ref, McMurry University, Bldg 1601 War Hawk Way, One McMurry University # 218, Abilene, TX, 79697. Tel: 325-793-4678. p. 2132

Waddy, Michelle, Br Mgr, San Francisco Public Library, Glen Park Branch Library, 2825 Diamond St, San Francisco, CA, 94131-3033. Tel: 415-355-2858. p. 228

Wade, Ann, Br Mgr, Caroline Library, Inc, Dawn Branch, 31046 Richmond Tpk, Hanover, VA, 23069. Tel: 804-632-8341. p. 2333

Wade, Brenna, Pub Serv Librn, Hillsdale College, 33 E College St, Hillsdale, MI, 49242. Tel: 517-607-2606. p. 1115

Wade, Charlene, Br Mgr, San Bernardino County Library, Bloomington Branch, 18028 Valley Blvd, Bloomington, CA, 92316. Tel: 909-820-0533. p. 212

Wade, Elizabeth J, Discovery, Systems & Digital Strategy Librarian, Guilford College, 5800 W Friendly Ave, Greensboro, NC, 27410. Tel: 336-316-2368. p. 1692

Wade, Kathleen, Libr Syst Adminr, Peoria Public Library, 8463 W Monroe St, Peoria, AZ, 85345. Tel: 623-773-7555. p. 68

Wade, Kathy, Librn, Washington County Historical Society Library, 307 E Market St, Salem, IN, 47167. Tel: 812-883-6495. p. 717

Wade, Kathy, Libr Asst, Tillamook Bay Community College Library, 4301 Third St, Tillamook, OR, 97141. Tel: 503-842-8222, Ext 1720. p. 1900

Wade, Kim, Librn, Montmorency County Public Libraries, Hillman Wright Branch, 121 W Second St, Hillman, MI, 49746-9024. Tel: 989-742-4021. p. 1081

Wade, LaShanta, Circ, Dundee Public Library, 202 E Main St, PO Box 1000, Dundee, FL, 33838. Tel: 863-439-9424. p. 394

Wade, Marcus, Br Mgr, District of Columbia Public Library, Capitol View Branch, 5001 Central Ave SE, Washington, DC, 20019. Tel: 202-645-0755. p. 364

Wade, Margaret, Res Mgt Librn, Western Theological Seminary, 101 E 13th St, Holland, MI, 49423. Tel: 616-392-8555, Ext 112. p. 1116

Wade, MaryAlice, Interim Dean, Libr Serv, Fort Hays State University, 502 S Campus Dr, Hays, KS, 67601. Tel: 785-628-4342. p. 812

Wade, Megan, Syst & Tech Serv Librn, University of Lynchburg, 1501 Lakeside Dr, Lynchburg, VA, 24501-3199. Tel: 434-544-8206. p. 2331

Wade, Shana, Assoc Dir, Mesa County Public Library District, 443 N Sixth St, Grand Junction, CO, 81501. Tel: 970-243-4442. p. 284

Wade, Steven, Instrul Serv Librn, Florida Southern College, 111 Lake Hollingsworth Dr, Lakeland, FL, 33801-5698. Tel: 863-616-6451. p. 417

Wadelius, Lauren, Adminr, The Pas Regional Library, 53 Edwards Ave, The Pas, MB, R9A 1R2, CANADA. Tel: 204-623-2023. p. 2591

Wadhwa, Meena, Coll Access, Libr Assoc, Marshall University Libraries, One John Marshall Dr, Huntington, WV, 25755-2060. Tel: 304-696-2320. p. 2405

Wadleigh, Deborah, Tech Serv Librn, Onslow County Public Library, 58 Doris Ave E, Jacksonville, NC, 28540. Tel: 910-455-7350, Ext 1415. p. 1697

Wadleigh, Jennifer, Libr Dir, Vinalhaven Public Library, Six Carver St, Vinalhaven, ME, 04863. Tel: 207-863-4401. p. 944

Wadley, Deborah, Br Mgr, Las Vegas-Clark County Library District, Sandy Valley Library, 650 W Quartz Ave, HCR 31 Box 377, Sandy Valley, NV, 89019. Tel: 702-723-5333. p. 1347

Wadman, Krista, Coord, Finance & Admin, Nova Scotia Provincial Library, 6016 University Ave, 5th Flr, Halifax, NS, B3H 1W4, CANADA. Tel: 902-424-2457. p. 2621

Waelchli, Paul, Sr Acad Librn, University of Wisconsin-Rock County Library, 2909 Kellogg Ave, Janesville, WI, 53546-5606. Tel: 608-758-6533. p. 2443

Waelchli, Paul, Dir, University of Wisconsin-Whitewater, 750 W Main St, Whitewater, WI, 53190-1790. Tel: 262-472-5516. p. 2488

Wagenaar, Larry J, Exec Dir, Historical Society of Michigan, 7435 Westshire Dr, Lansing, MI, 48917. Tel: 517-324-1828. p. 1124

Wagenaar, Sarah, Co-Librn, Archer Public Library, 203 Sanford St, Archer, IA, 51231. Tel: 712-723-5629. p. 732

Wagers, Ashley, Dir, Jackson County Public Library, 338 N Main St, McKee, KY, 40447. Tel: 606-287-8113. p. 869

Waggoner, Jessica, User Experience Librn, University of California, 1156 High St, Santa Cruz, CA, 95064. Tel: 831-459-5654. p. 243

Waggoner, Julia, Libr Dir, Northland College, 1411 Ellis Ave, Ashland, WI, 54806-3999. Tel: 715-682-1302. p. 2421

Wagh, Sulbha, Sci Outreach Librn, Benedictine University Library, 5700 College Rd, Lisle, IL, 60532-0900. Tel: 630-829-6054. p. 610

Wagler, Darla, Dir, Loogootee Public Library, 106 N Line St, Loogootee, IN, 47553. Tel: 812-295-3713. p. 704

Wagner, Alda, Br Mgr, Briggs Lawrence County Public Library, Southern, 317 Solida Rd, South Point, OH, 45680. Tel: 740-377-2288. p. 1791

Wagner, Bob, Librn, H J International Graduate School for Peace & Public Leadership, Four W 43rd St, New York, NY, 10036. Tel: 212-563-6647, Ext 106. p. 1587

Wagner, Charissa, Br Supvr, Kern County Library, Ridgecrest Branch, 131 E Las Flores Ave, Ridgecrest, CA, 93555-3648. Tel: 760-384-5870. p. 120

Wagner, Cheryl, Coordr, Prog, Youth Serv, Harrison Community Library, 105 E Main St, Harrison, MI, 48625. Tel: 989-539-6711, Ext 3. p. 1113

Wagner, Cheryl, Circ Mgr, Roanoke County Public Library, 6303 Merriman Rd, Roanoke, VA, 24018-6496. Tel: 540-772-7507. p. 2345

Wagner, Christina, Librn, Foley & Lardner LLP, 321 N Clark St, Ste 3000, Chicago, IL, 60654. Tel: 312-832-4500. p. 561

Wagner, Cindee, Dir, Palisade Public Library, 124 N Main St, Palisade, NE, 69040. Tel: 308-285-3525. p. 1332

Wagner, David, Circ & ILL, Drexel University Libraries, Queen Lane Library, 2900 Queen Lane, Philadelphia, PA, 19129. Tel: 215-991-8740. p. 1976

Wagner, Donna, Librn, Carnegie-Schuyler Library, 303 E Second St, Pana, IL, 62557. Tel: 217-562-2326. p. 632

Wagner, Gerald, ILL, Supvr, University of Cincinnati Libraries, Donald C Harrison Health Sciences Library, 231 Albert Sabin Way, Cincinnati, OH, 45267. Tel: 513-558-8389. p. 1765

Wagner, Heather, Digitization Coordr, University of California, Merced Library, 5200 N Lake Rd, Merced, CA, 95343. Tel: 209-205-0794. p. 176

Wagner, Jack, Cat, University of Oklahoma Health Sciences Center, 1105 N Stonewall Ave, Oklahoma City, OK, 73117-1220. Tel: 405-271-2285, Ext 48758. p. 1859

Wagner, Janet, Libr Mgr, Alcoma Community Library, Alcoma School, Rainer, AB, T0J 2M0, CANADA. Tel: 403-362-3741. p. 2551

Wagner, Jeffrey, Head, Ref, Hazleton Area Public Library, 55 N Church St, Hazleton, PA, 18201-5893. Tel: 570-454-2961. p. 1943

Wagner, Joan, Pres, Medical & Scientific Libraries of Long Island, Molloy College, 1000 Hempstead Ave, Rockville Centre, NY, 11571. p. 2771

Wagner, Joshua, Asst Librn, Operations Mgr, Crossroads Bible College, 3500 Depauw Blvd, Ste 1020, Indianapolis, IN, 46268. Tel: 317-789-8268. p. 691

Wagner, Julia, Asst Dir, Salt Spring Island Public Library, 129 McPhillips Ave, Salt Spring Island, BC, V8K 2T6, CANADA. Tel: 250-537-4666. p. 2575

Wagner, Julia, Librn, Salt Spring Island Public Library, 129 McPhillips Ave, Salt Spring Island, BC, V8K 2T6, CANADA. Tel: 250-537-4666. p. 2575

Wagner, Karen, Archivist, Wellington County Museum & Archives, 0536 Wellington Rd 18, RR 1, Fergus, ON, N1M 2W3, CANADA. Tel: 519-837-2600, Ext 5235. p. 2641

Wagner, Kaylee, Libr Tech, Saint Francis Medical Center College of Nursing, 511 NE Greenleaf St, Peoria, IL, 61603. Tel: 309-655-2180. p. 634

Wagner, Kurt, Univ Librn, Monmouth University Library, 400 Cedar Ave, West Long Branch, NJ, 07764. Tel: 732-571-4401. p. 1452

Wagner, Leah, Dir, Monroe Township Public Library, Four Municipal Plaza, Monroe Township, NJ, 08831-1900. Tel: 732-521-5000. p. 1419

Wagner, Lynne, Outreach Coordr, Youth Serv Coordr, Birchard Public Library of Sandusky County, 423 Croghan St, Fremont, OH, 43420. Tel: 419-334-7101. p. 1786

Wagner, Melissa, Br Mgr, Chicago Public Library, West Loop, 122 N Aberdeen St, Chicago, IL, 60607. Tel: 312-744-2995. p. 557

Wagner, Michael, Mgr, Nashville Public Library, Nashville Talking Library, 615 Church St, Nashville, TN, 37219. Tel: 615-862-5874. p. 2120

Wagner, Michelle, Local Hist/Genealogy, Indian River County Library System, 1600 21st St, Vero Beach, FL, 32960. Tel: 772-770-5060. p. 452

Wagner, Robin, Dean of Libr, Gettysburg College, 300 N Washington St, Gettysburg, PA, 17325. Tel: 717-337-6768. p. 1935

Wagner, Rod, Dir, Nebraska Library Commission, The Atrium, 1200 N St, Ste 120, Lincoln, NE, 68508-2023. Tel: 402-471-4001. p. 1322

Wagner, Sarah, Info Serv & Instrul Librn, Indiana University-Purdue University Fort Wayne, 2101 E Coliseum Blvd, Fort Wayne, IN, 46805-1499. Tel: 260-481-6511. p. 684

Wagner, Travis L, Asst Prof, University of Illinois at Urbana-Champaign, Library & Information Science Bldg, 501 E Daniel St, Champaign, IL, 61820-6211. Tel: 217-333-3280. p. 2784

Wagner, Victoria, Assoc Dir, Rutgers University Libraries, Robert Wood Johnson Library of the Health Sciences, One Robert Wood Johnson Pl, New Brunswick, NJ, 08903. p. 1425

Wagner, Wendy, Br Mgr, Mohave County Library District, Lake Havasu City Branch Library, 1770 N McCulloch Blvd, Lake Havasu City, AZ, 86403-8847. Tel: 928-453-0718. p. 65

Wagner-Hemmes, Kim, Br Mgr, Cochise County Library District, Elfrida Library, 10552 N Hwy 191, Elfrida, AZ, 85610-9021. Tel: 520-642-1744. p. 56

Wagnor, Margie, Br Mgr, Conejos County Library, Capulin Branch, 8047 Hwy 15, Capulin, CO, 81124. Tel: 719-274-0953. p. 287

Waheed, Jawadi, Supv Librn, California Department of Justice, CCI Forensic Library, 4949 Broadway, Rm A-107, Sacramento, CA, 95820. Tel: 916-227-3575. p. 207

Wahl, Andrew, Med Librn, Shirley Ryan AbilityLab, 355 E Erie St, 10th Flr, Chicago, IL, 60611. Tel: 312-238-5433. p. 568

Wahlstrom, Ann, Br Mgr, Ramsey County Library, North Saint Paul Branch, 2300 N St Paul Dr, North Saint Paul, MN, 55109. Tel: 651-747-2701. p. 1204

Wahlstrom, Nancy, Tech Serv, United States Army, MWR Library, Bldg 93, Wold Ave, Fort Benning, GA, 31905. Tel: 706-545-7141. p. 479

Wahlstrom, Rachel, Asst Librn, Meagher County City Library, 205 SW Garfield, White Sulphur Springs, MT, 59645. Tel: 406-547-2250. p. 1304

Wahnschaffe, Janae, Dir, Utah State Hospital, 1300 E Center St, Provo, UT, 84606-3554. Tel: 801-344-4264. p. 2270

Wai, Zoe, Mgr, NASA Goddard Institute for Space Studies Library, 2880 Broadway, Rm 710, New York, NY, 10025. Tel: 212-678-5613. p. 1592

Waibel, Sue, Dir, Remington-Carpenter Township Public Library, 105 N Ohio St, Remington, IN, 47977. Tel: 219-261-2543. p. 714

Waid, Bridgette, Adult Programming, Librn, Van Buren Public Library, 1409 Main St, Van Buren, AR, 72956. Tel: 479-474-6045. p. 111

Waide, John, Outreach Coordr, Saint Louis University, 3650 Lindell Blvd, Saint Louis, MO, 63108-3302. Tel: 314-977-9359. p. 1275

Wainwright, Amy, Co-Dir, Outreach & Student Engagement Librn, John Carroll University, One John Carroll Blvd, University Heights, OH, 44118. Tel: 216-397-4259. p. 1826

Wainwright, Christina, Br Mgr, San Diego Public Library, Pacific Beach/Taylor, 4275 Cass St, San Diego, CA, 92109. Tel: 858-581-9934. p. 220

Wainwright, Francesca, Regional Mgr, The Seattle Public Library, 1000 Fourth Ave, Seattle, WA, 98104-1109. Tel: 206-386-4636. p. 2379

Waiss, Gayle, Asst Libr Dir, Ch Serv, Siuslaw Public Library District, 1460 Ninth St, Florence, OR, 97439. Tel: 541-997-3132. p. 1879

Waite, Carolyn, Cataloger, Hellenic College-Holy Cross Greek Orthodox School of Theology, 50 Goddard Ave, Brookline, MA, 02445-7496. Tel: 617-850-1367. p. 1003

Waite, Lucy, Dir, Libr Serv, Villa Maria College Library, 240 Pine Ridge Rd, Buffalo, NY, 14225. Tel: 716-961-1863. p. 1511

Waites, Carolynn, Br Mgr, Brazoria County Library System, Manvel Branch, 20514B Hwy 6, Manvel, TX, 77578. Tel: 281-489-7596. p. 2135

Waites, Wills, Instruction & Access Services Librn, Roosevelt University, 430 S Michigan Ave, Chicago, IL, 60605. Tel: 312-341-3638. p. 567

Waits, Sondra, Dir, Bienville Parish Library, 2768 Maple St, Arcadia, LA, 71001. Tel: 318-263-7410. p. 881

Waitz, Emily, Dir, Libr Serv, Northwestern Health Sciences University, 2501 W 84th St, Bloomington, MN, 55431-1599. Tel: 952-300-3567. p. 1166

Waitz, Emily, Head, Tech Serv, Interim Co-Dir, Hamline University, School of Law Library, 1536 Hewitt Ave, Saint Paul, MN, 55104. Tel: 651-523-2379. p. 1199

Wake, Joelle, Ch, Whiting Public Library, 1735 Oliver St, Whiting, IN, 46394-1794. Tel: 219-659-0269. p. 726

Wake, Joelle, Libr Dir, Lincoln Township Public Library, 2099 W John Beers Rd, Stevensville, MI, 49127. Tel: 269-429-9575. p. 1152

Wakefield, Diane, Dir, Beaver Area Memorial Library, 100 College Ave, Beaver, PA, 15009-2794. Tel: 724-775-1132. p. 1908

Wakefield, Heather J, Dir, Saegertown Area Library, 325 Broad St, Saegertown, PA, 16433. Tel: 814-763-5203. p. 2002

Wakefield, Jessi, Br Mgr, White Oak Library District, Lockport Branch, 121 E Eighth St, Lockport, IL, 60441. Tel: 815-838-0755. p. 643

Wakefield, Sheila, Librn, Dothan Houston County Library System, Ashford Branch, 305 Sixth Ave, Ashford, AL, 36312. Tel: 334-899-3121. p. 15

Wakefield, Wesley H, Pres, Bible Holiness Movement Library, 311 Falcon Pl, Penticton, BC, V2A 8K6, CANADA. Tel: 250-492-3376. p. 2573

Wakeford, Leslie, Metadata & Archives Librn, Wake Forest University, Law Library, Worrell Professional Ctr, 1834 Wake Forest Rd, Winston-Salem, NC, 27109. Tel: 336-758-4520. p. 1726

Wakeman, Amanda, Dir, Jane Morgan Memorial Library, 109 W Edgewater St, Cambria, WI, 53923. Tel: 920-348-4030. p. 2426

Wakeman, Amanda, Dir, Columbus Public Library, 223 W James St, Columbus, WI, 53925-1572. Tel: 920-623-5910. p. 2429

Wakeman, Meghan, Res Sharing Librn, Capital District Library Council, 28 Essex St, Albany, NY, 12206. Tel: 518-438-2500. p. 2770

Wakeman, Milo, Asst Librn, Jackson Laboratory, 600 Main St, Bar Harbor, ME, 04609-1500. Tel: 207-288-6083. p. 916

Wakeman, Milo, Libr Asst, Hennepin County Medical Center, Mail Code R2, 701 Park Ave, Minneapolis, MN, 55415. Tel: 612-873-2710. p. 1183

Wakimoto, Diana, Assoc Librn, California State University, East Bay Library, CSU East Bay Library, 25800 Carlos Bee Blvd, Hayward, CA, 94542-3052. Tel: 510-885-4287. p. 150

Wakin, Eric, Dep Dir, Stanford University Libraries, Hoover Institution Library & Archives, 434 Galvez Mall, Stanford, CA, 94305. Tel: 650-725-7750. p. 248

Walaskay, Ann, Librn, Ref (Info Servs), Oakland Community College, Bldg K, 27055 Orchard Lake Rd, Farmington Hills, MI, 48334-4579. Tel: 248-522-3528. p. 1104

Walch, Amanda, Ref & Instruction Librn, University of Jamestown, 6070 College Lane, Jamestown, ND, 58405-0001. Tel: 701-252-3467. p. 1736

Walchak, Shelley, Dir, Pine River Public Library District, 395 Bayfield Center Dr, Bayfield, CO, 81122. Tel: 970-884-2222. p. 266

Walcott, Dennis M, Pres & Chief Exec Officer, Queens Library, 89-11 Merrick Blvd, Jamaica, NY, 11432. Tel: 718-990-0700. p. 1553

Walcott, Richard, Circ Mgr, Thiel College, 75 College Ave, Greenville, PA, 16125-2183. Tel: 724-589-2118. p. 1939

Walczak, Jerome, Ref Librn, Agawam Public Library, 750 Cooper St, Agawam, MA, 01001. Tel: 413-789-1550. p. 984

Wald, Juli, Br Mgr, Anythink Libraries, Anythink York Street, 8990 York St, Ste A, Thornton, CO, 80229. Tel: 303-405-3234. p. 296

Wald, Juli, Dir, Middlebury Community Public Library, 101 E Winslow St, Middlebury, IN, 46540. Tel: 574-825-5601. p. 706

Waldemer, Susan, Librn, Wilder Public Library District, 111 Second St, Wilder, ID, 83676. Tel: 208-482-7880. p. 533

Walden, Carolyn, Head, Cat & Coll Mgt, University of Alabama at Birmingham, Mervyn H Sterne Library, 917 13th St S, Birmingham, AL, 35205. Tel: 205-934-0633. p. 9

Walden, Diane, Regional Librn, Colorado Department of Corrections, 12750 Hwy 96, Lane 13, Crowley, CO, 81034. Tel: 303-866-6341. p. 273

Walden, Julia, Extended Serv, Mgr, Licking County Library, 101 W Main St, Newark, OH, 43055-5054. Tel: 740-349-5507. p. 1807

Walden, Melody, Dir, Spartan College of Aeronautics & Technology Library, 8820 E Pine St, Tulsa, OK, 74115. Tel: 918-831-8605. p. 1865

Walden, Robin, Lead Cataloger, The John P Holt Brentwood Library, 8109 Concord Rd, Brentwood, TN, 37027. Tel: 615-371-0090. p. 2089

Walden, Vanessa, Database Mgr, Peninsula Library System, 32 W 25th Ave, Ste 201, Suite 201, San Mateo, CA, 94403-4000. Tel: 650-349-5538. p. 2762

Waldera, Sarah, Libr Dir, Blair-Preston Public Library, 122 S Urberg Ave, Blair, WI, 54616. Tel: 608-989-2502. p. 2424

Waldin, Valerie, Ref Librn, Hudson Valley Community College, 80 Vandenburgh Ave, Troy, NY, 12180. Tel: 518-629-7319. p. 1652

Waldman, Becky, Marketing & Communications Coord, Peterborough Public Library, 345 Aylmer St N, Peterborough, ON, K9H 3V7, CANADA. Tel: 705-745-5382, Ext 2324. p. 2672

Waldo, Jacob, Pub Serv Librn, University of Mississippi, 481 Chuckie Mullins Dr, University, MS, 38677. Tel: 662-915-6824. p. 1234

Waldo, Suzy, Mgr, Carnegie Library of Pittsburgh, South Side, 2205 E Carson St, Pittsburgh, PA, 15203. Tel: 412-431-0505. p. 1992

Waldon, Johnna, Br Mgr, Lexington Public Library, Tates Creek, 3628 Walden Dr, Lexington, KY, 40517. p. 862

Waldon, Rachelle, Libr Dir, North Central University Library, 915 E 14th St, Minneapolis, MN, 55404. Tel: 612-343-4494. p. 1184

Waldrep, Sherry, Dir, Allerton Public Library District, 4000 Green Apple Lane, Monticello, IL, 61856. Tel: 217-762-4676. p. 619

Waldron, Everitt, Syst/Tech Serv, Cayuga County Community College, 197 Franklin St, Auburn, NY, 13021. Tel: 315-294-8596. p. 1488

Waldron, Marc, Managing Librn, Brooklyn Public Library, Bushwick, 340 Bushwick Ave, Brooklyn, NY, 11206. Tel: 718-602-1348. p. 1502

Waldron, Tamera, ILL, Idaho National Laboratory Research Library, 2251 North Blvd, MS 2300, Idaho Falls, ID, 83415. Tel: 208-526-1185. p. 523

Waldron, Tracy, Dir, East Kingston Public Library, 47 Maplevale Rd, East Kingston, NH, 03827. Tel: 603-642-8333. p. 1362

Waldrop, Jean, Libr Dir, Harding University, 915 E Market St, Searcy, AR, 72149-5615. Tel: 501-279-4011. p. 109

Waldrop, Jeffrey, Dean of Libr, Mercer University Atlanta, 3001 Mercer University Dr, Atlanta, GA, 30341. Tel: 678-547-6274. p. 465

Waldrop, Patricia, Ch, Tombigbee Regional Library System, Evans Memorial Library, 105 N Long St, Aberdeen, MS, 39730. Tel: 662-369-4601. p. 1235

Waldrop, Susan O, Libr Tech, United States Army, Martin Army Community Hospital Medical Library, Bldg 9200, Rm 010 MCXB-IL, 7950 Martin Loop, Fort Benning, GA, 31905-5637. Tel: 706-544-3533. p. 479

Walenta, Suzanne, Curator, Rolla A Clymer Research Library, 383 E Central, El Dorado, KS, 67042. Tel: 316-321-9333. p. 806

Walenter, Stacy, Librn, Lincoln County Public Libraries, Troy Branch, Third & Kalispell Ave, Troy, MT, 59935. Tel: 406-295-4040. p. 1299

Walgenbach, Penny, Library Contact, Colusa County Free Library, Arbuckle Branch, 610 King St, Arbuckle, CA, 95912. Tel: 530-476-2526. p. 131

Waligorski, Monica, Adult Serv Mgr, New Lenox Public Library District, 120 Veterans Pkwy, New Lenox, IL, 60451. Tel: 815-485-2605. p. 624

Walk, Margaret, Head, Tech Serv, Montgomery County-Norristown Public Library, 1001 Powell St, Norristown, PA, 19401-3817. Tel: 610-278-5100, Ext 118. p. 1971

Walker, Adrianne, Interim Archivist, University of West Florida Historic Trust, 117 E Government St, Pensacola, FL, 32502. Tel: 850-595-5840, Ext 126. p. 437

Walker, Adrienne, Librn, Mount San Jacinto College, 300 Bldg, 1499 N State St, San Jacinto, CA, 92583-2399. Tel: 951-487-3450. p. 230

Walker, Aimee, Chairperson, Librn, Joliet Junior College Library, Campus Ctr (A-Bldg), 2nd Flr, 1215 Houbolt Rd, Joliet, IL, 60431. Tel: 815-280-2626. p. 603

Walker, Alli, Circ Mgr, Tech Mgr, Manheim Township Public Library, 595 Granite Run Dr, Lancaster, PA, 17601. Tel: 717-560-6441. p. 1952

Walker, Amira, Res & Instruction Librn, Washington & Lee University, University Library, 204 W Washington St, Lexington, VA, 24450-2116. Tel: 540-458-8643. p. 2329

Walker, Andy, Assoc Prof, Dept Head, Utah State University, 2830 Old Main Hill, Education, Bldg 215, Logan, UT, 84322. Tel: 435-797-2614. p. 2794

Walker, Angela, Ref & Instruction Librn, Eastern Connecticut State University, 83 Windham St, Willimantic, CT, 06226-2295. Tel: 860-465-5566. p. 347

Walker, Angie, Br Mgr, Boonville Community Public Library, 121 W Main St, Boonville, NC, 27011. Tel: 336-367-7737. p. 1675

Walker, Aspen, Commun Engagement Mgr, Boulder Public Library, 1001 Arapahoe Rd, Boulder, CO, 80302. Tel: 303-441-3100. p. 266

Walker, Aubrey, Asst Dir, Jake Epp Library, 255 Elmdale Dr, Steinbach, MB, R5G 1N6, CANADA. Tel: 204-326-6841. p. 2590

Walker, Barbara, Br Mgr, Aiken-Bamberg-Barnwell-Edgefield Regional Library, Nancy Carson - North Augusta Library, 135 Edgefield Rd, North Augusta, SC, 29841-2423. Tel: 803-279-5767. p. 2045

Walker, Becky, Dir, Meherrin Regional Library, William E Richardson Jr Memorial Library, 100 Spring St, Emporia, VA, 23847. Tel: 434-634-2539. p. 2327

Walker, Becky S, Dir, Meherrin Regional Library, 133 W Hicks St, Lawrenceville, VA, 23868. Tel: 434-848-2418, Ext 301. p. 2327

Walker, Ben F, Assoc Dean, Faculty Affairs & Access & Tech Servs, University of Florida Libraries, 1545 W University Ave, Gainesville, FL, 32611-7000. Tel: 352-273-2545. p. 407

Walker, Bill, Br Librn, Stockton-San Joaquin County Public Library, Maya Angelou Branch, 2324 Pock Lane, Stockton, CA, 95205. p. 250

Walker, Billie, Head Librn, Pennsylvania State University, 30 E Swedesford Rd, Malvern, PA, 19355. Tel: 610 648-3228. p. 1957

Walker, Billie, Head Librn, Pennsylvania State University, 30 E Swedesford Rd, Malvern, PA, 19355. Tel: 610-648-3215. p. 1957

Walker, Brad, Dir, The W H & Edgar Magness Community House & Library, 118 W Main St, McMinnville, TN, 37110. Tel: 931-473-2428. p. 2111

Walker, Charlene, Librn, Luray City Library, 119 N Main St, Luray, KS, 67649. Tel: 785-698-2208. p. 822

Walker, Cindy, Br Asst, Cumberland Public Libraries, Parrsboro Library, 91 Queen St, Parrsboro, NS, B0M 1S0, CANADA. Tel: 902-254-2046. p. 2615

Walker, Connie, Libr Dir, Moniteau County Library, 501 S Oak St, California, MO, 65018. Tel: 573-796-2642. p. 1239

Walker, Corey, Dir, Paulding County Carnegie Library, 205 S Main St, Paulding, OH, 45879-1492. Tel: 419-399-2032. p. 1814

Walker, Cynthia, Exec Dir, The Brick Store Museum, 117 Main St, Kennebunk, ME, 04043. Tel: 207-985-4802. p. 928

Walker, Cynthia, Head, Children's Servx, Waterford Township Public Library, 5168 Civic Center Dr, Waterford, MI, 48329. Tel: 248-618-7684. p. 1158

Walker, Darlene, Interim Dir, Yeadon Public Library, 809 Longacre Blvd, Yeadon, PA, 19050. Tel: 610-623-4090. p. 2025

Walker, DauVeen, Br Mgr, Charles County Public Library, Potomac Branch, 3225 Ruth B Swann Dr, Indian Head, MD, 20640. Tel: 301-375-7375. p. 969

Walker, David, Dir, Albany Law School, 80 New Scotland Ave, Albany, NY, 12208. p. 1482

Walker, Debbie, Cat, Gadsden Public Library, 254 S College St, Gadsden, AL, 35901. Tel: 256-549-4699. p. 18

Walker, Debra Ann, Librn, Norman Wells Community Library, PO Box 97, Norman Wells, NT, X0E 0V0, CANADA. Tel: 867-587-3714. p. 2613

Walker, Demetra T, Dean, Francis Marion University, 4822 E Palmetto St, Florence, SC, 29506. Tel: 843-661-1300. p. 2059

Walker, Denise, Libr Mgr, Virginia Beach Public Library, Joint-Use Library, TCC Campus, Bldg L, 1700 College Crescent, Virginia Beach, VA, 23453. Tel: 757-822-7800. p. 2351

Walker, Diane Parr, Edward H Arnold Univ Librn, Hesburgh Libraries, 221 Hesburgh Library, University of Notre Dame, Notre Dame, IN, 46556. Tel: 574-631-5252. p. 711

Walker, Donna, Exec Dir, Jefferson County Public Library, 10200 W 20th Ave, Lakewood, CO, 80215. Tel: 303-275-2201. p. 288

Walker, Evelyn, Librn, Mountainair Public Library, 109 Roosevelt Ave, Mountainair, NM, 87036. Tel: 505-847-9676. p. 1473

Walker, Frazier, Communications Mgr, Develop Mgr, Cecil County Public Library, 301 Newark Ave, Elkton, MD, 21921-5441. Tel: 410-996-1055, Ext 129. p. 964

Walker, Helen, Mgr, Libr Serv, Burr & Forman Library, 420 N 20th St, Ste 3400, Birmingham, AL, 35203. Tel: 205-251-3000. p. 8

Walker, Jamie, Head, Tech Serv, Colorado Mesa University, 1100 North Ave, Grand Junction, CO, 81501. Tel: 970-248-1863. p. 283

Walker, Jane, Librn, Elm Creek Public Library, 241 N Tyler St, Elm Creek, NE, 68836. Tel: 308-856-4394. p. 1313

Walker, Janet, Dir, South Cheatham Public Library, 358 N Main St, Kingston Springs, TN, 37082. Tel: 615-952-4752. p. 2105

Walker, Jennifer, Libr Serv Mgr, Grand Prairie Public Library System, 901 Conover Dr, Grand Prairie, TX, 75051. Tel: 972-237-5700. p. 2185

Walker, Jennifer, Head Librn, County of Carleton Law Library, Ottawa Court House, 2004-161 Elgin St, Ottawa, ON, K2P 2K1, CANADA. Tel: 613-233-7386, Ext 225. p. 2666

Walker, Jill, Archives, Spec Coll Librn, Benedictine University Library, 5700 College Rd, Lisle, IL, 60532-0900. Tel: 630-829-6050. p. 610

Walker, Jill, Cat Librn, Wheaton College, Marion E Wade Center, 351 E Lincoln, Wheaton, IL, 60187-4213. Tel: 630-752-5908. p. 662

Walker, Jon, Exec Dir, Pueblo City-County Library District, 100 E Abriendo Ave, Pueblo, CO, 81004-4290. Tel: 719-562-5625. p. 293

Walker, Julie, State Librn, Georgia Public Library Service, 5800 Jonesboro Rd, Morrow, GA, 30260. Tel: 404-235-7140. p. 491

Walker, Julie, Exec Dir, Northern Lights Library System, 5615-48 St, Elk Point, AB, T0A 1A0, CANADA. Tel: 780-724-2596, Ext 2112. p. 2539

Walker, Karen, Br Mgr, Clay County Public Library System, Orange Park Public Library, 2054 Plainfield Ave, Orange Park, FL, 32073-5498. Tel: 904-278-4750. p. 396

Walker, Keri, Dir, St James Parish Library, 1879 W Main St, Lutcher, LA, 70071-5140. Tel: 225-869-3618. p. 895

Walker, Kim, Ser Tech, University of the District of Columbia, David A Clarke School of Law, Charles N & Hilda H M Mason Law Library, Bldg 39, Rm B-16, 4200 Connecticut Ave NW, Washington, DC, 20008. Tel: 202-274-7310. p. 380

Walker Knoot, Jennie, Librn, Debra S Fish Early Childhood Resource Library, Ten Yorkton Ct, Saint Paul, MN, 55117. Tel: 651-641-3544. p. 1199

Walker, Kristin, Doc Delivery, Librn, University of Texas Libraries, Interlibrary Services Department, PCL1-343, First Flr Dock, 101 E 21st St, Stop S5463, Austin, TX, 78712-1492. Tel: 512-495-4134. p. 2142

Walker, Larissa, Librn, Oliver Springs Public Library, 610 Walker Ave, Oliver Springs, TN, 37840. Tel: 865-435-2509. p. 2123

Walker, Laura, Librn, Tarkington Community Library, 3032 FM 163, Cleveland, TX, 77327. Tel: 281-592-5136. p. 2156

Walker, Laura Beth, Head Librn, First Regional Library, Lafayette County-Oxford Public Library, 401 Bramlett Blvd, Oxford, MS, 38655. Tel: 662-234-5751. p. 1220

Walker, Lauren, Asst Dir, Coventry Public Library, 1672 Flat River Rd, Coventry, RI, 02816. Tel: 401-822-9100. p. 2030

Walker, Lizzy, Metadata & Digital Initiatives Librn, Wichita State University Libraries, 1845 Fairmount, Wichita, KS, 67260-0068. Tel: 316-978-5138. p. 844

Walker, Loraine, Librn, Noxubee County Library System, 145 Dr Martin Luther King Jr Dr, Macon, MS, 39341. Tel: 662-726-5461. p. 1225

Walker, Lori, Ch Serv, Oostburg Public Library, 213 N Eighth St, Oostburg, WI, 53070. Tel: 920-564-2934. p. 2467

Walker, Lucinda H, Dir, Norwich Public Library, 368 Main St, Norwich, VT, 05055-9453. Tel: 802-649-1184. p. 2290

Walker, Mallory, Access Serv Librn, Loyola-Notre Dame Library, Inc, 200 Winston Ave, Baltimore, MD, 21212. Tel: 410-617-6801. p. 954

Walker, Mallory, Interim Libr Dir, Pine Manor College, 400 Heath St, Chestnut Hill, MA, 02467. Tel: 617-731-7081. p. 1011

Walker, Marianne M, Exec Ed, American Law Institute Library, 4025 Chestnut St, Philadelphia, PA, 19104. Tel: 215-243-1627. p. 1974

Walker, Marjorie, Prog Coordr, National Cotton Council of America Library, 7193 Goodlett Farms Pkwy, Cordova, TN, 38016. Tel: 901-274-9030. p. 2095

Walker, Martaire, Ref Librn, Atlanta-Fulton Public Library System, Evelyn G Lowery Library at Southwest, 3665 Cascade Rd SW, Atlanta, GA, 30331. Tel: 404-699-6363. p. 461

Walker, Martha, Dir, Cornell University Library, Mui Ho Fine Arts Library, Rand Hall, 921 University Ave, #235, Ithaca, NY, 14853. Tel: 607-255-3710. p. 1551

Walker, Mary, Resource Librn, Syst Librn, Butler Community College Library & Archives, Library 600 Bldg, 901 S Haverhill Rd, El Dorado, KS, 67042-3280. Tel: 316-322-3234. p. 805

Walker, Mary, Acq, Digital Res Coordr, Wichita State University Libraries, 1845 Fairmount, Wichita, KS, 67260-0068. Tel: 316-978-5792. p. 844

Walker, Mattie, Reader Serv Librn, Rust College, 150 E Rust Ave, Holly Springs, MS, 38635. Tel: 662-252-8000, Ext 4100. p. 1220

Walker, Melissa, Customer Serv Mgr, Barberton Public Library, 602 W Park Ave, Barberton, OH, 44203-2458. Tel: 330-745-1194. p. 1748

Walker, Melveta, Dir, Eastern New Mexico University - Portales, 1500 S Ave K, Portales, NM, 88130-7402. Tel: 575-562-2626. p. 1473

Walker, Michael C, Assoc Librn, Pub Serv, Virginia State University, One Hayden Dr, Petersburg, VA, 23806. Tel: 804-524-6946. p. 2337

Walker, Michelle, Dir, OSHA, 200 Constitution Ave NW, Rm N-2625, Washington, DC, 20210-2001. Tel: 202-693-2350. p. 374

Walker, Michelle, Librn, Knoxville Public Library, 200 E Main St, Knoxville, IL, 61448-1351. Tel: 309-289-2113. p. 605

Walker, Nancy, Br Supvr, Riverside Public Library, Arlington, 9556 Magnolia Ave, Riverside, CA, 92503-3698. Tel: 951-826-2291. p. 203

Walker, Nancy, Dir, Grafton Public Library, 201 Fourth Ave, Grafton, IA, 50440. Tel: 641-748-2735. p. 755

Walker, Nikki, Librn, Crittenden County Library, Horseshoe Branch, 3181 Horseshoe Circle, Hughes, AR, 72348. Tel: 870-339-3862. p. 104

Walker, Patricia, Br Mgr, Alexandria Library, Local History/Special Collections, 717 Queen St, Alexandria, VA, 22314-2420. Tel: 703-746-1719. p. 2302

Walker, Patricia Sue, Br Mgr, Knox County Public Library System, Corryton Branch, 7733 Corryton Rd, Corryton, TN, 37721. Tel: 865-688-1501. p. 2106

Walker, Patrisha, Asst Libr Dir, Interim Libr Dir, Plaquemines Parish Library, Bldg 203, Ste B-11, 333 F Edward Herbert Blvd, Belle Chasse, LA, 70037. Tel: 504-934-6765. p. 885

Walker, Philip, Dir, Vanderbilt University, Annette & Irwin Eskind Family Biomedical Library & Learning Center, 2209 Garland Ave, Nashville, TN, 37232-8340. Tel: 615-936-2200. p. 2122

Walker, Phillip Ira, Evening Supvr, Transylvania University Library, 300 N Broadway, Lexington, KY, 40508. Tel: 859-233-8225. p. 863

Walker, Quientell, Br Mgr, Oconee County Public Library, 501 W South Broad St, Walhalla, SC, 29691. Tel: 864-638-4133. p. 2072

Walker, Robin, Dir, Educ Serv, Librn & Archivist, International Longshore & Warehouse Union, 1188 Franklin St, 4th Flr, San Francisco, CA, 94109. Tel: 415-775-0533. p. 225

Walker, Rosie, Dir, Addison Township Public Library, 1440 Rochester Rd, Leonard, MI, 48367-3555. Tel: 248-628-4228, 248-628-7180. p. 1126

Walker, Sarah, Dept Head, Ref, State Historical Society of North Dakota, North Dakota Heritage Ctr, 612 E Boulevard Ave, Bismarck, ND, 58505-0830. Tel: 701-328-2091. p. 1730

Walker, Sharon, Tech Asst, Wallace Community College, 3000 Earl Goodwin Pkwy, Selma, AL, 36701. Tel: 334-876-9344, 334-876-9345. p. 35

Walker, Sharon, Libr Mgr, Vancouver Island Regional Library, Sidney/North Saanich Branch, 10091 Resthaven Dr, Sidney, BC, V8L 3G3, CANADA. Tel: 250-656-0944. p. 2571

Walker, Shaundra, Libr Dir, Georgia College, 221 N Clark St, Milledgeville, GA, 31061. Tel: 478-445-0987. p. 490

Walker, Sherry, Librn, Watertown Township Fostoria Library, 9405 Foster St, Fostoria, MI, 48435. Tel: 989-795-2794. p. 1107

Walker, Stacey, Customer Experience Supervisor, Douglas County Libraries, Castle Rock Branch, 100 S Wilcox St, Castle Rock, CO, 80104-2726. Tel: 303-791-7323. p. 270

Walker, Stephanie, Dean of Libr, University of Massachusetts at Boston, 100 Morrissey Blvd, Boston, MA, 02125-3300. Tel: 617-287-5927. p. 1000

Walker, Stephen, Access Serv Librn, Lehman College, City University of New York, 250 Bedford Park Blvd W, Bronx, NY, 10468. Tel: 718-960-7773. p. 1499

Walker, Steve, Dr, Pres, Seminole Nation Museum Library, 524 S Wewoka Ave, Wewoka, OK, 74884. Tel: 405-257-5580. p. 1869

Walker, Susan, Head, Pub Serv, Yale University Library, Lewis Walpole Library, 154 Main St, Farmington, CT, 06032. Tel: 860-677-2140. p. 328

Walker, Teresa, Assoc Dean, Res & Learning Serv, University of Tennessee, Knoxville, 1015 Volunteer Blvd, Knoxville, TN, 37996-1000. Tel: 865-974-4351. p. 2107

Walker, Theresa, Info Spec, PPG Industries, Inc, Chemicals Technical Information Center, 440 College Park Dr, Monroeville, PA, 15146. Tel: 724-325-5221. p. 1996

Walker, Thomas D, Dr, Assoc Dean, Wayne State University, 106 Kresge Library, Detroit, MI, 48202. Tel: 313-577-0350. p. 2787

Walker, Tiffany, Librn, Broward College, South Campus Library LRC, Bldg 81, 7300 Pines Blvd, Pembroke Pines, FL, 33024. Tel: 954-201-8825, 954-201-8896. p. 391

Walker, Virginia, Librn, Invermere Public Library, 646 Fourth St, Invermere, BC, V0A 1K0, CANADA. Tel: 250-342-6416. p. 2567

Walker, Wayne, Interim Exec Dir, Southern California Library Cooperative, 254 N Lake Ave, No 874, Pasadena, CA, 91101. Tel: 626-283-5949. p. 2762

Walker, Willis C, Librn, Bard College, Levy Economics Institute Library, Blithewood Ave, Annandale-on-Hudson, NY, 12504. Tel: 845-758-7729. p. 1487

Walker-Lanz, Jesse, Asst Dir, Pub Serv, County of Los Angeles Public Library, 7400 E Imperial Hwy, Downey, CA, 90242-3375. Tel: 562-940-8409. p. 134

Walker-Papke, Elizabeth, Online & Distance Learning Librn, Spring Arbor University, 106 E Main St, Spring Arbor, MI, 49283. Tel: 517-750-6443. p. 1152

Walko, Ellen, Coordr, ILL, Talbot County Free Library, 100 W Dover St, Easton, MD, 21601-2620. Tel: 410-822-1626. p. 964

Walkowiak, Julie, Acq, Libr Asst, The College of Saint Scholastica Library, 1200 Kenwood Ave, Duluth, MN, 55811-4199. Tel: 218-723-6649. p. 1172

Walkup, Danielle, Research Servs Librn, Adirondack Community College Library, Scoville Learning Ctr, 640 Bay Rd, Queensbury, NY, 12804. Tel: 518-743-2200,Ext 2384. p. 1625

Wall, Anne, Evening Fac Mgr, Wingate University, 110 Church ST, Wingate, NC, 28174. Tel: 704-233-8089. p. 1724

Wall, Brenda, Br Mgr, De Soto Trail Regional Library System, Lucy Maddox Memorial, 11880 Columbia St, Blakely, GA, 39823. Tel: 229-723-3079. p. 469

Wall, Carly, Br Mgr, Preble County District Library, Brooke-Gould Memorial, 301 N Barron St, Eaton, OH, 45320-1705. Tel: 937-456-4331. p. 1784

Wall, Cindy, Head, Children's Servx, Southington Public Library & Museum, 255 Main St, Southington, CT, 06489. Tel: 860-628-0947. p. 337

Wall, Dannaya, Tech Serv Coordr, Regent College, 5800 University Blvd, Vancouver, BC, V6T 2E4, CANADA. Tel: 604-221-3340. p. 2579

Wall, Diane R, Asst Dir, Head, Tech Serv, Melrose Public Library, 263 W Foster St, Melrose, MA, 02176. Tel: 781-665-2313. p. 1034

Wall, Jim, Mgr, County of Los Angeles Public Library, Acton Agua Dulce Library, 33792 Crown Valley Rd, Acton, CA, 93510. Tel: 661-269-7101. p. 135

Wall, Karen, Dir, Charlton Public Library, 40 Main St, Charlton, MA, 01507. Tel: 508-248-0452. p. 1009

Wall, Kathleen, Coordr, Coll Serv, Reynolds-Alberta Museum Reference Centre, 6426 40th Ave, Wetaskiwin, AB, T9A 2G1, CANADA. Tel: 780-312-2080. p. 2559

Wall, Kevin, Libr Dir, North Tonawanda Public Library, 505 Meadow Dr, North Tonawanda, NY, 14120. Tel: 716-693-4132. p. 1608

Wall, Patricia A, Librn, San Bernardino Valley College Library, 701 S Mount Vernon Ave, San Bernardino, CA, 92410. Tel: 909-384-8577. p. 214

Wall, Patrick, Dir, University City Public Library, 6701 Delmar Blvd, University City, MO, 63130. Tel: 314-727-3150. p. 1284

Wall, Raelene, Library Contact, Brigus Public Library, Seven S St, Brigus, NL, A0A 1K0, CANADA. Tel: 709-528-3156. p. 2607

Wall, Richard, Coll Develop, Queens College, Benjamin S Rosenthal Library, 65-30 Kissena Blvd, Flushing, NY, 11367-0904. Tel: 718-997-3700. p. 1534

Wall, Thomas, Univ Librn, Boston College Libraries, 140 Commonwealth Ave, Chestnut Hill, MA, 02467. p. 1010

Wallace, Breezy, Branch Lead, Saint Clair County Library System, Capac Branch Library, 111 N Main St, Capac, MI, 48014. Tel: 810-395-7000. p. 1142

Wallace, Carolyn, Sr Br Mgr, Alachua County Library District, Tower Road Branch, 3020 SW 75th St, Gainesville, FL, 32608. Tel: 352-333-2840. p. 406

Wallace, Christy, Computer Tech, Jacksonville Public Library, 200 Pelham Rd S, Jacksonville, AL, 36265. Tel: 256-435-6332. p. 23

Wallace, Dana, Br Librn, Plaquemines Parish Library, Belle Chasse Branch, 8442 Hwy 23, Belle Chasse, LA, 70037. Tel: 504-393-0449, 504-394-3570. p. 885

Wallace, Debra, Asst City Librn, Roanoke Public Library, 308 S Walnut St, Roanoke, TX, 76262. Tel: 817-491-2691. p. 2233

Wallace, Donna, Head, Ref & Adult Serv, Auburn Public Library, 49 Spring St, Auburn, ME, 04210. Tel: 207-333-6640. p. 913

Wallace, Ed, Satellite Librn, United States Court of Appeals, One Exchange Terrace, Rm 430, Providence, RI, 02903. Tel: 401-752-7240. p. 2041

Wallace, Edwin, Head, Per, Lehman College, City University of New York, 250 Bedford Park Blvd W, Bronx, NY, 10468. Tel: 718-960-7757. p. 1499

Wallace, Elisabeth, Librn, Mountain Area Health Education Center, 121 Hendersonville Rd, Asheville, NC, 28803. Tel: 828-257-4473. p. 1672

Walsh, John, Asst Dir, Syst Librn, Middleborough Public Library, 102 N Main St, Middleborough, MA, 02346. Tel: 508-946-2470. p. 1035

Walsh, John, Assoc Univ Librn, Coll Mgt Serv, George Mason University Libraries, 4348 Chesapeake River Way, Fairfax, VA, 22030. Tel: 703-993-3711. p. 2317

Walsh, Kara, Asst Dir, Columbia County Traveling Library, 702 Sawmill Rd, Ste 101, Bloomsburg, PA, 17815. Tel: 570-387-8782. p. 1913

Walsh, Lorraine, Libr Asst, Belmar Public Library, 517 Tenth Ave, Belmar, NJ, 07719. Tel: 732-681-0775. p. 1389

Walsh, Margaret, Assoc Mgr, Edmonton Public Library, Lois Hole Library, 17650 69 Ave NW, Edmonton, AB, T5T 3X9, CANADA. Tel: 780-442-0879. p. 2536

Walsh, Mary Alice, Dir, Ridley Park Public Library, 107 E Ward St, Ridley Park, PA, 19078. Tel: 610-583-7207. p. 2001

Walsh, Maryann, Librn, Middlefield Public Library, 188 Skyline Trail, Middlefield, MA, 01243. Tel: 413-623-6421. p. 1035

Walsh, Nicole, Asst Mgr, Saint Louis County Library, Eureka Hills Branch, 156 Eureka Towne Center Dr, Eureka, MO, 63025-1032. Tel: 314-994-3300, Ext 3200. p. 1273

Walsh, Robert, Libr Dir, University of Connecticut, Waterbury Regional Campus Library, 99 E Main St, Waterbury, CT, 06702. Tel: 203-236-9900. p. 340

Walsh, Sheila, Asst Dir, Bellevue Public Library, 106 N Third St, Ste 1, Bellevue, IA, 52031. Tel: 563-872-4991. p. 734

Walsh, Tara, Ch, Beaver Island District Library, 26400 Donegal Bay Rd, Beaver Island, MI, 49782. Tel: 231-448-2701. p. 1083

Walsh, Tiffany, Coordr, Instrul Serv, University at Buffalo Libraries-State University of New York, Charles B Sears Law Library, John Lord O'Brian Hall, 211 Mary Talbert Way, Buffalo, NY, 14260-1110. Tel: 716-645-1322. p. 1511

Walsh-O'Connor, Marcie, Dir, Whitman Public Library, 100 Webster St, Whitman, MA, 02382. Tel: 781-447-7613. p. 1069

Walster, Dian E, Dr, Prof, Wayne State University, 106 Kresge Library, Detroit, MI, 48202. Tel: 313-577-1825. p. 2787

Walter, Adam, Dir, Swanton Local School District Public Library, 305 Chestnut St, Swanton, OH, 43558. Tel: 419-826-2760. p. 1822

Walter, Bobby, Distance Educ, Ref Librn, Kentucky State University, 400 E Main St, Frankfort, KY, 40601-2355. Tel: 502-597-6855. p. 855

Walter, Catherine, Curator, Chancellor Robert R Livingston Masonic Library of Grand Lodge, 71 W 23rd St, 14th Flr, New York, NY, 10010-4171. Tel: 212-337-6620. p. 1581

Walter, Christopher S, Dir, Haddon Heights Public Library, 608 Station Ave, Haddon Heights, NJ, 08035-1907. Tel: 856-547-7132. p. 1406

Walter, Cora, Cat, Grant County Public Library District, 201 Barnes Rd, Williamstown, KY, 41097-9482. Tel: 859-824-2080. p. 877

Walter, Karon, Head Librn, Capital Area District Libraries, Holt-Delhi Library, 2078 Aurelius Rd, Holt, MI, 48842. Tel: 517-694-9351. p. 1124

Walter, Leisa, ILL Serv, A T Still University, Kirksville Campus, 800 W Jefferson St, Kirksville, MO, 63501. Tel: 660-626-2345. p. 1258

Walter, Marlene, Asst Librn, Dominy Memorial Library, 201 S Third St, Fairbury, IL, 61739. Tel: 815-692-3231. p. 587

Walter, Molly, Asst Libr Dir, Harlingen Public Library, 410 76 Dr, Harlingen, TX, 78550. Tel: 956-216-5800. p. 2188

Walter, Scott, PhD, Dean, Univ Libr Serv, San Diego State University, 5500 Campanile Dr, San Diego, CA, 92182-8050. Tel: 619-594-6728. p. 221

Walter, Thomas B, Computer Librn, Ref Librn, Mississippi College, 151 E Griffith St, Jackson, MS, 39201-1391. Tel: 601-925-7120. p. 1222

Walter-Smith, Lily, Libr Tech, Regina-Qu'Appelle Health Region, Pasqua Hospital Library, 4101 Dewdney Ave, Regina, SK, S4T 1A5, CANADA. Tel: 306-766-2370. p. 2747

Waltermire, Kyla, Exec Dir, Mississippi Valley Library District, 408 W Main St, Collinsville, IL, 62234. Tel: 618-344-1112. p. 573

Walters, Barbara, Exec Dir, North Central Washington Libraries, 16 N Columbia St, Wenatchee, WA, 98801. Tel: 509-663-1117, Ext 129. p. 2393

Walters, Carolyn, Dean, Univ Libr, Indiana University Bloomington, 1320 E Tenth St, Bloomington, IN, 47405. Tel: 812-855-3403. p. 670

Walters, Janine, Dir, Center Point Public Library, 720 Main St, Center Point, IA, 52213. Tel: 319-849-1509. p. 738

Walters, John, Head, Doc Serv, Utah State University, Regional Depository Collection of US Government Documents, 3000 Old Main Hill, Logan, UT, 84322-3000. Tel: 435-797-2683. p. 2265

Walters, Jorie, Research Coordr, Kankakee County Historical Society Museum Library, 801 S Eighth Ave, Kankakee, IL, 60901-4744. Tel: 815-932-5279. p. 604

Walters, Kim, Dir, Autry National Center, Braun Research Library, 234 Museum Dr, Los Angeles, CA, 90065. Tel: 323-221-2164, Ext 255. p. 160

Walters, Linda, Head Librn, New Straitsville Public Library, 102 E Main St, New Straitsville, OH, 43766. Tel: 740-394-2717. p. 1807

Walters, Lowell, Dir, Mississippi County Library System, 200 N Fifth St, Blytheville, AR, 72315-2709. Tel: 870-762-2431. p. 91

Walters, Mandy, Dir, Pend Oreille County Library District, 116 S Washington Ave, Newport, WA, 99156. p. 2372

Walters, Mark, Libr Dir, Kalamazoo Valley Community College Libraries, 6767 West O Ave, Rm 3210, Kalamazoo, MI, 49003. Tel: 269-488-4328, 269-488-4380. p. 1122

Walters, Megan, Libr Dir, United States Air Force, Base Library, 443 Cody Ave, Hurlburt Field, FL, 32544. Tel: 850-884-6266, 850-884-6947. p. 411

Walters, Michelle, Head, Tech Serv, Ela Area Public Library District, 275 Mohawk Trail, Lake Zurich, IL, 60047. Tel: 847-438-3433. p. 607

Walters, Robert, Ref Librn, Orange Public Library, 348 Main St, Orange, NJ, 07050. Tel: 973-786-3988. p. 1431

Walters, Sam, Dir, Hearst Free Library, 401 Main St, Anaconda, MT, 59711. Tel: 406-563-6932. p. 1287

Walters, Sheryl, Ref Librn, Logan University/College of Chiropractic Library, 1851 Schoettler Rd, Chesterfield, MO, 63006. Tel: 636-230-1781. p. 1242

Walters, Susan, Chief Librn, Richmond Public Library, 100-7700 Minoru Gate, Richmond, BC, V6Y 1R9, CANADA. Tel: 604-231-6422. p. 2575

Walters, Tyler, Dean of Libr, Virginia Polytechnic Institute & State University Libraries, 560 Drillfield Dr, Blacksburg, VA, 24061. Tel: 540-231-5595. p. 2307

Walters, William H, Dr, Exec Dir, Manhattan College, 4513 Manhattan College Pkwy, Riverdale, NY, 10471. Tel: 718-862-7743. p. 1627

Walthall, Brandy, Youth Serv Librn, Atlantic City Free Public Library, William K Cheatham Bldg, One N Tennessee Ave, Atlantic City, NJ, 08401. Tel: 609-345-2269, Ext 3051. p. 1388

Walthart, Carol, Libr Dir, Colesburg Public Library, 220 Main St, Colesburg, IA, 52035. Tel: 563-856-5800. p. 741

Walther, James H, Dr, Exec Dir, Tampa Bay Library Consortium, Inc, 1600 E 8th Ave, No A200, Tampa, FL, 33605. Tel: 813-622-8252, Ext 102. p. 2763

Waltje, Jorg, Dean, Learning Res, Macomb Community College Libraries, Center Campus, 44575 Garfield Rd, C-Bldg, Clinton Township, MI, 48038-1139. Tel: 586-286-2104, Ext 2. p. 1157

Waltman, Colleen, Libr Dir, Homewood Public Library, 17917 Dixie Hwy, Homewood, IL, 60430-1703. Tel: 708-798-0121. p. 601

Waltner, Dusty, Br Mgr, Meridian Library District, Silverstone Branch, 3531 E Overland Rd, Meridian, ID, 83642. Tel: 208-884-2616. p. 525

Walton, Dawn, Assoc Dir, User Serv, University of North Carolina Wilmington Library, 601 S College Rd, Wilmington, NC, 28403. Tel: 910-962-3272, 910-962-3760. p. 1723

Walton, Dean, Ref Librn, University of Oregon Libraries, Allan Price Science Commons & Research Library, Onyx Bridge, Lower Level, 1344 Franklin Blvd, Eugene, OR, 97403. Tel: 541-346-2871. p. 1879

Walton, Earlene, Head Librn, Daingerfield Public Library, 207 Jefferson St, Daingerfield, TX, 75638. Tel: 903-645-2823. p. 2162

Walton, Jennifer, Co-Dir, Marine Biological Laboratory, McLean MS 8, 360 Woods Hole Rd, Woods Hole, MA, 02543. Tel: 508-289-7452. p. 1071

Walton, Jennifer, Cataloger, Bob Jones University, 1700 Wade Hampton Blvd, Greenville, SC, 29614. Tel: 864-370-1800, Ext 6000. p. 2060

Walton, Jessica, Librn, Pocahontas County Free Libraries, Durbin Community Library, 4715 Stauton-Parkersburg Tpk, Durbin, WV, 26264. Tel: 304-456-3142. p. 2408

Walton, Kathy, Asst Librn, Shellsburg Public Library, 110 Main St, Shellsburg, IA, 52332. Tel: 319-436-2112. p. 781

Walton, Katie, Acq Mgr, Arkansas State Library, 900 W Capitol, Ste 100, Little Rock, AR, 72201-3108. Tel: 501-682-2266. p. 100

Walton, Kerry, Academic Services, Interim Assoc Dean of Libraries, West Chester University, 25 W Rosedale Ave, West Chester, PA, 19383. Tel: 610-436-3453. p. 2020

Walton, Lauren, Supv Librn, Alameda Free Library, 1550 Oak St, Alameda, CA, 94501. Tel: 510-747-7716. p. 115

Walton, Lauren, Supv Librn, Alameda Free Library, West End, 788 Santa Clara Ave, Alameda, CA, 94501-3334. Tel: 510-747-7767. p. 115

Walton, Linda, Dir, National Network of Libraries of Medicine Region 6, Univ of Iowa Hardin Libr for Health Sci, 600 Newton Rd, Iowa City, IA, 52242-1098. Tel: 319-335-6431. p. 2765

Walton, Lori, Dir, Algona Public Library, 210 N Phillips St, Algona, IA, 50511. Tel: 515-295-5476. p. 730

Walton, Maureen, Circ Supvr, Franklin Public Library, 9151 W Loomis Rd, Franklin, WI, 53132. Tel: 414-425-8214. p. 2436

Walton, Rachel, Digital Archivist, Rec Mgr, Rollins College, 1000 Holt Ave, Campus Box 2744, Winter Park, FL, 32789-2744. Tel: 407-691-1127. p. 456

Walton, Rachel, Libr Mgr, Ferrum College, 150 Wiley Dr, Ferrum, VA, 24088. Tel: 540-365-4424, 540-365-4426. p. 2318

Walton, Rosemary, Librn, Law Library of Chiesa, Shahinian & Giantomasi, 105 Eisenhower Pkwy, Roseland, NJ, 07068. Tel: 973-530-2146. p. 1440

Walton, Sue Anne, Libr Dir, Au Sable Forks Free Library, Nine Church Lane, Au Sable Forks, NY, 12912-4400. Tel: 518-647-5596. p. 1488

Walton, Tyler, Libr Asst, Aurora Public Library, Hoffman Library, 1298 Peoria St, Aurora, CO, 80011. Tel: 303-739-1572. p. 264

Walton, Wendi, Br Mgr, Lincoln County Library System, Alpine Branch, 243 River Circle, Alpine, WY, 83128. Tel: 307-654-7323. p. 2496

Walton-Cagle, Lisa, Mgr, West Georgia Regional Library, Warren P Sewell Memorial Library of Bremen, 315 Hamilton Ave, Bremen, GA, 30110. Tel: 770-537-3937. p. 470

Waltz, Erin, Pub Serv Mgr, Supreme Court of Ohio, 65 S Front St, 11th Flr, Columbus, OH, 43215-3431. Tel: 614-387-9668. p. 1777

Waltz, Erin N, Dir, Supreme Court of Ohio, 65 S Front St, 11th Flr, Columbus, OH, 43215-3431. Tel: 614-387-9680. p. 1777

Waltz, Natasha, Br Mgr, Mansfield-Richland County Public Library, Butler Branch, 21 Elm St, Butler, OH, 44822. Tel: 419-883-2220. p. 1798

Walvoord, Chantal, Ref Librn, Rockwall County Library, 1215 E Yellowjacket Lane, Rockwall, TX, 75087. Tel: 972-204-7700. p. 2234

Walvoord, Travis, Librn, Zula Bryant Wylie Public Library, 225 Cedar St, Cedar Hill, TX, 75104-2655. Tel: 972-291-7323, Ext 1313. p. 2154

Walworth, Carl, Dir, Mattoon Public Library, 1600 Charleston Ave, Mattoon, IL, 61938-3935. Tel: 217-234-1710. p. 615

Walz, Greg, Mgr, Res, Utah State Historical Society, 7292 S State St, Midvale, UT, 84047. Tel: 801-245-7227. p. 2266

Walz, Missy, Asst Librn, ILL, Granton Community Library, 217 N Main St, Granton, WI, 54436. Tel: 715-238-5250. p. 2437

Walz, Pam, Head Librn, Leola Public Library, 802 Main St, Leola, SD, 57456. Tel: 605-439-3383. p. 2078

Walzer-Grammatico, Alyson, Head, Info Serv, Head, Ref, Delray Beach Public Library, 100 W Atlantic Ave, Delray Beach, FL, 33444. Tel: 561-266-0194. p. 394

Wambach, Andrea, Br Librn, United States Court of Appeals, 1102 US Courthouse, 300 S Fourth St, Rm 1102, Minneapolis, MN, 55415. Tel: 612-664-5830. p. 1185

Wambach, Andrea, Librn, US Courts Library, 512 Federal Court Bldg, 316 N Robert St, Saint Paul, MN, 55101. Tel: 651-848-1320. p. 1202

Wamer, Tam, Br Mgr, Washington County Public Library, Belpre Branch, 2012 Washington Blvd, Belpre, OH, 45714. Tel: 740-423-8381. p. 1799

Wamhoff, Meredith, Programming, Walnut Public Library District, 101 Heaton St, Walnut, IL, 61376. Tel: 815-379-2159. p. 658

Wamsley, Gregg, Dir, Hutchinson Public Library, 901 N Main, Hutchinson, KS, 67501-4492. Tel: 620-663-5441. p. 814

Wamsley, Lori, Fac Librn, Mt Hood Community College Libraries, 26000 SE Stark St, Gresham, OR, 97030. Tel: 503-491-7150. p. 1881

Wan, Fang, Asst Librn, Alfred University, Scholes Library of Ceramics, New York State College of Ceramics at Alfred University, Two Pine St, Alfred, NY, 14802-1297. p. 1485

Wan, Ronglin, Commun Libr Mgr, Queens Library, Bellerose Community Library, 250-06 Hillside Ave, Bellerose, NY, 11426. Tel: 718-831-8644. p. 1554

Wanamaker, Becky, Libr Dir, Clymer Library, 115 Firehouse Rd, Pocono Pines, PA, 18350-9705. Tel: 570-646-0826. p. 1998

Wanamaker, Karen, Curric Mats Ctr, Kutztown University, 15200 Kutztown Rd, Bldg 5, Kutztown, PA, 19530. Tel: 610-683-4480. p. 1949

Wang, Alison, Dir, Libr Serv, Norwalk Community College, 188 Richards Ave, Norwalk, CT, 06854-1655. Tel: 203-857-7207. p. 331

Wang, Andrew, Head Librn, North Carolina Museum of Art, 2110 Blue Ridge Rd, Raleigh, NC, 27607-6494. Tel: 919-664-6770. p. 1709

Wang, Andrew, Head Librn, University of Oregon Libraries, Design Library, 200 Lawrence Hall, 1190 Franklin Blvd, Eugene, OR, 97403-1299. Tel: 541-346-3637. p. 1879

Wang, Cheng, Ref Librn, Columbia University, C V Starr East Asian Library, 300 Kent Hall, MC 3901, 1140 Amsterdam Ave, New York, NY, 10027. Tel: 212-854-4318. p. 1584

Wang, Congwen, Research Librn, Northwest Missouri State University, 800 University Dr, Maryville, MO, 64468-6001. Tel: 660-562-1193. p. 1261

Wang, Dave, Commun Libr Mgr, Queens Library, Laurelton Community Library, 134-26 225th St, Laurelton, NY, 11413. Tel: 718-528-2822. p. 1555

Wang, Dong, Assoc Prof, University of Illinois at Urbana-Champaign, Library & Information Science Bldg, 501 E Daniel St, Champaign, IL, 61820-6211. Tel: 217-333-3280. p. 2784

Wang, Fangmin, Head, Libr Info Tech, Ryerson University Library, 350 Victoria St, 2nd Flr, Toronto, ON, M5B 2K3, CANADA. Tel: 416-979-5000, Ext 557034. p. 2692

Wang, Hanrong, Ref Librn, Jacksonville State University Library, 700 Pelham Rd N, Jacksonville, AL, 36265. Tel: 256-782-5758. p. 23

Wang, Haohan, Asst Prof, University of Illinois at Urbana-Champaign, Library & Information Science Bldg, 501 E Daniel St, Champaign, IL, 61820-6211. Tel: 217-333-3280. p. 2784

Wang, Henry, Librn III/Ref, Joe A Guerra Laredo Public Library, 1120 E Calton Rd, Laredo, TX, 78041. Tel: 956-795-2400. p. 2209

Wang, Hongjie, Head, Res & Instrul Serv, UConn Health Sciences Library, 263 Farmington Ave, Farmington, CT, 06034-4003. Tel: 860-679-4053. p. 313

Wang, Ingrid, Dean, Univ Libr, Long Island University, One University Plaza, Brooklyn, NY, 11201. Tel: 718-780-4513. p. 1505

Wang, Ingrid, Dean, Univ Libr, Long Island University Post, 720 Northern Blvd, Brookville, NY, 11548. Tel: 516-299-2764. p. 1507

Wang, Ingrid, Dean, Univ Libr, Academic Libraries of Brooklyn, Long Island University Brooklyn Library-LLC 524A, One University Plaza, Brooklyn, NY, 11201. Tel: 718-488-1680. p. 2770

Wang, Jiangiang, Dr, Assoc Prof, University at Buffalo, The State University of New York, 534 Baldy Hall, Buffalo, NY, 14260. Tel: 716-645-2412. p. 2789

Wang, Jiannan, Assoc Librn, Syst, California State University, East Bay Library, CSU East Bay Library, 25800 Carlos Bee Blvd, Hayward, CA, 94542-3052. Tel: 510-885-2973. p. 150

Wang, Joan, Librn, Washington University Libraries, East Asian, January Hall, 2nd Flr, One Brookings Dr, Campus Box 1061, Saint Louis, MO, 63130-4862. Tel: 314-935-4816. p. 1277

Wang, John, Dean of Libr, University of Texas at Arlington Library, 702 Planetarium Pl, Arlington, TX, 76019. Tel: 817-272-5318. p. 2136

Wang, Jue, Tech Serv Librn, Leeward Community College Library, 96-045 Ala Ike St, Pearl City, HI, 96782. Tel: 808-455-0672. p. 514

Wang, Lan, Ms, Head Librn, Lane College Library, 545 Lane Ave, Jackson, TN, 38301-4598. Tel: 731-426-7593. p. 2102

Wang, Lei, Asst Dir, Tech, Asst Dir, Innovation & User Experience, Yale University Library, Harvey Cushing/John Hay Whitney Medical Library, Sterling Hall of Medicine, 333 Cedar St, New Haven, CT, 06510. Tel: 203-785-6485. p. 327

Wang, Lili, Library Contact, MacNeal Hospital, 3249 S Oak Park Ave, Berwyn, IL, 60402. Tel: 708-783-3089. p. 542

Wang, Lina, Tech Librn, Halliburton Energy Services, 3000 N Sam Houston Pkwy E, Houston, TX, 77032. Tel: 281-871-2699. p. 2191

Wang, Maggie, Adult Ref, AV, Monterey Park Bruggemeyer Library, 318 S Ramona Ave, Monterey Park, CA, 91754-3399. Tel: 626-307-1368. p. 180

Wang, Peiling, Prof, University of Tennessee, Knoxville, 451 Communications Bldg, 1345 Circle Park Dr, Knoxville, TN, 37996-0332. Tel: 865-974-2148. p. 2792

Wang, Ray, Dean of Libr, Info Serv, University of New Orleans, 2000 Lakeshore Dr, New Orleans, LA, 70148. Tel: 504-280-6556. p. 904

Wang, Ray, Dean, Univ Libr, Adelphi University, One South Ave, Garden City, NY, 11530. Tel: 516-877-3549. p. 1536

Wang, Rong, Asst Dir, Syst & Tech, Bergen Community College, 400 Paramus Rd, Paramus, NJ, 07652-1595. Tel: 201-612-5563. p. 1432

Wang, Sharon, Ref Librn, York University Libraries, Osgoode Hall Law School Library, 92 Scholar's Walk, Keele Campus, Toronto, ON, M3J 1P3, CANADA. Tel: 416-736-5893. p. 2662

Wang, Shumin, Br Head, Vancouver Public Library, Marpole Branch, 8386 Granville St, Vancouver, BC, V6P 4Z7, CANADA. Tel: 604-665-3978. p. 2581

Wang, Tianjia, Librn, Mary M Campbell Public Library, Tenth & Green Sts, Marcus Hook, PA, 19061-4592. Tel: 610-485-6519. p. 1958

Wang, Wendy, Library Contact, Metron Inc, 1818 Library St, Ste 600, Reston, VA, 20190. Tel: 703-787-8700. p. 2339

Wang, Wenlian, Libr Tech, Northern College, Kirkland Lake Campus Library, 140 Government Rd E, Kirkland Lake, ON, P2N 3H7, CANADA. Tel: 705-567-9291, Ext 3700. p. 2679

Wang, Wensheng, Head, Access Serv, Cameron University Library, 2800 W Gore Blvd, Lawton, OK, 73505-6377. Tel: 580-581-6710. p. 1851

Wang, Xuemao, Dean of Libr, Northwestern University Libraries, 1970 Campus Dr, Evanston, IL, 60208-2300. Tel: 847-491-7658. p. 586

Wang, Ya, Electronic Collections Coord, San Francisco State University, 1630 Holloway Ave, San Francisco, CA, 94132-4030. Tel: 415-405-2680. p. 228

Wang, Yan, Digital Res/Presv Librn, University of Alabama at Birmingham, Mervyn H Sterne Library, 917 13th St S, Birmingham, AL, 35205. Tel: 205-934-6357. p. 9

Wang, Yan, Br Librn, Boston Public Library, Chinatown Branch, Two Boylston St, Boston, MA, 02116. Tel: 617-807-8176. p. 992

Wang, Yan, Syst Librn, North Carolina Central University, 1801 Fayetteville St, Durham, NC, 27707-3129. Tel: 919-530-5240. p. 1685

Wang, Yang, Prof, University of Illinois at Urbana-Champaign, Library & Information Science Bldg, 501 E Daniel St, Champaign, IL, 61820-6211. Tel: 217-333-3280. p. 2784

Wang, Yanhong, E-Resources Librn, Head, Tech Serv, McDaniel College, 2 College Hill, Westminster, MD, 21157-4390. Tel: 410-857-2741. p. 981

Wang, YiPing, Media/Instruction Librn, Laney College, 900 Fallon St, Oakland, CA, 94607. Tel: 510-464-3495. p. 185

Wang, Yongming, Syst Librn, The College of New Jersey, 2000 Pennington Rd, Ewing, NJ, 08628-1104. Tel: 609-771-2311. p. 1402

Wang, Zheng, Assoc Librn, Hesburgh Libraries, 221 Hesburgh Library, University of Notre Dame, Notre Dame, IN, 46556. Tel: 574-631-5252. p. 711

Wang, Ziyan, Circ Supvr, Somerset County Library System of New Jersey, Hillsborough Public, Hillsborough Municipal Complex, 379 S Branch Rd, Hillsborough, NJ, 08844. Tel: 908-458-8420. p. 1392

Wangsgard, Lynnda, Dir, Weber County Library System, 2464 Jefferson Ave, Ogden, UT, 84401-2464. Tel: 801-337-2617. p. 2267

Wann, Jennifer, Mgr, Libr Develop, Arkansas State Library, 900 W Capitol, Ste 100, Little Rock, AR, 72201-3108. Tel: 501-682-5288. p. 100

Wanner, Amanda, Admin Serv Librn, Ad, McBride Memorial Library, 500 N Market St, Berwick, PA, 18603. Tel: 570-752-2241, Ext 204. p. 1910

Wanser, Margaret, Tech Serv, Oyster Bay-East Norwich Public Library, 89 E Main St, Oyster Bay, NY, 11771. Tel: 516-922-1212. p. 1614

Wantuch, Dana, Sr Law Librn, New York State Supreme Court Law Library, Schenectady County Judicial Bldg, 612 State St, Schenectady, NY, 12305. Tel: 518-285-8518. p. 1638

Wanza, Mary, Dir, Coppin State College, 2500 W North Ave, Baltimore, MD, 21216-3698. Tel: 410-951-3405. p. 952

Warburg, Helena, Head, Sci Libr, Williams College, 26 Hopkins Hall Dr, Williamstown, MA, 01267. Tel: 413-597-3085. p. 1069

Warburton, Sally, Libr Dir, Pulaski County Public Library System, 60 W Third St, Pulaski, VA, 24301. Tel: 540-980-7770. p. 2339

Ward, Anna, Libr Mgr, Wake County Public Library System, Green Road Community Library, 4101 Green Rd, Raleigh, NC, 27604. Tel: 919-790-3200. p. 1711

Ward, Antonella, Multimedia Support Librn, Angelo State University Library, 2025 S Johnson, San Angelo, TX, 76904-5079. Tel: 325-486-6540. p. 2235

Ward, Betty, Librn, Westmoreland County Law Library, Two N Main St, Ste 202, Greensburg, PA, 15601. Tel: 724-830-3266. p. 1938

Ward, Brad, Exec Dir, Northeast Florida Library Information Network, 2233 Park Ave, Ste 402, Orange Park, FL, 32073. Tel: 904-278-5620. p. 2763

Ward, Bria, Dir, Human Res, Denver Public Library, Ten W 14th Ave Pkwy, Denver, CO, 80204-2731. Tel: 720-865-1111. p. 275

Ward, Brooke, Archives, Ser Librn, Florida College, 119 N Glen Arven Ave, Temple Terrace, FL, 33617-5578. Tel: 813-988-5131, Ext 212. p. 451

Ward, Cassi, Exec Dir, Putnam Historical Museum, 63 Chestnut St, Cold Spring, NY, 10516. Tel: 845-265-4010, Ext 17. p. 1520

Ward, Crystal, Br Mgr, Vigo County Public Library, 12 Points Branch, 2200 N 13th St, Terre Haute, IN, 47804. Tel: 812-645-3625. p. 721

Ward, Dane, Dean of Libr, Appalachian State University, 218 College St, Boone, NC, 28608. Tel: 828-262-6725. p. 1674

Ward, Danielle, Mkt Librn, Wilmington Memorial Library, 175 Middlesex Ave, Wilmington, MA, 01887-2779. Tel: 978-658-2967. p. 1070

Ward, Darlene, Asst Libr Dir, Illinois College of Optometry Library, 3241 S Michigan Ave, Chicago, IL, 60616-3878. Tel: 312-949-7151. p. 562

Ward, Deborah, Dir, University of Missouri-Columbia, J Otto Lottes Health Sciences Library, One Hospital Dr, Columbia, MO, 65212. Tel: 573-882-0471. p. 1244

Ward, Denise, Doc Delivery, Marshall University Libraries, Joan C Edwards School of Medicine Health Science Libraries, 1600 Medical Center Dr, Ste 2400, Huntington, WV, 25701-3655. Tel: 304-691-1750. p. 2405

Ward, Donita, Libr Dir, Wells Branch Community Library, 15001 Wells Port Dr, Austin, TX, 78728. Tel: 512-989-3188. p. 2143

Ward, Doretha, Libr Spec, York Technical College Library, 452 S Anderson Rd, Rock Hill, SC, 29730. Tel: 803-323-5991. p. 2068

Ward, Gerald, Digital Serv Librn, High Point University, One University Pkwy, High Point, NC, 27268. Tel: 336-841-9103. p. 1697

Ward, Heath, Libr Dir, Saluda County Library, 101 S Main St, Saluda, SC, 29138. Tel: 864-445-4500, Ext 2264. p. 2069

Ward, Janet, Asst Dir, Limestone University Library, 1115 College Dr, Gaffney, SC, 29340. Tel: 864-488-8351. p. 2060

Ward, Jennifer, Outreach Serv Librn, University of Alaska Southeast, 11066 Auke Lake Way, BE1, Juneau, AK, 99801. Tel: 907-796-6285. p. 47

Ward, Jessica, Br Mgr, Sandhill Pisgah Library & Community Center, 727 Sandhill Rd, Brandon, MS, 39047. Tel: 601-829-1653. p. 1212

Ward, Jewel, Librn, National Oceanic & Atmospheric Administration, 151 Patton Ave, Asheville, NC, 28801-5001. Tel: 828-271-4335. p. 1673

Ward, Joan, Librn, McKellar Township Public Library, 701 Hwy 124, McKellar, ON, P0G 1C0, CANADA. Tel: 705-389-2611. p. 2657

Ward, Joe, Ref Librn, Holy Family University Library, 9801 Frankford Ave, Philadelphia, PA, 19114. Tel: 267-341-3584. p. 1981

Ward, Julie, County Libr Dir, York County Library, 138 E Black St, Rock Hill, SC, 29730. Tel: 803-981-5858. p. 2068

Ward, Kaila, Youth Serv Librn, Middlesex Public Library, 1300 Mountain Ave, Middlesex, NJ, 08846. Tel: 732-356-6602. p. 1418

Ward, Kari, Dir, Information Nevada, Nevada State Library, Archives & Public Records, 100 N Stewart St, Carson City, NV, 89701. Tel: 775-431-0097. p. 2769

Ward, Kathie, Br Mgr, Harrisville Public Library, 1767 Simpson Hwy 469, Harrisville, MS, 39082-4005. Tel: 601-847-1268. p. 1218

Ward, Kathie Jo, Ch Serv, Magee Public Library, 120 First St NW, Magee, MS, 39111. Tel: 601-849-3747. p. 1225

Ward, Kathy, Head, ILL, Hazleton Area Public Library, 55 N Church St, Hazleton, PA, 18201-5893. Tel: 570-454-2961. p. 1943

Ward, Keely, Res Analyst, Holland & Knight LLP, 150 N Riverside Plaza, Chicago, IL, 60606. Tel: 312-263-3600. p. 561

Ward, Kelly, Dir, Putnam County District Library, The Educational Service Ctr, 136 Putnam Pkwy, Ottawa, OH, 45875-1471. Tel: 419-523-3747. p. 1811

Ward, Kim, Dir, Pierce District Library, 208 S Main St, Pierce, ID, 83546. Tel: 208-464-2823. p. 528

Ward, Latia, Research Librn, University of Virginia, Arthur J Morris Law Library, 580 Massie Rd, Charlottesville, VA, 22903-1738. Tel: 434-297-9334. p. 2310

Ward, Laura, Librn, Stetson Public Library, 70 Village Rd, Stetson, ME, 04488. Tel: 207-296-2020. p. 942

Ward, Leslie, Emerging Tech Librn, Queensborough Community College, City University of New York, 222-05 56th Ave, Bayside, NY, 11364-1497. Tel: 718-281-5795. p. 1491

Ward, Luciano, Circ Serv, Wilmette Public Library District, 1242 Wilmette Ave, Wilmette, IL, 60091-2558. Tel: 847-256-6950. p. 663

Ward, Megan, Exec Dir, First Parish Church of Norwell, 24 West St, Norwell, MA, 02061. Tel: 781-659-7100. p. 1043

Ward, Michelle, Campus Librn, Okanagan College Library, 1000 KLO Rd, Kelowna, BC, V1Y 4X8, CANADA. Tel: 250-762-5445, Ext 4749. p. 2568

Ward Morris, Kaitlynne, Dir, State Archives, Pub Info Officer, Rhode Island State Library, State House, Rm 208, 82 Smith St, Providence, RI, 02903. Tel: 401-222-2473. p. 2040

Ward, Paul, Jr, Asst Dir, Gaston County Public Library, 1555 E Garrison Blvd, Gastonia, NC, 28054. Tel: 704-868-2164. p. 1690

Ward, Rick, Dir, Blue Ridge Regional Library, 310 E Church St, Martinsville, VA, 24112-2909. Tel: 276-403-5430. p. 2331

Ward, Samantha, Operations Mgr, University of Tennessee, Knoxville, Webster C Pendergrass Agriculture & Veterinary Medicine Library, A-113 Veterinary Medical Ctr, 2407 River Dr, Knoxville, TN, 37996-4541. Tel: 865-974-4728. p. 2108

Ward, Sarah, Visual & Performing Arts Librn, Butler University Libraries, 4600 Sunset Ave, Indianapolis, IN, 46208. Tel: 317-940-9218. p. 690

Ward, Sarah, Assoc Dir, Norfolk Public Library, Two Liberty Lane, Norfolk, MA, 02056. Tel: 508-528-3380. p. 1040

Ward, Sarah, Dir, Burlington Public Library, 820 E Washington Ave, Burlington, WA, 98233. Tel: 360-755-0760. p. 2360

Ward, Sarah Laleman, Outreach Librn, Hunter College Libraries, East Bldg, 695 Park Ave, New York, NY, 10065. Tel: 212-772-4108. p. 1588

Ward Smith, Angela, Chief, Library Services, Environment & Climate Change Canada, Queen Sq, 5th Flr, 45 Alderney Dr, Dartmouth, NS, B2Y 2N6, CANADA. Tel: 902-426-7232. p. 2617

Ward, Steven, Dir, Taylorville Public Library, 121 W Vine St, Taylorville, IL, 62568. Tel: 217-824-4736. p. 653

Ward, Tamara, Learning Res Ctr Coordr, Wayne County Community College District, John Conyers Jr LRC Library, Northwest Campus, 8200 W Outer Dr, Detroit, MI, 48219. Tel: 313-943-4080. p. 1099

Ward, Tamara, Learning Res Ctr Coordr, Wayne County Community College District, Health Science Resource Center, Northwest Campus, 8200 W Outer Dr, Detroit, MI, 48219. Tel: 313-943-4080. p. 1100

Ward, Tina, Teen Serv, Milton-Union Public Library, 560 S Main St, West Milton, OH, 45383. Tel: 937-698-5515. p. 1830

Ward-Nesbit, Caroline, Head Librn, Thomaston Public Library, 60 Main St, Thomaston, ME, 04861. Tel: 207-354-2453. p. 943

Ward-Smith, Angela, Head, Libr Serv, Environment & Climate Change Canada, 351 St Joseph Blvd, Place Vincent Massey Annex, 1st Flr, Gatineau, QC, K1A 0H3, CANADA. Tel: 902-426-7232. p. 2713

Warden, Donna, Asst Admin, Volunteer State Community College Library, 1480 Nashville Pike, Gallatin, TN, 37066-3188. Tel: 615-230-3407. p. 2099

Warden, Haley, Director of Engagement, Auburn Public Library, 49 Spring St, Auburn, ME, 04210. Tel: 207-333-6640. p. 913

Warden, Pam, Librn, Mingo County Library, 1481 Helena Ave, Delbarton, WV, 25670. Tel: 304-475-2749. p. 2402

Warden, Stephanie, Asst Libr Dir, University of Wisconsin-Superior, 907 N 19th St, Superior, WI, 54880. Tel: 715-394-8342. p. 2480

Wardle, Amy, Ref, Free Library of Northampton Township, 25 Upper Holland Rd, Richboro, PA, 18954-1514. Tel: 215-357-3050. p. 2001

Wardley, Lisa, Library Contact, Zama City Community Library, Zama Cornerstone Bldg, 1025 Aspen Dr, Zama City, AB, T0H 4E0, CANADA. Tel: 780-683-2888. p. 2560

Wardroper, Lawrence, Head, Libr Syst & Cat, Government of Canada, Federal Courts & Tax Court of Canada, Courts Administration Service-Library Services, 90 Sparks St, Ottawa, ON, K1A 0H9, CANADA. Tel: 613-996-8735. p. 2667

Ware, Aidan, Gallery Dir, Idea Exchange, One North Sq, Cambridge, ON, N1S 2K6, CANADA. Tel: 519-621-0460. p. 2635

Ware, David, Dir, State Historian, Arkansas State Archives, One Capitol Mall, Ste 215, Little Rock, AR, 72201. Tel: 501-682-6901. p. 100

Ware, Erica, Br Mgr, Clayton County Library System, Forest Park Branch, 696 Main St, Forest Park, GA, 30297. Tel: 404-366-0850. p. 483

Ware, Margaret, ILL, Ref, McCowan Memorial Library, 15 Pitman Ave, Pitman, NJ, 08071. Tel: 856-589-1656. p. 1435

Ware, Paige, Br Mgr, Botetourt County Libraries, Fincastle Branch, 11 Academy St, Fincastle, VA, 24090-3316. Tel: 540-473-8339. p. 2344

Ware, Roxanne, Dir, Chase Township Public Library, 8400 E North St, Chase, MI, 49623. Tel: 231-832-9511. p. 1090

Ware, Shelby, Dir, Dir, Archives, LeTourneau University, 2100 S Mobberly Ave, Longview, TX, 75602-3524. Tel: 903-233-3260. p. 2213

Wareham, John, Ref Librn, Star Tribune, 650 Third Ave S, Ste 1300, Minneapolis, MN, 55488. Tel: 612-673-7759. p. 1185

Wareham, Wendy, Mgr, Libr Serv, Brandon Regional Health Authority, 150 McTavish Ave E, Brandon, MB, R7A 2B3, CANADA. Tel: 204-578-4080. p. 2585

Warehime, Rosie, Dir, Weller Public Library, 212 Main St, Waitsburg, WA, 99361. Tel: 509-337-8149. p. 2391
Wares, Michael, Asst Dir, Tech Serv, Fordham University Libraries, 441 E Fordham Rd, Bronx, NY, 10458-5151. Tel: 718-817-3570. p. 1498
Warf, Kasey, Libr Dir, Metcalfe County Public Library, 200 S Main St, Edmonton, KY, 42129. Tel: 270-432-4981. p. 854
Warfield, Adrianna, Children's Serv Coordr, Somerset County Library System, 11767 Beechwood St, Princess Anne, MD, 21853. Tel: 410-968-0955. p. 973
Warga, Julia, Dir, Res & Instruction Serv, Kenyon College Library & Information Services, Olin & Chalmers Libraries, 103 College Dr, Gambier, OH, 43022. p. 1787
Warga, Melanie, Dir, Ohio County Public Library, 413 Main St, Hartford, KY, 42347. Tel: 270-298-3790. p. 858
Wargo, Dena, Human Res, Mishawaka-Penn-Harris Public Library, 209 Lincolnway E, Mishawaka, IN, 46544. Tel: 574-259-5277, Ext 1102. p. 706
Wargo, Diane F, Ad, Churchill County Library, 553 S Maine St, Fallon, NV, 89406-3387. Tel: 775-423-7581. p. 1345
Wargo, Terri, Dir, West Lebanon-Pike Township Public Library, 200 N High St, West Lebanon, IN, 47991. Tel: 765-893-4605. p. 726
Warhank, Anneliese, Archivist, Oral Historian, Montana Historical Society, 225 N Roberts St, Helena, MT, 59601-4514. Tel: 406-444-4774. p. 1296
Waring, Ashley, Asst Dir, Reading Public Library, 64 Middlesex Ave, Reading, MA, 01867-2550. Tel: 781-944-0840. p. 1049
Wark, Dawna, Dir, Pub Serv, Hamilton Public Library, 55 York Blvd, Hamilton, ON, L8R 3K1, CANADA. Tel: 905-546-3200, Ext 3285. p. 2645
Wark, Jennifer, Head, Circ, Ludington Public Library, Five S Bryn Mawr Ave, Bryn Mawr, PA, 19010-3471. Tel: 610-525-1776. p. 1916
Wark, Jonathan, Dir, East Albemarle Regional Library, 100 E Colonial Ave, Elizabeth City, NC, 27909. Tel: 252-335-2511. p. 1687
Wark, Jonathan, Dir, Dare County Library, 700 N Hwy 64-264, Manteo, NC, 27954. Tel: 252-473-2372. p. 1702
Wark, Laura, Chief Exec Officer, Essa Public Library, 8505 County Rd 10, Unit 1, Angus, ON, L0M 1B1, CANADA. Tel: 705-424-6531. p. 2628
Wark, Laura, Chief Exec Officer, Essa Public Library, Thornton Branch, 34 Robert St, Thornton, ON, L0L 2N0, CANADA. Tel: 705-458-2549. p. 2628
Warkentin, Bettina, Libr Dir, Cumberland University, One Cumberland Sq, Lebanon, TN, 37087. Tel: 615-547-1374. p. 2108
Warkentin, Martin, Colls Librn, University of the Fraser Valley, 33844 King Rd, Bldg G, Abbotsford, BC, V2S 7M8, CANADA. Tel: 604-504-7441, Ext 4460. p. 2562
Warlick, Stefanie, Interim Assoc Dean of Libraries, James Madison University Libraries, 880 Madison Dr, MSC 1704, Harrisonburg, VA, 22807. Tel: 540-568-4289. p. 2324
Warminski, Beverly, Br Librn, Carson County Public Library, White Deer Branch, 200 Fourth St, White Deer, TX, 79097. Tel: 806-883-7121. p. 2225
Warne, Amber, Asst Librn, Belle Plaine City Library, 222 W Fifth Ave, Belle Plaine, KS, 67013. Tel: 620-488-3431. p. 798
Warne-Peter, Sheila, Br Librn, Southeast Regional Library, Grenfell Branch, 710 Desmond St, Grenfell, SK, S0G 2B0, CANADA. Tel: 306-697-2455. p. 2753
Warnement, Mary, Head, Reader Serv, Boston Athenaeum, Ten 1/2 Beacon St, Boston, MA, 02108-3777. Tel: 617-227-0270. p. 991
Warner, Amanda, Asst Dir, Youth Serv, Plain City Public Library, 305 W Main St, Plain City, OH, 43064-1148. Tel: 614-873-4912, Ext 131. p. 1816
Warner, Beth, Assoc Dir, Info Tech, Ohio State University LIBRARIES, William Oxley Thompson Library, 1858 Neil Ave Mall, Columbus, OH, 43210-1286. Tel: 614-292-6785. p. 1776
Warner, Doris, Dir, Fairview Public Library, 43 Walnut St, Margaretville, NY, 12455. Tel: 845-586-3791. p. 1569
Warner, Elizabeth, Evening Supvr, Drexel University Libraries, Hahnemann Library, 245 N 15th St MS 449, Philadelphia, PA, 19102-1192. p. 1976
Warner, Jennifer, Dir, Weston Public Library, 87 School St, Weston, MA, 02493. Tel: 781-786-6150. p. 1068
Warner, Jenny, Mgr, Triodyne Inc, 3054 N Lake Terrace, Glenview, IL, 60026. Tel: 847-677-4730. p. 594
Warner, Kim, Youth Serv Librn, Wayne Public Library, Robert B & Mary Y Benthack Library-Senior Ctr, 410 Pearl St, Wayne, NE, 68787. Tel: 402-375-3135. p. 1340
Warner, Kristina, Archivist, Norwegian-American Historical Association Archives, 1510 St Olaf Ave, Northfield, MN, 55057. Tel: 507-786-3450. p. 1191
Warner, Laura, Mgr, Libr Res, Brantford Public Library, 173 Colborne St, Brantford, ON, N3T 2G8, CANADA. Tel: 519-756-2220. p. 2633
Warner, Lian, Instruction Librn, North Greenville University, 100 Donnan Blvd, Tigerville, SC, 29688. Tel: 864-977-7091. p. 2071
Warner, Mary, Exec Dir, Charles A Weyerhaeuser Memorial Museum, 2151 Lindbergh Dr S, Little Falls, MN, 56345. Tel: 320-632-4007. p. 1180
Warner, Mary Ann, Adult Serv Coordr, Schenectady County Public Library, 99 Clinton St, Schenectady, NY, 12305-2083. Tel: 518-388-4500. p. 1638
Warner, Miriam, Dir, Wendell Free Library, Seven Wendell Depot Rd, Wendell, MA, 01379. Tel: 978-544-3559. p. 1064
Warner, Nicole, Librn, Archives & Digital Coll Initiatives, Pennsylvania College of Technology, 999 Hagan Way, Williamsport, PA, 17701. Tel: 570-327-4523. p. 2023
Warner, Raven, Coll Maint & Preservation Tech, Maryland Institute College of Art, 1401 W Mount Royal Ave, Baltimore, MD, 21217. Tel: 410-225-2304, 410-225-2311. p. 955
Warner, Simeon, Dir, Informational Serv, Interim Assoc Univ Librn, Cornell University Library, 201 Olin Library, Ithaca, NY, 14853. Tel: 607-255-4144. p. 1551
Warner, Susan, Head, Youth Serv, Kalamazoo Public Library, 315 S Rose St, Kalamazoo, MI, 49007-5264. Tel: 269-553-7876. p. 1121
Warner, Susan, Dir, Wolverine Community Library, 5716 W Main St, Wolverine, MI, 49799-9403. Tel: 231-525-8800. p. 1160
Warner, Valerie, Libr Tech, Grantsville City Library, 42 N Bowery St, Grantsville, UT, 84029. Tel: 435-884-1670. p. 2264
Warnick, Mark, Libr Dir, Black River Technical College Library, 1410 Hwy 304 E, Pocahontas, AR, 72455. Tel: 870-248-4061. p. 108
Warnick, Shirley S, Dir, Gallatin County Public Library, 209 W Market St, Warsaw, KY, 41095. Tel: 859-567-2786. p. 876
Warnke, Robin, Customer Experience Supervisor, Douglas County Libraries, Lone Tree Branch, 10055 Library Way, Lone Tree, CO, 80124. Tel: 303-791-7323. p. 270
Warnke, Sue, Dir, Sayre Public Library, 113 E Poplar, Sayre, OK, 73662. Tel: 580-928-2641. p. 1861
Warnock, Doug, Supvr, Middlesex County Library, Ailsa Craig Branch, 147 Main St, Ailsa Craig, ON, N0M 1A0, CANADA. Tel: 519-293-3441. p. 2682
Warnock, Doug, Supvr, Middlesex County Library, Parkhill Branch, 229 B Main St, Parkhill, ON, N0M 2K0, CANADA. Tel: 519-294-6583. p. 2682
Warren, April, Colls Librn, Middle Georgia State University, Cochran Campus, 1100 Second St SE, Cochran, GA, 31014. Tel: 478-934-3071. p. 471
Warren, Brad, Dean of Libr, Augusta University, 1459 Laney-Walker Blvd, Augusta, GA, 30912-0004. Tel: 706-721-2856. p. 467
Warren, Brad, Dean of Libr, Augusta University, 2500 Walton Way, Augusta, GA, 30904-2200. Tel: 706-721-2856. p. 467
Warren, Brie, Librn, Redington-Fairview General Hospital, 46 Fairview Ave, Skowhegan, ME, 04976. Tel: 207-858-2321. p. 940
Warren, Christa, Acq & Coll, Sr Mgr, Tech, Salt Lake County Library Services, 8030 S 1825 W, West Jordan, UT, 84088. Tel: 801-943-4636. p. 2274
Warren, Christopher S, Libr Dir, Dothan Houston County Library System, 445 N Oates St, Dothan, AL, 36303. Tel: 334-793-9767. p. 14
Warren, Eric, Coordr, Instruction & Ref, Springfield Technical Community College Library, One Armory Sq, Bldg 27, Ste 1, Springfield, MA, 01105. Tel: 413-755-4555. p. 1057
Warren, Evelyn, Mgr, NASA Ames Research Center, Technical Library, Bldg 202, Mail Stop 202-3, Moffett Field, CA, 94035-1000. Tel: 650-604-5681. p. 178
Warren Foster, Chriss, Dr, Interim Dean, Merritt College Library, 12500 Campus Dr, Oakland, CA, 94619. Tel: 510-436-2461. p. 185
Warren, Jalyn, Electronic Res, Community College of Philadelphia Library, Mint Bldg, Level 1, 1700 Spring Garden St, Philadelphia, PA, 19130. Tel: 215-751-8394. p. 1975
Warren, Jessica, Dir, Clearwater Public Library, 109 E Ross St, Clearwater, KS, 67026-7824. Tel: 620-584-6474. p. 802
Warren, Julie, Libr Serv & Pub Relations Mgr, Palm Springs Public Library, 300 S Sunrise Way, Palm Springs, CA, 92262-7699. Tel: 760-416-6731. p. 191
Warren, Katy, Br Head, Harnett County Public Library, Angier Public, 28 N Raleigh St, Angier, NC, 27501-6073. Tel: 919-639-4413. p. 1701
Warren, Laura, Mgr, Libr Operations, Metropolitan Library System in Oklahoma County, Warr Acres Library, 5901 NW 63rd St, Warr Acres, OK, 73132-7502. p. 1858
Warren, Len, Dir, Park City Public Library, 2107 E 61st St N, Park City, KS, 67219. Tel: 316-744-6318. p. 830
Warren, Leslie A, Dean, Library & Instructional Support, Northern Michigan University, 1401 Presque Isle Ave, Marquette, MI, 49855-5376. Tel: 906-227-2260. p. 1130
Warren, Lynne, Curator, Museum of Contemporary Art Library, 220 E Chicago Ave, Chicago, IL, 60611. Tel: 312-397-3894. p. 565
Warren, Misty L, Cat, ILL, Lamar Public Library, 102 E Parmenter St, Lamar, CO, 81052-3239. Tel: 719-336-1292. p. 289
Warren, Pat, Br Librn, Wapiti Regional Library, Big River Public Library, 606 First St N, Big River, SK, S0J 0E0, CANADA. Tel: 306-469-2152. p. 2745
Warren, Scott, Assoc Dean, Res, Syracuse University Libraries, 222 Waverly Ave, Syracuse, NY, 13244-2010. Tel: 315-443-8339. p. 1650
Warren, Stephen, Libr Mgr, Vancouver Island Regional Library, Chemainus Branch, 2592 Legion St, Chemainus, BC, V0R 1K0, CANADA. Tel: 250-246-9471. p. 2570
Warren, Stephen, Libr Mgr, Vancouver Island Regional Library, Ladysmith Branch, 3-740 First Ave, Ladysmith, BC, V9G 1A3, CANADA. Tel: 250-245-2322. p. 2571
Warren, Tessia, Libr Mgr, Pikes Peak Library District, Ruth Holley Library, 685 N Murray Blvd, Colorado Springs, CO, 80915. Tel: 719-531-6333, Ext 6101. p. 271

Warren, Wes, Ref Librn, University of Mount Olive, 646 James B Hunt Dr, Mount Olive, NC, 28365-1699. Tel: 919-658-7869. p. 1705

Warrene, Carl, Syst Adminr, University of North Dakota, Thormodsgard Law Library, 215 Centennial Dr, Grand Forks, ND, 58202. Tel: 701-777-2204. p. 1735

Warrenger, Krissy, Dir, Head Librn, Derby Neck Library Association, 307 Hawthorne Ave, Derby, CT, 06418. Tel: 203-734-1492. p. 308

Warrick, Steve, Br Mgr, Montgomery County Public Libraries, Davis Library, 6400 Democracy Blvd, Bethesda, MD, 20817-1638. Tel: 240-777-0916. p. 974

Warrow, Jeannine, Libr Dir, Melvindale Public Library, 18650 Allen Rd, Melvindale, MI, 48122. Tel: 313-429-1090. p. 1131

Warsavage, Laina, Libr Dir, Orford Social Library, 573 NH Rte 10, Orford, NH, 03777. Tel: 603-353-9756. p. 1377

Wartenberg, Paul, Actg Dir, Ref Serv, Bartow Public Library, 2150 S Broadway Ave, Bartow, FL, 33830. Tel: 863-534-0131. p. 384

Warthen, Lee, Asst Dir, Head, Coll Develop, University of Utah, S J Quinney Law Library, 332 S 1400 East, Salt Lake City, UT, 84112-0731. Tel: 801-581-5344. p. 2272

Wascher, Karen, Circ Mgr, Morningside University, 1501 Morningside Ave, Sioux City, IA, 51106. Tel: 712-274-5245. p. 782

Wasemiller, Monica, Ch Serv, Prog Dir, Hustisford Community Library, 609 W Juneau St, Hustisford, WI, 53034. Tel: 920-349-4545. p. 2442

Washam, Linda, Br Mgr, Trails Regional Library, Odessa Branch, 204 S First, Odessa, MO, 64076. Tel: 816-633-4089. p. 1285

Washburn, Earl, Library Contact, Vermont Grand Lodge Library, 49 East Rd - Berlin, Barre, VT, 05641-5390. Tel: 802-223-1883. p. 2278

Washburn, Eileen, Ch & Youth Librn, Richmond Memorial Library, 15 School Dr, Marlborough, CT, 06447-1582. Tel: 860-295-6210. p. 321

Washburn, Elizabeth, Ref Librn, Fall River Public Library, 104 N Main St, Fall River, MA, 02720. Tel: 508-324-2700. p. 1018

Washburn, Mike, Dir, Linwood Community Library, 19649 Linwood Rd, Linwood, KS, 66052. Tel: 913-723-3208. p. 821

Washburn, Shannon, Asst Librn, Meagher County City Library, 205 SW Garfield, White Sulphur Springs, MT, 59645. Tel: 406-547-2250. p. 1304

Washburn, Vanessa, Circ Coordr, Ref Coordr, Southwestern Assemblies of God University, 1200 Sycamore St, Waxahachie, TX, 75165-2342. Tel: 972-825-4761. p. 2255

Washell, Nancy, Dir, Glendale Area Public Library Inc, Community Bldg, 961 Forest St, Coalport, PA, 16627. Tel: 814-672-4378. p. 1923

Washington, AlTonya R, Ref & Instruction Librn, Winston-Salem State University, 601 Martin Luther King Jr Dr, Winston-Salem, NC, 27110. Tel: 336-750-2037. p. 1726

Washington, Carolyn, Br Mgr, Winn Parish Library, Atlanta Branch, 110 School Rd, Atlanta, LA, 71404. Tel: 318-628-7657. p. 912

Washington, David, Dir, External Libr Serv, Temple University Libraries, 1210 W Berks St, Philadelphia, PA, 19122-6088. Tel: 215-204-8231. p. 1986

Washington, Helena, Med Librn, Corporal Michael J Crescenz VA Medical Center, 3900 Woodland Ave, Philadelphia, PA, 19104. Tel: 215-823-5860. p. 1975

Washington, Jessica, Mgr, Saint Mary Parish Library, Amelia Branch, 625 Lake Palourde, Amelia, LA, 70340. Tel: 985-631-2262. p. 890

Washington, Kellie, Br Mgr, Southeast Arkansas Regional Library, Dermott Branch, 117 S Freeman St, Dermott, AR, 71638. Tel: 870-538-3514. p. 104

Washington, Linda, Libr Tech, Phillips Community College of the University of Arkansas, 1000 Campus Dr, Helena, AR, 72342. Tel: 870-338-6474. p. 98

Washington, Madelyn, Head Music Libr, University of Houston, Music Library, 220 Moores School of Music Bldg, Houston, TX, 77204-4017. Tel: 713-743-4231. p. 2199

Washington, Marquita, Br Mgr, Atlanta-Fulton Public Library System, Hapeville Branch, 525 King Arnold St, Hapeville, GA, 30354. Tel: 404-762-4065. p. 461

Washington, Paulette, Learning Commons Mgr, California State University, East Bay Library, CSU East Bay Library, 25800 Carlos Bee Blvd, Hayward, CA, 94542-3052. Tel: 510-885-2651. p. 150

Washington, Robyn, ILL, Department of Veterans Affairs, Central Office Library, 810 Vermont Ave NW, Washington, DC, 20420. Tel: 202-273-8520. p. 363

Washington, Sheila, Law Librn, Lewis, Brisbois, Bisgaard & Smith, 633 W Fifth St, Ste 4000, Los Angeles, CA, 90071. Tel: 213-250-1800. p. 162

Washington, Shya N, Libr Mgr, Central Arkansas Library System, Esther DeWitt Nixon Branch, 703 W Main St, Jacksonville, AR, 72076. Tel: 501-457-5038. p. 101

Washington, Sylvia, Tech Serv, Pine Bluff & Jefferson County Library System, Main Library, 600 S Main St, Pine Bluff, AR, 71601. Tel: 870-534-4802. p. 107

Washington, Tabitha, Dir, Gadsden County Public Library, 732 S Pat Thomas Pkwy, Quincy, FL, 32351. Tel: 850-627-7106. p. 439

Wasiecko, Steve, Libr Operations Mgr, Aurora Public Library, 14949 E Alameda Pkwy, Aurora, CO, 80012. Tel: 303-739-6600. p. 264

Wasielewski, Alice, Sr Libr Tech, University of Kentucky Libraries, Science & Engineering Library, 211 King Bldg, 179 Funkhouser Dr, Lexington, KY, 40506-0039. Tel: 859-257-6217. p. 864

Wasielewski, Matt, Dir, Libr Serv, Denver Seminary, 6399 S Santa Fe Dr, Littleton, CO, 80120. Tel: 303-762-6955. p. 290

Wasielewski, Terrance, Coll Develop Librn, Tech Serv Librn, The Sage Colleges, 140 New Scotland Ave, Albany, NY, 12208. Tel: 518-244-2435. p. 1483

Wasilick, Michael J, Libr Dir, Wake County Public Library System, 4020 Carya Dr, Raleigh, NC, 27610-2900. Tel: 919-250-1200. p. 1710

Waskiewicz, Danielle, Libr Dir, Westhampton Free Library, Seven Library Ave, Westhampton Beach, NY, 11978-2697. Tel: 631-288-3335, Ext 116. p. 1664

Waskin, Lisa, Dir, Superior District Library, 541 Library Dr, Sault Sainte Marie, MI, 49783. Tel: 906-632-9331. p. 1149

Wasley, Patrick, PhD, Archivist, Ser, Averett University Library, 344 W Main St, Danville, VA, 24541-2849. Tel: 434-791-5692. p. 2314

Wassberg, Linda A, Libr Tech, United States Courts, 624 US Courthouse, 500 State Ave, Kansas City, KS, 66101. Tel: 913-735-2200. p. 817

Wassef, Maggy, Libr Mgr, Saint Mary's Hospital, 3830 Lacombe Ave, Montreal, QC, H3T 1M5, CANADA. Tel: 514-345-3511, Ext 3317. p. 2727

Wassenaar, Anna, Dir, Blue Island Public Library, 2433 York St, Blue Island, IL, 60406-2011. Tel: 708-388-1078, Ext 14. p. 543

Wasserman, Janet, Ch Serv, North Merrick Public Library, 1691 Meadowbrook Rd, North Merrick, NY, 11566. Tel: 516-378-7474. p. 1608

Wasserman, Mona, Dir, Libr Serv, St Francis College Library, 180 Remsen St, Brooklyn, NY, 11201. Tel: 718-489-5305. p. 1506

Wassick, Maddy, Med Librn/CME Coordr, McLaren Bay Region Health Sciences Library, 1900 Columbus Ave, Bay City, MI, 48708-6880. Tel: 989-894-3783. p. 1083

Wasson, Rebecca, Dir & Librn, Farmer Township Community Library, 500 S Main St, Ste 132, Bushton, KS, 67427-9749. Tel: 620-562-3217. p. 800

Wasterlain, Justin, Br Mgr, Santa Clara City Library, Mission Branch Library, 1098 Lexington St, Santa Clara, CA, 95050. Tel: 408-615-2957. p. 241

Wastlick, Carrie A, Library Contact, Sauk County Law Library, 515 Oak St, Baraboo, WI, 53913. Tel: 608-355-3287. p. 2422

Watanabe, Cynthia, Circ Librn, East Baton Rouge Parish Library, 7711 Goodwood Blvd, Baton Rouge, LA, 70806-7625. Tel: 225-231-3745. p. 882

Waterhouse, Janetta L, Dir, Libr Syst & Tech Serv, University at Albany, State University of New York, 1400 Washington Ave, Albany, NY, 12222-0001. Tel: 518-442-3631. p. 1484

Waterman, Edra, Dir/Chief Exec Officer, Hamilton East Public Library, One Library Plaza, Noblesville, IN, 46060. Tel: 317-773-1384. p. 710

Waterman, Edra L, Dir, Hamilton East Public Library, Fishers Branch, Five Municipal Dr, Fishers, IN, 46038. Tel: 317-579-0300. p. 710

Waterman, Tracy, Librn, Minnesota Department of Natural Resources Library, 500 Lafayette Rd, Saint Paul, MN, 55155. Tel: 651-259-5506. p. 1200

Waterous, Edward W, Chairperson, Librn, Collectors Club of Chicago Library, 1029 N Dearborn St, Chicago, IL, 60610. Tel: 312-642-7981. p. 559

Waters, Alica, Regional Librn, State of Rhode Island, Talking Books Library, One Capitol Hill, Providence, RI, 02908-5803. Tel: 401-574-9315. p. 2041

Waters, Alicia, Regional Librn, State of Rhode Island, Department of Administration, One Capitol Hill, 2nd Flr, Providence, RI, 02908. Tel: 401-574-9315. p. 2041

Waters, Austin, Student Serv Librn, University at Buffalo Libraries-State University of New York, Charles B Sears Law Library, John Lord O'Brian Hall, 211 Mary Talbert Way, Buffalo, NY, 14260-1110. Tel: 716-645-8595. p. 1511

Waters, Austin B, Ref Librn, Touro University, 225 Eastview Dr, Central Islip, NY, 11722-4539. Tel: 631-761-7150. p. 1516

Waters, Bill, Ch Serv Librn, Quincy Public Library, 526 Jersey St, Quincy, IL, 62301-3996. Tel: 217-223-1309, Ext 219. p. 637

Waters, Carolyn, Dir & Head Librn, The New York Society Library, 53 E 79th St, New York, NY, 10075. Tel: 212-288-6900, Ext 244. p. 1598

Waters, Chandra, Sr Librn, University of Illinois at Chicago, Library of the Health Sciences, Urbana, 102 Medical Sciences Bldg, MC-714, 506 S Mathews Ave, Urbana, IL, 61801. Tel: 312-996-8966. p. 570

Waters, Courtney, Teen Librn, Missouri River Regional Library, 214 Adams St, Jefferson City, MO, 65101. Tel: 573-634-2464. p. 1252

Waters, Emily, Asst Dean, Curtis Institute of Music, 1720 Locust St, Philadelphia, PA, 19103. Tel: 215-717-3123. p. 1976

Waters, Gina, Libr Dir, Hauge Memorial Library, 50655 Charles St, Osseo, WI, 54758. Tel: 715-597-3444. p. 2468

Waters, Jennifer, Libr Mgr, Chauvin Municipal Library, 5200 Fourth Ave N, Chauvin, AB, T0B 0V0, CANADA. Tel: 780-858-3746. p. 2531

Waters, Karen, Dir, Illinois Department of Transportation, 320 Harry Hanley Bldg, 2300 S Dirksen Pkwy, Springfield, IL, 62764-0001. Tel: 217-524-3834, 217-782-6680. p. 649

Waters, Linda, Dir, Desoto County Library, 125 N Hillsborough Ave, Arcadia, FL, 34266. Tel: 863-993-4851. p. 383

Waters, Lora, Acq, Libr Spec, Owensboro Community & Technical College Library, Learning Resource Ctr Bldg, 1st Flr, 4800 New Hartford Rd, Owensboro, KY, 42303. Tel: 270-686-4580. p. 871

Waters, Natalie, Head Librn, McGill University Libraries, Schulich Library of Physical Science, Life Sciences, & Engineering, Macdonald

Stewart Library Bldg, 809 Sherbrooke St W, Montreal, QC, H3A 2K6, CANADA. Tel: 514-398-1204. p. 2726
Waters, Thomas, Tech Serv Librn, Brenau University, 625 Academy St, Gainesville, GA, 30501-3343. Tel: 770-718-5303. p. 480
Waters, Tommy, Bus Librn, Howard University Libraries, 500 Howard Pl NW, Ste 203, Washington, DC, 20059. Tel: 202-806-1599. p. 369
Waters, Tommy, Bus Librn, Howard University Libraries, Business, 2600 Sixth St NW, Washington, DC, 20059. Tel: 202-806-1599. p. 369
Waters, Tommy, Interim Librn, Howard University Libraries, Social Work, 601 Howard Pl NW, Rm 200, Washington, DC, 20059. Tel: 202-806-7316. p. 369
Waters, Vern, Mgr, Salt Lake County Library Services, Columbus Branch, 2530 S 500 E, South Salt Lake, UT, 84106. p. 2274
Waters, Vicki, Dir, Grant County Library, 507 S Canyon Blvd, John Day, OR, 97845-1050. Tel: 541-575-1992. p. 1882
Waterstone, Marek, Head, Acq & Coll Serv, University of Houston, The O'Quinn Law Library, 12 Law Library, Houston, TX, 77204-6054. Tel: 713-743-2300. p. 2199
Wathen, Charlotte, Librn, Tombigbee Regional Library System, Wren Public Library, 32655 Hwy 45 N, Aberdeen, MS, 39730-9796. Tel: 662-256-4957. p. 1236
Wathen, LynnDee, Br Mgr, Mid-Continent Public Library, Buckner Branch, 19 E Jefferson St, Buckner, MO, 64016. Tel: 816-650-3212. p. 1250
Wathen, LynnDee, Br Mgr, Mid-Continent Public Library, Parkville Branch, 8815 Tom Watson Pkwy, Parkville, MO, 64152. Tel: 816-741-4721. p. 1251
Watkins, Ally, Youth Librn, First Regional Library, Lafayette County-Oxford Public Library, 401 Bramlett Blvd, Oxford, MS, 38655. Tel: 662-234-5751. p. 1220
Watkins, Angela, Libr Dir, Aztec Public Library, 319 S Ash, Aztec, NM, 87410. Tel: 505-334-7657. p. 1463
Watkins, April, Libr Mgr, Piedmont Regional Library System, Talmo Public Library, 45 A J Irvin Rd, Talmo, GA, 30575. Tel: 706-693-1905. p. 483
Watkins, Cathy, Libr Asst, Dora Bee Woodyard Memorial Library, 411 Mulberry St, Elizabeth, WV, 26143. Tel: 304-275-4295. p. 2402
Watkins, Faye, Dean, Florida Agricultural & Mechanical University Libraries, 525 Orr Dr, Tallahassee, FL, 32307-4700. Tel: 850-599-3370. p. 446
Watkins, Jim, Dir, Charlotte County Library, Phenix Branch, Charlotte St, Phenix, VA, 23959. Tel: 434-542-4654. p. 2309
Watkins, Jim, Librn, Charlotte County Library, 112-116 Legrande Ave, Charlotte Court House, VA, 23923. Tel: 434-542-5247. p. 2309
Watkins, Julia, Br Dir, Mountainburg Public Library, 225 Hwy 71 NW, Mountainburg, AR, 72946. Tel: 479-369-1600. p. 105
Watkins, Kathie, Dir, Linden-Carnegie Public Library, 102 S Main St, Linden, IN, 47955. Tel: 765-339-4239. p. 703
Watkins, Melinda, Ch Serv Librn, Valley Cottage Free Library, 110 Rte 303, Valley Cottage, NY, 10989. Tel: 845-268-7700, Ext 123. p. 1656
Watkins, Rick, Br Head, Winnipeg Public Library, Cornish, 20 West Gate, Winnipeg, MB, R3C 2E1, CANADA. Tel: 202-986-4680. p. 2596
Watkins, Rick, Br Head, Winnipeg Public Library, Sir William Stephenson, 765 Keewatin St, Winnipeg, MB, R2X 3B9, CANADA. Tel: 204-986-7070. p. 2596
Watkins, Rodney, Head, Access Serv, Morehead State University, 150 University Blvd, Morehead, KY, 40351. Tel: 606-783-9343. p. 869
Watkis, Errol, Fac Adminr & Head, Multimedia Serv, Howard University Libraries, 500 Howard Pl NW, Ste 203, Washington, DC, 20059. Tel: 202-806-7238. p. 368
Watkoskey, Kelsey, Br Mgr, Ocean County Library, Point Pleasant Borough Branch, 834 Beaver Dam Rd, Point Pleasant Beach, NJ, 08742-3853. Tel: 732-295-1555. p. 1447
Watney, Laurel, Dir, Sterling College, 125 W Cooper, Sterling, KS, 67579. Tel: 620-278-4234. p. 837
Watson, Allison, Br Asst, Cumberland Public Libraries, Springhill Miners Memorial Library, 85 Main St, Springhill, NS, B0M 1X0, CANADA. Tel: 902-597-2211. p. 2615
Watson, Amy, Info Spec, PPG Industries, Inc, Technical Information Center, 4325 Rosanna Dr, Allison Park, PA, 15101. Tel: 412-492-5268. p. 1996
Watson, Angie, Circ & ILL, Tremont District Public Library, 215 S Sampson St, Tremont, IL, 61568. Tel: 309-925-5432, 309-925-5597. p. 654
Watson, Ann M, Assoc State Librn, Libr Serv, State Library of Ohio, 274 E First Ave, Ste 100, Columbus, OH, 43201. Tel: 614-728-4988. p. 1777
Watson, Azusa, Asst Librn, Coronation Memorial Library, 5001 Royal St, Coronation, AB, T0C 1C0, CANADA. Tel: 403-578-3445. p. 2532
Watson, Barbara, Chmn, First Baptist Church Library, 2709 Monument Ave, Richmond, VA, 23220. Tel: 804-355-8637, Ext 120. p. 2340
Watson, Berrie, Asst Dir, Head, Libr Syst, University of South Florida Saint Petersburg, 140 Seventh Ave S, POY118, Saint Petersburg, FL, 33701-5016. Tel: 727-873-4402. p. 442
Watson, Carol A, Dir, University of Georgia, Alexander Campbell King Law Library, 225 Herty Dr, Athens, GA, 30602-6018. Tel: 706-542-1922. p. 459
Watson, Carrie, Librn, Varnum Memorial Library, 194 Main St, Jeffersonville, VT, 05464. Tel: 802-644-2117. p. 2287
Watson, Carrie E, Libr Dir, Farmland Public Library, 116 S Main St, Farmland, IN, 47340. Tel: 765-468-7292. p. 682
Watson, Cheyenne, Archivist, Staten Island Institute of Arts & Sciences, Snug Harbor Cultural Ctr, Bldg H, 1000 Richmond Terrace, Staten Island, NY, 10301. Tel: 718-727-1135. p. 1645
Watson, Diana, Supvr, Middlesex County Library, Newbury Branch, 22894 Hagerty St, Newbury, ON, N0L 1Z0, CANADA. Tel: 519-693-4275. p. 2682
Watson, Diane, Communications Mgr, Marion Public Library, 445 E Church St, Marion, OH, 43302-4290. Tel: 740-387-0992. p. 1799
Watson, Gwen, Dir, Libr Serv, Winston & Strawn LLP Library, 35 W Wacker Dr, Chicago, IL, 60601. Tel: 312-282-5404. p. 570
Watson, Gwen, Dir, Res, Winston & Strawn Library, 1111 Louisiana St, 25th Flr, Houston, TX, 77002-5242. Tel: 713-651-2600. p. 2200
Watson, Jamie, Coordr, Coll Develop, Baltimore County Public Library, 320 York Rd, Towson, MD, 21204-5179. Tel: 410-887-6100. p. 979
Watson, Jenny, Head, Access Serv, Oklahoma City University, School of Law Library, 2501 N Blackwelder, Oklahoma City, OK, 73106. Tel: 405-208-5271. p. 1858
Watson, Jessica, Dir, Coraopolis Memorial Library, 601 School St, Coraopolis, PA, 15108-1196. Tel: 412-264-3502. p. 1924
Watson, Jonathan, Librn, Solano County Library, Law Library, Hall of Justice, 600 Union Ave, Fairfield, CA, 94533. Tel: 707-421-6520. p. 142
Watson, Kate, Senior Coord, Toronto International Film Festival Inc, TIFF Bell Lightbox, 350 King St W, Toronto, ON, M5V 3X5, CANADA. Tel: 416-599-8433. p. 2693
Watson, Kathy, Dir, Estill County Public Library, 246 Main St, Irvine, KY, 40336-1026. Tel: 606-723-3030. p. 860
Watson, Kathy, Asst Dir, Head, Youth Serv, Kimball Library, Five Academy Ave, Atkinson, NH, 03811-2202. Tel: 603-362-5234. p. 1354
Watson, Kathy, Dir, Dr Nathan Porter Memorial Library, 228 N Front St, Greenfield, TN, 38230-9998. Tel: 731-235-9932. p. 2100
Watson, Kelvin, Dir, Broward County Libraries Division, 100 S Andrews Ave, Fort Lauderdale, FL, 33301. Tel: 954-357-7444. p. 396
Watson, Kelvin, Exec Dir, Las Vegas-Clark County Library District, 7060 W Windmill Lane, Las Vegas, NV, 89113. Tel: 702-507-6030, 702-734-7323. p. 1346
Watson, Kim, Supvr, Libr Access Serv, Rio Salado College, 2323 W 14th St, Tempe, AZ, 85281. Tel: 480-517-8428. p. 79
Watson, Laura, Dir, Libr Serv, Ref Librn, Highland Community College Library, 2998 W Pearl City Rd, Freeport, IL, 61032-9341. Tel: 815-599-3539. p. 590
Watson, Linda, Automation Syst Coordr, Marion County Public Library System, 2720 E Silver Springs Blvd, Ocala, FL, 34470. Tel: 352-671-8551. p. 430
Watson, Lois, Librn, Department of Veterans Affairs, 200 Veterans Ave, No 124D, Beckley, WV, 25801. Tel: 304-255-2121, Ext 4342. p. 2397
Watson, Lorie, Br Mgr, Neuse Regional Library, Comfort Public Library, 4889 Hwy 41 W, Trenton, NC, 28585. Tel: 910-324-5061. p. 1699
Watson, Marion, Commun Librn, Cariboo Regional District Library, McLeese Lake Branch, 6749 Hwy 97 N, McLeese Lake, BC, V0L 1P0, CANADA. Tel: 250-297-6533. p. 2584
Watson, Maurio J, Circ Tech, Delaware State University, 1200 N Dupont Hwy, Dover, DE, 19901-2277. Tel: 302-857-6133. p. 352
Watson, Melissa, Br Mgr, Washington County Public Library, Damascus Branch, 310 Water St, Damascus, VA, 24236. Tel: 276-475-3820. p. 2301
Watson, Merla, Librn, Dickens County-Spur Public Library, 412 E Hill St, Spur, TX, 79370-2511. Tel: 806-271-3714. p. 2245
Watson, Nathan, Asst Dir, Bedford Public Library, 1323 K St, Bedford, IN, 47421. Tel: 812-275-4471. p. 669
Watson, Pam, Asst Librn, Divernon Township Library, 221 S Second St, Divernon, IL, 62530. Tel: 217-628-3813. p. 578
Watson, Paul, Libr Tech, First Baptist Church of West Terre Haute Library, 205 S Fifth, West Terre Haute, IN, 47885. Tel: 812-533-2016. p. 726
Watson, Sheila, Dir, Avon Public Library, Garfield & Fifth Ave, Avon By The Sea, NJ, 07717. Tel: 732-502-4525. p. 1388
Watson, Stardust, Librn, First Baptist Church of West Terre Haute Library, 205 S Fifth, West Terre Haute, IN, 47885. Tel: 812-533-2016. p. 726
Watson-Phillips, Kaysha, Asst Dir, Head, Ad Ref Serv, Baldwin Public Library, 2385 Grand Ave, Baldwin, NY, 11510-3289. Tel: 516-223-6228. p. 1490
Watt, Beth, Cat Tech, University of Nevada-Reno, Lake Tahoe Prim Library, 999 Tahoe Blvd, Incline Village, NV, 89451. Tel: 775-881-7412. p. 1349
Watt, Nona, Head, Tech Serv, Indiana University, School of Law Library, Maurer School of Law, 211 S Indiana Ave, Bloomington, IN, 47405. Tel: 812-855-9666. p. 670
Watt, Sandy, Asst Librn, Nakusp Public Library Association, 92 Sixth Ave NW, Nakusp, BC, V0G 1R0, CANADA. Tel: 250-265-3363. p. 2570
Watters, Joyce "Petey", Mrs, Outreach Librn, Stewart County Public Library, 102 Natcor Dr, Dover, TN, 37058. Tel: 931-232-3127. p. 2097
Watters, Julie, Info Serv Mgr, Wilson, Sonsini, Goodrich & Rosati, 650 Page Mill Rd, Palo Alto, CA, 94304. Tel: 650-493-9300. p. 192

Watters, Peter, Coordr, Circ, Coordr, ILL, Luther Seminary Library, 2375 Como Ave, Saint Paul, MN, 55108. Tel: 651-641-3447. p. 1200

Watters, Susan, Early Literacy Coordr, Outreach Serv, Pender County Public Library, 103 S Cowan St, Burgaw, NC, 28425. Tel: 910-259-1234. p. 1676

Watters, Timothy, Ref Librn, Library of Michigan, 702 W Kalamazoo St, Lansing, MI, 48909. Tel: 517-373-0630. p. 1125

Watts, Amber, Univ Archivist, Fort Hays State University, 502 S Campus Dr, Hays, KS, 67601. Tel: 785-628-5282. p. 812

Watts, Angela, Dir, Jimmy Swaggart Bible College & Seminary Library, 8919 World Ministry Ave, Baton Rouge, LA, 70810-9000. Tel: 225-768-3890. p. 883

Watts, Christina, Br Mgr, Newberry County Library System, Whitmire Memorial, 303 Church St, Whitmire, SC, 29178. Tel: 803-694-3961. p. 2066

Watts, Doris, Libr Tech, Haskell Indian Nations University, 155 Indian Ave, Lawrence, KS, 66046-4800. Tel: 785-749-8470. p. 819

Watts, G Randall, Assoc Dir, University of Tennessee, Lamar Alexander Bldg, 877 Madison Ave, Memphis, TN, 38163. Tel: 901-448-4599. p. 2115

Watts, Jama, Genealogy Librn, Ref Librn, Marion County Public Library, 201 E Main St, Lebanon, KY, 40033-1133. Tel: 270-692-4698. p. 861

Watts, Jessica, Lead Librn, Greater Sudbury Public Library, Coniston Public Library-Mike Solski Branch, 30 Second Ave, Coniston, ON, P0M 1M0, CANADA. Tel: 705-688-3953. p. 2683

Watts, Jessica, Lead Librn, Greater Sudbury Public Library, Copper Cliff Public Library, 11 Balsam St, Copper Cliff, ON, P0M 1N0, CANADA. Tel: 705-688-3954. p. 2683

Watts, Jessica, Lead Librn, Greater Sudbury Public Library, Garson Public Library, Citizen Service Centre, 214 Orell St, Garson, ON, P3L 1V2, CANADA. Tel: 705-688-3957. p. 2683

Watts, Jessica, Lead Librn, Greater Sudbury Public Library, Lively Public Library-Earl Mumford Branch, Citizen Service Centre, 15 Kin Dr, Unit A, Lively, ON, P3Y 1M3, CANADA. Tel: 705-688-3959. p. 2683

Watts, Julie, Dir, Meade County Public Library, 996 Old Ekron Rd, Brandenburg, KY, 40108. Tel: 270-422-2094. p. 849

Watts, Karly, Archivist, Greenbrier Historical Society Archives & Library, 814 Washington St W, Lewisburg, WV, 24901. Tel: 304-645-3398. p. 2407

Watts, Nancy, Local Hist Librn, Lewistown Public Library, 701 W Main St, Lewistown, MT, 59457. Tel: 406-538-5212. p. 1298

Watts, Spencer, Dir, East Baton Rouge Parish Library, 7711 Goodwood Blvd, Baton Rouge, LA, 70806-7625. Tel: 225-231-3700. p. 882

Watts, Tasneem, Br Mgr, Anaheim Public Library, Euclid, 1340 S Euclid St, Anaheim, CA, 92802-2008. Tel: 714-765-3625. p. 116

Watwood, Carol, Health Sci Librn, Western Kentucky University Libraries, Helm-Cravens Library Complex, 1906 College Heights Blvd, No 11067, Bowling Green, KY, 42101-1067. Tel: 270-745-3912. p. 849

Waugh, Andrew, Research Coordr, Nova Scotia Legal Aid Library, 5475 Spring Garden Rd, Ste 401, Halifax, NS, B3J 3T2, CANADA. Tel: 902-420-6590. p. 2620

Waugh, Chairity, Tech Serv Librn, Louisiana State University Libraries, LSU School of Veterinary Medicine Library, Skip Bertman Dr, Baton Rouge, LA, 70803-8414. Tel: 225-578-9796. p. 884

Waugh, Joyce H, Librn, Pike-Amite-Walthall Library System, Gloster Branch, 229 E Main St, Gloster, MS, 39638. Tel: 601-225-4341. p. 1226

Waugh, Laura, Assoc Univ Librn, Digital Scholarship & Research, Texas State University, 601 University Dr, San Marcos, TX, 78666-4684. Tel: 512-408-2351. p. 2241

Waugh, Tammy Jo, Libr Coord, Hardin Memorial Hospital, 913 N Dixie Ave, Elizabethtown, KY, 42701-2503. Tel: 270-706-1688. p. 854

Waughtal, Hannah, ILL, Fort Nelson Public Library, Municipal Sq, 5315-50th Ave S, Fort Nelson, BC, V0C 1R0, CANADA. Tel: 250-774-6777. p. 2566

Wavrunek, Jeff, Dir, Libr Serv, Wasco County Library District, 722 Court St, The Dalles, OR, 97058. Tel: 541-296-2815. p. 1899

Wax, Laura, Dir, Friends of Historic Boonville, 614 E Morgan, Boonville, MO, 65233. Tel: 660-882-7977. p. 1238

Waxman, Carol, Ch Serv, West Hartford Public Library, 20 S Main St, West Hartford, CT, 06107-2432. Tel: 860-561-6950. p. 345

Waxman Kern, Wendy, Outreach & Vols Coordr, San Juan Island Library, 1010 Guard St, Friday Harbor, WA, 98250-9612. Tel: 360-378-2798. p. 2364

Waxton, Roddretta, Asst Dir, Pub Libr Serv, Lake County Public Library, 1919 W 81st Ave, Merrillville, IN, 46410-5488. Tel: 219-769-3541. p. 705

Way, Stephanie, Youth Serv, Southern Oklahoma Library System, 601 Railway Express St, Ardmore, OK, 73401. Tel: 580-223-3164. p. 1840

Waybright, Joyce, Librn, United States Army, Bruce C Clarke Library Community Services Division, Bldg 3202, 597 Manscen Loop, Ste 100, Fort Leonard Wood, MO, 65473-8928. Tel: 573-563-4113. p. 1246

Wayland, Jane, Dir, Princeton Public Library, 698 E Peru St, Princeton, IL, 61356. Tel: 815-875-1331. p. 636

Wayland, Randy, Mgr, Libr Operations, Metropolitan Library System in Oklahoma County, Midwest City Library, 8143 E Reno Ave, Midwest City, OK, 73110-3999. p. 1857

Wayman, Matthew, Head Librn, Pennsylvania State University, Schuylkill Campus, 240 University Dr, Schuylkill Haven, PA, 17972-2210. Tel: 570-385-6234. p. 2003

Wayman, Melissa, Mgr, Salt Lake County Library Services, Magna Branch, 2675 S 8950 W, Magna, UT, 84044. p. 2274

Wayment, Michelle, Prog Serv, United States Department of Agriculture, 3793 N 3600 E, Kimberly, ID, 83341-5776. Tel: 208-423-5582. p. 523

Wayne, Richard, Assoc Dir, University of Texas Southwestern Medical Center, 5323 Harry Hines Blvd, Dallas, TX, 75390-9049. Tel: 214-645-4957. p. 2169

Waynick, Joan, Librn/Mgr, Rockingham County Public Library, Madison Mayodan Branch, 140 E Murphy St, Madison, NC, 27025. Tel: 336-548-6553. p. 1686

Waynick, Joan, Librn, Rockingham County Public Library, Stoneville Branch, 201 E Main St, Stoneville, NC, 27048. Tel: 336-573-9040. p. 1686

Wayno, Jeffrey, Coll Serv Librn, Columbia University, The Burke Library at Union Theological Seminary, 3041 Broadway, New York, NY, 10027. Tel: 212-851-5608. p. 1583

Wcisel, Jennifer, Curator, Grand Rapids Art Museum, 101 Monroe Center St NW, Grand Rapids, MI, 49503. Tel: 616-831-1000. p. 1110

Weal, Linda, Libr Dir, Old Forge Library, 220 Crosby Blvd, Old Forge, NY, 13420. Tel: 315-369-6008. p. 1610

Wealand, Chieko, Br Mgr, San Francisco Public Library, Marina Branch Library, 1890 Chestnut St, San Francisco, CA, 94123-2804. Tel: 415-355-2823. p. 228

Wear, Jessica, Cat, Phillips Public Library, 286 Cherry St, Phillips, WI, 54555. Tel: 715-339-2868. p. 2469

Wear, Lori, Curator of Coll, Kern County Museum, 3801 Chester Ave, Bakersfield, CA, 93301-1395. Tel: 661-437-3330, Ext 213. p. 120

Weare, David W, Libr Dir, Ogunquit Memorial Library, 166 Shore Rd, Ogunquit, ME, 03907. Tel: 207-646-9024. p. 934

Wearly, Jason, Archivist, Circ Spec, Clark State Community College Library, 570 E Leffel Lane, Springfield, OH, 45505. Tel: 937-328-6022. p. 1821

Weast, Dana, ILL, Libr Tech, University of Arkansas-Monticello Library, 514 University Dr, Monticello, AR, 71656. Tel: 870-460-1080. p. 105

Weatherby, Melanie, Libr Mgr, Piedmont Regional Library System, Maysville Public Library, 9247 Gillsville Rd, Maysville, GA, 30558. Tel: 706-652-2323. p. 482

Weatherford, Coni, Br Mgr, Pima County Public Library, Kirk-Bear Canyon, 8959 E Tanque Verde Rd, Tucson, AZ, 85749. Tel: 520-594-5275. p. 82

Weatherholt, Jennie, Br Mgr, Spencer County Public Library, Grandview Branch, 403 Main St, Grandview, IN, 47615-0717. Tel: 812-649-9732. p. 716

Weatherly, Corrine, Sr Librn, Pierce County Library System, Graham Branch, 9202 224th St E, Graham, WA, 98338. Tel: 253-548-3322. p. 2386

Weatherly, Dixie, Br Mgr, Dillon County Library, Latta Branch, 101 N Marion St, Latta, SC, 29565-3597. Tel: 843-752-5389. p. 2058

Weathersbee, Mindy, Asst Dir, Amarillo College, 2201 S Washington, Amarillo, TX, 79109. Tel: 806-371-5462. p. 2134

Weatherwax, Sarah, Curator, Photog & Prints, Library Company of Philadelphia, 1314 Locust St, Philadelphia, PA, 19107. Tel: 215-546-3181. p. 1982

Weaver, Abigail, Teen Serv Librn, Mount Prospect Public Library, Ten S Emerson St, Mount Prospect, IL, 60056. Tel: 847-253-5675. p. 621

Weaver, Angela, Liaison Librn, University of Puget Sound, 1604 N Warner St, Upper Loading Dock, Tacoma, WA, 98416. Tel: 253-879-3229. p. 2387

Weaver, Benjamin, Dir, Libr Serv, State Correctional Institution, 189 Fyock Rd, Indiana, PA, 15701. Tel: 724-465-9630. p. 1946

Weaver, Bobbi, Foreign & Intl Law Ref Librn, California Western School of Law Library, 290 Cedar St, San Diego, CA, 92101. Tel: 619-525-1497. p. 215

Weaver, Brandi, Dir, Ohio University Chillicothe Campus, 101 University Dr, Chillicothe, OH, 45601-0629. Tel: 740-774-7201. p. 1759

Weaver, Breyanna, Dir, Robinson Public Library District, 606 N Jefferson St, Robinson, IL, 62454-2665. Tel: 618-544-2917. p. 640

Weaver, David, Dir, Ohioana Library, 274 E First Ave, Ste 300, Columbus, OH, 43201. Tel: 614-466-3831. p. 1777

Weaver, Deb, Ref Librn, SCLHS Saint Joseph Hospital, 1375 E 19th Ave, 3rd Flr, Denver, CO, 80218-1191. Tel: 303-812-3625. p. 277

Weaver, Diana, Dir, Basehor Community Library District 2, 1400 158th St, Basehor, KS, 66007. Tel: 913-724-2828. p. 798

Weaver, Elizabeth, Librn, New Brunswick Community College, 950 Grandview Ave, Saint John, NB, E2L 3V1, CANADA. Tel: 506-658-6727. p. 2605

Weaver, Erin, Asst Dir, South Fayette Township Library, 515 Millers Run Rd, Morgan, PA, 15064. Tel: 412-257-8660. p. 1966

Weaver, James, Fiscal Officer, Bluffton Public Library, 145 S Main St, Bluffton, OH, 45817. Tel: 419-358-5016. p. 1751

Weaver, Janet, Dir, Elliott Public Library, 401 Main St, Elliott, IA, 51532. Tel: 712-767-2355. p. 751

Weaver, Joan, Dir, Kinsley Public Library, 208 E Eighth St, Kinsley, KS, 67547-1422. Tel: 620-659-3341. p. 817

Weaver, Joyce, Dir, Libr & Archives, Mint Museum, 2730 Randolph Rd, Charlotte, NC, 28207. Tel: 704-337-2000, 704-337-2023. p. 1680

Weaver, Julie, Libr Dir, Beldon Noble Memorial Library, 2759 Essex Rd, Essex, NY, 12936. Tel: 518-963-8079. p. 1532
Weaver, Mary M, Librn, East Woodstock Library Association, 15 Prospect St, East Woodstock, CT, 06244. Tel: 860-928-0284. p. 310
Weaver, Paul L, Ser Librn, Owens Community College Library, 30335 Oregon Rd, Perrysburg, OH, 43551. Tel: 567-661-7234. p. 1815
Weaver, Roger, Dir, Curtis Laws Wilson Library, 400 W 14th St, Rolla, MO, 65409-0060. Tel: 573-341-4221. p. 1268
Weaver, Susan, Dir, Harrisville Public Library, Seven Canal St, Harrisville, NH, 03450. Tel: 603-827-2918. p. 1367
Weaver, Tabatha, Br Mgr, Chatham County Public Libraries, Wren Memorial Library, 500 N Second Ave, Siler City, NC, 27344. Tel: 919-742-2016. p. 1708
Weaver, Taryn, Dir, Wadena Public Library, 136 S Mill St, Wadena, IA, 52169. Tel: 563-774-2039. p. 788
Weaver, Todd, Librn, Jones Day, 51 Louisiana Ave NW, Washington, DC, 20001-2113. Tel: 202-879-3939, 202-879-3953. p. 370
Weaver-Pieh, Chri, Ms, Coll Res Mgr, Medina County District Library, 210 S Broadway, Medina, OH, 44256. Tel: 330-725-0588. p. 1801
Webb, Adam A, Dir, Garland County Library, 1427 Malvern Ave, Hot Springs, AR, 71901. Tel: 501-623-4161. p. 99
Webb, Alice, Head, Tech Serv, Apache County Library District, 30 S Second W, Saint Johns, AZ, 85936. Tel: 928-337-4923. p. 76
Webb, Alisha, Ref Serv Librn, Guilford Technical Community College, 601 E Main St, Jamestown, NC, 27282. Tel: 336-334-4822, Ext 50330. p. 1698
Webb, Andrew, Branch Lead, Saint Clair County Library System, Marine City Branch Library, 300 S Parker Rd, Marine City, MI, 48039. Tel: 810-765-5233. p. 1142
Webb, Annette, Tech Info Spec, Department of Veterans Affairs, One Medical Center Dr, Clarksburg, WV, 26301. Tel: 304-623-3461. p. 2401
Webb, Beth, Acad Librn, University of Wisconsin-Rock County Library, 2909 Kellogg Ave, Janesville, WI, 53546-5606. Tel: 608-898-5047. p. 2443
Webb, Caroline, Dir, Texas Chiropractic College, 5912 Spencer Hwy, Pasadena, TX, 77505. Tel: 281-998-6049. p. 2225
Webb, Catherine, Community Outreach, Mount Vernon Public Library, 28 S First Ave, Mount Vernon, NY, 10550. Tel: 914-668-1840, Ext 236. p. 1575
Webb, Charles, Br Mgr, Fairfax County Public Library, Patrick Henry Branch, 101 Maple Ave E, Vienna, VA, 22180-5794. Tel: 703-938-0405. p. 2316
Webb, David, Head, Ref, Roanoke County Public Library, 6303 Merriman Rd, Roanoke, VA, 24018-6496. Tel: 540-772-7507. p. 2345
Webb, Debbie, Supvr, Access Serv, Camosun College, Liz Ashton Campus Centre Library, 4461 Inteurban Rd, 3rd Flr, Victoria, BC, V9E 2C1, CANADA. Tel: 250-370-4531. p. 2582
Webb, Elizabeth, Dir, Tech Serv, Baldwin County Library Cooperative, Inc, PO Box 399, Robertsdale, AL, 36567-0399. Tel: 251-970-4010. p. 34
Webb, Galen, Ref Librn, Fort Smith Public Library, 3201 Rogers Ave, Fort Smith, AR, 72903. Tel: 479-783-0229. p. 96
Webb, Kathleen, Dean, Univ Libr, University of Dayton Libraries, 300 College Park Dr, Dayton, OH, 45469. Tel: 937-229-4221. p. 1780
Webb, Kathleen, Dir, Marvin Memorial Library, 29 W Whitney Ave, Shelby, OH, 44875-1252. Tel: 419-347-5576. p. 1820
Webb, Kyle, Access Serv Librn, Pacific University Libraries, Hillsboro Campus, 222 SE Eighth Ave, Hillsboro, OR, 97123. Tel: 503-352-7331. p. 1880
Webb, Laurie, Executive Asst, Long Beach Museum of Art Library, 2300 E Ocean Blvd, Long Beach, CA, 90803. Tel: 562-439-2119, Ext 226. p. 158
Webb, Lee, Theol & Ref LIbrn, Oklahoma City University, 2501 N Blackwelder, Oklahoma City, OK, 73106. Tel: 405-208-5068. p. 1858
Webb, Lester, Dir, Outreach & Tech, Kingston Frontenac Public Library, 130 Johnson St, Kingston, ON, K7L 1X8, CANADA. Tel: 613-549-8888. p. 2650
Webb, Linda, Circ Mgr, Missouri Baptist University, One College Park Dr, Saint Louis, MO, 63141-8698. Tel: 314-434-1115. p. 1271
Webb, Madison, Librn, Englewood Public Library, 35 Carroll St, Englewood, TN, 37329. Tel: 423-887-7152. p. 2098
Webb, Megan Miria, Dir, Clinton Public Library, 118 S Hicks St, Clinton, TN, 37716. Tel: 865-457-0519. p. 2093
Webb, Nikeda, Ch Serv, Matteson Area Public Library District, 801 S School St, Matteson, IL, 60443-1897. Tel: 708-748-4431. p. 615
Webb, Noreen, VPres, University of California, Los Angeles, 2320 Moore Hall, Mail Box 951521, Los Angeles, CA, 90095-1521. Tel: 310-825-8799. p. 2782
Webb, Paris E, Web/Digital Serv Librn, Marshall University Libraries, One John Marshall Dr, Huntington, WV, 25755-2060. Tel: 304-696-3511. p. 2405
Webb, Rachel, Acq, Colls Librn, Union County Public Library, 316 E Windsor St, Monroe, NC, 28112. Tel: 704-283-8184. p. 1703
Webb, Rebecca, Law Librn, Supvr, Danville Public Library, Law, 511 Patton St, Danville, VA, 24541. Tel: 434-799-5118. p. 2315
Webb, Thom, Customer Serv Coordr, Matteson Area Public Library District, 801 S School St, Matteson, IL, 60443-1897. Tel: 708-748-4431. p. 615
Webber, Adrienne C, Dean, Grambling State University, 403 Main St, Grambling, LA, 71245-2761. Tel: 318-274-3354. p. 890
Webber, Katherine, Lending Serv Supvr, Lewiston Public Library, 200 Lisbon St, Lewiston, ME, 04240. Tel: 207-513-3004. p. 929
Webber, Katherine, Dir, Topsham Public Library, 25 Foreside Rd, Topsham, ME, 04086. Tel: 207-725-1727. p. 943
Webber, Priscilla J, Ch, Adams Public Library System, 128 S Third St, Decatur, IN, 46733-1691. Tel: 260-724-2605. p. 678
Webber-Bey, Deimosa, Archives Mgr, Librn, Tech Serv, Scholastic Inc Library, 557 Broadway, New York, NY, 10012. Tel: 212-343-6171. p. 1601
Weber, Barbara, Ad, Bedford Park Public Library District, 7816 W 65th Pl, Bedford Park, IL, 60501. Tel: 708-458-6826. p. 540
Weber, Christine, Financial Mgr, Hamburg Township Library, 10411 Merrill Rd, Hamburg, MI, 48139. Tel: 810-231-1771. p. 1112
Weber, Christine, Dr, Asst Dean, Library & Archival Services, Illinois College of Optometry Library, 3241 S Michigan Ave, Chicago, IL, 60616-3878. Tel: 312-949-7153. p. 562
Weber, Cindy, Dir, Stowe Free Library, 90 Pond St, Stowe, VT, 05672. Tel: 802-253-6145, Ext 16. p. 2295
Weber, Connie A, Dir, Richmond Public Library, 107 E Central, Richmond, KS, 66080. Tel: 785-835-6163. p. 833
Weber, Darlene, Libr Mgr, Sno-Isle Libraries, Mill Creek Library, 15429 Bothell Everett Hwy, Mill Creek, WA, 98012-1212. Tel: 425-337-4822. p. 2370
Weber, Erin, Res & Instruction Librn, Salisbury University, 1101 Camden Ave, Salisbury, MD, 21801-6863. Tel: 410-543-6130. p. 976
Weber, Gary, Open Info Team Lead, Alberta Government Library, Capital Blvd, 11th Flr, 10044 - 108 St, Edmonton, AB, T5J 5E6, CANADA. Tel: 780-427-2985. p. 2534
Weber, Georgia, Coordr, Computer Serv, Easton Area Public Library & District Center, 515 Church St, Easton, PA, 18042-3587. Tel: 610-258-2917. p. 1928
Weber, Ivy, Dir, Elberon Public Library, 106 Main St, Elberon, IA, 52225. Tel: 319-439-5476. p. 750
Weber, Jeanine, Public Services & ILL Coord, Aquinas College, 1700 Fulton St E, Grand Rapids, MI, 49506. Tel: 616-632-2128. p. 1109
Weber, Jennifer, Head Librn, Austin Community College, Northridge Campus Library, 11928 Stone Hollow Dr, 2nd, Rm 1223, Austin, TX, 78758. Tel: 512-223-4741. p. 2138
Weber, Joshua, Assessment Librn, Virtual Serv Librn, SUNY Westchester Community College, 75 Grasslands Rd, Valhalla, NY, 10595. Tel: 914-606-6819. p. 1656
Weber, Kathleen S, Libr Assoc, Potomac State College of West Virginia University, 103 Fort Ave, Keyser, WV, 26726. Tel: 304-788-6907. p. 2406
Weber, Kelley A, Dir, Libr Serv, Kansas Wesleyan University, 100 E Claflin Ave, Salina, KS, 67401-6100. Tel: 785-833-4395. p. 835
Weber, Kelsey, Library Contact, O'Melveny & Myers LLP, 610 Newport Center Dr, 17th Flr, Newport Beach, CA, 92660-6429. Tel: 949-760-9600. p. 183
Weber, LaDonna Riddle, Librn, Virginia Davis Laskey Research Library, 1027 18th Ave S, Nashville, TN, 37212-2126. p. 2118
Weber, Liane, Library Contact, Beth El Temple Center, Two Concord Ave, Belmont, MA, 02478-4075. Tel: 617-484-6668. p. 988
Weber, Michael, Metadata Serv, Tech Serv, Kutztown University, 15200 Kutztown Rd, Bldg 5, Kutztown, PA, 19530. Tel: 610-683-4480. p. 1949
Weber, Nancy, Head, Adult Serv, Crystal Lake Public Library, 126 Paddock St, Crystal Lake, IL, 60014. Tel: 815-459-1687. p. 574
Weber, Nicholas, Libr Dir, Woodstock Public Library, 414 W Judd, Woodstock, IL, 60098-3195. Tel: 815-338-0542. p. 665
Weber, Nicolas, Dr, Asst Prof, University of Washington, Mary Gates Hall, Ste 370, Campus Box 352840, Seattle, WA, 98195-2840. Tel: 206-543-1794. p. 2794
Weber, Patrick, Interlibrary Loan & Course Reserves Coord, Shepherd University, 301 N King St, Shepherdstown, WV, 25443. p. 2414
Weber, Rebecca, Librn, Oklahoma State University Libraries, Mary L Williams Education & Teaching, 001 Willard Hall, Stillwater, OK, 74078. Tel: 405-744-9769. p. 1862
Weber, Ryan, Educational Resources & Tech, Libr Serv Spec, Indiana University South Bend, 1700 Mishawaka Ave, South Bend, IN, 46615. Tel: 574-520-5543. p. 718
Weber, Shelly, Library Contact, Fond Du Lac Circuit Court, 160 S Macy St, Fond du Lac, WI, 54935. Tel: 920-929-3040. p. 2435
Weber, Shilo, Ch, Platte County Public Library, 904 Ninth St, Wheatland, WY, 82201. Tel: 307-322-2689. p. 2500
Weber, Stephanie, Dir, Florence County Library, 400 Olive Ave, Florence, WI, 54121. Tel: 715-528-3094. p. 2435
Weber, Suzin, Br Mgr, Free Library of Philadelphia, Tacony Branch, 6742 Torresdale Ave, Philadelphia, PA, 19135-2416. Tel: 215-685-8755. p. 1980
Weber, Teresa, Dir, Bayfield Carnegie Library, 37 N Broad St, Bayfield, WI, 54814. Tel: 715-779-3953. p. 2422
Weber, Valerie, Br Librn, Yuma County Free Library District, Heritage Branch, 350 Third Ave, Yuma, AZ, 85364. Tel: 928-373-6507. p. 86
Weber-Mendham, Karen, Youth Serv, Land O'Lakes Public Library, 4242 County Hwy B, Land O'Lakes, WI, 54540. Tel: 715-547-6006. p. 2448

Webster, Berenika, Dr, Assoc Univ Librn for Colls & Organizational Effectiveness, University of Pittsburgh Library System, 3960 Forbes Ave, Pittsburgh, PA, 15260. Tel: 412-648-3330. p. 1996
Webster, Cissy, Dir, City County Library, 1717 Main St, Tahoka, TX, 79373. Tel: 806-561-4050. p. 2246
Webster, Donna-Jo, Dir, Eden Library, 2901 E Church St, Eden, NY, 14057. Tel: 716-992-4028. p. 1529
Webster, Jefferson, Coll Develop Librn, Dallas Theological Seminary, 3909 Swiss Ave, Dallas, TX, 75204. Tel: 214-887-5287. p. 2166
Webster, Jennifer, Teen Librn, Morley Library, 184 Phelps St, Painesville, OH, 44077-3926. Tel: 440-352-3383. p. 1812
Webster, Keith G, Dean, Univ Libr, Carnegie Mellon University, Hunt Library, 4909 Frew St, Pittsburgh, PA, 15213. Tel: 412-268-2444. p. 1992
Webster, Kim, Coordr, Libr Serv, Baker College of Clinton Township Library, 34950 Little Mack Ave, Clinton Township, MI, 48035-4701. Tel: 586-790-9584. p. 1092
Webster, Leslie, Assoc Dir, Finance & Operations, Salt Lake County Library Services, 8030 S 1825 W, West Jordan, UT, 84088. Tel: 801-943-4636. p. 2274
Webster, Lisa, Librn, Nora Sparks Warren Library, 210 N Willow St, Pauls Valley, OK, 73075. Tel: 405-238-5188. p. 1860
Webster, Marshall, Actg Libr Dir, Mary Riley Styles Public Library, 120 N Virginia Ave, Falls Church, VA, 22046. Tel: 703-248-5030. p. 2317
Webster, Peter, Assoc Univ Librn, Info Syst, Saint Mary's University, 923 Robie St, Halifax, NS, B3H 3C3, CANADA. Tel: 902-420-5507. p. 2621
Webster, Susan, Libr Asst, Gibbon Public Library, 116 LaBarre, Gibbon, NE, 68840. Tel: 308-468-5889. p. 1315
Webster, Wynell, Br Mgr, Mesa County Public Library District, Clifton Branch, Mesa Point Shopping Ctr, Ste 6F, 590 32 Rd, Clifton, CO, 81520. Tel: 970-434-6936. p. 284
Webster, Wynell, Head of Br Serv, Mesa County Public Library District, 443 N Sixth St, Grand Junction, CO, 81501. Tel: 970-243-4442. p. 284
Wechsler, Gail, Libr Dir, Law Library Association of Saint Louis, 1300 Civil Courts Bldg, Ten N Tucker Blvd, Saint Louis, MO, 63101. Tel: 314-622-4470. p. 1271
Weddle, Jackie, Librn, Maine Department of Corrections, Maine State Prison Library, 807 Cushing Rd, Warren, ME, 04864. Tel: 207-273-5300. p. 944
Weddle, Janice, Asst Librn, Pub Serv, Head, Instruction & Outreach, Hendrix College, 1600 Washington Ave, Conway, AR, 72032. Tel: 501-450-4560. p. 92
Weddle, Jeff, Dr, Assoc Prof, University of Alabama, 7035 Gorgas Library, Campus Box 870252, Tuscaloosa, AL, 35487-0252. Tel: 205-348-4610. p. 2781
Weddle, Liz, Access Serv Supvr, University of Northwestern-St Paul, 3003 Snelling Ave N, Saint Paul, MN, 55113. Tel: 651-631-5241. p. 1202
Wedeking, Lucile, Libr Dir, Stamford Carnegie Library, 600 E McHarg St, Stamford, TX, 79553. Tel: 325-773-2532. p. 2245
Wedig, Nick, Circulation Admin, Allegheny County Law Library, 921 City-County Bldg, 414 Grant St, Pittsburgh, PA, 15219-2543. Tel: 412-350-5353. p. 1990
Wee, Sandy, Access Serv Mgr, San Mateo County Library, Library Administration, 125 Lessingia Ct, San Mateo, CA, 94402-4000. Tel: 650-312-5276. p. 235
Weed, Virginia, Librn, Mid-Mississippi Regional Library System, Winona-Montgomery County, 115 N Quitman St, Winona, MS, 38967-2228. Tel: 662-283-3443. p. 1224
Weeden, Megan, Libr Dir, Coventry Public Library, 1672 Flat River Rd, Coventry, RI, 02816. Tel: 401-822-9100. p. 2030
Weedman, Barbara, Libr Dir, Henrico County Public Library, 1700 N Parham Rd, Henrico, VA, 23229. Tel: 804-501-1900. p. 2325
Weedman, Carol, Librn, Victoria Public Library District, 227 E Main St, Victoria, IL, 61485. Tel: 309-879-2295. p. 657
Weekes, Lisa, Mgr, Community Dev, Chinook Arch Regional Library System, 2902 Seventh Ave N, Lethbridge, AB, T1H 5C6, CANADA. Tel: 403-380-1500. p. 2546
Weekly, Nancy, Curator, Burchfield Penney Art Center, Burchfield Penney Art Center at Buffalo State College, 1300 Elmwood Ave, Buffalo, NY, 14222. Tel: 716-878-3216, 716-878-6011. p. 1509
Weeks, Cindy, Asst Dir, Bradford County Public Library, 456 W Pratt St, Starke, FL, 32091. Tel: 904-368-3911. p. 444
Weeks, Clarice, Dir, Paul Quinn College, 3837 Simpson Stuart Rd, Dallas, TX, 75241. Tel: 214-379-5576. p. 2167
Weeks, Dennis, Dr, Dir, Valencia College, East Campus Library, 701 N Econlockhatchee Trail, Orlando, FL, 32825. Tel: 407-582-2467. p. 432
Weeks, Dustin, Asst Chair, Library Services, Daytona State College Library, Bldg 115, Rm 314, 1200 W International Speedway Blvd, Daytona Beach, FL, 32114. Tel: 386-506-3593. p. 392
Weeks, Eddie, Legislative Librn, Tennessee General Assembly, Office of Legal Services, 804 Cordell Hull Bldg, 425 Rep John Lewis Way N, Nashville, TN, 37243. Tel: 615-741-5816. p. 2120
Weeks, Jamie, Head, Univ Archives & Digital Colls, Weber State University, 3921 Central Campus Dr, Dept 2901, Ogden, UT, 84408-2901. Tel: 801-626-6486. p. 2268
Weeks, Jeaneal C, Dir, Hiawatha Public Library, 150 W Willman St, Hiawatha, IA, 52233. Tel: 319-393-1414. p. 758
Weeks, Jennifer, County Librn, Santa Clara County Library District, 1370 Dell Ave, Campbell, CA, 95032. Tel: 408-293-2326. p. 126
Weeks, Jennifer, Br Mgr, Belmont County District Library, Shadyside Branch, 4300 Central Ave, Shadyside, OH, 43947. Tel: 740-676-0506. p. 1800
Weeks, Olivia L, Dir, Law Libr, Campbell University, Norman Adrian Wiggins School of Law Library, 225 Hillsborough St, Ste 203H, Raleigh, NC, 27603. Tel: 919-865-5870. p. 1676
Weeks, Pat, Curatorial Asst, Independence Seaport Museum Library, 211 S Columbus Blvd, Philadelphia, PA, 19106. Tel: 215-413-8640. p. 1981
Weeks, Roosevelt, Dir of Libr, Austin Public Library, 710 W Cesar Chavez St, Austin, TX, 78701. Tel: 512-974-7400. p. 2138
Weeks, Ruth, Asst Dir, University of Alabama, School of Law Library, 101 Paul Bryant Dr, Tuscaloosa, AL, 35487. Tel: 205-348-5925. p. 38
Weeks, Sherrill, Dir, Ransom Public Library, 411 S Vermont Ave, Ransom, KS, 67572. Tel: 785-731-2855. p. 833
Weeks, William, Libr Tech, Gulf Correctional Institution Library, Annex Branch, 699 Ike Steel Rd, Wewahitchka, FL, 32465. Tel: 850-639-1780. p. 455
Weeks-Wegner, Kathy, Br Mgr, Jackson County Library, Lakefield Branch, 410 Main St, Lakefield, MN, 56150-1201. Tel: 507-662-5782. p. 1179
Weems, Kelsey, ILL, Abilene Christian University, 221 Brown Library, ACU Box 29208, Abilene, TX, 79699-9208. Tel: 325-674-2316. p. 2131
Weerasinghe, Jean, Dir, Libr & Info Serv, Government of Canada, Federal Courts & Tax Court of Canada, Courts Administration Service-Library Services, 90 Sparks St, Ottawa, ON, K1A 0H9, CANADA. Tel: 613-995-1382. p. 2667
Weese, Bernadette, Libr Dir, Elizabethton-Carter County Public Library, 201 N Sycamore St, Elizabethton, TN, 37643. Tel: 423-547-6360. p. 2097
Weessies, Kathleen, Librn, Michigan State University Libraries, Map Library, W308 Main Library, 366 W Circle Dr, East Lansing, MI, 48824. Tel: 517-884-6467. p. 1102
Wegener, Brenda, Br Mgr, San Diego Public Library, Carmel Valley, 3919 Townsgate Dr, San Diego, CA, 92130. Tel: 858-552-1668. p. 219
Wegener, Darla, County Librn, Tulare County Library, 200 W Oak Ave, Visalia, CA, 93291-4993. Tel: 559-713-2700. p. 257
Weger, Kaitlyn, Libr Asst, Olney Central College, 305 N West St, Olney, IL, 62450. Tel: 618-395-777, ext 2262. p. 629
Wegmann, Mary, Coll Develop Librn, Sonoma State University Library, 1801 E Cotati Ave, Rohnert Park, CA, 94928. Tel: 707-664-3983. p. 204
Wegner, Heather, Dir, Spillman Public Library, 719 Wisconsin Ave, North Fond du Lac, WI, 54937-1335. Tel: 920-929-3771. p. 2465
Wegner, Kassandra, Ref Librn, Jamestown Community College, Cattaraugus County, 260 N Union St, Olean, NY, 14760. Tel: 716-376-7517. p. 1557
Wegner, Kathy, Ch, Neillsville Public Library, 409 Hewett St, Neillsville, WI, 54456-1923. Tel: 715-743-2558. p. 2464
Wegner, Lacey, Libr Operations Coordr, Fort Hays State University, 502 S Campus Dr, Hays, KS, 67601. Tel: 785-628-5837. p. 812
Wegner, Lisa, Librn, Kentucky Correctional Institution for Women Library, 3000 Ash Ave, Pewee Valley, KY, 40056. Tel: 502-241-8454, Ext 2302. p. 872
Wegner, Paul, Asst Dir, Institute for American Indian Studies, 38 Curtis Rd, Washington, CT, 06793. Tel: 860-868-0518. p. 343
Wehmeyer, Jacqueline, Libr Dir, Parkland Library, 6620 University Dr, Parkland, FL, 33067. Tel: 954-757-4200. p. 436
Wehr, Peggy, Br Mgr, Indianapolis Public Library, Fountain Square, 1066 Virginia Ave, Indianapolis, IN, 46203. Tel: 317-275-4395. p. 695
Wehrenberg, Tricia, Youth Serv Librn, Winona Public Library, 151 W Fifth St, Winona, MN, 55987. Tel: 507-452-4582. p. 1209
Wehrle, Kate Hamlin, Dir, Depauville Free Library, 32333 County Rte 179, Depauville, NY, 13632. Tel: 315-686-3299. p. 1525
Wehrle, Lacey, Br Mgr, Public Library of Cincinnati & Hamilton County, Mount Healthy, 7608 Hamilton Ave, Cincinnati, OH, 45231. Tel: 513-369-4469. p. 1763
Weibel, Mike, Br Mgr, Tulsa City-County Library, Peggy V Helmerich Library, 5131 E 91st St, Tulsa, OK, 74137. p. 1866
Weible, John, Sr Lecturer, University of Illinois at Urbana-Champaign, Library & Information Science Bldg, 501 E Daniel St, Champaign, IL, 61820-6211. Tel: 217-333-3280. p. 2784
Weible, Lisa, Activity Spec, Librn, Norfolk Regional Center, 1700 N Victory Rd, Norfolk, NE, 68701. Tel: 402-370-3290. p. 1326
Weible, Sue, Br Mgr, Jackson District Library, Grass Lake Branch, 130 W Michigan Ave, Grass Lake, MI, 49240. Tel: 517-522-8211. p. 1120
Weibley, Chelsea, Exec Dir, Palmyra Public Library, 50 Landings Dr, Ste B, Annville, PA, 17003. Tel: 717-838-1347. p. 1906
Weich, Orti, Libr Mgr, Alder Flats/Buck Lake Public Library, PO Box 148, Alder Flats, AB, T0C 0A0, CANADA. Tel: 780-388-3881. p. 2521
Weichel, Bri, Information Literacy Coord, Library Services, Hastings College, 705 E Seventh St, Hastings, NE, 68901. Tel: 402-461-7330. p. 1317

Weissbach, Shira, Educ Dir, Temple Sinai, 1401 N Limekiln Pike, Dresher, PA, 19025. Tel: 215-643-6510. p. 1927
Weisse, Laurinda, Univ Archivist, University of Nebraska at Kearney, 2508 11th Ave, Kearney, NE, 68849-2240. Tel: 308-865-8593. p. 1319
Weisser, Teresa, Cataloging & Metadata Librn, Millersville University, Nine N George St, Millersville, PA, 17551. Tel: 717-871-7111. p. 1963
Weissinger, Alison, Dir, DeKalb County Public Library, Darro C Willey Administrative Offices, 3560 Kensington Rd, Decatur, GA, 30032. Tel: 404-508-7190. p. 475
Weissman, Brittney, Library Contact, New York State Veterans Home Library, 4207 State Hwy 220, Oxford, NY, 13830. Tel: 607-843-3100. p. 1614
Weissman, Marc, Tech Librn, Derby Public Library, 313 Elizabeth St, Derby, CT, 06418. Tel: 203-736-1482. p. 309
Weissman, Neil B, Provost, Central Pennsylvania Consortium, c/o Franklin & Marshall College, Goethean Hall 101, Lancaster, PA, 17604. Tel: 717-358-4282. p. 2774
Weistling, Ripple, Fac Serv Librn, American University, 4300 Nebraska Ave NW, Washington, DC, 20016-8182. Tel: 202-274-4382. p. 360
Weitenhagen, Jesse, Br Mgr, Tulsa City-County Library, Glenpool Branch, 730 E 141st St, Glenpool, OK, 74033. p. 1866
Weiter, Stephen, Interim Dean, University of North Carolina at Charlotte, 9201 University City Blvd, Charlotte, NC, 28223-0001. Tel: 704-687-0494. p. 1681
Weitman, Helen, Br Supvr, Western Manitoba Regional Library, Hartney/Cameron Branch, 209 Airdrie St, Hartney, MB, R0M 0X0, CANADA. Tel: 204-858-2102. p. 2586
Weitzel, Karen, Dir, Human Res, The Kansas City Public Library, 14 W Tenth St, Kansas City, MO, 64105. Tel: 816-701-3517. p. 1255
Weitzel, Penny V, Asst Dir, Mason City Public Library, 225 Second St SE, Mason City, IA, 50401. Tel: 641-421-3668. p. 768
Weitzer, William, Dr, Exec Dir, Center for Jewish History, 15 W 16 St, New York, NY, 10011. Tel: 212-294-8340, 212-744-6400. p. 1580
Welaish, Andy, Dir of Libr Operations, Millersville University, Nine N George St, Millersville, PA, 17551. Tel: 717-871-7111. p. 1963
Welborn, Aaron, Dir, Communications, Duke University Libraries, 411 Chapel Dr, Durham, NC, 27708. Tel: 919-660-5800. p. 1684
Welborn, Jordan, Libr Dir, Campbell County Public Library, 684 Village Hwy, Lower Level, Rustburg, VA, 24588. Tel: 434-332-9560. p. 2346
Welch, Andrew, Librarian for Discovery Services & Tech, Drake University, 2725 University Ave, Des Moines, IA, 50311. Tel: 515-271-2862. p. 746
Welch, Bethany, Librn, Pike County Library, Delight Branch Library, 401 E Antioch St, Delight, AR, 71940. Tel: 870-379-2456. p. 106
Welch, Caroline, Ad, Wilbraham Public Library, 25 Crane Park Dr, Wilbraham, MA, 01095-1799. Tel: 413-596-6141. p. 1069
Welch, Cindy, Dr, Clinical Assoc Prof, University of Tennessee, Knoxville, 451 Communications Bldg, 1345 Circle Park Dr, Knoxville, TN, 37996-0332. Tel: 865-974-7918. p. 2792
Welch, Cynthia, Adminr, Embroiderers Guild of America, 1205 E Washington St, Ste 104, Louisville, KY, 40206. Tel: 502-589-6956. p. 864
Welch, Daniel, Dir, Learning Res, Dir, Technology, Lake Erie College of Osteopathic Medicine, 1858 W Grandview Blvd, Erie, PA, 16509. Tel: 814-866-8451. p. 1932
Welch, Janelle, Managing Librn, Brooklyn Public Library, Crown Heights, 560 New York Ave, Brooklyn, NY, 11225. Tel: 718-773-1180. p. 1502
Welch, Jim, Dir, Mill Memorial Library, 495 E Main St, Nanticoke, PA, 18634-1897. Tel: 570-735-3030. p. 1967
Welch, Kjersten, Admin Serv, Sioux City Art Center, 225 Nebraska St, Sioux City, IA, 51101-1712. Tel: 712-279-6272. p. 782
Welch, Linda, Libr Office Mgr, Montclair Public Library, 50 S Fullerton Ave, Montclair, NJ, 07042. Tel: 973-744-0500. p. 1420
Welch, Parks, Dir, Wake Forest University, Coy C Carpenter Medical Library, Bowman Gray Center for Medical Education, 475 Vine St, Winston-Salem, NC, 27101. Tel: 336-716-2299. p. 1726
Welch, Paula, Head, Circ, Morse Institute Library, 14 E Central St, Natick, MA, 01760. Tel: 508-647-6520. p. 1037
Welch, Rollie, Adult Coll Develop Librn, Principal Librn, Lee County Library System, Library Processing, 881 Gunnery Rd N, Ste 2, Lehigh Acres, FL, 33971-1246. Tel: 239-533-4170. p. 403
Welch, Sarah, Librn, Pearl River Community College, Forrest County Center Library, 5448 US Hwy 49 S, Hattiesburg, MS, 39401. Tel: 601-554-5522. p. 1230
Welch, Todd, Assoc Dean, Cat, Digital Serv, Spec Coll, Utah State University, 3000 Old Main Hill, Logan, UT, 84322-3000. Tel: 435-797-8268. p. 2265
Welcher, Belinda, Dir, Red Creek Free Library, 6817 Main St, Red Creek, NY, 13143. Tel: 315-754-6679. p. 1626
Welden, Avery, Access Serv Librn, Reserves Librn, Phillips Theological Seminary Library, 901 N Mingo Rd, Tulsa, OK, 74116. Tel: 918-270-6427. p. 1865
Welden, Marie, Br Mgr, Tulsa City-County Library, Broken Arrow Branch, 300 W Broadway Ave, Broken Arrow, OK, 74012. p. 1866
Weldon, LoriAnn, Patron Serv, Southwest Baptist University Libraries, Mercy College of Nursing & Health Sciences Library, 4431 S Fremont, Springfield, MO, 65804-7307. Tel: 417-893-7149. p. 1238
Weldon, Rhonda, Br Mgr, Tulsa City-County Library, Collinsville Branch, 1223 Main, Collinsville, OK, 74021. p. 1866
Weldon, Shawn, Curator of Ms, Rec Mgr, Catholic Historical Research Center of the Archdiocese of Philadelphia, 6740 Roosevelt Blvd, Philadelphia, PA, 19149. Tel: 215-904-8149. p. 1975
Weldon, Stephanie, Mgr, Libraries & Media Serv, SCLHS Saint Joseph Hospital, 1375 E 19th Ave, 3rd Flr, Denver, CO, 80218-1191. Tel: 303-812-3625. p. 277
Weleschuk, Roseann, Librn, Andrew Municipal Public Library, Village of Andrew Multiplex, 5021-50 St, Andrew, AB, T0B 0C0, CANADA. Tel: 587-957-2130. p. 2522
Weleski, Heather, Dir, Avalon Public Library, 317 S Home Ave, Avalon, PA, 15202. Tel: 412-761-2288. p. 1908
Welfare, Vicky, Libr Mgr, Sno-Isle Libraries, Langley Library, 104 Second St, Langley, WA, 98260. Tel: 360-221-4383. p. 2370
Welke, Ashley, Mgr, Libr Operations, Metropolitan Library System in Oklahoma County, Edmond Library, Ten S Blvd, Edmond, OK, 73034-3798. p. 1857
Welker, Margaret, Co-Dir, Coldspring Area Public Library, 14221 State Hwy 150 W, Coldspring, TX, 77331. Tel: 936-653-3104. p. 2157
Welko, Kathy, Head, Guest Serv, Addison Public Library, Four Friendship Plaza, Addison, IL, 60101. Tel: 630-543-3617. p. 535
Wellbaum, Janell, Asst to the Dean of Libraries, Baylor University Libraries, 1312 S Third St, Waco, TX, 76798. Tel: 254-710-3590. p. 2252
Wellborn, Renee, Libr Dir, Gilman-Danforth District Library, 715 N Maple St, Gilman, IL, 60938. Tel: 815-265-7522. p. 592
Wellikson, McKay, Coll Supvr, Tempe Public Library, 3500 S Rural Rd, Tempe, AZ, 85282. Tel: 480-350-5508. p. 80
Wellington, Jody, Circ/Adult Serv, Cary Library, 107 Main St, Houlton, ME, 04730. Tel: 207-532-1302. p. 927
Wellington, Laurel, Libr Mgr, Brooklyn Hospital Center, 121 DeKalb Ave, 3rd Flr, Brooklyn, NY, 11201. Tel: 718-250-6943, 718-250-8000. p. 1501
Welliver, Hilary, Dr, Dir, Kent County Public Library, 497 S Red Haven Ln, Dover, DE, 19901. Tel: 302-744-1919. p. 352
Wellman, Jared, Digital Res Librn, Lynn University Library, 3601 N Military Trail, Boca Raton, FL, 33431-5598. Tel: 561-237-7073. p. 385
Wellman, Kristen, Ad, Wayne Public Library, 3737 S Wayne Rd, Wayne, MI, 48184. Tel: 734-721-7832. p. 1158
Wellnitz, Kristen, Managing Librn, Bay County Library System, Alice & Jack Wirt Public Library, 500 Center Ave, Bay City, MI, 48708. Tel: 989-893-9566. p. 1083
Wells, Candace, Adult Serv Mgr, Libr Dir, Monticello-Union Township Public Library, 321 W Broadway St, Monticello, IN, 47960. Tel: 574-583-2665. p. 707
Wells, Carole, Asst Librn, Roodhouse Public Library, 220 W Franklin St, Roodhouse, IL, 62082. Tel: 217-589-5123. p. 643
Wells, Cathy, Libr Dir, Huxford Genealogical Society Inc, 20 S College St, Homerville, GA, 31634. Tel: 912-487-2310. p. 482
Wells, Chris, IT Mgr, Genesee District Library, 4195 W Pasadena Ave, Flint, MI, 48504. Tel: 810-732-0110. p. 1105
Wells, Connie, Tech Serv, Eastham Public Library, 190 Samoset Rd, Eastham, MA, 02642. Tel: 508-240-5950. p. 1016
Wells, Dan, Head, Tech, Calvin University & Calvin Theological Seminary, 1855 Knollcrest Circle SE, Grand Rapids, MI, 49546-4402. Tel: 616-526-7133. p. 1110
Wells, Danielle, Dir & Librn, Palco Public Library, 309 Main St, Palco, KS, 67657. Tel: 785-737-4286. p. 830
Wells, Deborah Jean, Syst Librn, West Virginia State University, Campus Box L17, Institute, WV, 25112. Tel: 304-766-3150. p. 2406
Wells, Dee Dee, Pub Serv, Hazard Community & Technical College Library, One Community College Dr, Hazard, KY, 41701. Tel: 606-487-3145. p. 858
Wells, Donna, Head, Tech Serv, Southeastern Baptist Theological Seminary Library, 114 N Wingate St, Wake Forest, NC, 27587. Tel: 919-863-2253. p. 1720
Wells, Elaine, Dir, State University of New York, State College of Optometry, 33 W 42nd St, New York, NY, 10036-8003. Tel: 212-938-5690. p. 1602
Wells, Elizabeth, Evening Librn, Copiah-Lincoln Community College, Simpson County Ctr, 151 Co-Lin Dr, Mendenhall, MS, 39114. Tel: 601-849-0116. p. 1226
Wells, Eunice F, ILL, Ref Librn, Lipscomb University, One University Park Dr, Nashville, TN, 37204-3951. Tel: 615-966-5836. p. 2119
Wells, Geraldine, Asst Mgr, Mobile Public Library, West Regional Library, 5555 Grelot Rd, Mobile, AL, 36609. Tel: 251-340-8555. p. 26
Wells, Jackie, Dir, Camargo Township District Library, 14 N Main St, Villa Grove, IL, 61956. Tel: 217-832-5211. p. 658
Wells, Jamie, Ms, Dir, Roxana Public Library District, 200 N Central Ave, Roxana, IL, 62084-1102. Tel: 618-254-6713. p. 643
Wells, Janet, Dir, M-C River Valley Public Library District, 304 Main St, Meredosia, IL, 62665. Tel: 217-584-1571. p. 617
Wells, Jennifer, Mgr, Cobb County Public Library System, West Cobb Regional Library, 1750 Dennis Kemp Lane, Kennesaw, GA, 30152. Tel: 770-528-4699. p. 489
Wells, Jonathan, Tech Serv, Dallas County Law Library, George Allen Courts Bldg, 600 Commerce St, Rm 760, Dallas, TX, 75202-4606. Tel: 214-653-6013. p. 2164

Wenzel, Duane, Br Mgr, Hawaii State Public Library System, Salt Lake-Moanalua Public Library, 3225 Salt Lake Blvd, Honolulu, HI, 96818. Tel: 808-831-6831. p. 510

Wenzel, Maria, Exec Dir, Carbon County Library System, 215 W Buffalo St, Rawlins, WY, 82301. Tel: 307-328-2618. p. 2498

Wenzel, Shealyn, Br Librn, Southeast Regional Library, Oxbow Branch, 516 Prospect Ave, Oxbow, SK, S0C 2B0, CANADA. Tel: 306-483-5175. p. 2754

Wenzl, Amy, Mgr, Omaha Public Library, Charles B Washington Branch, 2868 Ames Ave, Omaha, NE, 68111-2426. Tel: 402-444-4849. p. 1330

Wenzl, Amy, Mgr, Omaha Public Library, Saddlebrook Branch, 14850 Laurel Ave, Omaha, NE, 68116. Tel: 402-444-5780. p. 1330

Wenzler, John E, Dean of Libr, California State University, East Bay Library, CSU East Bay Library, 25800 Carlos Bee Blvd, Hayward, CA, 94542-3052. Tel: 510-885-3664. p. 150

Weppler-Van Diver, Mary, Archives & Spec Coll Librn, California State University, Stanislaus, One University Circle, Turlock, CA, 95382. Tel: 209-664-6538. p. 253

Wepryk, Rebecca, Libr Operations Mgr, Drayton Valley Municipal Library, 5120 52nd St, Drayton Valley, AB, T7A 1R7, CANADA. Tel: 780-514-2722. p. 2533

Werbach, John, Finance Mgr, Maricopa County Library District, 2700 N Central Ave, Ste 700, Phoenix, AZ, 85004. Tel: 602-652-3000. p. 70

Werbeloff, Marina D, Librn, Harvard Library, Physics Reading Room, 450 Jefferson Laboratory, 17 Oxford St, Cambridge, MA, 02138. Tel: 617-495-2878. p. 1007

Werden, Rose, Librn, Walpole Town Library, North Walpole, 70 Church St, North Walpole, NH, 03609. Tel: 603-445-5153. p. 1383

Werhane, David I, Dir, National Scouting Museum, Philmont Scout Ranch, 17 Deer Run Rd, Cimarron, NM, 87714. Tel: 575-376-1136, 575-376-2281, Ext 1256. p. 1465

Wermers, Sophia, Libr Asst, Edith B Siegrist Vermillion Public Library, 18 Church St, Vermillion, SD, 57069-3093. Tel: 605-677-7060. p. 2084

Werne, Ken, Br Mgr, Johnson County Library, Lenexa City Center Library, 8778 Penrose Lane, Lenexa, KS, 66219. p. 830

Werner, Dee, Dir, Hastings Public Library, 304 Beaver St, Hastings, PA, 16646. Tel: 814-247-8231. p. 1942

Werner, Lance M, Dir, Kent District Library, 814 West River Center Dr NE, Comstock Park, MI, 49321. Tel: 616-784-2007. p. 1093

Werner, Melissa A, Exec Dir, Hoyt Library, 284 Wyoming Ave, Kingston, PA, 18704. Tel: 570-287-2013. p. 1949

Werner, Rick, Dir, Willoughby-Eastlake Public Library, 35150 Lakeshore Blvd, Eastlake, OH, 44095. Tel: 440-943-2203. p. 1783

Werner, Rob, Pub Serv Librn, Bellingham Public Library, 210 Central Ave, Bellingham, WA, 98225. Tel: 360-778-7214. p. 2358

Werner, Shirley, Librn, Congregational Church of Patchogue, 95 E Main St, Patchogue, NY, 11772. Tel: 631-475-1235. p. 1615

Wernert, Betsy, Children's Mgr, Granville Public Library, 217 E Broadway, Granville, OH, 43023-1398. Tel: 740-587-0196. p. 1788

Wernet, Mary Linn, Archivist, Northwestern State University Libraries, 913 University Pkwy, Natchitoches, LA, 71497. Tel: 318-357-4585. p. 900

Wernett, Lisa, Dept Head, Ref, Berkeley Heights Public Library, 29 Park Ave, Berkeley Heights, NJ, 07922. Tel: 908-464-9333. p. 1390

Werosh, Keith, PhD, Dir, Libr Serv, Calumet College of Saint Joseph, 2400 New York Ave, Whiting, IN, 46394. Tel: 219-473-4373. p. 726

Werre, Pam, Pub Serv, Minnesota State University Moorhead, 1104 Seventh Ave S, Moorhead, MN, 56563. Tel: 218-477-2922. p. 1189

Wersching, Yolande, Head of Libr, Loyola University Chicago Libraries, Lewis Library, 25 E Pearson St, Chicago, IL, 60611. Tel: 312-915-6623. p. 563

Wersebe, Jeanna, Dr, Librn, Prog Coordr, California State University, Long Beach, Dept of Advanced Studies in Education & Counseling, 1250 Bellflower Blvd, Long Beach, CA, 90840-2201. Tel: 562-985-4517. p. 2782

Werth, Katie, Dep Dir, Enfield Public Library, 104 Middle Rd, Enfield, CT, 06082. Tel: 860-763-7510. p. 311

Wertheim, Carla, Exec VPres, Metropolitan Milwaukee Fair Housing Council Library, 600 E Mason St, Ste 401, Milwaukee, WI, 53202. Tel: 414-278-1240. p. 2459

Wertheim, Jan, Librn, Sweetser Services for Children & Families, 50 Moody St, Saco, ME, 04072-0892. Tel: 207-294-4945. p. 939

Wertheimer, Andrew, Dr, Assoc Prof, University of Hawaii, 2550 McCarthy Mall, Hamilton Library, Rm 002, Honolulu, HI, 96822. Tel: 808-956-7321. p. 2784

Werthmann, Eric, Dir, Woodbridge Town Library, Ten Newton Rd, Woodbridge, CT, 06525. Tel: 203-389-3435. p. 349

Werthmuller, Dianne, Libr Tech, University of Arkansas Fort Smith, 5210 Grand Ave, Fort Smith, AR, 72904. Tel: 479-788-7200. p. 96

Wertin, Libby, Librn/Acad Files, Academy of Motion Picture Arts & Sciences, 333 S La Cienega Blvd, Beverly Hills, CA, 90211. Tel: 310-247-3000, Ext 2208. p. 124

Wertkin, Jennifer, Dir, Wellfleet Public Library, 55 W Main St, Wellfleet, MA, 02667. Tel: 508-349-0310. p. 1064

Wertzberger, Janelle, Asst Dean, Dir, Scholarly Communications, Gettysburg College, 300 N Washington St, Gettysburg, PA, 17325. Tel: 717-337-7010. p. 1935

Wes-Hall, Heather, Outreach Serv, Goodnight Memorial Public Library, 203 S Main St, Franklin, KY, 42134. Tel: 270-586-8397. p. 856

Wesch, Debra, Librn, Arlington Public Library, 410 W Elm St, Arlington, NE, 68002. Tel: 402-478-4545. p. 1305

Wescott, Virginia, Head, Circ, Troy Public Library, 100 Second St, Troy, NY, 12180. Tel: 518-274-7071. p. 1653

Weseloh, Benjamin R, Dir, West Chicago Public Library District, 118 W Washington St, West Chicago, IL, 60185. Tel: 630-231-1552. p. 660

Wesley, Crystal, Acq, Centre College of Kentucky, 600 W Walnut St, Danville, KY, 40422. Tel: 859-238-5273. p. 853

Wesley, Holley, Ref Librn, Emmet O'Neal Library, 50 Oak St, Mountain Brook, AL, 35213. Tel: 205-879-0459. p. 31

Wesley, Threasa, Teaching & Learning Librn, Northern Kentucky University, University Dr, Highland Heights, KY, 41099. Tel: 859-572-5721. p. 859

Wesner, Kendra, Ad, Redford Township District Library, 25320 W Six Mile, Redford, MI, 48240. Tel: 313-531-5960. p. 1143

Wess, Susan, Dir, Milan Public Library, 151 Wabash St, Milan, MI, 48160. Tel: 734-439-1240. p. 1132

Wessel, Elizabeth, Acq, Circ, Martin Luther College Library, 1995 Luther Ct, New Ulm, MN, 56073-3965. Tel: 507-233-9131. p. 1190

Wessells, Robert S, Asst Librn, United States Navy, Academic Resources Information Center, 440 Meyerkord Rd, Newport, RI, 02841. Tel: 401-841-4352, 401-841-6631. p. 2035

Wessner, Lela, Library Contact, United States Navy, Resource Center, Naval Sta Bremerton Base-MWR, 120 S Dewey St, Bldg 502, Bremerton, WA, 98314-5000. Tel: 360-535-5932. p. 2360

Wesson, Cameron, Provost, Central Pennsylvania Consortium, c/o Franklin & Marshall College, Goethean Hall 101, Lancaster, PA, 17604. Tel: 717-358-4282. p. 2774

West, Andrea, Adult Serv Mgr, Brown County Library, 515 Pine St, Green Bay, WI, 54301. Tel: 920-448-4400, Ext 7. p. 2438

West, Belinda, Dir, Caldwell Public Library, 517 Spruce St, Caldwell, OH, 43724. Tel: 740-732-4506. p. 1754

West, Betsy, Librn, Grove Hill Public Library, 108 Dubose Ave, Grove Hill, AL, 36451-9502. Tel: 251-275-8157. p. 19

West, Brandon, Head, Instruction & Res, State University of New York College, SUNY Geneseo, One College Circle, Geneseo, NY, 14454-1498. Tel: 585-245-5594. p. 1537

West, Brittany M, Dir, Clyde W Roddy Library, 371 First Ave, Dayton, TN, 37321-1499. Tel: 423-775-8406. p. 2096

West, Deanna D, Dept Head, The MITRE Corporation, 202 Burlington Rd, Bedford, MA, 01730-1420. Tel: 781-271-7667. p. 988

West, Debbie, Humanities Librn, Troy University Library, 309 Wallace Hall, Troy, AL, 36082. Tel: 334-808-6344. p. 37

West, Deborah, Ref & Instruction, Gannon University, 619 Sassafras St, Erie, PA, 16541. Tel: 814-871-7557. p. 1931

West, George, Asst Dir, Knox County Public Library, 206 Knox St, Barbourville, KY, 40906. Tel: 606-546-5339. p. 848

West, Isaiah, YA Serv, Alexandria Library, Charles E Beatley Jr Central, 5005 Duke St, Alexandria, VA, 22304-2903. Tel: 703-746-1767. p. 2302

West, Jaci, Adult Serv, Paul Sawyier Public Library, 319 Wapping St, Frankfort, KY, 40601-2605. Tel: 502-352-2665. p. 856

West, Janet, Head, Res Serv, Port Washington Public Library, One Library Dr, Port Washington, NY, 11050. Tel: 516-883-3728, Ext 1402. p. 1622

West, Janet, Commun Libr Mgr, Wake County Public Library System, Fuquay-Varina Community Library, 271 Bramblehill Dr, Fuquay-Varina, NC, 27526. Tel: 919-557-2788. p. 1711

West, Janine, Dir, Libr Serv, Eleanor London Cote Saint Luc Public Library, 5851 Blvd Cavendish, Cote Saint-Luc, QC, H4W 2X8, CANADA. Tel: 514-485-6900, Ext 4202. p. 2711

West, Jeff, Fac Mgr, Boone County Public Library, 1786 Burlington Pike, Burlington, KY, 41005. Tel: 859-342-2665. p. 850

West, Joyce, Pub Serv Adminr, Alachua County Library District, 401 E University Ave, Gainesville, FL, 32601-5453. Tel: 352-334-3968. p. 406

West, Leslie, Head, Adult Serv, Homewood Public Library, 1721 Oxmoor Rd, Homewood, AL, 35209-4085. Tel: 205-332-6620. p. 21

West, Linda, Dir, Tinicum Memorial Public Library, 620 Seneca St, Essington, PA, 19029. Tel: 610-521-9344. p. 1932

West, Lori, Br Mgr, Fargo Public Library, Dr James Carlson Branch, 2801 32nd Ave S, Fargo, ND, 58103. Tel: 701-476-4040. p. 1733

West, Lori, Br Mgr, Fargo Public Library, Northport, 2714 Broadway, Fargo, ND, 58102. Tel: 701-476-4026. p. 1733

West, Lori, Mgr, Br Serv, Fargo Public Library, 102 N Third St, Fargo, ND, 58102. Tel: 701-241-1472. p. 1733

West, Maggie, Br Mgr, Athens Regional Library System, Lavonia-Carnegie Branch, 28 Hartwell Rd, Lavonia, GA, 30553. Tel: 706-356-4307. p. 458

West, Maggie, Br Mgr, Athens Regional Library System, Royston Branch, 634 Franklin Springs St, Royston, GA, 30662. Tel: 706-245-6748. p. 459

West, Mara, Ref & Instruction Librn, Minot State University, 500 University Ave W, Minot, ND, 58707. Tel: 701-858-3095. p. 1738

West, Melanie, Assoc Dir, Access Serv, Embry-Riddle Aeronautical University, One Aerospace Blvd, Daytona Beach, FL, 32114. Tel: 386-226-6591. p. 392

West Prichard, Laurie, Dir, Killingworth Library Association, 301 Rte 81, Killingworth, CT, 06419. Tel: 860-663-2000. p. 319

West, Retta, Educ Spec, Ref & Instruction, Southwest Virginia Community College Library, Russell Hall, 599 Community College Rd, Cedar Bluff, VA, 24609. Tel: 276-964-7265. p. 2309

West, Sandy, Dir, Rend Lake College, 468 N Ken Gray Pkwy, Ina, IL, 62846. Tel: 618-437-5321. p. 601

West, Sara, Br Mgr, Harris County Public Library, Octavia Fields Memorial Branch, 1503 S Houston Ave, Humble, TX, 77338. Tel: 832-927-5500. p. 2192

West, Sharon, Mgr, Saskatchewan Justice, Court of the Queen's Bench, Court House, 2425 Victoria Ave, Regina, SK, S4P 3V7, CANADA. Tel: 306-787-7809. p. 2747

West, Staci, Pub Relations Mgr, Milton-Union Public Library, 560 S Main St, West Milton, OH, 45383. Tel: 937-698-5515. p. 1830

West, Stuart, Superintendent, US National Park Service, 35110 Hwy 194 E, La Junta, CO, 81050. Tel: 719-383-5010. p. 287

West, Tammy, Br Mgr, Wayne County Public Library, Collinwood Depot, 101 E Depot St, Collinwood, TN, 38450. Tel: 931-724-2498. p. 2129

West, Timothy J, Ref/Tech Serv, Flat River Community Library, 200 W Judd St, Greenville, MI, 48838. Tel: 616-754-6359. p. 1112

West, Traci, Spec Coll Librn, Univ Archivist, Dallas Baptist University, 3000 Mountain Creek Pkwy, Dallas, TX, 75211-9299. Tel: 214-333-5210. p. 2163

West, Wayne, Libr Asst, New Mexico State University at Alamogordo, 2400 N Scenic Dr, Alamogordo, NM, 88310. Tel: 575-439-3653. p. 1459

West-Finkle, Pamela, Dir, Andes Public Library, 242 Main St, Andes, NY, 13731. Tel: 845-676-3333. p. 1487

West-Pawl, Victoria, Instruction & Ref Librn, Johnson & Wales University, College of Business, 7150 Montview Blvd, Denver, CO, 80220. Tel: 303-256-9378. p. 276

West-Pawl, Victoria, Libr Dir, Front Range Community College, 3645 W 112th Ave, Westminster, CO, 80031. Tel: 303-404-5505. p. 298

Westall, Samantha, Curric Librn, Framingham State University, 100 State St, Framingham, MA, 01701. Tel: 508-626-4657. p. 1019

Westberg, Kathy, Ch, ILL, Durand Public Library, 604 Seventh Ave E, Durand, WI, 54736. Tel: 715-672-8730. p. 2431

Westberry, Kim, First Year Experience Librn, University of Wisconsin-River Falls, 410 S Third St, River Falls, WI, 54022. Tel: 715-425-4918. p. 2474

Westborn, Nicole, Children's Librn, Circ Serv, Kellogg-Hubbard Library, 135 Main St, Montpelier, VT, 05602. Tel: 802-223-3338. p. 2289

Westbrock, Theresa, Dean, Libr Serv, University of Northern Iowa Library, 1227 W 27th St, Cedar Falls, IA, 50613-3675. Tel: 319-273-2737. p. 737

Westbrook, Joshua, Tech Serv, Columbia Basin College Library, 2600 N 20th Ave, Pasco, WA, 99301. Tel: 509-544-2263. p. 2373

Westbrook, Sandy, Ref, South Windsor Public Library, 1550 Sullivan Ave, South Windsor, CT, 06074. Tel: 860-644-1541. p. 337

Westbrooks, Elaine L, Vice Provost & Univ Librn, University of North Carolina at Chapel Hill, 208 Raleigh St, CB 3916, Chapel Hill, NC, 27515. Tel: 919-962-1053. p. 1678

Westcott, Anita, Dir, Americus Township Library, 710 Main St, Americus, KS, 66835. Tel: 620-443-5503. p. 796

Westcott, Joni, Commun Serv Supvr, Yavapai County Free Library District, Clark Memorial Library, 39 N Ninth St, Clarkdale, AZ, 86324. Tel: 928-634-5423. p. 74

Westcott, Stephanie, Learning Coordr, Virginia's Academic Library Consortium, George Mason University, 4400 University Dr, Fenwick 5100, Fairfax, VA, 22030. Tel: 703-993-4654. p. 2776

Westen, James, Head, Adult Serv, Dover Town Library, 56 Dedham St, Dover, MA, 02030-2214. Tel: 508-785-8113. p. 1014

Westenbroek, Tony, Br Mgr, Ottawa Public Library/Bibliothèque publique d'Ottawa, Rosemount Branch, 1207 Wellington West/Ouest, Ottawa, ON, K1Y 2Z8, CANADA. p. 2669

Westenbroek, Tony, Br Mgr, Ottawa Public Library/Bibliothèque publique d'Ottawa, Sunnyside, 1049 Bank St, Ottawa, ON, K1S 3W9, CANADA. p. 2669

Westenburg, Elizabeth, Ref Mgr, Idaho State Historical Society, Idaho History Ctr, 2205 Old Penitentiary Rd, Boise, ID, 83712-8250. Tel: 208-514-2324. p. 517

Westenfeld, Jane, Res & Instruction Librn, Spec Coll Librn, Allegheny College, 520 N Main St, Meadville, PA, 16335. Tel: 814-332-3769. p. 1959

Wester, Candle, Assoc Dir, Faculty Servs & Administration, University of South Carolina, Law Library, 1525 Senate St, Columbia, SC, 29208. Tel: 803-777-5942. p. 2055

Wester, Michelle, Outreach & Children's Serv, Harnett County Public Library, 601 S Main St, Lillington, NC, 27546-6107. Tel: 910-893-3446. p. 1700

Wester, Paul, Dir, United States Department of Agriculture, 10301 Baltimore Ave, Beltsville, MD, 20705-2351. Tel: 301-504-5755. p. 959

Westercamp, Christine, Libr Dir, Farmington Public Library, 205 Elm St, Farmington, IA, 52626. Tel: 319-878-3702. p. 753

Westerfield, Lindsey B, Dir, Russell County Public Library, 535 N Main St, Jamestown, KY, 42629. Tel: 270-343-7323. p. 861

Westerman, Casey, Archivist, Spec Coll, Agnes Scott College, 141 E College Ave, Decatur, GA, 30030-3770. Tel: 404-471-6344. p. 475

Westerman, Teresa, Br Mgr, Currituck County Public Library, Corolla Branch, 1123 Ocean Trail, Corolla, NC, 27927-9998. Tel: 252-453-0496. p. 1673

Westervelt, Jan, Ms, Br Mgr, Enoch Pratt Free Library, Light Street Branch, 1251 Light St, Baltimore, MD, 21230-4305. Tel: 443-984-4926. p. 953

Westfall Briggs, Amber, Regional Dir, Avery-Mitchell-Yancey Regional Library System, 289 Burnsville School Rd, Burnsville, NC, 28714. Tel: 828-682-4476. p. 1677

Westfall, Ruth, Asst Dir, Tech, Suffolk Cooperative Library System, 627 N Sunrise Service Rd, Bellport, NY, 11713. Tel: 631-286-1600. p. 1492

Westgate, Hilary, Outreach Librn, Ref & Instruction Librn, Ramapo College of New Jersey, 505 Ramapo Valley Rd, Mahwah, NJ, 07430-1623. Tel: 201-684-7570. p. 1415

Westgate, Susan, Dir, Carol Stream Public Library, 616 Hiawatha Dr, Carol Stream, IL, 60188. Tel: 630-344-6101. p. 549

Westhoff, Randall, Associ Vice Pres, Academic Affairs, Bemidji State University, 1500 Birchmont Dr NE, No 28, Bemidji, MN, 56601-2699. Tel: 218-755-2016. p. 1165

Westkamper, Joanne, Dir, Raymond Library, 832 Raymond Hill Rd, Oakdale, CT, 06370. Tel: 860-848-9943. p. 332

Westlake, Claire, Br Coordr, North Vancouver District Public Library, Parkgate, 3675 Banff Ct, North Vancouver, BC, V7H 2Z8, CANADA. Tel: 604-929-3727. p. 2573

Westlake, Matheson, Supv Librn, Holland Free Public Library, 129 Spring Mills Rd, Milford, NJ, 08848. Tel: 908-995-4767. p. 1419

Westley, David, Librn, Boston University Libraries, African Studies Library, 771 Commonwealth Ave, Boston, MA, 02215. Tel: 617-353-3726. p. 993

Westmoreland, Molly, Dir, Wilson County Public Library, 249 Nash St W, Wilson, NC, 27893-3801. Tel: 252-237-5355, Ext 5024. p. 1724

Weston, Andrea, Libr Dir, Rich County Library, 55 N Main St, Randolph, UT, 84064. Tel: 435-793-2122. p. 2270

Weston, Barbara, Commun Connections Librn, Mgr, Programming, Coquitlam Public Library, 575 Poirier St, Coquitlam, BC, V3J 6A9, CANADA. Tel: 604-937-4143. p. 2565

Weston, Kathleen, Law Librn, William H Miller Law Library, 207 City-County Courts Bldg, 825 Sycamore, Evansville, IN, 47708-1849. Tel: 812-435-5175. p. 682

Weston, Kim, Tech Serv, Rockland Community College Library, 145 College Rd, Suffern, NY, 10901. Tel: 845-574-4407. p. 1647

Weston, Kimberly, Dir, Dexter Free Library, 120 E Kirby St, Dexter, NY, 13634. Tel: 315-639-6785. p. 1525

Weston, Linda, Circ, Fiscal Officer, Andover Public Library, 142 W Main St, Andover, OH, 44003-9318. Tel: 440-293-6792. p. 1746

Weston, Matthew, Dir, Dowagiac District Library, 211 Commercial St, Dowagiac, MI, 49047-1728. Tel: 269-782-3826. p. 1101

Weston, Richard, Assoc Libr Dir, Saul Ewing Arnstein & Lehr, Centre Square West, 1500 Market St, 38th Flr, Philadelphia, PA, 19102. Tel: 215-972-7777. p. 1985

Weston, Rory, Mgr, Tech Innovation Librn, Coquitlam Public Library, 575 Poirier St, Coquitlam, BC, V3J 6A9, CANADA. Tel: 604-937-4251. p. 2565

Weston, Wil, Head, Coll Mgt, San Diego State University, 5500 Campanile Dr, San Diego, CA, 92182-8050. Tel: 619-594-6988. p. 221

Weston-Elchert, Laura, Library Contact, Fort Wayne News-Sentinel Library, 600 W Main St, Fort Wayne, IN, 46801. Tel: 260-461-8468. p. 684

Weston-Stoll, Keri, Asst Dir, Waukee Public Library, 950 S Warrior Lane, Waukee, IA, 50263. Tel: 515-978-7944. p. 789

Westphal, Aimie, Asst Dir, Amesbury Public Library, 149 Main St, Amesbury, MA, 01913. Tel: 978-388-8148. p. 984

Westphal, Kristine, Info Serv Mgr, Phillips, Lytle LLP Library, 125 Main St, Buffalo, NY, 14203-2887. Tel: 716-847-5470. p. 1509

Westphal, Robin, Dir, Missouri State Library, 600 W Main St, Jefferson City, MO, 65101. Tel: 573-751-8720. p. 1253

Westphal, Robin, Ms, State Librn, Missouri State Library, James C Kirkpatrick State Information Ctr, 600 W Main St, Jefferson City, MO, 65101. Tel: 573-751-0586. p. 1253

Westphalen, Peg, Cat Mgr, The Master's University, 21726 W Placerita Canyon Rd, Santa Clarita, CA, 91321-1200. Tel: 661-362-2277. p. 242

Westphall, Shaleigh, Ref & Instruction Librn, Willamette University, 900 State St, Salem, OR, 97301. Tel: 503-821-8966. p. 1897

Westrick, Jennifer, Res Info Spec, Library of Rush University Medical Center, Armour Academic Ctr, 600 S Paulina St, Ste 571, Chicago, IL, 60612. Tel: 312-563-2679. p. 563

Westwood, Karen, Dir, Hennepin County Law Library, C-2451 Government Ctr, 300 S Sixth St, Minneapolis, MN, 55487. Tel: 612-348-7977. p. 1183

Wethem, Sarah, Youth Librn, Douglas County Library, 720 Fillmore St, Alexandria, MN, 56308. Tel: 320-762-3014. p. 1163

Wetherbee, Hanna, Ch, Spillman Public Library, 719 Wisconsin Ave, North Fond du Lac, WI, 54937-1335. Tel: 920-929-3771. p. 2465

Wetherbee, Jimm, Network & Syst Adminr, Wingate University, 110 Church ST, Wingate, NC, 28174. Tel: 704-233-8089. p. 1724

Wetherby, Julie, Asst Librn, Cambridge Public Library, 21 W Main St, Cambridge, NY, 12816. Tel: 518-677-2443. p. 1512

Wetherington, Mark, Libr Dir, Bitterroot Public Library, 306 State St, Hamilton, MT, 59840. Tel: 406-363-1670. p. 1294
Wethington, Jessica, Communications Mgr, Louisville Metro Planning Commission, 444 S Fifth St, Ste 300, Louisville, KY, 40202. Tel: 502-574-5174. p. 866
Wetmore, Gayle, Supvr, Haliburton County Public Library, Stanhope Branch, 1109 N Shore Rd, Algonquin Highlands, ON, K0M 1J0, CANADA. Tel: 705-489-2402. p. 2644
Wetnight, Jill, Br Mgr, Indianapolis Public Library, Franklin Road, 5550 S Franklin Rd, Indianapolis, IN, 46239. Tel: 317-275-4385. p. 695
Wetta, Molly, Mgr, Libr Serv, Santa Barbara Public Library, 40 E Anapamu St, Santa Barbara, CA, 93101-2722. Tel: 805-564-5608. p. 240
Wetterauer, Don, Dir, Alpine Public Library, 805 W Ave E, Alpine, TX, 79830. Tel: 432-837-2621. p. 2133
Wettergreen, Brenda, Librn, Beverly Public Library, Beverly Farms, 24 Vine St, Beverly, MA, 01915-2208. Tel: 978-921-6066. p. 989
Wettergreen, Brenda, Ch, Reading Public Library, 64 Middlesex Ave, Reading, MA, 01867-2550. Tel: 781-944-0840. p. 1049
Wetterstrom, Daniel, Head, Tech, Librn, Westland Public Library, 6123 Central City Pkwy, Westland, MI, 48185. Tel: 734-326-6123. p. 1159
Wettstein, Chris, Ref Serv, Valencia College, East Campus Library, 701 N Econlockhatchee Trail, Orlando, FL, 32825. Tel: 407-582-2467. p. 432
Wewe, Boniface N, Managing Librn, Brooklyn Public Library, Washington Irving Branch, 360 Irving Ave, Brooklyn, NY, 11237. Tel: 718-628-8378. p. 1504
Weyeneth, Melissa, Ad, Dunlap Public Library District, 302 S First St, Dunlap, IL, 61525. Tel: 309-243-5716. p. 580
Weyrens, Angela, Libr Dir, Multnomah County Library, Central Library, 801 SW Tenth Ave, Portland, OR, 97205. p. 1892
Weyrick, Christina, Commun Relations Mgr, North Canton Public Library, 185 N Main St, North Canton, OH, 44720-2595. Tel: 330-499-4712. p. 1809
Whalen, Debbie, Spec Coll & Archives Librn, Eastern Kentucky University Libraries, 103 Crabbe Library, 521 Lancaster Ave, Richmond, KY, 40475. Tel: 859-622-1792. p. 873
Whalen, Ginny, Dir, Robertson County Public Library, 207 N Main St, Mount Olivet, KY, 41064. Tel: 606-724-5746. p. 870
Whalen, Kimberly, Assoc Professor of Library Science, Valparaiso University, 1410 Chapel Dr, Valparaiso, IN, 46383-6493. Tel: 219-464-5754. p. 723
Whalen, Tomi, Br Mgr, Kitsap Regional Library, Little Boston, 31980 Little Boston Rd NE, Kingston, WA, 98346-9700. Tel: 360-297-2670. p. 2360
Whalen-Nevin, Bridget, Dir, Morristown Public Library, 200 Main St, Morristown, NY, 13664. Tel: 315-375-8833. p. 1574
Whaley, Hunter, Ref Librn, Columbia University, Arthur W Diamond Law Library, 435 W 116th St, New York, NY, 10027. Tel: 212-854-3922. p. 1583
Whaley, Jennifer, Dir, Onslow County Public Library, 58 Doris Ave E, Jacksonville, NC, 28540. Tel: 910-455-7350. p. 1697
Whaley, Laura, Regional Mgr, Santa Cruz City-County Library System, 117 Union St, Santa Cruz, CA, 95060-3873. Tel: 831-427-7706, Ext 7734. p. 242
Whaley, Martha, Res Mgr, East Tennessee State University, James H Quillen College of Medicine Library, Maple St, Bldg 4, Johnson City, TN, 37614. Tel: 423-439-8069. p. 2103
Whalin, Kathleen, Ch, York Public Library, 15 Long Sands Rd, York, ME, 03909. Tel: 207-363-2818. p. 947
Whannell, Paula, Treas, Polk County Biomedical Consortium, c/o Unity Point Health Sciences Library, 1200 Pleasant St, Des Moines, IA, 50309. Tel: 515-241-6490. p. 2765
Wharton, Amy, Dir, University of Virginia, Arthur J Morris Law Library, 580 Massie Rd, Charlottesville, VA, 22903-1738. Tel: 434-924-1816. p. 2310
Wharton, April, Librn, Swan Hills Municipal Library, 5536 Main St, Swan Hills, AB, T0G 2C0, CANADA. Tel: 780-333-4505. p. 2556
Wharton, Carrie, Outreach Specialist, Programming Spec, Goddard Public Library, 201 N Main St, Goddard, KS, 67052. Tel: 316-794-8771. p. 810
Wharton, Jennifer, Youth Serv Librn, Matheson Memorial Library, 101 N Wisconsin, Elkhorn, WI, 53121. Tel: 262-723-2678. p. 2433
Wharton, Kira, Chief Librn, United States Marine Band, Marine Barracks Annex & Band Support Facility, Seventh & L Sts SE, Washington, DC, 20003. Tel: 202-433-4298. p. 379
Wharton, Nick, Head, Pub Serv, Head, Ref, University of Hartford Harrison Libraries, 200 Bloomfield Ave, West Hartford, CT, 06117. Tel: 860-768-4264. p. 345
Whatley, Edward, Res & Instruction Librn, Georgia College, 221 N Clark St, Milledgeville, GA, 31061. Tel: 478-445-4047. p. 490
Whatley, Joy, Libr Dir, Chula Vista Public Library, 365 F St, Chula Vista, CA, 91910. Tel: 619-691-5170. p. 129
Whatley, Kara, Univ Librn, California Institute of Technology, 1200 E California Blvd, M/C 1-43, Pasadena, CA, 91125-4300. Tel: 626-395-3805. p. 193
Whatley, Kara, Head, Sci & Eng, The NYU Tandon School of Engineering, Five MetroTech Ctr, Brooklyn, NY, 11201-3840. Tel: 646-997-3164. p. 1505
Whatley, Melissa, Asst Mgr, Saint Charles City-County Library District, Middendorf-Kredell Branch, 2750 Hwy K, O'Fallon, MO, 63368-7859. Tel: 636-272-4999, 636-978-7926. p. 1278
Whatley, Miriam, Asst Mgr, Saint Louis County Library, Samuel C Sachs Branch, 16400 Burkhardt Pl, Chesterfield, MO, 63017-4660. Tel: 314-994-3300, Ext 3800. p. 1274
Wheat, Curtis, Dir, Reform Public Library, 302 First St S, Reform, AL, 35481. Tel: 205-375-6240. p. 34
Wheatley, Gerald, Library Contact, Arusha Centre, c/o The Old Y Bldg, 233-12 Ave SW, No 106, Calgary, AB, T2R 0G9, CANADA. Tel: 403-270-3200. p. 2526
Wheatley, Jessica, Fed Libr Mgr, United States Environmental Protection Agency, 77 W Jackson Blvd (ML-16J), Chicago, IL, 60604. Tel: 312-886-6822. p. 569
Wheatley, Laura, Dir, Franklin County Library District, 109 S First E, Preston, ID, 83263. Tel: 208-852-0175. p. 529
Wheaton, Mike, Mgr, Libr Tech Serv, Middle Tennessee State University, 1611 Alumni Dr, Murfreesboro, TN, 37132. Tel: 615-898-5043. p. 2117
Wheaton, Nathalie, Archivist, Library of Rush University Medical Center, Armour Academic Ctr, 600 S Paulina St, Ste 571, Chicago, IL, 60612. Tel: 312-942-6358. p. 563
Wheaton, Rebekah, Libr Dir, Fundy Library Region, St Croix Public Library, 11 King St, Saint Stephen, NB, E3L 2C1, CANADA. Tel: 506-466-7529. p. 2605
Wheeler, Abraham, Pres, Michigan Health Sciences Libraries Association, 1407 Rensen St, Ste 4, Lansing, MI, 48910. Tel: 517-884-0893. p. 2767
Wheeler, Alisha, Librn, Franklin Correctional Facility Library, 62 Bare Hill Rd, Malone, NY, 12953. Tel: 518-483-6040. p. 1567
Wheeler, Amanda, Children's & Teen Serv, Lincoln County Public Library, 201 Lancaster St, Stanford, KY, 40484. Tel: 606-365-7513. p. 875
Wheeler, Amy, Finance Mgr, Orbis Cascade Alliance, PO Box 6007, Portland, OR, 97228. Tel: 541-246-2470. p. 2773
Wheeler, Angela, Librn, Oregon State Penitentiary Library, Coffee Creek Correctional Facility, 24499 SW Grahams Ferry Rd, Wilsonville, OR, 97070. Tel: 503-570-6783. p. 1896
Wheeler, Caitlin, Libr Supvr, Spokane County Library District, Moran Prairie Library, 6004 S Regal St, Spokane, WA, 99223-6949. Tel: 509-893-8340. p. 2384
Wheeler, Caitlin, Libr Supvr, Spokane County Library District, Otis Orchards Library, 22324 E Wellesley Ave, Otis Orchards, WA, 99027-9336. Tel: 509-893-8390. p. 2384
Wheeler, Eric, Reader & Digital Serv Librn, Simpson University, 2211 College View Dr, Redding, CA, 96003. Tel: 530-226-4117. p. 199
Wheeler, Jade, Br Mgr, Ouachita Parish Public Library, Ollie Burns Branch, 5601 Hwy 165 S, Richwood, LA, 71202. Tel: 318-327-1235. p. 898
Wheeler, Jessie, Dir, Exira Public Library, 114 W Washington St, Exira, IA, 50076. Tel: 712-268-5489. p. 752
Wheeler, John Mark, Library Contact, Arkansas Department of Correction, Pine Bluff Work Complex Chapel Library, 890 Freeline Dr, Pine Bluff, AR, 71603-1498. Tel: 870-267-6510. p. 107
Wheeler, Kate, Teen Serv Librn, Brighton District Library, 100 Library Dr, Brighton, MI, 48116. Tel: 810-229-6571. p. 1087
Wheeler, Kathleen, Dir, First Presbyterian Church Library, 21 Firelands Blvd, Norwalk, OH, 44857. Tel: 419-668-1923. p. 1810
Wheeler, Kathy, Asst Univ Librn, Coll, University of South Alabama Libraries, Marx Library, 5901 USA Drive N, Mobile, AL, 36688. Tel: 251-460-7938. p. 27
Wheeler, Katie, Ch, Exira Public Library, 114 W Washington St, Exira, IA, 50076. Tel: 712-268-5489. p. 752
Wheeler, Katie, Area Asst Dir, Mid-Plains Community College, Von Riesen Library Bldg, 1205 E Third St, McCook, NE, 69001. Tel: 308-345-8117. p. 1324
Wheeler, Katie, Asst Dir, Learning Res, Mid-Plains Community College, McDonald-Belton Bldg, 601 W State Farm Rd, North Platte, NE, 69101. Tel: 308-221-6433. p. 1327
Wheeler, Laurie, Dir, Arms Library, 60 Bridge St, Shelburne Falls, MA, 01370. Tel: 413-625-0306. p. 1052
Wheeler, Lisa, Supvry Librn, US Environmental Protection Agency Library, 75 Hawthorne St, San Francisco, CA, 94105. Tel: 415-947-4406. p. 230
Wheeler, Marcia, Libr Asst, Montgomery Memorial Library, 711 Main St, Jewell, IA, 50130. Tel: 515-827-5112. p. 762
Wheeler, Mary, Tech Coordr, Minot Public Library, 516 Second Ave SW, Minot, ND, 58701-3792. Tel: 701-852-1045. p. 1738
Wheeler, Maurice, Dr, Assoc Prof, University of North Texas, 3940 N Elm St, Ste E292, Denton, TX, 76207. Tel: 940-565-2445. p. 2793
Wheeler, Michelle, Dir, Dunkerton Public Library, 203 E Tower St, Dunkerton, IA, 50626. Tel: 319-822-4610. p. 749
Wheeler, Natalie, Br Mgr, Fauquier County Public Library, Bealeton Branch, 10877 Willow Dr N, Bealeton, VA, 22712. Tel: 540-422-8500, Ext 2. p. 2352
Wheeler, Pattie, Archivist, Columbia International University, 7435 Monticello Rd, Columbia, SC, 29203-1599. Tel: 803-807-5106. p. 2053
Wheeler, Ryan J, Dir, Phillips Academy, 180 Main St, Andover, MA, 01810. Tel: 978-749-4490. p. 985
Wheeler, Stephen, Br Mgr, San Diego Public Library, Logan Heights, 567 S 28th St, San Diego, CA, 92113-2498. Tel: 619-533-3968. p. 219

Wheeler, Stephen, Br Mgr, San Diego Public Library, Mission Hills-Hillcrest/Knox, 215 W Washington St, San Diego, CA, 92103. Tel: 619-692-4910. p. 220

Wheeler, Terrie, Dir, New York Presbyterian Hospital-Weill Cornell, 21 Bloomingdale Rd, White Plains, NY, 10605. Tel: 914-997-5897. p. 1664

Wheeler, Terry, Dir, Cornell University Library, Samuel J Wood Library & C V Starr Biomedical Information Center, 1300 York Ave, C115, Box 67, New York, NY, 10065-4896. Tel: 646-962-2469. p. 1552

Wheeler, Thomas, IT Serv Mgr, Charleston County Public Library, 68 Calhoun St, Charleston, SC, 29401. Tel: 843-805-6801. p. 2048

Wheelock, Meliss, Readers' Advisory Coordr, Kokomo-Howard County Public Library, 220 N Union St, Kokomo, IN, 46901-4614. Tel: 765-457-3242. p. 700

Whelan, David, Dir of Libr, San Diego Law Library, 1105 Front St, San Diego, CA, 92101-3904. Tel: 619-685-6567. p. 218

Whelan, Ellen, Interim Chief Exec Officer, North Perth Public Library, 260 Main St W, Listowel, ON, N4W 1A1, CANADA. Tel: 519-291-4621. p. 2653

Whelan, Heidi, Youth Serv Librn, Baxter Memorial Library, 71 South St, Gorham, ME, 04038. Tel: 207-222-1190. p. 926

Whelan, Holly, Libr Mgr, Arapahoe Library District, Eloise May Library, 1471 S Parker Rd, Denver, CO, 80231. p. 279

Whelan, Holly, Libr Mgr, Arapahoe Library District, Smoky Hill Public Library, 5430 S Biscay Circle, Centennial, CO, 80015. p. 279

Whelan, Jennifer, Coord, Research & Instruction, College of the Holy Cross, One College St, Worcester, MA, 01610. Tel: 508-793-2254. p. 1072

Whelan, John L, Librn III, College of the North Atlantic Library Services, Grand Falls-Windsor Campus, Five Cromer Ave, Grand Falls-Windsor, NL, A2A 1X3, CANADA. Tel: 709-292-5637. p. 2609

Whelan, Mariko, Youth/Teen Serv Coordr, Scottsdale Public Library, 3839 N Drinkwater Blvd, Scottsdale, AZ, 85251-4467. Tel: 480-312-7323. p. 77

Whelchel, Angela, Ch, Atlanta-Fulton Public Library System, Roswell Branch, 115 Norcross St, Roswell, GA, 30075. Tel: 770-640-3075. p. 461

Whelchel, Dana, Head, Tech Serv, Anderson University Library, 316 Boulevard, Anderson, SC, 29621. Tel: 864-231-2050. p. 2047

Whelchel, Debbie, Ch Serv, Ada Public Library, 124 S Rennie, Ada, OK, 74820. Tel: 580-436-8125. p. 1839

Whelpley, Ryan, Br Mgr, Ashtabula County District Library, Geneva Public Library, 860 Sherman St, Geneva, OH, 44041. Tel: 440-466-4521. p. 1747

Whewell, Jean, Operations Mgr, Southwestern University, 1100 E University Ave, Georgetown, TX, 78626. Tel: 512-863-1635. p. 2184

Whidden, Linda M, Assoc Librn, Head, Tech & Info Res, King's University College at the University of Western Ontario, 266 Epworth Ave, London, ON, N6A 2M3, CANADA. Tel: 519-433-3491, Ext 4506. p. 2653

Whipp, Ashleigh, Ch Serv, Youth Serv, Bracebridge Public Library, 94 Manitoba St, Bracebridge, ON, P1L 2B5, CANADA. Tel: 705-645-4171. p. 2632

Whipp, Ashleigh, Chief Librn, Grimsby Public Library, 18 Carnegie Lane, Grimsby, ON, L3M 1Y1, CANADA. Tel: 905-945-5142. p. 2643

Whipperling, Robin, Exec Dir, Goodhue County Historical Society Library, 1166 Oak St, Red Wing, MN, 55066. Tel: 651-388-6024. p. 1194

Whippey, Caroline, Dir, Libr Serv, Brescia University College, 1285 Western Rd, London, ON, N6G 1H2, CANADA. Tel: 519-432-8353, Ext 28250. p. 2653

Whipple, Jona, Digital History & Archives Mgr, Federal Reserve Bank of Saint Louis, One Federal Reserve Bank Plaza, Saint Louis, MO, 63102-2005. p. 1270

Whipps, Kimsey, Operations Mgr, University of Mississippi Medical Center, 2500 N State St, Jackson, MS, 39216-4505. Tel: 601-984-1291. p. 1223

Whisenhunt, Joann, County Librn, Montgomery County Library, 145A Whittington St, Mount Ida, AR, 71957-9404. Tel: 870-867-3812. p. 105

Whisler, Laurel, Assoc Dean, Libr & Learning Commons, Bristol Community College, 777 Elsbree St, Fall River, MA, 02720. Tel: 774-357-2062. p. 1017

Whisler, Laurel, Libr Dir, Columbia College, 1301 Columbia College Dr, Columbia, SC, 29203-9987. Tel: 803-786-3877. p. 2053

Whisman, Linda A, Assoc Dean, Libr Serv, Southwestern Law School, Bullock Wilshire Bldg, 1st Flr, 3050 Wilshire Blvd, Los Angeles, CA, 90010. Tel: 213-738-5771. p. 168

Whisner, Mary, Pub Serv Librn, University of Washington Libraries, Gallagher Law Library, William H Gates Hall, 4000 15th Ave NE, Seattle, WA, 98195-3020. Tel: 206-543-7672. p. 2382

Whistance-Smith, Doug, Libr Dir, Drayton Valley Municipal Library, 5120 52nd St, Drayton Valley, AB, T7A 1R7, CANADA. Tel: 780-514-2722. p. 2533

Whitacre, Lee Margaret, Libr Spec, University of Illinois Library at Urbana-Champaign, Architecture & Art Library, 208 Architecture Bldg, 608 E Lorado Taft Dr, Urbana, IL, 61801. Tel: 217-300-6250. p. 655

Whitacre, Lindsay, Asst Dir, Harvard Library, Monroe C Gutman Library, 6 Appian Way, Cambridge, MA, 02138. Tel: 617-495-3453. p. 1006

Whitaker, Alice, Dir, Cherokee Public Library, 118 Church St, Cherokee, AL, 35616. Tel: 256-359-4384. p. 12

Whitaker, Christine, Coll Develop Librn, University of South Carolina, School of Medicine Library, Bldg 101, 6311 Garners Ferry Rd, Columbia, SC, 29209. Tel: 803-216-3200. p. 2056

Whitaker, Courtney, Adminr, Wilderness Coast Public Libraries, 1180 W Washington St, Monticello, FL, 32344. Tel: 850-997-7400. p. 426

Whitaker, Dianne, Br Mgr, Montgomery County Public Libraries, Wheaton Library, 11701 Georgia Ave, Silver Spring, MD, 20902. Tel: 240-777-0686. p. 975

Whitaker, Elizabeth, Library Contact, St John's Medical Center, 625 E Broadway, Jackson, WY, 83001. Tel: 307-739-7370. p. 2495

Whitaker, J Noelene, Librn, Pulaski County Public Library, Nancy Branch, Mills Springs Plaza, Nancy, KY, 42544. Tel: 606-636-4241. p. 875

Whitaker, Jen, Youth Librn, Universal City Public Library, 100 Northview Dr, Universal City, TX, 78148-4150. Tel: 210-659-7048. p. 2250

Whitaker, Leslie, Dir, Richard S & Leah Morris Memorial Library, 605 High St, Claude, TX, 79019. Tel: 806-226-2341. p. 2156

Whitaker, Polly, Ref Serv, Miami University Libraries, Rentschler Library, 1601 University Blvd, Hamilton, OH, 45011. Tel: 513-785-3235. p. 1812

Whitaker, Shannon, Librn, Georgetown Public Library, 102 W West St, Georgetown, IL, 61846. Tel: 217-662-2164. p. 592

Whitaker, Sue, Coll Curator, Worthington Historical Society Library, 50 W New England Ave, Worthington, OH, 43085. Tel: 614-885-1247. p. 1833

Whitcomb, Glenny, Libr Dir, Chilton Public Library, 221 Park St, Chilton, WI, 53014. Tel: 920-849-4414. p. 2427

Whitcomb, Janine, Archives Mgr, University of Massachusetts Lowell Library, Center for Lowell History, Patrick J Mogan Cultural Ctr, 40 French St, Lowell, MA, 01852. Tel: 978-934-4997. p. 1030

Whitcomb, Patricia, Circ, Venice Public Library, 325 Broadway, Venice, IL, 62090. Tel: 618-877-1330. p. 657

White, Alice, Asst Dir, Midland County Public Library, Midland Centennial, 2503 W Loop 250 N, Midland, TX, 79705. Tel: 432-742-7400. p. 2219

White, Amanda, Head, Adult Serv, Shelby County Public Library, 57 W Broadway St, Shelbyville, IN, 46176. Tel: 317-398-7121, 317-835-2653. p. 718

White, Amy, Dir, Lisbon Public Library, 101 E Main St, Lisbon, IA, 52253. Tel: 319-455-2800. p. 766

White, Andrew, Dir, Rensselaer Libraries, Rensselaer Architecture Library, Greene Bldg 308, 3rd Flr, 110 Eighth St, Troy, NY, 12180-3590. Tel: 518-276-8310. p. 1652

White, Andrew W, Univ Librn, Wesleyan University, 252 Church St, Middletown, CT, 06459. Tel: 860-685-2570. p. 322

White, Angela, Br Mgr, Tippecanoe County Public Library, Klondike Branch, 3062 Lindberg Rd, West Lafayette, IN, 47906. Tel: 765-463-5893. p. 701

White, Angie, Bus Mgr, Public Library of Anniston-Calhoun County, 108 E Tenth St, Anniston, AL, 36201. Tel: 256-237-8501. p. 4

White, Ann, Dep Dir, Handley Regional Library System, 100 W Piccadilly St, Winchester, VA, 22601. Tel: 540-662-9041, Ext 25. p. 2354

White, Ann Marie, Libr Dir, Oliver Wolcott Library, 160 South St, Litchfield, CT, 06759-0187. Tel: 860-567-8030. p. 320

White, Anna, Mgr, Baltimore County Public Library, Owings Mills Branch, County Campus Metro Center, 10302 Grand Central Ave, Owings Mills, MD, 21117. Tel: 410-887-2092. p. 980

White, Ayoola, Teen Serv Librn, Maplewood Memorial Library, 129 Boyden Ave, Maplewood, NJ, 07040. Tel: 973-762-1688. p. 1416

White, Barbara, Dep Dir, Akron-Summit County Public Library, 60 S High St, Akron, OH, 44326. Tel: 330-643-9102. p. 1744

White, Becki, Ref (Info Servs), Pottsville Free Public Library, 215 W Market St, Pottsville, PA, 17901. Tel: 570-622-8105, 570-622-8880. p. 1999

White, Brenda Battleson, Dr, Clinical Asst Prof, University at Buffalo, The State University of New York, 534 Baldy Hall, Buffalo, NY, 14260. Tel: 716-645-2412. p. 2789

White, Briana, Youth Serv Librn, Pendleton Public Library, 502 SW Dorion Ave, Pendleton, OR, 97801-1698. Tel: 541-966-0380. p. 1890

White, Brook, Mr, Coll Develop Mgr, Volusia County Public Library, 1290 Indian Lake Rd, Daytona Beach, FL, 32124. Tel: 386-248-1745. p. 392

White, Charity, Dir, Coldwater-Wilmore Regional Library, 221 E Main, Coldwater, KS, 67029. Tel: 620-582-2333. p. 803

White, Cheryl, Libr Assoc II, Quinebaug Valley Community College Library, 742 Upper Maple St, Danielson, CT, 06239. Tel: 860-932-4171. p. 308

White, Chriss, Asst Dir, Centerburg Public Library, 49 E Main St, Centerburg, OH, 43011. Tel: 740-625-6538. p. 1757

White, Christina, Br Librn, Mingo County Library, Matewan Branch, Warm Hollow Rd, Matewan, WV, 25678. Tel: 304-426-6306. p. 2402

White, Christopher, ILL Librn, Syst Librn, The Sage Colleges, 140 New Scotland Ave, Albany, NY, 12208. Tel: 518-244-4521. p. 1483

White, Christopher, Libr Dir, Russell Sage College Libraries, 109 Second St, Troy, NY, 12180. Tel: 518-244-4521. p. 1653

White, Christopher C, Coordr, Libr Serv, Saint Louis Community College, Florissant Valley Campus Library, 3400 Pershall Rd, Ferguson, MO, 63135-1408. Tel: 314-513-4484. p. 1272
White, Cora, Circ, Olympic College, Poulsbo Campus, 1000 Olympic College Pl NW, Poulsbo, WA, 98370. Tel: 360-394-2720. p. 2360
White, Crystal, Exec Dir, Appaloosa Museum & Heritage Center, 2720 W Pullman Rd, Moscow, ID, 83843. Tel: 208-882-5578. p. 526
White, Danita, Info Res Librn, Hampton University, 129 William R Harvey Way, Hampton, VA, 23668. Tel: 757-727-5179. p. 2323
White, Deb, Youth Serv Librn, The Library of Hattiesburg, Petal, Forrest County, 329 Hardy St, Hattiesburg, MS, 39401-3496. Tel: 601-582-4461. p. 1218
White, Diane, Libr Dir, Somerset Public Library, 1464 County St, Somerset, MA, 02726. Tel: 508-646-2829. p. 1053
White, Dianne, Ref Librn, Walsh College, 3838 Livernois Rd, Troy, MI, 48083-5066. Tel: 248-823-1338. p. 1155
White, Dorene, Dir, Massena Public Library, 122 Main, Massena, IA, 50853. Tel: 712-779-3726. p. 769
White, Dottie, Dir, Nutter Fort Library, 1300 Buckhannon Pike, Nutter Fort, WV, 26301-4406. Tel: 304-622-7563. p. 2410
White, Eric, Adult Serv, Estes Valley Library, 335 E Elkhorn Ave, Estes Park, CO, 80517. Tel: 970-586-8116. p. 280
White, Eva, Dir, Crawford County Library System, 1409 Main St, Van Buren, AR, 72956. Tel: 479-471-3226. p. 111
White, Gail, Asst Librn, Valley Public Library, 232 N Spruce St, Valley, NE, 68064. Tel: 402-359-9924. p. 1339
White, Heather, Asst Dir, Libr Engagement Facilitator, East Carolina University, J Y Joyner Library, E Fifth St, Greenville, NC, 27858-4353. Tel: 252-328-2870. p. 1693
White, Holly, Instrul Tech Librn, Luther College, 700 College Dr, Decorah, IA, 52101. Tel: 563-387-1790. p. 745
White, Jacquelyn, Br Mgr, Forsyth County Public Library, Walkertown Branch, 2969 Main St, Walkertown, NC, 27051. Tel: 336-703-2990. p. 1725
White, Jason, Head, Tech Serv, Shelby County Public Library, 57 W Broadway St, Shelbyville, IN, 46176. Tel: 317-398-7121, 317-835-2653. p. 718
White, Jennifer, Dir, Linton Public Library, 95 SE First St, Linton, IN, 47441. Tel: 812-847-7802. p. 703
White, Jenny, Dir, Schuyler Public Library, 108 E 18th St, Schuyler, NE, 68661-1929. Tel: 402-352-2221. p. 1335
White, Jessica, Youth Serv Librn, Spalding Memorial Library, 724 S Main St, Athens, PA, 18810-1010. Tel: 570-888-7117. p. 1908
White, Joanne, Libr Asst, Coastal Pines Technical College, Baxley Learning Resource Center, 1334 Golden Isles Pkwy W, Rm 1110, Baxley, GA, 31513. Tel: 912-367-1700. p. 503
White, John, Dean of Libr, College of Charleston, 205 Calhoun St, Charleston, SC, 29401-3519. Tel: 843-953-5530. p. 2050
White, Karen J, ILL/Ref Librn, Library of Michigan, 702 W Kalamazoo St, Lansing, MI, 48915. Tel: 517-373-2985. p. 1125
White, Karen P, Dir, Elbridge Free Library, 241 E Main St, Elbridge, NY, 13060. Tel: 315-689-7111. p. 1529
White, Kashawna, Mgr, Circ & Br Serv, Laramie County Library System, 2200 Pioneer Ave, Cheyenne, WY, 82001-3610. Tel: 307-773-7210. p. 2492
White, Keisha, Presch Outreach Plus Mgr, Rapides Parish Library, Westside Regional, 5416 Provine Pl, Alexandria, LA, 71303. Tel: 318-442-2483, Ext 1905. p. 880
White, Kelvin, PhD, Dr, Assoc Prof, University of Oklahoma, Bizzell Memorial Library, 401 W Brooks, Rm 120, Norman, OK, 73019-6032. Tel: 405-325-3921. p. 2791
White, Kitty, Asst Librn, Van Zandt County Sarah Norman Library, 317 First Monday Lane, Canton, TX, 75103. Tel: 903-567-4276. p. 2152
White, Kyle, Br Mgr, Cabarrus County Public Library, 27 Union St N, Concord, NC, 28025. Tel: 704-920-2050. p. 1682
White, Lauren, Dir, Ruth Culver Community Library, 540 Water St, Prairie du Sac, WI, 53578. Tel: 608-643-8318. p. 2471
White, Laurie, ILL, Ela Area Public Library District, 275 Mohawk Trail, Lake Zurich, IL, 60047. Tel: 847-438-3433. p. 607
White, Leah, Dir of Organizational Dev, Skokie Public Library, 5215 Oakton St, Skokie, IL, 60077-3680. Tel: 847-673-7774. p. 647
White, Lely, Head, Cat, University of Dallas, 1845 E Northgate Dr, Irving, TX, 75062-4736. Tel: 972-721-5310. p. 2203
White, Lena, Dir, Buna Public Library, 1042 Hwy 62 S, Buna, TX, 77612. Tel: 409-994-5501. p. 2151
White, Linda, Cat, Keyano College Library, 8115 Franklin Ave, Fort McMurray, AB, T9H 2H7, CANADA. Tel: 780-791-4916. p. 2540
White, Lisa, Library Contact, Multnomah County Library, Albina, 3605 NE 15th Ave, Portland, OR, 97212. p. 1892
White, Lisa, Literacy Serv, Amarillo Public Library, 413 E Fourth Ave, Amarillo, TX, 79101. Tel: 806-378-3054. p. 2134
White, Lori, Librn, Northeast Alabama Community College, 138 Alabama Hwy 35, Rainsville, AL, 35986. Tel: 256-228-6001, Ext 2326. p. 34
White, Lynnda, Circ, Reserves, Florida Gateway College, 149 SE College Pl, Lake City, FL, 32025-2006. Tel: 386-754-4400. p. 415
White, M, Br Mgr, Tacoma Public Library, Moore Branch, 215 S 56th St, Tacoma, WA, 98408. Tel: 253-280-2930. p. 2387
White, Margaret, City Librn, Libr Mgr, Douglas Public Library, 560 E Tenth St, Douglas, AZ, 85607. Tel: 520-417-7352. p. 59
White, Meghan, Events & Outreach, Blue Island Public Library, 2433 York St, Blue Island, IL, 60406-2011. Tel: 708-388-1078, Ext 30. p. 543
White, Michael, Actg Head Librn, Queen's University, Engineering & Science Library, Douglas Library, 93 University Ave, Kingston, ON, K7L 5C4, CANADA. Tel: 613-533-6000, Ext 36785. p. 2651
White, Missi, Br Mgr, Carbon County Library System, Sinclair Branch, 604 Lincoln St, Sinclair, WY, 82334. Tel: 307-328-5299. p. 2498
White, Missi, Circ Mgr, Carbon County Library System, 215 W Buffalo St, Rawlins, WY, 82301. Tel: 307-328-2618. p. 2498
White, Nadine, Pub Serv Librn, Whistler Public Library, 4329 Main St, Whistler, BC, V8E 1B2, CANADA. Tel: 604-935-8433. p. 2584
White, Nancy, Mgr, User Serv, Winthrop University, 824 Oakland Ave, Rock Hill, SC, 29733. Tel: 803-323-2335. p. 2068
White, Nicole, Dir, Esmeralda County Public Libraries, Ten Montezuma St, Silverpeak, NV, 89047. Tel: 775-937-2215. p. 1351
White, Nicole M, Br Mgr, Santa Fe Public Library, Southside Branch Library, 6599 Jaguar Dr, Santa Fe, NM, 85707. Tel: 505-955-2822. p. 1477
White, Nina, Dir, Milford District Library, Two S Grant Ave, Milford, IL, 60953-1399. Tel: 815-889-4722. p. 617
White, Nina, Youth Serv Coordr, James V Brown Library of Williamsport & Lycoming County, 19 E Fourth St, Williamsport, PA, 17701. Tel: 570-326-0536. p. 2023
White, Pam, Asst Br Mgr, Chesterfield County Public Library, Meadowdale, 4301 Meadowdale Blvd, Richmond, VA, 23234. Tel: 804-751-2275. p. 2312
White, Pamela, Br Mgr, Shreve Memorial Library, Hollywood/Union Avenue, 2105 Hollywood Ave, Shreveport, LA, 71108. Tel: 318-636-5520. p. 909
White, Phoebe, Br Librn, Reynolds County Library District, Oates Branch, 8483 Hwy J, Black, MO, 63625. Tel: 573-269-1117. p. 1241
White, Rebecca, Dir, Clermont Public Library, 503 Larabee St, Clermont, IA, 52135. Tel: 563-423-7286. p. 740
White, Rebecca, Archivist, Dir, Pease Public Library, One Russell St, Plymouth, NH, 03264-1414. Tel: 603-536-2616. p. 1378
White, Robb, Tech Ctr Supvr, Lebanon Public Library, 101 S Broadway, Lebanon, OH, 45036. Tel: 513-932-2665. p. 1795
White, Robin, Chairperson, Oglala Lakota College, Nursing College Center, PO Box 861, Pine Ridge, SD, 57770. Tel: 605-867-5856. p. 2078
White, Robyn, Circ Supvr, Waco-McLennan County Library System, 1717 Austin Ave, Waco, TX, 76701-1794. Tel: 254-750-5947. p. 2254
White, Ruth, Mgr, Tri-County Regional Library, Dierks Public Library, 202 W Third St, Dierks, AR, 71833. Tel: 870-286-3228. p. 106
White, Sara, ILL Assoc, Traverse Des Sioux Library Cooperative, 1400 Madison Ave, Ste 622, Mankato, MN, 56001-5488. Tel: 833-837-5422. p. 1181
White, Sarah Beth, Ref Librn, Virginia Highlands Community College Library, 100 VHCC Dr, Abingdon, VA, 24210. Tel: 276-739-2542. p. 2301
White, Sarah Beth, Instruction & Res Serv Librn, Roanoke College, 220 High St, Salem, VA, 24153-3794. Tel: 540-375-2295. p. 2347
White, Scott, Chief Librn, Fiorello H LaGuardia Community College Library, 31-10 Thomson Ave, Long Island City, NY, 11101. Tel: 718-482-5421. p. 1565
White, Susan, Circ Serv Coordr, West Florida Public Library, 239 N Spring St, Pensacola, FL, 32502. Tel: 850-436-5060. p. 437
White, Suzanne, Dir, Catawba County Library, 115 West C St, Newton, NC, 28658. Tel: 828-465-8664. p. 1706
White Thunder, Ellen, Asst Archivist, Oglala Lakota College, Three Mile Creek Rd, Kyle, SD, 57752. Tel: 605-455-6063. p. 2077
White, Tim, Head, Adult Serv, Worth Public Library District, 6917 W 111th St, Worth, IL, 60482. Tel: 708-448-2855. p. 665
White, Todd, Asst Prof, Electronic Res, Head Ref Librn, The College of Saint Scholastica Library, 1200 Kenwood Ave, Duluth, MN, 55811-4199. Tel: 218-723-6140. p. 1171
White, Tony, Univ Librn, OCAD University, Bldg MCC, 2nd Flr, 113 McCaul St, Toronto, ON, M5T 1W1, CANADA. Tel: 416-977-6000, Ext 348. p. 2690
White, Trenita, Tech Serv Librn, Santa Fe College, 3000 NW 83rd St, Bldg Y, Gainesville, FL, 32606. Tel: 352-395-5771. p. 407
White, Ustadza, Tech Serv Mgr, Yavapai College Library, 1100 E Sheldon St, Bldg 3, Prescott, AZ, 86301. Tel: 928-776-2264. p. 74
White, Valerie, Youth Serv Spec, Canton Free Library, Eight Park St, Canton, NY, 13617. Tel: 315-386-3712. p. 1513
White, Vicky, YA Librn, West Springfield Public Library, 200 Park St, West Springfield, MA, 01089. Tel: 413-736-4561. p. 1066
White, Wendy, Dir, Libr Serv, Craven Community College, 800 College Ct, New Bern, NC, 28562. Tel: 252-638-7272. p. 1705
White, William, Dir, Troy Public Library, 500 E Walnut St, Troy, AL, 36081. Tel: 334-566-1314. p. 37
White, Zeke, Mgr, Baltimore County Public Library, Woodlawn Branch, 1811 Woodlawn Dr, Baltimore, MD, 21207-4074. Tel: 410-887-1336. p. 980
White-Busby, Shawna L, Br Mgr, Latimer County Public Library, 301 W Ada Ave, Wilburton, OK, 74578. Tel: 918-465-3751. p. 1869

White-Farnham, Jamie, Libr Dir, University of Wisconsin-Superior, 907 N 19th St, Superior, WI, 54880. Tel: 715-394-8201. p. 2480
White-Sellards, Phyllis, Libr Assoc, Marshall University Libraries, One John Marshall Dr, Huntington, WV, 25755-2060. Tel: 304-696-2320. p. 2405
Whiteaker, Shaun, Dir, Washington County Public Library, 333 W Main St, Springfield, KY, 40069. Tel: 859-336-7655. p. 875
Whited, Jon, Mgr, Info Tech, Bloomington Public Library, 205 E Olive St, Bloomington, IL, 61701. Tel: 309-828-6091. p. 543
Whitefield, Andrew, Br Supvr, Wellington County Library, Hillsburgh Branch, Nine Station St, Hillsburgh, ON, N0G 1Z0, CANADA. Tel: 519-855-4010. p. 2641
Whitehair, Alesha, Dir, Taylor County Public Library, 200 Beech St, Grafton, WV, 26354. Tel: 304-265-6121. p. 2403
Whitehead, Brad, Serials & Database Librarian, Midlands Technical College Library, 1260 Lexington Dr, West Columbia, SC, 29170-2176. Tel: 803-822-3535. p. 2072
Whitehead, Jennifer, Head, Children's Servx, Clapp Memorial Library, 19 S Main St, Belchertown, MA, 01007. Tel: 413-323-0417. p. 988
Whitehead, Julie, Ref Librn, Dixon Homestead Library, 180 Washington Ave, Dumont, NJ, 07628. Tel: 201-384-2030. p. 1399
Whitehead, Leslie, Asst Librn, Bevill State Community College, 2631 Temple Ave N, Fayette, AL, 35555. Tel: 205-932-3221, Ext 5141. p. 16
Whitehead, Marcia, Libr, Humanities & Soc Sci, University of Richmond, 261 Richmond Way, Richmond, VA, 23173. Tel: 804-289-8823. p. 2342
Whitehead, Martha, Univ Librn, Harvard Library, Wadsworth House, 1341 Massachusetts Ave, Cambridge, MA, 02138. Tel: 617-495-3650. p. 1005
Whitehead, Michael, Teen Serv Librn, Simi Valley Library, 2969 Tapo Canyon Rd, Simi Valley, CA, 93063. Tel: 805-526-1735. p. 246
Whitehead, Sola, Chief Librn, Portland VA Medical Center Library, 3710 SW US Veterans Hospital Rd, P6LIB, Portland, OR, 97239-2964. Tel: 503-220-8262, Ext 55955. p. 1894
Whitehill, Bobbi, Youth Serv Librn, Lied Public Library, 100 E Garfield St, Clarinda, IA, 51632. Tel: 712-542-2416. p. 740
Whitehorn, Lexi, Dir, Mayville Public Library, 52 Center Ave N, Mayville, ND, 58257. Tel: 701-788-3388. p. 1737
Whitehorn, Stanley, Head, Library Facilities, University of Mississippi, One Library Loop, University, MS, 38677. Tel: 662-915-7935. p. 1234
Whitehurst, Kellen, Head of Br Serv, East Albemarle Regional Library, 100 E Colonial Ave, Elizabeth City, NC, 27909. Tel: 252-335-2511. p. 1687
Whitehurst, Kellen, Dir, Pasquotank County Library, 100 E Colonial Ave, Elizabeth City, NC, 27909. Tel: 252-335-2473. p. 1687
Whiteing, Dhana, Libr Mgr, Community Libraries of Providence, Mt Pleasant Library, 315 Academy Ave, Providence, RI, 02908. Tel: 401-272-0106. p. 2038
Whiteman, Michael, Assoc Dean of Libr, Dir, Law Libr, University of Cincinnati, 2540 Clifton Ave, Cincinnati, OH, 45219. Tel: 513-556-0163. p. 1764
Whiteman, Teresa, Br Librn, Southeast Regional Library, Pangman Branch, 120 Mergen St, Pangman, SK, S0C 2C0, CANADA. Tel: 306-442-2119. p. 2754
Whitemore, Wendy, Adminr, Seltzer, Caplan, McMahon, Vitek, 750 B St, Ste 2100, San Diego, CA, 92101. Tel: 619-685-3009. p. 222
Whitesell, David, Curator, University of Virginia, Albert & Shirley Small Special Collections Library, 170 McCormick Rd, Charlottesville, VA, 22904. Tel: 434-243-1776. p. 2310
Whitesell, Melissa, Libr Dir, Dalton State College, 650 College Dr, Dalton, GA, 30720-3778. Tel: 706-272-4585. p. 474
Whiteside, Alice, Head of Libr, University of North Carolina at Chapel Hill, Joseph Curtis Sloane Art Library, 102 Hanes Art Ctr, CB 3405, Chapel Hill, NC, 27599-3405. Tel: 919-962-2397. p. 1679
Whiteside, Ann, Dir, Harvard Library, Frances Loeb Library, Harvard Graduate School of Design, 48 Quincy St, Gund Hall, Cambridge, MA, 02138. Tel: 617-495-9163. p. 1007
Whiteside, Dennis, Evening Coordr, ILL, City Colleges of Chicago, Malcolm X College - Carter G Woodson Library, 1900 W Jackson St, 2nd Flr, Chicago, IL, 60612. Tel: 312-850-7244. p. 558
Whiteside, Phyllis, Med Librn, United States Army, Irwin Army Community Hospital Medical Library, CDR USAMEDDAC-Med Libr, 600 Caisson Hill Rd, Fort Riley, KS, 66442-7037. Tel: 785-239-7874. p. 808
Whitesides, Robert, Dir, Shenandoah County Library, 514 Stoney Creek Blvd, Edinburg, VA, 22824. Tel: 540-984-8200, Ext 206. p. 2315
Whitesitt, Wendy, Libr Serv Mgr, McMinnville Public Library, 225 NW Adams St, McMinnville, OR, 97128. Tel: 503-435-5562. p. 1886
Whitfield, Bill, Archivist, Ravalli County Museum, 205 Bedford St, Hamilton, MT, 59840. Tel: 406-363-3338. p. 1295
Whitfield, Jan, Assoc Dir, Coll Develop, Fayetteville State University, 1200 Murchison Rd, Fayetteville, NC, 28301-4298. Tel: 910-672-1520. p. 1689
Whitfield, Kevin, Cat Librn, Youngstown State University, One University Plaza, Youngstown, OH, 44555-0001. Tel: 330-941-2922. p. 1836
Whitfield, Martin, Dep Dir, Mgt Serv, Phoenix Public Library, 1221 N Central Ave, Phoenix, AZ, 85004. Tel: 602-262-4636. p. 72
Whitfield, Sharon, Dr, Librn, Rider University, 2083 Lawrenceville Rd, Lawrenceville, NJ, 08648. p. 1411
Whitford, Adam, Actg Curator, Library Contact, Southern Alberta Art Gallery Library, 601 Third Ave S, Lethbridge, AB, T1J 0H4, CANADA. Tel: 403-327-8770, Ext 23. p. 2546
Whitford, Michelle, Dir, Hepburn Library of Edwards, 205 Main St, Edwards, NY, 13635. Tel: 315-562-3521. p. 1529
Whitham, Crystal, Librn, Allegheny Wesleyan College Library, 2161 Woodsdale Rd, Salem, OH, 44460. Tel: 330-337-6403, Ext 302. p. 1819
Whithaus, Rhonda, Electronic Res, University of Missouri-Columbia, Elmer Ellis Library, 104 Ellis Library, Columbia, MO, 65201-5149. Tel: 573-882-9164. p. 1243
Whiting, Peter, Scholarly Communications Librn, University of Southern Indiana, 8600 University Blvd, Evansville, IN, 47712. Tel: 812-465-1280. p. 682
Whitledge, Bryan, Archives Mgr, Central Michigan University, Clarke Historical Library, 250 E Preston, Mount Pleasant, MI, 48859. Tel: 989-774-2159. p. 1135
Whitley, Betsy, Ref & Instruction Librn, Dalton State College, 650 College Dr, Dalton, GA, 30720-3778. Tel: 706-272-4527. p. 474
Whitlock, Brandy, Instrul Serv Librn, Anne Arundel Community College, 101 College Pkwy, Arnold, MD, 21012-1895. Tel: 410-777-2211. p. 951
Whitlock, Carrie, Tech Serv Librn, Staunton Public Library, One Churchville Ave, Staunton, VA, 24401. Tel: 540-332-3902, Ext 4229. p. 2347
Whitlow, Michael, Ref Librn, University of Denver, Westminster Law Library, Sturm College of Law, 2255 E Evans Ave, Denver, CO, 80208. Tel: 303-871-6206. p. 278
Whitlow, Tammy, Mgr, Tri-County Regional Library, Foreman Public Library, 216 Schumann St, Foreman, AR, 71836. Tel: 870-542-7409. p. 106
Whitman, Connie, Asst Dir, Greene County Public Library, 120 N 12th St, Paragould, AR, 72450. Tel: 870-236-8711. p. 107
Whitman, Deirdre, City Librn, Watertown Regional Library, 160 Sixth St NE, Watertown, SD, 57201-2778. Tel: 605-882-6220. p. 2085
Whitmarsh, Fred, Br Mgr, Markham Public Library, Unionville Branch, 15 Library Lane, Unionville, ON, L3R 5C4, CANADA. Tel: 905-513-7977, Ext 5551. p. 2656
Whitmer, Sandra, Dir, Warrenville Public Library District, 28 W 751 Stafford Pl, Warrenville, IL, 60555. Tel: 630-393-1171. p. 659
Whitmill, Clint, Librn, Milton Public Library, 422 N Main St, Milton, IA, 52570. Tel: 641-656-4611. p. 770
Whitmire, Amanda L, Bibliographer, Head Librn, Stanford University Libraries, Harold A Miller Marine Biology Library, Hopkins Marine Sta, 120 Ocean View Blvd, Pacific Grove, CA, 93950-3094. Tel: 831-655-6228, 831-655-6229. p. 249
Whitmire, Dana, Electronic Res Librn, University of Texas Health Science Center at San Antonio Libraries, 7703 Floyd Curl Dr, MSC 7940, San Antonio, TX, 78229-3900. Tel: 210-567-2450. p. 2240
Whitmire, Emily, Br Mgr, Oconee County Public Library, Seneca Branch, 300 E South Second St, Seneca, SC, 29678. Tel: 864-882-4855. p. 2072
Whitmore, Emily, Asst Head, Circ Serv, Mount Prospect Public Library, Ten S Emerson St, Mount Prospect, IL, 60056. Tel: 847-253-5675. p. 621
Whitmore, Emily, Libr Dir, Spring Green Community Library, 230 E Monroe St, Spring Green, WI, 53588-8035. Tel: 608-588-2276. p. 2478
Whitmore, Gregory, Admin Technologies Librarian, University of Virginia, Arthur J Morris Law Library, 580 Massie Rd, Charlottesville, VA, 22903-1738. Tel: 434-924-4674. p. 2310
Whitmore, Keri, Asst Dir, Franklin Public Library, 9151 W Loomis Rd, Franklin, WI, 53132. Tel: 414-427-7548. p. 2436
Whitmore, Marcella, Br Mgr, Washington County Free Library, Leonard P Snyder Memorial, 12624 Broadfording Rd, Clear Spring, MD, 21722. Tel: 301-842-2730. p. 968
Whitmore, Tiffany, Br Mgr, Riverside Regional Library, Oran Branch, 120 Mountain St, Oran, MO, 63771. Tel: 573-262-3745. p. 1252
Whitney, Amy, Br Adminr, Frederick County Public Libraries, Emmitsburg Branch, 300-A S Seton Ave, Unit 2 J, Emmitsburg, MD, 21727. Tel: 301-600-7201. p. 966
Whitney, Amy, Br Adminr, Frederick County Public Libraries, Thurmont Regional Library, 76 E Moser Rd, Thurmont, MD, 21788. Tel: 301-600-7201. p. 966
Whitney, Christine, Librn, Des Moines Area Community College, 1125 Hancock Dr, Boone, IA, 50036-5326. Tel: 515-433-5043. p. 735
Whitney, Hilley, Head, Access Serv, Oklahoma State University Libraries, Athletic Ave, 216, Stillwater, OK, 74078. Tel: 405-744-9775. p. 1862
Whitney, Lisa, Br Head, Henderson County Public Library, Fletcher Branch, 120 Library Rd, Fletcher, NC, 28732. Tel: 828-687-1218. p. 1695
Whitney, Mechelle, Coll Develop, East Baton Rouge Parish Library, 7711 Goodwood Blvd, Baton Rouge, LA, 70806-7625. Tel: 225-231-3700. p. 882
Whitney, Missy, Librn, Albany Public Library, 302 S Main St, Albany, IL, 61230. Tel: 309-887-4193. p. 535
Whitney, Rebecca, Libr Dir, Somersworth Public Library, 25 Main St, Somersworth, NH, 03878-3198. Tel: 603-692-4587. p. 1381
Whitney, Tracy, Libr Mgr, Marion Public Library, 4036 Maple Ave, Marion, NY, 14505. Tel: 315-926-4933. p. 1569

Whiton, Tim, Libr Dir, Washburn Memorial Library, 1290 Main St, Washburn, ME, 04786. Tel: 207-455-4814. p. 944

Whitsitt, Kathleen, Authority Control Librn, Lone Star College System, 20515 State Hwy 249, Bldg 11, Rm 11437, Houston, TX, 77070-2607. Tel: 281-290-2842. p. 2196

Whitt, Bridgette, Distance Instruction Librn, Morehead State University, 150 University Blvd, Morehead, KY, 40351. Tel: 606-783-5287. p. 869

Whitt, Bridgette, Acq Librn, University of Tennessee at Martin, Ten Wayne Fisher Dr, Martin, TN, 38238. Tel: 731-881-7079. p. 2111

Whitt, James, Library Contact, Eastern Kentucky Correctional Complex Library, 200 Road to Justice, West Liberty, KY, 41472. Tel: 606-743-2800, Ext 2855. p. 876

Whitt, Julie, Human Res Mgr, Upper Arlington Public Library, 2800 Tremont Rd, Columbus, OH, 43221. Tel: 614-486-9621. p. 1778

Whitt, Kathleen, Dir, Upper Sandusky Community Library, 301 N Sandusky Ave, Upper Sandusky, OH, 43351-1139. Tel: 419-294-1345. p. 1826

Whittaker, Beth M, Head of Libr, University of Kansas Libraries, Spencer Research Library, 1450 Poplar Lane, Lawrence, KS, 66045-7616. Tel: 785-864-4275. p. 820

Whittaker, Carol, Archivist/Ref Librn, Delta College Library, 1961 Delta Rd, University Center, MI, 48710. Tel: 989-686-9006. p. 1155

Whittaker, Judith, Dir, Ellington Farman Library, 760 Thornten Rd, Ellington, NY, 14732. Tel: 716-287-2945. p. 1530

Whitted, John, Librn, Virginia University of Lynchburg, 2058 Garfield Ave, Lynchburg, VA, 24501. Tel: 434-528-5276. p. 2331

Whittemore, Gail, Ref Librn, Pace University, 78 N Broadway, White Plains, NY, 10603. Tel: 914-422-4273. p. 1665

Whittemore, Lory, Br Mgr, New Tecumseth Public Library, Pam Kirkpatrick Branch, 139 Queen St N, Tottenham, ON, L0G 1W0, CANADA. Tel: 905-936-2291. p. 2628

Whitten, Kit, Archivist/Librn, Carnegie Observatories, 813 Santa Barbara St, Pasadena, CA, 91101. Tel: 626-304-0228. p. 193

Whitten, Rebecca E, Librn, Bevill State Community College, Irma D Nicholson Library, Jasper Campus, 1411 Indiana Ave, Jasper, AL, 35501. Tel: 205-387-0511, Ext 5748. p. 17

Whitten, Tyler, Libr Dir, Auburn Public Library, 749 E Thach Ave, Auburn, AL, 36830. Tel: 334-501-3190. p. 5

Whittenmore, Lory, Br Mgr, New Tecumseth Public Library, D A Jones Branch, 42 Main St W, Beeton, ON, L0G 1A0, CANADA. Tel: 905-729-3726. p. 2628

Whittingham, Amy, Tech Librn, Genaire Ltd Library, 468 Niagara Stone Rd, Unit D, Niagara-on-the-Lake, ON, L0S 1J0, CANADA. Tel: 905-684-1165. p. 2661

Whittingham, Rachel, Libr Dir, Central Baptist College, 1501 College Ave, Conway, AR, 72034. Tel: 501-205-8878. p. 92

Whittington, Blair, Librn Spec, Glendale Library, Arts & Culture, Brand Library & Art Center, 1601 W Mountain St, Glendale, CA, 91201. Tel: 818-548-2050. p. 148

Whittington, Emily, Adminr, McManus & Felsen LLP, 1990 M St, Ste 600, Washington, DC, 20005. Tel: 202-296-9260. p. 371

Whittington, Lea, Assoc Dir, Tech Serv, Academy of Motion Picture Arts & Sciences, 333 S La Cienega Blvd, Beverly Hills, CA, 90211. Tel: 310-247-3000, Ext 2223. p. 124

Whittington, Linda, Asst Librn, Vinalhaven Public Library, Six Carver St, Vinalhaven, ME, 04863. Tel: 207-863-4401. p. 944

Whittington, Mariea Daniell, Exec Dir, Fuller Theological Seminary, 135 N Oakland Ave, Pasadena, CA, 91182. Tel: 626-584-5218. p. 193

Whittington-Hudspith, Renae, Libr Assoc, Ellsworth Community College, 1100 College Ave, Iowa Falls, IA, 50126-1199. Tel: 641-648-8560. p. 761

Whittle, Ashley, Interim Head, Spec Coll & Archives, University of North Carolina at Asheville, One University Heights, Ramsey Library, CPO 1500, Asheville, NC, 28804. Tel: 828-251-6645. p. 1673

Whittle, Augusta, Ad, Robert L F Sikes Public Library, 1445 Commerce Dr, Crestview, FL, 32539. Tel: 850-682-4432. p. 391

Whittle, Holly, Youth Librn, Elko-Lander-Eureka County Library System, 720 Court St, Elko, NV, 89801. Tel: 775-738-3066. p. 1344

Whittle, Susan S, Dir, Southwest Georgia Regional Library, 301 S Monroe St, Bainbridge, GA, 39819. Tel: 229-248-2665. p. 467

Whitton, Christie Carnahan, Asst Dir, Peabody Public Library, 1160 E State Rd 205, Columbia City, IN, 46725. Tel: 260-244-5541. p. 676

Whitton, Jesse, Archivist, Coordr, User Serv, Indiana University East Campus Library, Hayes Hall, 2325 Chester Blvd, Richmond, IN, 47374. Tel: 765-973-8309. p. 715

Whitwell, Kasey, Admin Coordr, Norfolk County Public Library, 46 Colborne St S, Simcoe, ON, N3Y 4H3, CANADA. Tel: 519-426-3506, Ext 1258. p. 2678

Whitworth, Candi, Exec Dir, Beaverhead County Museum Research Library, 15 S Montana St, Dillon, MT, 59725. Tel: 406-683-5027. p. 1292

Wiant, Julie, Exec Dir, Spring City Free Public Library, 245 Broad St, Spring City, PA, 19475-1702. Tel: 610-948-4130. p. 2009

Wichlacz, Stephanie, Pub Serv Librn, Youth Serv Librn, Virginia Public Library, 215 Fifth Ave S, Virginia, MN, 55792-2642. Tel: 218-748-7525. p. 1206

Wichman, Emily, Br Mgr, Clermont County Public Library, Bethel Branch, 611 W Plane St, Bethel, OH, 45106-1302. Tel: 513-734-2619. p. 1803

Wichman, Emily, Br Mgr, Clermont County Public Library, Williamsburg Branch, 594 Main St, Williamsburg, OH, 45176. Tel: 513-724-1070. p. 1803

Wichterman, Drew, Ad, Tipp City Public Library, 11 E Main St, Tipp City, OH, 45371. Tel: 937-667-3826. p. 1823

Wick, Amanda, Archivist, University of Minnesota Libraries-Twin Cities, Charles Babbage Institute, 211 Elmer L Andersen Library, 222 21st Ave S, Minneapolis, MN, 55455. Tel: 612-624-5050. p. 1185

Wick, Chris, Dir, Clermont County Public Library, 5920 Buckwheat Rd, Milford, OH, 45150. Tel: 513-732-2736. p. 1802

Wick, Michael, Dir, Burlington Public Library, 22 Sears St, Burlington, MA, 01803. Tel: 781-270-1690. p. 1003

Wick, Michael, Ref (Info Servs), Peabody Institute Library, 82 Main St, Peabody, MA, 01960-5553. Tel: 978-531-0100. p. 1045

Wick, Ryan, Info Tech, Oregon State University Libraries, Special Collections & Archives Research Center, 121 The Valley Library, 5th Flr, Corvallis, OR, 97331. Tel: 541-737-2075. p. 1877

Wick, Tiffanie, Dir, Libr Serv, Electronic Res Librn, Western Colorado University, One Western Way, Gunnison, CO, 81231. Tel: 970-943-2477. p. 285

Wicke, Heather, Libr Dir, Brandywine Community Library, 60 Tower Dr, Topton, PA, 19562-1301. Tel: 610-682-7115. p. 2013

Wickenheiser, Diane, Libr Mgr, Hays Public Library, 210 Second Ave, Hays, AB, T0K 1B0, CANADA. Tel: 403-725-3744. p. 2542

Wickens, Danita, Tech Serv Coordr, University of Jamestown, 6070 College Lane, Jamestown, ND, 58405-0001. Tel: 701-252-3467. p. 1736

Wicker, Kelsey, Asst Dir, Cardington-Lincoln Public Library, 128 E Main St, Cardington, OH, 43315. Tel: 419-864-8181. p. 1756

Wicker, Marci, Pub Serv Librn, University of Mississippi, 481 Chuckie Mullins Dr, University, MS, 38677. Tel: 662-915-6824. p. 1234

Wickers, Donna, Head, Circ, Harborfields Public Library, 31 Broadway, Greenlawn, NY, 11740. Tel: 631-757-4200. p. 1541

Wickes, Elizabeth, Lecturer, University of Illinois at Urbana-Champaign, Library & Information Science Bldg, 501 E Daniel St, Champaign, IL, 61820-6211. Tel: 217-333-3280. p. 2784

Wickett, Karen, Asst Prof, University of Illinois at Urbana-Champaign, Library & Information Science Bldg, 501 E Daniel St, Champaign, IL, 61820-6211. Tel: 217-333-3280. p. 2784

Wickett, Michele, Youth Serv Librn, Harrington Public Library, 110 E Center St, Harrington, DE, 19952. Tel: 302-398-4647. p. 353

Wickett, Sarah, Head of Libr, Queen's University, Bracken Health Sciences Library, Botterell Hall, Ground Flr, 18 Stuart St, Kingston, ON, K7L 3N6, CANADA. Tel: 613-533-6000, Ext 77078. p. 2651

Wickham, Kathy, Library Contact, Florida State University Libraries, John A Degen Resource Room, 239 Fine Arts Bldg, 540 W Call St, Rm 204, Tallahassee, FL, 32306-1160. Tel: 850-645-7247. p. 447

Wickham, Mary, Youth Programmer, La Grange Association Library, 1110 Route 55, 2nd Flr, LaGrangeville, NY, 12540. Tel: 845-452-3141. p. 1561

Wickham, Meredith, Dir, First Regional Library, 370 W Commerce St, Hernando, MS, 38632. Tel: 662-429-4439. p. 1219

Wickman, Donald, Librn, Essex County Historical Society / Adirondack History Museum, 7590 Court St, Elizabethtown, NY, 12932. Tel: 518-873-6466. p. 1529

Wicks, Emily, Dir, Chouteau County Library, 1518 Main St, Fort Benton, MT, 59442. Tel: 406-622-5222. p. 1293

Wicks, Stacy, Libr Adminr, Ohio Department of Rehabilitation & Correction, 1980 W Broad St, Columbus, OH, 43223. Tel: 419-726-7977, Ext 62247. p. 1774

Wicksall, Stacey, Dir, Macedon Public Library, 30 Main St, Macedon, NY, 14502-9101. Tel: 315-986-5932. p. 1566

Wickwire, Peggy, Ch, Canby Public Library, 220 NE Second Ave, Canby, OR, 97013-3732. Tel: 503-266-3394. p. 1875

Widdoes, Sheryl, Board Secretary, O'Brien Memorial Library, 51771 Blue River Dr, Blue River, OR, 97413. p. 1874

Widener, Mike, Rare Bk Librn, Yale University Library, Lillian Goldman Library Yale Law School, 127 Wall St, New Haven, CT, 06511. Tel: 203-432-4494. p. 328

Wider, Eve, Dir, University of Pittsburgh at Greensburg, Greensburg Campus, 150 Finoli Dr, Greensburg, PA, 15601-5804. Tel: 724-836-9688. p. 1938

Widera, Adam, Ref Librn, Finger Lakes Community College, 3325 Marvin Sands Dr, Canandaigua, NY, 14424-8405. Tel: 585-785-1371. p. 1512

Widger, Sarah, Head, Circ, Bozeman Public Library, 626 E Main St, Bozeman, MT, 59715. Tel: 406-582-2400. p. 1289

Widhalm, Mary Beth, Pub Serv Librn, Westbank Community Library District, 1309 Westbank Dr, Austin, TX, 78746. Tel: 512-327-3045. p. 2143

Widi, Karen, Librn, Skidmore, Owings & Merrill Library, 224 S Michigan Ave, Ste 1000, Chicago, IL, 60604. Tel: 312-554-9090, Ext 4660. p. 568

Widler, Stephanie, Librn, Enterprise Public Library, 202 S Factory, Enterprise, KS, 67441. Tel: 785-263-8351. p. 807

Widmer, Barbara, Ch, Wolfeboro Public Library, 259 S Main St, Wolfeboro, NH, 03894. Tel: 603-569-2428. p. 1384

Widmer, Jessica, Dep Dir, Operations, Pierce County Library System, Key Center, 8905 Key Peninsula Hwy NW, Lakebay, WA, 98349. Tel: 253-548-3309. p. 2386

Wilcox, Sallie, Patient Educ Librn, Bellevue Medical Library, Patients Library, 462 First Ave & 27th St, New York, NY, 10016. Tel: 212-263-8925. p. 1580

Wilcox, Taylor, Teen Librn, Waupaca Area Public Library, 107 S Main St, Waupaca, WI, 54981-1521. Tel: 715-258-4414. p. 2485

Wilcox, Tom, Ad, Leesburg Public Library, 100 E Main St, Leesburg, FL, 34748. Tel: 352-728-9790. p. 418

Wilczek, Keely, Mgr, User Serv, Harvard Library, John F Kennedy School of Government Library, 79 John F Kennedy St, Cambridge, MA, 02138. Tel: 617-495-1300. p. 1007

Wilczek, Nick, County Librn, Nevada County Community Library, 980 Helling Way, Nevada City, CA, 95959. Tel: 530-265-7050. p. 182

Wild, Elizabeth, Dir, Henry Public Library, 702 Front St, Henry, IL, 61537. Tel: 309-364-2516. p. 598

Wild, Judith, Assoc Librn, Tech Serv, Brooklyn College Library, 2900 Bedford Ave, Brooklyn, NY, 11210. Tel: 718-951-5426. p. 1501

Wild, Kimberley, Circ Librn, Herrin City Library, 120 N 13th St, Herrin, IL, 62948-3233. Tel: 618-942-6109. p. 598

Wild, Larry C, Cataloger, Judson University, 1151 N State St, Elgin, IL, 60123. Tel: 847-628-2030. p. 584

Wilde, Amber, Dir, Grace Balloch Memorial Library, 625 N Fifth St, Spearfish, SD, 57783. Tel: 605-642-1330. p. 2083

Wilde, Candace, Dir, Brownville-Glen Park Library, 216 Brown Blvd, Brownville, NY, 13615. Tel: 315-788-7889. p. 1507

Wilde, Jonah, Coordr, Rainbow Resource Centre Library, 545 Broadway, Winnipeg, MB, R3C 0W3, CANADA. Tel: 204-474-0212. p. 2594

Wilde, Michelle, Interim Head, Research & Community Engagement, Colorado State University Libraries, Morgan Library, 1201 Center Ave Mall, Fort Collins, CO, 80523. Tel: 970-491-1838. p. 280

Wilden, Rebecca, Asst Dir, Bucyrus Public Library, 200 E Mansfield St, Bucyrus, OH, 44820-2381. Tel: 419-562-7327, Ext 106. p. 1753

Wilden, Rebecca, Dir, Mechanicsburg Public Library, 60 S Main St, Mechanicsburg, OH, 43044. Tel: 937-834-2004. p. 1801

Wilder, Asa, Librn, Antioch University Library, 900 Dayton St, Yellow Springs, OH, 45387. Tel: 310-578-1080, Ext 338. p. 1835

Wilder, Baasil, Librn, Smithsonian Libraries, Anacostia Community Museum Library, 1901 Fort Pl SE, Rm 215, Washington, DC, 20020. Tel: 202-633-4862. p. 375

Wilder, Baasil, Librn, Smithsonian Libraries, Vine DeLoria, Jr Library, National Museum of the American Indian, Cultural Resource Ctr, MRC 538, 4220 Silver Hill Rd, Suitland, DC, 20746-0537. Tel: 301-238-1376. p. 375

Wilder, Heather, Br Mgr, Pueblo City-County Library District, Pueblo West Library, 298 S Joe Martinez Blvd, Pueblo West, CO, 81007. p. 293

Wilder, Paul, Mgr, Info & Libr Serv, Harness Racing Museum & Hall of Fame, 240 Main St, Goshen, NY, 10924-2157. Tel: 845-294-6330. p. 1540

Wilder, Sallie, Asst Librn, Norridgewock Public Library, 40 Mercer Rd, Norridgewock, ME, 04957. Tel: 207-634-2828. p. 933

Wilder, Stanley, Dean, Louisiana State University Libraries, 295 Middleton Library, Baton Rouge, LA, 70803. Tel: 225-578-2217. p. 884

Wilder, Ted, Chief Info Officer, Libr Dir, Beloit College, 731 College St, Beloit, WI, 53511. Tel: 608-363-2470. p. 2423

Wildermuth, Jane, Head, Spec Coll & Archives, Wright State University Libraries, 126 Dunbar Library, 3640 Colonel Glenn Hwy, Dayton, OH, 45435-0001. Tel: 937-775-3927. p. 1781

Wildermuth, Sue, Libr Assoc, Lima Public Library, Elida Branch, 500 E Kiracofe Ave, Elida, OH, 45807. Tel: 419-339-6097. p. 1796

Wildey, Laura, Cat/ILL Spec, Hopkinsville-Christian County Public Library, 1101 Bethel St, Hopkinsville, KY, 42240. Tel: 270-887-4362, Ext 108. p. 860

Wildhagen, Jen, Br Mgr, St Joseph Public Library, 927 Felix St, Saint Joseph, MO, 64501-2799. Tel: 816-232-7729. p. 1269

Wildman, Marc, Exec Dir, Central New York Library Resources Council, 5710 Commons Park Dr, East Syracuse, NY, 13057. Tel: 315-446-5446. p. 2770

Wildman, Tracy, Law Librn, James Crabtree Correctional Center, 216 N Murray St, Helena, OK, 73741. Tel: 572-568-6000. p. 1849

Wiles, Bradley, Head, Spec Coll & Archives, Northern Illinois University Libraries, 217 Normal Rd, DeKalb, IL, 60115-2828. Tel: 815-753-9392. p. 577

Wiles, Bradley, Head, Spec Coll & Archives, Northern Illinois University Libraries, Regional History Center, Founders Library, 217 Normal Rd, DeKalb, IL, 60115. Tel: 815-753-9392. p. 578

Wiley, Chip, Instruction/Coll Develop, College of the Ozarks, Lyons Memorial Library, One Opportunity Ave, Point Lookout, MO, 65726. Tel: 417-690-3411. p. 1266

Wiley, Chip, Res & Instruction Librn, Roberts Wesleyan College & Northeastern Seminary, 2301 Westside Dr, Rochester, NY, 14624-1997. Tel: 585-594-6893. p. 1629

Wiley, Elaine, Curator, Maturango Museum, 100 E Las Flores Ave, Ridgecrest, CA, 93555. Tel: 760-375-6900. p. 201

Wiley, Jack, Dean of Instruction, Trinidad State Junior College, 600 Prospect St, Trinidad, CO, 81082. Tel: 719-846-5593. p. 297

Wiley, Leigh, Dir, Worth County Library, 205 E Pope St, Sylvester, GA, 31791. Tel: 229-776-2096. p. 498

Wiley, Lucretia, Tech Serv, Warren-Trumbull County Public Library, 444 Mahoning Ave NW, Warren, OH, 44483. Tel: 330-399-8807. p. 1828

Wiley, Paula, Dir, Iowa Wesleyan University, 107 W Broad St, Mount Pleasant, IA, 52641. Tel: 319-385-6316. p. 771

Wiley, Stephanie, Tech Coordr, Training Coordr, Union County Public Library, 316 E Windsor St, Monroe, NC, 28112. Tel: 704-283-8184. p. 1703

Wiley-Smith, Christopher, ILL Spec, Washington State University Libraries, 14204 NE Salmon Creek Ave, Vancouver, WA, 98686. Tel: 360-546-9154. p. 2391

Wilford, Kathy, ILL, Smithers Public Library, 3817 Alfred Ave, Smithers, BC, V0J 2N0, CANADA. Tel: 250-847-3043. p. 2576

Wilhelm, Cori, Dir, Libr Serv, SUNY Canton, 34 Cornell Dr, Canton, NY, 13617. Tel: 315-386-7228. p. 1514

Wilhelm, Karen, Br Mgr, Rupp Ida Public Library, Erie Islands Library, 281 Concord Ave, Put-In-Bay, OH, 43456. Tel: 419-285-4004, p. 1816

Wilhelm, Ruth, Local Hist Librn, Putnam County District Library, The Educational Service Ctr, 136 Putnam Pkwy, Ottawa, OH, 45875-1471. Tel: 419-523-3747. p. 1811

Wilhelm, Tracy, Libr Mgr, Anne Chorney Public Library, 5111 52 Ave, Waskatenau, AB, T0A 3P0, CANADA. Tel: 780-358-2777. p. 2559

Wilhelmi, Chris, Asst Dir, Sandy Public Library, 38980 Proctor Blvd, Sandy, OR, 97055-8040. Tel: 503-668-5537. p. 1898

Wilhelms, Nicole, Libr Mgr, Arapahoe Library District, Castlewood Library, 6739 S Uinta St, Centennial, CO, 80112. p. 279

Wilhelms, Nicole, Libr Mgr, Arapahoe Library District, Southglenn Public Library, 6972 S Vine St, Centennial, CO, 80122-3270. p. 279

Wilhoit, Karen, Univ Librn, Wright State University Libraries, 126 Dunbar Library, 3640 Colonel Glenn Hwy, Dayton, OH, 45435-0001. Tel: 937-775-3039. p. 1781

Wilhoite, Jessica, Asst Dir, Youth Serv, Romulus Public Library, 11121 Wayne Rd, Romulus, MI, 48174. Tel: 734-955-4517. p. 1145

Wiljer, Christopher, Librn/Br Mgr, Allen County Public Library, Monroeville Branch, 115 Main St, Monroeville, IN, 46773. Tel: 260-421-1340. p. 683

Wilk, Alison, Libr Tech, Pennsylvania College of Optometry at Salus University, 8360 Old York Rd, Elkins Park, PA, 19027. Tel: 215-780-1261. p. 1930

Wilk, Carolyn, Copyright Librn, United States Naval War College Library, 686 Cushing Rd, Newport, RI, 02841-1207. Tel: 401-841-2641. p. 2035

Wilk, Jocelyn, Univ Archivist, Columbia University, Rare Book & Manuscript, Butler Library, 6th Flr E, 535 W 114th St, New York, NY, 10027. Tel: 212-854-5590. p. 1583

Wilk, Jocelyn K, Univ Archivist, Columbia University, Archives, Butler Library, 6th Flr, 535 W 114th St, MC 1127, New York, NY, 10027. Tel: 212-854-1338. p. 1582

Wilke, Janet Stoeger, Dean, University of Nebraska at Kearney, 2508 11th Ave, Kearney, NE, 68849-2240. Tel: 308-865-8546. p. 1319

Wilke, Melanie, Ch Serv, Terrace Public Library, 4610 Park Ave, Terrace, BC, V8G 1V6, CANADA. Tel: 250-638-8177. p. 2577

Wilke, Rebecca, Archives Asst, Field Museum of Natural History, 1400 S DuSable Lake Shore Dr, Chicago, IL, 60605-2496. Tel: 312-665-7892. p. 561

Wilken, Arin, Dir, Altoona Public Library, 1303 Lynn Ave, Altoona, WI, 54720-0278. Tel: 715-839-5029. p. 2419

Wilken, Arin, Dir, Genoa City Public Library, 126 Freeman St, Genoa City, WI, 53128-2073. Tel: 262-279-6188. p. 2437

Wilken, Cathy, Librn, Guilford Free Library, 4024 Guilford Center Rd, Guilford, VT, 05301. Tel: 802-254-6545. p. 2285

Wilken, Kevin, Pub Info Officer, Nebraska Department of Corrections, 2725 N Hwy 50, Tecumseh, NE, 68450. Tel: 402-335-5998. p. 1338

Wilken, Susan, Dir, Sterling Public Library, 150 Broadway St, Sterling, NE, 68443. Tel: 402-866-2056. p. 1337

Wilkening, Mary, Librn, Grant Park Public Library, 107 W Taylor St, Grant Park, IL, 60940. Tel: 815-465-6047. p. 595

Wilkerson, Matthew, Syst Adminr, Decatur Public Library, 130 N Franklin St, Decatur, IL, 62523. Tel: 217-424-2900. p. 576

Wilkerson, Veronica, Instrul Librn, Panola College, 1109 W Panola St, Carthage, TX, 75633. Tel: 903-693-1181. p. 2154

Wilkerson, Wendy, Circ Librn, Operations Mgr, West Falmouth Library, 575 W Falmouth Hwy, West Falmouth, MA, 02574. Tel: 508-548-4709. p. 1065

Wilkes, Georgia, Br Mgr, Neosho/Newton County Library, Seneca Branch, 1216 Cherokee, Seneca, MO, 64865. Tel: 417-776-2705. p. 1264

Wilkes, Hannah, Mgr, Baltimore County Public Library, Loch Raven Branch, 1046 Taylor Ave, Towson, MD, 21286. Tel: 410-887-4444. p. 979

Wilkes, Jamey, Dir, Libr Serv, North Georgia Technical College Library, 121 Meeks Ave, Blairsville, GA, 30512. Tel: 706-439-6326. p. 468

Wilkes, Jamey, Dir, Libr Serv, North Georgia Technical College Library, 1500 Hwy 197 N, Clarkesville, GA, 30523. Tel: 706-754-7720. p. 471

Wilkey, Cindy, Dir, Audrey Pack Memorial Library, 169 W Rhea Ave, Spring City, TN, 37381. Tel: 423-365-9757. p. 2127

Wilkie, Margaret, Br Mgr, Pima County Public Library, Mission, 3770 S Mission Rd, Tucson, AZ, 85713. Tel: 520-594-5325. p. 82

Wilkins, Carol, Dir, Wellman Scofield Public Library, 711 Fourth St, Wellman, IA, 52356. Tel: 319-646-6858. p. 790

Williams, Audrey, Circ Mgr, Williamsburg County Library, 215 N Jackson, Kingstree, SC, 29556-3319. Tel: 843-355-9486. p. 2063

Williams, Austin Martin, Dir, Law Libr, Prof, Georgetown University, Georgetown Law Library (Edward Bennett Williams Library), 111 G St NW, Washington, DC, 20001. Tel: 202-662-9162. p. 368

Williams, Barbara, Sister, Archivist/Librn, Georgian Court University, 900 Lakewood Ave, Lakewood, NJ, 08701-2697. Tel: 732-987-2441. p. 1411

Williams, Benjamin, Assoc Vice Chancellor, Univ Libr Syst, Keiser University Library System, 1500 NW 49th St, Fort Lauderdale, FL, 33309. Tel: 954-351-4035. p. 401

Williams, Beth, Assoc Dean, Stanford University Libraries, Robert Crown Law Library, Crown Quadrangle, 559 Nathan Abbott Way, Stanford, CA, 94305-8610. Tel: 650-725-0804. p. 248

Williams, Bethany, Pub Serv Librn, Bastrop Public Library, 1100 Church St, Bastrop, TX, 78602. Tel: 512-332-8880. p. 2144

Williams, Beverly, Libr Mgr, Wake County Public Library System, Richard B Harrison Community Library, 1313 New Bern Ave, Raleigh, NC, 27610. Tel: 919-856-5720. p. 1711

Williams, Brandon, Tech Adminr, Mesa Public Library, 64 E First St, Mesa, AZ, 85201-6768. Tel: 480-644-3100. p. 66

Williams, Brenda, Asst Dir, Bus Mgr, Kemper-Newton Regional Library System, 101 Peachtree St, Union, MS, 39365-2617. Tel: 601-774-9297. p. 1234

Williams, Brenda, Law Librn, Montgomery County Law Library, 505 Montgomery County Courts Bldg, 41 N Perry St, Dayton, OH, 45402. Tel: 937-225-4496. p. 1780

Williams, Brett, Ref Librn, Indian River State College, Ken Pruitt Campus Library, 500 NW California Blvd, Port Saint Lucie, FL, 34986. Tel: 772-336-6383. p. 404

Williams, Brett R, Tech Serv Librn, Indiana Tech, Academic Ctr, West Wing, 1600 E Washington Blvd, Fort Wayne, IN, 46803. Tel: 260-422-5561, Ext 2516. p. 684

Williams, Brittani, ILL Tech, Tulane University, Rudolph Matas Library of the Health Sciences, Tulane Health Sciences Campus, 1430 Tulane Ave, SL-86, New Orleans, LA, 70112-2699. Tel: 504-988-2413. p. 904

Williams, Brooke, Res & Instruction Librn, Northeastern University Libraries, 360 Huntington Ave, Boston, MA, 02115. Tel: 617-373-2363. p. 998

Williams, Bryon, Librn, United States Army, 332 Minnesota St, Ste E1500, Saint Paul, MN, 55101. Tel: 651-290-5304, 651-290-5727. p. 1202

Williams, Candis, Libr Tech, Farmville Public Library, 4276 W Church St, Farmville, NC, 27828. Tel: 252-753-3355. p. 1688

Williams, Carla, Libr Spec, Ohio University Libraries, Music-Dance, Robert Gidden Hall, Fifth Flr, Athens, OH, 45701-2978. Tel: 740-593-4255. p. 1748

Williams, Carmela, Sr Admin Assoc, Robeson County Public Library, 101 N Chestnut St, Lumberton, NC, 28359. Tel: 910-738-4859. p. 1702

Williams, Carol, Dir, Oak Lawn Public Library, 9427 S Raymond Ave, Oak Lawn, IL, 60453. Tel: 708-422-4990. p. 628

Williams, Carol L, Asst Dir, Hammond Public Library, 564 State St, Hammond, IN, 46320-1532. Tel: 219-931-5100, Ext 345. p. 689

Williams, Carole, Info Literacy Librn, Greenville Technical College Libraries, Bldg 102, 506 S Pleasantburg Dr, Greenville, SC, 29607. Tel: 864-236-6438. p. 2062

Williams, Carolyn, Head, Circ, Galveston County Library System, 2310 Sealy Ave, Galveston, TX, 77550. Tel: 409-763-8854, Ext 141. p. 2183

Williams, Cassandra, Br Mgr, Southwest Georgia Regional Library, Miller County-James W Merritt Jr Memorial Library, 259 E Main St, Colquitt, GA, 39837. Tel: 229-758-3131. p. 467

Williams, Cassi, Libr Asst, Lester Public Library of Rome, 1157 Rome Center Dr, Nekoosa, WI, 54457. Tel: 715-325-8990. p. 2464

Williams, Cecilia, ILL, Mercer University, Jack Tarver Library, 1300 Edgewood Ave, Macon, GA, 31207. Tel: 478-301-2102. p. 486

Williams, Chad, Dir, Res, Oklahoma Historical Society-Museum of the Western Prairie, 1100 Memorial Dr, Altus, OK, 73521. Tel: 580-482-1044. p. 1839

Williams, Chad A, Dir, Oklahoma Historical Society, Oklahoma History Ctr, 800 Nazih Zuhdi Dr, Oklahoma City, OK, 73105. Tel: 405-522-5207. p. 1859

Williams, Charles Matthew, Librn, Montgomery City-County Public Library System, Pike Road Branch Library, 9585 Vaughn Rd, Pike Road, AL, 36064-2292. Tel: 334-244-8679. p. 30

Williams, Chelsea, Dir, Hamburg Public Library, 35 N Third St, Hamburg, PA, 19526-1502. Tel: 610-562-2843. p. 1939

Williams, Cherry, Director, Distinctive Collections, University of California, Riverside, Special Collections & University Archives, 900 University Ave, Riverside, CA, 92521. Tel: 951-827-3233. p. 203

Williams, Cheryl, Br Supvr, Barry-Lawrence Regional Library, Cassville Branch, 301 W 17th St, Cassville, MO, 65625-1044. Tel: 417-847-2121. p. 1263

Williams, Chris, Assoc Librn, Ref Serv Coordr, Horry-Georgetown Technical College, 2050 Hwy 501 E, Conway, SC, 29526-9521. Tel: 843-349-5268. p. 2057

Williams, Cindy, Sr Admin Assoc, San Juan College Library, 4601 College Blvd, Farmington, NM, 87402. Tel: 505-566-3249. p. 1468

Williams, Clara R, Dr, Librn, Atlanta Botanical Garden, 1345 Piedmont Ave NE, Atlanta, GA, 30309-3366. Tel: 404-591-1546, 404-591-1725. p. 460

Williams, Clay, Dep Chief Librn, Hunter College Libraries, East Bldg, 695 Park Ave, New York, NY, 10065. Tel: 212-772-4143. p. 1588

Williams, Constance, Col Archivist, Coordr, Circ, Interim Chief Librn, Queensborough Community College, City University of New York, 222-05 56th Ave, Bayside, NY, 11364-1497. Tel: 718-281-6567. p. 1491

Williams, Coralie, Ch Serv, Henry Carter Hull Library, Inc, Ten Killingworth Tpk, Clinton, CT, 06413. Tel: 860-669-2342. p. 306

Williams, Cynthia, Sr Libr Asst, Gloucester, Lyceum & Sawyer Free Library, Two Dale Ave, Gloucester, MA, 01930. Tel: 978-325-5557. p. 1021

Williams, Cynthia, Asst Librn, Children's Prog, Lilly Pike Sullivan Municipal Library, 103 SE Railroad St, Enfield, NC, 27823. Tel: 252-445-5203. p. 1688

Williams, Daijai, Evening Libr Asst, Johnson C Smith University, 100 Beatties Ford Rd, Charlotte, NC, 28216. Tel: 704-371-6731, 704-371-6740. p. 1680

Williams, Dean, Libr Spec, Appalachian State University, William Leonard Eury Appalachian Collection, 218 College St, Boone, NC, 28608. Tel: 828-262-2186. p. 1675

Williams, Debbie A, Libr Dir, Mountaintop Public Library, 384 Second St, Thomas, WV, 26292. Tel: 304-463-4582. p. 2415

Williams, Delisa, Outreach Serv Spec, Youth Serv Spec, Lee County Library, 107 Hawkins Ave, Sanford, NC, 27330. Tel: 919-718-4665. p. 1715

Williams, Donald, Copyright & Scholarly Comms Mgr, Ball State University Libraries, 2000 W University Ave, Muncie, IN, 47306-1099. Tel: 758-285-5330. p. 708

Williams, Donna, Mgr, Tech Serv, Miller & Martin PLLC, Volunteer Bldg, Ste 1200, 832 Georgia Ave, Chattanooga, TN, 37402-2289. Tel: 423-756-6600. p. 2092

Williams, Door, Ref Librn, Virginia Museum of Fine Arts Library, 200 N Arthur Ashe Blvd, Richmond, VA, 23220-4007. Tel: 804-340-1495. p. 2344

Williams, Edna, Librn, Hightower Memorial Library, 630 Ave A, York, AL, 36925. Tel: 205-392-2004. p. 40

Williams, Edward, Fiscal Officer, Ashtabula County District Library, 4335 Park Ave, Ashtabula, OH, 44004. Tel: 440-997-9343, Ext 322. p. 1747

Williams, Eke, Libr Dir, Coney Island Hospital, 2601 Ocean Pkwy, Brooklyn, NY, 11235. Tel: 718-616-4159. p. 1504

Williams, Elaine, Br Mgr, Highland County District Library, Lynchburg Branch, 102 S Main St, Lynchburg, OH, 45142. Tel: 937-364-2511. p. 1789

Williams, Elizabeth, Br Mgr, San Bernardino County Library, Yucaipa Branch, 12040 Fifth St, Yucaipa, CA, 92399. Tel: 909-790-3146. p. 214

Williams, Emily, Br Mgr, Lonesome Pine Regional Library, Coeburn Community, 111 Third St, Coeburn, VA, 24230. Tel: 276-395-6152. p. 2354

Williams, Emily, Br Mgr, Lonesome Pine Regional Library, J Fred Matthews Memorial Library, 16552 Wise St, Saint Paul, VA, 24283-3522. Tel: 276-762-9702. p. 2355

Williams, Ethel J, Dir, White Hall Public Library, 640 Freedom Rd, Whitehall, AL, 36040. Tel: 334-874-7323. p. 40

Williams, Felicia, Libr Dir, Lamoni Public Library, 301 W Main St, Lamoni, IA, 50140. Tel: 641-784-6686. p. 764

Williams, Fredda, Br Mgr, Ch Serv, Knox County Public Library System, South Knoxville Branch, 4500 Chapman Hwy, Knoxville, TN, 37920. Tel: 865-573-1772. p. 2106

Williams, Gayle, Archives Dir, Syst Dir of Libr, Henry Ford Hospital, 2799 W Grand Blvd, Detroit, MI, 48202. Tel: 313-916-2550. p. 1098

Williams, Genevieve, Interim Libr Dir, Pacific Lutheran University, 12180 Park Ave S, Tacoma, WA, 98447-0001. Tel: 253-535-7443. p. 2386

Williams, Gloria, Br Mgr, Mobile Public Library, Parkway Branch, 1924-B Dauphin Island Pkwy, Mobile, AL, 36605-3004. Tel: 251-470-7766. p. 26

Williams, Greg, Libr Dir, Oregon City Public Library, 606 John Adams St, Oregon City, OR, 97045. Tel: 503-657-8269. p. 1890

Williams, Gregory, Dir, Archives & Spec Coll, California State University Dominguez Hills, 1000 E Victoria St, Carson, CA, 90747. Tel: 310-243-3013. p. 129

Williams, Harley, Teen Librn, Elizabethton-Carter County Public Library, 201 N Sycamore St, Elizabethton, TN, 37643. Tel: 423-547-6360. p. 2098

Williams Hart, Erin, Head, Adult Serv, Sun Prairie Public Library, 1350 Linnerud Dr, Sun Prairie, WI, 53590. Tel: 608-825-7323. p. 2480

Williams, Heather, Mgr, Mobile Public Library, Semmes Branch, 9150 Moffett Rd, Semmes, AL, 36575. Tel: 251-645-6840. p. 26

Williams, Heather, Outreach Serv, Shelby County Public Library, 309 Eighth St, Shelbyville, KY, 40065. Tel: 502-633-3803. p. 874

Williams, Heather, Ref Librn, Whatcom Community College Library, Heiner Bldg, 231 W Kellogg Rd, Bellingham, WA, 98226. Tel: 360-383-3300. p. 2359

Williams, Helene, Teaching Prof, University of Washington, Mary Gates Hall, Ste 370, Campus Box 352840, Seattle, WA, 98195-2840. Tel: 206-543-1794. p. 2794

Williams, Holly, Libr Dir, Pittsfield Public Library, 110 Library St, Pittsfield, ME, 04967. Tel: 207-487-5880. p. 935

Williams, Hope, Librn, Nevada State Library, Archives & Public Records, Regional Library for the Blind & Physically Handicapped, 100 N Stewart St, Carson City, NV, 89701-4285. Tel: 775-684-3354. p. 1344

Williams Huber, Sheree, Dean, Learning Commons, Jefferson Community & Technical College, 622 S First St, Louisville, KY, 40202. Tel: 502-213-2156. p. 865

Williams, Jacob, Youth Librn, Independence Public Library, 220 E Maple, Independence, KS, 67301. Tel: 620-331-3030. p. 815

Williams, Jami, Ch Serv, Marvin Memorial Library, 29 W Whitney Ave, Shelby, OH, 44875-1252. Tel: 419-347-5576. p. 1820

Williams, Jamie, Dir, Ericson Public Library, 702 Greene St, Boone, IA, 50036. Tel: 515-432-3727. p. 735

Williams, Jana Lu, Fac Librn, Walla Walla Community College Library, 500 Tausick Way, Walla Walla, WA, 99362-9267. Tel: 509-527-4292. p. 2392

Williams, Janene, Librn, Lost Rivers District Library, Howe Branch, 1523 Hwy 22, Howe, ID, 83244. Tel: 208-767-3018. p. 515

Williams, Janet L, Dir, Libr Serv, Tabor College Library, 400 S Jefferson St, Hillsboro, KS, 67063. Tel: 620-947-3121, Ext 1202. p. 813

Williams, Janice, Coordr, South Georgia State College, 2001 S Georgia Pkwy, Waycross, GA, 31503. Tel: 912-449-7519. p. 503

Williams, Jean, Asst Dir, Cat & Metadata, Hamilton College, 198 College Hill Rd, Clinton, NY, 13323. Tel: 315-859-4383. p. 1519

Williams, Jeanne, Libr Dir, Central Skagit Library District, 110 W State St, Sedro-Woolley, WA, 98284-1551. Tel: 360-755-3985. p. 2383

Williams, Jennifer, Acq & Coll Develop Librn, Athens State University, 407 E Pryor St, Athens, AL, 35611. Tel: 256-216-6667. p. 5

Williams, Jennifer, Asst Dir, Archives & Spec Coll, Emerson College, 120 Boylston St, Boston, MA, 02116-4624. Tel: 617-824-8679. p. 995

Williams, Jennifer, Pub Relations Coordr, Coshocton Public Library, 655 Main St, Coshocton, OH, 43812-1697. Tel: 740-622-0956. p. 1778

Williams, Jess, Dir, Teaching & Learning Services, Texas State University, 601 University Dr, San Marcos, TX, 78666-4684. Tel: 512-408-1812. p. 2241

Williams, Jessica, Dir, Mount Horeb Public Library, 105 Perimeter Rd, Mount Horeb, WI, 53572. Tel: 608-437-9378. p. 2463

Williams, Jillian, Ch Mgr, Saint Joseph County Public Library, 304 S Main St, South Bend, IN, 46601. Tel: 574-282-4646. p. 718

Williams, Joan, Libr Dir, Bennett College, 900 E Washington St, Greensboro, NC, 27401-3239. Tel: 336-517-2141. p. 1691

Williams, Joanna, Ref Librn, Alcorn State University, 1000 ASU Dr, Alcorn State, MS, 39096-7500. Tel: 601-877-2392. p. 1211

Williams, Jodie, Literacy Coordr, Manatee County Public Library System, 1301 Barcarrota Blvd W, Bradenton, FL, 34205-7522. Tel: 941-748-5555, Ext 3820. p. 386

Williams, Joe, Law Librn, Day Pitney LLP, One Jefferson Rd, Parsippany, NJ, 07054. Tel: 973-966-6300. p. 1432

Williams, Joe, Dir, Pub Serv, University of North Carolina at Chapel Hill, 208 Raleigh St, CB 3916, Chapel Hill, NC, 27515. Tel: 919-962-1053. p. 1678

Williams, John, Head, Cat, Fordham University Libraries, 441 E Fordham Rd, Bronx, NY, 10458-5151. Tel: 718-817-3570. p. 1498

Williams, Joi, Asst Dir, Tech Serv, Alabama A&M University, 4900 Meridian St N, Normal, AL, 35762. Tel: 256-372-4712. p. 31

Williams, Joseph, Dir, Greenwich Library, 101 W Putnam Ave, Greenwich, CT, 06830-5387. Tel: 203-622-7956. p. 314

Williams, Joshua, Archivist, Fisk University, 1000 17th Ave N, Nashville, TN, 37208-3051. Tel: 615-329-8838. p. 2118

Williams, Joyce, Dir, Virgil & Josephine Gordon Memorial Library, 917 N Circle Dr, Sealy, TX, 77474. Tel: 979-885-7469. p. 2242

Williams, Julie, Coordr, Minnesota West Community & Technical College, Granite Falls Campus, 1593 11th Ave, Granite Falls, MN, 56241. Tel: 320-564-5056. p. 1210

Williams, June S, Libr Mgt, Saint Louis Community College, Forest Park Campus Library, 5600 Oakland Ave, Saint Louis, MO, 63110-1316. Tel: 314-644-9209. p. 1273

Williams, K C, Dir, Blount County Public Library, 508 N Cusick St, Maryville, TN, 37804. Tel: 865-982-0981. p. 2111

Williams, Karen, Access Serv/ILL Librn, Auburn University, 7440 East Dr, Montgomery, AL, 36117. Tel: 334-244-3200. p. 28

Williams, Karnecia, Librn, Birmingham Public Library, Inglenook, 4100 N 40th Terrace N, Birmingham, AL, 35217-4162. Tel: 205-849-8739. p. 7

Williams, Katherine, Libr Support Spec, South Central Kansas Library System, 321 N Main St, South Hutchinson, KS, 67505. Tel: 620-663-3211. p. 837

Williams, Kathleen, Librn, Municipal Research Library, Zeidler Municipal Bldg, Rm B-2, 841 N Broadway, Milwaukee, WI, 53202-3567. Tel: 414-286-2299. p. 2460

Williams, Kathy, Libr Tech, Lakeland College Library, 5707 College Dr, Vermilion, AB, T9X 1K5, CANADA. Tel: 780-871-7509. p. 2558

Williams, Katie, Ref/Outreach Librn, Indian River State College, 3209 Virginia Ave, Fort Pierce, FL, 34981-5599. Tel: 772-462-7587. p. 404

Williams, Kayla, Librn, Avonmore Public Library, 437 Westmoreland Ave, Avonmore, PA, 15618. Tel: 724-697-4415, Ext 103. p. 1908

Williams, Kelly, Tech Serv Supvr, Central Texas College, Bldg 102, 6200 W Central Texas Expressway, Killeen, TX, 76549. Tel: 254-616-3307. p. 2206

Williams, Kevin, Dir, Colorado Mountain College, 1275 Crawford Ave, Steamboat Springs, CO, 80487. Tel: 970-870-4493. p. 295

Williams, Kime, Libr Dir, Palo Verde Valley Library District, 125 W Chanslorway, Blythe, CA, 92225. Tel: 760-922-5371. p. 124

Williams, Kirsten, Resource Sharing & Cataloging Librn, University of Southern Indiana, 8600 University Blvd, Evansville, IN, 47712. Tel: 812-464-1913. p. 682

Williams, Krista, Br Librn, Southeast Regional Library, Whitewood Branch, 731 Lalonde St, Whitewood, SK, S0G 5C0, CANADA. Tel: 306-735-4233. p. 2755

Williams, Kristin, Dir, Libr & Media Serv, Blue Mountain Community College Library, 2411 NW Carden Ave, Pendleton, OR, 97801. Tel: 541-278-5915. p. 1890

Williams, Kristy, Libr Dir, Saxton Community Library, 315 Front St, Saxton, PA, 16678-8612. Tel: 814-212-6925. p. 2003

Williams, Kyle, Reference Support Specialist, Bellevue University, 1028 Bruin Blvd, Bellevue, NE, 68005. Tel: 402-557-7304. p. 1308

Williams, La-Nita, Circ Serv, High Point University, One University Pkwy, High Point, NC, 27268. Tel: 336-841-9102. p. 1697

Williams, LaDelle, Librn, Colorado Territorial Correctional Facility Library, PO Box 1010, Canon City, CO, 81215-1010. Tel: 719-275-4181, Ext 3167. p. 269

Williams, LaShunda, Br Mgr, Gadsden Public Library, East Gadsden Branch, 809 E Broad St, Gadsden, AL, 35903. Tel: 256-549-4691. p. 18

Williams, Laura, Asst City Librn, Dike Public Library, 133 E Elder, Dike, IA, 50624-9612. Tel: 319-989-2608. p. 748

Williams, Laura, Ref Assoc, Holbrook Public Library, Two Plymouth St, Holbrook, MA, 02343. Tel: 781-767-3644. p. 1024

Williams, Laura, Head Music Libr, Duke University Libraries, 411 Chapel Dr, Durham, NC, 27708. Tel: 919-660-5952. p. 1684

Williams, Laura, Music Librn, Duke University Libraries, William R Perkins Music Library, 113 Mary Duke Biddle Music Bldg, Nine Brodie Gym Dr, Durham, NC, 27708. Tel: 919-660-5952. p. 1684

Williams, Laura, Med Librn, UPMC Passavant - McCandless, 9100 Babcock Blvd, Pittsburgh, PA, 15237-5842. Tel: 412-748-6320. p. 1997

Williams, Lee, Pres, Health Sciences Library Network of Kansas City, Inc, c/o Shook, Hardy & Bacon Medical Library & Scientific Resource Ctr - Joyce Sickel, 2555 Grand Blvd, Kansas City, MO, 64108. Tel: 816-235-1880. p. 2769

Williams, Leonette, Assoc Dir, Law Libr for Coll & Admin Serv, University of Southern California Libraries, Asa V Call Law Library, 699 Exposition Blvd, LAW 202, MC 0072, Los Angeles, CA, 90089-0072. Tel: 213-740-6482. p. 170

Williams, Lisa, Br Mgr, Lawrence County Library, Bobbi Jean Memorial, 102 Hendrix St, Imboden, AR, 72434. Tel: 870-869-2093. p. 112

Williams, Lisa Marie, Chief Librn/CEO, Oxford County Library, 21 Reeve St, Woodstock, ON, N4S 7Y3, CANADA. Tel: 519-539-9800, Ext 3260. p. 2705

Williams, Lisa W, Dir, Libr Serv, Parker, Poe, Adams & Bernstein, LLP, PNC Plaza, 301 Fayetteville St, Ste 1400, Raleigh, NC, 27601. Tel: 919-828-0564. p. 1710

Williams, Lois, Circ & ILL, Marion County Library System, 101 East Court St, Marion, SC, 29571. Tel: 843-423-8300. p. 2065

Williams, Lori, Br Serv Supvr, Inglewood Public Library, 101 W Manchester Blvd, Inglewood, CA, 90301-1771. Tel: 310-412-5397. p. 152

Williams, Lori, Asst Libr Mgr, White Pine County Library, 950 Campton, Ely, NV, 89301-1965. Tel: 775-293-6900. p. 1345

Williams, Louise, Circ Coordr, Scotland County Memorial Library, 312 W Church St, Laurinburg, NC, 28352-3720. Tel: 910-276-0563. p. 1700

Williams, Lynn, Reader Serv, Lewis & Clark College, Paul L Boley Law Library, Lewis & Clark Law School, 10015 SW Terwilliger Blvd, Portland, OR, 97219. Tel: 503-768-6776. p. 1891

Williams, Mabel, Br Mgr, Newark Public Library, Vailsburg, 75 Alexander St, Newark, NJ, 07106. Tel: 973-733-7755. p. 1427

Williams, Mackenzie, Librn, Cooper Union for Advancement of Science & Art Library, Seven E Seventh St, New York, NY, 10003. Tel: 212-353-4186. p. 1584

Williams, Marcie, Br Mgr, Cleveland Public Library, Union, 3463 E 93rd St, Cleveland, OH, 44104. Tel: 216-623-7088. p. 1769

Williams, Maren, Ref Coordr, University of Louisiana at Monroe Library, 700 University Ave, Monroe, LA, 71209-0720. Tel: 318-342-1065. p. 899

Williams, Marie, Supvr, Middlesex County Library, Wardsville Branch, 21935 Hagerty Rd, Wardsville, ON, N0L 2N0, CANADA. Tel: 519-693-4208. p. 2682

Williams, Marjorie, Tech Asst, University of Southern Mississippi-Gulf Coast Research Laboratory, 703 E Beach Dr, Ocean Springs, MS, 39564. Tel: 228-872-4213, 228-872-4253. p. 1228

Williams, Mark, Libr Dir, Philadelphia Public Library, 714 Thompson St, Philadelphia, TN, 37846. Tel: 865-657-9059. p. 2124

Williams, Marvin, Ser Tech, University of the District of Columbia, David A Clarke School of Law, Charles N & Hilda H M Mason Law Library, Bldg 39, Rm B-16, 4200 Connecticut Ave NW, Washington, DC, 20008. Tel: 202-274-7310. p. 380

Williams, Matthew R, Dir, Kearney Public Library, 2020 First Ave, Kearney, NE, 68847. Tel: 308-233-3280. p. 1319

Williams, Meg, Dir, Wynnewood Public Library, 108 N Dean A McGee Ave, Wynnewood, OK, 73098. Tel: 405-665-2512. p. 1869
Williams, Megan, Tech Serv Librn, Shenandoah University, 1460 University Dr, Winchester, VA, 22601. Tel: 540-665-4638. p. 2354
Williams, Melani, Supvr, Tech Serv, Coquitlam Public Library, 575 Poirier St, Coquitlam, BC, V3J 6A9, CANADA. Tel: 604-937-4149. p. 2565
Williams, Melissa, Asst Librn, Coll Mgt, Tech, Supreme Court of the United States Library, One First St NE, Washington, DC, 20543. Tel: 202-479-3037. p. 376
Williams, Michael, Area Res Mgr, Cent Libr, Indianapolis Public Library, 2450 N Meridian St, Indianapolis, IN, 46208. Tel: 317-275-4302. p. 694
Williams, Michael, Librn, Calhoun County Library, Point Comfort Branch, One Lamar St, Point Comfort, TX, 77978. Tel: 361-987-2954. p. 2228
Williams, Michael B, Dir, Harnett County Public Library, Dunn Public, 110 E Divine St, Dunn, NC, 28334. Tel: 910-892-2899. p. 1701
Williams, Mike, Area Res Mgr, Cent Libr, Indianapolis Public Library, Central Library, 40 E Saint Clair St, Indianapolis, IN, 46204. Tel: 317-275-4100. p. 694
Williams, Mindy, Dir, Bennett Public Library, 203 Main St, Bennett, IA, 52721. Tel: 563-890-2238. p. 734
Williams, Monica D, Managing Librn, Brooklyn Public Library, Saratoga, Eight Thomas S Boyland St, @ Macon St, Brooklyn, NY, 11233. Tel: 718-573-5224. p. 1504
Williams, Monique, Br Mgr, Presque Isle District Library, Millersburg Branch, 5561 Main St, Millersburg, MI, 49759. p. 1145
Williams, Natalie, Youth Serv, Indian Prairie Public Library District, 401 Plainfield Rd, Darien, IL, 60561-4207. Tel: 630-887-8760. p. 575
Williams, Nelle, Libr Dir, University of Alabama College of Community Health Sciences, 850 Peter Bryce Blvd, Tuscaloosa, AL, 35401. Tel: 205-348-1364. p. 38
Williams, Norma, Libr Assoc for Coll & Access Serv, Barton College, 400 Atlantic Christian College Dr NE, Wilson, NC, 27893. Tel: 252-399-6506. p. 1723
Williams, Paige, Dir, Portsmouth Public Library, 1220 Gallia St, Portsmouth, OH, 45662-4185. Tel: 740-353-5990. p. 1816
Williams, Pam, Interim Dir, Libr Serv, Three Rivers Community College, 574 New London Tpk, Norwich, CT, 06360-6598. Tel: 860-215-9306. p. 332
Williams, Pam, Libr Dir, Frankenmuth James E Wickson District Library, 359 S Franklin St, Frankenmuth, MI, 48734. Tel: 989-652-8323. p. 1107
Williams, Pam, Acq, Orange Public Library, 220 N Fifth St, Orange, TX, 77630. Tel: 409-883-1086. p. 2224
Williams, Patricia, Law Librn, Georgia Department of Corrections, Office of Library Services, 2978 Hwy 36 W, Jackson, GA, 30233. Tel: 770-504-2431. p. 482
Williams, Patricia, Info Spec, Danville Public Library, Westover, 94 Clifton St, Danville, VA, 24541. Tel: 434-799-5152. p. 2315
Williams, Patrick, Head, Info Tech, Middleton Public Library, 7425 Hubbard Ave, Middleton, WI, 53562-3117. Tel: 608-827-7422. p. 2457
Williams, Paula, Ref (Info Servs), Bergen Community College, 400 Paramus Rd, Paramus, NJ, 07652-1595. Tel: 201-612-5299. p. 1432
Williams, Pete, Media Librn, Metadata Librn, Curtis Institute of Music, 1720 Locust St, Philadelphia, PA, 19103. Tel: 215-717-3147. p. 1976
Williams, Peter, Librn, State Education Resource Center Library, 175 Union St, Waterbury, CT, 06706. Tel: 860-632-1485. p. 344
Williams, Peter, Libr Dir, Curtis Institute of Music, 1720 Locust St, Philadelphia, PA, 19103. Tel: 215-893-5265. p. 1976
Williams, Peter, PhD, Assoc Prof, Interim Dept Head, Texas A&M University - Commerce, Frank Young Education Bldg N, No 113, 2600 S Neal St, Commerce, TX, 75428. Tel: 903-886-5520. p. 2793
Williams, Pia, Exec Dir, Libr Mgr, Waterloo Region Law Association, 85 Frederick St, Kitchener, ON, N2H 0A7, CANADA. Tel: 519-742-0872. p. 2652
Williams, Rebecca, Ch & Youth Librn, Person County Public Library, 319 S Main St, Roxboro, NC, 27573. Tel: 336-597-7881. p. 1714
Williams, Rebekah, Dept Chair, Tacoma Community College Library, Bldg 7, 6501 S 19th St, Tacoma, WA, 98466-6100. Tel: 253-566-6028. p. 2387
Williams, Ricky, Libr Dir, Pine Bluff & Jefferson County Library System, Main Library, 600 S Main St, Pine Bluff, AR, 71601. Tel: 870-534-4802. p. 107
Williams, Ronald C, Dr, Archivist, Hawaii State Archives, Iolani Palace Grounds, 364 S King St, Honolulu, HI, 96813. Tel: 808-586-0329. p. 506
Williams, Roy L, Sr, Dir, Pub Relations, Birmingham Public Library, 2100 Park Pl, Birmingham, AL, 35203-2744. Tel: 205-226-3600. p. 7
Williams, Ryan, District Libr Mgr, Timberland Regional Library, 415 Tumwater Blvd SW, Tumwater, WA, 98501-5799. Tel: 360-943-5001. p. 2388
Williams, Sam, Ref & Instruction Librn, Idaho State Law Library, 514 W Jefferson St, 2nd Flr, Boise, ID, 83702. Tel: 208-364-4554. p. 518
Williams, Sandra, Pub Serv Coordr, Arlington Public Library System, Southeast, 900 SE Green Oaks Blvd, Arlington, TX, 76018. p. 2136
Williams, Sarah C, Head of Libr, University of Illinois Library at Urbana-Champaign, Funk Library, Agricultural, Consumer & Environmental Sciences, 1101 S Goodwin, MC-633, Urbana, IL, 61801. Tel: 217-333-8916. p. 656
Williams, Satasha, Access Serv Librn, William Paterson University, 300 Pompton Rd, Wayne, NJ, 07470. Tel: 973-720-3190. p. 1452
Williams, Sharalyn, Pub Serv Librn, Gonzaga University School of Law, 721 N Cincinnati St, Spokane, WA, 99220. Tel: 509-313-5792. p. 2383
Williams, Sheila, Library Contact, Proskauer Rose LLP, 2049 Century Park E, Ste 2400, Los Angeles, CA, 90067. Tel: 310-284-5683, 310-557-2900. p. 167
Williams, Shellie, Dir, Minerva Free Library, 116 Miller St, Sherman, NY, 14781. Tel: 716-761-6378. p. 1640
Williams, Shelly, Dir, Maclure Library, 840 Arch St, Pittsford, VT, 05763. Tel: 802-483-2972. p. 2291
Williams, Sheryl, Br Mgr, Mid-Continent Public Library, Smithville Branch, 120 Richardson St, Smithville, MO, 64089. Tel: 816-532-0116. p. 1251
Williams, Shugana, Librn, Mississippi Gulf Coast Community College, Hwy 49 S, Perkinston, MS, 39573. Tel: 601-928-6259. p. 1229
Williams, Stacie, Asst Prof of Practice, Simmons University, 300 The Fenway, Boston, MA, 02115. Tel: 617-521-2800. p. 2786
Williams, Stephanie, Libr Syst Adminr, Berks County Public Libraries, 1040 Berk Rd, Leesport, PA, 19533. Tel: 610-378-5260. p. 1954
Williams, Steven, Dir, Port Arthur Public Library, 4615 Ninth Ave, Port Arthur, TX, 77642. Tel: 409-985-8838. p. 2228
Williams, Susan, Dir, Del Norte Public Library, 790 Grand Ave, Del Norte, CO, 81132. Tel: 719-657-2633. p. 273
Williams, Susan, Ch, C E Brehm Memorial Public Library District, 101 S Seventh St, Mount Vernon, IL, 62864. Tel: 618-242-6322. p. 621
Williams, Tamica, Br Mgr, Assumption Parish Library, Belle Rose Branch, 7089 Hwy One, Belle Rose, LA, 70341. Tel: 225-473-1936. p. 899
Williams, Tanya, Dir, Collier County Public Library, 2385 Orange Blossom Dr, Naples, FL, 34109. Tel: 239-593-0334. p. 427
Williams, Tara, Libr Mgr, Kinchafoonee Regional Library System, Clay County Library, 208 S Hancock St, Fort Gaines, GA, 39851-9506. Tel: 229-768-2248. p. 475
Williams, Teressa, Libr Dir, Tuzzy Consortium Library, 5421 North Star St, Barrow, AK, 99723. Tel: 907-852-1711. p. 43
Williams, Tim, Ref & Instruction Librn, Peninsula College Library, 1502 E Lauridsen Blvd, Port Angeles, WA, 98362-6698. Tel: 360-417-6280. p. 2374
Williams, Tina, Outreach Serv Mgr, White Oak Library District, 201 W Normantown Rd, Romeoville, IL, 60446. Tel: 815-886-2030. p. 643
Williams, Tina, Asst Dir, Perry County Public Library, 289 Black Gold Blvd, Hazard, KY, 41701. Tel: 606-436-2475, 606-436-4747. p. 858
Williams, Tisha, Managing Librn, Brooklyn Public Library, Ryder, 5902 23rd Ave, Brooklyn, NY, 11204. Tel: 718-331-2962. p. 1504
Williams, Todd, Lead Doc Imaging/Application Spec, Knox Community Hospital, 1330 Coshocton Rd, Mount Vernon, OH, 43050. Tel: 740-393-9000. p. 1804
Williams, Tracy, Librn, Shelton State Community College, Martin Campus, 9500 Old Greensboro Rd, Tuscaloosa, AL, 35405. Tel: 205-391-2203. p. 37
Williams, Travis, Archivist & Spec Coll Librn, Saint Edwards University, 3001 S Congress Ave, Austin, TX, 78704-6489. Tel: 512-428-1047. p. 2140
Williams, Ursula, Access Services Assoc, The College of Wooster Libraries, 1140 Beall Ave, Wooster, OH, 44691-2364. Tel: 330-263-2442. p. 1833
Williams, Velma, Libr Spec, Shaw University, 118 E South St, Raleigh, NC, 27601. Tel: 919-582-8438. p. 1710
Williams, Virginia, Cat, Frostburg State University, One Susan Eisel Dr, Frostburg, MD, 21532. Tel: 301-687-4884. p. 967
Williams, Yoshieka, Mgr, Saint Mary Parish Library, Patterson Branch, 521 Catherine St, Patterson, LA, 70392. Tel: 985-395-2777. p. 890
Williams, Yvonne, Tech Serv Assoc, Huntingdon College, 1500 E Fairview Ave, Montgomery, AL, 36106. Tel: 334-833-4421. p. 29
Williams-Baig, Rosie, Dir, Nancy L McConathy Public Library, 21737 Jeffery Ave, Sauk Village, IL, 60411. Tel: 708-757-4771. p. 645
Williams-Bergen, Eric, Director, Research & Digital Scholarship, St Lawrence University, 23 Romoda Dr, Canton, NY, 13617. Tel: 315-229-5453. p. 1513
Williams-Curl, Jennifer, Libr Coord, Western Dakota Technical Institute Library, 800 Mickelson Dr, Rapid City, SD, 57703. Tel: 605-718-2904. p. 2081
Williams-Hart, Tiffany, Graduate Studies Programs, Mgr, University at Albany, State University of New York, Draper 015, 135 Western Ave, Albany, NY, 12203. Tel: 518-442-5258. p. 2789
Williamsen, Julie, Libr Dir, Stanford University Libraries, Graduate School of Business Library, Knight Management Ctr, 655 Knight Way, Stanford, CA, 94305-7298. Tel: 650-725-2002. p. 248
Williamson, Carla, Circ, The Parrott Centre, 376 Wallbridge-Loyalist Rd, Belleville, ON, K8N 5B9, CANADA. Tel: 613-969-1913, Ext 2249. p. 2631
Williamson, Chiara, Exec Dir, Ontario Archaeological Society Library, 1444 Queen St E, Ste 102, Toronto, ON, M4L 1E1, CANADA. Tel: 416-406-5959. p. 2691

Wilson, Bernice, Br Mgr, Columbus-Lowndes Public Library, Crawford Public, 320 Main St, Crawford, MS, 39743. Tel: 662-272-5144. p. 1215

Wilson, Betty, Digital Serv Dir, Idea Exchange, One North Sq, Cambridge, ON, N1S 2K6, CANADA. Tel: 519-621-0460. p. 2635

Wilson, Brad, Dir, St Francis of the Woods, 11414 W Hwy 33, Coyle, OK, 73027. Tel: 405-466-3774. p. 1845

Wilson, Brenton, Assoc Dir, Point Park University Library, 414 Wood St, Pittsburgh, PA, 15222. Tel: 412-392-3163. p. 1995

Wilson, Brian, Sr Mgr, Archives & Library, The Henry Ford, 20900 Oakwood Blvd, Dearborn, MI, 48124. Tel: 313-982-6081. p. 1095

Wilson, Britt, Br Supvr, University of Texas Libraries, Kuehne Physics-Mathematics-Astronomy Library, Robert L Moore Hall 4.200, S5441, 2515 Speedway, Austin, TX, 78713. Tel: 512-495-4610. p. 2142

Wilson, Brittany, Youth Serv, Cape Canaveral Public Library, 201 Polk Ave, Cape Canaveral, FL, 32920-3067. Tel: 321-868-1101. p. 388

Wilson, Candice, Librn, Federal Law Enforcement Training Center Library, Bldg 262, 1131 Chapel Crossing Rd, Glynco, GA, 31524. Tel: 912-267-2320. p. 481

Wilson, Candy, Libr Dir, Dr Sandor & Berthe Benedek Memorial Library, 7 McCoy St, Savona, NY, 14879. Tel: 607-583-4426. p. 1637

Wilson, Catherine, Br Mgr, Chicago Public Library, Northtown, 6800 N Western Ave, Chicago, IL, 60645. Tel: 312-744-2292. p. 557

Wilson, Chalanda, Coordr, Outreach Serv, Allen Parish Libraries, 320 S Sixth St, Oberlin, LA, 70655. Tel: 318-491-4543. p. 905

Wilson, Christine, Circ, Tech Serv, Pasquotank County Library, 100 E Colonial Ave, Elizabeth City, NC, 27909. Tel: 252-335-2473. p. 1687

Wilson, Cliff, Pres, Ashland Historical Society Library, Two Myrtle St, Ashland, MA, 01721. Tel: 508-881-8183. p. 986

Wilson, Connie, Br Mgr, Allegany County Library System, Frostburg Public, 65 E Main St, Frostburg, MD, 21532. Tel: 301-687-0790. p. 963

Wilson, Connie, Librn, Wilsonville Public Library, 203 Iva St, Wilsonville, NE, 69046. Tel: 308-737-7258. p. 1341

Wilson, Cris, Ad, Kershaw County Library, 1304 Broad St, Camden, SC, 29020. Tel: 803-425-1508, Ext 3209. p. 2048

Wilson, Dani, Dean, Libr & Learning Res, Fullerton College, 321 E Chapman Ave, Fullerton, CA, 92832-2095. Tel: 714-992-7040. p. 147

Wilson, Danielle, Libr Mgr, Alameda County Library, San Lorenzo Library, 395 Paseo Grande, San Lorenzo, CA, 94580-2453. Tel: 510-284-0640. p. 143

Wilson, David, Fac Librn, Austin Community College, Northridge Campus Library, 11928 Stone Hollow Dr, 2nd, Rm 1223, Austin, TX, 78758. Tel: 512-223-4743. p. 2138

Wilson, Deanna, Libr Dir, Charlotte E Hobbs Memorial Library, 227 Main St, Lovell, ME, 04051. Tel: 207-925-3177. p. 930

Wilson, Debbie, Library Contact, Schreeder, Wheeler & Flint LLP, 1100 Peachtree St NE, Ste 800, Atlanta, GA, 30309. Tel: 404-681-3450. p. 466

Wilson, Debbie, ILL Serv, Oil Creek District Library Center, Two Central Ave, Oil City, PA, 16301. Tel: 814-678-3054. p. 1973

Wilson, Del, Dir, Irondale Public Library, 105 20th St S, Irondale, AL, 35210. Tel: 205-951-1415. p. 23

Wilson, Dennis, Libr Dir, Naval History & Heritage Command, 805 Kidder-Breese St SE, Washington Navy Yard, DC, 20374-5060. Tel: 202-433-2060. p. 382

Wilson, Derek, Asst Br Mgr, Atlanta-Fulton Public Library System, East Point Branch, 2757 Main St, East Point, GA, 30344. Tel: 404-613-1050. p. 461

Wilson, Elaine, Acq, University of Texas, School of Public Health Library, 1200 Herman Pressler Blvd, Houston, TX, 77030-3900. Tel: 713-500-9121. p. 2200

Wilson, Eric, Br Mgr, Hampton Public Library, Phoebus Branch, One S Mallory St, Hampton, VA, 23663. Tel: 757-727-1149. p. 2322

Wilson, Erika, Curator of Coll, Nova Scotia Museum of Industry Library, 147 N Foord St, Stellarton, NS, B0K 1S0, CANADA. Tel: 902-755-5425. p. 2622

Wilson, Erin, Circ Mgr, Worthington Libraries, Worthington Park Library, 1389 Worthington Centre Dr, Worthington, OH, 43085. Tel: 614-807-2674. p. 1834

Wilson, Felicia, Asst Dir, Colls & Technology, Nashville Public Library, 615 Church St, Nashville, TN, 37219-2314. Tel: 615-862-5805. p. 2119

Wilson, Galen, Sr Law Librn, New Castle County Law Library, Leonard L Williams Justice Center, 500 N King St, Ste 2500, Wilmington, DE, 19801. Tel: 302-255-0847. p. 357

Wilson, Gay, Planning & Develop Librn, Springfield-Greene County Library District, 4653 S Campbell Ave, Springfield, MO, 65810-1723. Tel: 417-882-0714. p. 1281

Wilson, Gina, Mgr, Mobile Public Library, Theodore Oaks Branch, 5808 Hwy 90 W, Ste E, Theodore, AL, 36582. Tel: 251-653-5012. p. 26

Wilson, Ginger, Librn, Yoakum County / Cecil Bickley Library, 205 W Fourth St, Denver City, TX, 79323. Tel: 806-592-2754. p. 2170

Wilson, Gloria, Libr Mgr, Mayerthorpe Public Library, 4601 52nd St, Mayerthorpe, AB, T0E 1N0, CANADA. Tel: 780-786-2404. p. 2547

Wilson, Grady, Dir, McCreary County Public Library District, Six N Main St, Whitley City, KY, 42653. Tel: 606-376-8738. p. 877

Wilson, Gwen, Dir, Santa Rosa County Library System, 6275 Dogwood Dr, Milton, FL, 32570. Tel: 850-981-7323. p. 426

Wilson, Hannah, Access Serv Mgr, University of Washington Libraries, Tacoma Library, 1900 Commerce St, Box 358460, Tacoma, WA, 98402-3100. Tel: 253-692-4391. p. 2382

Wilson, Harold, Evening & Weekend Manager, Media Spec, Brooklyn College Library, 2900 Bedford Ave, Brooklyn, NY, 11210. Tel: 718-951-5327. p. 1501

Wilson, Janet, Dir, Rangeley Public Library, Seven Lake St, Rangeley, ME, 04970. Tel: 207-864-5529. p. 938

Wilson, Janice A, Dir, Libr Serv, Eastern Connecticut State University, 83 Windham St, Willimantic, CT, 06226-2295. Tel: 860-465-4466. p. 347

Wilson, Jessica, Assoc Dir, Roddenbery Memorial Library, 320 N Broad St, Cairo, GA, 39828-2109. Tel: 229-377-3632. p. 468

Wilson, Jessica, Ref Librn, South Kingstown Public Library, 1057 Kingstown Rd, Peace Dale, RI, 02879-2434. Tel: 401-783-4085, 401-789-1555. p. 2036

Wilson, Jim, Dir, Burke County Public Library, 204 S King St, Morganton, NC, 28655-3535. Tel: 828-764-9276. p. 1704

Wilson, Joan Meis, Br Mgr, San Bernardino County Library, Needles Branch, 1111 Bailey Ave, Needles, CA, 92363. Tel: 760-326-9255. p. 213

Wilson, John, Govt Info Coordr, Ref Librn, Georgia Southwestern State University, 800 Georgia Southwestern State University Dr, Americus, GA, 31709. Tel: 229-931-2850. p. 457

Wilson, John, Tech Coordr, Freed-Hardeman University, 158 E Main St, Henderson, TN, 38340-2399. Tel: 731-989-6067. p. 2101

Wilson, Julie, Br Mgr, Oldham County Public Library, South Oldham, 6720 W Hwy 146, Crestwood, KY, 40014. Tel: 502-241-1108. p. 861

Wilson, Karen, Br Mgr, Jackson/Hinds Library System, Margaret Walker Alexander Library, 2525 Robinson Rd, Jackson, MS, 39209-6256. Tel: 601-354-8911. p. 1221

Wilson, Kat, Pub Serv, Great Falls Public Library, 301 Second Ave N, Great Falls, MT, 59401-2593. Tel: 406-453-0181, Ext 213. p. 1294

Wilson, Kate, Archivist, Instruction Librn, Saint Mary's College Library, 1928 Saint Mary's Rd, Moraga, CA, 94575. Tel: 925-631-4229. p. 180

Wilson, Kathleen, Br Mgr, Kitsap Regional Library, Manchester Branch, 8067 E Main St, Manchester, WA, 98353. Tel: 360-871-3921. p. 2360

Wilson, Kathleen, Br Mgr, Kitsap Regional Library, Port Orchard Branch, 87 Sidney Ave, Port Orchard, WA, 98366-5249. Tel: 360-876-2224. p. 2360

Wilson, Kathy, Head, Circ, Derby Public Library, 313 Elizabeth St, Derby, CT, 06418. Tel: 203-736-1482. p. 309

Wilson, Kathy, Sr Libr Tech, Bibliotheque Publique de Pointe-Claire, Valois Branch, 68 Prince-Edward Ave, Pointe-Claire, QC, H9R 4C7, CANADA. Tel: 514-630-1218, Ext 1661. p. 2728

Wilson, Kelly, Br Mgr, Pima County Public Library, Sam Lena-South Tucson, 1607 S Sixth Ave, Tucson, AZ, 85713. Tel: 520-594-5265. p. 82

Wilson, Kitty, Br Operations Coordr, DeKalb County Public Library, Darro C Willey Administrative Offices, 3560 Kensington Rd, Decatur, GA, 30032. Tel: 404-508-7190. p. 475

Wilson, Kristina, Archivist, Curtis Institute of Music, 1720 Locust St, Philadelphia, PA, 19103. Tel: 215-717-3148. p. 1976

Wilson, Lana J, Asst Dir, Taylor University, 1846 Main St, Upland, IN, 46989. Tel: 765-998-5267. p. 722

Wilson, Lara, Dir, Spec Coll, Univ Archivist, University of Victoria Libraries, McPherson Library, PO Box 1800, Victoria, BC, V8W 3H5, CANADA. Tel: 250-472-4480. p. 2583

Wilson, Laura, Br Mgr, Sci Librn, College of the Holy Cross, O'Callahan Science Library, Swords Bldg, Worcester, MA, 01610. Tel: 508-793-2643. p. 1072

Wilson, Laura, Res, Instruction & Outreach Librn, College of the Holy Cross, One College St, Worcester, MA, 01610. Tel: 508-793-3886. p. 1072

Wilson, Laura Lee, Dir, Huron County Community Library, Six W Emerald St, Willard, OH, 44890. Tel: 419-933-8564. p. 1831

Wilson, Lauri, Tech Serv Spec, South Arkansas Community College, 300 S West Ave, El Dorado, AR, 71730. Tel: 870-864-7115. p. 94

Wilson, Laurie, Assoc Librn, Davis Polk & Wardwell LLP Library, 450 Lexington Ave, New York, NY, 10017. Tel: 212-450-4000. p. 1585

Wilson, Leslie, Ch Serv Librn, Anacortes Public Library, 1220 Tenth St, Anacortes, WA, 98221-1988. Tel: 360-293-1910, Ext 27. p. 2357

Wilson, Lisa, Libr Mgr, Granum Public Library, 310 Railway Ave, Granum, AB, T0L 1A0, CANADA. Tel: 403-687-3912. p. 2541

Wilson, Locord, Dr, Interim Dean, Library & Info Services, Jackson State University, 1325 J R Lynch St, Jackson, MS, 39217. Tel: 601-979-2123, 601-979-4270. p. 1222

Wilson, Lorelie, Asst Br Librn, Pottawatomie Wabaunsee Regional Library, Alma Branch, 115 W Third St, Alma, KS, 66401. Tel: 785-765-3647. p. 834

Wilson, Maegen, Asst Dir, Wayne County Public Library, 1001 E Ash St, Goldsboro, NC, 27530. Tel: 919-580-4014. p. 1691

Wilson, Margery, Br Mgr, Waterville Public Library, Deansboro Branch, Marshall Community Ctr, Deansboro, NY, 13328. Tel: 315-841-4888. p. 1660

Wilson, Marianne, Libr Dir, Corsicana Public Library, 100 N 12th St, Corsicana, TX, 75110. Tel: 903-654-4810. p. 2161

Wilson, Mark, Dir, Columbia University, Original & Special Materials Cataloging, 102 Butler Library, 535 W 114th St, New York, NY, 10027. Tel: 212-854-2714. p. 1583

Wilson, Mary, Head, Pub Serv, John Marshall Law School, 245 Peachtree Center Ave NE, 18th Flr, Atlanta, GA, 30303. Tel: 678-916-2663. p. 465

Wilson, Mary, Online Serv, Ref, Resources Librn, Shorter University, 315 Shorter Ave NW, Rome, GA, 30165. Tel: 706-233-7822. p. 495

Wilson, Mary, Dir, Harvard Public Library, Four Pond Rd, Harvard, MA, 01451-1647. Tel: 978-456-4114. p. 1023

Wilson, Mary, Asst Dir, Paterson Free Public Library, 250 Broadway, Paterson, NJ, 07501. Tel: 973-321-1223. p. 1433

Wilson, Mary Ellen, ILL Coordr, Patten Free Library, 33 Summer St, Bath, ME, 04530. Tel: 207-443-5141, Ext 24. p. 916

Wilson, Mat, Br Mgr, Montgomery County Memorial Library System, Charles B Stewart - West Branch, 202 Bessie Price Owen Dr, Montgomery, TX, 77356. Tel: 936-442-7718, 936-788-8314. p. 2159

Wilson, Megan, Br Mgr, Blackwater Regional Library, Carrollton Public, 14362 New Towne Haven Lane, Carrollton, VA, 23314. Tel: 757-238-2641. p. 2313

Wilson, Melissa, Librn, Northwest Regional Library, Roseau Public Library, 121 Center St E, Ste 100, Roseau, MN, 56751. Tel: 218-463-2825. p. 1205

Wilson, Mia, Human Res & Finance Coordr, South Central Kansas Library System, 321 N Main St, South Hutchinson, KS, 67505. Tel: 620-663-3211. p. 837

Wilson, Mia, Librn, Temple College, 2600 S First St, Temple, TX, 76504. Tel: 254-298-8622. p. 2247

Wilson, Michael W, Dr, Campus Librn, Art Institute of Atlanta Library, 6600 Peachtree Dunwoody Rd, 100 Embassy Row, Atlanta, GA, 30328-1635. Tel: 770-689-4885. p. 460

Wilson, Michella, Dir, Gleason Memorial Library, 105 College St, Gleason, TN, 38229. Tel: 731-648-9020. p. 2099

Wilson, Monica, Libr Mgr, Nelson, Mullins, Riley & Scarborough, 1320 Main St, Ste 1700, Columbia, SC, 29201. Tel: 803-255-9367. p. 2053

Wilson, Nancy, Dep Dir, Solano County Library, 1150 Kentucky St, Fairfield, CA, 94533. p. 142

Wilson, Nancy, Head Librn, Lewis Dana Hill Memorial Library, 2079 Main St, Center Lovell, ME, 04231-9702. Tel: 207-928-2301. p. 921

Wilson, Nancy, Dir, Lawrence Memorial Library, 40 North St, Bristol, VT, 05443. Tel: 802-453-2366. p. 2280

Wilson, Oceana, Dean of Libr, Bennington College, One College Dr, Bennington, VT, 05201-6001. Tel: 802-440-4610. p. 2279

Wilson, Pam, Pub Serv Mgr, Hoover Public Library, 200 Municipal Dr, Hoover, AL, 35216. Tel: 205-444-7810. p. 21

Wilson, Patty, Br Mgr, Ohoopee Regional Library System, Glennville Public, 408 E Barnard St, Glennville, GA, 30427. Tel: 912-654-3812. p. 502

Wilson, Patty, Cat/Ser Librn, Immaculata University, 1145 King Rd, Immaculata, PA, 19345-0705. Tel: 484-323-3839. p. 1945

Wilson, Phyllis, Libr Tech, Colorado Department of Corrections, Limon Correctional Facility Library-General, 49030 State Hwy 71, Limon, CO, 80826. Tel: 719-775-9221, Ext 3240. p. 289

Wilson, Reggie, Mgr, Springfield City Library, East Springfield Branch, 21 Osborne Terrace, Springfield, MA, 01104. Tel: 413-263-6840. p. 1056

Wilson, Reggie, Mgr, Springfield City Library, Sixteen Acres Branch, 1187 Parker St, Springfield, MA, 01129. Tel: 413-263-6858. p. 1056

Wilson, Sandra, Assoc Librn, Reference Services, University of Detroit Mercy Libraries, 4001 W McNichols Rd, Detroit, MI, 48221-3038. Tel: 313-578-0577. p. 1099

Wilson, Sara, Prog Coordr, Southwest Kansas Library System, Talking Books, 100 Military Ave, Ste 210, Dodge City, KS, 67801. Tel: 620-225-1231. p. 805

Wilson, Sara, Dir, Mill Pond Public Library, 140 N South St, Kingston, WI, 53939. Tel: 920-394-3281. p. 2445

Wilson, Sarah, Libr Dir, Elkhart Public Library District, 121 E Bohan St, Elkhart, IL, 62634. Tel: 217-947-2313. p. 584

Wilson, Sarah, Youth Serv Librn, Thomas Ford Memorial Library, 800 Chestnut St, Western Springs, IL, 60558. Tel: 708-246-0520. p. 661

Wilson, Scott, Librn, Los Angeles Times, 2300 E Imperial Hwy, El Segundo, CA, 90245. Tel: 213-237-5000. p. 140

Wilson, Shannon, Library District, Tribal Community Outreach Specialist, Courier, Navajo County Library District, 121 W Buffalo, Holbrook, AZ, 86025. Tel: 928-524-4745. p. 63

Wilson, Shatiqua, Dir, Southern University in New Orleans, 6400 Press Dr, New Orleans, LA, 70126. Tel: 504-286-5225. p. 903

Wilson, Silvia, Dir, Kezar Falls Circulating Library, Two Wadleigh St, Parsonsfield, ME, 04047. Tel: 207-625-2424. p. 935

Wilson, Staci, Dir, Libr Serv, Catawba Valley Community College Library, Cuyler A Dunbar Bldg, 2550 Hwy 70 SE, Hickory, NC, 28602. Tel: 828-327-7400, Ext 4525. p. 1696

Wilson, Stephanie, Ref (Info Servs), Seattle University, School of Law Library, Sullivan Hall, 901 12th Ave, Seattle, WA, 98122-4411. Tel: 206-398-4221. p. 2380

Wilson, Steve P, Outreach Librn, University of South Carolina, School of Medicine Library, Bldg 101, 6311 Garners Ferry Rd, Columbia, SC, 29209. Tel: 803-216-3200. p. 2056

Wilson, Susan, ILL Librn, Pub Serv Librn, Kilgore College, 1100 Broadway, Kilgore, TX, 75662. Tel: 903-983-8239. p. 2205

Wilson, Suzanne, Libr Tech & Res Dir, Illinois Wesleyan University, One Ames Plaza, Bloomington, IL, 61701-7188. Tel: 309-556-3144. p. 543

Wilson, Suzanne, Outreach & Prog Coordr, Rotary Club of Slave Lake Public Library, 50 Main St SW, Slave Lake, AB, T0G 2A0, CANADA. Tel: 780-849-5250. p. 2554

Wilson, Tamara L B, Cat/Syst Librn, US Customs & Border Protection Information Resources Center, 90 K St NE, Washington, DC, 20229. Tel: 202-325-0130. p. 380

Wilson, Tammie, Librn, South Carolina Attorney General's Office Library, 1000 Assembly St, Ste 519, Columbia, SC, 29201-3117. Tel: 803-734-3970. p. 2054

Wilson, Terri, Assoc Dir, Texas Tech University Health Sciences, Harrington Library, 1400 Wallace Blvd, Amarillo, TX, 79106. Tel: 806-414-9964. p. 2214

Wilson, Terrie, Head of Libr, Michigan State University Libraries, Fine Arts-Art, W403 Main Library, 366 W Circle Dr, East Lansing, MI, 48824. Tel: 517-884-6469. p. 1102

Wilson, Tiffany, Commun Coordr, Chattahoochee Valley Libraries, 3000 Macon Rd, Columbus, GA, 31906-2201. Tel: 706-243-2673. p. 471

Wilson, Tiffany, Br Mgr, Johnson County Public Library, Franklin Branch, 401 State St, Franklin, IN, 46131. Tel: 317-738-2833. p. 686

Wilson, Tracy, Adult Serv Coordr, Asst Dir, Roseville Public Library, 29777 Gratiot Ave, Roseville, MI, 48066. Tel: 586-445-5407. p. 1146

Wilson, W Blake, Asst Dir, Instrul Serv Librn, University of Kansas Libraries, Wheat Law Library, Green Hall, Rm 200, 1535 W 15th St, Lawrence, KS, 66045-7608. Tel: 785-864-3025. p. 820

Wilson, William, Br Head, United States Navy, Naval Explosive Ordnance Disposal Technology Division Technical Library, 2008 Stump Neck Rd, Code 2011, Indian Head, MD, 20640-5070. Tel: 301-744-6817. p. 969

Wilson, Yvette, Librn, Madison County Law Library, One N Main, Rm 205, London, OH, 43140-1068. Tel: 740-852-9515. p. 1797

Wilson-Cotey, Anne Elizabeth, Tech Serv Spec, Valparaiso University, 1410 Chapel Dr, Valparaiso, IN, 46383-6493. Tel: 219-464-5500. p. 723

Wilt, Laura, Librn, Oregon Department of Transportation Library, Mill Creek Bldg, 555 13th St NE, Salem, OR, 97301. Tel: 503-986-3280. p. 1896

Wilt, Richard, Dr, Dean, Libr Serv, Lehigh Carbon Community College Library, 4750 Orchard Rd, Schnecksville, PA, 18078. Tel: 610-799-1164. p. 2003

Wilting, Ben, Emerging Tech Librn, Amarillo Public Library, 413 E Fourth Ave, Amarillo, TX, 79101. Tel: 806-378-3054. p. 2134

Wilton, Brenda, Librn, Bonavista Memorial Public Library, 32 Church St, Bonavista, NL, A0C 1B0, CANADA. Tel: 709-468-2185. p. 2607

Wilton, Karen, Circ Mgr, William Jeanes Memorial Library, 4051 Joshua Rd, Lafayette Hill, PA, 19444-1400. Tel: 610-828-0441, Ext 102. p. 1950

Wiltrout, Richard, Mgr, Info Tech, Tuscarawas County Public Library, 121 Fair Ave NW, New Philadelphia, OH, 44663-2600. Tel: 330-364-4474. p. 1807

Wiltrout, Richard, IT Mgr, North Canton Public Library, 185 N Main St, North Canton, OH, 44720-2595. Tel: 330-499-4712. p. 1809

Wimberly, Ware W, III, Dir, Wabash Carnegie Public Library, 188 W Hill St, Wabash, IN, 46992-3048. Tel: 260-563-2972. p. 724

Wimbish, Michelle, Area Dir, Learning Res, Southern Union State Community College, Valley Campus Library, 321 Fob James Dr, Valley, AL, 36854. Tel: 334-756-4151. p. 39

Wimbish, Michelle, Dir, Learning Res Ctr, Southern Union State Community College, 750 Robert St, Wadley, AL, 36276. Tel: 256-395-2211. p. 39

Wimer, Aaron, Libr Dir, The Citadel, 171 Moultrie St, Charleston, SC, 29409-6140. p. 2050

Wimmer, Carly, Young Adult Coll Develop Librn, Kokomo-Howard County Public Library, 220 N Union St, Kokomo, IN, 46901-4614. Tel: 765-457-3242. p. 699

Wimsatt, Zebulon, Youth Serv Librn, Mansfield Public Library, 255 Hope St, Mansfield, MA, 02048-2353. Tel: 508-261-7380. p. 1031

Winans, Dawn, Head, Research & Discovery, Kettering University Library, 1700 W University Ave, Flint, MI, 48504. Tel: 810-762-9842. p. 1107

Winberry, Jennifer, Asst Dir, Hunterdon County Library, 314 State Rte 12, Bldg 3, Flemington, NJ, 08822. Tel: 908-788-1444. p. 1403

Winberry, Jennifer, Asst Dir, Hunterdon County Library, South County Branch, 1108 Old York Rd, Ringoes, NJ, 08551. Tel: 908-968-4611. p. 1403

Winbigler, Dayle, Libr Serv Coordr, The College of Idaho, 2112 Cleveland Blvd, Caldwell, ID, 83605. p. 518

Winborne, Wayne, Exec Dir, Rutgers University Libraries, Institute of Jazz Studies, John Cotton Dana Library, 185 University Ave, 4th Flr, Newark, NJ, 07102. Tel: 973-353-3796. p. 1428

Winchcombe, Terri, Mgr, Acq Serv, Saint Mary's University, 923 Robie St, Halifax, NS, B3H 3C3, CANADA. Tel: 902-420-5535. p. 2621

Winchell, John, Archives Curator, Western Michigan University, Zhang Legacy Collections Center, 1650 Oakland Dr, Kalamazoo, MI, 49008. Tel: 269-387-8485. p. 1122

Wind, Allyson A, Discovery Librn, Electronic Res Librn, East Stroudsburg University, 200 Prospect Ave, East Stroudsburg, PA, 18301-2999. Tel: 570-422-3597. p. 1928

Wind, Katherine, Digital Serv Librn, Bristol Community College, Taunton Campus, Two Hamilton St, 3rd Flr, Taunton, MA, 02780. Tel: 774-357-4001. p. 1017

Windham, Daphne L, Libr Dir, Briceville Public Library, 111 Slatestone Rd, Briceville, TN, 37710. Tel: 865-426-6220. p. 2089
Windham, Melody, Asst Br Mgr, Bossier Parish Libraries, Anna P Tooke Memorial Branch, 451 Fairview Point Rd, Elm Grove, LA, 71051. Tel: 318-987-3915. p. 886
Windhorst, Colin, Dr, Dir, Lincoln Memorial Library, 17 King St, Dennysville, ME, 04628. Tel: 207-726-4750. p. 923
Windish, Donna, Instrul Serv Librn, Randolph Community College Library, 629 Industrial Park Ave, Asheboro, NC, 27205-7333. Tel: 336-633-0204. p. 1671
Windle, Christy, Br Mgr, Shasta Public Libraries, Anderson Branch, 3200 W Center St, Anderson, CA, 96007. Tel: 530-365-7685. p. 199
Windsor, Michael, Circ Mgr, Scarborough Public Library, 48 Gorham Rd, Scarborough, ME, 04074. Tel: 207-396-6268. p. 939
Winecoff, Judith, Youth Serv Librn, Watauga County Public Library, 140 Queen St, Boone, NC, 28607. Tel: 828-264-8784. p. 1675
Winehart, Brandi, Youth Librn, Allen Park Public Library, 8100 Allen Rd, Allen Park, MI, 48101. Tel: 313-381-2425. p. 1077
Wines, Bill, Head, Circ & Tech Serv, Commerce Township Community Library, 180 E Commerce, Commerce Township, MI, 48382. Tel: 248-669-8101, Ext 102. p. 1093
Winfield, Carly, Ref & Instrul Design Librn, Richard Bland College Library, Commons Bldg, 11301 Johnson Rd, Petersburg, VA, 23805. Tel: 804-862-6226. p. 2337
Winfield, Lesley, Libr Mgr, Olds Municipal Library, 5217 52nd St, Olds, AB, T4H 1H7, CANADA. Tel: 403-556-6460. p. 2549
Winfield, Lynda, Libr Mgr, Longview Municipal Library, 128 Morrison Rd, Longview, AB, T0L 1H0, CANADA. Tel: 403-558-3927. p. 2547
Winfrey, Emily, Supvr, Youth Serv, Gaston County Public Library, 1555 E Garrison Blvd, Gastonia, NC, 28054. Tel: 704-868-2164. p. 1690
Winfrey, Laura, Dir, Somerville-Fayette County Library, 216 W Market St, Somerville, TN, 38068-1592. Tel: 901-465-5248. p. 2127
Wing, Erica, Dir, Johnstown Public Library, 38 S Market St, Johnstown, NY, 12095. Tel: 518-762-8317. p. 1558
Wing, Justin C, Budget Dir, Dir, Strategic Initiatives, University of Delaware Library, 181 S College Ave, Newark, DE, 19717-5267. Tel: 302-831-2965. p. 355
Wing, Natalie, Librn, Yukon Public Law Library, Yukon Law Courts, 2134 Second Ave, Whitehorse, YT, Y1A 2C6, CANADA. Tel: 867-667-3086. p. 2758
Wing, Tracy, Dir, Greenfield Public Library, 202 S First St, Greenfield, IA, 50849. Tel: 641-743-6120. p. 756
Wingard, Ben, Librn, Sierra College Library, Nevada County Campus, 250 Sierra College Dr, Grass Valley, CA, 95945. Tel: 530-274-5304. p. 203
Winger, Sara, Sr Acad Librn, University of Wisconsin-Platteville Baraboo Sauk County, 1006 Connie Rd, Baraboo, WI, 53913. Tel: 608-800-6817. p. 2422
Winger, Sarah, Acad Librn, University of Wisconsin-Platteville Richland Campus, 1200 US Hwy 14 W, Richland Center, WI, 53581. Tel: 608-800-6817. p. 2473
Winger, Tami, Libr Dir, Kountze Public Library, 800 S Redwood Ave, Kountze, TX, 77625. Tel: 409-246-2826. p. 2207
Wingertzahn, Marianne, Head, Circ, Bronxville Public Library, 201 Pondfield Rd, Bronxville, NY, 10708. Tel: 914-337-7680. p. 1500
Wingo, Tara, Electronic Res, Ser, Union University, 1050 Union University Dr, Jackson, TN, 38305-3697. Tel: 731-661-5414. p. 2102
Wingrove, Karen, ILL, Northland Public Library, 300 Cumberland Rd, Pittsburgh, PA, 15237-5455. Tel: 412-366-8100, Ext 119. p. 1994
Wings, Arron, Dean, Learning Serv, Kirkwood Community College, Benton Hall, 6301 Kirkwood Blvd SW, Cedar Rapids, IA, 52404-5260. Tel: 319-398-5553. p. 738
Winkelmann, Carrie, Librn, Petersburg Public Library, 220 S Sixth St, Petersburg, IL, 62675. Tel: 217-632-2807. p. 635
Winkelmann, Jeanie, Online Research Librn, University of Jamestown, 6070 College Lane, Jamestown, ND, 58405-0001. Tel: 701-252-3467. p. 1736
Winkers, Mona, Ch, Dwight T Parker Public Library, 925 Lincoln Ave, Fennimore, WI, 53809-1743. Tel: 608-822-6294. p. 2434
Winkler, Irene, Head, Adult Serv, Uniondale Public Library, 400 Uniondale Ave, Uniondale, NY, 11553. Tel: 516-489-2220. p. 1654
Winkler, Jennifer, Br Mgr, Lorain Public Library System, North Ridgeville Branch, 35700 Bainbridge Rd, North Ridgeville, OH, 44039. Tel: 440-327-8326. p. 1797
Winkler, Joy A, Librn, Immanuel Medical Center, 6901 N 72nd St, Omaha, NE, 68122. Tel: 402-572-2345. p. 1328
Winkler, Julia, Ch, Dailey Memorial Library, 101 Junior High Dr, Derby, VT, 05829. Tel: 802-766-5063. p. 2283
Winkler, Monica, Dir, Keokuk Public Library, 210 N Fifth St, Keokuk, IA, 52632. Tel: 319-524-1483. p. 762
Winland, Natalie, Pub Serv Mgr, University of Cincinnati, 4200 Clermont College Dr, Batavia, OH, 45103-1785. Tel: 513-732-5233. p. 1749
Winlock, Debbie, Libr Mgr, Page Public Library, 479 S Lake Powell Blvd, Page, AZ, 86040. Tel: 928-645-4270. p. 67
Winn, Beverly, Head, Tech Serv, Nevins Memorial Library, 305 Broadway, Methuen, MA, 01844-6898. Tel: 978-686-4080. p. 1035
Winn, Jade, Outreach Librn, University of San Diego, Helen K & James S Copley Library, 5998 Alcala Park, San Diego, CA, 92110. p. 222
Winn, Janis, Ref Librn, Utica University, 1600 Burrstone Rd, Utica, NY, 13502-4892. Tel: 315-792-3351. p. 1656
Winn, Trevor, Head, Adult Serv, Royal Oak Public Library, 222 E Eleven Mile Rd, Royal Oak, MI, 48067-2633. Tel: 248-246-3732. p. 1146
Winner, Cristina, Dir, Crowley Public Library, 409 Oak St, Crowley, TX, 76036. Tel: 817-297-6707. p. 2162
Winnicki, Debbie, Dir, Libr Serv, Head Librn, Brokenhead River Regional Library, 427 Park Ave, Beausejour, MB, R0E 0C0, CANADA. Tel: 204-268-7570. p. 2585
Winnigham, Laura, Dir, Pickett County Public Library, 79 Pickett Square Annex, Byrdstown, TN, 38549. Tel: 931-864-6281. p. 2090
Winograd, Catherine, Sr Res Librn, Russell Sage Foundation Library, 112 E 64th St, New York, NY, 10065. Tel: 212-752-8640. p. 1601
Winograd, Mary Beth, Circ Mgr, Fort Bend County Libraries, 1001 Golfview Dr, Richmond, TX, 77469-5199. Tel: 281-633-4748. p. 2232
Winrod, Michelle, Asst Librn, Craig Public Library, 504 Third St, Craig, AK, 99921. Tel: 907-826-3281. p. 44
Winslow, Dan, Coll Develop Librn, Syst Librn, Midwestern State University, 3410 Taft Blvd, Wichita Falls, TX, 76308-2099. Tel: 940-397-4169. p. 2257
Winslow, Nikki, District Dir, Altadena Library District, 600 E Mariposa St, Altadena, CA, 91001. Tel: 626-798-0833. p. 116
Winslow, Nikki, Asst Dir, Glendale Library, Arts & Culture, 222 E Harvard St, Glendale, CA, 91205. Tel: 818-548-2021. p. 148
Winslow, Nikki, Br Mgr, Las Vegas-Clark County Library District, Spring Valley Library, 4280 S Jones Blvd, Las Vegas, NV, 89103. Tel: 702-507-3820. p. 1347
Winslow, Tricia, Br Mgr, Southwest La Plata Library District, 75 County Rd 218, Durango, CO, 81303. Tel: 970-375-3816. p. 278
Winsor, John, Head, Tech Serv, Syst Librn, Northeastern University Libraries, 5000 MacArthur Blvd, Oakland, CA, 94613. Tel: 510-430-2066. p. 185
Winstead, Amber, Librn II, Sheppard Memorial Library, 530 S Evans St, Greenville, NC, 27858. Tel: 252-329-4580. p. 1694
Winstead, Jean, Librn, Beebe Healthcare, 424 Savannah Rd, Lewes, DE, 19958. Tel: 302-645-3100, Ext 5472. p. 353
Winstead, Leaha, Youth Librn, Neshoba County Public Library, 230 Beacon St, Philadelphia, MS, 39350. Tel: 601-656-4911. p. 1229
Winstead, Tina, Dir, Huntington Memorial Library, 62 Chestnut St, Oneonta, NY, 13820-2498. Tel: 607-432-1980. p. 1611
Winston, Andrew, Asst Dir, Pub Serv, George Washington University, Jacob Burns Law Library, 716 20th St NW, Washington, DC, 20052. Tel: 202-994-0028. p. 367
Winston, Comfort, Libr Coord, University of Arkansas Community College Batesville, 2005 White Dr, Batesville, AR, 72501. Tel: 870-612-2020. p. 90
Winston, Kyle, Gen Mgr, Corpus Christi Museum of Science & History, 1900 N Chaparral St, Corpus Christi, TX, 78401. Tel: 361-826-4667. p. 2160
Winston, Mark, Dir, J Lewis Crozer Library, 620 Engle St, Chester, PA, 19013-2199. Tel: 610-494-3454. p. 1921
Winter, Amy, Br Mgr, Willoughby-Eastlake Public Library, Eastlake Branch, 36706 Lake Shore Blvd, Eastlake, OH, 44095. Tel: 440-942-7880. p. 1783
Winter, Kathy, Libr Asst, Garden City Community College, 801 Campus Dr, Garden City, KS, 67846. Tel: 620-276-9656. p. 809
Winter, Ken, Assoc Libr Dir, Virginia Department of Transportation (VDOT) Research Library, 530 Edgemont Rd, Charlottesville, VA, 22903. Tel: 434-962-8979. p. 2310
Winter, Leah, Br Mgr, Annapolis Valley Regional Library, Isabel & Roy Jodrey Memorial Library - Hantsport, 10 Main St, Hantsport, NS, B0P 1P0, CANADA. Tel: 902-684-0103. p. 2616
Winter, Susan, Dr, Assoc Dean, Res, University of Maryland, Hornbake Library, Ground Flr, Rm 0220, 4130 Campus Dr, College Park, MD, 20742-4345. Tel: 301-405-2039. p. 2786
Winterbauer, Theresa, Head, Youth Serv, DeKalb Public Library, Haish Memorial Library Bldg, 309 Oak St, DeKalb, IL, 60115-3369. Tel: 815-756-9568. p. 577
Wintermute, Harriet, Head, Metadata Serv, Iowa State University Library, 302 Parks Library, 701 Morrill Rd, Ames, IA, 50011-2102. Tel: 515-344-4993. p. 731
Winterowd, Leigh Ann, Br Mgr, Kitsap Regional Library, Kingston Branch, 26159 Dulay Rd NE, Kingston, WA, 98346. Tel: 360-297-3330. p. 2360
Winters, Adam, Archivist, Southern Baptist Theological Seminary, 2825 Lexington Rd, Louisville, KY, 40280-0294. p. 866
Winters, Barbara, Head Librn, Bethlehem College & Seminary Library, 720 13th Ave S, Minneapolis, MN, 55415. Tel: 612-455-3420. p. 1183
Winters, Colleen, Dir, Forest Grove City Library, 2114 Pacific Ave, Forest Grove, OR, 97116. Tel: 503-992-3246. p. 1880
Winters, Kendra, Mgr, West Georgia Regional Library, Maude P Ragsdale Public Library, 1815 Hiram-Douglasville Hwy, Hiram, GA, 30141. Tel: 770-439-3964. p. 470
Winters, Laurie, Br Librn, Moundsville-Marshall County Public Library, Cameron Public, Benedum Bldg, 44 Main St, Cameron, WV, 26033. Tel: 304-686-2140. p. 2410
Winters, Rosemary, Libr Dir, Cutchogue-New Suffolk Free Library, 27550 Main Rd, Cutchogue, NY, 11935. Tel: 631-734-6360. p. 1524
Winters, Susan, Pub Serv Librn, University of Mississippi, 481 Chuckie Mullins Dr, University, MS, 38677. Tel: 662-915-6824. p. 1234

Witte-Walker, Deanna, Exec Dir, Southold Historical Society Museum Library, 54325 Main Rd, Southold, NY, 11971. Tel: 631-765-5500. p. 1643
Wittek, Lauren, Communications Spec, University of Arizona Libraries, Health Sciences Library, 1501 N Campbell Ave, Tucson, AZ, 85724. Tel: 520-626-6125. p. 83
Wittekind, Paul, Librn, Porzio, Bromberg & Newman Library, 100 Southgate Pkwy, Morristown, NJ, 07962-1997. Tel: 973-889-43628. p. 1422
Wittenberg, Jamie, Asst Dean, University of Colorado Boulder, 1720 Pleasant St, Boulder, CO, 80309. Tel: 303-492-8705. p. 267
Wittenberg, Ronda, Libr Operations Mgr, Humboldt County Library, 1313 Third St, Eureka, CA, 95501-0553. Tel: 707-269-1918. p. 141
Wittenborn, Katelyn, Digital Initiatives Librn, Wyoming State Library, 2800 Central Ave, Cheyenne, WY, 82002. Tel: 307-777-7282. p. 2493
Wittenborne, Lisa, Librn II, Chester Public Library, 733 State St, Chester, IL, 62233. Tel: 618-826-3711. p. 553
Wittenmyer, Eve, Br Mgr, Palos Verdes Library District, Malaga Cove, 2400 Via Campesina, Palos Verdes Estates, CA, 90274-3662. Tel: 310-377-9584, Ext 450. p. 205
Wittenmyer, Eve, Br Mgr, Palos Verdes Library District, Miraleste, 29089 Palos Verdes Dr E, Rancho Palos Verdes, CA, 90275. Tel: 310-377-9584, Ext 452. p. 205
Witter, Caitlin, Librn, Shawano County Library, Tigerton Branch, 221 Birch St, Tigerton, WI, 54486. Tel: 715-535-2194. p. 2476
Witteveen, April, Libr Dir, Oregon State University, Tykeson Hall 202, 1500 SW Chandler Ave, Bend, OR, 97702. Tel: 541-322-2079. p. 1874
Witteveen-Lane, Caralee, Librn, Mercy Health, Wege Center for Health & Learning, 300 Lafayette Ave SE, Grand Rapids, MI, 49503. Tel: 616-685-6243. p. 1111
Wittman, Jessica, Asst Dir, Acad Tech, The John Marshall Law School, 300 S State St, 6th Flr, Chicago, IL, 60604. Tel: 312-427-2737. p. 564
Wittmann, Stacy, Dir, Eisenhower Public Library District, 4613 N Oketo Ave, Harwood Heights, IL, 60706. Tel: 708-867-7828. p. 597
Wittorff, Amy Northrop, Exec Dir, Wethersfield Historical Society, 150 Main St, Wethersfield, CT, 06109. Tel: 860-529-7656. p. 347
Wittwer, Annett, Commun Librn, Cariboo Regional District Library, Tatla Lake Branch, 16451 Chilcotin Hwy, Tatla Lake, BC, V0L 1V0, CANADA. Tel: 250-476-1242. p. 2584
Witzki, Patricia, Library Contact, Long Beach Public Library, West End, 810 W Beech St, Long Beach, NY, 11561. Tel: 516-432-2704. p. 1565
Wivell, Tiffany, Asst Dir, Bosler Memorial Library, 158 W High St, Carlisle, PA, 17013-2988. Tel: 717-243-4642. p. 1918
Wixom, Jill, Circ Mgr/ILL, Franklin Pierce University Library, 40 University Dr, Rindge, NH, 03461-3114. Tel: 603-899-4140. p. 1379
Wladysiuk, Stefan, Librn, Polish Institute of Arts & Sciences Library, 4220 rue Drolet, Montreal, QC, H2W 2L6, CANADA. Tel: 514-379-4220. p. 2727
Wnek, Zavhary X, Curator, Latah County Historical Society Library, 327 E Second St, Moscow, ID, 83843. Tel: 208-882-1004. p. 526
Wochinske, Kelly, Youth Serv Coordr, Milwaukee Public Library, 814 W Wisconsin Ave, Milwaukee, WI, 53233-2309. Tel: 414-286-3000. p. 2459
Wodarczak, Erwin, Univ Archivist, University of British Columbia Library, University Archives, Irving K Barber Learning Ctr, 1961 East Mall, Vancouver, BC, V6T 1Z1, CANADA. Tel: 604-827-3954. p. 2580
Wodehouse, Kate, Coll, Dir, Libr Serv, Providence Athenaeum, 251 Benefit St, Providence, RI, 02903. Tel: 401-421-6970. p. 2039
Woessner, Jeanette, Dir, Libr & Res Serv, Fredrikson & Bryon, 200 S Sixth St, Ste 4000, Minneapolis, MN, 55402. Tel: 612-492-7000. p. 1183
Woetzel, Mary Denise, Ref Librn, J Sargeant Reynolds Community College Library, Parham Campus-Library & Information Services, Massey LTC, Rm 103, 1651 E Parham Rd, Richmond, VA, 23228. Tel: 804-523-5329. p. 2341
Wofford, Glenda, Dir, Salem Public Library, 403 N Jackson St, Salem, MO, 65560. Tel: 573-729-4331. p. 1278
Wofford, Jessica, Dir, Raymond A Sapp Memorial Township Library, 103 E Main St, Wyanet, IL, 61379. Tel: 815-699-2342. p. 665
Wogee, Alysha, Head, Youth Serv, Pahrump Community Library, 701 E St, Pahrump, NV, 89048. Tel: 775-727-5930. p. 1348
Wogen, Peggy, Dir, Malta Township Public Library, 203 E Adams St, Malta, IL, 60150. Tel: 815-825-2525. p. 612
Wohl, Helen, Asst Library Dir, Technical Services, University of Miami, 1311 Miller Dr, Coral Gables, FL, 33146. Tel: 305-284-2251. p. 390
Wohl, Jo, Br Mgr, Carbon County Library System, Hanna Branch, 303 Third St, Hanna, WY, 82327. Tel: 307-325-9357. p. 2498
Wohl, Jo, Br Mgr, Carbon County Library System, Medicine Bow Branch, 314 Sage St, Medicine Bow, WY, 82329. Tel: 307-379-2888. p. 2498
Wohleber, Barbara, Chief Librn, Britt Area Library, Britt Public School, 841 Riverside Dr, Britt, ON, P0G 1A0, CANADA. Tel: 705-383-2292. p. 2633
Wohler, Melissa, Dir, Frankfort Free Library, 123 S Frankfort St, Frankfort, NY, 13340. Tel: 315-894-9611. p. 1534
Wohlers, John, Tech Coordr, Waubonsee Community College, Collins Hall, 2nd Flr, State Rte 47 at Waubonsee Dr, Sugar Grove, IL, 60554. Tel: 630-466-2587. p. 652
Wohlford, Carol, Libr Dir, Eudora Public Library, 14 E Ninth St, Eudora, KS, 66025. Tel: 785-542-2496. p. 807
Wohlfort, Jordan, Coll Develop Librn, Maryland State Library for the Blind & Print Disabled, 415 Park Ave, Baltimore, MD, 21201-3603. Tel: 410-230-2424. p. 955
Wohnoutka, Jill, Exec Dir, Kandiyohi County Historical Society, 610 NE Hwy 71, Willmar, MN, 56201. Tel: 320-235-1881. p. 1208
Woitas, Christina, Dir, Sussex County Department of Libraries, Greenwood Public, 100 Mill St, Greenwood, DE, 19950. Tel: 302-349-5309. p. 353
Wojnowski, Amy, Ch Serv Librn, New London Public Library, 406 S Pearl St, New London, WI, 54961-1441. Tel: 920-982-8519. p. 2464
Wojtalewicz, Terri, Dir, Lansing Community Library, 730 First Terrace, Ste 1, Lansing, KS, 66043. Tel: 913-727-2929. p. 818
Wolak, Jody, Libr Dir, Wayne Public Library, 3737 S Wayne Rd, Wayne, MI, 48184. Tel: 734-721-7832. p. 1158
Wolaver, Lou Ann, Librn, S M Dunlap Memorial Library, 300 W Main St, Italy, TX, 76651. Tel: 972-483-6481. p. 2203
Wolbeck, Dixie, Libr Mgr, Heisler Municipal Library, 100 Haultain Ave, Heisler, AB, T0B 2A0, CANADA. Tel: 780-889-3925. p. 2542
Wolcott, Mandi, Asst Dir, Coburn Free Library, 275 Main St, Owego, NY, 13827. Tel: 607-687-3520. p. 1613
Wolcott, Peggy, Asst Librn, Madbury Public Library, Nine Town Hall Rd, Madbury, NH, 03823. Tel: 603-743-1400. p. 1371
Wold, Derrick, Dir, Davie County Public Library, 371 N Main St, Mocksville, NC, 27028-2115. Tel: 336-753-6030. p. 1703
Wold, Hailey, Dir, Otero Junior College, 20 Pinon Ave, La Junta, CO, 81050. Tel: 719-384-6882. p. 287
Woldo, Jane, Asst Prof of Law, Libr Dir, Vermont Law School, 164 Chelsea St, South Royalton, VT, 05068. Tel: 802-831-1461. p. 2295
Wolenetz, Alissa, Dir, Lewistown Public Library, 701 W Main St, Lewistown, MT, 59457. Tel: 406-538-5212. p. 1298
Wolf, Adriana, Dir, Libr Serv, West Virginia Northern Community College Library, 1704 Market St, Wheeling, WV, 26003-3699. Tel: 304-214-8952. p. 2417
Wolf, Christina, Archivist, Spec Coll Librn, Oklahoma City University, 2501 N Blackwelder, Oklahoma City, OK, 73106. Tel: 405-208-5068. p. 1858
Wolf, Ed, Circ Serv, West Liberty University, 208 University Dr, West Liberty, WV, 26074. p. 2417
Wolf, Eric, Dir of Coll, The New York Society Library, 53 E 79th St, New York, NY, 10075. Tel: 212-288-6900, Ext 247. p. 1598
Wolf, Jay, Head, Tech Serv, Englewood Public Library, 31 Engle St, Englewood, NJ, 07631. Tel: 201-568-2215, Ext 235. p. 1401
Wolf, Katherine, Librn, School for Advanced Research Library, 660 Garcia St, Santa Fe, NM, 87505. Tel: 505-954-7234. p. 1477
Wolf, Kathy, Br Mgr, Rochester Public Library, Winton, 611 Winton Rd N, Rochester, NY, 14609. Tel: 585-428-8204. p. 1630
Wolf, Molly, Head, Res & Instrul Serv, Widener University, One University Pl, Chester, PA, 19013. Tel: 610-499-4075. p. 1921
Wolf, Robert, University Librn for Technical Servs, Fairleigh Dickinson University, 285 Madison Ave, M-LAO-03, Madison, NJ, 07940. Tel: 973-443-8523. p. 1415
Wolf, Susan, Ref Mgr, Northbrook Public Library, 1201 Cedar Lane, Northbrook, IL, 60062-4581. Tel: 847-272-6224. p. 627
Wolfcale, Lidia, Circ Supvr, Saint Johns County Public Library System, Ponte Vedra Beach Branch, 101 Library Blvd, Ponte Vedra Beach, FL, 32082. Tel: 904-827-6956. p. 440
Wolfe, Arline, Arts Metadata Tech, Music Libr Supvr, Saint Lawrence University, Music Library, 21 Romoda Dr, Canton, NY, 13617. Tel: 315-229-5799. p. 1514
Wolfe, Ashley, Head, Adult Serv, Head, YA, Clinton Public Library, 313 S Fourth St, Clinton, IN, 47842-2398. Tel: 765-832-8349. p. 675
Wolfe, Carrie, Libr Dir, Abington Social Library, 536 Hampton Rd, Abington, CT, 06230. Tel: 860-974-0415. p. 301
Wolfe, Doug, Head Librn, Saint Peter Public Library, 601 S Washington Ave, Saint Peter, MN, 56082. Tel: 507-934-7420. p. 1203
Wolfe, Elaina, Br Mgr, Union County Public Library, Waxhaw Branch, 509 S Providence St, Waxhaw, NC, 28173. Tel: 704-843-3131. p. 1704
Wolfe, Heather, Dr, Curator of Ms, Folger Shakespeare Library, 201 E Capitol St SE, Washington, DC, 20003-1094. Tel: 202-675-0325. p. 366
Wolfe, Jean, Librn, Tunbridge Public Library, 289 Vt Rte 110, Tunbridge, VT, 05077. Tel: 802-889-9404. p. 2296
Wolfe, Jeanne M, Libr Dir, Ben Guthrie Lac Du Flambeau Public Library, 622 Peace Pipe Rd, Lac Du Flambeau, WI, 54538. Tel: 715-588-7001. p. 2447
Wolfe, Jennifer, Ref Librn, Athens State University, 407 E Pryor St, Athens, AL, 35611. Tel: 256-216-6668. p. 5
Wolfe, Jo, Dir, Skagit County Historical Museum, 501 S Fourth St, La Conner, WA, 98257. Tel: 360-466-3365. p. 2368
Wolfe, Julie, Chief Financial Officer, Saint Charles City-County Library District, 77 Boone Hills Dr, Saint Peters, MO, 63376. Tel: 636-441-2300. p. 1277
Wolfe, Katja, Libr Dir, Kenai Community Library, 163 Main St Loop, Kenai, AK, 99611. Tel: 907-283-4378. p. 48
Wolfe, Kay, Librn, Chetopa City Library, 312 Maple, Chetopa, KS, 67336. Tel: 620-236-7194. p. 801

Wolfe, Mark, Br Mgr, Free Library of Philadelphia, Bushrod Branch, 6304 Castor Ave, Philadelphia, PA, 19149-2731. Tel: 215-685-1471. p. 1977

Wolfe, Michael A, Circ Librn, The Edward Waters College Library, 1658 Kings Rd, Jacksonville, FL, 32209-6199. Tel: 904-470-8086. p. 411

Wolfe, Mikaela, Asst Dir, Head, Adult Serv, Sharon Public Library, 11 N Main St, Sharon, MA, 02067-1299. Tel: 781-784-1578. p. 1052

Wolfe, Patrick, Libr Spec, Spartanburg Community College Library, Downtown Campus, Evans Academic Ctr, 2nd Flr, 220 E Kennedy St, Spartanburg, SC, 29302. Tel: 864-592-4058. p. 2069

Wolfe, Rebecca, Librn/Br Mgr, Allen County Public Library, Dupont, 536 E Dupont Rd, Fort Wayne, IN, 46825. Tel: 260-421-1315. p. 683

Wolfe, Rebecca, Librn/Br Mgr, Allen County Public Library, Grabill Branch, 13521 State St, Grabill, IN, 46741. Tel: 260-421-1325. p. 683

Wolfe, Suellen, Law Librn, Pennsylvania Legislative Reference Bureau Library, Main Capitol Bldg, Rm 641, Harrisburg, PA, 17120-0033. Tel: 717-787-4816. p. 1941

Wolfe, Susan, Dir, Allen F Pierce Free Library, 34 Fenner Ave, Troy, PA, 16947-1125. Tel: 570-297-2745. p. 2014

Wolfe, Tyler, Mgr, Baltimore County Public Library, Towson Branch, 320 York Rd, Towson, MD, 21204-5179. Tel: 410-887-6166. p. 980

Wolff, Amy, Chief Librn, New Holstein Public Library, 2115 Washington St, New Holstein, WI, 53061-1098. Tel: 920-898-5165. p. 2464

Wolff, Erin, Head, Circ, Stevens Memorial Library, 345 Main St, North Andover, MA, 01845. Tel: 978-688-9505. p. 1040

Wolff, Jane, Circ Librn, Newbury Town Library, Zero Lunt St, Byfield, MA, 01922-1232. Tel: 978-465-0539. p. 1004

Wolff, Joan, Med Librn, Bryn Mawr Hospital Library, 130 S Bryn Mawr Ave, Bryn Mawr, PA, 19010. Tel: 484-337-3160. p. 1916

Wolff, Necia, Bibliog Instr, Ref (Info Servs), Saint Mary's University, Louis J Blume Library, One Camino Santa Maria, San Antonio, TX, 78228-8608. Tel: 210-436-3441. p. 2238

Wolff, Rich, Libr Adminr, Tinley Park Public Library, 7851 Timber Dr, Tinley Park, IL, 60477-3398. Tel: 708-532-0160. p. 653

Wolff, Sandra, Dir, Westgate Public Library, 180 Main St, Westgate, IA, 50681. Tel: 563-578-5151. p. 791

Wolfgang, Lesley, Libr Dir, HSHS Saint Mary's Hospital, 1800 E Lake Shore Dr, Decatur, IL, 62521. Tel: 217-464-2966. p. 576

Wolfgang, Lesley, Libr Dir, St John's Hospital, 800 E Carpenter, Springfield, IL, 62769. Tel: 217-544-6464, Ext 44567. p. 650

Wolfgram, Derek, Libr Dir, Redwood City Public Library, 1044 Middlefield Rd, Redwood City, CA, 94063-1868. Tel: 650-780-7018. p. 200

Wolfle, Tracey, Human Res Mgr, Licking County Library, 101 W Main St, Newark, OH, 43055-5054. Tel: 740-349-5501. p. 1807

Wolford, Linda, Br Mgr, Kansas City, Kansas Public Library, West Wyandotte, 1737 N 82nd St, Kansas City, KS, 66112. Tel: 913-295-8250, Ext 5. p. 817

Wolfram, Dietmar, Dr, Prof, University of Wisconsin-Milwaukee, NWQD, Rm 3860, 2025 E Newport, Milwaukee, WI, 53211. Tel: 414-229-4707. p. 2794

Wolfrom, Katelyn, Evening/Weekend Ref Librn, Drexel University Libraries, Hagerty Library, 33rd & Market Sts, Philadelphia, PA, 19104-2875. Tel: 215-895-2750. p. 1976

Wolfson, Chana, Assistant Judaica Librn, Hebrew Union College-Jewish Institute of Religion, 3101 Clifton Ave, Cincinnati, OH, 45220-2488. Tel: 513-487-3284. p. 1761

Wolfson, Gail, Sr Assoc, General Mills, Inc, Business Information Center, One General Mills Blvd, Minneapolis, MN, 55426-1347. Tel: 763-764-5461. p. 1183

Wolfson, Maxine, Librn, Temple Emanu-El Library, 99 Taft Ave, Providence, RI, 02906. Tel: 401-331-1616. p. 2041

Wolfson, Stephen, Copyright Librn, Research Librn, University of Georgia, Alexander Campbell King Law Library, 225 Herty Dr, Athens, GA, 30602-6018. Tel: 706-542-1922. p. 459

Wolinsky, Judi, Mgr, Homewood Public Library, 17917 Dixie Hwy, Homewood, IL, 60430-1703. Tel: 708-798-0121. p. 601

Wolke, Johanna, Asst Dir, Clark Memorial Library, Seven Pinehurst Dr, Carolina, RI, 02812. Tel: 401-364-6100. p. 2030

Wolkowicz, Nicholas, Head Librn, Massachusetts Trial Court, 50 State St, Springfield, MA, 01103-2021. Tel: 413-748-7923. p. 1056

Wollersheim, Sharon, Librn, Coutts Municipal Library, 218 First Ave S, Coutts, AB, T0K 0N0, CANADA. Tel: 403-344-3804. p. 2532

Wollerton, Wendy Tremper, Dir, Livingston Free Library, 90 Old Post Rd, Livingston, NY, 12541. Tel: 518-851-2270. p. 1564

Woloshyniuk, Tracy, Libr Mgr, Newbrook Public Library, 4805 50th St, Newbrook, AB, T0A 2P0, CANADA. Tel: 780-576-3772. p. 2549

Wolotira, Alena, Head, Pub Serv, University of Washington Libraries, Gallagher Law Library, William H Gates Hall, 4000 15th Ave NE, Seattle, WA, 98195-3020. Tel: 206-685-4812. p. 2382

Wolske, Martin, Assoc Teaching Prof, University of Illinois at Urbana-Champaign, Library & Information Science Bldg, 501 E Daniel St, Champaign, IL, 61820-6211. Tel: 217-333-3280. p. 2784

Wolsky, Katie, Circ Mgr, Reserves Mgr, Lexington Theological Seminary, 230 Lexington Green Circle, Ste 300, Lexington, KY, 40503. Tel: 859-280-1229. p. 863

Wolstein, Alexis, Information Literacy Coord, Colorado State University - Pueblo, 2200 Bonforte Blvd, Pueblo, CO, 81001-4901. Tel: 719-549-2363. p. 293

Wolstencroft, Pauline, Sr Librn, Los Angeles County Museum of Art, 5905 Wilshire Blvd, Los Angeles, CA, 90036-4597. Tel: 323-857-6121. p. 163

Wolstenholme, Gayle, Dir, Glocester Libraries, 1137 Putnam Pike, Chepachet, RI, 02814. Tel: 401-568-6077. p. 2030

Wolter, Barbara, Mgr, Bartram Trail Regional Library, Taliaferro County, 117 Askin St, Crawfordville, GA, 30631. Tel: 706-456-2531. p. 502

Wolter, Brad, Dir, Chelsea Public Library, St Joseph's Parish School, 201 Broad St, Chelsea, IA, 52215. Tel: 641-489-2921. p. 739

Wolter, June, Dir, Garnavillo Public Library, 122 Main St, Garnavillo, IA, 52049. Tel: 563-964-2119. p. 754

Woltjer, Gavin, Libr Dir, Billings Public Library, 510 N Broadway, Billings, MT, 59101. Tel: 406-657-8292. p. 1288

Woltkamp, Denise, Head Librn, J T & E J Crumbaugh Memorial Public Library, 405 E Center St, LeRoy, IL, 61752-1723. Tel: 309-962-3911. p. 608

Woltz, Jonathan, Electronic Res Librn, Syst Librn, Southwestern Oklahoma State University, 100 Campus Dr, Weatherford, OK, 73096-3002. Tel: 580-774-7074. p. 1868

Wolven, Laura, Libr Dir, Finkelstein Memorial Library, 24 Chestnut St, Spring Valley, NY, 10977. Tel: 845-352-5700, Ext 283. p. 1644

Wolven, Robin, Access Serv Librn, Crowder College, 601 Laclede Ave, Neosho, MO, 64850. Tel: 417-455-5606. p. 1264

Wolverine, Priscilla, Librn, Dave O'Hara Community Library, Bag Service, No 4, La Loche, SK, S0M 1G0, CANADA. Tel: 306-822-2151. p. 2741

Wolverton, Catherine, Dir, Cedar Grove Free Public Library, One Municipal Plaza, Cedar Grove, NJ, 07009. Tel: 973-239-1447, Ext 211. p. 1395

Wolynetz, Lubow, Curator, Ukrainian Museum & Library of Stamford, 39 Clovelly Rd, Stamford, CT, 06902-3004. Tel: 203-323-8866, 203-324-0488. p. 339

Wolynska, Ewa, Head, Spec Coll, Central Connecticut State University, 1615 Stanley St, New Britain, CT, 06050. Tel: 860-832-2086. p. 324

Womack, Jim, Coll Develop, Faulkner University, 5345 Atlanta Hwy, Montgomery, AL, 36109-3398. Tel: 334-386-7207. p. 28

Womack, Kathy, Libr Mgr, Tonto Basin Public Library, 415 Old Hwy 188, Tonto Basin, AZ, 85553. Tel: 928-479-2355. p. 80

Womack, Raven, Pub Serv, Mt Hood Community College Libraries, 26000 SE Stark St, Gresham, OR, 97030. Tel: 503-491-7161. p. 1881

Wonderly, Jessica, Dir, Ridgway Free Public Library, 329 Center St, Ridgway, PA, 15853. Tel: 814-773-7573. p. 2001

Wonderly, Susan, Dir, Pahrump Community Library, 701 E St, Pahrump, NV, 89048. Tel: 775-727-5930. p. 1348

Wondracek, Jennifer L, Libr Dir, Capital University, Law School Library, 303 E Broad St, Columbus, OH, 43215. Tel: 614-236-6448. p. 1772

Wong, Anna, Asst Dir, Patron Serv, Community Library of DeWitt & Jamesville, 5110 Jamesville Rd, DeWitt, NY, 13078. Tel: 315-446-3578. p. 1525

Wong, Cassandra, Commun Librn, Santa Clara County Library District, Gilroy Library, 350 W Sixth St, Gilroy, CA, 95020. Tel: 408-842-8207. p. 127

Wong, Ching, Br Supvr, Madison Public Library, Goodman South Madison Branch, 2222 S Park St, Madison, WI, 53713. Tel: 608-266-6395. p. 2449

Wong, Ching, Br Supvr, Madison Public Library, Monroe, 1705 Monroe St, Madison, WI, 53711. Tel: 608-266-6390. p. 2449

Wong, Cindy, Libr Tech, Arcadis Corporate Library, 55 St Clair Ave W, 7th Flr, Toronto, ON, M4V 2Y7, CANADA. Tel: 416-596-1930, Ext 61332. p. 2686

Wong, Connie, ILL Coordr, Tufts University, Hirsh Health Sciences Library, 145 Harrison Ave, Boston, MA, 02111. Tel: 617-636-3787. p. 1034

Wong, Elaine, Ref & Instruction, Mission College Library, 3000 Mission College Blvd, Santa Clara, CA, 95054-1897. Tel: 408-855-5162. p. 241

Wong, Elise, Scholarly Communications Librn, Tech Serv Librn, Saint Mary's College Library, 1928 Saint Mary's Rd, Moraga, CA, 94575. Tel: 925-631-4229. p. 180

Wong, Jason, Researcher, McCarthy Tetrault LLP Library, 421 Seventh Ave SW, Ste 4000, Calgary, AB, T2P 4K9, CANADA. Tel: 403-260-3697. p. 2528

Wong, Jason, Res Spec, McCarthy Tetrault LLP Library, 2400-745 Thurlow St, Vancouver, BC, V6E 0C5, CANADA. Tel: 604-643-7979. p. 2579

Wong, Jennifer, Librn, Estrella Mountain Community College Library, 3000 N Dysart Rd, Avondale, AZ, 85392. Tel: 623-935-8191. p. 55

Wong, Jenny, Cat Librn, Baton Rouge Community College, 201 Community College Dr, Baton Rouge, LA, 70806. Tel: 225-216-8590. p. 882

Wong, Jenny, Acq, East Baton Rouge Parish Library, 7711 Goodwood Blvd, Baton Rouge, LA, 70806-7625. Tel: 225-231-3700. p. 882

Wong, Karen, Br Supvr, Greater Victoria Public Library, Saanich Centennial Branch, G R Pearkes Recreation Ctr, 3110 Tillicum Rd, Victoria, BC, V9A 6T2, CANADA. Tel: 250-940-4875, Ext 864. p. 2583

Wong, Len, Br Mgr, Richmond Hill Public Library, Richmond Green Library, One William F Bell Pkwy, Richmond Hill, ON, L4S 2T9, CANADA. Tel: 905-780-0711. p. 2676

Wong Loock, Leslie, Head, Res & Instruction, Nassau Community College, One Education Dr, Garden City, NY, 11530-6793. Tel: 516-572-7400, 516-572-7401. p. 1537

Wong, Marlene M, Head Librn, Smith College Libraries, Werner Josten Performing Arts Library, Mendenhall Ctr for the Performing Arts, 122 Green St, Northampton, MA, 01063. Tel: 413-585-2931. p. 1043

Wong, Peggy, Ch Serv Librn, Piscataway Township Free Public Library, 500 Hoes Lane, Piscataway, NJ, 08854. Tel: 732-463-1633. p. 1435

Wong, Ryan, Circ Supvr, Hartland Public Library, 110 E Park Ave, Hartland, WI, 53029. Tel: 262-367-3350. p. 2441

Wong, Siu-Ki, Head, Tech Serv & Syst, Campbell University, 113 Main St, Buies Creek, NC, 27506. Tel: 910-893-1469. p. 1676

Wong, Tara, Chief Exec Officer, Oakville Public Library, 120 Navy St, Oakville, ON, L6J 2Z4, CANADA. Tel: 905-815-2042, Ext 2027. p. 2662

Wong, Violet, Librn, Chinook Regional Library, Maple Creek Branch, Town Office Complex, 205 Jasper St, Maple Creek, SK, S0N 1N0, CANADA. Tel: 306-662-3522. p. 2752

Wonsowicz, Jennifer, Human Res Mgr, Indian Trails Public Library District, 355 S Schoenbeck Rd, Wheeling, IL, 60090. Tel: 847-459-4100. p. 662

Woo Shue, Kelli, Client Serv Mgr, Nova Scotia Provincial Library, 6016 University Ave, 5th Flr, Halifax, NS, B3H 1W4, CANADA. Tel: 902-424-2457. p. 2621

Woo Shue, Lisa, Libr Tech, Nova Scotia Barristers' Society, The Law Courts, 7th Flr, 1815 Upper Water St, Halifax, NS, B3J 1S7, CANADA. Tel: 902-425-2665. p. 2619

Wood, Andrew, Librn III, College of the North Atlantic Library Services, One Prince Philip Dr, St. John's, NL, A1C 5P7, CANADA. Tel: 709-758-7448. p. 2609

Wood, Arleen, Commun Liaison Librn, Iosco-Arenac District Library, 120 W Westover St, East Tawas, MI, 48730. Tel: 989-362-2651. p. 1102

Wood, Barbara, Graduate Health & Human Services Librn, Kennesaw State University Library System, 385 Cobb Ave NW, MD 1701, Kennesaw, GA, 30144. Tel: 470-578-2560. p. 483

Wood, Beth, Dir, Robert W Rowe Public Library District, 120 E Si Johnson Ave, Sheridan, IL, 60551. Tel: 815-496-2031. p. 646

Wood, Betty, Dir, Elberta Public Library, 13052-A Main St, Elberta, AL, 36530. Tel: 251-986-3069. p. 15

Wood, Bonnie, Town Librn, Grainfield City Library, 242 Main, Grainfield, KS, 67737. Tel: 785-673-4770. p. 810

Wood, Brian, Chairperson, Bonnyville Municipal Library, 4804 49th Ave, Bonnyville, AB, T9N 2J3, CANADA. Tel: 780-826-3071. p. 2524

Wood, Carolyn, Libr Dir, West Deptford Free Public Library, 420 Crown Point Rd, West Deptford, NJ, 08086. Tel: 856-845-5593. p. 1452

Wood, Cassie, Br Supvr, Bruce County Public Library, Lucknow Branch, 526 Campbell St, Lucknow, ON, N0G 2H0, CANADA. Tel: 519-528-3011. p. 2673

Wood, Cassie, Br Supvr, Bruce County Public Library, Ripley Branch, 23 Jessie St, Ripley, ON, N0G 2R0, CANADA. Tel: 519-395-5919. p. 2674

Wood, Catt, Sr Libr Tech, Los Medanos College Library, 1351 Pioneer Sq, Brentwood, CA, 94513. Tel: 925-513-1646. p. 124

Wood, Charlotte, Asst Libr Dir, Wilmington Memorial Library, 175 Middlesex Ave, Wilmington, MA, 01887-2779. Tel: 978-658-2967. p. 1070

Wood, Dan, Principal Librn, Youth Serv, Escondido Public Library, 239 S Kalmia St, Escondido, CA, 92025. Tel: 760-839-5456. p. 141

Wood, Danielle, Spec Serv, Rapid City Public Library, 610 Quincy St, Rapid City, SD, 57701-3630. Tel: 605-394-6139. p. 2081

Wood, David, Curator, Concord Museum Library, 53 Cambridge Tpk, Concord, MA, 01742. Tel: 978-369-9763. p. 1012

Wood, Dean, Principal, Jackie Brannon Correctional Center Library, 900 N West St, McAlester, OK, 74501. Tel: 918-421-3350. p. 1853

Wood, Deborah, Spec Coll Librn, Richmond Memorial Library, 19 Ross St, Batavia, NY, 14020. Tel: 585-343-9550. p. 1491

Wood, Dianne, Curatorial Asst, Museum of American Glass, Wheaton Arts & Cultural Ctr, 1501 Glasstown Rd, Millville, NJ, 08332. Tel: 856-825-6800, Ext 142. p. 1419

Wood, Elaine, Br Mgr, Pamunkey Regional Library, West Point Branch, 721 Main St, West Point, VA, 23181. Tel: 804-843-3244. p. 2324

Wood, Elizabeth, Exec Dir, Stonington Historical Society, 40 Palmer St, Stonington, CT, 06378. Tel: 860-535-1131. p. 339

Wood, Emma, Asst Librn, Pub Serv, University of Massachusetts School of Law Library, 333 Faunce Corner Rd, North Dartmouth, MA, 02747. Tel: 508-985-1121. p. 1041

Wood, Hannah, Archives & Spec Coll Librn, Harding University, 915 E Market St, Searcy, AR, 72149-5615. Tel: 501-279-4205. p. 109

Wood, Jack Darrell, Spec Coll Librn, Jackson-Madison County Library, 433 E Lafayette St, Jackson, TN, 38301. Tel: 731-425-8600. p. 2102

Wood, Janie, Ch, Shelbina Carnegie Public Library, 102 N Center St, Shelbina, MO, 63468. Tel: 573-588-2271. p. 1279

Wood, Jason, Dep Libr Dir, Univ Archivist, Simmons University, 300 The Fenway, Boston, MA, 02115-5898. Tel: 617-521-2441. p. 999

Wood, Jennifer, Archivist, Albion District Library, 501 S Superior St, Albion, MI, 49224. Tel: 517-629-3993. p. 1076

Wood, Jennifer, Tech Coordr, Henrico County Public Library, 1700 N Parham Rd, Henrico, VA, 23229. Tel: 804-501-1900. p. 2325

Wood, Jessica, Librn, Texas Commission on Environment Quality, Bldg A, Rm 102, 12100 Park 35 Circle, Austin, TX, 78753. Tel: 512-239-0020. p. 2140

Wood, Joni, Ref Serv, Ozark Dale County Library, Inc, 416 James St, Ozark, AL, 36360. Tel: 334-774-2399, 334-774-5480. p. 32

Wood, Julie, Archives, Metadata Specialist, Illinois Wesleyan University, One Ames Plaza, Bloomington, IL, 61701-7188. Tel: 309-56-3620. p. 543

Wood, Julie, Mgr, Libr Serv, Franciscan Health Indianapolis, 8111 S Emerson Ave, Indianapolis, IN, 46237. Tel: 317-528-7136. p. 691

Wood, Julie, Network Adminr, Southern Utah University, 351 W University Blvd, Cedar City, UT, 84720. Tel: 435-586-8052. p. 2262

Wood, Kirsten, Youth Serv Librn, Plattsmouth Public Library, 401 Ave A, Plattsmouth, NE, 68048. Tel: 402-296-4154. p. 1333

Wood, Lisa, Br Mgr, Branch District Library, Quincy Branch, 11 N Main St, Quincy, MI, 49082-1163. Tel: 517-639-4001. p. 1093

Wood, Liz, Evening Res Serv Libr Spec, Landmark College Library, 19 River Rd S, Putney, VT, 05346. Tel: 802-387-1648. p. 2292

Wood, Luz, Br Mgr, Riverside County Library System, Norco Library, 3240 Hamner Ave, Ste 101B, Norco, CA, 92860. Tel: 951-735-5329. p. 202

Wood, Marg, Br Coordr, Lennox & Addington County Public Library, Napanee Branch, 25 River Rd, Napanee, ON, K7R 3S6, CANADA. Tel: 613-354-2525. p. 2660

Wood, Martin, Dir, Florida State University Libraries, Charlotte Edwards Maguire Medical Library, 1115 W Call St, Tallahassee, FL, 32306-4300. Tel: 850-645-7304. p. 447

Wood, Mary Anne, Youth Serv Coordr, London Public Library, 20 E First St, London, OH, 43140. Tel: 740-852-9543. p. 1796

Wood, Megan, Children's Coordr, Prairie Grove Public Library, 123 S Neal St, Prairie Grove, AR, 72753. Tel: 479-846-3782. p. 108

Wood, Megan, Dir, Mus & Libr Serv, Ohio History Connection, 800 E 17th Ave, Columbus, OH, 43211. Tel: 614-297-2576. p. 1774

Wood, Melanie, Dir, Aliceville Public Library, 416 Third Ave N, Aliceville, AL, 35442. Tel: 205-373-6691. p. 4

Wood, Michael, Librn, Bates Technical College Library, 2201 S 78th St, E201, Tacoma, WA, 98409-9000. Tel: 253-680-7550. p. 2386

Wood, Nancy, Br Mgr, Park County Public Libraries, Fairplay Branch, 400 Front St, Fairplay, CO, 80440. Tel: 719-836-4297. p. 265

Wood, Nancy M, Libr Dir, Richmond Memorial Library, 15 School Dr, Marlborough, CT, 06447-1582. Tel: 860-295-6210. p. 321

Wood, Nicole, Res Mgt Librn, Austin Peay State University, 601 College St, Clarksville, TN, 37044. Tel: 931-221-7387. p. 2092

Wood, Pamela R, Dir, Libr Serv, University of Mount Olive, 646 James B Hunt Dr, Mount Olive, NC, 28365-1699. Tel: 919-658-7753. p. 1705

Wood, Patricia, Dir, Head, Circ & Tech Serv, Ohio State University LIBRARIES, Marion Campus Library, 1469 Mount Vernon Ave, Marion, OH, 43302. Tel: 740-725-6254. p. 1776

Wood, Patti, Ch, Eckstein Memorial Library, 1034 E Dewey St, Cassville, WI, 53806. Tel: 608-725-5838. p. 2427

Wood, Rebecca, Youth Serv Librn, Robert W Barlow Memorial Library, 921 Washington Ave, Iowa Falls, IA, 50126. Tel: 641-648-2872. p. 761

Wood, Shelby, Libr Mgr, Olive G Pettis Memorial Library, 36 Mill Village Rd N, Goshen, NH, 03752. Tel: 603-863-6921. p. 1365

Wood, Sinai, Doc Librn, Baylor University Libraries, Jesse H Jones Library, 1301 S Second St, Waco, TX, 76798. Tel: 254-710-4606. p. 2253

Wood, Susan, Asst Dir, Elizabeth Titus Memorial Library, Two W Water St, Sullivan, IL, 61951. Tel: 217-728-7221. p. 652

Wood, Susan, Media Serv, Ref & Instruction, Suffolk County Community College, Montaukett Learning Center, 121 Speonk Riverhead Rd, Riverhead, NY, 11901-3499. Tel: 631-548-2544. p. 1627

Wood, Teri, Head Librn, Benewah County District Library, 46 Isaacson St, Fernwood, ID, 83830. Tel: 208-245-4883. p. 520

Wood, Vicki, Coordr, Youth Serv, Lincoln City Libraries, 136 S 14th St, Lincoln, NE, 68508-1899. Tel: 402-441-8565. p. 1321

Wood, William, Library Contact, Brown University, Sciences Library, 201 Thayer St, Providence, RI, 02912. Tel: 401-863-3333. p. 2037

Wood-Gramza, Heather, Dir, Howard Miller Public Library, 14 S Church St, Zeeland, MI, 49464-1728. Tel: 616-772-0874. p. 1161

Woodall, Christopher, Tech Librn, Salisbury University, 1101 Camden Ave, Salisbury, MD, 21801-6863. Tel: 410-543-6130. p. 976

Woodall, Jennifer, Cat Librn, Head, Access Serv, Emmanuel College, 400 The Fenway, Boston, MA, 02115. Tel: 617-264-7653. p. 995

Woodall, Joyce, Head Librn, Eva Public Library, 4549 Hwy 55 E, Eva, AL, 35621. Tel: 256-796-8638. p. 16

Woodard, Regi, Libr Asst, Riley City Library, 115 S Broadway St, Riley, KS, 66531. Tel: 785-485-2978. p. 833

Woodard, Susan, Dir, Cheney Public Library, 203 N Main St, Cheney, KS, 67025. Tel: 316-542-3331. p. 801

Woodard, Tracy, Mgr, Suwannee River Regional Library, White Springs Public Library, 16403 Jewett St, White Springs, FL, 32096. Tel: 386-397-1389. p. 419

Woodbridge, Ross, Br Mgr, Alachua County Library District, Alachua Branch, 14913 NW 140 St, Alachua, FL, 32615. Tel: 386-462-2592. p. 406

Woodburn, Chris, Dep Dir, Ocmulgee Regional Library System, 531 Second Ave, Eastman, GA, 31023. Tel: 478-374-4711. p. 477
Woodbury, Sandra, Circ, Burlington Public Library, 22 Sears St, Burlington, MA, 01803. Tel: 781-270-1690. p. 1004
Woodcock, Linda, Ser Librn, Tech Serv Librn, Kwantlen Polytechnic University Library, 12666 72nd Ave, Surrey, BC, V3W 2M8, CANADA. Tel: 604-599-2450. p. 2576
Woodcox, Jeff, Curator, Sloan Museum Archives, 1221 E Kearsley St, Flint, MI, 48503. Tel: 810-237-3421. p. 1107
Woodhouse, Anya, Circ Mgr, Lake Oswego Public Library, 706 Fourth St, Lake Oswego, OR, 97034-2399. Tel: 503-675-3996. p. 1884
Woodland, Alicia, YA Mgr, McMillan Memorial Library, 490 E Grand Ave, Wisconsin Rapids, WI, 54494-4898. Tel: 715-422-5136. p. 2489
Woodley, Chris, Educ Mgr, Mgr, Access Serv, Conestoga College, 299 Doon Valley Dr, Kitchener, ON, N2G 4M4, CANADA. Tel: 519-748-5220, Ext 3361. p. 2651
Woodley, Valerie, Ch, Dir, Warren Township Public Library, 210 Burnett Ave, Warren, IL, 61087. Tel: 815-745-2076. p. 658
Woodley, Victoria, Dir, Pollard Memorial Library, Senior Center Branch, 276 Broadway St, Lowell, MA, 01854. p. 1029
Woodmansee, Jeff, Research Support & Reference Librn, University of Arkansas at Little Rock, William H Bowen School of Law / Pulaski County Law Library, 1201 McMath Ave, Little Rock, AR, 72202. Tel: 501-916-5470. p. 102
Woodrow, Adam, Dean, Learning & Libr Serv, Westmoreland County Community College Library, Student Achievement Ctr, Youngwood Campus, 145 Pavilion Lane, Youngwood, PA, 15697-1814. Tel: 724-925-5852. p. 2027
Woodrow, Chris, Dir, Corporate Serv, Windsor Public Library, 850 Ouellette Ave, Windsor, ON, N9A 4M9, CANADA. Tel: 519-255-6770. p. 2704
Woodrow, Christine, Dir, New Boston Public Library, 127 N Ellis St, New Boston, TX, 75570-2905. Tel: 903-628-5414. p. 2222
Woodrow, Patricia, Libr Tech II, College of the North Atlantic Library Services, L A Bown Building Library, Bay St George Campus - L A Bown Bldg, Rm 29, 15 Washington Dr, Stephenville, NL, A2N 2V5, CANADA. Tel: 709-643-7787. p. 2609
Woodruff, Dawn, Librn, North Central Washington Libraries, Twisp Public Library, 201 N Methow Valley Hwy, Rm 1, Twisp, WA, 98856. Tel: 509-997-4681. p. 2394
Woodruff, Julie, Tech Serv Mgr, L E Phillips Memorial Public Library, 400 Eau Claire St, Eau Claire, WI, 54701. Tel: 715-839-1647. p. 2432
Woodruff, Kevin, Literacy Librn, Research Librn, Bryan College Library, 585 Bryan Dr, Dayton, TN, 37321. Tel: 423-775-7430. p. 2096
Woodruff, Margaret, Libr Dir, Charlotte Library, 115 Ferry Rd, Charlotte, VT, 05445. Tel: 802-425-3864. p. 2281
Woodruff, Mary E, Dir, Libr Serv, Mintz, Levin, Cohn, Ferris, Glovsky & Popeo, One Financial Ctr, Boston, MA, 02111. Tel: 617-348-1682. p. 997
Woodrum, Janet, Circ Mgr, Danville Public Library, 101 S Indiana St, Danville, IN, 46122-1809. Tel: 317-745-2604. p. 678
Woods, Alyssa, Ad, Park Falls Public Library, 121 N Fourth Ave, Park Falls, WI, 54552. Tel: 715-762-3121. p. 2468
Woods, Amy, Head, Circ, Oneonta Public Library, 221 Second St S, Oneonta, AL, 35121. Tel: 205-274-7641. p. 31
Woods, Anna, Curator, Kansas Historical Society, 6425 SW Sixth Ave, Topeka, KS, 66615-1099. Tel: 785-272-8681. p. 838
Woods, Christine, Asst Dir, Head, Ref Serv, Ventress Memorial Library, 15 Library Plaza, Marshfield, MA, 02050. Tel: 781-834-5535. p. 1032
Woods, Connee R, Dir, Ruthven Public Library, 1301 Gowrie St, Ruthven, IA, 51358. Tel: 712-837-4820. p. 780
Woods, Debra, Dir, Calumet Park Public Library, 1500 W 127th St, Calumet Park, IL, 60827. Tel: 708-385-5768. p. 548
Woods, Donna, Cat/Ref Librn, Westbank Community Library District, 1309 Westbank Dr, Austin, TX, 78746. Tel: 512-327-3045. p. 2143
Woods, Elin, Research & Instruction Librarian for Student Success, University of Scranton, 800 Linden St, Scranton, PA, 18510-4634. Tel: 570-941-7809. p. 2005
Woods, Eric, Br Mgr, Free Library of Philadelphia, Roxborough Branch, 6245 Ridge Ave, Philadelphia, PA, 19128-2630. Tel: 215-685-2550. p. 1980
Woods, Helen, Ref Serv Coordr, Alaska Resources Library & Information Services ARLIS, Library Bldg, 3211 Providence Dr, Ste 111, Anchorage, AK, 99508-4614. Tel: 907-786-7660. p. 41
Woods, Jean, Dr, Dir, Delaware Museum of Natural History Library, 4840 Kennett Pike, Wilmington, DE, 19807. Tel: 302-658-9111, Ext 314. p. 357
Woods, Joanne, Br Mgr, Free Library of Philadelphia, Andorra Branch, 705 E Cathedral Rd, Philadelphia, PA, 19128-2106. Tel: 215-685-2552. p. 1977
Woods, Julie, Asst Librn, Idabel Public Library, 103 E Main St, Idabel, OK, 74745. Tel: 580-286-6406. p. 1850
Woods, Katie, Communications Mgr, San Mateo County Library, Library Administration, 125 Lessingia Ct, San Mateo, CA, 94402-4000. Tel: 650-312-5274. p. 235
Woods, Natalie, Br Mgr, Louisville Free Public Library, Western, 604 S Tenth St, Louisville, KY, 40203. Tel: 502-574-1779. p. 866
Woods, Roberta Lian, Ref & Instrul Serv Librn, University of Hawaii, 2525 Dole St, Honolulu, HI, 96822-2328. Tel: 808-956-0478. p. 513
Woods, Sheila, Library Contact, Schenectady County Public Library, Rotterdam, 1100 N Westcott Rd, Schenectady, NY, 12306. Tel: 518-356-3440. p. 1638
Woods, Sonja, Coordr, Sagebrush Federation, One S Tenth St, Miles City, MT, 59301-3398. Tel: 406-234-1496. p. 1299
Woods, Sonja N, Archivist, Howard University Libraries, Moorland-Spingarn Research Center, 500 Howard Pl NW, Washington, DC, 20059. Tel: 202-806-7480. p. 369
Woods, Stephen, Data Spec, Govt Info Spec, Librn, Pennsylvania State University Libraries, Social Sciences & Education, 208 Paterno Library, 2nd & 5th Flrs, University Park, PA, 16802-1809. Tel: 814-865-0665. p. 2016
Woods, Tymmi A, Distance Learning Librn, Arizona Western College, 2020 S Ave 8E, Yuma, AZ, 85366. Tel: 928-317-6434. p. 85
Woods, Zoe, Library Intern, Hillsboro Public Library, 819 High Ave, Hillsboro, WI, 54634. Tel: 608-489-2192. p. 2441
Woodside, Carla, Dir, Sarah Stewart Bovard Memorial Library, 156 Elm St, Tionesta, PA, 16353. Tel: 814-755-4454. p. 2012
Woodside, Cathy, Info Res Mgr, Canada Department of Justice, EPCOR Tower, 300 10423 101 St, Edmonton, AB, T5H 0E7, CANADA. Tel: 780-495-2973. p. 2536
Woodstrup, Wendi, Br Mgr, Hawaii State Public Library System, Mililani Public Library, 95-450 Makaimoimo St, Mililani, HI, 96789. Tel: 808-627-7470. p. 509
Woodward, Chris, Tech Librn, Grapevine Public Library, 1201 Municipal Way, Grapevine, TX, 76051. Tel: 817-410-3407. p. 2186
Woodward, Gail, Instruction Librn, McLennan Community College Library, 1400 College Dr, Waco, TX, 76708-1498. Tel: 254-299-8390. p. 2253
Woodward, Kaitlin, Circ Mgr, Ida Public Library, 320 N State St, Belvidere, IL, 61008-3299. Tel: 815-544-3838. p. 541
Woodward, Krista, Children & Teen Librn, Osceola Public Library, 300 S Fillmore St, Osceola, IA, 50213. Tel: 641-342-2237. p. 775
Woodward, Susie, Library Contact, Multnomah County Library, St Johns, 7510 N Charleston Ave, Portland, OR, 97203. p. 1892
Woodward, Wade, Libr Dir, Converse College, 580 E Main St, Spartanburg, SC, 29302. Tel: 864-596-9020, 864-596-9071. p. 2069
Woodworth, Andy, Librn, Camden County College Library, 200 College Dr, Blackwood, NJ, 08012. Tel: 856-227-7200, Ext 4407. p. 1391
Woody, Gloria T, Spec Coll, Florida Agricultural & Mechanical University Libraries, 525 Orr Dr, Tallahassee, FL, 32307-4700. Tel: 850-599-3370. p. 446
Woody, Laura, Asst Dir, Sequatchie County Public Library, 227 Cherry St, Dunlap, TN, 37327. Tel: 423-949-2357. p. 2097
Woody, Stephen, First Year Experience Librn, Washburn University, 1700 SW College Ave, Topeka, KS, 66621. Tel: 785-670-2507. p. 839
Woody, Susan, Dir, Des Moines Public Library, 1000 Grand Ave, Des Moines, IA, 50309. Tel: 515-283-4103. p. 745
Woody, Whitney, Dir, Prog & Youth Serv, Mooresville Public Library, 220 W Harrison St, Mooresville, IN, 46158-1633. Tel: 317-831-7323. p. 707
Woofter, Valerie, Circ, Fairmont State University, 1201 Locust Ave, Fairmont, WV, 26554. Tel: 304-367-4733. p. 2402
Woolard, Karen, Bus Mgr, Sheppard Memorial Library, 530 S Evans St, Greenville, NC, 27858. Tel: 252-329-4580. p. 1694
Woolbright, Jacalyn, Librn, Lapeer District Library, Hadley Branch, 3556 Hadley Rd, Hadley, MI, 48440. Tel: 810-797-4101. p. 1126
Woolcott, Liz, Head, Cat, Head, Metadata Serv, Utah State University, 3000 Old Main Hill, Logan, UT, 84322-3000. Tel: 435-797-9458. p. 2265
Woolery, Emily, Ref Librn, Mt San Antonio College Library, 1100 N Grand Ave, Walnut, CA, 91789. Tel: 909-274-4260. p. 258
Wooley, Liz, Libr Mgr, Central Arkansas Library System, John Gould Fletcher Library, 823 N Buchanan St, Little Rock, AR, 72205-3211. Tel: 501-663-5457. p. 101
Woolley, Kelley, Assoc Dir, Libr Serv, San Diego Zoo Global Library, Beckman Ctr, 15600 San Pasqual Valley Rd, Escondido, CA, 92027. Tel: 760-747-8702, Ext 5736. p. 141
Woolridge, Carol, Exec Dir, Columbia County Historical & Genealogical Society Library, 225 Market St, Bloomsburg, PA, 17815. Tel: 570-784-1600. p. 1913
Woolridge, Elizabeth, Support Serv Coordr, Athens Technical College Library, Greene County Campus, 1051 Athens Tech Dr, Greensboro, GA, 30642. Tel: 706-453-0524. p. 459
Woolridge, Elizabeth, Support Serv Coordr, Athens Technical College Library, Walton County Campus, 212 Bryant Rd, Monroe, GA, 30655. Tel: 706-552-0922. p. 459
Woolstrum, Jennifer, Dir, Baden Memorial Library, 385 State St, Baden, PA, 15005-1946. Tel: 724-869-3960. p. 1908
Wooten, Ann, Librn, Southern Regional Technical College Library Services, Cairo Campus, 1550 Hwy 84 W, Cairo, GA, 39828. Tel: 229-378-2906. p. 499
Wooten, Carolyn, Asst Dir, Rainsville Public Library, 941 Main St E, Rainsville, AL, 35986. Tel: 256-638-3311. p. 34
Wooten, Craig, Dir, Syst Adminr, B S Ricks Memorial Library, 310 N Main St, Yazoo City, MS, 39194. Tel: 662-746-5557. p. 1236
Wooten, Howard, Libr Asst II, City Colleges of Chicago, Richard J Daley College Library, 7500 S Pulaski Rd, Chicago, IL, 60652-1200. Tel: 773-838-7667. p. 558

Wooten, Locrecia, Cat Librn, Digitization Librn, Louisiana State University Health Sciences Center, 1501 Kings Hwy, Shreveport, LA, 71130. Tel: 318-675-5458. p. 908

Wooten, Rodney, Libr Dir, Mid-Atlantic Christian University, 715 N Poindexter St, Elizabeth City, NC, 27909-4054. Tel: 252-334-2057. p. 1687

Wooton, Jimmy, Commun Engagement Mgr, Greenville County Library System, 25 Heritage Green Pl, Greenville, SC, 29601-2034. Tel: 864-527-9235. p. 2061

Word, Robin, Br Mgr, Bienville Parish Library, Castor Branch, 1955 Hwy 507, Castor, LA, 71016. Tel: 318-544-8451. p. 881

Worden, Jaye, Mrs, Dir, Adams Center Free Library, 18267 State Rte 177, Adams Center, NY, 13606. Tel: 315-583-5501. p. 1481

Wordofa, Kebede H, Syst Librn, Austin Peay State University, 601 College St, Clarksville, TN, 37044. Tel: 931-221-7959. p. 2092

Worford, Darlene, Librn, Birmingham Public Library, Titusville, Two Sixth Ave SW, Birmingham, AL, 35211-2909. Tel: 205-322-1140. p. 8

Worford, William, Cat/Syst Librn, Orange County Community College Library, 115 South St, Middletown, NY, 10940. Tel: 845-341-4256. p. 1571

Workinger, Doug, Asst Dir, Kokomo-Howard County Public Library, 220 N Union St, Kokomo, IN, 46901-4614. Tel: 765-457-3242. p. 699

Workman, Cal, Adult Prog Coordr, Manchester Community Library, 138 Cemetery Ave, Rte 7A, Manchester Center, VT, 05255. Tel: 802-362-2607. p. 2288

Workman, Catherine, Br Mgr, Santa Cruz City-County Library System, Garfield Park, 705 Woodrow Ave, Santa Cruz, CA, 95060. Tel: 831-427-7709. p. 243

Workman, Frances, Co-Dir, Table Rock Public Library, 511 Luzerne St, Table Rock, NE, 68447. p. 1338

Workman, Jacob, Br Mgr, Amarillo Public Library, East Branch, 2232 E 27th St, Amarillo, TX, 79103. Tel: 806-342-1589. p. 2134

Workman, Moira, Health Educator, Northwestern Memorial Hospital, Galter Pavilion, Ste 3-304, 251 E Huron St, Chicago, IL, 60611. Tel: 312-926-5465. p. 566

Worley, Debra, Pub Serv Asst, Indian Hills Community College, 721 N First St, Bldg CV06, Centerville, IA, 52544. Tel: 641-856-2143, Ext 2237. p. 739

Worman, Josh, Dir, Haston Library, 5167 Main St, Franklin, VT, 05457. Tel: 802-285-6505. p. 2284

Wornek, Lawral D, Head, Reference & Access Servs, Northeastern University Libraries, 5000 MacArthur Blvd, Oakland, CA, 94613. Tel: 510-430-2029. p. 185

Worrall, Bettina, Libr Mgr, Menno-Simons Community Library, 521 Cleardale Dr, Cleardale, AB, T0H 3Y0, CANADA. Tel: 780-685-2340. p. 2531

Worrell, Jennifer, Asst to the Dean of Libraries, Illinois Institute of Technology, 35 W 33rd St, Chicago, IL, 60616. Tel: 312-567-5136. p. 562

Worrell, Paul, Coord for Library Research & Instruction, Maryville University Library, 650 Maryville University Dr, Saint Louis, MO, 63141. Tel: 314-529-9492. p. 1271

Worsham, Jeremy, Assoc Dir, Berry College, 2277 Martha Berry Hwy, Mount Berry, GA, 30149. Tel: 706-368-6707. p. 492

Worso, Ed, Fiscal Officer, Burton Public Library, 14588 W Park St, Burton, OH, 44021. Tel: 440-834-4466. p. 1753

Worster, Carol, Supvr, Gas Technology Institute, 1700 S Mount Prospect Rd, Des Plaines, IL, 60018-1804. Tel: 847-768-0500. p. 578

Worstine, Martha, Law Librn, Clinton County Law Library, Clinton County Courthouse, 3rd Flr, 46 S South St, Wilmington, OH, 45177. Tel: 937-382-2428. p. 1832

Worth, Ben, Libr Mgr, Rocky Mountain House Public Library, 4922 52nd St, Rocky Mountain House, AB, T4T 1B1, CANADA. Tel: 403-845-2042. p. 2552

Worth, Claudia, Presv Spec, Wheat Ridge Historical Society Library, 4610 Robb St, Wheat Ridge, CO, 80033. Tel: 303-421-9111. p. 298

Worth, Diana, Acq & Tech Serv Mgr, Pennsylvania College of Technology, 999 Hagan Way, Williamsport, PA, 17701. Tel: 570-327-4523. p. 2023

Wortham, Shannon, Br Mgr, Springfield-Greene County Library District, Park Central Branch, 128 Park Central Sq, Springfield, MO, 65806-1311. Tel: 417-831-1342. p. 1281

Worthington, Debbie, Libr Dir, United States Air Force, Bldg 2610, Ste 100, 480 Fifth Ave, Mountain Home AFB, ID, 83648. Tel: 208-828-2326, 208-828-2743. p. 527

Worthington, Nancy, Librn, Worthington Biochemical Corp Library, 730 Vassar Ave, Lakewood, NJ, 08701. Tel: 732-942-1660. p. 1411

Worthy, Ryda, Dir, South Mississippi Regional Library, 900 Broad St, Columbia, MS, 39429. Tel: 601-736-5516. p. 1215

Worthy, Ryda, Dir, Longleaf Library Consortium, 100 S Jackson St, Brookhaven, MS, 39601. Tel: 601-833-5038. p. 2768

Wos, Cathy, Adult Coll, Adult Serv, Barbara S Ponce Public Library, 7770 52nd St, Pinellas Park, FL, 33781. Tel: 727-369-0676. p. 437

Wotton, Gwenda, Head Librn, Parkland Regional Library-Manitoba, Birch River & District Library, 116 Third St E, Birch River, MB, R0L 0E0, CANADA. Tel: 204-236-4419. p. 2586

Wotton, Pam, Asst Librn, Canaan Town Library, 1173 US Rte 4, Canaan, NH, 03741. Tel: 603-523-9650. p. 1356

Woughter, Kerrey, Dir, Libr Serv, Northwestern Michigan College, 1701 E Front St, Traverse City, MI, 49686-3061. Tel: 231-995-1060. p. 1154

Woukko, Larry, Dir, Republic-Michigamme Public Library, 227 Maple St, Republic, MI, 49879-9998. Tel: 906-376-2239, 906-376-2277. p. 1144

Wounick, John, Circ, Libr Asst II, Reserves, Pennsylvania Western University - California, 250 University Ave, California, PA, 15419-1394. Tel: 724-938-4091. p. 1917

Woychyshyn, Kim, Asst Librn, Minnedosa Regional Library, 45 First Ave SE, Minnedosa, MB, R0J 1E0, CANADA. Tel: 204-867-2585. p. 2588

Wozniak, Michael, Ref (Info Servs), Charlotte Mecklenburg Library, 310 N Tryon St, Charlotte, NC, 28202-2176. Tel: 704-416-0100. p. 1679

Woznica, Katarzyna (Kathy), Librn, Hartford Hospital, Education & Resource Ctr, 3rd Flr, 560 Hudson St, Hartford, CT, 06102. Tel: 860-845-5096. p. 317

Wrage, Jennifer, VPres, Sarah Hull Hallock Free Library, 56-58 Main St, Milton, NY, 12547. Tel: 845-795-2200. p. 1572

Wray, Christina, Librn, Indiana University, Indiana Institute on Disability & Community, 2853 E Tenth St, Bloomington, IN, 47408-2601. Tel: 812-855-0077. p. 670

Wray, Douglas, Mgr, Cat Serv, Westchester Library System, 570 Taxter Rd, Ste 400, Elmsford, NY, 10523-2337. Tel: 914-231-3243. p. 1531

Wray, Susan, Asst Dir, Mid-Continent Public Library, 15616 E US Hwy 24, Independence, MO, 64050. Tel: 816-521-7220. p. 1250

Wrede, Clint, Cat Librn, University of Northern Iowa Library, 1227 W 27th St, Cedar Falls, IA, 50613-3675. Tel: 319-273-2781. p. 737

Wren, Jan, Libr Dir, University of the Cumberlands, 821 Walnut St, Williamsburg, KY, 40769. Tel: 606-539-4329. p. 877

Wrench, Brittaney, Libr Asst, Sampson-Clinton Public Library, Miriam B Lamb Memorial, 144 S Church St, Garland, NC, 28441. Tel: 910-529-2441. p. 1681

Wrenn, George, Head, Info Res Mgt, Humboldt State University Library, One Harpst St, Arcata, CA, 95521-8299. Tel: 707-826-3412. p. 117

Wrigg, Annie M, Dir, Pelican Rapids Public Library, 25 W Mill Ave, Pelican Rapids, MN, 56572. Tel: 218-863-7055. p. 1192

Wright, Alyssa, Head, Res Serv, West Virginia University Libraries, 1549 University Ave, Morgantown, WV, 26506. Tel: 304-293-4040. p. 2409

Wright, Andrea, Clinical Librn, Tech Serv Librn, University of Alabama College of Community Health Sciences, 850 Peter Bryce Blvd, Tuscaloosa, AL, 35401. Tel: 205-348-1335. p. 38

Wright, Andrea, Assoc Dir, Pub Serv, United States Air Force Academy Libraries, 2354 Fairchild Dr, Ste 3A15, USAF Academy, CO, 80840-6214. Tel: 719-333-4406. p. 297

Wright, Andrea, Pres, Alabama Health Libraries Association, Inc, University of Alabama, Lister Hill Library, 1530 Third Ave S, Birmingham, AL, 35294-0013. Tel: 205-348-1335. p. 2761

Wright, Ashlee, Libr Dir, Harrison Memorial Library, Ocean Ave & Lincoln St, Carmel, CA, 93921. Tel: 831-624-4629. p. 128

Wright, Benedette, Supvr, Libr Serv, WellStar Library Services, 677 Church St, Marietta, GA, 30060. Tel: 770-793-7178. p. 490

Wright, Brenda, Assoc Dean, Florida Agricultural & Mechanical University Libraries, 525 Orr Dr, Tallahassee, FL, 32307-4700. Tel: 850-599-3370. p. 446

Wright, Brianne, Archivist, Kingsport Public Library & Archives, 400 Broad St, Kingsport, TN, 37660-4292. Tel: 423-224-2559. p. 2104

Wright, Cathy, Head, Pub Serv, H Grady Bradshaw Chambers County Library, 3419 20th Ave, Valley, AL, 36854. Tel: 334-768-2161. p. 39

Wright, Cherie, Dir, River East Public Library, 813 W Rte 120, McHenry, IL, 60051. Tel: 815-385-6303. p. 616

Wright, Cheryl, Mgr, Organizational Learning & Development, Indianapolis Public Library, 2450 N Meridian St, Indianapolis, IN, 46208. Tel: 317-275-4808. p. 694

Wright, Courtney, Dir, Edwards River Public Library District, 412 E Main St, Aledo, IL, 61231. Tel: 309-582-2032. p. 535

Wright, David, Dr, Assoc Dean, Learning Res, Surry Community College, R Bldg, 630 S Main St, Dobson, NC, 27017. Tel: 336-386-3259. p. 1683

Wright, Deborah, Dir, Prince William Public Libraries, 13083 Chinn Park Dr, Prince William, VA, 22192. Tel: 703-792-8150. p. 2338

Wright, Debra, Asst Librn, Glenwood & Souris Regional Library, 18-114 Second St S, Souris, MB, R0K 2C0, CANADA. Tel: 204-483-2757. p. 2590

Wright, Drew, Scholarly Communications Librn, Cornell University Library, Samuel J Wood Library & C V Starr Biomedical Information Center, 1300 York Ave, C115, Box 67, New York, NY, 10065-4896. Tel: 646-962-2554. p. 1552

Wright, Eileen, Ref Librn, Montana State University-Billings Library, 1500 University Dr, Billings, MT, 59101. Tel: 406-657-1656. p. 1288

Wright, Florencia, Dep County Librn, Tulare County Library, 200 W Oak Ave, Visalia, CA, 93291-4993. Tel: 559-713-2700. p. 257

Wright, Gretchen, Gen Mgr, Goodspeed Opera House Foundation, 20 Norwich Rd, East Haddam, CT, 06423-1344. Tel: 860-615-0347. p. 309

Wright, Haddon, Circ Spec, Virginia Peninsula Community College Library, 227C Kecoughtan Hall, 99 Thomas Nelson Dr, Hampton, VA, 23666. Tel: 757-825-3656. p. 2323

Wright, Jamie, Asst Librn, Central City Public Library, 1604 15th Ave, Central City, NE, 68826. Tel: 308-946-2512. p. 1309

Wuebker, Justina, Dir, Earlham Public Library, 120 S Chestnut Ave, Earlham, IA, 50072. Tel: 515-758-2121. p. 750

Wuepper, Jon, Br Mgr, Cass District Library, Local History Branch, 145 N Broadway St, Cassopolis, MI, 49031. Tel: 269-357-7823, Ext 500. p. 1089

Wuerker, Katy, Ref Librn, Teen Serv Librn, Ipswich Public Library, 25 N Main St, Ipswich, MA, 01938. Tel: 978-356-6648. p. 1026

Wukovitz, Laura, Campus Librn, Harrisburg Area Community College, 2010 Pennsylvania Ave, York, PA, 17404. Tel: 717-801-3335. p. 2026

Wulff, Meredith, Youth Spec, First Regional Library, Lafayette County-Oxford Public Library, 401 Bramlett Blvd, Oxford, MS, 38655. Tel: 662-234-5751. p. 1220

Wulff, Warren, Libr Mgr, Natural Resources Canada Library, 605 Robson St, Ste 1500, Vancouver, BC, V6B 5J3, CANADA. Tel: 604-666-1147. p. 2579

Wunderlich, Molly, Assoc Dir, Van Buren District Library, 200 N Phelps St, Decatur, MI, 49045. Tel: 269-423-4771. p. 1096

Wunsch, Deb, Adminr, Elizabeth Township Public Library, 210 E Myrtle St, Elizabeth, IL, 61028-9785. Tel: 815-858-2212. p. 584

Wuollet, Diane, Academic Specialist, Minnesota State Community & Technical College, Wadena Campus, 405 Colfax Ave SW, Wadena, MN, 56482. Tel: 218-631-7865. p. 1189

Wuolu, David, Coll Develop Librn, Saint John's University, 2835 Abbey Plaza, Collegeville, MN, 56321. Tel: 320-363-2128. p. 1170

Wurangian, Nelia, Tech Serv, Loma Linda University, 11072 Anderson St, Loma Linda, CA, 92350-0001. Tel: 909-558-4581. p. 157

Wurmann, Kirsten, Br Head, Winnipeg Public Library, Harvey Smith Library - West End, 999 Sargent Ave, Winnipeg, MB, R3E 3K6, CANADA. Tel: 204-806-1078. p. 2596

Wurr, Heather, Youth & Teen Serv Librn, Desert Foothills Library, 38443 N School House Rd, Cave Creek, AZ, 85331. Tel: 480-488-2286. p. 57

Wurster, Mark, Res Sharing Supvr, Catawba College, 2300 W Innes St, Salisbury, NC, 28144-2488. Tel: 704-637-4783. p. 1714

Wurtz, Mike, Head, Archives & Spec Coll, University of the Pacific Libraries, Holt-Atherton Special Collections & Archives, 3601 Pacific Ave, Stockton, CA, 95211. Tel: 209-946-3105. p. 250

Wurzer, Greg, Librn, University of Saskatchewan Libraries, Law, Law Bldg, Rm 8, 15 Campus Dr, Saskatoon, SK, S7N 5A6, CANADA. Tel: 306-966-6020. p. 2750

Wuthenow, Josephine, Head, Adult Serv, Head, Ref, Mastics-Moriches-Shirley Community Library, 407 William Floyd Pkwy, Shirley, NY, 11967. Tel: 631-399-1511. p. 1640

Wyatt, Brandy, Libr Adminr, Northwest Georgia Regional Library System, 310 Cappes St, Dalton, GA, 30720. Tel: 706-876-1360. p. 474

Wyatt, David, Br Mgr, Fort Vancouver Regional Library District, Stevenson Community Library, 120 NW Vancouver Ave, Stevenson, WA, 98648. p. 2391

Wyatt, David, Commun Librn, Fort Vancouver Regional Library District, North Bonneville Community Library, 214 CBD Mall (Inside City Hall), North Bonneville, WA, 98639. Tel: 509-427-4439. p. 2391

Wyatt, Judy, Librn, South Routt Library District, Yampa Public Library, 116 Main St, Yampa, CO, 80483. Tel: 970-638-4654. p. 292

Wyatt, Linda, Tech/Cat Librn, Benton County Public Library, 121 S Forrest Ave, Camden, TN, 38320-2055. Tel: 731-584-4772. p. 2090

Wyatt, Michelle, Librn, Northeast State Community College, 2425 Hwy 75, Blountville, TN, 37617. Tel: 423-354-2429. p. 2088

Wyatt, Naomi, Br Mgr, Bienville Parish Library, Ringgold Branch, 2078 Hall St, Ringgold, LA, 71068. Tel: 318-894-9770. p. 881

Wyatt, Patty, Circ, Decatur County Library, 20 W Market St, Decaturville, TN, 38329. Tel: 731-852-3325. p. 2096

Wyche, Floyd, Circ Supvr, Bristol Public Library, Five High St, Bristol, CT, 06010. Tel: 860-584-7787. p. 304

Wyche, Lynn, Dir, North Florida College Library, 325 NW Turner Davis Dr, Madison, FL, 32340. Tel: 850-973-1624. p. 419

Wyche, Paul, Text Librn, Journal Gazette Library, 600 W Main St, Fort Wayne, IN, 46802. Tel: 260-461-8258. p. 685

Wyckoff, Cammie, Admin Supvr, Cornell University Library, Library Annex, Palm Rd, Ithaca, NY, 14853. Tel: 607-253-3514. p. 1552

Wyckoff, Tanya, Dir, Bedford Public Library, 507 Jefferson St, Bedford, IA, 50833-1314. Tel: 712-523-2828. p. 734

Wyckoff, Wade, Assoc Univ Librn, McMaster University Library, 1280 Main St W, Hamilton, ON, L8S 4L6, CANADA. Tel: 905-525-9140, Ext 26557. p. 2647

Wydert, Greg, Dir, Creve Coeur Public Library, 311 N Highland St, Creve Coeur, IL, 61610. Tel: 309-699-7921. p. 574

Wykes, Shelly, Libr Dir, Litchfield District Library, 115 W Saint Joe St, Litchfield, MI, 49252. Tel: 517-542-3887. p. 1127

Wyld, Kira, Sci, Tech, Eng & Math Librn, University of Washington Libraries, Engineering Library, Engineering Library Bldg, Box 352170, Seattle, WA, 98195-2170. Tel: 206-543-0740. p. 2381

Wyld, Kira, Sci, Tech, Eng & Math Librn, University of Washington Libraries, Mathematics Research Library, Padelford Hall C-306, Box 354350, Seattle, WA, 98195-4350. Tel: 206-685-1469. p. 2382

Wylie, Micky, Mrs, Librn, Dickinson Wright LLP Library, 199 Bay St, Ste 2200, Toronto, ON, M5L 1G4, CANADA. Tel: 416-777-0101. p. 2688

Wylie, Tricia, Dir, New River Public Library Cooperative, 110 N Lake Ave, Lake Butler, FL, 32054. Tel: 386-496-2526. p. 415

Wyma, Heidi, Mgr, Support Serv, Chatham-Kent Public Library, 120 Queen St, Chatham, ON, N7M 2G6, CANADA. Tel: 519-354-2940. p. 2635

Wyman, Andrea, Dr, Research Servs Librn, Pennsylvania Western University - Edinboro, 200 Tartan Dr, Edinboro, PA, 16444. Tel: 814-732-2796. p. 1929

Wyman, Chelsea, Outreach Librn, University of Wisconsin-La Crosse, 1631 Pine St, La Crosse, WI, 54601-3748. Tel: 608-785-8396. p. 2446

Wymer, Becky, Syst Librn, Creighton University, 2500 California Plaza, Omaha, NE, 68178-0209. Tel: 402-280-2220. p. 1328

Wyneken, Rachel, Head, Children's Servx, Mastics-Moriches-Shirley Community Library, 407 William Floyd Pkwy, Shirley, NY, 11967. Tel: 631-399-1511. p. 1640

Wynn, Stephen, Assoc Dean, Tech Serv & Libr Syst, Truman State University, 100 E Normal, Kirksville, MO, 63501-4211. Tel: 660-785-4535. p. 1259

Wynn, Tammie, Library Contact, David Wade Correctional Center, 670 Bell Hill Rd, Homer, LA, 71040. Tel: 318-927-0424. p. 891

Wynne, Betty, Ch, Dudley-Tucker Library, Six Epping St, Raymond, NH, 03077. Tel: 603-895-7058. p. 1379

Wyrzykowski, Jake, Ch Serv, Phillips Public Library, 286 Cherry St, Phillips, WI, 54555. Tel: 715-339-2868. p. 2469

Wyse, Valerie, Br Mgr, Oscoda County Library, Fairview Branch, 2053 E Miller Rd, Fairview, MI, 48621. Tel: 989-848-0994. p. 1133

Xander, Stephanie, Coll Mgt Librn, United States Army, Van Noy Library, 5966 12th St, Bldg 1024, Fort Belvoir, VA, 22060-5554. Tel: 703-806-3273. p. 2319

Xavier, Patrick, Sr Librn, Los Angeles Public Library System, Cypress Park Branch Library, 1150 Cypress Ave, Los Angeles, CA, 90065-1144. Tel: 323-224-0039. p. 164

Xia, Jingfeng, Libr Dir, Gwynedd Mercy University, 1325 Sumneytown Pike, Gwynedd Valley, PA, 19437. Tel: 215-646-7300, Ext 21474. p. 1939

Xiao, Jingshan, Assoc Dir, Res Mgt, Assoc Dir, Tech, University of Houston - Clear Lake, Bayou Bldg 2402, 2700 Bay Area Blvd, Houston, TX, 77058-1002. Tel: 281-283-3912. p. 2199

Xie, Hongbo, Assoc Dir, Libr Serv, Head, Tech Serv, Coe College, 1220 First Ave NE, Cedar Rapids, IA, 52402. Tel: 319-399-8026. p. 738

Xie, Jiangjing, Commun Libr Mgr, Queens Library, Fresh Meadows Community Library, 193-20 Horace Harding Expressway, Fresh Meadows, NY, 11365. Tel: 718-454-7272. p. 1554

Xie, Wendy, Tech Serv Mgr, Orland Park Public Library, 14921 Ravinia Ave, Orland Park, IL, 60462. Tel: 708-428-5120. p. 630

Xie, Zhiwu, Chief Strategy Officer, Virginia Polytechnic Institute & State University Libraries, 560 Drillfield Dr, Blacksburg, VA, 24061. Tel: 540-231-4453. p. 2307

Xing, Sunan, Asst Librn, Mitchell Silberberg & Knupp LLP, 11377 W Olympic Blvd, Los Angeles, CA, 90064-1683. Tel: 310-312-2000. p. 166

Xiong, Anna, Govt Info Coordr, Rice University, 6100 Main, MS-44, Houston, TX, 77005. Tel: 713-348-6212. p. 2198

Xu, Gordon, Assoc Univ Librn, Scholarly Communications, New Jersey Institute of Technology, 186 Central Ave, Newark, NJ, 07103. Tel: 973-596-3205. p. 1426

Xu, Joe, Librn, Jones Walker, 190 E Capital St, Ste 800, Jackson, MS, 39201. Tel: 601-949-4792. p. 1222

XU, Xinhao, Asst Prof, University of Missouri-Columbia, 303 Townsend Hall, Columbia, MO, 65211. Tel: 573-882-4546. p. 2787

Xu, Yan, Mgr, Naperville Public Library, Naper Boulevard, 2035 S Naper Blvd, Naperville, IL, 60565-3353. Tel: 630-961-4100, Ext 2210. p. 623

Xue, Lijun, Coll Mgt Librn, Madonna University Library, 36600 Schoolcraft Rd, Livonia, MI, 48150-1173. Tel: 734-432-5683. p. 1127

Xue, Susan, Electronic Res Librn, Head, Info Serv, Head, Pub Serv, University of California, Berkeley, C V Starr East Asian Library, Berkeley, CA, 94720-6000. Tel: 510-642-2556. p. 123

Xue, Zhaohui, Curator of Coll, Stanford University Libraries, East Asia Library, Lathrop Library Bldg, 518 Memorial Way, Stanford, CA, 94305. Tel: 650-725-3435. p. 248

Yablonsky, Karen A, Dir, Sylvester Memorial Wellston Public Library, 135 E Second St, Wellston, OH, 45692. Tel: 740-384-6660. p. 1829

Yacobucci Farquhar, Kelly, County Historian, Rec Mgt Officer, Montgomery County Department of History & Archives, Nine Park St, Fonda, NY, 12068. Tel: 518-853-8186. p. 1534

Yacovelli, Leigh-Anne, Dir, Wernersville Public Library, 100 N Reber St, Wernersville, PA, 19565-1412. Tel: 610-678-8771. p. 2019

Yacovone, Maria, ILL, Agawam Public Library, 750 Cooper St, Agawam, MA, 01001. Tel: 413-789-1550. p. 984

Yacyshyn, Joanne, Br Librn, Wapiti Regional Library, Porcupine Plain Public Library, 302 Pine St W, Porcupine Plain, SK, S0E 1H0, CANADA. Tel: 306-278-2488. p. 2746

Yager, Ellice, Librn, Northeast Mississippi Community College, 101 Cunningham Blvd, Booneville, MS, 38829. Tel: 662-720-7584. p. 1212

Yager, Heather, Assoc Dir, Tech, Massachusetts Institute of Technology Libraries, Office of the Director, Bldg NE36-6101, 77 Massachusetts Ave, Cambridge, MA, 02139-4307. Tel: 617-253-3839. p. 1008
Yagerhofer, Jane, Cat, Lehigh Carbon Community College Library, 4750 Orchard Rd, Schnecksville, PA, 18078. Tel: 610-799-1150. p. 2003
Yahraus, Jeffrey A, Dir, Williams County Public Library, 107 E High St, Bryan, OH, 43506-1702. Tel: 419-636-6734. p. 1753
Yake, Matthew, Library Contact, Multnomah County Library, Belmont, 1038 SE Cesar E Chavez Blvd, Portland, OR, 97214. p. 1892
Yamada, Grace, Librn, Supvr, Carlsmith Ball LLP Library, ASB Tower, Ste 2200, 1001 Bishop St, Honolulu, HI, 96813. Tel: 808-523-2500. p. 505
Yamakawa, Linda, Librn, College of the Sequoias Library, 915 S Mooney Blvd, Visalia, CA, 93277. Tel: 559-730-3824. p. 257
Yamamoto, Helen, Libr Mgr, Wake County Public Library System, Morrisville Community Library, 310 Town Hall Dr, Morrisville, NC, 27560. Tel: 919-463-8460. p. 1711
Yamamoto, Sue, Mgr, County of Los Angeles Public Library, Rosemead Library, 8800 Valley Blvd, Rosemead, CA, 91770-1788. Tel: 626-573-5220. p. 137
Yamasaki, Margaret, Mgr, San Jose Public Library, Evergreen, 2635 Aborn Rd, San Jose, CA, 95121-1294. Tel: 408-808-3060. p. 231
Yamasaki, Margaret, Mgr, San Jose Public Library, Village Square Branch Library, 4001 Evergreen Village Sq, San Jose, CA, 95135. Tel: 408-808-3093. p. 232
Yan, Phil, Webmaster, Tennessee State University, 3500 John A Merritt Blvd, Nashville, TN, 37209. Tel: 615-963-5213. p. 2121
Yan, Ruth, Dr, Dir, Libr Serv, Allen College, 1990 Heath St, Waterloo, IA, 50703. Tel: 319-226-2080. p. 788
Yanagihara, Alicia, Instr, Librn, Honolulu Community College Library, 874 Dillingham Blvd, Honolulu, HI, 96817-4598. Tel: 808-845-9232. p. 512
Yancey, Doug, Exec Dir, Chemeketa Cooperative Regional Library Service, 4000 Lancaster Dr NE, Salem, OR, 97305. Tel: 503-399-5165. p. 2773
Yancey, Martha, Dir, West Virginia University Libraries, Evansdale Library, 1212 Evansdale Dr, Morgantown, WV, 26506. Tel: 304-293-4696. p. 2409
Yancey, Toni, Health Sci Librn, Department of Behavioral Health, St Elizabeths Hospital, 1100 Alabama Ave SE, Washington, DC, 20032. Tel: 202-299-5997. p. 363
Yanchick, Laura, Youth Serv, Joliet Public Library, 150 N Ottawa St, Joliet, IL, 60432. Tel: 815-740-2660. p. 603
Yancich, Jamie, Law Librn, Washington County Law Library, One S Main St, Ste G004, Washington, PA, 15301. Tel: 724-228-6747. p. 2018
Yanez, Maria, Libr Asst, Alexander Memorial Library, La Salle County Library - Encinal Branch, 201 Center St, Cotulla, TX, 78014. p. 2161
Yang, Andrea, Coll Develop Coordr, Montgomery County Memorial Library System, 104 I-45 N, Conroe, TX, 77301-2720. Tel: 936-522-2102. p. 2159
Yang, Changwoo, Dr, Assoc Prof, Valdosta State University, Odum Library, 1500 N Patterson St, Valdosta, GA, 31698. Tel: 229-333-7185. p. 2784
Yang, Grace, Mgr, County of Los Angeles Public Library, Sunkist Library, 840 N Puente Ave, La Puente, CA, 91746-1316. Tel: 626-960-2707. p. 138
Yang, Jainxin, Ref & Instruction Librn, Gateway Community College Library & Learning Commons, 20 Church St, New Haven, CT, 06510. Tel: 203-285-2158. p. 325
Yang, Jianshan, Syst Librn, Xavier University of Louisiana, One Drexel Dr, New Orleans, LA, 70125-1098. Tel: 504-520-7311. p. 904
Yang, Lan, Dir, Doc Delivery, Texas A&M University Libraries, 400 Spence St, College Station, TX, 77843. Tel: 978-862-1904. p. 2157
Yang, Lily, ILL, Brigham Young University-Hawaii, BYU-Hawaii, No 1966, 55-220 Kulanui St, Bldg 5, Laie, HI, 96762-1294. Tel: 808-675-3878. p. 514
Yang, Lucy, Circ Serv Coordr, Tompkins Cortland Community College Library, Baker Commons, 2nd Flr, 170 North St, Dryden, NY, 13053-8504. Tel: 607-844-8222, Ext 4361. p. 1526
Yang, Mai, Librn, Fresno City College Library, 1101 E University Ave, Fresno, CA, 93741. Tel: 559-442-4600, Ext 8918. p. 145
Yang, Pang H, Dep Dir, Ramsey County Library, 4570 N Victoria St, Shoreview, MN, 55126. Tel: 651-486-2200. p. 1203
Yang, Sharon Li-shiuan, Pub Serv Librn, Harvard Library, Harvard-Yenching Library, Two Divinity Ave, Cambridge, MA, 02138. Tel: 617-495-2756. p. 1006
Yang, Shengnan, Asst Prof, Western University, FIMS & Nursing Bldg, Rm 2020, London, ON, N6A 5B9, CANADA. Tel: 519-661-2111, Ext 84720. p. 2796
Yang, Tao, Librn, Rutgers University Libraries, East Asian Library, Alexander Library, 169 College Ave, New Brunswick, NJ, 08901-1163. Tel: 848-932-6086. p. 1425
Yang, Xiao Hua, Acq Librn, Western Connecticut State University, 181 White St, Danbury, CT, 06810. Tel: 203-837-9105. p. 307
Yang, Yuezeng Shen, Cat Librn, Cleveland State University, Michael Schwartz Library, Rhodes Tower, Ste 501, 2121 Euclid Ave, Cleveland, OH, 44115-2214. Tel: 216-687-5274. p. 1769
Yanicke, Joan, Regional Dir, Library Services, Saint Vincent Hospital, 123 Summer St, Worcester, MA, 01608. Tel: 508-363-6117. p. 1072
Yannarella, Patricia, Br Mgr, Boone County Public Library, Chapin Memorial, 6517 Market St, Petersburg, KY, 41080. Tel: 859-342-2665. p. 850
Yannarella, Patricia, Info Serv Coordr, Boone County Public Library, 1786 Burlington Pike, Burlington, KY, 41005. Tel: 859-342-2665. p. 850
Yannarella, Phil, Librn, Cincinnati Museum Center At Union Terminal, Geier Science Library, 760 W Fifth St, Cincinnati, OH, 45203. Tel: 513-455-7183. p. 1760
Yannarella, Philip, Govt Doc Librn, Northern Kentucky University, University Dr, Highland Heights, KY, 41099. Tel: 859-572-5455. p. 859
Yanniello, Allyssa, Librn, La Roche University, 9000 Babcock Blvd, Pittsburgh, PA, 15237. Tel: 412-536-1063. p. 1994
Yanusz, Elana, Curator, Seward Community Library & Museum, 239 Sixth Ave, Seward, AK, 99664. Tel: 907-224-4007. p. 50
Yao, Hong, Coll Develop Coordr, Queens Library, 89-11 Merrick Blvd, Jamaica, NY, 11432. Tel: 718-990-0700. p. 1553
Yao, Jennifer, Ref & Instrul Serv Librn, New School, Adam & Sophie Gimbel Design Library, Two W 13th St, 2nd Flr, New York, NY, 10011. Tel: 212-229-8914, Ext 4285. p. 1593
Yap, Derek, Cat/Syst Librn, Yukon College Library, 500 College Dr, Whitehorse, YT, Y1A 5K4, CANADA. Tel: 867-668-8870. p. 2758
Yap, Eric, Ref Librn, Brooklyn Law School Library, 250 Joralemon St, Brooklyn, NY, 11201. Tel: 718-780-7580. p. 1501
Yap, Jenny, Librn, Berkeley City College Library, 2050 Center St, Rm 131, Berkeley, CA, 94704. p. 121
Yarbro, Tracey, Librn, American Contract Bridge League, 6575 Windchase Blvd, Horn Lake, MS, 38637. Tel: 662-253-3106. p. 1220
Yarbrough, Dorothy, Asst Librn, Blountsville Public Library, 65 Chestnut St, Blountsville, AL, 35031. Tel: 205-429-3156. p. 10
Yarbrough Hawkins, Felita, Librn, Birmingham Public Library, Avondale, 509 40th St S, Birmingham, AL, 35222-3309. Tel: 205-226-4000. p. 7
Yarbrough, Shannon, Dir, Trinity Health, Health Ctr East, 1st Flr, Ste 103, 20 Burdick Expressway W, Minot, ND, 58701. Tel: 701-857-5435. p. 1738
Yarman, Don, Exec Dir, Ohio Public Library Information Network, 2323 W Fifth Ave, Ste 130, Columbus, OH, 43204. Tel: 614-728-5252. p. 2773
Yashgur, Rima, Librn, Congregation Beth Israel, Ellen Jeanne Goldfarb Community Learning Ctr, 701 Farmington Ave, West Hartford, CT, 06119. Tel: 860-233-8215. p. 345
Yasner, Jason, Dep Dir, Library of Congress, National Library Service for the Blind & Print Disabled, Library Collections & Services Group, 1291 Taylor St NW, Washington, DC, 20542. Tel: 202-707-5100. p. 370
Yasuda, Naoko, Libr Syst Coordr, Tech Serv, Highline College Library, 2400 S 240th St, MS 25-4, Des Moines, WA, 98198. Tel: 206-592-3726. p. 2363
Yatcilla, Jane S, Head of Libr, Purdue University Libraries, Veterinary Medical, Lynn Hall of Veterinary Medicine 1133, 625 Harrison St, West Lafayette, IN, 47907. Tel: 765-494-2856. p. 726
Yates, Christopher, Dep Dir, South Carolina State Library, 1500 Senate St, Columbia, SC, 29201. Tel: 803-734-4618. p. 2054
Yates, Darrell, Dir, Lloydminster Public Library, 5010 - 49 St, Lloydminster, AB, T9V 0K2, CANADA. Tel: 780-875-0850. p. 2547
Yates, Darrell, Dir, Lakeland Library Region, 1302 100 St, North Battleford, SK, S9A 0V8, CANADA. Tel: 306-445-6108. p. 2743
Yates, Evelyn, Assoc Librn, Coordr, Spec Serv, University of Arkansas-Pine Bluff, 1200 N University Dr, Pine Bluff, AR, 71601. Tel: 870-575-8411. p. 108
Yates, Gary, Mgr, Alexander Graham Bell Association for the Deaf & Hard of Hearing, 3417 Volta Pl NW, Washington, DC, 20007. Tel: 202-204-4683. p. 359
Yates, Jeremy, Coordr, Spec Projects, Putnam County Library System, 601 College Rd, Palatka, FL, 32177-3873. Tel: 386-329-0441. p. 433
Yates, Molly, Librn, Big Horn County Library, Deaver Branch, 180 W First St, Deaver, WY, 82421. p. 2491
Yates, Molly, Librn, Big Horn County Library, Frannie Branch, 305 Fifth St, Frannie, WY, 82423. p. 2491
Yates, Stephanie, Br Adminr, Frederick County Public Libraries, Urbana Reginal Library, 9020 Amelung St, Frederick, MD, 21704. Tel: 301-600-7000. p. 966
Yates, Steven, Dr, Asst Dir, Assoc Prof, University of Alabama, 7035 Gorgas Library, Campus Box 870252, Tuscaloosa, AL, 35487-0252. Tel: 205-348-4610. p. 2781
Yates, Vickie, ILL Coordr, Jackson Parish Library, 614 S Polk Ave, Jonesboro, LA, 71251-3442. Tel: 318-259-5697, 318-259-5698. p. 892
Yates, Will, Librn, United Hospital Fund of New York, 1411 Broadway, 12th Flr, New York, NY, 10018. Tel: 212-494-0720. p. 1603
Yatuzis, Sara, Asst Dir, Milford Public Library, 11 SE Front St, Milford, DE, 19963. Tel: 302-422-8996. p. 354
Yau, Yong-Le, Managing Librn, Brooklyn Public Library, Paerdegat, 850 E 59th St, Brooklyn, NY, 11234. Tel: 718-241-3994. p. 1503
Yaw, Matthew, Br Coordr, Erie County Public Library, Edinboro Branch, 413 W Plum St, Edinboro, PA, 16412-2508. Tel: 814-451-7081. p. 1931
Yawn, Amy E, Librn, Kelly Hart & Hallman, Wells Fargo Tower, 201 Main St, Ste 2500, Fort Worth, TX, 76102. Tel: 817-332-2500. p. 2180

Yaws, Rene, Mgr, Jefferson County Public Library, Columbine, 7706 W Bowles Ave, Littleton, CO, 80123. Tel: 303-403-5340. p. 288

Yax, Jared, Curator of Coll, Tri-Cities Historical Museum, 200 Washington Ave, Grand Haven, MI, 49417. Tel: 616-842-0700. p. 1109

Yaylor, Tamera, Bus Off Mgr, Glenwood-Lynwood Public Library District, 19901 Stony Island Ave, Lynwood, IL, 60411. Tel: 708-758-0090. p. 611

Yazel, Suzanne, Human Res Mgr, Mount Prospect Public Library, Ten S Emerson St, Mount Prospect, IL, 60056. Tel: 847-253-5675. p. 621

Yazzie, Doris, Libr Tech, Navajo County Library District, 121 W Buffalo, Holbrook, AZ, 86025. Tel: 928-524-4745. p. 63

Yazzie, Vananda, Librn, Glacier County Library, Browning Branch, 214 First St NW, Browning, MT, 59417. Tel: 406-338-7105. p. 1291

Ybarra, Dawnna, Libr Asst, Winslow Public Library, 420 W Gilmore St, Winslow, AZ, 86047. Tel: 928-289-4982. p. 85

Ybarra, Schiree, Librn, North Central Washington Libraries, Quincy Public Library, 208 Central Ave S, Quincy, WA, 98848-1203. Tel: 509-787-2359. p. 2394

Ye, Grace, Senior Digital Systems Librn, Pepperdine University Libraries, 24255 Pacific Coast Hwy, Malibu, CA, 90263. Tel: 310-506-4252. p. 171

Yeager, Janet, Br Mgr, San Diego Public Library, Carmel Mountain Ranch, 12095 World Trade Dr, San Diego, CA, 92128. Tel: 858-538-8181. p. 219

Yeager, Justine, Dir, North Pocono Public Library, 1315 Church St, Moscow, PA, 18444. Tel: 570-842-4700. p. 1966

Yeager, Lori, Circ Librn, Pulaski County Public Library, 304 S Main St, Somerset, KY, 42501. Tel: 606-679-8401. p. 875

Yeager, Michelle, Dir, Woodbury Public Library, 33 Delaware St, Woodbury, NJ, 08096. Tel: 856-845-2611. p. 1456

Yeager, Rebekah, Circ, Quitman Public Library, 202 E Goode St, Quitman, TX, 75783-2533. Tel: 903-763-4191. p. 2230

Yeaple Mann, Jennifer D, Librn, Massachusetts State Laboratory Institute Library, Dept of Public Health, 305 South St, Jamaica Plain, MA, 02130. Tel: 617-983-6290. p. 1026

Yearl, Mary, Head Librn, McGill University Libraries, Osler Library of the History of Medicine, McIntyre Medical Sciences Bldg, 3655 Promenade Sir William Osler, Montreal, QC, H3G 1Y6, CANADA. Tel: 514-398-4475, Ext 09873. p. 2726

Yearout, Teresa, Coordr, Libr Serv, Southwest Virginia Community College Library, Russell Hall, 599 Community College Rd, Cedar Bluff, VA, 24609. Tel: 276-964-7266. p. 2309

Yeatman, Jill, Chairperson, Elizabethtown-Kitley Township Public Library, 4103 County Rd 29, Addison, ON, K6V 5T4, CANADA. Tel: 613-498-3338. p. 2627

Yeckley, Pauline, Librn, De Anza College, 21250 Stevens Creek Blvd, Cupertino, CA, 95014-5793. Tel: 408-864-8303. p. 133

Yee, B, Tech Serv, College of New Caledonia Library, 3330 22nd Ave, Prince George, BC, V2N 1P8, CANADA. Tel: 250-561-5811, 250-562-2131, Ext 5298. p. 2574

Yee, Jason, Br Mgr, Cambridge Public Library, Valente Branch, 826 Cambridge St, Cambridge, MA, 02141. Tel: 617-349-4015. p. 1004

Yee, Karl, Syst Adminr, Northeastern University Libraries, 360 Huntington Ave, Boston, MA, 02115. Tel: 617-373-4904. p. 998

Yee, Shirley, Br Mgr, Chicago Public Library, Logan Square, 3030 W Fullerton Ave, Chicago, IL, 60647. Tel: 312-744-5295. p. 557

Yee, Warren, Coordr, Coll Serv, Media Coordr, Syst Coordr, Northeastern University School of Law Library, 416 Huntington Ave, Boston, MA, 02115. Tel: 617-373-3350. p. 999

Yeh, Felicia, Dep Dir, University of South Carolina, School of Medicine Library, Bldg 101, 6311 Garners Ferry Rd, Columbia, SC, 29209. Tel: 803-216-3200. p. 2056

Yeilding, Howard, IT Serv, San Jose Public Library, 150 E San Fernando St, San Jose, CA, 95112-3580. Tel: 408-808-2420. p. 231

Yelinek, Kathryn, Research Librn, Bloomsburg University of Pennsylvania, 400 E Second St, Bloomsburg, PA, 17815-1301. Tel: 570-389-4205. p. 1913

Yelk, Heidi, Dep Law Librn, Wisconsin State Law Library, 120 Martin Luther King Jr Blvd, 2nd Flr, Madison, WI, 53703. Tel: 608-261-7555. p. 2452

Yell, Cindy, Asst Dir, Libr Serv, Brazoria County Library System, 912 N Velasco, Angleton, TX, 77515. Tel: 979-864-1505. p. 2135

Yelverton, Randall, Exec Dir, Peoria Public Library, 107 NE Monroe St, Peoria, IL, 61602-1070. Tel: 309-497-2140. p. 634

Yelverton-Johnson, Teresa, Circ Supvr, Lake Superior State University, 906 Ryan Ave, Sault Sainte Marie, MI, 49783. Tel: 906-635-2815. p. 1149

Yeo, Sandra, Head Librn, Boyne Regional Library, 15 First St SW, Carman, MB, R0G 0J0, CANADA. Tel: 204-745-3504. p. 2586

Yeoman, Diane, Dir, Mason City Public Library District, 820 W Chestnut St, Mason City, IL, 62664. Tel: 217-482-3799. p. 615

Yeomans, Caroline, Med Librn, Grand River Hospital, 835 King St W, Kitchener, ON, N2G 1G3, CANADA. Tel: 519-749-4300, Ext 2235. p. 2651

Yeomans, Melinda, Dir of Teaching & Learning Center, Umpqua Community College Library, 1140 Umpqua College Rd, Roseburg, OR, 97470. Tel: 541-440-7657. p. 1895

Yerdon, Jessica, Libr Asst, Vernon Public Library, 4441 Peterboro St, Vernon, NY, 13476. Tel: 315-829-2463. p. 1657

Yerger, Maura, Tech Serv, Woodbury Public Library, 269 Main St S, Woodbury, CT, 06798. Tel: 203-263-3502. p. 349

Yerk, Becky, Tech Serv, Cherry Valley Public Library District, 755 E State St, Cherry Valley, IL, 61016-9699. Tel: 815-332-5161, Ext 34. p. 553

Yerkes, Kory, Mgr, Network Serv, Vols Coordr, Brighton Memorial Library, 2300 Elmwood Ave, Rochester, NY, 14618. Tel: 585-784-5300. p. 1628

Yerkey, Bob, Mgr, Auburn University, Ralph Brown Draughon Library, 231 Mell St, Auburn, AL, 36849. Tel: 334-844-2704. p. 5

Yerman, Roslyn F, Libr Dir, Madison Heights Public Library, 240 W 13 Mile Rd, Madison Heights, MI, 48071-1894. Tel: 248-837-2852. p. 1128

Yerramareddy, Indira, Libr Mgr, International Food Policy Research Institute Library, 1201 I St NW, Washington, DC, 20005. Tel: 202-862-5600. p. 370

Yersavich, Joe, Mgr, Columbus Metropolitan Library, Dublin Branch, 75 N High St, Dublin, OH, 43017. p. 1772

Yesowitch, Martha, Commun Partnerships Coordr, Charlotte Mecklenburg Library, 310 N Tryon St, Charlotte, NC, 28202-2176. Tel: 704-416-0100. p. 1679

Yetter, Amanda, Youth Serv Librn, H Leslie Perry Memorial Library, 205 Breckenridge St, Henderson, NC, 27536. Tel: 252-438-3316. p. 1695

Yetto, Sara, Dir, Cheney Library, 73 Classic St, Hoosick Falls, NY, 12090-1326. Tel: 518-686-9401. p. 1548

Yetwin, Hannah, Archivist, Georgia O'Keeffe Museum, 217 Johnson St, Santa Fe, NM, 87501. p. 1476

Yeung, Samantha, Div Mgr, Thousand Oaks Library, 1401 E Janss Rd, Thousand Oaks, CA, 91362-2199. Tel: 805-449-2660, Ext 7332. p. 252

Yevropina, Anna, Archivist/Librn, National Endowment for Democracy Library, 1201 Pennsylvania Ave NW, Ste 1100, Washington, DC, 20004. Tel: 202-378-9700. p. 372

Yi, Hua, Coll Mgt Librn, California State University, 333 S Twin Oaks Valley Rd, San Marcos, CA, 92096. Tel: 760-750-4368. p. 234

Yi, Hyokyoung, Interim Dir, University of Washington Libraries, Tateuchi East Asia Library, 322 Gowen Hall, Box 353527, Seattle, WA, 98195-3527. Tel: 206-543-6603. p. 2382

Yi, Ju Sun, Dep State Archivist, Hawaii State Archives, Iolani Palace Grounds, 364 S King St, Honolulu, HI, 96813. Tel: 808-586-0329. p. 506

Yilibuw, Dolores, Libr Dir, Lexington Theological Seminary, 230 Lexington Green Circle, Ste 300, Lexington, KY, 40503. Tel: 859-280-1224. p. 863

Yin, Crystal, E-Resources & Systems Librn, Justice Institute of British Columbia Library, 715 McBride Blvd, New Westminster, BC, V3L 5T4, CANADA. Tel: 604-528-5597. p. 2572

Yip, Monyee, Tech Serv Mgr, Weber County Library System, 2464 Jefferson Ave, Ogden, UT, 84401-2464. Tel: 801-337-2617. p. 2267

Yip, Teresa, Cataloger, Marymount Manhattan College, 221 E 71st St, New York, NY, 10021. Tel: 212-774-4818. p. 1591

Yisak, Ruddiyette, Br Mgr, Forsyth County Public Library, Malloy/Jordon East Winston Heritage Center, 1110 E Seventh St, Winston-Salem, NC, 27101. Tel: 336-703-2950. p. 1725

Yoas, Helen, Librn, Cat & Metadata Initiatives, Pennsylvania College of Technology, 999 Hagan Way, Williamsport, PA, 17701. Tel: 570-327-4523. p. 2023

Yob, Jaime, Dir, Priest Lake Public Library, 28769 Hwy 57, Priest Lake, ID, 83856. Tel: 208-443-2454. p. 529

Yockey, Brandon, Librn I, Illinois Department of Corrections, 10940 Lawrence Rd, Sumner, IL, 62466. Tel: 618-936-2064. p. 653

Yockey, Julie, Dir, Carthage Public Library, 612 S Garrison Ave, Carthage, MO, 64836. Tel: 417-237-7040. p. 1241

Yockey, Pam, Archivist, Plymouth Historical Museum Archives, 155 S Main St, Plymouth, MI, 48170-1635. Tel: 734-455-8940, Ext 3. p. 1141

Yocom, Laurie, Dir, Wilson Public Library, 910 Meridian Ave, Cozad, NE, 69130-1755. Tel: 308-784-2019. p. 1311

Yocum, Renee, Dir, Gleason Memorial Library, 101 E Main St, Ringling, OK, 73456. Tel: 580-662-2925. p. 1861

Yoder, Kathy, Libr Dir, Ohio State University LIBRARIES, Agricultural Technical Institute Library, Halterman Hall, 1328 Dover Rd, Wooster, OH, 44691-4000. Tel: 330-287-1294. p. 1774

Yoder, Kevin, Dir, Hollidaysburg Area Public Library, One Furnace Rd, Hollidaysburg, PA, 16648-1051. Tel: 814-695-5961. p. 1944

Yoder, Leanne, Dir, Arizona Superior Court in Pima County, 110 W Congress, Rm 256, Tucson, AZ, 85701-1317. Tel: 520-724-8456. p. 81

Yoder, Paige, Dir, Union City Public Library, 408 N Columbia St, Union City, IN, 47390-1404. Tel: 765-964-4748. p. 722

Yoder, Tab, Br Librn, Marinette County Library System, Crivitz Public Library, 606 Louisa St, Crivitz, WI, 54114. Tel: 715-854-7562. p. 2453

Yoder, Tillie K, Assoc Librn, Goshen College, Mennonite Historical Library, 1700 S Main, Goshen, IN, 46526. Tel: 574-535-7418. p. 687

Yohannes, Semhar, Sci Librn, University of Maryland, Baltimore County, 1000 Hilltop Circle, Baltimore, MD, 21250. Tel: 410-455-2356. p. 958

Yohn, Matt, Metadata Librn, Bridgewater College, 402 E College St, Bridgewater, VA, 22812. Tel: 540-828-5414. p. 2308

Yoke, Beth, Chief Strategy Officer, Public Library of Cincinnati & Hamilton County, 800 Vine St, Cincinnati, OH, 45202-2009. Tel: 513-369-4568. p. 1761
Yokota, Junko, Library Contact, National Louis University Library, North Shore, 5202 Old Orchard Rd, Skokie, IL, 60077. Tel: 224-233-2798. p. 565
Yonezawa, Pearl, Sr Librn, Los Angeles Public Library System, Los Feliz Branch Library, 1874 Hillhurst Ave, Los Angeles, CA, 90027-4427. Tel: 323-913-4710. p. 164
Yoo, Eun-Young, Prof, North Carolina Central University, 1801 Fayetteville St, Durham, NC, 27707. Tel: 919-530-6485. p. 2790
Yoo, Ming, Head, Libr Syst, Oklahoma State University Libraries, Athletic Ave, 216, Stillwater, OK, 74078. Tel: 405-744-5466. p. 1862
Yoon, Jung Won, Dr, Assoc Prof, University of South Florida, 4202 Fowler Ave, CIS 1040, Tampa, FL, 33620-7800. Tel: 813-974-3520. p. 2783
Yoon, Kyunghye, PhD, Assoc Prof, Saint Catherine University, 2004 Randolph Ave, Mailstop No 4125, Saint Paul, MN, 55105. Tel: 651-690-6802. p. 2787
Yopp, Amber, Youth Serv Coordr, Roanoke Public Libraries, 706 S Jefferson St, Roanoke, VA, 24016-5191. Tel: 540-853-2473. p. 2345
Yopp, Jessica, Libr Assoc, Roanoke Higher Education Center Library, 108 N Jefferson St, Ste 216, Roanoke, VA, 24016. Tel: 540-767-6016. p. 2345
York, Glenda, Ref Librn, Russell County Public Library, 535 N Main St, Jamestown, KY, 42629. Tel: 270-343-7323. p. 861
York, Laura, Ref & Ad Serv Librn, Andover Public Library, 142 W Main St, Andover, OH, 44003-9318. Tel: 440-293-6792. p. 1746
York, Maurice, Dir, Libr Initiatives, Big Ten Academic Alliance, 1819 S Neil St, Ste D, Champaign, IL, 61820-7271. Tel: 217-300-0945. p. 2764
York, Michael, Pres, Council of State Library Agencies in the Northeast, New Hampshire State Library, 20 Park St, Concord, NH, 03301. Tel: 603-271-2397. p. 2769
York, Priscilla, Librn, Mattawamkeag Public Library, 327 Main St, Mattawamkeag, ME, 04459. Tel: 207-736-7013. p. 931
York, Steven, Cat Librn, Christopher Newport University, One Avenue of the Arts, Newport News, VA, 23606. Tel: 757-594-8702. p. 2333
York, Sue, Librn, Fall River Public Library, 314 Merchant Ave, Fall River, KS, 67047. Tel: 620-658-4432. p. 808
York, Terri, Libr Dir, Webster County Library, 219 W Jackson St, Marshfield, MO, 65706. Tel: 417-468-3335. p. 1261
York, Tim, Mgr, Cherokee Regional Library System, 305 S Duke St, LaFayette, GA, 30728. Tel: 706-638-0288. p. 484
Yoshimura, Morgan, Interim Mgr, San Antonio Public Library, Potranco, 8765 State Hwy 151, Access Rd, San Antonio, TX, 78245. Tel: 210-207-9280. p. 2239
Yosifova, Maria, Libr Supvr, Bluegrass Community & Technical College, Newton Learning Commons, 120 Classroom Bldg, 500 Newton Pike, Lexington, KY, 40508. Tel: 859-246-6713. p. 862
Yoskosky, Kelly, Coordr, Programming, Rostraver Public Library, 700 Plaza Dr, Belle Vernon, PA, 15012. Tel: 724-379-5511. p. 1909
Yost, Brian, Head, Tech Serv & Syst, Hope College, Van Wylen Library, 53 Graves Pl, Holland, MI, 49422. Tel: 616-395-7492. p. 1115
Yost, Candace, Libr Dir, Philbrick-James Library, Four Church St, Deerfield, NH, 03037-1426. Tel: 603-463-7187. p. 1360
Yost, Janet, Dir, Kutztown Community Library, 70 Bieber Alley, Kutztown, PA, 19530-1113. Tel: 610-683-5820. p. 1949
Yost, Michelle, ILL Assoc, Hope College, Van Wylen Library, 53 Graves Pl, Holland, MI, 49422. Tel: 616-395-7794. p. 1115
Yott, Patrick, Assoc Dean, Digital Strategies & Serv, Northeastern University Libraries, 360 Huntington Ave, Boston, MA, 02115. Tel: 617-373-8778. p. 998
Youb, Laurie, Ch, Dawson Creek Municipal Public Library, 1001 McKellar Ave, Dawson Creek, BC, V1G 4W7, CANADA. Tel: 250-782-4661. p. 2565
Youle, Elizabeth, Assoc Dir, Reference & Public Services, Academy of Motion Picture Arts & Sciences, 333 S La Cienega Blvd, Beverly Hills, CA, 90211. Tel: 310-247-3000, Ext 2230. p. 124
Youles, Kathyrn, Regional Libr Dir, Screven-Jenkins Regional Library, 106 S Community Dr, Sylvania, GA, 30467. Tel: 912-564-7526. p. 498
Younce, Eldon, Dir, Anthony Public Library, 624 E Main, Anthony, KS, 67003-2738. Tel: 620-842-5344. p. 796
Young, Allison, Libr Dir, Marian Sutherland Kirby Library, 35 Kirby Ave, Mountain Top, PA, 18707. Tel: 570-474-9313. p. 1967
Young, Americus, Br Mgr, Marshall County Library System, Ruth B French Library, 161 S Hwy 309, Byhalia, MS, 38611. Tel: 662-838-4024. p. 1220
Young, Ammon, Libr Dir, Columbia County Traveling Library, 702 Sawmill Rd, Ste 101, Bloomsburg, PA, 17815. Tel: 570-387-8782. p. 1913
Young, Amy, Dir, Reed Memorial Library, 167 E Main St, Ravenna, OH, 44266-3197. Tel: 330-296-2827, Ext 101. p. 1817
Young, Anita, Campus Librn, Wake Technical Community College, Perry Health Sciences Library, Bldg C, Rm 123, 2901 Holston Lane, Raleigh, NC, 27610-2092. Tel: 919-747-0002. p. 1711
Young, Audrey, Asst Dir, Head, Ref, Easttown Library & Information Center, 720 First Ave, Berwyn, PA, 19312-1769. Tel: 610-644-0138. p. 1910
Young, Beth, Head, Ref, Christopher Newport University, One Avenue of the Arts, Newport News, VA, 23606. Tel: 757-594-7134. p. 2333
Young, Betsy, Fac Librn, Austin Community College, Northridge Campus Library, 11928 Stone Hollow Dr, 2nd, Rm 1223, Austin, TX, 78758. Tel: 512-223-4869. p. 2138
Young, Brian, Librn, Rio Hondo College Library, 3600 Workman Mill Rd, 2nd Flr, Whittier, CA, 90601. Tel: 562-908-3376. p. 259
Young, Brittany, Law Librn, Prog Supvr, Lane County Law Library, Lane County Public Service Bldg, 125 E Eighth Ave, Eugene, OR, 97401. Tel: 541-682-4337. p. 1879
Young, Carla, Cat, Dir, Teen Prog, Jackson County Public Library, 208 N Church St, Ripley, WV, 25271-1204. Tel: 304-372-5343. p. 2413
Young, Caroline, Assoc Dir, Rutgers University Library for the Center for Law & Justice, 123 Washington St, Newark, NJ, 07102-3094. Tel: 973-353-3151. p. 1428
Young, Charles, Libr Mgr, New Orleans Public Library, Nora Navra Library, 1902 St Bernard Ave, New Orleans, LA, 70116-1317. Tel: 504-596-3118. p. 903
Young, Chelsea, Instruction & Engagement Librn, University of Arkansas at Little Rock, 2801 S University Ave, Little Rock, AR, 72204. Tel: 501-916-6190. p. 102
Young, Cheryl, Libr Dir, Lakeside Public Library, 915 N Lake Rd, Lakeside, OR, 97449. Tel: 541-759-4432. p. 1884
Young, Courtney, Dir, Village of Avon Public Library, 105 S Main St, Avon, IL, 61415. Tel: 309-465-3933. p. 539
Young, Courtney, Univ Librn, Colgate University, 13 Oak Dr, Hamilton, NY, 13346-1398. Tel: 315-228-7362. p. 1543
Young, Cynthia, Exec Dir, SullivanMunce Cultural Center, 225 W Hawthorne St, Zionsville, IN, 46077. Tel: 317-873-4900. p. 728
Young, Cynthia C, Dir, Libr Serv, University of Maine at Augusta, 85 Texas Ave, Belfast Hall, Bangor, ME, 04401. Tel: 207-262-7900. p. 916
Young, Dana, Tech & Instruction Librn, Gavilan College Library, 5055 Santa Teresa Blvd, Gilroy, CA, 95020. p. 148
Young, Darlene, Acq, Cat, Buffalo River Regional Library, 230 E James Campbell Blvd, Ste 108, Columbia, TN, 38401-3359. Tel: 931-388-9282. p. 2094
Young, Darlene, Librn, Registrar, Orleans County Historical Society, Inc, 109 Old Stone House Rd, Brownington, VT, 05860. Tel: 802-754-2022. p. 2280
Young, David W, Research Librn, University of North Carolina at Pembroke, One University Dr, Pembroke, NC, 28372. Tel: 910-521-6516. p. 1707
Young, David W, Dr, Exec Dir, Delaware Historical Society Research Library, 505 N Market St, Wilmington, DE, 19801. Tel: 302-655-7161. p. 357
Young, Deb, Circ Mgr, Coventry Public Library, 1672 Flat River Rd, Coventry, RI, 02816. Tel: 401-822-9100. p. 2030
Young, Debbie, Bus Mgr, Daviess County Public Library, 2020 Frederica St, Owensboro, KY, 42301. Tel: 270-684-0211. p. 871
Young, Eric, Libr Dir, Northern Kentucky University, Nunn Dr, Highland Heights, KY, 41099. Tel: 859-572-6030. p. 859
Young, Eric, Asst Dean, Dir, University of South Dakota, McKusick Law Library, Knudson School of Law, 414 E Clark St, Vermillion, SD, 57069-2390. Tel: 605-658-3524. p. 2084
Young, Henry, Dr, Dean of Business, Law, & Academic Resources, Victor Valley College Library, 18422 Bear Valley Rd, Victorville, CA, 92395-5850. Tel: 760-245-4271, Ext 2262. p. 256
Young, Holly, Circ Asst, ILL, Bradford Public Library, 21 S Main St, Bradford, VT, 05033. Tel: 802-222-4536. p. 2280
Young, Jane, Head, Circ, Acorn Public Library District, 15624 S Central Ave, Oak Forest, IL, 60452-3204. Tel: 708-687-3700. p. 627
Young, Jane, Cat, Dept Chair, Century College Library, 3300 N Century Ave, White Bear Lake, MN, 55110. Tel: 651-779-3264. p. 1208
Young, Jeanne, Web Spec, University of Puget Sound, 1604 N Warner St, Upper Loading Dock, Tacoma, WA, 98416. Tel: 253-879-2663. p. 2387
Young, Jim B, Fac Mgr, Greensboro Public Library, 219 N Church St, Greensboro, NC, 27402. Tel: 336-373-2471. p. 1692
Young, Kara, Digital Serv & Emerging Tech Librn, Northwestern University Libraries, Pritzker Legal Research Center, 375 E Chicago Ave, Chicago, IL, 60611. Tel: 312-503-0252. p. 587
Young, Kate, Libr Mgr, Des Moines Public Library, 1000 Grand Ave, Des Moines, IA, 50309. Tel: 515-248-6413. p. 745
Young, Kathy, Librn, Manly Public Library, 127 S Grant, Manly, IA, 50456. Tel: 641-454-2982. p. 767
Young, Kelley, Br Mgr, East Baton Rouge Parish Library, Bluebonnet Regional, 9200 Bluebonnet Blvd, Baton Rouge, LA, 70810. Tel: 225-763-2280. p. 883
Young, Kristen, Lead Librn, United States Air Force School of Aerospace Medicine, USAFSAM/EDM, 2510 Fifth St, Bldg 840 E100, Wright-Patterson AFB, OH, 45433. Tel: 937-938-3592. p. 1834
Young, Lauren, Ad, Marion Public Library, 120 N Main St, Marion, WI, 54950. Tel: 715-754-5368. p. 2454
Young, Libby, Outreach Librn, Furman University Libraries, 3300 Poinsett Hwy, Greenville, SC, 29613-4100. Tel: 864-294-2260. p. 2061
Young, Lisa, Mgr, Access Serv, Lindenwood University Library, 209 S Kingshighway, Saint Charles, MO, 63301. Tel: 636-949-4670. p. 1268

Young, Lisa, Dr, Dir, Scottsdale Community College Library, 9000 E Chaparral Rd, Scottsdale, AZ, 85256. Tel: 480-423-6222. p. 77

Young, Lora, Libr Asst, Hamilton Public Library, 312 N Davis St, Hamilton, MO, 64644. Tel: 816-583-4832. p. 1247

Young, Lyn, Librn, Central Georgia Technical College Library, I Bldg, 2nd Flr, 3300 Macon Tech Dr, Macon, GA, 31206-3628. Tel: 478-757-3549. p. 486

Young, Marsha, Br Supvr, Marathon County Public Library, Hatley Branch, 435 Curtis Ave, Hatley, WI, 54440. Tel: 715-446-3537. p. 2486

Young, Martha, Dir, Margaret Carder Public Library, 201 W Lincoln Ave, Mangum, OK, 73554. Tel: 580-782-3185. p. 1852

Young, Mary, Admin Serv, Librn, Azalea Regional Library System, 1121 East Ave, Madison, GA, 30650. Tel: 706-342-4974, Ext 1026. p. 488

Young, Mary, Asst Librn, De Leon City County Library, 125 E Reynosa St, De Leon, TX, 76444-1862. Tel: 254-893-2417. p. 2169

Young, Michelle, Br Mgr, Hawaii State Public Library System, Waimea Public Library, 9750 Kaumualii Hwy, Waimea, HI, 96796. Tel: 808-338-6848. p. 511

Young, Michelle, Libr Dir, Island Trees Public Library, 38 Farmedge Rd, Levittown, NY, 11756. Tel: 516-731-2211. p. 1562

Young, Michelle L, Dean of Libr, Clarkson University Libraries, Andrew S Schuler Educational Resources Ctr, CU Box 5590, Eight Clarkson Ave, Potsdam, NY, 13699-5590. Tel: 315-268-4268. p. 1622

Young, Michelle L, Dir of Libr, Clarkson University Libraries, Health Sciences Library, 59 Main St, 1st Flr, Potsdam, NY, 13699. Tel: 315-268-4268. p. 1622

Young, Monica, Dir, Libr Serv, Guilford Technical Community College, 601 E Main St, Jamestown, NC, 27282. Tel: 336-334-4822, Ext 50587. p. 1698

Young, Monica Williamson, Librn, Moses Cone Health System, Women's Hospital of Greensboro Library, 801 Green Valley, Greensboro, NC, 27408. Tel: 336-832-6878. p. 1692

Young, Natalie, Ch Serv Librn, Shiawassee District Library, 502 W Main St, Owosso, MI, 48867-2607. Tel: 989-725-5134. p. 1139

Young, Paul, Libr Supvr, Rutgers University Libraries, James Dickson Carr Library, 75 Ave E, Piscataway, NJ, 08854-8040. Tel: 848-445-3607. p. 1424

Young, Rachel, Info Serv, Carrollton Public Library, 1700 N Keller Springs Rd, Carrollton, TX, 75006. Tel: 972-466-4800. p. 2153

Young, Rebecca, Dir, Libr Serv, Nova Scotia College of Art & Design University Library, 5163 Duke St, Halifax, NS, B3J 3J6, CANADA. Tel: 902-444-7212. p. 2619

Young, Rhea, Dir, Montgomery County Memorial Library System, 104 I-45 N, Conroe, TX, 77301-2720. Tel: 936-522-2123. p. 2159

Young, Richard, Dir, Brown County Public Library District, 143 W Main St, Mount Sterling, IL, 62353. Tel: 217-773-2013. p. 621

Young, Robert, Pub Serv Librn, Joe Barnhart Bee County Public Library, 110 W Corpus Christi St, Beeville, TX, 78102-5604. Tel: 361-362-4901. p. 2146

Young, Robert H, Dr, Dir, Massachusetts General Hospital, Tracy Burr Mallory Memorial Library, Dept of Pathology, 55 Fruit St, Boston, MA, 02114. Tel: 617-726-8892. p. 997

Young, Ross, Libr Dir, Dundee Public Library, 202 E Main St, PO Box 1000, Dundee, FL, 33838. Tel: 863-439-9424. p. 394

Young, Roxie, Dir, Montgomery Memorial Library, 711 Main St, Jewell, IA, 50130. Tel: 515-827-5112. p. 762

Young, Samuel R, Librn, United States Cavalry Association, 3220 N Jesse Reno St, El Reno, OK, 73036. Tel: 405-422-6330. p. 1847

Young, Sara, Dir, Anita Public Library, 812 Third St, Anita, IA, 50020. Tel: 712-762-3639. p. 731

Young, Sharon, Librn, Noxubee County Library System, 145 Dr Martin Luther King Jr Dr, Macon, MS, 39341. Tel: 662-726-5461. p. 1225

Young, Stephanie, Adult Serv Supvr, Info Serv Supvr, Seminole Community Library at St Petersburg College, 9200 113th St N, Seminole, FL, 33772. Tel: 727-394-6921. p. 444

Young, Stephanie, Youth Serv Librn, Whitman Public Library, 100 Webster St, Whitman, MA, 02382. Tel: 781-447-7613. p. 1069

Young, Stephanie, Librn, New York State Office of the State Comptroller Library, 110 State St, 15th Flr, Albany, NY, 12236. Tel: 518-473-4206. p. 1483

Young, Stephanie, Adult Serv, Ogdensburg Public Library, 312 Washington St, Ogdensburg, NY, 13669-1518. Tel: 315-393-4325. p. 1610

Young, Sue, Br Tech, Monroe County Library System, Newport Branch, 8120 N Dixie Hwy, Newport, MI, 48166. Tel: 734-586-2117. p. 1134

Young, Sue, Br Mgr, Wilson County Public Library, Elm City Branch, 114 N Railroad St, Elm City, NC, 27822-0717. Tel: 252-236-4269. p. 1724

Young, Susan Ramirez, Br Mgr, Rock Island Public Library, Southwest, 9010 Ridgewood Rd, Rock Island, IL, 61201. Tel: 309-732-7338. p. 641

Young, Susanne, Br Mgr, Davis Jefferson Parish Library, Jennings Headquarter Branch, 118 W Plaquemine, Jennings, LA, 70546-0356. Tel: 318-824-9530. p. 892

Young, Sydney, Principal Libr Asst/Youth serv, Glen Ridge Free Public Library, 240 Ridgewood Ave, Glen Ridge, NJ, 07028. Tel: 973-748-5482. p. 1405

Young, Teresa, Dir, Webster County Historical Museum Library, 721 W Fourth Ave, Red Cloud, NE, 68970. Tel: 402-746-2444. p. 1334

Young, Terry S, Dir, McMurry University, Bldg 1601 War Hawk Way, One McMurry University # 218, Abilene, TX, 79697. Tel: 325-793-4690. p. 2132

Young, Tonja, Libr Dir, Daphne Public Library, 2607 US Hwy 98, Daphne, AL, 36526. Tel: 251-620-2500. p. 13

Young, Virginia, Head, Pub Serv, Le Moyne College, 1419 Salt Springs Rd, Syracuse, NY, 13214. Tel: 315-445-4336. p. 1648

Young, Wyatt, Librn, Chester County History Center Library, 225 N High St, West Chester, PA, 19380. Tel: 610-692-4800, Ext 221. p. 2020

Young, Zach, Asst Dir, Libr Serv, Frontier Nursing University Library, 2050 Lexington Rd, 2nd Flr, Versailles, KY, 40383. Tel: 859-251-4730. p. 876

Young-Lenarz, Jackie, Sr Dir, Libr, Sullivan University Library, 2222 Wendell Ave, Louisville, KY, 40205. Tel: 502-456-6773. p. 867

Youngblood, Joshua, Spec Coll Res & Outreach Serv Librn, University of Arkansas Libraries, 365 N McIlroy Ave, Fayetteville, AR, 72701-4002. Tel: 479-575-7251. p. 95

Youngblood, Lisa D, Libr Dir, Harker Heights Public Library, 400 Indian Trail, Harker Heights, TX, 76548. Tel: 254-259-5491. p. 2187

Youngblood, Mandy, Libr Asst, New Mexico Junior College, One Thunderbird Circle, Hobbs, NM, 88240. Tel: 575-492-2870. p. 1469

Youngblood, Michelle L, Technician III, Colorado Department of Corrections, Sterling Correctional Facility Library- West - East, 12101 Hwy 61, Sterling, CO, 80751. p. 296

Younger, Lauren, Instrul Serv Librn, Outreach Librn, University of Dallas, 1845 E Northgate Dr, Irving, TX, 75062-4736. Tel: 972-721-4128. p. 2203

Younger, Susan, Asst Dir, Wautoma Public Library, 410 W Main St, Wautoma, WI, 54982-5415. Tel: 920-787-2988. p. 2486

Younger, William, Pub Serv Mgr, Lewiston City Library, 411 D St, Lewiston, ID, 83501. Tel: 208-798-2525. p. 524

Younggren, Kellyn, Sr Archivist, Montana Historical Society, 225 N Roberts St, Helena, MT, 59601-4514. Tel: 406-444-3317. p. 1296

Youngken, Jill, Dir, Libr & Archives, Lehigh County Historical Society, Lehigh Valley Heritage Museum, 432 W Walnut St, Allentown, PA, 18102. Tel: 610-435-1074, Ext 13. p. 1904

Youngmark, Fay, Libr Serv Mgr, Pennsylvania State University-Harrisburg Library, 351 Olmsted Dr, Middletown, PA, 17057-4850. Tel: 717-948-6566. p. 1963

Youngquest, Summer, Law Librn, Clark County Law Library, 309 S Third St, Ste 400, Las Vegas, NV, 89101. Tel: 702-455-4696. p. 1346

Youngs, Jill, Mgr, Northern Onondaga Public Library, 8686 Knowledge Lane, Cicero, NY, 13039. Tel: 315-699-2032. p. 1518

Youngs, Lila M, Dir, Richville Free Library, 87 Main St, Richville, NY, 13681-3102. Tel: 315-287-1481. p. 1627

Youngstrand, Keri, Dir, University of Minnesota Crookston, 2900 University Ave, Crookston, MN, 56716-0801. Tel: 218-281-8395. p. 1171

Youngstrom, Jason, Librn, Syst & Tech Planning, National Renewable Energy Laboratory Library, 15013 Denver West Pkwy, Golden, CO, 80401-3305. Tel: 303-275-4026. p. 283

Younkin, Roxanne, Librn, Dunbar Community Library, 60 Connellsville St, Dunbar, PA, 15431. Tel: 724-277-4775. p. 1928

Yousif, Ninous, Librn, Assyrian Universal Alliance Foundation, 4343 W Touhy Ave, Lincolnwood, IL, 60712. Tel: 773-863-3538. p. 609

Youssef, Yasser, Dr, Lecturer, University of Oklahoma, Bizzell Memorial Library, 401 W Brooks, Rm 120, Norman, OK, 73019-6032. Tel: 405-325-3921. p. 2791

Yowell, Linda, Support Serv Mgr, Fauquier County Public Library, 11 Winchester St, Warrenton, VA, 20186. Tel: 540-422-8500, Ext 1. p. 2351

Yu, Emma Lee, Ref Librn, Brooklyn College Library, 2900 Bedford Ave, Brooklyn, NY, 11210. Tel: 718-758-8204. p. 1501

Yu, Hsin-Han, Dir, Acad Tech, University of the Pacific Libraries, 3601 Pacific Ave, Stockton, CA, 95211. Tel: 209-932-3057. p. 250

Yu, Lifeng, Tallahassee Campus Libr Dir, Keiser University Library System, 1500 NW 49th St, Fort Lauderdale, FL, 33309. Tel: 954-351-4035. p. 401

Yu, Miranda, Libr Mgr, Vaughan Public Libraries, Maple Library, 10190 Keele St, Maple, ON, L6A 1G3, CANADA. Tel: 905-653-7323. p. 2701

Yu, Philip, Libr & Archives Asst, Audrey & Harry Hawthorn Library & Archives at the UBC Museum of Anthropology, 6393 NW Marine Dr, Vancouver, BC, V6T 1Z2, CANADA. Tel: 604-822-4834. p. 2579

Yu Schott, Melissa, Dir, Pub Libr Serv, Department of Community Services, Government of Yukon, 1171 First Ave, Whitehorse, YT, Y1A 0G9, CANADA. Tel: 867-667-5239. p. 2757

Yu, Yi, Syst Mgr, Tech Mgr, Nova Scotia Legislative Library, Province House, 2nd Flr, Halifax, NS, B3J 2P8, CANADA. Tel: 902-424-5932. p. 2620

Yu, Ying, Med Librn, Columbia Basin College Library, 2600 N 20th Ave, Pasco, WA, 99301. Tel: 509-544-8337. p. 2373

Yuan, Xiaojun, Dr, Assoc Prof, University at Albany, State University of New York, Draper 015, 135 Western Ave, Albany, NY, 12203. Tel: 518-591-8746. p. 2789

Yue, Paoshan, Acq, Electronic Res, University of Nevada-Reno, 1664 N Virginia St, Mailstop 0322, Reno, NV, 89557-0322. Tel: 775-682-5599. p. 1349

Yuen, Kandace, Med Librn, Connecticut Valley Hospital, Willis Royle Library, Silver St, Middletown, CT, 06457. Tel: 860-262-5520. p. 322

Yueping He, Helen, Head of Libr, University of Toronto Libraries, Dentistry Library, 124 Edward St, Rm 267, Toronto, ON, M5G 1G6, CANADA. Tel: 416-864-8213. p. 2698

Yuill, JoAnn, Librn, United States Department of Energy, 3610 Collins Ferry Rd, Morgantown, WV, 26507. Tel: 304-285-4184. p. 2409

Yukawa, Joyce, PhD, Assoc Prof, Saint Catherine University, 2004 Randolph Ave, Mailstop No 4125, Saint Paul, MN, 55105. Tel: 651-690-6802. p. 2787
Yulish, Jonathan, Exec Dir, Congregation Beth Emeth, 300 W Lea Blvd, Wilmington, DE, 19802. Tel: 302-764-2393. p. 356
Yun, Junkoo, Br Mgr, Chicago Public Library, Gage Park, 2807 W 55th St, Chicago, IL, 60632. Tel: 312-747-0032. p. 556
Yunker, Amelia, Head, Adult Serv, Salem-South Lyon District Library, 9800 Pontiac Trail, South Lyon, MI, 48178-7021. Tel: 248-437-6431. p. 1151
Yunker, Martie, Ch, Archbold Community Library, 205 Stryker St, Archbold, OH, 43502-1142. Tel: 419-446-2783. p. 1746
Yunko, Paula, Access & Ser Librn, Keystone College, One College Green, La Plume, PA, 18440-0200. Tel: 570-945-8332. p. 1950
Yuran, Robin, Ch, Head, Libr Serv, Hotchkiss Library of Sharon, Inc, Ten Upper Main St, Sharon, CT, 06069. Tel: 860-364-5041. p. 336
Yurgelonis, Chris, Libr Dir, Fort Lee Public Library, 320 Main St, Fort Lee, NJ, 07024. Tel: 201-592-3615. p. 1403
Yuschenkoff, Victoria, Library Contact, Ventura County Medical Center, 3291 Loma Vista Rd, Ventura, CA, 93003. Tel: 805-652-6030. p. 256
Zaarab, Nawal, Res Serv Spec, Borden Ladner Gervais LLP Library, 1000 de la Gauchetiere W, Ste 900, Montreal, QC, H3B 5H4, CANADA. Tel: 514-954-3159. p. 2721
Zabaly, Mary Jo, Libr Asst, Jonestown Community Library, 18649 FM 1431, Ste 10A, Jonestown, TX, 78645. Tel: 512-267-7511. p. 2204
Zabel, Diane W, Head of Libr, Librn, Pennsylvania State University Libraries, William & Joan Schreyer Business Library, 309 Paterno Library, 3rd Flr, University Park, PA, 16802-1810. Tel: 814-865-1013. p. 2016
Zabonick, Erin, Asst Dir, Three Rivers Public Library, 88 N Main St, Three Rivers, MI, 49093-2137. Tel: 269-273-8666. p. 1154
Zabonick, Erin, Libr Dir, Three Rivers Public Library, 88 N Main St, Three Rivers, MI, 49093-2137. Tel: 269-273-8666. p. 1154
Zaborowski, Barbara A, Dr, Dean, Learning Res, Pennsylvania Highlands Community College Library, 101 Community College Way, Johnstown, PA, 15904. Tel: 814-262-6425. p. 1948
Zabriskie, Stephanie, Head, Circ, Waltham Public Library, 735 Main St, Waltham, MA, 02451. Tel: 781-314-3425. p. 1062
Zabski, Heather, Asst Dir, Fox River Valley Public Library District, 555 Barrington Ave, East Dundee, IL, 60118-1496. Tel: 847-428-3661. p. 580
Zaccagnini, Jessica, Adult Serv, Gunn Memorial Library, Inc, Five Wykeham Rd, Washington, CT, 06793-1308. Tel: 860-868-7586. p. 343
Zaccardi, Sarah, Info Serv Librn, Post University, 800 Country Club Rd, Waterbury, CT, 06723-2540. Tel: 203-568-1631. p. 344
Zaccari, Helen, Dir, Admin Serv, University of California, Davis, 100 NW Quad, Davis, CA, 95616. Tel: 530-752-8792. p. 134
Zaccaria, Mary Grace, Dir, Tomkins Cove Public Library, 419 Liberty Dr N, Tomkins Cove, NY, 10986. Tel: 845-786-3060. p. 1652
Zaccone, Marie, Libr Dir, Carbondale Public Library, Five N Main St, Carbondale, PA, 18407. Tel: 570-282-4281. p. 1918
Zacharias, Anne, Social Sciences & Outreach Librn, Oakland University Library, 100 Library Dr, Rochester, MI, 48309-4479. Tel: 248-370-2475. p. 1144
Zacharias, Charlene, Libr Asst, Daysland Public Library, 5128 50th St, Daysland, AB, T0B 1A0, CANADA. Tel: 780-781-0005. p. 2532
Zachary, Warren, Head, Tech Serv, Calumet City Public Library, 660 Manistee Ave, Calumet City, IL, 60409. Tel: 708-862-6220, Ext 224. p. 548
Zacherl, Anna, Dir, Orangeburg County Library, 510 Louis St, Orangeburg, SC, 29115-5030. Tel: 803-531-4636. p. 2066
Zachery, Angela, Librn, Opelousas Public Library, 212 E Grolee St, Opelousas, LA, 70570. Tel: 337-948-3693. p. 905
Zachman, Jon B, Curator of Coll, Greensboro Historical Museum Archives Library, 130 Summit Ave, Greensboro, NC, 27401-3004. Tel: 336-373-4589. p. 1692
Zachwieja, Jeffrey, Coordr, Electronic Res, Oakland Community College, Library Systems, 2900 Featherstone Rd, MTEC A210, Auburn Hills, MI, 48326. Tel: 248-522-3488. p. 1082
Zaffarano, Sandra, Dir, Middleville Free Library, One S Main St, Middleville, NY, 13406. Tel: 315-891-3655. p. 1572
Zaffino, Lynn, Libr Dir, Easton Public Library, 691 Morehouse Rd, Easton, CT, 06612. Tel: 203-261-0134. p. 310
Zafrin, Vika, Institutional Repository Librn, Boston University Libraries, Mugar Memorial Library, 771 Commonwealth Ave, Boston, MA, 02215. Tel: 617-353-3710. p. 993
Zafron, Michelle, Ref Librn/Health Sci Liaison, University at Buffalo Libraries-State University of New York, Health Sciences Library, Abbott Hall, 3435 Main St, Bldg 28, Buffalo, NY, 14214-3002. Tel: 716-829-5746. p. 1510
Zaghloul, Raik, Govt Doc Librn, Head, Coll Develop, Union College, 807 Union St, Schenectady, NY, 12308. Tel: 518-388-6277. p. 1638
Zago, Sue, Dir, Law Libr, University of New Hampshire School of Law, Two White St, Concord, NH, 03301. p. 1360
Zagonel, April, Ch, Girard Public Library, 128 W Prairie Ave, Girard, KS, 66743-1498. Tel: 620-724-4317. p. 809
Zagorski, Megan, Asst to the Dir, C C Mellor Memorial Library, One Pennwood Ave, Edgewood, PA, 15218-1627. Tel: 412-731-0909. p. 1929
Zagurski, Salina, Asst Librn, Dobson Community Library, 113 S Crutchfield St, Dobson, NC, 27017. Tel: 336-386-8208. p. 1683
Zaharevich, Thomas, Collections & Tech Services Librarian, Elizabethtown College, One Alpha Dr, Elizabethtown, PA, 17022-2227. Tel: 717-361-1452. p. 1929
Zaher, Diane, Mgr, County of Los Angeles Public Library, Bell Library, 4411 E Gage Ave, Bell, CA, 90201-1216. Tel: 323-560-2149. p. 135
Zahid, Abdullah, Commun Libr Mgr, Queens Library, Hollis Community Library, 202-05 Hillside Ave, Hollis, NY, 11423. Tel: 718-465-7355. p. 1554
Zahn, Nora, Youth Serv Librn, North Adams Public Library, 74 Church St, North Adams, MA, 01247. Tel: 413-662-3133. p. 1040
Zahor, Theresa, Ref & Instruction, Farmingdale State College of New York, 2350 Broadhollow Rd, Farmingdale, NY, 11735-1021. Tel: 934-420-2040. p. 1532
Zahradnik, Tracy, Eng Librn, University of Toronto Libraries, Engineering & Computer Science Library, Sandford Fleming Bldg, Rm 2402, Ten King's College Rd, Toronto, ON, M5S 1A5, CANADA. Tel: 416-946-5966. p. 2698
Zahrt, Chad, Asst Dean, University of Wisconsin-Milwaukee, NWQD, Rm 3860, 2025 E Newport, Milwaukee, WI, 53211. Tel: 414-229-5421. p. 2794
Zaino, Jeff, Head, Infrastructure & Content, New Canaan Library, 151 Main St, New Canaan, CT, 06840. Tel: 203-594-5010. p. 324
Zajac, Ryan, Libr Dir, Roxbury Free Library, 1491 Roxbury Rd, Roxbury, VT, 05669. Tel: 802-485-6860. p. 2293
Zajkowski, Maureen, Prog Mgr, SUNYConnect, Office of Library & Information Services, SUNY Plaza, Albany, NY, 12246. Tel: 518-320-1477. p. 2771
Zakar, Kate, Asst Dir, Eureka Springs Carnegie Public Library, 194 Spring St, Eureka Springs, AR, 72632. Tel: 479-253-8754. p. 94
Zakharov, Wei S, Librn, Purdue University Libraries, Aviation Technology, Airport Terminal, Rm 163, 1501 Aviation Dr, West Lafayette, IN, 47907. Tel: 765-494-2872. p. 725
Zakharova, Yelizaveta, Spec Coll Librn, Frostburg State University, One Susan Eisel Dr, Frostburg, MD, 21532. Tel: 301-687-4889. p. 967
Zakhour, Diana, Asst Dir, Libr Serv, Pacifica Graduate Institute, 249 Lambert Rd, Carpinteria, CA, 93013. Tel: 805-969-3626, Ext 169. p. 128
Zaldivar, Nora, Archives Team Lead, Massachusetts Institute of Technology, 244 Wood St, Lexington, MA, 02420-9176. Tel: 781-981-3985. p. 1028
Zalduendo, Ines, Ref Librn, Spec Coll Archivist, Harvard Library, Frances Loeb Library, Harvard Graduate School of Design, 48 Quincy St, Gund Hall, Cambridge, MA, 02138. Tel: 617-495-9163. p. 1007
Zalecky, Richard A, Fiscal Officer, Wickliffe Public Library, 1713 Lincoln Rd, Wickliffe, OH, 44092. Tel: 440-944-6010. p. 1831
Zaleski, Toni, Dir, Edmeston Free Library, 26 East St, Edmeston, NY, 13335. Tel: 607-965-8208. p. 1529
Zaleta, Kathy, Circ, Hillside Public Library, 405 N Hillside Ave, Hillside, IL, 60162-1295. Tel: 708-449-7510. p. 599
Zalewski, Honor, Br Mgr, Henrico County Public Library, North Park Branch Library, 8508 Franconia Rd, Henrico, VA, 23227. Tel: 804-501-1970. p. 2326
Zalewski, JoLynn, Librn, Presque Isle District Library, Onaway Branch, 20774 State St, Onaway, MI, 49765. p. 1145
Zalewski, Laura, Dir, Topsfield Town Library, One S Common St, Topsfield, MA, 01983. Tel: 978-887-1528. p. 1060
Zalocki, Frank, Educ Supvr, New Jersey Department of Corrections, Eight Production Way, Avenel, NJ, 07001. Tel: 732-574-2250, Ext 8017. p. 1388
Zambito, Beth, Head, Adult Serv, Head, Ref Serv, Newburgh Free Library, 124 Grand St, Newburgh, NY, 12550. Tel: 845-563-3628. p. 1606
Zambrano, Diana, Br Mgr, Monmouth County Library, Ocean Township, 701 Deal Rd, Ocean, NJ, 07712. Tel: 732-531-5092. p. 1416
Zamietra, Kathleen, Healthcare Professions Librn, Instruction Coordr, DeSales University, 2755 Station Ave, Center Valley, PA, 18034. Tel: 610-282-1100, Ext 1346. p. 1920
Zammarelli, Mary, Librn, Roger Williams Medical Center, 825 Chalkstone Ave, Providence, RI, 02908. Tel: 401-456-2036. p. 2041
Zammarelli, Mary F, Dir, Libr Serv, Our Lady of Fatima Hospital, Marian Hall, First Flr, 200 High Service Ave, North Providence, RI, 02904. Tel: 401-456-2036. p. 2036
Zamon, Christina, Head, Spec Coll, University Archives, Georgia State University, 100 Decatur St SE, Atlanta, GA, 30303-3202. Tel: 404-413-2889. p. 464
Zamora, Ana, Asst Librn, Palacios Library, Inc, 326 Main St, Palacios, TX, 77465. Tel: 361-972-3234. p. 2224
Zamora, Cassandra, Dir, Santa Ana Pueblo Community Library, Two Dove Rd, Bernalillo, NM, 87004. Tel: 505-771-6736. p. 1464
Zamora, Julian, Mgr, County of Los Angeles Public Library, Florence Express Library, 7600 Graham Ave, Los Angeles, CA, 90001. Tel: 323-581-8028. p. 136
Zamora, Marie Leah, Ref, William Paterson University, 300 Pompton Rd, Wayne, NJ, 07470. Tel: 973-720-2663. p. 1452
Zampini, Louise, Chef de Div, Bibliotheques de Montreal, Pierrefonds, 13555 Blvd Pierrefonds, Pierrefonds, QC, H9A 1A6, CANADA. Tel: 514-258-5593. p. 2720

Zampini, Louise, Chef de Div, Bibliotheques de Montreal, William G Boll Library, 110 rue Cartier, Roxboro, QC, H8Y 1G8, CANADA. Tel: 514-626-0397. p. 2721

Zamudio, Dan, Access Serv Librn, Concordia University, 7400 Augusta St, River Forest, IL, 60305-1499. Tel: 708-209-3057. p. 639

Zamutt, Jeanne, Early Childhood Librn, Temple Emanu-El, 8500 Hillcrest Rd, Dallas, TX, 75225. Tel: 214-706-0000, Ext 185. p. 2168

Zana, Heather, Ad, Cameron Public Library, 304 E Third St, Cameron, TX, 76520. Tel: 254-697-2401. p. 2152

Zancanella, Jean-Louise, Asst Dir, Libr Serv, College of Western Idaho, Nampa Campus Multipurpose Bldg, 1st Flr, Rm 105/103, 6042 Birch Lane, Nampa, ID, 83687. Tel: 205-562-3118. p. 527

Zanders, Kenyotta, Br Mgr, Tangipahoa Parish Library, Loranger Branch, 19451 Hwy 40, Loranger, LA, 70446. Tel: 985-878-6224. p. 881

Zane, Katy, Head, Learning Resources, West Liberty University, 208 University Dr, West Liberty, WV, 26074. p. 2417

Zanger, Karen, Vols Librn, Rockdale Temple, 8501 Ridge Rd, Cincinnati, OH, 45236. Tel: 513-891-9900. p. 1763

Zani, Lisa, Circ Supvr, Westborough Public Library, 55 W Main St, Westborough, MA, 01581. Tel: 508-366-3050. p. 1066

Zanin-Yost, Alessia, Health Sci Librn, Slippery Rock University of Pennsylvania, 109 Campus Loop, Slippery Rock, PA, 16057. Tel: 724-738-2058. p. 2007

Zanish-Belcher, Tanya, Dir, Archives, Dir, Spec Coll, Wake Forest University, 1834 Wake Forest Rd, Winston-Salem, NC, 27109. Tel: 336-758-5755. p. 1726

Zanke, Anita, Libr Coord, Westmoreland County Historical Society, 809 Forbes Trail Rd, Greensburg, PA, 15601. Tel: 724-836-1800, Ext 100. p. 1938

Zannino, Cate, Ch, Reading Public Library, 64 Middlesex Ave, Reading, MA, 01867-2550. Tel: 781-944-0840. p. 1049

Zapata, Allan, Teen Coordr, Lawrence Public Library, 51 Lawrence St, Lawrence, MA, 01841. Tel: 978-620-3600. p. 1027

Zapor, Bobbie, Ms, Libr Supvr, Indiana University of Pennsylvania, Northpointe Regional Campus Library, Academic Bldg, 167 Northpointe Blvd, Freeport, PA, 16229. Tel: 724-294-3300. p. 1946

Zaporozhetz, Laurene E, Dir, United States Air Force, The D'Azzo Research Library, AFIT/ENWL, 2950 Hobson Way, Bldg 642, Wright-Patterson AFB, OH, 45433-7765. Tel: 937-255-6565, Ext 4216. p. 1834

Zappacosta, Joe, Dir, Hackley Public Library, 316 W Webster Ave, Muskegon, MI, 49440. Tel: 231-722-8003. p. 1135

Zappe, Christopher, Provost, Central Pennsylvania Consortium, c/o Franklin & Marshall College, Goethean Hall 101, Lancaster, PA, 17604. Tel: 717-358-4282. p. 2774

Zappitello, Joseph, Dir, Harbor-Topky Memorial Library, 1633 Walnut Blvd, Ashtabula, OH, 44004. Tel: 440-964-9645. p. 1748

Zappitello, Kathy, Exec Dir, Conneaut Public Library, 304 Buffalo St, Conneaut, OH, 44030-2658. Tel: 440-593-1608. p. 1778

Zarafonetis, Mike, Coordr, Digital Scholarship & Serv, Haverford College, 370 Lancaster Ave, Haverford, PA, 19041-1392. Tel: 610-896-4226. p. 1942

Zaragoza, Aide, Circ, California State University, Bakersfield, 9001 Stockdale Hwy, 60 LIB, Bakersfield, CA, 93311. Tel: 661-654-3234. p. 119

Zaragoza, Juan, Dir, Carlos Albizu University Library, 2173 NW 99 Ave, Miami, FL, 33172. Tel: 305-593-1223, Ext 3131. p. 421

Zarco, Brooke, Dir, Blair Public Library, 2233 Civic Dr, Blair, NE, 68008. Tel: 402-426-3617. p. 1308

Zareski, Sarah, Teen Serv Librn, Derby Neck Library Association, 307 Hawthorne Ave, Derby, CT, 06418. Tel: 203-734-1492. p. 308

Zarft, Kathy, Tech Serv, Tech, NorQuest College, 10215-108th St, 5th Flr, Edmonton, AB, T5J 1L6, CANADA. Tel: 708-644-6070. p. 2537

Zarin, Kate, Circ Asst, Co-Dir of Youth Services, Kent Library Association, 32 N Main St, Kent, CT, 06757. Tel: 860-927-3761. p. 319

Zarnowski, Shana, ILL Librn, Pease Public Library, One Russell St, Plymouth, NH, 03264-1414. Tel: 603-536-2616. p. 1378

Zaros, Christa, Colls Mgr, Long Island Museum of American Art, History & Carriages, Gerstenburg Carriage Reference Library, 1200 Rte 25A, Stony Brook, NY, 11790-1992. Tel: 631-751-0066, Ext 232. p. 1646

Zaros, Christa, Colls Mgr, Long Island Museum of American Art, History & Carriages, Kate Strong Historical Library, 1200 Rte 25A, Stony Brook, NY, 11790. Tel: 631-751-0066. p. 1646

Zarotsky, Tanya, Circ, University of Southern California Libraries, Von KleinSmid Center Library, Von KleinSmid Ctr, 3518 Trousdale Pkwy, Los Angeles, CA, 90089-0182. Tel: 213-740-8227. p. 170

Zarr, Jennifer, Libr Mgr, New York Public Library - Astor, Lenox & Tilden Foundations, St Agnes Branch, 444 Amsterdam Ave, (@ 81st St), New York, NY, 10024-5506. Tel: 212-621-0619. p. 1597

Zarriello, Cyndi, Library Asst, Children's, Grafton Public Library, 35 Grafton Common, Grafton, MA, 01519. Tel: 508-839-4649. p. 1021

Zarrillo, John, Archivist/Ref Librn, Georgetown University, Bioethics Research Library, Kennedy Institute of Ethics, 37th & O St NW, Washington, DC, 20057. Tel: 202-687-3885. p. 368

Zaskey, Melanie Lorraine, Dir, Res Sharing, Southeast Florida Library Information Network, Inc, Florida Atlantic University, Wimberly Library, Office 452, 777 Glades Rd, Boca Raton, FL, 33431. Tel: 561-208-0984. p. 2763

Zaslow, Barry, Music Librn, Miami University Libraries, Amos Music Library, Center for the Performing Arts, Oxford, OH, 45056. Tel: 513-529-2299. p. 1812

Zaspel, Jennifer, Dr, Dean, Acad Support, VPres, Milwaukee Public Museum, 800 W Wells St, Milwaukee, WI, 53233. Tel: 414-278-2728. p. 2460

Zataweski, Jacqueline, Dir, Nottoway County Public Libraries, 414 Tyler St, Crewe, VA, 23930. Tel: 434-645-8688. p. 2314

Zavala Garcia, Laura, Dir, Corpus Christi Public Libraries, 805 Comanche, Corpus Christi, TX, 78401. Tel: 361-826-7055. p. 2160

Zavalina, Oksana, Dr, Assoc Prof, University of North Texas, 3940 N Elm St, Ste E292, Denton, TX, 76207. Tel: 940-565-2445. p. 2793

Zavarella, Suzy, Head, Teen Serv, Ossining Public Library, 53 Croton Ave, Ossining, NY, 10562. Tel: 914-941-2416. p. 1613

Zavinski, Tamara, Sr Librn, Support Serv, Oxnard Public Library, 251 South A St, Oxnard, CA, 93030. Tel: 805-385-7519. p. 190

Zavinski, Tammy, Br Mgr, Portsmouth Public Library, Cradock, 28 Prospect Pkwy, Portsmouth, VA, 23702. Tel: 757-393-8759. p. 2338

Zawadzki, Shelley, Br Mgr, Chicago Public Library, Canaryville, 642 W 43rd St, Chicago, IL, 60609. Tel: 312-747-0644. p. 556

Zawodny, Kt, Ms, Br Mgr, Arundel Anne County Public Library, Brooklyn Park Library, One E 11th Ave, Baltimore, MD, 21225. Tel: 410-222-6260. p. 950

Zazelenchuk, Mary, Dir, High River Library, 909 First St SW, High River, AB, T1V 1A5, CANADA. Tel: 403-652-2917. p. 2543

Zbaraschuk, Tony, Pub Serv Librn, Southwestern Adventist University, 101 W Magnolia St, Keene, TX, 76059. Tel: 817-202-6480. p. 2204

Zbyl, Antoinette, Dir, Charleroi Area Public Library, 638 Fallowfield Ave, Charleroi, PA, 15022-1996. Tel: 724-483-8282. p. 1921

Zdinak, Zachariah, ILL Librn, Per Librn, Franciscan University of Steubenville, 1235 University Blvd, Steubenville, OH, 43952-1763. Tel: 740-283-6366. p. 1821

Zdravecky, Leanne, Coordr, Monroe County Public Library, 303 E Kirkwood Ave, Bloomington, IN, 47408. Tel: 812-349-3050. p. 671

Zdravecky, Leanne, Dir, Operations, Cambria County Library System & District Center, 248 Main St, Johnstown, PA, 15901. Tel: 814-536-5131. p. 1947

Zdravkovska, Nevenka, Head of Libr, University of Maryland Libraries, STEM Library, William E Kirwan Hall, Rm 1403, 4176 Campus Dr, College Park, MD, 20742. Tel: 301-405-9144. p. 963

Zdunkewicz, Catherine, Coordr, Texas Children's Hospital, West Tower 16th Flr, Rm 16265, 6621 Fannin St, Houston, TX, 77030. Tel: 832-826-1619. p. 2198

Zebrowski, Judith, Librn, Info Literacy Initiatives, Pennsylvania College of Technology, 999 Hagan Way, Williamsport, PA, 17701. Tel: 570-327-4523. p. 2023

Zebrowski, Kate, Libr Asst, Ingalls Memorial Library, 203 Main St, Rindge, NH, 03461. Tel: 603-899-3303. p. 1379

Zebula, Natalie, Ref & ILL Librn, Lawrence Technological University Library, 21000 W Ten Mile Rd, Southfield, MI, 48075-1058. Tel: 248-204-3000. p. 1151

Zeeb, Katie, Digital Serv, California Baptist University, 8432 Magnolia Ave, Riverside, CA, 92504. Tel: 951-343-4365. p. 201

Zeff, Oliver, Assoc Librn, Westfield State University, 577 Western Ave, Westfield, MA, 01085-2580. p. 1067

Zegel, Susan, Mgr, National Economic Research Associates, Inc, 360 Hamilton Ave, 10th Flr, White Plains, NY, 10601. Tel: 212-345-2272. p. 1664

Zegers, Judy, Dir, Sully Community Library, 318 Sixth Ave, Sully, IA, 50251. Tel: 641-594-4148. p. 785

Zeggane, Madjid, Data Res Assoc, Washington University Libraries, Kopolow Business Library, One Brookings Dr, Campus Box 1061, Saint Louis, MO, 63130. Tel: 314-935-6963. p. 1277

Zeh, Jessie, Dir, Cohocton Public Library, Eight Maple Ave, Cohocton, NY, 14826. Tel: 585-384-5170. p. 1520

Zeh, Justin, Dir, Avoca Free Library, 18 N Main St, Avoca, NY, 14809. Tel: 607-566-9279. p. 1489

Zeh, Justin, Dir, Prattsburg Free Library, 26 Main St, Prattsburgh, NY, 14873. Tel: 607-522-3490. p. 1624

Zeibak, Karen, Circ Serv Mgr, Wilton Library Association, 137 Old Ridgefield Rd, Wilton, CT, 06897-3000. Tel: 203-762-3950. p. 348

Zeidman-Karpinski, Ann, Librn, University of Oregon Libraries, Allan Price Science Commons & Research Library, Onyx Bridge, Lower Level, 1344 Franklin Blvd, Eugene, OR, 97403. Tel: 541-346-2663. p. 1879

Zeidman-Karpinski, Ann, Ref Librn, Sci Librn, University of Oregon Libraries, Mathematics, 218 Fenton Hall, Eugene, OR, 97403. Tel: 541-346-2663. p. 1879

Zeile, Carol A, Dir, Alma College Library, 614 W Superior St, Alma, MI, 48801. Tel: 989-463-7342. p. 1077

Zeiler, Patricia, Exec Dir, Fort Lauderdale Historical Society, 219 SW Second Ave, Fort Lauderdale, FL, 33301. Tel: 954-463-4431. p. 401

Zeinoun, Delaina, Syst & Electronic Res, Charleston Southern University, 9200 University Blvd, Charleston, SC, 29406. Tel: 843-863-7951. p. 2050

Zeitler, Courtnay, Head, Circ, University of the South, 178 Georgia Ave, Sewanee, TN, 37383-1000. Tel: 931-598-1837. p. 2126

Zelasko, Shannon, Lead Librn, Learning Res Spec, Kaskaskia College Library, 27210 College Rd, Centralia, IL, 62801. Tel: 618-545-3130. p. 551
Zelazny, Ilan, Head, Syst, Hunter College Libraries, East Bldg, 695 Park Ave, New York, NY, 10065. Tel: 212-772-4171. p. 1588
Zelazo, Cheryl, Ad, Joshua Hyde Public Library, 306 Main St, Sturbridge, MA, 01566-1242. Tel: 508-347-2512. p. 1058
Zeldman, Jessica, Info Serv, Wellington County Library, 190 Saint Andrews St W, Fergus, ON, N1M 1N5, CANADA. Tel: 519-787-7805. p. 2641
Zelenka, Betty, Librn, Milligan Public Library, 507 Main St, Milligan, NE, 68406. Tel: 402-629-4302. p. 1325
Zelinski-Gafford, Anna, Lead Librn, United States Navy Library for Innovation & Technology (LIT), 22269 Cedar Point Rd B407, Patuxent River, MD, 20670-1120. Tel: 301-342-1927. p. 972
Zell, Annmarie, Head, Res & Ref Serv, Interim Deputy Director, New York University School of Law, Vanderbilt Hall, 40 Washington Sq S, New York, NY, 10012-1099. Tel: 212-992-8863. p. 1599
Zeller, Josh, Head, Access Serv, Mount Saint Joseph University, 5701 Delhi Rd, Cincinnati, OH, 45233-1671. Tel: 513-244-4882. p. 1761
Zelner, Tisha, Head, Pub Serv, University of Southern Mississippi Library, 124 Golden Eagle Dr, Hattiesburg, MS, 39406. Tel: 601-266-6167. p. 1218
Zelten, Julie, Dir, Land O'Lakes Public Library, 4242 County Hwy B, Land O'Lakes, WI, 54540. Tel: 715-547-6006. p. 2448
Zelwietro, Joe, Chief Librn, Prince Rupert Library, 101 Sixth Ave W, Prince Rupert, BC, V8J 1Y9, CANADA. Tel: 250-627-1345. p. 2574
Zeman, Anne, Dir, Hopewell Public Library, 13 E Broad St, Hopewell, NJ, 08525. Tel: 609-466-1625. p. 1409
Zeman, Barbara, Dir, Paw Paw Public Library District, 362 Chicago Rd, Paw Paw, IL, 61353. Tel: 815-627-9396. p. 633
Zeman, Emily, Colls Mgr, St Joseph Museums Inc, 3406 Frederick Ave, Saint Joseph, MO, 64506. Tel: 816-232-8471. p. 1269
Zemke, Brianna, Librn, Deer Park Public Library, 112 Front St W, Deer Park, WI, 54007. Tel: 715-269-5464. p. 2430
Zemke, Karen, Librn, Deer Park Public Library, 112 Front St W, Deer Park, WI, 54007. Tel: 715-269-5464. p. 2430
Zemke, Marika, Adult Serv Mgr, Commerce Township Community Library, 180 E Commerce, Commerce Township, MI, 48382. Tel: 248-669-8101, Ext 108. p. 1093
Zemrock, Joy, Ref Librn, Loudonville Public Library, 122 E Main St, Loudonville, OH, 44842. Tel: 419-994-5531. p. 1797
Zender, Roger, Assoc Univ Librn, Curator, Case Western Reserve University, 11055 Euclid Ave, Cleveland, OH, 44106. Tel: 216-368-5637. p. 1766
Zenelis, John G, Dean, Libr & Univ Librn, George Mason University Libraries, 4348 Chesapeake River Way, Fairfax, VA, 22030. Tel: 703-993-2240. p. 2317
Zeng, Hao, Head, Digital & Web Serv, Yeshiva University Libraries, 2520 Amsterdam Ave, New York, NY, 10033. Tel: 646-592-4107. p. 1604
Zeng, Marcia, Dr, Prof, Kent State University, 314 University Library, 1125 Risman Dr, Kent, OH, 44242-0001. Tel: 330-672-2782. p. 2790
Zeng, Yang, Dir, Queens Library, Flushing Library, 41-17 Main St, Flushing, NY, 11355. Tel: 718-661-1200. p. 1554
Zengler, Keith, Asst Libr Dir, Butt-Holdsworth Memorial Library, 505 Water St, Kerrville, TX, 78028. Tel: 830-257-8422. p. 2205
Zenor, Michelle, Dir, Henderson County, 121 S Prairieville, Athens, TX, 75751. Tel: 903-677-7295. p. 2137
Zent, Alice, Br Mgr, Loudoun County Public Library, Law Library, 18 E Market St, Leesburg, VA, 20176. Tel: 703-777-0695. p. 2328
Zentner, Krystal, Libr Dir, Bridger Public Library, 119 W Broadway Ave, Bridger, MT, 59014. Tel: 406-662-3598. p. 1289
Zeoli, Julie, Adult Serv Mgr, Asst Libr Dir, Yorba Linda Public Library, 4852 Lakeview Ave, Yorba Linda, CA, 92886. Tel: 714-777-2873. p. 261
Zepeda Aguilar, Maria, Circ Mgr, Peach Public Libraries, 315 Martin Luther King Jr Dr, Fort Valley, GA, 31030. Tel: 478-825-1640. p. 480
Zepeda, Ofelia, Col Librn, Tohono O'odham Community College Library, Hwy 86 Milepost 111 W, Sells, AZ, 85634. Tel: 520-383-0032. p. 78
Zepeda, Sarah, Research Librn, Colorado Department of Transportation Library, Shumate Bldg, 4201 E Arkansas Ave, Denver, CO, 80222. Tel: 303-757-9972. p. 274
Zero, Marie, Tech Serv, Lake Wales Public Library, 290 Cypress Garden Lane, Lake Wales, FL, 33853. Tel: 863-678-4004. p. 416
Zerr, Diane, Teaching & Learning Librn, Saskatchewan Polytechnic, 4500 Wascana Pkwy, Regina, SK, S4P 3A3, CANADA. Tel: 306-775-7413. p. 2748
Zerrenner, Emily, Res & Instruction Librn, Salisbury University, 1101 Camden Ave, Salisbury, MD, 21801-6863. Tel: 410-543-6130. p. 976
Zervas, Emily, Libr Dir, Putney Public Library, 55 Main St, Putney, VT, 05346. Tel: 802-387-4407. p. 2292
Zeter, Mary Jo, Coordr, Area Studies, Librn, Michigan State University Libraries, Area Studies, Main Library, 366 W Circle Dr, East Lansing, MI, 48824. Tel: 517-884-6392. p. 1102
Zetterberg, Wynn, Programming Dir, Sheridan Public Library, 103 W First St, Sheridan, IN, 46069. Tel: 317-758-5201. p. 718
Zettwoch, Mary, ILL Supvr, University of Missouri-Saint Louis Libraries, Thomas Jefferson Library, One University Blvd, Saint Louis, MO, 63121-4400. Tel: 314-516-5060. p. 1276
Zetty, Janelle, Head, Cat, University of Louisiana at Lafayette, 400 E St Mary Blvd, Lafayette, LA, 70503. Tel: 337-482-6033. p. 893
Zevenbergen, Amy, Dir, Doon Public Library, 207 Barton Ave, Doon, IA, 51235. Tel: 712-726-3526. p. 748
Zeysing, Matt, Curator, Naismith Memorial Basketball Hall of Fame, 1000 Hall of Fame Ave, Springfield, MA, 01105. Tel: 413-781-6500. p. 1056
Zgiet-Ellis, Julie, Dir, Mercy Hospital, Tower B, Ste 1000, 621 S New Ballas Rd, Saint Louis, MO, 63141. Tel: 314-251-6340. p. 1271
Zgraggen, Cathy, Supvr, Deschutes Public Library District, La Pine Branch, 16425 First St, La Pine, OR, 97739. Tel: 541-312-1094. p. 1874
Zhang, Alex, Dir, Duke University Libraries, J Michael Goodson Law Library, 210 Science Dr, Durham, NC, 27708. Tel: 919-613-7115. p. 1684
Zhang, Junfang, Head, Syst Develop, Old Dominion University Libraries, 4427 Hampton Blvd, Norfolk, VA, 23529-0256. Tel: 757-683-5952. p. 2336
Zhang, Li, Head, Legal Data Lab, University of Virginia, Arthur J Morris Law Library, 580 Massie Rd, Charlottesville, VA, 22903-1738. Tel: 434-924-4730. p. 2310
Zhang, Mei, Asst Prof, Simmons University, 300 The Fenway, Boston, MA, 02115. Tel: 617-521-2800. p. 2786
Zhang, Peter, Assoc Univ Librn, University of Texas at Arlington Library, 702 Planetarium Pl, Arlington, TX, 76019. Tel: 817-272-1006. p. 2136
Zhang, Qiping, Dr, Assoc Prof, Long Island University, C W Post Campus, 720 Northern Blvd, Brookville, NY, 11548-1300. Tel: 516-299-2866, 516-299-2900. p. 2788
Zhang, Rongxiang, Evening/Weekend Supvr, Columbia University, C V Starr East Asian Library, 300 Kent Hall, MC 3901, 1140 Amsterdam Ave, New York, NY, 10027. Tel: 212-854-4318. p. 1584
Zhang, Shali, Dean of Libr, Auburn University, Ralph Brown Draughon Library, 231 Mell St, Auburn, AL, 36849. Tel: 334-844-1714. p. 5
Zhang, Tian, Head, Serials Management, St John's University Library, St Augustine Hall, 8000 Utopia Pkwy, Jamaica, NY, 11439. Tel: 718-990-5082. p. 1556
Zhang, Wen Wen, Mgr, County of Los Angeles Public Library, West Covina Library, 1601 W Covina Pkwy, West Covina, CA, 91790-2786. Tel: 626-962-3541. p. 138
Zhang, Wendy, Libr Asst, Columbia University, Mathematics, 303 Mathematics, 2990 Broadway, MC 4702, New York, NY, 10027. Tel: 212-854-4713. p. 1583
Zhang, Wenxian, Head, Archives & Spec Coll, Rollins College, 1000 Holt Ave, Campus Box 2744, Winter Park, FL, 32789-2744. Tel: 407-646-2231. p. 455
Zhang, Xiangmin E, Dr, Asst Prof, Wayne State University, 106 Kresge Library, Detroit, MI, 48202. Tel: 313-577-1825. p. 2787
Zhang, Xiwen, Ref Librn, California State University, San Bernardino, 5500 University Pkwy, San Bernardino, CA, 92407-2318. Tel: 909-537-5106. p. 212
Zhang, Yang, Asst Teaching Prof, University of Illinois at Urbana-Champaign, Library & Information Science Bldg, 501 E Daniel St, Champaign, IL, 61820-6211. Tel: 217-333-3280. p. 2784
Zhang, Yin, Dr, Prof, Kent State University, 314 University Library, 1125 Risman Dr, Kent, OH, 44242-0001. Tel: 330-672-2782. p. 2790
Zhang, Ying, Head, Acq & Coll Serv, University of Central Florida Libraries, 12701 Pegasus Dr, Orlando, FL, 32816-8030. Tel: 407-883-4253. p. 432
Zhang, Yingting, Info & Educ Librn, Rutgers University Libraries, Robert Wood Johnson Library of the Health Sciences, One Robert Wood Johnson Pl, New Brunswick, NJ, 08903. p. 1425
Zhang, Zhijiang, Acq & Cat, Manchester Community College Library, Great Path, Manchester, CT, 06040. Tel: 860-512-2875. p. 320
Zhao, Dangzhi, PhD, Prof, University of Alberta, 7-104 Education N, University of Alberta, Edmonton, AB, T6G 2G5, CANADA. Tel: 780-492-7625. p. 2795
Zhao, Rachel, Librn, Alberta Children's Hospital Knowledge Centre, 28 Oki Dr NW, A2-908, 2nd Flr, Calgary, AB, T3B 6A8, CANADA. Tel: 403-955-7077. p. 2525
Zhao, Shuzhen, Bibliog Serv, Head, Acq, University of Windsor, 401 Sunset Ave, Windsor, ON, N9B 3P4, CANADA. Tel: 519-253-3000, Ext 3162. p. 2704
Zhao, Taian, Head, Tech Serv, Borough of Manhattan Community College Library, 199 Chambers St, S410, New York, NY, 10007. Tel: 212-220-1452. p. 1580
Zhe-Heimerman, Kari, Instrul Serv, Sci Librn, Le Moyne College, 1419 Salt Springs Rd, Syracuse, NY, 13214. Tel: 315-445-4627. p. 1648
Zhilina, Jenya, Archivist, Rec Mgr, Sasaki Associates, Inc Library, 64 Pleasant St, Watertown, MA, 02472. Tel: 617-923-5336. p. 1063
Zhong, Jessie, Head, Acq, Head, Electronic Res, Head, Metadata Serv, Dallas Theological Seminary, 3909 Swiss Ave, Dallas, TX, 75204. Tel: 214-887-5289. p. 2166
Zhong, Ying, Web Serv Librn, California State University, Bakersfield, 9001 Stockdale Hwy, 60 LIB, Bakersfield, CA, 93311. Tel: 661-654-3119. p. 119

Zhorne, Mona, Adult Serv, Pocahontas Public Library, 14 Second Ave NW, Pocahontas, IA, 50574. Tel: 712-335-4471. p. 777

Zhou, Jian-zhong, Head, Res & Instruction, California State University, Sacramento, 6000 J St, Sacramento, CA, 95819-6039. Tel: 916-278-6708. p. 208

Zhou, June, Br Mgr, San Diego County Library, 4S Ranch Branch, 10433 Reserve Dr, San Diego, CA, 92127. Tel: 858-673-4697. p. 216

Zhou, Yuqing, Ref/Syst Librn, Central New Mexico Community College Libraries, 525 Buena Vista SE, Albuquerque, NM, 87106-4023. Tel: 505-224-4000, Ext 52540. p. 1460

Zhou, Yvonne, Managing Librn, Brooklyn Public Library, Bay Ridge, 7223 Ridge Blvd, Brooklyn, NY, 11209. Tel: 718-748-5709. p. 1502

Zhou, Zehao, Pub Serv, York College of Pennsylvania, 441 Country Club Rd, York, PA, 17403-3651. Tel: 717-815-1518. p. 2026

Zhu, Julie, Syst Librn, Bryant & Stratton College Library, 1259 Central Ave, Albany, NY, 12205. Tel: 518-437-1802. p. 1482

Zhu, Yin, Tech & Acq Librn, Board of Governors of The Federal Reserve System, Research Library, 20th & C St NW, MS 102, Washington, DC, 20551. Tel: 202-452-3333. p. 361

Ziadie, Ann Marie, Sr Asst Librn, Saint Peter's University, Hudson Terrace, Englewood Cliffs, NJ, 07632. Tel: 201-761-6459. p. 1402

Ziarko, Lauren, Univ Archivist, Manhattanville University Library, 2900 Purchase St, Purchase, NY, 10577. Tel: 914-323-5422. p. 1624

Ziarnik, Natalie, Dep Dir, Ela Area Public Library District, 275 Mohawk Trail, Lake Zurich, IL, 60047. Tel: 847-438-3433. p. 607

Ziarnik, Natalie, Head, Youth Serv, Ela Area Public Library District, 275 Mohawk Trail, Lake Zurich, IL, 60047. Tel: 847-438-3433. p. 607

Zick, Medina, Br Mgr, Scottsdale Public Library, Mustang Library, 10101 N 90th St, Scottsdale, AZ, 85258-4404. Tel: 480-312-6031. p. 77

Ziegler, Amanda, Libr Dir, Wauneta Public Library, 319 N Tecumseh Ave, Wauneta, NE, 69045. Tel: 308-394-5243. p. 1340

Ziegler, Annette, Head, Support Serv, Medicine Hat Public Library, 414 First St SE, Medicine Hat, AB, T1A 0A8, CANADA. Tel: 403-502-8539. p. 2548

Ziegler, Cheryl, Dir, Libr & Archives, Union League Club of Chicago Library, 65 W Jackson Blvd, Chicago, IL, 60604. Tel: 312-435-4818. p. 569

Ziegler, Roy, Univ Librn for External Relations, Florida State University Libraries, Strozier Library Bldg, 116 Honors Way, Tallahassee, FL, 32306. Tel: 850-644-2706. p. 446

Ziegman-Nye, Diana, Fiscal Officer, Kaubisch Memorial Public Library, 205 Perry St, Fostoria, OH, 44830-2265. Tel: 419-435-2813. p. 1786

Zielinski, Karen, Head, Children's Servx, Scarsdale Public Library, 54 Olmsted Rd, Scarsdale, NY, 10583. Tel: 914-722-1300. p. 1637

Zielinski, Marijo, Libr Asst, Saint Francis Seminary, 3257 S Lake Dr, Saint Francis, WI, 53235-0905. Tel: 414-747-6479. p. 2475

Zielke, David, Head, Tech Serv, Librn, Dixie State University Library, 225 S 700 E, Saint George, UT, 84770. Tel: 435-652-7716. p. 2270

Ziemak, Izzy, Adult Serv Supvr, Burton Public Library, 14588 W Park St, Burton, OH, 44021. Tel: 440-834-4466. p. 1753

Ziemer, Heidi, Circ, Albright College, 13th & Exeter Sts, Reading, PA, 19604. Tel: 610-921-7207. p. 2000

Zienta, Cyndi, Law Librn, Sandusky County Law Library, 100 N Park Ave, No 106, Fremont, OH, 43420. Tel: 419-334-6165. p. 1787

Zierke, Lisa, Tech Serv, Prescott Public Library, 215 E Goodwin St, Prescott, AZ, 86303. Tel: 928-777-1507. p. 73

Ziese, Carol, Head, Tech Serv, Decatur Public Library, 130 N Franklin St, Decatur, IL, 62523. Tel: 217-421-9739. p. 576

Zigadto, Janet, Law Librn II, Connecticut Judicial Branch Law Libraries, Waterbury Law Library, Waterbury Courthouse, 300 Grand St, Waterbury, CT, 06702. Tel: 203-591-3338. p. 316

Zigas, Mari, Head, Children's Servx, Johnson Free Public Library, 274 Main St, Hackensack, NJ, 07601-5797. Tel: 201-343-4169. p. 1406

Zigelbaum, Liza, Dir, Med Libr, Kingsbrook Jewish Medical Center, 585 Schenectady Ave, Brooklyn, NY, 11203. Tel: 718-504-5689. p. 1504

Zigrang, Todd, Pres, Health Capital Consultants, LLC Library, 2127 Innerbelt Business Center Dr, Ste 107, Saint Louis, MO, 63114-5700. Tel: 314-994-7641. p. 1271

Ziliotto, Diane, Assoc Libr Dir, Spec Coll Librn, Westmont College, 955 La Paz Rd, Santa Barbara, CA, 93108. Tel: 805-565-6147. p. 241

Zilka, Dave, Dir, Monessen Public Library, 326 Donner Ave, Monessen, PA, 15062. Tel: 724-684-4750. p. 1964

Zilli, Michelle, Libr Mgr, Timberland Regional Library, Naselle Branch, Four Parpala Rd, Naselle, WA, 98638. Tel: 360-484-3877. p. 2389

Zillner, Amy, Br Mgr, San Bernardino County Library, Barstow Branch, 304 E Buena Vista St, Barstow, CA, 92311-2806. Tel: 760-256-4850. p. 212

Zima, Hannah Good, Libr Office Mgr, Nicolet Federated Library System, 1595 Allouez Ave, Ste 4, Green Bay, WI, 54311. Tel: 920-448-4410. p. 2438

Zimba, Karen, Dir, Milford Free Library, 64 S Main St, Milford, NY, 13807. Tel: 607-286-9076. p. 1572

Zimble, Stephanie, Archivist/Ref Librn, Oakmont Carnegie Library, 700 Allegheny River Blvd, Oakmont, PA, 15139. Tel: 412-828-9532. p. 1972

Zimdars, Liz, Head, Adult Serv, Middleton Public Library, 7425 Hubbard Ave, Middleton, WI, 53562-3117. Tel: 608-827-7423. p. 2457

Zimerman, Martin, Electronic Serv Librn, Long Island University, One University Plaza, Brooklyn, NY, 11201. Tel: 718-780-4513. p. 1505

Zimkus, John J, Educ Dir, Historian, Warren County Historical Society, 105 S Broadway, Lebanon, OH, 45036. Tel: 513-932-1817. p. 1795

Zimmer, Jennifer Lammers, Digital Serv, University of Michigan, Kresge Library Services, Stephen M Ross School of Business, 701 Tappan St, Ann Arbor, MI, 48109-1234. Tel: 734-764-6845. p. 1079

Zimmer, Kimberly, Dir, Community Library, 110 Union St, Cobleskill, NY, 12043-3830. Tel: 518-234-7897. p. 1520

Zimmer, Scott, Univ Librn, Alliant International University, 1000 S Fremont Ave, Unit 5, Alhambra, CA, 91803. Tel: 626-270-3270. p. 115

Zimmer, Scott, Libr Dir, Alliant International University, 5130 E Clinton Way, Fresno, CA, 93727. Tel: 559-253-2265. p. 144

Zimmer, Scott, Dir, Libr Serv, Univ Librn, Alliant International University, 10455 Pomerado Rd, San Diego, CA, 92131-1799. Tel: 858-635-4553. p. 214

Zimmer, Scott, Dir, Libr Serv, Alliant International University, San Francisco Law School, One Beach St, Ste 100, San Francisco, CA, 94133-2221. Tel: 858-635-4553. p. 223

Zimmerli, Adam, Br Mgr, Richmond Public Library, East End, 1200 N 25th St, Richmond, VA, 23223. Tel: 804-646-4474. p. 2341

Zimmerman, Bill, Libr Team Lead, Bonneville Power Administration Library & Visitor Center, 905 NE 11th Ave, Portland, OR, 97232. p. 1890

Zimmerman, Cory, Asst Dir, Chatsworth Township Library, 501 E School St, Chatsworth, IL, 60921. Tel: 815-635-3004. p. 553

Zimmerman, D Edward, Asst Dean of Libr, Syst & Tech, Indiana University of Pennsylvania, 431 S 11th St, Rm 203, Indiana, PA, 15705-1096. Tel: 724-357-2330. p. 1946

Zimmerman, Ed, Libr Dir, DeSales University, 2755 Station Ave, Center Valley, PA, 18034. Tel: 610-282-1100, Ext 1253. p. 1919

Zimmerman, Erin, Tech Asst, Tech Serv, Heartland Community College Library, 1500 W Raab Rd, Normal, IL, 61761. Tel: 309-268-8273. p. 625

Zimmerman, Jessi, Br Librn, Waseca-Le Sueur Regional Library, Le Sueur Public, 118 E Ferry St, Le Sueur, MN, 56058. Tel: 507-665-2662. p. 1207

Zimmerman, Kathryn, Patron Experience Supvr, Hennepin County Library, Brooklyn Park, 8500 W Broadway Ave, Brooklyn Park, MN, 55445. Tel: 612-543-6228. p. 1186

Zimmerman, Kristie, Asst Librn, Freeport Area Library, 428 Market St, Freeport, PA, 16229-1122. Tel: 724-295-3616. p. 1934

Zimmerman, Lewis, Head, Access Serv, University of Denver, Westminster Law Library, Sturm College of Law, 2255 E Evans Ave, Denver, CO, 80208. Tel: 303-871-6364. p. 278

Zimmerman, Martha, Assoc Dean, Dir, Coll Mgt, Salisbury University, 1101 Camden Ave, Salisbury, MD, 21801-6863. Tel: 410-543-6130. p. 976

Zimmerman, Rochelle, Ref (Info Servs), Northwood University, 4000 Whiting Dr, Midland, MI, 48640-2398. Tel: 989-837-4275. p. 1132

Zimmerman, Stephanie, Human Res Coordr, Training & Develop Coordr, Library System of Lancaster County, 1866 Colonial Village Lane, Ste 107, Lancaster, PA, 17601. Tel: 717-207-0500. p. 1952

Zimmermann, Angela, Dir, Mukwonago Community Library, 511 Division St, Mukwonago, WI, 53149-1204. Tel: 262-363-6411, Ext 4100. p. 2463

Zimmermann, Michelle, Ch, North Mankato Taylor Library, 1001 Belgrade Ave, North Mankato, MN, 56003. Tel: 507-345-5120. p. 1190

Zimpelmann, Meagan, Libr Tech, Kenai Peninsula College Library, 156 College Rd, Soldotna, AK, 99669. Tel: 907-262-0384. p. 51

Zingarelli-Sweet, Desirae, Ref Librn, Colgate Rochester Crozer Divinity School, 1100 S Goodman St, Rochester, NY, 14620-2592. Tel: 585-340-9602. p. 1628

Zinger, Emily, Southeast Asia Digital Librarian, Cornell University Library, Division of Asia Collections (Carl A Kroch Library), Kroch Library, Level 1, Ithaca, NY, 14853. Tel: 607-255-8199. p. 1551

Zink, Chris, Asst Dir, Onawa Public Library, 707 Iowa Ave, Onawa, IA, 51040. Tel: 712-423-1733. p. 774

Zink, Paul, Head, IT, Bloomfield Township Public Library, 1099 Lone Pine Rd, Bloomfield Township, MI, 48302-2410. Tel: 248-642-5800. p. 1086

Zinkie, Lisa, Mgr, Dallas Public Library, Hampton-Illinois, 2951 S Hampton Rd, Dallas, TX, 75224. Tel: 214-670-7646. p. 2165

Zinn, Donna Heller, Librn, The Perry Historians, 763 Dix Hill Rd, New Bloomfield, PA, 17068. Tel: 717-582-4896. p. 1968

Zinnerman-Bethea, Darlene, Dir, Benedict College Library, 1600 Harden St, Columbia, SC, 29204. Tel: 803-705-4773. p. 2053

Zinnkosko, Suzanne, Dir, Gallison Memorial Library, 11 Center St, Harrington, ME, 04643. Tel: 207-483-4547. p. 927

Zino, Eric, Libr Dir, Haddonfield Public Library, 60 Haddon Ave, Haddonfield, NJ, 08033-2422. Tel: 856-429-1304. p. 1406

Zins, Tina, Exec Dir, Penn Hills Library, 1037 Stotler Rd, Pittsburgh, PA, 15235-2099. Tel: 412-795-3507. p. 1995

Zinser Bednarski, Diane, Exec Dir, Inland Library System, 254 N Lake Ave, No 874, Pasadena, CA, 91101. Tel: 626-283-5949. p. 193

Zinsou, Natasha, Interim Head, Acq, University of Texas at Dallas, 800 W Campbell Rd, Richardson, TX, 75080. Tel: 972-883-2630. p. 2231
Zinz, C, Archivist, Research Librn, Barkerville Historic Town Library & Archives, 14301 Hwy 26 E, Barkerville, BC, V0K 1B0, CANADA. Tel: 888-994-3332, Ext 26. p. 2563
Ziolkowska, Sarah, Librn, Halifax Public Libraries, Halifax North Memorial, 2285 Gottingen St, Halifax, NS, B3K 3B6, CANADA. Tel: 902-490-5723. p. 2617
Zion, Rebecca, Librn, North Central Washington Libraries, Brewster Public Library, 108 S Third St, Brewster, WA, 98812. Tel: 509-689-4046. p. 2393
Ziph, Sally, Instrul Serv Librn, University of Michigan, Kresge Library Services, Stephen M Ross School of Business, 701 Tappan St, Ann Arbor, MI, 48109-1234. Tel: 734-764-5532. p. 1079
Zippay, Vickie, Ch Serv, Williams County Public Library, 107 E High St, Bryan, OH, 43506-1702. Tel: 419-636-6734. p. 1753
Zirkle, Robin, Adminr, Centre County Library & Historical Museum, 200 N Allegheny St, Bellefonte, PA, 16823-1601. Tel: 814-355-1516. p. 1910
Zishka, Wendy, Ch Serv, Speedway Public Library, 5633 W 25th St, Speedway, IN, 46224-3899. Tel: 317-243-8959. p. 719
Zittlow, Todd, Archivist, Concordia Historical Institute, 804 Seminary Pl, Saint Louis, MO, 63105-3014. Tel: 314-505-7900. p. 1270
Zittrain, Jonathan, Vice Dean, Libr & Info Res, Harvard Library, Harvard Law School Library, Langdell Hall, 1545 Massachusetts Ave, Cambridge, MA, 02138. Tel: 617-495-3416, 617-495-3455. p. 1006
Zitzman, Rachel, Instruction Librn, Midlands Technical College Library, Beltline Library, 316 S Beltline Blvd, 2nd Flr, Columbia, SC, 29205. Tel: 803-738-7847. p. 2072
Zline, Samantha, Br Mgr, Arundel Anne County Public Library, Severna Park Library, 45 McKinsey Rd, Severna Park, MD, 21146. Tel: 410-222-6290. p. 950
Znamirowski, Barbara, Head, Maps, Data & Govt Info Ctr, Trent University, 1600 West Bank Dr, Peterborough, ON, K9J 7B8, CANADA. Tel: 705-748-1011, Ext 7470. p. 2672
Zobbi, Joanne, Circ Asst, Maynard Public Library, 77 Nason St, Maynard, MA, 01754-2316. Tel: 978-897-1010. p. 1033
Zobel, James W, Archivist, MacArthur Memorial Library & Archives, MacArthur Sq, Norfolk, VA, 23510. Tel: 757-441-2965. p. 2334
Zobel, Sherlonya, Assoc Dir, Ann Arbor District Library, 343 S Fifth Ave, Ann Arbor, MI, 48104. Tel: 734-327-4200. p. 1078
Zoberman, Emanuel, Libr Dir, William D Block Memorial Law Library, 18 N County St, Waukegan, IL, 60085-4359. Tel: 847-377-2267. p. 660
Zoccali, Tina, Ref Librn, Alston & Bird, LLP Library, 90 Park Ave, 12th Flr, New York, NY, 10016. Tel: 212-210-9526. p. 1578
Zody, Amanda, Circ, ILL, Indiana Wesleyan University, 4201 S Washington St, Marion, IN, 46953. Tel: 765-677-2383. p. 704
Zoellner, Alan F, Dr, Ref/Govt Doc Librn, College of William & Mary in Virginia, Earl Gregg Swem Library, One Landrum Dr, Williamsburg, VA, 23187. Tel: 757-221-3065. p. 2353
Zohn, Kristen, Curator, Lauren Rogers Museum of Art Library, 565 N Fifth Ave, Laurel, MS, 39440. Tel: 601-649-6374. p. 1225
Zola, Jim, Div Mgr, Children's Serv, High Point Public Library, 901 N Main St, High Point, NC, 27262. Tel: 336-883-3668. p. 1696
Zoleta, Kris, Asst to the Dean of Libraries, California State Polytechnic University Library, 3801 W Temple Ave, Bldg 15, Pomona, CA, 91768. Tel: 909-869-3074. p. 196
Zolkiewicz, Alyssa, Actg Dir, Crafton Public Library, 140 Bradford Ave, Pittsburgh, PA, 15205. Tel: 412-922-6877. p. 1993
Zollars, Scotty M, Dir, Libr Serv, Labette Community College Library, 1230 S Main St, Parsons, KS, 67357. Tel: 620-820-1167. p. 831
Zoller, Gabriela, Dir, Libr Serv, Head, Tech Serv, Science History Institute Museum & Library, 315 Chestnut St, Philadelphia, PA, 19106. Tel: 215-873-8205. p. 1985
Zoller, Karen, Dir, Notre Dame College, 4545 College Rd, South Euclid, OH, 44121. Tel: 216-373-5266. p. 1820
Zoller, Marya, Actg Dir, Hawaii State Public Library System, Hawaii State Library, 478 S King St, Honolulu, HI, 96813. Tel: 808-586-3500. p. 507
Zollman, Andrew, Bus Librn, Yuma County Free Library District, 2951 S 21st Dr, Yuma, AZ, 85364. Tel: 928-782-1871. p. 85
Zollo, Emily, Asst Dir, Latham Memorial Library, 16 Library Lane, Thetford, VT, 05074. Tel: 802-785-4361. p. 2296
Zoltai, Steve, Archivist, Coll Develop Librn, Canadian Memorial Chiropractic College, 6100 Leslie St, Toronto, ON, M2H 3J1, CANADA. Tel: 416-482-2340, Ext 206. p. 2687
Zondervan, Robyn, Librn, Kitchener Public Library, Grand River Stanley Park, 175 Indian Rd, Kitchener, ON, N2B 2S7, CANADA. Tel: 519-896-1736. p. 2651
Zonderwyk, Gary, CUL Adminr, New Jersey State Library, Talking Book & Braille Center, 2300 Stuyvesant Ave, Trenton, NJ, 08618. Tel: 609-406-7179, Ext 825. p. 1448
Zook, Christina L, Court Adminr, Perry County Law Library, Perry County Courthouse, Center Sq, Two E Main St, New Bloomfield, PA, 17068. Tel: 717-582-5143, Option 5. p. 1968
Zook, Jess, Youth Serv Coordr, Adamstown Area Library, 110 W Main St, Adamstown, PA, 19501. Tel: 717-484-4200. p. 1903
Zoppa, Jackie, Libr Tech, Capital Health/Nova Scotia Hospital, Hugh Bell Bldg, Rm 200, 300 Pleasant St, Dartmouth, NS, B2Y 3Z9, CANADA. Tel: 902-464-3146. p. 2617
Zoppel, Carol, Chairperson, Res & Instruction Librn, Salem State University, 352 Lafayette St, Salem, MA, 01970-5353. Tel: 978-542-6811. p. 1051
Zoran, Amy, Head, Circ, Chelsea District Library, 221 S Main St, Chelsea, MI, 48118-1267. Tel: 734-475-8732. p. 1090
Zorbas, John A, Dir, Butte County Public Law Library, 1675 Montgomery St, Oroville, CA, 95965. Tel: 530-538-7122. p. 190
Zorich, River, Access Services Lead, Shoreline Community College, 16101 Greenwood Ave N, Shoreline, WA, 98133-5696. Tel: 206-533-2548. p. 2383
Zorn, Christofer, Tech Serv Coordr, Ajax Public Library, 55 Harwood Ave S, Ajax, ON, L1S 2H8, CANADA. Tel: 905-683-4000, Ext 8838. p. 2627
Zou, Benhui, Co-Chair, Palomar College Library, 1140 W Mission Rd, San Marcos, CA, 92069-1487. Tel: 760-744-1150, Ext 2618. p. 234
Zou, Ning, Assoc Dir, Student Academic Servs & Learning Design, Harvard Library, Monroe C Gutman Library, 6 Appian Way, Cambridge, MA, 02138. Tel: 617-495-3453. p. 1006
Zou, Qing (Jason), Head, Digital Initiatives, Lakehead University, 955 Oliver Rd, Thunder Bay, ON, P7B 5E1, CANADA. Tel: 807-343-8251. p. 2685
Zou, Qiong, Syst Librn, Asnuntuck Community College Library, 170 Elm St, Enfield, CT, 06082-0068. Tel: 860-253-3172. p. 311
Zrubek, Kim, Ref Librn, Friendswood Public Library, 416 S Friendswood Dr, Friendswood, TX, 77546-3897. Tel: 281-482-7135. p. 2182
Zsulya, Carol, Head, Coll Mgt, Cleveland State University, Michael Schwartz Library, Rhodes Tower, Ste 501, 2121 Euclid Ave, Cleveland, OH, 44115-2214. Tel: 216-523-7373. p. 1769
Zubeck, Donna, Library Contact, Long Island Community Hospital, 101 Hospital Rd, Patchogue, NY, 11772. Tel: 631-447-3010, 631-654-7100. p. 1615
Zuber, Anne, Dir, Wenonah Free Public Library, 101 E Mantua Ave, Wenonah, NJ, 08090. Tel: 856-468-6323. p. 1452
Zuber, Wendy, Librn, Montana State Prison, 600 Conley Lake Rd, Deer Lodge, MT, 59722. Tel: 406-415-6410. p. 1292
Zubic, Dawn, Circ Supvr, Jefferson County Library, Windsor, 7479 Metropolitan Blvd, Barnhart, MO, 63012. Tel: 636-461-1914. p. 1249
Zubik, Jessica, Youth & Teen Serv Librn, Chelsea District Library, 221 S Main St, Chelsea, MI, 48118-1267. Tel: 734-475-8732. p. 1091
Zubrod, Danielle, Libr Tech, Colorado Department of Corrections, 0200 County Rd 219, Rifle, CO, 81650. Tel: 970-625-7587. p. 294
Zubrod, Nancy, Dept Chair, St Luke's College Library, 2800 Pierce St, Ste 202, Sioux City, IA, 51104. Tel: 712-279-4961. p. 782
Zuckerman, Jane, YA Serv, Floral Park Public Library, 17 Caroline Pl, Floral Park, NY, 11001. Tel: 516-326-6330. p. 1533
Zuckerman, Laura, Br Mgr, San Diego County Library, Valley Center Branch, 29200 Cole Grade Rd, Valley Center, CA, 92082-5880. Tel: 760-749-1305. p. 217
Zumwalt, Kelly, Dir, Pendleton County Public Library, 801 Robbins St, Falmouth, KY, 41040. Tel: 859-654-8535. p. 854
Zumwalt, Kim, Dir, Watseka Public Library, 201 S Fourth St, Watseka, IL, 60970. Tel: 815-432-4544. p. 659
Zumwalt, Sara, Dir, Litchfield Carnegie Public Library, 1205 S State St, Litchfield, IL, 62056. Tel: 217-324-3866. p. 610
Zuni, Jeremy, Proc Archivist, Texas A&M University-San Antonio, One University Way, San Antonio, TX, 78224. Tel: 210-784-1518. p. 2239
Zuniga, Andrea, Br Mgr, City of San Bernardino Library Services, Howard M Rowe Branch, 108 E Marshall Blvd, San Bernardino, CA, 92404. Tel: 909-883-3411. p. 212
Zuniga, Daniela, Mgr, Miami-Dade Public Library System, Shenandoah Branch, 2111 SW 19th St, Miami, FL, 33145. Tel: 305-250-4688. p. 424
Zuniga, Martin, Br Head, Monterey County Free Libraries, San Ardo Branch, 62350 College St, San Ardo, CA, 93450. Tel: 831-627-2503. p. 173
Zuniga, Norma, Dir of Libr, Arlington Public Library System, 100 S Center St, Arlington, TX, 76010. Tel: 817-459-6914. p. 2136
Zupkoff, Kim, Head, Circ Serv, Antioch Public Library District, 757 Main St, Antioch, IL, 60002. Tel: 847-395-0874, Ext 9064. p. 537
Zurgable, Penni, Regional Mgr, Kent District Library, Comstock Park Branch, 3943 West River Dr NE, Comstock Park, MI, 49321. p. 1094
Zurgable, Penni, Regional Mgr, Kent District Library, Plainfield Township Branch, 2650 Five Mile Rd NE, Grand Rapids, MI, 49525. p. 1094
Zurliene, Kelly, Dir, Breese Public Library, 530 N Third St, Breese, IL, 62230. Tel: 618-526-7361. p. 544
Zurmuehlen, Maryann, Head, Support Serv, Novi Public Library, 45255 W Ten Mile Rd, Novi, MI, 48375. Tel: 248-349-0720. p. 1138
Zuzzi, Jacqueline, Dir, Washington Township Free Public Library, 37 E Springtown Rd, Long Valley, NJ, 07853. Tel: 908-876-3596. p. 1414
Zverez, Cathy, Libr Tech - ILL, Alamosa Public Library, 300 Hunt Ave, Alamosa, CO, 81101. Tel: 719-587-2538. p. 263
Zvir, Taras, Relig Studies Librn, Catholic University of America, Religious Studies-Philosophy & Canon Law, 316A Mullen Library, 620 Michigan Ave NE, Washington, DC, 20064. Tel: 202-319-5071. p. 362

Zwald Costello, Stacy, County Librn, Colusa County Free Library, 738 Market St, Colusa, CA, 95932. Tel: 530-458-7671. p. 131

Zweibel, Stephen, Digital Scholarship Librn, City University of New York, 365 Fifth Ave, New York, NY, 10016-4309. Tel: 212-817-7067. p. 1582

Zweibohmer, Paula, Asst Librn, Elma Public Library, 710 Busti Ave, Elma, IA, 50628. Tel: 641-393-8100. p. 751

Zwicker, Susan, Librn, Smithsonian Libraries, Smithsonian Environmental Research Center Library, 647 Contees Wharf Rd, Edgewater, DC, 21037. Tel: 202-633-1675. p. 376

Zwickey, Lisa, Libr Dir, Redgranite Public Library, 135 W Bannerman Ave, Redgranite, WI, 54970. Tel: 920-566-0176. p. 2472

Zych, William, Access Serv, University of Saint Thomas, Charles J Keffer Library, 1000 LaSalle Ave, MOH 206, Minneapolis, MN, 55403. Tel: 651-962-4667. p. 1203

Zydek, Ann M, Dir, Warsaw Community Public Library, 310 E Main St, Warsaw, IN, 46580-2882. Tel: 574-267-6011. p. 724

Zydlewski, Diane, Assoc Librn, Ref & Instruction, Outreach Serv, Emmanuel College, 400 The Fenway, Boston, MA, 02115. Tel: 617-264-7654. p. 995

Zyglowicz, Daniel, Circ Supvr, ILL Tech, Pennsylvania Western University - California, 250 University Ave, California, PA, 15419-1394. Tel: 724-938-4044. p. 1917

Zyglowicz, Daniel, Cat, Monessen Public Library, 326 Donner Ave, Monessen, PA, 15062. Tel: 724-684-4750. p. 1964

Zykorie, Susan, Ch, Deer Park Public Library, 3009 Center St, Deer Park, TX, 77536. Tel: 281-478-7208. p. 2169

Zylman, Jake, Br Mgr, San Bernardino County Library, Newton T Bass Branch, 14901 Dale Evans Pkwy, Apple Valley, CA, 92307. Tel: 760-247-2022. p. 212

Zylstra, Tracy, Dir, Canton Public Library, 225 N Broadway, Canton, SD, 57013-1715. Tel: 605-987-5831. p. 2075